Directory of Business Information Resources

Directory of
Business
Information
Resources

2016

Twenty-Third Edition

Directory of
Business
Information
Resources

- Associations
- Newsletters
- Magazines & Journals
- Trade Shows
- Directories & Databases
- Web Sites

Grey House
Publishing

AMENIA, NY 12501

PUBLISHER: Leslie Mackenzie
EDITOR: Richard Gottlieb
EDITORIAL DIRECTOR: Laura Mars

PRODUCTION MANAGER & COMPOSITION: Kristen Thatcher
PRODUCTION ASSISTANT: Geoff Graves
MARKETING DIRECTOR: Jessica Moody

Grey House Publishing, Inc.
4919 Route 22
Amenia, NY 12501
518.789.8700
FAX 518.789.0545
www.greyhouse.com
e-mail: books@greyhouse.com

While every effort has been made to ensure the reliability of the information presented in this publication, Grey House Publishing neither guarantees the accuracy of the data contained herein nor assumes any responsibility for errors, omissions or discrepancies. Grey House accepts no payment for listing; inclusion in the publication of any organization, agency, institution, publication, service or individual does not imply endorsement of the editors or publisher.

Errors brought to the attention of the publisher and verified to the satisfaction of the publisher will be corrected in future editions.

First edition published 1992
Twenty-Third edition published 2015
Printed in Canada
The directory of business information resources. – 1992-2016

    v. ; 27.5 cm.
    Annual
    Other title: Business information resources

1. Business information services – United States – Directories. 2. Reference books – Business – Bibliography – Periodicals. 3. Association, institutions, etc. – United States – Directories. 4. Business – Databases – Directories. 5. Trade shows – Directories. I. Title: Business information resources.

HF54.52.U5 D56
016.65
ISBN: 978-1-61925-900-3 softcover
ISSN: 1549-7224

Introduction

Introduction

This twenty-third edition of *The Directory of Business Information Resources* has been the premier reference book for business researchers since 1992. With comprehensive coverage of 101 industries, it provides ways to find new customers, increase loyalty among existing customers, and improve the bottom line. As America's economy continues to improve, current, comprehensive business information is more valuable than ever.

Praise for previous editions:

> "...convenient, efficient vehicle for locating sources of information on U.S. businesses... recommended for academic libraries... ideal for collection development."

-American Reference Books Annual

> "...continues to be an essential reference source..."

-Choice

> "...a worthy addition to academic and large public libraries serving business researchers..."

-Booklist

> "...substantial reference, recommended for marketing and industry research collections..."

-Library Journal

This reference work offers an unequaled collection of valuable, industry-specific resources. Reach out to new customers through industry **Associations**, **Directories**, **Databases**, and **Trade Shows**. Find new ways to cut costs and improve efficiency through **Magazines**, **Journals** and **Newsletters**. Learn what your competitors are up to by visiting the latest, most important **Web Sites**.

New Content

The 101 industry chapters include 264 new listings, most of them added to **Alternative Energy**, **Environment & Conservation**, **Food & Beverage**, and **Healthcare**. Other chapters that saw significant additions are **Agriculture**, **Financial Services**, **Publishing**, **Aviation & Aerospace**, **Barbers & Beauty Shops**, **Journalism**, **Motion Pictures**, **Motorcycles**, **Performing Arts**, and **Restaurants**.

With 24,234 listings – hundreds more than before – this twenty-third edition is the most comprehensive guide to business information on the market today. All listings include name, address, phone, fax, web site, email, key contacts and a brief description, making your research focused and productive. When available, we have indicated an association's presence on Facebook, Twitter and LinkedIn.

Online-only information, however, is often confusing, unreliable, and outdated. The value of the focused, comprehensive data in *The Directory of Business Information Resources*, compiled with the business researcher in mind, cannot be overstated. This edition provides immediate assistance with your business: attend industry Trade Shows to **promote your product** and **find new customers**; subscribe to Publications to **stay competitive and ahead of the curve**; join Associations for **business support** and **educational opportunities**.

2016 Features

User Guide: Defines fields for entry type. In addition to name, address, phone, fax, web site, e-mail, and description, *Associations* include number of members, dues, founding year. *Publications* include cost, frequency. *Trade shows* include location, number of exhibitors, attendees.

Content Summary of Chapter Listings: Lists more than 1,600 specific businesses under each chapter name. For example, *Accounting* lists auditors, bookkeepers, payroll, and taxes; *Engineering* includes cost engineers, geologists, and robotics; *Restaurants* covers bakers, cookware, and caterers.

NAICS and SIC Reference Tables: Enable users to approach their topic based on the North American Industry Classification System (NAICS), or the Department of Labor's Standard Industrial Classification System (SIC).

Two Indexes:

Entry Index – Alphabetical list of all entries.

Publisher Index – Alphabetical list of publishers of industry literature, or sponsors of trade shows, etc. The entry number listed identifies the title of the published material/trade show listed in this directory. Note that publishers often offer additional material not included here.

The Directory of Business Information Resources answers the need for well-organized, accessible business information for market researchers, advertising agencies, job placement and career planning offices, public relations personnel, and business schools and colleges. And the amount of information in this edition is up: 6,430 Associations, 2,941 Newsletters, 4,996 Magazines and Journals, 3,376 Trade Shows, 3,741 Directories and Databases, 250 International Resources. Plus, 58,544 contact names, 18,649 fax numbers, 19,157 web sites, and 15,348 e-mail addresses.

The Directory of Business Information Resources is available for subscription online at http://gold.greyhouse.com for even faster, easier access to this vast array of information. With a subscription, users can search by keyword, geographic area, organization type, key contact name and so much more. Visit the site or call 800-562-2139 to set up a free trial of the Online Database.

User Guide

Descriptive listings in *The Directory of Business Information Resources* are organized into 98 industry chapters. You will find the following types of listings throughout the book: Associations; Newsletters; Magazines & Journals; Trade Shows; Directories & Databases; and Web Sites.

Below is a sample listing illustrating the kind of information that is or might be included in an Association entry, with additional fields that apply to publication and trade show listings. Each numbered item of information is described in the paragraphs on the following page.

---

(1) **12345**

(2) **National Association of Big Band Musicians**

(3) 2061 Ryders Avenue

Westerville, OH 43081

(4) 002-208-0843

(5) 800-208-0845

(6) 002-208-0844

(7) info@bigb.com

(8) www.bigb.com

(9) Linda Whare, Executive Director
Keith Fallon, Secretary
Bill Jenkins, Editor

(10) A national organization that supports those musicians and instructors whose main interest is big band music. Committed to furthering the art of big bands through teaching, performance, compositions and scholarly research. Also promotes the growth and establishment of big band literature and libraries, and offers musicians and teachers guidance in instrument maintenance and performing venues.

(11) 1M *Members*

(12) *Founded*: 1984

(13) Bi Monthly

(14) $59.00

(15) 110,000

(16) **Special Issues:**
Top 100 Music Dealers
January

(17) 3,000 Attendees

(18) April

Resources User Key

(1) Record Number: Entries are listed alphabetically within each category and numbered sequentially. Entry numbers, rather than page number, are used in the indexes to refer to listings.

(2) Title: Formal name of company or organization. Where organization names are completely capitalized, the listing will appear at the beginning of the alphabetized section.

(3) Address: Location or permanent address of the association.

(4) Phone Number: The listed phone number is usually for the main office, but may also be for the sales, marketing, or public relations office as provided.

(5) Toll-Free Number: This is listed when provided by the association.

(6) Fax Number: This is listed when provided by the association.

(7) E-Mail: This is listed when provided, and is generally the main office e-mail.

(8) Web Site: This is listed when provided, and is also referred to as an URL address. These web sites are accessed through the Internet by typing http:// before the URL address.

(9) Key Executives: Lists key contacts of the association, publication or sponsoring organization.

(10) Description: This paragraph contains a brief description of the association and their purpose and services.

(11) Members: Total number of association members.

(12) Founded: Year association was founded, or publication began.

(13) Frequency, if listing is a publication.

(14) Subscription price, if listing is a publication.

(15) Circulation, if listing is a publication.

(16) Scheduled special issues, if listing is a magazine.

(17) Attendees, if listing is a trade show.

(18) Month, if listing is a trade show.

Content Summary of Chapter Listings

Chapters in this directory often include a wide range of topics. The following list of keywords from the Association listings shows the subjects covered in each chapter.

Accounting
Accounting Historians
Accounting Standards
Accreditation
Auditors
Black Accountants
Bookkeepers
Broadcast Cable Financial
  Management
Budget & Program Analysis
Computerized Accounting
Construction Financial
  Management
Cost Estimating
Government Accountability
Government Financial Officers
Healthcare Financial Management
Hospitality Financial Management
Insolvency
Insurance
Latino Accountants
Military Comptrollers
Newspapers Financial Management
Payroll
Public Accountants
Taxes
Trucking Financial Management
Valuation
Women Accountants

Advertising
Advertising Agencies
Advertising Research
Cable TV Advertising
Children's Advertising
Commercials
Communications
E Marketing
Educational Advertising
Exhibition Management
Newspaper Advertising
Outdoor Advertising
Photographers
Point of Purchase
Public Opinion
Railroad Advertising
Signs
Transportation Advertising
Women in Advertising

Agriculture
4-H
Agricultural Aviation
Agricultural Communications
Agricultural Consultants
Agricultural County Agents
Agricultural Economics
Agricultural Education
Agricultural Engineers
Agricultural Fairs
Agricultural History
Agricultural Law
Agricultural Management
Agricultural Manufacturers
Agricultural Marketing
Agricultural Research
Agricultural Retail
Agricultural Teachers
Agronomy
Alfalfa

Angus
Animal Health
Animal Hides
Animal Science
Aquatics
Arid Lands
Bedding Plants
Bee Keeping
Beef
Bio-Dynamic Farming
Biomolecular Study
Blacksmiths
Blueberries
Brahman Beef
Canola
Cereal
Christmas Trees
Conservation
Corn
Cotton
Cottonseed
Cranberries
Crops
Dairy
Ecological Farming
Eggs
Enology
Entomology
Family Farming
Feed
Fertilizer
Fisheries
Florals
Foresters
Gardening
Grain
Grapes
Grasslands
Guernsey
Hay
Herbs
Hereford
Holstein
Horticulture
Irrigation
Jersey Cattle
Livestock
Maple Syrup
Millers
Oil Seed
Onions
Organic
Pesticides
Phytopathology
Pork
Potato
Poultry
Produce
Santa Gertrudis
Seeds
Sheep
Soil
Soybean
Sugar
Sunflowers
Veal
Walnuts
Weeds
Wheat

Alternative Energy
Biodiesel
Biogas
Biomass
Clean Energy
Energy Recovery
Ethanol
Geothermal Energy
Hydrogen
Lignite Energy
Low Impact Hydropower
Ocean Renewable Energy
Renewable Energy
Solar Energy
Sustainable Energy
Thermal Energy
Wind Energy

Amusement & Entertainment
Amusement Equipment
  Manufacturers
Amusement Equipment Rentals
Amusement Industry Marketing
Amusement Parks
Amusement Safety
Aquariums
Caves
Circus
Coin Operated
Concessions
Game Developers
Go-Karts
Haunted Attractions
Jugglers
Kiddie Rides
Laser Attractions
Motor Sports
Roller Coasters
Theaters
Themed Amusements
Ticketing
Water Parks
Zoos

Apparel & Accessories
Cashmere & Camel Hair
  Manufacturers
Clothing Contractors
Clothing Manufacturers
Costume Designers
Cotton
Cotton Shippers
Fashion Designers
Footwear
Fur Manufacturers
Fur Merchants
Headwear
Home Sewing/Crafts
Hosiery
Infant & Children Wear
Intimate Apparel
Knitting
Leather
Millners, Dressmakers & Tailors
Neckwear
Needlework
Sportswear
Sunglasses
Uniform Manufacturers

Union Manufacturers &
  Distributors
Western & English Tack Apparel

Appliances
Manufacturers
Parts Suppliers
Repair
Retail Dealers
Service

Architecture
Accessibility for the Disabled
Architectural Historians
Building Officials
Cast Stone
Code Administrators
Concrete
Conservation
Design Drafting
Education
Environmental Design
Impact Assessment
Insulated Cable Engineers
Intelligent Buildings
Landscape Architects
Livable Communities
Marine Engineers
Naval Architects
Precasts
Preservation
Schools of Architecture
Sustainable Buildings
Urban Design

Art & Antiques
Aesthetics
American History
Animal Artists
Antique Dealers
Appraisal
Art Dealers
Art Education
Art Libraries
Art Materials
Art Museums
Art Placement
Art Research
Art Therapy
Auctioneers
Blacksmiths
College Art
Collectors
Conservation
Fine Arts
Fine Print Dealers
Illustrators
Library Art
Limited Edition Dealers
Photography
Picture Framers
Preservation Technology
School Programs
State Art Agencies

Automotive
Aftermarkets
Air Conditioning
Antique Trucks
Auto Auctions
Autobody Work

Content Summary of Chapter Listings

Content Summary of Chapter Listings

Society of Arboriculture

Gifts
Christmas
Handmade
Holiday
International
Museums
Salespeople Association
Souvenirs
Toy and Hobby

Glass & Ceramics
China Clay Producers
Flint Glass Workers Union
Glazing Industry Code Committee
Industrial Sand Association
Insulating Glass
Porcelain Enamel Institute
Refractory Ceramic Fiber

Government
Access Professionals
Board of National Labor Relations
Border Patrol Council
Center for Neighborhood
Chiefs of Police
Citizens Against Government
  Waste
Community Development
Conference of Mayors
Council of State Housing
Council on the Homeless
Council on Water Policy
County and City Health Officials
Emergency Management
Fire Chiefs
Governmental Purchasing
Housing Law Project
Interstate Oil and Gas
League of Cities
Local Air Pollution
Milk Control Agencies
Procurement Round Table
Rural Housing Coalition
Search and Rescue
State Community Service Programs
Study of the Presidency
Trust for Public Land
Urban and Regional Information
Urban Economic Development
Weatherization Assistance
World Federalist Association

Graphic Design
Graphic Arts
Graphic Communications
Illustrators
Imaging
Printing
Publication Designers
Urban Art

Hardware
Doors
Equipment Lessors
Hand Tools
Locksmiths
Lumbermen
Metal Detectors

Healthcare
Applied Psychophysiology
Association for Worksite Health
  Promotion
Athletic Trainers
Blood Banks

Bone and Mineral Research
Breast Cancer
Cataract & Refractive Medicine
Cell Biology
Chiropractics
Cleft Palate Craniofacial
Clinical Nutrition
Compliance Packaging
Continuity of Care
Council on the Aging
County Health Facility
  Administration
Cremation
Dental
Gerantological Society
Headaches
Health Plans
Healthcare Recruitment
Home Care
Human Genetics
Human Services
Laser Medicine
Medical Imaging
Medical Instrumentation
Medical Libraries
Mental Retardation
Nonprescription Medicines
Nuclear Medicine
Pain
Pharmacology
Postgraduate Medicine
Psychiatry
Psychologyl
Radiology
Sleep Products
Speech-Language-Hearing
State Medicaid Directors
Suicidology
Textile Rental Services
Tissue Banks
Worksite Health

Heating & Air Conditioning
Air Balance Consultants
Flexible Air Duct
Gas Appliance Manufacturers
Masonry Heater
Microwave Power Institute
Mobile Air Conditioning
Power Engineers
Refrigeration
Solar Energy
Wholesalers

Hobbies & Games
American Craft Council
American Quilts
Archery
Camping
Home Sewing
Hooking Artists
Miniatures
Model Railroad
Philatelic Society
Society of Craft Designers

Hotels & Motels
Asian/American Hotel Owners
Executive Housekeepers
Facility Management
Hospitality Financial &
  Technology
Hotel and Motel Brokers
Hotel and Restaurant Employees
Resort Development
Small Luxury Hotels

Industrial Equipment
Abrasive Manufacturers
Asphalt Recycling and Reclaiming
Casting Industry Suppliers
Coatings
Composite Can and Tube Institute
Composite Fabricators
Corrugated Steel Pipe
Electroplaters Surface Finishers
Fluid Controls
Hack and Band Saw Manufacturers
Heat Processing Equipment
Hoist Manufacturers
Industrial Diamonds
Industrial Engineers
Industrial Security
Spray Equipment
Tribologists & Lubrication

Insurance
American Prepaid Legal Services
Arbitration Forums
Association of Retired Persons
Cargo War Risk Reinsurance
Certified Insurance Counselors
Committee for Arson Control
Crop Insurers
Defense & Corporate Counsel
Fire Investigators
Highway Loss Data Institute
Insurance Law
National Viatical Association
Property Insurance Loss Register
Registered Mail Insurance
Self Insurance Institute
Shipowners Claim
Transportation Consumer
  Protection
Underwriters Laboratories
Workers Compensation
  Reinsurance

Interior Design, Decorating & Lighting
Can Manufacturers
Carpets and Rugs
Decorative Fabric Distributors
Floor Covering
Florists
Home Furnishings
Illuminating Engineering
Kitchen and Bath
Lighting Association
Paint and Decorating
Picture Framers
Upholstery
Window Coverings

International Trade
Academy of International Business
American League for Exports
Security Assistance
Hong Kong Trade Development
International Chambers of
  Commerce
Latin American Studies
Oil and Gas of Russian Far East
US China Business Council

Jewelry & Watches
Appraisers Association
Cultured Pearl Information
Diamond Council
Estate Jewelry
Gemological Institute
Gold Prospectors
Goldsmiths

Indian Arts & Crafts
Jewelers Vigilance Committee
Silversmiths
Traveling Jewelers
World Gold Council

Journalism
Collegiate Press
Environmental Journalists
Gay and Lesbian Press
Hollywood Foreign Press
Investigative Reporters and Editors
Overseas Press Club of America
Society for News Design
Society of American Travel Writers

Law Enforcement & Public Safety
Academy of Criminal Justice
  Science
American Jail Association
American Polygraph Association
Arson Investigators
Bloodhounds
Bombs
Drug Enforcement Officers
Footprint Association
Forensic Dentists
Livestock Theft
National Constables Association
Society of Criminology

Leather Products
Pedorthic Footwear Association
Restorers
Saddle Markers
Sponge and Chamois Institute

Legal
American Bar Foundation
American Institute of
  Parliamentarians
American Society of Family &
  Conciliation
American Society for Legal
  History
American Society for Trial
  Consultants
Arbitration Association
Center on Children and the Law
Commission on Mental Retardation
  & Physical Disability Law
Council on Legal Education
  Opportunity
Council on State Government
Equal Justice Works
Family Mediators
First Amendment Lawyers
  Association
Japanese American Society for
  Legal Studies
Legal Investigators
Mineral Law
Native American Rights Fund
People Against Racist Terror
Psychiatry and the Law

Libraries
American Archivists
American Indian Library
Art Libraries Society
Asian/Pacific American Librarians
Center for Children's Books
Library Blinding Institute
Library Needs of Nurses
Population/Family Planning
Recorded Sound

The North American Industry Classification System (NAICS, pronounced Nakes) was developed as the standard for use by Federal statistical agencies in classifying business establishments for the collection, analysis, and publication of statistical data related to the business economy of the U.S. NAICS was developed under the auspices of the Office of Management and Budget (OMB), and adopted in 1997 to replace the old Standard Industrial Classification (SIC) system (see page xxiii). Below are all relevant NAICS codes and descriptions. For a more detailed explanation of the NAICS, visit www.naics.com.

11	**Agriculture, Forestry, Fishing and Hunting**
11141	Food Crops Grown Under Cover
11191	Tobacco Farming
114	Fishing, Hunting and Trapping
115	Support Activities for Agriculture and Forestry
21	**Mining**
211111	Crude Petroleum and Natural Gas Extraction
212	Mining (except Oil and Gas)
22	**Utilities**
22131	Water Supply and Irrigation Systems
23	**Construction**
236	Construction of Buildings
237	Heavy and Civil Engineering Construction
23815	Glass and Glazing Contractors
23821	Electrical Contractors
23822	Plumbing, Heating, and Air-Conditioning Contractors
2383	Building Finishing Contractors
31-33	**Manufacturing**
311	Food Manufacturing
3111	Animal Food Manufacturing
31121	Flour Milling and Malt Manufacturing
3113	Sugar and Confectionery Product Manufacturing
3114	Fruit and Vegetable Preserving and Specialty Food Manufacturing
3115	Dairy Product Manufacturing
3117	Seafood Product Preparation and Packaging
3118	Bakeries and Tortilla Manufacturing
31191	Snack Food Manufacturing
31192	Coffee and Tea Manufacturing
31193	Flavoring Syrup and Concentrate Manufacturing
31194	Seasoning and Dressing Manufacturing
312	Beverage and Tobacco Product Manufacturing
3141	Textile Furnishings Mills
315	Apparel Manufacturing
315211	Men's and Boys' Cut and Sew Apparel Contractors
315212	Women's, Girls', and Infants' Cut and Sew Apparel Contractors
315292	Fur and Leather Apparel Manufacturing
3159	Apparel Accessories and Other Apparel Manufacturing
316	Leather and Allied Product Manufacturing
3162	Footwear Manufacturing
321	Wood Product Manufacturing
322	Paper Manufacturing
323	Printing and Related Support Activities
324	Petroleum and Coal Products Manufacturing
325	Chemical Manufacturing
3252	Resin, Synthetic Rubber, and Artificial Synthetic Fibers and Filaments Manufacturing
3253	Pesticide, Fertilizer, and Other Agricultural Chemical Manufacturing
3254	Pharmaceutical and Medicine Manufacturing
3255	Paint, Coating, and Adhesive Manufacturing
3256	Soap, Cleaning Compound, and Toilet Preparation Manufacturing
32591	Printing Ink Manufacturing
32592	Explosives Manufacturing
325992	Photographic Film, Paper, Plate, and Chemical Manufacturing
326	Plastics and Rubber Products Manufacturing
3262	Rubber Product Manufacturing
32621	Tire Manufacturing
32622	Rubber and Plastics Hoses and Belting Manufacturing
32629	Other Rubber Product Manufacturing
327	Nonmetallic Mineral Product Manufacturing
32711	Pottery, Ceramics, and Plumbing Fixture Manufacturing
32712	Clay Building Material and Refractories Manufacturing

3272	Glass and Glass Product Manufacturing
3273	Cement and Concrete Product Manufacturing
3274	Lime and Gypsum Product Manufacturing
32791	Abrasive Product Manufacturing
331	Primary Metal Manufacturing
332	Fabricated Metal Product Manufacturing
3325	Hardware Manufacturing
333	Machinery Manufacturing
3331	Agriculture, Construction, and Mining Machinery Manufacturing
3333	Commercial and Service Industry Machinery Manufacturing
3334	Ventilation, Heating, Air-Conditioning, and Commercial Refrigeration Equipment Manufacturing
3335	Metalworking Machinery Manufacturing
3336	Engine, Turbine, and Power Transmission Equipment Manufacturing
334	Computer and Electronic Product Manufacturing
3342	Communications Equipment Manufacturing
33422	Radio and Television Broadcasting and Wireless Communications Equipment Manufacturing
3343	Audio and Video Equipment Manufacturing
3344	Semiconductor and Other Electronic Component Manufacturing
3345	Navigational, Measuring, Electromedical, and Control Instruments Manufacturing
334518	Watch, Clock, and Part Manufacturing
3346	Manufacturing and Reproducing Magnetic and Optical Media
335	Electrical Equipment, Appliance, and Component Manufacturing
3353	Electrical Equipment Manufacturing
336	Transportation Equipment Manufacturing
3361	Motor Vehicle Manufacturing
3363	Motor Vehicle Parts Manufacturing
3364	Aerospace Product and Parts Manufacturing
3365	Railroad Rolling Stock Manufacturing
3366	Ship and Boat Building
336991	Motorcycle, Bicycle, and Parts Manufacturing
336992	Military Armored Vehicle, Tank, and Tank Component Manufacturing
337	Furniture and Related Product Manufacturing
3372	Office Furniture (including Fixtures) Manufacturing
3391	Medical Equipment and Supplies Manufacturing
33991	Jewelry and Silverware Manufacturing
33992	Sporting and Athletic Goods Manufacturing
33993	Doll, Toy, and Game Manufacturing
33994	Office Supplies (except Paper) Manufacturing
33995	Sign Manufacturing
42	**Wholesale Trade**
423	Merchant Wholesalers, Durable Goods
424	Merchant Wholesalers, Nondurable Goods
425	Wholesale Electronic Markets and Agents and Brokers
44-45	**Retail Trade**
441	Motor Vehicle and Parts Dealers
442	Furniture and Home Furnishings Stores
443	Electronics and Appliance Stores
444	Building Material and Garden Equipment and Supplies Dealers
445	Food and Beverage Stores
446	Health and Personal Care Stores
451	Sporting Goods, Hobby, Book, and Music Stores
453	Miscellaneous Store Retailers
454	Nonstore Retailers
48-49	**Transportation and Warehousing**
481	Air Transportation
482	Rail Transportation
483	Water Transportation
484	Truck Transportation

485	Transit and Ground Passenger Transportation
486	Pipeline Transportation
487	Scenic and Sightseeing Transportation
4885	Freight Transportation Arrangement
493	Warehousing and Storage

51	**Information**
511	Publishing Industries (except Internet)
5111	Newspaper, Periodical, Book, and Directory Publishers
5121	Motion Picture and Video Industries
51223	Music Publishers
515	Broadcasting (except Internet)
516	Internet Publishing and Broadcasting
517	Telecommunications
518	Data Processing, Hosting and Related Services
51912	Libraries and Archives
51913	Internet Publishing and Broadcasting and Web Search Portals

52	**Finance and Insurance**
522	Credit Intermediation and Related Activities
52211	Commercial Banking
522292	Real Estate Credit
522293	International Trade Financing
52311	Investment Banking and Securities Dealing
52392	Portfolio Management
52399	All Other Financial Investment Activities
524	Insurance Carriers and Related Activities
525	Funds, Trusts, and Other Financial Vehicles
5251	Insurance and Employee Benefit Funds
52593	Real Estate Investment Trusts

53	**Real Estate and Rental and Leasing**
531	Real Estate
5321	Automotive Equipment Rental and Leasing
53212	Truck, Utility Trailer, and RV (Recreational Vehicle) Rental and Leasing
53221	Consumer Electronics and Appliances Rental
53223	Video Tape and Disc Rental
5324	Commercial and Industrial Machinery and Equipment Rental and Leasing
533	Lessors of Nonfinancial Intangible Assets (except Copyrighted Works)

54	**Professional, Scientific, and Technical Services**
5411	Legal Services
5412	Accounting, Tax Preparation, Bookkeeping, and Payroll Services
5413	Architectural, Engineering, and Related Services
54135	Building Inspection Services
54141	Interior Design Services
54143	Graphic Design Services
541613	Marketing Consulting Services
54162	Environmental Consulting Services
5418	Advertising and Related Services

54182	Public Relations Agencies
54183	Media Buying Agencies
541921	Photography Studios, Portrait

56	**Administrative and Support and Waste Management and Remediation Services**
561422	Telemarketing Bureaus
56145	Credit Bureaus
5615	Travel Arrangement and Reservation Services
5616	Investigation and Security Services
5617	Services to Buildings and Dwellings
56191	Packaging and Labeling Services
562	Waste Management and Remediation Services

| **61** | **Educational Services** |
| 6114 | Business Schools and Computer and Management Training |

71	**Arts, Entertainment, and Recreation**
711	Performing Arts, Spectator Sports, and Related Industries
713	Amusement, Gambling, and Recreation Industries
71321	Casinos (except Casino Hotels)
71394	Fitness and Recreational Sports Centers

72	**Accommodation and Food Services**
7211	Traveler Accommodation
72111	Hotels (except Casino Hotels) and Motels
72112	Casino Hotels
7212	RV (Recreational Vehicle) Parks and Recreational Camps
722	Food Services and Drinking Places
7221	Full-Service Restaurants

81	**Other Services (except Public Administration)**
8111	Automotive Repair and Maintenance
811211	Consumer Electronics Repair and Maintenance
8113	Commercial and Industrial Machinery and Equipment (except Automotive and Electronic) Repair and Maintenance
81141	Home and Garden Equipment and Appliance Repair and Maintenance
8121	Personal Care Services
81231	Coin-Operated Laundries and Drycleaners
813211	Grantmaking Foundations
813312	Environment, Conservation and Wildlife Organizations

92	**Public Administration**
921	Executive, Legislative, and Other General Government Support
922	Justice, Public Order, and Safety Activities
924	Administration of Environmental Quality Programs
92612	Regulation and Administration of Transportation Programs
92613	Regulation and Administration of Communications, Electric, Gas, and Other Utilities
92614	Regulation of Agricultural Marketing and Commodities
928	National Security and International Affairs

The Standard Industrial Classification (SIC) is a United States government system for classifying industries by a four-digit code. Established in 1937, it has been supplanted by the six-digit North American Industry Classification System (NAICS) (see page ixx), which was released in 1997; however certain government departments and agencies, such as the U.S. Securities and Exchange Commission (SEC), still use SIC codes. Below are all major SIC codes and descriptions. For a more detailed explanation of the SIC system, visit http://www.census.gov/epcd/www/sic.html.

01 Agricultural Production - Crops

07 Agricultural Services

09 Fishing, Hunting and Trapping

10 Metal Mining

12 Coal Mining

13 Oil and Gas Extraction

14 Mining and Quarrying of Nonmetallic Minerals, Except Fuels

15 Building Construction - General Contractors & Operative Builders

16 Heavy Construction, Except Building Construction - Contractors

17 Construction - Special Trade Contractors

20 Food and Kindred Products

21 Tobacco Products

22 Textile Mill Products

23 Apparel and Other Finished Products Made From Fabrics and Similar Materials

24 Lumber and Wood Products, Except Furniture

25 Furniture and Fixtures

26 Paper and Allied Products

27 Printing, Publishing, and Allied Industries

28 Chemicals and Allied Products

29 Petroleum Refining and Related Industries

30 Rubber and Miscellaneous Plastics Products

31 Leather and Leather Products

32 Stone, Clay, Glass, and Concrete Products

33 Primary Metal Industries

34 Fabricated Metal Products, Except Machinery and Transportation Equipment

35 Industrial and Commercial Machinery and Computer Equipment

36 Electronic and Other Electrical Equipment and Components, Except Computer Equipment

37 Transportation Equipment

38 Measuring, Analyzing, and Controlling Instruments; Photographic, Medical and Optical Goods; Watches

39 Miscellaneous Manufacturing Industries

41 Local and Suburban Transit and Interurban Highway Passenger Transportation

42 Motor Freight Transportation and Warehousing

44 Water Transportation

45 Transportation By Air

47 Pipelines, Except Natural Gas

47 Transportation Services

48 Communications

49 Electric, Gas and Sanitary Services

50 Wholesale Trade-Durable Goods

51 Wholesale Trade-Non-Durable Goods

60 Depository Institutions

61 Non-Depository Credit Institutions

63 Insurance Carriers

65 Real Estate

73 Business Services

75 Automotive Repair, Services, and Parking

76 Miscellaneous Repair Services

78 Motion Pictures

79 Amusement and Recreation Services

80 Health Services

81 Legal Services

82 Educational Services

84 Museums, Art Galleries, and Botanical and Zoological Gardens

87 Engineering, Accounting, Research, Management, and Related Services

92 Justice, Public Order, and Safety

94 Administration of Human Resource Programs

95 Administration of Environmental Quality and Housing Programs

96 Administration of Economic Programs

97 National Security and International Affairs

Associations

1 AGN International - North America
2851 S Parker Rd
Suite 850
Aurora, CO 80014-2744

303-743-7880
800-782-2272
FAX 303-743-7660
E-Mail: rhood@agn.org
Home Page: na.agn.org
Social Media: *Facebook, LinkedIn*

Rita J. Hood, Executive Director
Patsy Bowen, Director, Member Info Services
Mark Pigg, Director, Internal Info Systems
Nathalie Champagne, Director/Member Programs
Courtney Mino, Director, Meetings/Staff Dev.

Worldwide association of separate and independent accounting and consulting firms. Composed of CPA consulting firms who share information and resources via the association programs. AGN-NA operates under the premise that by sharing information and resources, members' growth and quality goals can be achieved more quickly.
53 Members
Founded in 1978

2 ARMA International
11880 College Blvd
Suite 450
Overland Park, KS 66210

913-341-3808
800-422-2762
FAX 913-341-3742
E-Mail: headquarters@armaintl.org
Home Page: www.arma.org
Social Media: *Facebook, Twitter, LinkedIn*

Peter Kurilecz, IGP, CRM, CA, President
Tera Ladner, J.D., IGP, CRM, President-Elect
Brenda Prowse, CRM, Treasurer
Fred Pulzello, IGP, CRM, Immediate Past President
Candace Daniels, Product Marketing Manager

ARMA International is a not-for-profit association and a source for authoritative education, the latest legislative updates, standards & best practices. The association was established in 1955. Its approximately 10,000 members include records managers, archivists, corporate librarians, imaging specialists, legal professionals, IT managers, consultants, and educators, all of whom work in a wide variety of industries.
27000 Members
Founded in 1955

3 Academy of Accounting Historians
Case Western Reserve University
10900 Euclid Avenue
Cleveland, OH 44106

216-368-2058
FAX 205-368-6244
E-Mail: acchistory@case.edu
Home Page: www.aahq.org
Social Media: *Facebook, Twitter, LinkedIn, YouTube*

Massimo Sargiacomo, President
Robert Colson, President Elect
Gary Spraakman, VP, Partnerships
Yvette Lazdowski, VP,Communications
Stephanie Moussalli, Secretary

Subjects include modern prespectives of accounting history.
600 Members
Founded in 1973

4 Accounting & Financial Women's Alliance
2365 Harrodsburg Road, A325
Lexington, KY 40504

859-219-3532
800-326-2163
FAX 859-219-3532
E-Mail: afwa@afwa.org
Home Page: www.afwa.org
Social Media: *Facebook, Twitter, LinkedIn*

Dianna M. Patton, CPA, CFP, President
Linda Harris, CPA, President Elect
Mary E. Duff, CPA, VP, Chapter Initiatives
Karyn Hartke, CPA, Vice President - Membership
Ericka Harney, Executive Director

To enable women in all accounting and related fields to achieve their full personal, professional and economic potential and to contribute to the future development of their profession.
Founded in 1938

5 Accreditation Council for Accountancy and Taxation
1330 Braddock Place
Suite 540
Alexandria, VA 22314

888-289-7763
FAX 703-549-2984
Home Page: www.acatcredentials.org

Michael P. Salazar, CPA, EA, ABA, President
Virginia Bruns, Vice President
Christine Giovetti, Secretary/Treasurer
Carla Rich, Education Director
Peter M. Berkery, Jr., JD, CFP, Public Director

To identify professionals in independent practice who specialize in providing financial, accounting and taxation services to individuals and small to mid-size businesses.
Founded in 1973

6 Advancing Government Accountability
2208 Mount Vernon Avenue
Alexandria, VA 22301-1314

703-684-6931
800-AGA-7211
FAX 703-548-9367
E-Mail: agamembers@agacgfm.org
Home Page: www.agacgfm.org
Social Media: *Facebook, Twitter, LinkedIn, Twitter, GovLoop*

John E. Homan, 2015-2016 AGA National President
Ann M. Ebberts, MS, PMP, Chief Executive Officer
Maryann Malesardi, Director of Comm/Journal Editor
Cristina Barbudo, MS, CPA, Director of Finance & Admin
Jerome Bruce, Director, Meetings & Expositions

AGA supports the careers and professional development of government finance professionals working in federal, state and local governments as well as the private sector and academia. Through education, research, publications, certification and conferences, AGA reaches thousands of professionals and offers more than 100,000 continuing professional education (CPE) hours annually.
15000 Members
Founded in 1950
Mailing list available for rent: 18,000 names

7 Affordable Housing Association of Certified Public Accountants
459 N 300 W
Suite 11
Kaysville, UT 84037

801-547-0809
800-532-0809
FAX 801-547-5070
E-Mail: info@ahacpa.org
Home Page: www.ahacpa.org

Les Sparks, President
Kathy Christensen, Contact
Mike Olsen, Contact
Susan Harris, Contact

AHACPA is a national association of CPAs and financial professionals providing financial services, support and education for the affordable housing and HUD-approved lender communities, informing members of financial requirements and provide specific guidance on how to efficiently implement those requirements.
500 Members
Founded in 1998
Mailing list available for rent

8 American Accounting Association
5717 Bessie Drive
Sarasota, FL 34233-2399

941-921-7747
FAX 941-923-4093
E-Mail: info@aaahq.org
Home Page: www.aaahq.org
Social Media: *Facebook, Twitter*

Tracey Sutherland, Executive Director
Julie Smith David, Chief Innovation Officer
Dave Frazier, Finance Director
Diane Hazard, Publications Director
Stephanie Austin, Publications Assistant

The American Accounting Association promotes worldwide excellence in accounting education, research and practice. The Association is a voluntary organization of persons interested in accounting education and research.
9000 Members
Founded in 1916

9 American Association for Budget and Program Analysis
PO Box 1157
Falls Church, VA 22041

703-828-4333
FAX 703-941-1535
E-Mail: aabpa@aabpa.org
Home Page: www.aabpa.org
Social Media: *Facebook, Twitter, LinkedIn, GovLoop*

Melissa Neuman, President
Ben Wilson, Vice President for Membership
Sandra Beattie, Vice President for Programs
Justin Ryan Riordan, Vice President for Communications
Darreisha Bates, Treasurer/Secretary

Helps federal, state, and local government managers and analysts, corporate executives and academic specialists meet the unique challenges of their careers. By helping members keep up with the latest developments in their fields, establish and maintain contacts with colleagues, represent their interests and share opportunities, AABPA serves the key difference between simply having a job and being part of a highly respected and well trained profession.
400 Members
Founded in 1976

10 American Association of Attorney-Certified Public Accountants
PO Box 706
Warrendale, PA 15095

703-352-8064
888-288-9272
FAX 703-352-8073
E-Mail: info@attorney-cpa.com
Home Page: www.attorney-cpa.com
Social Media: *Facebook, Twitter, LinkedIn*

John W. Pramberg, President
David M. Berger, President Elect/ Vice President
Jo Ann M. Koontz, Secretary
Melissa R. Benowitz, CMP, Director of Meetings
Kimmy Livingston, Director, Membership

The AAA-CPA is the only association in the nation whose members are comprised of professionals dually qualified as both attorneys and certified public accountants. Today, the AAA-CPA offers an array of products and services to help members succeed in their practice such as; networking and referral
1370 Members
Founded in 1964

11 American Association of Finance & Accounting
1702 E. Highland Ave
Suite 200
Phoenix, AZ 85016

602-277-3700
FAX 602-926-2629
E-Mail: mnolan@afpersonnel.com
Home Page: www.aafa.com

An alliance of executive search firms specializing in the recruiting of finance and accounting professionals.
Founded in 1978

12 American Association of Managing General Agents
610 Freedom Business Center
Suite 110
King of Prussia, PA 19406

610-992-0022
FAX 610-992-0021
E-Mail: mark@aamga.org
Home Page: www.aamga.org
Social Media: *Facebook, Twitter, LinkedIn*

Bernd G. Heinze, Esq, Executive Director
Roger Ware, Jr., ARM, President
Marty Bair, CFO
Caitlin Skelton, Director of Meetings and Projects
Jeff Henry, Director of Education

Trade association to international wholesale insurance professionals and leader in representing the interests of its members before federal, state,and local governments and regulatory agencies
Founded in 1926

13 American College of Trust and Estate Counsel
901 15th Street, NW
Suite 525
Washington, DC 20005

202-684-8460
FAX 202-684-8459
Home Page: www.actec.org
Social Media: *Facebook, Twitter, LinkedIn*

Bruce Stone, President
Cynda C. Ottaway, President Elect
Susan T. House, Vice President
Charles D. Fox, IV, Treasurer
John A. Terrill, II, Secretary

Nonprofit association of lawyers that advises clients on planning for tax efficient transfer of wealth during life and after death, preparing real estate planning documents, administering trusts, guardianships, planning for employee benefits, etc.
2700+ Members
Founded in 1949

14 American Council of Life Insurers
101 Constitution Avenue
Suite 700
Washington, DC 20001-2133

202-624-2000
877-674-4659
E-Mail: contact@acli.com
Home Page: www.acli.com
Social Media: *Facebook, Twitter, YouTube, RSS*

Deanna Mulligan, Chairman
Pete Schaefer, Chairman-Elect
Dirk Kempthorne, President & Chief Executive Officer
Brian Waidmann, Chief of Staff
Larry Burton, Chief Operating Officer

Trade association advocating federal, state, and international forums for public policy that supports the industry marketplace. ACLI members offer life insurance, annuities, retirement plans, long-term care, disability income insurance, and reinsurance.
300 Members

15 American Institute of Certified Public Accountants
1211 Avenue of the Americas
New York, NY 10036-8775

212-596-6200
888-777-7077
FAX 212-596-6213
E-Mail: service@aicpa.org
Home Page: www.aicpa.org
Social Media: *Facebook, Twitter, LinkedIn, RSS*

Tim L. Christen, CPA, CGMA, Chairman
Barry C Melancon, CPA, CGMA, President & Chief Executive Officer
Susan Coffey, CPA, CGMA, Senior Vice President
Mark Peterson, Senior Vice President
Anthony Pugliese, Senior Vice President

The American Institute of Certified Public Accountants is the national, professional organization for all Certified Public Accountants. Its mission is to provide members with the resources, information, and leadership that enable them to provide valuable services in the highest professional manner to benefit the public as well as employers and clients.
41200 Members
Founded in 1887

16 American Institute of Professional Bookkeepers
6001 Montrose Road
Suite 500
Rockville, MD 20852

800-622-0121
FAX 800-541-0066
E-Mail: info@aipb.org
Home Page: www.aipb.org

Stanley Hartman, Executive Director
Stephen Sahlein, Director of Publishing
Carol Watson, Director
Robin Merrill, Assistant Manager
Kenia Salgado, Manager

Achieve recognition of bookkeepers as accounting professionals, keep bookkeepers up to date on changes in bookkeeping, accounting and tax, answer questions on bookkeeping and accounting, and certify bookkeepers.
30000 Members
Founded in 1987

17 American Payroll Association
660 North Main Avenue
Suite 100
San Antonio, TX 78205-1217

210-226-4600
FAX 210-226-4027
E-Mail: apa@americanpayroll.org
Home Page: www.americanpayroll.org
Social Media: *Facebook, Twitter, LinkedIn*

Deborah Viers Traylor, President
Christine Avery, Managing Editor/Membership
Caren Jean Bennett, Editorial Assistant
Patricia Bowton, Director/Certification
Debbie Cervini, Production Coordinator

The American Payroll Association is the leading advocate for the advancement of payroll professionals and a catalyst for connecting the payroll industry with employers and government. Our vision is to create opportunities and forge a community by providing the education, skills, and resources necessary for payroll professionals to become successful leaders and strategic partners within their organizations.
20000 Members
Founded in 1982

18 American Property Tax Counsel
1970 East Grand Ave.
Suite 330
El Segundo, CA 90245

310-364-0193
844-227-0407
Home Page: www.aptcnet.com
Social Media: *LinkedIn*

Provides property tax services locally and nationally.

19 American Society of Military Comptrollers
415 N Alfred St
Alexandria, VA 22314-2269

703-549-0360
800-462-5637
FAX 703-549-3181
Home Page: www.asmconline.org
Social Media: *Facebook, Twitter, LinkedIn*

Craig Bennett, President
Gretchen Anderson, Vice President
Al Runnels, Executive Director
Riitta Silverman, Associate Director for Finance
Phara G. Rodrigue, Associate Director

ASMC is the non-profit educational and professional organization for persons, military and civilian, involved in the overall field of military comptrollership. ASMC promotes the education and training of its members, and supports the development and advancement of the profession of military comptrollership. The society sponsors research, provides professional programs to keep members abreast of current issues and encourages the exchange of techniques and approaches.
20000 Members
Founded in 1948

20 American Woman's Society of Certified Public Accountants
136 South Keowee Street
Dayton, OH 45402

713-893-5685
800-297-2721
FAX 937-222-5794
E-Mail: info@awscpa.org

Home Page: www.awscpa.org
Social Media: *Facebook, Twitter, LinkedIn*

Cynthia Cox, President
Christina Flynn, VP, Programs
Krista D. Saul, Secretary
Belicia Cespedes, Treasurer
Wendy Lewis, VP/Marketing

The American Woman's Society of Certified Public Accountants (AWSCPA) began in 1933 as a group of nine women CPAs united in facing the challenges affecting women in the profession at that time. Over the years, the organization has grown. Membership increased dramatically in 1982 when the membership amended the Society's bylaws to allow affiliated local groups. Today, AWSCPA has 25 affiliates located throughout the country with a membership of approximately 2,000.
1500 Members
Founded in 1933

21   Appraisers Association of America
212 West 35th Street
11th Floor South
New York, NY 10001

212-889-5404
FAX 212-889-5503
E-Mail: referrals@appraisersassociation.org
Home Page: www.appraisersassociation.org
Social Media: *Facebook, Twitter, LinkedIn*

Deborah G. Spanierman, AAA, President
Cynthia D. Herbert, AAA, First Vice President
Edward Yee, AAA, Second Vice President
Linda Selvin, Executive Director
Sharon Chrust, AAA, Recording Secretary

Develop and promote skills in the profession of appraising through education and professional practice.
Founded in 1949

22   Association for Accounting Administration
136 S Keowee Street
Dayton, OH 45402

937-222-0030
FAX 937-222-5794
E-Mail: info@cpafma.org
Home Page: www.cpafma.org
Social Media: *Facebook, Twitter, LinkedIn*

Kim Fantaci, President
Jim Fahey, AAAPM, Chair
Robert E. Biddle, Jr., AAAPM, Vice Chair
Sharon Trabbic, AAAPM, Director of Education
Larry Sheftel, PHR, Director of Membership & Growth

The Association of Accounting Administrators enables accounting firm administrators to communicate with one another and provide each other with the benefits of everyone's experiences in what was a new and emerging profession.
900 Members
Founded in 1984

23   Association for Accounting Marketing
9 Newport Drive
Suite 200
Forest Hill, MD 21050

443-640-1061
FAX 856-439-0525
E-Mail: info@accountingmarketing.org
Home Page: www.accountingmarketing.org
Social Media: *Facebook, Twitter, LinkedIn*

Jack Kolmansberger, President
Laura Snyder, Vice President
Lauren Clemmer, Executive Director
Amy Chetelat, Financial Director
Jessica Bialczak, Association Coordinator

The Association for Accounting Marketing (AAM) is a national organization and is the only trade association of its kind that provides resources, education, seminars, workshops, support and a global network to the accounting marketing industry. Our membership includes accounting firm marketers from Big Four and other national, regional, local and sole proprietor firms. Others include sales and business development professionals, accounting partners, firm administrators, and students.
843 Members
Founded in 1989

24   Association for Management Information in Financial Services
14247 Saffron Circle
Carmel, IN 46032

317-815-5857
E-Mail: ami2@amifs.org
Home Page: www.amifs.org
Social Media: *Facebook, Twitter, LinkedIn*

Jefferson Nathasingh, President
Robert McDonald, EVP
Lynn Courchaine, Conference Chair
Kevin Link, Executive Director
Krissa Hatfield, Asst. Executive Director

A nonprofit professional association dedicated to developing and advancing the profession of management information for the financial services industry.
Founded in 1980

25   Association of Accounting Administrators
136 South Keowee Street
Dayton, OH 45402

937-222-0030
E-Mail: info@cpafma.org
Home Page: www.cpafma.org
Social Media: *Facebook, Twitter, LinkedIn*

Kim Fantaci, President
Jim Fahey, AAAPM, Chair
Ginny Fedrich, AAAPM, Secretary
Jane Johnson, AAAPM, Treasurer
Sharon Trabbic, AAAPM, Director of Education
Founded in 1984

26   Association of Certified Fraud Examiners
716 West Ave
Austin, TX 78701-2727

512-478-9000
800-245-3321
FAX 512-478-9297
E-Mail: memberservices@acfe.com
Home Page: www.acfe.com
Social Media: *Facebook, Twitter, LinkedIn*

Joseph T Wells, Chairman
James D Ratley, President/CEO
John D Gill, VP/Education
John Warren, VP/General Counsel
Jeanette LeVie, VP/Administration

The ACFE is reducing business fraud world-wide and inspiring public confidence in the integrity and objectivity within the profession.
75000 Members
Founded in 1988

27   Association of Chartered Accountants in the United States
3887 Punahele Road
Princeville, HI 96722

508-395-0224
E-Mail: admin@acaus.org
Home Page: www.acaus.org
Social Media: *Facebook, LinkedIn*

David Powell FCA (ICAEW), President
Sasha Carlson, Executive Director
Timothy Clacket, Secretary

Robert McDonald, Treasurer
David Freeman, Board Member

ACAUS is a nonprofit professional and educational organization representing interests of U.S. based chartered accountants from the institutes of Chartered Accountants across the globe.
6000 Members
Founded in 1980

28   Association of College & University Auditors
PO Box 14306
Lenexa, KS 66285-4306

913-895-4620
FAX 913-895-4652
E-Mail: ACUA-info@goAMP.com
Home Page: www.acua.org
Social Media: *Facebook, Twitter, LinkedIn, YouTube*

Vijay Patel, President
Sandy Jansen, Immediate Past President
Stephanie Newman, Executive Director
Raven Hardin, Association Manager
Dede Gish Panjada, Education Director

The Association of College & University Auditors (ACUA) is a professional organization comprised of audit professionals from all over the globe. We strive to continually improve the internal operations and processes of the individual institutions we serve, through continued professional development and the dissemination of individual internal audit experiences in an open forum with friends and colleagues.
Founded in 1958

29   Association of Credit Union Internal Auditors
1727 King Street
Suite 300
Alexandria, VA 22314

703-688-2284
FAX 703-348-7602
E-Mail: acuia@acuia.org
Home Page: www.acuia.org
Social Media: *Facebook, Twitter, LinkedIn*

John Gallagher, Chairman
Kara Giano, CIA, CIDA, CRMA, Vice Chair
Margaret Chamberlain, CUERME, Secretary
Barry Lucas, Treasurer
Linda Goff, CUCE, Director

ACUIA is committed to being a quality provider of credit union internal audit resources. ACUIA is an international professional organization dedicated to the practice of internal auditing in credit unions. ACUIA's objectives are: to unify and encourage cooperative relationships among credit union internal auditors to facilitate the exchange of information and ideas; to provide educational opportunities for developing and enhancing audit and leadership skills; promote the IA profession.
600 Members
Founded in 1991

30   Association of Government Accountants
2208 Mount Vernon Ave
Alexandria, VA 22301-1314

703-684-6931
800-AGA-7211
FAX 703-548-9367
E-Mail: communications@agacgfm.org
Home Page: www.agacgfm.org
Social Media: *LinkedIn*

John E. Homan, National President
Susan Fritzlen, Chief Operating Officer
Cristina Barbudo, Director of Finance/Administration
Maryann Malesardi, Director of Comm/Journal Editor

Ann M. Ebberts, MS, PMP, Chief Executive Officer

AGA supports the careers and professional development of government finance professionals working in federal, state and local governments as well as the private sector and academia. Through education, research, publications, certification and conferences, AGA reaches thousands of professionals and offers more than 100,000 continuing professional education (CPE) hours annually.
Founded in 1950

31   Association of Healthcare Internal Auditors

10200 W 44th Avenue
Suite 304
Wheat Ridge, CO 80003

303-327-7546
888-ASK-AHIA
FAX 720-881-6101
E-Mail: info@ahia.org
Home Page: www.ahia.org
Social Media: *LinkedIn, YouTube*

Cavell Alexander, Chairman
David Richstone, Vice Chair
David Stumph, Executive Director
Michelle Cunningham, Account Executive
Bryon Neaman, CPA, CIA, Secretary/Treasurer

The Association of Internal Auditors (AHIA) is a network of experienced healthcare internal auditing professionals who come together to share tools, knowledge and insight on how to assess and evaluate risk within a complex and dynamic healthcare environment. AHIA is an advocate for the profession, continuing to elevate and champion the strategic importance of healthcare internal auditors with executive management and the Board.
885 Members
Founded in 1981

32   Association of Independent Accounting Professionals

E-Mail: staff@aiaponline.com
Home Page: www.aiaponline.com

An online resource designed for today's independent accountant—provides practice expansion opportunities, information, and resources.

33   Association of Insolvency Advisors and Restructuring Advisors

221 Stewart Avenue
Suite 207
Medford, OR 97501-3647

541-858-1665
FAX 541-858-9187
E-Mail: aira@aira.org
Home Page: www.aira.org
Social Media: *Twitter, LinkedIn*

Matthew Schwartz, CIRA, Chairman
Thomas Morrow, CIRA, President
David Payne, CIRA, CDBV, Vice President - Conferences
Teri Stratton, CIRA, Vice President - CIRA, CDBV
Joel Waite, Vice President - Development

AIRA is a nonprofit professional association serving the bankruptcy, restructuring and turn-around practice area. AIRA's membership consists of accountants, financial advisors, investment bankers, attorneys, workout consultants, trustees, and others in the field of business turnaround, restructuring and bankruptcy. AIRA members are among the most trusted and sought-after professionals in matters dealing with limited capital resources and deteriorating operating performance.
2000+ Members
Founded in 1982

34   Association of Insolvency and Reconstruction

221 W. Stewart Avenue
Suite 207
Medford, OR 97501

541-858-1665
FAX 541-858-9187
E-Mail: aira@aira.org
Home Page: www.aira.org

Matthew Schwartz, CIRA, Chairman
Thomas Morrow, CIRA, President
David Payne, CIRA, CDBV, Vice President - Conferences
Teri Stratton, CIRA, Vice President - CIRA, CDBV
Grant Newton, Executive Director
Founded in 1982

35   Association of Latino Professionals in Finance and Accounting

801 South Grand Avenue
Suite 400
Los Angeles, CA 90017

213-243-0004
FAX 213-243-0006
E-Mail: lori.ruff@national.alpfa.org
Home Page: www.alpfa.org
Social Media: *Facebook, Twitter, LinkedIn, YouTube, Instagram*

Charles P. Garcia, Chuief Executive Officer
Migdalia Diaz, Chief Operating Officer
Selene Benavides, Chief Financial Officer
Julio Carbonell, Chief Information Officer
Leni Delgado, General Counsel

ALPFA is the leading professsional association dedicated to enhancing opportunities for Latinos in the accounting, finance and related professions. ALPFA is a nonprofit entity registered with the IRS.
72000 Members
Founded in 1972

36   Association of Local Government Auditors

859-276-0686
E-Mail: kyoung@nasact.org
Home Page: algaonline.org
Social Media: *Twitter, LinkedIn, RSS*

Kymber Waltmunson, President
David Givans, President Elect
Corrie Stokes, Past President
Kristine Adams Wannberg, Treasurer
Tina Adams, Secretary

A professional organization committed to supporting and improving local government auditing through advocacy, collaboration, education, and training.
Founded in 1985

37   Association of Public Pension Fund Auditors

PO Box 16064
Columbus, OH 43216-6064

E-Mail: webmaster@appfa.org
Home Page: www.appfa.org

Ryan Babin, President
Greg Beck, Vice President
Amy L. Barett, Secretary
Mary Kay Howard, Treasurer
Dave McKnight, Board Member

A professional association consisting of internal auditors dedicated to providing comprehensive professional development and networking opportunities for its members.
100+ Members
Founded in 1991

38   BCCA

550 W. Frontage Road
Suite 3600
Northfield, IL 60093

847-881-8757
FAX 847-784-8059
E-Mail: info@bccacredit.com
Home Page: www.bccacredit.com
Social Media: *Twitter, LinkedIn*

Mary Collin, President & CEO
Jamie Smith, Director of Operations
Arcelia Pimentel, Sales/Membership
Susan Graves, Credit Investigator
Tracey Harris, Credit Investigator

BCCA is the media industry's credit association that functions as a central clearing house for credit information on advertisers, agencies and buying services, both locally and nationally. Also provides an Electronic Media Credit Application (EMCAPP.com) to members that helps streamline the application process. One app in one location!
545 Members
Founded in 1972

39   Beta Alpha Psi

220 Leigh Farm Road
Durham, NC 27707

919-402-4044
E-Mail: bap@bap.org
Home Page: www.bap.org
Social Media: *Facebook, Twitter, LinkedIn*

Shawn Harter, President
Margaret Fiorentino, Executive Director
Samantha Simunyu, Associate Manager - Marketing
George Gamble, Director of Administration
Lisa Wicker, Manager - Chapter Services

BETA ALPHA PSI is an honorary organization for Financial Information students and professionals. The primary objective of Beta Alpha Psi is to encourage and give recognition to scholastic and professional excellence in the business information field. This includes promoting the study and practice of accounting, finance and information systems; providing opportunities for self-development, service and association among members and practicing professionals.
300K Members
Founded in 1919

40   Broadcast Cable Credit Association

550 W Frontage Rd
Suite 3600
Northfield, IL 60093-1243

847-881-8757
FAX 847-784-8059
E-Mail: info@bccacredit.com
Home Page: www.bccacredit.com
Social Media: *Facebook, Twitter, LinkedIn*

Mary Collin, President/CEO
Jamie Smith, Director/Operations
Arcelia Pimentel, BCCA Sales/Membership
Susan Graves, Credit Investigator
Tracey Harris, Credit Investigator

BCCA, a subsidiary of Media Financial Management Association, represents credit and collection professionals from TV, radio, cable, system operators, newspaper, and magazine organizations in the U.S. and Canada. BCCA functions as a central clearinghouse for credit information on advertisers, agencies and buying services, both locally and nationally.
600 Members
Founded in 1972

41 **CPA Associates International**
Meadows Office Complex
301 Route 17 North
Rutherford, NJ 07070-2599

201-804-8686
FAX 201-804-9222
E-Mail: homeoffice@cpaai.com
Home Page: www.cpaai.com

Hans van den Besselaar, Chairman
Hans van den Besselaar, Chairman-Elect
James F. Flynn, President
Ted A. Carnevale, Treasurer
Claudio Cifali, Secretary

CPA Associates International was established
as a global group of high-quality independent
CPA and chartered accounting firms; it is market exclusive, with members in major cities
throughout the world. The organized association provides members with the capabilities of
the largest firm, yet allows each to maintain its
local practice while avoiding costly overhead
and unnecessary controls.
148 Members
Founded in 1960

42 **CPAsNET.com**
PO Box 7648
Princeton, NJ 8543

609-890-0800
FAX 609-689-9720
E-Mail: solutions@cpasnet.com
Home Page: www.cpasnet.com

An association of accounting and business consulting firms who have pooled their resources to
provide their clients with the local, national,
and international perspective needed to prosper.
500 Members

43 **Construction Financial Management Association**
100 Village Blvd
Suite 200
Princeton, NJ 08540-5783

609-452-8000
888-421-9996
FAX 609-452-0474
E-Mail: info@cfma.org
Home Page: www.cfma.org
Social Media: *Facebook, Twitter, LinkedIn, YouTube*

Stuart Binstock, President/CEO
Brian Summers, VP, Content Strategy &
Education
Robert Rubin, CPA, VP, Finance &
Administration
Michael Verbanic, Director/Member
Experience
Stacy Williams, Admin Assistant, Membership

CFMA is the only organization dedicated to
bringing together construction financial professionals and those partners serving their unique
needs. CFMA has 89 chapters located throughout the US and Canada.
7000 Members
Founded in 1981

44 **Construction Industry CPA/Consultants Association**
15011 East Twilight View Drive
Fountain Hills, AZ 85268

480-836-0300
800-864-0491
FAX 480-836-0400
E-Mail: info@cicpac.com
Home Page: www.cicpac.com
Social Media: *Facebook, LinkedIn*

Chris Iannuzzi, President
Jacquelyn Daenen, Vice President
Kathleen Baldwin, Secretary/ Treasurer
Ken Gardiner, President Elect
John J. Corcoran, CPA, Executive Director

The Construction Industry CPAs/Consultants
Association (CICPAC) is a national association
of CPA firms recognized in their respective
markets for providing high quality financial
and consulting services. Each firm is the exclusive member in its area and must demonstrate
proficiency in construction industry services
and a reputation for high-quality work and
integrity.
7500 Members
Founded in 1989

45 **Construction Industry CPAs/Consultants Association**
15011 East Twilight View Drive
Fountain Hills, AZ 85268

480-836-0300
FAX 480-836-0400
E-Mail: info@cicpac.com
Home Page: www.cicpac.com
Social Media: *Facebook, LinkedIn*

Chris Iannuzzi, President
Ken Gardiner, President Elect
Jacquelyn Daenen, Vice President
Kathleen Baldwin, Secretary/Treasurer
John J. Corcoran, CPA, Executive Director
Founded in 1989

46 **Federal Accounting Standards Advisory Board**
441 G St. NW
Mailstop 6H19
Washington, DC 20548

202-512-7350
FAX 202-512-7366
E-Mail: fasab@fasab.gov
Home Page: www.fasab.gov
Social Media: *Twitter, LinkedIn*

Tom Allen, Chairman
Wendy Payne, Executive Director
Robin Gillam, Assistant Director
Melissa Batchelor, Assistant Director
Domenic Savini, Assistant Director

Establishes accounting standards for financial
reporting entities of the United States Government.
Founded in 1990

47 **Federation of Schools of Accountancy**
220 Leigh Farm Road
Durham, NC 27707-8110

919-402-4825
E-Mail: mtarasi@aicpa.org
Home Page: www.thefsa.org

Michael Roberts, President
Rebecca Shortridge, Vice President/ President
Elect
Michael Akers, Secretary
Parveen Gupta, Treasurer
Robert Ricketts, Past President

Promotes and supports high-quality graduate
accounting programs and achieves public trust
in the accounting profession through leadership
in supporting and shaping high quality accounting education.
169 Members
Founded in 1978

48 **Federation of Tax Administrators**
444 N. Capitol Street NW
Suite 348
Washington, DC 20001

202-624-5890
FAX 202-624-7888
Home Page: www.taxadmin.org

Linda Tanton, Chief Counsel
Verenda Smith, Deputy Director
Darrell Reeves, Office Manager
Gale Garriott, Executive Director
John Feldmann, Senior Manager of
Compliance

A nonprofit corporation designed to improve
the quality of state tax administration by providing services to state tax authorities and administrators. These services include research
and information exchange, training, and intergovernmental and interstate coordination.
Founded in 1937

49 **Financial Accounting Standards Board**
401 Merritt Boulevard
PO Box 5116
Norwalk, CT 06856-5116

203-847-0700
FAX 203-849-9714
E-Mail: director@fasb.org
Home Page: www.fasb.org
Social Media: *Facebook, LinkedIn, RSS, YouTube*

Russell G. Golden, Chairman
Jeffrey D. Mechanick, Assistant Director
Susan M Cosper, Technical Director
Suzanne Q. Bielstein, Director-Planning and
Support
Matthew Esposito, Assistant Director

The mission of the FASB is to establish and
improve standards of financial accounting and
reporting that foster financial reporting by
nongovernmental entities that provides deci-
sion-useful information to investors and other
users of financial reports. That mission is accomplished through a comprehensive and independent process that encourages broad
participation, objectively considers all stakeholder views, and is subject to oversight by the
Financial Accounting Foundation's Board of
Trustees.
Founded in 1973

50 **Financial Executives International**
1250 Headquarters Plaza
West Tower, 7th Floor
Morristown, NJ 07960

973-765-1000
FAX 973-765-1018
E-Mail: membership@financialexecutives.org
Home Page: www.financialexecutives.org
Social Media: *Facebook, Twitter, LinkedIn, YouTube, Google+*

Mitch Danaher, Chairman
Andrej Suskavcevic, President/CEO
Lili DeVita, VP & Chief Operating Officer
Paul Chase, VP and CFO
Jamie Cherkas, Executive Assistant to the CEO

FEI strives to be recognized globally as the
leading organization for senior-level financial
executives. Connects members through: interaction: providing local and international forums for connecting with peers, information:
providing insight to assist with informed business decisions, influence: providing authoritative representation for members' interests, and
integrity: providing the tools to advance the
profession through ethical leadership.
15M Members
Founded in 1931

51 **Financial Management Association International**
University of South Florida
4202 E Fowler Ave
BSN 3331
Tampa, FL 33620-5500

813-974-2084
FAX 813-974-3318
E-Mail: fma@coba.usf.edu
Home Page: www.fma.org
Social Media: *Facebook, Twitter*

Jay R. Ritter, President
David Denis, President Elect
Brad Barber, VP Program

Ronald Masulis, VP Global Services
Andrea J. Heuson, Secretary/Treasurer

Serving the global finance community by: Promoting the development of high-quality research that extends the frontier of financial knowledge; Promoting the understanding of basic and applied research and of sound financial practices; Enhancing the quality and relevance of education in finance; Providing opportunities for professional interaction between and among academics, practitioners, and students.
Founded in 1970

52   Financial Managers Society

1 North LaSalle Street
Suite 3100
Chicago, IL 60602-4003

312-578-1300
800-275-4367
FAX 312-578-1308
E-Mail: info@fmsinc.org
Home Page: www.fmsinc.org
Social Media: *Facebook, Twitter, LinkedIn*

Sydney K. Garmong, CPA, Chairman
John Westwood, Vice Chairman
Dick Yingst, President
Tom King, Director, Professional Dev
Mark Loehrke, Editor/Writer

Provides service to financial personnel such as savings and loan financial officers, and to community commercial banks and credit unions.
Founded in 1948

53   Government Finance Officers Association

203 N. LaSalle Street
Suite 2700
Chicago, IL 60601-1210

312-977-9700
FAX 312-977-4806
Home Page: www.gfoa.org
Social Media: *Facebook, Twitter, LinkedIn, YouTube*

Heather A. Johnston, President
Marc Gonzales, President Elect
Jeffrey Esser, Executive Director/CEO
John Jurkash, Chief Financial Officer
Tami Garrett, Secretary

Represents public finance officials throughout the United States and Canada and promotes the professional management of governmental financial resources by indentifying, developing, and advancing fiscal strategies, policies, and practices for the public benefit.
Founded in 1906

54   Government Officers Finance Association

203 North Lasalle Street
Suite 2700
Chicago, IL 60601-1210

312-977-9700
FAX 312-977-4806
Home Page: www.gfoa.org
Social Media: *Facebook, Twitter, LinkedIn, YouTube*

Heather A. Johnston, President
Marc Gonzales, President-Elect
Jeffrey L. Esser, Executive Director CEO
John Jurkash, Chief Financial Officer
Tami Garrett, Secretary

The purpose of the Government Finance Officers Association is to enhance and promote the professional management of governments for the public benefit by identifying and developing financial policies and best practices and promoting their use through education, training, facilitation of member networking, and leadership.
16000 Members
Founded in 1906

55   Healthcare Financial Management Association

3 Westbrook Corporate Center
Suite 7600
Westchester, IL 60154-5723

708-531-9600
800-252-4362
FAX 708-531-0032
E-Mail: jfifer@hfma.org
Home Page: www.hfma.org
Social Media: *Facebook, Twitter, LinkedIn, YouTube*

Joseph J. Fifer, FHFMA, CPA, President & Chief Executive Officer
Edwin P. Czopek, Executive Vice President & CFO
Susan Brenkus, VP, HR & Chapter Relations
Richard L. Gundling, VP, Healthcare Financial Practices
Todd Nelson, VP, Education & Org Solutions

HFMA is the nation's leading membership organization for healthcare financial management executives and leaders. HFMA's vision is to be the indispensable resource for healthcare finance.
40000 Members
Founded in 1950

56   Hospitality Financial and Technology Professionals

11709 Boulder Lane
Suite 110
Austin, TX 78726

512-249-5333
800-646-4387
FAX 512-249-1533
E-Mail: Membership@hftp.org
Home Page: www.hftp.org
Social Media: *Facebook, Twitter, LinkedIn*

Daniel N. Conti, Jr., CHAE, CAM, President
Arlene Ramirez, Vice President
Frank I Wolfe, Ex Officio
Lyle Worthington, CHTP, Treasurer
Jerry M. Trieber, Immediate Past President

HFTP is an international, professional association providing a global network, continuing education and resources to the hospitality, finance and technology communities.
4600 Members
Founded in 1952

57   INPACT Americas

PO Box 495
Frederick, MD 21705-0495

301-694-8580
FAX 301-694-5804
E-Mail: Mara@inpactam.org
Home Page: www.inpactam.org

Reynold P. Cicalese, President
Mara Ambrose, Executive Director
Kevin R. Hessler, Treasurer / President-Elect
Loraine Koepenick, Coordinator of Member Services
James A. Ruzon, Immediate Past President

A nonprofit association focused on contributing to the profitability and success of North America's accounting and consulting firms through management and marketing programs and resources.

58   Information Resources Management Association

701 E Chocolate Ave
Suite 200
Hershey, PA 17033-1240

717-533-8845
FAX 717-533-8661

E-Mail: member@irma-international.org
Home Page: www.irma-international.org

Jan Travers, Executive Director
Sherif Kamel, Communications Director
Lech Janczewski PhD, IRMA World Representative Director
Gerald Grant, IRMA Doctoral Symposium Director
Paul Chalekian, IRMA United States Representative

An international professional organization dedicated to advancing the concepts and practices of information resources management in modern organizations. The primary objective of IRMA is to assist organizations and professionals in enhancing the overall knowledge and understanding of effective information resource management in the early 21st century and beyond.

59   Information Systems Audit & Control Association (ISACA)

3701 Algonquin Rd
Suite 1010
Rolling Meadows, IL 60008-3124

847-253-1545
FAX 847-253-1443
E-Mail: news@isaca.org
Home Page: www.isaca.org
Social Media: *Facebook, Twitter, LinkedIn, Google+*

Tony Hayes, International President
Allan Boardman, International Vice President
Juan Luis Carselle, International Vice President
Rams,s Gallego, International Vice President
Theresa Grafenstine, International Vice President

With members in more than 160 countries, ISACA is a recognized worldwide leader in IT governance, control, security and assurance. Sponsors international conferences, publishes the thw ISACA Journal and develops international information systems auditing and control standards.
14000 Members
Founded in 1969

60   Institute for Professionals in Taxation

600 Northpark Town Center
1200 Abernathy Rd., Suite L-2
Atlanta, GA 30328-1040

404-240-2300
FAX 404-240-2315
E-Mail: website@ipt.org
Home Page: www.ipt.org

Margaret C. Wilson, CMI, Esq., President
Chris G. Muntifering, CMI, First Vice President
Kellianne N. Nagy, CMI, CAE, Second Vice President
Margaret Dickson, Chief Financial Officer
Cass D. Vickers, Executive Director

A nonprofit educational association that provides educational programs, certifies, and establishes strict codes of conduct for state and local income, property, and sales.
4100+ Members
Founded in 1976

61   Institute of Internal Auditors

247 Maitland Ave
Altamonte Springs, FL 32701-4201

407-937-1111
FAX 407-937-1101
E-Mail: CustomerRelations@theiia.org
Home Page: na.theiia.org
Social Media: *Facebook, Twitter, LinkedIn, Auditchannel.tv*

Lawrence J. Harrington, Chairman
Angela Witzany, Senior Vice Chairman of the Board
Frank M. O'Brien, CIA, QIAL, Vice Chairman

- Research
Harold C. Silverman, Vice Chairman
Naohiro Mouri, CIA, Vice Chairman

Independent, objective assurance and consulting activity designed to add value to an organization's operations. It helps an organization accomplish its objectives by bringing a systematic, disciplined approach to evaluate and improve the effectiveness of risk management, control and governance processes. Representation from more than 100 countries.
18000 Members
Founded in 1941

62   Institute of Management Accountants
10 Paragon Dr
Suite 1
Montvale, NJ 07645-1760

201-573-9000
800-638-4427
FAX 201-474-1600
E-Mail: ima@imanet.org
Home Page: www.imanet.org
Social Media: *Facebook, Twitter, LinkedIn, YouTube*

Benjamin R. Mulling, Chair
Jeffrey C. Thomson, President and CEO
Marc P. Palker, CMA, Chair-Elect
Joseph A. Vincent, CMA, Chair-Emeritus

Professional organization devoted exclusively to management accounting and financial management. Goals are to help members develop both personally and professionally, by means of education, certification and association with other business professionals.
70,00 Members
Founded in 1919

63   Institute of Management and Administration
3 Bethesda Metro Center
Suite 250
Bethesda, MD 20814-5377

800-372-1033
703-341-3500
FAX 800-253-0332
E-Mail: blawhelp@bna.com
Home Page: www.bna.com
Social Media: *Facebook, Twitter, LinkedIn, YouTube*

Gregory C. McCaffery, CEO & President
Sue Martin, Chief Operating Officer
Paul Albergo, Bureau Chief
Joe Breda, EVP, Product
Daniel M. Fine, EVP, Strategy

An independent source of exclusive business management information for experienced senior and middle management proessionals.

64   Insurance Accounting & Systems Association, Inc.
3511 Shannon Road
Suite 160
Durham, NC 27707

919-489-0991
FAX 919-489-1994
E-Mail: info@iasa.org
Home Page: www.iasa.org
Social Media: *Facebook, Twitter, LinkedIn, YouTube*

Forrest Mills, Jr., Chairman
Tim Morgan, President
Joe Pomilia, Executive Director
Tom Ewbank, CFO
Carlos A Correa, CIO

A nonprofit, education association that strives to enhance the knowledge of insurance professionals and participants from similar organizations closely allied with the insurance industry by facilitating the exchange of ideas and information.

65   International Cost Estimating and Analysis Association
8221 Old Courthouse Rd
Suite 106
Vienna, VA 22182

703-938-5090
FAX 703-938-5091
E-Mail: iceaa@iceaaonline.org
Home Page: www.iceaaonline.org
Social Media: *Facebook, Twitter*

Paul R. Marston, President
Michael J. Thompson, Executive Vice President
Peter Braxton, VP, Professional Development
Greg Kiviat, Secretary
Bob Hunt, Treasurer

A non-profit organization dedicated to improving cost estimating and analysis in government and industry by enhancing the competence and achievements of its professional members
2015 Members
Founded in 2012

66   International Federation of Accountants
529 Fifth Avenue
6th Floor
New York, NY 10017

212-286-9344
FAX 212-286-9570
E-Mail: communications@ifac.org
Home Page: www.ifac.org
Social Media: *Facebook, Twitter, LinkedIn, YouTube*

Olivia Kirtley, President
Rachel Grimes, Deputy President
Fayezul Choudhury, CEO
Russell Guthrie, Executive Director
Alta Prinsloo, Executive Director

IFAC is the global organization for the accountancy profession. It works with members and associates in 123 countries and jurisdictions to protect the public interest by encouraging high quality practices by the world's accountants.
173 Members
Founded in 1977

67   National Academy of Public Administration
1600 K Street NW
Suite 400
Washington, DC 20006

202-347-3190
FAX 202-223-0823
E-Mail: feedback@napawash.org
Home Page: www.napawash.org
Social Media: *Facebook, Twitter, LinkedIn, Vimeo*

Robert J. Shea, Chair
Nancy R. Kingsbury, Vice Chair
Dan G Blair, President and CEO
B.J Reed, Secretary
Sallyanne Harper, Treasurer

An independent, nonprofit, and non-partisan organization that helpsthe Federal government address its critical management challenges through in-depth studies and analyses, advisory services and technical assistance, Congressional testimony, forums and conferences, and online stakeholder engagement.
800 Members
Founded in 1967

68   National Association of Black Accountants
7474 Greenway Center Drive
Suite 1120
Greenbelt, MD 20770

301-474-6222
888-571-2939

FAX 301-474-3114
E-Mail: customerservice@nabainc.org
Home Page: www.nabainc.org
Social Media: *Facebook, Twitter, LinkedIn, YouTube*

Jina Etienne, CPA, CGMA, President/CEO
Lauren Yost, SPHR, Chief Operating Officer
Kenneth E. Cooke, CPA, Chairman
Rhonda Johnson Adams, Controller
Stephen Schultz, Director of Conferences

Nationwide professional association with the primary purpose of developing, encouraging and serving as a resource for greater participation by African-Americans and other minorities in the accounting and finance professions.
Founded in 1969

69   National Association of Certified Valuators and Analysts (NACVA)
5217 South State Street
Suite 400
Salt Lake City, UT 84107

801-486-0600
800-677-2009
FAX 801-486-7500
E-Mail: nacva1@nacva.com
Home Page: www.nacva.com
Social Media: *Facebook, Twitter, YouTube*

Terry A. Isom, WA, Chairman
Brien K. Jones, COO/EVP
Melissa Cardwell, Director of Project Management
Parnell Black, CEO
Pam Bailey, Executive Director

Global, professional association that supports the business valuation and litigation consulting disciplines within the CPA and professional communities. Along with its training and certification progams, NACVA offers a range of support services, reference materials, software, and customized databases to enahnce the professional capabilities and capacities of its members.
6500 Members
Founded in 1990

70   National Association of Computerized Tax Processors
H&R Block
4400 Main Street
Kansas City, MO 64111

816-328-8485
FAX 800-996-3526
Home Page: www.nactp.org
Social Media: *Facebook*

Rebecca McCaulley, President
Zeke Gikas, Vice President
Mary Zuroske, Treasurer
Vicki Massey, Secretary
Angela Camp, Webmaster

Nonprofit association that represents tax processing software and hardware developers, electronic filing processors, tax form publishers and tax processing service bureaus. The association promotes standards in tax processing and works closely with the Internal Revenue Service and state governments to promote efficient and effective tax filing.
14100 Members
Founded in 1969

71   National Association of Construction Auditors
7305 Hancock Village Drive
Suite 519
Chesterfield, VA 23832

804-608-8703
FAX 888-702-1059
E-Mail: info@thenaca.org

Home Page: www.thenaca.org
Social Media: *Facebook, Twitter, LinkedIn*

Brian D. Felix, Chairman/Founder
Carl E. Hansen, Vice Chairman
Larry G. Baker, Secretary/Treasurer

Provides resources, information, and leadership for NACA members, their clients, and the public to ensure the highest standard of construction control environments possible.

72   National Association of Enrolled Agents
1730 Rhode Island Avenue, NW
Suite 400
Washington, DC 20036-3953

202-822-6232
855-880-6232
FAX 202-822-6270
E-Mail: info@naea.org
Home Page: www.naea.org
Social Media: *Facebook, Twitter, LinkedIn, YouTube*

Terry Durkin, EA, MBA, President
John L. Fiegel, CAE, Interim Executive Vice President
Katrina Holland, Director of Membership
Gloriel Rodriguez, Membership Coordinator
Maya English, Senior Program Coordinator

Members are individuals who are enrolled to represent taxpayers before the Internal Revenue Service. We advise, represent and prepare tax returns for individuals, partnerships, corporations, estates, trusts and any entities with tax reporting requirements.
11000 Members
Founded in 1972

73   National Association of Insurance and Financial Advisors
2901 Telestar Court
Falls Church, VA 22042-1205

877-866-2432
Home Page: www.naifa.org
Social Media: *Facebook, Twitter, LinkedIn, YouTube*

Jules O. Gaudreau, Jr., President
Paul R. Dougherty, President Elect
Keith M. Gillies, Secretary
Matthew S. Tassey, Treasurer
Kevin M. Mayeux, CAE, Chief Executive Officer

Serves and represents insurance and financial advisors, advocates for a positive legislative and regulatory environment, enhances business and professional skills, and promotes the ethical conduct of its members.
Founded in 1890

74   National Association of Mutual Insurance Companies
3601 Vincennes Road
Indianapolis, IN 46268

317-875-5250
FAX 317-879-8408
Home Page: www.namic.org
Social Media: *Facebook, Twitter, LinkedIn, YouTube, RSS*

Paul G. Stueven, PFMM, Chairman
Steve Linkous, Chairman Elect
Paul A. Ehlert, J.D., Vice Chairman
Charles Chamness, President/CEO
Christopher P. Taft, CIC, CPA, Secretary/Treasurer

The largest property/casualty insurance trade association that has educational and advocacy programs to promote public policy solutions that benefit policyholders and the NAMIC member companies that exist to serve them.
Founded in 1920

75   National Association of Personal Financial Advisors
8700 W. Bryn Mawr Avenue
Suite 700N
Chicago, IL 60631

847-483-5400
888-333-6659
FAX 847-483-5415
E-Mail: info@napfa.org
Home Page: www.napfa.org
Social Media: *Facebook, Twitter, LinkedIn, YouTube*

Frank Moore, Chair
Tim Kober, Vice Chair
J. David Lewis, Treasurer
Geoffrey Brown, CEO
Chris Hale, Managing Editor

Professional association of Fee-Only financial advisors who advocate for client-focused financial planning with a Fee-Only compensation.
Founded in 1983

76   National Association of State Auditors, Comptrollers and Treasurers
449 Lewis Hargett Circle
Suite 290
Lexington, KY 40503-3590

859-276-1147
FAX 859-278-0507
Home Page: www.nasact.org

Calvin McKelvogue, President
Richard K. Ellis, First Vice President
Debbie Davenport, Second Vice President
R. Kinney Poynter, CPA, Executive Director
D. Clark Partridge, Secretary

Serves as the premier organization working to bring together state auditors, state comptrollers and state treasurers to cooperatively address government financial management issues.

77   National Association of State Boards of Accountancy
150 Fourth Ave. North
Ste. 700
Nashville, TN 37219-2417

615-880-4200
FAX 615-880-4290
E-Mail: cpe@nasba.org
Home Page: nasba.org
Social Media: *Facebook, Twitter, LinkedIn, YouTube, RSS*

Walter C. Davenport, Chairman
Donald H. Burkett, Vice Chairman
Ken L. Bishop, President/CEO
Laurie J. Tish, Secretary
E. Kent Smoll, Treasurer

Enhances the effectiveness and advances the common interests of theBoards of Accountancy by creating a forum for accounting regulators and practitioners to address issues relevant to the viability of the accounting profession.
Founded in 1908

78   National Association of State Budget Officers
444 North Capitol Street NW
Suite 642
Washington, DC 20001

202-624-5382
FAX 202-624-7745
E-Mail: nasbo-direct@nasbo.org
Home Page: www.nasbo.org
Social Media: *Facebook, Twitter, LinkedIn, Google+*

Tom Mullaney, President
Margaret Kelly, President Elect
Scott D. Pattison, Executive Director
Stacey Mazer, Senior Staff Associate
Brian Sigritz, Director of State Fiscal Studies

Provides a range of publications, services, and knowledge-sharing opportunities for its members and others interested in state finance issues.

79   National Association of Tax Professionals
PO Box 8002
Appleton, WI 54912-8002

800-558-3402
FAX 800-747-0001
E-Mail: natp@natptax.com
Home Page: www.natptax.com
Social Media: *Facebook, Twitter, LinkedIn, MySpace, YouTube*

Jean Millerchip, EA, CFP, President
Kelly A. Nokleby, EA, Vice President
Gerard F. Cannito, CPA, CFP, Interim CEO
Matt Bone, CPA, Director of Finance/Administration
Nancy Kasten, Director, Marketing & BD

NATP members have access to a wide range of the most reliable industry resources, which ultimately save time and money. Members enjoy the support and knowledge that comes from joining the only professional organization that is 100% devoted to tax expertise.
Founded in 1979

80   National CPA Health Care Advisors Association
1801 West End Avenue
Suite 800
Nashville, TN 37203

615-373-9880
800-231-2524
FAX 615-377-7092
E-Mail: info@hcaa.com
Home Page: www.hcaa.com
Social Media: *Twitter*

Hal (Buzz) Coons, III, President
James White, Vice President
Brian Bourke, Secretary
William Rooney, Treasurer
Greg Papineau, Past President

HCAA is an association of CPA firms that provide services to health care providers beyond traditional compliance work. Members are admitted on a territorial exclusive basis, one member in each territory.

81   National Conference of CPA Practitioners
22 Jericho Turnpike
Suite 110
Mineola, NY 11501

516-333-8282
888-488-5400
FAX 516-333-4099
Home Page: go.nccpap.org/
Social Media: *Facebook, Twitter, LinkedIn, Flickr, YouTube*

NCCAP is a group of CPA professionals that allows small CPA firms and the sole practitioner to have a greater community impact and presence. This organization also gives back through its local chapters and at the national level.

82   National Society of Accountants
1330 Braddock Place
Suite 540
Alexandria, VA 22314-1574

703-549-6400
800-966-6679
FAX 703-549-2984
E-Mail: members@nsacct.org
Home Page: www.nsacct.org
Social Media: *Facebook, Twitter, LinkedIn*

Kathy R. Hettick, President
Alfred Giovetti, First Vice President

Brian Thompson, Second Vice President
John G. Ams, Executive Vice President
Jodi Goldberg, Vice President

Professional society of practicing accountants and tax practitioners that sponsors the Accreditation Council for Accountancy and Taxation and supports the National Society of Public Accountants Political Action Committee and NSPA Scholarship Foundation.
30000 Members
Founded in 1945

83 National Society of Accountants for Cooperatives
136 South Keowee Street
Dayton, OH 45402

937-222-6707
FAX 937-222-5794
E-Mail: info@nsacoop.org
Home Page: www.nsacoop.org
Social Media: *Facebook*

Kim Fantaci, Executive Director
Carrie Parrish, President
Stanley Mitchell, CFO, Vice President
Jeff Roberts, Association Executive
Krista Saul, Client Accounting Manager

A professional society involved with the financial management and planning of cooperative business. It also provides educational programming, networking opportunities, and a directory of other professionals.
2000 Members
Founded in 1936

84 National Tax Association
725 15th St. NW
Ste. 600
Washington, DC 20005-2109

202-737-3325
FAX 202-737-7308
E-Mail: natltax@aol.com
Home Page: www.ntanet.org

Alan Auerbach, President
Peter Brady, Vice President
Victoria Perry, Vice President
Charmaine J. Wright, Secretary
Eric Toder, Treasurer

A nonpartisan, nonpolitical educational association of tax professionals dedicatd to advancing understanding of the theory and practice of public finance.
Founded in 1907

85 PKF North America
1745 N. Brown Road
Suite 350
Lawrenceville, GA 30043

770-279-4560
FAX 770-279-4566
E-Mail: tsnyder@pkfna.org
Home Page: www.pkfna.org
Social Media: *Facebook, Twitter, LinkedIn, YouTube*

Terry Snyder, President
Debbie Kuhl, Vice President

An association of legally independently-owned accounting and consulting firms with offices in North America and throughout the world through its affiliation with PKF International.
402 Members

86 PrimeGlobal
3235 Satellite Bvld Bldg. 400
Suite 300
Duluth, GA 30096

678-417-7730
FAX 678-999-3959
E-Mail: kmead@primeglobal.net
Home Page: www.primeglobal.net

Social Media: *Facebook, Twitter, LinkedIn, YouTube*
Michelle Arnold, Chief Regional Officer
Kevin Mead, President/CEO
Anne Hampson, CFO
Stacey Sanchez, Director, Global Events
Kathy Sautters, Communications Director

PrimeGlobal is an international affiliation of independent accounting and consulting firms.
200 Members
Founded in 1978

87 Society of Actuaries
475 N Martingale Rd
Suite 600
Schaumburg, IL 60173-2252

847-706-3500
888-697-3900
FAX 847-706-3599
E-Mail: customerservice@soa.org
Home Page: www.soa.org
Social Media: *Twitter, LinkedIn, YouTube*

Greg Heidrich, Executive Director
Stacy Lin, Deputy Executive Director/CFO
Tiffany Berger, Director of Finance & Facilities
Richard Veys, General Counsel
Michael Boot, Managing Director of Sections

An educational, research and professional organization dedicated to serving the public and society members. The vision is for actuaries to be recognized as the leading professional in the modeling and management of risk.
17000 Members
Founded in 1889
Mailing list available for rent: 17000 names at $300 per M

88 Society of Financial Examiners
12100 Sunset Hills Rd
Suite 130
Reston, VA 20190-3221

703-234-4140
800-787-7633
FAX 888-436-8686
E-Mail: sofe@sofe.org
Home Page: www.sofe.org
Social Media: *Facebook, LinkedIn*

Annette Knief, CFE, President
Joanne Campanelli, CFE, Vice President
Susan Bernard, CFE, AES, Vice President
Mark Murphy, CFE, Secretary
Colette Hogan Sawyer, CFE, Vice President

The Society of Financial Examiners is a professional society for examiners of insurance companies, banks, savings and loans, and credit unions.
1700+ Members
Founded in 1973

89 Society of Financial Service Professionals
3803 West Chester Pike
Suite 225
Newtown Square, PA 19073-3239

610-526-2500
800-392-6900
FAX 610-359-8115
E-Mail: Info@FinancialPro.org
Home Page: www.financialpro.org
Social Media: *Facebook, Twitter, LinkedIn, YouTube, Flickr, RSS*

Michael P. Dow, President
James M. Christian, Immediate Past President
Anthony R. Bartlett, President Elect
James S. Aussem, JD, AEP, Secretary
Joseph E. Frack, Chief Executive Officer

Provides financial products and planning services in order to help individuals, families, and businesses achieve financial security.
11000 Members
Founded in 1928

90 The American Society of IRS Problem Solvers
170 South River Road
Bedford, NH 3110

800-322-0933
Home Page: www.irsproblemsolvers.com

A select group of licensed tax professionals located in communities across the United States to help taxpayers end individual and business IRS problems.

91 The Professional Accounting Society of America
Home Page: www.thepasa.org

A professional organization designed specifically for entry-level and mid-level associates working at accounting firms across America.
Founded in 2005

Newsletters

92 AAA Report
Association for Accounting Administration
136 S Keowee Street
Dayton, OH 45402

937-222-0030
FAX 937-222-5794
E-Mail: aaainfo@cpaadmin.org
Home Page: www.cpaadmin.org

Dennis Lemieux, President
Norman Saale, Vice President
Janine Zirrith, Secretary
Jim Fahey, Treasurer
Jane Johnson, Director of Education

Qarterly newsletter for the professional manager.
12 Pages
Frequency: Four/Year
Founded in 1984
Printed in 4 colors

93 AGA Today
Association of Government Accountants
2208 Mount Vernon Ave
Alexandria, VA 22301-1314

703-562-0900
800-242-7211
FAX 703-548-9367
E-Mail: agacgfm@agacgfm.org
Home Page: www.agacgfm.org

Relmond Van Daniker, Executive Director
Evelyn Brown, National President

This publication acts as a clearinghouse for current government financial management information.
Frequency: Bi-Weekly
Circulation: 12,000

94 ARCH
Society of Actuaries
475 N Martingale Rd
Suite 600
Schaumburg, IL 60173-2252

847-706-3500
FAX 847-706-3599
E-Mail: webmaster@soa.org
Home Page: www.soa.org

Greg Heidrich, Executive Director
Stacy Lin, Deputy Executive Director/CFO
Tiffany Berger, Director of Finance
Richard Veys, General Counsel

ARCH is an informal communication providing current actuarial research to friends and members of the actuarial community. Its primary goal is the speedy dissemination of current thinking and aids to research.

95 ASMC Connections
415 N Alfred St
Alexandria, VA 22314-2269

703-549-0360
800-462-5637
FAX 703-549-3181
Home Page: www.asmconline.org
Social Media: *Facebook, Twitter, LinkedIn*

Marilyn Thomas, President
Art Hagler, VP
Kathy Watern, VP
Nancy Phillips, Treasurer

Provides insight into defense financial news, chapter spot lights, and other society news.
19m+ Members
Founded in 1948

96 AWSCPA News
American Woman's Society of CPAs
136 South Keowee Street
Dayton, OH 45402

937-222-1872
800-297-2721
FAX 937-222-5794
E-Mail: info@awscpa.org
Home Page: www.awscpa.org

Amy Knowles-Jones, President
Kelly Welter, President Elect
Alexandra Miller, Secretary/Treasurer
Cynthia Cox, VP - Member Services

Available electronically.
Frequency: Quarterly
Circulation: 1500
Founded in 1933
Printed in 4 colors

97 AcSEC Update
American Institute of Certified Public Accountants
1211 Avenue of the Americas
Suite 6
New York, NY 10036-8701

212-596-6200
FAX 212-596-6213
E-Mail: service@aicpa.org
Home Page: www.aicpa.org
Social Media: *Facebook, Twitter, LinkedIn*

Barry C Melancon, CEO
Susan Coffey, Senior Vice President
Lawson Carmichael, SVP - Strategy, People, Innovation
Arleen Thomas, SVP - Mgmt Accounting

Provides information about recently issued AcSEC pronouncments and current AcSEC projects.
Frequency: 4 Times/Year
Founded in 1887

98 Accounting Alerts
Grant Thornton
175 W Jackson Blvd
20th Floor
Chicago, IL 60604-2687

312-856-0001
FAX 312-602-8099
Home Page: www.grantthornton.com
Social Media: *Twitter*

Stephen Chipman, CEO
Lou Grabowsky, COO
Russ Wieman, Chief Financial Officer

Periodic newsletter that highlights important accounting developments.
Founded in 1924

99 Accounting Education News
American Accounting Association
5717 Bessie Dr
Sarasota, FL 34233-2399

941-921-7747
FAX 941-923-4093

E-Mail: info@aaahq.org
Home Page: aaahq.org

Tracey Sutherland, Executive Director
Deirdre Harris, Publication Contact
Diane Hazard, Publications Director

Information on industry development and associations, the newsletter is only available to members.
8600 Members
Frequency: Quarterly
Circulation: 8500
Founded in 1916
Printed in 3 colors on matte stock

100 Accounting Historians Notebook
Academy of Accounting Historians
10900 Euclid Avenue
Cleveland, OH 44106-7235

216-368-2058
FAX 216-368-6244
E-Mail: acchistory@case.edu
Home Page: www.aahhq.org

Joanne Cross, President
Robert Colson, President Elect
Yvette Lazdowski, VP, Communications
Robert Colson, VP Communications
Stephanie Moussalli, Secretary

Published by the Academy of Accounting Historians, the Notebook provides information about the Academy, its members, conference, and publications. Subscription to the semi-annual publication is included in membership to the Academy.
600 Members
8 Pages
Frequency: Semi-Annual
Founded in 1973
Printed in one color

101 Accounting Office Management & Administration Report
Institute of Management and Administration
3 Bethesda Metro Center
Suite 250
Bethesda, MD 20814-5377

800-372-1033
703-341-3500
FAX 800-253-0332
E-Mail: customercare@bna.com
Home Page: www.ioma.com

Designed for use by anyone responsible for the day-to-day management of a CPA firm. Provides actionable information that readers can use to manage their firms efficiently and profitably.
Cost: $469.00
Frequency: Monthly
Founded in 1984

102 Accounting and Auditing Update Service
Thomson Reuters
2395 Midway Rd
Carrollton, TX 75006

817-332-3709
800-431-9025
FAX 888-216-1929
E-Mail: trta.lei-support@thomsonreuters.com
Home Page: www.ria.thomsonreuters.com

Elaine Yadlon, Plant Manager
Thomas H Glocer, CEO & Director
Robert D Daleo, Chief Financial Officer
Kelli Crane, Senior Vice President & CIO

Analyzes FASB and AICPA pronouncements.
Cost: $465.00
Frequency: Bi-Weekly
Founded in 1935

103 Attorney/CPA Newsletter
American Association of Attorney-CPAs

8647 Richmond Highway
Suite 639
Alexandria, VA 22309

703-352-8064
888-288-9272
FAX 703-352-8073
E-Mail: info@attorney-cpa.com
Home Page: www.attorney-cpa.com

Robert Driegert, President
Domenick Lioce, President Elect
Joseph Cordell, Treasurer
John Pramberg, Secretary

To promote the study and understanding of law and accounting and those related professions.
Frequency: Quarterly
Founded in 1964

104 Behavioral Research in Accounting
American Accounting Association
5717 Bessie Dr
Sarasota, FL 34233

941-921-7747
FAX 941-923-4093
E-Mail: info@aaahq.org
Home Page: www.aaahq.org

Tracey Sutherland, Executive Director
Julie Smith David, CIO
Diane Ledger, Director of Finance

To promote the wide dissemination of the results of systematic scholarly inquiries into the broad field of accounting.
Cost: $20.00
Frequency: Twice per Year
Circulation: 1400

105 BusIndNews
American Institute of Certified Public Accountants
1211 Avenue of the Americas
Suite 6
New York, NY 10036-8701

212-596-6200
FAX 212-596-6213
E-Mail: service@aicpa.org
Home Page: www.aicpa.org
Social Media: *Facebook, Twitter, LinkedIn*

Barry C Melancon, CEO
Susan Coffey, Senior Vice President
Lawson Carmichael, SVP - Strategy
Arleen Thomas, SVP - Mgmt Accounting

The AICPA e-newsletter for members in business and industry, contains timely information on current issues and developments in areas related to business and industry.
Frequency: Monthly
Founded in 1887

106 Business Valuation Monitor
Grant Thornton
175 W Jackson Blvd
20th Floor
Chicago, IL 60604-2687

312-856-0001
FAX 312-602-8099
Home Page: www.grantthornton.com
Social Media: *Twitter, LinkedIn*

Stephen Chipman, CEO
Lou Grabowsky, COO
Russ Wieman, CFO

Newsletter covering value creation perspectives for corporate executives and the investment community in the areas of financial reporting, transaction support, damage calculations in disputes, intellectual property, bankruptcy proceedings and corporate tax planning.
Founded in 1924

107 CAE Bulletin
Institute of Internal Auditors

247 Maitland Ave
Altamonte Spgs, FL 32701-4201

407-830-7600
FAX 407-937-1101
E-Mail: custserv@theiia.org
Home Page: www.theiia.org

J. Michael Pepper, Chairman
Carolyn Saint, Senior Vice President
John Wxzelaki, Vice Chairman -
Finance/Security

Newsletter that alerts members to news, guidance and information that helps professionals become as effective as possible in their jobs.
Frequency: Twice Monthly

108   CPA Insider
American Institute of Certified Public Accountants
1211 Avenue of the Americas
Suite 6
New York, NY 10036-8701

212-596-6200
FAX 212-596-6213
E-Mail: service@aicpa.org
Home Page: www.aicpa.org
Social Media: *Facebook, Twitter, LinkedIn*

Barry C Melancon, CEO
Susan Coffey, Senior Vice President
Lawson Carmichael, SVP - Strategy
Arleen Thomas, SVP - Mgmt Accounting

Delivers need-to-know news of the profession, hard-hitting commentary, recommended products and professional development resources.
Frequency: Weekly
Founded in 1887

109   Chapter Weekly
National Association of Tax Professionals
PO Box 8002
Appleton, WI 54912-8002

800-558-3402
FAX 800-747-0001
E-Mail: natp@natptax.com
Home Page: www.natptax.com
Social Media: *Facebook, Twitter, MySpace*

Jo Ann Schoen, President
Jean Millerchip, Vice President
Gerard Cannito, Treasurer
Patricia M. McNeer, Secretary

E-Newsletter features Chapter events and updates.
Frequency: Weekly

110   Client Information Bulletin
WPI Communications
55 Morris Ave
Springfield, NJ 07081-1422

973-467-8700
800-323-4995
FAX 973-467-0368
E-Mail: info@wpicommunications.com
Home Page: www.wpicomm.com

Steve Klinghoffer, Owner
Lori Klinghoffer, Executive Vice President
Marilyn Lang, Circulation Manager
Sandy McMurray, Sales Manager
Anna Cooley, Managing Editor

This monthly newsletter covers important new tax developments, general business principles, financial planning, estate planning and other related topics.
4 Pages
Frequency: Monthly
Founded in 1952
Printed in 2 colors

111   Controller's Report
Institute of Management and Administration

3 Bethesda Metro Center
Suite 250
Bethesda, MD 20814-5377

800-372-1033
7033413500
FAX 800-253-0332
E-Mail: customercare@bna.com
Home Page: www.ioma.com

Aimed at corporate controllers in companies of all sizes.
Cost: $437.00
20 Pages
Frequency: Monthly
Founded in 1984
Printed in 2 colors

112   Controller's Tax Letter
Institute of Management and Administration
3 Bethesda Metro Center
Suite 250
Bethesda, MD 20814-5377

800-372-1033
7033413500
FAX 800-253-0332
E-Mail: customercare@bna.com
Home Page: www.ioma.com

Focuses on the tax implications of business decisions and provides readers in corporate finance/accounting details on recently settled cases from US Tax Court, with full citations for those who want to know more. CTL also shows controllers, accounting managers and tax managers the effects of business decisions as they relate to a company's strategic planning for new sales efforts, expanding their overseas or foreign presence, and exemptions and deductions available where laws have changed.
Cost: $259.00
Frequency: Monthly
Founded in 1984

113   Controllers Update
Institute of Certified Management Accountants
10 Paragon Drive
Suite 1
Montvale, NJ 07645-1718

800-638-4427
FAX 201-474-1600
E-Mail: ima@imanet.org
Home Page: www.imanet.org
Social Media: *Facebook, Twitter, LinkedIn*

Jeffrey C. Thomson, President and CEO
Brian L. McGuire, Chair
John C. Macaulay, Chair-Elect
Sandra B. Richtermeyer, Chair-Emeritus

Monthly newsletter with useful information for chief financial officers, plant controllers and financial management personnel.
Frequency: Monthly
Circulation: 2,200

114   Corporate Finance Insider
American Institute of Certified Public Accountants
1211 Avenue of the Americas
Suite 6
New York, NY 10036-8701

212-596-6200
FAX 212-596-6213
E-Mail: service@aicpa.org
Home Page: www.aicpa.org
Social Media: *Facebook, Twitter, LinkedIn*

Barry C Melancon, CEO
Susan Coffey, Senior Vice President
Lawson Carmichael, SVP - Strategy
Arleen Thomas, SVP - Mgmt Accounting

Covers financial management and corporate compliance issues, nationwide job opportunities, plus career advancement strategies from the experts, self assessment tools, compensa-

tion research and hiring trends for those who recruit, train and manage CPAs and other financial professionals.
Frequency: Monthly
Founded in 1887

115   Corporate Taxation Insider
American Institute of Certified Public Accountants
1211 Avenue of the Americas
Suite 6
New York, NY 10036-8701

212-596-6200
FAX 212-596-6213
E-Mail: service@aicpa.org
Home Page: www.aicpa.org
Social Media: *Facebook, Twitter, LinkedIn*

Barry C Melancon, CEO
Susan Coffey, Senior Vice President
Lawson Carmichael, SVP - Strategy
Arleen Thomas, SVP - Mgmt Accounting

Delivers need-to-know news of the profession, hard-hitting commentary, recommended products and professional development resources to its subscribers.
Frequency: Monthly
Founded in 1887

116   Currency
Grant Thornton
175 W Jackson Blvd
20th Floor
Chicago, IL 60604-2687

312-856-0001
FAX 312-602-8099
Home Page: www.grantthornton.com
Social Media: *Twitter, LinkedIn*

Stephen Chipman, CEO
Lou Grabowsky, COO
Russ Wieman, Chief Financial Officer

Electronic newsletter for bank executives that covers issues and trends in the financial institutions industry.
Founded in 1924

117   E@lert
National Association of Enrolled Agents
1120 Connecticut Avenue NW
Suite 460
Washington, DC 20036-3922

202-822-6232
FAX 202-822-6270
E-Mail: info@naea.org
Home Page: www.naea.org
Social Media: *Facebook, Twitter, LinkedIn*

Frank I Degen, President
Betsey Buckingham, president-elect
Robert Reedy, Treasurer/Secretary

Newsletter that provides brief updates on the latest tax news affecting clients and practices.
11000 Members

118   FSA Times
Institute of Internal Auditors
247 Maitland Ave
Altamonte Spgs, FL 32701-4201

407-937-1100
FAX 407-937-1101
E-Mail: custserv@theiia.org
Home Page: www.theiia.org

J. Michael Pepper, Chairman
Carolyn Saint, Senior Vice President
John Wxzelaki, Vice Chairman -
Finance/Security

Quarterly publication provided to members of the Institute of Internal Auditors' Financial Services Auditor Group to support knowledge development for financial services auditors.
Frequency: Quarterly

119 Financial Bulletin
Grant Thornton
175 W Jackson Blvd
20th Floor
Chicago, IL 60604-2687

312-856-0001
FAX 312-602-8099
Home Page: www.grantthornton.com
Social Media: *Twitter, LinkedIn*

Stephen Chipman, CEO
Lou Grabowsky, COO
Russ Wieman, Chief Financial Officer

Electronic publication that covers regulations
and developments affecting financial services
industry.
Founded in 1924

120 Focus on Forensics
Grant Thornton
175 W Jackson Blvd
20th Floor
Chicago, IL 60604-2687

312-856-0001
FAX 312-602-8099
Home Page: www.grantthornton.com
Social Media: *Twitter, LinkedIn*

Stephen Chipman, CEO
Lou Grabowsky, COO
Russ Wieman, Chief Financial Officer

Periodic newsletter providing valuable forensic
accounting insights into some of the most complex and critical challenges that businesses and
legal counsel face today.
Founded in 1924

121 General Ledger
American Institute of Professional
Bookkeepers
6001 Montrose Rd
Suite 500
Rockville, MD 20852-4873

800-622-0121
FAX 800-541-0066
E-Mail: info@aipb.org
Home Page: www.aipb.org

Stan Hartman, Owner

The latest bookkeeping, accounting and tax
news, keep current on bookkeeping and reporting techniques, time and money-saving charts,
practical tips, sharpen skills with a Bookkeeper's Quiz in every issue, and monthly and
annual rates and numbers are included.
Frequency: Monthly
Circulation: 30000
Founded in 1987
Mailing list available for rent

**122 Government Accounting and
Auditing Update**
Thomson Reuters
2395 Midway Rd
Carrollton, TX 75006

817-332-3709
800-431-9025
FAX 888-216-1929
E-Mail: trta.lei-support@thomsonreuters.com
Home Page: www.ria.thomsonreuters.com

Elaine Yadlon, Plant Manager
Thomas H Glocer, CEO & Director
Robert D Daleo, Chief Financial Officer
Kelli Crane, Senior Vice President & CIO

Includes changes taking place in government
accounting and financial reporting, analysis of
the latest developments, explanations of how
they affect work and practical guidance on
adapting to these changes.
Cost: $370.00
8 Pages
Frequency: Monthly
Founded in 1935

Mailing list available for rent: 5000 names
Printed in 2 colors on glossy stock

**123 Government Financial Management
TOPICS**
2208 Mount Vernon Avenue
Alexandria, VA 22301

703-684-6931
800-AGA-7211
FAX 703-548-9367
E-Mail: agacgfm@agacgfm.org
Home Page: www.agacgfm.org
Social Media: *Facebook, Twitter, LinkedIn,
GovLoop*

Evelyn A. Brown, President
Relmond P Van Daniker, Executive Director

An AGA member service, designed to give national exposure to chapter events, community
service projects and member accomplishments
while offering the most up-to-date Association
news.
15000 Members
Frequency: Bi-Weekly
Founded in 1950
Mailing list available for rent: 18,000 names

**124 Governmental Accounting Standards
Board Action Report**
401 Merritt 7
PO Box 5116
Norwalk, CT 06856-5116

203-847-0700
FAX 203-849-9714
E-Mail: webmaster@gasb.org
Home Page: www.gasb.org

Robert Attmore, Chairman
David Bean, Director Research/Technical
Active

Action Report newsletter that includes developments in the standards-setting process and the
status of technical projects.
Cost: $155.00
Frequency: Monthly

125 IIA Insight
Institute of Internal Auditors
247 Maitland Ave
Altamonte Spgs, FL 32701-4201

407-937-1100
FAX 407-937-1101
E-Mail: custserv@theiia.org
Home Page: www.theiia.org
Social Media: *Facebook, Twitter, LinkedIn*

J. Michael Pepper, Chairman
Carolyn Saint, Senior Vice President
John Wxzelaki, Vice Chairman -
Finance/Security

Member newsletter designed to instruct members on using IIA services, products, and training opportunities.
Frequency: Monthly

126 IIA Today
Institute of Internal Auditors
247 Maitland Ave
Altamonte Spgs, FL 32701-4201

407-830-7600
FAX 407-937-1101
E-Mail: custserv@theiia.org
Home Page: www.theiia.org

J. Michael Pepper, Chairman
Carolyn Saint, Senior Vice President
John Wxzelaki, Vice Chairman -
Finance/Security

Provides relevent and timely information on internal audit news. In print and electronic formats available.
Frequency: Twice Monthly

127 IMA Educational Case Journal
Institute of Management Accountants
10 Paragon Dr
Suite 1
Montvale, NJ 07645-1760

800-638-4427
FAX 201-474-1600
E-Mail: ima@imanet.org
Home Page: www.imanet.org
Social Media: *Facebook, Twitter, LinkedIn*

Jeffrey C. Thomson, President and CEO
Brian L. McGuire, Chair
John C. Macaulay, Chair-Elect
Sandra B. Richtermeyer, Chair-Emeritus

The journal publishes teaching cases and research related to case writing or teaching with
cases in management accounting and related
fields.
Cost: $250.00
60000 Members
Frequency: Quarterly

128 IOMA's Report on Salary Surveys
Institute of Management and Administration
3 Bethesda Metro Center
Suite 250
Bethesda, MD 20814-5377

800-372-1033
7033413500
FAX 800-253-0332
E-Mail: customercare@bna.com
Home Page: www.ioma.com

Analyzes data from major salary surveys released during the year by the biggest compensation survey companies, WorldatWork,
SHRM, state HR societies, and the Big Four
accounting firms, to give readers an overview
of those expensive, hard-to-manage services.
Cost: $445.00
Founded in 1984

129 Infoline
Hospitality Financial & Technology
Professionals
11709 Boulder Lane
Suite 110
Austin, TX 78726-1832

512-249-5333
800-646-4387
FAX 512-249-1533
E-Mail: membership@hftp.org
Home Page: www.hftp.org

Frank I Wolfe, Executive VP/CEO
Lucinda Hart, COO
Thomas Atzenhofer, CFO
Eliza Selig, Director of Communications

Provides information regarding chapter and of-
ficer activities.
Frequency: Monthly
Founded in 1952

130 Information Management Newsletter
Information Resources Management
Association
701 E Chocolate Ave
Suite 200
Hershey, PA 17033-1240

717-533-8845
FAX 717-533-8861
E-Mail: member@irma-international.org
Home Page: www.irma-international.org

Jan Travers, Executive Director
Sherif Kamel, Communications Director
Lech Janczewski PhD, IRMA World
Representative Director
Gerald Grant, IRMA Doctoral Symposium
Director
Paul Chalekian, IRMA United States
Representative

This practical, informative newsletter is a leading publication of information technology re-

sources management. Short, concise articles give objective, professional views of newly emerging technologies and trends.
Cost: $60.00
Frequency: Semi-Annually
ISSN: 1080-286X

131 Internal Auditing Report
Thomson Reuters
2395 Midway Rd
Carrollton, TX 75006

817-332-3709
800-431-9025
FAX 888-216-1929
E-Mail: trta.lei-support@thomsonreuters.com
Home Page: www.ria.thomsonreuters.com

Elaine Yadlon, Plant Manager
Thomas H Glocer, CEO & Director
Robert D Daleo, Chief Financial Officer
Kelli Crane, Senior Vice President & CIO

Perfect for keeping up to date on new auditing standards and developments. Offers guidance on managing internal auditing departments, covers new audit technology, offers new audit techniques used by successful audit management practices, and provides practitioner level feedback on current Institute of Internal Auditors standards.
Cost: $320.00
12 Pages
Frequency: Six Times/Year
Circulation: 5000
Founded in 1935
Mailing list available for rent: 5000 names
Printed in 2 colors on glossy stock

132 Jacobs Report
Offshore Press
PO Box 8137
Prairie Village, KS 66208-2824

913-362-9667
888-516-3177
FAX 913-432-7174
E-Mail: jacobs@offshorepress.com
Home Page: www.offshorepress.com

Vernon K Jacobs, President

Contains International tax news.
Frequency: Daily
Founded in 1981

133 Letter Ruling Review
Tax Analysts
400 S Maple Ave
Suite 400
Falls Church, VA 22046-4245

703-533-4400
800-955-2444
FAX 703-533-4444
E-Mail: cservice@tax.org
Home Page: www.taxanalysts.com

Chris Bergin, CEO
Martin Lobel, Chairman of the Board

Publication analyzes significant private letter rulings issued by the Internal Revenue Service during the month.
4 Pages
Frequency: Monthly
Founded in 1970
Printed in one color on matte stock

134 Management & Administration Report (ADMAR)
Institute of Management and Administration
3 Bethesda Metro Center
Suite 250
Bethesda, MD 20814-5377

800-372-1033
7033413500
FAX 800-253-0332

E-Mail: customercare@bna.com
Home Page: www.ioma.com

How to manage corporate accounting departments more effectively, boost staff productivity, reduce operation costs and adopt new systems and technology, and take charge of your dealings with auditors and lenders.
Founded in 1984

135 Managing Accounts Payable
Institute of Management and Administration
3 Bethesda Metro Center
Suite 250
Bethesda, MD 20814-5377

800-372-1033
7033413500
FAX 800-253-0332
E-Mail: customercare@bna.com
Home Page: www.ioma.com

The source of information for accounts payable and those responsible for the function. Each issue contains 5-7 articles, 6-10 short news clips, a manager's forum on the back page and calendar of upcoming seminars and conferences.
Cost: $419.00
Frequency: Monthly
Founded in 1984

136 Managing the General Ledger
Institute of Management and Administration
3 Bethesda Metro Center
Suite 250
Bethesda, MD 20814-5377

800-372-1033
7033413500
FAX 800-253-0332
E-Mail: customercare@bna.com
Home Page: www.ioma.com

Aimed at controllers and corporate accounting managers and shows the most current techniques for efficient monthly closings and AICPA approved methods for general ledger entries.
Cost: $308.14
Frequency: Monthly
Founded in 1984

137 NSPA Washington Reporter
National Society of Public Accountants
1010 N Fairfax St
Alexandria, VA 22314-1574

703-549-6400
800-966-6679
FAX 703-549-2984
E-Mail: members@nsacct.org
Home Page: www.nsacct.org
Social Media: *Facebook, Twitter, LinkedIn*

Harlan Rose, President
Steven Hanson, First Vice President
Marilyn Niwao, Second Vice President
Brian Thompson, Secretary-Treasurer

Coverage of NSPA activity with the government, and news on members in various states.
Frequency: Monthly
Founded in 1955

138 National Estimator
Society of Cost Estimating and Analysis
8221 Old Courthouse Rd
Suite 106
Vienna, VA 22182

703-938-5090
FAX 703-938-5091
E-Mail: scea@sceaonline.org
Home Page: www.sceaonline.org

Erin Whittaker, Executive Director
Sharon Burger, Certification Program Admin
Brittany Walker, Membership Coordinator
Debra Lehman, Treasurer

Information on cost estimating and analysis, earned value management, budget and financial

analysis, and program control.
Cost: $55.00
2015 Members
Frequency: Biannual
Founded in 1990

139 National Newsletter
415 N Alfred St
Alexandria, VA 22314-2269

703-549-0360
800-462-5637
FAX 703-549-3181
Home Page: www.asmconline.org
Social Media: *Facebook, Twitter, LinkedIn*

Marilyn Thomas, President
Art Hagler, VP
Kathy Watern, VP
Nancy Phillips, Treasurer

Focuses on society information such as training, events, and other issues related to supporting the membership of ASMC.
19m+ Members
Frequency: Monthly
Founded in 1948

140 New Developments Summary
Grant Thornton
175 W Jackson Blvd
20th Floor
Chicago, IL 60604-2687

312-856-0001
FAX 312-602-8099
Home Page: www.grantthornton.com
Social Media: *Twitter, LinkedIn*

Stephen Chipman, CEO
Lou Grabowsky, COO
Russ Wieman, Chief Financial Officer

Periodic bulletin providing a detailed summary of a recent technical development or accounting pronouncement.
Founded in 1924

141 News Plus
National Association of Black Accountants
7474 Greenway Center Dr
Suite 1120
Greenbelt, MD 20770-3504

301-474-6222
888-571-2939
FAX 301-474-3114
E-Mail: newsplus@nabainc.org
Home Page: www.nabainc.org
Social Media: *Facebook, Twitter, LinkedIn, YouTube*

Calvin Harris Jr., President/CEO
Guillermo Hysaw, Executive Director and COO
Veda Stanley, Executive Vice President
Sheila Taylor-Clark, CPA
Ronald Walker, Chairman, Division of Firms

Updates on accounting proposals and regulations.
Cost: $20.00
Frequency: Quarterly
Founded in 1969

142 Nonprofit Report: Accounting, Taxation Management
Thomson Reuters
2395 Midway Rd
Carrollton, TX 75006

817-332-3709
800-431-9025
FAX 888-216-1929
E-Mail: trta.lei-support@thomsonreuters.com
Home Page: www.ria.thomsonreuters.com

Elaine Yadlon, Plant Manager
Thomas H Glocer, CEO & Director
Robert D Daleo, Chief Financial Officer
Kelli Crane, Senior Vice President & CIO

Offers CPAs with nonprofit clients, and professionals working in the nonprofit sector. A prac-

tical, timely look at today's key nonprofit issues, including IRS rulings and pronouncements, AICPA changes and legislation governing the financial management of most nonprofit organizations.
Cost: $250.00
Frequency: Monthly
Founded in 1935
Mailing list available for rent
Printed in 2 colors on glossy stock

143 On the Horizon
Grant Thornton
175 W Jackson Blvd
20th Floor
Chicago, IL 60604-2687

312-856-0001
FAX 312-602-8099
Home Page: www.grantthornton.com
Social Media: *Twitter, LinkedIn*

Stephen Chipman, CEO
Lou Grabowsky, COO
Russ Wieman, Chief Financial Officer

Updates on announcements, meetings and proposals from the accounting standards-setting bodies and industry regulators.
Frequency: Weekly
Founded in 1924

144 Partner's Report for Law Firm Owners
Institute of Management and Administration
3 Bethesda Metro Center
Suite 250
Bethesda, MD 20814-5377

800-372-1033
703-341-3500
FAX 800-253-0332
E-Mail: customercare@bna.com
Home Page: www.ioma.com

Keeps partners up-to-date on salary guidelines and benefits, as well as provides the reader with tips on increasing profit margins and exercising leadership skills.
Cost: $464.00
Frequency: Monthly
Founded in 1984

145 Payroll Currently
American Payroll Association
660 N Main Ave
Suite 100
San Antonio, TX 78205-1217

210-226-4600
FAX 210-226-4027
E-Mail: apamail@mindspring.com
Home Page: www.payroll.org
Social Media: *Facebook, Twitter, LinkedIn*

Daniel Maddux, President

Member newsletter containing breaking payroll compliance news and updates.
Frequency: Bi-Weekly

146 Payroll Manager's Report
Institute of Management and Administration
3 Bethesda Metro Center
Suite 250
Bethesda, MD 20814-5377

800-372-1033
703-341-3500
FAX 800-253-0332
E-Mail: customercare.bna.com
Home Page: www.ioma.com

Written for payroll practitioners working with small and large employers. Provides how-to information on managing a payroll department cost effectively and service-efficiently.
Cost: $399.00
Frequency: Monthly
Founded in 1984

147 Payroll Practitioner's Monthly
Institute of Management and Administration
3 Bethesda Metro Center
Suite 250
Bethesda, MD 20814-5377

800-372-1033
703-341-3500
FAX 800-253-0332
E-Mail: customercare@bna.com
Home Page: www.ioma.com

Shows payroll professionals what they need to do and how to do it when it comes to the many rules, regulations and laws they must follow to prepare and distribute a corporate payroll.
Cost: $399.00
16 Pages
Frequency: Monthly
Founded in 1984

148 Payroll Tax Alert
Institute of Management and Administration
3 Bethesda Metro Center
Suite 250
Bethesda, MD 20814-5377

800-372-1033
703-341-3500
FAX 800-253-0332
E-Mail: customercare@bna.com
Home Page: www.ioma.com

Used by payroll managers and professionals in accounting or human resources. Provides quick, hard hitting updates on changes to federal and state payroll policy (wage-hour rules, industrial orders, new posting requirements and tax issues) from every agency that has a hand in corporate payroll & benefits administration.
Cost: $240.00
Frequency: Monthly
Circulation: 2000
Founded in 1984

149 Pocket MBA
Practising Law Institute
810 Seventh Avenue
21st Floor
New York, NY 10019-5818

212-824-5700
800-260-4754
FAX 212-581-4670
E-Mail: info@pli.edu
Home Page: www.pli.edu
Social Media: *Facebook, Twitter*

Victor J Rubino, President
Nickola Francis, Subscription Manager

Provides information every lawyer needs to know about business and finance.
Cost: $1295.00
Frequency: Weekly
Founded in 1933

150 Polaris International Newsletter
Polaris International
9200 South Dadeland Boulevard
Suite 510
Miami, FL 33156

305-670-0580
FAX 305-670-3818
E-Mail: info@accountants.org
Home Page: www.accountants.org
Social Media: *Facebook, Twitter, LinkedIn, Youtube*

Kevin Mead, President
Lydie Jubin, Chief Regional Officer
Anne Hampson, CFO
Pedro Figueroa, Administrative Manager

Newsletter containing information regarding events, activities and recent news for accounting and consulting firms.
Frequency: Quarterly
Founded in 1978

151 Practicing CPA
American Institute of Certified Public Accountants
1211 Avenue of the Americas
Suite 6
New York, NY 10036-8701

212-596-6200
FAX 212-596-6213
E-Mail: service@aicpa.org
Home Page: www.aicpa.org
Social Media: *Facebook, Twitter, LinkedIn*

Barry C Melancon, CEO
Susan Coffey, Senior Vice President
Lawson Carmichael, SVP - Strategy
Arleen Thomas, SVP - Mgmt Accounting

Articles on development and management of firms.
Frequency: Monthly
Founded in 1887

152 Public Accounting Desk Book
Strafford Publications
590 Dutch Valley Road
PO Box 13729
Atlanta, GA 30324-0729

404-881-1141
800-926-7926
FAX 404-881-0074
E-Mail: customerservice@straffordpub.com
Home Page: www.straffordpub.com
Social Media: *Twitter*

Richard Ossoff, President
Jon McKenna, Executive Editor

Provides public accounting firms with authoritative news and analysis of developments in the accounting profession today and emerging trends for the future. Also reports SEC auditor changes, mergers, acquisitions, personnel changes and related events.
Cost: $39.00
Frequency: Annual
ISSN: 0161-309X
Founded in 1984

153 Public Accounting Report
CCH
2700 Lake Cook Rd
Riverwoods, IL 60015-3867

847-940-4600
800-835-5224
FAX 773-866-3095
Home Page: www.cch.com

Mike Sabbatis, President
Douglas M Winterrose, Vice President & CFO
Jim Bryant, EVP Software Products

Written for public accounting firm partners and professionals, it is renowned for its straight reporting and analysis of the news, developments, and trends that have influenced the profession for more than 20 years.
Cost: $449.00
8 Pages
Frequency: Bi-Weekly

154 SEC Accounting Report
Thomson Reuters
2395 Midway Rd
Carrollton, TX 75006

817-332-3709
800-431-9025
FAX 888-216-1929
E-Mail: trta.lei-support@thomsonreuters.com
Home Page: www.ria.thomsonreuters.com

Elaine Yadlon, Plant Manager
Thomas H Glocer, CEO & Director
Robert D Daleo, Chief Financial Officer
Kelli Crane, Senior Vice President & CIO

For senior executives needing monthly news and insights on emerging SEC issues. The SEC Accounting Report can help you to understand

SEC changes and their subsequent compliance requirements.
Cost: $365.00
8 Pages
Frequency: Monthly
Circulation: 5000
Founded in 1935
Mailing list available for rent: 5000 names
Printed in 2 colors on glossy stock

155 Strategic TechNotes
Institute of Management Accountants
10 Paragon Dr
Suite 1
Montvale, NJ 07645-1774

201-573-9000
800-638-4427
FAX 201-474-1600
E-Mail: ima@imanet.org
Home Page: www.imanet.org
Social Media: *Facebook, Twitter, LinkedIn*

Jeffrey C. Thomson, President and CEO
Brian L. McGuire, Chair
John C. Macaulay, Chair-Elect
Sandra B. Richtermeyer, Chair-Emeritus

Award-winning technology e-newsletter designed for IMA members and others who want a look into the world of today's and tomorrow's technological trends and tools.
60000 Members
Frequency: 2 Times/Month

156 TAXPRO Monthly
National Association of Tax Professionals
PO Box 8002
Appleton, WI 54912-8002

800-558-3402
FAX 800-747-0001
E-Mail: natp@natptax.com
Home Page: www.natptax.com
Social Media: *Facebook, Twitter, MySpace*

Jo Ann Schoen, President
Jean Millerchip, Vice President
Gerard Cannito, Treasurer
Patricia M. McNeer, Secretary
Kathy Stanek, CEO

Covers the latest news in detail and explores critical new developments in federal tax laws while providing practical applications of tax laws and procedures.
Frequency: Monthly

157 TAXPRO Weekly
National Association of Tax Professionals
PO Box 8002
Appleton, WI 54912-8002

800-558-3402
FAX 800-747-0001
E-Mail: natp@natptax.com
Home Page: www.natptax.com
Social Media: *Facebook, Twitter, MySpace*

Jo Ann Schoen, President
Jean Millerchip, Vice President
Gerard Cannito, Treasurer
Patricia M. McNeer, Secretary
Kathy Stanek, CEO

Members receive e-Newsletter featuring tax alerts and news briefs hot off the press.
Frequency: Weekly

158 TOPICS Newsletter
Association of Government Accountants
2208 Mount Vernon Ave
Alexandria, VA 22301-1314

703-684-6931
800-AGA-7211
FAX 703-548-9367
E-Mail: agacgfm@agacgfm.org
Home Page: www.agacgfm.org

Relmond Van Daniker, Executive Director
Evelyn Brown, National President

Designed to give national exposure to chapter events, community service projects and member accomplishments while offering the most up-to-date Association news, released every other Monday morning by e-mail to members.
Frequency: 2x/Month

159 Tax Hot Topics
Grant Thornton
175 W Jackson Blvd
20th Floor
Chicago, IL 60604-2687

312-856-0001
FAX 312-602-8099
Home Page: www.grantthornton.com
Social Media: *Twitter, LinkedIn*

Stephen Chipman, CEO
Lou Grabowsky, COO
Russ Wieman, Chief Financial Officer

Electronic newsletter addressing a wide range of tax issues, including Internal Revenue Service rulings, tax-related litigation, and state, local and international tax developments
Frequency: Biweekly
Founded in 1924

160 Tax Incentives Alert
Strafford Publications
590 Dutch Valley Road NE
PO Box 13729
Atlanta, GA 30324-0729

404-881-1141
800-926-7926
FAX 404-881-0074
E-Mail: customerservice@straffordpub.com
Home Page: www.straffordpub.com

Richard Ossoff, President
Jon McKenna, Executive Editor

Reports on the new and ever-evolving array of federal and state tax credits, exemptions, deductions, abatements and other incentives.
Cost: $467.00
Frequency: Monthly
ISSN: 0161-309X
Founded in 1984

161 Tax Insider
American Institute of Certified Public Accountants
1211 Avenue of the Americas
Suite 6
New York, NY 10036-8701

212-596-6200
FAX 212-596-6213
E-Mail: service@aicpa.org
Home Page: www.aicpa.org
Social Media: *Facebook, Twitter, LinkedIn*

Barry C Melancon, CEO
Susan Coffey, Senior Vice President
Lawson Carmichael, SVP - Strategy
Arleen Thomas, SVP - Mgmt Accounting

Delivers need-to-know news of the profession, hard-hitting commentary, recommended products and professional development resources to tax and financial planning professionals.
Frequency: 2x/Month
Founded in 1887

162 Tax Letter and Social Security Report
Scott Peyron & Associates
209 Main Street
Suite 200
Boise, ID 83702-7356

208-388-3800
FAX 208-388-8898
E-Mail: info@peyron.com
Home Page: www.peyron.com

Scott Peyron, Owner

Covers taxes, social security tax, benefit tips and information for middle income individuals

and professionals.
Cost: $56.00
4 Pages
Frequency: Monthly
Circulation: 2000
Printed in one color on matte stock

163 The CPA Letter
American Institute of Certified Public Accountants
1211 Avenue of the Americas
Suite 6
New York, NY 10036-8701

212-596-6200
FAX 212-596-6213
E-Mail: service@aicpa.org
Home Page: www.aicpa.org
Social Media: *Facebook, Twitter, LinkedIn*

Barry C Melancon, CEO
Susan Coffey, Senior Vice President
Lawson Carmichael, SVP - Strategy
Arleen Thomas, SVP - Mgmt Accounting

A news source for certified public accountants.
Frequency: Monthly
Founded in 1887

164 The Gaming Auditorium
Institute of Internal Auditors
247 Maitland Ave
Altamonte Spgs, FL 32701-4201

707-937-1100
FAX 407-937-1101
E-Mail: custserv@theiia.org
Home Page: www.theiia.org

J. Michael Pepper, Chairman
Carolyn Saint, Senior Vice President
John Wxzelaki, Vice Chairman - Finance/security

Quarterly publication provided to members of the Institute of Internal Auditors' Gaming Audit Group to support knowledge development for gaming audit professionals.
Frequency: Quarterly

165 Tone at the Top
Institute of Internal Auditors
247 Maitland Ave
Altamonte Spgs, FL 32701-4201

407-937-1100
FAX 407-937-1101
E-Mail: custserv@theiia.org
Home Page: www.theiia.org

J. Michael Pepper, Chairman
Carolyn Saint, Senior Vice President
John Wxzelaki, Vice Chairman - Finance/security

Newsletter that provides executive management, boards of directors, and audit committees with concise, leading-edge information in issues such as risk, internal control, governance, ethics, and the changing role of internal auditing.
Frequency: Quarterly

166 Wealth Management Insider
American Institute of Certified Public Accountants
1211 Avenue of the Americas
Suite 6
New York, NY 10036-8701

212-596-6200
FAX 212-596-6213
E-Mail: service@aicpa.org
Home Page: www.aicpa.org
Social Media: *Facebook, Twitter, LinkedIn*

Barry C Melancon, CEO
Susan Coffey, Senior Vice President
Lawson Carmichael, SVP - Strategy
Arleen Thomas, SVP - Mgmt Accounting

Delivers need-to-know news of the profession, hard-hitting commentary, recommended prod-

ucts and professional development resources to CPAs who currently provide financial planning services or are looking to expand their practice.
Frequency: 2x/Month
Founded in 1887

Magazines & Journals

167 AIRA Journal
Association of Insolvency & Restructuring Advisors
221 W Stewart Ave
Suite 207
Medford, OR 97501-3647

541-858-1665
FAX 541-858-9187
E-Mail: aira@aira.org
Home Page: www.airacira.org

Anthony Sasso, President
Thomas Morrow, Vice President
Mathew Schwartz, Treasurer
Joel Waite, VP

Publication provides accurate and authoritative information in regard to current issues and developments relevant to the insolvency and restructuring practice, as well as to inform members of upcoming Association events.
Frequency: Bi-Monthly

168 Accountants SEC Practice Manual
CCH
2700 Lake Cook Rd
Riverwoods, IL 60015-3867

847-940-4600
800-835-5224
FAX 773-866-3095
Home Page: www.cch.com

Mike Sabbatis, President
Douglas M Winterrose, Vice President & CFO
Jim Bryant, EVP Software Products

Offers guidance for preparing and filing financial statements with the SEC, including regulations, forms and helpful summaries and checklists.
Cost: $819.00
Frequency: Annual
Founded in 1913

169 Accounting Historians Journal
Academy of Accounting Historians
10900 Euclid Avenue
Cleveland, OH 44106-7235

216-368-2058
FAX 216-368-6244
E-Mail: acchistory@case.edu
Home Page: www.aahhq.org

Joanne Cross, President
Robert Colson, President Elect
Yvette Lazdowski, VP, Communications
Robert Colson, VP Communications
Stephanie Moussalli, Secretary

Published by the Academy of Accounting Historians, the Journal provides research on the evolution of accounting thought and accounting practice. Subscription to the semi-annual publication is included in membership to the Academy.
600 Members
200 Pages
Frequency: Semi-Annual
Founded in 1973
Printed in one color

170 Accounting Horizons
American Accounting Association

5717 Bessie Dr
Sarasota, FL 34233-2399

941-921-7747
FAX 941-923-4093
E-Mail: info@aaahq.org
Home Page: aaahq.org
Social Media: *Facebook*

Tracey Sutherland, Executive Director
Deirdre Harris, Publications Contact

Accounting and business information.
Cost: $100.00
8600 Members
Frequency: Quarterly
Circulation: 6000
Founded in 1916
Printed in 3 colors on matte stock

171 Accounting Today
Accountants Media Group & SourceMedia, Inc.
1 State Street Plaza
25th Floor
New York, NY 10004

212-258-8445
800-221-1809
FAX 212-292-5216
E-Mail: william.carlino@sourcemedia.com
Home Page: www.accountingtoday.com
Social Media: *Facebook, Twitter, LinkedIn*

Michael Cohn, Editor-in-Chief
Tamika Cody, Managing Editor
Daniel Hood, Editor in Chief
Seth Fineberg, Technology Editor

Covers accounting and auditing standards, taxation and practice management.
Cost: $99.00
48 Pages
Circulation: 34991
ISSN: 1044-5714
Founded in 1987
Printed in 4 colors on glossy stock

172 Accounting and Tax Highlights
Thomson Reuters
2395 Midway Rd
Carrollton, TX 75006

817-332-3709
800-431-9025
FAX 888-216-1929
E-Mail: trta.lei-support@thomsonreuters.com
Home Page: www.ria.thomsonreuters.com

Elaine Yadlon, Plant Manager
Thomas H Glocer, CEO & Director
Robert D Daleo, Chief Financial Officer
Kelli Crane, Senior Vice President & CIO

Covers current news and developments in the field. Audiocassette program for CPAs for continuing professional education. Accepts advertising.
Cost: $112.00
28 Pages
Frequency: Monthly
Founded in 1935

173 Accounting and the Public Interest
American Accounting Association
5717 Bessie Dr
Sarasota, FL 34233-2399

941-921-7747
FAX 941-923-4093
E-Mail: deirdre@aaahq.org
Home Page: aaahq.org

Tracey Sutherland, Executive Director
Deirdre Harris, Publications Contact

An academic journal taking the view that accounting is a social activity with far-ranging consequences for every citizen, welcoming innovation and eclecticism, alternative theories and methodologies, as well as the more traditional ones. The common element in this diversity is the requirement that the study and its

findings be linked to the public interest by situating them within a historical, social, and political context, and ultimately providing guidance.
8600 Members
Frequency: Periodically
Circulation: 400
Founded in 1916

174 Achieve
National Association of Black Accountants
7474 Greenway Center Dr
Suite 1120
Greenbelt, MD 20770-3504

301-474-6222
888-571-2939
FAX 301-474-3114
E-Mail: customerservice@nabainc.org
Home Page: www.nabainc.org
Social Media: *Facebook, Twitter, LinkedIn, YouTube*

Calvin Harris Jr., President/CEO
Guillermo Hysaw, Executive Director and COO
Veda Stanley, Executive Vice President
Sheila Taylor-Clark, CPA
Ronald Walker, Chairman, Division of Firms

Magazine for NABA student members. Discussed are issues relevant to student academic, career, and personal aspirations.
Frequency: 2 Times/Year
Founded in 1969

175 Actuary Magazine
Society of Actuaries
475 N Martingale Rd
Suite 600
Schaumburg, IL 60173-2252

847-706-3500
FAX 847-706-3599
E-Mail: webmaster@soa.org
Home Page: www.soa.org

Greg Heidrich, Executive Director
Stacy Lin, Deputy Executive Director/CFO

Provides informative feature articles that focus on a variety of actuarial topics, plus career information, SOA education initiatives and trends in international business.
Frequency: Bimonthly
Printed in 4 colors on glossy stock

176 Armed Forces Comptroller
415 N Alfred St
Alexandria, VA 22314-2269

703-549-0360
800-462-5637
FAX 703-549-3181
Home Page: www.asmconline.org
Social Media: *Facebook, Twitter, LinkedIn*

Robert Hale, Executive Director
John Bunnell, Associate Director of Certification
Jennifer Sizemore, Chapter Management
Don W Fox, General Counsel

Leading industry journal, is one of the Society's means of sharing professional information. Articles are received from a variety of sources, such as academia, the government, and our members.
18000 Members
Founded in 1948

177 Audit Report
Association of Credit Union Internal Auditors
PO Box 150908
Alexandria, VA 22315

703-688-2284
866-254-8128
FAX 703-683-0295
E-Mail: acuia@acuia.org

Home Page: www.acuia.org
Social Media: *Facebook, Twitter, LinkedIn*

Samuel Capuano, Chairman of the Board
Jill Chase, Vice Chair

Articles of interest to those in the auditing profession.
800 Members
Frequency: Quarterly
Founded in 1989
Printed in 4 colors

178 Auditing: A Journal of Practice & Theory
American Accounting Association
5717 Bessie Dr
Sarasota, FL 34233-2399

941-921-7747
FAX 941-923-4093
E-Mail: deirdre@aaahq.org
Home Page: aaahq.org

Tracey Sutherland, Executive Director
Deirdre Harris, Publications Contact

The journal is distributed to members of the Auditing section of the Association, as well as libraries.
8600 Members
Frequency: Twice/Year
Circulation: 2000
Founded in 1916

179 CFMA Building Profits
Construction Financial Management
Association
100 Village Blvd
Suite 200
Princeton, NJ 08540-5783

609-452-8000
888-421-9996
FAX 609-452-0474
E-Mail: info@cfma.org
Home Page: www.cfma.org
Social Media: *Facebook, Twitter, LinkedIn, YouTube*

Stuart Binstock, President and CEO
Brian Summers, COO
Robert Rubin, CPA

Information for financial managers and CPAs concerned with financial management.
7000 Members
Frequency: Bi-Monthly
Circulation: 7,000
Founded in 1981

180 CPA Practice Management Forum
CCH
2700 Lake Cook Rd
Riverwoods, IL 60015-3867

847-940-4600
800-835-5224
FAX 773-866-3095
Home Page: www.cch.com

Mike Sabbatis, President
Douglas M Winterrose, Vice President & CFO
Jim Bryant, EVP Software Products

Mini-journal that includes articles featuring best practices, tips and advice from the nation's leading practice management experts.
Cost: $529.00
24 Pages
Frequency: Monthly

181 CPA Technology Advisor
Cygnus Publishing
1233 Janesville Avenue
Fort Atkinson, WI 53538-0803

800-547-7377
E-Mail: shari.dodgen@cygnuspub.com
Home Page: www.cygnusb2b.com

John French, CEO
Paul Bonaiuto, CFO

Ed Wood, VP
Kris Flitcroft, EVP

The magazine is a resource for accountants and managers that features a Buyer's Guide that lists hundreds of businesses, manufacturers and professionals that can assist public accounting firms in delivering a variety of services to their clients in various industries.
Cost: $48.00
Circulation: 50,000+
Founded in 1991
Printed in 4 colors on glossy stock

182 CPA Wealth Provider
Accountants Media Group & SourceMedia, Inc.
One State Street Plaza
25th Floor
New York, NY 10004

212-258-8445
800-221-1809
FAX 212-292-5216
E-Mail: howard.wolosky@sourcemedia.com
Home Page: www.accountingtoday.com
Social Media: *Facebook*

Michael Cohn, President and CEO
Joseph Wells, Chairman
John Gill, VP of Education
John Warren, VP and General Counsel

Offers financial planning strategies, product information and practivve-building advice in an environment that recognizes the special needs of accountants.
Frequency: Quarterly
Circulation: 37000
Founded in 1968
Printed in 4 colors on glossy stock

183 Computers in Accounting
Thomson Reuters
2395 Midway Rd
Carrollton, TX 75006

817-332-3709
800-431-9025
FAX 888-216-1929
E-Mail: trta.lei-support@thomsonreuters.com
Home Page: www.ria.thomsonreuters.com

Elaine Yadlon, Plant Manager
Thomas H Glocer, CEO & Director
Robert D Daleo, Chief Financial Officer
Kelli Crane, Senior Vice President & CIO

Contains the latest information on accounting, tax and business software, electronic spreadsheets, and available hardware.
Cost: $58.00
40 Pages
Founded in 1935

184 Controller's Cost & Profit Report
Thomson Reuters
2395 Midway Rd
Carrollton, TX 75006

817-332-3709
800-431-9025
FAX 888-216-1929
E-Mail: trta.lei-support@thomsonreuters.com
Home Page: www.ria.thomsonreuters.com

Elaine Yadlon, Plant Manager
Thomas H Glocer, CEO & Director
Robert D Daleo, Chief Financial Officer
Kelli Crane, Senior Vice President & CIO

Targets cash flow issues, risk/reward decisions, personnel trends, ways to increase productivity while reducing overhead costs, and technology updates for the new millennium.
Cost: $195.50
Frequency: SemiMonthly
Founded in 1935

185 Current Issues in Auditing
American Accounting Association

5717 Bessie Dr
Sarasota, FL 34233-2399

941-921-7747
FAX 941-923-4093
E-Mail: info@aaahq.org
Home Page: www.aaahq.org

Tracey Sutherland, Executive Director
Julie Smith David, CIO
Diane Ledger, Director of Finance

This open-access journal offers free access to AAA members, non-members, and libraries.
Frequency: Periodically

186 EA Journal
National Association of Enrolled Agents
1120 Connecticut Avenue NW
Suite 460
Washington, DC 20036-3922

202-822-6232
FAX 202-822-6270
E-Mail: info@naea.org
Home Page: www.naea.org
Social Media: *Facebook, Twitter, LinkedIn*

Frank I Degen, President
Betsey Buckingham, President-elect
Robert Reedy, Treasurer/Secretary
Gigi Jarvis, Sr. Dir. Marketing/Communication
William Grutzkuhn, Director
Finance/Administration

EA Journal brings information that helps set professionals apart from other tax practitioners.
12000 Members
Frequency: Every Other Month
Founded in 1972

187 Financial Executive
Financial Executives International
1250 Headquarters Plaza
West Tower, 7th Floor
Morristown, NJ 07960

973-765-1000
FAX 973-765-1018
E-Mail: membership@financialexecutives.org
Home Page: www.financialexecutives.org
Social Media: *Facebook, Twitter, LinkedIn, YouTube*

Marie N Hollein, President & CEO
Marsha Hunt, VP
Mitch Danaher

Addresses accounting and treasury subjects, as well as overall strategies in corporate financial management.
Cost: $69.00
72 Pages
Frequency: 10x/yr
Circulation: 17000
ISSN: 0895-4186
Founded in 1931
Printed in 4 colors on glossy stock

188 Financial Executive Magazine
200 Campus Drive
PO Box 674
Florham Park, NJ 07932

973-360-0177
FAX 973-898-4649
Home Page: www.financialexecutives.org

Marie N Hollein, President & CEO
Marsha Hunt, VP
Mitch Danaher
Paul Chase, VP/Chief Financial Officer
Christopher Allen, VP/Chief Marketing Officer

Award-winning flagship publication of FEI, providing senior-level financial executives with financial, business and management news, trends and strategies to help them work better, faster and smarter. Covers professional, strategic and technological practices and developments that affect financial executives' day-to-day and longer-term issues, reflecting the financial executive's increasing involve-

ment in the general management of their companies.
15M Members
Frequency: 10x/ Year
Founded in 1931

189 Financial Management

Financial Management Association International
College of Business Administration
4202 East Fowler Avenue BSN 3331
Tampa, FL 33620-5500

813-974-2084
FAX 813-974-3318
E-Mail: fma@coba.usf.edu
Home Page: www.fma.org

William G Christie, Executive Editor

Financial Management serves the profession by publishing significant new scholarly research in finance that is of the highest quality. The principal criteria for publishability are originality, rigor, timeliness, practical relevance and clarity.
Frequency: Quarterly

190 ISACA Journal

Information Systems Audit & Control Association
3701 Algonquin Rd
Suite 1010
Rolling Meadows, IL 60008-3124

847-253-1545
FAX 847-253-1443
E-Mail: news@isaca.org
Home Page: www.isaca.org
Social Media: *Facebook, Twitter, LinkedIn*

Susan Caldwell, CEO
Kristen Kessinger, Manager Of Media Relations

Provides professional development information to those spearheading IT governance and those involved with information systems audit, control and security.
Cost: $75.00
10000 Members
Frequency: Bimonthly
Circulation: 86000
Founded in 1969

191 Information Management

ARMA International
11880 College Blvd
Suite 450
Overland Park, KS 66215

913-341-3808
800-422-2762
FAX 913-341-3742
E-Mail: hq@arma.org
Home Page: www.arma.org
Social Media: *Facebook, Twitter, LinkedIn*

Komal Gulich, President
Julie Colgan, President-elect
Brenda Prowse, Treasurer

ARMA International is a not-for-profit association and a source for authoritative education, the latest legislative updates, standards & best practices.
11000 Members
Founded in 1955

192 Information Management Magazine

ARMA International
11880 College Blvd
Suite 450
Overland Park, KS 66215

913-341-3808
800-422-2762
FAX 913-341-3742
E-Mail: hq@arma.org

Home Page: www.arma.org
Social Media: *Facebook, Twitter, LinkedIn*

Komal Gulich, President
Julie Colgan, President-elect
Brenda Prowse, Treasurer

The leading source of information on topics and issues central to the management of records and information worldwide. Each issue features insightful articles written by experts in the management of records and information.
Cost: $115.00
Frequency: Bi-monthly
Circulation: 11000
ISSN: 1535-2897
Mailing list available for rent: 9000 names
Printed in 4 colors on glossy stock

193 Insight

Illinois CPA Society
550 W Jackson Blvd
Suite 900
Chicago, IL 60661-5742

312-993-0407
800-993-0407
FAX 312-993-9954
E-Mail: jwinn@stametine.com
Home Page: www.icpas.org
Social Media: *Facebook, Twitter, LinkedIn, YouTube*

Elaine Weiss, President & CEO
Todd Shapiro, CFO & VP Finance & Administration
Judy Giannetto, INSIGHT Director

Editorial content focuses on practical issues affecting professional development.
Frequency: Monthly
Circulation: 23000
Founded in 1980

194 Internal Auditing

Thomson Reuters
2395 Midway Rd
Carrollton, TX 75006

817-332-3709
800-431-9025
FAX 888-216-1929
E-Mail: trta.lei-support@thomsonreuters.com
Home Page: www.ria.thomsonreuters.com

Elaine Yadlon, Plant Manager
Thomas H Glocer, CEO & Director
Robert D Daleo, Chief Financial Officer
Kelli Crane, Senior Vice President & CIO

Provides solutions to internal auditing problems. Only professional resource written exclusively by leading practitioners.
Cost: $275.00
Frequency: Annual+
Founded in 1935

195 Internal Auditor Magazine

Institute of Internal Auditors
247 Maitland Ave
Altamonte Spgs, FL 32701-4201

407-937-1100
FAX 407-937-1101
E-Mail: iia@theiia.org
Home Page: www.theiia.org
Social Media: *Facebook, Twitter, LinkedIn*

J. Michael Pepper, Chairman
Carolyn Saint, Senior Vice President
John Wxzelaki, Vice Chairman - Finance/security

World's leading publication covering the internal audit profession. Shares timely, helpful- indispensable -information for professionals who want to keep pace with the diverse, dynamic field of internal auditing.
160M Members
Founded in 1941

196 International Journal of Business Data Communications and Networking

Information Resources Management Association
701 E Chocolate Ave
Suite 200
Hershey, PA 17033-1240

717-533-8845
FAX 717-533-8661
E-Mail: member@irma-international.org
Home Page: www.irma-international.org

Jan Travers, Executive Director
Sherif Kamel, Communications Director
Lech Janczewski PhD, IRMA World Representative Director
Gerald Grant, IRMA Doctoral Symposium Director
Paul Chalekian, IRMA United States Representative

This journal examines the impact of data communications and networking technologies, policies, and management on business organizatios, capturing their effect on IT-enabled management practices.
Cost: $545.00
Frequency: Quarterly
ISSN: 1548-0631

197 Interpreter Magazine

Insurance Accounting Systems Association
PO Box 51340
Durham, NC 27717-1340

919-489-0991
FAX 919-489-1994
E-Mail: info@iasa.org
Home Page: www.iasa.org
Social Media: *Facebook, Twitter*

Ruth Estrich, President
Elizabeth Mercier, CIO
Ernie Pearson, Board Chair
Joseph Pomilia, Executive Director

This magazine includes reports on actions by the NAIC, interviews with business leaders, reports on industry trends and news about IASA activities.
Cost: $45.00
12 Pages
Frequency: Quarterly
Founded in 1940

198 Issues in Accounting Education

American Accounting Association
5717 Bessie Dr
Sarasota, FL 34233-2399

941-921-7747
FAX 941-923-4093
E-Mail: deirdre@aaahq.org
Home Page: aaahq.org

Tracey Sutherland, Executive Director
Deirdre Harris, Publications Contact

Provides a forum for exchange of education-related ideas and techniques among accounting professors. A widley cited resource for academic members of the Association.
8600 Members
Frequency: Quarterly
Circulation: 5500
Founded in 1983

199 Journal of Accountancy

American Institute of Certified Public Accountants
1211 Avenue of the Americas
New York, NY 10036-8701

212-596-6200
FAX 212-596-6213
E-Mail: service@aicpa.org
Home Page: www.aicpa.org

Social Media: *Facebook, Twitter, LinkedIn, RSS*

Barry C Melancon, CEO
Susan Coffey, Senior Vice President
Lawson Carmichael, SVP - Strategy
Arleen Thomas, SVP - Mgmt Accounting and Global

AICPA publication that focuses on the latest news and developments related to the field of accounting
Frequency: Monthly
Founded in 1887

200 Journal of Accounting Research
University of Chicago Booth School of Business
5807 S Woodlawn Ave
Chicago, IL 60637-1656

773-702-7743
FAX 773-702-2225
E-Mail: jar@chicagobooth.edu
Home Page: www.chicagobooth.edu
Social Media: *Facebook, Twitter, LinkedIn, YouTube*

Ted Snyder, Manager
Nicholas Dopuch, Consulting Editor

Publishes original research using analytical, empirical, experimental, and field study methods in accounting research.
Cost: $49.00
Frequency: 5 Times/Year
Circulation: 2800
Founded in 1963

201 Journal of Accounting and Public Policy
Elsevier
3251 Riverport Lane
Maryland Heights, MO 63043

314-447-8878
877-839-7126
FAX 314-447-8077
E-Mail: journalcustomerservice-usa@elsevier.com
Home Page: www.elsevier.com

Ron Mobed, CEO
David Lomas, CFO
Gavin Howe, EVP, Human Resources

Publishes research papers that focus on the intersection between accounting and public policy. It offers articles on accounting including public administration, political science and the law.
Cost: $126.00
Frequency: 6x Yearly
ISSN: 0278-4254
Founded in 1997

202 Journal of Applied Finance
Financial Management Association International
College of Business Administration
4202 East Fowler Avenue BSN 3331
Tampa, FL 33620-5500

813-974-2084
FAX 813-974-3318
E-Mail: fma@coba.usf.edu
Home Page: www.fma.org

Betty J Simkins, Editor
Ramesh P Rao, Editor
Charles W Smithson, Editor

The Journal of Applied Finance's goal is to be the leading bridging journal between practitioners and academics. The mission is to publish well-crafted papers of interest to practitioners and of use to academics in stimulating research and in their teaching function.
Frequency: 2 Times/Year

203 Journal of Construction Accounting & Taxation
Thomson Reuters
2395 Midway Rd
Carrollton, TX 75006

817-332-3709
800-431-9025
FAX 888-216-1929
E-Mail: trta.lei-support@thomsonreuters.com
Home Page: www.ria.thomsonreuters.com

Elaine Yadlon, Plant Manager
Thomas H Glocer, CEO & Director
Robert D Daleo, Chief Financial Officer
Kelli Crane, Senior Vice President & CIO

Authoritative, targeted articles and experience-based columns cover several areas, including job-costing, risk assessment, dispute resolution, financial reporting, and benchmarking contractor performance.
Cost: $270.00
Frequency: 6 Times/Year
Circulation: 3400
Founded in 1935

204 Journal of Cost Analysis and Parametrics
Society of Cost Estimating and Analysis
8221 Old Courthouse Rd
Suite 106
Vienna, VA 22182

703-938-5090
FAX 703-938-5091
E-Mail: scea@sceaonline.org
Home Page: www.sceaonline.org

Erin Whittaker, Executive Director
Sharon Burger, Certification Program Admin
Brittany Walker, Membership Coordinator

The Journal of Cost Analysis and Parametrics is a joint publication with the International Society of Parametric Analysts. It is dedicated to promoting excellence in cost estimating, cost analysis, and cost management.
Cost: $ 55.00
2015 Members
Frequency: Twice/Year
Founded in 1990

205 Journal of Cost Management
Thomson Reuters
2395 Midway Rd
Carrollton, TX 75006

817-332-3709
800-431-9025
FAX 888-216-1929
E-Mail: trta.lei-support@thomsonreuters.com
Home Page: www.ria.thomsonreuters.com

Elaine Yadlon, Plant Manager
Thomas H Glocer, CEO & Director
Robert D Daleo, Chief Financial Officer
Kelli Crane, Senior Vice President & CIO

Journal of modern cost management (including cost and managerial accounting topics), especially activity-based costing, activity-based management, performance measurement, target costing and investment justification. Accepts advertising.
Cost: $275.00
64 Pages
Founded in 1935

206 Journal of Emerging Technologies in Accounting
American Accounting Association
5717 Bessie Dr
Sarasota, FL 34233-2399

941-921-7747
FAX 941-923-4093
E-Mail: info@aaahq.org

Home Page: aaahq.org
Social Media: *Facebook, Twitter*

Tracey Sutherland, Executive Director
Deirdre Harris, Publications Contact

This journal is distributed to members of the AI/Emerging Technologies section of the Association, as well as libraries.
8600 Members
Frequency: Annually
Circulation: 300
Founded in 1916

207 Journal of Government Financial Management
Association of Government Accountants
2208 Mount Vernon Ave
Alexandria, VA 22301-1314

703-684-6931
800-242-7211
FAX 703-548-9367
E-Mail: agacgfm@agacgfm.org
Home Page: www.agacgfm.org

Relmond Van Daniker, Executive Director
Evelyn Brown, National President

Provides valuable information for governmental decision makers. Examines budgeting, accounting, auditing and data process developments.
Cost: $60.00
Frequency: Quarterly
Circulation: 14,769
Mailing list available for rent: 18,000 names

208 Journal of Information Systems
American Accounting Association
5717 Bessie Dr
Sarasota, FL 34233-2399

941-921-7747
FAX 941-923-4093
E-Mail: deirdre@aaahq.org
Home Page: aaahq.org

Tracey Sutherland, Executive Director
Deirdre Harris, Publications Contact

Covers developments relating to information systems in use in the accounting industry.
Cost: $35.00
8600 Members
Frequency: Twice/Year
Founded in 1916

209 Journal of International Accounting Research
American Accounting Association
5717 Bessie Dr
Sarasota, FL 34233-2399

941-921-7747
FAX 941-923-4093
E-Mail: deirdre@aaahq.org
Home Page: aaahq.org

Tracey Sutherland, Executive Director
Deirdre Harris, Publications Contact

Has a diverse readership and is interested in articles in auditing, financial accounting, managerial accounting, systems, tax, and other specialties within the field of accounting.
8600 Members
Frequency: Twice/Year
Circulation: 1300
Founded in 1916

210 Journal of Legal Tax Research
American Accounting Association
5717 Bessie Dr
Sarasota, FL 34233-2399

941-921-7747
FAX 941-923-4093
E-Mail: deirdre@aaahq.org
Home Page: aaahq.org

Tracey Sutherland, Executive Director
Deirdre Harris, Publications Contact

Publishes creative and innovative studies employing legal research methodologies that logically and clearly identify, decribe and illuminate important current tax issues, propose improvements in tax systems and unique solutions to problems, and critically analyze proposed or recent tax rule changes from both technical and policy perspectives.
8600 Members
Frequency: Twice/Year
Circulation: 900
Founded in 1916

211   Journal of Management Accounting Research
American Accounting Association
5717 Bessie Dr
Sarasota, FL 34233-2399

941-921-7747
FAX 941-923-4093
E-Mail: deirdre@aaahq.org
Home Page: aaahq.org

Tracey Sutherland, Executive Director
Deirdre Harris, Publications Contact

Devoted exclusively to management accounting research. Contributingto the expansion of knowledge related to the theory and practice of management accounting. Covers all areas of management accounting including, budgeting, internal reporting, incentives, performance evaluation, and the interface between internal and external reporting.
8600 Members
Frequency: Annually, December
Circulation: 2000
Founded in 1916

212   Journal of Organizational and End User Computing
Information Resources Management Association
701 E Chocolate Ave
Suite 200
Hershey, PA 17033-1240

717-533-8845
FAX 717-533-8661
E-Mail: member@irma-internationa.org
Home Page: www.irma-international.org

Jan Travers, Executive Director
Sherif Kamel, Communications Director
Lech Janczewski PhD, IRMA World Representative Director
Gerald Grant, IRMA Doctoral Symposium Director
Paul Chalekian, IRMA United States Representative

The Journal of Organizational and End User Computing (JOEUC) provides a forum to information technology educators, researchers, and practitioners to advance the practice and understanding of organizational and end user computing. The journal features a major emphasis on how to increase organizational and end user productivity and performance, and how to achieve organizational, strategic and competitive advantage.
Cost: $125.00
Frequency: Quarterly
ISSN: 1546-2234

213   Journal of the American Taxation Association
American Accounting Association
5717 Bessie Dr
Sarasota, FL 34233-2399

941-921-7747
FAX 941-923-4093
E-Mail: info@aaahq.org
Home Page: aaahq.org

Tracey Sutherland, Executive Director
Deirdre Harris, Publications Contact

Dedicated to disseminating a wide variety of tax knowledge and publishes research that employs quantitative, analytical, experimental, and descriptive methods to address tax topics of interest to its readership.
8600 Members
Frequency: Twice/Year
Circulation: 1100
Founded in 1916

214   National Public Accountant
National Society of Accountants
1010 N Fairfax St
Alexandria, VA 22314-1574

703-549-6400
800-966-6679
FAX 703-549-2984
E-Mail: members@nsacct.org
Home Page: www.nsacct.org
Social Media: *Facebook, Twitter, LinkedIn*

Harlan Rose, President
Steven Hanson, First Vice President
Marilyn Niwao, Second Vice President
Brian Thompson, Secretary-Treasurer

News for practicing accountants and tax practitioners.
48 Pages
Circulation: 20000
ISSN: 0027-9978
Founded in 1945

215   New Accountant
REN Publishing
3550 W Peterson Avenue
Suite 403
Chicago, IL 60659

773-866-9900
FAX 773-866-9881
E-Mail: inquiries@RenPublishing.com
Home Page: www.renpublishing.com/

Steven N Polydoris, President/Publisher/Editor

A professional publication for accounting students and the accounting profession. Each issue includes articles to introduce students to the many and diverse career opportunities available to accounting majors and to prepare college accounting students and recent graduates to sit for the CPA exam. Also available in an online format.
Cost: $85.00
17 Pages
Frequency: Monthly
Circulation: 68000
Founded in 1883

216   Newspaper Financial Executive Journal
Interactive & Newsmedia Financial Executives
550 W. Frontage Road
Suite 3500
Northfield, IL 50093

847-715-7000
FAX 847-715-7004
Home Page: www.infe.org
Social Media: *Facebook, Twitter, LinkedIn*

Trade publication for financial management of newspapers. More than 800 members.
Frequency: Weekly
Circulation: 1000
Founded in 1947

217   North American Actuarial Journal
Society of Actuaries
475 N Martingale Rd
Suite 600
Schaumburg, IL 60173-2252

847-706-3500
FAX 847-706-3599

E-Mail: webmaster@soa.org
Home Page: www.soa.org

Greg Heidrich, Executive Director
Stacy Lin, Deputy Executive Director/CFO
Harry H Panjer, Editor

Scientically addresses domestic and international problems, interests and concerns of actuaries, their customers, and public policy decision makers.
Frequency: Quarterly
Circulation: 22800
ISSN: 1092-0277
Founded in 1997
Mailing list available for rent: 17000 names at $105 per M

218   PayState Update
American Payroll Association
660 N Main Ave
Suite 100
San Antonio, TX 78205-1217

210-226-4600
FAX 210-226-4027
E-Mail: apamail@mindspring.com
Home Page: www.payroll.org
Social Media: *Facebook, Twitter, LinkedIn*

Daniel Maddux, President

Newsletter dedicated exclusively to state and local payroll compliance news and issues.
Cost: $289.00
Frequency: Bi-Weekly

219   Payroll Administration Guide
Bureau of National Affairs
3 Bethesda Metro Center
Suite 250
Bethesda, MD 20814

800-372-1033
FAX 800-253-0332
E-Mail: customercare@bna.com
Home Page: www.bna.com

Gregory McCaffery, President and CEO
John Camp, VP and CTO
Lisa Fitzpatrick, VP and CMO

A notification and reference service for payroll professionals. Covers federal and state employment tax, wage-hour and wage-payment laws.
Cost: $896.00
Frequency: Bi-Weekly
Founded in 1929

220   Paytech
American Payroll Association
660 N Main Ave
Suite 100
San Antonio, TX 78205-1217

210-226-4600
FAX 210-226-4027
E-Mail: apa@americanpayroll.org
Home Page: www.payroll.org
Social Media: *Facebook, Twitter, LinkedIn*

Daniel Maddux, President

Member magazine that includes case studies, topical articles, themed issues and comprehensive Buyer's Guides.
Cost: $200.00
Frequency: Monthly
Circulation: 40000
Founded in 1982

221   Practical Tax Strategies
Thomson Reuters
2395 Midway Rd
Carrollton, TX 75006

817-332-3709
800-431-9025
FAX 888-216-1929

E-Mail: trta.lei-support@thomsonreuters.com
Home Page: www.ria.thomsonreuters.com

Elaine Yadlon, Plant Manager
Thomas H Glocer, CEO & Director
Robert D Daleo, Chief Financial Officer
Kelli Crane, Senior Vice President & CIO

Features offer in-depth articles and technical
notes on taxation.
Cost: $185.00
64 Pages
Frequency: Monthly
Circulation: 12000
Founded in 1935

222 Public Budgeting and Finance
American Association for Budget and
Program
PO Box 1157
Falls Church, VA 22041

703-941-4300
FAX 703-941-1535
E-Mail: aabpa@aol.com
Home Page: www.aabpa.org
Social Media: *Facebook, Twitter, LinkedIn,
GovLoop*

Judy Thomas, President
Melissa Neuman, President Elect
Anthony Rainey, VP
Patrick Vallely, Treasurer

Budget and program analysis professionals.
Frequency: Quarterly

223 Real Estate Taxation
Thomson Reuters
2395 Midway Rd
Carrollton, TX 75006

817-332-3709
800-431-9025
FAX 888-216-1929
E-Mail: trta.lei-support@thomsonreuters.com
Home Page: www.ria.thomsonreuters.com

Elaine Yadlon, Plant Manager
Thomas H Glocer, CEO & Director
Robert D Daleo, Chief Financial Officer
Kelli Crane, Senior Vice President & CIO

Timely source of new ideas, trends and legal
developments in real estate taxation. This journal gives you complete, ongoing coverage of
all aspects of real estate tax planning.
Cost: $350.00
Frequency: Quarterly
Founded in 1935

224 Review of Taxation of Individuals
Thomson Reuters
2395 Midway Rd
Carrollton, TX 75006

817-332-3709
800-431-9025
FAX 888-216-1929
E-Mail: trta.lei-support@thomsonreuters.com
Home Page: www.ria.thomsonreuters.com

Elaine Yadlon, Plant Manager
Thomas H Glocer, CEO & Director
Robert D Daleo, Chief Financial Officer
Kelli Crane, Senior Vice President & CIO

Offers information on the taxation of individu-
als, legislation, etc.
Cost: $58.00
Frequency: Monthly
Founded in 1935

225 Sales & Use Tax Monitor
Strafford Publications
590 Dutch Valley Road NE
PO Box 13729
Atlanta, GA 30324-0729

404-881-1141
800-926-7926
FAX 404-881-0074
E-Mail: customerservice@straffordpub.com

Home Page: www.straffordpub.com
Social Media: *Twitter*

Richard Ossoff, President
Jon McKenna, Executive Editor

Provides updates on compliance requirements
and tax avoidance opportunities in every state.
Cost: $487.00
Frequency: 2 Times/Month
ISSN: 0161-309X
Founded in 1984

226 Spectrum Magazine
National Association Of Black Accountants
7474 Greenway Center Dr
Suite 1120
Greenbelt, MD 20770-3504

301-474-6222
888-571-2939
FAX 301-474-3114
Home Page: www.nabainc.org
Social Media: *Facebook, Twitter, LinkedIn,
YouTube*

Calvin Harris Jr., President/CEO
Guillermo Hysaw, Executive Director and COO
Veda Stanley, Executive Vice President
Sheila Taylor-Clark, CPA
Ronald Walker, Chairman, Division of Firms

Provides a communication mechanism whereby
readers are kept abreast of key topics of interest
within the accounting, finance, and business
professions.
Frequency: Annual

227 State Income Tax Monitor
Strafford Publications
590 Dutch Valley Road NE
PO Box 13729
Atlanta, GA 30324-0729

404-881-1141
800-926-7926
FAX 404-881-0074
E-Mail: customerservice@straffordpub.com
Home Page: www.straffordpub.com

Richard Ossoff, President
Jon McKenna, Executive Editor

This journal is a comprehensive briefing on the
latest revenue rulings, tax codes, regulations,
court decisions and more in every state.
Cost: $467.00
Frequency: 2 Times/Month
ISSN: 0161-309X
Founded in 1984

228 Strategic Finance
Institute of Management Accountants
10 Paragon Dr
Suite 1
Montvale, NJ 07645-1774

201-573-9000
800-638-4427
FAX 201-474-1600
E-Mail: ima@imanet.org
Home Page: www.imanet.org
Social Media: *Facebook, Twitter, LinkedIn*

Jeffrey C. Thomson, President and CEO
Brian L. McGuire, Chair
John C. Macaulay, Chair-Elect
Sandra B. Richtermeyer, Chair-Emeritus

IMA's award winning magazine that provides
the latest information about practices and
trends in finance, accounting, and information
management that will impact members and
their jobs.
Cost: $195.00
Frequency: Monthly
Printed in 4 colors on glossy stock

229 TAXPRO Journal
National Association of Tax Professionals

PO Box 8002
Appleton, WI 54912-8002

800-558-3402
FAX 800-747-0001
E-Mail: natp@natptax.com
Home Page: www.natptax.com
Social Media: *Facebook, Twitter, MySpace*

Jo Ann Schoen, President
Jean Millerchip, Vice President
Gerard Cannito, Treasurer
Patricia M. McNeer, Secretary
Kathy Stanek, CEO

In-depth tax information and timely feature articles on such issues as new tax acts, practical
tax applications, and solutions to the
day-to-day challenges of running a tax practice.
Frequency: Quarterly

**230 Tax Management Estates, Gifts and
Trusts Journal**
Bureau of National Affairs
3 Bethesda Metro Center
Suite 250
Bethesda, MD 20814

800-372-1033
FAX 301-294-6760
E-Mail: www.customercare@bna.com
Home Page: www.bna.com

Gregory McCaffery, President and CEO
John Camp, VP and CTO
Lisa Fitzpatrick, VP and CMO

Provides articles by leading tax practitioners
and proven techniques for estate planning and
planning opportunities. It also features reviews
of legislative, administrative and judicial
developments.
Frequency: Bimonthly

231 Tax and Business Advisor
Grant Thornton
175 W Jackson Blvd
Suite 20
Chicago, IL 60604-2687

312-856-0001
FAX 312-602-8099
Home Page: www.grantthornton.com
Social Media: *Twitter, LinkedIn*

Stephen Chipman, CEO
Lou Grabowsky, COO
Russ Wieman, Chief Financial Officer

Current tax and general business issues.
Founded in 1924

232 The Accounting Review
American Accounting Association
5717 Bessie Dr
Sarasota, FL 34233-2399

941-921-7747
FAX 941-923-4093
E-Mail: info@aaahq.org
Home Page: aaahq.org
Social Media: *Facebook, Twitter*

Tracey Sutherland, Executive Director
Deirdre Harris, Publications Contact

A respected journal covering accounting theory
and research, business problems and the teaching of business and accounting subjects. Read
by businessmen, teachers, and students of accounting, as well as practicing accountants
throughout the world.
Cost: $275.00
8600 Members
Frequency: 6/Year
Circulation: 8000
Founded in 1916

233 The Bottom Line
PO Box 1157
Falls Church, VA 22041

703-941-4300
FAX 703-941-1535
E-Mail: aabpa@aabpa.org
Home Page: www.aabpa.org
Social Media: *Facebook, Twitter, LinkedIn, GovLoop*

Judy Thomas, President
Melissa Neuman, President Elect
Anthony Rainey, VP
Patrick Vallely, Treasurer

Helps federal, state, and local government managers and analysts, corporate executives and academic specialists meet the unique challenges of their careers. By helping members keep up with the latest developments in their fields, establish and maintain contacts with colleagues, represent their interests and share opportunities, AABPA serves the key difference between simply having a job and being part of a highly respected and well trained profession.
400 Members
Frequency: Monthly
Founded in 1976

234 The Bottomline
Hospitality Financial & Technology
Professionals
11709 Boulder Lane
Suite 110
Austin, TX 78726-1832

512-249-5333
800-646-4387
FAX 512-249-1533
E-Mail: membership@hftp.org
Home Page: www.hftp.org

Frank I Wolfe, Executive VP/CEO
Lucinda Hart, COO
Thomas Atzenhofer, CFO
Eliza Selig, Director of Communications

The Bottomline chronicles the most important industry news with focuses on both finance, technology and general management in hospitality.
4800 Members
Frequency: 10x/Year
Founded in 1952

235 The Compass
American Society of Women Accountants
1760 Old Meadow Road
Suite 500
McLean, VA 22102

703-506-3265
800-326-2163
FAX 703-506-3266
E-Mail: aswa@aswa.org
Home Page: www.aswa.org
Social Media: *Facebook, Twitter, LinkedIn*

Cheryl E Heitz, President
Catherine Mulder, President-elect
Berranthia Brown, VP

Each e-magazine includes content in the areas of accounting & auditing, controllership, leadership, and tax and quick and easy links to the popular sections of the American Society of Women Accountants web site.
Frequency: Monthly
Founded in 1938

236 The Tax Adviser
American Institute of Certified Public
Accountants
1211 Avenue of the Americas
New York, NY 10036-8701

212-596-6200
FAX 212-596-6213
E-Mail: service@aicpa.org
Home Page: www.aicpa.org
Social Media: *Facebook, Twitter, LinkedIn*

Barry C Melancon, CEO
Susan Coffey, Senior Vice President
Lawson Carmichael, SVP - Strategy
Arleen Thomas, SVP - Mgmt Accounting

Monthly tax journal for CPAs and other tax professionals. It includes tax-planning techniques and tax-saving methods which make it a premier source of cutting-edge tax strategies.
Frequency: Monthly
Founded in 1887

237 Today's CPA
Texas Society of CPAs
14651 Dallas Pkwy
Suite 700
Dallas, TX 75254-7408

972-687-8500
800-428-0272
FAX 972-687-8646
Home Page: www.tscpa.org
Social Media: *Facebook, Twitter, LinkedIn*

Fred Timmons, Chairman
William Hornberger, Chairman/Elect
Stephen W Parker, Treasurer
Roxie Samaniego, Secretary

Includes articles, news and professional tips.
Cost: $28.00
27000 Members
Frequency: Bimonthly

Trade Shows

238 AAA Annual Meeting
American Accounting Association
5717 Bessie Dr
Sarasota, FL 34233-2399

941-921-7747
FAX 941-923-4093
E-Mail: info@aaahq.org
Home Page: aaahq.org

Tracey Sutherland, Executive Director
Karen Pincus, President
Deirdre Harris, Publications Contact

Highlighting the difference made when members are actively engaged in the profession. Striving for thought leadership through research, teaching, involvement in practice, and standard setting. 70 booths of accounting equipment, supplie and services. Accounting and business education, research and practice textbooks, publishers, software, etc.
8600 Members
Frequency: Annual/Summer
Founded in 1916

239 AAH Research Conference
Academy of Accounting Historians
10900 Euclid Avenue
Cleveland, OH 44106-7235

216-368-2058
FAX 216-368-6244
E-Mail: acchistory@case.edu
Home Page: www.aahhq.org

Joanne Cross, President
Robert Colson, President Elect
Yvette Lazdowski, VP, Communications
Robert Colson, VP Communications
Stephanie Moussalli, Secretary

Subjects include modern perspectives of accounting history.
600 Members
Founded in 1973

240 ACUA Annual Conference
Association of College and University
Auditors

PO Box 14306
Lenexa, KS 66285-4306

913-895-4620
FAX 913-895-4652
E-Mail: acua-info@goamp.com
Home Page: www.acua.org

M Kevin Robinson, President
J Richard Dawson, Vice President
Karen R Hinen, Executive Director

Annual conference for professionals in the auditing profession.
Frequency: Annual

241 ACUA Midyear Conference
Association of College and University
Auditors
PO Box 14306
Lenexa, KS 66285-4306

913-895-4620
FAX 913-895-4652
E-Mail: acua-info@goamp.com
Home Page: www.acua.org
Social Media: *Facebook, Twitter, LinkedIn*

M Kevin Robinson, President
J Richard Dawson, Vice President
Karen R Hinen, Executive Director

The Midyear Conference was designed to offer a more intense type of training with two-and-a-half days spent on a particular subject matter.
273 Attendees
Frequency: Annual

242 ACUIA Annual Conference & One-Day Seminar
Association of Credit Union Internal
Auditors
PO Box 150908
Alexandria, VA 22315

703-688-2284
866-254-8128
FAX 703-683-0295
E-Mail: acuia@acuia.org
Home Page: www.acuia.org
Social Media: *Facebook, Twitter, LinkedIn*

Brad Feldman, Executive Director
Barry Lucas, Director

This four-day event covers the latest developments and features some of the industry's most popular speakers.

243 AGA's Professional Development Conference & Exposition
Association of Government Accountants
2208 Mount Vernon Avenue
Alexandria, VA 22301

703-684-6931
800-242-7211
FAX 703-548-9367
E-Mail: agacgfm@agacgfm.org
Home Page: www.agacgfm.org

Relmond Van Daniker, Executive Director
Evelyn Brown, National President

Worth 24 CPE hours, the conferenc covers the latest research and information about the American Recovery Act, the constantly changing rules and standards, new management techniques, technological advances and practical tips for bringing greater efficiency to government operations. $800 for members, $1000 for nonmembers
Frequency: Annual

244 AHIA Annual Conference
The Association of Healthcare Internal
Auditors

10200 W 44th Avenue
Suite 304
Wheat Ridge, CO 80033

888-275-2442
FAX 303-422-8894
E-Mail: ahia@ahia.org
Home Page: www.ahia.org

Mark Eddy, Director
Pat Bogusz, Executive Director

Exhibits concerning cost containment and increased productivity in health care institutions through internal auditing.
1000 Attendees
Founded in 1981

245 AM&AA Summer Conference
Alliance of Merger and Acquisition Advisors
200 E. Randolph Street
24th Floor
Chicago, IL 60601

312-856-9590
877-844-2535
FAX 312-729-9800
E-Mail: info@amaaonline.org
Home Page: www.amaaonline.com

Matthew C Hawkins, Conference Chairman

Hosts many of the world's leading mid-market M&A executives, top tier speakers, as well as an invaluable networking opportunity.
Frequency: Semi-Annual

246 AM&AA Winter Conference
Alliance of Merger and Acquisition Advisors
200 E. Randolph Street
24th Floor
Chicago, IL 60601

312-856-9590
877-844-2535
FAX 312-729-9800
E-Mail: info@amaaonline.com
Home Page: www.amaaonline.com

Matthew C Hawkins, Conference Chairman

The conference covers a wide range of current topics of interest to members, such as new accounting and tax regulations, value-added intermediary services, financing, licensure, marketing and business development services and networking opportunities.
Frequency: Semi-Annual

247 ARMA International Conference & Expo
ARMA International
11880 College Blvd.
Suite 450
Overland Park, KS 66210

913-341-3808
800-422-2762
FAX 913-341-3742
E-Mail: hq@arma.org
Home Page: www.arma.org/conference
Social Media: *Facebook, Twitter, LinkedIn*

Carol Jorgenson, Meetings/Education Coordinator
Wanda Wilson, Senior Manager, Conferences
Elizabeth Zlitni, Exposition Manager

Conference, seminar, workshop, banquet, award ceremony and 175 exhibits of micrographics, optical disk, automated document storage and retrieval systems and more technology of interest to information professionals.
3500 Attendees
Frequency: Annual
Founded in 1956

248 ASWA/AWSCPA Joint Annual Conference
American Woman's Society of CPAs
136 S Keowee Street
Dayton, OH 45402

937-222-1872
800-297-2721
FAX 937-222-5794
E-Mail: info@awscpa.org
Home Page: www.awscpa.org
Social Media: *Facebook, Twitter, LinkedIn*

Amy Knowles-Jones, President
Kelly Welter, President Elect
Alexandra Miller, Secretary/Treasurer
Cynthia Cox, VP - Member Services

The conference presents an opportunity to learn from leading experts on ways to develop a variety of your skills, leadership development, networking, education and fun.
Frequency: Annual/September
Founded in 2001

249 ASWA/AWSCPA Joint National Conference
American Society of Women Accountants
1760 Old Meadow Road
Suite 500
McLean, VA 22102

703-506-3265
800-326-2163
FAX 703-506-3266
E-Mail: aswa@aswa.org
Home Page: www.aswa.org
Social Media: *Facebook, Twitter, LinkedIn*

Julia Merrill, Annual Conference Contact

Banquet, luncheon, tours and exhibits of accounting, business and employment opportunities. In conjunction with American Women's Society of CPAs
400 Attendees
Frequency: Annual

250 Academy of Accounting Historians Annual Research Conference
Academy of Accounting Historians
10900 Euclid Avenue
Cleveland, OH 44106-7235

216-368-2058
FAX 216-368-6244
E-Mail: acchistory@case.edu
Home Page: www.aahhq.org

Joanne Cross, President
Robert Colson, President Elect
Yvette Lazdowski, VP, Communications
Robert Colson, VP Communications
Stephanie Moussalli, Secretary

Encourages research, publication, teaching and personal interchanges in all phases of accounting history and its inter-relation with business and economic history. Members are individuals and institutional affiliates with business and economic history.
600 Members
Frequency: Annual
Founded in 1973

251 Accounting Technology New York Show & Conference
Flagg Management
353 Lexington Avenue
New York, NY 10016

212-286-0333
FAX 212-286-0086
E-Mail: flaggmgmnt@msn.com
Home Page: www.flaggmgmt.com

Russell Flagg, President

The free Show focuses on new computer-savvy systems for accounting practices and client operations. See new products offered for the first time. The Conference offers CPE sessions with

more than 100 exhibitors and nationally recognized speakers.
Frequency: Annual

252 All Star Conference
Institute of Internal Auditors
247 Maitland Avenue
Altamonte Springs, FL 32701-4201

407-371-1100
FAX 407-937-1101
E-Mail: iia@theiia.org
Home Page: www.theiia.org

J. Michael Pepper, Chairman
Carolyn Saint, Senior Vice President
John Wxzelaki, Vice Chairman - Finance/security

Event features concurrent sessions in tracks focusing on strategies for excellence, risk management, emerging issues, organization best practices, and preventing fraud.
400 Members
Frequency: October/Annual

253 Alliance of Merger & Acquisition Advisors Semi-Annual Conference
200 E Randolph St
24th Floor
Chicago, IL 60601-6435

312-856-9590
877-844-2535
FAX 312-729-9800
E-Mail: info@amaaonline.org
Home Page: www.amaaonline.com

Michael Nall, Owner

AM&AA is the premier International Organization serving the educational and resource needs of the middle market M&A profession. Conferences cover a wide range of current topics of interest to our members, such as new accounting and tax regulations, value-added intermediary services, financing, licensure, marketing and business development services and networking.
Frequency: Semi-Annual
Founded in 1998

254 American Association of Attorney-Certified Public Accountants Convention
American Association of Attorney-CPAs
8647 Richmond Highway
Suite 639
Alexandria, VA 22309

703-352-8064
888-288-9272
FAX 703-352-8073
E-Mail: info@attorney-cpa.com
Home Page: www.attorney-cpa.com

Robert Driegert, President
Domenick Lioce, President Elect
Joseph Cordell, Treasurer
John Pramberg, Secretary

Exhibits for persons licensed both as attorneys and CPAs.
Frequency: July/Annual
Founded in 1964

255 American Payroll Association Annual Congress
American Payroll Association
660 North Main Avenue
Suite 100
San Antonio, TX 78205

210-226-4600
FAX 210-224-6038
E-Mail: apamail@mindspring.org
Home Page: www.americanpayroll.org
Social Media: *Facebook, Twitter, LinkedIn, YouTube*

Dave Maddux, Executive Director

The Annual Congress is the premier payroll event of the year. With over 190 workshops and special programs and entertainment, Congress is an excellent opportunity for payroll and other financial professionals to learn and network.
1500 Attendees
Frequency: Annual
Founded in 1982

256 American Payroll Association Fall Forum
American Payroll Association
660 North Main Avenue
Suite 100
San Antonio, TX 78205

210-226-4600
FAX 210-224-6038
E-Mail: apamail@mindspring.org
Home Page: www.americanpayroll.org
Social Media: *Facebook, Twitter, LinkedIn, YouTube*

Dave Maddux, Executive Director

APA's Fall Forum is conducted under the auspices of APA's Strategic Payroll Leadership Task Force. This conference includes APA's Payroll Best Practices Survey and the presentation of APA's Prism Award winners.
1500 Attendees
Frequency: Annual
Founded in 1982

257 Annual ACFE Fraud Conference and Exhibition
716 West Ave
Austin, TX 78701-2727

512-478-9070
800-245-3321
FAX 512-478-9297
E-Mail: accounting@acfe.com
Home Page: www.acfe.com
Social Media: *Facebook, Twitter, LinkedIn*

James D Ratley, President and CEO
Scott Grossfeld, Chief Executive Officer

The ACFE is the world's largest anti-fraud organization and premier provider of anti-fraud training and education.
50000 Members

258 Annual Conference for Women in Accounting
1760 Old Meadow Road
Suite 500
McLean, VA 22102

703-506-3265
800-326-2163
FAX 703-506-3266
E-Mail: aswa@aswa.org
Home Page: www.aswa.org
Social Media: *Facebook, Twitter, LinkedIn, ASWA Presidents Blog*

Barbara W Cornington, President
Monika P Miles CPA, VP of Membership
Tracy L Johnson CPA, VP of Chapter Partnering
Vivian L Moller CPA, VP of Communications

Provides a program that offers a myriad of opportunities to help you meet your continuing education goals, whether technical or soft-skills focused, as well as an opportunity to network with other women of similar backgrounds.
4000 Members
Founded in 1938

259 BCCA Media Credit Seminar
550 W Frontage Rd
Suite 3600
Northfield, IL 60093-1243

847-881-8757
FAX 847-784-8059

E-Mail: info@bccacredit.com
Home Page: www.bccacredit.com
Social Media: *Facebook, Twitter*

Cherryl Ingram, Chairman
Chad Richardson, Vice Chairman
Dalton Lee, Secretary
Ralph Bender, Treasurer

Subsidiary of the Media Financial Management Association. BCCA provides credit information, education, and networking opportunities which enables members to efficiently manage credit risk and increase profitability.
600 Members
Founded in 1972

260 CPAAI Regional Meetings
301 State Rt 17
Rutherford, NJ 07070-2599

201-804-8686
FAX 201-804-9222
E-Mail: homeoffice@cpaai.com
Home Page: www.cpaai.com

James F Flynn, President
Glenda Nixon, Chairman
Ted Carnevale, Secretary

CPA Associates International was established as a global group of high-quality independent CPA and chartered accounting firms; it is market exclusive, with members in major cities throughout the world. The organized association provides members with the capabilities of the largest firm, yet allows each to maintain its local practice while avoiding costly overhead and unnecessary controls.
2050 Members
Founded in 1960

261 Capital Summit
American Payroll Association
660 North Main Avenue
Suite 100
San Antonio, TX 78205

210-226-4600
FAX 210-226-4027
E-Mail: apamail@mindspring.org
Home Page: www.americanpayroll.org
Social Media: *Facebook, Twitter, LinkedIn, YouTube*

Dave Maddux, Executive Director

APA hosts the Capital Summit in Washington, D.C. This conference offers attendees the opportunity to meet with government officials and learn about the latest compliance initiatives.
Frequency: Annual
Founded in 1982

262 Club and Hotel Controllers Conference
11709 Boulder Lane
Suite 110
Austin, TX 78726

512-249-5333
800-646-4387
FAX 512-249-1533
Home Page: www.hftp.org
Social Media: *Facebook, Twitter, LinkedIn*

Frank I Wolfe, Executive VP/CEO
Lucinda Hart, COO
Thomas Atzenhofer, CFO
Eliza Selig, Director of Communications

The program offers a range of sessions that reflect diverse responsibilities, from technology to taxes, human resource management to personal inspiration.
4600 Members
Founded in 1952

263 Current Financial Reporting Issues Conference
200 Campus Drive
PO Box 674
Florham Park, NJ 07932

973-360-0177
FAX 973-898-4649
Home Page: www.financialexecutives.org

Marie N Hollein, President & CEO
Marsha Hunt, VP
Mitch Danaher
Paul Chase, VP/Chief Financial Officer
Christopher Allen, VP/Chief Marketing Officer

Get updated in all the areas of financial reporting critical to the sustainability of your company. FASB/IASB technical accounting, revenue recognition, accounting for leases by lessors and lessees, financial instruments-recognition, measurement, hedging and expected loss model, Washington tax update, and the latest SEC happenings.
15M Members
Founded in 1931

264 Detecting & Deterring Financial Reporting Fraud
200 Campus Drive
PO Box 674
Florham Park, NJ 07932

973-360-0177
FAX 973-898-4649
Home Page: www.financialexecutives.org

Marie N Hollein, President & CEO
Marsha Hunt, VP
Mitch Danaher
Paul Chase, VP/Chief Financial Officer
Christopher Allen, VP/Chief Marketing Officer

Executive workshop for exploring strategies for building an ethical philosophy that deters fraud, employs skepticism-an enemy of fraud-in management's attitude and developing a culture of collaboration and knowledge sharing to deter and detect fraud.
15M Members
Frequency: 10x/Year
Founded in 1931

265 Distance Learning Seminar
550 W Frontage Rd
Suite 3600
Northfield, IL 60093-1243

847-881-8757
FAX 847-784-8059
E-Mail: info@bccacredit.com
Home Page: www.bccacredit.com
Social Media: *Facebook, Twitter*

Cherryl Ingram, Chairman
Chad Richardson, Vice Chairman
Dalton Lee, Secretary
Ralph Bender, Treasurer

Credit & Collections 101 for the New Credit Professional
600 Members
Founded in 1972

266 Educational Institutions Payroll Conference
American Payroll Association
660 North Main Avenue
Suite 100
San Antonio, TX 78205

210-226-4600
FAX 210-226-4027
E-Mail: apamail@mindspring.org
Home Page: www.americanpayroll.org
Social Media: *Facebook, Twitter, LinkedIn, YouTube*

Dave Maddux, Executive Director

This conference focuses on compliance issues impacting payroll professionals working in the higher education community.
Frequency: Annual
Founded in 1982

267 FMA Annual Meeting
University of South Florida
4202 E Fowler Ave
BSN 3331
Tampa, FL 33620-9951

813-974-2084
FAX 813-974-3318
E-Mail: fma@coba.usf.edu
Home Page: www.fma.org

Jack S Rader, Executive Director
Douglas R Emery, President Elect
Franklin Allen, VP Program
Alexander J Triantis, VP Global Services
Ajay Patel, Secretary/Treasurer

The Financial Management Association International (FMA) is the global leader in developing and disseminating knowledge about financial decision making. FMA's members include adademicians and practitioners worldwide.
Founded in 1970

268 Financial Leadership Forum
200 Campus Drive
PO Box 674
Florham Park, NJ 07932

973-360-0177
FAX 973-898-4649
Home Page: www.financialexecutives.org

Marie N Hollein, President & CEO
Marsha Hunt, VP
Mitch Danaher
Paul Chase, VP/Chief Financial Officer
Christopher Allen, VP/Chief Marketing Officer

Forum to help advance the success of senior-level financial executives.
15M Members
Frequency: 10x/Year
Founded in 1931

269 Gaming Conference
Institute of Internal Auditors
247 Maitland Avenue
Altamonte Springs, FL 32701-4201

407-371-1100
FAX 407-937-1101
E-Mail: iia@theiia.org
Home Page: www.theiia.org

J. Michael Pepper, Chairman
Carolyn Saint, Senior Vice President
John Wxzelaki, Vice Chairman -
Finance/security

A must attend event for knowledge-seeking auditors, compliance officers, regulators, and professionals from gaming sectors.
300 Members
Frequency: April/Annual

270 General Audit Management Conference
Institute of Internal Auditors
247 Maitland Avenue
Altamonte Springs, FL 32701-4201

407-371-1100
FAX 407-937-1101
E-Mail: iia@theiia.org
Home Page: www.theiia.org

J. Michael Pepper, Chairman
Carolyn Saint, Senior Vice President
John Wxzelaki, Vice Chairman -
Finance/security

The premiere opportunity for chief audit executives (CAEs), audit directors, and audit leaders to network with peers, benchmark against best

practices, and tap into the knowledge of the profession's highest-level practitioners.
800 Members
Frequency: March/Annual

271 Governance, Risk and Control Conference
Institute of Internal Auditors
247 Maitland Avenue
Altamonte Springs, FL 32701-4201

407-371-1100
FAX 407-937-1101
E-Mail: iia@theiia.org
Home Page: www.theiia.org

J. Michael Pepper, Chairman
Carolyn Saint, Senior Vice President
John Wxzelaki, Vice Chairman -
Finance/security

Develop and enhance your auditing skills.
400 Members
Frequency: August/Annual

272 HITEC
11709 Boulder Lane
Suite 110
Austin, TX 78726

512-249-5333
800-646-4387
FAX 512-249-1533
Home Page: www.hftp.org
Social Media: *Facebook, Twitter, LinkedIn*

Frank I Wolfe, Executive VP/CEO
Lucinda Hart, COO
Thomas Atzenhofer, CFO
Eliza Selig, Director of Communications

Attend HITEC and network with the industry's innovators, gain knowledge from an expert-led education program and find technology products and services to take your organization to the next level.
4600 Members
Founded in 1952

273 Hall of Fame Gala
200 Campus Drive
PO Box 674
Florham Park, NJ 07932

973-360-0177
FAX 973-898-4649
Home Page: www.financialexecutives.org

Marie N Hollein, President & CEO
Marsha Hunt, VP
Mitch Danaher
Paul Chase, VP/Chief Financial Officer
Christopher Allen, VP/Chief Marketing Officer

Providing recognition to senior-level financial executives who have epitomized the performance, leadership and integrity of the most exemplary financial professionals throughout their careers and in doing so, have made significant contributions to the betterment of their respective organizations and to the profession as a whole.
15M Members
Founded in 1931

274 IASA Annual Conference
Insurance, Accounting & Systems Association
PO Box 51340
Durham, NC 27717-1340

919-489-0991
FAX 919-489-1994
E-Mail: info@iasa.org
Home Page: www.iasa.org
Social Media: *Facebook, Twitter*

Ruth Estrich, President
Joseph Pomilia, Executive Director
Ernie Pearson, Board Chair
H. Louise Ziemann, president-elect
Tom Ewbank, CFO

Provides comprehensive education programs targeted for financial and technology professionals in the industry.
1800 Attendees
Frequency: Annual

275 IFRS Boot Camp
200 Campus Drive
PO Box 674
Florham Park, NJ 07932

973-360-0177
FAX 973-898-4649
Home Page: www.financialexecutives.org

Marie N Hollein, President & CEO
Marsha Hunt, VP
Mitch Danaher
Paul Chase, VP/Chief Financial Officer
Christopher Allen, VP/Chief Marketing Officer

Provides an update on various recent convergence and regulatory/ statutory matters impacting U.S. GAAP and IFRS reporting companies. Provides financial executives with practical information for addressing global accounting convergence in their organizations, including potential operational considerations rellated to topics such as leases and revenue recognition.
15M Members
Frequency: 10x/Year
Founded in 1931

276 IMA's Annual Conference & Exposition
10 Paragon Dr
Suite 1
Montvale, NJ 07645-1774

201-573-9000
800-638-4427
FAX 201-474-1600
E-Mail: ima@imanet.org
Home Page: www.imanet.org
Social Media: *Facebook, Twitter, LinkedIn*

Jeffrey C. Thomson, President and CEO
Brian L. McGuire, Chair
John C. Macaulay, Chair-Elect
Sandra B. Richtermeyer, Chair-Emeritus

Offers three days of knowledge building, education, networking, optional pre-conference workshops, and opportunities to earn NASBA-approved credits.
67000 Members
Founded in 1919

277 IMA's Student Leadership Conference
10 Paragon Dr
Suite 1
Montvale, NJ 07645-1774

201-573-9000
800-638-4427
FAX 201-474-1600
E-Mail: ima@imanet.org
Home Page: www.imanet.org
Social Media: *Facebook, Twitter, LinkedIn*

Jeffrey C. Thomson, President and CEO
Brian L. McGuire, Chair
John C. Macaulay, Chair-Elect
Sandra B. Richtermeyer, Chair-Emeritus

Offers three days of learning and career networking opportunities for college students and educators. Accounting, finance, and business students will learn from veteran practitioners about the critical role of accountants and financial professionals within business.
67000 Members
Founded in 1919

278 Information Resources Management Association Conferences
Information Resources Management Association

701 E Chocolate Avenue
Suite 200
Hershey, PA 17033

717-533-8845
FAX 717-533-8861
E-Mail: member@irma-international.org
Home Page: www.irma-international.org

Jan Travers, Executive Director
Sherif Kamel, Communications Director
Lech Janczewski PhD, IRMA World
Representative Director
Gerald Grant, IRMA Doctoral Symposium
Director
Paul Chalekian, IRMA United States
Representative

Provides forums for researchers and practitioners to share leading-edge knowledge in the global information resource management area. Various seminars, conventions, conferences and other training programs are offered by IRMA throughout the year.

279   Joint ISPA/SCEA Conference & Workshop
Society of Cost Estimating & Analysis
8221 Old Courthouse Rd
Suite 106
Vienna, VA 22182

703-938-5090
FAX 703-938-5091
E-Mail: scea@sceaonline.org
Home Page: www.sceaonline.net

Erin Whittaker, Executive Director
Sharon Burger, Certification Program Admin
Brittany Walker, Membership Coordinator
Debra Lehman, Treasurer

Speakers and panel sessions, integrated training tracks, informative workshops and vendor exhibits. Three of every four years, the annual conference is a joint conference with the International Society of Parametric Analysts (ISPA). Certification exams are offered at the conference for a separate fee.
2015 Members
400 Attendees
Frequency: Annual/June
Founded in 1990

280   NATP National Conference and Expo
National Association of Tax Professionals
PO Box 8002
Appleton, WI 54912-8002

800-558-3402
FAX 800-747-0001
E-Mail: natp@natptax.com
Home Page: www.natptax.com
Social Media: *Facebook, Twitter, MySpace*

Jo Ann Schoen, President
Jean Millerchip, Vice President
Gerard Cannito, Treasurer
Patricia M. McNeer, Secretary
Kathy Stanek, CEO

Four days filled with top-notch tax education, fun social events, networking, and much more.
Frequency: Annual

281   National Leadership Conference
Association of Government Accountants
2208 Mount Vernon Avenue
Alexandria, VA 22301

703-684-6931
800-242-7211
FAX 703-548-9367
E-Mail: agacgfm@agacgfm.org
Home Page: www.agacgfm.org

Relmond Van Daniker, Executive Director
Evelyn Brown, National President

Presents new tools, and innovations, insights from financial management and accountability leaders, their strategies, mistakes, new management techniques, and the most current standards and regulations updates.
Frequency: Annual/February

282   Performance Management Conference (PMC)
Association of Government Accountants
2208 Mount Vernon Avenue
Alexandria, VA 22301

703-684-6931
800-242-7211
FAX 703-548-9367
E-Mail: agacgfm@agacgfm.org
Home Page: www.agacgfm.org

Relmond Van Daniker, Executive Director
Evelyn Brown, National President

Leaders in performance reporting from all levels of goverment, the private sector and academia share how-tos, lessons learned and cooperative initiatives among governments. Registration begins at $395 for Members, $450 for nonmembers.
Frequency: Annual/November

283   Practice Management Conference
Association for Accounting Administration
136 S Keowee Street
Dayton, OH 45402

937-222-0030
FAX 937-222-5794
E-Mail: aaainfo@cpaadmin.org
Home Page: www.cpaadmin.org
Social Media: *Twitter, LinkedIn*

Dennis Lemieux, President
Norman Saale, Vice President
Janine Zirrith, Secretary
Jim Fahey, Treasurer
Jane Johnson, Director of Education

Information and displays of accounting administration equipment and products.
200 Attendees
Frequency: Annual/June

284   SCEA/ISPA Joint Annual Conference & Training Workshop
Society of Cost Estimating and Analysis
8221 Old Courthouse Rd
Suite 106
Vienna, VA 22182

703-938-5090
FAX 703-938-5091
E-Mail: scea@sceaonline.org
Home Page: www.sceaonline.org

Erin Whittaker, Executive Director
Sharon Burger, Certification Program Admin
Brittany Walker, Membership Coordinator

Features training sessions to help attendees enhance their skill set or prepare for the CCEA or CPP exams, study sessions, Professional Papers give attendees the chance to hear about best practices, lessons learned and the latest developments in the field.
2015 Members
500+ Attendees
Frequency: Annual
Founded in 1990

285   Society of Actuaries Annual Meeting & Exhibit
Society of Actuaries
475 N Martingale Road
Suite 600
Schaumburg, IL 60173

847-697-3900
E-Mail: customerservice@soa.org
Home Page: www.soa.org

Greg Heidrich, Executive Director
Stacy Lin, Deputy Executive Director/CFO

Sessions and keynote presentations about cutting edge research, and discussions, networking opportunities, the latest and greatest technologies, sponsorship opportunities; sometimes held in conjunction with the Academy Luncheon. Registration fees begin at $55 for the luncheon and go to $995 for full meeting attendance.
1,700 Attendees
Frequency: Annual/November

286   SourceMedia Conferences & Events
SourceMedia
One State Street Plaza
27th floor
New York, NY 10004

212-803-6093
800-803-3424
FAX 212-803-8515
E-Mail: abconferences@sourcemedia.com
Home Page: www.sourcemedia.com/

James M Malkin, Chairman & CEO
William Johnson, CFO
Steve Andreazza, VP, Sales & Customer Service
Celie Baussan, SVP, Operations
Anne O'Brien, EVP Marketing & Strategic Planning

SourceMedia Conferences & Events attract over 20,000 attendees worldwide. The content embraces a variety of formats, including: conferences, executive roundtables, expositions, Web seminars, custom events and pod casts. With over 70 events annually, participants are provided with premier content as well as access to the industry's top solution providers. Markets served include: accounting; banking; capital markets; financial services; information technology; insurance; and real estate.

287   Technology and Office Productivity (TOP) Conference
National Association of Tax Professionals
PO Box 8002
Appleton, WI 54912-8002

800-558-3402
FAX 800-747-0001
E-Mail: natp@natptax.com
Home Page: www.natptax.com
Social Media: *Facebook, Twitter, MySpace*

Jo Ann Schoen, President
Jean Millerchip, Vice President
Gerard Cannito, Treasurer
Patricia M. McNeer, Secretary
Kathy Stanek, CEO

Two days filled with valuable education on what it takes to run a small business, fun social events, networking, and more.
Frequency: Annual

288   The IIA's International Conference
The Institute of Internal Auditors
247 Maitland Avenue
Altamonte Springs, FL 32701-4201

407-937-1100
FAX 407-937-1101
E-Mail: iia@theiia.org
Home Page: www.theiia.org

William J Mulcahy, Conference Chairman
Richard Chambers, President & CEO

Annual conference that features and unprecedented number of concurrent sessions on today's top issues, industry best practices, and unique challenges to help you add value to your organization.
84000 Attendees
Frequency: Annual
Founded in 1941

289 The World Congress Annual Leadership Summit on Mergers & Acquisitions
200 E Randolph St
24th Floor
Chicago, IL 60601-6435

312-856-9590
877-844-2535
FAX 312-729-9800
E-Mail: info@amaaonline.org
Home Page: www.amaaonline.com

Michael Nall, Owner

AM&AA is the premier International Organization serving the educational and resource needs of the middle market M&A profession.
Founded in 1998

290 Valcon
Association of Insolvency & Restructuring Advisors
221 Stewart Avenue
Suite 207
Medford, OR 97501

541-858-1665
FAX 541-858-9187
E-Mail: aira@aira.org
Home Page: www.airacira.org

Anthony Sasso, President
Thomas Morrow, Vice President
Mathew Schwartz, Treasurer
Joel Waite, VP
Matthew Schwartz, Treasurer

Join leading restructuring and valuation experts - attorneys, private equity investors, bankers, financial advisors and workout specialists - to discuss cutting-edge valuation issues and market developments.
Frequency: Annual/February
Founded in 1984

Directories & Databases

291 ARMA International's Buyers Guide
ARMA International
11880 College Blvd
Suite 450
Overland Park, KS 66215

913-341-3808
800-422-2762
FAX 913-341-3742
E-Mail: hq@arma.org
Home Page: www.arma.org/conference
Social Media: *Facebook, Twitter, LinkedIn*

75-100 companies listed. Free.

292 Accountancy: A Professional Reference Guide
Georgia State University
35 Broad Street
5th Floor
Atlanta, GA 30302-3991

404-413-7200
FAX 404-413-7203
E-Mail: admissions@gsu.edu
Home Page:
robinson.gsu.edu/accountancy/index.html

Carla Hines, Administrative Coordinator
Allison Jacobs, Director of Student Services

Listings of accounting firms, associations, regulatory agencies and schools offering accredited accounting programs.
Cost: $99.95
450 Pages
Frequency: Hardcover

293 Accounting Research Directory
Markus Wiener Publishing

231 Nassau St
Princeton, NJ 08542-4601

609-921-1141
FAX 609-921-1140
E-Mail: info@markusweiner.com
Home Page: www.markuswiener.com
Social Media: *Facebook*

Markus Wiener, Owner
Lawrence D Brown, Editor
Markus Wiener, President

Quick guide arranged by author's names for key articles. It can enable those interested in quantitative literature analysis to test and verify much of the work in this area by the authors in this book.
Cost: $79.95
Frequency: Hardcover
ISBN: 1-558760-68-7

294 Accounting and Tax Database
ProQuest Information and Learning
789 E Eisenhower Parkway
PO Box 1346
Ann Arbor, MI 48106-1346

734-761-4700
800-889-3358
FAX 800-864-0019
E-Mail: support@il.proquest.com
Home Page: www.il.proquest.com
Social Media: *Facebook, Twitter, LinkedIn*

Offers comprehensive indexing and informative abstracts of articles in prominent accounting, taxation and financial management publications from the US and other countries. Over 260,000 citations.

295 American Association of Attorney-Certified Public Accountants Directory
American Association of Attorney-CPAs
8647 Richmond Highway
Suite 639
Alexandria, VA 22309

703-352-8064
888-288-9272
FAX 703-352-8073
E-Mail: info@attorney-cpa.com
Home Page: www.attorney-cpa.com

Robert Driegert, President
Domenick Lioce, President Elect
Joseph Cordell, Treasurer
John Pramberg, Secretary
Driegert, Secretary

Offers names, addresses and biographical data on 1,400 individuals licensed as both attorneys and CPAs.
100 Pages
Frequency: Annual
Founded in 1964
Printed in one color

296 Directory of Actuarial Memberships
Society of Actuaries
475 N Martingale Rd
Suite 600
Schaumburg, IL 60173-2252

847-706-3500
FAX 847-706-3599
E-Mail: webmaster@soa.org
Home Page: www.soa.org
Social Media: *Twitter, LinkedIn*

Greg Heidrich, Executive Director
Stacy Lin, Deputy Executive Director/CFO
Tiffany Berger, Director of Finance
Richard Veys, General Counsel
Francis P. Sabatini, Vice President

Lists member names, affiliations and contact information for major US and international ac-

tuarial professional associations.
Cost: $150.00
Mailing list available for rent: 17000 names at $300 per M

297 Federal Tax Coordinator 2D
Thomson Reuters
2395 Midway Rd
Carrollton, TX 75006

817-332-3709
800-431-9025
FAX 888-216-1929
E-Mail: trta.lei-support@thomsonreuters.com
Home Page: www.ria.thomsonreuters.com

Elaine Yadlon, Plant Manager
Thomas H Glocer, CEO & Director
Robert D Daleo, Chief Financial Officer
Kelli Crane, Senior Vice President & CIO

Provides verbatim text of the Internal Revenue Code and IRS Regulations. Information is arranged by subject rather than in Code order. Professional tax preparers are heavy users of this service because of the thorough authoritative analysis it provides.
Cost: $2460.00
Founded in 1935

298 Future Actuary
Society of Actuaries
475 N Martingale Rd
Suite 600
Schaumburg, IL 60173-2252

847-706-3500
FAX 847-706-3599
E-Mail: webmaster@soa.org
Home Page: www.soa.org

Greg Heidrich, Executive Director
Stacy Lin, Deputy Executive Director/CFO

Full coverage on topics like career development, non-traditional careers, grading systems, study tips, professional conduct and ethics and the structure of actuarial organizations.
Mailing list available for rent: 17000 names at $300 per M

299 International Guide to Accounting Journals
Markus Weiner Publishers
231 Nassau St
Princeton, NJ 08542-4601

609-921-1141
FAX 609-921-1140
E-Mail: info@markuswiener.com
Home Page: www.markuswiener.com

Markus Wiener, Owner
Surendra Agrawal, Editor

Approximately 300 journals in accounting and related areas, including about 150 published in the US and 150 from 33 other countries that are published in English.
Cost: $49.95
ISBN: 1-558760-67-9

300 National Society of Public Accountants Yearbook
National Society of Public Accountants
1010 N Fairfax St
Alexandria, VA 22314-1574

703-549-6400
800-966-6679
FAX 703-549-2984
E-Mail: members@nsacct.org
Home Page: www.nsacct.org
Social Media: *Facebook, Twitter, LinkedIn*

Harlan Rose, President
Steven Hanson, First Vice President
Marilyn Niwao, Second Vice President
Brian Thompson, Secretary-Treasurer

Association members and committees, lists of affiliated state organizations and members of governing board.
Frequency: Annual

Industry Web Sites

301 www.aabpa.org
American Assoc for Budget and Program Analysis
Social Media: *LinkedIn*
The American Association for Budget and Program Analysis helps federal, state and local government managers and analysts, corporate executives and academic specialists meet the unique challenges of their careers related to the fields of public budgeting and program analysis.

302 www.acatcredentials.org
Accreditation Council for Accountancy and Taxation
Identifies and accredits specialists in accountancy and federal taxation who serve the financial needs of individuals and small to mid-sized business entities. Offers 3 credentials: Accreditation in Accountancy/Accredited Business Accountant, Accredited Tax Preparer and Accredited Tax Advisor.

303 www.acaus.org
Association of Chartered Accountants in the U.S.
ACAUS is a nonprofit professional and educational organization representing interests of over 6,000 U.S. based chartered accountants from the institutes of Chartered Accountants across the globe.

304 www.accountants.org
IGAF Polaris
Association of over 136 independent accounting firms located throughout the world. We developed this comprehensive search site as a means of helping people locate an accounting or consulting firm anywhere in the world.

305 www.acfe.com
Association of Certified Fraud Examiners
The ACFE is the world's largest anti-fraud organization and premier provider of anti-fraud training and education.

306 www.agacgfm.org
Advancing Government Accountability
Educational organization dedicated to the enhancement of public financial management.

307 www.agn.org
Accountants Global Network International
Composed of CPA consulting firms who share information and resources via the associated programs.

308 www.ahia.org
Association of Healthcare Internal Auditors
Promotes cost containment and increased productivity in health care institutions through internal auditing. Serves as a forum for the exchange of experience, ideas, and information among members; provides continuing professional education courses and informs members of developments in health care internal auditing. Offers employment clearinghouse services.

309 www.aicpa.org
American Institute of Certified Public Accountants
The American Institute of Certified Public Accountants is the national, professional organiza-

tion for all Certified Public Accountants. Its mission is to provide members with the resources, information, and leadership that enable them to provide valuable services in the highest professional manner to benefit the public as well as employers and clients.

310 www.aipb.org
American Institute of Professional Bookkeepers
Achieve recognition of bookkeepers as accounting professionals, to keep bookkeepers up-to-date on changes in bookkeeping, accounting and tax, to answer bookkeepers everyday bookkeeping and accounting questions, and to certify bookkeepers who meet high national standards.

311 www.amaaonline.com
Alliance of Merger & Acquisition Advisors
AM&AA is the premier International Organization serving the educational and resource needs of the middle market M&A profession.

312 www.americanpayroll.org
American Payroll Association
American Payroll Association provides numerous opportunities for payroll education and information.

313 www.aswa.org
American Society of Women Accountants
Organization for networking and information exchange in pursuit of professional development.

314 www.attorney-cpa.com
American Association of Attorney-CPAs
Seeks to safeguard the professional and legal rights of CPA attorneys.

315 www.awscpa.org
American Woman's Society of CPAs
Provides supportive environment that promotes equity and provides opportunities for the achievement of career goals in a competitive and rapidly changing profession.

316 www.bap.org
Beta Alpha Psi
Beta Alpha Psi is an honorary organization for Financial Information students and professionals. The primary objective is to encourage and give recognition to scholastic and professional excellence in the business information field.

317 www.bccacredit.com
Broadcast Cable Credit Association
Information on Credit Inquiry Service, credit and collection seminars yearly, credit personnel directories, surveys and on-line services.

318 www.bna.com
Bureau of National Affairs
A national organization that has a broad range of employment topics, designed for the small to medium-sized organization.

319 www.computercpa.com
Accountant's Home Page
Provides information on general accounting for manufacturing, contstruction, service, not-for-profit, e-commerce and more.

320 www.cpa.net
Mark Dietrich, CPA, PC
Includes information on social security and alternatives, bill presentation and payment.

321 www.cpaadmin.org
Association for Accounting Administration

Enables accounting firm administrators to communicate with one another and share experiences in the profession.

322 www.cpaai.com
CPA Associates International
CPA Associates International was established as a global group of high-quality independent CPA and chartered accounting firms; it is market exclusive, with members in major cities throughout the world. The organized association provides members with the capabilities of the largest firm, yet allows each to maintain its local practice while avoiding costly overhead and unnecessary controls.

323 www.cpatechadvisor.com
The CPA Technology Advisor
Online resource for accountants and managers. The Web site features a Buyer's Guide that lists hundreds of businesses, manufacturers, and professionals that can assist public accounting firms in delivering a variety of services to their clients in various industries.

324 www.expresscarriers.com
Express Carriers Association
A member organization of chief financial officers within the American Trucking Association.

325 www.gasb.org
Governmental Accounting Standards Board
Establishes and improves standards of state and local governmental accounting and financial reporting that will result in useful information for users of financial reports and guide and educate the public, including issuers, auditors and users of those financial institutions.

326 www.grantthornton.com
Grant Thornton LLP
Grant Thornton LLP is the U.S. member firm of Grant Thornton International Ltd., one of the six global audit, tax and advisory organizations.

327 www.greyhouse.com
Grey House Publishing
Authoritative reference directories for business information and general reference, including accounting, banking and financial markets. Users can search the online databases with varied search criteria allowing for custom searches by product category, geographic area, sales volume, keyword, subject and more. Full Grey House catalog and online ordering also available.

328 www.hftp.org
Hospitality Financial & Technology Professionals
HFTP is the global professional association for financial and technology personnel working in hotels, clubs, and other hospitality-related businesses.

329 www.iasa.org
Insurance, Accounting & Systems Association
The Insurance Accounting & Systems Association Web site offers information about membership in the organization, accounting seminars, events, publications and textbooks.

330 www.ifac.org
International Federation of Accountants
IFAC is the global organization for the accountancy profession. It works with its 157 members and associates in 123 countries and jurisdictions to protect the public interest by encouraging high quality practices by the world's accountants.

331 www.igafworldwide.org

International Group of Accounting Firms

IGAF Worldwide is one of the oldest, largest, and most well-respected accounting associations in the world. It was founded for the purpose of providing member firms with the tools and resources they need to furnish a broad spectrum of efficient, cost-effective accounting, auditing and management services to clients around the globe.

332 www.imanet.org

Institute of Management Accountants

Professional organization devoted exclusively to management accounting and financial management. Goals are to help members develop both personally and professionally, by means of education, certification, and association with other business professionals.

333 www.infe.org

Interactive & Newsmedia Financial Executives

Controllers, chief accountants, auditors, business managers, treasurers, secretaries and related newspaper executives, educators and public accountants.

334 www.nabainc.org

National Association of Black Accountants

Nationwide professional association with the primary purpose of developing, encouraging and serving as a resource for greater participation by African-Americans and other minorities in the accounting and finance professions.

335 www.nactp.org

Nat'l Association of Computerized Tax Processors

A nonprofit association that represents tax processing software and hardware developers, electronic filing processors, tax form publishers and tax processing service bureaus. The association promotes standards in tax processing and works closely with the Internal Revenue Service and state governments to promote efficient and effective tax filing.

336 www.nacva.com

National Assoc of Certified Valuation Analysts

Global, professional association that supports the business valuation and litigation consulting disciplines within the CPA and professional communities. Along with its training and certification programs, NACVA offers a range of support services, marketing tools, software programs, reference materials and customized databases to enhance the professional capabilities of its members.

337 www.naea.org

National Association of Enrolled Agents

Members are enrolled to represent taxpayers before the Internal Revenue Service. We advise, represent and prepare tax returns for individuals, partnerships, corporations, estates, trusts and any entities with tax reporting requirements.

338 www.nsacct.org

National Society of Accountants

Professional society of practicing accountants and tax practitioners that sponsors the Accreditation Council for Accountancy and Taxation and supports the National Society of Public Accountants Political Action Committee and NSPA Scholarship Foundation.

339 www.sceaonline.org

Society of Cost Estimating and Analysis

Dedicated to improving cost estimating and analysis in government and industry. Offers a unique collection of educational and training materials on cost estimating, cost analysis, earned value management and related disciplines through its professional development program.

340 www.taxsites.com

Tax and Accounting Sites Directory

A comprehensive index of internet resources, designed to be a starting point for people who are searching for tax and accounting information and services.

341 www.theiia.org

Institute of Internal Auditors

International organization of internal auditors, corporate executives and board members. Contact and current development information.

Associations

342 Ad Council
815 Second Avenue
9th Floor
New York, NY 10017-4503

212-922-1500
FAX 212-962-1676
E-Mail: info@adcouncil.org
Home Page: www.adcouncil.org
Social Media: *Facebook, Twitter, LinkedIn, YouTube, Tumblr, Pinterest, In*

David Christopher, Chairman
Lisa Sherman, President and CEO
Jon Fish, Executive Vice President/CFO
Priscilla Natkins, EVP, Director of Client Services
Paula Veale, EVP, Corporate Communications

Our mission is to identify a select number of significant public issues and stimulate action on those issues through communications programs that make a measurable difference in our society. To that end, the Ad Council marshals volunteer talent from the advertising and communications industries, the facilities of the media, and the resources of the business and non-profit communities to create awareness, foster understanding and motivate action.
100 Members
Founded in 1941

343 Advertising Council Inc
1707 L Street NW
Suite 600
Washington, DC 20036

202-331-9153
FAX 202-331-9186
E-Mail: kpastre@adcouncil.org
Home Page: www.adcouncil.org
Social Media: *Facebook, Twitter, LinkedIn, YouTube, Tumblr, Pinterest, In*

David Christopher, Chairman
Lisa Sherman, President and CEO
Jon Fish, Executive Vice President/CFO
Priscilla Natkins, EVP, Director of Client Services
Paula Veale, EVP, Corporate Communications

The Ad Council marshals volunteer talent from the advertising and communications industries, the facilities of the media, and the resources of the business and non-profit communities to create awareness, foster understanding and motivate action.
Founded in 1941

344 Advertising Educational Foundation
220 E 42nd St
Suite 3300
New York, NY 10017-5806

212-986-8060
FAX 212-986-8061
E-Mail: pa@aef.com
Home Page: www.aef.com
Social Media: *Facebook, Twitter*

Gordon McLean, Chairman
Sharon Hudson, VP/Manager
Paula Alex, President/CEO
Janice Spector, EVP, Managing Director
Marcia Solling, VP, Content Manager

The AEF is supported by ad agencies, advertisers and media companies. The AEF acknowledges that advertising is a vital and highly visible force in American society. Thus, a realistic understanding of how advertising is created, how it works and what it contributes to our social and economic life is important for all who play active roles in our complex society.
48 Members
Founded in 1983

345 Advertising Media Credit Executives Association
PO Box 740031
Louisville, KY 40201-7431

502-582-4327
FAX 502-582-4330
E-Mail: myounger@gannett.com
Home Page: www.amcea.org

Norman TaylorNorman Taylor, President
Kimberly Archibald Russell, Vice President
Newt Collins, Secretary/Treasurer
Vickie Bolinger, Immediate Past President
Sandra Lawson, Director

The objectives of the AMCEA: To improve the professionalism, principles, understanding and techniques of media credit management by encouraging the exchange of ideas, methods and procedures within the membership; To provide additional education and training in the business fundamentals of media credit and credit policies; and in the related areas of finance, accounting, law and economics for the purpose of enhancing the career development of the members.
Founded in 1953

346 Advertising Photographers of America
2221-D Peachtree Rd, NE
Suite 553
Atlanta, GA 30309

800-272-6264
888-889-7190
FAX 888-889-7190
E-Mail: info@apaatlanta.com
Home Page: www.apaatlanta.com

Harold Daniels, Chairman
Juliette Wolf-Robin, National Executive Director
David Fine, Treasurer
Jason Fobart, Board Member
Nate Dorn, Board Member

APA's mission is Successful Professional Photographers. Our goal is to establish, endorse, and promote professional practices, standards, and ethics in the photographic and advertising community. We seek to mentor, motivate, educate, and inspire in the pursuit of excellence. Our aim is to champion and speak as one common voice for advertising photographers and image makers to the advertising industry in the United States and the World.
Founded in 1981

347 Advertising Research Foundation
432 Park Ave South
6th Floor
New York, NY 10016-8013

212-751-5656
FAX 212-319-5265
E-Mail: info@thearf.org
Home Page: www.thearf.org
Social Media: *Facebook, Twitter, LinkedIn, YouTube, Flickr*

David Poltrack, Chairman
Gayle Fuguitt, CEO & President
Rachael Feigenbaum, SVP, Events Program Producer
Michael Heitner, EVP, Member Needs & Value
Navarrow Wright, Chief Technology Officer

The Advertising Research Foundation (ARF) is an open forum where the best and brightest from every avenue of advertising gather to exchange ideas and research strategies. Together, we challenge conventional maxims, take on the latest issues, and discover new insights that benefit us all. This collaboration yields something invaluable: knowledge. Knowledge that is meaningful, actionable, and indispensable. Knowledge that empowers our members to

have a true impact on their marketing programs.
Founded in 1936

348 Advertising Self-Regulatory Council
112 Madison Avenue
3rd Floor
New York, NY 10016

212-705-0104
E-Mail: lbean@asrc.bbb.org
Home Page: www.asrcreviews.org
Social Media: *Facebook, Twitter, RSS*

C. Lee Peeler, President & CEO
Linda Bean, Director of Communication
Reshma Persaud, Marketing Manager
Sarah Agler, Administrative Coordinator
Camille Sasena, Office Coordinator

Establishes the policies and procedures for advertising industry self-regulation. The self-regulatory system is administered by the Council of Better Business Bureaus.

349 Advertising Specialty Institute
4800 Street Rd
Trevose, PA 19053

215-953-4000
800-546-1350
FAX 215-953-3045
E-Mail: customerservice@asicentral.com
Home Page: www.asicentral.com
Social Media: *Facebook, Twitter, LinkedIn, YouTube, Instagram, Pinterest*

Norman Unger Cohn, Chairman
Timothy Andrews, President/CEO
Steve Bright, EVP/General Counsel
Rob Watson, SVP, Marketing
Vince Bucolo, Chief Operating Officer

The Advertising Specialty Institute, or ASI, has been providing award-winning products and services to the advertising specialty and promotional products industry for over 50 years. ASI publishes print and online business magazines, product catalogs, Web sites and informational directories. ASI's mission, then, is to bring together these participants by providing catalogs, information directories, newsletters, magazines, Web sites and databases, and offering interactive e-commerce, and marketing
26000 Members
Founded in 1950

350 Advertising Women of New York
28 West 44th Street
Suite 912
New York, NY 10036-4910

212-221-7969
FAX 212-221-8296
E-Mail: lynn.branigan@awny.org
Home Page: www.awny.org
Social Media: *Facebook, Twitter, LinkedIn, YouTube, Bloggr*

Amy Wilkins, President
Sheila Buckley, First Vice President
Nadine McHugh, Second Vice President
Lynn Branigan, Executive Director
Suzanne Hogan, Associate Director, Events

AWNY was founded as the first women's association in the communications industry. It's active affiliate of the American Advertising Federation. Provides a forum for personal and professional growth; to serve as a catalyst for the advancement of women in the communications field.
1700 Members
Founded in 1912

351 Alliance for Audited Media
48 W. Seegers Road
Arlington Heights, IL 60005-3913

224-366-6939
FAX 224-366-6949

Home Page: auditedmedia.com
Social Media: *Facebook, Twitter, LinkedIn, YouTube, Instagram*

Christina Meringolo, Chairwoman
Scott Kruse, Vice Chair
Evan Ray, Vice Chair
Chris Daly, Secretary
Liberta Abbondante, Treasurer

A nonprofit, member-based organization that works with media companies, advertising technology providers, ad agencies, and advertisers to provide them with independently verified data and information critical to evaluating and purchasing media.
Founded in 1914

352 **American Academy of Advertising**
24710 Shaker Blvd.
Beachwood, OH 44122

786-393-3333
E-Mail: director@aaasite.org
Home Page: www.aaoa.wildapricot.org
Social Media: *Facebook, Twitter*

Karen M. Lancendorfer, President
Michelle Renee Nelson, Vice President
Patricia B. Rose, Executive Director
Jami Fullerton, Secretary
Gayle Kerr, Treasurer

The American Academy of Advertising (AAA) is an organization of advertising scholars and professionals with an interest in advertising and advertising education. The Academy fosters research that is relevant to the field and provides a forum for the exchange of ideas among its academic and professional members.
600 Members
Founded in 1957

353 **American Advertising Federation**
1101 Vermont Ave NW
Suite 500
Washington, DC 20005-6306

202-898-0089
800-999-2231
FAX 202-898-0159
E-Mail: aaf@aaf.org
Home Page: www.aaf.org
Social Media: *Facebook, Twitter, YouTube, RSS*

Jim Norton, Chairman
James Edmund Datri, President & CEO
Joanne Schecter, EVP/Club Services
Karen Cohn, SVP, Conference & Meeting Logistics
Lisa Rubin, EVP, Special Events & Corp Services

The AAF is the oldest national advertising trade association, and protects and promotes the well-being of advertising. The AAF accomplishes this through a unique, nationally coordinated grassroots network of advertisers, agencies, media companies, local advertising clubs and college chapters.
40000 Members
Founded in 1967

354 **American Association for Public Opinion Research**
One Parkview Plaza
Suite 800
Oakbrook Terrace, IL 60181

847-686-2230
FAX 847-686-2251
E-Mail: athocher@aapor.org
Home Page: www.aapor.org
Social Media: *Facebook, Twitter, LinkedIn, YouTube*

Mollyann Brodie, President
Roger Tourangeau, Vice President
Adam Thocher, Executive Director

Heidi Diederich, Administrative Director
Crystal Stone, Administrator

The AAPOR community includes producers and users of survey data from a variety of disciplines. Our members span a range of interests including election polling, market research, statistics, research methodology, health related data collection and education.
1700 Members
Founded in 1947
Mailing list available for rent: 1000 names at $400 per M

355 **American Association of Advertising Agencies**
1065 Avenue of the Americas
16th Floor
New York, NY 10018

212-682-2500
FAX 212-682-8391
E-Mail: nhill@aaaa.org
Home Page: www.aaaa.org
Social Media: *Facebook, Twitter, LinkedIn, YouTube, Google+*

Nancy Hill, President/CEO
Michael D Donahue, Executive VP
Laura J. Bartlett, CFO & COO
Tom Finneran, EVP, Agency Management Services
Mike Donahue, EVP, Strategic Partnerships

The national trade association reprsenting the advertising volume placed by agencies nationwide.
600 Members
Founded in 1917

356 **American Marketing Association**
311 S Wacker Dr
Suite 5800
Chicago, IL 60606-6629

312-542-9000
800-262-1150
FAX 312-542-9001
Home Page: www.ama.org
Social Media: *Facebook, Twitter, LinkedIn, Youtube, Pinterest, Google+*

Rob Malcolm, Chairperson
Valarie Zeithaml?, Chairman-Elect
Mary Garrett, VP/Finance/Secretary
Russ Klein?, Chief Executive Officer
Beth Taylor, Chief Operations Officer

The AMA is a professional association for individuals and organizations leading the practice, teaching and development of marketing knowledge worldwide. Our principle role is to serve as a forum to connect like-minded individuals and foster knowledge sharing, provide resources, tools and training and support marketing practice and thought leadership around the globe.
40000 Members
Founded in 1953

357 **Asian American Advertising Federation**
6230 Wilshire Blvd
Suite 1216
Los Angeles, CA 90048

E-Mail: ghomfranzen@3af.org
Home Page: www.3af.org
Social Media: *Facebook, Twitter*

Edward Chang, President
Jay Kim, Vice President
Iris Yim, Secretary
Sandra Lee, Treasurer
Genny Hom-Franzen, Executive Director

Consists of Asian American advertising agency principals, media, advertisers and strategic partners that seek to grow the Asian American advertising and marketing industry, raise public

awareness of the Asian community, and increase professionalism within the industry.

358 **Association of Canadian Advertisers**
95 St Clair Avenue West
Suite 1103
Toronto, ON M4V 1N6

416-964-3805
800-565-0109
FAX 416-964-0771
E-Mail: rlund@acaweb.ca
Home Page: www.acaweb.ca
Social Media: *Twitter, LinkedIn*

Patrick Dickinson, Chair
Ron Lund, President, CEO
Paul Hetu, Vice President, Montreal
Susan Charles, Vice President, Member Services
Christina Wang, Communications Specialist

The Association of Canadian Advertisers (ACA) is a national, not-for-profit association exclusively dedicated to serving the interests of companies that market and advertise their products and services in Canada. Membership in the ACA is restricted to client marketers only, making it the premier Canadian marketing association. It cuts across all products and service sectors, and speaks on behalf of over 200 companies.
Founded in 1914

359 **Association of Hispanic Advertising Agencies**
8280 Willow Oaks Corporate Drive
Suite 600
Fairfax, VA 22031

703-745-5531
FAX 703-610-0227
E-Mail: info@ahaa.org
Home Page: www.ahaa.org
Social Media: *Facebook, Twitter, LinkedIn, YouTube, Storify*

Aldo Quevedo, Chairman
Horacio Gavilan, Executive Director
Fulvia Lee, Program Manager
Carlos Santiago, Secretary
Gabriela Alcantara-Díaz, Treasurer

Our mission is to grow, strengthen and protect the Hispanic marketing and advertising industry by providing leadership in raising awareness of the value of the Hispanic market opportunities and enhancing the professionalism of the industry.
100 Members
Founded in 1996

360 **Association of Marketing Service Providers**
1800 Diagonal Road
Suite 320
Alexandria, VA 22314-2862

703-836-9200
FAX 703-548-8204
E-Mail: webmaster@epicomm.org
Home Page: epicomm.org
Social Media: *Facebook, Twitter, LinkedIn, Pinterest, Google+, YouTube*

Ken Garner, President/CEO
Leo Raymond, VP-Postal & Member Relations
Tyler T. Keeney, Director of Member Satisfaction
Dean D'Ambrosi, Executive Vice President
Mike Philie, SVP/Managing Director

MFSA is the national trade association for the mailing and fulfillment services industry and works to improve the business environment for mailing and fulfillment companies and to provide opportunities for the learning and professional development of the managers of these companies. MFSA provides: instant postal info; periodicals, surveys, and manuals unique to the

industry; networking opportunities; and management education and information.
Founded in 2014

361 Association of National Advertisers
Association of National Advertisers
708 Third Avenue
33 Floor
New York, NY 10017

212-697-5950
FAX 212-687-7310
E-Mail: info@ana.net
Home Page: www.ana.net
Social Media: *Facebook, Twitter, LinkedIn, Instagram*

Christine Manna, Chief Operating Officer
Robert D Liodice, President and CEO
Marni Gordon, Senior Vice President
Nick Primola, Senior Vice President
Kristen McDonough, Vice President

The Association of National Advertisers (ANA) is the advertising industry's oldest trade association. Currently, the ANA leads the marketing community by providing its members insights, collaboration, and advocacy. ANA's membership includes 10,000 brands that collectively spend over $250 billion in marketing communications and advertising.
450 Members
Founded in 1910

362 Better Business Bureau
3033 Wilson Blvd
Suite 600
Arllington, VA 22201

703-276-0100
FAX 703-525-8277
Home Page: www.bbb.org
Social Media: *Facebook, Twitter, LinkedIn, YouTube, Google+, Pinterest, F*

Mary E. Power, CAE, President
Beverly Baskin, SVP/Chief Mission Officer
David Diedrich, Chief Operating Officer
Bill Fanelli, CISSP, Chief Security Officer
Bennie F. Johnson, Chief Strategy Officer

The BBB is a leader in public services related to ethical business practices and dispute resolution. It is our passion to promote honesty and integrity in the marketplace. We are committed to and guided by trust, respect and fairness.
Founded in 1912

363 Brand Activation Association
650 First Avenue
Suite 2-SW
New York, NY 10016

212-420-1100
FAX 212-533-7622
E-Mail: bcarlson@pmalink.org
Home Page: www.baalink.org
Social Media: *Facebook, Twitter, LinkedIn, Flickr*

Bonnie J. Carlson, President & CEO
Edward M. Kabak, Chief Legal Officer
Lana Mavreshko, Chief Financial Officer
Christine Goonan, Director of Membership
Mike Kaufman, VP, Marketing & Events

Organization that advocates networking, recognition, and provides educational resources to help brand marketers overcome the significant challengesthey face in a rapidly changing marketplace.
Founded in 1911

364 Cabletelevision Advertising Bureau
830 3rd Avenue
2nd Floor
New York, NY 10022

212-508-1200
FAX 212-832-3268
E-Mail: ChuckT@theVAB.com

Home Page: www.thecab.tv
Social Media: *Facebook, Twitter, LinkedIn*

Sean Cunningham, President & CEO
Charles (Chuck) Thompson, EVP, Strategic Operations
Danielle DeLauro, SVP, Strategic Sales Insights
Gary Tietjen, VP, Local Sales & Initiatives
Evelyn Skurkovich, Sr. Director

365 Eight-Sheet Outdoor Advertising Association
PO Box 582096
Elk Grove, CA 95758

209-251-7622
800-874-3387
FAX 209-251-7658
E-Mail: ddjesoaa@comcast.net
Home Page: www.juniorbillboard.org
Social Media: *Facebook*

Carla Osmus, Chairman
Peter Maloney, President
David Jacobs, Executive Director
Mike Cossota, Vice President
Billboard Guru, Secretary/Treasurer

The Association has helped establish size, structure and location standards, has adopted a code of ethics and standards of business practices. These self-policing efforts have helped stabilize the industry and added the standardization needed for planning
140 Members
Founded in 1953

366 Insurance and Financial Communications Association
515 East Grant Rd Ste 141
Box 250
Tucson, AZ 85705

602-350-0717
FAX 866-402-7336
E-Mail: info@ifcaonline.org
Home Page: www.ifcaonline.com
Social Media: *Facebook, Twitter, LinkedIn, YouTube*

Jaimee Niles, President
Ralph Chaump, Vice President
Laurie Swinton, Past President
Katherine Gebhardt, Director, Communications
Tara Haselden, Director, Social Media

IFCA's primary objective is to encourage and promote the exchange of experience and ideas among its members through an extensive program of formal schools, workshops, seminars, Newsletters, research studies, networking, international awards competition and IFCA's showcase event: the three-day annual meeting. The IFCA name reflects the diversity of our members and helps us recruit new members from more companies.
700 Members
Founded in 1933

367 Interactive Advertising Bureau
116 E 27th Street
7th Floor
New York, NY 10016

212-380-4700
Home Page: www.iab.net
Social Media: *Facebook, Twitter, LinkedIn, YouTube, Instagram, Google+*

Carl Kalapesi, VP, Industry Initiatives
Randall Rothenberg, President & Chief Executive Officer
Patrick Dolan, EVP/COO
Sherrill Mane, SVP, Research, Analytics
David Doty, EVP/Chief Marketing Officer

The Interactive Advertising Bureau (IAB) is comprised of leading media and technology companies that are responsible for selling 86% of online advertising in the United States. On

behalf of its members, the IAB is dedicated to the growth of the interactive advertising marketplace, of interactive's share of total marketing spend, and of its members' share of total marketing spend. The IAB educates marketers, agencies, and media companies about the value of interactive advertising.
500 Members
Founded in 1996

368 Intermarket Advertising Network
5307 S 92nd Street
Hales Corners, WI 53130

414-425-8800
FAX 414-425-0021
E-Mail: camg@greenrubino.com
Home Page: www.intermarketnetwork.com
Social Media: *LinkedIn*

Deborah Pfluger, President
Joe Erwin, Vice President
Tom Wilson, Co-Chairman
Dan Borgmeyer, Co-Chairman

IAN (Intermarket Agency Network) is a forum for leaders of noncompetitive marketing agencies to openly exchange knowledge in a collaborative setting. A nationwide association of carefully selected agencies, its members meet twice annually to freely discuss important issues like new business, financials, HR, creativity, growth and much more. No topic is off limits.
19 Members
Founded in 1967

369 International Advertising Association
747 Third Ave.
2nd Fl.
New York, NY 10017

646-722-2612
FAX 646-722-2501
E-Mail: iaa@iaaglobal.org
Home Page: www.iaaglobal.org
Social Media: *Facebook, Twitter, LinkedIn*

Michael Lee, Managing Director
Marie Scotti, Director, Membership Services

International network comprising thousands of members working in all areas of marketing communications.
Founded in 1938

370 International Communications Agency Network
P.O. Box 3417
Nederland, CO 80466

808-965-8240
FAX 303-484-4087
E-Mail: info@icomagencies.com
Home Page: www.icomagencies.com
Social Media: *Facebook, Twitter, Pinterest*

Emma Keenan, Executive Director
Galina Epishkina, Eurasia Regional Director
Patrick Gaulon, Director Finance
Alice Lemoine, Finance Manager
DeAnna Moxley, Manager of Administration

One of the world's largest networks of independent advertising and marketing communications agencies. Our mission is: To provide effective integrated communications resources to clients internationally; To provide a free exchange of ideas, information & support for members.
80+ Members
Founded in 1950

371 International Sign Association
1001 N Fairfax Street
Suite 301
Alexandria, VA 22314

703-836-4012
866-WHY-SIGN
FAX 703-836-8353

E-Mail: info@signs.org
Home Page: www.signs.org
Social Media: *Facebook, Twitter, LinkedIn, YouTube*

Lori Anderson, President & CEO
Brandon Hensley, COO
David Hickey, Vice President, Government Relation
Bill Winslow, Vice President, Finance
Alison Kent, Director, Workforce Development

The International Sign Association (ISA) is devoted to supporting, promoting and improving the sign industry through government advocacy, education and training programs, technical resources, stakeholder outreach and industry networking events. Our members are manufacturers, users and suppliers of on-premise signs and other visual communications systems.
2600 Members
Founded in 1944

372   Internet Marketing Association
10 Mar Del Rey San
Clemente, CA 92673

949-443-9300
FAX 949-443-2215
E-Mail: info@imanetwork.org
Home Page: imanetwork.org
Social Media: *Facebook, Twitter, LinkedIn, YouTube, Google+, RSS*

Sinan Kanatsiz, Chairman & Founder
Matthew Langie, Vice Chairman
Lei Lani Fera, Chief Creative Officer
Rachel Reenders, Executive Director
Vince Walden, Chief Accountant
Founded in 2001

373   League of Advertising Agencies
915 Clifton Avenue
Clifton, NJ 07013

973-473-6643
FAX 973-473-0685
E-Mail: info@weinrichadv.com
Home Page: www.theweinrichgroup.com

Andy Weinrich, Executive Vice President
Robert Weinrich, Marketing Director

Provides marketing solutions that maximize success.

374   MAGNET: Marketing & Advertising Global Network
1017 Perry Hwy
Suite 5
Pittsburgh, PA 15237-2173

412-366-6850
FAX 412-366-6840
E-Mail: cheri@magnetglobal.org
Home Page: www.magnetglobal.org
Social Media: *Facebook, Twitter, RSS Feed*

Mark Lethbridge, President
Joanne Kim, Vice President
Scott Morgan, Vice President - Membership
Gary Leopold, Vice President
Kevin Flynn, Vice President - Programs

Today, MAGNET is a group of non-competing, independently owned advertising agencies in major markets throughout the world. The network is comprised of leading agencies, with billings ranging from 8 million to 200 million US dollars, sharing a desire to pursue and achieve excellence in this profession we call marketing.
40 Members
Founded in 1999

375   Newspaper Association of America
4401 Wilson Blvd
Suite 900
Arlington, VA 22203

571-366-1000
FAX 571-366-1009
Home Page: www.naa.org
Social Media: *Facebook, Twitter, LinkedIn, YouTube, Google+, RSS*

Donna Barrett, Chairman
Stephen P. Hills, Vice Chairman
Robert J. Dickey, Past Chairman
Tony W. Hunter, Secretary
Michael J. Klingensmith, Treasurer

376   Outdoor Advertising Association of America
1850 M St NW
Suite 1040
Washington, DC 20036-5821

202-833-5566
FAX 202-833-1522
E-Mail: nfletcher@oaaa.org
Home Page: www.oaaa.org
Social Media: *Facebook, Twitter, LinkedIn, YouTube, Pinterest*

William Reagan, Chairman
Nancy J Fletcher, President/CEO
Ken Klein, EVP, Government Affairs
Marci Werlinich, VP, Membership & Admin
Kerry Yoakum, Vice President, Government Affairs
1000 Members
Founded in 1891

377   Point of Purchase Advertising International
440 N. Wells Street
Suite 740
Chicago, IL 60654

312-863-2900
FAX 312-229-1152
E-Mail: todddittman@retailenvironments.org
Home Page: www.popai.com
Social Media: *Facebook, Twitter, LinkedIn, Pinterest*

Michelle Adams, Chairman
Scott Eisen, Treasurer
Madeline Baumgartner, Market Research Manager
Nancy Carpenter, Director of Member Relations
Chelsea Kidd-Edie, Communications Coordinator

Education, globalization, technology, advocacy and elevating marketing at retail as a measured medium on a par with print, broadcast, and other advertising mediums are the driving strategies behind POPAI's direction. Throughout the years we have focused on strengthening global partnerships, enriching our research and educational programs, and utilizing technology to better serve our members.
1400+ Members
Founded in 1936

378   Promotional Products Association International
3125 Skyway Circle North
Irving, TX 75038-3526

972-252-0404
888-426-7724
FAX 972-258-3004
E-Mail: steves@ppa.org
Home Page: www.ppai.org
Social Media: *Facebook, Twitter, YouTube, RSS*

Paul Bellantone, President and CEO
Bob McLean, EVP
Lisa Beck, Member Engagement Programs Manager

Sara Besly, Foundation Manager
Sandy Mendoza, Business Analytics Manager

Offers credibility, viability, visibility, community and opportunity to individuals and companies in the promotional products industry.
PPAI's Mission: The Promotional Products Association International advocates the power and value of promotional products in the marketing and advertising professions to ensure the success of its members and the global industry.
7500 Members
Founded in 1904

379   Retail Advertising and Marketing Association
1101 New York Ave NW
Washington, DC 20005

202-783-7971
800-673-4692
FAX 202-737-2849
E-Mail: gattim@nrf.com
Home Page: nrf.com
Social Media: *Facebook, Twitter, LinkedIn, Youtube, Instagram*

Kip Tindell, Chairman
Carleen Kohut, EVP/COO
Vicki Cantrell, SVP/ Executive Director
Mallory Duncan, SVP/General Counsel
David French, SVP, Government Relations

Provides visionary leadership that promotes creativity, innovation and excellence within all marketing disciplines that strategically elevates our members and our industry.
1600 Members
Founded in 1952

380   The Outdoor Advertising Association of America, Inc.
1850 M St. NW
Suite 140
Washington, DC 20036

202-833-5566
FAX 202-833-1522
Home Page: www.oaaa.org
Social Media: *Facebook, Twitter, LinkedIn, Pinterest, YouTube*

William Reagan, Chairman
Nancy Fletcher, President & CEO
Ken Klein, EVP, Govt. Affairs
Stephen Freitas, Chief Marketing Officer

Out-of-home advertising industry association.
Founded in 1891

381   Traffic Audit Bureau for Media Measurement
271 Madison Ave
Suite 1504
New York, NY 10016-1012

212-972-8075
FAX 212-972-8928
E-Mail: inquiry@tabonline.com
Home Page: www.tabonline.com

Joseph Philport, President/CEO
Larry Hennessey, VP, Audit Policy & Member Services
Jeff Casper, Senior Vice President
Sean McCarthy, Senior Vice President - Information
Shawn Ballard, Vice President - Finance

The Traffic Audit Bureau for Media Measurement Inc. is a non-profit organization whose historical mission has been to audit the circulation of out of home media in the United States. Recently TAB's role has been expanded to lead and/or support other major out of home industry research initiatives.
450 Members
Founded in 1933

382   Transworld Advertising Agency Network: TAAN
814 Watertown Street
Newton, MA 02465

617-795-1706
FAX 419-730-1706
E-Mail: info@taan.org
Home Page: www.taan.org
Social Media: *Twitter*

Jon Bailey, Chairman
Peter Gerritsen, President
Peter Colee, Governor - International/Europe
Marcy Tessmann, US Governor
John McCallum, Governor - International/Europe

TAAN exists to enhance the intelligence, expertise, reach and personal effectiveness of the owners of its member agencies: Intelligence, through the sharing of best practices, management information, processes and technologies; Expertise, through cooperative utilization of the talents, skills and experience of each member; Reach, through hands-on affiliations with local independent agencies around the world; Personal Effectiveness, through education and close, confidential, trusted relations.
47+ Members
Founded in 1936

383   eMarketing Association
40 Blue Ridge Dr.
Charlestown, RI 2813

800-496-2950
FAX 408-884-2461
E-Mail: admin@emarketingassociation.com
Home Page: www.emarketingassociation.com
Social Media: *Facebook, Twitter, LinkedIn*

International association of emarketing professionals committed to enriching the marketing community and its members through recognition, research, advocacy, education, and service.
Founded in 1997

Newsletters

384   A Formula for Fueling Ad Agency New Business Through Social Media
American Association of Advertising Agencies
1065 Avenue of the Americas
16th Floor
New York, NY 10018

212-682-2500
FAX 212-682-8391
Home Page: www.aaaa.org
Social Media: *Facebook, Twitter, LinkedIn*

Nancy Hill, President
Michael D. Donahue, Executive Vice President
Laura J. Bartlett, CFO & COO
Michele Adams, Board Secretary

Designed to focus and kick-start your agency's understanding, participation, credibility and leadership in social media with less expense, time and frustration. Created for C level and senior executives charged with the responsibility of new business development.

385   AAA Newsletter
American Academy of Advertising
24710 Shaker Blvd.
Beachwood, OH 44122

786-393-3333
E-Mail: director@aaasite.org
Home Page: www.aaasite.org
Social Media: *Facebook, Twitter*

Debbie Treise, President
Kim Sheehan, President Elect

Margie Morrison, Vice President
Nancy Mitchell, Treasurer
Glen Griffin, Secretary

The newsletter is designed to keep members up-to-date on activities of the Academy and to share information between members regarding their activities.
600 Members
Frequency: Quarterly
Founded in 1957

386   ACT Newsletter
Advertising Communications Times
29 Bala Ave
Suite 114
Bala Cynwyd, PA 19004

484-562-0063
FAX 484-562-0068
E-Mail: adcomtimes@aol.com
Home Page: www.phillybizmedia.com

Joseph H. Ball, Publisher/Executive Editor
Elena Cruz, Executive Assistant

Business to business newsletter for company owners and executives in Philadelphia, Eastern Pennsylvania, Southern New Jersey & Delaware.
Frequency: Monthly
Circulation: 40000

387   Associated Spring Newsletter
Associated Spring
18 Main St
Bristol, CT 06010-6581

860-582-9581
800-528-3795
FAX 860-589-3122
E-Mail: springs@asbg.com
Home Page: www.asbg.com

Paulo Coit, Manager

Offers news, conferences and seminars.
Frequency: Quarterly

388   Business Owner
Mailing & Fulfillment Service Association
1421 Prince Street
Suite 410
Alexandria, VA 22314-2806

703-836-9200
FAX 703-548-8204
Home Page: www.mfsanet.org
Social Media: *Facebook, Twitter, LinkedIn*

Ken Garner, President/CEO
Leo Raymond, Vice President
Karen Loveridge, Executive Assistant

Distributed to the owner or CEO of all member companies as a dues-supported benefit of membership. Developed specifically to communicate with owners and CEOs on issues unique to them.
Frequency: Bi-Monthly

389   Conexion Newsletter
Association of Hispanic Advertising Agencies
8400 Westpark Drive
2nd Floor
McLean, VA 22102

703-610-9014
FAX 703-610-0227
E-Mail: info@ahaa.org
Home Page: www.ahaa.org
Social Media: *Facebook, Twitter, LinkedIn, YouTube*

Ingrid Otero-Smart, President/CEO
Leo Olper, CEO
Roberto Orci, Chair

AHAA represents the best minds and resources dedicated to Hispanic-specialized marketing.
Frequency: Monthly

390   Counselor
Advertising Specialty Institute
4800 E Street Rd
Langhorne, PA 19053-6698

215-953-4000
800-546-1350
FAX 215-953-3045
E-Mail: info@asicentral.com
Home Page: www.asicentral.com
Social Media: *Facebook*

Timothy M Andrews, CEO
Norman Cohn, Chairman
Matthew Cohn, Vice Chairman
Carol Albright, SVP-Human Resources

The voice of the promotional products industry, Counselor keeps you up to date with industry news and trends.
Frequency: 13x/Year
Circulation: 40000

391   DMA Daily Digest
Direct Marketing Association
1120 Avenue of the Americas
New York, NY 10036-6700

212-768-7277
FAX 212-302-6714
E-Mail: customerservice@the-dma.org
Home Page: www.the-dma.org
Social Media: *Facebook, Twitter, LinkedIn*

Lawrence M Kimmel, CEO

A summary of today's industry news from trade publications and national media. Also available as an e-mail newsletter.

392   Direct Hit
Midwest Direct Marketing Association
PO Box 75
Andover, MN 55304

763-607-2943
FAX 763-753-2240
E-Mail: mdma@mdma.org
Home Page: www.mdma.org

Beth Gervais, President
Vicki Erickson, Secretary/Treasurer

Brings members news of meetings, activities, local and regional events, pertinent articles and changes in legislation and postal requirements that affect the direct marketing industry.
Frequency: Bi-Monthly
Circulation: 600

393   Display Newsletter
Eight-Sheet Outdoor Advertising Association
1244 Lake Park Ave
Galt, CA 95632

209-251-7622
800-847-3387
FAX 209-251-7658
E-Mail: ddjesoaa@comcast.net
Home Page: www.esoaa.com
Social Media: *Facebook*

David Jacobs, Executive Director
Nick Sr. Keyes, Chairman
Carla Osmus, President
Deb Justus, Vice President
Stuart Rayburn, Secretary/ Treasurer

Includes updates and supplements to the Rates and Allotments book.
Frequency: Monthly
Circulation: 350

394   Dos and Dont's in Advertising
Council of Better Business Bureaus
4200 Wilson Blvd
Suite 800
Arlington, VA 22203-1838

703-276-0100
FAX 703-525-8277

E-Mail: webmaster@bbb.org
Home Page: www.bbb.org

Stephen A Cox, CEO

Provides in-depth coverage of the laws and regulations governing the advertising industry. Helps you to write, place and manage ads that foster consumer trust and confidence, follow federal and state ad rules, regulations and laws. It has helped legal and advertising professionals produce advertising that is ethical and correct for 50 years.
4000 Pages
Frequency: Monthly
Founded in 1970

395   Education Adviser
Advertising Specialty Institute
4800 E Street Rd
Langhorne, PA 19053-6698

215-953-4000
800-546-1350
FAX 215-953-3045
E-Mail: info@asicentral.com
Home Page: www.asicentral.com

Timothy M Andrews, CEO
Norman Cohn, Chairman
Matthew Cohn, Vice Chairman
Carol Albright, SVP-Human Resources

Professional development and insight each month.
Frequency: Monthly

396   Employment Points
Mailing & Fulfillment Service Association
1421 Prince Street
Suite 410
Alexandria, VA 22314-2806

703-836-9200
FAX 703-548-8204
E-Mail: mfsa-mail@mfsanet.org
Home Page: www.mfsanet.org

The content is written for business owners and operators who want to stay informed about current employment issues. The editorial is targeted on human resource issues and employment practices in the mailing and fulfillment services industry.
Frequency: 4x/Year
Circulation: 2000

397   Globe Newsletter
International Communications Agency Network
1649 Lump Gulch Road
PO Box 490
Rollinsville, CO 80474-0490

303-258-9511
FAX 303-484-4087
E-Mail: info@icomagencies.com
Home Page: www.icomagencies.com
Social Media: *Facebook, Twitter*

Bob Morrison, Director
Joe Phelps, North American Member at Large

A review of industry trends, member agency news and network happenings.
Frequency: Monthly
Circulation: 150

398   IAB Informer
Interactive Advertising Bureau
116 E 27th Street
7th Floor
New York, NY 10016

212-380-4700
Home Page: www.iab.net
Social Media: *Facebook, Twitter, LinkedIn*

Randall Rothenberg, President/CEO

Features the latest need-to-know information from the IAB as well as research and other

highlights from the world of Internet advertising and marketing
Frequency: Monthly

399   IAB SmartBrief
Interactive Advertising Bureau
116 E 27th Street
7th Floor
New York, NY 10016

212-380-4700
Home Page: www.iab.net
Social Media: *Facebook, Twitter, LinkedIn*

Randall Rothenberg, President/CEO

Designed specifically for advertising, marketing and media executives, providing the latest need-to-know news and industry information that maximizes your time, giving you and edge over your competition.
Frequency: Monthly

400   ISA SmartBrief
International Sign Association
1001 N Fairfax Street
Suite 301
Alexandria, VA 22314

703-836-4012
866-WHY-SIGN
FAX 703-836-8353
E-Mail: info@signs.org
Home Page: www.signs.org

Duane Laska, Chairman
Harry Niese, Vice Chairman
Chad Jones, Secretary/Treasurer

ISA SmartBrief is a weekly e-newsletter, providing industry developments, new technology, and special offers from ISA.
2600 Members
Frequency: Weekly/Online

401   InsideAPA Newsletter
Advertising Photographers of America
27 W 20th Street
Suite 601
New York, NY 10011

212-807-0399
FAX 212-727-8120
E-Mail: jocelyn@apany.com
Home Page: www.apanational.com

Theresa Raffetto, National President
Michael Grecco, VP
George Simian, Treasurer

InsideAPA is a blog style newsletter focused on photographers and the membership of the Advertising Photographers of America, APA.

402   PPB Newslink
Promotional Products Association International
3125 Skyway Cir N
Irving, TX 75038-3539

972-252-0404
FAX 972-258-3004
E-Mail: ppb@ppai.org
Home Page: www.ppai.org
Social Media: *Facebook, Twitter, LinkedIn, YouTube*

Paul Bellantone, President
Steven Meyer, Chairman of the Board
Marc Simon, Chair-Elect

Electronic newsletter providing news and information about PPAI and the industry with links to articles in the online version of PPB Magazine.
Frequency: Weekly

403   PostScripts
Mailing & Fulfillment Service Association

1421 Prince Street
Suite 410
Alexandria, VA 22314-2806

703-836-9200
FAX 703-548-8204
E-Mail: mfsa-mail@mfsanet.org
Home Page: www.mfsanet.org
Social Media: *Facebook, Twitter, LinkedIn*

Leo Raymond, Editor

Each issue of PostScripts highlights a theme relevant to mailing or fulfillment operations, such as production management or information technology.
Frequency: 18x/Year
Circulation: 2800

404   Postal Points
Mailing & Fulfillment Service Association
1421 Prince Street
Suite 410
Alexandria, VA 22314-2806

703-836-9200
FAX 703-548-8204
E-Mail: mfsa-mail@mfsanet.org
Home Page: www.mfsanet.org
Social Media: *Facebook, Twitter, LinkedIn*

Leo Raymond, Editor

Deals exclusively with current and pending postal and delivery issues. Here you will find the facts and analysis of developing postal issues.
Frequency: 18x/Year

405   STORES First Edition
Retail Advertising & Marketing International
325 7th St Nw
Suite 1100
Washington, DC 20004-2818

202-661-3052
FAX 202-737-2849
Home Page: www.rama-nrf.org
Social Media: *Facebook, Twitter*

Kevin Brown, RAMA Chairman
Rob Gruen, Vice Chairman
Gwen Morrison, CEO
Julie Gardner, CMO

E-newsletter alerting readers to new stories including web only content as well as STORES and NRF events taking place in the upcoming month.
Frequency: Monthly

406   STORES Retail Deals
Retail Advertising & Marketing International
325 7th St Nw
Suite 1100
Washington, DC 20004-2818

202-661-3052
FAX 202-737-2849
Home Page: www.rama-nrf.org

Kevin Brown, RAMA Chairman
Rob Gruen, Vice Chairman
Gwen Morrison, CEO
Julie Gardner, CMO

Provides coverage of retail industry product and service provider news.
Frequency: Semi-Monthly

407   Shopping Center Ad Trends
National Research Bureau
320 Valley St
Burlington, IA 52601-5513

319-752-5415
FAX 319-752-3421
E-Mail: contactus@supervisionmagazine.com

35

Home Page:
www.national-research-bureau.com

Diane M Darnall, President
Nancy Heinzel, Editor

Advertising and marketing information for the clothing and furniture industry.
Frequency: Monthly
Founded in 1993

408   Signals
International Sign Association
1001 N Fairfax Street
Suite 301
Alexandria, VA 22314

703-836-4012
866-WHY-SIGN
FAX 703-836-8353
E-Mail: info@signs.org
Home Page: www.signs.org

Duane Laska, Chairman
Harry Niese, Vice Chairman
Chad Jones, Secretary/Treasurer

ISA's legislative newsletter.
2600 Members
Frequency: Weekly/Online

409   Signline
International Sign Association
1001 N Fairfax Street
Suite 301
Alexandria, VA 22314

703-836-4012
866-WHY-SIGN
FAX 703-836-8353
E-Mail: info@signs.org
Home Page: www.signs.org

Duane Laska, Chairman
Harry Niese, Vice Chairman
Chad Jones, Secretary/Treasurer

ISA's newsletter developed especially for sign users, sign companies, planners, building and zoning officials, and other government groups connected with the sign industry. Find important legal and planning information on signage, as well as information on traffic safety, amortization, the economic value of on-premise signs, and other related topics.
2600 Members
Frequency: Weekly/Online

410   Weekly Information Newsletter
MAGNET: Marketing & Advertising Global Network
1017 Perry Hwy
Suite 5
Pittsburgh, PA 15237-2173

412-366-6850
FAX 412-366-6840
E-Mail: cheri@magnetglobal.org
Home Page: www.magnetglobal.org
Social Media: *Facebook, Twitter*

Jim Nash, President

Keeps members alert to such items as new business activities, personnel information, purchases of new equipment and software, industry trends and projections.
Frequency: Weekly

Magazines & Journals

411   Advantages
Advertising Specialty Institute
4800 E Street Rd
Langhorne, PA 19053-6698

215-953-4000
800-546-1350
FAX 215-953-3045
E-Mail: info@asicentral.com

Home Page: www.asicentral.com
Social Media: *Facebook*

Timothy M Andrews, CEO
Norman Cohn, Chairman
Matthew Cohn, Vice Chairman
Carol Albright, SVP-Human Resources

Written especially for the promotional products sales professional, Advantages can help you sell more.
Frequency: 13x/Year
Circulation: 40000

412   Advertiser
The Pohly Company
253 Summer Street
Floor 3
Boston, MA 02210

617-451-1700
800-383-0888
FAX 617-338-7767
E-Mail: info@pohlyco.com
Home Page: www.pohlyco.com
Social Media: *Facebook, Twitter, LinkedIn*

Diana Pohly, President & CEO
Bill Pryor, Media Sales General Manager
Kevin Miller, Chief Creative Officer
Bill Dugan, VP/General Manager, FuelNet
Matt Thorsen, Director of Operations & Production

Reports on today's most critical marketing issues such as measuring brand equity, using emerging technologies and global marketing. It also contains articles on key benchmarks and industry trends.
Frequency: 6x/Year

413   Advertising & Society Review
Advertising Educational Foundation
220 E 42nd St
Suite 3300
New York, NY 10017-5813

212-986-8060
FAX 212-986-8061
Home Page: www.aef.com
Social Media: *Facebook*

John Partilla, Chairman
Paula Alex, CEO

Directed to professors and students in liberal arts colleges, universities and professional schools, Advertising & Society Review is an academic publication that publishes articles, essays and other scholarships about advertising in society, culture, history and the economy.

414   Advertising Age
Ad Age Group/Division of Crain Communications
711 3rd Ave
New York, NY 10017-4014

212-210-0785
FAX 212-210-0465
E-Mail: kwheaton@adage.com
Home Page: www.adage.com
Social Media: *Facebook, Twitter, LinkedIn*

Norm Feldman, President

Editorial insights, exclusive analysis and proprietary data take readers beyond the day's news, helping our audience understand ongoing and emerging trends.
Frequency: Weekly
Circulation: 56650

415   Adweek
Prometheus Global Media
770 Broadway
7th Floor
New York, NY 10003-9595

212-493-4100
FAX 646-654-5368

Home Page: www.prometheusgm.com
Social Media: *Facebook, Twitter*

Richard D. Beckan, CEO
James A. Finkelstein, Chairman
Madeline Krakowsky, Vice President Circulation
Tracy Brater, Executive Director Creative Service

Adweek is the source for advertising and agency news, information and opinion. Covering the industry from an agency perspective, Adweek focuses on the image makers and those who create the strategy and the ads as well as those who buy the media and handle client relations.
Cost: $149.00
Frequency: Weekly
Circulation: 36000
Founded in 1978

416   Billboard Magazine
Prometheus Global Media
770 Broadway
7th Floor
New York, NY 10003-9595

212-493-4100
FAX 646-654-5368
Home Page: www.prometheusgm.com
Social Media: *Facebook, Twitter, RSS*

Richard D. Beckman, CEO
James Finkelstein, Chairman
Madeline Krakowsky, Vice President Circulation
Tracy Brater, Executive Director Creative Service

Packed with in-depth music and entertainment features including the latest in new media and digital music, global coverage, music and money, touring, new artists, radio news and retail reports.
Cost: $149.00
Frequency: Weekly
Founded in 1894

417   Brandweek
Prometheus Global Media
770 Broadway
7th Floor
New York, NY 10003-9595

212-493-4100
FAX 646-654-5368
Home Page: www.prometheusgm.com

Richard D. Beckman, CEO
James A. Finkelstein, Chairman
Madeline Krakowsky, Vice President Circulation
Tracy Brater, Executive Director Creative Service

Focuses on marketing strategy and services, brand identity, sponsorships, licensing, media usage and distribution and promotions.
Frequency: Weekly
Circulation: 26000
Founded in 1991

418   BtoB Magazine
Crain Communications, Inc.
1155 Gratiot Ave
Detroit, MI 48207-2732

313-446-6000
E-Mail: info@crain.com
Home Page: www.crain.com

Keith Crain, Chairman
Rance Crain, President
Mary Kay Crain, Treasurer/Assistant Secretary
Merrilee P. Crain, Secretary/Assistant Treasurer
Robert Felsenthal, Vice President/Publisher

Dedicated to integrated business to business marketing. Every page is packed with substance news, reports, technologies,

benchmarks, and best practices served up by the most knowledgeable journalists.
Frequency: Monthly
Circulation: 45000

419   Corporate Logo Magazine
Virgo Publishing LLC
3300 N Central Ave
Suite 300
Phoenix, AZ 85012-2532

480-675-9925
FAX 480-990-0819
E-Mail: kkennedy@vpico.com
Home Page: www.vpico.com

Jenny Bolton, President

Provides promotional products distributors with tools to grow their businesses in a competitive marketplace.
Circulation: 20000
Founded in 1986
Printed in on glossy stock

420   Counselor
Advertising Specialty Institute
4800 E Street Rd
Langhorne, PA 19053-6698

215-953-4000
FAX 215-953-3045
E-Mail: info@asicentral.com
Home Page: www.asicentral.com
Social Media: *Facebook*

Timothy M Andrews, CEO
Norman Cohn, Chairman
Matthew Cohn, Vice Chairman
Carol Albright, SVP-Human Resources

Counselor's coverage of marketing trends and new products is a must read for distributor principals.
Frequency: Monthly
Circulation: 11000

421   Creativity
Ad Age Group/Division of Crain Communications
1155 Gratiot Ave
Detroit, MI 48207-2732

313-446-6000
E-Mail: info@crain.com
Home Page: www.crain.com

Norm Feldman, Manager

Information, insight and inspiration in the brand creativity world. Each month we showcase the best work and take readers inside the making of ground breaking brand communications and experiences, while exploring the issues facing those in the idea business.
Frequency: Monthly
Circulation: 33000

422   Government Relations: How To Guide for Clubs & Federations
American Advertising Federation
1101 Vermont Ave NW
Suite 500
Washington, DC 20005-6306

202-898-0089
800-999-2231
FAX 202-898-0159
E-Mail: aaf@aaf.org
Home Page: www.aaf.org
Social Media: *Facebook, Twitter, YouTube*

James Edmund Datri, President
Constance Cannon Frazier, COO
Joanne Schecter, Executive Vice President

The purpose of this manual is to help reduce the anxiety level that many feel when dealing with lawmakers.

423   Hispanic Business Magazine
Hispanic Business Inc

425 Pine Ave
Santa Barbara, CA 93117-3709

805-964-4554
FAX 805-964-5539
E-Mail: info@hispanstar.com
Home Page: www.hirediversity.com

Jesus Chavarria, President

Our feature stories highlight significant trends in the US Hispanic market and include profiles of successful entrepreneurs, analysis of economic trends and news and data on such topics as government procurement, workplace diversity, politics, advertising, entertainment and events.
Frequency: Monthly
Circulation: 225000
Founded in 1979

424   Hospitality Style
ST Media Group International
11262 Cornell Park Dr
Cincinnati, OH 45242-1812

513-421-2050
800-421-1321
FAX 513-421-5144
E-Mail: customer@stmediagroup.com
Home Page: www.stmediagroup.com

Tedd Swormstedt, CEO
Brian Foos, CFO

Publication for design and architecture of hotels, restaurants, spas, resorts, casinos, complexes or convention centers. Covers hospitality design with the eye of a fashion magazine, identifying trends and showcasing them seasonally in a photo-rich format.
Frequency: Monthly
Circulation: 17000
Founded in 1906

425   IQ News Adweek
Prometheus Global Media
770 Broadway
7th Floor
New York, NY 10003-9595

212-493-4100
FAX 646-654-5368
Home Page: www.prometheusgm.com
Social Media: *Facebook, Twitter, RSS*

Richard D. Beckman, CEO
James A. Finkelstein, Chairman
Madeline Krakowsky, Vice President Circulation
Tracy Brater, Executive Director Creative Service

Adweek IQ Daily goes out every weekday morning with a briefing of the most important news on interactive advertising, the latest moves by major brands and agencies in terms of content creation, media partnerships and distribution strategies in the digital realm.
Frequency: Daily

426   In-Store Marketer
In-Store Marketing Institute
7400 Skokie Blvd
Skokie, IL 60077-3339

847-675-7400
FAX 847-675-7494
E-Mail:
pdproducts_editor@instoremarketer.org
Home Page: www.instoremarketer.org
Social Media: *Facebook, Twitter, LinkedIn*

Peter Hoyt, President

Members-only e-newsletter highlights new content added to the Institute's website, including research, audio-enabled presentations, image galleries and trends articles.
Frequency: Bi-Monthly
Circulation: 15000
Printed in 4 colors on glossy stock

427   Industrial + Specialty Printing
ST Media Group International
11262 Cornell Park Dr
Cincinnati, OH 45242-1812

513-421-2050
800-421-1321
FAX 513-421-5144
E-Mail: customer@stmediagroup.com
Home Page: www.stmediagroup.com

Tedd Swormstedt, CEO
Brian Foos, CFO

Covers functional and decorative printing done as part of the manufacturing process, examining the challenges printers face when setting up and maintaining efficient workflows and provides the solutions to keep production on track in industrial printing operations.
Frequency: Monthly
Circulation: 17000
Founded in 1906

428   Insight Briefs
Association of National Advertisers
708 Third Avenue
33 Floor
New York, NY 10017

212-697-5950
FAX 212-661-8057
E-Mail: info@ana.net
Home Page: www.ana.net
Social Media: *Facebook, Twitter, LinkedIn, YouTube*

Bob Liodice, President & CEO
Christine Manna, COO
William Zengel, EVP

Association of National Advertisers collections of their best materials on a given subject. These resources incorporate information gathered from ANA's vast archive of proprietary information, including: best practices, case studies, charts, data, and quotes from client-side marketers. The purpose of the Briefs is to give high-level insights on a range of timely and important marketing topics.
Frequency: Monthly

429   International Archive Magazine
Luerzer's Archive Inc
106 West 29th St
New York, NY 10001

212-643-4297
FAX 646-619-4264
E-Mail: office@luezersarchive.net
Home Page: www.luezersarchive.net

Sandra Lehnst, CEO
Michael Weinzettl, Publisher
Christina Hrdlicka, Managing Editor
Michael Weinzettl, Editor in Chief

Presents new and innovative TV, magazine, poster and newspaper ads from 20 countries. Devoted to presentation of ads. Translations are provided.
Frequency: Bi-Monthly

430   Journal of Advertising (JA)
American Academy of Advertising
24710 Shaker Blvd.
Beachwood, OH 44122

512-471-8149
FAX 512-471-7018
E-Mail: jaeditor@austin.utexas.edu
Home Page: www.journalofadvertising.org
Social Media: *Facebook, Twitter*

Herbert J Rotfeld, President
Debbie Treise, President Elect
Steve Edwards, Vice President
Margie Morrison, Treasurer
Wei-Na Lee, Ph.D, Editor

The premier academic publication covering significant intellectual development pertaining to advertising theories and their relationship with

practice. The goal is to provide a public forum that reflects the current understanding of advertising as a process of communication, its role in the changing environment, and the relationships between these and other components of the advertising business and practice.
600 Members
Frequency: Quarterly
Founded in 1957

431 Journal of Advertising Research
World Advertising Research Center Ltd
2233 Wisconsin Ave NW
Suite 535
Washington, DC 20007-4144

202-778-4544
FAX 202-778-4546
E-Mail: americas@warc.com
Home Page: www.noralgroup.com
Social Media: *Facebook, Twitter*

Eva Kasten, President

The mission of the Journal of Advertising Research is to act as the research and development vehicle for professionals in all areas of marketing including media, research, advertising and communications
Frequency: Quarterly
Circulation: 1850

432 Journal of Current Issues and Research in Advertising
CTC Press
PO Box 290159
Columbia, SC 29229-0159

803-754-3112
800-382-8856
FAX 803-754-3013
E-Mail: j-leigh@tamu.edu
Home Page: www.ctcpress.com

James H Leigh, Co-Editor

Educates advertising students, professionals and all others interested in advertising.

433 Journal of Euromarketing
Taylor & Francis Inc
325 Chestnut St
Suite 800
Philadelphia, PA 19106-2614

215-625-8900
800-354-1420
FAX 215-625-2940
Home Page: www.taylorandfrancis.com

Kevin Bradley, President

Aims to meet the needs of academicians, practitioners, and public policymakers in the discussion of marketing issues pertaining to Europe. It helps to increase our understanding of the strategic planning aspects of marketing in Europe and the marketing aspects of the trading relationship between European and foreign firms.
Frequency: Quarterly
ISSN: 1049-6483

434 Journal of Interactive Advertising
American Academy of Advertising
24710 Shaker Blvd.
Beachwood, OH 44122

786-393-3333
E-Mail: patrose@aaasite.org
Home Page: www.aaasite.org
Social Media: *Facebook, Twitter*

Debbie Treise, President
Kim Sheehan, President Elect
Margie Morrison, Vice President
nancy Mitchell, Treasurer
Glen Griffin, Secretary

A refereed online publication designed to promote our understanding of interactive advertis-

ing, marketing and communication in a networked world.
600 Members
Frequency: 2x/Year
Founded in 1957

435 Media
Media Index Publishing
PO Box 24365
Seattle, WA 98124-0365

206-382-9220
800-332-1736
FAX 206-382-9437
E-Mail: media@media-inc.com
Home Page: www.media-inc.com

Katie Sauro, Editor
James Baker, President

Contains the most up-to-date information and issues that are important to you as a member of the marketing, advertising, broadcast, film and video production, multimedia and creative services industries, along with special focus segments and lists each issue, helpful advice from industry leaders and insightful reporting.
Frequency: Bi-Monthly
Circulation: 10,000
Mailing list available for rent: 35M names

436 Mediaweek
Prometheus Global Media
770 Broadway
7th Floor
New York, NY 10003-9595

212-493-4100
FAX 646-654-5368
Home Page: www.prometheusgm.com
Social Media: *Facebook, Twitter, RSS*

Richard D. Beckman, CEO
James A. Finkelstein, Chairman
Madeline Krakowsky, Vice President Circulation
Tracy Brater, Executive Director Creative Service

Highly targeted circulation covers media decision makers at the top 350 ad agencies in America, all top buying services and client media departments.
Frequency: Weekly
Circulation: 21000
Founded in 1991

437 News & Views
Advertising Media Credit Executives Association
8840 Columbia 100 Parkway
Columbia, MD 21045-2158

410-992-7609
FAX 410-740-5574
E-Mail: amcea@amcea.org
Home Page: www.amcea.org

Sheila Wroten, President
Mary Younger, Vice President
Josie Salazar, Secretary/ Treasurer
Vickie Bolinger, Director
Grace Carter, Director

Our magazine reports on current trends and legal issues while offering tips on customer service, time management and collections.
Frequency: Quarterly

438 Outdoor Advertising Magazine
Outdoor Advertising Magazine
Rapid City, SD 57702

877-926-5406
E-Mail: publisher@oam.net
Home Page: www.oam.net
Social Media: *Facebook, Twitter, LinkedIn*

Randall Williamson, Publisher

A major source for the outdoor and out-of-home advertising industry. Contains the latest information on products, services, sup-

plies, technology, creative ideas, financial and industry news.
Cost: $24.95
Founded in 1920

439 PC Today
Promotional Products Association International
3125 Skyway Cir N
Irving, TX 75038-3539

972-252-0404
FAX 972-258-3004
E-Mail: ppb@ppai.org
Home Page: www.ppai.org
Social Media: *Facebook, Twitter, LinkedIn, YouTube*

Paul Bellantone, President
Steven Meyer, Chairman of the Board
Marc Simon, Chair-Elect

Quick-read, daily, electronic newsletter serves the unique educational needs of distributor salespeople.
Frequency: Weekly

440 POP Design
In-Store Marketing Institute
7400 Skokie Blvd
Skokie, IL 60077-3339

847-675-7400
FAX 847-675-7494
E-Mail: pdproducts_editor@instoremarketer.org
Home Page: www.instoremarketer.org
Social Media: *Facebook, Twitter, LinkedIn*

Peter Hoyt, President

Serves the news and product information needs of producers and designers of in-store displays, signs and fixtures. Each issue features the latest trends and technologies vital to building and designing successful in-store merchandising.
Frequency: Bi-Monthly
Circulation: 15000
Printed in 4 colors on glossy stock

441 PPB Magazine
Promotional Products Association International
3125 Skyway Cir N
Irving, TX 75038-3539

972-252-0404
888-426-7724
FAX 972-258-3004
E-Mail: ppb@ppai.org
Home Page: www.ppai.org
Social Media: *Facebook, Twitter, YouTube*

Paul Bellantone, President
Steven Meyer, Chairman of the Board
Marc Simon, Chair-Elect

Coverage concentrates on news activities and events of the promotional products industry.
Cost: $62.00
Frequency: Monthly

442 Package Design Magazine
ST Media Group International
11262 Cornell Park Dr
Cincinnati, OH 45242-1812

513-421-2050
800-421-1321
FAX 513-421-5144
E-Mail: customer@stmediagroup.com
Home Page: www.stmediagroup.com

Tedd Swormstedt, CEO
Brian Foos, CFO

Full of the news and information professional package designers need to stay abreast of the latest innovations, materials, and technology driving the packaging industry. Presents read-

ers with the useful insights they need to succeed in competitive retail markets.
Frequency: Monthly
Circulation: 17000
Founded in 1906

443 Politically Direct
Direct Marketing Association
1120 Avenue of the Americas
New York, NY 10036-6713

212-768-7277
FAX 212-302-6714
E-Mail: customerservice@the-dma.org
Home Page: www.the-dma.org
Social Media: *Facebook, Twitter, LinkedIn*

Matt Blumberg, Chairman
Glenn Eisen, Vice Chairman
Rick Erwin, Treasurer

Published in both print and digital versions, this newsletter on DMA advocacy efforts keeps DMA members informed and involved in the politics and policies that impact them today and ahead of the curve on developments that will affect them tomorrow.
Frequency: Quarterly

444 Promotional Consultant Magazine
Promotional Products Association
International
3125 Skyway Cir N
Irving, TX 75038-3539

972-252-0404
FAX 972-258-3004
E-Mail: ppb@ppai.org
Home Page: www.ppai.org
Social Media: *Facebook, Twitter, YouTube*

Paul Bellantone, President
Steven Meyer, Chairman of the Board
Marc Simon, Chair-Elect

Featuring short, sales-specific articles, relevant trends, targeted strategies, expert voices and compelling case studies.
Frequency: Bi-Monthly
Circulation: 20000

445 Public Opinion Journal
American Association for Public Opinion
Research
111 Deer Land Road
Suite 100
Deerfield, IL 60015-4943

913-895-4601
FAX 913-895-4652
E-Mail: aapor-info@goamp.com
Home Page: www.aapor.org
Social Media: *Facebook, Twitter, LinkedIn*

Paul Lavrakas, President
Rob Santos, VP/President-Elect
Scott Keeter, Secretary-Treasurer

Offers articles about the science and practice of survey and opinion research to give people a voice in the decisions that affect their daily lives.
Frequency: Quarterly
Founded in 1948
Mailing list available for rent: 1000 names at $400 per M

446 Public Relations Unplugged: PR Strategies For AAF Ad Clubs and Members
American Advertising Federation
1101 Vermont Ave NW
Suite 500
Washington, DC 20005-6306

202-898-0089
800-999-2231
FAX 202-898-0159

E-Mail: aaf@aaf.org
Home Page: www.aaf.org

James Edmund Datri, President
Constance Cannon Frazier, COO
Joanne Schecter, Executive Vice President

In this text you will find guidance, instructions and examples to help your ad club deflect legislative threats and become a more prominent voice within your community.

447 Response
201 Sandpointe Ave
Suite 500
Santa Ana, CA 92707-8700

714-338-6700
800-854-3112
FAX 714-513-8482
E-Mail: thaire@questex.com
Home Page: www.responsemagazine.com
Social Media: *Facebook, Twitter, LinkedIn, YouTube*

Thomas Haire, Editor
Don Rosenberg, VP
Kristina Kronenberg, Marketing Director

Magazine of direct response television reporting. Educates marketers and advertising executives on how to sell products, generate leads and drive store sales through infomercials, short-form commercials, televised shopping and multi-media retailing.
Frequency: Monthly
Circulation: 12000
Founded in 1987

448 STORES Magazine
Retail Advertising & Marketing
International
325 7th St NW
Suite 1100
Washington, DC 20004-2818

202-661-3052
FAX 202-737-2849
Home Page: www.rama-nrf.org

Kevin Brown, RAMA Chairman
Rob Gruen, Vice Chairman
Gwen Morrison, CEO
Julie Gardner, CMO

A publication devoted to retail news and trends as well as notification of conferences and meetings.
Frequency: Monthly

449 Screen Printing Magazine
ST Media Group International
11262 Cornell Park Dr
Cincinnati, OH 45242-1812

513-421-2050
800-421-1321
FAX 513-421-5144
E-Mail: customer@stmediagroup.com
Home Page: www.stmediagroup.com

Tedd Swormstedt, CEO
Brian Foos, CFO

Leading publication and trusted source of information for the screen-printing industry. Landmark coverage of the latest techniques and technologies that save time, energy and money.
Frequency: Monthly
Circulation: 17000
Founded in 1906

450 Shopper Marketing
In-Store Marketing Institute
7400 Skokie Blvd
Skokie, IL 60077-3339

847-675-7400
FAX 847-675-7494
E-Mail:
pdproducts_editor@instoremarketer.org

Home Page: www.instoremarketer.org
Social Media: *Facebook, Twitter, LinkedIn*

Peter Hoyt, President

The leading information source for news and information surrounding the shopper marketing industry. Each month, more than 18000 marketers, manufacturers, agencies and retailers of consumer products or services who buy and specify in-store marketing solutions turn to Shopper Marketing to learn about the latest insights, data and trends surrounding the industry.
Frequency: Bi-Monthly
Circulation: 15000
Printed in 4 colors on glossy stock

451 Shopper Marketing Newswire
In-Store Marketing Institute
7400 Skokie Blvd
Skokie, IL 60077-3339

847-675-7400
FAX 847-675-7494
E-Mail:
pdproducts_editor@instoremarketer.org
Home Page: www.instoremarketer.org
Social Media: *Facebook, Twitter, LinkedIn*

Peter Hoyt, President

Delivered to a powerful audience of brands, retailers, agencies and solution providers. Offering personnel updates, company news, research/ data reports, path-to-purchase innovations, co-marketing initiatives across FDM and specialty chains and more.
Frequency: Bi-Monthly
Circulation: 15000
Printed in 4 colors on glossy stock

452 Sign & Digital Graphics
National Business Media Inc
2800 W Midway Boulevard
PO Box 1416
Broomfield, CO 80020

303-469-0424
800-669-0424
FAX 303-469-5730
E-Mail: mdixon@nbm.com
Home Page: www.nbm.com/sb
Social Media: *Facebook, Twitter*

James Kochevar, Publisher
Ken Mergentime, Executive Editor
Matt Dixon, Managing Editor

A comprehensive monthly trade publication covering the business of visual communications offering a broad range of in-depth reporting for professionals. Topics covered include commercial signage, wide-format commercial printing, electric signs and letters, architectural signage, electronic displays, vehicle wraps and graphics and much more.
Cost: $38.00
120 Pages
Frequency: Monthly
Circulation: 18300
Founded in 1986
Mailing list available for rent: 1000 names at $225 per M
Printed in 4 colors

453 Sign Builder Illustrated
Simmons-Boardman Publishing Corporation
345 Hudson St
12th Floor
New York, NY 10014-7123

212-620-7200
FAX 212-633-1165
E-Mail: jwoten@sbpub.com
Home Page: www.simmonsboardman.com

Arthur J McGinnis Jr, President

How-to magazine featuring the latest products, technology and techniques to enhance the sign maker's craft.
Frequency: Monthly
Circulation: 19055

454 **Sign Business**
National Business Media Inc
2800 W Midway Boulevard
PO Box 1416
Broomfield, CO 80020

303-469-0424
800-669-0424
FAX 303-469-5730
E-Mail: mdixon@nbm.com
Home Page: www.nbm.com/sb

James Kochevar, Publisher
Ken Mergentime, Executive Editor
Matt Dixon, Managing Editor

Contains information on electrical illuminated signage, outdoor advertising and commercial sign shops.
Cost: $38.00
120 Pages
Frequency: Monthly
Circulation: 18348
Founded in 1986
Mailing list available for rent: 1000 names at $225 per M
Printed in 4 colors

455 **SignCraft Magazine**
SignCraft Publishing Company
PO Box 60031
Fort Myers, FL 33906

239-939-4644
800-204-0204
FAX 239-939-0607
E-Mail: signcraft@signcraft.com
Home Page: www.signcraft.com

Tom McIltrot, Editor

Each issue includes an inside look at several sign shops, plus articles on techniques, materials, pricing, sales and computer aided sign making and puts hundreds of layout ideas at your fingertips.
Frequency: Monthly
Circulation: 14000
Mailing list available for rent: 25M names

456 **Signs of the Times Magazine**
ST Media Group International
11262 Cornell Park Dr
Cincinnati, OH 45242-1812

513-421-2050
800-421-1321
FAX 513-421-5144
E-Mail: customer@stmediagroup.com
Home Page: www.stmediagroup.com

Tedd Swormstedt, CEO
Brian Foos, CFO

It is our mission to educate and inspire signage and graphics professionals worldwide through award winning editorial perspectives, technology updates, CAS reports, new product reviews, one of a kind Electric, CAS and Commercial State of the Industry reports, graphics techniques and much more.
Frequency: Monthly
Circulation: 17000
Founded in 1906

457 **Supplier Global Resource**
Advertising Specialty Institute
4800 E Street Rd
Langhorne, PA 19053-6698

215-953-4000
800-546-1350
FAX 215-953-3045
E-Mail: info@asicentral.com

Home Page: www.asicentral.com
Social Media: *Facebook*

Timothy M Andrews, CEO
Norman Cohn, Chairman
Matthew Cohn, Vice Chairman
Carol Albright, SVP-Human Resources

The buying power of Supplier Global Resource readers is large-scale and powerful.
Frequency: 13x/Year
Circulation: 40000

458 **Survey Practice**
American Association for Public Opinion Research
111 Deer Land Road
Suite 100
Deerfield, IL 60015-4943

913-895-4601
FAX 913-895-4652
E-Mail: aapor-info@aapor.com
Home Page: www.aapor.org
Social Media: *Facebook, Twitter, LinkedIn*

Paul Lavrakas, President
Rob Santos, VP/President-Elect
Scott Keeter, Secretary-Treasurer

AAPOR's e-journal with public opinion and survey research articles and commentary.
Frequency: Quarterly
Founded in 1948
Mailing list available for rent: 1000 names at $400 per M

459 **TelevisionWeek**
Crain Communications
1155 Gratiot Ave
Detroit, MI 48207-2732

313-446-6000
E-Mail: info@crain.com
Home Page: www.crain.com

Norm Feldman, Manager
Chuck Ross, Managing Director

Covers all aspects of the business programming and production, distribution and talent, broadcast, cable and satellite, advertising and media, government and regulation, finance and emerging technologies.
Founded in 1982

460 **The Advertiser Magazine**
Pohly Company
99 Bedford Street
Floor 5
Boston, MA 02111

617-457-3938
E-Mail: bliodice@ana.net
Home Page: www.ana.net

Kristina Sweet, Assoc Publisher, Director Sales

Reports on today's most critical marketing issues such as measuring brand equity, using emerging technologies and digital marketing. It also contains articles on key benchmarks and industry trends. Offers news and events in the advertising industry. Produced by Association of National Advertisers.
Frequency: 6x/Year
Circulation: 25000

461 **The Big Picture**
ST Media Group International
11262 Cornell Park Dr
Cincinnati, OH 45242-1812

513-421-2050
800-421-1321
FAX 513-421-5144
E-Mail: customer@stmediagroup.com
Home Page: www.stmediagroup.com

Tedd Swormstedt, CEO
Brian Foos, CFO

Provides real-world solutions to today's design and production challenges. This publication re-

ports on digital printing of visual communications with coverage of digital printing from image capture and processing to finishing and display.
Frequency: Monthly
Circulation: 17000
Founded in 1906

462 **VMSD**
ST Media Group International
11262 Cornell Park Dr
Cincinnati, OH 45242-1812

513-421-2050
800-421-1321
FAX 513-421-5144
E-Mail: customer@stmediagroup.com
Home Page: www.stmediagroup.com

Tedd Swormstedt, CEO
Brian Foos, CFO

Leading magazine for retail designers and store display professionals, showcasing the latest store designs and visual presentations, presents merchandising strategies and new products, and reports on industry news and events.
Frequency: Monthly
Circulation: 17000
Founded in 1906

463 **Wearables**
Advertising Specialty Institute
4800 E Street Rd
Langhorne, PA 19053-6698

215-953-4000
800-546-1350
FAX 215-953-3045
E-Mail: info@asicentral.com
Home Page: www.asicentral.com
Social Media: *Facebook*

Timothy M Andrews, CEO
Norman Cohn, Chairman
Matthew Cohn, Vice Chairman
Carol Albright, SVP-Human Resources

Serves the apparel and accessories segment of the advertising specialty industry.
Frequency: 13x/Year
Circulation: 40000

464 **Winning at Retail**
In-Store Marketing Institute
7400 Skokie Blvd
Skokie, IL 60077-3339

847-675-7400
FAX 847-675-7494
E-Mail: pdproducts_editor@instoremarketer.org
Home Page: www.instoremarketer.org
Social Media: *Facebook, Twitter, LinkedIn*

Peter Hoyt, President

Shares insights, case studies and lessons learned from thousands of studies conducted by Perception Research Services, the leading company in packaging and shopper marketing research.
Frequency: Bi-Monthly
Circulation: 15000
Printed in 4 colors on glossy stock

Trade Shows

465 **AAPOR Annual Conference**
American Association for Public Opinion Research
111 Deer Lake Road
Suite 100
Deerfield, IL 60015

847-205-2651
FAX 847-480-9282
E-Mail: aapor-info@goamp.com

Home Page: www.aapor.org
Social Media: *Facebook, Twitter, LinkedIn*

Paul Lavrakas, President
Rob Santos, VP/President-Elect
Scott Keeter, Secretary-Treasurer

Features cutting edge research and informal access to leaders in the fields.
850 Attendees
Frequency: Annual
Mailing list available for rent: 1000 names at $400 per M

466 ADMERICA!
American Advertising Federation
1101 Vermont Ave NW
Suite 500
Washington, DC 20005-6306

202-898-0089
800-999-2231
FAX 202-898-0159
E-Mail: aaf@aaf.org
Home Page: www.aaf.org
Social Media: *Facebook, Twitter, YouTube*

James Edmund Datri, President
Constance Cannon Frazier, COO
Joanne Schecter, Executive Vice President

Connects all aspects of the advertising industry. Influential agencies, clients, media companies, suppliers, and colleges from across the country will address how to thrive in a recovering economy and how the changing culture of business and consumers is impacting our industry.

467 AMCEA Conference
Advertising Media Credit Executives Association
8840 Columbia 100 Parkway
Columbia, MD 21045-2158

410-992-7609
FAX 410-740-5574
E-Mail: amcea@amcea.org
Home Page: www.amcea.org

J Dee Stevenson, President
Kimberly Riley, VP
Vickie Bolinger, Director

The conference encompasses four days and is a networking extravaganza. Top attorneys discuss bankruptcy and legal issues. We invite advertising agencies to discuss network buying and liability problems.
Frequency: Annual

468 ANA Advertising Financial Management Conference
Association of National Advertisers
708 Third Avenue
33 Floor
New York, NY 10017

212-697-5950
FAX 212-661-8057
E-Mail: info@ana.net
Home Page: www.ana.net
Social Media: *Facebook, Twitter, LinkedIn, YouTube*

Bob Liodice, President & CEO
Christine Manna, COO
William Zengel, EVP

Brings together top marketing finance and procurement professionals from the client side with agency CFOs and other key industry stakeholders interested in efficiencies, cost savings, return on investment, and delivering greater value to organizations.

469 ANA Advertising Law & Public Policy Conference
Association of National Advertisers

708 Third Avenue
33 Floor
New York, NY 10017

212-697-5950
FAX 212-661-8057
E-Mail: info@ana.net
Home Page: www.ana.net
Social Media: *Facebook, Twitter, LinkedIn, YouTube*

Bob Liodice, President & CEO
Christine Manna, COO
William Zengel, EVP

Keeping up with the digital revolution is becoming a nearly impossible task. This conference enters the battlefield by putting together a stellar faculty, including leading regulators, top practitioners, and serious critics, capped off by a session that puts it all together led by a leading law professor.

470 ANA Annual Conference - The Masters of Marketing
Association of National Advertisers
708 Third Avenue
33 Floor
New York, NY 10017

212-697-5950
FAX 212-661-8057
E-Mail: info@ana.net
Home Page: www.ana.net
Social Media: *Facebook, Twitter, LinkedIn, YouTube*

Bob Liodice, President & CEO
Christine Manna, COO
William Zengel, EVP

The conference offers an opportunity to learn from and engage with the leaders of the industry as they build brands, leverage the expanding array of media, make marketing more accountable and improve the quality of their marketing organizations.

471 ANA Digital & Social Media Conference
Association of National Advertisers
708 Third Avenue
33 Floor
New York, NY 10017

212-697-5950
FAX 212-661-8057
E-Mail: info@ana.net
Home Page: www.ana.net
Social Media: *Facebook, Twitter, LinkedIn, YouTube*

Bob Liodice, President & CEO
Christine Manna, COO
William Zengel, EVP

Discussing how to use social media to impact the consumer decision journey and how to effectively partner with other companies to maximize social media reach and more.

472 ANA TV & Everything Video Forum Presented by Google
Association of National Advertisers
708 Third Avenue
33 Floor
New York, NY 10017

212-697-5950
FAX 212-661-8057
E-Mail: info@ana.net
Home Page: www.ana.net
Social Media: *Facebook, Twitter, LinkedIn, YouTube*

Bob Liodice, President & CEO
Christine Manna, COO
William Zengel, EVP

The forum recognizes that the role of television in the media mix is being redefined and broadened. In addition to traditional television, the

TV & Everything Video Forum will explore the use of video on any type of screen or device: the computer, Internet, mobile, point-of-purchase, gaming, and more. Registration starts at $595.
Frequency: Annual

473 ANA/WFA Global Marketing Conference
Association of National Advertisers
708 Third Avenue
33 Floor
New York, NY 10017

212-697-5950
FAX 212-661-8057
E-Mail: info@ana.net
Home Page: www.ana.net
Social Media: *Facebook, Twitter, LinkedIn, YouTube*

Bob Liodice, President & CEO
Christine Manna, COO
William Zengel, EVP

Offers tips on marketing on a worldwide scale.

474 Ad:tech Adweek
Prometheus Global Media
770 Broadway
7th Floor
New York, NY 10003-9595

212-493-4100
FAX 646-654-5368
Home Page: www.prometheusgm.com
Social Media: *Facebook, Twitter, RSS*

Richard D. Beckman, CEO
James A. Finkelstein, Chairman
Madeline Krakowsky, Vice President Circulation
Tracy Brater, Executive Director Creative Service

An interactive advertising and technology conference and exhibition. Worldwide shows blend keynote speakers, topic driven panels and workshops to provide attendees with the tools and techniques they need to compete in a changing world.

475 Advertising Financial Management Conference
Association of National Advertisers
708 Third Avenue
33 Floor
New York, NY 10017

212-697-5950
FAX 212-661-8057
E-Mail: info@ana.net
Home Page: www.ana.net
Social Media: *Facebook, Twitter, LinkedIn, YouTube*

Bob Liodice, President & CEO
Christine Manna, COO
William Zengel, EVP

The agenda is developed with input from members of the Advertising Financial Management Committee and topics focus on efficiency, return on investment, cost savings and new ideas to bring greater value to organizations. Registration begins at $1,095.
Frequency: Annual

476 Advertising Law & Public Policy Conference
Association of National Advertisers
708 Third Avenue
33 Floor
New York, NY 10017

212-697-5950
FAX 212-661-8057
E-Mail: info@ana.net
Home Page: www.ana.net

Social Media: *Facebook, Twitter, LinkedIn, YouTube*

Bob Liodice, President & CEO
Christine Manna, COO
William Zengel, EVP

Discuss new policy initiatives and how they will transform advertising; recent court decisions, regulatory changes reshaping the legal environment for advertising. Hear from FCC, FTC, and FDA experts and representatives. Registration begins at $795.
Frequency: Annual

477 Advertising Media Credit Executives Association Annual Conference
Advertising Media Credit Executives Association
PO Box 433
Louisville, KY 40201

502-582-4327
FAX 502-582-4330
E-Mail: amcea@amcea.org
Home Page: www.amcea.org

Cheryl E Szluzer, President
Sheila Wroten, Vice President

Media credit managers, editors, business mangers and other professionals gather for exhibits of advertising media such as newspapers, magazines, radio and television.
400 Attendees
Frequency: Annual
Founded in 1896

478 Annual Action Taker Series
Retail Advertising & Marketing International
325 7th Street NW
Suite 1100
Washington, DC 20004

202-661-3052
FAX 202-737-2849
Home Page: www.rama-nrf.org

Kevin Brown, RAMA Chairman
Rob Gruen, Vice Chairman
Gwen Morrison, CEO
Julie Gardner, CMO

Come hear real case studies and inspiring concepts from today's retail creative leaders.
400 Attendees
Frequency: Annual

479 Annual Advertising Conference
Advertising Women of New York
25 W 45th Street
Suite 403
New York, NY 10036

212-221-7969
FAX 212-221-8296
E-Mail: awny@awny.org
Home Page: www.awny.org
Social Media: *Facebook, Twitter, LinkedIn, You tube*

Carol Watson, President
Melissa Goidel, VP

To meet some of the top people in the field of advertising; to discover techniques of career planning that can help you get the job of your choice with greater ease; to network with some of the most influential advertising executives of the time from a variety of disciplines.
600 Attendees

480 Annual Conference and Mailing & Fulfillment Expo
Mailing & Fulfillment Service Association
1421 Prince Street
Suite 410
Alexandria, VA 22314-2806

703-836-9200
FAX 703-548-8204

E-Mail: mfsa-mail@mfsanet.org
Home Page: www.mfsanet.org

Ken Garner, President
Jennifer Root, Director
Bill Stevenson, Director Marketing

Quality educational sessions, industry specific exhibit hall, networking and more.
Frequency: Annual

481 Annual Global Marketing Summit
International Advertising Association - NY Chapter
World Serivce Center
275 Madison Avenue Suite 2102
New York, NY 10016

212-338-0222
FAX 212-983-0455
E-Mail: coordinator@iaany.org
Home Page: www.iaany.org
Social Media: *Facebook, Twitter, LinkedIn*

Tom Brookbanks, President
Larry Levy, Treasurer
Sean Lough, Secretary

Designed to provide participants with the knowledge, tools and inspiration needed to market global brands. Various registration options. Visit website for details.
1000 Attendees
Frequency: Annual

482 Annual MAPOR Conference- Public Opinion Frontiers
American Association for Public Opinion Research
111 Deer Lake Road
Suite 100
Deerfield, IL 60015

847-205-2651
FAX 847-480-9282
E-Mail: aapor-info@goamp.com
Home Page: www.aapor.org
Social Media: *Facebook, Twitter, LinkedIn*

Paul Lavrakas, President
Rob Santos, VP/President-Elect
Scott Keeter, Secretary-Treasurer

Focusing on emerging methods in data collection and analysis and research into attitude formation.
850 Attendees
Frequency: Annual
Mailing list available for rent: 1000 names at $400 per M

483 Annual Proceedings Conference
American Academy of Advertising
24710 Shaker Blvd.
Beachwood, OH 44122

786-393-3333
E-Mail: patrose@aaasite.org
Home Page: www.aaasite.org
Social Media: *Facebook, Twitter*

Debbie Treise, President
Kim Sheehan, President Elect
Margie Morrison, Vice President
nancy Mitchell, Treasurer
Glen Griffin, Secretary

Every year the American Academy of Advertising holds a conference at which advertising research findings and theories are presented, as well as papers concerning methods of teaching advertising.
600 Members
Founded in 1957

484 Asian-Pacific Conference
American Academy of Advertising
24710 Shaker Blvd.
Beachwood, OH 44122

786-393-3333
E-Mail: patrose@aaasite.org

Home Page: www.aaasite.org
Social Media: *Facebook, Twitter*

Debbie Treise, President
Kim Sheehan, President Elect
Margie Morrison, Vice President
nancy Mitchell, Treasurer
Glen Griffin, Secretary

Focusing on issues in the Asian-Pacific region, this conference welcomes research on any aspect of advertising as broadly defined in one or more Asian-Pacific countries or in multiple countries involving at least one Asian-Pacific country. This conference is co-sponsored by China Advertising Association of Commerce and Communication University of China.
600 Members
Founded in 1957

485 Audience Measurement 7.0
Advertising Research Foundation
432 Park Avenue S
6th Floor
New York, NY 10016-8013

212-751-5656
FAX 212-319-5265
E-Mail: info@thearf.org
Home Page: www.thearf.org
Social Media: *Facebook, Twitter, LinkedIn, youtube*

Colleen Fahey Rush, Chief Research Officer
David Poltrack, Secretary
Bernard Bradpiece, Treasurer

Knowing the latest developments in audience composition and measurement across platforms is critical to ensuring your company's money is spent most effectively. Get up-to-the-minute on the latest evaluation approaches and technology.
400 Members
Founded in 1936

486 Cable Advertising Conference
Cabletelevision Advertising Bureau
830 3rd Avenue
2nd Floor
New York, NY 10022

212-508-1200
FAX 212-832-3268
Home Page: www.thecab.tv

Sean Cunningham, President

Annual conference and exhibits of advertising-supported cable television networks and services to support local advertising sales.
2000 Attendees
Frequency: Annual/April

487 Cannes Lion Advertising Festival Screening
American Association of Advertising Agencies
1065 Avenue of the Americas
16th Floor
New York, NY 10018

212-682-2500
FAX 212-682-8391
E-Mail: kipp@aaaa.org
Home Page: www.aaaa.org
Social Media: *Facebook, Twitter, LinkedIn*

Nancy Hill, President
Chris Weil, Chair
Andrew Bennett, Director at Large
Sharon Napier, Secretary/Treasurer

The screening will bring together hundreds of industry professionals to view the winning work of Cannes and celebrate the Philadelphia advertising community.

488 Channel Partners Conference & Expo
Virgo Publishing LLC

3300 N Central Ave
Suite 300
Phoenix, AZ 85012-2532

480-675-9925
FAX 480-990-0819
E-Mail: kkennedy@vpico.com
Home Page: www.vpico.com

John Siefert, CEO
Kelly Ridley, CFO
Jon Benninger, VP
John LyBarger, Director of IT

The communications industry's only event designed exclusively for indirect sales organizations - agents, VARs, systems integrators, interconnects and consultants - focused on transforming their businesses to become converged solutions providers.
Circulation: 20000
Founded in 1986
Printed in on glossy stock

489 Co-Creation and the Future of Agencies
American Association of Advertising Agencies
1065 Avenue of the Americas
16th Floor
New York, NY 10018

212-682-2500
FAX 212-682-8391
E-Mail: kipp@aaaa.org
Home Page: www.aaaa.org
Social Media: *Facebook, Twitter, LinkedIn*

Nancy Hill, President
Chris Weil, Chair
Andrew Bennett, Director at Large
Sharon Napier, Secretary/Treasurer

Learn how to be part of the trend toward the disintermediation of agents, marketers are increasing going around agencies to work directly with the media, production companies, and even directly to creative talent via crowdsourcing.

490 Comprehensive CRM & Database Marketing
Direct Marketing Association
1120 Avenue of the Americas
New York, NY 10036-6700

212-768-7277
FAX 212-302-6714
E-Mail: customerservice@the-dma.org
Home Page: www.the-dma.org
Social Media: *Facebook, Twitter, LinkedIn*

Lawrence M Kimmel, CEO

In an increasingly digital marketing landscape, metrics and ROI are being scrutinized and recalibrated like never before. Whether interested in classic database statistics or emerging trends in web analytics, the insights gained in our classes will add up to success.

491 DMA Annual Conference & Exhibition
Direct Marketing Association
1120 Avenue of Americas
New York, NY 10036-6700

212-768-7277
FAX 212-302-6714
E-Mail: dmaconferences@the-dma.org
Home Page: www.the-dma.org
Social Media: *Facebook, Twitter, LinkedIn*

Lawrence M Kimmel, CEO
Julie A Hogan, SVP Conferences/Education Services

Offers a progressive marketers to help better engage customers and improve bottom line re-

sults in all channels, including social, search, monile, video and more.
12000 Attendees
Frequency: Annual/October

492 Direct Marketing Institute
Direct Marketing Association
1120 Avenue of the Americas
New York, NY 10036-6700

212-768-7277
FAX 212-302-6714
E-Mail: customerservice@the-dma.org
Home Page: www.the-dma.org
Social Media: *Facebook, Twitter, LinkedIn*

Lawrence M Kimmel, CEO

A three-day intensive direct marketing seminar, the DMI iwll give step-by-step tactics to maximize the ROI of your campaigns.

493 Effective Email Marketing
Direct Marketing Association
1120 Avenue of the Americas
New York, NY 10036-6700

212-768-7277
FAX 212-302-6714
E-Mail: customerservice@the-dma.org
Home Page: www.the-dma.org
Social Media: *Facebook, Twitter, LinkedIn*

Lawrence M Kimmel, CEO

The online world presents a myriad of options for establishing and developing customer and community relationships. If you want to segment and target your email database or launch a mobile campaign, we can teach you the best practices and strategies you need to meet and exceed your goals.

494 Email Evolution Conference
Direct Marketing Association
1120 Avenue of Americas
New York, NY 10036-6700

212-768-7277
FAX 212-302-6714
E-Mail: www.dmaconference@the-dma.org
Home Page: www.the-dma.org
Social Media: *Facebook, Twitter, LinkedIn*

Lawrence M Kimmel, CEO
Julie A Hogan, SVP Conferences/Education Services

Focuses on the ever-changing and evolving world of email marketing, providing attendees with the best ways to capitalize on the high ROI this low-cost communication tool can provide both on its own, and integrated with social, search, mobile, video and other email enhancers.
10M Attendees
Frequency: Annual/February

495 Giving and Receiving Feedback with Grace & Style
American Association of Advertising Agencies
1065 Avenue of the Americas
16th Floor
New York, NY 10018

212-682-2500
FAX 212-682-8391
E-Mail: kipp@aaaa.org
Home Page: www.aaaa.org
Social Media: *Facebook, Twitter, LinkedIn*

Nancy Hill, President
Chris Weil, Chair
Andrew Bennett, Director at Large
Sharon Napier, Secretary/Treasurer

The majority of professionals cringe when it comes time for performance evaluations, self assessments, and even everyday feedback. Participants learn how to speak assertively and deliver constructive criticism while also

understanding how to receive feedback openly and grow professionally from the experience.

496 Global Shop Conference
Nielsen Business Media
1145 Sanctuary Parkway
Suite 355
Alpharetta, GA 30074

770-569-1540
FAX 770-569-5105
E-Mail: kara.kobrzycki@nielsen.com
Home Page: www.globalshop.org
Social Media: *Facebook, Twitter, LinkedIn*

David Loechner, President
Michael Alicea, SVP/Human Resources
Denise Bashem, VP/Finance

Retail designers and brand marketers find the most innovative concepts, newest products and services to create unique store design and in-store marketing solutions.
50000 Attendees
Frequency: Annual/March

497 Government Affairs Conference
American Advertising Federation
1101 Vermont Avenue NW
Suite 500
Washington, DC 20005

800-999-2231
FAX 202-898-0159
E-Mail: aaf@aaf.org
Home Page: www.aaf.org

James Edmund Datri, President
Constance Cannon Frazier, COO
Joanne Schecter, Executive Vice President

The conference is held annually in conjunction with the Association of National Advertisers and the American Association of Advertising Agencies.
807 Attendees
Frequency: Annual

498 Hospitality Match
ST Media Group International
11262 Cornell Park Dr
Cincinnati, OH 45242-1812

513-421-2050
800-421-1321
FAX 513-421-5144
E-Mail: customer@stmediagroup.com
Home Page: www.stmediagroup.com

Tedd Swormstedt, CEO
Brian Foos, CFO

A series of targeted and exclusive invitation-only events that bring key decision makers from top design firms, purchasing companies and hotel groups together with relevan suppliers, face-to-face for a weekend of serious business and exceptional networking events. Suppliers will meet with pre-qualified hospitality buyers through pre-arranged one-on-one meetings.
Frequency: Monthly
Circulation: 17000
Founded in 1906

499 IAA World Congress
International Advertising Association
747 Third Ave.
2nd Fl.
New York, NY 10017

646-722-2612
FAX 646-722-2501
E-Mail: iaa@iaaglobal.org
Home Page: www.iaaglobal.org

Bi-annual event attracts more than a thousand marketing communications professionals from all over the world.
1200 Attendees
Frequency: Bi-annual

500 IAB Annual Leadership Meeting
Interactive Advertising Bureau
116 E 27th Street
7th Floor
New York, NY 10016

212-380-4700
Home Page: www.iab.net
Social Media: *Facebook, Twitter, LinkedIn*

Randall Rothenberg, President/CEO

Addresses head-on issues taking place right
now in the digital industry.
Frequency: Monthly

**501 ICOM International World
Management Conference**
International Communications Agency
Network
1649 Lump Gulch Road
PO Box 490
Rollinsville, CO 80474-0490

303-258-9511
FAX 303-484-4087
E-Mail: info@icomagencies.com
Home Page: www.icomagencies.com
Social Media: *Facebook, Twitter, LinkedIn,
YouTube*

Bob Morrison, Director
Joe Phelps, North American Member at Large

Members will network and share ideas and success stories. Members will share learned information from the worst global economic crisis
since 1929, what they learned about their businesses, their clients and their staffs and what
they will do differently going forward.
80 Attendees
Frequency: Annual

502 IFCA Annual Conference
Insurance and Financial Communications
Association
1037 N 3rd Ave
Tucson, AZ 85705

602-350-0717
E-Mail: info@ifcaonline.com
Home Page: www.ifcaonline.com
Social Media: *Facebook, Twitter, LinkedIn,
YouTube*

Susan o'Neill, President
Ralph Chaump, VP
Kim Schultz, Secretary

Offers networking among peers, education
through platform speeches and practical workshops, display of the best industry communications work being done and volunteer
opportunities.

503 ISA International Sign Expo
International Sign Association
1001 N Fairfax Street
Suite 301
Alexandria, VA 22314

703-836-4012
866-WHY-SIGN
FAX 703-836-8353
E-Mail: info@signs.org
Home Page: www.signs.org

Duane Laska, Chairman
Harry Niese, Vice Chairman
Chad Jones, Secretary/Treasurer

ISA's annual internation sign Expo is a premier
platform for the sign industry to conduct business. 500 exhibitors. Admission from $15 to
$40.
12800 Attendees

**504 ISA Supplier & Distributor
Conference**
International Sign Association

1001 N Fairfax Street
Suite 301
Alexandria, VA 22314

703-836-4012
866-WHY-SIGN
FAX 703-836-8353
E-Mail: info@signs.org
Home Page: www.signs.org

Duane Laska, Chairman
Harry Niese, Vice Chairman
Chad Jones, Secretary/Treasurer

The conference featured a slate of experts
speaking on a wide range of topics specifically
of interest to companies that sell to sign manufacturers.
Frequency: Annual

**505 Integrated Marketing Members Only
Conference by Microsoft Advertising**
Pohly Company
99 Bedford Street
Floor 5
Boston, MA 02111

617-457-3938
E-Mail: ksweet@pohlyco.com
Home Page: www.ana.net

Kristina Sweet, Assoc Publisher, Director Sales

The development of new communications and
the evolution of traditional communications
have shifted power from the marketer to the
consumer, which created enormous opportunities, providing marketers with the ability to
better target their customers. Discover how top
marketers develop, execute, and evaluate their
overall marketing communications strategy
based on consumer insight.
Frequency: 6x/Year
Circulation: 25000

**506 International Career Developmemt
Conference**
DECA Inc
1908 Association Drive
Reston, VA 20191

703-860-5000
FAX 703-860-4013
Home Page: www.deca.org

Jacklyn Schiller, President
Jim Brock, President-elect
Lynore Levenhagen

Gathering of members, advisors,
businesspersons and alumni who attend. Most
of the participants are competitors in one of
DECA's competency based competitive events.
15000 Attendees

**507 MFSA Midwinter Executive
Conference**
Mailing & Fulfillment Service Association
1421 Prince Street
Suite 410
Alexandria, VA 22314-2806

703-836-9200
FAX 703-548-8204
E-Mail: mfsa-mail@mfsanet.org
Home Page: www.mfsanet.org

Ken Garner, President
Jennifer Root, Director
Bill Stevenson, Director Marketing

Addresses financial operations and business
valuation, marketing your own company, the
changing world of postal regulations, technology in fulfillment, building a sales team, being
strong in digital printing and the landscape of
employment law.

508 MIXX Conference & Expo
Interactive Advertising Bureau

116 E 27th Street
7th Floor
New York, NY 10016

212-380-4700
E-Mail: lisa@iab.net
Home Page: www.iab.net

Lisa Milgram, Events Director
Margaret Southwell, Events Coordinator

The preeminet event for marketing and agency
professionals-and the publishers and technology firms who help drive their efforts. Brings
together the industry's most prominent and influential figures to share insights on the most
pressing topics in advertising.
Frequency: Annual

509 Mailer Strategies Conference
Mailing & Fulfillment Service Association
1421 Prince Street
Suite 410
Alexandria, VA 22314-2806

703-836-9200
FAX 703-548-8204
E-Mail: mfsa-mail@mfsanet.org
Home Page: www.mfsanet.org

Ken Garner, President
Jennifer Root, Director
Bill Stevenson, Director Marketing

This conference will focus solely on postal issues that are important to your operations.

510 Media Conference & Tradeshow
American Association of Advertising
Agencies
1065 Avenue of the Americas
16th Floor
New York, NY 10018

212-682-2500
FAX 212-682-8391
E-Mail: kipp@aaaa.org
Home Page: www.aaaa.org
Social Media: *Facebook, Twitter, LinkedIn*

Nancy Hill, President
Chris Weil, Chair
Andrew Bennett, Director at Large
Sharon Napier, Secretary/Treasurer

Empowered consumers will be featured center
stage in live focus groups during the conference.

**511 Media and Account Management
Conference**
Association of Hispanic Advertising
Agencies
8400 Westpark Drive
2nd Floor
McLean, VA 22102

703-610-9014
FAX 703-610-0227
E-Mail: info@ahaa.org
Home Page: www.ahaa.org
Social Media: *Facebook, Twitter*

Horacio Gavilan, Executive Director
Melissa Chen, Membership/Directory
Ayanna Wiggins, Marketing

Examines the myriad of changes facing Hispanic agencies in and beyond including shifts
in approaches to communications planning, demographics and client needs.

512 Multicultural Council Meeting
Interactive Advertising Bureau
116 E 27th Street
7th Floor
New York, NY 10016

212-380-4700
Home Page: www.iab.net
Social Media: *Facebook, Twitter, LinkedIn*

Randall Rothenberg, President/CEO

IAB members contributing information on the interactive advertising marketplace.
Frequency: Monthly

513   NCDM Conference
Direct Marketing Association
1120 Avenue of Americas
New York, NY 10036-6700

212-768-7277
FAX 212-302-6714
E-Mail: dmaconferences@the-dma.org
Home Page: www.the-dma.org
Social Media: *Facebook, Twitter, LinkedIn*

Julie A Hogan, SVP Conferences/Events

Presents industry experts and hard-hitting case studies from a variety of verticles, such as financial services, retail, automotive, publishing, non-profit and many more, who will share the latest strategies and methodologies in gathering, analyzing, leveraging and protecting the most valuable business asset, customer data.
10M Attendees
Frequency: Annual/December

514   NRF Annual Convention & EXPO
Retail Advertising & Marketing
International
325 7th Street NW
Suite 1100
Washington, DC 20004

202-661-3052
FAX 202-737-2849
Home Page: www.rama-nrf.org

Kevin Brown, RAMA Chairman
Rob Gruen, Vice Chairman
Gwen Morrison, CEO
Julie Gardner, CMO

RAMA is undertaking in important transformation to become an organization that's representative of the changes that are affecting the retail marketing community with a strategic view that includes the integration of mobile, digital and traditional media.
400 Attendees
Frequency: Annual

515   National Conference on Operations & Fulfillment (NCOF)
Direct Marketing Association
1120 Avenue of Americas
New York, NY 10036-6700

212-768-7277
FAX 211-302-6714
E-Mail: dmaconferences@the-dma.org
Home Page: www.the-dma.org
Social Media: *Facebook, Twitter, LinkedIn*

Julie A Hogan, SVP Conference/Events
Lawrence M Kimmel, CEO

Focuses on innovative solutions for the warehouse, distribution, operations, and ecommerce needs in the ever-changing world of operations and fulfillment.
10M Attendees

516   New York Nonprofit Confernce
Direct Marketing Association
1120 Avenue of Americas
New York, NY 10036-6700

212-768-7277
FAX 212-302-6714
E-Mail: dmaconferences@the-dma.org
Home Page: www.the-dma.org
Social Media: *Facebook, Twitter, LinkedIn*

Lawrence M Kimmel, CEO
Julie A Hogan, SVP Conferences/Education Services

Discover which acknowledgement problems work best and why, increase revenue with membership options-as well as traditional fundraising appeals, learn how the internet and

e-mail campaigns can improve fundraising, lowering costs and increase advocacy.
10M Attendees

517   OAAA National Convention
Outdoor Advertising Association of
America
1850 M Street NW
Suite 1040
Washington, DC 20036

202-833-5566
FAX 202-833-1522
E-Mail: nfletcheter@oaaa.org
Home Page: www.oaaa.org

Nancy Fletcher, President
Willliam reagan, Secretary
Kevin Reily, Treasurer

The national convention program will offer depth of content and a diverse schedule of activities with something important for everyone engaged in the out of home business.
Frequency: Biennial

518   OAAA\TAB National Convention + Expo
Outdoor Advertising Association of
America
1850 M St. NW
Suite 140
Washington, DC 20036

202-833-5566
FAX 202-833-1522
Home Page: www.oaaa.org

Responsibility for the program alternates between the Outdoor Advertising Association of America (OAAA) and Traffic Audit Bureau (TAB).
Frequency: Annual

519   PPAI Brand
Promotional Products Association
International
3125 Skyway Cir N
Irving, TX 75038-3539

972-252-0404
FAX 972-258-3004
E-Mail: ppb@ppai.org
Home Page: www.ppai.org
Social Media: *Facebook, Twitter, LinkedIn, YouTube*

Steve Slagel, President

The industry's most highly regarded incentive products showcase, gives an all-access pass to the $46 billion incentives market.

520   PPAI Decorate
Promotional Products Association
International
3125 Skyway Cir N
Irving, TX 75038-3539

972-252-0404
FAX 972-258-3004
E-Mail: ppb@ppai.org
Home Page: www.ppai.org
Social Media: *Facebook, Twitter, LinkedIn, YouTube*

Paul Bellantone, President
Steven Meyer, Chairman of the Board
Marc Simon, Chair-Elect

The best in screen printing, embroidery and digital technology. Experience demonstrations of the newest products and equipment.

521   PPAI Expo
Promotional Products Association
International
3125 Skyway Circle N
Irving, TX 75038-3526

972-258-3104
FAX 972-258-3012

E-Mail: ppb@ppai.org
Home Page: www.ppa.org

Paul Bellantone, President
Steven Meyer, Chairman of the Board
Marc Simon, Chair-Elect

Offering you the tools, opportunities and innovative ideas you need to excel, to grow your business beyond expectation and become the example to be followed.

522   PPAI MASCAS
Promotional Products Association
International
3125 Skyway Cir N
Irving, TX 75038-3539

972-252-0404
FAX 972-258-3004
E-Mail: ppb@ppai.org
Home Page: www.ppai.org
Social Media: *Facebook, Twitter, LinkedIn, YouTube*

Paul Bellantone, President
Steven Meyer, Chairman of the Board
Marc Simon, Chair-Elect

Master Advertising Specialist (MAS) and Certified Advertising Specialist (CAS) are the promotional products industry's professional designations.

523   Powering Creativity Outside the Creative Department
American Association of Advertising
Agencies
1065 Avenue of the Americas
16th Floor
New York, NY 10018

212-682-2500
FAX 212-682-8391
E-Mail: kipp@aaaa.org
Home Page: www.aaaa.org
Social Media: *Facebook, Twitter, LinkedIn*

Nancy Hill, President
Chris Weil, Chair
Andrew Bennett, Director at Large
Sharon Napier, Secretary/Treasurer

The success of any communication, any campaign, any brand, any company or community depends on smarter, more creative, more impactful thinking from everyone involved. Young professionals who work in account management, media, research and production disciplines should look to attend.

524   RAMA CMO Summit
Retail Advertising & Marketing
International
325 7th Street NW
Suite 1100
Washington, DC 20004

202-661-3052
FAX 202-737-2849
Home Page: www.rama-nrf.org

Kevin Brown, RAMA Chairman
Rob Gruen, Vice Chairman
Gwen Morrison, CEO
Julie Gardner, CMO

To provide a networking and discussion forum for senior retail marketing executives.
50 Attendees

525   RAMACON: Thoughtful Topics, Fearless Ideas Remarkable People
Retail Advertising & Marketing
International

325 7th Street NW
Suite 1100
Washington, DC 20004

202-661-3052
FAX 202-737-2849
Home Page: www.rama-nrf.org

Kevin Brown, RAMA Chairman
Rob Gruen, Vice Chairman
Gwen Morrison, CEO
Julie Gardner, CMO

RAMA is undertaking in important transformation to become an organization that's representative of the changes that are affecting the retail marketing community with a strategic view that includes the integration of mobile, digital and traditional media.
400 Attendees
Frequency: Annual

526 Re:Think The ARF Annual Convention & Expo
Advertising Research Foundation
432 Park Avenue S
6th Floor
New York, NY 10016-8013

212-751-5656
FAX 212-319-5265
E-Mail: info@thearf.org
Home Page: www.thearf.org
Social Media: *Facebook, Twitter, LinkedIn, YouTube*

Colleen Fahey Rush, Chief Research Officer
David Poltrack, Secretary
Bernard Bradpiece, Treasurer

Re:Think is a research forum where the ad industry gathers to dispense, explore and challenge the latest knowledge driving the advertising and marketing industry. Showcases innovative market research services and products, high-level networking, free education, and leading-edge industry resources. Various registration options are available. Visit the ARF website for details.
400 Members
Founded in 1936

527 Reinventing Account Management
American Association of Advertising Agencies
1065 Avenue of the Americas
16th Floor
New York, NY 10018

212-682-2500
FAX 212-682-8391
E-Mail: kipp@aaaa.org
Home Page: www.aaaa.org
Social Media: *Facebook, Twitter, LinkedIn*

Nancy Hill, President
Chris Weil, Chair
Andrew Bennett, Director at Large
Sharon Napier, Secretary/Treasurer

Next Practices for Senior Agency Professionals. The traditional account management function at advertising agencies and other marketing communications firms is changing dramatically to meet the needs of a 24/7 digitally connected multichannel marketplace.

528 Response Expo
201 Sandpointe Ave
Suite 500
Santa Ana, CA 92707-8700

714-338-6700
800-854-3112
FAX 714-513-8482
E-Mail: thaire@questex.com
Home Page: www.responsemagazine.com

Social Media: *Facebook, Twitter, LinkedIn, YouTube*

Thomas Haire, Editor
Don Rosenberg, VP
Kristina Kronenberg, Marketing Director

Focuses on the evolution of consumers from passive watchers to active and empowered brand evangelists. Technology and social media have enabled and encouraged consumers to engage and interact with content. Learn how to take DR marketing from traditional campaign management to the future of customer engagement.
Frequency: Monthly
Circulation: 12000
Founded in 1987

529 Shopper Marketing Expo
In-Store Marketing Institute
7400 Skokie Blvd
Skokie, IL 60077-3339

847-675-7400
FAX 847-675-7494
E-Mail: pdproducts_editor@instoremarketer.org
Home Page: www.instoremarketer.org
Social Media: *Facebook, Twitter, LinkedIn*

Peter Hoyt, President

The premier annual event in the in-store industry filled with symposia, seminars, exhibits and awards dedicated to integrating the wide variety of solutions, tools and expertise needed to influence decision-making along the path to purchase.
Circulation: 15000
Printed in 4 colors on glossy stock

530 Shopper Marketing Summit
In-Store Marketing Institute
7400 Skokie Blvd
Skokie, IL 60077-3339

847-675-7400
FAX 847-675-7494
E-Mail: pdproducts_editor@instoremarketer.org
Home Page: www.instoremarketer.org
Social Media: *Facebook, Twitter, LinkedIn*

Peter Hoyt, President

A world-class senior level conference offering ideas and solutions to retailers, manufacturers and marketers of consumer products and services, agencies and other solution providers who are looking to achieve new heights at retail.
Printed in 4 colors on glossy stock

531 Signage and Graphics Summit
ST Media Group International
11262 Cornell Park Dr
Cincinnati, OH 45242-1812

513-421-2050
800-421-1321
FAX 513-421-5144
E-Mail: customer@stmediagroup.com
Home Page: www.stmediagroup.com

Tedd Swormstedt, CEO
Brian Foos, CFO

Three days of education and networking for high-volume sign companies, screen printers and digital print shops.
Founded in 1906

532 Speak to Be Heard! Influencing Others to Take Action
American Association of Advertising Agencies
1065 Avenue of the Americas
16th Floor
New York, NY 10018

212-682-2500
FAX 212-682-8391

E-Mail: kipp@aaaa.org
Home Page: www.aaaa.org
Social Media: *Facebook, Twitter, LinkedIn*

Nancy Hill, President
Chris Weil, Chair
Andrew Bennett, Director at Large
Sharon Napier, Secretary/Treasurer

Eliminate the static that plagues communicative delivery- to persuade, sell your ideas, motivate, influence or simply effectively communicate face-to-face with a clear message. Account executives, media directors, senior managers should attend.

533 Stratconn
In-Store Marketing Institute
7400 Skokie Blvd
Skokie, IL 60077-3339

847-675-7400
FAX 847-675-7494
E-Mail: pdproducts_editor@instoremarketer.org
Home Page: www.instoremarketer.org
Social Media: *Facebook, Twitter, LinkedIn*

Peter Hoyt, President

Gathering the leading designers/producers of displays, signs and fixtures together with teams of merchandising experts from leading CPG manufacturers and retailers.
Printed in 4 colors on glossy stock

534 Strategy for Account Managers
American Association of Advertising Agencies
1065 Avenue of the Americas
16th Floor
New York, NY 10018

212-682-2500
FAX 212-682-8391
E-Mail: kipp@aaaa.org
Home Page: www.aaaa.org
Social Media: *Facebook, Twitter, LinkedIn*

Nancy Hill, President
Chris Weil, Chair
Andrew Bennett, Director at Large
Sharon Napier, Secretary/Treasurer

Workshop is designed for mid-an-higher-level account managers at marketing communication firms of all types who have clients that want them to think more strategically.

535 SupplySide International Tradeshow and Conference
Virgo Publishing LLC
3300 N Central Ave
Suite 300
Phoenix, AZ 85012-2532

480-675-9925
FAX 480-990-0819
E-Mail: kkennedy@vpico.com
Home Page: www.vpico.com

John Siefert, CEO
Kelly Ridley, CFO
Jon Benninger, VP
John LyBarger, Director of IT

The world's largest event for healthy and innovative ingredients. Food, beverage, dietary supplement and cosmeceutical manufacturers, marketers and formulators attend to source cutting edge ingredients and learn from outstanding educational presentations at the largest event of its kind.
Founded in 1986

536 Transformation LA
American Association of Advertising Agencies

1065 Avenue of the Americas
16th Floor
New York, NY 10018

212-682-2500
FAX 212-682-8391
E-Mail: kipp@aaaa.org
Home Page: www.aaaa.org
Social Media: *Facebook, Twitter, LinkedIn*

Nancy Hill, President
Chris Weil, Chair
Andrew Bennett, Director at Large
Sharon Napier, Secretary/Treasurer

Talent recruitment and retention; regulatory updates; mobility; social media; and growing your business are a few of the sessions scheduled. Tour some of the entertainment capital's most creative facilities, including innovative 4A's member agencies.

537 VMSD International Retail Design Conference
ST Media Group International
11262 Cornell Park Dr
Cincinnati, OH 45242-1812

513-421-2050
800-421-1321
FAX 513-421-5144
E-Mail: customer@stmediagroup.com
Home Page: www.stmediagroup.com

Tedd Swormstedt, CEO
Brian Foos, CFO

The premier educational event created especially for members of the retail design community.
Circulation: 17000
Founded in 1906

Directories & Databases

538 AMCEA Member Handbook & Roster
Advertising Media Credit Executives Association
8840 Columbia 100 Parkway
Columbia, MD 21045-2158

410-992-7609
FAX 410-740-5574
E-Mail: amcea@amcea.org
Home Page: www.amcea.org

J Dee Stevenson, President
Kimberly Riley, VP
Vickie Bolinger, Director

Inside you will find direct telephone numbers to every credit manager in our association along with numbers for credit references and fax inquiries. We also include their e-mail addresses and computer hardware and software information.

539 Advertisers and Agency Red Book Plus
Canon Communications Pharmaceutical Medial Group
300 American metro Bvld
Newtown, PA 18940

215-944-9800
FAX 215-867-0053
E-Mail: sandra.baker@cancom.com
Home Page: www.pharmalive.com

Karl Engel, President
Styli Engel, Executive VP/Editor-in-Chief
James Hannan, CEO/Group Publisher
Lisa Aberman, CFO/COO

Advertising information.
Cost: $1788.00
Frequency: Quarterly
Founded in 1982

540 Advertising Age: Leading National Advertisers Issue
Ad Age Group/Crain Communications
711 3rd Ave
New York, NY 10017-4014

212-210-0785
FAX 212-210-0200
E-Mail: subs@crain.com
Home Page: www.adage.com
Social Media: *Facebook, Twitter, LinkedIn*

Keith E Crain, Chairman/Publisher
Rance E Crain, President/Editor-In-Chief
David S Klein, VP Publishing/Editorial Director

Featuring comprehensive ad spending estimates on 100 elite, company profiles and sales and earnings reports for our annual 100 Leading National Advertisers Report.
Cost: $5.00
Frequency: Annual
Circulation: 59,000
Founded in 1930

541 Advertising Growth Trends
Schonfeld & Associates Inc
1931 Lynn Circle
Libertyville, IL 60048-1323

847-816-4870
800-205-0030
FAX 847-816-4872
E-Mail: saiinfo@saibooks.com
Home Page: www.saibooks.com

Carol Greenhut, Publisher

Information on publicly owned corporations that spend on advertising. Measures of profitability and effectiveness of the company's advertising expenditures are shown.
Cost: $395.00
230 Pages
Frequency: Annual
ISBN: 1-932024-84-0

542 Advertising Ratios & Budgets
Schonfeld & Associates Inc
1931 Lynn Circle
Libertyville, IL 60048-1323

847-816-4870
800-205-0030
FAX 847-816-4872
E-Mail: saiinfo@saibooks.com
Home Page: www.saibooks.com

Carol Greenhut, Publisher

The detailed annual report covers over 5,000 companies and 300 industries with information on current advertising budgets, ad-to-sales ratios and ad-to-gross margin ratios, as well as budgets and growth rate forecasts. Use it to track competition, win new ad agency clients, set and justify ad budgets, sell space and time or plan new media ventures and new products. Includes industry and advertiser ad spending rankings.
Cost: $395.00
190 Pages
Frequency: Annual
ISBN: 1-932024-80-8

543 Advertising Red Books
PO Box 1514
Summit, NJ 07902

800-908-5395
E-Mail: info@redbooks.com
Home Page: www.redbooks.com

Advertising Red Books has been providing competitive intelligence and prospecting data to media companies, advertising agencies, manufacturers, libraries, advertising service and suppliers.
Founded in 1922

544 Advertising and Marketing Intelligence
New York Times
1719 State Route 10
#A
Parsippany, NJ 07054-4507

E-Mail: hartman-center@duke.edu
Home Page: www.library.duke.edu

Contains abstracts of articles from over 75 publications on advertising, marketing and the media.

545 Adweek Directory
Prometheus Global Media
770 Broadway
7th Floor
New York, NY 10003-9595

212-493-4100
FAX 646-654-5368
Home Page: www.prometheusgm.com
Social Media: *Facebook, Twitter*

Richard D. Beckman, CEO
James A. Finkelstein, Chairman
Madeline Krakowsky, Vice President Circulation
Tracy Brater, Executive Director Creative Service

Adweek Directories Online is where you will find searchable databases with comprehensive information on ad agencies, brand marketers and multicultural media.
Frequency: Annual
Circulation: 800
Founded in 1981

546 Brands and Their Companies
Gale/Cengage Learning
PO Box 09187
Detroit, MI 48209-0187

248-699-4253
800-877-4253
FAX 248-699-8049
E-Mail: galee.galeord@cengage.com
Home Page: www.gale.com
Social Media: *Facebook, Twitter, LinkedIn, YouTube*

Patrick C Sommers, President

This source lists manufacturers and distributors from small businesses to large corporations, from both the public and private sectors offering complete coverage of more than 426,000 US consumer brands.
Frequency: Annual
ISBN: 1-414434-26-X

547 Buyers Guide to Outdoor Advertising
DoMedia LLC
247 Marconi Boulevard
Suite 400
Columbus, OH 43215

866-939-3663
E-Mail: contact@domedial.com
Home Page: www.domedia.com

FC Miller, Publisher
Robert Gainey, Circulation Manager

Offers valuable information on outdoor advertising companies and their markets.

548 Circulation
Standard Rate & Data Services
1700 E Higgins Rd
Des Plaines, IL 60018-5610

847-375-5000
800-851-7737
FAX 847-375-5001
E-Mail: contact@srds.com
Home Page: www.srds.com

George Carens, Executive Vice President
Trish Delaurier, Publisher

This print service provides complete circulation, penetration and consumer demographic information on your newspaper options so you can make objective comparisons in multi newspaper markets and across markets. You'll be able to analyze circulation, number of households, retail sales, average household income and market rankings to determine what papers deliver your target audience.
Frequency: Annual
Circulation: 1000+

549 Co-op Advertising Programs Sourcebook
National Register Publishing
430 Mountain Ave.
Suite 400
New Providence, NJ 07974

800-473-7020
FAX 908-673-1189
E-Mail: nrpeditorial@marquiswhoswho.com
Home Page: www.co-opsourcebook.com

The best source for media companies, wholesalers, retailers and others for finding available advertising dollars to fund co-op programs. Includes 52 product classifications.
Frequency: Semi-Annual

550 Consumer Magazine Advertising Source
Standard Rate & Data Services
1700 E Higgins Rd
Des Plaines, IL 60018-5610

847-375-5000
800-851-7737
FAX 847-375-5001
E-Mail: contact@srds.com
Home Page: www.srds.com

George Carens, Executive Vice President
Joseph Hayes, Publisher

This service provides complete planning information on US consumer magazines, including standardized ad rates, dates, contact information and links to online media kits, Web sites and audit statements that provide additional facts on readership information and positioning.
Frequency: Semi-Annual
Circulation: 2000+

551 Creative Industry Director
Black Book Inc
740 Broadway
Suite 202
New York, NY 10003-9518

212-979-6700
800-841-1246
FAX 212-673-4321
E-Mail: eryder@blackbook.com
Home Page: www.blackbook.com

Joe Resudek, Janet

Designed to meet the needs of professionals who seek creative services in every aspect of media, advertising, production and the fashion industry.
Frequency: Annual

552 Fashion and Print Directory: Madison Avenue Handbook
Peter Glenn Publications
777 E Atlantic Ave
Suite C2337
Delray Beach, FL 33438

561-404-4209
888-332-6700
FAX 561-892-5786
E-Mail: gjames@pgdirect.com
Home Page: www.pgdirect.com

Gregory James, Publisher
Todd Heustess, Editor

The most reliable and comprehensive entertainment resource includes over 400 pages of national information including everyone you need to know within the advertising, fashion and print industries.
Frequency: Annual
Founded in 1956

553 IQ Directory Adweek
Prometheus Global Media
770 Broadway
7th Floor
New York, NY 10003-9595

212-493-4100
FAX 646-654-5368
Home Page: www.prometheusgm.com

Richard D. Beckman, CEO
James A. Finkelstein, Chairman
Madeline Krakowsky, Vice President Circulation
Tracy Brater, Executive Director Creative Service

Profile of companies at the leading edge of digital marketing, has the specifics you'll need to investigate, launch and/or expand your digital presence. Profiles over 2,200 interactive agencies, web developers, brand marketers, online media, CD-ROM developers, POP/Kiosk designers and multimedia creative companies
Founded in 1981

554 IRS Corporate Financial Ratios
Schonfeld & Associates Inc
1931 Lynn Circle
Libertyville, IL 60048-1323

847-816-4870
800-205-0030
FAX 847-816-4872
E-Mail: saiinfo@saibooks.com
Home Page: www.saibooks.com

Carol Greenhut, Publisher

An ideal reference for CPAs, controllers, bankers, CFOs, tax lawyers, financial analysts, investment advisors and corporate planners, this reference book features 70-plus key financial ratios calculated from the latest income statement and balance sheet data available from the IRS.
Cost: $225.00
300 Pages
Frequency: Annual
ISBN: 1-932024-79-4

555 ISA Membership & Buyer's Guide
International Sign Association
1001 N Fairfax Street
Suite 301
Alexandria, VA 22314

703-836-4012
866-WHY-SIGN
FAX 703-836-8353
E-Mail: info@signs.org
Home Page: www.signs.org

Duane Laska, Chairman
Harry Niese, Vice Chairman
Chad Jones, Secretary/Treasurer

Discover a new supplier or distributor. Use our database to search members by company, location, products, services or equipment.
2600 Members

556 Illustrated Guide to P.O.P. Exhibits and Promotion
Creative Magazine
31 Merrick Avenue
Merrick, NY 11566

516-378-0800
FAX 516-378-0884
E-Mail: info@creativemag.com
Home Page: www.creativemag.com

Larry Flasterstein, Publisher

The Illustrated Guide serves over 15,000 P.O.P buyers, sales promotion and event managers in the leading corporations in North America with quick, up to the minute information about the resources in this industry.
Frequency: Annual

557 Infomercial Marketing Sourcebook
Prometheus Global Media
770 Broadway
7th Floor
New York, NY 10003-9595

212-493-4100
FAX 646-654-5368
Home Page: www.prometheusgm.com

Richard D. Beckman, CEO
James A. Finkelstein, Chairman
Madeline Krakowsky, Vice President Circulation
Tracy Brater, Executive Director Creative Service

A complete resource guide for everyone involved in the infomercial industry.

558 Internship Directory
American Advertising Federation
1101 Vermont Ave NW
Suite 500
Washington, DC 20005-6306

202-898-0089
800-999-2231
FAX 202-898-0159
E-Mail: aaf@aaf.org
Home Page: www.aaf.org

James Edmund Datri, President
Constance Cannon Frazier, COO
Joanne Schecter, Executive Vice President

More than 1,500 advertising and marketing internships are listed in this valuable resource.
Circulation: 50000

559 Mediaweek Multimedia Directory
Prometheus Global Media
770 Broadway
7th Floor
New York, NY 10003-9595

212-493-4100
FAX 646-654-5368
Home Page: www.prometheusgm.com

Richard D. Beckman, CEO
James A. Finkelstein, Chairman
Madeline Krakowsky, Vice President Circulation
Tracy Brater, Executive Director Creative Service

Focuses on the most powerful segments covering 9,000 media companies from the top 100 media markets for radio, broadcast TV, cable TV and daily newspapers. Also includes the top 300 consumer magazines, the top 150 trade magazines, networks, syndicators, sales representatives, multi-media holding companies, trade associations and rating organizations.
Frequency: Annual
Circulation: 800

560 Medical Marketing and Media
Haymarket Media Inc
114 W 26th St
4th Floor
New York, NY 10001-6812

212-206-0606
FAX 212-638-6117
E-Mail: custserv@haymarketmedia.com
Home Page: www.haymarket.com

William Bekover, Chief Executive Officer

Offers a comprehensive editorial resource to leaders, thinkers and executives dedicated to the promotion and commercialization of pre-

scription drugs and other medical products and services in the US.
Frequency: Monthly
Circulation: 15000
Founded in 1996

561 Navigator
Promotional Products Association
International
3125 Skyway Circle N
Irving, TX 75038-3539

972-252-0404
FAX 972-258-3004
E-Mail: ppb@ppai.org
Home Page: www.ppai.org

Paul Bellantone, President
Steven Meyer, Chairman of the Board
Marc Simon, Chair-Elect

An invaluable resource designed to educate distributors about PPAI supplier and business services members and the products they offer.
Frequency: Annual

562 Online Advertising Playbook
John Wiley & Sons
111 River St
Hoboken, NJ 07030-5790

201-748-6000
FAX 201-748-6088
E-Mail: info@wiley.com
Home Page: www.wiley.com

Stephen Smith, President & Chief Executive Officer
Vincent Marzano, Vice President

The book focuses on the enduring strategies necessary for marketers to have the knowledge base necessary to execute winning campaigns.

563 Planning for Out of Home Media
Traffic Audit Bureau for Media
Measurement
271 Madison Ave
Suite 1504
New York, NY 10016-1012

212-972-8075
FAX 212-972-8928
E-Mail: inquiry@tabonline.com
Home Page: www.tabonline.com

Joseph Philport, President
Larry Hennessy, Vice President

Reference book contains up-to-date descriptions of O-O-H media and their production specifications, O-O-H local and national case history success stories and creative guidelines, travel trend data, new technologies and a glossary of O-O-H terminology.

564 Print Media Production Source
Standard Rate & Data Services
1700 E Higgins Rd
Des Plaines, IL 60018-5610

847-375-5000
800-851-7737
FAX 847-375-5001
E-Mail: contact@srds.com
Home Page: www.srds.com

Trish Delaurier, Publisher
George Carens, Executive Vice President

This service provides complete data on all critical ad production specifications for business and consumer magazines and newspapers. Production, traffic and graphic design personnel use this current, accurate resource to confirm essential production information so they can control production deadlines and budgets.
Frequency: Quarterly
Circulation: 800+

565 R&D Ratios & Budgets
Schonfeld & Associates Inc

1931 Lynn Circle
Libertyville, IL 60048-1323

847-816-4870
800-205-0030
FAX 847-816-4872
E-Mail: saiinfo@saibooks.com
Home Page: www.saibooks.com

Carol Greenhut, Publisher

The comprehensive annual report covers over 4,700 companies and 280 industries with information on current R&D budgets, R&D-to-sales ratios and R&D-to-gross margin ratios. Use it to track competition, set and justify R&D budgets, screen potential acquisitions, sell the laboratory and technology markets or plan new ventures and develop new products. Includes industry and R&D spender rankings.
Cost: $395.00
186 Pages
Frequency: Annual
ISBN: 1-932024-81-6

566 Radio Creative Resources Directory
Radio Advertising Bureau
1320 Greenway Dr
Suite 500
Irving, TX 75038-2547

972-753-6700
800-232-3131
FAX 972-753-6727
E-Mail: jhaley@rab.com
Home Page: www.rab.com

Erica Farber, President
Van Allen, EVP and CFO
Beverly Fraser, SVP

A list of radio production companies and studios in response to advertisers and agencies who want to find companies that specialize in writing, casting and producing great radio spots. Our current edition contains over 60 companies including many Radio-Mercury Award winners.
Frequency: Annual

567 Research & Development Growth Trends
Schonfeld & Associates Inc
1931 Lynn Circle
Libertyville, IL 60048-1323

847-816-4870
800-205-0030
FAX 847-816-4872
E-Mail: saiinfo@saibooks.com
Home Page: www.saibooks.com

Carol Greenhut, Publisher

Information on publicly owned corporations that spend on R&D.
Cost: $395.00
277 Pages
Frequency: Annual
ISBN: 1-932024-85-9

568 Standard Industry Directory
Association of Hispanic Advertising
Agencies
8400 Westpark Drive
2nd Floor
McLean, VA 22102

703-610-9014
FAX 703-610-0227
E-Mail: info@ahaa.org
Home Page: www.ahaa.org
Social Media: *Facebook, Twitter*

Horacio Gavilan, President
Melissa Chen, Membership/Directory
Ayanna Wiggins, Marketing

AHAA represents the best minds and resources that are dedicated to Hispanic-specialized marketing.

569 Suppliers Directory
Eight-Sheet Outdoor Advertising
Association
1244 Lake Park Ave
Galt, CA 95632

209-251-7622
800-847-3387
FAX 209-251-7658
E-Mail: ddjesoaa@comcast.net
Home Page: www.esoaa.com

Rebecca Lambert, Editor

Lists suppliers to the Eight-Sheet outdoor billboard industry; arranged by specialty. Includes definitions of basic industry terms.
Frequency: Annual
Circulation: 800

570 The Art & Science of Managing a Content Marketing Strategy
Direct Marketing Association
1120 Avenue of the Americas
New York, NY 10036-6700

212-768-7277
FAX 212-302-6714
E-Mail: customerservice@the-dma.org
Home Page: www.the-dma.org
Social Media: *Facebook, Twitter, LinkedIn*

Lawrence M Kimmel, CEO

Effective Search Engine Optimization and Search Engine Marketing can have a dramatic effect on a website's performance and ROI. From optimization techniques to keyword bidding, our Search course offerings will give the insights and strategies to improve search results and efficiency.

571 Tie-In Promotion Service
Association of National Advertisers
708 Third Avenue
33 Floor
New York, NY 10017

212-697-5950
FAX 212-661-8057
E-Mail: info@ana.net
Home Page: www.ana.net
Social Media: *Facebook, Twitter, LinkedIn, YouTube*

Bob Liodice, President & CEO
Christine Manna, COO
William Zengel, EVP

Brand names listed by their companies as available for possible tie-in promotions with other companies.
Frequency: Annual/December

572 U.S. Sourcebook of R&D Spenders
Schonfeld & Associates Inc
1931 Lynn Circle
Libertyville, IL 60048-1323

847-816-4870
800-205-0030
FAX 847-816-4872
E-Mail: saiinfo@saibooks.com
Home Page: www.saibooks.com

Carol Greenhut, Publisher

A directory of publicly owned corporations that spend on R&D, published annually. Corporate name, address, telephone number, and website are provided along with the names and titles of three senior executives, R&D budgets, sales, fiscal year closing, and more. Organized by state and ZIP code. The ideal reference for sales people who call on R&D centers and for economic development agencies.
Cost: $395.00
180 Pages
Frequency: Annual
ISBN: 1-932024-83-2

573 US Source Book of Advertisers
Schonfeld & Associates Inc
1931 Lynn Circle
Libertyville, IL 60048-1323

847-816-4870
800-205-0030
FAX 847-816-4872
E-Mail: saiinfo@saibooks.com
Home Page: www.saibooks.com

Carol Greenhut, Publisher

A directory of publicly owned corporations that advertise. Corporate name, address, telephone number and website are provided along with the names and titles of three senior executives, ad budgets, sales, fiscal year closing and more. The ideal reference for media sales, ad agency new business development and selling corporate services.
Frequency: Annual
ISBN: 1-932024-55-7

574 Who's Who: MASA Buyer's Guide to Blue Ribbon Mailing Services
Mailing & Fulfillment Service Association
1421 Prince Street
Suite 410
Alexandria, VA 22314-2806

703-836-9200
FAX 703-548-8204
E-Mail: mfsa-mail@mfsanet.org
Home Page: www.mfsanet.org

Ken Garner, President
Bill Stevenson, Director Marketing

Offers a detailed listing of suppliers of equipment, products and services to the direct mail industry, most containing a description of the specific products they provide.
Frequency: Annual

575 Workbook
Scott & Daughters Publishing
6762 Lexington Avenue
Los Angeles, CA 90038-2482

323-856-0008
800-547-2688
FAX 323-856-4368
E-Mail: contributors@workbookstock.com
Home Page: www.workbook.com
Social Media: *Facebook, Twitter*

Alexis Scott, Owner
Susan Haller, Managing Editor
Bill Daniels, Publisher

This directory, offered in four volumes, lists over 25,000 advertising agencies, art directors and freelance illustrators in the United States.
Frequency: Annual
Circulation: 35,000

576 Workforce Growth Trends
Schonfeld & Associates Inc
1931 Lynn Circle
Libertyville, IL 60048-1323

847-816-4870
800-205-0030
FAX 847-816-4872
E-Mail: saiinfo@saibooks.com
Home Page: www.saibooks.com

Carol Greenhut, Publisher

Information on all publicly owned corporations. Study is ordered by U.S. Department of Commerce SIC(Standard Industrial Classification) and alphabetically by company name within each SIC. Each companys historical information, average annual percent change, sales and shares are displayed.
Cost: $395.00
580 Pages
Frequency: Annual
ISBN: 1-932024-87-5

577 Workforce Ratios & Forecasts
Schonfeld & Associates Inc
1931 Lynn Circle
Libertyville, IL 60048-1323

847-816-4870
800-205-0030
FAX 847-816-4872
E-Mail: saiinfo@saibooks.com
Home Page: www.saibooks.com

Carol Greenhut, Publisher

This comprehensive annual study by Schonfeld & Associates covers over 6,600 companies and 420 industries. The information reported includes current number of employees, a forecast of projected employee headcount and growth rates, as well as sales per employee and gross margin per employee. Use it to track competition, set and justify manpower budgets, screen potential acquisitions, plan new ventures and develop new businesses. Includes rankings by size and growth rate.
Cost: $395.00
250 Pages
Frequency: Annual
ISBN: 1-932024-86-7

Industry Web Sites

578 www.aaaa.org
American Association of Advertising Agencies
To improve and strengthen the advertising agency business in the United States by counseling members on operations and management.

579 www.aaasite.org
American Academy of Advertising
An organization of advertising scholars and professionals with an interest in advertising and advertising education.

580 www.aaf.org
American Advertising Federation
The American Advertising Federation protects and promotes the wellbeing of advertising.

581 www.aapor.org
American Association for Public Opinion Research
The American Advertising Federation protects and promotes the wellbeing of advertising.

582 www.adcouncil.org
Advertising Council
The Ad Council is a private, non-profit organization that marshals volunteer talent from the advertising and communications industries, the facilities of the media, and the resources of the business and non-profit communities to deliver critical messages to the American public.

583 www.aef.com
Advertising Educational Foundation
The advertising industry's provider and distributor of educational content to enrich the understanding of advertising and it's role in culture, society and the economy.

584 www.ahaa.org
Association of Hispanic Advertising Agencies
Mission to grow, strengthen and protect the Hispanic marketing and advertising industry by providing leadership in raising awareness of the value of the Hispanic market opportunities and enhancing the professionalism of the industry.

585 www.ana.net
Association of National Advertisers
Provides indispensable leadership that drives marketing excellence and champions, promotes and defends the interests of the marketing community.

586 www.apanational.com
Advertising Photographers of America
Our goal is to establish, endorse and promote professional practices, standards and ethics in the photographic and advertising community.

587 www.awny.org
Advertising Women of New York
The organization now consists of influential women and men representing the advertising, marketing, media, promotion and public relations fields.

588 www.bbb.org
Better Business Bureau
To be the leader in advancing marketplace trust.

589 www.biznetis.net
Biznet Internet Solutions
Biznet Internet Solutions is a full-service Web solutions company that focuses on business and mobile Web sites, provides advertising agency support, and Internet marketing.

590 www.esoaa.com
Eight-Sheet Outdoor Advertising Association
To provide leadership, services and standards to promote, protect and advance the eight sheet industry.

591 www.greyhouse.com
Grey House Publishing
Authoritative reference directories for business information and general reference including advertising, communications, marketing and media markets. Users can search the online databases with varied search criteria allowing for custom searches by product category, geographic area, sales volume, keyword, subject and more. Full Grey House catalog and online ordering also available.

592 www.iaany.org
International Advertising Association
Promoting the value of advertising globally, advocacy of freedom of commercial speech and consumer choice and encouraging industry self regulation.

593 www.iab.net
Interactive Advertising Bureau
Dedicated to the growth of the interactive advertising marketplace, of interactive's share of total marketing spend, and of its members' share of total marketing spend

594 www.icomagencies.com
International Communications Agency Network
The international organization of museums and museum professionals which is committed to the conservation, continuation and communication to society of the world's natural and cultural heritage, present and future, tangible and intangible.

595 www.ifcaonline.com
Insurance and Financial Communicators Association
An international association for insurance and financial communicators offering professional development and networking.

596 www.magnetglobal.org
MAGNET: Marketing & Advertising Global Network
Provides a way for member agencies to share their experience, knowledge and ideas with other agencies in other parts of the world.

597 www.marketingpower.com
American Marketing Association
It is a professional association for individuals and organizations involved in the practice, teaching and study of marketing and advertising worldwide.

598 www.mfsanet.org
Mailing & Fulfillment Service Association
The national trade association for the mailing and fulfillment services industry.

599 www.oaaa.org
Outdoor Advertising Association of America
To provide leadership, services and standards to promote, protect and advance the outdoor advertising industry.

600 www.popai.com
Point of Purchase Advertising International
Dedicated to promoting Marketing at Retail as a powerful advertising medium being rapidly integrated into the strategic marketing mix as retail programs deliver a critical combination of brand messaging and information at the critical moment of the consumer purchase decision.

601 www.ppa.org
Promotional Products Association International
To lead the industry by expanding the market, providing indispensable products and services, and enhancing our members' professionalism and success.

602 www.rama-nrf.com
Retail Advertising & Marketing International
Provides visionary leadership that promotes creativity, innovation and excellence within all marketing disciplines that strategically elevates our members and our industry.

603 www.signs.org
International Sign Association
Supports, promotes and improves the sign industry, which sustains the nation's retail industry.

604 www.taan.org
Transworld Advertising Agency Network
A network of independently owned advertising agencies that work closely together in the exchange of management information, reciprocal services and personal local contact.

605 www.tabonline.com
Traffic Audit Bureau for Media Measurement
An independent third party provider of standardized and valid circulation measures for out of home media.

606 www.thearf.org
Advertising Research Foundation
An open forum where the best and brightest from every avenue of advertising can gather to exchange ideas and research strategies

607 www.thecab.tv
Cabletelevision Advertising Bureau
Dedicated to providing advertisers and agencies with the most current, complete and actionable cable television media insights at the national, DMA and local levels.

608 www.tradepromo.org
Trade Promotion Management Association
Provides members with information, education and research on the dynamic world of trade promotion, including co op advertising, market development funds, slotting fees, off invoice deductions, channel promotions and more.

Associations

609   4-H
7100 Connecticut Ave.
Chevy Chase, MD 20815

301-961-2800
Home Page: www.4-h.org
Social Media: *Facebook, Twitter, LinkedIn,
Instagram, Pinterest, YouTube*

Lisa A. Lauxman, Contact

A global network of youth development organizations operating independently in more than 50 countries. The club's slogan is "Learn by doing."
Founded in 1902

610   AACC International
3340 Pilot Knob Road
St. Paul, MN 55121-2055

651-454-7250
800-328-7560
FAX 651-454-0766
E-Mail: aacc@scisoc.org
Home Page: www.aaccnet.org
Social Media: *Facebook, Twitter, LinkedIn,
Pinterest*

Gerard Downey, Chair of the Board
Lydia Tooker Midness, President
Dave L. Braun, Treasurer
Samuel Millar, Director
Matthew K. Morell, Director

Formerly the American Association of Cereal Chemists, a non-profit organization of members who are specialists in the use of cereal grains in foods.
154 Members
Founded in 1915

611   Agribusiness Council(ABC)
PO Box 5565
Washington, DC 20016

202-296-4563
FAX 202-887-9178
E-Mail: info@agribusinesscouncil.org
Home Page: www.agribusinesscouncil.org

Nicholas E Hollis, President/CEO

The Agribusiness Council (ABC) is a private, nonprofit/tax-exempt, membership organization dedicated to strengthening U.S. agro-industrial competitiveness through programs which highlight international trade and development potentials as well as broad issues which encompass several individual agribusiness sectors and require a food systems approach. Examples of such issues are commercialization of new tech/crops, environmental impacts, human resource development, trade and investment policy.
Founded in 1967

**612   Agricultural & Applied Economics
Association**
555 E Wells Street
Suite 1100
Milwaukee, WI 53202-6600

414-918-3190
FAX 414-276-3349
E-Mail: info@aaea.org
Home Page: www.aaea.org
Social Media: *Facebook, Twitter, LinkedIn,
Blogger, Google+*

Jill McCluskey, President
Jayson Lusk, President-Elect
Barry Goodwin, Past President
Michael Boland, Director
Ani Katchova, Director

The Agricultural & Applied Economics Association (AAEA) is a not-for-profit association serving the professional interests of members working in agricultural and broadly related fields of applied economics. Members of the AAEA are employed by academic or government institutions, as well as in industry and not-for-profit organizations, and engage in a variety of teaching, research, and extension/outreach activities.
3000 Members
Founded in 1910

**613   Agricultural Communicators of
Tomorrow**
PO Box 110180
Gainesville, FL 32611-0180

352-392-1971
FAX 352-392-9589
Home Page: www.ifas.ufl.edu
Social Media: *Facebook, Twitter*

Dr Jack Payne, Senior Vice President

A national organization of college students professionally interested in communications related to agriculture, food, natural resources and allied fields. The Mission of UF/IFAS is to develop knowledge in agricultural, human and natural resources and to make that knowledge accessible to sustain and enhance the quality of human life.
Founded in 1853

614   Agricultural Retailers Association
1156 15th St NW
Suite 500
Washington, DC 20005-1745

202-457-0825
FAX 202-457-0864
E-Mail: info@aradc.org
Home Page: www.aradc.org
Social Media: *Facebook, Twitter*

Dave DuFault, Chairman
Daren Coppock, President & CEO
Richard Gupton, SVP, Public Policy & Counsel
Donnie Taylor, VP, Membership & Corp
Relations
Brian Reuwee, Dir., Comm. & Marketing

The Agricultural Retailers Association (ARA) is a nonprofit trade association that serves as the political voice of agricultural retailers and distributors. We're advocates, educators, and champions for the American ag retailer. The Agricultural Retailers Association (ARA) is a nonprofit trade association that serves as the political voice of agricultural retailers and distributors. We're advocates, educators, and champions for the American ag retailer.
Frequency: Annual
Founded in 1993

615   Agriculture Council of America
11020 King St
Suite 205
Overland Park, KS 66210-1201

913-491-1895
FAX 913-491-6502
E-Mail: info@agday.org
Home Page: www.agday.org
Social Media: *Facebook, Twitter, Flickr,
YouTube*

Curt Blades, Chair
Annette Degnan, Vice Chair
Curt Blades, Secretary/Treasurer
Lynn Henderson, Board Member
Nancy Barcus, Bard Member

The Agriculture Council of America (ACA) is an organization uniquely composed of leaders in the agriculture, food and fiber communities dedicated to increasing the public awareness of agriculture's vital role in our society.
75 Members
Founded in 1973

616   Agriculture Federal Credit Union
1400 Independence Ave SW
Room SM2
Washington, DC 20250

202-479-2270
800-368-3552
FAX 202-479-3877
E-Mail: members@agriculturefcu.org
Home Page: www.agfed.org
Social Media: *Facebook, Twitter*

Margie Click, President/CEO
Theodora Ezekwerre, Senior Vice President
Tom Bowles, Senior Vice President
Clifton Jeter, Chair
Stephen J Hawkins, Vice Chair

Agriculture Federal Credit Union meets the highest standards for long term financial soundness. AgFed's workplace environment motivates and empowers employees to provide quality service to our members. AgFed offers a wide range of financial services and products to satisfy the diverse needs of our members throughout their lifetimes. AgFed has state-of-the-art technology designed to meet our members' needs.
23000 Members
Founded in 1934

**617   American Agricultural Law
Association**
P.O. Box 5861
Columbia, SC 29250

803-728-3200
FAX 360-423-2287
E-Mail: ellenberg@aglaw-assn.org
Home Page: www.aglaw-assn.org

Jesse J. Richardson, Jr., President
Kristy Thomason Ellenberg, Executive Director
Anne 'Beth' Crocker, President-Elect
Justin Schneider, Director
Amber Miller, Director

The AALA is a membership organization that focuses on the legal needs of the agricultural community.
600 Members
Founded in 1980

618   American Agriculture Movement
AAM National Secretary/Treasurer
11232 Road K
Liberal, KS 67901

620-482-6306
E-Mail: jrice@swko.net
Home Page: www.aaminc.org

Larry Matlack, President
Arthur Chaney, Executive Vice President
John Willis, Vice President
Lynn Kirkpatrick, Vice President of Marketing
Marc Wetzel, Vice President of Membership

The creation of the AAM has provided a farmer-created, farmer-built organization within which farmers themselves have been the leaders, speakers and organizers; empowering farmers as they had not been in the past, to speak for and advocate for themselves.
Founded in 1977

619   American Angus Association
3201 Frederick Ave
St Joseph, MO 64506-2997

816-383-5100
FAX 816-233-9703
E-Mail: angus@angus.org
Home Page: www.angus.org
Social Media: *Facebook, Twitter, Pinterest,
Youtube, Vimeo*

Richard Wilson, Iinterim CEO
Jim Sitz, Vice President
Charlie Boyd II, Treasurer
Diane Strahm, Administrative Assistant
Richard Wilson, CFO

The American Angus Association is the nation's largest beef registry association. Our goal is to serve the beef cattle industry, and increase the production of consistent, high quality beef that will better satisfy consumers throughout the world.
36000 Members
Founded in 1873

620 American Association of Crop Insurers

1 Massachusetts Ave NW
Suite 800
Washington, DC 20001-1401

202-789-4100
FAX 202-408-7763
E-Mail: aaci@mwmlaw.com
Home Page: www.cropinsurers.com

Michael R. McLeod, Executive Director
David Graves, President
Bill O'Conner, Senior Government Relations
Laura Phelps, Senior Government Relations

The American Association of Crop Insurers is a nonprofit industry service organization representing the interests of insurance companies, agents, and adjusters involved in the Federal crop insurance program. AACI's reinsured company members write more than 80 percent of the crop insurance sold by private companies nationwide. AACI's primary purpose is governmental relations with Congress, the U.S. Department of Agriculture, and other executive agencies whose decisions influence the program.
25 Members
Founded in 1980

621 American Beekeeping Federation

3525 Piedmont Rd NE
Bldg 5 Suite 300
Atlanta, GA 30305-1509

404-760-2875
FAX 404-240-0998
E-Mail: info@abfnet.org
Home Page: www.abfnet.org

Regina Robuck, Executive Director
Valerie Lake, Membership Coordinator
Tara Zeravsky, Sr Conference Planner
Tim Tucker, President
Gene Brandi, Vice President

The ABF is a national organization that continually works in the interest of all beekeepers, large or small, and those associated with the industry to ensure the future of the honey bee. Our members share a common interest to work toward better education and information for all segments of the industry in the hope of increasing our chances for survival in today's competitive world.
1200+ Members
Founded in 1943

622 American Brahman Breeders Association

3003 South Loop West
Suite 520
Houston, TX 77054

713-349-0854
FAX 713-349-9795
E-Mail: abba@brahman.org
Home Page: www.brahman.org
Social Media: *Facebook, Twitter, YouTube, Instagram*

J. D. Sartwelle, Jr., President
George Kempfer, Vice President
Loren Pratt, Secretary/Treasurer
Chris Shivers, Executive Vice President
Armelinda Ibarra, Recording Secretary / Office Mgr

American Brahman Breeders is a beef crossbreeding organization that plays a big role in the United States and beyond.
Founded in 1924

623 American Dairy Science Association

1800 South Oak Street
Suite 100
Champaign, IL 61820-6974

217-356-5146
FAX 217-398-4119
E-Mail: adsa@assochq.org
Home Page: www.adsa.org
Social Media: *RSS*

Susan Duncan, President
Lou Armentano, Vice President
Peter Studney, Executive Director
Matt Lucy, Editor-in-Chief
Vicki Paden, Administrative Assistant

The American Dairy Science Association (ADSA) is an international organization of educators, scientists, and industry representatives who are committed to advancing the dairy industry and keenly aware of the vital role the dairy sciences play in fulfilling the economic, nutritive, and health requirements of the world's population. Together, ADSA members have discovered new methods and technologies that have revolutionized the dairy industry.
3000 Members
Founded in 1998
Mailing list available for rent

624 American Farm Bureau Federation

600 Maryland Ave SW
Suite 1000W
Washington, DC 20024-2555

202-484-3600
FAX 202-484-3604
E-Mail: bstallman@fb.org
Home Page: www.fb.org
Social Media: *Facebook, Twitter, RSS, You Tube, Google+, Pinter*

Bob Stallman, President
Don Lipton, Executive Director
Julie Anna Potts, Executive Vice President/Treasurer
Ellen Steen, General Counsel & Secretary
Mace Thornton, Acting Director

Farm Bureau is an independent, non-governmental, voluntary organization governed by and representing farm and ranch families united for the purpose of analyzing their problems and formulating action to achieve educational improvement, economic opportunity and social advancement and, thereby, to promote the national well-being. Farm Bureau is local, county, state, national and international in its scope and influence and is non-partisan, non-sectarian and non-secret in character.
3M Members
Founded in 1919

625 American Feed Industry Association

American Feed Industry Association
2101 Wilson Blvd
Suite 916
Arlington, VA 22201-3047

703-524-0810
FAX 703-524-1921
E-Mail: afia@afia.org
Home Page: www.afia.org
Social Media: *Facebook, Twitter, LinkedIn, YouTube*

Rob Sheffer, Chairman
Joel G. Newman, President & Treasurer
Shakera Daley, Accounting and Admin Coordinator
Sarah Novak, VP/Membership
Richard Sellers, AFIA, SVP/Corporate Secretary

AFIA is the world's largest organization devoted exclusively to representing the business, legislative and regulatory interests of the U.S. animal feed industry and its suppliers. AFIA also is the recognized leader on international industry developments. Members include more than 500 domestic and international companies and state, regional and national associations.
690 Members
Founded in 1909

626 American Forage and Grassland Council

PO Box 867
Berea, KY 40403

800-944-2342
E-Mail: tina.bowling@afgc.org
Home Page: www.afgc.org
Social Media: *Facebook, Twitter, YouTube*

Tina Bowling, Executive Director
Howard Straub, President
Ray Smith, Senior Vice President
Roger L Staff, Treasurer
Coy Fitch, Director

The American Forage and Grassland Council (AFGC) is an international organization made up of 20 affiliate councils in the United States and Canada. Our primary objective is to promote the profitable production and sustainable utilization of quality forage and grasslands. Mission is to be recognized as the leader and voice of economically and environmentally sound forage agriculture.
2700 Members

627 American Guernsey Association

1224 Alton Darby Creeek Road
Suite G
Columbus, OH 43228

614-864-2409
FAX 614-864-5614
E-Mail: info@usguernsey.com
Home Page: www.usguernsey.com

David Trotter, President
Duane Schuler, 1st Vice President
David Coon, 2nd Vice President
Brian Schnebly, Executive Secretary
Deb Hoffman, Office Manager

The AGA's mission is to provide and promote programs and services to enhance the value and profitability of the Guernsey breed for the members, owners and dairy industry worldwide.
900 Members
Founded in 1877

628 American Hereford Association

PO Box 014059
Kansas City, MO 64101

816-842-3757
FAX 816-842-6931
E-Mail: aha@hereford.org
Home Page: www.hereford.org
Social Media: *Facebook*

Craig Huffhines, Executive Vice President
Jack Ward, COO
Angie Stump Denton, Communications Director
Amy Cowen, Youth Activities Director
Joe Rickabaugh, Field Mgmt Director

Association for people in the Hereford cattle industry.
Founded in 1910

629 American Jersey Cattle Association

6486 E Main Street
Reynoldsburg, OH 43068-2362

614-861-3636
FAX 614-861-8040

Home Page: www.usjersey.com
Social Media: *Facebook, Twitter*

Neal Smith, CEO/Executive Secretary
Vickie J. White, Treasurer
Cherie L Bayer, Director
Cari Wolfe, Director/Research
Kristin Paul, Director of Field Service

They improve and promote the Jersey cattle breed.
2178 Members
Founded in 1868

630 American Livestock Breeds Convervancy (ALBC)

PO Box 477
33 Hillsboro St
Pittsboro, NC 27312

919-542-5704
FAX 919-545-0022
Home Page: www.livestockconservancy.org
Social Media: *Facebook, Twitter, LinkedIn, Blogger, YouTube*

Charles Bassett, Executive Director
Terry Wollen, President
Angelique Thompson, Operations Manager
James McConnell, Treasurer
Anneke Jakes, Manager of Breed Registry

The American Livestock Breeds Conservancy is a nonprofit membership organization working to protect over 180 breeds of livestock and poultry from extinction. Included are asses, cattle, goats, horses, sheep, pigs, rabbits, chickens, ducks, geese, and turkeys.
Founded in 1977

631 American Meat Science Association

201 W Springfield Ave
Ste 1202
Champaign, IL 61822-7676

217-356-5370
800-517-AMSA
FAX 888-205-5834
FAX 217-356-5370
E-Mail: information@meatscience.org
Home Page: www.meatscience.org
Social Media: *Facebook, Twitter, LinkedIn, Vimeo*

Bucky Gwartney, Ph.D., President
Thomas Powell, Executive Director
Deidrea Mabry, Director, Scientific Communications
Jen Persons, Membership and Marketing Manager
Rachel Adams, M.S., Youth Programs Coordinator

The American Meat Science Association is a broad-reaching organization of individuals that discovers, develops, and disseminates its collective meat science knowledge to provide leadership, education, and professional development. Our passion is to help meat science professionals achieve previously unimaginable levels of performance and reach even higher goals.
Founded in 1964

632 American Phytopathological Society

3340 Pilot Knob Road
Saint Paul, MN 55121-2097

651-454-7250
800-328-7560
FAX 651-454-0766
E-Mail: aps@scisoc.org
Home Page: www.apsnet.org
Social Media: *Facebook, Twitter, LinkedIn, YouTube, Pinterest*

Michelle Bjerkness, Operations/Membership
Amy Hope, Exeutive Vice President
Kim Davis, Finance
Erik Uner, IT
Betty Ford, Meetings

APS is a diverse global community of scientists that: provides credible and beneficial information related to plant health; advocates and participates in the exchange of knowledge with the public, policy makers, and the larger scientific community; and promotes and provides opportunities for scientific communication, career preparation, and professional development for its members.
4500 Members
Founded in 1908

633 American Seed Trade Association

1701 Duke Street
Suite 275
Alexandria, VA 22314-3415

703-837-8140
FAX 703-837-9365
E-Mail: info@amseed.com
Home Page: www.amseed.org
Social Media: *Facebook, Twitter, YouTube, Google+*

Risa DeMasi, Chairman
Andrew LaVigne, President/CEO
Bernice Slutsky, SVP, Domestic and Intl. Policy
Jane DeMarchi, VP, Gov & Regulatory Affairs
Ric Dunkle, Ph.D., Senior Dir., Seed Health & Trade

ASTA's mission is to be an effective voice of action in all matters concerning the development, marketing and movement of seed, associated products and services throughout the world. ASTA promotes the development of better seed to produce better crops for a better quality of life.
700+ Members
Founded in 1883

634 American Sheep Industry Association

9785 Maroon Circle
Suite 360
Englewood, CO 80112

303-771-3500
FAX 303-771-8200
E-Mail: eatlamb@wildblue.net
Home Page: www.sheepusa.org
Social Media: *Facebook, Twitter*

Burton Pfliger, President
Mike Corn, Vice President
Peter Orwick, Executive Director
Larry Kincaid, Chief Financial Officer
Paul Rodgers, Deputy Director of Policy

ASI is the national organization representing the interests of sheep producers located throughout the United States. From East to West, farm flocks to range operations, ASI works to represent the interests of all producers. ASI is a federation of 45 state sheep associations as well as individual members.
82000 Members
Founded in 1865

635 American Society for Enology and Viticulture

PO Box 1855
Davis, CA 95617-1855

530-753-3142
FAX 530-753-3318
E-Mail: society@asev.org
Home Page: www.asev.org
Social Media: *Twitter, LinkedIn, Picasa*

Mark Greenspan, President
Nichola Hall, 1st Vice President
James Harbertson, 2nd Vice President
Tom Collins, Secretary/Treasurer
Dan Howard, Executive Director

The American Society for Enology and Viticulture (the sciences of winemaking and grape growing) is a 501 (c)(6), tax exempt professional society dedicated to the interests of enologists, viticulturists, and others in the

fields of wine and grape research and production throughout the world. Our membership includes professionals from wineries, vineyards, academic institutions and organizations.
2400+ Members
Founded in 1950

636 American Society for Horticultural Science

1018 Duke Street
Alexandria, VA 22314

703-836-4606
FAX 703-836-2024
E-Mail: webmaster@ashs.org
Home Page: www.ashs.org
Social Media: *Facebook, Twitter, LinkedIn, Pinterest*

Michael A. Arnold, Chairman
Curt Rom, President
Cynthia McKenney, Education Division Vice President
Angela Davis, Industry Division Vice President
Susan Barton, VP/Extension Division

A cornerstone of research and education in horticulture and an agent for active promotion of horticultural science.
1200 Members
ISSN: 0018-5345
Founded in 1903

637 American Society of Agricultural Consultants

605 Columbus Ave South
New Prague, MN 56071

952-758-5811
FAX 952-758-5813
E-Mail: asac@gandgcomm.com
Home Page: www.agconsultants.org
Social Media: *Facebook, Twitter, LinkedIn, YouTube*

Den Gardner, Executive Vice President
Kristy Mach, Associate
Gary Wagner, VP/Secretary

An association representing the full range of agricultural consultants which serves as an information, resource, and networking base for its members. The specific purpose of ASAC is to foster the science of agricultural consulting in all its varied fields; to promote the profession and maintain high standards under which the members conduct their service to the public; hold meetings for the exchange of ideas and the study of the profession of agricultural consulting;
181 Members
Founded in 1963

638 American Society of Agricultural and Biological Engineers

2950 Niles Rd
St Joseph, MI 49085-8607

269-429-0300
800-371-2723
FAX 269-429-3852
E-Mail: hq@asabe.org
Home Page: www.asabe.org
Social Media: *Facebook, Twitter, LinkedIn, YouTube*

Darrin Drollinger, Executive Director
Joe Walker, Publication Director
Dolores Landeck, Director/Public Affairs
Scott Cedarquist, Dir., Standards & Tech Activities
Mark Crossley, Director/Membership

The American Society of Agricultural and Biological Engineers is an educational and scientific organization dedicated to the advancement of engineering applicable to agricultural, food, and biological systems. With members in more than 100 countries. The Society's Agricultural,

Food and Biological Engineers develop efficient and environmentally sensitive methods of producing food, fiber, timber, and renewable energy sources.
8000 Members
Founded in 1907
Mailing list available for rent: 10000 names at $120 per M

639   American Society of Agronomy
5585 Guilford Road
Madison, WI 53711-5801

608-273-8080
FAX 608-273-2021
E-Mail: membership@agronomy.org
Home Page: www.agronomy.org
Social Media: *Facebook, Twitter, LinkedIn, RSS*

Jean L. Steiner, President
Wes Meixelsperger, Chief Financial Officer
Sara Uttech, Senior Manager - Governance
Wes Meixelsperger, Director of Meetings
Ian Popkewitz, Director of IT and Operations
Promote human welfare through advancing the acquisition and dissemination of scientific knowledge concerning the nature, use improvement and interrelationships of plants, soils, water and environment. The society shall promote effective research, disseminate scientific information, facilitate technology transfer, foster high standards of education, strive to maintain high standards of ethics, promote advancements in this profession and cooperate with other organizations of similar objectives.
11000 Members
Founded in 1907

640   American Society of Animal Science
PO Box 7410
Champaign, IL 61826-7410

217-356-9050
FAX 217-568-6070
E-Mail: asas@asas.org
Home Page: www.asas.org
Social Media: *Facebook, Twitter, LinkedIn, YouTube*

Dr. Michael L. Looper, President
Jacelyn Hemmelgarn, Chief Operations Officer
Meghan Wulster-Radcliffe, Chief Executive Officer
Melissa Burnett, Membership Manager
Samantha Walker, Program Director

The American Society of Animal Science is a membership society that supports the careers of scientists and animal producers in the United States and internationally. The American Society of Animal Science fosters the discovery, sharing and application of scientific knowledge concerning the responsible use of animals to enhance human life and well-being.
ISSN: 0021-8812
Founded in 1908

641   American Society of Consulting Arborists
9707 Key West Ave
Suite 100
Rockville, MD 20850-3992

301-947-0483
FAX 301-990-9771
E-Mail: asca@mgmtsol.com
Home Page: www.asca-consultants.org
Social Media: *Facebook, Twitter, LinkedIn, Pinterest*

Barbara Neal, President
Grace L. Jan, Vice President, Meetings
Beth W. Palys, Executive Director
Shannon Sperati, Senior Member Services Manager
Julie Hill, Marketing Director

The industry's premier professional association focusing solely on arboricultural consulting.

Consulting Arborists are authoritative experts on trees, consulting property owners, municipalities, attorneys, insurance professionals and others on tree disease, placement, preservation and dispute resolution in addition to providing consulting and expert testimony in the legal, insurance and environmental arenas.

642   American Society of Farm Managers and Rural Appraisers (ASFMRA)
950 S Cherry St
Suite 508
Denver, CO 80246-2664

303-758-3513
FAX 303-758-0190
E-Mail: info@asfmra.org
Home Page: www.asfmra.org
Social Media: *Facebook, Twitter, LinkedIn, Plaxo*

Fred L. Hepler, AFM, AAC, President
Merrill E. Swanson, President-Elect
LeeAnn E. Moss, Academic Vice President
Debe Alvarez, Manager/Education
Cheryl Cooley, Manager/Meetings & IT
The ASFMRA provides members with the resources, information, and leadership that enable them to provide valuable services to the agricultural community. The focus of the ASFMRA is providing education and networking opportunities for a professional group of members providing farm and ranch management, rural and real property appraising, review appraisal, and agricultural consulting services to the private and public sectors and to the governmental and lending communities.
1900 Members
Founded in 1929
Mailing list available for rent

643   American Soybean Association
12125 Woodcrest Executive
Suite 100
St. Louis, MO 63141-5009

314-576-1770
800-688-7692
FAX 314-576-2786
E-Mail: membership@soy.org
Home Page: www.soygrowers.com
Social Media: *Facebook, Twitter, LinkedIn, YouTube, RSS*

Ray Gaesser, Chairman
Wade Cowan, President
Richard Wilkins, 1st Vice President
Steve Censky, CEO
Julie Hawkins, Meeting Planner/Executive Asst.

The American Soybean Association (ASA) is recognized by the majority of U.S. soybean growers and industry for its vital role as their domestic and international policy advocate. ASA is clearly leading an expanding soybean value-chain, with farmers capturing a growing percentage. ASA's development of influential and effective grower leaders is recognized throughout the agriculture industry.
22000 Members
Founded in 1920

644   Animal Agriculture Alliance
2101 Wilson Blvd
Suite 916-13
Arlington, VA 22201

703-562-5160
FAX 703-524-1921
E-Mail: info@animalagalliance.org
Home Page: www.animalagalliance.org
Social Media: *Facebook, Twitter*

Sherrie Webb, Chairman
Kay Johnson Smith, President and CEO
Hannah Thompson, Communications Director
Casey Whitaker, Communications Coordinator
Morgan Hawley, Project Manager

The Animal Agriculture Alliance, is a broad based coalition of individual farmers, ranchers, producer organizations, suppliers, packer-processors, scientists, veterinarians and retailers. The Alliance with its members are interested in helping consumers better understand the role animal agriculture plays in providing a safe, abundant food supply to a hungry world.
3000 Members
Founded in 1987

645   Aquatic Plant Management Society
7922 NW 71st Street
Gainesville, FL 32653

FAX 601-634-5502
E-Mail: webmaster@apms.org
Home Page: www.apms.org
Social Media: *Facebook, Twitter, LinkedIn, Bloggr*

Mike Netherland, President
Rob Richardson, Vice-President
Jeff Schardt, Secretary
Jason Ferrell, Editor
Sherry Whitaker, Treasurer

The Aquatic Plant Management Society, Inc. is an international organization of scientists, educators, students, commercial pesticide applicators, administrators, and concerned individuals interested in the management and study of aquatic plants. The Aquatic Plant Management Society (APMS) strives to promote environmental stewardship through scientific innovation and development of technology related to integrated plant management in aquatic and riparian systems.
Founded in 1961

646   Association for Arid Lands Studies
601 Indiana Avenue
PO Box 45004
Lubbock, TX 79409-5004

806-742-3667
FAX 806-742-1286
E-Mail: gay.riggan@ttu.edu
Home Page: www.iaff.ttu.edu
Social Media: *Facebook*

Tibor Nagy, VP
Dr. A C Correa, International Director/ICASALS
Bob Crosier, Director
Dawn Cepica, International Faculty Counselor
Stephanie Cloninger, Special Projects Coordinator

To promote the university's special mission of the interdisciplinary study of arid and semi-arid environments and the human relationship to these environments from an international perspective.
200 Members
Founded in 1977

647   Association of American Feed Control Officials
1800 South Oak Street
Suite 100
Champaign, IL 61820-6974

217-356-4221
FAX 217-398-4119
E-Mail: aafco@aafco.org
Home Page: www.aafco.org
Social Media: *Facebook*

Tim Darden, President
Doug Lueders, President Elect
Ali Kashani, Secretary/Treasurer
Mark LeBlanc, Senior Director
Ken Bowers, Junior Director

The Association of American Feed Control Officials (AAFCO) is a voluntary membership association of local, state and federal agencies charged by law to regulate the sale and distribution of animal feeds and animal drug remedies.Although AAFCO has no regulatory

authority, the Association provides a forum for the membership and industry representation to achieve two main goals: Ensure consumer protection and safeguarding the health of animals and humans.
Founded in 1909

648   Association of American Seed Control Officials
Utah Department of Agriculture
350 N Redwood Road
PO Box 146500
Salt Lake City, UT 84114-6500

801-848-8543
FAX 801-538-7189
E-Mail: walshm@purdue.edu
Home Page: www.seedcontrol.org

Jim Drews, President
Johnny Zook, First Vice President
Greg Stordahl, Second Vice President
Greg Helmbrecht, Treasurer
John Heaton, Secretary

The Association of American Seed Control Officials is an organization of seed regulatory officials from the United States and Canada. The members meet to discuss mutual concerns of seed law enforcement, to be updated on new developments in the seed industry, and to update the Recommended Uniform State Seed Law which the organization developed and maintains as model law.
Founded in 1949

649   Association of Equipment
6737 W Washington Street
Suite 2400
Milwaukee, WI 53214-5647

414-272-0943
FAX 414-272-1170
E-Mail: aem@aem.org
Home Page: www.aem.org
Social Media: *Twitter*

John Patterson, Chairman
Nick Yaksich, VP, Government & Industry Relations
Megan Tanel, VP, Exhibitions & Events
Anne Forristall Luke, VP, Political & Public Affairs
Al Cervero, VP, Construction, Mining & Utility
850 Members
Founded in 1946

650   Association of Equipment Manufacturers
6737 W Washington St
Suite 2400
Milwaukee, WI 53214-5647

414-272-0943
866-236-0442
FAX 414-272-1170
E-Mail: aem@aem.org
Home Page: www.aem.org
Social Media: *Facebook, Twitter, LinkedIn, StumbleUpon, Google+*

John Patterson, Chairman
Dennis Slater, President
Anne Forristall Luke, Vice President
Renee Peters, Chief Financial Officer
Judy Gaus, VP, HR & Admin Affairs

A trade association that provides services on a global basis for companies that manufacture equipment, products and services used worldwide in the following industries: Agriculture, Construction, Forestry, Mining and Utility. AEM's membership and represents 200+ product lines.
850 Members
Founded in 1894

651   Bio-Dynamic Farming and Gardening Association
1661 North Water Street
Suite 307
Milwaukee, WI 53202

262-649-9212
FAX 262-659-9213
FAX new
E-Mail: info@biodynamics.com
Home Page: www.biodynamics.com

Steffen Schneider, President
Janet Gamble, Vice President and Secretary
Greg Georgaklis, Treasurer
Zachary Krebs, Technology
Penny Molina, Business Relationships

The Bio-Dynamic Farming and Gardeing Association (BDA) is an association of individuals and organizations in North America who are committed to the transformation of the whole food system.
Founded in 1938

652   Biodynamic Farming and Gardening Association
1661 N Water Street
Suite 307
Milwaukee, WI 53202

262-649-9212
FAX 262-649-9213
E-Mail: info@biodynamics.com
Home Page: www.biodynamics.com
Social Media: *Facebook*

Steffen Schneider, President
Janet Gamble, Vice President and Secretary
Greg Georgaklis, Treasurer
Zachary Krebs, Technology
Penny Molina, Business Relationships

The Biodynamic Farming and Gardening Association (BDA) is an association of individuals and organizations in North America who are committed to the transformation of the whole food system, from farm to table, and who draw inspiration from the spiritual-scientific insights of Rudolf Steiner. Biodynamics is a worldwide movement for the renewal of agriculture based on an understanding of the spiritual forces at work in nature and in human social life.
Founded in 1938

653   Cape Cod Cranberry Growers' Association
1 Carver Square Boulevard
PO Box 97
Carver, MA 02330

508-866-7878
FAX 508-866-4220
E-Mail: info@cranberries.org
Home Page: www.cranberries.org
Social Media: *Facebook*

Brad Morse, President
Gary Garretson, 1st Vice President
Keith Mann, 2nd Vice President
Brian Wick, Executive Director
Henry Gillet, Jr,, Government Affairs Director

Promotes the success of US and Canadian cranberry growers through health, agricultural and environmental stewardship research and education.
Founded in 1888

654   Committee on Organic and Sustainable Agriculture
5585 Guilford Road
Madison, WI 53711-5801

608-273-8080
FAX 608-273-2021
E-Mail: queries@dl.sciencesocieties.org
Home Page: dl.sciencesocieties.org
Social Media: *Facebook, Twitter, LinkedIn*

Ann-Marie Fortuna, Chair

Develops programming for members and divisions interested in sustainable and organic agriculture for the Societies' annual meeting; obtain input and develop recommendations on ways to better serve members interested in sustainable and organic agriculture beyond the activities ata the annual meeting
Founded in 2003

655   Communicating for AMERICA
112 E Lincoln Avenue
PO Box 677
Fergus Falls, MN 56537

218-739-3241
800-432-3276
FAX 218-739-3832
E-Mail: memberbenefits@cainc.org
Home Page: www.communicatingforamerica.org
Social Media: *Facebook*

Milt Smedsrud, Chairman
Patty Strickland, President/ Chief Operations Officer
Stephen Rufer, Vice President/General Counsel
Ben Shierer, Vice President of Government Rel
David Ramey, Owner

Strives to promote health, well-being and advancement of people in agriculture and agribusiness.
40M Members
Founded in 1972

656   Community Alliance with Family Farmers
36355 Russell Boulevard
PO Box 363
Davis, CA 95616

530-756-8518
800-892-3832
FAX 530-756-7857
E-Mail: info@caff.org
Home Page: www.caff.org
Social Media: *Facebook, Twitter, YouTube, Flickr*

Rich Collins, Board Chair
David Runsten, Policy Director
Diane Del Signore, Executive Director
Diana Aberella, Chief Operating Officer
Megan Sabato, Director of Communications

Mission is to build a movement of rural and urban people to foster family-scale agriculture that cares for the land, sustains local economies and promotes social justice.
Cost: $47.95
Founded in 1978

657   Corn Refiners Association
1701 Pennsylvania Ave NW
Suite 950
Washington, DC 20006-5806

202-331-1634
FAX 202-331-2054
E-Mail: comments@corn.org
Home Page: www.corn.org
Social Media: *Facebook, Twitter, LinkedIn, StumbleUpon, Google+*

Audrae Erickson, President
Thomas D Malkoski, Vice Chairman of the Board
J Patrick Mohan, Treasurer

Supports carbohydrate research programs through grants to colleges, government laboratories and private research centers.
8 Members
Founded in 1913

658 Council for Agricultural Science and Technology
4420 Lincoln Way
Ames, IA 50014-3447

515-292-2125
FAX 515-292-4512
E-Mail: cast@cast-science.org
Home Page: www.cast-science.org
Social Media: *Facebook, Twitter, LinkedIn, YouTube, Blogspot, Schooltube*

David Songstad, President
Kent G. Schescke, Executive Vice President
Dan Gogerty, Managing Communications Editor
Carol Gostele, Managing Scientific Editor
Melissa Sly, Director of Council Operations

Assembles, interprets and communicates science based information regionally, nationally and internationally on food, fiber, agriculture, natural resources, and related societal and environmental issues.
2000+ Members
Founded in 1972

659 Crop Insurance and Reinsurance Bureau Inc.
440 First St NW
Suite 500
Washington, DC 20001

202-544-0067
FAX 202-330-5255
E-Mail: mtorrey@cropinsurance.org
Home Page: www.cropinsurance.org

Sheri Bane, Chairwoman
Mike Torrey, Executive Vice President
Tara Smith, Federal Affairs Vice President
Sarah Hubbart, Director of Communications
Stephanie Butler, Director of Operations

The Crop Insurance Research Bureau is a national trade association made up of insurance providers and related organizations that provide a variety of insurance products to farmers. CIRB companies are big and small and offer private hail/fire coverage on growing crops, as well as participate in the federal crop insurance program which offers a greater variety of subsidized insurance products from yield based coverages to revenue products.
Founded in 1964

660 Crop Science Society of America
5585 Guilford Road
Madison, WI 53711-1086

608-273-8086
FAX 608-273-2021
E-Mail: membership@agronomy.org
Home Page: www.agronomy.org
Social Media: *Facebook, Twitter, LinkedIn*

Jean L. Steiner, President
Wes Meixelsperger, Chief Financial Officer
Sara Uttech, Senior Manager - Governance
Wes Meixelsperger, Director of Meetings
Luther Smith, Dir, Prof Dev& Buss. Relations

Seeks to advance research, extension, and teaching of all basic and applied phases of the crop sciences.
4700 Members
Founded in 1955

661 CropLife America
1156 15th St NW
Suite 400
Washington, DC 20005-1752

202-296-1585
FAX 202-463-0474
E-Mail: Info@croplifeamerica.org
Home Page: www.croplifeamerica.org

Social Media: *Facebook, Twitter, LinkedIn, YouTube, RSS Feeds*

Jay Vroom, President and CEO
Beau Greenwood, EVP, Gov Relations & Public Affairs
William Kuckuck, EVP/COO
Rachel G. Lattimore, SVP/General Counsel
Douglas T. Nelson, Senior Advisor

A trade association of the manufacturers, formulators, and distributors of agricultural crop protection, pest control, and biotechnology products. Membership is composed of companies that produce, sell and distribute virtually all the active ingredients used in crop protection chemicals.
86 Members
Founded in 1933

662 Ecological Farming Association
2901 Park Ave.
Suite D-2
Soquel, CA 95073

831-763-2111
E-Mail: info@eco-farm.org
Home Page: eco-farm.org
Social Media: *Facebook, Twitter, Instagram*

Ken Dickerson, Executive Director
Isabelle Jenniches, Programs & Operations Manager
Deborah Yashar, Communications Manager
Allie Wilson, Conference Production
Emily Summerlin, Communications Coordinator

EcoFarm is a nonprofit educational organization that promotes sustainable agriculture.
Founded in 1981

663 Equipment Marketing & Distribution Association (EMDA)
PO Box 1347
Iowa City, IA 52244

319-354-5156
FAX 319-354-5157
E-Mail: pat@emda.net
Home Page: www.emda.net
Social Media: *Facebook, Twitter, LinkedIn*

Patricia A Collins, Executive VP

EMDA members are devoted to the marketing of specialized eqipment: agricultural, outdoor power, light industrial, forestry, irrigation, turf and grounds maintenance, lawn and garden and parts/components for those segments of industry.
250 Members
Founded in 1945

664 Farm Equipment Manufacturers Association
1000 Executive Parkway Dr
Suite 100
St Louis, MO 63141-6369

314-878-2304
FAX 314-732-1480
E-Mail: info@farmequip.org
Home Page: www.farmequip.org

Mike Kloster, President
Richard Kirby, 1st Vice President
Paul Jeffrey, 2nd Vice President
Vernon Schmidt, Executive Vice President
Kristi Ruggles, Publications Editor

An information gathering and distributing organization for farm equipment manufacturers and suppliers. The Farm Equipment Manufacturers Association shall provide industry leadership to enhance business opportunities and profitability to the Membership by providing a forum for marketing shortline equipment through networking, communications, and technology, and a forum for purchasing

materials and services required by the Members.
730+ Members
Founded in 1950

665 Farm Foundation
1301 W 22nd St
Suite 615
Oak Brook, IL 60523-2197

630-571-9393
FAX 630-571-9580
E-Mail: mary@farmfoundation.org
Home Page: www.farmfoundation.org
Social Media: *Facebook, Twitter, YouTube, RSS Feeds, Blogger*

Mark Scholl, Chairman
Neilson C. Conklin, President
Sheldon R. Jones, VP, Finance and Programs
Mary Thompson, VP, Communications and Operations
Tim Brennan, Director of Development

A publicly supported nonprofit organization working to improve the economic health and social well-being of US agriculture, the food system and rural people by helping private and public sector decision makers identify and understand forces that will shape the future.
Founded in 1993

666 Fertilizer Institute
425 Third Street, SW
Suite 950
Washington, DC 20024

202-962-0490
FAX 202-962-0577
E-Mail: information@tfi.org
Home Page: www.tfi.org
Social Media: *Facebook, Twitter, LinkedIn, YouTube*

Chris Jahn, President
Bradley Cheng, Director, Accounting
Monica Conway, Executive Assis to the President
Ener Cunanan, Manager, Office Services
Kathy Mathers, Vice President, Public Affairs

TFI is the leading voice in the fertilizer industry, representing the public policy, communication and statistical needs of producers, manufacturers, retailers and transporters of fertilizer. Issues of interest to TFI members include security, international trade, energy, transportation, the environment, worker health and safety, farm bill and conservation programs to promote the use of enhanced efficiency fertilizer.
325 Members
Founded in 1883

667 Foundation for Agronomic Research
107 S State St
Suite 300
Monticello, IL 61856-1968

605-692-6280
E-Mail: pfixen@ipni.net
Home Page: www.farmresearch.com

Harold Reetz, President
Dr Paul Fixen, Senior Vice President

The Foundation for Agronomic Research (FAR) is a non-profit (501(c)(3) research and education foundation, created in 1980 by the Board of Directors of the Potash & Phosphate Institute (PPI), now the International Plant Nutrition Institute (IPNI), to expand its research efforts beyond that possible with PPI's resources and mandate. The mission of FAR is to improve the economic vigor and sustainability of agriculture in N.A. and around the world, while protecting and enhancing the environment.
Founded in 1980

668 Fresh Produce Association of the Americas

590 East Frontage Road
PO Box 848
Nogales, AZ 85628

520-287-2707
FAX 520-287-2948
E-Mail: info@freshfrommexico.com
Home Page: www.freshfrommexico.com

Matt Mandel, Chairman
Lance Jungmeyer, President
Paula Beemer, Communications Coordinator
Georgina Felix, International Affairs Director
Allison Moore, Dir., Legislative & Reg. Affairs

The Fresh Produce Association of the Americas and its members help to ensure North America's uninterrupted access to fresh, high-quality, healthy and delicious Mexican-grown fruits and vegetables. The FPAA is the leading agent of produce trade at the U.S.-Mexico border and across the country.
125+ Members
Founded in 1944

669 Fresh Produce and Floral Council

2400 E. Katella Ave.
Ste. 330
Anaheim, CA 92806

714-739-0177
FAX 714-739-0226
E-Mail: info@fpfc.org
Home Page: www.fpfc.org

Brad Martin, Chairman
Carissa Mace, President
Amy Wun, Manager Member Programs
Angela Steier, Events and Marketing Consultant
Connie Stukenberg, Secretary/Treasurer

Promotes through communication and education, fresh fruit, vegetable and floral products. Acts as a trade organization providing an environment for better communication within the industry.
600+ Members
Founded in 1965

670 Herb Growing and Marketing Network

PO Box 245
Silver Springs, PA 17575-0245

717-393-3295
FAX 717-393-9261
E-Mail: herbworld@aol.com
Home Page: www.herbworld.com

Maureen Rogers, Director

The Herb Growing & Marketing Network is the largest trade association for the herb industry. We are an information service. We have a library of over 3000 books, subscribe to over 200 periodicals, monitor blogs of all types and search the Web looking for resources and research on the herb industry that we can pass on to our members.
Cost: $48.00
1000 Members
Founded in 1990

671 Holstein Association USA

1 Holstein Place
PO Box 808
Brattleboro, VT 05302-0808

802-254-4551
800-952-5200
FAX 802-254-8251
E-Mail: info@holstein.com
Home Page: www.holsteinusa.com
Social Media: *Facebook, Twitter, You Tube*

John Meyer, CEO
Lisa Perrin, Marketing

Holstein Association USA maintains records on over 22 million Registered Holsteinsr, collect-ing and analyzing production, type and genetic data to provide useable information that enables dairy producers to improve their businesses by breeding better cows. The Holstein Association works to help dairy producers recognize the full potential of their herds.
30000 Members
Founded in 1885

672 International Association of Fairs and Expositions

3043 E Cairo Street
PO Box 985
Springfield, MO 65802

417-862-5771
800-516-0313
FAX 417-862-0156
E-Mail: iafe@fairsandexpos.com
Home Page: www.fairsandexpos.com
Social Media: *Facebook, Twitter, You Tube*

Jim Tucker, President/CEO
Steve Siever, Director of Sales
Max Willis, CFO
Missy McCormack, Comm. Design and Prod. Manager
Rebekah Lee, Director of Comm. and Editor

The International Association of Fairs and Expositions (IAFE) is a voluntary, non-profit corporation whose members provide services and products that promote the overall development and improvement of fairs, shows, expositions, and allied fields. Mission is to lead in representing and facilitating the evolving interests of agricultural fairs, exhibitions and show associations.
1300 Members
Founded in 1885

673 International Association of Operative Millers

12351 w. 96th Terrace
Suite 100
Lenexa, KS 66215

913-338-3377
FAX 913-338-3553
E-Mail: info@iaom.info
Home Page: www.iaom.info
Social Media: *Facebook, Twitter, LinkedIn*

Roy Loepp, President
Brad Allen, Vice President
Melinda Farris, Executive Vice President
Shannon Henson, Director of Meetings and Exhibits
Annette Peterson, Administrative Assistant

The International Association of Operative Millers (IAOM) is comprised of grain millers and allied trades representatives devoted to the advancement of education and training opportunities in the grain milling industries. Among its members, IAOM promotes a spirit of fellowship and cooperation, enhances their proficiency, and advances their interests in industry activities.
1500 Members
Founded in 1896

674 International Fruit Tree Association

16020 Swingley Ridge Rd.
Suite 300
Chesterfield, MO 63017

636-449-5083
FAX 636-449-5051
E-Mail: dungey@ifruittree.org
Home Page: www.ifruittree.org
Social Media: *Facebook, Twitter*

Tim Welsh, President
Rod Farrow, Vice President
Chris Hedges, Treasurer

The association promotes research on, and understanding of, Intensive Orchard Systems.
Founded in 1958

675 International Maple Syrup Institute

5072 Rock St.
RR#4
Spencerville, ON KOE 1XO

860-974-1235
FAX 802-868-5445
E-Mail: agrofor@ripnet.com
Home Page: www.internationalmaplesyrupinstitute.com

Dave Chapeskie, Executive Director
Alfred Bolduc, Board Member
Roger Palmer, Board Member
Tim Perkins, Advisor
Steve Childs, Advisor

The International Maple Syrup Institute (IMSI) was founded to promote and protect pure maple syrup and other pure maple products. The organization provides an important international framework for communication, information exchange and cooperation on a variety of issues related to the production, sale and marketing of pure maple syrup. In addition, the Institute has been a strong monitor for adulteration around the world, protecting the integrity of maple products.
15M Members
Founded in 1975

676 International Weed Science Society

University of Arkansas
1366 W. Altheimer Drive
Fayetteville, AR 72704

479-575-3984
FAX 479-575-3975
E-Mail: secretary@iwss.info
Home Page: www.iwss.info

Dr Albert Fischer, President
Dr Nilda Burgos, Vice President
Dr Frank Dayan, Treasurer
Dr Baruch Rubin, Past President
Dr Bernal Valverde, Ex-Officio

The International Weed Science Society (IWSS) was formed in 1975, by individuals from Europe, North America, South America, and the Asian-Pacific area, to deal with global weed science issues. The IWSS is a worldwide scientific organization, open to all who are interested in weeds and their control. The formation of IWSS was promoted actively by the six existing regional weed science societies. The purpose of IWSS is to supplement and complement their vital role.
Founded in 1975

677 Irrigation Association

8280 Willow Oaks Corporate Drive
Suite 400
Fairfax, VA 22031

703-536-7080
FAX 703-536-7019
E-Mail: info@irrigation.org
Home Page: www.irrigation.org

Aric J. Olson, President
Gregory R. Hunter, Vice President
Deborah M. Hamlin, CAE, FASAE, Chief Executive Officer
John R. Farner, Jr, Government & PA Director
Rebecca J. Bayless, Finance Director

The Irrigation Association is the leading membership organization for irrigation equipment and system manufacturers, dealers distributors, designers, consultants, contractors and end users.
1600 Members
Founded in 1949

678 Livestock Marketing Association

10510 NW Ambassador Drive
Kansas City, MO 64153-1278

816-891-0502
800-821-2048

FAX 816-891-0552
E-Mail: lmainfo@lmaweb.com
Home Page: www.lmaweb.com
Social Media: *Facebook, Twitter, YouTube, Instagram*

Tim Starks, Chairman of the Board
Dan Harris, President
Neal Brosnan, Facilities Manager
Mark Mackey, CEO
Vincent Nowak, CFO

We are committed to the support and protection of the local livestock auction markets. Auctions are a vital part of the livestock industry, serving producers and assuring a fair, competitive price through the auction method of selling.
800 Members
Founded in 1947

679   Maryland and Virginia Milk Producers Cooperative
1985 Isaac Newton Square West
Reston, VA 20190-5094

703-742-6800
FAX 703-742-7459
Home Page: www.mdvamilk.com

Richand Mosemann, Second VP
Dwayne Meyers, NC President

Known for being a leader in the dairy industry, the Eastern Milk Producers Cooperative has a reputation for integrity, service and high quality products.
Founded in 1920

680   Midwest Equipment Dealers Association
5330 Wall St
Suite 100
Madison, WI 53718-7929

608-240-4700
FAX 608-240-2069
E-Mail: gmanke@medaassn.com
Home Page: www.medaassn.com

Gary W. Manke, Executive Vice President, CEO
Antoniewicz Gaugert, Wisconsin & Illinois Legal Counsel
Julie Roisum, Executive Assistant
Jerry Deblaey, Vice President

Our mission is to promote the farm, industrial, outdoor power equipment, dairy and farmstead mechanization industry and to provide services that will assist Association members in becoming more profitable and better equipped to operate in today's business environment.
Founded in 1991

681   NCBA CLUSA
1401 New York Ave NW
Suite 1100
Washington, DC 20005-2160

202-638-6222
FAX 202-638-1374
E-Mail: ncba@ncba.coop
Home Page: www.ncba.coop
Social Media: *Facebook, Twitter, YouTube, Google+*

Andrew Jacob, Chair
Michael Beall, President & Chief Executive Officer
Patricia Brownell Sterner, Chief Operating Officer, NCBA
Amy Coughenour Betancourt, Chief Operating Officer
Valeria Roach, Chief Financial Officer

Leading US organization strengthening the cooperative form of business to empower people and improve quality of life worldwide. To make cooperatives a strong, distinct and unified sector, recognized by the American public. Our member co-ops operate in the areas including, agricultural supply and marketing, chil-

dren, energy, food distribution, healthcare and housing.
1800 Members
Founded in 1916

682   National 4-H Council
7100 Connecticut Ave
Chevy Chase, MD 20815-4934

301-961-2800
FAX 301-961-2894
E-Mail: info@fourhcouncil.edu
Home Page: www.4-h.org
Social Media: *Facebook, Twitter, LinkedIn, Google+, Pinterest, YouTube*

Donald Floyd, President/CEO
Jennifer Sirangelo, EVP/COO
Andy Ferrin, Senior Vice President
Paul Koehler, Senior Vice President
Jill Bramble, Senior Vice President

Works to advance the 4-H youth development movement, building a world in which youth and adults learn, grow, and work together as catalysts for positive change. National 4-H Council partners with the Cooperative Extension System and other organizations to provide technical support and training, develop curricula, create model programs and promote positive youth development to fulfill its mission. National 4-H Council also manages the National 4-H Conference.
7M Members
Founded in 1902

683   National Agri-Marketing Association
11020 King St
Suite 205
Overland Park, KS 66210-1201

913-491-6500
FAX 913-491-6502
E-Mail: agrimktg@nama.org
Home Page: www.nama.org
Social Media: *Facebook, Twitter, LinkedIn, Flicker, You Tube*

Marvin Kokes, President
Matt Coniglio, First VP/ President Elect
Amy Bradford, Secretary/Treasurer
Amy Bugg, Vice President
Amber Harrison, Vice President

Marketing and communication suppliers, including trade publications, radio and television broadcast sales organizations, premium/incentive manufacturers, printers, marketing research firms, photographers and related professionals.
3500 Members
Founded in 1957

684   National Agricultural Aviation Association
1440 Duke Street
Alexandria, VA 22314

202-546-5722
FAX 202-546-5726
E-Mail: information@agaviation.org
Home Page: www.agaviation.org
Social Media: *Facebook*

Rick Boardman, President
Harley Curless, Vice President
Andrew D. Moore, Executive Director
Jay Calleja, Manager of Communications
Lindsay Barber, Manager of Meetings, Marketing

NAAA supports the interests of small business owners and pilots licensed as professional commercial aerial applicators who use aircraft to enhance food, fiber and bio-fuel production, protect forestry and control health-threatening pests. NAAA provides networking, educational, government relations, public relations,

recruiting and informational services to its members.
1900 Members
Founded in 1966

685   National Alliance of Independent Crop Consultants
349 E Nolley Dr
Collierville, TN 38017-3538

901-861-0511
FAX 901-861-0512
E-Mail: AllisonJones@NAICC.org
Home Page: www.naicc.org

Gary Coukell, P.Ag., President
Debra Keenan, President Elect
Marla Siruta, Secretary
Nathan Goldschmidt, Treasurer
James E. Todd, Past President

The national society of agricultural professionals who provide research and advisory services. Memebers comprise 40 states and several foreign countries, and have expertise in the production of most crops grown around the world.
500+ Members
Founded in 1978

686   National Association of Agricultural Educators (NAAE)
300 Garrigus Building
University of Kentucky
Lexington, KY 40546-0215

859-257-2224
800-509-0204
FAX 859-323-3919
E-Mail: jay_jackman@ffa.org
Home Page: www.naae.org
Social Media: *Facebook, Twitter, YouTube, Pinterest, Flickr*

Charlie Sappington, President
Wm. Jay Jackman, Executive Director
Alissa Smith, Associate Executive Director
Katie Wood, Meeting Planner/Program Assistant
Julie Fritsch, Comm. & Marketing Director

Professionals providing agricultural education for the global community through visionary leadership, advocacy and service. NAAE seeks to advance agricultural education and promote the professional interests and growth of agriculture teachers as well as recruit and prepare students who have a desire to teach agriculture.
7800+ Members
Founded in 1948

687   National Association of Agricultural Fairs
Tennessee Department of Agriculture
440 Hogan Road
PO Box 40627
Nashville, TN 37220

615-837-5160
800-342-8206
FAX 615-837-5194
E-Mail: pick.tn@tn.gov
Home Page: www.picktnproducts.org
Social Media: *Facebook, Twitter, Pinterest*

Ed Harlan, Agribusiness Coordinator
Dan Strasser, Director of Market Development
Nelson Owen, Livestock Grading/Market News

US and Canadian representatives of state/provincial agencies that are responsible for the support of educational and agricultural fairs.
35 Members
Founded in 1966

688   National Association of Animal Breeders
PO Box 1033
Columbia, MO 65205-1033

573-445-4406
FAX 573-446-2279

E-Mail: naab-css@naab-css.org
Home Page: www.naab-css.org

Dr Charles Brown II, Chairman
Dr Gordon Doak, Secretary - Treasurer - President
Dr Roger Weigle, Vice Chairman
Jere R Mitchell, Service Director
Dr Roger Weigle, Vice Chairman

The purpose of the National Association of Animal Breeders (NAAB) as defined by its By-Laws is to unite those individuals and organizations engaged in the artificial insemination of cattle and other livestock into an affiliated federation operating under self-imposed standards of performance and to conduct and promote the mutual interest and ideals of its members.

20 Members
Founded in 1975

689 National Association of County Agricultural Agents

6584 W Duroc Road
Maroa, IL 61756

217-794-3700
FAX 217-794-5901
E-Mail: exec-dir@nacaa.com
Home Page: www.nacaa.com
Social Media: *Facebook, Twitter*

Cynthia Gregg, President
Mark Nelson, President-Elect
Alan Galloway, Vice President
Matt Herring, Secretary
Alan Galloway, Treasurer

The NACAA strives to: Advance the professional status of Extension agents and specialists with agriculture-related Extension appointments. Encourage, promote, and provide professional improvement for all members. Provide for the exchange of ideas, methods, and techniques. Represent professional interests of members in matters of public policy and affairs. Promote public confidence, esteem, and respect for Cooperative Extension. Recognize excellence in Cooperative Extension nationwide.

3850 Members
Founded in 1917
Mailing list available for rent: 3500 names at $500 per M

690 National Association of Extension 4-H Agents

University of Georgia
3801 Lake Boone Trail
Suite 190
Raleigh, NC 27607

919-232-0112
FAX 919-779-5642
E-Mail: execdir@nae4ha.com
Home Page: www.nae4ha.org
Social Media: *Facebook, Twitter*

Kimberly Gressley, President
Shawn Tiede, VP, Finance & Operations
Kori Myers, Vice President for Professional Dev
Casey Mull, VP, Marketing & Outreach
Linda Tripp, VP, Programs

Designed to meet the needs of youth development professionals by maximizing the use of technology, provide progressive levels of professional development, elevate the quality of youth development work through scholarship, research and practice, advocate for the 4-H youth development profession.

3600 Members
Founded in 1946

691 National Association of State Departments of Agriculture

4350 North Fairfax Drive
#910
Arlington, VA 22203

202-296-9680
FAX 703-880-0509
E-Mail: nasda@nasda.org
Home Page: www.nasda.org
Social Media: *Facebook, Twitter*

Greg Ibach, President
Michael Strain, Vice President
Steven Reviczky, Second Vice President
DeWitt Ashby, Director, Trade Shows & Grants
Carol Black, Project Manager, Pesticide Workers

Represents the state departments of agriculture in the development, implementation and communication of sound public policy and programs which support and promote the American agricultural industry, while protecting consumers and the environment.

Founded in 1916

692 National Association of Wheat Growers

415 2nd Street NE
Suite 300
Washington, DC 20002-4993

202-547-7800
FAX 202-546-2638
E-Mail: wheatworld@wheatworld.org
Home Page: www.wheatworld.org
Social Media: *Facebook, Twitter, RSS Feed, Youtube*

Brett Blankenship, President
Gordon Stoner, Vice President
David Schemm, Treasurer
Jim Palmer, Chief Executive Officer
Hugh Whaley, Director of Corporate Relations

Nonprofit partnership of US wheat growers, by combining their strengths, voices and ideas are working to ensure a better future for themselves, their industry and the general public. NAWG's mission statement is: NAWG unites U.S. wheat growers to create beneficial policies for wheat growers; effective relationships with industry; and profitable opportunities through research and technology.

Founded in 1950

693 National Bison Association

8690 Wolff Court
Suite 200
Westminster, CO 80031

303-292-2833
FAX 303-845-9081
E-Mail: david@bisoncentral.com
Home Page: www.bisoncentral.com
Social Media: *Facebook*

Bruce Anderson, President
Roy Liedtke, Vice President
Dave Carter, Executive Director
Jim Matheson, Assistant Director
Marilyn Wentz, Bison World Editor

Formed to promote the production, marketing and preservation of bison. The mission of the National Bison Association is to bring together stakeholders to celebrate the heritage of American bison/buffalo, to educate, and to create a sustainable future for our industry.

1100+ Members
Founded in 1995

694 National Christmas Tree Association

16020 Swingley Ridge Rd
Suite 300
Chesterfield, MO 63017-6030

636-449-5070
FAX 636-449-5051
E-Mail: info@realchristmastrees.org

Home Page: www.realchristmastrees.org
Social Media: *Facebook, Twitter, YouTube, Blogger*

Blake Rafeld, President
Paul Schroeder, Vice President
Bob Schaefer, Vice President
Tom Dull, President-Elect
Rick Dungey, Executive Director

The National Christmas Tree Association (NCTA) is the national trade association representing the Christmas tree industry. NCTA represents more than 700 active member farms, 29 state and regional associations, and more than 4,000 affiliated businesses that grow and sell Christmas trees or provide related supplies and services.

700 Members
Founded in 1955
Mailing list available for rent: 5100 names

695 National Cotton Council of America

National Cotton Council of America
PO Box 2995
7193 Goodlett Farms Pkwy
Cordova, TN 38088-2995

901-274-9030
FAX 901-725-0510
Home Page: www.cotton.org

Sledge Taylor, Chairman
Gary Adams, President & Chief Executive Officer
Dr. Jody Campiche, VP, Economy and Policy Analysis
Dr Bill M. Norman, VP, Technical Services
Craig Brown, VP Producer Affairs

The National Cotton Council is a unifying force of the U.S. cotton industry, bringing together representatives from the seven industry segments in the 17 cotton-producing states of the Cotton Belt to work out common problems and develop programs of mutual benefit.

35 Members

696 National Cottonseed Products Association

866 Willow Tree Circle
Cordova, TN 38018-6376

901-682-0800
FAX 901-682-2856
E-Mail: info@cottonseed.com
Home Page: www.cottonseed.com

Ben Morgan, BS, MBA, EVP/Secretary
Bobby Crum, Vice President
Sandi Stine, Treasurer

National association of cottonseed products. NCPA is an organization of firms and individuals engaged in the processing of cottonseed and the marketing of cottonseed products, as well as cottonseed. These include oil mills, refiners, product dealers and product brokers.

200 Members
Founded in 1929

697 National Council of Agricultural Employers

525 9th Street, NW
Suite 800
Washington, DC 20004

202-629-9320
FAX 202-728-0303
E-Mail: info@ncaeonline.org
Home Page: www.ncaeonline.org
Social Media: *Facebook*

Luawanna Hallstrom, President
Fred Leitz, Eastern Vice President
Ray Prescott, Western Vice President
Joe Young, Treasurer
Bryan Little, Secretary

NCAE represents Agricultural Employer interests before Congress and Regulatory/Administrative bodies such as the Departments of

Labor, Homeland Security, Agriculture, the Occupational Safety and Health Administration, and the Environmental Protection Agency.
250 Members
Founded in 1964

698 National Crop Insurance Services
8900 Indian Creek Pkwy
Suite 600
Overland Park, KS 66210-1567

913-685-2767
800-951-6247
FAX 913-685-3080
E-Mail: webmaster@ag-risk.org
Home Page: www.ag-risk.org
Social Media: *Facebook, Twitter*

Dr. Thomas P. Zacharias, President and CEO
Linda Kovelan, Director Executive Services
Laurie Langstraat, V.P. Public Relations
Sherri Scharff, V.P. Membership Services
Jim Crist, CFO/COO

NCIS is an association of insurance companies writing insurance for damage by hail, fire and other weather perils to growing crops.
60+ Members
Founded in 1915

699 National Dairy Herd Information Association
PO Box 930399
Verona, WI 53593-0399

608-848-6455
FAX 608-260-7772
E-Mail: jmattison@requestltd.com
Home Page: www.dhia.org

Kent Buttars, President
Susan Lee, Vice President
Jay Mattison, CEO/Administrator
Leslie Thoman, Accounting/Bookkeeping
Steven Sievert, Quality Certification Services

The objective is to promote accuracy, credibility and uniformity of DHI records. To represent the DHI system on issues involving other National and International organizations
65M Members

700 National Farmers Organization
528 Billy Sunday Road
Suite 100, PO Box 2508
Ames, IA 50010-2508

515-292-2000
800-247-2110
FAX 866-629-3976
E-Mail: nfo@nfo.org
Home Page: www.nfo.org
Social Media: *Facebook, Twitter, YouTube*

Paul Olson, President, Chairman of the Board
Paul Riniker, Vice President
Perry Gainer, Communications Director

National Farmers defines itself by its sophisticated commodity marketing and ag risk management programs and services. Through National Farmers MaximumMarketing, producers market their commodities in pooled groups, and their bank accounts benefit.
30M Members
Founded in 1955

701 National Farmers Union
20 F Street NW
Suite 300
Washington, DC 20001

202-554-1600
800-347-1961
FAX 202-554-1654
E-Mail: info@nfudc.org
Home Page: www.nfu.org
Social Media: *Facebook, Twitter, YouTube, Instagram*

Roger Johnson, President
Donn Teske, Vice President

Jeff Knudson, SVP, Operations
Chandler Goule, Senior Vice President of Programs
Ethan Whitmore, Director of Information Services

Farmers Union helped shape national policy, organized cooperative businesses that thrive today, delivered educational programs designed to build rural leaders, and provided farmers and ranchers with opportunities to be at the table.
25000 Members
Founded in 1902

702 National Fisheries Institute
7918 Jones Branch Dr
Suite 700
Mc Lean, VA 22102-3319

703-752-8880
FAX 703-752-7583
E-Mail: bsb@nfi.org
Home Page: www.aboutseafood.com
Social Media: *Facebook, Twitter, LinkedIn, Pinterest, google+*

John Connely, President
Gavin Gibbons, Director, Media Relations

The National Fisheries Institute is a non-profit organization dedicated to education about seafood safety, sustainability, and nutrition. From vessels at sea to your favorite seafood restaurant, our diverse member companies bring delicious fish and shellfish to American families. NFI promotes the US Dietary Guidelines that suggest Americans include fish and shellfish in their diets twice per week for longer, healthier lives.
241 Members
Founded in 1945

703 National Future Farmers of America Organization
6060 FFA Drive
P.O. Box 68960
Indianapolis, IN 46268-0960

317-802-6060
800-772-0939
FAX 317-802-6051
E-Mail: shop@ffa.org
Home Page: www.ffa.org
Social Media: *Facebook, Twitter, LinkedIn, Instagram, YouTube*

Steve A. Brown, Board Chair
Andy Paul, President
W. Dwight Armstrong, Ph.D., Chief Executive Officer
Joshua Bledsoe, Chief Operating Officer
David Schapker, Chief Financial Officer

Headquarters of the National FFA Organization, the organization's mission is to prepare students for successful careers and a lifetime of informed choices in the global agriculture, food, fiber and natural resources systems.
507M Members
Founded in 1928

704 National Grain and Feed Association
1250 I St NW
Suite 1003
Washington, DC 20005-3939

202-289-0873
FAX 202-289-5388
E-Mail: ngfa@ngfa.org
Home Page: www.ngfa.org
Social Media: *Facebook, Twitter, LinkedIn, Flickr*

Randall C Gordon, President
Todd E. Kemp, Vice President of Marketing
Charles M. Delacruz, VP/General Counsel/Secretary
David A. Fairfield, Vice President of Feed Services
Sarah Gonzalez, Dir. Comm & Digital Media

NGFA is the national trade association of grain elevators, feed and feed ingredient manufacturers, grain and oilseed processors, exporters, livestock and poultry integrators, and firms providing products and services to the industry.
Founded in 1896

705 National Grange
1616 H St NW
Suite 10
Washington, DC 20006-4999

202-628-3507
888-447-2643
FAX 202-347-1091
E-Mail: eluttrell@nationalgrange.org
Home Page: www.nationalgrange.org
Social Media: *Facebook, Twitter, YouTube, RSS Feeds*

Ed Luttrell, President/Master
Stephanie Tiller, Executive Assistant/Event Planner
Burton Eller, Legislative Director
Charlene Shupp Espenshade, Youth and Young Adult Director
Sandor Szima, Building Engineer

Promotes general welfare and agriculture through local organizations. Presides over the advancement and promotion of the farming and agriculture industry.
300K Members
Founded in 1867

706 National Hay Association
Ellington Agricultural Center
432 Hogan Rd.
Nashville, TN 37220

615-837-5560
800-707-0014
FAX 615-523-1385
E-Mail: NHAExecOffice@gmail.com
Home Page: www.nationalhay.org
Social Media: *Facebook*

Bob Eckenberg, President
Terry Button, First Vice President
Amy Freeburg, Second Vice President
Paul Dugger, Executive Director
Carl Blackmer, Director

The National Hay Association is made up of people that are involved in the production, sale and transportation of forage products across the United States and the world. As an organization we work for the good of the hay industry through knowledge among members, to following government legislation. We operate as an independent organization with no commitments or ties to any government groups.
750 Members
Founded in 1895

707 National Institute for Animal Agriculture
13570 Meadowgrass Dr
Suite 201
Colorado Springs, CO 80921-3058

719-538-8843
FAX 719-538-8847
E-Mail: niaa@animalagriculture.org
Home Page: www.animalagriculture.org
Social Media: *Facebook, Twitter, LinkedIn, YouTube*

Glenn K. Fischer, Chairman of the Board
Katie Ambrose, Chief Operating Officer
R. Scott Stuart, Chief Executive Officer
Mona Wolverton, Event Coordinator
Polly Welden, Marketing

NIAA is an organization that satisfies your needs, concerns and interests about the animal agriculture industry. NIAA's purpose is quite simple - to provide a source for individuals, organizations, and the entire animal agriculture industry to obtain information, education and

Agriculture / Associations

solutions for challenges facing animal agriculture.
250 Members

708 National Oilseed Processors Association
1300 L St NW
Suite 1020
Washington, DC 20005-4168

202-842-0463
FAX 202-842-9126
E-Mail: thammer@nopa.org
Home Page: www.nopa.org

Thomas A. Hammer, President
David J. Hovermale, EVP, Gov. Relations
David C. Ailor, EVP, Regulatory Affairs
Jeanne L. Seibert, Office Administrator
Mark Sandeen, Secretary-Treasurer

NOPA now represents oilseed crushers of soybeans, canola, flaxseed, safflower seed and sunflower seed. NOPA represents twelve (12) regular member firms engaged in the actual processing of oilseeds, and eight (8) associate member firms who are consumers of vegetable oil or oilseed meal, including some refiners.
Founded in 1989

709 National Onion Association
822 7th St
Suite 510
Greeley, CO 80631-3941

970-353-5895
FAX 970-353-5897
E-Mail: kreddin@onions-usa.org
Home Page: www.onions-usa.org
Social Media: *Twitter, LinkedIn, Pinterest, RSS*

Shawn Hartley, President
John Rietveld, Vice President
Doug Stanley, 2nd Vice President
Wayne Mininger, Executive VP
Kim Reddin, Director of Public & Industry Rel

The National Onion Association (NOA) is the official organization representing growers, shippers, brokers, and commercial representatives of the U.S. onion industry.
500 Members
Founded in 1913
Mailing list available for rent: 600 names

710 National Pork Producers Council
122 C Street NW
Suite 875
Washington, DC 20001

202-347-3600
800-937-7675
FAX 202-347-5265
E-Mail: news@nppc.org
Home Page: www.nppc.org
Social Media: *Facebook, Twitter, LinkedIn, Pinterest, Flickr, Swinecast*

Ron Prestage, DVM, President
Ken Maschhoff, Vice President
Neil Dierks, Chief Executive Officer
Dallas Hockman, VP, Industry Relations
Pete Houska, Regional Dir. Producer Services

The National Pork Producers Council conducts public-policy outreach on behalf of its affiliated state associations, enhancing opportunities for the success of U.S. pork producers and other industry stakeholders by establishing the U.S. pork industry as a consistent and responsible supplier of high-quality pork to the domestic and world markets.
44 Members

711 National Potato Council
1300 L St NW
Suite 910
Washington, DC 20005-4107

202-682-9456
FAX 202-682-0333

E-Mail: spudinfo@nationalpotatocouncil.org
Home Page: www.nationalpotatocouncil.org
Social Media: *Facebook, Twitter, YouTube*

Dan Lake, President
Jim Tiede, First Vice President
Larry Alsum, VP, Finance & Office Procedures
John Keeling, EVP/CEO
Hollee Alexander, Senior Director, Programs & Events

The National Potato Council is the advocate for the economic well-being of U.S. potato growers on federal legislative, regulatory, environmental, and trade issues.
45000 Members
Founded in 1948

712 National Potato Promotion Board
4949 S. Syracuse St.
#400
Denver, CO 80237

303-369-7783
FAX 303-369-7718
E-Mail: info@uspotatoes.com
Home Page: www.uspotatoes.com
Social Media: *Facebook, Twitter, YouTube, Pinterest, Instagram*

Carl Hoverson, Chairman
Blair Richardson, President & CEO
Diana LeDoux, VP, Finance & IT
David Fraser, VP, Industry Comm. & Policy
John Toaspern, Chief Marketing Officer

Also known as the US Potato Board. Organized to operate a national marketing program to position potatoes as low calorie, nutritious vegetables and to facilitate market expansion into domestic and export sales.
2500+ Members
Founded in 1971

713 National Sunflower Association
2401 46th Avenue SE
Suite 206
Mandan, ND 58554-4829

701-328-5100
888-718-7033
FAX 701-328-5101
E-Mail: larryk@sunflowernsa.com
Home Page: www.sunflowernsa.com
Social Media: *Facebook, YouTube*

John Sandbakken, Executive Director
Tina Mittelsteadt, Business & Office Manager
Lerrene Kroh, Meeting Planner & Advertising Sales

Trade association for the sunflower industry.
20000 Members
Founded in 1981
Printed in 4 colors on glossy stock

714 National Turkey Federation
1225 New York Avenue NW
Suite 400
Washington, DC 20005

202-898-0100
FAX 202-898-0203
E-Mail: info@turkeyfed.org
Home Page: www.eatturkey.com
Social Media: *Facebook, Twitter, YouTube, Pinterest*

John Burkel, Chairman
Joel Brandenberger, President
Damon Wells, Vice President, Gov Relations
Lisa Wallenda Picard, Vice President, Sceintific Reg

(NTF) is the national Advocate for all segments of the $8 billion turkey industry, providing services and conducting activities that increase demand for its members' products. The federation also protects and enhances its members' ability

to effectively and profitably provide wholesome, high quality, nutritious turkey products.
264 Members
Founded in 1939

715 National Young Farmer Educational Association
PO Box 20326
Montgomery, AL 36120

334-546-9951
888-332-2668
FAX 334-213-0421
E-Mail: nyfea-main@nyfea.org
Home Page: www.nyfea.org
Social Media: *Facebook, Twitter, Google+*

Allen Tyler, President
Tim Kelley, President-Elect
Denise Sanner, Secretary

To promote the personal and professional growth of all people involved in agriculture.

716 Nebraska Alfalfa Dehydrators Association
8810 Craig Dr
Overland Park, KS 66212-2916

913-341-0562
800-678-9192
FAX 913-341-0564
E-Mail: wcobbkc@sbcglobal.net
Home Page: www.nebada.org

Carlton Bert, President
David Rhea, Vice President
Chris Healey, Director

Information for the processors and suppliers in the alfalfa industry.
Founded in 1941

717 North American Farm Show Council
590 Woody Hayes Drive
Columbus, OH 43210

614-292-4278
FAX 614-292-9448
E-Mail: gamble.19@osu.edu
Home Page: www.farmshowcouncil.org

Doug Wagner, President
Dennis Alford, First Vice President
Chip Blalock, Second Vice President
Chuck Gamble, Secretary-Treasurer

Members are agriculture trade show sponsors and suppliers of services to these shows. Provides members with education, communication and evaluation. Provides the best possible marketing showcase for exhibitors and related products to the farmer/rancher/producer customer.
37 Members
Founded in 1972

718 North American Millers' Association
600 Maryland Ave SW
Suite 825 W
Washington, DC 20024

202-484-2200
FAX 202-488-7416
E-Mail: generalinfo@namamillers.org
Home Page: www.namamillers.org
Social Media: *Facebook, Twitter, LinkedIn, Flickr*

Dan Dye, Chairman
James A McCarthy, President and CEO
Christopher Clark, CAE, VP, Communications & Administration
Paul B. Green, Export Consultant
Benjamin Boroughs, Dir., Reg. & Technical Affairs

Trade association representing the wheat, corn, oat and rye milling industry. NAMA members operate one hundred and seventy mills in thirty-eight states and Canada. Their aggregate production of more than one hundred and sixty

million pounds per day is approximately ninety-five percent of the industry capacity in the U.S.
45 Members
Founded in 1902

719 Northeastern Weed Science Society

P.O. Box 25
Woodstown, NJ 08098

315-209-7580
E-Mail:
northeasternweedscience@hotmail.com
Home Page: www.newss.org

Rakesh Chandran, President
Randy Prostak, Vice President
Erin Hitchner, Treasurer
Art Gover, Editor
Todd Mervosh, Public Relations

Serves the Northeastern US by bringing together those who are concerned with the knowledge of weeds and their control, cooperates with other scientific societies to promote research, education and outreach activities and publishes scientific and practical information of value concerning weed sciences and other fields.
Founded in 1946

720 Oregon Tilth

2525 SE 3rd Street
Corvallis, OR 97333

503-378-0690
877-378-0690
FAX 541-753-4924
E-Mail: organic@tilth.org
Home Page: www.tilth.org
Social Media: *Facebook, Twitter, Instagram*

Lynn Youngbar, President
Chris Schreiner, Executive Director
Susan Schechter, Secretary
Ryan Wist, Treasurer
Connie Karr, Certification Director

Oregon Tilth is a nonprofit research and education membership organization dedicated to biologicaly sound and socially equitable agriculture. Oregon Tilth offers educational events throughout the state of Oregon, and provides organic certification services to organic growers, processors and handlers internationally.
Founded in 1974

721 Organic Crop Improvement Association

1340 North Cotner Boulevard
Lincoln, NE 68505-1838

402-477-2323
FAX 402-477-4325
E-Mail: info@ocia.org
Home Page: www.ocia.org
Social Media: *Facebook, Twitter*

Jack Geiger, President
Susan Linkletter, First Vice-President
Joel Koskan, Second Vice-President
Demetria Stephens, Secretary
Jeff Kienast, Treasurer

OCIA International is a farmer owned international program of certification, which adheres to strict organic standards. It currently certifies thousands of farmers and processors in North, Central and South America and Asia. OCIA International is IFOAM accredited and adheres to the USDA ISO Guide 65, Japan Agriculture Standards and the Quebec Accreditation Council. OCIA has also been accredited from the USDA National Organic Program and Costa Rica Ministry of Agriculture.
3500 Members
Founded in 1985
Mailing list available for rent: 3500 names at $50 per M

722 Organic Seed Alliance

PO Box 772
Port Townsend, WA 98368

360-385-7192
FAX 360-385-7455
E-Mail: info@seedalliance.org
Home Page: www.seedalliance.org
Social Media: *Facebook, Twitter*

Sebastian Aguilar, President
Micaela Colley, Executive Director
Atina Diffley, Vice President
Sean Schmidt, Secretary
Zea Sonnabend, Treasurer

Supports the ethical development and stewardship of the genetic resources of agricultural seed.
Founded in 2003

723 Produce Marketing Association

Po Box 6036
Newark, DE 19714-6036

302-738-7100
FAX 302-731-2409
E-Mail: solutionctr@pma.com
Home Page: www.pma.com
Social Media: *Facebook, Twitter, YouTube, Flickr, Pinterest*

Bryan Silbermann, CEO
Tony Parassio, Chief Operating Officer
Yvonne Bull, Chief Financial Officer
Robert J Whitaker, Chief Science/Technology Officer
Margi Prueitt, Senior Vice President

The Produce Marketing Association is a not-for-profit trade association serving members who market fresh fruits, vegetables, and floral products worldwide. Its members are involved in the production, distribution, retail, and foodservice sectors of the industry.
2500 Members
Founded in 1949

724 Professional Farmers of America

1818 Market Street 31st Floor
Philadelphia, PA 19103

319-277-1278
800-772-0023
E-Mail: editors@profarmer.com
Home Page: www.agweb.com/profarmer
Social Media: *Facebook, Twitter, LinkedIn*

Chip Flory, Editor/Publisher
Julianne Johnston, Sr. Markets Editor
Meghan Pederson, Pro Farmer Reporter
Brian Grete, Senior Market Analyst
Jim Wiesemeyer, Washington Consultant

Provides farmers with marketing strategies and market-trend data, as well as seminars and home study courses.
25M Members
Founded in 1973

725 Santa Gertrudis Breeders International

PO Box 1257
Kingsville, TX 78364-1257

361-592-9357
FAX 361-592-8572
E-Mail: jford@santagertrudis.com
Home Page: santagertrudis.com/
Social Media: *Facebook*

John E Ford, Executive Director
Diana L. Ruiz, Association Services

America's First Beef Breed developed in 1918 at the famous King Ranch in Texas. Recognized in 1940 by the USDA. Famous for raid and efficient growth, solid red color, hardiness and good disposition. They are adaptable to many environments and are present throughout the US and in other countries.

726 Society of American Foresters

5400 Grosvenor Ln
Bethesda, MD 20814-2198

301-897-8720
866-897-8720
FAX 301-897-3690
E-Mail: membership@safnet.org
Home Page: www.safnet.org
Social Media: *Facebook, Twitter, LinkedIn*

Michael T Goergen Jr, Executive VP/CFO
Louise Murgia, Interim Executive Vice-President
Jorge Esguerra, Chief Financial Officer
Christopher Whited, Senior Director, Marketing
Elaine Cook, Office Manager, Marketing & Members

Provides access to information and networking opportunities to prepare members for the challenges and the changes that face natural resource professionals.
Founded in 1900

727 Society of Commercial Seed Technologists

653 Constitution Avenue NE
Washington, DC 20002

202-870-2412
FAX 607-273-1638
E-Mail: scst@seedtechnology.net
Home Page: www.seedtechnology.net
Social Media: *Facebook, Twitter*

Barbara Cleave, President
David Stimpson, Vice President
Steve Beals, Director-at-Large
DaNell Jamieson RST, RGT, Director-at-Large
Heidi Jo Larson, RST, Director-at-Large

Professionals involved in the testing and analysis of seeds, including research, production and handling based on botanical and agricultural sciences.
250 Members
Founded in 1922

728 Soil and Plant Analysis Council

347 North Shores Circle
Windsor, CO 80550

970-686-5702
FAX 402-476-0302
E-Mail: rmiller@lamar.colostate.ed
Home Page: www.spcouncil.com

Rao Mylavarapu, President
Robert Mikkelsen, Vice President International Plant
Robert Miller, Secretary/Treasurer
Rigas Karamanos, Past President

Promotes uniform soil test and plant analysis methods, use, interpretation and terminology.
250 Members
Founded in 1969

729 Southern Cotton Ginners Association

874 Cotton Gin Pl
Memphis, TN 38106-2588

901-947-3104
FAX 901-947-3103
E-Mail:
andrea.steadman@southerncottonginners.or
Home Page: www.southerncottonginners.org
Social Media: *Facebook*

Riley James, Chairman of Board
Holt Shoaf, President
Henry G. Tri Watkins, Vice President
Timothy L. Price, Executive Vice President
Andrea Steadman, Marketing Communications Specialist

Operates in a five state area as an information center covering safety and governmental regulations. Serves its members by providing safety, training and regulatory representation.

Sponsors certification programs and hosts the industry's leading trade show, The Mid-South Farm & Gin Show.
700 Members
Founded in 1967

730   Texas Agribusiness Market Research Center

600 John Kimbrough Blvd.
Suite 371 - 2124 TAMU
College Station, TX 77843

979-845-5911
FAX 979-845-6378
E-Mail: AFCER@tamu.edu
Home Page: afcerc.tamu.edu
Social Media: *Facebook, LinkedIn*

Loren Schroeder, Program Manager
Senarath Dharmasena, Assistant Professor
Robin Hanselman, Graphic Design/Data Specialist

Provide a single point to all agricultural resources on the internet. Objective is to promote agribusiness and to enhance agricultural product marketing and research.

731   The William H. Miner Agricultural Research Institute

1034 Miner Farm Road
PO Box 90
Chazy, NY 12921

518-846-7121
FAX 518-846-8445
Home Page: www.whminer.com
Social Media: *Facebook, Google+*

Dr Joseph C Burke, Chairman
Richard J. Grant, Ph.D., President
Kirk Beattie, VP/Administration
Catherine S. Ballard, Director of Research
Steve J. Fessette, Director of Physical Plant

Miner Institute conducts integrated, cutting-edge education, research, and demonstration programs that optimize the biological and economic relationships among forage-crop production, dairy and equine management, and environmental stewardship. We envision a vital agricultural community in northern New York and surrounding regions built on effective use of forage crops and management technologies that optimize animal production and well-being while sustaining the natural environment.
Founded in 1903

732   USA Dry Pea & Lentil Council

2780 W. Pullman Road
Moscow, ID 83843

208-882-3023
FAX 208-882-6406
E-Mail: pulse@pea-lentil.com
Home Page: www.pea-lentil.com

Tim D. McGreevy, CEO
Pete Klaiber, VP, Marketing
Jessie Hunter, Director of Domestic Marketing
Drex Rhoades, Director of Communications
Tayebeh Soltani, Assistant Marketing Manager

The USA Dry Pea & Lentil Council(USADPLC) is a non-profit organization to promote and protect the interests of growers, processors, warehousemen and sellers of dry peas, lentils and chickpeas in the United States.
Founded in 1965

733   USA Rice Federation

USA Rice Federation
2101 Wilson Bvld
Suite 610
Arlington, VA 22201

703-226-2300
FAX 703-236-2301
E-Mail: riceinfo@usarice.com
Home Page: www.usarice.com

Social Media: *Facebook, Twitter, LinkedIn, Pinterest, YouTube, Google+*

Johnny Broussard, Director, Legislative Affairs
Lauren Echols, Manager, Government Affairs/PAC
Reece Langley, Vice President, Government Affairs
Steve Hensley, Senior Director, Regulatory Affairs

The global advocate for all segments of the U.S. rice industry with a mission to promote and protect the interests of producers, millers, merchants and allied businesses. USA Rice is made up of the USA Rice Grower's Assoc, USA Rice Millers' Assoc, USA Rice Council, and the USA Rice Merchants' Association.

734   United Fresh Produce Association

1901 Pennsylvania Ave NW
Suite 1100
Washington, DC 20006-3412

202-303-3400
FAX 202-303-3433
E-Mail: united@unitedfresh.org
Home Page: www.unitedfresh.org
Social Media: *Facebook, Twitter, LinkedIn, YouTube*

Tom Stenzel, President/CEO
Jeff Oberman, Vice President, Trade Relations
Victoria Backer, Executive Vice President
Jessica Mosley, Director, Education
Lorelei DiSogra, Ed.D., R.D., Vice President Nutrition & Health

Equipment, supplies, cartons, packaging machinery, computers, sorting and sizing equipment, harvesting equipment, film wrap manufacturing and commodity organizations.
1000+ Members
Founded in 1904

735   United Producers

8351 N High St
Sute 250
Columbus, OH 43235-1440

614-890-6666
800-456-3276
FAX 614-890-4776
E-Mail: webmaster@uproducers.com
Home Page: www.uproducers.com
Social Media: *Facebook, LinkedIn*

Dennis Bolling, President/CEO
Joe Werstak, CFO

A cooperative marketing organization owned by farmers and ranchers in the United States' corn belt, midwest and southeast.
36000 Members
Frequency: Annual Meetings
Founded in 1962

736   United States Animal Health Association

4221 Mitchell Ave.
St Joseph, MO 64507

816-671-1144
FAX 816-671-1201
E-Mail: usaha@usaha.org
Home Page: www.usaha.org
Social Media: *Facebook, Twitter*

Dr. David Meeker, President
Dr. Bruce King, President
Barbara Determan, Second Vice President
Dr. Kristin Haas, Third Vice President
Dr. Annette Jones, Treasurer

Seeks to prevent, control and eliminate livestock diseases.
1400 Members
Founded in 1897

737   United States Canola Association

600 Pennsylvania Ave SE
Suite 320
Washington, DC 20003-6300

202-969-8113
FAX 202-969-7036
E-Mail: info@uscanola.com
Home Page: www.uscanola.com
Social Media: *Facebook, Twitter, YouTube*

John Gordley, Executive Director
Dale Thorenson, Assistant Director
Angela Dansby, Communications Director
Mary O'Donohue, Advertising Sales Representative

USCA members are producers and processors of canola and grapeseed.
Founded in 1989

738   United States Egg Marketers

4500 Hugh Howell Road
Suite 270
Tucker, GA 30084

770-360-9220
FAX 770-360-7058
E-Mail: info@unitedegg.org
Home Page: www.unitedegg.org
Social Media: *Facebook, Twitter, RSS Feed*

Chad Gregory, President & CEO
David Inall, Senior Vice President
Sherry Shedd, Vice President of Finance
Derreck Nassa, Director of Operations
Oscar Garrison, Director of Food Safety

A producer cooperative established specifically for the purpose of exporting large quantities of U.S. Shell Eggs.

739   United States Grains Council

20 F Street NW
Suite 600
Washington, DC 20001

202-789-0789
FAX 202-898-0522
E-Mail: grains@grains.org
Home Page: www.grains.org
Social Media: *Facebook, Twitter, LinkedIn, YouTube, Flickr, Pinterest*

Alan Tiemann, Chairman
Thomas Sleight, President and CEO
Debra Keller, Secretary/Treasurer
Chip Councell, Vice Chairman
Mark Seastrand, Barley Sector Director

Motivated by the grain sorghum, barley and corn producer associations and representatives of the agricultural community. Provides commodity export market development.
175 Members
Founded in 1960

740   United States Hide, Skin & Leather Association

1150 Connecticut Ave, NW
12th Floor
Washington, DC 20036

202-587-4250
E-Mail: ssothmann@meatinstitute.org
Home Page: www.ushsla.org

Jamie Zitnik, Chairman
Stephen Sothmann, President
Henry Bank, Vice Chairman
Chris Mullally, Secretary

Exclusive representative of the hides and skin industry in the United States. Members range in size from small family-owned businesses to large corporations. Participates in two annual trade shows in Asia as a cooperator through the US Department of Agriculture's Foreign Agriculture Service.
35 Members

741 Veal Quality Assurance Program & Veal Issues Management Program
7501 NW Tiffany Springs Parkway
Suite 200
Kansas City, MO 64153

717-823-6995
E-Mail: info@vealfarm.com
Home Page: www.vealfarm.com

Members include veal producers and processors.
1300 Members
Founded in 1984

742 Walnut Council
Wright Forestry Center
1007 N 725 W
West Lafayette, IN 47906-9431

765-583-3501
FAX 765-583-3512
E-Mail: walnutcouncil@walnutcouncil.org
Home Page: www.walnutcouncil.org

Jerry Van Sambeek, President
Dan Harris, VP
Liz Jackson, Executive Director
Bill Hoover, Treasurer
John Katzke, Quartermaster

A science based organization that encourages research, discussion, and application of knowledge about growing hardwood trees.
1000 Members
Founded in 1970

743 Weed Science Society of America
810 East 10th St.
Lawrence, KS 66044-7065

785-865-9250
800-627-0326
FAX 785-843-1274
E-Mail: jlancaster@allenpress.com
Home Page: www.wssa.net
Social Media: *Facebook, Twitter, LinkedIn, RSS, YouTube*

Joyce Lancaster, Executive Secretary
Beverly Lindeen, Managing Editor
John Madsen, Secretary
Ian Burkel, Treasurer

Promotes research, education and extension outreach activities related to weeds, provides science-based information to the public and policy makers; and fosters awareness of weeds and their impacts on managed and natural ecosystems.
2000 Members
Founded in 1956

744 Western Fairs Association
1776 Tribute Rd
Suite 210
Sacramento, CA 95815-4495

916-927-3100
FAX 916-927-6397
E-Mail: info@fairsnet.org
Home Page: www.fairsnet.org
Social Media: *Facebook, Twitter, YouTube, Instagram*

Troy Bowers, President
Barbara Quaid, VP
Stephen Chambers, Executive Director
Tami Davis Triggs, Accounting Manager
Jessica Boudevin, Communications Manager

A non-profit association with members throughout the Western United States and Canada that strives to promote industry standards. Membership includes access to conventions and trade shows, educational training programs as well as legislative advocacy support.
2000 Members
Founded in 1922

745 Western United States Agricultural Trade Association
4601 NE 77th Avenue
Suite 240
Vancouver, WA 98662-2697

360-693-3373
FAX 360-693-3464
E-Mail: export@wusata.org
Home Page: www.wusata.org
Social Media: *Facebook, Twitter, LinkedIn*

Andy Anderson, Executive Director
Janet Kenefsky, Deputy Director/Intl. Mark. Dir.
Tricia Walker, FundMatch Manager
Terri Curtis, Office Coordinator
Becky Rein, Executive Administrator

The Western United States Agricultural Trade Association (WUSATAr) is a non-profit trade association whose members are the thirteen western state departments of agriculture. WUSATA is administered by the USDA 's Foreign Agricultural Service (FAS) and funded through the Market Access Program (MAP) with a mission to support and assist members and agribusinesses in the thirteen Western States in developing and enhancing international markets for U.S. food and agricultural products.
Founded in 1980

Newsletters

746 AAM Newsletter
American Agriculture Movement
24800 Sage Creek Road
Scenic, SD 57780

605-993-6201
FAX 605-993-6185
E-Mail: jjobgen@hotmail.com
Home Page: www.aaminc.org

Larry Matlack, President
Arthur Chaney, Executive Vice President
John Willis, Vice President
Jim Rice, Secretary/Treasurer
John Willis, Vice President

The creation of the AAM has provided a farmer-created, farmer-built organization within which farmers themselves have been the leaders, speakers and organizers; empowering farmers as they had not been in the past, to speak for and advocate for themselves. Updates about events, news, articles and letters to the editor.
Founded in 1977
Mailing list available for rent

747 ALBC News
American Livestock Breeds Conservancy
PO Box 477
Pittsboro, NC 27312

919-542-5704
FAX 919-545-0022
Home Page: www.albc-usa.org
Social Media: *Facebook, Blogger*

Charles Bassett, Executive Director

Provides in-depth information about current ALBC activities, breed information, member updates, and more.
Frequency: Bi-Monthly

748 ARA Retailer Facts
Agricultural Retailers Association
1156 15th St Nw
Suite 500
Washington, DC 20005-1745

202-457-0825
FAX 202-457-0864
E-Mail: ara@aradc.org

Home Page: www.aradc.org
Social Media: *Facebook, Twitter, RSS Feed*

Daren Coppock, President and CEO
Richard Gupton, SVP
Donnie Taylor, VP of Membership
Gary Baise, General Counsel

The Agricultural Retailers Association advocates before Congress and the Executive Branch to ensure a profitable business environment for members.
Frequency: Daily

749 ARClight
National Agri-Marketing Association
11020 King St
Suite 205
Overland Park, KS 66210-1201

913-491-6500
FAX 913-491-6502
E-Mail: agrimktg@nama.org
Home Page: www.nama.org
Social Media: *Facebook, Twitter, LinkedIn, Flicker, You Tube*

Jennifer Pickett, CEO
Vicki Henrickson, President
Paul Redhage, Secretary/Treasurer
Matt Coniglio, Vice President

Agricultural Relations Council - a national association with members involved in agricultural public relations. Electronic newsletter of interest to association members.

750 ASA Today
American Soybean Association
12125 Woodcrest Executive
Suite 100
Saint Louis, MO 63141-5009

314-576-1770
800-688-7692
FAX 314-576-2786
E-Mail: bcallanan@soy.org
Home Page: www.soygrowers.com
Social Media: *Facebook, Twitter, RSS Feed*

Steve Censky, CEO
Cassandra Schlef, Communications Coordinator

For members only
Frequency: Weekly

751 ASAC News
American Society of Agricultural Consultants
N78W14573 Appleton Ave
#287
Menomonee Falls, WI 53051

262-253-6902
FAX 262-253-6903
E-Mail: cmerry@countryside-marketing.com
Home Page: www.agconsultants.org
Social Media: *Facebook, LinkedIn*

~the American Society of Agricultural Consultants (ASAC) is a non-profit organization oriented around raising the standards and image of professional agricultural consultants. ASAC is the only association representing the full range of agricultural consultants.
Frequency: Quarterly
Founded in 1963

752 Agri Times Northwest
PO Box 1626
Pendleton, OR 97801

541-276-6202
FAX 541-278-4778
E-Mail: editor@agritimesnw.com
Home Page: www.agritimesnw.com

Sterling Allen, Publisher
Jim Eardley, Editor
Brianna Walker, Graphics

Contains news stories and columns pertaining to rural life and agri-business, designed to keep farmers and ranchers up to date with agriculture in their backyard.
Cost: $20.00
Frequency: Bi-Monthly
Founded in 1981

753 AgriMarketing Weekly
Henderson Communications LLC
1422 Elbridge Payne Rd
Suite 250
Chesterfield, MO 63017-8544

636-728-1428
FAX 636-777-4178
E-Mail: info@agrimarketing.com
Home Page: www.agrimarketing.com

Lynn Henderson, Publisher/Editorial Director
Stephanie Wobbe, Editorial Assistant
Audrey Evans, Customer Service Manager

It includes a recap of the most important news within the industry during the prior week.
Frequency: Weekly
Circulation: 4500

754 Agricultural Law Update
American Agricultural Law Association
127 Young Rd
Kelso, WA 98626

360-200-5699
FAX 360-432-2287
E-Mail: RobertA@aglaw-assn.org
Home Page: www.aglaw-assn.org

Amy Swanson, President
Robert Achenbach, Jr., Executive Director
David K Waggoner, Director
Ruth A Moore, Director
Beth Crocker, Director

Articles written about environmental and agricultural issues.

755 Agweek
Grand Forks Herald
375 2nd Avenue N
Grand Forks, ND 58206-6008

701-780-1100
FAX 701-780-1211
E-Mail: kdeats@gfherald.com
Home Page: www.gfherald.com
Social Media: *RSS Feed*

Matthew C Cory, Managing Editor
Tom Dennis, Editorial/Opinion Page Editor
Mary Jo Hotler, Editor

Features classifieds, weather information, farming, ranch news and opinion for the Upper Midwest
Cost: $32.00
Frequency: Weekly

756 Alliance Link Newsletter
Animal Agriculture Alliance
2101 Wilson Blvd
Suite 916-B
Arlington, VA 22201

703-562-5160
FAX 703-524-1921
E-Mail: info@animalagalliance.org
Home Page: www.animalagalliance.org
Social Media: *Facebook, Twitter*

Kay Johnson, Executive VP
Sarah Hubbart, Communications Coordinator

Helps members and industry stakeholders stay informed about the key issues impacting animal agriculture
Frequency: Monthly

757 American Beekeeping Federation Newsletter
American Beekeeping Federation

3525 Piedmont Rd NE
Bldg 5 Suite 300
Atlanta, GA 30305-1509

404-760-2875
FAX 404-240-0998
E-Mail: info@abfnet.org
Home Page: www.abfnet.org

Robin D Lane, Executive Director
Grayson Daniels, Membership Coordinator
Troy Fore, Director of Government Relations

Newsletter for members of the American Beekeeping Federation.
Cost: $35.00
24 Pages
Frequency: Bi-Monthly
Circulation: 1750
Founded in 1943

758 American Feed Industry Newlsetter
American Feed Industry Association
2101 Wilson Boulevard
Suite 916
Arlington, VA 22201

703-524-0810
FAX 703-524-1921
E-Mail: afia@afia.org
Home Page: www.afia.org
Social Media: *Facebook, Twitter, LinkedIn*

Al Gunderson, Chairman of the Board
Jeff Cannon, Chair/Elect
Joel Newman, President and Treasurer
Richand Sellers, VP and Corporate Security

Newsletter published every two weeks by the American Feed Industry for members only.
Frequency: Bi-Monthly
Circulation: 700
Founded in 1909

759 Aquatic Plant News
Aquatic Plant Management Society
PO Box 821265
Vicksburg, MS 39182-1265

FAX 601-634-5502
E-Mail: dpetty@ndrsite.com
Home Page: www.apms.org
Social Media: *Facebook, LinkedIn*

Terry Goldsby, President
Mike Netherland, President-elect
Sherry Whitaker, Treasurer

Aquatic Plant News is produced 3 times each year, and is distributed primarily by email.
Frequency: 3x Yearly
Founded in 1961

760 Association of American Seed Control Officials Bulletin
Utah Department of Agriculture
350 N Redwood Road
PO Box 146500
Salt Lake City, UT 84114-6500

801-538-7100
FAX 801-538-7126
E-Mail: agriculture@utah.gov
Home Page: www.ag.utah.gov
Social Media: *Facebook, Twitter, YouTube*

Stephen T Burningham, Control Officer
Leonard Blachham, Commissioner
Jed Christenson, Marketing

Seed laws in the United States and Canada.
Frequency: Annual+
Circulation: 5000

761 CSA News
5585 Guilford Road
Madison, WI 53711-1086

608-273-8080
FAX 608-273-2021
E-Mail: headquarters@agronomy.org

Home Page: www.agronomy.org
Social Media: *Facebook, Twitter, LinkedIn*

Ellen E Bergfeld, Executive VP
Luther Smith, Executive Director
Michela Cobb, Director Financial Services
Audrey Jankowski, Analyst/Programmer
Ian Popkewitz, Director IT/Operations

The official magazine for members of the American Society of Agronomy, Crop Science Society of America, and Soil Science Society of America.
11000 Members
Founded in 1907

762 Chaff Newsletter
American Association of Grain Inspection
PO Box 26426
Kansas City, MO 64196

816-569-4020
FAX 816-221-8189
E-Mail: info@aagiwa.org
Home Page: www.aagiwa.org

Larry Kitchen, President
Mark Fulmer, VP

Welcomes member information about new products, business changes, personnel changes and other items that may be of interest to AAGIWA members.
Frequency: Monthly

763 Council for Agricultural Science and Technology Newsletter
Council For Agricultural Science and Technology
4420 Lincoln Way
Ames, IA 50014-3447

515-292-2125
FAX 515-292-4512
E-Mail: info@cast-science.org
Home Page: www.cast-science.org
Social Media: *Facebook, Twitter, LinkedIn, YouTube*

Phillip Stahlman, President
Lowell Midla, President-elect
Turner Sutton, Treasurer

Identifies food, fiber, environmental and other agricultural issues for all stake holders, including legislators, policy makers and the public.
Founded in 1972

764 Country Folks
Lee Publications
6113 State Highway 5
PO Box 121
Palatine Bridge, NY 13428

518-673-3237
800-836-2888
FAX 518-673-3245
E-Mail: info@leepub.com
Home Page: www.leepub.com
Social Media: *Facebook, Twitter*

Frederick Lee, Publisher
Scott Duffy, Sales Manager

Agricultural news from national, state and local levels. Some features on farm and agricultural industry, rural interest, etc.
75 Pages
Frequency: Weekly
Circulation: 27000
Founded in 1973

765 Country World Newspaper
Echo Publishing Company
401 Church St
Sulphur Springs, TX 75482-2681

903-885-0861
800-245-2149
FAX 903-885-8768

E-Mail: scott@ssecho.com
Home Page: www.countryworldnews.com

Scott Key, President
Kari Arnold, Editor

A newspaper offering agricultural information to farmers, ranchers, dairyfarmers, and agri-businesses.
Frequency: Weekly
Founded in 1981

766 Dair-e-news
American Dairy Science Association
1800 S. Oak Street
Suite 100
Champaign, IL 61820-6974

217-356-5146
FAX 217-398-4119
E-Mail: adsa@assochq.org
Home Page: www.adsa.org
Social Media: *Facebook*

Peter Studney, Executive Director
Cara Tharp, Executive Assistant

Timely topics and important announcements, industry calendar of events, and news of the Association.

767 DairyProfit Weekly
6437 Collamer Road
East Syracuse, NY 13057-1031

315-703-7979
800-334-1904
FAX 315-703-7988
E-Mail: dgarno@dairybusiness.com
Home Page: www.dairybusiness.com
Social Media: *Facebook, Twitter, YouTube*
Keeps readers up to date with a quick, timely summary of news, markets and trends that impact your business.
Frequency: Weekly
Founded in 1904

768 Decision Support Systems for Agrotechnology Transfer
ICASA
2440 Campus Road
PO Box 527
Honolulu, HI 96822

808-956-2713
FAX 808-956-2711
E-Mail: icasa@icasa.net
Home Page: www.icasa.net

Jeffrey White, Co-Chair
Martin Ittersum, Co-Chair
Gordon Tsuji, Secretariat

Systems analysis and crop simulation models for agrotechnology transfers and risk assessment. Reference guides and models for maize, wheat, rice, sorghum, millet, barley, soybean, peanut and potato are included. Linked to GIS software.

769 Doane's Agricultural Report
Doane Agricultural Services
77 Westport Plz
Suite 250
St Louis, MO 63146-3121

314-569-2700
866-647-0918
FAX 314-569-1083
Home Page: www.doane.com

Rich Pottorff, Chief Economist
Marty Foreman, Senior Economist
Sam Funk, Senior Economist

Provides information to US farmers and agricultural professionals. Doane keeps you up to date on factors affecting your farm program benefits and production costs too.
Frequency: Weekly

770 Farm Managers & Rural Appraisers News
Amer. Society of Farm Managers & Rural Appraisers
950 S Cherry St
Suite 508
Denver, CO 80246-2664

303-758-3513
FAX 303-758-0190
E-Mail: asfmra@asfmra.org
Home Page: www.asfmra.org
Social Media: *Facebook, Twitter, LinkedIn, Plaxo*

Paul Joerger, President
Jim Rickert, President-elect
Fred Hepler, First Vice President

Provides members and other agricultural professionals with current information relative to the industry and educational offerings.
Frequency: Bi-Monthly
Founded in 1929

771 Farm and Ranch Guide
2401 46th Avenue SE
Mandan, ND 58554

701-255-4905
FAX 701-255-2312
E-Mail: office@farmandranchguide.com
Home Page: www.farmandranchguide.com
Social Media: *Facebook, Twitter, RSS Feed*

Brian Kroshus, Group Publisher
Mark Conlon, Editor
Patrick Sitter, General Manager
Andrea Johnson, Assistant Editor

Inform and entertain while serving as a conduit between our valued advertising customers and our loyal readers
Cost: $32.95
Frequency: Bi-Monthly
Circulation: 38,000

772 Farmer's Friend
116 Main Street
Towanda, PA 18846

570-265-2151
800-253-3662
FAX 570-265-6130
E-Mail: kandrus@thedailyreview.com
Home Page: www.farmers-friend.com

Ronald W Hosie, Editor
Kelly Andrus, Managing Editor
Debbie Bump, Circulation

Farming news.
Frequency: Weekly
Founded in 1977

773 Feedstuffs
The Miller Publishing Company
5810 W. 78th St
Suite 200
Bloomington, MN 55339

952-931-0211
FAX 952-938-1832
E-Mail: smuirhead@feedstuffs.com
Home Page: www.feedstuffs.com

Sarah Muirhead, Publisher/Editor
Rod Smith, Staff Editor/Livestock & Poultry
Tim Lundeen, Staff Editor/Nutrition & Health
Jacqui Fatka, Staff Editor/Policy
Kristin Bakker, Editorial Production Manager

A newspaper for agribusiness, each week of the month focuses on a different animal species. Topics include nutrition, health, marketing issues and the popular Bottom Line of Nutrition section.
Cost: $144.00
24 Pages
Frequency: Weekly
Circulation: 16600
Founded in 1895

774 Fencepost
The Fencepost
423 Main Street
Windsor, CO 80550-5129

970-686-5691
FAX 970-686-5694
E-Mail: gloftus@thefencepost.com
Home Page: www.thefencepost.com

Gary Loftus, Publisher
Amiella Diaz, Editor
Robyn Scherer, Staff Reporter

Farming news and reports.
Cost: $39.00
Frequency: Weekly
Founded in 1980

775 Forestry Source
Society of American Foresters
5400 Grosvenor Ln
Bethesda, MD 20814-2198

301-897-8720
866-897-8720
FAX 301-897-3690
E-Mail: safweb@podi.com
Home Page: www.safnet.org
Social Media: *Facebook, Twitter, LinkedIn*

Joe Smith, Editor
Michael T Goergen, Jr., Executive Vice President
Patricia Adadevoh, Leadership Services Manager

Offers the latest information on national forestry trends, the latest developments in forestry policy at the federal, state, and local levels, the newest advances in forestry-related research and technology, and up-to-date information about SAF programs and activities
Cost: $35.00
Frequency: Monthly
Founded in 1990

776 Friday Notes
Council For Agricultural Science and Technology
4420 West Lincoln Way
Ames, IA 50014-3447

515-292-2125
FAX 515-292-4512
E-Mail: cast@cast-science.org
Home Page: www.cast-science.org

John Bonner, Executive VP/CEO
Phillip Stahlman, President
Turner Sutton, Treasurer

E-Newsletter featuring lead articles on current topics being discussed in agriculture, congressional updates, announcements of upcoming CAST publications and activities, and information about CAST's scientific society, company, and nonprofit members.
Frequency: Quarterly
Circulation: 4000
Founded in 1972

777 Global Dairy Update
DairyBusiness Communications
6437 Collamer Road
East Syracuse, NY 13057-1031

315-703-7979
800-334-1904
FAX 315-703-7988
E-Mail: dgarno@dairybusiness.com
Home Page: www.dairybusiness.com
Social Media: *Facebook, Twitter, YouTube*

Dave Natzke, Editor
Scott Smith, Chairman/Co-CEO
John Montandon, President/Co-CEO
Joel Hastings, President, Dairy Business

Focuses on dairy developments throughout the world.
Founded in 1904

778 Goats on the Move
Meat & Livestock Australia
1401 K Street NW
Suite 602
Washington, DC 20005

202-521-2551
FAX 202-521-2699
E-Mail: info@mla.com.au
Home Page: www.mla.com.au
Social Media: *Facebook, Twitter, YouTube*

Don Heatley, Chairman
David Palmer, Managing Director
Bernie Bindon, Director
Chris Hudson, Director

eNewsletter providing information on the latest
developments in MLA's goat program and the
broader Australian goatmeat industry.
Frequency: Quarterly
Founded in 1998

779 Greenhouse Product News
Scranton Gillette Communications
3030 W Salt Creek Lance
Suite 201
Arlington Heights, IL 60005-5025

847-391-1000
FAX 847-390-0408
E-Mail: bbellew@sgcmail.com
Home Page: www.gpnmag.com

Bob Bellew, VP/Group Publisher
Tim Hodson, Editorial Director
Jasmina Radjevic, Managing Editor

Features the industry's leading Buyer's Guide
directory, the PGR table and the bookstore are
just a few reasons the industry's buyers keep
coming back to GPN.
Frequency: Monthly
Mailing list available for rent: 19,000 names

780 Hay Market News
US Department of Agriculture
1400 Independence Ave., S.W.
Washington, DC 20250-0506

202-690-7650
FAX 509-457-7132
E-Mail: shessman2@kda.state.ks.us
Home Page: www.usda.gov

Tom Vilsack, Secretary
Chris Smith, Chief Information Officer
Matt Paul, Director of Communications
Ramona Romero, General Counsel

Federal newsletter offering information and up-
dates on crops and farming.
Cost: $40.00
8 Pages
Circulation: 180
Founded in 1862

781 Holstein Association News
Holstein Association
1 Holstein Place
PO Box 808
Brattleboro, VT 05302-0808

802-254-4551
800-952-5200
FAX 802-254-8251
E-Mail: info@holstein.com
Home Page: www.holsteinusa.com

John Meyer, CEO/Executive Secretary
Chuck Worden, President
Glenn E Brown, Vice President
Barbara Casna, CFO/Treasurer

Bimonthly newsletter provides active customers with information on the association programs and services and how to integrate them
into their dairy operations.
Founded in 1885

782 Holstein Pulse
Holstein Association USA Inc

1 Holstein Place
PO Box 808
Brattleboro, VT 05302-0808

802-254-4551
800-052-5200
FAX 802-254-8251
E-Mail: info@holstein.com
Home Page: www.holsteinusa.com

Chuck Worden, President
Glenn E Brown, Vice President
Barbara Casna, Treasurer

Includes information relevant to our members,
new developments in the industry, as well as
updates from the CEO and President.
Cost: $2.00
Frequency: Quarterly
Founded in 1885

783 Irrigation Association E-Newsletter
Irrigation Association
6540 Arlington Blvd
Falls Church, VA 22042-6638

703-536-7080
FAX 703-536-7019
E-Mail: info@irrigation.org
Home Page: www.irrigation.org

Deborah Hamlin, Executive Director
Noreen Rich, Foundation Manager
Kathleen Markey, Marketing Director

Published on a quarterly basis, this e-newsletter
provides updates on Foundation activities and
accomplishments.
Frequency: Monthly
Founded in 1949

784 Irrigation Association IA Times
Irrigation Association
6540 Arlington Blvd
Falls Church, VA 22042-6638

703-536-7080
FAX 703-536-7019
E-Mail: info@irrigation.org
Home Page: www.irrigation.org

Deborah Hamlin, Executive Director
Kathleen Markey, Marketing Director

Reports on federal and state policies and legislation that affect the irrigation industry. Status
updates on industry initiatives, and information
on the latest association events, programs,
services and awards.
1600 Members
Frequency: Monthly
Founded in 1949

785 Kiplinger Agricultural Letter
Kiplinger Washington Editors
1100 13th St. NW
Washington, DC 20005

202-887-6400
800-544-0155
FAX 202-778-8976
E-Mail: sub.services@kiplinger.com
Home Page: www.kiplinger.com
Social Media: *Facebook, Twitter, RSS*

Knight A Kiplinger, President, Editor-in-Chief
Ed Maixner, Editor

Forecasts and judgments on wages, income,
food packaging, processing and marketing
techniques.
Cost: $137.00
Frequency: Biweekly
Founded in 1929

786 NAMA Newsletter
North American Millers' Association
600 Maryland Ave SW
Suite 825 W
Washington, DC 20024

202-484-2200
FAX 202-488-7416

E-Mail: generalinfo@namamillers.org
Home Page: www.namamillers.org

Mary Waters, President
James Bair, Vice President
Paul B Green, Export Consultant
Sherri Lehman, Director of Government
Relations
Mary Waters, President

Trade association representing the wheat, corn,
oat and rye milling industry. NAMA members
operate one hundred and seventy mills in
thirty-eight states and Canada. Their aggregate
production of more than one hundred and sixty
million pounds per day is approximately
ninety-five percent of the industry capacity in
the U.S.
Frequency: Monthly
Circulation: 250

787 NASDA News
1156 15th St NW
Suite 1020
Washington, DC 20005-1711

202-296-9680
FAX 202-296-9686
E-Mail: nasda@nasda.org
Home Page: www.nasda.org
Social Media: *Facebook, Twitter*

Stephen Haterius, CEO
Steve Troxler, President
Chuck Ross, Vice President

Represents the state departments of agriculture
in the development, implementation and communication of sound public policy and programs which support and promote the
American agricultural industry, while protecting consumers and the environment.
Founded in 1915

788 NBA Weekly Update
National Bison Association
8690 Wolff Ct
200
Westminster, CO 80031

303-292-2833
FAX 303-845-9081
E-Mail: marilyn@bisoncentral.com
Home Page: www.bisoncentral.com

Dave Carter, Executive Director
Jim Matheson, Assistant Director
Marilyn Wentz, Bison World Editor

Mailed exclusively to all Life, Active and Allied Industry members. Contains the most up to
date information available on the bison
industry.
Frequency: Weekly

789 NCPA Newsletter
National Cottonseed Products Association
866 Willow Tree Cir
Cordova, TN 38018-6376

901-682-0800
FAX 901-682-2856
E-Mail: info@cottonseed.com
Home Page: www.cottonseed.com

Ben Morgan, Executive VP & Secretary
Sandi Stine, Treasurer

Providing members with information on legislation, administrative rulings, federal regulations and court decisions affecting their
business.
Founded in 1897

790 National Honey Report
Federal Market News Service
1400 Independence Avenue SW
STOP 0238
Washington, DC 20250

202-720-2175
FAX 202-720-0547

Home Page:
www.ams.usda.gov/mnreports/fvmhoney.pdf
Billy Cox, Director
Becky Unkenholz, Deputy Director
Joan Shaffer, Senior Public Affairs Specialist
Current honey market information and colony conditions in the United States and other countries.
16 Pages
Frequency: Monthly
Founded in 1915

791 National Onion Association Newsletter
National Onion Association
822 7th St
Suite 510
Greeley, CO 80631-3941

970-353-5895
FAX 970-353-5897
E-Mail: wmininger@onions-usa.org
Home Page: www.onions-usa.org
Social Media: *Twitter*

Mike Meyer, President
Gary Mayfield, Vice President
Kim Reddin, Director of Public & Industry
Newsletter published by and only for the National Onion Association.
Frequency: Monthly
Circulation: 600
Founded in 1913
Mailing list available for rent: 600 names

792 Nebraska Alfalfa Dehydrators Bulletin
Nebraska Alfalfa Dehydrators Association
8810 Craig Dr
Overland Park, KS 66212-2916

913-648-6800
FAX 913-648-2648
E-Mail: wcobbkc@sbcglobal.net
Home Page: www.nebada.org

Jon Montgomery, President
David Rhea, Vice President
Dallas Buck, Director
Wanda Cobb, Executive Director/Secretary
Information for the processors and suppliers in the alfalfa industry.
Frequency: Weekly
Founded in 1941

793 New England Farm Bulletin and Garden
Jacob's Meadow Inc.
PO Box 67
Townton, MA 02780

E-Mail: kimberlee@jacobsmeadow.org
Home Page: www.jacobsmeadow.org

Articles explore relevant topics; extensive farm clasifieds, doings around New England, book reviews and discount prices.

794 News of the Association of Official Seed Analysts
Association of Official Seed Analysts (AOSA)
101 East State Street
#214
Ithaca, NY 14850

607-256-3313
FAX 607-273-1638
E-Mail: aosa.office@twcny.rr.com
Home Page: www.aosaseed.com

Dan Curry, President
Michael Stahr, Vice President
Janine Maruschak, Secretary/Treasurer
News items, technical reports, rules changes for testing seeds, surveys, identification and tax news, legislative updates and updates on the Association and publications in progress.

795 No-Till Farmer
Lessiter Publications
225 Regency Court
Suite 200
Brookfield, WI 53045

262-782-4480
800-645-8455
FAX 262-782-1252
E-Mail: info@lesspub.com
Home Page: www.no-tillfarmer.com
Social Media: *Facebook, Twitter, LinkedIn, YouTube*

Frank Lessiter, Editor
Mike Lessiter, President
Darrell Bruggink, Executive Editor/Publisher
Amy Johnson, Production Manager
Management information for farmers interested in conservation tillage.
Frequency: Monthly
Circulation: 8000
Founded in 1972

796 North American Millers' Association Newsletter
600 Maryland Ave SW
Suite 825 W
Washington, DC 20024

202-484-2200
FAX 202-488-7416
E-Mail: generalinfo@namamillers.org
Home Page: www.namamillers.org

Mary Waters, President
James Bair, VP

Trade association representing the wheat, corn, oat and rye milling industry. NAMA members operate one hundred and seventy mills in thirty-eight states and Canada. Their aggregate production of more than one hundred and sixty million pounds per day is approximately ninety-five percent of the industry capacity in the U.S.
45 Members
Founded in 1902

797 Northeastern Weed Science Society Newsletter
PO Box 307
Fredericksburg, PA 17026

814-574-4067
E-Mail: northeasternweedscience@hotmail.com
Home Page: www.newss.org

Antonio DiTommaso, President
Greg Armel, Vice President
Melissa Bravo, Secretary/Treasurer
Darren Lycan, Editor
Javier Vargas, Public Relations
Serves the Northeastern US by bringing together those who are concerned with the knowledge of weeds and their control, cooperates with other scientific societies to promote research, education and outreach activities and publishes scientific and practical information of value concerning weed sciences and other fields.
Founded in 1946

798 OCIA Communicator Newletter
1340 North Cotner Boulevard
Lincoln, NE 68505-1838

402-477-2323
FAX 402-477-4325
E-Mail: info@ocia.org
Home Page: www.ocia.org

Kevin Koester, President/ First Vice President
Jack Geiger, Second Vice President
Demetria Stephens, Secretary
Terrence Sheehan, Treasurer
Amy Krasne, Secretary

A quarterly newsletter published by the Organic Crop Improvement Association International (OCIA).
Cost: $50.00
Frequency: Quarterly
Circulation: 300
Mailing list available for rent: 3500 names at $50 per M

799 Organic Report
Organic Trade Association
28 Vernon Street
Suite 413
Brattleboro, VT 05301

802-275-3800
FAX 802-275-3801
E-Mail: info@ota.com
Home Page: www.ota.com
Social Media: *Facebook, Twitter, LinkedIn*

Matthew McLean, President
Sarah Bird, Vice President
Tony Bedard, Treasurer
Kelly Shea, Secretary
Targets an audience of manufacturers, growers, retailers, importers, distributors, and consultants in the organic food and fiber industry.
Frequency: Monthly
Circulation: 2500
Founded in 1985

800 Peterson Patriot
Peterson Patriot Printers-Publishers
202 Main Street
PO Box 126
Peterson, IA 51047-0126

712-295-7711
E-Mail: patriot@iowatelecom.net

Roger Stoner, Publisher
Jane Stoner, Editor/Circulation Manager
Agricultural news.
Cost: $18.00
12 Pages
Frequency: Weekly
Circulation: 549

801 Pro Farmer
Farm Journal Media
1550 N Northwest HW
Suite 403
Park Ridge, IL 60068

215-578-8900
800-320-7992
FAX 215-568-6782
E-Mail: rmurray@farmjournal.com
Home Page: www.farmjournalmedia.com

Andy Weber, Chief Executive Officer
Steve Custer, Executive Vice President/Publishing
Jeff Pence, Division President
Chuck Roth, Senior Vice President
Mitch Rouda, President, eMedia
Farm market news, analysis and management advice.
8 Pages
Frequency: Weekly
Founded in 1973

802 SHORTLINER
Farm Equipment Manufacturers Association
1000 Executive Parkway Dr
Suite 100
St Louis, MO 63141-6369

314-878-2304
FAX 314-732-1480
E-Mail: info@farmequip.org
Home Page: www.farmequip.org
Social Media: *Twitter*

Andrew Cummings, President
Bob Atkinson, Treasurer
Marc McConnell, 1st Vice President

Mike Kloster, 2nd Vice President
Richard Kirby, Secretary

A review of news stories, press reports, and government actions affecting the industry.
Frequency: Bi-Monthly

803 Salt & Trace Mineral Newsletter
Salt Institute
700 N Fairfax Street
Suite 600
Alexandria, VA 22314-2040

703-549-4648
FAX 703-548-2194
E-Mail: info@saltinstitute.org
Home Page: www.saltinstitute.org

Lori Roman, President
Morton Satin, VP/Science & Research

Information on animal nutrition.
Frequency: Quarterly
Founded in 1914

804 Seed News
PO Box 772
Port Townsend, WA 98368

360-385-7192
FAX 360-385-7455
E-Mail: info@seedalliance.org
Home Page: www.seedalliance.org
Social Media: *Facebook, Twitter*

Sebastian Aguilar, President
Atina Diffley, Vice President
Zea Sonnabend, Treasurer

Information covering events, seminars and meetings.
Cost: $8.00
8 Pages

805 Seed Technologist Newsletter
Association of Official Seed Analysts (AOSA)
101 East State Street
#214
Ithaca, NY 14850

607-256-3313
FAX 607-273-1638
E-Mail: aosa.office@twcny.rr.com
Home Page: www.aosaseed.com

Dan Curry, President
Michael Stahr, Vice President
Janine Maruschak, Secretary/Treasurer

News items, technical reports, rules changes for testing seeds, surveys, identification and tax news, legislative updates and updates on the Association and publications in progress.
Cost: $20.00
Frequency: TriAnnual
Circulation: 500

806 Signals Newsletter
Association for Communication Excellence
ACE Headquarters
59 College Road, Taylor Hall
Durham, NH 03824

603-862-1564
FAX 603-862-1585
E-Mail: ace.info@unh.edu
Home Page: www.aceweb.org

Faith Peppers, President
Joanne Littlefield, Vice President
Elaine Edwards, Treasurer
Emily Eubanks, Professional Development Director
Jason Ellis, Research Director

The newsletter includes articles with a professional development focus; updates from special interest groups, states and regions; announcements about upcoming workshops and conferences; and write-ups about members' awards

and accomplishments, job changes and more.
Cost: $75.00
Frequency: Bimonthly

807 Smart Choices Newsletter
Communicating for America
112 E Lincoln Avenue
Fergus Falls, MN 56537

218-739-3241
80- 43- 327
FAX 218-739-3832
E-Mail: info@cabenefits.org
Home Page: www.cabenefits.org

Milt Smedsrud, CEO
Wayne Nelson, President

Filled with updates on legislative accomplishments and advocacy, articles about healthy living and first-hand accounts from those participating in CA Education Programs.
40M Members
Founded in 1972

808 Society for Laboratory Automation and Screening
100 Illinois Street
Suite 242
St. Charles, IL 60174

630-256-7527
877-990-7557
FAX 630-741-7527
E-Mail: slas@slas.org
Home Page: www.slas.org
Social Media: *Facebook, Twitter, LinkedIn, YouTube*

Greg Dummer, CEO
Mary Geismann, Manager
Carol Brady, Coordinator

Provides forums for education and information exchange to encourage the study of and advance science and technology for the drug discovery, agrochemical, biotechnology, chemical, clinical diagnostic, consumer product, energy, forensic, pharmaceutical, security and other industries.
Frequency: Bi-Monthly

809 Southern Cotton Ginners Association Newsletter
874 Cotton Gin Pl
Memphis, TN 38106-2588

901-947-3104
FAX 901-947-3103
E-Mail:
carmen.griffin@southerncottonginners.org
Home Page: www.southerncottonginners.org
Social Media: *Facebook*

George LaCour, President
Robert Royal, Vice President
Sledge Taylor, Treasurer
Timothy Price, Secretary

Operates in a five state area as an information center covering safety and governmental regulations. Serves its members by providing safety, training and regulatory representation. Sponsors certification programs and hosts the industry's leading trade show, The Mid-South Farm & Gin Show.
Founded in 1950

810 TecAGRInews
Clark Consulting International
435 Root Street
PO Box 68
Park Ridge, IL 60068-0068

847-836-5100
FAX 847-589-8889
E-Mail: warren.clark@ccimarketing.com
Home Page: www.ccimarketing.com

Warren E Clark, President & Chief Executive Officer

News on new technology in agriculture reaching large computerized family farmers.
Frequency: Weekly
Circulation: 100000+
Founded in 1988

811 The Agrarian Advocate
36355 Russell Boulevard
P.O. Box 363
Davis, CA 95617

530-756-8518
800-892-3832
FAX 530-756-7857
E-Mail: judith@fullbellyfarm.com
Home Page: www.caff.org
Social Media: *Facebook, Twitter, YouTube*

Carol Presley, Board Chair
Pete Price, Vice President
Judith Redmond, Secretary
Vicki Williams, Treasurer

Provides timely reporting on the food and farming issues
Cost: $47.95
Frequency: 3x/Year
Founded in 1978

812 The Alliance Link
Animal Agriculture Alliance
2101 Wilson Blvd
Suite 916-B
Arlington, VA 22201

703-562-5160
E-Mail: info@animalagalliance.org
Home Page: www.animalagalliance.org
Social Media: *Facebook, Twitter*

Kay Johnson, President and CEO
Emily Meredith, Communications Director

Provides information about specific animal rights organizations and their campaigns, referenced quotes by the activists themselves, as well as information to help with security at your facilities.
Frequency: Monthly

813 The Exchange
American Agricultural Economics Association
555 E Wells Street
Suite 1100
Milwaukee, WI 53202-6600

414-918-3190
FAX 414-276-3349
E-Mail: info@aaea.org
Home Page: www.aaea.org
Social Media: *Facebook*

Richard Sexton, President
Julie Caswell, President-elect

Electronic newsletter for members of AAEA. Includes association announcements, membership news, and updates from the profession.
Frequency: Bi-Monthly
Founded in 1910

814 USA Rice Daily
USA Rice Federation
2101 Wilson Blvd
Suite 610
Arlington, VA 22201

703-226-2300
FAX 703-236-2301
E-Mail: riceinfo@usarice.com
Home Page: www.usarice.com
Social Media: *Facebook, Twitter, RSS, You Tube*

Betsy Ward, President/CEO
Ann Banville, Vice President Domestic Promotion
Patricia Alderson, Vice President Member Services
Jim Guinn, Vice President International
Bob Cummings, Chief Operating Officer

The latest news on issues and activities for the U.S. rice industry.

815 Update
6060 FFA Drive
PO Box 68960
Indianapolis, IN 46268-0960

317-802-6060
888-332-2668
Home Page: www.ffa.org

Important news, information and program updates.
12 Pages
Frequency: Monthly
Circulation: 45,000
Founded in 1928

816 Vegetarian Journal
Vegetarian Resource Group
PO Box 1463
Baltimore, MD 21203

410-366-8343
FAX 410-366-8804
E-Mail: vrg@vrg.org
Home Page: www.vrg.org
Social Media: *Facebook, Twitter, RSS*

Charles Stahler, President
Jeannie McStay, Catalog Manager
Debra Wasserman, Treasurer
Keryl Cryer, Senior Editor
Sonja Helman, Coordinator

Informative articles, recipes, book reviews, notices about vegetarian events, product evaluations, where to find vegetarian products and services. All nutrition information based on scientific studies.
Frequency: Quarterly
Circulation: 15000

817 WSSA Newsletter
P.O.Box 7065
Lawrence, KS 66044-7065

785-429-9622
800-627-0629
FAX 785-843-1274
E-Mail: wssa@allenpress.com
Home Page: www.wssa.net

Rod Lym, President
Joe DiTomaso, Vice President
John Madsen, Secretary
Ian Burke, Treasurer
James Anderson, Director Publications

Promotes research, education and extension outreach activities related to weeds, provides science-based information to the public and policy makers; and fosters awarenes of weeds and their impacts on managed and natural ecosystems.
Founded in 1956

818 Webster Agricultural Letter
Webster Communications Corporation
3835 9th St N
Suite 401W
Arlington, VA 22203-5812

703-525-4512
FAX 703-852-3534
E-Mail: editor@agletter.com
Home Page: www.agletter.com

James C Webster, President
Marilyn Webster, Vice President

Agricultural politics and policy issues.
Cost: $397.00
6 Pages
Frequency: 2x Monthly
ISSN: 1073-4813
Founded in 1980
Printed in one color on matte stock

819 Weekly Livestock Reporter
PO Box 7655
Fort Worth, TX 76111-0655

817-831-3147
FAX 817-831-3117
E-Mail: service@weeklylivestock.com
Home Page: www.weeklylivestock.com

Ted Gouldy, Publisher
Phil Stoll, CEO/President
Mickey Schwarz, Circulation Manager

Offers comprehensive weekly information for cattle farmers and livestock agricultural professionals.
Cost: $18.00
Frequency: Weekly
Circulation: 10000
Founded in 1897

820 Weekly Weather and Crop Bulletin
NOAA/USDA Joint Agricultural Weather Facility
1400 Independence Ave SW
Washington, DC 20250

202-720-2791
E-Mail: jawfweb@oce.gov
Home Page: www.usda.gov

Douglas LeComte, Publisher
Annette Holmes, Secretary

Provides a vital source of information on weather, climate and agricultural developments worldwide, along with detailed charts and tables of agrometeorological information that are appropriate for the season.
Cost: $60.00
Frequency: Weekly
Circulation: 1,500
Founded in 1862

Magazines & Journals

821 AFIA Journal
American Feed Industry Association
2101 Wilson Boulevard
Suite 916
Arlington, VA 22201

703-524-0810
FAX 703-524-1921
E-Mail: afia@afia.org
Home Page: www.afia.org
Social Media: *Facebook, Twitter, LinkedIn*

Joel Newman, President
Richard Sellers, VP and Corporate Secretary
Keith Epperson, Vice President
Sarah Novak, Vice President

Variety of topics about the animal feed industry and its suppliers.
Frequency: Quarterly
Founded in 1909

822 Acreage Magazine
Heartland Communications Group
1003 Central Avenue
Fort Dodge, IA 50501

515-955-1600
800-247-2000
Home Page: www.acreagelife.com
Social Media: *Facebook*

Francis McLean, Publisher

Cultural news and features edited for rural farm producers magazine.
Cost: $5.00
40 Pages
Frequency: Monthly
Founded in 1985

823 Acres USA
5321 Industrial Oaks Boulevard
Suite 128
Austin, TX 78735

51- 8-2 44
800-355-5315
FAX 512-892-4448
E-Mail: info@acresusa.com
Home Page: www.acresusa.com
Social Media: *Facebook, Twitter, LinkedIn*

Fred C Walters, CEO/President

Commercial-scale organic/ sustainable farming news.
Cost: $27.00
Frequency: Monthly
Circulation: 19000
ISSN: 1076-4968
Founded in 1970

824 Agri Marketing Magazine
Henderson Communications LLC
1422 Elbridge Payne Rd
Suite 250
Chesterfield, MO 63017-8544

636-728-1428
FAX 636-777-4178
E-Mail: info@agrimarketing.com
Home Page: www.agrimarketing.com

Lynn Henderson, Editorial Director
Audrey Evans, Customer Service Manager
Stephanie Wobbe, Editorial Assistant
Judy Henderson, Artist

Covers the unique interests of corporate agribusiness executives, their marketing communications agencies, the agricultural media, ag trade associations and other ag-related professionals.
Circulation: 8000
Founded in 1962

825 AgriSelling Principles and Practices
Henderson Communications LLC
1422 Elbridge Payne Rd
Suite 250
Chesterfield, MO 63017-8544

636-728-1428
FAX 636-777-4178
E-Mail: info@agrimarketing.com
Home Page: www.agrimarketing.com

Lynn Henderson, Editorial Director
Audrey Evans, Customer Service Manager
Stephanie Wobbe, Editorial Assistant
Judy Henderson, Artist

This 448-page book is utilized by many major agribusiness corporations and academic institutions for training its sales and marketing staff and or students.
Founded in 1962

826 Agribusiness Fieldman
Western Agricultural Publishing Company
4969 E Clinton Way
Suite 104
Fresno, CA 93727-1549

559-252-7000
E-Mail: westag@psnw.com
Home Page: www.westagpubco.com

For the professional agricultural consultant, featuring the latest information on chemical regulation, pest control techniques and feature stories on PCA and PCO community.

827 Agrichemical Age
Farm Progress Publishers
191 S Gary Ave
Carol Stream, IL 60188-2024

630-690-5600
800-441-1410
FAX 630-462-2869

E-Mail: transf.tovm
Home Page: www.farmprogress.com

Jeffry M Lapin, President
John Vogel, Editor
Willie Vogt, Corporate Editorial Director
John Otte, Economics Editor
Dan Crummett, Executive Editor

Information for fertilizer/pesticide dealers, distributors, commercial applicators and crop consultants.

828   Agricultural Aviation
National Agricultural Aviation Association
1440 Duke Street
Alexandria, VA 22314

202-546-5722
FAX 202-546-5726
E-Mail: information@agaviation.org
Home Page: www.agaviation.org

Dana Ness, President
Rick Boardman, Vice President
Doug Davidson, Secretary
Brenda Watts, Treasurer

Official publication for legislative updates, industry trends, new products and more.
Frequency: 6x Yearly
Founded in 1978

829   Agricultural History
The Sheridan Press
MSU History Department
PO Box H
Mississippi State, MS 39762

662-268-2247
E-Mail: aimarcus@history.msstate.edu
Home Page: www.aghistorysociety.org

Claire Strom, Editor
James C Giesen, Executive Secretary
Alan I Marcus, Treasurer

Traces historical lineage of agriculture in the US.
Cost: $47.00
Frequency: Quarterly
Circulation: 900
Founded in 1924

830   Agriculture Research Magazine
Agricultural Research Service
George Washington Carver Center
5601 Sunnyside Avenue
Beltsville, MD 20705-5130

301-504-1651
FAX 301-504-1641
E-Mail: info@ars.usda.gov
Home Page: www.ars.usda.gov/ar

Robert Sowers, Editor/Circulation Manager
William Johnson, Art Director
Edward Knipling, CEO
Carol Durflinger, Secretary
Cost: $50.00
27 Pages
Frequency: Monthly
Circulation: 45000
Founded in 1954

831   Agronomy Journal
5585 Guilford Road
Madison, WI 53711-1086

608-273-8080
FAX 608-273-2021
E-Mail: headquarters@agronomy.org
Home Page: www.agronomy.org
Social Media: *Facebook, Twitter, LinkedIn*

Ellen E Bergfeld, Executive VP
Luther Smith, Executive Director
Michela Cobb, Director Financial Services
Audrey Jankowski, Analyst/Programmer
Ian Popkewitz, Director IT/Operations

Journal of agriculture and natural resource sciences. Articles convey original research in soil science, crop science, agroclimatology, agronomic modeling, production agriculture, instrumentation, and more.
Founded in 1907

832   Agweek
Grand Forks Herald
375 2nd Avenue N
Grand Forks, ND 58203

701-780-1100
800-477-6572
FAX 701-780-1123
E-Mail: onlineteam@gfherald.com
Home Page: www.agweek.com
Social Media: *RSS*

Michael Jacobs, Publisher/Editor
Tom Dennis, Editorial/Opinion Page Editor
Dawn Zimney, Circulation Director
Cory Matt, Managing Editor

Agweek features classified, weather information, farming, ranch news and opinions for the Upper Midwest.
Cost: $32.00
80 Pages
Frequency: Weekly
Circulation: 25,000
Founded in 1879
Printed in 4 colors

833   Alimentos Balanceados Para Animales
WATT Publishing Company
303 N Main Street
Rockford, IL 61101

815-966-5400
FAX 815-966-6416
E-Mail: gill@wattmm.com
Home Page: www.wattnet.com

Jim Watt, Chairman/CEO
Clayton Gill, Editorial Director
Christina Karmer, Human Resources Consultant

For feed industry professionals in Latin America.
Founded in 1994

834   American Agriculturist
Farm Progress Companies
5227 B Baltimore Park
Littlestown, PA 17340

717-359-0150
800-441-1410
FAX 717-359-0250
E-Mail: jvogel@farmprogress.com
Home Page: www.farmprogress.com

John Vogel, Editor
Willie Vogt, Corporate Editorial Director
Dan Crummett, Executive Editor

Serves Northeast producers with information to help them maximize their productivity and profitability. Each issue is packed with information, ideas, news and analysis.
Cost: $26.95
Frequency: Monthly
Founded in 1842

835   American Bee Journal
Dadant and Sons
51 S 2nd St
Hamilton, IL 62341-1397

217-847-3324
888-922-1293
FAX 217-847-3660
E-Mail: editor@americanbeejournal.com
Home Page: www.americanbeejournal.com
Social Media: *Facebook, Twitter*

Tim C Dadant, President
Marta Menn, Advertising
Dianne Behnke, Publisher
Joe Graham, Editor

Read by commercial and hobby beekeepers and entomologists.
Cost: $22.95
80 Pages
Frequency: Monthly
Circulation: 11000
ISSN: 0002-7626
Founded in 1861
Printed in 4 colors on glossy stock

836   American Christmas Tree Journal
National Christmas Tree Association
16020 Swingley Ridge Rd
Suite 300
Chesterfield, MO 63017-6030

636-449-5070
FAX 636-449-5051
E-Mail: info@realchristmastrees.org
Home Page: www.realchristmastrees.org

Cline Church Ciocci, President
DeLaine Bender, Executive Director
Becky Rasmussen, Assistant Director
Rick Dungey, PR/Marketing Director
Lauren Mangnall, Project Coordinator

Covers production and research topics, marketing advice, feature stories, legislative updates, tax and business management info, NCTA news and more
Cost: $57.00
Frequency: Quarterly
Circulation: 1500
ISSN: 0569-3845

837   American Feed Industry Association Journal
2101 Wilson Blvd
Suite 916
Arlington, VA 22201-3047

703-524-0810
FAX 703-524-1921
E-Mail: afia@afia.org
Home Page: www.afia.org
Social Media: *Facebook, Twitter, LinkedIn*

Joel Newman, President
Richard Sellers, VP/Feed Regulation & Nutrition
Keith Epperson, VP/Manufacturing & Training
Sarah Novak, VP/Membership & Public Relations
Leanna Nail, Director of Administration

Includes a variety of topics about the animal feed industry and its suppliers.
Founded in 1909

838   American Fruit Grower
Meister Media Worldwide
37733 Euclid Ave
Willoughby, OH 44094-5992

440-942-2000
800-572-7740
FAX 440-975-3447
E-Mail: info@meistermedia.com
Home Page: www.meistermedia.com

Gary Fitzgerald, Chairman and CEO
Michael Deluca, President
Donald Hohmeier, VP and CFO

Specialized production and marketing information and industry-wide support for fruit growers.
Cost: $19.95
66 Pages
Frequency: Monthly
Circulation: 14000
Founded in 1880

839   American Journal of Agricultural Economics (AJAE)
American Agricultural Economics Association

555 E Wells Street
Suite 1100
Milwaukee, WI 53202-6600

414-918-3190
FAX 414-276-3349
E-Mail: info@aaea.org
Home Page: www.aaea.org
Social Media: *Facebook*

Richard Sexton, President
Julie Caswell, President-elect

The leading journal for agricultural economics.
3000 Members
Frequency: 5x Yearly
Founded in 1910

**840   American Journal of Enology and
Viticulture**
1784 Picasso Avenue, Suite D
PO Box 1855
Davis, CA 95617-1855

530-753-3142
FAX 530-753-3318
E-Mail: society@asev.org
Home Page: www.asev.org
Social Media: *Twitter, LinkedIn*

Lyndie Boulton, Executive Director
Dan Howard, Assistant Executive Director
Leticia Chacon-Rodriguez, President
James Kennedy, First Vice President

The official journal of the American Society
for Enology and Viticulture and is the premier
journal dedicated to scientific research on
winemaking and grapegrowing.
Frequency: Quarterly
Founded in 1950

841   American Small Farm Magazine
Back 40 Group
P.O. Box 8
Hartshorn, MO 65479

573-858-3244
866-284-9844
FAX 573-858-3245
E-Mail: Publisher@SmallFarm.com
Home Page: www.smallfarm.com

Paul Berg, Editor
Herman Beck-Chenoweth, Publisher

Published for the owner/operator of farms from
5 to 300 acres. Focuses on production agricul-
ture including alternative and sustainable farm-
ing ideas and technology, case studies, small
farm lifestyle and tradition.
Cost: $18.00
Frequency: Monthly
Circulation: 62,444
ISSN: 1064-7473
Founded in 1992

842   American Vegetable Grower
Meister Media Worldwide
37733 Euclid Ave
Willoughby, OH 44094-5992

440-942-2000
800-572-7740
FAX 440-975-3447
Home Page:
www.growingproduce.com/americanvegetableg
rower/

Gary Fitzgerald, President
Rosemary Gordon, Editor
Jo Monahan, Publisher
Brian Sparks, Group Editor
Paul Rusnak, Managing Editor

American Vegetable Grower magazine provides
insight on field, greenhouse and organic pro-
duction, marketing, and new varieties and
products.
Cost: $19.95
Frequency: Monthly
Circulation: 26000
Founded in 1908

843   Animal & Dairy News
American Dairy Science Association
2441 Village Green Pl
Champaign, IL 61822-7676

217-356-5146
FAX 217-398-4119
E-Mail: adsa@assochq.org
Home Page: www.adsa.org

Donald C Beitz, President
Philld C Tongz, VP
Peter Studney, Executive Director
William R Aimutis, Treasurer
A Publication of ADSA
Founded in 1898
Mailing list available for rent

**844   Applied Economic Perspectives and
Policy (AEPP)**
American Agricultural Economics
Association
555 E Wells Street
Suite 1100
Milwaukee, WI 53202-6600

414-918-3190
FAX 414-276-3349
E-Mail: info@aaea.org
Home Page: www.aaea.org
Social Media: *Facebook*

Richard Sexton, President
Julie Caswell, President-elect

Formerly the Review of Agricultural Economics, each issue includes both featured and submitted articles.
3000 Members
Frequency: Quarterly
Founded in 1910

845   Beef Today
Farm Journal Media
1818 Market Street
31st Floor
Philadelphia, PA 19103-3654

215-578-8900
800-331-9310
FAX 215-568-6782
E-Mail: jstruyk@farmjournal.com
Home Page: www.agweb.com/livestock/beef
Social Media: *Facebook, Twitter, YouTube*

Andy Weber, Chief Executive Officer
Steve Custer, Executive Vice President
Jeff Pence, President, Electronic Media
Chuck Roth, Senior Vice President
Boyce Thompson, Editorial Director

This is the only nationwide publication that
currently serves beef producers of all
sizes-large and small. It delivers the tools cattlemen need to make sustainable and profitable
choices to transition their herd to the next generation. Topics include genetics, animal health,
business planning, pasture management, wildlife management and market analysis.
Frequency: Weekly
Founded in 1973

846   Belt Pulley
Belt Pulley Pub Company
PO Box 58
Jefferson, WI 53549-1341

920-674-9732
Home Page: www.beltpulley.com

Katie Elmore, Publisher
Jane Aumann, Managing Editor

Covers antique tractors and farm machinery of
all makes and models.
Cost: $20.00
Frequency: Monthly
Circulation: 3500
Founded in 1987

847   Better Crops International Magazine
Potash and Phosphate Institute
3500 Parkway Lane
Suite 550
Norcross, GA 30092-2844

770-447-0335
FAX 770-448-0439
E-Mail: info@ipni.net
Home Page: http://www.ipni.net/wave

Terry Roberts, President
Steve Couch, VP Administration
Gavin Sulewski, Editor

Researchers report on nutrient-related topics
for corn, wheat, groundnut, oil palm, sugarcane, rice, crop rotations, and fish ponds. The
issue concludes with a back cover commentary
explaining why support of agricultural development is the right thing to do.

848   Biodynamics Journal
PO Box 944
East Troy, WI 53120-0944

26- 6-9 92
888-516-7797
FAX 26- 6-9 92
E-Mail: info@biodynamics.com
Home Page: www.biodynamics.com
Social Media: *Facebook*

Jean-Paul Courtens, President
Janet Gamble, Secretary
Steffen Schneider, Treasurer
Robert Karp, Executive Director

Provides a thoughtful collection of original articles centered on a theme of interest to the
biodynamic community. Recent themes have
included urban agriculture, biodynamic community, earth healing, raw milk, and the
biodynamic preparations.

849   Capital Press
Press Publishing Company
1400 Broadway NE
PO Box 2048
Salem, OR 97308-2048

503-364-4431
800-882-6789
FAX 503-370-4383
E-Mail: bnipp@capitalpress.com
Home Page: www.capitalpress.com
Social Media: *Facebook, Twitter, LinkedIn,
MySpace, Stumble Upon*

Mike Forrester, President
John Perry, COO
Michael O'Brien, Publisher
Joe Beach, Editor

For the agricultural and forest community of
the Pacific Northwest.
Cost: $44.00
60 Pages
Frequency: Weekly
Circulation: 37000
Founded in 1928
Printed in 4 colors

850   Carrot Country
Columbia Publishing
8405 Ahtanum Rd
Yakima, WA 98903-9432

509-248-2452
800-900-2452
FAX 509-248-4056
E-Mail: dbrent@columbiapublications.com
Home Page: www.carrotcountry.com

Brent Clement, Editor/Publisher
Mike Stoker, Publisher

Includes information on carrot production,
grower and shipper feature stories, carrot research, new varieties, market reports, spot reports on overseas production and marketing
and other key issues and trends of interest to

US and Canadian carrot growers.
Cost: $10.00
Frequency: Quarterly
Circulation: 2500
ISSN: 1071-6653
Founded in 1993
Printed in 4 colors on glossy stock

851 Cattle Guard
Colorado Cattlemen's Agricultrual Land Trust
8833 Ralston Road
Arvada, CO 80002-2239

303-431-6422
FAX 303-431-6446
E-Mail: ccaglt@aol.com
Home Page: www.coloradocattle.org

T Wright Dickinson, President
Frank Daley, First VP
Tim Canterbury, Treasurer
Terry Frankhauser, Executive VP
Heidi Brown, Membership and Operations Manager

A full overview of information is given through this magazine for cattle farmers and breeders.
Founded in 1867

852 Cattleman
Texas & Southwestern Cattle Raisers Association
1301 W 7th St
Suite 201
Fort Worth, TX 76102-2665

817-332-7064
800-242-7820
FAX 817-332-8523
E-Mail: tscra@tscra.org
Home Page: www.texascattleraisers.org
Social Media: Facebook, Twitter

Joe Parker, President
Eldon White, Executive VP and CEO
Clay Birdwell, First VP
Pete Bonds, Second VP
Matt Brockman, Manager

Full overview of information for the cattle producer in Texas and Oklahoma.
Cost: $25.00
130 Pages
Frequency: Monthly
Circulation: 16000
Founded in 1877
Printed in 4 colors on glossy stock

853 Cereal Foods World
AACC International
3340 Pilot Knob Rd
St. Paul, MN 55121-2055

651-454-7250
FAX 651-454-0766
E-Mail: akohn@scisoc.org
Home Page: www.aaccnet.org

David H Hahn, President
Debi E Rogers, Chair of Board
Laura Hansen, Treasurer

Articles on scientific studies that focus on advances in grain based food science.
Founded in 1915

854 Choices
Agricultural & Applied Economics Association
1709 Darien Club Drive
Darien, IL 60561

630-271-1679
FAX 630-908-3384
E-Mail: Walt@farmfoundation.org
Home Page: www.choicesmagazine.org

Walter J Armbruster, Editor
James Novak, Associate Editor

Provides current coverage regarding economic implications of food, farm, resource, or rural community issues directed toward a broad audience. Publishes thematic groupings of papers and individual papers.
Frequency: Quarterly
ISSN: 0886-5558
Founded in 1910
Printed in 4 colors on glossy stock

855 Choices Magazine
American Agricultural Economics Association
555 E Wells Street
Suite 1100
Milwaukee, WI 53202-6600

414-918-3190
FAX 414-276-3349
E-Mail: info@aaea.org
Home Page: www.aaea.org
Social Media: Facebook

Richard Sexton, President
Julie Caswell, President-elect

Designed to provide current coverage regarding economic implications of food, farm, resource, or rural community issues directed toward a broad audience. Online only.
3000 Members
Frequency: Quarterly
Founded in 1910

856 Christmas Tree Lookout
Pacific Northwest Christmas Tree Association
4093 12th Street SE
PO Box 3366
Salem, OR 97302

503-364-2942
FAX 503-581-6819
E-Mail: info@christmas-tree.com
Home Page: www.nwtrees.com

Bruce Wiseman, President
John Tillman, VP- Washington
Jan Hupp, Secretary/Treasurer
Mike Ramsby, V.P. Oregon
Bryan Ostlund, Executive Director

Marketing research and industry information for Christmas tree growers. Mailing list available.
Cost: $25.00
80 Pages
Frequency: Quarterly
Circulation: 1500
Founded in 1955
Printed in 4 colors on glossy stock

857 Christmas Trees
Tree Publishers
PO Box 107
Lecompton, KS 66050-0107

785-887-6324
E-Mail: ctreesmag@gmail.com
Home Page: www.christmastreesmagazine.com
Social Media: Facebook, Twitter

Catherine Howard,
Publisher/Editor/Advertising

Magazine of plantation management for Christmas tree growers, shearing, shaping and marketing. Accepts advertising.
Cost: $16.00
44 Pages
Frequency: Quarterly
Circulation: 3200
ISSN: 0149-0217
Founded in 1973
Printed in 4 colors on glossy stock

858 Citrus & Vegetable Magazine
Vance Publishing
400 Knightsbridge Pkwy
Lincolnshire, IL 60069

847-634-2600
FAX 847-634-4379
E-Mail: info@vancepublishing.com
Home Page: www.vancepublishing.com

Shawn Etheridge, VP and Publishing Director
Matthew Morgan, Director
Greg Johnson, Editorial Director
Vicky Boyd, Editor

Devlivers profitable production and management strategies to commercial citrus and vegetable growers in Florida.
Cost: $45.00
Frequency: Monthly
Circulation: 12000
Founded in 1937
Printed in 4 colors on glossy stock

859 Citrus Industry
Southeast AgNet Publications
5053 NW Hwy 225-A
Ocala, FL 34482

352-671-1909
FAX 888-943-2224
E-Mail: office@southeastagent.com
Home Page: www.citrusindustry.net

William Cooper, President
Robin Loftin, Vice President
Ernie Neff, Editor

News, facts and data of interest to citrus growers, processors and shippers.
Cost: $24.00
64 Pages
Frequency: 6 issues per year
Circulation: 9900
Founded in 1920
Printed in 4 colors on glossy stock

860 Cotton Farming
One Grower Publishing, LLC
Collierville, TN 38117-5710

901-853-5067
FAX 901-853-2197
E-Mail: lguthrie@onegrower.com
Home Page: www.cottonfarming.com
Social Media: Twitter, RSS, Flickr

Mike Rolfs, President
Lia Guthrie, Publisher
Tommy Horton, Editor
Carroll Smith, Senior Writer
Debbie Gibbs, Sales Manager

For commercial cotton growers across the United States Cotton Belt.
52 Pages
Frequency: Monthly
Circulation: 36300
Founded in 1993
Printed in 4 colors on glossy stock

861 Country Living
Arens Publications
395 S High Street
Covington, OH 45318-0069

937-473-2028
FAX 937-473-2500
E-Mail: garyg@arenspub.com
Home Page: www.arenspub.com

Gary Godfrey, Owner
Connie Didier, Manager
Don Selanders, Sales Manager

Current news and features devoted to the agricultural industry.
Cost: $13.95
Frequency: Monthly
Circulation: 17000
Founded in 1954

862 Country Woman
Reiman Publications
5400 S 60th St
Greendale, WI 53129-1404

414-423-0100
888-861-1264
FAX 414-423-1143

E-Mail: editors@countrywomenmagazine.com
Home Page: www.reimanpub.com
Social Media: *Facebook, Twitter*

Barbara Newton, President
Marylin Kruse, Editor
Lisa Karpinski, Director/Marketing
Reese Ludewig, Marketing Manager

Offers recipes, stories, profiles and articles pertaining to the country woman.
Cost: $14.98
68 Pages
Frequency: 6 issues in a year
Circulation: 50,000 +
Founded in 1970

863 Countryside and Small Stock Journal
Countryside Publications
145 Industrial Dr
Medford, WI 54451-1711

715-785-7979
800-551-5691
FAX 715-785-7414
E-Mail: customerservice@countrysidemag.com
Home Page: www.countrysidemag.com

Mike Campbell, Publisher
Anne-Marie Belanger, Managing Editor
Elen Grunseth, Circulation & Fulfillment

Offers information for homesteaders seeking a self-reliant lifestyle.
Cost: $18.00
132 Pages
Circulation: 115000
ISSN: 8750-7595
Founded in 1917
Printed in on newsprint stock

864 County Agents
National Association of County Agricultural Agents
6584 W Duroc Road
Maroa, IL 61756

217-794-3700
FAX 217-794-5901
E-Mail: exec-dir@nacaa.com
Home Page: www.nacaa.com
Social Media: *Facebook, Twitter*

Paul Craig, President
Henry Dorough, President-elect
Mike Hogan, Vice President
Richard Fetcher, Secretary
Parman Green, Treasurer

Members receive professional improvement, news of association activities, shared education efforts from other states and reports from NACAA leadership and member states.
Cost: $10.00
Frequency: Quarterly
Circulation: 5000
Founded in 1916
Mailing list available for rent: 3850 names at $125 per M
Printed in 4 colors on matte stock

865 Cranberries Magazine
Cranberries Magazine
PO Box 190
Rochester, MA 02770

508-763-8080
FAX 508-763-4141
E-Mail: cranberries@comcast.net

Carolyn Gilmore, Editor/Publisher

Containing up-to-date news, technical articles, new product information, grower profiles, economic data and other related features regarding the cranberry industry. Accepts advertising.
Cost: $25.00
28 Pages
Frequency: Monthly
Circulation: 850
Founded in 1936

866 Crop Insurance Today
National Crop Insurance Services
8900 Indian Creek Pkwy
Suite 600
Overland Park, KS 66210-1567

913-685-2767
FAX 913-685-3080
E-Mail: webmaster@ag-risk.org
Home Page: www.ag-risk.org

Thomas Zacharias, President

A quarterly magazine published by the National Crop Insurance Services. Includes current rate information, tips and advice, industry news, forecasts, and resources.
Cost: $13.00
Frequency: Quarterly
Circulation: 18000
Founded in 1915
Printed in 4 colors on glossy stock

867 Crop Science
Crop Science Society of America
5585 Guilford Road
Madison, WI 53711-5801

608-273-8080
FAX 608-273-2021
E-Mail: headquarters@crops.org
Home Page: www.crops.org
Social Media: *Facebook, Twitter, LinkedIn*

Ellen Bergfeld, CEO
Wes Meixelsperger, CFO

Publishes original research in crop breeding and genetics, crop physiology and metabolism, crop ecology, production and management, and much more.
Founded in 1955

868 DVM Magazine
Advanstar Communications
8033 Flint St
Lenexa, KS 66214-3335

913-492-4300
800-225-6864
FAX 913-871-3808
E-Mail: dverdon@advanstar.com
Home Page: www.dvm360.com
Social Media: *Facebook, Twitter*

Margaret Rampey, Editor
Marnette Falley, Principal
Sabrina Wilcox, COO
Dot Theisen, Sales Manager
Mindy Valcarcel, Senior Editor

The leading news in veterinary medicine covering news, features, practice management and new products and services.
Cost: $48.00
Frequency: Monthly
Circulation: 20000+
ISSN: 0012-7337
Founded in 1992

869 Dairy Herd Management
Vance Publishing
400 Knightsbridge Parkway
Lincolnshire, IL 60069

847-634-2600
FAX 847-634-4379
E-Mail: info@vancepublishing.com
Home Page: www.vancepublishing.com

Tom Quaife, Editor/Associate Publisher
Matthew Morgan, Director

Helps top dairy producers prepare for and adapt to the different management skills needed in this increasingly evolving industry
Cost: $60.00
Frequency: Monthly
Circulation: 61638

870 Dairy Today
Farm Journal

30 S 15th Street
Suite 900
Philadelphia, PA 19102-4803

215-578-8900
800-320-7992
E-Mail: dcrisafulli@farmjournal.com
Home Page: www.farmjournal.com
Social Media: *Facebook, Twitter, RSS, You Tube*

Charlene Finck, Editor
Katie Humphreys, Managing Editor
Beth Snyder, Art Director
Sara Schafer, Business & Crops Online Editor

Award-winning editorial covers the broad spectrum of production, nutrition and marketing information. It serves dairy producers who milk 40+ cows or are members of the Dairy Herd Improvement Association.
Frequency: Monthly
Circulation: 125000
Founded in 1989

871 Dealer & Applicator
Vance Publishing
400 Knightsbridge Pkwy
Lincolnshire, IL 60069-3628

847-634-2600
FAX 847-634-4379
Home Page: www.vancepublishing.com

Peggy Walker, President
Dean Horowitz, VP eMedia & Marketing
Steve Reiss, VP Salon & Woodworking
William C. Vance, CEO
Shawn Etheridge, VP Produce & Raw Crop

Serves as the reader's business partner to provide full-service dealers and custom applicators with management and business strategies to increase profitability.
Founded in 1937

872 Drovers
Vance Publishing
400 Knightsbridge Parkway
Lincolnshire, IL 60069

847-634-2600
FAX 847-634-4379
E-Mail: info@vancepublishing.com
Home Page: www.vancepublishing.com

William C Vance, Chairman
Peggy Walker, President

Recognized as the beef industry leader for more than 130 years, valued for its management, production and marketing information.
Cost: $60.00
Frequency: Monthly
Circulation: 92000
Founded in 1873

873 Eastern DairyBusiness
DairyBusiness Communications
6437 Collamer Road
East Syracuse, NY 13057-1031

315-703-7979
800-334-1904
FAX 315-703-7988
E-Mail: kjentz@dairybusiness.com
Home Page: www.dairybusiness.com
Social Media: *Facebook, Twitter, YouTube*

Joel P Hastings, President
John Montandon, President & Co-CEO
Scott A Smith, Chairman / Co-CEO

Reports on milk production and prices, quotes on hay and feed markets, animal health and nutrition, and the newest innovations in dairying technology, specifically tailored to the Eastern parts of the United States
Cost: $49.95
67 Pages
Frequency: Monthly
Circulation: 14000
ISSN: 1528-4360

874 Egg Industry
WATT Publishing Company
303 N Main Street
Suite 500
Rockford, IL 61101

815-966-5400
FAX 815-966-6416
E-Mail: tokeefe@wattnet.net
Home Page: www.wattnet.com

James Watt, Chairman/CEO
Greg Watt, President/COO
Terrance O'Keefe, Editor

Regarded as the standard for information on current issues, trends, production practices, processing, personalities and emerging technology. A pivotal source of news, data and information for decision-makers in the buying centers of companies producing eggs and further-processed products.
Cost: $36.00
Frequency: Monthly
Circulation: 2500

875 Executive Guide to World Poultry Trends
WATT Publishing Company
303 N Main Street
Suite 500
Rockford, IL 61101

815-966-5400
FAX 815-966-6416
Home Page: www.wattnet.com

James Watt, Chairman/CEO
Greg Watt, President/COO
Jeff Swanson, Publishing Director

Offers detailed analysis on a country-by-country and market-by-market basis.

876 FFA New Horizons
National FFA Organization
6060 FFA Drive
P.O. Box 68960
Indianapolis, IN 46268

317-802-6060
800-772-0939
FAX 317-802-6051
E-Mail: newhorizons@ffa.org
Home Page: www.ffanewhorizons.org
Social Media: *Facebook, Twitter*

Jessy Yancey, Association Editor
Christina Carden, Associate Production Director
Julie Woodard, FFA Publications Manager

The official member magazine of the FFA contains information about agricultural education, career possibilities, chapter and individual accomplishments and news on FFA. Now available online.
100 Pages
Frequency: Bi-Monthly
Circulation: 525000
ISSN: 1069-806x
Founded in 1928
Printed in 4 colors

877 FRONTIER
Meat & Livestock Australia
1401 K Street NW
Suite 602
Washington, DC 20005

202-521-2551
FAX 202-521-2699
E-Mail: info@mla.com.au
Home Page: www.mla.com.au
Social Media: *Facebook, Twitter, YouTube*

Don Heatley, Chairman
David Palmer, Managing Director

Bernie Bindon, Director
Chris Hudson, Director

Offers northern beef producers practical information on how to best manage their cattle enterprise and improve on-property profits and sustainability.
30000 Members
Frequency: Quarterly
Founded in 1998

878 Farm Chemicals International
Meister Media Worldwide
65 Germantown Ct.
Suite 202
Cordova, TN 38018

901-756-8822
800-572-7740
E-Mail: fci.circ@meistermedia.com
Home Page:
www.farmchemicalsinternational.com
Social Media: *Facebook, Twitter, RSS*

William Miller II, President
Rosemary Gordon, Editor
Robert White, COO
Roger Hercl, CFO
Richard Meister, Director

Information on production, marketing and application of crop protection chemicals and fertilizers.
Circulation: 8000
Founded in 1986

879 Farm Equipment
Cygnus Publishing
1233 Janesville Avenue
PO Box 803
Fort Atkinson, WI 53538-0803

920-000-1111
800-547-7377
FAX 920-563-1699
E-Mail: editor@cpasn.com
Home Page: www.cygnus.com

John French, Chief Executive Officer
Paul Bonaiuto, Chief Financial Officer
Kathy Scott, Director of Public Relations
Ed Wood, Vice President, Human Resources
Kris Flitcroft, Executive Vice President

An industry-wide information and product news curriculum for farm equipment dealers that enhances their knowledge of business management principles.
Cost: $48.00
Frequency: Monthly
Circulation: 10000
Founded in 1937
Printed in 4 colors on glossy stock

880 Farm Equipment Guide
Heartland Communications
1003 Central Avenue
PO Box 1115
Fort Dodge, IA 50501-1115

515-955-1600
800-247-2000
FAX 515-574-2182
E-Mail: dustin@agdeal.com
Home Page: www.farmershotline.com
Social Media: *Facebook, Twitter*

Sandra J Simonson, Group Publisher
Tracy Roper, Production Manager
Tammy Sweeney, Operational Manager
Dustin Hector, Sales Manager
Chet Frahm, Advertising Sales Associate

A subscription that includes an annual blue book of specifications, serial numbers and average pricing on farm machinery with monthly updates that list thousands of pieces for sale and thousands of actual auction values.
120 Pages
Frequency: Monthly
Circulation: 20,000
ISSN: 1047-725X

Founded in 1981
Printed in 4 colors on glossy stock

881 Farm Impact
314 E Church Street
Mascoutah, IL 62258-2100

618-566-8282
FAX 618-566-8283

Greg Hoskins, Publisher
Michael King, Advertising Manager

Offers information to farmers.
Frequency: Monthly

882 Farm Journal
30 S 15th Street
Suite 900
Philadelphia, PA 19102-4803

215-557-8900
800-523-1538
FAX 215-568-4436
E-Mail: scuster@farmjournal.com
Home Page: www.farmjournalmedia.com

Andrew J Weber Jr, CEO/President
Crain Freiberg, Editor
Steve Custer, President/Publishing
Chuck Roth, Senior Vice President/Project Dev

Published for operators and owners of commercial farms and ranches. Provides timely, useful marketing and management information to help them produce more efficiently, buy more wisely, sell their products at the highest possible prices, and retain as much of their income as possible.
Cost: $24.75
182 Pages
Frequency: Monthly
Circulation: 440,000
Founded in 1878

883 Farm Reporter
Meridian Star
814 22nd Avenue
PO Box 1591
Meridian, MS 39302

601-693-1551
FAX 601-485-1210
Home Page: www.meridianstar.com
Social Media: *Facebook, Twitter*

Michael Stewart, Executive Editor
Steve Gillespie, Assistant Editor
Ida Brown, Staff Writer
Briand Livingston, Staff Writer
Otha Barham, Outdoors Page

Reports on every phase of farming including timber, cattle, poultry and all growing crops.
Cost: $2.00
Frequency: Monthly

884 Farm Review
Lewis Publishing Company
PO Box 153
Lynden, WA 98264-0153

360-354-4444
FAX 360-354-4445
E-Mail: tribune@lyndentribune.com
Home Page: www.lyndentribune.com

Michael D Lewis, Publisher
Calvin Bratt, Editor
Diane Partlow, Circulation Manager

Offers a review of farming techniques and trends nationwide.
Cost: $30.00
Frequency: Quarterly
Circulation: 7000
Founded in 1888

885 Farm Show Magazine
Farm Show Publishing

Johnson Building
PO Box 1029
Lakeville, MN 55044-1029

952-469-5572
800-834-9665
FAX 952-469-5579
Home Page: www.farmshow.com/
Social Media: *Facebook*

Mark Newhall, Editor/Publisher
Bill Gergen, Associate Editor

Focuses on latest agricultural products, and
product evaluation. Contains no advertising.
Cost: $17.95
Founded in 1977

886 Farm Talk
Farm Talk
1801 S Highway 59
PO Box 601
Parsons, KS 67357-4900

620-421-9450
800-356-8255
FAX 620-421-9473
E-Mail: farmtalk@terraworld.net
Home Page: www.farmtalknewspaper.com

Mark Parker, Publisher
Ted Gum, Manager

Agriculture for Eastern Kansas, Western Mis-
souri, Northeast Oklahoma and Northwest Ar-
kansas.
Cost: $30.00
60 Pages
Frequency: Weekly
Circulation: 10000
Founded in 1974

887 Farm World (Farm Week)
Mayhill Publications
27 N Jefferson Street
PO Box 90
Knightstown, IN 46148-1242

317-326-2235
800-876-5133
FAX 765-345-3398
E-Mail: webmaster@mayhill-publications.com
Home Page: www.mayhill-publications.com/

Dave Blower Jr, Editor
Richard Lewis, Publisher
Diana Scott, Marketing Manager

Agriculture, farming, and related areas in Indiana, Ohio and Kentucky. Accepts advertising.
Cost: $28.50
84 Pages
Frequency: Monthly

888 Farm and Dairy
Lyle Printing and Publishing Company
185 E State Street
PO Box 38
Salem, OH 44460

330-337-3419
800-837-3419
FAX 330-337-9550
E-Mail: farmanddairy@aol.com
Home Page: www.farmanddairy.com

Scot Darling, Chief Executive Officer,
Publisher
Susan Crowell, Editor
Billy Sekely, Advertising Manager
Howard Marsh, Circulation Manager

Briefs of research reports from experiment stations in agriculture, success stories concerning
farmers of Ohio, Pennsylvania and West Virginia, sale and livestock market reports, auctions and more. Accepts advertising.
Cost: $ 28.00
132 Pages
Circulation: 33500
ISSN: 0014-7826
Founded in 1914
Printed in 4 colors on n stock

889 Farm and Ranch Living
Reiman Publications
5400 S 60th St
Greendale, WI 53129-1404

414-423-0100
888-858-5417
FAX 414-423-1143
E-Mail: editors@farmandranchliving.com
Home Page: www.reimanpub.com

Barbara Newton, President
Catherine Cassidy, SVP/Editor-in-Chief
Ann Kaiser, Editor
Lisa Karpinski, Marketing & Circulation
Manager
Gretchen Trautman, Membership Director

Includes stories written by working farm families, antique tractor events and rural photo contests.
Cost: $3.99
68 Pages
Frequency: Bimonthly
Founded in 1978

890 FarmWorld
DMG World Media
27 N Jefferson Street
PO Box 90
Knightstown, IN 46148-1242

765-345-5133
800-876-5133
FAX 765-345-5133
E-Mail: webmaster@farmworldonline.com
Home Page: www.farmworldonline.com

Tony Gregory, Publisher
David Blower Jr, Editor
Meggie Foster, Assistant Editor
Toni Hodson, Advertising Manager

Agriculture, farming, and related areas in Indi-
ana, Ohio and Kentucky. Accepts advertising.
Cost: $38.95
84 Pages
Frequency: Weekly
Founded in 1955
Printed in 4 colors on newsprint stock

891 Farmers Digest
Heartland Communications
1003 Central Avenue
PO Box 1115
Fort Dodge, IA 50501-1115

515-955-1600
800-247-2000
FAX 515-574-2182
E-Mail: fd@farmersdigest.com
Home Page: www.agdeal.com

Sandra J Simonsoa, Group Publisher
Melanie Filloon, Subscription Coordinator

Straightforwarded, commonsense articles on
every aspect of farming and ranching edited
with one goal in mind - to make you a better
farmer or rancher.
Founded in 1941

892 Farmers Hot Line
Heartland Communications
1003 Central Avenue
Fort Dodge, IA 50501-1052

515-955-1600
800-247-2000
FAX 515-955-1668
E-Mail: dustin@agdeal.com
Home Page: www.agdeal.com
Social Media: *Facebook, Twitter*

Gale W McKinney II, President/CFO
Mary Gonnerman, Vice President
Sandy Simonson, Publisher
Dustin Hector, Sales Manager
Chet Frahm, Advertising Sales Associate

Distributed to manufacturers, farmers, auctioneers and service companies nationwide. De-

signed to help buyers and sellers of new and
used farm machinery, auctions, farm real estate,
services and supplies.
Cost: $9.95
Circulation: 50000
Founded in 1988

893 Farmers' Advance
Camden Publications
331 E Bell Street
PO Box 130
Camden, MI 49232

517-368-0365
800-222-6336
FAX 517-368-5131
E-Mail: transfer@ca.homecomm.net
Home Page: www.farmersadvance.com/
Social Media: *Facebook*

Don Lee, Circulation Manager
Richard Aginian, President
Ken Ungar, Senior Vice President
Kyle Hupfer, Director

Farming technology magazine.
Cost: $25.00
Frequency: Weekly
Circulation: 20000
Founded in 1898

894 Farmers' Exchange
Exchange
PO Box 490
Fayetteville, TN 37334

931-433-9737
FAX 931-433-0053
E-Mail: exchange@vallnet.com
Home Page: www.fexonline.com

William Thomas, Publisher/Editor/CEO
Jim Bowers, Sales/Marketing Manager

Magazine offers a forum for the exchange of
farming ideas and information country-wide.
56 Pages
Frequency: Monthly
Circulation: 30000
Founded in 1987

895 Farmshine
Dieter Krieg
State and Main Streets
PO Box 219
Brownstown, PA 17508

717-656-8050
866-724-6455
FAX 717-656-8188
E-Mail: advertise@farmshine.com
Home Page: www.farmshine.com

Dieter Krieg, Publisher/Editor
Tammy Krieg, Ad Sales

Information pertaining to the farming commu-
nity.
Cost: $12.00
Frequency: Weekly
ISSN: 0745-7553
Founded in 1979
Printed in on newsprint stock

896 Fastline Productions
Fastline Publications
4900 Fox Run Road
PO Box 248
Buckner, KY 40010

502-222-0146
800-626-6409
FAX 502-222-0615
Home Page: www.fastline.com
Social Media: *Facebook, Twitter, YouTube,
Flickr*

William G Howard, President/Editor
Gail Olzewski, Owner
Clifford Wolfe, CIO
Melanie Combs, Vice President
Crysten Minzenberger, Marketing Manager

Nationwide and regional picture buying guides for the farming industry.
Cost: $12.00
Frequency: Monthly
Founded in 1978

897 Feed & Grain
Cygnus Business Media
1233 Janesville Ave
Fort Atkinson, WI 53538

631-845-2700
800-547-7377
E-Mail: info@cygnus.com
Home Page: www.cygnusb2b.com

John French, CEO
Paul Bonaiuto, CFO
Edward Wood, Vice President, HR & Communications

Provides techniques and solutions on ways yo increase productivity and profitability for the commercial feed, grain and allied processing industry.
Frequency: Bi-Monthly
Circulation: 16,500

898 Feed Additive Compendium
The Miller Publishing Company
5810 W 78th St
Suite 200
Bloomington, MN 55439

952-931-0211
FAX 952-938-1832
E-Mail: smuirhead@feedstuffs.com
Home Page: www.feedstuffs.com

Sarah Muirhead, Publisher
Rod Smith, Staff Editor/Livestock & Poultry
Sally Schuff, Staff Editor/Washington Bureau
Jacqui Fatka, Staff Editor/Grains & Ingredients
Kristin Baker, Editorial Production Manager

This magazine takes a closer look at the food additives and agriculture industries.
Cost: $260.00
Frequency: Weekly
Founded in 1935

899 Feed International
WATT Publishing Company
303 N Main Street
Suite 500
Rockford, IL 61101

815-966-5400
FAX 815-966-6416
E-Mail: kjennison@wattnet.net
Home Page: www.wattnet.com

James Watt, Chairman/CEO
Greg Watt, President/COO
Ken Jennison, Editor

Provides feed formulators and manufacturers outside North America with the latest feed and grain market developments, management strategies, and information on nutrition and regulations to efficiently and safely formulate, process and market animal feeds and become more competitive in the world market.
Cost: $48.00
Frequency: Monthly
Circulation: 19191
ISSN: 9274-5771
Founded in 1980
Mailing list available for rent: 19,191 names at $225 per M
Printed in 4 colors

900 Feed Management
WATT Publishing Company
303 N Main Street
Suite 500
Rockford, IL 61101

815-966-5400
FAX 815-966-6416

E-Mail: kjennison@wattnet.net
Home Page: www.wattnet.com

Jim Watt, Chairman/CEO
Greg Watt, President/COO
Ken Jennison, Editor

Covers the latest news in feed production, nutritional developments and trends, food safety and regulatory developments, grain markets, management strategies and new products.
Cost: $48.00
Circulation: 20,250
ISSN: 0014-956X
Founded in 1950
Mailing list available for rent: 20,249 names at $155 per M
Printed in 4 colors on glossy stock

901 Flue Cured Tobacco Farmer
Tabacco Farmer.Com
3101 Poplarwood Court
Suite 115
Raleigh, NC 27604

91- 8-2 47
FAX 919-876-6531
E-Mail: publisher@tobaccofarmer.com
Home Page: www.tobaccofarmer.com

Dayton Matlick, Chairman
Taco Tuinstra, Editor in Chief
Noel Morris, Publisher

Business of farming publication for commercial tobacco producers. Feature articles deal with the research-backed production, harvesting and marketing aspects of the flue cured tobacco.
Cost: $25.00
Circulation: 14000
ISSN: 0015-4512
Founded in 1964
Printed in 4 colors on glossy stock

902 Food Aid Needs Assessment
US Department of Agriculture
1400 Independence Avenue SW
Washington, DC 20250

202-690-7650
800-999-6779
FAX 202-720-2030
Home Page: www.usda.gov
Social Media: *Facebook, Twitter, LinkedIn, YouTube, Flickr*

Gene Mathia, Branch Chief

This annual report assesses the food situation in 60 developing countries. Most of the data are presented by region; crisis countries are covered individually.
Cost: $30.00
Founded in 1862

903 Forest Science
5400 Grosvenor Ln
Bethesda, MD 20814-2198

301-897-8720
866-897-8720
FAX 301-897-3690
E-Mail: safweb@podi.com
Home Page: www.safnet.org
Social Media: *Facebook, Twitter, LinkedIn*

Michael T Goergen Jr, Executive VP/CFO
Brittany Brumby, Assistant to the CEO/Council
Amy Ziadi, Information Technology Manager
Larry D Burner CPA, Sr. Director Finance

Provides access to information and networking opportunities to prepare members for the challenges and the changes that face natural resource professionals.
Founded in 1900

904 Fresh Cut Magazine
Great American Publishing

75 Applewood Drive, Suite A
PO Box 128
Sparta, MI 49345

616-887-9008
FAX 616-887-2666
E-Mail: fcedit@freshcut.com
Home Page: www.freshcut.com

Matt McCallum, Publisher
Kimberly Baker, Director of Media Services
Beecky Bosserd, Circulation Manager
Lee Dean, Editorial Director

Covers all sectors of the international value-added produce industry. Features industry profiles, research reports, governmental legislation coverage, industry columnists, news reports, new equipment showcases and much more.
Cost: $15.00
40 Pages
Frequency: Monthly
ISSN: 1072-2831
Founded in 1993
Printed in 4 colors on glossy stock

905 Fresh Digest
Fresh Produce & Floral Council
16700 Valley View Ave
Suite 130
La Mirada, CA 90638-5844

714-739-0177
FAX 714-739-0226
E-Mail: info@fpfc.org
Home Page: www.fpfc.org

Carissa Mace, President
Pauleen Yoshikane, Director of Operations

Addresses issues concerning the Western US, with heavy emphasis on the important California market, read by thousands of professionals in the produce and floral industries.
600+ Members
Founded in 1965

906 Fruit Country
Clintron Publishing
PO Box 547
Yakima, WA 98907-0547

509-248-2452
800-869-7923
FAX 509-248-4056

Clintke Withers, Publisher
John M Dahlin, Editor

Written for and about growers, their operations and their needs. Stories on growers and shippers, developments and trends in the fruit industry, human interest stories and politics, new products, chemicals and supplies, avant garde management techniques, cultural practices and tips on profitability. Advertising equipment and services to the fruit industry and distribution system.
Cost: $12.00
Frequency: Monthly
Circulation: 11,500

907 Futures Magazine
Futures Magazine
111 W Jackson Blvd
7th Floor
Chicago, IL 60604-4139

312-977-0999
FAX 312-846-4638
Home Page: www.aip.com

Steve Lown, Manager
James T Holter, Editor

Agriculture commodities charted by various technical studies, plus analysis.
Cost: $39.00
24 Pages
Frequency: Monthly
Founded in 1972

908 Game Bird Breeders, Agiculturists, Zoologists and Conservationists
Game Bird Breeders
1155 W 4700 S
Salt Lake City, UT 84123
George Allen, Editor

Articles on how to keep and breed all types of game birds.
Cost: $18.00
45 Pages
Frequency: Monthly
Founded in 1974

909 Glimpsing Kentucky's Forgotten Heroes: Profiles & Lessons from an American
Agribusiness Council
PO Box 5565
Washington, DC 20016

202-296-4563
FAX 202-887-9178
E-Mail: info@agribusinesscouncil.org
Home Page: www.agribusinesscouncil.org
Cost: $10.00

910 Grape Grower
Western Agricultural Publishing Company
4969 E Clinton Way
Suite 104
Fresno, CA 93727

559-252-7000
FAX 559-252-7387
E-Mail: westag@psnw.com
Home Page: www.westagpubco.com

Paul Baltimore, Co Publisher
Jim Baltimore, Co Publisher
Randy Bailey, Editor
Robert Fujimoto, Assistant Editor

The West's most widely read authority on the cultivation of table grapes, raising grapes and wine grapes. All aspects of production are covered with the most current university, government and private research.

911 Greenhouse Grower
Meister Media Worldwide
37733 Euclid Ave
Willoughby, OH 44094-5992

440-942-2000
800-572-7740
FAX 440-975-3447
E-Mail: gg.circ@meistermedia.com
Home Page: www.meistermedia.com

Gary Fitzgerald, President
Rick T Melnick, Corporate Editorial Director

Industry-leading voice for the commercial floriculture industry in the United States. Compiles buyers' directories and annual reports on the largest growers in the nation, produces vibrant emedia products and manages industry-leading events and awards programs.
Frequency: Monthly
Circulation: 20000
Founded in 1932

912 Grower
Vance Publishing
400 Knightsbridge Parkway
Lincolnshire, IL 60069

847-634-2600
FAX 847-634-4379
E-Mail: info@vancepublishing.com
Home Page: www.vancepublishing.com

William C Vance, Chairman
Peggy Walker, President

Positioned as the key source of profitable production and management strategies to commercial producers who control 90% of the U.S.

fruit and vegetable market.
Cost: $45.00
Frequency: Monthly
Circulation: 22,000
Founded in 1937

913 Growertalks Magazine
Ball Publishing
622 Town Road
PO Box 1660
West Chicago, IL 60186

630-231-3675
888-888-0013
FAX 630-231-5254
E-Mail: info@ballpublishing.com
Home Page: www.growertalks.com

Chris Beytes, Editor/Publisher
Jennifer Zurko, Managing Editor

Specializes in the publishing of horticulture information, primarily related to floriculture production and marketing.
Frequency: Monthly
Circulation: 12000
Founded in 1937

914 Guernsey Breeders' Journal
Purebred Publishing Inc
1224 Alton Darby Creeek Road
Suite G
Columbus, OH 43228

614-864-2409
FAX 614-864-5614
E-Mail: info@usguernsey.com
Home Page: www.usguernsey.com

Seth Johnson, Executive Secretary-Treasurer
Brian Schnebly, Programs Coordinator
Katie Hensen, Editor
Ashley Shaffer, Assistant Editor

The journal discusses breeder stories, management trends and events in the Guernsey industry.
Frequency: 10x Yearly

915 Gulf Coast Cattleman
EC Larkin
11201 Morning Ct
San Antonio, TX 78213-1300

21-3-4 77
FAX 210-344-4258
E-Mail: info@gulfcoastcattleman.com
Home Page: www.gulfcoastpub.com

E C Larkin Jr, President
Joan Dover, Circulation
M'Lys Lloyd, Managing Editor

Services commercial cattlemen along the Gulf Coast states with industry news, management and herd health related articles.
Cost: $15.00
64 Pages
Frequency: Monthly
Circulation: 16000
ISSN: 0017-5552
Founded in 1935
Printed in 4 colors on glossy stock

916 Hereford World
American Hereford Association
PO Box 014059
Kansas City, MO 64101

81-8-2 37
FAX 816-842-6931
E-Mail: aha@hereford.org
Home Page: www.hereford.org

Craig Huffhines, Executive VP
Mary Ellen Hummel, Executive Assistant

Trade magazine for breeders of registered Polled Hereford cattle.
Frequency: Monthly
Circulation: 9500
Founded in 1742

917 High Country News
High Country Foundation
119 Grand Avenue
PO Box 1090
Paonia, CO 81428

970-527-4898
800-905-1155
FAX 970-527-4897
E-Mail: circulation@hcn.org
Home Page: www.hcn.org

Paul Larmer, Executive Director
Greg Hanscom, Editor
Mike Maxwell, Director of Operations
Cindy Wehling, Art Director

Covers environmental and public lands issues.
Cost: $32.00
Circulation: 23000
Founded in 1970

918 High Plains Journal/Midwest Ag Journal
High Plains Publishing Company
1500 E Wyatt Earp Boulevard
PO Box 760
Dodge City, KS 67801

620-227-1834
800-452-7171
FAX 620-227-7173
E-Mail: journal@hpj.com
Home Page: www.hpj.com

Tom Tayor, Publisher/CEO
Holly Martin, Editor
John Seatvet, Sales Manager
Sarah Farlee, Marketing Director

Farming news for the central states.
Cost: $46.00
Frequency: Weekly
Circulation: 50000
Printed in 4 colors on glossy stock

919 Hoard's Dairyman The National Dairy Farm Magazine
PO Box 801
Fort Atkinson, WI 53538-0801

920-563-5551
FAX 920-563-7298
E-Mail: hoards@hoards.com
Home Page: www.hoards.com
Social Media: *Facebook, Twitter*

Steve A. Larson, Managing Editor
Corey A. Geiger, Senior Associate Editor
Demmos J. Hallady, Western Editor
Lucas S. Sjostrom, Associate Editor
Amanda C. Smith, Associate Editor

News aimed at the dairy farmer.
Cost: $18.00
5000 Members
Frequency: 20x/Year
Circulation: 63,000
Founded in 1885
Printed in 4 colors on glossy stock

920 Hog Producer
Farm Progress
6200 Aurora Avenue
Suite 609 E
Urbandale, IA 50322-2838

515-278-6693
FAX 515-278-7797
E-Mail: jotte@farmprogress.com
Home Page: www.farmprogress.com

Sara Wyant, Publisher
John Otte, Editor

Management publication to help pork producers in the production, housing, genetics, health care and marketing of hogs.

921 Holstein Pulse
Holstein Association USA

PO Box 808
Brattleboro, VT 05302-0808

802-254-4551
800-965-5200
FAX 802-254-8251
E-Mail: info@holstein.com
Home Page: www.holsteinusa.com

John Meyer, CEO
Lisa Perrin, Marketing
Frequency: Quarterly
Circulation: 19000

922 Holstein World
Dairy Business Communications
6437 Collamer Road
East Syracuse, NY 13057

315-703-7979
800-334-1904
FAX 315-703-7988
Home Page: www.holsteinworld.com

Joel P Hastings, Publisher/Editor
Janice Barrett, Associate Editor

Showcases breeders who own America's genet-
ically superior cattle. Elite group of progressive
dairymen who have income, herd size, and milk
production considerably above the national av-
erages.
Cost: $38.95
123 Pages
Frequency: Monthly
Circulation: 12000
ISSN: 0199-4239
Founded in 1904
Printed in 4 colors on glossy stock

923 HortScience
American Society for Horticultural Science
1018 Duke Street
Alexandria, VA 22314-2851

703-836-4606
FAX 703-836-2024
E-Mail: webmaster@ashs.org
Home Page: www.ashs.org

Michael Neff, Executive Director
Ruth Guamond, Managing Editor

HortScience is a bimonthly journal concentrat-
ing on significant research, education, exten-
sion findings, and methods.
Cost: $55.00
160 Pages
Frequency: Monthly
Circulation: 2500
ISSN: 0018-5345
Founded in 1903
Mailing list available for rent: 2500 names at
$100 per M

924 IMPACT Magazine
Agricultural Communicators of Tomorrow
P.O. Box 110180
Gainesville, FL 32611-0180

352-392-1971
FAX 352-392-9589
Home Page: www.ifas.ufl.edu
Social Media: *Facebook, Twitter*

Jack Payne, Senior Vice President

Features news about the statewide teaching, research and extension programs of the University of Florida's Institute of Food and
Agricultural Sciences.
Founded in 1970

925 Implement & Tractor
Farm Journal Media
1818 Market Street
31st Floor
Philadelphia, PA 19103-3654

215-578-8900
800-331-9310
FAX 215-568-6782

E-Mail: jstruyk@farmjournal.com
Home Page:
www.agweb.com/machinery/implement_tractor
.aspx

Andy Weber, Chief Executive Officer
Steve Custer, Executive Vice President
Jeff Pence, President, Electronic Media
Chuck Roth, Senior Vice President

Implement & Tractor is a bimonthly publication providing news and insights for dealers,
distributors, OEMs, engineers and the associations that make up the more than $40 billion
dealer and wholesaler equipment industry.
Frequency: Bimonthly
Founded in 1885

**926 International Journal of Vegetable
Science**
Taylor & Francis Group LLC
325 Chestnut St
Suite 800
Philadelphia, PA 19106-2614

215-625-8900
800-354-1420
FAX 215-625-2940
E-Mail: haworthorders@taylorandfrancis.com
Home Page: www.taylorandfrancis.com

Vincent M. Russo, Editor

Features innovative articles on all aspects of
vegetable production, including growth regulation, pest management, sustainable production,
harvesting, handling, storage, shipping and
final consumption.
Frequency: Quarterly

**927 International Poultry Exposition
Guide**
WATT Publishing Company
122 S Wesley Ave
Mt Morris, IL 61054-1451

815-734-7937
FAX 815-734-4201
E-Mail: olentine@wattmm.com
Home Page: www.wattnet.com

Jim Watt, Chairman/CEO
Lisa Thornton, Managing Editor
Clay Schreiber, Publisher

**928 Invasive Plant Science and
Management Journal**
P.O.Box 7065
Lawrence, KS 66044-7065

785-429-9622
800-627-0326
FAX 785-843-1274
E-Mail: wssa@allenpress.com
Home Page: www.wssa.net

Dale Shaner, President
Jeff Derr, VP
Tom Mueller, Secretary
Dave Gealy, Treasurer
Michael Foley, Director Publications

Promotes research, education and extension
outreach activities related to weeds, provides
science-based information to the public and
policy makers; and fosters awarenes of weeds
and their impacts on managed and natural
ecosystems.
2000 Members
Founded in 1956

929 Jojoba Happenings
John S Turner Public Relations
805 N 4th Avenue
Unit 404
Phoenix, AZ 85003-1304

FAX 602-252-5722

John Turner, Publisher
Ken Lucas, Editor

Jojoba farming. Accepts advertising.
8 Pages
Frequency: Bi-Monthly

**930 Journal of Agricultural & Food
Chemistry**
American Chemical Society
1155 16th St NW
Washington, DC 20036-4892

202-872-4600
800-227-9919
FAX 202-872-4615
E-Mail: jafc@ucdavis.edu
Home Page: www.pubs.acs.org

Madeleine Jacobs, CEO
John W Finley, Associate Editor
Elizabeth Waters, Associate Editor

Research results in pesticides, fertilizers, agri-
cultural and food processing chemistry.
Cost: $146.00
Frequency: Monthly
Circulation: 159000
Founded in 1856

931 Journal of Animal Science (JAS)
PO Box 7410
Champaign, IL 61826

217-356-9050
FAX 217-398-4119
E-Mail: asas@assochq.org
Home Page: www.asas.org
Social Media: *Facebook, Twitter, RSS*

Meghan Wulster-Radcli, CEO
Jacelyn Hemmelgarn, COO

Premier journal for animal science and serves
as the leading source of new knowledge and
perspective in this area. JAS consistently ranks
as on of the top journals in the category of Agriculture, Dairy, and Animal Sciences.
Frequency: Monthly
ISSN: 0021-8812
Founded in 1908

932 Journal of Applied Communications
Association for Communications Excellence
University of Florida
407 Rolfs Hall
Gainesville, FL 32611-0540

352-273-2094
FAX 352-392-8583
E-Mail: rwtelg@ufl.edu
Home Page: www.aceweb.org

Holly Young, Interim Executive Director
Faith Peppers, President
Joanne Littlefield, Vice President

A referred journal offering professional development for educational communicators who
emphasize agriculture, natural resources, and
life and human sciences.
Frequency: Quarterly
ISSN: 1051-0834

**933 Journal of Applied Communications
(JAC)**
ACE
448 Agricultural Hall
Stillwater, OK 74078

40- 7-4 04
866-941-3048
E-Mail:
editor@journalofappliedcommunications.or
Home Page:
www.journalofappliedcommunications.org

Dwayne Cartmell, Executive Editor
Ricky Telg, Editorial Board Chair

The Journal of Applied Communications is a
refereed journal offering professional development for educational communicators who em-

phasize agriculture, natural resources, and life and human sciences.
Frequency: Quarterly
Founded in 1970

934   Journal of Aquatic Plant Management
PO Box 821265
Vicksburg, MS 39182-1265

FAX 601-634-5502
E-Mail: webmaster@apms.org
Home Page: www.apms.org
Social Media: *Facebook, LinkedIn*

Terry Goldsby, President
Cody Gray, VP
Sherry Whitaker, Treasurer
Jeff Schardt, Secretary
Robert J. Richardson, Editor

A publication of the Aquatic Plant Management Society, Inc.
Founded in 1961

935   Journal of Biomolecular Screening
36 Tamarack Ave
Suite 348
Danbury, CT 06811

203-778-8828
FAX 203-748-7557
E-Mail: email@aol.com
Home Page: www.sbsonline.org

Jeff Paslay, President
Michelle Palmer, Executive Director
Christine Giordano, Executive Director

The leading peer-reviewed journal focusing on drug-discovery sciences. Delivers the latest advancements in quantitative biomolecular sciences.
Cost: $175.00
Frequency: 10x/Year

936   Journal of Dairy Science
American Dairy Science Association
2441 Village Green Pl
Champaign, IL 61822-7676

217-356-5146
FAX 217-398-4119
E-Mail: adsa@assochq.org
Home Page: www.adsa.org

Donald C Beitz, President
Philld C Tongz, VP
Peter Studney, Executive Director
William R Aimutis, Treasurer

Official Journal of the American Dairy Science Association
3000 Members
Founded in 1898
Mailing list available for rent

937   Journal of Environmental Quality
5585 Guilford Road
Madison, WI 53711-1086

608-273-8080
FAX 608-273-2021
E-Mail: headquarters@agronomy.org
Home Page: www.agronomy.org
Social Media: *Facebook, Twitter, LinkedIn*

Ken Barbarick, President
Sharon Clay, President Elect
Ellen Bergfeld, CEO

Published by ASA, CSSA, and SSSA. Papers are grouped by subject matter and cover water, soil, and atmospheric research as it relates to agriculture and the environment.
11000 Members
Founded in 1907

938   Journal of Forestry
Society of American Foresters

5400 Grosvenor Ln
Bethesda, MD 20814-2198

301-897-8720
866-897-8720
FAX 301-897-3690
E-Mail: safweb@podi.com
Home Page: www.safnet.org
Social Media: *Facebook, Twitter, LinkedIn*

Michael T Goergen Jr, Executive VP/CEO
Matthew Walls, Publications Dir./Managing Editor

To advance the profession of forestry by keeping professionals informed about significant developments and ideas in the many facets of forestry: economics, education and communication, entomology and pathology, fire, forest ecology, geospatial technologies, history, international forestry, measurements, policy, recreation, silviculture, social sciences, soils and hydrology, urband and community forestry, utilization and engineering, and wildlife management.
Cost: $85.00
Frequency: 8x Yearly
ISSN: 0022-1201
Founded in 1902

939   Journal of Natural Resources & Life Sciences Education
5585 Guilford Road
Madison, WI 53711-1086

608-273-8080
FAX 608-273-2021
E-Mail: headquarters@agronomy.org
Home Page: www.agronomy.org
Social Media: *Facebook, Twitter, LinkedIn*

Ellen E Bergfeld, CEO
Wes Meixelsperger, CFO
Alexander Barton, Director of Business Development
Lisa Al-Moodi, Managing Editor

Today's educators look here for the latest teaching ideas in the life sciences, natural resources, and agriculture.
11000 Members
Founded in 1907

940   Journal of Plant Registrations
Crop Science Society of America
5585 Guilford Road
Madison, WI 53711-5801

608-273-8080
FAX 608-273-2021
E-Mail: headquarters@crops.org
Home Page: www.crops.org
Social Media: *Facebook, Twitter, LinkedIn*

Maria Gallo, President
Jeffrey Volenec, President-elect

Publishes cultivar, germplasm, parental line, genetic stock, and mapping population registration manuscripts.
4700 Members
Founded in 1955

941   Journal of Soil and Water Conservation
Soil and Water Conservation Society
945 SW Ankeny Rd
Ankeny, IA 50021

515-289-2331
800-843-7645
FAX 515-289-1227
E-Mail: pubs@swcs.org
Home Page: www.swcs.org

Oksana Gieseman, Editor
Jorge Delgado, Research Editor

The JSWC is a multidisciplinary journal of natural resource conservation research, practice, policy, and perspectives. The journal has two sections: the A Section containing various departments and features and the Research Section containing peer-reviewed research papers.
Cost: $99.00
Frequency: 6x Yearly
Circulation: 2000
ISSN: 0022-4561
Founded in 1945

942   Journal of Sustainable Agriculture
Taylor & Francis Group LLC
325 Chestnut St
Suite 800
Philadelphia, PA 19106-2614

215-625-8900
800-354-1420
FAX 215-625-2940
Home Page: www.taylorandfrancis.com

Stephen R. Gliessman, Editor

Focuses on new and unique systems in which resource usage and environmental protection are kept in balance with the needs of productivity, profits, and incentives that are necessary for the agricultural marketplace. It increases professional and public awareness and gains support for these necessary changes in our agricultural industry.
Frequency: 8x Yearly

943   Journal of Vegetable Science
Taylor & Francis Group LLC
825 Chestnut Street
Suite 800
Philadelphia, PA 19106

215-625-8900
800-354-1420
FAX 215-625-2940
Home Page: www.haworthpress.com

Vincent M Russo PhD, Editor

Features innovative articles on all aspects of vegetable production, including growth regulation, pest management, sustainable production, harvesting, handling, storage, shipping and final consumption.
Frequency: Quarterly
ISSN: 1931-5260

944   Journal of the American Society of Farm Managers and Rural Appraisers
950 S Cherry St
Suite 508
Denver, CO 80246-2664

303-758-3513
FAX 303-758-0190
E-Mail: nhardiman@agri-associations.org
Home Page: www.asfmra.org
Social Media: *Facebook, Twitter, LinkedIn*

Nancy Hardiman, Director Education
Brian Stockman, Executive VP
Debe L Alvarez, Manager Education/Faculty

Provides the most up-to-date studies, research, practices, and methodologies proposed by the leading academic, management, appraisal and consulting members of our professions.
2300 Members
Founded in 1929
Mailing list available for rent

945   Land
Free Press Company
418 S 2nd Street
PO Box 3169
Mankato, MN 56001

507-344-6395
800-657-4665
Home Page: www.the-land.com

Kevin Schulz, Editor
Lynnae Schrader, Assistant Editor
Kim Henrickson, Advertising Manager
Ken Lingen, Manager

Agricultural news
Cost: $20.00
48 Pages
Frequency: Weekly
Circulation: 40000
ISSN: 0279-1633
Founded in 1976
Printed in 4 colors on newsprint stock

946 Landscape Management
Advanstar Landscape Group
7500 Old Oak Blvd
Cleveland, OH 44130-3343

440-243-8100
800-225-4569
FAX 440-891-2740
Home Page: www.act-europe.org

Ron Hall, Editor-in-Chief
Jason Stahl, Managing Editor

Covers news, market trends, business and operations management, technical information on horticulture and agronomy for professional landscape contractors, lawncare operators and in-house grounds managers.
Cost: $3.83
Circulation: 60014
Founded in 1962
Printed in 4 colors on glossy stock

947 Meat Science Journal
American Meat Science Association
2441 Village Green Pl
Champaign, IL 61822-7676

217-356-5368
800-517-AMSA
FAX 888-205-5834
FAX 217-356-5370
E-Mail: information@meatscience.org
Home Page: www.meatscience.org

Thomas Powell, Executive Director

The official journal of AMSA. Peer-reviewed resource is the best way to stay current on the latest research in meat science across all meat products and in all aspects of meat production and processing.

948 MidAmerican Farmer Grower
MidAmerica Farm Publications
19 N Main Street
PO Box 323
Perryville, MO 63775

573-547-2244
877-486-6997
FAX 573-547-5663
E-Mail: publisher@mafg.net
Home Page: www.mafg.net

John M LaRose, CEO/Publisher
Barbara Galeski, Editor
Jack Thompson II, Marketing

Offers farming news for the middle states.
Cost: $19.00
Frequency: Weekly

949 Midwest DairyBusiness
DairyBusiness Communications
6437 Collamer Road
East Syracuse, NY 13057-1031

315-703-7979
FAX 315-703-7988
Home Page: www.dairybusiness.com/midwest

Dave Natzke, Editorial Director
Joel P Hastings, Publisher
JoDee Sattler, Associate Editor
Tom Vilsack, Secretary

Business resource for successful milk producers. Only business-oriented dairy publication exclusively for the large herd, Midwest milk producer.
Cost: $45.00
43 Pages
Frequency: Monthly

Circulation: 27500
ISSN: 1087-7096
Founded in 1904
Printed in 4 colors on glossy stock

950 Milling Journal
3065 Pershing Court
Decatur, IL 62526

217-877-9660
800-728-7511
FAX 217-877-6647
E-Mail: webmaster@grainnet.com
Home Page: www.grainnet.com

Mark Avery, Publisher
Arvin Donley, Editor
Jody Sexton, Production Manager

Mailed to all active AOM members in the US, Canada, and internationally, including wheat flour/corn mills and corn/oilseed processors in US and Canada.
Frequency: Quarterly
Circulation: 1224

951 Mushroom News
American Mushroom Institute
1284 Gap Newport Pike
Suite 2
Avondale, PA 19311-9503

610-268-7483
FAX 610-268-8015
E-Mail: ami@mwmlaw.com
Home Page: www.americanmushroom.org

For growers and scientists in the mushroom production.
Cost: $275.00
Frequency: Monthly
Founded in 1955

952 NWAC News: National Warmwater Aquaculture Center
127 Experiment Station Road
PO Box 197
Stoneville, MS 38776

662-686-3302
FAX 662-686-3568
E-Mail: sharris@drec.msstate.edu
Home Page: www.msstate.edu/dept/tcnwac

Jammy Avery, Publisher
J Charles Lee, President
Frequency: Bi-annually
Circulation: 1000
Founded in 1993
Printed in 3 colors on matte stock

953 National Farmers Union News
National Farmers Union
11900 E Cornell Ave
Aurora, CO 80014-6201

303-368-7300
800-347-1961
FAX 303-368-1390
Home Page: www.nfu.org

Dave Frederickson, President
Rae Price, Editor

Grass roots structure in which policy positions are initiated locally. The goal is to sustain and strengthen family farm and ranch agriculture.
Cost: $10.00
Frequency: Monthly
Circulation: 250000
Founded in 1902

954 National Hog Farmer
7900 International Dr
Suite 300
Minneapolis, MN 55425-2562

952-851-4710
FAX 952-851-4601
Home Page: www.nationalhogfarmer.com

Dale Miller, Manager
Steve May, Publisher
John Frinch, President
Robert Moraczewski, Senior Vice President
Susan Rowland, Marketing Manager

Offers production information for hog farming business managers.
Cost: $35.00
Frequency: Monthly
Circulation: 31000
Founded in 1956
Mailing list available for rent: 84M names
Printed in 4 colors on glossy stock

955 National Wheat Growers Journal
National Association of Wheat Growers
415 2nd St NE
Suite 300
Washington, DC 20002-4993

202-547-7800
FAX 202-546-2638
E-Mail: wheatworld@wheatworld.org
Home Page: www.wheatworld.org
Social Media: *Facebook, Twitter*

David Cleavinger, Publisher
Karl Scronce, Second Vice President
Dana Peterson, Second Vice President
Melissa George Kessler, Director of Communications

Information for wheat growers.
Founded in 1950

956 North Africa and Middle East Int'l Agricultural and Trade Report
US Department of Agriculture
200 Independence Ave SW
Washington, DC 20201-0007

202-690-7650
800-999-6779
FAX 202-512-2250
Home Page: www.usda.gov

Michael Kurrzig, Editor
Chris Smith, Chief Information Officer
Matt Paul, Director of Communications
Ramona Romero, General Counsel

Information on current and projected agriculture production and trade in North Africa and the Middle East. Reports include trade and production data, highlights United States and European trade with the region.
Frequency: Annual
Founded in 1862

957 North American Deer Farmers Magazine
North American Deer Farmers Association
4501 Hills and Dales Rd NW
Suite C
Canton, OH 44708

330-454-3944
FAX 330-454-3950
E-Mail: info@nadefa.org
Home Page: www.nadefa.org

Shawn Schafer, Executive Director
Tim Condict, First VP
Bill Pittenger, Second VP

National association of deer farming and ranching. Membership dues include this quarterly magazine.
Cost: $15.00
32 Pages
Frequency: Quarterly
Circulation: 1000

ISSN: 1084-0583
Founded in 1983
Printed in 4 colors on glossy stock

958   Northeast Dairy Business
DairyBusiness Communications
6437 Collamer Road
East Syracuse, NY 13057-1031

315-703-7979
800-334-1904
FAX 315-703-7988
Home Page: www.dairybusiness.com/northeast

Eleanor Jacobs, Editor
Susan Harlow, Managing Editor
Joel Hasting, CEO/Publisher
Tom Vilsack, Secretary
Sue Miller, Circulation Manager

Business resource for successful milk producers. Devoted exclusively to the business and dairy management needs of milk producers in the 12 northeastern states.
Cost: $3.00
51 Pages
Frequency: Monthly
Circulation: 17500
ISSN: 1523-7095
Founded in 1904
Printed in 4 colors on glossy stock

959   Nut Grower
Western Agricultural Publishing Company
4969 E Clinton Way
Suite 119
Fresno, CA 93727-1549

559-252-7000
FAX 559-252-7387
E-Mail: westag@psnw.com
Home Page: www.westagpubco.com

Paul Baltimore, Co Publisher
Jim Baltimore, Co Publisher
Randy Bailey, Editor
Robert Fujimoto, Assistant Editor

Covers production topics, the latest in research developments, and crop news on almonds, walnuts, pistachios, pecans and chestnuts.

960   OEM Off-Highway
1233 Janesville Avenue
Fort Atkinson, WI 53538-2738

920-563-6388
800-547-7377
FAX 920-563-1701
E-Mail: Leslie.Shalabi@cygnuspub.com
Home Page: www.cygnusb2b.com

Richard Reiff, President
Leslie Shalabi, Publisher
Chad Elmore, Associate Editor
James S. Rank, VP
Kathy Scott, Director of Public Relations

Offers information on off-road machinery and farm equipment.
Founded in 1966

961   Onion World
Columbia Publishing
8405 Ahtanum Rd
Yakima, WA 98903-9432

509-248-2452
800-900-2452
FAX 509-248-4056
Home Page: www.onionworld.net

Brent Clement, Editor
Mike Stoker, Publisher

Includes information on onion production and marketing, grower and shipper feature stories, onion research, from herbicide and pesticide studies to promising new varieties, martket reports, feedback from major onion meetings and conventions, spot reports on overseas production and marketing, and other key issues and trends of interest to US and Canadian onion

growers.
Cost: $16.00
32 Pages
Circulation: 6500
Founded in 1984
Printed in 4 colors on glossy stock

962   Organic World
Loft Publishing
3939 Leary Way NW
Seattle, WA 98107-5043

206-632-2767
FAX 206-632-7055

Covers the news of organic gardening.
Cost: $15.00
Frequency: Quarterly

963   Pacific Farmer-Stockman
999 W Riverside
PO Box 2160
Spokane, WA 99201

509-595-5385
800-624-6618
FAX 509-459-5102
Home Page:
www.farmerstockmaninsurance.com

Michael R Craigen, General Manager
Tracy Sikes, Manager
Kathy Bergloff, Manager
Michelle Musgrave, Administrative Assistant

Offers farming news and information for farmers and herdsmen located in the Pacific states.

964   Peanut Farmer
Specialized Agricultural Publications
5808 Faringdon Place
Suite 200
Raleigh, NC 27609

919-872-5040
FAX 919-876-6531
E-Mail: publisher@peanutfarmer.com
Home Page: www.peanutfarmer.com

Dayton H Matlick, Chairman
Mary Evans, Publisher/Sales Director
Mary Ann Rood, Editor

Offers peanut farmers profitable methods of raising, marketing and promoting peanuts, plus key related issues.
Cost: $15.00
24 Pages
Frequency: Monthly January-July
Circulation: 18,500
Founded in 1965
Printed in 4 colors on glossy stock

965   Peanut Grower
Vance Publishing
10901 W 84th Ter
Suite 200
Lenexa, KS 66214-1631

913-438-5721
FAX 913-438-0697
E-Mail: mweeks@vancepublishing.com
Home Page: www.vancepublishing.com

Cliff Becker, VP
William C Vance, CEO

Written for the US peanut farmers. Covers disease, weed and insect control, legislation, farm equipment, marketing and new research.

966   Pesticide Chemical News Guide
FCN Publishing
2200 Clarendon Blvd
Suite 1401
Arlington, VA 22201

888-732-7070
Home Page: www.agra-net.com

Jason Huffman, Editor-in-Chief

Reference tool on pesticides and chemicals.
Frequency: Monthly

967   Pig International
WATT Publishing Company
303 N Main Street
Suite 500
Rockford, IL 61101

815-966-5400
FAX 815-966-6416
E-Mail: rabbott@wattnet.net
Home Page: www.wattnet.com

James Watt, Chairman/CEO
Greg Watt, President/COO
Roger Abbott, Editor

Covers nutrition, animal health issues, feed procurement, and how producers can be profitable in the world pork market.
Frequency: Monthly
Circulation: 17600
ISSN: 0191-8834
Founded in 1971
Mailing list available for rent
Printed in 4 colors on glossy stock

968   Plant Disease
American Phytopathological Society
3340 Pilot Knob Road
St. Paul, MN 55121-2097

651-454-7250
800-328-7560
FAX 651-454-0766
E-Mail: aps@scisoc.org
Home Page: www.apsnet.org
Social Media: *Facebook, Twitter, LinkedIn, YouTube*

R. Michael Davis, Editor-in-Chief

Published to stimulate plant disease research and to enable those throughout the world to benefit from the advances made in this environmentally important science.
Frequency: Monthly
Circulation: 1200
ISSN: 0191-2917

969   Pork
Vance Publishing
400 Knightsbridge Parkway
Lincolnshire, IL 60069

847-634-2600
FAX 847-634-4379
E-Mail: info@vancepublishing.com
Home Page: www.vancepublishing.com

William C Vance, Chairman
Peggy Walker, President

Delivers practical, how-to information on production management, business techniques, industry trends and market analysis to the pork industry.
Cost: $50.00
Frequency: Monthly
Circulation: 16,000
Mailing list available for rent

970   Pork Report
PO Box 10383
Clive, IA 50325

515-223-6186
FAX 515-223-2646

Charles Harness, Publisher

Hog farming news and information.

971   Potato Country
Columbia Publishing
8405 Ahtanum Rd
Yakima, WA 98903-9432

509-248-2452
800-900-2452
FAX 509-248-4056
Home Page: www.potatocountry.com

Brent Clement, Editor/Publisher
Mike Stoker, Publisher

Edited for potato growers and allied industry people throughout the Western fall-production states. Editorial material covers production, seed, disease forecast, equipment, fertilizer, irrigation, pest/weed management, crop reports and annual buyers guide.
Cost: $18.00
32 Pages
Frequency: Daily
Circulation: 7500
ISSN: 0886-4780
Founded in 1993
Printed in 4 colors on glossy stock

972   Potato Grower
Harris Publishing Company
360 B Street
Idaho Falls, ID 83402

208-524-4217
FAX 208-522-5241
Home Page: www.potatogrower.com

Jason Harris, Publisher
Gary Rawlings, Editor

Current news on growing potatoes, market trends, technology.
Cost: $20.95
48 Pages
Frequency: Monthly
Founded in 1971
Printed in on glossy stock

973   Poultry Digest
WATT Publishing Company
122 S Wesley Ave
Mt Morris, IL 61054-1451

815-734-7937
FAX 815-734-4201
E-Mail: olentine@wattmm.com
Home Page: www.wattnet.com

Jim W Watt, Chairman/CEO
Charles G Olentine Jr PhD, VP/Publisher
Clay Schreiber, Publisher
Jim Wessel, Circulation Director

A magazine serving the production side of the entire poultry industry.

974   Poultry International
WATT Publishing Company
303 N Main Street
Suite 500
Rockford, IL 61101

815-966-5400
FAX 815-966-6416
E-Mail: mclements@wattnet.net
Home Page: www.wattnet.com

James Watt, Chairman/CEO
Greg Watt, President/COO
Mark Clements, Editor

Viewed by commercial poultry integrators as the leading international source of news, data and information for their businesses.
68 Pages
Frequency: Monthly
Circulation: 20,000
ISSN: 0032-5767
Founded in 1962
Printed in 4 colors

975   Poultry Times
Poultry & Egg News
345 Green Street NW
PO Box 1338
Gainesville, GA 30503

770-536-2476
FAX 770-532-4894
Home Page: www.poultrytimes.net
Social Media: *Facebook*

Christopher Hill, Publisher/Editor
David Strickland, Editor
Barbara Olejnik, Associate Editor

Dinah Winfree, National Sales Representative
Stacy Louis, National Sales Representative

The only newspaper in the poultry industry. We deliver the most up to date news in teh poultry industry.
Cost: $22.00
Frequency: Twice Monthly
Circulation: 13000
Founded in 1954

976   Poultry USA
WATT Publishing Company
303 N Main Street
Suite 500
Rockford, IL 61101

815-966-5400
FAX 815-966-6416
Home Page: www.wattnet.com

James Watt, Chairman/CEO
Greg Watt, President/COO
Jeff Swanson, Publishing Director

The only resource focused on the entire integrated poultry market, delivering relevant and timely information to industry professionals across the entire poultry supply chain - from farm to table.
Frequency: Monthly

977   Practical Winery & Vineyard
58 Paul Dr
Suite D
San Rafael, CA 94903-2054

415-479-5819
FAX 415-492-9325
E-Mail: Office@practicalwinery.com
Home Page: www.practicalwinery.com

A bi-monthly magazine of wine-growing and winemaking news and reviews.
Cost: $31.00
Circulation: 7500
Founded in 1985

978   Prairie Farmer
Prairie Farm Dairy
300 E Washington St
PO Box 348
Pana, IL 62557-1239

217-562-3956
FAX 217-877-9695
E-Mail: info@prairiefarms.com
Home Page: www.prairiefarms.com

James R Smith, Manager
Mike Wilson, Editor

Agricultural news.

979   Progressive Farmer
2100 Lakeshore Drive
Birmingham, AL 35209-6721

205-445-6000
FAX 205-445-6422
E-Mail: bruce_thomas@timeinc.com
Home Page: www.progressivefarmer.com

Bruce Thomas, Publisher
Jack Odle, Editor
Allen Vaughan, Business Manager

Farming news with regional focus on the midwest, midsouth and southwest.
Cost: $18.00
106 Pages
Frequency: 6 issues/Year
Circulation: 610000
ISSN: 0033-0760
Founded in 1886

980   RF Design
RFD News

131 E Main Street
Bellevue, OH 44811-1449

419-483-7410
FAX 419-483-3737

Barry LeCerf, Publisher

Comprehensive source of rural agricultural news and information for farmers and the general public.
Frequency: Weekly

981   Rice Farming
Vance Publishing
400 Knightsbridge Pkwy
Lincolnshire, IL 60069-3628

847-634-2600
800-888-9784
FAX 847-634-4379
E-Mail: vlboyd@worldnet.att.net
Home Page: www.vancepublishing.com

Peggy Walker, President
William Vance, Chairman
Judy Riggs, Director
Vicky Boyd, Editor

Profitable production strategies for commercial rice growers.
Founded in 1937

982   Rice Journal
Specialized Agricultural Publications
3000 Highwoods Boulevard
Suite 300
Raleigh, NC 27604-1029

919-878-0540
FAX 919-876-6531
E-Mail: publisher@ricejournal.com
Home Page: www.ricejournal.com

Dayton H Matlick, President
Mary Evans, Publisher

Offers rice growers profitable methods of producing, marketing and promoting rice, plus key related issues.
Founded in 1897

983   RuraLife
William Johnston
1172 Orangeburg Mall Circle
Orangeburg, SC 29115-3439

803-534-1980

Jaun Maults, Executive Director
Gary Grimmond, Editor

Farm and agricultural news.

984   Rural Heritage
Allan Damerow
281 Dean Ridge Ln
Gainesboro, TN 38562-5039

931-268-0655
E-Mail: info@ruralheritage.com
Home Page: www.ruralheritage.com

Gail Damerow, Owner

Publication for people who farm and log with horses and other draft animals.
Cost: $26.00
100 Pages
Frequency: Bi-Monthly
Circulation: 8500
ISSN: 0889-2970
Founded in 1976
Printed in 4 colors on matte stock

985   Rural Living
Michigan Farm Bureau
7373 W Saginaw Highway
PO Box 30960
Lansing, MI 48909-8460

517-323-7000
FAX 517-323-6793

E-Mail: mifarmnews@michfb.com
Home Page: www.michiganfarmbureau.com

Dennis Rudat, Editor
Paul W Jackson, President
Brigette Leach, Director
Earl Butz, Secretary

Editorial emphasis on consumer food news, travel information and issue analysis.
24 Pages
Frequency: Quarterly
Circulation: 200000

986 Santa Gertrudis USA
Caballo Rojo Publishing
PO Box 1257
Kingsville, TX 78364-1257

361-592-9357
FAX 361-592-8572
Home Page: www.santagertrudis.com

Ervin Kaatz, Executive Director

Official Journal of the Breed developed in 1918 at the famous King Ranch in Texas. Famous solid red color, hardiness and good disposition. They are adaptable to many environments and are present throughout the US and in other countries.

987 Seed Industry Journal
Freiberg Publishing Company
2701 Minnetonka Dr
PO Box 7
Cedar Falls, IA 50613-1531

319-553-0642
FAX 319-277-3783
Home Page: www.care4elders.com

Bill Freiberg, Owner
Carol Cutler, Editor

International seed industry news.

988 Seed Technology Journal
Society of Commerical Seed Technologists
101 E State Street
Suite 214
Ithaca, NY 14850

607-256-3313
FAX 607-256-3313
E-Mail: scst@twcny.rr.com
Home Page: www.seedtechnology.net

Brent Reschly, President
Neal Foster, Vice President

Published jointly with the Association of Official Seed Analysts. an international journal containing scientific and technological papers in all areas of seed science and technology. The emphasis is on applied and basic research in seed physiology, pathology and biology that may relate to seed development, maturation, germination, dormancy and deterioration.
Cost: $125.00
Frequency: Members Cost: $75.00
Founded in 1922

989 Seed Today
Grain Journal Publishing Company
3065 Pershing Ct
Decatur, IL 62526-1564

217-877-9660
800-728-7511
FAX 217-877-6647
E-Mail: webmaster@grainnet.com
Home Page: www.grainnet.com

Mark Avery, Publisher
Joe Funk, Editor
Kay Merryfield, Circulation Administrator
Ayanna Green, Manager

Information for individuals related to seeds.
Frequency: Quarterly
Circulation: 4000
Founded in 1978

990 Seed World
Scranton Gillette Communications
380 E Northwest Highway
Suite 200
Des Plaines, IL 60016-2282

847-298-6622
FAX 847-390-0408
Home Page: www.seedworld.com

E S Gillette, Publisher
Angela Dansby, Editor

Seed marketers.
Cost: $30.00
48 Pages
Frequency: Monthly
Circulation: 5000
ISSN: 0037-0797
Founded in 1915

991 Seed and Crops Industry
Freiberg Publishing Company
2701 Minnetonka Dr
Cedar Falls, IA 50613-1531

319-553-0642
800-959-3276
FAX 319-277-3783
E-Mail: informa@cfu.net
Home Page: www.care4elders.com

Bill Freiberg, Owner

Offers information for farmers related to crop protection.
Frequency: Monthly

992 Self Employed Country
Communicating for Agriculture & the Self Employed
112 E Lincoln Ave
Fergus Falls, MN 56537-2217

218-739-3241
800-432-3276
FAX 218-739-3832
Home Page: www.selfemployedcountry.org

Milt Smedsrud, Owner
Jerry Barney, Production Manager

For members of Communicating for Agriculture, including legislation relating to CA activities, exchange program activities, rural seniors news, health and insurance material, feature stories and columns.
Cost: $6.00
Frequency: Quarterly
Founded in 1985

993 Shorthorn Country
Durham Management Company
5830 S 142nd St
Siote A
Omaha, NE 68137-2894

402-827-8003
FAX 402-827-8006
Home Page:
www.durhamstaffingsolutions.com

Machael Durham, President
Tracy Duncan, Editor
Peggy Gilliland, Circulation Manager

Magazine published for cattle producers who breed and sell registered Shorthorn and Polled Shorthorn cattle.
Cost: $24.00
Circulation: 3000
ISSN: 0149-9319
Founded in 1956

994 Soil Science
Lippincott Williams & Wilkins
351 W Camden St
Baltimore, MD 21201-2436

410-949-8000
800-638-6423

FAX 410-528-4414
Home Page: www.lww.com

J Arnold Anthony, Operations

Covers investigations in environmental soils.
Cost: $205.00
Frequency: Monthly
Circulation: 2800
ISSN: 0038-075X

995 Soil Science of America Journal
Soil Science Society of America
677 S Segoe Rd
Madison, WI 53711-1086

608-273-8095
FAX 608-273-2021
E-Mail: headquarters@soils.org
Home Page: www.soils.org

Ellen Bergfeld, CEO

For those involved in research, teaching and extension activities in physics, chemistry, mineralogy, microbiology, soil fertility and plant nutrition
Cost: $600.00
Circulation: 4000
Founded in 1961

996 Southeast Farm Press
14920 US Highway 61
Clarksdale, MS 38614

662-624-8503
866-505-7173
FAX 662-627-1977
Home Page: www.southeastfarmpress.com

Grey Frey, Publisher
Paul Hollis, Editor

Offers farming news for the southeastern states.
Founded in 1989

997 Southeastern Peanut Farmer
Southern Peanut Farmer's Federation
110 E 4th Street
Po Box 706
Tifton, GA 31794

229-386-3470
FAX 229-386-3501
E-Mail: info@gapeanuts.com
Home Page: www.gapeanuts.com

Joy Carter, Editor

Offers information to peanut farmers.
Cost: $25.00
20 Pages
Frequency: Monthly
Circulation: 8400
ISSN: 0038-3694
Founded in 1961
Printed in 4 colors on glossy stock

998 Southwest Farm Press
Farm Press Publications
2104 Harvell Circle
Bellevue, NE 68005

402-505-7173
866-505-7173
FAX 402-293-0741
E-Mail: sscs@pbsub.com
Home Page: southwestfarmpress.com

Greg Frey, Publisher
Ron Smith, Editor
Hembree Brandon, Editorial Director
Forrest Laws, Executive Editor
Darrah Parker, Marketing Manager

Farming news.
Cost: $40.00
Frequency: Fortnightly
Circulation: 33,100
Founded in 1974

999 Soybean South
6263 Poplar Avenue
Suite 540
Memphis, TN 38119-4736

901-385-0595
FAX 901-767-4026

John Sowell, Publisher
Jeff Kehl, Circulation Director

Profitable prediction strategies for soybean farmers.
Frequency: 5 per year
Printed in 4 colors on glossy stock

1000 Speedy Bee
American Beekeeping Federation
3525 Piedmont Road NE
Bldg 5 Suite 300
Atlanta, GA 30305-1509

404-760-2875
FAX 404-240-0998
E-Mail: info@abfnet.org
Home Page: www.abfnet.org

Troy Fore, Publisher/Editor

The latest news affecting the beekeeping and honey industry.
Cost: $17.95
16 Pages
Frequency: Monthly
Circulation: 1500
ISSN: 0190-6798
Founded in 1972
Printed in on newsprint stock

1001 Spudman Magazine
Great American Publishing
Po Box 128
Suite A
Sparta, MI 49345-0128

616-887-9008
FAX 616-887-2666
Home Page: www.spudman.com

Matt McCallum, Owner
Kimberly Warren, Managing Editor
Erica Bernard, Circulation Manager
Marnie Draper, Advertising Manager
Jill Peck, Creative Director

Information for potato farming and marketing.
Circulation: 15500
Printed in on glossy stock

1002 Successful Farming
Meredith Corporation
1716 Locust St
Des Moines, IA 50309-3023

515-284-3000
800-678-2659
FAX 515-284-3563
E-Mail: shareholderhelp@meredith.com
Home Page: www.meredith.com

Stephen M Lacy, CEO
Sandy Williams, Production Manager
William Kerr, CEO
Tom Davis, Publisher

U.S. commerical farmers, ranchers and those employed in those operations or a directly related occupation.
Cost: $15.95
Frequency: Monthly
Circulation: 442000
Founded in 1902
Mailing list available for rent: 500M names at $75 per M
Printed in 4 colors on glossy stock

1003 Sugar: The Sugar Producer Magazine
Harris Publishing Company
360 B Street
Idaho Falls, ID 83402

208-524-4217
800-638-0135

FAX 208-522-5241
Home Page: www.sugarproducer.com

Jason Harris, Publisher
David FairBourn, Editor
Rob Erickson, Marketing
Eula Endecott, Circulation Manager

Sugar beet industry information.
Cost: $15.95
Frequency: Monthly
Circulation: 16000
Founded in 1975

1004 Sugarbeet Grower
Sugar Publications
503 Broadway
Fargo, ND 58102-4416

701-476-2111
FAX 701-476-2182
Home Page: www.sugarpub.com

Provides news and feature articles pertaining to sugarbeet production practices, research, legislation and marketing, along with profiles of industry leaders and outstanding producers. Primary audience is United States and Canadian sugarbeet growers.
Cost: $12.00
Circulation: 11,300
Founded in 1963

1005 Sunflower Magazine
National Sunflower Association
Ste 206
2401 46th Ave SE
Mandan, ND 58554-4829

701-328-5100
888-718-7033
FAX 701-328-5101
Home Page: www.sunflowernsa.com

John Sandbakken, Executive Director
Sonia Mullally, Communications Director

Magazine geared to sunflower products.
Cost: $9.00
Circulation: 29300
Founded in 1981
Printed in 4 colors

1006 Sunflower and Grain Marketing Magazine
Sunflower World Publishers
3307 Northland Drive
Suite 130
Austin, TX 78731-4964

512-407-3434
FAX 512-323-5118

Ed R Allen, Editor

Offers news and information on the sunflower and grain industries.
Circulation: 15,000

1007 Super Hay Today Magazine
Mt Adams Publishing and Design
14161 Fort Road
White Swan, DC 98552-9786

509-848-2706
800-554-0860
FAX 509-848-3896
Home Page: www.hortexponw.com

Vee Graves, Editor
Julie LaForge, Advertising Manager

1008 Swine Practitioner
10901 W 84th Terrace
Suite 200
Lenexa, KS 66214-1649

913-438-8700
800-255-5113
FAX 913-438-0695

E-Mail: info@vancepublishing.com
Home Page: www.vancepublishing.com

Kristal Arnold, Editor
Kevin Murphy, Sales/Marketing Manager
Bill Newham, Publishing Director
Cliff Becker, Group Publisher
Lori Eppel, Chief Financial Officer

Offers technical information, primarily on swine health and related production areas, to veterinarians and related industry professionals.
Frequency: Monthly
Circulation: 4800
Mailing list available for rent

1009 The Forestry Source
5400 Grosvenor Ln
Bethesda, MD 20814-2198

301-897-8720
FAX 301-897-3690
E-Mail: safweb@safnet.org
Home Page: www.safnet.org
Social Media: *Facebook, Twitter, LinkedIn*

Michael T Goergen Jr, Executive VP/CFO
Brittany Brumby, Assistant to the CEO/Council
Amy Ziadi, Information Technology Manager
Larry D Burner CPA, Sr Director Finance

Provides access to information and networking opportunities to prepare members for the challenges and the changes that face natural resource professionals.
Founded in 1900

1010 The Grower
Vance Publishing
400 Knightsbridge Parkway
Lincolnshire, IL 60069

847-634-2600
FAX 847-634-4379
E-Mail: info@vancepublishing.com
Home Page: www.vancepublishing.com
Social Media: *Facebook, Twitter*

William C Vance, Chairman
Peggy Walker, President

The key source of profitable production and management strategies to commercial producers who control 90% of the U.S. fruit and vegetable market.
Cost: $45.00
Frequency: Monthly
Circulation: 22,004
Founded in 1937
Printed in 4 colors on glossy stock

1011 The Plant Genome
Crop Science Society of America
5585 Guilford Road
Madison, WI 53711-5801

608-273-8080
FAX 608-273-2021
E-Mail: headquarters@crops.org
Home Page: www.crops.org
Social Media: *Facebook, Twitter, LinkedIn*

Maria Gallo, President
Jeffrey Volenec, President-Elect

Electronic journal that provides readership with a short publication of the latest advances and breakthroughs in plant genomics research.
Founded in 1955

1012 The Sunflower Magazine
2401 46th Avenue SE
Suite 206
Mandan, ND 58554-4829

701-328-5100
888-718-7033
FAX 701-663-8652

Home Page: www.sunflowernsa.com
Social Media: *Facebook, YouTube*

Larry Kleingartner, Executive Director
John Sandbakken, Marketing Director

Contains fresh, current and important articles on production strategies, ongoing research and market information.
Founded in 1981
Printed in 4 colors on glossy stock

1013 Today's Farmer
MFA
201 Ray Young Dr
Columbia, MO 65201-3599

573-874-5111
FAX 573-876-5521
E-Mail: hr@mfa-inc.com
Home Page: www.mfa-inc.com

William Streeter, CEO
J Brian Griffith, Senior Vice President of Operations

Management and marketing news.
Cost: $12.00
Founded in 1914

1014 Tomato Country
Columbia Publishing
8405 Ahtanum Rd
Yakima, WA 98903-9432

509-248-2452
800-900-2452
FAX 509-248-4056
Home Page: www.tomatomagazine.com

Brent Clement, Editor/Publisher
Mike Stoker, Publisher

Includes information on tomato production and marketing, grower and shipper feature stories, tomato research, from herbicide and pesticide studies to new varieties, market reports, feedback from major tomato meetings and conventions, along with other key issues and points of interest for USA and Canada tomato growers.

1015 Top Producer
Farm Journal Media
1818 Market Street
31st Floor
Philadelphia, PA 19103-3654

215-578-8900
800-320-7992
FAX 215-568-6782
E-Mail: topproducer@farmjournal.com
Home Page: www.agweb.com/topproducer

Andy Weber, Chief Executive Officer
Steve Custer, Executive Vice President
Jeff Pence, President, Electronic Media
Chuck Roth, Senior Vice President

Top Producer is the premier magazine devoted to the business of farming. The focus on industry leaders, entrepreneurs and innovators in agriculture make this magazine the authoritative business resource for commercial farm operators.
Frequency: Weekly
Founded in 1973

1016 Tree Farmer Magazine, the Guide to Sustaining America's Family Forests
American Forest Foundation
1111 19th St NW
Suite 780
Washington, DC 20036

202-463-2700
FAX 202-463-2785
E-Mail: info@forestfoundation.org
Home Page: www.forestfoundation.org

Tom Martin, President & CEO
Brigitte Johnson APR, Director Communications, Editor

The official magazine of ATFS, this periodical provides practical, how-to and hands-on information and techniques, and services to help private fore landowners to become better stewards, save money and time, and add to the enjoyment of their land.

1017 Tree Fruit
Western Agricultural Publishing Company
4969 E Clinton Way
Suite 104
Fresno, CA 93727-1546

559-252-7000
FAX 559-252-7387
E-Mail: westag@psnw.com
Home Page: www.westagpubco.com

Paul Baltimore, Co Publisher
Jim Baltimore, Co Publisher
Randy Bailey, Editor
Robert Fujimoto, Assistant Editor

For tree fruit growers in California.

1018 Valley Potato Grower
420 Business Highway 2
PO Box 301
East Grand Forks, MN 56721

218-773-7783
FAX 218-773-6227
E-Mail: vpgsales@nppga.org
Home Page: www.nppga.org

Todd Phelph, CEO
Duane Maatz, Chairman

Information on potato farming.
Circulation: 10600
Founded in 1946

1019 Vegetable Growers News
Great American Publishing
75 Applewood Drive Suite A
PO Box 128
Sparta, MI 49345

616-887-9008
FAX 616-887-2666
Home Page: www.vegetablegrowersnews.com

Matt McCallum, Executive Publisher
Brenda Bradford, Advertising
Kimberly Warren, Managing Editor
Erica Bernard, Circulation Department
Jill Peck, Creative Director

Market and marketing news.
Cost: $12.00
Frequency: Monthly

1020 Vegetables
Western Agricultural Publishing Company
4969 E Clinton Way
#104
Fresno, CA 93727-1549

559-252-7000
FAX 559-252-7387
E-Mail: westag@psnw.com
Home Page: www.westagpubco.com

Paul Baltimore, Co Publisher
Jim Baltimore, Co Publisher
Randy Bailey, Editor
Robert Fujimoto, Assistant Editor

The definitive source for information on all aspects of western vegetable production.

1021 Vineyard and Winery Management
PO Box 2358
Winsdor, CA 95492

707-366-6820
800-535-5670
FAX 607-535-2998
E-Mail: rmerletti@vwm-online.com
Home Page: www.vwm-online.com

Robert Merletti, Publisher
Tom Loid, General Manager

Dennis Black, General Manager
Suzanne Webb, Marketing Director

To be the bottom line resource for growers and vintners; to keep our readers tuned and primed for profit.
Cost: $37.00
100 Pages
Circulation: 6000
ISSN: 1047-4951
Founded in 1975
Printed in 4 colors on glossy stock

1022 Wallaces Farmer
Farm Progress Companies
255 38th Avenue
Suite P
St Charles, IL 60174-5410

630-462-2224
800-441-1410
E-Mail: rswoboda@farmprogress.com
Home Page: www.farmprogress.com

Rod Swoboda, Editor
Willie Vogt, Corporate Editorial Director
Frank Holdmeyer, Executive Editor

Serves Iowa farmers and ranchers with information to help them maximize their productivity and profitability. Each issue is packed with information, ideas, news and analysis.
Cost: $26.95
ISSN: 0043-0129
Founded in 1855

1023 Weed Science Journal
P.O.Box 7065
Lawrence, KS 66044-7065

785-429-9622
800-627-0629
FAX 785-843-1274
E-Mail: wssa@allenpress.com
Home Page: www.wssa.net

Dale Shaner, President
Jeff Derr, VP
Tom Mueller, Secretary
Dave Gealy, Treasurer
Michael Foley, Director Publications

Promotes research, education and extension outreach activities related to weeds, provides science-based information to the public and policy makers; and fosters awarenes of weeds and their impacts on managed and natural ecosystems.
2000 Members
Founded in 1956

1024 Weed Technology Journal
P.O.Box 7065
Lawrence, KS 66044-7065

785-429-9622
800-627-0629
FAX 785-843-1274
E-Mail: wssa@allenpress.com
Home Page: www.wssa.net

Dale Shaner, President
Jeff Derr, VP
Tom Mueller, Secretary
Dave Gealy, Treasurer
Michael Foley, Director Publications

Promotes research, education and extension outreach activities related to weeds, provides science-based information to the public and policy makers; and fosters awarenes of weeds and their impacts on managed and natural ecosystems.
Founded in 1956

1025 Western DairyBusiness
DairyBusiness Communications
6437 Collamer Road
East Syracuse, NY 13057-1031

315-703-7979
800-334-1904

FAX 315-703-7988
E-Mail: bbaker@dairyline.com
Home Page: www.dairybusiness.com

Joel P Hastings, Editor
John Montandon, President & Co-CEO
Debbie Morneau, Marketing Coordinator

Business resource for successful milk producers. Covers 13 Western states. Provides information and news that is helpful in the daily operations of dairymen.
Cost: $49.95
67 Pages
Frequency: Monthly
Circulation: 14000
ISSN: 1528-4360
Founded in 1904
Printed in 4 colors on glossy stock

1026 Western Farm Press
Penton Media
249 W 17th Street
New York, NY 10011

212-204-4200
E-Mail: hbrandon@farmpress.com
Home Page: westernfarmpress.com

Greg Frey, VP
Hembree Brandon, Editorial Director
Harry Cline, Editor

Provides growers and agribusiness with in-depth coverage of the region's major crops plus the legislative, environmental and regulatory issues that affect their businesses.

1027 Western Fruit Grower
Meister Media Worldwide
37733 Euclid Ave
Willoughby, OH 44094-5992

440-942-2000
800-572-7740
FAX 440-975-3447
E-Mail: rljones@meistermedia.com
Home Page: www.meisternet.com

Gary Fitzgerald, President
John Monahan, Publisher
Richard Jones, Editor

Edited for commercial growers of deciduous crops, citrus fruit and nut grape crops in the Western US.
Cost: $19.95
66 Pages
Frequency: Monthly
Circulation: 36000
Founded in 1933

1028 Western Livestock Journal
Crow Publications
7355 E Orchard Road
Suite 300
Greenwood Village, CO 80111

303-722-7600
800-850-2769
FAX 303-722-0155
E-Mail: editorial@wlj.net
Home Page: www.wlj.net

Pete Crow, Publisher

Offers its readers the best coverage of timely, necessary news and information that affects the livestock industry, particularly cattle.
Cost: $45.00
Frequency: Weekly
Circulation: 30000+
Founded in 1922

Trade Shows

1029 AACC International Annual Meeting
3340 Pilot Knob Road
St. Paul, MN 55121-2055

651-454-7250
800-328-7560
FAX 651-454-0766
E-Mail: aacc@scisoc.org
Home Page: www.aaccnet.org
Social Media: *Facebook, Twitter, LinkedIn*

Betty Ford, Director of Meetings
Rhonda Wilkie, Meetings Coordinator
Deborah Rogers, Chair
David Hahn, President
Steven C. Nelson, Executive Vice President

Formerly the American Association of Cereal Chemists, the AACC meeting offers a chance to come together, network with peers, discuss critical issues in the science and discover the methods of others.
Founded in 1915

1030 AAEA Annual Meeting
Agricultural & Applied Economics Association
415 S Duff Avenue
Suite C
Ames, IA 50010-6600

515-233-3202
FAX 515-233-3101
E-Mail: nknight@iastate.edu
Home Page: www.aaea.org

Per Pinstrup-Anderson, President
Yvonne C Bennett, Executive Director
Nancy Knight, Manager Meetings
Joan Greiner, Events Coordinator

Annual meeting and trade show of 25 exhibitors.
1700 Attendees
Frequency: Annual/August
Founded in 1985

1031 AAEA Symposia
555 E Wells Street
Suite 1100
Milwaukee, WI 53202-6600

414-918-3190
FAX 414-276-3349
E-Mail: info@aaea.org
Home Page: www.aaea.org

Otto C Doering III, President
Yvonne C Bennett, Executive Director

Providing a platform for research on the economics related to the role of consumers' food environments on their choices and health outcomes. The conference is aimed at providing insights into the influence of the food environment on the quality, price, and availability of food, associatec health or environmental impacts, and to uncover the impact of policies aimed at influencing the food production and choice.
3000 Members
Frequency: Annual
Founded in 1910
Mailing list available for rent

1032 AAFCO Meeting
Association of American Feed Control Officers
PO Box 478
Oxford, IN 47971

765-385-1029
FAX 765-385-1032

E-Mail: sharon@aafco.org
Home Page: www.aafco.org

Sharon Krebs, Assistant Secretary/Treasurer
Frequency: Annual/July/August

1033 AAW Annual Convention
American Agri-Women
2103 Zeandale Road
Manhattan, KS 66502

785-537-6171
FAX 785-537-9727
Home Page: www.americanagriwomen.org
Social Media: *Facebook, Twitter*

Karen Yost, President
Jody Elrod, Secretary
Peggy Clark, Treasurer

Tradeshow consisting of products of interest to women in agribusiness, farms and ranches.
350 Attendees
Frequency: Annual/November
Founded in 1974

1034 AEM Annual Conference
Association of Equipment Manufacturers
6737 W Washington St
Suite 2400
Milwaukee, WI 53214-5650

414-272-0943
866-236-0442
FAX 414-272-1170
E-Mail: info@aem.org
Home Page: www.aem.org

Dennis Slater, President
Frequency: Annual/November

1035 AFIA Pet Food Conference
American Feed Industry Association
2101 Wilson Blvd
Suite 916
Arlington, VA 22201-3047

703-524-0810
FAX 703-524-1921
E-Mail: afia@afia.org
Home Page: www.afia.org
Social Media: *Facebook, Twitter, LinkedIn*

Joel Newman, President
Richard Sellers, VP
Donald E Orr, Chairman
Anne Keller, Communications Director

Organization devoted to representing companies in the animal feed industry and its suppliers.
690 Members
Founded in 1909

1036 ALBC Conference
American Livestock Breeds Conservancy
PO Box 477
Pittsboro, NC 27312

919-542-5704
FAX 919-545-0022
Home Page: www.albc-usa.org
Social Media: *Facebook*

Charles Bassett, Executive Director

An educational opportunity where members can share their knowledge with other members by sharing posters at the annual conference, subtting articles to the newsletter and more.
Frequency: Annual

1037 AMSA Reciprocal Meat Conference
American Meat Science Association
2441 Village Green Place
Champaign, IL 61822

217-356-5370
800-517-AMSA
FAX 888-205-5834
FAX 217-356-5370

E-Mail: information@meatscience.org
Home Page: www.meatscience.org\rmc

William Mikel, President
Scott J. Eilert, President-Elect
Casey B. Frye, Treasurer

RMC is the annual meeting for AMSA, featuring an interactive program tailored to bring attendees the very best and inspiring educational experience. Attendees are professionals in academia, government and industry, as well as students in the meat, food and animal science fields.

1038 AOSA/SCST Annual Meeting-Association of Official Seed Analysts
PMB #411
101 East State Street
Suite 214
Ithaca, NY 14850

607-256-3313
FAX 607-273-1638
E-Mail: aosa.office@twcny.rr.com
Home Page: www.aosaseed.com

Ellen Chirco, President
Wayne Guerke, VP
Dan Curry, Secretary/Treasurer
Aaron Palmer, Certificate/Analysis
Larry Nees, Membership

Seed testing and laboratory equipment, supplies and services; workshops and discussions.
Frequency: Annual/June

1039 ARA Conference & Expo
1156 15th St NW
Suite 500
Washington, DC 20005-1745

202-457-0825
FAX 202-457-0864
E-Mail: info@aradc.org
Home Page: www.aradc.org

Jack Eberstacher, CEO
Jon Nienas, Secretary/Treasurer
Stacy Mayuga, Marketing Director

Advocates in the ag retail and distribution industry.
Frequency: Annual
Founded in 1993

1040 ARBA National Convention
American Rabbit Breeders Association
8 Westport Court
Bloomington, IL 61704

309-664-7500
FAX 309-664-0941
Home Page: www.arba.net

Mike Avesing, President
Erik Bengtson, Vice-President
Eric Stewart, Executive Director
David Freeman, Treasurer

Seminar, banquet, luncheon and 1500 rabbit breeders exhibits.
3000 Attendees
Frequency: Annual/April
Founded in 1910

1041 ASA-CSSA-SSSA International Annual Meeting
American Society of Agronomy
5585 Guilford Road
Madison, WI 53711-5801

608-273-8080
FAX 608-273-2021
E-Mail: pscullion@agronomy.org
Home Page: www.agronomy.org
Social Media: *Facebook, Twitter, LinkedIn*

Newell Kitchen, President
Kenneth Barbarick, President-Elect

Society members are dedicated to the conservation and wise use of natural resources to pro-

duce food, feed and fiber crops while maintaining and improving the environment. Annual meeting and exhibits of agricultural equipment, supplies and services.
Frequency: Annual/Fall

1042 ASABE Annual International Meeting
American Society of Agricultural & Bio-Engineers
2950 Niles Road
St. Joseph, MI 49085-9659

269-429-0300
800-371-2723
FAX 269-429-3852
Home Page: www.asabe.org
Social Media: *Facebook, Twitter, YouTube*

Melissa Moore, Exec VP/Meetings & Conference Dir
Donna Hull, Publication Director

A forum to expand awareness of industry trends, promote and acknowledge innovations in design and technology, and provide opportunities for professional development. Networking, trade show, technical workshops and presentations, specialty sessions, and career fair.
Frequency: Annual/June
Founded in 1907

1043 ASAS-ADSA Annual Meeting
American Society of Animal Science
1800 S. Oak Street
Suite 100
Champaign, IL 61820-6974

217-356-9050
FAX 217-398-4119
Home Page: www.asas.org
Social Media: *Facebook, Twitter*

Dr. Margaret E. Benson, President
Dr. James L. Sartin, President-Elect
Dr. Meghan Wulster-Radcliffe, CEO
Jacelyn Friedrich, COO

Professional organization for animal scientists designed to help members provide effective leadership through research, extension, teaching and service for the dynamic and rapidly changing livestock and meat industries. Containing 45 booths. Always a joint meeting with ADSA, and usually with one or more of these organizations: CSAS, AMPA, WSASAS, and PSA.
2000 Attendees
Frequency: Annual/July
Founded in 1908

1044 ASCA Annual Conference
American Society of Consulting Arborists
9707 Key West Ave
Suite 100
Rockville, MD 20850-3992

301-947-0483
FAX 301-990-9771
E-Mail: asca@mgmtsol.com
Home Page: www.asca-consultants.org

Beth Palys, Executive Director

Recognized as a high quality, in depth conference with cutting edge speakers. Combining the best forum for discussion of current and relevant arboricultural issues, as well as consulting practice management issues and key consulting topics such as the role of the expert witness, risk assessment and tree appraisal
300 Attendees
Frequency: Annual/November/December

1045 ASEV National Conference
American Society for Enology and Vinticulture

PO Box 1855
Davis, CA 95617-1855

530-753-3142
FAX 530-753-3318
E-Mail: society@asev.org
Home Page: www.asev.org
Social Media: *LinkedIn*

Dr. Sara Spayd, President
Leticia Chacon-Rodriguez, 1st Vice President
Dr. James Kennedy, 2nd Vice President
Dr. James Harbertson, Secretary/Treasurer

Provides a forum for the presentation of research in the fields of enology and viticulture or related sciences.
Frequency: Annual/June
Founded in 1950

1046 ASFMRA Annual Meeting
American Socitey of Farm Mgrs & Rural Appraisers
950 S Cherry Street
Suite 508
Denver, CO 80246-2664

303-758-3513
FAX 303-758-0190
E-Mail: meetings@asfmra.org
Home Page: www.asfmra.org
Social Media: *Facebook, Twitter, LinkedIn*

Jeffrey Berg, President
Paul Joerger, President-Elect
Jim Rickert, 1st Vice President

Twenty-five exhibits of agricultural equipment, supplies and services; educational seminars and program sessions.
375 Attendees
Frequency: Annual/November

1047 ASHS Annual Conference
American Society for Horticultural Science
1018 Duke Street
Alexandria, VA 22314-2851

703-836-4606
FAX 703-836-2024
E-Mail: webmaster@ashs.org
Home Page: www.ashs.org
Social Media: *Facebook*

Fred T Davies, Chair
Dewayne Ingram, President
Paul Bosland, President-Elect
Curt R. Rom, Treasurer

Facilitating the mutual exchange of ideas and information concerning horticultural research, extension, education, and industry.
Frequency: Annual/August

1048 ATA Annual Conference
Animal Transportation Association
12100 Sunset Hills Road
Suite 130
Reston, VA 20190

703-437-4377
FAX 703-435-4390
E-Mail: info@animaltransportationassociation.org
Home Page: www.animaltransportationassociation.org

Robin Turner, Association Director
Lisa Schoppa, AATA President
Erik Liebegott, President-Elect
Chris Santarelli, Secretary/Treasurer

The latest information and technology relating to the transportation of animals. Subtopics include welfare, stress, meat quality, environmental control, biosecurity guidelines, training programs, and new transport designed crates and trailers.
150 Attendees
Frequency: Annual

1049 AVMA Annual Convention
American Veterinary Medical Association

1931 N Meacham Road
Suite 100
Schaumburg, IL 60173

800-248-2862
FAX 847-925-1329
E-Mail: avmaininfo@avma.org
Home Page: www.avma.org
Social Media: *Facebook, Twitter, Flickr, YouTube*

Rene Carlson, President
Douglas Aspros, President-Elect
Jan Strother, Vice President
Barbara Schmidt, Treasurer
W. Ron DeHaven, Executive Vice President

Seminar and more than 300 exhibits of products, materials, equipment, data, and services for veterinary medicine. Education and hands-on labs, exhibit hall, charitable events and networking.
10000 Attendees
Frequency: Annual/July

1050 Acres USA Conference
5321 Industrial Oaks Boulevard
Suite 128
Austin, TX 78735

512-892-4446
800-355-5315
FAX 512-892-4448
E-Mail: info@acresusa.com
Home Page: www.acresusa.com
Social Media: *Facebook, Twitter, LinkedIn*

Fred C Walters, Publisher/Editor
1300 Attendees
Founded in 1970
Printed in on newsprint stock

1051 Ag Progress Days
College of Agricultural Sciences
Penn State University
420 Agricultural Admin Building
University Park, PA 16802

814-865-2081
FAX 814-865-1677
E-Mail: agprogressdays@psu.edu
Home Page: www.apd.psu.edu

Bob Oberheim, Manager

Agricultural trade show focusing on the innovations and progress made in the agricultural industry. More than 400 commercial exhibitors, interactive educational exhibits, guided tours and workshops, machinery and field demonstrations, live animals and equine seminars and demonstrations.
50M Attendees
Frequency: Annual/August
Founded in 1976

1052 Agri News Farm Show
Agri News
18 1st Avenue SE
Rochester, MN 55904-6118

507-857-7707
800-533-1727
FAX 507-281-7436
Home Page: www.agrinew.com

John Losness, Publisher
Rosie Allen, Advertsising Manager
Mychal Wilmes, Managing Editor

Annual show of 123 exhibitors of farming equipment, supplies and services.
7,500 Attendees
Frequency: Annual/March

1053 Agricultural Retailers Association Convention and Expo
Agricultural Retailers Association

1156 15th Street
Suite 302
Washington, DC 20005

202-570-0825
800-535-6272
FAX 314-567-6808
E-Mail: kelly@aradc.org
Home Page: www.aradc.org
Social Media: *Facebook, Twitter*

Daren Coppock, President/CEO
Richard Gupton, Sr, VP, Public Policy
Michelle Hummel, VP Marketing/Communications

Annual show of 120 manufacturers, suppliers and distributors of agricultural chemicals and fertilizers. Seminar, conference and banquet.
1200 Attendees
Frequency: Annual/December
Founded in 1993

1054 Allied Social Sciences Association Annual Meeting
555 E Wells Street
Suite 1100
Milwaukee, WI 53202-6600

414-918-3190
FAX 414-276-3349
E-Mail: info@aaea.org
Home Page: www.aaea.org

Otto C Doering III, President
Yvonne C Bennett, Executive Director

The professional association for agricultural economists and related fields.
3000 Members
Frequency: Annual
Founded in 1910
Mailing list available for rent

1055 America Trades Produce Conference
590 East Frontage Road
PO Box 848
Nogales, AZ 85628

520-287-2707
FAX 520-287-2948
E-Mail: info@freshfrommexico.com
Home Page: www.fpaota.org

Lee Frank, President
Alicia Bon Martin, Vice Chair
Allison Moore, Communications Director
Jose Luis Obregon, Deputy Director
Martha Rascon, Public Affairs Director

Represents companies involved in growing, harvesting, marketing and importing of Mexican produce entering the US.
125+ Members
Founded in 1944

1056 American Farriers Association Annual Convention Marketplace
American Farriers Association
4059 Iron Works Parkway
Suite 1
Lexington, KY 40511

859-233-7411
FAX 859-231-7862
E-Mail: info@americanfarriers.org
Home Page: www.americanfarriers.org
Social Media: *Facebook*

Buck McClendon, President
Thomas Trosin, President Elect
John Blombach, Vice President
Alan Larson, Treasurer
Jason Knight, Secretary

One-hundred and seventy exhibits of equipment and supplies for farriers, seminar, banquet, luncheon and tours.
1500 Attendees
Frequency: Annual/February
Founded in 1971

1057 American Livestock Breeds Convervancy ALBC Conference
PO Box 477
Pittsboro, NC 27312

919-542-5704
FAX 919-545-0022
Home Page: www.albc-usa.org
Social Media: *Facebook, Blogger*

Charles Bassett, Executive Director

Ensuring the future of agriculture through genetic conservation and the promotion of endangered breeds of livestock and poultry. A nonprofit membership organization working to protect over 180 breeds of livestock and poultry from extinction.

1058 American Seed Trade Association Annual Conference
1701 Duke Street
Suite 275
Alexandria, VA 22314-2878

703-837-8140
FAX 703-837-9365
Home Page: www.amseed.com

Andy Lavigna, CEO

Producers of seeds for planting purposes. Consists of companies involved in seed production and distribution, plant breeding and related industries in North America.
850 Members
Founded in 1883

1059 Americas Food & Beverage Show
4601 NE 77th Avenue
Suite 200
Vancouver, WA 98662-2697

360-693-3373
FAX 360-693-3464
Home Page: www.wusata.org

Andy Anderson, Executive Director
Eliza Lane, Outreach Coordinator

A nonprofit organization that promotes the export of food and agricultural products from the Western region of the US Comprised of 13 state funded agricultural promotion agencies.

1060 Annual Agricultural Law Symposium
127 Young Rd.
Kelso, WA 98626

360-200-5699
FAX 360-423-2287
E-Mail: roberta@aglaw-assn.org
Home Page: www.aglaw-assn.org

Patricia A. Jensen, President
Amy Swanson, President-Elect
Robert P. Achenbach Jr., Executive Director

Bringing opportunities and ideas.
Frequency: Annual/October
Founded in 1980

1061 Annual Board of Delegates Meeting
1400 K St NW
Suite 1200
Washington, DC 20005-2449

202-789-0789
FAX 202-898-0522
E-Mail: grains@grains.org
Home Page: www.grains.org

Kenneth Hobbie, President
Michael T Callahan, Director International Operations
Cheri Johnson, Manager Communications
Valerie Smiley, Manager Membership
Andrew Pepito, Director Finance/Administration

Motivated by the grain sorghum, barley and corn producer associations and representatives

of the agricultural community. Provides commodity export market development.
Founded in 1960

1062 Annual Convention of the American Assoc. of Bovine Practitioners
American Association of Bovine Practicioners
PO Box 3610
Auburn, AL 36831-3610

334-821-0442
FAX 334-821-9532
E-Mail: aabphq@aabp.org
Home Page: www.aabp.org

Brian J. Gerloff, President
Nigel B. Cook, President-Elect
Daniel L. Grooms, Vice President
Brian K. Reed, Treasurer
Charles W. Hatcher, Exhibits Chairman

130 exhibits of pharmaceutical and biological manufacturers, equipment and agricultural companies, computer programs and supplies.
1905 Attendees
Frequency: Annual/September
Founded in 1967

1063 Annual Meeting and Professional Improvement Conferences (AM/PIC)
6584 W Duroc Road
Maroa, IL 61756
217-794-3700
FAX 217-794-5901
E-Mail: exec-dir@nacaa.com
Home Page: www.nacaa.com
Social Media: *Facebook, Twitter*

Rick Gibson, President
Hundreds of NACAA members from all over the country, every one relates to the same challenges faced every day on the job. Networking with other professional organizations.
Founded in 1917
Mailing list available for rent: 3500 names at $500 per M

1064 Aquatic Plant Management Society Annual Meeting
Aquatic Plant Management Society
PO Box 821265
Vicksburg, MS 39182-1265

FAX 601-634-5502
E-Mail: dpetty@ndrsite.com
Home Page: www.apms.org
Social Media: *Facebook, LinkedIn*

Tyler Koschnick, President
Mike Netherland, VP
Sherry Whitaker, Treasurer
Jeff Schardt, Secretary
Craig Aguillard, Director

An international organization of educators, scientists, commercial pesticide applicators, administrators and individuals interested in aquatic plant species and plant management.
Founded in 1961

1065 Argi-Marketing Conference
11020 King St
Suite 205
Overland Park, KS 66210-1201

913-491-6500
FAX 913-491-6502
E-Mail: agrimktg@nama.org
Home Page: www.nama.org
Social Media: *Facebook, Twitter, LinkedIn, YouTube, Flickr*

Jennifer Pickett, CEO
Vicki Henrickson, Vice President

Marketing and communication suppliers, including trade publications, radio and television broadcast sales organizations, premium/incentive manufacturers, printers, marketing re-

search firms, photographers and related professionals.
Founded in 1957

1066 Asia Pacific Leather Fair
1150 Connecticut Ave, NW
12th Floor
Washington, DC 20036

202-587-4250
E-Mail: jreddington@meatami.com
Home Page: www.ushsla.org

John Reddington, President
Susan Hogan, Manager
John Hochstein, Chairman

Exclusive representative of the hides and skin industry in the United States. Members range in size from small family-owned businesses to large corporations. Participates in two annual trade shows in Asia as a cooperator through the US Department of Agriculture's Foreign Agriculture Service.

1067 Beltwide Cotton Conference
National Cotton Council of America
7193 Goodlett Farms Parkway
Cordova, TN 38016

901-274-9030
FAX 901-725-0510
Home Page: www.cotton.org

Dr. Mark D. Lange, President & CEO
A. John Maguire, Sr, Vice President
Charles H. Parker, Chairman
Chuck Coley, Vice Chairman
Meredith B. Allen, Vice President

Offers a forum for agricultural professionals.
Frequency: Annual/January

1068 Big Iron Farm Show and Exhibition
Red River Valley Fair Association
1201 West Main Avenue
PO Box 797
West Fargo, ND 58078-0797

701-282-2200
800-456-6408
FAX 701-282-6909
E-Mail: info@redrivervalleyfair.com
Home Page: www.bigironfarmshow.com
Social Media: *Facebook*

Bryan Schulz, General Manager

Annual show of 750 manufacturers of agricultural machinery and related products with over 1,000 exhibit spaces.
70M Attendees
Frequency: Annual/September

1069 Breeders of the Carolinas Field Day
PO Box 1257
Kingsville, TX 78364-1257

361-592-9357
FAX 361-592-8572
Home Page: www.santagertrudis.com

Ervin Kaatz, Executive Director

Devoted to the interests and the needs of the breed developed in 1918 at the famous King Ranch in Texas. Recognized in 1940 by the USDA, and famou for efficient growth, solid red color, hardiness and good disposition. They areadaptable to many environments and are present throughout the US and in other countries.

1070 COSA Annual Meeting
Committee on Organic and Sustainable Agriculture
5585 Guilford Road
Madison, WI 53711-5801

608-273-8080
FAX 608-273-2021
Home Page: www.cosagroup.org

Ann-Marie Fortuna, Chair

COSA is a committee of the Tri-Societies for agronomy. The annual committee meeting is held in conjunction with the ASA-CSSA-SSSA Annual Meeting.
Frequency: Annual/Fall

1071 CPMA Convention
590 East Frontage Road
PO Box 848
Nogales, AZ 85628

520-287-2707
FAX 520-287-2948
E-Mail: info@freshfrommexico.com
Home Page: www.fpaota.org

Lee Frank, President
Alicia Bon Martin, Vice Chair
Allison Moore, Communications Director
Jose Luis Obregon, Deputy Director
Martha Rascon, Public Affairs Director

Represents more than 125 member companies involved in growing, harvesting, marketing and importing of mexican produce entering the US at Nogales, Arizona.
125+ Members
Founded in 1944

1072 Citrus Expo
Southeast AgNet Publications/Citrus Industry Mag
5053 NW Hwy 225-A
Ocala, FL 34482

352-671-1909
FAX 888-943-2224
E-Mail: CitrusExpo@southeastagnet.com
Home Page: www.citrusexpo.net

Maryann Holland, Show Manager

Citrus Trade Show with seminars, containing 150 exhibits. Complimentary attendance and lunch are provided to bona-fide grove owners & managers, citrus production managers, professional crop advisors, association execs & board members, government & legislative officials and the citrus research community.
1500 Attendees
Frequency: Annual/August
Founded in 1992

1073 Commodity Classic
Commodity Classic: ASA, NWGA, NCGA, NSP
632 Cepi Drive
Chesterfield, MO 63005-6397

636-733-9004
FAX 636-733-9005
E-Mail: corninfo@ncga.com
Home Page: www.commodityclassic.com

Dave Burmeister, Registration Information
Kristi Burmeister, Exhibitor Information
Susan Powers, Media/Press Information
Beth Musgrove, General Information
Peggy Findley, Sponsorship Information

550 booths of equipment, seed and chemicals. Lecture series, classes, entertainment, awards, annual meetings of several agri-organziations/associations, and the trade show.
4000 Attendees
Frequency: February

1074 Contractor Summit
6540 Arlington Blvd
Falls Church, VA 22042-6638

703-536-7080
FAX 703-536-7019
E-Mail: info@irrigation.org
Home Page: www.irrigation.org

Deborah Hamlin, Executive Director
Denise Stone, Meetings Director

Promotes education and use of irrigation in many areas of agriculture.
1600 Members
Founded in 1949

1075 Country Elevator Conference & Trade Shows
1250 I St NW
Suite 1003
Washington, DC 20005-3939

202-289-0873
FAX 202-289-5388
E-Mail: ngfa@ngfa.org
Home Page: www.ngfa.org

Kendell Keith, President
Ronald D Olson, Chairman
Tom Coyle, Second Vice Chair
Randall Gordon, Vice President

NGFA is the national trade association of grain elevators, feed and feed ingredient manufacturers, grain and oilseed processors, exporters, livestock and poultry integrators, and firms providing products and services to the industry.
Founded in 1896

1076 EMDA Industry Showcase
Equipment Marketing & Distribution Association
PO Box 1347
Iowa City, IA 52244

319-354-5156
FAX 319-354-5157
E-Mail: pat@edma.net
Home Page: www.edma.net

Patricia A Collins, Executive VP

Annual convention and 130 exhibits of equipment, supplies and services for wholesaler-distributors and independent manufacturer's representatives of shortline and specialty farm equipment, light industrial, lawn and garden, turf care equipment, estate and park maintenance equipment.
600 Attendees
Frequency: November

1077 Eastern Milk Producers Cooperative Annual Meeting
1985 Isaac Newton Square West
Reston, VA 20190-5094

703-742-6800
FAX 703-742-7459
Home Page: www.mdvamilk.com

Known for being a leader in the dairy industry, the Eastern Milk Producers Cooperative has an 85-plus year reputation for integrity, service and high quality products.
ISSN: west-

1078 EcoFarm Conference
Ecological Farming Association
2901 Park Ave.
Suite D-2
Soquel, CA 95073

831-763-2111
E-Mail: info@eco-farm.org
Home Page: eco-farm.org

Allie Wilson, Conference Production

The largest sustainable agriculture conference in the western US, with a technical focus.
Frequency: Annual
Founded in 1980

1079 El Foro
WATT Publishing Company
122 S Wesley Avenue
Mount Morris, IL 61054

815-734-4171
FAX 815-734-4201

E-Mail: olentine@wattmm.com
Home Page: www.wattnet.com

Jim Watt, Chairman/CEO

A trade show and technical symposium for the Latin American poultry, pig and feed industries. Containing 50 booths and 150 exhibits.
275 Attendees
Frequency: July

1080 Equipment Manufacturers Conference
American Feed Industry Association
2101 Wilson Blvd
Suite 916
Arlington, VA 22201-3047

703-524-0810
FAX 703-524-1921
E-Mail: afia@afia.org
Home Page: www.afia.org
Social Media: *Facebook, Twitter, LinkedIn*

Joel Newman, President
Richard Sellers, VP
Donald E Orr, Chairman
Anne Keller, Communications Director

Organization devoted to representing companies in the animal feed industry and its suppliers.
690 Members
Founded in 1909

1081 European Seafood Exposition
4601 NE 77th Avenue
Suite 200
Vancouver, WA 98662-2697

360-693-3373
FAX 360-693-3464
Home Page: www.wusata.org

Andy Anderson, Executive Director
Eliza Lane, Outreach Coordinator

A nonprofit organization that promotes the export of food and agricultural products from the Western region of the US Comprised of 13 state funded agricultural promotion agencies.

1082 FFA National Agricultural Career Show
National FFA Organization
PO Box 68960
6060 FFA Drive
Indianapolis, IN 46268-0960

888-332-2589
FAX 800-366-6556
E-Mail: careershow@ffa.org
Home Page: www.ffa.org

850 booths encouraging high school youth to select careers in the agricultural industry. Held during the National FFA Convention.
45M Attendees
Frequency: Fall, Annually

1083 FPAA Convention & Golf Tournament
590 East Frontage Road
PO Box 848
Nogales, AZ 85628

520-287-2707
FAX 520-287-2948
E-Mail: info@freshfrommexico.com
Home Page: www.fpaota.org

Lee Frank, President
Alicia Bon Martin, Vice Chair
Allison Moore, Communications Director
Jose Luis Obregon, Deputy Director
Martha Rascon, Public Affairs Director

Represents companies involved in growing, harvesting, marketing and importing of Mexican produce entering the US.
125+ Members
Founded in 1944

1084 Farm Bureau Showcase
American Farm Bureau Federation
1850 Howard Avenue
Suite C
Elk Grove, IL 60007

224-656-6600
FAX 847-685-8696
E-Mail: webmaster@fb.org
Home Page: www.fb.org

Bob Stallman, President

Two-hundred plus booths featuring exhibits of agricultural equipment, supplies and services.
6-8M Attendees
Frequency: January

1085 Farm Equipment Manufacturers Association Spring Management Clinic
1000 Executive Parkway
Suite 100
St Louis, MO 63141-6369

314-878-2304
FAX 314-732-1480
E-Mail: info@farmequip.org
Home Page: www.farmequip.org

Robert K Schnell, Executive VP
James Bearden, First VP
Richard W Heiniger, Second VP

An information gathering and distributing organization for farm equipment manufacturers and suppliers.
Founded in 1950

1086 Farm Progress Show
Farm Progress Companies
255 38th Avenue
Suite P
St Charles, IL 60174-5410

630-462-2224
800-441-1410
E-Mail: mjungmann@farmprogress.com
Home Page: www.farmprogressshow.com

Matt Jungman, National Shows Manager

Annual farm show of 400 exhibitors representing various types of agricultural products and services for farmers and agribusiness, including small operations to top producers.
Frequency: August/September

1087 Farm Science Review
Ohio State University
590 Woody Hayes Drive
232 Ag Engineering Building
Columbus, OH 43210-1057

614-926-6691
800-644-6377
FAX 614-292-9448
E-Mail: gamble.18@osu.edu
Home Page: fsr.osu.edu

Chuck Gamble, Manager
Mattk Sullivan, Assistant Manager
Suzanne Steel, Media Coordinator

Annual show of 600 exhibitors of agricultural equipment, supplies and services.
140M Attendees
Frequency: Annual/September

1088 Farm/Ranch Expo
Bacon Hedland Management
475 S Frontage Road
Suite 101
Burr Ridge, IL 60527

630-323-6880
FAX 630-898-3550

Gene Bacon, Show Manager

160 booths
7M Attendees
Frequency: January

1089 Farmfest
Farm Fairs
Highway 60 West
PO Box 731
Lake Crystal, MN 56055

507-726-6863
FAX 507-726-6750

Annual show of 450 manufacturers, suppliers and distributors of farm equipment and machinery, computers and software products, chemicals, seeds and crops, and techniques of planting, tillage and harvesting.
50M Attendees

1090 Fertilizer Outlook and Technology Conference
425 Third Street SW
Suite 950
Washington, DC 20002-8037

202-962-0490
FAX 202-962-0577
E-Mail: information@tfi.org
Home Page: www.tfi.org

Ford West, President
Ener Cunanan, Office Manager
Harry L Vroomen PhD, VP
Kathy Mathers, VP
Pamela D Guffain, Director/Government Relations
Gain perspective on the outlook for agriculture and major fertilizer materials and inputs from industry experts.
Founded in 1970

1091 Fresh Summit International Convention & Expo
1500 Casho Mill Road
PO Box 6036
Newark, DE 19714-6036

302-738-7100
FAX 302-731-2409
E-Mail: pma@pma.com
Home Page: www.pma.com
Social Media: *Facebook, Twitter, Flickr, YouTube, Xchange*

Bryan Silbermann, President
Lorna Christie, VP/Industry Products & Services
Julie Stewart, Director Communications
Nancy Tucker, VP Global Business Development
Rayne Yori, VP Finance
PMA brings together leaders from around the world and from every segment of the supply chain. Participants throughout the global fresh produce and floral supply chains come together as a community to learn, network, build relationships, and do business.
Founded in 1949

1092 GEAPS Operations, Management, & Technology Seminar
Grain Elevator & Processing Society
4248 Park Glen Road
Minneapolis, MN 55416

952-928-4640
FAX 952-929-1318
E-Mail: info@geaps.com
Home Page: www.geaps.com

David Krejci, Executive VP/Secretary
Darren Grahsl, Manager/Member & Chapter Services
Chuck House, Manager/Comm & Professional Dev
Amy McGarrigle, Manager/Member Ser & Information
Jason Stones, Manager/Member Ser & Publications
Offered in collaboration with the National Grain and Feed Association, boasted a faculty

of industry experts covering topics including contamination, purity and salvage; handling, storage and incident response; theft protection and inventory management beset practices; and natural disaster response and preparedness
2,000 Attendees
Frequency: March
Founded in 1937

1093 GIE+EXPO - Green Industry & Equipment Expo
Professional Lawncare Network, Inc
222 Pearl Street
Suite 300
New Albany, IN 47150

812-949-9200
800-558-8767
FAX 812-949-9600
E-Mail: info@gie-expo.com
Home Page: www.gie-expo.com
Social Media: *Facebook, Twitter*

Annual show of 400 manufacturers, suppliers and distributors of lawn care equipment, supplies and services, including fertilizers, weed control materials, insurance information and power equipment, plus education sessions and presentations and demos.

1094 Government Affairs Conference
USA Rice Federation
4301 N Fairfax Drive
Suite 425
Arlington, VA 22203

703-226-2300
FAX 703-236-2301
E-Mail: riceinfo@usarice.com
Home Page: www.usarice.com

Jamie Warshaw, Chairman
Discuss issues and activities for the U.S. rice industry, legislation, training, and seminars.
Frequency: Annual

1095 Grain Feed Association Trade Show
National Grain and Feed Association
1250 I Street NW
Suite 1003
Washington, DC 20005-3922

202-289-0873
FAX 202-289-5388
E-Mail: ngfa@ngfa.org
Home Page: www.ngfa.org

Randall Gordon, President
Dave Hoogmoed, Chairman
One hundred and thirty booths exhibiting agribusiness products, supplies and services.
1.3M Attendees
Frequency: March

1096 Grange Growth Summit
1616 H St NW
Suite 10
Washington, DC 20006-4999

202-628-3507
888-447-2643
FAX 202-347-1091
Home Page: www.nationalgrange.org

Ed Luttrell, President
Jennifer Dugent, Communications Manager
Leroy Watson, Legislative Director
Cindy Greer, Director Youth\Young Adult
DoriAnn Gedris, Marketing Director
Promotes general welfare and agriculture through local organizations. Presides over the advancement and promotion of the farming and agriculture industry.
300k Members
Founded in 1960

1097 Grape Grower Magazine Farm Show
Western Agricultural Publishing Company

4974 E Clinton Way
Suite 123
Fresno, CA 93727-1520

559-261-0396
FAX 559-252-7387
Home Page: www.westagpubco.com

Phill Rhoads, Manager
Seminars, exhibits and prizes for grape growers. Contianing 80 booths and exhibits.

1098 Green Industry Conference - GIC
Professional Lawncare Network, Inc (PLANET)
950 Herndon Parkway
Suite 450
Herndon, VA 20170

703-736-9666
800-395-2522
FAX 703-736-9668
E-Mail: info@gic-expo.com
Home Page:
www.landcarenetwork.org/events/greenindustryconf/index.cfm

Held in conjunction with the GIE+EXPO, the conference offers leadership series, workshops, educational opportunities, events, and new member orientation.
Frequency: Annual

1099 GrowerExpo
Ball Publishing
335 N River Street
PO Box 9
Batavia, IL 60510-0009

630-208-9080
800-456-5380
FAX 630-208-9350
E-Mail: info@ballpublishing.com

Diane Blazek, President
A trade show devoted to horticulture and floriculture production and marketing. 200 booths.
2M Attendees
Frequency: January

1100 Hawkeye Farm Show
Midwest Shows
PO Box 737
Austin, MN 55912

507-437-7969
FAX 507-437-7752
E-Mail: salesfsu@farmshowsusa.com
Home Page: www.farmshowsusa.com

Penny Swank, Show Manager
18000 Attendees
Frequency: March

1101 Holstein Association USA Regional Meeting
1 Holstein Place
PO Box 808
Brattleboro, VT 05302-0808

802-254-4551
800-965-5200
FAX 802-254-8251
E-Mail: info@holstein.com
Home Page: www.holsteinusa.com

John Meyer, CEO
Lisa Perrin, Marketing
Dairy cattle breed association with a membership base of people with strong interests in breeding, raising and milking Holstein cattle.
Founded in 1885

1102 IAOM Conferences and Expos
International Association of Operative Millers

10100 West 87th Street
Suite 306
Overland Park, KS 66212

913-338-3377
FAX 913-338-3553
E-Mail: info@iaom.info
Home Page: www.aomillers.org
Social Media: *Facebook, LinkedIn*

Joe Woodard, President
Aaron Black, Vice President
Joel Hoffa, Treasurer
Melinda Farris, Executive Vice President

Premier educational events for grain milling and seed processing professionals. The annual events gather milling and allied trade professionals from around the world for several days of education, networking and fellowship.
Frequency: Annual/May
Founded in 1896

1103 IFTA Annual Conference
International Fruit Tree Association
16020 Swingley Ridge Rd.
Suite 300
Chesterfield, MO 63017

636-449-5083
FAX 636-449-5051
E-Mail: dungey@ifruittree.org
Home Page: www.ifruittree.org

Tim Welsh, President
Rod Farrow, Vice President
Chris Hedges, Treasurer

Distinguished speakers, workshops and a regional orchard tour are highlights of the association's annual conference.
Frequency: Annual
Founded in 1958

1104 International Feed Expo
American Feed Industry Association
2101 Wilson Blvd
Suite 916
Arlington, VA 22201-3047

703-524-0810
FAX 703-524-1921
E-Mail: afia@afia.org
Home Page: www.afia.org
Social Media: *Facebook, Twitter, LinkedIn*

Joel Newman, President
Richard Sellers, VP
Donald E Orr, Chairman
Anne Keller, Communications Director

Organization devoted to representing companies in the animal feed industry and its suppliers.
Founded in 1909

1105 International Hoof-Care Summit
American Farriers Journal
223 Regency Court, PO Box 624
Suite 200
Brookfield, WI 53008-0624

262-782-4480
800-645-8455
FAX 262-782-1252
E-Mail: info@lesspub.com
Home Page: www.americanfarriers.com

Alice Musser, Conference Manager

Conference held for America's leading most innovative hoof-care professionals.
800 Attendees
Frequency: January

1106 International Marketing Conference & Annual Membership Meeting
1400 K St NW
Suite 1200
Washington, DC 20005-2449

202-789-0789
FAX 202-898-0522

E-Mail: grains@grains.org
Home Page: www.grains.org

Kenneth Hobbie, President
Michael T Callahan, Director International Operations
Cheri Johnson, Manager Communications
Valerie Smiley, Manager Membership
Andrew Pepito, Director Finance/Administration

Motivated by the grain sorghum, barley and corn producer associations and representatives of the agricultural community. Provides commodity export market development.
Founded in 1960

1107 International Off-Highway and Power Plant Meeting and Exposition
Society of Automotive Engineers
400 Commonwealth Drive
Warrendale, PA 15096-0001

724-776-4841
FAX 724-776-4026
Home Page: www.sae.org

Diane Rogne, Show Manager
Sam Barill, Treasurer
Andrew Brown, Treasurer

Annual show of 270 suppliers of parts, components, materials and systems utilized in farm and industrial machinery and off-road and recreational vehicles.
5000 Attendees
Circulation: 84,000

1108 International Sweets & Biscuits Fair (ISM)
4601 NE 77th Avenue
Suite 200
Vancouver, WA 98662-2697

360-693-3373
FAX 360-693-3464
Home Page: www.wusata.org

Andy Anderson, Executive Director
Eliza Lane, Outreach Coordinator

A nonprofit organization that promotes the export of food and agricultural products from the Western region of the US Comprised of 13 state funded agricultural promotion agencies.

1109 Irrigation Show
Irrigation Association
6540 Arlington Blvd
Falls Church, VA 22042-6638

703-536-7080
FAX 703-536-7019
E-Mail: info@irrigation.org
Home Page: www.irrigation.org

Phil A. Burkart, President
Robert D. Dobson, President-Elect
Warren C. Thoma, Vice President
John E. Vikupitz, Treasurer

The Irrigation Show is the industry's one-stop event. Discover innovations on the show floor and in technical sessions, make connections with industry experts, business partners, and peers and build expertise with targeted education and certification.
3.5M Attendees
Frequency: Annual/November

1110 KFYR Radio Agri International Stock & Trade Show
KFYR Radio
3500 East Rosser Avenue
PO Box 1658
Bismarck, ND 58501

701-580-0550
800-472-2170
FAX 701-255-8155

E-Mail: mwall@clearchannel.com
Home Page: www.kfyr.com

Syd Stewart, General Manager
Neil Cary, Manager
Jim Lowe, Manager

Annual show of 400 exhibitors of agricultural equipment, livestock and services.
15M Attendees
Frequency: February

1111 Kentucky Grazing Conference
151 Treasure Island Cswy. #2
St. Petersburg, FL 33706-4734

727-367-9702
800-707-0014
FAX 727-367-9608
E-Mail: darthay@yahoo.com
Home Page: www.nationalhay.org

Ron Bradtmueller, President
Gary Smith, First VP
Richard Larsen, Second VP
Rollie Bernth, Director
Don Kieffer, Executive Director

NHA is the trade group that represents the interests of the hay industry throughout the United States and internationally.
Founded in 1895

1112 Kosherfest
4601 NE 77th Avenue
Suite 200
Vancouver, WA 98662-2697

360-693-3373
FAX 360-693-3464
Home Page: www.wusata.org

Andy Anderson, Executive Director
Eliza Lane, Outreach Coordinator

A nonprofit organization that promotes the export of food and agricultural products from the Western region of the US Comprised of 13 state funded agricultural promotion agencies.

1113 Legislative Action Conference National Pork Producers Council
122 C Street NW
Suite 875
Washington, DC 20001

202-347-3600
800-937-7675
FAX 202-347-5265
E-Mail: warnerd@nppc.org
Home Page: www.nppc.org
Social Media: *Facebook, Twitter*

Don Butler, President
Sam Carney, President-Elect
Doug Wolf, Vice President
Neil Dierks, CEO

National Pork Producers Council hosts a legislative action conference twice a year for pork producers from around the nation to learn about, discuss and lobby on agriculture legislation important to the U.S. pork industry.

1114 Legislative Conference
6540 Arlington Blvd
Falls Church, VA 22042-6638

703-536-7080
FAX 703-536-7019
E-Mail: info@irrigation.org
Home Page: www.irrigation.org

Deborah Hamlin, Executive Director
Denise Stone, Meetings Director

Promotes education and use of irrigation in many areas of agriculture.
Founded in 1949

1115 Liquid Feed Symposium
American Feed Industry Association

2101 Wilson Blvd
Suite 916
Arlington, VA 22201-3047

703-524-0810
FAX 703-524-1921
E-Mail: afia@afia.org
Home Page: www.afia.org
Social Media: *Facebook, Twitter, LinkedIn*

Joel Newman, President
Richard Sellers, VP
Donald E Orr, Chairman
Anne Keller, Communications Director

Organization devoted to representing companies in the animal feed industry and its suppliers.
Founded in 1909

1116 Mid South Farm Gin Supply Exhibit

Southern Cotton Ginners Association
874 Cotton Gin Place
Memphis, TN 38106

901-947-3104
FAX 901-947-3103
Home Page: www.southerncottonginners.org

Chris Clegg, Chairman
Will Wade, President/Tennessee
Tim Price, Executive VP
Richard Kelly, VP/Tennessee
Allen Espey, Vice President/Tenessee

Exhibits new technology and practices for those in the cotton industry.
Frequency: Annual/February

1117 Mid-America Farm Show

Salina Area Chamber of Commerce
120 W Ash St.
PO Box 586
Salina, KS 67401

785-827-9301
FAX 785-827-9758
Home Page: www.salinakansas.org

Don Weiser, Show Manager

Annual show of 325 exhibitors of agricultural equipment, supplies and services, including irrigation equipment, fertilizer, farm implements, hybrid seed, agricultural chemicals, tractors, feed, farrowing crates and equipment, silos and bins, storage equipment and farm buildings.
13M Attendees
Frequency: Annual/March
Founded in 1911

1118 Mid-America Horticulture Trade Show

Mid Am Trade Show
401 N. Michigan Ave.
Suite 2200
Chicago, IL 60611

312-321-5130
800-300-6103
FAX 312-673-6882
E-Mail: mail@midam.org
Home Page: www.midam.org
Social Media: *Facebook, Twitter, LinkedIn, YouTube*

Barbara Rosborough, President
Bill Vogel, Vice President
Jim Melka, Secretary
Dave Story, Treasurer

Mid-Am is a green-industry event featuring more than 650 leading suppliers offering countless products, equipment, and services for the horticulture industry. Mid-Am also offers a variety of educational seminars featuring the best and the brightest in the horticultural and business communities to help keep you informed of the latest trends.
Frequency: Annual/January

1119 Midwest Ag Expo: OH

590 Woody Hayes Drive
Room 232
Columbus, OH 43210

614-292-4278
FAX 614-292-9448
E-Mail: gamble.19@osu.edu
Home Page: www.farmshows.org

Doug Wagner, President
Dennis Alford, 1st Vice President
Chip Blalock, 2nd Vice President
Chuck Gamble, Secretary-Treasurer

Members are agriculture trade show sponsors and suppliers of services to these shows. Provides members with education, communication and evaluation. Provides the best possible marketing showcase for exhibitors and related products to the farmer/rancher/producer customer.
Founded in 1972

1120 Midwest Expo: IL

Illinois Fertilizer & Chemical Association
130 W Dixie Highway
PO Box 186
Saint Anne, IL 60964-0186

815-939-1566
800-892-7122
FAX 815-427-6573

Jean Trobec, President

Annual show of 130 manufacturers, suppliers and distributors of agricultural chemical and fertilizer application equipment, supplies and services.
2500 Attendees
Frequency: August, Danville

1121 Midwest Farm Show

North Country Enterprises
5330 Wall St
Suite 100
Madison, WI 53718

608-240-4700
FAX 608-240-2069
Home Page: medaassn.com

Bill Henry, President
Massey Ferguson, Vice-President
Julie Roisum, Executive Assistant

250 booths. Top farm show exhibiting dairy and Wisconsin's tillage equipment, feed and seed.
175 Members
11M+ Attendees
Frequency: January

1122 NCTA Convention & Trade Show

National Christmas Tree Association
16020 Swingley Ridge Rd
Suite 300
Chesterfield, MO 63017-6030

636-449-5070
FAX 636-449-5051
E-Mail: info@realchristmastrees.org
Home Page: www.realchristmastrees.org

Steve Drake, CEO
Pam Helmsing, Executive Director
Becky Rasmussen, Assistant Director
Rick Dungey, PR/Marketing Director

Draws christmas tree growers, retailers and suppliers from around the world for education, contests, networking and the trade show.
500 Attendees
Frequency: Annual/August

1123 NDHIA Annual Meeting

National Dairy Herd Improvement Association

421 S Nine Mound Round
PO Box 930399
Verona, WI 53593-0399

608-848-6455
FAX 608-848-7675
E-Mail: info@dhia.org
Home Page: www.dhia.org

Jay Mattison, CEO
Dan Sheldon, President
Lee Maassen, VP
250 Attendees

1124 NHA Annual Convention

National Hay Association
151 Treasure Island Cswy
#2
St. Petersburg, FL 33706

727-367-9702
800-707-0014
FAX 727-367-9608
E-Mail: darthay@yahoo.com
Home Page: www.nationalhay.org

Information and technology affecting the Hay industry.
Frequency: Annual/September

1125 National 4-H Conference

4-H
National 4-H Conference Center
7100 Connecticut Ave.
Chevy Chase, MD 20815

Home Page: www.4-h.org/4-h-conference

Annual leadership and personal development event for 4-H members, 15 to 19 years old.
Frequency: Annual
Founded in 1927

1126 National Agri-Marketing Association Conference

National Agri-Marketing Association
11020 King Street
Suite 205
Overland Park, KS 66210

913-491-6500
FAX 913-491-6502
E-Mail: agrimktg@nama.org
Home Page: www.nama.org

Paul Redhage, President
Kenna Rathai, 1st Vice President

Annual show of 60 exhibitors of marketing and communication suppliers, including trade publications, radio and television broadcast sales organizations, premium/incentive manufacturers, printers, marketing research firms and photographers.
1400 Attendees
Frequency: April

1127 National Agricultural Plastics Congress

American Society for Plasticulture
526 Brittany Drive
State College, PA 16803

814-238-7045
FAX 814-238-7051
E-Mail: contact@plasticulture.org
Home Page: www.plasticulture.org

William Tietjen, President
Jodi Fleck-Arnold, VP
Edward Cary, Secretary/Treasurer
Patricia Heuser, Executive Director

Congress of research presentations, with exhibit area of equipment, supplies and services relating to greenhouse production and mulch film production of agricultural and horticultural crops.
225 Attendees
Frequency: March

1128 National Alliance of Independent Crop Consultants Annual Meeting

349 E Nolley Dr
Collierville, TN 38017-3538

901-861-0511
FAX 901-861-0512
E-Mail: jonesnaicc@aol.com
Home Page: www.naicc.org

Allison Jones, Executive VP
Shannon Gomes, Secretary

Represents individual crop consultants and contract researchers.
500+ Members
Founded in 1978

1129 National Association Extension 4-H Agents Convention

University of Georgia
Hoke Smith Annex
Athens, GA 30602

706-542-8804
E-Mail: freemand@vt.edu

Bo Ryles, State 4-H Leader
Heather Schultz, Live Stock Coordinator

50 booths for young people, youth staff and volunteers involved in 4-H.
1.2M Attendees
Frequency: November

1130 National Association of Agricultural Educators (NAAE) Convention

300 Garrigus Building
University of Kentucky
Lexington, KY 40545

859-257-2224
800-509-0204
FAX 859-323-3919
E-Mail: jay_jackman@ffa.org
Home Page: www.naae.org

Greg Curlin, President
Ken Couture, President-elect
Jay Jackman PhD, CAE, Executive Director
Alissa Smith, Associate Executive Director
Julie Fritsch, Com. and Marketing Coordinator

A federation of 50 affiliated state vocational agricultural teacher associations.
7600 Members
Founded in 1948

1131 National Association of County Agricultural Agents Conference

National Association of County Agricultural Agents
6584 W Duroc Road
Maroa, IL 61756

217-794-3700
FAX 217-794-5901
E-Mail: exec-dir@nacaa.com
Home Page: www.nacaa.com
Social Media: *Facebook, Twitter*

Paul Wigley, President
Paul Craig, President-Elect
Henry Dorough, Vice President
Richard Fechter, Secretary
Parman Green, Treasurer

Annual conference and exhibits for county agricultural agents and extension workers.
Frequency: Annual

1132 National Association of Wheat Growers Convention

National Association of Wheat Growers
415 2nd St NE
Suite 300
Washington, DC 20002-4993

202-547-7800
FAX 202-546-2638
E-Mail: wheatworld@wheatworld.org

Home Page: www.wheatworld.org
Social Media: *Facebook, Twitter*

Brett Blankenship, President
Jim Palmer, Chief Executive Officer

Convention and trade show for the wheat, corn, soybean and sorghum industries.
Frequency: Annual/February
Founded in 1950

1133 National Cotton Council Annual Meeting

7193 Goodlett Farms Parkway
Cordova, TN 38016

901-274-9030
FAX 901-725-0510
Home Page: www.cotton.org

Mark Lange, President/CEO
A. John Maguire, Senior Vice President

Membership consists of approximately 300 delegates named by cotton interests in the cotton-producing states.
35 Members

1134 National Custom Applicator Exposition

Agribusiness Association of Iowa
900 Des Moines Street
Suite 150
Des Moines, IA 50309-5549

515-262-8323
FAX 515-262-8960
E-Mail: info@agribiz.org
Home Page: www.agribiz.org

Ed Beaman, President/CEO

Annual show of 70 manufacturers, suppliers and distributors of agrichemicals, fertilizers, spray equipment, tanks, agriplanes and agricomputer and flotation equipment.
2500 Attendees
Frequency: August

1135 National Farm Machinery Show & Tractor Pull

590 Woody Hayes Drive
Room 232
Columbus, OH 43210

614-292-4278
FAX 614-292-9448
E-Mail: gamble.19@osu.edu
Home Page: www.farmshows.org

Doug Wagner, President
Dennis Alford, 1st Vice President
Chip Blalock, 2nd Vice President
Chuck Gamble, Secretary-Treasurer

Members are agriculture trade show sponsors and suppliers of services to these shows. Provides members with education, communication and evaluation. Provides the best possible marketing showcase for exhibitors and related products to the farmer/rancher/producer customer.
37 Members
Founded in 1972

1136 National Farm Machinery Show and Championship Tractor Pull

Kentucky Fair and Exposition Center
937 Phillips Lane
PO Box 37130
Louisville, KY 40233-7130

502-367-5000
FAX 502-367-5299
Home Page: www.farmmachineryshow.org

Harold Workman, President/CEO

Annual show of 800 plus exhibitors of agricultural products, equipment, supplies and services.
293M Attendees
Frequency: February

1137 National Farmers Union Convention

20 F Street NW
Suite 300
Washington, DC 20001

202-554-1600
800-347-1961
FAX 202-554-1654
Home Page: www.nfu.org
Social Media: *Facebook, Twitter, YouTube*

Roger Johnson, President
Claudia Svarstad, Vice President
Jeff Knudson, VP of Operations
Chandler Goule, VP of Government Relations

Promotes educational, cooperative and legislative activities of farm families in 26 states.
25000 Members
Founded in 1902

1138 National Grain Feed Association Annual Convention

National Grain Feed Association
1250 I Street NW
Suite 1003
Washington, DC 20005

202-289-0873
FAX 202-289-5388
E-Mail: ngfa@ngfa.org
Home Page: www.ngfa.org

Kendall Keith, NGFA President
Todd Kemp, Director Marketing/Treasurer
Rachel Lyon, Meetings Manager
Marion Wimbush, Pressman

Committee meetings addressing issues essential to the business; Ag Village exhibitors and speakers.
1.3M Attendees
Frequency: March/April
Founded in 1896

1139 National Grange Convention

1616 H St NW
Suite 10
Washington, DC 20006-4999

202-628-3507
888-447-2643
FAX 503-622-0343
Home Page: www.nationalgrange.org

Ed Luttrell, President
Jennifer Dugent, Communications Manager
Leroy Watson, Legislative Director
Cindy Greer, Director Youth\Young Adult
DoriAnn Gedris, Marketing Director

Promotes general welfare and agriculture through local organizations. Presides over the advancement and promotion of the farming and agriculture industry.
300k Members
Founded in 1960

1140 National No-Tillage Conference

No-Till Farmer
225 Regency Court, PO Box 624
Suite 200
Brookfield, WI 53008-0624

262-782-4480
800-645-8455
FAX 262-782-1252
E-Mail: info@lesspub.com
Home Page: www.no-tillfarmer.com

Mike Lessitor, Executive VP
Alice Musser, Conference Manager

Conference held for America's leading most innovative no-till farmers.
Frequency: January

1141 National Orange Show Fair

National Orange Show

689 South E Street
San Bernardino, CA 92408

909-888-6788
FAX 909-889-7666
Home Page: http://nationalorageshow.com
Social Media: Facebook

Five days of entertainment, art, exhibits, music, food and rides celebrating and educating the community on the California orange.
80000 Attendees
Frequency: Annual/May
Founded in 1889

1142 National Potato Council Annual Meeting
1300 L St NW
Suite 910
Washington, DC 20005-4107

202-682-9456
FAX 202-682-0333
E-Mail: spudinfo@nationalpotatocouncil.org
Home Page: www.nationalpotatocouncil.org
Social Media: Twitter

John Keeling, Executive VP/CEO
Hollee Stubblebine, Director Industry Communications
Keith Masser, President
Jim Wysocki, VP Finance
Dan Elmore, VP Grower/Public Relations

Connect with other grower leaders from across the country on shaping national public policy impacting potato production and distribution. Such issues as keeping potatoes in schools, finalizing free trade agreements, and gearing up for the next Farm Bill will be reviewed and strategies will be developed.
45000 Members
Founded in 1948

1143 National Potato Council's Annual Meeting
National Potato Council
1300 L Street
Suite 910
Washington, DC 20005

202-682-9456
E-Mail: spudinfo@nationalpotatocouncil.org
Home Page: www.nationalpotatocouncil.org

John Keeling, CEO
Holly Stubblebine, Director of Public Relations
Mark Szymanski, Director of Public Relations

Annual meeting and exhibits of potato growing equipment, supplies and services.

1144 New England Grows
New England Grows
8-D Pleasant Street South
Natick, MA 01760

508-653-3009
FAX 508-653-4112
E-Mail: info@newenglandgrows.org
Home Page: www.negrows.org

M. Virginia Wood, Executive Director
Jennifer A. Barich, Event Manager
Diane A. Zinck, Exhibit Sales & Marketing Manager
Owen J. Regan, Director of Operations
Elaine A. Kiesewetter, Conference Assistant

One of the largest and most visited horticulture and green industry events in North America, this event is known for its progressive educational conference and world-class trade show.
13000 Attendees
Frequency: Annual/February

1145 North American Beekeeping Conference
American Beekeeping Federation

3525 Piedmont Road
Bldg 5 Suite 300
Atlanta, GA 30305-1509

404-760-2875
FAX 404-240-0998
E-Mail: info@abfnet.com
Home Page: www.abfnet.com

Robin D. Lane, Executive Director
Tara Zeravsky, Senior Conference Planner

Expert talks and discussions about beekeeping hot topics; exhibits and introduction of new products; and workshops.
1500 Attendees
Frequency: Annual/January
Founded in 1943

1146 North American Deer Farmers Association Annual Conference & Exhibit
North American Deer Farmers Association
104 S Lakeshore Drive
Lake City, MN 55041-1266

651-345-5600
FAX 651-345-5603
E-Mail: info@nadefa.org
Home Page: www.nadefa.org

Carolyn Laughlin, President
Dave McQuaig, First VP
Glenn Dice Jr, Second VP

Annual show of 30+ exhibitors of deer farming equipment, supplies and services.
300 Attendees
Frequency: February
Founded in 1983

1147 North American Farm and Power Show
Tradexpos
811 W Oakland Avenue
PO Box 1067
Austin, MN 55912

507-437-4697
800-949-3976
FAX 507-437-8917
E-Mail: steve@tradexpos.com
Home Page: www.tradexpos.com

Steve Guenthner, Show Director

Agri-business farm show for the 5-state region. Free admission and parking.
28M Attendees
Frequency: March

1148 North American Fertilizer Transportation Conference
425 Third Street SW
Suite 950
Washington, DC 20002-8037

202-962-0490
FAX 202-962-0577
E-Mail: information@tfi.org
Home Page: www.tfi.org

Ford West, President
Ener Cunanan, Office Manager
Harry L Vroomen PhD, VP
Kathy Mathers, VP
Pamela D Guffain, Director/Government Relations

Co-hosted by The Fertilizer Institute and the Canadian Fertilizer Institute. Provides and opportunity for shippers and carriers to discuss issues of concern and work to reach mutually-beneficial solutions to logistical problems.
325 Members
Founded in 1970

1149 North American International Livestock Exposition
Kentucky Fair and Exposition Center

937 Phillips Lane
PO Box 37130
Louisville, KY 40209-7130

502-367-5000
FAX 502-367-5139
Home Page: www.livestockexpo.org

Debbie Burda, Booking/Events
Ellen Anderson, Event Contact

Purebred livestock show with more than 20,000 entries in eight major divisions: dairy cattle, dairy goats, llamas, quarter horses, draft horses, market swine, beef cattle, sheep. Held at Kentucky Fair and Exposition Center in Louisville, Kentucky.
Frequency: November

1150 Northwest Agricultural Congress
4991 Drift Creek Rd SE
Sublimity, OR 97385-9764

503-769-8940
FAX 503-769-8946
Home Page: www.nwagshow.com

Jim Heater, Show Manager

Second largest agricultural show on the west coast. Show is produced by the Northwest Horticultural Congress which is a partnership between Oregon Horticultural Society, the Oregon Association of Nurseries and Northwest Nut Growers Association. Show held in conjunction with annual meetings and seminars by all three of the horticultural groups.
21000 Members

1151 Nut Grower Magazine Farm Show
Western Agricultural Publishing Company
4974 E Clinton Way
Suite 123
Fresno, CA 93727-1520

559-252-7000
FAX 559-252-7387

Phill Rhoads, Manager

Productions seminars, guest speakers, prizes and exhibits for nut growers. Containing 80 booths and exhibits.

1152 Organic Seed Growers Conference
PO Box 772
Port Townsend, WA 98368

360-385-7192
FAX 360-385-7455
E-Mail: info@seedalliance.org
Home Page: www.seedalliance.org
Social Media: Facebook, Twitter

Dan Hobbs, Executive Director
Matthew Dillon, Executive Director

Supports the ethical development and stewardship of the genetic resources of agricultural seed.
Founded in 1975

1153 Ozark Fall Farmfest
Ozark Empire Fair
3001 North Grant Street
PO Box 630
Springfield, MO 65308

417-833-2660
FAX 417-833-3769
Home Page: www.ozarkempirefair.com

Pat Lloyd, Manager

Annual show of 700 exhibitors with about 600 booths of agricultural products and services, including livestock.
40M Attendees
Frequency: October

1154 PMA Convention & Exposition
Produce Marketing Association

1500 Casho Mill Road
Newark, DE 19711-3547

302-738-7100
FAX 302-731-2409
E-Mail: pma@pma.com
Home Page: www.pma.com
Social Media: *Twitter, Flickr, YouTube*

Bryan Silbermann, President & CEO
Lorna D. Christie, Vice President & COO
Yvonne Bull, CFO

A trade association of companies engaged in
the marketing of fresh and safe produce and
floral products. Show will inlcude 600 exhibitors with 1,600 booths.
16000 Attendees
Frequency: Annual/October
Founded in 1949

1155 PMA Fresh Summit

590 East Frontage Road
PO Box 848
Nogales, AZ 85628

520-287-2707
FAX 520-287-2948
E-Mail: info@freshfrommexico.com
Home Page: www.fpaota.org

Lee Frank, President
Alicia Bon Martin, Vice Chair
Allison Moore, Communications Director
Jose Luis Obregon, Deputy Director
Martha Rascon, Public Affairs Director

Represents more than 125 member companies
involved in growing, harvesting, marketing and
importing of mexican produce entering the US
at Nogales, Arizona.
125+ Members
Founded in 1944

1156 Pest World

National Pest Management Association
9300 Lee Highway
Suite 301
Fairfax, VA 22031

703-738-8330
FAX 703-352-3031
Home Page: www.pestworld.org

Robert Lederer, Executive VP
Dominique Broyles, Director
Conventions/Meetings

240 booths.
4000 Attendees
Frequency: October

1157 Potato Expo

1300 L St NW
Suite 910
Washington, DC 20005-4107

202-682-9456
FAX 202-682-0333
E-Mail: spudinfo@nationalpotatocouncil.org
Home Page: www.nationalpotatocouncil.org
Social Media: *Twitter*

John Keeling, Executive VP/CEO
Hollee Stubblebine, Director Industry
Communications
Keith Masser, President
Jim Wysocki, VP Finance
Dan Elmore, VP Grower/Public Relations

Largest conference and tradeshow for the potato industry held in North America. Offers educational programming covering the top issues
facing the potato industry, provides networking
opportunities with key decision makers and
showcases the latest products and services for
potato production and distribution.
45000 Members
Founded in 1948

1158 Power Show

590 Woody Hayes Drive
Room 232
Columbus, OH 43210

614-292-4278
FAX 614-292-9448
E-Mail: gamble.19@osu.edu
Home Page: www.farmshows.org

Doug Wagner, President
Dennis Alford, 1st Vice President
Chip Blalock, 2nd Vice President
Chuck Gamble, Secretary-Treasurer

Members are agriculture trade show sponsors
and suppliers of services to these shows. Provides members with education, communication
and evaluation. Provides the best possible marketing showcase for exhibitors and related
products to the farmer/rancher/producer
customer.
37 Members
Founded in 1972

1159 Prairie Farmer Farm Progress Show

Farm Progress Publishers
1301 E Mound Road
Decatur, IL 62526-9394

217-877-9070
FAX 217-877-9695

Sherry Stout, Editor
Jeffrey Smith, Advertising

One of the largest farm shows in the country.

1160 Pro Farmer Midwest Crop Tour

1818 Market Street 31st Floor
Philadelphia, PA 19103

800-772-0023
E-Mail: editors@profarmer.com
Home Page: www.profarmer.com
Social Media: *Twitter*

Sue King, Contact

Join the Pro Farmer editors at these seminars to
discuss commodity markets, world economy,
farm policy, land prices and more.
25M Members
Founded in 1973

**1161 Produce Executive Development
Program**

1901 Pennsylvania Ave NW
Suite 1100
Washington, DC 20006-3412

202-303-3400
FAX 202-303-3433
E-Mail: united@unitedfresh.org
Home Page: www.uffva.org
Social Media: *Facebook, Twitter, YouTube*

Thomas E Stenzel, CEO
Nicholas J Tompkins, Chair
Robert A Grimm, Executive Committee
Daniel G Vache, Secretary/Treasurer

Equipment, supplies, cartons, packaging machinery, computers, sorting and sizing equipment, harvesting equipment, film wrap
manufacturing and commodity organizations.
1000+ Members
Founded in 1904

1162 Produce Inspection Training Program

1901 Pennsylvania Ave NW
Suite 1100
Washington, DC 20006-3412

202-303-3400
FAX 202-303-3433
E-Mail: united@unitedfresh.org
Home Page: www.uffva.org
Social Media: *Facebook, Twitter, YouTube*

Thomas E Stenzel, CEO
Nicholas J Tompkins, Chair

Robert A Grimm, Executive Committee
Daniel G Vache, Secretary/Treasurer

Equipment, supplies, cartons, packaging machinery, computers, sorting and sizing equipment, harvesting equipment, film wrap
manufacturing and commodity organizations.
1000+ Members
Founded in 1904

**1163 Produce for Better Health Annual
Meeting**

590 East Frontage Road
PO Box 848
Nogales, AZ 85628

520-287-2707
FAX 520-287-2948
E-Mail: info@freshfrommexico.com
Home Page: www.fpaota.org

Lee Frank, President
Alicia Bon Martin, Vice Chair
Allison Moore, Communications Director
Jose Luis Obregon, Deputy Director
Martha Rascon, Public Affairs Director

Represents companies involved in growing,
harvesting, marketing and importing of Mexican produce entering the US.
125+ Members
Founded in 1944

**1164 Profit Briefing Professional Farmers
of America**

1818 Market Street 31st Floor
Philadelphia, PA 19103

800-772-0023
E-Mail: editors@profarmer.com
Home Page: www.profarmer.com
Social Media: *Twitter*

Sue King, Contact

Join the Pro Farmer editors at these seminars to
discuss commodity markets, world economy,
farm policy, land prices and more.
25M Members
Founded in 1973

**1165 Purchasing & Ingredient Suppliers
Conference**

American Feed Industry Association
2101 Wilson Blvd
Suite 916
Arlington, VA 22201-3047

703-524-0810
FAX 703-524-1921
E-Mail: afia@afia.org
Home Page: www.afia.org
Social Media: *Facebook, Twitter, LinkedIn*

Joel Newman, President
Richard Sellers, VP
Donald E Orr, Chairman
Anne Keller, Communications Director

Organization devoted to representing companies in the animal feed industry and its
suppliers.
690 Members
Founded in 1909

1166 SAF National Convention

5400 Grosvenor Ln
Bethesda, MD 20814-2198

301-897-8720
FAX 301-897-3690
E-Mail: safweb@safnet.org
Home Page: www.safnet.org

Michael T Goergen Jr, Executive VP/CFO
Brittany Brumby, Assistant to the CEO/Council
Amy Ziadi, Information Technology Manager
Larry D Burner CPA, Sr Director Finance

Provides access to information and networking
opportunities to prepare members for the chal-

lenges and the changes that face natural resource professionals.
Founded in 1900

1167 SBS Conference & Exhibition
Society for Biomolecular Sciences
100 Illinois Street
Suite 242
St. Charles, IL 60174

630-256-7527
877-990-7527
FAX 630-741-7527
E-Mail: slas@slas.org
Home Page: www.slas.org
Social Media: *Facebook, Twitter, LinkedIn*

Michelle Palmer, Ph.D, President
David Dorsett, Vice President
Erick Rubin, Ph.D, Treasurer
Andy Zaayenga, Secretary

Scientists, innovators, researchers and industry analysts from around the world will converge to learn about the latest trends and basic and applied research that are transforming the way new pharmaceuticals are developed.
2000 Attendees
Frequency: Annual

1168 Santa Gertrudis Breeders International Annual Meeting
PO Box 1257
Kingsville, TX 78364-1257

361-592-9357
FAX 361-592-8572
Home Page: www.santagertrudis.com

Ervin Kaatz, Executive Director

Information and issues regarding America's First Beef Breed developed in 1918 at the famous King Ranch in Texas. Recognized in 1940 by the USDA. Famous for rapid and efficient growth, solid red color, hardiness and good disposition. They are adaptable to many environments and are present throughout the US and in other countries.

1169 Society for Biomolecular Screening
Society for Biomolecular Screening
36 Tamarack Avenue
Suite 348
Danbury, CT 06810

203-788-8828
FAX 203-748-7557
E-Mail: sbsemail@aol.com
Home Page: www.sbsonline.org

Al Kolbh, President
Christine Giordano, Executive Director
Larry Walker, Editor-in-Chief
Marietta Manono, Manager
Meetings/Exhibitions

Technical sessions, exhibits, exhibitor tutorials, short courses, discussion groups related to discovery in the pharmaceutical and agrochemical industry and 181 exhibits.

1170 Soil and Water Conservation Society Annual International Conference
Soil and Water Conservation Society
945 SW Ankeny Road
Ankeny, IA 50021-9764

515-289-2331
800-843-7645
FAX 515-289-1227
E-Mail: swcs@swcs.org
Home Page: www.swcs.org

Bill Boyer, President
Dan Towery, Vice-President
Clark Gantzer, Secretary
Jerry Pearce, Treasurer

Explores ways to improve the linkages among conservation science, policy and application at local, national, and international scales. The conference will provide participants an opportunity to teach skills, learn techniques, compare successes, and improve understanding.
1200 Attendees
Frequency: Annual

1171 Southern Farm Show
590 Woody Hayes Drive
Room 232
Columbus, OH 43210

614-292-4278
FAX 614-292-9448
E-Mail: gamble.19@osu.edu
Home Page: www.farmshows.org

Doug Wagner, President
Dennis Alford, 1st Vice President
Chip Blalock, 2nd Vice President
Chuck Gamble, Secretary-Treasurer

Members are agriculture trade show sponsors and suppliers of services to these shows. Provides members with education, communication and evaluation. Provides the best possible marketing showcase for exhibitors and related products to the farmer/rancher/producer customer.
37 Members
Founded in 1972

1172 St. Louis All Equipment Expo
SouthWestern Association
P.O. Box 419264
Kansas City, MO 64141

816-762-5616
800-561-5323
FAX 816-561-1249
E-Mail: oholcombe@swassn.com
Home Page: www.swassn.com

Jeffrey Flora, CEO
Cory Hayes, Director of Education

Manufacturers, suppliers and distributors of farm equipment, outdoor power equipment, supplies and agriculture products. Containing 350 booths.
15M Attendees
Frequency: December

1173 State Masters Conference
1616 H St NW
Suite 10
Washington, DC 20006-4999

202-628-3507
888-447-2643
FAX 202-347-1091
Home Page: www.nationalgrange.org

Ed Luttrell, President
Jennifer Dugent, Communications Manager
Leroy Watson, Legislative Director
Cindy Greer, Director Youth\Young Adult
DoriAnn Gedris, Marketing Director

Promotes general welfare and agriculture through local organizations. Presides over the advancement and promotion of the farming and agriculture industry.
300k Members
Founded in 1960

1174 Sunbelt Agricultural Exposition
Sunbelt Ag Expo
290-G Harper Boulevard
Moultrie, GA 31788-2157

229-985-1968
FAX 229-890-8518
E-Mail: info@sunbeltexpo.com
Home Page: www.sunbeltexpo.com
Social Media: *Facebook*

Over 1,200 exhibitors showing the latest agricultural technology in products and equipment plus harvesting and tillage demonstrations in the field. Largest farm show in North America's premier farm show.
200M Attendees
Frequency: Annual/October

1175 Sustainable Foods Summit
1340 North Cotner Blvd
Lincoln, NE 68505

402-477-2323
FAX 402-477-4325
E-Mail: info@ocia.org
Home Page: www.ocia.org

Jeff See, Executive Director

OCIA International is a farmer owned international program of certification, which adheres to strict organic standards. It currently certifies thousands of farmers and processors in North, Central and South America and Asia. OCIA International is IFOAM accredited and adheres to the USDA ISO Guide 65, Japan Agriculture Standards and the Quebec Accreditation Council. OCIA has also been accredited from the USDA National Organic Program and Costa Rica Ministry of Agriculture.
3500 Members
Founded in 1985
Mailing list available for rent: 3500 names at $50 per M

1176 Sweetener Symposium
2111 Wilson Blvd
Suite 600
Arlington, VA 22201-3051

703-351-5055
FAX 703-351-6698
E-Mail: info@sugaralliance.org
Home Page: www.sugaralliance.org

James Johnson, President
Jack Roney, Director Economics/Policy Analysis
Luther Markwart, Executive Vice President
Carolyn Cheney, Vice President

Covering a broad range of timely issues affecting the industry.
Founded in 1983

1177 TFI Fertilizer Marketing & Business Meeting
425 Third Street SW
Suite 950
Washington, DC 20002-8037

202-962-0490
FAX 202-962-0577
E-Mail: information@tfi.org
Home Page: www.tfi.org

Ford West, President
Ener Cunanan, Office Manager
Harry L Vroomen PhD, VP
Kathy Mathers, VP
Pamela D Guffain, Director/Government Relations

Brings together members from each sector of the fertilizer industry for two days of networking and conducting business leading up to the spring planting season.
325 Members
Founded in 1970

1178 TFI World Fertilizer Conference
425 Third Street SW
Suite 950
Washington, DC 20002-8037

202-962-0490
FAX 202-962-0577
E-Mail: information@tfi.org
Home Page: www.tfi.org

Ford West, President
Ener Cunanan, Office Manager
Harry L Vroomen PhD, VP
Kathy Mathers, VP

Pamela D Guffain, Director/Government Relations

Provides two days of networking and conducting business with industry leaders from as many as 60 different countries that represent all sectors of the fertilizer industry.
325 Members
Founded in 1970

1179 Tree Fruit Expo
Western Agricultural Publishing Company
4974 E Clinton Way
Suite 123
Fresno, CA 93727-1520

559-252-7000
FAX 559-252-7387

Phill Rhoads, Manager

Productions seminars, dessert contest, guest speakers, prizes and exhibits for tree fruit growers. Containing 80 booths and exhibits.

1180 USA Rice Outlook Conference
USA Rice Federation
4301 N Fairfax Drive
Suite 425
Arlington, VA 22203

703-226-2300
FAX 703-236-2301
E-Mail: riceinfo@usarice.com
Home Page: www.usarice.com

Jamie Warshaw, Chairman
Jeannette Davis, Conference Contact

Discuss issues and activities for the U.S. rice industry, legislation, training, and seminars.
Frequency: Annual

1181 USHSLA Annual Convention
United States Hide, Skin & Leather Association
1150 Connecticut Avenue, NW
12th Floor
Washington, DC 20036

202-587-4250
Home Page: www.ushsla.org

John Hochstein, Chairman
John Reddington, President

Represents the hide, skin and leather industries. Members range from small family-owned businesses to large corporations.
Frequency: Annual

1182 United Fresh Convention
590 East Frontage Road
PO Box 848
Nogales, AZ 85628

520-287-2707
FAX 520-287-2948
E-Mail: info@freshfrommexico.com
Home Page: www.fpaota.org

Lee Frank, President
Alicia Bon Martin, Vice Chair
Allison Moore, Communications Director
Jose Luis Obregon, Deputy Director
Martha Rascon, Public Affairs Director

Represents companies involved in growing, harvesting, marketing and importing of Mexican produce entering the US.
125+ Members
Founded in 1944

1183 United Fresh Fruit and Vegetable Association Annual Convention
United Fresh Fruit & Vegetable Association
1901 Pennsylvania Avenue NW
Suite 1100
Washington, DC 20006

202-624-4989
FAX 202-303-3433

E-Mail: united@uffva.org
Home Page: www.uffva.org

Thomas Stenzel, CEO
Mark Overbay, Manager Communications
30000 Attendees

1184 United States Animal Health Association Annual Meeting
4221 Mitchell Ave.
St Joseph, MO 64508

816-671-1144
FAX 816-671-1201
E-Mail: usaha@usaha.org
Home Page: www.usaha.org

Benjamin Richey, Executive Director
Kelly Janicek, Executive Assistant

Seeks to prevent, control and eliminate livestock diseases.
1400 Members
Founded in 1897

1185 United States Hide, Skin & Leather Assoc. - Asia Pacific Leather Fair
1150 Connecticut Ave, NW
12th Floor
Washington, DC 20036

202-587-4250
E-Mail: jreddington@meatami.com
Home Page: www.ushsla.org

John Reddington, President
Susan Hogan, Manager
John Hochstein, Chairman
Stephen Sothmann, Director/International Affairs
Stephen Sothmann, Event Coordinator

Buyers will see the complete spectrum of the leather sector featuring the latest technology and products for leather making and footwear, as well as the widest range of leathers from around the globe displayed under one roof.
35 Members

1186 Virginia Farm Show
Lee Publications
6113 State Highway 5
PO Box 121
Palatine Bridge, NY 13428-0121

518-673-2269
800-218-5586
FAX 518-673-3245
E-Mail: kmaring@leepub.com
Home Page: www.leepub.com

Ken Maring, Trade Show Manager

This show caters to the full-time farmer, with exhibits of all the major lines of equipment and services, and seminars presented by industry experts in dairy, beef and crop production.
Frequency: January
Founded in 1982

1187 Walnut Council Annual Meeting
1011 N 725 W
West Lafayette, IN 47906-9431

765-583-3501
FAX 765-583-3512
E-Mail: walnutcouncil@walnutcouncil.org
Home Page: www.walnutcouncil.org

Liz Jackson, Executive Director
Larry R Frye, VP
William Hoover, Treasurer

Inviting scientists with the latest research on hardwood forestry, black walnut in particular, to present.
1000 Members
Founded in 1970

1188 Washington Public Policy Conference
United Fresh Produce Association

1901 Pennsylvania Ave NW
Suite 1100
Washington, DC 20006-3412

202-303-3400
FAX 202-303-3433
E-Mail: united@unitedfresh.org
Home Page: www.uffva.org
Social Media: *Facebook, Twitter, YouTube*

Thomas E Stenzel, CEO
Nicholas J Tompkins, Chair
Robert A Grimm, Executive Committee
Daniel G Vache, Secretary/Treasurer

Equipment, supplies, cartons, packaging machinery, computers, sorting and sizing equipment, harvesting equipment, film wrap manufacturing and commodity organizations.
1000+ Members
Founded in 1904

1189 Water Conference
6540 Arlington Blvd
Falls Church, VA 22042-6638

703-536-7080
FAX 703-536-7019
E-Mail: info@irrigation.org
Home Page: www.irrigation.org

Deborah Hamlin, Executive Director
Denise Stone, Meetings Director

Promotes education and use of irrigation in many areas of agriculture.
1600 Members
Founded in 1949

1190 Western Fairs Association Convention & Trade Show
1776 Tribute Rd
Suite 210
Sacramento, CA 95815-4495

916-927-3100
FAX 916-927-6397
E-Mail: stephenc@fairsnet.org
Home Page: www.fairsnet.org

Stephen J Chambers, Executive Director
Jon Baker, VP

A non-profit association with members throughout the Western United States and Canada that strives to promote industry standards. Membership includes access to conventions and trade shows, educational training programs as well as legislative advocacy support.
2000 Members
Founded in 1922

1191 Western Farm Show
Investment Recovery Association
638 W 39th Street
Kansas City, MO 64111

816-561-5323
800-728-2272
FAX 816-561-1991

Annual show of 700 manufacturers, suppliers and distributors of equipment, supplies and services relating to the agricultural industry.
35M Attendees
Frequency: February
Founded in 1962

1192 Wheat Industry Conference
415 2nd Street NE
Washington, DC 20002-4993

202-547-7800
FAX 202-546-2638
E-Mail: wheatworld@wheatworld.org
Home Page: www.wheatworld.org
Social Media: *Facebook, Twitter, YouTube*

David Cleavinger, First Vice President
Karl Scronce, Second Vice President
Dana Peterson, CEO
Melissa George Kessler, Director of Communications

Nonprofit partnership of US wheat growers, by combining their strengths, voices and ideas are working to ensure a better future for themselves, their industry and the general public.
Founded in 1950

1193 Winter Fancy Food Show
4601 NE 77th Avenue
Suite 200
Vancouver, WA 98662-2697

360-693-3373
FAX 360-693-3464
Home Page: www.wusata.org

Andy Anderson, Executive Director
Eliza Lane, Outreach Coordinator

A nonprofit organization that promotes the export of food and agricultural products from the Western region of the US Comprised of 13 state funded agricultural promotion agencies.

1194 World Dairy Expo
151 Treasure Island Cswy. #2
St. Petersburg, FL 33706-4734

727-367-9702
800-707-0014
FAX 727-367-9608
E-Mail: darthay@yahoo.com
Home Page: www.nationalhay.org

Ron Bradtmueller, President
Gary Smith, First VP
Richard Larsen, Second VP
Rollie Bernth, Director
Don Kieffer, Executive Director

NHA is the trade group that represents the interests of the hay industry throughout the United States and internationally.
750 Members
Founded in 1895

1195 World Pork Expo
122 C Street NW
Suite 875
Washington, DC 20001

202-347-3600
800-937-7675
FAX 202-347-5265
E-Mail: warnerd@nppc.org
Home Page: www.nppc.org
Social Media: *Facebook, Twitter*

Don Butler, President
Sam Carney, President-Elect
Doug Wolf, Vice President
Neil Dierks, CEO

The world's largest pork-specific trade show featuring business seminars, hundreds of exhibitors, breed shows and sales, and plenty of food and entertainment for everyone.
44 Members

Directories & Databases

1196 AGRICOLA
US National Agricultural Library
10301 Baltimore Ave
Beltsville, MD 20705-2351

301-504-5755
FAX 301-504-5675
E-Mail: director@nalusda.gov
Home Page: www.agricola.nal.usda.gov/

Simon Y Liu, Director
Chris Cole, Acting Deputy Director

A database containing more than 3.3 million citations to journal literature, government reports, proceedings, books, periodicals, theses, patents, audiovisuals, electronic information, and other materials related to agriculture and its allied sciences.
Founded in 1962

1197 ARI Network
Ari Network Services
10850 W Park Pl
Suite 1200
Milwaukee, WI 53224-3636

414-973-4300
800-558-9044
FAX 414-973-4619
Home Page: www.arinet.com
Social Media: *Facebook, Twitter, LinkedIn, YouTube*

Roy W. Olivier, President & CEO
Darin R. Janecek, CFO
Brian E. Dearing, Chairman

Offers current information on agricultural business, financial and weather information as well as statistical information for farmers.

1198 Ag Ed Network
ARI Network Services
10850 W Park Pl
Suite 900
Milwaukee, WI 53224-3636

414-973-4300
800-558-9044
FAX 414-973-4619
E-Mail: info@arinet.com
Home Page: www.arinet.com

Roy W Olivier, Chief Executive Officer
John C Bray, New Market Development

Offers access to more than 1500 educational agriculture lessons covering farm business management and farm production.
Frequency: Full-text

1199 AgriMarketing Services Guide
Henderson Communications LLC
1422 Elbridge Payne Rd
Suite 250
Chesterfield, MO 63017-8544

636-728-1428
FAX 636-777-4178
E-Mail: info@agrimarketing.com
Home Page: www.agrimarketing.com

Richard A Herrett, Executive Director

AgriMarketing Services Guide is published each December and is commonly referred to as the Who's Who in the North American ag industry sector.
Frequency: Annual/December

1200 Agricultural Research Institute: Membership Directory
Agricultural Research Institute
9650 Rockville Pike
Bethesda, MD 20814-3998

301-530-7122
FAX 301-571-1816

Richard A Herrett, Executive Director

125 member institutions; also lists study panels and committees interested in environmental issues, pest control, agricultural meteorology, biotechnology, food irradiation, agricultural policy, research and development, food safety, technology transfer and remote sensing.
Cost: $50.00
Frequency: Annual

1201 American Feed Industry Association: Software Directory
American Feed Industry Association
2101 Wilson Blvd
Suite 916
Arlington, VA 22201-3047

703-524-0810
FAX 703-524-1921

E-Mail: afia@afia.org
Home Page: www.afia.org

Joel Newman, President/CEO
Richard Sellers, Vice President
Anne Keller, Communications Director
Donald E Orr, Chairman

Companies that design software programs applicable to the feed industry.
Cost: $25.00

1202 American Fruit Grower: Source Book Issue
Meister Media Worldwide
37733 Euclid Ave
Willoughby, OH 44094-5992

440-942-2000
800-572-7740
FAX 440-975-3447
E-Mail: joe_monahan@meistermedia.com
Home Page: www.meistermedia.com

Richard T Meister, Chairman
Gary T Fitzgerald, President
Joe Monahan, Group Publisher

Offers a list of manufacturers and distributors of equipment and supplies for the commercial fruit growing industry.
Cost: $19.95
66 Pages
Circulation: 35,143

1203 American Meat Science Association Directory of Members
American Meat Science Association
2441 Village Green Place
Champaign, IL 61822

217-356-5370
800-517-AMSA
FAX 888-205-5834
FAX 217-356-5370
E-Mail: information@meatscience.org
Home Page: www.meatscience.org

William Mikel, President
Scott J. Eilert, President Elect
Casey B. Frye, Treasurer

Directory for American Meat Science members only.
Cost: $20.00
230 Pages
Frequency: Biennial

1204 American Society of Consulting Arborists: Membership Directory
American Society of Consulting Arborists
9707 Key West Ave
Suite 100
Rockville, MD 20850-3992

301-947-0483
FAX 301-990-9771
E-Mail: asca@mgmtsol.com
Home Page: www.asca-consultants.org

James R. Clark, Ph.D, President
Gordon Mann, President-Elect
Beth W. Palys, Executive Director

About 270 persons specializing in the growth and care of urban shade and ornamental trees; includes expert witnesses and monetary appraisals.
Frequency: Annual

1205 Biological & Agricultural Index
HW Wilson Company
950 Dr Martin Luther King Jr Blvd
Bronx, NY 10452-4297

718-588-8405
800-367-6770
FAX 718-590-1617
Home Page: www.hwwilson.com

Harold Regan, President & CEO
Ann Case, Vice President, Editorial
Phillip Taylor, Customer Service Director

Amy Rosenbaum, Senior Manager
Kathleen McEvoy, Director of Public Relations

Provides fast access to core literature. In addition to citations to research and feature articles, users finding indexing of reports of symposia and conferences, and citations to current book reviews. Available on Web and disc.
359 Pages
Founded in 1898

1206 Citrus & Vegetable Magazine: Farm Equipment Directory Issue
Vance Publishing
10901 W 84th Ter
Suite 200
Lenexa, KS 66214-1631

913-438-5721
FAX 913-438-0697
E-Mail: cvmscott@compuserve.com
Home Page: www.vancepublishing.com

Michael H Ross, President, Chief Operating Officer
William C Vance, Chairman, Chief Executive Officer
Judy Riggs, Director/Research Marketing

Offers information on a list of manufacturers of produce and citrus growing, handling, picking and packaging equipment.
Cost: $25.00
48 Pages
Frequency: Annual
Circulation: 12,000
ISSN: 0009-7586
Founded in 1938

1207 Complete Guide to Gardening and Landscaping by Mail
Mailorder Gardening Association
5836 Rockburn Woods Way
Elkridge, MD 21075-7302

410-540-9830
FAX 410-540-9827
Home Page: www.mailordergardening.com

Bruce Frasier, President
Jim Bryant, First Vice President
Roberta Simpson, Second Vice President
Jean Vivlamore Norton, Treasurer
Camille Cimino, Executive Director

Member catalogers who sell gardening and nursery stock and supplies to consumers.
Cost: $2.00
Frequency: Annual
Founded in 1934

1208 Contemporary World Issues: Agricultural Crisis in America
ABC-CLIO
130 Cremona Drive
PO Box 1911
Santa Barbara, CA 93117-1911

805-681-1911
800-422-2546
FAX 805-685-9685
E-Mail: CustomerService@abc-clio.com
Home Page: www.abc-clio.com

Ron Boehm, President/CEO

List of agencies and organizations in the US concerned with agricultural issues.
Cost: $50.00
Founded in 1953

1209 Crop Protection Reference
Vance Communications Corporation
315 W 106th St
Suite 504
New York, NY 10025-3473

212-932-1727
800-839-2420
FAX 646-733-6010
E-Mail:

GreenbookCustomerService@Greenbook.net
Home Page: www.greenbook.net

Hilda Vazquez, Director Marketing, Sales

A single comprehensive source of up-to-date label information of crop protection products marketed in the United States by basic manufacturers and formulators. Extensive product indexing helps to locate products by: brand name, manufacturer crop site, mode of action, disease, insect, week, product category, common name, tank mix.
Cost: $50.00
Frequency: Annual

1210 Directory for Small-Scale Agriculture
US Department of Agriculture
Secretary oF Agriculture
Whitten Building/Room 200A
Washington, DC 20250-0001

202-012-2000

Offers information on persons involved with projects and activities relating to small-scale agriculture.
Cost: $5.50
119 Pages

1211 Directory of American Agriculture
Agricultural Resources & Communications
P.O.Box 283
Wamego, KS 66547-0283

785-456-9705
800-404-7940
FAX 785-456-1654
E-Mail: chris@agresources.com
Home Page: www.agresources.com

Christina Wilson, President

This directory lists over 7,000 state and national associations involved in providing products and services related to food and fiber industries, in 27 categories. There are categorical indexes as well. Includes guide to Washington, D.C. offices, USDA listings, and guide to ag commodity commissions. Available on CD for $99.
Cost: $64.95
350 Pages
ISSN: 0897-1919
Founded in 1988
Printed in on matte stock

1212 EMDA Membership Directory
Equipment Marketing & Distribution Association
PO Box 1347
Iowa City, IA 52244-1347

319-354-5156
FAX 319-354-5157
E-Mail: pat@edma.net
Home Page: www.emda.net

Patricia A Collins, Executive VP

Annual directory of FEWA-AIMRA members, includes address, phone, fax, web, e-mail, territory covered (with map) product descriptions, key personneland descriptive paragraph.
Cost: $50.00

1213 Electronic Pesticide Reference: EPR II
Vance Communications Corporation
315 W 106th St
Suite 504
New York, NY 10025-3473

212-932-1727
FAX 646-733-6020
E-Mail:
GreenbookCustomerService@Greenbook.net
Home Page: www.greenbook.net

Hilda Vazquez, Director Marketing, Sales

Complete electronic reference to our 1,500 crop protection products; a full range of product information: full text labels and supplemental labels, full text MSDS's, product summaries, list of labeled tank mixes, worker protection information, DOT shipping information, SARA Title III reporting information. Search by brand name, manufacturer, common name crop, plant, site, weed, disease, insect plus much more. All versions of EPR II are provided on CD-ROM for windows.

1214 Food & Beverage Marketplace
Grey House Publishing
4919 Route 22
PO Box 56
Amenia, NY 12501

518-789-8700
800-562-2139
FAX 845-373-6390
E-Mail: books@greyhouse.com
Home Page: www.greyhouse.com
Social Media: *Facebook, Twitter*

Richard Gottlieb, President
Leslie Mackenzie, Publisher

The most comprehensive resource in the food and beverage industry. Available in a three-volume printed directory, a subscription-based Online Database, as well as mailing list and database formats.
Cost: $595.00
2000 Pages
ISBN: 1-592373-61-5
Founded in 1981

1215 Food & Beverage Marketplace: Online Database
Grey House Publishing
4919 Route 22
PO Box 56
Amenia, NY 12501

518-789-8700
800-562-2139
FAX 845-373-6390
E-Mail: gold@greyhouse.com
Home Page: www.gold.greyhouse.com
Social Media: *Facebook, Twitter*

Richard Gottlieb, President
Leslie Mackenzie, Publisher

This complete updated Food & Beverage Market Place: Online Database is the go-to source for the food and beverage industry. Anyone involved in the food and beverage industry needs this 'industry bible' and the important contacts to develop critical research data that can make for successful business growth.
Frequency: Annual
Founded in 1981

1216 Food and Agricultural Export Directory
National Technical Information Service
5285 Port Royal Rd
Springfield, VA 22161-0001

703-605-6000
800-553-6847
FAX 703-605-6900
E-Mail: info@ntis.gov
Home Page: www.ntis.gov

Linda Davis, Vice President
Patrik Ekstr"m, Business Development Manager
Reuel Avila, Managing Director

Includes up to date listings of federal and state agencies, trade associations and a host of other organizations that can help you penetrate foreign markets. Includes phone and fax numbers.
100 Pages
Frequency: Annual

1217 Food, Hunger, Agribusiness: A Directory of Resources
Center For Third World Organizing

1218 E 21st St
Oakland, CA 94606-3132

510-533-7583
FAX 510-533-0923
Home Page: www.ctwo.org

Lian Cheun, MAAP Director
Dan Ringer-Barwick, Operations Director

Offers information on organizations and publishers of books and other materials on food, hunger and agribusiness overseas.
Cost: $12.95
160 Pages

1218 Grain & Milling Annual

Sosland Publishing Company
4800 Main St
Suite 100
Kansas City, MO 64112-2513

816-756-1000
FAX 816-756-0494
E-Mail: web@sosland.com
Home Page: www.sosland.com

Gordon Davidson, President

Offers a list of milling companies, mills, grain companies and cooperatives.
Cost: $115.00
Frequency: Annual
Circulation: 6,000
ISSN: 1098-4615

1219 Guernsey Breeders' Journal: Convention Directory Issue

Purebred Publishing Inc
7616 Slate Ridge Blvd
Reynoldsburg, OH 43068-3126

614-575-4620
FAX 614-864-5614
E-Mail: sjohnson@usguernsey.com
Home Page: www.usguernsey.com

Seth Johnson, Manager
Dale Jensen, President
Tom Ripley, VP

A convention directory offering a list of officers and national members of the American Guernsey Cattle Association.
Cost: $20.00
Frequency: 10x Yearly

1220 Hort Expo Northwest

Mt Adams Publishing and Design
14161 Fort Road
White Swan, WA 98952-9786

509-848-2706
800-554-0860
FAX 509-848-3896
Home Page: www.hortexponw.com

Vee Graves, Editor
Julie LaForge, Advertising Manager

The directory is mailed to subscribers and is also available complimentary at horticulture shows in the Northwest.
32 Pages
Frequency: Annually
Circulation: 8,700
Founded in 1989
Printed in 4 colors on glossy stock

1221 Industrial Economic Information

Global Insight
800 Baldwin Tower
Eddystone, PA 19022

610-490-4000
800-933-3374
FAX 610-490-2557
E-Mail: info@globalinsight.com
Home Page: www.globalinsight.com

Joseph E Kasputys, Chair/President/CEO
Pricella Trumbull, Chief Operations Officer
Vicki Van Mater, VP
Kenneth J McGill, Product Management

Global Insight's unique perspective provides the most comprehensive economic and financial coverage of countries, regions and industries from any source.

1222 International Green Front Report

Friends of the Trees Society
PO Bo 253
Twisp, WA 98856

509-997-9200
FAX 509-997-4812
Home Page: www.friendsofthetrees.net

Michael Pilarski, Director

Organizations and periodicals concerned with sustainable forestry and agriculture and related fields.
Cost: $7.00
192 Pages
Frequency: Irregular
Circulation: 8,000
Founded in 1978

1223 International Soil Tillage Research Organization

International Soil Tillage Research
1680 Madison Avenue
Wooster, OH 44691-4114

330-263-3700
FAX 330-263-3658

A Franzluebbers, Editor-in-Chief

More than 750 individuals and institutions in 72 countries involved in the research or application of soil tilage and related subjects.
Cost: $100.00
Frequency: 10 per year

1224 Journal of the American Society of Farm Managers and Rural Appraisers

ASFMRA
950 S Cherry St
Suite 508
Denver, CO 80246-2664

303-758-3513
FAX 303-758-0190
E-Mail: asfmra@agri-associations.org
Home Page: www.asfmra.org

Cheryl L Cooley, Manager
Communications/PR
Frequency: Annually
Mailing list available for rent: 2500 names at $1M per M

1225 Landscape & Irrigation: Product Source Guide

Adams Business Media
11 Hanover Square
Suite 501
New York, NY 10005

212-566-7600
FAX 212-566-7877
E-Mail: lenadams@acgresources.com
Home Page: www.acgresources.com

Len Adams, CEO

Offers information on suppliers, distributors and manufacturers serving the professional agriculture and landscaping community.
Circulation: 37,000

1226 Material Safety Data Sheet Reference

Vance Communications Corporation
315 W 106th St
Suite 504
New York, NY 10025-3473

212-932-1727
FAX 646-733-6020
E-Mail:

GreenbookCustomerService@Greenbook.net
Home Page: www.greenbook.net

Susan J Vannucci, Manager

Regulatory and product safety requirements. Contains full text MSDS's for products listed in the 1999 15th Edition Crop Protection Reference plus additional safety information such as DOT shipping information, SARA Title III regulations, Hazardous Chemical inventory reporting information plus much more.

1227 Meat and Poultry Inspection Directory

US Department of Agriculture
Administration Building
Room 344
Washington, DC 20250-0001

202-690-7650
FAX 202-512-2250
Home Page: www.access.gpo.gov

Offers valuable information on all meat and poultry plants that ship meat interstate and therefore come under the US Department of Agriculture inspection.
Cost: $16.00
600 Pages
Frequency: SemiAnnual

1228 NASDA Directory

National Association of State Dept of Agriculture
1156 15th St NW
Suite 1020
Washington, DC 20005-1711

202-296-9680
FAX 202-296-9686
E-Mail: nasda@nasda.org
Home Page: www.nasda.org

Stephen Haterius, Executive Director
Richard Kirchoff, Executive VP/CEO

Top agricultural officials in 50 states and four territories.
Cost: $100.00
Frequency: Annual

1229 National Agri-Marketing Association Directory

11020 King St
Suite 205
Overland Park, KS 66210-1201

913-491-6500
FAX 913-491-6502
E-Mail: agrimktg@nama.org
Home Page: www.nama.org
Social Media: Facebook, Twitter, LinkedIn, Flickr, YouTube

Vicki Henrickson, President
Beth Burgy, 1st VP/ President-Elect
Paul Redhage, Secretary/Treasurer

Orginated as the Chicago Area Agricultural Advertising Association with 39 charter members. In 1963 the name was changed to the National Agricultural Advertising and Marketing Association and the present name was assumed in 1973.
Cost: $150.00
2500 Pages
Frequency: Annual
Founded in 1956

1230 National Organic Directory

Community Alliance with Family Farmers
36355 Russell Boulevard
PO Box 363
Davis, CA 95617-0363

530-756-8518
800-892-3832
FAX 530-756-7857

E-Mail: info@caff.org
Home Page: www.caff.org

Judith Redmond, President
George Davis, VP
Pete Price, Secretary
Poppy Davis, Treasurer
Leland Swendon, Executive Director

Wriiten for all sectors of the booming organic food and fiber industry. Offers international listing with full contact information and extensive, cross-referenced index. Also provides regulatory updates, essays by industry leaders and other ressources.
Cost: $47.95
400 Pages
Frequency: Annual
Circulation: 2,500
ISBN: 1-891894-04-8
Founded in 1983

1231 Organic Pages Online North American Resource Directory
Organic Trade Association
28 Vernon St.
Suite 413
Brattleboro, VT 05301

802-275-3800
FAX 802-275-3801
E-Mail: info@ota.com
Home Page: www.ota.com
Social Media: *Facebook, Twitter, LinkedIn*

Matt McLean, President
Sarah Bird, Vice President
Todd Linsky, Secretary
Kristen Holt, Treasurer

Provides over 1,300 listings by company name, brand name, business type, supply chain, product and service.

1232 Produce Marketing Association Membership Directory and Buyer's Guide
Produce Marketing Association
PO Box 6036
Newark, DE 19714-6036

302-738-7100
FAX 302-731-2409
E-Mail: pma@pma.com
Home Page: www.pma.com

Bryan Silbermann, President
Julie Koch, Production Manager

A list of over 2,000 members that are involved in retail grocery and foodservice marketing businesses, including international companies.
Cost: $70.00
280 Pages
Frequency: Annual

1233 Professional Workers in State Agricultural Experiment Stations
US Department of Agriculture
200 Independence Ave SW
Whitten Bldg/Room 200A
Washington, DC 20201-0007

202-690-7650
FAX 202-512-2250
Home Page: www.access.gpo.gov

Mike Johanns, Secretary of Agriculture

This directory offers information on academic and research personnel in all agricultural, forestry, aquaculture and home economics industries.
Cost: $15.00
289 Pages
Frequency: Annual
Founded in 1963

1234 Turf & Ornamental Reference
Vance Communications Corporation

315 W 106th St
Suite 504
New York, NY 10025-3473

212-932-1727
FAX 646-733-6020
E-Mail:
GreenbookCustomerService@Greenbook.net
Home Page: www.greenbook.net

Susan J Vannucci, Manager

Professional guide to plant protection problems. Provides the turf and ornamental industry with a single comprehensive source of up to date label and MSDS information of plant protection products marketed in the United States by basic manufacturers and formulators. Extensive product indexing helps to locate products by: brand name; manufacturer; plant site; mode of action; disease, insect, weed; product category; common name; tank mix.
Cost: $159.00

1235 USAHA Report of the Annual Meeting
United States Animal Health Association
4221 Mitchelle Ave.
St Joseph, MO 64507

816-671-1144
FAX 816-671-1201
E-Mail: usaha@usaha.org
Home Page: www.usaha.org

Benjamin Richey, Executive Director
Kelly Janicek, Executive Assistant

Held in conjunction with the American Association of Veterinary Laboratory Diagnosticians. (AAVLD)
Founded in 1897

1236 Warehouses Licensed Under US Warehouse Act
Farm Service Agency-US Dept. of Agriculture
1400 Independence Avenue SW
Stop Code 0506
Washington, DC 20013-2415

202-720-7809
FAX 202-690-0014

Eric Parsons, Chief Public Affairs

Agricultural warehouses voluntarily licensed under the US Warehouse Act governing public storage facilities.
Frequency: Annual

1237 Who's Who International
WATT Publishing Company
303 N Main Street
Suite 500
Rockford, IL 61101

815-966-5400
FAX 815-966-6416
Home Page: www.wattnet.com

James Watt, Chairman/CEO
Greg Watt, President/COO
Jeff Swanson, Publishing Director

Contains a detailed statistical section of key contacts in the industry. Includes industry phone book, genetic hatcheries and products, company directories, poultry marketers by city and state, refrigerated warehouses and federal agencies and associations.
310 Pages

1238 Who's Who in the Egg & Poultry Industry in the US and Canada
WATT Publishing Company

303 N Main Street
Suite 500
Rockford, IL 61101

815-966-5400
FAX 815-966-6416
Home Page: www.wattnet.com

James Watt, Chairman/CEO
Greg Watt, President/CEO
Jeff Swanson, Publishing Director

Contains a detailed statistical section of key contacts in the industry. Includes industry phone book, genetic hatcheries and products, company directories, poultry marketers by city and state, refrigerated warehouses and federal agencies and associations.
Cost: $105.00
Frequency: Annual
ISSN: 0510-4130

1239 World Databases in Agriculture
National Register Publishing
430 Mountain Ave.
Suite 400
New Providence, NJ 07974

800-473-7020
FAX 908-673-1189
E-Mail: nrpeditorial@marquiswhoswho.com
Home Page: www.nationalregisterpub.com

Agricultural information on databases, including CD-ROM, magnetic tape, diskette, online, fax or databroadcast worldwide.

Industry Web Sites

1240 http://gold.greyhouse.com
G.O.L.D Grey House OnLine Databases

Grey House Publishing's online database platform, GOLD, includes Quick Search, Keyword Search and Expert Search for most business sectors including agriculture and food markets. The GOLD platform makes finding the information you need quick and easy. All of Grey House's directory products are available for subscription on the GOLD platform.

1241 www.aaccnet.org
AACC International

A non-profit organization of members who are specialists in the use of cereal grains in foods.

1242 www.aaea.org
Agricultural & Applied Economics Association

A not-for-profit association serving the professional interests of members working in agricultural and boradly related fields of applied economics.

1243 www.aafco.org
Association of American Feed Control Officials

Provides a mechanism for develping and implementing uniform and equitab;e laws, regulations, standrads and enforcement policies for regulating the manufacture, distribution and sale of animal feeds; resulting in safe, effective, and useful feeds.

1244 www.aagiwa.org
American Assoc of Grain Inspection & Weighing

The national association representing grain inspection and weighing agencies. These agencies provide official inspection services to measure the quantity of grain being bough and sold in the United States.

1245 www.aaminc.org
American Agriculture Movement

An umbrella organization composed of state organizations representing family farm producers.

1246 www.aapausa.org
AFIA Alfalfa Processors Council

Information for the processors and suppliers in the alfalfa industry.

1247 www.abfnet.org
American Beekeeping Federation

A national organiation with baout 1,000 members that continually works in the interest of all beekeepers, large or small, and those associated with the industry to ensure the future of the honeybee.

1248 www.aceweb.org
Agricultural Communicators in Education

An international association of communicators and information technologists. Develops professional skills of its members to extend knowledge about agriculture, natural resources and life and human sciences to people worldwide.

1249 www.adsa.org
American Dairy Science Association

Provides leadership in scientific and technical support to sustain and grow the global dairy through generation, dissemination, and exchange of information and services.

1250 www.aem.org
Association of Equipment Manufacturers

A trade association that provides services on a global basis for companies that manufacture equipment, products and services used worldwide in the following industries: Agriculture, Construction, Forestry, Mining and Utility. AEM's membership is made up of more than 750 companies and represents 200+ product lines.

1251 www.afgc.org
American Forage and Grassland Council

Dedicated to advancing the use of forage as a prime feed resource. Members present the academic community, producers, private industry, institutes and foundations.

1252 www.afia.org
American Feed Industry Association

Represents the total feed industry, as a key segment of the food chain, and member copmanies' interests, with one industry leadership voice on matters involving federal/state legislation and regulation

1253 www.ag.ohio-state.edu/~farmshow
North American Farm Show Council/Ohio State Univ

Strives to improve the value of its member shows through education, communication and evaluation. Provides the best possible marketing showcase for exhibitors of agricultural equipment and related products to the farmer/rancher/producer customer.

1254 www.agconsultants.org
American Society of Agricultural Consultants

A non-profit organization oriented around raising the standards and image of professional agricultural consultants.

1255 www.agday.org
Agriculture Council of America

A nonprofit organization composed of leaders in the agricultural, food and fiber community, dedicating its efforts to increasing the public's awareness of agriculture's role in modern society.

1256 www.agnic.org
Agriculture Network Information Center

A voluntary alliance of members based on the concept of centers of excellence. The member institutions are dedicated to enhancing collective information and services among the members and their partners for all those seeking agriculture information over the Internet.

1257 www.agribusiness.com
National Agri-Marketing Association

The nation's largest professional association for professionals in marketing and agribusiness

1258 www.amseed.com
American Seed Trade Association

Promotes the development of better seed to produce better crops for a better quality of life.

1259 www.angus.org
American Angus Association

The nation's largest beef registry association with over 30,000 adult and junior members. The goal is to serve the beef cattle industry, and increase the production of consistent, high quality beef that will better satisfy consumers throughout the world.

1260 www.animalalliance.org
Animal Agricultural Alliance

A non-profit organization that is dedicated to the protection of wildlife, the alleviation of animal suffering and the preservation of our environment.

1261 www.aomillers.org
International Association of Operative Millers

An international organization, comprised of flour millers, cereal grain and seed processors and allied trades representatives and companies devoted to the advancement of technology in the flour milling and cereal grain processing industries.

1262 www.apms.org
Aquatic Plant Management Society

An international organization of scientists, educators, students, commercial pedticide applicators, administrators, and concerned individuals interested in the management and study of aquatic plants.

1263 www.asabe.org
American Society of Agricultural & Biological Eng

An educational and scientific organization dedicated to the advancement of engineering applicable to agriculture, food, and biological systems.

1264 www.asas.org
American Society of Animal Science

Discover, disseminate and apply knowledge for sustainable use of animals for food and other human needs.

1265 www.asca-consultants.org
American Society of Consulting Arborists

The industry's premier professional association focusing solely on arboricultural consulting. Consulting Arborists are authoritative experts on trees, consulting property owners, municipalities, attorneys, insurance professionals and others on tree disease, placement, preservation and dispute resolution in addition to providing consulting and expert testimony in the legal, insurance and environmental arenas.

1266 www.asev.org
American Society for Enology and Viticulture

A tax exempt professional society dedicated to the interests of enologists, viticulturists, and others in the fields of wine and grape research and production throughout the world.

1267 www.biodynamics.com
Biodynamic Farming and Gardening Association

A non-profit, membership organization that fosters tknowledge of the practices and principles of the biodynamic method of agriculture, horticulture, and forestry in the North American continent

1268 www.cast-science.org
Council for Agricultural Science and Technology

A nonprofit organization composed of scientific societies an many individual, student, copmany, nonprofit, and associate society members.

1269 www.christmastree.org
National Christmas Tree Association

Strives to be one voice representing Christmas Tree Professionals and promoting the use of Real Christmas Trees

1270 www.corn.org
Corn Refiners Association

The national trade association representing the corn refining (wet milling) industry of the United States.

1271 www.cottonseed.com
National Cottonseed Products Association

An organization of firms and individuals engaged in the processing of cottonseed and the marketing of cottonseed products, as well as cottonseed. These include oil mills, refiners, product dealers and product brokers.

1272 www.cropinsurance.org
Crop Insurance Research Bureau

Working to improve crop insurance through unity and leadership

1273 www.croplifeamerica.org
CropLife America

Represents the developers manufacturers, formulators and distributors of plant science solutions for agriculture and pest management in the Unted States.

1274 www.crops.org
Crop Science Society of America

Seeks to advance research, extension, and teaching of all basic and applied phases of the crop sciences.

1275 www.dhia.org
National Dairy Herd Improvement Association

Promote accuracy, credibility, and uniformity of DHI records; represent the DHIA system on issues involving other National and International organizations; organize industry activities that benefit members of National DHIA

1276 www.eap.mcgill.ca/cfbmc.htm
Canadian Farm Business Management Council

To share and co-ordinate informatio non farm business management in order to help prevent duplication, encourage cost-sharing and build partnerships; to act as a forum for dialogue on farm business management issues of concern nationally or in more than on province of the country; to develop, adapt and distribute information products in farm business management to help increase the competitiveness of Canadian Agriculture.

1277 www.fairsandexpos.com
International Association of Fairs & Expositions

A voluntary, non-profit corporation, organizing state, provincial, regional, and county agricultural fairs, shows, exhibitions and expositions.

1278 www.farmers-friend.com
Farmers Friend
Farming news.

1279 www.fb.org
American Farm Bureau Federation

The unified national voice of agriculture, working through our grassroots organization to enhance and strengthen the lives of rural American and to build strong, prosperous agricultural communities

1280 www.fewa-aimra.org
FEWA-AIMRA Marketing & Distribution Association

Merged with AIMRA to form the leading association devoted to the marketing of specialized equipment.

1281 www.fourhcouncil.edu
National 4-H Council

Empowers youth to reach their full potential, working and learning in partnership with caring adults.

1282 www.fpaota.org
Fresh Produce Association of the Americas

A non-profit trade group of more than 100 members who are involved in the growth, harvest, import and distribution of the finest produce from Mexico.

1283 www.fpfc.org
Fresh Produce and Floral Council

Stimulates the promotion and sale of fresh fruit, vegetables and floral products; improves communications between all segments of the fresh produce and floral industries; and to exchange ideas on better and more economical handling of fresh fruit, vegetables and floral products from the farm to table.

1284 www.freshcut.com
Great American Publishing

Information on carrot production, growers and shippers.

1285 www.grains.org
US Grains Council

Develops export markets for U.S. barley corn, grain sorghum and related products. A private, non-profit corporation with nine international offices and programs in more than 50 countries.

1286 www.greyhouse.com
Grey House Publishing

Authoritative reference directories for business information and general reference, including agriculture and food markets. Users can search the online databases with varied search criteria allowing for custom searches by product category, geographic area, sales volume, keyword, subject and more. Full Grey House catalog and online ordering also available.

1287 www.hereford.org
American Hereford Association

For the raising and breeding of stock in the hereford cattle industry.

1288 www.holsteinusa.com
Holstein Association USA

The largest breed organization in the world, comprised of members who have a strong interest in breeding, raising and milking Holstein cattle.

1289 www.iaff.ttu.edu/aals
Association for Arid Land Studies

1290 www.iaom.info
International Association of Operative Millers

An international organization, comprised of flour millers, cereal grain and seed processors and allied trades representatives and companies devoted to the advancement of technology in the flour milling and cereal grain processing industries.

1291 www.ifas.ufl.edu
Institute of Food & Agriculture/Univ of Florida

For college students professionally interested in communications related to agriculture, food, natural resources and allied fields.

1292 www.ipaa.net
International Pesticide Applicators Association

Provides education and information for the professional horticultural applicator. Legislative work involves the states of Washington, Oregon, Idaho in the area of laws and regulations.

1293 www.irrigation.org
Irrigation Association

Membership organization for irrigation equipment and system manufacturers, dealers, distributors, designers, consultants, contractors and end users.

1294 www.mailordergardening.com
Mailorder Gardening Association

nonprofit organization serving the needs of companies involved in marketing gardening products to consumers

1295 www.meatami.org
American Meat Institute

Dedicated to increasing the efficiency, profitability and safety of meat and poultry worldwide.

1296 www.naab-css.org
National Association of Animal Breeders

To unite thos individuals and organizations engaged in the artificial insemination of cattle and other livestock into an affiliated federation operating under self-imposed standards of performance and to conduct and promote the mutual interest and ideals of its members.

1297 www.nacaa.com
National Association County Agricultural Agents

For agents focusing on educational programs for the youth of the community.

1298 www.naicc.org
National Alliance of Independent Crop Consultants

A professional society that represents the nation's crop porduction and research consultants.

1299 www.nama.org
National Agri-Marketing Association

Professional association for professionals in marketing and agribusiness.

1300 www.nationalgrange.org
Nat'l Grange of the Order of Patrons of Husbandry

Provides opportunities for individuals and families to develop to their highest potential in order to build stronger communities and states, as well as a stronger nation.

1301 www.nationalplantboard.org
National Plant Board

A non-profit organization of the plant pest regulatory agencies opf each of the staes and Commonwealth of Puerto Rico.

1302 www.nationalpotatocouncil.Org
National Potato Council

The advocate for the economic well-being of U.S. potato growers on federal legislative, regulatory, environmental and trade issues.

1303 www.nfu.org
National Farmers Union

Protects and enhances the economic well-being and quality of life for family farmers and ranchers and their rural communities

1304 www.nppc.org
National Pork Producers Council

Conducts public-policy outreach on behalf of its 43 affiliated state associations, enhancing opportunities for the success of U.S. pork producers and other industry stakeholders by establishing the U.S. pork industry as a consistent and responsible supplier of high-quality pork to the domestic and world markets.

1305 www.ocia.com
Organic Crop Improvement Association International

Dedicated to providing the highest quality organic certification serices and access to global organic markets

1306 www.onions-usa.org
National Onion Association

The official organization representing growers, shippers, brokers, and commerical representatives of the U.S. onion industry.

1307 www.ota.com
Organic Trade Association

A membership-based business association that focuses on the organic business community in North America. Promotes and protects the growth of organic trade to benefit the environment, farmers, the public and the economy.

1308 www.pma.com
Produce Marketing Association

Global trade association serving the entire produce and floral supply chains by enhancing the marketing of produce, floral, and related products and services worldwide.

1309 www.profarmer.com
Professional Farmers of America

Gives customers a competitive edge in marketing and financial management through timely delivery and accurate analysis of market-sensitive news and views.

1310 www.sbsonline.org
Society for Biomolecular Sciences

Non-profit scientific society dedicated to drug discovery and its related disciplines. Provides a forum for global educationand information exchange among professionals in the chemical, pharmaceutical, biotech and agrochemical industries.

1311 www.seedtechnology.net
Society Commercial Seed Technologists

An organization comprised of commercial, independent and government seed technologists.

1312 www.sheepusa.org
American Sheep Industry Association

The national organization representing the interests of sheep producers located throughout the United States.

1313 www.southerncottonginners.org
Southern Cotton Ginners Association
Serves its members by providing safety, training, and regulatory representation.

1314 www.southwesternassn.com
SouthWestern Association
Established by a progressive group of independent hardware and farm implement/mercantile dealers to help increase their profitability and solve common problems.

1315 www.soygrowers.com
American Soybean Association
Represents U.S. soybean farmers through policy advocacy and international market development.

1316 www.sugaralliance.org
American Sugar Alliance
A natinoal coalition of sugarcane and sugarbeet farmers, processoris, refiners, suppliers, workers and others dedicated to preserving a strong domestic sugar industry.

1317 www.sunflowernsa.com
National Sunflower Association

A non-profit commodity organization working on problems and opportunities for the improvement of all members.

1318 www.tfi.org
Fertilizer Institute
The leading voice in the fertilizer industry, representing the public policy, communication and statistical needs of producers, manufacturers, retailers and transporters of fertilizer.

1319 www.turfweeds.net
Turfgrass Weed Science/Virginia Polytech Institute
Provides weed management information and research reports to turfgrass managers.

1320 www.unitedfresh.org
United Fresh Produce Association
Commited to driving the growth and success of produce companies and their partners. Represents the interests of member companies throughout the global, fresh produce supply chain, including family-owned, private and publicly traded businesses as well as regional, national and international companies.

1321 www.usguernsey.com
American Guernsey Association
Register and deliver guernsey cattle throughout the United States.

1322 www.uspotatoes.com
United States Potato Board
The central organizing force in implementing programs that will increase demand for potatoes.

1323 www.vealfarm.com
Veal Quality Association Program
For veal producers and processors.

1324 www.wawgg.org
Washington Association of Wine Grape Growers
Advocates for the Washington wine growing industry by educating, promotin, representing, and unifying the industry and fostering a positive business environment for continued growth and production of world-class, Washington-grown wines.

1325 www.wildblueberries.com
Wild Blueberry Association of North America
For processors and growers of wild blueberries in Eastern Canada and Maine.

107

Associations

1326 Advanced BioFuels USA
507 North Bentz Street
Frederick, MD 21701

301-644-1395
E-Mail: info@AdvancedBiofuelsUSA.or
Home Page: advancedbiofuelsusa.info

Joanne M. Ivancic, President/Executive Director
Robert E. Kozak, Treasurer
Dr. Craig Laufer, Secretary

A nonprofit organization that advocates for the adoption of advanced biofuels as an energy security, military flexibility, economic development andclimate change mitigation/pollution control solution though its promotion of public understanding, acceptance, and research.

1327 Advanced Biofuels Association
800 17th Street, NW
Suite 1100
Washington, DC 20006

Home Page:
www.advancedbiofuelsassociation.com
Social Media: *Facebook, Twitter, LinkedIn, YouTube*

Wayne Simmons, Chairman
Chris Ryan, Vice Chairman
Michael McAdams, President
Andrew Rojeski, Secretary
Christopher Higby, Treasurer

Organization that seeks to help America transform to a low carbon economy by supporting and advocating for public policies that are technology neutral, use sustainable feedstocks, and offering financial support to its member companies to bring products to market that are competitive and compatible with petroleum-based fuels and byproducts.
40 Members

1328 Alliance for Affordable Energy
P.O. Box 751133
New Orleans, LA 70175

504-208-9761
E-Mail: casey@all4energy.com
Home Page: all4energy.org
Social Media: *Facebook, Twitter, LinkedIn, YouTube, Instagram, Flickr*

Casey DeMoss, Chief Executive Officer
Logan Atkinson Burke, Manager, Admin & Reg. Affairs
John Williams, Treasurer
Logan Atkinson, Office Development Manager
Logan Williams, Volunteer & Intern Manager

An environmental advocacy organization that promotes fair, affordable, environmentally responsible energy.
Founded in 1985

1329 Alliance to Save Energy
1850 M Street, NW
Suite 610
Washington, DC 20036

202-857-0666
Home Page: www.ase.org
Social Media: *Facebook, Twitter, LinkedIn, YouTube, Google+, Flickr*

Sen Mark Warner, Chairman
Jane Palmieri, Co-Chairman
Kateri Callahan, President
William Von Hoene, 1st Vice Chair
Frank Murray, Secretary

Organization that leads worldwide energy efficiency initiatives in policy advocacy, research, education and technology deployment.

1330 Alternative Energy Association
1061 East Indiantown Road
Suite 400
Jupiter, FL 33477

561-776-8600
E-Mail: alternativeenergyassn@gmail.com
Home Page: www.alternativeenergyassn.com

Organization that uses marketing campaigns, seminars, and eduactional activities to promote awareness of clean, renewable sources of power generation as alternatives to the use of fossil fuels for energy production.

1331 Alternative Energy Resources Organization
432 N. Last Chance Gulch
Helena, MT 59601

406-443-7272
FAX 406-442-9120
E-Mail: aero@aeromt.org
Home Page: www.aeromt.org
Social Media: *Facebook, Twitter, Myspace, Pinterest, Google+*

Jennifer Hill-Hart, Executive Director
Corrie Williamson, Comm. & Membership Director
Rosie Goldich, Abundant Montana Intern

A grassroots nonprofit organization dedicated to solutions that promote resource conservation and local economic vitality. By bringing people together, AERO offers a vehicle for collective action and a sense of common purpose for citizens within their communities to shape a more sustainable future.
Founded in 1974

1332 American Biogas Council
1211 Connecticut Ave NW
Suite 600
Washington, DC 20036-2701

202-640-6595
E-Mail: info@americanbiogascouncil.org
Home Page: www.americanbiogascouncil.org
Social Media: *Twitter, LinkedIn, YouTube, Flickr*

Bernie Sheff, PE, Chairman
Paul Greene, Vice-Chair
Melissa VanOrnum, Treasurer
Mark Stoermann, Vice-Chair
Patrick Serfass, Executive Director (ex-officio)

Mission is to create jobs, environmental sustainability and energy independence by growing the American biogas industry.
Mailing list available for rent

1333 American Coalition for Ethanol
5000 South Broadband Lane
Suite 224
Sioux Falls, SD 57108

605-334-3381
E-Mail: cbeck@ethanol.org
Home Page: ethanol.org
Social Media: *Facebook, Twitter*

Ron Alverson, President
Duane Kristensen, Vice President
Brian Jennings, Executive Vice President
Ron Lamberty, Senior Vice President
Chuck Beck, Director of Communications

Environmental advocacy organization that promotes the use of ethanol as the most successful renewable energy platform in the world.
Founded in 1987

1334 American Council for an Energy-Efficient Economy
529 14th Street N.W
Suite 600
Washington, DC 20045-1000

202-507-4000
FAX 202-429-2248

Home Page: www.aceee.org
Social Media: *Facebook, Twitter, RSS*

Alison Silverstein, President
Timothy M Stout, Treasurer
Peter A. Molinaro, Secretary
Roland J. Risser, Special Advisor
Jim Barrett, Chief Economist

A nonprofit organization that seeks to advance energy efficiency policies, programs, technologies, investments, and behaviors.

1335 American Council on Renewable Energy
1600 K Street NW
Suite 650
Washington, DC 20006

202-393-0001
E-Mail: weirich@acore.org
Home Page: www.acore.org
Social Media: *Facebook, Twitter, LinkedIn, YouTube*

Michael R. Brower, Interim President and CEO
Todd Foley, Senior VP of Policy and Government
Dawn Butcher, Director of Event Planning
Cindi Ec, Director, Leadership Programs
Kevin Haley, Strategic Communications Manager

Works to bring all forms of renewable energy into the mainstream of America's economy and lifestyle. Members include every aspect and sector of the renewable energy industries and their trade associations, including wind, solar, geothermal, biomass and biofuels, hydropower tidal/current energy and waste energy.
Founded in 2001

1336 American Hydrogen Association
P.O. Box 4205
Mesa, AZ 85201

480-234-5070
E-Mail: help@clean-air.org
Home Page:
www.americanhydrogenassociation.org
Social Media: *Facebook, YouTtube*

Roy McAlister, President
Ben Ferguson, Vice President
Douglas Hawley, Secretary/Treasurer

Providing information on the use of hydrogen as a fuel.

1337 American Solar Energy Society
2525 Arapahoe Ave
Ste E4-253
Boulder, CO 80302

303-443-3130
FAX 303-443-3212
E-Mail: info@ases.org
Home Page: www.ases.org
Social Media: *Facebook, Twitter, LinkedIn, Digg*

David Panich, Chair
Tiffiny Harrower, Finance & Accounting Manager
Carly Rixham, Executive Director
Richard Behlmann, Secretary
Lauren Harrower, Membership Manager/Data Analyst

The nation's leading association of solar professionals & advocates. Mission is to inspire an era of energy innovation and speed the transition to a sustainable energy economy. Advancing education, research and policy.
13M Members
Founded in 1954

1338 American Water Works Association
6666 W. Quincy Ave.
Denver, CO 80235-3098

303-794-7711
800-926-7337

FAX 303-347-0804
Home Page: www.awwa.org
Social Media: *Facebook, Twitter, LinkedIn, YouTube*

Gene C. Koontz, President
Jeanne M. Bennett-Bailey, President Elect
John J. Donahue, Immediate Past President
David E. Rager, Treasurer
Jon Eaton, VP/Minnesota Section Director

The largest nonprofit, scientific and educational association dedicated to managing and treating water.
Founded in 1881

1339 American Wind Energy Association
1501 M Street NW
Suite 1000
Washington, DC 20005

202-383-2500
FAX 202-383-2505
E-Mail: windmail@awea.org
Home Page: www.awea.org
Social Media: *Facebook, Twitter, LinkedIn, YouTube, Flickr*

Mike Garland, Chair
Pam Poisson, SVP Operations/CFO
Matthew Fuller, Director, Finance
Chi Wei, Director, Information Technology
Tom Kiernan, Chief Executive Officer

Promotes wind energy as a clean source of electricity for consumers around the world. Representing wind power project developers, equipment suppliers, services providers, parts manufacturers, utilities, researchers, and others involved in the wind industry - one of the world's fastest growing energy industries.
2500+ Members

1340 Association of Energy Engineers
3168 Mercer University Drive
Atlanta, GA 30341

770-447-5083
E-Mail: al@aeecenter.org
Home Page: www.aeecenter.org
Social Media: *Facebook, Twitter, LinkedIn, YouTube*

Dr. Scott Dunning, President
Asit Patel, President Elect
Randy Haines, Past President
Ian Boylan, Secretary
Paul Goodman, Treasurer
17500 Members
Founded in 1977

1341 Association of Energy Engineers (AEE)
3168 Mercer University Drive
Atlanta, GA 30341

770-447-5083
FAX 770-446-3969
E-Mail: al@aeecenter.org
Home Page: www.aeecenter.org
Social Media: *Facebook, Twitter, YouTube*

Dr. Scott Dunning, President
Albert Thumann, Executive Director
Kate Feltgen, Information Services Director
Lauren Lake, Event and Marketing Director
Patricia Ardavin, Membership Director

Information and networking in the dynamic fields of energy engineering and energy management, renewable and alternative energy, power generation, energy services, sustainability, and all related areas.
17500 Members
Founded in 1977

1342 Biomass Energy Research Association
901 D Street, S.W
Suite 100
Washington, DC 20024

410-953-6202
FAX 410-290-0377
E-Mail: bera@beraonline.org
Home Page: beraonline.org

Joan Pellegrino, President/Treasurer
Phillip C. Badger, Secretary/Director
Mark A. Paisley, Director
Janis L. Tabor, Director
Dr. Evan Hughes, Director

An association of bioenergy researchers, companies, and advocates that promotes education and research on renewable biomass energy and waste-to-energy systems.

1343 Biomass Power Association
100 Middle St.
PO Box 9729
Portland, ME 04104-9729

202-494-2493
E-Mail: carrie@usabiomass.org
Home Page: www.usabiomass.org

Bob Cleaves, President & CEO
Carrie Annand, VP of External Affairs
Nicholas Mazuroski, Director of Operations and Research
Katherine A. Peña, Web Director

The nation's leading organization working to expand and advance the use of clean, renewable biomass power. Educates policymakers at the state and federal level about the benefits of biomass and provides regular briefings and research to keep members fully informed about public policy impacting the biomass industry. Members include local owners and operators of existing biomass facilities, suppliers, plant developers and others.
80 Members

1344 Biomass Thermal Energy Council
1211 Connecticut Avenue NW
Suite 600
Washington, DC 20036-2701

202-596-3974
FAX 202-223-5537
E-Mail: info@biomassthermal.org
Home Page: www.biomassthermal.org
Social Media: *Facebook, Twitter, LinkedIn, SlideShare, Vimeo*

Dan Wilson, Chairman
Joel Stronberg, Executive Director
Dayanita Ramesh, Project Assistant
Emanuel Wagner, Programs Director
Ben Bell Walker, Technical Affairs

An association of biomass fuel producers, appliance manufacturers and distributors, supply chain companies and non-profit organizations that view biomass thermal energy as a renewable, responsible, clean and energy-efficient pathway to meeting America's energy needs. BTEC engages in research, education, and public advocacy for the fast growing biomass thermal energy industry.
Founded in 2009

1345 Business Council for Sustainable Energy
805 15th Street, NW
Suite 708
Washington, DC 20005

202-785-0507
FAX 202-785-0514
E-Mail: bcse@bcse.org
Home Page: www.bcse.org
Social Media: *Facebook, Twitter, LinkedIn*

Mark Wagner, Chair
Rob Gramlich, Vice Chair
Scott Crider, Vice Chair

Lisa Jacobson, President
Ruth McCormick, Director, Federal and State Affairs

A coalition of companies and trade associations from the energy efficiency, natural gas and renewable energy sectors, and includes independent electric power producers, investor-owned utilities, public power, commercial end-users and project developers and service providers for environmental markets.

1346 Canadian Renewable Fuels Association(CRFA)
350 Sparks Street
Suite 605
Ottawa, ON K1R 7S8

613-594-5528
FAX 613-594-3076
E-Mail: a.kent@greenfuels.org
Home Page: www.greenfuels.org
Social Media: *Facebook, Twitter, LinkedIn, Instagram*

Andrea Kent, President
Deborah Elson, VP, Public Affairs & Membership
Tyler Bjornson, Executive Director
William Meyer, Manager, Communication
Jim Grey, Chair

Promotes and advances the use of renewable fuels for transporation- to protect our environment by reducing harmful emissions and to grow our economy by creating the good, green-energy jobs of the future.
Founded in 1984

1347 Center for Energy Efficiency and Renewable Technologies
1100 11th Street
Suite 311
Sacramento, CA

916-442-7785
E-Mail: info@ceert.org
Home Page: ceert.org
Social Media: *Facebook, Twitter, LinkedIn*

Jonathan M. Weisgall, Chairman
Ralph Cavanagh, Vice Chair
V. John White, Executive Director
John Shahabian, Director of Operations
Kevin Lynch, Secretary/Treasurer

A partnership of major environmental groups and private-sector clean energy companies that advocate for policies that promote global warming solutions and increased reliance on clean, renewable energy sources for California and the West.
Founded in 1990

1348 Clean Energy Group
50 State St.
Suite 1
Montpelier, VT 05602

802-223-2554
FAX 802-223-4967
E-Mail: Lmilford@cleanegroup.org
Home Page: www.cleanegroup.org
Social Media: *Facebook, Twitter*

Lewis Milford, President & Founder
Warren Leon, Executive Director, Clean Energy
Robert Sanders, Senior Finance Director
Valerie Stori, Project Director
Anthony Vargo, Chief Financial Officer

A leading nonprofit advocacy organization working in the US and internationally on innovative clean energy technology, finance, and policy programs. Supported by major foundations, as well as state, federal and international energy agencies.
Founded in 1998

1349 Distributed Wind Energy Association
1065 Main Ave
Suite 209
Durango, CO 81301

928-380-6012
E-Mail: jjenkins@distributedwind.org
Home Page: distributedwind.org
Social Media: *Facebook, Twitter, LinkedIn*

Mike Bergey, President
Chris Diaz, Vice President
Roger Dixon, Acting Secretary
Kevin Schulte, Acting Treasurer
Jennifer Jenkins, Executive Director

A collaborative group comprised of manufacturers, distributors, project developers, dealers, installers, and advocates, whose primary mission is to promote and foster all aspects of the American distributed wind energy industry.

1350 Ducks Unlimited
One Waterfowl Way
Memphis, TN 38120

901-758-3825
800-45D-UCKS
Home Page: www.ducks.org
Social Media: *Facebook, Twitter, YouTube, Instagram*

George Dunklin, Jr., Chairman
Paul R. Bonderson, Jr., President
Dale Hall, Chief Executive Officer
Rogers Hoyt, Jr., First Vice President
Wendell Weakley, Treasurer

Conserves, restores, and manages wetlands and associated habitats for North America's waterfowl.
Founded in 1937

1351 Efficient Windows Collaborative
21629 Zodiac Street NE
Wyoming, MN 55092

E-Mail:
efficientwindowscollaborative@gmail.com
Home Page: www.efficientwindows.org
Social Media: *Facebook, Twitter, LinkedIn*

A nonprofit organization that partners with window, door, skylight,and component manufacturers, research organizations, federal, state and local government agencies, and others interested in expanding the market for high-efficiency fenestration products.

1352 Energy Recovery Council
2200 Wilson Boulevard
Suite 310
Arlington, VA 22201

202-467-6240
E-Mail: tmichaels@energyrecoverycouncil.org
Home Page: www.energyrecoverycouncil.org

Ted Michaels, President

Represents the waste-to-energy industry and communities that own waste-to-energy facilities. Current ERC members own and operate modern waste-to-energy facilities that operate nationwide, safely disposing of municipal solid waste, while at the same time generating renewable electricity using modern combustion technology equipped with state-of-the-art emission control systems.

1353 Environmental and Energy Study Institute
1112 16th Street, NW
Suite 300
Washington, DC 20036-4819

202-628-1400
FAX 202-204-5244
E-Mail: info@eesi.org
Home Page: www.eesi.org

Social Media: *Facebook, Twitter, LinkedIn, Vimeo*

Jared Blum, Chairman
Carol Werner, Executive Director
David Robison, Director of Finance & Admin
Susan Williams, Director of Development
Alison Alford, Programs & Administrative
Assistant

A nonprofit organization that advances innovative policy solutions that set us on a cleaner, more secure and sustainable energy path.
Founded in 1984

1354 Export Council for Energy Efficiency
E-Mail: laura@solarcities.org
Home Page: www.ecee.org

Laura Gubisch, Executive Director

A nonprofit association that promotes the export of energy efficient products, services, and technologies worldwide.
Founded in 1994

1355 Florida Solar Energy Center
1679 Clearlake Rd.
Cocoa, FL 32922-5703

321-638-1000
FAX 321-638-1010
Home Page: www.fsec.ucf.edu
Social Media: *Facebook*

James Fenton, Director

Created by the State of Florida in 1975, FSEC is the largest publicly-supported alternative energy research institute in the United States.
Founded in 1975

1356 Fuel Cell and Hydrogen Energy Association
1211 Connecticut Avenue Northwest
#600
Washington, DC 20036

202-261-1337
E-Mail: info@fchea.org
Home Page: www.fchea.org
Social Media: *Facebook, Twitter, LinkedIn, Google+*

Morry B. Markowitz, President
Bud DeFlaviis, Director of Government Affairs
Jennifer Gangi, Director of Comm. & Outreach
Sandra Curtin, Research & Comm. Manager
Connor Dolan, Director Of External Affairs

A trade association for the fuel cell and hydrogen energy industry,and is dedicated to the commercialization of fuel cells and hydrogen energy technologies.
Founded in 2010

1357 Geothermal Energy Association
209 Pennsylvania Avenue SE
Washington, DC 20003

202-454-5261
FAX 202-454-5265
E-Mail: jgreco@terra-genpower.com
Home Page: www.geo-energy.org
Social Media: *Facebook, Twitter, LinkedIn, YouTube, Wordpress*

Karl Gawell, Executive Director
Leslie Blodgett, Geothermal News Specialist
Kathy Kent, Sr. Director of Marketing
Mihaela-Daniela Lobontiu, Business Manager
Yoram Bronicki, President

Advocates for public policies that will promote the development and utilization of geothermal resources, provides a forum for the industry to discuss issues and problems, encourages research and development to improve geothermal technologies, presents industry views to governmental organizations, and conducts education and outreach projects.

1358 Geothermal Exchange Organization
312 S. Fourth St
Suite 100
Springfield, IL 62701

888-255-4436
Home Page: www.geoexchange.org
Social Media: *Facebook, Twitter, LinkedIn, Google+*

Douglas Dougherty, President & CEO
Ted Clutter, Manager of Outreach

A nonprofit trade association that promotes the manufacture, designand installation of GeoExchange systems—an energy efficient and environmentallyfriendly heating and cooling technology.

1359 Geothermal Resources Council
630 Pe¤a Dr.
Ste. 400
Davis, CA 95618-5476

530-758-2360
FAX 530-758-2839
E-Mail: grc@geothermal.org
Home Page: www.geothermal.org
Social Media: *Facebook, Twitter, LinkedIn, YouTube, Flickr, Pinterest, Bl*

Steve Ponder, Executive Director
Ian Crawford, Director of Communications,
Editor
Estela M. Smith, GRC Office Manager
Anh Lay, Office Associate
Chi-Meng Moua, Graphic Designer

Nonprofit, educational association actively seeking to expand its role as a primary professional educational association for the international geothermal community.
1300+ Members
Founded in 1970

1360 Intergovernmental Renewable Energy Organization
884 2nd Avenue, UN Centre
No. 20050
New York, NY 10017

917-862-6444
FAX 212-202-4100
E-Mail: ireo@ireoigo.org
Home Page: www.ireoigo.org
Social Media: *Facebook, Twitter*

Dr. Anthony James Watson, Chairman
Heidi Walters, Chief Protocol Officer
Diane Mello, Executive Director Operations
John Hill, Secretary-General
Michael Rubin, Under Secretary

Promotes the urgent transition to renewable energy sources and sustainable development through collaborative effort and the implementation of projects that improve the lives of people while preserving the environment and our resources for future generations of humans.
Founded in 2008

1361 International Association for Energy Economics
28790 Chagrin Blvd
Suite 350
Cleveland, OH 44122-4642

216-464-5365
FAX 216-464-2737
E-Mail: iaee@iaee.org
Home Page: www.iaee.org
Social Media: *Facebook, LinkedIn*

David Newbery, President
Jacques Percebois, Vice President for
Publications
Christophe Bonnery, Vice President for
Business & Govt.
G⬜rkan Kumbaroglu, Vice President for
Conferences

Ricardo B. Raineri, Vice President for Academic Affairs

Association for those involved in energy economics including publications, consultants, energy database software.
3400 Members
Founded in 1977
Mailing list available for rent

1362 International Association for Hydrogen Energy
5794 SW 40 St.
#303
Miami, FL 33155

E-Mail: info@iahe.org
Home Page: www.iahe.org

Dr. T. Nejat Veziroglu, President
John W. Sheffield, Vice President
Juan Carlos Bolcich, Vice President for South America
Ibrahim Din‡er, Vice President for Strategy
Bruno Pollet, Vice President for South Africa

An association that stimulates the exchange of information in the Hydrogen Energy field through its publications and sponsorship of international workshops, short courses and conferences and endeavors to inform the general public of the important role of Hydrogen Energy in the planning of an inexhaustible and clean energy system.

1363 International District Energy Association
24 Lyman Street
Suite 230
Westborough, MA 1581

508-366-9339
FAX 508-366-0019
E-Mail: idea@districtenergy.org
Home Page: www.districtenergy.org
Social Media: *Facebook, Twitter, YouTube, Flickr, RSS*

Bruce Ander, Chair
Tim Griffin, Vice Chair
Chris Lyons, Second Vice Chair
James Adams, Secretary/Treasurer
Ken Smith, Past Chair

An organization that actively works to foster the success of its members as leaders in providing reliable, economical, efficient and environmentally sound district heating, district cooling and cogeneration (combined heat and power) services.
Founded in 1909

1364 International Ground Source Heat Pump Association
1201 S. Innovation Way Dr.
Suite 400
Stillwater, OK 74074

405-744-5175
800-626-4747
FAX 405-744-5283
E-Mail: igshpa@okstate.edu
Home Page: www.igshpa.okstate.edu
Social Media: *Facebook, Twitter, Youtube, Google+*

John Turley, President
Gail Ezepek, Conference and Membership Assistant
Janet Reeder, Technical Writer
Ben Champlin, Graphic Designer
Roshan Revankar, Manager

Member-driven organization established to advance ground source heat pump technology on local, state, national and international levels. IGSHPA utilizes state-of-the-art facilities for conducting GSHP system installation training and geothermal research. Mission is to promote the use of ground source heat pump technology

worldwide through education and communication.
Founded in 1987

1365 Interstate Renewable Energy Council
PO Box 1156
Latham, NY 12110-1156

518-458-6059
E-Mail: info@irecusa.org
Home Page: www.irecusa.org
Social Media: *Facebook, Twitter, LinkedIn, Pinterest, YouTube*

Larry Shirley, Chair
Jane Weissman, President and CEO
Larry Sherwood, Vice President, COO
Maryteresa Colello, Administrative Coordinator
Louise Urgo, Administration

Works with industry, government, educators and other stakeholders to ensure that the broader use of renewable energies is possible, safe, affordable and practical, particularly for the individual consumer.
Founded in 1982

1366 Lignite Energy Council
1016 E. Owens Avenue
PO Box 2277
Bismarck, ND 58502-2277

701-258-7117
800-932-7117
FAX 701-258-2755
E-Mail: lec@lignite.com
Home Page: www.lignite.com
Social Media: *Facebook, Twitter, YouTube, RSS Feeds*

Jason Bohrer, President/CEO
Marie Hoerner, Dir., Finance & Benefit Resources
Mike Jones, Ph. D., VP, Research and Development
Steve Van Dyke, Vice President of Communications
Kay LaCoe, Director of Membership Marketing

Regional Trade Association - promotes policies and activities that maintain a viable lignite industry and enhance development of our regions' lignite resources.
355 Members
Founded in 1974

1367 Low Impact Hydropower Institute
PO Box 194
Harrington Park, NJ 07640

201-906-2189
FAX 206-984-3086
E-Mail: mjsale@lowimpacthydro.org
Home Page: www.lowimpacthydro.org
Social Media: *Facebook, Twitter, Google+ Pinterest*

Julie Keil, Chair
John Seebach, Vice-Chair
Michael J. Sale, PhD, Executive Director
Dana Hall, Deputy Director
Jacob Palmer, Treasurer

Dedicated to reducing the impacts of hydropower generation through the certification of hydropower projects that have avoided or reduced their environmental impacts pursuant to the Low Impact Hydropower Institute's criteria. Mission is to reduce the impacts of hydropower dams through market incentives.

1368 NABCEP
56 Clifton Country Rd.
Suite 202
Clifton Park, NY 12065

800-654-0021
FAX 518-899-1092
E-Mail: info@nabcep.org

Home Page: www.nabcep.org
Social Media: *Facebook*

Don Warfield, Chair
Richard Lawrence, Executive Director
Kathryn Casey, Program Manager
Sue Pratt, Business Manager
Melissa Bell, Program Assistant

Mission is to support, and work with, the renewable energy and energy efficiency industries, professionals, and stakeholders. Goal is to develop voluntary national certification programs that will; promote renewable energy, provide value to practitioners, promote worker safety and skill, and promote consumer confidence.
Founded in 2002

1369 National Association of Energy Service Companies
1615 M Street, NW
Suite 800
Washington, DC 20036

202-822-0950
FAX 202-822-0955
E-Mail: info@naesco.org
Home Page: www.naesco.org
Social Media: *Facebook, LinkedIn*

David Weiss, Chairman
Mike Kearney, Vice Chair
Terry E. Singe, Executive Director
Donald Gilligan, President
Scott Ririe, Secretary

An organization that promotes energy efficiency at state, federal, and international facilities; ensures the key role of ESCOs in delivering energyefficiency resources; and builds new market opportunities while growing existingmarkets.

1370 National Association of State Energy Officials
2107 Wilson Boulevard
Suite 850
Arlington, VA 22201

703-299-8800
FAX 703-299-6208
E-Mail: energy@naseo.org
Home Page: www.naseo.org
Social Media: *Facebook, Twitter, LinkedIn, YouTube, Flickr*

Janet Streff, Chair
Robert Jackson, Vice Chair
David Terry, Executive Director
Jeffrey C. Genzer, General Counsel
Marion Gold, Treasurer

A national nonprofit association that facilitates peer learning among state energy officials, serves as a resource for and about state energy offices, and advocates the interests of the state energy offices to Congress and federal agencies.
Founded in 1986

1371 National Biodiesel Board
605 Clark Ave
PO Box 104898
Jefferson City, MO 65101

573-635-3893
800-929-3437
FAX 573-635-7913
E-Mail: info@biodiesel.org
Home Page: www.biodiesel.org
Social Media: *Facebook, Twitter, YouTube, RSS Feeds, Google+*

Gary Haer, Chairman
Ed Ulch, Vice-Chair
Jim Conway, Treasurer
Ron Marr, Secretary

Mission is to advance the interests of its members by creating sustainable biodiesel industry growth. NBB serves as the industry's central coordinating entity and will be the single voice for its diverse membership base.

1372 National Fenestration Rating Council
6305 Ivy Lane
Suite 140
Greenbelt, MD 20770

301-589-1776
FAX 301-589-3884
E-Mail: info@nfrc.org
Home Page: www.nfrc.org
Social Media: *Facebook, Twitter, LinkedIn, YouTube*

James C. Benney, Chief Executing Officer
Deborah Callahan, Chief Operating Officer
Jessica Finn, Membership Coordinator
Cheryl Gendron, Meeting Manager
Scott Hanlon, Program Director

A nonprofit organization that administers an independent rating andlabeling system for the energy performance of windows, doors, skylights, and attachment products.
Founded in 1989

1373 National Hydropower Association
25 Massachusetts Ave, NW
Suite 450
Washington, DC 20001

202-682-1700
FAX 202-682-9478
E-Mail: help@hydro.org
Home Page: www.hydro.org
Social Media: *Facebook, Twitter*

Linda Church Ciocci, Executive Director
Steve Wenke, Vice President
John McCormick, President
Debbie Mursch, Treasurer
John Suloway, Secretary

Dedicated to promoting the growth of clean, affordable US hydropower. Seeks to secure hydropower's place as a climate-friendly, renewable and reliable energy source that serves national environmental, energy, and economic policy objectives. Members are involved in projects throughout the US hydropower industry, including both federal and non-federal hydroelectric facilities.

1374 National Renewable Energy Association
629 North Main Street
Hattiesburg, MS 39401

601-582-3330
FAX 601-582-3354
E-Mail: nrea@megagate.com
Home Page:
www.nationalrenewableenergyassociation.org

A nonprofit organization dedicated to helping Americans use less energy and to use more renewable energy in the future.
Founded in 2007

1375 National Renewable Energy Laboratory
15013 Denver West Parkway
Golden, CO 80401

303-275-3000
Home Page: www.nrel.gov
Social Media: *Facebook, Twitter, LinkedIn, YouTube*

Dr. Dan Arvizu, President
Dr. Dana Christensen, Deputy Laboratory Director
Bobi Garrett, Deputy Laboratory Director
David Post, Acting Deputy Lab Director/COO
Howard Branz, Research Fellow

Develops renewable energy and energy efficiency technologies and practices, advances related science and engineering, and transfers knowledge and innovations to address the nation's energy and environmental goals.

1376 National Wind Coordinating Collaborative
1110 Vermont Ave NW
Suite 950
Washington, DC 20005

202-656-3303
E-Mail: info@awwi.org
Home Page: nationalwind.org

Lauren Flinn, Facilitator
Abby Arnold, Senior Mediator

Provides a neutral forum for various stakeholders to pursue the shared objective of developing environmentally, economically, and politically sustainable commercial markets for wind power in the United States.
Founded in 1994

1377 Natural Resources Defense Council
40 West 20th Street
New York, NW 10011

212-727-2700
FAX 212-727-1773
E-Mail: webmaster@nrdc.org
Home Page: www.nrdc.org
Social Media: *Facebook, Twitter, YouTube, Tumblr, RSS*

Daniel R. Tishman, Chairman
Frederick A.O. Schwarz, Chair Emeritus
Patricia Bauman, Vice Chair
Mary Moran, Treasurer
Alan F. Horn, Vice Chair

A nonprofit environmental action group that works to restore the natural elements, defend endangered species, and strives to safeguard the Earth: its people, its plants and animals and the natural systems on which all life depends.
14000 Members

1378 North American Board of Certified Energy Practitioners
56 Clifton Country Rd
Suite 202
Clifton Park, NY 12065

800-654-0021
FAX 518-899-1092
E-Mail: info@nabcep.org
Home Page: www.nabcep.org
Social Media: *Facebook*

Don Warfield, Chair
Richard Lawrence, Executive Director
Kathryn Casey, Program Manager
Sue Pratt, Business Manager
Melissa Bell, Program Assistant

Offers entry level knowledge assessment, professional certification, and company accreditation programs to renewable energy professionals throughout North America.
Founded in 2002

1379 Northeast Sustainable Energy Association
50 Miles Street
Greenfield, MA 01301-3255

413-774-6051
FAX 413-774-6053
E-Mail: nesea@nesea.org
Home Page: www.nesea.org
Social Media: *Facebook, Twitter, LinkedIn, YouTube*

Jennifer Marrapese, Executive Director
Miriam Aylward, Director of Program Development
Mary Biddle, Deputy Executive Director
Gina Sieber, Business manager
Jenny Goldberg, Outreach & Event Coordinator

The nation's leading regional membership organization focused on promoting the understanding, development and adoption of energy

conservation and non-polluting, renewable energy technologies.
1802 Members
Founded in 1974

1380 Ocean Renewable Energy Coalition
12909 Scarlet Oak Drive
Darnestown, MD 20878

301-869-3790
FAX 301-869-5637
E-Mail: info@oceanrenewable.com
Home Page: www.oceanrenewable.com
Social Media: *Facebook, Twitter, RSS*

Sean O'Neill, President
Carolyn Elefant, General and Regulatory Counsel

Exclusively dedicated to promoting marine and hydrokinetic energy technologies from clean, renewable ocean resources. Organization embraces a wide range of renewable technologies; including wave, tidal, current, offshore wind, ocean thermal, marine biomass and all other technologies that utilize renewable resources from oceans, tidal areas and other unimpounded water bodies to produce electricity, desalinized water, hydrogen, mariculture and other by products.
40+ Members
Founded in 2005

1381 Office of Energy Efficiency & Renewable Energy
Forrestal Building
1000 Independence Avenue, SW
Washington, DC 20585

202-586-8302
Home Page: apps3.eere.energy.gov
Social Media: *Facebook, Twitter, LinkedIn*

David Danielson, Assistant Secretary
David Friedman, Principal Deputy Assis Secretary
Michael Budney, Director of Business Operations
John Lushetsky, Strategic Programs Director
Kathleen Hogan, Deputy Assistant Secretary

Leads the U.S. Department of Energy's efforts to develop and deliver market-driven solutions for energy-saving homes, buildings, and manufacturing;sustainable transportation; and renewable electricity generation.

1382 One Sky
One Sky
1635 Grandview Road
Gibsons, BC V0N 1V5

604-886-0508
Home Page: www.onesky.ca

Michael S. Smithers, Executive Director
Lisa Gibson, Nigeria Integral Leadership Coord.
Gail Hochachka, Integral Program Coordinator

Explores and promotes practical solutions and appropriate technologies for our environmental. social and economic challenges in a global setting.
Founded in 2000

1383 Pellet Fuels Institute
1901 North Moore St
Suite 600
Arlington, VA 22209

703-522-6778
FAX 703-522-0548
E-Mail: hedrick@pelletheat.org
Home Page: www.pelletheat.org
Social Media: *Facebook, Twitter, LinkedIn*

Stephen Faehner, Chairman
Jennifer Hedrick, Executive Director
Andrew Estep, Association Executive
John Crouch, Director of Public Affairs
Chris Amey, Vice Chairman

Promotes energy independence throught the effiecient use of clean, renewable, densified biomass fuel.
Founded in 1985

1384 Portable Rechargeable Battery Association
1776 K Street
4th Floor
Washington, DC 20006

202-719-4978
Home Page: www.prba.org

Charlie Monahan, Chairman
Stephen P. Victor, President & COO
Chris Carlson, Vice President of Logistics
Andrew J. Sirjord, Vice President
Mark HickoK, Director

A nonprofit trade association that develops plans for workable battery recycling programs to be used industry wide and that serves as the voice of the Rechargeable Power Industry, representing its members on legislative, regulatory and standards issues at the state, federal and international level.
Founded in 1991

1385 Renewable Energy Markets Association (REMA)
1211 Connecticut Ave NW
Suite 650
Washington, DC 20036-2701

202-640-6597
FAX 202-223-5537
E-Mail: info@renewablemarketers.org
Home Page: www.renewablemarketers.org
Social Media: *Facebook, Twitter*

Richard Anderson, President
Ian McGowan, Vice President
Patrick Serfass, General Manager
Joel Stronberg, Director - Policy and Gov. Affairs
Kevin Maddaford, Treasurer

A nonprofit association dedicated to maintaining and growing strong markets for renewable energy in the United States. Representing organizations that sell, purchase, or promote renewable energy products.

1386 Renewable Energy and Efficiency Business Association, Inc.
185 Asylum Street
CityPlace I
Hartford, CT 06103-3469

E-Mail: pmichaud@murthalaw.com
Home Page: www.reeba.org

Jim Daylor, Chairman/Treasurer
John Michael Callahan, Vice Chairman
Christopher F. Haplin, President
Paul Michaud, Executive Director/Founder
Jackie Rowe, Director of Operations & Membership

An active business organization that promotes the sustainable deployment of renewable energy, DSM and energy efficiency advocacy, collaboration, networking, and information sharing.
Founded in 2010

1387 Renewable Fuels Association (RFA)
425 Third Street SW
Suite 1150
Washington, DC 20024

202-289-3835
FAX 202-289-7519
Home Page: www.ethanolrfa.org
Social Media: *Facebook, Twitter, LinkedIn, YouTube, Google+, Instagram*

Randall Doyal, RFA Chairman
Bob Dinneen, President & CEO
Kelly Davis, Director of Regulatory Affairs

Samantha Slater, Vice President, Government Affairs
Tony Jackson, Communications Director

The national trade association for the US ethanol industry promoting policies, regulations and research and development initiatives that will lead to the increased production and use of fuel ethanol. Membership includes a broad cross-section of businesses, individuals and organizations dedicated to the expansion of the US fuel ethanol industry.
181 Members
Founded in 1981

1388 Rocky Mountain Institute
1820 Folsom Street
Boulder, CO 80302

303-245-1003
E-Mail: bet@rmi.org
Home Page: www.rmi.org
Social Media: *Facebook, Twitter, YouTube*

Amory B. Lovins, Chief Scientist/Chair Emeritus
Marty Pickett, JD, Managing Director
Jules Kortenhorst, Chief Executive Officer
Robert Hutchinson, Senior Fellow
Kathy Wight, Executive Assistant

Emphasizes integrative design, advanced technologies working with the private sector as well as civil society and government to drive the transition from coal and oil to efficiency and renewables.
Founded in 1982

1389 Solar Electric Light Fund
1612 K Street NW
Suite 300
Washington, DC 20006

202-234-7265
E-Mail: info@self.org
Home Page: self.org
Social Media: *Facebook, Twitter, YouTube*

Robert A. Freling, Executive Director
Jeff Lahl, Project Director
John Alejandro, Communications Director
Darren Anderson, Project Manager
Lisa Esler, Finance Director

Designs and implements solar energy solutions to assist people living in energy poverty with their economic, educational, health care, and agricultural development.
Founded in 1990

1390 Solar Electric Power Association
1220 19th Street, NW,
Suite 800
Washington, DC 20036-2405

202-857-0898
Home Page: www.solarelectricpower.org
Social Media: *Facebook, Twitter, LinkedIn, YouTube*

Steve Malnight, Chair
Joseph Forline, Chair Elect
Julia Hamm, President & CEO
John Hewa, Secretary
Ervan Hancock, Treasurer

An educational nonprofit association dedicated to advancing utilityintegration of solar through collaborative solutions, objeive information and shared benefits to the utility, its customers, and the public good.
Founded in 1992

1391 Solar Energy Industries Association
600 14th Street, NW
Suite 400
Washington, DC 20005

202-682-0556
E-Mail: info@seia.org
Home Page: www.seia.org

Social Media: *Facebook, Twitter, LinkedIn, YouTube, Pinterest*

Nat Kreamer, Chair
Tom Starrs, Vice Chair
Rhone Resch, President & CEO
Laura Stern, Treasurer
Scott Hennessey, Secretary

Works with its member companies to make solar a mainstream and significant energy source by expanding markets, removing market barriers, strenghtening the industry and educating the public on the benefits of solar energy.
1000 Members

1392 Solar Energy International
39845 Mathews Lane
Paonia, CO 81428

970-527-7657
Home Page: www.solarenergy.org
Social Media: *Facebook, Twitter, LinkedIn, YouTube*

Ed Marston, Chairperson
Sarah Bishop, President

A nonprofit educational organization that provides industry-leadingtechnical training and expertise in renewable energy to empower people, communities, and businesses worldwide.
Founded in 1991

1393 Solar Living Institute
PO Box 836
13771 S. Hwy 101
Hopland, CA 95449

707-472-2450
FAX 707-472-2498
E-Mail: sli@solarliving.org
Home Page: solarliving.org
Social Media: *Facebook, Twitter, LinkedIn, YouTube*

John Schaeffer, Founder/Board President
Karen Kallen, Managing Director
Miranda Mott, Programs Coordinator
Caleb Gordon, Farm & Garden Manager
Everardo Dominguez, Landscaper

A nonprofit solar training and sustainability organization. Mission is to promote sustainable living through inspirational environmental education.
Founded in 1998

1394 The Sustainable Biodiesel Alliance
P.O. Box 1677
Kahului, HI 96732

512-410-7841
FAX 512-410-7841
E-Mail: infoadmin@fuelresponsibly.org
Home Page:
test.sustainablebiodieselalliance.com/SBA/
Social Media: *Facebook, Twitter*

Kelly King, Chair
Annie Nelson, Vice-Chair
Mike Nasi, Treasurer
Ed Zwick, Secretary

An organization founded to support and encourage sustainable production and use of the renewable fuel biodiesel. Its primary mission is the completion of an independent sustainability certification system for U.S. Biodiesel Feedstock.
Founded in 2006

1395 UNEP SEF Alliance
Clean Energy Group
50 State St.
Suite 1
Montpelier, VT 05602

802-223-2554
FAX 802-223-4967

E-Mail: RTyler@cleanegroup.org
Home Page: www.unepsefalliance.org

The only convening body in the international system for public finance agencies in the clean energy sector. Members are visionary organizations from various countries pushing the forefront of how to do public finance for clean energy.

1396 US Renewable Energy Association, LLC.
PO Box 0550
Lexington, MI 48450

810-359-2250
E-Mail: sales@usrea.org
Home Page: www.usrea.org
Social Media: *Facebook, Twitter, LinkedIn, Google+, Pinterest, YouTube*

Gerald Zack, Founder/ President / CEO

A volunteer renewable energy advocacy group working to educate and promote advanced technologies in the R.E. industry.

1397 United States Clean Heat & Power Association
1875 Connecticut Ave. NW
10th Floor
Washington, DC 20009

202-888-0708
E-Mail: information@chpassociation.org
Home Page: www.chpassociation.org
Social Media: *Facebook, Twitter, Rss Feeds*

Chrissy Borskey, Chair
Dale Louda, Executive Director
Debbie Chance, Vice Chair
Jim Kerrigan, Secretary
Paul Lemar, Treasurer

Providing superior advocacy, networking, education and market information to companies in the business of clean, local energy generation. Documents the benefits of clean heat and power to the public and to decision-makers. Also participates in federal agency programs to promote clean distributed energy.
Founded in 1999

1398 United States Energy Association
1300 Pennsylvania Avenue, NW
Suite 550
Washington, DC 20004-3022

202-312-1230
FAX 202-682-1682
E-Mail: reply@usea.org
Home Page: www.usea.in
Social Media: *Facebook, Twitter, LinkedIn*

Vickey A. Bailey, Chairman
Will Polen, Senior Director
Sheila Slocum Hollis, Treasurer
Barry K. Worthington, Executive Director
Brian Kerans, Chief Financial Officer

An association of public and private energy-related organizations, corporations, and government agencies that represent the broad interests of the U.S. energy sector by increasing the understanding of energy issues, both domestically and internationally.

1399 Wind Energy Foundation
1501 M Street, NW
Suite 900
Washington, DC 20005

202-580-6440
E-Mail: info@windenergyfoundation.org
Home Page: www.windenergyfoundation.org
Social Media: *Facebook, Twitter, YouTube*

Steven Dayney, Chair
Edward Zaelke, Vice-Chair
Jayshree Desai, Treasurer
Tom Kiernan, Secretary
John Kostyack, Executive Director

A nonprofit organization dedicated to raising public awareness of wind as a clean, domestic energy source through communication, research, and education.
Founded in 1970

1400 Women's Council on Energy and the Environment
816 Connecticut Ave NW
Suite 200
Washington, DC 20006

202-997-4512
FAX 202-478-2098
Home Page: www.wcee.org
Social Media: *Facebook, Twitter, LinkedIn*

Robin Cantor, President
Mary Brosnan-Sell, Vice President
Joyce Chandran, Executive Director
Barbara Tyran, Treasurer
Alice Grabowski, Secretary

Supports women involved in the environmental community with education, research, new trend information and several publications.

1401 World Resources Institute(WRI)
10 G Street NE
Suite 800
Washington, DC 20002

202-729-7600
FAX 202-729-7686
E-Mail: cpotochny@gmail.com
Home Page: www.wri.org
Social Media: *Facebook, Twitter, LinkedIn, YouTube, RSS*

James A. Harmon, Chair
Andrew Steer, President & CEO
Steve Barker, CFO/Chief Administrative Officer
Manish Bapna, EVP/Managing Director
Lawrence MacDonald, VP, Communications

WRI takes research and puts ideas into action, working globally with governments, business and civil society to build transformative solutions that protect the earth and improve people's lives.
Founded in 1982

Newsletters

1402 BTEC Newsletter
Biomass Thermal Energy Council
1211 Connecticut Avenue NW
Suite 600
Washington, DC 20036-2701

202-596-3974
FAX 202-223-5537
E-Mail: info@biomassthermal.org
Home Page: www.biomassthermal.org
Social Media: *Facebook, Twitter*

Joseph Seymour, Executive Director
Charlie Niebling, Chairman
T.J. Morice, Vice-Chairman
Jon Strimling, Secretary
Bob Sourek, Treasurer

Provides member news, industry updates, upcoming events, and breaking BTEC news.
Frequency: Monthly
Founded in 2009

1403 Biogas News
American Biogas Council
1211 Connecticut Ave NW
Suite 600
Washington, DC 20036-2701

202-596-3974
FAX 202-223-5537

E-Mail: info@americanbiogascouncil.org
Home Page: www.americanbiogascouncil.org

Paul Greene, Chairman
Norma McDonald, Vice-Chair
Melissa VanOrnum, Treasurer
Nora Goldstein, Secretary

Members only publication includes everything from legislative updates to industry news and funding opportunities.
Frequency: Bi-Weekly

1404 Clean Energy Direct
IHS, Inc.

855-417-4155
E-Mail: energy@omeda.com
Home Page: www.theenergydaily.com
Social Media: *RSS*

George Lobsenz, Executive Editor
Sabrina Ousmaal, Associate Publisher
Eric Lindeman, Contributing Editor

Get analysis of regulation, technology and industry news of renewables, top news in the clean energy industry as well as access to clean energy articles and archives.
Cost: $695.00
Frequency: Weekly

1405 Climate Change News
Environmental and Energy Study Institute
1112 16th Street, NW
Suite 300
Washington, DC 20036-4819

202-628-1400
FAX 202-204-5244
E-Mail: cwerner@eesi.org
Home Page: www.eesi.org
Social Media: *Facebook, Twitter, YouTube*

Carol Werner, Executive Director
Jared Blum, Chair
Shelley Fidler, Treasurer
Richard L. Ottinger, Chair Emeritus

Recounts the top climate science, business, and politics stories of the week and includes a list of upcoming events and pending federal legislation.
Frequency: Weekly
Founded in 1984

1406 Coal Outlook
Pasha Publications
1600 Wilson Boulevard
Suite 600
Arlington, VA 22209-2509

703-528-1244
800-424-2908
FAX 703-528-1253

Harry Baisden, Group Publisher
Michael Hopps, Editor
Kathy Thorne, Circulation Manager

Primary strategic information source that keeps coal marketing executives and utilities up-to-date on who's getting coal contracts and at what price.
Cost: $795.00
Frequency: Weekly

1407 Coal Week International
McGraw Hill
2 Penn Plz
Suite 25
New York, NY 10121-0101

212-904-2000
800-752-8878
FAX 720-548-5701
E-Mail: support@platts.com
Home Page: www.mcgraw-hill.com

Peter C Davis, President
David Stellfox, Editor
Harry Sachinis, CEO
Larry Barth, Marketing Manager

A market management intelligence service for executives concerned with world trade metal-lurgical and steam coal.
Cost: $987.00
8 Pages
Frequency: Weekly
Founded in 1888

1408   Coal and Synfuels Technology
Pasha Publications
1600 Wilson Boulevard
Suite 600
Arlington, VA 22209-2510

703-528-1244
800-424-2908
FAX 703-528-1253

Harry Baisden, Group Publisher
Michael Hopps, Editor
Reports on the US and international advances in clean coal technologies, synthetic fuels and clean air issues.
Cost: $790.00
Frequency: Weekly
Founded in 1985

1409   Connecting to the Grid
Interstate Renewable Energy Council
PO Box 1156
Latham, NY 12110-1156

518-458-6059
E-Mail: info@irecusa.org
Home Page: www.irecusa.org

Laurel Varnado, Editor
Ken Jurman, Chair
David Warner, Vice Chair
Jane Pulaski, Secretary
Jennifer Szaro, Treasurer
Focusing on the latest news on interconnection and net metering in the US.
Frequency: Monthly

1410   Council on Women in Energy and Environmental Leadership Newsletter
Association of Energy Engineers
4025 Pleasantdale Rd
Suite 420
Atlanta, GA 30340-4264

770-447-5083
FAX 770-446-3969
E-Mail: info@aeecenter.org
Home Page: www.aeecenter.org
Social Media: *Facebook, Twitter, LinkedIn, YouTube*

Eric A. Woodroof, President
Gary Hogsett, President Elect
Bill Younger, Secretary
Paul Goodman, C.P.A., Treasurer
Addressing the high cost of energy, present and future sources of energy, and the impact of energy on the environment.
8.2M Members
Founded in 1977

1411   EESI Update
Environmental and Energy Study Institute
1112 16th Street, NW
Suite 300
Washington, DC 20036-4819

202-628-1400
FAX 202-204-5244
E-Mail: cwerner@eesi.org
Home Page: www.eesi.org
Social Media: *Facebook, Twitter, YouTube*

Carol Werner, Executive Director
Jared Blum, Chair
Shelley Fidler, Treasurer
Richard L. Ottinger, Chair Emeritus
Updating supporters about the current work of EESI.
Frequency: 3x Yearly
Founded in 1984

1412   Energy Insight
Association of Energy Engineers (AEE)
4025 Pleasantdale Rd.
Suite 420
Atlanta, GA 30340

770-447-5083
FAX 770-446-3969
E-Mail: al@aeecenter.org
Home Page: www.aeecenter.org
Social Media: *Facebook, Twitter, YouTube*

Albert Thumann, Executive Director
Written by, about and for the AEE member. Electronic publication includes information on AEE news, officers, award programs, nominations, certification, chapter news, operations report, presidents' message, study missions, upcoming events, and more.
15M Members
Frequency: Tri-Annually
Founded in 1977
Mailing list available for rent

1413   GRC Bulletin
Geothermal Resources Council
20001 Second Street
Suite 5
Davis, CA 95618-5476

530-758-2360
FAX 530-758-2839
E-Mail: grc@geothermal.org
Home Page: www.geothermal.org
Social Media: *Facebook, Twitter, LinkedIn, YouTube, Flickr*

Curt Robinson, Ph.D, Executive Director
Features articles on technical topics and geothermal development issues, as well as commentaries and news briefs.
Frequency: 6x Yearly
Founded in 1970

1414   Geothermal Energy Weekly
Geothermal Energy Association
209 Pennsylvania Avenue SE
Washington, DC 20003

202-454-5241
E-Mail: jgreco@terra-genpower.com
Home Page: www.geo-energy.org

Karl Gawell, Executive Director
Leslie Blodgett, Editor-in-Chief
Paul Thomsen, President
Jonathan M. Weisgall, Chairman

Electronic newsletter providing updates on the national, state, and international levels, and includes news from GEA member companies. Upcoming events, job opportunities, and Requests for Proposals are also found here.
Frequency: Weekly

1415   NABCEP News
56 Clifton Country Rd.
Suite 202
Clifton Park, NY 12065

800-654-0021
FAX 518-899-1092
E-Mail: info@nabcep.org
Home Page: www.nabcep.org

Ezra Auerbach, Executive Director
Don Warfield, Chair
Jane Weissman, Vice Chair
Les Nelson, Treasurer
Jeff Spies, Secretary
Newsletter from the North American Board of Certified Energy Practitioners featuring news, updates, technical issues and accomplishments of their certificants. Available electronically only.
Frequency: Bi-Monthly
Founded in 2000

1416   NHA Today
National Hydropower Association
25 Massachusetts Ave, NW
Suite 450
Washington, DC 20001

202-682-1700
FAX 202-682-9478
E-Mail: help@hydro.org
Home Page: www.hydro.org
Social Media: *Facebook, Twitter*

Linda Church Ciocci, Executive Director
David Moller, President
James Crew, Treasurer
John Ragonese, Vice President
Tim Oakes, Secretary
Offers the latest information on regulatory and legislative policy, regional concerns, and issues on the horizon. Available electronically to members of NHA only.
Frequency: Bi-Weekly

1417   OREC Newsletter
Ocean Renewable Energy Coalition

301-869-3790
E-Mail: info@oceanrenewable.com
Home Page: www.oceanrenewable.com

Sean O'Neill, President
Carolyn Elefant, General Counsel
Striving to keep members, legislators, regulators, the media and the public at large up to date with OREC's activities as well as ongoing developments in this emerging industry.
40+ Members
Frequency: Weekly
Founded in 2005

1418   Pellet Fuels Institute
Pellet Fuels Institute.
1901 North Moore Street
Suite 600
Arlington, VA 22209

703-522-6778
FAX 703-522-0548
E-Mail: pfimail@pelletheat.org
Home Page: www.pelletheat.org

Jennifer Hedrick, Executive Director
Jason Berthiaume, Membership/Gov't Affairs
John Crouch, Director of Public Affairs
Newsletter with industry news, updates published quarterly

1419   Renewable Energy in the 50 States
American Council on Renewable Energy(ACORE)
1660 K Street NW
Suite 650
Washington, DC 20006

202-393-0001
Home Page: www.acore.org

Dennis V. McGinn, President/CEO
Tom Weirich, VP of Corporate Relations
Dawn Butcher, Director of Event Planning/Mktg.
Executive summary on the status of renewable energy implementation at the state-level. A two-page overview on key developments including installed and planned projects.
Founded in 2001

1420   Small Wind Energy
Interstate Renewable Energy Council
PO Box 1156
Latham, NY 12110-1156

518-458-6059
E-Mail: info@irecusa.org
Home Page: www.irecusa.org

Larry Sherwood, Editor
Ken Jurman, Chair
David Warner, Vice Chair

Jane Pulaski, Secretary
Jennifer Szaro, Treasurer

Featuring updates and news about small wind energy issues.
Frequency: Quarterly

1421 Solar@Work

American Solar Energy Society
4760 Walnut Street
Suite 106
Boulder, CO 80301

303-443-3130
FAX 303-443-3212
E-Mail: ases@ases.org
Home Page: www.ases.org
Social Media: *Facebook, Twitter, LinkedIn*

Susan Greene, President
David G. Hill, Chair
Bill Poulin, Treasurer
Jason Keyes, Secretary

Get the latest business and market analysis, technology breakthroughs and career advice from ASES professionals.
13M Members
Frequency: Bi-Monthly
Founded in 1954

1422 Sun Times

Alternative Energy Resources Organization
432 N. Last Chance Gulch
Helena, MT 59601

406-443-7272
FAX 406-442-9120
E-Mail: aero@aeromt.org
Home Page: www.aeromt.org
Social Media: *Facebook, Twitter, Myspace*

Bryan von Lossberg, Executive Director

Stay up to date on AERO news and events.
Frequency: Monthly
Founded in 1974

1423 Sustainable Bioenergy, Farms, and Forests

Environmental and Energy Study Institute
1112 16th Street, NW
Suite 300
Washington, DC 20036-4819

202-628-1400
FAX 202-204-5244
E-Mail: cwerner@eesi.org
Home Page: www.eesi.org
Social Media: *Facebook, Twitter, YouTube*

Carol Werner, Executive Director
Jared Blum, Chair
Shelley Fidler, Treasurer
Richard L. Ottinger, Chair Emeritus

A look at sustainable bioenergy, farm, and forest policy issues.
Frequency: Weekly
Founded in 1984

1424 The Biodiesel Bulletin

National Biodiesel Board
605 Clark Ave
PO Box 104898
Jefferson City, MO 65110-4898

573-635-3893
FAX 573-635-7913
E-Mail: info@biodiesel.org
Home Page: www.biodiesel.org
Social Media: *Facebook, Twitter, YouTube*

Gary Haer, Chairman
Ed Ulch, Vice-Chair
Jim Conway, Treasurer
Ron Marr, Secretary

Electronic publication keeping members up to date on the biodiesel industry and technology.
Frequency: Monthly
Mailing list available for rent

1425 The Energy Daily

IHS, Inc.

855-417-4155
E-Mail: energy@omeda.com
Home Page: www.theenergydaily.com

George Lobsenz, Executive Editor
Sabrinal Ousmaal, Associate Publisher
Erica Lengermann, Manager, Sales

Keeping readers at the forefront of all major developments in the energy industry. Through in-depth analysis of issues, cutting-edge reporting and unbiased journalism, The Energy Daily continues to deliver the news readers need for business success.
Cost: $2497.00
Frequency: Daily

1426 The Energy Roundup

IHS, Inc.

855-417-4155
E-Mail: energy@omeda.com
Home Page: www.theenergydaily.com

George Lobsenz, Executive Editor
Sabrinal Ousmaal, Associate Publisher
Erica Lengermann, Manager, Sales

The most important developing stories delivered weekly.
Frequency: Weekly

1427 The IREC Report

Interstate Renewable Energy Council
PO Box 1156
Latham, NY 12110-1156

518-458-6059
E-Mail: info@irecusa.org
Home Page: www.irecusa.org

Jane Pulaski, Editor
Ken Jurman, Chair
David Warner, Vice Chair
Jane Pulaski, Secretary
Jennifer Szaro, Treasurer

A monthly recap of the latest news about IREC's programs, policies and best practices in renewable energy.
Frequency: Monthly

1428 The ISPQ Insider

Interstate Renewable Energy Council
PO Box 1156
Latham, NY 12110-1156

518-458-6059
E-Mail: info@irecusa.org
Home Page: www.irecusa.org

Jane Pulaski, Editor
Ken Jurman, Chair
David Warner, Vice Chair
Jane Pulaski, Secretary
Jennifer Szaro, Treasurer

A monthly recap of the latest news, policies and best practices from the ISPQ credentialing program for renewable energy, weatherization and the energy retrofit sector.
Frequency: Monthly

1429 The SITN Quarterly

Interstate Renewable Energy Council
PO Box 1156
Latham, NY 12110-1156

518-458-6059
E-Mail: info@irecusa.org
Home Page: www.irecusa.org

Jane Pulaski, Editor
Ken Jurman, Chair
David Warner, Vice Chair
Jane Pulaski, Secretary
Jennifer Szaro, Treasurer

Summary of the latest news, policies and best practices from the Solar Instructor Training Network.
Frequency: Quarterly

1430 Utility Reporter: Fuels, Energy and Power

InfoTeam
PO Box 15640
Plantation, FL 33318-5640

954-473-9560
FAX 954-473-0544
E-Mail: infoteamma@aol.com

Randy M Allen CPA, Editor

Focuses on activities involving: power generation, combustion, delivery and transmission; alternative energy devices and systems; heat transfer, storage and utilization; and myriad of related topics.
Cost: $289.00
20 Pages
Frequency: Monthly
ISBN: 0-890298-4-
Printed in one color on matte stock

1431 Wind Energy SmartBrief

American Wind Energy Association
1501 M Street NW
Suite 1000
Washington, DC 20005

202-383-2500
FAX 202-383-2505
E-Mail: windmail@awea.org
Home Page: www.awea.org
Social Media: *Facebook, Twitter, YouTube, Flickr*

Ned Hall, Chair
Thomas Carnahan, Chair-Elect
Gabriel Alonso, Secretary
Don Furman, Treasurer
Denise Bode, CEO

Delivers quickly digestible summaries of the day's wind energy-related stories from across the media, as well as links to those stories. SmartBrief not only keeps readers informed about the industry, it allows them to stay on top of what's being said about it.
2500+ Members
Frequency: Daily

1432 Wind Energy Weekly

American Wind Energy Association
1501 M Street NW
Suite 1000
Washington, DC 20005

202-383-2500
FAX 202-383-2505
E-Mail: windmail@awea.org
Home Page: www.awea.org
Social Media: *Facebook, Twitter, YouTube, Flickr*

Ned Hall, Chair
Thomas Carnahan, Chair-Elect
Gabriel Alonso, Secretary
Don Furman, Treasurer
Denise Bode, CEO

Packed with detailed and up-to-date information on the world of wind energy that simply can't be obtained elsewhere. Readers have a professional interest in wind energy, need to keep up with wind energy development news or late-breaking legislative, economic, and environmental developments.
2500+ Members
Frequency: Weekly

Magazines & Journals

1433 Biodiesel Magazine

National Biodiesel Board

605 Clark Ave
PO Box 104898
Jefferson City, MO 65110-4898

573-635-3893
FAX 573-635-7913
E-Mail: info@biodiesel.org
Home Page: www.biodieselmagazine.com
Social Media: *Facebook, Twitter, YouTube*

Gary Haer, Chairman
Ed Ulch, Vice-Chair
Jim Conway, Treasurer
Ron Marr, Secretary

Trade journal dedicated to objective, independent coverage of biodiesel news, events and information relevant to the global industry. With editorial focus on US and international methyl ester manufacturing, trade, distribution and markets, Biodiesel Magazine also provides valuable insight into feedstock and market share competition from the non-ester renewable diesel sector.
Frequency: Monthly
Mailing list available for rent

1434 Biomass Power & Thermal
Biomass Thermal Energy Council
1211 Connecticut Avenue NW
Suite 600
Washington, DC 20036-2701

202-596-3974
FAX 202-223-5537
E-Mail: info@biomassthermal.org
Home Page: www.biomassthermal.org
Social Media: *Facebook, Twitter*

Joseph Seymour, Executive Director
Charlie Niebling, Chairman
T.J. Morice, Vice-Chairman
Jon Strimling, Secretary
Bob Sourek, Treasurer

Tailored for industry professionals engaged in utilizing biomass for the generation of electricity, thermal energy, or both (CHP). Maintains a core editorial focus on biomass logistics; generating, cultivating, collecting, transporting, processing, marketing, procuring and utilizing sustainable biomass for power and heat.
Frequency: Monthly
Founded in 2009

1435 Distributed Generation & Alternative Energy Journal
Association of Energy Engineers (AEE)
4025 Pleasantdale Rd.
Suite 420
Atlanta, GA 30340

770-447-5083
FAX 770-446-3969
E-Mail: al@aeecenter.org
Home Page: www.aeecenter.org
Social Media: *Facebook, Twitter, YouTube*

Albert Thumann, Executive Director
Jorge B. Wong, Ph.D, Editor-in-Chief

An authoritative publication which provides readers with detailed information on the latest innovations and developments in the distributed generation and related alternative energy fields.
15M Members
Frequency: Quarterly

1436 Energy Engineering
Association of Energy Engineers (AEE)
4025 Pleasantdale Rd.
Suite 420
Atlanta, GA 30340

770-447-5083
FAX 770-446-3969
E-Mail: al@aeecenter.org

Home Page: www.aeecenter.org
Social Media: *Facebook, Twitter, YouTube*

Albert Thumann, Executive Director
Jorge B. Wong, Ph.D, Editor-in-Chief

The oldest journal exclusively written for engineers, energy managers, facility managers, utility professionals, VP's of operations, governmental energy managers and plant engineers involved in the design and application of energy management and facility improvement technologies.
15M Members
Frequency: Monthly
Founded in 1904

1437 Energy Law Journal
Federal Energy Bar Association
1990 M St Nw
Suite 350
Washington, DC 20036-3429

202-223-5625
FAX 202-833-5596
E-Mail: admin@eba-net.org
Home Page: www.eba-net.org

Lorna Wilson, Administrator
Clinton A. Vince, Editor-in-Chief

Lawyers and consultants engaged in energy and public utility law.
Cost: $35.00
Frequency: Monthly
Circulation: 2600
ISSN: 0270-9163
Founded in 1946
Printed in 2 colors on matte stock

1438 Geo Outlook
International Ground Source Heat Pump Association
1201 S Innovation Way
Suite 400
Stillwater, OK 74074

405-744-5175
800-626-4747
FAX 405-744-5283
E-Mail: igshpa@okstate.edu
Home Page: www.igshpa.okstate.edu

Jim Bose, Ph.D, Executive Director
Shelly Fitzpatrick, Conference & Membership Coordinator
John Turley, Chairman
Jack Henrich, Vice Chairman

The official publication of the geoexchange industry.
Frequency: Quarterly
Circulation: 50000

1439 Home Power Magazine
312 N. Main Street
Phoenix, OR 97535

541-512-0201
800-707-6585
Home Page: www.homepower.com
Social Media: *Facebook, Twitter*

Claire Anderson, Associate Editor

For renewable energy and sustainable living enthusiasts- homeowners and industry professionals alike. Specializing in hands-on, practical information about RE technologies, and presenting technical material in an easy-to-use format.
Frequency: Bi-Monthly

1440 IEEE Power and Energy Magazine
IEEE
PO Box 1331
Piscataway, NJ 08855

732-981-0061
FAX 732-981-9667

E-Mail: custome-service@ieee.org
Home Page: www.ieee.org

Mel Olken, Editor
Susan Schneiderman, Business Development

Dedicated to disseminating information on all matters of interest to electric power engineers and other professionals involved in the electric power industry. Feature articles focus on advanced concepts, technologies, and practices associated with all aspects of electric power from a technical perspective in synergy with nontechnical areas such as business, environmental, and social concerns.
Cost: $260.00
82 Pages
Frequency: Monthly
Circulation: 23000
ISSN: 1540-7977
Founded in 2003
Mailing list available for rent
Printed in on glossy stock

1441 Renewables Global Status Report
REN21
REN21 Secretariat c/o UNEP
15, Rue de Milan 75441
Paris, France CEDEX 09

+33 1 44 3714 5090
E-Mail: secretariat@ren21.net
Home Page: www.new.ren21.net

Mohamed El-Ashry, Chair-UN Foundation
Michael Eckhart, VP- Citygroup
Kevin Nassiep, VP
Christine Lins, Executive Secretary

The Global Status Report(GSR) is the collaborative effort of over 400 authors, contributors and reviewers and is today the most frequently referenced report on renewable energy market, industry and policy trends, it provides testimony of the undeterred growth of electricity, heat and fuel production capacities from renewable energy sources including solar PV, wind power, solar hot water/heating, biofuels, hydropower and geothermal.

1442 SOLAR TODAY
American Solar Energy Society
4760 Walnut Street
Suite 106
Boulder, CO 80301

303-443-3130
FAX 303-443-3212
E-Mail: ases@ases.org
Home Page: www.ases.org
Social Media: *Facebook, Twitter, LinkedIn*

Susan Greene, President
David G. Hill, Chair
Bill Poulin, Treasurer
Jason Keyes, Secretary

With the renewable energy industry changing at an unprecedented pace, SOLAR TODAY helps readers understand the changes, where the industry is headed, and how it's affecting the country.
13M Members
Frequency: 9x Yearly
Founded in 1954

1443 Solar Energy
Elsevier Science
655 Avenue of the Americas
PO Box 945
New York, NY 10010-5107

212-633-3800
FAX 212-633-3850
Home Page: www.elsevier.com

Young Suk Chi, Manager

Devoted exclusively to the science and technology of solar energy applications. Presents information not previously published in journals

on any aspect of solar energy research, development, application, measurement or policy.
Frequency: Monthly
Circulation: 6400

1444 Strategic Planning for Energy and the Environment
Association of Energy Engineers (AEE)
4025 Pleasantdale Rd.
Suite 420
Atlanta, GA 30340

770-447-5083
FAX 770-446-3969
E-Mail: al@aeecenter.org
Home Page: www.aeecenter.org
Social Media: *Facebook, Twitter, YouTube*

Albert Thumann, Executive Director
Dr. Wayne C. Turner, Editor

Concentrates on the background, new developments and policy issues which impact corporate planning for energy savings, operational efficiency, and environmental concerns.
15M Members
Frequency: Quarterly

1445 The Ally
BlueGreen Alliance
1020 19th Street NW
Suite 600
Washington, DC 20036

202-706-6910
E-Mail: ashley@bluegreenallliance.org
Home Page: www.bluegreenalliance.org
Social Media: *Facebook, Twitter, flickr, YouTube*

David Foster, Executive Director

A biweekly update providing reports, letters, press releases and other publications along with clean energy industry news.

1446 The Energy Journal
International Association for Energy Economics
28790 Chagrin Blvd
Suite 350
Cleveland, OH 44122-4642

216-464-5365
FAX 216-464-2737
E-Mail: iaee@iaee.org
Home Page: www.iaee.org
Social Media: *Facebook, LinkedIn*

Mine Yucel, President
Lars Bergman, President-Elect
David L. Williams, Executive Director

Promotes the advancement and dissemination of new knowledge concerning energy and related topics. Publishing a blend of theoretical, empirical and policy related papers in energy economics.
3400 Members
Founded in 1977

Trade Shows

1447 AERO Annual Meeting
Alternative Energy Resources Organization
432 N. Last Chance Gulch
Helena, MT 59601

406-443-7272
FAX 406-442-9120
E-Mail: aero@aeromt.org
Home Page: www.aeromt.org
Social Media: *Facebook, Twitter, Myspace*

Bryan von Lossberg, Executive Director
Sustainability Begins at Home.
Frequency: Annual/ October
Founded in 1974

1448 AWEA Offshore Windpower Conference & Exhibition
American Wind Energy Association
1501 M Street NW
Suite 1000
Washington, DC 20005

202-383-2500
FAX 202-383-2505
E-Mail: windmail@awea.org
Home Page: www.awea.org
Social Media: *Facebook, Twitter, YouTube, Flickr*

Ned Hall, Chair
Thomas Carnahan, Chair-Elect
Gabriel Alonso, Secretary
Don Furman, Treasurer
Denise Bode, CEO

Brings together exhibitors and attendees from all over the world who are interested in becoming players in this new and highly promising market.
2500+ Members
1700 Attendees
Frequency: Annual/October

1449 AWEA Windpower Conference & Exhibition
American Wind Energy Association
1501 M Street NW
Suite 1000
Washington, DC 20005

202-383-2500
FAX 202-383-2505
E-Mail: windmail@awea.org
Home Page: www.awea.org
Social Media: *Facebook, Twitter, YouTube, Flickr*

Ned Hall, Chair
Thomas Carnahan, Chair-Elect
Gabriel Alonso, Secretary
Don Furman, Treasurer
Denise Bode, CEO

Recognized as one of the world's premier wind energy trade shows, bringing together attendees and exhibitors from every aspect of the industry. Exhibitors display the latest industry products and services from manufacturing leaders, component suppliers, and other wind energy organizations. This conference combines education, exhibition, and networking creating a perfect venue for business development.
2500+ Members
16000 Attendees
Frequency: Annual/June

1450 Annual Algae Biomass Summit
Biomass Power Association
100 Middle St.
PO Box 9729
Portland, ME 04104-9729

703-889-8504
E-Mail: info@biomasspowerassociation.com
Home Page: www.usabiomass.org
Social Media: *Facebook*

Bob Cleaves, President & CEO
Gary Melow, State Projects Coordinator

This dynamic event unites industry professionals from all sectors of the world's algae utilization industries including, but not limited to; financing, algal ecology, genetic systems, carbon partitioning, engineering & analysis, biofuels, animal feeds, fertilizers, bioplastics, supplements and foods.
80 Members
Frequency: Annual/October

1451 Annual National Ethanol Conference
Renewable Fuels Association

425 Third Street SW
Suite 1150
Washington, DC 20024

202-289-3835
FAX 202-289-7519
E-Mail: necregistration@bbiinternational.com
Home Page: www.ethanolrfa.org
Social Media: *Facebook, Twitter, YouTube, Flickr*

Bob Dinneen, President & CEO
Christina Martin, Executive Vice President
Alex Obuchowski, CFO

Recognized as the preeminent conference for delivering accurate, timely information on marketing, legislative and regulatory issues facing the ethanol industry. Meet and interact with key stakeholders and take part in shaping the future of the ethanol industry.
1250+ Attendees
Frequency: Annual/February
Founded in 1981

1452 Annual North American Waste-to-Energy Conference
Solid Waste Association of North America - SWANA

800-GOS-WANA
FAX 301-589-7068
Home Page: www.nawtec.org

Co-sponsored by ERC, ASME and SWANA, in partnership with WTERT, the conference and trade show focuses on municipal waste-to-energy operational issues and policy, technology and research initiatives.

1453 Annual Renewable Energy Technology Conference & Exhibition (RETECH)
American Council on Renewable Energy
1600 K Street NW
Suite 700
Washington, DC 20006

202-393-0001
E-Mail: vay@acore.org
Home Page: www.refindirectory.com
Social Media: *Facebook, Twitter, LinkedIn, YouTube*

Dennis V. McGinn, President

Conference sessions deliver unparalleled educational content including business development opportunities, topical professional development, current trends, the newest technologies and important up-to-date information on the changing legislative and regulatory landscapes. Exhibition offers the best opportunity to meet, network and connect with companies and organizations in the renewable energy industry.
3000+ Attendees
Frequency: Annual/October
Founded in 2001

1454 Bioenergy Fuels & Products Conference & Expo
Biomass Thermal Energy Council
1211 Connecticut Avenue NW
Suite 600
Washington, DC 20036-2701

202-596-3974
FAX 202-223-5537
E-Mail: info@biomassthermal.org
Home Page: www.biomassthermal.org
Social Media: *Facebook, Twitter*

Joseph Seymour, Executive Director
Charlie Niebling, Chairman
T.J. Morice, Vice-Chairman
Jon Strimling, Secretary
Bob Sourek, Treasurer

Speakers and moderators who will address a range of topics including raw material, product

and market developments and bio-process technologies.
Frequency: Annual/March
Founded in 2009

1455 Biomass Thermal DC Summit
Biomass Thermal Energy Council
1211 Connecticut Avenue NW
Suite 600
Washington, DC 20036-2701

202-596-3974
FAX 202-223-5537
E-Mail: info@biomassthermal.org
Home Page: www.biomassthermal.org
Social Media: *Facebook, Twitter*

Joseph Seymour, Executive Director
Charlie Niebling, Chairman
T.J. Morice, Vice-Chairman
Jon Strimling, Secretary
Bob Sourek, Treasurer

Summit participants engage policy makers and renewable energy - related groups on the substantial benefits of biomass thermal energy use; increased rural economic activity, energy independence, healthier forests, and effective tax policy.
Frequency: Annual/November
Founded in 2009

1456 Building Energy
Northeast Sustainable Energy Association
50 Miles St
Greenfield, MA 01301-3255

413-774-6051
FAX 413-774-6053
E-Mail: nesea@nesea.org
Home Page: www.nesea.org
Social Media: *Facebook, Twitter, LinkedIn*

David Barclay, Executive Director
Sonia Hamel, Vice Chair
Daniel Sagan, Secretary
Michael Skelly, Treasurer

Oldest and largest regional renewable energy event in the country, known for showcasing next-generation thinkers and game-changing ideas.
1802 Members
Founded in 1974
Mailing list available for rent

1457 Energy Innovation Summit
National Biodiesel Board
605 Clark Ave
PO Box 104898
Jefferson City, MO 65110-4898

573-635-3893
FAX 573-635-7913
E-Mail: info@biodiesel.org
Home Page: www.biodiesel.org
Social Media: *Facebook, Twitter, YouTube*

Gary Haer, Chairman
Ed Ulch, Vice-Chair
Jim Conway, Treasurer
Ron Marr, Secretary

Designed to bring together key players from across the energy ecosystem - researchers, entrepreneurs, investors, corporate executives, and government officials - to share ideas for developing and deploying the next generation of clean energy technologies.
Frequency: Annual/February

1458 Geothermal Energy Expo
Geothermal Energy Association
209 Pennsylvania Avenue SE
Washington, DC 20003

202-454-5261
FAX 202-454-5265

E-Mail: jgreco@terra-genpower.com
Home Page: www.geo-energy.org

Karl Gawell, Executive Director
Leslie Blodgett, Editor-in-Chief
Paul Thomsen, President
Jonathan M. Weisgall, Chairman
Kathy Kent, Director of Events

The world's largest gathering of vendors providing support for geothermal resource exploration, characterization, development, production and management. Provides a unique opportunity for exhibitors to showcase their projects, equipment, services and state of the art technology to the geothermal community.
Frequency: Annual/October

1459 GlobalCon Conference & Expo
Biomass Thermal Energy Council
1211 Connecticut Avenue NW
Suite 600
Washington, DC 20036-2701

202-596-3974
FAX 202-223-5537
E-Mail: info@biomassthermal.org
Home Page: www.biomassthermal.org
Social Media: *Facebook, Twitter*

Joseph Seymour, Executive Director
Charlie Niebling, Chairman
Dan Arnett, Vice-Chairman
John Ackerly, Secretary
Mike Jostrom, Treasurer

Designed specifically to facilitate those seeking to expand their knowledge of fast-moving developments in the energy field, explore promising new technologies, compare energy supply options, and learn about innovative and cost-conscious project implementation strategies.
Frequency: Annual/March
Founded in 2009

1460 IGSHPA Conference & Expo
International Ground Source Heat Pump Association
1201 S Innovation Way
Suite 400
Stillwater, OK 74074

405-744-5175
800-626-4747
FAX 405-744-5283
E-Mail: igshpa@okstate.edu
Home Page: www.igshpa.okstate.edu

Jim Bose, Ph.D, Executive Director
Shelly Fitzpatrick, Conference & Membership Coordinator
Jack Henrich, Chairman
Greg Wells, Vice Chairman
Jim Bose, Executive Director

The largest technical conference in the US dedicated solely to geothermal. Conference features technical classes, which attract many industry newcomers each year.
Frequency: Annual/October

1461 International Bioenergy and Bioproducts Conference (IBBC)
Technical Association of the Pulp & Paper Industry
15 Technology Parkway S
Norcross, GA 30092

770-446-1400
800-322-8686
FAX 770-446-6947
E-Mail: webmaster@tappi.org
Home Page: www.tappi.org

Norman F. Marsolan, Chair
Thomas J. Garland, Vice Chair
Larry N. Montague, President & CEO

Focusing on technical advancements and commercialization of bioconversion technologies that leverage the forest products manufacturing

infrastructure and will include technical presentations, expert panels, case studies, and reports from projects that address feedstock and harvesting improvements to increase yield and quality of biomass, and much more.
500 Attendees
Frequency: Annual/October

1462 International Biomass Conference & Expo
Biomass Thermal Energy Council
1211 Connecticut Avenue NW
Suite 600
Washington, DC 20036-2701

202-596-3974
FAX 202-223-5537
E-Mail: info@biomassthermal.org
Home Page: www.biomassthermal.org
Social Media: *Facebook, Twitter*

Joseph Seymour, Executive Director
Charlie Niebling, Chairman
Dan Arnett, Vice-Chairman
John Ackerly, Secretary
Mike Jostrom, Treasurer

This dynamic event unites industry professionals from all sectors of the world's interconnected biomass utilization industries - biobased power, thermal energy, fuels and chemicals. Where future and existing producers of biobased power, fuels and thermal energy products go to network with waste generators and other industry suppliers and technology providers.
Frequency: Annual/April
Founded in 2009

1463 International Topical Meeting on Advances in Reactor Physics
555 N Kensington Ave
La Grange Park, IL 60526-5592

708-352-6611
800-323-3044
FAX 708-352-0499
E-Mail: advertising@ans.org
Home Page: www.ans.org
Social Media: *Facebook, Twitter, LinkedIn*

Jack Tuohy, Executive Director
James S Tulenko, VP
William F Naughton, Treasurer

Advances in reactor physics being the main topic of discussion. Promoting the awareness and understanding of the application of nuclear science and technology.
10500 Members
Founded in 1954

1464 NABCEP Continuing Education Conference
NABCEP
56 Clifton Country Rd.
Suite 202
Clifton Park, NY 12065

800-654-0021
FAX 518-899-1092
E-Mail: CEconference@nabcep.org
Home Page: www.nabcep.org

Ezra Auerbach, Executive Director
Don Warfield, Chair
Jane Weissman, Vice Chair
Les Nelson, Treasurer
Jeff Spies, Secretary

The objective of this conference is to offer NABCEP certified installers and technical sales professionals an opportunity that allows them to fulfill the majority of their CE requirements at a single event. In combination with manufacturer's training sessions, conference registrants will be able to attend workshops on the NEC,

financial analysis, safety, and emerging fire codes.
Frequency: Annual/March
Founded in 2000

1465   National Biodiesel Conference & Expo

National Biodiesel Board
605 Clark Ave
PO Box 104898
Jefferson City, MO 65110-4898

573-635-3893
FAX 573-635-7913
E-Mail: info@biodiesel.org
Home Page: www.biodiesel.org
Social Media: *Facebook, Twitter, YouTube*

Gary Haer, Chairman
Ed Ulch, Vice-Chair
Steven J. Levy, Treasurer
Ron Marr, Secretary

The only event that gathers biodiesel decision-makers from across the United States, and the world. Opportunities abound for attendees and exhibitors to network connect and learn. Event explores the topics of governmental policy, technical issues and marketing trends in the biodiesel industry.
Frequency: Annual/February

1466   National Hydropower Association Annual Conference

National Hydropower Association
25 Massachusetts Ave, NW
Suite 450
Washington, DC 20001

202-682-1700
FAX 202-682-9478
E-Mail: help@hydro.org
Home Page: www.hydro.org
Social Media: *Facebook, Twitter*

Linda Church Ciocci, Executive Director
David Moller, President
Eric Van Deuren, Treasurer
Cherise Oram, Vice President
Suzanne Grassell, Secretary

Program will provide a unique opportunity to hear first-hand from the Administration, Congress, federal regulators and resource agencies on the issues and policies that directly affect individual businesses and projects.
Frequency: Annual/April

1467   Pellet Fuels Institute Annual Conference

1901 North Moore Street
Suite 600
Arlington, VA 22209

703-522-6778
FAX 703-522-0548
E-Mail: pfimail@pelletheat.org
Home Page: www.pelletheat.org

Jennifer Hedrick, Executive Director
Jason Berthiaume, Membership/ Gov't Affairs Associate
John Crouch, Director of Public Affairs

Conference educates industry members on the latest information including new program development and what to expect in upcoming months. Speakers, roundtable panels, annual golf tournament and a beach bash.

1468   Renewable Energy Finance Forum (REFF) -Wall Street

American Council on Renewable Energy
1600 K Street NW
Suite 700
Washington, DC 20006

202-393-0001
E-Mail: vay@acore.org
Home Page: www.refindirectory.com

Social Media: *Facebook, Twitter, LinkedIn, YouTube*

Dennis V. McGinn, President
Estelle Lloyd, Managing Editor & Co-Founder
Tom, Naylor, Ronan
Murphy Managing Editor

Bringing together the top leaders of the USA's renewable energy industry, drawing attendees from the entire value chain, including financiers, manufacturers and developers.
700 Attendees
Frequency: Annual/June
Founded in 2001

1469   Renewable Energy Markets Conference

Renewable Energy Markets Association
1211 Connecticut Ave NW
Suite 600
Washington, DC 20036-2701

202-640-6597
FAX 202-223-5537
E-Mail: info@renewablemarketers.org
Home Page: www.renewablemarketers.org
Social Media: *Facebook, Twitter*

Richard Anderson, President
Ian McGowan, Vice President
Kevin Maddaford, Treasurer
Sarah Smith, Secretary
Josh Lieberman, General Manager

Bridging the interests of renewable energy generators, sellers, and utilities with those of purchasers, policymakers, and the communities that benefit from clean energy, this is the nation's premier forum for the energy community to gather, learn from each other, and recognize best practices for promoting renewable energy.
400 Attendees
Frequency: Annual/November

1470   Solar Thermal

Interstate Renewable Energy Council
PO Box 1156
Latham, NY 12110-1156

518-458-6059
E-Mail: info@irecusa.org
Home Page: www.irecusa.org

Jane Weissman, Executive Director
Lary Sherwood, Vice Chaie
David Warner, Chair
Jane Pulaski, Secretary
Jennifer Szaro, Treasurer

A two-day conference and networking event for industry professionals including; installers, manufacturers, distributors, engineers, designers, policy makers, code officials, and trainers. A national solar heating and cooling conference.
Frequency: Annual/December

1471   U.S. Clean Heat & Power Association's Annual Spring CHP Forum

U.S. Clean Heat & Power Association
105 North Virginia Avenue
Suite 204
Falls Church, VA 22046

703-436-2257
E-Mail: info@uschpa.org
Home Page: www.uschpa.org
Social Media: *Twitter*

Jessica Bridges, Executive Director
Joe Allen, Chair
Warren Ferguson, Vice Chair
John Rathbun, Secretary
Paul Lemar, Treasurer

Showcasing a series of knowledgeable speakers sharing their expertise on policies and best practices that have facilitated CHP deployment in overseas markets and offering advice on how to break down barriers to CHP deployment and

replicate those successes stateside. Listen to national and international trade and policy authorities, US government officials, and CHP business leaders discuss CHP challenges, success stories, and market expansion opportunities.
Frequency: Annual/May
Founded in 1999

1472   UNEP SEF Alliance Annual Meeting

Clean Energy Group/ UNEP SEF Alliance
50 State St.
Suite 1
Montpelier, VT 05602

802-223-2554
FAX 802-223-4967
E-Mail: RTyler@cleangroup.org
Home Page: www.unepsefalliance.org

Members engage in candid discussion with peer agencies about current challenges faced, latest programme developments, and plans for future programme design. Experts speak about specialized topics, and proposals for new areas of collaboration are presented and discussed.
Frequency: Annual/September

1473   World Renewable Energy Forum

American Solar Energy Society
4760 Walnut Street
Suite 106
Boulder, CO 80301

303-443-3130
FAX 303-443-3212
E-Mail: ases@ases.org
Home Page: www.ases.org
Social Media: *Facebook, Twitter, LinkedIn*

Susan Greene, President
David G. Hill, Chair
Bill Poulin, Treasurer
Jason Keyes, Secretary

American Solar Energy Society annual conference and the bi-annual World Renewable Energy Congress have combined, providing a unique opportunity for renewable energy enthusiasts from around the world to share experiences.
13M Members
Frequency: Annual/May
Founded in 1954

1474   World Shale Gas Conference & Exhibition

Institute of Gas Technology
1700 S Mount Prospect Rd
Des Plaines, IL 60018-1804

847-768-0664
FAX 847-768-0669
Home Page: www.gastechnology.org
Social Media: *Facebook, Twitter, LinkedIn, YouTube*

David Carroll, President & CEO
Ronald Snedic, Vice President/ Corporate Devel.
Paul Chromek, General Counsel & Secretary

Unique platform to uncover the real impact of shale on the global gas market. Provides a valuable opportunity to develop business, explore future prospects and unlock the potential of shale gas globally. Share knowledge and experience among industry professionals, government operators and solution providers.

Directories & Databases

1475 American Solar Energy Society Membership Directory
4760 Walnut Street
Suite 106
Boulder, CO 80301-2843

303-443-3130
FAX 303-443-3212
E-Mail: ases@ases.org
Home Page: www.ases.org

Susan Greene, President
David G. Hill, Chair
Bill Poulin, Treasurer
Jason Keyes, Secretary

Offers information on over 2,000 manufacturers, professors, architects, engineers and others in the solar energy field.

1476 Association of Energy Service Companies Directory
Association of Energy Service Companies
6060 N Central Expy
Dallas, TX 75206-5209

214-692-0771
800-692-0771
FAX 214-692-0162
Home Page: www.aesc.net

Patty Jordan, Publisher
About 750 energy service companies and industry suppliers.
Frequency: Bi-Monthly
Circulation: 10,000

1477 Database of State Incentives for Renewables & Efficiency (DSIRE)
North Carolina State University
Campus Box 7504
Raleigh, NC 27695-7504

919-515-3470
FAX 919-515-2556
E-Mail: DSIREinfo@ncsu.edu
Home Page: www.dsireusa.org
Social Media: *Facebook, Twitter*

Amanda Vanega, Program Manager
Funded by the US Department of Energy's Office of Energy Efficiency and Renewable Energy. A comprehensive source of information on state, local, utility and federal incentives and policies that promote renewable energy and energy efficiency.
Founded in 1995

1478 Energy
WEFA Group
800 Baldwin Tower Boulevard
Eddystone, PA 19022-1368

610-490-4000
FAX 610-490-2770
E-Mail: info@wefa.com
Home Page: www.wefa.com

Peter McNabb
This database covers energy supply and demand, including weekly rig count and gasoline prices by states; reserves, stocks, production, consumption and trade of petroleum products.

1479 Energy Science and Technology
US Department of Energy
PO Box 62
Oak Ridge, TN 37831-0062

865-574-1000
FAX 865-576-2865

E-Mail: OSTIWebmaster@osti.gov
Home Page: www.osti.gov

This large database offers over 3 million citations, with abstracts, to literature pertaining to all fields of energy.

1480 Handbook: Solar Energy System Design
American Society of Plumbing Engineers
2980 S River Rd
Des Plaines, IL 60018-4203

847-296-0002
FAX 847-296-2963
E-Mail: info@aspe.org
Home Page: www.aspe.org

Tom Govedarica, Executive Publisher
Richard Albrecht, Publication Coordinator
Gretchen Pienta, Managing Editor

This manual provides the know-how on solar hot-water systems, collectors, thermal storage and much more.
Cost: $20.00

1481 Membership Roster and Registry of Geothermal Services & Equipment
Geothermal Resources Council
20001 Second Street
Suite 5
Davis, CA 95618-5476

530-758-2360
FAX 530-758-2839
E-Mail: grc@geothermal.org
Home Page: www.geothermal.org
Social Media: *Facebook, Twitter, LinkedIn, YouTube, Flickr*

Curt Robinson, Ph.D, Executive Director
Steve Ponder, Interim Executive Director
Estela M. Smith, Office Manager
Ian Crawford, Managing Editor
Chi-Meng Moua, Library Associate

A unique publication that provides business, consulting and research contacts throughout the international geothermal community.
Frequency: Annual
Founded in 1970

1482 REFIN Directory
American Council on Renewable Energy
1600 K Street NW
Suite 700
Washington, DC 20006

202-393-0001
E-Mail: vay@acore.org
Home Page: www.refindirectory.com
Social Media: *Facebook, Twitter, LinkedIn, YouTube*

Dennis V. McGinn, President
Douglas Llyod, CEO and Co-Founder
Estelle Llyod, Managing Editor
Connects suppliers of capital and expertise with industry participants engaged in the scale-up of renewable energy.
Frequency: Annually
Founded in 2001

1483 The Source for Renewable Energy
Momentum Technologies, LLC
PO Box 460813
Glendale, CO 80246

303-229-4841
FAX 408-705-2031
E-Mail: energy@mtt.com
Home Page: energy.sourceguides.com

A comprehensive buyer's guide and business directory to more than 18,000 renewable energy businesses and organizations worldwide.

1484 Wind Energy Conversion Systems
South Dakota Renewable Energy
Association

PO Box 491
Pierre, SD 57501-0491

605-224-8641

Offers valuable information for electrical-output wind machine manufacturers.
Cost: $2.00
45 Pages
Frequency: Annual

Industry Web Sites

1485 energy.sourceguides.com
Momentum Technologies, LLC

A comprehensive buyer's guide and business directory to more than 18,000 renewable energy businesses and organizations worldwide.

1486 http://gold.greyhouse.com
G.O.L.D Grey House OnLine Databases
Grey House Publishing's online database platform, GOLD, offers Quick Search, Keyword Search and Expert Search for most business sectors including mining, petroleum and alternative energy markets. The GOLD platform makes finding the information you need quick and easy. All of Grey House's directory products are available for subscription on the GOLD platform.

1487 www.acore.org
American Council on Renewable Energy
Works to bring all forms of renewable energy into the mainstream of America's economy and lifestyle. Members include every aspect and sector of the renewable energy industries and their trade associations, including wind, solar, geothermal, biomass and biofuels, hydropower tidal/current energy and waste energy.

1488 www.aeecenter.org
Association of Energy Engineers (AEE)
Information and networking in the dynamic fields of energy engineering and energy management, renewable and alternative energy, power generation, energy services, sustainability, and all related areas.

1489 www.aeromt.org
Alternative Energy Resources Organization
A grassroots nonprofit organization dedicated to solutions that promote resource conservation and local economic vitality. By bringing people together, AERO offers a vehicle for collective action and a sense of common purpose for citizens within their communities to shape a more sustainable future.

1490 www.americanbiogascouncil.org
American Biogas Council
Mission is to create jobs, environmental sustainability and energy independence by growing the American biogas industry.

1491 www.americanhydrogenassociation.org
American Hydrogen Association
Providing information on the use of hydrogen as a fuel.

1492 www.ases.org
American Solar Energy Society
The nation's leading association of solar professionals & advocates. Mission is to inspire an era of energy innovation and speed the transition to a sustainable energy economy. Advancing education, research and policy.

1493 www.awea.org
American Wind Energy Association

Promotes wind energy as a clean source of electricity for consumers around the world. Representing wind power project developers, equipment suppliers, services providers, parts manufacturers, utilities, researchers, and others involved in the wind industry - one of the world's fastest growing energy industries.

1494 www.biodiesel.org
National Biodiesel Board

Mission is to advance the interests of its members by creating sustainable biodiesel industry growth. NBB serves as the industry's central coordinating entity and will be the single voice for its diverse membership base.

1495 www.biogaspower.org
Bio-Gas Power Association

Dedicated to providing the industry with the knowledge needed to operate and maintain these facilities by providing a common ground to learn from each others' experiences. Developed as a way for owners, operators, technicians, and dealerships alike to come together and share ideas, experience, opinions, and tackle the tough issues that come with owning and operating Bio-Gas to Energy Facilities.

1496 www.biomassthermal.org
Biomass Thermal Energy Council

An association of biomass fuel producers, appliance manufacturers and distributors, supply chain companies and non-profit organizations that view biomass thermal energy as a renewable, responsible, clean and energy-efficient pathway to meeting America's energy needs. BTEC engages in research, education, and public advocacy for the fast growing biomass thermal energy industry.

1497 www.cleanegroup.org
Clean Energy Group

A leading nonprofit advocacy organization working in the US and internationally on innovative clean energy technology, finance, and policy programs. Supported by major foundations, as well as state, federal and international energy agencies.

1498 www.dsireusa.org
DSIRE Database

Funded by the US Department of Energy's Office of Energy Efficiency and Renewable Energy. A comprehensive source of information on state, local, utility and federal incentives and policies that promote renewable energy and energy efficiency.

1499 www.eesi.org
Environmental and Energy Study Institute

A nonprofit organization that advances innovative policy solutions that set us on a cleaner, more secure and sustainable energy path.

1500 www.energyrecoverycouncil.org
Energy Recovery Council

Represents the waste-to-energy industry and communities that own waste-to-energy facilities. Current ERC members own and operate modern waste-to-energy facilities that operate nationwide, safely disposing of municipal solid waste, while at the same time generating renewable electricity using modern combustion technology equipped with state-of-the-art emission control systems.

1501 www.ethanolrfa.org
Renewable Fuels Association

The national trade association for the US ethanol industry promoting policies, regulations and research and development initiatives that will lead to the increased production and use of fuel ethanol. Membership includes a broad cross-section of businesses, individuals and or-

ganizations dedicated to the expansion of the US fuel ethanol industry.

1502 www.geo-energy.org
Geothermal Energy Association

Advocates for public policies that will promote the development and utilization of geothermal resources, provides a forum for the industry to discuss issues and problems, encourages research and development to improve geothermal technologies, presents industry views to governmental organizations, and conducts education and outreach projects.

1503 www.geothermal.org
Geothermal Resources Council

Nonprofit, educational association actively seeking to expand its role as a primary professional educational association for the international geothermal community.

1504 www.greyhouse.com
Grey House Publishing

Authoritative reference directories for business information and general reference, including alternative energy, mining and petroleum markets. Users can search the online databases with varied search criteria allowing for custom searches by product category, geographic area, sales volume, keyword, subject and more. Full Grey House catalog and online ordering also available.

1505 www.hydro.org
National Hydropower Association

Dedicated to promoting the growth of clean, affordable US hydropower. Seeks to secure hydropower's place as a climate-friendly, renewable and reliable energy source that serves national environmental, energy, and economic policy objectives. Members are involved in projects throughout the US hydropower industry, including both federal and non-federal hydroelectric facilities.

1506 www.iaee.org
International Association for Energy Economics

Association for those involved in energy economics including publications, consultants, energy database software.

1507 www.igshpa.okstate.edu
International Ground Source Heat Pump Association

Member-driven organization established to advance ground source heat pump technology on local, state, national and international levels. IGSHPA utilizes state-of-the-art facilities for conducting GSHP system installation training and geothermal research. Mission is to promote the use of ground source heat pump technology worldwide through education and communication.

1508 www.irecusa.org
Interstate Renewable Energy Council

Works with industry, government, educators and other stakeholders to ensure that the broader use of renewable energies is possible, safe, affordable and practical, particularly for the individual consumer.

1509 www.ireoigo.org
Intergovernmental Renewable Energy Organization

Promotes the urgent transition to renewable energy sources and sustainable development through collaborative effort and the implementation of projects that improve the lives of people while preserving the environment and our resources for future generations of humans.

1510 www.lignite.com
Lignite Energy Council

Regional Trade Association - promotes policies and activities that maintain a viable lignite industry and enhance development of our regions' lignite resources.

1511 www.nabcep.org
N. American Board of Cert. Energy Practitioners

Mission is to support, and work with, the renewable energy and energy efficiency industries, professionals, and stakeholders. Goal is to develop voluntary national certification programs that will; promote renewable energy, provide value to practitioners, promote worker safety and skill, and promote consumer confidence.

1512 www.nationalrenewableenergyassociation.org
National Renewable Energy Association

A nonprofit organization dedicated to helping Americans use less energy and to use more renewable energy in the future.

1513 www.nesea.org
Northeast Sustainable Energy Association

The nation's leading regional membership organization focused on promoting the understanding, development and adoption of energy conservation and non-polluting, renewable energy technologies.

1514 www.oceanrenewable.com
Ocean Renewable Energy Coalition

Striving to keep members, legislators, regulators, the media and the public at large up to date with OREC's activities as well as ongoing developments in this emerging industry.

1515 www.renewablemarketers.org
Renewable Energy Markets Association

A nonprofit association dedicated to maintaining and growing strong markets for renewable energy in the United States. Representing organizations that sell, purchase, or promote renewable energy products.

1516 www.seia.org
Solar Energy Industries Association

Works with its member companies to make solar a mainstream and significant energy source by expanding markets, removing market barriers, strenghtening the industry and educating the public on the benefits of solar energy.

1517 www.solarliving.org
Solar Living Institute

A nonprofit solar training and sustainability organization. Mission is to promote sustainable living through inspirational environmental education.

1518 www.unepsefalliance.org
UNEP SEF Alliance

The only convening body in the international system for public finance agencies in the clean energy sector. Members are visionary organizations from various countries pushing the forefront of how to do public finance for clean energy.

1519 www.usabiomass.org
Biomass Power Association

The nation's leading organization working to expand and advance the use of clean, renewable biomass power. Educates policymakers at the state and federal level about the benefits of biomass and provides regular briefings and research to keep members fully informed about public policy impacting the biomass industry. Members include local owners and operators of existing biomass facilities, suppliers, plant developers and others.

1520 www.uschpa.org

US Clean Heat & Power Association

Providing superior advocacy, networking, education and market information to companies in the business of clean, local energy generation. Documents the benefits of clean heat and power to the public and to decision-makers. Also participates in federal agency programs to promote clean distributed energy.

1521 www.wcee.org

Women's Council on Energy and the Environment

Supports women involved in the environmental community with education, research, new trend information and several publications.

Associations

1522 Academy of Science Fiction Fantasy and Horror Films
334 W 54th St
Los Angeles, CA 90037-3806

323-752-5811
FAX 323-752-5811
E-Mail: saturn.awards@ca.rr.com
Home Page: www.saturnawards.org
Social Media: *Facebook, Twitter*

Robert Holguin, CEO & President
David Bilbrey, Executive Administrator
Michael Laster, Director of Operations
Jeff Rector, Official Spokesperson
Kurt Reichenbach, Art Designer

Honors, recognizes and promotes genre films. Annually presents the prestigious Saturn Awards. In recent years, have added television and home entertainment categories to the media mix. Widened the scope of our awards by celebrating achievement in additional genres including action, adventure, and thrillers as well as international cinema.
Founded in 1972

1523 American Alliance for Health, Physical Education, Recreation and Dance
1900 Association Drive
Reston, VA 20191-1598

703-476-3400
800-213-7193
FAX 703-476-9527
E-Mail: info@aahperd.org
Home Page: www.shapeamerica.org
Social Media: *Facebook, Twitter, Instagram*

Steve Jefferies, President
E. Paul Roetert, Chief Executive Officer
Dolly D. Lambdin, President-Elect
Frances Cleland, Member-at-Large
Neil Dougherty, Member-at-Large

Organization that provides educational programs, resources and support for professionals within the fields of health, physical education, recreation and dance. AAHPERD's mission is to promote and support leadership, research, education, and best practices in the professions that support creative, healthy, and active lifestyles.
25000 Members
Founded in 1885

1524 American Amusement Machine Association
450 E Higgins Rd
Suite 201
Elk Grove Vlg, IL 60007-1417

847-290-9088
866-372-5190
FAX 847-290-9121
E-Mail: information@coin-op.org
Home Page: www.coin-op.org
Social Media: *Facebook, Twitter, LinkedIn*

Chris Felix, President
Tina Schwartz, Business & Finance Manager
Holly Hampton, Vice President
Frank Consentino, Secretary
Rich Babich, Treasurer

Non profit trade association representing the manufacturers, distributors and part suppliers to the coin-operated and out of home amusement industry.
Founded in 1981

1525 American Association of Cheerleading Coaches and Administration
6745 Lenox Center Court
Suite 318
Memphis, TN 38115

800-533-6583
FAX 901-251-5851
E-Mail: jimlord@aacca.org
Home Page: www.aacca.org
Social Media: *Facebook, Twitter*

Jim Lord, Executive Director
Mike Nordengran, Administration
Sheila Noone, Media Relations

AACCA,is a non-profit educational association for cheerleading coaches across the United States. Members of the association include: youth, junior high school, high school, all star, and college or university coaches/advisors, as well as leading national cheerleading instructional companies dedicated to the safe and responsible practice of student cheerleading.
70000 Members
Founded in 1987

1526 American Coaster Enthusiasts
P.O. Box 540261
Grand Prairie, T 75054-0261

469-278-6223
FAX 740-452-2552
E-Mail: info@aceonline.org
Home Page: www.aceonline.org
Social Media: *Facebook, Twitter, RSS*

Dave Altman, President
Jerry Willard, Vice President
David Lipnicky, Public Relations Director
Lee Ann Draud, Publications Director
Brian Peters, Information Services Director

ACE is the world's largest ride enthusiast organization, and its members are the most educated, dedicated, and passionate amusement park guests. ACE's activities include publications, action-packed events, and preservation efforts. ACE is highly visible in the mainstream media. Local television stations and newspapers often consider ACE events in their area to be major news items.
7000 Members
Founded in 1978

1527 American Disc Jockey Association
20118 N 67th Avenue
Suite 300-605
Glendale, CA 85308

888-723-5776
FAX 866-310-4676
E-Mail: office@adja.org
Home Page: www.adja.org
Social Media: *Facebook, Twitter, YouTube*

Rob Snyder, Director

An association of professional mobile entertainers. Encourages success for its members through continuous education, camaraderie, and networking. The primary goal is to educate Disc Jockeys so that each member acts ethically and responsibly.

1528 Amusement Industry Manufacturers & Suppliers International
P.O. Box 92366
Nashville, TN 37209

714-425-5747
FAX 714-276-9666
E-Mail: info@aimsintl.org
Home Page: www.aimsintl.org
Social Media: *Facebook*

Brian D King, President

The Amusement Industry Manufacturers and Suppliers (AIMS) Trade Association evolved from the American Recreational Equipment Association. The Associations purpose is to establish communications and foster working relations using the highest degree of professionalism with other Amusement Industry Trade Associations, Local, State, and Federal Government entities in order to promote and preserve the prosperity of the Amusement Industry.
Founded in 1994

1529 Amusement and Music Operators Association
600 Spring Hill Ring Road
Suite 111
West Dundee, IL 60118

847-428-7699
800-937-2662
FAX 847-428-7719
E-Mail: amoa@amoa.com
Home Page: www.amoa.com
Social Media: *Facebook*

Jerry Johnston, President
Gaines C. Butler, 1st Vice President
Jack Kelleher, Executive Vice President
Lori Schneider, Deputy Director
Claudia Kaczmarek, Office Manager

AMOA was created when 68 jukebox owners from around the country banded together to fight the repeal of the jukebox royalty exemption. The modest beginning, created by a common cause, revealed a fierce passion-shared by many-about their business. Harnessing the collective strength, energy, knowledge and entrepreneurial spirit of a growing number of volunteer members, AMOA quickly established itself as a major force.
Founded in 1948

1530 Association of College Unions International
120 W Seventh Street
One City Centre, Suite 200
Bloomington, IN 47404

812-245-2284
FAX 812-245-6710
E-Mail: acui@acui.org
Home Page: www.acui.org
Social Media: *Facebook, Twitter, YouTube*

Sarah Aikman, President
John Taylor, Chief Executive Officer
Elizabeth Beltramini, Content Curation Director
Jake Dawes, Events and Operations Coordinator
Jason Cline, Strategic Initiatives Executive

The association is a non-profit organization and has member institutions in a number of countries. ACUI members work at and attend urban and rural campuses at both the two and four year levels and are dedicated to building community on campus through programs, services and publications with the common goal of unifying the union and activities fields.
1000 Members
Founded in 1914

1531 Association of Zoos and Aquariums
8403 Colesville Rd
Suite 710
Silver Spring, MD 20910-3314

301-562-0777
FAX 301-562-0888
E-Mail: membership@aza.org
Home Page: www.aza.org
Social Media: *Facebook, Twitter, Pinterest, Instagram, YouTube*

Kris Vehrs, J.D., Executive Director
Jim Maddy, President & CEO
Jill Nicoll, Chief Operating Officer
Phil Wagner, Senior Vice President, Finance
Ana Maria Sanchez, Controller

A nonprofit organization dedicated to the advancement of accredited zoos and aquariums in the areas of animal care, wildlife conservation, education and science.
200 Members
Founded in 1924

1532 Circus Fans Association of America

2704 Marshall Avenue
Lorain, OH 44052-4315

360-452-1919
E-Mail: circusvern@aol.com
Home Page: www.circusfans.org

Gary C. Payne, President
Cheryl Deptula, Executive Secretary-Treasurer
Peter Wagner, President Elect
Connie Thomas, Central Vice President
Mort Gamble, Public Relations Director

Established to enjoy and preserve the circus as an institution. CFA offers you an opportunity interact with fellow circus enthusiasts in many ways. Local geographic groups (called TENTS) provide a chance for folks who live in the same geographic area to attend shows together and to meet to discuss the circus scene. State organizations (called TOPS) organize larger gatherings and special events.
Founded in 1926

1533 Circus Historical Society

3100 Parkside Lane
Williamsburg, VA 23185

757-259-0412
E-Mail: CircusHistoricalSociety@gmail.com
Home Page: www.circushistory.org
Social Media: *Facebook, Twitter*

Deborah Walk, President
Don Covington, Vice President
Robert Cline, Secretary/Treasurer
Chris Berry, Trustee
Maureen Brunsdale, Trustee

The Circus Historical Society, Inc. (CHS) is a tax-exempt, not-for-profit educational organization dedicated to recording the history of the American circus from the first one in Philadelphia during 1793 to today. Membership includes historians, scholars, circus personnel, memorabilia collectors, Americana specialists who share both a love of the circus and a desire to preserve and disseminate its great heritage.
1000 Members
Founded in 1939

1534 Clowns of America International

PO Box 112
Eustis, FL 32727

352-357-1676
877-816-6941
E-Mail: coaioffice@aol.com
Home Page: www.coai.org

Glenn Kohlberger, President
Michael B. Cox, Vice-President
Dan Fitzwilly' Langwell, Secretary
Paddee Embrey, Treasurer
Sandra Winstead, Sergeant-at-Arms

The purpose of Clowns of America International Website is to share, educate, and act as a gathering place for serious minded amateurs, semiprofessionals, and professional clowns. COAI provides its membership with necessary resources that allow them to further define and improve their individual clown character. Visitors who are interested in the clown arts will find a variety of resources that will stimulate their interest, foster their curiosity and offer pathways to valuable information.

1535 Council for Amusement & Recreational Equipment Safety

PO Box 8236
Des Moines, IO 50301-8236

617-727-3200
217-558-7194
E-Mail: doug.rathbun@illinois.gov
Home Page: www.caresofficials.org

Rob Gavel, President
Mike Triplett, 1st Vice President
Dean McKernon, 2nd Vice President
Chad Halsey, Secretary/Treasurer
Mike Triplett, ASTM Liaison

CARES is a voluntary organization of chief government officials who are responsible for the enforcement of amusement ride and recreational equipment regulations within their jurisdiction. Fosters cooperation among regulatory officials and amusement equipment industries to promote public safety. CARES membership has grown to more than two dozen regulatory agencies in the United States and Canada, and includes the informal participation of the U.S. Consumer Product Safety.

1536 Game Manufacturers Association

240 North Fifth Street
Suite 340
Columbus, OH 43215

614-255-4500
FAX 614-255-4499
E-Mail: ed@gama.org
Home Page: www.gama.org
Social Media: *Facebook*

Travis Severance, Retail Chair
Bob Maher, Distributor Chair
Justin Ziran, President
Jamie Chambers, Vice President
John Ward, Executive Director

The Game Manufacturers Association (GAMA) is the non-profit trade organization dedicated to serving the tabletop game industry. Strengthens and supports industry professionals by advancing their interests, providing educational programs and opportunities, and promoting their form of quality social entertainment. Led by publishers and manufacturers, GAMA promotes the interests of all persons involved in the commerce of games and game-related products.
450 Members
Founded in 1977

1537 International Amusement & Leisure Defense Association

PO Box 4563
Louisville, KY 40204

502-473-0956
FAX 502-473-7352
E-Mail: info@ialda.org
Home Page: www.ialda.org
Social Media: *LinkedIn*

Kurt A. Anselmi, Esq., Board Member/Emeritus
David M. Bennett, Esq., Vice-President
Gaylee W. Gillim, Esq., Secretary
Sean P. Hannon, Esq., Treasurer
Thomas Sheehan, Esq., Board Member/Emeritus

The International Amusement & Leisure Defense Association, Inc. is a non-profit association of lawyers and other professionals who are actively engaged in representing the interests of the amusement and leisure industries. IALDA members work closely with those in the amusement and water park industries as well as those involved in the bowling, roller skating, and other leisure industries.

1538 International Association of Amusement Parks and Attractions (IAAPA)

1448 Duke St
Alexandria, VA 22314-3403

703-836-4800
FAX 703-836-4801
E-Mail: iaapa@iaapa.org
Home Page: www.iaapa.org
Social Media: *Facebook, Twitter, LinkedIn*

Gerardo Arteaga Cerda, Chairman
Paul Noland, President and CEO
Susan Mosedale, Executive Vice President
June Ko, Vice President
David Mandt, SVP, Marketing and Communications

A non-profit organization with a membership consisting of fixed-site enterainment and attractions facilities and suppliers. The association is dedicated to the preservation and prosperity of the amusement industry worldwide.
4100 Members
Founded in 1918

1539 International Association of Fairs Expositions

3043 East Cairo St.
PO Box 985
Springfield, MO 65802

417-862-5771
800-516-0313
FAX 417-862-0156
E-Mail: iafe@fairsandexpos.com
Home Page: www.fairsandexpos.com
Social Media: *Facebook, Twitter, You Tube*

Jim Tucker, President/CEO
Max Willis, CFO
Steve Siever, Director of Sales
Missy McCormack, Comm. Design and Prod. Manager
Rebekah Lee, Director of Comm. and Editor

The International Association of Fairs and Expositions (IAFE) is a voluntary, non-profit corporation, serving state, provincial, regional, and county agricultural fairs, shows, exhibitions, and expositions. Its associate members include state and provincial associations of fairs, non-agricultural expositions and festivals, associations, corporations, and individuals engaged in providing products and services to its members, all of whom are interested in the improvement of fairs, and expositions.
1300 Members
Founded in 1885

1540 International Association of Haunted Attractions

1001 Greenbay Road
Winnetka, IL 60093

888-320-8494
FAX 609-799-7032
E-Mail: admin@iahaweb.com
Home Page: www.iahaweb.com
Social Media: *Facebook*

Patrick Konopelski, President
Gene Schopf, Vice President
John Eslich, Treasurer
Brett Bertolino, Secretary
Lore Callahan, Board Member

The Haunted Attraction Association assists and advances the thriving haunt industry through communication, education, and information. Our worldwide network of members exchange ideas, information, experiences and concerns via our conferences, exclusive networking events, message boards, newsletters, magazines and more. HAA members have been featured on national television shows such as Good Morning America, the Today Show, and our at-

tractions have been featured in national publications.
400 Members
Founded in 1998

1541 International Brotherhood of Magicians

13 Point West Blvd
St Charles, MO 63301-4431

636-724-2400
FAX 636-724-8566
E-Mail: info@magician.org
Home Page: www.magician.org
Social Media: *Facebook, Twitter, YouTube*

Joe M. Turner, International President
Becki Wells, International Vice President
Donald E. Wiberg, International Secretary
Charles Arkin, International Treasurer
Oscar Munoz, International President-Elect

The International Brotherhood of Magicians is the world's largest organization dedicated to the art of magic, with members in 88 countries. Our official publication, The Linking Ring, has linked magicians throughout the world. Local branches of the I.B.M., known as Rings, meet each month in hundreds of locations. Our Annual Convention features top professional magicians in our spectacular evening shows.
12000 Members
Founded in 1922

1542 International Festivals and Events Association (IFEA)

2603 W. Eastover Terrace
Boise, ID 83706-2800

208-433-0950
FAX 208-433-9812
E-Mail: nia@ifea.com
Home Page: www.ifea.com
Social Media: *Facebook, Twitter, LinkedIn, YouTube*

Cindy Lerick, Chair
Steven Wood Schmader, CFEE, President & CEO
Nia Forster Hovde, CFEE, VP/Dir. of Marketing & Comm.
Beth Peterson, Director of Membership Services
Craig Sarton, Creative & Publications Director

The IFEA exists to serve the needs of our entire industry, who produce and support quality celebrations for the benefit of their respective 'communities' and all those who share our core values of excellence & quality; the sharing of experience, knowledge, creativity and best practices; and the importance of 'community' building both locally and globally. Our success lies in the success of those we serve through professional education, programming, products and resources, and networking.
2000 Members
Founded in 1956
Mailing list available for rent

1543 International Game Developers Association

19 Mantua Road
Mt Royal, NJ 08061

856-423-2990
FAX 856-423-3420
E-Mail: contact@igda.org
Home Page: www.igda.org
Social Media: *Facebook, Twitter, LinkedIn, YouTube, Flickr, Kickstarter,*

Jon Grande, Chair
Kate Edwards, Executive Director
Tristin Hightower, Director of Operations
Jillian Mood, Partner & Member Relations Manager
Dr. Farhad Javidi, Secretary

The International Game Developers Association is the largest non-profit membership organization serving individuals who create video games. We bring together developers at conferences, in local chapters and in special interest groups to improve their lives and craft. The IGDA is dedicated to improving developers' careers and lives through: Community, Professional Development, and Advocacy.
Founded in 1994

1544 International Jugglers' Association

PO Box 7307
Austin, TX 78713-7307

702-798-0099
FAX 702-248-2550
E-Mail: webmaster@juggle.org
Home Page: www.juggle.org
Social Media: *Facebook, YouTube*

Nathan Wakefield, Chair
Art Jennings, Chairman Emeritus
Martin Frost, Communications Director
Kyle Johnson, Marketing Director
Marilyn Sullivan, Membership Director

An organization of individuals dedicated to promoting juggling.
Founded in 1947

1545 International Laser Display Association

7062 Edgeworth Drive
Orlando, FL 32819-2700

407-797-7654
FAX 503-344-3770
E-Mail: mail@laserist.org
Home Page: www.laserist.org

Christine Jenkin, President
Patrick Murphy, ILDA Executive Director
Olga Eser, Vice President
Dan Goldsmith, Secretary
Alex Henning, Treasurer

The International Laser Display Association (ILDA) is the world's leading organization dedicated to advancing the use of laser displays in the fields of art, entertainment and education. Promotes the use of laser displays in the international marketplace through awards programs, publications, technology standards and a code of ethics. ILDA also represents the industry on safety issues and provides forums for members to exchange ideas, forge partnerships and explore.
Founded in 1986

1546 International Laser Tag Association: ILTA

5351 E Thompson Road
Suite 236
Indianapolis, IN 46237

317-786-9755
FAX 317-786-9757
E-Mail: info@lasertag.org
Home Page: www.lasertag.org

Ryan McQuillen, Executive Director
Eric Gaizat, Membership Director

The International Laser Tag Association (ILTA) is the non-profit developer and operator association for the laser tag industry. Help members become better informed through our research, services, and communications with all levels of the industry. Since the creation of the ILTA, no other source has been more reliable for information about our industry. Assist members by providing them with the most accurate infor available to date.
350 Members
Founded in 1996

1547 International Magicians Society

581 Ellison Avenue
Westbury, NY 11590

516-333-2377
FAX 516-333-0018
E-Mail: info@imsmagic.com
Home Page: www.magicims.com

Tony Hassini, Chairman/CEO
Anthony Emin, World President
Remington Scott, Creative Director
William H. Mellhany, Magic Historian
John M. Caluwaert, Legal Counsel

Promotes and preserves the art of magic. IMS helps create new magicians in order to pass the torch to the next generation of magicians.
37000 Members
Founded in 1968

1548 International Ticketing Association

5868 East 71st Street
Suite E 367
Indianapolis, IN 46220

212-629-4036
FAX 212-628-8532
E-Mail: info@intix.org
Home Page: www.intix.org
Social Media: *Facebook, Twitter, LinkedIn, YouTube*

Jena L Hoffman, President/CEO
Tiffany Kelham, Membership Associate
Jane, Pelletier, Meeting Manager
Dorothea Heck, Sales & Service Manager
Mary Leaton, Accounting Associate

The International Ticketing Association is a nonprofit membership organization committed to leading the forum for the entertainment ticketing industry. INTIX represents ticketing, sales, technology, finance, and marketing professionals who work in arts, sports, and entertainment as well as a full range of public venues and institutions. Members represent organizations from across the United States, Canada and 20 countries from around the globe.
1000 Members
Founded in 1980

1549 National Association of Amusement Ride Safety Officials

PO Box 638
Brandon, FL 33509-0638

813-661-2779
800-669-9053
FAX 813-685-5117
E-Mail: naarsoinfo@aol.com
Home Page: www.naarso.com

Jack S. Silar, Chairman and Membership Chairman
Jonathan R. Brooks, President
Rick Smith, Vice President
Leonard Cavalier, Executive Director
Tony Rossi, Treasurer

NAARSO is dedicated to the advancement of amusement ride and device safety through the doctrine of Safety Through Communication. NAARSO is a non-profit organization that provides resources for amusement industry professionals dedicated to the safety of the industry and its patrons.
800 Members
Founded in 1987

1550 National Association of Teachers of Singing

9957 Moorings Dr
Suite 401
Jacksonville, FL 32257-2416

904-992-9101
FAX 904-262-2587
E-Mail: info@nats.org
Home Page: www.nats.org

Social Media: *Facebook, Twitter, LinkedIn, YouTube, Flickr, Pinterest*

Norman Spivey, President
Carole Blankenship, Vice President (Auditions)
Dan Johnson-Wilmot, Vice President (Membership)
Kathleen H. Arecchi, Vice President (Workshops)
Lloyd Mims, Secretary/Treasurer

Encourages the highest standards of the vocal art and of ethical principals in the teaching of singing; and promote vocal education and research at all levels, both for the enrichment of the general public and for the professional advancement of the talented.
7000 Members
Founded in 1944

1551 National Caves Association
PO Box 625
Cobleskill, NY 12043

270-492-2228
FAX 931-688-3988
E-Mail: info@cavern.com
Home Page: www.cavern.com
Social Media: *Facebook, Twitter*

Susan Berdeaux, Executive Director

Nonprofit organization of publicly and privately owned caves and caverns - caves developed for public visitation.
Founded in 1965

1552 National Independent Concessionaires Association, Inc.
1043 E. Brandon Blvd.
Brandon, FL 33511

813-438-8926
FAX 813-438-8928
E-Mail: nica@nicainc.org
Home Page: www.nicainc.org
Social Media: *Facebook, RSS Feeds*

Joe Potillo, Jr., President
Paulette Keene, 2nd Vice President
Yachika Smith, Office Manager
Rey O'Day, Interim Executive Manager
Stacia Markowitz, Treasurer

Striving towards better communication between fairs, festivals and independent concessionaires nationwide.
1200 Members
Founded in 1993

1553 National Recreation and Park Association
22377 Belmont Ridge Road
Ashburn, VA 20148-4501

703-858-0784
800-626-6772
FAX 703-858-0794
E-Mail: customerservice@nrpa.org
Home Page: www.nrpa.org
Social Media: *Facebook, Twitter, LinkedIn, YouTube, Pinterest*

Robert F. Ashcraft, Chairman/Executive Director
Barbara Tulipane, President/CEO
Ted Mattingly, Director, Facilities
Kevin Conley, Director Information Technology
David Wenner, Administrator

NRPA is the leading advocacy organization dedicated to the advancement of public parks and recreation opportunities. Advances parks, recreation and environmental conservation efforts that enhance the quality of life.
Founded in 1965

1554 New England Association of Amusement Parks and Attractions
774 Portland Road
PO Box 85
Saco, ME 04072

877-999-8740
FAX 207-283-4716
E-Mail: secretary@neaapa.com
Home Page: www.neaapa.com
Social Media: *Facebook, Twitter, LinkedIn, YouTube*

Ryan DeMaria, President
Dorothy Lewis, 1st VP
Eric Anderson, Second Vice President
Charlene Conway, Treasurer

NEAAPA is the premier regional association representing amusement parks, attractions, and their suppliers. NEAAPA works with its members on education opportunities, legislative and policy issues, as well as promotion of the Association's members.
Founded in 1912

1555 Outdoor Amusement Business Association
1035 S Semoran Blvd
Suite 1045A
Winter Park, FL 32792-5512

407-681-9444
800-517-6222
FAX 407-681-9445
E-Mail: oaba@oaba.org
Home Page: www.oaba.org
Social Media: *Facebook, Twitter, YouTube, Instagram*

Michael Wood, Chairman
Robert W Johnson, President
Dee Dee Alford, Vice President
Al DeRusha, Senior Vice President
Brenda Ruiz, Manager of Programs and Services

The OABA manages and influences concerns for its members. OABA believes that all business owners and members of the trade association should continue to raise the level of safety and quality in the mobile amusement industry.
4000 Members
Founded in 1964

1556 PLASA
630 Ninth Avenue
Suite 609
New York, NY 10036

212-244-1505
FAX 212-244-1502
E-Mail: info@plasa.org
Home Page: www.plasa.org
Social Media: *Facebook, Twitter*

Christopher Toulmin, Director of Events
Matthew Griffiths, Chief Executive Officer
Shane McGreevy, Chief Finance Officer
Lori Rubenstein, Director of Membership
Jackie Tien, Group Publisher

PLASA is the lead international membership body for those who supply technologies and services to the event, entertainment and installation industries. As the worldwide voice for those who supply and service the entertainment, event and installation markets, PLASA will develop, promote, support and grow our industry.
1200+ Members

1557 Roller Skating Association International
6905 Corporate Dr
Indianapolis, IN 46278-1927

317-347-2626
FAX 317-347-2636
E-Mail: rsa@rollerskating.com
Home Page: www.rollerskating.org

Social Media: *Facebook, Twitter, LinkedIn, YouTube, Pinterest, Google+*

Robert Bentley, President
Michael Jacques, Vice President
Jim McMaho, Executive Director
Tina Robertson, Director of Conventions
Lynette Rowland, Director of Comm./Editor/Publisher

The Roller Skating Association (RSA) is a trade association that serves commercial (for-profit) skating center owner/operators. It also serves those involved in various facets of the roller related industry such as teachers, coaches, manufacturers, distributors and other elements of the family entertainment industry. Promotes the success of members through education and advancing the roller skating business.
1000 Members
Founded in 1937

1558 Showmen's League of America
1023 W. Fulton Market
Chicago, IL 60607

312-733-9533
800-350-9906
FAX 312-733-9534
E-Mail: office@showmensleague.org
Home Page: www.showmensleague.org
Social Media: *Facebook, Twitter*

Paul Kasin, President
Ron Porter, 1st Vice President
Debbie Powers, 2nd Vice President
Guy Leavitt, 3rd Vice President
Cindy Henning, Executive Secretary

It seeks to promote the success of our members through education and advancing the roller skating business.elp those in need through one of its many programs.
Founded in 1913

1559 Society of Broadcast Engineers
9102 N Meridian St
Suite 150
Indianapolis, IN 46260-1896

317-846-9000
FAX 317-846-9120
Home Page: www.sbe.org
Social Media: *Facebook, Twitter, LinkedIn, YouTube*

Jerry Massey, President
James E. Leifer, Vice President
John L Poray CAE, Executive Director
Megan Clappe, Certification Director
Debbie Hennessey, Sustaining Member Manager

Committed to serving broadcast engineers. From the studio operator to the maintenance engineer and the chief engineer to the vice president of engineering, SBE members come from commercial and non-commercial radio and television stations and cable facilities. A growing segment of members are engaging the industry on their own as consultants and contractors, field and sales engineers.
5100+ Members
Founded in 1964
Mailing list available for rent: 5700 names at $170 per M

1560 Society of Camera Operators
PO Box 2006
Toluca Lake, CA 91610

818-563-9110
818-382-7070
FAX 818-563-9117
E-Mail: socoffice@soc.org
Home Page: www.soc.org
Social Media: *Facebook, Twitter*

Mark August, President
Michael Scott, First Vice President
Mitch Dubin, Second Vice President

Lisa Stacilauskas, Third Vice President
Bill McClelland, Treasurer

Advances the art and creative contribution of the operating cameraman in the Motion Picture and Television Industries. The Society serves the purpose of bringing into the closest confederation Industry leaders in their fields.
Founded in 1979

1561 Tennessee Department of Agriculture, Market Development Division
Tennessee Department of Agriculture
440 Hogan Road
PO Box 40627
Nashville, TN 37204

615-837-5160
800-342-8206
FAX 615-837-5194
E-Mail: pick.tn@tn.gov
Home Page: www.picktnproducts.org
Social Media: *Facebook, Twitter, Pinterest*

Ed Harlan, Assistant Commissioner
Debbie Ball, Director of Marketing
Nelson Owen, Livestock Grading/Market News
Erica Alexander, TAEP Producer Diversification Coor
Art Colebank, Digital Media Specialist

US and Canadian representatives of state/provincial agencies that are responsible for the support of educational and agricultural fairs.
35 Members
Founded in 1966

1562 Themed Entertainment Association
150 East Olive Avenue
Suite 306
Burbank, CA 91502-1850

818-843-8497
FAX 818-843-8477
E-Mail: info@teaconnect.org
Home Page: www.teaconnect.org
Social Media: *Facebook, Twitter, LinkedIn, YouTube*

Steve Birket PE, President
Melissa Townsend, Vice President
Michael Mercadante, Treasurer
Jennie Nevin, Chief Operating Officer
Marie Brennan, Intern

The Themed Entertainment Association (TEA) is an international non-profit association representing the world's leading creators, developers, designers and producers of compelling places and experiences.
Founded in 1991

1563 Western Fairs Association
1776 Tribute Rd
Suite 210
Sacramento, CA 95815-4495

916-927-3100
FAX 916-927-6397
E-Mail: info@fairsnet.org
Home Page: www.fairsnet.org
Social Media: *Facebook, Twitter, YouTube, Instagram*

Troy Bowers, President
Barbara Quaid, Vice President
Stephen J Chambers, Executive Director
Tami Davis Triggs, Accounting Manager
Jessica Boudevin, Communications Manager

Western Fairs Association (WFA) serves the fair industry throughout the Western United States and Canada. Assists in maintaining the highest professional standards within the fair industry through a voluntary network of individuals and organizations. Promotes the prosperity of fairs through education and training programs.
2000 Members
Founded in 1922

1564 World Waterpark Association
8826 Santa Fe Drive
Suite 310
Overland Park, KS 66212-3676

913-599-0300
FAX 913-599-0520
E-Mail: wwamemberinfo@waterparks.org
Home Page: www.waterparks.org
Social Media: *Facebook, Twitter, LinkedIn, YouTube, Instagram*

Mark Moore, Chair
Rick Root, President
Kelly Harris, Dir. of Ops & Member Services
Aleatha Ezra, Director of Park Member Development
Patty Miller, Dir. of Trade Show & Advertising

Provides forum for exchange of ideas related to the water amusement park industry.
1200 Members
Founded in 1982

Newsletters

1565 ACE News
American Coaster Enthusiasts
1100-H Brandywine Boulevard
Zanesville, OH 43701-7303

740-450-1560
FAX 740-452-2552
E-Mail: info@aceonline.org
Home Page: www.aceonline.org

Lee Ann Draud, Publications Director
Mike Thompson, Editor
Dave Altman, President
Jerry Willard, Vice President
Susan Shick, Secretary

Up-to-date information about ACE, the events, roller coasters, and amusement parks.
20 Pages
Frequency: Bimonthly

1566 Adams Gaming Report
Casino City Press
95 Wells Ave
Newton, MA 02459-3299

617-332-2850
800-490-1715
FAX 617-964-2280
E-Mail: customerservice@casinocitypress.com
Home Page: www.casinopromote.com

Michael A Corfman, CEO

Focuses on the gaming industry with nationwide coverage.
Cost: $149.00
Frequency: Monthly

1567 Affiliate Connection
International Festivals and Events Association
2603 W Eastover Ter
Boise, ID 83706-2800

208-433-0950
FAX 208-433-9812
E-Mail: craig@ifea.com
Home Page: www.ifea.com

Steven Schmader, President
Nia Hovde, VP/Marketing
Craig Sarton, Creative &Publications Director
Bette Monteith, Director Of Finance

The IFEA newsletter provides information and news 24 hours a day, 7 days a week, keeping members, suppliers and affiliates up-to-date and current.
2000 Members
Circulation: 2,700
Founded in 1956

Mailing list available for rent: 20000 names at $235 per M

1568 Celebrity Bulletin
Celebrity Service
252 West 37th St
Suite 1204
New York, NY 10017-3632

212-757-7979
FAX 212-582-7701
E-Mail: mark@celebrityservice.com
Home Page: www.celebrityservice.com

Mark Kerrigan, Manager
Nicole Bagley, COO
Nancy R. Bagley, President
Soroush Shehabi, CEO

A daily guide on the whereabouts and vital information of the famous. Includes celebrity contacts including agents, business managers, publicists, and record companies. Gives advanced notice of who's coming to town, what projects they're working on and how to get in touch with them. Features an International Page noting arrivals in cities worldwide.
Cost: $2245.00
4 Pages
Frequency: Daily
Founded in 1939

1569 Connector
Society of Broadcast Engineers
9102 N Meridian St
Suite 150
Indianapolis, IN 46260-1896

317-846-9000
FAX 317-846-9120
Home Page: www.sbe.org

John L Poray CAE, Executive Director
Ralph Hogan, President
Joseph Snelson, Vice President
James Leifer, Secretary
Jerry Massey, Treasurer

To youth members and high schools across the country that have radio or television stations. Provides students with information on careers in broadcast engineering, post-secondary education, high school student stations, scholarships and technical information.
Frequency: 3x/Year
Circulation: 300

1570 Entertainment Marketing Letter
EPM Communications
19 W.21st St, # 303
New York, NY 10012-3208

212-941-0099
888-852-9467
FAX 212-941-1622
E-Mail: info@epmcom.com
Home Page: www.epmcom.com

Ira Mayer, Owner
Michele Khan, Marketing
Terence Keegan, Editor

Covers marketing techniques used in the entertainment industry, and by others who link their goods and services marketing through entertainment properties.
Cost: $449.00
Frequency: 24x Year
ISSN: 1048-5112
Printed in on matte stock

1571 INTIX e-Newsletter
330 W 38th Street
Suite 605
New York, NY 10018

212-629-4036
FAX 212-629-8532

E-Mail: info@intix.org
Home Page: www.intix.org

Jena L Hoffman, President/CEO
Kathleen O'Donnell, Deputy Director
Kevin McDonnell, Sales Manager
Mary Leaton, Accounting Associate
Tiffany Kelham, Membership Associate

E-mail bulletin which includes news from the
association, promotions, replacements, clips
from industry news sources; vendor updates,
conferences and exhibitions, the latest job post-
ings, and listings of members searching for a
job.
Frequency: Monthly

1572 SBE-News
Society of Broadcast Engineers
9102 N Meridian St
Suite 150
Indianapolis, IN 46260-1896

317-846-9000
FAX 317-846-9120
Home Page: www.sbe.org

John L Poray CAE, Executive Director
Ralph Hogan, President
Joseph Snelson, Vice President
James Leifer, Secretary
Jerry Massey, Treasurer

Email subscription of timely news and updates
sent from the National Office.
Frequency: Semimonthly
Circulation: 4,000

1573 Signal
Society of Broadcast Engineers
9102 N Meridian St
Suite 150
Indianapolis, IN 46260-1896

317-846-9000
FAX 317-846-9120
Home Page: www.sbe.org

John L Poray CAE, Executive Director
Ralph Hogan, President
Joseph Snelson, Vice President
James Leifer, Secretary
Jerry Massey, Treasurer

Provides members with timely articles on various broadcast-related topics, information on
upcoming events, recognition of members' activities and achievements and details of SBE
services.
Frequency: Bimonthly
Circulation: 5,500

1574 Theme and Museum Index Report
Themed Entertainment Association/AECOM
150 E. Olive Ave.
Suite 306
Burbank, CA 91502-1850

818-843-8497
FAX 818-843-8477
E-Mail: judy@teaconnect.org
Home Page:
www.aecom.com/What+We+Do/Economics/Th
eme+Index+Report

Judith Rubin, TEA Publications, PR & Social
Media
Jennie Nevin, TEA COO

Annual attendance figures for the global attractions industry.
Frequency: Annual

Magazines & Journals

1575 Amusement Business
VNU Business Media

49 Music Sq W
Suite 300
Nashville, TN 37203-3213

615-321-4251
888-900-3782
FAX 615-327-1575
E-Mail: mshear@amusementbusiness.com
Home Page: www.amusementbusiness.com

Michael Marchesano, President/CEO
Karen Oertley, Publisher
James Zoltak, Editor
Lisa Krugel, Classified Ad Manager

Serves the management of more than 10,000
mass entertainment and amusement facilities.
Cost: $129.00
Frequency: Monthly
Founded in 1894

1576 Amusement Today
Amusement Today
2012 E Randol Mill Rd
Suite 203
Arlington, TX 76011-8222

817-460-7220
FAX 817-265-6397
E-Mail: gslade@amusementtoday.com
Home Page: www.amusementtoday.com

Gary Slade, Publisher
Bill Rea, Director
Sammy Piccola, Accounting/Circulation
Sue Nicholas, Advertising

Keeps decision makers in the amusement in-
dustry up-to-date with current events, business,
international developments and new attractions
at amusement parks and waterparks.
Cost: $50.00
Frequency: Monthly
Circulation: 36000
Mailing list available for rent: 3000 names

1577 Balloons and Parties
PartiLife Publications
65 Sussex Street
Hackensack, NJ 07601

201-441-4224
FAX 201-342-8118
E-Mail: info@balloonsandparties.com
Home Page: www.balloonsandparties.com
Social Media: *Facebook, Twitter*

Andrea P Zettler, Editor
Janet Slowik, Director

A decorating resource offering tips and suggestions for parties, special occasions, holidays,
banquets and events. Targeted, informative and
practical ideas for the event decorating industry. Motivates readers to produce professional,
innovative party services.
Cost: $9.95
2 Members
Frequency: 4x/Year
Circulation: 7000
Founded in 1986
Printed in 4 colors on glossy stock

1578 Bandwagon
Circus Historical Society
3100 Parkside Lane
Williamsburg, VA 23185

757-259-0412
E-Mail: rfsabia@widomaker.com
Home Page: www.circushistory.org

Judith L. Griffin, President
Neil C. Cockerline, Vice President
Robert Cline, Secretary/Treasurer

Publishes articles relating to circus history.
Cost: $5.00
Frequency: Bimonthly
Founded in 1939

1579 Baseline
Ziff Davis Media

28 E 28th St
Suite 1
New York, NY 10016-7914

212-503-3500
FAX 212-503-5696
E-Mail: baseline@ziffdavisenterprise.com
Home Page: www.ziffdavis.com

Jason Young, CEO
Eileen Feretic, Editor
Stephanie McCarthy, Marketing

Publication that offers practical information
and guidance on the management of informa-
tion technology.
Cost: $205.00
Frequency: Monthly
Circulation: 125100

1580 Billboard Magazine
Prometheus Global Media
770 Broadwaye Blvd.
New York, NY 10003-9595

212-493-4100
FAX 646-654-5368
Home Page: www.prometheusgm.com
Social Media: *Facebook, Twitter*

Richard D. Beckman, CEO
James A. Finkelstein, Chairman
Madeline Krakowsky, Vice President
Circulation
Tracy Brater, Executive Director Creative
Service

Packed with in-depth music and entertainment
features including the latest in new media and
digital music, global coverage, music and
money, touring, new artists, radio news and retail reports.
Cost: $149.00
Frequency: Weekly
Founded in 1894

1581 BoxOffice Magazine
BoxOffice Media
9107 Wilshire Blvd.
Suite 450
Beverly Hills, CA 90210-4241

310-876-9090
Home Page: www.boxoffice.com

Peter Crane, Publisher
Kenneth James Bacon, Creative Director
Phil Contrino, Editor
Amy Nicholson, Editor

The premier trade magazine covering the latest
developments in the movie industry, from films
in production to digital cinema and everything
in between.
Founded in 1948

1582 Camera Operator
Society of Camera Operators
PO Box 2006
Toluca Lake, CA 91610

818-382-7070
FAX 323-856-9155
E-Mail: camopmag@soc.org
Home Page: www.soc.org

Chris Tufty, President
Steve Fracol, Vice President
Dan Turrett, Treasurer
Dan Gold, Recording Secretary

Features articles written by and about SOC
members, presented from the camera operator's
point of view. Encompassing the latest technological trends while reviewing historical productions, the Camera Operator seeks to
enlighten and educate readers on the motion
picture, television and commerical industries.
Cost: $20.00
Frequency: Semi-Annual
Printed in 4 colors

1583 Carnival Magazine
PO Box 4138
Salisbury, NC 28145-4138

704-638-0878
FAX 704-636-1051
E-Mail: vicky@carnivalmag.com
Home Page: www.carnivalmag.com

Charles Dabbs, Publisher
Kevin Freese, Editor

Chronicles contemporary outdoor amusement
history providing readers with information and
news on carnivals, events, people, trade shows,
manufacturers, suppliers and more.
Cost: $40.00
Frequency: Monthly

1584 Carousel News and Trader
11001 Peoria Street
Sun Valley, CA 91352

818-332-7944
FAX 818-332-7944
E-Mail: roland@carouselnews.com
Home Page: www.carouselnews.com

Dan Horenberger, Publisher
Roland Hopkins, Editor
Ted McDonald, Webmaster

Articles devoted to the collecting, restoration
and selling of carousel art.
Cost: $35.00
48 Pages
Frequency: Monthly
Founded in 1985

1585 Casino Journal
BNP Media
2401 W Big Beaver Rd
Suite 700
Troy, MI 48084-3333

248-362-3700
FAX 248-332-0317
E-Mail: davidsonl@bnpmedia.com
Home Page: www.bnp.com

Taggert Henderson, CEO
Marian Green, Editor
Lynn Davidson, Marketing

A primary information source for the key decision makers in the worldwide casino, lottery,
parimutuel, bingo and emerging internet wagering markets.
Frequency: Monthly
Circulation: 13034
Founded in 1995

1586 Connect Magazine
8403 Colesville Rd
Suite 710
Silver Spring, MD 20910-6331

301-562-0777
FAX 301-562-0888
E-Mail: membership@aza.org
Home Page: www.aza.org
Social Media: *Facebook, Twitter*

Jim Maddy, President & CEO
Kris Vehrs JD, Executive Director
Jill Nicoll, SVP, Marketing & Corp Strategies
Laura Benson, SVP, Finance & Administration

Your window to the professional zoo and
aquarium world. Each month, the magazine
features fascinating stories that explore trends,
educational initiatives, member achievements
and conservation efforts.
200 Members
Founded in 1924

1587 Daily Variety
5900 Wilshire Blvd
Suite 3100
Los Angeles, CA 90036-7209

323-617-9100
FAX 323-965-5375

E-Mail: dana.harris@variety.com
Home Page: www.variety.com

Jay Penske, President
Abe Burns, Marketing
Millie Chiavelli, Managing Director
Steve Gaydos, Executive Editor
Paula Taylor, Creative Director

Focuses on film, television, video, cable, music
and theater. Includes coverage of financial, regulatory and legal matters pertaining to the entertainment industry.
Cost: $329.00
Frequency: Daily
Circulation: 38248

**1588 Entertainment, Publishing and the
Arts Handbook**
Thomson West Publishing
610 Opperman Dr
St Paul, MN 55123-1340

651-687-7000
800-344-5008
FAX 651-687-5581
Home Page: www.west.thomson.com

Charles B Cater, Executive VP
Laurie Zenner, VP

Provides information on the latest development
in the expanding legal field of entertainment,
publishing, and the arts. The articles focus on
such issues as books, copyrights, right-of-pub-
licity and more.
Cost: $538.00
Frequency: Annual

1589 Fair Dealer
Western Fairs Association
1776 Tribute Rd
Suite 210
Sacramento, CA 95815-4495

916-927-3100
FAX 916-927-6397
E-Mail: stephenc@fairsnet.org
Home Page: www.fairsnet.org

Stephen J Chambers, Executive Director
Jon Baker, VP
Nichole Farley, Marketing

Offers information for fairground owners, man-
agers and workers, fair related businesses.
Cost: $35.00
2000 Members
Frequency: Quarterly
Circulation: 1500
Founded in 1922
Printed in on glossy stock

1590 Fairs & Expos
International Association of Fairs &
Expositions
3043 E Cairo
PO Box 985
Springfield, MO 65802

417-862-5771
800-516-0313
FAX 417-862-0156
E-Mail: iafe@fairsandexpos.com
Home Page: www.fairsandexpos.com

Jim Tucker, President
Steve Siever, Director
Max Willis, CFO
Marla Calico, Director Of Education
Rachel Mundhenke, Director Of technology

The source for information on fair trends, inno-
vative ideas, and association activities.
Circulation: 3250
Founded in 1885
Printed in 4 colors on glossy stock

1591 Hollywood Reporter
Prometheus Global Media

770 Broadway
New York, NY 10003-9595

212-493-4100
FAX 646-654-5368
Home Page: www.prometheusgm.com
Social Media: *Facebook, Twitter, YouTube*

Richard D. Beckman, CEO
James A. Finkelstein, Chairman
Madeline Krakowsky, Vice President
Circulation
Tracy Brater, Executive Director Creative
Service

Gives fresh ideas for film and TV. Covers the
full spectrum of craft and commerce in the en-
tertainment industry.
Cost: $199.00
Frequency: Weekly
Circulation: 34770

1592 Inside Arts
Association of Performing Arts Presenters
1211 Connecticut Ave NW
Suite 200
Washington, DC 20036-2716

202-833-2787
888-820-2787
FAX 202-833-1543
E-Mail: editor@artspresenters.org
Home Page: www.artspresenters.org

Mario Durham, President
Sean Handerhan, Marketing
Alicia Anstead, Editor
Margaret Stevens, Director
Laura Benson, Programme Manager

This publication explores issues critical to the
performing arts, presenting and touring field.
Cost: $42.00
1900 Members
Frequency: Bi-Monthly
Founded in 1957
Printed in 4 colors

**1593 International Gaming and Wagering
Business**
BNP Media
PO Box 1080
Skokie, IL 60076-9785

847-763-9534
FAX 847-763-9538
E-Mail: igwb@halldata.com
Home Page: www.igwb.com

James Rutherford, Editor
Lynn Davidson, Marketing
Tammie Gizicki, Director

Focuses on business strategy, legislative infor-
mation, food service and promotional concerns.
Frequency: Monthly
Circulation: 25000

1594 JUGGLE
International Jugglers' Association
3315 E Russell Road
Suite 203
Las Vegas, NV 89120

702-798-0099
FAX 709-248-2550
E-Mail: editor@juggle.org
Home Page: www.juggle.org

Alan Howard, Editor
Scott Krause, Treasurer
Marilyn Sullivan, Membership Director
Martin Frost, Store Manager
Dave Pawson, Chair

Offers readers a variety of colorful articles and
features on the art of juggling including interviews, a listing of jugggling clubs, upcoming
events and more.
Cost: $30.00
Frequency: Quarterly
Founded in 1947

1595 Journal of Leisure Research
22377 Belmont Ridge Road
Ashburn, VA 20148

703-858-0784
800-626-6772
FAX 703-858-0794
E-Mail: customerservice@nrpa.org
Home Page: www.nrpa.org
Social Media: *Facebook, Twitter, LinkedIn, YouTube*

Jodie H Adams, President
Jessica Lytle, Director
John Crosby, Marketing
Advancing parks, recreation and environmental conservation efforts that enhance the quality of life for all people.
Founded in 1965

1596 Journal of Physical Education, Recreation & Dance (JOPERD)
1900 Association Dr
Reston, VA 20191-1502

703-476-3400
800-213-7193
FAX 703-476-9527
E-Mail: info@aahperd.org
Home Page: www.aahperd.org
Social Media: *Facebook, Twitter, YouTube*

Monica Mize, President
Judith C Young, VP
Paula Kun, Marketing
Provides a variety of information on health, physical education, recreation, and dance issues than any other publication in the field.
25000 Members
Founded in 1885

1597 Journal of Singing
National Association of Teachers of Singing
9957 Moorings Dr
Suite 401
Jacksonville, FL 32257-2416

904-992-9101
FAX 904-262-2587
E-Mail: info@nats.org
Home Page: www.nats.org

Richard Dale Sjoerdsma, Editor-in-Chief
Provides current information regarding the teaching of singing as well as results of recent research in the field. A refereed journal, it serves as a historical record and is a venue for teachers of singing and other scholars to share the results of their work in areas such as history, diction, voice science, medicine, and especially voice pedagogy.
Frequency: 5x times/year

1598 Laserist
International Laser Display Association
7062 Edgeworth Drive
Orlando, FL 32819

407-797-7654
FAX 503-344-3770
E-Mail: president@laserist.org
Home Page: www.laserist.org

Christine Jenkin, President
Patrick Murphy, Executive Director
Providing the latest news about the art and technology of laser displays.
Frequency: Quarterly
Founded in 1986
Printed in 4 colors

1599 Linking Ring Magazine
International Brotherhood of Magicians
11155 S Towne Square
Suite C
St Louis, MO 63123

314-845-9200
FAX 314-845-9220

E-Mail: info@magician.org
Home Page: www.magician.org

Joan Pye, President
Shawn Farquhar, VP
Don Wiberg, Secretary
Roger Miller, Treasurer
Keeps IBM members informed about what's happening in the world of magic.
13000 Members
Frequency: Monthly
Founded in 1922

1600 Magic-Unity-Might: MUM Magazine
Society of American Magicians
7566 John Avenue
PO Box 510260
Saint Louis, MO 63129

314-846-5659
FAX 314-846-5659
E-Mail: webmaster@magicsam.com
Home Page: www.magicsam.com

John Apperson, President
David Goodsell, National Secretary
Marlene Clark, National Secretary
You will find articles dealing with the business of magic, publicity, showmanship and the history of magic and the lives of famous magicians. Many of the creative minds in the business are regular contributors.
60 Pages
Frequency: Monthly
Circulation: 30,000
Founded in 1902

1601 NRPA Express
22377 Belmont Ridge Road
Ashburn, VA 20148

703-858-0784
800-626-6772
FAX 703-858-0794
E-Mail: customerservice@nrpa.org
Home Page: www.nrpa.org
Social Media: *Facebook, Twitter, LinkedIn, YouTube*

Jodie H Adams, President
Jessica Lytle, Director
John Crosby, Marketing
Membership publication delivering the latest news and information about upcoming events, research projects, educational opportunities, grants, and initiatives about NRPA and the parks and recreation community.
Founded in 1965

1602 New Calliope
Clowns of America International
PO Box C
Richeyville, PA 15358-0532

724-938-8765
888-522-5696
FAX 724-938-8765
Home Page: www.coai.org

Tom King, President
Pamela Bacher, VP
Contains informative articles regarding the art of clowning, such as make-up, costuming, props, skit development, etc. News of regional and local clown alley activities; resources for your clowning needs; information on the annual international conventions; information on the various regional conventions through the year.
Frequency: Bi-Monthly

1603 Park & Rec Trades
Trades Publishing Company
20 Our Way Dr
Crossville, TN 38555-5790

931-484-8819
FAX 931-484-8825

E-Mail: subscribe@thetrades.com
Home Page: www.parktrades.com

Tim Wilson, Owner
Kristie Irvin, Marketing
Event calendar and buying guides for amusement and recreation park professionals.
Frequency: Monthly
Circulation: 32000
Printed in 4 colors on newsprint stock

1604 Parks and Recreation Magazine
National Recreation and Park Association
22377 Belmont Ridge Road
Ashburn, VA 20148

703-858-0784
FAX 703-858-0794
E-Mail: info@nrpa.org
Home Page: www.nrpa.org

Douglas Vaira, Editor
Jessica Lytle, Director
John Crosby, Marketing
Barbara Tulipane, President
Michele White, Executive Assistant
NRPA's magazine keeps members informed about parks, recreation and envrionmental conservation efforts.
Circulation: Monthly
Founded in 1965

1605 Play Meter
Skybird Publishing Company
PO Box 337
Metairie, LA 70004-0337

504-488-7003
888-473-2376
FAX 504-488-7083
E-Mail: news@playmeter.com
Home Page: www.playmeter.com

Bonnie Theard, Editor
Trade publication that provides members with information on the coin-operated entertainment industry, including upcoming trade shows, new products, ongoing trends and more.
Cost: $60.00
Frequency: Monthly
Circulation: 60000
Founded in 1974

1606 Pollstar: Concert Hotwire
4697 W Jacquelyn Ave
Fresno, CA 93722-6443

559-271-7900
FAX 559-271-7979
E-Mail: info@pollstar.com
Home Page: www.pollstar.com

Gary Smith, COO
Shari Rice, VP
Gary Bongiovanni, CEO
Trade publication for the concert industry offering global coverage and information including concert tour schedules, ticket sales information and more.
Cost: $449.00
Frequency: Weekly
Circulation: 20000
Printed in 4 colors

1607 Protocol
Entertainment Services and Technology Association
875 Sixth Avenue
Suite 1005
New York, NY 10001

212-244-1505
FAX 212-244-1502
E-Mail: info@esta.org
Home Page: www.esta.org

Beverly Inglesby, Editor
Lori Rubinstein, Executive Director
Bill Groener, President

Featuring columns and articles of interest to professionals in the entertainment technology industry on business and technical topics, current standards issues, certification developments, and trade shows.
550 Members
Frequency: Quarterly
Printed in 4 colors

1608 RePlay Magazine

PO Box 572829
Tarzana, CA 91357-7004

818-776-2880
FAX 818-776-2888
E-Mail: editor@replaymag.com
Home Page: www.replaymag.com

Edward Adlum, Owner
Barry Zweben, Marketing

A trade publication for those within the coin-operated amusement machine industry, primarily distributors, manufacturers and operators of jukeboxes and games.
Cost: $65.00
Frequency: Monthly
Circulation: 36000
ISSN: 1534-2328
Founded in 1975
Printed in 4 colors on glossy stock

1609 Research Quarterly for Exercise and Sport (RQES)

1900 Association Dr
Reston, VA 20191-1502

703-476-3400
800-213-7193
FAX 703-476-9527
E-Mail: info@aahperd.org
Home Page: www.aahperd.org
Social Media: *Facebook, Twitter, YouTube*

Monica Mize, President
Judith C Young, VP
Paula Kun, Marketing

Publishes research in the art and science of human movement that contributes to the knowledge and development of theory either as new information, reviews, substantiation or contradiction of previous findings, or as application of new or improved techniques.
25000 Members
Founded in 1885

1610 Rollercoaster!

American Coaster Enthusiasts
1100-H Brandywine Boulevard
Zanesville, OH 43701-7303

740-450-1560
FAX 740-452-2552
E-Mail: info@aceonline.org
Home Page: www.aceonline.org

Dave Altman, President
Jerry Willard, VP
Paul Blick, Events Director

Magazine featuring in-depth articles of parks and coasters of the past along with profiles of today's coaster, parks, people, and places.
7000 Members
Founded in 1978

1611 Souvenirs, Gifts & Novelties Magazine

10 E Athens Avenue
Suite 208
Ardmore, PA 19003

610-645-6940
FAX 610-645-6943
E-Mail: sgnmag@kanec.com
Home Page: www.sgnmag.com

Scott C Borowsky, President
Tony DeMasi, Editor

Trade magazine for the resort-gift, souvenir industry. Articles cover merchandising trends, profile successful operations, new products, trade show calendar, plus buyer's guide issue.
Cost: $40.00
Circulation: 42,362
Printed in 4 colors on glossy stock

1612 Strategies: A Journal for Physical and Sport Educators

1900 Association Dr
Reston, VA 20191-1502

703-476-3400
800-213-7193
FAX 703-476-9527
E-Mail: info@aahperd.org
Home Page: www.aahperd.org
Social Media: *Facebook, Twitter, YouTube*

Monica Mize, President
Judith C Young, VP
Paula Kun, Marketing

Delivers practical ideas, how-to information, and tips for sport and physical educators.
25000 Members
Founded in 1885

1613 The Bulletin

120 W Seventh Street
One City Centre, Suite 200
Bloomington, IN 47404

812-245-2284
FAX 812-245-6710
E-Mail: acui@acui.org
Home Page: www.acui.org
Social Media: *Facebook, Twitter, YouTube*

Rich Steele, President
Marsha Herman-Betzen, Executive Director
Andrea Langeveld, Marketing

Features everything from research analyses to best practices to practical reports about trends in the field.
1000 Members
Founded in 1914

1614 The New Calliope

PO Box 1171
Englewood, FL 34295-1171

941-474-4351
877-816-6941
Home Page: www.coai.org

Pamela Bacher, President
Michael B. Cox, Vice-President
Catherine Hardebeck, Secretary
Candyce Will, Treasurer

Contains informative articles regarding the art of clowning such as; makeup, costuming, props, skit development, etc. News of regional and local clown alley activities, resources for your clowning needs, information on the annual international convention, and information on various regional conventions through the year.

1615 Therapeutic Recreation Journal

22377 Belmont Ridge Road
Ashburn, VA 20148

703-858-0784
800-626-6772
FAX 703-858-0794
E-Mail: customerservice@nrpa.org
Home Page: www.nrpa.org
Social Media: *Facebook, Twitter, LinkedIn, YouTube*

Jodie H Adams, President
Jessica Lytle, Director
John Crosby, Marketing

Advancing parks, recreation and environmental conservation efforts that enhance the quality of life for all people.
Founded in 1965

1616 Tourist Attractions & Parks

10 E Athens Avenue
Suite 208
Ardmore, PA 19003

610-645-6940
FAX 610-645-6943
E-Mail: tapmag@kanec.com
Home Page: www.tapmag.com
Social Media: *Facebook, Twitter*

Scott C Borosky, President/Ex Editor
Caroline Burns, Managing Editor
Larry White, Publisher
Kittey White, Account Executive
Laurie O'Malley, Account Executive

Trade magazine for amusement, national & waterparks, zoos, and aquariums, bowling, skating + family entertainment centers, forest festivals.
Cost: $49.00
28124 Members
Circulation: 31,388
Founded in 1972

1617 Vending Times

Vending Times
55 Maple Avenue
Suite 102
Rockville Centre, NY 11570

212-302-4700
FAX 212-221-3311
Home Page: www.vendingtimes.com

Alicia Lavay, President/Publisher
Nick Montano, VP/Executive Editor
Tim Sanford, Editor-in-Chief
Maria Ackies, Production Manager

Addresses the business, legal, legislative and regulatory concerns of companies providing industrial, institutional and public vending, refreshment, feeding and recreational services
Cost: $40.00
Frequency: Monthly
Circulation: 16,000
Founded in 1962

1618 White Tops

Circus Fans Association of America
1515 S Butler Street
Port Angeles, WA 98363

360-452-1919
E-Mail: feedback@circusfan.org
Home Page: www.circusfans.org

Vern Mendonca, President

Articles about the illustrious history of circus, including the greatest performers, famous acts and feats, logistical facts and figures, management and marketing, and the shows of yesteryear.
Circulation: 2000
Founded in 1926

Trade Shows

1619 ACE Coaster Con

American Coaster Enthusiasts
1100-H Brandywine Boulevard
Zanesville, OH 43701-7303

740-450-1560
FAX 740-452-2552
E-Mail: info@aceonline.org
Home Page: www.aceonline.org

Dave Altman, President
Jerry Willard, VP
Susan Shick, Secretary
Cheri Armstrong, Treasurer
David Lipnicky, Public Relation Director

An annual convention, a great opportunity for fellow ACEers to gather together to ride coasters.
7000 Attendees
Frequency: Annual
Founded in 1978

1620 ACUI Conference
Association of College Unions International
120 W 7th Street
One City Centre, Suite 200
Bloomington, IN 47404-3925

812-245-ACUI
FAX 812-245-6710
E-Mail: acui@acui.org
Home Page: www.acui.org

Michelle Smith, Director, Educational Prgms & Svcs
Marsha Herman, Executive Director
Tim Arth, Event and Corporate Sales Manager
Karen Keith, Financial Service Manager
Julie Sylvester, Office Administrator

Tours and outings, peer learning network, leadership meetings, orientation for new members, education sessions, seminars, networking fair, keynote speakers.
Frequency: Annual
Founded in 1914

1621 AIMS International Safety Seminar
Amusement Industry Manufacturers & Suppliers Intl
3026 S Orange
Santa Ana, CA 92707

714-425-5747
FAX 714-276-9666
E-Mail: info@aimsintl.org
Home Page: www.aimsintl.org

Brian D King, President

This AIMS event is a comprehensive week of hands-on instruction taught by today's top industry professionals, for individuals responsible for the care and safety of the amusement industry's guests. Certification testing also available.
Frequency: January

1622 APAP Conference
Association of Performing Arts Presenters
1211 Connecticut Avenue NW
Suite 200
Washington, DC 20036

202-833-2787
888-717-APAP
FAX 202-833-1543
E-Mail: info@apapconference.org
Home Page: www.apapconference.org

Sandra Gibson, President
Sean Handerhan, Marketing
Leah Yoon, Director
Judy Moore, Conference Manager

Providing valuable networking resources and opportunities for performing arts presenters, artists and artist managers throughout the world. Hundreds of exhibitors and performances: see who is doing what in the world of performing arts. Educational tracks are offered; special events; special interests; and clinics.
1900 Members
4000 Attendees
Frequency: January
Founded in 1957

1623 Amusement Expo
American Amusement Machine Association
450 E. Higgins Road
Suite 201
Elk Grove Village, IL 60007-1417

847-290-9088
866-372-5190
FAX 847-290-9121

E-Mail: information@coin-op.org
Home Page: www.coin-op.org
Social Media: *Facebook, Twitter, LinkedIn*

John Schultz, President
Tina Schwartz, Business and Finance Manager
John Margold, Chairman
Frank Consentino, Secretary
Rich Babich, Treasurer

Featuring the latest in video games, digital-jukeboxes, dartboards, redemption games, plush toys, smart cards and more, as well as educational programs and seminars.

1624 Amusement Industry Expo
I-X Center
One I-X Center Drive
Cleveland, OH 44135

216-676-6000
800-897-3942
FAX 216-265-2621
E-Mail: info@ixamusementpark.com
Home Page: www.ixcenter.com

John O'Brien, Director

Supplies and products for the amusement industry.
4100 Attendees
Frequency: March/April

1625 Amusement Showcase International: ASI
William T Glasgow Inc
10729 W 163rd Place
Orland Park, IL 60467

708-226-1300
FAX 708-226-1310
E-Mail: info@asi-show.com
Home Page: www.asi-show.com

William T Glasgow, Executive Director
Features exhibits and seminars for the coin-operated amusement industry.
4000 Attendees
Frequency: Annual/March

1626 Amusement and Music Operators Association International Expo
William T Glasgow Inc
10729 W 163rd Place
Orland Park, IL 60467

708-226-1300
FAX 708-226-1310
E-Mail: info@amoashow.com
Home Page: www.amoashow.com

William T Glasgow, Executive Director

The AMOA International Expo is designed for professionals from the amusement, music and vending industries.
8000 Attendees
Frequency: Annual/September
Founded in 1948

1627 BPAA Convention
PO Box 4563
Louisville, KY 40204

502-473-0956
FAX 502-473-7352
E-Mail: info@ialda.org
Home Page: www.ialda.org

Lambert J. Hassinger, Jr., President
Bryan T. Pope, Vice-President

Nonprofit association of lawyers and other professionals who are actively engaged in representing the interests of the amusement and leisure industries.

1628 Broadcast Engineering Conference (BEC)
Society of Broadcast Engineers

9102 N Meridian Street
Suite 150
Indianapolis, IN 46260

317-846-9000
FAX 317-846-9120
Home Page: www.sbe.org

John L Poray CAE, Executive Director
Vincent A Lopez CEV, CBNT, President

Held in conjunction with the National Association of Broadcasters, features SBE Ennes Workshop followed by sessions covering the latest in broadcast technology.
500 Attendees
Frequency: Annual/Spring
Mailing list available for rent: 4700 names

1629 COAI Annual Spring International Convention
Clowns of America International
PO Box C
Richeyville, PA 15358-0532

724-938-8765
888-522-5696
FAX 724-938-8765
Home Page: www.coai.org

Glenn Kohlberger, President
Michael Cox, VP
Catherine Hardebeck, Secretary
Padee Embrey, Treasurer

The purpose of these conventions is to provide educational seminars, competitions for individuals and group skits, make up and costume competitions, as well as competitions in balloons and parade ability.
Frequency: Annual/Spring

1630 COAI Convention
PO Box 1171
Englewood, FL 34295-1171

941-474-4351
877-816-6941
Home Page: www.coai.org

Pamela Bacher, President
Michael B. Cox, Vice-President
Catherine Hardebeck, Secretary
Candyce Will, Treasurer

Offering classes, shows and competitions, theme party and banquet.

1631 CinemaCon
National Association of Theatre Owners
750 1st St NE
Suite 1130
Washington, DC 20002-4241

202-962-0054
FAX 202-962-0370
Home Page: www.cinemacon.com
Social Media: *Facebook*

Mitch Neuhauser, Managing Director

A gathering of cinema owners and operators.
4000 Members
3500 Attendees
Frequency: Annual/March/ Las Vegas
Founded in 2010

1632 CoasterCon
American Coaster Enthusiasts
1100-H Brandywine Boulevard
Zanesville, OH 43701-7303

740-450-1560
FAX 740-452-2552
E-Mail: info@aceonline.org
Home Page: www.aceonline.org

Dave Altman, President
Jerry Willard, VP
Susan Shick, Secretary
Cheri Armstrong, Treasurer
David Lipnicky, Public Relation Director

The flagship event of American Coaster.
Frequency: Annual/June

1633 Digital Out-of-Home Interactive Entertainment Conference (DNA)
450 E Higgins Rd
Suite 201
Elk Grove Vlg, IL 60007-1417

847-290-9088
866-372-5190
FAX 847-290-9121
E-Mail: information@coin-op.org
Home Page: www.coin-op.org
Social Media: *Facebook, Twitter, LinkedIn*

John Schultz, President
Tina Schwartz, Business & Finance Manager
David Cohen, Chairman
Frank Consentino, Secretary
John Margold, Treasurer

Six dedicated sessions that speak directly to the industry and new opportunities, with a leading selection of speakers with direct experience in the sector and its future.
Founded in 1981

1634 Fun Expo
William T Glasgow
10729 W 163rd Place
Orland Park, IL 60467

708-226-1300
FAX 708-226-1310
E-Mail: info@funexpo.com
Home Page: www.funexpo.com

William T Glasgow, Executive Director

Devoted to the family and location based entertainment industry and the trends that drive it. A focused and efficient event bringing buyers and sellers together in an atmosphere that allows industry professionals to conduct business.
Frequency: Annual/March

1635 GAMA Trade Show
Game Manufacturers Association
240 N.Fifth St
Suite 340
Columbus, OH 43215

614-255-4500
FAX 614-255-4499
E-Mail: ops@gama.org
Home Page: www.gama.org

John Ward, Executive Director
John Kaufeld, Marketing/Sales
Rick Loomis, President
Jamie Chambers, Vice President
Aaron Witten, Treasurer

For retailers, manufacturers, and industry professionals to network, see the newest products, and learn from others about ways to make their stores and businesses successful.
15000 Attendees

1636 IAAPA Attractions Expo
1035 S Semoran Blvd
Suite 1045A
Winter Park, FL 32792-5512

407-681-9444
800-517-6222
FAX 407-681-9445
E-Mail: oaba@aol.com
Home Page: www.oaba.org
Social Media: *Facebook, Twitter, YouTube*

Robert W Johnson, President
Al DeRusha, VP
Anita Rockett, Director

The OABA manages and influences concerns for its members. OABA believes that all business owners and members of the trade association should continue to raise the level of safety and quality in the mobile amusement industry.
4000 Members
Founded in 1964

1637 IAFE Annual Convention
3043 East Cairo St.
PO Box 985
Springfield, MO 65802

417-862-5771
800-516-0313
FAX 417-862-0156
E-Mail: iafe@fairsandexpos.com
Home Page: www.fairsandexpos.com
Social Media: *Facebook, Twitter*

Jim Tucker, President
Steve Siever, Director

The International Association of Fairs and Expositions (IAFE) is a voluntary, non-profit corporation whose members provide services and products that promote the overall development and improvement of fairs, shows, expositions, and allied fields.
1300 Members
Founded in 1885

1638 IFEA Annual Convention & Expo
International Festivals and Events Association
2603 W Eastover Terrace
Boise, ID 83706

208-433-0950
FAX 208-433-9812
E-Mail: schmader@ifea.com
Home Page: www.ifea.com

Steven Wood Schmader, President
Nia Forster, VP/Marketing
Shauna Spencer, Director
Bette Monteith, Director Of Finance
Beth Petersen, Director Of Membership Services

Unites the world's leading festivals and events, suppliers, media, sponsors and related industry professionals to share information on every aspect of event production through in depth workshops, round table discussions and networking.
2000 Members
Frequency: Annual/Sept
Founded in 1956
Mailing list available for rent: 20000 names at $235 per M

1639 IISF Trade Show
1035 S Semoran Blvd
Suite 1045A
Winter Park, FL 32792-5512

407-681-9444
800-517-6222
FAX 407-681-9445
E-Mail: oaba@aol.com
Home Page: www.oaba.org
Social Media: *Facebook, Twitter, YouTube*

Robert W Johnson, President
Al DeRusha, VP
Anita Rockett, Director

The OABA manages and influences concerns for its members. OABA believes that all business owners and members of the trade association should continue to raise the level of safety and quality in the mobile amusement industry.
4000 Members
Founded in 1964

1640 ILDA Conference
International Laser Display Association
7062 Edgeworth Drive
Orlando, FL 32819

407-797-7654
FAX 503-344-3770
E-Mail: president@laserist.org
Home Page: www.laserist.org

Christine Jenkin, President
Patrick Murphy, Executive Director

One of the world's largest exhibitions of entertainment technology. Features international exhibitors from the fields of lighting, lasers, audio, video and staging.
70000 Attendees
Founded in 1986

1641 INTIX Annual Conference & Exhibition
INTIX
330 W 38th Street
Suite 605
New York, NY 10018

212-629-4036
FAX 212-629-8532
E-Mail: info@intix.org
Home Page: www.intix.org

Jena L Hoffman, President
Kathleen O'Donnell, Deputy Director
Kevin McMacdonnell, Sales Manager

Combines educational workshops, committee and business meetings, networking and social events. Every major supplier serving he entertainment ticketing industry is represented at the exhibition. Launch new products and conduct user meetings for existing clients
Frequency: January

1642 International Association of Amusement Parks and Attractions Expo
Int'l Association of Amusement Parks & Attractions
1448 Duke Street
Alexandria, VA 22314

703-836-4800
FAX 703-836-4801
Home Page: www.iaapa.org

Chip Cleary, President/CEO
Susan Mosedale, Executive VP
Jan MacCool, Executive Assistant

Features diverse entertainment exhibitions from high tech, to games, rides, food and beverage and much more. IAAPA showcases products and services for amusement parks, water parks, family entertainment centers, zoos, aquariums, museums — any company in the business of entertainment.
30M Attendees
Frequency: Annual/Nov
Founded in 1918

1643 International Association of Fairs and Expositions Annual Convention
International Association of Fairs & Expositions
3043 E Cairo
PO Box 985
Springfield, MO 65802

417-862-5771
800-516-0313
FAX 417-862-0156
E-Mail: iafe@fairsandexpos.com
Home Page: www.fairsandexpos.com

Jim Tucker, President
Steve Siever, Director
Max Willis, CFO
Marla Calico, Director Of Education
Rachel Mundhenke, Director Of Technology

Largest event serving fairs and expositions. Convention attendees are able to network and learn from each other during the intensive four days of workshops, special seminars, and round table discussions. Companies showcase themselves while serving as a one-stop shop for all of a fair's booking, product, and service needs.
5000 Attendees
Frequency: Nov

1644 International Brotherhood of Magicians Annual Convention
International Brotherhood of Magicians
11155 S Towne Square
Suite C
St Louis, MO 63123

314-845-9200
FAX 314-845-9220
E-Mail: info@magician.org
Home Page: www.magician.org

John Pye, President
Shawn Farquhar, VP
Jack White, Marketing
Don Wiberg, Secretary
Roger Miller, Treasurer

A place where members can meet and network with others sharing an interest in the art of magic.
13000 Members
Frequency: July
Founded in 1922

1645 International Ticketing Association Annual Conference & Exhibition
330 W 38th Street
Suite 605
New York, NY 10018

212-629-4036
FAX 212-628-8532
E-Mail: info@intix.org
Home Page: www.intix.org
Social Media: *Facebook, Twitter, LinkedIn, YouTube*

Jena L Hoffman, President/CEO
Kathleen O'Donnell, Deputy Director

Non-profit association committed to the improvement, progress and advancement of ticket management. Provides educational programs, trade shows, conducts surveys, conference proceedings, and its valuable membership directory.
1000 Members
Founded in 1979

1646 Laser Tag Convention
International Laser Tag Association
5351 E Thompson Road
Suite 236
Indianapolis, IN 46237

317-786-9755
FAX 317-786-9757
E-Mail: info@lasertag.org
Home Page: www.lasertag.org

Shane Zimmerman, Executive Director

The source for all things laser tag. Co-located with the Roller Skating Trade Show, this provides an opportunity to meet suppliers and manufacturers of laser tag equipment, video games, kitchen equipment and more.
Frequency: May

1647 Laughter Works
Laughter Works Seminars
PO Box 1220
Folsom, CA 95763-1220

916-985-6570
E-Mail: info@laughterworks.com
Home Page: www.laughterworks.com

Jim Pelley, President

Seminars and keynote speeches on humor, create positive team environment, unleash creativity and enhance productivity in the workplace.

1648 NATS National Conference
National Association of Teachers of Singing
9957 Moorings Dr
Suite 401
Jacksonville, FL 32257-2416

904-992-9101
FAX 904-262-2587

E-Mail: info@nats.org
Home Page: www.nats.org

Allen Henderson, Executive Director
Deborah L Guess, Director of Operations
Tom Strother, Marketing & Communication
Elizabeth Zettler, Program Administrator
Frequency: June/July

1649 National Recreation and Park Association's Congress and Exposition
National Recreation and Park Association
22377 Belmont Ridge Road
Ashburn, VA 20148

703-858-0784
FAX 703-858-0794
E-Mail: info@nrpa.org
Home Page: www.nrpa.org

Britt Esen, Director
Jodie H Adams, President
John Crosby, Marketing

Education and training opportunity plus a tradeshow for the park and recreation industry.
4000 Attendees
Frequency: October
Founded in 1965

1650 OABA Annual Meeting & Chairman's Reception
Outdoor Amusement Business Association
1035 S Semoran Blvd
Suite 1045A
Winter Park, FL 32792-5512

407-681-9444
800-517-6222
FAX 407-681-9445
E-Mail: oaba@oaba.org
Home Page: www.oaba.org
Social Media: *Facebook, Twitter, YouTube*

Bill Johnson, Chairman
Jeanne McDonagh, 1st Vice Chair
Rober Johnson, President

The OABA manages and influences concerns for its members. OABA believes that all business owners and members of the trade association should continue to raise the level of safety and quality in the mobile amusement industry.
4000 Members
Founded in 1965

1651 Origins Game Fair
280 N High Street
Suite 230
Columbus, OH 43215

614-255-4500
FAX 614-255-4499
E-Mail: ops@gama.org
Home Page: www.gama.org
Social Media: *Facebook*

John Ward, Executive Director
John Kaufeld, Marketing/Sales
Rick Loomis, President

A non-profit trade association dedicated to the advancement of the tabletop game industry
450 Members
Founded in 1977

1652 Pinball Expo
Pinball Expo
3869 Niles Road SE
Warren, OH 44484

330-369-1192
800-323-3547
FAX 330-369-6279
E-Mail: brkpinball@aol.com
Home Page: www.pinballexpo.org

Robert Berk, Expo Chairman
Mike Pacak, Co-Expo Chairman

Annual show of manufacturers and related suppliers of pinball machines and supplies; tournaments and tours with over 50 exhibitors.
1,000 Attendees
Frequency: October

1653 RSA Convention and Trade Show
Roller Skating Association International
6905 Corporate Drive
Indianapolis, IN 46278

317-347-2626
FAX 317-347-2636
E-Mail: rsa@rollerskating.com
Home Page: www.rollerskating.org

Bobby Braun, President
Ron Liette, VP
John Purcell, Executive Director

Helping roller skating industry professionals discover ways to build strong foundations for their businesses.
1000 Members
Frequency: Annual/August
Founded in 1937

1654 SLA Annual Meeting & Convention
Showmen's League of America
1023 W Fulton Market
Chicago, IL 60607

312-733-9533
800-350-9906
FAX 312-733-9534
E-Mail: joeb@showmensleague.org
Home Page: www.showmensleague.org
Social Media: *Twitter*

Sam Johnston, President
Chris Atkins, 1st Vice President
Ron Porter, 2nd Vice President
Joe Burum, Executive Secretary
John Hanschen, Treasurer

Promotes friendship and fellowship between its members and the outdoor amusement industry, and pledges to help those in need through one of its many programs.
Founded in 1913

1655 World Waterpark Association Annual Tradeshow
World Waterpark Association
8826 Santa Fe Drive
Suite 310
Overland Park, KS 66212

913-599-0300
FAX 913-599-0520
E-Mail: aezra@waterparks.org
Home Page: www.waterparks.org

Rick Root, President
Patty Miller, Director
Aleatha Ezra, Marketing

Exhibits include waterpark attractions, water quality equipment and apparel, with more than 300 booths.
1000 Members
2600 Attendees
Frequency: October
Founded in 1981

Directories & Databases

1656 American Casino Guide
Casino Vacations
PO Box 703
Dania, FL 33004-0703

954-989-2766
800-741-1596
FAX 954-966-7048
Home Page: www.americancasinoguide.com

Steve Bourie, Author

A guide to every casino/resort, riverboat and Indian casino in the United States.
Cost: $16.95
448 Pages
Frequency: Annually
ISBN: 1-883768-11-X
Founded in 1992
Printed in one color

1657 Association of Performing Arts Presenters Membership Directory
1211 Connecticut Ave NW
Suite 200
Washington, DC 20036-2716

202-833-2787
888-820-2787
FAX 202-833-1543
E-Mail: info@artspresenters.org
Home Page: www.artspresenters.org

Sandra Gibson, President
Sean Handerhan, Marketing

An invaluable resource for members to keep in touch with colleagues. Puts more than 1,450 presenters, service organizations, artists, management consultants, and vendors at your fingertips. An excellent networking tool for everyone on your staff.
1900 Members
Frequency: Annual
Founded in 1957

1658 Celebrity Access Directory
Celebrity Access
2430 Broadway St
Suite 200
Boulder, CO 80304-4118

303-350-1700
FAX 303-339-6877
E-Mail: sales@celebrityaccess.com
Home Page: www.celebrityaccess.com

Peter Denholtz, President
Marc Gentilella, Editor
Keri Mullin, Marketing

Database directory of more than 35,000 performers that includes contact information for agents as well as links to websites, record companies, touring schedules, box office info and more.
Cost: $899.00
Frequency: Annual
Founded in 1998

1659 Data List & Membership Directory
Western Fairs Association
1776 Tribute Rd
Suite 210
Sacramento, CA 95815-4495

916-927-3100
FAX 916-927-6397
E-Mail: stephenc@fairsnet.org
Home Page: www.fairsnet.org

Stephen J Chambers, Executive Director
Jon Baker, Vice President
Nichole Farley, Marketing

A premier source of fair industry information for the Western United States and Canada. Referred to as the Bible of the fair industry, this directory contains a complete listing of every member fair, festival, special event, fair-related business, fair association, and agriculture-related organization.
2000 Members
Frequency: Annual
Founded in 1922
Printed in on glossy stock

1660 Dinner Theatre: A Survey and Directory
Greenwood Publishing Group

88 Post Road W
PO Box 5007
Westport, CT 06881-5007

203-226-3571
800-225-5800
FAX 203-222-1502
E-Mail: customer-service@greenwood.com
Home Page: www.greenwood.com

Debra Adams, Editor

Listings of dinner theaters, including in-depth profiles are offered in this comprehensive directory.
Cost: $82.95
160 Pages
Frequency: Hardcover
ISBN: 0-313284-42-3

1661 Directory of Historic American Theatres
Greenwood Publishing Group
88 Post Road W
PO Box 5007
Westport, CT 06881-5007

203-226-3571
800-225-5800
FAX 203-222-1502
E-Mail: customer-service@greenwood.com
Home Page: www.greenwood.com

Debra Adams, Editor

Directory of theaters built before 1915.
Cost: $86.95
367 Pages
Frequency: Hardcover
ISBN: 0-313248-68-0

1662 EPM Entertainment Marketing Sourcebook
EPM Communications
19 W.21st St,# 303
3rd Floor
New York, NY 10012-3208

212-941-0099
888-852-9467
FAX 212-941-1622
E-Mail: info@epmcom.com
Home Page: www.epmcom.com

Ira Mayer, Owner
Michele Khan, Marketing

Over 4,000 media companies, sponsors and retailers that provide products and services to entertainment marketers.
Cost: $95.00
278 Pages
Frequency: Annual
Printed in on matte stock

1663 Grey House Performing Arts Directory
Grey House Publishing
4919 Route 22
PO Box 56
Amenia, NY 12501

518-789-8700
800-562-2139
FAX 845-373-6390
E-Mail: books@greyhouse.com
Home Page: www.greyhouse.com
Social Media: *Facebook, Twitter*

Leslie Mackenzie, Publisher
Richard Gottlieb, Editor

The most comprehensive resource covering the Performing Arts. This directory provides current information on over 8,500 dance companies, instrumental music programs, opera companies, choral groups, theater companies, performing arts series and performing arts facilities.
Cost: $185.00
1200 Pages
Frequency: Annual

ISBN: 1-592373-76-3
Founded in 1981

1664 Grey House Performing Arts Directory - Online Database
Grey House Publishing
4919 Route 22
PO Box 56
Amenia, NY 12501

518-789-8700
800-562-2139
FAX 845-373-6390
E-Mail: gold@greyhouse.com
Home Page: www.gold.greyhouse.com
Social Media: *Facebook, Twitter*

Leslie Mackenzie, Publisher
Richard Gottlieb, President

The Grey House Performing Arts Directory - Online Database provides immediate access to dance companies, orchestras, opera companies, choral groups, theater companies, series, festivals and perfoming arts facilities across the country, or in their region, state, or in your own backyard. It offers unequaled coverage of the Performing Arts - over 8,500 listings - of the major performance organization, facilities, and information resources.
Frequency: Annual
Founded in 1981

1665 IAAPA Directory & Buyers Guide
Int'l Association of Amusement Parks & Attractions
1448 Duke St
Alexandria, VA 22314-3403

703-836-3677
FAX 703-836-2824
E-Mail: iaapa@iaapa.org
Home Page: www.iaapa.org

Will Morey, Chairman
Marion Mamon, Vice Chair

Directory of amusement parks, the attraction industry and related topics.
Founded in 1918

1666 SBE Membership Directory & Buyer's Guide
Society of Broadcast Engineers
9102 N Meridian St
Suite 150
Indianapolis, IN 46260-1896

317-846-9000
FAX 317-846-9120
Home Page: www.sbe.org

Ralph Hogan, President
Joseph Snelson, VP

Provides a quick reference to all members and Sustaining Members' services. Offers a yellow-page guide section that contains categorical listings of all SBE Substaining Members and advertisements from leading equipment and service suppliers.
Frequency: Annually
Circulation: 5,500

1667 Travel and Entertainment Policies and Procedures Guide
Institute of Management & Administration
1 Washington Park
Suite 1300
Newark, NJ 07102

973-718-4700
FAX 973-622-0595
E-Mail: rcochran@ioma.com
Home Page: www.ioma.com

Joe Bremner, President
Perry Patterson, VP
Andy Dzamba, Editor
James Bell, Marketing

The report offers tips and suggestions to improve T&E operations, information on reimbursement policies and benchmark data, current trends, and more.
Cost: $329.00
Frequency: Annual
Circulation: 185,000

1668 Who's Who in Festivals and Events Membership Directory & Buyers Guide
International Festivals and Events Association
2603 W Eastover Terrace
Boise, ID 83706-2800

208-433-0950
FAX 208-433-9812
E-Mail: craig@ifea.com
Home Page: www.ifea.com

Steven Schmader, President
Nia Forster, VP/Marketing
Craig Sarton, Director

Membership directory list hundreds of festivals and vendor members.
2000 Members
2000 Pages
Founded in 1956
Mailing list available for rent: 2000 names at $235 per M

Industry Web Sites

1669 http://gold.greyhouse.com
G.O.L.D Grey House OnLine Databases

Grey House Publishing's online database platform, GOLD, provides Quick Search, Keyword Search and Expert Search for most business sectors, including amusement, entertainment and recreation markets. The GOLD platform makes finding the information you need quick and easy. All of Grey House's directory products are available for subscription on the GOLD platform.

1670 www.aceonline.org
American Coaster Enthusiasts

ACE is a non-profit organization with members across the United States that promotes the roller coaster industry through a variety of events and publications.
7000 Members

1671 www.acui.org
Association of College Unions International

Nonprofit educational organization. Dedicated to building community on campus through programs, services and publications with the common goal of unifying the union and activities fields.

1672 www.amoa.com
Amusement and Music Operators Association

Providing leadership for the amusement, music, entertainment and vending industry. AMOA works vigorously to protect and promote industry interests. Members include operators, manufacturers, suppliers, distributors, and consultants.

1673 www.cavern.com
National Caves Association

Nonprofit organization of publicly and privately owned show caves and caverns developed for public visitation. Provides access to a directory of caves for those seeking out adventure, fun and education.

1674 www.circushistory.org
Circus Historical Society

The Circus Historical Society is a not-for-profit educational organization whose mission is to record the history of the American circus. Members have the opportunity to meet and network at circus conventions where there are presentations, films and more.

1675 www.coin-op.org
American Amusement Machine Association

Non-profit trade association representing the manufacturers, distributors and part suppliers to the coin-operated and out of home amusement industry.

1676 www.fairsnet.org
Western Fairs Association

A non-profit association with members throughout the Western United States and Canada that strives to promote industry standards. Membership includes access to conventions and trade shows, educational training programs, as well as legislative advocacy support.

1677 www.greyhouse.com
Grey House Publishing

Reference directories for most business sectors, including amusement, entertainment and recreation markets. Users can search the online databases with varied search criteria allowing for custom searches by product category, geographic area, sales volume, keyword, subject and more. Full Grey House catalog and online ordering also available.

1678 www.iaapa.org
International Association of Amusement Parks & Attractions

An international trade association that seeks to improve and support professional industry standards at permanently situated amusement facilities worldwide.
4,500 Members

1679 www.ifea.com
International Festivals and Events Association

A voluntary association of events, event producers, event suppliers and related professionals and organizations whose common purpose is the production and presentation of festivals, events, and civic and private celebrations.

1680 www.intix.org
International Ticket Association

Not-for-profit association representing 22 countries worldwide. Committed to the improvement, progress and advancement of ticket management through educational programs, trade shows, conducts surveys, conference proceedings, and produces a membership directory.
1,200 Members

1681 www.laserist.org
International Laser Display Association

Dedicated to advancing the use of laser displays, in art, entertainment and education. ILDA supports high industry standards, promotes safety and provides the opportunity for members to meet and network at trade shows and conventions.

1682 www.lasertag.org
International Laser Tag Association: ILTA

The ILTA helps individuals and companies start or add a lasertag facility.

1683 www.magicsam.com
Society of American Magicians

Promote and maintain harmonious fellowship among those interested in magic as an art, im-

prove ethics of the magical profession, and foster, promote and improve the advancement of magical arts in the field of amusement and entertainment. Membership includes professional and amateur magicians, manufacturers of magical apparatus and collectors.

1684 www.merchandisegroup.com
Nielsen Business Media's Merchandise Group ASD/AMD

Leading producer of trade shows and publications in the variety and general merchandise industry.

1685 www.music-rights.com
Ad Producer.com

Provides music rights providers with the highest quality platform to leverage the Web to market your services around the world around the clock.

1686 www.natoonline.org
National Association of Theatre Owners

Exhibition trade organization, representing more than 30,000 movie screens in all 50 states, and additional cinemas in 50 countries worldwide.

1687 www.nats.org
National Association of Teachers of Singing

Encourage the highest standards of the vocal art and of ethical principals in the teaching of singing; and promote vocal education and research at all levels, both for the enrichment of the general public and for the professional advancement of the talented.

1688 www.oaba.org
Outdoor Amusement Business Association

Promotes interest of the outdoor amusement industry. Provides members with public relations and safety services as well as it's monthly Show Time magazine and annual publication The Midway Marquee.
4,000 Members

1689 www.rollerskating.org
Roller Skating Association International

A trade association representing skating center owners, operators; teachers, coaches and judges of roller skating; and manufacturers and suppliers of roller skating equipment.

1690 www.sbe.org
Society of Broadcast Engineers

Professional organization of television and radio engineers and those in the related fields. SBE has members in 114 chapters across the United States and Hong Kong.

1691 www.toyassociation.org
Toy Industry Association

National organization for U.S. producers and importers of toys, games and children's entertainment products. Represents more than 500 member companies including designers, safety consultants, testing laboratories, licensors, communication professionals and inventors.

1692 www.waterparks.com
World Waterpark Association

Official Web site for the waterpark and water-leisure industries provides a comprehensive listing of waterparks around the world. It was developed and is maintained by the World Waterpark Association, the international organization created to further safety and business effectiveness in the waterpark industry.

Associations

1693 American Apparel & Footwear Association (AAFA)

American Apparel & Footwear Association
1601 N Kent Street
Suite 1200
Arlington, VA 22209

703-524-1864
800-520-2262
FAX 847-522-6741
E-Mail: mrhowell@apparelandfootwear.org
Home Page: www.wewear.org
Social Media: *Facebook, Twitter, LinkedIn, YouTube, Instagram*

Rick Helfenbein, Chairman
Juanita Duggan, President/CEO
Stephen E Lamar, Executive Vice President
Ashley Stewart Bailey, Chief of Staff
Susan Lapetine, VP/Industry Relations

The American Apparel & Footwear Association (AAFA) is the national trade association representing apparel, footwear and other sewn products companies, and their suppliers which compete in the global market. AAFA's mission is to promote and enhance its members' competitiveness, productivity and profitability in the global market by minimizing regulatory, legal, commercial, political, and trade restraints.
Founded in 2000

1694 American Cotton Shippers Association

88 Union Ave
Suite 1204
Memphis, TN 38103-5150

901-525-2272
FAX 901-527-8303
E-Mail: bmay@acsa-cotton.org
Home Page: www.acsa-cotton.org
Social Media: *RSS Feeds*

Bobby Walton, Chairman
William E May, President
Vaniece C. Boone, Vice President/Memphis Operations
Linda Colston, Administrative Assistant/Accounting
Laura Skillern, Bookkeeper

ACSA members are engaged in a great enterprise, the purchasing, storing, tansporting and merchandising of America's most valuable cash crop and it's most abundant natural fiber.
Founded in 1924

1695 American Flock Association

PO Box 1090
Cherryville, NC 28021

617-303-6288
FAX 704-671-2366
E-Mail: info@flocking.org
Home Page: www.flocking.org
Social Media: *LinkedIn, Pinterest, YouTube*

Steve Rosenthal, Managing Director

AFA members include manufacturers of roll-to-roll coated textiles, papers, and films as well as coaters of three dimensional objects and printers of apparel decoration and graphics art products. Industry suppliers are a key sector of the membership. The AFA is affiliated with the National Textile Association, a non-profit trade organization representing over 150 textile manufacturers and industry suppliers with operations in the U.S., and Canada.
Founded in 1984

1696 American Sewing Guild

9660 Hillcroft St
Suite 510
Houston, TX 77096-3866

713-729-3000
FAX 713-721-9230
E-Mail: margo@asg.org
Home Page: www.asg.org
Social Media: *Facebook, Twitter, YouTube*

Betty Brees, Chairman
Jeanette Swanson, Secretary
Jodell Larkin, Treasurer
Margo Martin, Executive Director

ASG is a membership organization that welcomes sewing enthusiasts of all skill levels. Chapters are located in cities all across the country and members meet monthly to learn new sewing skills, network with others who share an interest in sewing and participate in community service sewing projects.
20000 Members
Founded in 1993

1697 Cashmere and Camel Hair Manufacturers Institute

3 Post Office Square
8th Floor
Boston, MA 02110

617-542-7481
FAX 617-542-2199
E-Mail: info@cashmere.org
Home Page: www.cashmere.org

Karl Spilhaus, President

The Cashmere & Camel Hair Manufacturers Institute (CCMI) is an international trade association representing the interests of producers and manufacturers of camel hair and cashmere fiber, yarn, fabric and garments throughout the world.
25 Members
Founded in 1984

1698 Chemical Fabrics and Film Association

1300 Sumner Avenue
Cleveland, OH 44115-2851

216-241-7333
FAX 216-241-0105
E-Mail: cffa@chemicalfabricsandfilm.com
Home Page: www.chemicalfabricsandfilm.com

Charles M Stockinger, Executive Secretary

International trade association representing manufacturers of polymer-based fabric and film products, used in the building and construction, automotive, fashion and many other industries.
40 Members
Founded in 1927

1699 Color Association of the United States

33 Whitehall Street
Suite M3
New York, NY 10004

212-947-7774
FAX 212-594-6987
E-Mail: info@colorassociation.com
Home Page: www.colorassociation.com
Social Media: *Facebook, Twitter, LinkedIn, YouTube, Pinterest, Instagram*

Sherrie Donghia, Chairman
Marcella Echavarria, Interior/Forecast
Linda De Franco, Fashion/Forecast
Kelly Kovak, Beauty/Forecast
Sal Cesarani, Men's Fashion/Forecast

The Color Association of The United States creates and delivers global color intelligence across industries. The Color Association serves as premier forecast agent, specialized educator, and trusted advisor to color professionals whose responsibility is to ensure marketplace success for their color decisions in the realm of brands, product and service, and spatial environments.
Founded in 1915

1700 Costume Designers Guild

11969 Ventura Boulevard
First Floor
Studio City, CA 91604-3570

818-752-2400
FAX 818-752-2402
E-Mail: cdgia@cdgia.com
Home Page: www.costumedesignersguild.com
Social Media: *Facebook, Twitter*

Ivy Thaide, Secretary
Nanrose Buchman, Treasurer
Salvador Perez, President
Cate Adair, Vice President
Rachael M. Stanley, Executive Director

The Costume Designers Guild (CDG) is Local 892 of the International Alliance of Theatrical and Stage Employees (I.A.T.S.E.). The Guild represents Costume Designers, Assistant Costume Designers and Costume Illustrators working at the highest levels of skill and expertise in motion pictures, television and commercials. The CDG promotes and protects the economic status of its members while improving working conditions and raising standards for our craft.
810 Members
Founded in 1953

1701 Cotton Incorporated

6399 Weston Pkwy
Cary, NC 27513

919-678-2220
FAX 919-678-2230
Home Page: www.cottoninc.com
Social Media: *Facebook, Twitter, Youtube, RSS Feeds*

J. Berrye AnkenyWorsham, President and CEO
Michael Watson, VP of Fiber Competition
Kater D. Hake, Ph.D., Vice President Agriculture
Edward M. Barnes, Senior Director of Agriculture
Linda De Franco, Director of Product Trend Analysis

To ensure that cotton remains the first choice among consumers in apparel and home products, Cotton Incorporated helps companies manufacture, market, and sell cotton products more efficiently and more profitably.
Founded in 1970

1702 Council of Fashion Designers of America

65 Bleecker St
11th Floor
New York, NY 10012

212-302-1821
FAX 212-768-0515
E-Mail: info@cfda.com
Home Page: www.cfda.com
Social Media: *Facebook, Twitter, Youtube, Google+, Pinterest, T*

Diane von Furstenberg, Chairman
Steven Kolb, President/CEO
Lisa Smilor, Executive Vice President
CaSandra Diggs, Deputy Director
Marc Karimzadeh, Editorial & Comm. Director

The CFDA's goals are: to further the position of fashion design as a recognized branch of American art and culture, advance its artistic and professional standards, establish and maintain a code of ethics and practices of mutual benefit in professional, public, and trade relations, and promote and improve public understanding and appreciation of the fashion arts through leadership in quality and taste.
250 Members
Founded in 1962

1703 Custom Tailors and Designers Association of America

229 Forest Hills Road
Rochester, NY 14625

888-248-2832
FAX 866-661-1240
E-Mail: info@ctda.com
Home Page: www.ctda.com
Social Media: *Facebook, Twitter, LinkedIn*

Peter Roberti, President
Mitch Gambert, 1st Vice President
Craig Wertheim, 2nd Vice President
Jeff Landis, Treasurer
Gordon Goldstein, Secretary

Established as a venue through which ideas and techniques for design, pattern making, fitting, cutting and tailoring could be shared and exchanged.
300 Members
Founded in 1880

1704 Fashion Footwear Association of New York

274 Madison Avenue
Suite 1701
New York, NY 10016

212-751-6422
FAX 212-751-6404
E-Mail: info@ffany.org
Home Page: www.ffany.org
Social Media: *Facebook, Twitter, Instagram, Pinterest*

Jim Issler, Chairman
Ronald A. Fromm, President/CEO
Phyllis Rein, Executive Vice President
Liz Carroll, Executive Assistant
Shelley Berquist, SVP, Operations & Marketing

FFANY's mission is to promote and assist the common business interests of its members. FFANY is committed to supporting New York City as the recognized national center of fashion trade and commerce and aims to ensure the city continues to be the best venue for both national and international footwear industry events.
300 Members
Founded in 1980

1705 Fashion Scholarship Fund

1501 Broadway
Suite 1810
New York, NY 10036

212-278-0008
FAX 212-279-6241
E-Mail: hharrison@fashionscholarshipfund.org
Home Page: www.ymafsf.org
Social Media: *Facebook, Twitter, Instagram, Pinterest, Vimeo*

Debra Malbin, Co-Chairman
Paul Rosengard, Co-Chairman
Peter Sachse, President
Michael Setola, Treasurer
Doug Evans, Secretary

The YMA Fashion Scholarship Fund(FSF) is a national association dedicated to promoting education of the fashion arts and business by granting scholarships to talented students and facilitating internships, mentorships and career programs.
800+ Members
Founded in 1937

1706 Hosiery Association

7421 Carmel Executive Park Drive
Suite 200
Charlotte, NC 28226

704-365-0913
FAX 704-362-2056
E-Mail: thainfo@hosieryassociation.com
Home Page: www.hosieryassociation.com

Social Media: *Facebook, Twitter, LinkedIn, Pinterest*

Sally Kay, President/CEO
Sheila Simpson, Director/Finance
Vicki Camp, Office Manager

The Hosiery Association(THA) is the only international nonprofit trade association exclusively representing the specific needs of legwear companies that produce and sell more than 90 percent of the products in the US. Supplier companies to the industry also play a major role in membership and sponsorship of THA.
Founded in 1905

1707 International Glove Association

PO Box 146
Brookville, PA 15825

814-328-5208
FAX 814-328-2308
E-Mail: gloves@windstream.net
Home Page: www.iga-online.com

Kim O'Leary, President
Brent Fidler, Vice President
Bill Trainer, Past President
Matt Reid, Member
Larry Garner, Member

Our mission is to further build an association that improves manufacturing and distribution of hand protection. Studying, clarifying, and recommending government action to help promote proper glove selection and use, and the interests of glove manufacturers and distributors, will help association members achieve success with customers and maintain a financially sound organization.
Founded in 2003

1708 Leather Apparel Association

19 W 21st Street
Suite 403
New York, NY 10010

212-727-1210
FAX 212-727-1218
Home Page: www.leatherassociation.com

Morris Goldfarb, President
Richard Harrow, Executive Director
Fran Harrow, Marketing

Represents the nation's leading leather retailers, manufacturers, cleaners and other businesses in promoting leather apparel in the US.
Founded in 1990

1709 National Luggage Dealers Association

1817 Elmdale Avenue
Glenview, IL 60026

847-998-6869
FAX 847-998-6884
E-Mail: inquiry@nlda.com
Home Page: www.nlda.com

Alex Shapiro, President
George Morri, CEO
Felicia Libbin, Marketing Director

The National Luggage Dealers Association (NLDA) improves the buying power of the many stores it represents, giving the individual store owners the ability to compete with larger companies and department stores. Many of the founding members continue to be represented today by successive generations of family members.
130+ Members
Founded in 1925

1710 National NeedleArts Association

1100-H Brandywine Boulevard
Zanesville, OH 43701-7303

740-455-6773
800-889-8662
FAX 740-452-2552
E-Mail: info@tnna.org

Home Page: www.tnna.org
Social Media: *Facebook, Twitter, LinkedIn, Pinterest, Instagram*

Ewe Count, Chair & Board Representative
Dave VanStralen, Board President
Don Lynch, Board Vice President
Barbara Bergstan, Director
Claudia Dutcher, Director

TNNA is an international trade organization representing retailers, manufacturers, distributors, designers, manufacturers' representatives, publishers, teachers and wholesalers of products and supplies for the specialty needlearts market. These businesses create and market hand painted needlepoint canvases, hand-dyed and specialty crochet and knitting yarns, embroidery, needlepoint and cross-stitch materials, kits, tools and more.
2650 Members
Founded in 1975

1711 North American Association of Uniform Manufacturers & Distributors

6800 Jericho Turnpike
Suite 120W
Syosset, NY 11791

516-393-5838
FAX 516-393-5878
E-Mail: rjlerman@naumd.com
Home Page: www.naumd.com

Aviva Tavel, Chairman
Richard J Lerman, President & CEO
Jackie Rosselli, Director of Communications
Lee Galperin, Vice Chair
Brian Garry, Treasurer

The North-American Association of Uniform Manufacturers & Distributors (NAUMD) is a trade association representing the interests of all parties in the uniform & image apparel industry.
450+ Members
Founded in 1933

1712 Private Label Manufacturers Association

630 Third Avenue
New York, NY 10017-6506

212-972-3131
FAX 212-983-1382
E-Mail: info@plma.com
Home Page: www.plma.com

John Shields, Former Chairman & CEO
Myra Rosen, VP

PLMA has steadily grown in size, reflecting the increasing importance of store brands to retailers and consumers. As you will see, PLMA member services have mirrored store brands new role in the marketplace, too.
3200+ Members
Founded in 1979

1713 The Fashion Group International, Inc.

8 W. 40th St.
7th Fl.
New York, NY 10018

212-302-5511
FAX 212-302-5533
E-Mail: pmaffei@fgi.org
Home Page: www.fgi.org
Social Media: *Facebook, Twitter, LinkedIn, YouTube*

Margaret Hayes, President
Patricia Maffei, Managing/Membership Director

Global, nonprofit organization supporting the professional development of its members in the fashion and lifestyle industries.
5000 Members
Founded in 1930

1714 The Knitting Guild Association (TKGA)
1100-H Brandywine Boulevard
Zanesville, OH 43701-7303

740-452-4541
FAX 740-452-2552
E-Mail: tkga@tkga.com
Home Page: www.tkga.com
Social Media: *Facebook, Twitter, Pinterest*

Penny Sitler, Executive Director

Membership organization for knitters with focus on knitting education and enhancing knitters skills. TKGA seeks to advance creativity, knowledge and the quality of workmanship in knitting through education and communication.
11000 Members
Founded in 1984

1715 The Vision Council of America
Sunglass and Reader Division
225 Reinekers Lane
Suite 700
Alexandria, VA 22314-2846

703-548-4560
866-826-0290
FAX 703-548-4580
E-Mail: info@thevisioncouncil.org
Home Page: www.thevisioncouncil.org
Social Media: *Facebook, Twitter, LinkedIn, YouTube*

Mike Daley, Chief Executive Officer
Maureen Beddis, Vice President of Marketing
Deborah Malakoff-Castor, Vice President of Shows
Greg Chavez, Vice President of Member Services
Brian Carroll, Chief Operating Officer

Serving as the global voice for vision care products and services, The Vision Council represents the manufacturers and suppliers of the optical industry. We position our members to be successful in a competitive marketplace through education, advocacy, consumer outreach, strategic relationship building and industry forums.
263 Members
Founded in 1999

1716 Tri-State Linen Supply Association
1800 Diagonal Rd
Suite 200
Alexandria, VA 22314-2842

703-519-0029
877-770-9274
FAX 703-519-0026
E-Mail: trsa@trsa.org
Home Page: www.trsa.org
Social Media: *Facebook, Twitter, LinkedIn, YouTube, RSS Feeds*

Roger Cocivera, President/CEO
George Ferencz, VP

Provides hygienic sustainable laundering services that offer cost-effective, energy-efficient solutions while protecting the environment and employing hundreds of thousands of individuals in highly safety-conscious workplaces nationwide.
1400 Members
Founded in 1913

1717 Uniform Code Council
Princeton Pike Corporate Center
1009 Lenox Drive Suite 202
Lawrenceville, NJ 08648

609-620-0200
FAX 609-620-1200
Home Page: www.gs1us.org
Social Media: *Facebook, Twitter, LinkedIn*

W. Rodney McMullen, Chairman
Bob Carpenter, President and CEO
Laura DiSciullo, Senior Vice President,

Solutions
Bernie Hogan, Senior Vice President
Yegneswaran Kumar, Senior Vice President

Barcodes, eCommerce and data synchronization, to EPC/RFID and business process automation standards.
Frequency: Members 280,000
Founded in 1974

1718 Unite Here International Union
275 Seventh Avenue
New York, NY 10001-6708

212-265-7000
FAX 212-265-3415
E-Mail: ccarrera@unitehere.org
Home Page: www.unitehere.org
Social Media: *Facebook, Twitter, Google+, RSS Feeds*

D. Taylor, President
Tho Thi Do, General VP, Immigration
Sherri Chiesa, Secretary/Treasurer
Peter Ward, Recording Secretary

UNITE HERE represents workers throughout the U.S. and Canada who work in the hotel, gaming, food service, manufacturing, textile, distribution, laundry, and airport industries.
850k Members
Founded in 2004

1719 United States Fashion Industry Association
1140 Connecticut Ave.
Suite 950
Washington, DC 20036

202-419-0444
FAX 202-783-0727
E-Mail: info@usfashionindustry.com
Home Page: www.usfashionindustry.com
Social Media: *Facebook, Twitter, LinkedIn, Google+*

Julia K. Hughes, President
Samantha Sault, VP, Communications

Representing brands, retailers, importers and wholesalers, the association works to eliminate tariffs, quotas and other impediments to the free movement of textiles and apparel globally.
Founded in 1989

1720 Western and English Sales Association
451 E 58th Avenue
Suite 4128
Denver, CO 80216

303-295-1040
800-295-1041
FAX 303-295-0941
E-Mail: info@denver-wesa.com
Home Page: www.denver-wesa.com
Social Media: *Facebook*

Gene House, Chairman
Mark Broughton, President
Scott Piper, Vice President
Gerald Adame, Treasurer
Jay Phillips, Secretary

WESA began under the corporate name Men's Apparel Club of Colorado. The goal was to create a forum where retailers, manufacturers, and sales representatives could conduct business in an atmosphere of fair trade and fellowship.
1200 Members
Founded in 1921

Newsletters

1721 AAFA Newsletter
American Apparel & Footwear Association

1601 N Kent Street
Suite 1200
Arlington, VA 22209

703-524-1864
800-520-2262
FAX 847-522-6741
Home Page: www.apparelandfootwear.org

Kevin M Burke, President
Stephen E Lamar, VP
Scott Elmore, Marketing

The nationwide trade association representing apparel, footwear and other sewn products companies and their suppliers which compete in the global market.
Founded in 2000

1722 Barbara's View/Shopping Guides
Barbara's View

PO Box 531006
Miami, FL 33153-1006

305-757-7638
FAX 305-756-5353
E-Mail: barbara@barbarasview.com
Home Page: www.barbarasview.com

Barbara Wexner Levy, President

Shopping guides for fashion cities around the world.
Cost: $18.00
Frequency: Monthly
Founded in 1976

1723 Clothing Manufacturers Association of the USA
Clothing Manufacturers Association of the USA

770 Broadway
10th Floor
New York, NY 10003-9559

646-654-5000
FAX 646-654-5001

David L Calhoun, CEO

Statistical report on profit sales, production and marketing trends for the men's and boy's tailored clothing industry.
Cost: $30.00
Frequency: Annual
Circulation: 300
Founded in 1933
Mailing list available for rent: 100 names at $200 per M

1724 DNR-Daily News Record
Fairchild Publications

7 W 34th St
New York, NY 10001-8100

212-630-3880
800-360-1700
FAX 212-630-3868
E-Mail: info@dnrnews.com
Home Page: www.dnrnews.com

Samuel Farrel, President/CEO
John Birmingham, Editor-in-Chief
Jim Rossi, Marketing
Don Miller, Circulation Manager
Tom Beebe, Creative Director

Supplies retail fashion, product merchandising and marketing news for men's and boys' fashion.
Cost: $85.00
Frequency: Weekly
Circulation: 15755

1725 International Association of Clothing Designers & Executives Newsletter
475 Park Avenue South
Floor 9 No. 9
New York, NY 10016-6901

212-685-6602
E-Mail: newyorkiacde@cox.net
Home Page: www.iacde.com

Joachim Hensch, President
Mina Henry, Director

1726 The Vision Voice
The Vision Council Of America
225 Reinekers Lane
Suite 700
Alexandria, VA 22314

703-548-4560
866-826-0290
FAX 703-548-4580
E-Mail: info@thevisioncouncil.org
Home Page: www.thevisioncouncil.org
Social Media: *Facebook, Twitter*

Ed Greene, CEO
Brian Carroll, CFO
Maureen Beddis, VP of Marketing & Communications
Greg Chavez, VP of Member Services

Newsletter for the membership of The Vision Council of America. A nonprofit association of manufacturers and distributors of sunglasses and sunglass parts.
12 Pages
Founded in 1940

1727 Uniformer
Professional Apparel Association
994 Old Eagle School Road
Suite 1019
Wayne, PA 19087-1802

610-971-4850
FAX 610-971-4859

Sharon Tannahill, Executive Director

Seeks to enhance the growth of the professional apparel industry by educating uniform retailers.
1200+ Members
16 Pages
Frequency: Quarterly
Circulation: 500

1728 UpFront Newsletter
Embroidery Trade Association
P O Box 794534
Dallas, TX 75379-4534

888-628-2545
FAX 972-755-2561
E-Mail: info@embroiderytrade.org
Home Page: www.embroiderytrade.org

John Swinburn, Executive Director
Dolores Cheek, Manager Of Member Services

A newsletter with advice and information on topics such as marketing, business operations and problem solving
1200 Members
Frequency: Weekly
Founded in 1990

Magazines & Journals

1729 Accessories
Business Journals

50 Day Street
Norwalk, CT 06854

203-853-6015
FAX 203-852-8175
Home Page: www.busjour.com

Britton Jones, President/CEO
Stuart Nifoussi, VP
Mac Brighton, Chairman & COO
Christone Sullivan, Controller

This magazine profiles the national fashion trade for women's accessories.
Cost: $35.00
Frequency: Monthly
Circulation: 100000
Founded in 1931

1730 Apparel Magazine
Susan S. Nichols
801 Gervais St.
Suite 101
Columbia, SC 29201

803-771-7500
800-845-8820
FAX 803-799-1461
E-Mail: cdeberry@apparelmag.com
Home Page: www.apparel.edgl.com

Susan S. Nichols, Publisher
Jordan Speer, Editor in Chief
Cindy DeBerry, Sales Manager

Trade publication for apparel/sewn products, manufacturing executives. Accepts advertising. Covers topics ranging from new products and technology to production management, sourcing, fabrics and financial news.
Cost: $48.00
180 Pages
Frequency: Monthly
Circulation: 18752
Printed in 4 colors on matte stock

1731 California Apparel News
MnM Publishing Corp
110 E 9th Street
Suite A-777
Los Angeles, CA 90079-1777

213-627-3737
E-Mail: info@apparelnews.net
Home Page: www.apparelnews.net

Alison A Nieder, Executive Editor
N Jayne Seward, Fashion Editor
Deborah Belgum, Senior Editor

News and analysis on the largest manufacturing center in the country, special supplements on denim, lingerie, trade shows, textiles and more. Contains the only comprehensive coverage of Los Angeles Fashion Week.
Cost: $89.00
450 Pages
Frequency: Weekly
Founded in 1945

1732 Children's Business
Fairchild Publications
Po Box 5121
New York, NY 10087-5121

212-630-3880
800-932-4724
FAX 212-630-3868
E-Mail: debra.goldberg@fairchildpub.com
Home Page: www.fairchildmediakit.com

Debra Goldberg, Publisher
Tracy R Mitchell, Executive Editor
Ralph Erardy, Senior VP

Infants' and toddlers' wear, juvenile merchandise, footwear and toys.
Cost: $5.00
45 Pages
Frequency: Monthly
Circulation: 30458
ISSN: 0884-2280
Founded in 1985

1733 Clothing & Textile Research Journal
International Textile & Apparel Association
PO Box 70687
Knoxville, TN 37938-0687

865-992-1535
FAX 916-722-8149
E-Mail: info@itaaonline.org
Home Page: www.itaaonline.org
Social Media: *Facebook*

Jana Hawley, President
Laurel E Wilsonn, VP
Nancy Rutherford,Ph.D, Executive Director

Offers the latest information on all areas of clothing and textiles.
Cost: $85.00
64 Pages
Frequency: Quarterly
Circulation: 1300
ISSN: 0887-3020
Founded in 1944
Printed in one color on matte stock

1734 Costume! Business
Gift Basket Review
815 Haines Street
Jacksonville, FL 32206-6025

904-634-1902
800-729-6338
FAX 904-633-8764
Home Page: www.festivities-pub.com

Debra Paulk, Publisher
Kathy Horak, Editor

News and current issues in the costume retailing business.
Cost: $29.95
Frequency: Quarterly
Circulation: 8,000

1735 Dress
Costume Society of America
390 Amwell Road
Suite 402
Hillsborough, NJ 08844

908-359-1471
800-272-9447
FAX 908-450-1118
Home Page: www.costumesocietyamerica.com/
Social Media: *Facebook, Twitter*

Sally Halverston, Associate Editor
Rosalyn M Lester, President
Linda Welters, Editor-in-Chief
Margaret Ordonez, Managing Editor

Journal of the Costume Society of America. The Costume Society of America advances the global understanding of all aspects of dress and appearance.
ISSN: 0361-2112
Founded in 1973
Printed in on matte stock

1736 Fashion Accessories Magazine
SCM Publications
10 DeGraaf Court
PO Box 859
Mahwah, NJ 07430

201-684-9222
FAX 201-684-9228
Home Page: www.accessoriesmagazine.com

Lorrie Frost, Publisher
Lauren Parker, Editor

Offers information on the latest in fashion, jewelry and accessories.
Founded in 1951

1737 Fashion Market Magazine
Fashion Market Magazine Group
617 West 46th Street
New York, NY 10036

212-541-9350
FAX 212-541-9340

Home Page: www.fmmg.com
Social Media: *Facebook, Twitter*

Victoria Monjo, Editor
Nicole Phillip, Fashion Editor

News for the apparel industry in New York, with original pictures and news in fashion, technology, finance and real estate.
Cost: $84.74
64 Pages
Frequency: Monthly
Circulation: 80000
Founded in 1985

1738 Footwear Plus
Symphony Publishing
36 Cooper Square
4th Floor
New York, NY 10003

646-278-1550
FAX 646-278-1553
Home Page: www.footwearplusmagazine.com
Social Media: *Facebook, Twitter*

Greg Dutter, Editor-in-Chief
Pauline Lee, Associate Editor

Focuses on fashion, merchandising, trends and ideas in the retail footwear industry.
Cost: $50.58
Founded in 1989
Printed in on glossy stock

1739 Hosiery News
Home Sewing Association
105 Mall Boulevard
Po Box 369
Monroeville, PA 15146

412-372-5950
FAX 412-372-5953
Home Page: www.sewing.org

Dotty Grexa, President
Dale Sutherland, Treasurer
Jenna Sheldon, Director Trade Show/Meetings
Jenny Prevatte, Director Information Services

It covers all THA activities, industry news, personnel changes, statistics, legislative and regulatory concerns, marketing, technology, financial reports and new product information.
Cost: $69.00
Frequency: Monthly
Founded in 1915

1740 Impressions Magazine
1145 Sanctuary Parkway
Suite 355
Alpharetta, GA 30009-4772

800-241-9034
E-Mail: impressions@bill.com
Home Page: www.impressionsmag.com

Chris Casey, Publisher
Marcia Derryberry, Editor-in-Chief
Jamar Laster, Senior Editor

Offers news and information on the development or imprintable and imprinted sportswear and textiles.
Cost: $69.00
Circulation: 30000

1741 Industrial Fabric Products Review
U.S. Industrial Fabrics Association International
1801 County Road BW
Roseville, MN 55113-4061

651-222-2508
800-225-4324
FAX 651-631-9334
E-Mail: generalinfo@ifai.com
Home Page: www.ifai.com

Stephen M Warner, President
JoAnne Ferris, Director Of Marketing

Keeps individuals up to date on the information needed to keep their business growing.
Cost: $69.00
Frequency: Monthly
Founded in 1915

1742 Juvenile Merchandising
EW Williams Publications Company
2125 Center Ave
Suite 305
Fort Lee, NJ 07024-5898

201-592-7007
FAX 201-592-7171
E-Mail: philpl@ewwpi.com
Home Page: www.williamspublications.com

Andrew Williams, President
Phillip Russo, Publisher
Peter Berlinski, Editor-in-Chief

Offers news on the juvenile clothing, accessories and furniture industry.
Cost: $85.00
Circulation: 8000
Founded in 1938

1743 Knit Ovations Magazine
Woolknit Associates
267 5th Avenue
Suite 806-807
New York, NY 10016

212-683-7785
FAX 212-683-2682

Eleanor Kairalla, Publisher

Fashions in knitwear for men and women trends in market; fashion color forecasts; guest features on knitwear by retail executives.

1744 Made to Measure
Halper Publishing Company
633 Skokie Blvd
Suite 490
Northbrook, IL 60062

224-406-8850
FAX 224-406-8850
E-Mail: news@uniformmarket.com
Home Page: www.madetomeasuremag.com
Social Media: *Facebook, Twitter*

Rick Levine, President

Serves the uniform and career apparel industry.
Frequency: Bi-annually
Circulation: 25000
Founded in 1930
Printed in 4 colors on glossy stock

1745 Market Maker
Advanstar Communications
6200 Canoga Avenue
2nd Floor
Woodland Hills, CA 91367

818-593-5000
FAX 818-593-5020
E-Mail: info@advanstar.com
Home Page: www.advanstar.com

Chirs DeMoulin, VP
Susannah George, Marketing Director
Joseph Loggia, President

Industry fashions
Cost: $2.00
Circulation: 14900
Founded in 1987

1746 Menswear Retailing Magazine
Business Journals Inc
1384 Broadway
Suite 11
New York, NY 10018-6111

212-686-4412
FAX 212-686-6821
E-Mail: karena@mrketplace.com
Home Page: www.mrketplace.com

Bethany Raborn, Manager
Stuart Nifoussi, VP
Karen Alberg, Editor

Includes accurate information on the menswear retailing business, insightful analysis, bold ideas and real world fashion.
Circulation: monthly

1747 Needle's Eye
Union Special Corporation
1 Union Special Plz
Huntley, IL 60142-7007

847-669-5101
FAX 847-669-4535
E-Mail: dkanies@unionspecial.com
Home Page: www.unionspecial.com

Terence A Hitpas, President

Industry events, developments in machine-sewed products, informs about improved manufacturing methods, and promotes interest in Union Special machinery.
Frequency: Monthly
Circulation: 28595
Founded in 1881

1748 Notions
American Sewing Guild
9660 Hillcroft St
Suite 510
Houston, TX 77096-3866

713-729-3000
FAX 713-729-9230
Home Page: www.asg.org

Margo Martin, Executive Director

Contains articles written exclusively for us by the world's leading sewing experts, messages from the ASG Board of Directors and ASG National Headquarters, information about the latest sewing products and books.
Frequency: Quarterly

1749 Outerwear
Creative Marketing Plus
213-37 39th Avenue
Suite 228
Bayside, NY 11361

718-606-0767
FAX 718-606-6345
E-Mail: rharrow@creativemarketingplus.com
Home Page: www.creativemarketingplus.com

Richard Harrow, Presidetn/CEO
Duke Wollsoncoft, Creative Director

Focuses on outerwear buyers' needs, fashion trends, as well as leading buying offices and promotional plans.
Cost: $62.00
30 Pages
Frequency: Monthly
Circulation: 16000
Founded in 1983
Printed in 4 colors on glossy stock

1750 Printwear Magazine
National Business Media Inc
PO Box 1416
Broomfield, CO 80038-1416

303-469-0424
800-669-0424
FAX 303-465-3424
E-Mail: pweditor@nbm.com
Home Page: www.nbm.com

Bob Wieber, President
Mark Buchanan, Editor

Screen printing and embroidery equipment and technique, apparel styles and trends, heat-applied graphics, special effects printing and embroidery, business management and sales/marketing skills, digital transfers and sublimation, promotional products, embroidery digitizing, new products and the latest industry literature.
Frequency: Monthly
Circulation: 25000

1751 Promotional Sportswear
520 W Foothill Pkwy
Corona, CA 92882-6305

951-279-9327
FAX 909-279-9327
E-Mail: customerservice@promowear.com
Home Page: www.promowear.com

Ted Taylor, Owner

Commercial direct screen printing, embroidery and complete art services on the highest quality sportswear available.

1752 Promowear
National Bussines Media Inc
P.O Box 1416
Broomfield, CO 80038

303-469-0424
800-669-0424
FAX 303-469-5730
E-Mail: pweditor@nbm.com
Home Page: www.nbm.com/pr
Social Media: Facebook, Twitter

Bob Wieber, President
Mark Buchanan, Editor

The latest style trends, detailed product and sourcing information, sales and marketing tips, industry news.
Frequency: 6 Issues/Year
Founded in 1990

1753 Stitches
4800 Street Road
Trevose, PA 19053

800-546-1350
800-546-1350
FAX 215-953-3107
E-Mail: mrollender@asicentral.com
Home Page: www.asipublications.com/stitches
Social Media: Facebook, Twitter

Nicole Rollender, Editor
Ed Koehler, Advertising Director

Information and the latest technology for embroidery professionals.
Circulation: 17233
Founded in 1987

1754 Tack N' Togs Merchandising
The Miller Publishing Company
12400 Whitewater Dr
Suite 160
Minnetonka, MN 55343-4590

952-931-0211
FAX 952-938-1832
Home Page: www.tackntogs.com
Social Media: Facebook, Twitter

Sarah Muirhead, Publisher
Julie Golson-Richards, Associate Editor
Cindy Miller-Johnson, Adverting Sales Manager
Michelle Adaway, Advertising Account Excutive

Providing the latest news and information on equine retailing.
Frequency: Monthly
Circulation: 20424
Founded in 1970

1755 Textile Rental Magazine
Textile Rental Services Association
1800 Diagonal Rd
Suite 200
Alexandria, VA 22314-2842

703-519-0029
877-770-9274
FAX 703-519-0026
E-Mail: trsa@trsa.org
Home Page: www.trsa.org

Roger Cocivera, President/CEO
Jack Morgan, Editor

Packed with valuable tips and ideas.
Frequency: Monthly

1756 Uniformer
Professional Apparel Association
994 Old Eagle School Road
Suite 1019
Wayne, PA 19087-1866

610-971-4850
FAX 771-261-4859

Hope Silverman, Executive Director
Frequency: Quarterly

1757 Vows Magazine
Peter Grimes
24 Daisy St
Ladera Ranch, CA 92694-0709

949-388-4848
FAX 949-388-8448
E-Mail: info@vowsmagazine.com
Home Page: www.vowsmagazine.com

Kori Grimes, Owner
Karlnon Nazarro, Director

Bridal retail, including how to survive as an independent retailer, how to merchandise and promote your business, how to effectively sell and train a sales staff, as well as identifying fashion and consumer shopping trends and preferences.
Founded in 1990

1758 Wearables Business
Advertising Specialty Institute
4800 E Street Rd
Langhorne, PA 19053-6698

215-953-4000
800-546-1350
FAX 215-953-3045
E-Mail: nrollender@asicentral.com
Home Page: www.asicentral.com

Timothy M Andrews, President
Richard Fairfield, Publisher

Educational resource for promotional apparel distributors.
Cost: $1320.00
Frequency: Monthly
Circulation: 13533
Founded in 1987

1759 Women's Wear Daily
Fairchild Publications
750 3rd Ave
New York, NY 10017-2703

212-630-3500
800-289-0273
FAX 212-630-3566
E-Mail: wwd@pubservice.com
Home Page: www.wwd.com
Social Media: Twitter

Mary G Berner, CEO
Christine Guilfoyle, Publisher
Edward Nardoza, Editor in Chief

Serves as the voice of authority, international newswire and agent of change for the fashion, beauty and retail industries.
Cost: $195.00
Frequency: Daily
Circulation: 43618
Founded in 1892

Trade Shows

1760 ASD/AMD Las Vegas Trade Show
ASD/AMD Group

6255 W. Sunset Blvd
19th Floor
Los Angeles, CA 90028

323-817-2200
800-421-4511
FAX 310-481-1900
Home Page: www.asdonline.com

Greg Farrar, President
Mark Hosbein, Marketing

Provides a portfolio of innovative face to face, print and online products for the wholesale industry.
10000 Attendees
Frequency: BiAnnual/August/March

1761 ASG Conference
American Sewing Guild
9660 Hillcroft
Suite 510
Houston, TX 77096

713-729-3000
FAX 713-729-9230
Home Page: www.asg.org

Martha Ramey, President

Gives all Guild members the opportunity to meet sewing professionals, industry representatives, and other sewing enthusiasts from around the country, and to participate in sewing seminars and sewing related special events and tours.
20000 Attendees
Frequency: Annual/July

1762 AccessoriesTheShow
Accessories Magazine
50 Day Street
Norwalk, CT 06854

203-853-6015
800-358-6678
FAX 203-852-8175
E-Mail: sharon@busjour.com
Home Page: www.accessoriestheshow.com

Britton Jonese, President
Sharon Enright, VP

All accessories trade event in the fashion capital of the US attracts thousands of fine specialty buyers
22k + Attendees

1763 Action Sports Retailer Trade Exposition
Miller Freeman Publications
PO Box 1899
Laguna Beach, CA 92652

847-296-6742
FAX 847-391-9827
E-Mail: info@nsga.org
Home Page: www.nsga.org

Matt Carlson, President & Ceo

Manufacturers, suppliers, retailers, buyers, guides, outfitters, distributors, importers, exporters, press and industry influencers have converged at Fly-Fishing Retailer to chart the future of their business.

1764 American Flock Association Annual Meeting
American Flock Association
6 Beacon Street
Suite 1125
Boston, MA 02108

617-303-6288
FAX 704-671-2366
E-Mail: info@flocking.org
Home Page: www.flocking.org

Karl Spilhaus, President
Steve Rosenthal, Managing Director

Provides positive leadership to foster a strong flock industry in North America.
60 Members
Founded in 1984

1765 Apparel Importers Trade and Transportation Conference
United States Fashion Industry Association (USFIA)
1140 Connecticut Ave.
Suite 950
Washington, DC 20036

202-419-0444
FAX 202-783-0727
Home Page: www.importersapparelconference.com
Social Media: *Facebook, Twitter, LinkedIn, Google+*

Julia K. Hughes, President

Hot topics from the apparel products supply chain.
Frequency: Annual
Founded in 1989

1766 Apparel Show of the Americas
Bobbin Publishing/Miller Freeman
PO Box 279
Euless, TX 76039

817-215-1600
800-693-1363
FAX 817-215-1666
E-Mail: bobbin.expoinfo@mfi.com
Home Page: www.mfi.com

Betty Webb, Trade Show Director

Conference, seminar and 329 exhibits of equipment, fabrics, accessories and services for sewn products and apparel.
Founded in 1992

1767 Arnold Sports Festival
Arnold Sports Festival
1215 Worthington Woods Blvd.
Worthington, OH 43805

614-431-2600
FAX 516-625-1023
E-Mail: lpinney@arnoldexpo.com
Home Page: www.arnoldsportsfestival.com
Social Media: *Facebook, Twitter*

Lucy Pinneyr, Event Chair
Brent LaLonda, Media Contact

Five days of fitness equipment, sports entertainment, supplements, apparel and athletic stars, with more than 17,000 competitive athletes in 40 sporting events. Over 500 exhibitors.
150M+ Attendees
Frequency: March
Founded in 1976

1768 Bead and Button Show
Kalmbach Publishing Company
21027 Crossroads Circle
PO Box 1612
Waukesha, WI 53187-1612

262-796-8776
800-533-6644
FAX 262-796-1615
Home Page: www.beadandbuttonshow.com
Social Media: *Facebook*

Gerald Boettcher, President

The biggest bead show in the country.
3500 Attendees
Frequency: Annual/May
Founded in 1985

1769 Big and Tall Men's Apparel Needs Show
Specialty Trade Show

3939 Hardie Road
Coconut Grove, FL 33133-6437

305-663-6635
FAX 305-661-8118
E-Mail: info@spectrade.com
Home Page: www.spectrade.com

A gathering of buyers and vendors of apparel and accessories for tall and plus sized men. 200 Exhibitors.
1,500 Attendees
Frequency: February/August

1770 Chicago Men's Collective: Winter
Merchandise Mart Properties Inc
222 Merchandise Mart Plaza
Suite 470
Chicago, IL 60654

312-527-7635
800-677-6278
E-Mail: bschedler@mmart.com
Home Page: www.mmart.com

Bruce Schedler, VP

Approximately 300 exhibitors and over 1,000 lines of product featuring men's fashion business attire.
5000 Attendees
Frequency: August

1771 Convergence
Handweavers Guild of America
1255 Buford Highway
Suite 211
Suwanee, GA 30024-1701

678-730-0010
FAX 678-730-0836
E-Mail: hga@weavespindye.org
Home Page: www.weavespindye.org

Nancy Peck, President
Mary Ann Sanborn, VP
Elaine Bradley, Marketing
Sandra Bowles, Executive Director

Conference for everyone who loves and works in fiber.
3000 Attendees
Frequency: June, Biennial

1772 E-Sports & Business Services Show at the Super Show
Communications & Show Management
1450 NE 123rd Street
North Miami, FL 33161

305-893-8771
FAX 305-893-8783
Home Page: www.bizbash.com
Social Media: *Facebook, Twitter*

Tom Cove, President

Retailers, distributors, wholesalers, importers/exporters and other buyers of sports related products come for 10,000 exhibits of sports apparel, footwear, accessories and e-commerce products and services.
100k Attendees
Frequency: Annual/January

1773 EGA National Seminar
Embroiderers' Guild of America
1355 Bardstown Road
Suite 157
Louisville, KY 40204

502-589-6956
FAX 502-584-7900
E-Mail: sem2010@egausa.org
Home Page: www.egausa.org

Lorie Welker, President
Barbara Harrison, VP

Lectures, workshops and networking.
20000 Attendees

1774 Eastern Men's Market/Collective
AmericasMart Atlanta

240 Peachtree Street NW
Suite 2200
Atlanta, GA 30303-1327

404-220-3000
800-285-6278
FAX 404-220-3030
E-Mail: webmaster@americasmart.com
Home Page: www.americasmart.com
Social Media: *Facebook, Twitter*

Jeff Portman, President/COO
Hank Almquist, VP

An outlet for the latest trends and designs in products and services.
500 Attendees

1775 Embroidery Trade Association Convention
Embroidery Trade Association
PO Box 794534
Dallas, TX 75379-4534

972-247-0415
888-628-2545
FAX 972-755-2561
E-Mail: info@embroiderytrade.org
Home Page: www.embroiderytrade.org

John Swinburn, Executive Director

An organization with the objective to continually strengthen the commercial embroidery business.
1200 Members
Founded in 1990

1776 FFANY Collections
Fashion Footwear Association of New York
274 Madison Avenue
Suite 1701
New York, NY 10016

212-751-6422
FAX 212-751-6404
E-Mail: info@ffany.org
Home Page: www.ffany.org
Social Media: *Facebook, Twitter*

Joseph C Moore, President/CEO
Phyllis Rein, Senior VP

The essential venue for fashion footwear. Held at FFANY participating show rooms.
300 Attendees
Frequency: August
Founded in 1980

1777 Fabric Exhibition
Advanstar Communications
2501 Colorado Avenue
Suite 280
Santa Monica, CA 90404

310-857-7500
FAX 310-857-7500
E-Mail: info@advanstar.com
Home Page: www.advanstar.com

Joseph Loggia, President
Chris DeMoulin, VP
Susannah George, Marketing Director

Conference and exhibition of interest to those in the fabric and garment industry.
7000 Attendees

1778 Fitness Show at the Super Show
Communications & Show Management
1450 NE 123rd Street
North Miami, FL 33161

305-893-8771
FAX 305-893-8783
Home Page: www.bizbash.com

Tom Cove, President

Retailers, distributors, wholesalers, importers/exporters and other buyers of sports related products come for 10,000 exhibits of sports ap-

parel, footwear, accessories and e-commerce products and services.
100k Attendees
Frequency: Annual/January

1779 Gatlinburg Apparel & Jewelry Market
Norton Shows
PO Box 265
Gatlinburg, TN 37738

865-436-6151
FAX 865-436-6152
Home Page: www.nortonshows.com

Tom Norton, Show Manager/Owner
Linda Norton, Owner

Trade show that has wholesale, cash-and-carry, ladies, men's, and children's apparel, fashion jewelry, accessories, fine jewelry and gifts from around the world. There are 500-700 booths.
20000 Attendees
Frequency: March/June/Sept/Nov
Founded in 1987
Mailing list available for rent: 70,000 names

1780 Global Leather
American Apparel & Footwear Association
1601 N Kent Street
Suite 1200
Arlington, VA 22205

703-524-1864
800-520-2262
FAX 847-522-6741
E-Mail: info@globalleathers.com
Home Page: globalleathers.com

Kevin M Burke, President
Stephen E Lamar, VP
Dawn Van Dyke, Marketing

Showcases the best in new leather materials and components for footwear leather, needle and allied trades of North America. Brings together hundreds of exhibitors from the major sourcing cities around the world, showcasing thousands of products.
1500 Attendees
Frequency: February/August
Founded in 1981

1781 Holiday Sample Sale
San Francisco Design Center
635 8th Street
San Francisco, CA 94103

415-490-5800
FAX 415-490-5885
Home Page: www.sfdesigncenter.com

Dianne Travalini, Show Director
Aruex Dalmacio, Show Manager

Open to the public and offers jewelry, accessories and leather items, gift items, home accessories, housewares, toys and apparel.
11000 Attendees
Frequency: November

1782 Hospitality Design Expo
American Flock Association
6 Beacon Street
Suite 1125
Boston, MA 02108

617-303-6288
FAX 617-542-2199
E-Mail: info@flocking.org
Home Page: www.flocking.org

Steve Rosenthal, Director

Provides positive leadership to foster a strong flock industry in North America.
Frequency: May

1783 IACDE Convention
Internatl Assoc of Clothing Designers & Executives

835 NW 36th Terrace
Oklahoma City, OK 73118

405-602-8037
FAX 405-602-8038
Home Page: www.iacde.com

Joachim Hensch, President
Mina Henry, Director

Focus is on the retail link in the apparel supply chain. The students and faculty of the Fashion Institute of Technology are involved in the planning and presentation of many of the convention programs.
Frequency: Annual
Founded in 1910

1784 ISAM: International Swimwear and Activewear Market
California Market Center
110 E 9th Street
Los Angeles, CA 90079

213-303-3688
800-225-6278
FAX 213-630-3708
E-Mail: info@californiamarketcenter.com

Barbara Brady, Director

Serves the swimwear and resortwear industry.
Frequency: August/September
Founded in 1978

1785 Imprinted Sportswear Shows (ISS)
Imprinted Sportswear Shows (ISS)
Nielson Business Media
1145 Sanctuary Parkway, Ste 355
Alpharetta, GA 30004-4756

800-933-8735
FAX 770-777-8700
E-Mail: issshows@xpressreg.net
Home Page: www.issshows.com

David Loechner, President
Michael Alicea, Senior VP

Shows in: Long Beach, Orlando, Atlantic City, Atlanta and Fort Worth. Showcases the newest products, apparel, and equipment featuring new technology, sublimation, and techniques with hands-on demos. There are new conferences at every show providing learning and networking opportunities. Discuss business opportunities, best practices, artistic trends, and techniques.
Founded in 1981

1786 International Fashion Boutique Show
Advanstar Communications
757 3rd Ave
New York, NY 10017-2013

212-951-6600
FAX 212-951-6793
E-Mail: info@advanstar.com
Home Page: www.advanstar.com

Offers a variety of fashion trade shows throughout each year at the Javitz Convention Center in New York.
25000 Attendees

1787 International Fashion Fabric Exhibition
Advanstar Communications
641 Lexington Avenue
8th Floor
New York, NY 10022

212-951-6600
FAX 212-951-6793
E-Mail: info@advanstar.com
Home Page: www.advanstar.com

Joseph Loggia, CEO
Tony Calanca, Executive Vice President
Steven Sturm, Executive Vice President

Conference and exhibits of interest to those in the fabric and garment industries.
15000 Attendees

1788 International Hosiery Exposition
Home Sewing Association
105 Mall Boulevard
PO Box 369
Monroeville, PA 15146

412-372-5950
FAX 412-372-5953
Home Page: www.sewing.org

Dotty Grexa, President
Jenna Sheldon, Director Trade Show/Meetings
Jenny Prevatte, Director Information Services

Specialize in the latest hosiery and sewn products industries' supplies and services. 250 Exhibitors.
10000 Attendees

1789 International Intimate Apparel Lingerie Show
Specialty Trade Show
3939 Hardle Road
Coconut Grove, FL 33133-6437

305-663-6635
FAX 305-661-8118
E-Mail: info@spectrade.com
Home Page: www.lingerieshow.cc

Jeff Yunis, President

Specializing in lingerie and adult products.
2,000 Attendees
Frequency: October

1790 International Kids Fashion Show
Advanstar Communications
641 Lexington Avenue
8th Floor
New York, NY 10022

212-951-6600
FAX 212-951-6793
E-Mail: info@advanstar.com
Home Page: www.advanstar.com

Joseph Loggia, CEO
Thomas Ehardt, Executive Vice President

Children's fashions, accessories, gift items, and footwear.
3500 Attendees
Frequency: Jan/March/August/October

1791 International Show at the Super Show
Communications & Show Management
1450 NE 123rd Street
North Miami, FL 33161

305-808-3531
FAX 305-893-8783
Home Page: www.bizbash.com

Richard Aaron, President
David Adler, CEO, Founder
Ann Keusch, COO

Retailers, distributors, wholesalers, importers/exporters and other buyers of sports related products come for 10,000 exhibits of sports apparel, footwear, accessories and e-commerce products and services.
100k Attendees
Frequency: January

1792 International Vision Expo
The Vision Council of America
225 Reinekers Lane
Suite 700
Alexandria, VA 22314

703-548-4560
866-826-0290
FAX 703-548-4580
E-Mail: info@thevisioncouncil.org
Home Page: www.thevisioncouncil.org

Ed Greene, President
Brian Carroll, VP
Maureen Beddis, Marketing Director

Learn about new market information, statistics, training and industry trends.
Frequency: Biennial
Founded in 1999

1793 International Western Apparel and Accessories Market

Dallas Market Center
2100 Stemmons Freeway
Dallas, TX 75207

214-655-6100
800-325-6587
FAX 800-637-6833
Home Page: www.dallasmarketcenter.com

Bill Winsor, President/CEO
Pat Zajac, Contact Home Expo

Offers array of services geared toward helping retailers expand business and increase profits.
200M Attendees
Frequency: March/August
Founded in 1957

1794 Licensed Sports Show at the Super Show

Communications & Show Management
1450 NE 123rd Street
North Miami, FL 33161

305-808-3531
FAX 305-893-8783
Home Page: www.bizbash.com

Richard Aaron, President
David Adler, CEO, Founder
Ann Keusch, COO

Retailers, distributors, wholesalers, importers/exporters and other buyers of sports related products come for 10,000 exhibits of sports apparel, footwear, accessories and e-commerce products and services.
100k Attendees
Frequency: January

1795 MAGIC International Show

MAGIC International
2501 Colorado Avenue
Suite 280
Santa Monica, CA 90404

310-857-7500
FAX 310-593-5020
E-Mail: cs@MAGIConline.com
Home Page: www.magiconline.com

Joe Loggia, President/CEO
Francine Rich, Womens Sales Contact
Christopher Giffin, Vice President Sales
Pam Thompson, Attendee Relations

Fashion trade show in Las Vegas. 3,000 exhibitors.
75000 Attendees
Frequency: February/August
Founded in 1933

1796 Management Conference & Team Dealer Summit

National Sporting Goods Association
1601 Feehanville Drive
Suite 300
Mount Prospect, IL 60056

847-296-6742
800-815-5422
FAX 847-391-9827
E-Mail: info@nsga.org
Home Page: www.nsga.org

Bob Dickman, Chairman of the Board
Matt Carlson, President/CEO
Dustin Dobrin, Research and Information Director

The goal is to stimulate fresh, agile thinking. How you and your company can create a culture that encourages and stimulates action, focus on the solution and fresh thinking.

1797 Manufacturers Wholesalers Outerwear Sportswear Show

I. Spiewak & Sons
463 7th Avenue
10th Floor
New York, NY 10018-6505

212-695-1620
800-223-6850
FAX 212-629-4803
E-Mail: jerry@spiewak.com
Home Page: www.spiewak.com

Gerald Spiewak, Executive Director
Roy Spiewak, President

180 booths for manufacturers and importers of outerwear and rainwear.
3M Attendees
Frequency: January

1798 Material World

Urban Expositions
1395 S Marietta Parkway
Building 400, Suite 210
Marietta, GA 30067

770-180-0972
800-318-2238
FAX 678-285-7469
Home Page: www.material-world.com

Doug Miller, President
Tim von Gal, Executive VP
Suzanne Pruitt, Contact

From design to delivery, Material World is the international full package, sourcing and fashion information event for the fabric related industries.
10600 Attendees
Frequency: May

1799 Men's and Boy's Apparel Show

Miami International Merchandise Mart
777 NW 72nd Avenue
Miami, FL 33126

305-665-5630
FAX 305-261-3659
Home Page: www.miamimart.net

Martiza Agudo, President
Glorys Covo, Administrator

This is a three-day show where wholesale buyers will find an extensive display of apparel lines including Calvin Klein, Perruzo, Supreme, just to name a few.
1000 Attendees
Frequency: April/May

1800 National Bridal Market: Fall

Merchandise Mart Properties Inc
222 Merchandise Mart Plaza
Suite 470
Chicago, IL 60654

312-527-4141
800-677-6278
FAX 312-527-7971
E-Mail: mmailand@mmart.com
Home Page: www.mmart.com

Christopher Kennedy, President
Stephanie Ambuehl, Marketing

Specializing in leading bridal and special occasion resources for department and specialty stores.
3000 Attendees
Frequency: October

1801 National Halloween & Costume & Party Show

Transworld Exhibits
1850 Oak Street
Northfield, IL 60093

847-784-6905
800-323-5462

FAX 847-446-3523
Home Page: www.tweshows.com

Joe Thaler, CEO
Paul O'Connor, Executive Director

Attracts people from across the US and over 50 foreign countries to see what over 700 manufacturers and distributors are showcasing as new and exciting for parties, shops and haunted houses. Free educational seminars and workshops.
10000 Attendees
Frequency: February

1802 National Needlework Market

The National NeedleArts Association
1100-H Brandywine Blvd
Zanesville, OH 43701

740-455-6773
800-889-8662
FAX 740-452-2552
E-Mail: info@tnna.org
Home Page: www.tnna.org

Enabling professionals to come together to share knowledge, products and experiences.
5M Attendees
Frequency: Annual

1803 National Sewing Show

Home Sewing Association
PO Box 369
Monroeville, PA 15146

412-372-5950
FAX 412-372-5953
Home Page: www.sewing.org

Dotty Grexa, President

Offers free sewing projects, guidelines and also a chat room where you can share with other about your ideas and collaborate on others.
Frequency: September

1804 New England Apparel Club

New England Apparel Club
75 McNeil Way
Suite 207
Dedham, MA 02026

781-326-9223
FAX 781- 32- 689
E-Mail: neacrlg@aol.com
Home Page: www.neacshow.com

Richard Usherwood, President
Donald Hurowitz, Vice President
Rhonda Goldberg, Executive Director

2500 regional sales reps exhibiting clothing and related equipment, supplies and services.
2000 Attendees
Frequency: October, Boston

1805 Northstar Fashion Exhibitors

Northstar Fashion Exhibitors
175 Kellogg Blvd West
St Paul, MN 55102

763-546-8717
800-272-6972
FAX 763-546-9176
E-Mail: northstarfashion@aol.com
Home Page: northstarfashion.com

Rick Siegel, President
Stanley Kaye, Show Coordinator
Debi Higgins, Manager

Trade show collections for men's, women's, Childrens apparel, accessories and textiles. 250 Booths.
1,260 Attendees
Frequency: 5/Year

1806 Northwest Shoe Traveler's Buying Shoe Market

Northwest Shoe Traveler's

12630 12th Street N
Lake Elmo, MN 55042

651-436-2709
FAX 651-436-2028

Teri Tompkins, Show Manager

Trade show collections for men's, women's and Childrens.
250 Attendees
Frequency: January

1807 Off-Price Specialist Show
Off Price Specialist Center
16985 W Bluemound Road
Suite 210
Brookfield, WI 53005

262-782-1600
FAX 262-782-1601
E-Mail: info@offpriceshow.com
Home Page: www.offpriceshow.com
Social Media: *Facebook, Twitter*

Stephen Krogulski, President/CEO
David Lapidos, Executive Vice President
Faye Osvatic, Buyers Contact
Kevin Redlich, Product Manager

Premiere show for off-price apparel and accessories.
12000 Attendees
Frequency: May 8-10
Founded in 1995

1808 Outdoor Retailer Summer Market
Nielsen Sports Group
31910 Del Obispo
Suite 200
San Juan Capistrano, CA 92675

949-226-5722
Home Page: www.outdoorretailer.com

Kenji Haroutunian, Director
Margle Lelvis, Marketing
Krista Dill, Account Executive
Jennifer Holcomb, Marketing Manager
Kenji Haroutunian, Show Director

The leading growth vehicle for brands that are interested in progressing and advancing into multiple channels of the outdoor marketplace.
17000 Attendees
Frequency: August

1809 Outdoor Retailer Winter Market
VNU Expositions
PO Box 1899
Laguna Beach, CA 92652

949-226-5722
FAX 949-226-5625
Home Page: www.outdoorretailer.com

Marisa Nicholson, National Sales Manager
Paul Dillman, Senior Account Executive
Peter Devin, Group Show Director
David Lockner, Manager

Features the most comprehensive collection of outdoor apparel, gear, equipment, climbing technology, footwear, ski mountaineering, hunting, rescue outerwear and accessory companies from which to buy products.

1810 PGA Merchandise Show
Reed Exhibition Companies
383 Main Avenue
Suite 3
Norwalk, CT 06851

203- 84- 562
800-840-5628
FAX 203-840-9628
E-Mail: inquiry@pga.reedexpo.com
Home Page: www.pgaexpo.com

Andre Smith, Director Marketing/Special Events
Marc Simon, Group Sales Director
Sherry Major, Media Contact

World's largest golf industry trade event. Open to retail buyers and golf industry professionals. Not open to the public.
38500 Attendees
Frequency: January
Founded in 1954

1811 Performance & Lifestyle Footwear Show at the Super Show
Communications & Show Management
1450 NE 123rd Street
North Miami, FL 33161

305-893-8771
FAX 305-893-8783
Home Page: www.bizbash.com

Richard Aaron, President
David Adler, CEO/President
Chad Kaydo, Editor in Chief
Dana Price, COO

Retailers, distributors, wholesalers, importers/exporters and other buyers of sports related products come for 10,000 exhibits of sports apparel, footwear, accessories and e-commerce products and services.
100k Attendees
Frequency: January

1812 Printwear Show
National Business Media Inc
PO Box 1416
Broomfield, CO 80038

303-469-0424
800-669-0424
FAX 303-465-3424
Home Page: www.nbmshows.com
Social Media: *Twitter*

Bob Wieber, President

The event for buyers involved in screen printing, embroidery, heat applied graphics, digital textile printing, sublimation and apparel.
Frequency: August

1813 Professional Apparel Association Trade
Professional Apparel Association
994 Old Eagle School Road
Suite 1019
Wayne, PA 19087-1866

610-971-4850
FAX 610-971-4859

Dr. Sharon Tannahill, Executive Director

Exhibitors display health care and hospitality uniforms, shoes, and accessories, and career apparel. Workshops and seminars for uniform retailers are also available. Biennial.

1814 Seattle Trend Show
Pacific Northwest Apparel Association
P.O. Box 3050
Issaquah, WA 98027

206-767-9200
FAX 206-767-0707
E-Mail: pnaa@nwtrendshow.com
Home Page: www.nwtrendshow.com

Jane Powell, Director
Gary Morgan, President

Show and exhibits of apparel and related accessories.
2000 Attendees
Frequency: Jan/Apr/Jun/Aug/Oct

1815 Shoe Market of America
Miami Merchandise Mart
2335 NW 107 Ave
Suite 2M31 Box 120
Miami, FL 33172

786-331-9000
FAX 786-331-9955

E-Mail: info@smota.com
Home Page: www.smota.com

Dianne Travalini, Executive Director
Alex Meme, Manager

Features the entire spectrum of footwear companies.
2500 Attendees
Frequency: 3x per year

1816 Southwestern Shoe Traveler's
Southwestern Shoe Traveler's Association
1024 Oxfordshire Dr.
Cannollton, TX 75007

972-446-4089
FAX 214-292-9691
E-Mail: southwestshoeexpo@verizon.net

Mona Bennight, Executive Director

Definitive footwear trade site for footwear retailers.
1800 Attendees
Frequency: June

1817 Syracuse Super Show
Oncenter Complex
800 So. State Street
Syracuse, NY

315-488-4201
E-Mail: abc43@juno.com
Home Page: www.syracusesupershow.com

Carol Sweet, Menswear Contact
Dick Pirozzolo, Footwear Contact
Rhonda Goldberg, Women's & Children's Contact

Largest assortment of fashions in Upstate New York. The show is open to the wholesale trade only - sales representatives, manufacturers and retailers.

1818 THA Annual Convention
The Hosiery Association
7421 Carmel Executive Park Drive
Suite 200
Charlotte, NC 28226

704-365-0913
FAX 704-362-2056
E-Mail: THAinfo@hosieryassociation.com
Home Page: www.hosieryassociation.com
Social Media: *Facebook, Twitter*

Sally Kay, President/CEO

Promotes leg wear manufacturers & suppliers
Founded in 1905

1819 TNNA Trade Shows
National Needlework Association
1100-H Brandywine Boulevard
Zanesville, OH 43701

740-455-6773
800-889-8662
FAX 740-452-2552
E-Mail: info@tnna.org
Home Page: www.tnna.org
Social Media: *Facebook, Twitter*

A market for serious needleart buyers and sellers learn about trends in fashion, color and design. With over 800 booths.
Frequency: 4x per year

1820 Team Sports Show at the Super Show
Communications & Show Management
1450 NE 123rd Street
North Miami, FL 33161

305-893-8771
FAX 305-893-8783
Home Page: www.bizbash.com

Richard Aaron, President
David Adler, CEO/founder
Chad Kaydo, Editor in Chief
Dana Price, COO

Retailers, distributors, wholesalers, importers/exporters and other buyers of sports related products come for 10,000 exhibits of sports apparel, footwear, accessories and e-commerce products and services.
100k Attendees
Frequency: January

1821 Tennis & Golf Show at the Super Show
Communications & Show Management
1450 NE 123rd Street
North Miami, FL 33161

305-893-8771
FAX 305-893-8783
Home Page: www.bizbash.com

Richard Aaron, President
David Adler, CEO/Founder
Chad Kaydo, Editor in Chief
Dana Price, COO

Retailers, distributors, wholesalers, importers/exporters and other buyers of sports related products come for 10,000 exhibits of sports apparel, footwear, accessories and e-commerce products and services.
100k Attendees
Frequency: January

1822 Trimmings, Accessories, Fabrics Expo
National Knitwear & Sportswear
Association
386 Park Avenue S
Suite 5741
New York, NY 10016-8804

212-683-7520
FAX 212-532-0766

Seth Bodner, Executive Director

The only all-inclusive trimmings show in the United States. 160 booths.
6M Attendees
Frequency: November

1823 WAM: Western Apparel Manufacturers Show
Dallas Market Center
2300 Stemmons Freeway
Dallas, TX 75207

214-556-6100
FAX 214-638-7221
E-Mail: info@dmcmail.com
Home Page: www.dallasmarketcenter.com
Social Media: *Facebook, Twitter*

Apparel manufacturing equipment. Held to meet the needs of the TOLA retailers who take advantage of the early fall buying opportunities.
3.2M Attendees
Frequency: April

1824 WSA: Western Shoe Associates
Western Shoe Associates
20281 SW Birch Street
Newport Beach, CA 92660

949-851-8451
FAX 949-851-8523

Mitch Fisherman, President
Steve Katz, VP
Marie Mussabini, Exhibitor Coordinator
Dave Darling, Treasurer

Trade show held twice a year and featuring footwear.

1825 WWD Magic
MAGIC International
2501 Colorado Avenue
Suite 280
Santa Monica, CA 90404

310-857-7500
FAX 310-857-7510
E-Mail: cs@magiconline.com

Home Page: www.magiconline.com
Social Media: *Facebook, Twitter*

Joe Loggia, President/CEO
Laura McConnell, VP

WWD Magic, a joint venture with Women's Wear Daily, is the recognized leader in women's apparel and accessories expositions in the world. WWD Magic offers the opportunity to discover new resources, network with industry peers, attend trend seminars and fashion shows, and meet with major manufacturers in an exciting and efficient forum. Containing over 1,000 exhibitors and 2,000 booths.
85000 Attendees
Frequency: August
Founded in 1933

1826 Western Shoe Associates International
Western Shoe Associates
20281 SW Birch Street
Suite 100
Newport Beach, CA 92660

949-851-8451
FAX 949-851-8523

Mitch Fisherman, President
Marie Mussabini, Exhibitor Coordinator

Footwear trade market.

1827 Western and English Sales Association Trade Show
Western and English Sales Association
451 E 58th Avenue
Suite 4128
Denver, CO 80216

303-295-1040
800-295-1041
FAX 303-295-0941
E-Mail: info@denver-wesa.com
Home Page: www.denver-wesa.com

Toni High, Executive Director
Amy Thomas, Trade Show Director

Trade shows for Equestrian-related products; wholesalers to retailers
10000 Attendees
Frequency: 2x/Year

1828 Women and Children's Market
AMC Trade Shows/DMC Expositions
2140 Peachtree Street NW
Suite 2200
Atlanta, GA 30303

404-220-3000
800-285-6278
FAX 404-220-3030

Sarah Adamson, Show Manager

Women and children's apparel.
9000 Attendees

1829 Women's and Children's Apparel Market
Dallas Market Center
2100 Stemmons Freeway
Dallas, TX 75207

214-556-6100
800-325-6587
E-Mail: ahood@dmcmail.com
Home Page: www.dallasmarketcenter.com
Social Media: *Facebook, Twitter*

Pat Zajac, Home Expo

Features the most comprehensive variety of apparel and accessories lines.
20000 Attendees
Frequency: October
Founded in 1957

1830 Women's and Children's Fall Market
Merchandise Mart Properties Inc

222 Merchandise Mart Plaza
Suite 470
Chicago, IL 60654

312-527-4141
800-677-6278
FAX 312-527-7782
Home Page: www.merchandisemart.com

Christopher Kennedy, President

Hundreds of designers featuring women's and children's clothing and accessories
5000 Attendees
Founded in 1950

1831 Women's and Children's Summer/Fall Preview Market
Merchandise Mart Properties
222 Merchandise Mart Plaza
Suite 470
Chicago, IL 60654

312-527-4141
800-677-6278
FAX 312-527-7782
Home Page: www.merchandisemart.com

H Brennen III, Executive VP

Women's and children's apparel.
5000 Attendees
Frequency: June

1832 Wonderful World of Weddings and Occasions
Expo Productions
510 Hartbrook Drive
Hartland, WI 53029

262-367-5500
800-367-5520
FAX 262-367-9956
E-Mail: monica@epishows.com
Home Page: www.weddingshowepi.com

Monica Seeger, Sales Manager

Wedding and other special occasion products, services, ideas including live and recorded music, still and video photography, cakes and catering, formal wear, gifts and much more.
6000 Attendees
Frequency: January
Founded in 1967

1833 X-treme Sports Show at the Super Show
Communications & Show Management
1450 NE 123rd Street
North Miami, FL 33161

305-893-8771
FAX 305-893-8783
Home Page: www.bizbash.com

Richard Aaron, President
David Adler, CEO/Founder
Chad Kaydo, Editor in Chief
Dana Price, COO

Retailers, distributors, wholesalers, importers/exporters and other buyers of sports related products come for 10,000 exhibits of sports apparel, footwear, accessories and e-commerce products and services.
100k Attendees
Frequency: January

Directories & Databases

1834 Action Sports Retailer Buyer's Guide Issue
Miller Freeman Publications

2655 Seely Avenue
San Jose, CA 95134

408-943-1234
FAX 408-943-0513

Pat Cochran, Editor

Guide to 1,600 manufacturers and distributors of specialty watersports, beach, skateboarding, snowboarding, volleyball and bicycling equipment and clothing.
Cost: $25.00

1835 American Apparel Contractors Association Directory - American Made Apparel

4870 Nome Street
Denver, CO 80239-2728

303-373-2924
FAX 703-522-6741

Sue C Strickland, Executive Director
Sunny Park, Owner

Over 300 listings are offered pertaining to contractors, manufacturers and suppliers to the apparel industry.
30 Members
100 Pages
Frequency: Annual
Founded in 1981

1836 Apparel Specialty Stores Directory

Chain Store Guide
10117 Princess Palm Dr
Tampa, FL 33610

813-627-6700
800-927-9292
FAX 813-627-6888
E-Mail: webmaster@chainstoreguide.com
Home Page: www.csgis.com

Mike Jarvis, Publisher
Chris Leedy, Advertising Sales
Shami Choon, Manager

The facts on more than 4,800 companies operating more than 70,700 stores all involved in the sale of women's, men's, family and children's wear. Also included are sporting goods stores that offer apparel and active wear as well as related merchandise. Includes more than 15,000 key buyers and executives.
Cost: $335.00

1837 Bobbin-Suppliers Sourcing Issue

Bobbin Blenheim Media Corporation
1110 Shop Road
PO Box 1986
Columbia, SC 29201-4743

800-845-8820
FAX 803-799-1461

Offers information on over 8,000 suppliers to the apparel/sewn products industry.

1838 College Store Executive: Emblematics Directory Issue

Executive Business Media
825 Old Country Road
Westbury, NY 11590

516-334-3030
FAX 516-334-3059
E-Mail: ebm-mail@ebmpubs.com
Home Page: www.ebmpubs.com

Murry Greenwald, President

List of distributors of products with emblems or insignia; coverage includes Canada.
Cost: $5.00
Frequency: Annual, February

1839 Complete Directory of Apparel

Sutton Family Communications & Publishing Company

155 Sutton Lane
Fordsville, KY 42343

270-740-0870
E-Mail: jlsutton@apex.net
Home Page: www.fleamarketeer.net

Theresa Sutton, Editor
Lee Sutton, General Manager

Print-out from database of wholesalers, manufacturers, distributors, importers and close-out houses. Database is updated daily to guarantee the most current sources available.
Cost: $77.65
100+ Pages

1840 Complete Directory of Apparel Close-Outs

Sutton Family Communications & Publishing Company
155 Sutton Lane
Fordsville, KY 42343

270-740-0870
E-Mail: jlsutton@apex.net
Home Page: www.fleamarketeer.net

Theresa Sutton, Editor
Lee Sutton, General Manager

Print-out from database of wholesalers, manufacturers, distributors, importers and close-out houses. Database is updated daily to guarantee the most current sources available to the close-out apparel industry.
Cost: $55.20
100+ Pages

1841 Complete Directory of Baby Goods and Gifts

Sutton Family Communications & Publishing Company
155 Sutton Lane
Fordsville, KY 42343

270-740-0870
E-Mail: jlsutton@apex.net
Home Page: www.fleamarketeer.net

Theresa Sutton, Editor
Lee Sutton, General Manager

Print-out from database of wholesalers, manufacturers, distributors, importers and close-out houses for baby goods and gifts. Database is updated daily to guarantee the most current sources available.
Cost: $57.65
100+ Pages

1842 Complete Directory of Belts, Buckles & Boots

Sutton Family Communications & Publishing Company
155 Sutton Lane
Fordsville, KY 42343

270-740-0870
E-Mail: jlsutton@apex.net
Home Page: www.fleamarketeer.net

Theresa Sutton, Editor
Lee Sutton, General Manager

Print-out from database of wholesalers, manufacturers, distributors, importers and close-out houses. Database is updated daily to guarantee the most current sources available.
Cost: $55.20
100+ Pages

1843 Complete Directory of Brand New Surplus Merchandise

Sutton Family Communications & Publishing Company

155 Sutton Lane
Fordsville, KY 42343

270-740-0870
E-Mail: jlsutton@apex.net
Home Page: www.fleamarketeer.net

Theresa Sutton, Editor
Lee Sutton, General Manager

Print-out from database of wholesalers, manufacturers, distributors, importers and close-out houses. Database is updated daily to guarantee the most current sources available.
Cost: $92.70
100+ Pages

1844 Complete Directory of Caps & Hats

Sutton Family Communications & Publishing Company
155 Sutton Lane
Fordsville, KY 42343

270-740-0870
E-Mail: jlsutton@apex.net
Home Page: www.fleamarketeer.net

Theresa Sutton, Editor
Lee Sutton, General Manager

Print-out from database of wholesalers, manufacturers, distributors, importers and close-out houses. Database is updated daily to guarantee the most current sources available.
Cost: $55.20
100+ Pages

1845 Complete Directory of Clothing & Uniforms

Sutton Family Communications & Publishing Company
155 Sutton Lane
Fordsville, KY 42343

270-740-0870
E-Mail: jlsutton@apex.net
Home Page: www.fleamarketeer.net

Theresa Sutton, Editor
Lee Sutton, General Manager

Print-out from database of wholesalers, manufacturers, distributors, importers and close-out houses. Database is updated daily to guarantee the most current sources available.
Cost: $55.20
100+ Pages

1846 Complete Directory of Hat Pins, Feathers and Fads

Sutton Family Communications & Publishing Company
155 Sutton Lane
Fordsville, KY 42343

270-740-0870
E-Mail: jlsutton@apex.net
Home Page: www.fleamarketeer.net

Theresa Sutton, Editor
Lee Sutton, General Manager

Print-out from database of wholesalers, manufacturers, distributors, importers and close-out houses. Database is updated daily to guarantee the most current sources available.
Cost: $67.70
100+ Pages

1847 Complete Directory of Purses & Handbags

Sutton Family Communications & Publishing Company
155 Sutton Lane
Fordsville, KY 42343

270-740-0870
E-Mail: jlsutton@apex.net
Home Page: www.fleamarketeer.net

Theresa Sutton, Editor
Lee Sutton, General Manager

Print-out from database of wholesalers, manufacturers, distributors, importers and close-out houses. Database is updated daily to guarantee the most current sources available.
Cost: $55.20
100+ Pages

1848 Complete Directory of Sunglasses & Eye Weather
Sutton Family Communications & Publishing Company
155 Sutton Lane
Fordsville, KY 42343

270-740-0870
E-Mail: jlsutton@apex.net
Home Page: www.fleamarketeer.net

Theresa Sutton, Editor
Lee Sutton, General Manager

Print-out from database of wholesalers, manufacturers, distributors, importers and close-out houses. Database is updated daily to guarantee the most current sources available.
Cost: $55.20
100+ Pages

1849 Complete Directory of T-Shirts, Heat Transfers & Supplies
Sutton Family Communications & Publishing Company
155 Sutton Lane
Fordsville, KY 42343

270-740-0870
E-Mail: jlsutton@apex.net
Home Page: www.fleamarketeer.net

Theresa Sutton, Editor
Lee Sutton, General Manager

Print-out from database of wholesalers, manufacturers, distributors, importers and close-out houses. Database is updated daily to guarantee the most current sources available.
Cost: $55.20
100+ Pages

1850 Complete Directory of Western Wear
Sutton Family Communications & Publishing Company
155 Sutton Lane
Fordsville, KY 42343

270-740-0870
E-Mail: jlsutton@apex.net
Home Page: www.fleamarketeer.net

Theresa Sutton, Editor
Lee Sutton, General Manager

Print-out from database of wholesalers, manufacturers, distributors, importers and close-out houses. Database is updated daily to guarantee the most current sources available.
Cost: $55.20
100+ Pages

1851 Complete Directory of Women's Accessories
Sutton Family Communications & Publishing Company
155 Sutton Lane
Fordsville, KY 42343

270-740-0870
E-Mail: jlsutton@apex.net
Home Page: www.fleamarketeer.net

Theresa Sutton, Editor
Lee Sutton, General Manager

Print-out from database of wholesalers, manufacturers, distributors, importers and close-out houses. Database is updated daily to guarantee the most current sources available.
Cost: $55.20
100+ Pages

1852 Directory of Active Sportswear
Sutton Family Communications & Publishing Company
155 Sutton Lane
Fordsville, KY 42343

270-740-0870
E-Mail: jlsutton@apex.net
Home Page: www.fleamarketeer.net

Theresa Sutton, Editor
Lee Sutton, General Manager

Print-out from database of wholesalers, manufacturers, distributors, importers and close-out houses. Database is updated daily to guarantee the most current sources available. Approximately 740 wholesale sources in a 3-ring binder.
Cost: $67.20
100+ Pages

1853 Directory of Apparel Specialty Stores
AKTRIN Textile Information Center
164 S Main Street
PO Box 898
High Point, NC 27261

336-418-8583
FAX 336-841-5435
E-Mail: aktrin@aktrin.com
Home Page: www.textile-info.com

Information resource for people seeking in-depth, up-to-date data on the apparel specialty stores marketplace. Fully searchable database, either in form of a CD-ROM or downloadable over the Internet.
Cost: $780.00
Frequency: Annual

1854 Directory of Hosiery Manufacturers
Hosiery Association
7421 Carmel Executive Park Drive
Suite 200
Charlotte, NC 28226

704-365-0913
FAX 704-362-2056
E-Mail: thainfo@hosieryassociation.com
Home Page: www.hosieryassociation.com
Social Media: *Facebook, Twitter*

Sally Kay, President/CEO

Over 700 hosiery manufacturers and distributors.
Founded in 1905

1855 Directory of Mail Order Catalogs
Grey House Publishing
4919 Route 22
PO Box 56
Amenia, NY 12501

518-789-8700
800-562-2139
FAX 518-789-0556
E-Mail: books@greyhouse.com
Home Page: www.greyhouse.com
Social Media: *Facebook, Twitter*

Leslie Mackenzie, Publisher
Richard Gottlieb, President

The premier source of information on the mail order catalog industry. Covers over 13,000 consumer and business catalog companies with 44 different product chapters including clothing and sportswear.
Cost: $395.00
1900 Pages
Frequency: Annual
ISBN: 1-592373-96-8
Founded in 1981

1856 Directory of Mail Order Catalogs - Online Database
Grey House Publishing

4919 Route 22
PO Box 56
Amenia, NY 12501

518-789-8700
800-562-2139
FAX 518-789-0556
E-Mail: gold@greyhouse.com
Home Page: http://gold.greyhouse.com
Social Media: *Facebook, Twitter*

Leslie Mackenzie, Publisher
Richard Gottlieb, President

Reach over 10,000 consumer catalog companies in one easy-to-use source with The Directory of Mail Order Catalogs - Online Database. Filled with business-building detail, each company profile gives you the information you need to access that organization quickly and easily. Listings provide key contacts, sales volume, employee size, printing information, circulation, list data, product descriptions and much more.
Frequency: Annual
Founded in 1981

1857 Earnshaw's Buyer's Guide to the New York Market
Earnshaw Publications
36 Cooper Square
4th Floor
New York, NY 10003

646-278-1550
FAX 646- 27- 155
Home Page: www.earnshaws.com

Noelle Heffernan, Publisher

A children's wear guide offering over 1,200 manufacturers and suppliers of clothing for infants, boys and girls apparel.
200 Pages
Frequency: Annual
Circulation: 10,000

1858 Earnshaw's Infants', Girls', Boys' Wear Review: Children's Wear Directory
Earnshaw Publications
36 Cooper Square
4th Floor
New York, NY 10003

646-278-1550
FAX 646-278-1553
Home Page: www.earnshaws.com

Noelle Heffernan, Publisher

A directory of over 1,500 children's apparel and accessory firms with offices or showrooms in the United States.
Cost: $10.00
Frequency: Annual
Circulation: 10,000

1859 Financial Performance Profile of Public Apparel Companies
Kurt Salmon Associates
650 Fifth Avenue
New York, NY 10019

212-319-9450
Home Page: www.kurtsalmon.com

John Karonis, CEO

Information on over 60 publicly held apparel manufacturers are available.
Cost: $400.00
300 Pages
Frequency: Annual
Founded in 1935

1860 Garment Manufacturers Index
Klevens Publications

411 S Main Street
Suite 209
Los Angeles, CA 90013

213-625-9000
FAX 213-625-5002
E-Mail: editor@klevenspub.com
Home Page: www.garmentindex.com

Herbert Schwartz, Editor

A list of over 5,000 manufacturers and suppliers of products and services such as fabrics, trimmings, factory equipment and sewing contractors used in the manufacture of apparel and other sewn products.
Cost: $105.00
264 Pages
Frequency: Annual
Circulation: 29,495
ISSN: 1065-1330
Founded in 1938
Printed in 4 colors on matte stock

1861 Hosiery and Bodywear: Buyer's Guide to Support and Control Top Pantyhose
Advanstar Communications
641 Lexington Ave
8th Floor
New York, NY 10022-4503

212-951-6600
FAX 212-951-6793
E-Mail: info@advanstar.com
Home Page: www.advanstar.com

Joseph Loggia, CEO

List of about 50 hosiery manufacturers.
Cost: $3.00
Frequency: Annual September
Circulation: 10,500

1862 Impressions: Directory Issue
Miller Freeman Publications
501 W. President George Bush Hwy. #150
Richardson, TX 75080

813-366-2877
800-697-8859
E-Mail: nimp@omeda.com
Home Page: www.impressionsmag.com

Marcia Derrberry, Editor in Chief

A list of more than 1,500 suppliers of products, services and equipment used in the imprinted sportswear industry including textile screen print equipment, supplies, embroidery equipment and supplies, and all types of imprintables.
Cost: $18.00
Frequency: Annual
Circulation: 60,000

1863 International Nonwovens Directory
1100 Crescent Green Suite 115
PO Box 1288
Cary, NC 27518

919-233-1210
FAX 919-233-1282
Home Page: www.inda.org

Rory Holmes, President
Annette Balint, Director Finance
Ian Butler, Director Market Research/Stats

A Who's Who directory of services and supplies to the nonwovens industry.
300 Members
750 Pages
Frequency: Biennial
Circulation: 2,000

1864 Nationwide Directory of Men's & Boys' Wear Buyers
Reed Reference Publishing RR Bowker

630 Central Ave
New Providence, NJ 07974-1544

908-286-1090
888-269-5372
FAX 908-464-3553
E-Mail: info@bowker.com
Home Page: www.bowker.com

A who's who directory of services and supplies to the industry.
Cost: $147.00
700 Pages
Frequency: Annual
Circulation: 1,000

1865 Outerwear Sourcebook: Directory Issue
Creative Marketing Plus
213-37 39th Avenue
Suite 228
Bayside, NY 11361

718-606-0767
FAX 718-606-6345
E-Mail: rharrow@creativemarketingplus.com
Home Page: www.creativemarketingplus.com

Richard Harrow, President

List of more than 3,500 outerwear manufacturers in the US and Canada; 1,000 companies providing products and services to the outerwear trade.
Cost: $40.00
Frequency: Annual

1866 WWD Buyers Guide: Womens Apparel and Accessories Manufacturers
Fairchild Publications
750 3rd Ave
New York, NY 10017-2703

212-630-4000
FAX 212-630-3563

Mary G Berner, Chief Executive Officer
Christine Guilfoyle, Publisher

Over 5,500 apparel and accessory manufacturers.
Founded in 1892

1867 WWD Suppliers Guide
Fairchild Books and Visuals
750 3rd Ave
New York, NY 10017-2700

212-630-4320
FAX 212-630-3566

Mary G Berner, Chief Executive Officer
Christine Guilfoyle, Publisher

Over 5,500 apparel and accessory manufacturers in the US. Supplement to WWD Magazine.
Founded in 1892

Industry Web Sites

1868 http://gold.greyhouse.com
G.O.L.D Grey House OnLine Databases

Grey House Publishing's online database platform, GOLD, offers Quick Search, Keyword Search and Expert Search in most business sectors, including apparel and accessories markets. The GOLD platform makes finding the information you need quick and easy - whether you're a novice searcher or an experienced database user. All of Grey House's directory products are available for subscription on the GOLD platform.

1869 www.apparelandfootwear.org
American Apparel & Footwear Association

The national trade association for the apparel and footwear industries. Conducts seminars,

compiles statistics and produces industry reports.

1870 www.cashmere.org
Cashmere and Camel Hair Manufacturers Institute

For cashmere and camel hair product manufacturers.

1871 www.chemicalfabricsandfilm.com
Chemical Fabrics and Film Association

An international trade association representing manufacturers of polymer-based fabric and film products, used in the building and construction, automotive, fashion and many other industries.

1872 www.colorassociation.com
Color Association of the US

Information on color/design issues; issues color charts two years in advance of selling seasons in order to profile popular American colors. Forecasts are issued in women's fashions and men's and children's clothing.

1873 www.costumedesignersguild.com
Costume Designers Guild

Works to promote employment and to create improved working conditions for costume designers.

1874 www.ctda.com
Custom Tailors and Designers Assn of America

Seeks to promote awareness of designers and makers of men's custom tailored clothing.

1875 www.embroiderytrade.org
Embroidery Trade Association

An organization with the objective to continually strengthen the commercial embroidery business.

1876 www.formalwear.org
International Formalwear Association

For the formal wear industry.

1877 www.greyhouse.com
Grey House Publishing

Authoritative reference directories for most industries, including apparel and accessories. Users can search the online databases with varied search criteria allowing for custom searches by product category, geographic area, sales volume, keyword, subject and more. Full Grey House catalog and online ordering also available.

1878 www.ifai.com
Industrial Fabrics Association International

For geosynthetics, fabricators, installers, equipment manufacturers, suppliers, testing firms, consultants, and educators, who produce textiles, nets, mats, grids, and other products.

1879 www.itaaonline.org
Int'l Textile & Apparel Assn Membership Directory

For college professors of clothing and textile studies.

1880 www.naumd.com
North American Assoc. of Uniform Manufacturers

For manufacturers and distributors of uniforms and career wear.

1881 www.sewing.org
American Home Sewing and Craft Association

Handicraft and collectibles forum.

1882 www.uc-council.org
GS1 US

Members rely on the standards and services of GS1 US for the effective management and control of their supply chains. Everyday we strive to keep a leader's pace in developing, maintaining, supporting and expanding the services we offer to fulfill our mission.

1883 www.uniteunion.org
Union of Needletrade Industrial Textile Employees
A union fighting for working people.

1884 www.vowsmag.com
Grimes & Associates
Information on the business specifics necessary for today's wedding professional.

Associations

1885 Air Conditioning Contractors of America

2800 S Shirlington Rd
Suite 300
Arlington, VA 22206-3607

703-575-4477
E-Mail: info@acca.org
Home Page: www.acca.org
Social Media: *Facebook, Twitter, LinkedIn, YouTube, RSS Feeds, Flickr*

Paul T. Stalknecht, President & CEO
Kevin W. Holland, Senior Vice President
Chris Hoelzel, Vice President, Product Fulfillment
Kimya Bailey Cajchun, Vice President of Membership
Craig Gotthardt, Vice President of Information

ACCA is a non-profit association serving the HVACR community, working to promote professional contracting, energy efficiency, and healthy, comfortable indoor environments.
64000 Members
Founded in 1914

1886 Air-Conditioning, Heating and Refrigeration Institute

2111 Wilson Boulevard
Suite 500
Arlington, VA 22201

703-524-8800
FAX 703-562-1942
E-Mail: ahri@ahrinet.org
Home Page: www.ahrinet.org
Social Media: *Facebook, Twitter, RSS Feeds*

Stephen Yurek, President and CEO
Stephanie Murphy, Chief Financial Officer
Francis Dietz, Vice President of Public Affairs
Bob Johnston, Director/Accounting
Doug Burkes, Manager/Office Operations

AHRI is one of the largest trade associations in the nation, representing heating, water heating, ventilation, air conditioning and commercial refrigeration manufacturers within the global HVACR industry.
300 Members
Founded in 1953

1887 American Boiler Manufacturers Association

8221 Old Courthouse Rd
Suite 207
Vienna, VA 22182-3839

703-356-7172
FAX 703-356-4543
Home Page: www.abma.com
Social Media: *Facebook, Twitter, LinkedIn*

Robert Stemen, Chairman
W. Randall Rawson, President & CEO
Geoffrey Hailey, Director of Technical Affairs
Hugh K. Webster, General Counsel
Cheryl Jamall, Director of Meetings

The American Boiler Manufacturers Association (ABMA) is the national, nonprofit trade association of commercial, institutional, industrial and electricity-generating boiler system manufacturing companies (400,000 Btuh heat input), dedicated to the advancement and growth of the boiler and combustion equipment industry.
Founded in 1888

1888 American Society of Heating, Refrigeration & Air-Conditioning Engineers

1791 Tullie Cir NE
Atlanta, GA 30329-2398

404-636-8400
800-527-4723
FAX 404-321-5478
E-Mail: ashrae@ashrae.org
Home Page: www.ashrae.org
Social Media: *Facebook, Twitter, LinkedIn, YouTube*

William P. Bahnfleth, President
Jeff H Littleton, Executive VP
Darryl K. Boyce, P.Eng., Vice President
Bjarne W. Olesen, Ph.D., Vice President
Daniel C. Pettway, Vice President

An international organization that fulfills its mission of advancing heating, ventilation, air conditioning and refrigeration to serve humanity and promote a sustainable world through research, standards writing, publishing and continuing education.
55000 Members
Founded in 1894

1889 American Society of Mechanical Engineers

Two Park Avenue
New York, NY 10016-5900

973-882-1170
800-843-2763
FAX 202-429-9417
E-Mail: infocentral@asme.org
Home Page: www.asme.org
Social Media: *Facebook, Twitter, LinkedIn*

Madiha El Mehelmy Kotb, President
Thomas G. Loughlin, Executive Director
Chitra Sethi, Managing Editor
David Walsh, Editor
John Kosowatz, Senior Editor

ASME is a not-for-profit membership organization that enables collaboration, knowledge sharing, career enrichment, and skills development across all engineering disciplines, toward a goal of helping the global engineering community develop solutions to benefit lives and livelihoods.
12000 Members
Founded in 1880

1890 American Vacuum Society (AVS)

125 Maiden Lane
15th Floor
New York, NY 10038

212-248-0200
FAX 212-248-0245
Home Page: www.avs.org
Social Media: *Facebook, Twitter, LinkedIn, RSS Feeds*

Susan B. Sinnott, President
Jeannette DeGennaro, Exhibition & Sales Manager
Yvonne Towse, Managing Director
Ricky Baldeo, Office Services Coordinator
Angela Klink, Member Services Administrator

As an interdisciplinary, professional Society, AVS supports networking among academic, industrial, government, and consulting professionals involved in a variety of disciplines - chemistry, physics, biology, mathematics, business, sales, etc through common interests related to the basic science, technology development and commercialization of materials, interfaces, and processing areas.
4500 Members
Founded in 1953

1891 Association of Home Appliance Manufacturers

1111 19th Street NW
Suite 402
Washington, DC 20036

202-872-5955
FAX 202-872-9354
E-Mail: info@aham.org
Home Page: www.aham.org

Paul V. Sikir, Board Chair
Joseph M. McGuire, President
Peter Frank, Vice President, Finance
Nick Baker, Manager, Communications
Jennifer Cleary, Director/Regulatory Affairs

A not-for-profit trade association representing manufacturers of major and portable home appliance, floor care appliances and suppliers to the industry .
Founded in 1915

1892 Industrial Heating Equipment Association

5040 Old Taylor Mill Rd.
PMB 13
Taylor Mill, KY 41015

859-356-1575
FAX 859-356-0908
E-Mail: ihea@ihea.org
Home Page: www.ihea.org
Social Media: *Facebook*

Tim Lee, President
Bill Pasley, 1st Vice President
Mike Shay, 2nd Vice President
Jay Cherry, Treasurer
Anne Goyer, Executive Vice President

The Industrial Heating Equipment Association (IHEA) is a voluntary national trade association representing the major segments of the industrial heat processing equipment industry.
Founded in 1929

1893 International Housewares Association

6400 Shafer Ct
Suite 650
Rosemont, IL 60018-4929

847-292-4200
FAX 847-292-4211
E-Mail: pbrandl@housewares.org
Home Page: www.housewares.org
Social Media: *Facebook, Twitter, LinkedIn, YouTube*

Richard L. Boynton, Chairman
Phil J. Brandl, President
Dean Kurtis, Vice President, Finance
Mia Rampersad, Vice President, Trade Show
Perry Reynolds, Vice President, Marketing

A full-service trade association dedicated to promoting the sales and marketing of housewares.
Founded in 1938

1894 International Institute of Ammonia Refrigeration

1001 N. Fairfax Street
Suite 503
Alexandria, VA 22314

703-312-4200
FAX 703-312-0065
E-Mail: info@iiar.org
Home Page: www.iiar.org
Social Media: *Facebook, Twitter, LinkedIn, YouTube, Google+*

Robert Port, Jr., Chairman
David L. Rule, President
Bruce Badger, Chief Operating Officer
Marcos Braz, Chair-Elect
Tom Leighty, Vice Chair

IAR is an organization providing advocacy, education, standards, and information for the benefit of the ammonia refrigeration industry

worldwide. IIAR's vision is to be recognized as the world's leading advocate for the safe, reliable and efficient use of ammonia and other natural refrigerants for industrial applications.
1200 Members
Founded in 1971

1895   International Kitchen Exhaust Cleaning Association
100 North 20th Street
Suite 400
Philadelphia, PA 19103

215-320-3876
FAX 215-564-2175
E-Mail: information@ikeca.org
Home Page: www.ikeca.org
Social Media: *Facebook, Twitter, LinkedIn, YouTube, Blog*

Kathy Slomer, President
Sarah Hagy, Executive Director
Lisa Chester, Associate Director
Hanna Linn, Administrative Director
Gina Marinilli, Standard Development Director

Promotes fire safety in restaurants and professionalism in the kitchen exhaust cleaning industry. This not for profit trade association, has established stringent standards and practices for contractors engaged in kitchen exhaust cleaning, conducted a variety of educational programs, and worked with influential code setting bodies such as the National Fire Protection Association to improve existing codes and regulations.
Founded in 1989

1896   International Microwave Power Institute
PO Box 1140
PO Box 1140
Mechanicsville, VA 23111-5007

804-559-6667
FAX 804-559-4087
E-Mail: info@impi.org
Home Page: www.impi.org
Social Media: *Facebook, Twitter*

Molly Poisant, Executive Director
Ben Wilson, Executive Committee
John Gerling, Executive Committee
Ric Gonzalez, Executive Committee
Bob Schiffman, Executive Committee

The International Microwave Power Institute (IMPI) was founded in 1966 in Canada to serve the information needs of specialists working with microwave and RF heating systems. In 1977, the Institute reorganized to expand its industrial and scientific base to meet the information needs evolving in consumer microwave ovens and related products.
Founded in 1966

1897   National Air Duct Cleaners Association
1120 Route 73
Suite 200
Mt Laurel, NJ 08054

856-380-6810
FAX 856-439-0525
E-Mail: info@nadca.com
Home Page: www.nadca.com
Social Media: *Facebook, Twitter, LinkedIn, YouTube*

Michael Vinick, President
Richard Lantz,ÿASCS, 1st Vice President
Ric MacDonald,ÿASCS, 2nd Vice President
Mike Dwyer, CAE, Chief Relationship Officer
Jodi Araujo, Executive Director

NADCA: The HVAC Inspection, Maintenance and Restoration Association, otherwise known as the National Air Duct Cleaners Association (NADCA), was formed in 1989 as a non-profit association of companies engaged in the clean-

ing of HVAC systems. Its mission was to promote source removal as the only acceptable method of cleaning and to establish industry standards for the association.
1000 Members
Founded in 1989

1898   National Kitchen and Bath Association
687 Willow Grove St
Hackettstown, NJ 07840-1731

908-850-1206
800-843-6522
FAX 908-852-1695
E-Mail: feedback@nkba.org
Home Page: www.nkba.org
Social Media: *Facebook, Twitter, LinkedIn, Pinterest*

John K. Morgan, President
Carolyn F. Cheetham, CMKBD, Vice President
Bill Darcy, Chief Executive Officer
Stephen Graziano, Senior Director of Finance
Nancy Barnes, Director of Learning

The NKBA enhances the success of its members in the kitchen and bath industry through networking, education, certification, marketing and business tools, leadership opportunities, and the annual Kitchen/Bath Industry Show.
40000 Members
Founded in 1963

1899   North American Retail Dealers Association
222 South Riverside Plaza
Suite 2100
Chicago, IL 60606

312-648-0649
800-621-0298
FAX 312-648-1212
E-Mail: nardasvc@narda.com
Home Page: www.narda.com
Social Media: *Facebook, LinkedIn*

Leon Barbachano, Chairman
Timothy W. Seavey, First Vice Chairman
Otto Papasadero, Executive Director
Pam Clark, Administrative Assistant
Bob Goldberg, Legal Counsel

To enhance the ability of independent appliance retailers to build progressive, profitable businesses. NARDA members sell and serve kitchen and laundry appliances, consumer home and mobile electronics, computers and other home and small office products, furniture, sewing machines, vacuum cleaners, room air conditioners, and other consumer home products.
3000 Members
Founded in 1943

1900   Professional Service Association
71 Columbia Street
Cohoes, NY 12047-2939

518-237-7777
888-777-8851
FAX 518-237-0418
E-Mail: psaworld@aol.com
Home Page: www.psaworld.com

Don Holman, President
Carmine D'Alessandro, Vice President
Linda Knudsen, Administrative Vice President
Randy Carney, Executive Director
Ralph Wolff, Director

PSA is an independent trade association dedicated to the highest standards of quality service. The purpose of PSA is to be the voice of the independent service provider and to assess and identify industry related problems and provide solutions. PSA is dedicated to providing educational training, certification, business management training, support and fairness to the independent service industry. PSA encourages professionalism and honesty identifies

those techs who provide that kind of service.
Cost: $150.00
1105 Members
Frequency: Membership Fee
Founded in 1989

1901   Refrigeration Service Engineers Society
1911 Rohlwig Road
Suite A
Rolling Meadows, IL 60008-1397

847-297-6464
800-297-5660
FAX 847-297-5038
E-Mail: general@rses.org
Home Page: www.rses.org
Social Media: *Facebook, Twitter, LinkedIn, RSS Feeds, Pinterest, Tumblr,*

Roger M. Hensley, CMS, E&E, Board Chairman
Harlan Krepcik, International President
Michael Thompson, International Vice President
Nick Reggi, CMS, RCT, International Secretary/Treasurer
Roger M.ÿ Hensley, CMS, RCT, International Sergeant at Arms

To provide opportunities for enhanced technical competence by offering comprehensive, cutting-edge education and certification to our members and the HVACR industry. To advance the professionalism and proficiency of our industry through alliances with other HVACR associations. To be the definitive industry leader in all segments of the HVACR industry by providing superior educational training.
15231 Members
Founded in 1933

1902   Silicon Valley Compucycle
1096 Pecten Ct
Milpitas, CA 95035

408-432-1239
866-989-2970
FAX 408-432-1249
E-Mail: svcinfo@svc.com
Home Page: www.svc.com
Social Media: *Facebook, Twitter*

Vivienne Harwood Mattox, Executive Director
Yvonne Swartz, Executive Manager
Beth Strong, Marketing & Communications Manager

Association dedicated to promote technical excellence by providing a global forum to inform, educate, and engage the members, the technical community, and the public on all aspects of vacuum coating, surface engineering and related technologies.
Founded in 2001

1903   United Servicers Association
3501 N. Southport Ave.
Suite 199
Chicago, IL 60657

800-683-2558
FAX 855-290-5366
E-Mail: administration@unitedservicers.com
Home Page: www.unitedservicers.com
Social Media: *Facebook, LinkedIn*

James Dolbeare, President
Bob Dougherty, Vice President
Jennifer Webert, Secretary
Manny Ortega Jr., Treasurer
Paul MacDonald, Executive Director

Organization provides technical and service process training and education for appliance service professionals.

Newsletters

1904 ACCA Insider
Air Conditioning Contractors of America
2800 Shirlington Rd
Suite 300
Arlington, VA 22206-3607

703-575-4477
E-Mail: info@acca.org
Home Page: www.acca.org
Social Media: *Facebook, Twitter, LinkedIn, YouTube*

Paul T Stalknecht, President & CEO

Each issue contains association and industry news, boiled down into a brief, easy to read format that will keep you up to date in just five minutes each Monday.
Frequency: Weekly

1905 AVEM Newsletter
Association of Vacuum Equipment Manufacturers
International
201 Park Washington Court
Falls Church, VA 22046-4527

703-538-3543
FAX 703-241-5603
E-Mail: aveminfo@avem.org
Home Page: www.avem.org

Dennis S. Pellegrino, President

Association news, member company news and informational articles regarding government programs, standards, economics, international trade and other issues affecting business operations.
49 Members
Frequency: Quarterly
Founded in 1969
Mailing list available for rent

1906 Insights
1791 Tullie Cir NE
Atlanta, GA 30329-2398

404-636-8400
800-527-4723
FAX 404-321-5478
E-Mail: ashrae@ashrae.org
Home Page: www.ashrae.org
Social Media: *Facebook, Twitter*

Lee Burgett, President
Jeff H Littleton, Executive VP

ASHRAE Insights is the Society's newsletter with articles of interest to members, including Chapter News, Obituaries, Membership Advancement and other news.
55000 Members
Frequency: 6x/Year
Founded in 1894

1907 SVC Bulletin
Society of Vacuum Coaters
71 Pinon Hill Place NE
Albuquerque, NM 87122

505-856-7188
FAX 505-856-6716
E-Mail: svcinfo@svc.com
Home Page: www.svc.com
Social Media: *Facebook, Twitter*

Vivienne Harwood Mattox, Executive Director
Yvonne Swartz, Executive Manager
Beth Strong, Marketing & Communications Manager

The SVC bulletin is distributed to professionals working in the vacuum coating community and related sciences and technologies. Each issue contains contributed articles, previews, or reviews of the TechCon; SVC committee activi-

ties; technical articles from the Conference Proceedings; book reviews, Corporate Sponsor news and profiles; and Society news.
Frequency: 3x/Year
Circulation: 15000

1908 The Buzz
Air Conditioning Contractors of America
2800 Shirlington Rd
Suite 300
Arlington, VA 22206-3607

703-575-4477
E-Mail: info@acca.org
Home Page: www.acca.org
Social Media: *Facebook, Twitter, LinkedIn, YouTube*

Paul Stalknecht, President & CEO

Roundup of latest news and interesting links for HVACR professionals.
Frequency: Weekly
Founded in 1984

1909 Your Business
Air Conditioning Contractors of America
2800 Shirlington Rd
Suite 300
Arlington, VA 22206-3607

703-575-4477
E-Mail: info@acca.org
Home Page: www.acca.org
Social Media: *Facebook, Twitter, LinkedIn, YouTube*

Paul Stalknecht, President & CEO

Contains management advice for small business owners.
Frequency: Bi-Weekly
Founded in 1984

1910 eSociety
1791 Tullie Cir NE
Atlanta, GA 30329-2398

404-636-8400
800-527-4723
FAX 404-321-5478
E-Mail: ashrae@ashrae.org
Home Page: www.ashrae.org
Social Media: *Facebook, Twitter*

Lee Burgett, President
Jeff H Littleton, Executive VP

The official electronic newsletter of ASHRAE. Contains monthly news form the society about its activities and chapters.
55000 Members
Frequency: Monthly
Founded in 1894

Magazines & Journals

1911 ACCA Contractor Excellence
Air Conditioning Contractors of America
2800 Shirlington Rd
Suite 300
Arlington, VA 22206-3607

703-575-4477
E-Mail: info@acca.org
Home Page: www.acca.org
Social Media: *Facebook, Twitter, LinkedIn, YouTube*

Paul T Stalknecht, President & CEO

Representing the HVACR contracting industry. We help our members acquire and satisfy customers while upholding the most stringent requirements for professional ethics, and advocating for improvements to the industry overall.
Founded in 1914

1912 ACR Standard: Assessment, Cleaning & Restoration of HVAC Systems
National Air Duct Cleaners Association
1518 K St NW
Suite 503
Washington, DC 20005-1203

202-737-2926
FAX 202-347-8847
E-Mail: info@nadca.com
Home Page: www.nadca.com

Ken Sufka, Owner

1913 AHRI Trends Magazine
Air Conditioning & Refrigeration Institute
2111 Wilson Boulevard
Suite 500
Arlington, VA 22201

703-524-8800
FAX 703-528-3816
E-Mail: ahri@ahri.net
Home Page: www.ari.org

A resource for HVAC contractors and technicians.

1914 ASHRAE Journal
American Society of Heating, Refrigeration & AC
1791 Tullie Cir NE
Atlanta, GA 30329-2398

404-636-8400
800-527-4723
FAX 404-321-5478
E-Mail: ashrae@ashrae.org
Home Page: www.ashrae.org

Lee Burgett, President
Jeff H Littleton, Executive VP

Explores topical technical issues, such as: indoor air quality, energy management, thermal storage, alternative refrigerants, fire and life safety and more.
Cost: $59.00
Frequency: Monthly

1915 ASME International Journal
American Society of Mechanical Engineers
3 Park Ave
Floor 22
New York, NY 10016-5902

212-591-7000
800-843-2763
FAX 212-591-8676
E-Mail: infocentral@asme.org
Home Page: www.asme.org

David Walsh, Editor
Chitra Sethi, Managing Editor

Provides advanced scientific and technological information for the mechanical engineering industry to facilitate the international exchange and transfer of technology.
Cost: $375.00
Frequency: Monthly

1916 Appliance
Dana Chase Publications
1110 Jorie Boulevard
PO Box 90919
Oak Brook, IL 60522-9019

630-990-3484
FAX 630-990-0078
E-Mail: lisa@appliance.com
Home Page: www.appliancemagazine.com

George Shurtleff, Production Manager
Maria Nigro, Circulation Director
Dana Chase Jr, Chairman

Devoted to serving the appliance industry worldwide, producers of consumer, commercial, business and medical appliances. Editorial material serves product engineering and design, production management and supervision, purchasing, management, marketing, sales and ser-

vice. Accepts advertising.
Cost: $75.00
90 Pages
Frequency: Monthly
Circulation: 34500
ISSN: 0003-6781
Founded in 1944

1917 Appliance Design
Business News Publishing
2401 W Big Beaver Rd
Suite 700
Troy, MI 48084-3333

248-362-3700
877-747-1625
FAX 248-362-0317
E-Mail: info@asnews.com
Home Page: www.bnpmedia.com
Social Media: *Facebook, Twitter*

Mitchell Henderson, CEO
Richard Babyak, Editor-in-Chief
Amy Alef, Production Manager
Mary Lowe, Associate Editor

Devoted to providing solutions for design and engineering teams in the global, commercial, and medical appliance/durable goods industry.
Circulation: 25,000
ISSN: 0003-6803
Founded in 1955
Printed in 4 colors on glossy stock

1918 Appliance Service News
Gamit Enterprises
1917 S Street
PO Box 808
St Charles, IL 60174

630-845-9481
877-747-1625
FAX 630-845-9483
E-Mail: info@asnews.com
Home Page: www.applianceservicenews.com

William Wingstedt, Editor/Publisher
Peggy Wingstedt, Sales Representative

Published for owners, managers and technicians of appliance repair dealers. Accepts advertising.
Cost: $59.95
36 Pages
Frequency: Monthly
Circulation: 33000
ISSN: 0003-6803
Founded in 1950
Printed in 4 colors on glossy stock

1919 Boiler Systems Engineering Magazine
American Boiler Manufacturers Association
8221 Old Courthouse Rd
Suite 202
Vienna, VA 22182-3839

703-356-7172
FAX 703-522-2665
E-Mail: randy@abma.com
Home Page: www.abma.com
Social Media: *Facebook, Twitter, LinkedIn*

Randell Rawson, President
Diana McClung, Executive Assistant
Cheryl Jamall, Director Of Meetings
Frequency: Monthly
Founded in 1888

1920 Contractor Excellence
Air Conditioning Contractors of America
2800 S Shirlington Rd
Suite 300
Arlington, VA 22206-3607

703-575-4477
E-Mail: info@acca.org
Home Page: www.acca.org

Paul Stalknecht, President

A quality source of business information for the HVAC industry, available to members.
Frequency: Quarterly
Founded in 2002

1921 HPE Magazine
American Boiler Manufacturers Association
8221 Old Courthouse Rd
Suite 202
Vienna, VA 22182-3839

703-356-7172
FAX 703-522-2665
E-Mail: randy@abma.com
Home Page: www.abma.com
Social Media: *Facebook, Twitter, LinkedIn*

Randell Rawson, President
Diana McClung, Executive Assistant
Cheryl Jamall, Director Of Meetings
Founded in 1888

1922 HVAC&R Research Journal
American Society of Heating, Refrigeration & AC
1791 Tullie Circle NE
Atlanta, GA 30329-2398

404-636-8400
800-527-4723
FAX 404-321-5478
E-Mail: ashrae@ashrae.org
Home Page: www.ashrae.org

Tom Watson, President
Jeff H Littleton, Executive VP

Offers the most comprehensive reporting of archival research in the fields of environmental control for the built environment. Also covers cooling technologies for a wide range of applications and related processes and concepts, including underlying thermodynamics, fluid dynamics, and heat transfer.
Frequency: Bi-Monthly
ISBN: 1-883413-98-2

1923 Indoor Comfort News Magazine
Institute of Heating and Air Conditioning
454 W Broadway
Glendale, CA 91204-1209

818-551-1555
FAX 818-551-1115
E-Mail: ihaci@ihaci.org
Home Page: www.ihaci.org

Susan Evans, Senior VP

A tool for attaining the trade association's goal of educating and promoting the HVAC/R/SM industry. Readers are top buyers and decision makers. They service and install new construction and replacement/retrofit projects.
Frequency: Monthly
Founded in 1955

1924 Journal of Microwave Power and Electromagnetic Energy
International Microwave Power Institute
7076 Drinkard Way
P O Box 1140
Mechanicsville, VA 23111-5007

804-559-6667
FAX 804-559-4087
E-Mail: info@impi.org
Home Page: www.impi.org

Molly Poisant, Executive Director

Designed for the information needs of professionals specializing in the research and design of industrial and bio-medical applications, the Journal exemplifies the highest standards of scientific and technical information on the theory and application of electromagnetic power.
Cost: $250.00
Frequency: Quarterly

1925 RSES Journal
Refrigeration Service Engineers Society

1911 Rohlwing Road
Suite A
Rolling Meadows, IL 60008-1397

847-297-6464
800-297-5660
FAX 847-297-5038
E-Mail: general@rses.org
Home Page: www.rses.org
Social Media: *Facebook, Twitter, LinkedIn*

Mark Lowry, Executive Vice President
Lori A Kasallis, Editor

Providing quality technical content in digital and printed forms that can be applied on the job site.
Frequency: Monthly
Circulation: 15231

1926 Today's Boiler
American Boiler Manufacturers Association
8221 Old Courthouse Rd
Suite 202
Vienna, VA 22182-3839

703-356-7172
FAX 703-522-2665
Home Page: www.abma.com

W Randy Rawson, President & CEO

Trends, Technologies & Innovations, The Official Magazine of the American Boiler Manufacturers Association.
Founded in 1888

Trade Shows

1927 ABMA Annual Meeting
American Boiler Manufacturers Association
8221 Old Courthouse Road
Suite 207
Vienna, VA 22182-3839

703-356-7172
FAX 703-356-4543
Home Page: www.abma.com

Jack Rentz, Chairman
W Randall Rawson, President/CEO
Kevin Hoey, Vice Chairman
Tom Giaier, Secretary

The association's premier membership networking event where members have the opportunity to learn about developments and trends inside and outside the industry, and have the opportunity, through committee and product/market group meetings to focus on issues and concerns of specific relevance to their product and market segments.
Frequency: Bi-Annual

1928 ABMA Manufacturers Conference
American Boiler Manufacturers Association
8221 Old Courthouse Road
Suite 207
Vienna, VA 22182-3839

703-356-7172
FAX 703-356-4543
Home Page: www.abma.com

Jack Rentz, Chairman
W Randall Rawson, President/CEO
Kevin Hoey, Vice Chairman
Tom Giaier, Secretary

Designed to bring together manufacturing plant, office and others concerned with the design, fabrication, sales and distribution of ABMA products and services to network, discuss trends and developments, and problem solve with others in the industry and with outside experts.
Frequency: Annual/October

1929 ACCA Conference & Indoor Air Expo
Air Conditioning Contractors of America

2800 Shirlington Rd
Suite 300
Arlington, VA 22206

703-575-4477
E-Mail: info@acca.org
Home Page: www.acca.org
Social Media: *Facebook, Twitter, LinkedIn, YouTube*

Paul Stalknecht, President & CEO
Rosemary Graeme, Executive Assistant
Kevin W. Holland, Senior Vice President

Workshops and learning opportunities for HVAC contractors.
Frequency: Annual/March

1930 AHAM Annual Meeting
Association of Home Appliance Manufacturers
1111 19th Street NW
Suite 402
Washington, DC 20036

202-872-5955
FAX 202-872-9354
E-Mail: info@aham.org
Home Page: www.aham.org

Edward V McAssey III, Chairman
Nick Baker, Manager
Alan M Holaday, Treasurer
Joseph M McGuire, President
Kevin Messner, Vice President

Provides ideas for the solution of problems and concerns of the Cross Functional Design.
Frequency: Annual/April

1931 AHRI Annual Meeting
Air-Conditioning, Heating & Refrigeration Inst
2111 Wilson Boulevard
Suite 500
Arlington, VA 22201

703-524-8800
FAX 703-528-3816
E-Mail: ahri@ahrinet.org
Home Page: www.ahrinet.org

Stephen R Yurek, President
Stephanie Murphy, CFO
AmandaE. Donahue, Executive Assistant

The premiere networking experience of the heating, ventilation, air conditioning and commercial refrigeration manufacturing industry addresses the topics and issues you want most. Offers opportunities to learn about the top issues facing the industry, network with industry leaders and colleagues, and participate in product section business
480+ Attendees
Frequency: November

1932 ASME International Mechanical Engineering Congress and Exposition
American Society of Mechanical Engineers
Three Park Avenue
New York, NY 10016-5990

973-882-1170
800-843-2763
E-Mail: infocentral@asme.org
Home Page: www.asme.org

Sam Y Zamrik PhD, President
David Walsh, Editor
Chitra Sethi, Managing Editor
John Kosowatz, Senior Editor

Hundreds of sessions, forums, exhibits, tours and social events keep you current on the latest trends in technology and industry, and provide the opportunity to trade tips and share ideas with engineers in different industries and companies around the world.
Frequency: Annual/Fall

1933 Fall Tech Conference
15000 Commerce Parkway
Suite C
Mt. Laurel, NJ 08054

856-380-6810
FAX 856-439-0525
E-Mail: info@nadca.com
Home Page: www.nadca.com

Kenneth M Sufka, Executive Vice President
Jodi Araujo, Executive Director
Leanne Murray, Director Membership
Jess Madden, Director Publications
Claire MacNab, Director Meetings

One-stop shop for training and certification. Designed to help members stand out from the competition. NADCA's trainers are highly experienced and know what it takes to be ultra successful in the HVAC cleaning industry.
1000 Members
Founded in 1989

1934 GAMA Annual Meeting
Gas Appliance Manufacturers Association
2107 Wilson Boulevard
Suite 600
Arlington, VA 22201

703-525-7060
FAX 703-525-6790
E-Mail: sheit@gamanet.org
Home Page: www.gamanet.org

Stacy Heit, Manager of Meetings/Events

National trade association whose members manufacture space and water heating appliances, components and related products.
405 Attendees
Frequency: Annual
Founded in 1935

1935 HARDI Annual Fall Conference
15000 Commerce Parkway
Suite C
Mt. Laurel, NJ 08054

856-380-6810
FAX 856-439-0525
E-Mail: info@nadca.com
Home Page: www.nadca.com

Kenneth M Sufka, Executive Vice President
Jodi Araujo, Executive Director
Leanne Murray, Director Membership
Jess Madden, Director Publications
Claire MacNab, Director Meetings

Conference offers information on profitability, confidence in navigating the economic waters, and finding the most effective and efficient means to achieve the market and profit objectives.
1000 Members
Founded in 1989

1936 IIAR
1001 N. Fairfax Street
Suite 503
Alexandria, VA 22314

703-312-4200
FAX 703-312-0065
E-Mail: iiar_request@iiar.org
Home Page: www.iiar.org

David L. Rule, President

IIAR provides advocacy, education, and standards for the benefit of the global community in the safe and sustainable installation and operation of ammonia and other natural refrigerant systems.
2086 Members
Founded in 1971

1937 IMPI Annual Symposium
International Microwave Power Institute

7076 Drinkard Way
P O Box 1140
Mechanicsville, VA 23111

804-596-6667
FAX 804-559-4087
E-Mail: info@impi.org
Home Page: www.impi.org

Molly Poisant, Executive Director
Neal Cooper, Treasurer

Brings together researchers from across the globe to share the latest findings related to non-communications uses of microwave energy.
Frequency: Annual/June

1938 International Air Conditioning, Heating & Refrigerating Expo
International Exposition Company
15 Franklin Street
Westport, CT 06880

203-221-9232
FAX 203-221-9260
E-Mail: info@ahrexpo.com
Home Page: www.ahrexpo.com

Mark Stevens, VP
Jeff Stevens, Sales VP
Kelley Stevens, Sales Manager

Co-sponsored by American Society of Heating, Refrigeration and Air Conditioning Engineers and the Air Conditioning and Refrigeration Institute, this expo features exhibits that include equipment and services of industrial, commercial and residential heating, refrigeration, air conditioning and ventilation.
37292 Attendees
Frequency: Annual/January
Founded in 1930

1939 International CES Show
1111 19th Street NW
Suite 402
Washington, DC 20036

202-872-5955
FAX 202-872-9354
E-Mail: info@aham.org
Home Page: www.aham.org

Paul Sikir, Chairman
Jennifer Mintman, First Vice Chairperson
Jennifer Mintman, Treasurer
Joseph M McGuire, President

World's largest consumer technology tradeshow.
Founded in 1915

1940 International Home & Housewares Show
International Housewares Associaton
6400 Shafer Court
Suite 650
Rosemont, IL 60018

847-292-4200
FAX 847-292-4211
E-Mail: sjanota@houseares.org
Home Page: www.housewares.org

Mia Rampersad, VP, Trade Shows
Sharon Janota, Manager, Trade Show Operations
David Reeves, Manager, Information Technology
Dean Kurtis, Finance & Information Technology
Judy Colitz, Manager Special Events

International housewares marketplace, showcasing thousands of new products and designs.
18500 Attendees
Frequency: March

1941 International Housewares Show
1111 19th Street NW
Suite 402
Washington, DC 20036

202-872-5955
FAX 202-872-9354
E-Mail: info@aham.org
Home Page: www.aham.org

Paul Sikir, Chairman
Jennifer Mintman, First Vice Chairperson
Jennifer Mintman, Treasurer
Joseph M McGuire, President

The center of the IHA's yearly activities. One
of the top 20 largest trade shows in the U.S.
and in the top 10 in Chicago.
Founded in 1915

1942 Kitchen & Bath Industry Show
1111 19th Street NW
Suite 402
Washington, DC 20036

202-872-5955
FAX 202-872-9354
E-Mail: info@aham.org
Home Page: www.aham.org

Paul Sikir, Chairman
Jennifer Mintman, First Vice Chairperson
Jennifer Mintman, Treasurer
Joseph M McGuire, President

The ultimate Kitchen & Bath destination. The
freshest designs, products and technology from
500 leading manufacturers and suppliers. The
brightest and best in the industry assemble to
spot trends, see and experience product introductions, acquire knowledge and find the practical solutions and valuable connections.
Founded in 1915

**1943 Kitchen/Bath Industry Show and
Conference**
National Kitchen & Bath Association
687 Willow Grove Street
Hackettstown, NJ 07840

800-843-6522
FAX 908-852-1695
E-Mail: feedback@nkba.org
Home Page: www.nkba.org

Alan Zielinski, CEO & President
Timothy Captain, PR Manager
John A Petrie, Vice President
Carolyn Cheetham, Treasurer
Bill Darcy, CEO

Showcases the latest products and cutting-edge
design ideas of the kitchen and bath industry.
40000 Attendees
Frequency: May

**1944 NADCA's Annual Meeting &
Exposition**
15000 Commerce Parkway
Suite C
Mt. Laurel, NJ 08054

856-380-6810
FAX 856-439-0525
E-Mail: info@nadca.com
Home Page: www.nadca.com

Kenneth M Sufka, Executive Vice President
Jodi Araujo, Executive Director
Leanne Murray, Director Membership
Jess Madden, Director Publications
Claire MacNab, Director Meetings

Promises educational sessions, live equipment
demonstrations, and opportunities to meet
peers.
1000 Members
Founded in 1989

1945 NASA Convention & Trade Show
National Appliance Service Association

3407 Williams Drive
PO Box 2514
Kokomo, IN 46904

765-453-1820
FAX 765-453-1895
E-Mail: nasahq2011@gmail.com
Home Page: www.nasa1.org

Scott Kopin, President
Gordon Daniels, VP/Treasurer
Carrie Giannakos, Executive Director
Mike Hanika, Director
Don Kehoe, Director

Classes on marketing, advertising, customer
service, machine repair by experienced professionals in the industry. Attendees are informed
about industry trends and products, and have
the opportunity to take advantage of show spe-
cials offered by exhibitors.
Frequency: Annual

1946 NCCA Annual Meeting
National Coil Coaters Association
1300 Sumner Avenue
Cleveland, OH 44115

216-241-7333
FAX 216-241-0105
E-Mail: ncca@coilcoating.org
Home Page: www.coilcoating.org

Jeff Alexander, President
Jeff Widenor, Vice President
John Favilla, Treasurer
Frequency: April

1947 National Appliance Parts Suppliers
National Appliance Parts Suppliers
Association
4015 W MARSHALL AVE
Longview, TX 75604

903- 75- 398
E-Mail: board11@napsaweb.org
Home Page: www.napsaweb.org

Jim Bossman, President
Sherry Harrell, Secretary, Treasurer
Jason Cunningham, Secretary

For those in the appliance parts replacement
business. Containing 62 booths and 60 exhibits.

**1948 RSES Annual Conference and HVAC
Technology Expo**
Refrigeration Service Engineers Society
1911 Rohlwing Road
Suite A
Rolling Meadows, IL 60008-1397

847-297-6464
800-297-5660
E-Mail: general@rses.org
Home Page: www.rses.org
Social Media: *Facebook, Twitter, LinkedIn*

Mark Lowry, Executive Vice President
Lori Kasallis, Publisher Editor
Jean Birch, Conference & Seminar Manager

80 booths consisting primarily of products and
services.

1949 SMACNA Annual Convention
15000 Commerce Parkway
Suite C
Mt. Laurel, NJ 08054

856-380-6810
FAX 856-439-0525
E-Mail: info@nadca.com
Home Page: www.nadca.com

Kenneth M Sufka, Executive Vice President
Jodi Araujo, Executive Director
Leanne Murray, Director Membership
Jess Madden, Director Publications
Claire MacNab, Director Meetings

Business and skill tips for HVAC and Contractor professionals.
1000 Members
Founded in 1989

**1950 The International Roundtable of
Household Appliance Manufacturer
Associations**

E-Mail: jnotini@aham.org
Home Page: www.irhma.org

Jill A. Notini, VP, Communications &
Marketing

Informal forum for discussion of issues facing
global appliance manufacturer associations.
Founded in 2014

**1951 VDTA/SDTA International Trade
Show**
1111 19th Street NW
Suite 402
Washington, DC 20036

202-872-5955
FAX 202-872-9354
E-Mail: info@aham.org
Home Page: www.aham.org

Paul Sikir, Chairman
Jennifer Mintman, First Vice Chairperson
Jennifer Mintman, Treasurer
Joseph M McGuire, President

Featuring exhibits, and seminars for the vacuum and sewing business.
Founded in 1915

**1952 World Educational Congress for
Laundering and Drycleaning (Clean
Show)**
Riddle & Associates
3098 Piedmont Road NE
Suite 350
Atlanta, GA 30305

404-876-1988
FAX 404-876-5121
E-Mail: info@cleanshow.com
Home Page: www.cleanshow.com
Social Media: *Facebook, Twitter*

John Riddle, Manager
Ann Howell, Communications

World's largest exposition for laundry,
drycleaning and textile services industry featuring working equipment and educational program. Draws international attendance.
11000 Attendees
Frequency: Biennial, Odd Years
Founded in 1977

Directories & Databases

**1953 A Portrait of the US Appliance
Industry**
UBM Canon
11444 W. Olympic Blvd.
Los Angeles, CA 90064

310-445-4200
FAX 310-445-4299
E-Mail: www.ubm.com
Home Page: www.appliancemagazine.com

David J Chase, President
Susan Chase Korin, CEO

Appliance companies in the US.
Cost: $45.00
Frequency: Annual
Founded in 1944

**1954 Complete Directory of Small
Appliances**
Sutton Family Communications &
Publishing Company

920 State Route 54 East
Elmitch, KY 42343

270-276-9500
E-Mail: jlsutton@apex.net

Theresa Sutton, Publisher
Lee Sutton, Editor

Print-out from database of wholesalers, manufacturers, distributors, importers and close-out houses. Database is updated daily to guarantee the most current and up-to-date sources available.

Cost: $55.20
100 Pages

1955 Directory of Certified Performance (Online)
Air Conditioning & Refrigeration Institute
Ste 500
2111 Wilson Blvd
Arlington, VA 22201-3036

703-524-8800
FAX 703-528-3816
E-Mail: ari@ari.org
Home Page: www.ari.org

Stephen R Yurek, President

The trusted source of performce certified heating, ventilation, air-conditioning, and commercial refrigeration equipment and components.

Industry Web Sites

1956 http://gold.greyhouse.com
G.O.L.D Grey House OnLine Databases
Grey House Publishing's online database platform, GOLD, offers Quick Search, Keyword Search and Expert Search for most business sectors including appliances and small electroincs. The GOLD platform makes finding the information you need quick and easy. All of Grey House's directory products are available for subscription on the GOLD platform.

1957 www.abma.com
American Boiler Manufacturers Association
Represents companies involved in utility, industrial and commercial steam generation.

1958 www.acca.org
Air Conditioning Contractors of America
Representing the HVACR contracting industry. We help our members acquire and satisfy customers while upholding the most stringent requirements for professional ethics, and advocating for improvements to the industry overall.

1959 www.aga.org
American Gas Association
Represents local energy utility companies that deliver natural gas to more than 56 million homes, businesses and industries throughout the United States.

1960 www.aham.org
Association of Home Appliance Manufacturers
Statistical information and summaries on appliances.

1961 www.apda.com
Appliance Parts Distributors Association
Promotes the sale of appliance parts through independent distributors.

1962 www.appliancemagazine.com
Dana Chase Publications

Appliance industry information content focused into 20 industry zones for targeted editorial coverage.

1963 www.ari.org
Air Conditioning & Refrigeration Institute
Representing manufacturers of central air-conditioning and commercial refrigeration equipment.

1964 www.ashrae.org
American Society of Heating, Refrigeration & A/C
Serving the heating, ventilation, air conditioning and refrigeration industries.

1965 www.asme.org
American Society of Mechanical Engineers
Focuses on technical, educational and research issues of the engineering and technology community.

1966 www.bema.org
Bakery Equipment Manufacturers Association
Serves the baking and snack food industries.

1967 www.gamanet.org
Gas Appliance Manufacturers Association
Serves the residential, commercial and industrial gas and oil fired appliance industries.

1968 www.ge.com
General Electric
Information on home appliances, lighting, home solutions, corporate trends and customer service.

1969 www.greyhouse.com
Grey House Publishing
Authoritative reference directories for most business sectors including appliances and small electronics markets. Users can search the online databases with varied search criteria allowing for custom searches by product category, geographic area, sales volume, keyword, subject and more. Full Grey House catalog and online ordering also available.

1970 www.housewares.org
International Housewares Association
Provides information on the international home & housewares industry, with search tools, consumer purchase trend data, and access to global opportunities and discount business services.

1971 www.ihea.org
Industrial Heating Equipment Association
A voluntary national trade association representing the major segments of the industrial heat processing equipment industry.

1972 www.impi.org
International Microwave Power Institute
A forum for the exchange of information on all aspects of microwave and RF heating technologies.

1973 www.napsaweb.org
National Appliance Parts Suppliers Association
Provides distributors of replacement parts for major home appliances with information and services.

1974 www.narda.com
North American Retail Dealers Association
Serves the independent retailer industry.

1975 www.nasa1.org
National Appliance Service Association

Promotes interests of portable and commercial appliance service repair and sales to industry owners.

1976 www.nkba.com
National Kitchen & Bath Association
Protects the interests of members by fostering a better business climate, awarding certification, and conducting training and seminars.

1977 www.psaworld.com
Professional Service Association
Information for companies that service and repair electronics and appliances.

1978 www.repairclinic.com
RepairClinic
Installation tips and how-to information on all appliances.

1979 www.reta.com
Refrigerating Engineers & Technicians Association
Seeks to upgrade the skills and knowledge of experienced members. Offers home-study courses on refrigeration and air conditioning.

1980 www.rses.org
Refrigeration Service Engineers Society
The world's leading education, training and certification association for heating, ventilation, air conditioning and refrigeration professionals.

1981 www.supco.com
Sealed Unit Parts
Serves the precision electronic test and service instruments, and refrigeration & air conditioning components industries; dedicated to producing high quality, innovative products at affordable prices to a wide range of customers.

Associations

1982 American Architectural Foundation

740 15th Street NW
Suite 225
Washington, DC 20005

202-787-1001
FAX 202-787-1002
E-Mail: info@archfoundation.org
Home Page: www.archfoundation.org
Social Media: *Facebook, Twitter, RSS*

G. Sandy Diehl, III, Chair
Ron Bogle, Hon. AIA, President & CEO
John Syvertsen, Vice Chair & Secretary
James R. Tolbert, III, Treasurer

The American Architectural Foundation (AAF) is dedicated to the vibrant social, economic, and environmental future of cities. In the past decade alone, AAF has worked directly with local leaders through more than 500 city engagements. During this time, AAF has served every major metropolitan region and most second-tier cities in the United States.

1983 American Architectural Manufacturers Association

1827 Walden Office Square
Suite 550
Schaumburg, IL 60173-4268

847-303-5664
FAX 847-303-5774
E-Mail: customerservice@aamanet.org
Home Page: www.aamanet.org
Social Media: *Facebook, Twitter, LinkedIn, YouTube, Flickr, RSS*

Rich Walker, President and CEO
Dean Lewis, Technical Information Manager
Maureen Knight, Government Affairs
Jannine Klemencic, Executive Assistant
Melissa McCord, Staff Accountant

Advocate for manufacturers and professionals in the fenestration industry with respect to product certification, standards development, education and training, legislative regulations, and building and energy codes.

1984 American College of Healthcare Architects

18000 W.105th St.
Olathe, KS 66061-7543

913-895-4604
FAX 913-895-4652
E-Mail: acha-info@goamp.com
Home Page: www.healtharchitects.org
Social Media: *Twitter, YouTube*

Anthony J. Haas, President
Mark A.ÿ Nichols, President-Elect
John W.ÿ Rogers, Secretary/Treasurer
Vince G. Avallone, Regent
Ellen Belknap, Regent

Provides certificate holders with networking, educational, and marketplace opportunities and distinguishes healthcare architects through certification, experience, and rigorous standards.

1985 American Design Drafting Association & American Digital Design Association

105 East Main Street
Newbern, TN 38059-1526

731-627-0802
FAX 731-627-9321
Home Page: www.adda.org
Social Media: *Facebook, Twitter, LinkedIn, Google+*

Rick Frymyer, Chairman of the Board
Richard Button, Governor - CFO
Danny G. Lewis, Governor

Bruce Nielsen, Governor
H. Duane Moore, Governor

The American Design Drafting Association was conceived by a dedicated and enthusiastic group of oil and gas piping drafters who were involved in various phases of design drafting. This group consisted of highly specialized industry drafters, educational instructors, piping designers, and engineering personnel.
1000+ Members
Founded in 1948

1986 American Institute of Architects (AIA)

1735 New York Ave Nw
Washington, DC 20006-5292

202-626-7300
800-242-3837
FAX 202-626-7547
E-Mail: infocentral@aia.org
Home Page: www.aia.org
Social Media: *Facebook, Twitter, LinkedIn, Youtube, RSS Feeds, Instagram,*

Christine McEntee, Executive Vice President

Based in Washington, D.C., the AIA is the leading professional membership association for licensed architects, emerging professionals, and allied partners.
83000 Members
Founded in 1857

1987 American Institute of Architects (AIAA)

1735 New York Ave Nw
Washington, DC 20006-5292

202-626-7300
800-242-3837
FAX 202-626-7547
E-Mail: infocentral@aia.org
Home Page: www.aia.org
Social Media: *Facebook, Twitter, LinkedIn, YouTube, RSS, Instagram, Flick*

Christine McEntee, Executive Vice President
83000 Members
Founded in 1857

1988 American Institute of Architecture Students

1735 New York Ave, NW
Suite 300
Washington, DC 20006-5209

202-808-0075
FAX 202-626-7414
E-Mail: mailbox@aias.org
Home Page: www.aias.org
Social Media: *Facebook, Twitter, Instagram, YouTube*

Charlie Klecha, President
Obi Okolo, Vice President
Nick Serfass, AIA, CAE, Executive Director

An independent, non-profit, student-run organization dedicated to providing unmatched programs, information, and resources on issues critical to architectural education.
Founded in 1956

1989 American Planning Association

205 N. Michigan Ave.
Suite 1200
Chicago, IL 60601

312-431-9100
FAX 312-786-6700
E-Mail: customerservice@planning.org
Home Page: www.planning.org
Social Media: *Facebook, Twitter, LinkedIn, YouTube, Flickr, RSS, Google+*

William Anderson, President
Carol Rhea, President Elect
Lee Brown, Director

James Drinan, Executive Director
Ann Simms, Chief Operating Officer

An independent, nonprofit educational organization that provides leadership in the development of vital communities.
Founded in 1978

1990 American Society for Aesthetics

1550 Larimer Streetÿ
#644
Denver, CO 0202-1602

912-961-3189
FAX 912-961-1395
E-Mail: asa@aesthetics-online.org
Home Page: www.aesthetics-online.org
Social Media: *Facebook, Twitter*

Robert Stecker, Editor
Theodore Gracyk, Editor
James Harold, Book Review Editor
Dominic McIver Lopes, Past President
Sondra Bacharach, Member

The American Society for Aesthetics promotes study, research, discussion, and publication in aesthetics. Aesthetics, in this connection, is understood to include all studies of the arts and related types of experience from a philosophic, scientific, or other theoretical standpoint, including those of psychology, sociology, anthropology, cultural history, art criticism, and education. The arts include the visual arts, literature, music, and theater arts.
Founded in 1942

1991 American Society for Healthcare Engineering

155 N. Wacker Drive
Suite 400.
Chicago, IL 60606

312-422-3800
FAX 312-422-4571
E-Mail: ashe@aha.org
Home Page: www.ashe.org
Social Media: *Facebook, Twitter, YouTube*

Philip C. Stephens, President
David A. Dagenais, President Elect
Dale Woodin, Senior Executive Director
Patrick J. Andrus, Deputy Executive Director
Susan B. McLaughli, Associate Member Director

One of the largest associations devoted to optimizing the health care built environment and is a personal membership organization of the American Hospital Association.

1992 American Society of Architectural Illustrators

294 Merrill Hill Road
Hebron, ME 4238

207-966-2062
E-Mail: HQ@asai.org
Home Page: www.asai.org
Social Media: *Facebook*

Jon Soules, President
Carlos Cristerna, Vice President
W. Daniel Church, Secretary
Columbus Cook, Treasurer
Tina Bryant, Executive Director

An international, nonprofit organization dedicated to the advancement and recognition of the art, science, and profession of architectural illustration. Through communication, education, and advocacy, this society strives to redefine and emphasize the role of illustration in the practice and appreciation of architecture.
Founded in 1986

1993 American Society of Concrete Contractors

2025 S. Brentwood Blvd.
Suite 105
St. Louis, MO 63144

314-962-0210
866-788-2722
FAX 314-968-4367
E-Mail: questions@ascconline.org
Home Page: www.ascconline.org
Social Media: *Facebook, LinkedIn, Pinterest*

Mike Poppoff, President
Scott M. Anderson, First Vice President
Rocky R. Geans, Vice President
Beverly Garnant, Executive Director
Bruce Suprenant, Technical Director

Provides knowledge on technical production and distribution of concrete construction, educates the industry on constructability, develops business savvy members, and helps them deliver a high quality product.
500 Members

1994 American Society of Golf Course Architects

125 N. Executive Drive
Suite 302
Brookfield, WI 53005

262-786-5960
FAX 262-786-5919
Home Page: www.asgca.org
Social Media: *Facebook, Twitter, LinkedIn, Instagram*

Lee Schmidt, President
Steve Smyers, Vice President
Greg Martin, Treasurer
John Sanford, Secretary
Chad Ritterbusch, Executive Director

The leader in advancing the interests of golf course architects andthe profession of golf course architecture for the benefit of ASGCA members and their clients, the golf industry, and the game of golf.
Founded in 1946

1995 American Society of Landscape Architects

636 Eye St NW
Washington, DC 20001-3736

202-898-2444
888-999-2752
FAX 202-898-1185
E-Mail: info@asla.org
Home Page: www.asla.org
Social Media: *Facebook, Twitter, LinkedIn, RSS Feeds, Pinterest, Instagra*

K. Richard Zweifel, FASLA, President
Jeffery A. Townsend, ALSA, VP Finance
Hunter L. Beckham, FALSA, VP Professional Practice
Keith P. Wilson, ASLA, VP Membership
Pamela J. Linn, ALSA, VP Communication

Residential and commercial real estate developers, federal and state agencies, city planning commissions and individual property owners are all among the thousands of people and organizations in America and Canada that will retain the services of a landscape architect this year.
15000 Members
Founded in 1899

1996 Applied Technology Council

201 Redwood Shores Parkway
Suite 240
Redwood City, CA 94065

650-595-1542
FAX 650-593-2320
Home Page: www.atcouncil.org

James A. Amundson, President
Victoria Arbitrio, Vice President
William Staehlin, Secretary/Treasurer
Roberto Leon, Past President
Chris Rojahn, Executive Director

A nonprofit, tax-exempt corporation that develops and promotes state-of-the-art, user-friendly engineering resources and applications for use in mitigating the effects of natural and other hazards on the built enviroment. ATC also identifies and encourages needed research and develops consensus opinions onstructural engineering issues in a nonproprietary format.

1997 Architectural League

594 Broadway
Suite 607
New York, NY 10012

212-753-1722
FAX 212-486-9173
E-Mail: info@archleague.org
Home Page: www.archleague.org
Social Media: *Facebook, Twitter, YouTube, Instagram, Vimeo*

Annabelle Selldorf, President
Paul Lewis, Vice President
Leo Villareal, Vice President
Michael Bierut, Vice President
Kate Orff, Vice President
Founded in 1881

1998 Architectural Precast Association

325 John Knox Rd
Ste L103
Tallahassee, FL 32303ÿ

850-205-5637
FAX 850-222-3019
E-Mail: info@archprecast.org
Home Page: www.archprecast.org

Paul Rossi, President
Chris Cox, Vice President
Fred L. McGee, Executive Director
Cari Renfro, Project Manager & Event Planner
Chris Leonhardt, Associate Director

A national trade association organized to advance the interests of architectural precast in North America.
Founded in 1966

1999 Architectural Research Centers Consortium, Inc.

Home Page: www.arccweb.org
Social Media: *Facebook, Twitter, LinkedIn, Google+*

Keith Diaz-Moore, President
Hazem RashdAli, Vice President
Saif Haq, Treasurer
Leonard Bachman, Secretary
Michael D. Kroelinger, Past President

An international association of architectural research centers committed to the expansion of the research culture and a supporting infrastructure in architecture and related design disciplines.
Founded in 1976

2000 Association for Computer Aided Design in Architecture

E-Mail: membership@acadia.org
Home Page: acadia.org

Michael Fox, President
Aron Temkin, Vice President
Greg Luhan, Secretary

Michael Christenson, Treasurer
Wei Yan, Membership

An international network of digital design researchers and professionals that facilitate critical investigations into the role of computation in architecture, planning, and building science, encouraging innovation in design creativity, sustainability, and education.

2001 Association for Environment Conscious Building

PO Box 32
Llandysul, SA

845-456-9773
Home Page: www.aecb.net
Social Media: *Facebook, Twitter*

Keith & Sally Hall, Founder
Chris Baines, Honorary President
Andy Simmonds, Chief Executive Officer
Sally Hall, Finance and Administration Officer
Gill Rivers, Business Operations Manager

A network of individuals, students, educational establishments, andcompanies with a common aim of promoting sustainable building. It brings together builders, architects, designers, manufacturers, housing associations, and local authorities to develop, share, and promote best practice in environmentally sustainable building.
Founded in 1989

2002 Association for Preservation Technology International

3085 Stevenson Drive
Suite 200
Springfield, IL 62703

217-529-9039
FAX 888-723-4242
E-Mail: info@apti.org
Home Page: www.apti.org
Social Media: *Facebook, LinkedIn*

Gretchen Pfaehler, President
John Diodati, Vice President, Co-chair Conference
Michael Schuller, Vice-President, Co-chair Training
Nathela Chatara, CAEAdministrative Director
Lesley Gilmore, Treasurer

The Association for Preservation Technology (APT) is a cross-disciplinary, membership organization dedicated to promoting the best technology for conserving historic structures and their settings.
Founded in 1968

2003 Association for Women in Architecture + Design

1315 Storm Pkwy.
Torrance, CA 90501

310-534-8466
FAX 310-257-1942
Home Page: awaplusd.org
Social Media: *Facebook, Twitter, LinkedIn, Instagram, Pinterest*

Kishani De Silva, President
Christina Monti, Vice President
Anna Harris, Parliamentarian
Linda Daley, Chief Financial Officer
Terri Moore, Secretary

Organization dedicated to the professional development of women working in the fields of architecture and design.
Founded in 1915

2004 Association of Architecture Organizations
224 South Michigan Avenue
Suite 116
Chicago, IL 60604

312-561-2159
FAX 312-922-2607
Home Page: www.aaonetwork.org
Social Media: *Facebook, Twitter, RSS*

Lynn Osmond, Hon. AIA, President & CEO
Margie O'Driscoll, Hon. AIACC, Vice Chair
Nate Eudaly, Treasurer
Linda Sylvan, Secretary
Michael Wood, Executive Director

A member-based network that connects organizations around the worlddedicated to enhancing public dialogue about architecture and design.
Founded in 2005

2005 Association of Collegiate Schools of Architecture
1735 New York Ave NW
3rd Floor
Washington, DC 20006-5209

202-785-2324
FAX 202-628-0448
E-Mail: info@acsa-arch.org
Home Page: www.acsa-arch.org
Social Media: *Facebook, Twitter, LinkedIn, Vimeo*

Norman R. Millar, President
Hsin-Ming Fung, Vice President/President-Elect
Michael J Monti, PhD, Executive Director
Eric Wayne Ellis, Director of Operations and Programs
Pascale J. Vonier, Director of Communications

Nonprofit membership association founded to advance the quality of architectural education.
500 Members
Founded in 1912

2006 Association of Licensed Architects
One East Northwest Hwy.
Suite 200
Palatine, IL 60067

847-382-0630
FAX 847-382-8380
E-Mail: ala@alatoday.org
Home Page: www.alatoday.org
Social Media: *Facebook, Twitter, LinkedIn*

Jeffrey Budgell, President
James K. Zahn, Esq, Vice President
Patrick C. Harris, Treasurer
Mark V. Spann, Secretary
Joanne Sullivan, Executive Director

An organization open to all architects and professions related to architecture and it represents architects registered or licensed in any state, territory, or possession of the United States or foreign country.

2007 Association of Professional Landscape Designers
2207 Forest Hills Drive
Harrisburg, PA 17112

717-238-9780
FAX 717-238-9985
Home Page: www.apld.com
Social Media: *Facebook, Twitter, LinkedIn, Pinterest*

Denise Calabrese, Executive Director
Lisa M. (Frye) Ruggiers, Associate Executive Director
Angela Burkett, Membership Director
Michelle Keyser, Director of Communications
Jennifer Swartz, Bookkeeper

An international organization dedicated to advancing the professionof landscape design and promoting the recognition of landscape designers as qualified and dedicated professionals.
Founded in 1986

2008 Association of University Architects
17595 S Tamiami Trail
Fort Myers, FL 33908-4570

FAX 239-590-1010
E-Mail: information@auaweb.net
Home Page: www.auaweb.net

Evie Asken, Director Campus Planning
Steven Thweatt, President

Purpose is to achieve more effective planning in the field of higher education, improve the design and construction standards of university buildings and to develop common bonds and establish standards which will ensure clarity of communications and render effective the exchange of information.
Founded in 1955

2009 Business Architecture Guild
E-Mail: info@businessarchitectureguild.org
Home Page:
www.businessarchitectureguild.org

Bob Carlston, Director of Business Management
John Machiski, Treasurer
Neal McWhorter, Founder
Jim Rhyne, Founder
Kathy Ulrich, Founder/ Executive Director

A professional association that offers exclusive content to its members. Additional benefits include a private online community, opportunities to provide feedback and collaborate with them on content, a knowledge repository, newsletters, webinars, and more.

2010 Cast Stone Institute
813 Chestnut Street
PO Box 68
Lebanon, PA 17042-7218

717-272-3744
FAX 717-272-5147
E-Mail: staff@caststone.org
Home Page: www.caststone.org

Jesse Hawthorne, President
Scott Mathews, Vice President
Jan Boyer, Executive Director
Tim Michael, Director
David Owen, Director

An organization of cast stone manufacturers, associates, professional architects, engineers and concrete technologists formed for the purpose of improving the quality of cast stone and disseminating information regarding its use.
70 Members
Founded in 1927

2011 Center for Environmental Design Research
University of California at Berkeley
390 Wurster Hall
Suite 1839
Berkeley, CA 94720-1839

510-642-2896
FAX 510-643-5571
E-Mail: earens@berkeley.edu
Home Page: www.cedr.berkeley.edu
Social Media: *Facebook, Twitter, LinkedIn, Flickr, Youtube*

Tom J. Buresh, M.Arch., Chair, Department of Architecture
Paul Waddell, M.S., Ph.D, Chair, Department of City
G. Mathias Kondolf, M.S., Ph.D., Chair, Department of Landscaping
Jennifer Wolch, Ph.D., Dean
Gary Brown, M.Arch, Associate Dean for Faculty Affairs

Mission is to foster research in environmental planning and design

2012 Construction Sciences Research Foundation, Inc.
E-Mail: info@csrf.org
Home Page: www.csrf.org

Raymond K. Best, President
Kurt T. Preston, VP Finance and Administration
Michael D. Dell'Isola, Vice President
Charles Chief Boyd, Secretary/Treasurer
Julie K Brown, Director

An independent, nonprofit construction industry research organization dedicated to unifying and integrating communication between programs and design/communications processes used in facilities design and construction.

2013 Council on Tall Buildings and Urban Habitat
SR Crown Hall, Illinois Institute of Technology
3360 S State Street
Chicago, IL 60616-3796

312-567-3487
FAX 312-567-3820
E-Mail: info@ctbuh.org
Home Page: www.ctbuh.org
Social Media: *Facebook, Twitter, YouTube*

David Malott, Chairman
Antony Wood, Executive Director
Patti Thurmond, Operations
Carissa Devereux, Membership
Steven Henry, Design & Production

Supported by architecture, engineering, planning development and construction professionals, designed to facilitate exchanges among those involved in all aspects of the planning, design, construction and operation of tall buildings.
Founded in 1969

2014 Environmental Design Research Association
7918 Jones Branch Drive
Suite 300
McLean, VA 22102

703-506-2895
FAX 703-506-3266
E-Mail: headquarters@edra.org
Home Page: www.edra.org
Social Media: *Facebook, Twitter, LinkedIn, YouTube, Flickr, Instagram*

Gowri Betrabet Gulwadi, Chair
Lynne Manzo, Chair Elect
Paula Horrigan, Secretary
Shanuna Mallery-Hill, Treasurer
Kate O Donnell, Executive Director

An organization dedicated to advancing and distributing environmental design research, thereby improving understanding of the interrelationships between people, their built and natural surroundings. EDRA's goal is also to facilitate the creation of environments that are responsive to human needs.
Founded in 1968

2015 Green Building Alliance
33 Terminal Way
Suite 331
Pittsburgh, PA 15219

412-431-0709
E-Mail: info@gbapgh.org
Home Page: www.go-gba.org
Social Media: *Facebook, Twitter, LinkedIn, YouTube*

Michael Kuhn, President
Christine Mondor, Vice President
Mike Schiller, CEO

Kevin Clarke, Secretary
Mark Smith, Treasurer

An organization that promotes healthy, high performing places for everyone by inspiring and leading the market, demonstrating and proving value, and equipping the community with knowledge and resources.
1200 Members
Founded in 1993

2016 Historic New England
Soc for Preservation of New England Antiquities
141 Cambridge St
Boston, MA 02114-2702

617-227-3956
FAX 617-227-9204
Home Page: www.historicnewengland.org
Social Media: *Facebook, Twitter, YouTube, Tumblr, Zazzle*

Carl R. Nold, President/CEO
Diane Viera, Executive Vice President/COO
Kimberlea Tracey, Vice President for Advancement
Wendy Gus, Director of Finance
Benjamin Haavik, Team Leader for Property Care

Focuses on buildings, landscapes and objects reflecting New England life from the 17th century to the present. Also publishes a magazine about the organizations objects, architectural holdings and activities.
6000 Members
Founded in 1910

2017 Institute for Urban Design
17 West 17th Street, 7th Floor
New York, NY 10014-3731

212-366-0780
FAX 212-633-0125
E-Mail: info@ifud.org
Home Page: www.ifud.org
Social Media: *Facebook, Twitter, LinkedIn, RSS Feeds, vimeo*

Anne Guiney, Executive Director
Alexandra Sutherland-Brown, Program Coordinator

Responsible for city planning.
1M Members
Founded in 1979

2018 Insulated Cable Engineers Association
P.O. Box 2694
Alpharetta, GA 30023

Home Page: www.icea.net

R.O. Bristol, President
Rick Williamson, 1st VP
Kim Nuckles, 2nd VP

A professional organization dedicated to developing cable standardsfor the electric power, control, and telecommunications industries.
Founded in 1925

2019 Interior Design Educators Council
One Parkview Plaza
Suite 800
Oakbrook Terrace, IL 60181ÿ

630-544-5057
E-Mail: info@idec.org
Home Page: www.idec.org
Social Media: *Facebook, Twitter, LinkedIn, YouTube, Flickr, Yahoo, Google*

Cynthia Mohr, President
Katherine Ankerson, Past President
Migette Kaup, President Elect
Cindy Martimo, Secretary/Treasurer
Jill Pable, Director

An organization dedicated to the advancement of interior design education, scholarship, and service.
Founded in 1972

2020 International Association for Impact Assessment
1330 23rd Street S
Suite C
Fargo, ND 58103-3705

701-297-7908
FAX 701-297-7917
E-Mail: info@iaia.org
Home Page: www.iaia.org
Social Media: *Facebook, Twitter, YouTube*

Rita Hamm, CEO
Jennifer Howell, Publications/Meetings Specialist
Bridget John, Marketing/Financial Specialist
Shelli LaPlante, Member Liaison/Conference Registrar
Loreley Fortuny, Special Project Associate

A forum for advancing innovation, development, and communication of best practice in impact assessment. Exists to improve and better inform the decision-making of today that has environmental consequences for tomorrow.
2500 Members
Founded in 1980

2021 International Association of Innovation Professionals
4422 Castle Wood Street
Sugar Land, TX 77479

925-858-0905
E-Mail: hello@iaoip.org
Home Page: iaoip.org
Social Media: *Facebook, Twitter, LinkedIn, Instagram, Vimeo*

Brett Trusko, President/ CEO
Lewis Archer, Webmaster
Charisma Aggarwal, Development Manager
Dana J. Landry, VP Certification Programs
Marco D. Mancin, Director

Creates events and provides resources to help professionals learn the latest innovation methodologies, and offer certification testing to help themadvance in their careers.

2022 International Code Council
500 New Jersey Avenue, NW
6th Floor
Washington, DC 20001

708-799-4981
888-422-7233
FAX 708-799-4981
E-Mail: members@iccsafe.org
Home Page: www.iccsafe.org
Social Media: *Facebook, Twitter, LinkedIn, Youtube*

C.P. Ramani, President
Pat Nathan, Vice President
Mark Johnson, Executive VP and Director, Business
Hamid Naderi, Sr. VP, Product Development
Laurence Genest, VP, Sales Marketing

A nonprofit membership association dedicated to preserving the public health, safety and welfare in the built environment through the promulgation of model codes suitable for adoption by governmental entities and assisting code enforcement officials, design professionals, builders, manufacturers and others involved in the design, construction and regulatory processes.
16000 Members
Founded in 1915

2023 International Interior Design Association
222 Mechandise Mart
Suite 567
Chicago, IL 60654

312-467-1950
888-799-4432
312-467-1950
E-Mail: iidahq@iida.org
Home Page: www.iida.org
Social Media: *Facebook, Twitter, LinkedIn, YouTube, Instagram*

Julio Braga, President
Scott Hierlinger, President Elect
Viveca Bissonnette, Vice President
Dennis Krause, Senior Vice President
Cheryl Dust, Executive Vice President

Association that provides its members with sources, knowledge, and contacts necessary in the interior design field.

2024 Marine Engineers' Beneficial Association
444 N. Capitol Street, NW
Suite 800
Washington, DC 20001

202-638-5355
FAX 202-638-5369
Home Page: www.mebaunion.org
Social Media: *Facebook, Twitter, YouTube*

Marshall Ainley, President
Bill Van Loo, Secretary/ Treasurer
Mark Gallagher, Contracts Rep
Eric C. Pittman, Comptroller

The oldest maritime trade union that represents licensed mariners, deck and engine officers and has a training plan to provide further technical training. It has worked hard in Washington, DC to ensure proper examination and licensing of engineers and the abolition of controversial license fees.
Founded in 1875

2025 Marine Technology Society
1100 H St., NW
Suite LL-100
Washington, DC 20005

202-717-8705
FAX 202-347-4302
E-Mail: membership@mtsociety.org
Home Page: www.mtsociety.org

Drew Michel, President
Jerry Boatman, Immediate Past President
Ray Toll, Vice President
Richard lawson, Executive Director
Chris Barett, Director

A growing organization with a membership that includes businesses, institutions, individual professionals, and students who are ocean engineers, technologists, policy makers, and educators. This group works to promote awareness, understanding, advancement, and the application of marine technology.
Founded in 1963

2026 National Academy of Environmental Design

E-Mail: info@naedonline.org
Home Page: www.naedonline.org

Daniel Friedman, President
Thomas R. Fisher, Vice President
Frederick Steiner, Immediate Past President
James F. Palmer, Secretary
Claudia Phillips, Treasurer

A nonprofit organization that provides the public with expertise and leadership in the creation of healthier, greener, safer, and more resilient American communitites through environmental design.

163

2027   National Architectural Accrediting Board

1101 Connecticut Avn., NW
Suite 410
Washington, DC 20036

202-783-2007
FAX 202-783-2822
E-Mail: info@naab.org
Home Page: www.naab.org
Social Media: *Facebook, Twitter*

Shannon B. Kraus, President
Scott Veazey, President Elect
Patricia Kucker, Treasurer
Brian R. Kelly, Secretary
Andrea S. Rutledge, Executive Director

Develops and maintains a system of accreditation in professional architecture education that is responsive to the needs of society and allows institutions with varying resources and circumstances to evolve according to their individual needs.

2028   National Association of Home Builders

1201 15th Street NW
Washington, DC 20005

202-266-8200
800-368-5242
FAX 202-266-8400
Home Page: www.nahb.org
Social Media: *Facebook, Twitter, LinkedIn, Google+, Pinterest*

Kevin Kelly, Chairman
Tom Woods, Chairman-Elect
Ed Brady, Second Vice Chairman
Granger MacDonald, Third Vice Chairman
Gerald M. Howard, Chief Executive Officer

A trade association that helps promote the policies that make housing a national priority.
Founded in 1940

2029   National Council of Architectural Registration Boards

1801 K St NW
Suite 700k
Washington, DC 20006-1320

202-783-6500
FAX 202-783-0290
Home Page: www.ncarb.org
Social Media: *Facebook, Twitter, LinkedIn, YouTube*

Blakely C. Dunn, Vice President
Michael Armstrong, CEO

Committed to protecting the health, safety, and welfare of the public through effective regualtion and exemplary service.
Founded in 1919

2030   National Organization of Minority Architects

1735 New York Avenue
NW #357
Washington, DC ÿ20006

202-586-6682
E-Mail: president@noma.net
Home Page: www.noma.net
Social Media: *Facebook, Twitter, LinkedIn*

Kathy Dixon, President
Kevin M. Holland, President Elect
Aminah Wright, Secretary
Walter Wilson, Treasurer
Gianna Pigford, Recording Secretary

A national organization that strives to minimize the effects of racism in the architecture profession and also battles against apathy, bigotry, and abuse of the natural environment.

2031   Organization of Women Architects and Designers

PO Box 10078
Berkeley, CA 94709

Home Page: www.owa-usa.org
Social Media: *Facebook*

Janet Crane, President
Mui Ho, Secretary
Bill Hocker, Webmaster
Anne Jakiemiec, Health Plan Consultant
Judy L. Rowe, FAIA, Treasurer

A nonprofit organization that is an active support network for women involved in architecture, engineering, planning, landscape architecture, interior and graphic design, and related environmental design fields.
Founded in 1970

2032   Partners for Livable Communities

1429 21st St Nw
Washington, DC 20036-5902

202-887-5990
FAX 202-466-4845
E-Mail: livability@livable.org
Home Page: www.livable.com
Social Media: *RSS*

Robert H. McNulty, President
Penny Cuff, Vice President of Programs
Irene Garnett, Vice President of Finance
Faith Koleszar, Executive Assistant
Arianna Koudounas, Program Officer

A non-profit leadership organization working to improve the livability of communities by promoting quality of life, economic development, and social equity.
Founded in 1977

2033   Society for Environmental Graphic Design

1900 L Street NW
Suite 710
Washington, DC ÿ20036ÿ

202-638-5555
FAX 202-478-2286
E-Mail: segd@segd.org
Home Page: www.segd.org
Social Media: *Facebook, Twitter, LinkedIn, RSS Feeds*

Clive Roux, CEO
Ann Makowski, COO
Pat Matson Knapp, Director of Communications
Justin Molloy, Director of Education
Sara Naegelin, Director of Sponsorship

The global community of people who work at the intersection of communication design and the built environment.
Founded in 1974

2034   Society of American Registered Architects

14 E. 38th Street
New York, NY 10016

888-385-7272
FAX 888-385-7272
E-Mail: cmoscato@sara-national.org
Home Page: www.sara-national.org
Social Media: *Facebook*

Ron Knabb, Jr., FARA, President
Gaetano Ragusa, FARA, President-Elect
John J. Di Benedetto, FARA, Vice-President
Francisco J. Urrutia, FARA, Treasurer
Cathie Moscato, Executive Director

A professional society that includes the participation of all architects, regardless of their roles in the architectural community, the opportunity to share information and ideas.
Founded in 1956

2035   Society of Architectural Historians

1365 N Astor St
Chicago, IL 60610-2144

312-573-1365
FAX 312-573-1141
E-Mail: info@sah.org
Home Page: www.sah.org
Social Media: *Facebook, Twitter, LinkedIn, YouTube, Instagram, RSS*

Kenneth Breish, President
Ken Tadashiÿ Oshima, Vice President
Sandy Isenstadt, 2nd Vice President
Pauline Saliga, Executive Director
Michael J. Gibson, Treasurer

A not-for-profit membership organization and learned society that promotes the study and preservation of the built environment worldwide.
2500 Members
Founded in 1940

2036   Society of Naval Architects and Marine Engineers

99 Canal Center Plaza
Suite 310
Alexandria, VA 22314

703-997-6701
800-798-2188
FAX 703-997-6702
Home Page: www.sname.org

Edward N. Comstock, President
Erik Seither, Executive Director

Internationally recognized nonprofit technical, professional society of individual members serving the maritime and offshore industries and their suppliers. Dedicated to advancing the industry by recording information, sponsoring research, offering career guidance and supporting education.
10000 Members
Founded in 1893

2037   Sustainable Buildings Industry Council

1090 Vermont Avenue NW
Suite700
Washington, DC 20005

202-289-7800
FAX 202- 28- 109
E-Mail: nibs@nibs.org
Home Page: www.sbicouncil.org
Social Media: *Facebook, Twitter, LinkedIn, Pinterest*

Bud DeFlaviis, Executive Director
Kimberly Lowry, Executive Assistant

Mission is to unite and inspire the building industry toward higher performance through education, outreach, advocacy and the mutual exchange of ideas.
Founded in 1980

2038   The Architectural League of New York

594 Broadway
Suite 607
New York, NY 10012

212-753-1722
FAX 212-486-9173
E-Mail: info@archleague.org
Home Page: archleague.org
Social Media: *Facebook, Twitter, YouTube, Instagram, Vimeo*

Rosalie Genevro, Executive Director
Anne Rieselbach, Program Director
Nicholas Anderson, Communications Director

The League provides a forum for debate about current issues in architecture, design and urbanism.
Founded in 1881

2039 The National Institute of Building Sciences
1090 Vermont Avenue, NW
Suite 700
Washington, DC 20005-4950

202-289-7800
FAX 202-289-1092
E-Mail: nibs@nibs.org
Home Page: www.nibs.org
Social Media: *RSS*

James T. Ryan, Chairman
Stephen Ayers, Vice Chairman
Henry L. Green, President
John G Lloyrd, Vice President
John Marshall Ortiz, AIA, Secretary

A nonprofit, non-governmental organization that brings together representatives of government, the professions, industry, labor and consumer interests, and regulatory agencies to focus on the identification and resolution of problems that hamper the contruction of safe, affordable structures for housing, commerce, and industry throughout the United States.

2040 U.S. Green Building Council
2101 L Street, NW
Suite 500
Washington, DC 20037

202-742-3792
800-795-1747
E-Mail: info@usgbc.org
Home Page: www.usgbc.org
Social Media: *Facebook, Twitter, LinkedIn, YouTube, Instagram, Google+*

Kunal Gulati, Product Marketing Specialist
Mark de Groh, Director, Philanthropy
Aline Peterson, Media & Communications Specialist
Lee Brown, Account Manager
Alex Hammack, Operations Associate

This organization is made up of tens of thousands of member organizations, chapters, and student and community volunteers that strive to transform the way buildings and communities are operated, enabling an environmentally and socially responsible, healthy, and prosperous environment that improves the quality of life.
Founded in 1973

2041 United States Access Board
Access Board
1331 F St Nw
Suite 1000
Washington, DC 20004-1111

202-272-0080
800-872-2253
FAX 202-272-0081
E-Mail: info@access-board.gov
Home Page: www.access-board.gov
Social Media: *Facebook, Twitter, Vimeo*

Karen L. Braitmayer, FAIA, Chair
David M. Capozzi, Executive Director
Neil Melick, Director
James J. Raggio, General Counsel
Lisa Fairhall, Deputy General Counsel

Independent federal agency devoted to accessibility for people with disabilities. Its key missions include developing and maintaining guidelines for the built environment, transit vehicles, telecommunications equipment and standards for electronic and information technology; providing technical assistance and training on these guidelines and standards and enforcing design standards for federally funded facilities.
Founded in 1968

2042 Urban Design Associates
3 PPG Place
3rd Floor
Pittsburgh, PA 15222

412-263-5200
FAX 844-270-8374
Home Page: www.urbandesignassociates.com
Social Media: *Facebook, Twitter, Vimeo*

Designs resilient neighborhoods, towns, villages, districts, places, and buildings.
Founded in 1964

Newsletters

2043 A/E Business Review
6524 E Rockaway Hills Drive
PO Box 4808
Cave Creek, AZ 85331-7609

480-488-0311
FAX 480-488-0311

Clare Ross, Publisher
The management and marketing newsletter of architects, engineers and planners.
7 Pages
Frequency: Monthly

2044 AIA Architect
American Institute of Architects
1735 New York Ave Nw
Washington, DC 20006-5292

202-626-7300
800-242-3837
FAX 202-626-7547
E-Mail: infocentral@aia.org
Home Page: www.aia.org

Robert Ivy, CEO
Jeff Potter, President

News of America's community of architects
Frequency: Weekly

2045 Access Currents
Access Board
1331 F St Nw
Suite 1000
Washington, DC 20004-1135

202-272-0080
800-872-2253
FAX 202-272-0081
E-Mail: info@access-board.gov
Home Page: www.access-board.gov

David Capozzi, Executive Director
Frequency: Bi-Monthly

2046 Certifier
Nat'l Council of Architectural Registration Boards
1801 K St Nw
Suite 700K
Washington, DC 20006-1320

202-879-0520
FAX 202-783-0290
Home Page: www.ncarb.org

Michael Armstrong, CEO
Blakely Dunn, Vice President

State architectural registration boards.
Frequency: Annual
Founded in 1919

2047 Design Drafting News
American Design Drafting Association
105 E Main Street
Newbern, TN 38059-1526

731-627-0802
FAX 731-627-9321

E-Mail: corporate@adda.org
Home Page: www.adda.org

Ron McDonald, President
Dennis Schwartz, Executive VP

Newsletter for the American Design Drafting Association and American Digital Design Association.
Frequency: Bi-Monthly
Circulation: 1800

2048 Design Firm Management & Administration Report
Institute of Management and Administration
3 Bethesda Metro Center
Suite 250
Bethesda, MD 20814-537

703-341-3500
800-372-1033
FAX 800-253-0332
Home Page: www.ioma.com

Provides practical, hands-on, timely information to design firm managers and administrators about the marketing and management aspects of operating a firm.
Cost: $429.00
Frequency: Monthly

2049 Designline
American Institute of Building Design
529 14th St NW
Suite 750
Washington, DC 20045

202-249-1407
800-366-2423
FAX 866-204-0293
E-Mail: info@aibd.org
Home Page: www.aibd.org

Dan Sater, President
Alan Kent, Vice President

Focuses on issues, education, and events as they happen in the building design industry.
Frequency: Quarterly

2050 Direct Connection
Nat'l Council of Architectural Registration Boards
1801 K St NW
Suite 700K
Washington, DC 20006-1301

202-870-0520
FAX 202-782-0290
E-Mail: customerservice@ncarb.org
Home Page: www.ncarb.org

Ron McDonald, CEO
Blakely Dunn, Vice President

Offers information and news on licensing, board certification, architectural trends and more for the professional architect and intern architect.
16 Pages
Circulation: 50000
Printed in 2 colors on glossy stock

2051 Energy Design Update
Aspen Publishers
76 Ninth Avenue
7th Floor
New York, NY 10011

212-771-0600
800-638-8437
Home Page: www.aspenpublishers.com

Mark Dorman, CEO
Gustavo Dobles, VP Operations

For professionals concerned with residential load management and energy efficient design and construction in housing.
Cost: $297.00
16 Pages
Frequency: Monthly

2052 Guidelines Letter: New Directions and Techniques in the Design Profession
Guidelines
PO Box 2590
Alameda, CA 94501

510-235-5174
800-634-7779
FAX 510-523-5175
E-Mail: info@sfia.net
Home Page: www.sfia.net

Fred Stitt, Director/Editor
Chandler Vienneau, Circulation Director

Business and technical information for design professionals including comprehensive survey information regarding fees and client costs. The Guidelines Letter is in its 28th year of publication.
Cost: $70.00
4 Pages
Frequency: Monthly
ISSN: 1089-2141
Founded in 1992

2053 Landscape Architectural News Digest
American Society of Landscape Architects
636 Eye St NW
Washington, DC 20001-3736

202-898-2444
800-787-2752
FAX 202-898-1185
E-Mail: membership@asla.org
Home Page: www.asla.org

Jonathan Mueller, President
Seck Hardi, Editor

Provides a comprehensive view of the latest developments in regional, residential and corporate architecture.
Cost: $42.00
16 Pages
Frequency: Monthly

2054 Memo
American Institute of Architects
1735 New York Ave Nw
Washington, DC 20006-5292

202-626-7300
800-242-3837
FAX 202-626-7547
E-Mail: infocentral@aia.org
Home Page: www.aia.org

Robert Ivy, CEO
Jeff Potter, President
Norman Koonce, Editor
Scott Frank, Director

Architectural news and information.
Frequency: Monthly
Circulation: 85000

2055 SARAscope
Society of American Registered Architects
P.O. Box 280
Newport, TN 37822

888-385-7272
E-Mail: cmoscato@sara-national.org
Home Page: www.sara-national.org

Suzette Stoler, President
Cathie Moscato, Executive Director

Listing society conventions, meetings and other activities. Discusses news about the Society of interest to members.
Frequency: BiWeekly
Founded in 1956

2056 SBIC Newsletter
Sustainable Buildings Industry Council

1090 Vermont Avenue NW
Suite 700
Washington, DC 20005

202-289-7800
FAX 202-289-1092
E-Mail: nibs@nibs.org
Home Page: www.sbicouncil.org

Henry Green, President
John Lloyd, Vice President
Gretchen Hesbacher, Editor

Published to inform the members of the mission to advance the design, affordability, energy performance and environmental soundness of residential, institutional and commercial buildings. Newsletter is free to members.
6-8 Pages
Frequency: 2-3 per year
Circulation: 400
Founded in 1995
Printed in 2 colors on matte stock

2057 Society of Architectural Historians Newsletter
Society of Architectural Historians
1365 N Astor St
Chicago, IL 60610-2144

312-573-1365
FAX 312-573-1141
E-Mail: info@sah.org
Home Page: www.sah.org

Dr. Abigail Van Slyck, President
Prof. Ken Breisch, Vice President

Keeps readers informed about upcoming SAH events, conferences, tours, awards, publications and exhibitors.
Frequency: Bi-Monthly

2058 Times
Council of Tall Buildings and Urban Habitat
Illinois Institute of Technology SR Crown
3360 S State Street
Chicago, IL 60616-3793

312-567-3487
FAX 312-567-3820
E-Mail: info@ctbuh.org
Home Page: www.ctbuh.org

Patti Thurmond, Operations Manager
Antony Wood, Executive Director
Tansri Muliani, News Editor
Steven Henry, Publications

Newsletter for members of CTBUH.
Cost: $75.00
Frequency: Monthly
Circulation: 1200
ISSN: 1061-5121
Founded in 1969
Printed in 2 colors on matte stock

Magazines & Journals

2059 AI Communications
AIAA
1735 New York Ave NW
Washington, DC 20006-5209

202-626-7300
800-242-3837
FAX 202-626-7547
E-Mail: infocentral@aia.org
Home Page: www.aia.org

Jeffery Potter, President
Mickey Jacob, Vice President

Student programs and issues dealing with architectural education.
Founded in 1857

2060 APT Bulletin: The Journal of Preservation Technology
Association for Preservation Technology Int'l
3085 Stevenson Drive
Suite 200
Springfield, IL 62705

217-529-9039
FAX 888-723-4242
E-Mail: info@apti.org
Home Page: www.apti.org

Joan Berkowitz, President
Gretchen Pfaehler, Vice President

Articles showcase cutting-edge preservation techniques, as well as innovative applications of established restoration technologies.

2061 Adobe Magazine
Adobe Systems
345 Park Ave
San Jose, CA 95110-2704

408-536-6000
FAX 408-537-6000
Home Page: www.adobe.com

Shantanu Narayen, CEO
Mark Garrett, SVP

Devoted to adobe and earthen architecture. Showing both old and new traditions of building the earth.
Cost: $4.00
Circulation: 4,500

2062 American School & University
PRIMEDIA Intertec Publication
9800 Metcalf Ave.
Overland Park, KS 66212

913-341-1300
FAX 913-967-1898
E-Mail: jagron@primediabusiness.com
Home Page: www.penton.com

Nicola Alais, Senior VP
Gregg Herring, Publisher
David KIESELSTEIN, CEO

The industry's definitive educational facilities publication.
Cost: $50.00
508 Pages
Frequency: Monthly
Circulation: 63540
Founded in 1928
Printed in 4 colors on glossy stock

2063 Architectural Design
John Wiley & Sons
111 River St
Hoboken, NJ 07030-5790

201-748-6000
FAX 201-748-6088
E-Mail: info@wiley.com
Home Page: www.wiley.com

Matthew Kissner, CEO/President
Jean-Lou Chameau, President

Continues to publish a vigorous and wide range treatment of architectural trends of topical importance.
Cost: $145.00
Founded in 1807

2064 Architectural Digest
4 Times Square
Suite 15
New York, NY 10036-6518

212-286-2860
FAX 212-286-6790
Home Page: www.architecturaldigest.com

Giulio Capua, Publisher
Margaret Russell, Editor-in-Chief

For the connoisseur of interior design. The purpose is to cultivate an appreciation of excel-

lence in the luxury world of design and furnishing.
Cost: $39.95
Frequency: Monthly
Circulation: 840,995
Founded in 1999

2065 Architectural Record
McGraw Hill
2 Penn Plaza
9th Floor
New York, NY 10121-2298

212-904-2594
FAX 212-904-4256
E-Mail: william_hanley@mcgraw-hill.com
Home Page: archrecord.construction.com

William Hanley, Web Editor
Cathleen McGuigan, Editor in Chief
Ilan Kapla, Sr. Manager, Web Production
Rama Bandu, Web Producer
Elisabeth Broome, Managing Editor

Provides a compelling editorial mix of design ideas and trends, building science, business and professional strategies, exploration of key issues, news products and computer-aided practice.
Cost: $49.00
Frequency: Monthly

2066 Architecture Magazine
American Institute of Architects
One Thomas Circle, NW
Suite 600
Washington, DC 20005

202-452-0800
FAX 202-785-1974
E-Mail: info@architecturemag.com
Home Page: www.architecturemag.com

Ned Cramer, Editor-in-Chief
Greig O'Brien, Managing Editor
Katie Gerfen, Senior Editor

Evaluation of new and existing buildings and related news that affects the profession.
Frequency: Monthly
Circulation: 63449

2067 Ballast Quarterly Review
Ballast
2022 X Avenue
Dysart, IA 52224-9767

E-Mail: ballast@netins.net

Roy Behrens, Editor

Examines an eclectic assortment of publications with an emphasis on graphic design and architecture.
16 Pages
Frequency: Quarterly

2068 Building Design & Construction
Reed Business Information
360 Park Ave S
New York, NY 10010-1737

1 -46 -46 6
FAX 646-756-7583
E-Mail: submail@reedbusiness.com
Home Page: www.reedbusiness.com

Mark Kelsey, CEO
James Reed, President

Serves the needs of the design and construction professionals of commercial, industrial and institutional buildings that include new and retrofit projects. Geared towards the building team that includes professionals from building firms, owning firms and design firms.
Frequency: Monthly
Founded in 1946

2069 CRIT: Journal of the American Institute of Architecture Students
American Institute of Architecture Students

1735 New York Ave NW
Washington, DC 20006-5292

202-626-7472
FAX 202-626-7414
E-Mail: mailbox@aias.org
Home Page: www.aias.org

Joshua Caulfield, CEO
Joshua Caulfield, Executive Director
Yurly Napelenok, Programs & Membership
Laura Meader, Editor in Chief

The premier source of and the only international journal of student design work.
Frequency: Bi-Annual
Circulation: 13,000
Founded in 1976

2070 CTBUH Review Journal
Council on Tall Buildings and Urban Habitat
S.R.Crown Hall,
3360 South State Street
Chicago, IL 60616

312-567-3487
FAX 312-567-3820
E-Mail: info@ctbuh.org
Home Page:
www.ctbuh.org/Publications/Journal/tabid/72/language/en-GB/Defaul

Marshall Ali, Editor
Anthony Wood, Executive Director
Robert Lau, Associate Editor

CTBUH Review is the Professional Journal of the Council on Tall Buildings and Urban Habitat. It includes refereed papers submitted by researchers, scholars, suppliers, and practicing professionals engaged in the planning, design, construction, and operation of tall buildings and the urban environment throughout the world. Membership benefits include monthly e-updates, access to on-line buildings database, discounts on selected publications and registration at Council-sponsored activities.
Cost: $150.00
1400 Pages
Frequency: Quarterly

2071 Classicist
Transaction Publishing Rutgers
35 Berrue Circle
Piscataway, NJ 08854-8042

732-445-2280
888-999-6778
FAX 732-445-3138
E-Mail: trans@transactionpub.com
Home Page: www.transactionpub.com

Mary Curtis, President
Prof. David Shulman, Editor

Dedicated to the theory and practice of architecture and artistic classicism.
Cost: $39.95
164 Pages

2072 Computer-Aided Engineering
Penton Media
1300 E 9th St
Suite 316
Cleveland, OH 44114-1503

216-696-7000
FAX 216-696-1752
E-Mail: information@penton.com
Home Page: www.penton.com

David Kieselstein, CEO
Nicola Allais, EVP
Jasmine Alexander, Senior VP & CIO

Database applications in design and manufacturing.
Cost: $50.00
96 Pages
Founded in 1982

2073 Concrete Masonry Designs
13750 Sunrise Valley Drive
Herndon, VA 20171-4662

703-713-1900
FAX 703-713-1910
E-Mail: ncma@ncma.org
Home Page: www.ncma.org

Mary Arntson-Terrell, Director of Sales
Robert Thomas, President

Highlights concrete masonry applications, best practice tips, specifications and details. Also showcases concrete masonry landscape products.
Cost: $2.50
Frequency: Monthly
Circulation: 25000
Founded in 1918
Printed in 4 colors on glossy stock

2074 Contemporary Stone & Tile Design
BNP Media
210 E State Rt 4
Suite 203
Paramus, NJ 07652-5103

201-291-9001
FAX 201-291-9002
E-Mail: info@stoneworld.com
Home Page: www.stoneworld.com

Alex Bachrach, Publisher
Michael Reis, Editor
Jennifer Adams, Editor

Focuses on stone and ceramic tile use in interior design for architects, interior designers, specifiers and consumrs with the buying influence for stone or stone materials and a variety of architectural and construction products and services.

2075 Design Issues
MIT Press
55 Hayward Street
Cambridge, MA 02142-1315

617-253-5646
FAX 617-258-6779
Home Page: www.mitpress.mit.edu

Michael Sims, Managing Editor
Ellen Faran, Director

Provokes inquiry into the cultural and intellecutual issues surrounding design. Regular features include theoretical and critical articles by professional and scholarly contributions, extensive book reviews, and illustrations.
110 Pages
Frequency: Quarterly
ISSN: 0747-9360
Founded in 1984

2076 Design Journal
Journal Communications Group
1720 20th St #201
Santa Monica, CA 90404

310-394-4394
FAX 310-394-0966
E-Mail: customer.services@benjamins.nl
Home Page: designjournalmag.com

Kees Vaes, Editor
Karin Plijnaar, Marketing Manager

Focuses on the design and architecture marketplace. Includes newsbites and a calendar, as well as designer and lighting resources.
Frequency: Monthly
Circulation: 34000
Founded in 1982

2077 Design Solutions Magazine
Architectural Woodwork Institute

46179 Westlake Drive
Suite 120
Potomac Falls, VA 20165

571-323-3636
FAX 571-323-3630
E-Mail: adsales@awinet.org
Home Page: www.awinet.org

Teresa McCain, Director of Operations
Philip Duvic, Executive VP

Featuring beautiful woodwork projects manu-
factured by members of the Architectural
Woodwork Institute (AWI). Many other related
publications, including woodworking quality
standards used by woodwork manufacturers
and design professionals.
Cost: $25.00
Frequency: Quarterly
Circulation: 25000
Founded in 1953

2078 Design/Build Business
Cygnus Publishing
12735 Morris Road
Bldg. 200
Alpharetta, GA 30152-0803

770-427-5290
800-547-7377
FAX 404-935-9290
E-Mail: kathy.scott@cygnusb2b.com
Home Page: www.cygnusb2b.com

John French, CEO
Michael Martin, President

Serves builders, architects and designing and
remodeling firms, nationwide. Edited to these
professions serving the residential and light
commercial marketplaces.
Cost: $24.00
72 Pages
Frequency: Monthly
Circulation: 60424
ISSN: 1068-9433
Founded in 1935

2079 Dodge Construction News
McGraw Hill
PO Box 182604
Columbus, OH 43272

614-866-5769
877-833-5524
FAX 614-759-3749
E-Mail: customer.service@mcgraw-hill.com
Home Page: www.mcgraw-hill.com

Jennifer Hayes, Editor
Harold McGraw III, President/CEO

Consists of program edition and proceedings
and recap edition for the National Conventions
of the American Institute of Architects and
Construction Specifications Institute.
Circulation: 86400
Founded in 1958

2080 Fabrics Architecture
U.S. Industrial Fabrics Association
International
1801 County Road NW
Roseville, MN 55113-4061

651-222-2508
800-225-4324
FAX 651-631-9334
E-Mail: fabarch@ifai.com
Home Page: www.usifi.com

Ruth Stephens, Executive Director

Strives to inform architects, designers, landscape architects, engineers and other specifiers
about architectural fabric structures, the fibers
and fabrics used to make them, their design
possibilities, their construction, and issues regarding their applicability and acceptance.
Cost: $39.00
Frequency: Bi-Monthly

2081 Glass Magazine
National Glass Association
1945 Old Gallows Rd
Suite 750
Vienna, VA 22182

703-442-4890
866-342-5642
FAX 703-442-0630
E-Mail: editorialinfo@glass.org
Home Page: www.glass.org

Phil James, CEO
Nicole Harris, Vice President

Offers readers experienced editorial direction
and informative coverage including market
segment surveys, resource guides, reader polls,
industry profiles, industry states, and industry
products.
Frequency: Monthly

2082 Harvard Design Magazine
Harvard University Graduate School of
Design
48 Quincy St
Gund Hall
Cambridge, MA 02138-3000

617-495-5453
FAX 617-495-8949
E-Mail: hdm@gsd.harvard.edu
Home Page: www.gsd.harvard.edu
Social Media: *Facebook, Twitter, LinkedIn*

Mohsen Mostafavi, Dean

Aims to provide a forum for thoughtful and articulate practitioners, journalists, and academics, primarily from architecture, landscape
architecture and urban design and planning.
Frequency: Bi-Annual

**2083 Impact Assessment and Project
Appraisal (IAPA)**
International Association for Impact
Assessment
1330 23rd Street S
Suite C
Fargo, ND 58103-3705

701-297-7908
FAX 701-297-7917
E-Mail: info@iaia.org
Home Page: www.iaia.org

Rita Hamm, CEO
Jennifer Howell, Publications

IAPA is an international refereed journal. It
welcomes papers on the environmental, social,
health, technology, integrated, sustainability,
etc. assessment of projects, programs, plans
and policies.
Frequency: Quarterly
Circulation: 1600
ISSN: 1461-5517

2084 Inland Architect
Real Estate News Corporation
3500 West Peterson Avenue
Suite 403
Chicago, IL 60659

773-866-9900
888-641-3169
FAX 773-866-9881
E-Mail: rencorpil@aol.com
Home Page: www.inlandarchitectmag.com

Steven Polydoris, Publisher/Editor

Covers distinguished and historical buildings.
Cost: $27.00
120 Pages
Founded in 1883
Printed in 4 colors on glossy stock

2085 Journal of Architectural Education
Blackwell Publishing Inc

350 Main St
Suite 6
Malden, MA 02148-5089

781-388-8598
800-835-6770
FAX 781-388-8210
E-Mail: cs-journals@wiley.com
Home Page: www.blackwellpublishing.com

Vincent Marzano, VP
Stephen Smith, CEO

Enhances architectural design education, theory
and practice.
Frequency: Quarterly
ISBN: 0-262753-24-3
Founded in 1947

**2086 Journal of Architectural and Planning
Research**
Locke Science Publishing
332 S. Michigan Avenue
Suite 1032 #L221
Chicago, IL 60604

E-Mail: japr@lockescience.com
Home Page: www.lockescience.com

Andrew Seidel, Editor-in-Chief
Ajay Garde, Editor

The major international disciplinary resource
for professionals and scholars in architecture,
design, and planning. Also provides a link between theory and practice for researchers and
practicing professionals.

2087 Journal of Urban Technology
New York City Technical College
300 Jay St
Brooklyn, NY 11201-1909

718-260-5250
FAX 718-260-5524
E-Mail: connect@citytech.cuny.edu
Home Page: www.cuny.edu

Russell Hotzler, President
Miguel Cairol, VP

Covers technological developments in the ar-
chitecture and transporatation fields.
Circulation: 10000
Founded in 1946

**2088 Journal of the Society of
Architectural Historians**
Society of Architectural Historians
1365 N Astor St
Chicago, IL 60610-2144

312-573-1365
FAX 312-573-1141
E-Mail: info@sah.org
Home Page: www.sah.org

Prof. Ken Breisch, Vice President
Abigail Van Slyck, President

Offers three to four scholarly articles on American and International topics, reviews of re-
cently-published books, reviews of architecture
exhibitions, and a variety of editorials designed
to place the discipline of architectural history
within a larger intellectual context.
Frequency: Quarterly

2089 Metal Architecture
Modern Trade Communications
7450 Skokie Blvd
Suite 200
Skokie, IL 60077-3374

847-674-2200
FAX 847-674-3676
E-Mail: circulation@moderntrade.com
Home Page: www.moderntrade.com
Social Media: *Facebook, Twitter, LinkedIn*

Paul Deffenbaugh, Editorial Director
Mark Robins, Senior Editor

John S. Lawrence, CEO
John Paul Lawrence, President
Low-rise construction involving architects, engineers and specifiers.
Frequency: Monthly
Circulation: 33000
Founded in 1980

2090 Metropolis Magazine
Bellerophon Publications
61 W 23rd St
4th Floor
New York, NY 10010-4246

212-627-9977
FAX 212-627-9988
E-Mail: edit@metropolismag.com
Home Page: www.metropolismag.com
Social Media: *Facebook, Twitter, LinkedIn*

Horace Havemeyer, Publisher
Susan Szenasy, Editor-in-Chief

The only magazine that covers all facets of design: architecture, interiors, furniture, preservation, urban design, graphics and crafts.
Cost: $27.95
Circulation: 61000
Founded in 1980

2091 Old House Interiors
Gloucester Publishers Corporation
10 Harbor Rd
Gloucester, MA 01930-3222

978-283-3200
800-356-9313
FAX 978-283-4629
E-Mail: info@oldhouseinteriors.com
Home Page: www.oldhouseinteriors.com

Regina Cole, Editor
Covers restoration techniques for the pre-1939 home.
Cost: $26.00
116 Pages
Circulation: 100000
Founded in 1995
Printed in 4 colors on glossy stock

2092 Places: A Forum of Environmental Design
Journal of Environmental Design
100 Higgans Hall
Brooklyn, NY 11205

FAX 718-399-4332

James F Fulton, Publisher
Covers architecture, landscape architecture, urban design, with a multidisciplinary view of all aspects of public and private places.
Cost: $35.00

2093 Preservation Magazine
National Trust for Historic Preservation
1785 Massachusetts Ave NW
Washington, DC 20036-2189

202-588-6000
800-944-6847
FAX 202-588-6038
E-Mail: info@savingplaces.org
Home Page: www.preservationnation.org

Stephanie Meeks, CEO
David Brown, EVP
Offers lively writing by the nation's best journalists on controversies, trends, accomplishments, and events of importance to cities, towns, suburbs, and rural communities.

2094 Professional Builder
Reed Business Information
360 Park Ave S
New York, NY 10010-1737

646-746-6845
FAX 646-756-7583
E-Mail:

corporatecommunications@reedbusiness.com
Home Page: www.reedbusiness.com

Mark Kelsey, CEO
James Reed, President
New residential construction magazine with a tradition of providing builders the solutions they need to maximize profits.
Frequency: Monthly
Founded in 1936

2095 Reed Bulletin
Reed Business Informtion
30 Technology Parkway South
Suite 100
Norcross, GA 30092

800-424-3996
E-Mail: talisha.jackson@reedbusiness.com
Home Page: www.reedconstructiondata.com

Talisha Jackson, Media Contact

Provides contractors with project news and tools suppliers.

2096 Residential Architect
Hanley-Wood
1 Thomas Circle NW
Suite 600
Washington, DC 20005-5811

202-452-0800
888-269-8410
FAX 202-785-1974
E-Mail: cconroy@hanleywood.com
Home Page: www.residentialarchitect.com

Claire Conroy, Editorial Director
Jennifer Lash, Managing Editor
Bruce Snider, Senior Editor

It delivers substantive editorial on marketing, presentation, products, technology and business management to architects and designers.
Cost: $39.95
Frequency: 9x Yearly
Circulation: 22000
Founded in 1976

2097 Society of Architectural Administrators News Journal
Society of Architectural Administrators
15 E 7th Street NW
Cincinatti, OH 45202

513-684-3451

Patsy Frost, Publisher
Society news for professionals in the architectural community.

2098 Urban Omnibus
The Architectural League of New York
594 Broadway
Suite 607
New York, NY 10012

212-753-1722
E-Mail: info@urbanomnibus.net
Home Page: urbanomnibus.net
Social Media: *Facebook, Twitter, Vimeo, YouTube*

Jonathan Tarleton, Senior Editor
Emily Schmidt, Senior Editor
Online publication exploring new ideas and projects for the built environment of New York.
Frequency: Weekly
Founded in 2009

2099 World Monuments Fund
350 Fifth Avenue
Suite 2412
New York, NY 10118

646-424-9594
FAX 646-424-9593

E-Mail: wmf@wmf.org
Home Page: www.wmf.org

Bonnie Burnham, President
Jonathan Foyle, Chief Executive
Darlene McCloud, VP
Lisa Ackerman, Executive VP, COO

This magazine offers information on the latest architectural trends, specifically landmarks, monuments, antiquities.
Cost: $17.95
16 Pages
Frequency: Quarterly
Founded in 1965
Printed in 4 colors on glossy stock

Trade Shows

2100 AIA National Convention and Design Exposition
American Institute of Architects
1735 New York Avenue NW
Washington, DC 20006-5292

202-626-7300
800-242-3837
FAX 202-626-7547
E-Mail: infocentral@aia.org
Home Page: www.aia.org

Christine McEntee, CEO

Offers the chance to meet with more than 800 exhibitors and discover new products and technologies that can be used in future projects.
Frequency: Annual/April

2101 ASLA Annual Meeting & EXPO
American Society of Landscape Architects
636 Eye Street NW
Washington, DC 20001-3736

202-988-2444
800-787-2752
FAX 202-898-1185
E-Mail: info@asla.org
Home Page: www.asla.org

Thomas Tavella, President
Mark Hough, VP

Landscape architect educational session and workshop plus 500 exhibits of outdoor lighting, playground and park equipment, landscape maintenance equipment, computer hardware and software and much more.
6000 Attendees

2102 American Institute of Architects Minn. Convention & Products Exhibition
American Institute of Architects, Minnesota Chap.
275 Market Street
Suite 54
Minneapolis, MN 55405

612-339-6904
FAX 612-338-7981
E-Mail: infocentral@aia.org
Home Page: www.aia-mn.org

Christine McEntee, CEO

175 exhibits of windows, concrete, roofing, millwork, tile and more, plus conference, seminar and dinner.
2500 Attendees
Frequency: Annual
Founded in 1934

2103 American Institute of Building Design Annual Convention
American Institute of Building Design

529 14th St NW
Suite750
Washington, DC 20045

800-366-2423
FAX 866-204-0293
E-Mail: info@aibd.org
Home Page: www.aibd.org

Dan Sater, President
Alan Kent, VP

A four day convention and trade show for residential design professionals
Frequency: Annual/July

2104 American Society for Aesthetics Annual Conference
American Society for Aesthetics
PO Box 915
Pooler, GA 31322

912-921-3189
FAX 912-961-1395
E-Mail: asa@aesthetics-online.org
Home Page: www.aesthetics-online.org

Paul Guyer, President
Dabney Townsend, Treasurer
Dominic McLver Lopes, VP

Seminar, conference, and exhibits related to the study of the arts, all disciplines.
500 Attendees
Frequency: Annual/October
Founded in 1942

2105 Annual Technical & Educational Conference
American Design Drafting Association
105 E Main St
Newbern, TN 38059-1526

731-627-0802
FAX 731-627-9321
E-Mail: corprorate@adda.org
Home Page: www.adda.org

Ron McDonald, President
Dennis Schwartz, Executive VP

Annual professional educational conference dedicated to serve the professional growth and advancement of the individuals working in the extremely fast paced, professional graphic community.
100 Members
Frequency: Annual/April

2106 Computers for Contractors and A/E/C Systems Fall
AEC Systems International/Penton Media
1300 E 9th St
Suite 316
Cleveland, OH 44114

216-696-7000
FAX 216-696-6662
E-Mail: information@penton.com
Home Page: www.aecsystems.com

Sharon Rowlands, CEO
Nicola Allais, EVP

Computers for construction is the only tradeshow and conference dedicated exclusively to computer use by contractors. A/E/C SYSTEMS Fall is the regional technology event for the entire design and construction industry.
7000 Attendees
Frequency: Annual/November

2107 Council on Tall Buildings & Urban Habitat Congress
Lehigh University
11 East Packer Avenue
Bethlehem, PA 18015

610-583-3000
FAX 610-758-4522

E-Mail: inctbuh@lehigh.edu
Home Page: www.ctbuh.orh

Antony Wood, Executive Director

Brings the world's leading decision makers together. For additional information visit our website or email us.
600+ Attendees
Frequency: Annual/February
Founded in 1969
Mailing list available for rent: 4500 names

2108 EDM/PDM Expo
AEC Systems International/Penton Media
1300 E 9th St
Suite 316
Cleveland, OH 44114

216-696-7000
FAX 216-696-7000
E-Mail: info@aecsystems.com
Home Page: www.aecsystems.com

Sharon Rowlands, CEO
Nicola Allais, EVP

Showcases ways to manage technical/engineering documents, product management, and drawing conversion. Over 500 exhibits are shown.
20M Attendees
Frequency: Annual/May

2109 International Manufacturing & Engineering Technology Congress
AEC Systems International/Penton Media
1300 E 9th St
Suite 316
Cleveland, OH 44114

216-696-7000
FAX 216-696-6662
E-Mail: info@aecsystems.com
Home Page: www.aecsystems.com

Sharon Rowlands, CEO
Nicola Allais, EVP

Automotive, aeronautics, and aerospace, electrical and electronics, consumer products, industrial, heavy equipment, and process industries. 1000 exhibits.
15M Attendees
Frequency: Annual/November

2110 LightFair
AMC
120 Wall Street
17th Floor
New York, NY 10005

212-248-5000
FAX 212-248-5017
E-Mail: ies@ies.org
Home Page: www.iesna.org

Chip Israel, President
Daniel Salinas, Vice President

A major lighting trade show in North America featuring architectural lighting products from all spectrons of the industry. Containing 600 booths and 400 exhibits.
17M Attendees
Frequency: Annual/June
Mailing list available for rent: 10M names at $100 per M

2111 Lightfair International
Atlanta Market Center
240 Peachtree Street NW
Suite 2200
Atlanta, GA 30303-1327

404-220-3000
800-ATL-MART
FAX 404-220-3030
E-Mail: webmaster@americasmart.com
Home Page: www.americasmart.com

John Portman, CEO
Jeffery Portman, COO

The world's largest annual architectural/commercial lighting trade show and conference program. Lightfair International features the latest technology, products, education, information, awards and industry association events. 600 booths.
20M Attendees
Frequency: Annual/May

2112 M/Tech
AEC Systems International/Penton Media
1300 E 9th Street
Suite 316
Cleveland, OH 44114

216-696-7000
FAX 216-696-6662
E-Mail: info@aecsystems.com
Home Page: www.aecsystems.com

Sharon Rowlands, CEO
Nicola Allais, EVP

Focuses on applications to improve every phase of the product development cycle including CAD/CAM/CAE, Internet/intra/extranct, rapid prototyping and tooling, project/financial management, simulation and analysis, EDM/PDM and much more. 300 exhibits.
15M Attendees
Frequency: Annual/November

2113 M/Tech West
AEC Systems International/Penton Media
1300 E 9th St
Suite 316
Cleveland, OH 44114

216-696-7000
FAX 216-696-6662
E-Mail: info@aecsystems.com
Home Page: www.acesystems.com

Sharon Rowlands, CEO
Nicola Allais, EVP

Explores concurrent engineering practices, computer integrated manufacturing, and mechanical engineering applications. 50 exhibits.
20M Attendees
Frequency: Annual/May

2114 National Council of Architectural Registration Boards Annual Meeting
Natl. Council of Architectural Registration Boards
1801 K Street NW
Suite 700K
Washington, DC 20006

202-783-6500
FAX 202-783-0290
E-Mail: customerservice@ncarb.org
Home Page: www.ncarb.org

Ronald Biltch, President
Blakely Dunn, VP

Annual meeting and exhibits of architecture equipment, supplies and services.

2115 Retail Design & Construction Conference & Expo
Primedia
3585 Engineering Drive
Suite 100
Norcross, GA 30092

678-421-3000
800-216-1423
FAX 913-967-1898
Home Page: www.primedia.com

Charles Stubbs, President
Kim Payne, SVP

Annual show of 145 exhibitors of equipment, supplies and services for retail design, construction, development, operations and maintenance, including signage, building equipment and materials, fixtures, floor coverings, furnishings, lighting, landscaping, store fronts,

roofing, HVAC, maintenance materials and contractor services.
1000 Attendees

2116 SARA National Conference
Society Of American Registered Architects
P.O. Box 280
Newport, TN 37822

888-385-7272
FAX 888-385-7272
E-Mail: cmoscato@sara-national.org
Home Page: www.sara-national.org
Social Media: *LinkedIn*

Guy Ragusa, Membership Chair
Cathie Moscato, Executive Director
Suzette Stoler, President
Gaetano Ragusa, Vice President

Annual conference holding the National Board Meeting, Architecture & Design Banquet, President's Celebration Banquet & Installation of Officers, and the International & Distinguished Building Award Presentations
503 Members
Founded in 1956

2117 TCAA Convention
Tile Contractors Association of America
10434 Indiana Avenue
Kansas City, MO 64137

816- 86- 930
800-655-8453
FAX 816-767-0194
E-Mail: info@tcaainc.org
Home Page: www.tcaainc.org

Chris Pattavina, Associate Director
Carole Damon, Executive Director

Architect/designer learning exchange, speakers, business meetings, new products and technology
Founded in 1903

2118 Technology for Construction
Hanley-Wood
6191 N State Hwy 161
Suite 500
Irving, TX 75038

972-366-6300
866-962-7469
FAX 972-536-6301
E-Mail: rmcconnell@hanleywood.com
Home Page:
www.technologyforconstruction.com

Rick McConnell, President
Tom Cindric, Group Director

Annual forum that showcases the technology, tools and solutions for the design, construction, maintenance and modification of commercial buildings, institutions and other structures. These tools and education are essential for the seamless collaboration and communication between all those involved throughout the asset lifecycle.
72M Attendees
Frequency: Annual
Founded in 1976

Directories & Databases

2119 Akron School Design Institute
American Architectural Foundation
1020 19th Street NW
Suite 525
Washington, DC 20036

202-787-1001
FAX 202-78 -002

E-Mail: info@archfoundation.org
Home Page: www.archfoundation.org
Ron Bogie, President/CEO
Scott Lauer, VP of Programs
Frequency: Annual

2120 Dodge Building Stock
DRI/McGraw-Hill
148 Princeton Heights Town Road
Height Town, NJ 08520

609- 42- 500
800-393-6343
E-Mail: support@construction.com
Home Page: www.dodge.construction.com
Social Media: *Facebook, Twitter, LinkedIn*

Keith Fox, President
Linda Brennan, VP of Operations

This database contains more than 18,000 historical and forecast quarterly time series on US buildings, including total square footage, number of buildings, and roof area for groups of structures in the categories of commercial, institutionals, manufacturing and residential.

2121 Pro File/Official Directory of the American Institute of Architects
American Institute of Architects (AIAA)
1735 New York Avenue NW
Washington, DC 20006-5292

202-783-6500
800-242-3837
FAX 202-626-7364
E-Mail: infocentral@aia.org
Home Page: www.aia.org

Christine McEntee, CEO

Over 18,000 architectural firms are listed. These listings have one or more principals who is a member of the American Institute of Architects.
Cost: $225.00
1800 Pages
Frequency: Annual

2122 Progressive Architecture: Information Sources Issue
Penton Media
1300 E 9th St
Suite 316
Cleveland, OH 44114-1503

216-696-7000
FAX 216-696-1752
E-Mail: information@penton.com
Home Page: www.penton.com

David Rowlands, CEO
Nicola Allais, EVP

List of trade and professional architecture associations.
Cost: $48.00

2123 Sweets Directory
Grey House Publishing/McGraw Hill Construction
1221 Avenue of the Americas
New York, NY 10020-1095

212-512-2000
800-442-2258
FAX 212-512-3840
E-Mail: webmaster@mcgraw-hill.com
Home Page: www.mcgraw-hill.com
Social Media: *Facebook, Twitter*

Harold W McGraw III, CEO
Jack Callahan, Vice President

The leading desktop reference and preliminary research guide, featuring more than 10,000 building product manufacturers and their products.
Cost: $145.00
950 Pages
Frequency: Annual

ISBN: 1-592378-50-1
Founded in 1906

2124 ThomasNet
Thomas Publishing Company, LLC
User Services Department
5 Penn Plaza
New York, NY 10001

212-695-0500
800-699-9822
FAX 212-290-7362
E-Mail: contact@thomaspublishing.com
Home Page: www.thomasnet.com
Social Media: *Facebook, Twitter, LinkedIn*

Carl Holst-Knudsen, President
Robert Anderson, VP, Planning
Mitchell Peipert, VP, Finance
Ivy Molofsky, VP, Human Resources

A way to reach qualified businesses that list their company information on ThomasNet.com. Detailed profiles promote their products, services, capabilities and brands carried. The ThomasNet.com web site is the most up-to-date compilation of 650,000 North American manufacturers, distributors, and service companies in 67,000 industrial categories.
Founded in 1898

2125 Visual Merchandising and Store Design
ST Media Group International
P.O. Box 1060
Skokie, IL 60076

847-763-4938
800-421-1321
FAX 847-763-9030
E-Mail: customer@stmediagroup.com
Home Page: www.stmediagroup.com

Steve Duccilli, Group Publisher
Wade Swormstedt, Editor/Publisher
Ted Swormstedt, President/CEO

Visual Merchandising and Store Design showcases the latest store designs and visual presentations, presents merchandising strategies and new products and reports on industry news and events.
Frequency: Monthly
Circulation: 27000
Founded in 1922

Industry Web Sites

2126 http://gold.greyhouse.com
G.O.L.D Grey House OnLine Databases

Grey House Publishing's online database platform, GOLD. offers Quick Search, Keyword Search and Expert Search for most business sectors including architecture, buidling and construction markets. The GOLD platform makes finding the information you need quick and easy. All of Grey House's directory products are available for subscription on the GOLD platform.

2127 www.access-board.gov
Architectural & Transportation Barriers Compliance
Devoted to accessibility for people with disabilities.

2128 www.acsa-arch.org
Association of Collegiate Schools of Architecture
A nonprofit, membership association founded to advance the quality of architectural education.

2129 www.adda.org
American Design Drafting Association

The premier professional organization for drafters, designers, engineers, architects, ilustrators, graphics artist, digital technicians, digitial imaging, visual communications and multimedia

2130   www.aecsystems.com.au
A/E/C Systems International/Penton Media
Focuses on Internet/Intranet for the design, engineering and construction industries.

2131   www.aia.org
American Institute of Architects
A professional membership association for licensed, emerging professionals, and allied partners.

2132   www.apti.org
Association for Preservation Technology Int'l
A cross-disciplinary, membership organization dedicated to promoting the best technology for conserving historic structures and their settings.

2133   www.archprecast.org
Architectural Precast Association
A national trade association organized to advance the interests of architectural precast concrete in North America.

2134   www.asla.org
American Society of Landscape Architects
The national professional association representing landscape architects.

2135   www.builderspace.com
BuilderSpace.com
An online directory for the building industry and resources created to help users find the services and information they need.

2136   www.construction.com
McGraw-Hill Construction
McGraw-Hill Construction (MHC), part of The McGraw-Hill Companies, connects people and projects across the design and construction industry, serving owners, architects, engineers, general contractors, subcontractors, building product manufacturers, suppliers, dealers, distributors and adjacent markets.

2137   www.ctbuh.org
Council on Tall Buildings and Urban Habitat
Studies and reports on all aspects of the planning, design, and construction of tall buildings.

2138   www.greyhouse.com
Grey House Publishing
Authoritative reference directories for most business sectors including architecture, building and construction markets. Users can search the online databases with varied search criteria allowing for custom searches by product category, geographic area, sales volume, keyword, subject and more. Full Grey House catalog and online ordering also available.

2139   www.historicnewengland.org
Soc. for Preservation of New England Antiquities
Focuses on buildings, landscapes and objects reflecting New England life from the 17th century to the present.

2140   www.icea.net
Insulated Cable Engineers Association
Professional organization dedicated to developing cable standards for the electric power, control and telecommunications industries. Ensures safe, economical and efficient cable systems utilizing proven state-of-the-art materials and concepts. ICEA documents are of interest to cable manufacturers, architects and engineers, utility and manufacturing plant personnel, telecommunication engineers, consultants and OEMs.

2141   www.ihs.com
International Code Council
Nonprofit membership association with more than 16,000 members who span the building community, from code enforcement officials to materials manufacturers. Dedicated to preserving the public health, safety and welfare in the built environment through the effective use and enforcement of model codes.

2142   www.ncarb.org
Nat'l Council of Architectural Registration Boards
For state registration boards in the United States regulating the practice of architecture.

2143   www.reedconstructiondata.com
Architects First Source Online
Comprehensive building products information.

2144   www.sah.org
Society of Architectural Historians
Provides an international forum for those who care about architecture and its related arts.

2145   www.sara-national.org
Society of American Registered Architects
Architects helping Architects by sharing ideas and information.

2146   www.sarc.msstate.edu
Small Town Center
To maintain and improve the quality of life in American small towns.

2147   www.sbicouncil.org
Sustainable Buildings Industry Council
Information on the design, affordability, energy performance, and enviromental soundness of residential, institutional and commercial buildings.

2148   www.sname.org
Society of Naval Architects and Marine Engineers
Internationally recognized nonprofit, technical, professional society of individual members serving the maritime and offshore industries and their suppliers. Dedicated to advancing the industry by recording information, sponsoring research, offering career guidance and supporting education.

2149   www.sweets.construction.com
McGraw Hill Construction
In depth product information that lets you find, compare, select, specify and make purchase decisions in the industrial product marketplace.

Associations

2150 American Academy of Equine Art
117 North Water Street
PO Box 1364
Georgetown, KY 40324

502-570-8567
FAX 859-281-6043
E-Mail: fcconner@aaea.net
Home Page: www.aaea.net

Xochitl Barnes, AAEA Vice President
Frances Clay Conner, Executive Director

The AAEA serves to educate and encourage a broad awareness and appreciation of contemporary equine art as a specific and distinctively worthy segment of fine art in America.
90 Members
Founded in 1980

2151 American Alliance of Museums
2451 Crystal Dr.
Suite 1005
Arlington, VA 22202

202-289-1818
FAX 202-289-6578
E-Mail: membership@aam-us.org
Home Page: www.aam-us.org
Social Media: *Facebook, Twitter, LinkedIn*

Laura L. Lott, President & CEO
Kyle Ange, VP, Finance & Operations
Brent Mundt, VP, Development
Janet Vaughan, VP, Membership & Programs
Elizabeth Merritt, VP, Strategic Foresight

Dedicated to promoting excellence within the museum community. Through advocacy, professional education, information exchange, accreditation and guidance on current professional standards of performance, AAM assists museum staff, boards and volunteers across the country to better serve the public.
16000 Members
Founded in 1906

2152 American Art Therapy Association
4875 Eisenhower Avenue
Suite 240
Alexandria, VA 22304-3302

703-212-2238
888-290-0878
E-Mail: info@arttherapy.org
Home Page: www.arttherapy.org
Social Media: *Facebook, Twitter, LinkedIn, RSS*

Donna Betts, PHD, ATR-BC, President
Susan Corrigan, Executive Director
Michele Basham, Director, Membership Information
Julia Connell, Communications Manager
Barbara Florence, Director, Communication, Education

An organization of professionals dedicated to the belief that the creative process involved in art making is healing and life enhancing. Its mission is to serve its members and the general public by providing standards of professional competence, and developing and promoting knowledge in, and of, the field of art therapy.
4500 Members
Founded in 1969

2153 American Association of Museums
2451 Crystal Drive
Suite 1005
Arlington, VA 22202

202-289-1818
FAX 202-289-6578
E-Mail: membership@aam-us.org

Home Page: www.aam-us.org
Social Media: *Facebook, Twitter, LinkedIn*

Meme Omogbai, Chairman
Ford W. Bell, President
Laura Lott, COO
Canan Abayhan, Senior Director, Information
Carol Constantine, Director, Finance & Administration
16000 Members
Founded in 1906

2154 American Society for Aesthetics
1550 Larimer Street
#644
Denver, CO 80202-1602

912-921-2124
E-Mail: secretary-treasurer@aesthetics-online.or
Home Page: www.aesthetics-online.org
Social Media: *Facebook, Twitter*

Robert Stecker, Editor
Theodore Gracyk, Editor
James Harold, Book Review Editor
James Harold, Book Review Editor

Promotes study, research, discussion and publication in aesthetics, which includes all studies of the arts and related experience including philosophic, scientific and theoretical viewpoints.
Founded in 1942

2155 American Society of Bookplate Collectors & Designers
5802 Bullock Loop
Suite C1 #84404
Laredo, TX 78041-8807

414-228-7831
E-Mail: info@bookplate.org
Home Page: www.bookplate.org
Social Media: *Facebook, Twitter, LinkedIn, YouTube, Flickr, Pinterest, In*

For designers, owners and collectors of bookplates.
Founded in 1977

2156 Antique Appraisal Association of America
1403 Gloria Lane
Boulder City, NV 89005

702-629-4502
888-791-0033
E-Mail: aaaofamerica@att.net
Home Page: www.antiqueappraisalassn.com

Helen Nolan, Executive Director

Members are well known for their Code of Ethics in their dealing with their customers. Our qualified professional appraisers have expertise in all types of appraisals and appraisal-related services, including insurance damage claims, estate probate, estate liquidation, estate auctions, court testimony, consultants and much more.
Founded in 1972

2157 Antique Coin Machine Collectors Association

E-Mail: diermanor@gmail.com

Association for collectors and enthusiasts of antique coin-operated devices.
Founded in 1985

2158 Antiques & Collectibles National Association
PO Box 4389
Davidson, NC 28036

704-895-9088
800-287-7127

FAX 704-895-0230
Home Page: www.antiqueandcollectible.com

Angie Becker, President
Mike Becker, Vice President

Association founded in 1991 for the benefit of antique dealers and collectors.
Founded in 1991

2159 Antiques Council
PO Box 1508
Warren, MA 01083

413-436-7064
FAX 413-436-0448
E-Mail: info@antiquescouncil.com
Home Page: www.antiquescouncil.com

Marty Shapiro, President
Alan Cunha, VP
John Copenhaver, Education Director
David Bernard, Facilities Director
Joel Fletcher, Communications Director

A nonprofit organization created by professional antique dealers to improve the confidence of the public in antiques and their dealers through education, service and example.
100 Members
Founded in 1990

2160 Art Dealers Association of America
205 Lexington Avenue
Suite 901
New York, NY 10016

212-488-5550
FAX 646-688-6809
E-Mail: adaa@artdealers.org
Home Page: www.artdealers.org
Social Media: *Facebook, Twitter, Instagram*

Dorsey Waxter, President
Mary Sabbatino, Vice President
Adam Sheffer, Vice President
Laurence Shopmaker, Secretary
Mark Brady, Treasurer

Nonprofit organzation that works to improve the stature and standing of the art gallery business. Members deal primarily with paintings, sculpture, prints, drawings and photographs from the Renaissance to the present day. We have more than 160 member galleries in more than 25 US cities.
160 Members
Founded in 1962

2161 Art Libraries Society of North America
7044 S. 13th St.
Oak Creek, WI 53154

414-768-8000
800-817-0621
FAX 414-768-8001
E-Mail: customercare@arlisna.org
Home Page: www.arlisna.org
Social Media: *Facebook, Twitter, LinkedIn, Pinterest*

Kristen Regina, President
Heather Gendron, Vice-President/President Elect
Jamie Lausch Vander Broek, Secretary
Mark Pompelia, Treasurer
Robert J. Kopchinski, Association & Conference Manager

Devoted to fostering excellence in art librarianship, visual resources and curatorship for the advancement of visual arts. See website for available publications.
1000 Members
Founded in 1972
Mailing list available for rentat $200 per M

2162 Art and Antique Dealers League of America

PO Box 2066
Lenox Hill Station
New York, NY 10021

212-879-7558
FAX 212-772-7197
E-Mail:
secretary@artantiquedealersleague.com
Home Page: www.artantiquedealersleague.com

Clinton Howell, President
Robert Simon, VP
David Mayer, Secretary-Executive Director
Susan Kaplan Jacobson, Treasurer
109 Members
Founded in 1926

2163 Art and Creative Materials Institute/ACMI

99 Derby Street
Suite 200
Hingham, MA 02043

781-556-1044
FAX 781-207-5550
E-Mail: debbieg@acminet.org
Home Page: www.acminet.org

Michael Storei, President
Joan Lilly, Vice President
Timothy Gomez, Treasurer
Debbie Gustafson, Associate Director
Debbie Munroe, Certification Director

A non-profit association of manufacturers of art, craft and other creative materials, ACMI sponsors a certification program for both children's and adult's art materials and products, certifying that these products are non-toxic and meet voluntary standards of quality and performance. ACMI seeks to create and maintain a positive environment for art, craft and other creative materials usage, promoting safety in the materials and providing information and service resources on such products.
210 Members
Founded in 1936
Mailing list available for rent: 199 names

2164 Arts Midwest

2908 Hennepin Ave.
Suite 200
Minneapolis, MN 55408-1954

612-341-0755
Home Page: www.artsmidwest.org
Social Media: *Facebook, Twitter, YouTube, Flickr*

David J. Fraher, President & CEO
Peter Capell, Chair

One of six regional arts organizations established with funding from the National Endowment for the Arts, Arts Midwest provides access to performing, visual and literary arts programs in Illinois, Indiana, Iowa, Michigan, Minnesota, North Dakota, Ohio, South Dakota and Wisconsin.

2165 Association for Preservation Technology International

3085 Stevenson Drive
Suite 200
Springfield, IL 62703

217-529-9039
FAX 888-723-4242
E-Mail: info@apti.org
Home Page: www.apti.org
Social Media: *Facebook, LinkedIn*

Gretchen Pfaehler, President
John Diodati, Vice President
Dean Koga, Vice President
Lesley Gilmore, Treasurer
Nathela Chatara, CAE, Administrative Director

The Association for Preservation Technology (APT) is a cross-disciplinary, membership organization dedicated to promoting the best technology for conserving historic structures and their settings.
Founded in 1968

2166 Association of Historians of American Art

E-Mail: info@ahaaonline.org
Home Page: www.ahaaonline.org
Social Media: *Facebook, LinkedIn*

Anna Marley, Chair
Ellery Foutch, Co-Chair
Akela Reason, Chair Emerita
Jillian Russo, Secretary
Monica Jovanovich-Kelley, Treasurer

An association for the promotion of scholarship in American art.
Founded in 1979

2167 Association of Restorers

8 Medford Place
New Hartford, NY 13413

315-733-1952
800-260-1829
FAX 315-724-7231
Home Page: www.assoc-restorers.com

Andrea Daley, Founder

It is the mission of the AOR, Association of Restorers Inc, to increase the awareness of choice to consere, refurbish or restore historical works of art, household furnishings and architectural constructions
Founded in 1997

2168 College Art Association

TERRA Foundation
50 Broadway
21st Floor
New York, NY 10004

212-691-1051
FAX 212-627-2381
E-Mail: nyoffice@collegeart.org
Home Page: www.collegeart.org
Social Media: *Facebook, Twitter, YouTube*

DeWitt Godfrey, President
John Richardson, Vice President for External Affairs
Charles A. Wright, Vice President for Committees
Doralynn Pines, Secretary
John Hyland Jr., Treasurer

Promotes excellence in scholarship and technology in the criticisim of the visual arts and in the creativity and technical skill in the teaching and practices of art.
13000 Members
Founded in 1911

2169 Indian Arts & Crafts Association

4010 Carlisle NE
Suite C
Albuquerque, NM 87107

505-265-9149
FAX 505-265-8251
E-Mail: info@iaca.com
Home Page: www.iaca.com
Social Media: *Facebook, Twitter*

Joseph P. Zeller, President
Cliff Fragua, Vice President
Beth Hale, Secretary
Kathi Ouellet, Treasurer

Nonprofit trade association whose mission is to promote, protect and preserve Indian arts.
700 Members
Founded in 1974

2170 International Fine Print Dealers Association (IFPDA)

250 W 26th St
Suite 405
New York, NY 10001-6737

212-674-6095
FAX 212-674-6783
E-Mail: info@ifpda.org
Home Page: www.ifpda.org
Social Media: *Facebook, Twitter*

Paula McCarthy Panczenko, President
David Cleaton-Roberts, Vice President
Barbara Krakow, Vice President
Joni Moisant Weyl, Treasurer
Armin Kunz, Secretary

A nonprofit organzation that aspires to create a greater awareness and appreciation of fine prints among collectors and the general public. Povides funding for a variety of print-related educational programs, including pubications, lectures and symposia.
160 Members
Founded in 1987

2171 International Foundation for Art Research

500 5th Avenue
Suite 935
New York, NY 10110

212-391-6234
FAX 212-391-8794
E-Mail: kferg@ifar.org
Home Page: www.ifar.org

Jack A Josephson, Chairman
Sharon Flescher, Executive Director

Nonprofit educational and research organization working for the interests of art scholarship, law and the public interest.
Founded in 1969

2172 Mid Atlantic Arts Foundation

201 N. Charles St.
Suite 401
Baltimore, MD 21201

410-539-6656
FAX 410-837-5517
Home Page: www.midatlanticarts.org
Social Media: *Facebook, Twitter, YouTube, Pinterest*

Alan W. Cooper, Executive Director
E. Scott Johnson, Chair

One of six regional arts organizations established with funding from the National Endowment for the Arts, Mid Atlantic Arts Foundation promotes access to and participation in the arts in Delaware, the District of Columbia, Maryland, New Jersey, New York, Pennsylvania, the US Virgin Islands, Virginia and West Virginia.
Founded in 1979

2173 Mid-America Arts Alliance

2018 Baltimore Ave.
Kansas City, MO 64108

816-421-1388
Home Page: www.maaa.org
Social Media: *Facebook, Twitter, Flickr*

Mary Kennedy, Chief Executive Officer
C. Kendrick Fergeson, Chair

One of six regional arts organizations established with funding from the National Endowment for the Arts, Mid-America Arts Alliance supports artists, cultural organizations and traveling exhibitions in underserved communities in Arkansas, Kansas, Missouri, Nebraska, Oklahoma and Texas.
Founded in 1972

2174 National Antique & Collectible Association
PO Box 4389
Davidson, NC 28036

704-895-9088
800-287-7127
FAX 704-895-0230
E-Mail: info@acna.us
Home Page: www.acna.us
Social Media: *Facebook, Twitter*

Angie Becker, President
Mike Becker, Vice President

The largest trade association for antique dealers & private collectors in the country. Our association has members in all 50 states. We offer an array of benefits including our insurance programs, merchant services, quarterly newsletter, educational seminars, travel, supply discounts and many more.
4300 Members
Founded in 1991

2175 National Antique Doll Dealers Association (NADDA)
Home Page: www.nadda.org
Social Media: *Facebook*

Lynette Gross, President
Ed Kolibaba, Vice President
Diane Costa, Secretary
Richard K. Saxman, Treasurer

NADDA was formed to promote honesty and integrity in the increasingly popular antique doll trade.
Founded in 1986

2176 National Art Education Association
901 Prince Street
Suite 300
Alexandria, VA 22314

703-860-8000
800-299-8321
FAX 703-860-2960
E-Mail: info@arteducators.org
Home Page: www.arteducators.org/
Social Media: *Facebook, Twitter, LinkedIn*

Dennis Inhulson, President
Patricia Franklin, President Elect
Deborah B Reeve, Executive Director

Promote art education through professional development, service, advancment of knowledge and leadership.
22000 Members
Founded in 1947
Mailing list available for rent: 22,000 names at $95 per M

2177 National Art Materials Trade Association
20200 Zion Ave.
Cornelius, NC 28031

704-892-6244
E-Mail: info@namta.org
Home Page: www.namta.org
Social Media: *Facebook, Twitter, LinkedIn*

Hayley Prendergast, President
Kevin P Lavin, Executive VP & CFO
Howard Krinsky, Vice President
Reggie Hall, Executive Director
Rick Munisteri, Director of Meetings

International association of manufacturers, importers, wholesalers and retailers of art materials.
2.1M Members

2178 National Assembly of State Arts Agencies
1200 18th St NW
Suite 1100
Washington, DC 20036

202-347-6352
202-347-5948
FAX 202-737-0526
E-Mail: nasaa@nasaa-arts.org
Home Page: www.nasaa-arts.org
Social Media: *Facebook*

Gary Gibbs, President
Jonathan Katz, Chief Executive Officer
Laura S. Smith, CFRE, Chief Advancement Officer
Kelly J Barsdale, Chief Planning Officer
Sharon Gee, Director of Meetings and Events

NASAA's mission is to advance and promote a meaningful role for the arts in the lives of individuals, families and communities throughout the United States. We empower state art agencies through strategic assistance that fosters leadership, enhances planning and decision making, and increases resources. TDD 202-347-5948.
56 Members
Founded in 1968

2179 National Association of Fine Arts
1155 F Street NW
Suite 1050
Washington, DC 20004

414-332-9306
FAX 888-884-6232
E-Mail: info@artmarketing.com
Home Page: www.nafa.com
Social Media: *Facebook, Twitter, LinkedIn*

Kim O'Brien, President & CEO
Chip Anderson, Vice Chair
S Christopher Johnson, Secretary
Nathan Zuidema, Treasurer

Seeks to provide services and networking opportunities to individuals in the arts community.
100 Members
Founded in 1986

2180 National Auctioneers Association
8880 Ballentine St
Overland Park, KS 66214

913-541-8084
FAX 913-894-5281
E-Mail: support@auctioneers.org
Home Page: www.auctioneers.org
Social Media: *Facebook, Twitter, LinkedIn, YouTube*

Spanky Assiter, CAI, AARE, President
John S. Nicholls, AARE, VP
James Devin Ford, CAI, CES, Treasurer
Hannes Combest, CEO
Thomas W. Saterly, Past President

NAA promotes the auction method of marketing and enhances the professionalism of its practitioners
6,000 Members
Founded in 1948

2181 National Guild of Community Schools of the Arts
520 8th Avenue
3rd Floor, Suite 302
New York, NY 10018

212-268-3337
FAX 212-268-3995
E-Mail: guildinfo@nationalguild.org
Home Page: www.nationalguild.org
Social Media: *Facebook, Twitter, LinkedIn, YouTube, Instagram, RSS*

Jonathan Herman, Executive Director
Ken Cole, Assosiate Director

Claire Wilmoth, Membership Associate
James Harton, Program Director
Traci Horgen, Business Manager

Arts Management in Community Institutions (AMICI) Summer Institute trains administrators to meet needs of growing and emerging arts schools. Other programs, services, guildnotes newsletter, job opportunities listings, and publications catalog available upon request on online. Mailing list $25 for non-members, free for members.
300 Members
Founded in 1937

2182 National Network for Art Placement
935 W Avenue 37
Los Angeles, CA 90065

323-222-4035
800-354-5348
E-Mail: NNAPnow@aol.com
Home Page: www.artistplacement.com
Social Media: *Facebook, Pinterest, RSS*

Warren Christensen, Consultant

An organization that helps any artist with start up capital and services for small businesses.

2183 National Trust for Historic Preservation
2600 Virginia Avenue
Suite 1000
Washington, DC 20037

202-588-6000
800-944-6847
FAX 202-588-6038
E-Mail: info@savingplaces.org
Home Page: www.savingplaces.org
Social Media: *Facebook, Twitter, Pinterest, Instagram, YouTube*

Stephanie K. Meeks, President &CEO
David J. Brown, Vice President & CPO
Paul Edmondson, Chief Legal Officer
Terry Richey, Chief Marketing Officer
Rosemarie Rae, Chief Financial Officer

A private, nonprofit membership organization dedicated to saving historic places and revitlizing America's communities. Also provides leadership, education, advocacy, and resources to save America's diverse historic places and revitalize the communities.
270k Members
Founded in 1949

2184 New England Foundation for the Arts
145 Tremont St.
7th Fl.
Boston, MA 02111

617-951-0010
Home Page: www.nefa.org

Cathy Edwards, Executive Director
Lawrence J. Simpson, Chair

One of six regional arts organizations established with funding from the National Endowment for the Arts, New England Foundation for the Arts supports artists and their endeavours in Connecticut, Maine, Massachusetts, New Hampshire, Rhode Island and Vermont.
Founded in 1976

2185 Professional Picture Framers Association
2282 Springport Road
Suite F
Jackson, MI 49202

517-788-8100
800-762-9287
FAX 517-788-8371
E-Mail: ppfa@ppfa.com

Home Page: www.ppfa.com
Social Media: *Facebook*

John Pruitt, President
Stuart M Altschuler, VP
Jim Esp, Secretary & Executive Director
Robin Gentry, Treasurer

A trade association of manufacturers, wholesalers, print publishers, importers and retailers selling art, framing and related supplies.
3000 Members
Founded in 1971

2186 Society of Animal Artists

5451 Sedona Hills Drive
Berthoud, CO 80513

970-532-3127
FAX 970-532-2537
E-Mail: admin@societyofanimalartists.com
Home Page: www.societyofanimalartists.com
Social Media: *Facebook*

Diane Mason, President
Allen Bragden, VP
Marilyn Newmark, VP
Douglas Allen, VP
Renee Headings-Bemis, Treasurer

Devoted to promoting excellence in the portrayal of the creatures sharing our planet and to the education of the public through informative art seminars, lectures and teaching demonstrations.
360 Members
Founded in 1960

2187 Society of Illustrators

128 E 63rd St
New York, NY 10065

212-838-2560
FAX 212-838-2561
E-Mail: info@societyillustrators.org
Home Page: www.societyillustrators.org
Social Media: *Facebook, Twitter*

Tim O'Brien, President
Karen Green, Vice President
Victor Juhasz, Executive VP
Leslie Cober-Gentry, Secretary
David Ruess, Treasurer

A professional society of illustrators and art directors.
950 Members
Founded in 1901

2188 South Arts

1800 Peachtree St. NW
Suite 808
Atlanta, GA 30309

404-874-7244
FAX 404-873-2148
Home Page: www.southarts.org
Social Media: *Facebook, Twitter, LinkedIn*

Suzette M. Surkamer, Executive Director
Ted Abernathy, Chair

One of six regional arts organizations established with funding from the National Endowment for the Arts, South Arts assists state arts agencies in Alabama, Florida, Georgia, Kentucky, Louisiana, Mississippi, North Carolina, South Carolina and Tennessee with the production, promotion and presentation of southern arts and culture.
Founded in 1975

2189 The American Institute for Conservation of Historic & Artistic Works

1156 15th Street
Suite 320
Washington, DC 20005-1714

202-452-9545
FAX 202-452-9328
E-Mail: info@conservation-us.org

Home Page: www.conservation-us.org
Social Media: *Facebook, Twitter, YouTube, Flickr*

Eryl P. Wentworth, Executive Director
Ruth Seyler, Membership & Meetings Director
Eric Pourchot, Institutional Advancement Director
Sandy T. Nguyen, Finance Director
Abigail Choudhury, Development and Education

Conservators of artistic and cultural property.
3500 Members
Founded in 1961

2190 The Art Students League of New York

215 W 57th Street
New York, NY 10019

212-247-4510
FAX 212-541-7024
E-Mail: info@artstudentsleague.org
Home Page: www.theartstudentsleague.org
Social Media: *Facebook, Twitter, YouTube, Pinterest, Instagram*

Salvatore Barbieri, President
Susan Matz, Vice President
Howard A. Friedman, Vice President
Ira Golberg, Executive Director
Ken Park, Director of Communications

Educational organization that provides space, studios and offices to members.
Founded in 1875

2191 The Art and Antique Dealers League of America, Inc.

PO Box 2066
Lenox Hill Station
New York, NY 10021

212-879-7558
FAX 212-772-7197
E-Mail:
secretary@artantiquedealersleague.com
Home Page: www.artantiquedealersleague.com

Clinton Howell, President
Robert Simon, Vice President
David Mayer, Secretary-Executive Director
Susan Kaplan Jacobson, Treasurer

Nonprofit organization promotes interests of retailers and wholesalers of antiques and art objects.
110 Members
Founded in 1926

2192 The Maven Co.

Maven Company
PO Box 937
Plandome, NY 11020-0937

51 -62 -880
FAX 914-248-0800
E-Mail: fasttrack@erols.com
Home Page: www.mavencompany.com

N Chittenden, VP

An innovator of new and unique programs to help antique dealers sell their merchandise and to make their shows more successful.
5,000 Attendees
Frequency: January/Annual
Founded in 1970

2193 The National Antique & Art Dealers Association of America

220 E 57th St
New York, NY 10022

212-826-9707
FAX 212-832-9493
Home Page: www.naadaa.org

James R McConnaughy, President
Mark Jacoby, VP
Arlie Sulka, Secretary
Steven J Chait, Treasurer

Works to promote the best interests of the antique art exhibitions and to promote just, honorable and ethical trade practices.
38 Members
Founded in 1954

2194 Train Collectors Association

PO Box 248
Strasburg, PA 17579-0248

717-687-8623
Home Page: www.traincollectors.org

Wayne S. Sheriff, President

The worldwide organization for tinplate train collectors and enthusiasts.
30000 Members
Founded in 1954

2195 Volunteer Committees of Art Museums

5139 Thorncroft Court
Royal Oak, MI 48073

504-488-2631
FAX 504-484-6662
E-Mail: co_presidents@vcam.org
Home Page: www.vcam.org
Social Media: *Facebook, Twitter, LinkedIn, YouTube*

Peter Milne, President
Linda McGinty, Co President
Julie George, Secretary
Victoria Cather, Treasurer

An internationally recognized non-profit organization. VCAM is committed to provide a forum for information exchange, mutual education and enhancement of services to its art museum volunteer committee members through international conferences, regional meetings, published comprehensive conference reports, resource files and the VCAM NEWS publication.
19 Members
Founded in 1952

2196 Western States Arts Federation (WESTAF)

1743 Wazee St.
Suite 300
Denver, CO 80202

303-629-1166
Home Page: www.westaf.org
Social Media: *Facebook, Twitter*

Anthony Radich, Executive Director
Virginia Gowski, Chair

One of six regional arts organizations established with funding from the National Endowment for the Arts, WESTAF advances the preservation and development of the arts in Alaska, Arizona, California, Colorado, Hawaii, Idaho, Montana, Nevada, New Mexico, Oregon, Utah, Washington and Wyoming.

Newsletters

2197 ARTnewsletter

ARTnews Associates
48 W 38th Street
New York, NY 10018-6211

212-398-1690
800-284-4625
FAX 212-819-0394
E-Mail: info@artnewsonline.com
Home Page: www.artnewsonline.com

Milton Esterow, Publisher/CEO
Robin Cembalest, Executive Editor
Debra Melson, Marketing
Elizabeth McNamara, Circulation Manager

Business report on the world art market. Targeted to private collectors, dealers, gallery owners, museum directors and curators, tax and estate buyers.
Cost: $279.00
Frequency: Bi-weekly
Circulation: 83375
Founded in 1902

2198 ASA Newsletter
P.O. Box 915
Pooler, GA 31322

912-921-2124
E-Mail: asa@aesthetics-online.org
Home Page: www.aesthetics-online.org

Paul Guyer, President
Dominic McIver Lopes, VP
Dabney Townsend, Secretary/Treasurer

Promotes study, research, discussion and publication in aesthetics, which includes all studies of the arts and related experience including philosophic, scientific and theoretical viewpoints.
Founded in 1942

2199 Antique Appraisal Association of America Newsletter
Antique Appraisal Association of America
1403 Gloria Lane
Boulder City, NV 89005

702-629-4502
888-791-0033
E-Mail: aaaofamerica@att.net
Home Page: www.antiqueappraisalassn.com

Marge Swenson, Publisher

Supplies members with additional knowledge of antiques from research.

2200 Art Hazards Newsletter
New York Foundation for the Arts
155 Avenue of the Americas
14th Floor
New York, NY 10013

212-366-6900
FAX 212-366-1778
E-Mail: csa@tmn.com

Theodore Berger, Executive Director
Toni Lewis, Director Administration

Contains information on all hazardous materials; art materials and articles.
Cost: $24.00
Frequency: Quarterly
Founded in 1977

2201 Art Research News
500 5th Avenue
Suite 935
New York, NY 10110

212-391-6234
FAX 212-391-8794
E-Mail: kferg@ifar.org
Home Page: www.ifar.org

Sharon Flescher, Executive Director

The latest news on authenticity, ownership, theft, and other artistic, legal and ethical issues concerning art objects.
Founded in 1969

2202 Arts & Culture Funding Report
Capitol City Publishers
4416 East West Hwy
Suite 400
Bethesda, MD 20814-4568

301-916-1800
800-637-9915
FAX 301-528-2497
Home Page: www.capitolcitypublishers.com

A monthly newsletter on federal, state, private and nonprofit sector funding and financial as-

sistance to arts and cultural organizations.
Cost: $198.00
Frequency: Monthly
ISSN: 1047-3297

2203 Arts Management
Radius Group
545 5th Ave
New York, NY 10017-3647

212-972-2929
FAX 212-972-7581
E-Mail: postmaster@trflaw.com
Home Page: www.trflaw.com

Leonard A Rodes, Partner
David Trachtenberg, Partner
Barry Friedberg, Partner

The national news service for those who finance, manage and communicate the arts.
Cost: $18.00
Frequency: 5 per year

2204 Artsfocus
Colorado Springs Fine Arts Center
30 W Dale St
Colorado Spring, CO 80903-3249

719-634-5581
FAX 719-634-0570
E-Mail: info@csfineartscenter.org
Home Page: www.csfineartscenter.org

Sam Gappmayer, CEO
Kari Torgerson, COO
Tom Jackson, Director of Development

Museum members publication.
Cost: $5.00
24 Pages
Frequency: Quarterly
Founded in 1936
Printed in 2 colors on matte stock

2205 Aviso
American Association of Museums
1575 Eye Street NW
Suite 400
Washington, DC 20005-1113

202-289-1818
FAX 202-289-6578
E-Mail: membership@aam-us.org
Home Page: www.aam-us.org

Ford W Bell, President
Douglas Myers, CEO Executive Director

Reports on museums in the news, federal legislation affecting museums, upcoming seminars and workshops, federal grant deadlines and AAM activities and services.
Frequency: Monthly

2206 Bookplates in the News
Amer. Society of Bookplate Collectors & Designers
605 N Stoneman Avenue
Suite F
Alhambra, CA 91801-1406

626-579-9147
E-Mail: exlibris@att.net
Home Page: www.artisanale@hotmail.com

Audrey Spencer Arellanes, Publisher
Victor Amor, Owner

Collectors' news for designers, owners and collectors of bookplates.
Cost: $25.00
200 Pages
Frequency: Quarterly
Circulation: 250

2207 Communique
Association for Preservation Technology Int'l

3085 Stevenson Drive
Suite 200
Springfield, IL 62703

217-529-9039
FAX 888-723-4242
E-Mail: info@apti.org
Home Page: www.apti.org

Joan Berkwitz, President
Gretchen Pfaehler, Vice President
Kyle Normandin, Treasurer
Nathela Chatara,CAE, Administrative Director

APT's electronic newsletter, enables APT members to exchange preservation information, publicize their news and awards, share project experience with colleagues, post calls for papers, and submit preservation queries to the readership.
Frequency: Quarterly

2208 Cotton & Quail Antique Gazette
F+W Media
38 E. 29th Street
New York, NY 10016

212-447-1400
FAX 212-447-5231
E-Mail: contact_us@fwmedia.com
Home Page: www.fwpublications.com

Greg Smith, Publisher
Linda Kunkel, Editor
Dave Paul, Marketing

Contains articles about various collecting topics, announcements of upcoming shows, reviews of shows and auctions, a Q & A column on antiques, 'how-to' articles, regular features about collecting and selling, an extensive show and auction calendar.
Cost: $20.00
Frequency: Monthly
Circulation: 25000
Founded in 1965

2209 Encouraging Rejection
Noforehead Press
Box 55
Kearsarge, NH 03847-0130

Home Page: www.reuben.org

Mark Heath, Editor/Publisher

To inspire and encourage artists in the face of rejection.
Cost: $19.00
Frequency: Bi-Monthly
Founded in 1994

2210 Folk Art Finder
Gallery Press
117 N Main Street
Essex, CT 06426-1302

860-767-0313
Home Page: folkart.com

Florence Laffal, Editor/Publisher

Contains feature stories, a calendar of events, a readers exchange, news items, book reviews, and classified and display ads relating to 20th century American folk art. Other issues addressed are folk art preservation, laws affecting the arts and funding for the arts.
Cost: $14.00
24 Pages
Frequency: Quarterly
Mailing list available for rent
Printed in one color on matte stock

2211 IFAR Journal
International Foundation for Art Research
500 5th Avenue
Suite 935
New York, NY 10110

212-391-6234
FAX 212-391-8794
E-Mail: kferg@ifar.org

Home Page: www.ifar.org
Social Media: *Facebook*

Sharon Flescher PhD, CEO
Jack A. Josephson, Chairman

Listings of stolen art and the legal developments of articles on art recovery, art law, cultural property and art authentication.
Cost: $65.00
32 Pages
Frequency: Quarterly
ISSN: 1098-1195
Founded in 1969

2212 Indian Arts & Crafts Association Newsletter
4010 Carlisle NE
Suite C
Albuquerque, NM 87107

505-265-9149
FAX 505-265-8251
E-Mail: info@iaca.com
Home Page: www.iaca.com

Joseph Zeller, President
Don Standing Bear Forest, VP
Gail Chehak, Executive Director
Susan Pourian, Secretary
Kathi Ouellet, Treasurer

2213 International Association of Auctioneers Newsletter
Butterfield & Butterfield Auctioneers
220 San Bruno Ave
San Francisco, CA 94103-5018

415-861-7500
800-222-2854
FAX 415-861-8951
E-Mail: appraisals.us@bonhams.com
Home Page: www.butterfields.com

Melcolm Barbar, CEO

A news bulletin with descriptions of upcoming auctions around the world.
8 Pages
Frequency: Quarterly
Circulation: 6500
Founded in 1865

2214 Kovels on Antiques and Collectibles
Antiques
2135 N Milwaukee Ave
Chicago, IL 44122

773-360-8162
FAX 216-752-3115
Home Page: www.kovels.com
Social Media: *Facebook, Twitter*

Terry Kovel, Co-Publisher
Ralph Kovel, Co-Publisher

Newsletter for dealers, investors and collectors.
Cost: $27.00
12 Pages
Frequency: Monthly
Founded in 1995
Printed in 4 colors on matte stock

2215 National Association of Antiques Bulletin
National Association of Dealers in Antiques
PO Box 421
Barrington, IL 60011-0421

847-381-3101
FAX 815-877-4282

Shirley Kowing, Publisher

Educational and association news.

2216 Professional Picture Framers Association Newsletter
4305 Sarellen Road
Richmond, VA 23231-4311

804-226-0430
FAX 804-222-2175
E-Mail: framers@gnn.com

Rex P Boynton, Executive Director

Trade association news for manufacturers, wholesalers, print publishers, importers and retailers selling art, framing and related supplies.

2217 Stolen Art Alert
500 5th Avenue
Suite 935
New York, NY 10110

212-391-6234
FAX 212-391-8794
E-Mail: kferg@ifar.org
Home Page: www.ifar.org

Sharon Flescher, Executive Director

Reports on art thefts and recoveries and also covered major art forgery cases.
Founded in 1969

2218 VCAM NEWS
Volunteer Communities of Art Museums
New Orleans Museum of Art
PO Box 19123
New Orleans, LA 70179

504-488-2631
FAX 504-484-6662
E-Mail: president@vcam.org
Home Page: www.vcam.org

Peter Milne, President
Susan Colangelo, Secretary
Victoria Cather, Treasurer

Informs and invigorates the volunteers.
19 Members
Founded in 1952

2219 World Fine Art
Art Baron Management Corporation
1356 Cherry Bottom Road
Colombos, OH 43230-6771

614-476-9708

Jeffrey Coffin, Publisher
Steve Shipp, Editor
John Blackburn, Manager
Art history, values and projections regarding artists and movements.
Cost: $95.00
10 Pages
Frequency: 9 per year
Printed in one color

Magazines & Journals

2220 A History of Art Therapy
American Art History
4875 Eisenhower Avenew
Suite 240
Alexandria, VA 22304-3302

703-212-2238
888-290-0878
E-Mail: info@arttherapy.org
Home Page: www.arttherapy.org

Mercedes ter Maat, President
Charlotte Boston,MA,ATR, Secretary
Joseph Jaworek ATR-BC, Treasurer
Frequency: Yearly

2221 AIC Guide to Digital Photography and Conservation Documentation
American Institute for Conservation

1156 15th St NW
Suite 320
Washington, DC 20005-1714

202-452-9545
FAX 202-452-9328
E-Mail: info@aic-faic.org
Home Page: www.aic-faic.org

Eryl Wentworth, Executive Director
Adam Allen, Meetings Associate
Steve Charles, Membership Assistant

2222 Advocacy and Lobbying: Speaking up for the Arts
National Assembly of State Arts Agencies
1029 Vermont Ave NW
2nd Floor
Washington, DC 20005-3517

202-347-6352
FAX 202-737-0526
E-Mail: nasaa@nasaa-arts.org
Home Page: www.nasaa-arts.org

Dennis Dewey, Manager
Arlynn Fishbaugh, President
Pam Breaux, VP
Bobby Kadis, Treasurer
John Bracey, Secretary

2223 Airbrush Action
3209 Atlantic Avenue
PO Box 438
Allenwood, NJ 08720

732-223-7878
800-876-2472
FAX 732-223-2855
E-Mail: customerservice@airbrushaction.com
Home Page: www.airbrushaction.com

Clifford S Stieglitz, President/Publisher

Offers information on the art and graphic design community. Airbrush Action's editorial includes features/coverage on: automotive customizing, hobby applications, illustration, signs, t-shirts, body art, home decorative and more.
Cost: $26.95
Circulation: 35000
Printed in 4 colors on glossy stock

2224 Airbrush Art and Action
Paisano Publishers
28210 Dorothy Drive
PO Box 3000
Agoura Hills, CA 91301

818-889-8740
800-247-6246
FAX 818-889-1252
Home Page: www.paisanopub.com/

Joseph Teresi, Publisher

A look at new products, step by step instruction features, profiles of professionals in the airbrushing field, and examples of airbrushed artworks.
Frequency: Bi-annually
Circulation: 68500

2225 American Artist
Billboard
770 Broadway
New York, NY 10003-9589

646-654-4400
800-562-2706
FAX 646-654-5514
E-Mail: billboard@espcomp.com
Home Page: www.billboard.com

Jessica Letkemann, Managing Editor
Lisa Ryan Howard, Publisher

A magazine devoted to the best of the best in the art industry.
Cost: $43.45
Frequency: Monthly
Circulation: 71,435
Founded in 1894

2226 Antique Trader
F+W Media
38 E. 29th Street
New York, NY 10016

212-447-1400
FAX 212-447-5231
E-Mail: contact_us@fwmedia.com
Home Page: www.fwpublications.com

Jim Ogle, CFO
Sara Domville, President
Chad Phelps, Chief Digital Officer
David Nussbaum, CEO

For the antiques and collectibles hobby industry. Accepts advertising.
Cost: $38.00
100 Pages
Frequency: Weekly
Circulation: 27363
Founded in 1957

2227 Antique Week
Mayhill Publications
27 N Jefferson Street
PO Box 90
Knightstown, IN 46148

765-345-5133
800-876-5133
FAX 800-695-8153
E-Mail: tony@antiqueweek.com
Home Page: www.antiqueweek.com

Gary Thoe, President
David Blower, Senior Editor

Antique dealers.
Cost: $38.95
Frequency: Weekly
Circulation: 65000
Founded in 1968

2228 Aristos
Aristos Foundation
PO Box 20845
Park West Station
New York, NY 10025

212-678-8550
E-Mail: aristos@aristos.org
Home Page: www.aristos.org

Louis Torres, Editor
Michelle Marder Kamhi, Editor

Independent online journal advocating objective standards in arts scholarship and criticism. Our aim is to present well-reasoned commentary on the arts and on the philosophy of art, for a broad audience of general readers and scholars.
Cost: $25.00
Frequency: Monthly
Founded in 1982

2229 Art & Antiques
Art & Antiques Worldwide Media LLC
1319-cc Military Cutoff Road #192
Wilmington, NC 28405

910-679-4402
888-350-0951
FAX 919-869-1864
E-Mail: info@artandantiquesmag.com
Home Page: www.artandantiquesmag.com

Jon Dorfman, Senior Editor

Magazine for collectors of the fine and decorative arts.
Frequency: Monthly

2230 Art & Auction
Art & Auction

601 West 26th Street
Suite 410
New York, NY 10001

212-447-9555
800-777-8718
FAX 212-447-5221
E-Mail: info@artandauction.com
Home Page: www.artinfo.com

Louise T Blouin, President/Owner
Benjamin Genocchio, Editor-in-Chief

Editorial covers the art market from antiquities to contemporary art, monthly calendar of gallery exhibitions and auction sales.
Cost: $80.00
Frequency: Monthly
Circulation: 38500
Founded in 1996

2231 Art Business News
Advanstar Communications
600 Unicorn Park Drive
Suite 400
Woburn, MA 01801

339-298-4200
800-552-4346
FAX 781-939-2490
E-Mail: info@advanstar.com
Home Page: www.advanstar.com/

Julie MacDonald, Editor
Joseph Loggia, CEO

Publication addressing the business aspect of art and framing. Editorial covers everything from trends and sales to new colors and the latest tax changes.
Cost: $43.00
Frequency: Monthly
ISSN: 0273-5652
Founded in 1992

2232 Art Materials Retailer
Fahy-Williams Publishing
171 Reed Street
PO Box 1080
Geneva, NY 14456-2137

315-789-0458
800-344-0559
FAX 315-789-4263
E-Mail: kfahy@fwpi.com
Home Page: www.fwpi.com

J Kevin Fahy, Publisher
Tina Manzer, Editorial Director
Bradley G. Gordner, Senior Editor
Frequency: Quarterly
Circulation: 12000
Printed in 4 colors on glossy stock

2233 Art in America
Brant Publications
575 Broadway
5th Floor
New York, NY 10012-3227

212-941-2900
FAX 212-941-2885
E-Mail: interview_ad@brantpub.com
Home Page: www.interviewmagazine.com

Sandra Brant, Publisher
Elizabeth Baker, Editor

Includes show reviews, event schedules, profiles of artists and genres and updates on literature and materials.
Cost: $24.95
Frequency: Monthly
Circulation: 64,182
Founded in 1984

2234 Arts and Activities
Publishers' Development Corporation

12345 World Trade Dr
San Diego, CA 92128-3743

858-605-0200
FAX 858-605-0247
E-Mail: promo@artsandactivities.com
Home Page: www.gunsmagazine.com

Tom Von Rosen, Owner
Maryellen Bridge, Editor

Offers information and news on the latest in the visual arts.
Cost: $24.95
Frequency: Monthly
Founded in 1932

2235 Artweek
PO Box 485
Hilo, HI 96721-0485

800-733-2916
800-733-2916
FAX 262-495-8703
E-Mail: info@artweek.com
Home Page: www.artweek.com

Debra Koppman, Editor
Laura Richar Janku, Editor

Critical reviews of contemporary West Coast art as well as news, features, articles, interviews, special sections and opinion pieces.
Cost: $34.00
Frequency: Monthly
Founded in 1968

2236 Breakthrough Magazine
Breakthrough Magazine
2271 Old Baton Rouge Highway
PO Box 2945
Hammond, LA 70404-2945

985-345-7266
800-783-7266
FAX 985-542-1831
E-Mail: info@breakthroughmagazine.com
Home Page: www.breakthroughmagazine.com

Larry Blomquist, Publisher

Artist profiles, tips, previews, and a calendar of events. Incorporates similar techniques related to wildlife carvings, sculpture and photography.
Cost: $32.00
Frequency: Quarterly
Circulation: 8932

2237 CNA
F+W Media
38 E. 29th Street
New York, NY 10016

212-447-1400
FAX 212-447-5231
E-Mail: contact_us@fwmedia.com
Home Page: www.fwpublications.com

Jim Ogle, CFO
Sara Domville, President
Chad Phelps, Chief Digital Officer
David Nussbaum, CEO

A craft industry trade magazine reaching retailers and industry leaders. Readers turn to CNA each month in search of trends, innovative products, partnerships, corporate accomplishments, and retail strategies that positively impact their businesses. Regular editorial includes timely product showcases and special sections that target arts, crafts, scrapbooking, children's activities, sewing and needlework products. The editorial team has much experience in the industry.
Cost: $30.00
112 Pages
Circulation: 21777
Founded in 1945

2238 Christie's International Magazine
Christies Publications

20 Rockefeller Plaza
New York, NY 10020

212-636-2000
800-395-6300
FAX 212-636-2399
E-Mail: info@christies.com
Home Page: www.christies.com

Mark Wrey, Publisher
Victoria Tremlett, Editor
John L Vogelstein, Chairman

Devoted to the promotion of Christie's fine art auctions worldwide.
Cost: $70.00
Circulation: 60000
Founded in 1766

2239 Craft and Needlework Age
F+W Media
38 E. 29th Street
New York, NY 10016

212-447-1400
FAX 212-447-5231
E-Mail: contact_us@fwmedia.com
Home Page: www.fwpublications.com

Jim Ogle, CFO
Sara Domville, President
Chad Phelps, Chief Digital Officer
David Nussbaum, CEO

Trade magazine serving the crafts and needlework industry. Accepts advertising.
Cost: $20.00
Frequency: Monthly
Founded in 1952

2240 Decorative Artist's Workbook
F+W Media
38 E. 29th Street
New York, NY 10016

212-447-1400
FAX 212-447-5231
E-Mail: contact_us@fwmedia.com
Home Page: www.fwpublications.com

Jim Ogle, CFO
Sara Domville, President
Chad Phelps, Chief Digital Officer
David Nussbaum, CEO

The leading how-to magazine for decorative painters, because it offers detailed step-by-step instruction and illustrations for fabulous projects, plus problem-solving tips, and articles on new techniques, products and books. Readers find a full range of decorative painting subjects and styles painted in a whole range of skill levels and mediums and on a variety of surfaces...and all designed by the most well known artists and instructors in decorative painting!
Cost: $27.00
72 Pages
Frequency: Quarterly
Circulation: 111573
Founded in 1987

2241 Folk Art
American Folk Art Museum
2 Lincoln Square
Columbus Avenue at 66th Street
New York, NY 10023

212-595-9533
FAX 212-265-2350
E-Mail: info@folkartmuseum.org
Home Page: www.folkartmuseum.org

Irene Kreney, Manager
Linda Dune, Acting Director
Edward Blanchard, President, Treasurer

An award winning publication. The editorial content is geared toward collectors, scholars, and the museum community interested in traditional and contemporary American folk and decorative arts. A benefit of membership, and is delivered to a targeted national and international readership.

2242 HOW Magazine
F&W Publications
10151 Carver Road
Blue Ash, OH 45242

513-531-2690
FAX 513-531-1843
E-Mail: contact_us@fwmedia.com
Home Page: www.fwpublications.com
Social Media: *Facebook, Twitter, LinkedIn*

David Nussbaum, CEO
Jim Ogle, COO/CFO
Sara Domville, President

The industry's leading creativity, business and technology magazine for graphic design professionals. Each issue provides a mix of essential business information, up-to-date technology tips, the creative whys and hows behind noteworthy projects, and profiles of professionals who are influencing design.
Cost: $27.73
140 Pages
Frequency: Monthly
Circulation: 44883
Founded in 1985

2243 Hammer's Blow
259 Muddy Fork Road
Jonesborough, TN 37659

423-913-1022
FAX 423-913-1023
E-Mail: centraloffice@abana.org
Home Page: www.abana.org

David Hutchinson, President
Jack Parks, First VP
Peter Renzetti, Second VP
Bill Clemens, Secretary

Journal of the Artist-Blacksmiths' Association of North America
4500 Members
Frequency: Quarterly
Circulation: 2 Mag.
Founded in 1973

2244 I.D. Magazine
F+W Media
38 E. 29th Street
New York, NY 10016

212-447-1400
FAX 212-447-5231
E-Mail: contact_us@fwmedia.com
Home Page: www.fwpublications.com

Jim Ogle, CFO
Sara Domville, President
Chad Phelps, Chief Digital Officer
David Nussbaum, CEO
Andr,a Pellegrino, Advertising Director

The international design magazine, showcases innovative products and technologies for sophisticated readers who are at the forefront of shaping the world through design. The multi-disciplinary coverage embraces design trends, theories, experiments and innovators.
Cost: $59.96
96 Pages
Frequency: 1 Year 8 Issues
Circulation: 31,424
Founded in 1954

2245 IFAR Journal
500 5th Avenue
Suite 935
New York, NY 10110

212-391-6234
FAX 212-391-8794
E-Mail: kferg@ifar.org
Home Page: www.ifar.org

Sharon Flescher, Executive Director
Jack Josephson, Chairman

Emphasizes education and research regarding the ethical, legal and scholarly issues concerning art objects. In addition to news stories and

book reviews, the Journal contains feature articles on art authenticity and attribution; forgery and fraud; art law and ethics; World War II-era art restitution issues; conserving, restoring and caring for art; and art theft.
Founded in 1969

2246 Journal of Aesthetics and Art Criticism
P.O. Box 915
Pooler, GA 31322

912-921-2124
E-Mail: asa@aesthetics-online.org
Home Page: www.aesthetics-online.org

Paul Guyer, President
Dominic McIver Lopes, VP
Dabney Townsend, Secretary/Treasurer

Promotes study, research, discussion and publication in aesthetics, which includes all studies of the arts and related experience including philosophic, scientific and theoretical viewpoints.
Founded in 1942

2247 Journal of the American Institute for Conservation (JAIC)
1156 15th Street
Suite 320
Washington, DC 20005-1714

202-452-9545
FAX 202-452-9328
E-Mail: info@conservation-us.org
Home Page: www.conservation-us.org

Eryl Wentworth, Executive Director
Meg Loew Craft, President
Pamela Hatchfield, VP

Publication of peer-reviewed technical studies, research papers, treatment case studies and ethics and standards discussions relating to the broad field of conservation and preservation of historic and cultural works.
3500 Members
Founded in 1961

2248 Magazine Antiques
Brant Publications
575 Broadway
5th Floor
New York, NY 10012-3227

212-941-2900
FAX 212-941-2885
E-Mail: interview_ad@brantpub.com
Home Page: www.interviewmagazine.com

Sandra Brant, Publisher
Allison Ledes, Editor
Donald Liebling, Circulation Manager
Jennifer Norton, Marketing Executive

Articles on American and European decorative and fine arts, architecture, historic preservation, and collecting.
Cost: $24.95
Frequency: Monthly
Circulation: 64402
Founded in 1969

2249 Memory Makers
F+W Media
38 E. 29th Street
New York, NY 10016

212-447-1400
FAX 212-447-5231
E-Mail: contact_us@fwmedia.com
Home Page: www.fwpublications.com

Jim Ogle, CFO
Sara Domville, President
Chad Phelps, Chief Digital Officer
David Nussbaum, CEO
Buddy Redling, Editor in Chief

Entertains, informs, and inspires the burgeoning number of scrapbook enthusiasts. Features

the ideas and stories of its readers - people who believe in keeping scrapbooks and the tradition of the family photo historian alive. Two special newsstand-only issues are dedicated to specific areas of interest including holidays, heritage albums, and more.
Cost: $45.00
144 Pages
Frequency: Bi-annually
Circulation: 203287
Founded in 1996

2250 Michaels Create!
F+W Media
38 E. 29th Streett
New York, NY 10016

212-447-1400
FAX 212-447-5231
E-Mail: contact_us@fwmedia.com
Home Page: www.fwpublications.com

Jim Ogle, CFO
Sara Domville, President
Chad Phelps, Chief Digital Officer
David Nussbaum, CEO

Features contemporary designs reflecting the latest trends with clear instructions. The home decorating, fashion, and gift ideas will inspire experienced crafters as well as seasonal crafters to explore new possibilities. Step-by-step instructions, tips, and techniques will engage crafters of all ages - including kids - with the creative skills of crafting to be enjoyed as a year-round activity.
Cost: $21.97
116 Pages
Frequency: Monthly
Circulation: 24991
Founded in 1975

2251 Military Trader
F+W Media
38 E. 29th Street
New York, NY 10016

212-447-1400
FAX 212-447-5231
E-Mail: contact_us@fwmedia.com
Home Page: www.fwpublications.com
Social Media: *Facebook, Twitter, LinkedIn*

David Nussbaum, CEO
Jim Ogle, CFO/COO
Sara Domville, President

Monthly publication for collectors of military memorabilia.
Cost: $19.00
Frequency: Monthly
Founded in 1952

2252 Museum
American Association of Museums
1575 Eye Street NW
Suite 400
Washington, DC 20005-1113

202-289-1818
FAX 202-289-6578
E-Mail: membership@aam-us.org
Home Page: www.aam-us.org

John Strand, Publisher
Susan Breitkopf, Editor In Chief
Ford Bell, President
Frequency: Bi-Monthly

2253 Panorama
Association of Historians of American Art

Home Page: journalpanorama.org

Ross Barrett, Executive Editor
Sarah Burns, Executive Editor
Jennifer Jane Marshall, Executive Editor

The online journal of the Association of Historians of American Art.
Frequency: Biannual

2254 Pastel Journal
F+W Media
38 E. 29th Street
New York, NY 10016

212-447-1400
FAX 212-447-5231
E-Mail: contact_us@fwmedia.com
Home Page: www.fwpublications.com

Jim Ogle, CFO
Sara Domville, President
Chad Phelps, Chief Digital Officer
David Nussbaum, CEO

Written by pastel artists for pastel artists. Content is geared toward artists, amateur & professional alike, who already work in pastels and who want to further develop their skills through in-depth information on pastel painting processes and thought-provoking ideas from successful pastel artists. Also included is information on workshops and exhibitions, as well as articles providing details on the business aspects of art - creating prints, creating Web sites, framing prints, and shipping.
Cost: $27.00
84 Pages
Circulation: 19167
Founded in 1999

2255 Picture Framing Magazine
Hobby Publications
83 South Street
Unit 307
Freehold, NJ 07728

732-536-5160
800-969-7176
FAX 732-536-5761
E-Mail: www.pictureframingmagazine.com
Home Page:
www.pictureframingmagazine.com

David Gherman, President
Patrick Sarver, Editor
Bruce Gherman, Executive Publisher

News and trends in the picture framing trade, marketing strategies, and economic developments.
Cost: $20.00
Frequency: Monthly
Circulation: 25000
ISSN: 1052-9977
Founded in 1955

2256 Postcard Collector
F+W Media
38 E. 29th Street
New York, NY 10016

212-447-1400
FAX 212-447-5231
E-Mail: contact_us@fwmedia.com
Home Page: www.fwpublications.com

Jim Ogle, CFO
Sara Domville, President
Chad Phelps, Chief Digital Officer
David Nussbaum, CEO

Monthly publication for postcard collectors.
Cost: $29.98
Frequency: Monthly
Founded in 1982

2257 SchoolArts
Davis Publications
50 Portland Street
Worcester, MA 01618

508-754-7201
800-533-2847
FAX 508-753-3834
E-Mail: contactus@davis-art.com
Home Page: www.davisart.com
Social Media: *Facebook, Twitter, LinkedIn*

Wyatt Wade, Owner
John Carr, Marketing

For art educators.
Cost: $23.95
60 Pages
Frequency: Monthly
Circulation: 23717
Founded in 1901
Printed in 4 colors on matte stock

2258 Sotheby's Preview Magazine
Sotheby's
1334 York Ave
New York, NY 10021-4806

212-606-7000
541-312-5682
FAX 212-606-7107
E-Mail: preview@sothebys.com
Home Page: www.sothebys.com

William F Ruprecht, CEO
Bruno Vinciguerra, Chief Operating Officer

Auction schedule listings, exhibition dates and catalogue pricing.
Cost: $75.00
48 Pages
Circulation: 80,000
Founded in 1976
Printed in 4 colors on newsprint stock

2259 Style: 1900
199 George Street
Lambertville, NJ 08530

609-397-4104
FAX 609-397-4409
E-Mail: fred@style1900.com
Home Page: www.style1900.com
Social Media: *Facebook, Twitter, LinkedIn*

Fred Albert, Editor
Jennifer Strauss, Director Advertising
David Rago, Publisher

The only publication devoted solely to the works and thoughts of the arts and crafts movement.
Cost: $6.95
88 Pages
Frequency: Quarterly
Circulation: 20000
ISSN: 1080-451X
Founded in 1987
Mailing list available for rent: 7,000 names at $250 per M
Printed in 4 colors on glossy stock

2260 The Anvil's Ring
259 Muddy Fork Road
Jonesborough, TN 37659

423-913-1022
FAX 423-913-1023
E-Mail: centraloffice@abana.org
Home Page: www.abana.org

David Hutchison, President
Jack Parks, First VP
Peter Renzetti, Second VP

The most comprehensive overview on what's happening in the artist- blacksmithing world or the inspiration to get you out to the forge.
4500 Members
Frequency: Quarterly
Circulation: 2 Mag.
Founded in 1973

2261 The Chronicle of the Horse
American Academy of Equine Art
117 North Water Street
PO Box 1364
Georgetown, KY 40324

859-281-6031
FAX 859-281-6043
E-Mail: fcconner@aaea.net
Home Page: www.aaea.net

Frances Clay Conner, Executive Director
Xochitl Barnes, AAEA President

The official magazine of the American Academy of Equine Art.
90 Members
Founded in 1980

2262 Visual Anthropology Review
American Anthropoligical Association
2200 Wilson Blvd
Suite 600
Arlington, VA 22201-3357

703-528-1902
FAX 703-528-3546
E-Mail: najwa@optonline.net
Home Page: www.aaanet.org

Bill Davis, Executive Director
Oona Schmid, Director of Publishing
Leith Mullings, President

Directed toward the study of visual aspects of human behavior including anthropology of art and museology and the use of media in anthropological research, representation, and teaching.
Cost: $25.00
Circulation: 1000
ISSN: 1053-7147
Founded in 1902
Mailing list available for rent
Printed in one color on glossy stock

2263 Watercolor Magic
F+W Media
38 E. 29th Street
New York, NY 10016

212-447-1400
FAX 212-447-5231
E-Mail: contact_us@fwmedia.com
Home Page: www.fwpublications.com

Jim Ogle, CFO
Sara Domville, President
Chad Phelps, Chief Digital Officer
David Nussbaum, CEO

Offers valuable how-to instruction and creative inspiration for artists who work in water-based media. From page after page of inspirational ideas, to illustrations of the best techniques, to must-have painting tools and materials, watercolorists will find everything they need to know to help them create art from the inside out. Plus, each issue includes special reports and tons of tips from the foremost experts in the field. The definitive source of creative inspiration and technical info.
Cost: $27.00
72 Pages
Frequency: Monthly
Circulation: 94636
Founded in 1993

Trade Shows

2264 AAM Annual Meeting & MuseumExpo
American Alliance of Museums
2451 Crystal Dr.
Suite 1005
Arlington, VA 22202

202-289-1818
FAX 202-289-6578
E-Mail: membership@aam-us.org
Home Page: www.aam-us.org

Andrea Streat, Director, Meetings & Events

The largest gathering of museum professionals in the world.
Frequency: Annual/May

2265 ABANA International Conferences
Artist-Blacksmith's Association of North America

259 Muddy Fork Road
Jonesborough, TN 37659

423-913-1022
FAX 423-913-1023
E-Mail: conference@abana.org
Home Page: www.abana.org

David Hutchison, President
Peter Renzetti, 2nd Vice President
Linda Tanner, Treasurer

Held biennially in the United States for members. Demonstrations, panel discussions and lectures by experts in the field from around the globe. Share knowledge of technical, aesthetic and business areas of the craft for beginners to established professionals.
1000 Attendees
Frequency: Biennial
Founded in 1975

2266 AHAA Symposium
Home Page:
www.ahaaonline.org/?page=Symposium

Anna Marley, Chair
Ellery Foutch, Co-Chair

Biennial syposium (even-numbered years) of the Association of Historians of American Art.
Frequency: Biennial
Founded in 2010

2267 AIGA Design Conference
American Institute of Graphic Arts (AIGA)
233 Broadway
17th Fl.
New York, NY 10279

212-807-1990
Social Media: *Facebook, Twitter, Instagram*

Stefan Bucher, Chair
Roman Mars, Conference Committee
Debbie Millman, Conference Committee
Nathan Shedroff, Conference Committee

Speakers, exhibitions, roundtables, professional development and a live, head-to-head design competition for up-and-comers.
Frequency: Annual

2268 American Art Therapy Association Conference
American Art Therapy Association
4875 Eisenhower Avenue
Sute 240
Alexandria, VA 22304

703-548-5860
888-290-0878
FAX 703-783-8468
E-Mail: info@arttherapy.org
Home Page: www.arttherapy.org

Mercedes ter Maat, President
Susan Corrigan, Executive Director

Over 20 exhibitors of art supplies, books, therapeutic materials and schools.
800 Attendees
Frequency: Annual
Founded in 1969

2269 American Institute for Conservation Annual Meeting
Amer Institute for Conservation of Historic Works
1156 15th Street NW
Suite 320
Washington, DC 20005

202-452-9545
FAX 202-452-9328
E-Mail: info@conservation-us.org
Home Page: www.aic-faic.org

Eryl P Wentworth, Executive Director
Adam Allen, Meeting Manager
Meg Loew Craft, President

Annual meeting of conservators of artistic and cultural property, which includes seminars and workshops with over 1,000 members attending yearly. 50 booths.
1000 Attendees
Frequency: June
Founded in 1971

2270 American Society for Aesthetics Annual Conference
American Society for Aesthetics
11935 Abersorn Street
Savannah, GA 31419

912-921-2124
E-Mail: asastcar@vms.csd.mu
Home Page: www.aestheticsonline.org

Carolyn Korsmeyer, President
Stephen Davies, VP

Seminar, conference, and exhibits related to the study of the arts, all disciplines.
500 Attendees
Frequency: Annual
Founded in 1942

2271 Antique Arms Show
Beinfeld Productions
72 Sunrise Drive
Rancho Mirage, CA 92270

760-202-4489
FAX 760-202-4793
Home Page: www.antiquearmsshow.com

Wallace Beinfeld, Show Manager

Public show with 1000 booths of antiques and collectibles.
5M/6M Attendees
Frequency: January

2272 Art Expo New York
Advanstar Communications
641 Lexington Avenue
8th Floor
New York, NY 10022

212-951-6600
FAX 212-951-6793
E-Mail: info@advanstar.com
Home Page: www.advanstar.com

Joseph Loggia, CEO
Thomas Ehardt, Vice President
Tom Florio, CFO

Five hundred and eighty exhibitors of artwork including: paintings, sculpture, prints and graphics.
15000 Attendees
Frequency: Annual
Founded in 1985

2273 Art Libraries Society of North America Annual Conference
Art Libraries Society of North America
7044 S. 13th St.
Oak Creek, WI 53154

414-768-8000
800-817-0621
FAX 414-768-8001
E-Mail: arlisna@mercury.interpath.com
Home Page: www.arlisna.org

Deborah Kempe, President
Gregory Most, VP

Annual conference and show of publishers, book dealers, library suppliers and visual resources suppliers.
500 Attendees
Frequency: April
Founded in 1977

2274 Art Miami: International Art Fair
Advanstar Communications

641 Lexinton Avenue
8th Floor
New York, NY 10022

212-951-6600
FAX 212-951-6793
E-Mail: info@advanstar.com
Home Page: www.advanstar.com

Joseph Loggia, CEO
Thomas Ehardt, Vice President
Tom Florio, CFO

99 exhibits of fine arts, attended by professionals.
44500 Attendees

2275 Art Supply Expo
Marketing Association Services
1516 Pontius Avenue
Floor 2
Los Angeles, CA 90025-3306

310-478-0074

Randy Bauler, Executive Director

Exhibits consist of art and drafting equipment and computer graphics supplies.
10M Attendees
Frequency: October

2276 Art and Creative Materials Institute/ACMI Annual Meeting
99 Derby St.
Suite 200
Hingham, MA 02043

781- 55- 104
FAX 781- 20- 555
E-Mail: debbief@acminet.org
Home Page: www.acminet.org

Van Foster, President
Deborah S Gustafson, Associate Director
Debbie Munroe, Certification Director
Carol Rourke, Program Director

A non-profit association of manufacturers of art, craft and other creative materials, ACMI sponsors a certification program for both children's and adult's art materials and products, certifying that these products are non-toxic and meet voluntary standards of quality and performance. ACMI seeks to create and maintain a positive environment for art, craft and other creative materials usage, promoting safety in the materials and providing information and service resources on such products.
210 Members
Founded in 1940
Mailing list available for rent: 199 names

2277 Conference of the Volunteer Committees of Art Museums of Canada and the US
Volunteer Committees of Art Museums
Philbrook Museum
2727 S Rockford
Tulsa, OK 74114

FAX 918-743-4230

Grace Robin, VCAM President

Triennial conference and exhibits of art museum equipment, supplies and services.
Founded in 1952

2278 Consumer Show
Maven Company
PO Box 937
Plandome, NY 11030-0937

51- 62- 880
E-Mail: fasttrack@erols.com
Home Page: www.mavencompany.com

N Chittenden, VP

Specialty show, doll, toy and teddy bear.
5,000 Attendees
Frequency: Semi-Annual
Founded in 1970

2279 Craftsmen's Christmas Classic Arts and Crafts Festival
Gilmore Enterprises
3514-A Drawbridge Pkwy
Greensboro, NC 27410-8584

336-282-5550
FAX 336-274-1084
E-Mail: Contact@GilmoreShows.com
Home Page: www.gilmoreshows.com

Jennifer Palmer, Show Manager
Clyde Gilmore, Executive Director

Features work from over 305 talented artists and craftspeople. All juried exhibitors work has been hand made by the exhibitors and must be original design and creation. Visit Christmas Tree Village to view the uniquely decorated Christmas Trees by some of our exhibitors. Something from every taste and budget with items from the most contemporary to the most traditional.
Founded in 1982

2280 Craftsmen's Classic Arts and Crafts Festival
Gilmore Enterprises
3514-A Drawbridge Pkwy
Greensboro, NC 27410-8584

336-282-5550
FAX 336-274-1084
E-Mail: Contact@GilmoreShows.com
Home Page: www.gilmoreshows.com

Jennifer Palmer, Show Manager
Clyde Gilmore, Executive Director

Features work from over 305 talented artists and craftspeople. All work has been hand made by the juried exhibitors and must be original design and creation. See the creative process in action with several exhibitors demonstrating their craft in their booths. Something from every style, taste and budget with items from the most contemporary to the most traditional.
15000 Attendees
Frequency: March/April/Aug/Sept/Oct.
Founded in 1982

2281 Decor Expo
Pfingsten Publishing
6000 Lombardo Center Drive
Suite 420
Seven Hills, OH 44131

216-328-8926
888-772-8926
FAX 216-328-9452
E-Mail: iafg-info@pfpublish.com
Home Page: www.decor-expo.com

Hugh T Tobin, Group Show Director
Rob Spademan, Marketing Director

Five hundred booths exhibiting fine art, limited edition prints, graphics, oil paintings and reproductions. Three shows a year in Orlando (January), New York City (March), and Atlanta (September).
4M Attendees
Frequency: September

2282 Gilmore Shows
Craftsmen's Classic Art & Craft Festivals
3514-A Drawbridge Pkwy
Greensboro, NC 27410-8584

336-282-5550
FAX 336-274-1084
E-Mail: contact@gilmoreshows.com
Home Page: www.gilmoreshows.com
Social Media: *Facebook*

Jennifer Palmer, Show Manager
Clyde Gilmore, Executive Director
Jan Donovon, Marketing Manager

10 shows annually in North Carolina, South Carolina and Virginia. Each show features work from 250-450 talented artists and craftspeople from across the nationa. All juried exhibitors work has been hand made by the exhibitors and must be original design and creation. There is something from every taste and budget with items from traditional to contemporary, functional to whimsical, decorative to fun & funky. Visit Christmas Tree Village to view the trees decorated by some or our exhibitors.
20000 Attendees
Frequency: October/November
Founded in 1973

2283 IACA Markets
Indian Arts & Crafts Association
4010 Carlisle NE
Suite C
Albuquerque, NM 87107

505-265-9149
FAX 505-265-8251
E-Mail: info@iaca.com
Home Page: www.iaca.com

Joseph Zeller, President
Don Standing Bear Forest, VP
Susan Pourian, Secretary
Kathy Ouellet, Treasurer

Wholesale and retail markets of authentic, handmade Indian arts & crafts.
300 Attendees
Frequency: Semi-Annually

2284 IFPDA Print Fair
International Fine Print Dealers Association
250 W 26th St
Suite 405
New York, NY 10001-6737

212-674-6095
FAX 212-674-6783
E-Mail: info@ifpda.org
Home Page: www.ifpda.org

Michele Senecal, Executive Director
Laura Beth Gencarella, PR/Marketing Manager
Tara Reddi, President
Elizabeth Fodde-Reguer, Executive Assistant

The largest and most celebrated art fair dedicated to fine prints.

2285 Morristown Antiques Show
Wendy Management
PO Box 222
Harrison, NY 10528

914-316-4700
FAX 914-698-6273
Home Page: www.wendyantiquesshows.com

Meg Wendy, President
Perry Grosser, Marketing and Finance

Three day show of 85 important dealers from the Northeast. Covers the key periods of antiques for budget minded collectors.
Frequency: November/Annual
Founded in 1930

2286 NAMTA's World of Art Materials
National Art Materials Trade Association
20200 Zion Ave.
Cornelius, NC 28031

704-926-6244
FAX 702-892-6247
E-Mail: info@namta.org
Home Page: www.namta.org

Reggie Hall, Executive Director
Richard Goodban, President

Seven hundred and fifty booths including educational programs to advance the welfare of the art materials and framing industry.
5M Attendees
Frequency: May

2287 National Art Education Association Convention
National Art Education Association

1806 Robert Fulton Drive
Suite 300
Reston, VA 20191-1590

703-860-8000
800-299-8321
FAX 703-860-2960
E-Mail: info@arteducators.org
Home Page: www.naea-reston.org

Kathy Duse, Show Manager
Dr. Deborah Reeve, Executive Director
Dr. Robert Sabol, President

Annual show of 140-200 exhibitor booths displaying manufacturers, suppliers, distributors, publishing companies and universities latest art textbooks and high-tech software. Show draws approximately 4,000 or more attendees.
Frequency: April

2288 National Guild of Community Schools of the Arts Conference
National Guild of Community Schools of the Arts
520 Eighth Avenue, 3rd Floor
Suite 302
New York, NY 10018-8018

212-268-3337
FAX 212-268-3995
E-Mail: guildinfo@nationalguild.org
Home Page: www.nationalguild.org

Jonathan Herman, Executive Director
Kenneth Cole, Director

Exhibits of equipment, supplies and services for the advancement of education in the performing and visual arts. Arts Management in Community Institutions (AMICI) Summer Institute trains administrators to meet needs of growing and emerging arts schools. Other programs, services, guildnotes newsletter, job opportunities listings, and publications catalog available upon request on online.
350 Attendees
Frequency: Annual

2289 New York Antiques Show
Wendy Management
PO Box 222
Harrison, NY 10528

914-316-4700
FAX 914-698-6273
Home Page: www.wendyantiquesshows.com

Meg Wendy, President
Perry Grosser, Marketing and Finance

This unique, sophisticated show is an important convenient source for trend setting decorators. There are quality antiques for new, young, collectors as well as seasoned pros. This show is filled with 17th, 18th, and 19th Century American, English, French, Oriental and Continental furniture and decorative accessories, including rare books, clocks, silver, brass, paintings, prints, maps, porcelain, rugs, glass, lighting devices, sconces, candlesticks, garden urns, and so much more. 80/90 Dealers
Frequency: September
Founded in 1930

2290 Professional Picture Framers Association Show
Professional Picture Framers Association
4305 Sarellen Road
Richmond, VA 23231

517-788-8100
FAX 517-788-8100
E-Mail: ppfa@ppfa.com
Home Page: www.ppfa.com

Mark Klostermeyer, President

Source for manufacturers, wholesalers, print publishers, importers and retailers selling art, framing and related supplies.
Frequency: Annual
Founded in 1971

2291 Surtex
George Little Management
1133 Westchester Avenue
White Plains, NY 10606-3547

914-421-3200
800-272-7469
FAX 914-948-6180
Home Page: www.surtex.com

George(Jeff) Little II, President/COO
Penny Sikalis, VP, Show Manager
Rita Malek, Show Manager

In addition to providing the art and design component of this market we also include important home products.
5000 Attendees
Frequency: May/October

2292 The AADLA Spring Show
PO Box 2066
Lenox Hill Station
New York, NY 10021

212-879-7558
FAX 212-772-7197
E-Mail:
secretary@artantiquedealersleague.com
Home Page: www.artantiquedealersleague.com

Clinton Howell, President
Robert Simon, VP
Susan Caplan Jacobson, Treasurer
David Mayer, Secretary/Executive Director
Ira Spanierman, Vice Chairperson

The best choice of the very best in fine art. Unique chances to view and buy paintings as well as objects reflecting excellence in the applied arts.
109 Members
Frequency: November/50 Attendees
Founded in 1926

Directories & Databases

2293 AADA Membership Directory
Art Dealers Association of America
205 Lexington Avenue
Suite 901
New York, NY 10016

212-488-5550
FAX 64- 68- 680
E-Mail: straussnatt.net
Home Page: www.artdealers.org

Lucy Mitchell-Innes, President
Michael Findlay, Vice President
Jeffery Fraenkel, Secretary

An annual directory listing the AADA members. Published by the Art Dealers Association of America.
77 Pages
Founded in 1962

2294 ARTWEEK Gallery Calendar Section
Spaulding Publishing
PO Box 52100
Palo Alto, CA 94303-0751

800-733-2916
FAX 262-495-8703
E-Mail: info@artweek.com
Home Page: www.artweek.com

Richard J O'Brien, Chairman
John T Bourger, Vice Chairman

A screened list of galleries on the West coast and other Western states are profiled.
Cost: $34.00
Circulation: 14,500

2295 American Art Directory
National Register Publishing
430 Mountain Ave.
Suite 400
New Providence, NJ 07974

800-473-7020
FAX 908-673-1189
E-Mail: nrpeditorial@marquiswhoswho.com
Home Page: www.nationalregisterpub.com

Provides important information on museums, art organizations, art schools, libraries, art editors and critics, scholarships, fellowships, exhibitions and state art countils as well as funding sources and booking agencies.

2296 Art Index
HW Wilson Company
10 Estes Street
Ipswich, MA 01938

800-653-2726
FAX 978-356-6565
E-Mail: information@ebscohost.com
Home Page: www.hwwilson.com

Tim Collins, President
Michael Gorrell, EVP of Technology, CIO

Offers more than 500,000 citations to articles and book reviews in over 300 periodicals, yearbooks and museum bulletins.
Founded in 1929

2297 Art Museums of the World
Greenwood Publishing Group
88 Post Road W
PO Box 5007
Westport, CT 06881-5007

203-226-3571
800-225-5800
FAX 203-222-1502
E-Mail: customer-service@greenwood.com
Home Page: www.greenwood.com

Debra Adams, Editor

National and international art museum list.
Cost: $259.00
1696 Pages
ISBN: 0-313213-22-4

2298 Art in America: Guide to Galleries, Museums, and Artists
Brant Publications
575 Broadway
New York, NY 10012-3227

212-941-2900
FAX 212-941-2885
E-Mail: interview_ad@brantpub.com
Home Page: www.interviewmagazine.com

David Nussman, CEO

A list of over 4,000 museums, galleries and other display areas.
Cost: $15.00
Frequency: Annual
Circulation: 70,000
Founded in 1969

2299 Arts and Humanities Search
Institute for Scientific Information
1500 Spring Garden St
Philadelphia, PA 19130-4067

215-386-0100
800-386-4474
FAX 215-386-2911

Offers data from more than 1100 arts and humanities journals.

2300 Directory of MA and PhD Programs in Art and Art History
College Art Association
50 Broadway
21 Floor
New York, NY 10004

212-691-1051
FAX 212-627-2381
E-Mail: nyoffice@collegeart.org
Home Page: www.collegeart.org
Social Media: *Facebook, Twitter, LinkedIn*

Linda Downs, Executive Director
Alan Gilbert, Editor
Anne Collins Goodyear, President

Institutions are profiled that offer M.A. and Ph.D. programs in art and art history.
Cost: $12.50
152 Pages
Founded in 1911

2301 Films and Videos on Photography
Program for Art on Film
200 Willoughby Avenue
Brooklyn, NY 11205

718-399-4506
FAX 718-399-4507
E-Mail: info@artfilm.org
Home Page: www.artfilm.org

Nadine Covert, Executive Director

An annotated directory of over 500 films and videos on photography, photographers, and photographic techniques.
Cost: $15.00
132 Pages
ISBN: 0-870995-75-1
Founded in 1990

2302 IACA Directory
Indian Arts & Crafts Association
4010 Carlisle NE
Suite C
Albuquerque, NM 87107

505-265-9149
FAX 505-265-8251
E-Mail: info@iaca.com
Home Page: www.iaca.com

Joseph Zeller, President
Don Standing Bear Forest, VP
Susan Pourian, Secretary
Kathy Ouellet, Treasurer

Directory of all IACA members (wholesalers, retailers, artists/craftspeople, collectors, museums and ancillary organizations)
Cost: $15.00

2303 Illustrators Annual
Society of Illustrators
128 E 63rd St
New York, NY 10065-7392

212-838-2560
FAX 212-838-2561
E-Mail: info@societyillustrators.org
Home Page: www.societyillustrators.org

Denis Dittrich, President
Tim O'Brien, Executive Vice President
Victor Juhasz, Vice President
David Reuss, Treasurer

Published by the Society of Illustrators
Cost: $49.95
320 Pages
Circulation: 7000
Founded in 1959
Mailing list available for rent: 1000 names at $600 per M
Printed in 4 colors

2304 Key Guide to Electronic Resources: Art and Art History
Information Today

143 Old Marlton Pike
Medford, NJ 08055-8750

609-654-6266
800-300-9868
FAX 609-654-4309
E-Mail: custserv@infotoday.com
Home Page: www.infotoday.com

Thomas H Hogan, President
Roger R Bilboul, Chairman of the Board

An evaluative directory of electronic reference in the fields of art and art history.
Cost: $39.50
120 Pages
ISBN: 1-573870-22-6

2305 NAMTA International Convention & Trade Show Directory
National Art Materials Trade Association
20200 Zion Ave.
Cornelius, NC 28031

704-892-6244
FAX 704-892-6247
E-Mail: info@namta.org
Home Page: www.namta.org
Social Media: *Facebook, Twitter, LinkedIn*

Richard Fjordbotten, President
Reggie Hall, Executive Director

National Art Materials Trade Association directory.

2306 Official Museum Directory
National Register Publishing
430 Mountain Ave.
Suite 400
New Providence, NJ 07974

800-473-7020
FAX 908-673-1189
E-Mail: nrpeditorial@marquiswhoswho.com
Home Page: www.nationalregisterpub.com

Comprehensive reference for those seeking information on the country's museums. Features profiles and statistics on more than 7,700 museums in the US.

2307 The Artful Home: Furniture, Sculpture and Objects
Kraus Sikes
931 E Main Street
Suite 106
Madison, WI 53703-2955

608-572-2590
877-223-4600
FAX 608-257-2690
E-Mail: info@artfulhome.com
Home Page: www.guild.com

Lisa Bayne, CEO
Bill Lathrop, Vice President

A wealth of information on craft artists working in furniture, wall decor and accessories are listed.
Cost: $29.95
256 Pages
Frequency: Annual
Circulation: 15,000

2308 What Museum Guides Need To Know: Access For Blind & Visually Impaired Visitors
American Foundation for the Blind
2 Penn Plaza
Suite 1102
New York, NY 10121

212-502-7600
800-232-5463
FAX 888- 54- 833
E-Mail: afbinfo@afb.net
Home Page: www.afb.org

Carl R Augusto, President/CEO
Paul Schroeder, Vice President, Programs

Provides practical, easy-to-use guidelines on how to greet blind and visually impaired museum goers. This handbook also covers aesthetics and visual impairment and a training outline for museum requirements for accessibility.
Cost: $16.95
64 Pages

2309 Who's Who in Art Materials
National Art Materials Trade Association
20200 Zion Ave.
Cornelius, NC 28031

704-892-6244
FAX 704-892-6247
E-Mail: info@namta.org
Home Page: www.namta.org
Social Media: *Facebook, Twitter, LinkedIn*

Richard Fjordbotten, President
Reggie Hall, Executive Director

Membership directory of the National Art Materials Trade Association.

Industry Web Sites

2310 http://gold.greyhouse.com
G.O.L.D Grey House OnLine Databases

Grey House Publishing's online database platform, GOLD, offers Quick Search, Keyword Search and Expert Search for most business sectors including art, antique and renovation markets. The GOLD platform makes finding the information you need quick and easy - whether you're a novice searcher or an experienced database user. All of Grey House's directory products are available for subscription on the GOLD platform.

2311 www.aam-us.org
American Association of Museums

For the museum community, enhances the ability of museums to serve the public interest, works on behalf of museums in educating federal legislators, assists museums in improving technical standards.

2312 www.acminet.org
Art and Creative Materials Institute

For art and craft product makers who encourage safe use of materials and proper labeling through certification.

2313 www.albemarle-nc.com/camden
Watermark Association of Artisans

Provides marketing assistance to craft producers.

2314 www.aristos.org/aristos2.htm
Aristos Foundation

The Foundation's purpose is to deepen public understanding of the nature of art as well as to foster the understanding and appreciation of humanistic values in the arts. Publishes an online journal.

2315 www.artantiquedealersleague.com
Art and Antique Dealers League of America

Nonprofit organization promotes interests of retailers and wholesalers of antiques and art objects.

2316 www.artdealers.org
Art Dealers Association of America

Works to improve the stature and standing of the art gallery business. Members deal primarily in paintings, sculpture, prints, drawings and photographs from the Renaissance to the present day. We have over 160 member galleries in more than 25 US cities.

2317 **www.artnet.com**
Art Net United States
The place to buy, sell and research fine art on-line.

2318 **www.collegeart.org**
College Art Association
Association for institutions that offer MA and PhD programs in art and art history.

2319 **www.greyhouse.com**
Grey House Publishing
Authoritative reference directories for most business sectors, including art, antique and restoration markets. Users can search the online databases with varied search criteria allowing for custom searches by product category, geographic area, sales volume, keyword, subject and more. Full Grey House catalog and online ordering also available.

2320 **www.iaca.com**
Indian Arts & Crafts Association
Not for profit trade association. Our mission is to promote, protect and preserve Indian arts.

2321 **www.naadaaa.org**
National Association of Dealers in Antiques
Nonprofit trade association of America's leading dealers mutually pledged to safeguard the interests of those who buy, sell or collect antiques and works of art.

2322 **www.naao.net**
National Association of Artist's Organizations
For artists within nonprofit organizations. Dedicated to the presentation of alternative visual arts, media, literature, new music and performing arts.

2323 **www.naea-reston.org**
National Art Education Association
Manufacturers, suppliers, distributors, publishing companies and universities.

2324 **www.naled.com**
National Association of Limited Edition Dealers
For dealers, vendors and publishers involved with collectibles and gifts.

2325 **www.namta.org**
National Art Materials Trade Association
For manufacturers, importers, wholesalers and retailers of art materials.

2326 **www.nasaa-arts.org**
National Assembly of State Arts Agencies
For those in the arts agency field in the US.

2327 **www.societyillustrators.com**
Society of Illustrators
For professional illustrators and art directors.

2328 **www.sothebys.com**
Sotheby's
Auction schedule listings, exhibition dates and catalogue pricing.

Associations

2329 AERA Engine Builders Association
500 Coventry Lane
Suite 180
Crystal Lake, IL 60014

815-526-7600
888- 26-2372
FAX 815-526-7601
E-Mail: info@aera.org
Home Page: www.aera.org
Social Media: *Facebook, Twitter*

Rex B. Crumpton, Chairman
Steve Edmondson, First Vice Chairman
Bobby Kammerer, Second Vice Chairman
Steve Schoeben, Treasurer
Kevin Frische, Director

A specialized network of professional engine
builders, rebuilders, production engine
remanufacturers and installers.
Founded in 1922

2330 AUTOMOTIVE WHO'S WHO, Inc.
AUTOMOTIVE WHO'S WHO, Inc
2899 East Big Beaver Road
#400
Troy, MI 48083

248-368-0200
FAX 248-368-0202
E-Mail: info@automotivewhoswho.com
Home Page: www.automotivewhoswho.com

David M Bennett, Managing Director

Publishes an automotive original equipment
suppliers directory and database for users by a
wide range of industry professionals including
top executives, site managers, engineers, buyers, consultants and researchers. The comprehensive directory covers the automotive
manufacturing supply chain comprised of Tier
I, II and III suppliers of parts, components,
assemblies and related services.
Founded in 1999

**2331 Advocates for Highway and Auto
Safety**
750 1st St NE
Suite 901
Washington, DC 20002

202-408-1711
FAX 202-408-1699
E-Mail: advocates@saferoads.org
Home Page: www.saferoads.org
Social Media: *Facebook, Twitter*

Judith Lee Stone, President
Jacqueline Gillan, VP
Judie Pasquini, Director

An organization whose members advocate the
support and advancement of highway and auto
safety through the implementation of state and
federal laws, programs and policies.
Founded in 1989

**2332 Alliance of Automobile
Manufacturers**
803 7th Street, N.W
Suite 300
Washington, DC 20001

202-326-5500
Home Page: www.autoalliance.org
Social Media: *Facebook, Twitter, YouTube,
Google+, RSS*

Mitch Bainwol, President/ CEO

An association of 12 of the largest car manufacturers, and is the leading advocacy group for
the auto industry.

**2333 Alliance of State Automotive
Aftermarket Associations**
5330 Wall Street
Suite 100
Madison, WI 53718

608-240-2066
FAX 608-240-2069
E-Mail: info@asaaa.com
Home Page: www.asaaa.com
Social Media: *Facebook, Twitter, Google+,
Pinterest*

Skip Potter, President
Randy Lisk, VP
Gary Manke, Executive Director
Ben Welch-Bolen, CEO & Co-Owner
Tom Sepper, Chief Operating Officer

ASAAA consists of more than 10,000 members
from both regional and state associations that
support and represent the automotive aftermarket industry including that of parts and accessories, supplies and services.
10000 Members
Founded in 1953

**2334 American Association of Motor
Vehicle Administrators**
4301 Wilson Blvd
Suite 400
Arlington, VA 22203

703-522-4200
FAX 703-522-1553
E-Mail: info@aamva.org
Home Page: www.aamva.org
Social Media: *Facebook, Twitter, LinkedIn,
YouTube, Flickr*

Neil D Schuster, President
Mark Saitta, VP
Claire O'Brian, Marketing

A nonprofit association that supports both state
and provincial official members throughout
North America who oversee the administration
and enforcement of motor vehicle laws. Services include development and research in motor vehicle administration, law enforcement and
highway safety as well as being an information
clearinghouse.
Founded in 1933

**2335 American Autoimmune Related
Diseases Association**
22100 Gratiot Ave.
Eastpointe, MI 48021

586-776-3900
800-598-4668
FAX 586-776-3900
Home Page: www.aarda.org
Social Media: *Twitter, LinkedIn, YouTube*

Betty Diamond, Chairperson
Noel R. Rose, Chairman Emeritus
Stanley M. Finger, Vice Chairperson
Virginia T. Ladd, President
John Kaiser, Treasurer

Includes patient information about
autoimmunity and autoimmune related diseases.
Founded in 1991

2336 American Automobile Association
1000 AAA Drive
Heathrow, FL 32746

407-444-4240
800-222-4357
FAX 800-444-4247
Home Page: www.aaa.com

Robert Darbelnet, President
Jerry Cheske, Director Public Relations

Nation's largest motoring and leisure travel organization. AAA provides travel, insurance, financial and automotive related services. The
not-for-profit, fully tax paying AAA has been a
leader and advocate for the safety and security
of all travelers.
45MM Members
Founded in 1902

**2337 American Automotive Leasing
Association**
675 North Washington Street
Suite 410
Alexandria, VI 22314

703-548-0777
FAX 703-548-1925
E-Mail: sederholm@aalafleet.com
Home Page: www.aalafleet.com

Pamela Sederholm, Executive Director
Traci Peters, Account Manager
Courtney Groff, Legislative Associate

A national industry association composed of
commercial automotive fleet leasing and management companies.
Founded in 1955

2338 American Bus Association
111 K Street NE
9th Floor
Washington, DC 20002

202-842-1645
800-283-2877
FAX 202-842-0850
E-Mail: abainfo@buses.org
Home Page: www.buses.org
Social Media: *Facebook, Twitter, LinkedIn,
YouTube*

Thomas JeBran, Chair
John Meier, Vice Chair
Peter Pantuso, President & CEO
Frank Henry, Secretary/Treasurer

ABA supports 3,800 members consisting of
motorcoach and tour companies in addition to
organizations that represent the tourism and
travel industry. ABA strives to educate consumers on the importance of highway and
motorcoach safety.
Founded in 1926

2339 American Coatings Association
1500 Rhode Island Ave., NW
Washington, DC 20005

202-462-6272
FAX 202-462-8549
E-Mail: members@paint.org
Home Page: www.paint.org
Social Media: *Facebook, Twitter, LinkedIn,
Hangout*

J. Andrew Doyle, President/ CEO
Thomas J. Graves, Vice President
Allen Irish, Counsel/ Director
Jeff Wasikowski, Counsel
Nathan Perrine, CFO

2340 American Highway Users Alliance
1101 14th St NW
Suite 750
Washington, DC 20005-5608

202-857-1200
FAX 202-857-1220
E-Mail: info@highways.org
Home Page: www.highways.org
Social Media: *Facebook, Twitter*

Bill Graves, Chairman
Richard A. Coon, Vice Chairman
Thomas F. Jensen, Secretary
Roy E.ÿ Littlefield, Treasurer

A nonprofit trade association that actively advocates and promotes safe and uncongested
highways and America's freedom of mobility.
Founded in 1932

2341 American International Automobile Dealers Association
500 Montgomery Street
Suite 800
Alexandria, VA 22314

703-519-7800
800-462-4232
FAX 703-519-7810
E-Mail: goaiada@aiada.org
Home Page: www.aiada.org
Social Media: *Facebook, Twitter, LinkedIn, YouTube*

Jenell Rose, Chairwoman
Larry Kull, Chairman Elect
Bradley Hoffman, Vice Chair
Greg Kaminsky, Secretary/Treasurer

Lobbying and communications organization for American automobile dealerships that sell and service international nameplate brands.
11000 Members
Founded in 1970

2342 American Public Transportation Association
1300 I Street NW
Suite 1200 East
Washington, DC 20005

202-496-4800
FAX 202-496-4324
E-Mail: meetings2@apta.com
Home Page: www.apta.com
Social Media: *Facebook, Twitter, YouTube, Flickr, Blog*

Michael Melaniphy, President & CEO
Petra Mollet, Chief of Staff
Rosemary Sheridan, VP, Marketing
Jeff Popovich, Chief Information Officer
Mary L. Childress, Chief Financial Officer

APTA is an international organization that supports and represents the transportation industry. Membership benefits include an annual association meeting, an international expo, membership directory, access to online publications, newsletters and electronic news service.
Founded in 1882

2343 American Society for Quality
600 N Plankinton Avenue
PO Box 3005
Milwaukee, WI 53201-3005

414-272-8575
800-248-1946
FAX 414-272-1734
E-Mail: help@asq.org
Home Page: www.asq.org
Social Media: *Facebook, Twitter, LinkedIn, YouTube, Google+*

John C Timmerman, Chair
Paul E Borawski, CEO
Chava Scher, Treasurer
Fay Spano, Communications/Media Relations

An international organization with more than 90,000 members, the ASQ is an authoritative resource on quality that strives for improvement within the workplace and communities alike worldwide through the usage of advanced technology and training programs.
90M Members
Founded in 1946

2344 American Society of Body Engineers
2122 15 Mile Rd
Suite F
Sterling Height, MI 48310-4853

586-268-8360
FAX 586-268-2187
E-Mail: asbe@asbe.com
Home Page: www.asbe.com

William Bonner, President
Jeff Grundy, Director

The American Society of Body Engineers is a non-profit corporation consisting of about 1,000 members within the industry including engineers, designers and suppliers. The organization strives to keep members current on the latest technological advancements within the field of automotive body engineering.
1000 Members
Founded in 1945

2345 American Trucking Association
950 North Glebe Road
Suite 210
Arlington, VA 22203-4181

E-Mail: media@trucking.org
Home Page: www.trucking.org
Social Media: *Facebook, Twitter, YouTube, Flickr*

Duane Long, Chairman
Pat Thomas, First Vice Chairman
Kevin W. Burch, Second Vice Chairman
Barry Pottle, Vice Chairman
Bill Graves, President
Founded in 1933

2346 Antique Automobile Club of America
501 W. Governor Rd
P.O. Box 417
Hershey, PA 17033

717-534-1910
FAX 717-534-9101
E-Mail: lgawel@aaca.org
Home Page: www.aaca.org
Social Media: *Facebook, YouTube*

Don Barlup, President
Bob Parrish, Executive Vice President
Micky Bohne, Immediate Past President
John McCarthy, VP - Finance & Budget
Mel Carson, Secretary / Treasurer

America's premiere resource for the collectible vehicle community—includes publications, calendars, membership information, merchandise, photos, and forum.
Founded in 1935

2347 Antique Truck Club of America
85 S Walnut St
PO Box 31
Boyertown, PA 19512

610-367-2567
FAX 610-367-9712
E-Mail: office@antiquetruckclubofamerica.org
Home Page:
www.antiquetruckclubofamerica.org
Social Media: *Facebook*

Fred Chase, President
Dave Lewis, Vice President
Tom Oehme, Treasurer
Mike Fowler, Secretary

An organization of persons who own or have an interest in antique commercial vehicles, and who wish to promote the preservation, restoration, operation and history of antique commercial vehicles.
Cost: $36.00
Frequency: Membership Fee
Founded in 1971

2348 Association for the Advancement of Automotive Medicine
35 E Wacker Drive
Ste. 850
Chicago, IL 60601

847-844-3880
FAX 312-644-8557
E-Mail: info@aaam.org
Home Page: www.aaam.org
Social Media: *LinkedIn*

Frank A. Pintar, President
Brian N. Fildes, Immediate Past President
Gary A. Smith, President-Elect

Federico E. Vaca, Secretary
Kristy B. Arbogast, Treasurer

A professional multidisciplinary organization dedicated to limiting injuries from motor vehicle crashes.
Founded in 1957

2349 Association for the Advancement of
PO Box 4176
Barrington, IL 60011-4176

847-844-3880
FAX 847-844-3884
E-Mail: info@aaam.org
Home Page: www.aaam.org

Frank A. Pintar, President
Gary A Smith, President Elect
Federico E Vaca, Secretary
Kristy B Arbogast, Treasurer
Founded in 1957

2350 Association of Diesel Specialists
400 Admiral Boulevard
Kansas City, MO 64106

816-285-0810
888-401-1616
FAX 847-770-4952
E-Mail: info@diesel.org
Home Page: www.diesel.org

Chuck Oliveros, President
Carl Fergueson, VP
Al Roerts, Secretary
Laura Roundtree, Treasurer

The worldwide diesel industry's leading trade association, dedicated to the highest level of service on diesel fuel injection and related systems.
700+ Members
Founded in 1956

2351 Association of International Automobile Manufacturers
1050 K Street, NW
Suite 650
Washington, DC 20001

202-650-5555
FAX 703-525-8817
E-Mail: info@globalautomakers.org
Home Page: www.globalautomakers.org
Social Media: *Facebook, Twitter, RSS*

Michael J Stanton, President
Ellen J Gleberman, Vice President/General Counsel
Jim Lentz, Chairman
John Mendel, Vice Chairman
Scott Becker, Treasurer

An international trade association that supports original equipment suppliers, automobile trade organizations and motor vehicle manufacturers. AIAM monitors government regulations and provides information and advocacy support relative to regulatory and legislative issues that directly affect the auto industry.

2352 Auto Body Parts Association
400 Putnam Pike
Suite J 503
Smithfield, RI 02917-2442

401-531-0809
800-323-5832
FAX 401-262-0193
E-Mail: info@autobpa.com
Home Page: www.autobpa.com

Dan Morrissey, Chairman
Jim Smith, President
Eric Taylor, Vice President
Michael Koren, Secretary
Dolores Richardson, Treasurer

An association of manufacturers, distributors, insurance and repair professionals which pro-

vide the collision repair industry with quality replacement parts.
140 Members
Founded in 1980

2353 Auto Care Association

7101 Wisconsin Ave
Suite 1300
Bethesda, MD 20814-3415

301-654-6664
FAX 301-654-3299
E-Mail: info@autocare.org
Home Page: www.autocare.org
Social Media: *Facebook, Twitter, Google+,YouTube*

Richard Jago, Chairman
Michael Klein, Vice Chairman
Kathleen Schmatz, President & CEO
Mark Finestone, Vice President
Ira Davis, Secretary

Provides advocacy, educational, networking, technology, market intelligence and communications resources on auto care to its members.

2354 Auto International Association

7101 Wisconsin Avenue
Suite 1300
Bethesda, MD 20814

301-654-6664
FAX 301-654-3299
E-Mail: aia@aftermarket.org
Home Page: www.aiaglobal.org
Social Media: *Facebook, Twitter, LinkedIn*

Steve Bearden, Chair
Peter Klotz, Vice Chair

The Auto International Association (AIA) segment of the Automotive Aftermarket Industry Association promotes global trade in automotive products by providing a bridge between the international automotive community and the North American aftermarket.
Founded in 1981

2355 Automatic Transmission Rebuilders Association

2400 Latigo Avenue
Oxnard, CA 93030

805-604-2000
866-464-2872
FAX 805-604-2003
E-Mail: webmaster@atra.com
Home Page: www.atra.com
Social Media: *Facebook, Twitter, Google+*

Dennis Madden, CEO
Jim Lyons, VP
Lance Wiggins, Director

Not-for-profit professional organization dedicated to the improvement and welfare of the automatic transmission repair industry for the benefit of the motoring public.
2000 Members
Founded in 1954

2356 Automotive Aftermarket Industry Association

7101 Wisconsin Avenue
Suite 1300
Bethesda, MD 20814-3415

301-654-6664
FAX 301-654-3299
E-Mail: info@autocare.org
Home Page: www.autocare.org
Social Media: *Facebook, Twitter, LinkedIn, Google+*

Kathleen Schmatz, President
Susan Medick, COO & CFO
Rich White, Senior VP
Aaron Lowe, AAP, SVP, Regulatory & Gov. Affairs
Paul Fiore, Director, Government Affairs

A trade association consisting of more than 23,000 member companies and affiliates representing over 100,000 repair shops, distribution outlets, and parts stores.
23000 Members
Founded in 1999

2357 Automotive Aftermarket Suppliers Association

PO Box 13966
Research Triangle Park, NC 27709-3966

919-549-4800
FAX 919-549-4824
E-Mail: media@mema.org
Home Page: www.aftermarketsuppliers.org

Steve Handschuh, President
Bill Hanvey, Senior Vice President
Chris Gardner, Vice President
Ann Wilson, Senior Vice President
Margaret Beck, Senior Director

Automotive aftermarket supplier industry that provides a forum to address issues and resources that highlight the importance of purchasing quality parts backed by full-service suppliers.
Founded in 1971

2358 Automotive Body Parts Association

400 Putnam Pike
Suite J 503
Smithfield, RI 02917-2442

401-531-0809
800-323-5832
FAX 401-262-0193
E-Mail: info@autobpa.com
Home Page: www.autobpa.com

Dan Morrissey, Chairman
Jim Smith, President
Eric Taylor, Vice President
Michael Koren, Secretary
Dolores Richardson, Treasurer

Members are companies that distribute, supply or manufacture automotive replacement body parts.
140 Members
Founded in 1980

2359 Automotive Consulting Group

Automotive Consulting Group
4370 Varsity Dr.
Suite D
Ann Arbor, MI 48108

734-973-1110
FAX 734-973-1118
E-Mail: acg@autoconsulting.com
Home Page: www.autoconsulting.com

Dennis Virag, President

Management consulting firm providing top line and bottom line business performance improvement services to the worldwide automotive industry.
Founded in 1986

2360 Automotive Engine Rebuilders Association

500 Coventry Ln
Suite 180
Crystal Lake, IL 60014

815-526-7600
888-326-2372
FAX 815-526-7601
E-Mail: info@aera.org
Home Page: www.aera.org
Social Media: *Facebook, Twitter*

Rex B. Crumpton, Chairman
Steven Edmondson, First VC
Paul Hauglie, President
Steve Schoeben, Treasurer
Dwayne J. Dugas, Advisory Board Chairman

Network of specialists including production engine remanufacturers, installers, and professional engine rebuilders, provide services and support for the engine rebuilding industry.
Founded in 1922

2361 Automotive Fleet & Leasing Association

N83 W13410 Leon Road
Menomonee Falls, WI 53051

414-386-0366
FAX 414-359-1671
E-Mail: info@afla.org
Home Page: www.afla.org
Social Media: *Facebook, LinkedIn*

Brian Barber, President
Steve Gibson, Executive Vice President
Michael Bieger, Vice President
Bill Elliott, Executive Director
Theresa Belding, Secretary

Provides an advanced forum for corporate fleet professionals to work with industry leaders.
400 Members
Founded in 1969

2362 Automotive Fleet and Leasing Association

11950 W. Lake Park Drive
Milwaukee, WI 53224

414-386-0366
FAX 414-359-1671
E-Mail: info@aflaonline.com
Home Page: www.aflaonline.com

John Dmochowsky, Executive VP
Tom Callahan, President
Bill Elliot, Executive Director

An organization consisting of more than 300 members that provides information, education and research on the fleet industry. Member benefits include annual conferences, educational seminars, the AFLA membership directory and more. The best source of information and contacts for automotive fleet and leasing professionals.
300 Members
Founded in 1969

2363 Automotive Industry Action Group

26200 Lahser Road
Suite 200
Southfield, MI 48033-7100

248-358-3003
FAX 248-799-7995
E-Mail: order_inquiry@aiag.org
Home Page: www.aiag.org
Social Media: *Facebook, Twitter*

John Batchik, Chairman
David Kneisler, Vice Chairman
Scot Sharland, Executive Director

Composed of major North American vehicle manufacturers and their suppliers. Provides an open forum where members cooperate to develop and promote solutions that enhance prosperity in the automotive industry.
1000 Members
Founded in 1982

2364 Automotive Lift Institute

80 Wheeler Ave
PO Box 85
Cortland, NY 13045

607-756-7775
FAX 607-756-0888
E-Mail: info@autolift.org
Home Page: www.autolift.org
Social Media: *Facebook, Twitter, YouTube*

Bob O'Gorman, President
Jeff Kritzer, Board of Directors

An association of manufacturers and distributors of automotive lifts used to raise motor ve-

hicles for undercarriage work. Promotes awareness of safety measures used in operating lifts.
20 Members
Founded in 1945

2365 Automotive Maintenance & Repair Association
725 E Dundee Road
Suite 206
Arlington Heights, IL 60004

847-947-2650
FAX 202-318-0378
Home Page: amra.org
Social Media: *Facebook*

Bill Ihnken, CEO
Chuck Abbott, Vice President, US Sales
Greg Dunkin, Vice President, Key Accounts
Amy Bonder, Vice President of Sales
Dennis Johndrow, Director of Compliance

A nonprofit trade association formally organized to represent the interests, common policies, and purposes of companies engaged in providing automotive maintenance and repair services, their suppliers, and related companies in the automotive industry when dealing with consumers.
Founded in 1994

2366 Automotive Oil Change Association
330 N. Wabash Ave.
Suite 2000
Chicago, IL 60611

312-321-5132
800-230-0702
FAX 312-673-6832
E-Mail: info@aoca.org
Home Page: www.aoca.org
Social Media: *Facebook*

Len Minco, President
David Haney, VP
Bob Falter, Treasurer
Dave Jensen, Secretary
Jim Grant, Past President

AOCA is a non-profit trade association that supports and represents more than 3,500 member facilities within the convenient automotive service industry. AOCA strives to educate consumers on the benefits of preventative auto maintenance, and the reliability of fast lube service centers.
3500 Members
Founded in 1987

2367 Automotive Parts Remanufacturers Association
4460 Brookfield Corporate Drive
Suite H
Chantilly, VA 20151-1671

703-968-2772
FAX 703-968-2878
E-Mail: mail@apra.org
Home Page: www.apra.org
Social Media: *Facebook, Twitter, LinkedIn, YouTube*

William C Gager, President
Mark Kothe, CEO
Jeanie Magathan, Senior VP

Mission is to address the needs of the automotive and truck parts remanufacturing industry and to serve members by providing a wide range of quality products, services, workshops and education, through legislative advocacy, offering technical services, as well as arranging many networking opportunities for members of the remanufacturing community.
1000 Members
Founded in 1941

2368 Automotive Public Relations Council
Original Equipment Suppliers Association (OESA)

25925 Telegraph Rd.
Ste. 350
Southfield, MI 48033-2553

248-952-6401
FAX 248-952-6404
E-Mail: info@oesa.org
Home Page: www.oesa.org

Neil De Koker, President & CEO
Greg Janicki, Executive Director, Marketing

APRC is a professional organization for those within public relations that work in the automotive industry. Member benefits include access to industry news, discounted vendor services, and APRC conferences where members have the opportunity to meet and network with colleagues and practitioners in the automotive industry.
Founded in 1998

2369 Automotive Recyclers Association
9113 Church St.
Manassas, VA 20110

571-208-0428
888-385-1005
FAX 571-208-0430
Home Page: www.a-r-a.org
Social Media: *Facebook, Twitter, Blog*

Ricky Young, President
Mike Swift, First Vice President
RD Hooper, Second Vice President
Michael E. Wilson, Chief Executive
David Gold, Secretary

ARA is an international non-profit trade association with more than 3,000 members that supply equipment and services within the automotive recycling industry.
1000 Members
Founded in 1943

2370 Automotive Service Association
8209 Mid Cities Blvd.
Suite 100
North Richland Hill, TX 76182-4712

817-514-2900
800-272-7467
FAX 817-514-0770
E-Mail: asainfo@ASAshop.org
Home Page: www.asashop.org
Social Media: *Facebook, Twitter, LinkedIn*

Donny Seyfer, AAM, Chairman
Roy Schnepper, Chairman Elect
Bill Moss, AAM, Secretary/Treasurer
Darrell Amberson, AAM, Immediate Past Chairman
John Cochrane, General Director

Leading organization for owners and managers of independent automotive service businesses that strive to deliver excellence in service and repairs to consumers.
8000 Members
Founded in 1951

2371 Automotive Specialty Products Alliance
1667 K Street
NW Suite 300
Washington, DC 20006

202-862-3902
FAX 202-223-2636
E-Mail: qbradley@consumered.org
Home Page: www.inhalant.org
Social Media: *Facebook, Twitter, YouTube*

Colleen Creighton, Executive Director

Provides a unified industry voice for its members engaged in the automotive chemical and vehicle appearance product markets before state, regional and federal legislators and regulators.
Founded in 1966

2372 Automotive Warehouse Distributors Association
7101 Wisconsin Avenue
Suite 1300
Bethesda, MD 20814-3415

301-654-6664
FAX 301-654-3299
E-Mail: aaia@aftermarket.org
Home Page: www.autocare.org
Social Media: *Facebook, Twitter, LinkedIn, Google+*

Kathleen Schmatz, President
Richard Jago, Chairman
Michael Klein, Vice Chairman
Mark Finestone, Treasurer
Ira Davis, Secretary

A trade association consisting of more than 600 members who are manufacturers and warehouse distributors, affiliates, marketing associations and others actively involved in the production, distribution and installation of motor vehicle parts, tools, services, accessories, equipment, materials and supplies. A segment of the Automotive Aftermarket Industry Association.
600 Members
Founded in 1947

2373 Battery Council International
330 N Wabash Ave
Suite 2000
Chicago, IL 60611

312-644-6610
FAX 312-527-6640
E-Mail: info@batterycouncil.org
Home Page: www.batterycouncil.org

Mark O. Thornsby, CAE, Executive Vice President

A not-for-profit trade association formed to promote the interests of an international lead-acid battery industry.
265 Members
Founded in 1924

2374 Bearing Specialists Association
800 Roosevelt Rd
Bldg C, Suite 312
Glen Ellyn, IL 60137

630-858-3838
FAX 630-790-3095
E-Mail: info@bsahome.org
Home Page: www.bsahome.org
Social Media: *Twitter, LinkedIn, RSS*

Jack Simpson, President
Brian Negri, VP
Tim Breen, Treasurer
Jerilyn J. Church, Executive Secretary

BSA is a not-for-profit association that consists of companies that distribute factory-warranted ball, roller, and anti-friction bearings through authorized dealers. BSA provides members with the opportunity to network with others in the industry through meetings, seminars and educational programs at their annual convention.
100 Members
Founded in 1966

2375 Brake Manufacturers Council
PO Box 13966
Research Triangle Park, NC 27709-3966

919-549-4800
FAX 919-549-4824
E-Mail: media@mema.org
Home Page: www.aftermarketsuppliers.org

Frank Oliveto, Chairman
Walt Britland, Vice Chair
Terry Heffelfinger, Second Vice Chair
Jack Carney, Secretary
Bob Wilkes, Immediate Past Chairman

Obtaining and disseminating to members information on topics of interest to the brake parts industry.
Founded in 1971

2376 California Autobody Association
P.O. Box 660607
Sacramento, CA 95866-0607

916-557-8100
FAX 916-405-3529
Home Page: www.calautobody.com
Social Media: *Facebook, LinkedIn*

David Picton, 1st VP
Chuck Reyes, President

CAA is a non-profit trade association consisting of more than 1,000 members that support collision repair industry training and education with the goal of providing quality consumer repairs at reasonable prices.
1000+ Members
Founded in 1967

2377 Car Care Council
7101 Wisconsin Ave
Suite 1300
Bethesda, MD 20814

240-333-1088
FAX 301-654-3299
E-Mail: webmaster@aftermarket.org
Home Page: www.carcare.org
Social Media: *Facebook, Twitter, Pinterest, Instagram*

Rich White, Executive Director
Ruth Elhinger, President

A nonprofit 501 (c) (3) educational foundation whose purpose is to educate motorists about the importance of maintenance repairs and entertainment for safer, cleaner, better-performing vehicles. Provides editorial and public service material for media use.
2000 Members
Founded in 1968

2378 Center for Auto Safety
1825 Connecticut Ave NW
Suite 330
Washington, DC 20009-5708

202-328-7700
FAX 202-387-0140
Home Page: www.autosafety.org

Clarence M Ditlow III, Executive Director

Provides consumers with advocacy support in Washington for auto quality and safety in addition to helping owners of unreliable vehicles by providing information relative to lemon laws, recalls, defect investigations, legislative issues in Congress and more.
15000 Members
Founded in 1970

2379 Driving School Association of the Americas
3125 Wilmington Pike
Kettering, OH 45429

800-270-3722
FAX 937-290-0696
E-Mail: info@thedsaa.org
Home Page: www.thedsaa.org
Social Media: *Facebook, Twitter*

Charles Chauncy, President
Sheila Varnado, Executive VP
Robert Cole, Treasurer
Anthony Caracci, Secretary

A nonprofit organization for the purpose of raising the standards of educational methods in teaching drivers education, to promote traffic safety on the highways and streets, to publicize, inform and educate the general public to

the need for more intensive driver training, safer roadways and all things relating there to.
58000 Members
Founded in 1973

2380 Electric Auto Association
323 Los Altos Drive
Aptos, CA 95003

831-688-8669
E-Mail: contact@eaaev.org
Home Page: www.electricauto.org
Social Media: *Facebook*

Ron Freund, Chairman
Marc Geller, Co-Chairman
Howard Clearfield, Treasurer
Guy Hall, Board Member
Terry Hershner, Board Member

A nonprofit educational organization that promotes the advancement and widespread adoption of battery electric vehicles.
Founded in 1967

2381 Filter Manufacturers Council
10 Laboratory Drive
PO Box 13966
Research Triangle Park, NC 27709-3966

919-406-8846
FAX 919-549-4824
E-Mail: jburkhart@mema.org
Home Page: www.aftermarketsuppliers.org
Social Media: *Facebook*

Steve Handschuh, President
Jack Cameron, VP

For manufacturers of vehicular and industrial filtration products in North America. Active in efforts to educate people on proper disposal of used oil filters.
Founded in 1971

2382 Ford Dealers Alliance
401 Hackensack Avenue
Continental Plaza
Hackensack, NJ 07601

201-342-4542
FAX 201-342-3997
E-Mail: fda@dealersalliance.org
Home Page: www.dealersalliance.org

A Michell Van Vorst, Executive Director
Edwin Mullane, President

Organization that strives to protect dealers against factory encroachment into retail.
15000 Members
Founded in 1969

2383 Formula & Automobile Racing Association
786-571-6965
E-Mail: info@farausa.com
Home Page: www.farausa.com
Social Media: *Facebook, Twitter, YouTube, Instagram*

Reinaldo "Tico Almeida, President
Carlos Mendez, Chief Operating Officer
Victor Leo, Driver Academy Director
Randy Almeida, Vice President
Bob Van Epps, Race Director

Provider of motorsports events for auto enthusiasts.

2384 Global Auto Makers
1050 K Street, NW
Suite 650
Washington, DC 20001

202-650-5555
E-Mail: info@globalautomakers.org
Home Page: www.globalautomakers.org
Social Media: *Facebook, Twitter, RSS*

Michael J Stanton, President & CEO
Ellen J Gleberman, Vice President/General Counsel

Scott Becker, Treasurer
David Zuchowski, Secretary
Michael J. Stanton, President & CEO

Working with industry leaders, legislators, regulators, and other stakeholders to create the kind of public policy that improves vehicle safety, encourages technological innovation, and protects the planet. Goal is to foster an open and competitive automotive marketplace that encourages investment, job growth, and development of more vehicles that enhance Americans' quality of life.
Founded in 1961

2385 Global Automakers
1050 K Street, NW
Suite 650
Washington, DC 20001

202-650-5555
E-Mail: info@globalautomakers.org
Home Page: www.globalautomakers.org
Social Media: *Facebook, Twitter, RSS*

Jim Lentz, Chairman
John Mendel, Vice Chairman
John Bozella, Chief Executive Officer
David Zuchowski, Secretary
Scott Becker, Treasurer

A Washington, D.C.-based trade association and Lobby group whose members include international automobile and light duty truck manufacturers that design, build, and sell products in the United States.

2386 Golden Era Automobile Association
18021-150th Avenue East
Orting
Washington 98360

360-893-4227
E-Mail: AGW1886@aol.com
Home Page: www.geaaonline.org

Henry Moebius, President

A car club that celebrates original cars, trucks, and motorcycles from 1915-1942 and World War II.

2387 Heavy Duty Manufacturers Association
10 Laboratory Drive
PO Box 13966
Research Triangle Park, NC 27709-3966

919-549-4800
FAX 919-506-1465
E-Mail: info@hdma.org
Home Page: www.hdma.org

Timothy R. Kraus, President
Jennifer Hjalmquist, Senior Director
Beth Barkovich, Director
Richard Anderson, Senior Market Research Analyst
Katelyn Litalien, Manager

Represents companies participating in the classes 4-8 medium and heavy truck original equipment and aftermarket parts manufacturing industry.
Founded in 1983

2388 Independent Automotive Damage Appraisers Association
P.O. Box 12291
Columbus, GA 31917-2291

800-369-IADA
FAX 888-IAD- NOW
E-Mail: admin@iada.org
Home Page: www.iada.org

Mark Nathan, President
Bill Ambrosino, First Vice President
Michael E. Sellman, Secretary/ Treasurer
John Williams, Executive Vice President

Leader in the insurance/automotive industry in providing its members and the entire industry a

forum for exchange of ideas and solutions to common problems in automotive appraisal and repair.
Founded in 1947

2389 International Association of Auto Theft Investigators
PO Box 223
PO Box 223
Clinton, NY 13323-0223

315-853-1913
FAX 315-883-1310
E-Mail: webmaster@iaati.org
Home Page: www.iaati.org

John P O Byrne, President
John V Abounader, Executive Director
John V. Abounader, Executive Director

Formed to improve communication and coordination among the growing family of professional auto theft investigators.
4904 Members
Founded in 1952

2390 International Automotive Technician's Network
640 W Lambert Road
Brea, CA 92821

714-257-1335
E-Mail: dmca-copyright@iatn.net
Home Page: www.iatn.net
Social Media: *Facebook, Twitter, LinkedIn*

Monica Buchholz, Marketing

A group of professional automotive technicians from 153 countries who exchange technical knowledge and information with other members from around the world.
64601 Members

2391 International Carwash Association
230 East Ohio Street
uite 603
Chicago, IL 60611

888-422-8422
E-Mail: info@carwash.org
Home Page: www.carwash.org
Social Media: *Facebook, Twitter, LinkedIn*

Gary Dennis, President
Pam Piro, Vice President
Eric Wulf, Chief Executive Officer
Claire Moore, Chief Operating Officer
Charnann Cox, Treasurer

A nonprofit trade group representing the retail and supply segmentsof the professional car wash industry in North America and around the globe.

2392 International Motor Press Association
4 Park Street
Harrington Park, NJ 07640

201-750-3533
FAX 201-750-2010
Home Page: www.impa.org
Social Media: *Facebook, Twitter*

David Kiley, President
Mike Allen, First VP
Karl Greenberg, Second VP
Lisa Barrow, Secretary
Mike Geylin, Treasurer

Professional group of writers and editors producing auto articles for the press, radio or TV.

2393 International Show Car Association
1092 Centre Rd
Auburn Hills, MI 48326-2657

248-373-1700
Home Page: www.theisca.com
Social Media: *Facebook, Twitter*

Bob Larivee, Owner
Bob Millard, General Manager

An organization of automotive enthusiasts who enjoy building, showing and viewing customs (cars, bikes and trucks), hot rods, competition cars, street machines and antique/restored vehicles.
Founded in 1963

2394 Manufacturers of Emission Controls Association
2200 Wilson Blvd
Suite 310
Arlington, VA 22201

202-296-4797
FAX 202-331-1388
E-Mail: asantos@meca.org
Home Page: www.meca.org

Joseph Kubsh, Executive Director
Dr. Rasto Brezny, Deputy Director

Nonprofit association of the world is leading manufacturers of mobile source emission control manufacturers. Serves as a source of technical information on motor vehicle emission control technology.
Founded in 1976

2395 Metropolitan Parking Association
1112 16th St NW
Suite 840
Washington, DC 20036

202-296-4336
800-647-7275
FAX 202-296-3102
E-Mail: nfo@weareparking.org
Home Page: weareparking.org
Social Media: *Facebook, Twitter, LinkedIn, YouTube*

Mark Muglich, Chairman
Alan B. Lazowski, Chair Elect
Nicolle Judge, Vice Chair
Robert A Zuritsky, Treasurer
David Damus, Secretary

To promote and encourage ethical business practices among the operators of parking facilities, and to instill in public and non-public users of parking services confidence in the integrity and skills of parking operators.
400 Members
Founded in 1981

2396 Micro-Reality Motorsports
PO 25 102 South Main Street
Cumberland, IA 50843

712-774-2577
FAX 712-243-8552
E-Mail: nsei@metc.net
Home Page: www.microreality.com

Kerry Namanny, President

Manufactures and promotes NASCAR micro-reality racing centers, plus several other sports and entertainment/promotions.
321 Members
Founded in 1986

2397 Mobile Air Conditioning Society Worldwide
225 S Broad Street
PO Box 88
Lansdale, PA 19446

215-631-7020
FAX 215-631-7017
E-Mail: macsworldwide@macsw.org
Home Page: www.macsw.org
Social Media: *Facebook, Twitter, LinkedIn, YouTube, Google+*

Andrew Fiffick, Chairman
Gus Swensen, Vice Chair
Elvis Hoffpauir, President/COO
David Jack, Secretary
Peter Coll, Treasurer

Provides technical training, information and communication for the professionals in the automotive air conditioning industry.
1700 Members
Founded in 1981

2398 Motor & Equipment Manufacturers Association
10 Laboratory Drive
PO Box 13966
Research Triangle Park, NC 27709-3966

919-549-4800
FAX 919-406-1465
E-Mail: info@mema.org
Home Page: www.mema.org
Social Media: *Flickr*

Steve Handschuh, President
Wendy Earp, Senior Vice President
Paul McCarthy, Vice President
Jo Anne Farr, Vice President
Leigh Merino, Senior Director

Represents more than 1,000 companies that manufacture motor vehiclecomponents and systems for the original equipment and aftermarket segments of the light vehicle and heavy-duty industries.

2399 Motor & Equipment Remanufacturers Association
25925 Telegraph Road
Suite 350
Southfield, MI 48033

248-750-1280
FAX 248-750-1281
E-Mail: info@mera.org
Home Page: www.mera.org
Social Media: *Twitter, LinkedIn, YouTube, Instagram, Flickr*

Shawn K. Zwicker, Chairman
Peter M. Butterfield, Vice Chairman
Michael Cardone Jr, Immediate Past Chairman
John R. Chalifoux, President & COO
Jack Vollbrecht, Senior Vice President

A trade group of many businesses, both large and small, in the remanufacturing industry.
Founded in 1904

2400 Motor and Equipment Manufacturers Association
10 Laboratory Drive
PO Box 13966
Research Triangle Park, NC 27709-3966

919-549-4800
FAX 919-406-1465
E-Mail: info@mema.org
Home Page: www.mema.org
Social Media: *Facebook, Twitter, LinkedIn, Flickr*

Steve Handschuh, President
Robert E McKenna, CEO
Wendy Earp, CFO, Treasurer & Senior VP
Jo Ann Farr, VP, Human Resource

Serves manufacturers of all types of automotive and truck products through market research, legislative and regulatory representation and reporting, information services, industry networking and commercial services.
2000 Members
Founded in 1904

2401 Motorcycle Industry Council
2 Jenner Street
Suite 150
Irvine, CA 92618-3806

949-727-4211
FAX 949-727-3313

E-Mail: memberservices@mic.org
Home Page: www.mic.org

A nonprofit, national trade association representing manufacturers and distributors of motorcycles, scooters, motorcycle/ATV parts and accessories.
Founded in 1914

2402 NAFA Fleet Management Association
125 Village Boulevard Princeton Forrestal Villa
Suite 200
Princeton, NJ 08540

609-720-0882
FAX 609-452-8004
E-Mail: info@nafa.org
Home Page: www.nafa.org
Social Media: *Facebook, Twitter, LinkedIn*

Cluade T Masters, President
Ruth A Wolfson, Senior VP
Joanne Marsh, Director Marketing & Communications

Serving the needs of those managing fleets of automobiles, light duty trucks and/or vans for US and Canadian organizations. Offers statistical research, publications, including NAFA's Fleet Executive monthly magazine, regional meetings, government representation, conferences, trade shows and seminars.
3000+ Members
Founded in 1957

2403 NARSA - The International Heat Transfer Association
3000 Village Run Road
Suite 103
Wexford, PA 15090-6315

724-799-8415
FAX 724-799-8416
E-Mail: info@narsa.org
Home Page: www.narsa.org

Maarten Taal, Chairman
Pat O' Connor, President
Mark Hicks, Vice President
Darlene Barlow, Secretary
Angelo Miozza, Treasurer

An association that has provided focus for the business of thermal management for transportation by providing commercial and technical forums that lead business development and product innovation for more than 58 years.
Founded in 1954

2404 National Association of Automobile Museums
P.O. Box 271
Auburn, IN 46706

260-925-1444
FAX 260-925-6266
Home Page: www.naam.museum

Terry Ernest, President
Mary Ann Porinchak, President Elect
Matthew G. Anderson, Secretary
Judy Endelman, Treasurer
Laura Brinkman, Executive Director

A professional center for automobile museums and affiliated organizations that supports, educates, and encourages members to operate according to professional standards of the museum industry.
Founded in 1994

2405 National Auto Auction Association
5320 Spectrum Dr
Suite D
Frederick, MD 21703

301-696-0400
FAX 301-631-1359
E-Mail: naaa@naaa.com

Home Page: www.naaa.com
Social Media: *Facebook, Twitter*

Jack Neshe, President
Ellie Johnson, President-Elect
Mike Browning, Vice President
Frank Hackett, CEO
Steve McCannoughey, CFO

NAAA represents more then 317 auto auctions both domestic and international. With more than 8.9 million units sold each year. If there is one dominant theme that runs through the colorful history and phenomenal success of this entrepreneurial industry it is that auction business is all about people. NAAA is the net result of the people who pioneered and built it into one of the most respected trade associations in the world.
Founded in 1948

2406 National Auto Body Council
7044 S. 13th St.
Oak Creek, WI 53154

414-908-4957
FAX 414-768-8001
Home Page: www.nationalautobodycouncil.org
Social Media: *Facebook, Twitter, YouTube*

Nick Notte, President
Elizabeth Stein, Vice President
Brandon Devis, Past President
Rick E. Tuuri, Treasurer
Elizabeth Clark, Vice President

A nonprofit organization dedicated to promoting the professionalismand integrity of the collision industry through community service initiatives.
Founded in 1990

2407 National Auto Sport Association
P.O. Box 2366
Napa Valley, CA 94558

510-232-6272
FAX 510-277-0657
E-Mail:
bizdev@drivenasa.com.prx2.unblocksit.es
Home Page: www.nasaproracing.com

An American motorsports organization promoting road racing and high-performance driver education.
Founded in 1991

2408 National Automobile Dealers Association
8400 Westpark Drive
McLean, VA 22102

703-821-7000
800-252-6232
E-Mail: help@nada.org
Home Page: www.nada.org
Social Media: *Facebook, Twitter, LinkedIn, YouTube, Flickr*

Forest McConnell, Chairman
William C Fox, Vice Chairman
Peter K Welch, President
Jeffrey B. Carlson, Secretary
George E. Nahas, Treasurer

Represents more than 19,700 new car and truck dealers, both domestic and international, with more than 43,000 separate franchises.
Founded in 1917

2409 National Automotive Finance Association
7037 Ridge Road
Suite 300
Hanover, MD 21076-1343

410-712-4036
800-463-8955
FAX 410-712-4038
E-Mail: inquire@nafassociation.com

Home Page: www.nafassociation.com
Social Media: *LinkedIn*

Asbel Perez-Viciedo, Chairman
Steve Hall, President
Scot Seagrave, Vice President
Ian Anderson, Vice President
Laurie Kight, Secretary
Founded in 1996

2410 National Automotive Radiator Service Association
3000 Villiage Run Road
Suite 103, #221
Wexford, PA 15090-6315

724-799-8415
800-551-3232
FAX 724-799-8416
E-Mail: info@narsa.org
Home Page: www.narsa.org

Wayne Juchno, Executive Director
Douglas Shymoniak, Manager, Sales & New Business
Laressa Davis, Member Services Coordinator

Trade association serving the cooling system service industry and the public.
1500 Members
Founded in 1953

2411 National Glass Association
1945 Old Gallows Rd
Suite 750
Vienna, VA 22182

703-442-4890
866-342-5642
FAX 703-442-0630
E-Mail: administration@glass.org
Home Page: www.glass.org
Social Media: *Facebook, Twitter, LinkedIn*

Nicole Harris, President & CEO
Nicole Harris, Vice President/Publisher
Tom Howhannesian, Chairman-Elect
Ken Mairotti, Treasurer
Michael Albert, Chairman

Provides information and education, as well as promote quality workmanship, ethics, and safety in the architectural, automotive and window and door glass industries. Acts as a clearinghouse for industry information, a catalyst in education and training matters, and a powerful voice on behalf of the members.
4000 Members
Founded in 1948

2412 National Independent Automobile Dealers Association
2521 Brown Boulevard
Arlington, TX 76006-5203

817-492-2377
800-682-3837
FAX 817-649-5866
E-Mail: mike@naida.com
Home Page: www.niada.com

Karen Barbee, President
Michael R Linn, President
Steve Jordan, COO

Representing quality independent automobile dealers for almost 60 years. NIADA is here to assist members in becoming more successful within the used motor vehicle industry.
19000 Members
Founded in 1946

2413 National Locksmith Automobile Association

630-837-2044
E-Mail:
customerservice@thenationallocksmith.com

Home Page: www.thenationallocksmith.com
Social Media: *Facebook*

An organization of automotive specialists that service mechanical locks, produce duplicate keys of all types, and program transponders.

2414 National Motorists Association
402 W 2nd St
Waunakee, WI 53597

608-849-6000
800-882-2785
FAX 888-787-0381
E-Mail: nma@motorists.org
Home Page: www.motorists.org
Social Media: *Facebook, Twitter*

James Baxter, President
Gary Biller, Executive Director

Advocates, represents and protects the interests of North American motorists.
Cost: $35.00
Frequency: Annual Membership Dues
Founded in 1982

2415 National Parking Association
1112 16th St NW
Suite 840
Washington, DC 20036

202-296-4336
800-647-7275
FAX 202-296-3102
E-Mail: info@weareparking.org
Home Page: weareparking.org
Social Media: *Facebook, Twitter, LinkedIn, YouTube*

Mark Muglich, Chairman
Alan B. Lazowski, Chair Elect
Nicolle Judge, Vice Chair
David Damus, Secretary
Robert A Zuritsky, Treasurer

Our members are comprised of parking professionals in both the public and private sectors from across the country and around the world. NPA members are private operators, parking consultants, colleges and universities, municipalities, parking authorities, hospitals and medical centers and industry vendors.
2400 Members
Founded in 1951

2416 National Truck Equipment Association
37400 Hills Tech Dr
Farmington Hill, MI 48331-3414

248-489-7090
800-441-6832
FAX 248-489-8590
E-Mail: info@ntea.com
Home Page: www.ntea.com
Social Media: *Facebook, Twitter, LinkedIn, YouTube, Flickr, Instagram*

James Carney, Executive Director
Frank Livas, First Vice President

Represents small to mid-sized companies that manufacture, distribute, install, buy, sell and repair commercial trucks, truck bodies, truck equipment, trailers and accessories.
1600 Members
Founded in 1964

2417 National Wheel and Rim Association
3943-2 Baymeadows Road
Jacksonville, FL 32217

904-737-2900
FAX 904-636-9881
E-Mail: info@cvsn.org
Home Page: www.nationalwheelandrim.org

Dave Willis, President
Edward Neeley, Vice President
Andy Robblee, Treasurer
Angelo Volpe, Sectretary/Executive VP

Represents warehouse distributors of wheels, rims and related parts.
230 Members
Founded in 1924

2418 North American Automobile Trade Association
10 Four Seasons Place
10th Floor
Etobicoke, ON M9B 6H7

877-227-8878
E-Mail: naata@naata.org
Home Page: naata.org
Social Media: *Facebook, Twitter, LinkedIn, Flickr*

Tahverlee Dunlop, President/ CEO
George Sahakian, Vice President
Andrew Pilsworth, Director
Jan Zurek, Director
Wouter VanEssen, Treasurer

Promotes the export of motor vehicles.
Founded in 1996

2419 North American Council of Automotive Teachers (NACAT)
1820 Shiloh Road
Suite 1403
Tyler, TX 75703

903-747-8234
FAX 843-556-7068
E-Mail: office@nacat.com
Home Page: www.nacat.com
Social Media: *Facebook, LinkedIn*

Curt Ward, President
Patrick Brown-Harrison, Vice President/President Elect
Jim Voth, Secretary
Randy Nussler, Treasurer

Supports all educators in the automotive industry, with training and education, publications and seminars.
750 Members
Founded in 1974

2420 Original Equipment Suppliers Association
25925 Telegraph Rd
Ste. 350
Southfield, MI 48033-2553

248-952-6401
FAX 248-952-6404
E-Mail: info@oesa.org
Home Page: www.oesa.org
Social Media: *Facebook, LinkedIn, RSS*

Julie A Fream, President &CEO
Neil De Koker, President Elect
Margaret Baxter, Senior VP, Operations
Dave Andrea, Senior VP, Industry Analysis
Glenn Stevens, Senior VP, Membership & Sales

Dedicated to advancing the business interests of companies supplying components, systems, modules, equipment, materials and services used in and by the original equipment automotive industry and to engage in activities in support of the welfare of the association membership. OESA is an affiliate of the Motor and Equipment Manufacturers Association.
340 Members
Founded in 1998

2421 Overseas Automotive Council
10 Laboratory Drive
PO Box 13966
Research Triangle Park, NC 27709-3966

919-406-8854
FAX 919-549-4824
E-Mail: bbrucato@aasa.mema.org

Home Page: www.aftermarketsuppliers.org
Social Media: *Facebook, Twitter, LinkedIn*

Mick Jordan, Chairman
Tim Vehlewald, 1st Vice Chair
Sharmila Kakac, Second Vice Chair
Ben Brucato, Executive Director
Bill Long, Managing Director

One of the oldest and most unique organizations in the global automotive aftermarket. Mission is to promote the sale of automotive products and services exported from North America, to enhance the prestige and goodwill of the global automotive aftermarket industry, to promote friendly trade relationships, cultural understanding and mutually beneficial cooperation among those engaged in the automotive aftermarket industry.
500+ Members
Founded in 1923

2422 Performance Warehouse Association
41-701 Corporate Way
Suite 1
Palm Desert, CA 92260

760-346-5647
FAX 760-346-5847
Home Page: www.pwa-par.org

Larry Pacey, Chairman
Ken Woomer, Chairman Elect
Trent Lowe, Treasurer

An organization of specialty automotive parts wholesalers joined together and dealing with management, financial and legislative matters.
10000 Members
Founded in 1971

2423 Production Engine Remanufacturers Association
PO Box 250
Colleyville, TX 76034-0250

817-243-2646
FAX 417-998-5056
E-Mail: jeopolich@pera.org
Home Page: www.pera.org
Social Media: *Facebook, LinkedIn*

Nancie J. Boland, Executive VP
Robert P. McGraw, President

The Production Engine Remanufacturers Association is an association of individual and firm who remanufacture internal combustion enhgines or their major components or supply necessay components, supplies and eqipment required in the manufacturing process. The goal of PERA is to provide members with the opportunity to exchange ideas, methods and procedures necessary to efficiently produce remanufactured products which are equal or superior to origianl products in quality and performance.
Founded in 1946

2424 Recreation Vehicle Dealers Association
3930 University Dr
Suite 300
Fairfax, VA 22030-2515

703-591-7130
FAX 703-359-0152
E-Mail: info@rvda.org
Home Page: www.rvda.org
Social Media: *Facebook, Twitter, LinkedIn, YouTube*

Mike Molino, President
Ronnie Hepp, VP of Administration
Hank Fortune, Director of Finance
Susan Charter, Associate Services Manager
John McCluskey, Chairman

National association advances the best interests of RV retailers through education, services, leadership and programs of market expansion that promote increased use and sale of RVs while enhancing their image.

2425 Recreational Vehicle Aftermarket Association

54 Westerly Road
Camp Hill, PA 17011

717-730-0300
FAX 630-544-5055
E-Mail: ellenkietzmann@blueox.us
Home Page: www.rvaftermarket.org

Ellen Kietzmann, President
Ron Dempster, VP
Jess Fowler, Secretary
Bill Fudale, Treasurer

An organization for the suppliers, distributors and agents that represent the aftermarket segment of the RV industry.
110 Members
Founded in 1969

2426 Retread and Repair Information Bureau

1013 Birch Street
Falls Church, VA 22046

703-533-7677
877-394-6811
FAX 703-533-7678
E-Mail: info@retread.org
Home Page: www.retread.org
Social Media: *Facebook, Twitter, LinkedIn*

David Stevens, Managing Director
Bob Majewski, President

Serving as the public relations arm of the retread industry. Gathering and disseminating information on retread passenger and truck tires to members and the general public.
500 Members
Founded in 1973

2427 Rubber Manufacturers Association

1400 K St NW
Suite 900
Washington, DC 20005

202-682-4800
FAX 202-682-4854
E-Mail: info@rma.org
Home Page: www.rma.org
Social Media: *Facebook, Twitter, YouTube*

Charlie Cannon, President, CEO
Tracey Norberg, Senior VP
Dan Zielinski, Senior VP

National trade association for makers of tires and other rubber products.
100 Members

2428 Service Specialists Association

1221 Candlewick Dr NW
Suite 2B
Poplar Grove, IL 61065

847-760-0067
800-763-5717
FAX 330-722-5638
E-Mail: trucksvc@aol.com
Home Page: www.truckservice.org
Social Media: *Facebook*

Matt Thompson, President
Sean Ryan, Vice President
Toni Nastali, Treasurer
Billy Burkholder, Director
Nancy Hodges, Director

Members are persons, firms or corporations who have operated a full line heavy duty repair service shop for at least one year with sufficient inventory to service market area, having rebuilding department capable of making all necessary repairs.
140 Members
Founded in 1981

2429 Society of Automotive Engineers

SAE Automotive Headquarters
755 W Big Beaver
Suite 1600
Troy, MI 48084-4906

724-776-4841
877-606-7323
FAX 248-273-2494
E-Mail: CustomerService@sae.org
Home Page: www.sae.org
Social Media: *Facebook, Twitter, LinkedIn, Google+*

Donald J Hillebrand, President
Mircea Gradu, VP, Automotive
Carol Story, Treasurer
David Schutt, CEO

Offers automotive engineers the technical information and expertise used in building, maintaining and operating self propelled vehicles for use on land, sea, air or space.
84000 Members
Founded in 1905

2430 Society of Automotive Historians

E-Mail: webmaster@autohistory.org
Home Page: www.autohistory.org

Andrew Beckman, President
Edward Garten, Vice President
Bob Ebert, Secretary
Robert G. Barr, Director
Vince Wright, Director

Encourages research, preservation, recording, compilation, and publication of historical facts concerning the development of the automobile and related items throughout the world.
Founded in 1969

2431 Society of Collision Repair Specialists

PO Box 909
Prosser, WA 99350

877-841-0660
877-841-0660
FAX 877-851-0660
E-Mail: info@scrs.com
Home Page: www.scrs.com
Social Media: *Facebook, Twitter*

Andy Dingman, Chairman
Kye Yeung, Vice Chair
Bruce Halcro, Treasurer
Brett Bailey, Secretary
Aaron Schulenburg, Executive Director

For owners and managers of auto collision repair shops, suppliers, insurance and educational associates and suppliers in the US, Canada, Australia and New Zealand. Distributes technical, management, marketing and sales information. Works to promote professionalism within the collision repair industry.
Founded in 1983

2432 Society of Independent Gasoline Marketers of America

3930 Pender Drive
Suite 340
Fairfax, VA 22030

703-709-7000
FAX 703-709-7007
E-Mail: sigma@sigma.org
Home Page: www.sigma.org

Kenneth Doyle, Executive VP
Thomas Schmidt, First VP
Brian Beaver, Second VP

Supports independent fuel marketers and suppliers, providing training and education, publications and seminars.
250 Members
Founded in 1958

2433 Specialty Equipment Market Association

1575 South Valley Vista Drive
Diamond Bar, CA 91765-0289

909-610-2030
FAX 909-860-0184
E-Mail: sema@sema.org
Home Page: www.sema.org
Social Media: *Facebook, Twitter, Google+, Tumblr*

Doug Evans, Chairman
Wade Kawasaki, Chair Elect
Christopher J Kirsting, President & CEO

This trade association consists of a diverse group of manufacturers, distributors, retailers, publishing companies, auto restorers, street rod builders, restylers, car clubs, race teams and more.
5700+ Members
Founded in 1963

2434 The Aluminum Association

1400 Crystal Dr.
Suite 430
Arlington, CA 22202

703-358-2960
E-Mail: info@aluminum.org
Home Page: www.aluminum.org
Social Media: *Facebook, Twitter, LinkedIn*

Heidi Brock, President
Karen Bowden, VP, Finance & Administration
Joe Quinn, VP, Public Affairs
Charles Johnson, VP, Policy
Ryan Olsen, VP, Business Info. & Statistics

The Aluminum Association's Aluminum Transportation Group promotes the use of aluminum in automobile and commercial vehicle manufacturing.

2435 The Recreation Vehicle Industry Association

1896 Preston White Drive
Reston, VA 20191

703-620-6003
FAX 703-620-5071
Home Page: www.rvia.org

Derald Bontrager, Chairman
Robert L. Parish, First Vice Chairman
Garry Enyart, Second Vice Chairman
Kevin Phillips, Secretary
Matthew Miller, Treasurer
Founded in 1963

2436 Tire Industry Association

1532 Pointer Ridge Pl
Suite G
Bowie, MD 207161883

301-430-7280
800-876-8372
FAX 301-430-7283
E-Mail: info@tireindustry.org
Home Page: www.tireindustry.org
Social Media: *Facebook, Twitter, LinkedIn*

Jason Littlefield, Executive VP
Bob Bignell, Executive Director

Representing all segments of the tire industry, including those that manufacture, repair, recycle, sell, service or use new or retreaded tires, and also those suppliers or individuals who furnish equipment, material or services to the industry.
5000 Members
Founded in 2002

2437 Tire and Rim Association

175 Montrose West Ave
Suite 150
Copley, OH 44321-2793

330-666-8121
FAX 330-666-8340

E-Mail: tra@us-tra.org
Home Page: www.us-tra.org

Joseph Pacuit, Executive VP

Technical standardizing organization for tire, rim and valve manufacturers.
110 Members
Founded in 1903

2438 Triangle Electric Auto Association
3702 Burwell Rollins CIR
Raleigh, NC 27612-5239

E-Mail: pppayments@rtpnet.org
Home Page: www.rtpnet.org

An association focused on the conversion of gas cars into electric cars.
Founded in 1990

2439 United States Auto Club
USAC National Office
4910 West 16th Street
Speedway, IN 46224-0001

317-247-5151
FAX 317-248-5584
Home Page: www.usacracing.com
Social Media: *Facebook, Twitter*

Kevin Miller, President

Supports all driving professionals and consumers with education, publications, driving and vacation tips. Publishes monthly magazine.

2440 United States Council for Automotive Research
1000 Town Center Drive
Suite 300
Southfield, MI 48075

248-223-9000
Home Page: www.uscar.org

Steve Zimmer, Executive Director
Matt Liddane, Vice President
Paul Mascarenas, Chief Technical Officer
Jon Lauckner, Council Member

The collaborative automotive technology company for Chrysler Group LLC, Ford Motor Company, and General Motors.
Founded in 1992

2441 Womens Automotive Association International
PO Box 2535
Birmingham, MI 48012

248-646-5250
FAX 248-387-3550
E-Mail: lhswaai@aol.com
Home Page: www.waai.com

Lorraine H Schultz, Founder/CEO
Lynn M. Wilhelm, Executive Director
Jennifer Michael, Treasurer
Ellen Mckoy, Vice President
Jody DeVere, Vice President

Dedicated to the development and advancement of women as automotive industry leaders. Today, the organization continues to thrive throughout the United States and Canada as the leading women's global organization dedicated to this purpose.
600 Members
Founded in 1995

Newsletters

2442 AIAG e-News Brief
Automotive Industry Action Group

26200 Lahser Road
Suite 200
Southfield, MI 48033-7100

248-358-3570
FAX 248-358-3253
E-Mail: inquiry@aiag.org
Home Page: www.aiag.org

John Batchik, Chairman
David Kneisler, Vice Chairman
J. Scot Sharland, Executive Director

Global automotive industry news, member succes stories and need to know information on AIAG products and events.
1000 Members
Frequency: Monthly
Founded in 1982

2443 Automotive Market Report
Automotive Auction Publishing
607 Laurel Drive
Monroeville, PA 15146-4405

412-373-6383
FAX 412-373-6388

Clyde K Hillwig, Publisher

News items pertinent to auto auctions and the auto industry.
Frequency: BiWeekly
Circulation: 10000

2444 Automotive Week: Greensheet
Molinaro Communications
PO Box 355
Munroe Falls, OH 44262-0355

330-688-4960
877-694-6076
FAX 866-926-0452
E-Mail: gary@thegreensheetonline.com
Home Page: www.thegreensheetonline.com

Gary Molinaro, Publisher/Editor
Marc Vincent, Managing Editor

Intelligence concerning the $270 billion independent automotive aftermarked. Breaking news & analysis not available anywhere else in the industry. Key moves in the retail and wholesale distribution channels, mergers & acquisitions; financial analysis of publicly-traded entities. Classified, non-product advertising accepted.
Cost: $225.00
4 Pages
Frequency: 48 issues
ISSN: 0889-3918
Founded in 1975
Printed in on matte stock

2445 Car Dealer Insider
United Communications Group
9737 Washingtonian Blvd.
Suite 100
Gaithersburg, MD 20878-7364

301-287-2700
FAX 301-287-2039
Home Page: www.ucg.com

Jill Gardner, Publisher
Donna Lawrence, Editor
Bruce Levenson, Co-Founder
Nancy Becker, Partner, President

Marketing intelligence for new car dealers includes dealer-tested tactics, best management practices and breaking news stories.
Frequency: Bi-Monthly
Founded in 1977

2446 Chek-Chart Service Bulletin
Motor Information Systems/Chek-Chart

1301 W Long Lake Rd
Suite 200
Troy, MI 48098-6349

248-828-0000
800-426-6867
FAX 248-828-0215

Paul M Eckstein, Manager
Anthony Mattar, Owner

Up-to-date information on all the new automotive developments from the car manufacturers. Information bulletin for service station dealers, mechanics, and instructors. Chek/Chart is part of MotorInformation Systems.

2447 EngiNEWS
Production Engine Remanufacturers Association
28203 Woodhaven Road
Edwards, MO 65326

417-998-5057
FAX 417-998-5056
E-Mail: nancieboland@pera.org
Home Page: www.pera.org
Social Media: *Facebook, LinkedIn*

Nancie J. Boland, Exutive VP
Robert P. McGraw, President

An semi-annual e-newsletter covering problems from airline fees to the amount of cars on the road and postives of new businesses involved in remanufacturing.
Frequency: Quarterly
Founded in 1946
Mailing list available for rent: 200 names

2448 Executive Directors Report
Society of Collision Repair Specialists
PO Box 909
Prosser, WA 99350

509-735-0607
877-841-0660
FAX 877-851-0660
E-Mail: info@scrs.com
Home Page: www.scrs.com

Aaron Schulenburg, Executive Director
Luis Alonso, Treasurer
Linda Atkins, Administrative Assistant

Newsletter for owners and managers of auto collision repair shops, suppliers, insurance and educational associates and suppliers in the US, Canada, Australia and New Zealand. Technical, management, marketing and sales information. Free to members.
Frequency: Bi-Annually
Circulation: 6000
Founded in 1982

2449 FirstUp: Daily News
American Int'l Automobile Dealers Association
211 N Union St
Suite 300
Alexandria, VA 22314-2643

703-519-7800
800-462-4232
FAX 703-519-7810
E-Mail: goaiada@aiada.org
Home Page: www.aiada.org
Social Media: *Twitter*

Jim Smail, Chairman
Ray Mungenast, Chairman-Elect
Jenell Ross, Vice Chair
Larry Kull, Secretary/ Treasurer
Cody Lusk, President

Conveys the day's auto-related news quickly, concisely, and accurately. Topics covered in FirstUp range from new vehicle releases, to the latest legislation concerning the auto industry.
11M+ Members
Frequency: Daily
Circulation: 30000
Founded in 1970

2450 Fleet Administration News
PO Box 159
Litchfield Park, AZ 85340

623-772-9096
FAX 623-772-9098
Home Page: ncsfa.state.ut.us

Joe O'Neill, Executive Director

NCSFA members are state government administrators responsible for vehicle fleet management.
Cost: $50.00
Frequency: Quarterly
Printed in on matte stock

2451 Fleet Perspectives
National Association of Fleet Administrators
125 Village Boulevard
Suite 200
Princeton, NJ 08540

609-720-0882
FAX 609-452-8004
E-Mail: info@nafa.org
Home Page: www.nafa.org
Social Media: *Facebook, Twitter, LinkedIn*

Phillip E. Russo, Executive Director
Patrick McCarron, Deputy Executive Director
Joanne Marsh, Director Marketing &
Communications

Official e-newsletter for Public Service and
Corporate fleet managers. Contains special profiles on NAFA Members, important fleet news, and informative articles that won't be found anywhere else.
3000+ Members
Frequency: Quarterly
Founded in 1957

2452 FleetFOCUS
National Association of Fleet Administrators
125 Village Boulevard
Suite 200
Princeton, NJ 08540

609-720-0882
FAX 609-452-8004
E-Mail: info@nafa.org
Home Page: www.nafa.org
Social Media: *Facebook, Twitter, LinkedIn*

Phillip E. Russo, Executive Director

The focus for quick-reading highlights designed to give professional fleet managers the latest industry news.
2600+ Members
Frequency: Bi-Weekly

2453 Highway & Vehicle/Safety Report
Stamler Publishing Company
178 Thimble Island Road
PO Box 3367
Branford, CT 06405-1967

203-488-9808
800-422-4121
FAX 203-488-3129
Home Page: www.trafficsafetynews.com

S Paul Stamler, Publisher
Suzanne Reutenauer, Circulation Manager

Business to business newsletter on the latest developments in transportation safety, regulations and new legislation, and new technology in the automotive industry.
Cost: $467.00
Frequency: Monthly
Founded in 1973

2454 Highway Users In Action
American Highway Users Alliance
1101 14th St NW
Suite 750
Washington, DC 20005

202-857-1200
FAX 202-857-1220

E-Mail: info@highways.org
Home Page: www.highways.org
Social Media: *Facebook, Twitter, YouTube*

Bill Graves, Chairman
Richard A. Coon, Vice Chairman
Thomas F. Jensen, Secretary
Roy E. Littlefield, Treasurer

e-Newsletter with the latest, most recent Highway Users work on behalf of membership. Offers information affecting members.
Frequency: Bi-Annually
Founded in 1932

2455 Hybrid & Electric Vehicle Progress
Alexander Communications Group
1916 Park Ave
8th Floor
New York, NY 10037-3733

212-281-6099
800-232-4317
FAX 212-283-7269
Home Page: www.evprogress.com

Romauld Alexander, Owner
Laurence Alexander, CEO

News of hybrid and electric vehicle commercialization. Worldwide coverage focuses on news and data on both the technical and business aspects of the hybrid or electric vehicle industry.
Cost: $477.00
8 Pages
Frequency: Fortnightly
Circulation: 800
ISSN: 0190-4175
Founded in 1954
Printed in 2 colors on matte stock

2456 IMPACT
International Motor Press Association
4 Park Street
Harrington Park, NJ 07640

201-750-3533
FAX 201-750-2010
E-Mail: mike@jalopnik.com
Home Page: www.impa.org

Mike Spinelli, President
John Matras, First VP
Mike Allen, Second VP
Frequency: Monthly

2457 Independent Gasoline Marketing (IGM)
Soc. of Independent Gasoline Marketers of America
3930 Pender Drive
Suite 340
Fairfax, VA 22030

703-709-7000
FAX 703-709-7007
E-Mail: sigma@sigma.org
Home Page: www.sigma.org

Kenneth Doyle, Executive VP
Marilyn Selvitelle, VP

Information for independent fuel marketers and suppliers on legislative issues, new market trends, equipment use and management techniques.
32 Pages
Circulation: 4000
Founded in 1958
Printed in 4 colors on glossy stock

2458 Lemon Times
Center for Auto Safety

1825 Connecticut Ave NW
Suite 330
Washington, DC 20009-5725

202-328-7700
FAX 202-387-0140
Home Page: www.autosafety.org

Clarence M Ditlow III, Executive Director
Sanja Pesek, Editor

Reports on the auto safety world of CAS, as well as covering safety litigation, secret warranties, crash tests, lemon laws, recalls, federal and state investigations.
Cost: $20.00
15000 Members
Frequency: Quarterly
Founded in 1970

2459 Market Watch
AIADA
211 N Union St
Suite 300
Alexandria, VA 22314-2643

800-462-4232
FAX 703-519-7810
E-Mail: goaiada@aiada.org
Home Page: www.aiada.org
Social Media: *Twitter*

Jim Smail, Chairman
Ray Mungenast, Chairman-Elect
Jenell Ross, Vice Chair
Larry Kull, Secretary/ Treasurer
Cody Lusk, President

Emailed report providing a succinct rundown of the latest industry sales numbers and data. A summary of monthly trends, accompanied by easy-to-read charts and graphs, allows readers to track trends, note milestones, and react quickly to a shifting auto market.
11M+ Members
Frequency: Monthly
Founded in 1970

2460 Motor
Hearst Business Communications
567 Robbins Dr
Suite 200
Troy, MI 48083-4515

248-585-1700
FAX 248-828-7004
E-Mail: jlypen@motor.com
Home Page: www.motor.com

Duane Harrison, Owner
Kevin Carr, President
Paul Moszak, Vice President/General Manager
Lori Aemiseqger, Marketing
Richard Laimbeer, Publisher

Articles to keep readers up to date on the latest diagnostic techniques and service procedures. Management articles to help shop owners increase profitability, latest tools available, new products and industry news.
Cost: $48.00
Frequency: Monthly
Circulation: 138941
Founded in 1903

2461 NACAT News
North American Council of Automotive Teachers
PO Box 80010
Charleston, SC 29416

843-556-7068
FAX 843-556-7068
E-Mail: office@nacat.com
Home Page: www.nacat.com

Patrick Brown Harrison, President
Rob Thompson, Vice President

Cutting edge automotive information for automotive educators. Also news of the organization and the automotive industry.
Circulation: 750
Founded in 1974

2462 NAFA Fleetfocus
National Association of Fleet Administrators
125 Village Boulevard
Suite 200
Princeton, NJ 08540

609-720-0882
FAX 732-494-6789
E-Mail: info@nafa.org
Home Page: www.nafa.org

Philip Russo, Executive Director
Patrick McCarren, Deputy Executive Director
Joanne Marsh, Director Marketing

The focus for quick rading highlights designed to give professional fleet managers the latest industry news.
3000+ Members
Frequency: Weekly
Circulation: 3600
Founded in 1946
Printed in one color on matte stock

2463 News & Views
Bearing Specialists Association
800 Roosevelt Road
Building C, Suite 312
Glen Ellyn, IL 60137

630-858-3838
FAX 630-790-3095
E-Mail: info@bsahome.org
Home Page: www.bsahome.org
Social Media: *LinkedIn*

Linda Miller, President
Richard W Church, Executive Director
Jerilyn J Church, Executive Secretary

Monthly newlsetter of BSA, the forum to enhance networking and knowledge sharing to promote the sale of bearings through authorized distributors. Available to members only.
100 Members
Frequency: E-Newlsetter for Members
Circulation: 400
Founded in 1966

2464 Nozzle Chatter
Association of Diesel Specialists
400 Admiral Boulevard
Kansas City, MO 64106

816-285-0810
FAX 847-770-4952
E-Mail: info@diesel.org
Home Page: www.diesel.org
Social Media: *Facebook, LinkedIn*

Chuck Hess, President
Andy Girres, Vice President
Chuck Oliveros, Treasurer
Carl Fergueson, Secretary
David Fehling, Executive Director

Member benefit focusing on a variety of news, tips and information on the diesel industry. Contains information that will encourage the exchange of ideas among members; provides a forum for discussion and debate; allow for the fostering of new relationships and contacts; provide members with the knowledge and expertise of colleagues; and provide immediate access to information concerning training materials and publications through monthly reviews.
700+ Members
Frequency: Monthly
Founded in 1956

2465 OAC Global Report
Overseas Automotive Council

PO Box 13966
Research Triangle Park, NC 27709-3966

919-549-4800
FAX 919-549-4824
E-Mail: media@mema.org
Home Page: www.tune-up.org

Margaret Beck, Senior Director
Steve Handschuh, President

Free to members.
Frequency: Monthly
Founded in 1923

2466 Passenger Transport
American Public Transit Association
1666 K St NW
Suite 1100
Washington, DC 20006-1215

202-496-4800
FAX 202-496-4324
E-Mail: ptsubscriptions@apta.com
Home Page: www.apta.com

Michael Melaniphy, President/CEO
Petra Mollet, VP
Rosemary Sherid, Marketing

Information on federal legislative, administrative and regulatory developments, management and operations, new technology, and state and local developments in public transit,
Frequency: Bi-Weekly
Circulation: 5000
Founded in 1882

2467 Power Report
JD Power and Associates Publications Division
2625 Townsgate Rd
Suite 100
Westlake Villag, CA 91361-5737

805-418-8000
888-537-6937
FAX 805-418-8900
E-Mail: information@jdpa.com
Home Page: www.jdpower.com

Finbarr O'Neill, CEO
Mary Ann Maskery, Editor
JD Power, Chairman

Focuses on what car buyers and owners feel about their current vehicles.
Cost: $299.00
Frequency: Monthly
Founded in 1968

2468 Quality
BNP Media Company
155 N. Pfingsten Rd.
Suite 205
Deerfield, IL 60015

847-405-4044
FAX 248-358-1024
E-Mail: dalpozzod@bnpmedia.com
Home Page: www.qulitymag.com
Social Media: *Twitter*

Taggart Henderson, Co-CEO
Darrell O. Dal Pozzo, Group Publisher
Chistopher Sheehy, Senior Audience Development Manager

A monthly business publication serving the quality assurance and process improvement needs of more than 64,000 manufacturing professionals. the magazine reports on the use of sound metrology methods, statistical analysis and process improvement techniques to significantly improve quality on the shop floor and in manufacturing planning.
1000 Members
Frequency: Monthly
Founded in 1962

2469 Safety & Environment/ Working Conditions
Automotive Industry Action Group

26200 Lahser Road
Suite 200
Southfield, MI 48033-7100

248-358-3570
FAX 248-358-3253
E-Mail: inquiry@aiag.org
Home Page: www.aiag.org

John Batchik, Chairman
David Kneisler, Vice Chairman
J. Scot Sharland, Executive Director

Addresses emerging and global issues in safety, health and the environment affecting member companies and employees worldwide.
1000 Members
Frequency: Monthly
Founded in 1982

2470 Service Executive
Automotive Week Publishing
PO Box 3495
Wayne, NJ 07474-3495

973-694-7792
Home Page: www.auto-week.com

Marketing information for the independent automotive aftermarket. Fast-breaking news of new market entries and strategies; key retail and wholesale developments; merger, acquisition, bankruptcy reports; regular charts of the Top 25 market leaders in various segments (parts, chains, tune-up specialists, brake specialists, tire, fast lube, etc.). The market's sole weekly. Classified non-product advertising accepted.
Cost: $130.00
4 Pages
Frequency: Monthly
Founded in 1975
Printed in on matte stock

2471 Shop Talk
IMACA Education Foundation
6410 Southwest Boulevard
Suite 212
Fort Worth, TX 76109-3920

817-732-4600
FAX 817-732-9610
Home Page: www.imaca.org

Joan M Jones, Circulation Director

Technical and industry information for the mobile air conditioning industry.
Cost: $20.00
Founded in 1958

2472 Show Stopper
International Show Car Association
1092 Centre Rd
Auburn Hills, MI 48326-2657

248-373-1700
Home Page: www.theisca.com

Bob Larivee, Owner

Car association report about shows.

2473 Supply Chain Solutions
Automotive Industry Action Group
26200 Lahser Road
Suite 200
Southfield, MI 48033-7100

248-358-3570
FAX 248-358-3253
E-Mail: inquiry@aiag.org
Home Page: www.aiag.org

John Batchik, Chairman
David Kneisler, Vice Chairman
J. Scot Sharland, Executive Director

Important information on customs and supply chain security regulation; materials manage-

ment and logistics best practices; and automatic identifications/ RFID standards.
1000 Members
Frequency: Monthly
Founded in 1982

2474 The Insider
American Bus Association
111 K Street NE
9th Floor
Washington, DC 20002

202-842-1645
FAX 202-842-0850
E-Mail: abainfo@buses.org
Home Page: www.buses.org
Social Media: *Facebook, Twitter, LinkedIn*

James Jalbert, Chairman
Thomas JeBran, Vice Chairman
Frank Henry, Secretary/ Treasurer
Peter Pantuso, President & CEO
Brandon Buchanan, Director of Operations

First source of information for bus and tour operators, travel partners, manufacturers, suppliers, and policy-makers seeking original coverage on the motorcoach, tous, and travel industry, from legislation and regulation to news to grow readers' business.
Frequency: Bi-Monthly
Circulation: 10000
Founded in 1926

2475 Tire Business
Crain Communications Inc
1725 Merriman Rd
Suite 300
Akron, OH 44313-5283

330-836-9180
FAX 330-836-2831
E-Mail: info@crain.com
Home Page: www.crain.com

William Morrow, Executive VP, Operations
Peter Brown, VP

Besides reporting on breaking news, Tire Business also compiles numerous rankings and industry statistics relating to the North American tire and automotive service markets, independent tire dealers, tire manufacturers, tire retreaders and the global tire market.
Frequency: Bi-Weekly
Circulation: 30000
Founded in 1983

2476 Today's Tire Industry
Tire Industry Association
1532 Pointer Ridge Pl
Suite G
Bowie, MD 20716-1874

301-430-7280
800-876-8372
FAX 301-430-7283
E-Mail: info@tireindustry.org
Home Page: www.tireindustry.org

Kevin Rohlwing, Senior Vice President Of Training
Sandra Martinez, Director Operations
Dr.Roy Littlefield, Executive Vice President
Chris Marnett, Director Of Training

Features retail, management, personnel and industry related information.
Cost: $13.00

2477 UPdate: Society of Automotive Engineers
Society of Automotive Engineers
400 Commonwealth Dr
Warrendale, PA 15086-7511

724-776-4841
877-606-7323
FAX 724-776-5760

E-Mail: update@sae.org
Home Page: www.saesections.org

Richard O Schaum, President
Martha Schanno, Circulation Manager

Published to enhance communications with and among SAE members on such non-technical issues as society activities, meetings and members. Recruitment advertising is accepted.
Frequency: Monthly
Circulation: 65000
Founded in 1905
Printed in 2 colors on newsprint stock

2478 USAC News
United States Auto Club
PO Box 24001
Indianapolis, IN 46224-0001

317-247-5151
FAX 317-247-0123
Home Page: www.usacracing.com

Kevin Miller, President

Contains schedules and news from USAC divisions.
8 Pages
Frequency: Monthly
Founded in 1982

2479 Ward's Automotive Reports
Ward's Communications
3000 Town Center
Suite 2750
Southfield, MI 48075-1245

248-799-2622
877-825-1815
FAX 248-357-9747
E-Mail: wards@wardsauto.com
Home Page: www.wardsauto.com

Tom Duncan, Publisher
Steve Finlay, Senior Editor
Jim Bush, Business Manager
Chris Lamphear, Marketing Manager

Automotive sales, production and inventory statistics, news and analysis.
Cost: $1195.00
8 Pages
Frequency: Weekly
Founded in 1924
Printed in 2 colors on matte stock

2480 Ward's Dealer Business
PRIMEDIA Intertec-Technology & Transportation
3000 Town Center
Suite 2750
Southfield, MI 48075-1245

248-799-2622
877-778-2512
FAX 248-357-9747
E-Mail: wards@wardsauto.com
Home Page: www.wardsauto.com

Thomas Duncan, Group Publisher
Steve Finlay, Senior Editor
Steve Sindly, Editor
James Bush, Managing Director

Information for the management of US new car dealerships by covering profit building techniques and business expansions. Includes analysis of current automotive trends.
Cost: $36.00
Frequency: Monthly
Circulation: 32635

2481 Ward's Engine and Vehicle Technology Update
Ward's Communications
3000 Town Center
Suite 2750
Southfield, MI 48075-1245

248-799-2622
FAX 248-357-9747

E-Mail: wards@wardsauto.com
Home Page: www.wardsauto.com

Thomas Duncan, Group Publisher
Steve Finlay, Senior Editor
Barbara McClellan, Senior International Edit
James Bush, Managing Director
John Sousanis, Publication Manager

Review of the latest advances in engine and vehicle technology.
Cost: $935.00
8 Pages
Printed in 2 colors on ³ stock

Magazines & Journals

2482 ACTION Magazine
Mobile Air Conditioning Society Worldwide
225 S Broad Street
Lansdale, PA 19446

215-631-7020
FAX 215-631-7017
E-Mail: info@macsw.org
Home Page: www.macsw.org
Social Media: *Facebook, Twitter, LinkedIn*

The journal of record for the professional in the growing global mobile AC industry and changing heat transfer and engine cooling system marketplace. has access to the global design and service and repair experts in automotive, heavy-duty, off-road, and bus mobile A/C, heat transfer and engine cooling system industry.
1700 Members
Frequency: 8x Yearly
Circulation: 13000
Founded in 1981

2483 AGRR
Key Communications
PO Box 569
Garrisonville, VA 22463

540-720-5584
FAX 540-720-5687
E-Mail: news@glassbytes.com
Home Page: www.agrrmag.com

Debra Levy, Publisher
Charles Cumpston, Editor

Source of unbiased, accurate information about the auto glass repair and replacement industry.
Frequency: Monthly
Circulation: 10,000
Founded in 2001

2484 Accident Analysis & Prevention
AAAM
PO Box 4176
Barrington, IL 60011-4176

847-844-3880
FAX 847-844-3884
E-Mail: info@aaam.org
Home Page: www.aaam.org

Brian N. Fildes, Ph.D, President
Mary Pat McKay, MD, President-Elect
Kristy B. Arbogast, Ph.D, Secretary
Frances D. Bents, Treasurer

Provides wide coverage of the general areas relating to accidental injury and damage, including the pre-injury and immediate post-injury phases. Published papers deal with medical, legal, economic, educational, behavioral, theoretical or empirical aspects of transportation accidents, as well as with accidents at other sites.
Frequency: 6x Yearly
Founded in 1957

2485 Aftermarket Business Magazine
Advanstar Communications

6200 Canoga Avenue
2nd Floor
Woodland Hills, CA 91367

81 -22 -403
FAX 818-593-5020
E-Mail: jsavas@advanstar.com
Home Page: aftermarketbusiness.com

Larry Silvey, Editor
Jim Savas, VP

Specializing in providing news, trends, research and analysis on aftermarket auto parts
Cost: $5.00
Frequency: Monthly
Circulation: 41,077
Founded in 1936
Printed in on glossy stock

2486 Alt Fuels Advisor
Alexander Communications Group
1916 Park Ave
8th Floor, Suite 501
New York, NY 10037-3733

212-281-6099
800-232-4317
FAX 212-283-7269
Home Page: www.altfuels.com

Romauld Alexander, Owner
Laurence Alexander, CEO

News and developments in alternative fuel vehicles, including natural gas, propane, CNG, ethanol, electric, hybrid and fuel cells. Alt Fuels brings together news of technical and business developments, usage, infrastructure and regulations for all types of alternative and clean fuel vehicles.
Cost: $367.00
Frequency: Monthly
ISSN: 1528-6746

2487 American Rodder
Buckaroo Communications
701 Arcturus Avenue
Oxnard, CA 93033

805-986-0400
866-515-5600
FAX 810-735-6765
Home Page: www.superrod.com

Gerry Burgel, Editor
Debby Wheeler, Customer Service

Covers the street-rod and custom-car industries. Accepts advertising.
Cost: $39.99
100 Pages

2488 Auto Laundry News
EW Williams Publications
2125 Center Ave
Suite 305
Fort Lee, NJ 07024-5898

201-592-7007
FAX 201-592-7171
E-Mail: philpl@ewwpi.com
Home Page: www.williamspublications.com

Andrew Williams, President
Stefan Budricks, Editor
Janys Kuznier, Circulation Director

Provides technical, operational, marketing, advertising, and managerial information for owners, operators, and investors in self services and automatic carwashes, as well as auto detailing information.
Cost: $56.00
Frequency: Monthly
Circulation: 17292
Founded in 1953

2489 Auto Remarketing
Cherokee Publishing Company

301 Cascade Pointe Ln
Cary, NC 27513-5778

919-674-6020
800-608-7500
FAX 919-674-6027
Home Page: www.autoremarketing.com

Ron Smith, CEO

Reports on changes in the automotive industry and their effects on the buying and selling of cars.
Cost: $24.95
Frequency: Monthly
Circulation: 22000
Founded in 1990

2490 Auto Rental News
Bobit Business Media
3520 Challenger St
Torrance, CA 90503-1640

310-533-2400
FAX 310-533-2500
Home Page: www.bobit.com

Edward J Bobit, CEO
Cathy Stephens, Executive Editor

For those involved in the renting of cars and trucks.
Cost: $30.00
Frequency: Monthly
Circulation: 16000

2491 Auto Trim and Restyling News
Bobit Publishing
3520 Challenger St
Torrance, CA 90503-1640

310-533-2400
800-241-9034
FAX 310-533-2500
Home Page: www.bobit.com

Edward J Bobit, CEO
Travis Weeks, Group Publisher

Latest information on enhancing the appearance of cars with new upholstery, convertible tops and more.
Cost: $19.95
Frequency: Monthly
Founded in 1955

2492 AutoDealer
AIADA
211 N Union St
Suite 300
Alexandria, VA 22314-2643

800-462-4232
FAX 703-519-7810
E-Mail: goaiada@aiada.org
Home Page: www.aiada.org
Social Media: Twitter

Jim Smail, Chairman
Ray Mungenast, Chairman-Elect
Jenell Ross, Vice Chair
Larry Kull, Secretary/ Treasurer
Cody Lusk, President

Offers members an in-depth look at America's international auto industry and provides thoughtful analysis of everything from cutting edge vehicle technology to legislation making its way through the halls of Congress. Features include exclusive interviews with auto executives, detailed political coverage, vehicle reviews, and member spotlights.
11M+ Members
Frequency: Quarterly
Founded in 1970

2493 AutoInc
Automotive Service Association

8191 Precinct Line Road
Suite 100
Colleyville, TX 76034-7675

817-514-2900
800-272-7467
FAX 817-514-0770
E-Mail: asainfo@ASAshop.org
Home Page: www.asashop.org

Ron Nagy, Chairman
Darrell Amberson, Chairman-Elect
Frequency: Monthly
Founded in 1951

2494 AutoSmart
Aegis Group-Publishers
30400 Van Dyke Avenue
Warren, MI 48093-2368

586-574-3400
FAX 248-447-7566
E-Mail: campbell-ewald@c-e.com
Home Page: www.campbell-ewald.com

Jim Palmer, President
Bill Ludwig, Chairman, CEO
Jeremy Morris, Publisher

Published for Delco Electronics for car company decision makers who deal with such systems.
Frequency: Monthly

2495 Autoglass
National Glass Association
1945 Old Gallows Rd
Suite 750
Vienna, VA 22182

703-442-4890
866-342-5642
FAX 703-442-0630
E-Mail: nicole@glass.org
Home Page: www.glass.org

Phil James, CEO
Nancy Davis, Editor-in-Chief

Forum for owners, managers and distributors in glass replacement, repair, tinting, and also auto security fields. News and reports on insurance and legislative regulations. New product updates, news and technology information.
Cost: $24.95
Circulation: 7000
ISSN: 1047-2061
Founded in 1948

2496 Automotive Cooling Journal
National Automotive Radiator Service Association
3000 Villiage Run Road
Suite 103, #221
Wexford, PA 15090-6315

724-799-8415
800-551-3232
FAX 724-799-8416
E-Mail: info@narsa.org
Home Page: www.narsa.org

Wayne Juchno, Executive Director
Douglas Shymoniak, Manager
Maarten Taal, President
Pat O'Connor, Vice President
Darlene Barlow, Secretary

Auto cooling system service data. Free to members.
Cost: $30.00
60 Pages
Frequency: Monthly
Circulation: 10000
Founded in 1956

2497 Automotive Design & Production
Gardner Publications

705 S Main St
Suite 200
Plymouth, MI 48170-2089

734-416-9705
FAX 734-416-9707
E-Mail: daver@autofieldguide.com
Home Page: www.adp.com

Mike Vohland, Publisher
Lawrence S Gould, Contributing Editor
Rick Kline Jr, Publisher

Coverage of the automotive industry: suppliers, manufacturers from design through delivery.
Cost: $65.00
Frequency: Monthly
Circulation: 60,404
Founded in 1928

2498 Automotive Engineering International Magazine
Society of Automotive Engineers
400 Commonwealth Dr
Warrendale, PA 15096-0001

724-772-8509
877-606-7323
FAX 724-776-9765
E-Mail: customerservice@sae.org
Home Page: www.sae.org

David Schutt, CEO
Kevin Jost, Editor
Brian Kaleida, Chief Information Officer

Cars, aircraft, trucks, off highway equipment, engines, materials, manufacturing and fuels have the Society of Engineers in common. The SAE is your one stop resource for technical information and expertise used in building, maintaining and operating self propelled vehicles for use on land, sea, air or space.
Cost: $120.00
125 Pages
Frequency: Monthly
Circulation: 124451
Founded in 1905

2499 Automotive Executive Magazine
National Auto Dealers Association
8400 Westpark Dr
Mc Lean, VA 22102-3591

703-821-7150
800-252-6232
FAX 703-821-7234
E-Mail: msaldana@nada.org
Home Page: www.aemag.com

Tom Choy, Owner
Mark Stertz, President

Devoted exclusively to the automotive executive. Features that take on the new topics in the industry, and columns filled with practical, solid business advice for each dealership department.
Cost: $24.00
40 Pages
Frequency: Monthly
Circulation: 23000
Founded in 1917

2500 Automotive Fleet
Bobit Publishing Company
3520 Challenger St
Torrance, CA 90503-1640

310-533-2400
847-647-9780
FAX 310-533-2500
E-Mail: Bobitpubs@halldata.com
Home Page: www.bobit.com

Edward J Bobit, CEO
Ty Bobit, President

Improvements in operational, purchasing and management responsibilities.
Cost: $35.00
Frequency: Monthly
Circulation: 21037
Founded in 1961

2501 Automotive Industries
Worldwide Purchasing Ltd
Versailles, KY 40383

313-262-5702
E-Mail: jal@autoindustry.us
Home Page: www.ai-online.com

John Larkin, Publisher
Ed Richardson, Editor
Ben Adler, Finance
Nick Palmen, Associate Publisher

Offers information for vehicle producers and suppliers worldwide.
Cost: $70.00
Frequency: Monthly
Circulation: 85000
Founded in 1895
Printed in on glossy stock

2502 Automotive Manufacturing & Production
Gardner Publications
6915 Valley Ln
Cincinnati, OH 45244-3153

513-527-8800
800-950-8020
FAX 513-527-8801
E-Mail: rkline2@autofieldguide.com
Home Page: www.gardnerweb.com

Rick Kline Sr, CEO/Publisher
Richard Kline, VP

For engineers and managers who are concerned with improving manufacturing.
Cost: $89.00
110 Pages
Frequency: Monthly
Founded in 1934

2503 Automotive News
Crain Communications
1155 Gratiot Ave
Detroit, MI 48207-2732

313-446-0450
877-812-1584
FAX 313-446-1680
E-Mail: customerservice@autonews.com
Home Page: www.autonews.com

Richard Johnson, Managing Editor
Jason Stein, Editor
Tony Merpi, Director Of Marketing
Victor Galvan, Web Editor

Covers the manufacturing side of the automotive industry, including engineering, design, production and suppliers, with equal emphasis on the retail side of the industry, including the marketing, sales, service and resale of vehicles.
Frequency: Weekly
Circulation: 79000

2504 Automotive Recycling
Automotive Recyclers Association
9113 Church Street
Suite 1
Manassas, VA 20110-5457

571-208-0428
888-385-1005
FAX 571-208-0430
E-Mail: michael@a-r-a.org
Home Page: www.a-r-a.org

Michael E Wilson, CEO
Linda Pitman, President
Randy Reitman, Secretary

Offers information on the recycling of automobiles and automotive parts.
Cost: $40.00
Frequency: Bi-Monthly
Circulation: 1100
ISSN: 1058-9376
Founded in 1943
Printed in on glossy stock

2505 Body Language
Automotive Body Parts Association
1510 Eldridge Parkway
Suite 110-168
Houston, TX 77077

281-531-0809
800-323-5832
FAX 281-531-9411
E-Mail: info@autobpa.com
Home Page: www.autobpa.com

Stanley Rodman, Executive Director
Nicholas Scheid, President

Published six times per year by the Automotive Body Parts Association, this newsletter keeps body shop operators and insurance industry executives up-to-date on the latest information concerning the manufacturing, distribution and importing of aftermarket body parts.
Cost: $80.00
146 Members
167 Pages
Circulation: 400
Founded in 1980

2506 BodyShop Business
Babcox Publications
3550 Embassy Pkwy
Akron, OH 44333-8318

330-670-1234
FAX 330-670-0874
Home Page: www.babcox.com

Bill Babcox, Owner
Georgina Carson, Editor
Bob Bissler, Senior Editor

Devoted to helping collision-repair shop owners and managers run more profitable businesses. Editorially, BodyShop business covers all aspects of collision repair, with a focus on how-to topics include management, dimensioning, straightening, welding, refinishing, law and technology.
Cost: $64.00
Frequency: Monthly
Circulation: 60145
Founded in 1920

2507 Brake & Front End
Babcox Publications
3550 Embassy Pkwy
Akron, OH 44333-8318

330-670-1234
FAX 330-670-0874
E-Mail: amarkel@babcox.com
Home Page: www.babcox.com

Bill Babcox, Owner
Andrew Markel, Editor
Brad Mitchell, Circulation/IT Director

Has monthly service articles that feature the latest information on brake, chassis, exhaust, front end, front-wheel drive and wheel alignment. Each issue also profiles the newest product and service offerings from aftermarket suppliers.
Cost: $64.00
Frequency: Monthly
Circulation: 40,310
Founded in 1920

2508 Cars & Parts
Amos Press

PO Box 4129
Sidney, OH 45365-4129

937-498-2111
800-448-3611
FAX 937-498-0807
E-Mail: editorial@carsandparts.com
Home Page: www.amospress.com

Bruce D Boyd, CEO
Margie Bruns, Advertising Manager
Mark Kaufman, Associate Publisher

Focused to the serious collector car lobbyist. Each issue has an array of how-to articles, detailed coverage of feature cars and intriguing historical views of the auto companies and their most influential players. Additionally there are reports on major collector car shows and auctions including analysis of price trends on major categories of cars. Also included is a calendar of upcoming events: shows, auctions and swap meets. Finally, each issue has an extensive classified section.
Cost: $31.95
124 Pages
Frequency: Monthly
Founded in 1957
Printed in 4 colors on glossy stock

2509 Counterman
Babcox Publications
3550 Embassy Pkwy
Akron, OH 44333-8318

330-670-1234
FAX 330-670-0874
Home Page: www.babcox.com

Bill Babcox, Owner
Jon Owens, Publisher

Targeted at the needs of the jobber sales team — those who buy and sell parts, services, equipment, build brand awareness, preference and loyalty by recommending parts to the DIY customer and professional technician.
Cost: $ 110.00
Frequency: Monthly
Circulation: 50,000
Founded in 1920

2510 Dealer
Horizon Communications
5201 Great America Pkwy
Floor 20, Suite 320
Santa Clara, CA 95054-1122

408-969-4888
FAX 408-969-4895
E-Mail: jh@horizonpr.com
Home Page: www.horizonpr.com

Mike Roscoe, Publisher

Information for automobile dealers on service, parts, used car merchandising, financing, body shop, planning and risk management.
Cost: $35.00
Frequency: Monthly
Circulation: 21178
Founded in 1995

2511 Destinations
American Bus Association
111 K Street NE
9th Floor
Washington, DC 20002

202-842-1645
FAX 202-842-0850
E-Mail: abainfo@buses.org
Home Page: www.buses.org

Peter J Pantuso, CEO
Brandon Buchanan, Director of Operations
Clyde J. Hart Jr, Senior Vice President
Eric Braendel, CFO

Motorcoach travel across North America and Association news.
80 Pages
Frequency: Monthly

Circulation: 6000
Founded in 1926
Printed in 4 colors on glossy stock

2512 Diesel Progress: North American Edition
Diesel & Gas Turbine Publications
20855 Watertown Rd
Suite 220
Waukesha, WI 53186-1873

262-754-4100
FAX 262-754-4175
E-Mail: mosenga@dieselpub.com
Home Page: www.dieselspec.com

Michael Osenga, President
S Bollwahn, Circulation Manager

Geared towards readers interested in state-of-the-art systems technology. Features include new product listings, systems design, research and product testing as well as systems maintenance and rebuilding.
Frequency: Monthly
Circulation: 26,011
Founded in 1837

2513 Double Clutch
Antique Truck Club of America
PO Box 91
Imgomar, PA 15127

412-366-0392
FAX 724-727-9768
Home Page: www.atca-inc.net/

Bill Powell, Publisher
Greg Matecko, Publisher

Magazine for antique truck enthusiasts.
Cost: $50.00
Founded in 1971

2514 Dual News Magazine
Driving School Association of the Americas
3125 Wilmington Pike
Kettering, OH 45429

800-270-3722
FAX 937-290-0696
E-Mail: info@thedsaa.org
Home Page: www.thedsaa.org
Social Media: Facebook, Twitter

Sharon Postigo Fife, President
Robert Cole, Treasurer
Sheila Varnado, Executive VP
Debbie Prudhomme, Secretary

Keeping all driving school professionals informed of upcoming educational seminars, sharing ideas & opinions and introducing products and the like to driving educators. Represents a continuing commitment to the driving school industry.
58000 Members
Founded in 1973

2515 Engine Builder
Babcox Publications
3550 Embassy Pkwy
Akron, OH 44333-8318

330-670-1234
FAX 330-670-0874
Home Page: www.babcox.com

Bill Babcox, Owner
Doug Kaufman, Editor

Business magazine serving the machine shop, custom engine, production engine and small parts rebuilding markets. It delivers editorial excellence that reflects the growing sophistication of the rebuilding industry and aids its readers in the profitable operation of their businesses.
Cost: $64.00
72 Pages
Frequency: Monthly
Circulation: 19500

Founded in 1920
Printed in 4 colors on glossy stock

2516 Engine Professional
Automotive Engine Rebuilders Association
500 Coventry Ln
Suite 180
Crystal Lake, IL 60014-7592

815-526-7600
866-326-2372
FAX 815-526-7601
E-Mail: info@aera.org
Home Page: www.aera.org
Social Media: Facebook, Twitter

David Bianchi, Chairman
John Goodman, President
Dean Yatchyshyn, Treasurer
Dwayne J. Dugas, 1st Vice Chairman
Ron McMorris, 2nd Vice Chairman

Packed with highly technical, application-driven articles that will help you and your business thrive.
Frequency: Quarterly
Founded in 1922

2517 FLEETSolutions
National Association of Fleet Administrators
125 Village Boulevard
Suite 200
Princeton, NJ 08540

609-720-0882
FAX 609-452-8004
E-Mail: info@nafa.org
Home Page: www.nafa.org
Social Media: Facebook, Twitter, LinkedIn

Phillip E. Russo, Executive Director

Contains educational articles based on the eight disciplines of the fleet management profession.
2600+ Members
Frequency: Bi-Monthly

2518 Family Motor Coaching Magazine
8291 Clough Pike
Cincinnati, OH 45244-2796

513-474-3622
800-543-3622
FAX 513-474-2332
E-Mail: membership@fmca.com
Home Page: www.fmca.com

Don Eversman, Executive Director

Official publication of the Family Motor Coach Association, an organization for owners of self-contained motor homes. Publishes articles regarding motor home maintenance and repair, new products, travel destinations of interest to RV travelers and association news.
Cost: $24.00
Frequency: Monthly
Circulation: 98000

2519 Fleet Financials
Bobit Publishing Company
23210 Crenshaw Blvd
Suite 101
Torrance, CA 90505-3181

310-539-1969
FAX 310-539-4329
E-Mail: mike.antich@bobit.com
Home Page: www.fleet-central.com

John Bebout, Owner

Features profiles of successfully managed fleets and analysis of lease verses company ownership.
Cost: $28.00
Frequency: Monthly
Circulation: 15500

2520 Global Connection
Automotive Parts Remanufacturers Association

4215 Lafayette Center Dr
Suite 3
Chantilly, VA 20151-1243

703-968-2772
FAX 703-968-2878
E-Mail: mail@apra.org
Home Page: www.apra.org

William Gager, President
Jeanie Magathan, Sr. VP
Morris Spector, Director, Advertising &
Marketing
Marlene Koskinas, Executive Assistant

Association newsletter provides members with
information on the remanufacturing industry
including product updates, news features and
more.
Cost: $35.00
1000 Members
Frequency: Monthly
Circulation: 10000+
Founded in 1941

2521 Global Insight

Motor and Equipment Manufacturers
Association
10 Laboratory Drive
PO Box 13966
Research Triangle Park, NC 27709-3906

919-549-4800
FAX 919-406-1465
E-Mail: info@mema.org
Home Page: www.mema.org

Bob McKenna, President
Wendy Earp, VP
Frank Hampshire, Marketing

Member publication examines critical issues
and challenges facing today's original equip-
ment, aftermarket and heavy duty suppliers.
Subscriptions and advertising available.
Frequency: Quarterly
Circulation: 2400
Founded in 1904

2522 Hemmings Classic Car

Hemmings Motor News
PO Box 4317
Bennington, VT 05201

802-442-3101
800-227-4373
FAX 802-447-9631
E-Mail: hmnmail@hemmings.com
Home Page: www.hemmings.com

Formerly the Special Interest Auto magazine,
features contemporary road tests and in-depth
automobile profiles, automotive design, engineering, styling and historical exposes, how-to
restoration and technical articles, and profiles
on specialists and shops specializing in the
collector-car industry.
Frequency: Monthly
Founded in 1954

2523 Hemmings Motor News

PO Box 100
Bennington, VT 05201

802-442-3101
800-227-4373
FAX 802-447-9631
E-Mail: hmnmail@hemmings.com
Home Page: www.hemmings.com

Terry Ehrich, Publisher
Eileen Desmarais, Marketing

The bible of the car collector, this monthly
magazine serves to enhance the experience of
the car collector-enthusiast. Regular departments include vehicle and parts search, price
checkers, dealers tips, hobby directory and

more.
Cost: $31.95
Frequency: Monthly
Circulation: 210000
Founded in 1954

2524 ImportCar

Babcox Publications
3550 Embassy Pkwy
Akron, OH 44333-8318

330-670-1234
FAX 330-670-0874
E-Mail: mdellavalle@babcox.com
Home Page: www.babcox.com

Bill Babcox, Owner
David Wooldridge, Publisher

Complete import service magazine. It is geared
exclusively to the vehicle repair needs of import specialist technicians. The in-depth, technical nature of the magazine's editorial content
helps technicians of all abilities do their jobs
more efficiently and effectively.
Cost: $64.00
Frequency: Monthly
Circulation: 29190
Founded in 1979

2525 Independent Battery Manufacturers

401 North Michigan Avenue
24th Floor
Chicago, IL 60611

312-644-6610
FAX 312-527-6640
E-Mail: info@thebatteryman.com
Home Page: www.thebatteryman.com

Founded in 1921

**2526 International Collision Parts Industry
Suppliers Guide**

Automotive Body Parts Association
1510 Eldridge Parkway
Suite 110-168
Houston, TX 77077

281-531-0809
800-323-5832
FAX 281-531-9411
E-Mail: info@autobpa.com
Home Page: www.autobpa.com

Stanley Rodman, Executive Director
Nicholas Scheid, President

Covers the collision replacement parts industry.
146 Members
64 Pages
Frequency: Quarterly
Circulation: 2300
Founded in 1980
Printed in 4 colors on glossy stock

2527 Journal of Quality Technology

American Society for Quality
600 N Plankinton Avenue
PO Box 3005
Milwaukee, WI 53201-3005

414-272-8575
800-248-1946
FAX 414-272-1734
E-Mail: help@asq.org
Home Page: www.asq.org

Roberto M Saco, President
Paul E Borawski, Executive Director
Erica Gumieny, Sales
Fay Spano, Communications/Media Relations

Published by the American Society for Quality,
the JQT is a quarterly, peer-reviewed journal
that focuses on the subject of quality control
and the related areas of reliability and similar
disciplines.
Cost: $30.00
100M Members
Frequency: Quarterly
Founded in 1946

2528 LCT Magazine

Bobit Publishing Company
3520 Challenger St
Torrance, CA 90503-1640

310-533-2400
800-380-8335
FAX 310-533-2500
E-Mail: webmaster@bobit.com
Home Page: www.bobit.com

Edward J Bobit, CEO

Serves the limousine agency owner.
Cost: $28.00
Frequency: Monthly
Circulation: 10000
Founded in 1961

2529 Limousine Digest

Digest Publications
29 Fostertown Road
Medford, NJ 08055

609-953-4900
FAX 609-953-4905
E-Mail: info@limodigest.com
Home Page: www.limodigest.com

Chris Weiss, Publisher
Susan Rose, Assistant Publisher
Iric Cohen, President

Information for owners and operators of limou-
sine, livery and transportation fleets, including
day to day operational information, industry
trends, product reviews, technical advances, as
well as success stories.
Cost: $24.95
100 Pages
Frequency: Monthly
Circulation: 12500
ISSN: 1095-8436
Founded in 1990
Printed in 4 colors on glossy stock

2530 Locator

John Holmes Publishing Company
521 Main Street
PO Box 286
Whiting, IA 51063

712-458-2213
800-831-0820
FAX 712-458-2687
E-Mail: sales@partslocator.com
Home Page: www.partslocator.com

John Holmes, President
Charis Lloyd, VP
Wendy Lloyd, Marketing Director
Stacy Phillips, Editor

Nation's leading auto and truck parts magazine.
Cost: $29.00
250 Pages
Frequency: Monthly
Circulation: 18500
Founded in 1957
Printed in 4 colors on newsprint stock

2531 Lubes-N-Greases

LNG Publishing Company
6105 Arlington Blvd
Suite G
Falls Church, VA 22044-2708

703-536-0800
FAX 703-536-0803
E-Mail: info@Lngpublishing.com
Home Page: www.lngpublishing.com

Gloria Stienberg Briskin, Advertising Director
Nancy DeMarco, Publisher
Lisa Tocci, Managing Editor

The magazine of industry in motion.
Frequency: Monthly
Circulation: 17300
ISSN: 1080-9449
Founded in 1995
Printed in 4 colors on glossy stock

2532 Lubricants World
4545 Post Oak Place
Suite 230
Houston, TX 77027

713-840-0378
FAX 713-840-8585

Kathryn B Carnes, Editor
Professional journal for those in the oil and
grease industry.

2533 MOVE
AAMVA
4301 Wilson Blvd
Suite 400
Arlington, VA 22203-1867

703-522-4200
FAX 703-522-1553
E-Mail: info@aamva.org
Home Page: www.aamva.org

Neil D. Schuster, President & CEO
Marc Saitta, Vice President & CFO

Provides members with practical and in-depth
how-to information on a wide range of topics.
Provides feature articles and departments that
tackle issues facing today's administrators.
Frequency: Quarterly
Founded in 1933
Printed in 4 colors

2534 MOVE Magazine
American Assn. of Motor Vehicle
Administrators
Executive Plaza, 11350 McCormick Rd
Suite 900
Hunt Valley, MD 21031

410-584-1955
FAX 410-584-1998
Home Page: www.aamva.org

Linda Lewis-Pickett, President/CEO
Bonnie L Rutledge, Editor

Journal of the voluntary, nonprofit, educational
organization. AAMVA represents the state and
provincial officials in the US, Canada and
Mexico, who are responsible for the adminis-
tration and enforcement of laws pertaining to
the motor vehicle and its use.
Cost: $26.00
Frequency: Quarterly
Circulation: 32000
Founded in 1996
Printed in 4 colors on glossy stock

2535 Market Analysis
Motor and Equipment Manufacturers
Association
10 Laboratory Drive
PO Box 13966
Research Triangle Park, NC 27709-3966

919-549-4800
FAX 919-406-1465
E-Mail: info@mema.org
Home Page: www.mema.org

Bob McKenna, President
Wendy Earp, VP
Frank Hampshire, Marketing

Provides an analysis of how the vehicles parts
industry is affected by the economy including
informative news topics such as producer price
indexes for parts and accessories, market data
and more.
Frequency: Monthly
Founded in 1904

2536 Modern Car Care
Virgo Publishing LLC
3300 N Central Ave
Suite 300
Phoenix, AZ 85012-2532

480-990-1101
FAX 480-990-0819

E-Mail: jsiefert@vpico.com
Home Page: www.vpico.com
John Seifert, CEO
Kelly Ridley, Executive VP, CFO
Heather Wood, VP,Human Resources
Magazine for automotive professionals.
Frequency: Monthly
Circulation: 20000
Founded in 1986

2537 Motor Age
Chilton Company
300 Park Ave
Suite 19
New York, NY 10022-7409

212-751-3596
888-527-7008
FAX 212-371-4058
E-Mail: info@advanstar.com
Home Page: www.chiltonfunds.com

Richard L Chilton Jr, Chairman, CEO
Michael Clark, President, COO

Features developments in the auto industry.
Cost: $14.00
Frequency: Monthly
Circulation: 143,000
Founded in 1992

2538 Motor Magazine
Hearst Business Communications
1301 Long Lake Road
Suite 300
Troy, MI 48098

248-585-1700
800-288-6828
FAX 248-879-8603
E-Mail: motorbookscallcenter@motor.com
Home Page: www.motor.com

Duane Harrison, Owner
John Lypen, Editor
Richard Laimbeer, Publisher

Emphasis on repair and service end of automo-
bile business for owners and managers.
Cost: $63.00
Frequency: Monthly
Circulation: 140000
Founded in 1903

2539 Motor Trend
Primedia
6420 Wilshire Boulevard
Los Angeles, CA 90048-5502

323-822-2201
FAX 323-782-2467
Home Page: www.motortrend.com

Tom Rogers, CEO
Eric Schwab, Advertising Manager
Peter Clancey, Marketing Executive

Comprehensive magazine offers the latest in-
formation and news on the automotive industry.
Cost: $47.88
Frequency: Monthly
Circulation: 999999
Founded in 1988
Printed in 4 colors on glossy stock

2540 NADA'S Automotive Executive
National Automobile Dealers Association
8400 Westpark Dr
9th Floor, Suite 1
Mc Lean, VA 22102-3591

703-821-7000
800-252-6232
FAX 703-821-7075
E-Mail: nadainfo@nada.org
Home Page: www.nada.org

Phillip D Brady, President
Rick Wagoner, CEO

Provides up to the minute legislative, regulatory and state association news, also includes

product development and implementation, la-
bor relations and the economic climate.
Cost: $24.00
Frequency: Monthly
Circulation: 21850
Founded in 1975

2541 NAPA Outlook
National Auto Parts Association
2999 Circle 75 Pkwy SE
Atlanta, GA 30339-3050

770-956-2200
877-794-9511
FAX 770-956-2211
E-Mail: customersupport@napaonline.com
Home Page: www.napaautocare.com

Thomas C Gallagher, CEO

Ideas for business procedures for jobber store
owners.
28 Pages
Frequency: Monthly
Founded in 1925

2542 NASCAR Performance
Babcox Publications
3550 Embassy Pkwy
Akron, OH 44333-8318

330-670-1234
FAX 330-670-0874
E-Mail: dkaufman@babcox.com
Home Page: www.babcox.com

Bill Babcox, Owner
Doug Kaufman, Editor

Focuses on what goes on behind the scenes in
NASCAR racing, and how that advanced technology transfers to automotive aftermarket applications. Professional NASCAR Garage is a
quarterly supplement to all Babcox
publications.
Founded in 1920

2543 National Oil & Lube News
National Oil & Lube News
4418 74th St
Suite 66
Lubbock, TX 79424-2336

806-762-4464
800-796-2577
FAX 806-762-4023
E-Mail: info@noln.net
Home Page: www.noln.net

Garrett McKinnon, Editor
Steve Hurt, Co Publisher

Geared towards fast oil change and lubrication
shop owners and managers. Information on the
latest technology and environment concerns,
also provides a link between shops and suppli-
ers.
Cost: $29.00
76 Pages
Frequency: Monthly
Circulation: 17000
ISSN: 1071-1260
Founded in 1986
Printed in 4 colors on glossy stock

2544 New England Automotive Report
Thomas Greco Publications
PO Box 734
Neptune, NJ 07753

732-922-8909
FAX 732-922-9821
E-Mail: setlit4u@msn.com
Home Page: www.aaspnj.org

Thomas Greco, Owner
Alicia D'Aquila, Editor
Charles Bryant, Executive Director

Provides reports on ideas, products and services to enhance collision repair productivity,

also identifies insurance issues.
Cost: $48.00
85 Pages
Frequency: Monthly
Circulation: 4500
Founded in 1996
Printed in 4 colors on glossy stock

2545 Old Cars Weekly
F+W Media
38 E. 29th Street
New York, NY 10016

212-447-1400
FAX 212-447-5231
E-Mail: contact_us@fwmedia.com
Home Page: www.fwpublications.com

Jim Ogle, CFO
Sara Domville, President
Chad Phelps, Chief Digital Officer
David Nussbaum, CEO

Covers the entire field of collectible automobiles - from classic touring cars and roadsters of the early 1900s to the popular muscle cars of the 1960s and 1970s. Includes historical perspectives and facts on cars and their manufacturers, and reports on attractions at upcoming shows. Regular columns include 'New Products,' 'Questions & Answers,' 'Show Biz,' 'Bookmobile,' 'Restoration Basics,' and an extensive classified word ad section. Hundreds of car show listings are included.
Cost: $41.98
64 Pages
Frequency: Weekly
Circulation: 63104
Founded in 1971

2546 PWA Conference
Performance Warehouse Association
41-701 Corporate Way
Suite 1
Palm Desert, CA 92260

760-346-5647
FAX 760-346-5847
E-Mail: donnie@pedistributors.com
Home Page: www.pwa-par.org

Donnie Eatherly, President
John Towle, Executive Director
Larry Pacey, Chairman
Trent Lowe, Treasurer
Frequency: September

2547 Parking Magazine
National Parking Association
1112 16th St NW
Suite 840
Washington, DC 20036-4880

202-296-4336
800-647-7275
FAX 202-296-3102
E-Mail: info@npapark.org
Home Page: www.npapark.org

Jeff Wolfe, Chairman
Mark Muglich, Chair Elect
Christine Banning, President

Published by the National Parking Association.
Cost: $99.00
2500 Members
Frequency: Monthly
Circulation: 4000
ISSN: 0031-2193
Founded in 1952
Mailing list available for rent: 2600 names at $250 per M
Printed in 4 colors

2548 Parts & People
Automotive Counseling & Publishing

899 Logan Street
Denver, CO 80203

303-765-4664
FAX 303-765-4650
Home Page: www.partsandpeople.com

Lance Buchner, Owner
Rob Merwin, Editor

Collision and mechanical local and national news.
Cost: $36.00
Frequency: Monthly
Circulation: 59000
Founded in 1986

2549 Parts Plus Magazine
3085 Fountainside Drive
#210
Germantown, TN 38138

901-727-8112
800-727-8112
FAX 901-682-9098
E-Mail: info@networkhq.com
Home Page: www.partsplus.com

Alan Bostwick, Executive VP

Published by the Association of Automotive Aftermarkets Distributors.
Cost: $29.95
Frequency: Monthly
Circulation: 5000
Founded in 1965

2550 Professional Carwashing and Detailing
National Trade Publications
19 British American Blvd. West
Latham, NY 12110-2197

518-783-1281
FAX 518-783-1386
Home Page: www.carwash.com

Tracy Aston-Martin, Vice President
Sandy Murphy, Publisher

Provides technical and marketing information to professional vehicle washing owners, managers and investors. Accepts advertising.
Cost: $42.00
76 Pages
Frequency: Monthly
Circulation: 19000
Founded in 1976
Mailing list available for rent: 18M names at $125 per M
Printed in 4 colors on matte stock

2551 Professional Tool & Equipment News
1233 Janesville Avenue
Fort Atkinson, WI 53538

920-563-6388
888-966-3976
FAX 920-563-1699
E-Mail: sales@pten.com
Home Page: www.vehicleservicepros.com

Larry Greenberger, Publisher
Jacques Gordon, Editor
Sara Shelstrom, Publisher

Information for personnel and owners of general and specialty repair shops, including buying tools and equipment, technological innovations, new systems, time saving ideas and product releases.
Cost: $32.00
Frequency: Monthly
Circulation: 105044
Founded in 1996

2552 Quality Engineering
American Society for Quality

600 N Plankinton Avenue
PO Box 3005
Milwaukee, WI 53201-3005

414-272-8575
800-248-1946
FAX 414-272-1734
E-Mail: help@asq.org
Home Page: www.asq.org

James Rooney, Chair
Paul E Borawski, CEO
Erica Gumieny, Sales
Brian LeHouillier, Managing Director

Co-published with Taylor and Francis, this journal is for professional practitioners and researchers whose goal is quality engineering improvements and solutions.
Cost: $34.75
100M Members
Frequency: Quarterly/Members Price
Founded in 1946

2553 Quality Management Journal
American Society for Quality
600 N Plankinton Avenue
PO Box 3005
Milwaukee, WI 53201-3005

414-272-8575
800-248-1946
FAX 414-272-1734
E-Mail: help@asq.org
Home Page: www.asq.org

James Rooney, Chair
Paul E Borawski, CEO
Erica Gumieny, Sales
Brian LeHouillier, Managing Director

Published by the American Society for Quality, the QMT is a quarterly, peer-reviewed journal that focuses on the subject of quality management practice and provides a discussion forum for both practitioners and academics in the area of research.
Cost: $50.00
100M Members
Frequency: Quarterly
Founded in 1946

2554 Quality Progress
American Society for Quality
600 N Plankinton Avenue
PO Box 3005
Milwaukee, WI 53201-3005

414-272-8575
800-248-1946
FAX 414-272-1734
E-Mail: help@asq.org
Home Page: www.asq.org

James Rooney, Chair
Paul E Borawski, CEO
Erica Gumieny, Sales
Brian LeHouillier, Managing Director

Published by the American Society for Quality, the QP is a peer-reviewed journal that focuses on the subject of quality control, discussing the usage and implementation of quality principles including the subject areas of organizational behavior, knowledge management and process improvement.
Cost: $55.00
100M Members
Founded in 1946

2555 RV Trade Digest
Cygnus Publishing
1233 Janesville Avenue
Fort Atkinson, WI 53538

920-000-1111
800-547-7377
FAX 920-563-1699

E-Mail: editor@rvtradedigest.com
Home Page: www.cygnusb2b.com

John French, CEO
Tom Kohn, Executive Vice President
Paul Caplan, Senior Vice President
Paul Bonaiuto, CFO

Offers in-depth information to a trade audience of business professionals actively engaged in the manufacture, distribution and sales of RVs, supplies and accessories.
Cost: $40.00
Frequency: 9 issues (1year
Circulation: 16055
Founded in 1966
Printed in 4 colors on glossy stock

2556 Recyclers Power Source
PO Box 556
Spirit Lake, IA 51360

712-336-5614
800-336-5614
FAX 712-336-5617
E-Mail: jstahly@qwestoffice.net
Home Page: www.rpowersource.com

Laura Kabele
Julie Stahly

Purchasing guide for automotive recycling.
Frequency: Monthly

2557 SAE Off-Highway Engineering
Society of Automotive Engineers
400 Commonwealth Dr
Warrendale, PA 15096-0001

724-776-4841
877-606-7323
FAX 724-776-0790
E-Mail: sohe@sae.org
Home Page: www.sae.org

David Schutt, CEO
Brian Kaleida, Chief Information Officer

Member services and news, as well as activities including meetings, professional development seminars, publication introductions and education programs.
Cost: $70.00
Frequency: Monthly
Circulation: 58263
Founded in 1905

2558 SEMA News
Performance Aftermarket Publishers
1575 South Valley Vista Drive
Diamond Bar, CA 91765

909-860-2030
FAX 909-860-0184
E-Mail: editors@semanews.com
Home Page: www.sema.org

Christopher Kersting, President
Peter MacGillivray, VP Communications

Covers specialty and performance segment of autos with the Auto Aftermarket, Specialty Equipment and Marketing Association.
Cost: $39.95
96 Pages
Frequency: Monthly
Circulation: 35000
Founded in 1988
Printed in 4 colors on matte stock

2559 School Bus Fleet
Bobit Publishing Company
3520 Challenger St
Torrance, CA 90503-1640

310-533-2400
FAX 310-533-2500
E-Mail: sbf@bobit.com
Home Page: www.bobitbusinessmedia.com;

www.schoolbusfleet.com
Social Media: Facebook, Twitter, LinkedIn

Edward J Bobit, CEO
Mark Hollenbeck, Associate Publisher
Frank DiGiacomo, Publisher

Published for persons involved with the transportation of school children grades K-12, includes articles on lowering costs, improving fleet operations, scheduling techniques, vehicle maintenance and federal regulatory issues.
Cost: $25.00
Frequency: Monthly
Circulation: 22000
Founded in 1961

2560 Software Quality Professional
American Society for Quality
600 N Plankinton Avenue
PO Box 3005
Milwaukee, WI 53201-3005

414-272-8575
800-248-1946
FAX 414-272-1734
E-Mail: help@asq.org
Home Page: www.asq.org

James Rooney, Chair
Paul E Borawski, ASQ CEO
Erica Gumieny, Sales
William Mc Bee III, Treasurer
Brian Houillier, Managing

Published by the American Society for Quality, the SQP is a quarterly, peer-reviewed journal for software development professionals that focuses on the subject of quality practice principles in the implementation of software and the development of software systems.
Cost: $45.00
100M Members
Frequency: Quarterly
Founded in 1946

2561 Specialty Automotive Magazine
Meyers Publishing
799 Camarillo Springs Rd
Camarillo, CA 93012-9468

805-445-8881
FAX 805-445-8882
E-Mail: len@meyerspublishing.com
Home Page: www.meyerspublishing.com

Len Meyers, Owner
Len Meyers, Publisher
Andrew Meyers, Associate Publisher
Harriet Kaplan, Assistant Editor

For accessories and performance specialists, dedicated for car and truck product suppliers and installers. Various fatermaker segments are covered: street, track, van, truck, and off-road. Features cover: technology and trends, performance retailing, new product showcases, upgrade news, trade shows, legislation, advertising, OEM's industry news, and people on the move.
Cost: $10.00
Frequency: Monthly
Circulation: 25000
ISSN: 0894-7414
Founded in 1983
Printed in 4 colors on glossy stock

2562 Sport Truck & SUV Accessory Business
Cygnus Publishing
1233 Janesville Avenue
Fort Atkinson, WI 53538

920-000-1111
800-547-7377

FAX 920-563-1699
Home Page: www.cygnusb2b.com

John French, CEO
Pat Walker, Editor
Tom Kohn, Executive Vice President
Founded in 1966

2563 Supercharger
Detroit Section Society of Automotive Engineers
28535 Orchard Lake Road
Suite 200
Farmington Hills, MI 48334

248-324-4445
FAX 248-324-4449
E-Mail: jjablonski@sae-detroit.org
Home Page: www.sae-detroit.org

Charon Morgan, Chair
Terry Rhoades, Treasurer

The official publication of SAE Detroit Section that brings members together with news of upcoming tours, technical meetings, events and more.
Circulation: 16000
Printed in on glossy stock

2564 Tire Retread Information Packet & Buyers Guide
Tire Retread and Repair Information Bureau
1013 Birch Street
Falls Church, VA 22046

703-533-7677
877-394-6811
FAX 703-533-7678
E-Mail: info@retread.org
Home Page: www.retread.org

David Stevens, Managing Director
Bob Majewski, President
Eddie Burleson, Vice President
Phil Boarts, Secretary/Treasurer
Norm Ball, Director

Published by the Tire Retread Information Bureau.
380 Pages
Frequency: Weekly
Founded in 1972

2565 Tire Review
Babcox Publications
3550 Embassy Pkwy
Akron, OH 44333-8318

330-670-1234
FAX 330-670-0874
E-Mail: bbabcox@babcox.com
Home Page: www.babcox.com

Bill Babcox, Owner
David Modiz, Group Publisher
Dave Wooldridge, Publisher

Designed to assist the independent retail tire dealer in his number one concern — profitability. It focuses on pricing strategies, marketing and effective advertising to meet the challenges of today's industry.
Cost: $64.00
84 Pages
Frequency: Monthly
Founded in 1902

2566 Tow Times
TT Publications
203 West SR 434
Winter Springs, FL 32708

407-327-4817
800-308-3745
FAX 407-327-2603
E-Mail: news@towtimes.com
Home Page: www.towtimes.com

Clarissa Powell, Publisher
Tim Jackson, Editor
Dave Jones, President

Edited to review various aspects of the towing and road services. Accepts advertising.
Cost: $34.00
56 Pages
Frequency: Monthly
Founded in 1983

2567 Toy Cars & Models
F+W Media
38 E. 29th Street
New York, NY 10016

212-447-1400
FAX 212-447-5231
E-Mail: contact_us@fwmedia.com
Home Page: www.fwmedia.com

Jim Ogle, CFO
Sara Domville, President
Chad Phelps, Chief Digital Officer
David Nussbaum, CEO

Provides comprehensive coverage of the model car hobby without bias toward scale, subject, manufacturer or material. Offers columns and news stories featuring models made of die-cast, white metal, plastic, resin and more while getting readers in touch with the manufacturers, distributors and retailers who sell these model cars. Monthly giveaways, reader polls and an active letters column give readers a chance to participate in their hobby.
Cost: $29.98
88 Pages
Frequency: Monthly
Circulation: 17916
Founded in 1998

2568 Traffic Injury Prevention
AAAM
PO Box 4176
Barrington, IL 60011-4176

847-844-3880
FAX 847-844-3884
E-Mail: info@aaam.org
Home Page: www.aaam.org

Brian N. Fildes, Ph.D, President
Mary Pat McKay, MD, President-Elect
Kristy B. Arbogast, Ph.D, Secretary
Frances D. Bents, Treasurer

Bridging the disciplines of medicine, engineering, public health and traffic safety in order to foster the science of traffic injury prevention. The journal focuses on research, interventions and evaluations within the areas of traffic safety, crash causation, injury prevention and treatment.
Frequency: 6x Yearly
ISSN: 1538-9588
Founded in 1957

2569 Truck & SUV Performance
Bobit Publishing Company
3520 Challenger St
Torrance, CA 90503-1640

310-533-2400
FAX 310-533-2500
E-Mail: travis.weeks@bobit.com
Home Page: www.bobit.com

Edward J Bobit, CEO
John Jeffries, Editor
Circulation: 32,000
Founded in 1961

2570 Underhood Service
Babcox Publications
3550 Embassy Pkwy
Akron, OH 44333-8318

330-670-1234
FAX 330-670-0874

E-Mail: bbabcox@babcox.com
Home Page: www.babcox.com

Bill Babcox, CEO
Jeff Stankard, VP/ Group Publisher
Jennifer McMullen, Managing Editor

Meets the special needs of those technicians where most of their jobs involve the service and repair of under-the-hood systems. Answers the challenge of a continuing expansion of automotive technology.
Cost: $64.00
Frequency: Monthly
Circulation: 40500
Founded in 1920

2571 Used Car Dealer Magazine
Nat'l Independent Automobile Dealers Association
2521 Brown Boulevard
Arlington, TX 76006-5203

817-492-2377
800-682-3837
FAX 817-649-5866
Home Page: www.niada.com/

Michael R Linn, CEO/Publisher
Michael Harbour, Editor
Angela Ledbetter, Executive Assistant
Adrianne Argumaniz, Publication Manager

Information on auctions, profit center opportunities, trends in used car market, and updates on legislation. Coverage on association membership and the entire used vehicle industry.
Cost: $36.00
Circulation: 15000
Founded in 1946
Printed in 4 colors on glossy stock

2572 Ward's Autoworld
Ward's Communications
3000 Town Center
Suite 2750
Southfield, MI 48075-1245

248-799-2622
FAX 248-357-9747
E-Mail: wards@wardsauto.com
Home Page: www.wardsauto.com

Thomas Duncan, Publisher
Drew Winter, Editor

News and analysis for automotive OEM professionals.
Cost: $55.00
130 Pages
Frequency: Monthly
Circulation: 102000
ISSN: 0043-0315
Founded in 1924
Mailing list available for rent: 99,000 names
Printed in 4 colors on glossy stock

2573 Ward's Dealer Business
Ward's Communications
3000 Town Center
Suite 2750
Southfield, MI 48075-1245

248-799-2622
FAX 248-357-9747
E-Mail: wards@wardsauto.com
Home Page: www.wardsdealer.com

Thomas Duncan, Group Publisher
Drew Winter, Editor
Tony Noland, CEO
James Bush, Managing Director

News and analysis for auto dealership professionals.
80 Pages
Frequency: Monthly
Circulation: 27000
ISSN: 1086-1629
Founded in 1924
Mailing list available for rent: 98,861 names
Printed in 4 colors

Trade Shows

2574 AAIW: Automotive Aftermarket Industry Week Expo
Overseas Automotive Council
10 Laboratory Drive
Po Box 13966
Reserach Triangle, NC 27709-3966

919-549-4800
FAX 919-549-4824
E-Mail: media@mema.org
Home Page: www.oac-intl.org

Jeremy Denton, Show Management

Containing 2,500 exhibits.
100M+ Attendees
Frequency: November

2575 AAMVA Annual International Conference
American Assoc. of Motor Vehicle Administrators
4301 Wilson Boulevard
Suite 400
Arlington, VA 22203

703-522-4200
FAX 703-522-1553
E-Mail: info@aamva.org
Home Page: www.aamva.org

Neil D Schuster, President
Marc Saitta, VP &CFO
Kathy King, Director Business Services

The annual conference of the American Association of Motor Vehicle Administrators during August that provides numerous exhibits, programs and presentations and the opportunity for members to meet and network with colleagues.
800 Attendees
Frequency: August
Founded in 1933

2576 ABPA Trade Show Fair
Automotive Body Parts Association
1510 Eldridge Parkway
Suite 110-168
Houston, TX 77077

281-531-0809
800-323-5832
FAX 281-531-9411
E-Mail: info@autobpa.com
Home Page: www.autobpa.com

Stanley Rodman, Executive Director
Dolores Richardson, President

Trade show with 35 exhibitors and over 43 booths.
146 Members
Frequency: September
Founded in 1980

2577 AFLA Annual Meeting and Conference
Automotive Fleet and Leasing Association
1000 Westgate Drive
St Paul, MN 55114

651-203-7247
FAX 651-290-2266
E-Mail: info@aflaonline.com
Home Page: www.aflaonline.com

Theresa Belding, President
John Dmochowsky, VP
Edward Bobit, Executive Director

Providing the opportunity and a forum for the exchange of information and ideas between related segments of the fleet industry.
300 Members
300 Attendees

Frequency: September
Founded in 1969

2578 AIAG AutoTech Conference
Automotive Industry Action Group
26200 Lahser Road
Suite 200
Southfield, MI 48033

248-358-3003
FAX 248-799-7995
E-Mail: inquiry@aiag.org
Home Page: www.aiag.org

Jhon Batchik, Chairman
David Kneisler, Vice Chairman

It's a venue where the collaboration between
OEMs and suppliers is showcased through educational sessions, product and service exhibits
and demonstrations, and networking
opportunities.
3000 Attendees
Founded in 1982

**2579 AOCA Annual Convention & Fast
Lube Expo**
Automotive Oil Change Association
1701 North Greenville Avenue
Suite 404
Richardson, TX 75081

972-458-9468
800-331-0329
FAX 972-458-9539
E-Mail: info@aoca.org
Home Page: www.aoca.org

Pat Wirth, President
Randy Groover, VP
Bob Falter, Director
LeeAnn Stump, Executive Director

Brings hundreds of vendors offering thousands
of products and services to the fast lube industry and ancillary profit centers.
3000 Members
Frequency: Annual/April-May
Founded in 1987

**2580 ARA Annual Convention &
Exposition**
Automotive Recyclers Association
9113 Church Street
Manassas, VA 20110

571-208-0428
888-385-1005
FAX 571-208-0430
E-Mail: michael@a-r-a.org
Home Page: www.a-r-a.org

Michael Wilson, CEO
Kim Glasscock, Meetings & Expositions

Automotive recycling trade show. Containing
over 150 booths and more than 100 exhibits.
The 2006 trade show is scheduled for September 27th to September 30th in Indianapolis, Indiana and the 2007 trade show is scheduled for
September 26th to September 29th in Orlando,
Florida.
800 Attendees
Frequency: Annual/September

2581 ARTA Powertrain Expo
Automatic Transmission Rebuilders
Association
2400 Latigo Avenue
Oxnard, CA 93030

805-604-2000
866-464-2872
FAX 805-604-2003
E-Mail: dmadden@atra.com
Home Page: www.atra.com

Dennis Madden, CEO
Jim Lyons, VP
Lance Wiggins, Director

Speakers on many subjects, providing information and tips for those within the transmission
repair industry. Event provides the opportunity
for members to meet and network.
2000 Members
Frequency: September
Founded in 1954

2582 ASA Annual Convention
Automotive Service Association
8190 Precinct Line Road
Suite 100
Colleyville, TX 76034-7675

817-514-2900
800-272-7467
FAX 817-514-0770
E-Mail: asainfo@ASAshop.org
Home Page: www.asashop.org

Ron Pyle, President/Chief Staff Executive
Toni Slanton, Executive Director
Jhon Scully, Senior Vice President
Linda Ferguson, Program Administrator
Frequency: April/May

**2583 American Engine Rebuilders
Association Expo**
American Engine Rebuilders Association
500 Coventry Lane
Suite 180
Crystal Lake, IL 60014

815-526-7600
888-326-2372
FAX 815-526-7601
E-Mail: info@aera.org
Home Page: www.aera.org

John Goodman, President
Dwayne J. Dugas, Chairman
Ron McMorris, First Vice Chairman
David Bianchi, Treasurer

550 exhibits with automotive services equipment, parts, tools, supplies and services. Seminar and dinner also offered.
6000 Attendees
Frequency: Annual
Founded in 1974

**2584 American Public Transportation
Association Expo**
American Public Transit Association
1666 K Street NW
Suite 1100
Washington, DC 20006

202-496-4800
FAX 202-496-4324
E-Mail: meetings2@apta.com
Home Page: www.apta.com

Michael Melaniphy, President
Gary Thomas, Chair
Rosemary Sherid, Marketing
Karen W. Harvey, Director Human Resources

Industry leaders from around the globe attend
to meet suppliers of the latest public transportation products, services, and technologies designed to enhance the passenger experience and
make your transit system more efficient and
profitable.
15000 Attendees
Frequency: October 2008/2011
Founded in 1882

2585 Annual Lean Six Sigma Conference
American Society for Quality
600 N Plankinton Avenue
PO Box 3005
Milwaukee, WI 53201-3005

414-272-8575
800-248-1946
FAX 414-272-1734

E-Mail: help@asq.org
Home Page: www.asq.org

James Rooney, Chair
Paul E Borawski, Executive Director
Erica Gumieny, Sales
Fay Spano, Communications/Media Relations

An exclusive two-day briefing and networking
event designed by and for the top practitioners
in the Six Sigma community.
100M Members
Frequency: Annual/February
Founded in 1946

2586 Annual Quality Audit Conference
American Society for Quality
600 N Plankinton Avenue
PO Box 3005
Milwaukee, WI 53201-3005

414-272-8575
800-248-1946
FAX 414-272-1734
E-Mail: help@asq.org
Home Page: www.asq.org

James Rooney, Chair
Paul E Borawski, Executive Director
Erica Gumieny, Sales
Fay Spano, Communications/Media Relations

Topics of interest include: new innovating au-
dit/process approaches, value added involvement, corporate expectations, corporate/social
responsibility, auditing in the overall corporate
scheme.
100M Members
Frequency: Annual/October
Founded in 1946

2587 Annual Service Quality Conference
American Society for Quality
600 N Plankinton Avenue
PO Box 3005
Milwaukee, WI 53201-3005

414-272-8575
800-248-1946
FAX 414-272-1734
E-Mail: help@asq.org
Home Page: www.asq.org

James Rooney, Chair
Paul E Borawski, Executive Director
Erica Gumieny, Sales
Fay Spano, Communications/Media Relations

The sessions we plan will help you to navigate
through unpredictable consumer behavior and
increasing competition to build a strong foundation for reaching superior levels of quality
service.
100M Members
Frequency: Annual/September
Founded in 1946

**2588 Annual World Conference on Quality
and Improvement**
American Society for Quality
600 N Plankinton Avenue
PO Box 3005
Milwaukee, WI 53201-3005

414-272-8575
800-248-1946
FAX 414-272-1734
E-Mail: help@asq.org
Home Page: www.asq.org

James Rooney, Chair
Paul E Borawski, Executive Director
Erica Gumieny, Sales
Fay Spano, Communications/Media Relations

Conference focuses on quality and improvement with more than 2,000 exhibits and attendees. Keynote speakers and sessions discuss
quality tools, techniques and methodologies.

Provides the opportunity for members to meet and network with colleagues in the industry.
100M Members
Frequency: Annual/May
Founded in 1946

2589 Atlantic City Classic Car Show & Auction
Atlantic City Convention Center
One Convention Center Boulevard
Atlantic City, NJ 04801

609-449-2000
FAX 609-449-2090
Home Page: www.acclassiccars.com
Social Media: *Facebook, Twitter*

Held annually, the AC Classic Car Show and Auction is the east coast's largest classic car show and auction.
60000 Attendees

2590 Auto Remarketing Convention
Auto Remarketing
Westview At Weston
301 Cascade Pointe Lane # 101
Cary, NC 27513

800-608-7500
FAX 919-674-6027
Home Page: www.autoremarketing.com

Ron Smith, President

Executive conference focused on remarketing strategies for manufacturer, bank, finance, commercial and rental fleet/lease vehicles.
Frequency: February
Founded in 1996

2591 Automotive Aftermarket Products Expo
Automotive Aftermarket Industry Association
7101 Wisconsin Avenue
Suite 1300
Bethesda, MD 20814-3415

301-654-6664
FAX 301-654-3299
E-Mail: aaia@aftermarket.org
Home Page: www.aftermarket.org

Kathleen Schmatz, President

Largest aftermarket trade show in North America, featuring over 1700 exhibitors of auto parts, accessories and services.
100M Attendees
Frequency: November

2592 Automotive Engine Rebuilders Association Expo
Automotive Engine Rebuilders Association
500 Coventry Lane
Suite 180
Crystal Lake, IL 60014-7592

815-526-7600
888-326-2372
FAX 815-526-7601
E-Mail: info@aera.org
Home Page: www.aera.org

John Goodman, President
Dwayne J. Dugas, Chairman
Ron McMorris, First Vice Chairman
David Bianchi, Treasurer

Demonstrations of the industry's latest technology in equipment, tools, supplies, parts, and services for automotive, heavy-duty, industrial, high-performance, marine, and specialty engines. Featuring the leading national and international companies showcasing the latest new products and services in the world of engine building, remanufacturing, and installation.

2593 BCI Annual Convention
Battery Council International

401 N Michigan Avenue
24th Floor
Chicago, IL 60611-4267

312-644-6610
FAX 312-527-6640
E-Mail: info@batterycouncil.org
Home Page: www.batterycouncil.org

Maurice A Desmarais, Executive VP
Ann Noll, Account Manager

Offers members the opportunity to exchange ideas and views with industry members from around the world in a working meeting atmosphere.
Frequency: Annual/Spring

2594 BSA Convention
Bearing Specialists Association
800 Roosevelt Road
Building C, Suite 312
Glen Ellyn, IL 60137

630-858-3838
FAX 630-790-3095
E-Mail: info@bsahome.org
Home Page: www.bsahome.org
Social Media: *LinkedIn*

Linda Miller, President
Richard W Church, Executive Director
Jerilyn J Church, Executive Secretary
Kathy Fatz, Association Manager
Janet Arden, Publications Editor

The world's premier bearing industry event for authorized distributors of bearing products and services and the manufacturers of those products.
100 Members
Frequency: Annual
Founded in 1966

2595 BSA Winter Meeting
Bearing Specialists Association
800 Roosevelt Road
Building C, Suite 312
Glen Ellyn, IL 60137

630-858-3838
FAX 630-790-3095
E-Mail: info@bsahome.org
Home Page: www.bsahome.org

Linda Miller, President
Jack Simpson, Vice President
Brian Negri, Treasurer
Kathy Fatz, Association Manager
Janet Arden, Publications Editor

BSA committees will be addressing many important issues and association projects at the Winter Meeting. Attending this meeting will help to influence the direction the industry takes over the coming years.
Frequency: Annual

2596 Chicago Auto Show
Chicago Automobile Trade Association
McCormick Place
2301 S Lake Shore Drive
Chicago, IL 60616

630-495-2282
FAX 630-495-2260
Home Page: www.chicagoautoshow.com
Social Media: *Facebook, Twitter, YouTube*

Paul Brian, Director of Communications, CATA
Mark Bilek, Internet Director, CATA
Michelle Ferm, Communications Specialist, CATA
Dave Sloan, Auto Show General Manager
Sandi Potempa, Dir., Special Events & Exhibits

The Chicago Auto Show is the largest auto show in North America and has been held more times than any other auto exposition on the continent.
Frequency: Annual
Founded in 1901

2597 Convergence Conference and Exhibition
Society of Automotive Engineers
755 W Big Beaver
Suite 1600
Troy, MI 48084

248-273-2455
FAX 24- 27- 249
E-Mail: pkreh@sae.org
Home Page: www.sae.org/convergence

Patti Kreh, Meetings, Exhibits Contact
Nori Fought, Meetings, Exhibits Contact
David Schutt, Chief Executive Officer

Serving the automotive and transportation electronics community by delivering relevant technology solutions and an electrifying line-up invited speakers and presenters.
8900+ Attendees
Frequency: October

2598 Dayton Auto Show
Hart Productions
60 N Second Street
Batavia, OH 45103

513-797-7900
877-704-8190
FAX 513-797-1013
E-Mail: vicki@hartproductions.com
Home Page: www.hartproductions.com

Chip Hart, Show Management
Vicki Hart, Show Management
Vicki Diebold, Show Management
Trisha Marshall, Production Assistant
Victoria Hart, CFO

Annual auto show presented by the Dayton area Auto Dealers Association.
Frequency: March

2599 Heavy Duty Aftermarket Week
Association of Diesel Specialists
400 Admiral Boulevard
Kansas City, MO 64106

816-285-0810
FAX 847-770-4952
E-Mail: info@diesel.org
Home Page: www.diesel.org
Social Media: *Facebook, LinkedIn*

Chuck Hess, President
Andy Girres, Vice President
Chuck Oliveros, Treasurer
Carl Fergueson, Secretary
David Fehling, Executive Director

A distributor-focused business conference created by the industry's leading trade associations and marketing groups with a long-term goal of consolidating the many annual events on the industry calendar and to create the most valuable annual event for the heavy duty aftermarket. Heavy Duty Aftermarket Week is the largest North American gathering of the independent heavy-duty industry.
700+ Members
1800+ Attendees
Frequency: Annual/January
Founded in 1956

2600 IAATI Annual Training Seminar
International Association of Auto Theft Investigators
PO Box 223
Clinton, NY

315-853-1913
FAX 315-883-1310
E-Mail: jvabounader@iaati.org
Home Page: www.iaati.org
Social Media: *LinkedIn*

Joe Broslus, President
John O'Byrne, VP
John V. Abounader, Executive Director
Marianne Finney, Marketing

Provides members who are auto theft investigators with resources to develop and maintain professional standards within the industry. Some of the topics covered range from arson and marine investigations to staged accident investigations. The 2012 seminar is in Kansas City, MO.
4904 Members
350 Attendees
Founded in 1952

2601 International Autobody Congress and Exposition
Hanley-Wood
8600 Freeport Parkway
Suite 200
Irving, TX 75063

972-366-6324
888-529-1641
FAX 972-536-6445
E-Mail: krobinson@hanleywood.com
Home Page: www.naceexpo.com

Linsay Roberts, Director
Ellen Pipkin, Show Manager

Specifically created for professionals involved in all aspects of the collision repair industry.
15M Attendees
Frequency: November

2602 International Big R Show
Automotive Parts Remanufacturers Association
4215 Lafayette Center Drive
Suite 3
Chantilly, VA 20151-1243

703-968-2772
FAX 703-968-2878
E-Mail: mail@apra.org
Home Page: www.bigrshow.com

William Gager, President
Jeanie Magathan, Sr. VP
Morris Spector, Director, Advertising & Marketing
Marlene Koskinas, Executive Assistant

Designed to attract rebuilders of a wide range of automotive and truck parts, exposing them to the key suppliers in this industry. Rebuilders specializing in electrical, c.v. joints, brake, clutch, transmissions, mechanical hydraulic, fuel systems, rack and pinion and air conditioning products will visit the show.
1000 Members
3000 Attendees
Frequency: November / Las Vegas, NV
Founded in 1941

2603 LA Auto Show
Los Angeles Convention Center
1201 S Figueroa Street
Los Angeles, CA 90015

213-741-1151
Home Page: www.laautoshow.com

The Los Angeles Auto Show is one of the top automotive events worldwide, bringing together the latest new vehicles from auto manufacturers around the world.

2604 MACS Convention and Trade Show
Mobile Air Conditioning Society Worldwide
225 S Broad Street
PO Box 88
Lansdale, PA 19446

215-631-7020
FAX 215-631-7017
E-Mail: macsworldwide@macsw.org
Home Page: www.macsw.org

David Jack, Secretary
Elvis Hoffpauir, President, CEO
Mary Koban, Director

Andrew Fiffick, Chairman
Peter Coll, Treasurer
2000 Attendees
Frequency: Annual

2605 NAAA Annual Conference
National Auto Auction Association
5320 Spectrum Drive
Suite D
Frederick, MD 21703

301-696-0400
FAX 301-631-1359
E-Mail: naaa@naaa.com
Home Page: www.naaa.com

Frank Hackett, Executive Director
Tom Dozier, Meetings Manager

Annual convention and exhibits of automobile and truck auction equipment, supplies and services.
Frequency: Fall

2606 NADA Convention & Expo
National Automobile Dealers Association
8400 Westpark Drive
Mc Lean, VA 22102-3522

703-217-7000
800-252-6232
FAX 703-821-7075
E-Mail: nadainfo@nada.org
Home Page: www.nada.org

Gary Heimes, Convention Director
Stephen R Pitt, Executive Director, Convention
Phillip Brady, President

Providing automobile dealers with the latest in cutting edge technology, products and services they need to impact the future success of their businesses.
25000 Attendees
Frequency: January/February

2607 NAFA Fleet Management Seminar
National Association of Fleet Administrators
125 Villiage Boulevard
Suite 200
Princeton, NJ 08540

609-720-0882
FAX 609-452-8004
E-Mail: info@nafa.org
Home Page: www.nafa.org

Phillip E Russo, Executive Director
Patrick McCarren, Deputy Executive Director
Joanne Marsdh, Director Marketing & Membership

Designed to provide comprehensive education to fleet managers like you who seek the fundamental principles and practices of successful fleet management.
3000+ Members
Founded in 1957
Printed in on glossy stock

2608 NAFA Institute & Expo
National Association of Fleet Administrators
125 Villiage Boulevard
Suite 200
Princeton, NJ 08540

609-720-0882
FAX 609-452-8004
E-Mail: info@nafa.org
Home Page: www.nafa.org

Phillip E Russo, Executive Director
Patrick McCarren, Deputy Executive Director
Joanne Marsh, Director Marketing & Communications

To provide attendees and exhibitors alike with a more dynamic interaction on the exhibit hall floor and within concurrent sessions. An excellent opportunity to attend valuable education courses designed to benefit the veteran fleet

professional as well as challenge first-time attendees!
3000+ Members
Frequency: April
Founded in 1957
Printed in on glossy stock

2609 NARSA Annual Convention & Trade Show
National Automotive Radiator Service Association
3000 Villiage Run Road
Suite103, #221
Wexford, PA 15090-6315

724-799-8415
800-551-3232
FAX 724-799-8416
E-Mail: info@narsa.org
Home Page: www.narsa.org

Wayne Juchno, Executive Director
Douglas Shymoniak, Manager, Sales & New Business
Maarten Taal, President
Pat O'Connor, Vice President
Angelo Miozza, Treasurer

180 booths featuring seminars and workshops of parts, equipment and supplies.
1.8M Attendees
Frequency: Annual/November

2610 NPA Annual Parking, Transportation and Services Convention & Expo
National Parking Association
1112 16th Street NW
Suite 300
Washington, DC 20036

202-296-4336
800-647-7275
FAX 202-296-3102
E-Mail: info@npapark.org
Home Page: www.npapark.org

Lawrence McFadden, Director Mktg/Business Development
Christine Banning, President
Heather Seiber, VP Marketing and Communications

Bringing together parking professionals from around the world with leading experts from business and industry to explore the latest trends and developments. The Convention also affords members an opportunity to share ideas and experiences and to explore the latest equipment and technologies at the Exposition.
Frequency: Annual
Founded in 1955
Mailing list available for rent: 1700 names at $250 per M

2611 National Auto Glass Conference & Expo
National Glass Association
1945 Old Gallows Rd
Suite 750
Vienna, VA 22182

703-442-4890
FAX 703-442-0630
E-Mail: attend@glass.org
Home Page: www.glass.org

Phil James, President/CEO

Visit with over 50 companies and get informed about the latest technology and see products demonstrated live. Get answers to your technical questions and find out which solutions are right for your business.
800 Attendees
Frequency: Annual/May

2612 National Independent Automobile Dealers Association Convention & Expo
National Independent Automobile Dealers Assoc.
2521 Brown Boulevard
Arlington, TX 76006-5203

817-492-2377
800-682-3837
FAX 817-649-5866
E-Mail: kimberly@niada.com
Home Page: www.niada.com

Ginger Barrientez, Director of Events
Michael R Linn, President/CEO
Steven Jordan, COO

75 booths including automobile aftermarkets and finance companies.
Frequency: June

2613 National Quality Education Conference
American Society for Quality
600 N Plankinton Avenue
PO Box 3005
Milwaukee, WI 53201-3005

414-272-8575
800-248-1946
FAX 414-272-1734
E-Mail: help@asq.org
Home Page: www.asq.org

James Rooney, Chair
Paul E Borawski, CEO
Erica Gumieny, Sales
Fay Spano, Communications/Media Relations

Provides teachers, administrators, and support personnel opportunities to examine continuous improvement principles used in education. It provides resources and best practices to help you address requirements of No Child Left Behind, while helping you increase student achievement and improve overall performance.
100M Members
Frequency: Annual/November
Founded in 1946

2614 New York International Auto Show
Jacob Javits Center
655 West 34th Street
New York, NY 10001

718-746-5300
800-282-3336
FAX 718-746-9333
Home Page: www.autoshowny.com
Social Media: *Facebook, Twitter, YouTube*

The show offers virtually every make and model vehicle sold in the US under one roof giving consumers the unique opportunity to see everything the auto industry has to offer. From fuel-sipping economy cars to million dollar supercars, NYIAS has something for everyone.
Frequency: Annual

2615 North American Council of Automotive Teachers International Conference
North American Council of Automotive Teachers
PO Box 80010
Charleston, SC 29416

843-556-7068
FAX 843-556-7068
E-Mail: office@nacat.com
Home Page: www.nacat.com

Patrick Brown Harrison, President
Rob Thompson, Vice President
Curt Ward, Secretary
Chuck Ginther, Treasurer

Annual show of 70 exhibits and 50 seminars, suppliers, distributors, publishing companies and other trade organizations.
Frequency: July
Mailing list available for rent: 750 names at $165 per M

2616 North American International Auto Show
Detroit Auto Dealers Association
1900 W Big Beaver
Troy, MI 48084

248-643-0250
FAX 248-637-0784
E-Mail: naiasmail@dada.org
Home Page: www.naias.com

Rod Alberts, Executive Director
William Perkins, Chair

Annual show and exhibits of new automobiles and trucks, concept cars and van conversions.
808M Attendees
Frequency: January
Founded in 1907

2617 PERA Annual Conference
Production Engine Remanufacturers Association
28203 Woodhave Road
Edwards, MO 65326

417-998-5057
FAX 417-998-5056
E-Mail: nancieboland@pera.org
Home Page: www.pera.org
Social Media: *Facebook, LinkedIn*

Nancie J. Boland, Executive VP
Robert P. McGraw, President

An opportunity to exchange ideas, methods and procedures necessary to efficiently produce remanufactured products which are equal or superior to original products in quality and performance. PERA adheres to and supports the premise that its members are dedicated to the highest business ethics, customer satisfaction, employee consideration and to the continual up-grading of the engine remanufacturing industry.
150 Attendees
Frequency: September / Seatle, WA
Founded in 1946

2618 PWA Annual Conference
Performance Warehouse Association
41-701 Corporate Way
Suite 1
Palm Desert, CA 92260

760-346-5647
FAX 760-346-5847
E-Mail: christina@pwa-par.org
Home Page: www.pwa-par.org

John Towle, President
Larry Pacey, Chairman
Trent Lowe, Treasurer

This is an exclusive opportunity for manufacturers and distributors to meet in a private, businesslike environment to discuss sales and marketing policies and programs.
165 Attendees
Frequency: Annual/September
Founded in 1974

2619 Performance Racing Industry Trade Show
Performace Racing Industry
31706 South Coast Highway
Laguna Beach, CA 92651

949-499-5413
FAX 949-499-0410

E-Mail: mail@performanceracing.com
Home Page: www.performanceracing.com

John Kilroy, Publisher/General Manager
Dan Schechner, Editor
Merredith Kaplan Burns, Managing Editor

Annual show. Features the latest in motorsports technology from 1400 companies with 4000 booths.
42000 Attendees
Frequency: Annual

2620 Philadelphia Auto Show
Philadelphia Convention Center
1101 Arch Street
Philadelphia, PA 19107

215-418-4700
Home Page: www.phillyautoshow.com
Social Media: *Facebook, Twitter*

Recognized by the industry as one of the top shows in the country, the Philly Auto Show displays more than 700 vehicles from a variety of manufacturers.
Frequency: Annual

2621 RV Dealers International Convention & Expo
Recreation Vehicle Dealers Association
3930 University Drive
Fairfax, VA 22030-2515

703-591-7130
FAX 703-359-0152
E-Mail: info@rvda.org
Home Page: www.rvda.org

Mike Molino, CAE, President
Mary Anne Shreve, Editor

For RV retailers from across the U.S. and Canada.
Frequency: September
Mailing list available for rent: 1500 names

2622 RVAA Executive Conference
Recreational Vehicle Aftermarket Association
1833 Centre Point Circle
Suite 123
Naperville, IL 60563-9306

630-596-9004
E-Mail: info@rvaahq.org
Home Page: www.rvaahq.org
Social Media: *Facebook, Twitter*

Patrick Farrey, Executive Director
Laura Hallen, Account Executive
Michael Greskiewicz, Expo Sales Manager
Meg Pawelski, Events & Awards Manager
Danielle Griffin, Communications Manager

An event which allows members to meet with each other to develop strategies for the coming year. It's the perfect opportunity for you to make the contacts and have the important face to face meeting time, with the potential partners that will enhance your success.
Frequency: October
Founded in 1969

2623 SAE International Truck & Bus Meeting and Exhibition
Society of Automotive Engineers
755 W Big Beaver
Suite 1600
Troy, MI 48084

248-273-2455
877-606-7323
FAX 248-273-2494
E-Mail: automotive_hq@sae.org
Home Page: www.sae.org
Social Media: *Facebook, Twitter, LinkedIn, YouTube, Google +*

Dr. Rodica Baranescu, President
David Schutt, CEO
Nori Fought, Conference Service

Representative
John Miller, Program Developer
Jack Pokrzywa, Operations Director

100 booths featuring suppliers of parts and components.
2.5M Attendees
Frequency: November

2624 SEMA International Auto Salon Trade Show
Specialty Equipment Market Association
1575 South Valley Vista Drive
Diamond Bar, CA 91765

909-610-2030
E-Mail: showinfo@sema.org
Home Page: www.sema.org
Social Media: *Facebook, Twitter, Google+*

Christopher Kersting, President and CEO
Gary Vigil, Trade Show Director
Marel Del Rio, Trade Show Coordinator

When the sport-compact scene was just beginning, the show was launched to educate members about the growing market and to bring new buyers and opportunities to manufacturers.
Frequency: May
Founded in 1998

2625 SEMA Offroad Convention
Specialty Equipment Market Association
1575 South Valley Vista Drive
Diamond Bar, CA 91765-0910

909-610-2030
E-Mail: sema@sema.org
Home Page: www.phillyautoshow.com

Chris Kersting, President/CEO
Geoege Afremow, Vice President & CFO
Scooter Brothers, Chairman

Designed as a companion event to the well established SEMA Spring Expo, and as an extension of the SEMA Show, will target companies serving the recreational and performance off-road segments and aims to create new opportunities for this growing market.
Frequency: February

2626 SEMA Show
Specialty Equipment Market Association
1575 South Valley Vista Drive
Diamond Bar, CA 91765-0910

909-610-2030
FAX 909-860-0184
E-Mail: sema@sema.org
Home Page: www.sema.org

Chris Kersting, President/CEO
Geoege Afremow, Vice President & CFO
Scooter Scooter, Chairman

The premier automotive specialty performance products trade event in the world featuring performance, accessories, restoration and motorsports products.
100M Attendees
Frequency: November

2627 SEMA Spring Expo
Specialty Equipment Market Association
1575 South Valley Vista Drive
Diamond Bar, CA 91765-0910

909-610-2030
E-Mail: sema@sema.org
Home Page: www.sema.org

Chris Kersting, President/CEO
Geoege Afremow, Vice President & CFO
Scooter Scooter, Chairman

The only trade show delivering the SEMA Show experience to the doorsteps of regional auto and truck parts and accessory businesses. We feature the leading companies that produce truck caps and accessories, automotive trim and

restyling products, wheels and tires, gauges and instruments, performance parts and more.
Frequency: February

2628 SIGM Annual Meeting
Society of Independent Gasoline Marketers
3930 Pender Drive
Suite 340
Fairfax, VA 22030

703-709-7000
FAX 703-709-7007
E-Mail: sigma@sigma.org
Home Page: www.sigma.org

Kenneth Doyle, Executive Vice President
Susan Crosby, Director, Communication & Education
Mary Alice Kutyn, Director of Meetings
Nancy Muskett, Director, Advertising & Sponsorship
Marilyn Selvitelle, Director, Business Development

SIGMA meetings are valuable and varied, addressing topics of interest for branded or unbranded motor fuel marketers, those interested in alternative fuels, fuel suppliers, and of course administrative and financial discussions for all types of organizations.
Frequency: October

2629 SOUTHCON
Wescon
1230 Rosecrans Avenue
Suite 100
Manhattan Beach, CA 90266

310-524-4100
800-877-2668
FAX 310-643-7328
E-Mail: j.cruz@ecishow.com
Home Page: www.southcon.org

Joey Quesada Cruz, Show Management
Rod Mann, Conference Management

Issues that concern design, manufacturing and test departments. Instructors are leading experts in the topics they present.
10M Attendees
Frequency: February

2630 Supernationals Custom Auto Show
TNT Promotions Inc
PO Box 50386
Albuquerque, NM 87181-0386

505-480-0056
800-300-9381
Home Page: www.thesupernationals.com

The premier annual automotive event in New Mexico. Attracts prominent street rods and customs from throughout the country, as well as local and regional vehicles for both show and competition display.
25000 Attendees
Frequency: Annual/February
Founded in 1992

2631 TIA World Tire Expo
Tire Industry Association
1532 Pointer Ridge Place
Suite G
Bowie, MD 20716-1883

301-430-7280
800-876-8372
FAX 301-430-7283
E-Mail: info@tireindustry.org
Home Page: www.tireindustry.org

Gary Albright, President & CEO
Lary Brandt, CEO
Mike Berra Jr, Vice President
Eddie Burleson, General Manager

Providing an ideal forum for diverse individuals to meet, network and advance new business and marketing opportunities. This world-class exhibition is the number one showcase dedi-

cated to those who have an interest in tire, rubber and transportation services.
Frequency: April

2632 WMDA Mega Show Annual Convention
WMDA Service Station & Automotive Repair Assoc.
1532 Pointer Ridge Place
Suite G
Bowie, MD 20716

301-390-0900
800-492-0329
FAX 301-390-3161
E-Mail: mgates@wmda.net
Home Page: www.wmda.net
Social Media: *Facebook*

Rick Agoris, President
Marta Gates, Director of Operations
Kirk McCauley, Director of Member Relations
Tirika Williams, Director of Finance

Featuring Over 225 Exhibits for the service station, automotive repair, car wash, convenience store & tire industries.
1500 Attendees

Directories & Databases

2633 American Bus Association's Motorcoach Marketer
American Bus Association
111 K Street NE
9th Floor
Washington, DC 20002

202-842-1645
FAX 202-842-0850
E-Mail: abainfo@buses.org
Home Page: www.buses.org

Thomas JeBran, President
John Meier, Vice Chairman
Frank Henry, Secretary/Treasurer

This directory is a comprehensive guide of the bus and travel industry offering information on hotels and sightseeing services, attractions, museums, restaurants and more.
500 Pages
Frequency: Annual
Founded in 1926

2634 American Public Transit Association Membership Directory
American Public Transit Association
1666 K St NW
Suite 1100
Washington, DC 20006-1215

202-496-4800
FAX 202-496-4324
E-Mail: hbrett@apta.com
Home Page: www.apta.com

Michael Melaniphy, President/CEO
Petra Mollet, VP
Rosemary Sheridan, VP Communications and Marketing

A who's who directory of services and supplies within the public transportation industry.
Founded in 1882

2635 Automotive Aftermarket Suppliers
Automotive Aftermarket Suppliers Association
10 Laboratory Drive
PO Box 13966
Research Triangle Park, NC 27709-3966

919-549-4800
FAX 919-549-4824

E-Mail: media@mema.org
Home Page: www.aftermarketsuppliers.org

Steve Handschuh, President
Chris Gardner, VP
Margaret Beck, Marketing and
Communications

Directory of automotive supply chains and job-
bers/retailers in North America. Also, warehouse distributors and major programmed
distribution groups.
Founded in 1974

**2636 Automotive Parts Rebuilders
Association Membership Directory**
Automotive Parts Remanufacturers
Association
4460 Brookfield Corporate Drive
Suite H
Chantilly, VA 20151-1671

703-968-2772
FAX 703-968-2878
E-Mail: magathan@buyreman.com
Home Page: www.bigrshow.com

William Gager, President
Morris Spector, Marketing

Lists member companies and their products,
addresses, phone and fax numbers, key personnel and sometimes even internet information.
Keep this directory, your network resource for
the automotive parts rebuilding industry, on
your desk throughout the year.
Cost: $35.00
Frequency: Annual
Founded in 1941

**2637 ELM Guide to Automakers in North
America**
ELM International
PO Box 1740
East Lansing, MI 48826-1740

517-332-4900
FAX 517-351-3032
E-Mail: contact_us@automotivesuppliers.com

The third edition of this guide contains more
than 400 profiles that highlight the North
American manufacturing operations of Chrysler, Ford, GM and all of the foreign owned
automakers.
Cost: $350.00
Frequency: Semiannual

**2638 ELM Guide to Japanese Affiliated
Suppliers in North America**
ELM International
PO Box 1740
East Lansing, MI 48826-1740

517-332-4900
FAX 517-351-3032
E-Mail: contact_us@automotivesuppliers.com
Home Page: www.automotivesuppliers.com

Mark Santucci

Offers information on approximately 290 Japanese owned automotive original equipment
components manufacturers that operate in
North America.
Cost: $350.00

**2639 ELM Guide to US Automotive
Sourcing**
ELM International
PO Box 1740
East Lansing, MI 48826-1740

517-332-4900
FAX 517-351-3032
E-Mail: contact_us@automotivesuppliers.com

Mark Santucci, Executive Director

Two volumes offering information on automotive original equipment manufacturer parts and
components suppliers and profiles of plants be-

longing to 576 companies.
Cost: $775.00
1200 Pages

2640 NAFA's Professional Directory
National Association of Fleet Administrators
125 Village Boulevard
Suite 200
Princeton, NJ 08540

609-720-0882
FAX 609-452-8004
E-Mail: info@nafa.org
Home Page: www.nafa.org
Social Media: *Facebook, Twitter, LinkedIn*

Phillip E. Russo, Executive Director
Patrick McCarren, Executive Director
Mary Sticha, Vice President
Joanne Marsh, Director of Marketing
Gladys Reyes, Meeting & Event Planners

NAFA Member and Affiliate contact information.
2600+ Members
Frequency: Quarterly

2641 Old Cars Price Guide
F+W Media
38 E. 29th Street
New York, NY 10016

212-447-1400
FAX 212-447-5231
E-Mail: contact_us@fwmedia.com
Home Page: www.fwpublications.com

Rick Groth, Publisher
Ron Kowalke, Editor
David Nussbaum, CEO
Sara Domville, President

The nation's most respected authority for pricing antique and collectible automobiles. The
extensive price-guide section covers makes and
models of domestic cars, from AMC to Willys,
from model years 1901 to 1994. Also included
are light-duty trucks and selected makes of imported cars. Cars are valued in six conditions -
from 'Excellent' down to 'Parts Car.' Also includes columns and features on collectible cars.
Cost: $19.98
148 Pages
Frequency: Monthly
Circulation: 61000
Founded in 1978

2642 PXN Parts Exchange New
15030 Avenue of Science
Suite 100
San Diego, CA 92128

858-946-1900
800-669-4237
FAX 858-946-1073
E-Mail: ICSCUser@audatex.com
Home Page: www.adpclaims.com
Social Media: *Facebook, Twitter, LinkedIn,
YouTube*

Tony Aquila, Chairman, President & CEO
Jack Sanders, COO
Kamal Hamid, Director Investor Relations
Lisa Collins, Marketing Coordinator

Provides an electronic link from your ADP estimating system to comprehensive database of
new replacement parts. Data on over three and
a half million parts facilitates the writing of
complete, cost-effective damage reports.

2643 RV Trade Digest
Cygnus Publishing
1233 Janesville Avenue
Fort Atkinson, WI 53538

920-000-1111
800-547-7377
FAX 920-563-1699

E-Mail: info@cygnus.com
Home Page: www.cygnus.com

John French, CEO
Paul Bonaiuto, CFO
Ed Wood, VP, HR and Communications
Kris Flitcroft, EVP-Residential, Construction,
Mfg.
Blair Johnson, SVP, Business Development

Propriety BASE technology connecting busi-
nesses with multi-media content.
Cost: $40.00
40 Pages
Frequency: Bi-Monthly
Circulation: 15,000
Founded in 1983
Printed in 4 colors on glossy stock

**2644 Transmission Digest Buyer's Guide
Issue**
MD Publications
PO Box 2210
3057 E Cairo Street
Springfield, MO 65801-2210

417-866-3917
800-274-7890
FAX 417-866-2781
E-Mail: bmace@mdpublications.com
Home Page: www.mdpublications.com

Carol Langsford, President
Michelle Dickeman, Vice President
Bob Mace, Publisher
Gary Sifford, Editor
Mike Anderson, Advertising Sales

List of over 500 manufacturers and distributors
of products and services for the motor vehicle
transmission repair industry.
Cost: $15.00
Printed in 4 colors on glossy stock

2645 Ward's Automotive Yearbook
Ward's Communications
3000 Town Center
Suite 2750
Southfield, MI 48075-1245

248-799-2622
FAX 248-357-9747
E-Mail: tduncan@wardsauto.com
Home Page: www.wardsauto.com
Social Media: *Facebook, Twitter*

Thomas Duncan, Group Publisher
James Bush, Managing Editor
David Zoia, Editorial Director
Drew Winter, Senior Editor
Chris Lamphear, Marketing Director

Directory of suppliers to the vehicle manufac-
turing industry. New vehicle sales, production
and inventory data and new vehicle product in-
formation and statistics.
Cost: $475.00
500 Pages
Frequency: Annual
Circulation: 26,000
ISBN: 0-910589-15-1
Founded in 1938

2646 Who Makes It and Where Directory
Tire Guides
1101 S Rogers Circle
Suite 6
Boca Raton, FL 33487-2748

561-997-9229
FAX 561-997-9233
E-Mail: tireinfo@tireguides.com
Home Page: www.tireguides.com

Nancy Garfield, Owner
James Garfield, Editor-in-Chief
Al Snyder, Contributing Editor
Jeff Chychrun, Associate Editor

Brand listings with manufacturer & distributor
information; worldwide listing of web site ad-

dresses, fax numbers & U.S. toll free numbers.
Cost: $7.00
62 Pages
Frequency: Annual
Founded in 1950

2647 Worldwide Automotive Supplier Directory

Society of Automotive Engineers
400 Commonwealth Drive
Warrendale, PA 15086-7511

724-776-4841
877-606-7323
FAX 724-776-0790
E-Mail: customerservice@sae.org
Home Page: www.sae.org
Social Media: *Facebook, Twitter, LinkedIn, YouTube, Google+*

David Schutt, President
Michael Thompson, Publisher
Melissa Bachman, Marketing
Peggy Bartlett, Corporate Sales

Directory features 10,000+ supplier listings from every major vehicle-producing region. And, it is the ONLY directory to provide information on a company's technical capabilities.
Cost: $329.00
Frequency: Annual
Circulation: 60,550
ISBN: 0-768015-36-7

Industry Web Sites

2648 http://gold.greyhouse.com
G.O.L.D Grey House OnLine Databases

Grey House Publishing's online database platform, GOLD, offers Quick Search, Keyword Search and Expert Search for most business sectors including automotive and transportation markets. The GOLD platform makes finding the information you need quick and easy - whether you're a novice searcher or an experienced database user. All of Grey House's directory products are available for subscription on the GOLD platform.

2649 www.aaam.org
Assn for the Advancement of Automotive Medicine

A professional multidisciplinary organization dedicated entirely to motor vehicle crash prevention and control.

2650 www.aamva.org
American Assn. of Motor Vehicle Administrators

Nonprofit organization represents state and provincial officials in the US and Canada who administer and enforce motor vehicle laws. Strives to develop model programs in motor vehicle administration, police traffic services and highway safety.

2651 www.aflaonline.com
Automotive Fleet & Leasing Association

Designed to improve communications among buyers, sellers, fleet administrators, lending institutions, lessors, used vehicle marketers and allied automotive service companies.

2652 www.aftermarket.org
Automotive Aftermarket Industry Association

For those involved in the motor vehicle replacement parts industry.

2653 www.aiada.org
American Int'l Automobile Dealers Assocation

Lobbying and communications organization for American automobile dealerships that sell and service international nameplate brands.

2654 www.aiag.org
Automotive Industry Action Group

Composed of major North American vehicle manufacturers and their suppliers. Provides an open forum where members cooperate to develop and promote solutions that enhance prosperity in the automotive industry.

2655 www.aoca.org
Automotive Oil Change Association

Representing the convenient automotive service industry. Dedicated to enhancing the competency of fast lube owners, educating the public about services our members offer and maintaining a favorable business environment for the industry as a whole.

2656 www.apra.org
Automotive Parts Rebuilders Association

Association of more than 1,500 member companies engaged in the rebuilding of automotive related hard parts, including starters, alternators, clutches, transmissions, brakes, drive shafts and other parts for passenger cars, trucks, off road, equipment and industrial uses.

2657 www.asq.org
American Society for Quality

The world's leading authority on quality that creates better workplaces and communitites worldwide by advancing learning, quality improvement, and knowledge exchange to improve business results.

2658 www.atra-gears.com
Automatic Transmission Rebuilders Association

Not for profit professional organization dedicated to the improvement and welfare of the automatic transmission repair industry for the benefit of the motoring public.

2659 www.autobpa.com
Automotive Body Parts Association

Members are companies that distribute, supply or manufacture automotive replacement body parts.

2660 www.autoconsulting.com
Automotive Consulting Group

Management consulting firm providing top line and bottom line business performance improvement services to the worldwide automotive industry.

2661 www.automotivefleetmgt.com
Automotive Fleet Management Corporation

Formed in order that financial institutions such as banks, credit unions and finance companies could repossess and dispose of their automotive collateral in a manner that is quick, efficient and cost effective.

2662 www.awda.org
Automotive Warehouse Distributors Association

Oldest organized group of warehouse distributors and their respective suppliers of parts, accessories tools and other supplies for the automotive aftermarket. In January 2004, AWDA joined forces with the Automotive Aftermarket Industry Association.

2663 www.buses.org
American Bus Association

Trade association for the North American bus industry.

2664 www.busesintl.com
Buses International Association

An organization of persons throughout the world who are professionally involved in the management of companies or organizations which operate or manufacture buses.

2665 www.carcare.org
Car Care Council

A nonprofit 501 (c) (3) educational foundation whose purpose is to educate motorists about the importance of maintenance repairs and entertainment for safer, cleaner better performing vehicles. Provides editorial and public service material for media use.

2666 www.classiccar.com
ClassicCar.Com

Offers classic car enthusiasts around the world an online community with chats, forums and discussion groups.

2667 www.diesel.org
Association of Diesel Specialists

The worldwide diesel industry's leading trade association, dedicated to the highest level of service on diesel fuel injection and related systems.

2668 www.edmunds.com
Edmunds.Com

Founded in 1966 for the purpose of publishing new and used automotive pricing guides for automobile buyers.

2669 www.filtercouncil.org
Filter Manufacturers Council

For manufacturers of vehicular and industrial filtration products in North America. Active in efforts to educate people on proper disposal of used oil filters.

2670 www.forecast1.com
Forecast International

An electronic information/data service sourced from thousands of worldwide publications, in 15 languages. Provides concise passenger vehicles e-mail news and analysis summaries, news, trends and contract information with hyper-links to the source or a related website. Delivered 100 times a year.

2671 www.greyhouse.com
Grey House Publishing

Authoritative reference directories for most business sectors including automotive and transportation markets. Users can search the online databases with varied search criteria allowing for custom searches by product category, geographic area, sales volume, keyword, subject and more. Full Grey House catalog and online ordering also available.

2672 www.hemmings.com
Hemmings Motor News

Hemmings Motor News for the car collector and enthusiast.

2673 www.iaati.org
Int'l Association of Auto Theft Investigators

To improve communication and coordination among the growing family of professional auto theft investigators.

2674 www.impa.org
International Motor Press Association

Professional group of writers and editors producing auto articles for the press, radio or TV.

2675 www.macsw.org
Mobile Air Conditioning Society Worldwide

Provides technical training, information and communication for the professionals in the automotive air conditioning industry.

2676 www.mema.org
Motor and Equipment Manufacturers Association

Serves manufacturers of all types of automotive and truck products through market research, legislative and regulatory representation and reporting, information services, EDI network and credit reporting.

2677 www.naaa.com
National Auto Auction Association

Represents dealer wholesale auto auctions. Promotes exchange of ideas and public relations in the used car merchandising industry.

2678 www.nada.com
National Automobile Dealers Association

Provides representation for franchised new car and truck dealers in government, industry and public affairs. Provides counsel on legal and regulatory and political representation on Capital Hill.

2679 www.nafa.org
National Association of Fleet Administrators

Serving the needs of those managing fleets of automobiles, light duty trucks and/or vans for US and Canadian organizations. Offers statistical research, publications, regional meetings, government representation, conferences, trade shows and seminars.

2680 www.narsa.org
National Automotive Radiator Service Association

Trade association serving the cooling system service industry and the public.

2681 www.nascar.com
Turner Sports Interactive

Providing up-to-the-minute coverage on a 24-hour basis, NASCAR.COM delivers news, statistics and information on races, drivers, teams and industry events.

2682 www.nationalwheelandrim.org
National Wheel and Rim Association

Represents warehouse distributors of wheels, rims and related parts in the US and Canada.

2683 www.ncsfa.state.ut.us
National Conference of State Fleet Administrators

For state government administrators responsible for vehicle fleet management.

2684 www.ntea.com
National Truck Equipment Association

Represents small to mid-sized companies that manufacture, distribute, install, buy, sell and repair commercial trucks, truck bodies, truck equipment, trailers and accessories.

2685 www.partsplus.com
Association of Automotive Aftermarkets

Purchases and markets automotive replacement parts. Headquarters office for Parts Plus program distributors.

2686 www.pera.org
Production Engine Remanufacturers Association

The goal of the Production Engine Remanufacturers Association is to provide it's members with the opportunity to exchange the ideas, methods and procedures necessary to efficiently produce remanufactured products which are equal or superior to original products in quality and performance.

2687 www.pwa-par.com
Performance Warehouse Association

An organization of specialty automotive parts wholesalers joined together and dealing with management, financial and legislative matters.

2688 www.retread.org
Tire Retread Information Bureau

Serving as the public relations arm of the retread industry. Gathering and disseminating information on retread passenger and truck tires to members and the general public.

2689 www.rma.org
Rubber Manufacturers Association

National trade association for makers of tires and other rubber products.

2690 www.rvda.org
National RV Dealers Association

National association advances the best interests of RV retailers through education, services, leadership and programs of market expansion that promote increased use and sale of RVs as well as enhancement of the RV's image.

2691 www.scrs.com
Society of Collision Repair Specialists

For owners and managers of auto collision repair shops, suppliers, insurance and educational associates and suppliers in the US, Canada, Australia and New Zealand. Distributes technical, management, marketing and sales information. Works to promote professionalism within the collision repair industry.

2692 www.theautochannel.com
Auto Channel

Auto news, commentary and other useful information.

2693 www.tireindusty.org
Tire Industry Association

Representing all segments of the tire industry, including those that manufacture, repair, recycle, sell, service or use new or retreaded tires and also those suppliers or individuals who furnish equipment, material or services to the industry.

Associations

2694 Aero Safety & Maintenance Association
P.O. Box 182604
Columbus, OH 43272

202-383-2378
877-833-5524
FAX 614-759-3749
E-Mail: customer.service@mcgraw-hill.com
Home Page: www.mcgrawhill.com

Herald McGraw, President
Jim Mathews, Publisher

A nonprofit research organization that depends primarily upon tax-deductible contributions.

2695 Aeronautical Radio & Research Incorporated
400 Collins Road N.E.
Cedar Rapids, IA 52498

319-295-1000
800-633-6882
FAX 410-266-2020
E-Mail: corpcomm@arinc.com
Home Page: www.arinc.com
Social Media: *Facebook, Twitter, LinkedIn, YouTube, Google+, Instagram*

John M Belcher, Chairman & CEO
Stephen L Waechter, VP & CFO

Provider of communications, engineering and integration solutions, we help our customers in the defense, commercial and government industries mitigate risk, improve operational and systems performance and meet program requirements.
Founded in 1929

2696 Aeronautical Repair Station Association
121 N Henry St
Alexandria, VA 22314-2903

703-739-9543
FAX 703-299-0254
E-Mail: arsa@arsa.org
Home Page: www.arsa.org
Social Media: *Facebook, Twitter, LinkedIn, RSS, Google+*

Gary Hudnall, President
Warner Calvo, Vice President
Basil Barimo, Executive VP
Marshall S Filler, General Counsel/Managing Director
Sarah MacLeod, Executive Director

Helps develop guidance, policy and interpretations that are clear, concise and consistent, and applied uniformly to all similarly situated companies and individuals.
700 Members
Founded in 1984

2697 Aerospace Industries Association
2310 E El Segundo Blvd
El Segundo, CA 90245-4609

310-336-5000
FAX 310-336-7055
E-Mail: membership@aia-aerospace.org
Home Page: www.aero.org
Social Media: *Facebook, Twitter, Youtube, Google+*

W M Austin, President & CEO
R Clinton, Senior VP/General Counsel/Secretary
H J Mitchell, Vice President
M H Goodman, Principal Director

The Aerospace Industries Association shapes public policy that ensures the US aerospace, defense and homeland security industry remains preeminent and that its members are suc-

cessful and profitable in a changing global market.
283 Members
Founded in 1919

2698 Aerospace Medical Association
320 S Henry St
Alexandria, VA 22314-3579

703-739-2240
FAX 703-739-9652
E-Mail: jsventek@asma.org
Home Page: www.asma.org
Social Media: *Facebook, Twitter, LinkedIn*

Jeffery C. Sventek,MS,CASp, Executive Director
Gisselle Vargas, Operations manager
Gloria Carter, Director

Our mission is to apply and advance scientific knowledge to promote and enhance the health, safety and performance of those involved in aerospace and related activities.
3200 Members
Founded in 1929
Mailing list available for rent

2699 Air Force Association
1501 Lee Hwy
Suite 400
Arlington, VA 22209-1198

703-247-5800
800-727-3337
FAX 703-247-5853
E-Mail: membership@afa.org
Home Page: www.afa.org
Social Media: *Facebook, Twitter, LinkedIn, Youtube, Blogger*

George Muellner, Chairman
Jerry E White, Vice Chairman
Craig R McKinley, President
Len Vernamonti, Treasurer
Marvin L Tooman, Secretary

Independent nonprofit, civilian organization promoting public understanding of aerospace power and the pivotal role it plays in the security of the nation.
1400 Members
Founded in 1946

2700 Air Taxi Association
300 Galleria Parkway
Atlanta, GA 30339

770-563-7400
Home Page: www.atxa.com
Social Media: *Twitter, LinkedIn, Youtube*

Gordon Wilson, President & CEO
Eric Bock, Executive VP/CLO/CAO
Philip Emery, Executive VP/CFO
Mark Ryan, Executive VP/CIO
Bryan Conway, Chief Marketing Officer

Backed by leading air taxi companies, ATXA's mission is to speed the adoption of the air taxi model so that more business, individuals, and communities can enjoy the benefits of direct, personal flights.
Founded in 2006

2701 Air Traffic Control Association
1101 King St
Suite 300
Alexandria, VA 22314

703-299-2430
FAX 703-299-2437
E-Mail: info@atca.org
Home Page: www.atca.org
Social Media: *Facebook, Twitter, LinkedIn, RSS,YouTube*

Neil Planzer, Chairman
Charles Keegan Planzer, Chair Elect
Peter F Dumont, President & CEO
Rachel Jackson, Treasurer
Rachel Jackson, Secretary

Works to establish and maintain a safe and efficient air traffic control system.
2400+ Members
Founded in 1956

2702 Air Transport Association of America
1301 Pennsylvania Ave NW
Suite 1100
Washington, DC 20004-1738

202-626-4000
800-497-3326
FAX 202-626-4166
E-Mail: a4a@airlines.org
Home Page: www.airlines.org
Social Media: *Facebook, Twitter, LinkedIn, YouTube, Instagram*

Nicholas E. Calio, President/CEO
Paul R Archambeault, Senior VP/CFO/COO
David A Berg, SVP/General Counsel/Secretary
Christine M. Burgeson, SVP, Global Government Affairs
Sean D. Kennedy, SVP, Global Government Affairs

Supports and assists its members by promoting the air transport industry and the safety, cost effectiveness, and technical advancement of its operators; advocating common industry positions before state and local governments; conducting designated industry-wide programs; and assuring governmental and public understanding of all aspects of air transport.
25 Members
Founded in 1936

2703 Aircraft Electronics Association
3570 NE Ralph Powell Rd
Lees Summit, MO 64064

816-347-8400
FAX 816-347-8405
E-Mail: info@aea.net
Home Page: www.aea.net
Social Media: *Facebook, Twitter, LinkedIn, Youtube, Flickr*

David Loso, Chairman
Michael Kus, Vice Chair
Paula Derks, President
Debra McFarland, Executive Vice President
Kim Stephenson, Secretary

Persons interested in aviation and avionics.
1200 Members

2704 Aircraft Owners & Pilots Association
421 Aviation Way
Frederick, MD 21701-4756

301-695-2000
800-872-2672
FAX 301-695-2375
E-Mail: phil.boyer@aopa.org
Home Page: www.aopa.org
Social Media: *Facebook, Twitter, LinkedIn, Google+, Instagram*

Mark Baker, President & CEO
George Perry, CDR USN (Ret), SVP
Bruce Landsberg, Senior Safety Advisor

AOPA has achieved its prominent position through effective advocacy, enlightened leadership, technical competence, and hard work. Providing member services that range from representation at the federal, state, and local levels to legal services, advice, and other assistance, we have built a service organization that far exceeds any other in the aviation community. AOPA ePilot and AOPA ePilot Flight Training Edition unique e-mail newsletters issued every Friday morning only to AOPA members.
405k Members
Founded in 1939

2705 Airline Pilots Association International
1625 Massachusetts Ave NW
Suite 800
Washington, DC 20036

703-689-2270
FAX 202-797-4052
Home Page: www.alpa.org
Social Media: *Facebook, Twitter, LinkedIn, YouTube, Instagram, Flickr*

Lee Moak, President
Sean Cassidy, First VP
Bill Couette, VP Administration
Randolph Helling, VP Finance

Promotes airplane use and co-operates with government agencies and private and public flying organizations to increase general safety.
64000 Members
Founded in 1931

2706 Airport Consultants Council
908 King St
Suite 100
Alexandria, VA 22314

703-683-5900
FAX 703-683-2564
E-Mail: info@acconline.org
Home Page: www.acconline.org
Social Media: *Facebook, Twitter, LinkedIn, Google+*

Paula P Hochstetler, President
T.J. Schulz, Executive VP
John B Reynolds, Manager of Communicatons
Colleen Flood, Manager, Marketing & Membership
Chris Spaulding, Assistant

Represents the majority of airport consulting firms in the United States.
200+ Members
Founded in 1978

2707 Airports Association Council International
1615 L Street NW
Suite 300
Washington, DC 20036

202-293-8500
888-424-7767
FAX 202-331-1362
Home Page: www.aci-na.com
Social Media: *Facebook, Twitter, LinkedIn, Youtube*

Deborah McElroy, Interim President
Nancy Zimini, Senior VP
Kent George, Chairman
Ian A Redhead, VP Airport Services
Patricia Hahn, EVP Operations/General Counsel

Members are boards, commissions, local governmental entities operating public airport facilities and more.
240 Members
Founded in 1947

2708 Allied Pilots Association
14600 Trinity Blvd
Suite 500
Fort Worth, TX 76155-2512

817-302-2272
FAX 817-302-2119
E-Mail: public-comment@alliedpilots.org
Home Page: www.alliedpilots.org
Social Media: *Facebook, Twitter, Youtube*

Dave Ahles, Executive Director
Captian Dave Bates, President
Officer Anthony Chapman, Vice President

Provides all the traditional union representation services for its members. This includes the lobbying of airline pilots views to Congress and government agencies. In addition, it devotes

more than 20 percent of its dues income to support aviation safety.
11500 Members
Founded in 1963

2709 American Astronautical Society
6352 Rolling Mill Place
Suite 102
Springfield, VA 22152-2370

703-866-0020
FAX 703-866-3526
E-Mail: aas@astronautical.org
Home Page: www.astronautical.org
Social Media: *Facebook, Twitter, Youtube*

Lyn D Wigbels, President
J. Walter Faulconer, EVP
David B. Spencer, VP Publications
Harley A Thronson, VP Programs

Independent scientific and technical group in the United States exclusively dedicated to the advancement of space science and exploration.
1400 Members
Founded in 1954

2710 American Bonanza Society
Mid-Continent Airport
PO Box 12888
Wichita, KS 67277

316-945-1700
FAX 316-945-1710
E-Mail: bonanza2@bonanza.org
Home Page: www.bonanza.org
Social Media: *Facebook, Twitter, LinkedIn*

Nancy Johnson, Executive Director
Tom Turner, Technical Manager

We are nearly 10,000 owners and pilots of Bonanza, Baron and Travel Air type aircraft who have banded together to share information and experiences involving the operation and maintenance of the Beech produced aircraft. Together, we offer an underwriter recognized flight proficiency program, and service clinics scheduled throughout the year at various locations. These clinics provide members the opportunity to have their aircraft evaluated by highly experienced ABS technical personnel.
10K Members
Founded in 1967

2711 American Helicopter Society
2701 Prosperity Avenue
Suite 210
Fairfax, VA 22031

703-684-6777
855-247-4685
FAX 703-739-9279
E-Mail: staff@vtol.org
Home Page: www.vtol.org
Social Media: *Facebook, Twitter, LinkedIn*

Mike Hirschberg, Executive Director
Kay Yosua Brackins, Deputy Director
Randy Johnson, Director Of Information Resource
David Renzi, Director Of Meetings & Advertising
Holly Cafferelli, Director Of Administration

Promotes the interests of designers, engineers and manufacturers of the vertical flight industry. Serving as a clearinghouse for technical information, the society publishes several periodicals, organizes the largest vertical flight technology display in the world, and maintains a comprehensive library.
6000 Members
Founded in 1944

2712 American Institute of Aeronautics and Astronautics
1801 Alexander Bell Dr
Suite 500
Reston, VA 20191-4344

703-264-7500
800-639-2422
FAX 703-264-7551
E-Mail: custserv@aiaa.org
Home Page: www.aiaa.org
Social Media: *Facebook, Twitter, LinkedIn, YouTube, Flickr, Instagram*

Jim Albaugh, President
Mark J Lewis, President-Elect
Laura McGill, VP Finance
Steven E. Gorrell, VP Education
Annalisa Weigel, VP Member Services

Advancing the arts, sciences and technology of aeronautics and astronautics and promotes the professionalism of those engaged in these pursuits.
31,00 Members
Founded in 1930

2713 Army Aviation Association of America
593 Main Street
Monroe, CT 06468-2830

203-268-2450
FAX 203-268-5870
E-Mail: aaaa@quad-a.org
Home Page: www.quad-a.org
Social Media: *Facebook, Twitter, LinkedIn, Youtube*

Bill Harris, Executive Director
Barbara McCann, Executive Assistant
Mark Albertson, Historian
Jennifer Chittem, Marketing Communications
Janis Arena, Manager

A professional force that holds the aviation community, both military and industry together.

2714 Association of Air Medical Services
909 N Washington Street
Suite 410
Alexandria, VA 22314

703-836-8732
FAX 703-836-8920
E-Mail: jfiegel@aams.org
Home Page: www.aams.org

John Fiegel, Executive Director/CEO
Rick Sherlock, President &CEO
Kristin Discher, Office Manager

Voluntary nonprofit organization, encourages and supports its members in maintaining a standard of performance reflecting safe operations and efficient, high quality patient care. Built on the idea that representation from a variety of medical transport services and businesses can be brought together to share information, collectively resolve problems and provide leadership in the medical transport community. We provide a e-mail newsletter called Capitol Watch for AAMS Members.
581 Members
Founded in 1980

2715 Association of Flight Attendants-CWA
501 3rd St NW
Suite 1
Washington, DC 20001

202-434-1300
800-424-2401
FAX 202-434-1411
E-Mail: info@afacwa.org
Home Page: www.afacwa.org
Social Media: *Facebook, Twitter, Youtube*

Saraý Saraý, International President
Debora Sutor, International VP

Kevin Creighan, International Secretary/Treasurer

Represents over 50,000 flight attendants at 26 airlines, serving as a voice for flight attendants at their workplace, in the industry, the media and on Capitol Hill.
55M Members
Founded in 1930

2716 Association of Naval Aviation

6551 Loisdale Road
Suite 222
Springfield, VA 22150

703-960-6806
FAX 703-960-6807
E-Mail: anahqtr@aol.com
Home Page: www.anahq.org
Social Media: *Facebook, Twitter, LinkedIn*

James L Holloway, Chairman
David L Philman, President
Michael E Field, Secretary/Treasurer
Linda Bubien, Advertising Director
R M Rausa, Editor

Professional, nonprofit, educational and fraternal society of Naval Aviation, whose main purpose is to educate the public and our national leaders on the vital roles of the Navy, Marine Corp and Coast Guard Aviation as key elements of our national defense posture. ANA continuously seeks to elucidate the key current issues impacting Naval Aviation through published writing, symposia, speeches and discussions with various interest groups.

2717 Aviation Development Council

141-07 20th Ave
Suite 404
Whitestone, NY 11357

718-746-0212
FAX 718-746-1006
E-Mail: root@aviationdevelopmentcouncil.org
Home Page: www.adcnynj.org

William Huisman, Executive Director
Addresses noise problems from air carriers in the New York - New Jersey region.
Founded in 1962

2718 Aviation Distributors and Manufacturers

Fernley & Fernley Inc
100 North 20th Street
Suite 400
Philadelphia, PA 19103-1462

215-320-3872
FAX 215-564-2175
E-Mail: adma@fernley.com
Home Page: www.adma.org
Social Media: *Facebook*

Steve Langston, President
Lise Pearson, VP
Craig Lockerbie, VP
Trudie Bruner, Management Liaison
Kristen Olszewski, Executive Director

Promotes interests of wholesalers and manufacturers of general aviation aircraft parts and supplies.
Founded in 1943

2719 Aviation Insurance Association

7200 W 75th Street
Overland Park, KS 66204

913-627-9632
FAX 913-381-2515
E-Mail: mandie@aiaweb.org
Home Page: www.aiaweb.org
Social Media: *Facebook, Blog*

David Sales, President
Paul Herbers, Vice President
Herbers Gardner, Secretary
Christopher R. Zanette, Treasurer
Mandie Bannwarth, Executive Director

A not-for-profit association dedicated to expanding the knowledge of and promoting the general welfare of the aviation insurance industry through numerous educational programs and events.
900 Members
Founded in 1976

2720 Aviation Suppliers Association

2233 Wisconsin Ave. NW
Suite 503
Washington, DC 20007

202-347-6899
FAX 202-347-6894
Home Page: www.aviationsuppliers.org
Social Media: *Facebook, Twitter, LinkedIn*

Michele Dickstein, President
Tony Brigham, Coordinator, Programs & Services

The voice of the aviation parts supply industry on regulatory and legal matters.
570+ Members
Founded in 1993

2721 Aviation Technician Education Council

117 North Henry Street
Alexandria, VA 22314-2903

703-548-2030
E-Mail: atec@atec-amt.org
Home Page: www.atec-amt.org

Goertzen Ryan, President
Kienast Amy, Vice President
Hoyle Gary, Treasurer

Organization of Federal Aviation Administration approved Aviation Maintenance Technician schools and supporting industries.
Founded in 1961

2722 Cessna Owner Organization

N7450 Aanstad Road
PO Box 5000
Iola, WI 54945

715-445-5000
888-692-3776
FAX 715-445-4053
E-Mail: help@cessnaowner.org
Home Page: www.cessnaowner.org
Social Media: *Facebook*

Daniel Weiler, Executive Director
Joe Jones, Publisher
Ryan Jones, Executive Publisher
Dennis Piotrowski, Editor
Kara Grundman, Graphic Designer

Membership support organization for Cessna aircraft owners.
5000 Members
Founded in 1973

2723 Civil Aviation Medical Association

PO Box 2382
Peachtree City, GA 30269-2382

770-487-0100
FAX 770-487-0080
E-Mail: civilavmed@yahoo.com
Home Page: www.civilavmed.com

Mark Eidson, President
Clawton T Cowl, President-Elect
Gordon L Ritter, Secretary/Treasurer
David P Millet, Executive VP
James Carpenter, VP Communications & Representation

Aviation medical equipment, supplies and services. Working on behalf of physicians engaged in the practice of aviation medicine and dedicated to civil aviation safety.
Cost: $5.00
800+ Members
Founded in 1948

2724 Experimental Aircraft Association

3000 Poberezny Road
3000 Poberezny road
Oshkosh, WI 54902

920-426-4800
800-564-6322
FAX 920-426-6761
E-Mail: webmaster@eaa.org
Home Page: www.eaa.org
Social Media: *Facebook, Twitter*

Tom Poberezny, President
David Berkley, Communications Director
Adam Smith, VP Member Services

Works to keep aviation history alive. Members are active restorers and enthusiasts working to keep vintage aircraft in the air and flying for the pleasure and education of themselves and the public at large. EAA's weekly electronic newsletter e-Hot Line.
170M Members
Founded in 1953

2725 Flight Safety Foundation

801 N Fairfax Street
Suite 400
Alexandria, VA 22314-1774

703-739-6700
FAX 703-739-6708
E-Mail: wahdan@flightsafety.org
Home Page: www.flightsafety.org
Social Media: *Facebook, Twitter, LinkedIn*

David McMillan, Chairman
Kevin L Hiatt, President & CEO
Kenneth P Quinn, Secretary/General Counsel
David Barger, Treasurer

Supported by airlines, aerospace manufacturers, aviation professionals, corporate flight departments and others interested in flight safety.
900 Members
Founded in 1947

2726 Forecast International

Forecast International
22 Commerce Rd
Newtown, CT 06470

203-426-0800
800-451-4975
FAX 203-426-0223
E-Mail: info@forecast1.com
Home Page: www.forecastinternational.com
Social Media: *Facebook, Twitter, LinkedIn, Google+*

Ray Peterson, VP, Research & Editorial Svcs.
Raymond Jaworowski, Senior Aerospace Analyst
Richard Pettibone, Senior Government Analyst
Rebecca Barnett Edwards, Latin America & Caribbean Analyst
Nicole Loeser, Middle East & Africa Analyst

Premier provider of market intelligence, forecasting, proprietary research and consulting services.
Cost: $495.00
24 Pages
Frequency: Weekly
Founded in 1973
Printed in 4 colors on matte stock

2727 Future Aviation Professionals of America (FAPA)

4959 Massachusetts Boulevard
Atlanta, GA 30337

404-997-8097
FAX 770-997-8111
Home Page: www.fapa.info/

Linda Nelson, Chairman

Provides career information for those seeking careers in aviation, publications, newsletter, interview briefings and Aviation Job Bank. Also

provides personal financial planning for airline pilots.
15M Members
Founded in 1974

2728 General Aviation Manufacturers Association
1400 K St NW
Suite 801
Washington, DC 20005-2485

202-393-1500
FAX 202-842-4063
E-Mail: bforan@GAMA.aero
Home Page: www.gama.aero

Pete Bunce, President & CEO
Mary Lynn J Rynkiewicz, Director of Communications
Jens Hennig, VP Operations
Paul H Feldman, VP Government Affairs
bree J Foran, Meeting/Office Coordinator

Manufacturers of general aviation aircraft and related equipment. Members also operate fleets of aircraft, fixed based operations and pilot training facilities.
50 Members
Founded in 1970

2729 Helicopter Association International
1920 Ballanger Ave
Alexandria, VA 22314-2898

703-683-4646
800-435-4976
FAX 703-683-4745
E-Mail: rotor@rotor.org
Home Page: www.rotor.com
Social Media: *Facebook, Twitter, LinkedIn*

Anthony W Burson, Chairman
Gale Wilson, Vice Chairman
Matthew S Zuccaro, President
Max Lyons, Treasurer
Edward F DiCampli, Executive VP/Secretary

Nonprofit organization provides members with services that directly benefit their operations and advances the civil helicopter industry by providing programs to enhance safety, encourage professionalism and promote the unique societal contributions made by the rotary flight industry.
2500 Members
Founded in 1948

2730 Helicopter Safety Advisory Conference
Marathon Oil Company
PO Box 60136
Houston, TX 77205

281-892-4088
E-Mail: mark.fontenot@bp.com
Home Page: www.hsac.org

Mark Fontenot, Chairman
Joseph Gross, Treasurer
Ron Domonique, Secretary
Robert Hall, Vice Chair

Promotes safety and seeks to improve operations through establishment of standards of practice.
115 Members
Founded in 1978

2731 International Association of Machinists and Aerospace Workers
9000 Machinists Place
Upper Marlboro, MD 20772-2687

301-967-4500
E-Mail: websteward@iamaw.org
Home Page: www.goiam.org
Social Media: *Facebook, Twitter*

R Thomas Buffenbarger, International President
Richard Michalski, VP

Dave Ritchie, General VP
Bill Trbovitch, Director Communications
Warren L Mart, General Secretary/Treasurer

Has an annual budget of approximately $101.3 million.
700K Members

2732 International Coordinating Council of Aerospace Industries Associations
1000 Wilson Blvd.
Suite 1700
Arlington, VA 22209-3928

703-358-1064
Home Page: www.iccaia.org
Social Media: *LinkedIn*

David F. Melcher, Chairman
Jim Quick, Vice-Chairman

The voice of the world's aerospace manufacturers in matters concerning international standards and regulations for air transport safety and security.
Founded in 1972

2733 International Council of Aircraft Owner and Pilot Associations
421 Aviation Way
Frederick, MD 21701

301-695-2220
FAX 301-695-2375
E-Mail: iaopa@aopa.org
Home Page: www.iaopa.org

Mark Baker, President
Craig Spence, Secretary General
Jeremy DeLaTorre, Administrator

Nonprofit federation of 53 autonomous, nongovernmental, national general aviation organizations. Facilitates the movement of general aviation aircraft.
40000 Members
Founded in 1962

2734 International Flight Services Association
1100 Johnson Ferry Road
Suite 300
Atlanta, GA 30342

404-252-3663
FAX 404-252-0774
E-Mail: ifsanet@gmail.com
Home Page: www.ifsanet.org
Social Media: *Facebook, Twitter, Youtube*

Vicky Stennes, President
Kenneth Samara, Chairman
Pam Chumley, Executive Administrator
Ellen Hoy, Membership Manager
Michelle Moore, Meetings Manager

The International Flight Services Association is a global professional association created to serve the needs and interests of airline and railway personnel, in-flight and rail caterers and suppliers responsible for providing passenger foodservice on regularly scheduled travel routes.
Founded in 1966

2735 International Society of Women Airline Pilots
ISA + 21
723 S. Casino Center Blvd.
2nd Floor
Las Vegas, NV 89101-6716

E-Mail: chairwoman@iswap.org
Home Page: www.iswap.org

Liz Jennings Clark, Chair
Maria Haddad, Human Performance
Liana B Hart, Treasurer
Eva Marie Brock, Secretary
Kathy A McCullough, Communications Director

Fosters cooperation and exchange among women airline pilots employed as flight crew members (Captain, First Officer or Second Officer) and holding seniority numbers with an air carrier which operates at least one aircraft with a gross weight of 90,000 pounds or more.
4000 Members
Founded in 1978

2736 Light Aircraft Manufacturers Association
2001 Steamboat Ridge Ct
Daytona Beach, FL 32128-6918

651-592-7565
301-693-2223
FAX 651-226-1825
E-Mail: info@lama.bz
Home Page: www.lama.bz

Dan Johnson, Chairman/President

Promotes interests of kit-built light aircraft. Membership dues are $125 for voting members and $25 for non-voting members.
50 Members
Founded in 1984

2737 Lighter Than Air Society
Lighter Than Air Society
526 S. MAIN ST
Suite 406
Akron, OH 44311-3311

330-535-5827
E-Mail: suggest@blimpinfo.com
Home Page: www.blimpinfo.com

Joseph Huber, President
Ron Browning, Director Business Development

Nonprofit organization whose members are devoted to the study of the history, science and techniques of all forms of buoyant flight.
1000 Members
Founded in 1952

2738 Mount Diablo Pilots Association
PO Box 6632
Concord, CA 94524

925-370-0828
E-Mail: president@mdpa.org
Home Page: www.mdpa.org
Social Media: *Facebook, Twitter*

Stewart Bowers, President
Natasha Lantsor, VP, Activities
Madeleine Ferguson, VP Communications
Steve Mink, VP Programs
Elaine Yeary, Treasurer

To promote good public relations between general aviation enthusiasts and the local community; to encourage participation in fly-ins and other aviation activities; to promote safety and educational activities for pilots; to provide mutual resources of information on flying for members; to furnish information and support to the Contra Costa Airport Advisory Committee and other governmental agencies concerned with aviation; to be a proxy on aviation matters of community concern for its membership

2739 National Aeronautic Association
1 Reagan National Airport
Hangar 7, Suite 202
Washington, DC 20001-6015

703-416-4888
800-644-9777
FAX 703-416-4877
E-Mail: naa@naa.aero
Home Page: www.naa.aero

Jonathan Gaffney, President
Natasha Clark, Director, Administration
Art Greenfield, Contest & Records Director

A non-profit association that is dedicated to the advancement of the art, sport and science of aviation in the United States.
3000 Members
Founded in 1905

2740 National Agricultural Aviation Association

1440 Duke Street
Alexandria, VA 22314

202-546-5722
FAX 202-546-5726
E-Mail: information@agaviation.org
Home Page: www.agaviation.org
Social Media: *Facebook*

Brian Rau, President
Leif Isaacson, Vice President
Marký Hartz, Secretary
Harley Curless, Treasurer

Voice of the aerial application industry, we work to preserve aerial application's place in the protection and production of America's food and fiber supply. Aerial application is one of the safest, fastest, most efficient and economical ways to apply pesticides. It is also the most environmentally friendly tool of modern agriculture.
1,300 Members
Founded in 1966

2741 National Air Traffic Controllers Association

1325 Massachusetts Ave Nw
Washington, DC 20005-4171

202-628-5451
800-266-0895
FAX 202-628-5767
E-Mail: web_staff@list.natca.net
Home Page: www.natca.org
Social Media: *Facebook, Twitter, LinkedIn, Youtube, Instagram*

Paul Rinaldi, President
Trish Gilbert, Executive VP
Clint Lancaster, Alaskan Regional Vice President
Kevin Peterson, Central Regional Vice President
Dean Iacopelli, Eastern Regional Vice President

Founded to ensure safety and longevity of air traffic controller positions around the nation. Represents over 15,000 air traffic controllers throughout the US, Puerto Rico and Guam, along with 2,508 other bargaining unit members that span all areas from engineers and architects to nurses and health care professionals to members of the accounting community.
15000 Members
Founded in 1987

2742 National Air Transportation Association

818 Connecticut Avenue
NW Suite 900
Washington, DC 20006

202-774-1535
800-808-6282
FAX 202-452-0837
E-Mail: dgleason@NATA.aero
Home Page: www.nata.aero
Social Media: *Facebook, Twitter, LinkedIn, RSS*

Andy Priester, Chairman
Priester Hiller, Vice Chair
Priester Aviation, President & CEO
Diane Gleason, Director, Meetings and Conferences

Aggressively promotes safety and the success of aviation service businesses through its advocacy efforts before government, the media and the public as well as by providing valuable pro-

grams and forums to further its members' prosperity.
Founded in 1940

2743 National Association of Flight Instructors

EAA Aviation Center
3101 E Milham Ave
Portage, MI 49002

866-806-6156
FAX 920-426-6865
E-Mail: nafi@nafinet.org
Home Page: www.nafinet.org
Social Media: *Facebook, Twitter, LinkedIn, Google+*

Robert Meder, Chairman
John Niehas, Program Coordinator
David Hipschman, Mentor Editor
Phil Poynor, VP, Government & Industry Relations
John Gibson, Director Of Sponsorship

Dedicated exclusively to raising and maintaining the professional standing of the flight instructor in the aviation community. Maintains a benefits package available for everyone from the independent instructor to those teaching at flight schools. Every other week we'll send NAFI members with access to e-mail and electronic eMentor.
Founded in 1967

2744 National Business Aviation Association

1200 G St NW
Suite 1100
Washington, DC 20005

202-783-9000
FAX 202-331-8364
E-Mail: info@nbaa.org
Home Page: www.nbaa.org
Social Media: *Facebook, Twitter, LinkedIn, instagram,youtube,itunes*

Ronald Duncan, Chairman
Paul Anderson, ViceChair
Edward M Bolen, President & CEO
Dan Hubbard, Senior VP
Todd Wormington, Director

An organization for companies that rely on general aviation aircraft to help make their businesses more efficient, productive and successful.
8000 Members
Founded in 1947

2745 National EMS Pilots Association

PO Box 2128
Layton, UT 84041-9128

801-436-7505
877-668-0430
FAX 866-906-6023
E-Mail: contactus@nemspa.org
Home Page: www.nemspa.org
Social Media: *Facebook, Twitter*

Kurt Williams, President
Stuart Buckingham, Treasurer

A professional organization dedicated to serving pilots involved in the air-medical transport industry, and to improving the quality and safety of those services
Founded in 1984

2746 Ninety-Nines

4300 Amelia Earhart Drive
Suite A
Oklahoma City, OK 73159

405-685-7969
800-994-1929
FAX 405-685-7985
E-Mail: 99s@ninety-nines.org
Home Page: www.ninety-nines.org

Social Media: *Facebook, Twitter, Google+, Skype*

Martha Phillips, President
Jan McKenzie, Vice President
Cynthia Madsen, Secretary
Leslie Ingham, Treasurer
Lin Caywood, Director

International organization of licensed women pilots from 35 countries. We are a nonprofit, charitable membership corporation holding 501(c)(3) US tax status. Members are professional pilots for airlines, industry and government; we are pilots who teach and pilots who fly for pleasure; we are pilots who are technicians and mechanics. First and foremost, we are women who love to fly.
5500 Members
Founded in 1929

2747 Piper Owners Society

N7450 Aanstad Rd
Iola, WI 54945

715-445-5000
866-697-4737
FAX 715-445-4053
E-Mail: help@piperowner.org
Home Page: www.piperowner.org
Social Media: *Facebook*

Dan Weiler, Executive Director
Joe Jones, Publisher
Ryan Jones, Executive Publisher
Dennis Piotrowski, Editor
Kara Grundman, Graphic Designer

To support private owners of all models of Piper light aircraft. Members receive a full color monthly magazine which includes flying experiences, aircraft parts explained and historical features.
Founded in 1987

2748 Popular Rotorcraft Association

PO Box 68
Mentone, IN 46539

574-353-7227
FAX 574-353-7021
E-Mail: praofficemgr@gmail.com
Home Page: www.pra.org
Social Media: *Facebook, Youtube*

Scott Lewis, President
Douglas Barker, Vice President
Stan Foster, Secretary
Robert Rymer, Treasurer

A nonprofit organization dedicated to the advancement of knowledge, public education and safety among Rotorcraft enthusiasts worldwide.
2000 Members
Founded in 1962

2749 Professional Aeromedical Transport

PO Box 7519
Alexandria, VA 22307

800-541-7517

Purpose is to standardize and upgrade services of aeromedical transport operations. Membership is open to companies and individuals active in the industry.
170 Members
Founded in 1986

2750 Professional Aviation Maintenance Association

400 North Washington Street
Suite 300
Alexandria, VA 22314

87- 90- 541
800-356-1671
FAX 616-527-1327
E-Mail: info@pama.org
Home Page: www.pama.org

Social Media: *Facebook, Twitter, LinkedIn, Google+*

Roger Sickler, Chairman
Jeff Gruber, Vice Chairman
Clark Gordon, Secretary

Enhances professionalism and recognition of the Aviation Maintenance Technician through communication, education, representation and support for continuous improvement in aviation safety.
3300 Members
Founded in 1972

2751 Regional Airline Association
2025 M St NW
Suite 800
Washington, DC 20036-3309

202-367-1170
FAX 202-367-2170
E-Mail: raa@raa.org
Home Page: www.raa.org
Social Media: *Facebook, Twitter, YouTube*

Roger Cohen, President
Scott Foose, Vice President
Faye Malarkey Black, Senior VP, Legislative Affairs
Liam Connolly, Senior Director
Kelly Murphy, Media Relations

Membership consists of more than 70 airlines, plus 350 Associate members provide goods and services.
510 Members
Founded in 1975

2752 Reliability Engineering & Management Institute
University Of Arizona
1130 N Mountian Avenue
Building 119 Room N 517
Tucson, AZ 85721

520-621-6120
FAX 520-621-8191
E-Mail: dimitri@u.arizona.edu
Home Page: www.u.arizona.edu/~dimitri/

Dr Dimitri Kececioglu PE, Prof Aerospace/Mech Engineering

An institute to help provide a working knowledge in reliability engineering.
Frequency: November
Founded in 1971

2753 Seaplane Pilots Association
3859 Laird Blvd
Lakeland, FL 33811

863-701-7979
888-772-8923
FAX 863-701-7588
E-Mail: spa@seaplanes.org
Home Page: www.seaplanes.org
Social Media: *Facebook, Twitter, YouTube*

Walter Windus, Chairman
Stephen Williams, President
Lyle Panepinto, VP
Gordon Richardson, Treasurer
John Touchett, Secretary

Represents members in dozens of seaplane access issues annually and provides numerous exclusive benefits. Members who have provided SPA with a valid email address receive Water Flying Update, a bimonthly e-newsletter that provides recent news, advocacy updates, technical tips, upcoming events, and a tip for using SPA's web site.
375 Members
Founded in 1971

2754 Soaring Society of America
PO Box 2100
Hobbs, NM 88241-2100

505-392-1177
FAX 505-392-8154

E-Mail: membership@ssa.org
Home Page: www.ssa.org
Social Media: *Facebook, Twitter*

Dennis Layton, Chief Operating Officer
Eric Bick, Editor
Kathey Pope, Accounting Manager
Misty Dodson, Merchandise/Membership Services
Melinda Hughes, Magazine Adv./Membership Services

Fosters and promote all phases of gliding and soaring, nationally and internationally.
16K Members
Founded in 1932

2755 Society of Experimental Test Pilots
44814 N Elm Avenue
Lancaster, CA 93534

661-942-9574
FAX 661-940-0398
E-Mail: setp@setp.org
Home Page: www.setp.org

Timothy R. Morey, President
Todd Ericson, President Elect
Art Tomassetti, Vice President
John Tougas, Secretary
Dan Wells, Treasurer

International organization that seek to promote air safety and contributes to aeronautical advancement by promoting sound aeronautical design and development; interchanging ideas, thoughts and suggestions of the members, assisting in the professional development of experimental pilots, and providing scholarships and aid to members and the families of deceased members.
2000 Members
Founded in 1955

2756 Society of Flight Test Engineers
44814 N Elm Avenue
Lancaster, CA 93534

661-949-2095
FAX 661-949-2096
E-Mail: sfte@sfte.org
Home Page: www.sfte.org
Social Media: *Facebook, LinkedIn, RSS*

Peter Scheidler, President
Douglas Bell, Vice President

Members are engineers whose principal professional interest is the flight testing of aircraft. Purpose is to improve communications in the fields of flight test operations, analysis, instrumentation and data systems. We offer an online newsletter called SFTE Flight Test News.
900 Members
Founded in 1968

2757 Space Enterprise Council
3500 Lacey Rd.
Suite 100
Downers Grove, IL 60515

630-678-8300
866-835-8020
Social Media: *Facebook, Twitter, LinkedIn, Google+, YouTube, Pinterest*

Earl Madison, Chair
Rosanna Sattler, Vice Chair
Joe Cassady, Executive Director

Represents interests of commercial, military and civil sectors of space industry to policymakers.
Founded in 2000

2758 Space Foundation
4425 Arrowswest Drive
Colorado Spring, CO 80907

719-576-8000
800-691-4000
FAX 719-576-8801
E-Mail: web@spacefoundation.org

Home Page: www.spacefoundation.org
Social Media: *Facebook, Twitter, LinkedIn, Instagram, Google+, RSS, Pinte*

Elliot H. Pulham, CEO
Holly Roberts, CFO
Kevin C Cook, VP, Marketing & Communications
Steve Eisenhart, Senior VP, Strategy
Art Rakewitcz, VP, Operations

To advance space-related endeavors to inspire, enable, and propel humanity.
- Members
Founded in 1983

2759 Tailhook Association
9696 Businesspark Ave
San Diego, CA 921313-164

858-689-9223
800-322-4665
E-Mail: jrdavis@tailhook.net
Home Page: www.tailhook.org
Social Media: *Facebook, LinkedIn, Google+*

Gregory Keithley, President
Capt. J R Davis, Executive Director
Capt. Dennis Irelan, Editor
CDR Mike Dechemedy, Managing Editor

An independent, fraternal, nonprofit organization internationally recognized as the premier supporter of the aircraft carrier and other sea-based aviation.

2760 The Aerospace States Association
202-257-4872
E-Mail: huettner@aerostates.org
Home Page: www.aerostates.org
Social Media: *Facebook, Twitter*

Lt. Gov. Kay Ivey (AL), Chair
Lt. Gov. Mark Hutchison (NV), Vice Chair

Represents perspective of states with aerospace industries to the federal government as it defines national aerospace policy.
Founded in 1991

2761 Transportation-Communications International Union
3 Research Place
Rockville, MD 20850

301-948-4910
E-Mail: websteward@tcunion.org
Home Page: www.tcunion.org
Social Media: *Facebook, Twitter*

Robert A Scardelletti, President
Russell C Oathout, National General Counsel

Members come from diverse transportation industries. In addition to bargaining and representation of its members, provides mortgage and bankcard programs and other services to its members.
Founded in 1899

2762 Tripoli Rocketry Association
PO Box 87
Bellevue, NE 68005

402-884-9530
FAX 402-884-9531
E-Mail: info@tripoli.org
Home Page: www.tripoli.org
Social Media: *Facebook, Twitter, LinkedIn, YouTube, Google+*

Stu Barrett, President
Bob Brown, VP
Bruce Lee, Treasurer
David Wilkins, Secretary

This is a non-profit organization dedicated to the advancement and operation of non-professional high power rocketry.
Founded in 1964

2763 United States Parachute Association
5401 Southpoint Centre Boulevard
Fredricksburg, VA 22407

540-604-9740
FAX 540-604-9741
E-Mail: uspa@uspa.org
Home Page: www.uspa.org
Social Media: *Facebook, Twitter, LinkedIn, YouTube, Google+*

Sherry Butcher, President
Randy Allison, Vice President
Ray Lallo, Secretary
Albert Berchtold, Treasurer

The USPA is a voluntary membership organization of individuals who enjoy and support the sport of skydiving. The purpose of USPA is three-fold: to promote safe skydiving through training, licensing, and instructor qualification programs; to ensure skydiving's rightful place on airports and in the airspace system; and to promote competition and record-setting programs.
33000 Members

2764 United States Pilots Association
1652 Indian Point Road
Branson, MO 65616

417-338-2225
E-Mail: jan@uspilots.org
Home Page: www.uspilots.org

Arnold Zimmerman, Owner
Jan Hoynacki, Executive Director

Works to promote aviation safety and pilot education and also acts as a forum for exchange of ideas.
5000 Members

2765 United States Ultralight Association
16192 Coastal Highway
Lewes, DE 19958

717-339-0200
FAX 717-339-0063
E-Mail: usua@usua.org
Home Page: www.usua.org

Dale Hooper, Executive VP
Reginald E DeLoach, President

Annual meeting and exhibits of ultralight and microlight aviation equipment, supplies and services. There will be 20 booths.
3000 Members
Founded in 1985

2766 University Aviation Association
2415 Moore's Mill Road
Suite 265-216
Auburn, AL 36830

334-528-0300
FAX 334-844-2432
E-Mail: uaamail@uaa.aero
Home Page: www.uaa.aero
Social Media: *Facebook, Twitter, Youtube*

Carolyn Williamson, Executive Director
David McAlister, Member Services Coordinator
Mary Chandler, Coordinator Office Administration

The voice of collegiate aviation education to its members, the industry, government and the general public. Through the collective expertise of its members, this nonprofit organization plays a pivotal role in the advancement of degree-granting aviation programs that represent all segments of the aviation industry.
625+ Members
Founded in 1947

2767 Vintage Aircraft Association
P.O. Box 3086
Oshkosh, WI 54903-3086

920-426-6110
FAX 920-426-6579
E-Mail: membership@eaa.org
Home Page: www.vintageaircraft.org
Social Media: *Facebook, Twitter, LinkedIn, Instagram, Google+, Tumblr, Vi*

Geoff L Robison, President
Dave Clark, Vice President
Steve Nesse, Secretary
Jerry Brown, Treasurer
Ron Alexander, Director

Brings together people from around the world who share an interest in the aircraft of yesterday.
8000 Members
Founded in 1971

2768 World Airline Historical Society
P.O. Box 489
Ocoee, FL 34761

904-221-1446
FAX 407-522-9352
E-Mail: Information@WAHSOnline.com
Home Page: www.wahsonline.com
Social Media: *Facebook, Twitter, LinkedIn, Youtube, RSS*

Chris Slimmer, President
Don Levine, VP
William Demarest, Treasurer
Bill Demarest, Secretary/Editor

Open to all persons and groups interested in collecting airline memorabilia and the study of the airline industry, past and current.
500 Members
Founded in 1977

Newsletters

2769 AIA Update
Aerospace Industries Association
15049 Conference Center Drive
Suite 600
Chantilly, VA 20151-3824

571-307-0000
FAX 571-307-1001
E-Mail: membership@aia-aerospace.org
Home Page: www.aero.org

Wanda Austin, President
Peter B. Teets, Chairman
Thomas S. Moorman, Vice chairman
Barbara M. Barrett, Ambasador
Frequency: 9x/Year

2770 ATCA Bulletin
Air Traffic Control Association
1101 King St
Suite 300
Alexandria, VA 22314-2963

703-299-2430
FAX 703-299-2437
E-Mail: info@atca.org
Home Page: www.atca.org
Social Media: *Facebook, Twitter, LinkedIn*

Peter F Dumont, President
Monte Belger, Chairman
William Cotton, Director South Central
Jeff Greffith, Secretary

Provides information on activities of the association, important developments in the air traffic control industry.
Frequency: Monthly
ISSN: 0400-1915
Founded in 1956
Printed in on matte stock

2771 ATXA Newsletter
Air Taxi Association
400 Galleria Parkway
Suite 1500
Atlanta, GA 30339

678-390-0001
Home Page: www.atxa.com

Offers information and association news for professionals in the aviation industry.
Frequency: Bimonthly, E-Newsletter

2772 Accident Prevention
Flight Safety Foundation
801 N Fairfax Street
Suite 400
Alexandria, VA 22314-1774

703-739-6700
FAX 703-739-6708
E-Mail: apparao@flightsafety.org
Home Page: www.flightsafety.org

J.A. Donoghue, Director Publications
Mark Lacagnina, Senior Editor
Wayne Rosenkrans, Senior Editor
Linda Werfelman, Senior Editor
Rick Darby, Associate Editor

Focuses on the flight deck, including in-depth reviews of accident reports. Authors offer tips and descriptions on pilot incapacitation, outlines techniques to prevent runway overrun and addresses a wide variety of other subjects aimed at the experienced cockpit crew. Subscription included with FSF membership. Others will be $280.00/year.
4-16 Pages
Frequency: Monthly
Circulation: 3,000
Founded in 1948
Printed in 2 colors

2773 Aerospace Daily
AviationNow
1200 G St Nw
Suite 900
Washington, DC 20005-3821

202-383-2378
800-525-5003
FAX 202-383-2438
E-Mail: aviationdaily@aviationnow.com
Home Page: www.aviationnow.com

Lee Ewing, Editor-in-Chief
Brett Davis, Managing Editor
Mark Lipowicz, Publisher
George Hamilton, President

Daily intelligence on the defense and space industries. If you're a prime or subcontractor, an aviation, defense or space official, a consultant or analyst, or an engineering or research and development manager, you'll benefit from our news on policy and programs.
8 Pages
Frequency: Daily
Founded in 1963

2774 Air Safety Week
Phillips Publishing
7811 Montrose Road
Potomac, MD 20854

703-522-8502
Home Page: www.phillips.com

Dan Cook, Publisher

Weekly newsletter dealing with aviation safety, security, recreation, certification and accident investigation.
Cost: $695.00
10 Pages
Frequency: Monthly

2775 Airport Consultants Council News
Airport Consultants Council

908 King St
Suite 100
Alexandria, VA 22314-3067

703-683-5900
FAX 703-683-2564
E-Mail: info@acconline.org
Home Page: www.acconline.org

Paula Hochstetler, President
Anthony Mavrogiannis, Editor
Sharon Brown, Operations Manager
Cassandra Lamar, Marketing Manager

Council newsletter offering information on important and relevant issues for the aviation consulting community.
Frequency: Quarterly
Circulation: 300
Founded in 1978

2776 Airport Operations
Flight Safety Foundation
801 N Fairfax Street
Suite 400
Alexandria, VA 22314-1774

703-396-6700
FAX 703-739-6708
E-Mail: apparao@flightsafety.org
Home Page: www.flightsafety.org

J.A. Donaghue, Director Publications
Mark Lacagnina, Senior Editor
Wayne Rosenkrans, Senior Editor
Linda Werfelman, Senior Editor
Rick Darby, Associate Editor

Directs attention to ground operations that involve aircraft and other equipment, airport personnel and services, air traffic control and passengers. Subscription included with FSF membership. Others will be $280.00/year.
4-8 Pages
Frequency: Bi-Monthly
Founded in 1974
Printed in 2 colors on glossy stock

2777 Annual Conference Proceedings
Air Traffic Control Association
1101 King St
Suite 300
Alexandria, VA 22314-2963

703-299-2430
FAX 703-299-2437
E-Mail: info@atca.org
Home Page: www.atca.org
Social Media: *Facebook, Twitter, LinkedIn*

Peter F Dumont, President
Monte Belger, Chairman
William Cotton, Director South Central
Jeff Greffith, Secretary

A compendium of fifty or more air traffic control technical papers, covering the entire range of ATC subjects, authored by ATC experts from the full spectrum of public and private organizations engaged in advancement of the science of air traffic control.

2778 Antique Airplane Association Newsletter
Antique Airplance Association
22001 Bluegrass Rd
Ottumwa, IA 52501-8569

641-938-2773
FAX 641-938-2093
E-Mail: antiqueairfield@sirisonline.com
Home Page: www.antiqueairfield.com

Robert L Taylor, CEO
Lucinda Reis, Editor

Air museums, US and abroad historical aviation societies, for AAA chapters, flying aircraft company histories, etc. - For AAA Digest: antique and classic aircraft restorations, mystery aircraft, etc.
Founded in 1953
Printed in 4 colors on glossy stock

2779 Aviation Accident Law & Practice
LexisNexis Matthew Bender & Company
PO Box 933
Dayton, OH 45401-0933

212-448-2000
800-253-5624
FAX 518-487-3584

R Kaye Esq., Publisher
Domestic and international laws.

2780 Aviation Consumer
Belvoir Publishers
PO Box 2626
Greenwich, CT 06836-2626

203-422-7300
FAX 203-661-4802

Robert Englander, Publisher
Richard Weeghman, Editor

Offers valuable information to the consumer regarding airports, airlines, safety and values.

2781 Aviation Daily
Aviation Week
1200 G Street NW
Suite 922
Washington, DC 20005

202-383-2374
800-525-5003
FAX 888-385-1428
E-Mail: aviationdaily@aviationnow.com
Home Page: www.aviationnow.com

Anthony Velocci, Editor-in-Chief
James Asker, Executive Editor
Gregory Hamilton, President
Guy Norris, Senior Editor

Daily intelligence information on the commercial aviation and air transportation industry worldwide.
Cost: $1985.00
10 Pages
Frequency: Daily
Founded in 1939
Printed in on n stock

2782 Aviation Education News Bulletin
Aviation Distributors & Manufacturers Association
100 North 20th Street
4th-Floor
Philadelphia, PA 19103-1443

215-320-3872
FAX 215-564-2175
E-Mail: adma@fernley.com
Home Page: www.adma.org

F. Charles Elkins, President
Michael Shaw, VP
Kristen Olszewski, Executive Director
Meg Taft, Meeting Manager

Association news pertaining to suppliers, distributors and manufacturers of aviation materials.
Frequency: Monthly
Founded in 1943

2783 Aviation Law Reports
CCH
2700 Lake Cook Rd
Riverwoods, IL 60015-3867

847-940-4600
800-835-5224
FAX 773-866-3095
Home Page: www.cch.com

Mike Sabbatis, President
Douglas M Winterrose, Vice President & CFO
Jim Bryant, EVP Software Products

News covering aviation law and regulations.
Cost: $2495.00
Frequency: Weekly
Founded in 1913

2784 Aviation Maintenance
Professional Aviation Maintenance Association
972 E Tuttle Road
Building 204
Ionia, MI 48846

724-772-4092
800-356-1671
FAX 616-527-1327
E-Mail: hq@pama.org
Home Page: www.pama.org

Dale Forton, President
Roger Sickler, Chairman
Jeff Gruber, Vice Chairman
John Wicht, Secretary
Richard Wellman, Treasurer

The source for information on the worldwide aviation aftermarket. Covers the latest new business trends, regulatory developments, technical advancements, and new products and services

2785 Aviation Mechanics Bulletin
Flight Safety Foundation
801 N Fairfax Street
Suite 400
Alexandria, VA 22314-1774

703-739-6700
FAX 703-739-6708
E-Mail: apparao@flightsafety.org
Home Page: www.flightsafety.org

William Voss, President/CEO
Roger Rozelle, Publisher
Jerry Lederer, Founder

Directed to the aviation maintenance technician, with an emphasis on airline and corporate operations. Other regular sections include maintenance safety alerts, mechanical-incident reports and reviews of new products of interest to maintenance technicians.
Cost: $24.00
16 Pages
Frequency: Bi-Monthly
Founded in 1953

2786 Aviation Medical Bulletin
Aviation Insurance Agency
475 N Central Avenue
PO Box 20787
Atlanta, GA 30320

404-767-7501
800-241-6103
FAX 404-761-8326
E-Mail: Pilot@harveywatt.com
Home Page: www.harveywatt.com

Pat Hiebel, President
Sean Daigre, Claims Director

Health education for the professional airline pilot.
Cost: $13.95
Frequency: Monthly
Founded in 1951

2787 Aviators Hot Line
Heartland Communications
PO Box 1052
Fort Dodge, IA 50501-1052

515-955-1600
800-247-2000
FAX 515-955-1668
Home Page: www.hlipublishing.com

Gale W McKinney Ii, CEO
Joseph W Peed, Chairman
Mary Gonnerman, VP

Airline Trade Magazine.
Cost: $24.95
Frequency: Monthly
Founded in 1968

2788 Buoyant Flight
Lighter Than Air Society
526 S Main Street
Suite 232
Akron, OH 44311

E-Mail: suggest@blimpinfo.com
Home Page: www.blimpinfo.com

Articles on the history, science and techniques of buoyant flight.
Founded in 1954

2789 Cabin Crew Safety
Flight Safety Foundation
801 N Fairfax Street
Suite 400
Alexandria, VA 22314-1774

703-739-6700
FAX 703-739-6708
E-Mail: ostrega@flightsafety.org
Home Page: www.flightsafety.org

William Voss, President
Roger Rozelle, Publisher
Rick Derby, Editor
Patzy Sepezy, Circulation Manager

Focuses attention on the cabin crew, especially in airline operations, but the special requirements of corporate operations are also presented. Explanations on how to deal with hijackers, advocates of child restraints, emergency action plans and tips to reduce stress. Subscription included with FSF membership. Others will be $280.00/year.
Cost: $240.00
4 Pages
Printed in 2 colors

2790 Captain's LOG
World Airline Historical Society
P.O. Box 489
Ocoee, FL 34761

904-221-1446
FAX 407-522-9352
E-Mail: president@wahsonline.com
Home Page: www.wahsonline.com

Duane Young, President
Craig Morris, Vice President
Jay Prall, Treasurer
Bill Demarest, Secretary/Editor
Frequency: Quarterly

2791 Command, Control, Communications and Intelligence
American Defense Preparedness Association
22 Commerce Road
Newtown, CT 22201-3062

203-426-0800
800-451-4975
FAX 203-426-1964
E-Mail: info@forecast1.com
Home Page: www.forecast1.com

Ray Peterson, Vice President
Andrew Briney, Editor

Programs and funding information.
Cost: $1640.00
Founded in 1973

2792 Federal Air Surgeons Medical Bulletin
US Federal Aviation Administration
800 Independence Avenue SW
Washington, DC 20591

866-835-5322
Home Page: www.faa.gov

Michael Huerta, Acting Administrator
David Grizzle, Chief Operating Officer
David Weingart, Chief of Staff
Victoria B. Wessmer, Assistant Administrator Of Finance

Published for aviation medical examiners and others interested in aviation safety and aviation medicine.
Frequency: Quarterly
Circulation: 8000
Founded in 1967

2793 Flight Safety Foundation NEWS
Flight Safety Foundation
801 N Fairfax Street
Suite 400
Alexandria, VA 22314-1774

703-396-6700
FAX 703-739-6708
E-Mail: apparao@flightsafety.org
Home Page: www.flightsafety.org

William Voss, President/CEO
Roger Rozelle, Publisher
Allen Smith, Marketing Manager

A primary tool for communicating the Foundation's activities through seminars, workshops, special projects, committee actions, awards to its members.
Cost: $480.00
Frequency: Monthly

2794 Flight Test News
Society of Flight Test Engineers
44814 N Elm Avenue
PO Box 4037
Lancaster, CA 93539-4037

661-949-2095
FAX 661-949-2096
E-Mail: sfte@sfte.org
Home Page: www.sfte.org

Peter Donath, President
Michael Barrlett, Vice President
Mark Mondt, Secretary
Steve Martin, Treasurer
Barbara A. Wood, Director

Offers specific information for flight test engineers.

2795 Flightlog
Association of Flight Attendants
501 3rd St NW
Washington, DC 20001

202-434-1300
FAX 202-712-9792
E-Mail: info@afacwa.org
Home Page: www.afanet.org
Social Media: *Facebook, Twitter, YouTube*

Elliott Kindred, Manager
Veda Shook, International President
Sara Nelson, International President

Offers updated information and news for flight attendants.
Frequency: Monthly

2796 General Aviation Accident Report
Andrews Communications
175 Stafford Street Building 4
Suite 140
Wayne, PA 19087

610-225-0510
800-345-1101
FAX 610-225-0501
Home Page: www.andrewspub.com

Robert Maroldo, Publisher
Nicholas Sullivan, Editor

General aviation laws.
20 Pages
Founded in 1972

2797 Helicopter News
Phillips Business Information

1201 Seven Locks Road
Potomac, MD 20854

301-354-1400
FAX 301-309-3847

Thomas Phillips, Publisher
Holly Yeager, Editor

Information on the rapidly changing helicopter industry.
Cost: $797.00
Frequency: 25 Issues

2798 Helicopter Safety
Flight Safety Foundation
801 N Fairfax Street
Suite 400
Alexandria, VA 22314-1774

703-396-6700
FAX 703-739-6708
E-Mail: apparao@flightsafety.org
Home Page: www.flightsafety.org

J.A. Donaghue, Director Publications
Mark Lacagnina, Senior Editor
Wayne Rosenkrans, Senior Editor
Linda Werfelman, Senior Editor
Rick Darby, Associate Editor

Highlights the broad spectrum of real-world helicopter operations. Subscription included with FSF membership. Others will be $280.00/year.
4-8 Pages
Frequency: Bi-Monthly
Founded in 1974
Printed in 2 colors

2799 Hotline
Aeronautical Repair Station Association
121 N Henry St
Alexandria, VA 22314-2903

703-739-9543
FAX 703-739-9488
E-Mail: arsa@arsa.org
Home Page: www.arsa.org
Social Media: *Facebook, Twitter, LinkedIn, YouTube*

Gary M. Fortner, President
Gary Jordan, VP
Jim Perdue, Treasurer

Devoted to regulatory compliance in aircraft design, production and maintenance.
Frequency: Monthly

2800 Human Factors & Aviation Medicine
Flight Safety Foundation
801 N Fairfax Street
Suite 400
Alexandria, VA 22314-1774

703-396-6700
FAX 703-739-6708
E-Mail: apparao@flightsafety.org
Home Page: www.flightsafety.org

J.A. Donaghue, Director Publications
Mark Lacagnina, Senior Editor
Wayne Rosenkrans, Senior Editor
Linda Werfelman, Senior Editor
Rick Darby, Associate Editor

Presents information important to the training and performance of all aviation professionals. Subscription included with FSF membership. Others will be $280.00/year.
4-8 Pages
Frequency: Bi-Monthly
Founded in 1953
Printed in 2 colors

2801 IE News: Aerospace and Defense
Institute of Industrial Engineers

3577 Parkway Lane
Suite 200
Norcross, GA 30092

770-449-0460
800-494-0460
FAX 770-441-3295
E-Mail: boyeyemi@iienet.org
Home Page: www.iienet.org

Jane Gaboury, Editorial Director
Don Greene, Vice President
Michael Hughes, Editor

Offers information and updates for industrial engineers.

2802 Inside the Air Force

Inside Washington Publishers
PO Box 7167
Washington, DC 20044-7167

703-685-5009
800-424-9068
FAX 703-416-8543

Donna Haseley, Editor

An executive weekly report on Air Force programs, procurement and policymaking.
Cost: $980.00
Frequency: Weekly
Printed in one color on matte stock

2803 International Operations Bulletin

National Business Aviation Association
1200 18th St Nw
Suite 400
Washington, DC 20036-2527

202-783-9000
FAX 202-331-8364
E-Mail: info@nbaa.org
Home Page: www.ebace.com

Ed Bolen, President/CEO

Flight information for international business flight crews.
Frequency: Quarterly
Circulation: 4000
Founded in 1947

2804 Jet Fuel Intelligence

Energy Intelligence Group
5 E 37th St
Suite 5
New York, NY 10016-2807

212-532-1112
FAX 212-532-4479
E-Mail: info@energyintel.com
Home Page: www.energyintel.com

Ivan Sandrea, President
Thomas Wallin, Executive Vice President and Editor
Raja W Sidawi, Chairman
Peter Kemp, Editor
Sarah Miller, Editor-at-Large

Offers the latest information on jets, fuel, cargo, safety and legislation.
Cost: $2595.00
Frequency: Weekly
Founded in 1951

2805 Light Aircraft Manufacturers Association Newsletter

Light Aircraft Manufacturers Association
2001 Steamboat Ridge Ct
Dayton Beach, FL 32128-6918

651-592-7565
FAX 65- 22- 182
E-Mail: info@lama.bz
Home Page: www.lama.bz

Larry Burke, President
Dave Martin, Editor

Manufacturers, distributors and suppliers receive the latest information and news pertain-

ing to light aircraft, including updated news from Washington, DC.
Frequency: Quarterly
Circulation: 66
Founded in 1984
Printed in 2 colors on glossy stock

2806 Light Plane Maintenance

Belvoir Publishers
PO Box 5656
Norwalk, CT 06856-5656

203-422-7300
800-829-9085
FAX 203-661-4802
Home Page: www.lightplane-maintenance.com

John Likakis, Publisher

Articles of interest for light aircraft owners.
Cost: $19.97
24 Pages

2807 Mx Newsletter

Professional Aviation Maintenance Association
972 E Tuttle Road
Building 204
Ionia, MI 48846

724-772-4095
800-356-1671
FAX 724-772-4064
E-Mail: hq@pama.org
Home Page: www.pama.org
Social Media: *Facebook, Twitter, LinkedIn*

Roger Sickler, Chairman
Jeff Gruber, Vice Chairman
John Wicht, Secretary

Features news for and about members, relevant articles and hot legislative information.
Frequency: Six/Year
Printed in one color

2808 NAA Record

National Aeronautic Association
1 Reagan National Airport
Hangar 7
Washington, DC 20001-6015

703-416-4888
FAX 703-416-4877
E-Mail: naa@naa.aero
Home Page: www.naa.aero

Jonathan Gaffney, President
Nancy Sack, Administration Director
Arthur W Greenfield, Contest & Records Director
Frequency: Monthly
Circulation: 3000

2809 NBAA Management Guide

National Business Aviation Association
1200 18th St Nw
Suite 400
Washington, DC 20036-2527

202-783-9000
FAX 202-331-8364
E-Mail: info@nbaa.org
Home Page: www.nbaa.org

Ed Bolen, President
Steven Brown, Sr VP Operations/Administration

Designed to assist existing flight departments with their operational and administrative requirements and to provide overall guidance for operating a flight department. Available to members only.

2810 National Aeronautics

National Aeronautic Association

1737 King Street
Suite 220
Alexandria, VA 22314

703-527-0226
800-644-9777
FAX 703-416-4877
Home Page: www.naa-usa.org

Shannon Chambers, Editor
David L Ivey, Publisher
Nancy Sack, Office Manager

Information on industry events for the aviation community, also opinion articles, records and awards, technology developments, education, and future events.
8 Pages
Circulation: 3500
Founded in 1905
Printed in 2 colors on glossy stock

2811 National Transportation Safety Board Digest Service

Hawkins Publishing Company
103 River Rd
Edgewater, MD 21037-3824

410-798-1098
FAX 410-798-1098
Home Page: www.ntsb.gov

Mark V Rosenker, Chairman

Loose-leafed indexed-digested-analysis of the decisions of the National Transportation Safety Board and its predecessor (the CAB), dealing with Aviation Safety Enforcement matters.
Cost: $390.00
Frequency: Monthly

2812 News & Views

Association of Air Medical Services
909 N Washington Street
Suite 410
Alexandria, VA 22314

703-836-8732
FAX 703-836-8920
E-Mail: information@aams.org
Home Page: www.aams.org

John Fiegel, Executive Director
David J Dries, Editor
Gloria Dow, Editor

This faxed/e-mailed newsletter contains information on association activity updates, community and member news, crew fitness and survival, member survey data, member profiles, editorials, and classifieds.
Frequency: Monthly

2813 Ninety-Nines News

Ninety-Nines
4300 Amelia Earhart Dr
Suite A
Oklahoma City, OK 73159-1106

405-685-7969
800-994-1929
FAX 405-685-7985
E-Mail: 99s@ninety-nines.org
Home Page: www.ninety-nines.org

Laura Ohrenberg, Manager
Susan Larson, President
Pat Prentiss, VP
Donna Moore, Secretary
Liz Lundin, Headquarters Manager

News and events for licensed women pilots.
Founded in 1929

2814 Operations Update

Helicopter Association International
1635 Prince St
Alexandria, VA 22314-2898

703-683-4646
FAX 703-683-4745
Home Page: www.rotor.com

Matthew Zuccaro, President

Provides useful information to helicopter owners and operators regarding issues, events and new technologies that may effect or enhance the operator's ability to conduct business with helicopters.
Frequency: Monthly

2815 Parachutist
United States Parachute Association
5401 Southpoint Centre Boulevard
Fredricksburg, VA 22407

540-604-9740
FAX 540-604-9740
E-Mail: uspa@uspa.org
Home Page: www.uspa.org
Social Media: *Facebook, Twitter, LinkedIn, YouTube, RSS*

Elijah Florio, Editor in Chief
Laura Sharp, Managing Editor
Guilherme Cunha, Advertising Manager, Web Developer
David Cherry, Graphic Designer

The official newsletter of the USPA.
33000 Members
Founded in 1946

2816 Preliminary Accident Reports
Helicopter Association International
1635 Prince St
Alexandria, VA 22314-2898

703-683-4646
FAX 703-683-4745
Home Page: www.rotor.com

Matthew Zuccaro, President

PARs summarize civil helicopter accident reports as received from the National Transportation Safety Board and the Transportation Safety Board of Canada. One subscription included upon request in Regular and Associate member dues.
Frequency: Quarterly

2817 Rotor Breeze
Bell Helicopter Textron
600 E Hurst Boulevard
PO Box 482
Hurst, TX 76053

817-280-2011
FAX 817-280-2321
Home Page: www.bellhelicopter.com

Mike Redenbaugh, Chairman/CEO
Brandon Battles, Editor

Newsletter on Bell Helicopter products and customer support.
Frequency: Quarterly
Founded in 1935

2818 Space Calendar
Space Age Publishing Company
65-1230 Mamalahoa Hwy
Suite D-20
Kamuela, HI 96743-7301

808-885-3473
FAX 808-885-3475
E-Mail: news@spaceagepub.com
Home Page: www.spaceagepub.com

Steve Durst, Owner

Publication for the space industry.
Cost: $59.00
Frequency: Weekly

2819 Space Fax Daily
Space Age Publishing Company
65-1230 Mamalahoa Hwy
Suite D-20
Kamuela, HI 96743-7301

808-885-3473
FAX 808-885-3475

E-Mail: news@spaceagepub.com
Home Page: www.spaceagepub.com

Steve Durst, Owner
Charles Bohannan, Associate Editor
Michelle Gonella, Marketing Manager
Information covering the space industry.
Cost: $59.00
Frequency: Weekly
Founded in 1988

2820 Space Letter
Callahan Publications
6220 Nelway Drive
PO Box 1173
Mclean, VA 22101

703-356-1925

Vincent F Callahan Jr, Editor

Information from Washington on the US multi-billion dollar National Space Program. Legislation, budgets, marketing trends and contracting.
Cost: $190.00
8 Pages
Frequency: 24/Yr
Printed in one color

2821 Space Station News
Phillips Publishing
7811 Montrose Road
Potomac, MD 20854-3363

301-208-6787
FAX 301-340-0877

Tom Phillips, President/CEO/Publisher
Information pertaining to the space station program.
Founded in 1974

2822 Speednews
Speednews
17383 W. Sunset Boulevard
Suite A 220
Pacific Palisades, CA 90272

310-203-9603
FAX 310-203-9352
E-Mail: admin@speednews.com
Home Page: www.speednews.com

William Freeman III, Publisher
Stephen Costley, Editor
Joanna Speed, VP, Circulation
Stephen A. Costley, VP, Managing Editor
Pamela Leven, Subscription Sales

Market intelligence newsletter for the aviation industry.
Cost: $687.00
Frequency: Weekly
Circulation: 50000
ISSN: 0271-2598
Founded in 1979

2823 The NAA Record
1 Reagan National Airport
Hangar 7
Washington, DC 20001-6015

703-416-4888
800-644-9777
FAX 703-416-4877
E-Mail: naa@naa.aero
Home Page: www.naa.aero

Jonathan Gaffney, President
Nancy Sack, Administration Director
Arthur W Greenfield, Contest & Records Director

A non-profit association that is dedicated to the advancement of the art, sport and science of aviation in the United States.
3000 Members
Frequency: Monthly
Circulation: 3000
Founded in 1905

2824 World Airline News
Phillips Publishing
7811 Montrose Road
Potomac, MD 20854

301-354-1400
FAX 301-340-0877
Home Page: www.phillips.com

Tom Phillips, President/CEO/Publisher

Provides airline executives with news and analysis on route developments, codesharing agreements, and traffic statistics as well as aviation entertainment.
Cost: $697.00
Frequency: Weekly/Newsletter
Circulation: 1,850
Founded in 1974

2825 World Airport Week
Phillips Publishing
7811 Montrose Road
Potomac, MD 20854

301-354-1400
FAX 301-340-0877
Home Page: www.phillips.com

Tom Phillips, CEO

Focuses on commercialization and privatization of airports around the world.
Cost: $597.00
Frequency: Weekly
Circulation: 1800

Magazines & Journals

2826 ABS Magazine
American Bonanza Society
PO Box 12888
Wichita, KS 67277

316-945-1700
FAX 316-945-1710
E-Mail: ABSMail@bonanza.org
Home Page: www.bonanza.org

Nancy Johnson, Executive Director
Peggy L Fuksa, Events Coordinator

Offers a treasury of practical information on such topics as maintenance, piloting techniques, aircraft restoration, aircraft insurance and ot her important subjects especially chosen for those with a specific interest in Bonanza, Baron, and Travel Air models of aircraft. This colorful magazine also features aircraft owned by an ABS members on its cover every month, as well as schedules of the numerous member activities which are conducted all around the nation.
Frequency: Monthly

2827 AIAA Technical Reports
American Institute of Aeronautics and Astronautics
1801 Alexander Bell Dr
Suite 500
Reston, VA 20191-4344

703-264-7500
800-639-2422
FAX 703-264-7551
E-Mail: tammym@aiaa.org
Home Page: www.aiaa.org

Cort Durocher, President
Kathy Watkins, Maketing Manager
Dr David S Dolling, VP Publications

Each year AIAA sponsors approximately 25 national meetings where professionals present technical papers on subjects such as guidance and control Computers in Aerospace, etc.
Cost: $3.00
Circulation: 1925
Founded in 1963

2828 AOPA Flight Training Magazine
Aircraft Owners & Pilots Association
421 Aviation Way
Frederick, MD 21701-4756

301-695-2000
800-872-2672
FAX 301-695-2375
Home Page: www.aopa.org

Craig Fuller, President

Provides up-to-date aviation news and safety
tips for student pilots and CFIs.

2829 AOPA Pilot Magazine
Aircraft Owners & Pilots Association
421 Aviation Way
Frederick, MD 21701-4756

301-695-2000
800-872-2672
FAX 301-695-2375
Home Page: www.aopa.org

Craig Fuller, President
Phil Boyer, President

Will keep you up to date on all the hottest issues in general aviation from the newest technologies in avionics to the latest safety and
techniques to enhance your flying. Available
only to AOPA members. Membership costs
only $39.00/annually.
Frequency: Monthly
Circulation: 34,000

2830 AUSA News
Association of the United States Army
2425 Wilson Boulevard
Arlington, VA 22201-3326

703-841-4300
800-336-4570
FAX 703-525-9039
E-Mail: ausa-info@ausa.org
Home Page: www.ausa.org

Peter Murphy, Editor
Gordon R Sullivan, President

AUSA represents every American soldier by:
being the voice for all components of Amer-
ica's army; fostering public support of the
Army's role in national security; providing pro-
fessional education and information programs.
Frequency: Monthly
Circulation: 10000
Founded in 1950

2831 Aerospace Engineering
400 Commonwealth Drive
Warrendale, PA 15096-1

724-776-4841
877-606-7323
FAX 724-776-0790
E-Mail: magazines@sae.org
Home Page: www.sae.org

Richard Klien, President
Mircea Gradu, Executive VP

Serves the international aerospace design and
manufacturing field which consists of producers of airliners, helicopters, spacecraft, missiles; their powerplants, propulsion systems,
avionics, electronic/electrical systems, parts
and components.
Cost: $75.00
Frequency: 10 issues
Circulation: 28440
Founded in 1905

2832 Agricultural Aviation
National Agricultural Aviation Association
1005 E St SE
Washington, DC 20003-2847

202-546-5722
FAX 202-546-5726

E-Mail: information@agaviation.org
Home Page: www.agaviation.org

Andrew Moore, Executive Director
Peggy Knizer, Assistant Executive Director

Official publication of the National Agricultural Aviation Association. Typical subject matter includes information on agricultural
aviation business, agricultural aircraft, legislative issues, pesticides, new products and services, safety, maintenance, people profiles.
Cost: $30.00
Circulation: 5200
Founded in 1921

2833 Air Classics
Challenge Publications
9509 Vassar Ave
Unit A
Chatsworth, CA 91311-0883

818-700-6868
800-562-9182
FAX 818-700-6282
E-Mail: customerservice@challengeweb.com
Home Page: www.challengeweb.com

Edwin Schnepf, Owner

Magazine of military aviations.
Cost: $36.95
76 Pages
Frequency: Monthly
Founded in 1963

2834 Air Force Magazine
Air Force Association
1501 Lee Hwy
Suite 400
Arlington, VA 22209-1198

703-247-5800
800-727-3337
FAX 703-247-5853
E-Mail: letters@afa.org
Home Page: www.afa.org

Michael Dunn, President
Robert S. Dudney, Editor in Chief
Stephen P. Condon, National President
Suzann Chapman, Editor
John A. Tirpak, Executive Editor

Analysis of all aspects of aerospace power,
from military and scientific advances to politi-
cal ramifications. Includes reports on new tech-
nology and studies missile management.
Cost: $36.00
Frequency: Monthly
Circulation: 202718
Founded in 1946

2835 Air Line Pilot
Air Lines Pilot Association International
1625 Massachusetts Ave NW
Suite 800
Washington, DC 20036-2204

703-689-2270
FAX 202-797-4052
Home Page: www.alpa.org

Captain Lee Moak, President
Mary Jo McPherson, Associate Editor
Captain Sean Cassidy, Vice President

Emphasizes advances in air safety, flight tech-
nology, industry developments and aviation
history.
Cost: $32.00
56 Pages
Frequency: Monthly
Circulation: 86,656
Founded in 1931

2836 Air Line Pilot Magazine
Airline Pilots Association International

1625 Massachusetts Ave NW
Suite 800
Washington, DC 20036-2204

703-689-2270
FAX 202-797-4052
Home Page: www.alpa.org

Captain Lee Moak, President
Captain Sean Cassidy, Vice President
Frequency: Monthly

2837 Air Medical Journal
Elsevier, Health Sciences Division
3251 Riverport Lane
Maryland Heights, MO 63043

314-447-8000
800-401-9962
FAX 314-447-8033
E-Mail: elspcs@elsevier.com
Home Page: www.elsevier.com

Ron Mobed, CEO
David J Dries, Editor
Adriaan Roosen, Executive Vice President

Is the industry's combined trade and research
journal. Each issue contains research articles,
abstracts and book reviews designed to keep
you up-to-date on the latest discoveries. Membership benefits includes a complimentary subscription.
Cost: $82.00
Founded in 1986

2838 Air Progress
Challenge Publications
9509 Vassar Ave
Unit A
Chatsworth, CA 91311-0883

818-700-6868
FAX 818-700-6282
E-Mail: customerservice@challengeweb.com
Home Page: www.challengeweb.com

Edwin Schnepf, Owner
Taccy Kruger, Editor

Covers all phases of aviation.
Cost: $36.95
84 Pages
Frequency: Monthly
Founded in 1963

2839 Air Progress - Warbirds International
Challenge Publications
9509 Vassar Ave
Unit A
Chatsworth, CA 91311-0883

818-700-6868
800-562-9182
FAX 818-700-6282
E-Mail: customerservice@challengeweb.com
Home Page: www.challengeweb.com

Edwin Schnepf, Owner
Michael O'Leary, Editor
Tim Baudler, Associate Publisher

The magazine of veteran and vintage military
aircraft.
Cost: $22.00
80 Pages
Frequency: Quarterly
Circulation: 3836
Founded in 1963

2840 Air Transport World
Penton Media
8380 Colesville Rd
Suite 700
Silver Spring, MD 20910

301-755-0200
FAX 913-514-3909
Home Page: www.atwonline.com

JA Donoghue, Editorial Director
William A Freeman III, Publisher

Lists nationwide and international information on airports, airlines and the latest technology in the aviation industry.
Cost: $65.00
85 Pages
Frequency: Monthly
Circulation: 40000
Founded in 1964
Printed in 4 colors on glossy stock

2841 Air and Space/Smithsonian
National Air and Space Museum
Smithsonian Institution
PO Box 37012 ,Victor Bldg 7100 MRC
Washington, DC 20013-7012

202-633-6070
800-513-3081
FAX 202-275-1886
Home Page: www.airspacemag.com/

Joseph Bonsignore, Publisher
George C Larson, Editor

Smithsonian magazine offering information on the latest developments, technology, and historical news of the aviation industry.
Cost: $24.00
124 Pages
Founded in 1986

2842 Aircraft Maintenance Technology
Cygnus Business Media
1233 Janesville Avenue
Fort Atkinson, WI 53538

800-547-7377
FAX 920-563-1699
E-Mail: jjezo@amtonline.com
Home Page: www.cygnusb2b.com

Jon Jezo, Publisher
Ronald Donner, Editor

Provides in depth coverage of the critical technical and professional issues facing today's technicians.
Cost: $90.00
98 Pages
Frequency: Monthly
Circulation: 39000
ISSN: 1072-3145
Founded in 1989
Mailing list available for rent: 41M names
Printed in 4 colors on glossy stock

2843 Airline Pilot Careers
Aviation Information Resources
1029 Peachtree Parkway N
Suite 352
Peachtree City, GA 30269

404-592-6500
87- 33- 293
FAX 770-487-6617
E-Mail: KitDarby@gmail.com
Home Page: www.jet-jobs.com

Kit Darby, President/Publisher

Information to assist pilots in their career development as a airline pilot. Includes feature airline news, personnel announcements, aviation medical information, classifieds and calendar events.
Cost: $29.95
40 Pages
Frequency: Monthly
ISSN: 1095-4317
Founded in 1989

2844 Airliners
World Transport Press
2854 Sterling Road
Hollywood, FL 33020

954-923-4474
800-875-6711
FAX 954-923-4541

E-Mail: airlinesonline@earthlink.net
Home Page: www.airlinersonline.com

Jon Proctor, Editor

Dedicated solely to the exciting world of airlines and airliners, past, present, and future. Airline histories, travel adventures, color photos of the latest airlines, humorous articles and much more. Accepts advertising.
Cost: $26.95
80 Pages
Circulation: 80000

2845 Airport Business
Cygnus Business Media
1233 Janesville Avenue
Fort Atkinson, WI 53538

800-547-7377
E-Mail: john.infanger@cygnuspub.com
Home Page: www.cygnusb2b.com

John Infanger, Editorial Director

Targets professionals who manage aitports, airport-based businesses, and corporate flight facilities in North America. Helps managers more effectively operate their operations by sharing case studies of what others are doing successfully, combined with expert analysis, industry news, and product information.
Cost: $60.00
44 Pages
Frequency: Monthly
Circulation: 14100
ISSN: 1072-1797
Founded in 1986

2846 Airport Equipment & Technology
8380 Colesville Rd
Suite 700
Silver Spring, MD 20910-6257

301-755-0200
FAX 913-514-3909
Home Page: www.atwonline.com

William A Freeman III, Publisher
Geoffrey Thomas, Editor-in-Chief

Related to airport and airport operations.
Cost: $65.00
Frequency: Quarterly
Circulation: 40000
Founded in 1965

2847 Airport Journal
Airport Journal
551 Revere Avenue
PO Box 66001
Westmont, IL 60559

630-986-8132
FAX 630-986-5010
Home Page: www.airportjournal.com

John Andrews, Editor

This journal offers news, information, statistics and reviews pertaining to airports across the globe.
Cost: $13.00
Frequency: Monthly

2848 Airports
Aviation Week
1200 G St NW
Suite 900
Washington, DC 20005-3821

202-383-2378
800-525-5003
FAX 202-383-2438
E-Mail: aw_intelligence@aviationnow.com
Home Page: www.aviationnow.com

Christopher Fotos, Editor
Kimberley Johnson, Associate Editor
Mark Lipowicz, Publisher

Airports, the weekly for airport managers, users and suppliers, gives you exclusive insider intelligence to meet business challenges with

your eyes open.
Cost: $98.00
Frequency: Weekly
Founded in 1920

2849 Airpower
Sentry Books
Republic Press
PO Box 881526
San Diego, CA 92168

818-368-2012
E-Mail: support@airwingmedia.com
Home Page: www.wingsairpower.com

Joseph Mizrahi, Publisher
Mike Machat, Editor/Publisher

Military and commercial aviation history, contains photos, drawings and interviews.
Cost: $44.00
56 Pages
Frequency: Monthly
Circulation: 45000
ISSN: 1067-1048
Founded in 1971

2850 Airways
Airways International
120 McGhee Road
PO Box 1109
Sandpoint, ID 83864

360-457-6485
800-440-5166
FAX 208-263-5906
E-Mail: airways@airwaysmag.com
Home Page: www.airwaysmag.com

John Wegg, Editor-in-Chief
Seija Wegg, VP Marketing

Written for airline and air travel professionals, and the consumer. Focuses on the current air transport industry: the airliner, manufacturers, the people, technologies, the airports and the airways. Plus takes a nostalgic look at the past.
Cost: $39.95
80 Pages
Frequency: Monthly
Circulation: 43000
ISSN: 1074-4320
Founded in 1994

2851 America's Flyways
United States Pilots Association
1652 Indian Point Road
Brandson, MO 65616

417-338-2225
FAX 309-215-6323
E-Mail: jan@hoynacki.com
Home Page: www.uspilots.org

Arnold Zimmerman, Owner
Jan Hoynacki, Executive VP
Frequency: Monthly

2852 Army Aviation
Army Aviation Publications
755 Main St
Suite 4D
Monroe, CT 06468-2830

203-268-2450
FAX 203-268-5870
E-Mail: aaaa@quad-a.org
Home Page: www.quad-a.org

William R Harris, Publisher
Maryann Stirling, Circulation Manager
Daniel Petrosky, President

Is a professional military publication reporting on news and developments pertinent to the field of U.S. Army Aviation and is the official publication of the Army Aviation Association of America. Each issue offers in-depth coverage of a specific development or program within U.S. Army Aviation along with dynamic, easy-to-read feature articles from key offices, agencies, and operational units world-

wide.
Cost: $30.00
Frequency: Monthly
Founded in 1957
Printed in 4 colors on glossy stock

2853 Aviation Business Journal
National Air Transportation Association
4226 King St
Alexandria, VA 22302-1507

703-845-9000
800-808-6282
FAX 703-845-8176
E-Mail: rmulholland@NATA.aero
Home Page: www.nata.aero
Social Media: *Facebook, Twitter, LinkedIn*

James K Coyne, President
Tim Heck, VP/CFO
Eric R Byer, Gov't & Industry Affairs

Authored by experienced aviation journalists
and industry experts
Frequency: Quarterly

2854 Aviation Digest Associates
P.O. Box 2231
Danbury, CT 06810

203-264-3727

Robert Dorr, Publisher
Sharon Simmons, Associate Publisher

Newsmagazine/shopper distributed to owners
of general aviation (private and corporate) air-
craft.
Cost: $20.00
Frequency: Monthly
Circulation: 12,000

2855 Aviation Equipment Maintenance
Phillips Business Information
7811 Montrose Road
Potomac, MD 20854

301-354-1400
FAX 301-309-3847
Home Page: www.phillips.com

Richard Koulbanis, Publisher
Clif Stroud, Editor
John J. Coyle, President

Produced monthly and is the leading publication for airline and general aviation maintenance managers. AEM provides information on
maintenance techniques, management procedures, new products and ground support
equipment.
Frequency: Monthly
Founded in 1974

2856 Aviation International News
Convention News Company
81 Kenosia Avenue
Danbury, CT 06810

203-798-2400
FAX 203-798-2104
E-Mail: jhartford@ainonline.com
Home Page: www.ainonline.com

Anthony Ramodo, Publisher
Charles Alcock, Editor
Jeff Hartford, Circulation Manager
Wilson Leach, Executive Director

Update on business aviation, equipment and
services, and business aviation news and
events.
Cost: $74.98
116 Pages
Frequency: Monthly
Circulation: 39,000
ISSN: 0887-9877
Founded in 1972
Printed in 4 colors on glossy stock

2857 Aviation Safety
Belvoir Publishers

800 Connecticut Avenue
PO Box 5656
Norwalk, CT 06856

203-857-3100
FAX 203-857-3103
E-Mail: customer_service@belvoir.com
Home Page: www.belvoir.com

Ken Ibold, Editor-in-Chief
Robert Englander, CEO
Tom Canfield, VP

Journal on risk management and accident pre-
vention, includes interviews with officials of
the FFA.
Cost: $65.00
Frequency: Monthly
Founded in 1972

2858 Aviation Week & Space Technology
Aviation Week
1200 G St NW
Suite 900
Washington, DC 20005-3821

202-383-2378
800-525-5003
FAX 202-383-2438
Home Page: www.aviationnow.com

Anthony L Velocci Jr, Editor-in-Chief
James R Asker, Manager Editor
Jim Mathews, Publisher

Articles and features on the aviation/aerospace
industry, including aircraft rockets, missiles,
space vehicles, powerplants, avionics and re-
lated components and equipment.
Cost: $5.00
Frequency: Weekly
Circulation: 140000
Founded in 1884

**2859 Aviation, Space and Environmental
Medicine**
Aerospace Medical Association
320 S Henry St
Alexandria, VA 22314-3579

703-739-2240
FAX 703-739-9652
E-Mail: inquiries@asma.org
Home Page: www.asma.org

Gisselle Vargas, Manager

Provides contact with physicians, life scientists, bioengineers and medical specialists
working in both basic medical research and in
its clinical applications.
Frequency: Monthly

2860 Avionics News
Aircraft Electronics Association
3570 Ne Ralph Powell Rd
Lees Summit, MO 64064-2360

816-347-8400
FAX 816-347-8405
E-Mail: info@aea.net
Home Page: www.aea.net
Social Media: *Facebook, Twitter, LinkedIn*

Gregory Vall, President/Publisher
Gary Harp, Chairman
Jenneie Flattery, Treasurer

A magazine devoted exclusively to persons in-
terested in aviation and avionics. Complimen-
tary within North America.
Cost: $132.00
Frequency: Monthly
Circulation: 8500
Founded in 1975

**2861 Avionics: The Journal of Global
Airspace**
PBI Media

1201 Seven Locks Road
Potomac, MD 20854

301-354-1400
847-559-7314
FAX 301-340-0542
Home Page: www.avionicsmagazine.com

Daniel E Comiskey, Publisher
Stuart Bonner, Circulation Manager
Don Pazour, CEO
David Jensen, Editor-In-Chief

Covers electronics carried aboard aircraft,
ground navigational and systems for air traffic
control.
Cost: $89.00
Frequency: Monthly
Founded in 1999
Printed in 4 colors on glossy stock

2862 Balloon Life
Balloon Life Magazine
9 Madelaine Avenue
Westport, CT 06880

203-629-1241
FAX 206-935-3326
E-Mail: bill_armstrong@balloonlife.com
Home Page: www.balloonlife.com

Bill Armstrong, Publisher/Editor

Dedicated to the sport of hot air ballooning.
Four-color magazine contains articles on major
events, safety, education, news, calendar and
special reports to bring alive the life of bal-
looning.
Cost: $21.00
40 Pages
Frequency: Bi-Monthly
Circulation: 4000
ISSN: 0887-6061
Founded in 1986
Printed in 4 colors on glossy stock

2863 Business & Commercial Aviation
McGraw Hill
4 International Drive
Suite 260
Rye Brook, NY 10573

914-939-0300
800-257-9402
FAX 914-939-1184
E-Mail: p02cs@mcgraw-hill.com
Home Page: www.aviationnow.com

William Garvey, Editor-in-Chief
Mark Lipowicz, Publisher
Richard Aarons, Safety Editor

Information for the management and executive
levels of aircraft companies on improvements
in operations and news of today's general aviation industry.
Cost: $60.00
Frequency: Monthly
Circulation: 52329

2864 Captain's Log
World Airline Historical Society
PO Box 489
Ocoee, FL 34761

904-221-1446
FAX 407-522-9352
E-Mail: president@WAHSOnline.com
Home Page: www.wahsonline.com
Social Media: *Facebook, Twitter*

Duane Young, President
Craig Morris, VP

The premiere magazine for collectors of airline
memorabilia.
Frequency: Quarterly
Circulation: 500

2865 Cessna Owner Magazine
Cessna Owner Organization

N7450 Aanstad Rd
Iola, WI 54945-5000

715-445-5000
888-692-3776
FAX 715-445-4053
E-Mail: help@cessnaowner.org
Home Page: www.cessnaowner.org

Dan Weller, Executive Director
Joe Jones, Publisher

The official publication of the Cessna Owner Organization, it includes pilot tips, owner/aircraft articles, alerts, maintenance tips, new product information, SDR summaries, AD's, insurance updates, and much more.
Cost: $9.95
Frequency: Monthly
Circulation: 5000

2866 Controller

Sandhills Publishing
PO Box 82545
Lincoln, NE 68501-5310

402-479-2181
800-331-1978
FAX 402-479-2195
E-Mail: human-resources@sandhills.com
Home Page: www.sandhills.com

Tom Peed, Publisher

A magazine designed and edited to provide a means of communication between buyer and seller in today's general aviation marketplace.
Cost: $52.00
60 Pages
Frequency: Weekly
Circulation: 20,000 +
Founded in 1978

2867 EAA Sport Aviation

Experimental Aircraft Association
3000 Poberezny Road
PO Box 3086
Oshkosh, WI 54902

920-426-4800
800-564-6322
FAX 920-426-6761
E-Mail: webmaster@eaa.org
Home Page: www.eaa.org

Tom Poberezny, President
David Berkley, Communications Director
Adam Smith, VP Member Services

For pilots, designers, and enthusiasts of sport and homebuilt aircraft.
Cost: $40.00
100 Pages
Frequency: Monthly
Circulation: 165000
ISSN: 0038-7835
Founded in 1953
Printed in 4 colors on glossy stock

2868 EAA Sport Pilot Magazine

Experimental Aircraft Association
3000 Poberezny Road
PO Box 3086
Oshkosh, WI 54902

920-426-4800
800-564-6322
FAX 920-426-6761
E-Mail: webmaster@eaa.org
Home Page: www.eaa.org

Tom Poberezny, President
David Berkley, Communications Director
Adam Smith, VP Member Services

Dedicated to those to fly, buy, build/assemble, maintain, and have fun with light-sport aircraft, sport pilot eligible aircraft, and ultralights, as well as the full spectrum of member activities that give people the opportunity to participate in recreational aviation.

2869 EAA Vintage Aircraft Association

Experimental Aircraft Association
PO Box 3086
Oshkosh, WI 54903-3086

920-426-4825
800-564-6322
FAX 920-426-6579
E-Mail: vintageaircraft@eaa.org
Home Page: www.vintageaircraft.org

Geoff Robison, President

Devoted to all aspects of antique, classic and contemporary aircraft. (All aircraft cinstructed by the original manufacturer, or its licensee on or before 12/31/1970).
Cost: $36.00
6000+ Members
32 Pages
Frequency: Monthly
Circulation: 10,000
Founded in 1971

2870 FAA Aviation News

Government Printing Office
AFS-805 Room 832
800 Independence Avenue, S.W.
Washington, DC 20591

202-512-0000
866-835-5322
E-Mail: webmasteravnews@faa.gov
Home Page: www.faa.gov/

Phyllis Duncan, Editor
Michael Huerta, Administrator
David Weingart, Chief of Staff
Daniel J. Mehan, Chief Information Officer

Contains regulations and approved operational techniques, also in depth accident and incident reports.
Cost: $21.00
Frequency: Bi-monthly
Circulation: 50,000
Founded in 1966

2871 Flight Physician

Civil Aviation Medical Association
P.O. Box 2382
Peachtree City, GA 30269-2382

770-487-0100
FAX 770-487-0080
E-Mail: david.millett@yahoo.com
Home Page: www.civilavmed.com

David Millett MD, Executive VP
James Heins MD, President
Gordon L Ritter, Secretary/Treasurer
Cost: $5.00
Frequency: Bi-Monthly

2872 Flight Safety Digest

Flight Safety Foundation
801 N Fairfax Street
Suite 400
Alexandria, VA 22314-1774

703-247-0700
FAX 703-739-6708
E-Mail: Marshall@flightsafety.org
Home Page: www.flightsafety.org

William Voss, President/CEO
Roger Rozelle, Publisher
Mark Lacagnina, Senior Editor

Analyzes controversial industry issues; and authors have shared observations of important, but sometimes subtle influences that affect the airline industry. Authors have described the latest innovations in training, technology and management. Monthly sections present analyses of aviation statistics, brief accident reports and abstracts of information received at FSF Jerry Lederer Aviation Safety Library. Subscription included with FSF membership. Oth-

ers will be $520.00.
Cost: $520.00
Frequency: Monthly
Circulation: 1000
Founded in 1982
Printed in one color

2873 Flight Training

Aircraft Owners & Pilots Association
421 Aviation Way
Frederick, MD 21701-4756

301-695-2000
800-872-2672
FAX 301-695-2375
E-Mail: flighttraining@aopa.org
Home Page: www.aopa.org

Craig Fuller, President
Thomas B Haines, Editor-in-Chief

Offers information to new pilots and their instructors as well as flight school managers and owners.
Cost: $21.00
Frequency: Monthly
Circulation: 40000+
Founded in 1939

2874 Flightline Magazine

Allied Pilots Association
14600 Trinity Blvd
Suite 500
Fort Worth, TX 76155-2559

817-302-2272
FAX 817-302-2119
E-Mail: public-comment@alliedpilots.org
Home Page: www.alliedpilots.org

Dave Ahles, Executive Director
Captain Dave Bates, President
James Eaton, Secretary/Treasurer

2875 Flyer

Flyer Media
5611 76th Street W
PO Box 39099
Lakewood, WA 98439

253-471-9888
800-426-8538
FAX 253-471-9911
E-Mail: comments@generalaviationnews.com
Home Page: www.generalaviationnews.com

Janice Wood, Editor
Ben Sclair, Publisher
Roy McGhee, Production Manager
Ron Boydston, Circulation Manager

For general and business aviation.
Cost: $35.00
72 Pages
Frequency: Monthly
Circulation: 50000
ISSN: 1052-9136
Founded in 1949
Printed in 4 colors on newsprint stock

2876 Flying

460 N Orlando Avenue
Suite 20
Winter Park, FL 32789

407-628-4802
FAX 407-628-7061
E-Mail: flying@neodata.com
Home Page: www.flyingmag.com

J Mac McClellan, Editor-in-Chief
Wayne Lincourt, Associate Publisher
Rachel Goldstein, Sales Development Manager

Dedicated to general aviation and includes industry news, products, reports on every aircraft category, the latest new products, technology and photography.
Cost: $54.00
116 Pages
Frequency: Monthly
Circulation: 310321

Founded in 1918
Printed in 4 colors

2877 Flying Magazine
National Association of Flight Instructors
EAA Aviation Center
730 Grand Street
Allegan, MI 49010

920-426-6801
866-806-6156
FAX 920-426-6865
E-Mail: nafi@eaa.org
Home Page: www.nafinet.org

Sean Elliot, President
Jason Blair, Executive Director

Provided to all NAFI members, this highly respected general aviation magazine is a great source of information. NAFI and Flying have entered into a partnership that directly benefits you - the NAFI member! Flying is the perfect compliment to the technical flight instruction how-to's contained in NAFI Mentor.

2878 GPS World
Advanstar Communications
201 Sandpointe Ave
Suite 500
Santa Ana, CA 92707-8700

714-513-8400
FAX 714-513-8680
E-Mail: info@gpsworld.com
Home Page: www.gpsworld.com

Mike Weldon, Plant Manager
Alan Cameron, Editor in Chief
Tracy Cozzen, Managing Editor

Covers current news and developments in the area of GPS (global positioning system) technology.
Cost: $54.00
Frequency: Monthly
Circulation: 35010
Founded in 1987

2879 Helicopter Association International Magazine
1635 Prince St
Alexandria, VA 22314-2898

703-683-4646
800-435-4976
FAX 703-683-4745
E-Mail: marty.lenehan@rotor.com
Home Page: www.rotor.com

Matthew Zuccaro, President
Edward DiCampli, Executive Vice President

Dedicated exclusively to the civil helicopter industry. It covers pertinent helicopter operational safety and regulatory issues, including FAA question and answer column, legislative and lobbying issues, and HAI committee and member activities. Accepts advertising.
Cost: $15.00
48 Pages
Frequency: Quarterly
ISSN: 0897-831X
Founded in 1988
Printed in 4 colors on matte stock

2880 Hook Magazine
Tailhook Association
9696 Businesspark Ave
San Diego, CA 92131

858-689-9223
800-322-4665
E-Mail: thookassn@aol.com
Home Page: www.tailhook.org

Dennis Trelan, Editor
Jan Jacobs, Managing Editor

Dedicated to telling the story of US Navy carrier aviation, both past and person. Contains a selection of carrier and squadron histories balanced with departments containing the latest

news of current units and aerospace industry developments affecting carrier aviation.
Frequency: Quarterly

2881 IAM Journal
International Association of Machinists and
9000 Machinists Pl
Upper Marlboro, MD 20772-2675

301-967-4500
FAX 301-967-4588
E-Mail: websteward@goiam.org
Home Page: www.goiam.org
Social Media: *Facebook, Twitter*

R Thomas Buffenbarger, CEO

This advocacy magazine addresses the trends and forces that affect us all. It covers stories provide an indepth analysis of today's hot issues and are meant to spark discussion among IAM members. Its feature stories provide a glimpse of the men and women who belong to the IAM. IAM represents works primarily in the air transport, aerospace, metalworking, machinery, manufacturing and automotive industries.

2882 Journal of Aerospace Engineering
American Society of Civil Engineers
9000 Machinists Pl
Upper Marlboro, MD 20772-2675

301-967-4500
800-548-2723
FAX 703-295-6222
E-Mail: marketing@asce.org
Home Page: www.goiam.org

R Thomas Buffenbarger, President
Bill Henry, Publisher
Richard Michalski, General Vice President

Covers lunar soil mechanics, aerospace structures, and materials, extraterrestrial construction, robotics, remote sensing, applications, and real time data collection systems. Defines the role of civil engineering in space and emphasizes the practical applications of civil engineering in space and on earth.
Cost: $140.00
Frequency: Quarterly
Founded in 1852

2883 Journal of Air Traffic Control
Air Traffic Control Association
1101 King St
Suite 300
Alexandria, VA 22314-2963

703-299-2430
FAX 703-299-2437
E-Mail: info@atca.org
Home Page: www.atca.org

Peter F Dumont, President
Brian Courter, Meetings and Program Coordinator
Michele Townes, Communications Director

Devoted to developments in air traffic control. It contains articles on current issues involving ATC operations, innovative concepts and applications of technology to ATC, public policy debates impacting ATC, commentary by noted aviation experts and policy makers, ATC historical material, and reviews of books and videos of interest to the aviation community.
Frequency: Quarterly
Founded in 1956

2884 Journal of Astronautical Sciences
American Astronautical Society
6352 Rolling Mill Place
Suite 102
Springfield, VA 22152-2370

703-866-0020
FAX 703-866-3526

E-Mail: aas@astronautical.org
Home Page: www.astronautical.org

Frank Slazer, President
James Kirkpatrick, Executive Director

An archival publication devoted to the sciences and technology of astronautics.
Cost: $170.00
Frequency: Quarterly
ISSN: 0021-9142

2885 Journal of Guidance, Control & Dynamics
American Institute of Aeronautics and Astronautics
1801 Alexander Bell Dr
Suite 500
Reston, VA 20191-4344

703-264-7500
800-639-2422
FAX 703-264-7551
E-Mail: custserv@aiaa.org
Home Page: www.aiaa.org

Dr. Brian Dailey, President
George T Schmidt, Editor-in-Chief

Offers information on guidance control, navigation, electronics and more related to astronautical and aeronautical systems.
Cost: $675.00
Frequency: Fortnightly
Circulation: 3000
Founded in 1930

2886 Journal of Propulsion & Power
American Institute of Aeronautics and Astronautics
1801 Alexander Bell Dr
Suite 500
Reston, VA 20191-4344

703-264-7500
800-639-2422
FAX 703-264-7551
E-Mail: custserv@aiaa.org
Home Page: www.aiaa.org

Dr. Brian Dailey, President
Vigor Yang MD, Editor

Offers information on new advances and technology in airbreathing, propulsion systems, fuels, power generation and more.
Cost: $730.00
Frequency: Fortnightly
Circulation: 1900
Founded in 1930

2887 Journal of Rocket Motor and Propellant Developers
California Rocketry Publishing
PO Box 1242
Claremont, CA 91711-1242

626-974-9417
FAX 626-974-9407
E-Mail: 01rocket@gte.net
Home Page: www.v-serv.com/dpt

Jerry Irvine, Publisher

Technical journal covering propellant formulations, motor design, performance results and methods. Back issues available.
Cost: $499.00
16 Pages
Frequency: Annual
Circulation: 500
Founded in 1994
Printed in on matte stock

2888 Journal of the American Helicopter Society
American Helicopter Society International
217 N Washington St
Alexandria, VA 22314-2538

703-684-6777
855-247-4685

FAX 703-739-9279
E-Mail: webmaster@vtol.org
Home Page: www.vtol.org

Mike Hirschberg, Executive Director
Ashis Bagai, Associate Editor

The scope of the Journal covers the full range of research, analysis, design, manufacturing, test, operations, and support. A constantly growing list of specialty areas is included within that scope. Is distributed to the AHS membership for $20.00 and is also available for subscription.
Cost: $95.00
Frequency: Quarterly

2889 KITPLANES

Light Aircraft Manufacturers Association
2001 Steamboat Ridge Ct
Daytona Beach, FL 94588-8233

65- 59- 756
FAX 925-426-0771
E-Mail: info@lama.bz
Home Page: www.lama.bz

Dan Johnson, President

Experimental-category homebuilt aircraft.
Frequency: Monthly

2890 Maintenance Update

Helicopter Association International
1635 Prince St
Alexandria, VA 22314-2898

703-683-4646
FAX 703-683-4745
Home Page: www.rotor.com

Matthew Zuccaro, President
Edward DiCampli, Executive Vice President

Provides a forum for mechanics and technicians to exchange information. It includes regulatory issues, airworthiness directives, aircraft alerts and items of special interest.
Cost: $50.00
Frequency: Quarterly

2891 Midwest Flyer Magazine

Flyer Publications
PO Box 199
Oregon, WI 53575-199

608-835-7063
FAX 608-835-7063
E-Mail: info@midwestflyer.com
Home Page: www.midwestflyer.com

Dave Weinman, Publisher/Editor

Reaches all aircraft owners in the Upper Midwest. Articles include flying travel destinations, fly-in restaurants and the issues affecting general aviation in the Midwest and nationwide.
Cost: $15.00
32 Pages
Founded in 1978

2892 NAFI Magazine

National Association of Flight Instructors
730 Grand Street
Allegan, MI 49010

920-426-6801
866-806-6156
FAX 920-426-6865
E-Mail: nafi@nafinet.org
Home Page: www.nafinet.org

Jason Blair, Executive Director

A monthly magazine published by the National Association of Flight Instructors.
Cost: $39.00
18 Pages
Frequency: Monthly
Circulation: 5400
Founded in 1967

2893 NAFI Mentor

National Association of Flight Instructors
730 Grand Street
Allegan, MI 49010

920-426-6801
866-806-6156
FAX 920-426-6865
E-Mail: nafi@nafinet.org
Home Page: www.nafinet.org

Jason Blair, Executive Director
Rusty Sachs, Executive Director

Membership includes this magazine created exclusively for flight instructors.
20 Pages
Frequency: Monthly

2894 NASA Tech Briefs

Associated Business Publications International
261 5th Avenue
Suite 1901
New York, NY 10016

212-490-3999
FAX 212-986-7864
E-Mail: linda@techbriefs.com
Home Page: www.techbriefs.com

Dominic Mucchetti, CEO
Linda Bell, Editor
Marie Claussell, Circulation Manager
Domenic Mucchetti, CEO
Zoe Wai, Manager

Features exclusive reports of innovations developed by NASA and its partners that can be applied to develop new and improved products and solve engineering or manufacturing problems.
Cost: $49.00
Frequency: Monthly
Circulation: 30000
Founded in 1985

2895 Naval Aviation News

Naval Historical Center
805 Kidder Breese Street SE
Washington Navy Yard
Washington, DC 20374-5060

202-433-4882
FAX 202-433-8200
E-Mail: navymuseum@navy.mil
Home Page: www.history.navy.mil

Wendy Lelend, Managing Editor
Admiral Jay A. DeLoach, Director

Professional magazine of naval aviation.
Cost: $21.00
42 Pages
Frequency: Monthly
Circulation: 25,000
ISSN: 0028-1417
Founded in 1917
Printed in 4 colors on glossy stock

2896 Ninety-Nines News

Ninety-Nines
4300 Amelia Earhart Dr
Suite A
Oklahoma City, OK 73159-1106

405-685-7969
800-994-1929
FAX 405-685-7985
Home Page: www.ninety-nines.org

Laura Ohrenberg, Manager
Susan Larson, President
Boby Row, Editor
Pat Theberge, Vice President

A bi-monthly magazine published by Ninety-Nines.
Cost: $20.00
Circulation: 6500
Founded in 1929

2897 Northwest Airlifter

PO Box 98801
Tacoma, WA 98498

253-584-1212
800-293-1216
FAX 253-581-5962

Tom Swarner, CEO

Features news, mission stories and entertainment for military personnel and families of McChord AFB.
Frequency: Weekly

2898 Overhaul & Maintenance

McGraw Hill
1221 Avenue of the Americas
New York, NY 10020-1095

212-512-2000
800-525-5003
FAX 212-512-3840
E-Mail: p18cs@mcgraw-hill.com
Home Page: www.mcgraw-hill.com

Harold W McGraw III, CEO

Information for people in airlines, flight departments, maintenance operations, maintenance bases, military logistics, issues on safety, quality, and compliance in the aviation aftermarket.
Cost: $54.00
Frequency: Monthly
Circulation: 35000
ISSN: 0031-1588

2899 PRA Rotorcraft E-Zine

Popular Rotorcraft Association
PO Box 68
Mentone, IN 46539

574-353-7227
FAX 574-353-7021
E-Mail: prahq@medt.com
Home Page: www.pra.org

Igor Bensen, Founder
Douglas Barker, President
Tim O'Connor, VP
Cost: $42.00
Frequency: Monthly
Circulation: 1500

2900 Parachutist Magazine

United States Parachute Association
5401 Southpoint Centre Blvd
Fredericksburg, VA 22407-2612

540-604-9740
FAX 540-604-9741
E-Mail: uspa@uspa.org
Home Page: www.uspa.org
Social Media: *Facebook, Twitter*

Jay Stokes, President
Ed Scott, Executive Director

Supporting safe skydiving and those who enjoy it.
Cost: $4.50
112 Pages
Frequency: Monthly
Circulation: 35000
Founded in 1946

2901 Pipers

Pipers Owner Society
N7450 Aanstad Rd
Iola, WI 54945

715-445-5000
866-697-4737
FAX 715-445-4053
E-Mail: help@piperowner.org
Home Page: www.piperowner.org

Keith Mathiowetz, Editor
Daniel Weiler, Executive Director
Joe Jones, Publisher

The official magazine of the Piper Owners Society.
Cost: $9.95
55 Pages
Frequency: Monthly
Circulation: 8400
Mailing list available for rent: 2750 names
Printed in 4 colors

2902 Plane and Pilot
Werner Publishing
12121 Wilshire Blvd
12th Floor
Los Angeles, CA 90025-1168

310-820-1500
FAX 310-826-5008
E-Mail: editors@planeandpilotmag.com
Home Page: www.wernerpublishing.com

Steve Werner, Owner

Articles on general aviation from light single-engine planes to medium weight twins and related products.
Cost: $11.97
Frequency: Monthly
Founded in 1965

2903 Powered Sport Flying Mangazine
Popular Rotorcraft Association
PO Box 68
Mentone, IN 46539

574-353-7227
FAX 574-353-7021
E-Mail: prahq@medt.com
Home Page: www.pra.org

Igor Bensen, Founder
B Scott Lewis, President
Tim O'Connor, VP

Devoted exclusively to homebuilt rotorcraft. Also has information, technical articles, photos of autogyros and helicopters, safety tips and news of new products for rotorcraft builders and pilots.
2000 Attendees
Frequency: August

2904 Professional Pilot
Queensmith Communications
30 S Quaker Ln
Suite 300
Alexandria, VA 22314-4596

703-370-0606
FAX 703-370-7082
E-Mail: editorial@propilotmag.com
Home Page: www.propilotmag.com

Murray Smith, Owner
Anthony Herrera, General Manager
Phil Rose, Managing Editor
Ivor Tafro, Communications Manager

Offers information for career pilots.
Cost: $50.00
Frequency: Monthly
Circulation: 35000
ISSN: 0191-6238
Founded in 1966
Printed in 4 colors on glossy stock

2905 ROTOR Magazine
Helicopter Association International
1635 Prince St
Alexandria, VA 22314-2898

703-683-4646
FAX 703-683-4745
Home Page: www.rotor.com

Matthew Zuccaro, President

Dedicated to exclusively to the civil helicopter industry. It covers pertinent helicopter operations, safety and regulatory issues including an FAA question and answer column, legislative and lobbying issues, and HAI committee and member activities. Advertising space is available is this publication. Subscription included

with membership.
Cost: $15.00
Frequency: Quarterly

2906 Rotor & Wing
Access Intelligence
4 Choke Cherry Rd
2nd Fl
Rockville, MD 20850-4024

301-354-2000
FAX 301-340-0542
E-Mail: asteinebach@pbimedia.com
Home Page: www.aviationtoday.com
Social Media: *Facebook, Twitter, LinkedIn*

Don Pazour, CEO
Julian Clover, Managing Editor
Jim McKenna, Manager

Semitechnical information for helicopter industry, both civil and military. Includes pilot reports, features, news and product section.
Cost: $90.99
88 Pages
Frequency: Monthly
Circulation: 33,400
Founded in 1977

2907 Rotorcraft Magazine
Popular Rotorcraft Association
PO Box 68
Mentone, IN 46539

574-353-7227
FAX 574-353-7021
E-Mail: prahq@medt.com
Home Page: www.pra.org

B Scott Lewis, President
Tim O'Connor, VP

Devoted exclusively to homebuilt rotorcraft. Free to members.
Cost: $26.00
60 Pages
Founded in 1963

2908 Russian Aeronautics
Allerton Press
250 W 57th St
New York, NY 10107-2099

212-459-0535
FAX 646-424-9695
E-Mail: journals@allertonpress.com
Home Page: www.allertonpress.com

W Shalof, Publisher
Vyacheslav A Firsov, Editor-in-Chief

The sole scientific-technical journal in Russia publishing articles on fundamental research, application, and developments in the field of aeronautical, space, rocket science and engineering that are carried out at institutes of higher education, research institutes, design bureaus, and branch enterprises.Published in English and Russian.
Cost: $1945.00
Frequency: Quarterly
ISSN: 1068-7998
Founded in 1971

2909 Soaring Magazine
Soaring Society of America
5425 W Jack Gomez Boulevard
PO Box 2100
Hobbs, NM 88241-2100

505-392-1177
FAX 505-392-8154
E-Mail: dlayton@ssa.org
Home Page: www.ssa.org

Susan Dew, Staff Writer
Amaris Bradford, Editorial Assistant
Denise Layton, Managing Editor
Dennis Wright, Executive Director

Each issue brings you the latest developments on safety issues, delightful accounts of individual soaring accomplishments, a sharing of ideas

and experiences, tips from the great soaring pilots of our times, and much more.
Cost: $26.00
60 Pages
Frequency: Monthly
Founded in 1932

2910 Space News
Army Times Publishing Company
6883 Commercial Dr
Springfield, VA 22151-4202

703-750-7400
800-368-5718
FAX 703-750-8622
E-Mail: cust-svc@gannettgov.com
Home Page: www.armytimes.com

Elaine Howard, CEO
Tobias Naegele, Editor-in-Chief
Alex Neill, Managing Editor
Judy McCoy, Publisher

For top level executives in government and industry worldwide. Devoted exclusively to issues for military government and commercial space.
Cost: $55.00
Frequency: Weekly
Circulation: 360000
Founded in 1990

2911 Space Times
American Astronautical Society
6352 Rolling Mill Place
Suite 102
Springfield, VA 22152-2370

703-866-0020
FAX 703-866-3526
E-Mail: aas@astronautical.org
Home Page: www.astronautical.org

Frank Slazer, President
James Kirkpatrick, Executive Director
Lin D. Wigbels, Executive Vice President

The voice of the AAS, presenting thought provoking ideas and opinions, features articles on salient issues in space policy and future exploration, and reviews and notes of interest to both the professional and popular community of space flight advocates.
Cost: $85.00
Frequency: Bi-Monthly
Circulation: 1300
ISSN: 1933-2793

2912 The Airline Handbook
Air Transport Association of America
1301 Pennsylvania Ave NW
Suite 1100
Washington, DC 20004-1738

202-626-4000
800-497-3326
FAX 202-626-4166
E-Mail: a4a@airlines.org
Home Page: www.airlines.org
Social Media: *Twitter, LinkedIn*

Nicholas Calio, President
Steve Lott, VP Communications

2913 Trade-A-Plane
TAP Publishing Company
174 4th St
Crossville, TN 38555-4303

931-484-5137
800-337-5263
FAX 931-484-2532
E-Mail: info@trade-a-plane.com
Home Page: www.trade-a-plane.com

Cosby A Stone, CEO
L Stone, Circulation Manager

World's largest advertising periodical for general aviation.
Cost: $14.95
Frequency: Monthly
Circulation: 118000
Founded in 1937

2914 Ultralight Flying
Glider Rider
1085 Bailey Avenue
Chattanooga, TN 37404

423-629-5375
FAX 423-629-5379
Home Page: www.ultralightflying.com

Tracy Knauss, Publisher
Sharon Hill, Editor

Conventional and motorized ultralight flying.
Cost: $36.95
48 Pages
Frequency: Monthly
Circulation: 50000+
Founded in 1973
Printed in on newsprint stock

2915 Vertiflite
American Helicopter Society International
217 N Washington St
Alexandria, VA 22314-2538

703-684-6777
855-247-4685
FAX 703-739-9279
E-Mail: staff@vtol.org
Home Page: www.vtol.org

Michael Hirschberg, Executive Director
Kim Smith, Editor
Mike Hirschberg, Managing Editor

Magazine published for the vertical flight industry, pursuing excellence within the business, stimulating research, debate and expert opinion.
Cost: $80.00
72 Pages
Frequency: Monthly
Circulation: 12000
ISSN: 0042-4455
Founded in 1943
Printed in 4 colors on glossy stock

2916 Water Flying
Seaplane Pilots Association
3859 Laird Blvd
Lakeland, FL 33811

863-701-7979
888-772-8923
FAX 863-701-7588
E-Mail: spa@seaplanes.org
Home Page: www.seaplanes.org

Steve McCaughey, Executive Director
Randy Juen, Vice President
J.J. Frey, President

Features articles covering everything from pilot technique and safety to destinations and personalities. Each issue includes industry news and an update on regulatory issues across the country. The March/April issue is our Directory Special, with flight school and float directories.
Cost: $45.00
32 Pages
Circulation: 7500
ISSN: 0733-1754
Founded in 1972
Mailing list available for rent
Printed in on glossy stock

2917 Western Flyer
Northwest Flyer

PO Box 98786
Tacoma, WA 98498-0786

253-968-3422
FAX 253-588-4005

Dave Sinclair, Publisher
Kirk Gormley, Editor

Covering general aviation, including all aspects of business and sport aviation.
Cost: $24.00
84 Pages
Frequency: BiWeekly
Circulation: 38,000

2918 Wings
Sentry Books
P.O. Box 881526
San Diego, CA 92168

818-368-2012
E-Mail: support@airwingmedia.com
Home Page: www.wingsairpower.com

Mike Machat, Publisher/Editor

Historic aviation, heavy on photos, artwork, drawings, interviews with aviation designers, pilots, engineers.
Cost: $44.00
56 Pages
Frequency: Monthly
Circulation: 30000
ISSN: 1067-0637
Founded in 1971

2919 Wings West
Wiesner Publishing
6160 South Syracuse
Suite 300
Greenwood Village, CO 80111

303-662-5200
FAX 303-397-7619
Home Page: www.wiesnerpublishing.com

Babette Andre, Editor
Becky Stairs, Advertising Executive
Dan Wiesner, CEO

Information for the mountain aviation community on various facets of western flying, including travel and safety for active pilots.
Cost: $17.97
72 Pages
Frequency: Bi-Monthly

2920 Wings of Gold Magazine
Association of Naval Aviation
2550 Huntington Avenue
Suite 201
Alexandria, VA 22303-1400

703-960-6806
FAX 703-960-6807
E-Mail: anahqtr@aol.com
Home Page: www.anahq.org

R M Rausa, Editor
Linda Bubien, Advertising Director
Walter Massenburg, President
Jacqueline M Hayes, Editorial Assistant

Articles and commentary designed to inform the public of the value of a strong maritime air posture to US national policy. Also, articles on subjects related to Navy, Marine Corps and Coast Guard aviation, such as personnel technology, history, readiness, aircraft and weapon systems and budgetary issues within DOD and before the Congress.
Cost: $25.00

2921 World Airshow News
Flyer Publications
PO Box 975
East Troy, WI 53120-0975

262-642-2450
FAX 262-642-4374
E-Mail: jeffparnau@gmail.com

Home Page: www.airshowmag.com
Social Media: Facebook, Twitter, LinkedIn

Jim Froneberger, Editor
Sandra Ruka, Advertising Sales
Jim Froneberger, Editor
Cost: $24.95
Frequency: Nine Times a Year
Circulation: 6000

Trade Shows

2922 AAC Annual Conference & Exposition
Airport Consultants Council
908 King Street
Suite 100
Alexandria, VA 22314-3121

703-683-5900
FAX 703-583-2564
E-Mail: info@acconline.org
Home Page: www.acconline.org
Social Media: Facebook, Twitter, LinkedIn

Paula P Hochstetler, President
Emily VanderBush, Marketing & Membership Coordinator
John B Reynolds, Coordinator of Communications
Sharon Brown, Director, Programs & Finance

Enhanced networking programs; workshops; keynote speakers; exhibitors.
Frequency: July

2923 AAC/AAAE Airport Planning, Design & Construction Symposium
Airport Consultants Council
908 King Street
Suite 100
Alexandria, VA 22314-3121

703-683-5900
FAX 703-683-2564
E-Mail: info@acconline.org
Home Page: www.acconline.org
Social Media: Facebook, Twitter, LinkedIn

Paula P Hochstetler, President
Emily VanderBush, Marketing & Membership Coordinator
John B Reynolds, Coordinator of Communications
Sharon Brown, Director, Programs & Finance

Planning and development, land side/terminal facilities development, airside/airfield facility development, program and construction management, and information technology are the focus of the symposium.
600 Attendees
Frequency: Spring

2924 AAS National Conference
American Astronautical Society
6352 Rolling Mill Place
Suite 102
Springfield, VA 22152-2370

703-866-0020
FAX 703-866-3526
E-Mail: aas@astronautical.org
Home Page: www.astronautical.org

Frank Slazer, President
James Kirkpatrick, Executive Director
350 Attendees
Frequency: Annual, November

2925 ADMA International Fall Conference
Aviation Distributors & Manufacturers Association

100 North 20th Street
Suite 400
Philadelphia, PA 19103-1442

215-320-3872
FAX 215-564-2175
E-Mail: adma@fernley.com
Home Page: www.adma.org

Michael Shaw, President
F Charles Elkins, Past President
Kristen Olszewski, Executive Director
Meg Taft, Meeting Manager

Educational and informational presentations, group activities, and planned networking functions, including Private Conference Sessions.
Frequency: May, November

2926 AEA International Convention & Trade Show
Aircraft Electronic Association
3570 NE Ralph Powell Road
Lee's Summit, MO 64064

816-347-8400
FAX 816-347-8405
E-Mail: info@aea.net
Home Page: www.aea.net
Social Media: *Facebook, Twitter, LinkedIn, Youtube*

Paula Derks, President
Debra McFarland, Executive Vice President
Aaron Ward, Information Services Director
Mike Adamson, VP, Member Training & Education

Workshops, training sessions, keynote speakers, and hundreds of exhibitors in the field of aviation electronics.
Frequency: April

2927 AHS International Annual Forum & Tech Display
American Helicopter Society
217 N Washington Street
Alexandria, VA 22314

703-684-6777
FAX 703-739-9279
E-Mail: staff@vtol.org
Home Page: www.vtol.org
Social Media: *Facebook, Twitter, LinkedIn, RSS, YouTube*

Michael Hirschberg, Executive Director
Kay Brackins, Deputy Director/Production Mgr
David Renzi, Director of Meetings & Marketing

Exhibits for technical professionals in aircraft design, engineering, government, operators and industry executives. Over 200 presentations on aerodynamics, acoustics, dynamics, operations, product support, propulsion, testing and evaluation, and other areas. Technology display is concurrent with the Forum and is presented by leading manufacturers, service providers, defense contractors, universities and r&d organizations.
Founded in 1943

2928 AIAA New Horizons Forum & Expo at the Aerospace Science Meeting
American Institute of Aeronautics & Astronautics
1801 Alexander Bell Drive
Suite 500
Reston, VA 20191-4344

703-264-7500
800-639-2422
FAX 703-264-7551
E-Mail: tammym@aiaa.org
Home Page: www.aiaa.org

Social Media: *Facebook, Twitter, LinkedIn, Youtube*

Cort Durocher, President
Tammy Marko, Director
Lawrence Garrett, Editor

A forum for scientists and engineers from industry, government and academia to share and disseminate knowledge and research. New Horizons will feature speakers sharing about new technology, challenges, opportunities, and trends, as well as panel discussions. The Aerospace Expo will showcase exhibits from industry, government and small businesses with hardware and software demos, discussions, and opportunities for side meetings.
Frequency: Annual
Founded in 1930

2929 ASA Annual Conference
Aviation Suppliers Association
2233 Wisconsin Ave. NW
Suite 503
Washington, DC 20007

202-347-6899
FAX 202-347-6894
Home Page:
www.aviationsuppliers.org/Annual-Conference
Social Media: *Facebook, Twitter*

Michele Dickstein, President
Tony Brigham, Coordinator, Programs & Services

Annual event for the aviation distribution industry featuring workshops, networking opportunities and a vendor showcase.
Frequency: Annual

2930 Aerofast SAE Aerospace Automated Fastening Conference & Exposition
Society of Automotive Engineers
400 Commonwealth Drive
Warrendale, PA 15096-0001

72- 77- 484
877-606-7323
FAX 724-776-0790
Home Page: www.sae.org

Diane Applegate, Meetings/Exhibits
David Shutt, CEO

Annual show of 45 manufacturers or suppliers of fasteners, assembly systems, CNC's, tooling and fixtures, fully automated systems.
400 Attendees
Frequency: September
Founded in 1990

2931 Aerospace Atlantic
Society of Automotive Engineers
400 Commonwealth Drive
Warrendale, PA 15096-0001

724-776-4841
877-606-7323
FAX 724-776-0790
Home Page: www.sae.org

David Shutt, President

Annual show of 30 exhibitors of aircraft systems and components, engineering services, electronics, power systems and computer services.
700 Attendees
Frequency: 84,000 Members

2932 Aerospace Medical Association Meeting
Aerospace Medical Association
320 S Henry Street
Alexandria, VA 22314-3579

703-739-2240
FAX 703-739-9652

E-Mail: inquiries@asma.org
Home Page: www.asma.org

Jeffrey Sventek, Executive Director
Gisselle Vargas, Operations Manager

Provides a multi-faceted forum for all aerospace medical disciplines and concurrently provides continuing education credits for those attending the meeting. Lectures, seminars, panels, poster presentations, workshops, film reports, and technical and scientific exhibits present data on the latest results of clinical and research studies.
Frequency: Annual

2933 Aerospace Testing Expo
Society of Flight Test Engineers
44814 N Elm Avenue
Lancaster, CA 93534

661-949-2095
FAX 661-949-2096
E-Mail: sfte@sfte.org
Home Page: www.sfte.org
Social Media: *Facebook, Twitter, LinkedIn, Youtube*

Peter Donath, President
Michael Barrlett, Vice President
Frequency: April

2934 Aerotech: Society of Automotive Engineers Aerospace Technology Congress
Society of Automotive Engineers
400 Commonwealth Drive
Warrendale, PA 15096-0001

724-776-4841
877-606-7323
FAX 724-776-0790
E-Mail: advertising@sae.org
Home Page: www.sae.org

David Shutt, President

Annual show of 80 suppliers to aerospace engineers and designers.
2500 Attendees
Frequency: October

2935 Agricultural Aviation Convention
National Agricultural Aviation Association
1440 Duke Street
Alexandria, VA 22314

202-546-5722
FAX 202-546-5726
E-Mail: information@agaviation.org
Home Page: www.agaviation.org

Andrew Moore, Executive Director
Jay Calleja, Manager,Programs, & Events

Information on agricultural aviation business, agricultural aircraft, legislative issues, pesticides, new products and services, safety, maintenance, people, state and regional association news. 135 booths.
1300 Attendees

2936 Air Cargo Forum and Exposition
The International Air Cargo Association
PO Box 661510
Miami, FL 33266-1510

786-265-7011
FAX 786-265-7012
E-Mail: secgen@tiacca.org
Home Page: www.tiaca.org

Tom Davis, Deputy Director, Exhibits
Michael Steen, Chairman
Oliver Evans, Vice Chairman

This is the premier show for the Air Cargo Industry.
3000 Attendees
Frequency: September

2937 Air Medical Transport Conference
Association of Air Medical Services

909 N Washington Street
Suite 410
Alexandria, VA 22314

703-836-8732
FAX 703-836-8920
E-Mail: information@aams.org
Home Page: www.aams.org

John Fiegel, Executive Director/CEO
Blair Marie Beggan,
Communications/Marketing Director
Natasha Ross, Education/Meetings Manager
Elena Sierra, Membership Manager

Attendees are emergency medical and critical care professionals from both hospital and independent providers of air and ground medical transport services. CEO's, program directors, medical directors, physicians, nurses, respiratory therapists, paramedics, pilots, communication specialists and mechanics.
1800 Attendees
Frequency: Annual/Fall
Founded in 1980
Mailing list available for rent: 1600 names

2938 Air Medical Transport Conference (AMTC)

Association of Air Medical Services
909 N Washington Street
Suite 410
Alexandria, VA 22314

703-836-8732
FAX 703-836-8920
E-Mail: information@aams.org
Home Page: www.aams.org

Rick Sherlock, President
Natasha Ross, Education & Meeetings Manager
Elena Sierra, Membership Manager
Blair Marie Beggan, Communication & Marketing Manager

Provides up-to-date information on the latest techniques and innovative approaches to air medical practice from community experts, and continuing education credits opportunities; keynote speakers and educational offerings, plus technology demos and networking opportunities; and the largest trade show of the industry with exhibits from hundreds of providers.
Frequency: March

2939 Air Show Trade Expo International

Dayton International Airport
3800 Wright Drive
Suite A
Vandalia, OH 45377

937-898-5901
877-359-3291
FAX 937-898-5121
E-Mail: info@daytonairshow.com
Home Page: www.daytonairshow.com

Terry Greivous, Executive Director
Brenda Kerfoot, General Manager

One hundred and thirty three booths that encompass all aspects of the global aerospace industry. Commercial and military aircraft and equipment, plus major suppliers' products and services display.
12M Attendees
Frequency: July

2940 Air Traffic Control Association Convention

Air Traffic Control Association
1101 King St
Suite 300
Alexandria, VA 22314

703-299-2430
FAX 703-299-2437

E-Mail: info@atca.org
Home Page: www.atca.org

Peter Dumont, President
Kenneth Carlisle, Director of Meetings & Expositions

Containing over 325 booths and exhibits of air traffic control products and services.
4,500 Attendees
Frequency: 3 times per year

2941 Aircraft Electronics Association Annual Convention & Trade Show

Aircraft Electronics Association
3570 NE Ralph Powell Road
Lee's Summit, MO 64064

816-347-8400
FAX 816-347-8405
E-Mail: info@aea.net
Home Page: www.aea.net

Paula Derks, President
Debra McFarland, VP

Annual show of 131 exhibitors of industry related equipment and supplies.
1500 Attendees
Frequency: March/April Annual
Founded in 1980

2942 Aircraft Owners & Pilots Association Expo

Aircraft Owners & Pilots Association
421 Aviation Way
Frederick, MD 21701

301-695-2000
800-872-2672
FAX 301-695-2375
E-Mail: aopahq@aopa.org
Home Page: www.aopa.org

Craig Fuller, President
Robert Moran, COO

From the latest technology, to tools and flight gear, you'll find today's best products. 500 Exhibit Booths.
Frequency: June

2943 Aircraft Owners Pilots Association Expo

Aircraft Owners & Pilots Association
421 Aviation Way
Frederick, MD 21701

301-695-2000
888-462-3976
FAX 301-695-2375
Home Page: www.aopa.org

Craig Fuller, President
Robert Moran, COO

Annual exhibits of single-engine and multi-engine aircraft, avionics, financing information and related equipment, supplies and services. Expo offers 75 seminar hours covering the latest safety, medical, proficiency, ownership, and technology issues. Over 500 booths.
Frequency: November

2944 Airliners International

World Airline Historical Society
PO Box 489
Ocoee, FL 34761

904-221-1446
FAX 407-522-9352
E-Mail: president@WAHSOnline.com
Home Page: www.wahsonline.com
Social Media: *Facebook, Twitter*

Duane Young, President
Craig Morris, VP
1000 Attendees
Frequency: Annual/August
Founded in 1977

2945 Airlines Electronic Engineering Committee Conference

Airlines Electronic Engineering Committee
2551 Riva Road
Annapolis, MD 21401-7435

410-266-4000
FAX 410-266-2047
Home Page: www.arinc.com

Daniel A Martinec, Chairman
Roger S Goldberg, Show Contact

Annual show and exhibit of air transport avionics equipment and systems.
Frequency: October

2946 Airport Systems Action Planning Meeting

ARINC
2551 Riva Road
Annapolis, MD 21401

410-664-4000
80 -63 -688
FAX 410-266-2329
E-Mail: flightops@arinc.com
Home Page: www.arinc.com
Social Media: *Facebook, Twitter, LinkedIn*

Lee Suarez, Staff VP
John M Belcher, Chairman/CEO
Stephen Waechter, VP Business Operations/CFO
Linda Hartwig, Sr Dir Corporate Communications

The meeting format will include organizational, technical, and project updates from the ARINC management team.
Frequency: September
Founded in 1920

2947 Airports Council International - North America Annual Conference & Expo

Airports Council International
1775 K Street NW
Suite 500
Washington, DC 20006

202-293-8500
FAX 202-331-1362
E-Mail: apeters@aci-na,org
Home Page: www.aci-na.org
Social Media: *Facebook, Twitter, LinkedIn, Youtube*

Gregory Principato, President
Deborah McElroy, VP
Nancy Zimini, SVP Administration and Operations

Representatives from more than 100 airports around the world attend this exhibition and conference; seminars, discussions and speakers about air travel and the industry, developing legal affairs, challenges and best practices; hundreds of exhibitors.
Frequency: September
Founded in 1948

2948 Airports Council International: North America Convention

Airports Council International-North America
1775 K Street NW
Suite 500
Washington, DC 20006

202-293-8500
FAX 202-331-1362
Home Page: www.aci-na.org

Deborah McElroy, Vice President
Nancy Zimini, SVP Administration & Operations
Juliet Wright, Senior Director Public Relations
Gregory Principato, President

Annual show and exhibit of air transportation equipment, supplies and services.
Frequency: Annual

2949 American Bonanza Society Convention
Midcontinent Airport
PO Box 12888
Wichita, KS 67277

316-945-1700
FAX 316-945-1710
E-Mail: ABSMail@bonanza.org
Home Page: www.bonanza.org

Nancy Johnson, Executive Director
Peggy L Fuksa, Events Coordinator

Annual convention featuring educational seminars and 75-100 exhibits of equipment, supplies and services for the aviation industry, including aftermarket products, safety items and computer weather services.
1200 Attendees
Frequency: September
Founded in 1967

2950 Annual Repair Symposium
Aeronautical Repair Station Association
121 N Henry Street
Alexandria, VA 22314-2903

703-739-9543
FAX 703-739-9488
E-Mail: arsa@arsa.org
Home Page: www.arsa.org
Social Media: *Facebook, Twitter, LinkedIn, Youtube*

Craig Fabian, VP
Daniel Fisher, VP

The Symposium will include a variety of sessions on topical subjects. Legislative Day will inform you about the issues that affect your business, and includes the opportunity for you to arrange Capitol Hill meetings with your representatives, senators and congressional staff.
Frequency: Annual/March

2951 Annual Scientific Meeting
Aerospace Medical Association
320 S Henry Street
Alexandria, VA 22314-3579

703-739-2240
FAX 703-739-9652
E-Mail: rrayman@asma.org
Home Page: www.asma.org

Jeffrey Sventek, Executive Director
Gisselle Vargas, Operations Manager
Russell Rayman MD, Executive Director

Provides a multi-faceted forum for all aerospace medical disciplines and concurrently provides continuing education credits for those attending the meeting.
3000 Attendees
Frequency: Annual/May
Founded in 1929
Mailing list available for rent

2952 Army Aviation Association of America Convention
Army Aviation Association of America
755 Main Street
Suite 4D
Monroe, CT 06468-2830

203-268-2450
FAX 203-268-5870
E-Mail: aaaa@quad-a.org
Home Page: www.quad-a.org
Social Media: *Facebook, Twitter, Youtube*

Daniel J Petrosky, President
Howard Yellen, Senior Vice President
E.J. Sinclair, Secretary

A show of 275 or more exhibitors both military and industry displaying technology and material pertinent to the army aviation community.
6000 Attendees
Frequency: Annual/May
Founded in 1978

2953 Arnic Aviation Customer Meeting
British Telecommunications
2551 Riva Road
Annapolis, MD 21401

410-266-4000
800-633-6882
FAX 410-266-2329
E-Mail: flightops@arinc.com
Home Page: www.arinc.com
Social Media: *Facebook, Twitter, LinkedIn, Youtube*

Lee Suarez, Staff VP
John M Belcher, Chairman/CEO
Stephen Waechter, VP Business Operations/CFO
Linda Hartwig, Sr Dir Corporate Communications

Up to date information on the current and future products and services of Arnic and its strategic partners in Asia.
Frequency: May
Founded in 1920

2954 Arnic Global Communications Workshop
British Telecommunications
2551 Riva Road
Annapolis, MD 21401

410-266-4000
800-633-6882
FAX 410-266-2329
E-Mail: flightops@arinc.com
Home Page: www.arinc.com
Social Media: *Facebook, Twitter, LinkedIn, Youtube*

Lee Suarez, Staff VP
John M Belcher, Chairman/CEO
Stephen Waechter, VP Business Operations/CFO
Linda Hartwig, Sr Dir Corporate Communications

Concentrates on the communications needs of the airlines serving the Latin America/Caribbean region, and provides information on the benefits of implementing a data link program and associated applications.
Frequency: May
Founded in 1920

2955 Aviation Insurance Association Conference
Aviation Insurance Association
400 Admiral Blvd
Kansas City, MO 64106

816-221-8488
FAX 816-472-7765
E-Mail: mandie@aiaweb.org
Home Page: www.aiaweb.org
Social Media: *Facebook*

Trevor Light, President
Paul Herbers, Vice President
Meredith Carr, Director, Marketing & Membership

Provides a forum for the biggest names and best minds in the aviation insurance industry. Offers top-notch speakers, continuing education classes, time with vendors and opportunities to network and develop relationships that last a lifetime.
Frequency: Annual
Founded in 1976

2956 Aviation Services and Suppliers Supershow
National Air Transportation Association
4226 King Street
Alexandria, VA 22302

703-845-9000
800-808-6282
FAX 703-845-8176
Home Page: www.nata.aero

James K Coyne, President
Eric Byer, VP
Diane Gleason, Manager Meetings/Conventions
Eric R Byer, Dir Government/Industry Affairs

Workshop, conference, seminar and 700 exhibits of aviation products & services for fixed base and air charter operators.
5000 Attendees
Frequency: May/Annual

2957 Aviation Show South America
American Aerospace & Defense Industries
212 Carengie Center
Suite 203
Princeton, NJ 08540

609-987-9050
FAX 609-987-0277
E-Mail: info@aadi.net
Home Page: www.aadi.net

Marianne Ferrandi, Show Contact

One hundred and seven exhibitors of areospace information.
90000 Attendees
Frequency: July

2958 Aviation Technician Education Council Conference
Aviation Technician Education Council
2090 Wexford Court
Harrisburg, PA 17112-1579

717-540-7121
FAX 717-540-7121
E-Mail: info@atec-amt.org
Home Page: www.atec-amt.org

Vince Jones, President
Richard Dumaresq, Executive Director

Annual conference and exhibits of aviation maintenance equipment, supplies and services.
150 Attendees
Frequency: April

2959 Business Information Technology Conference
Airports Council International - North America
1775 K Street NW
Suite 500
Washington, DC 20036-2463

202-293-8500
FAX 202-331-1362
E-Mail: meetings@aci-na.org
Home Page: www.aci-na.org

Gregory Principato, President
Diedre Clemmons, Director, Conferences
Cassandra Jackson, Manager, Conferences

Hear from industry experts and peers on the latest way to deal with IT challenges, maximize the value of your IT infrastructure and anticipate new technologies.
Frequency: Annual

2960 Civil Air Patrol Annual Conference
Civil Air Patrol
105 S Hansell Street
Building 714
Maxwell AFB, AL 36112-6332

334-834-2236
877-227-9142

FAX 334-953-4262
Home Page: www.capmembers.com

Brig Gen Amy Courter, Interim National
Commander
1.2M Attendees
Frequency: August
Founded in 1930

**2961 Civil Aviation Medical Association
Conference**
Civil Aviation Medical Association
PO Box 2382
Peachtree City, GA 30269-2382

77- 48- 010
FAX 77- 48- 008
E-Mail: david.millett@yahoo.com
Home Page: www.civilavmed.com

James Heins MD, President
David Millet MD, Executive VP
Gordon Ritter, Secretary/Treasurer

Annual conference and exhibits of aviation
medical equipment, supplies and services. Containing 15 booths.
250 Attendees
Frequency: October
Founded in 1948

2962 Defense & Security Symposium
International Society for Optical
Engineering
PO Box 10
Bellingham, WA 98227-0010

360-676-3290
888-504-8171
FAX 360-647-1445
E-Mail: CustomerService@SPIE.org
Home Page: www.spie.org

Dr John C Carrano, Contact Person
Dr Larry B Stotts, Contact Person
Dr. Katarina Svanberg, President
William Arnold, Vice President

A large, unclassified international symposium
related to sensors and sensor networks.
5700 Attendees
Frequency: March

2963 Economic Specialty Conference
Airports Association Council International
1775 K Street NW
Suite 500
Washington, DC 20006

202-293-8500
FAX 202-331-1362
Home Page: www.aci-na.org

Gregory Principato, President
Nancy Zimini, VP
Christopher Oswald, SVP Technical Affairs
Ian A Redhead, VP Airport Services
Patricia Hahn, EVP Operations/General
Counsel

Provided with information on the latest economic trends for airports and the airport industry. Attendees include executive directors and
CFOs from airports throughout North America,
plys representatives from insurance companies
and airport concessionaires.
Frequency: May

**2964 Experimental Aircraft Association
AirVenture**
Experimental Aircraft Association
3000 Poberezny Road
PO Box 3086
Oshkosh, WI 54902

920-426-4800
800-236-4800
FAX 920-232-7772

E-Mail: webmaster@eaa.org
Home Page: www.airventure.org

Tom Poberezny, President
David Berkley, Communications Dirctor
Adam Smith, VP Member Services

Recreational aviation event, with more than
765,000 people and 10,000 airplanes attending.
Containing 900 booths and 730 exhibits.
765M Attendees
Founded in 1953

2965 Fall Education Conference
University Aviation Association
3410 Skyway Drive
Auburn, AL 36830-6444

334-844-2434
FAX 334-844-2432
E-Mail: uaamail@uaa.aero
Home Page: www.uaa.aero

Carolyn Williamson, Executive Director
Mary Chandler, Coordinator Office
Administration
Founded in 1947

2966 GTO Annual Convention & Fly In
Pipers Owner Society & Cessna Owner
Organization
PO Box 5000
Iola, WI 54945

715-445-5000
888-692-3776
FAX 715-445-4053
E-Mail: help@piperowner.org
Home Page: www.gto.aircraftownersgroup.com

Dan Weiler, Executive Director
Joe Jones, Publisher

Annual fly in prior to the EAA AirVenture.
150 Attendees
Frequency: Annual

2967 Gate Way to Oshkosh
Cessna Owner Organization
N7450 Aanstad Rd
Iola, WI 54945

715-445-5000
888-692-3776
FAX 715-445-4053
E-Mail: help@cessnaowner.org
Home Page: www.cessnaowner.org

Dan Weiler, Executive Director
Joe Jones, Publisher
150 Members
Frequency: Annual

2968 Heli-Expo
Helicopter Association International
1635 Prince Street
Alexandria, VA 22314-2818

703-683-4646
FAX 703-683-4745
E-Mail: heliexpo@rotor.com
Home Page: www.rotor.com

Matthew Zuccaro, President
Edward DiCampli, Executive Vice President
Elaine Little, Administrative Services Manager

The world's largest tradeshow dedicated to the
international helicopter community. Attend for
new ideas, business solutions, products and services, and networking. Over 550 exhibiting
companies offering engines, avionics, instruments, modifications, helicopters for every
mission, finance, insurance, software, uniforms
and safety gear, mechanic and pilot training,
parts, and accessories.
16000 Attendees
Frequency: February

**2969 IFSA Annual Conference &
Exhibition**
Inflight Food Service Association

304 W Liberty Street
Suite 201
Louisville, KY 40202-3011

502-583-3783
FAX 502-589-3602
Home Page: www.ifsanet.com

Pam Chumley, Executive Administrator
Jim Fowler, Executive Director
Jacqueline Petty, Manager of Communications
Caitlin Ellery, Membership Manager

An opportunity to experience excellent educational speakers, panel discussions, culinary demos, and general sessions focused on important
issues in the in-flight and onboard foodservice
industry. An exhibition is held in conjunction
with the conference to exhibit the latest innovations while providing network opportunities
with key leaders and decision makers in
in-flight and railway catering.
Frequency: Annual

**2970 International Air Cargo Forum &
Exposition**
International Air Cargo Association
5600 NW 36th Street
Suite 620
Miami, FL 33266-1510

786-265-7011
FAX 786-265-7012
E-Mail: secgen@tiaca.org
Home Page: www.tiaca.org

Michael Steen, Chairman
George F Johnson, Treasurer
Daniel F Fernandez, Secretary General

Biennial trade show of the air cargo industry
featuring services and products from aircraft
manufacturers, airlines, airports, freight forwarders trade publications logistics
consultants.
4,000 Attendees
Frequency: September
Founded in 1960

**2971 Joint Airports
Environmental/Technical Committee
Meeting**
Airports Association Council International
1615 L Street
Suite 300
Washington, DC 20006

202-293-8500
888-424-7767
FAX 202-331-1362
E-Mail: memberservices@aci-na.org
Home Page: www.aci-na.org
Social Media: *Facebook, Twitter, LinkedIn*

Gregory Principato, President
Nancy Zimini, VP
Christopher Oswald, SVP Technical Affairs
Frequency: May
Founded in 1948

2972 NATA FBO Leadership Conference
National Air Transportation Association
4226 King Street
Alexandria, VA 22302

703-845-9000
800-808-6282
FAX 703-845-8176
E-Mail: info@nata-online.org
Home Page: www.nata.aero
Social Media: *Facebook, Twitter, LinkedIn*

James Sweeney, Chairperson
Thomas Hendricks, President

An opportunity for business leaders to meet
with their customers and learn about the latest
challenges and opportunities facing their industry. d seminars. The Conference will focus on
the changing climate of the industry and the developing environment. Opportunities to learn

service and marketing techniques, network and exchange best practices.
Frequency: Annual

2973 NBAA Annual Meeting & Convention
National Business Aviation Association
1200 18th Street NW
Suite 400
Washington, DC 20036

202-783-9000
FAX 702-331-8364
E-Mail: info@nbaa.org
Home Page: www.nbaa.org

Ed Bolen, President/CEO

Learning sessions, networking opportunities, 1,000 exhibitors, demonstrations and displays.
32000 Attendees
Frequency: September

2974 National Space Symposium
Space Foundation
4425 Arrowswest Drive
Colorado Springs, CO 80907

719-768-8000
800-691-4000
FAX 719-576-8801
E-Mail: web@spacefoundation.org
Home Page: www.spacefoundation.org
Social Media: *Facebook, Twitter, LinkedIn*

Martin Faga, Chairman
Elliot G Pulham, President/CEO

The National Space Symposium is the premier U.S. policy and program forum, providing an opportunity for information and interaction on all sectors of space - civil, commercial, and national security. The conference is attended by industry leaders, military and government officials and general space enthusiasts, and covered locally and nationally by broadcast, print and industry trade media.
Frequency: Annually/April

2975 Ninety Nines International Conference
International Organization of Women Pilots
4300 Amelia Earhart Road
Oklahoma City, OK 73159-1140

405-685-7969
800-994-1929
FAX 405-685-7985
E-Mail: 99s@ninety-nines.org
Home Page: www.ninety-nines.org

Susan Larson, President
Pat Theberge, VP
Corbi Bulluck, Director
Laura Ohrenberg, Headquarters Manager
Frances Luckhart, Secretary
Frequency: August

2976 PAMA Aviation Maintenance & Management Symposium
Professional Aviation Maintenance Association
972 E Tuttle Road
Building 204
Ionia, MI 48846

724-772-4092
800-356-1671
FAX 616-527-1327
E-Mail: hq@pama.org
Home Page: www.pama.org
Social Media: *Facebook, Twitter, LinkedIn*

Roger Sickler, Chairman
Jeff Gruber, Vice Chairman
John Wicht, Secretary
Frequency: March
Founded in 1972

2977 PRA International Conference
Popular Rotorcraft Association

PO Box 68
Mentone, IN 46539

574-353-7227
FAX 574-353-7021
E-Mail: prahq@medt.com
Home Page: www.pra.org

B Scott Lewis, President
Tim O'Connor, VP

Exhibits, flight demonstrations, contests, commercial exhibits, great food, forums on rotorcraft topics, and unlimited fun! There are also many other events sanctioned by PRA and its local chapters.
2000 Attendees
Frequency: August

2978 PRA International Convention Fly-In
Popular Rotorcraft Association
PO Box 68
Mentone, IN 46539

574-353-7227
FAX 574-353-7021
Home Page: www.pra.org

Igor Bensen, Founder
Scott Lewis, President
Tim O'Connor, VP

The largest gathering of homebuilt rotorcraft in the world. It has exhibits, flight demonstrations, contests, commercial exhibits, great food, forums on rotorcraft topics, and unlimited fun.
3500 Attendees
Frequency: Annual/Summer

2979 Professional Aviation Maintenance Symposium and Trade Show
Professional Aviation Maintenance Association
972 E Tuttle Road
Building 204
Ionia, MI 48846

202-300-0258
800-356-1671
FAX 616-527-1327
E-Mail: hq@pama.org
Home Page: www.pama.org

Dale Forton, President

Annual show of 200 exhibitors of aviation and aerospace products for the aviation maintenance industry.
2000 Attendees
Frequency: March

2980 Regional Airline Association Convention
Regional Airline Association
2025 M Street NW
Suite 800
Washington, DC 20036

202-367-1170
FAX 202-367-2170
E-Mail: raa@raa.org
Home Page: www.raa.org
Social Media: *Facebook, Twitter*

Roger Cohen, President
Scott Foose, Vice President

A forum for airport and airline professionals held twice a year in the spring and fall.
Frequency: May/October

2981 Regional Airline Association Spring Meeting
Regional Airline Association
2025 M Street NW
Suite 800
Washington, DC 20036

202-367-1170
FAX 202-367-2170
E-Mail: raa@raa.org

Home Page: www.raa.org
Social Media: *Facebook, Twitter*

Roger Cohen, President
Scott Foose, Vice President

Forum for airport and airline professionals.
1.6M Attendees
Frequency: May

2982 Reliability Engineering and Management Institute Conference
Univ of Arizona, Aerospace & Mechanical Engin Dept
1130 N Mountain Avenue
Building 119 Room N 517
Tucson, AZ 85721

520-621-6120
FAX 520-621-8191
E-Mail: dimitri@u.arizona.edu
Home Page: www.u.arizona.edu/~dimitri/

Dr Dimitri B Kececioglu, Manager

Provides all engineers, and particularly Reliability Managers and Engineers, and Products Assurance Managers and Engineers in government and Industry, with a working knowledge of Reliability Engineering Theory and Practice; Mechanical Reliability Prediction; Reliability Testing and Demonstration; Failure Analysis (FAMECA); Complete Industry Product Assurance strategies; Maintainability Engineering; Reliability and Quality Management; Manufacturing Techniques, and more.
Frequency: Nov Arizona

2983 Reliability Testing Institute
University Of Arizona
1130 N Mountain Avenue
Tucson, AZ 85721

520-621-6120
FAX 520-621-8191
E-Mail: dimitri@u.arizona.edu
Home Page: www.u.arizona.edu/~dimitri/

Dr Dimitri Kececioglu PE, Prof
Aerospace/Mech Engineering

An institute to help provide a working knowledge in reliability engineering.
Frequency: May

2984 SAE AeroTech Congress & Exhibition
Society of Automotive Engineers
400 Commonwealth Drive
Warrendale, PA 15086-7511

724-776-4841
877-606-7323
FAX 724-776-0790
E-Mail: jhudson@sae.org
Home Page: www.sae.org
Social Media: *Facebook, Twitter, LinkedIn, Youtube*

David Shutt, President

Provides a forum for the aerospace community to meet and discuss current and future challenges, opportunities and requirements of next-generation R&D, products, and systems, and to develop professional relationships among the worldwide community. Technical sessions, panel discussions, keynote speakers, presentations and demonstrations.
3M Attendees
Frequency: Annual

2985 SAE Government/Industry Event
Society of Automotive Engineers
400 Commonwealth Drive
Warrendale, PA 15086-7511

724-776-4841
877-606-7323
FAX 724-776-0790
E-Mail: mjena@sae.org
Home Page: www.sae.org

Social Media: *Facebook, Twitter, LinkedIn, Youtube*

David Shutt, President

Awards and presentations, technical sessions, network receptions, and exhibits.
Frequency: Annual

2986 SAE World Congress
Society of Automotive Engineers
400 Commonwealth Drive
Warrendale, PA 15096-0001

724-776-4841
877-606-7323
FAX 724-776-0790
E-Mail: agrech@sae.org
Home Page: www.sae.org
Social Media: *Facebook, Twitter, LinkedIn, Youtube*

David Shutt, President

Reinvented in 2010, the World Conference provides a highly relevant and engaging technical program, expanded and improved opportunities for networking and information exchange, and innovative exhibits.
3.5M Attendees
Frequency: Annual

2987 SAFE Symposium
SAFE Association
PO Box 130
Creswell, OR 97426

541-895-3012
FAX 541-895-3014
E-Mail: safe@peak.org
Home Page: www.safeassociation.com
Social Media: *Facebook*

Robert Billings, President
Marcia Baldwin, President-Elect

The Symposium provides an internationally attended marketplace for the exchange of technical information, product and service exhibitions, and the showcasing of industry capabilities for meeting challenges in vehicular occupant protection and personnel worn safety equipment.
Frequency: October

2988 SAMPE Fall Technical Conference
Society for the Advancement of Material & Process
1161 Park View Drive
Suite 200
Covina, CA 91724

626-331-0616
800-562-7360
FAX 626-332-8929
E-Mail: sampeibo@sampe.org
Home Page: www.sampe.org
Social Media: *Facebook, LinkedIn*

Priscilla Heredia, Conference & General Information
Karen Chapman, Exhibit Information

The Society for the Advancement of Material and Process Engineering's Fall event showcases the latest technology, applications and materials for the advanced manufacturing marketplace; educational sessions, and exhibits.
Frequency: Annual/Fall

2989 SAMPE Spring Conference & Exhibition
Society for the Advancement of Material & Process
1161 Park View Drive
Suite 200
Covina, CA 91724

626-331-0616
800-562-7360
FAX 626-332-8929
E-Mail: sampeibo@sampe.org

Home Page: www.sampe.org
Social Media: *Facebook, LinkedIn*

Priscilla Heredia, Conference & General Information
Karen Chapman, Exhibit Information

The Society for the Advancement of Material and Process Engineering's Spring event showcases the latest technology, applications and materials for the advanced manufacturing marketplace; educational sessions, and exhibits.
Frequency: Annual/Spring

2990 Sea-Air-Space
Navy League of the United States
11208 Waples Mill Road
Suite 112
Fairfax, VA 22030

703-631-6200
800-564-4220
FAX 703-818-9177
E-Mail: sales@jspargo.com
Home Page: www.jspargo.com

Paul doCarmo, Assistant Director/Exhibit Sales
Connie Shaw, Exhibit Sales Account Manager

Annual event to help promote and develop a technologically advanced naval force.
6000 Attendees
Frequency: April

2991 Seaplane Pilots Association Conference
Seaplane Pilots Association
3859 Laird Blvd
Lakeland, FL 33811

863-701-7979
888-772-8923
FAX 863-701-7588
E-Mail: spa@seaplanes.org
Home Page: www.seaplanes.org

Steve McCaughey, Executive Director
Randy Juen, Vice President

Thirty booths and conference.
1.5M Attendees
Frequency: September

2992 Soaring Society of America Annual Convention
Soaring Society of America
5425 W Jack Gomez Boulevard
PO Box 2100
Hobbs, NM 88241-2100

505-392-1177
FAX 505-392-8154
E-Mail: merchandise@ssa.org
Home Page: www.ssa.org

Meetings, exhibits, and displays.
Frequency: Annual

2993 Society of Automotive Engineers: Aerotech Expo
Society of Automotive Engineers
400 Commonwealth Drive
Warrendale, PA 15096-0001

772- 77- 484
877-606-7323
FAX 248-273-2494
E-Mail: advertising@sae.org
Home Page: www.sae.org

David Shutt, President

Exhibits of commercial, military, business and general aviation.

2994 Society of Experimental Test Pilots
Society of Experimental Test Pilots
44814 Elm Avenue
Lancaster, CA 93534

661-942-9574
FAX 661-940-0398

E-Mail: setp@setp.org
Home Page: www.setp.org

Steve Rainey, President
Paula Smith, Executive Director

These conferences provide major forums for the discussion of aspects of tax, accounting, administration, statute and case law, which are of general concern to practitioners, as well as providing advance knowledge of developments affecting trusts, estates and subjects of allied subjects. Twenty Booths.
1.5M Attendees
Frequency: September

2995 Strategic Space and Defense
Space Foundation
4425 Arrowswest Drive
Colorado Springs, CO 80907

719-576-8000
FAX 719-576-8801
E-Mail: web@spacefoundation.org
Home Page: www.spacefoundation.org

Elliot G Pullman, President/CEO
Chuck Zimkas, Chief Operating Officer
Holly Roberts, CFO

The definitive global security conference where the senior leadership of U.S. Strategic Command, component and supported commands, and the executive leadership of the national security industrial base gather to gain insight on the Command's mission, global activities and relationships.
Frequency: October

2996 United States Pilots Association Meeting
United States Pilots Association
1652 Indian Point Road
Branson, MO 65616

417-338-2225
E-Mail: jan@hoynacki.com
Home Page: www.uspilots.org

Paul Hough, Chairman
Jan Hoynacki, Executive Director

Holds two meetings a year — in the spring and fall.
Frequency: June/Septemter

2997 United States Ultralight Association
United States Ultralight Association
PO Box 3501
Gettysburg, PA 17325-1810

717-339-0200
FAX 717-339-0063
E-Mail: usua@usua.com
Home Page: www.usua.com

Steve McCaughey, Executive Director
Dale Hooper, Executive VP

Annual meeting and exhibits of ultralight and microlight aviation equipment, supplies and services. There will be 20 booths.
3000 Attendees
Frequency: February
Founded in 1998

2998 World Airline Historical Society Convention
World Airline Historical Society
PO Box 489
Ocoee, FL 34761

904-221-1446
FAX 407-522-9352
E-Mail: Information@WAHSOnline.com
Home Page: www.wahsonline.com

Duane Young, President
Craig Morris, Vice President

Convention and exhibits of airline memorabilia, including airplane models, airline sched-

ules, postcards, posters, photos and publications from airlines.
500 Members
Frequency: Annual
Founded in 1977

Directories & Databases

2999 AAMS Resource Guide
Association of Air Medical Services
909 N Washington Street
Suite 410
Alexandria, VA 22314

703-836-8732
FAX 703-836-8920
E-Mail: information@aams.org
Home Page: www.aams.org

John Fiegel, Executive Director
Blair Marie Beggan, Communications & Marketing
Gloria Dow, Editor

The directory contains information on the association and its products and services; pertinent details on members, including demographic and historical information; and special crew listings that help community members perform their jobs better through enhanced networking opportunities. It also provides decision makers with a buyer's guide of community vendors and suppliers and the services they supply.

3000 ABD: Aviation Buyer's Directory
Air Service Directory
116 Radio Circle
Suite #302
Mt Kisco, NY 10549

914-242-8700
FAX 914-242-5422
E-Mail: abd@abdonline.com
Home Page: abdonline.com/

Manufacturers and dealers of aviation equipment and aircraft are the focus of this directory.
Cost: $25.00
400 Pages
Frequency: Quarterly
Circulation: 17,000

3001 AOPA's Airport Directory
Aircraft Owners & Pilots Association
421 Aviation Way
Frederick, MD 21701-4756

301-695-2000
800-872-2672
FAX 301-695-2375
Home Page: www.aopa.org

Craig Fuller, President

Includes information on over 7,400 airports, seaplane bases and heliports. Also covers more than 2,200 private use airports. In addition to basic airport information such as runways, lighting, approaches, frequencies, identifiers and lat/long, you'll also find listings of nearby hotels, transportation, restaurants, etc. Paperback.
Cost: $29.95
680 Pages
Frequency: Annual
Circulation: 300,000
Founded in 1962
Printed in one color on glossy stock

3002 Address List for Regional Airports Divisions and Airport Districts
US Federal Aviation Administration
800 Independence Avenue SW
Washington, DC 20591-0001

202-366-4000
866-835-5322

FAX 202-493-5032
Home Page: www.faa.gov

David Grizzle, COO
David Weingart, Chief of Staff

Offers district offices and airports.
20 Pages

3003 Aerospace Database
Cambridge Scientific Abstracts
Aerospace Access
59 John Street, 7th Floor
New York, NY 10038

212-349-1120
FAX 212-349-1283

Tony Lenti, Managing Editor
Earl Spencer, Owner

Provides bibliographic coverage of basic and applied research in aeronautics, astronautics, and space sciences. The database also covers technology development and applications in complementary and supporting fields such as chemistry, geosciences, physics, communications, and electronics. In addition to periodic literature, the database also includes coverage of reports issued by NASA, other US government agencies, international institutions, universities, and private firms.

3004 Airline Handbook
Air Transport Association
1301 Pennsylvania Ave NW
Suite 1100
Washington, DC 20004

202-626-4000
800-497-3326
FAX 301-206-9789
E-Mail: a4a@airlines.org
Home Page: www.airlines.org

Nicholas Calio, President/CEO

Overview of the history, structure, economics and operations of the airline industry. Includes a glossary of commonly used airline terminology.
Cost: $10.00
Frequency: Hardcover
Founded in 2001

3005 Airport Operators Council International
1775 K St NW
Suite 500
Washington, DC 20006-1529

202-293-8500
FAX 202-331-1362
E-Mail: webmaster@aci-na.org
Home Page: www.aci-na.com

Gregory Principato, President
Deborah McElroy, Executive VP External Affairs
Nancy Zimini, Senior Vice President

Contains an annual time series of aviation and airport data for more than 580 airports from the Worldwide Airport Traffic Report.
Founded in 1948

3006 Airports
CTB/McGraw Hill
20 Ryan Ranch Rd
Monterey, CA 93940-5770

831-393-0700
FAX 831-393-6528

Ellen Haley, President

Offers information on airport management issues, including funding. Congressional and regulatory activities, legal matters, noise and capacity problems are offered as well.
Frequency: Full-text

3007 Aviation Businesses and the Service they Provide
National Air Transportation Association
4226 King St
Alexandria, VA 22302-1507

703-845-9000
800-808-6282
FAX 703-845-8176
E-Mail: csipes@nata-online.org
Home Page: www.nata.aero
Social Media: *Facebook, Twitter, LinkedIn*

Thomas Hendricks, President
Timothy Heck, Financial Officer, VP
Shannon Chambers, Director Mktg/Communications

A detailed fact book, complete with statistical data, on the aviation services industry.

3008 Aviation Telephone Directory
Aviation Telephone Directory
6619 Tumbleweed Ridge Lane
Suite 102
Henderson, NV 89015

800-437-2962
FAX 702-943-8982
Home Page: www.aviationfinder.com

Is the leading source for General Aviation information with more than 14,000 Companies and 10,000 airports. Yellow pages, White pages, and Blue pages(by airport). Thousands of phone numbers.
Cost: $19.95
790 Pages
Frequency: BiAnnually
Circulation: 20000
ISSN: 1075-1378
Founded in 1949
Printed in 4 colors on newsprint stock

3009 Collegiate Aviation Guide
University Aviation Association
3410 Skyway Dr
Auburn, AL 36830-6444

334-844-2434
FAX 334-844-2432
Home Page: www.uaa.aero

Carolyn Williamson, Executive Director
Mary Chandler, Coordinator Office Administration

A comprehensive guide of regionally accredited colleges and universities with aviation offerings ranging from academic completion certificates and associate degrees to doctoral programs. Contains listings of institutions throughout the United States, with some located in Canada.
Cost: $29.95
Founded in 1947

3010 Commuter Flight Statistics and Online Origin & Destination Data
US Department of Transportation
Kendall Square
Cambridge, MA 02142-1093

617-494-5906

Robin A Caldwell, Director

Covers all areas of the commuter airline flight industry, including statistical information on flights by commuter airlines.
Frequency: Statistical

3011 Flying Annual and Buyers Guide
Hachette Filipacchi Magazines

1633 Broadway
42nd Floor
New York, NY 10019-6708

212-767-6000
FAX 212-767-5600
Home Page: www.hfmnewsstand.com/index

Alain Lemarchand, CEO
Richard Collins, Editor at Large

This substantial guide lists manufacturers, dealers, suppliers and professionals in the aviation industry.
Cost: $18.00

3012 General Aviation Statistical DataBook
General Aviation Manufacturers Association
1400 K St NW
Suite 801
Washington, DC 20005-2402

202-393-1500
FAX 202-842-4063
E-Mail: bforan@gama.aero
Home Page: www.gama.aero

Pete Bunce, President, Chief Executive Officer

Statistics on US general aviation shipments, aircraft fleet, international trade, safety and the most current data on airport statistics and pilot population.
Cost: $10.00
Frequency: Annual

3013 Guide to Selecting Airport Consultants and Membership Directory
Airport Consultants Council
908 King Street
Suite 100
Alexandria, VA 22314-3067

703-683-5900
FAX 703-683-2564
E-Mail: info@acconline.org
Home Page: www.acconline.org

Paula Hochstetler, President
T.J. Shultz, Executive VP

A full nationwide listing of airport consultants and association news.
Frequency: Annual

3014 Helicopter Annual
Helicopter Association International
1635 Prince St
Alexandria, VA 22314-2898

703-683-4646
FAX 703-683-4745
Home Page: www.rotor.com

Matthew Zuccaro, President

A comprehensive reference guide for th civil helicopter industry. Includes specifications, industry statistics, HAI membership directories by class and geographic matrix, listings of international civil aviation contacts, key FAA personnel, association committees, and more. First copy included free with membership.
Cost: $50.00
360 Pages
Frequency: Annual
Circulation: 25,000

3015 International Aerospace Abstracts
American Institute of Aeronautics and Astronautics
1801 Alexander Bell Dr
Suite 500
Reston, VA 20191-4344

703-264-7500
800-639-2422
FAX 703-264-7551
E-Mail: tammym@aiaa.org
Home Page: www.aiaa.org

Dr. Brian Dailey, President

This database contains more than 2 million references and abstracts of journal and monograph literature relating to aerospace science and technology.
Frequency: Monthly

3016 Light Aircraft Manufacturers Association Directory
2001 Steamboat Ridge Ct
Daytona Beach, FL 94588

651-592-7565
FAX 925-426-0771
E-Mail: info@lama.bz
Home Page: www.lama.bz

Don Johnson, President
Jan Fridrich, Secretary General

A list of over 400 member manufacturers of light and ultralight aircraft and suppliers of related products and services.

3017 Living with Your Plane
Flyer Media
5611 76th Street W
PO Box 39099
Lakewood, WA 98499-0099

253-471-9888
800-426-8538
FAX 253-471-9911
Home Page: www.flyer-online.com/airparks

Dave Sclair, Editor
Janice Wood, Editorial Coordinator

Offers a large amount of information including 400 residential airports with phones, addresses and contact names.
Cost: $20.00
Frequency: Annual
Circulation: 1,000

3018 NBAA Directory of Member Companies, Aircraft & Personnel
National Business Aviation Association
1200 18th St NW
Suite 400
Washington, DC 20036-2527

202-783-9000
FAX 202-331-8364
E-Mail: info@nbaa.org
Home Page: www.nbaa.org

Ed Bolen, President

Furnished to members only and contains a comprehensive listing of NBAA Member companies with their aircraft and flight department personnel.

3019 Space Law
Oceana Publications
198 Madison Avenue
New York, NY 10016

800-334-4249
FAX 212-726-6476
E-Mail: custserv.us@oup.com
Home Page: www.oceanalaw.com

Paul Stephen Dempsey, Editor

Provides in-depth expert coverage by today's preeminent export of the most pressing issues currently being faced by international regulators in this dynamic and growing area of the law.
Cost: $625.00
40 Pages
Frequency: 5 Volume Set
Circulation: 2,000
ISBN: 0-379012-92-8
Printed in 4 colors

3020 United States Civil Aircraft Registry
Insured Aircraft Title Service

PO Box 19527
Oklahoma City, OK 73144-0527

405-681-6663
800-654-4882
FAX 405-681-9299
E-Mail: iats@earthlink.net
Home Page: www.insuredaircraft.com

Matthew Kelly, Owner

This directory covers owners of over 275,000 aircraft.
Cost: $600.00
190 Pages
Frequency: Monthly
Founded in 1963

3021 Water Landing Directory
Seaplane Pilots Association
3859 Laird Blvd
Lakeland, FL 33811

863-701-7979
888-772-8923
FAX 863-701-7588
E-Mail: spa@seaplanes.org
Home Page: www.seaplanes.org

Steve McCaughey, Executive Director

Is the only publication that combines federal, state, provincial and special agency regulations affecting seaplane operators. The directory includes waterway closures and restrictions, seaplane bases listed by state and city, informative seaplane base diagrams, customs information, flight planning charts and other miscellaneous quick reference materials.

3022 World Aviation Directory and Aerospace Database
McGraw Hill
1200 G St NW
Suite 922
Washington, DC 20005-3821

202-343-2300
FAX 202-383-2347
Home Page:
www.mcgraw-hillhomelandsecurity.com

John McNicholas, Marketing Director

Aviation and the aerospace industry are covered in this global directory offering information on manufacturers, subcontractors, support services and associations.
2500 Pages

Industry Web Sites

3023 http://gold.greyhouse.com
G.O.L.D Grey House OnLine Databases

Grey House Publishing's online database platform, GOLD, offers Quick Search, Keyword Search and Expert Search for most business sectors including aviation and aerospace markets. The GOLD platform makes finding the information you need quick and easy - whether you're a novice searcher or an experienced database user. All of Grey House's directory products are available for subscription on the GOLD platform.

3024 www.aams.org
Association of Air Medical Services

Air medical transport equipment, supplies and services.

3025 www.aci-na.org
Airports Council International-North America

Represents local, regional and state governing bodies that own and operate commercial airports throughout the United States and Canada.

3026 **www.aeronet.com**
Aeronet Worldwide

Specializes in urgent shipping solutions. From computer and technical supplies, to medical equipment, to odd size, one of a kind machine parts, we have always been there for our clients, one shipment at a time.

3027 **www.afa.org**
Air Force Association

Independent nonprofit, civilian organization promoting public understanding of aerospace power and the pivotal role it plays in the security of the nation.

3028 **www.afanet.org**
Association of Flight Attendants

Represents over 50,000 flight attendants at 26 airlines, serving as a voice for flight attendants at their workplace, in the industry, the media and on Capitol Hill.

3029 **www.agaviation.org**
National Agricultural Aviation Association

Voice of the aerial application industry, we work to preserve aerial application's place in the protection and production of America's food and fiber supply. Aerial application is one of the safest, fastest, most efficient and economical ways to apply pesticides. It is also the most environmentally friendly tool of modern agriculture.

3030 **www.aia-aerospace.org**
Aerospace Industries Association

The Aerospace Industries Association shapes public policy that ensures the US aerospace, defense and homeland security industry remains preeminent and that its members are successful and profitable in a changing global market.

3031 **www.aiaa.org**
American Institute of Aeronautics and Astronautics

Advances the arts, sciences, and technology of aeronautics and astronautics and promotes the professionalism of those engaged in these pursuits.

3032 **www.airlines.org**
Air Transport Association

Supports and assits its members by promoting the air transport industry and the safety, cost effectiveness, and technical advancement of its operators; advocating common industry positions before state and local governments; conducting designated industry-wide programs; and assuring governmental and public understanding of all aspects of air transport.

3033 **www.airship-association.org**
Airship Association

Circulates information on all matters affecting airships.

3034 **www.anahq.org**
Association of Naval Aviation

Professional, nonprofit, educational and fraternaL society of Naval Aviation, whose main purpose is to educte the public and our national leaders on the vital roles of the Navy, Marine Corp and Coast Guard Aviation as key elements of our national defense posture. ANA continuosly seeks to elucidate the key current issues impacting Naval Aviation through published writing, symposia, speeches and discussions with various interest groups.

3035 **www.aopa.org**
Aircraft Owners & Pilots Association

Works to make flying safer, more economical and enjoyable for private aircraft owners.

3036 **www.arinc.com**
Aeronautical Radio

Aeronautical Radio provides transportation communications and systems engineering solution for five major industries: aviation, airports, defense, government, and transportation

3037 **www.arsa.org**
Aeronautical Repair Station Association

Helps develop guidance, policy and interpretations that are clear, concise and consistent, and applied uniformly to all similarly situated companies and individuals.

3038 **www.asma.org**
Aerospace Medical Association

Our mission is to apply and advance scientific knowledge to promote and enhance the health, safety and performance of those involved in aerospace and related activities.

3039 **www.astronautical.org**
American Astronautical Society

Independent scientific and technical group in the United States exclusively dedicated to the advancement of space science and exploration.

3040 **www.atec-amt.org**
Aviation Technician Education Council

Organization of Federal Aviation Administration approved Aviation Maintenance Technician schools and supporting industries.

3041 **www.blimpinfo.com**
Lighter Than Air Society

Nonprofit organization whose members are devoted to the study of the history, science and techniques of all forms of buoyant flight.

3042 **www.bonanza.org**
American Bonanza Society

ABS is a group of members who own, fly or have a sincere interest in Bonanza, Baron, and Travel air type aircraft. Because of this common interest we share information and experiences involving the operation and maintenance of the Beech produced aircraft.

3043 **www.cessnaowner.org**
Cessna Owner Organization

Membership support organization for Cessna aircraft owners.

3044 **www.civilavmed.com**
Civil Aviation Medical Association

Aviation medical equipment, supplies and services. Working on behalf of physicians engaged in the practice of aviation medicine, dedicated to civil aviation safety.

3045 **www.eaa.org**
Experimental Aircraft Association

Equipment, supplies and services for sport and recreational flying.

3046 **www.generalaviation.org**
General Aviation Manufacturers Association

Manufacturers of general aviation aircraft, and related equipment.

3047 **www.greyhouse.com**
Grey House Publishing

Authoritative reference directories for most business sectors including aviation and aerospace markets. Users can search the online databases with varied search criteria allowing for custom searches by product category, geographic area, sales volume, keyword, subject and more. Full Grey House catalog and online ordering also available.

3048 **www.iaopa.org**
Int'l Council of Aircraft Owner & Pilot Assns.

Nonprofit federation of 53 autonomous, nongovernmental, national general aviation organizations. Facilitates the movement of general aviation aircraft.

3049 **www.ifsanet.com**
International Inflight Food Service Association

For airline and railway personnel, caterers and suppliers responsible for providing passenger food service.

3050 **www.iswap.org**
International Society of Women Airline Pilots

Organization for all women pilots who are employed as flight crew members (Captain, First Officer, or Second Officer) and hold seniority numbers with an airline carrier that operates at least one aircraft with a gross wieght of 90,000 pounds or more.

3051 **www.naa.usa.org**
National Aeronautic Association

For aerospace corporations, aero clubs, affiliates and major national sporting aviation organizations.

3052 **www.nafinet.org**
National Association of Flight Instructors

Dedicated to raising and maintaining the professional standing of the flight instructor in the aviation community. Maintains a benefits package available for everyone from the independent instructor to those teaching at flight schools.

3053 **www.nata.aero**
National Air Transportation Association

National association of aviation business service providers.

3054 **www.natca.org**
National Air Traffic Controllers Association

Founded to ensure the safety and longetivity of air traffic controller positions around the nation. Represents over 15,000 air traffic controllers throughout the US, Puerto Rico and Guam, along with 2,508 other bargaining unit members that span the areas of engineers and architects to nurses and health care professionals to members of the accounting community.

3055 **www.nbaa.org**
National Business Aviation Association

Not-for-profit, nonpartisan corporation dedicated to the success of the business aviation community.

3056 **www.ninety-nines.org**
Ninety-Nines

International organization of licensed women pilots from 35 countries. We are a nonprofit, charitable membership corporation holding 501(c)(3) US tax status. Members are professional pilots for airlines, industry, government; we are pilots who teach and pilots who fly for pleasure; we are pilots who are technicians and mechanics. First and foremost, we are women who love to fly.

3057 **www.ofainc.com.**
Organization of Flying Adjusters

Dedicated to the highest standard of professional ethics in handling aviation insurance claims, investigating causes of aircraft accidents objectively and promoting every aspect of air safety.

3058 www.piperowner.org
Pipers Owner Society

Independent group of Piper owners, pilots, and enthusiasts, the POS is committed to the goal of safe, fun, and affordable flying. Membership benefits include: pre-buy referral service; free STC summaries, free parts locating and a referral service. Pipers magazine is exclusively for POS members.

3059 www.pra.org
Popular Rotorcraft Association

A nonprofit organization dedicated to the advancement of knowledge, public education and safety among Rotorcraft enthusiasts worldwide.

3060 www.quad-a.org
Army Aviation Association of America

Aerospace products, helicopters, rotor blades, engines, tires, helmets and related aviation equipment. Representing membership interests to the Army and the Legislative Branch.

3061 www.rotor.com
Helicopter Association International

Receives and disseminates information concerning the use, operation, hiring, contracting and leasing of helicopters.

3062 www.safeassociation.com
SAFE Association

Website of the nonprofit organization dedicated to the preservation of human life. It provides a common meeting ground for the sharing of problems, ideas and information.

3063 www.seaplanes.org
Seaplane Pilots Association

Represents our members in dozens of seaplane access issues annually and provides numerous exclusive benefits.

3064 www.ssa.org
Soaring Society of America

Fosters and promote all phases of gliding and soaring, nationally and internationally.

3065 www.tcunion.org
Transportation-Communications International Union

Members come from diverse transportation industries. In addition to bargaining and representation of its members, provides mortgage and bankcard programs and other services to its members.

3066 www.tiaca.org
International Air Cargo Association

For air cargo industry services and products from aircraft manufacturers, airlines, airports, freight forwarders trade publications logistics consultants, etc.

3067 www.ussf.org
Space Foundation

Nonprofit organization advancing the exploration, development and use of space and space education for the benefit of humankind.

3068 www.vtol.org
AHS International

For designers, engineers and manufacturers of the vertical flight industry.

3069 www.wahsonline.com
World Airline Historical Society

Open to all persons and groups interested in collecting airline memorabilia and the study of the airline industry, past and current.

Associations

3070 ARMA International
11880 College Blvd
Suite 450
Overland Park, KS 66210

913-341-3808
800-422-2762
FAX 913-341-3742
E-Mail: headquarters@armaintl.org
Home Page: www.arma.org
Social Media: *Facebook, Twitter, LinkedIn*

Peter Kurilecz, President
Tera Ladner, President Elect
Brenda Prowse, Treasurer
Fred Pulzello, IGP, CRM, Immediate Past
President

A not-for-profit professional association and
the authority on managing records and information.
11000 Members
Founded in 1955

**3071 Advancing Financial Crime
Professionals Worldwide**
80 Southwest 8th Street
Suite 2350
Miami, FL 33130

305-373-0020
866-459-CAMS
FAX 305-373-5229
E-Mail: info@acams.org
Home Page: www.acams.org
Social Media: *Facebook, Twitter, LinkedIn*

Ted Weissberg, Chief Executive Officer
John Byrne, Executive Vice President
Ari House, Chief Financial Officer
Ms. Hue Dang, Head of Asia
Geoffrey Fone, Director of Sales

The largest international membership organization dedicated to enhancing the knowledge and
expertise of financial crime detection and prevention professionals from a wide range of industries in both public and private sectors.

**3072 American Association of Bank
Directors**
1250 24th Street, NW
Suite 700
Washington, DC 20037

202-463-4888
FAX 202-349-8080
E-Mail: info@aabd.org
Home Page: aabd.org
Social Media: *Twitter, LinkedIn*

David Baris, President
Richard M. Whiting, Executive Director
Charles J. Thayer, Chairman Emeritus
Andrew Baris, VP and Director of Marketing
Betty Pelton, Membership Director

Devoted to serving the information, education
and advocacy needs of individual bank and
savings institution directors. This nonprofit organization has members nationwide.
Founded in 1989

**3073 American Association of Residential
Mortgage Regulators**
1025 Thomas Jefferson Street, NW
Suite 500 East
Washington, DC 20007

202-521-3999
FAX 202-833-3636
E-Mail: efreundel@aarmr.org
Home Page: www.aarmr.org

Rod Carnes, President
Tony Florence, Vice President
Robert Niemi, Treasurer

Stacey Valerio, Secretary
David Saunders, Executive Director

Promotes the exchange of information and education concerning the licensing, supervision,
and regulation of the residential mortgage
industry.

3074 American Bankers Association
1120 Connecticut Avenue NW
Washington, DC 20036

202-663-5000
800-226-5377
FAX 202-828-4540
E-Mail: custserv@aba.com
Home Page: www.aba.com
Social Media: *Facebook, Twitter, LinkedIn,
Google+, YouTube, Instagram*

John A Ikard, Chairman
R. Daniel Blanton, Chair Elect
Dorothy A. Savarese, Vice Chair
Frank Keating, President & CEO
G. William Beale, Treasurer

Brings together all categories of banking institutions to best represent the interests of this
rapidly changing industry. Its membership includes community, regional and money center
banks and holding companies, as well as savings associations, trust companies and savings
banks.
Founded in 1875

**3075 American Bankers Insurance
Association**
American Bankers Association
1120 Connecticut Avenue NW
Washington, DC 20036

202-663-5163
800-226-5377
FAX 202-828-4546
E-Mail: vbarton@aba.com
Home Page: www.theabia.com
Social Media: *Facebook, Twitter, LinkedIn*

Paul Petrylak, President/Chairman
Neal Aton, Vice President
David Cissell, Secretary
Val Teagarden, Treasurer

The American Bankers Insurance Association
(ABIA) is the insurance subsidiary of the
American Bankers Association (ABA). The
ABIA's mission is to develop policy and provide advocacy for banks in insurance and to
support bank insurance operations through research, education, compliance assistance, and
peer group networking opportunities.
300 Members
Founded in 2001

3076 American Bankruptcy Institute
66 Canal Center Plaza
Suite 600
Alexandria, VA 22314

703-739-0800
FAX 703-739-1060
E-Mail: support@abiworld.org
Home Page: www.abiworld.org
Social Media: *Facebook, Twitter, LinkedIn,
Google+, Flickr*

Patrica A Redmond, Chairman
James Patrick Shea, President
Jeffery N Pomerantz, President Elect
John Tittle Jr., Treasurer
Hon. Dennis R. Dow, Secretary

Multidisciplinary, non-partisan organization
dedicated to research and education on matters
related to insolvency. Engaged in numerous educational and research activities as well as the
production of a number of publications both for
the insolvency practitioner and the public.
12000 Members
Founded in 1982

3077 American Payroll Association
660 North Main Avenue
Suite 100
San Antonio, TX 78205-1217

210-226-4600
FAX 210-226-4027
E-Mail: APA@americanpayroll.org
Home Page: www.americanpayroll.org
Social Media: *Facebook, Twitter, LinkedIn*

Dan Maddux, Executive Director

Conducts payroll training conferences and seminars across the country and publishes a complete library of resource texts and newsletters.
21000 Members
Founded in 1982

**3078 Arab Bankers Association of North
America**
150 West 28th Street
Suite 801
New York, NY 10001

212-599-3030
FAX 212-599-3131
E-Mail: info@arabbankers.org
Home Page: www.arabbankers.org

Mona Aboelnaga Kanaan, President
Susan Peters, Executive Director/COO
Ryah Aqel, Communications Coordinator
Zainab Al Dabbagh, Development Associate
Gabby Elhilow, Administrative Associate

Provides news, job listings, and resources for
financial institutions in the U.S. and the Middle
East.
Founded in 1983

**3079 Association For Financial
Professionals**
4520 East West Highway
Suite 750
Bethesda, MD 20814

301-907-2862
FAX 301-907-2864
E-Mail: afp@afponline.org
Home Page: www.afponline.org
Social Media: *Facebook, Twitter, LinkedIn,
Youtube, RSS*

Anthony Scaglione, Chairman
Roberta Eiseman, Vice Chairman
Jeff Johnson, Vice Chairman
Ann Anthony, Director
Terry Crawford, Director

The Association for Financial Professionals
(AFP) serves a network of more than 16,000
treasury and finance professionals. Headquartered in Bethesda, MD, AFP provides members
with breaking news, economic research and
data on the evolving world of treasury and finance, as well as world-class treasury certification programs, networking events, financial
analytical tools, training, and public policy representation to legislators and regulators.

3080 Association for Financial Technology
10813 Pleasant Valley Road
Frazeysburg, OH 43822

614-895-1208
FAX 614-895-3466
E-Mail: aft@aftweb.com
Home Page: www.aftweb.com
Social Media: *Facebook, Twitter, LinkedIn*

Wade Arnold, President
Xan Kasprzak, Vice President & Program Chair
Andrew Grinstead, Treasurer
James R Bannister, Executive Director
Susan Hurley, Managing Director

Association founded to promote high standards
of professionalism in the planning, development, implementation and application of technology to the financial services industry.
Founded in 1972

3081 Association for Management in Financial Services
14247 Saffron Circle
Carmel, IN 46032-7769

317-815-5857
FAX 317-815-5877
E-Mail: ami2@amifs.org
Home Page: www.amifs.org
Social Media: *Facebook, Twitter, LinkedIn*

Jefferson Nathasingh, President
Robert McDonald, Executive Vice President
Meg Foster, Treasurer
Kevin Link, Executive Director
Krissa Hatfield, Asst. Executive Director

The Association for Management Information in Financial Services is the preeminent organization for management information professionals in the financial services industry, and counts among its members individuals who set the policies and advance the concepts of management information at major financial institutions worldwide.
300 Members
Founded in 1980

3082 Association of Independent Trust Companies
2213 North Broadway
Ada, OK 74820

405-680-7869
FAX 580-332-4714
E-Mail: ato@trustorgs.com
Home Page: www.trustorgs.com
Social Media: *Facebook, Twitter*

Bond Payne, President
Tony Guthrie, Treasurer
Thomas Blank, General Counsel/Secretary
Somerlyn Cothran, Executive Director
Jamie Whitefield, Administration

To provide a forum of leaders, owners and operators of trust companies and wealth management providers.
150 Members
Founded in 1989

3083 Association of Military Banks of America (AMBA)
PO Box 3335
Warrenton, VA 20188

540-347-3305
FAX 540-347-5995
E-Mail: info@ambahq.org
Home Page: www.ambahq.org
Social Media: *Facebook, Twitter*

Terry Tuggle, Chairman
Raleigh A Trovillion, Vice Chairman
Steven Lepper, President/CEO
James A Cerrone, Chairman Elect
Steven Lepper, President and CEO

AMBA is a not-for-profit association of banks operating on military installations, banks not located on military installations but serving military customers, and military banking facilities designated by the US Treasury.
130 Members
Founded in 1959

3084 Association of Residential Mortgage Compliance Professionals
167 West Hudson Street
Suite 200
Long Beach, NY 11561

516-442-3456
Home Page: armcp.org
Social Media: *LinkedIn*

The first and only national organization in the Unites States devoted exclusively to residential mortgage compliance professionals offering discussion groups, educational forums, panels,

lectures, and other venues for residential mortgage compliance professionals.
Founded in 2010

3085 Bank Administration Institute
115 S LaSalle St
Suite 3300
Chicago, IL 60603-3801

312-683-2464
888-224-0037
FAX 312-683-2373
E-Mail: info@bai.org
Home Page: www.bai.org
Social Media: *Facebook, Twitter, LinkedIn, YouTube*

Scott M Peters, Chairman
Christopher J McComish, Vice Chair
Deborah L Bianucci, President & CEO
Charles G Kim, Secretary
Rilla S Delorier, Treasurer

The financial services industry's partner for breakthrough information and intelligence needed to innovate and stay relevant in an evolving marketplace. Serves a wide segment of the financial services industry, from the largest multinational banks to community-based institutions.

3086 Bank Insurance and Securities Association
2025 M Street NW
Suite 800
Washington, DC 20036

202-367-1111
FAX 202-367-2111
E-Mail: bisa@BISAnet.org
Home Page: www.bisanet.org
Social Media: *Facebook, Twitter, StumbleUpon*

Dan Overbey, President
Daniel J McCormack, President Elect
Frank A Consalo, VP
James B Nonnegard, VP
Thomas N Howe, Treasurer/Secretary

Dedicated to serving the needs of those responsible for marketing securities, insurance and other investment and risk management products through commercial banks, trust companies, savings institutions, and credit unions.
Founded in 2002

3087 Bankers' Association for Finance & Trade
1120 Connecticut Avenue NW
Washington, DC 20036

202-663-7575
FAX 202-663-5538
E-Mail: info@baft-ifsa.com
Home Page: www.baft.org
Social Media: *Facebook, Twitter*

John Ahearn, Chairman
Michael Quinn, Vice Chairman
Tod R Burwell, CEO
Daniel J Scanlan, Treasurer/Secretary
Rita Gonzalez, Managing Director

A financial services trade association headquartered in Washington, DC, whose membership primarily represents a broad range of financial institutions and service members that provide services throughout the global financial community.
180 Members
Founded in 1921

3088 Community Development Bankers Association
1444 Eye Street NW
Suite 201
Washington, DC 20005

202-689-8935
E-Mail: info@cdbanks.org

Home Page: www.cdbanks.org
Social Media: *Facebook, Twitter, LinkedIn*

Brian Argrett, Chairman
Robert Jones III, Vice-Chair
Huey Townsend, Treasurer
Robert Patrick Cooper, Secretary
Robert McGill, Emeritus Director

The national trade association of the community development bank sector.

3089 Conference of State Bank Supervisors
1129 20th Street, N.W.
9th Floor
Washington, DC 20036

202-296-2840
FAX 202-296-1928
E-Mail: drodgers@csbs.org
Home Page: www.csbs.org

Melanie G Hall, Chairman
Katherine E Hoyle, Administrative Assistant
Mick Thompson, Vice Chairman
John Ryan, Secretary
Charles J Dolezal, Treasurer

The nationwide organization of banking regulators from all 50 states, the District of Columbia, Guam, Puerto Rico, and the U.S. Virgin Islands.
Founded in 1902

3090 Consumer Bankers Association
1225 Eye St., NW
Suite 550
Washington, DC 20005

202-552-6382
E-Mail: rhunt@cbanet.org
Home Page: www.cbanet.org
Social Media: *Facebook, Twitter, LinkedIn*

Richard Hunt, President/ Chief Executive Officer
Janet Pike, Executive Assistant
Steven I. Zeisel, General Counsel/ EVP
Tiffany Haas, VP, Congressional Affairs
Kristen Fallon, VP, Congressional Affairs

The recognized voice on retail banking issues in the nation's capital.

3091 Council for Electronic Billing and Payment
13450 Sunrise Valley Drive
Suite 100
Herndon, VA 20171

703-561-1100
E-Mail: runger@nacha.org
Home Page: cebp.nacha.org
Social Media: *LinkedIn*

Robert Unger, Senior Director
Liz Millard, Assistant Director

Promotes electronic consumer and business-to-business billing and payment programs and services across any delivery channel. It also provides an open forum for education, resource development, solution innovation, research and the exchange of information about the electronic billing and the electronic payment industries.
416 Members
Founded in 2008

3092 Credit Union National Association
5710 Mineral Point Rd
Madison, WI 53705

800-356-8010
800-356-9655
FAX 608-231-4333
E-Mail: ccsorders@cuna.coop
Home Page: www.cuna.org
Social Media: *Facebook, Twitter, LinkedIn, YouTube*

Susan Streifel, Chairman
Rodney Staatz, Vice Chairman

Patrick Jury, Secretary
Maurice Smith, Treasurer
Jim Nussle, President Ex Officio

A national trade association for both state and federally chartered credit unions located in the United States.

3093 Electronic Funds Transfer Association

4000 Legato Road
Suite 1100
Fairfax, VA 22033

571-318-5556
FAX 571-318-5557
Home Page: www.efta.org
Social Media: *Twitter*

Kurt Helwig, President & CEO
Pat O'Donnell, Chairman
Melanie Renner, Meeting Coordinator
Lynne Barr, Secretary
Keith Harrison, Treasurer

The Electronic Funds Transfer Association (EFTA) is the nation's leading inter-industry professional association promoting the adoption of electronic payment systems and commerce.
Founded in 1977

3094 Electronic Payments Association NACHA

2550 Wasser Terrace
Suite 400
Herndon, VA 20171

703-561-1100
FAX 703-787-0996
E-Mail: info@nacha.org
Home Page: www.nacha.org
Social Media: *Facebook, Twitter, LinkedIn, YouTube*

Donna Schwartze, Media Contact
Joshua Maze, Sponsorship
Janet O Estep, President & CEO

NACHA manages the development, administration, and governance of the ACH Network, the backbone for the electronic movement of money and data. The ACH Network provides a safe, secure, and reliable network for direct account-to-account consumer, business, and government payments. Annually, it facilitates billions of Direct Deposit via ACH and Direct Payment via ACH transactions. Used by all types of financial institutions, the ACH Network is governed by the fair and equitable NACHA Operating Rules
Founded in 1974

3095 Electronic Transactions Association

1101 16th STREET NW #402
WASHINGTON, DC 20036

202-828-2635
800-695-5509
Home Page: www.electran.org
Social Media: *Facebook, LinkedIn, YouTube, Flickr*

Debra Rossi, President
Greg Cohen, President-Elect
Jeff Rosenblatt, Treasurer
Jeff Sloan, Secretary
Kim Fitzsimmons, Immediate Past-President

A trade organization representing independent sales organizations, merchant service providers and those help them serve their merchant clients.
Founded in 1990

3096 Environmental Bankers Association

1827 Powers Ferry Rd, Building 14
Suite 100
Atlanta, GA 30339

678-619-5045
FAX 678-229-2777
E-Mail: eba@envirobank.org

Home Page: www.envirobank.org
Social Media: *Facebook, Twitter, LinkedIn, YouTube*

Sharon Valverde, President
Geogina Dannatt, Vice President
Richard Belyea, Secretary & Communication
David Lambert, Treasurer
Dan Richardson, General Counsel

EBA voting members are banks, trust companies, credit unions, savings and loan associations, and other financial services organizations with an interest in environmental risk management and related issues. Active participants are bankers from Trust or Credit offices with responsibility for environmental liability, and financial services officers with environmental interests. Affiliate members are from law firms, consulting and insurance organizations.
Founded in 1994

3097 Financial Managers Society

1 North LaSalle Street
Suite 3100
Chicago, IL 60602-4003

312-578-1300
800-275-4367
FAX 312-578-1308
E-Mail: info@fmsinc.org
Home Page: www.fmsinc.org
Social Media: *Facebook, Twitter, LinkedIn, Instagram*

Dick Yingst, President/ CEO
Sydney K Garmong, Chairman
John Westwood, Vice Chairman
Darrell E Blocker, Director-at-Large
Diane DelLella, Director-at-Large

A nonprofit professional society serving the financial services industry.
Founded in 1948

3098 Financial Services Roundtable

600 13th Street, NW
Suite 400
Washington, DC 20005

202-289-4322
E-Mail: info@fsroundtable.org
Home Page: www.fsround.org
Social Media: *Twitter, LinkedIn, YouTube*

Frederick H. Waddell, Chairman
Ajaypal S Banga, Chairman-Elect
Larry Zimpleman, Immediate-Past Chairman
Kessel Stelling, Treasurer
Richard K. Davis, Director

The leading advocacy organization for America's financial services industry. Its members include banking, insurance, asset management, finance, and credit card companies.

3099 Financial Women International

1027 W Roselawn Avenue
Roseville, MN 55113

651-487-7632
866-807-6081
FAX 651-489-1322
E-Mail: info@fwi.org
Home Page: www.fwi.org

Melissa Curzon, President
Cindy Hass, VP
Carleen DeSisto, Secretary

FWI is dedicated to developing leaders, accelerating careers, and generating results for professionals in the banking and financial services industry.
1000 Members
Founded in 1921

3100 Financial Women's Association

215 Park Avenue South
Suite 1712
New York, NY 10003

212-533-2141
E-Mail: FWAoffice@FWA.org
Home Page: fwa.org
Social Media: *Facebook, Twitter, LinkedIn*

Katrin Dambrot, President
Ria Davis, President-Elect
Maureen Adolf, Pat President
Amy Geffen, Executive Director
Ilene Moskowitz, Secretary

A nonprofit organization established by a group of Wall Street Women to support the role and development of women in the financial services industry.
Founded in 1956

3101 Global Association of Risk Professionals

111 Town Square Place
14th Floor
Jersey City, NJ 07310

201-719-7210
FAX 201-222-5022
E-Mail: info@garp.com
Home Page: www.garp.com
Social Media: *Facebook, Twitter, LinkedIn, YouTube, Google+*

Richard Apostolik, President & CEO
Ken Abbott, Chief Risk Officer
William Martin, Chief Risk Officer
Ben Golub, Chief Risk Officer
Laura Dottori, Senior Executive VP & CRO

To be the leading professional association for risk managers, managed by and for its members dedicated to the advancement of the risk profession through education, training and the promotion of best practices globally. Members come from over 100 countries.
52330 Members
Founded in 1996

3102 Impact Mortgage Management Advocacy & Advisory Group

2740 S. Newland Street
Lakewood, CO 80227

303-674-1200
FAX 303-674-1664
E-Mail: bill@immaag.com
Home Page: www.immaag.com

Provides thousands of state licensed mortgage loan originators the information and advocacy support necessary for the industry to deal with absorbing the results of the financial crisis being dealt with by the nation.

3103 Independent Community Bankers of America

1615 L St NW
Suite 900
Washington, DC 20036

202-659-8111
866-843-4222
FAX 202-659-9216
E-Mail: info@icba.org
Home Page: www.icba.org
Social Media: *Facebook, Twitter, LinkedIn, YouTube, Pinterest, Tumblr*

Jack A Hartings, Chairman
Rebeca Romero Rainey, Chairman Elect
R. Scott Heitkamp, Vice Chair
Mike Ellenburg, Secretary
Preston Kennedy, Treasurer

Trade association for the nations community banks.
5000 Members

3104 Institute of Certified Bankers

American Bankers Association
1120 Connecticut Avenue NW
Washington, DC 20036

202-663-5092
800-226-5377
FAX 202-828-4540
E-Mail: icb@aba.com
Home Page: www.aba.com/ICB/default.htm
Social Media: *Facebook, Twitter, LinkedIn*

Frank Keating, President/CEO

A national association of certified professionals in the financial services industry whose mission is to provide financial services professionals with confidence, credibility and recognition through its certifications.
Founded in 1990

3105 Institute of International Bankers

299 Park Avenue
17th Floor
New York, NY 10171

212-421-1611
FAX 212-421-1119
E-Mail: iib@iib.org
Home Page: www.iib.org
Social Media: *Facebook, Twitter, LinkedIn*

Roger Blissett, Chairman
Sarah Miller, CEO
Angelo R Aldana, Vice Chair
John Geremia, Secretary
Joseph Cervelli, Treasurer

To help resolve the many special legislative, regulatory and tax issues confronting internationally headquartered financial institutions that engage in banking, securities and/or insurance activities in the United States.
Founded in 1966

3106 International Financial Services Association

9 Sylvan Way
Suite 130
Parsippany, NJ 07054-3817

973-656-1900
FAX 973-656-1915
E-Mail: info@intlbanking.org
Home Page: www.ifsaonline.org

Tod Burwell, Vice President
Colleen Kennedy, Manager, Programs & Events

Represents the international operations areas of financial services providers, their customers, suppliers and partners. Dedicates itself to meeting the specific needs of those who provide, use, and support trade and payments with particular focus on documentary credits, funds transfer, treasury operations, compliance, and regulatory reporting.
Founded in 1924

3107 Investment Bankers Association

E-Mail: info2@investmentbankersassociation.org
Home Page: www.investmentbankersassociation.org

A national organization for businesses that want to go public and raise capital to meet small regional and independent brokerage firms, investment bankers, capital sources and other capital market service providers.

3108 MasterCard Worldwide

2000 Purchase St
Purchase, NY 10577-2405

914-249-2000
FAX 914-249-4135

Home Page: www.mastercardinternational.com
Social Media: *Facebook, Twitter, LinkedIn*

Robert W Selander, CEO
Sharon Gamsin, VP
Chris Harral, Director
Chris A McWilton, Chief Financial Offcier
Lawrence Flanagan, Chief Marketing Officer

Administers the MasterCard credit and other MasterCard products fo member financial institutions around the world.
25000 Members
Founded in 1940

3109 Mortgage Bankers Association

1919 M Street NW
5th Floor
Washington, DC 20036

202-557-2700
800-793-6222
FAX 202-721-0248
E-Mail: membership@mba.org
Home Page: www.mortgagebankers.org
Social Media: *Facebook, Twitter, LinkedIn, Youtube*

Bill Emerson, Chairman
Rodrigo Lopez, Chair Elect
J David Motley, Vice Chair
David H. Stevens, President & CEO
Jeffrey M Schummer, VP Education/Business Development

Seeks to improve methods of originating, servicing and marketing loans.
2900 Members
Founded in 1914

3110 Mortgage Bankers Association of America

1919 M Street NW
5th Floor
Washington, DC 20036

202-557-2700
800-793-6222
Home Page: www.mbaa.org

Bill Cosgrove, CMB, Chairman
Bill Emerson, Chairman-Elect
Rodrigo Lopez, CMB, Vice Chairman
David H. Stevens, President/ CEO
Marcia Davies, Chief Operating Officer

A national association representing the entire real estate finance industry. This association develops innovative business tools and provides education and training for industry professionals.

3111 NACHA: Electronic Payments Association

2550 Wasser Terrace
Suite 400
Herndon, VA 20171

703-561-1100
FAX 703-787-0996
E-Mail: info@nacha.org
Home Page: www.nacha.org
Social Media: *Facebook, Twitter, LinkedIn, YouTube*

Robert Garinger, President/CEO
Janet C Boyst, Executive VP
Deb Evans-Doyle, Senior Director Conference Mktg
Julie Hedlund, Senior Director Electronic Commerce
Michael Herd, Director Public Relations

To promote the development of electronic solutions that improve the payments for the benefit of its members and their customers.
11000 Members
Founded in 1974

3112 National Association of Affordable Housing Lenders

1667 K Street NW
Suite 210
Washington, DC 20006

202-293-9850
FAX 202-293-9852
E-Mail: naahl@naahl.org
Home Page: www.naahl.org
Social Media: *Twitter, YouTube*

Buzz Roberts, President/CEO
Paul Haaland, COO
Sara Olson, Administrator

Represents America's leaders in moving private capital to those in need. Encompasses 200 organizations committed to increasing private lending and investing in low and moderate-income communities.
Founded in 1990

3113 National Association of Bankruptcy Trustees

One Windsor Cove
Suite 305
Columbia, SC 29223

803-252-5646
800-445-8629
FAX 803-765-0860
E-Mail: info@nabt.com
Home Page: www.nabt.com

Richard D Nelson, President
Dwayne Murray, President-Elect
Ronald R Peterson, Vice President
Brian L.Budsberg, Treasurer
Raymond J Obuchowski, Secretary

A non profit association formed to address the needs of bankruptcy trustees throughout the country and to promote the effectiveness of the bankruptcy system as a whole.
Founded in 1982

3114 National Association of Chapter 13 Trustees

1 Windsor Cove
Suite 305
Columbia, SC 29223

803-252-5646
800-445-8629
FAX 803-765-0860
E-Mail: Info@NACTT.com
Home Page: www.nactt.com

Mary Ida Townson, President
D Sims Crawford, President Elect
Joyce Bradley Babin, VP
David G Peake, Secretary
O. Byron Meredith, Treasurer

Provides a forum within which Chapter 13 Trustees will act as an information and communication resource to advance education, leadership, and continuous improvement in the administration of bankruptcy. We will provide the means to establish and implement professional standards and participate in the national legislative and administrative processes while promoting the highest ethical principles.
1000 Members
Founded in 1965

3115 National Association of Credit Union Supervisory & Auditing Committees

PO Box 160
Del Mar, CA 92014

800-287-5949
FAX 858-792-3884
E-Mail: nacusac@nacusac.org
Home Page: www.nacusac.org

Celeste Shelton, Executive Director
Lauren Clark, Associate Director
Bob Spinder, Associate Director

Michael MacFeeters, Chairman
Cecil Short, Vice Chairman

A unique organization of, by and for credit union supervisory committee members. Provides leadership, support and education to enhance the capability of credit union supervisory and auditing committee members to fulfill their responsibilities.
Founded in 1985

3116 National Association of Federal Credit Unions
3138 10th St N
Arlington, VA 22201-2149

703-522-4770
800-336-4644
FAX 703-524-1082
E-Mail: msc@nafcu.org
Home Page: www.nafcu.org
Social Media: *Facebook, Twitter, LinkedIn, YouTube*

Ed Templeton, Chairman
Richard L Harris, Vice Chairman
Jeanne Kuckey, Treasurer
Debra Schwartz, Secretary
B Dan Berger, President & CEO

A respected and influential trade association that exclusively represents the interests of federal credit unions before the federal government and the public.
Founded in 1967

3117 National Association of Government Guaranteed Lenders
215 East 9th Avenue
Stillwater, OK 74074

405-377-4022
FAX 405-377-3931
E-Mail: info@naggl.org
Home Page: www.naggl.org
Social Media: *Facebook, Twitter, LinkedIn, YouTube*

Anthony Wilkinson, President/CEO
Jane Butler, EVP
Jennifer Shaklee, Assistant VP Marketing
Jennifer Sterret-O'Neill, COO
Larry Conley, Chairman

Promotes professional and governmental affairs interests of financial institutions and small businesses who participate in Small Business Administration guaranteed lending and secondary market programs.
600 Members
Founded in 1984

3118 National Association of Independent Housing Professionals
601 Pennsylvania Ave. NW
South Building, Suite 900
Washington, DC 20004

202-587-9300
FAX 304-267-9046
Home Page: www.naihp.org

Marc Savitt, CRMS, President
Peter Gallo, Vice President
Kate Crawford, Secretary/Treasurer
Brian Benjamin, Legislative Chair
William Howe, Director

A legislative and regulatory organization comprised of all housing industry professionals.

3119 National Association of Mortgage Professionals
2701 W. 15th Street
Suite 536
Plano, TX 75075

972-758-1151
FAX 530-484-2906
E-Mail: membership@namb.org
Home Page: www.namb.org

Social Media: *Facebook, Twitter, LinkedIn, YouTube, RSS*

John Councilman, President
Rocke Andrews, President Elect
Fred Kreger, Vice President
Rick Bettencourt, Secretary
Andy W. Harris, Treasurer

The only national trade association representing the mortgage professional industry. It promotes the industry through programs and services such aseducation, professional certification and government affairs representation.
Founded in 1973

3120 National Association of Mortgage Brokers
2701 West 15th Street
Suite 536
Plano, TX 75075

972-758-1151
FAX 530-484-2906
E-Mail: membership@namb.org
Home Page: www.namb.org
Social Media: *Facebook, Twitter, LinkedIn, Youtube, RSS*

John Councilman, President
Rocke Andrews, President Elect
Fred Kreger, VP
Rick Bettencourt, Secretary
Andy W Harris, Treasurer

Mortgage brokers who seek to increase professionalism and to foster business relationships among members.
27000 Members
Founded in 1973

3121 National Association of Professional Mortgage Women
705 North Mountain Business Center
Suite E-104
Newington, CT 06111

800-827-3034
FAX 469-524-5121
E-Mail: napmw1@napmw.org
Home Page: www.napmw.org
Social Media: *Facebook, LinkedIn, Google+, RSS*

Kelly Hendricks, President
Nikki Bell, President Elect
Windee Falla, Secretary
Judy Alderson, Treasurer
Laurel Knight, Vice President

Serves all mortgage professionals and employers who want to excel. Provides business, personal, and leadership development opportunities advancing women in mortgage-related professions.
4500 Members
Founded in 1964

3122 National Association of State Credit Union Supervisors
1655 Fort Myer Dr
Suite 650
Arlington, VA 22209

703-528-8351
800-728-7927
FAX 703-528-3248
E-Mail: offices@nascus.org
Home Page: www.nascus.org
Social Media: *Facebook, Twitter, LinkedIn*

Steve Pleger, Chairman
Mary Ellen O'Neil, Chair Elect
Jay Bienvenu, Secretary/Treasurer
John Fields, Director
Linda K Jekel, Past President

State chartered credit unions and state credit union supervisors.
900 Members
Founded in 1965

3123 National Bankers Association
1513 P St NW
Washington, DC 20005

202-588-5432
FAX 202-588-5443
E-Mail: mgrant@nationalbankers.org
Home Page: www.nationalbankers.org
Social Media: *Facebook, Twitter*

Michael Grant, President
Preston Pinkett III, Chairman
Neill S Wright, Treasurer
Cynthia Day, Secretary
B Doyle Mitchell Jr, Past President

Members are minority and women's banking institutions, minority individuals employed by majority banks and institutions.
16000 Members
Founded in 1927

3124 National Credit Union Administration
1775 Duke St
Suite 4206
Alexandria, VA 22314-6115

703-518-6300
800-755-1030
FAX 703-518-6539
E-Mail: pacamsil@ncua.gov
Home Page: www.ncua.gov
Social Media: *Facebook, Twitter, LinkedIn*

Deborah Matz, Chairman
David Marquis, Executive Director

Governed by a three member board appointed by the President and confirmed by the US Senate, this independent federal agency charters and supervises federal credit unions. NCUA, with the backing of the full faith and credit of the US government, operates the National Credit Union Share Insurance Fund, insuring the savings of 80 million account holders in all federal credit unions and many state chartered credit unions.
700 Members
Founded in 1909

3125 National Investment Banking Association
422 Chesterfield Road
Bogart, GA 30622

706-208-9620
FAX 706-993-3342
E-Mail: emily@nibanet.org
Home Page: www.nibanet.org
Social Media: *Facebook, Twitter, LinkedIn, Youtube, RSS*

James E Hock, Chairman
Carlo Corzine, Chairman
William Jordan, Treasurer
Gerald A Adler, Chairman , Govt & Legal Committee
Lynne Bolduc, Secretary

A national trade association of regional and independent brokerages, investment banking firms, and related capital market service providers.
Founded in 1932

3126 National Marine Bankers Association
231 South LaSalle Street
Suite 2050
Chicago, IL 60604

312-946-6260
E-Mail: info@marinebankers.org
Home Page: www.marinebankers.org

Micheal Bryant, President
Peggy Bodenreider, VP
Willialm B Otto, Treasurer
Jayme B Yates, Secretary
Jackie Forese, Director

Created to educate current and prospective lenders in marine financing procedures and to

promote the extension of credit to consumer and trade borrowers.
70 Members
Founded in 1980

3127 National Mitigation Banking Association
107 S. West Street # 573
Alexandria, VA 22314

202-457-8409
E-Mail: info@mitigationbanking.org
Home Page: www.mitigationbanking.org

Michael Sprague, President
Donald H Ross, Vice President
Donna Collier, Secretary
Randy Vogel, Treasurer
Wayne White, Immediate Past-President

Promotes federal legislation and regulatory policy that encourages mitigation banking and conservation banking as a means of compensating for adverse impacts to America's wetlands and other natural resources.

3128 National Reverse Mortgage Lenders Association
1400 16th St., NW
Suite 420
Washington, DC 20036

202-939-1760
FAX 202-265-4435
E-Mail: dhicks@dworbell.com
Home Page: www.nrmlaonline.org
Social Media: *Facebook, Twitter, LinkedIn*

Joe DeMarkey, Co-Chairman
Reza Jahangiri, Co-Chairman
Sherry Apanay, Vice-Chairwoman
Mark Browning, Vice-Chairman
Steve McClellan, Secretary

Trade association that serves as an educational resource, policy advocate and public affairs center for reverse mortgage lenders and related professionals.
Founded in 1997

3129 Nonprofit Risk Management Center
204 South King Street
Leesburg, VA 20175

703-777-3504
FAX 202-785-3891
Home Page: www.nonprofitrisk.org
Social Media: *Twitter*

Peter Andrew, President
Lisa Prinz, Treasurer
Carolyn Hayes-Gulston, Secretary
Melanie L Herman, Executive Director
Erin Gloeckner, Project Manager

Provides risk management assistance and resources for community-serving nonprofit organizations.

3130 Public Risk Management Association
700 S. Washington St.
Suite 218
Alexandria, VA 22314

703-528-7701
FAX 703-739-0200
E-Mail: info@primacentral.org
Home Page: www.primacentral.org

Dean Coughenour, President
Regan Rychetsky, Past-President
Terri Evans, President-Elect
Scott Kramer, Director
Lori J Gray, Director

Member based organization which is dedicated to providing practicaleducation, training, and information for public sector risk management practitioners.

3131 Risk Management Association
1801 Market Street
Suite 300
Philadelphia, PA 19103-1628

215-446-4000
800-677-7621
FAX 215-446-4101
E-Mail: customers@rmahq.org
Home Page: www.rmahq.org
Social Media: *Facebook, Twitter, LinkedIn, WordPress*

J Tol Broome Jr, Chairman
Helga Houston, Vice Chair
William F Githens, CEO
H Lynn Harton, Director
C Matthew Lusco, Director

A not-for-profit, member driven professional association whose sole purpose is to advance the use of sound risk principles in the financial services industry.
3000 Members
Founded in 1914

3132 Securities Industry and Financial Markets Association (SIFMA)
1101 New York Ave Nw
Suite 800
Washington, DC 20005-4279

202-962-7300
FAX 202-962-7305
Home Page: www.fisma.org
Social Media: *Facebook, Twitter, LinkedIn*

T Timothy Ryan Jr, President/CEO
Randy Snook, Senior Managing Director/EVP
Donald D Kittell, CFO

SIFMA's mission is to champion policies and practices that benefit investors and issuers, expand and perfect global capital markets, and foster the development of new products and services. SIFMA provides an enhanced member network of access and forward-looking services, as well as premiere educational resources for the professionals within the industry and the investors whom they serve.

3133 Society of Financial Examiners
12100 Sunset Hills Rd
Suite 130
Reston, VA 20190-3221

703-234-4140
800-787-7633
FAX 888-436-8686
E-Mail: sofe@sofe.org
Home Page: www.sofe.org

L. Brackett, Executive Director
Judy Estus, Administrator
William Latza, General Counsel
Annette Knief, President
James Kattman, Treasurer

Professional society for examiners of insurance companies, banks, savings and loans, and credit unions.
Founded in 1973

3134 Society of Risk Management Consultants
621 North Sherman Avenue
Madison, WI 53704

Home Page: www.srmcsociety.org

Michael E Norek, President
David L Stegall, President-Elect
Benjamin C Few III, Treasurer
Christopher J Franki, Secretary
Marie E Piccininni, Director

An international organization of professionals engaged in risk management, insurance and employee benefits consulting.
Founded in 1984

3135 The Association of Executives in Finance, Credit, & International Business
8840 Columbia 100 Parkway
Columbia, MD 21045-2158

410-423-1840
888-256-3242
FAX 410-740-5574
E-Mail: fcib_global@fcibglobal.com
Home Page: www.fcibglobal.com
Social Media: *Twitter, LinkedIn, RSS*

Marta Chacon, Director, The Americas
Ron Shepherd, Director, Business Dev.
Noelin Hawkins, Director, Europe, Middle East
Barry Norton, Advisory Board Chairman
Tim Bastian, Board Member

The premier Association for Finance, Credit and International business professionals. The leading resource for global credit information, professional development and education.
1000+ Members
Founded in 1919

3136 The Bankers Association for Finance and Trade
1120 Connecticut Avenue, NW
Washington, DC 20036

202-663-7575
FAX 202-663-5538
E-Mail: info@baft.org
Home Page: www.baft.org
Social Media: *Facebook, Twitter*

Rita Gonzalez, Managing Director
Michael Quinn, Vice chair
Tod R. Burwell, CEO
Daniel J Scanlan, Secretary-Treasurer
Ian Stewart, Director

3137 The Fiduciary and Investment Risk Management
Post Office Box 507
Stockbridge, GE 30281

678-565-6211
FAX 678-565-8788
E-Mail: info@thefirma.org
Home Page: www.thefirma.org
Social Media: *Facebook, Twitter, LinkedIn, RSS*

Bruce K. Goldberg, President
Jennifer De Vries, Vice President
David Jonke, Secretary
Bradley F. Beshea, SVP, Fiduciary Compliance Officer
John L Clark, Director

Provider of current and relevant fiduciary and investment risk management education and networking opportunities to risk management professionals.

3138 The First
7054 Jefferson Highway
Baton Rouge, LA 70806

225-228-7275
FAX 225-228-7276
Home Page: www.thefirstbank.com
Social Media: *Facebook, Twitter*

Personal and commercial banking. Offers information about services,products, and locations.

3139 University Risk Management and Insurance Association
PO Box 1027
Bloomington, IN 47402

812-855-6683
FAX 812-856-3149
E-Mail: urmia@urmia.org
Home Page: www.urmia.org

Social Media: *Facebook, Twitter, LinkedIn, Flickr. YouTube*

Donna McMahon, President
Kathy E Hargis, President-Elect
Cheryl Lloyd, Secretary
Tish Gade-Jones, Treasurer
Sally Alexander, Director

Advances the discipline of risk management in higer education.

3140 Urban Financial Services Coalition
1200 G St NW
Suite 800
Washington, DC 20005

202-289-8335
800-996-8335
FAX 202-434-8707
E-Mail: ufsc@ufscnet.org
Home Page: www.ufscnet.org
Social Media: *Facebook, Twitter, LinkedIn, Youtube*

Roderick Hayes, President
Dorothy Reed, Vice President
Ola Truelove, Treasurer
Delores Blake, Secretary
Walter Brown, Immediate Past President

Formerly known as the National Association of Urban Bankers is an organization of minority professionals in the financial services industry and related fields.
Founded in 1974

3141 Western Independent Bankers
555 Montgomery Street
Suite 750
San Francisco, CA 94111

415-352-2323
FAX 415-352-2314
E-Mail: info@wib.org
Home Page: www.wib.org
Social Media: *Facebook, Twitter, LinkedIn, YouTube*

Russell A. Colombo, Chair
Bryan Luke, Chair-elect
J David Joves, Secretary
Richard T Beard, Immediate Past Chair
Bruce Lowry, Treasurer

A trade association that informs, educates, and connects community banks with the resources and services to achieve the highest standards of personal and organizational performance.
Founded in 1937

3142 Women's World Banking
122 East 42nd Street
42nd Floor
New York, NY 10168

212-768-8513
FAX 212-768-8519
Home Page: www.womensworldbanking.org
Social Media: *Facebook, Twitter, LinkedIn, YouTube, Google +, Flickr*

Jennifer Riria, Chair
Mary Houghton, Vice Chair
Connie Collingsworth, Secretary
Mary Ellen Iskenderian, President and CEO
J. Thomas Jones, Chief Operating Officer

A global nonprofit organization devoted to giving more low-income women access to the financial tools and resources they require to build security and prosperity.

Newsletters

3143 ABA Bank Directors Briefing
American Bankers Association

1120 Connecticut Avenue NW
Washington, DC 20036

202-663-5000
800-226-5377
FAX 202-828-4548
Home Page: www.aba.com
Social Media: *Facebook, Twitter, LinkedIn*

Frank Keating, President/CEO
Stephen Crowe, Treasurer

Published by the editors of ABA Banking Journal in cooperation with the American Bankers Association. Focuses on keeping bank directors informed about legislative and regulatory developments, summarizing important banking industry trends, updating all directors on the latest thinking in corporate governance, educating new directors in the basics of community bank directorship
Frequency: Monthly

3144 ABA Bankers News
American Bankers Association
1120 Connecticut Avenue NW
Washington, DC 20036-3902

202-635-5000
800-226-5377
FAX 202-663-7543
E-Mail: custserv@aba.com
Home Page: www.aba.com
Social Media: *Facebook, Twitter, LinkedIn*

Frank Keating, President/CEO
Stephen Crowe, Treasurer

For everyone in the banking industry especially CEOs and compliance officers. Learn to use the internet effectively, retain your best customers, reduce risk, nurture a sales culture and more.
Cost: $450.00
Frequency: Bi-Weekly
Founded in 1875

3145 ABIA Insurance News
American Bankers Association
1120 Connecticut Avenue NW
Washington, DC 20036

202-663-5163
800-226-5377
FAX 202-828-4546
E-Mail: vbarton@aba.com
Home Page: www.theabia.com

Paul Petrylak, President/Chairman
Neal Aton, Vice President
David Cissell, Secretary
Val Teagarden, Treasurer

The American Bankers Insurance Association (ABIA) is the insurance subsidiary of the American Bankers Association (ABA). The ABIA's mission is to develop policy and provide advocacy for banks in insurance and to support bank insurance operations through research, education, compliance assistance, and peer group networking opportunities.
300 Members
Frequency: Bi-Weekly
Founded in 2001

3146 AITCO Advisor
Association of Independent Trust Companies
8 S Michigan Ave
Suite 802
Chicago, IL 60603-3452

312-223-1611
FAX 312-580-0165
E-Mail: atico@gss.net
Home Page: www.aitco.net

Marcia Williams, Treasurer
Doug Nunn, President
Tom Blank, General Counsel/Secretary

Features professionally written articles on marketing and legislative issues as well as association updates.
Frequency: Quarterly

3147 AMI Bulletin
Assn for Management Information in Financial Svcs
14247 Saffron Circle
Carmel, IN 46032

317-518-5857
FAX 317-518-5877
E-Mail: ami2@amifs.org
Home Page: www.amifs.org

Andy Schrieff, President
Jeff Nathasingh, Executive VP
Lynn Courchaine, Treasurer

News, calendars, events, and industry articles.
Frequency: Quarterly

3148 Access
American Safe Deposit Association
5433 S 200 E
Franklin, IN 46131-8982

317-738-4432
FAX 317-738-5267
E-Mail: jmclin@aol.com
Home Page: www.tasda.com

Bill Lee, Publisher
Thomas Cullinan, President
J Wayne Merrill, First VP
Winnifred Howard-Hommack, Second Vice President
Kevin Fanning, Treasurer

A newsletter full of timely articles on safe deposit procedures, policies, problems and solutions.
Cost: $10.00

3149 Advocacy Bulletins
CFA Institute
Po Box 3668
Charlottesville, VA 22903-0668

434-951-5499
800-247-8132
FAX 434-951-5262
E-Mail: info@amir.org
Home Page: www.cfainstitute.org

Alan Meder, Chair
John Rogers, President

To communicate time-sensitive information to interested AIMR/CFA Member Societies and members.
Frequency: Periodically

3150 Allied News
Allied Finance Adjusters Conference
P.O.Box 41368
Raleigh, NC 27629

800-621-3016
800-843-1232
FAX 888-949-8520
E-Mail: alliedfinanceadjusters@gmail.com
Home Page: www.alliedfinanceadjusters.com
Social Media: *Facebook, Twitter, LinkedIn*

George Badeen, President

Trade Association of recovery specialists.
Cost: $200.00
Founded in 1936

3151 American Banker
SourceMedia
1 State Street Plaza
27th floor
New York, NY 10004-1561

212-803-8200
800-803-3424
FAX 212-843-9608

E-Mail: custserv@sourcemedia.com
Home Page: www.sourcemedia.com

Douglas Manoni, CEO
Richard Antoneck, CFO
Cost: $99.00
Frequency: Monthly
Founded in 2005

3152 BNA's Banking Report

Bureau of National Affairs
3 Bethesda Metro Center
Suite 250
Bethesda, MD 20814

800-372-1033
FAX 800-253-0332
E-Mail: customercare@bna.com
Home Page: www.bna.com

Donna Ives, VP Operations
Gregory McCaffery, President

Legal and regulatory developments in the financial services industry.
Cost: $1780.00
Frequency: Weekly
ISSN: 1522-5984
Founded in 1929

3153 Bank Alerts

Consumer Bankers Association
1000 Wilson Blvd
Suite 2500
Arlington, VA 22209-3912

703-276-1750
FAX 703-528-1290
E-Mail: research@cbanet.org
Home Page: www.cbanet.org
Social Media: *Facebook, Twitter, LinkedIn*

Richard Hunt, President
Janet Pike, Executive Assistant

Federal legislative developments.
Frequency: Monthly
Circulation: 10,000
Founded in 1919
Printed in on newsprint stock

3154 Bank Directors Briefing

American Bankers Association
1120 Connecticut Avenue NW
Washington, DC 20036-3902

202-635-5000
800-226-5377
FAX 202-663-7597
Home Page: www.aba.com

Matthew Williams, Chair
John Ikard, Vice Chairman

Newsletter reporting on legislative developments and management issues affecting community banks and their boards of directors.
Frequency: Monthly
Circulation: 33130

3155 Bank Rate Monitor

Bank Rate
11760 US Highway 1
Suite 500
North Palm Beach, FL 33408-8888

561-630-2400
FAX 561-625-4540
Home Page: www.bankrate.com

Don Munsell, Production Director

Independent national source for the financial industry.
Cost: $499.00
4 Pages
Frequency: Weekly
Mailing list available for rent: 750 names
Printed in 3 colors

3156 Bank Technology News

SourceMedia

1 State Street Plaza
27th floor
New York, NY 10004-1561

212-803-8200
800-803-3424
FAX 212-843-9608
E-Mail: custserv@sourcemedia.com
Home Page: www.sourcemedia.com

Douglas Manoni, CEO
Richard Antoneck, CFO
Cost: $99.00
Frequency: Monthly
Founded in 2005

3157 Bank Tellers Report

Sheshunoff Information Services
4120 Freidrich Lane
Suite 100
Austin, TX 78744

512-305-6500
800-456-2340
FAX 512-305-6575
E-Mail: customercare.sis@sheshunoff.com
Home Page: www.sheshunoff.com

Bob Mate, CEO
Marge Simmons, Author

General interest publication for bank tellers.
Cost: $449.00
Frequency: Monthly
Founded in 1975

3158 Bank and S&L Quarterly Rating Service

Sheshunoff Information Services
4120 Freidrich Lane
Suite 100
Austin, TX 78744

512-305-6500
800-456-2340
FAX 512-305-6575
E-Mail: customercare.sis@sheshunoff.com
Home Page: www.sheshunoff.com

Bob Mate, CEO

Statistical reports and research on savings and loan institutions.
Cost: $580.00
Frequency: Quarterly
Circulation: 5000
Mailing list available for rent: 5000 names

3159 Banks in Insurance Report

John Wiley & Sons
111 River St
Hoboken, NJ 07030-5790

201-748-6000
800-225-5945
FAX 201-748-6088
E-Mail: info@wiley.com
Home Page: www.wiley.com

Mari Baker, CEO
Jean-Lou Chameau, President
Linda Katehi, Chancellor

Highlights the steps necessary for expansion into insurance products and services through articles that report on legislative activities, regulatory concerns, business and strategies.
Cost: $745.00
16 Pages
Frequency: Monthly
ISSN: 8756-6079
Founded in 1807
Printed in one color on matte stock

3160 Cheklist

BKB Publications

98 Greenwich Avenue
1st Floor
New York, NY 10011-7743

212-807-7933
FAX 212-807-1821
E-Mail: bkbpub1@ix.netcom.com

Brian Burkart, Publisher
Charlene Komar Storey, Editor

Features general news, feature articles, legislative updates, reports on trends, legal advice, marketing ideas, product information and news of state and national association activities.
Cost: $35.00
Frequency: Quarterly
Circulation: 16,000
ISSN: 1066-3029

3161 Client Quarterly

WPI Communications
55 Morris Ave
Suite 300
Springfield, NJ 07081-1422

973-467-8700
800-323-4995
FAX 973-467-0368
E-Mail: info@wpicommunications.com
Home Page: www.wpicomm.com

Steve Klinghoffer, Owner/Publisher
Lori Klinghoffer, Executive Vice President

Information and advice on financial, business and tax matters.
Frequency: Quarterly
Founded in 1952

3162 Community Bank President

Siefer Consultants
525 Cayuga Street
PO Box 1384
Storm Lake, IA 50588-1384

712-660-1026
FAX 866-680-5866
E-Mail: info@siefer.com
Home Page: www.siefer.com

Dan Siefer, Publisher

Profit making opportunities for financial institutions.
Cost: $297.00
8 Pages
Frequency: Monthly

3163 Compliance & Management Bulletin

American Bankers Association
1120 Connecticut Avenue NW
Washington, DC 20036-3902

202-663-5000
800-226-5377
FAX 202-828-4540
E-Mail: custserv@aba.com
Home Page: www.aba.com

Frank Keating, President/CEO
Albert Kelly, Chair

Includes the information you need to keep up with and respond to the latest in new and revised laws and regulations affecting your institution's management and operations.
Cost: $375.00
Frequency: Published, As Needed
Circulation: 2000
Founded in 1992

3164 Consumer Bankers Association

Consumer Bankers Association
1000 Wilson Blvd
Suite 2500
Arlington, VA 22209-3912

703-276-1750
FAX 703-528-1290

E-Mail: webmaster@cbanet.org
Home Page: www.cbanet.org

Richard Hunt, President
Janet Pike, Executive Assistant

Legislative newsletter on retail banking for association members.
Founded in 1919

3165 Credit Card Management
Thomson Financial Publishing
1 State St
27th Floor
New York, NY 10004-1481

212-825-8445
800-328-9378
FAX 212-292-5216
E-Mail: general.info@thomson.com
Home Page: www.sourcemedia.com

Douglas Manoni, CEO
Richard Antoneck, CFO

Information on the major developments in the credit card industry.
Cost: $98.00
74 Pages
Frequency: Monthly
Circulation: 19000
Printed in 4 colors on glossy stock

3166 Credit Union Journal
SourceMedia
1 State St
27th Floor
New York, NY 10004-1561

212-803-8200
800-803-3424
FAX 212-843-9608
E-Mail: custserv@sourcemedia.com
Home Page: www.sourcemedia.com

Douglas Manoni, CEO
Richard Antoneck, CFO
Cost: $99.00
Frequency: Monthly
Founded in 2005

3167 Current Issues in Bank Auditing
Bank Research Associates
5866 Kootenai Lane
PO Box 7812
Boise, ID 83707-1812

208-322-3508
Home Page: www.bankresearchassociates.com

Don L Raymond CPA, Editor

Offers information and updates on auditing of financial institutions.
Cost: $98.00
6 Pages
Frequency: Monthly
Founded in 1979

3168 DTCC Newsletter
Depository Trust Company
55 Water St
New York, NY 10041-0024

212-855-1000
FAX 212-855-2350
E-Mail: info@dtcc.com
Home Page: www.dtcc.com

Robert Druskin, Chairman
Michael Bodson, President

Information for the banking and securities industry.
Frequency: Monthly
Circulation: 7000
Founded in 1999

3169 Daily Treasury Statement
Financial Management Service

3700 E West Highway
Room 502A
Hysttaville, MD 20782

202-874-9790
800-826-9434
FAX 202-874-8447
E-Mail: dts.Questions@fms.treas.gov
Home Page: www.fms.treas.gov

Richard L Gregg, Commissioner
Melanie Rigney, Editor

This report offers the latest news of the Treasury Department.
Frequency: Daily
Founded in 1974

3170 Digest for Corporate & Securities Lawyers
Bowne & Company
55 Water Street
New York, NY 10041

212-924-500
212-229-3400
Home Page: www.bowne.com

Bruce Brumberg, Editor-in-Chief
Johanna McKenzie, Editor
Susan Koffman, Editor
Karen Axelrod, Managing Editor
David Shea, Chairman/CEO

Summaries of articles on corporate finance, mergers acquisitions, initial public offerings (ipos) and restructuring. Selects articles from hundreds of publications focusing on articles trends, strategies and advice on deal structuring.
2700 Members
Frequency: Monthly
Founded in 1775

3171 Direct Deposit Authorization Forms
NACHA: Electronic Payments Association
13450 Sunrise Valley Drive
Suite 100
Herndon, VA 20171

703-561-1100
FAX 703-787-0996
E-Mail: info@nacha.org
Home Page: www.nacha.org

Janet O Estep, CEO
Maurice Haitema, Chairperson

These authorizations are for companies looking for generic authorization forms that market ACH benefits to consumers.
Cost: $30.00
Frequency: Monthly

3172 Directors & Trustees Digest
American Bankers Association
1120 Connecticut Avenue NW
Washington, DC 20036-3902

202-663-5000
FAX 202-828-4540
E-Mail: custserv@aba.com
Home Page: www.aba.com

Frank Keating, President/CEO
Albert Kelly, Chairman
Steven Crowe, Treasurer
Monique Hanis, Marketing/Business Development

Provides corporate governance guidance, outlines board legal and fiduciary responsibilities and offers resourceful information on board management relations.
Frequency: Monthly

3173 Examiner
Conference of State Bank Supervisors

1129 20th Street, N.W.
9th Floor
Washington, DC 20036-4327

202-296-2840
FAX 202-296-1928
Home Page: www.csbs.org

Neal Milner, CEO
Thomas Harlow, CFO
Cecelia Smith, Senior Manager, Administration
John Gorman, General Counsel

Provides news, analysis and commentary on the important events affecting the state banking system.
Frequency: Weekly

3174 FSPA Newsletter
Financial & Security Products Association
Plaza Ladera, 5300 Sequoia NW
Suite 205
Albuquerque, NM 87120

505-839-7958
800-843-6082
FAX 505-839-0017
E-Mail: info@fspa1.com
Home Page: www.fspa1.com

Mark Thatcher, Chairman
Bill Mercer, President
John M Vrabec, Executive Director

Offers timely ideas and techniques to help you compete and run your business more effectively. Also provides low-cost opportunities for members to advertise their products and/or services within the body of the newsletter, or in an insert included with the newsletter mailing.
Frequency: Monthly

3175 Federal Reserve Bulletin
Board of Governors of the Federal Reserve System
20th St & Constitution Ave N
Washington, DC 20551-0001

202-452-3284
FAX 202-452-3101
Home Page: www.federalreserve.gov
Social Media: *Facebook, Twitter, LinkedIn*

Ben S Bernanke, Chairman
Janet Yellen, Vice Chairman

Reports on analysis on economic developments, regulatory issues and new data. The quarterly version will no longer be published, however the Board will print an annual compendium.
Frequency: Annual
Founded in 1913

3176 Federal Reserve Regulatory Service
Federal Reserve Board Publishers
20th St & Constitution Ave N
Washington, DC 20551-0001

202-452-3000
FAX 202-452-3819
E-Mail: publication-bog@frbog.frb.gov
Home Page: www.federalreserve.gov
Social Media: *Facebook, Twitter, LinkedIn*

Ben S Bernanke, Chairman
Janet Yellen, Vice Chairman

Consumer and community affairs.
Cost: $200.00
Frequency: Monthly

3177 Financial Services Daily
SNL Securities
One SNL Plaza
PO Box 2124
Charlottesvle, VA 22902

434-977-1600
FAX 434-977-4466

E-Mail: CustomerService@snl.com
Home Page: www.snl.com

Mike Chinn, President/CEO
Nick Cafferillo, COO

Comprehensive daily coverage of the financial services and technology sectors.
Cost: $795.00
40 Pages
Frequency: Monthly
Founded in 1987

3178   Funds Transfer Report
Bankers Research
PO Box 431
Westport, CT 06881-0431
Ted Volckhausen Sr, Publisher/Co-Editor
Ted Volckhausen Jr, Editor

Offers banking and financial information to professionals and consumers.
Cost: $324.00
Frequency: Monthly

3179   Global Investment Technology
Global Investment Technology
909 Third Avenue
27th Floor
New York, NY 10022

212-370-3700
FAX 212-370-4606
E-Mail: info@globalinv.com
Home Page: www.globalinv.com

Micheal Horton, Publisher
Paven Saeghel, Editor-in-Chief

Focuses exclusively on strategic business trends, operations, and automation issues facing US and non-US investment institutions and banks.
Cost: $695.00
Frequency: Bi-Weekly
Circulation: 1800
Founded in 1991

3180   Global Survey of Regulatory & Market Developments in Banking
Institute of International Bankers
299 Park Ave
17th Floor
New York, NY 10171-3896

212-421-1611
FAX 212-421-1119
E-Mail: iib@iib.org
Home Page: www.iib.org
Social Media: *Facebook, Twitter, LinkedIn*

Sarah ""sally"" Miller, CEO
Richard Coffman, General Counsel
William Goodwin, Communications Director

The study documents the economic contributions that international banks make to the United States, and also addresses the benefits that other countries enjoy from the extensive activities of United States and other non-domestic banks in their markets.
Frequency: Annual

3181   IBES Monthly Comments
Lynch, Jones and Ryan
1633 Broadway
48th Floor
New York, NY 10019

212-310-9500
800-992-7526
FAX 646-223-9081
E-Mail: ljrinfo@ljr.com
Home Page: www.ljr.com

Stanley Chamberlin, Publisher
Todd W Burns, President

Monitors changes in global earning estimates database.
Founded in 1966

3182   ICBA Washington Report
Independent Community Bankers of American
1615 L Street NW
Suite 900
Washington, DC 20036

202-659-8111
E-Mail: info@icba.org
Home Page: www.icba.org

Camden R Fine, President/CEO
Rachael Solomon, Advertising Contact

Provides detailed coverage of important federal legislative and regulatory developments specifically for community bankers.
Cost: $60.00
Frequency: Monthly

3183   IFSA Newsletter
International Financial Services Association
1120 Connecticut Avenue, NW
Washington, DC 20036

20 -66 -757
FAX 202-663-5538
E-Mail: info@baft-ifsa.com
Home Page: www.ifsaonline.org
Social Media: *Facebook, Twitter, LinkedIn*

Tod Burwell, Vice President
250 Pages
Frequency: Quarterly
Founded in 1924

3184   In Focus
National Assn of Government Guaranteed Lenders
215 East 9th Avenue
Stillwater, OK 74074

405-377-4022
FAX 405-377-3931
E-Mail: bfortune@naggl.com
Home Page: www.naggl.com

Tony Wilkinson, President/CEO
Jennifer Sterrett O'Neill, EVP/COO
Jenifer Brake, Assistant VP Marketing
Jennifer Sterrett-O'Neill, Assistant VP Communications

Practical tips that will help you build the little efficiencies that make a big difference.
Frequency: Monthly

3185   Inside Mortgage Compliance
Inside Mortgage Finance Publishers
7910 Woodmont Ave
Suite 1000
Bethesda, MD 20814-7019

301-951-1240
FAX 301-656-1709
E-Mail: imce@imfpubs.com
Home Page: www.imfpubs.com

Guy Cecala, Owner/Publisher

Keeps executives on top of crucial and evolving legal and regulatory issues. Covers fair housing, predatory lending, consumer protection, RESPA, TILA, lawsuits. Features monthly CRA ratings.
Cost: $571.00
14 Pages
Frequency: Monthly
ISSN: 1093-605X
Founded in 1990
Mailing list available for rent: 750 names
Printed in 2 colors on matte stock

3186   Inside Strategy
Strategy Research Corporation
100 NW 37th Avenue
Miami, FL 33125

305-649-5400
FAX 305-643-5584

E-Mail: strategy@canect.net
Home Page: www.strategyresearch.com

Johanna Strouss, Editor
Richard Tobin, President

Inside Strategy is a newsletter that covers trends and developments in Latin America and the US Hispanic market mostly obtained from SRC, studies, products services and reports.
38511 Pages
Frequency: Monthly
Founded in 1998

3187   Inside The GSEs
Inside Mortgage Finance Publishers
7910 Woodmont Ave
Suite 1000
Bethesda, MD 20814-7019

301-951-1240
FAX 301-656-1709
E-Mail: service@imfpubs.com
Home Page: www.imfpubs.com

Guy Cecala, Owner
Greg Johnson, Editor
John Bancroft, Managing Editor
Mary L Probka, Director Marketing/Circulation

Subscribers know the latest on GSE finance, products, political contributions, their critics and supporters, and news on potential reform, controversies and regulatory activities.
Cost: $763.00
14 Pages
Frequency: Bi-Weekly
ISSN: 1093-605X
Founded in 1985
Mailing list available for rent: 400 names
Printed in 2 colors on matte stock

3188   MSRB Manual
Municipal Securities Rulemaking Board
1900 Duke St
Suite 600
Alexandria, VA 22314-3461

703-797-6600
FAX 703-797-6700
E-Mail: MSRBsupport@msrb.org
Home Page: www.msrb.org

Lynnette Hotkis, Executive Director
Marcelo Vieira, Director Research

Rules of the Municipal Rule-Making Board.
Cost: $7.00
Founded in 1975

3189   NACHA: Electronic Payments Association Newsletter
NACHA: The Electronic Payments Association
13450 Sunrise Valley Drive
Suite 100
Herndon, VA 20171

703-561-1100
FAX 703-787-0996
E-Mail: info@nacha.org
Home Page: www.nacha.org

Marcie Haitema, Chairperson
Janet O Estep, CEO

Articles on industry self regulatory organizations for automated clearing house payment systems and other electronic payments.
Cost: $120.00
Printed in 2 colors on matte stock

3190   NAGGL News Flash
National Assn of Government Guaranteed Lenders
215 East 9th Avenue
Stillwater, OK 74074

405-377-4022
FAX 404-377-3931

E-Mail: bfortune@naggl.com
Home Page: www.naggl.org

Tony Wilkinson, President/CEO
Jennifer Sterrett O'Neill, EVP/COO
Jenifer Brake, Assistant VP Marketing
Jennifer Sterrett-O'Neill, Assistant VP
Communications

This email is an at-a-glance review of recent industry news.
Frequency: Bi-Monthly

3191 Nilson Report
HSN Consultants
1110 Eugenia Place
Suite 100
Carpinteria, CA 930113-992

805-684-8800
FAX 805-684-8825
E-Mail: info@nilsonreport.com
Home Page: www.nilsonreport.com

H Spencer Nilson, Publisher

Credit card newsletter.
Cost: $945.00
12 Pages
Frequency: BiWeekly

3192 Opportunities for Banks in Life Insurance
American Association of Bank Directors
1250 24th Street, NW
Suite 700
Washington, DC 20037

20 -46 -488
FAX 202-349-8080
E-Mail: info@aabd.org
Home Page: www.aabd.org

David Baris, Executive Director

The guide reviews best insurance sales practices, distribution strategies, selling through investment brokers, using licensed branch bankers, referrals from investment specialists, referrals from licensed branch bankers, stand alone life specialists, direct sales and more.
Cost: $12.50

3193 Origination News
Thomson Financial
One State Street Plaza
27th floor
New York, NY 10004

212-803-8760
FAX 212-292-5216
Home Page: www.originationnews.com

Elaine Yadlon, Plant Manager
Richard J Harrington, President/CEO

Information for mortgage industry executives on mortgage brokers, mortgage bankers and mortgage executives in commercial banks, savings banks, savings and loan associations and credit unions.
Cost: $78.00
Frequency: Monthly

3194 Payments System Report
National Automated Clearing House Association
13450 Sunrise Valley Drive
Suite 100
Herndon, VA 20171-4607

703-561-1100
800-487-9180
FAX 703-787-0996
E-Mail: info@nacha.org
Home Page: www.nacha.org
Social Media: *Facebook, Twitter, LinkedIn*

Janet O Estep, CEO

Official source for Automated Clearing House (ACH) news and information. Contains reports on rule changes, legislative and regulatory de-

velopments, policy issues, market research, product developments and marketing solutions.
Frequency: Monthly

3195 Peer News
American Bankers Association
1120 Connecticut Avenue NW
Washington, DC 20036

202-635-5000
800-226-5377
FAX 202-828-4540
E-Mail: icb@aba.com
Home Page: www.aba.com/icbcertifications

Frank Keating, President/CEO
Albert Kelly, Chairman
Steven Crowe, Treasurer
Monique Hanis, Marketing/Business Development
Mark DeBaugh, Marketing/Communications Manager

ICB members receive a newsletter that shares program developments, member career notes, insights from ICB leadership, the latest continuing education opportunities, and more.
Frequency: Quarterly

3196 Pratt's Bank Security Report
AS Pratt & Sons
805 15th St. NW
Third Floor
Washington, DC 20005-2207

800-572-2797
E-Mail: customercare.sis@sheshunoff.com
Home Page: www.aspratt.com

Peter Knopp, Editor

Security officers and consultants can keep up with the latest developments affecting bank security by subscribing to Pratt's Bank Security Report.
Cost: $455.00
Frequency: Monthly
Founded in 1867

3197 RTC Suits Against Savings Institution Directors and Officers
American Association of Bank Directors
1250 24th Street, NW
Suite 700
Washington, DC 20037

20 -46 -488
FAX 202-349-8080
E-Mail: info@aabd.org
Home Page: www.aabd.org

David Baris, Executive Director

This study reviews all 90 of the cases in the RTC's public files that were filed by the RTC against directors and officers.
Cost: $85.00

3198 Regional Mortgage Market Report
Mortgage Bankers Association
1717 Rhode Island Avenue, NW
Suite 400
Washington, DC 20036

202-557-2700
E-Mail: membership@mortgagebankers.org
Home Page: www.mortgagebankers.org
Social Media: *Facebook, Twitter, LinkedIn*

The Regional Mortgage Market Report for MSAs and/or states has been designed to provide mortgage professionals with a primary source of information to help identify mortgage lending opportunities and manage the risks associated with mortgage servicing.
Cost: $395.00
Frequency: Quarterly
Founded in 1914

3199 Report of Task Force on Asset Freezes of Bank Directors and Officers
American Association of Bank Directors

1250 24th Street, NW
Suite 700
Washington, DC 20037

20 -46 -488
FAX 202-349-8080
E-Mail: info@aabd.org
Home Page: www.aabd.org

David Baris, Executive Director
Cost: $25.00

3200 SCOR Report
Stewart Gordon Associates
PO Box 781992
Dallas, TX 75378-1992

972-620-2489
FAX 972-406-0213
E-Mail: tsg@scor-report.com
Home Page: www.scor-report.com

Tom Stewart Gordon, Publisher
C Delton Simmons, Circulation Manager
Anne D Hall, Production Manager

Capital information alternatives for small business. Target audience: small business, their lawyers and accountants.
Cost: $280.00
Founded in 1994

3201 SNL Bank & Thrift Daily
SNL Securities
212 7th Street NE
Charlottesville, VA 22902-2124

434-977-1600
FAX 434-977-4466
E-Mail: subscriptions@snl.com
Home Page: www.snl.com
Social Media: *Twitter, Youtube*

Michael Chinn, President/CEO
Nick Cafferillo, COO

Summary of previous week's acquisition announcements, branch sales, merger conversions, FDIC transactions and deal updates and perspectives.
Cost: $1700.00
Frequency: Weekly
Founded in 1987

3202 SNL REIT Weekly
SNL Securities
212 7th Street NE
Charlottesvle, VA 22902

434-977-1600
FAX 434-977-4466
E-Mail: subscriptions@snl.com
Home Page: www.snl.com
Social Media: *Twitter, Youtube*

Michael Chinn, President/CEO
Nick Cafferillo, COO

Fax newsletter that summarizes the previous week's activity involving REITs. Includes comprehensive articles on current industry trends, condensed news stories, recent capital offerings and the latest market information.
Cost: $496.00
15 Pages
Frequency: Weekly
Founded in 1987

3203 Secondary Mortgage Markets
Federal Home Loan Mortgage Corporation
8200 Jones Branch Drive
McLean, VA 22102-3110

703-903-2000
800-424-5401
FAX 703-903-4045
E-Mail: smm@frediemac.com
Home Page: www.freddiemac.com

Charles E. Haldeman, CEO
Ralph Boyd, Executive VP Community Relations

Covers buying and selling residential and commercial mortgage-backed and asset-backed loans, marketing, and risk management.
Frequency: Monthly
Circulation: 15000
Founded in 1970

3204   Securities & Investments M&A
SNL Securities
212 7th Street NE
Charlottesvle, VA 22902

434-977-1600
FAX 434-977-4466
E-Mail: CustomerService@snl.com
Home Page: www.snl.com
Social Media: *Twitter, Youtube*

Michael Chinn, President/CEO
Nick Cafferillo, COO

Fully devoted to M&A in the securities and asset management sectors.
Cost: $795.00
40 Pages
Frequency: Monthly
Founded in 1987

3205   Specialty Finance M&A
SNL Securities
212 7th Street NE
Charlottesvle, VA 22902

434-977-1600
FAX 434-977-4466
E-Mail: CustomerService@snl.com
Home Page: www.snl.com
Social Media: *Twitter, Youtube*

Michael Chinn, President/CEO
Nick Cafferillo, COO

A unique source dedicated exclusively to specialty finance M&A.
Cost: $795.00
40 Pages
Frequency: Monthly
Founded in 1987

3206   Study of Leading Banks in Insurance
American Bankers Insurance Association
1120 Connecticut Avenue NW
Washington, DC 20036

202-663-5163
800-226-5377
FAX 202-828-4546
E-Mail: vbarton@aba.com
Home Page: www.aba.com

Frank Keating, President/Chairman
Albert Kelly, Chairman
David Cissell, Secretary
Neal Aton, Treasurer

Presents the findings from the eighth research of the current and planned insurance activities of U.S. banks. Designed as a management tool for executives who need to understand how the bank-insurance industry is developing.
300 Members
Frequency: Annual
Founded in 2001

3207   Thrift Insider
Inside Mortgage Finance Publishers
7910 Woodmont Ave
Suite 1000
Bethesda, MD 20814-7019

301-951-1240
FAX 301-656-1709
E-Mail: service@imfpubs.com
Home Page: www.imfpubs.com

Guy Cecala, Owner

Complete coverage of regulatory, legislative, legal, accounting, and market issues in the thrift industry.
Cost: $485.00
Frequency: Bi-Weekly

3208   U.S. Banker
SourceMedia
1 State St
27th Floor
New York, NY 10004-1561

212-803-8200
800-803-3424
FAX 212-843-9608
E-Mail: custserv@sourcemedia.com
Home Page: www.sourcemedia.com

Douglas Manoni, CEO
Richard Antoneck, CFO
Cost: $99.00
Frequency: Monthly
Founded in 2005

3209   World Bank News
World Bank
1818 H St Nw
Room U11-147
Washington, DC 20433-0002

202-473-1000
FAX 202-477-6391
Home Page: www.mehr.org

Graeme Wheeler, CEO
Paul Wolfowitz, President
Cynthia Delgadillo, Production Manager

For journalists and the developing community
Frequency: Fortnightly
Circulation: 9000
Founded in 1980

Magazines & Journals

3210   A Guide to Implementing Direct Payment
NACHA: Electronic Payments Association
13450 Sunrise Valley Drive
Suite 100
Herndon, VA 20171

703-561-1100
FAX 703-787-0996
E-Mail: info@nacha.org
Home Page: www.nacha.org
Social Media: *Facebook, Twitter, LinkedIn*

Janet O Estep, CEO

A complete overview of these popular ACH applications. Also discussed are benefits, costs, operational/implementation concerns and promotional efforts. Included are sample promotional materials and implementation checklists.

3211   A Profile of State Chartered Banking
1129 20th Street, N.W.
9th Floor
Washington, DC 20036-4327

202-296-2840
800-886-2727
FAX 202-296-1928
E-Mail: rstromberg@csbs.org
Home Page: www.csbs.org

John Ryan, President/CEO
Cecelia Smith, Senior Manager, Administration
54 Pages
Frequency: Monthly
Founded in 1902

3212   ABA Bank Compliance
American Bankers Association
1120 Connecticut Avenue NW
Washington, DC 20036-3971

202-635-5000
800-226-5377
FAX 202-663-7543

E-Mail: custserv@aba.com
Home Page: www.aba.com

Frank Keating, President
Albert Kelly, Chairman

The source for timely, authoritative analysis of the ever-changing regulatory environment. Covers all the current regulatory issues, such as Privacy and E-Commerce, and perennial Compliance focus areas, such as lending, the Community Reinvestment Act, risk management, training and technology.
Cost: $450.00
Frequency: Bi-Monthly
Founded in 1875

3213   ABA Bank Marketing
American Bankers Association
1120 Connecticut Avenue NW
Washington, DC 20036-3971

202-635-5000
800-226-5377
FAX 202-828-4540
E-Mail: custserv@aba.com
Home Page: www.aba.com

Frank Keating, President
Albert Kelly, Chairman

A designed package of marketing intelligence, featuring essential industry news, in-depth articles, award-winning columnists and opinions, useful case studies and time-saving advice.
Cost: $120.00
Frequency: Monthly
Founded in 1875

3214   ABA Bank Marketing Survey Report
ABA Marketing Network
1120 Connecticut Avenue NW
Washington, DC 20036-3971

202-663-5000
800-226-5377
FAX 202-828-4540
E-Mail: marketingnetwork@aba.com
Home Page: www.aba.com/marketingnetwork/

Frank Keating, President
Albert Kelly, Chairman

The ABA Bank Marketing Survey Report provides comprehensive detailed benchmarks of bank marketing in such areas as marketing expenditures, marketing functions, market segmentation strategies, cross-selling/sales incentives, direct marketing, Internet marketing and advertising agency use.

3215   ABA Banking Journal
Simmons-Boardman Publishing Corporation
345 Hudson St
12th Floor
New York, NY 10014-7123

212-620-7200
FAX 212-633-1165
E-Mail: bstreeter@sbpub.com
Home Page: www.simmonsboardman.com

Arthur J McGinnis Jr, President

The official journal of the American Bank Association, reporting on the banking industry.
Frequency: Monthly
Circulation: 32867
Founded in 1908
Mailing list available for rent

3216   ABA Consumer Banking Digest
American Bankers Association
1120 Connecticut Avenue NW
Washington, DC 20036-3902

202-635-5000
800-226-5377
FAX 202-828-4547

E-Mail: drhodes@aba.com
Home Page: www.aba.com

Frank Keating, President
Albert Kelly, Chairman

Provides perspectives on the latest developments, shifts and changes in the e-commerce sector. The goal is to provide a comprehensive, yet concise, description of current events shaping the rapidly emerging world of e-commerce and banking.
Cost: $450.00
Frequency: Bi-Monthly
Founded in 1875

3217 ABA Reference Guide for Regulatory Compliance
American Bankers Association
1120 Connecticut Avenue NW
Washington, DC 20036-3200

202-635-5000
800-226-5377
FAX 202-663-7597
Home Page: www.aba.com

Frank Keating, President
Albert Kelly, Chairman

Ideal source for Compliance Managers, Department Managers and Staff, Product Managers, and Retail/Branch Managers and those preparing for the Certified Regulatory Compliance Manager Exam.
Cost: $350.00
Frequency: Annual

3218 ABA Trust & Investments
American Bankers Association
1120 Connecticut Avenue NW
Washington, DC 20036

202-635-5000
800-226-5377
FAX 202-828-4540
E-Mail: custserv@aba.com
Home Page: www.aba.com

Frank Keating, President
Albert Kelly, Chairman

Brings current, authoritative, wide-ranging coverage and updates on all aspects of the trust and investments industry
Cost: $120.00
15 Pages
Frequency: Bi-Monthly

3219 ACH Marketing Handbook: A Guide for Financial Institutions & Companies
NACHA: The Electronic Payments Association
13450 Sunrise Valley Drive
Suite 100
Herndon, VA 20171

703-561-1100
FAX 703-787-0996
E-Mail: info@nacha.org
Home Page: www.nacha.org

Marcie Haitema, Chairperson
Janet O Estep, CEO

Designed for financial institutions and companies to assist them in understanding ACH products and services-their benefits, risk management considerations, and consumer perspectives.
Cost: $70.00
Frequency: Annual+

3220 ACH Operating Rules & Guidelines
NACHA: Electronic Payments Association
13450 Sunrise Valley Drive
Suite 100
Herndon, VA 20171

703-561-1100
FAX 703-787-0996

E-Mail: info@nacha.org
Home Page: www.nacha.org

Janet O Estep, CEO
Marcie Haitema, Chairperson

Reflects the results of the Rules Simplifications initiative.
Cost: $78.00

3221 ACH Operating Rules, Corporate Edition
NACHA: Electronic Payments Association
13450 Sunrise Valley Drive
Suite 100
Herndon, VA 20171

703-561-1100
FAX 703-787-0996
E-Mail: info@nacha.org
Home Page: www.nacha.org

Janet O Estep, CEO
Marcie Haitema, Chairperson

Reflects the results of the Rules Simplification initiative. Previously organized around major topics, the simplified Rules framework is structured around the rights and responsibilities of participants in the ACH Network.
Cost: $46.00

3222 ACH Settlement Guide
NACHA: Electronic Payments Association
13450 Sunrise Valley Drive
Suite 100
Herndon, VA 20171

703-561-1100
FAX 703-787-0996
E-Mail: info@nacha.org
Home Page: www.nacha.org
Social Media: *Facebook, Twitter, LinkedIn*

Janet O Estep, CEO

Designed to provide a thorough working knowledge of how money flows through the ACH Network and to equip financial institutions with the necessary tools to reconcile the daily ACH. Included in this publication are examples of statements, ACH advices and a sample balancing worksheet that financial institutions can use as a model for daily reconciling. This document was written as a direct result of financial institutions losing money due to the mismanagement of the ACH settlement function.

3223 AFP Exchange
Association for Financial Professionals
4520 East West Hwy
Suite 750
Bethesda, MD 20814-3319

301-907-2862
FAX 301-907-2864
E-Mail: afp@afponline.org
Home Page: www.afponline.org

Michael Connolly, Chairman of the Board
Susan Glass, Vice Chairman
James Kaitz, President & CEO

AFP Exchange is published for financial professionals. Editorial highlights include case studies and practical business information. Regular departments include outlook, new products and services, calendar and book reviews.
Cost: $90.00
80 Pages
Frequency: Bi-Monthly
Circulation: 12000
Founded in 1979
Printed in 4 colors on glossy stock

3224 AITCO Membership Directory
Association of Independent Trust Companies

8 S Michigan Ave
Suite 1000
Chicago, IL 60603-3452

312-223-1611
FAX 312-580-0165
E-Mail: aitco@gss.net
Home Page: www.aitco.net

Douglas Nunn, President
Marcia Williams, Treasurer
Tom Blank, General Counsel/Secretary

Provides members with contact information on peers as well as industry vendors. This reference tool also include a listing of key officers as well as detailed descriptions of the company's product line and specialty areas.
50+ Pages

3225 American Banker
American Banker/SourceMedia
1 State St
27th Floor
New York, NY 10004-1561

212-803-8450
800-221-1809
FAX 212-843-9600
E-Mail: adam.silverstone@sourcemedia.com
Home Page: www.sourcemedia.com

Douglas Manoni, CEO
Richard Antoneck, CFO

Focuses on the continuing changes in banking, including lending, money market shifts, developments in operations and technology, marketing, mortgages and mergers.
Cost: $945.00
Circulation: 18754
Founded in 1835

3226 BAI Banking Strategies
Bank Administration Institute
115 S. LaSalle Street
Suite 3300
Chicago, IL 60603-3801

312-683-2464
888-284-4078
FAX 312-683-2373
E-Mail: info@bai.org
Home Page: www.bai.org
Social Media: *Facebook, Twitter, LinkedIn, Youtube*

Lewis Fischer, Chairman of the Board
Scott Peters, Vice Chairman

Offers insightful editorial perspective in-depth unbiased coverage of important strategic issues and industry best practices.
Frequency: Monthly

3227 Bank Director News
American Association of Bank Directors
1250 24th Street, NW
Suite 700
Washington, DC 20037

202-463-4888
FAX 202-349-8080
E-Mail: info@aabd.org
Home Page: www.aabd.org

David Baris, Executive Director
Frequency: quarterly

3228 Bank Insurance & Securities Marketing
Bank Insurance and Securities Association
2025 M Street NW
Suite 800
Washington, DC 20036

202-367-1111
FAX 202-367-2111
E-Mail: bisa@BISAnet.org
Home Page: www.bisanet.org

Jim McNeil, Executive Director
Marc A Vosen, President

The official publication of the Bank Insurance & Securities Association, sets the standard for in-depth industry reporting. Offers readers expert advice, exemplary editorials, in-depth articles and timely news updates.
Founded in 2002

3229 Bank News
Bank News Publications
PO Box 29156
Shawnee Mission, KS 66205-9156

913-261-7000
800-336-1120
FAX 913-261-7010
E-Mail: info@banknews.com
Home Page: www.banknews.com

Janet Holman, President & Publisher
Joel Holman, CEO & Publisher

News and features for banks and bankers.
Cost: $79.00
64 Pages
Frequency: Monthly
Circulation: 7000
Founded in 1901
Printed in 4 colors on glossy stock

3230 Bank Notes
510 King Street
Suite 410
Alexandria, VA 22314

703-549-0977
800-966-7475
FAX 703-548-5945
E-Mail: eba@envirobank.org
Home Page: www.envirobank.org

Rick Ferguson, President
Scott Beckerman, Treasurer
76 Pages
Frequency: Bi-Monthly
Founded in 1994

3231 Bank Systems & Technology
CMP Media
240 West 35th Street
New York, NY 10001

212-928-8400
FAX 212-600-3080
E-Mail: siannuz@cmp.com
Home Page: www.cmp.com

David Leven, CEO
Dame Helen Alexander, Chairman

In-depth look into the new age of banking where total integration of technology is the driving force of new product business growth. Features deliver critical information on the strategic use of technology for increased profitability and productivity, in turn providing bankers with the tools to gain the competitive advantage on today's changing financial services landscape.
Cost: $52.00
Frequency: Monthly
Circulation: 23753
Founded in 1918

3232 Bank Technology News
Thomson Media
1 State St
27th Floor
New York, NY 10004-1481

212-803-8200
FAX 212-843-9600
E-Mail: custserv@sourcemedia.com
Home Page: www.banktechnews.com
Social Media: *Facebook, Twitter*

Penny Crosman, Editor in Chief
Douglas J. Manoni, CEO

The leading source for financial services technology coverage, written for those individuals who are responsible for the front, middle and back office technology needs of their financial institutes.
52 Pages
Frequency: Monthly
Founded in 1987
Mailing list available for rent

3233 Bankers Digest
P.O. Box 743006
Dallas, TX 75374-3006

214-221-4544
FAX 214-221-4546
E-Mail: bankersdigest@bankersdigest.com
Home Page: www.bankersdigest.com

Bonnie J Blackman, Owner
R Blackman Jr, Managing Editor

A weekly news magazine devoted to the southwest banking news. Accepts advertising.
Cost: $29.00
16 Pages
Frequency: Weekly
Circulation: 3100
ISSN: 0140-1800
Founded in 1942
Printed in 2 colors on glossy stock

3234 Bankers' Magazine
Thomson Reuters
195 Broadway
Suite 4
New York, NY 10007-3124

646-822-2000
800-231-1860
FAX 646-822-2800
E-Mail: trta.lei-support@thomsonreuters.com
Home Page: www.ria.thomsonreuters.com

Elaine Yadlon, Plant Manager
Thomas H Glocer, CEO & Director
Robert D Daleo, Chief Financial Officer
Kelli Crane, Senior Vice President & CIO

Written by bank professionals who offer urgent information about the banking industry to the banking community.
Cost: $115.00
Frequency: Bi-Monthly
Founded in 1935

3235 Banking Strategies
Bank Administration Institute
115 S. LaSalle Street
Suite 3300
Chicago, IL 60603

312-683-2464
800-224-9889
FAX 312-683-2373
E-Mail: info@bai.org
Home Page: www.bai.org
Social Media: *Facebook, Twitter, LinkedIn, Youtube*

Lewis Fischer, Chairman of the Board
Scott Peters, Vice Chairman

Includes information on finance, economics, planning, operations, regulations, retail, technology and human resources management.
Cost: $66.50
66 Pages
Circulation: 42175
ISSN: 1091-6385

3236 Banking Strategies Magazine
Bank Administration Institute
115 S LaSalle St
Suite 3300
Chicago, IL 60603

312-683-2464
888-284-4078
FAX 312-683-2373
E-Mail: info@bai.org
Home Page: www.bai.org

Social Media: *Facebook, Twitter, LinkedIn, Youtube*

Lewis Fischer, Chairman of the Board
Scott Peters, Vice Chairman

To present the latest in best practices and thought leadership through high-quality, in-depth, unbiased editorial coverage of strategic and managerial issues in today's complex and dynamic financial services business.
Frequency: Annual

3237 Broker Magazine
Thomson Media
1 State St
27th floor
New York, NY 10004-1481

212-825-8445
888-501-8850
FAX 212-292-5216
E-Mail: Custserv@thomsonmedia.com
Home Page: www.brokermagazine.com

Mark Fogarty, Editorial Director
Brad Finkelstein, Editor
Timothy Murphy, Group Publisher

Features on training, motivation, technology, legislation and marketing
Cost: $60.00
Frequency: Bi-Monthly

3238 Business Credit
Assn of Executives in Finance, Credit & In'tl Bus
8840 Columbia 100 Parkway
Columbia, MD 21045-2158

410-423-1840
888-256-3242
FAX 410-740-5574
E-Mail: fcib_info@fcibglobal.com
Home Page: www.fcibglobal.com
Social Media: *Twitter, LinkedIn*

Kelly Bates, Chairperson
Robin Schauseil, President
Tom Demovic, Director

For professionals responsible for extending credit and collecting receivables. Topics include business law, lien law, technology, credit management, collections, deductions, fraud, credit risk, credit scoring, outsourcing, information services, trade finance and more.
Cost: $54.00
72 Pages
Frequency: 10x/Year
Circulation: 32000
Founded in 1896
Printed in 4 colors on matte stock

3239 Business Credit Magazine
8840 Columbia 100 Parkway
Columbia, MD 21045-2158

410-423-1840
888-256-3242
FAX 410-740-5574
Home Page: www.fcibglobal.com
Social Media: *LinkedIn*

Marta Chacon, Director, The Americas
Ron Shepherd, Director, Business Dev.
Noelin Hawkins, Director, Europe, Middle East
Business Credit
1000+ Members
Frequency: Monthly
Circulation: 38000
Founded in 1919

3240 CFA Digest
CFA Institute
PO Box 3668
Charlottesville, VA 22903-0668

434-951-5499
800-247-8132
FAX 434-951-5262
E-Mail: info@cfainstitute.org

Home Page: www.cfainstitute.org
Social Media: *Facebook, Twitter, LinkedIn*

John Rogers, CEO
Daniel J Larocco, Co-Editor

Distills selected current industry research into short, easy-to-read summaries.
Frequency: Quarterly
Founded in 1971

3241 CFA Magazine
CFA Insitute
Po Box 3668
Charlottesville, VA 22903-0668

434-951-5499
800-247-8132
FAX 434-951-5262
E-Mail: info@cfainstitute.org
Home Page: www.cfainstitute.org
Social Media: *Facebook, Twitter, LinkedIn*

John Rogers, CEO
Roger Mitchell, Associate Editor

A practice-based, professional member magazine. Created on the feedback from a series of worldwide focus groups and a member survey.
Frequency: Bi-Monthly
Founded in 2003

3242 CMBS World
30 Broad Street
28th Floor
New York, NY 10004

212-509-1844
FAX 212-509-1895
E-Mail: info@crefc.org
Home Page: www.cmbs.org
Social Media: *Facebook, Twitter, LinkedIn*

Stephen Renna, CEO
Ed DeAngelo, VP

To inform, educate and stimulate meaningful discussions and exchanges among CMBS members on the risks and benefits of commercial mortgage-backed securities.
309 Pages
Frequency: Quarterly
Founded in 1994

3243 Commercial Mortgage Insight
Zackin Publications
PO Box 2180
Waterbury, CT 06722-2180

800-325-6745
FAX 203-262-4680
E-Mail: info@cmi-online.com
Home Page: www.cmi-online.com/cmi

Paul Zackin, Publisher
Jessica Lillian, Editor

For decision-making executives in commercial mortgage banking and brokerage firms, commercial banks and community/savings institutions. Provides professionals with timely and comprehensive market news, trends and know-how needed to make informed decisions and choices.
Cost: $48.00
32 Pages
Frequency: Monthly
Circulation: 16089
ISSN: 1095-0729
Founded in 1997
Printed in 4 colors on glossy stock

3244 Community Bank President
Siefer Consultants
PO Box 1384
Storm Lake, IA 50588-1384

712-732-7340
FAX 712-732-7906
E-Mail: siefer@ncn.net

Dan Siefer, Publisher

Analysis of trends, new ideas and implementation strategies, regulatory compliance, and bank profitability. Provides a glimpse at the latest deposit and loan statistics, marketing and new technology updates and bank management issues.
Frequency: Monthly
Circulation: 1800

3245 Community Banker Magazine
America's Community Bankers
1120 Connecticut Avenue NW
Washington, DC 20036

202-857-3100
80- 22- 537
FAX 202-296-8716
E-Mail: info@acbankers.org
Home Page:
www.americascommunitybankers.org

Frank Keating, President
Monique Hanis, Senior VP Marketing
Leann Shepp, Circulation Manager
Diane Casey-Landry, President

Community Banker presents engaging, practical and timely reporting and analysis on industry issues. Enhanced coverage of major interest to community bank leaders includes mortgages, management, technology and wealth.
Cost: $66.00
Frequency: Monthly
Circulation: 10500+
ISSN: 1529-1332
Printed in 4 colors on glossy stock

3246 Community Banking Advisor
624 Grassmere Park Drive
Suite 15
Nasville, TN 37211

615-377-3392
800-231-2524
FAX 615-377-7092
E-Mail: info@bankingcpas.com
Home Page: www.bankingcpas.com

Brian Blaha, President

A publication for banking professionals that features articles on management, tax, operational, and other issues confronting community banks.
24 Pages
Frequency: Quarterly
Founded in 1995

3247 Compliance Manual
NACHA: The Electronic Payments Association
13450 Sunrise Valley Drive
Suite 100
Herndon, VA 20171

703-561-1100
FAX 703-787-0996
E-Mail: info@nacha.org
Home Page: www.nacha.org

Janet O Estep, CEO
Marcie Haitema, Chairperson

Covers authorizations, disclosures, processing, funds availability, settlement, error resolution, returns, reversals, retention, audit, all Standard Entry Class Codes and much, much more.
Cost: $90.00

3248 Credit Union Journal
Thomson Media
1 State St
27th Floor
New York, NY 10004-1481

212-803-8200
800-221-1809
FAX 800-843-9600

E-Mail: Richard.Scalise@sourcemedia.com
Home Page: www.cujournal.com

Frank J Diekmann, Editor/Co-Publisher
Lisa Freeman, Managing Publisher

A surging economy, combined with competitive pricing policies and regulatory changes allowing credit unions to expand their field of membership.
Cost: $119.00
Frequency: Weekly

3249 Credit Union Management Magazine
Credit Union Executives Society
5510 Research Park Drive
PO Box 14167
Madison, WI 53708-167

608-271-2664
800-252-2664
FAX 608-271-2303
E-Mail: cues@cues.org
Home Page: www.cues.org
Social Media: *Facebook, Twitter, LinkedIn*

Fred Johnson, President/CEO
Mary Arnold, VP Publications
George Hofheimer, VP Professional Development
Barbara Kachelski, CAE, SVP/CIP

Published for credit union CEOs and senior management, the magazine focuses each month on general management, operations, marketing and human resource functions. Includes in-depth coverage of technology, facilities, finance, lending, staffing and card services, among other topics.
Cost: $129.00
11067 Members
Frequency: Monthly
Circulation: 8000
Founded in 1962

3250 Documentary Credit World
International Financial Services Association
1120 Connecticut Avenue NW
Washington, DC 20036

20 -66 -757
FAX 202-663-5538
E-Mail: info@baft-ifsa.com
Home Page: www.ifsaonline.org

Frank Keating, President
Albert Kelly, Chairman

Published jointly by the Institute of International Banking Law and Practice and the IFSA. DCW is your source for information on LCs.
Cost: $595.00
Frequency: 10x/Year

3251 Electronic Payments Journal
NACHA: Electronic Payments Association
13665 Dulles Technology Dr
Suite 300
Herndon, VA 20171-4607

703-561-1100
FAX 703-787-0996
E-Mail: info@nacha.org
Home Page: www.nacha.org

Janet O Estep, CEO

Helps industry professionals to track the latest developments in electronic payments and provides in-depth coverage of a broad array of payment issues.
Founded in 1978

3252 Electronic Payments Review and Buyer's Guide
NACHA: Electronic Payments Association
13450 Sunrise Valley Drive
Suite 100
Herndon, VA 20171

703-561-1100
FAX 703-787-0996

E-Mail: info@nacha.org
Home Page: www.nacha.org

Janet O Estep, CEO
Marcie Haitema, Chairperson

A directory of payment services with listings for ACH Services, Authentication & Security Solutions, B2B Invoicing & Presentment Services, Card Services, Check/Electronic Check Services, Consultants & Industry Associations, Consumer-Based Bill Payment & Presentment, Electronic Government Services, Electronic Consumer Services, International Payment Resources, Payment & Processing Software & Hardware, Thrid-Party Service Providers, and Wireless Payment & Commerce
Cost: $3.50
Frequency: Annual

3253 Federal Credit Union Magazine

National Association of Federal Credit Unions
3138 10th St N
Suite 3
Arlington, VA 22201-2160

703-522-4770
800-336-4644
FAX 703-524-1082
E-Mail: tfcu@nafcunet.org
Home Page: www.nafcu.org

Fred Becker, President

Written for CEOs, senior staff and volunteers of Federal Credit Unions. Offers legislative and regulatory news, as well as technology and operational issues.
Cost: $99.00
80 Pages
Frequency: Bi-Monthly
Circulation: 11136
ISSN: 1043-7789
Founded in 1967
Printed in 4 colors on glossy stock

3254 Finance and Development

International Monetary Fund
700 19th St NW
Washington, DC 20431-0002

202-623-7000
FAX 202-623-6220
E-Mail: publicaffairs@imf.org
Home Page: www.imf.org

David Lipton, First Deputy Managing Director
Christine Lagarde, Managing Director

Analysis of financial and economic developments and explanation of the policies and work of the International Monetary Fund and the World Bank.
Cost: $10.00
Frequency: Quarterly
Circulation: 130000
Founded in 1945
Mailing list available for rent: 120M names
Printed in 4 colors

3255 Financial Analyst

CFA Institute
PO Box 3668
Charlottesville, VA 22903-0668

434-951-5499
800-247-8132
FAX 434-951-5262
E-Mail: info@cfainstitute.org
Home Page: www.cfainstitute.org

John Rogers, CEO
Rodney N Sullivan, Associate Editor

Is to advance the knowledge and understanding of the practice of investment management through the publication of high-quality, practitioner-relevant research.

3256 Financial Review

Blackwell Publishing

350 Main St
Commerce Place
Malden, MA 02148-5089

781-388-8200
FAX 781-388-8210
Home Page: www.blackwellpublishing.com

Steven Smith, President/CEO
Vincent Marzano, Vice President, Treasurer

Publishes original empirical, theoretical and methodological research providing new insights into issues of importance in financial economics.
Frequency: Quarterly
ISSN: 0732-8516

3257 Financial Women Today Magazine

Financial Women International
1027 W Roselawn Avenue
Roseville, MN 55113

651-487-7632
866-807-6081
FAX 651-489-1322
E-Mail: info@fwi.org
Home Page: www.fwi.org

Melissa Curzon, President
Cindy Hass, VP
Carleen DeSisto, Secretary

Serves nearly 10,000 female financial service professionals, helping them to attain their economic, professional and personal goals.
Cost: $24.00
Frequency: Quarterly
Circulation: 19000
ISSN: 1059-3950
Founded in 1921
Mailing list available for rent
Printed in 4 colors on matte stock

3258 Global Custodian

Asset International
1055 Washington Blvd
Stamford, CT 06901

203-295-5015
888-374-3722
FAX 203-595-3201
E-Mail: education@globalcustodian.com
Home Page: www.globalcustodian.com

Dominic Hobson, Editor-in-Chief
Charles Ruffel, Founder/CEO
Maredith Hughes, VP

Written for international institutional investors. Stories cover engineering markets, cross border investing, securities lending and more.
Cost: $185.00
Frequency: 5x/Year
Circulation: 20000
Founded in 1989

3259 Government Affairs Bulletin

Financial Services Roundtable
1001 Pennsylvania Ave NW
Suite 500 S
Washington, DC 20004-2508

202-289-4322
FAX 202-289-1903
E-Mail: info@fsround.org
Home Page: www.fsround.org
Social Media: *Facebook, Twitter*

Tim Pawlenty, CEO
Richard Whiting, Executive Director

This bulletin keeps the members of the Roundtable informed on issues in the financial services industry and how the Roundtable views them.
100 Pages
Frequency: Weekly
Founded in 1993

3260 ICBA Independent Banker Magazine

Independent Community Bankers of America

518 Lincoln Road
PO Box 267
Sauk Centre, MN 56378

320-526-6546
800-422-7285
FAX 320-352-5766
E-Mail: info@icba.org
Home Page: www.icba.org

Camden R Fine, President/CEO
Rachael Solomon, Advertising Contact

ICBA members rely on for community banking news.
Cost: $60.00
Frequency: Monthly

3261 Independent Banker

Inside Mortgage Finance Publishers
7910 Woodmont Ave
Suite 1000
Bethesda, MD 20814-7019

301-951-1240
800-422-8439
FAX 301-656-1709
E-Mail: service@imfpubs.com
Home Page: www.imfpubs.com
Social Media: *Twitter, LinkedIn, Youtube*

John Bancroft, VP
George Brooks, Editor

Features strategies for high-performance community banks. Also includes profiles of success stories in community banks and assesses developments in legislation and regulation.
Frequency: Monthly
Circulation: 9,800
Mailing list available for rent

3262 Information Management Magazine

ARMA International
11880 College Blvd
Suite 450
Overland Park, KS 66215

913-341-3808
800-422-2762
FAX 913-341-3742
E-Mail: hq@arma.org
Home Page: www.arma.org

Komal Gulch, President
Brenda Prowse, Treasurer

The leading source of information on topics and issues central to the management of records and information worldwide. Each issue features insightful articles written by experts in the management of records and information.
Cost: $115.00
Frequency: Bi-monthly
Circulation: 11000
ISSN: 1535-2897
Mailing list available for rent: 9000 names
Printed in 4 colors on glossy stock

3263 International Banking Focus

Institue of International Bankers
299 Park Ave
17th Floor
New York, NY 10171-3896

212-421-1611
FAX 212-421-1119
E-Mail: iib@iib.org
Home Page: www.iib.org

Sarah ""sally"" Miller, Chief Executive Officer
Richard Coffman, General Counsel
Robin Wilks, Chief Administrative Officer

The Focus describes the latest legislative, regulatory and tax developments in Washington and various states, along with the Institute's efforts to address particular problems that affect international banks.
Frequency: Bi-Monthly
Founded in 1966

3264 Journal of Performance Management
Assn for Management Information in
Financial Svcs
14247 Saffron Circle
Carmel, IN 46032

317-815-5857
FAX 317-815-5877
E-Mail: ami2@amifs.org
Home Page: www.amifs.org

Andy Streiff, President
Jeff Nathasingh, Executive VP
Cost: $200.00
Frequency: 3/year
Circulation: 350

3265 Mortgage Banking
Mortgage Bankers Association
1717 Rhode Island Avenue, NW
Suite400
Washington, DC 20036

202-557-2700
E-Mail: membership@mortgagebankers.org
Home Page: www.mortgagebankers.org

Janet Reilley Hewett, Editor-in-Chief
Michael Young, Chairman

Provides in-depth coverage of the real estate fi-
nance industry. Intelligent analysis of news and
the most important issues and trends affecting
the industry. Association discount available.
Cost: $60.00
120 Pages
Frequency: 14x/Year
Circulation: 6000
ISSN: 0730-0212
Founded in 1914
*Mailing list available for rent: 2800 names at
$100 per M*
Printed in 4 colors on glossy stock

3266 Mortgage Servicing News
Thomson Media
1 State Street Plaza
27th Floor
New York, NY 10004-1481

212-825-8445
800-221-1809
FAX 212-292-5216
E-Mail: custserv@thomsonmedia.com
Home Page:
www.mortgageservicingnews.com/

Mark Fogarty, Editor
Timothy Murphy, Group Publisher
Timothy Reifschneider, Marketing Manager
Virginia Wiese, Custom Publishing

Information on cross serving techniques, legis-
lative decisions, management strategies, and
professional profiles.
Cost: $98.00
Frequency: Monthly
Circulation: 20,000

3267 NABTalk It
National Association of Bankruptcy
Trustees
One Windsor Cove
Suite 305
Columbia, SC 29223

803-252-5646
800-445-8629
FAX 803-765-0860
E-Mail: info@nabt.com
Home Page: www.nabt.com

Nancy H Cooper, Staff Editor
Neil Gordon, President
Frequency: Quarterly

3268 NACTT Quarterly
National Association of Chapter 13 Trustees

1 Windsor Cove
Suite 305
Columbia, SC 29223

803-252-5646
800-445-8629
FAX 803-765-0860
E-Mail: info@nactt.com
Home Page: www.nactt.com

Debra Miller, President
Margaret Burks, VP

The Quarterly emphasizes current local and national developments in Chapter 13. Each Quarterly provides a summary of the most recent
Chapter 13 Bankruptcy court decisions.

3269 NACUSAC News
NACUSAC
PO Box 160
Del Mar, CA 92014

800-287-5949
FAX 858-792-3884
E-Mail: nacusac@nacusac.org
Home Page: www.nacusac.org

Gerald Dunning, Chairman
Robert Butler, Director

Official magazing of the National Association
of Credit Union Supervisory & Auditing Committees that keeps you up to date on the latest
developments and events affecting supervi-
sory/auditing committee members.
Frequency: Quarterly

3270 NMB Magazine
National Association of Mortgage Brokers
2701 West 15th Street
Suite536
Plano, TX 75075

972-758-1151
FAX 530-484-2906
E-Mail: pr@nmpmediacorp.com
Home Page: www.namb.org
Social Media: *Facebook, Twitter, LinkedIn,
Youtube*

Mike Anderson, VP
Donald Frommeyer, President
Debbie Maxwell, Production Manager
Cost: $59.95
Frequency: Monthly
Founded in 1973

3271 National Mortgage Broker Magazine
Banat Communications
23425 N 39th Drive
104-193
Glendale, AZ 85310

623-516-2723
FAX 623-516-7738
E-Mail: jon@banatcommunications.com
Home Page: www.nationalmortgagebroker.com

Mike Anderson, VP
Donald Frommeyer, President
Debbie Maxwell, Production Manager
Cost: $59.95
Frequency: Monthly
Founded in 1984

3272 New England Economic Indicators
Federal Reserve Bank of Boston
600 Atlantic Avenue
Suite 100
Boston, MA 02210-2204

617-973-3000
FAX 617-973-5918
E-Mail: boston.library@bos.frb.org
Home Page: www.bos.frb.org

Eric S Rosengren, President/CEO
Kenneth Montgomery, VP COO

Contains current and historical economic data
for the states of CT, ME, MA, NH, RI, and VT,

as well as the US data include employment, un-
employment, prices and construction activity.
80 Pages
Frequency: Monthly
Circulation: 7000
Founded in 1914

3273 North Western Financial Review
NFR Communications
7400 Metro Blvd
Suite 217
Minnieapolis, MN 55439

952-835-2275
FAX 612-831-1464
E-Mail:
info@northwesternfinancialreview.com
Home Page:
www.northwesternfinancialreview.com

Tom Bengston, Publisher

Provides useful information and useful data re-
garding developments without trade association
bias.
Frequency: Annual+
Circulation: 9,000
Founded in 1989

3274 RMA Journal
Risk Management Association
1801 Market Street
Suite 300
Philadelphia, PA 19103-1628

215-446-4000
800-677-7621
FAX 215-446-4101
E-Mail: customers@rmahq.org
Home Page: www.rmahq.org
Social Media: *Facebook, Twitter, LinkedIn*

William Githens, President/CEO
Linda O'Loughlin, Director Marketing
Dwight Overturf, CFO

Expanded both format and content to address
an array of risk management issues while re-
specting and preserving essentials of commer-
cial lending
Cost: $95.00
Frequency: Monthly
Founded in 1914
Printed in 4 colors on glossy stock

3275 Reg/Ops
America's Community Bankers
1120 Connecticut Ave NW
Washington, DC 20036

202-857-3100
800-226-5377
FAX 202-296-8716
E-Mail: custserv@aba.com
Home Page:
www.americascommunitybankers.com

Frank Keating, President
Albert Kelly, Chairman

Offers detailed reporting and analysis of the
latest banking legislation, regulations, and
agency compliance guidance.
Cost: $405.00
16 Pages
Frequency: Monthly
Founded in 1950

3276 Regional Review
Federal Reserve Bank of Boston
600 Atlantic Ave
Boston, MA 02210-2204

617-973-3000
800-409-1333
FAX 617-973-4292
E-Mail: bostonlibrary@bos.frb.org
Home Page: www.bos.frb.org

Erin Rosengren, President/CEO

Magazine on economics, banking, business topics, designed for the busy professional.
Frequency: Quarterly
Circulation: 15000
ISSN: 1062-1865
Founded in 1913
Printed in 5 colors on glossy stock

3277 Regulatory Report
America's Community Bankers
1120 Connecticut Avenue NW
Washington, DC 20036

202-857-3100
80- 22- 537
FAX 202-296-8716
E-Mail: info@acbankers.org
Home Page:
www.americascommunitybankers.com

Frank Keating, President
Harry P Doherty, Editor

Dedicated to thoroughly analyzing regulations and laws of key importance to banks.
Cost: $680.00
38702 Pages
Frequency: Monthly

3278 SNL Quarterly Bank & Thrift Digest
SNL Securities
212 7th Street NE
Charlottesvle, VA 22902

434-977-1600
FAX 434-977-4466
E-Mail: customerservice@snl.com
Home Page: www.snl.com
Social Media: *Facebook, Twitter, LinkedIn, Youtube*

Mike Chinn, President & CEO

Contains all relevant information on every publicly traded bank and thrift providing insight into each individual institution and allowing quick and accurate comparisons with both peer institutions and industry benchmarks.
Cost: $799.00
600 Pages
Frequency: Quarterly
Founded in 1987
Mailing list available for rent

3279 SNL Real Estate Securities Quarterly
SNL Securities
212 7th Street NE
Charlottesville, VA 22902

434-977-1600
FAX 434-977-4466
E-Mail: subscriptions@snl.com
Home Page: www.snl.com
Social Media: *Facebook, Twitter, LinkedIn, Youtube*

Mike Chinn, President & CEO

This data digest provides comprehensive corporate, market, and financial information and portfolio level property data on more than 240 publicly traded and privately held real estate companies. SNL Real Estate Securities Quarterly is the industry's most comprehensive publication for evaluating real estate company performance at both a property and financial level.
Cost: $696.00
Frequency: Quarterly
Founded in 1987
Mailing list available for rent

3280 Secondary Marketing Executive
Zackin Publications
70 Edwin Avenue
PO Box 2180
Waterbury, CT 6708

203-755-0158
800-325-6745
FAX 203-262-4680

E-Mail: info@sme-online.com
Home Page: www.sme-online.com/sme

Vanessa Williams, Account Executive
John Clapp, Editor
June Han, Marketing

Offers how-to information for buyers and sellers of mortgage loans.
Cost: $48.00
48 Pages
Frequency: Monthly
Circulation: 95000
ISSN: 0891-2947
Founded in 1970

3281 Servicing Management
LDJ Corporation
70 Edwin Avenue
PO Box 2180
Waterbury, CT 06722-2330

203-755-0158
800-325-6745
FAX 203-262-4680
E-Mail: info@sm-online.com
Home Page: www.sm-online.com

Paul Zackin, Publisher
John Clapp, Editor
June Han, Marketing

Includes updates on industry and regulatory trends, and advise on operating their departments more profitably and efficiently.
Cost: $48.00
Frequency: Monthly
Circulation: 22500
Founded in 1989

3282 US Banker
Thomson Media
1 State St
27th Floor
New York, NY 10004-1481

212-803-8200
800-221-1809
FAX 212-843-9600
E-Mail: ustserv@sourcemedia.com
Home Page: www.americanbanker.com

Neil Weinberg, Editor-in-Chief
John Ceasar, Group Publisher
James Malkin, Chairman/CEO

Features on news and technological developments in the banking industry. Includes reports on companies, personalities and industry trends.
Cost: $109.00
Frequency: Monthly
Circulation: 80000
Founded in 1955

3283 Washington Perspective
America's Community Bankers
1120 Connecticut Avenue NW
Washington, DC 20036

202-857-3100
800-226-5377
FAX 202-296-8716
E-Mail: info@acbankers.org
Home Page:
www.americascommunitybankers.com

Frank Keating, President
Albert Kelly, Chairman

Zeroes in on the issues developing on Capital Hill and at the regulatory agencies that affect community banking.
Cost: $595.00
4 Pages
Frequency: Weekly
Circulation: 2200
Founded in 1992

Trade Shows

3284 ABA National Conference for Community Bankers
American Bankers Association
1120 Connecticut Avenue NW
Washington, DC 20036

800-226-5377
800-226-5377
E-Mail: custserv@aba.com
Home Page: www.aba.com

Frank Keating, President
Albert Kelly, Chairman

Features educational sessions, exceptional speakers, networking opportunities and world class exhibit hall.
2 mil Members
1500 Attendees
Frequency: Annual, February
Founded in 1875

3285 ABA Sales Management Workshop
American Bankers Association
1120 Connecticut Avenue NW
Washington, DC 20036

202-635-5000
800-226-5377
E-Mail: custserv@aba.com
Home Page: www.apa.com

Frank Keating, President
Albert Kelly, Chairman

Workshop on creating and keeping customers, over 13 exhibitors, visited by community bank executives, managers, sales and marketing staff.
Frequency: Annual, September

3286 ABA Wealth Management & Trust Conference
American Bankers Association
1120 Connecticut Avenue NW
Washington, DC 20036

800-226-5377
E-Mail: custserv@aba.com
Home Page: www.aba.com

Frank Keating, President
Albert Kelly, Chairman

Delivers practical, inventive ideas for wealth management and trust professionals.
Frequency: Annual, May

3287 AMIFS Annual Profitability & Performance Measurement Conference
Assn for Management Information in Financial Svcs
14247 Saffron Circle
Carmel, IN 46032

317-815-5857
FAX 317-815-5877
E-Mail: ami2@amifs.org
Home Page: www.amifs.org

Andy Streiff, President
Jeff Nathasingh, EVP
Kevin W Link, Executive Director

3-day conference consisting of one day of workshops, and two days of educational sessions. 10 exhibitors.
Frequency: April

3288 ARMA International Conference & Expo
ARMA International

11880 College Blvd
Suite 450
Overland Park, KS 66215

913-341-3808
800-422-2762
FAX 913-341-3742
E-Mail: Conference@armaintl.org
Home Page: www.arma.org/conference

Carol Jorgenson, Meetings/Education Coordinator
Wanda Wilson, Senior Manager, Conferences
Elizabeth Zlitni, Exposition Manager

Conference, seminar, workshop, banquet, award ceremony and 175 exhibits of micrographics, optical disk, automated document storage and retrieval systems and more technology of interest to information professionals.
3500 Attendees
Frequency: Annual
Founded in 1956

3289 American Bankers Insurance Association Annual Conference
American Bankers Insurance Association
1120 Connecticut Avenue NW
Washington, DC 20036

202-663-5163
800-226-5377
FAX 202-828-4546
E-Mail: vbarton@aba.com
Home Page: www.aba.com

Paul Petrylak, President/Chairman
Thomas Anderson, VP
David Cissell, Secretary
Neal Aton, Treasurer

The Conference highlights Best Practices Panel presentations as well as numerous break-out sessions with case studies by bankers and providers of insurance products and services.
300 Members
Frequency: September
Founded in 2001

3290 American League of Financial Institutions Annual Conference
America's Community Bankers
900 19th Street NW
Suite 400
Washington, DC 20006

202-857-3176
FAX 202-296-8716
E-Mail: webmaster@alfi.org
Home Page: www.businessfinance.com

William W Zuppe, Chairman
Mark Macomber, First Vice Chairman
Edwin R Maus, Second Vice Chairman
Diane Casey-Landry, President/CEO
Monique Hanis, Marketing/Business Development

Exhibits for financial institutions, federal and state chartered minority savings and loan associations in 25 states and DC.
Frequency: Annual

3291 American Safe Deposit Association Conference
American Safe Deposit Association
PO Box 519
Franklin, IN 46131-0519

317-738-4432
FAX 317-738-5267
Home Page: www.tasda.com

Thomas Cullinan, President
J Wayne Merrill, First VP
Winnifred Howard-Hammack, Second VP
Joyce A McLin, Executive Director
Kevin Fanning, Treasurer

Offers jam-packed sessions full of information and ideas that can be implemented immediately after conference.
200 Attendees
Frequency: June

3292 Association for Financial Professionals Annual Conference
Association for Financial Professionals
4520 East West Highway
Suite 750
Bethesda, MD 20814

301-907-2862
FAX 301-907-2864
E-Mail: AFP@AFPonline.org
Home Page: www.AFPonline.org
Social Media: *Facebook, Twitter, LinkedIn, Youtube*

Susan Glass, Chairman
Anita Patterson, Vice Chairman

Workshop and 642 exhibits of lockboxes, check processing systems, computers, investments, pensions, foreign exchange, consulting, mergers, acquisitions and more information of interest to financial professionals.
6000 Attendees
Frequency: October
Founded in 1979

3293 Association of Independent Trust Companies Conference
Association of Independent Trust Companies
8 South Michigan Avenue
Suite802
Chicago, IL 60603

312-223-1611
FAX 312-580-0615
E-Mail: aitco@gss.net
Home Page: www.aitco.net

Douglas Nunn, President
Marcia Williams, Treasurer
Tom Blank, General Counsel/Secretary

Typically attracts more than 50 financial executive to an information-packed program which addresses the practical issues and challenges of doing business within the trust and financial advisory industry.
Frequency: Annual

3294 Association of Military Banks of America Conference
Association of Military Banks of America(AMBA)
PO Box 3335
Warrenton, VA 20188

540-347-3305
FAX 540-347-5995
E-Mail: christiane.jacobs@ambahq.org
Home Page: www.ambahq.org

Andrew Egeland, President
John Mitchell, Chairman
Terry Tuggle, Vice Chairman
Frequency: September

3295 Bank Insurance and Securities Association Annual Conference
Bank Insurance and Securities Association
2025 M Street, NW
Suite 800
Washington, DC 20036

202-367-1111
FAX 20 -36 -211
E-Mail: bisa@BISAnet.org
Home Page: www.bisanet.org

Jim McNeil, Executive Director
Marc A Vosen, President

Focus on the internal administration of the supervisory and compliance functions of the bank broker-dealer and its related activities.
Frequency: June
Founded in 2002

3296 Bankers' Association for Finance & Trade Annual Conference
Bankers' Association for Finance & Trade
1120 Connecticut Avenue NW
6th Floor
Washington, DC 20036-3902

202-663-7575
FAX 202-663-5538
E-Mail: info@baft-ifsa.com
Home Page: www.baft.org

Tom Burwell, Vice President
Colleen Kennedy, Manager,Programs, & Events
Donna K Alexander, President

Focused on the global environment and the impact of economic developments in specifications and markets including consecutive breakouts on compliance, risk mitigation and key issues.
Frequency: April

3297 Boot Camp for BSA Professionals
Conference of State Bank Supervisors
1129 20th Street, N.W.
9th Floor
Washington, DC 20036

202-296-2840
FAX 202-296-1928
E-Mail: rstromberg@csbs.org
Home Page: www.csbs.org

Greg Gonzales, Chairman
Candace Franks, Vice Chairman
David Cotney, Secretary

Will provide BSA Compliance knowledge and value to your regulatory agency, financial institution or money service business.
Frequency: May

3298 CPSA Annual Meeting
Check Payment Systems Association
2025 M Street NW
Suite 800
Washington, DC 20036-2422

202-671-1144
FAX 202-367-2144
E-Mail: info@cpsa-checks.org
Home Page: www.cpsa-checks.org

Steven Antolick, Executive Director
Renee Lurker, Senior Associate

In addition to the business meeting, there are presentations from top industry performers and innovators.
Frequency: May

3299 CSBS Annual Meeting & Conference
Conference of State Bank Supervisors
1129 20th Street NW
9th Floor
Washington, DC 20036

202-296-2840
FAX 202-296-1928
E-Mail: mbquist@csbs.org
Home Page: www.csbs.org

Mary Beth Quist, Meetings/Conference Contact
Neil Milner, President

The largest gathering of State 7 Federal banking regulators, state bank CEOs, industry policy makers and representatives of companies who support the banking industry.
Frequency: May

3300 Combating Payments & Check Fraud Conference
Bank Administration Institute

115 S LaSalle St
Suite 3300
Chicago, IL 60603-3801

312-683-2464
888-224-0037
FAX 312-683-2373
E-Mail: info@bai.org
Home Page: www.bai.org
Social Media: *Facebook, Twitter, LinkedIn, Youtube*

Lewis Fischer, Chairman of the Board
Scott Peters, Vice Chairman
Frequency: September

3301 Commercial Mortgage Securities Association Conference

Commercial Mortgage Securities
Association
900 7th Street, NW
Suite 820
New York, NY 10004-2304

212-509-1844
FAX 212-509-1895
E-Mail: info@crefc.org
Home Page: www.cmbs.org
Social Media: *Facebook, Twitter, LinkedIn*

Steven Renna, CEO

Intensive educational offerings and presentations on the CMBS industry's biggest challenges.
Frequency: June

3302 Commerical Real Estate Finance/Multifamily Housing Convention & Expo

Mortgage Bankers Association
1717 Rhode Island Avenue NW
Suite 400
Washington, DC 20036

202-557-2700
E-Mail: meetiings@mortgagebankers.org
Home Page: www.mortgagebankers.org

David H Stevens, President/CEO
Elaine Howard, VP Meetings/Conferences

Thousands of commerical real estate industry professionals gathered from across the country to do business with and learn the latest in industry trends, regulatory develoments and strategies to succeed in today's dynamic marketplace.
Frequency: Annual/February

3303 Community & Regional Bank Forum

Bank Insurance and Securities Association
2025 M Street, NW
Suite 800
Washington, DC 20036

202-367-1111
FAX 202-367-2111
E-Mail: bisa@BISAnet.org
Home Page: www.bisanet.org

Jim McNeil, Executive Director
Marc A Vosen, President
Frequency: September
Founded in 2002

3304 Community Bank Director's Conference

American Association of Bank Directors
1250 24th Street, NW
Suite 700
Washington, DC 20037

202-463-4888
FAX 20 -34 -808
E-Mail: info@aabd.org
Home Page: www.aabd.org

Keith Dalrymple, President/CEO
David Baris, Executive Director

Sponsored by the AABD and Bank CEO Network, designed to provide information community bank directors need
Frequency: Annual

3305 Community Banking Advisory Network Super Conference

HCAA
624 Grassmere Park Drive
Suite 15
Nasvhile, TN 37211

615-377-3392
800-231-2524
FAX 615-377-7092
E-Mail: info@hcaa.com
Home Page: www.hcaa.com

Keith Kamperschroer, President

3306 Credit Congress

8840 Columbia 100 Parkway
Columbia, MD 21045-2158

410-423-1840
888-256-3242
FAX 410-740-5574
Home Page: www.fcibglobal.com
Social Media: *LinkedIn*

Marta Chacon, Director, The Americas
Ron Shepherd, Director, Business Dev.
Noelin Hawkins, Director, Europe, Middle East

Business Credit
1000+ Members
1500 Attendees
Founded in 1919

3307 Eastern Finance Association Meeting

Eastern Finance Association
220 Holman Hall
PO Box 1848
University, MS 38677

404-498-8937
FAX 404-498-8956
E-Mail: admin@easternfinance.org
Home Page: www.easternfinance.org

Mark Lion, President
Jacqueline Garner, VP Local Arrangements

Annual meeting and exhibits relating to any aspect of finance, including financial management, investments and banking.
Frequency: April

3308 Environmental Bankers Association Membership Meeting

Environmental Bankers Association
510 King Street
Suite 410
Alexandria, VA 22314

703-549-0977
800-966-7475
FAX 703-548-5945
E-Mail: eba@envirobank.org
Home Page: www.envirobank.org

Rick Ferguson, President
Scott Beckerman, Treasurer
Frequency: January/June
Founded in 1994

3309 Federal Reserve Board Conference

Federal Reserve Board Publishers
20th Street & Constitution Avenue NW
Washington, DC 20551

202-452-3000
FAX 202-728-5886
Home Page: www.federalreserve.gov

Lucrezia Reichlin, Conference Organizer
Dale Henderson, Conference Organizer
Deborah Lagomarsino, Media Contact

Organized by the International Research Forum on Monetary Policy. Its purpose is to encourage research on monetary policy issues that are rel-

evant for monetary policy making in interdependent economies.
Frequency: December

3310 Financial & Security Products Association Annual Conference

Financial & Security Products Association
Plaza Ladera, 5300 Sequoia NW
Suite 205
Albuquerque, NM 87120

505-839-7958
800-843-6082
FAX 919-648-0670
E-Mail: info@fspa1.com
Home Page: www.fspa1.com

Mark Thatcher, Chairman
Bill Mercer, President
John M Vrabec, Executive Director
Frequency: June
Founded in 1973

3311 Financial Women International Annual Conference

Financial Women International
1027 W Roselawn Avenue
Roseville, MN 55113

651-487-7632
866-807-6081
FAX 651-489-1322
E-Mail: info@fwi.org
Home Page: www.fwi.org

Melissa Curzon, President
Cindy Hass, VP
Carleen DeSisto, Secretary
Frequency: September

3312 GARP Annual Risk Management Convention & Exhibit

Global Association of Risk Professionals
111 Town Square Place
Suite 1215
Jersey City, NJ 07310

201-719-7210
FAX 201-222-5022
E-Mail: rich.apostolik@garp.com
Home Page: www.garp.com
Social Media: *Facebook, Twitter, LinkedIn*

Richard Apostolik, President/CEO
Kenneth Abbott, Managing Director
Mark Wallace, Chief Operating Officer
Thomas Daula, Chief Risk Officer
Frequency: February
Founded in 1996

3313 Global Association of Risk Professionals Annual Exhibition

111 Town Square Place
Suite 1215
Jersey City, NJ 07310

201-719-7210
FAX 201-222-5022
E-Mail: rich.apostolik@garp.com
Home Page: www.garp.com
Social Media: *Facebook, Twitter, LinkedIn*

Richard Apostolik, President/CEO
Kenneth Abbott, Managing Director
Mark Wallace, Chief Operating Officer
Thomas Daula, Chief Risk Officer

GARP's flagship event for Asia, with Keynote presentations, multi-track forum and separate workshops.
Frequency: Annual
Founded in 1996

3314 Independent Community Bankers of America National Convention and Techworld

Independent Community Bankers of
America

518 Lincoln Road
PO Box 267
Sauk Centre, MN 56378

320-526-6546
800-422-7285
FAX 320-352-5766
E-Mail: mark_traeger@icba.org
Home Page: www.icba.org

Jan Meyer, Director Conferences
Mark Traeger, Associate Dir
Conferences/Exhibits
Sandy Zehrer, Supervisor Conference/Exhibits
Greg Martinson, Executive Director

Only national trade show exclusively representing America's independent/community banks. Containing 200+ booths and 175+exhibitors.
3000 Attendees
Frequency: March

3315 Institute of International Bankers Annual Washington Conference
Institute of International Bankers
299 Park Avenue
17th Floor
New York, NY 10171

212-421-1611
FAX 212-421-1119
E-Mail: iib@iib.org
Home Page: www.iib.org

Sarah Miller, CEO
Maura Christ, Executive Assistant
William Harris, Controller
Andy Lebron, Membership Associate

A two-day conference featuring senior U.S. and international government policy makers and financial industry leaders. As part of the conference, which is widely attended by general manager and other senior officers of Institute member banks, there is an evening reception for the Washington community, including Administration officials, Members of Congress, banking regulators and senior staff.
Frequency: March
Founded in 1966

3316 International Financial Services Association Annual Conference
International Financial Services Association
1120 Connecticut Avenue NW
Washington, DC 20036

202-66-757
FAX 202-663-5538
E-Mail: info@baft-ifsa.com
Home Page: www.ifsaonline.org

Renee Wigfall, Manager, Meetings/Events
Todd Burwell, Vice President
Frequency: September

3317 Legal Issues and Regulatory Compliance Conference
Mortgage Bankers Association
1717 Rhode Island Avenue NW
Suite 400
Washington, DC 20036

202-557-2700
E-Mail: meetings@mortgagebankers.org
Home Page: www.mortgagebankers.org

David H Stevens, President/CEO
Elaine Howard, VP Meetings/Conferences

Learn about all the legal and regulatory developments facing the industry.
Frequency: Annual/May

3318 Microbanker
Microbanker
PO Box 708
Lake George, NY 12061

518-745-7071
FAX 518-745-7071

E-Mail: webmaster@microbanker.com
Home Page: www.microbanker.com

Annual show and exhibits of microcomputer software, hardware and services for banking, savings and loans, and credit unions.
200 Attendees

3319 Mid-Year Technical Conference
National Assn of Government Guaranteed Lenders
424 South Squires Street
Stillwater, OK 74074

405-377-4022
FAX 405-377-3931
E-Mail: bfortune@naggl.com
Home Page: www.naggl.com

Tony Wilkinson, President/CEO
Karen High, EVP/COO
Jenifer Brake, Assistant VP Marketing
Jennifer Sterrett-O'Neill, Assistant VP Communications
Cheryl Stone, VP Conferences
Frequency: May

3320 NACUSAC Annual Conference & Exposition
NACUSAC
PO Box 160
Del Mar, CA 92014

800-287-5949
FAX 858-792-3884
E-Mail: nacusac@nacusac.org
Home Page: www.nacusac.org

Celeste Shelton, Executive Director
Laura Clark, Associate Director
Bob Spindler, Associate Director

These events sponsored by the National Association of Credit Union Supervisory & Auditing Committees offer second-to-none networking and educational opportunities for supervisory and auditing committees.
Frequency: June

3321 National Association of Bankruptcy Trustees Annual Convention
National Association of Bankruptcy Trustees
One Windsor Cove
Suite 305
Columbia, SC 29223

803-252-5646
800-445-8629
FAX 803-765-0860
E-Mail: info@nabt.com
Home Page: www.nabt.com

Christina Hicks, President
Kelly Hagen, VP
Frequency: September

3322 National Association of Chapter 13 Trustees Annual Seminar
National Association of Chapter 13 Trustees
1 Windsor Cove
Suite 305
Columbia, SC 29223

803-252-5646
800-445-8629
FAX 803-765-0860
E-Mail: info@nactt.com
Home Page: www.nactt.com

Debra Miller, President
Margaret Burks, VP

This seminar is NAACO's educational highlight. National experts discuss complex issues and recent developments in the Chapter 13 areas.

3323 National Association of Federal Credit Unions Conference
National Association of Federal Credit Unions
3138 10th Street N
Suite 300
Arlington, VA 22201-2149

703-522-4770
800-336-4644
FAX 703-524-1082
E-Mail: fbecker@nafcu.org
Home Page: www.nafcu.org

Fred Becker, President/CEO
Patrick Morris, Executive Vice President/COO

Stands as a national forum for the federal credit union community where new ideas, issues, concerns and trends can be identified, discussed and resolved.
Frequency: July

3324 National Association of Mortgage Brokers Annual Conference
National Association of Mortgage Brokers
2701 West 15th Street
Suite 536
Plano, TX 75075

972-758-1151
FAX 530-484-2906
E-Mail: membership@namb.org
Home Page: www.namb.org

Donald Frommyer, President
George Hanzimanolis CRMS, VP
Frequency: June

3325 National Association of Professional Mortgage Women Annual Conference
National Assn of Professional Mortgage Women
PO Box 451718
Garland, TX 75045

425-778-6162
800-827-3034
FAX 425-771-9588
E-Mail: napmw1@napmw.org
Home Page: www.napmw.org

Laurie Abshier, President
Candice Smith, President-Elect
Liz Roberts, Senior Vice President
Patricia Hull, Executive Director
Frequency: May

3326 National Fraud Issues Conference
Mortgage Bankers Association
1717 Rhode Island Avenue NW
Suite 400
Washington, DC 20036

202-557-2700
E-Mail: meetings@mortgagebankers.org
Home Page: www.mortgagebankers.org

David H Stevens, President/CEO
Elaine Howard, VP Meetings/Conferences

Where industry professionals can learn about the issues related to the growing incidence and complexity of mortgage fraud.
Frequency: Annual/March

3327 National Investment Banking Association Annual Conference
National Investment Banking Association
PO Box 6625
Athens, GA 30604

706-208-9620
FAX 706-993-3342
E-Mail: emily@nibanet.org
Home Page: www.nibanet.org

James Hock, Co Chair
Gerald Alder, Director
Emily Foshee, Executive Director

D Scott Foshee, Chief Technology Officer
Vicki Barone, Treasurer/Secretary

Provides member firms with regularly scheduled forums where they are able to exchange ideas and information, evaluate presentations made by companies being underwritten or sponsored by member firms, collectively voice their positions on issues impacting their livelihood, and enhance their knowledge and expertise through ongoing educational programs designed to enable them to remain competitive.
Frequency: May

3328   National Marine Bankers Association Annual Conference
National Marine Bankers Association
231 South LaSalle Street
Suite 2050
Chicago, IL 60604

312-946-6260
E-Mail: bmcardle@nmma.org
Home Page: www.marinebankers.org

Bernice McArdle, Associate Manager

A three-day member conference where the latest trends issues relating to the marine industry are discussed in detail.
Frequency: September

3329   National Mortgage Servicing Conference & Expo
Mortgage Bankers Association
1717 Rhode Island Avenue NW
Suite 400
Washington, DC 20036

202-557-2700
E-Mail: meetings@mortgagebankers.org
Home Page: www.mortgagebankers.org

David H Stevens, President/CEO
Elaine Howard, VP Meetings/Conferences

Gives companies the opportunity to reach key servicing executives from residential mortgage companies. Showcase the product offerings, network with key decision makers, and obtain qualified leads.
Frequency: Annual/February

3330   National Policy Conference
Mortgage Bankers Association
1717 Rhode Island Avenue NW
Suite 400
Washington, DC 20036

202-557-2700
E-Mail: meetings@mortgagebankers.org
Home Page: www.mortgagebankers.org

David H Stevens, President/CEO
Elaine Howard, VP Meetings/Conferences

Brings togethers key officials, cabinet members and special guest speakers to address issues of what is happening in the community as well as the practical effect proposed changes may have on the business and industry
Frequency: Annual/March

3331   National Technology in Mortgage Banking Conference
Mortgage Bankers Association
1717 Rhode Island Avenue NW
Suite 400
Washington, DC 20036

202-557-2700
E-Mail: meetings@mortgagebankers.org
Home Page: www.mortgagebankers.org

David H Stevens, President/CEO
Elaine Howard, VP Meetings/Conferences

Forum to learn about the newest industry solutions and how they can increase the company's competitive edge. Focuses on relevant topics, including legal/regulatory updates, eMortgages, investor reporting changes adn

technology advances such as mobile computing.
Frequency: Annual/March

3332   Payments
NACHA: Electronic Payments Association
13450 Sunrise Valley Drive
Suite 100
Herndon, AV 20171

703-561-1100
FAX 703-787-0996
E-Mail: info@nacha.org
Home Page: www.nacha.org

Marcie Haitema, Chairperson
Janet O Estep, CEO

The premier source for payments professionals from across industries and around the globe to get the most vital and actionable information needed to help address the myriad of issues and opportunities in today's rapidly changing environment.
Frequency: Annual/April-May

3333   RMA Annual Conference of Lending & Credit Risk Management
Risk Management Association
1801 Market Street
Suite 300
Philadelphia, PA 19103-1628

215-446-4000
800-677-7621
FAX 215-446-4100
E-Mail: customers@rmahq.org
Home Page: www.rmahq.org

William Githens, President/CEO
Sonny B Lyles, Vice Chair

Containing 31 booths and 28 exhibits.
600 Attendees
Frequency: October

3334   Retail Delivery Conference & Expo
Bank Administration Institute
115 S. LaSalle Street
Suite 3300
Chicago, IL 60603-3801

312-683-2464
888-284-4078
FAX 312-683-2373
E-Mail: info@bai.org
Home Page: www.bai.org
Social Media: *Facebook, Twitter, LinkedIn, Youtube*

Lewis Fischer, Chairman of the Board
Scott Peters, Vice Chairman
2M Attendees
Frequency: November

3335   Sales Management Workshop
Bank Insurance and Securities Association
2025 M Street NW
Suite 800
Washington, DC 20036

202-367-1111
FAX 20 -36 -211
E-Mail: bisa@BISAnet.org
Home Page: www.bisanet.org

Jim McNeil, Executive Director
Marc A Vosen, President
Frequency: May/October/December
Founded in 2002

3336   Securities Industry and Financial Markets Association (SIFMA) Annual Meeting
SIFMA

1101 New York Avenue NW
8th Floor
Washington, DC 20005

202-962-7300
FAX 202-962-7305
Home Page: www.sifma.org/

Timothy Ryan, President/CEO
Cheryl Crispen, Executive Vice President

The Securities Industry and Financial Markets Association/SIFMA Annual Meeting and Conference program addresses a variety of topics that may include competitiveness of the U.S. capital markets, global exchange consolidation, regulatory and legal initiatives, and trends in the fixed-income and capital markets.

3337   TransPay Conference & Expo
Bank Administration Institute
115 S LaSalle St
Suite 3300
Chicago, IL 60603

312-683-2464
800-375-5543
FAX 312-683-2373
E-Mail: info@bai.org
Home Page: www.bai.org
Social Media: *Facebook, Twitter, LinkedIn, Youtube*

Lewis Fischer, Chairman of the Board
Scott Peters, Vice Chairman

Offers top solutions providers, innovators and your peers at BAY TransPay - focused on your financial institution profitability in payments.
Frequency: May

3338   Treasury & Risk Management Conference
Bank Administration Institute
115 S LaSalle St
Suite 3300
Chicago, IL 60603

312-683-2464
800-375-5443
FAX 312-683-2373
E-Mail: info@bai.org
Home Page: www.bai.org
Social Media: *Facebook, Twitter, LinkedIn, Youtube*

Lewis Fischer, Chairman of the Board
Scott Peters, Vice Chairman
Frequency: May

3339   Urban Financial Services Coalition Annual Conference
Urban Financial Services Coalition
1200 G Street NW
Suite 800
Washington, DC 20005

202-289-8335
800-996-8335
FAX 202-434-8707
E-Mail: ufsc@ufscnet.org
Home Page: www.ufscnet.org

Diane Evans, President
Brenda Joseph, Vice President
Linda Smith, Treasurer
Audrey Williams, Secretary
Frequency: June

Directories & Databases

3340   ABA Directory of Trust Banking
4709 Golf Road
Skokie, IL 60076

847-676-9600
800-321-3373
FAX 847-933-8101

E-Mail: custserv@accuitysolutions.com
Home Page: www.accuitysolutions.com

Hugh Jones, President
Kerry Hewson, VP

An official publication of the American Bankers Association. Listings include information such as national and state rankings, collective investment funds and corporate trusts.
Cost: $403.00
Circulation: 2800
ISBN: 1-563103-53-2

3341 ABA Financial Institutions Directory
4709 Golf Road
Skokie, IL 60076

847-676-9600
800-321-3373
FAX 847-933-8101
E-Mail: custserv@accuitysolutions.com
Home Page: www.accuitysolutions.com

Hugh Jones, President
Kerry Hewson, VP

This two-volume Executive Desktop Edition includes a special ABA Resource Guide with a Quick Reference Guide to Banking Regulations.
Cost: $500.00
Frequency: January/July
Circulation: 31850

3342 ABA Key to Routing Numbers
4709 Golf Road
Skokie, IL 60076

847-676-9600
800-321-3373
FAX 847-933-8101
E-Mail: custserv@accuitysolutions.com
Home Page: www.accuitysolutions.com

Hugh Jones, President
Kerry Hewson, VP
Cost: $184.00
Frequency: January/July
Circulation: 83300
Founded in 1911

3343 ACH Participant Directory
4709 Golf Road
Skokie, IL 60076

847-676-9600
800-321-3373
FAX 847-933-8101
E-Mail: custserv@accuitysolutions.com
Home Page: www.accuitysolutions.com

Hugh Jones, President
Kerry Hewson, VP
Cost: $207.00
Frequency: February/August
Circulation: 54600

3344 American Financial Directory
4709 Golf Road
Skokie, IL 60076

847-676-9600
800-321-3373
FAX 847-933-8101
E-Mail: custserv@accuitysolutions.com
Home Page: www.accuitysolutions.com

Hugh Jones, President
Kerry Hewson, VP
Cost: $558.00
Frequency: January/July
Circulation: 41300
ISBN: 1-563103-47-8
Founded in 1836

3345 Annual Membership Directory & Buyers' Guide
Financial & Security Products Association

Plaza Ladera, 5300 Sequoia NW
Suite 205
Albuquerque, NM 87120

505-839-7958
800-843-6082
FAX 505-839-0017
E-Mail: info@fspa1.com
Home Page: www.fspa1.com

Mark Thatcher, Chairman
Bill Mercer, President

Who's Who of independent firms serving financial institutions hleps readers locate new dealers, products/service suppliers and strategic business partners.

3346 Annual Report of the Board of Governors of the Federal Reserve System
Board of Governors
20th St & Constitution Ave N
Washington, DC 20551-0001

202-452-3284
FAX 202-452-3101
Home Page: www.federalreserve.gov

Rick McKinney, Manager
Janet Yellen, Vice Chair

Listing of directors, advisory councils and officers of banks and branches involved in mergers and acquisitions.
Frequency: Annual

3347 Annual Software Guide
Financial & Security Products Association
Plaza Ladera, 5300 Sequoia NW
Suite 205
Albuquerque, NM 87120

505-839-7958
800-843-6082
FAX 505-839-0017
E-Mail: info@fspa1.com
Home Page: www.fspa1.com

Mark Thatcher, Chairman
Bill Mercer, President
John Vrabec, Executive Director

This detailed evaluation of the latest software to enhance business performance is provided by Brown Smith Wallace (BSW) only to members of participating associations, including FSPA.

3348 BankNews Montain States Bank Directory
BankNews Publications
PO Box 29156
Shawnee Mission, KS 66201-9156

913-261-7000
800-336-1120
FAX 913-261-7010
Home Page: www.banknews.com

Janet Holman, President & Publisher
Joel Holman, CEO & Publisher

Over 600 commercial banks, savings and loans, and holding companies are listed in this directory, state banking and regulatory agencies are also studied in the areas of Colorado, Wyoming, New Mexico, Montana and Utah.
Cost: $ 35.00
350 Pages
Frequency: Annual
Circulation: 3,500

3349 BankRoll II
US Federal Reserve System, Board of Governors

20th Street & Constitution Avenue NW
Washington, DC 20551-0001

Home Page: www.federalreserve.gov/
Social Media: *Twitter, LinkedIn*

This database contains descriptive information and financial information from the Financial Report Bank Holding Companies (Y9) submitted to the Federal Reserve Board.

3350 Bankcard Barometer
RAM Research Corporation
1230 Avenue of the Americas
7th Floor, Rockefeller Center
New York, MD 21702-0700

301-954-4660
FAX 301-695-0160
Home Page: www.ramresearch.com

Robert B McKinley, Publisher/Editor

Database of nation's capital largest bank credit card issuers.
Cost: $1295.00
600 Pages
Frequency: Monthly
Founded in 1986
Printed in one color on matte stock

3351 Branches of Your State: Banks, Savings & Loans, Credit Unions & Savings
Sheshunoff Information Services
901 South Mopac
Suite 140
Austin, TX 78746-7970

512-472-4000
800-477-1772
FAX 512-305-6575
E-Mail: sales@smslp.com
Home Page: www.smslp.com
Social Media: *Facebook, Twitter, LinkedIn*

Gabrielle Sheshunoff, CEO

State editions list banks, savings and loan branches and credit unions. Individual banks are listed for states without branch banking.
Cost: $345.00
Frequency: Annual

3352 Data Book
FDIC Public Information Center
550 17th St Nw
Washington, DC 20429-0001

202-898-3631
877-275-3342
FAX 202-898-3984
E-Mail: publicinfo@fdic.gov
Home Page: www.fdic.gov
Social Media: *Facebook, Twitter, LinkedIn*

Martin Gruenberg, Chairman
Thomas Hoenig, Vice Chairman
Jeremiah Norton, Director

Offers information on bank names, locations, bank numbers and branches for each banking office, in seven volumes, divided geographically and aggregate bank deposits also known as Summary of Deposits.
Frequency: Quarterly

3353 Directory of Minority and Women-Owned Investment Bankers
San Francisco Redevelopment Agency
1 S Van Ness Avenue
Suite 5
San Francisco, CA 94103-5416

415-749-2400
FAX 415-749-2565
Home Page: www.sanfranciscofcu.org

Marcia Rosen, Executive Director
Erwin Tanjuaquio, Director Public Affairs

Lists 18 minority-owned investment banking firms.
Frequency: Biennial

3354 Directory of Venture Capital & Private Equity Firms - Online Database
Grey House Publishing
4919 Route 22
PO Box 56
Amenia, NY 12501

518-789-8700
800-562-2139
FAX 518-789-0556
E-Mail: gold@greyhouse.com
Home Page: www.gold.greyhouse.com
Social Media: *Facebook, Twitter*

Leslie Mackenzie, Publisher
Richard Gottlieb, Editor

Packed with need-to-know information, this database offers immediate access to 2,300 VC firms, over 10,000 managing partners, and over 11,500 VC investments.
Frequency: Annual

3355 Directory of Venture Capital and Private Equity Firms
Grey House Publishing
4919 Route 22
PO Box 56
Amenia, NY 12501

518-789-8700
800-562-2139
FAX 845-373-6390
E-Mail: books@greyhouse.com
Home Page: www.greyhouse.com
Social Media: *Facebook, Twitter*

Leslie Mackenzie, Publisher
Richard Gottlieb, Editor

Offers access to over 2,300 domestic and international venture capital and private equity firms, including detailed contact information and extensive data on investments and funds.
Cost: $685.00
1,200 Pages
Frequency: Annual
ISBN: 1-592372-72-4

3356 Financial Institutions Directory of New England
4709 Golf Road
Skokie, IL 60076

847-676-9600
800-321-3373
FAX 847-933-8101
E-Mail: custserv@accuitysolutions.com
Home Page: www.accuitysolutions.com

Hugh Jones, President
Kerry Hewson, VP
Cost: $114.00
Frequency: January/July

3357 Financial Management
University of South Florida COBA
3821 Holly Drive
Tampa, FL 33620-7360

813-974-4133
FAX 813-974-5130
E-Mail: caminfo@arts.usf.edu
Home Page: www.ira.usf.edu

Margaret Miller, Director
Alexa Favata, Associate Director

Financial management of individual firm, governmental unit or nonprofit institution, as opposed to financial structure of whole economy for practitioners and professors of financial management.
Cost: $20.00
Circulation: 11,500
Founded in 1970

3358 National Credit Union Administration Directory
National Credit Union Administration
1775 Duke St
Alexandria, VA 22314-6115

703-518-6300
800-755-1030
FAX 703-518-6539
E-Mail: consumerassistance@ncua.gov
Home Page: www.ncua.gov

J Leonard Skiles, Executive Director
Robert Fenner, Director/General Counsel
Jane Walters, Deputy Executive Director

Directory of credit unions governed by a three member board appointed by the President and confirmed by the US Senate, by the independent federal agency that charters and supervises federal credit unions. NCUA, with the backing of the full faith and credit of the US government, operates the National Credit Union Share Insurance Fund, insuring the savings of 80 million account holders in all federal credit unions and many state chartered credit unions.

3359 North American Financial Institutions Directory
4709 Golf Road
Skokie, IL 60076

847-676-9600
800-321-3373
FAX 847-933-8101
E-Mail: custserv@accuitysolutions.com
Home Page: www.accuitysolutions.com

Hugh Jones, President/CEO
Cost: $495.00
Frequency: January/July
Circulation: 31850
Founded in 1895

3360 Ranking the Banks
American Banker
1 State St
27th Floor
New York, NY 10004-1561

212-803-8450
FAX 212-843-9600
Home Page: www.sourcemedia.com

Douglas Manoni, President/CEO
David Longobardi, Editor-in-Chief
Richard Melville, Managing Editor
Timothy Reifschneider, Advertising Director

A comprehensive database of banking and financial services rankings, league tables, and vital statistics. Includes all tables published in the print edition of American Banker, and more. Organized by category with historical data.
Cost: $945.00
128 Pages

3361 State and Local MBA Directory
Mortgage Bankers Association of America
1717 Rhode Island Avenue, NW
Suite 400
Washington, DC 20036

202-557-2700
E-Mail: membership@mortgagebankers.org
Home Page: www.mortgagebankers.org

Michael Young, Chairman

All state and local MBA officers and a calendar of significant meeting dates.
Cost: $50.00
Frequency: SemiAnnual

3362 Thomson Bank Directory
4709 Golf Road
Skokie, IL 60076

847-676-9600
800-321-3373
FAX 847-933-8101

E-Mail: custserv@accuitysolutions.com
Home Page: www.accuitysolutions.com

Hugh Jones, President
Kerry Hewson, VP
Cost: $684.00
Frequency: June/December
Circulation: 35000
ISBN: 1-563103-45-1

3363 Thomson Credit Union Directory
4709 Golf Road
Skokie, IL 60076-1231

847-676-9600
800-321-3373
FAX 847-933-8101
E-Mail: custserv@accuitysolutions.com
Home Page: www.accuitysolutions.com

Hugh Jones, President
Kerry Hewson, VP

Semi-annual directory that includes valuable industry statistics, a quick telephone lookup index of all credit unions and a resource guide featuring vendors within the credit union marketplace. Includes over 12,500 major credit unions and 5,500 branches, with asset rankings, membership totals and more. Published in partnership with the Credit Union National Association.
Cost: $247.00
Frequency: January/July
ISBN: 1-563103-24-9

3364 Thomson Regulation CC Directory
4709 Golf Road
Skokie, IL 60076

847-676-9600
800-321-3373
FAX 847-933-8101
E-Mail: custserv@accuitysolutions.com
Home Page: www.accuitysolutions.com

Hugh Jones, President
Kerry Hewson, VP
Cost: $144.00
Frequency: January/July
Circulation: 30100

3365 Thomson Savings Directory
4709 Golf Road
Skokie, IL 60076-1231

847-676-9600
800-321-3373
FAX 847-933-8101
E-Mail: custserv@accuitysolutions.com
Home Page: www.accuitysolutions.com

Hugh Jones, President
Kerry Hewson, VP

Semi-annual directory dedicated to the thrift industry. Listings include primary correspondent information, national industry statistics and breakdowns of mortgage portfolios.
Cost: $316.00
Frequency: January/July

3366 World Bank Directory
4709 Golf Road
Skokie, IL 60076-1231

847-676-9600
800-321-3373
FAX 847-933-8101
E-Mail: custserv@accuitysolutions.com
Home Page: www.accuitysolutions.com

Hugh Jones, President
Kerry Hewson, VP

Contains detailed listings for 10,000 international banks and their branches worldwide plus the top 1,000 US banks. The information in this annual directory includes world and country rankings, international and correspondent contact information, principal correspondent insti-

tutions an standard settlement instructions.
Cost: $495.00
Frequency: September
Founded in 1895

3367 Worldwide Correspondents & Resource Guide
4709 Golf Road
Skokie, IL 60076-1231

847-676-9600
800-321-3373
FAX 847-933-8101
E-Mail: custserv@accuitysolutions.com
Home Page: www.accuitysolutions.com

Hugh Jones, President
Kerry Hewson, VP

A convenient one-volume directory listing the principal correspondent relationships for banks worldwide.
Cost: $184.00
Frequency: June/December

3368 Y-9 Report Analyzer
Sheshunoff Information Services
901 South Mopac
Suite 140
Austin, TX 78746-7970

512-472-4000
800-477-1772
FAX 512-305-6575
E-Mail: sales@smslp.com
Home Page: www.smslp.com
Social Media: *Facebook, Twitter, LinkedIn*

Gabrielle Sheshunoff, CEO

Sheshunoff Information Services provides bank holding companies (BHC) a tool to prepare and electronically file the following government forms: Y-9C, Y9-LP, Y11Q, and Y11I. Built in edit checks ensure the BHC's file the most accurate report possible.
Cost: $495.00
Frequency: Annual w/Quarterly Update

Industry Web Sites

3369 http://gold.greyhouse.com
G.O.L.D Grey House OnLine Databases
Grey House Publishing's online database platform, GOLD, offers Quick Search, Keyword Search and Expert Search, for most business sectors including banking and financial markets. The GOLD platform makes finding the information you need quick and easy - whether you're a novice searcher or an experienced database user. All of Grey House's directory products are available for subscription on the GOLD platform.

3370 www.aabd.org
American Association of Bank Directors
Devoted to serving the information, education and advocacy needs of individual bank and savings institution directors. This non-profit organization has members nationwide.

3371 www.aba.com
American Bankers Association
Brings together all categories of banking institutions to best represent the interests of this rapidly changing industry. It's membership — which includes community, regional and money center banks and holding companies, as well as savings associations, trust companies and savings banks makes ABA one of the largest banking trade associations in the country.

3372 www.aba.com/ICB/default.htm
Institute Of Certified Bankers

A national association of certified professionals in the financial services industry whose mission is to provide financial services professionals with confidence, credibility and recognition through its certifications.

3373 www.abiworld.org
American Bankruptcy Institute
Dedicated to research and education on matters related to insolvency.

3374 www.aftweb.com
Association for Financial Technology
Association founded in 1972 to promote high standards of professionalism in the planning, development, inplemtation and application of technology to the financial services industry.

3375 www.aitco.net
Association of Independent Trust Companies
Dedicated to provide a forum of leaders, owners and operators of trust companies and wealth management providers.

3376 www.ambahq.org
Association of Military Banks of America (AMBA)
Non-profit association of banks operating on military installments serving military customers and military banking facilities designated by the U.S. Treasury.

3377 www.baft.org
Bankers' Association for Finance & Trade
Financial trade association whose membership represents a broad range of internationally active financial institutions and companies that provide important services to the global financial community. BAFT serves as a forum for analysis, discussion and action among international financial professionals on a wide range of topics affecting international trade and finace, including legislative/regulatory issues.

3378 www.bai.org
Bank Administration Institute
The financial services industry's partner for breakthrough information and intelligence needed to innovate and stay relevant in an evolving marketplace. Serves a wide segment of the financial services industry, from the largest multinational banks to community-based institutions.

3379 www.bisanet.org
Bank Insurance and Securities Association
Dedicated to serving the needs of those responsible for marketing securities, insurance and other investment and risk management products.

3380 www.bmaatlanta.com
Business Marketing Association: Atlanta
BMA offers an information-packed website, online skills-building, marketing, certification programs and industry surveys and papers.

3381 www.cbanet.org
Consumer Bankers Association
Recognized voice on retail banking issues in the nation's capital. Member institutions are the leaders in consumer financial services, including auto finance, home equity lending, card products, education loans, small business services, community development, investments, deposits, and delivery.

3382 www.cfainstitute.org
CFA Institute
The CFA Institute is the global, non-profit professional association that administers the Char-

tered Financial Analyst curriculum and examination program.

3383 www.envirobank.org
Environmental Bankers Association
Dedicated to providing services for individuals with an interest in environmental risk management and related issues.

3384 www.freddiemac.com
Freddie Mac
Freddie Mac is a stockholder-owned corporation chartered by Congress to create a continuous flow of funds to mortgage lenders in support of homeownership and rental housing.

3385 www.fwi.org
Financial Women International
Formerly the National Association of Bank Women, the Association was founded in 1921 - one year after women won the right to vote, by a group of New York City women bankers. FWI serves women in the financial services industry that seeks to expand their personal and professional capabilities through self-directed growth in a supportive environment.

3386 www.garp.org
Global Association of Risk Management
This association is dedicated to being the leading professional association for risk managers, managed by and for its members.

3387 www.greyhouse.com
Grey House Publishing
Authoritative reference directories for most business sectors including banking and financial markets. Users can search the online databases with varied search criteria allowing for custom searches by product category, geographic area, sales volume, keyword, subject and more. Full Grey House catalog and online ordering also available.

3388 www.icba.org
Independent Community Bankers of America
Dedicated exclusively to enhancing the franchise value of the nation's community banks for the benefit of their customers and the communities they serve.

3389 www.ifsaonline.org
International Financial Services Association
Represents the international operations areas of financial services provider, their customers, suppliers and partners.

3390 www.iib.org
Institute of International Bankers
Created to help resolve the many special legislative, regulatory and tax issues confronting internationally headquartered financial institutions.

3391 www.jpmorganchase.com
JPMorgan Chase
A leading global financial services firm with assets of $1.3 trillion and operations in more than 50 countries.

3392 www.marinebankers.org
National Marine Bankers Association
Formed in 1980 in response to a request by the National Marine Manufacturers Association - NMMA - for additional sources of financing for it's members products. The purpose of the NMBA is to educate prospective lenders in marine finacing procedures, create new lenders to help finance the sales of the manufacturers products, and to create an information exchange for its members.

3393 www.mastercardinternational.com
MasterCard Worldwide

Administers the MasterCard credit card and other products for 25,000 member institutions around the world.

3394 www.mbaa.org
Mortgage Bankers Association of America

Representing the real estate finance industry, MBA serves its membership by representing their legislative and regulatory interests before the US Congress and federal agencies; by meeting their educational needs through programs and a range of periodicals and publications; and by supporting their business interests with a variety of research initiatives and other products and services.

3395 www.mortgagebankers.org
Mortgage Bankers Association

Seeks to improve methods of originating, servicing and marketing loans.

3396 www.naahl.org
National Association of Affordable Housing Lenders

For financial institutions and others with an interest in affordable housing and development lending.

3397 www.nabt.com
National Association of Bankruptcy Trustees

Nonprofit association formed in 1982 to address the needs of the bankruptcy trustees throughout the country and to promote the effectiveness of the bankruptcy system as a whole. While the majority of trustees who are members of the NABT are Chapter 7 trustees who primarily liquidate nonexempt assets for the benefit of creditors, many Chapter 7 trustees also serve as Chapter 11 trustees, who operate and reorganize companies. Some of our members are also Chapter 12 or Chapter 13 trustees.

3398 www.nacha.org
NACHA: Electronic Payments Association

Organization developing electronic solutions to improve the payments system. Representing more than 12,000 financial institutions through direct memberships and a network of regional payments associations, and 650 organizations through its industry councils, NACHA develops operating rules and business practices for the Automated Clearing House network and for electronic payments in the areas of internet commerce, electronic bill and invoice presentment and payment and other electronic payments.

3399 www.nactt.com
National Association of Chapter 13 Trustees

Provides a forum within which Chapteer 13 trustees will act as an information and communication resource to advance education, leadership, and continuous improvement in the administration of bankruptcy.

3400 www.nacusac.org
Nat'l Assoc. of Credit Union Super. & Audit. Comm.

A unique organization of, by and for credit union supervisory committee members.

3401 www.nafcu.org
National Association Of Federal Credit Unions

A respected and influential trade association that exclusively represents the interests of federal credit unions before the federal government and the public.

3402 www.naggl.com
Nat'l Assoc. of Government Guaranteed Lenders

Promotes professional and governmental affairs interests of financial institutions and small businesses who participate in the Small Business Administration guaranteed lending and secondary market programs.

3403 www.namb.org
National Association of Mortgage Brokers

Mortgage brokers who seek to increase professionalism and to foster business relationships among members.

3404 www.napmw.org
Nat'l Association of Professional Mortgage Women

Serves all mortgage professionals and employers who want to excel.

3405 www.nascus.org
Nat'l Assoc. of State Credit Union Supervisors

State chartered credit unions and state credit union supervisors.

3406 www.nationalbankers.org
National Bankers Association

Members are minority and women's banking institutions, minority individuals employed by majority banks and institutions.

3407 www.ncua.gov
National Credit Union Administration

Charters and supervises federal credit unions.

3408 www.nibanet.org
National Investment Banking Association

A national trade association of regional and independent brokerages, investment banking firms, and related capital market service providers.

3409 www.rmahq.org
Risk Management Association

Topics relating to all aspects of commercial lending, financial statement analysis and credit information exchange and managerial aspects of consumer lending.

3410 www.sifma.org/
Securities Industry and Financial Markets Assoc.

SIFMA's mission is to champion policies and practices that benefit investors and issuers, expand and perfect global capital markets, and foster the development of new products and services.

3411 www.snl.com
SNL Securities

News articles on banks and thrifts, insurance and other financial services. Also features vital company information.

3412 www.sourcemedia.com
SourceMedia

Provides market information, including news, analysis, and insight to the financial services and related industries.

3413 www.ufscnet.org
Urban Financial Services Coalition

An organization of minority professionals in the financial services industry and related fields.

3414 www.wiley.com
John Wiley & Sons

Wiley is a global publisher of print and electronic products, specializing in science, technical, and material books and journals, professional and consumer books and subscription services, textbooks and other educational materials for undergraduate and graduate students as well as lifelong learners. Wiley has approximately 22,700 active titles and about 400 journals, and publishes about 2000 new titles in a variety of print and electronic formats each year.

Associations

3415 Aesthetics' International Association

310 E. Interstate 30
Suite B107
Garland, TX 75043

972-203-8530
877-968-7539
FAX 972-226-2339
E-Mail: AIAthekey@aol.com
Home Page: www.aestheticsassociation.com/

Patricia Strunk, President
Michelle D'Allaird, Vice President
Melissa Lawrence, Membership Director

International professional organization for aestheticians that represents every facet of the aesthetics industry. We offer something for the student, aesthetician, make-up artist, reflexologist, aromatherapist, massage therapist, nutritionist, nurse, holistic practitioner and physician to the day spa and salon owner.
Founded in 1972

3416 American Association of Cosmetology Schools

9927 East Bell Road
Suite 110
Scottsdale, AZ 85260

480-281-0431
800-831-1086
FAX 480-905-0993
E-Mail: jim@beautyschools.org
Home Page: www.beautyschools.org
Social Media: *Facebook, Twitter*

Jim Cox, CEO
Lisa Zarda, General Manager
Geoff Gerard, Controller
Ashley Morris, Communications Manager
Linda Williams, Membership Manager

National non-profit association open to all privately owned schools of Cosmetology Arts and Sciences. AACS specializes in updating our members with information about new teaching methods, current industry events, and Washington, DC updates.
1100 Members
Founded in 1924

3417 American Beauty Association

15825 N 71st St
Suite 100
Scottsdale, AZ 85254-1521

480-281-0431
E-Mail: info@probeautyassociation.org
Social Media: *Facebook, Twitter, LinkedIn*

James Cox, Executive Director
Bruce Selan, VP
George Schaeffer, Secretary/Treasurer

ABA members are manufacturers, manufacturer reps and consultants in the professional beauty industry. Associate members are made up of trade publications, distributors and salons. The ABA's mission is to expand, serve and protect the interests of the professional beauty industry.
250 Members
Founded in 1985

3418 American Electrology Association

1616 Cherry Street
Wenatchee, WA 98801

509-663-6874
FAX 509-663-6874
E-Mail: infoaea@electrology.com
Home Page: www.electrology.com
Social Media: *Facebook*

Pearl Warner, CPE, President
Sandra K Jackson, 1st VP
Deborah Cassin, CPE, Treasurer

Mary Kaye Johnson, 2nd VP
Julia A Hamilton, 3rd VP

The American Electrology Association (AEA), is the largest international nonprofit membership organization for permanent hair removal professionals. Promotes the highest standards in Electrology education, practice and ethics and champions state licensing and regulation of the profession to protect the public interest.
1500 Members
250 Attendees
Frequency: 3 times a year
Circulation: 1500
Founded in 1958

3419 American Hair Loss Council

30 South Main
Shenandoah, PA 17976

412-765-3666
FAX 412-765-3669
E-Mail: info@ahcl.org
Home Page: www.ahlc.org
Social Media: *Facebook, Twitter, LinkedIn*

Susan Kettering, Executive Director
Peggy Thornhill, President
Marsha Scott, Vice President
Joseph Ellis, Board Member
Betty Ann Bugden, Treasurer

A not-for-profit agency, dedicated to sorting through this information, discovering what works and what doesn't, and presenting findings to the consumer.

3420 American Society of Hair Restoration Surgery

225 W. Wacker Drive
Suite 650
Chicago, IL 60606

312-981-6760
FAX 312-981-6787
E-Mail: info@cosmeticsurgery.org
Home Page: www.cosmeticsurgery.org
Social Media: *Facebook, Twitter, LinkedIn*

Michael J Will, President
Robert A Shumway, President-Elect
Robert H Burke, Treasurer
Joe Niamtu, Secretary
Jane Petro, Immediate Past President
1600 Members

3421 Associated Bodywork & Massage Professionals

25188 Genesee Trail Rd.
Suite 200
Golden, CO 80401

303-674-8478
800-458-2267
FAX 800-667-8260
E-Mail: expectmore@abmp.com
Home Page: www.abmp.com
Social Media: *Facebook, Twitter, LinkedIn*

Leslie Young, VP, Communication

Practice support and liability insurance for massage/bodywork professionals.
80000 Members
Founded in 1987

3422 Association of Cosmetologists and Hairdressers

15825 N. 71st Street
Suite 100
Scottsdale, AZ 85254-1521

480-281-0424
800-468-2274
FAX 480-905-0708
E-Mail: info@probeauty.org

Home Page: www.ncacares.org
Social Media: *Facebook, Twitter, Google+*

Scott Buchanan, Chariman
Reuben Carranza, Vice Chair
Steve Sleeper, Executive Director

Association of Cosmetologists membership includes salon owners, hairdressers, nail technicians, estheticians, educators, and students, and is the world's largest association of salon professionals.
3910 Members
Founded in 1985

3423 Association of Cosmetology Salon Professionals

PO Box 207
Chapin, SC 29036

803-345-2909
E-Mail: contact@mycosmetology.org
Home Page: www.mycosmetology.org

Linda Green, President
Sandra Mullins, Vice-President
Terry Frick, Secretary

Association for the promotion of professional standards in the cosmetology, esthetics and nail industries.

3424 Cosmetologists Chicago

440 S LaSalle Street
Suite 2325
Chicago, IL

312-321-6809
800-883-7808
FAX 312-673-6612
E-Mail: info@americasbeautyshow.com
Home Page:
www.chicagomidwestbeautyshow.com
Social Media: *Facebook, Twitter, Youtube, Pinterest, WordPress*

Denise Provenzano, President
Larry Silvestri, First VP
Robert Passage, 2nd VP
Lorrene Conino, Treasurer
Karen Gordon, Secretary

Voice of the salon industry, a beauty authority and presenter of the Chicago Midwest Beauty Show, stylists, estheticians, color technicians, salon owners, educators and nail technicians.
35000 Members

3425 Cosmoprof North America (CPNA)

15825 N 71st Street
Suite 100
Scottsdale, AZ 85254

480-281-0424
800-468-2274
FAX 480-905-0708
E-Mail: info@cosmoprofnorthamerica.com
Home Page: www.cosmoprofnorthamerica.com
Social Media: *Facebook, Twitter, LinkedIn, Pinterest, YouTube*

Max Wexler, Chariman
Scott Buchanan, Vice Chair
Bruce Selan, Treasurer

Supports all those involved with industry related equipment, supplies and services.
Frequency: Annual
Founded in 1892

3426 Intercoiffure of America

1645 Downtown West Blvd
Suite 18
Knoxville, TN 37919

614-457-7712
800-442-3007
FAX 614-457-7794
E-Mail: info@intercoiffure.com

Home Page: www.intercoiffure.com
Social Media: *Facebook, Twitter, Google+*

Frank Gambuzza, President
Sheila Zaricor-Wilson, VP
Andreas Zafiriadis, 2nd VP
Inge Handing, Secretary
Darlene Gage, Treasurer

Sponsors semiannual hair fashion shows in New York City.
260 Members
Founded in 1933

3427 International Guild of Hair Removal Specialists
1918 Bethel Road
Columbus, OH 43220

800-830-3247
Home Page: www.ighrs.org

Formerly known as the International Guild of Professional Electrologists. A non-profit organization dedicated to providing the latest information about permanent and long-term hair removal to the consumer.
2000 Members
Founded in 1979

3428 International Nail Technicians Association
330 N Wabash Ave
Chicago, IL 60611

312-321-6809
800-883-7808
FAX 312-245-1080
E-Mail: info@americasbeautyshow.com
Home Page: www.isnow.com
Social Media: *Facebook, Twitter, Youtube, Pinterest, WordPress*

Joseph Cartagena, President
Denise Provenzano, First VP
Larry Silvestri, 2nd VP
Karen Gordon, Treasurer
Robert Passage, Secretary

An international organization for nail professionals. In 2001 it was acquired by Cosmetologists Chicago with the purpose of providing an association 'home' to nail care professionals that is dedicated to the needs of technicians and the industry

3429 International Salon Spa Business Network
207 E Ohio Street
#361
Chicago, IL 60611

440-846-6022
866-444-4272
FAX 866-444-5139
E-Mail: margie@salonspanetwork.org
Home Page: www.icsa.cc
Social Media: *Facebook, Twitter*

Jason Volk, President
Paul Brown, Vice President
Scott Colabuono, Vice President
Larry Walt, Treasurer
Philip Gould, Secretary

Dedicated to helping its members grow their business, effect positive change politically, provide a forum for members to share their views and ideas and interface with the professional beauty industry on behalf of the chain salons and spas.
70 Members
Founded in 1973

3430 National Association of Barber Boards of America
870-230-0777
E-Mail: samdabarberman@yahoo.com

Sam Barcelona, President

Association for the promotion of professional standards in the barbering industry.
110 Members
Founded in 1926

3431 National Beauty Culturists' League
25 Logan Circle NW
Washington, DC 20005-3725

202-332-2695
FAX 202-332-0940
E-Mail: nbcl@bellsouth.net
Home Page: www.nbcl.org

Katie B Catalon, President

Established as the National Hair System Culture League, members are black beauticians and cosmetologists who embrace diversity.
3000 Members
Founded in 1919

3432 National Cosmetology Association
15825 N. 71st Street
Suite 100
Scottsdale, AZ 85254

480-281-0424
800-468-2274
FAX 480-905-0708
E-Mail: info@probeauty.org
Home Page: www.ncacares.org

Max Wexler, Chariman
Scott Buchanan, Vice Chair
Bruce Selan, Treasurer

Membership includes salon owners, hairdressers, nail technicians, estheticians, educators, and students. Members live and work in all 50 states, and also have the option to participate in the state and local affiliate, along with national activities.
25000 Members
Founded in 1921

3433 Professional Beauty Association
15825 N 71st Street
Suite 100
Scottsdale, AZ 85254-1521

480-281-0424
800-468-2274
FAX 480-905-0708
E-Mail: info@probeauty.org
Home Page: www.probeauty.org
Social Media: *Facebook, Twitter, LinkedIn, YouTube, Pinterest, Instagram*

Reuben Carranza, Chariman
Beth Hickey, Vice Chair
Steve Sleeper, Executive Director
Rachel Molepske, Manager, Leadership Operations
Toni Davis, Director

The Professional Beauty Association (PBA) is a non-profit trade association that represents the interests of the professional beauty industry from manufacturers and distributors to salons and spas. PBA serves the industry through five core competencies: education, government advocacy, commerce opportunities, research/statistics and public relations/image building.
1400 Members
Founded in 1904

3434 Society of Clinical and Medical Hair Removal
2424 American Lane
Madison, WI 53704-3102

608-443-2470
FAX 608-443-2474
E-Mail: homeoffice@scmhr.org
Home Page: www.scmhr.org
Social Media: *Facebook, Twitter, Google+*

William A Moore, President
Fadia Hoyek, Exectuive VP
Sandra Ysassi, Treasurer

Sarikhi Chaffin, Secretary
Ruth G Bayer, Vice President

An international non profit organization with members in the United States, Canada, Australia, Japan and beyond. Supports all methods of hair removal and is dedicated to the research of new technology that will keep its members at the pinnacle of their profession, offering safe, effective hair removal to their clients.
600 Members
Founded in 1985

Newsletters

3435 AEA Newsletter
American Electrology Association
1616 Cherry Street
Wenatchee, WA 98801

509-663-6874
FAX 509-663-6874
E-Mail: presaea@electrology.com
Home Page: www.electrology.com

Sharon Ortiz, CPE, President
Barbara Greathouse, CPE, 1st VP
Deborah Cassin, CPE, Treasurer

The largest international not for profit membership organization. Promotes the highest standards in Electrology education, practice and ethics and champions state licensing and regulation of the profession to protect public interest.
1500 Members
Frequency: Three/Year
Circulation: 1200
Founded in 1958

3436 ISNOW Cosmetologists Chicago
401 N Michigan Avenue
Chicago, IL 60611-4255

312-321-6809
800-883-7808
FAX 312-245-1080
E-Mail: info@americasbeautyshow.com
Home Page: www.isnow.com

Frank Gironda, President
Joseph Cartagena, First VP
Denise Provenzano, Secretary
Larry Silvestri, Treasurer

Represents the industries various constituencies and salon owners.
Cost: $18.95
Frequency: Monthly
Circulation: 5000
Founded in 2004

3437 National Beauty News
10405 E 55th Place
Suite B
Tulsa, OK 74146-6502

918-627-8000
FAX 918-627-8660

Douglas Von Allmen, Owner

Offers news of shows, seminars, product information and columns for the professional beauty industry.
Cost: $12.00
Frequency: Monthly
Circulation: 35,500

3438 Pink Sheet
685 Route 202/206
Bridgewater, NJ 08807

800-332-2181
908-547-2159
FAX 908-547-2200
E-Mail: custcare@elsevier.com

Home Page: www.elsevierbi.com
Social Media: *RSS*

Mike Squires, President
Cathy Kelly, Executive Editor
Brooke McManus, Managing Editor
Jim Chicca, Executive Director
Melissa Carlson, Editorial Operations Manager

Chronicles regulatory and legal news, major scientific developments and testing methodologies, and their effect on these industries. Product marketing news, new product launches, and promotions and advertising at the retail level, are also included.
Cost: $1050.00
Frequency: Weekly
Founded in 1939

Magazines & Journals

3439 AEA Journal of Electrology
American Electrology Association
1616 Cherry Street
Wenatchee, WA 98801

509-663-6874
FAX 509-663-6874
E-Mail: presaea@electrology.com
Home Page: www.electrology.com

Sharon Ortiz, CPE, President
Barbara Greathouse, CPE, 1st VP
Deborah Cassin, CPE, Treasurer

The Journal of Electrology is a membership news publication, published twice per year and is designed to inform and educate the professional electrologist by offering articles of interest and value by reputable authors who are well qualified in the topic area.
Cost: $40.00
1500 Members
Frequency: Semi-Annual
Circulation: 1200
Founded in 1958

3440 Beauty Store Business
Creative Age Publications
7628 Densmore Ave
Van Nuys, CA 91406-2042

818-782-7328
800-442-5667
FAX 818-782-7450
E-Mail: webmaster@creativeage.com
Home Page: www.creativeage.com

Deborah Carver, President/CEO
Mindy Rosiejka, Vice President/COO
Karie Frost, Executive Director

Industry trends and valuable tips concerning real estate, banking, insurance, product liability, advertising, merchandising, and more.
Frequency: Monthly
Circulation: 15000
ISSN: 1098-0660
Founded in 1971

3441 BeautyLink
American Association of Cosmetology Schools
9927 E. Bell Road
Suite 110
Scottsdale, AZ 85260

480-281-0431
800-831-1086
FAX 480-905-0993
E-Mail: jim@beautyschools.org
Home Page: www.beautyschools.org

Jim Cox, Executive Director
Lisa Zarda, General Manager

Quarterly magazine of the AACS, with cosmetology industry updates and features on new trends and best practices.
Frequency: Quarterly
Circulation: 7000

3442 Cosmetic World
Ledes Group
16 East 40th Street
Suite 700
New York, NY 10016

212-840-8800
FAX 212-840-7246
Home Page: www.cosmeticworld.com

Debra Davis, Advertising Director
Brittany Burhop, Executive Editor
Debbie Ward, Managing Editor

Current industry events, legislation, management changes and corporate activities, as well as marketing developments and financial analysis.
Cost: $175.00
Circulation: 5397
Printed in on glossy stock

3443 DaySpa Magazine
Creative Age Publications
7628 Densmore Ave
Van Nuys, CA 91406-2042

818-782-7328
FAX 818-782-7450
E-Mail: sverba@creativeage.com
Home Page: www.creativeage.com

Deborah Carver, President/CEO
Mindy Rosiejka, Vice President/COO
Karie Frost, Executive Director

DaySpa is dedicated to helping premium salon and spa owners better serve their client enhance their bottom line. Presents the most accurate, up-to-date information available on trends, products, equipment, services, and management and management tools in easy-to-read, entertaining articles.
Cost: $17.50
Frequency: Annual+
Circulation: 24,000+
Founded in 1972

3444 Dermascope Magazine
Aesthetics International Association
310 East I-30,
SuiteB107
Garland, TX 75043

469-429-9300
800-961-3777
FAX 469-429-9301
E-Mail: press@dermascope.com
Home Page: www.dermascope.com

William Strunk, Publisher
Amy McKay, Editor
Wes Wynne, Marketing Director

Provides education for skin care professionals. One of the oldest magazines in the industry.
Cost: $45.00
148 Pages
Frequency: Monthly
Circulation: 16000
ISSN: 1075-055X
Founded in 1972

3445 Looking Fit Magazine
Virgo Publishing LLC
3300 N Central Ave
Suite 300
Phoenix, AZ 85012-2532

48 - 9 - 11
FAX 480-990-0819
E-Mail: swhitley@vpico.com
Home Page: www.vpico.com

John Siefert, CEO
Kelly Ridley, Executive VP/ CFO

Educational resource for professionals in the indoor tanning industry.
Cost: $70.00
300 Pages
Frequency: Monthly
Founded in 1986

3446 Modern Salon
Vance Publishing
400 Knightsbridge Pkwy
Lincolnshire, IL 60069

847-634-2600
FAX 847-634-4379
E-Mail: info@vancepublishing.com
Home Page: www.vancepublishing.com

William C Vance, Chairman
Peggy Walker, President

The constant leader and voice of the professional salon industry. Delivers step-by-step education for the stylist and paid circulation for the advertiser.
Frequency: Monthly
Circulation: 117000
Founded in 1924
Printed in 4 colors on glossy stock

3447 NW Stylist and Salon
Porter Publishing
1750 Sw Skyline Blvd
Suite 8
Portland, OR 97221-2543

503-296-4889
888-297-7010
FAX 503-296-4893
Home Page: www.portlandpsinc.com

James Pettigrove, President
Lisa Kind, Managing Editor
Joel Holland, VP
Marcy Avenson, Advertising Director

Business trade journal mailed free to every salon school and practitioner in Oregon. Accepts advertising.
Cost: $20.00
36 Pages
Frequency: Monthly
Circulation: 22000
Founded in 1983

3448 NailPro
Creative Age Publications
7628 Densmore Ave
Van Nuys, CA 91406-2042

818-782-7328
800-442-5667
FAX 818-782-7450
E-Mail: webmaster@creativeage.com
Home Page: www.creativeage.com

Deborah Carver, President/CEO
Mindy Rosiejka, Vice President/COO
Karie Frost, Executive Director

Nail care how-to's, business related articles, information on nail anatomy and pathology, as well as new products, trends, profiles and a calendar of events.
Cost: $21.95
Frequency: Monthly
Circulation: 50713
Founded in 1971

3449 Nails Magazine
Bobit Publishing Company
3520 Challenger St
Torrance, CA 90503-1640

310-533-2400
FAX 310-533-2500
E-Mail: Hannah.Lee@bobit.com
Home Page: www.bobit.com

Edward J Bobit, CEO
Hannah Lee, Executive Editor
Uyonna Beckham, Sales Assistant

Sarah Paredes, Senior Production Manager
Ty Bobit, CEO

Offers business information on products and
application techniques for professional mani-
curists and salon owners.
Cost: $20.00
Frequency: Monthly
Circulation: 62274
Founded in 1961

3450 Salon News

Fairchild Publications
750 3rd Ave
New York, NY 10017-2703

212-630-4000
FAX 212-630-3563
Home Page: www.fairchildpub.com

Mary G Berner, CEO

Profitability and stability, salon services and re-
sale, and on motivation and education.
Frequency: Monthly
Circulation: 77,603

3451 Salon Today

Vance Publishing
400 Knightsbridge Pkwy
Lincolnshire, IL 60069

847-634-2600
FAX 847-634-4379
E-Mail: info@vancepublishing.com
Home Page: www.vancepublishing.com

William C Vance, Chairman
Peggy Walker, President

Content is modeled as a monthly exchange of
ideas on how to grow salon business. Special
issues include annual Salon Today 200, Salon
of the Year, Technology and Spa Business.
Frequency: Monthly
Circulation: 25000

3452 Skin Magazine

Allured Publishing Corporation
PO Box 50
Congers, NY 10920

845-267-3008
866-616-3008
FAX 845-267-3478
E-Mail: skininc@cambeywest.com
Home Page: www.skininc.com

Janet Ludwig, President
Lin Getner, Controller

The business magazine preferred by owners
and managers of salons and spas and the offi-
cial publication of the American Aestheticians
Education Association. Recently awarded a
Gold award for editorial from the American
Business Publication editors association.
Cost: $49.00
120 Pages
Frequency: Monthly
Circulation: 16000
Founded in 1988

3453 WWD Beauty Biz

Fairchild Publications
7 W 34th St
New York, NY 10001-8100

212-630-3880
FAX 212-630-3868
E-Mail: summits@fairchildpub.com
Home Page: www.fairchildpub.com

Mary Berner, President/CEO
Patrick McCarthy, Chairman/Editorial Director
Jenny B. Fine, Editor-in-Chief
Sarah Murphy, Publisher

The premier guide to the beauty industry. Provides in-depth coverage and analysis on all aspects of the industry, including trends, brands,
retailers, and personalities driving both the
general consumer and insider sides of the busi-

ness.
Cost: $60.00
Frequency: Monthly
Circulation: 40,056
Founded in 1892

Trade Shows

3454 AACS Annual Convention & Expo

American Association of Cosmetology
Schools
9927 E. Bell Road
Suite 110
Scottsdale, AZ 85260

480-281-0431
800-831-1086
FAX 480-905-0993
E-Mail: jim@beautyschools.org
Home Page: www.beautyschools.org

Jim Cox, Executive Director
Lisa Zarda, General Manager

An opportunity to bring your professional team
together to lead your school into the future. Education tracks, classes, social events, and the
expo hall complete the experience.
800 Attendees
Frequency: November

3455 ACSP Annual Meeting

Association of Cosmetology Salon
Professionals
PO Box 207
Chapin, SC 29036

803-345-2909
E-Mail: contact@mycosmetology.org
Home Page: www.mycosmetology.org

Linda Green, President
Sandra Mullins, Vice-President
Terry Frick, Secretary

Competitions, continuing education and annual
meeting.
Frequency: Annual

3456 AEA Annual Convention

American Electrology Association
1616 Cherry Street
Wenatchee, WA 98801

509-663-6874
FAX 509-663-6874
E-Mail: presaea@electrology.com
Home Page: www.electrology.com

Sharon Ortiz, CPE, President
Barbara Greathouse, CPE, 1st VP
Deborah Cassin, CPE, Treasurer

Annual convention usually in October. Includes
15 hours of CEUs as well as exhibitors.
1500 Members
300 Attendees
Frequency: Annual/Fall
Founded in 1958

3457 Aesthetics' World Expositions

Aesthetics' International Association
2611 N Belt Line Road
Suite 140
Sunnyvale, TX 75182-9357

972-203-8530
877-968-7539
FAX 972-226-2339
Home Page: www.beautyworks.com/aia

150-250 exhibits of skin care, body therapy
products make up and equipment. Salon owners, body massage therapists, and dermatologists attend.
3000 Attendees
Frequency: Biennial
Founded in 1979

**3458 American Electrology Association
Convention**

American Electrology Association
1616 Cherry Street
Wenatchee, WA 98801

509-663-6874
FAX 509-663-6874
E-Mail: presaea@electrology.com
Home Page: www.electrology.com

Sharon Ortiz, CPE, President
Barbara Greathouse, CPE, 1st VP
Deborah Cassin, CPE, Treasurer

AEA is the largest international nonprofit membership organization for permanent hair removal. The convention features the largest
number of exhibitors with the latest state of the
art equipment.
1500 Members
300 Attendees
Frequency: Annual
Founded in 1958

3459 Big Show Expo

Big Show Expo
1841 Broadway
Room 812
New York, NY 10023-7603

212-580-1407
FAX 212-757-3611

Bernice Calvin, President
Maggie Smallwood, Conference Coordinator

Largest group of ethnic beauty shows. 200
booths updating the skills and expertise of hairdressers with ethnic clientele and spotlighting
new trends in hair fashions, with all new styles
for today's fashion looks.
15M Attendees
Frequency: August, September

3460 COSMOPROF North America

COSMOPROF North America
15825 North 71st Street
Suite 100
Scottsdale, AZ 85254

480-281-0424
800-468-2274
FAX 480-905-0708
E-Mail: cpnainfo@probeauty.org
Home Page: www.cosmoprofnorthamerica.com

Eric Horn, Show Director
Ebony King, Show Manager
Wendy Forakis, Business Relations Manager

The most comprehensive and international professional beauty industry show on the continent. Attendees include manufacturers to
distributors , salon owners to spa professionals,
importers to retail buyers with hundreds of
exhibitors.
25000 Attendees
Frequency: July
Mailing list available for rent

3461 Hairworld

National Cosmetology Association
15825 North 71st Street
Suite 100
Scottsdale, AZ 85254

480-281-0424
800-468-2274
FAX 480-905-0708
E-Mail: info@probeauty.org
Home Page: www.ncacares.org

Max Wexler, Chairman
Scott Buchanan, Vice Chair
Bruce Selan, Treasurer

Annual show of 125 exhibitors of hair products, cosmetics and jewelry.
3000 Attendees
Frequency: July
Circulation: 30,000

3462 International Congress of Esthetics
Aesthetics' International Association
310 East I-30
Suite B107
Garland, TX 75043

469-429-9300
800-961-3777
FAX 469-429-9301
E-Mail: press@dermascope.com
Home Page: www.dermascope.com

Will Strunk, Publisher
Amy McKay, Editor

Biennial show of skin care, makeup and body therapy products and equipment.
3000 Attendees
Frequency: February
Founded in 1977

3463 NABBA Annual Conference
National Association of Barber Boards of America

870-230-0777
E-Mail: samdabarberman@yahoo.com

Sam Barcelona, President
Frequency: Annual

Directories & Databases

3464 AEA Online Directory
American Electrology Association
1616 Cherry Street
Wenatchee, WA 98801

509-663-6874
FAX 509-663-6874
E-Mail: presaea@electrology.com
Home Page: www.electrology.com

Sharon Ortiz, CPE, President
Barbara Greathouse, CPE, 1st VP
Deborah Cassin, CPE, Treasurer

Available on the AEA Web site.
1500 Members
Founded in 1958

3465 Drug Store and HBC Chains Database
Chain Store Guide
3922 Coconut Palm Dr
Tampa, FL 33619-1389

813-627-6700
800-927-9292
FAX 813-627-6888
E-Mail: webmaster@chainstoreguide.com
Home Page: www.csgis.com

Mike Jarvis, Publisher
Arthur Sciarrotta, Senior VP

Tap into the lucrative drug industry with profiles on more than 1,700 US and Canadian companies operating two or more retail drug stores, deep discount stores, health and beauty care (HBC) stores, cosmetic stores or vitamin stores that have industry sales of at least $250,000. This powerful database empowers you to sell and market your products successfully by reaching more than 8,300 key decision-makers.
Cost: $335.00
Circulation: 8,300

3466 Hayes Chain Drug Store Directory
Hayes Directories
PO Box 3436
Mission Viejo, CA 92690

949-583-0537
FAX 949-583-7419
E-Mail: enhayes@pacbell.net
Home Page: www.hayesdir.com

James Edward Hayes, Editor

Comes in two volumes and contains information for 34,773 chain pharmacies in the United States, 8 stores or more. First volume lists the chain headquarters, and includes the total count of stores with pharmacies. The second volume groups the individual chain stores alphabetically by chain name followed by the name and address information for the headquarters of the parent company.
Cost: $250.00
Frequency: Annual,November

3467 Hayes Drug Store Directory
Hayes Directories
PO Box 3436
Mission Viejo, CA 92690

949-583-0537
FAX 949-583-7419
E-Mail: enhayes@pacbell.net
Home Page: www.hayesdir.com

James Edward Hayes, Editor

Contains information for the 53,821 retail drug stores in the United States.
Cost: $335.00
Frequency: Annual,November

3468 Hayes Independent Drug Store Directory
Hayes Directories
PO Box 3436
Mission Viejo, CA 92690

949-583-0537
FAX 949-583-7419
E-Mail: enhayes@pacbell.net
Home Page: www.haynesdir.com

James Edward Hayes, Editor

Published annually and contains information for 19,048 independent retail pharmacies in the United States. Independent stores are 7 stores or less.
Cost: $300.00
Frequency: Annual,November

Industry Web Sites

3469 http://gold.greyhouse.com
G.O.L.D Grey House OnLine Databases

Grey House Publishing's online database platform, GOLD, offers Quick Search, Keyword Search and Expert Search for most business sectors including beauty and cosmetics markets. The GOLD platform makes finding the information you need quick and easy - whether you're a novice searcher or an experienced database user. All of Grey House's directory products are available for subscription on the GOLD platform.

3470 www.bbsi.org
Beauty and Barber Supply Institute

Our members are wholesaler-distributors, manufacturers and manufacturers' representatives from around the world. Our mission is to maximize the potential of the professional salon industry.

3471 www.beautyschools.org
American Association of Cosmetology Schools

Serves privately owned schools of Cosmetology Arts & Sciences.

3472 www.dermascope.com
Aesthetics' International Association

International professional organization for aestheticians representing every facet of the aesthetics industry. From the student, aesthetician, make-up artist, reflexologist, aromatherapist, massage therapist, nutritionist, nurse, holistic practitioner and physician to the day spa/salon owner.

3473 www.electrology.com
American Electrology Association

Organization of professional hair removal practitioners promoting the highest standards of electrology education through our annual and state conventions with seminars following a prescribed learning standard.

3474 www.greyhouse.com
Grey House Publishing

Authoritative reference directories for most business sectors including beauty and cosmetics markets. Users can search the online databases with varied search criteria allowing for custom searches by product category, geographic area, sales volume, keyword, subject and more. Full Grey House catalog and online ordering also available.

3475 www.isnow.com
Cosmetologists Chicago

Voice of the salon industry. Presenter of the Chicago Midwest Beauty Show, we are stylists, estheticians, color technicians, salon owners, educators and nail technicians.

3476 www.oneroof.org
American Beauty Association

Serves the interests of the professional beauty industry.

3477 www.salons.org
The Salon Association

Non-profit organization representing 7,000 employment-based salons and spas across the United States and Canada

Associations

3478 American Association for Medical Chronobiology & Chronotherapeutics

E-Mail: editorial@aamcc.org
Home Page: www.aamcc.net

Erhard Haus, President
Michael Smolensky, Vice President
Linda Sackett-Lundeen, Secretary-Treasurer
Molly Bray, Director
Martin Young, Director

Provides a forum for the exchange and discussion of new findings, methods, and applications in medical chronobiology and chronotherapeutics.

3479 American Association of Bioanalysts

906 Olive Street
Suite 1200
St Louis, MO 63101

314-241-1445
FAX 314-241-1449
E-Mail: aab@aab.org
Home Page: www.aab.org

Mark S Birenbaum PhD, Administrator

AAB is committed to the pursuit of excellence in clinical laboratory services by enhancing the professional skills of each of its members; promoting more efficient and productive operations; offering external quality control programs; collaborating with other professional associations and government agencies; promoting safe laboratory practices; and educating legislators, regulators, and the general public about clinical laboratory tests and procedures.
Founded in 1956

3480 American Association of Immunologists

9650 Rockville Pike
Bethesda, MD 20814

301-634-7178
FAX 301-634-7887
E-Mail: infoaai@aai.org
Home Page: www.aai.org
Social Media: *Facebook*

Marc K Jenkins, President
M Michele Hogan, Executive Director
David G Jakson, Director of Finance
Vivian Chin, Senior Accountant
Chhanda Das, Accounting Assistant

AAI is a professional organization founded to advance the knowledge of immunology and related disciplines, foster interchange of ideas and information among scientists, and promote understanding of the field of immunology.
Cost: $50.00
6500 Members
Founded in 1954

3481 American Geophysical Union

2000 Florida Ave Nw
Washington, DC 20009

202-462-6900
800-966-2481
FAX 202-328-0566
E-Mail: service@agu.org
Home Page: www.agu.org
Social Media: *Facebook, Twitter, LinkedIn, Youtube, RSS*

Robin E Bell, President
Eric A Davidson, President Elect
Susan Webb, International Secretary
Christine W McEntee, Executive Director/CEO
Louise Pellerin, General Secretary
52000 Members
Founded in 1919
Mailing list available for rent

3482 American Institute of Biological Sciences

1800 Alexander Bell Drive
Suite 400
Reston, VA 20191

703-674-2500
800-992-2427
FAX 703-674-2509
E-Mail: rogrady@aibs.org
Home Page: www.aibs.org
Social Media: *Facebook, Twitter, LinkedIn, Youtube, RSS*

Joseph Travis, President
John Tobin, Treasurer
Judith Skog, Secretary
Karen Schmaling, Vice President
John Burris, Member

Supports professionals involved with the biological sciences, including research, products, education; sponsors annual conference.
Mailing list available for rent

3483 American Registry of Magnetic Resonance Imaging Technologists

8815 Commonwealth Blvd.
Bellerose, NY 11426

718-347-8690
FAX 718-347-8691
E-Mail: ARMRIT@msn.com
Home Page: armrit.org

James F. Coffin, President & Executive Director
Thomas K. Schrack, Director
Charles G. Fiore, Senior Director & Legal Counsel
William J. Woodward, Director
Charles W. Kreines, Director

MRI schools, educational resources, certified tech resumes, practice tests, and verification of a tech's certification.
Founded in 1991

3484 American Society for Biochemistry and Molecular Biology

11200 Rockville Pike
Suite 302
Rockville, MD 20852-3110

240-283-6600
FAX 301-881-2080
E-Mail: asbmb@asbmb.org
Home Page: www.asbmb.org
Social Media: *Facebook, Twitter, LinkedIn, YouTube, Google+*

Steven McKnight, President
Karen Allen, Secretary
Toni M Antalis, Treasurer
Natalie Ahn, President-Elect
Barbara A Gordon, Executive Director

A professional and educational association for biochemists and molecular biologists which seeks to extend and utilize the field of biochemistry and molecular biology.
Cost: $18.50
11900 Members
Founded in 1906
Mailing list available for rent: 11000 names

3485 American Society for Reproductive Medicine

1209 Montgomery Highway
Birmingham, AL 35216-2809

205-978-5000
FAX 205-978-5005
E-Mail: asrm@asrm.org
Home Page: www.asrm.org
Social Media: *Facebook, Twitter, LinkedIn, Tumblr*

Rebecca Sokol, President
Owen K. Davis, President Elect
Richard Paulson, Vice President

Linda Giudice, Past President
Richard H. Reindollar, Executive Director

Organization devoted to advancing knowledge and expertise in the study of reproduction and reproductive disorders.
Founded in 1944

3486 American Society of Plant Biologists

15501 Monona Drive
Rockville, MD 20855-2768

301-251-0560
FAX 301-279-2996
E-Mail: info@aspb.org
Home Page: my.aspb.org

Crispin Taylor, Executive and Governance
Jotee Pundu, Administrative Staff
Melanie Binder, Member Services
Susan Cato, Member Services
Annette Kessler, Publications

A professional society devoted to the advancement of the plant sciences. It publishes research and organizes conferences that are key to the advancement of plant biology.

3487 American Soybean Association

12125 Woodcrest Executive Drive
Suite 100
St. Louis, MO 63141-5009

314-576-1770
800-688-7692
FAX 314-576-2786
E-Mail: membership@soy.org
Home Page: soygrowers.com
Social Media: *Facebook, Twitter, RSS*

Sam Butler, Director
Ted Glaub, Director
Richard Wilkins, Director
Wade Cowan, President
Ray Gaesser, Chairman

Domestic and international policy advocate of increasing market opportunities and value for U.S. soybean farmers.

3488 Association for Women Geoscientists

12000 N. Washington St.
Suite 285
Thornton, CO 80241-3134

303-412-6219
FAX 303-253-9220
E-Mail: office@awg.org
Home Page: www.awg.org

Blair Schneider, President
Roxy Frary, President Elect
Molly Long, Secretary
Bevin Bailey, Treasurer
Denise Cox, Past President

A professional organization which promotes the professional development of its members, provides geoscience outreach to girls, and encourages womento become geoscientists.
Founded in 1977

3489 Association for Women in Science

1321 Duke Street,
Suite 210
Alexandria, VA 22314

703-894-4490
FAX 703-894-4489
E-Mail: awis@awis.org
Home Page: www.awis.org
Social Media: *Facebook, Twitter, LinkedIn*

Ann Lee Karlon, President
Bahija Jallal, President Elect
Gail Gasparich, Secretary
Pamela Marrone, Treasurer
Janet Bandows, Executive Director & CEO

Provides support for female scientists and bioengineers. Also dedicated to achieving eq-

uity and full participation for women in science, mathematics, engineering and technology.
5000 Members
Founded in 1971
Mailing list available for rent

3490 Association of Biomolecular Resource Facilities
9650 Rockville Pike
Bethesda, MD 20814

301-634-7306
FAX 301-634-7455
E-Mail: abrf@abrf.org
Home Page: www.abrf.org
Social Media: *Facebook, LinkedIn, Flickr, YouTube, Google+*

Bill Hendrickson, President
Paula Turpen, Secretary/Treasurer
George Grills, Director
Tim Hunter, Director
Anoja Perera, Director

Dedicated to advancing core and research biotechnology laboratoriesthrough research, communication, and education.
700 Members
Founded in 1988

3491 Association of Women Soil Scientists
9611 S. Riverbend Ave.
Parlier, CA 93648

E-Mail: Suduan.Gao@ars.usda.gov
Home Page: www.womeninsoils.org

Wendy Greenberg, Chair

A nonprofit organization of women and men in soil science that promotes a better understanding of the role of soil scientists and that provides assistance and encouragement for women in non-traditional fields and for women seeking employment in the field of soil science.

3492 BioSpace
6465 South Greenwood Plaza
Suite 400
Centennial, CO 80111

877-277-7585
FAX 800-595-2929
E-Mail: support@biospace.com
Home Page: www.biospace.com
Social Media: *Facebook, Twitter, LinkedIn*

The leading online community for industry news and careers for lifescience professionals.

3493 Biotechnology Industry Organization
1201 Maryland Ave SW
Suite 900
Washington, DC 20024

202-962-9200
E-Mail: info@bio.org
Home Page: www.bio.org
Social Media: *Facebook, Twitter, LinkedIn, Youtube*

James C Greenwood, President
Scott Whitaker, COO
Joanne Duncan, CFO/SVP, Finance & Administration
Tom DiLenge, General Counsel/SVP, Legal
Daniel M Junius, Treasurer

Provides support for all those involved in biotechnology from a government, corporate, and trade viewpoint. Also represents biotechnology companies, academic institutions, biotechnology centers and related organizations in all 50 US states and 31 other nations. Researchers expand the boundaries of science to benefit mankind by providing better healthcare, enhanced agriculture, and a cleaner and safer environment.
1100+ Members
Founded in 1993
Mailing list available for rent

3494 Biotechnology Institute
1201 Maryland Avenue, SW
Suite 900
Washington, DC 20024

202-312-9269
FAX 202-355-6706
E-Mail: info@biotechinstitute.org
Home Page: www.biotechinstitute.org
Social Media: *Facebook, Twitter, LinkedIn, YouTube*

Thomas G. Wiggans, Chairman
Scott W. Morrison, Treasurer
Lawrence Mahan, Ph.D., President
Bianca Blanks, Director of Programs
Quinta Jackson, VP Finance & Administration

An independent nonprofit organization founded to teach the public about the benefits of biotechnology.

3495 Council for Biotechnology Information
1201 Maryland Ave SW
Suite 900
Washington, DC 20024-2149

202-962-9200
FAX 202-589-2547
E-Mail: cbi@whybiotech.com
Home Page: www.whybiotech.com
Social Media: *Facebook, Twitter*

James C Greenwood, CEO
Scott Whitaker, COO
Joanne Duncan, CFO/SVP, Finance & Administration
Tom DiLenge, General Counsel/SVP, Legal

A coalition of six of the world's leading biotechnology companies and two trade associations. Its mission is to improve the understanding and acceptance of biotechnology by collecting balanced, science-based information and communicating it through a variety of channels.
Founded in 2000
Mailing list available for rent

3496 Council of State Bioscience Associations
Home Page:
www.bio.org/council-state-bioscience-associations

Russell Allen, Chair
Nathan Tinker, Vice Chair

The council is comprised of 48 state-based trade organizations. It calls for public policy to support the bioscience industry.

3497 Crop Science Society of America
5585 Guilford Rd.
Madison, WI 53711-5801

608-273-8080
FAX 608-273-2021
E-Mail: membership@crops.org
Home Page: www.crops.org
Social Media: *Facebook, Twitter, LinkedIn*

Roch Gaussoin, President
Michael Grusak, President-Elect
Ellen Bergfeld, Member, Ex Officio
Mark Brick, Member, Ex Officio
E Charles Brummer, Member, Ex Officio

An educational and scientific organization comprised of more than 4,700 members dedicated to the advancement of crop science.
Founded in 1956

3498 CropLife America
1156 15th St. NW
Washington, DC 20005

202-296-1585
FAX 202-463-0474
E-Mail: info@croplifeamerica.org

Home Page: www.croplifeamerica.org
Social Media: *Facebook, Twitter, YouTube*

Jay Vroom, President &CEO
Beau Greenwood, EVP Government Relations
William F. Kuckuck, EVP/ COO
Rachel G. Lattimore, SVP & General Counsel
Priscilla Hammett, CFO

U.S. trade association representing the major manufacturers, formulators, and distributors of crop protection and pest control products.
Founded in 1933

3499 Electrophoresis Society
1202 Ann Street
Madison, WI 53713

608-258-1565
FAX 608-258-1569
E-Mail: matt-aes@tds.net
Home Page: www.aesociety.org
Social Media: *Facebook, Twitter, LinkedIn*

Mark A Hayes, President
Christa Hestekin, VP
Rodrigo Martinez-Duarte, Executive VP
Phil Beckett, Secretary
Lawrence I Grossman, Treasurer

Unique international organization founded to improve and promote technologies necessary for biomolecular separation and detection.
200 Members
Founded in 1972
Mailing list available for rent

3500 Enzyme Technical Association
1111 Pennsylvania Avenue, NW
Washington, DC 20004-2541

202-739-5613
FAX 202-739-3001
E-Mail: abegley@morganlewis.com
Home Page: www.enzymeassociation.org

Ann M Begley, General Counsel and Secretary
Robert Zega, Chairman
Vincent Sewalt, Treasurer
Gary L Yingling, C0-General Counsel
Scott Ravech, Member

Promotes the development, preservation, maintenance and general welfare of the industry to the world of manufacturing and distributing enzyme preparations from any source for direct and indirect addition or application to foods, drugs, and other articles of use by humans or animals.
Founded in 1970

3501 Federation of American Societies for Experimental Biology
9650 Rockville Pike
Bethesda, MD 20814

301-634-7000
FAX 301-634-7001
E-Mail: info@faseb.org
Home Page: www.faseb.org
Social Media: *Facebook, Twitter, LinkedIn, YouTube*

Parker B. Antin, PhD, President
Hudson H. Freeze, PhD, President-Elect
Thomas O Baldwin, Vice President for Science Policy
Mark O. Lively, PhD, Treasurer
Guy Fogleman, PhD, CFA, Federation Secretary

A nonprofit organization that is the principal umbrella organization of U.S. societies in the field of biological and medical research.
Founded in 1912

3502 International Society for Biomedical Polymeric Biomaterials
42 Broad Street
Rd # 217
Manakin Sabot, VA 23103

804-708-3010
FAX 804-708-0603
E-Mail: info@isbppb.org
Home Page: isbppb.org
Social Media: *Facebook, Twitter, Google +*

Mia Galijasevic, Executive Director
Munmaya Mishra, Founding Chairman
Gary L. Bowlin, President

An organization engaged in educating, networking, advocating, and advancing the field of biomedical polymers and polymeric biomaterials internationally.
Founded in 2011

3503 International Society for Chronobiology
University of Texas-Medical Branch
301 University Boulevard
Galveston, TX 77555

409-611-1011
E-Mail: prf@unife.it
Home Page: www.chronoint.org

Promotes studies on temporal parameters of biological variables and pursues related scientific and educational purposes. Encourages research centers and the establishment of chronobiology as an academic discipline in its own right.
300 Members
Founded in 1937
Mailing list available for rent

3504 International Society for Magnetic Resonance in Medicine
2300 Clayton Road
Suite 620
Concord, CA 94520

510-841-1899
FAX 510-841-2340
E-Mail: info@ismrm.org
Home Page: www.ismrm.org
Social Media: *Facebook, Twitter, LinkedIn, RSS*

Roberta A Kravitz, Executive Director
Kerry Crockett, Associate Executive Director
Anne-Marie Kahrovic, Director of Meetings
Mariam Barzin, Finance Director
Candace Spradley, Education Director

Nonprofit professional association devoted to furthering the development and application of magnetic resonance techniques in medicine and biology. Also holds annual scientific meeting and sponsors other major educational and scientific workshops.
5000 Members
Founded in 1994
Mailing list available for rent

3505 International Union of Biochemistry and Molecular Biology
3330 Hospital Drive N.W.
Calgary, AB T2N4N1

403-220-3021
FAX 403-270-2211
E-Mail: walsh@ucalgary.ca
Home Page: www.iubmb.org

Michael P. Walsh, General Secretary
Joan J Guinovart, President
Andrew H J Wang, President Elect
Francesco Bonomi, Treasurer
Avadhesha Surolia, Member for Publications

An international non-governmental organization concerned with biochemistry and molecular biology.
Founded in 1955

3506 Massachusetts Biotechnology Council
300 Technology Sq
8th Floor
Cambridge, MA 02139

617-674-5100
FAX 617-674-5101
E-Mail: info@massbio.org
Home Page: www.massbio.org
Social Media: *Facebook, Twitter, LinkedIn, Youtube*

Glenn Batchelder, Chairman
Dr. Abbie Celniker, Vice Chair
Michael Ohara, Treasurer
David Lucchino, Clerk
Geoff MacKay, Immediate past Chairman

Not for profit organization that provides services and support for the Massachusetts biotechnology industry. Committed to advancing the development of critical new science technology and medicines that benefit people worldwide.
400+ Members
Founded in 1985
Mailing list available for rent

3507 National Association of Wheat Growers
415 Second St. NE
Suite 300
Washington, DC 20002

202-547-7800
E-Mail: wheatworld@wheatworld.org
Home Page:
www.wheatworld.org/issues/biotech

Brett Blankenship, President
Jim Palmer, Chief Executive Officer

The association advocates for the use of biotechnology to increase crop variety and productivity, and meet the growing food requirements of the planet.
Founded in 1950

3508 National Center for Biotechnology Information
US National Library of Medicine
8600 Rockville Pike
Building 38A
Bethesda, MD 20894

301-496-2475
FAX 301-480-9241
E-Mail: info@ncbi.nlm.nih.gov
Home Page: www.ncbi.nlm.nih.gov
Social Media: *Facebook, Twitter, LinkedIn, YouTube, RSS, Google+*

To develop new information technologies to aid in the understanding of fundamental molecular and genetic processes that control health and disease.
Founded in 1988

3509 National Corn Growers Association
632 Cepi Drive
Chesterfield, MO 63005

636-733-9004
FAX 636-733-9005
E-Mail: corninfo@ncga.com
Home Page: www.ncga.com
Social Media: *Facebook, Twitter, Pinterest, RSS*

Chris Novak, Chief Executive Officer
Kathy Baker, Executive Assistant
Susan Claiborne, Receptionist
Martin Barbre, Chairman
Chip Bowling, President

News, facts, and information for growers, media, educators, and anyone else interested in corn.
Founded in 1957

3510 New York Biotechnology Association
205 East 42nd St
14th Floor
, NY 10017

212-433-2623
FAX 212-433-0779
E-Mail: info@nyba.org
Home Page: www.newyorkbio.org
Social Media: *Facebook, LinkedIn*

Robert Easton, Chairman
Nathan Tinker, Executive Director
Joseph Tortorice, VP, Operations
Patricia Wadington, Director, Membership Services
Cynthia Green, Secretary

NYBA has been an active & vocal champion for New York's life science industry. Through the Association's education & advocacy efforts in both Albany and Washington DC, NYBA has focused it's resources on building a powerful innovation force in New York state by working to create an economic atmosphere that rewards entrepreneurism, expands access to capital, invests in the industry's future, and protects patient access to life saving therapies.
250 Members
Founded in 1990

3511 North American Benthological Society
5400 Bosque Blvd.
Suite 680
Waco, TX 76710

254-399-9636
FAX 785-843-1274
E-Mail: webmaster@benthos.org
Home Page: www.benthos.org

The Society for Freshwater Science (SFS) is an international scientific organization whose purpose is to promote further understanding of freshwater ecosystems (rivers, streams, lakes, reservoirs, and estuaries) and ecosystems at the interface between aquatic and terrestrial habitats. The society fosters exchange of scientific information among the membership, and with other professional societies, resource managers, policy makers, educators, and the public.
Founded in 1953

3512 North Carolina Biotechnology Center
15 TW Alexander Drive
PO Box 13547
Research Triangle Park, NC 27709-3547

919-541-9366
FAX 919-990-9544
E-Mail: info@ncbiotech.org
Home Page: www.ncbiotech.org
Social Media: *Facebook, Twitter, LinkedIn, Youtube*

John L Atkins III, Chairman
Doug Edgeton, President & CEO
Judy Orchard, Senior Executive Assistant
Kenneth R Tindall, SVP, Science & Business Dev
Lynne Runyan, VP, Human Resource

To provide long-term economic and societal benefits to North Carolina through support of biotechnology research, business and education.
65 Members
Founded in 1981

3513 Pan American Marine Biotechnology Association

E-Mail: info@pamba.ca
Home Page: www.pamba.ca

Heather Manuel, President
Sergio Marshall, Vice President
Brian Dixon, Treasurer

Association for the promotion of sustainable use of marine resources in the Americas.
Founded in 1999

3514 Pennsylvania Biotechnology Association
650 East Swedesford Road
Suite 190
Wayne, PA 19087

610-947-6800
FAX 610-947-6801
E-Mail: president@pennsylvaniabio.org
Home Page: www.pabio.org

Christopher Molineaux, President & CEO
Vin Milano, Treasurer
Robert Bazemore, Chairman
Jeffrey Libson, Secretary
Christian Manders, COO

A catalyst to ensure Pennsylvania is a global leader in the biosciences by developing a cohesive community that unites the region's biotechnology, pharmaceutical research, and financial strategies.

3515 Protein Society
1450 S Rolling Road
Suite 3.007
Baltimore, MD 21227

443-543-5450
FAX 443-543-5453
E-Mail: staff@proteinsociety.org
Home Page: www.proteinsociety.org
Social Media: *Facebook, Twitter, LinkedIn*

Carol B Post, President
Jacquelyn Fetrow, Secretary/Treasurer
James U Bowie, Past President
Charles Brooks III, Councilor
Carlos Bustamante, Councilor

The Protein Society is a not-for-profit scientific and educational membership organization. Our mission is to provide international forums to facilitate communication and collaboration with respect to all aspects of the study of protein molecules, the building blocks of life.
2100 Members
Founded in 1986
Mailing list available for rent: 3,000 names at $200 per M

3516 Section for Magnetic Resonance Technologists
2300 Clayton Road
Suite 620
Concord, CA 94520

510-841-1899
FAX 510-841-2340
E-Mail: info@ismrm.org
Home Page: www.ismrm.org
Social Media: *Facebook, Twitter, LinkedIn*

Roberta A. Kravitz, Executive Director
Kerry Crockett, Associate Executive Director
Mariam Barzin, Director of Finance
Julia White, Accounting Coordinator
Mary Day, Office Manager

A professional organization in the medical imaging community providing education, professional advice and support for magnetic resonance (MR) technologists and radiographers throughout the world.

3517 Sino-American Pharmaceutical Professionals Association
P. O. Box 282
Nanuet, NY 10954

E-Mail: information@sapaweb.org
Home Page: www.sapaweb.org
Social Media: *Twitter, LinkedIn, YouTube*

Dr. Weiguo Dai, President
Dr. Jiwen Chen, Director
Dr. Lei Tang, President-elect

Li Chen, Director
Baoguo Huang, Director

An independent, nonprofit and professional organization with over 4,000 members in the U.S.A., China, Hong Kong, Taiwan, and Japan. It promotes pharmaceutical science and technology.
Founded in 1993

3518 Society for Biological Engineering
120 Wall Street
FL 23
New York, NY 10005-4020

FAX 203-775-5177
E-Mail: bio@aiche.org
Home Page: www.aiche.org/sbe
Social Media: *Facebook, LinkedIn, YouTube*

Georges Belfort, Director
Bill Bentley, Director
Brian Davison, Director
Paula T. Hammond, Director
Pankaj Mohan, Director

A global organization of leading engineers and scientists dedicatedto advancing the integration of biology with engineering.

3519 Society for Biomaterials
1120 Route 73
Suite 200
Mt Laurel, NJ 08054

856-439-0826
FAX 856-439-0525
E-Mail: info@biomaterials.org
Home Page: www.biomaterials.org
Social Media: *Facebook, Twitter, LinkedIn*

Antonios Mikos, President
Nicholas Ziats, President Elect
David Kohn, Secretary/Treasurer

Promotes advances in all phases of materials, research and development by encouragement of cooperative educational programs, clinical applications, and professional standards in the biomaterials field.
1550 Members
Founded in 1969

3520 Society for Biomolecular Screening
100 Illinois Street
Suite 242
St. Charles, IL 60174

630-256-7527
877-990-7527
E-Mail: slas@slas.org
Home Page: www.slas.org
Social Media: *Facebook, Twitter, LinkedIn, Youtube*

Dean Ho, President
Christine Giordano, Executive Director
Richard Eglen, Vice President
Mike Snowden, Treasurer
Michele A Cleary, Secretary

Provides a forum for education and information exchange among professionals within drug discovery and related disciplines.
2000+ Members
Founded in 1994

3521 Society for Cardiovascular Magnetic Resonance
19 Mantua Road
Mt. Royal, NJ 8061

856-423-8955
FAX 856-423-3420
E-Mail: hq@scmr.org
Home Page: www.scmr.org
Social Media: *Facebook, Twitter*

Victor A. Ferrari, MD, President
Jeanette Schulz-Menger, Vice-President
Matthias G. Friedrich, MD, Treasurer
Matthias Stuber, Vice Secretary-Treasurer
Orlando Simonetti, Immediate Past President

The leading international society for physicians, scientists, and technologists working in cardiovascular magnetic resonance.

3522 Society for Freshwater Science, Formerly NABS
5400 Bosque Blvd
Suite 680
Waco, TX 76710-4446

254-399-9636
FAX 254-776-3767
E-Mail: membership@benthos.org
Home Page: www.freshwater-science.org

Dave Strayer, President
Michelle Baker, President Assistant
Matt Whiles, President Elect
Sue Norton, Secretary
Mike Swift, Treasurer

International Scientific organization with the purpose to promote better understanding of the biotic communitites of lake and stream bottoms and their role in aquatic ecosystems, by providing media and disseminating new investigation results , new interpretations and other benthological informatoin to aquatic biologists and the scientific community. Also publishes a journal.
Founded in 1953

3523 Society for Industrial Microbiology and Biotechnology
3929 Old Lee Highway
Suite 92A
Fairfax, VA 22030

703-691-3357
FAX 703-691-7991
Home Page: www.simbhq.org
Social Media: *Facebook, Twitter, LinkedIn, RSS*

Christine Lowe, Executive Director
Jennifer Johnson, Director of Member Services
Suzannah Citrenbaum, Web Manager
Espie Montesa, Accountant
Katherine Devins, Publications Coordinator

A nonprofit international association dedicated to the advancement of microbiology sciences, especially as they apply to industrial products, biotechnology, materials, and processes.
Founded in 1949

3524 Society for Laboratory Automation and Screening
100 Illinois Street
Ste. 242
St. Charles, IL 60174

630-256-7527
877-990-7527
E-Mail: slas@slas.org
Home Page: www.slas.org
Social Media: *Facebook, Twitter, LinkedIn, YouTube*

Dean Ho, President
Richard Eglen, Vice President
Mike Snowden, Treasurer
Michele A Cleary, Secretary
Alastair Binnie, Director

A global community of more than 18,000 life science research and development professionals.
2000+ Members
Founded in 1994

3525 Strategic Information for the Life Sciences
BioAbility™
PO Box 14569
Research Triangle Park, NC 27709-4569

919-544-5111
FAX 919-544-5401

E-Mail: info@bioability.com
Home Page: www.bioability.com

Mark D Dibner, President/Founder
Tracey V du Laney, Research Director

BioAbility has provided the knowledge and experience to evaluate any area of the life sciences or biotechnology markets. Partnered with expert life science affiliates to bring a world-class level of expertise to our service offerings.
Founded in 1994

3526 The American Society for Cell Biology

8120 Woodmont Avenue
Suite 750
Bethesda, MD 20814

301-347-9300
FAX 301-347-9310
E-Mail: ascbinfo@ascb.org
Home Page: ascb.org
Social Media: *Facebook, Twitter, LinkedIn*

Shirley M Tilghman, President
Jennifer Lippincott-Schwartz, Past President
Peter Walter, President-Elect
Kathleen Green, Secretary
Gary J Gorbsky, Treasurer

A professional society that provides the exchange of scientific knowledge in the area of cell biology.

3527 Virginia Biotechnology Association

800 E Leigh St
Suite 14
Richmond, VA 23219-1534

804-643-6360
FAX 804-643-6361
E-Mail: questions@vabio.org
Home Page: www.vabio.org
Social Media: *Facebook, Twitter*

Jeffrey M Gallagher, CEO
Sherry Halloran, Director, Membership Services
Susan Moore, Senior Administrative Assistant
Jeff Conroy, Chairman
Crystal Icenhoue, Vice Chairman

Promotes the biotechnology industry in Virginia, to expand the knowledge and expertise of Virginia's businesses concerning biotechnology through seminars, educational publications and other means.
200 Members
Founded in 1992

3528 Women in Cognitive Science

Home Page: womenincogsci.org
Social Media: *Facebook*

Laurie Feldman, Officer
Judith Kroll, Officer
Suparna Rajaram, Officer
Debra Titone, Officer
Natasha Tokowicz, Officer

Organization that works to create an environment that encourages young women to join the field of cognitive psychology/science, particularly in cognitive neuroscience and computational modeling areas.

Newsletters

3529 AAI Newsletter

American Association of Immunologists
9650 Rockville Pike
Bethesda, MD 20814-3999

301-634-7178
FAX 301-634-7887

E-Mail: infoaai@aai.org
Home Page: www.aai.org

Leslie Berg, President
Gail Bishop, Vice President
Mitchell Kronenberg, Treasurer/Secretary
Frequency: Bi-Monthly

3530 BioPeople Magazine

PO Box 5778
Walnut Creek, CA 94596

925-932-6364
Home Page: www.biotechmedia.com

Lisa Wagner, Advertising Executive
Charlene Carpentier, Production Manager
Sukaini Virji-Jeganathan, Editor

Provides information and analysis of the international biotechnology industry, including corporate agreements, product status, financial transactions and new technologies.
Cost: $675.00
Frequency: Quarterly
Circulation: 10,000
Printed in on glossy stock

3531 BioWorld Financial Watch

BioWorld
3525 Piedmont Road
Building 6, Suite 400
Atlanta, GA 30305-4031

404-262-5476
800-688-2421
FAX 404-814-0759
E-Mail: customerservice@bioworld.com
Home Page: www.bioworld.com

Donald R Johnston, Publisher
Brady Huggett, Managing Editor
Chris Walker, Marketing Manager

Tracks public financing and portfolio performance offering expert analysis. The weekly source for biotechnology financial news.
Cost: $1197.00
Frequency: Weekly

3532 Biotechnology News

CTB International Publishing
PO Box 218
Maplewood, NJ 07040-218

973-966-0997
FAX 973-966-0242
Home Page: www.ctbintl.com

F G Racioppi, Marketing Director

A leading biotechnology publication for executives. Provides incisive intelligence on the ever-changing biotechnology industry and includes news on research, product development and corporate doings.
Cost: $634.00
Founded in 1985
Printed in one color on newsprint stock

3533 Biotechnology Newswatch

McGraw Hill
1221 Avenue of the Americas
Suite C3A
New York, NY 10020-1095

212-512-2000
FAX 212-512-3840
E-Mail: customer.service@mcgraw-hill.com
Home Page: www.mcgraw-hill.com

Harold W McGraw III, CEO
Mara Bovsun, Editor
Kenneth M Vittor, VP

Covers the business and technical news affecting companies engaged in serving the biotechnology sciences.
Cost: $737.00
12 Pages
Frequency: Monthly
Founded in 1910

3534 Genetic Technology News

John Wiley & Sons
111 River St
Hoboken, NJ 07030-5790

201-748-6000
FAX 201-748-6088
E-Mail: info@wiley.com
Home Page: www.wiley.com

William J Pesce, CEO

Covers technical and business developments in every area of genetic engineering and related techniques, analyzing their applications in the chemical, pharmaceutical and energy industries as well as in agriculture, animal breeding and medicine.
Cost: $585.00
18 Pages
Frequency: Monthly
Founded in 1807

3535 Industrial Bioprocessing

John Wiley & Sons
111 River St
Hoboken, NJ 07030-5790

201-748-6000
FAX 201-748-6088
E-Mail: info@wiley.com
Home Page: www.wiley.com

William J Pesce, CEO

Focuses on industrial processes involving biological routes to produce chemicals/energy; the conversion of biomaterials via fermentation, process monitoring and more.
Cost: $545.00
10 Pages
Frequency: Monthly
Founded in 1807
Mailing list available for rentat $180 per M
Printed in one color on matte stock

3536 J Biomolecular Screening

Society for Biomolecular Screening
100 Illinois Street
Suite 242
St.Charles, IL 60174

630-256-7527
FAX 630-741-7527
E-Mail: slas@slas.org
Home Page: www.sbsonline.org

Michelle Palmer, President
David Dorsett, Vice President
Erik Rubin, Treasurer
Andy Zaayenga, Secretary

Biomolecular industry news and information.
Cost: $478.00
Founded in 1992

3537 Life Sciences & Biotechnology Update

InfoTeam
PO Box 15640
Plantation, FL 33318-5640

954-473-9560
FAX 954-473-0544

Merton Allen, Editor

Medical and biological technology; health and disease; genetics and genetic engineering; bodily fluids, bones, tissues and organs, cancer, medical diagnoisis and treatment; medical instrumentation and procedures; medical care systems; public health; mental health; child care; medical costs; research; and more.
Frequency: Monthly

3538 Technotrends Newsletter

Burrus Research Associates
PO Box 47
Hartland, WI 53029-2347

262-367-0949
800-827-6770
FAX 262-367-7163

E-Mail: office@burrus.com
Home Page: www.burrus.com/

Dan Burrus, CEO
Patti A Thomsen, Editor
Jennifer Metcalf, Marketing

This newsletter researches the latest innovations in science and technology. Provides access to information that can give an edge on tomorrow, today and shows how you might benefit from each innovation.
Cost: $39.95
Frequency: Monthly
Circulation: 1000
Founded in 1984
Printed in 4 colors on matte stock

Magazines & Journals

3539 AWIS Magazine
Association for Women in Science
1200 New York Avenue
Suite 650
Washington, DC 20005

202-326-8940
FAX 202-326-8960
E-Mail: awis@awis.org
Home Page: www.awis.org

Janet Bandows, Executive Director

Focuses on issues relevant to women scientists. Contains articles about current events, career advancement, financial planning, work-life balance, and creating a diverse work environment.
Frequency: Quarterly
Circulation: 3500

3540 American Biotechnology Laboratory
International Scientific Communications
PO Box 870
Shelton, CT 06484-0870

203-926-9300
FAX 203-926-9310
E-Mail: webmaster@iscpubs.com
Home Page: www.iscpubs.com

Brian Howard, Publisher
Robert G Sweeny, Publisher

American Biotechnology Laboratory serves Industry, Universities, Government and others allied to the field with special interest in life science research.
Cost: $173.12
64 Pages
Frequency: Monthly
Circulation: 60058
Mailing list available for rent: 60M names at $170 per M
Printed in 4 colors on glossy stock

3541 Antiretroviral Resistance in Clinical Practice
National Center for Biotechnology Information
8600 Rockville Pike
Bethesda, MD 20894

301-496-2475
FAX 301-480-9241
E-Mail: info@ncbi.nlm.nih.gov
Home Page: www.ncbi.nlm.nih.gov

Anna Maria Geretti, Editor

3542 Applied Biochemistry and Biotechnology
Humana Press

999 Riverview Drive
Suite 208
Totowa, NJ 07512-1165

973-256-1699
FAX 973-256-8341
Home Page: www.humanapress.com

David Watt, Editor
Ashok Mulchandani, Editor-in-Chief
Paul Dolgert, Director
Fran Lipton, Production Manager

Reports on new techniques and original research in biotechnology and biochemistry with a focus on the application of new technologies.
Cost: $1505.00
Frequency: Monthly
Circulation: 373
Founded in 1977

3543 BioTechniques
52 Vanderbilt Avenue
7th Floor
New York, NY 10017

212-520-2777
FAX 212-520-2705
E-Mail: webmaster@biotechniques.com
Home Page: www.biotechniques.com

Nathan Blow, Editor in Chief
Bill Moran, Director of Sales
John C. Yarosh, Production Manager

Serves the biotechnical and pharmaceutical industries.
Cost: $145.00
254 Pages
Frequency: Monthly
Circulation: 85,000
Founded in 1983
Printed in 4 colors on glossy stock

3544 Biotechnology Progress
American Chemical Society
1155 16th St NW
Suite 600
Washington, DC 20036-4892

202-872-4600
80 - 2 - 55
FAX 202-872-4615
E-Mail: service@acs.org
Home Page: www.acs.org

Nancy Jackson, President

Information on new technology.
Cost: $924.00
Founded in 1876

3545 Biotechnology and Bioengineering
John Wiley & Sons
111 River St
Hoboken, NJ 07030-5790

201-748-6000
FAX 201-748-6088
E-Mail: info@wiley.com
Home Page: www.wiley.com

William J Pesce, CEO
Richard M Hochhauser, CEO

A scientific journal publishing new papers in the field of biotechnology and bioengineering.
Cost: $750.00
Frequency: 1 Year 28 Issue
Founded in 1807

3546 CleanRooms Magazine
PennWell Publishing Company
98 Spit Brook Rd
Suite L11
Nashua, NH 03062-5737

603-891-0123
80 - 2 - 05
FAX 603-891-9294

E-Mail: mikel@pennwell.com
Home Page: www.pennwell.com

Christine Shaw, VP
Mark A Desorbo, Associate Editor
James Enos, Publisher

Serves the contamination control and ultrapure materials and process industries. Written for readers in the microelectronics, pharmaceutical, biotech, health care, food processing and other user industries. Provides technology and business news and new product listings.
Frequency: Monthly
Circulation: 35031
Founded in 1987

3547 Engineering in Medicine and Biology
3 Park Avenue
17th Floor
New York, NY 10016

212-419-7900
800-272-6657
FAX 212-752-4929
E-Mail: jenderle@bme.uconn.edu
Home Page: www.ieee.org

Dr. John D Enderle, Editor
Desir,e de Myer, Managing Editor
Susan Schneiderman, Advertising Sales Manager

Focuses on up-to-date biomedical engineering applications for engineers who are at the forefront of electrotechnology innovation.
Cost: $300.00
Circulation: 7983
ISSN: 0739-5175
Founded in 1963

3548 Freshwater Science
Society for Freshwater Science
5400 Bosque Blvd.
Suite 680
Waco, TX 76710-4446

254-399-9636
FAX 254-776-3767
Home Page: www.freshwater-science.org

Pamela Silver, Editor
Rosemary J. Mackay, Managing Editor
Irwin Polls, Business Manager

Publishes timely, peer-reviewed scientific research that promotes a better understanding and environmental stewardship of biological communities living on the bottom of streams, rivers, lakes, and wetlands, with an emphasis on freshwater inland habitats. Theoretical discussions, speculative and philosophical articles, and critical appraisals of rapidly developing research fields.
Cost: $65.00
Frequency: Quarterly

3549 Journal of Biological Chemistry
American Society for Biochemistry
11200 Rockville Pike
Suite 302
Rockville, MD 20852-3110

240-283-6620
FAX 301-881-2573
E-Mail: asbmb@asbmb.org
Home Page: www.asbmb.org

Martha Fedor, Editor-in-Chief
Herbet Tabor, Co-Editor

3550 Journal of Biomolecular Screening
Sage Publications
2455 Teller Rd
Newbury Park, CA 91320-2234

805-499-9774
800-818-7243
FAX 805-499-0871

E-Mail: journals@sagepub.com
Home Page: www.sagepub.com

Blaise R Simqu, CEO
Mark Beggs, Associate Editor
Stein Roaldset, Advertising Editor
Christine Giordano, Society Updates Editor
Charles Hart, New Products Editor

An official publication of the Society for Biomolecular Sciences. Peer-reviewed publication on drug discovery sciences, with an emphasis on screening methods and technologies; Information on the latest biomolecular sciences, with regular topics including: target identification/validation assay development methods, and technologies, lead generation/optimization, virtual screening/chemo-informatics, data and image analysis, sample management, biomarkers and legal/licensing issues.
Cost: $610.00
Frequency: 10x year/Price Varies
ISSN: 1087-0571
Founded in 1994

3551 Journal of the North American Benthological Society
The North American Benthological Society
PO Box 7065
Lawrence, KS 66044-7065

254-399-9636
FAX 785-843-1274
E-Mail: info@freshwater-science.org
Home Page: www.benthos.org

Pamela Silver, Managing Editor
Irwin Polls, Business Manager

Articles that will promote further understanding of benthic communities and their role in aquatic ecosystems

3552 Lab Animal
Nature Publishing Group
1270 Broadway
6th Floor, Suite 807
New York, NY 10001-3224

212-278-8600
FAX 212-564-0217
E-Mail: info@labanimal.com
Home Page: www.labanimal.com

Angelo Notaro, Partner
Rachel Burley, Publisher
Richard Charkin, CEO

A peer-reviewed journal for professionals in animal research, emphasizing proper management and care. Offers the latest on animal models, breeds, breeding practices, in vitro and computer models, lab care, nutrition, and improved animal handling techniques. Offers timely and informative material, reaching both the academic research world and applied research industries, including genetic engineering, human therapeutics and pharmaceutical companies.
Cost: $159.00
Founded in 1869

3553 Molecular Plant: Microbe Interactions
American Phytopatholgical Society
3340 Pilot Knob Road
Saint Paul, MN 55121-2097

651-454-7250
800-328-7560
FAX 651-454-0766
E-Mail: aps@scisoc.org
Home Page: www.apsnet.org

Steve Nelson, Executive VP
Amy Hope, VP of Operations
Barbara Mock, VP Finance

Molecular biology and molecular genetics of pathological, symbiotic and associative interactions of microbes with plants, including plant response.
Frequency: Monthly
ISSN: 0894-0282
Mailing list available for rent

3554 Nature
Nature Publishing Group
1270 Broadway
Suite 807
New York, NY 10001-3224

212-278-8600
800-221-2123
FAX 212-564-0217
E-Mail: nature@natureny.com
Home Page: www.nature.com

Angelo Notaro, Partner
Josie Natori, CEO

A reliable source of up-to-date scientific information. Publishes papers from any area of science with great potential impact. Also publishes a broad range of informal material in the form of opinion articles, news stories, briefings and recruitment features, and contributed material.
Frequency: Monthly
Circulation: 60289

3555 Nature Biotechnology
Nature America
345 Park Avenue S
10th Floor
New York, NY 10010-1707

212-726-9200
800-221-2123
FAX 212-696-9635
E-Mail: biotech@natureny.com
Home Page: www.biotech.nature.com

Andrew Marshall, Editor
Richard Charkin, CEO
Annette Thomas, Managing Director
Philip Campbell, Editor-in-Chief
Peter Collins, Publishing Director

A monthly magazine of biotechnology news and research.
Cost: $178.00
550 Pages
Frequency: Monthly
Circulation: 18798
ISSN: 1054-0156
Founded in 1983
Printed in 4 colors on glossy stock

3556 Protein Science
Protein Society
9650 Rockville Pike
Bethesda, MD 20814-3999

301-634-7240
800-992-6466
FAX 301-634-7271
E-Mail: cyablonski@proteinsociety.org
Home Page: www.proteinsociety.org

Cynthia A Yablonski, Executive Officer
Arthur G Palmer III, President
Jean Baum, Secretary/Treasurer
2100 Members
Founded in 1986
Mailing list available for rent: 3,000 names at $200 per M

3557 Science Illustrated
Communications Solutions
8428 Holly Leaf Drive
McLean, VA 22102-2224

703-356-1688
FAX 202-296-1857
Home Page: http://www.scienceillustrated.com/

Tod Herbers, Editor

Provides physicians with information on research and development in the fields of science related to medicine.
Cost: $18.00
Circulation: 103200
Printed in 4 colors on glossy stock

Trade Shows

3558 AAB Annual Meeting and Education Conference
American Association of Bioanalysts
906 Olive Street
Suite 1200
Saint Louis, MO 63101-1448

314-241-1445
FAX 314-241-1449
E-Mail: aab@aab.org
Home Page: www.aab.org
Social Media: *Facebook, Twitter, LinkedIn*

Mark S Birenbaum PhD, Administrator

Educational programs, abstract presentations, poster presentations and exhibits
Founded in 1956

3559 Biometrics Technology Expo and Consortium Conference
J Spargo & Associates
11208 Waples Mill Road
Suite 112
Fairfax, VA 22030

703-631-6200
800-564-4220
FAX 703-654-6931
E-Mail: info@biometrics.org
Home Page: www.biometrics.org

Jeffrey Dunn, Chair
Fernando Podio, Chair

Co-located with the Biometric Consortium Conference, this event offers unparalleled opportunities to reach top buyers, federal and state agencies and leading industry corporations.
2000 Attendees
Frequency: September

3560 Biophysical Society Annual Meeting
Biophysical Society
11400 Rockville Pike
Suite 800
Bethesda, MD 20852

240-290-5600
FAX 240-290-5555
E-Mail: society@biophysics.org
Home Page: www.biophysics.org

Ro Kampman, Executive Officer
Harris Povich, Director of Finance and Operations
Vida Ess, Programs Coordinator

Includes 3,000 poster presentations, 200 exhibits, 20 symposias, workshops, platform sessions, and subgroup meetings. It is also the worlds largest meeting for biophysicists.
6M Attendees
Frequency: February/March
Mailing list available for rent

3561 Biotechnology Investment Conference
Massachusetts Biotechnology Council
One Cambridge Center
Cmabridge, MA 02142

617-674-5100
FAX 617-674-5101
E-Mail: inforequest@massbio.org
Home Page: www.massbio.org
Social Media: *Facebook, Twitter, LinkedIn, Youtube*

Geoffrey Cox, Chairman
Geoff McKay, Vice Chair
Michael Ohara, Treasurer

New England's largest biotechnology investor forum. Allows more than 70 local public and private companies to showcase their technologies and products in front of portfolio managers, analysts, venture capitalists and other investment professionals.
700 Attendees
Frequency: November

3562 Int'l Conference on Strategic Business Information in Biotechnology
Institute for Biotechnology Information
3200 Chapel Hill/Nelson Boulevard Suite 201
PO Box 14569
Research Triangle Park, NC 27709-4569

919-544-5111
FAX 919-544-5401
E-Mail: info@bioability.com
Home Page: www.biotechinfo.com

For strategists, company managers, information specialists, financial analysts or users of strategic business information in biotechnology.
150 Attendees
Frequency: October

Directories & Databases

3563 BioWorld Online
3525 Piedmont Road
Building 6, Suite 400
Atlanta, GA 30305

404-262-5476
800-688-2421
FAX 404-814-0759
E-Mail: customerservice@bioworld.com
Home Page: www.bioworld.com

Randy Osborne

This database contains a variety of information on biotechnology companies, products, and services.
Frequency: Full-text

3564 Biosis/Thomson Scientific
BIOSIS
1500 Spring Garden St
Fourth Floor
Philadelphia, PA 19130-4067

215-386-0100
800-336-4474
FAX 215-386-2911
Home Page: www.biosis.org/support;
scientific.thomson.com
Social Media: *Facebook, Twitter, LinkedIn*

Vin Caraher, President/CEO
Keith MacGregor, Executive VP
Andrea Degutis, Senior VP/Communications

A bibliographic database covering worldwide research on all biological and biomedical topics. Records contain bibliographic data, indexing information, and abstracts for most references. Biosis joined with the Thomson Corporation in early 2006 to expand its global presence.
Frequency: Updated Weekly

Industry Web Sites

3565 http://gold.greyhouse.com
G.O.L.D Grey House OnLine Databases
Grey House Publishing's online database platform, GOLD, offers Quick Search, Keyword Search and Expert Search for most business sectors, including scientific, technical and biotechnical markets. The GOLD platform makes finding the information you need quick and easy - whether you're a novice searcher or

an experienced database user. All of Grey House's directory products are available for subscription on the GOLD platform.

3566 www.aesociety.org
Electrophoresis Society
International organization founded to improve and promote technologies necessary for biomolecular separation and detection.

3567 www.asbmb.org
American Society for Biochemistry and Molecular
Serves members who teach and conduct research at colleges and universities and in various government laboratories, nonprofit research institutions and industry.

3568 www.asrm.org
American Society for Reproductive Medicine
Organization devoted to advancing knowledge and expertise in reproductive medicine and biology. Members of this voluntary nonprofit organization must demonstrate the high ethical principals of the medical profession, evince an interest in reproductive medicine and biology, and adhere to the objectives of the Society.

3569 www.benthos.org
North American Benthological Society
International scientific organization whose purpose is to promote better understanding of the biotic communities of lake and stream bottoms and their role in aquatic ecosystems, by providing media and disseminating new investigation results, new interpetations, and other benthological information to aquatic biologists and to the scientific community at large.

3570 www.bio.org
Biotechnology Industry Organization
For firms involved in the use of recombinant DNA, hybridoma and immulogical technologies in a wide range of applications including human health care, animal husbandry, agriculture and specialty chemical production.

3571 www.greyhouse.com
Grey House Publishing
Authoritative reference directories for most business markets including science, technical and biotechnical markets. Users can search the online databases with varied search criteria allowing for custom searches by product category, geographic area, sales volume, keyword, subject and more. Full Grey House catalog and online ordering also available.

3572 www.ismrm.org
Int'l Society for Magnetic Resonance in Medicine
For physicians and scientists promoting the applications of magnetic resonance techniques to medicine and biology. The Society holds annual scientific meetings and sponsors other major educational and scientific workshops.

3573 www.massbio.org
Massachusetts Biotechnology Council
Organization that provides services and support for the Massachusets biotechnology industry.

3574 www.proteinsociety.org
Protein Society
Formed in 1986 to promote international interactions among investigators in order to explore all aspects of the building blocks of life, protien molecules. Members come from universities, foundations, institutes and corporations to provide leadership in this broad field of research. The Society and its members are mak-

ing a strong impact on the advancements of protien science.

3575 www.whybiotech.com
Council for Biotechnology Information
Serves to improve understanding and acceptance of biotechnology by collecting balanced, credible and science based information, then communicating this information through a variety of channels.

Associations

3576 American Boat Builders and Repairers Association
1 Washington Street
Newport, RI 02840

401-236-2466
FAX 954-239-2600
E-Mail: info@abbra.org
Home Page: www.abbra.org
Social Media: *Facebook, Twitter, LinkedIn*

Graham Wright, President
Kirk Ritter, VP
Peter Sabo, Treasurer
Ron Helbig, Secretary
Cathy Cope, Director

Trade association for marinas, boat builders and repairers. Also offers a monthly newsletter and training seminars.
300 Members
Founded in 1943

3577 American Boat and Yacht Council Association
613 Third Street
Suite 10
Annapolis, MD 21403

410-990-4460
FAX 410-990-4466
E-Mail: info@abycinc.org
Home Page: www.abycinc.org
Social Media: *Facebook, Twitter, LinkedIn, Youtube*

John Adey, President
David Marlow, Chairman
F Steven Herb, Vice Chairman
Larry Akins, Treasurer
David Slobodien, Secretary

A not-for-profit membership organization that has been developing and updating the safety standards for boat building and repair.
4000+ Members
Founded in 1954

3578 American Boatbuilders Association, Inc.
The Brumby Building, Marietta Stn.
127 Church St., Suite 210
Marietta, GA 30060

770-792-3070
FAX 770-792-3073
Home Page: www.ababoats.com

Jay Patton, President

Volume materials purchasing group for independent boat builders.
Founded in 1992

3579 American Boating Association
PO Box 690
New Market, MD 21774

614-497-4088
E-Mail: admin@americanboating.org
Home Page: www.americanboating.org
Social Media: *Facebook, RSS*

Bill Condon, Founder/President

Through their membership in the American Boating Association, boaters and boating enthusiasts from across the nation share a common mission - working together to improve the safety, affordability, environmental cleanliness, growth and fun of our sport.
Cost: $10.00
30000 Members

3580 American Power Boat Association
17640 E. Nine Mile Road
Po Box 377
Eastpointe, MI 48021-0377

586-773-9700
FAX 586-773-6490
E-Mail: apbahq@apba.com
Home Page: www.apba-racing.com
Social Media: *Facebook, Twitter, LinkedIn, Youtube, RSS*

Dan Wiener, Executive Director
John Flynn, Creative Director
Sabrina Haudek, Membership Coordinator
Mark Wheeler, President
Dutch Squires, Vice President

The nation's authority on power boat racing which sanctions over 200 races each year.
6000 Members
Founded in 1903

3581 American Sail Training Association
221 3rd Street, Building 2, Ste. 101
PO Box 1459
Newport, RI 02840

401-846-1775
FAX 401-849-5400
E-Mail: asta@tallshipsamerica.org
Home Page: www.tallships.sailtraining.org
Social Media: *Facebook, Twitter, LinkedIn*

Mike Rauworth, Chairman
Caleb Pifer, Vice Chair
Eric Shaw, Vice Chair
Dexter Donham, Treasurer
Capt. Christoph Rowsom, Secretary

Supports all those involved with sail training ships and programs, as well as ships under construction or renovation.
300 Members
Founded in 1973

3582 American Society of Marine Artists
P.O.Box 247
Smithfield, VA 23430

757-357-3785
E-Mail: asma1978@verizon.net
Home Page:
www.americansocietyofmarineartists.com
Social Media: *Facebook, Twitter, LinkedIn*

Russ Kramer, President
Kim Shaklee, Vice President
Mike Killelea, Secretary
Peter Maytham, Managing Director
Sheri Farabaugh, Treasurer

A non-profit, tax exempt organization, whose objective is to recognize and promote marine art and history, and to encourage cooperation among artists, historians, marine enthusiasts and others in activities related to marine art and maritime history.
500+ Members
Founded in 1978

3583 Antique & Classic Boat Society
422 James St
Clayton, NY 13624

315-686-2628
FAX 315-686-2680
E-Mail: hqs@acbs.org
Home Page: www.acbs.org
Social Media: *Facebook, Twitter, LinkedIn*

Jeff Funk, President
John Howard, Senior VP
Rich Lepping, Second VP
Kathy Parker, Secretary
Timothy Bush, Treasurer

Society devoted to disseminating information on building and restoring wooden and antique boats.
12000 Members
Founded in 1975

3584 Association of Marina Industries
50 Water Street
Warren, RI 02885

866-367-6622
FAX 401-247-0074
E-Mail: info@marinaassociation.org
Home Page: www.marinaassociation.org
Social Media: *Facebook, Twitter, LinkedIn*

Jeff Rose, Chairman
Brad Gross, Vice Chairman
Joe Riley, Treasurer
Mick Webber, Secretary
Gary Groenewold, Immediate Past Chairman

The Association of Marina Industries is the international trade marine association for the marina industry.
800+ Members
Founded in 1986

3585 Boat Owners Association of the US
880 South Pickett Street
Alexandria, VA 22304

703-461-2878
800-395-2628
FAX 703-461-2847
E-Mail: mail@baotus.com
Home Page: www.boatus.com
Social Media: *Facebook, Twitter, Youtube*

Richard Schwartz, Chairman/Founder
Bill Oakerson, CEO
Margaret Podlich, President
Adam Wheeler, VP & Director of Towing
Heather Lougheed, VP, Membership

Supports all who are involved with legislation, regulations and consumer aspects of the industry.
62500 Members
Founded in 1966

3586 Boating Writers International
108 Ninth Street
Wilmette, IL 60091

847-736-4142
E-Mail: info@bwi.org
Home Page: www.bwi.org
Social Media: *LinkedIn*

Alan Wendt, President
Lenny Rudow, 1st VP
Lindsey Johnson, 2nd VP
Alan Jones, Director
Zuzana Prochazka, Director

A non-profit professional organization consisting of writers, broadcasters, editors, photgraphers, public relations specialists and others in the communications profession associated with the boating industry.
Founded in 1970

3587 Coastal Yachting Academy
PO Box 10441
St. Petersburg, FL 33733

727-867-9466
E-Mail: info@yachtdeliveries.com
Home Page:
www.charternet.com/charters/donharper/index.html

Don Harper, Captain/Owner

To provide the recreational boater reasonably priced training equal to the training of professional mariners.
Founded in 1970

3588 Marine Retailers Association of America
8401 73rd Ave N
Suite 71
Minneapolis, MN 55428

763-315-8043
E-Mail: matt@mraa.com

Home Page: www.mraa.com
Social Media: *Facebook, Twitter, LinkedIn*

Randy Wattenbarger, Chairman
Joe Lewis, Vice Chair
Joe Hoffmaster, Secretary/Treasurer
Steve Baum, Immediate Past Chairman
Rob Soucy, Director

Manufacturers and dealers of boats, equipment, supplies and services.
3000 Members
Founded in 1971

3589 Marine Safety Foundation
5050 Industrial Rd
Suite 2
Wall Township, NJ 07727-4044

732-751-0295
FAX 732-751-0508
E-Mail: msf@marinesafety.org
Home Page: www.marinesafety.org

Burt Thompson, Executive Director

Advances the safety of life at sea through research, education and coordination.
131 Members
Founded in 1993

3590 National Association of Charterboat Operators
PO Box 1070
Hurley, MS 39555

866-981-5136
FAX 877-263-8548
E-Mail: info@nacocharters.org
Home Page: www.nacocharters.org
Social Media: *Facebook*

Capt. Robert F Zales II, President
Capt. Tom Baker, Vice President
Capt. Ed O'Brien, Second Vice President
Capt Charlie Phillips, Secretary
Ron Maglio, Treasurer

A national association of charterboat owners and operators that represent thousands of individuals across the United States.
3600+ Members
Founded in 1991

3591 National Association of Sailing
15 Maritime Drive
Portsmouth, RI 02871

401-683-0800
800-877-2451
FAX 401-683-0840
E-Mail: info@ussailing.org
Home Page: www.ussailing.org
Social Media: *Facebook, Twitter, LinkedIn*

Bruce Burton, President
Cory Sertl, Vice President
Martine R Zurinskas, Secretary
Stephen T Freitas, Treasurer
Jack Gierhart, Executive Director

Accredits sailing schools, certifies instructors and provides teaching and management information. Publishes a newsletter and directory of American sailing schools and charter operators. Provides free consulting services for start-ups of new schools.
100 Members
Frequency: Quarterly
Founded in 1980
Mailing list available for rent

3592 National Association of State Boating Law Administrators
1648 McGrathiana Parkway
Suite 360
Lexington, KY 40511

859-225-9487
FAX 859-231-6403
E-Mail: info@nasbla.org
Home Page: www.nasbla.org

Social Media: *Facebook, Twitter, LinkedIn, Flickr, Foursquare, YouTube*

John Johnson, Executive Director & CEO
Tom Hayward, CFO
Ron Sarver, Deputy Director
Darren Rider, VP
Tom Guess, Treasurer

Representing the recreational boating authorities of all 50 States and U.S. territories. To strengthen the ability of the State and territorial boating authorities to reduce death, injury and property damage associated with recreational boating.
56 Members
Founded in 1960

3593 National Marine Bankers Association
231 South LaSalle St
Suite 2050
Chicago, IL 60604

312-946-6260
E-Mail: info@marinebankers.org
Home Page: www.marinebankers.org
Social Media: *LinkedIn*

Michael Bryant, President
Peggy Bodenreider, VP
William B Otto, Treasurer
Jayme B Yates, Secretary
Jackie Forese, Executive Director

Created for the purpose of educating current and prospective lenders in marine financing procedures, promoting the extension of credit to consumer and trade borrowers.
81 Members
Founded in 1979

3594 National Marine Distributors Association
37 Pratt St
Suite 3
Essex, CT 06426-1159

860-767-7898
FAX 860-767-7932
E-Mail: executivedirector@nmdaonline.com
Home Page: www.nmdaonline.com

Nancy Cueroni, Executive Director
Ryan Barber, President
Laura Leon, Vice President
Mike Connors, Secretary/Treasurer
Rick Chang, Past President

Wholesale distributors of marine accessories and hardware.
200 Members
Mailing list available for rent

3595 National Marine Electronics Association
7 Riggs Ave
Severna Park, MD 21146

410-975-9425
800-808-6632
FAX 410-975-9450
E-Mail: info@nmea.org
Home Page: www.nmea.org
Social Media: *Facebook*

David Gratton, Chairman
Johnny Lindstrom, Vice Chairman
Christopher Harley, Secretary
Marilyn S Quarders, Treasurer
Ken Harrison, International Executive Director

Is the unifying force behind the entire marine electronics industry, bringing together all aspects of the industry for the betterment of all in our business.
400 Members
Founded in 1957

3596 National Marine Manufacturers Association
231 South LaSalle St
Suite 2050
Chicago, IL 60604

312-946-6200
Home Page: www.nmma.org
Social Media: *Twitter, LinkedIn*

Thomas Dammrich, President
Ben Wold, EVP
Craig Boskey, VP Finance, CFO
Carl Blackwell, VP, Marketing & Communications
John McKnight, VP, Government Relations

Dedicated to creating, promoting and protecting an environment where members can achieve financial success through excellence in manufacturing, selling and service for their customers.
1400+ Members
Founded in 1979

3597 National Marine Representative Association
PO Box 360
Gurnee, IL 60031

847-662-3167
FAX 847-336-7126
E-Mail: info@nmraonline.org
Home Page: www.nmraonline.org

Rob Gueterman, President
Keith LaMarr, VP
Neal Tombley, Treasurer
Clayton Smith, Secretary
Brandon Flack, Past President

A national organization serving marine industry independent sales reps and the marine manufacturers who sell through reps.
300 Members
Founded in 1960

3598 National Safe Boating Council
9500 Technology
Suite 104
Manassas, VA 20110

703-361-4294
FAX 703-361-5294
Home Page: www.safeboatingcouncil.org
Social Media: *Facebook, Twitter, LinkedIn, Youtube*

Richard Moore, Chairman
Chris Stec, Vice Chairman
Pam Doty, Treasurer
Betsy Woods, Secretary
Rachel Johnson, Executive Director

NSBC has an interest in boating safety and education to reduce accidents and enhance the boating experience.
350 Members
Founded in 1958
Mailing list available for rent

3599 Northwest Marine Trade Association
1900 N Northlake Way
Suite 233
Seattle, WA 98103

206-634-0911
FAX 206-632-0078
E-Mail: info@nmta.net
Home Page: www.nmta.net
Social Media: *Facebook, Twitter, LinkedIn, Youtube, Pinterest, RSS*

Patricia Segulja-Lau, Chairman
Craig Perry, Vice Chair
James Baker, Secretary/Treasurer
Bruce Hedrick, Past Chairman
700+ Members
Founded in 1947

3600 Offshoreonly
PO Box 10868
St Petersburg, FL 33733

954-463-1101
FAX 727-394-2451
E-Mail: offshoreonly@offshoreonly.com
Home Page: www.offshoreonly.com
Social Media: *Facebook, Twitter*

Kathe Walker, President
Scott Ryerson, VP

OSO is a nonprofit organization catering to fun
loving boaters in the Tampa/Clearwater/St. Petersburg areas of Florida.
Mailing list available for rent

**3601 Personal Watercraft Industry
Association**
National Marine Manufacturers Association
231 South Lasalle Street
Suite 2050
Chicago, IL 60604

202-737-9761
FAX 866-861-2931
E-Mail: ddickerson@nmma.org
Home Page: www.pwia.org

David Dickerson, VP, State Govt Relations
Libby Yranski, Manager, State Govt Relations

Trade association representing manufacturers
of personal watercraft.
Founded in 1987

3602 Propeller Club of the United States
3927 Old Lee Hwy
Suite 101A
Fairfax, VA 22030

703-691-2777
FAX 703-691-4173
E-Mail: shannon@propellerclubhq.com
Home Page: www.propellerclubhq.com

Rick Schiappacasse, President
William Van Voorhis, Vice President
Tim Shusta, Secretary
Jack Crockett, Treasurer
Andrew Riester, Executive VP

Dedicated to the enhancement and well-being
of all interests of the maritime community on a
national and international basis.
10000 Members
Founded in 1927
Mailing list available for rent

3603 Recreational Boaters of California
925 L Street
Suite 260
Sacramento, CA 95814

916-441-4166
E-Mail: rboc@rboc.org
Home Page: www.rboc.org
Social Media: *Facebook, Twitter*

Greg Gibeson, President
Otis Brock, Secretary/Treasurer
Jerry Desmond Jr., Director Govt. Relations
Jerry Desmond, EVP
Ralph Longfellow, Vice President

Monitors the proceedings in the State Capitol,
reviewing each of the bills that are introduced
and/or amended as to whether they would have
an impact on boating.
Founded in 1968

3604 Sail America
50 Water St.
Warren, RI 02885

401-289-2540
FAX 401-247-0074
E-Mail: membership@sailamerica.com

Home Page: www.sailamerica.com
Social Media: *Facebook, Twitter, Vimeo*

Scot West, President
Greg Emerson, VP, Shows
Erin Schanen, VP, Association
Jay Stockmann, VP, Marketing

Trade association for sailing segment of recreational boating industry.
200+ Members
Founded in 1990

3605 Shipbuilders Council of America
20 F Street, NW
Suite 500
Washington, DC 20001

202-737-3234
FAX 202-737-0264
E-Mail: preever@balljanik.com
Home Page: www.shipbuilders.org
Social Media: *Facebook, Twitter*

Matt Paxton, President
Courtney Jowers, Director of Operations
Ashley Godwin, Senior Defense Advisor
Stephen Woodring, Government Relations
Manager
Joe Carnevale, Senior Defense Advisor

Represents the U.S. shipyard industry. SCA
members build, repair and service America's
fleet of commercial vessels.
73 Members
Founded in 1920

**3606 Society of Accredited Marine
Surveyors**
7855 Argyle Forest Blvd
Suite 203
Jacksonville, FL 32244

904-384-1494
800-344-9077
FAX 904-388-3958
E-Mail: samshq@marinesurvey.org
Home Page: www.marinesurvey.org

Lloyd E Kittredge, President
Rovert V Horvath, Executive Vice President
Bill Trenkle, Secretary/Treasurer
George J Sepel, Vp, Membership
Kenneth Weinbrecht, VP, Education

Dedicated to the advancement of the profession
of marine surveying
1000 Members
Founded in 1986

3607 Texas Dragon Boat Association
PO Box 980972
Houston, TX 77098

713-205-7373
E-Mail: webmaster@texasdragonboat.com
Home Page: www.houstondragonboat.com
Social Media: *Facebook, Twitter*

Michael Jhin, Chairman
David Mandell, President/Executive Director
Caroline Long, Secretary
Jim Travlos, Board Chairman

Promotes the tradition and sport of dragon
boating; increases the awareness of Asian and
Asian-American culture; and enhances
cross-cultural understanding.

3608 Traditional Small Craft Association
PO Box 350
Mystic, CT 06355

Home Page: www.tsca.net
Social Media: *Facebook*

Mary Loken, President
Roger Allen, Vice President
Pete Mathews, Secretary
Bill Meier, Treasurer
John Weiss, Chapter & Membership
Coordinator

Nonprofit, tax-exempt educational organization
which works to preserve and continue the living traditions, skills, lore and legends surrounding working and pleasure watercraft
whose origins predate the marine gasoline
engine.

**3609 U.S. Industrial Fabrics Association
International**
1801 County Road B W
Roseville, MN 55113-4061

651-222-2508
800-225-4324
FAX 651-631-9334
E-Mail: generalinfo@ifai.com
Home Page: www.ifai.com
Social Media: *Facebook, Twitter, LinkedIn,
YouTube*

Mary J Hennessy, President & CEO
Steve Schiffman, VP, Media & Sales
Sheila Sumner, Director of
Finance/Administration
Pam Egan-Blahna, Director, Human Resource
Andrew M Aho, Vice President of Operations

The mission of the United States Industrial
Fabrics Institute (USIFI) is to build a strong
coalition of US fiber, fabric, and end product
manufacturers and to serve member company
interests both domestically and internationally.
USIFI is part of the not-for-profit Industrial
Fabrics Association International
(www.ifai.com), the global association for the
specialty fabrics industry.
2000 Members
Founded in 1912

3610 United States Power Squadrons
1504 Blue Ridge Rd
Raleigh, NC 27607

919-821-0281
888-367-8777
FAX 888-304-0813
E-Mail: contactme@HQ.USPS.org
Home Page: www.usps.org
Social Media: *Facebook, Twitter, LinkedIn,
Youtube*

Mary Catherine Berube, Executive Director
Tammy Brown, Marketing Director
Stephanie Ford, Administrative Assistant
Lena Padro, Manager
Kathy Kesterson, Manager

A non-profit, educational organization dedicated to making boating safer and more enjoyable by teaching classes in seamanship,
navigation and related subjects.
45000 Members
Founded in 1914

3611 United States Rowing Association
2 Wall Street
Princeton, NJ 08540

609-751-0700
800-314-4769
FAX 609-924-1578
E-Mail: members@usrowing.org
Home Page: www.usrowing.org
Social Media: *Facebook, Twitter, Flickr,
Youtube*

Erin O'Connell, President
Jim Dietz, VP
Gary Caldwell, Treasurer
Frances Mennone, Secretary
Daniel Herbert, At-Large Representative

Non-profit membership organization, recognized by the U.S. Olympic Committee as the
national governing body for the sport of rowing
in the United States.
16000 Members
Founded in 1982

3612 United States Sailing Association
15 Maritime Drive
Portsmouth, RI 02871

401-683-0800
800-877-2451
FAX 401-683-0840
E-Mail: info@ussailing.org
Home Page: www.ussailing.org
Social Media: *Facebook, Twitter, LinkedIn, Youtube, RSS*

Bruce J Burton, Us Sailing President
Jack Gierhart, Executive Director
Cory Sertl, Vice President
Martine R Zurinskas, Secretary
Stephen T Freitas, Treasurer

National governing body for the sport of sailing.
100 Members
Founded in 1897

3613 Yacht Brokers Association of America
105 Eastern Avenue
Suite 104
Annapolis, MD 21403

410-940-6345
FAX 410-263-1659
E-Mail: info@ybaa.com
Home Page: www.ybaa.com
Social Media: *Facebook, Twitter, LinkedIn*

Hal Slater, President
David Benson, VP
Jean-Pierre Skov, Treasurer
Vincent J Petrella, Executive Director
Joseph Thompson, General Manager

Sets the standards for professional yacht brokers throughout North America
250 Members
Founded in 1920

3614 Yachting Club of America
PO Box 1040
Marco Island, FL 34146

239-642-4448
FAX 239-642-5284
E-Mail: bill@ycaol.com
Home Page: www.ycaol.com

David Martin, Owner

A membership organization dedicated to the advancement of yachting.
30000 Members
Founded in 1963

Newsletters

3615 ASMA News
American Society of Marine Artists
P.O.Box 247
Smithfield, VA 23430

757-357-3785
E-Mail: asma1978@verizon.net
Home Page:
www.americansocietyofmarineartists.com

Keeps you up to date with all of the Society's activities, along with providing space where artists like yourself can share ideas, inspirations, tips and even frustrations. Provides you access to the Society's network of members, local and national marine art news and information about art exhibitions and exhibition opportunities.
Frequency: Quarterly

3616 American Boat & Yacht Council News
American Boat and Yacht Council
613 Third Street
Suite 10
Annapolis, MD 21403

410-990-4460
FAX 410-990-4466
E-Mail: info@abycinc.org
Home Page: www.abycinc.org

George Bellwoar, Chairman
Jack Horner, Vice Chair
F. Steven Herb, Treasurer

News and technical information of interest to ABYC members.
4000+ Members
8 Pages
Frequency: Quarterly
Founded in 1954
Mailing list available for rent

3617 American Boat Builders and Repairers Association Newsletter
American Boat Builders and Repairers Association
50 Water Street
Warren, RI 02885

401-247-0318
866-367-6622
FAX 401-247-0074
Home Page: www.abbra.org

Jonathan Jones Haven, President
Peter Sabo, VP
Mark Amaral, Managing Director
Charles Teran, Treasurer/Secretary

Accepts advertising.
300 Members
4 Pages
Frequency: Monthly
Founded in 1943

3618 Anchor Line Newsletter
National Safe Boating Council
PO Box 509
Bristow, VA 20136

703-361-4294
FAX 703-361-5294
Home Page: www.safeboatingcouncil.org
Social Media: *Facebook, Twitter*

Joyce Shaw, Chairman
Lynda Nutt, Vice Chairman
Virgil Chambers, Executive Officer
Sandy Smith, Chief Financial Officer
350 Members
Founded in 1958

3619 Business of Pleasure Boats
National Marine Bankers Association
231 South LaSalle St
Suite 2050
Chicago, IL 60604

312-946-6260
E-Mail: bmcardle@nmma.org
Home Page: www.marinebankers.org
Social Media: *LinkedIn*

Karen Trostle, President
Jackie Forese, Director
Mike Ryan, Vice President
Bernice McArdlen, Manager
81 Members
Frequency: Quarterly
Founded in 1979

3620 MRAA Bearings
Marine Retailers Association of America
P.O.Box 725
Boca Grande, FL 33921-0725

941-964-2534
FAX 941-531-6777
E-Mail: mraa@mraa.com
Home Page: www.mraa.com

Phil Keeter, President
Marge Eckenroad, Executive Administrator

Larry Innis, Director Government Affairs
Marge Eckenroad, Executive Administrator

A publication encompassing issues that you need to know about, issues such as legislation, environment and compliance, legal, association and industry news, and much more.
3000 Members
Frequency: Monthly
Circulation: 2000
Founded in 1971

3621 Mainsheet
Rhodes 19 Class Association
174 Walnut Street
Reading, MA 01867

781-944-2697
E-Mail: info@rhodes19.org
Home Page: www.rhodes19.org
Social Media: *Facebook*

Steve Uhl, President
Mary Kovats, Secretary
Tom Carville, Treasurer

Newsletter concerning the Rhodes 19 design sailboat. Our mission is to promote Rhodes 19 racing by encouraging and supporting local fleet development nationally, and by working to maintain the one-design integrity of the boat.
Founded in 1965

3622 Marine Safety and Security Report
Stamler Publishing Company
178 Thimble Islands Rd
PO Box 3367
Branford, CT 06405-1967

203-488-9808
800-422-4121
FAX 203-488-3129
E-Mail: sstamler@ix.netcom.net

S Paul Stamler, President/CEO

Business-to-business newsletter providing information on boating and shipping safety and enforcement issues, including federal regulations and Coast Guard Actions, state safety programs, IMO activity, classification studies, vessel recalls, and safety equipment. Accepts no advertising and is solely supported by subscribers worldwide.
Cost: $77.00
4 Pages
Founded in 1973
Printed in 2 colors on matte stock

3623 Maritime Reporter and Engineering News
118 East 25th Street
New York, NY 10010

212-477-6700
FAX 212-254-6271
E-Mail: jomalley@marinelink.com
Home Page: www.marinelink.com

John O'Malley, Publisher
Greg Trauthwein, Associate Publisher
Michael Martino, Owner
Lucia M Annunziata, VP
Jennifer Rabulan, Technical Editor

Provides unparalleled coverage of the maritime industry covering the inland, Coastal and Great Lakes region.
95000 Members
Frequency: Monthly
Circulation: 50000
Founded in 1999

3624 NACO Newsletter
National Association of Charterboat Operators
PO Box 2990
Orange Beach, AL 36561

251-981-5136
FAX 251-981-8191

E-Mail: info@nacocharters.org
Home Page: www.nacocharters.org

Bob Zales II, President
Ed O'Brien, Vice President
Tom Becker, Second Vice President
Gary Krein, Secretary
3600+ Members
Frequency: Quarterly
Circulation: 3500
Founded in 1991

3625 Propeller Club Newsletter
Propeller Club of the United States
3927 Old Lee Hwy
Suite 101A
Fairfax, VA 22030-2422

703-691-2777
FAX 703-691-4173
E-Mail: shannon@propellerclubhq.com
Home Page: www.propellerclubhq.com

Thomas Allegretti, President/CEO
Niels Aalund, Sr. Vice President
Shannon Hendrickson-Pluta, Admin Asst
Virgil R Allen, VP Development

Features expanded coverage of Propeller Club
activities, including legislative and regulatory
reports, feature-length member profiles, regional news and expanded coverage of national
maritime issues.
10000 Members
Frequency: Quarterly
Founded in 1927

3626 Rudder
Antique & Classic Boat Society
422 James St
Clayton, NY 13624-1136

315-686-2628
FAX 315-686-2680
E-Mail: hqs@acbs.org
Home Page: www.acbs.org
Social Media: *Facebook, Twitter*

Jim Mersman, President
Dunc Hawkins, First VP
Teresa Hoffman, Second VP
Dick Winn, Treasurer
Brian Gagnon, Secretary

Historical news and how-to-restore wooden
and antique boats.
12000 Members
Frequency: Quarterly
Founded in 1975
Printed in 4 colors

3627 SAMS Newsletter
Society of Accredited Marine Surveyors
7855 Argyle Forest Blvd
Suite 203
Jacksonville, FL 32244

904-384-1494
800-344-9077
FAX 904-388-3958
E-Mail: samshq@marinesurvey.org
Home Page: www.marinesurvey.org

Joseph B Lobley, President
Stuart J. McLea, Executive Vice President
Llyod E. Kittredge, Secretary/Treasurer

For members.
1000 Members
Frequency: 4/Year
Circulation: 1000
Founded in 1986

3628 Seamanship Training
American Boating Association
PO Box 456
Centerville, MA 02632

508-534-9893
E-Mail: admin@americanboating.org

Home Page: www.americanboating.org
Social Media: *Facebook*

Bill Condon, Founder/President

Free to all ABA (American Boating Association) members as well as all boaters. Informative content on boating skills and safety issues.
30000 Members
Frequency: Bi-Monthly

3629 Shipyard Chronicle Newsletter
Shipbuilders Council of America
655 Fifteenth St NW
Suite 225
Washington, DC 20005

202-347-5462
FAX 202-347-5464
E-Mail: preever@balljanik.com
Home Page: www.shipbuilders.org
Social Media: *Facebook*

Matt Paxton, President, Vice Chairman
Allen Walker, President
Irene Ringwood, Manager

The publication is devoted to keeping members
up to date on the latest legislative and regulatory developments. It also includes a schedule
of upcoming association and industry related
government meetings, as well as news regarding SCA member companies.
73 Members
Founded in 1920

3630 Soundings Trade Only
Soundings Publications
10 Bokum Rd
Essex, CT 06426-1536

860-767-3200
FAX 860-767-1048
E-Mail: info@soundingspub.com
Home Page: www.soundingsonline.com
Social Media: *Facebook*

Ian Bowen, Manager
Peter Mitchel, Publisher

Nation's boating business newspaper. Coverage
of the recreational boating business; for marine
dealers, marine operators, distributors and manufacturers. BPA audited.
Cost: $13.97
15500 Members
33 Pages
Frequency: Monthly
Circulation: 34,000
Founded in 1965

3631 Tidings
National Marine Representatives
Association
1333 Delany Road #500
PO Box 360
Gurnee, IL 60031

847-662-3167
FAX 847-336-7126
E-Mail: info@nmraonline.org
Home Page: www.nmraonline.org

Chris Kelly, President
Kathy Munzinger, VP
Ken Smaga, Treasurer
Brandon Flack, Secretary
Chris Kelly, Secretary

Contains informative articles to help manufacturers develop sound and profitable relationships with independent sales representatives
and keep informed about the marine market in
general.
300 Members
500+ Pages
Frequency: Quarterly
Founded in 1960

3632 Water Life
Northwest Marine Trade Association

1900 N Northlake Way
Suite 233
Seattle, WA 98103-9087

206-634-0911
FAX 206-632-0078
E-Mail: info@nmta.net
Home Page: www.nmta.net
Social Media: *Facebook, Twitter, LinkedIn*

George Harris, President
Laura Snodgrass, Finance Director
John Thorburn, Vice President
Liz Manning, Membership Director

Provides industry information, member benefits, committee activity and new member announcements and anniversaries. Water Life
continues to evolve into a valuable tool for Pacific Northwest marine leaders.
700+ Members
Founded in 1947

3633 Yacht Broker News
Yacht Brokers Association of America
105 Eastern Avenue
Suite 104
Annapolis, MD 21403

410-940-6345
FAX 410-263-1659
E-Mail: info@ybaa.com
Home Page: www.ybaa,com

Vincent J. Petrella, Executive Director
Rod Rowan, President
Amy Luckado, Membership Director

Reports on latest business issues, industry concerns, legislation, regulatory activities and includes a member-to-member
section(WayPoints), where members can report
on their own company news, personnel updates
and business expansion.
250 Members
Frequency: Quarterly
Founded in 1920

Magazines & Journals

3634 American Sailor
US Sailing Association
15 Maritime Drive
PO Box 1260
Portsmouth, RI 02871-0907

401-683-0800
800-877-2451
FAX 401-683-0840
E-Mail: info@ussailing.org
Home Page: www.ussailing.org
Social Media: *Facebook, Twitter, LinkedIn*

Tom Hubbell, Us Sailing President
Jack Gierhart, Executive Director
Fred Hagedorn, Secretary
Jack Gierhart, Executive Director

Boating news.
100 Members
Frequency: Monthly
Founded in 1980

3635 Ash Breeze
Traditional Small Craft Association
PO Box 350
Mystic, CT 06355

E-Mail: drathmarine@rockisland.com
Home Page: www.tsca.net

Mike Wick, Co-Editor
Ned Asplundh, Co-Editor

Devoted to topics ranging from reports from
the chapters to technical details and specific designs with lines and offsets. You may find an-
ecdotal accounts of experiences in traditional
boats, and tips on how to spile a plank.
Frequency: Quarterly

3636 Boat & Motor Dealer
Preston Publications
6600 W Touhy Ave
PO Box 48312
Niles, IL 60714-4516

847-647-2900
FAX 847-647-1155
E-Mail: circulation@boatmotordealer.com
Home Page: www.prestonpub.com

Tinsley Preston, Owner
Jerome Koncel, Editorial Director

Dedicated to providing businesses in the recreational marine industry with the information, commentary and analysis needed to expand their businesses and improve profitability.
Founded in 1959
Mailing list available for rent: 30000 names at $100 per M

3637 BoatUS Magazine
Boat Owners Association of the US
880 South Pickett Street
Alexandria, VA 22304-4606

703-461-2864
FAX 703-461-2845
E-Mail: emagazine@boatus.com
Home Page: www.boatus.com
Social Media: *Facebook, Twitter*

Michael Vatalaro, Executive Editor
Richard Schwartz, Chairman/Founder
Chris Landers, Associate Editor

Boating magazine includes legislative, travel, safety, DIY, and consumer news of interest to recreational boat owners.
Cost: $19.00
62500 Members
Frequency: Annual/6
Circulation: 500K+
Founded in 1966

3638 Boatbuilder
Belvoir Publishers
PO Box 5656
Norwalk, CT 06856-5656

203-857-4880
FAX 203-661-4802
E-Mail: customer_service@belvoir.com
Home Page: www.belvoir.com

Robert Englander, Owner/CEO

The magazine is for those who build, modify and repair boats.
Founded in 1972

3639 Boating Industry
Ehlert Publishing Group
6420 Sycamore Ln N
Suite 100
Maple Grove, MN 55369-6014

763-383-4400
800-848-6247
FAX 763-383-4499
E-Mail: acollins@ehlertpublishing.com
Home Page: www.boatingindustry.com
Social Media: *Facebook, Twitter, LinkedIn*

Jonathan Sweet, Editor in Chief
Tom Kaiser, Senior Editor

Links together all sectors of the boating market from boat and motor dealers to marinas, boatyards, builders and suppliers. It also provides strategic analysis, in-depth coverage and proprietary research of the most critical issues.
Frequency: 8 Issues/2 Special Issues

3640 Boating Magazine
Bonnier Corporation
460 N. Orlando Ave
Suite 200
Winter Park, FL 32789

407-628-4802
FAX 407-628-7061

E-Mail: editor@boatingmag.com
Home Page: www.boatingmag.com
Social Media: *Facebook, Twitter*

John McEver, Publisher
Glenn Hughes, VP
Jonas Bonnier, Chairman

Offers up-to-date information on boats, manufacturers, suppliers, distributors related to the boating industry.
Cost: $17.95
Frequency: Monthly

3641 Canoe & Kayak Magazine
Canoe & Kayak
12025 115th Ave. NE
Suite D200
Kirkland, WA 98034

425-827-6363
800-692-2663
FAX 425-827-1893
E-Mail: letters@canoekayak.com
Home Page: www.canoekayak.com
Social Media: *Facebook, Twitter*

Jeff Moag, Editor
Dave Shively, Managing Editor

Published by the Canoe American Associates.
Cost: $17.95
Frequency: 7 Issues
Circulation: 62000
Founded in 1973
Mailing list available for rent

3642 Dry Stack Marina Handbook
Association of Marina Industries
50 Water Street
Warren, RI 02885

866-367-6622
FAX 401-247-0074
E-Mail: info@marinaassociation.org
Home Page: www.marinaassociation.org
Social Media: *Twitter, LinkedIn*

Jim Frye, CMM, Chairman/President
Gary Groenewold, Vice Chairman
Jeff Rose, Treasurer
Keith Boulais, Secretary

This book covers: Dry stack buildings and racks, Boat handling equipment, Statistics, Site planning, Typical costs, Fire protection problems & solutions, Comparision of dry stack vs. wet slip demand, Marketing, Facility operations, Lease or purchase decision, Loss control considerations.
Cost: $90.00
800+ Members
Frequency: 61 Illustrations
Founded in 1986

3643 Ensign
United States Power Squadrons
1504 Blue Ridge Rd
Raleigh, NC 27607-3906

919-821-0281
888-367-8777
FAX 888-304-0813
Home Page: www.usps.org
Social Media: *Facebook, Twitter*

Frank A. Dvorak, Executive Officer

Ensign magazine is the official magazine of United States Power Squadrons. The mission is to promote recreational boating safety through education and civic activities while providing fellowship for our members.
Cost: $10.00
45000 Members
48 Pages
Frequency: Monthly
Circulation: 35,000
Founded in 1914
Printed in 4 colors on glossy stock

3644 Fabric Architecture
U.S. Industrial Fabrics Association International
1801 County Road B W
Roseville, MN 55113-4061

651-222-2508
800-225-4324
FAX 651-631-9334
E-Mail: generalinfo@ifai.com
Home Page: www.usifi.com

Stephen Warner, CEO
JoAnne Ferris, Marketing Director

Targets architects, designers, specifiers, contractors and developers promoting the architectural advantages of fabric. Educates the industry about designing with fabric and promoting it as an environmentally-responsible choice.
Frequency: Bimonthly
Circulation: 8,000

3645 Fabric Graphics
Industrial Fabrics Association International
1801 County Road B W
Roseville, MN 55113-4061

651-222-2508
800-225-4324
FAX 651-631-9334
E-Mail: generalinfo@ifai.com
Home Page: www.ifai.com
Social Media: *Facebook, Twitter, LinkedIn*

Mary J. Hennessy, Executive VP
JoAnne Farris, Marketing Director
Steven C. Rider, CFO, VP

Created to educate and inspire professionals to use fabric to expand their business. Promotes the use of textiles as a printing medium, showcasing the numerous applications for fabric and the technology needed to achieve good results.
Frequency: Bimonthly
Circulation: 8,000
Founded in 1912

3646 Geosynthetics
Industrial Fabrics Association International
1801 County Road B W
Roseville, MN 55113-4061

651-222-2508
800-225-4324
FAX 651-631-9334
E-Mail: generalinfo@ifai.com
Home Page: www.ifai.com
Social Media: *Facebook, Twitter, LinkedIn*

Mary J. Hennessy, Executive VP
JoAnne Farris, Marketing Director
Steven C. Rider, CFO, VP

Targeting those who rely on the publication for the most professional presentation of Geosynthetic products, design, and applications.
Frequency: Bimonthly
Circulation: 14,000
Founded in 1912

3647 InTents
Industrial Fabrics Association International
1801 County Road B W
Roseville, MN 55113-4061

651-222-2508
800-225-4324
FAX 651-631-9334
E-Mail: generalinfo@ifai.com
Home Page: www.ifai.com
Social Media: *Facebook, Twitter, LinkedIn*

Mary J. Hennessy, Executive VP
JoAnne Farris, Marketing Director
Steven C. Rider, CFO, VP

Focuses on tents, fabric structures, and accessories that tent renters need to operate a profitable business. The magazine and its website

work together to deliver the total tent experience to readers and visitors.
Frequency: Bimonthly
Circulation: 11,000
Founded in 1912

3648 Marina/Dock Age
Preston Publications
6600 W Touhy Ave
Niles, IL 60714-4516

847-647-2900
FAX 847-647-1155
E-Mail: atownshend@marinadockage.com
Home Page: www.marinadockage.com/
Social Media: *Twitter, LinkedIn*

Tinsley Preston, Owner
Anna Townshend, Editor

Provide marina/boatyard owners and managers with the information they need to meet ever-changing government regulations, operate more efficiently, expand their business, and improve their profitability.
Cost: $50.00
16500 Members
Frequency: Monthly
Circulation: 24000
Founded in 1989

3649 Marinas and Small Craft Harbors
Association of Marina Industries
50 Water Street
Warren, RI 02885

866-367-6622
FAX 401-247-0074
E-Mail: info@marinaassociation.org
Home Page: www.marinaassociation.org
Social Media: *Twitter, LinkedIn*

Jim Frye, CMM, Chairman/President
Gary Groenewold, Vice Chairman
Jeff Rose, Treasurer
Keith Boulais, Secretary

The new edition includes updated and redrawn tables, charts, figures and text editing and additions, as well as newly created information on marina design characteristics of megyachts and test data, design loads, and recommendations on design and performance of dock cleats.
Cost: $89.95
800+ Members
Founded in 1986

3650 Marine Fabricator
Industrial Fabrics Association International
1801 County Road B W
Roseville, MN 55113-4061

651-222-2508
800-225-4324
FAX 651-631-9334
E-Mail: generalinfo@ifai.com
Home Page: www.ifai.com
Social Media: *Facebook, Twitter, LinkedIn*

Mary J. Hennessy, Executive VP
JoAnne Farris, Marketing Director
Steven C. Rider, CFO, VP

Educates professionals in the techniques of quality marine craftsmanship and upholstery. Marine shop professionals rely on the magazine to stay informed on the latest techniques, technologies, business management and news. .
Cost: $34.00
Frequency: Bi-Monthly
Circulation: 5,000
Founded in 1912

3651 Marine Log
Simmons-Boardman Publishing Corporation
345 Hudson St
12th Floor, Suite 1201
New York, NY 10014-7123

212-620-7200
FAX 212-633-1165

E-Mail: marinelog@sbpub.com
Home Page: www.marinelog.com
Social Media: *Facebook, Twitter, LinkedIn*

Arthur J McGinnis Jr, President
John Snyder, Publisher/Editor in Chief

For more than 130 years, maritime executives worldwide have turned to Marine Log as the source for news and analysis on issues impacting vessel design, construction and operations.
Frequency: Monthly
Circulation: 29934
Founded in 1878

3652 Marine News
Maritime Activity Reports
118 East 25th Street
New York, NY 10010

212-477-6700
FAX 212-254-6271
E-Mail: jomalley@marinelink.com
Home Page: www.marinelink.com

John O'Malley, Publisher
Greg Trauthwein, Associate Publisher
Michael Martino, Owner
Lucia M Annunziata, Owner
Jennifer Rabulan, Technical Editor

Features marine industry news and issues effecting maritime activity. Includes updates on vessel building and acquisitions as well as regular columns on research and devlepoment, equipment reports and an events calendar.
95000 Members
Frequency: Monthly
Circulation: 23000
Founded in 1999

3653 Motor Boating
Time4 Media Marine Group
460 N. Orlando Ave
Suite 200
Winter Park, FL 32789

407-628-4802
FAX 407-628-7061
E-Mail: editor@motorboating.com
Home Page: www.motorboating.com
Social Media: *Facebook, Twitter*

Ed Baker, Associate Publisher
John McEver, Publisher
Glenn Hughes, VP

Helps its readers buy, maintain and get the most out of their powerboats. It focuses on powerboats, people, products, destinations, trends and technological developments in the boating market, as well as cruising, water sports and safety.
Frequency: Monthly
Founded in 1907
Printed in on glossy stock

3654 National Numbering & Titling
National Association of State Boating Law
1500 Leestown Rd
Suite 330
Lexington, KY 40511-2047

859-225-9487
FAX 859-231-6403
E-Mail: info@nasbla.org
Home Page: www.nasbla.org
Social Media: *Facebook, Twitter, LinkedIn, Flickr, Foursquare*

John Johnson, Executive Director
Tom Hayward, Finance & Administration
Ron Sarver, Deputy Director

Facilitate ongoing efforts to evaluate and improve the programs' internal procedures and external interactions in the face of resource constraints and in preparation for implementing

the Coast Guard's Vessel Identification System.
Cost: $14.95
56 Members
Founded in 1960
Mailing list available for rent: 56 names

3655 Paddle Magazine
Paddle Sport Publishing
12025 115th Ave. NE
Suite D200
Kirkland, WA 98034

970-879-1450
FAX 970-870-1404
E-Mail: Eugene@paddlermagazine.com
Home Page: www.paddlermagazine.com
Social Media: *Facebook, Twitter*

Eugene Buchanan, Publisher/Editor
Jeff Moag, Editor
Kevin Thompson, Account Manager

Information to keep the paddle sport equipment dealer up-to-date on issues that will effect their business, industry trends in boats, apparel and accessories, how to articles to assist the reader in selling boats.
Cost: $18.00
Circulation: 5527
Printed in 4 colors on glossy stock

3656 Paddlesports Business
Canoe & Kayak
12025 115th Ave. NE
Suite D200
Kirkland, WA 98034

425-827-6363
800-692-2663
FAX 425-827-1893
E-Mail: letters@canoekayak.com
Home Page: www.canoekayak.com
Social Media: *Facebook, Twitter*

Jeff Moag, Editor
Dave Shively, Managing Editor

Trade publication for the paddlesports industry.
Founded in 1973
Mailing list available for rent

3657 Professional BoatBuilder
WoodenBoat Publications
41 Wooden Boat La
PO Box 78
Brooklin, ME 04616-0078

207-359-4651
800-877-5284
FAX 207-359-8920
E-Mail: proboat@proboat.com
Home Page: www.proboat.com
Social Media: *Facebook*

Paul Lazarus, Sr. Editor
Aaron Porter, Editor
Carl Cramer, Co-Director

Focuses on materials, design, and construction techniques and repair solutions chosen by marine professionals. Regular technical articles provide detailed, real-world examples to improve the efficiency and quality of their work.
Cost: $35.95
76 Pages
Circulation: 27500
ISSN: 1043-2035
Founded in 1974
Printed in 4 colors on glossy stock

3658 Propeller
American Power Boat Association
17640 E. Nine Mile Road
PO Box 377
Eastpointe, MI 48021-0377

586-773-9700
FAX 586-773-6490

E-Mail: propeller@apba-racing.com
Home Page: www.apba-racing.com

Mark Weber, President
Gloria Urbin, Executive Director
Tana Moore, News, Propellor

Propeller magazine is the mouthpiece of the American Power Boat Association, the nation's leading authority on power boat racing which sanctions over 200 races each year.
Cost: $2.50
22 Pages
Frequency: Monthly
ISSN: 0194-6218
Printed in 4 colors on glossy stock

3659 Small Craft Advisory
National Association of State Boating Law Admnstrs
1500 Leestown Rd
Suite 330
Lexington, KY 40511-2047

859-225-9487
FAX 859-231-6403
E-Mail: info@nasbla.org
Home Page: www.nasbla.org
Social Media: *Facebook, Twitter, LinkedIn, Flickr, Foursquare*

John Johnson, Executive Director
Tom Hayward, Finance & Administration
Ron Sarver, Deputy Director

Small Craft Advisory, published bimonthly, is for and about the nation's boating law administration professionals. Authoritative articles featuring practices, procedures, and research in recreational boating safety, marine law enforcement, and boating safety education are presented to enhance the efficiency and effectiveness of recreational boating safety. Each issue highlights successful recreational boating safety programs, NASBLA activities, professional news, and legislative updates
Cost: $14.00
56 Members
Frequency: Bi-Monthly
Circulation: 11000
Founded in 1960
Mailing list available for rent: 56 names

3660 Southern Boating Magazine
330 N Andrews Ave
Suite 200
Fort Lauderdale, FL 33301-1025

954-522-5515
888-882-6284
FAX 954-522-2260
E-Mail: sboating@southernboating.com
Home Page: www.southernboating.com
Social Media: *Facebook, Twitter*

Skip Allen, Owner/Chairman/Publisher/Editor
L.J. Wallace, Executive Editor
Cathryn Allen-Zubi, VP
Rain Hernandez Rouveroy, VP of Finance
Kellie Mackenroth, Circulation Manager

Focus is on boating in the southern US, Bahamas, and Caribbean.
Cost: $22.95
Frequency: Monthly
Circulation: 42000
Founded in 1972
Printed in 4 colors on matte stock

3661 Specialty Fabrics Review
Industrial Fabrics Association International
1801 County Road B W
Roseville, MN 55113-4061

651-222-2508
800-225-4324
FAX 651-631-9334
E-Mail: generalinfo@ifai.com

Home Page: www.ifai.com
Social Media: *Facebook, Twitter, LinkedIn*

Mary J. Hennessy, Executive VP
JoAnne Farris, Marketing Director
Steven C. Rider, CFO, VP

In print since 1915, this international publication targets specialty fabric professionals. Each issue brings timely reporting on industry topics, helpful business articles and a review of global news and market updates.
Frequency: Monthly
Circulation: 13000
Founded in 1912

3662 The Reference Point
American Boat and Yacht Council
Association
613 Third Street
Suite 10
Annapolis, MD 21403

410-990-4460
FAX 410-990-4466
E-Mail: info@abycinc.org
Home Page: www.abycinc.org
Social Media: *Facebook*

George Bellwoar, Chairman
Jack Horner, Vice Chair
F. Steven Herb, Treasurer

ABYC's technical professional quarterly journal.
4000+ Members
Frequency: Quarterly
Founded in 1954

3663 US Yacht Racing Union
US Sailing
15 Maritime Drive
PO Box 1260
Portsmouth, RI 02871-0907

401-683-0800
800-877-2451
FAX 401-683-0840
E-Mail: info@ussailing.org
Home Page: www.ussailing.org
Social Media: *Facebook, Twitter, LinkedIn*

Gary Jobson, Us Sailing President
Tom Hubbell, Vice President
Fred Hagedorn, Secretary
Jack Gierhart, Executive Director

National news of the Union, the latest in yacht racing, and dealers of yachts are covered.
100 Members
Founded in 1986

3664 UnderWater Magazine
Naylor, LLC
5950 NW 1st Place
Gainesville, FL 32607

800-369-6220
E-Mail: sgarrity@naylor.com
Home Page: www.underwater.com

Jamie Williams, Publication Director
Sean Garrity, Editorial
Rebecca Roberts, Marketing Manager

It covers the entire spectrum of underwater contracting, vehicles and technology.
Cost: $50.00
500 Members
Founded in 1968

3665 WoodenBoat
WoodenBoat Publications
41 Wooden Boat La
PO Box 78
Brooklin, ME 04616-0078

207-359-4651
800-877-5284
FAX 207-359-8920
E-Mail: info@woodenboat.com

Home Page: www.woodenboat.com
Social Media: *Facebook*

Tom Jackson, Sr. Editor
Carl Cramer, Publisher
Matt Murphy, Editor

Provides readers with a dynamic editorial environment that combines technologies with traditional methods of boat design, construction and repair. The magazine is about craftmanship in wood, and its active boating audience works at all levels of expertise to build, restore, and maintain their boats.
Cost: $29.95
160 Pages
Frequency: Bi-Monthly
Circulation: 98000
Founded in 1974

3666 WorkBoat
Diversified Business Communications
121 Free Street
Portland, ME 04101

207-842-5600
FAX 207-842-5611
E-Mail: info@divcom.com
Home Page: www.workboat.com
Social Media: *Facebook, Twitter*

Mike Lodato, VP
Ken Hocke, Senior Editor
David Krapf, Editor In Chief
Jerry Fraser, Publisher

Commercial marine publication serving the North American inland and coastal waterways — the most active sector in the commercial marine market today. Consisting of captains, owners, managers, operators, chief engineers and other industry professionals, the Workboat audience represents important and influential purchasing power in the commercial marine industry.
Cost: $39.00
Frequency: Monthly
Circulation: 25000
ISSN: 0043-8014
Founded in 1949

3667 Yachting Magazine
Time4 Media Marine Group
PO Box 420235
Palm Coast, FL 32142-0235

386-597-4382
800-999-0869
E-Mail: letters@yachtingmagazine.com
Home Page: www.yachtingmagazine.com
Social Media: *Facebook, Twitter*

Ed Baker, Associate Publisher
Rich Rasor, East Coast Sales Director

Covers the finest boats, electronics and equipment, including large yachts and yacht charters. It also covers the passions, adventures and lifestyles of active, affluent boat owners.
Frequency: Monthly
Founded in 1907

3668 Young Mariners Guide
Yachting Club of America
PO Box 1040
Marco Island, FL 34146

239-642-4448
FAX 239-642-5284
E-Mail: ycaol@hotmail.com
Home Page: www.ycaol.com

David Martin, Owner

Designed to inform and teach young people about boating in simple and handy pocket book to help them on their way to becoming the future of the yachting fraternity in America.
Cost: $5.00
30000 Members
32 Pages
Frequency: Softbound

Founded in 1963
Mailing list available for rent

Trade Shows

3669 Annual American and Canadian Sport, Travel and Outdoor Show
Expositions, Inc.
Edgewater Branch
PO Box 550
Cleveland, OH 44107-0550

216-529-1300
FAX 216-529-0311
E-Mail: showinfo@expoinc.com
Home Page: www.expoinc.com

Chris Fassnacht, President
Robert Attewell, Vice President
David Rosar, CFO, VP

975 exhibits of hunting and fishing equipment, travel services, boats, recreational vehicles and related equipment, supplies and services.
300k Attendees
Frequency: March
Founded in 1937

3670 Annual Boat & Fishing Show at the Lansing Center
Show Span, Inc
2121 Celebration Drive NE
Grand Rapids, MI 49525

616-447-2860
800-328-6550
FAX 616-447-2861
E-Mail: events@showspan.com
Home Page: www.showspan.com

John Loeks, President
Henri Boucher, Vice President
Mike Wilbraham, VP, Show Producer

Held in Lansing, Michigan.
Frequency: March
Founded in 1945

3671 Annual Boat Show
General Sports Shows/NMMA
231 S. LaSalle St
Suite 2050
Chicago, IL 60604

312-946-6200
800-777-4766
E-Mail: bmcardle@nmma.org
Home Page: www.generalsportshows.com

Jennifer Thompson, Show Manager
Bonnie Schuenemann, Special Events Coordinator
Patty Gibbs, Media Contact

Enjoy 5 days of boating fun, education and one-stop shopping with hundreds of boats and exhibits and special attractions all under one roof.
Frequency: January

3672 Annual Boat Show & Fishing Exposition
Greenband Enterprises
3450 South Highland Drive
Suite 105
Salt Lake City, UT 84106

801-485-7399
800-657-3050
FAX 801-485-0687
E-Mail: showinfo@greenband.com
Home Page: www.greenband.com
Social Media: *Facebook*

Jonathan D Greenband, Show Manager
Debra Greenband, Sales Manager

See the latest in Ski Boats, Cruisers, Fishing Boats, everything for boating fun.
45000 Attendees
Frequency: Annual, February
Founded in 1965

3673 Annual Boat, Vacation and Outdoor Show
Showtime Productions, Inc.
PO Box 4372
Rockford, IL 61110

815-877-8043
FAX 815-877-9037
E-Mail: brenda@showtimeproduction.net
Home Page: showtimeproduction.net

Tom Pellant, President
Brenda Rotoco, Event Coordinator

Boat, travel, outdoor equipment, supplies, and services plus demonstrations.
28000 Attendees
Frequency: February
Founded in 1970

3674 Annual Conference & Educational Symposia
Society of Accredited Marine Surveyors
7855 Argyle Forest Blvd
Suite 203
Jacksonville, FL 32244

904-384-1494
800-344-9077
FAX 904-388-3958
E-Mail: samshq@marinesurvey.org
Home Page: www.marinesurvey.org

Joseph B Lobley, President
Stuart J. McLea, Executive Vice President
Llyod E. Kittredge, Secretary/Treasurer
1000 Members
350 Attendees
Frequency: Annual/Fall
Founded in 1986

3675 Annual Conference on Sail Training and Tall Ships
American Sail Training Association
29 Touro Street
PO Box 1459
Newport, RI 02840

401-846-1775
FAX 401-849-5400
E-Mail: asta@sailtraining.org
Home Page: www.tallships.sailtraining.org
Social Media: *Facebook, Twitter, LinkedIn, Youtube*

Mike Rauworth, Chairman
Robert Rogers, Executive Director
Caleb Pifer, Vice Chair
300 Members
Frequency: November
Founded in 1973

3676 Annual Iowa Boat and Vacation Show
Iowa Show Productions
PO Box 2460
Waterloo, IA 50704-2460

319-232-0218
FAX 319-235-8932
E-Mail: info@iowashows.com
Home Page: www.iowashows.com

John Bunge, Show Manager

Over 25 dealers, 40 brands, 100's of models. Family runabouts, fishing boats, cabin cruisers, cuddies, power boats, waterski boats, personal watercraft, jet boats, bass boats, walleye boats, deck boats, pontoons, fish/ski boats, and marine accessories.
Frequency: January
Founded in 1975
Mailing list available for rent

3677 Annual Lido Yacht Expo
Duncan McIntosh Company
17782 Cowan, Ste A
Irvine, CA 92614

949-757-5959
FAX 949-660-6172
E-Mail: boatshow@goboating.com
Home Page: www.lidoyachtexpo.com
Social Media: *Facebook*

Duncan McIntosh, President
Jeff Fleming, Associate Publisher

An upscale in-the-water show of yachts and big boats. More than 2,000 feet of floating dock.
Frequency: May
Founded in 1973

3678 Annual National Capital Boat Show
Royal Productions
PO Box 4197
Chester, VA 23831

804-256-6556
FAX 804-288-7132
E-Mail: info@royalshows.com
Home Page: www.royalshows.com

David Posner, President

Nearly 40 dealers form throughout Maryland and Virginia bring a wide range of boats to the National Capital Boat Show including saltware fishing boats, ski boats, runabouts, motor yachts, jet boats, jon boats, PWC, bass boats, inflatables, deck boats and pontoons.
20000 Attendees
Frequency: March

3679 Annual Spring Boat Show
Southern California Marine Association
1006 East Chapman Ave
Orange, CA 92866

714-633-7581
FAX 714-633-9498
E-Mail: scma@scma.com
Home Page: www.scma.com
Social Media: *Facebook, Twitter*

Richard Tressler, President
Renee Acencio, Vice President

You'll find an assortment of marine accessory booths featuring the latest and newest products filled with everything that floats, affordable family runabouts, ski boats, fishing boats, cruisers, pontoons, performance sportboats and personal watercraft.
Frequency: June
Founded in 1956

3680 Annual Spring New Products Show
Pacific Expositions c/o Tihati Productions
3615 Harding Ave
Suite 506
Honolulu, HI 96816

808-732-6037
FAX 808-732-6039
E-Mail: info@pacificexpos.com
Home Page: www.pacificexpos.com

Tara Chanel-Thompson, Director/General Manager

The newest and most exciting products on land and sea with 320 exhibits for trade professionals, buyers, and the general public.
17000 Attendees
Frequency: Annual, April
Founded in 1974

3681 Association of Marina Industries Annual Conference
Association of Marina Industries
50 Water Street
Warren, RI 02885

866-367-6622
FAX 401-247-0074
E-Mail: info@marinaassociation.org

Home Page: www.marinaassociation.org
Social Media: *Twitter, LinkedIn*

Jim Frye, CMM, Chairman/President
Gary Groenewold, Chairman
Brad Gross, Treasurer
Keith Boulais, Secretary
800+ Members
Frequency: May
Founded in 1986

3682 Atlanta Boat Show
National Marine Manufacturers Association
200 E Randolph Drive
Suite 1500
Chicago, IL 60601

954-441-3228
E-Mail: lberryman@nmma.org
Home Page: www.atlantaboatshow.com
Social Media: *Facebook, Twitter*

Larry Berryman, Show Manager
Scott Cohens, Relationship Manager
Sarah Ryser, PR Manager
Venus Berryman, Show Administrator
Debbie Harewood, Director, Shows
Administration

Showcases the latest in boating products and
marine technology. 225 exhibitors.
Frequency: January
Founded in 1961

**3683 Atlantic City In-Water Power Boat
Show**
In-Water Power Boat Show
1650 Market St
36th Floor
Philadelphia, PA 19103

215-732-8001
FAX 215-732-8266
E-Mail: info@acinwaterboatshow.com
Home Page: www.acinwaterboatshow.com
Social Media: *Facebook, Twitter*

Jerry Flaxman, Executive VP

This show provides space for over 700 boats on
land and in-water and over 200 booths in the
marine marketplace, including 2 tents and
walkways along the piers. Showcases the new
models for each coming year.
Frequency: September
Founded in 1983

**3684 Atlantic City International Power
Boat Show**
National Marine Manufacturers Association
37-18 Northern Blvd
Suite 311
Long Islang City, NY 11101

718-707-0719
FAX 888-649-7786
E-Mail: jpritko@nmma.org
Home Page: www.acboatshow.com
Social Media: *Facebook, Twitter*

Jon Pritko, Show Manager
Josh Rosales, Operations Manager

Showcases more than 700 all-new models of
motor and express yachts, sports fisherman,
cruisers and sport boats. Attracts boaters from
all of the East Coast.
50000 Attendees
Frequency: February

3685 Boat Show of Grand Rapids
Show Span
2121 Celebration Drive NE
Grand Rapids, MI 49525

616-472-2860
800-328-6550
FAX 616-447-2861

E-Mail: events@showspan.com
Home Page: www.showspan.com

John Loeks, President
Henri Boucher, Vice President
Mike Wilbraham, VP, Show Producer

Over 400 exhibits of power and sail boats, ac-
cessories, clocks, dockominiums and vacation
destinations. Held at the Grand Center in Grand
Rapids, Michigan.
Frequency: February
Founded in 1945

3686 Boat Show of New England
North America Expositions Company
33 Rutherford Avenue
Boston, MA 02129-3795

617-472-1442
800-225-1577
FAX 617-242-1817
E-Mail: joneal@nmma.org
Home Page: www.naexpo.com
Social Media: *Facebook, Twitter*

Joseph B O'Neal, Managing Partner
Bob McAlpine, Operations Manager

Over 600 boats on display, both power and sail-
boats ranging from dinghies to 45 foot yachts,
along with every conceivable accessory for
your new or present boat.
215M Attendees
Frequency: February

3687 Brokerage Yacht Show
Yachting Promotions
1115 NE 9th Avenue
Fort Lauderdale, FL 33304-2110

954-764-7642
800-940-7642
FAX 954-462-4140
E-Mail: info@showmanagement.com
Home Page: www.showmanagement.com
Social Media: *Facebook, Twitter*

Steve Sheer, Director Advertising
Kaye Pearson, President

The totally in-water presentation features over
500 new and pre-owned vessels.
Frequency: February
Founded in 1976
Mailing list available for rent

3688 Education Under Sail Forum
American Sail Training Association
29 Touro Street
PO Box 1459
Newport, RI 02840

401-846-1775
FAX 401-849-5400
E-Mail: asta@sailtraining.org
Home Page: www.tallships.sailtraining.org
Social Media: *Facebook, Twitter, Youtube*

Mike Rauworth, Chairman
Robert Rogers, Executive Director
300 Members
Frequency: Biennial
Founded in 1973

3689 IBEX Annual Conference
National Marine Manufacturers Association
231 S. LaSalle St
Suite 2050
Chicago, IL 60604

312-946-6200
FAX 312-946-0401
Home Page: www.nmma.org

Thomas Dammrich, President
Ben Wold, Executive Vice President
Craig Boskey, VP Finance/CFO

Exhibition features the products and processes
now available that will streamline your
boatbuilding business. See the advanced technologies ready for the upcoming model-year.

Featuring 800 OEMs and suppliers, the exhibit
halls offer you an opportunity to source and
compare every tool available to boatbuilders.
Frequency: November
Founded in 1979

3690 IFAI Expo Americas
Internationl Fabrics Association
International
1801 County Road B W
Roseville, MN 55113-4061

651-222-2508
800-225-4324
FAX 651-631-9334
E-Mail: generalinfo@ifai.com
Home Page: www.ifaiexpo.com
Social Media: *Facebook, Twitter, LinkedIn*

Mary J. Hennessy, Executive VP
JoAnne Farris, Marketing Director
Steven C. Rider, CFO, VP

A trade event in the Americas for the technical
textiles and specialty fabrics industry.
Frequency: Annual/October
Founded in 1912

**3691 International Boating and Water
Safety Summit**
National Safe Boating Council
PO Box 509
Bristow, VA 20136

703-361-4294
FAX 703-361-5294
E-Mail: office@safeboatingcouncil.org
Home Page: www.safeboatingcouncil.org
Social Media: *Facebook, Twitter, Youtube*

Joyce Shaw, Chair
Chris Edmonston, Vice Chair
Veronica Floyd, Past Chair
Frequency: April

**3692 International Conference of
Professional Yacht Brokers**
Yacht Brokers Association of America
105 Eastern Avenue
Suite 104
Annapolis, MD 21403

410-940-6345
FAX 410-263-1659
E-Mail: info@ybaa.com
Home Page: www.ybaa.com
Social Media: *Facebook, Twitter, LinkedIn*

Vincent J. Petrella, Executive Director
Rod Rowan, President
250 Members
Frequency: Annual
Founded in 1920

**3693 International Marina & Boatyard
Conference**
American Boat Builders and Repairers
Association
50 Water Street
Warren, RI 02885

401-247-0318
866-367-6622
FAX 401-247-0074
E-Mail: info@marinaassociation.org
Home Page: www.abbra.org
Social Media: *Twitter, LinkedIn*

Jim Frye, CMM, Chairman/President
Gary Groenewold, Chairman
Brad Gross, Treasurer
Keith Boulais, Secretary

The conference is designed to meet the growing demand among those delivering the boating
experience for an international forum for education and exposition.
800+ Members
Frequency: Annual
Founded in 1986

3694 International WorkBoat Show
The International WorkBoat Show
121 Fine Street
PO Box 7437
Portland, ME 04101-7437

207-842-5500
FAX 207-842-5503
E-Mail: customerservice@divcom.com
Home Page: www.workboatshow.com
Social Media: *Facebook, Twitter*

Chris Dimmerling, Sales Director
Bob Callahan, Show Director
Denielle Christensen, Marketing Manager

The largest commercial marine tradeshow in
North America, serving people in coastal, inland and offshore waters. It features 1000 exhibiting companies and is produced in
partnership with WorkBoat magazine.
Frequency: Annual
Founded in 1978

3695 MEGATEX
Industrial Fabrics Association International
1801 County Road B W
Roseville, MN 55113-4061

651-222-2508
800-225-4324
FAX 651-631-9334
E-Mail: generalinfo@ifai.com
Home Page: www.ifai.com
Social Media: *Facebook, Twitter, LinkedIn*

Mary J. Hennessy, Executive VP
JoAnne Farris, Marketing Director
Steven C. Rider, CFO, VP
Jeffrey W Kirk, President

Will be held at the Georgia World Congress
Center in Atlanta, Georgia, and is anchored by
the IFAI Expo and the ATMW-I shows. Together, the shows are expected to have more
than 1,000 exhibitors.
20000 Attendees
Founded in 1912

**3696 Marine Retailers Association of
America Annual Convention**
Marine Regtailers Association of America
PO Box 1127
Oak Park, IL 60304

708-763-9210
FAX 708-763-9236
E-Mail: mraa@mraa.com
Home Page: www.mraa.com

Matt Gruhn, President
Liz Walz, Director
Larry Innis, Legislative Affairs
Frequency: November

**3697 Mid-America Sail & Power Boat
Show**
Lake Erie Marine Trade Association
1269 Bassett Road
Cleveland, OH 44145-1116

440-899-5009
FAX 440-899-5013
E-Mail: lemta@aol.com
Home Page: www.clevelandboatshow.com
Social Media: *Facebook*

Norm Schultz, President Emeritus

Annual show of 325 manufacturers and suppliers of pleasure boats and related marine equipment, supplies and services.
140M Attendees
Frequency: January

3698 Midwest Boat Show
Lake Erie Marine Trade Association

1269 Bassett Road
Cleveland, OH 44145-1116

440-899-5009
FAX 440-899-5013

Norm Schultz, President
Annual show and exhibits of boats, equipment,
supplies and services.
23M Attendees
Frequency: August
Founded in 1980

3699 NMBA Annual Conference
National Marine Bankers Association
231 South LaSalle Street
Suite 2050
Chicago, IL 60604

312-812-2777
E-Mail: bmcardle@nmma.org
Home Page: www.marinebankers.org
Social Media: *LinkedIn*

Michael Bryant, President
Jayme Yates, Secretary
Jackie Forese, Director

NMBA hosts a three day member conference
where the latest trends relating to marine industry are discussed in detail.
180 Attendees
Frequency: September

**3700 National Association of State Boating
Law Administrators Annual
Conference**
National Association of State Boating Law
1500 Leestown Road
Suite 330
Lexington, KY 40511

859-225-9487
FAX 859-231-6403
E-Mail: info@nasbla.org
Home Page: www.nasbla.org/

Toby Velasquez, President
Herb Angell, VP
Kevin Bergeron, Treasurer

Conference provides information that focuses
on boating education, industry trends, workshops, and programs that discuss the history of
recreational boating safety programs including
an overview of state-by-state regulatory laws.
Frequency: September

3701 National Capital Boat Show
Royal Productions
PO Box 4197
Chester, VA 23831-8475

804-425-6556
FAX 804-425-6563
Home Page: www.royalshows.com

Serving the Washington DC and suburban Vir-
ginia/Maryland markets. 40 dealers.
Frequency: March

3702 National Dry Stack Conference
Association of Marina Industries
444 North Capitol Street NW
Suite 645
Washington, DC 20001

202-379-9768
FAX 202-628-8679
E-Mail: info@imimarina.org
Home Page: www.imimarina.org

Gregg Kenney, Chairman
Alex Laidlaw, Vice Chairman
Maureen Healey, Executive Director
Cris McSparen, Treasurer
Brooke Fishel, Manager Communications

The Dry Stack is a three-day hybrid school
which combines an educational program along

with networking among leading operations, developers and vendors.
Frequency: October

**3703 National Marine Bankers Association
Annual Conference**
National Marine Bankers Association
231 South LaSalle Street
Suite 2050
Chicago, IL 60604

312-812-2777
E-Mail: bmcardle@nmma.org
Home Page: www.marinebankers.org
Social Media: *LinkedIn*

Michael Bryant, President
Jayme Yates, Secretary
Jackie Forese, Director

A three-day member conference where the latest trends issues relating to the marine industry
are discussed in detail.
Frequency: September

3704 North American Sail & Power Show
Lake Erie Marine Trade Association
1269 Bassett Road
Cleveland, OH 44145-1116

440-899-5009
FAX 440-899-5013
E-Mail: lemta@aol.com

Norm Schultz, President

Annual show and exhibits of marine equipment, supplies and services.
31M Attendees
Frequency: September

3705 Portland Boat Show
O'Loughlin Trade Shows
3600 SW Multnomah Boulevard
PO Box 80750
Portland, OR 97219-1750

503-246-8291
FAX 503-246-1066
E-Mail: otssport@earthlink.net
Home Page: www.oloughlintradeshows.com

Peter O'Loughlin, Show Manager
Robert O'Loughlin Sr, President

Offers hundreds of makes and models, accessories and plenty of expert advice through seminars and hands on demonstrations.
Frequency: January

**3706 Professional Boatbuilder:
International Boatbuilders Expo and
Conference**
WoodenBoat Publications
86 Great Cove Drive
PO Box 78
Brooklin, ME 04616

207-359-4651
FAX 207-359-8920
E-Mail: info@bibexshow.com
Home Page: www.ibexshow.com

Carl Cramer, Publisher
Anne Dunbar, Show Director
Joanne Miller, Registration Manager

Over 450 booths offering products for boat
builders, designers, repairers, surveyors, and
boatyard/marina operators.
2.5M Attendees
Frequency: November
Founded in 1989

3707 SCA Spring Safety Seminar
Shipbuilders Council of America
655 Fifteenth St NW
Suite 225
Washington, DC 20005

202-347-5462
FAX 202-347-5464
E-Mail: preever@balljanik.com

Home Page: www.shipbuilders.org
Social Media: *Facebook*

Matt Paxton, President

Represents the U.S. shipyard industry. SCA members build, repair and service America's fleet of commercial vessels.
73 Members
Frequency: March
Founded in 1920

3708 Sail America Industry Conference
Sail America
50 Water St.
Warren, RI 02885

401-289-2540
FAX 401-247-0074
Home Page: www.sailamerica.com/events/saic

Scot West, President

A two-day event for sailing industry professionals featuring seminars, workshops and networking events.
Frequency: Annual

3709 Seattle Boat Show
Northwest Marine Trade Association
1900 North Northlake Way
Suite 233
Seattle, WA 98103

206-634-0911
FAX 206-632-0078
E-Mail: info@seattleboatshow.com
Home Page: www.nmta.net
Social Media: *Facebook, Twitter, LinkedIn*

George Harris, President
John Thorburn, VP

The ten-day event features more than 1,000 recreational watercraft, seminars and the latest innovations in accessories at Qwest Field Event Center, plus 200 world-class boats in their natural habitat on South Lake Union.
Frequency: January-February
Founded in 1947

3710 St. Petersburg Boat Show
Show Management
1115 NE 9th Avenue
Fort Lauderdale, FL 33304

954-764-7642
800-940-7642
FAX 954-462-4140
E-Mail: info@showmanagement.com
Home Page: www.showmanagement.com
Social Media: *Facebook, Twitter*

Kaye Pearson, Owner/Promoter
Elise Lipoff, Director Public Relations
Steve Sheer, Director Advertising

More than 600 boats of all types and sizes, electronics, engines and a vast selection of marine accessories will be displayed on land and in water.
10000 Attendees
Frequency: December
Founded in 1977
Mailing list available for rent

3711 Suncoast Boat Show
Show Management
1115 NE 9th Avenue
Fort Lauderdale, FL 33304

954-764-7642
800-940-7642
FAX 954-462-4140
E-Mail: info@showmanagement.com
Home Page: www.showmanagement.com
Social Media: *Facebook, Twitter*

Kaye Pearson, Owner/Promoter
Elise Lipoff, Director Public Relations
Steve Sheer, Director Advertising
Chuck Bolt, Director Sales

Annual show and exhibits of boats and marine equipment, supplies and services.
30000 Attendees
Frequency: April
Founded in 1982
Mailing list available for rent

3712 U.S. Rowing Association Annual Convention
United States Rowing Association
2 Wall Street
Princeton, NJ 08540

609-751-0700
800-314-4769
FAX 609-924-1578
E-Mail: members@usrowing.org
Home Page: www.usrowing.org
Social Media: *Facebook, Twitter, Youtube*

Elizabeth Webb, Events Manager

Coaching programs and information, referee clinics, speakers, and competitions.
Frequency: December

3713 US Sailboat Show
Annapolis Boatshows
100 Severn Drive
PO Box 4997
Annapolis, MD 21401-4997

410-268-8828
FAX 410-280-3903

Dee Newman, Show Manager
Jim Barthold, General Manager

In-water sailboat show offering over 350 booths.
150M Attendees
Frequency: October

Directories & Databases

3714 American Boat and Yacht Council
613 Third Street
Suite 10
Annapolis, MD 21403

410-990-4466
FAX 410-956-2737
E-Mail: info@abycinc.org
Home Page: www.abycinc.org

George Bellwoar, Chair
Jack Horner, Vice Chair
Steven Herb, Treasurer

Marine suppliers, engineers and underwriters, as well as architects and designers for the marine industry are listed.
105 Pages
Frequency: Biennial
Founded in 1954

3715 Boater's Source Directory
Boat US Foundation
880 S Pickett St
Alexandria, VA 22304-4606

703-461-8952
800-336-2628
FAX 703-461-2855
Home Page: www.boatus.com/foundation
Social Media: *Facebook, Twitter, LinkedIn, Youtube*

Richard Schwartz, President

Pocket guide for boaters containing safety and regulatory information and resources.
Cost: $5.00
Frequency: Paperback, SemiAnnual
Founded in 1966

3716 Boating Industry: Marine Buyers' Guide Issue
Ehlert Publishing Group

6420 Sycamore Ln N
Suite 100
Maple Grove, MN 55369-6014

763-383-4400
800-848-6247
FAX 763-383-4499
E-Mail: dvoll@ehlertpublishing.com
Home Page: www.bowhuntingworld.com
Social Media: *Facebook, Twitter, Youtube*

Steven Hedlund, President
Liz Walz, Senior Editor
Jon Mohrm, Associate Editor
Tammy Galvin, Group Publisher

A who's who directory of services and supplies for the industry.
Cost: $29.95
Frequency: Annual
Circulation: 30,000
Mailing list available for rent

3717 Confined Space Entry Video and Manual
Shipbuilders Council of America
655 Fifteenth St NW
Suite 225
Washington, DC 20004-1166

202-347-5462
FAX 202-347-5464
E-Mail: preever@balljanik.com
Home Page: www.shipbuilders.org
Social Media: *Facebook*

Matt Paxton, President

This manual, in combination with the video program, covers some of the more common hazards associated with confined space entry. It also provides you with the information you will need to prevent accidents and injuries.
Cost: $ 50.00
73 Members
Founded in 1920

3718 Consumer Protection Database
Boat Owners Association of the US
800 South Pickett Street
Alexandria, VA 22304

703-412-2770
FAX 703-461-2847
Home Page: www.boatus.com
Social Media: *Facebook, Twitter, LinkedIn, Youtube*

Richard Schwartz, Chairman/Founder
Jim Ellis, President/CEO

Contains consumer complaints and safety information reported by boat owners, the US Coast Guard, manufacturers, marine surveyors and marine technicians.
Founded in 1966

3719 ISSPA Sports and Vacation Show Directory and Calendar
International Sport Show Producers Association
PO Box 480084
Denver, CO 80248-0084

303-892-6800
800-457-2434
FAX 303-892-6322
E-Mail: dseymour@iei-expos.com
Home Page: www.sportshow.org

Dianne Seymour, Executive Secretary

Products of outdoor recreation shows which include boating, travel, RV, hunting, and fishing.
Frequency: Annual

3720 Marine Products Directory
Underwriters Laboratories

12 Laboratory Drive
PO Box 13995
Research Triangle Park, NC 27709-3995

919-549-1400
FAX 919-547-6363
E-Mail: paul.r.ouellette@us.ul.com
Home Page: www.ul.com/marine
Social Media: *Facebook, Twitter, Youtube*

Keith E. Williams, President
Sanjeev Jesudas, President

UL has been testing and certifying products for marine use since 1969. With a UL Marine Mark on your product, you can show consumers, retailers, surveyors, insurers, government agencies, regulatory and ABTC, NFPA and UL Safety Standards.
Cost: $10.00
176 Pages
Frequency: Annual

3721 Membership Directory: Boating Industry Administration
National Association of State Boating Laws
1500 Leestown Road
Suite 300
Lexington, KY 40511-2047

859-225-9487
FAX 859-231-6403
E-Mail: info@nasbla.org
Home Page: www.nasbla.org

Toby Velasquez, President
Herb Angell, VP
Kevin Bergerson, Treasurer

Published by the National Association of State Boating Law Administration.

3722 NMRA Membership Directory
National Marine Representative Association
1333 Delany Road #500
PO Box 360
Gurnee, IL 60031

847-662-3167
FAX 847-336-7126
E-Mail: info@nmraonline.org
Home Page: www.nmraonline.org

Norm McLeod, Past President
Tim Luehmann, President
Jeff Gueterman, VP
Rick Silverlake, Treasurer
Chris Kelly, Secretary

Provides a complete listing of all NMRA sales representatives. Includes contact information for their main and associate offices, the territories they cover, the markets they represent, and the list of companies they represent.
Cost: $10.00

3723 National Marine Manufacturers Association Membership List
231 S. LaSalle St
Suite 2050
Chicago, IL 60601-6539

312-946-6200
FAX 312-946-0388
Home Page: www.nmma.org

Thomas Dammrich, President
Ben Wold, Executive Vice President
Craig Boskey, VP Finance/CFO

Directory of services and supplies to the industry.
160 Pages
Frequency: Quadrennial

3724 Pacific Boating Almanac
ProStar Publications
3416 Wesley Street
Suite B
Culver City, CA 90232-2901

310-280-1010
800-481-6277

FAX 310-280-1025
E-Mail: editor@prostarpublications.com
Home Page: www.prostarpublications.com

Peter Griffes, Owner

Consists of three regional volumes. This information includes the latest Coast Pilot, Tide & Current Tables, First Aid, Electronics, Navigation and Safety, Weather, and Yacht Club Burgees.
Cost: $26.95
Frequency: Annual
Circulation: 20,000
ISBN: 1-577857-05-4
Mailing list available for rent: 19,000 names
Printed in on matte stock

3725 Portbook of Marine Services
Portbook Publications
PO Box 462
Belfast, ME 04915

207-338-1619
FAX 207-338-6025
E-Mail: info@portbook.net
Home Page: www.portbook.net

Sandra Squire, Publisher

Marinas, yacht clubs, boatyards, dealers, marine supply stores, repair facilities, and other services for yachtsmen. For Annapolis, Maryland and Newport/Narragansett Bay, Rhode Island. Distributed free through advertisers, or four dollars by mail.
Cost: $40.00
100 Pages
Frequency: Annual
Circulation: 35M
Founded in 1982
Printed in on matte stock

3726 Register of American Yacht Clubs
Yachting Club of America
PO Box 1040
Marco Island, FL 34146-1040

239-642-4448
FAX 239-642-5284
E-Mail: info@ycaol.com
Home Page: www.ycaol.com

A reciprocity guide for yacht and sailing clubs in the United States, Hawaii, Alaska, and the Virgin Islands registered with the Yachting Club of America. 800 yacht clubs registered with the Yachting Club of America.
Cost: $35.00
200 Pages
Frequency: Softbound
Founded in 1963
Printed in on glossy stock

3727 Sail Tall Ships: Directory of Sail Training and Adventure at Sea
American Sail Training Association
240 Thames Street
PO Box 1459
Newport, RI 02840

401-846-1775
FAX 401-849-5400
E-Mail: asta@sailtraining.org
Home Page: www.ycaol.com

Lori Aguiar, Editor
Peter A Mello, Executive Director

Offers information on sail training ships, shoreside sail training programs and ships under construction or restoration.
Cost: $50.00
400 Pages
Frequency: Annual
Circulation: 15,000
ISBN: 0-963648-36-5
Founded in 1963

3728 Seafarers
Admiralty Insurance

6353 Argyle Forest Boulevard
Jacksonville, FL 32244

904-777-0042
800-456-8936
FAX 904-777-0279
Home Page: www.seafarers.com

Searchable database of boating associations, yacht clubs, boating clubs and source of nautical information and links.

3729 Ship Agents, Owners, Operators
Maritime Association of the Port of New York
17 Battery Place
Suite 913
New York, NY 10004-1194

212-747-1284
FAX 212-635-9498
E-Mail: themaritimeassoc@erols.com
Home Page: www.nymaritime.org

Edward Morgan, President
Brian McAllister, VP
Edward J Kelly, Executive Director

Directory of Atlantic, Gulf and West Coasts listing every steamship, owner, and operator in the major ports with lines that they represent and the countries that they serve.
Cost: $50.00
Frequency: Annual
Circulation: 2,000
Mailing list available for rent

3730 Shipyard Ergonomics Video and Workbook CD
Shipbuilders Council of America
655 Fifteenth St NW
Suite 225
Washington, DC 20004-1166

202-347-5462
FAX 202-347-5464
E-Mail: awalker@vesselalliance.com
Home Page: www.shipbuilders.org
Social Media: *Facebook*

Matt Paxton, President

Designed to instruct shipyard employees, supervisors and trainers in identifying ergonomic risks and providing tools to allow the development of creative solutions to reduce the hazards.
Cost: $75.00
73 Members
Founded in 1920

Industry Web Sites

3731 http://gold.greyhouse.com
G.O.L.D Grey House OnLine Databases

Grey House Publishing's online database platform, GOLD, offers Quick Search, Keyword Search and Expert Search, for most business sectors including boating manufacture and service markets. GOLD is quick and easy - whether you're a novice searcher or an experienced database user. All of Grey House's directory products are available for subscription on the GOLD platform.

3732 www.acbs.org
Antique & Classic Boat Society

Dedicated to the preservation and enjoyment of historic, antique and classic boats. ACBS brings people with this common interest together to share fellowship, information, experiences and ideas.

3733 www.americanboating.org
American Boating Association

ABA's mission is to promote boating safety, affordability, growth, and a clean environment. It provides exclusive services and benefits for boaters and boating enthusiasts.

3734 www.apba-racing.com
American Power Boat Association
The sole authority for UIM approved powerboat racing ine United States.

3735 www.by-the-sea.com
By the Sea
Everything for the boat professional and enthusiast alike. News of sales and events, message boards and contact information.

3736 www.greyhouse.com
Grey House Publishing
Authoritative reference directories for most business segments incluidng boat manufacturing and service markets. Users can search the online databases with varied search criteria allowing for custom searches by product category, geographic area, sales volume, keyword, subject and more. Full Grey House catalog and online ordering also available.

3737 www.ifai.com
Industrial Fabrics Association International
The only trade association in the world representing the entire specialty fabrics/technical textiles industry. Member products range from fiber and fabric suppliers to manufacturers of end products, equipment and hardware.

3738 www.imimarina.org
International Marina Institute
International Marina Institute's educational resources include specialized training courses and seminars on fundamental and advanced levels, workshops, conferences the advanced marina management school and the Certified Marina Manager program along with a wide selection of publications.

3739 www.lemta.com
Lake Erie Marine Trade Association
Trade association of more than 100 recreational boat dealers, marina operators and pleasure boat service companies located across northern Ohio; also plays the key role in looking out for the consumer.

3740 www.marinebankers.org
National Marine Bankers Association
The purpose of the NMBA is to educate prospective lenders in marine financing procedures, create new lenders to help finance the sales of the manufacturers products, and to create an information exchange for its members.

3741 www.mraa.com
Marine Retailers Association of America
Manufacturers and dealers of boats, equipment, supplies and services.

3742 www.nauticalworld.com
Dedicated to bringing all related web sites within easy access to watersports enthusiasts, including advertiser's information. Offers sections on marine electronics and hardware, sailing, boats, dock supplies, fishing accessories, diving accessories, industry news, watersports, weather forecasting and more.

3743 www.nauticexpo.com
NauticExpo
This Virtual Boat Show is accessible in five languages and presents all the boats and nautical equipment available on the international market. It offers an accurate and up-to-date source of information to yachtsmen and professionals.

3744 www.nmdaonline.com
National Marine Distributors Association
Engages in exclusively nonprofit activities designed to promote the common business interests and improve the business conditions of wholesale distributors of marine accessories and of the marine industry in general.

3745 www.nmraonline.org
National Marine Representatives Association
Members are independent boat and marine accessory sales representatives national association.

3746 www.nmta.net
Northwest Marine Trade Association
Oldest and largest regional boating trade organization in the nation representing the interests of approximately 800 member companies. Each year it produces the Seattle Boat Show at the Stadium Exhibition Center and the Seattle Boat Show at Shilshole Bay Marina on behalf of its members.

3747 www.propellerclubhq.com
Propeller Club of the United States
Grassroots, nonprofit organization, whose membership resides throughout the United States and the world. It is dedicated to the enhancement and well-being of all interests of the maritime community on a national and international basis.

3748 www.pwia.org
Personal Watercraft Industry Association
Ensuring that personal watercraft and personal watercraft users are treated fairly when local, state, and federal government officials consider boating regulations. PWIA supports and actively advocates for reasonable regulations, strong enforcement of boating and navigation laws, and mandatory boating safety education for all personal watercraft operators.

3749 www.rbbi.com
Polson Enterprises
Offering research tools and papers on new product development and new product development services for boat builders, plus experience in the fields of marine drives, engine, marine vessels, propellar guards, boating safety. Industry and regulation updates are also available on this site.

3750 www.tsca.com
Traditional Small Craft Association
Nonprofit, tax-exempt educational organization which works to preserve and continue the living traditions, skills, lore and legends surrounding working and pleasure watercraft including construction and use of boats.

3751 www.ussailing.org
United States Sailing Association
Encourages participation and promotes excellence in sailing and racing in the US.

Associations

3752 Academy of Canadian Cinema & Television
49 Ontario Street
Suite 501
Toronto, ON M5A 2V1

416-366-2227
800-644-5194
FAX 416-366-8454
E-Mail: academie@acct.ca
Home Page: www.academy.ca
Social Media: *Facebook, Twitter, LinkedIn, Flickr, YouTube*

Martin Katz, Chair
Robin Mirsky, Vice Chair
Anita McOuat, Treasurer
Julie Bristow, President & CEO
Scott Henderson, Vice President

A national non-profit, professional association dedicated to the promotion, recognition, and celebration of exceptional achievements in Candian film, television, and digital media.
Founded in 1949

3753 Academy of Television Arts and Science
5200 Lankershim Blvd
North Hollywood, CA 91601

818-754-2800
FAX 818-761-2827
E-Mail: lewis.kay@pmkbnc.com
Home Page: www.emmys.com
Social Media: *Facebook, Twitter, YouTube, Instagram, Pinterest*

Robert Cook, Chairman
David Eun, Vice Chair
Thomas W Sarnoff, Chair Emeritus
Margaret Loesch, Secretary
Marc Graboff, Treasurer

Nonprofit corporation devoted to the advancement of telecommunications arts and sciences and to fostering creative leadership in the telecommunications industry. In addition to recognizing outstanding programming and individual achievements for Primetime and Los Angeles area programming, ATAS sponsors meetings, conferences and activities for collaboration on a variety of topics involving traditional broadcast interests, new media and emerging digital technology.
12000 Members
Founded in 1959

3754 Alaska Broadcasters Association
700 W 41st Street
Suite 102
Anchorage, AK 99503

907-258-2424
FAX 907-258-2414
E-Mail: akba@gci.net
Home Page: www.alaskabroadcaster.org
Social Media: *Facebook*

Matt Wilson, President
Charlie Ellis, VP
Ric Schimdt, Secretary/Treasurer
Dick Olson, VP, Sales Manager
Darlene Simono, Executive Director

To provide assistance, which enables members to serve their communities of license through education, representation and advocacy.
Founded in 1964

3755 Alliance for Community Media
4248 Park Glen Road
Minneapolis, MN 55416

952-928-4643
FAX 202-393-2653
E-Mail: info@allcommunitymedia.org

Home Page: www.alliancecm.org
Social Media: *Facebook, Twitter, LinkedIn, Youtube, Flickr*

Mary Van Sickle, Chair
Jon Funfar, Chair Elect
Alan Bushong, Treasurer
Keri Stokstad, Secretary
Mike Wassenaar, President

Participants include cable access television and community programmers. Individual membership dues are $70.00, organization $350.00.
1000 Members
Founded in 1976
Mailing list available for rent: 1000 names at $200 per M

3756 Alliance for Women in Media
1250 24th St NW
Suite 300
Washington, DC 20037

202-750-3664
FAX 703-506-3266
E-Mail: info@allwomeninmedia.org
Home Page: www.allwomeninmedia.org
Social Media: *Facebook, Twitter, LinkedIn, Youtube*

Kristen Welch, Chair
Sarah Foss, Chair Elect
Keisha Sutton-James, Treasurer
Christine Travaglini, Treasurer Elect
Robin Alston, Director

Leverages the promise, passion, and power of women in all forms of media carrying forth with its mission by educating, advocating, and acting as a resource to its members and the industry at large via inspired thought leadership that illuminates areas of social need.
Founded in 1951

3757 Alliance of Motion Picture and Television Producers
15301 Ventura Blvd
Building E
Sherman Oaks, CA 91403

818-995-3600
FAX 818-382-1793
Home Page: www.amptp.org

Nick Counter, President

Trade association with respect to labor issues in the motion picture and television industry. Negotiate industry wide collective bargaining agreements that cover actors, craftspersons, directors, musicians, technicians and writers.
350 Members
Founded in 1982

3758 American Auto Racing Writers and Broadcasters Association
922 North Pass Avenue
Burbank, CA 91505-2703

818-842-7005
FAX 818-842-7020
E-Mail: dusty@aarwba.org
Home Page: www.aarwba.org
Social Media: *Facebook*

Norma Brandel, President/Executive Director
Kathy Seymour, VP
Rhonda Williams, Treasurer
Patrick Reynolds, Secretary
Ross R Olney, Past President

The American Auto Racing Writers & Broadcasters Association is the oldest and largest organization devoted to auto racing coverage.
400 Members
Founded in 1955

3759 American Center for Children and Media
5400 North St Louis Avenue
Chicago, IL 60625

703-509-5510
FAX 773-509-5303
E-Mail: info@centerforchildrenandmedia.org
Home Page:
www.centerforhildrenandmedia.org

David Kleeman, President
James Fellows, President Emeritus

Mission is to support a vibrant children's media industry by convening key constituencies to develop, implement and promote policies and practices that respect young people's well being, and are sustainable.
Founded in 1985

3760 American Disc Jockey Association
20118 N 67th Avenue
Suite 300-605
Glendale, CA 85308

888-723-5776
FAX 866-310-4676
E-Mail: office@adja.org
Home Page: www.adja.org
Social Media: *Facebook, Twitter, Youtube*

Rob Snyder, Director

An association of professional mobile entertainers. Encourages success for its members through continuous education, camaraderie, and networking. The primary goal is to educate Disc Jockeys so that each member acts ethically and responsibly.

3761 American Federation of Television and Radio Artists
5757 Wilshire Blvd
7th Floor
Los Angeles, CA 90036

323-954-1600
855-724-2387
FAX 212-532-2242
E-Mail: info@aftra.com
Home Page: www.aftra.com
Social Media: *Facebook, Twitter, Youtube, RSS*

David White, Executive Director
Mathis Dunn, Associate Executive Director
Duncan Crabtree-Ireland, CAO/General Counsel
Arianna Ozzanto, CFO
Daniel Inukai, Chief Information Officer

Represents its members in four major areas: news and broadcasting; entertainment programing; the recording business; and commercials and non-broadcast, industrial, educational media.
80000 Members
Founded in 1952

3762 American Private Radio Association (APRA)
PO Box 4221
Scottsdale, AZ 85261-4221

480-661-5000

Association members are from private radio stations.

3763 American Public Media
480 Cedar St.
St. Paul, MN 55101

800-562-8440
Home Page: www.americanpublicmedia.org

Jon McTaggart, President & CEO
Sylvia Strobel, SVP & General Counsel
David Kansas, SVP & COO
Morris Goodwin, SVP & CFO

Leading producer and distributor of public radio programming in the Upper Midwest, Cali-

fornia and Florida, reaching 19 million listeners weekly.
Founded in 1967

3764 American Sportscasters Association
225 Broadway
Suite 2030
New York, NY 10007

212-227-8080
FAX 212-571-0556
E-Mail: lschwa8918@aol.com
Home Page:
www.americansportscastersonline.com

Louis O Schwartz, President/Founder
Dick Enberg, Chairman
Jim Nantz, Board of Directors
Jon Miller, Board of Directors
Bill Walton, Board of Directors

National Association of Sportscasters, radio, television and cable covering the US, Puerto Rico and Canada. Very active web site. Offers seminars, compiles statistics and operates a placement service, maintains a Hall of Fame and biographical archives and library.
500 Members
Founded in 1980

3765 American Sportscasters Association, Inc.
225 Broadway
Suite 2030
New York, NY 10007-3742

212-227-8080
FAX 212-571-0556
E-Mail: lschwa8918@aol.com
Home Page:
www.americansportscastersonline.com

Louis O Schwartz, President/Founder
Dick Enberg, Chairman
Jim Nantz, Board of Directors
Jon Miller, Board of Directors
Bill Walton, Board of Directors

National Association of Sportscasters, radio, television and cable covering the US, Puerto Rico and Canada. Very active web site. Offers seminars, compiles statistics and operates a placement service, maintains a Hall of Fame and biographical archives and library.
500 Members
Founded in 1980

3766 Associated Press Broadcasters
1825 K Street NW
Suite 800
Washington, DC 20006-1202

212-621-1500
FAX 202-736-1107
E-Mail: info@ap.org
Home Page: www.apbroadcast.com
Social Media: *Facebook, Twitter, LinkedIn, Youtube*

Mary E Junck, Chairman
Gary Pruitt, President & CEO
Kathleen Carroll, Senior VP/Executive Editor
Jessica Bruce, VP/Director, Human Resource
Ken Dale, CFO/Senior VP

Seeks to advance journalism through radio and television, and cooperates with the AP to promote accurate and impartial news.
5.9m Members
Founded in 1846

3767 Association for Maximum Service Television
4100 Wisconsin Avenue NW
PO Box 9897
Washington, DC 20036-2224

202-966-1956
FAX 202-966-9617

E-Mail: mstv@mstv.org
Home Page: www.mstv.org

David Donovan, President

Assures the maintenance of an effective nationwide system of free television and seeks to meet present and future needs of the VHF and UHF system.
400+ Members
Founded in 1956

3768 Association of Independent Commercial Producers
3 W 18th St
5th Floor
New York, NY 10011

212-929-3000
FAX 212-929-3359
E-Mail: mattm@aicp.com
Home Page: www.aicp.com
Social Media: *Facebook, Twitter, LinkedIn, Youtube, Flickr, RSS*

Matt Miller, President & CEO
Jerry Solomon, Chairman
Ralph Laucella, Vice Chairman
Mark Andrew, Treasurer
Robert L Sacks, Secretary

The national trade association of television commercial producers who account for in excess of 80% of the commercial production done in the United States annually.
500 Members
Founded in 1972

3769 Association of Local Television Stations
1320 19th Street NW
Washington, DC 20036

202-887-1970
Home Page: www.altv.com

3770 Association of Public Television Stations
2100 Crystal Drive
Suite 700
Arlington, VA 22202

202-654-4200
FAX 202-654-4236
Home Page: www.apts.org
Social Media: *Facebook, Twitter*

Patrick Butler, President & CEO
Lonna Thompson, Executive VP/COO & General Counsel
Jennifer Kieley, VP, Government Relations
Stacey Karp, VP, Communications
Emil Mara, VP, Finance & Administration

Nonprofit membership organization that supports the continued growth and development of a strong and financially sound noncommercial television service for the American public. Provides advocacy for public television interests at the national level, as well as consistent leadership and information in marshaling grassroots and congressional support for its members: the nation's public television stations.
153 Members
Founded in 1979

3771 Audio Engineering Society
551 Fifth Avenue
Room 1225
New York, NY 10176

212-661-8528
FAX 212-682-0477
E-Mail: HQ@aes.org
Home Page: www.aes.org
Social Media: *Facebook, Twitter, LinkedIn, Youtube, Google+, RSS*

Roger Furness, Executive Director
Andres Mayo, President

Ron Streicher, Secretary
Garry Margolis, Treasurer
John Krivit, Past President

Professional society devoted to audio technology. Membership includes leading engineers, scientists and other authorities in the field. Serves its members, the industry and the public by stimulating and facilitating advances in the constantly changing field of audio.
Founded in 1948

3772 Broadcast Designers' Association International
145 W 45th Street
Room 1100
New York, NY 10036-4008

212-376-6222
FAX 212-376-6202

Association for manufacturers or suppliers of broadcast design equipment, supplies and services.

3773 Broadcast Education Association
1771 N St NW
Washington, DC 20036-2891

202-429-5355
888-380-7222
FAX 202-609-9940
E-Mail: help@beaweb.org
Home Page: www.beaweb.org
Social Media: *Facebook, Twitter, LinkedIn*

Heather Birks, Executive Director
J D Boyle, Director, Sales & Marketing
Traci Bailey, Manager, Business Operations
John Allen Hendricks, President
Michael Bruce, Secretary/Treasurer

Serves as a higher education association of professors and industry professionals who teach college students worldwide and prepares them to go into the broadcasting and related emerging technologies professions upon graduation from college.
1400 Members
Founded in 1955
Mailing list available for rent: 1300 names at $100 per M

3774 Broadcast Pioneers
7 World Trade Center
250 Greenwich Street
New York, NY 10007-0030

212-220-3000
FAX 212-246-2163
Home Page: www.bmi.com
Social Media: *Facebook, Twitter, YouTube, Pinterest, Google+*

Michael O'Neill, President & CEO
Bruce A Esworthy, Senior Vice President
Phillip R Graham, Senior Vice President
Catherine Brewton, Vice President
Mark Mason, Executive Director

Honors radio or television stations for excellence in art and community service. Maintains library documents on television broadcasting history.
1.4M Members
Founded in 1942

3775 Broadcasters Foundation of America
125 West 55th Street
4th Floor
New York, NY 10019-5366

212-373-8250
FAX 212-373-8254
E-Mail: info@thebfoa.org
Home Page: www.broadcastersfoundation.org

George G Beasley, Chairman & CEO
Richard A Foreman, President & CEO
James B Thompson, President
Peter Doyle, VP
Jeff Haley, VP

Provides financial assistance to radio and television broadcasters who are in financial need.

3776 Cable & Telecommunications Association for Marketing
120 Waterfront Street
Suite 200
National Harbor, MD 20745

301-485-8900
FAX 301-560-4964
E-Mail: info@ctam.com
Home Page: www.ctam.com
Social Media: *Facebook, Twitter, LinkedIn, Youtube*

Matrk Greatrex, Chair
Jamia Bigalow, Vice Chair
Jonathan Hargis, Secretary
Antoinette Allen, Director of Meetings
Dana Fragnoli-Piteo, Director of Marketing

Dedicated to the discipline and development of consumer marketing excellence in cable television, news media and telecommunications services. Members have the advantage of progressive research, insightful publications and forward thinking conferences all designed to help you and your company gain a competitive edge.
5500 Members
Founded in 1976

3777 Canadian Association of Broadcast Consultants
130 Cree Crescent
Winnepeg, MB R3J 3W1

204-889-9202
FAX 204-831-6650
E-Mail: jsadoun@yrh.com
Home Page: www.cabc-accr.ca

Joseph Sadoun, Ing P Eng, President
Kerry Pelser, Secretary/Treasurer

Prepares technical briefs, coverage studies and frequencies.

3778 Canadian Association of Broadcasters
770-45 O'Connor St
Ottawa, ON K1P 1A4

613-233-4035
FAX 613-233-6961
E-Mail: sbissonette@cab-acr.ca
Home Page: www.cab-acr.ca

Kevin Goldstein, Chairman
Susan Wheeler, Vice Chair
Sylvie Courtemanche, Secretary
Glenda Spenrath, Treasurer
Paul Cowling, VP, Regulatory Affairs

Serves as the eyes and ears of the private broadcasting community to advocate and lobby on its behalf and to act as a cebtral point on matters of joint interest.

3779 Canadian Association of Ethnic Broadcasters (Radio)
622 College Street
Toronto, ON M6G 1B6

416-531-9991
FAX 416-531-5274
E-Mail: info@chinradio.com
Home Page: www.chinradio.com
Social Media: *Facebook, Twitter*

Johnny Lombardi, Founder, President

Pioneer in multicultural radio broadcasting and has lead the way for similar briadcast operations to be established.

3780 Caribbean Broadcasting Union
Suite 1B, Building 6A
Harbor Industrial Estate
St Michael, BB 11145

246-430-1006
FAX 242-228-9524

E-Mail: patrick.cozier@caribsurf.com
Home Page: www.caribunion.com

Patrick Cozier, President

Stimulates the flow of broadcast material among the radio and television systems in the Caribbean region.
Founded in 1970
Mailing list available for rent

3781 Coalition Opposing Signal Theft
25 Massachusetts Ave NW
Suite 100
Washington, DC 20001

202-222-2300
E-Mail: webmaster@ncta.com
Home Page: www.ncta.com
Social Media: *Facebook, Twitter, LinkedIn*

Michael Powell, President & CEO
James M Assey, Executive VP
K Dane Snowden, Chief of Staff
Bruce Carnes, Senior VP, Finance & Administration
William Check, Senior VP, Science & Technology

Acts as a clearinghouse of information regarding cable signal theft.

3782 Community Antenna Television Association
PO Box 1005
Fairfax, VA 22030-1005

202-775-3550

An association of over 3,000 cable television systems.
3M Members

3783 Content Delivery & Security Association
39 N Bayles Ave
Port Washington, NY 11050

516-767-6720
FAX 516-883-5793
E-Mail: info@CDSAonline.org
Home Page: www.cdsaonline.org

Richard Atkinson, Chairman
Paul W Scott, VP
Tom Moran, Secretary/Treasurer
Joel Bigley, Executive VP

International trade association dealing with every facet of recording, media and related industries. Membership includes raw material providers, manufacturers, replicators, duplicators, packagers, and copyright holders.

3784 Corporation for Public Broadcasting
401 9th St NW
Washington, DC 20004-2129

202-879-9600
800-272-2190
FAX 202-879-9700
E-Mail: oigemail@cpb.org
Home Page: www.cpb.org
Social Media: *Facebook, Twitter*

Elizabeth Sembler, Chair
Vincent Curren, EVP & COO
William P Tayman Jr., CFO/Treasurer
Westwood Smithers Jr., Senior VP/General Counsel
Michael Levy, Executive VP

Facilitate the development of, and ensure universal access to, non-commercial high-quality programming and telecommunications services. It does this in conjunction with non-commercial educational telecommunications licensees across the country.
Founded in 1967

3785 Country Radio Broadcasters
1009 16th Ave South
Nashville, TN 37212

615-327-4487
FAX 615-329-4492
E-Mail: info@crb.org
Home Page: www.countryradioseminar.com
Social Media: *Facebook, Twitter*

Bill Mayne, Executive Director
Chasity Crouch, Business Manager
Carole Bowem, Secretary
R J Curtis, VP
Kristen England, Creative Director

Broadcasting forum.
Founded in 1969

3786 Educational Broadcasting Association
825 Eighth Ave
New York, NY 10019

212-560-1313
FAX 212-560-1314
E-Mail: programming@thirteen.org
Home Page: www.thirteen.org
Social Media: *Facebook, Twitter, Pinterest, YouTube*

Neal Shapiro, President & CEO
Claude Johnson, VP Communication
Caroline C Croen, VP, CFO, Treasurer
Robert A Feinberg, VP, General Counsel, Secretary
Carole Wacey, VP, Education

Association members are producers and directors of public educational programming, channel 13, PBS.
500 Members
Mailing list available for rent

3787 Enterprise Wireless Alliance
2121 Cooperative Way
Suite 255
Herndon, VA 20171

703-524-1074
800-482-8282
E-Mail: info@EnterpriseWireless.org
Home Page:
www.enterprisewirelessalliance.org

Catherine Leonard, Chairman
Davis Reeves, Vice Chair
Mark E Crosby, President/CEO
Gordon Day, Treasurer
Kenny Adams, Director

Provides a license renewal reminder service. Maintains liaison with major radio manufacturers and mediates problems between licensees.
15 Members
Founded in 1953

3788 Geospatial Information and Technology Association
1360 University Ave W
Suite 455
St. Paul, MN 55104-4086

844-447-4482
FAX 844-223-8218
E-Mail: bsamborski@gita.org
Home Page: www.gita.org
Social Media: *Facebook, Twitter, LinkedIn, YouTube*

Mark Limbruner, President
Matthew Thomas, President-Elect
Eric Hoogenraad, Secretary
Elizabeth Bialek, Treasurer
Talbot J Brooks, Past President

Provides unbiased educational programs, forums and publications for professionals involved with geospatial information and technology.
2200 Members
Founded in 1960

3789 Hollywood Radio and Television Society
16530 Ventura Blvd
Suite 411
Encino, CA 91436

818-789-1182
FAX 818-789-1210
E-Mail: info@hrts.org
Home Page: www.hrts.org
Social Media: *Facebook, Twitter, LinkedIn*

Bela Bajaria, President
Jennie Nevin, Director of Operations
Ruzzo Martinelli, Events
Meshak Vallesillas, Marketing &
Communications
Elvia Gonzalez, Member Services

Sponsors monthly luncheons featuring top industry and government speakers and seminars about broadcasting, maintains film and audio library.
100 Members
Founded in 1947
Mailing list available for rent

3790 Intercollegiate Broadcasting Systems
367 Windsor Highway
New Windsor, NY 12553-7900

845-565-0003
FAX 845-565-7446
E-Mail: ibs@ibsradio.org
Home Page: www.ibsradio.org
Social Media: *Facebook, Twitter*

Len Mailloux, Chairman
Norman Prusslin, President/Chair Emeritus
Fritz Kass, CEO
Tom Gibson, Executive VP
Allen Myers, EVP, FCC Licensing

Nonprofit association of student staffed radio stations based at schools and colleges across the country. Some 800 member stations operate all sizes and types of facilities including Internet-Webcasting, closed circuit, AM carrier-current, cable radio and FCC-licensed FM and AM stations.
800 Members
Founded in 1940

3791 International Association of Broadcast Monitors
PO Box 986
Irmo, SC 29063

803-749-9833
800-236-1741
FAX 888-732-9004
E-Mail: iabm@iabm.com
Home Page: www.iabm.com

Mike Ross, Executive Director
Kevin Repka, President
Ron Coucil, VP International
John Croll, Secretary
Holly Wine, Treasurer

Worldwide trade association made up of news retrieval services which monitor television, radio, internet and print news mediums. It acts as a clearinghouse or forum for discussion on topics of collective concerns and acts as a united voice for the news monitoring industry.
Founded in 1981

3792 International Council-National Academy
25 W 52nd Street
New York, NY 10019

212-489-6969
FAX 212-489-6557
E-Mail: iemmys@iemmys.tv
Home Page: www.iemmys.tv
Social Media: *Facebook, Twitter, LinkedIn*

Fred Cohen, Chairman
Bruce Paisner, President & CEO

Larry Gershman, VP
Simon Sutton, Secretary
Rainer Siek, Nominating Committee Chairman

Furthers the arts and sciences by bestowing International Emmy Awards, George Movshon Fellowship and the Joan Wilson memorial scholarship.
250+ Members
Founded in 1969

3793 International Radio and Television Society Foundation
1697 Broadway
10th Floor
New York, NY 10019

212-867-6650
FAX 212-867-6653
Home Page: www.irts.org

Joyce M. Tudrynff, President & CEO
Jim Cronin, Dir, Member Prgms &
Development
Marilyn L. Ellis, Director, Program
Administration
Lauren Kruk-Winokur, Dir, Academic Prgms &
Communication
Jack Myers, Chairman

The lines between broadcast televison and radio, cable, telephony and the computer industry may be blurring, but one thing remains clear, we all have an affinity for a business that entertains, informs, educates and serves the American public in a meaningful way. The foundation provides a unique common forum for all segments of the communication industry. Members can enjoy sharing insight and ideas with colleagues during the season's numerous events.
750 Members
Founded in 1939

3794 International Television Academy
25 W 52nd Street
New York, NY 10019

212-489-6969
FAX 212-489-6557
E-Mail: iemmys@iemmys.tv
Home Page: www.iemmys.tv
Social Media: *Facebook, Twitter, LinkedIn*

Bruce Paisner, President
Fred Cohen, Chairman
Larry Gershman, VP
Simon Sutton, Secretary
Rainer Siek, Nominating Committee Chairman

Organization of global broadcasters, with representatives from over 50 countries based outside of the US, and represents the world's largest production, distribution and broadcast companies.
Founded in 1969

3795 Jones/NCTI-National Cable Television Institute
9697 E Mineral Ave
Centennial, CO 80112

303-792-3111
800-525-7002
FAX 303-797-0829
E-Mail: info@jones.com
Home Page: www.jones.com

Glenn R Jones, CEO
Michael Guilfoyle, Director Market Strategy
Jerry Neese, Director Sales
Mary Bliss, Vice President
Stacey Slaughter, CEO/CFO

Workforce performance products, services and education.
30 Members
Founded in 1969
Mailing list available for rent

3796 Library of American Broadcasting
University of Maryland
Mckeldin Library
College Park, MD 20742-7011

301-405-0800
FAX 301-314-2634
E-Mail: bp50@umail.umed.edu
Home Page: www.lib.umd.edu
Social Media: *Facebook, Twitter, YouTube, Flickr*

Malachy Wienges, Chair
Barbara Williams Perry, 1st Vice Chair
Alison Gibson, 2nd Vice Chair
Jamie Jensen, Secretary
Terry D Peterson, Treasurer

Holds a wide ranging collection of audio and video recordings, books, pamphlets, periodicals, personal collections, oral histories, photographs, scripts and vertical files devoted exclusively to the history of broadcasting.
Founded in 1972

3797 Manufacturers Radio Frequency Advisory Committee
616 E 34th Street N
Wichita, KS 67219

316-832-9213
800-262-9206
E-Mail: info@mrfac.com
Home Page: www.mrfac.com

Joe Cramer, President
Danny Hankins, VP
Nate Miler, Secretary
Rich Elersich, Treasurer

Representing the voice of the manufacturing industry and private land mobile radio users before the Federal Communications Commision, the responsibe federal regulatory agency for the nation's industrial communications. The leaders of the manufacturing industry, individually and collectively, have an obligation to influence the policies, plans, and procedures which govern the growth, structure and use of our national radio spectrum and telecommunications systems.
14000 Members
Founded in 1954

3798 Media Communications Association International
P.O.Box 5135
Madison, WI 53705-0135

608-826-0722
800-899-6224
FAX 888-899-6224
E-Mail: loiswei@aol.com
Home Page: www.mca-i.org
Social Media: *Facebook, Twitter, LinkedIn, Google +*

Jim Dufek, President
Brian Alberth, President Elect
Art Kirsch, Treasurer
Liz De Nesnera, Secretary
Brian Alberth, Past President

The Media Communications Association-International is a global community that provides professional development seminars and events, opportunities for networking, members-only benefits, forums for education, and information resources for media communications professionals.
Founded in 1968

3799 Media Financial Management Association
550 W Frontage Road
Suite 3600
Northfield, IL 60093

847-716-7000
FAX 847-716-7004
E-Mail: info@mediafinance.org

Home Page: www.mediafinance.org
Social Media: *Twitter, LinkedIn*

Mary M Collins, President/CEO
Ed O'Connor, Director of Operations
Arcelia Pimentel, Membership Manager &
Sales
Andy Holdgate, Public Relations Consultant
Ralph Bender, Chairman

Professional society of media's top financial,
MIS Credit and HR executives, plus associates
in auditing, data processing, software development, law, tax and credit and collections
1300 Members
Founded in 1961
Mailing list available for rent

3800 Museum of Broadcast Communications
360 North State Street
Chicago, IL 60654-5411

312-245-8200
FAX 312-245-8207
E-Mail: info@museum.tv
Home Page: www.museum.tv
Social Media: *Facebook, Twitter*

Bruce DuMont, President, CEO
David Plier, VP, Secretary
Jack Weinberg, VP

Collects, preserves, and presents historic and
contemporary radio and television content as
well as educate, inform, and entertain the public through its archives, public programs,
screenings, exhibits, publications, and online
access to its resources.

3801 National Academy of Television Arts and Sciences
1697 Broadway
Suite 404
New York, NY 10019

212-586-8424
FAX 212-246-8129
Home Page: www.emmyonline.tv
Social Media: *Facebook, Twitter, LinkedIn, Google +*

Brent Stanton, Executive Director
David Winn, Director
Christine Chin, Manager

Dedicated to the advancement of the arts and
sciences of television and the promotion of creative leadership for artistic, educational and
technical achievements within the television industry. It recognizes excellence in television
with the coveted Emmy Award.
12M Members
Founded in 1957
Printed in on glossy stock

3802 National Alliance of State Broadcasters Associations
2333 Wisconsin St. NE
Albuquerque, NM 87110

505-881-4444
Home Page: www.nasbaonline.net
Social Media: *Twitter*

Kent Cornish, President
Oscar Rodriguez, President-Elect
Vance Harrison, Vice President
David Donovan, Secretary/Treasurer
Michelle Vetterkind, Past President

The Alliance represents the interests of the 50
state broadcast associations in Washington.

3803 National Association of Black Owned Broadcasters (NABOB)
1201 Connecticut Avenue NW
Suite 200
Washington, DC 20036

202-463-8970
FAX 202-429-0657

E-Mail: nabobinfo@nabob.org
Home Page: www.nabob.org

Micheal L Carter, VP
Karen E Slade, Treasurer
James L Winston, President

Largest trade organization representing the interests of African-American owners of radio
and television stations across the country.
Founded in 2001

3804 National Association of Broadcasters
1771 N St Nw
Washington, DC 20036

202-429-5300
FAX 202-429-4199
E-Mail: nab@nab.org
Home Page: www.nab.org
Social Media: *Facebook, Twitter, LinkedIn, YouTube*

David K Rehr, CEO
Philip J Lombardo, Chairman
Dean Goodman, COO
Ann Young-Orr, Executive Director
Michelle Duke, Development Director

Full service trade association that represents
the interests of free, over-the-air radio and television broadcasters. Offers seminars and workshops to members and holds local meetings that
offer support on legal and industry issues.
Sponsors the National Association of Broadcasters Educational Foundation, dedicated to
serving the public interest via education and
training programs, strategies to increase diverse
initiatives, community support and
philanthropy.
7000 Members
Founded in 1923

3805 National Association of College Radio/TV Stations
71 George Street
Providence, RI 02912-1824

401-863-2225
FAX 401-863-2221
E-Mail: nacb@aol.com

Members are student radio/TV stations and interested individuals. Has an annual budget of
approximately $300,000.
1600 Members
Founded in 1988

3806 National Association of Farm Broadcasters
1100 Platte Falls Road
PO Box 500
Platte City, MO 64079

816-431-4032
FAX 816-431-4087
E-Mail: info@nafb.com
Home Page: www.nafb.com
Social Media: *Facebook, Twitter*

Janet Adkison, President
Susan Littlefield, President Elect
Brian Winnekins, VP

Works to improve quantity and quality of farm
programming and serves as a clearinghouse for
new ideas in farm broadcasting.
600 Members
Founded in 1944

3807 National Association of Television Program Executives
5757 Wilshire Blvd
Penthouse 10
Los Angeles, CA 90036

210-857-1601
FAX 310-453-5258
E-Mail: info@natpe.org

Home Page: www.natpe.org
Social Media: *Facebook, Twitter, Youtube*

Rod Perth, President/CEO
Olivia Thomas, Executive Assistant to
President
Eric Low, Director, Registration
Jordan Ryder, VP, Event Programming
Dann Novak, Programming Producer

A global, non-profit organization dedicated to
the creation, development and distribution of
televised programming in all forms across all
mature and emerging media platforms.
2800 Members
Founded in 1963
Mailing list available for rent

3808 National Cable & Telecommunications Association
25 Massachusetts Ave. NW
Suite 100
Washington, DC 20001

202-222-2300
E-Mail: webmaster@ncta.com
Home Page: www.ncta.com
Social Media: *Facebook, Twitter, LinkedIn*

Michael Powell, President & CEO
Neil Smit, Chairman

Trade association for U.S. cable industry.
200+ Members
Founded in 1940

3809 National Cable Television Association
25 Massachusetts Ave NW
Suite 100
Washington, DC 20001

202-222-2300
FAX 202-775-3604
E-Mail: webmaster@ncta.com
Home Page: www.ncta.com
Social Media: *Facebook, Twitter, LinkedIn*

Michael Powell, President & CEO
Brian Dietz, VP
James E Assey, Executive VP
K Dane Snowden, Chief of Staff
Bruce Carnes, Senior VP, Finance &
Administration
200+ Members
Founded in 1940

3810 National Council for Families & TV
3801 Barham Boulevard
Los Angeles, CA 90068-1000

323-953-7300
FAX 310-208-5984
Home Page: www.salonprofessionals.org

Advances and promotes television awareness
for family television shows.

3811 National Federation of Community Broadcasting
PO Box 16
1308 Clear Fork Road
Crawford, CO 81415

970-279-3411
FAX 510-451-8208
E-Mail: comments@nfcb.org
Home Page: www.nfcb.org

Sonya Green, President
Lackisha Freeman, VP
Ann Alquist, Secretary
Ernesto Aguilar, Treasurer
Sally Kane, CEO

A national alliance of stations, producers, and
others committed to community radio. NFCB
advocates for national public policy, funding,
recognition, and resources on behalf of its
membership while providing services to empower and strengthen community broadcasters
through the core values of localism, diversity,
and public service.

3812 National Public Radio Association
1111 North Capitol Street NW
Washington, DC 20002

202-686-0516
FAX 202-513-3329
Home Page: www.npr.org
Social Media: *Facebook, Twitter*

Gary E Knell, President/CEO
Joyce MacDonald, Chief of Staff/Vice President
Jeff Perkins, Chief People Officer
Robert Kempf, General Manager
Deborah Cowan, VP/Chief Financial Officer

Works in partnership with member stations to create a more informed public, one challenged and invigorated by a deeper understanding and appreciation of events, ideas, and cultures.
750 Members
Founded in 1970

3813 National Religious Broadcasters
9510 Technology Dr
Manassas, VA 20110

703-330-7000
FAX 703-330-7100
E-Mail: info@nrb.org
Home Page: www.nrb.org
Social Media: *Facebook, Twitter, LinkedIn, YouTube, Google+ RSS*

Jerry A Johnson, President/CEO
Linda Smith, Executive VP & COO
Craig Parshall, Senior VP/General Counsel
Aaron Mercer, VP of Government Relations
Jennifer Gregorin, President Assistant

Represents evangelical Christian radio and television stations, program producers, multimedia developers and related organizations around the worldMembers are responsible for much of the world's Christian radio and television.
1700 Members
Founded in 1944
Mailing list available for rent

3814 National Sportscasters and Sportswriters Association
PO Box 1545
Salisbury, NC 28145

704-633-4275
FAX 704-633-2027
E-Mail: nssahalloffame@aol.com
Home Page: www.nssahalloffame.com
Social Media: *Facebook, Twitter*

Dave Goren, Executive Director
Katy Temple, Adminstrative Assistant

Meet annually.
1000 Members
Founded in 1959
Mailing list available for rent

3815 New England Cable & Telecommunications Associatoin Inc
Ten Forbes Road
Suite 440W
Braintree, MA 02184

781-843-3418
FAX 781-849-6267
E-Mail: ckillian@necta.info
Home Page: www.necta.info

Paul R Cianelli, President
Mark Reilly, Vice Chair
John Sutich, Treasurer
Jay Allbaugh, Secretary
William D Durand, Executive VP/Chief Counsel

NECTA is a six state regional trade association representing sbtstantially all private cable telecommunications companies in Connecticut, Maine, Massachusetts, New Hampshire, Rhode Island and Vermont.

3816 North American Broadcasters Association (N ABA)
205 Wellington Street West
Suite 6C300
Toronto, ON M5V 3G7

416-598-9877
FAX 416-598-9774
E-Mail: contact@nabanet.com
Home Page: www.nabanet.com

Michael McEwan, Director General
Anh Ngo, Director, Administration
Jason Paris, Senior Coordinator
Jenn Hadfield, Executive Assistant
Vineet Mathur, IT & Web Administrator

A non-profit association of broadcasting organizations in the United States, Mexico, and Canada committed to advancing the interests of broadcasters at home and internationally.

3817 North American Network
3700 Crestwood Pkwy NW
Suite 350
Duluth, GA 30096-7154

770-279-4560
FAX 770-279-4566
E-Mail: rbeilfuss@pkfnan.org
Home Page: www.pkfnan.org

Terry Snyder, President

Radio broadcasting agency that provides news and programming services to radio stations and organizations. Programming is sponsored by the corporations, government angencies, associations and nonprofit organizations who are indentified in the program notes and scripts.

3818 Public Broadcasting Service (PBS)
2100 Crystal Dr.
Arlington, VA 22202

Home Page: www.pbs.org
Social Media: *Facebook, Twitter, YouTube*

Paula Kerger, President & CEO
Barbara Landes, Chief Financial Officer
Jonathan Barzilay, Chief Operating Officer
Mary L. Plantamura, Assoc. General Counsel
Tom Tardivo, SVP, Finance & Business Development

PBS is a private, nonprofit association of public TV stations providing arts content, ecucational programs for children, documentaries and non-commercial news programs to all Americans.
Founded in 1969

3819 Public Radio in Mid-America (PRIMA)
3651 Olive Street
St Louis, MO 63108

314-516-5968
FAX 307-766-6184
E-Mail: info@kmwu.org
Home Page: www.kmwu.org

Tim Eby, General Manager
Terrence Dupuis, Chief Engineer
Shelley Kerley, Director, Development

Trusted source of informationa nd entertainment that opens minds and nourishes the spirit.

3820 Radio Advertising Bureau
1320 Greenway Dr
Suite 500
Irving, TX 75038-2547

972-753-6700
800-232-3131
FAX 972-753-6727
E-Mail: jhaley@rab.com
Home Page: www.rab.com
Social Media: *Facebook, Twitter*

Hartley AdkinsII, Chairman
Steve Newberry, Secretary

Ginny Morris, Vice Chair
Susan Larkin, Finance Chairman
Erica Farber, Executive Committee

Our mission is to lead industry initiatives and provide organizational, educational, research and advocacy programs and services that benefit the RAB membership and the Radio industry as a whole.
7000 Members

3821 Radio Television Digital News Assn.
529 14th Street NW
Suite 425
Washington, DC 20045

800-807-8632
FAX 202-223-4007
E-Mail: mikec@rtdna.org
Home Page: www.rtdna.org
Social Media: *Facebook, Twitter, LinkedIn*

Mike Cavender, Executive Director
Derrick Hinds, Communications, Marketing & Digital
Katie Switchenko, Programs
Karen Hansen, Membership & Program Manager
Jon Ebinger, International Program Consultant

An association dedicated to setting new standards for newsgathering and reporting.

3822 Radio Television Digital News Association (Canada)
529 14th Street NW
Suite 1240
Washington, DC 20045

800-807-8632
FAX 202-223-4007
E-Mail: mikec@rtdna.org
Home Page: www.rtdna.org
Social Media: *Facebook, Twitter, LinkedIn*

Mike Cavender, Executive Director
Derrick Hinds, Communications, Marketing & Digital
Katie Switchenko, Programs
Karen Hansen, Membership & Program Manager
Jon Ebinger, International Program Consultant

An association dedicated to setting new standards for newsgathering and reporting.

3823 Radio Television News Directors Association
529 14th Street NW
Suite 1240
Washington, DC 20045

800-807-8632
FAX 202-223-4007
E-Mail: barbarac@rtnda.org
Home Page: www.rtnda.org
Social Media: *Facebook, Twitter, LinkedIn*

Mike Cavender, Executive Director
Derrick Hinds, Communications, Marketing & Digital
Katie Switchenko, Programs
Karen Hansen, Membership & Program Manager
Jon Ebinger, International Program Consultant

Largest professional organization exclusively serving the electronic news profession. Dedicated to setting standards for newsgathering and reporting. Represents electronic journalists in radion, television and all digital media, as well as journalism educators and students.
3000+ Members
Founded in 1946

3824 Radio Television News Directors Assn. - Canada

439 University Avenue
5th Floor
Toronto, ON M5G 1Y8

437-836-3088
877-257-8632
FAX 416-364-8896
E-Mail: admin@rtndacanada.com
Home Page: www.rtndacanada.com
Social Media: *Facebook, Twitter*

Ian Koenigsfest, President
Andy LeBlanc, Past President
Michelle McEachern, Secretary/Treasurer
Marissa Nelson, VP, Digital Media
Kym Geddes, International Representative

Progressive organization offering a forum for open discussion and action in the broadcast news industry. Speaks for the leaders of Canada's radio and television news operations on the issues that impact the newsroom.

3825 Radio and Television Research Council

234 5th Ave
#417
New York, NY 10001

212-028-8933
FAX 212-481-3071

Robert M Purcell, Executive Director

Members are professionals actively engaged in radio/television research.
200 Members
Founded in 1941

3826 Satellite Broadcasting and Communication Association (SBCA)

1100 17th Street NW
Suite 1150
Washington, DC 20036

202-349-3620
800-541-5981
FAX 202-349-3621
E-Mail: info@sbca.org
Home Page: www.sbca.com
Social Media: *Facebook, Twitter, LinkedIn*

Jeffrey Blum, Chairman
Andrew Reinsdorf, Vice Chair
Joseph Widoff, Executive Director

National trade organization representing all segments of the satellite consumer services industry. The association is committed to expanding the utilization of satellite technology for the delivery of video, data, voice, interactive and broadband services.
1000 Members
Founded in 1986

3827 Society of Broadcast Engineers

9102 N Meridian St
Suite 150
Indianapolis, IN 46260

317-846-9000
FAX 317-846-9120
E-Mail: mclappe@sbe.org
Home Page: www.sbe.org
Social Media: *Facebook, Twitter, LinkedIn, YouTube*

Jerry Massey, President
James E Leifer, VP
Ted Hand, Secretary
Andrea Cummins, Treasurer
Tim Anderson, Director

SBE provides members with the opportunity to network and share ideas and information in keeping current with the ongoing changes within the industry. Members can attend annual conferences and expositions, have access to ed-

ucational opportunities and obtain professional certification.
5500 Members
Founded in 1964
Mailing list available for rent: 5700 names at $170 per M

3828 Society of Motion Picture & Television Engineers

3 Barker Ave
5th Floor
White Plains, NY 10601

914-761-1100
FAX 914-761-3115
Home Page: www.smpte.org
Social Media: *Facebook, Twitter, LinkedIn, YouTube, Flickr*

Robert P. Seidel, President
Matthew Goldman, Executive VP
Alan Lambshead, Standards VP
Peter Wharton, Secretary/Treasurer
Paul Michael Stechly, Finance VP

The Society of Motion Picture and Television Engineers (SMPTE), is the leading technical society for the motion imaging industry. SMPTE members are spread throughout 64 countries worldwide. Sustaining (institutional) Members belong to SMPTE, allowing networking and contacts to occur on a larger scale. Touching on every discipline, our members include engineers, technical directors, cameramen, editors, technicians, manufacturers, designers, educators, consultants and field users.
6000 Members
Founded in 1916

3829 Statenets National Association of State Radio Networks

17911 Harwood Avenue
Homewood, IL 60430

708-799-6676
804-364-3075
FAX 708-799-6698
E-Mail: idobrez@statenets.com
Home Page: www.statenets.com
Social Media: *Facebook, Twitter, LinkedIn, RSS*

Tom Dobrez, Executive Director
Sharon Kitchell, Deputy Director
Angle Martin, Account Executive
Jason Price, Administrative Coordinator
Carla Litton, Controller

Works with hundreds of regional and national marketers and political campaigns solve marketing challenges.

3830 Syndicated Network Television Association

One Penn Plaza
Suite 5310
New York, NY 10119

212-259-3740
FAX 212-259-3770
E-Mail: mburg@snta.com
Home Page: www.snta.com

Mitch Burg, President
Jordan Harris, Director, Marketing
Hadassa Gerber, Director, Research

Communicates to advertisers, their agencies and media planners and buyers the benefits of syndication, from the wide range of programming choices to their high ratings and national reach, and the reliability and cost effectiveness of advertising in syndicated programming.

3831 Television Bureau of Advertising

120 Wall Street
15th Floor
New York, NY 10005-3908

212-486-1111
FAX 212-935-5631
E-Mail: info@tvb.org
Home Page: www.tvb.org

Steve Lanzano, President
Abby Auerbach, Executive VP/CMO
Brad Seitter, EVP, Business Development
Jack Poor, VP, Marketing Insights
Scott Roskowski, SVP, Business Development

Not-for-profit trade association of America's broadcast television industry. TVB provides a diverse variety of tools and resources to support its members and to help advertisers make the best use of local television.
600 Members
Founded in 1954

3832 Television Bureau of Canada

160 Bloor Street East
Suite 1005
Toronto, ON M4W 1B9

416-923-8813
800-231-0051
FAX 416-413-3879
E-Mail: tvb@tvb.ca
Home Page: www.tvb.ca

Catherine MacLeod, President, CEO
Duncan Robertson, Director, Media Insights
Rhonda Lynn Bagnall, Director, Telecaster Services
Alan Dark, Chairman
Perry MacDonald, Vice Chairman

TVB markets the benefits and effectiveness of the TV medium in all its forms to advertisers and agencies. TVB collects, interprets, develops, identifies, and communicates information and data to be used.

3833 Television Critics Association

825 East Douglas Avenue
Witchita, KS 67202

316-268-6394
FAX 316-288-6627
E-Mail: info@tvcritics.org
Home Page: www.tvcritics.org
Social Media: *Facebook, Twitter*

Amber Dowling, President
Daniel Fienberg, Vice President
Sarah Rodman, Secretary
Melanie MacFarland, Treasurer
Todd VanDerWerff, Director

Represents journalists writing about television for print and online outlets.
220 Members

3834 Television Operators Caucus

1176 K Street NW
9th Floor
Washington, DC 20006

202-719-7090
FAX 202-719-7548
E-Mail: info@fundraise.com
Social Media: *Facebook, Twitter, Google+*

Nate Drouin, Founder/CEO
Kurt Schneider, COO
Kevin Bedell, CTO

Non-profit group of memebers that support television issues and its impacts on the world today.

3835 The Alliance for Community Media

4248 Park Glen Road
Minneapolis, MN 55416

952-928-4643
FAX 703-506-3266
E-Mail: info@allcommunitymedia.org

Home Page: www.allcommunitymedia.org
Social Media: *Facebook, Twitter, RSS,
YouTube, Flickr*

Keri Stokstad, Chair
Michael Heylin, Vice Chair
Alan Bushong, Treasurer
Mike Wassenaar, President
Melissa Serres, Assistant Director

Promotes civic engagement through community medias.
*1000 Members
Founded in 1976*

**3836 The Association for Maximum Service
Televi sion**
4100 Wisconsin Avenue NW
PO Box 9897
Washington, DC 20016

202-966-1956
FAX 202-966-9617
E-Mail: lmillory@mstv.org
Home Page: www.mstv.org
Social Media: *Twitter, RSS*

Craig Dubow, CEO
MSTV has endeavored to insure that American
public receive the highest quality, interference
free, over-the-air local television signals. Recognized as the industry leader in broadcasting
technology and spectrum policy issues.

3837 The Broadcasters Hall of Fame
1240 Ashford Lane, 1A
PO Box 8247
Akron, OH 44320

330-867-3779
FAX 330-867-4907
E-Mail: info@briadcastershalloffame.com
Home Page: www.broadcastershalloffame.com

C S (Doc) Williams, Founder, CEO
Henry Dunn, Chairman
Jeannette Camak, Secretary
Dollis Rogers, Assistant Secretary
Melvin L Brown, Trustee

A wealth of memorabilia from the early days of
broadcasting, clippings from newspapers and
magazines, taped recorded portions of early radio shows and other gems of broadcasting
history.
Founded in 1982

3838 WGBH Educational Foundation
One Guest Street
Boston, MA 02135

617-300-5400
Home Page: www.wgbh.org
Social Media: *Facebook, Twitter*

Jonathan C Abbott, President/CEO
Benjamin Godley, Executive VP & COO
Vinay Mehra, CFO/VP, Finance &
Administration
Susan L Kantrowitz, VP & General Counsel
Stacey Decker, CTO

Make knowledge and the creative life of the
arts, sciences, and humanities available to the
widest possible public
Founded in 1836

Newsletters

**3839 American Sportscasters Association
Insiders Newsletter**
American Sportscasters Association
225 Broadway
Suite 2030
New York, NY 10007-3742

212-227-8080
FAX 212-571-0556

E-Mail: lschwa8918@aol.com
Home Page:
www.americansportscastersonline.com
Social Media: *Facebook, Twitter*

Louis O Schwartz, CEO
Dick Enberg, Chairman Of The Board

Newsletter keeps sportscasters up to date on
important issues for the profession.
*24 Pages
Frequency: Quarterly
Circulation: 2500
Founded in 1980*

3840 Bandwidth Investor
Kagan World Media
126 Clock Tower Place
Carmel, CA 93923-8746

831-624-1536
FAX 831-625-3225
E-Mail: sgoldberg@kagan.com
Home Page: www.kagan.com

George Niesen, Editor
Harvy Carft, Marketing Manager
Tim Baskerville, CEO/President
Harvy Carft, Circulation Manager
*Cost: $945.00
Frequency: Monthly
Founded in 1969*

3841 Broadband Fixed Wireless
Kagan World Media
126 Clock Tower Place
Carmel, CA 93923-8746

831-624-1536
FAX 831-625-3225
E-Mail: info@kagan.com
Home Page: www.kagan.com

George Niesen, Editor
Tom Johnson, Marketing Manager
*Cost: $845.00
Frequency: Monthly*

3842 Broadband Systems & Design
Gordon Publications
301 Gibraltar Drive
#650
Morris Plains, NJ 07950-3400

973-292-5100
FAX 973-539-3476

Terry McCoy Jr, Publisher
Andrea Frucci, Editor

The only product tabloid serving buying
influencers, engineers, corporate managers and
purchasing professionals in the cable television
marketplace.
Circulation: 26,400

3843 Broadband Technology
Kagan World Media
126 Clock Tower Place
Carmel, CA 93923-8746

831-624-1536
FAX 831-625-3225
E-Mail: info@kagan.com
Home Page: www.kagan.com

George Niesen, Editor
Tom Johnson, Marketing Manager
*Cost: $1450.00
Frequency: Monthly
Founded in 1969*

3844 Broadcast Banker/Broker
Kagan World Media
126 Clock Tower Place
Carmel, CA 93923-8746

831-624-1536
800-307-2529
FAX 831-625-3225

E-Mail: info@kagan.com
Home Page: www.kagan.com

George Niesen, Editor
Tom Johnson, Marketing Manager

A readers guide to equity deals and debt financing for radio and TV Station buying and selling
analyzed. Key details on station trades with
critical yardsticks of value. Three month trial is
available.
*Cost: $925.00
Frequency: Monthly
Founded in 1969*

3845 Broadcast Investor
Kagan World Media
1 Lower Ragsdale Drive
Building One, Suite 130
Monterey, CA 93940-5749

831-624-1536
800-307-2529
FAX 831-625-3225
E-Mail: info@kagan.com
Home Page: www.kagan.com/

Tim Baskerville, President
Tom Johnson, Marketing Manager

The newsletter on investments in radio and TV
stations and publicly held companies. Comprehensive analysis of cash flow multiples and
trends that impact value. Three month trial
available.
*Cost: $1295.00
Frequency: Monthly
Founded in 1969*

3846 Broadcast Stats
Kagan World Media
126 Clock Tower Place
Carmel, CA 93923-8746

831-624-1536
800-307-2529
FAX 831-624-5882
E-Mail: info@kagan.com
Home Page: www.kagan.com

George Niesen, Editor
Tom Johnson, Marketing Manager

The numbers behind the broadcast companies.
Exclusive data, analysis and projections of radio and TV market billings, revenues, and cash
flows, plus complete data on the buy-sell market. The industry's key reference source. Three
month trial available.
*Cost: $795.00
Frequency: Monthly
Founded in 1969*

3847 Business Radio
Nt'l Association of Business & Educational
Radio
500 Montgomery Street
Alexandria, VA 22314

703-548-1500
FAX 703-836-1608

AE Goetz, Publisher

Association news for professionals, owners and
consumers regarding radio stations.
*Cost: $65.00
Circulation: 3,000*

3848 Cable Program Investor
Kagan World Media
1 Lower Ragsdale Dr
Building One, Suite 130
Monterey, CA 93940-5749

831-624-1536
800-307-2529
FAX 831-625-3225
E-Mail: info@kagan.com
Home Page: www.kagan.com/

Tim Baskerville, President
Tom Johnson, Marketing Manager

Robin Flynn, Senior VP
Sharon Armbrust, Senior Consultant
Derek Baine, Senior Vice President

Covers the economics of basic cable programming networks. Numbers, perspective unavailable from any other source. Programmers applaud its accuracy. Three month trial available.
Cost: $1045.00
Frequency: Monthly
Founded in 1969

3849 Cable TV Advertising
Kagan World Media
126 Clock Tower Place
Carmel, CA 93923-8746

831-624-1536
FAX 831-624-5882
E-Mail: info@kagan.com
Home Page: www.kagan.com

George Niesen, Editor
Tom Johnson, Marketing Manager

Analysis of sales of commercial time by cable TV networks, interconnects and local systems. Detailed reports on national and local spot sales. Case studies and projections, all about the industry's upside. Three month trial available.
Cost: $795.00
Frequency: Monthly

3850 Cable TV Finance
Kagan World Media
126 Clock Tower Place
Carmel, CA 93923-8746

831-624-1536
800-307-2529
FAX 831-624-5882
E-Mail: info@kagan.com
Home Page: www.kagan.com

George Niesen, Editor
Tom Johnson, Marketing Manager
Larry Gerbrandt, CEO/President
Judy Pinney, Circulation Manager
Tim Baskerville, Publisher

Cable's financial bible. Analyzes sources of funding for cable TV. Selling and buying of cable systems. Financing strategies and trends. Exclusive surveys of capital sources. Three month trial available.
Cost: $795.00
Frequency: Monthly
Founded in 1969

3851 Cable TV Investor
Kagan World Media
1 Lower Ragsdale Dr
Building One, Suite 130
Monterey, CA 93940-5749

831-624-1536
800-307-2529
FAX 831-625-3225
E-Mail: info@kagan.com
Home Page: www.kagan.com

Tim Baskerville, President
Tom Johnson, Marketing Manager

Readers road map to cable stock trends. Chart service tracking stock price movements of 37 publicly held cable TV companies. Each graph shows two years of stock price activity. Three month trial available.
Cost: $1295.00
Frequency: Monthly
Founded in 1969

3852 Cable TV Law Reporter
Kagan World Media

1 Lower Ragsdale Dr
Building One, Suite 130
Monterey, CA 93940-5749

831-624-1536
800-307-2529
FAX 831-625-3225
E-Mail: info@kagan.com
Home Page: www.kagan.com

Tim Baskerville, President
Tom Johnson, Marketing Manager

The quintessential library of cable court cases, arbitrations, legal precedents. Labeled and catalogued for easy reference. Required reading for attorneys, government regulators and top executives. Three month trial available.
Cost: $995.00
Frequency: Monthly
Founded in 1969

3853 Cable TV Technology
Kagan World Media
1 Lower Ragsdale Dr
Building One, Suite 130
Monterey, CA 93940-5749

831-624-1536
800-307-2529
FAX 831-625-3225
E-Mail: info@kagan.com
Home Page: www.kagan.com

Tim Baskerville, President
Tom Johnson, Marketing Manager

Incisive, thorough reports on technical advances in cable TV, in terms operating executives can grasp and use to implement strategies. Analyzes growth in addressable converters, high definition TV, fiber optics and other advancements. Three month trial available.
Cost: $925.00
Frequency: Monthly
Founded in 1969

3854 Community Radio News
National Federation of Community
Broadcasting
1970 Broadway
Suite 1000
Oakland, CA 94612

510-451-8200
FAX 510-451-8208
E-Mail: comments@nfcb.org
Home Page: www.nfcb.org
Social Media: *Facebook, Twitter*

Ryan Bruce, Publications Manager

Contains calendar of events and information on public broadcasting, job listings, and legislative and regulatory updates. Annual Community Radio Conference and Community Radio Program Awards Competition.
Cost: $75.00
12-16 Pages
Frequency: Monthly
Circulation: 400
Founded in 1975
Mailing list available for rent: 300 names at $25 per M
Printed in one color on matte stock

3855 Community Television Review
National Federation of Local Cable
Programmers
666 11th Street NW
Suite 806
Washington, DC 20001

202-393-2650
FAX 202-393-2653

Andrew Lewis, Publisher

Issues of importance to community programming on cable and other areas of telecommunications.
Cost: $15.00
36 Pages

3856 DBS Report
Kagan World Media
1 Lower Ragsdale Dr
Building One, Suite 130
Monterey, CA 93940-5749

831-624-1536
800-307-2529
FAX 831-625-3225
E-Mail: info@kagan.com
Home Page: www.kagan.com

Tim Baskerville, President
Tom Johnson, Marketing Manager
Cost: $1045.00
Frequency: Monthly
Founded in 1969

3857 Dance on Camera Journal
Dance Films Association
48 W 21st St
Suite 907
New York, NY 10010-6989

212-727-0764
FAX 212-727-0764
E-Mail: christy@dancefilms.org
Home Page: www.dancefilms.org

Deidra Towers, Executive Director
Louise Spain, President

The only service organization in the world dedicated to both the dance and the film community.
ISSN: 1098-8084
Founded in 1956
Printed in on matte stock

3858 Digital Television
Kagan World Media
126 Clock Tower Place
Carmel, CA 93923-8746

831-624-1536
800-307-2529
FAX 831-624-5882
E-Mail: info@kagan.com
Home Page: www.kagan.com

George Niesen, Editor
Tom Johnson, Marketing Manager

News of the Digital Television. Three month trial available.
Cost: $945.00
Frequency: Monthly
Founded in 1969

3859 Hearsay
Association of Radio Reading Services
600 Forbes Ave
Pittsburgh, PA 15219-3002

412-488-3944
FAX 412-488-3953
E-Mail: info@readingservice.org
Home Page: www.readingservice.org
Social Media: *Facebook, Twitter*

Andy Ai, President
Erica Hacker, Vice President

Newsletter for the Radio Reading industry.

3860 Inside Sports Letter
American Sportscasters Association
225 Broadway
Suite 2030
New York, NY 10007-3742

212-227-8080
FAX 212-571-0556
E-Mail: lschwa8918@aol.com
Home Page:
www.americansportscastersonline.com
Social Media: *Facebook*

Louis O Schwartz, President/Editor
Dick Enberg, Chairman
Elaine Graifer, Associate Editor
Patrick Turturro, Assistant Editor

A quarterly newsletter published by the American Sportscasters Association.
38513 Pages
Frequency: Quarterly
Circulation: 2000
Founded in 1980

3861 Interactive Mobile Investor
Kagan World Media
1 Lower Ragsdale Dr
Building One, Suite 130
Monterey, CA 93940-5749

831-624-1536
800-307-2529
FAX 831-625-3225
E-Mail: info@kagan.com
Home Page: www.kagan.com

Tim Baskerville, President
Tom Johnson, Marketing Manager
Cost: $945.00
Frequency: Monthly
Founded in 1969

3862 Interactive TV Investor
Kagan World Media
1 Lower Ragsdale Dr
Building One, Suite 130
Monterey, CA 93940-5749

831-624-1536
FAX 831-625-3225
E-Mail: info@kagan.com
Home Page: www.kagan.com

Tim Baskerville, President
Tom Johnson, Marketing Manager
Cost: $895.00
Frequency: Monthly
Founded in 1970

3863 Interactive Television
Kagan World Media
1 Lower Ragsdale Dr
Building One Suite 130
Monterey, CA 93940-5749

831-624-1536
800-307-2529
FAX 831-625-3225
E-Mail: info@kagan.com
Home Page: www.kagan.com

Tim Baskerville, President
Tom Johnson, Marketing Manager
News of the Interactive Television. Three month trial available.
Cost: $795.00
Frequency: Monthly
Founded in 1969

3864 Internet Media Investor
Kagan World Media
126 Clock Tower Place
Carmel, CA 93923-8746

831-624-1536
FAX 831-625-3225
E-Mail: info@kagan.com
Home Page: www.kagan.com

George Niesen, Editor
Tom Johnson, Marketing Manager
Cost: $945.00
Frequency: Monthly
Founded in 1969

3865 Interval
Society of Cable Telecommunications Engineers
140 Philips Road
Exton, PA 19341-1318

610-363-6888
800-542-5040
FAX 610-363-5898

E-Mail: scte@scte.org
Home Page: www.scte.org

Howard Whitman, Senior Editor
Marci Dodd, President

A monthly member newsletter. Subscription price of $25.00 is for non-members.
Cost: $25.00
Frequency: Monthly
Circulation: 16000
Founded in 1969

3866 Kagan Broadband
Kagan World Media
1 Lower Ragsdale Dr
Building One, Suite 130
Monterey, CA 93940-5749

831-624-1536
800-307-2529
FAX 831-625-3225
E-Mail: info@kagan.com
Home Page: www.kagan.com

Tim Baskerville, President/CEO
Harvy Craft, Marketing Manager
Robert Nayoor, Circulation Manager
Sandie Borthwick, Executive Director

Daily e-mail or fax.
Cost: $1295.00
Frequency: Monthly
Founded in 1970

3867 Kagan Media Money
Kagan World Media
1 Lower Ragsdale Dr
Building One, Suite 130
Monterey, CA 93940-5749

831-624-1536
800- 30- 252
FAX 831-625-3225
E-Mail: info@kagan.com
Home Page: www.kagan.com

Tim Baskerville, President
Tom Johnson, Marketing Manager
Sandie Borthwick, Executive Director

Analysts dissect deals, anticipate trends, project revenues, track financings, and value the debt and equity of hundreds of priovately held and publicly traded advertising, broadcasting, cable TV digital TV, home video, Internet media, motion picture, newspaper, pay TV, professional sports and wireless telecommunications companies in the US and abroad.
Cost: $1245.00
Frequency: Monthly
Founded in 1970

3868 Kagan Music Investor
Kagan World Media
1 Lower Ragsdale Dr
Building One,Suite 130
Monterey, CA 93940-5749

831-624-1536
800-307-2529
FAX 831-625-3225
E-Mail: info@kagan.com
Home Page: www.kagan.com

Tim Baskerville, President
Tom Johnson, Marketing Manager
Sandie Borthwick, Executive Director

News and analysis of the music industry for investors.
Cost: $945.00
Frequency: Monthly
Founded in 1969

3869 Marketing New Media
Kagan World Media
1 Lower Ragsdale Dr
Building One, Suite 130
Monterey, CA 93940-5749

831-624-1536
800-307-2529
FAX 831-625-3225

E-Mail: info@kagan.com
Home Page: www.kagan.com

Tim Baskerville, President
Tom Johnson, Marketing Manager
News of the Marketing New Media. Three month trial available.
Cost: $795.00
Frequency: Monthly
Founded in 1969

3870 Media Communications Association News
Media Communications Association International
P.O.Box 5135
Madison, WI 53705-0135

608-836-0722
FAX 888-899-6224
E-Mail: loiswei@aol.com
Home Page: www.mca-i.org
Social Media: *Facebook, Twitter, LinkedIn*

Gary Shifflet, President
Lois Weiland, Executive Director
Mike Brown, Treasurer
Jim Powell, Secretary
John Coleman, Board Member

Coverage of the multimedia industry and association activities.
Frequency: Quarterly
Circulation: 3,000
Founded in 1968
Printed in on glossy stock

3871 Media Mergers & Acquisitions
Kagan World Media
126 Clock Tower Place
Carmel, CA 93923-8746

831-624-1536
FAX 831-624-5882
E-Mail: info@kagan.com
Home Page: www.kagan.com

George Niesen, Editor
Tom Johnson, Marketing Manager
Where it all comes together. Exclusive scorecard of deals done by media companies. Dollar amounts, multiples paid, trends captured in succinct summaries of complex transactions. Three month trial available.
Cost: $795.00
Frequency: Monthly

3872 Media Sports Business
Kagan World Media
1 Lower Ragsdale Dr
Building One, Suite 130
Monterey, CA 93940-5749

831-624-1536
800-307-2529
FAX 831-625-3225
E-Mail: info@kagan.com
Home Page: www.kagan.com

Tim Baskerville, President
Tom Johnson, Marketing Manager
Cost: $945.00
Frequency: Monthly
Founded in 1969

3873 Monitoring Times
Grove Enterprises
7540 Highway 64 W
Brasstown, NC 28902-8079

828-837-9200
800-438-8155
FAX 828-837-2216
E-Mail: order@grove-ent.com
Home Page: www.grove-ent.com

Bob Grove, President
Judy Grove, Office Manager
Belinda McDonald, Office Manager

News on radio communication, scanner monitoring, international radio broadcasts and technical advice.
Cost: $28.95
92 Pages
Frequency: Monthly
Circulation: 50000
ISSN: 0889-5341
Founded in 1970
Printed in 4 colors on glossy stock

3874 Motion Picture Investor
Kagan World Media
1 Lower Ragsdale Dr
Building One Suite 130
Monterey, CA 93940-5749

831-624-1536
FAX 831-625-3225
E-Mail: info@kagan.com
Home Page: www.kagan.com

Tim Baskerville, President
Tom Johnson, Marketing Manager
Cost: $845.00
Frequency: Monthly
Founded in 1969

3875 Multichannel News
360 Park Ave S
New York, NY 10010-1710

212-887-8387
FAX 212-463-6703
E-Mail: crucker@nbmedia.com
Home Page: www.multichannel.com

Lawrence Oliver, Publisher
Marianne Paskowski, Editorial Director
Kent Gibbons, Editor
Heather Tatrow, Production Manager
Michael Demenchuk, Managing Editor

News of the electronic media industries.
Frequency: Weekly
Circulation: 18,875
Founded in 1980

3876 NRB Today
National Religious Broadcasters
9510 Technology Dr
Manassas, VA 20110-4149

703-330-7100
FAX 703-330-7100
E-Mail: info@nrb.org
Home Page: www.nrb.org
Social Media: *Facebook*

Frank Wright, President/CEO
Linda Smith, EVP/COO
Kenneth Chan, Director of Communications

This weekly newsletter by National Religious Broadcasters covers the latest news from the association and NRB's member organizations. The newsletter also serves as a source for tips, trends, and insights relevant to Christian communicators across the spectrum. Topics include audience building, branding, business strategy, innovation, job hunting, leadership, management, marketing, social media, and web strategy. NRB Today also features occasional columns, movie reviews, and product reviews.
Founded in 1944

3877 Networks
Geospatial Information & Technology Association
14456 E Evans Ave
Aurora, CO 80014-1409

303-337-0513
FAX 303-337-1001
E-Mail: bsamborski@gita.org
Home Page: www.gita.org

Bob Samborski, Executive Director
Lisa Connor, Membership Services Manager
Elizabeth Roberts, Marketing

A bi-monthly newsletter published by the Geospatial Information & Technology Association.
Cost: $125.00
28 Pages
Frequency: Monthly
Circulation: 2200
Founded in 1978

3878 Pay TV Newsletter
Kagan World Media
126 Clock Tower Place
Carmel, CA 93923-8746

831-624-1536
FAX 831-624-5882
E-Mail: info@kagan.com
Home Page: www.kagan.com

George Niesen, Editor
Tom Johnson, Marketing Manager

The pay TV industry's publication of record since 1973. Exclusive estimates of network subscribers and economics. The pay-per-view business, event-by-event, film-by-film. Three month trial available.
Cost: $795.00
Frequency: Monthly

3879 Public Broadcasting Report
Warren Communications News
2115 Ward Ct Nw
Washington, DC 20037-1209

202-872-9200
800-771-9202
FAX 202-318-8350
E-Mail: info@warren-news.com
Home Page: www.warren-news.com

Brig Easley, Manager
Daniel Warren, President/Editor

Industry news, personnel announcements and calendar listings for public broadcasting, digital TV, congress, FCC, and allied friends.
Cost: $575.00
Founded in 1945
Mailing list available for rent

3880 Radio & Records
Radio & Records
10100 Santa Monica Boulevard
3rd Floor
Los Angeles, CA 90067-4003

310-553-4330
FAX 310-203-8450
E-Mail: radioandrecords@billboard.biz
Home Page: www.radioandrecords.com

Erica Farber, Publisher/CEO
Henry Mowry, Director Sales

A music newspaper that covers all aspects of the radio and recording industry.
Cost: $325.00
100 Pages
Frequency: Weekly
Circulation: 8006
Printed in 4 colors on n stock

3881 Radio Business Report
2050 Old Bridge Rd
Suite B-01
Woodbridge, VA 22192-2481

703-492-8191
FAX 703-997-8601
Home Page: www.rbr.com

Jim Carnegie, Publisher
Jack Messmer, Executive Editor
Cathy Carnegie, VP Administration
Carl Marcucci, MD/Senior Editor
June Barnes, Sales

Focuses on radio business issues, inside news on people and controversial topics.
Cost: $220.00
Frequency: Daily
Circulation: 5100

Founded in 1983
Printed in 4 colors on matte stock

3882 Radio Ink
Streamline Publishing
224 Datura St
Suite 1015
West Palm Beach, FL 33401-5638

561-655-8778
800-610-5771
FAX 561-655-6164
Home Page: www.radioink.com

Eric Rhoads, Owner
Reed Bunzel, Editor
Marty Sacks, Marketing
Tom Elmo, Circulation

Geared toward radio broadcast management professionals contains information on marketing trends, special reports, sales and programming issues.
Cost: $199.00
Circulation: 5000
Founded in 1992

3883 Radio World
Industrial Marketing Advisory Services
5827 Columbia Pike
Suite 310
Falls Church, VA 22041-2027

703-998-7600
800-336-3045
FAX 703-998-2966
Home Page: www.totse.com

Steve Dana, President/Publisher
Lucia Cobo, Editor

A technical trade newspaper for the broadcast radio industry. Accepts advertising.
48 Pages
Circulation: 18000
Founded in 1978
Printed in 4 colors on newsprint stock

3884 Streaming Media Investor
Kagan World Media
126 Clock Tower Place
Carmel, CA 93923-8746

831-624-1536
FAX 831-624-5882
E-Mail: info@kagan.com
Home Page: www.kagan.com

George Niesen, Editor
Harvy Craft, Marketing Manager
Tim Baskerville, CEO/President

News of the Streaming Media Investor. Three month trial available.
Cost: $895.00
Frequency: Monthly
Founded in 1969

3885 TV Program Investor
Kagan World Media
1 Lower Ragsdale Dr
Building One, Suite 130
Monterey, CA 93940-5749

831-624-1536
800-307-2529
FAX 831-625-3225
E-Mail: info@kagan.com
Home Page: www.kagan.com

Tim Baskerville, President
Tom Johnson, Marketing Manager

More than just a newsletter, practically a seminar on how much programs cost and what they are worth. Exclusive spreadsheets with estimates of what goes between the commercials. Three month trial available.
Cost: $895.00
Frequency: Monthly
Founded in 1969

3886 Television Digest with Consumer Electronics
Warren Communications News
2115 Ward Ct Nw
Washington, DC 20037-1209

202-872-9200
800-771-9202
FAX 202-318-8350
E-Mail: info@warren-news.com
Home Page: www.warren-news.com

Brig Easley, Manager
Daniel Warren, President/Editor

A weekly newsletter providing continuous coverage of broadcasting, cable, consumer electronics and related industries.
Cost: $943.00
12 Pages
Frequency: Weekly
Mailing list available for rent

3887 The Signal
Society of Broadcast Engineers
9102 N Meridian St
Suite 150
Indianapolis, IN 46260-1896

317-846-9000
FAX 317-846-9120
E-Mail: mclappe@sbe.org
Home Page: www.sbe.org
Social Media: *Facebook, Twitter, LinkedIn*

John Poray, Executive Director
Vincent A Lopez, President

Provides members with timely articles on various broadcast-related topics, information on upcoming events, recognition of members' activities and achievements and details of SBE services.
Frequency: Bi-Monthly
Circulation: 5500
Mailing list available for rent: 4700 names at $100 per M
Printed in 4 colors on glossy stock

3888 Video Investor
Kagan World Media
126 Clock Tower Place
Carmel, CA 93923-8746

831-624-1536
FAX 831-624-5882
E-Mail: info@kagan.com
Home Page: www.kagan.com

George Niesen, Editor
Harvy Craft, Marketing Manager
Tim Baskerville, CEO/President

Authoritative look inside the business of renting and selling video cassettes. Exclusive estimates of retail and wholesale transactions and inventories. Tracking movies into the home. Three month trial is available.
Cost: $ 795.00
Frequency: Monthly
Founded in 1969

3889 Warren Communications News
Warren
2115 Ward Ct Nw
Washington, DC 20037-1209

202-872-9200
800-771-9202
FAX 202-318-8350
E-Mail: info@warren-news.com
Home Page: www.warren-news.com
Social Media: *Facebook, Twitter, LinkedIn*

Brig Easley, Manager
Daniel Warren, President/Editor

Commercial and noncommercial television stations and networks, including educational, low-power and instructional TV stations, and translators. Lists over 11,000 operating cable systems including subscribers, channel capaci-

ties, programming, fees and personnel.
Cost: $6.45
Mailing list available for rent

3890 Wireless Market Stats
Kagan World Media
1 Lower Ragsdale Dr
Building One, Suite 130
Monterey, CA 93940-5749

831-624-1536
800-307-2529
FAX 831-625-3225
E-Mail: info@kagan.com
Home Page: www.kagan.com

Tim Baskerville, President
Tom Johnson, Marketing Manager

News of the Wireless Market Stats. Three month trial available.
Cost: $995.00
Frequency: Monthly
Founded in 1969

3891 Wireless Telecom Investor
Kagan World Media
1 Lower Ragsdale Dr
Building One, Suite 130
Monterey, CA 93940-5749

831-624-1536
800-307-2529
FAX 831-625-3225
E-Mail: info@kagan.com
Home Page: www.kagan.com

Tim Baskerville, President
Tom Johnson, Marketing Manager

Exclusive analysis of private and public values of wireless telecommunications companies, including cellular telephone, ESMR and PCS. Exclusive databases of subscribers, market penetrations, market potential, industry growth. Catching super-fast growth in a capsule. Three month trial available.
Cost: $895.00
Frequency: Monthly
Founded in 1969

3892 Wireless/Private Cable Investor
Kagan World Media
1 Lower Ragsdale Dr
Building One, Suite 130
Monterey, CA 93940-5749

831-624-1536
800-307-2529
FAX 831-625-3225
E-Mail: info@kagan.com
Home Page: www.kagan.com/

Tim Baskerville, President
Tom Johnson, Marketing Manager

The original bible of the wireless cable, multipoint distribution pay TV industry. Published continuously since 1972, this newsletter is the window on cable competition. Three month trial available.
Cost: $1095.00
Frequency: Monthly
Founded in 1969

Magazines & Journals

3893 ARRL The National Association for Amateur Radio
American Radio Relay League
225 Main St
Newington, CT 06111-1494

860-594-0200
800-326-3942
FAX 860-594-0259

E-Mail: hq@arrl.org
Home Page: www.arrl.org

David Sumner, CEO
Kay Craigie, President
Bob Inderbitzen, Marketing Manager

Devoted to amateur radio information.
156M Members
Frequency: Monthly
Circulation: 146000
Founded in 1914

3894 Album Network
110 Spazier
Burbank, CA 91502-1852

818-842-2600
FAX 818-972-2899
Home Page: www.musicbiz.com

Steve Smith, Publisher

Editorial emphasis on chart ratings, sales performances, music reviews, and industry news.
Cost: $400.00
Frequency: Weekly
Circulation: 2,500

3895 Alliance for Community Media
1100 G St NW
Suite 740
Washington, DC 20005-7415

202-393-2650
FAX 202-393-2653
E-Mail: info@allcommunitymedia.org
Home Page: www.alliancecm.org

Hellen Soule, Executive Director
Denise M Woodson, Treasurer
Todd Thayer, Treasurer

Participants include cable access television and community programmers. Individual membership dues are $60.00, organization $305.00.
Cost: $35.00
36 Pages
Frequency: Quarterly
Circulation: 1500
ISSN: 1074-9004
Founded in 1985

3896 Almanac
International Council of NATAS
888 7th Avenue
5th floor
New York, NY 10019-3300

212-489-6969
FAX 212-489-6557
E-Mail: info@iemmys.tv
Home Page: www.iemmys.tv/

Camille Bide Roizen, Executive Director
Eva Obadia, Marketing Manager
Georges Leclere, Senior VP

An annual publication with highlights of the International Emmy Program, global preference guides, articles on various facets in and around television today.
Founded in 1969

3897 BE Radio
Primedia
98 Metcalf Avenue
PO Box 12901
Shawnee Mission, KS 66282-2901

913-341-1300
800-441-0294
FAX 913-514-6895
E-Mail: CorporateCustomerService@penton.com
Home Page: www.penton.com

Eric Jacobson, Senior VP
Chriss Scherer, Editor
Kirby Asplund, Marketing Director

Provides radio station managers and engineers the information they need to make critical equipment purchase decisions. Presents

need-to-know technical information to help readers solve the challenges of technology and the equipment problems they face. BE Radio serves the needs of radio engineers, managers and owners who need to make informed equipment and services buying decisions.
Cost: $30.00
Frequency: Monthly
Circulation: 12000
Founded in 1959

3898 Broadband Advertising
Kagan World Media
1 Lower Ragsdale Dr
Building One, Suite 130
Monterey, CA 93940-5749

831-624-1536
800-307-2529
FAX 831-625-3225
E-Mail: sgoldberg@snl.com
Home Page: www.kagan.com

Tim Baskerville, President

Reports and analysis of the sale of commercial time by cable TV networks, interconnects and local spot sales.
Cost: $1095.00
Frequency: Monthly
Founded in 1969
Printed in 2 colors on n stock

3899 Broadcast Engineering
Primedia
PO Box 12914
Overland Park, KS 66282-2914

913-341-1300
800-441-0294
FAX 913-967-1903
E-Mail: emily.kalmus@penton.com
Home Page: www.broadcastengineering.com
Social Media: *Facebook, Twitter, LinkedIn*

Brad Dick, Editor

Aimed at the market that includes corporate management, engineers/technicians and other management personnel at commercial and public TV stations, post-production and recording studios, broadcast networks, cable, telephone and satellite production centers and networks.
Circulation: 35000
Founded in 1960

3900 Broadcasting
Reed Business Information
2000 Clearwater Dr
Oak Brook, IL 60523-8809

630-574-0825
800-446-6551
FAX 630-288-8781
E-Mail: webmaster@reedbusiness.com
Home Page: www.reedbusiness.com

Jeff Greisch, President
Larry Dunn, Publishing Director
Jim Casella, CEO

Offers comprehensive coverage of television, radio, cable, satellite and the attendant equipment and emerging technologies. Accepts advertising.
Cost: $189.00
Founded in 1894

3901 CQ Amateur Radio
CQ Communications
25 Newbridge Rd
Suite 405
Hicksville, NY 11801-2887

516-681-2922
FAX 516-681-2926
E-Mail: cq@cq-amateur-radio.com
Home Page: http://www.cq-amateur-radio.com

Richard Ross, CEO
Rich Moseson, Managing Editor

Gail Sheehan, Managing Editor
Mellisa Gillgan, Circulation

Information for people interested in the developments of in the field radio communications and electronics. Coverage includes reviews of new operating programs, new products and seasonal promotional ideas.
Cost: $32.00
Frequency: Monthly
Circulation: 87000
Founded in 1950

3902 CTAM Quarterly Marketing Journal
Cable Television Administration & Marketing
201 N Union Street
Suite 440
Alexandria, VA 22314-2642

703-549-4200
FAX 703-684-1167
E-Mail: info@ctam.com
Home Page: www.ctam.com/

Char Beales, President
Patrick Dougherty, Marketing Manager

A journal offering financial information to persons in the cable television management and executives.
Cost: $295.00
Frequency: Quarterly

3903 Cable Plus/Cable TV Publications
Cable TV Publications/TV Host
PO Box 1665
Harrisburg, PA 17105-1665

800-922-4678
FAX 610-687-2965

Frank Dillahey, Sales Manager
Bob Newell, Marketing Director

Custom cable TV listing guides incorporating exclusive cable programming, editorial, movie reviews and TV listings that are sold to cable subscribers nationally. Circulation of this guide is over 1.75 million.
Cost: $24.00
Frequency: Monthly

3904 Communicator
Radio Television News Directors Association
1025 Thomas Jefferson St
7th Floor, Suite 700E
Washington, DC 20007-5214

202-625-3500
800-807-8632
FAX 202-223-4007
E-Mail: barbarac@rtnda.org
Home Page: www.rtnda.org
Social Media: *Facebook*

The latest information on technological breakthroughs, cutting edge newsroom practices, and contemporary management techniques.
Cost: $75.00
Frequency: 11x/yr
Circulation: 4,000

3905 DV Digital Video Magazine
Miller Freeman Publications
PO Box 1212
Skokie, IL 60076

888-776-7002
888-776-7002
FAX 847-763-9614
E-Mail: dv@halldata.com
Home Page: www.dv.com

Dominic Milano, Editorial Director
Armand DerHacobian, Associate Publisher
Jarett Cory, Sales Manager

Video production, animation and audio film, broadcast and new media. Includes discussions on training and communications.
Frequency: Monthly
Circulation: 64382
Founded in 1993

3906 Digital TV/Television Broadcast
United Entertainment Media
810 7th Avenue
27th Fl
New York, NY 10019

212-378-0400
FAX 212-378-2160
E-Mail: sedorusa@optonline.net
Home Page: www.governmentvideo.com
Social Media: *Facebook*

Gary Rhodes, International Sales Manager

Digital TV/Television Broadcast is an in depth analysis and insider views of the business of television. It discusses the individuals, market trends, technology, products and policies that drive the television industry in the digital age.
Frequency: Monthly
Circulation: 22000
Founded in 1978
Mailing list available for rent

3907 EQ Magazine
Miller Freeman Publications
810 7th Ave
27th Fl, Suite 4
New York, NY 10019-5818

212-636-2700
FAX 212-636-2750
E-Mail: sedorusa@optonline.net
Home Page: www.governmentvideo.com
Social Media: *Facebook*

Gary Rhodes, International Sales Manager

Articles on recording techniques and tips for musicians, producers, and engineers in the broadcast industry.
Frequency: Monthly
Circulation: 40000
Mailing list available for rent

3908 Emmy Magazine
Academy of Television Arts & Sciences
5200 Lankershim Blvd
North Hollywood, CA 91601-3155

818-754-2800
818-754-2860
FAX 818-761-2827
E-Mail: emmymag@emmys.org
Home Page: www.emmys.com/

John Shaffner, CEO
Laurel Whitcomb, VP Marketing
Barbara Chase, Director Membership
Juan Morales, Editor
Gail Polevoi, Manager

This magazine tells of association news, EMMY information and awards for the broadcasting and media industries.
Cost: $28.00
Founded in 1995

3909 FTTX
Information Gatekeepers
1340 Soldiers Field Rd
Suite 302
Brighton, MA 02135-1000

617-782-5033
800-323-1088
FAX 617-782-5735
E-Mail: info@igigroup.com
Home Page: www.igigroup.com

Paul Polishuk, CEO
Beverly Wilson, Controller
Yesim Taskor, Controller
Brian Mark, Editor

Covers developments, products, competition, technology, and standards for the use of fiber optics and related techniques in the cable TV industry.
Cost: $695.00
Frequency: Monthly
Circulation: 2000
Founded in 1977

3910 Financial Manager
Broadcast Cable Financial Management Association
550 W Frontage Rd
Suite 3600
Northfield, IL 60093-1243

847-716-7000
FAX 847-784-8059
E-Mail: info@bccacredit.com
Home Page: www.bcfm.com

Mary Collins, President
Jamie Smith, Director of Operations
Rachelle Brooks, BCCA Sales

A bi-monthly magazine published by the Broadcast Cable Financial Management Association.
Cost: $69.00
36 Pages
Frequency: 6 issues per ye
Circulation: 2000
Mailing list available for rent: 1100 names at $495 per M

3911 Folio
Pacifica Foundation
1925 Martin Luther King Jr Way
Berkeley, CA 94704-1037

510-849-2590
FAX 510-849-2617
E-Mail: contact@pacifica.org
Home Page: www.pacificafoundation.org

Lonnie Hicks, Manager
Dan Coughlin, Executive Director
Listing of programs heard on Pacific Radio Stations.
Cost: $40.00
28 Pages
Frequency: Monthly
Founded in 1949

3912 GBH: Member's Magazine
WGBH Educational Foundation
PO Box 55875
Boston, MA 02205-5875

617-300-5400
FAX 617-300-1026
E-Mail: feedback@wgbh.org
Home Page: www.wgbh.org

Diane Dion, Editor
Jon Abbott, Owner
Mary Cotton, Owner

Offers information on station programming, personalities and more for members of WGBH, Boston's PBS and NPR station.
Cost: $50.00
Frequency: Monthly
Circulation: 175000
Founded in 1951

3913 Hits Magazine
Color West
3405 Pacific Avenue
Burbank, CA 91505

818-840-8881
FAX 818-840-2753
E-Mail: info@colorwestprinting.com
Home Page: www.colorwestprinting.com

Dennis Lavinthal, Publisher
Lynn Jensen, President
Karen Jensen, Controller
Chartmakers and hits in contemporary pop music, industry news and happenings, also in-

cludes radio news and playlists.
Cost: $300.00
Frequency: Weekly
Circulation: 10000
Founded in 1971

3914 Inside Radio
Inside Radio
365 Union St
Littleton, NH 03561-5619

603-444-5720
800-248-4242
FAX 603-444-2872
E-Mail: info@insideradio.com
Home Page: www.insideradio.com

Cathy Devine, Research Director
Kelli Grisez, Operations Manager
Features issues that effect the radio industry and individuals involved in it.
Cost: $455.00
Frequency: Daily
Circulation: 7000

3915 International Cable
Phillips Business Information
1201 Seven Locks Road
Potomac, MD 20854-2931

301-354-1400
FAX 301-340-0542
E-Mail: edmerson@internationalcable.tv
Home Page: www.phillips.com

Nancy Umberger-Maynard, Publisher

Articles on technological advances internationally and the businesses that are making it possible.
Cost: $73.75
Frequency: Monthly
Circulation: 11,000

3916 Journal of Broadcasting and Electronic Media
Broadcast Education Association
1771 N St NW
Washington, DC 20036-2800

202-429-5355
888-380-7222
FAX 301-869-8608
E-Mail: Don.Godfrey@asu.edu
Home Page: www.beaweb.org

Heather Birks, Executive Director
Steven D Anderson, President
Donald G Godfrey, Editor
Cost: $50.00
Frequency: Quarterly
ISSN: 0883-8151
Founded in 1955
Printed in one color on matte stock

3917 Journal of College Radio
Intercollegiate Broadcasting System
367 Windsor Highway
New Windsor, NY 12553-7900

845-534-0003
FAX 845-565-7446
E-Mail: IBSHQ@aol.com
Home Page: www.collegeradio.tv/

Norman Prusslin, President
Jeff Tellis, VP

Magazine of the nonprofit association of student staffed radio stations based at schools and colleges across the country. Accepts advertising.
Cost: $20.00
24 Pages
Frequency: Quarterly
Founded in 1940

3918 Journal of Radio & Audio Media
Broadcast Education Association

1771 N St NW
Washington, DC 20036-2800

202-429-5355
FAX 202-775-2981
E-Mail: beamemberservices@nab.org
Home Page: www.beaweb.org

Heather Birks, Executive Director
Traci Bailey, Manager, Business Operations
Phylis Johnson, Editor
Mary Schaffer, President
Cost: $30.00
Frequency: Bi-annually
Founded in 1955

3919 Journal of the Audio Engineering Society
Audio Engineering Society
60 E 42nd Street
Room 2520
New York, NY 10165-2520

212-661-8528
FAX 212-682-0477
E-Mail: hq@aes.org
Home Page: www.aes.org
Social Media: *Facebook, Twitter*

Roger Furness, Executive Director
William T McQuaide, Managing Editor
The Journal contains state-of-the-art technical papers and engineering reports; feature articles covering timely topics; ore and post reports of AES conventions and society activities; news from AES sections; Standards and Education Committee work; membership news, patents, new products, and noteworthy developments. Subscriptions available in print, electronic and combination options.
Cost: $280.00
Frequency: 10/Year
Circulation: 12000
ISSN: 0004-7554
Printed in 4 colors on glossy stock

3920 Ku-Band World Magazine
Opportunities Publishing
305 Jackson Avenue W
Oxford, MS 38655-2154

FAX 662-236-5541

Ed Meek, Editor
Business application of developing Ku-band satellite communications systems.
Cost: $25.00
52 Pages
Frequency: Monthly
Founded in 1985

3921 Millimeter Magazine
2104 Harvell Circle
Bellevue, NE 68005

402-505-7100
866-505-7173
FAX 402-293-0741
E-Mail: llcs@pbsub.com
Home Page: www.millimeter.com

Cynthia Wisehart, Editorial Director
Gayle Grooms, Audience Marketing
Christina Heil, Marketing
Jeff Victor, Associate Editor

Authoritative resource for more than 33,000 qualified professionals in production, postproduction, animation, streaming and visual effects for motion pictures, television and commercials.
Cost: $25.00
150 Pages
Frequency: Monthly

3922 NRB Magazine
National Religious Broadcasters

9510 Technology Dr
Manassas, VA 20110-4149

703-330-7100
FAX 703-330-7100
E-Mail: info@nrb.org
Home Page: www.nrb.org
Social Media: *Facebook, Twitter*

Frank Wright, President
Linda Smith, President Assistant

Trade publication for Christian communicators, including radio, TV, Internet and international media.
Cost: $24.00
56 Pages
Frequency: Monthly
Circulation: 9000
ISSN: 1521-1754
Founded in 1969
Printed in 4 colors on glossy stock

3923 RPM Weekly
Novasound Productions
PO Box 630071
Irving, TX 75063-71

972-432-8100
FAX 972-432-8102
E-Mail: jv@rapmag.com
Home Page: www.rapmag.com

Jerry Vigil, Publisher
Shardan Azat, Manager

Information on radio stations and independent production houses, engineering and production directors that manage these studios, industry news and latest technology information.
Cost: $115.00
Frequency: Monthly
Circulation: 7500
Founded in 1988

3924 Radio
1930 Century Park W
Los Angeles, CA 90067-6803

323-263-6991
FAX 310-203-8450

Dwight Case, Editor

A magazine covering all aspects of the radio communications industry.
Cost: $215.00
Frequency: Monthly
Founded in 1973

3925 Radio Science
American Geophysical Union
2000 Florida Ave NW
Washington, DC 20009-1231

202-462-6900
800-966-2481
FAX 202-328-0566
E-Mail: service@agu.org
Home Page: www.agu.org
Social Media: *Facebook, Twitter*

Fred Spilhaus, Executive Director

Coverage of radio propagation, communication, and upper atmospheric physics.
Cost: $10.00
Circulation: 1200
Founded in 1919

3926 Radio-TV Interview Report
Bradley Communications
135 E Plumstead Avenue
PO Box 1206
Lansdowne, PA 19050-8206

610-591-1070
FAX 610-284-3704
E-Mail: Circ@rtir.com
Home Page: www.rtir.com

Bill Harrison, President

A source for finding authors and experts to interview about a wide variety of subjects.
88 Pages
Frequency: Monthly
Circulation: 4000
Founded in 1986

3927 SMPTE Motion Imaging Journal
Society of Motion Picture & Television Engineers
3 Barker Ave
Floor 5
White Plains, NY 10601-1509

914-761-1100
FAX 914-761-3115
Home Page: www.smpte.org

Barbara Lange, Executive Director

The gateway to the world of motion imaging featuring industry-leading papers and standards, the Journal keeps its members on the cutting edge of this ever-changing industry.
Cost: $140.00
Frequency: Monthly

3928 Satellite Retailer
Triple D Publishing
1300 S Dekalb St
Shelby, NC 28152-7210

704-482-9673
FAX 704-484-6976

Douglas G Brown Sr, President

Edited for the satellite industry.
Cost: $12.00
72 Pages
Frequency: Monthly
Founded in 1985

3929 Satvision Magazine
Satellite Broadcasting/Communications Association
1730 M St NW
Suite 600
Washington, DC 20036-4557

202-349-3620
FAX 202-349-3621
E-Mail: info@sbca.org
Home Page: www.sbca.com

Joseph Widoff, Executive Director

Offers information for television satellite dealers.
Cost: $35.00
Frequency: Monthly
Circulation: 10000

3930 Teleguia USA: Novedades USA - Buscando Amor
Echo Media
900 Circle 75 Pkwy SE
Suite 1600
Atlanta, GA 30339-6014

770-955-3346
E-Mail: salesinfo@echo-media.com
Home Page: www.echo-media.com

Michael Puffer, CEO
Kelly Elarbee, Media Director
Frequency: Weekly
Circulation: 100,000
Founded in 1986
Mailing list available for rent
Printed in 4 colors on newsprint stock

3931 Via Satellite
Phillips Business Information
1201 Seven Locks Rd
Suite 300
Potomac, MD 20854

301-541-1400
FAX 301-309-3847

Home Page:
www.kftv.com/company-30086.html

Scott Chase, Publisher
Richard Summers, Managing Editor

Covers voice, video and data in global commercial communications, including company profiles, market analysis and new products.
Cost: $49.00
Frequency: Monthly
Circulation: 17446

3932 WNYC Wavelength
1 Centre St
Suite 2453
New York, NY 10007-1699

212-669-7800
FAX 212-669-3312
Home Page: www.wnyc.org

Lori Krushefski, Marketing
Laura Walker, President

Relays broadcasting news. Accepts advertising.
16 Pages
Frequency: Monthly

3933 Women on the Job: Careers in the Electronic Media
American Women in Radio and Television
1760 Old Meadow Rd
Suite 800
Mc Lean, VA 22102-4306

703-506-3290
FAX 703-506-3266
E-Mail: info@awrt.org
Home Page: www.awrt.org

Maria Brennan, President

Association news focusing on women in the workplace, particularly media and communications industries.

3934 World Screen News
1123 Broadway
Suite 1201
New York, NY 10010-2007

212-924-7620
FAX 212-924-6940
E-Mail: mdaswani@worldscreen.com
Home Page: www.worldscreen.com

Ricardo Duise, Manager
Anna Carugati, Managing Editor
Kristin Brzoznowski, Managing Editor
Rafael Blanco, Executive Editor
Cesar Suero, Advertising Sales Director

Serves the international television cable and satellite industries including advertising agencies within the industry and others allied to the field. Also publishes the following supplements; TV Kids, TV Europe, TV Docs, TV Latina.
Cost: $50.00
Frequency: Monthly
Circulation: 4038
Founded in 1985

Trade Shows

3935 AES Convention
Audio Engineering Society
60 E 42nd Street
Room 2520
New York, NY 10165-2520

212-661-8528
FAX 212-682-0477
E-Mail: HQ@aes.org
Home Page: www.aes.org

Bob Moses, Executive Director
Roger Furness, Deputy Director
Jan Pederson, President

Frank Wells, President-Elect
Robert Breen, Vice President

An international organization that unites audio engineers, creative artists, scienists and students worldwide by promoting advances in audio and desseminating new knowledge and research.
Frequency: October

3936 Alaska Broadcasters Association Conference
Alaska Broadcasters Association
700 W 41st Street
Suite 102
Anchorage, AK 99503

907-258-2424
FAX 907-258-2414
E-Mail: akba@gci.net
Home Page: www.alaskabroadcaster.org
Social Media: *Facebook*

Gary Donovan, President
Matt Wilson, Vice President

Provides assistance which enables members to serve their communities of license through educations, representation and advocacy.
225 Attendees
Frequency: Annual

3937 Annual Community Radio Conference
National Federation of Community Broadcasters
1970 Broadway
Suite 1000
Oakland, CA 94612

510-451-8200
FAX 510-451-8208
E-Mail: comments@nfcb.org
Home Page: www.nfcb.org

Carol Pierson, President/CEO
Virginia Z Berson, VP Federation Services

National conference for public community radio stations offering opportunities for staff development, skill building, networking, affinity group, inspiration, new ideas, discussion and exchanges; exhibit area; programming awards. Business meetings for National Federation of Community Broadcasters.
300 Attendees
Frequency: April

3938 Annual IBS Broadcasting & Webcasting Conference
Intercollegiate Broadcasting System
367 Windsor Highway
New Windsor, NY 12553-7900

845-565-0003
FAX 845-565-7446
E-Mail: ibshq@aol.com
Home Page: www.ibsradio.org

Norman Prusslin, President
Fritz Kass, Chief Operating Officer

Over 110 seminars, live music, over 250 top broadcasting professionals, and 1,200 student radio & webcasters from around the world. Live webstream during conference.
1.2M Attendees
Frequency: March

3939 Audio Engineering Society Meeting
Audio Engineering Society
60 E 42nd Street
Room 2520
New York, NY 10165-2520

212-661-8528
FAX 212-682-0477
Home Page: www.aes.org

Roger K Furness, Executive Director

250 booths, held in the fall and spring of each year.
5M Attendees
Frequency: October

3940 Broadcast Designers' Association International Conference & Expo
Broadcast Designers' Association International
145 W 45th Street
Room 1100
New York, NY 10036-4008

212-376-6222
FAX 212-376-6202

Annual show and exhibits of broadcast design equipment, supplies and services.

3941 Broadcast Engineering Conference (BEC)
Society of Broadcast Engineers
9102 N Meridian Street
Suite 150
Indianapolis, IN 46260

317-846-9000
FAX 317-846-9120
E-Mail: mclappe@sbe.org
Home Page: www.sbe.org

John Poray, Executive Director
Vincent A Lopez, President

Offers broadcast engineers the opportunity to attend educational sessions, see the latest equipment and supplies, and meet with peers.
500 Attendees
Frequency: Annual/Spring

3942 CRS - Country Radio Show
Country Radion Broadcasters
819 18th Avenue South
Nashville, TN 37203

615-327-4487
FAX 615-329-4492
E-Mail: info@crb.org
Home Page: www.crb.org

Ed Salamon, Executive Director
Chasity Crouch, Business Manager

Jams, discussions, introduction of new comers, Hall of Fame presentations.
2,000 Attendees
Frequency: March

3943 Cable Television Trade Show and Convention: East
Convention Show Management Company
6175 Barfield Road NE
Suite 220
Atlanta, GA 30328-4327

404-252-2454
FAX 404-252-0215

Nancy Horne, Show Manager
Nine hundred booths.
6M Attendees
Frequency: August

3944 Cable and Satellite: European Broadcasting/Communications Show
Reed Exhibition Companies
255 Washington Street
Newton, MA 02458-1637

617-584-4900
FAX 617-630-2222

Elizabeth Hitchcock, International Sales
Communications forum for professionals in the broadcasting industry.
7.9M Attendees
Frequency: April

3945 MFMA/BCCA Annual Conference
Media Financial Management Association

550 W Frontage Road
Suite 3600
Northfield, IL 60093

847-716-7000
FAX 847-716-7004
E-Mail: info@mediafinance.org
Home Page: www.bcfm.com

Mary Collins, President/CEO
Jamie Smith, Director of Operations

Offers professional education targeting media financial and business executives; CPE opportunities; exhibitors; roundtables; and networking opportunities.
800 Attendees
Frequency: Annual
Mailing list available for rent: 1,200 names at $495 per M

3946 MIP-TV: International Television Program Market
Reed Exhibition Companies
255 Washington Street
Newton, MA 02458-1637

617-584-4900
FAX 617-630-2222

Elizabeth Hitchcock, International Sales

Spring market for the television industry to buy, sell and distribute television programming.
9M Attendees
Frequency: April

3947 NAB Radio Show
National Association of Broadcasters
1771 N Street NW
Washington, DC 20036

202-429-5300
888-140-4622
301-682-7962
FAX 202-429-4199
E-Mail: NABSHOW@expressreg.net
Home Page: www.nabshow.com

David Wharton, EVP Media Relations
Jennifer Landry-Jackson, Exhibit Sales
Kelly Bryant, Event Operations

A unique networking opportunity for station professionals representing all format and market sizes, with exhibits showcasing technologies, tools and solutions for the industry.
Frequency: Annual

3948 NAB Show
National Association of Broadcasters
1771 N Street NW
Washington, DC 20036

202-429-5300
800-342-2460
202-429-3189
FAX 202-429-4199
E-Mail: NABSHOW@expressreg.net
Home Page: www.nabshow.com

David Wharton, EVP Media Relations
Jennifer Landry-Jackson, Exhibit Sales
Kelly Bryant, Event Operations

A global event for broadcasting news, legislation, networking, education and technology. Over 150 countries represented by 85,000+ attendees and exhibitors; conferences, and training sessions, and over 1,500 exhibitors.
85M Attendees
Frequency: April

3949 NATPE Market & Conference
National Association of TV Program Executives
5757 Wilshire Boulevard
Penthouse 10
Los Angeles, CA 90036-3681

310-453-4440
FAX 310-453-5258

E-Mail: info@natpe.org
Home Page: www.natpe.org

Nick Orfanopoulos, Senior VP Exhibitions
Beth Braen, Senior VP Marketing

The National Association of Television Program Executives (NATPE) is a global alliance of business professionals engaged in the creation, development and distribution of content as well as advertising and financial activities. NATPE is the world's largest non-profit association dedicated to facilitating the continued growth and convergence of all content across all distribution platforms.
8000 Attendees
Frequency: Annual
Founded in 1963

3950 NATPE: The Alliance of Media Content
National Association of TV Program Executives
6868 Wilshire Boulevard
Penthouse 10
Los Angeles, CA 90036-3681

310-453-4440
800-NAT-PEGO
FAX 310-453-5258
E-Mail: info@natpe.org
Home Page: www.natpe.org

Pam Silverman, Exhibition & Advertising
Linda Nichols, Exhibitor Services
Eric Low, Registration & Membership

The National Association of Television Program Executives (NATPE) is a global alliance of business professionals engaged in the creation, development and distribution of content as well as advertising and financial activities. NATPE is the world's largest non-profit association dedicated to facilitating the continued growth and convergence of all content across all distribution platforms.
1000 Attendees
Frequency: January
Founded in 1963

3951 NECTA Convention & Exhibition
New England Cable And Telecommunications Assn
10 Forbes Road
Suite 440W
Braintree, MA 02184-2648

781-843-3418
FAX 781-849-6267
E-Mail: info@necta.info
Home Page: www.necta.info

Paul Cianelli, President
William Durand, Executive Vice President
Donna Nolan, Office Manager

A six state regional trade association representing substantially all private cable telecommunications companies in Connecticut, Maine, Massachusetts, New Hampshire, Rhode Island, and Vermont.
1.1M Attendees
Frequency: July

3952 National Public Radio Association
National Public Radio Association
635 Massachusetts Avenue NW
Washington, DC 20001-3753

202-513-2000
FAX 202-513-3329
Home Page: www.npr.org

Vivian Schiller, President & CEO
Howard Stevenson, Chair of the Board of Directors
Mitch Praver, COO

Seventy five booths for public radio professionals and providers of resource materials for public radio.
1.2M Attendees
Frequency: April/May

3953 National Religious Broadcasters Annual Convention and Exposition
National Religious Broadcasters
9510 Technology Drive
Manassas, VA 20110

703-330-7000
FAX 703-330-7100
E-Mail: info@nrb.org
Home Page: www.nrb.org

Dr Frank Wright, President/CEO
Linda Smith, President Assistant
David Keith, VP Operations

Containing 280 exhibits. Broadcast and communications emphasis.
5,700 Attendees
Frequency: February

3954 OAB Broadcast Engineering Conference
Society of Broadcast Engineers
9102 N Meridian Street
Suite 150
Indianapolis, IN 46260

317-846-9000
FAX 317-846-9120
E-Mail: mclappe@sbe.org
Home Page: www.sbe.org

Vincent A Lopez, President
John Poray, Executive Director

Offers broadcast engineers the opportunity to attend educational sessions, see the latest equipment and supplies, and meet with peers.
5500 Members
Frequency: Annual/November
Founded in 1964
Mailing list available for rent: 5700 names at $170 per M

3955 RAB2009 Conference
Radio Advertising Bureau
1320 Greenway Drive
Suite 500
Irving, TX 75038

972-536-6700
800-232-3131
FAX 972-753-6727
E-Mail: jhaley@rab.com
Home Page: www.rab.com

Erica Ferber, President
Van Allen, CFO

Learn about new media opportunities from new digital platforms and monetizing streams to HD strategies that will empower you to compete at a new level and be an innovator at your station.
1600 Attendees
Frequency: Annual/March

3956 Recruiting Conference and Expo
Kennedy Information
1 Phoenix Mill Lane
Floor 3
Peterborough, NH 03458

603-924-1006
800-531-0007
E-Mail: conferences@kennedyinfo.com
Home Page: www.recruiting2006.com

Matt Lyons, Director, Recruiting Group

Learn about the winning strategies, best practices, and tools ou will need to succeed in a challenging talent market.
Frequency: Nov New York

3957 SCTE Cable-Tec EXPO
Society of Cable Telecommunication Engineers
140 Philips Road
Exton, PA 19341-1318

610-363-6888
800-542-5040
FAX 610-363-5898
E-Mail: scte@scte.org
Home Page: www.scte.org

Lori Bower, Director
John Clark, CEO

Five hundred booths and, exhibits featuring telecommunications and programming equipment; dozens of workshops, with new technologies showcased.
12M Attendees
Frequency: Annual
Mailing list available for rent

3958 SMPTE Annual Tech Conference & EXPO
Society of Motion Picture & Television Engineers
3 Barker Avenue
5th Floor
White Plains, NY 10601

914-761-1100
FAX 914-761-3115
E-Mail: smpte@smpte.org
Home Page: www.smpte.org
Social Media: *Facebook, Twitter, LinkedIn*

Barbara Lange, Executive Director
Sally Ann D'Amato, Director, Operations
Roberta Gorman, Manager, Member Relations
Aimee Ricca, Product Marketing Manager

The Technical Conference and Exhibition which is held in the fall. This alternates between the east and west coasts, usually in Pasadena and New York.
Frequency: Annual

3959 Satellite Broadcasting and Communication Association (SBCA)
Show Management & Services
900 Jorie Boulevard
Suite 200
Oak Brook, IL 60523-3835

800-654-9276
FAX 630-990-2077

Diana Bubalo, Show Manager

Four hundred fifty booths.
2.5M Attendees

3960 Television Bureau of Advertising Annual Meeting
Television Bureau of Advertising
3 E 54th Street
New York, NY 10022

212-486-1111
FAX 212-935-5631
E-Mail: info@tvb.org
Home Page: www.tvb.org

Steve Lanzano, President
Abby Auerbach, EVP
Gary Bellis, VP/Communications

Annual show of 20-25 exhibitors of services for television stations, including research, sales and management training programs, incentives, collection agencies, advertiser contests and computer software.

3961 Western Cable Television Conference and Expo
Trade Associates

11820 Parklawn Drive
Suite 250
Rockville, MD 20852-2505

301-519-1610

Susan Rosenstock, Expo Director

One thousand three hundred booths featuring exhibits of programming, mobile aerial devices, video equipment and products and services for the communications and related industry fields.
10M Attendees
Frequency: November/December

3962 Western Show
Trade Associates
11820 Parklawn Drive
Suite 250
Rockville, MD 20852-2505

301-519-1610
FAX 301-468-3662

Susan Rosenstock, Director

One thousand booths featuring exhibits from cable operators and suppliers to the cable industry. The California Cable Television Association and the Arizona Cable Television Association sponsor this annual event.
10M Attendees
Frequency: December

Directories & Databases

3963 AES E-Library
Audio Engineering Society
60 E 42nd St
Room 2520
New York, NY 10165

212-661-8528
FAX 212-682-0477
E-Mail: HQ@aes.org
Home Page: www.aes.org
Social Media: *Facebook*

Bob Moses, Executive Director
Roger K Furness, Deputy Director

The library contains over 12,000 fully searchable PDF files documenting the progression of audio research from 1953 to the present, and includes every AES paper published at a convention, conference or in the Journal. Available as a subscription or pay per paper download: $135 for members, $245 for non, or $5 per paper for members or $20 for non.
Cost: $5.00
Frequency: Annual or Per-Paper

3964 Arbitron Radio County Coverage
Arbitron Company
142 5th Ave
New York, NY 10011-4312

212-887-1300
FAX 212-887-1558
Home Page: www.arbitron.com

Stephen Morris, CEO
Marilou Legge, Executive Vice President

This database offers access to audience listening estimates by county.
Frequency: Statistical

3965 Audio Engineering Society: Directory of Educational Programs
Audio Engineering Society
60 E 42nd St
Room 2520
New York, NY 10165

212-661-8528
FAX 212-682-0477
E-Mail: HQ@aes.org

Home Page: www.aes.org
Social Media: *Facebook*

Bob Moses, Executive Director
Roger K Furness, Deputy Director

Institutions offering postsecondary programs and seminars in audio technology and engineering are searchable by program type or geographic area. Available free online. Educators are asked to confirm the information for their institutions.
Frequency: Free Online

3966 Bacon's Newspaper & Magazine Directories
Cision U.S., Inc.
322 South Michigan Avenue
Suite 900
Chicago, IL 60604

312-263-0070
866-639-5087
E-Mail: info.us@cision.com
Home Page: us.cision.com

Joe Bernardo, President & CEO
Heidi Sullivan, VP & Publisher
Valerie Lopez, Research Director
Jessica White, Research Director
Rachel Farrell, Research Manager

Two volume set listing all daily and community newspapers, magazines and newsletters, news service and syndicates, syndicated columnists, complete editorial staff listings of each publication provided, covers U.S., Canada, Mexico, and Carribean.
Cost: $350.00
4,700 Pages
Frequency: Annual
ISSN: 1088-9639
Founded in 1951
Printed in one color on matte stock

3967 Bacon's Radio/TV/Cable Directory
Cision U.S., Inc.
332 South Michigan Avenue
Suite 900
Chicago, IL 60604

312-263-0070
866-639-5087
E-Mail: info.us@cision.com
Home Page: www.us.cision.com

Joe Bernardo, President & CEO
Heidi Sullivan, VP & Publisher
Valerie Lopez, Research Director
Jessica White, Research Director
Rachel Farrell, Research Manager

Includes comprehensive coverage for contact and programming information for more than 3,500 televsion networks, cable networks, television syndicators, television stations, and cable systems in the United States and Canada.
Cost: $350.00
Frequency: Annual
ISSN: 1088-9639
Printed in one color on matte stock

3968 Broadcast Engineering Equipment Reference Manual
Penton
249 W 17th Street
New York, NY 10011

212-204-4200
E-Mail:
corporatecustomerservice@penton.com
Home Page: www.penton.com

Sharon Rowlands, Chief Executive Officer

Offers a list of more than 1,400 manufacturers and distributors of communications equipment for radio, television and recording applications.
Cost: $20.00
Frequency: Annual
Circulation: 35,500
ISSN: 0007-1994

3969 Burrelle's Media Directory
BurrellesLuce
75 E Northfield Rd
Livingston, NJ 07039-4532

973-992-6600
800-631-1160
FAX 973-992-7675
Home Page: www.burrellesluce.com
Social Media: *Facebook, Twitter, LinkedIn*

Robert C Waggoner, CEO

Offers media outreach, media monitoring and media reporting products.
Cost: $795.00

3970 CPB Public Broadcasting Directory
Corporation for Public Broadcasting
401 9th St NW
Suite 200
Washington, DC 20004-2129

202-879-9600
FAX 202-879-9700
E-Mail: oigemail@cpb.org
Home Page: www.cpb.org
Social Media: *Twitter*

Robert T Coonrod, CEO

Offers information on public television stations, national and regional public broadcasting association and networks.
Cost: $15.00
152 Pages
Frequency: Annual
Circulation: 14,000

3971 Cable Online Data Exchange
Prometheus Global Media
770 Broadway
New York, NY 10003-9595

212-493-4100
FAX 646-654-5368
Home Page: www.prometheusgm.com

Richard D. Beckman, CEO
James A. Finkelstein, Chairman
Madeline Krakowsky, Vice President Circulation
Tracy Brater, Executive Director Creative Service

This database contains information on more than 10,000 US cable television system franchises.

3972 Complete Television, Radio and Cable Industry Directory
Grey House Publishing
4919 Route 22
PO Box 56
Amenia, NY 12501

518-789-8700
800-562-2139
FAX 845-373-6390
FAX new
E-Mail: books@greyhouse.com
Home Page: www.greyhouse.com

Richard Gottlieb, President
Leslie Mackenzie, Publisher

The most comprehensive industry data on the US and Canadian Televison, Radio and Cable Industries. Can also subscibe to the database found online.
Cost: $350.00
2000 Pages
ISBN: 9-781619-25-1
Founded in 1981

3973 Directory of Field Contacts for the Coordination of the Use of Radio
Federal Communications Commission
445 12th Street SW
Washington, DC 20554

202-180-0450
FAX 866-418-0232

E-Mail: fccinfo@fcc.gov
Home Page: www.fcc.com

Radio frequency coordinating agencies are listed.
170 Pages
Frequency: Annual

3974 Directory of Religious Media
National Religious Broadcasters
9510 Technology Dr
Manassas, VA 20110-4149

703-330-7100
FAX 703-330-7100
E-Mail: info@nrb.org
Home Page: www.nrb.org

Frank Wright, President
Linda Smith, President Assistant
David Keith, VP Operations

Comprehensive guide to radio, television, music and book publishers.
Frequency: 10 per year

3975 Editors Guild Directory
Motion Picture Editors Guild
7715 Sunset Boulevard
Suite 200
Hollywood, CA 90046

323-876-4770
FAX 323-876-0861
E-Mail: info@editorsguild.com
Home Page: www.editorsguild.com

Lisa Churgin, Guild President
Dede Allen, VP
Diane Adler, Secretary
Rachel Igel, Treasurer
Tris Carpenter, Manager

An invaluable resource for producers, directors and post production professionals alike. It lists contact, credit, award and classification information for all of the Guild's active members at the time of publication, as well as a list of Oscar and Emmy winners for every year since the awards began. It also include a retirees section.
Cost: $25.00

3976 GMRS National Repeater Guide
Personal Radio Steering Group
PO Box 2851
Ann Arbor, MI 48106-2851

734-662-4533
Home Page: gmrs.org

Corwin Moore, Administrative Director

Lists the 3,500 GMRS repeaters nationally, along with names and addresses of station licensees.
Frequency: Monthly

3977 Gale Directory of Publications and Broadcast Media
Gale/Cengage Learning
PO Box 09187
Detroit, MI 48209-0187

248-699-4253
800-877-4253
FAX 248-699-8049
E-Mail: gale.galeord@cengage.com
Home Page: www.gale.com

Patrick C Sommers, President

This media directory contains thousands of listings for radio and television stations and cable companies.
Frequency: Annual
ISBN: 1-414434-71-5
Founded in 2008

3978 International Motion Picture Almanac Intern Television & Video Almanac
Quigley Publishing Company, Incorporated

64 Wintergreen Lane
Groton, MA 01450

978-448-0272
FAX 978-448-9325
E-Mail: quigleypub@aol.com
Home Page: www.quigleypublishing.com

William J Quigley, President/Publisher
Jayme Kulesz, Editor
Michael Quigley, Associate Editor/Ops Manager
Dee Quigley, Associate Editor

Invaluable completely updated information to the most sucsessful people in the business. Are you one of them? With thousands of corporations, 5,000 plus career profiles and the most comprehensive information available on the second largest industry in the US.
Cost: $250.00
780 Pages
Frequency: Annual
ISBN: 0-900610-74-3
ISSN: 0074-7084
Founded in 1915

3979 Kagan Media Index
Kagan World Media
126 Clock Tower Place
Carmel, CA 93923-8746

831-624-1536
FAX 831-625-3225
E-Mail: info@kagan.com
Home Page: www.kagan.com

George Niesen, Editor
Tom Johnson, Marketing Manager

The most comprehensive collection of media industry databases found anywhere. Current estimates of industry growth for a dozen different media businesses, shown on a 145-line spreadsheet, projected forward and updated monthly. Three month trial available.
Cost: $795.00
Frequency: Monthly

3980 National Radio Publicity Outlets
Volt Directory Marketing
1800 Byberry Road
Suite 800
Huntingdon Valley, PA 19006-3520

800-677-3839
FAX 610-832-0878

Offers valuable information on over 7,000 radio stations in all major United States and Canadian markets.
Cost: $188.00
640 Pages
Frequency: SemiAnnual

3981 Radio & Records
Radio & Records
10100 Santa Monica Boulevard
5th Floor
Los Angeles, CA 90067-4003

310-553-4330
FAX 310-203-8450
Home Page: www.rronline.com

Erica Farber, Publisher/CEO
Sky Daniels, Vice President
Ron Rodriguez, Editor-in-Chief
Page Beaver, Operations Manager
Henry Mowry, Sales Executive

A music newspaper that covers all aspects of the radio and recording industry.
Cost: $299.00
Frequency: BiAnnual
Circulation: 10,000

3982 Radio Marketing Guide
Radio Advertising Bureau

1320 Greenway Dr
Suite 500
Irving, TX 75038-2547

972-753-6700
800-232-3131
FAX 972-753-6727
E-Mail: jhaley@rab.com
Home Page: www.rab.com

Mike Mahone, VP
Leah Kamon, SVP Marketing

A multi dimensional tool for Radio sales management and advertising professionals.
1600 Attendees

3983 Radio Talk Shows Need Guests
Pacesetter Publications
PO Box 101330
Denver, CO 80250-1330

303-722-7200
FAX 303-733-2626
Home Page: www.joesabah.com

Over 950 radio talk shows that interview guests over the telephone are profiled.
Cost: $198.00
Frequency: SemiAnnual
Founded in 1992

3984 SBE Members Directory
Society of Broadcast Engineers
9102 N Meridian St
Suite 150
Indianapolis, IN 46260-1896

317-846-9000
FAX 317-846-9120
E-Mail: mclappe@sbe.org
Home Page: www.sbe.org

John Poray, Executive Director
Vincent A Lopez, President

List of all members of SBE, Includes a history, awards earned, leadership, suppliers and other information. Free to members.
108 Pages
Mailing list available for rent: 4700 names at $170 per M

3985 TV Cable Publicity Guide
Volt Directory Marketing
1 Sentry Pkwy E
Blue Bell, PA 19422-2310

610-825-7720
FAX 610-941-6874
Home Page: www.volt.com

Jerry Di Pippo, CEO
Ronald Kochman, Vice President
Bruce Goodman, General Counsel

Over 5,000 cable and broadcast television stations and systems are profiled.
Cost: $188.00
545 Pages
Frequency: SemiAnnual

3986 TV Facts
Cabletelevision Advertising Bureau
830 3rd Ave
2nd Floor
New York, NY 10022-7523

212-508-1200
FAX 212-832-3268
Home Page: www.onetvworld.org

Sean Cunningham, President

An essential pocketsized media planning tool that contains 120 pages of essential data, graphs and charts highlighting the extraordinary growth and value of Cable in the changing TV landscape.
Frequency: Annual
Circulation: 20000

3987 Talk Show Selects
Broadcast Interview Source

2233 Wisconsin Ave NW
Suite 301
Washington, DC 20007-4132

202-333-5000
800-932-7266
FAX 202-342-5411
Home Page: www.expertclick.com

Mitchell Davis, Owner

More than 700 contacts at radio and television talk shows.
Cost: $185.00
240 Pages
Frequency: Annual
ISBN: 0-934333-35-1
Founded in 1984
Printed in on matte stock

3988 Television Yearbook
BIA Research
15120 Enterprise Ct
Suite 100
Chantilly, VA 20151-1275

703-818-8115
800-331-5086
FAX 703-803-3299
E-Mail: pob@bia.com
Home Page: www.bia.com

Tom Bruno, Owner

US television markets and their inclusive stations, television equipment manufacturers and related service providers and trade associations.
Cost: $64.00
Frequency: Annual

3989 Television and Cable Factbook
Warren Communications News
2115 Ward Ct NW
Washington, DC 20037-1209

202-872-9200
800-771-9202
FAX 202-318-8350
E-Mail: info@warren-news.com
Home Page: www.warren-news.com

Brig Easley, Manager
Daniel Warren, President/Editor

Commercial and noncommercial television stations and networks are profiled in this comprehensive directory. Educational and instructional stations are also included as one of the many categories of information.
Cost: $595.00
10M Pages
Frequency: 5 Volumes
Founded in 1932

3990 Top 200 National TV, News, Talk and Magazine Shows
Todd Publications
PO Box 635
Nyack, NY 10960-0635

845-358-6213
800-747-1056
FAX 845-358-6213

B Klein, Publisher

The 200 most popular information shows on US television.
Cost: $40.00
Frequency: Annual

3991 World Broadcast News: International 500 Issue
Penton
PO Box 12901
Shawnee Mission, KS 66282-2901

913-341-1300
FAX 913-514-6895
Home Page: www.penton.com

Eric Jacobson, Senior VP

Directory of services and supplies to the industry.
Cost: $10.00
Frequency: Annual

Industry Web Sites

3992 http://gold.greyhouse.com
G.O.L.D Grey House OnLine Databases
Grey House Publishing's online database platform, GOLD, offers Quick Search, Keyword Search and Expert Search for most business sectors including broadcasting, communications and media markets. The GOLD platform makes finding the information you need quick and easy - whether you're a novice searcher or an experienced database user. All of Grey House's directory products are available for subscription on the GOLD platform.

3993 www.aicp.com
Association of Independent Commercial Producers
Represents exclusively, the interests of US companies that specialize in producing commercials on various media - film, video, computer- for advertisers and their agencies. AICP members account for 85 percent of all domestic commercials aired nationally, whether produced for traditional braodcast channels or nontraditional use.

3994 www.alliancecm.org
Alliance for Community Media
Committed to assuring everyone's access to electronic media, through public education, a progressive legislative and regulatory agenda, coalition building and grassroots organizing. A nonprofit, national membership organization founded in 1976, the Alliance represents over 1,000 Public, Educational and Govermental access organizations and community media centers.

3995 www.americansportscasters.com
American Sportscasters Association
Covers the U.S., Puerto Rico, and Canada. Offers seminars, compiles statistics and operates a placement service, maintains a Hall of Fame and biographical archives and library.

3996 www.amptp.org
Alliance of Motion Picture & Television Producers
Trade association with respect to labor issues in the motion picture and television industry. We negotiate 80 industry wide collective bargaining agreements and represents over 350 production companies and studios.

3997 www.apts.org
Association of Public Televsion Stations
Nonprofit membership organization established in 1980 to support the continued growth and development of a strong and financially sound noncommercial television service for the American public. We provide advocacy for public television interests at the national level, as well as consistent leadership and information in marshalling grassroots and congressional support.

3998 www.bcfm.com
Broadcast Cable Financial Management Association
A professional society of over 1,200 of television, radio and cable TV's top financial, MIS and HR executives, plus associates in auditing, data processing, software development, credit and collections.

3999 www.bdaonline.org
Broad Designers Association
For broadcast designers. Conferences annually in Asia, Australia, Europe, South and North America.

4000 www.ctam.com
Cable Telecommunications Association for Marketing
Dedicated to the discipline and development of consumer marketing excellence in cable television, new media and telecommunication services. Members have the advantage of progressive research, insightful publications and forward thinking conferences.

4001 www.emmyonline.org
National Academy of Television Arts & Sciences
Dedicated to the advancement of the arts and sciences of television and the promotion of creative leadership for artistic, educational and technical achievements within the television industry. Bestows the Emmy Award.

4002 www.genehrts.com
Hollywood Radio and Television Society
Featuring top industry and government speakers and seminars about broadcasting, maintains film and audio library.

4003 www.gita.org
Geospatial Information & Technology Association
A variety of information and useful references for your professional and technical needs, with descriptions of new programs and services, and a stable source of important member contacts, industry news and association related ongoing programs.

4004 www.greyhouse.com
Grey House Publishing
Authoritative reference directories for most business sectors including broadcasting, communications and media markets. Users can search the online databases with varied search criteria allowing for custom searches by product category, geographic area, sales volume, keyword, subject and more. Full Grey House catalog and online ordering also available.

4005 www.halloffame.com
National Sportscasters & Sportswriters Association

4006 www.i-newsrelease.com
Tellmedia Communications
Media research, Internet news, satelite media tours and video news releases.

4007 www.iabm.com
International Association of Broadcast Monitors
Website of world wide trade association made up of news retrieval services which monitor television, radio, Internet and print news mediums.

4008 www.ibsradio.org
Intercollegiate Broadcasting System
For college and university broadcasting stations.

4009 www.iemmys.tv
International Television Academy
Organization of global broadcasters, with representatives from over 50 countries. Sixty percent of the 100-member board of directors come from countries outside the US, and represent the world's largest production, distribution and broadcast companies.

4010 **www.irts.org**
Int'l Radio & Television Society Foundation

For professionals in radio, broadcast and cable televison, corporate video production, collaborative communication, DVD and new media production, marketing and advertising plus related areas, as well as interested laypeople.

4011 **www.kagan.com**
Kagan World Media

For those interested in investments in radio and TV stations and publicly held companies.

4012 **www.lib.umd.edu/LAB**
Library of American Broadcasting

Devoted to television and radio broadcasting materials and archives.

4013 **www.lostremote.com**
Lost Remote

Television industry news, job listings and resources.

4014 **www.mca-i.org**
Media Communications Association International

Website of the global community of professional devoted to the business and art of visual communication.

4015 **www.mediabistro.com**
Media Bistro

News and articles especially for those in broadcasting and publishing.

4016 **www.millimeter.com**
Millimeter Magazine

Authoritative resource for more than 33,000 qualified professionals in production, postproduction, animation, streaming and visual effects for motion pictures, television and commercials.

4017 **www.mrfac.com**
Manufacturer's Radio Frequency Advisory Committee

Representing the voice of the manufacturing industry and private land mobile radio users before the FCC.

4018 **www.nab.org**
National Association of Broadcasters

Full service trade association that represents the interests of free, over-the-air radio and television broadcasters.

4019 **www.naed.org**
National Association of Electrical Distributors

Nonprofit organization dedicated to serving and protecting the electrical distribution channel; provides networking opportunities through approximately 50 meetings and conferences a year, training, industry information and research through TED Magazine, and a marketing campaign for the industry through the NAED Advocacy Initiative.

4020 **www.nafb.org**
National Association of Farm Broadcasters

Works to improve quantity and quality of farm programming and serves as a clearinghouse for new ideas in farm broadcasting.

4021 **www.natpe.org**
Nat'l Association of Television Program Executives

Our mission is a commitment to furthering the quality and quantity of content, offering the wealth of our resources and experience to every content creator, no matter what the medium. Because the industry encompasses so much more today than ever before, NATPE too is ex-

panding to accommodate this change and encourage progress while continuing to keep our members constantly appraised of changes.

4022 **www.ncta.com**
National Cable & Telecommunications Asssociation

National Cable and Telecommunications Association, formerly the National Cable Television Association, is the principal trade association of the cable television industry in the United States. Provides a strong national presence by providing a single, unified voice on issues affecting the cable and telecommunications industry.

4023 **www.ncti.com**
National Cable Television Institute

Independent provider of broadband communications training. Broadband cable system operators, contractors and industry vendors have turned to NCTI to train their employees who construct, operate and maintain broadband systems.

4024 **www.necta.info**
New England Cable & Telecommunications Association

NECTA is a six state regional trade association representing sbtstantially all private cable telecommunications companies in Connecticut, Maine, Massachusetts, New Hampshire, Rhode Island and Vermont.

4025 **www.nrb.org**
National Religious Broadcasters

For religious broadcasters and religious media. Hosts national convention featuring trade show and educational workshops.

4026 **www.pcia.com**
Personal Communications Industry Association

Represents companies that develop, own, manage and operate towers, commercial rooftops and other facilities for the provision of all types of wireless, broadcasting and telecommunications services. PCIA is dedicated to advancing an understanding of the benefits of wireless services and required infrastructure.

4027 **www.productionhub.com**
Production Hub

Television producers' news, listings, classifieds, casting notices and events.

4028 **www.rab.cpm**
Radio Advertising Bureau

For marketing personnel and raises awareness of radio among advertising and business communities.

4029 **www.radiospace.com**
North American Network

All information contained is provided to radio stations and networks for their free and unrestricted use.

4030 **www.rtndf.org**
Radio Television News Directors Association

Provides training programs, seminars, scholarship support and research in areas of critical concern to electronic news professionals and their audience. Offers professional development opportunities for working and aspiring journalists and journalism educators.

4031 **www.sacredheartprofram.org**
Sacred Heart Hour

Producers and syndicators of Public Service Radio Programs, Contact Radio available in,

thirty minute, fifteen minute, five minute versions, Pathways, one minute radio spots.

4032 **www.sbca.com**
Satellite Broadcasting/Communications Association

National trade association representing all segments of the satellite consumer services industry. The association is committed to expanding the utilization of satellite technology for the delivery of video, data, voice, interactive and broadband services.

4033 **www.sbe.org**
Society of Broadcast Engineers

Offers a cooperative educational program intended to assist in the ongoing rollout of digital television.

4034 **www.smpte.org**
Society of Motion Picture & Television Engineers

Serves the needs of film and TV engineers.

4035 **www.thirteen.org**
Educational Broadcasting Association

For producers and directors of public educational programming, channel 13, PBS.

4036 **www.tvspy.com**
TVSpy

Television industry news, articles and links to other sites of interest.

Associations

4037 ADSC: The International Association of Foundation Drilling

8445 Freeport Parkway
Suite 325
Irving, TX 75063

469-359-6000
FAX 469-359-6007
E-Mail: adsc@adsc-iafd.com
Home Page: www.adsc-iafd.com
Social Media: *Facebook, Twitter, LinkedIn*

Tom Tuozzolo, President
Al Rasband, VP
Martin McDermott, Treasurer

ADSC seeks to advance technology in the foundation of drilling and anchored earth retention industries. Represents drilled shaft, anchored earth retention, micropile contractors, civil engineers and manufacturing firms world wide.
Founded in 1972

4038 Adhesive & Sealant Council

7101 Wisconsin Ave
Suite 990
Bethesda, MD 20814

301-986-9700
FAX 301-986-9795
E-Mail: info@ascouncil.org
Home Page: www.ascouncil.org
Social Media: *Twitter, LinkedIn, RSS*

C Russell Thompson Jr., President & CEO
Charles R Williams Jr, Treasurer
Christine A Bryant, Director
John P Carroll, Director
Traci Jensen, Chairman

A North American trade association dedicated to representing the adhesive and sealant industry. ASC is bound by the collective efforts of its members, and strives to improve the industry operating environment and strengthen its member companies.
124 Members
Founded in 1958

4039 American Architectural Manufacturers Association

1827 Walden Office Square
Suite 550
Schaumburg, Il 60173-4268

847-303-5664
FAX 847-303-5774
E-Mail: customerservice@aamanet.org
Home Page: www.aamanet.org
Social Media: *Facebook, Twitter, LinkedIn, YouTube, Flickr, SlideShare*

Rich Walker, President, CEO
Dean Lewis, Educational Information Mgr.
Maureen Knight, Govt. Affairs Manager
Jannine Klemencic, Executive Assistant
Karen Allen, Accounting/HR Mgr.

Trade association that advocates for manufacturers and professionals in the fenestration industry and is dedicated to the promotion of quality window, door, curtain wall, storefront and skylight products.
Founded in 1936

4040 American Bar Association Forum on Construction Law

321 N Clark St.
Chicago, IL 60654

Home Page:
www.americanbar.org/groups/construction_ind
ustry.html
Social Media: *Facebook, Twitter, LinkedIn*

Steven B. Lesser, Chair

An association focused on the professional development of construction lawyers and enhancing perception of the role construction lawyers perform in the broader industry.
6000 Members
Founded in 1976

4041 American Concrete Pipe Association

8445 Freeport Parkway
Suite 350
Irving, TX 75063-2595

972-506-7216
FAX 972-506-7682
E-Mail: info@concrete-pipe.org
Home Page: www.concrete-pipe.org
Social Media: *Facebook, Twitter, LinkedIn, Youtube*

Matt Childs, President
Josh Beakley, PE, Technical Services Director
Kim Spahn, PE, Engineering Services Director

The American Concrete Pipe Association (ACPA) is a nonprofit organization, composed primarily of manufacturers of concrete pipe and related conveyance products located throughout the United States, Canada and in over 40 foreign countries. ACPA provides members with research, technical and marketing support to promote and advance the use of concrete pipe for drainage and pollution control applications.
145 Members
Founded in 1907

4042 American Concrete Pressure Pipe Association

4122 E Chapman Avenue
Suite 27
Orange, CA 92869

714-801-0298
FAX 703-273-7230
E-Mail: support@acppa.org
Home Page: www.acppa.org
Social Media: *Facebook, Twitter, LinkedIn*

Mark Carpenter, Chairman
Alexander Narcise, Vice Chaiman
David Tantalean, Secretary
Jim Tully, Treasurer
Richard I Mueller, President &Ceo

The American Concrete Pressure Pipe Association (ACPPA) is a nonprofit trade association representing manufacturers of concrete pressure pipe around the world. ACPPA sponsors research projects and conducts educational programs to promote and advance the use of concrete pressure pipe in water and wastewater applications. We also manage an independent audit program to certify compliance with all applicable American Water Works Association (AWWA) standards for the manufacturers.
5 Members
Founded in 1949

4043 American Concrete Pumping Association

606 Enterprise Drive
Lewis Center, OH 43035

614-431-5618
FAX 614-431-6944
E-Mail: christi@concretepumpers.com
Home Page: www.concretepumpers.com
Social Media: *Facebook, Twitter, LinkedIn, Youtube, Flickr, RSS*

Carl Walker, President
Beth Langhauser, Vice President
Scott Savage, Treasurer
Matt Kaminsky, Secretary
Dennis Andrews, Past President

The American Concrete Pumping Association promotes concrete pumping as the choice method of placing concrete, and to encourage and educate the concrete pumping industry on safe concrete pumping procedures. The ACPA

Operator Certification Program is the only industry-recognized certification program for testing concrete pumping practices.
270 Members
Founded in 1974

4044 American Congress on Surveying and Mapping

5119 Pagasus Court
Suite Q
Frederick, MD 21704

240-439-4615
FAX 240-439-4952
E-Mail: curtis.summer@acsm.net
Home Page: www.acsm.net
Social Media: *Facebook, Twitter, Blogger*

Curtis W Sumner, Executive Director
Bob Jupin, Accounting Manager
Sara Maggi, CST Program
Trish Milburn, Office Manager/Membership Services

A professional organization representing those who communicate the earth's spatial information using precisely prepared plats, charts, maps, and digital cartographic and related data systems.
7000 Members
Founded in 1941

4045 American Council for Construction Education

1717 N Loop 1604 East
Suite 320
San Antonio, TX 78232-1570

210-495-6161
FAX 210-495-6168
E-Mail: acce@acce-hq.org
Home Page: www.acce-hq.org
Social Media: *LinkedIn*

Michael M Holland, President
Allan J Hauck, VP
Michael M Holland, Executive VP
Jim Carr, Treasurer
Dr. Norma Jean Anderson, Secretary

The accrediting agency for postsecondary construction education programs. The mission of ACCE is to be a global advocate for programs of post-secondary construction higher education. To accomplish this mission, ACCE will develop, periodically update, and promulgate comprehensive standards for programs of construction higher education and aAccredit programs meeting these standards through a rigorous, formal process of peer review.
Cost: $150.00
115 Members
Founded in 1974

4046 American Fence Association

6404 International Parkway
Suite 2250-A
Plano, TX 75093

630-942-6598
800-822-4342
FAX 314-480-7118
E-Mail:
memberservices@americanfenceassociation.
Home Page:
www.americanfenceassociation.com
Social Media: *Facebook, Twitter*

Nate Prewitt, President
David Gregg, President Elect
Jamie R Turrentine, VP
Eddie Clark, Secretary
Susan Colson, Treasurer

The American Fence Association benefits the fence, deck and railing industry - as well as the consumer - by promoting the highest levels of professionalism, ethics and product standards by disseminating information and educating its members. With 31 member chapters serving the association, AFA offers several educational,

certification options and networking opportunities to keep its members above and beyond their competition.
Cost: $365.00
2400 Members
Founded in 1962

4047   American Institute of Building Design
7059 Blair Road NW
Suite 400
Washington, DC 20012

202-750-4900
800-366-2423
FAX 866-204-0293
E-Mail: info@aibd.org
Home Page: www.aibd.org
Social Media: *Facebook, Twitter, LinkedIn, RSS*

Steven Mickley, Executive Director
Whit Peterson, General Manager
David Pillsbury, President
Kevin Holdridge, Internal Vice President
Karen Kassik-Michelsohn, External Vice President

AIBD provides building designers with educational resources, and has developed nationwide design standards and a code of ethics for the building design profession. Today, AIBD is a nationally recognized association with professional and associate members in 48 states, throughout Canada and in Europe, Asia, Australia and the Bahamas. Its chartered state societies are active in their respective legislative arenas and work to promote public awareness of the bldg design profession.
Founded in 1950

4048   American Institute of Constructors
700 North Fairfax Street
Suite 510
Alexandria, VA 22314

703-683-4999
FAX 703-683-5480
E-Mail: info@professionalconstructor.org
Home Page: www.professionalconstructor.org
Social Media: *Facebook, Twitter, LinkedIn*

Joe Rietman, President
Joseph Sapp, Executive Director
Charles L Sapp, Director, Association Management
Bradley Monson, Treasurer
David Dominguez, Secretary

AIC is the organization that seeks to give Constructors the professional status they deserve. The Institute is the constructor's counterpart of professional organizations found in architecture, engineering, law and other fields. As such, the Institute serves as the national qualifying body of professional constructor. AIC membership identifies the individual as a true professional.
Founded in 1971

4049   American Institute of Steel Construction
One East Wacker Drive
Suite 700
Chicago, IL 60601-1802

312-670-2400
FAX 312-670-5403
E-Mail: ferch@aisc.org
Home Page: www.aisc.org

Roger Ferch, President
Jacques Cattan, VP, Certification
John Cross, VP, Market Development & Finance
Scott Melnick, VP, Communications, Member Services
Charlie Carter, VP & Chief Structural Engineer

The American Institute of Steel Construction (AISC), headquartered in Chicago, is a not-for-profit technical institute and trade asso-

ciation serving the structural steel design community and construction industry in the United States. AISC's mission is to make structural steel the material of choice by being the leader in structural-steel-related technical and market-building activities, including: specification and code development, research, education, and tech assistance.
2.7M Members
Founded in 1921

4050   American Iron and Steel Institute
25 Massachusetts Ave., NW
Suite 800
Washington, DC 20001

202-452-7100
Home Page: www.steel.org
Social Media: *Facebook, Twitter*

Chuck Schmmit, Chairman
John Ferriola, Vice Chairman
Thomas J. Gibson, President, CEO
Lisa Harrison, SVP, Communications
David E. Bell, VP, Finance & Admin.

An association of North American steel producers that features steel information for consumers, engineers, and other professionals.
145 Members

4051   American Public Works Association
2345 Grand Blvd
Suite 700
Kansas City, MO 64108-2625

816-472-6100
800-848-2792
FAX 816-472-1610
E-Mail: ddancy@apwa.net
Home Page: www.apwa.net
Social Media: *Facebook, Twitter, Youtube*

Brian R Usher, President
Ann Daniels, Director/Credentialing
Brad Patterson, Chapter Membership Manager
Mark Leinwetter, Lead Development Manager
David Dancy, Director/Marketing

APWA exists to develop and support the people, agencies, and organizations that plan, build, maintain, and improve our communities. Just as communities count on their public works professionals, APWA strives to be the organization those professionals know they can count on. APWA offers the most comprehensive resources available in the areas of professional development tools, advocacy efforts, networking opportunities, and outreach activities.
26000 Members
Founded in 1937

4052   American Society for Nondestructive Testing
1711 Arlingate Lane
PO Box 28518
Columbus, OH 43228-0518

614-274-6003
800-222-2768
FAX 614-274-6899
E-Mail: wholliday@asnt.org
Home Page: www.asnt.org
Social Media: *Facebook, Twitter, LinkedIn, Youtube*

Wayne Holliday, President
Mike Boggs, Quality Manager
Michael O'Toole, Manger/Conferences
Betsy Blazar, Manager/Marketing
Tim Jones, Manager/Publications

Technical society which is involved in nondestructive testing. ASNT publishes journals, including materials evaluation. The fall conference and quality testing show of this association is the society's largest annual show.
12000 Members
Founded in 1941

4053   American Society of Heating, Refrigerating and Air-Conditioning Engineers
1791 Tullie Circle NE
Atlanta, GA 30329

404-636-8400
800-527-4723
FAX 404-321-5478
E-Mail: ashrae@ashrae.org
Home Page: www.ashrae.org
Social Media: *Facebook, Twitter*

T David Underwood, President
Timothy G Wentz, President Elect
Bjarne W Olesen, Treasurer
Walid Chakroun, Vice President
Jeff Littleton, Secretary

ASHRAE is a building technology society. The Society and its members focus on building systems, energy efficiency, indoor air quality and sustainability within the industry. Through research, standards writing, publishing and continuing education, ASHRAE shapes tomorrow's built environment today.
55000 Members
Founded in 1894

4054   American Society of Professional Estimators
2525 Perimeter Place Dr
Suite 103
Nashville, TN 37214

615-316-9200
888-378-6283
FAX 615-316-9800
E-Mail: SBO@aspenational.org
Home Page: www.aspenational.org
Social Media: *Facebook, Twitter*

Patsy Smith, Executive Director
Tina Cooke, Membership Database, Bookkeeper
Tanya Graham, Certification Program
Doyle T Phillips, President
Marcene N Taylor, 1st VP

The American Society of Professional Estimators was created with dedication and commitment to the idea of providing its members with tangible benefits.
2500 Members
Founded in 1956

4055   American Subcontractors Association, Inc.
1004 Duke St.
Alexandria, VA 22314ÿ

703-684-3450
FAX 703-836-3482
E-Mail: ASAoffice@asa-hq.com
Home Page: www.asaonline.com
Social Media: *Facebook, Twitter, LinkedIn, YouTube, Google+, RSS*

Richard Bright, Chief Operating Officer
Colette Nelson, Chief Advocacy Officer
Marc Ramsey, Director, Communications
Linda Wilson, Director, Chapter Services
Robert Abney, Board of Directors

A nonprofit, national, membership trade association of constructionspecialty trade contractors, suppliers, and service providers in the United States and Canada.

4056   Asbestos Information and Training Centers
Georgia Institute of Real Estate
5784 Lake Forrest Drive
Atlanta, GA 30328

404-252-6768
800-633-3583
FAX 404-257-0354
E-Mail: gire@learningrealestate.com

Home Page: www.learningrealestate.com
Social Media: *Facebook, Twitter, RSS*

Rebecca Fletcher, School Director
Mendalyn Harper, Information Central
Manager
Jackie Townsend, Finance Director
Phil Avery, Finance Coordinator
Ned Kandul, Director, Art & Marketing

Sponsors the Regional Asbestos Information and Training Centers. The Centers provide information and training in identification and abatement of asbestos hazards with the ultimate goal of training contractors for eventual certification. Each center offers a variety of specialized courses including identification of asbestos hazards and possible remedies of problems and solutions for those involved in the asbestos hazard abatement process.
Founded in 1959

4057 Asphalt Emulsion Manufacturers Association

Three Church Circle
PO Box 250
Annapolis, MD 21401

410-267-0023
FAX 410-267-7546
E-Mail: krissoff@aema.org
Home Page: www.aema.org
Social Media: *Facebook*

Archie Reynolds, President
Mark Ishee, Vice President
Todd Ryne, Secretary/Treasurer
Mark McCollough, Past President
Diane Franson, Director

The Asphalt Emulsion Manufacturers Association is the International Organization representing the asphalt emulsion industry. AEMA's mission is to expand the use and applications of asphalt emulsions. Asphalt emulsions are the most environmentally sound, energy efficient and cost effective products used in pavement maintenance and construction.
150 Members
Founded in 1973

4058 Asphalt Institute

2696 Research Park Dr
Lexington, KY 40511-8480

859-288-4960
FAX 859-288-4999
E-Mail: info@asphaltinstitute.org
Home Page: www.asphaltinstitute.org
Social Media: *Facebook, Twitter, LinkedIn, YouTube*

Peter T Grass, President
Alexander Brown, Regional Director
Bob Horan, Regional Director
Mark Blow, Senior Regional Director
Bob Humer, Senior Regional Director

The Asphalt Institute is the international trade association of petroleum asphalt producers, manufacturers and affiliated businesses. Our mission is to promote the use, benefits and quality performance of petroleum asphalt, through engineering, research, marketing and educational activities, and through the resolution of issues affecting the industry.
113 Members
Founded in 1919

4059 Associated Builders & Contractors, Inc.

440 1st St., N.W.
Ste., 200
Washington, DC 20001

202-595-1505
E-Mail: gotquestions@abc.org
Home Page: www.abc.org

Social Media: *Facebook, Twitter, LinkedIn, YouTube*

Pamela Volm, Chairman
David Chapin, Chairman-Elect
Dan Brodbeck, Immediate Past Chairman
Anthony Stagliano, Treasurer
Michael Bellaman, President, CEO

A national construction industry trade association representing nearly 21,000 chapter members and whose activities include government representation, legal advocacy, education, workforce development, communications, technology,etc.
21000 Members
Founded in 1950

4060 Associated Builders and Contractors

440 1st St., N.W.
Ste., 200
Washington, DC 20001

202-595-1505
E-Mail: gotquestions@abc.org
Home Page: www.abc.org
Social Media: *Facebook, Twitter, LinkedIn, Youtube*

Pamela Volm, Chairman
David Chapin, Chairman-Elect
Dan Brodbeck, Immediate Past Chairman
Anthony Stagliano, Treasurer
Michael Bellaman, President, CEO

A national association representing merit shop construction and construction-related firms. ABC's membership represents all specialties within the U.S. construction industry and is comprised primarily of firms that perform work in the industrial and commercial sectors of the industry.
23000 Members
Founded in 1950

4061 Associated Construction Distributors

1605 SE Deleware Avenue, Suite B
PO Box 14552
Ankeny, IA 50021

515-964-1335
FAX 515-964-7668
E-Mail: acdi@acdi.net
Home Page: www.acdi.net

Tom Goetz, Executive VP
Dave Hill, Director/Sales/Marketing
Jane Zieser, Controller
Linda Phipps, Meeting Manager

Associated Construction Distributors International, Inc. (ACDI) was founded when a group of independent, entrepreneurial businessmen came together and realized they had much to offer and much to learn. Sharing business information continues today at the core of the organization. It has allowed the members to succeed individually and as group. ACDI distributors account for nearly one billion dollars in the sale of materials and equipment to the construction industry.
34 Members
Founded in 1968

4062 Associated Construction Publications

1200 Madison Ave
LL20
Indianapolis, IN 46225

317-423-7080
800-486-0014
FAX 317-423-7094
Home Page: www.acppubs.com
Social Media: *Facebook, Twitter, LinkedIn, RSS*

Wayne Curtis, Publisher
Royce Morse, Production Director

Strives to assist the heavy construction industry with local and regional news on a nationwide basis.
14 Members
Founded in 1938

4063 Associated Equipment Distributors

600 22nd Street
Suite 220
Oak Brook, IL 60523

630-574-0650
800-388-0650
FAX 630-574-0132
E-Mail: info@aednet.org
Home Page: www.aednet.org
Social Media: *Facebook, Twitter, Google+, YouTube*

Bob Henderson, EVP/COO
Jon Cruthers, VP, Sales/Publisher
Janet L Dixon, Director, Meetings & Conferences
Kim Phelan, Programs Director
Jenny Choe, Communications Director

Associated Equipment Distributors (AED) is an international trade association representing companies involved in the distribution, rental and support of equipment used in construction, mining, forestry, power generation, agriculture and industrial applications.
1200 Members
Founded in 1919

4064 Associated General Contractors of America

2300 Wilson Blvd
Suite 300
Arlington, VA 22201

703-548-3118
FAX 703-548-3119
E-Mail: info@agc.org
Home Page: www.agc.org
Social Media: *Facebook, Twitter, LinkedIn, RSS*

Charles L Greco, President
Mark Knight, Senior Vice President
Art Daniel, Vice President
Joseph Stella, Treasurer
Stephen E Sandherr, Chief Executive Officer

The Associated General Contractors of America (AGC) is the leading association for the construction industry. Operating in partnership with its nationwide network of 95 chartered Chapters, AGC provides a full range of services satisfying the needs and concerns of its members, thereby improving the quality of construction and protecting the public interest.
33000 Members
Founded in 1918

4065 Association of Equipment Manufacturers

6737 W Washington St
Suite 2400
Milwaukee, WI 53214-5647

414-272-0943
FAX 414-272-1170
E-Mail: aem@aem.org
Home Page: www.aem.org
Social Media: *Twitter*

John Patterson, Chair
Leif J Magnusson, Vice Chair
Dennis J Slater, Secretary
Goran Lindgren, Treasurer
Dennis Slater, President

Formed from the consolidation of the Construction Industry Manufacturers Association and Equipment Manufacturers Institute. The international trade and business development resource for companies that manufacture equipment, products and services used world-

wide in the construction, agricultural, mining, forestry, and utility fields.
Founded in 2002

4066 Association of Union Constructors (TAUC)

1501 Lee Highway
Suite 202
Arlington, VA 22209-1109

703-524-3336
FAX 703-524-3364
Home Page: www.tauc.org

Steven Lindauer, Chief Executive Officer
David Acord, Communications Manager
Ben Cahoon, Data Systems Manager
Wayne Creasap, Health Director
Michael Dorsey, Industrial Relations Director

TAUC's mission is to act as an advocate for union contractors and enhance cooperation between the three entities involved in the successful completion of construction projects: the union, the contractor and the owner-client, the company for which the work is being completed. By encouraging this tripartite dialogue, many potential issues and delays are eliminated before work even begins.
5000+ Members
Founded in 1969

4067 Association of the Wall and Ceiling Industry

513 West Broad Street
Suite 210
Falls Church, VA 22046

703-538-1722
FAX 703-534-8307
E-Mail: info@awci.org
Home Page: www.awci.org
Social Media: *Facebook, Twitter, LinkedIn, Youtube*

Steven Etkin, EVP/CEO
Brenton C Stone, Associate Publisher
Karen Bilak, Convention Director
Laura Porinchak, Communications Director
Annemarie Selvitelli, Education Director

Represents acoustics systems, ceiling systems, drywall systems, exterior insulation and finishing systems, fireproofing, flooring systems, insulation, and stucco contractors, suppliers and manufacturers and those in allied trades. The mission of the Association of the Wall and Ceiling Industry is to provide services and undertake activities that enhance the members' ability to operate a successful business.
2400 Members
Founded in 1918

4068 Barre Granite Association

PO Box 481
Barre, VT 05641

802-476-4131
FAX 802-476-4765
E-Mail: BGA@barregranite.org
Home Page: www.barregranite.org
Social Media: *Facebook, Twitter, LinkedIn, Pinterest*

Robert Couture, President
John Castaldo, VP/Executive Directors

Manufacturers of cemetery monuments, mausoleums, statuary, landscape and architectural granite products. It has been estimated that one-third of the public and private monuments and mausoleums in America — and they are millions in number — are products of the Barre quarries and Barre's international community of sculptors, artisans, mechanics and laborers. All this has been largely accomplished since the closing decades of the last century.
35 Members
Founded in 1889

4069 Brick Industry Association

1850 Centennial Park Drive
Suite 301
Reston, VA 20191

703-620-0010
FAX 703-620-3928
E-Mail: brickinfo@bia.org
Home Page: www.gobrick.com
Social Media: *Facebook, Twitter, LinkedIn, Youtube, Pinterest*

Ray Leonhard, President & CEO & CFO
Stephen Sears, COO & VP, Marketing
Sandy Speer, Executive Assistant
Judy Grandinetti, Accounting Manager
Susan Miller, VP, Environment, Health & Safety

National trade association representing distributors and manufacturers of clay brick and suppliers of related products and services. The Association is involved in a broad range of technical, research, marketing, government relations and communications activities. It is the recognized national authority on brick construction.
175 Members
Founded in 1934

4070 Bridge Grid Flooring Manufacturers Association

201 Castle Drive
West Mifflin, PA 15122

412-469-3985
FAX 419-257-0332
Home Page: www.abcdpittsburgh.org

Bill Ferko, President
Todd Carroll, Secretary
Jessica Saleh, Treasurer
Bill Ferko, Awards
Roxanne Podlipsky, Scholarships

Comprised of companies who manufacture steel grid flooring systems for bridges, and other companies with an interest in the steel grid market. The role of the Association is to promote the use of Grid Reinforced Concrete Bridge Decks through data collection, research/development, and education.

4071 Building Industry Association of Southern California

24 Executive Park
Suite 100
Irvine, CA 92614

949-553-9500
FAX 949-769-8943
Home Page: www.biasc.org
Social Media: *Facebook, Twitter, LinkedIn*

Michael Battaglia, President
Leonard Miller, Secretary/Treasurer
Daniel W Boyd, Immediate Past President

The Building Industry Association of Southern California is a nonprofit trade association representing companies involved in planning and building Southern California's communities. Our members are involved in all aspects of construction and green building - from architecture to roofing to landscape design.
1850 Members
Founded in 1923

4072 Building Material Dealers Association

1006 SE Grand Street
Suite 301
Portland, OR 97214

503-208-3763
888-960-6329
FAX 971-255-0790

E-Mail: bmda@bmda.com
Home Page: www.bmda.com

Gwyn Matras, Executive Director, Executive Assistant, Supervisor, Research Department, Customer Service

BMDA provides Notice of Right to a Lien service for all states and Construction Lien service for Oregon and Washington. We offer current lien law manuals for Oregon and Washington, which assists our members with all areas of the construction lien laws. At BMDA, we believe attorneys who specialize in construction lien law are your best choice for answering legal questions. Therefore, we offer attorney referrals for Oregon and Washington. BMDA will not provide legal advice at any time.
3500 Members
Founded in 1915

4073 Building Stone Institute

5 Riverside Drive, Bldg 2
PO Box 419
Chestertown, NY 12817

518-803-4336
866-786-6313
FAX 518-803-4338
E-Mail: jane@buildingstoneinstitute.org
Home Page: www.buildingstoneinstitute.org
Social Media: *Facebook*

Jane Bennett, Executive Vice President
Kayla Carlozza, Association Services Coordinator
Gina De Nardo, Communications
Robert Barnes III, President
Aaron Hicken, Vice President

The Building Stone Institute works on behalf of the quarries, fabricators, retailers, importers, exporters, carvers, sculptors, restorers, designers, and installers that comprise our diverse membership. BSI provides programs and services that empower our member companies to offer the highest level of quality products and services. BSI is a not-for-profit trade association dedicated to serving its member firms, and providing educational materials and continuing education.
350 Members
Founded in 1919

4074 Building Trades Association

6353 W. Rogers Circle
Unit 3
Boca Raton, FL 33487

800-326-7800
E-Mail: info@buildingtrades.com
Home Page: www.buildingtrades.com
Social Media: *Facebook*

An association made up of thousands of companies involved in all phases of the building and construction industries.

4075 California Redwood Associates

818 Grayson Road
Suite 201
Pleasant Hill, CA 94523

925-935-1499
888-225-7339
FAX 925-935-1496
E-Mail: info@calredwood.org
Home Page: www.calredwood.org
Social Media: *Youtube*

Christopher Grover, President

A trade association for redwood lumber producers.

4076 Cedar Shake and Shingle Bureau

PO Box 1178
Sumas, WA 98295-1178

604-820-7700
FAX 604-820-0266

E-Mail: info@cedarbureau.org
Home Page: www.cedarbureau.org

Lynne Christensen, Director of Operations
Barbara Enns, Accountant
Kelly Vaille, Marketing Coordinator
Christine Inglis, Customer Service
Sharron Beauregard, Project Coordinator

The Cedar Shake and Shingle Bureau is a non-profit organization that promotes the use of Certi-label cedar roofing and sidewall products. On June 9, 1915, at a meeting of the Trustees of the West Coast Lumber Manufacturers Association, it was agreed to establish a branch of the association to serve those members who manufactured shingles. Our influence grew, and as we survived both the Great Depression and World War II, manufacturers continued their quality commitment.
350 Members
Founded in 1915

4077 Construction Financial Management Association

100 Village Blvd
Suite 200
Princeton, NJ 08540

609-452-8000
888-421-9996
FAX 609-452-0474
E-Mail: info@cfma.org
Home Page: www.cfma.org
Social Media: *Facebook, Twitter, LinkedIn, Youtube*

Stuart Binstock, President & CEO
Erica O'Grady, VP, Operations
Robert Rubin, VP, Finance & Administration
Brian Summers, VP, Content Management & Education
Brigitte Meinders, Director, Marketing

CFMA is the only organization dedicated to bringing together construction financial professionals and those partners serving their unique needs. CFMA serves members located throughout the US and Canada.
7000 Members
Founded in 1981

4078 Construction Industry Service Corporation

2000 Spring Road
Suite 110
Oak Brook, IL 60523

630-472-9411
877-562-9411
FAX 630-472-9413
E-Mail: Julia@cisco.org
Home Page: www.cisco.org
Social Media: *Facebook, Twitter, LinkedIn*

Mark Maher, President
Joseph Benson, VP
Frank Furco, Treasurer
Loretta Molter, Secretary
Dan Allen, Executive Director

The Construction Industry Service Corporation (CISCO) is a non-profit labor management association bringing union construction labor and management representatives together to work cooperatively in order to better the construction industry as a whole. CISCO currently represents union contractors and workers in Cook, DuPage, Lake, Kane, Kendall and McHenry Counties.
14800 Members
Founded in 1988

4079 Construction Owners Association of America

5000 Austell Powder Springs Rd
Suite 217
Austell, GA 30106

770-433-0820
800-994-2622
FAX 404-577-3551
E-Mail: coaa@coaa.org
Home Page: www.coaa.org
Social Media: *Facebook, Twitter, LinkedIn*

Kevin Lewis, President
Dean McCormick, Vice President
Gwen Glattes, Secretary/Treasurer
Ted Argyle, Past President
Stuart Adler, Director

National association dedicated to supporting project Owners' success in the design and construction of buildings and facilities through education, information and developing relationships within the industry. Comprised of public and private owners who manage facilities development and capital improvement projects.
530 Members
Founded in 1994

4080 Construction Specifications Institute

110 South Union Street
Suite 100
Alexandria, VA 22314

703-684-0300
800-689-2900
FAX 703-236-4600
E-Mail: csi@csinet.org
Home Page: www.csinet.org
Social Media: *Facebook, Twitter, LinkedIn, Youtube, Flickr*

Lane J Beougher, President
Ronald L. Geren, President Elect
Ellen Kay Crews, Vice President
Kirby M. Davis, Vice President
Gary L. Beimers, Secretary

A national association dedicated to creating standards and formats to improve construction documents and project delivery. The organization is unique in the industry in that its members are a cross section of specifiers, architects, engineers, contractors and building materials suppliers.
15000 Members
Founded in 1948

4081 Continental Automated Buildings Association (CABA)

1173 Cyrville Road
Suite 210
Ottawa, Canada, ON K1J 7S6

613-686-1814
888-798-2222
FAX 613-744-7833
E-Mail: caba@caba.org
Home Page: www.caba.org
Social Media: *Facebook, Twitter, LinkedIn, YouTube*

Ronald J Zimmer, President & CEO
Rawlson O'Neil King, Communications Director
Greg Walker, Research Director
George Grimes, Marketing & BD Consultant
Brenda Williamson, Database Administrator

An association for the furtherance of automated buildings.
Founded in 1988

4082 Deep Foundations Institute

326 Lafayette Avenue
Hawthorne, NJ 07506

973-423-4030
FAX 973-423-4031
E-Mail: staff@dfi.org

Home Page: www.dfi.org
Social Media: *Facebook, LinkedIn*

John Wolosick, President
Dan Brown, Vice President
Matthew Janes, Treasurer
Mike Wysockey, Secretary
Robert B. Bittner, Immediate Past President

DFI gathers professionals in the deep foundations sector of the construction industry, to create a place for discussion, inquiry and debate. In so doing, DFI brings the disciplines together where they have learned from each other, creating a better informed, more communicative foundations industry.
3000 Members
Founded in 1976

4083 Design-Build Institute of America

1331 Pennsylvania Ave., NW
4th Floor
Washington, DC 20004

202-682-0110
FAX 202-682-5877
E-Mail: dbia@dbia.org
Home Page: www.dbia.org/Pages/default.aspx
Social Media: *Facebook, Twitter, LinkedIn*

Timothy J. Heck, Chief Financial Officer
Louis J. Jenny, VP, Advocacy & Outreach
Lisa Washington, CAE, Executive Director/CEO
Allison Leisner, Coordinator
Richard Thomas, Dir., State/Local Legis. Affairs

An organization that defines, teaches, and promotes best practices in design-build and represents the entire design and construction industry.
Founded in 1993

4084 Door & Access Systems Manufacturers Association International

1300 Sumner Avenue
Cleveland, OH 44115-2851

216-241-7333
FAX 216-241-0105
E-Mail: dasma@dasma.com
Home Page: www.dasma.com

John H. Addington, Executive Director
R. Christopher Johnson, Assistant Executive Director
Joseph R. Hetzel, Technical Director
Louise M. Shellhammer, Administrative Assistant
Eva Brunk, Technical Assistant

Trade association of manufacturers of garage doors, rolling doors, high performance doors, garage door operators, vehicular gate operators, and access control products.
Founded in 1996

4085 Elberton Granite Association

1 Granite Plaza
PO Box 640
Elberton, GA 30635

706-283-2551
FAX 706-283-6380
E-Mail: granite@egaonline.com
Home Page: www.egaonline.com

Manuel Fernadez, President

The Elberton Granite Association, Inc. is the largest trade association of granite quarriers and manufacturers in the United States. More than 250,000 granite memorials are manufactured annually by E.G.A. firms and shipped throughout the United States.
150 Members
Founded in 1951

4086 Expanded Metal Manufacturers Association

800 Roosevelt Rd. Bldg. C
Suite 312
Glen Ellyn, IL 60137

630-942-6591
FAX 630-790-3095
E-Mail: wlewis7@cox.net
Home Page: www.emma-assoc.org

Randall Schievelbein, President
Jeff Church, Executive Vice President
Chris Steward, Immediate Past President
Wes Lewis, Technical Consultant
Mike Fernie, Secretary/Treasurer

Educational resources that promote the use of
Expanded Metal which reduces scrap materials.
Founded in 1938

4087 Hollow Metal Door and Buck Association

National Assn of Architectural Metal
Manufacturer
800 Roosevelt Rd
Bldg C Suite 312
Glen Ellyn, IL 60137

630-942-6591
FAX 630-790-3095
E-Mail: wlewis7@cox.net
Home Page: www.naamm.org

Randall Schievelbein, President
Mike Fernie, Secretary/Treasurer
Tony Leto, Division Chair
Joseph Karpen, Division Vice Chair
Briana Gunn, Association Coordinator

The largest of four operating divisions of the
National Association of Architectural Metal
Manufacturers. HMMA is a group composed of
companies that manufacture, distribute and
promote the use of hollow metal door and
frame products.
60 Members
Founded in 1938

4088 Hollow Metal Manufacturers Association

800 Roosevelt Rd. Bldg. C
Suite 312
Glen Ellyn, IL 60137

630-942-6591
FAX 630-790-3095
E-Mail: wlewis7@cox.net
Home Page: www.hollowmetal.org

Randall Schievelbein, President
Jeff Church, Executive Vice President
Chris Steward, Immediate Past President
Wes Lewis, Technical Consultant
Mike Fernie, Secretary/Treasurer

Develops standards, conducts product performance testing and delivers education to promote the use of hollow metal doors and frames.
Founded in 1938

4089 ICC: International Code Council

500 New Jersey Avenue, NW
6th Floor
Washington, DC 20001

888-422-7233
202-370-1800
FAX 202-783-2348
E-Mail: webmaster@iccsafe.org
Home Page: www.iccsafe.org
Social Media: *Facebook, Twitter, LinkedIn, RSS, YouTube*

Alex Olszowy III, President
M. Dwayne Garriss, VP
Jay Elbettar, P.E., CBO, Secretary/Treasurer
Guy Tomberlin, CBO, Immediate Past
President
William Jeff Bechtold, Senior Building Official

The International Code Council is a mem-
ber-focused association dedicated to helping
the building safety community and construction
industry provide safe, sustainable and affordable construction through the development of
codes and standards used in the design, build
and compliance process. Mission: To provide
the highest quality codes, standards, products
and services for all concerned with the safety
and performance.
Founded in 1994

4090 Interlocking Concrete Pavement Institute

14801 Murdock Stree
Suite 230
Chantilly, VA 20151

703-657-6900
800-241-3652
FAX 703-657-6901
E-Mail: icpi@icpi.org
Home Page: www.icpi.org
Social Media: *Facebook, Twitter, LinkedIn, Youtube, Pinterest*

David Pitre, Chairman
Matt Lynch, Chair-Elect
Mike Mueller, Secretary/Treasurer
Dave Carter, Immediate Past Chair
Elliot Bender, Member

Self governed, self funded autonomous association representing the interlocking concrete
pavement industry in North America. Membership is open to producers, contractors, suppliers, consultants and others who have an interest
in the industry.
900+ Members
Founded in 1993

4091 International Door Association

PO Box 246
West Milton, OH 45383

937-988-8042
800-355-4432
FAX 937-698-6153
E-Mail: info@longmgt.com
Home Page: www.doors.org
Social Media: *Facebook, Twitter, LinkedIn, Youtube*

Randy Oliver, President
Bill Gibson, Immediate Past President
Tim Mattews, Treasure, Industry Director
Flossie Mohler, Industry Member Vice
President
Paul Peloquin, Dealer Member Vice President

The International Door Association plays an
important role in the process of quality creation
and control by providing helpful programs and
services to those who sell, install, and service
the superb products produced by the industry's
list of manufacturers. Door and access systems
dealers are the front line businesses that serve
the customer face-to-face.
750 Members
Founded in 1995

4092 International Slurry Surfacing Association

Three Church Circle
PO Box 250
Annapolis, MD 21401-1933

410-267-0023
FAX 410-267-7546
E-Mail: krissoff@slurry.org
Home Page: www.slurry.org
Social Media: *Facebook, Twitter*

Rusty Price, President
Carter Dabney, Vice President
Rex Eberly, Secretary
Eric Reimschiisel, Treasurer
Christine Deneuvillers, Immediate Past
President

The International Slurry Surfacing Association
(ISSA) is an international non-profit trade association comprised of contractors, equipment
manufacturers, research personnel, consulting
engineers and other industry professionals,
working together to promote the concept of
pavement preservation. ISSA promotes the
highest standards of ethics and quality while
providing its members with information, tech
assistance and ongoing opportunities for networking and professional development.
Cost: $500.00
220+ Members
Founded in 1963

4093 International Zinc Association

1822 East NC Highway 54
Suite 120
Durham, NC 27713

919-361-4647
FAX 919-361-1957
E-Mail: contact@zinc.org
Home Page: www.zinc.org
Social Media: *Facebook, Twitter*

A nonprofit global organization dedicated to
the interests of zinc and its users.
Founded in 1991

4094 Interstates Construction Services

1520 North Main
PO Box 260
Sioux Center, IA 51250

712-722-1662
FAX 712-722-1667
E-Mail: bdev@interstates.com
Home Page: www.interstates.com

Larry Den Herder, Chairman
Dave Crumrine, President
Catherine Bloom, Chief Financial Officer
Doug Post, President/Interstate Engineering
Jack Woelber, President/Control Systems

Combine the strengths of teams with processing industry expertise to develop the best solutions for clients' project needs. From the
planning table to the plant floor, Interstates is
with clients every step of the way. Assists with
preliminary budgeting and help develop cost
effective designs, setting the stage for a quick
and efficient startup.
Founded in 1953

4095 Manufactured Housing Institute

1655 North Fort Myer Road
Suite 104
Arlington, VA 22209

703-558-0400
FAX 703-558-0401
E-Mail: info@mfghome.org
Home Page: www.manufacturedhousing.org
Social Media: *Facebook, Twitter*

Richard Jennison, President/CEO
Phyllis Knight, Vice Chair
Kevin Clayton, Secretary
Howard Walker, Treasurer
Lois Starkey, VP/Regulatory Affairs

MHI is the national trade organization representing all segments of the factory-built housing industry. MHI serves its membership by
providing industry research, promotion, education and government relations programs, and
by building and facilitating consensus within
the industry.

4096 Mason Contractors Association of America: Advancing the Masonry Industry

1481 Merchant Drive
Algonquin, IL 60102

224-678-9709
800-536-2225
FAX 224-678-9714

Home Page: www.masoncontractors.org
Social Media: *Facebook, Twitter, LinkedIn*

Mark Kemp, Chairman
Michael Sutter, Vice Chair
Paul Odom, Treasurer
Paul Oldham, Secretary
Michael Schmerbeck, Regional Vice President

The Mason Contractors Association of America (MCAA) is the national trade association representing mason contractors. The MCAA is committed to preserving and promoting the masonry industry by providing continuing education, advocating fair codes and standards, fostering a safe work environment, recruiting future manpower, and marketing the benefits of masonry materials.
1000 Members
Founded in 1950

4097 Masonry Society
105 South Sunset Street
Suite Q
Longmont, CO 80501-6172

303-939-9700
FAX 303-541-9215
E-Mail: info@masonrysociety.org
Home Page: www.masonrysociety.org
Social Media: *LinkedIn*

Scott Walkowicz, President
Jerry M Painter, President-Elect
Darrell McMillian, Vice President
Christine A. Subasic, Secretary/Treasurer
Phillip J. Samblanet, Executive Director

Dedicated to the advancement of scientific engineering, architechtural and construction knowledge of masonry. Promotes research and education and disseminates information on masonry materials, design, construction. Publishes newsletters, codes & specifications and material on masonry design.
700 Members
Founded in 1977

4098 Mechanical Contractors Association of America
1385 Piccard Drive
Rockville, MD 20850

301-869-5800
FAX 301-990-9690
Home Page: www.mcaa.org

Provides high-quality educational materials and programs for 2,500 firms involved in heating, air conditioning, refrigeration, plumbing, piping, and mechanical service.

4099 Metal Building Manufacturers Association
1300 Sumner Avenue
Cleveland, OH 44115-2851

216-241-7333
FAX 216-241-0105
Home Page: www.mbma.com
Social Media: *Twitter, LinkedIn*

John H. Addington, General Manager
W. Lee Shoemaker, Ph.D., P.E., Dir., Research & Engineering
Jay D. Johnson, LEED AP, Dir., Architectural Services
Daniel J. Walker, P.E., Assistant General Manager
Vincent E. Sagan, P.E., Senior Staff Engineer

Promotes the design and construction of metal building systems in the low-rise, non-residential building marketplace.

4100 Metal Construction Association
8735 W. Higgins Rd.
Suite 300
Chicago, IL 60631

847-375-4718
FAX 847-375-6488

E-Mail: mca@metalconstruction.org
Home Page: www.metalconstruction.org
Social Media: *Facebook, Twitter, LinkedIn*

Karl Hielscher, Chair
Norbert Schneider, Chair Elect
Todd E. Miller, Past Chair
Dale Nelson, Treasurer
Jim Bush, Director

An organization of manufacturers and suppliers whose metal products are used in structures.
Founded in 1983

4101 Metal Framing Manufacturers Association
330 N Wabash Ave
Chicago, IL 60611

312-644-6610
FAX 312-321-4098
E-Mail: MFMAstats@smithbucklin.com
Home Page: www.metalframingmfg.org

Mark Thorsby, Executive Director
Amanda Frjelich, Member Services

The Members of the Metal Framing Manufacturers Association (MFMA) focus on the manufacture of ferrous and nonferrous metal framing (continuous slot metal channel systems) which consist of channels with in-turned lips and associated hardware for fastening to the channels (Strut) at random points.
Founded in 1981

4102 Mississippi Valley Equipment Association
11140 E Woodmen Rd
Falcon, CO 80831-8127

719-495-2283
800-388-9881
FAX 719-495-3014
E-Mail: oholcombe@swassn.com
Home Page: www.mvea.com
Social Media: *Facebook*

Jim C Herron, CEO
Olivia Holcombe, Director of Marketing
Cheinette Van Wyk, Administrative Manager
Jaclyn Parmer, Accounting Supervisor
Marge Tracy, Consumer Relations Supervisor

A regional affiliate of the North American Equipment Dealers Association provides members with a multitude of services designed to assist them in maintaining a profitable business operation.
165 Members
Founded in 1941

4103 Modular Building Institute
944 Glenwood Station Ln
Suite 204
Charlottesville, VA 22901-1480

434-296-3288
888-811-3288
FAX 434-296-3361
E-Mail: info@modular.org
Home Page: www.mbinet.org
Social Media: *Facebook, Twitter, LinkedIn, Youtube, Google+, Pinterest*

Michael Bollero Sr., President
Harry Klukas, VP
Kathy Wilmot, VP Elect
Kelly Williams, Secretary
Christopher Peterson, Treasurer

The Modular Building Institute (MBI) is the international non-profit trade association serving modular construction. Members are manufacturers, contractors, and dealers in two distinct segments of the industry - permanent modular construction (PMC) and relocatable buildings (RB). Associate members are companies supplying building components, services, and financing.
211 Members
Founded in 1983

4104 National Asphalt Pavement Association
5100 Forbes Blvd
Suite 200
Lanham, MD 20706—440

301-731-4748
888-468-6499
FAX 301-731-4621
E-Mail: mcervarich@hotmix.org
Home Page: www.asphaltpavement.org
Social Media: *Facebook, Twitter*

Mike Acott, President
Ester Magorka, VP Awards/Marketing Programs
Audrey Copeland Ph.D., P.E., VP/Engineering
Jay Hansen, Executive Vice President
Kent Hansen P.E., Director/Engineering

The only trade association that represents the interests of the asphalt pavement producer and paving contractor on the national level with Congress, government agencies, and other national trade and business organizations. NAPA supports an active research program designed to answer questions about environmental issues and to improve the quality of asphalt pavements and paving techniques used in the construction of roads, streets, highways, parking lots, and environmental facilities.
1200 Members
Founded in 1955

4105 National Association of Architectural Metal Manufacturers
800 Roosevelt Rd. Bldg. C
Suite 312
Glen Ellyn, IL 60137

630-942-6591
FAX 630-790-3095
E-Mail: wlewis7@cox.net
Home Page: www.naamm.org

Randall Schievelbein, President
Jeff Church, Executive Vice President
Chris Steward, Immediate Past President
Wes Lewis, Technical Consultant
Mike Fernie, Secretary/Treasurer

An association that represents a wide variety of architectural metal products for building construction.
Founded in 1938

4106 National Association of Church Design Builders
1000 Ballpark Way
Suite 306
Arlington, TX 76011

817-200-2622
866-416-2232
FAX 817-275-4519
Home Page: www.nacdb.com
Social Media: *Facebook, Twitter*

Dale Reiser, President
Steve Shehorn, Vice President
Amanda McFerren, Executive Director
Alexandria Gruhlkey, Administrator

An established, board-certified, nationwide association of firms committed to focusing on the ministry needs and styles of the churches they serve.

4107 National Association of Elevator Contractors
1298 Wellbrook Cir Ne
Suite A
Conyers, GA 30012-8031

770-760-9660
800-900-6232
FAX 770-760-9714
E-Mail: info@naec.org

Home Page: www.naec.org
Social Media: *Facebook*

Brian Farley, President
Bret Abels, Vice President
David Smarte, Secretary
Cory Hussey, Treasurer
Hugh Bertschin, Director

NAEC is an association of elevator contractors and suppliers serving primarily the interests of independent elevator contractors and independent suppliers of products and services; promoting safe and reliable elevator, escalator and short-range transportation and promoting excellence in the management of member companies.
634 Members
Founded in 1950

4108 National Association of Home Builders

1201 15th Street NW
Washington, DC 20005

202-822-0200
800-368-5242
FAX 202-266-8400
E-Mail: info@nahb.com
Home Page: www.nahb.org
Social Media: *Facebook, Twitter, LinkedIn, Google+, Pinterest*

Rick Judson, Chairman
Kevin Kelly, First Vice Chair
Tom Woods, Second Vice Chair
Ed Brady, Third Vice Chair
Gerald M Howard, CEO

Represents the building industry by serving its members and affiliated state and local builders associations.
2200 Members
Founded in 1942

4109 National Association of Women in Construction

327 S Adams Street
Fort Worth, TX 76104

817-877-5551
800-552-3506
FAX 817-877-0324
E-Mail: nawic@nawic.org
Home Page: www.nawic.org

Riki F. Lovejoy, CBT, CIT, President
Stephanie Crane, CIT, VP
Dede Hughes, EVP
Diana Sterrett, Bookkeeper
Lauri McCullough, Membership Coordinator

Founded by women working in the construction industry. The founders organized NAWIC to create a support network for women in construction.
5800 Members
Founded in 1953

4110 National Association of the Remodeling Industry

PO Box 4250
Des Plaines, IL 60016

847-298-9200
800-611-6274
FAX 847-298-9225
E-Mail: info@nari.org
Home Page: www.nari.org
Social Media: *Facebook, Twitter, YouTube, Pinterest*

Fred Ulreich, CEO
Kevin Anundson, Chairman
Judy Mozen, President
Tom Miller, Treasurer
David Pekel, Secretary

NARI has an inclusive, encompassing purpose to; establish and maintain a firm commitment to developing and sustaining programs that expand and unite the remodeling industry; to en-

sure the industry's growth and security; to encourage ethical conduct, sound business practices and professionalism in the remodeling industry; and to present NARI as the recognized authority in the remodeling industry.
Founded in 1935

4111 National Concrete Masonry Association

13750 Sunrise Valley Dr
Herndon, VA 20171-4662

703-713-1900
FAX 703-713-1910
E-Mail: info@ncma.org
Home Page: www.ncma.org
Social Media: *Facebook, Twitter, LinkedIn, Pinterest*

Robert Thomas, President
Brittaney R. Kamhong Thompson, Executive Administrator

Consists of manufacturers of concrete masonry products and suppliers of products to the industry. Offers a variety of technical of technical services and design aids through publications, computer programs, slide presentations and technical training.
Founded in 1918

4112 National Conference of States on Building Codes & Standards

505 Huntmar Park Dr
Suite 210
Herndon, VA 20170-5103

703-437-0100
FAX 703-481-3596
E-Mail: dbecker@ncsbcs.org
Home Page: www.ncsbcs.org

Kevin Egilmez, Project Manager
Debbie Becker, Administrative Assistant

Serves as a forum for the interchange of information and provides technical services, education and training to our members to enhance the public's social, economic well-being through safe, durable, accessible and efficient buildings.
Founded in 1967

4113 National Council of Acoustical Consultants

9100 Purdue Rd
Suite 200
Indianapolis, IN 46268

317-328-0642
FAX 317-328-4629
E-Mail: info@ncac.com
Home Page: www.ncac.com

Kenric Van Wyk P.E., President
Eric Reuter, VP Membership
Kerrie G. Standlee P.E., Immediate Past President
David Braslau, Director-at-Large

Strives to safeguard the interests of professional acoustical consulting firms. Managing physics and psychoacoustics to provide optimum lisning environments.
130 Members
Founded in 1962

4114 National Demolition Association

2025 M Street NW
Suite 800
Washington, DC 20036

202-367-1152
800-541-2412
FAX 202-367-2152
E-Mail: info@demolitionassociation.com
Home Page: www.demolitionassociation.com
Social Media: *Facebook, Twitter, LinkedIn*

Peter Banks, President
Scott Knightly, VP

Christopher Godek, Secretary
John Adamo, Treasurer

Represents the demolition industry including demolition contractorsto foster goodwill and the exchange of ideas with the public, governmental agencies and contractors engaged in the demolition industry, and for manufacturers or suppliers of demolition equipment, supplies and services.
900 Members
Founded in 1972

4115 National Electrical Contractors Association

3 Bethesda Metro Ctr
Suite 1100
Bethesda, MD 20814

301-657-3110
FAX 301-215-4500
E-Mail: beth.margulies@necanet.org
Home Page: www.necanet.org
Social Media: *Facebook, Twitter, LinkedIn, Youtube, Flickr*

John M Grau, CEO
Daniel G Walter, VP & COO
Traci Pickus, Secretary/Treasurer
Geary Higgins, VP, Labor Relations
Russell J Alessi, President, ELECTRI International

Represents a segment of the construction market comprised of electrical contracting firms.
70000 Members
Founded in 1879

4116 National Environmental Balancing Bureau

8575 Grovemont Cir
Gaithersburg, MD 20877

301-977-3698
866-497-4447
FAX 301-977-9589
E-Mail: jhuber@completecx.com
Home Page: www.nebb.org

James Huber, President
Jean Paul Le Blance, President Elect
Robert , Linder, Past President
Jim Kelleher, Treasurer

NEBB is an international certification assocaition for firms that deliver high performance building systems. Members perform testing, adjusting and balancing (TAB) of heating, ventilating and air-conditioning systems, commission and retro-commission building systems commissioning, execute sound and vibration testing, and test and certify lab fume hoods and electronic and bio clean rooms. NEBB holds the highest standards in certification.
Founded in 1971

4117 National Finishing Contractors Association

1 Parkview Plaza
Suite 610
Oakbrook Terrace, IL 60181

630-537-1042
866-322-3477
FAX 630-590-5272
E-Mail: fca@finishingcontractors.org
Home Page: www.finishingcontractors.org
Social Media: *Facebook, Twitter, LinkedIn*

Anthony (Tony) Darkangelo, Chief Executive Officer

The Association represents contractors performing glazing work, flooring, drywalling and painting, among other finishing trades.

4118 National Hispanic Construction Association
1330 Locust Rd. NW
Washington, DC 20012-1319

214-566-2410
E-Mail: info@builtbylatinos.org
Home Page: www.builtbylatinos.org
Social Media: *Facebook*

John H. Martinez-D., Chairman

Association serving the interests of Hispanic construction professionals.

4119 National Housing Endowment
1201 15th St Nw
Washington, DC 20005

202-293-9072
800-368-5242
FAX 202-266-8177
E-Mail: nhe@nahb.org
Home Page:
www.nationalhousingendowment.org
Social Media: *Facebook, Twitter, LinkedIn, Pinterest*

Robert L Mitchell, Chairman
Roger Pastore, Chair-Elect
Robert Camp, Treasurer
Patsy R Smith, Secretary

Provides a permanaent source of funds to address long-term industry concerns at the national level including: supporting scholarship progams that encourage students to select home building and related fields as their life's work, assisting colleges and universities in the development of housing related curricula and activities, revitalizing the industry's labor pool and enhancing its professionalism through apprenticeship programs, seminars and continuing education.
Founded in 1987

4120 National Lumber & Building Material Dealers Association
2025 M St NW
Suite 800
Washington, DC 20036-3309

202-367-1169
800-634-8645
FAX 202-367-2169
E-Mail: info@dealer.org
Home Page: www.dealer.org
Social Media: *Facebook, Twitter, LinkedIn*

JD Saunders, Chair
Scott Yates, Chair Elect
Scott Engquist, Treasurer
Chris Yenrick, Immediate Past Chair
Jonathan Paine, President

To advance the national agenda for America's building material suppliers.
6000 Members
Founded in 1916

4121 National Organization of Minority Architects
1735 New York Avenue, NW
Suite 357
Washington, DC 20006

202-568-6682
Home Page: www.noma.net
Social Media: *Facebook, Twitter, LinkedIn*

Kevin M Holland, President
Bryan Hudson, President Elect
Anzilla Gilmore, Vice President - South
Andrew Thompson, Vice President - Northÿ
Rod Henmi, Vice President - West

A national organization that strives to minimize the effects of racism in the architecture profession and also battles against apathy, bigotry, and abuse of the natural environment.
Founded in 1971

4122 National Paint and Coatings Association
1500 Rhode Island Ave Nw
Washington, DC 20005

202-462-6272
FAX 202-462-8549
E-Mail: npca@paint.org
Home Page: www.paint.org
Social Media: *Facebook, Twitter, LinkedIn*

J Andrew Doyle, President
Thomas J Graves, VP, General Counsel
Allen Irish, Counsel/Director, Industry Affairs

Manufacturers of paints and industrial coatings and suppliers to the industry.
400+ Members
Founded in 1887

4123 National Railroad Construction & Maintenance Association
500 New Jersey Ave NW
Suite 400
Washington, DC 20001

202-715-1264
FAX 202-318-0867
E-Mail: info@nrcma.org
Home Page: www.nrcma.org
Social Media: *Facebook, Twitter, LinkedIn*

Bill Dorris, Chairman
Chris Daloisio, Vice Chair
Mike Choat, Secretary/Treasurer
Chuck Baker, President
Keith Hartwell, Government Affairs

Members are railroad construction and maintenance contractors, engineering firms, manufacturing suppliers and professional associate firms.
100+ Members
Founded in 1978

4124 National Ready Mixed Concrete Association
900 Spring St
Silver Spring, MD 20910-4015

301-587-1400
888-846-7622
FAX 301-585-4219
E-Mail: info@nrmca.org
Home Page: www.nrmca.org
Social Media: *Facebook, Twitter, LinkedIn, YouTube*

Allen Hamblen, Chairman
Ted Chandler, Vice Chair
Scott Parson, Secretary/Treasurer
Ric Suzio, Immediate Past Chairman

Our mission is to provide exceptional value for our members by responsibly representing and serving the entire ready mixed concrete industry through leadership, promotion, education and partnering; to ensure ready mixed concrete is the building material of choice.
1200 Members
Founded in 1930

4125 National Roofing Contractors Association
10255 W. Higgins Road
Suite 600
Rosemont, IL 60018-5607

847-299-9070
FAX 847-299-1183
Home Page: www.nrca.net
Social Media: *Facebook, Twitter, LinkedIn, YouTube, Instagram, Google+*

Richard M. Nugent, President
Lindy Ryan, Senior Vice President
Scott Baxter, Vice President
Dennis Conway, Vice President
Bob Kulp, Vice President

An association of roofing, roof deck, and waterproofing contractors; industry-related associ-

ate members; and international members worldwide.
3500 Members
Founded in 1886

4126 National Slag Association
P.O Box 1197
Pleasant Grove, UT 84062

801-785-4535
FAX 801-785-4539
E-Mail: info@nationalslag.org
Home Page: www.nationalslag.org

Members are processors of iron and steel slags for use as a aggregate in construction and manufacturing applications.
77 Members
Founded in 1918

4127 National Stone, Sand & Gravel Association
1605 King St
Alexandria, VA 22314

703-525-8788
800-342-1415
FAX 703-525-7782
E-Mail: jwilson@nssga.org
Home Page: www.nssga.org
Social Media: *Facebook, Twitter, LinkedIn, YouTube*

Michael W Johnson, President & CEO
Gus Edwards, President Emeritus
Dennis F. Coker, Treasurer
Randy Lake, Secretary of the Board
Jennifer Lewis, Executive Administrator

Represents the crushed stone, sand and gravel — or aggregate — industries. Our members account for 90 percent of the crushed stone and 70 percent of the sand and gravel produced annually in the US.
570 Members
Founded in 1985

4128 National Systems Contractors Association
3950 River Ridge DR NE
Suite B
Cedar Rapids, IA 52402

319-366-6722
800-446-6722
FAX 319-366-4164
E-Mail: nsca@nsca.org
Home Page: www.nsca.org
Social Media: *Facebook, Twitter, LinkedIn, YouTube*

Michael Hester, President
Ray Bailey, VP
Josh Shanahan, Treasurer
David Ferlino, Secretary
Chuck Wilson, Executive Director

A not for profit association representing the commercial electronic systems industry. Also a powerful advocate of all who work within the low voltage industry, including systems contractors/integrators, product manufacturers, consultants, sales representatives, a growing number of architects, specifying engineers and others.
2800 Members
Founded in 1980

4129 National Terrazzo and Mosaic Association
P.O. Box 2605
Fredericksburg, TX 78624

800-323-9736
FAX 888-362-2770
E-Mail: info@ntma.com
Home Page: www.ntma.com

George Hardy, Executive Director

The association establishes national standards for all terrazzo floor and wall systems and provides complete specifications, color plates and general information to architects and designers at no cost.

4130 National Tile Contractors Association

626 Lakeland E Drive
PO Box 13629
Jackson, MS 39232

601-939-2071
FAX 601-932-6117
E-Mail: webmaster@tile-assn.com
Home Page: www.tile-assn.com
Social Media: *Facebook, Twitter, LinkedIn, YouTube*

James Woelfel, President
Martin Howard, First VP
Chris Walker, Second VP
Bart Bettiga, Executive Director
Jim Olson, Ass. Executive Director

Serving every segment of the industry, and is recognized as the largest and most respected tile contractors association in the world.
1000 Members
Founded in 1947
Mailing list available for rent

4131 National Utility Contractors Association

3925 Chain Bridge Road
Suite 300
Fairfax, VA 22230

703-358-9300
FAX 703-358-9307
E-Mail: nuca@nuca.com
Home Page: www.nuca.com
Social Media: *Facebook, Twitter, LinkedIn*

Bonnie Williams, VP, Marketing & Communications
Eben Wyman, VP, Government Relations
Bill Hillman, CEO

A national association that provides a forum for continuing education and promotes effective public policy, through its grassroots network, to protect and enhance your industry.
1400 Members
Founded in 1964

4132 North American Insulation Manufacturers Association

11 Canal Center Plaza
Suite 103
Alexandria, VA 22314-1548

703-684-0084
FAX 703-684-0427
Home Page: www.naima.org

Kate Offringa, President/CEO
Angus Crane, EVP

Manufacturers of fiber glass, rock wool, and slag wool insulation products. NAIMA members manufacture the vast majority of fiber glass, rock and slag wool insulations produced and used in North America.
Founded in 1933

4133 Northeastern Retail Lumber Association

585 N Greenbush Rd
Rensselaer, NY 12144

518-286-1010
800-292-6752
FAX 518-286-1755
E-Mail: rferris@nrla.org
Home Page: www.nrla.org

Jonas Kelly, Chair
Rita Ferris, President
Joe Miles, Chair Elect
Charles Handley, Vice Chair
Richard Tarr, Treasurer

A resource for industry members, consumers, and public officials independent lumber and

building material suppliers and associated businesses in New York and the six New England states.
1150 Members
Founded in 1894

4134 Operative Plasterers' and Cement Masons' International Association

11720 Beltsville Dr
Suite 700
Beltsville, MD 20705

301-623-1000
FAX 301-623-1032
E-Mail: opcmiaintl@opcmia.org
Home Page: www.opcmia.org

Patrick D Finley, General President
Earl F Hurd, General Secretary/Treasurer
Daniel E Stepano, EVP
Roger Bettermann, Vice President
Todd Lair, Vice President

Represents and trains plasterers and cement masonsn for the purpose of protecting and promoting the quality of the industry and the livelihood of the members.
Founded in 1864

4135 Outdoor Power Equipment Institute

341 S Patrick St
Alexandria, VA 22314

703-549-7600
FAX 703-549-7604
E-Mail: info@opei.org
Home Page: www.opei.org
Social Media: *Facebook, Twitter, LinkedIn*

Kris Kiser, President & CEO
Lee Sowell, Chairman
Tim Merrett, Vice Chair
Daniel Ariens, Secretary/Treasurer

International trade association whose members are manufacturers of powered lawn and garden maintenance products, components and attachment supplies, as well as industry related services.
85 Members
Founded in 1952

4136 Painting and Decorating Contractors of America

2316 Millpark Drive
Maryland Heights, MO 63043

314-514-7322
800-332-7322
FAX 314-890-2068
Home Page: www.pdca.org
Social Media: *Facebook, Twitter, LinkedIn, YouTube*

David Ryker, Chair
Tony Severino, Vice Chair
Mark Adams, Treasurer
Richard Greene, MBA, CAE, CEO
Libby Loomis, Special Projects

PDCA exists to lead the industry by providing quality products, programs, services, and opportunities essential to the success of our members.
5M Members
Founded in 1884

4137 Perlite Institute

2207 Forest Hills Drive
Suite A
Harrisburg, PA 17112

717-238-9723
FAX 717-238-9985
E-Mail: info@perlite.org
Home Page: www.perlite.org
Social Media: *Facebook, LinkedIn*

Matt Goecker, President
Matthew Malaghan, VP
Keith Hoople, Treasurer
Linda Chirico, Past President/Advisor

An international trade association which establishes product standards and specifications, and which encourages the development of new product uses through research.
183 Members
Founded in 1949

4138 Pile Driving Contractors Association

33 Knight Boxx Road
Suite 1
Orange Park, FL 32065

904-215-4771
888-311-7322
FAX 904-215-2977
E-Mail: execdir@piledrivers.org
Home Page: www.piledrivers.org
Social Media: *Facebook, Twitter, LinkedIn*

Eric Alberghini, President
Marty Corcoran, VP
Bill Marczewski, Treasurer
Eric Albergini, Secretary

An organization of pile driving contractors that advocates the incresed use of driven piles for deep foundations and earth retention systems. Promotes the use of driven pile solutions in all cases where they are effective, support educational programs for engineers on the design and efficiency of driven piles and for contractors on improving installation procedures and give contractors a larger voice in establishing procedures and standards for pile installation and design.
450 Members
Founded in 1996

4139 Pipe Fabrication Institute

511 Ave Of Americas
#601
New York, NY 10011

514-634-3434
866-913-3434
FAX 514-634-9736
E-Mail: pfi@pfi-institute.org
Home Page: www.pfi-institute.org

Jeff Huggard, Chairman
Tim Monday, Vice Chair
Greg Howell, Treasurer
Guy Fortin, Executive Director
Robert B Cottington, Legal Counsel

Members are companies producing sophisticated high temperature, high pressure piping systems that employ specialists from the United Association of Journeymen and Apprentices of the Plumbing and Pipe Fitting Industry. We exist solely for the purpose of ensuring a level of quality in the pipe fabrication industry that is without compromise.
65-70 Members
Founded in 1913

4140 Portable Sanitation Association International

2626 E 82nd Street
Suite 175
Bloomington, MN 55425

952-854-8300
800-822-3020
FAX 952-854-7560
E-Mail: info@psai.org
Home Page: www.psai.org
Social Media: *Facebook, Twitter, LinkedIn*

Tim Petersen, President
Karen Holm, VP
Matt Sola, Secretary
Dwayne Siegmann, Treasurer

International trade association that represents firms engaged in the leasing, renting, selling and manufacturing of portable sanitation equipment, services and supplies for construction, recreation, emergency and other uses. Devoted to the proper handling of human waste by the most modern, sanitary means, giving the great-

est concern to the preservation of an unspoiled environment.
550+ Members
Founded in 1971

4141 Portland Cement Association

5420 Old Orchard Road
Skokie, IL 60077-1083

847-966-6200
FAX 847-966-9781
E-Mail: info@cement.org
Home Page: www.cement.org
Social Media: *Facebook, Twitter, LinkedIn, YouTube*

John Stull, Chair
Karl Watson Jr, Vice-Chair
James G Toscas, President/CEO
Steve Ambrose, Vice President, Sales and Marketing

The Portland Cement Association represents cement companies in the United States and Canada. It conducts market development, engineering, research, education, and public affairs programs.
Founded in 1916

4142 Precast Prestressed Concrete Institute

200 W Adams St
Suite 2100
Chicago, IL 60606

312-786-0300
FAX 312-621-1114
E-Mail: info@pci.org
Home Page: www.pci.org
Social Media: *Facebook, Twitter, LinkedIn, RSS*

Robert Risser PE, President
Michelle Burgess, Managing Editor
Roger Becker PE, SE, Managing Director, R&D
Jeff Appel, Controller

Dedicated to fostering understanding and use of precast and prestressed concrete, maintains a full staff of techniocal and marketing specialists.
1400 Members
Founded in 1954

4143 Professional Construction Estimators Association of America

PO Box 680336
Charlotte, NC 28216

704-484-1494
877-521-7232
FAX 704-489-1495
E-Mail: pcea@pcea.org
Home Page: www.pcea.org
Social Media: *Facebook*

Bill Barton, President
Glenn Hessee, President Elect
Derek Lanning, VP
Matt Solomon, Secretary
Wesley Ferree, Treasurer

Promotes construction estimating as a profession by upholding the code of ethics, and expanding public awareness.
1000 Members
Founded in 1956

4144 Resilient Floor Covering Institute

115 Broad Street
Sutie 201
La Grange, GA 30240

301-340-8580
E-Mail: info@rfci.org
Home Page: www.rfci.com
Social Media: *Facebook, Pinterest*

Douglas Wiegand, Executive Director

Industry trade association of North American manufacturers who produce resilient flooring products. Associate members of RFCI supply

raw materials to the industry and manufacture installation and maintenance products.
21 Members
Founded in 1975

4145 Retail Contractors Association

400 North Washington Street
Suite 300
Alexandria, VA 22314ÿ

800-847-5085
703-683-5637ÿ
FAX 703-683-0018
Home Page: www.retailcontractors.org

Mike Wolffÿ, President
Robert Moore, Vice President
Brad Bogart, Secretary/Treasurer
Steve Bachman, Director
Jack Grothe, Director

A national organization of retail contractors united to provide a solid foundation of ethics, quality, and professionalism within the retail construction industry.

4146 Roof Coatings Manufacturers Association

750 National Press Building
529 14th Street NW
Washington, DC 20045

202-207-0919
FAX 202-223-9741
E-Mail: questions@roofcoatings.org
Home Page: www.roofcoatings.org
Social Media: *LinkedIn*

John Ferraro, Executive Director
Mike Fischer, Codes & Standard Director
Shawn Richardson, Communications Coordinator
Kelly Franklin, Industry Affairs Coordinator

Represents the interests of manufacturers of cold applied roof coatings, cements and waterproofing agents, as well as the suppliers of products, equipment and services to and for the industry.
70+ Members
Founded in 1983

4147 Rubber Pavements Association

10000 N. 31st. Ave.
Suite D-408
Phoenix, AZ 85281-5738

480-517-9944
877-517-9944
FAX 480-517-9959
E-Mail: mbelshe@rubberpavements.org
Home Page: www.rubberpavements.org

Cliff Ashcroft, VP
Mark Belshe, Executive Director
Guadalupe Dickerson, Office Manager

Dedicated to encouraging greater usage of high quality, cost effective asphalt pavements containing recycled tire rubber. Conducts national and international seminars.
20 Members
Founded in 1985

4148 SPRI: Single Ply Roofing Industry

465 Waverley Oaks Road
Suite 421
Waltham, MA 02452

781-647-7026
FAX 781-647-7222
E-Mail: info@spri.org
Home Page: www.spri.org

Al Janni, President
Linda King, Managing Director

Comprised of manufacturers and marketers of sheet applied membrane roofing systems and components to the commercial roofing industry.
58 Members
Founded in 1981

4149 Safety Glazing Certification Council

P.O. Box 730
Sackets Harbor, NY 13685

315-646-2234
FAX 315-646-2297
E-Mail: erin@amscert.com
Home Page: www.igcc.org

Don Boutelle, President
Bruce Kaskel, Vice President
Brian Burnet, Secretary
Bruce Kaskel, Treasurer

Nonprofit corporation that provides for the certifacation of safety glazing materials, comprised of safety glazing manufacturers and other parties concerned with public safety. SGCC is managed by a board of directors comprised of representatives from the safety glazing industry and the public interest sector.
105 Members
Founded in 1977

4150 Scaffold Industry Association

400 Admiral Blvd
Kansas City, MO 64106-1508

602-257-1144
816-595-4860
FAX 602-257-1166
E-Mail: info@scaffold.org
Home Page: www.scaffold.org
Social Media: *Facebook, Twitter, LinkedIn*

Mike Russell, President
Frank Frietsch, Treasurer

Promotes safety by developing educational and informational material, conducting educational seminars and training courses, providing audio-visual programs and codes for safe practices, and other training and safety aids; to work with state, federal and other agencies in developing more effective safety standards; to reduce accidents, thereby reducing insurance costs; and to assist members in becoming more efficient and profitable in their businesses.
1000 Members
Founded in 1972

4151 Screen Manufacturers Association

2850 S Ocean Boulevard
Suite 114
Palm Beach, FL 33480-6242

733-636-0672
FAX 561-533-7466
E-Mail: Kathryn@SMAinfo.org
Home Page: www.smainfo.org
Social Media: *Twitter*

Alan Gray, VP
Michael White-RiteScreen, President
Tammy Groft, Sales Manager

Manufacturers of insect screens, screen frames, window screens, detention screens, sliding screen doors, swinging screen doors, fiberglass insect screening and aluminum insect screening.
Cost: $1000.00
20 Members
Founded in 1955

4152 Specialty Tools and Fasteners Distributors Association

500 Elm Grove Rd.
Suite 210
Elm Grove, WI 53122

262-784-4774
800-352-2981
FAX 262-784-5059
E-Mail: info@stafda.org
Home Page: www.stafda.org
Social Media: *Facebook, LinkedIn*

Rick Lamb, President
Rod Gowett, VP
Georgia Foley, Executive Director

International trade association composed of distributors and manufacturers and rep agents of light construction, industrial and related products. Members also include publishers of industry press serving the construction and industrial trades.
Cost: $350.00
2603 Members
Founded in 1976

4153 Spray Polyurethane Foam Alliance
3827 Old Lee Hwy
Suite 101B
Fairfax, VA 22030

800-523-6154
FAX 703-222-5816
E-Mail: info@sprayfoam.org
Home Page: www.sprayfoam.org
Social Media: *Facebook, Twitter*

Bonnie Strickler, Chair
Dennis Vandewater, President
John Achille, VP
Richard Spiess, Secretary/Treasurer

A trade association representing interests associated with rigid and semi-rigid polyurethane foam products that are typically applied with spray equipment as roofing and insulation.
Founded in 1987

4154 Steel Door Instituteÿ
30200 Detroit Road
Westlake, OH 44145

440-899-0010
FAX 440-892-1404
E-Mail: info@steeldoor.org
Home Page: www.steeldoor.org

Jeff Wherry, Managing Director

A voluntary, nonprofit business association that develops quality and performance standards for steel doors and frames.
Founded in 1954

4155 Steel Joist Institute
234 W Cheves Street
Florence, SC 29501

843-407-4091
FAX 843-626-5565
E-Mail: sji@steeljoist.org
Home Page: www.steeljoist.org
Social Media: *Twitter, LinkedIn*

J Kenneth Charles III, Managing Director

Composed of active manufacturers, the SJI cooperates with government and business agencies to establish steel joint standards.
40 Members
Founded in 1928

4156 Steel Window Institute
1300 Sumner Ave
Cleveland, OH 44115-2851

216-241-7333
FAX 216-241-0105
E-Mail: swi@steelwindows.com
Home Page: www.steelwindows.com

John Addington, Executive Director

An association of the leading manufacturers of windows made from either solid or formed sections of steel, and such related products as casings, trim, mechanical operators, screens, and moldings when manufactureed and sold by members of the industry for use in conjunction with windows.
6 Members

4157 Structural Insulated Panel Association
P.O. Box 39848
Fort Lauderdale, FL 33339

253-858-7472
FAX 253-858-0272

E-Mail: info@sips.org
Home Page: www.sips.org
Social Media: *Facebook, Twitter, RSS*

Ard Smits, President
Tom Harrison, First VP
Mike Tobin, Second VP
Charlie Ewalt, Secretary/Treasurer

A trade association representing manufacturers, suppliers, fabricators, distributors, design professionals and builders committed to providing quality structural insulated panels for all segments of the construction industry.
250 Members
Founded in 1990

4158 Stucco Manufacturers Association
2402 Vista Nobleza
Newport Beach, CA 92660-3545

949-640-9902
FAX 949-701-4476
E-Mail: info@stuccomfgassoc.com
Home Page: www.stuccomfgassoc.com
Social Media: *Facebook, Youtube*

Kevin Wensel, President
Nick Brown, VP
Buck Buchanan, Secretary
Rui Bronze, Treasurer
Norma S Fox, Executive Director

Our main purpose is to promote the advantage of 3 coat colored cementitious stucco by educating the building industry and consumers.
50 Members
Founded in 1957

4159 Subcontractors Trade Association
1430 Broadway
Suite 1600
New York, NY 10018

212-398-6220
FAX 212-398-6224
E-Mail: hkita@stanyc.com
Home Page: www.stanyc.com
Social Media: *Facebook, Twitter, LinkedIn*

Jerry Liss, President
Robert J Ansbro, VP
Robert Weiss, VP
Peter Cafiero, Treasurer
John A Finamore, Secretary

Members are specialty and supply companies in the construction industry. Our goal is to improve the economic well being of our members through representation, support and assistance through the process of legislation, legal action, public relations, education and other public information programs.
350+ Members
Founded in 1966

4160 Textile Care Allied Trades Association
271 Route 46 West
Suite C-106
Fairfield, NJ 07004-2432

973-244-1790
FAX 973-244-4455
E-Mail: info@tcata.org
Home Page: www.tcata.org
Social Media: *Facebook, Twitter, LinkedIn*

Bryant Dunivan, President
Bryant Dunivan, President-Elect
David Cotter, Chief Executive Officer
Cheryl Paglia, Office Manager

Represents the interests of distributors and manufacturers of equipment and supplies for the cleaning industry.
Founded in 1920

4161 The American Institute of Architects
1735 New York Ave., NW
Washington, DC 20006-5292

800-AIA-3837
FAX 202-626-7547

E-Mail: docstechsupport@aia.org
Home Page: www.aia.org
Social Media: *Facebook, Twitter, LinkedIn, YouTube, RSS, Flickr*

Based in Washington D.C., the AIA is the leading professional membership association for licensed architects, emerging professionals, and allied partners.
Founded in 1857

4162 The Construction Specifications Institute
110 South Union Street
Suite 100
Alexandria, VA 22314ÿ

800-689-2900
FAX 703-236-4600
E-Mail: csi@csinet.org
Home Page: www.csinet.org
Social Media: *Facebook, Twitter, LinkedIn, YouTube, Flickr*

An organization that keeps and changes the standardization of construction language as it pertains to building specifications. It provides technical information and products, continuing education, professional conferences, and product shows.
Founded in 1948

4163 Tile Contractors' Association of America
10434 Indiana Avenue
Kansas City, MO 64137

816-868-9300
800-655-8453
FAX 816-767-0194
E-Mail: info@tcaainc.org
Home Page: www.tcaainc.org

Ronald Schwartz, President/Chairman
Brian Castro, President Elect/Vice-Chairman
Lucinda Noel, Treasurer
Jennifer Panning, Immediate Past President
Brad Trostrud, Director

Union contractor association featuring; Architect/designer learning exchange, speakers, business meetings, new products and technology.
175 Members
Founded in 1903

4164 Tile Roofing Institute
23607 Highway 99
Suite 2C
Edmonds, WA 98026

425-778-6162
FAX 425-771-9588
E-Mail: info@tileroofing.org
Home Page: www.tileroofing.org
Social Media: *Facebook, Twitter, LinkedIn*

Kevin Burlingame, Chairman
Chris Fenwick, Vice Chairman
Terry Johnson, Secretary/Treasurer
Cliff Taylor, Director

Manufacturers of clay and concrete roof tiles. Emphasis is on technical issues and codes that involve tile.
Founded in 1971

4165 Timber Frame Business Council
46 Chambersburg
PO Box 60
Becket, MA 01223

413-623-8759
855-598-1803
FAX 413-623-8759
E-Mail: info@timberframe.org
Home Page: www.timberframe.org
Social Media: *Facebook, Twitter*

Jeff Arvin, Executive Director
Bruce Bode, President

Advances the business, communications and research interests of companies engaged in the timber framing industry.
Founded in 1995

4166 Timber Framers Guild
12100 Sunset Hills Rd
PO Box 60
Becket, MA 01223

413-623-8759
855-598-1803
FAX 413-623-8759
E-Mail: info@tfguild.org
Home Page: www.tfguild.org
Social Media: *Facebook, Twitter*

Joel McCarty, Executive Director
The Guild is dedicated to establishing training programs for dedicated timber framers, disseminating information about timber framing and timber frame building design, displaying the art of timber framing to the public, and generally serving as a center of timber framing information for the professional and general public alike.
Cost: $85.00
1700 Members
Founded in 1984

4167 Truck Mixer Manufacturers Bureau
900 Spring St
Silver Spring, MD 20910-4015

301-587-1400
888-846-7622
FAX 301-587-1605
E-Mail: nmaher@cpmb.org
Home Page: www.cpmb.org

Robert Garbini, President
Deana Angelastro, Executive Administrator
An association of ready mixed concrete truck manufacturers who have joined together in support of the ready mixed industry. TMMB members are required to manufacture equipment in accordance to the TMMB Standards.
Founded in 1958

4168 Western Building Material Association
909 Lakeridge Drive SW
PO Box 1699
Olympia, WA 98507

360-943-3054
888-551-9262
FAX 360-943-1219
E-Mail: wbma@wbma.org
Home Page: www.wbma.org
Social Media: *Facebook, Twitter, LinkedIn*

Casey Voorhees, Executive Director
Stephanie Masters, Office Manager
Tom Rider, Manager Member Services

Regional trade association serving material dealers throughout the states of Alaska, Idaho, Montana, Oregon and Washington and a federated association of the National Lumber and Building Material Dealers Association.
600 Members
Founded in 1903

Newsletters

4169
American Bar Association
321 N Clark St.
Chicago, IL 60654

Home Page:
www.americanbar.org/publications/under_cons
truction

4170 ACSM Bulletin
American Congress on Surveying and Mapping
6 Montgomery Village Ave
Suite 403
Gaithersburg, MD 20879-3557

240-632-9716
FAX 240-632-1321
E-Mail: ilse.genovese@acsm.net
Home Page: www.acsm.net

Ilse Genovese, Editor
A bi-monthly professional magazine published by ACSM to inform the public about current developments taking place within the geospatial community.
Frequency: Bi-Monthly

4171 AHW Reporter
Duane Publishing
51 Park St
Dorchester, MA 02122-2643

617-282-4885
FAX 617-282-0320
Home Page: www.rubblemakers.com

Herb Duane, Owner
Toby Duane, Director
Asbestos and hazardous waste information.

4172 Asbestos & Lead Abatement Report
Business Publishers
2222 Sedwick Dr
Suite 101
Durham, NC 27713

800-223-8720
FAX 800-508-2592
E-Mail: custserv@bpinews.com
Home Page: www.bpinews.com

Tracks the major legislative, regulatory and technological developments in asbestos and lead abatement industries. Includes highlights of major research studies on the effect of lead and asbestos on human health.
Cost: $371.54
Frequency: BiWeekly

4173 Brick News
Brick Industry Association
1850 Centennial Park Drive
Suite 301
Reston, VA 20191-1542

703-620-0010
FAX 703-620-3928
E-Mail: brickinfo@bia.org
Home Page: www.gobrick.com

Richard Jennison, President/CEO
News, information and programs of interest to brick distributors.

4174 Building Products News
Palgrave Macmillan
175 5th Ave
Suite 4
New York, NY 10010-7728

212-982-3900
888-330-8477
FAX 212-307-5035
Home Page: www.macmillan.com

Winston Jeune, Director
A unique publication researching the commercial renovation and retrofit market.

4175 Building Stone
Building Stone Institute
5 Riverside Dr
Building 2
Chestertown, NY 12817

518-803-4336
866-786-6313

FAX 518-803-4336
Home Page: www.buildingstoneinstitute.org
Duffe Elkins, President
Rob Teel, VP
State of the industry publication for architects, designers and people in the natural stone industries: granite, marble, limestone, etc.
Cost: $65.00
Frequency: Quarterly
Circulation: 17,000
Founded in 1919

4176 Building and Construction Market Forecast
Reed Business Information
360 Park Ave S
New York, NY 10010-1737

646-746-6400
FAX 646-756-7583
E-Mail:
corporatecommunications@reedbusiness.com
Home Page: www.reedbusiness.com

Mark Kelsey, CEO
Stuart Whayman, CFO

Forecasts and analysis on the construction industry.
Cost: $187.00
6 Pages
Frequency: Monthly
Founded in 1946

4177 Catalyst Newsletter
Adhesive & Sealant Council
7101 Wisconsin Ave
Suite 990
Bethesda, MD 20814-4805

301-986-9700
FAX 301-986-9795
E-Mail: info@ascouncil.org
Home Page: www.ascouncil.org

Matt Croson, President

4178 Concrete Pipe News
American Concrete Pipe Association
8445 Freeport Parkway
Suite 350
Irving, TX 75063

972-506-7216
FAX 972-506-7682
E-Mail: info@concrete-pipe.org
Home Page: www.concrete-pipe.org

Matt Childs, President
Josh Beakley, Technical Services Director
Wanda Cochran, Events Manager

Concrete Pipe News is designed to provide information on the use and installation of precast concrete pipe products for a wide variety of applications, including drainage and pollution control systems. Industry technology, research and trends are also important subjects of the publication. Readers include engineers, specifiers, public works officials, contractors, suppliers, vendors and members of the American Concrete Pipe Association.
Cost: $3.50
16 Pages
Frequency: Quarterly
Founded in 1907

4179 Construction Company Strategist
Brownstone Publishers
149 5th Ave
10th Floor
New York, NY 10010

212-473-8200
FAX 212-564-0465

Douglas Lowey, CEO
Andrew Shapiro, VP

Strategies, legal tips, and how-to advice for successfully managing a construction company

in the 1990's. Features model contract language, forms, guidelines and more.
Cost: $269.00
Frequency: Monthly
Circulation: 180000
Founded in 1971
Printed in 2 colors on matte stock

4180 Construction Contractor
Federal Publications
1100 13th Street NW
Washington, DC 20005

202-772-8295
888-494-3696
FAX 202-772-8298
Home Page: fedpubseminars.com

Michael Canavan, Director

Bi-weekly newsletter providing in-depth legal insight and analysis for all construction professionals.
Cost: $592.00
Frequency: BiWeekly

4181 Construction Equipment Monthly
Heartland Communications
1003 Central Avenue
PO Box 1052
Fort Dodge, IA 50501-1052

515-955-1600
800-247-2000
FAX 515-574-2107
E-Mail: personnel@hlipublishing.com
Home Page: www.hlipublishing.com

Patrick Van Arnam, President
Gale McKinney, CFO

Listings by category, equipment and parts for sale.
Cost: $125.00
Frequency: Annual+
Founded in 1988

4182 Construction Labor Report
Bureau of National Affairs
3 Bethesda Metro Center
Suite 250
Bethesda, MD 20814

800-372-1033
FAX 800-253-0332
E-Mail: customercare@bna.com
Home Page: www.bna.com

Donna Ives, VP Operations
Gregory McCaffery, President

A weekly information service that covers union-management relations in the construction industry, reporting on significant legislative, judicial, economic, management and union developments.
Cost: $1543.00
Frequency: Weekly
Circulation: 1600
ISSN: 0010-6836

4183 Constructor Newsletter
Associated General Contractors of America
2300 Wilson Blvd
Suite 400
Arlington, VA 22201

703-548-3118
FAX 703-837-5400
E-Mail: info@agc.org
Home Page: www.agc.org

Kristine Young, President
Joe Jarboe, SVP

Reports on contractors and items of interest to the construction community.
Frequency: Monthly
Circulation: 33000
Founded in 1918

4184 Crow's Weekly Letter
CC Crow Publications

3635 N Farragut St
Portland, OR 97217-5954

503-241-7382
FAX 503-646-9971
E-Mail: info@chadcrowe.com
Home Page: www.chadcrowe.com

Chad Crowe, President

Weekly report on trends and prices in the wood products industry.
Cost: $285.00
12 Pages
Frequency: Weekly
Founded in 1921
Printed in 4 colors on matte stock

4185 Demo-Memo
Duane Publishing
51 Park Street
PO Box 130
Dorchester, MA 02122

617-282-4885
FAX 617-282-0320
Home Page: www.demolitionconsulting.com

Herbert Duane, President
Demolition news and information.

4186 Dodge Report & Bulletins
McGraw Hill
PO Box 182604
Columbus, OH 43272-1095

614-866-5769
877-833-5524
FAX 614-759-3749
E-Mail: customer.service@mcgraw-hill.com
Home Page: www.mcgraw-hill.com

Jennifer Hayes, Editor
Harold McGraw III, President/CEO

Dodge Reports gives you the information you need to prepare a bid or enter negotiations. The detailed project information will also enable you to sell products or services.
Frequency: Daily
Founded in 1884

4187 Environmental Building News
BuildingGreen
122 Birge St
Suite 30
Brattleboro, VT 05301-6703

802-257-7300
FAX 802-257-7304
E-Mail: info@buildinggreen.com
Home Page: www.buildinggreen.com

Alex Wilson, Owner
Nadav Malin, President
Tristan Roberts, Editorial Director
Jennifer Atlee, Research Director

Featuring comprehensive, practical information on a wide range of topics related to sustainable building—from energy efficiency and recycled-content materials to land-use planning and indoor air quality.
Cost: $99.00
Frequency: Monthly
Founded in 1992

4188 Hard Hat News
Lee Publications
6113 State Highway 5
PO Box 121
Palatine Bridge, NY 13428

518-673-3237
800-218-5586
FAX 518-673-2699
E-Mail: info@leepub.com
Home Page: www.leepub.com

Fred Lee, Owner
Wendell Jennings, Sales Manager

Construction and heavy equipment.
72 Pages
Frequency: Monthly

4189 Housing Marketing Report
CD Publications
8204 Fenton St
Silver Spring, MD 20910-4571

301-588-6380
800-666-6380
FAX 301-588-6385
E-Mail: info@cdpublications.com
Home Page: www.cdpublications.com

Michael Gerecht, President
Charles Wisniowski, Editor

Concise analysis of national and regional housing markets, materials and supplies.
Cost: $469.00
Founded in 1961
Mailing list available for rent: 2,000 names at $160 per M
Printed in on matte stock

4190 Indoor Air Quality Update
Aspen Publishers
76 Ninth Avenue
7th Floor
New York, NY 10011

212-771-0600
800-638-8437
FAX 301-695-7931
Home Page: www.aspenpublishers.com

Mark Dorman, CEO
Gustavo Dobles, VP Operations

A guide to the practical control of building materials.
Cost: $440.00
Circulation: 20000
ISSN: 1040-5313

4191 Industry News
Modular Building Institute
944 Glenwood Station Ln
Suite 204
Charlottesville, VA 22901-1480

434-296-3288
888-811-3288
FAX 434-296-3361
E-Mail: info@mbinet.org
Home Page: www.mbinet.org

Tom Hardiman, Executive Director
Steven Williams, Operations Director

For members only.
Circulation: 650

4192 Machinery Outlook
Manfredi & Associates
20934 W Lakeview Pkwy
Mundelein, IL 60060-9502

847-949-9080
FAX 847-949-9910
E-Mail: frank@manfredi.com
Home Page: www.machineryoutlook.com

Frank Manfredi, President
James Manfredi, Editor

A newsletter about and for the construction and mining machinery industry.
Cost: $550.00
14 Pages
Frequency: Monthly
Founded in 1984
Printed in one color on matte stock

4193 Manufactured Structures Newsletter
Bobbitt Group

1710 S Gilbert Rd
Ste 1167
Mesa, AZ 85204

480-982-6173
E-Mail: wsbobbitt@hotmail.com
Home Page: www.thebobbittgroup.com

William Bobbitt, Editor/Publisher
Marci Bobbitt, Associate Editor/Business
Manager

Covers all aspects of the automated building industry with a monthly collection of original
feature stories profiling leading and emerging
companies in the industry as well as other informative information on the industry, business
tips, proven sales and marketing and featured
editorials.
Frequency: Monthly
ISSN: 1068-4962
Founded in 1969

4194 NAWIC Image
National Association of Women in
Construction
327 S Adams Street
Fort Worth, TX 76104

817-877-5551
800-552-3506
FAX 817-877-0324
E-Mail: nawic@nawic.org
Home Page: www.nawic.org

Debra Gregoire, Presdient
Cindy Johnsen, VP

Management, trends and techniques in the con-
struction business.
Cost: $50.00
Frequency: Bi-Monthly
Circulation: 6000

4195 NRCMA Biweekly Email Bulletin
National Railroad Construction &
Maintenance Assoc
500 New Jersey Ave NW
Suite 400
Washington, DC 20001-2065

202-715-2919
FAX 202-318-0867
E-Mail: info@nrcma.org
Home Page: www.nrcma.org

Chuck Baker, President
Matt Ginsberg, Director of Operations
Frequency: Biweekly

4196 News Brief
Granite State Designers & Installers
Association
53 Regional Drive
Ste 1
Concord, NH 03301-3520

603-228-1231
FAX 603-228-2118
E-Mail: info@gsdia.org
Home Page: www.gsdia.org

Carl Hagstrom, Director
Randy Orvis, Director

Newsletter for members of GSD1 relative to
septic system design, installation and maintenance.
Cost: $150.00
Frequency: Monthly

4197 RCMA Newsletter
Roof Coatings Manufacturers Association
750 National Press Building
529 14th Street NW
Washington, DC 20045

202-207-0919
FAX 202-223-9741

E-Mail: questions@roofcoatings.org
Home Page: www.roofcoatings.org

Steve Heinje, Director
Frequency: Quarterly

4198 Redwood Reporter
California Redwood Association
818 Grayson Road
Suite 201
Pleasant Hill, CA 94523

925-935-1499
FAX 925-935-1496
E-Mail: info@calredwood.org
Home Page: www.calredwood.org

Pamela Allsebrook, Publisher
Christopher Grover, President

Information about the redwood business of interest to redwood dealers.
8 Pages
Circulation: 8000

4199 Reed Construction Data
700 Longwater Drive
Norwell, MA 02061

770-209-3730
800-334-3509
FAX 800-632-6732
Home Page: www.rsmeans.com

Offers statistical information for building contractors.

4200 SPEC-DATA Program
Construction Specifications Institute
110 S Union St
Ste 100
Alexandria, VA 22314-3351

703-684-0300
800-689-2900
FAX 703-684-8436
E-Mail: csi@csinet.org
Home Page: www.csinet.org

Walter Marlowe, CEO
Stacy Vail, Operations Director
Cost: $75.00
Frequency: Monthly

**4201 Scaffold Industry Association
Newsletter**
Scaffold Industry Association
400 Admiral Blvd
Kansas City, MO 64106-1508

602-257-1144
866-687-7115
FAX 602-257-1166
E-Mail: info@scaffold.org
Home Page: www.scaffold.org

Steve Smith, President
Daryl Hare, Treasurer

Information on scaffold safety in the construc-
tion industry. Offers safe training programs for
competent person and hazard awareness.
Cost: $65.00
Frequency: Monthly
Circulation: 1600
Founded in 1972

4202 Scantlings
Timbers Framers Guild
PO Box 295
Alstead, NH 03602

559-834-8453
888-453-0879
FAX 888-453-0879
E-Mail: info@tfguild.org
Home Page: www.tfguild.org

Joel McCarty, Executive Director

It is a member benefit that is not available by
subscription. Reports on timber framing events,
news, business, and people.
Circulation: 1700
Founded in 1984

**4203 Specialty Tools and Fasteners
Distributors Association Newsletter**
Specialty Tools and Fasteners Distributors
PO Box 44
Elm Grove, WI 53122

262-784-4774
800-352-2981
FAX 262-784-5059
E-Mail: info@stafda.org
Home Page: www.stafda.org

Georgia Foley, President
Catherine Usher, Member Service Director

Members distribute or manufacture power
equipment, anchors, fastening systems, drilling
equipment and other related industrial supplies.
Circulation: 4,500
Founded in 1976

4204 TAUC About Construction
The Association of Union Constructors
1501 Lee Highway
Suite 202
Arlington, VA 22209-1109

703-524-3336
FAX 703-524-3364
E-Mail: dacord@tauc.org
Home Page: www.tauc.org

Stephen R Lindauer, CEO
Kevin J Hilton, Senior VP

E-Newsletter containing exclusive TAUC content, with the latest collective bargaining agreements, wage rates, OSHA directives, legislative
activity on Capitol Hill, and much more.
Frequency: Annual/May
Founded in 1970

4205 TIDINGS Newsletter
Textile Care Allied Trades Association
271 Route 46 West
#D203
Fairfield, NJ 07004-2432

973-244-1790
FAX 973-244-4455
E-Mail: info@tcata.org
Home Page: www.tcata.org
Social Media: *LinkedIn*

Lawton Jones, President
Bryant Dunivan, President-Elect

Keeps members informed about relevant news
in and affecting the industry, such as legisla-
tive/ regulatory developments, benefits and
services.

4206 Tilt-Up eNews
Tilt-Up Concrete Association
113 First Street W
PO Box 204
Mount Vernon, IA 52314-0204

319-895-6911
FAX 320-213-5555
E-Mail: info@tilt-up.org
Home Page: www.tilt-up.org

Ed Sauter, Executive Director
James Baty, Technical Director

A monthly newsletter published by the Tilt-Up
Concrete Association, Tilt-Up eNews is free for
members, however non-members can also sign
up to receive these publications. The mission of
the Tilt-Up Concrete Association is to expand
and improve the use of Tilt-Up as the preferred
construction method by providing education
and resources that enhance quality and perfor-

mance.
Cost: $25.00
Frequency: Quarterly
Circulation: 5500
Founded in 1986
Printed in 4 colors on glossy stock

4207 Trade News
Specialty Tools and Fasteners Distributors
Assn.
500 Elm Grove Rd.
Suite 210
Elm Grove, WI 53122

262-784-4774
800-352-2981
FAX 262-784-5059
E-Mail: info@stafda.org
Home Page: www.stafda.org
Social Media: *Facebook, LinkedIn*

Mike Kangas, President
Kramer Darragh, Vice President

Provides insight into the construction and industrial world, member news, Convention details, Trend Reports, and more.
4000 Attendees
Frequency: Monthly

4208 Under Construction
American Bar Assocation
321 N Clark St.
Chicago, IL 60654

Home Page:
www.americanbar.org/publications/under_cons
truction

Jayne Czik, Editor
Ridgely Jackson, Associate Editor

Current legal topics in the construction industry and highlights from the ABA's Forum on Construction Law.
Frequency: 3x/year

**4209 Western Building Material
Association Newsletter**
Western Building Material Association
PO Box 1699
Olympia, WA 98507-1699

360-943-3054
888-551-9262
FAX 360-943-1219
E-Mail: wbma@wbma.org
Home Page: www.wbma.org

38511 Pages
Frequency: Monthly
Circulation: 700
Printed in on matte stock

4210 World Fence News
World Fencing Data Center
6101 W Courtyard Dr
Building 3 Suite 115
Austin, TX 78730-5031

512-349-2536
800-231-0275
FAX 512-349-2567
E-Mail: editor@worldfencenews.com
Home Page: www.worldfencenews.com

Roger Duke, Publisher
Rick Henderson, Editor

Includes the most up to date information on events, products, trends, and services that effect the industry.
Cost: $29.95
Frequency: Monthly
Circulation: 12500
Founded in 1983

Magazines & Journals

4211 ABC Today
Associated Builders and Contractors
4250 Fairfax Dr
9th Floor
Arlington, VA 22203-1665

703-812-2000
FAX 703-812-8201
Home Page: www.abc.org

Mike Bellaman, CEO
Todd Mann, COO

The purpose of this magazine is to offer industry updates on the latest trends and developments that affect general construction, labor, management, legislation, education, products and techniques for the building industry.
Cost: $36.00
Frequency: Monthly
Circulation: 25000
Founded in 1950

4212 American Painting Contractor
Douglas Publications
2807 N Parham Road
Suite 200
Richmond, VA 23294

703-519-2341
800-223-1797
E-Mail: ehoward@douglaspublications.com
Home Page: www.douglaspublications.com

Emily Howard, Editor
Jaimy Ford, Executive Editor

Features include business management, market research, decorating trends, techniques and developments in preparation and specialty coatings. News includes association activities, personnel changes and government actions.
Frequency: Monthly
Circulation: 25000
Founded in 1985

4213 American Public Works Magazine
2345 Grand Blvd
Suite 700
Kansas City, MO 64108-2625

816-472-6100
800-848-2792
FAX 816-472-1610
E-Mail: ddancy@apwa.net
Home Page: www.apwa.net

Brian Van Norman, Director
David Dancy, Director of Marketing
Kevin Clark, Editor

International educational and professional association of public agencies, private sector companies, and individuals dedicated to providing high quality public works goods and services. The magazine is a forum for public works professionals, agencies and companies. It includes public works-related topics to public attention in local, state and federal areas.
Cost: $100.00
40 Pages
Frequency: Monthly
ISSN: 0092-4873
Founded in 1937

4214 Architectural Record
McGraw-Hill Construction
2 Penn Plz
9th Floor
New York, NY 10121-2298

212-904-2594
FAX 212-904-4256

E-Mail: william_hanley@mcgraw-hill.com
Home Page: www.mcgraw-hill.com

William Hanley, Editor
Lamar Clarkson, Editor

Provides original, reliable and useful information to the architectural marketplace worldwide, setting the standards for excellence in architectural design and presenting insights and practical solutions for current challenges in the design, building construction and business practices.
Cost: $49.00
Frequency: Monthly
Circulation: 102,000
ISSN: 0003-858X

4215 Asphalt Magazine
Asphalt Institute
2696 Research Park Dr
Lexington, KY 40511-8480

859-288-4960
FAX 859-288-4999
E-Mail: info@asphaltinstitute.org
Home Page: www.asphaltinstitute.org
Social Media: *Facebook, Twitter, LinkedIn*

Peter Grass, President
Frequency: 3x/Year
Circulation: 18000

4216 Automated Builder
CMN Associates
2401 Grapevine Dr
Oxnard, CA 93036

805-351-5931
800-344-2537
FAX 805-351-5755
Home Page: www.automatedbuilder.com/

Donald Carlson
Agnes Carlson, Circulation

Distributed free of charge in the US to executive and management personnel upon written request in companies that are production (big volume) site builders, panelized home manufacturers, modular home manufacturers, special unit manufacturers, component manufacturers and HUD-Code, modular, panelized and commercial building dealers.
Cost: $50.00
Frequency: Monthly
Circulation: 25000
ISSN: 0899-5540
Founded in 1964
Printed in 4 colors on glossy stock

4217 BUILDER
Hanley-Wood
1 Thomas Cir NW
Suite 600
Washington, DC 20005-5811

202-452-0800
FAX 202-785-1974
E-Mail: bthompson@hanleywood.com
Home Page: www.builderonline.com

Frank Anton, CEO
Hanley Wood, Publisher
Boyce Thompson, Editoral Director

BUILDER is the leading brand in residential new construction and serves as the magazine of the National Association of Home Builders (NAHB). For more than three decades, BUILDER has provided essential news, information and resources about products, technologies, trends, regulatory requirements and best practices to help home building professionals navigate challenges for success. BUILDER is the trusted source for top builders, architects and other industry professionals across the country.
Cost: $29.95
Frequency: Monthly
Circulation: 104852
ISSN: 0744-N93

Founded in 1977
Mailing list available for rent: 100M names
Printed in 4 colors on glossy stock

4218 Bonded Builders News
Richard K Nicholson Enterprises
2201 Corporate Boulevard
Suite 100
Boca Raton, FL 33431-7337

561-278-6968
800-749-0381
FAX 561-368-1781
Home Page: www.bondedbuilders.com

Whit Ward, President
Howard Head, Editor-in-Chief

Provides builders and developers with information involving new technologies and changing trends in the home building industry.
Cost: $18.00
Frequency: Quarterly
Circulation: 7000

4219 Builder Insider
PO Box 191125
Dallas, TX 75219-8105

214-988-9181
866-930-1950
FAX 214-871-2931
Home Page: www.builderinsider.com

Michael Anderson, Editor

Independent trade publications covering the residential and light commercial building industry.
Cost: $12.00
28 Pages
Frequency: Monthly
Circulation: 5200
Founded in 1976

4220 Builders Trade Journal
Lee Publications
6113 State Highway 5
PO Box 121
Palatine Bridge, NY 13428

518-673-3237
800-836-2888
FAX 518-673-3245
E-Mail: info@leepub.com
Home Page: www.leepub.com

Fred Lee, Editor
Wendell Jennings, Sales Manager

Edited for the building industry.
Frequency: Monthly
Founded in 1982

4221 Building Design & Construction
Reed Business Information
360 Park Ave S
New York, NY 10010-1737

646-746-6400
FAX 646-756-7583
E-Mail:
corporatecommunications@reedbusiness.com
Home Page: www.reedbusiness.com

Mark Kelsey, CEO
Stuart Whayman, CFO
James Reed, Owner

Serves the needs of the design and construction professionals of commercial, industrial and institutional buildings that include new and retrofit projects. Geared towards the building team that includes professionals from building firms, owning firms and design firms.
Frequency: Monthly
Circulation: 76,005
Founded in 1993

4222 Building Environment Report
IAQ Publications

7920 Norfolk Ave
Suite 900
Bethesda, MD 20814-2539

301-913-0115
FAX 301-913-0119
Home Page: www.eschoolnews.com

Robert Morrow, Owner
Nancy David, Editor

Covers information to help manage building environmental hazards, meet environmental compliance requirements, protect building occupants, conference coverage and meetings of note.
Cost: $325.00
Frequency: Monthly
Circulation: 1,500

4223 Building Material Dealer
National Lumber & Building Material Dealers Assoc.
2025 M Street Nw
Ste 800
Washington, DC 20036

202-367-1169
FAX 202-367-2169
E-Mail: info@dealer.org
Home Page: www.dealer.org

Michael O'Brien, President
Scott Lynch, EVP

Content focuses on a mixture of regional and national news relating to governmental regulations, dealer and supplier news, meetings and seminars affecting the independent building retailer.
Frequency: Monthly
Circulation: 24,647

4224 Building Operating Management
Trade Press Publishing Corporation
2100 W Florist Avenue
Milwaukee, WI 53209-3799

414-228-7701
FAX 414-228-1134
Home Page: www.tradepress.com

Brad Ehlert, Group Publisher
Brian Terry, Publisher

Serves the field of facilities management, encompassing commercial building: office buildings, real estate/property management firms, developers, financial institutions, insurance companies, apartment complexes, civic/convention centers, including members of the Building Owners and Managers Association
Cost: $120.00
Frequency: Monthly
Circulation: 70000
Founded in 1954
Printed in 4 colors on glossy stock

4225 Building Stone Magazine
Building Stone Institute
5 Riverside Dr
Building 1
Chestertown, NY 12817

518-803-4336
866-786-6313
FAX 518-803-4336
Home Page: www.buildingstoneinstitute.org
Social Media: *Facebook*

Duffe Elkins, President
Rob Teel, VP

State of the industry publication for architects, designers and people in the natural stone industries: granite, marble, limestone, etc.
Cost: $65.00
350 Members
Circulation: 18000
Founded in 1919
Printed in 4 colors on glossy stock

4226 Building Supply Home Centers
Reed Business Information
360 Park Ave S
New York, NY 10010-1737

646-746-6400
FAX 646-756-7583
Home Page: www.reedbusiness.com

Mark Kelsey, CEO
James Reed, Owner

For owners, manufacturers and other executives of the retail building market.
Cost: $60.00
Frequency: Monthly
Founded in 1917

4227 Buildings: Facilities Construction & Management Magazine
Stamats Communications
PO Box 1888
Cedar Rapids, IA 52406-1888

319-364-6167
800-553-8878
FAX 319-365-5421
E-Mail: info@stamats.com
Home Page: www.stamats.com

Guy Wendler, CEO
Peter Stamats, EVP/CFO

Information on construction costs, building design, space planning, fire safety, environment solutions, energy effiency, accessibilty, security, and strategic facilities planning.
Cost: $70.00
Frequency: Monthly
Circulation: 56500
Founded in 1906

4228 CIM Construction Journal
Construction Industries of Massachusetts
1500 Providence Highway Suite 14
PO Box 667
Norwood, MA 02062

781-551-0182
FAX 781-551-0916
E-Mail: info@cimass.org
Home Page: www.cimass.org

Mark Drummey, Editor/Publisher
John Pourbaix, Executive Director

Digest of horizontal public works projects.
Frequency: Weekly
Circulation: 2000
Founded in 1921

4229 Carpenter
United Brotherhood of Carpenters & Joiners
6801 Placid St
Las Vegas, NV 89119-4205

702-938-1111
FAX 702-938-1122
E-Mail: dshoemaker@carpenters.org
Home Page: www.ubcmillwrights.com

William Irwin, Executive Director

Contains news and information on the union and its members, the craft, and the construction industry as a whole.
Founded in 1881

4230 Catholic Cemetery
National Catholic Cemetery Conference
1400 S Wolf Rd
Building # 3
Hillside, IL 60162

708-202-1242
888-850-8131
FAX 708-202-1255
Home Page: www.ntriplec.com

Christine Kohut, Editor
Dennis Fairbank, Executive Director

News on products and manufacturers and also gives information on cemetery maintenance and repairs.
Frequency: Monthly
Circulation: 2100
Founded in 1949

4231 Commerical Modular Construction
Emlen Publications/Modular Building Institute
1241 Andersen Dr
North Suite
San Rafael, CA 94901-5374

415-460-6185
800-965-8876
FAX 415-460-6288
E-Mail: info@emlenmedia.com
Home Page: www.emlenmedia.com

Eli Gage, Publisher
Ahavah Revis, Managing Editor

Contains articles on modular for architects, engineering and spec writers who need building product, specification and address information.

4232 Computer-Aided Engineering
Penton Media
1300 E 9th St
Suite 316
Cleveland, OH 44114-1503

216-696-7000
FAX 216-696-6662
E-Mail: information@penton.com
Home Page: www.penton.com

Sharon Rowlands, CEO

Database applications in design and manufacturing.
Cost: $50.00
96 Pages
Founded in 1982

4233 Concrete InFocus
National Ready Mixed Concrete Association
900 Spring St
Silver Spring, MD 20910-4015

240-485-1139
FAX 301-585-4219
E-Mail: info@nrmca.org
Home Page: www.nrmca.org
Social Media: *Facebook, LinkedIn, YouTube*

Robert Garbini, President
Deana Angelastro, Executive Administrator

The top resource for industry news, trends, research, legislative articles and company profiles.
1200 Members
Frequency: Quarterly
Circulation: 5000+
Founded in 1930

4234 Concrete Pressure Pipe Digest
American Concrete Pressure Pipe Association
3900 University Drive
Suite 110
Fairfax, VA 22030-2513

703-273-7227
FAX 703-273-7230
Home Page: www.acppa.org

Richard Mueller, Chair
Mike Leathers, Vice Chair

4235 Concrete Pumping Magazine
American Concrete Pumping Association
606 Enterprise Dr
Lewis Center, OH 43035-9432

614-431-5618
FAX 614-431-6944
Home Page: www.concretepumpers.com

Carl Walker, President
Christi Collins, Executive Director

Packed with articles on industry leaders, new products, and on-site examples.
Frequency: Quarterly
Circulation: 2,100

4236 Construction Bulletin
1200 Madison Ave
Indianapolis, IN 46225

317-423-7080
FAX 317-422-7034
Home Page: www.acppubs.com

Greg Sitek, Editor
Kenny Veach, Advertising Sales Manager

Serves heavy highway and building construction.
Cost: $199.00
Frequency: Weekly
Circulation: 4000
ISSN: 0010-6720
Founded in 1893

4237 Construction Dimensions
Association of the Wall and Ceiling Industry
513 W Broad St
Suite 210
Falls Church, VA 22046-3257

703-538-1600
FAX 703-534-8307
E-Mail: info@awci.org
Home Page: www.awci.org

Tim Wies, President
Jeffrey Burley, VP

A monthly magazine for manufacturers and suppliers in the wall and ceiling, and related industries. Construction Dimensions is the official publication of the Association of the Wall and Ceiling Industries International.
Cost: $ 40.00
115 Pages
Frequency: Monthly
Circulation: 23000
Founded in 1918

4238 Construction Distribution
Cygnus Business Media
1233 Janesville Avenue
Fort Atkinson, WI 53538

800-547-7377
E-Mail: nancy.terrill@cygnusb2b.com
Home Page: www.cygnusb2b.com

Nancy Terrill, Publisher
Rebecca Wasieleski, Editor

Resource for product, marketing and management information for construction supply distributors and the manufacturers and reps who serve them.
Frequency: Quarterly
Circulation: 14,800
Founded in 1966

4239 Construction Equipment Distribution
Associated Equipment Distributors
615 W 22nd St
Oak Brook, IL 60523-8807

630-574-0650
800-388-0650
FAX 630-574-0132
E-Mail: info@aednet.org
Home Page: www.aednet.org

Toby Mack, President
Mike Quirk, SVP

Offers valuable information for executives who sell and rent construction equipment.
Cost: $71.40
72 Pages
Frequency: Monthly
Circulation: 5500
Founded in 1918

4240 Construction Equipment Operation and Maintenance
Construction Publications
PO Box 1689
Cedar Rapids, IA 52406-1689

319-366-1597
FAX 319-362-8808

Clark Parks, Editor

Use and maintenance of construction equipment.
Cost: $10.00
24 Pages
Frequency: Monthly
Founded in 1948

4241 Construction Executive
Associated Builders and Contractors
4250 Fairfax Drive
9th Floor
Arlington, VA 22203-1665

703-812-2000
FAX 703-812-8201
Home Page: www.abc.org

Lisa A Nardone, Editor-in-Chief
Lauren Pinch, Assistant Editor
Mike Bellaman, CEO

Focus on commercial and industrial construction.
Cost: $24.00
Frequency: Monthly
Circulation: 49,000

4242 Construction Industry International
Quarto International
10 Whirling Dun
Collinsville, CT 06022-1239
Andrew Webster, Editor

Serves the administrative construction industry.
80 Pages
Frequency: Monthly
Founded in 1975

4243 Construction News West
McGraw Hill
PO Box 182604
Columbus, OH 43272-1095

614-866-5769
877-833-5524
FAX 614-759-3749
E-Mail: customer.service@mcgraw-hill.com
Home Page: www.mcgrawhill.com/

Jennifer Hayes, Editor
Harold McGraw III, President/CEO

Provides F.W. Dodge information for general contractors, suppliers, architects and owners in Arizona, Nevada and New Mexico.
Cost: $368.00
Frequency: Weekly
Circulation: 3000
Founded in 1902

4244 Construction Specifier
266 Elmwood Ave
Suite 289
Buffalo, NY 14222

716-572-5633
866-572-5633
FAX 866-572-5677
E-Mail: sales@constructionspecifier.com
Home Page: www.constructionspecifier.com

Jill Kaletha, Editor

The offical magazine of Construction Specifications Institute. Focused on the job functions of its core readership-professionals involved in the specification process. Offers insight and analysis on industry topics through news, product announcements, legal columns, case studies

and other research as well as providing in-depth features on industry-related issues.
Frequency: Monthly
Founded in 1956
Printed in on glossy stock

4245 Constructioneer
Associated Construction Publication
30 Technology Pkwy S
Suite 100
Norcross, GA 30092-2925

770-209-3730
800-424-3996
FAX 770-209-3712
E-Mail: rcdwebmaster@reedbusiness.com
Home Page: www.reedconstructiondata.com

Iain Melville, CEO
Steve Ritchie, VP Marketing
Marco Piovesan, VP Data

Information directed to construction industry of New York, Pennsylvania, New Jersey, and Delaware.
100 Pages
Frequency: Bi-Monthly
Circulation: 18889
Founded in 1975
Printed in 4 colors on matte stock

4246 Constructor Magazine
Associated General Contractors of America
2300 Wilson Blvd
Suite 400
Arlington, VA 22201-5426

703-548-3118
FAX 703-837-5400
E-Mail: info@agc.org
Home Page: www.agc.org

Kristine Young, President
Joe Jarboe, SVP

Voice of the construction industry.
Frequency: Monthly
Circulation: 40,000
Founded in 1918

4247 Contractors Guide
Painting and Decorating Contractors of America
1801 Park 270 Drive
Suite 220
St Louis, MO 63146-4020

314-514-7322
800-332-7322
FAX 314-514-9417
Home Page: www.pdca.org

Darylene Dennon, Chair

What every painting and decorating contractor needs to know, organized for easy use by painting and decorating contractors of all sizes.
Cost: $68.00

4248 Custom Home
Hanley-Wood
1 Thomas Cir NW
Suite 600
Washington, DC 20005-5811

202-452-0800
FAX 202-785-1974
E-Mail: fanton@hanleywood.com
Home Page: www.residentialarchitect.com

Frank Anton, CEO
Matt Flynn, CFO

Features materials, products, trends and the latest in designs for custom home construction.
Cost: $24.00
Frequency: 7 issues yearly
Circulation: 40000
Founded in 1976

4249 DBA Automated Builder Magazine
CMN Associates

2401 Grapevine Dr
Oxnard, CA 93036

805-351-5931
800-344-2537
FAX 805-351-5755
E-Mail: info@automatedbuilder.com
Home Page: www.automatedbuilder.com/

Don O Carlson, Editor/Publisher
Agnes Carlson, Circulation Manager

Magazine for manufacturers and suppliers who have a product line that is of interest to the factory-built housing industry. Covering all seven segments of US, Canadian and foreign housing industry, including: production builders; panelizers; component producers; modular; commercial modular; hud code; and all builder/dealers.
Frequency: Monthly
Circulation: 25000
ISSN: 0899-4450
Founded in 1964

4250 DFI Journal
Deep Foundations Institute
326 Lafayette Avenue
Hawthorne, NJ 07506

973-423-4030
FAX 973-423-4031
E-Mail: staff@dfi.org
Home Page: www.dfi.org

Publishes practice-oriented, high quality papers related to broad area of Deep Foundations Engineering.
Frequency: Bi-Annual

4251 Daily Construction Service
Construction Market Data
142 Arena Street
El Segundo, CA 90245

310-322-9990
FAX 858-573-0485

Jeanne Peterson, Editor

Offers valuable information for construction workers.
Cost: $365.00
Frequency: Monthly
Founded in 1933

4252 Daily Journal of Commerce
Dolan Media Company/New Orleans Publishing Grp
111 Veterans Memorial Blvd., Suite 1440
3445 North Causeway Blvd., Suite 90
Metairie, LA 70005-3028

504-834-9292
FAX 504-832-3435
E-Mail: djc@nopg.com
Home Page: www.djcgulfcoast.com

Lisa Blossman, Publisher
Christian Moises, Editor
Anne Lovas, General Manager
Becky Naquin, Assistance Editor

Reports on building and engineering industries.
Cost: $456.00
Frequency: Monthly
Founded in 1922

4253 Deep Foundations Magazine
Deep Foundations Institute
326 Lafayette Avenue
Hawthorne, NJ 07506

973-423-4030
FAX 973-423-4031
E-Mail: dfihq@dfi.org
Home Page: www.dfi.org

James Morrison, President
Virginia Fairweather, Executive Editor

Distributed to members.
Frequency: Quarterly
Circulation: 2753

4254 Demolition
National Demolition Association
16 N Franklin St
Suite 203
Doylestown, PA 18901-3536

215-348-4949
800-541-2412
FAX 215-348-8422
E-Mail: info@demolitionassociation.com
Home Page: www.demolitionassociation.com

Don Rachel, President
Jeff Kroeker, VP

Trade publication for the demolition industry.
Cost: $40.00
Circulation: 5000
ISSN: 1522-5690
Founded in 1972
Printed in 4 colors on matte stock

4255 Design Build
144 Lexington Street
Woburn, MA 01801

781-937-9265
FAX 781-937-9241
Home Page:
www.designbuild.construction.com

Gary Merrill, Sales Director
William Angelo, Editor-in-Chief

Received by all subscribers of Engineering News Record plus 7,500 owners identified by FW Dodge as having an interest in the design-build project delivery system, and 1,000 members of the Design-Build Institute of America.
84 Pages
Frequency: Quarterly
Circulation: 20000
ISSN: 1096-7095
Founded in 1953

4256 Design Cost & Data
Rector Communications
2300 Chestnut St
Suite 340
Philadelphia, PA 19103-4398

215-963-9661
FAX 215-963-9672
Home Page: www.rector.com

Marion Rector, Owner

Cost estimating magazine for architects, builders, developers, appraisers, specifiers, insurers and construction financiers.

4257 Design Lines
American Institute of Building Design
7059 Blair Rd NW
Suite 201
Washington, DC 20012

800-366-2423
FAX 866-204-0293
E-Mail: info@aibd.org
Home Page: www.aibd.org
Social Media: *Facebook, Twitter, LinkedIn*

Dan Sater, President
Alan Kent, Internal Vice President
Viki Wooster, External Vice President
Kerry Dick, Secretary/ Treasurer

Publication that focuses on issues, education, and events as they happen in the building design industry.
1500 Attendees
Frequency: Monthly
Founded in 1950

4258 Design Solutions Magazine
Architectural Woodwork Institute

46179 Westlake Dr
Suite 120
Potomac Falls, VA 20165

571-323-3636
FAX 571-323-3630
E-Mail: info@awinet.org
Home Page: www.awinet.org

Robert Stout, President
Mike Bell, Vice President

Each issue showcases beautiful examples of
fine architectural woodwork manufactured by
AWI Manufacturing Member companies. With
beautiful four-color images, crisp detailed
drawings and thought provoking articles, Design Solutions offers our readers a bountiful resource that's sure to inspire and delight all.
Cost: $25.00
Frequency: Quarterly
Circulation: 27,000

4259 Dodge Construction News
McGraw Hill
2 Penn Plaza
9th Floor
New York, NY 10121-1299

212-904-3507
FAX 212-904-2820
E-Mail: customerservice@mcgraw-hill.com
Home Page: www.mcgraw-hill.com

Jennifer Hayes, Editor
Harold McGraw, III, CEO/President

Consists of program edition and proceedings
and recap edition for the National Conventions
of the American Institute of Architects and
Construction Specifications Institute.
Circulation: 86400
Founded in 1884

4260 Door & Window Maker
Key Communications
PO Box 569
Garrisonville, VA 22463-0569

540-720-5584
FAX 540-720-5687
E-Mail: key-com@glass.com
Home Page: www.glass.com

Debra Levy, Owner
Brigid O'Leary, Assistant Editor
Frequency: 9 issues yearly
Circulation: 23,947
Founded in 1993

4261 Engineering News Record
McGraw Hill
2 Penn Plaza
9th Floor
New York, NY 10121-2298

212-904-3507
FAX 212-904-2820
E-Mail: scott_lewis@mcgraw-hill.com
Home Page: www.enr.com

Richard Korman, Managing Senior Editor
Ilan Kapla, Senior Manager
Keith Wallace, Production Editor

Provides the news, analysis, commentary and
data that construction industry professionals
need to do their jobs more effectively. ENR is
the national news magazine for the construction industry.
Cost: $82.00
Frequency: Weekly
Circulation: 60000
Founded in 1874

**4262 Environmental Design &
Construction**
Business News Publishing Company

2401 W Big Beaver Rd
Suite 700
Troy, MI 48084-3333

248-362-3700
FAX 248-362-0317
E-Mail: brownd@bnpmedia.com
Home Page: www.edcmag.com

Derrick Teal, Editor
Diana Brown, Publisher
Laura Zielinski, Associate Editor

Magazine dedicated to integrated high-performance buildings, and efficient and sustainable
design and construction.
Founded in 1926

4263 Equipment Today
Cygnus Business Media
1233 Janesville Avenue
Fort Atkinson, WI 53538

800-547-7377
E-Mail: becky.schultz@cygnuspub.com
Home Page: www.cygnusb2b.com

Becky Schultz, Editor

Contractors and other users of construction machinery. Editorial is focused on the selection,
application and maintenance of equipment as
well as new and improved product introductions. Accepts advertising.
Cost: $60.00
54 Pages
Frequency: Monthly
Circulation: 77,000
Founded in 1966

4264 FW Dodge Northwest Construction
McGraw Hill
800 S Michigan St
Seattle, WA 98108-2655

206-378-4715
800-393-6343
FAX 206-378-4741
E-Mail: support@construction.com
Home Page: www.construction.com

Keith Fox, President
Linda Brennan, VP Operations

Project news, plans, specifications and analysis
data for the construction professional.
Cost: $40.00
Frequency: Monthly
Founded in 1884

4265 Fabric Architecture
Industrial Fabrics Association International
1801 County Road B W
Roseville, MN 55113-4061

651-222-2508
800-225-4324
FAX 651-631-9334
E-Mail: generalinfo@ifai.com
Home Page: www.ifai.com

Stephen Warner, President
Chris Tschida, Editorial Manager

Strives to inform architects, designers, landscape architects, engineers and other specifiers
about architectural fabric structures, the fibers
and fabrics used to make them, their design
possibilities, their construction, and issues regarding their applicability and acceptance.
Cost: $39.00
Frequency: Bi-monthly

4266 Facility Management Journal
International Facility Management
Association
1 Greenway Plz
Suite 1100
Houston, TX 77046-0194

713-623-4362
FAX 713-623-6124

E-Mail: ifma@ifma.org
Home Page: www.ifma.org

Andrea Sanchez, Editor-in-Chief
Laurie Steiner, Senior Associate Editor

Covers industry economic, financial trends and
the industries legislative, special emphasis on
developments in technology.
Cost: $75.00
Circulation: 14000
Founded in 1990

4267 Facility News Magazines
National Lead Abatement Council
PO Box 535
Olney, MD 20830

301-924-5490
800-590-6522
FAX 301-924-0265

Stephen Weil, Publisher
Wendy Faxon, Editor

Information on facility maintenance manage-
ment.
Cost: $36.00
20 Pages
Frequency: Monthly
Circulation: 7500
Founded in 1981

4268 Fenestration Magazine
Ashlee Publishing
18 E 41st Street
20th Floor
New York, NY 10017-6009

212-376-7722
FAX 212-376-7723
Home Page: www.fenestrationmagazine.com

Joel Bruinooge, Editor

Windows and door industry.
Cost: $40.00
80+ Pages
Frequency: 10x yearly
Circulation: 17,000
ISSN: 0895-450X

4269 Fine Homebuilding
Taunton Press
63 S Main St
Box 5506
Newtown, CT 06470-2344

203-426-8171
FAX 203-426-3434
E-Mail: fh@tauton.com
Home Page: www.taunton.com

Harrison McCampbell, Editor
Rob Yagid, Assistant Editor

Reviews of new equipment and related building
materials and guidelines to successful work
techniques and general industry news.
Cost: $37.95
Circulation: 308,000
Founded in 1980

4270 Floor Covering Installer
Business News Publishing Company
22801 Ventura Blvd
#115
Woodland Hills, CA 91364

818-224-8035
818-224-8042
Home Page: www.fcimag.com

John Moore, Editor
Jennifer Allen, Production Manager

Provides the varied information needed by
those who engage in floor covering installation
with how-to and skill-building articles,
how-to-do-it photographic presentations, new
installation product information, news of the
industry, as well as how and where to get fur-

ther training in various aspects of floor covering installation.
Frequency: Bi-Monthly
Circulation: 40,000

4271 Foundation Drilling
ADSC
8445 Freeport Parkway
Suite 325
Irving, TX 75063

469-359-6000
FAX 469-359-6007
E-Mail: adsc@adsc-iafd.com
Home Page: www.adsc-iafd.com

Tim Wies, President
Jeffrey Burley, VP

Written for foundation drilling and anchored earth retention contractors and their project managers, superintendents, foremen, civil and structural engineers, soils engineers, public engineering officials, architects, manufacturers and distributors of industry related equipments.
Frequency: 8x yearly
Circulation: 5000

4272 Frame Building News
F+W Media
38 E. 29th Street
New York, NY 10016

212-447-1400
FAX 212-447-5231
E-Mail: contact_us@fwmedia.com
Home Page: www.fwpublications.com

David Nussbaum, CEO
Sara Domville, President

Edited for the diversified town & country builders of light-industrial, commercial, agricultural, and residential structures. The majority of the coverage is about post-frame structures. Readers look for the latest in post-frame research and techniques, building code information, equipment, and materials. Regular features include 'Builder Spotlight,' 'New Products,' 'Supplier News,' 'OSHA Updates,' 'Legal Issues,' 'Business Strategies,' and 'Calendar of Events.' Official magazine of NFBA.
56 Pages
Circulation: 19211
Founded in 1952

4273 Glass Digest
Ashlee Publishing
18 E 41st Street
New York, NY 10017-6009

212-376-7722
FAX 212-376-7723
Home Page:
www.glassdigestmagazine.com/ashlee/glassdigest/index.html

Jordan Wright, Publisher

Merchandising/technical publication for the flat glass industry.
Cost: $25.00
140 Pages
Frequency: Monthly
Founded in 1922

4274 Hanley-Wood's Tools of the Trade
Hanley Wood
1 Thomas Cir NW
Suite 600
Washington, DC 20005-5803

202-452-0800
FAX 202-785-1974
Home Page: www.hanleywood.com

Frank Anton, CEO
Matt Flynn, CFO

The wide array of tools and equipment in the construction and renovation industries.
Cost: $36.00
Circulation: 65,000
Founded in 1976

4275 Home Builders Magazine
Work-4 Projects
4819 Saint Charles Boulevard
Pierrefonds, QC H9H-3C7

514-620-2200
FAX 514-620-6300
E-Mail: editor@work4.ca
Home Page: www.homebuildercanada.com/

Nachmi Artzy, Publisher
Cheryl Carvery, Sales

Specializes in educating readers on the latest installation tips, building techniques and materials that can be put into on-site practice everyday.
Cost: $30.00
Frequency: Bi-Monthly
Circulation: 23265
Founded in 1988

4276 Hot Mix Asphalt Technology
National Asphalt Pavement Association
5100 Forbes Blvd
Suite 200
Lanham, MD 20706-4407

301-731-4748
888-468-6499
FAX 301-731-4621
E-Mail: mcervarich@hotmix.org
Home Page: www.hotmix.org

Mike Acott, President
Margaret Cervarich, VP Marketing/Public Affairs

The leading journal for the asphalt pavement contractor
Frequency: Bi-Monthly
Circulation: 10000

4277 IEEE Power and Energy Magazine
IEEE
PO Box 1331
Piscataway, NJ 08855-1331

732-981-0060
FAX 732-981-1721
E-Mail: customer-service@ieee.org
Home Page: www.ieee.org

Fran Zappulla, Staff Director, Publishing
Susan Hassler, Editor

Network analysis, system stability studies, fault protection and construction management.
Cost: $285.00
82 Pages
Frequency: Monthly
Circulation: 23000
ISSN: 1540-7977
Founded in 1885
Mailing list available for rent
Printed in on glossy stock

4278 InTents
Industrial Fabrics Association International
1801 County Road B W
Roseville, MN 55113-4061

651-222-2508
800-225-4324
FAX 651-631-9334
E-Mail: generalinfo@ifai.org
Home Page: www.ifai.com

Stephen Warner, CEO
Chris Tschida, Editorial Manager

Promotes the use of tents and accessories to the special-event and general-rental industries.
Cost: $39.00
Frequency: Bi-Monthly
Circulation: 12,000

4279 Insulation Outlook
National Insulation Association
12100 Sunset Hills Road
Suite 330
Reston, VA 20190-3295

703-683-6422
FAX 703-549-4838
E-Mail: editor@insulation.org
Home Page: www.insulation.org

Michele Jones, EVP/CEO
Julie McLaughlin, Director of Publications

Contains information on new products, industry trends, asbestos abatement and installation practices.
Cost: $45.00
Frequency: Monthly
Circulation: 7000
Founded in 1973
Printed in 4 colors on glossy stock

4280 Interior Construction
Ceilings & Interior Systems Construction Assn
1010 Jorie Boulevard
Suite 30
Oak Brook, IL 60223

630-584-1919
FAX 866-560-8537
Home Page: www.cisca.org

Shirley Wodynski, Executive Director
Rick Reuland, Editor

Offers information designed to keep contractors abreast of the changes in interior construction.
Cost: $35.00
Frequency: Monthly
Circulation: 10000
Founded in 1950

4281 Interlocking Concrete Pavement Magazine
Interlocking Concrete Pavement Institute
13921 Park Center Road
Suite 270
Herndon, VA 20171-3269

202-080-0285
800-241-3652
FAX 202-408-0285
E-Mail: icpi@icpi.org
Home Page: www.icpi.org

Ericka Giles, Editor
Charles McGrath, Executive Director
Cost: $5.00
32 Pages
Frequency: Quarterly
Circulation: 20,000
Founded in 1993
Printed in 4 colors

4282 Intermountain Contractor
McGraw Hill
1114 W 7th Avenue
Suite 100
Denver, CO 80204

303-756-9995
800-393-6343
FAX 303-756-4465
E-Mail: mark_shaw@mcgraw-hill.com
Home Page:
www.intermountain.construction.com

Seth Horositz, Publisher
Mark Shaw, Editor

For general contractors. Serves Colorado, Idaho, Montana, Utah and Wyoming.
Cost: $40.00
88 Pages
Frequency: Weekly
Circulation: 5,247

4283 International Construction
Primedia

3585 Engineering Drive
Suite 100
Norcross, GA 30092

678-421-3000
800-216-1423
Home Page: www.primedia.com

Charles Stubbs, President
Kim Payne, SVP

Provides valuable information to help readers succeed in every aspect of their jobs, from planning strategies to targeting growth, from solving engineering problems to selecting the right equipment and materials.

4284 Job-Site Supervisor
FMI Corporation
5171 Glenwood Ave
Suite 200
Raleigh, NC 27612-3266

919-787-8400
FAX 919-785-9320
E-Mail: webmasters@fminet.com
Home Page: www.fminet.com

Hank Harris, President

Delivers articles on safety, regulations and management; with a special section that examines a challenging construction project. Editorial is presented from a field manager's point-of-view, including charts, graphs, illustrations and industry advice.
Cost: $179.00
Circulation: 4000
Founded in 1953

4285 Journal of Light Construction
Hanley-Wood
186 Allen Brook Lane
Williston, VT 05495

802-879-3335
800-552-1951
FAX 802-879-9384
E-Mail: jlc-cs@hanley-wood.com
Home Page: www.jlconline.com

Don Jackson, Editor
Rick Strachan, Publisher

Written for builders, remodelers, contractors and architects involved in the design and construction of residential and light commercial buildings. Accepts advertising.
Cost: $39.95
150 Pages
Frequency: Monthly
Circulation: 73000
ISSN: 1040-5224
Founded in 1982
Mailing list available for rent: 70,000 names at $120 per M
Printed in 4 colors on glossy stock

4286 Journal of Protective Coatings & Linings
Technology Publishing Company
2100 Wharton St
Suite 310
Pittsburgh, PA 15203-1951

412-431-8300
800-837-8303
FAX 412-431-5428
E-Mail: webmaster@paintsquare.com
Home Page: www.paintsquare.com

Marian Welsh, Publisher
Mary Chollet, Editor-in-Chief

The right tools to help you reach the protective and marine coatings industry.
Cost: $80.00
Frequency: Monthly
Circulation: 15,000
ISSN: 8755-1985

4287 Kitchen & Bath Design News
Cygnus Business Media

2 University Plaza
Suite 310
Hackensack, NJ 07601

201-487-7800
FAX 201-487-1061
E-Mail: kathy.scott@cygnusb2b.com
Home Page: www.cygnusb2b.com

Eliot Sefrin, Editorial Director/Publisher
Scott, Director of Public Relations

Serving the kitchen and bath industry, a key niche within the residential construction and remodeling marketplace.
Frequency: Monthly
Circulation: 48667
Founded in 1966

4288 Manufactured Home Merchandiser
RLD Group
PO Box 269149
Suite 800
Chicago, IL 60626-9149

312-236-3529
FAX 312-236-4024

Herb Tider, President
Wayne Beamer, Editor

Offers information for home builders and professionals in the manufactured home industry.
Cost: $36.00
Frequency: Monthly
Circulation: 18600
Founded in 1952

4289 Masonry Magazine
Mason Contractors Association of America
1481 Merchant Drive
Algonquin, IL 60102

224-678-9709
800-536-2225
FAX 224-678-9714
Home Page: www.masoncontractors.org

Jeff Buczkiewicz, Executive Director
Tim O'Toole, Marketing Director

This periodical covers every aspect of the mason contractor profession, not only equipment and techniques but topics such as building codes and stanards.
Cost: $29.00
Frequency: Monthly
Circulation: 17,000

4290 Metal Roofing
F+W Media
38 E. 29th Street
New York, NY 10016

212-447-1400
FAX 212-447-5231
E-Mail: contact_us@fwmedia.com
Home Page: www.fwpublications.com

David Nussbaum, CEO
Sara Domville, President
Circulation: 25000
ISSN: 1533-8711
Founded in 1900
Printed in 4 colors on glossy stock

4291 Midwest Contractor
Associated Construction Publication
1200 Madison Ave
LL20
Indianapolis, IN 46225

317-423-7080
800-486-0014
FAX 317-423-7094
Home Page: www.acppubs.com

Tad Smith, CEO
Greg Sitek, Managing Editor

Annual equipment buyers' guide, a complete cross reference listing of manufacturers, area distributors and their construction equipment

lines.
Cost: $96.00
Founded in 1905

4292 Muir's Original Log Home Guide for Builders and Buyers
Gary J Schroder
1101 SE 7th Ave
Grand Rapids, MN 55744-4087

218-326-4434
800-359-6614
FAX 218-326-2529
Home Page: www.loghelp.com

Gary Schroeder, Owner
Allan Muir, Author

Log home industry.
Cost: $12.95
Frequency: Monthly
ISBN: 0-967786-90-8
Founded in 1978

4293 National Association of Demolition Contactors
National Demolition Association
16 N Franklin Street
Suite 203
Doylestown, PA 18901

215-348-4949
800-541-2412
FAX 215-348-8422
E-Mail: info@demolitionassociation.com
Home Page: www.demolitionassociation.com

Don Rachel, President
Jeff Kroeker, VP

Bimonthly magazine.
Cost: $40.00
Circulation: 5000
ISSN: 1522-5690
Founded in 1969
Printed in 4 colors on matte stock

4294 New England Construction
Associated Construction Publication
1200 Madison Ave
LL20
Indianapolis, IN 46225

317-423-7080
800-486-0014
FAX 317-423-7094
Home Page: www.acppubs.com

Tad Smith, CEO
Greg Sitek, Managing Editor

Complete reports on contracts awarded, low bids and proposed work; features on highway construction and earthmoving, land development projects, utility construction, industrial building construction in the six-state New England region.
Cost: $96.00
Frequency: Monthly
Circulation: 10490
Founded in 1975

4295 Northwest Construction
McGraw Hill
800 S Michigan St
Seattle, WA 98108-2655

206-378-4715
800-393-6343
FAX 206-378-4741
E-Mail: support@construction.com
Home Page: www.construction.com

Jeff Greisch, President
Heather McCune, Editor-in-Chief

A regional, monthly magazine with features on Washington and design construction projects. Accepts advertising.
Cost: $60.00
64 Pages
Frequency: Monthly

Circulation: 6,200
Founded in 1997

4296 Occupational Hazards
Penton Media
1300 E 9th St
Suite 316
Cleveland, OH 44114-1503

216-696-7000
FAX 216-696-6662
E-Mail: information@penton.com
Home Page: www.penton.com

Sharon Rowlands, CEO

Analysis of qualified recipients who have indicated that they recommend, select and/or buy the safety equipment, fire protection and other occupational health products.
65 Pages
Frequency: Monthly
Circulation: 65,777
ISSN: 0029-7909
Founded in 1892
Printed in 4 colors on glossy stock

4297 Old House Journal
Old House Journal Group
PO Box 420235
Palm Coast, FL 32142-235

800-826-3893
FAX 978-283-4629
E-Mail: daposporos@homebuyerpubs.com
Home Page: www.oldhousejournal.com

Demetra Aposporos, Editor-in-Chief
Danielle Small, Advertising Manager

Covers restoration techniques for the pre-1939 home.
Cost: $27.00
Circulation: 140119
Founded in 1999

4298 Pacific Builder & Engineer
Associated Construction Publication
30 Technology Pkwy S
Suite 100
Norcross, GA 30092-2925

770-209-3730
800-424-3996
FAX 770-209-3712
Home Page: www.acppubs.com

Tad Smith, CEO
Greg Sitek, Managing Editor

For management level personnel in the highway and heavy construction and non-residential building industries in Washington, Oregon, Idaho, Montana and Alaska. Includes notice of bid calls, low bidders, contract awards on area projects; cost cutting construction methods, unusual techniques and equipment applications, analysis of market conditions and industry trends, new products and literature, general industry news and views, personal news and legal advice. Accepts advertising.
Cost: $50.00
Circulation: 100000
Founded in 1902

4299 Pavement
Cygnus Business Media
1233 Janesville Avenue
Fort Atkinson, WI 53538

E-Mail: amy.schwandt@cygnusb2b.com
Home Page: www.cygnusb2b.com

Amy Schwandt, Publisher
Allan Heydorn, Editor/Associate Publisher

Reaches contractors in the pavement maintenance and commercial paving sector. Covers the four main segments of the market in each issue: sealcoating, striping, paving and sweeping.
Circulation: 18,500
Founded in 1985

4300 Period Homes
Restore Media
5185 MacArthur Blvd NW
Suite 725
Washington, DC 20016

202-339-0744
FAX 202-339-0749
E-Mail: info@restoremedia.com
Home Page: www.restoremedia.com

Michael Tucker, Chairman/CEO
Paul Kitzke, EVP
Peter Miller, President/Publisher

Lists sources of products for restoration and new construction of residential architecture.
Cost: $18.00
120 Pages
Circulation: 24,600
ISSN: 0898-0284

4301 Products Finishing
Scott Walker/Gardner Publications
6915 Valley Ln
Cincinnati, OH 45244-3153

513-527-8800
800-950-8020
FAX 513-527-8801
Home Page: www.gardnerweb.com

Rick Kline, CEO

Serves the finishing field, including educational services, public administration and other manufacturing industries.
Cost: $89.00
Frequency: Monthly
Circulation: 42000
Founded in 1928
Printed in 4 colors on glossy stock

4302 Professional Builder
Reed Business Information
2000 Clearwater Dr
Oak Brook, IL 60523-8809

630-288-8000
FAX 630-288-8781
Home Page: www.reedbusiness.com

Iain Melville, CEO
Andrew Rak, SVP

New residential construction magazine with a more than 63 year tradition of providing builders the solutions they need to maximize profits.
Frequency: Monthly
Circulation: 127002
Founded in 1931

4303 Professional Door Dealer Magazine
Virgo Publishing LLC
3300 N Central Ave
Suite 300
Phoenix, AZ 85012-2532

480-675-9925
FAX 480-990-0819
E-Mail: danielle@vpico.com
Home Page: www.vpico.com

Jenny Bolton, President

Educational resource for residential and commercial door and access-control professionals.
Circulation: 20000
Founded in 1986
Printed in on glossy stock

4304 Professional Remodeler
Reed Business Information
360 Park Ave S
New York, NY 10010-1737

646-746-6400
FAX 646-756-7583
E-Mail:
corporatecommunications@reedbusiness.com
Home Page: www.reedbusiness.com

Iain Melville, CEO
Andrew Rak, SVP

Designed to accomodate the needs of residential remodelers and light commercial renovators and focuses on news, features, new products, tech-takes, and management and marketing approaches.
Frequency: Monthly
Circulation: 18131
Founded in 2002

4305 Professional Roofing
National Roofing Contractors Association
10255 W Higgins Rd
Suite 600
Rosemont, IL 60018-5613

847-299-9070
800-323-9545
FAX 847-299-1183
E-Mail: nrca@nrca.net
Home Page: www.professionalroofing.net

William Good, EVP
Ambika-Punia Bailey, Editor
Chrystine Hanus, Associate Editor
Carl Good, Publisher

Articles on both technical and business aspects of professional roofing.
Cost: $35.00
3500 Members
Frequency: Monthly
Circulation: 16000
ISSN: 0896-5552
Founded in 1886

4306 Professional Spraying
88-11th Avenue NE
Minneapolis, MN 55413

612-623-6000
FAX 612-623-6580
E-Mail: CustomerService@graco.com
Home Page: www.graco.com

Patrick McHale, President/CEO
James Graner, CFO

Targets new products, industry news, and trade literature.
Frequency: Monthly
Circulation: 40000
Founded in 1926

4307 Qualified Remodeler
Cygnus Publishing
1233 Janesville Avenue
Fort Atkinson, WI 53538

920-563-6388
FAX 920-563-1704
E-Mail: john.huff@cygnusb2b.com
Home Page: www.cygnusb2b.com

John Huff, Publisher

Serving contractors who specialize in residential and light commercial remodeling.
72 Pages
Frequency: Monthly
Circulation: 82000
Founded in 1975
Mailing list available for rent: 84,000 names
Printed in 4 colors on glossy stock

4308 RSI
7300 N Linder Ave
Skokie, IL 60077

847-983-2000
E-Mail: roofingsidinginsulation@halldata.com
Home Page: www.rsimag.com

Delivers timely news, technical and business management information, including a monthly analysis of key industry trends and techniques to help roofing, siding and insulation contractors run progressive, profitable businesses
Cost: $36.00
64 Pages
Frequency: Monthly
Circulation: 23658
Founded in 1945

4309 Reed Bulletin

Reed Business Informtion
30 Technology Parkway South
Suite 100
Norcross, GA 30092

800-424-3996
E-Mail: talisha.jackson@reedbusiness.com
Home Page: www.reedconstructiondata.com

Talisha Jackson, Media Contact

Provides contractors with project news and tools suppliers.

4310 Reeves Journal

Business News Publishing Company
23421 South Pointe Dr.
Suite 280
Laguna Hills, CA 92653

949-830-0881
FAX 949-859-7845
E-Mail: ellyn@reevesjournal.com
Home Page: www.reevesjournal.com

Souzan Azar, Production
Ellyn Fishman, Publisher/Sales
Kati Larson, Advertising Sales
Jack Sweet, Editor

Reeves Journal, has been an invaluable tool for contractors & plumbing industry professionals for the last 85 years. Their goal is to address the regional opportunities and challenges facing PHC contractors, wholesalers and engineers in the 14 western United States.
Cost: $55.00
Frequency: Monthly
Circulation: 15,535
Founded in 1922

4311 Remodeling

Hanley-Wood
1 Thomas Cir NW
Suite 600
Washington, DC 20005-5811

202-452-0800
FAX 202-785-1974
E-Mail: rm@omeda.com
Home Page: www.residentialarchitect.com

Frank Anton, CEO
Claire Conroy, Editorial Director
Jennifer Lash, Managing Editor

News on state-of-the-art in remodeling management, products, construction and techniques. Appeals to the residential and light commercial remodeling contractor.
Cost: $44.95
Frequency: Monthly
Circulation: 93612
Founded in 1955

4312 Rental Equipment Register

17383 W Sunset Blvd
Suite A220
Pacific Plsds, CA 90272-4187

310-230-7160
FAX 310-230-7169
E-Mail: michael.roth@penton.com
Home Page: rermag.com

Michael Roth, Editor
Brandey Smith, Managing Editor

Edited for owners and managers of equipment rental and sales centers.
Cost: $45.00
125 Pages
Frequency: Monthly
Circulation: 21000
Founded in 1886

4313 Residential Architect

Hanley-Wood

1 Thomas Cir NW
Suite 600
Washington, DC 20005-5811

202-452-0800
888-269-8410
FAX 202-785-1974
E-Mail: jlash@hanleywood.com
Home Page: www.residentialarchitect.com

Frank Anton, CEO
Jennifer Lash, Managing Editor
Bruce Snider, Senior Editor

An award-winning national magazine focusing exclusively on the residential architecture profession.
Cost: $39.95
Frequency: 9x Yearly
Circulation: 22000
Founded in 1976

4314 Rock and Dirt

174 4th St
Crossville, TN 38555-4303

931-484-5137
800-251-6776
FAX 931-484-2532
E-Mail: subs@rockanddirt.com
Home Page: www.rockanddirt.com

Mike Stone, Publisher

Comprehensive buy/sell publications for heavy construction. Primary target audiences worldwide are contractors and other heavy equipment buyers. A non-editorial tabloid, each issue contains display and classified ads that feature thousand of pieces of heavy machinery and related products and services. The magazine also has a large auction section.
Cost: $14.33
Circulation: 170,000
Founded in 1950
Printed in 4 colors on newsprint stock

4315 Roofing Contractor

BNP Media
PO Box 5125
Naperville, IL 60540

630-554-2200
FAX 630-554-3817
E-Mail: mward@illinoisroofing.com
Home Page: www.illinoisroofing.com

Focuses on coverage of new technology and its implementation in the field. Regular issues include equipment comparisons, new product information, safety tips and legal advice.
Frequency: Monthly
Circulation: 27205
Founded in 1926

4316 Rural Builder

F+W Media
38 E. 29th Street
New York, NY 10016

212-447-1400
FAX 212-447-5231
E-Mail: contact_us@fwmedia.com
Home Page: www.fwpublications.com

Scott Tappa, Editor

Focuses on the post frame and metal frame industry.
Cost: $18.94
64 Pages
Circulation: 32000
Founded in 1952
Printed in 4 colors on glossy stock

4317 Scaffold & Access

Scaffold Industry Association

2001 E Campbell Avenue
Suite 101
Phoenix, AZ 85016

602-257-1144
866-687-7115
FAX 602-257-1166
Home Page: www.scaffold.org

Steve Smith, President
Marty Coughlin, President Elect
Daryl Hare, Treasurer
Mike Russell, Secretary

The official publication of the SAIA. Striving to elevate the standard of practice in the scaffold and access industry by educating professionals on safety issues, better business practices and innovative solutions to difficult problems.
Frequency: Monthly

4318 Services Magazine

Building Service Contractors Association Int'l
401 N Michigan Avenue
22nd Floor
Chicago, IL 60611

312-321-5167
800-368-3414
FAX 312-673-6735
E-Mail: info@bscai.org
Home Page: www.bscai.org

Sally Schopmeyer, President
Kevin Rohan, VP

The Building Service Contractors Association International is the trade association serving the facility services industry through education, leadership, and representatiion.
Cost: $30.00
56 Pages
Frequency: Monthly
Circulation: 20,504
ISSN: 0279-0548
Founded in 1981
Printed in 4 colors on glossy stock

4319 Shelter

Association Publications
1168 Vickery Ln
Suite 3
Cordova, TN 38016-1664

901-843-8226

James Powell, Editor

For the national distribution and retail segments of the building products industry.
Cost: $6.00
Frequency: Monthly
Founded in 1962

4320 Southern Building

Southern Building Code Congress International
900 Montclair Rd
Birmingham, AL 35213-1206

205-591-1853
888-422-7233
FAX 205-599-9871
E-Mail: webmaster@iccsafe.org
Home Page: www.iccsafe.org

Gary Nichols, VP Operations

Publishes and maintains a set of model building codes called the Standard Codes. Also provides educational and technical support to the codes enforcement industry.
Cost: $25.00
40 Pages
Circulation: 12000
Founded in 1943

4321 Southwest Contractor

McGraw Hill

4747 E Elliot Rd
Suite 29-339
Phoenix, AZ 85044

602-274-2155
800-393-6343
FAX 602-631-3073
E-Mail: scott_blair@mcgraw-hill.com
Home Page: www.southwest.construction.com

Seth Horowitz, Publisher
Scott Blair, Editor

We cover all aspects of the commercial construction industry in Arizona, Nevada and New Mexico. Our mission is to provide news about the projects, the people and the events that affect the building and highway/heavy segments market.
Cost: $40.00
48 Pages
Frequency: Monthly
Circulation: 7000
Founded in 1938

4322 State of Seniors Housing
American Seniors Housing Association
5225 Wisconsin Ave NW
Suite 502
Washington, DC 20015

202-237-0900
FAX 202-237-1616
Home Page: www.seniorshousing.org

David Schless, President
Doris Maultsby, VP
Frequency: Yearly

4323 Structural Insulated Panel
Structural Insulated Panel Association
PO Box 1699
Gig Harbor, WA 98335

253-858-7472
FAX 253-858-0272
Home Page: www.sips.org

Terry Dieken, President
Al Cobb, VP

A comprehensive, full color book on building with energy efficient SIPs.
Frequency: Quarterly
Circulation: 5000
Founded in 1990

4324 Structures
Business Journal of Portland
851 Sw 6th Ave
Suite 500
Portland, OR 97204-1342

503-274-8733
866-246-0424
FAX 503-219-3450
E-Mail: portland@bizjournals.com
Home Page: www.bizjournals.com/portland

Craig Wessel, Publisher

Special edition of The Business Journal that spotlights top construction projects and highlights the design, architecture and construction
Cost: $89.00
52 Pages
Frequency: Daily
Circulation: 400000
ISSN: 0742-6550
Printed in 4 colors on newsprint stock

4325 Subcontractor
Subcontractors Education Trust
1004 Duke St
Alexandria, VA 22314-3588

703-684-3450
800-221-0415
FAX 703-836-3482

E-Mail: asaoffice@asa-hq.com
Home Page: www.asaonline.com

Colette Nelson, EVP
Franklin Davis, Director Government Relations

News from the construction industry, including up-to-date information on legislative and regulatory affairs, and business news concerning the subcontracting industry.
24 Pages
Frequency: Quarterly
Circulation: 9000
Founded in 1966
Printed in 2 colors

4326 The Construction User
The Association of Union Constructors
1501 Lee Highway
Suite 202
Arlington, VA 22209-1109

703-524-3336
FAX 703-524-3364
E-Mail: dacord@tauc.org
Home Page: www.tauc.org

Stephen R Lindauer, CEO
Kevin J Hilton, Senior VP

TAUC's official magazine, giving readers a fresh and thought-provoking perspective on union construction and the issues contractors, labor and owner-clients face on a daily basis.
Frequency: Monthly
Founded in 1970

4327 Tileletter
National Tile Contractors Association
626 Lakeland E Drive
PO Box 13629
Jackson, MS 39232

601-939-2071
FAX 601-932-6117
E-Mail: bart@tile-assn.com
Home Page: www.tile-assn.com

Bart Bettiga, Executive Director
Lesley Goddin, Editor

A trade publication to the tile industry: contractors, distributors and manufacturers.
Cost: $35.00
100 Pages
Frequency: Monthly
Circulation: 20000
Mailing list available for rent: 20,000 names at $150 per M
Printed in on matte stock

4328 Tiling & Decorative Surfaces
Ashlee Publishing
18 E 41st Street
New York, NY 10017

212-376-7722
FAX 212-376-7723
Home Page: www.ashlee.com

Jordan M Wright, President

Provides information about industry trends and events throughout the world including interviews with manufacturers, distributors and contractors, offering tips on successful merchandising and sales techniques. Issues include product listings and project articles.
Cost: $50.00
Frequency: Monthly
Circulation: 27181
Founded in 1950

4329 Tilt-Up TODAY
Tilt-Up Concrete Association
113 First Street West
PO Box 204
Mount Vernon, IA 52314-0204

319-895-6911
FAX 320-213-5555
E-Mail: info@tilt-up.org

Home Page: www.tilt-up.org
Social Media: *Facebook*

Ed McGuire, President
Glenn Doncaster, President-Elect
Kimberly Corwin, Vice-President
Shane Miller, Treasurer
David Tomasula, Secretary

With continuing advancements in Tilt-Up innovation and architectural achievement, Tilt-Up TODAY highlights the wide variety of outstanding Tilt-Up construction that is taking place all across the world.
Frequency: Monthly
Founded in 2005
Printed in 4 colors on glossy stock

4330 Timber Framing
Timbers Framers Guild
PO Box 295
Alstead, NH 03602

559-834-8453
888-453-0879
FAX 888-453-0879
E-Mail: info@tfguild.org
Home Page: www.tfguild.org

Joel McCarty, Executive Director

Contains in-depth articles on timber framing history, technology, theory, practice, design, and engineering, as well as the work of the guild and its members
Cost: $25.00
Frequency: Quarterly
Founded in 1984

4331 Timber Home Living
Home Buyer Publications
4200 Lafayette Center Drive
Suite 100
Chantilly, VA 20151-1239

703-222-6951
800-850-7279
FAX 703-222-3209
E-Mail: store@homebuyerpubs.com
Home Page: www.loghomeliving.com
Social Media: *Facebook, LinkedIn*

Lara Sloan, Publisher

For individuals wishing to plan, build, decorate, or design a log or timber frame home.
Cost: $3.99
Frequency: Bi-Monthly

4332 Traditional Building
Restore Media
45 Main Street
Suite 411
Brooklyn, NY 11201

718-636-0788
FAX 718-636-0750
E-Mail: theditors@restoremedia.com
Home Page: www.traditional-building.com

Ray Shepherd, Production Manager
Clem Labine, Editor

Lists sources of products for restoration and new construction of traditional buildings.
Cost: $19.95
Frequency: Bi-Monthly
Circulation: 29,000
ISSN: 0898-0284
Founded in 1988
Printed in on glossy stock

4333 Underground Construction
Oildom Publishing Company of Texas
PO Box 941669
Houston, TX 77094-8669

281-558-6930
FAX 281-558-7029

E-Mail: oklinger@oildompublishing.com
Home Page: www.oildompublishing.com

Oliver Klinger, President & Publisher
Robert Carpenter, Editor
Cost: $25.00
Frequency: Monthly
Printed in 4 colors on glossy stock

4334 Underground Focus
Canterbury Communications
411 South Evergreen
Manteno, IL 60950

815-468-7814
FAX 815-468-7644
Home Page: www.underspace.com

Ron Rosencrans, Editor-in-Chief
Paula Miller, Advertising Manager
People read Underground Focus magazine because it documents the importance of their work and helps them get the budgets to do the job. It powerfully dramatizes the need for underground damage prevention and excavation safety.
Cost: $25.00
46 Pages
Circulation: 18,000
ISSN: 1090-400X
Founded in 1986
Printed in 2 colors

4335 Utility Contractor
3925 Chain Bridge Road
Suite 300
Fairfax, VA 22030

703-358-9300
FAX 703-358-9307
E-Mail: bill@nuca.com
Home Page: www.nuca.com

Bill Hillman, CEO
Serves the underground utility construction industry, including contractors, manufacturers, suppliers, engineering firms, municipal/public/private utilities, and others allied to the field.
Frequency: Monthly
Circulation: 20983
ISSN: 1098-0342
Founded in 1967

4336 Walls & Ceilings
Business News Publishing Company
2401 West Big Beaver Road
Suite 700
Troy, MI 48084

248-362-3700
FAX 248-362-5103
E-Mail: mark@wwcca.org
Home Page: www.wconline.com

Lynette Barwin, Production Manager
John Wyatt, Editor
Mark Fowler, Editorial Directort
Information regarding management, building methods, technology, government regulations, consumer trends, and product information for the contractor involved in exterior finishes, waterproofing, insulation, metal framing, drywall, fireproofing, partitions, stucco and plaster.
Cost: $49.00
140 Pages
Frequency: Monthly
Circulation: 30000
Founded in 1938
Printed in 4 colors

4337 Welding Journal
American Welding Society
550 NW 42nd Ave
Miami, FL 33126-5699

305-443-9353
800-443-9353
FAX 305-443-7559

E-Mail: info@aws.org
Home Page: www.aws.org

Annette O'Brien, Senior Editor
Mary Ruth Johnsen, Editor
Serves the metal working field, individuals and organizations engaged in welding, cutting or related processes and equipment for the fabrication, maintenance, design or repair of metal products.
Cost: $80.00
Frequency: Monthly
Circulation: 50,000
ISSN: 0043-2296
Founded in 1919

4338 Western Builder
Western Builder Publishing Company
30 Technology Pkwy S
Suite 100
Norcross, GA 30092-2925

770-209-3730
FAX 770-209-3712
Home Page: www.acppubs.com

Tad Smith, CEO
Greg Sitek, Editorial Director
Regional construction publication serving the heavy, highway and non-residential construction industry in Wisconsin and the Upper Peninsula of Michigan.
Cost: $53.00
Frequency: Monthly
Circulation: 100,000
Founded in 1905

4339 Window & Door
National Glass Association
1945 Old Gallows Rd
Suite 750
Vienna, VA 22182

703-442-4890
866-342-5642
FAX 703-442-0630
Home Page: www.glass.org

Philip James, President/CEO
Nicole Harris, VP
The focus is on technical, new product information, business management and industry issues which focus on manufacturing both new and replacement windows and doors.
Cost: $29.95
Circulation: 20000
Founded in 1948

4340 Window Film Magazine
Key Communications
PO Box 569
Garrisonville, VA 22463

540-720-5584
FAX 540-720-5687
E-Mail: boleary@glass.com
Home Page: www.windowfilmmag.com/

Debra Levy, Publisher
Penny Beverage, Assistant Editor
Katie Hodge, Editor
Provides industry news, supplier and film manufacturer profiles, technical and installation tips, as well as state-by-state legislative breakdowns and consumer marketing issues relevant to the film industry.
Cost: $35.00
Frequency: Monthly
Circulation: 7000

4341 Window World Magazine
Work-4 Projects
4819 St. Charles Boulevard
Pierrefonds, Quebec H9H-3C7

514-620-2200
FAX 514-620-6300

E-Mail: editor@work4.ca
Home Page: www.homebuildercanada.com

Nachmi Artzy, Publisher
Provides new products, announcements, calendar events, and coverage of industry news, technical and maketing information to small and medium window and door manufacturers of North America.
Cost: $30.00
Frequency: Bi-Monthly
Circulation: 9,877

4342 Wrecking and Salvage Journal
Duane Publishing
51 Park St
Dorchester, MA 02122-2643

617-282-4885
FAX 617-282-0320
Home Page: www.rubblemakers.com

Herb Duane, Owner
Toby Duane, Director
Business related information for those engaged in demolition and urban renewal.
Cost: $35.00
Frequency: Monthly
Circulation: 2500
Founded in 1967

Trade Shows

4343 ACSM Annual Spring Conference
American Congress on Surveying and Mapping
6 Montgomery Village Avenue
Suite 403
Gaithersburg, MD 20879

240-632-9716
FAX 240-632-1321
E-Mail: info@acsm.net
Home Page: www.acsm.net

Curtis Sumner, Executive Director
Colleen Campbell, Conference Director
Four hundred booths of products and services offered by companies involved in the aerial mapping industry.
2000 Attendees
Frequency: Annual/April

4344 ACSM/APLS Annual Conference & Technology Exhibition
American Congress on Surveying & Mapping
6 Montgomery Village Avenue
Gaithersburg, MD 20879

240-632-9716
FAX 240-632-1321
E-Mail: curtis.sumner@acsm.net
Home Page: www.acsm.net

Curtis Sumner, Executive Director
Colleen Campbell, Conference Director
The American Congress on Surveying & mapping and the Arizona Professional Land Surveyors organizations have come together to produce this exhibition with four hundred booths of products and services offered by companies involved in the aerial mapping industry.
1500 Attendees
Frequency: Annual

4345 AEMA Annual Meeting
Asphalt Emulsion Manufacturers Association

3 Church Circle
PO Box 250
Annapolis, MD 21401-1933

410-267-0023
FAX 410-267-7546
E-Mail: krissoff@aema.org
Home Page: www.aema.org

Michael Krissoff, Executive Director

Representing close to 150 of the world's leading companies in the pavement preservation and rehabilitation industry. A combined annual meeting with the International Slurry Surfacing Association and the Asphalt Recycling & Reclaiming Association.
400 Attendees
Frequency: Annual/March

4346   AGC Building Contractors Conference

Associated General Contractors of America
2300 Wilson Blvd
Suite 400
Arlington, VA 22201

703-548-3119
FAX 703-837-5405
E-Mail: meetings@agc.org
Home Page: www.agc.org

Carolyn Coker, Executive Director
Joe Jarboe, SVP

One hundred and seventy-five exhibiors of heavy and light construction equipment, trucks, building materials, management services, computer hardware and software. Contractors, subcontractors and trade professionals attend.
4500+ Attendees
Frequency: Annual

4347   AIBD Annual Convention

American Institute of Building Design
7059 Blair Rd NW
Suite 201
Washington, DC 20012

800-366-2423
FAX 866-204-0293
E-Mail: info@aibd.org
Home Page: www.aibd.org
Social Media: *Facebook, Twitter, LinkedIn*

Dan Sater, President
Alan Kent, Internal Vice President
Viki Wooster, External Vice President
Kerry Dick, Secretary/ Treasurer

Exhibition of 25 manufacturers, suppliers, distributors and plan publishers of building products including: roofing, windows, doors, floor covering, fire places, spas/jacuzzis, lumber, intercom systems, alarm systems and appliances; computer-aid design technology, computer hardware/software and plan publishers. Containing 30 booths and 30 exhibits.
1500 Attendees
Frequency: Annual/July
Founded in 1950

4348   AIC Annual Forum

American Institute of Constructors
PO Box 26334
Alexandria, VA 22314

703-683-4999
FAX 703-683-5480
E-Mail: dwright@professionalconstructor.org
Home Page: www.aicnet.org

David Wright, Executive Director
Andy Wasiniak, President
Paul Mattingly, Treasurer

Educational presentations from leading practitioners and educators in the world of construction, panel discussions with major voices in the industry, opportunities to network with other emerging leaders in the construction profession as they fine-tune their leadership skills.
Frequency: Annual/April

4349   AISC Annual Meeting

American Institute of Steel Construction
1 E Wacker Drive
Suite 700
Chicago, IL 60601-2000

312-670-2400
FAX 312-670-5403
E-Mail: ferch@aisc.org
Home Page: www.aisc.org

Roger Ferch, President
Katey Lenihan, Meeting Planner

One hundred booths attended by structural engineers, steel fabricators, educators and construction managers. Those interested in the design fabrication and erection of structural steel for non-residential buildings and bridges.
100 Attendees
Frequency: Annual/September

4350   APWA International Public Works Congress & Expo

American Public Works Association
2345 Grand Boulevard
Suite 700
Kansas City, MO 64108-2625

816-472-6100
800-848-2792
FAX 816-472-1610
E-Mail: ddancy@apwa.net
Home Page: www.apwa.net

Brian Van Norman, Director
David Dancy, Director of Marketing

Offers the benefit of a variety of educational sessions, depth of the exhibit program and endless opportunities for networking. The latest cutting-edge technologies, managerial techniques and regulatory trends designed to keep you focused on the right solutions at the right time.
6500 Attendees
Frequency: Annual/September

4351   APWA North American Snow Conference

American Public Works Association
2345 Grand Boulevard
Suite 700
Kansas City, MO 64108-2625

816-472-6100
800-848-2792
FAX 816-472-1610
E-Mail: ddancy@apwa.net
Home Page: www.apwa.net

Brian Van Norman, Director
David Dancy, Director of Marketing

Education, technical and hands-on for snow and ice management.
1000 Attendees
Frequency: Annual/April
ISSN: 0092-4873

4352   ASPE Estimating Academy & Annual Convention

American Society of Professional Estimators
2525 Perimeter Place Drive
Suite 103
Nashville, TN 37214

615-316-9200
888-378-6283
FAX 615-316-9800
E-Mail: sbo@aspenational.org
Home Page: www.aspenational.com

Karen Hinen, Executive Director
Patsy Smith, Convention Planning

Provides two days of presentations by nationally known speakers in the construction industry. ASPE's Technical Documents Committee prepares a book for each convention attendee

that contains papers submitted by the speakers at these educational sessions.
Frequency: Annual/July

4353   AWI Annual Meeting/Convention

Architectural Woodwork Institute
46179 Westlake Dr
Suite 120
Potomac Falls, VA 20165

571-323-3636
FAX 571-323-2330
E-Mail: info@awinet.org
Home Page: www.awinet.org

Kimberly Kennedy, Meeting/Conventions Director
Robert Stout, President

Seminar, workshop and woodwork products such as casework, fixtures and panelings, equipment and supplies.
Frequency: Annual/October

4354   Adhesive and Sealant Council Fall Convention

Adhesive & Sealant Council
7101 Wisconsin Avenue
Suite 990
Bethesda, MD 20814

301-986-9700
FAX 301-986-9795
E-Mail: bob.willis@ascouncil.org
Home Page: www.ascouncil.org

Bob Willis, Senior Manager Conventions/Meetings
Frequency: October

4355   AeroMat Conference and Exposition

ASM International
9639 Kinsman Road
Materials Park, OH 44073-0002

440-338-5151
800-336-5152
FAX 440-338-4634
E-Mail: natalie.nemec@asminternational.org
Home Page: www.asminternational.org

Stanley Theobald, Managing Director
Kelly Thomas, Exposition Account Manager
Natalie Nemec, Event Programming Manager

Conference for Aerospace Meterials Engineers, Structural Engineers and Designers. The annual event focuses on affordable structures and low-cost manufacturing, titanium alloy technology, advanced intermetallics and refractory metal alloys, materials and processes for space applications, aging systems, high strength steel, NDT evaluation, light alloy technology, welding and joining, and engineering technology.
150 exhibitors.
1500 Attendees
Frequency: Annual/June
Founded in 1984

4356   American Institute of Building Design Annual Convention

American Institute of Building Design
7059 Blair Road NW
Suite 201
Washington, DC 20012

202-249-1407
800-366-2423
FAX 202-249-2473
E-Mail: info@aibd.org
Home Page: www.aibd.org

Dan Sater, President

A four day convention and trade show for residential design professionals.
Frequency: Annual/July

4357   Annual Conference on Deep Foundations

Deep Foundations Institute

326 Lafayette Avenue
Hawthorne, NJ 07506

973-423-4030
FAX 973-423-4031
E-Mail: dfihq@dfi.org
Home Page: www.dfi.org

James Morrison, President
Katie Criqui, Event Coordinator

The premier event for industry members from across the globe to gather and share experiences, exchange ideas and learn the current state-of-the-practice from various disciplines such as engineers, contractors, suppliers, manufacturers and academicians.
600 Attendees
Frequency: Annual/October
Founded in 1975

4358 Arrowhead Home and Builders Show

Shamrock Productions
14552 Judicial Rd
Suite 111
Burnsville, MN 55306

952-431-9630
FAX 952-431-9633
E-Mail: info@shamrockprod.com
Home Page: www.shamrockprod.com/dh.htm

Randy Schauer, President/CEO

Home building, remodeling, landscaping and more.
41960 Attendees
Frequency: Annual/April

4359 Associated Builders and Contractors National Convention

Associated Builders and Contractors
4250 N Fairfax Dr
9th Floor
Arlington, VA 22203

703-812-2000
FAX 703-812-8200
E-Mail: meetings@abc.org
Home Page: www.abc.org

Michael Bellaman, President/CEO
Tina Schneider, Meetings/Conventions Director

Exhibits for construction contractors, subcontractors, and associated trades.

4360 Brick Show

Brick Industry Association
1850 Centennial Park Drive
Suite 301
Reston, VA 20191-1525

703-620-0100
FAX 703-620-3928
E-Mail: brickinfo@bia.org
Home Page: www.bia.org

Susan Ludwig, Show Manager

The only national tradeshow and conference for the clay brick industry.
950 Attendees
Frequency: Annual/March

4361 Builders Trade Show

Maryland National Capital Building Industry Assn.
1738 Elton Road
Suite 200
Silver Spring, MD 20903-5730

301-445-5400
FAX 301-445-5499
E-Mail: building@mncbia.org
Home Page: www.mncbia.org

Jean Mathis, Events Director
Diane Swenson, EVP

Annual show and exhibits of construction equipment, supplies and more.

4362 Building Industry Show

Building Industry Assn. of Southern California
17444 Sky Park Circle
Irvine, CA 92614

949-553-9500
FAX 949-769-8942
E-Mail: sfrias@biasc.org
Home Page: www.buildingindustryshow.com

Wes Keusder, President

Annual show of about 400 exhibitors of products and services for the building industry.
8000+ Attendees
Frequency: Annual/November

4363 Business Administration Conference

National Ready Mixed Concrete Association
900 Spring Street
Silver Spring, MD 20910

301-587-1400
888-846-7622
FAX 301-585-4219
E-Mail: info@nrmca.org
Home Page: www.nrmca.org

Robert Garbini, President
Deana Angelastro, Executive Administrator

A 3-day educational program for financial, information technology, and human resources professionals in the construction and construction materials business.
Frequency: Annual/October

4364 CFMA Annual Conference & Exhibition

Construction Financial Management Association
100 Village Blvd
Suite 200
Princeton, NJ 08540

609-452-8000
FAX 609-452-0474
E-Mail: info@cfma.org
Home Page: www.cfma.org

Joseph Burkett, Chairman
Pat Cebelak, Treasurer

The source and resource for construction financial professionals.
6000 Attendees
Frequency: Annual/May

4365 CONEXPO-CON/AGG

Association of Equipment Manufacturers
6737 W Washington St
Suite 2400
Milwaukee, WI 53214-5647

414-272-0943
800-867-6060
FAX 414-272-1170
Home Page: www.conexpoconagg.com

Ken Snover, Expo Managing Director
Jim Eldredge, Exhibits Coordinator

The international gathering place for the worldwide construction, aggregates and ready mixed concrete industries.
124M Attendees
Frequency: March/Every 3 Years
Founded in 2002

4366 Composites & Polycon

American Composites Manufacturers Association
1010 North Glebe Road
Suite 450
Arlington, VA 22201

703-525-0511
FAX 703-525-0743
E-Mail: info@acmanet.org
Home Page: www.acmashow.org

Lori Luchak, President

World's largest trade association serving the composites industry. Provides education and support for composites fabricators in the successful operation of businesses, and offers leading-edge services in regulatory compliance and formulation, education and training, management, and market expansion.
1.5M Attendees
Frequency: Annual/September

4367 Coverings: The Ultimate Tile & Stone Experience

NTP, Coverings Show Management
313 S Patrick Street
Alexandria, VA 22314

703-683-8500
800-687-7469
FAX 703-836-4486
E-Mail: coverings@ntpshow.com
Home Page: www.coverings.com

Karin Fendrich, COO

Showcasing the newest in tile and natural stone, the event provides opportunities for: continuing education, live demonstrations, networking and new business. 1200 international exhibitors, attracting 33,000+ distributors, retailers, fabricators, contractors, and design professionals.
33M Attendees
Frequency: Annual
Mailing list available for rent

4368 Delmarva Ag & Construction Show

Lee Publications
6113 State Highway 5
Palatine Bridge, NY 13428

518-732-2269
800-218-5586
FAX 518-673-3237
E-Mail: info@leepub.com
Home Page: www.leepub.com

Ken Maring, Trade Show Manager

Hundreds of agriculture and construction exhibitors with products and equipment. Skid steer rodeo for fun. Held at the Wicomico Youth and Civic Center in Maryland.
Frequency: Annual/December

4369 Design & Construction Exposition

Construction Association of Michigan
43636 Woodward
PO Box 3204
Bloomfield Hills, MI 48302

248-972-1000
FAX 248-972-1001
E-Mail: marketing@cam-online.com
Home Page: www.cam-online.com

Ron Riegel, Exposition Manager
Jeanny Snowden, Marketing Coordinator

Annual show of 250 manufacturers, suppliers and distributors of construction industry equipment, supplies and services.
11M Attendees
Frequency: Annual/February
Founded in 1985

4370 EdCon & Expo

Associated Builders and Contractors
4250 Fairfax Drive
9th Floor
Arlington, VA 22203-1665

703-812-2000
FAX 703-812-8201
E-Mail: meetings@abc.org
Home Page: www.abc.org

Michael Bellaman, CEO
Todd Mann, COO
Jason Daisey, CFO
1700 Attendees
Frequency: Annual/April

4371 Elevator Escalator Safety Awareness Annual Meeting
Elevator World
356 Morgan Avenue
Mobile, AL 36606

251-479-4514
800-730-5093
FAX 251-479-7043
E-Mail: admin@elevator-world.com
Home Page: www.elevator-world.com

Linda Williams, Director of Administration
Patricia Cartee, Director of Operations

Meetings, discussions and exhibits on the safety of elevators.
Frequency: Annual/February

4372 Environmental Management Conference and Exposition
Environmental Information Association
6935 Wisconsin Avenue
Suite 306
Chevy Chase, MD 20815-6112

301-961-4999
888-343-4342
FAX 301-961-3094
E-Mail: info@eia-usa.org
Home Page: www.eia-usa.org

Kelly Rutt, Developement Manager
Brent Kynoch, Managing Director

Annual conference of 85-100 exhibitors of equipment, supplies and services for quantifying, managing or remediating environmental hazards in buildings and facilities.
1200 Attendees

4373 Equipment Distributors Association Annual Meeting
Associated Equipment Distributors
600 Hunter Dr
Suite 220
Oak Brook, IL 60523-8807

630-574-0650
FAX 630-574-0132
E-Mail: info@aednet.org
Home Page: www.aednet.org

Toby Mack, President/CEO
Janet Dixon, Convention & Meetings Director

A place where distributor, manufacturer and supplier executives meet, build relationships, do business, and learn new skills.
3.5M Attendees
Frequency: Annual/January

4374 FENCETECH Convention & Expo
American Fence Association
800 Roosevelt Rd
Building C-312
Glen Ellyn, IL 60137-5899

630-942-6598
FAX 630-790-3095
E-Mail: afa@mindspring.com
Home Page:
www.americanfenceassociation.com

Rod Wilson, President
Mike Robinson, Vice President

Four hundred and eighty booths for the fence industry. Educational opportunities that will inform you of the most up-to-date technology.
5883 Attendees
Frequency: Annual/January/February

4375 GlassBuild America: Glass, Window & Door Expo
National Glass Association
1945 Old Gallows Rd
Suite 750
Vienna, VA 22182

703-424-4890
866-342-5642

FAX 703-442-0630
Home Page: www.glass.org

Philip James, President
Nicole Harris, VP

Provides one central showcase for the class processing equipment, window and door manufacturing equipment, and the latest technology for all types of glass and fenestration products used in residential and commercial construction and related applications.
Frequency: Annual/October

4376 Great Lakes Building Products Exposition
Michigan Lumber & Building Materials Association
5815 Executive Drive
Suite B
Lansing, MI 48911

517-394-5225
FAX 517-394-5228
E-Mail: assn@mlbma.org
Home Page: www.mlbma.org

Jodi Barber, VP
Rick Seely, President

Offering new products and presentations on industry topics for the building material dealer and builders/contractors.
Frequency: Annual/January

4377 Hard Hat Show
Lee Publications
6113 State Highway 5
Palatine Bridge, NY 13428-0121

518-732-2269
800-218-5586
FAX 518-673-3237
E-Mail: kmaring@leepub.com
Home Page: www.leepub.com

Ken Maring, Trade Show Manager
Larry Price, Sales Manager
Beth Snyder, Trade Show Manager

The premier showcase for heavy construction in the Northeast sharing information about the latest innovations in the construction industry!
3.5M Attendees
Frequency: Annual/March
Founded in 1989

4378 Home Improvement & Remodeling Exposition
Dmg World Media
325 Essjay Road
Suite 100
Williamsville, NY 14221

716-631-2266
800-274-6948
FAX 716-631-2425
Home Page: www.dmgevents.com

Mark Carr, President

Featuring a spectacular garden, the latest in home technology, thousands of products, celebrity appearances and over 350 exhibits where consumers can find what they need to create their own unique spaces and put their special style to work.
60000 Attendees
Frequency: Annual/March

4379 IDA International Garage Door Expo
International Door Association
PO Box 246
West Milton, OH 45383-0246

937-988-8042
800-355-4432
FAX 937-698-6153
E-Mail: info@longmgt.com
Home Page: www.doors.org

Chris Long, Managing Director
Steve Smith, Accounting Manager

Workshops and Exhibits featuring the latest product innovations as well as the traditional products and services for which the industry is known for.
Frequency: Annual/April

4380 INTEX Expo System Construction Association
Association of the Wall and Ceiling Industry
513 W Broad Street
Suite 210
Falls Church, VA 22046

703-538-1600
FAX 703-534-8307
E-Mail: info@awci.org
Home Page: www.awci.org

Tim Wies, President
Jeffrey Burley, VP

The premier interior/exterior wall and ceiling commercial construction trade show. This annual show host exhibitors such as, wall and ceiling contractors, general contractors, architects, specifiers, suppliers, and distributors.
3000 Attendees
Frequency: Annual/April

4381 Independent Electrical Contractors National Convention
Independent Electrical Contractors
4401 Ford Avenue
Suite 1100
Alexandria, VA 22302

703-549-7351
FAX 703-549-7448
E-Mail: info@ieci.org
Home Page: www.ieci.org

Tim Welsh, Executive VP
Trayvia Watson, Meetings Manager

One hundred booths of electrical equipment, products and services.
1000 Attendees
Frequency: Annual/October

4382 International Builders Show
National Association of Home Builders
1201 15th Street NW
Washington, DC 20005

202-266-8200
800-368-5242
FAX 202-266-8400
E-Mail: info@nahb.com
Home Page: www.nahb.org

Gerald Howard, CEO

More than 1,600 suppliers, representing the most comprehensive showcase of home building products and services, are ready to demonstrate how their offerings can help you to corner the market.
90000 Attendees
Frequency: Annual/January

4383 International Conference Building Official
International Code Council
5360 Workman Mill Road
Whittier, CA 90601-2298

888-422-7233
FAX 562-908-5524
Home Page: www.iccsafe.org

Jay Peters, Executive Director
Mark Johnson, SVP
1,2M Attendees
Frequency: Annual/September

4384 International Construction and Utility Equipment Exposition
Association of Equipment Manufacturers

6737 W Washington Street
Suite 2400
Milwaukee, WI 53214-5647

414-272-0943
FAX 414-272-1170
E-Mail: aem@aem.org
Home Page: www.aem.org

Sara Mooney Truesdale, Show Director
Paul Flemming, Exhibits Sales Manager

The only exposition for outdoor demonstrations of utility and construction equipment. Experience the newest technologies for their electric, phone, cable, water, sewer, gas, general construction, landscape, and government jobs.
15000 Attendees
Frequency: Annual/September

4385 International Thermal Spray Conference & Exposition
ASM International
9639 Kinsman Road
Materials Park, OH 44073

440-338-5151
800-336-5152
FAX 440-338-4634
E-Mail: natalie.nemec@asminternational.org
Home Page: www.asminternational.org

Charles Hayes, Executive Director
Pamela Kleinman, Senior Event Manager

Global annual event attracting professional interested in thermal spray technology focusing on advances in HVOF, plasma and detonation gun, flame spray and wire arc spray processes, performance of coatings, and future trends. 150 exhibitors.
1000 Attendees
Frequency: Annual/May

4386 Lumber and Building Material Expo
Northeastern Retail Lumber Association
585 N Greenbush Road
Rensselaer, NY 12144

518-286-1010
800-292-6752
FAX 518-286-1755
E-Mail: rferris@nrla.org
Home Page: www.nrla.org

Donna Berger, Events Coordinator
Rita Ferris, President

Largest regional trade show in the lumber and building material industry. Retail lumber dealers in the Northeast are afforded the opportunity to interact with manufacturers, wholesalers, and distributors of lumber, building materials, and related technologies.
7000 Attendees
Frequency: Annual/February

4387 MBI World of Modular Conference
Modular Building Institute
944 Glenwood Station Ln
Suite 204
Charlottesville, VA 22901-1480

434-296-3288
888-811-3288
FAX 434-296-3361
E-Mail: info@modular.org
Home Page: www.modular.org

Steven Williams, Operations Director
Tom Hardiman, Executive Director

High-profile speakers, educational sessions, exhibits, discussion on trends in commercial modular, entertainment and prizes
500 Attendees
Frequency: Annual

4388 MCAA Annual Convention & Masonry Showcase
Mason Contractors Association of America

1481 Merchant Drive
Algonquin, IL 60102

224-678-9709
800-536-2225
FAX 224-678-9714
Home Page: www.masoncontractors.org

Tim O'Toole, Marketing Director
Jeff Buczkiewicz, Executive Director

Featuring in-depth education seminars, high-profile international skills competitions and exhibit display. Attendees includes masonry contracting firms representing all facets of masonry installation, including the largest commercial, residential, institutional, landscape, paving, retaining, glass block, and stone contractors.
Frequency: Annual/March

4389 MIACON Construction, Mining & Waste Management Show
Finocchiaro Enterprises
2921 Coral Way
Miami, FL 33145

305-441-2865
FAX 305-529-9217
Home Page: www.miacon.com

Michael Finocchiaro, President
Jose Garcia, VP
Justine Finocchiaro, Chief Operations

Annual show of 650 manufacturers, suppliers, distributors and exporters of equipment, machinery, supplies and services for the construction, mining and waste managment industries. There will be 600 booths.
10M Attendees
Frequency: Annual/October
Founded in 1994

4390 Metalcon International
PSMJ Resources
10 Midland Avenue
Newton, MA 02458-1021

617-965-0055
FAX 617-928-1670
E-Mail: metalcon@psmj.com
Home Page: www.metalcon.com

Claire Kilcoyne, Show Manager
Suzanne Maher, Conference Director
Paula Parker, Exhibit Sales

Architects, builders, craftspeople, designers, framers, contractors, and other industry leaders will share their expertise, hone their skills, and make connections that will help their businesses reach new heights.
8000 Attendees
Frequency: Annual/October

4391 NCSBCS/AMCBO Annual Conference
Int'l Conference of State Bldg Codes & Standards
505 Huntmar Park Drive
Suite 210
Herndon, VA 20170

703-437-0100
FAX 703-481-3596
E-Mail: dbecker@ncsbcs.org
Home Page: www.ncsbcs.org

Kevin Egilmez, Project Manager
Carolyn Fitch, Membership Services

Providing a wide variety of technical and administrative information of immediate value to the nation's construction and code enforcement community, trade associations, information technology firms and professional societies, academicians, students, and elected officials regarding building codes administration and public safety.
Frequency: Annual/Sept-Oct

4392 NECA Convention
National Electrical Contractors Association
3 Bethesda Metro Center
Suite 1100
Bethesda, MD 20814

301-657-3110
FAX 301-215-4500
Home Page: www.necanet.org

Russell Alessi, President
Katie Nolan, Convention Manager

The event brings the largest manufacturers, utilities, contractors, engineers, consultants, plant engineers, and distributors from all over North America and 31 foreign countries.
8000 Attendees
Frequency: Annual/September

4393 NRCMA Conference
National Railroad Construction & Maintenance Assoc
500 New Jersey Avenue NW
Suite 400
Washington, DC 20001

202-715-2919
FAX 202-318-0867
E-Mail: info@nrcma.org
Home Page: www.nrcma.org

Chuck Baker, President
Matt Ginsberg, Director of Operations

For railroad personnel, managers and purchasers in design, construction and maintenance. Information on breakthrough innovations in rail construction, railroad safety, new rail projects of national significance and more. 60-80 exhibitors.
750 Attendees
Frequency: Annual/January

4394 NSSGA Dredging Seminar & Expo
National Stone, Sand & Gravel Association
1605 King Street
Alexandria, VA 22314

703-525-8788
800-342-1415
FAX 703-525-7782
E-Mail: jwilson@nssga.org
Home Page: www.nssga.org

Jennifer Wilson, President/CEO
Cynthia McDowell, Conventions Director

Created to specifically meet the needs of aggregate producers who use dredges or have an interest in using dredges in the future. This seminar uses educational seminars, plant tours and manufacturer's exhibits to provide information useful to both novice and experienced dredgers.
Frequency: Annual/June

4395 National Congress & Expo for Manufactured and Modular Housing
Manufactured Housing Institute
2111 Wilson Boulevard
Suite 100
Arlington, VA 22201-3040

703-558-0400
FAX 703-558-0401
E-Mail: info@mfghome.org
Home Page: www.manufacturedhousing.org

Thayer Long, President/CEO
Lisa Quinn Brechtel, VP/Executive Director

The opporunity to network with over 1500 industry captains who make a positive difference in the modular and manufactured housing industries.
Frequency: Annual/April

4396 National Demolition Association Conference and Trade Show
National Demolition Association

16 North Franklin Street
Suite 203
Doylestown, PA 18901

215-348-4949
800-541-2412
FAX 215-348-8422
E-Mail: info@demolitionassociation.com
Home Page: www.demolitionassociation.com

Don Rachel, President
Jeff Kroeker, VP
1700 Attendees
Frequency: Annual

4397 National Hardware Show
Reed Exhibitions
383 Main Avenue
Norwalk, CT 06851

203-404-4800
888-425-9377
FAX 203-840-9622
E-Mail: inquiry@hardware.reedexpo.com
Home Page: www.nationalhardwareshow.com

Richard Russo, Event Director
Juliana Van Der Beek, Sales Manager
The only housing after-market show, bringing together manufacturers and resellers of all products used to remodel, repair, maintain and decorate the home and its surroundings.
3M Attendees
Frequency: Annual/May

4398 New England Home Show
Dmg World Media
45 Braintree Hill Office Park
Suite 302
Braintree, MA 02184

781-849-0990
800-469-0990
FAX 781-849-7544
E-Mail: lauriemyette@us.dmgworldmedia.com
Home Page: www.newenglandhomeshow.com

Laurie Myette, Show Manager
Amy Kimball, Administrative Assistant

Annual show of 379 exhibitors of homebuilding and improvement equipment, supplies and services, including bathroom and kitchen supplies, building materials, appliances, doors and windows, swimming pools, hot tubs and spas.
100M Attendees
Frequency: Annual/February

4399 North American Quarry Recycling Show
Lee Publications
6113 State Highway 5
PO Box 121
Palatine Bridge, NY 13428-0121

518-732-2269
800-218-5586
FAX 518-673-3245
Home Page: www.leepub.com

Ken Maring, Trade Show Manager
Matt Stanley, Sales Manager

The North American Quarry Show is the largest trade show in North America for the aggregates industry.
Frequency: Annual/October

4400 North American Steel Construction Conference
American Institute of Steel Construction
One East Wacker Drive
Suite 700
Chicago, IL 60601

312-670-2400
FAX 312-670-5403
Home Page: www.aisc.org

David Ratterman, General Counsel
Roger Ferch, President

A premier education event aimed at providing structural engineers, steel fabricators, erectors, and detailers with practical information and the latest design and construction techniques.
2300 Attendees
Frequency: Annual/April

4401 Northwestern Building Products Expo
Northwestern Lumber Association
5905 Golden Valley Road
Suite 110
Minneapolis, MN 55422-4528

763-544-6822
888-644-6822
FAX 763-595-4060
Home Page: www.nlassn.org

Jodie Fleck, Director of Conventions
Paula Siewert, President
Building materials and their contractors attend this trade show and conference for continuing educataion and cammeraderie
1200 Attendees
Frequency: Annual

4402 PACE: Paint and Coatings Expo
Painting and Decorating Contractors of America
1801 Park 270 Drive
Suite 220
St Louis, MO 63146-4020

314-514-7322
800-332-7322
FAX 314-514-9417
Home Page: www.pdca.org

Richard Greene, CEO
Libby Loomis, Event Coordinator

This mega show is the culmination of months of research and planning by members of the two professional associations (PDCA & SSPC), who joined forces in search of a 'one-stop shop' solution for convening the maximum number of industry professionals in the most cost-effective and productive way.
Frequency: Annual/January

4403 PowerGen
Scaffold Industry Association
2001 E Campbell Avenue
Suite 101
Phoenix, AZ 85016

602-257-1144
866-687-7115
FAX 602-257-1166
Home Page: www.scaffold.org

Steve Smith, President
Marty Coughlin, President Elect
Daryl Hare, Treasurer
Mike Russell, Secretary

Companies from all sectors of the industry exhibit and attendees come together for a look at the industry with key emphasis on new solutions and innovations for the future.
Frequency: Annual/July

4404 RCMA Meeting
Roof Coatings Manufacturers Association
750 National Press Building
529 14th Street NW
Washington, DC 20045

202-207-0919
FAX 202-223-9741
E-Mail: questions@roofcoatings.org
Home Page: www.roofcoatings.org

Steve Heinje, Director

An educational program focusing on Technical, Marketing, and regulatory updates regarding roof coatings.
100 Attendees
Frequency: Annual

4405 SIA Annual Convention & Exposition
Scaffold Industry Association
2001 E Campbell Avenue
Suite 101
Phoenix, AZ 85016

602-257-1144
866-687-7115
FAX 602-257-1166
Home Page: www.scaffold.org

Steve Smith, President
Marty Coughlin, President Elect
Daryl Hare, Treasurer
Mike Russell, Secretary

Exhibits and classes on scaffold safety and education.
Frequency: Annual/July

4406 SIPA Annual Meeting & Conference
Structural Insulated Panel Association
PO Box 1699
Gig Harbor, WA 98335

253-858-7472
FAX 253-858-0272
Home Page: www.sips.org
Social Media: *Facebook, Twitter*

Frank Baker, President

A valuable networking event for both longtime veterans and newcomers to the SIP industry. If you're a builder, architect, developer or entrepreneur interested in employing SIPs in your next commercial or residential project, you'll be interested in this conference
Frequency: Annual/April

4407 STAFDA Annual Convention & Trade Show
Specialty Tools and Fasteners Distributors Assn.
500 Elm Grove Rd.
Suite 210
Elm Grove, WI 53122

262-784-4774
800-352-2981
FAX 262-784-5059
E-Mail: info@stafda.org
Home Page: www.stafda.org
Social Media: *Facebook, LinkedIn*

Mike Kangas, President
Kramer Darragh, Vice President

Members distribute or manufacture power equipment, anchors, fastening systems, drilling equipment and other related industrial supplies.
4000 Attendees
Frequency: Annual/November

4408 Spray Foam Conference & EXPO
Spray Polyurethane Foam Alliance
4400 Fair Lakes Court
Suite 105
Fairfax, VA 22033

800-523-6154
FAX 703-222-5816
Home Page: www.sprayfoam.org

Sig Hall, President
Bob Duke, Vice President
Peter Davis, Secretary/ Treasurer

Training and accreditation programs, general and breakout sessions, awards, networking receptions, and the exhibit hall
Frequency: Yearly
Founded in 1987

4409 TAUC Annual Meeting
The Association of Union Constructors
1501 Lee Highway
Suite 202
Arlington, VA 22209-1109

703-524-3336
FAX 703-524-3364

E-Mail: dacord@tauc.org
Home Page: www.tauc.org

Stephen R Lindauer, CEO
Kevin J Hilton, Senior VP

The prime meeting of the year, bringing together our membership from around the country in a relaxed and informal setting. The meeting will provide an opportunity to network and meet our union contractors.
Frequency: Annual/May
Founded in 1970

4410 TCA Annual Convention
Tilt-Up Concrete Association
113 First Street West
PO Box 204
Mount Vernon, IA 52314-0204

319-895-6911
FAX 320-213-5555
E-Mail: info@tilt-up.org
Home Page: www.tilt-up.org
Social Media: *Facebook*

Ed McGuire, President
Glenn Doncaster, President-Elect
Kimberly Corwin, Vice-President
Shane Miller, Treasurer
David Tomasula, Secretary

Tilt-up Concrete Association/TCA's annual convention that features intensive training and education seminars for contractors and engineers, as well as a trade show, building tour and focused sessions on marketing and architecturald design.
Frequency: Annual/October
Founded in 2005

4411 Technology for Construction
Hanley-Wood
8600 Freeport Parkway
Suite 200
Irving, TX 75063

972-366-6300
866-962-7469
FAX 972-536-6402
E-Mail: TCindric@hanleywood.com
Home Page:
www.technologyforconstruction.com

Tom Cindric, Show Director
Jackie James, Show Manager
Todd Gilmore, Sales Manager

International conference and tradeshow focused on the technology needs and interests of architects and interior designers; civil engineers, contractors, builders, and construction managers, facility managers, building engineers, owners, GIS, surveyors and mapping professionals for private, commercial, institutional and government sectors.
33M Attendees
Frequency: Annual/January

4412 Utility Construction Expo
National Utility Contractors Association
3925 Chain Bridge Road
Suite 300
Fairfax, VA 22030

703-358-9300
FAX 703-358-9307
E-Mail: bill@nuca.com
Home Page: www.nuca.com

Bill Hillman, CEO
Bonnie Williams, VP

The latest technologies, products, and services being offered by the leading manufacturers and suppliers in the underground utility construction industry. Next trade show is scheduled to take place in Las Vegas, Nevada.
Frequency: Annual/February

4413 WBMA Annual Convention
Western Building Material Association

909 Lakeridge Drive SW
PO Box 1699
Olympia, WA 98507

360-943-3054
888-551-9262
FAX 360-943-1219
E-Mail: wbma@wbma.org
Home Page: www.wbma.org

One hundred and fourty booths of products stocked and sold by building material dealers.
1.6M Attendees
Frequency: Annual/November

4414 World Adhesive Conference & Expo
Adhesive & Sealant Council
7101 Wisconsin Avenue
Suite 990
Bethesda, MD 20814

301-986-9700
FAX 301-986-9795
E-Mail: bob.willis@ascouncil.org
Home Page: www.ascouncil.org

Bob Willis, Senior Manager
Conventions/Meetings
Frequency: April

4415 World of Asphalt Show & Conference
National Asphalt Pavement Association
5100 Forbes Boulevard
Suite 200
Lanham, MD 20706

301-731-4748
888-468-6499
FAX 301-731-4621
E-Mail: mcervarich@hotmix.org
Home Page: www.hotmix.org

Mike Acott, President
Margaret Cervarich, VP Marketing/Public Affairs

The leading trade show for the asphalt pavement industry, bringing together the Asphalt Pavement Conference and the People, Plants and Paving training program.
6000 Attendees

Directories & Databases

4416 ANSI/SPRI Standard Field Test Procedure
Single Ply Roofing Institute
411 Waverley Oaks Road
Suite 331B
Waltham, MA 02542

781-647-7026
FAX 781-647-7222
E-Mail: info@spri.org
Home Page: www.spri.org

Linda King, Managing Director

Standard Field Test Procedure for determining the withdrawal resistance of roofing fasteners.
Cost: $5.00
Frequency: Free to members

4417 ANSI/SPRI Wind Design Standard
Single Ply Roofing Institute
411 Waverley Oaks Road
Suite 331B
Waltham, MA 02452

781-647-7026
FAX 781-647-7222
E-Mail: info@spri.org
Home Page: www.spri.org

Linda King, Managing Director

Written for those who design, specify and install smooth-surfaced, low-slope flexible mem-

brane roof systems.
Cost: $5.00
23 Pages

4418 Affirmative Action Compliance Manual for Federal Contractors
Bureau of National Affairs
1801 S Bell St
Arlington, VA 22202-4501

703-341-3000
800-372-1033
FAX 800-253-0332
E-Mail: customercare@bna.com
Home Page: www.bnabooks.com

Paul N Wojcik, CEO
Gregory C McCaffery, President

Employers and attorneys can more easily monitor and measure affirmative action requirements, implement policies, and quickly access other compliance information with this complete resource guide.
Cost: $611.00
Frequency: Monthly

4419 Automated Builder: Top Component Producers Survey Issue
Automated Builder
2401 Grapevine Dr
Oxnard, CA 93036

805-351-5931
FAX 805-351-5755
E-Mail: info@automatedbuilder.com
Home Page: www.automatedbuilder.com

Don Carlson, Publisher

Over 100 leading industrialized building producers are profiled on the basis of sales. Top HUD-Code home producers, TOP pakelizers, TOP commercial modular builders. Features articles on technology, methods and machinery, sales and marketing for in-plant building.
Cost: $6.00
48 Pages
Frequency: Monthly
Circulation: 25000
ISSN: 0899-5540
Founded in 1964

4420 Blue Book of Building and Construction
Contractors Register
PO Box 500
Jefferson Valley, NY 10535

914-450-0200
800-431-2584
FAX 914-243-0287
E-Mail: info@thebluebook.com
Home Page: www.thebluebook.com
Social Media: *YouTube*

Jeff Fandl, Editor

Regional construction directories in most major markets throughout the US. Online, thebluebook.com provides easy access to continually updated information for each of our regional editions.
4500 Pages
Frequency: Annual
Circulation: 615,000
Founded in 1913

4421 Building & Construction Trades Department
815 16th St NW
Suite 209
Washington, DC 20006-4101

202-347-1461
FAX 202-628-0724
Home Page: www.bctd.org
Social Media: *Facebook*

Mark Ayers, President
Joseph Maloney, Secretary/Treasurer

Coordinates activity and provides resources to 15 affiliated trades unions in the construction industry.
386 Pages
Founded in 1908

4422 Building Materials Directory
Underwriters Laboratories
333 Pfingsten Rd
Northbrook, IL 60062-2096

847-412-0136
877-854-3577
FAX 847-272-8129
E-Mail: cec@us.ul.com
Home Page: www.ul.com

Keith E Williams, CEO
John Drengenberg, Manager Consumer Affairs

Offers information on companies that have qualified to use the UL listing mark or classification marking on products that have been found to be in compliance with UL requirements.
Cost: $30.00
512 Pages
Frequency: Annual/February

4423 Cedar Shake and Shingle Bureau Membership Directory/Buyer's Guide
Cedar Shake & Shingle Bureau
PO Box 1178
Sumas, WA 98295-1178

604-820-7700
FAX 604-820-0266
Home Page: www.cedarbureau.org

Jim Tuffin, Chairman
Len Taylor Jr., Vice-Chairman
Rav Dhaliwal, Secretary/Treasurer

About 102 member manufacturing mills in the Pacific Northwest and British Columbia, Canada; approximately 163 affiliated roofing applicators, builders, architects, remodelers and suppliers of related products and services.
Cost: $17.00
Frequency: SemiAnnual
Circulation: 450

4424 Cement Americas
Penton Media Inc
249 W 17th St
New York, NY 10011-5390

212-204-4200
FAX 212-206-3622
E-Mail: steven.prokopy@penton.com
Home Page: www.penton.com

Sharon Rowlands, CEO

Offers 100 cement manufacturing companies in the United States, Canada, Mexico, Central and South America.
Cost: $78.00
225 Pages
Frequency: Annual
Circulation: 300
Mailing list available for rent
Printed in on glossy stock

4425 Construction Equipment: Construction Giants Issue
Reed Business Information
2000 Clearwater Dr
Oak Brook, IL 60523-8809

630-574-0825
FAX 630-288-8781
Home Page: www.reedbusiness.com

Mark Kelsey, CEO
Stuart Whayman, CFO
Dan Olley, CIO

Listing of approximately 250 of the largest equipment-owning heavy construction contractors, engaged in earthmoving, paving, building

and materials production owning over $10 million in equipment.
Frequency: Monthly
Circulation: 77010
Founded in 1949

4426 Construction Planning & Scheduling Manual
National Insulation Association
Ste 330
12100 Sunset Hills Rd
Reston, VA 20190-3295

703-683-6422
FAX 703-549-4838
E-Mail: niainfo@insulation.org
Home Page: www.insulation.org

Melissa Jackson, Director of Publications
Beth Michaels, Vice President
Kristin DiDomenico, Vice President

This manual from the Associated General Contractors (AGC) was written to provide guidance to the contractor in the effective use of modern project management techniques. Its primary objective is to provide an educational tool that can be used within the construction industry to teach the concepts of construction planning and scheduling. The content of the book is written for all project personnel, from the working foreman to the project executive.
Cost: $155.00

4427 Construction Specifier: Member Directory Issue
Construction Specifications Institute
990 Canal Center Plaza
Suite 300
Alexandria, VA 22314

703-684-0300
800-689-2900
FAX 703-684-8436
E-Mail: csi@csinet.org
Home Page: www.csinet.org

Eugene A Valentine, President
W Richard Cooper, VP

Roster of construction specifiers certified by the institute and approximately 17,200 members.
Cost: $203.00
Frequency: Annual/January
Circulation: 19500

4428 Constructor: AGC Directory of Membership and Services Issue
Associated General Contractors of America
333 John Carlyle Street
Sutie 200
Alexandria, VA 22314

703-548-3118
FAX 703-548-3119
E-Mail: constructinfo@riagc.org
Home Page: www.agc.org

Donald Scott, Production Manager
Michael Kennedy, General Counsel
Norman Walton, Treasurer

List of more than 8,500 member firms and 24,000 national associate member firms engaged in building, highway, heavy, industrial, municipal utilities and railroad construction.
Frequency: Annual/July
Circulation: 34,000
ISSN: 0162-6191

4429 Directory of Architectural and Construction Information Resources
Grey House Publishing
4919 Route 22
PO Box 56
Amenia, NY 12501

518-789-8700
800-562-2139
FAX 845-373-6390

E-Mail: books@greyhouse.com
Home Page: www.greyhouse.com
Social Media: *Facebook, Twitter*

Richard Gottlieb, President
Leslie Mackenzie, Publisher

The leading desktop reference and preliminary research guide, featuring more than 10,000 building product manufacturers and their products.
194 Pages
Frequency: Annual
ISBN: 1-519250-00-0

4430 Directory of Building Codes & Regulations
National Conference of States on Building Codes
505 Huntmar Park Dr
Herndon, VA 20170-5103

703-437-0100
800-362-2633
FAX 703-481-3596

Robert Wible, Executive Director
Carolyn Fitch, Membership Services

This directory is a comprehensive guide to the building codes and regulations adopted and enforced in each of the 50 states, Puerto Rico, the District of Columbia, and 53 major U. S. cities in 14 different code areas - building, mechanical, plumbing, electrical, energy conservation, gas, fire prevention, life safety, accessibility, one & two family, modular, ventilation/indoor air quality, manufactured home installation, and elevator.
Cost: $78.00
Frequency: Annual

4431 Dodge Construction Analysis System
McGraw-Hill
1221 Avenue of the Americas
New York, NY 10020-1095

212-512-2000
800-393-6343
FAX 212-512-3840
E-Mail: webmaster@mcgraw-hill.com
Home Page: www.mcgraw-hill.com

Harold W McGraw III, CEO
Joseph A Scott, National Marketing Director

This database lists over 4 million time series for construction projects involving more than 200 structural types.

4432 Dodge DataLine
McGraw-Hill
1221 Avenue of the Americas
New York, NY 10020-1095

212-512-2000
800-393-6343
FAX 212-512-3840
E-Mail: webmaster@mcgraw-hill.com
Home Page: www.mcgraw-hill.com

Harold W McGraw III, CEO
Joseph A Scott, National Marketing Director

Dodge DataLine offers the most advanced searching of project leads in the industry. You can search the largest U.S. database of 500,000+ active construction projects.
Frequency: Daily

4433 ENR Top 100 Construction Managers
Engineering News Record/McGraw Publishing
2 Penn Plaza
9th Floor
New York, NY 10121-2298

212-512-2000
888-877-8208
FAX 212-512-4039

351

E-Mail: support@construction.com
Home Page: www.construction.com

Gary Graizzaro, Plant Manager
John J Kosowatz, Managing Editor
William G. Krizan, Assistant Managing Editor

List of the top 100 leading construction and program management firms with the largest dollar volume in new construction management contracts on a for-fee only basis and an at-risk basis in the previous year.
Cost: $250.00
Frequency: Annual/June
Circulation: 90000

4434 ENR Top 400 Contractors Sourcebook
Engineering News Record/McGraw Publishing
2 Penn Plaza
9th Floor
New York, NY 10121-2298

212-512-2000
888-877-8208
FAX 212-512-4039
E-Mail: support@construction.com
Home Page: www.construction.com

Gary Graizzaro, Plant Manager
Joann Gonchar, Associate Editor
William G. Krizan, Assistant Managing Editor
Debra K. Rubin, Managing Senior Editor

Market analysis rankings of the largest U.S.-based general contractors in eight major industry sectors: general building, transportation, manufacturing, industrial process, petroleum, power, environmental and telecommunications.
Cost: $85.00
112 Pages

4435 ENR Top 600 Specialty Contractors Issue
Engineering News Record/McGraw Hill
2 Penn Plaza
9th Floor
New York, NY 10121-2298

212-512-2000
FAX 212-512-4039
E-Mail: support@construction.com
Home Page: www.construction.com

Gary Graizzaro, Plant Manager
John J Kosowatz, Managing Editor

Lists of the 600 largest US specialty subcontractors with sub-lists of top firms in mechanical contracting, electrical, excavation-foundation, steel erection, rofing, sheet metal, demolition-wrecking, glazing curtain wall, masonry, concrete, utilities, painting, wall/ceiling and asbestos abatement.
Cost: $350.00
Frequency: Annual/September
Circulation: 90000

4436 ENR Top Owners Sourcebook
Engineering News Record/McGraw Hill
2 Penn Plaza
9th Floor
New York, NY 10121-2298

212-512-2000
FAX 212-512-4039
E-Mail: constructioninfo@ecnext.com
Home Page: www.construction.com

Gary Graizzaro, Plant Manager
John J Kosowatz, Managing Editor

List of 700 companies that had the largest expenditures for building construction and building acquisition in the previous year.
Cost: $300.00
Frequency: Annual/December
Circulation: 90000

4437 Electrical Construction Materials Directory
Underwriters Laboratories
333 Pfingsten Rd
Northbrook, IL 60062-2096

847-412-0136
877-854-3577
FAX 847-272-8129
E-Mail: cec@us.ul.com
Home Page: www.UL.com

Keith E Williams, CEO
John Drengenberg, Manager Consumer Affairs

Companies that have qualified to use the UL listing mark or classification marking on or in connection with products which have been found to be in compliance with UL's requirements.
Cost: $30.00
Frequency: Annual
Printed in on glossy stock

4438 Fastener Selection Guide
Single Ply Roofing Institute
411 Waverley Oaks Road
Suite 331B
Waltham, MA 02452

781-647-7026
FAX 781-647-7222
E-Mail: info@spri.org
Home Page: www.spri.org

Linda King, Managing Director

Identifies the various fastener options for each desk type and typical pullout values.
Cost: $15.00

4439 Flexible Membrane Roofing: Guide to Specifications
Single Ply Roofing Institute
411 Waverley Oaks Road
Suite 331B
Waltham, MA 02452

781-647-7026
FAX 781-647-7222
E-Mail: info@spri.org
Home Page: www.spri.org

Linda King, Managing Director

Now in it's 7th edition, this is the most complete reference guide on materials, systems and designs for commerical roofing.
Cost: $50.00

4440 GreenSpec Directory
BuildingGreen
122 Birge Street
Suite 30
Brattleboro, VT 05301-6703

802-257-7300
FAX 802-257-7304
E-Mail: info@buildinggreen.com
Home Page: www.buildinggreen.com

Alex Wilson, Owner
Nadav Malin, Editor
Daniel Woodbury, Publisher
Charlotte Snyder, Circulation Manager

Information on more than 1,850 green building products carefully screened by the editors of Environmental Building News. Directory listings cover more than 250 categories, from access flooring to zero-VOC paints. Included are product descriptions, environmental characteristics and considerations, and manufacturer contact information with internet addresses.
Cost: $89.00
464 Pages
ISBN: 1-929884-15-X

4441 MasterFormat
Construction Specifications Institute

110 South Union Street
Suite 100
Alexandria, VA 22314-3351

800-689-2900
FAX 703-236-4600
E-Mail: csi@csinet.org
Home Page: www.csinet.org
Social Media: *Facebook, Twitter, LinkedIn, YouTube*

Paul R. Bertram Jr., President
Gregory J. Markling, President-Elect
Mitch A. Miller, Vice President
Casey F. Robb, Vice President
Lane J. Beougher, Secretary

The reengineering of this industry standard sets the present and future pace for organizing construction communication. MasterFormat 2004 Edition simplifies the process of determining where specific subject matter is located.
Cost: $159.00
516 Pages
ISBN: 0-976239-90-6
Founded in 2004

4442 NRCMA Membership Directory
National Railroad Construction & Maintenance Assoc
500 New Jersey Ave NW
Suite 400
Washington, DC 20001-2065

202-715-2919
FAX 202-318-0867
E-Mail: info@nrcma.org
Home Page: www.nrcma.org
Social Media: *Facebook, Twitter, LinkedIn*

Chuck Baker, President
Matt Ginsberg, Director of Operations
Jim Perkins, Chairman
Terry Benton, Vice Chairman

A book of the railroad contracting industry, lists all members of the NRC, including their technical specialities ang geographic regions of operation.
Cost: $35.00
Frequency: Free to Members

4443 Public Works Manual
Hanley-Wood
426 S Westgate Street
Addison, IL 60101

630-543-0870
800-524-2364
FAX 630-543-3112
E-Mail: arozgus@hanleywood.com
Home Page: www.pwmag.com

William D Palmer Jr., Editor-in-Chief
Amara Rozgus, Managing Editor
Sharon Glorioso, Associate Editor
Colette Palait, Editorial Assistant

Over 4,000 manufacturers and distributors of equipment, materials, services, computers and software used in the design, construction and maintenance of streets and highways, water systems, wastewater and solid wastes processing and recreation areas.
Cost: $30.00
Frequency: Annual
Circulation: 55000

4444 Roofing/Siding/Insulation: Trade Directory Issue
PO Box 1269
Skokie, IL 60076-8269

847-763-9594
FAX 847-763-9694
E-Mail: roofingsidinginsulation@halldata.com
Home Page: www.rsimag.com

Thomas Skernivitz, Editor
Jacke Lyttle, Publisher

Lists thousands of contractors, manufacturers and distributors of equipment and products.
Cost: $20.00
Frequency: Annual
Circulation: 22,000

4445 STAFDA Directory
Specialty Tools & Fasteners Distributors Assn
500 Elm Grove Rd.
Suite 210
Elm Grove, WI 53122

262-784-4774
800-352-2981
FAX 262-784-5059
E-Mail: info@stafda.org
Home Page: www.stafda.org
Social Media: *Facebook, LinkedIn*

Mike Kangas, President
Kramer Darragh, Vice President

This is a Who's Who of the industry. Listings include who makes over 900 different products: nearly 2,570 member addresses and contacts; brand names; fax numbers: 800 numbers; e-mail; www; and a recap of association services and activities.
500 Pages
Frequency: Annual
Circulation: 4500

4446 Scaffold Industry Association Directory & Handbook
Scaffold Industry Association
400 Admiral Blvd.
Kansas City, MO 64106-1508

816-595-4860
E-Mail: info@saiaonline.org
Home Page: www.scaffold.org
Social Media: *Facebook, Twitter, LinkedIn*

Steve Smith, President
Marty Coughlin, President-Elect
Daryl Hare, Treasurer
Mike Russell, Secretary

The SIA Directory and Handbook contains complete membership information, company and individual listings. It also includes federal OSHA scaffold standards for general industry, construction and maritime, scaffold plank grading rules, map and listing of OSHA regional and area offices, scaffold standards for the state of California, glossary of scaffold terms, illustrations of various types of scaffolds, and codes of safe practices.
Cost: $125.00
355 Pages
Circulation: 5000

4447 Source: Buyer's Guide & Dealer Directory
Northeastern Retail Lumber Association
585 N Greenbush Rd
Rensselaer, NY 12144-9615

518-286-1010
800-292-6752
FAX 518-286-1755
E-Mail: rferris@nrla.org
Home Page: www.nrla.org
Social Media: *Facebook*

Rita Ferris, President
Tony Shepley, Chair
Jon Hallgren, Chair Elect
Jonas Kelly, Vice Chair

The industry's guide to names, addresses, phone numbers, fax numbers, and product lines of companies that comprise the independent retail lumber dealers of the Northeast.
Cost: $89.95
Frequency: Annual

4448 Sourcebook
Ray Publishing

P.O.Box 992
Morrison, CO 80465-0992

303-467-1776
FAX 303-467-1777
Home Page: www.compositesworld.com

Judith Hazen, Publisher
Mike Mussleman, Managing Editor

A comprehensive directory of composites industry suppliers, manufacturers and service companies for the entire composites industry.
60 Pages
Founded in 1993
Printed in 4 colors on glossy stock

4449 Store Fixture Buyers' Guide and Membership Directory
Nat'l Association of Store Fixture Manufacturers
3595 Sheridan
Suite 200
Hollywood, FL 33322

954-893-7300
FAX 954-893-7500
E-Mail: nasfm@nasfm.org
Home Page: www.nasfm.org
Social Media: *Facebook, Twitter, LinkedIn*

Jo Rossman, Senior Editor
Klein Merriman, Executive Director

This buyers' guide features the products and services of some 400 store fixture manufacturers. Contact information, plant size, number of employees, and company descriptions of all member manufacturers, plant listings by location, and contact and company information on products and services of 200 supplier members is included.
Cost: $175.00
80 Pages
Frequency: Free to Members

4450 Sweets Directory
Grey House Publishing/McGraw Hill Construction
1221 Avenue of the Americas
New York, NY 10020-1095

212-512-2000
800-442-2258
FAX 212-512-3840
E-Mail: webmaster@mcgraw-hill.com
Home Page: www.mcgraw-hill.com
Social Media: *Facebook, Twitter*

Harold W McGraw III, CEO

The leading desktop reference and preliminary research guide, featuring more than 10,000 building product manufacturers and their products.
Cost: $145.00
950 Pages
Frequency: Annual
ISBN: 1-592378-50-1
Founded in 1906

4451 ThomasNet
Thomas Publishing Company, LLC
User Services Department
5 Penn Plaza
New York, NY 10001

212-695-0500
800-699-9822
FAX 212-290-7362
E-Mail: contact@thomaspublishing.com
Home Page: www.thomasnet.com
Social Media: *Facebook, Twitter, LinkedIn*

Carl Holst-Knudsen, President
Robert Anderson, VP, Planning
Mitchell Peipert, VP, Finance
Ivy Molofsky, VP, Human Resources

A way to reach qualified businesses that list their company information on ThomasNet.com. Detailed profiles promote their products, services, capabilities and brands carried. The

ThomasNet.com web site is the most up-to-date compilation of 650,000 North American manufacturers, distributors, and service companies in 67,000 industrial categories.
Founded in 1898

4452 Wind Design Guide
Single Ply Roofing Institute
411 Waverley Oaks Road
Suite 331B
Waltham, MA 02452

781-647-7026
FAX 781-647-7222
E-Mail: info@spri.org
Home Page: www.spri.org

Linda King, Managing Director

Wind Design Guide for Edge Systems Used with Low Slope Roofing Systems outlines design and construction of edge details for wind resistance, including test methods, calculations of design pressures and commentary.
Cost: $20.00

Industry Web Sites

4453 http://gold.greyhouse.com
G.O.L.D Grey House OnLine Databases
Grey House Publishing's online database platform, GOLD, offers Quick Search, Keyword Search and Expert Search for most business sectors including architecture, building and construction markets. The GOLD platform makes finding the information you need quick and easy - whether you're a novice searcher or an experienced database user. All of Grey House's directory products are available for subscription on the GOLD platform.

4454 www.abc.org
Associated Builders and Contractors
National trade association representing about 23,000 contractors, subcontractors, material suppliers and related firms from across the country and from all specialties in the construction industry.

4455 www.acdi.net
Associated Construction Distributors International
Cooperative association of independently owned and locally operated distributors of specialty construction products and equipment.

4456 www.acesystems.com
AEC Systems International/Penton Media
Focuses on Internet/Intranet for the design, engineering and construction industries.

4457 www.aednet.org
Associated Equipment Distributors
Membership association of 1,200 independent distributors, manufacturers, and other organizations involved in the distribution of construction equipment and related products and services in North America and throughout the world.

4458 www.agc.org
Associated General Contractors of America
The voice of the construction industry, an organization of qualified construction contractors and industry related companies dedicated to skill, integrity and responsibility.

4459 www.aibd.org
American Institute of Building Design
Our members consist of professional building designers and architects, who have for the most part chosen residential design as the focus of their practice.

353

4460 www.aisc.org
American Institute of Steel Construction

Serving the structural steel industry in the US. Our purpose is to promote the use of structural steel through research activities, market development, education, codes and specifications, technical assistance, quality certifacation and standardization.

4461 www.akropolis.net
Akropolis

To enable firms at all levels of the design and building industry to operate more efficiently with the help of cutting edge technology solutions.

4462 www.anodizing.org
Aluminum Anodizers Council

Represents the interests of aluminum anodizers worldwide and is the principal trade organization for the anodizing industry in North America. It promotes the interests of its members through technical exchange, ongoing education, statistical data, market promotion, and industry representation.

4463 www.apwa.net
American Public Works Association

An international educational and professionals association of public agencies, private sector companies, and individuals dedicated to providing high quality public works goods and services.

4464 www.aspenational.com
American Society of Professional Estimators

Serving the construction estimators by providing education, fellowship and opportunity for professional development. ASPE represents individual members involved in the construction industry.

4465 www.asphaltinstitute.org
Asphalt Institute

Conducts education, research and engineering services related to asphaltic products; conducts seminars and sells publications and videos on asphalt technology.

4466 www.asphaltpavement.org
National Asphalt Pavement Association

The only trade association that exclusively represents the interest s of the Hot Mix Asphalt producer and paving contractor on the national level with Congress, government agencies, and other national trade and business organizations.

4467 www.automatedbuilder.com
CMN Associates

Association of manufacturers and suppliers who have a product line that is of interest to the manufactured and pre-fabricated housing industry.

4468 www.awci.org
Association of the Wall and Ceiling Industries

Represents acoustics systems, ceiling systems, drywall systems, exterior insulation and finishing systems, fireproofing, flooring systems, insulation, and stucco contractors, suppliers and manufacturers and those in allied trades.

4469 www.build.com
Build.com

Providing consumers, contractors and industry professionals with a valuable resource of products, service and information related to the building and home improvement industry.

4470 www.buildingstone.org
Building Stone Institute

Quarries, fabricators, dealers, installers and restorers of all types of natural stone. Membership dues based on sales volume.

4471 www.calredwood.org
California Redwood Association

A trade association for redwood lumber producers.

4472 www.cfma.org
Construction Financial Management Association

Non-profit organization dedicated to serving the financial professional in the construction industry.

4473 www.cisco.org
Construction Industry Service Corporation

Labor management association that promotes union construction, union contractors and union apprenticeship programs throughout Northeastern Illinois.

4474 www.coaa.org
Construction Owners Association of America

To act as a focal point and voice for the interests of owners in construction. Comprised of a diverse group of men and women representing construction owners.

4475 www.concretepumpers.com
American Concrete Pumping Association

Provides education, insurance, marketing and much more to companies involved with the concrete pumping industry. Our dedication to the concrete pumping industry has led us to become a key part in the education of safety and business management to everyone involved, from the operators to the management.

4476 www.construction.com
McGraw-Hill Construction

McGraw-Hill Construction (MHC), part of The McGraw-Hill Companies, connects people and projects across the design and construction industry, serving owners, architects, engineers, general contractors, subcontractors, building product manufacturers, suppliers, dealers, distributors and adjacent markets.

4477 www.csinet.org
Construction Specifications Institute

Our mission is to continuously improve the process of creating and sustaining the built environment. We do this by facilitating communication among all those involved in that process.

4478 www.demolitionassociation.com
National Association of Demolition Contractors

Representing the demolition industry including demolition contractors, formed to foster goodwill and the exchange of ideas with the public, governmental agencies and constractors engaged in the demolition industry. Also for manufacturers or suppliers of demolition equipment, supplies and services.

4479 www.dfi.org
Deep Foundations Institute

We can best be described as being a technical association of firms and individuals in the deep foundations and related industry. DFI covers the gamut of deep foundation construction and earth retention systems.

4480 www.ebmda.org
Eastern Building Material Dealers Association

Established to foster, protect and promote the welfare and best interest of its members engaged in the retail lumber and building materials business.

4481 www.floorbiz.com
Floor Biz

Internet's leading creator and operator of a vertical business community for the flooring industry. FloorBiz leverages the interactive features and global reach of the Internet to create a multi-national, targeted business community vertically integrated from consumer to manufacturer.

4482 www.gobrick.com
Brick Industry Association

A national trade association representing distributors and manufacturers of clay brick and suppliers of related products and services.

4483 www.greyhouse.com
Grey House Publishing

Authoritative reference directories for most business sectors including architecture, building and construction markets. Users can search the online databases with varied search criteria allowing for custom searches by product category, geographic area, sales volume, keyword, subject and more. Full Grey House catalog and online ordering also available.

4484 www.homeimprovement.com
Hometime

Hometime is a home-improvement television show broadcast on public television, The Learning Channel and in syndication. A comprehensive online resource for your remodeling and home-improvement needs.

4485 www.iccsafe.org
International Code Council

Formerly known as the Building Officials and Code Administrators International, we publish codes that establish minimum performance requirements for all aspects of the construction industry.

4486 www.icpi.org
Interlocking Concrete Pavement Institute

Self governed, self funded, autonomous association representing the interlocking concrete pavement industry in North America. Membership is open to producers, contractors, suppliers, consultants and others who have an interest in the industry. As an industry voice, the membership represents a majority of concrete paver production in North America.

4487 www.iilp.org
International Institute for Lathe and Plaster

Federation of organizations representing contractors, unions and makers of lathing and manufacturing.

4488 www.manufacturedhousing.org
Manufactured Housing Institute

National trade organization representing all segments of the factory built housing industry. MHI serves its membership by providing industry research, promotion, education, and government relations programs, and by building and facilitating consensus within the industry.

4489 www.masoncontractors.org
Mason Contractors Association of America

Through strong programs, publications and services, the MCAA avtively promotes the interests of its members. By promoting the use of masonry, influencing resonable codes and standards, work force development and public affairs, the association advances the use of masonry.

4490 www.masonrysociety.org

Masonry Society

Dedicated to the advancement of scientific engineering, architechtural and construction knowledge of masonry. Promotes research and education and disseminates information on masonry materials, design, construction. Publishes a newsletter.

4491 www.mbinet.org

Modular Building Institute

Serving the commercial factory-built buildings industry on an international scale. Our regular members are manufacturers and dealers of commercial modular structures, while our associate members are companies supplying building components, services, and financing.

4492 www.naamm.org

Nat'l Assn of Architectural Metal Manufacturers

The largest of four operating divisions of the National Association of Architectural Metal Manufacturers. HMMA is a group composed of companies that manufacture, distribute and promote the use of hollow metal door and frame products.

4493 www.nahb.org

National Association of Home Builders

Represents the interests of concrete, log, modular, and panel manufacturers, builders, and suppliers.

4494 www.nam.org

National Association of Manufacturers

The nation's largest industrial trade association, representing small and large manufacturers in every industrial sector and in all 50 states.

4495 www.nari.org

National Association of the Remodeling Industry

A voice in the remodeling industry, NARI has an exclusive, encompasing purpose to; establish and maintain a firm commitment to developing and sustaining programs that expand and unite the remodeling industry; to ensure the industry's growth and security; to encourage ethical conduct, sound business practices and professionalism in the remodeling industry; and to present NARI as the recognized authority in the remodeling industry.

4496 www.nationalslag.org

National Slag Association

Members are processors of iron and steel slags for use as a aggregate in construction and manufacturing applications.

4497 www.nawic.org

National Association of Women in Construction

Founded by 16 women working in the construction industry. The founders organized NAWIC to create a support network for women in construction.

4498 www.ncac.com

National Council of Acoustical Consultants

Strives to safeguard the interests of professional acoustical consulting firms. Managing physics and psychoacoustics to provide optimum listning environments.

4499 www.ncma.org

National Concrete Masonry Association

Manufacturers of concrete masonry products and suppliers of products to the industry. Offers a variety of technical services and design aids through publications, computer programs, slide presentations and technical training.

4500 www.ncsbcs.org

National Conference of States on Building Codes

Serving as a forum for the interchange of information and provides technical services, education and training to our members to enhance the public's social, economic well-being through safe, durable, accessible and efficient buildings.

4501 www.necanet.org

National Electrical Contractors Association

Represents a segment of the construction market comprised of over 70,000 electrical firms.

4502 www.newhomes.move.com

HomeBuilder.com

The web's leading provider of information on newly built homes, with listings for over 125,000 new home and planned developments throughout the US. Supplier of media and technology solutions that promote and connect real estate professionals to consumers before, during and after a move.

4503 www.nrcma.org

National Railroad Construction & Maintenance Assn

Railroad construction and maintenance contractors, engineering firms, manufacturing suppliers and professional associate firms.

4504 www.nrla.org

Northeastern Retail Lumber Association

A resource for industry members, consumers, and public officials in dependent lumber and building material suppliers and associated businesses in New York and the six New England states.

4505 www.nrmca.org

National Ready Mixed Concrete Association

Our mission is to provide exceptional value for our members by responsibly representing and serving the entire ready mixed concrete industry through leadership, promotion, education and partnering; to ensure ready mixed concrete is the building material of choice.

4506 www.nssga.org

National Stone, Sand & Gravel Association

Represents the crushed stone, sand and gravel — or aggregate — industries. Our members account for 90 percent of the crushed stone and 70 percent of the sand and gravel produced annually in the US.

4507 www.ntma.com

National Terrazzo and Mosaic Association

Full service nonprofit trade association headquartered in Northern Virginia. The association establishes national standards for all terrazzo floor and wall systems and provides complete specifications, color plates and general information to architects and designers at no cost.

4508 www.nuca.com

National Utility Contractors Association

A national association that provides a forum for continuing education and promotes effective public policy, through its grassroots network, to protect and enhance your industry.

4509 www.oikos.com

Oikos

Devoted to serving professionals whose work promotes sustainable design and construction. Oikos is a Greek word meaning house. Oikos serves as the root for two English words: ecology and economy.

4510 www.opcmia.org

Operative Plasterers' & Cement Masons' Int'l Assn

Represents and trains plasterers and cement masons for the purpose of protecting and promoting the quality of our industry and the livelihood of our members.

4511 www.opei.org

Outdoor Power Equipment Institute

International trade association whose members are manufacturers of powered lawn and garden maintenance products, components and attachment supplies, as well as industry related services.

4512 www.pbmdf.com

Composite Panel Association

The association of North American wood and agrifiber based particle board and medium density fiberboard producers, to broaden the base of participation in industry outreach programs.

4513 www.pci.org

Precast Prestressed Concrete Institute

Dedicated to fostering greater understanding and use of precast and prestressed concrete, maintains a full staff of technical and marketing specialists.

4514 www.perlite.org

Perlite Institute

International trade association which establishes product standards and specifications, and which encourages the development of new product uses through research.

4515 www.pfi-institute.org

Pipe Fabrication Institute

Members are companies producing sophisticated high temperature, high pressure piping systems that employ specialists from the United Association of Journeymen & Apprentices of the Plumbing & Pipe Fitting Industry. We exist solely for the purpose of ensuring a level of quality in the pipe fabrication indusrty that is without compromise.

4516 www.piledrivers.org

Pile Driving Contractors Association

Organization of pile driving contractors that advocates the increased use of driven piles for deep foundations and earth retention systems. To do this we promote the use of driven pile solutions in all cases where they are effective, support educational programs for engineers on the design and efficiency of driven piles and for contractors on improving installation procedures. We also give contractors a larger voice in establishing procedures and standards for pile installation and design.

4517 www.pipefitters537.org

American Pipe Fittings Association

Trade association for any domestic corporation, firm or individual engaged in manufacture in the US or Canada of piping components and accessories, including pipe hangers and supports.

4518 www.psai.org

Portable Sanitation Association International

International trade association that represents firms engaged in the leasing, renting selling and manufacturing of portable sanitation equipment, services and supplies for construction, recreation, emergency and other uses. devoted to the proper handling of human waste by the most modern, sanitary means, giving the greatest concern to the preservation of an unspoiled environment.

4519 www.reedconstructiondata.com
First Source Online

Provides A/E/C professionals free access to the industry's most comprehensive, up-to-date library of formatted commercial building product information, plus manufacturers' addresses, telephone numbers, trade names, and regional distributors.

4520 www.rfci.com
Resilient Floor Covering Institute

Industry trade association of North American manufacturers who produce resilient flooring products. Associate members of RFCI supply raw materials to the industry and manufacture installation and maintenance products.

4521 www.roofcoatings.org
Roof Coatings Manufacturers Association

Represents the interests for manufacturers of cold applied roof coatings, cements and waterproofing agents, as well as the suppliers of products, equipment, and services to and for the industry. Currently RCMA boasts more than 70 member companies.

4522 www.rubberpavements.org
Rubber Pavements Association

Dedicated to encouraging greater usage of high quality, cost effective asphalt pavements containing recycled tire rubber. Conducts national and international seminars.

4523 www.saiaonline.org
Scaffold Industry Association

Promotes scaffold safety and education through its publications, conventions, tradeshows and training programs. Marketing of your product is available through the monthly magazine, convention and trade show.

4524 www.sgcc.org
Safety Glazing Certification Council

Provides for the certification of safety glazing materials, comprised of safety glazing manufacturers and other parties concerned with public safety. SGCC is managed by a board of directors comprised of representatives from the safety glazing industry and the public interest sector.

4525 www.sips.org
Structural Insulated Panel Association

A trade association representing manufacturers, suppliers, fabricators, distributors, design professionals and builders committed to providing quality structural insulated panels for all segments of the construction industry.

4526 www.spri.org
Single Ply Roofing Institute

Comprised of manufacturers and marketers of sheet applied membrane roofing systems and components to the commerical roofing industry.

4527 www.stafda.org
Specialty Tools & Fasteners Distributors Assn

International trade association composed of distributors and manufacturers and rep agents of light construction, industrial and related products. Members also include publishers of industry press serving the construction and industrial trades.

4528 www.stanyc.com
Subcontractors Trade Association

Members are specialty and supply companies in the construction industry. Our goal is to improve the economic well being of our members through representation, support and assistance through the process of legislation, legal action, public relations, education and other public information programs.

4529 www.steelwindows.com
Steel Window Institute

For United States manufacturers of windows made from hot-rolled, solid steel sections and such related products as castings, trim, mechanical operators, screens and moldings.

4530 www.sweets.construction.com
McGraw Hill Construction

In depth product information that lets you find, compare, select, specify and make purchase decisions in the industrial product marketplace.

4531 www.swensongranite.com
Swenson Granite Works

Family owned business that has been quarrying and cutting granite in New England since 1883.

4532 www.tcaainc.org
Tile Contractors Association of America

TCAA is an organization representing the finest union tile contractors in the United States. Founded in 1903, it is the only association which serves the needs of the union tile contractor.

4533 www.tfguild.org
Timber Framers Guild of North America

Dedicated to establishing training programs for dedicated timber framers, disseminating information about timber framing and timber frame building design, displaying the art of timber framing to the public, and generally serving as a center of timber framing information for the professional and general public alike.

4534 www.thebluebook.com
Contactors Register

Regional construction directories in most major markets throughout the US. Provides easy online access to continually updated information for each of our regional editions.

4535 www.tile-assn.com
National Tile Contractors Association

Serving every segment of the industry, and is recognized as the largest and most respected tile contractors association in the world.

4536 www.tilt-up.org
Tilt-up Concrete Association

Represents builders, engineers and suppliers involved with tilt-up concrete construction. Makes a continuing and increasingly important contribution to the success of each member through the most imaginative and efficient application of every appropriate skill, tool and service of the association.

4537 www.wbma.org
Western Building Material Association

Regional trade association serving building material dealers throughout the states of Alaska, Idaho, Montana, Oregon and Washington and a federated association of the National Lumber and Building Material Dealers Association.

4538 www.wfca.org
World Floor Covering Association

Shapes and defines public policy through agressive, national legislative advocacy on behalf of our members. Provides continuing professional educational programming through educational forums and the Regional Installation and Training Education (RITE) program.

4539 www.windowanddoor.com
WindowDoor.net

Anyone who is interested in window and door products can find the latest information on products, components and how-to information here.

Associations

4540 AACC International
3340 Pilot Knob Road
St. Paul, MN 55121

651-454-7250
800-328-7560
FAX 651-454-0766
E-Mail: aacc@scisoc.org
Home Page: www.aaccnet.org
Social Media: *Facebook, Twitter, LinkedIn, Pinterest*

Jan A Delcour, President
David H Hahn, Chair
Gerard Downey, President Elect
Dave L Braun, Treasurer
Marta S Izydorczyk, Director

Formerly the American Association of Cereal Chemists, a non-profit organization of members who are specialists in the use of cereal grains in foods.
Founded in 1915

4541 AOAC International
2275 Research Blvd
Suite 300
Rockville, MD 20850-3250

301-924-7077
800-379-2622
FAX 301-924-7089
E-Mail: aoac@aoac.org
Home Page: www.aoac.org
Social Media: *Facebook, Twitter, LinkedIn*

E James Bradford, CEO & Executive Director
Joyce L Schumacher, CFO
Delia A Boyd, Program Manager

Serves the communities of analytical sciences by providing the tools and porcesses necessary for community stakeholders to collaborate and through, consensus building, develop fit for purpose methods and services for assuring quality measurments.
3700 Members
Founded in 1884

4542 Acrylonitrile Group
1250 Connecticut Ave NW
Suite 700
Washington, DC 20036-2657

202-419-1500
FAX 202-659-8037
E-Mail: angroup@regnet.com
Home Page: www.angroup.org

Robert J Fensterheim, Group Executive Director, President

Affiliated with the Synthetic Organic Chemical Manufacturers, (TAG) was formed under the Chemical manufacturers Association to do research. TAG represents producers and users of the industrial chemical used to make plastics, fibers and synthetic rubber products.
Founded in 1960

4543 Adhesion Society
7101 Wisconsin Avenue
Suite 990
Bethesda, MD 20814

301-986-9700
FAX 301-986-9795
E-Mail: Adhesionsociety@ascouncil.org
Home Page: www.adhesionsociety.org
Social Media: *Twitter, LinkedIn*

Anand Jagota, President
Gregory Schueneman, Vice President
Charles Shuster, Treasurer
Leonardo Lopez, Secretary

Supports all those who are involved in adhesion's role in coatings, compostie materials, biological tissues and bonded structures.
400 Members
Founded in 1978

4544 Alkyl Amines Council
1850 M St NW
Suite 700
Washington, DC 20036

202-721-4100
FAX 202-296-8120
E-Mail: info@socma.com
Home Page: www.socma.com
Social Media: *Facebook, Twitter, LinkedIn, YouTube*

Lawrence D Sloan, President/CEO
Todd Brown, Director
Dolores Alonso, Senior Director

Data relating to production, processing and application.
6 Members
Founded in 1921

4545 Alkylphenols and Ethoxylates Research Council
1250 Connecticut Ave NW
Suite 700
Washington, DC 20036

202-419-1500
866-273-7262
FAX 202-659-8037
E-Mail: info@aperc.org
Home Page: www.alkylphenol.org

Robert J Fensterheim, Executive Director

Monitors regulatory developments affecting manufacturers in the chemical industry
5 Members
Founded in 1998

4546 Alliance for Responsible Atmospheric Policy
2111 Wilson Blvd
Suite 850
Arlington, VA 22201

703-243-0344
FAX 703-243-2874
E-Mail: fay@alliancepolicy.org
Home Page: www.alliancepolicy.org
Social Media: *Twitter*

John Hurst, Chair
William McQuade, Vice Chair
Nanette Lockwood, Treasurer
Kevin Fay, Executive Director
Tonya Hunt, Finance & Membership Director

Made up of companies who rely on alternatives to ozone depleting chlorofluorocarbons(CFCs). Theses alternatives are HCPCs and HFCs, used primarily as refrigerants, speciality solvents, agents for foamed plastics.
300 Members
Founded in 1980

4547 American Association Textile Chemists and Colorists
PO Box 12215
Research Triangle Park, NC 27709-2215

919-549-8141
800-360-5380
FAX 919-549-8933
E-Mail: danielsj@aatcc.org
Home Page: www.aatcc.org
Social Media: *Facebook, Twitter, LinkedIn, Youtube*

John Y Daniels, Executive VP
Debra Hibbard, Executive Assistant
Amy Holland, Office Manager
Bonnie Green, Membership Services
Suzanne Holmes, Program Manager/Technical Product

Supports all those working with colorants and chemical finishes for textile and related industries.
3000 Members

4548 American Association for Clinical Chemistry
900 Seventh Street, NW
Suite 400
Washington, DC 20001

202-857-0717
800-892-1400
FAX 202-887-5093
Home Page: www.aacc.org
Social Media: *Facebook, Twitter, LinkedIn, YouTube*

Robert H Christensen, President
Steven H Wong, President Elect
Elizabeth L Frank, Secretary
Michael Bennett, Treasurer
Dennis J Dietzen, Director

AACC is an international scientific/medical society of clinical laboratory professionals, physicians, research scientists and other individuals involved with clinical chemistry and other clinical laboratory science related disciplines.
Founded in 1948

4549 American Association for Crystal Growth
10922 Main Range Trail
Littleton, CO 80127

303-539-6907
888-506-1271
FAX 303-600-5144
E-Mail: AACG@comcast.net
Home Page: www.crystalgrowth.org

Robert Biefeld, President
Joan M Redwing, VP
Luis Zepeda-Ruiz, Treasurer
Mariya Zhuravleva, Secretary

Provides support for all professionals in the field of crystal and crystal growth.

4550 American Association of Bioanalysts
906 Olive Street
Suite 1200
Saint Louis, MO 63101-1448

314-241-1445
FAX 314-241-1449
E-Mail: aab@aab.org
Home Page: www.aab.org

Mark S Birenbaum PhD, Administrator

Professional association whose members are clinical laboratory directors, owners, supervisors, managers, medical technologists, medical laboratory technicians, physician office laboratory technicians, and phlebotomists.
Founded in 1956

4551 American Chemical Society
1155 16th St NW
Washington, DC 20036

202-872-4600
800-227-5558
FAX 202-872-4615
E-Mail: help@acs.org
Home Page: www.acs.org
Social Media: *Facebook, Twitter, LinkedIn, Google+*

Madeleine Jacobs, CEO

Self-governed individual membership organization that provides a range of opportunities for peer interaction and career development, regardless of professional or scientific interests.
15900 Members
Founded in 1876

4552 American Chemistry Council
700 Second St. NE
Washington, DC 20002

202-249-7000
FAX 202-249-6100
Home Page: www.americanchemistry.com
Social Media: *Facebook, Twitter, LinkedIn, Youtube*

Calvin M Dooley, President & CEO
Raymond J O'Bryan, CFO & CAO
Dell Perelman, Chief of Staff & General Counsel
Anne Womack Kolton, VP, Communications
Roger D Bernstein, VP, State Affairs

Committed to improved environmental, health and safety performance through responsible care, common sense advocacy designed to address major public policy issues, health and environmental research and product testing.
190 Members

4553 American Coatings Association
1500 Rhode Island Ave Nw
Washington, DC 20005

202-462-6272
FAX 202-462-8549
E-Mail: members@paint.org
Home Page: www.paint.org
Social Media: *Facebook*

J. Andrew Doyle, President & CEO
Thomas J. Graves, Vice President, General Counsel
Allen Irish, Counsel/Director, Industry Affairs
Alison Keane, Vice President, Government Affairs
Robin Eastman Caldwell, Senior Government Affairs

Supports all those involved in the manufacturer of chemicals.
Founded in 1903

4554 American Coke & Coal Chemicals Institute
25 Massachusetts Ave NW
Suite 800
Washington, DC 20001

724-772-1167
FAX 866-422-7794
E-Mail: information@accci.org
Home Page: www.accci.org

Ronald Schoen, Chairman
David Smith, Vice Chairman
Paul Saffrin, Secretary/Treasurer
David C. Ailor, President
Janis R. Deitch, Director of Administration

Formed by companies interested in establishing a forum to discuss and act upon issues of common concern to their industry. Today, ACCI represents 7 of the 8 independently owned and operated US merchant coke producers; several integrated steel companies which produce coke; and all 4 of the US and 1 Canadian coal chemical companies which refine coal tar. Nearly 50 companies contribute their knowledge and expertise to enhance the effectiveness of the Institute.
160 Members
Founded in 1944

4555 American College of Toxicology Annual Meeting
1821 Michael Faraday Drive
Suite 300
Reston, VA 20190

703-547-0875
FAX 703-438-3113
E-Mail: acthx@actox.org

Home Page: www.actox.org
Social Media: *Facebook, Twitter, LinkedIn*

Mary Ellen Cosenza, President
Tracey Zoetis, MS, VP
Timothy McGovern, PhD, Treasurer
Timothy McGovern, PhD, Secretary
Carol C Lemire, Executive Director

Multidisciplinary society composed of professionals having a common interest in toxicology. Our mission is to educate and lead professionals in industry, government and related areas of toxicology and actively promote the exchange of information and perspectives on the current status of safety assessment and the application of new developments in toxicology. Annual meeting,education courses, symposia and exhibits.
500 Members
Founded in 1979

4556 American Fiber Manufacturers Association
1530 Wilson Blvd
Suite 690
Arlington, VA 22209-2418

703-875-0432
FAX 703-875-0907
E-Mail: afma@afma.org
Home Page: www.afma.org

Paul O'Day, President
Robert Baker, VP
Frank Horn, President Economics Bureau Div

Trade association for US companies that manufacture synthetic and cellulosotic fibers.
33 Members
Founded in 1933

4557 American Hydrogen Association
PO Box 4205
Mesa, AZ 85211

480-234-5070
E-Mail: webmaster@clean-air.org
Home Page: www.clean-air.org
Social Media: *Facebook, YouTube*

Roy McAlister, President
Ben Ferguson, Vice President
Douglas Hawley, Secretary/Treasurer

Stimulates interest and helping to establish the renewable hydrogen energy economy.
Founded in 1966

4558 American Institute of Chemical Engineers
120 Wall Street
FL 23
New York, NY 10005-4020

212-591-7338
800-242-4363
FAX 203-775-5177
E-Mail: xpress@aiche.org
Home Page: www.aiche.org
Social Media: *Facebook, Twitter, LinkedIn*

John Sofranko, Executive Director
William D Byers, President
Cathy Diana, Director Human Resources
Ken Gruber, Finance/IT Manager

A professional association of members that provide leadership in advancing the chemical engineering profession.
50000 Members
Founded in 1908

4559 American Institute of Chemists
315 Chestnut St
Philadelphia, PA 19106-2702

215-873-8224
FAX 215-629-5224

E-Mail: info@theaic.org
Home Page: www.theaic.org

David Manuta, President
E Ray McAfee, President Elect
E Gerry Meyer, Secretary
J Stephen Duerr, Treasurer
Jerry Jasinski, Chairman

Supports all individual chemists and chemical engineers involved in the chemical industry.
Founded in 1923

4560 American Leather Chemists Association
1314 50th Street
Suite 103
Lubbock, TX 79412

806-744-1798
FAX 806-744-1785
E-Mail: alca@leatherchemists.org
Home Page: www.leatherchemists.org

Sarah Drayna, President
David Peters, VP
David Peters, VP Elect
Carol Adcock, Executive Secretary

Group of leather chemists interested in the development of methods that could be utilized to standardize both the supply and application of the tanning agents utilized by the industry
500 Members
Founded in 1903

4561 American Society Biochemistry and Molecular Biology
11200 Rockville Pike
Suite 302
Rockville, MD 20852-3110

240-283-6600
FAX 301-881-2080
E-Mail: asbmb@asbmb.org
Home Page: www.asbmb.org
Social Media: *Facebook, Twitter, LinkedIn, YouTube, Google+*

Barbara A Gordon, Executive Director
Jennifer Dean, Director, Marketing
Ben Corb, Director, Public Affairs
Mary Ann Gunselman, Executive Assistant
Steve Miller, Deputy Executive Director and CFO

A professional and educational association for biochemists and molecular biologists which seeks to extend and utilize the fields of biochemistry and molecular biology.
13000 Members
Founded in 1906
Mailing list available for rent

4562 American Society for Mass Spectrometry
2019 Galisteo Street, Building I-1
Santa Fe, NM 87505

505-989-4517
FAX 505-989-1073
E-Mail: office@asms.org
Home Page: www.asms.org
Social Media: *Facebook, Twitter, LinkedIn*

Jennifer Brodbelt, President
Vicki H. Wysocki, VP, Programs
Jack Henion, VP, Arrangements
Patrick R. Griffin, Treasurer
Yu Xia, Secretary

Formed to promote and disseminate knowledge of mass spectrometry and allied topics. Members come from academic, industrial and govermental laboratories. Their interests include advancement of techniques and instrumentation in mass spectrometry, as well as fundamental research in chemistry, geology, biological sciences and physics.
3500 Members
Founded in 1969

4563 American Society for Neurochemistry
9037 Ron Den Lane
Windermere, FL 34786

407-909-9064
FAX 407-876-0750
E-Mail: asnmanager@asneurochem.org
Home Page: www.asneurochem.org

Babette Fuss, PhD, President
Babette Fuss, President Elect
Sandra Hewett, Phd, Secretary
Jean Harry, PhD, Treasurer

Organized by US, Canadian and Mexican members of the International Society for Neurochemistry and incorporated in the District of Columbia. Membership dues are $75/year.
1000 Members
Founded in 1969

4564 American Society of Brewing Chemists
3340 Pilot Knob Rd
St. Paul, MN 55121-2055

651-454-7250
800-328-7560
FAX 651-454-0766
E-Mail: asbc@scisoc.org
Home Page: www.asbcnet.org
Social Media: *Facebook, Twitter, LinkedIn, Pinterest*

Christina Schoenberger, President
Christine S White, President-Elect
Chris D Powell, Vice President
Thomas H Shellhammer, Past President
Robert Christiansen, Secretary
700 Members
Founded in 1934

4565 Analytical, Life Science, and Diagnostics Association
500 Montgomery Street
Suite 400
Alexandria, VA 22314

703-647-6214
FAX 703-647-6368
E-Mail: cstarke@alssa.org
Home Page: www.alssa.org
Social Media: *Facebook, Twitter, LinkedIn*

Joseph D. Keegan, Chair
Timy Harkness, Vice Chair & Chair-Elect
Greg Herrema, Past Chairman
Michael J. Duff, President

ALSSA is the primary trade association for companies that supply instruments, chemical reagents, consumables and software used for analysis and measurement in chemistry and the life sciences.

4566 Association of Consulting Chemists and Chemical Engineers Inc.
A C C & C E
P.O. Box 902
Murray Hill, NJ 07974-0902

908-464-3182
FAX 908-464-3182
E-Mail: accce@chemconsult.org
Home Page: www.chemconsult.org

Linda Townsend, Executive Secretary
Dr John Bonacci, Executive Director

The only organization of its kind that attracts qualified technical consultants of all kinds who assist their clients in creating and using chemical knowledge and technology.
150 Members
Founded in 1928

4567 Association of Defensive Spray Manufacturers
906 Olive Street
Suite 1200
St Louis, MO 63101-1448

314-241-1445
FAX 314-241-1449
E-Mail: ADSM@pepperspray.org
Home Page: www.pepperspray.org

Mark S Birenbaum, Executive Director

To permit manufacturers of non lethal chemical weapons to join together to promote the industry as well as to address safety, quality control, marketing and other issues relevant to the industry
6 Members
Founded in 1992

4568 Association of Official Racing Chemists
1021 Storrs Rd
Storrs, CT 06268

860-487-3755
FAX 860-487-3756
Home Page: www.aorc-online.org

Dennis Hill, Executive Director

The international membership consits of individuals concerned with detection of drugs in racing samples.
200 Members
Founded in 1947

4569 Basic Acrylic Monomer Manufacturers
17260 Vannes Court
Hamilton, VA 20158

540-751-2093
FAX 540-751-2094
E-Mail: ehunt@adelphia.net
Home Page: www.bamm.net

Elizabeth K Hunt, Executive Director

Addresses the issues facing the basic acrylates. Also represents manufacturers and importers of acrylic acid and its esters.
5 Members
Founded in 1986
Mailing list available for rent

4570 CIIT Centers for Health Research
Six Davis Drive
PO Box 12137
Research Triangle Park, NC 27709-2137

919-581-1200
FAX 919-558-1400
E-Mail: wgreenlee@ciit.org
Home Page: www.thehamner.org
Social Media: *Twitter*

John G. Dent, Ph.D., Chair & Treasurer
Charles E. Hamner, Jr., D.V.M., P, Vice Chair
William F. Greenlee, Ph.D., President/CEO
Joseph S. Pagano, M.D., Secretary
Jamie H. Wilkerson, CPA, CGMA, Assistant Treasurer

Studies toxicological and human health risk issues associated with the manufacture, distribution and disposal of industrial chemicals.
130 Members
Founded in 1974

4571 Center for the Polyurethanes Industry
700 Second St., NE
Washington, DC 20002

202-249-7000
FAX 202-249-6100
Home Page: polyurethane.americanchemistry.com
Social Media: *Facebook, Twitter*

Calvin M. Dooley, President/CEO
Dell Perelman, Chief of Staff & General

Council
Raymond J. O'Bryan, CFO/ Chief Administrative Officer
Bryan Zumwalt, Vice President of Federal Affairs
Nacole B. Hinton, Managing Director, HR

CPI of the American Chemistry Council promotes the sustainable growth of the polyurethane industry, by identifying and managing issues that could impact the industry, in cooperation with user groups. Members are producers and distributors of chemicals and equipment used to make polyurethane and manufacture polyurethane products.

4572 Chemical Coaters Association International
5040 Old Taylor Mill Rd
PMB 13
Taylor Mill, KY 41015

859-356-1030
800-926-2848
FAX 513-624-0601
E-Mail: aygoyer@one.net
Home Page: www.ccaiweb.com

Anne Goyer, Executive Director

A technical and professional organization that provides information and training on surface coating technologies. Users and suppliers of industrial cleaners, paints, coatings, and equipment.
1000 Members
Founded in 1970
Mailing list available for rent

4573 Chemical Development and Marketing Association (CDMA)
330 N. Wabash Avenue
Suite 2200
Chicago, IL 60611

312-321-5145
800-232-5241
FAX 312-673-6885
E-Mail: pdma@pdma.org
Home Page: www.cdmaonline.org/home.html

Theodre D. Goldman, President/Treasurer
Tom Regino, Executive Vice President
Eileen Strauss, Vice President/Webmaster
Maricy Bourgis, Vice President

A forum for networking, learning and sharing best practices in business development and marketing for the chemical and allied industries. Keeps members informed on commercial/business development and marketing as well as industrial marketing research via its two meetings per year (spring and fall), seminars and business schools.
Founded in 1999

4574 Chemical Fabrics and Film Association
1300 Sumner Avenue
Cleveland, OH 44115-2851

216-241-7333
FAX 216-241-0105
E-Mail: cffa@chemicalfabricsandfilm.com
Home Page: www.chemicalfabricsandfilm.com

Charles Stockinger, Executive Secretary

International trade association representing manufacturers of polymer-based fabric and film products, used in the building and construction, automotive, fashion and many other industries.
40 Members
Founded in 1927

4575 Chemical Heritage Foundation
315 Chestnut St
Philadelphia, PA 19106

215-925-2222
FAX 215-925-1954
E-Mail: info@chemheritage.org

Home Page: www.chemheritage.org
Social Media: *Facebook, Twitter, LinkedIn, Pinterest*

Tom Tritton, President/CEO
Miriam Schaefer, Special Advisor to the President
Michael Meyer, Editor-in-Chief

An independent, nonprofit organization, CHF maintains major collections of instruments, fine art, photographs, papers, and books. We host conferences and lectures, support research, offer fellowships, and produce educational materials.
29 Members
Founded in 1992

4576　Chemical Industry Data Exchange

401 North Michigan Avenue
Chicago, IL 60611-4267

312-321-5145
FAX 312-212-5971
E-Mail: memberservices@cidx.org
Home Page: www.cidx.org

JoAnne Norton, Executive Director
Laura Field, Communications

Promotes standards to improve the efficiency of transactions across the chemical industry supply chain. Members include chemical producers and companies active in the chemicals industry.

4577　Chemical Strategies Partnership

423 Washington St
4th Floor
San Francisco, CA 94111

415-421-3405
FAX 415-421-3304
Home Page: www.chemicalstrategies.org

Jill Kauffman Johnson, Executive Director
Angeline Kung, Senior Associate
Aarthi Ananthanarayanan, Associate
Max Pike, Communications Associate
Mark Stoughton, Ph.D., Research Advisor

CSP seeks to reduce chemical use, waste, risks and cost through the transformation of the chemical supply chain by redefining the way chemicals are used and sold.
Founded in 1978
Mailing list available for rent

4578　Chemtrec

1300 Wilson Blvd
Arlington, VA 22209-2323

703-741-5500
800-262-8200
FAX 703-741-6086
E-Mail: chemtrec@chemtrec.com
Home Page: www.chemtrec.com

A 24 hour emergency communication service center that helps fire fighters and emergency responders protect the public and helps shippers of hazardous materials comply with the US Department of Transportation regulations.
Founded in 1971

4579　Chlorinated Paraffins Industry Association

1250 Connecticut Ave NW
Suite 700
Washington, DC 20036

202-419-1500
FAX 202-659-8037
E-Mail: info@regnet.com
Home Page: www.regnet.com/cpia

Robert J Fensterheim, Executive Director

Composed of manufacturers, distributors, and users of chlorinated paraffins, used in lubricants, plastics and flame retardants.
Founded in 1970

4580　Chlorine Chemistry Division of the American Chemistry Counsil

700 Second St., NE
Washington, DC 20002

202-249-7000
FAX 202-249-6100
Home Page:
www.americanchemistry.com/s_chlorine/index.asp
Social Media: *Facebook, Twitter*

Calvin M. Dooley, President/CEO
Raymond J. O'Bryan, CFO & CAO
Robert J. Simon, Vice President, Chemical Products
Bryan Zumwalt, Vice President, Federal Affairs
Nacole B. Hinton, Managing Director, HR

This division represents major producers and users of chlorine in North America, working to promote and protect the sustainability of chlorine chemsitry processes, products and applications in accordance with the Responsible Care initiative.

4581　Chlorine Free Products Association

1304 S Main St
Algonquin, IL 60102-2757

847-658-6104
FAX 847-658-3152
E-Mail: info@chlorinefreeproducts.org
Home Page: www.chlorinefreeproducts.org
Social Media: *YouTube*

Archie Beaton, Executive Director

A nonprofit association that's primary purpose is to promote total chlorine free policies, programs and technologies throughtout the world.

4582　Chlorine Institute

1300 Wilson Blvd
Suite 525
Arlington, VA 22209

703-894-4140
FAX 703-894-4130
E-Mail: info@cl2.com
Home Page: www.chlorineinstitute.org

Frankÿ Reiner, President
Henry Ward, VP, Emergency Preparedness
Terry Cirone, VP Health, Environment
Robyn Kinsley, Director, Transportation
Anna Belousovitch, Project Coordinator

Supports the chlo-alkali industry and serves the public by promoting the safe handling of chlorine and caustic materials.
204 Members
Founded in 1924

4583　Chlorobenzene Producers Association

1850 M St Nw
Suite 700
Washington, DC 20036-5810

202-721-4100
FAX 202-296-8120
E-Mail: helmest@socma.com
Home Page: www.socma.com
Social Media: *Facebook, Twitter, LinkedIn, YouTube*

Larry Sloan, President/CEO
David Doles, Treasurer
Gene Williams, Secretary

Addresses health and environmental issues in response to Environmental Protection Agency.
40 Members
Founded in 1921

4584　Color Pigments Manufacturers Association

1850 M Street NW
Suite 730
Washington, DC 20036

202-465-4900
FAX 202-296-8120

E-Mail: cpma@cpma.com
Home Page: www.pigments.org

J Lawrence Robinson, President

An industry trade association representing color pigment companies in Canada, Mexico and the US. Represents small, medium, and large color pigments manufacturers accounting for 95% of the production of color pigments in North America
50 Members
Founded in 1925

4585　Combustion Institute

5001 Baum Blvd
Suite 644
Pittsburgh, PA 15213-1851

412-687-1366
FAX 412-687-0340
E-Mail: office@combustioninstitute.org
Home Page: www.combustioninstitute.org

Prof. Katrina Kohse-Hoinghaus, President
Prof. James F. Driscoll, VP, President Elect
Prof. Marcus Alden, Vice President Section Affairs
Prof. Reginald Mitchell, Secretary
Prof. Derek Dunn-Rankin, Treasurer

International organizaton with sections in several foreign countries including Canada. A non profit, educational organization with the purpose of promoting and disseminating knowledge in the field of combustion science.
4000 Members
Founded in 1954

4586　Consumer Specialty Products Association

1667 k street,NW
Suite 300
Washington, DC 20006

202-872-8110
FAX 202-223-2636
E-Mail: info@cspa.org
Home Page: www.cspa.org
Social Media: *Facebook, Twitter, LinkedIn, Flickr, Google+*

Christopher Cathcart, President and CEO
Keith Fulk, Senior Vice President, Controller
Holly Schroeder SPHR, Director, Administrative Services
Phil Klein, Executive Vice President
Laura Madden, Director, Government Affairs

Supports all professionals involved in the manufacturer of chemical specialties.
Founded in 1914
Mailing list available for rent

4587　Consumer Specialty Products Association

1667 K Street, NW
Suite 300
Washington, DC 20006-2501

202-872-8110
FAX 202-223-2636
E-Mail: info@cspa.org
Home Page: www.cspa.org
Social Media: *Facebook, Twitter, LinkedIn, Flickr, Google+*

Christopher Cathcart, President
Phil Klein, Executive Vice President
Colleen Creighton, Executive Director
Susan Little, Executive Director
Keith Fulk, Senior VP & Controller

Nonprofit organization composed of many companies involved in the formulation, manufacture, testing and marketing of chemical specialty products. Its line includes disinfectants that kill germs in homes, hospitals and restaurants, candles and fragrances that eliminate

odors, pest management products for home and garden, cleaning products and much more.
200 Members
Founded in 1914

4588 Council for Chemical Research
1120 Route 73
Suite 200
Mount Laurel, NJ 08054

856-439-0500
FAX 856-439-0525
E-Mail: info@ccrhq.org
Home Page: www.ccrhq.org
Social Media: *Facebook, LinkedIn*

Dr. Jeffrey A Reimer, Chair
Dr. Eriv Lin, 1st Vice Chair
Dr. Jeff Robert, 2nd Vice Chair
Dr. Seth W. Snyder, President
Dr. Kelly O. Sullivan, Treasurer

Promotes cooperation in basic research and encourage high quality education in the chemical sciences and engineering. Membership represents industry, academia, and government.
200 Members
Founded in 1980

4589 Council of Producers & Distributors of Agrotechnology
1730 Rhode Island Avenue
Suite 812
Washington, DC 20036

202-386-7407
FAX 202-386-7409
Home Page: www.cpda.com

Dr Susan Ferenc, President
Diane Schute, Director of Communications
John Boling, Director of Legislative Affairs
Dr. Michael C White, Ph.D., J.D., Director, Regulatory Affairs
Melvin A. Moore-Adams, Administrative Coordinator

The voice of the generic pesticide, inert, adjuvant and surfactant manufacturer, as well as crop protection product formulators and distributors on federal legislative and regulatory issues affecting the crop protection industry.
56 Members
Founded in 1975

4590 CropLife America
1156 15th St NW
Suite 400
Washington, DC 20005-1752

202-296-1585
FAX 202-463-0474
E-Mail: Info@croplifeamerica.org
Home Page: www.croplifeamerica.org
Social Media: *Facebook, Twitter, LinkedIn, Youtube*

Jay Vroom, President and CEO
Beau Greenwood, Executive VP
Bill Kuckuck, Executive Vice President
Dr. Barbara Glenn, Senior Vice President, Science
Rachel Lattimore, Senior Vice President

A trade association of the manufacturers, formulators, and distributors of agricultural crop protection, pest control, and bitechnology products. Membership is composed of companies that produce, sell and distribute virtually all the active ingredients use in crop protection chemicals.
86 Members
Founded in 1933
Mailing list available for rent

4591 Drug, Chemical & Associated Technologies Association
One Union St
Suite 208
Robbinsville, NJ 08691-3162

609-208-1888
800-640-3228
FAX 609-208-0599
E-Mail: info@dcat.org
Home Page: www.dcat.org
Social Media: *Facebook, LinkedIn*

George Svokos, President
Dr. Folker Ruchatz, First Vice President
Milton Boyer, Second Vice President
Joe Sutton, Third Vice President
David Beattie, Director

The not for profit, member supported business development association whose membership is comprimsed of companies that manufacture, distribute or provide services to the pharmaceutical, chemical, nutritional and related industries.
350 Members
Founded in 1890

4592 Embalming Chemical Manufacturers
1370 Honeyspot Road Ext
Stratford, CT 06615-7115

Works to develop scientific, technological, and economic data about safety issues of the product.
Founded in 1951

4593 Emulsion Poylmers Council
1250 Connecticut Ave NW
Suite 700
Washington, DC 20036-2657

202-419-1500
FAX 202-659-8037
E-Mail: epc@regnet.com
Home Page: www.regnet.com/epc/

Robert J Fensterheim, Executive Director

Represents regulatory professionals at companies which produce emulsion polymers, chemical compounds used in a variety of coating and other industril applications.
7 Members
Founded in 1995

4594 Ethylene Oxide Sterlization Association, Inc.
PO Box 33361
Washington, DC 20033

866-235-5030
FAX 202-557-3836
E-Mail: eosainfo@eosa.org
Home Page: www.eosa.org

Jonathan Bull, President
Fenil Sutaria, Vice President
Robert Bogart, Treasurer
Chris Klosen, Secretary

EOSA is a non-profit organization that works to educate industry, regulators, and the public on the uses and benefits of ethylene oxide. EOSA also works to improve safety standards, foster industry communication, and provide a forum for issues related to ethylene oxide sterilization.
23 Members
Founded in 1995

4595 Federation of Analytical Chemistry and Spectroscopy Societies
2019 Galisteo St
Building I-1
Santa Fe, NM 87505

505-820-1653
FAX 505-989-1073
E-Mail: facssc@facssc.org

Home Page: www.facss.org
Social Media: *Facebook, Twitter, LinkedIn*

Greg Klunder, Governing Board Chairperson
Steven Ray, Governing Board Chairperson Elect
Cindy Lilly, Executive Assistant
Christopher Palmer, Secretary 2009-2013
Mark Druy, Treasurer 2013 - 2015

Exists to combine many small meetings previously organized bythe individual societies into one joint meeting that covers the whole field of Analytical Chemistry.
12 Members
Founded in 1972

4596 Federation of Societies for Coatings Technology
1500 Rhode Island Ave., NW
Washington, DC 20005

202-462-6272
FAX 202-462-8549
E-Mail: aca@paint.org
Home Page: www.paint.org
Social Media: *Facebook, Twitter, LinkedIn*

J Andrew Doyle, President & CEO
Thomas J Graves, VP/General Counsel/Corporate Sec.
Allen Irish, Counsel / Director
Alison Keane, Vice President, Government Affairs
Jeff Wasikowski, Counsel

Provides technical education and professional development to its members and to the global industry through its multi-national constituent societies and collectively as a federation.
6000 Members
Founded in 1922

4597 Independent Liquid Terminals Association
1005 North Glebe Road
Suite 600
Arlington, VA 22201

703-875-2011
FAX 703-875-2018
E-Mail: info@ilta.org
Home Page: www.ilta.org

Wayne N Driggers, Chairman
Jamie Coleman, Vice Chairman
Gregory J Pound, Treasurer/Secretary
Kim Breaux, Director
Sam Brown, Director

Provides members with essential informational tools to facilitate regulatory compliance and improve operations, safety and environmental performance.
80 Members
Founded in 1974

4598 Independent Lubricant Manufacturers Association
400 N Columbus St
Suite 201
Alexandria, VA 22314

703-684-5574
FAX 703-836-8503
E-Mail: ilma@ilma.org
Home Page: www.ilma.org
Social Media: *Facebook, Twitter*

Frank H Hamilton III, President
Beth Ann Jones, Vice President
Dave Croghan, Treasurer
Barbara Kudis, Secretary
Barbara A Bellanti, Immediate Past President

Supports all those involved in the US and international independent lubricant industry.
Founded in 1948

4599 Institute for Polyacrylate Absorbents
1850 M St NW
Suite 700
Washington, DC 20036

202-721-4100
FAX 202-296-8120
Home Page: www.superabsorbents.com

C. Tucker Helmes Ph.D., Executive Director

Represents manufacturers and users of absorbent polymers made of cross-linked polyacrylates and manufacturers and users of acrylic acid or its salts. It addresses the scientific, regulatory and related issues which are likely to impact the manufacture, use and disposal of fluid-absorbing polyacrylates.
Founded in 1985

4600 International Cadmium Association
168 Avenue de Tervuren BOX4
Brussels, VA 22066

202-776-0073
FAX 202-776-0092
E-Mail: contact@cadmium.org
Home Page: www.cadmium.org

Hugh Morrow, Consultant

Provides marketing research and promotion to the industry. Hosts seperate annual meetings in the United States and Europe.
30 Members
Mailing list available for rent

4601 International Ozone Association: Pan American Group Branch
PO Box 97075
Las Vegas, NV 89193

480-529-3787
FAX 480-522-3080
E-Mail: infO3zone@io3a.org
Home Page: www.ioa-pag.org

Robert Jarnis, Executive Director

Represents the interests of environmental and other scientific communities, application engineers, users, and manufacturers of ozone generation and contacting equipment.
810 Members
Founded in 1973

4602 Materials Technology Institute, Inc.
1215 Fern Ridge Pkwy
Suite 206
St Louis, MO 63141

314-576-7712
FAX 314-576-6078
E-Mail: mtiadmin@mti-global.org
Home Page: www.mtiproducts.org

James Macki, Executive Director
Deborah Ehret, Operations Director
Albert Krisher, President

Provides leadership in materials technology for chemical processing to improve reliability, profitability and safety.
52 Members
Founded in 1977

4603 Methanol Institute
225 Reinekers Lane
Suite 205
Alexandria, VA 22314

703-248-3636
FAX 703-248-3997
E-Mail: MI@methanol.org
Home Page: www.methanol.org
Social Media: *Facebook, Twitter, LinkedIn*

Gregory A. Dolan, CEO
Christopher D Chatterton, COO
Dom LaVigne, Director of Gov. & Public Affairs
Lawrence Navin, Sr. Manager, External Affairs

& Ops
April Chan, Executive Manager

Our mission is to expand markets for the use of methanol as a chemical commodity and an energy fuel.
35 Members
Founded in 1989

4604 National Aerosol Association
PO Box 5510
Fullerton, CA 92838

714-525-1518
FAX 714-526-1295
E-Mail: NAA@nationalaerosol.com
Home Page: www.nationalaerosol.com

Harry Zechman, President
Steve Cook, Vice President
Bart Bastian, Past Presidentÿÿ
Craig Autry, Treasurer

Individuals, firms and agencies engaged in the development, manufacture, packaging, sale or distribution of aerosol products.
30 Members
Founded in 1986

4605 National Association of Chemical Recyclers
1900 M Street NW
Washington, DC 20036

202-296-1725
FAX 202-296-2530
E-Mail: 103612.514@compuserve.com

Christopher Goebel, Executive Director

Members are companies whose primary business is the reclamation of solvents and other chemicals from industrial waste streams and recycling.
Founded in 1979

4606 National Chemical Credit Association
500 Seneca Street
Suite 400
Buffalo, NY 14204-1963

844-462-6342
FAX 716-878-0479
E-Mail: robert.gagliardi@abc-amega.com
Home Page: www.abc-amega.com
Social Media: *Twitter, LinkedIn, YouTube, Google+*

Don Peters, Contact
Glenn Lifrieri, Executive Board Co-Chair
Pam Kelley, Executive Board Past-Chair
Paulo Menezes, Treasurer
Gordon Miller, Member at Large

Members are major producers of basic chemicals and allied products.
100 Members
Founded in 1938

4607 National Pest Management Association
10460 North Street
Fairfax, VA 22030

703-352-6762
800-678-6722
FAX 703-352-3031
Home Page: www.npmapestworld.org
Social Media: *Facebook, Twitter*

H Russell Ives, President
Chuck Tindol, President-Elect
Bryan Cooksey, Jr., Treasurer
Dennis Jenkins, Secretary
William A Tesh, Immediate Past President

Represents the interests of its members and the structural pest control industry.
7000 Members
Frequency: October
Founded in 1933

4608 North American Catalysis Society
PO Box 80262
Wilmington, DE 19880

302-695-2488
FAX 302-695-8347
E-Mail: michael.b.damore@usa.dupont.com
Home Page: www.nacatsoc.org

Enrique Igle-sia, President
Bruce R. Cook, VP
Hong-Xin Li, Secretary
C. Y Chen, Treasurer

Fosters an interest in heterogeneous and homogeneous catalysis. Organizes national meetings. Members are chemists and chemical engineers engaged in the study and use of reactions involving catalysts. Publishes a newsletter.
1400 Members
Founded in 1956
Mailing list available for rent: 3400 names

4609 Pine Chemicals Association
PO Box 17136
Fernandina Beach, FL 32035

404-994-6267
FAX 404-994-6267
E-Mail: wjones@pinechemicals.org
Home Page: www.pinechemicals.org
Social Media: *Facebook, Twitter, LinkedIn, YouTube*

Charles W Morris, President/COO
Steve Violette, Chairman/CEO
Amanda Young, Executive Director
Mike Roberts, Vice-Chairman
Lee Godina, Chairman & CEO

An association of producers, processors and consumers of pine chemicals. Promotes innovative, safe and environmentally responsible practices to assure a reliable supply of high quality products.
50 Members
Founded in 1947

4610 Polyisocyanurate Insulation Manufacturers Association
529 14th Street NW
Suite 750
Washington, DC 20045

301-654-0000
FAX 301-951-8401
E-Mail: pima@pima.org
Home Page: www.pima.org
Social Media: *Facebook, Twitter*

Renee Lamura, Director of Member Services
Jared O Blum, President

Represents the interests of polyisocyanurate manufacturers and suppliers to the industry. Efforts include education, environmental responsibility, government partnerships and energy conservation.
32 Members
Founded in 1970
Mailing list available for rent

4611 Polyurethane Foam Association
334 Lakeside Plz
Loudon, TN 37774

865-657-9840
FAX 865-381-1292
E-Mail: rluedeka@pfa.org
Home Page: www.pfa.org

Pat Martin, Chairman
Robert Luedeka, Executive Director

Suppliers of raw material and equipment. Associate members are manufacturers of flexible polyurethane foam. Our mission is to educate customers and other groups about flexible polyurethane foam and promote its use in manufactured and industrial products. This includes providing facts on environmental, health and safety issues related to polyurethane foam to

the membership of PFA, polyurethane foam users, regulatory officials, business leaders and the media.
63 Members
Founded in 1980

4612 Powder Coating Institute
5040 Old Taylor Mill Rd
PMB 13
Taylor Mill, KY 41015

859-525-9988
800-988-COAT
FAX 859-356-0908
E-Mail: pci-info@powdercoating.org
Home Page: www.powdercoating.org
Social Media: *Facebook, Twitter, LinkedIn, Pinterest*

John Cole, President
John Sudges, Vice President
Ron Cudzilo, Secretary/Treasurer
Bob Allsop, Director
John Cole, Secretary/ treasurer

A trade association representing suppliers of powder coating materials, equipment, and related products and services in North America.
325 Members
Founded in 1981
Mailing list available for rent

4613 Process Equipment Manufacturers Association
201 Park Washington Ct
Falls Church, VA 22046

703-538-1796
FAX 703-241-5603
E-Mail: info@pemanet.org
Home Page: www.pemanet.org

Susan A. Denston, Executive Director & Secretary
Harry W. Buzzerd, Management Counsel
Charlie Ingram, Treasurer
Chuck Weilbrenner, President
Jay Brown, Vice-President

Manufacturers and suppliers of equipment for food, chemical, pulp and paper, water, wastewater processing.
50 Members
Founded in 1960

4614 Society of Chemical Manufacturers and Affiliates
1850 M St Nw
Suite 700
Washington, DC 20036-5810

202-721-4100
FAX 202-296-8120
E-Mail: info@socma.com
Home Page: www.socma.com
Social Media: *Facebook, Twitter, LinkedIn, YouTube*

J. Steel Hutchinson, Chairman
Larry Sloan, President/ CEO
Tracy Devore, Manager
Tima Good, Account Executive
Sandra Lehrer, Senior Manager

Conducts workshops and seminars. Maintains a library on cancer policies and related subjects. Its member companies have more than 2,000 manufacturing sites and 100,000 employees.
300 Members
Founded in 1921

4615 Society of Cosmetic Chemists
120 Wall St
Suite 2400
New York, NY 10005-4088

212-668-1500
FAX 212-668-1504
E-Mail: scc@scconline.org

Home Page: www.scconline.org
Social Media: *Facebook, Twitter, LinkedIn*

Guy Padulo, President
Dawn Burke-Colvin, Vice President
David Smith, Executive Director
Dawn Thiel Glaser, Secretary
Peter Tsolis, Treasurer

Supports all those involved in working with and developing cosmetic chemicals.
4000 Members
Founded in 1945

4616 Society of Toxicology
1821 Michael Faraday Drive
Suite 300
Reston, VA 20190

703-438-3115
FAX 703-438-3113
E-Mail: sothq@toxicology.org
Home Page: www.toxicology.org
Social Media: *Facebook, Twitter, LinkedIn, Pinterest, Google+*

Peter L Goering, President
Patricia E Ganey, Vice President-Elect

Members are scientists concerned with the effects of chemicals on man and the environment. Promotes the acquisition and utilization of knowledge in toxicology, aids in the protection of public health and facilitates disciplines. The society has a strong commitment to education in toxicology and to the recruitment of students and new members into the profession.
5000 Members
Founded in 1961

4617 Spray Polyurethane Foam Alliance
3827 Old Lee Hwy.
#101B
Fairfax, VA 22030

800-523-6154
FAX 703-222-5816
E-Mail: info@sprayfoam.org
Home Page: www.sprayfoam.org
Social Media: *Facebook, Twitter*

Robert Duke, President
Dennis Vandewater, Vice President
Peter Davis, Secretary/Treasurer
Bill Baley, Board Member
Mac Sheldon, Board Member

A trade association representing interests associated with rigid and semi-rigid polyurethane foam products that are typically applied with spray equipment as roofing and insulation.
Founded in 1987
Mailing list available for rent

4618 The Electrochemical Society
65 South Main St
Building D
Pennington, NJ 08534-2839

609-737-1902
FAX 609-737-2743
E-Mail: esc@electrochem.org
Home Page: www.electrochem.org
Social Media: *Facebook, Twitter, LinkedIn*

Roque J Calvo, Executive Director
Mary E. Yess, Deputy Executive Director
Dinia Agarwala, Interface Production manager
Karen Chmielewski, Finance Associate
Paul B. Cooper, Editorial Manager

An international nonprofit, educational organization concerned with a broad range of phenomena relating to electrochemical and solid-state science and technology. The Electrochemical Society has scientists and engineers in over 70 countries worldwide who hold individual membership, as well as roughly 100 corporations and laboratories that hold corporate membership.
8000 Members
Founded in 1902

Newsletters

4619 AAB Bulletin
American Association of Bioanalysts
906 Olive Street
Suite 1200
Saint Louis, MO 63101-1448

314-241-1445
FAX 314-241-1449
E-Mail: aab@aab.org
Home Page: www.aab.org

Mark S Biernbaum PhD, Administrator

Newsletter that provides the latest information on meetings, conferences, legislative and regulatory issues and developments.
Frequency: Quarterly
Founded in 1956

4620 AACG Newsletter
American Association for Crystal Growth
25 4th Street
Somerville, NJ 08876-3205

908-575-0649
FAX 908-575-0794
E-Mail: aacg@att.net
Home Page: www.crystalgrowth.org

Candace Lynch, Chief Editor
Lara Keefer, Editor
Peter Schunemann, President
Robert Biefeld, Vice President

Technical articles and includes calendar of upcoming meetings.
Circulation: 600
ISSN: 1527-2389
Founded in 1966
Printed in 4 colors on glossy stock

4621 AATCC News
PO Box 12215
Research Triangle Park, NC 27709-2215

919-549-8141
800-360-5380
FAX 919-549-8933
E-Mail: danielsj@aatcc.org
Home Page: www.aatcc.org
Social Media: *Facebook, Twitter, LinkedIn*

John Daniels, Executive VP
Debra Hibbard, Executive Assistant
Chris Leonard, Technical Director

Free, emailed newsletter providing up-to-date news and feature articles.
3000 Members

4622 APE Newsletter
Alkylphenois & Ethoxylates Research Council
1250 Connecticut Ave Nw
Suite 700
Washington, DC 20036-2657

202-419-1506
866-273-7262
FAX 202-659-8037
E-Mail: angroup@regnet.com
Home Page: www.angroup.org

Robert J Fensterheim, Editor

4623 Adhesion Society Newsletter
Adhesion Society
2 Davidson Hall
Blacksburg, VA 24061-0001

540-231-7257
FAX 540-231-3971
E-Mail: adhesoc@vt.edu
Home Page: www.adhesionsociety.org

Esther Brann, Manager

4624 Advanced Coatings and Surface Technology
John Wiley & Sons
111 River St
Hoboken, NJ 07030-5790

201-748-6000
FAX 201-748-6088
E-Mail: info@wiley.com
Home Page: www.wiley.com

William J Pesce, CEO

Provides intelligence service reports and puts into perspective significant developments in coatings and surface modification across a broad range of industry lines. ACT interprets developments ranging from traditional coating processes to chemical vapor deposition and iron beam methods, which offers interdisciplinary analyses of those that have true commercial potential.
Cost: $530.00
10 Pages
Frequency: Monthly
Founded in 1807

4625 Amber-Hi-Lites
Rohm And Haas Company
100 S Independence Mall W
Suite 1A
Philadelphia, PA 19106-2399

215-592-3000
FAX 215-592-3377
Home Page: www.rohmhaas.com

Raj L Gupta, CEO

Offers discussions of ion exchange resin use in fields of water conditioning.

4626 Analytical Chemistry
American Chemical Society
1155 16th St Nw
Suite 600
Washington, DC 20036-4892

202-872-4600
800-227-5558
FAX 202-872-4615
E-Mail: service@acs.org
Home Page: www.acs.org

Madeleine Jacobs, CEO
Elizabeth Zubritsky, Manager

Information and news on the chemical industry.
Founded in 1876

4627 Biochemistry
American Chemical Society
1155 16th St Nw
Suite 600
Washington, DC 20036-4892

202-872-4600
800-333-9511
FAX 202-872-4615
E-Mail: service@acs.org
Home Page: www.acs.org

Madeleine Jacobs, CEO

News and information for the scientific community.
Cost: $137.00
Frequency: Weekly
Founded in 1876

4628 ChemEcology
Chemical Manufacturers Association
1300 Wilson Boulevard
Arlington, VA 22209-2307

703-741-5502
FAX 703-741-6807

Rebecca Swinehart, Editor
Issues on health, safety and the environment.

4629 ChemWeek Association
ChemWeek

110 William St
Suite 11
New York, NY 10038-3910

212-621-4900
FAX 212-621-4800
E-Mail: ltattum@chemweek.com
Home Page: www.chemweek.com

John Rockwell, VP
Joe Mennella, Global Sales Director

Comprehensive coverage of the latest developments, uses, production, distribution, and manufacturing of chemicals for all industries.
Cost: $159.00
Frequency: Monthly
Circulation: 20779
Founded in 1977

4630 Chemical Bond
American Chemical Society
1155 16th St Nw
Suite 600
Washington, DC 20036-4892

202-872-4600
800-227-5558
FAX 202-872-4615
E-Mail: service@acs.org
Home Page: www.acs.org

Madeleine Jacobs, CEO

Covers organization activities.

4631 Chemical Bulletin
American Chemical Society
Ste 312
1400 Renaissance Dr
Park Ridge, IL 60068-1336

847-647-8405
FAX 847-647-8364
E-Mail: chicagoacs@ameritech.net
Home Page: www.chicagoacs.org

Gail Wilkening, Office Manager

Highlights events and meetings of local chapters, profiles prominent society members, and reports on research and technological advancements in the field.
Cost: $20.00
Frequency: Monthly
Circulation: 5700

4632 Chemical Economics Handbook Program
SRI Consulting
4300 Bohannon Dr
Suite 200
Menlo Park, CA 94025-1042

650-384-4300
FAX 650-330-1190
Home Page: www.sriconsulting.com

John Pearson, President/CEO

Ongoing multiclient program focusing on the chemical and allied products industries. History, status and projected trends for hundreds of chemicals, chemical raw materials, and end-use products. Service includes access to on-line data base and client inquiry privileges.
Cost: $12000.00
Frequency: Monthly
Founded in 1946

4633 Chemical Industries Newsletter
SRI International
333 Ravenswood Ave
Menlo Park, CA 94025-3493

650-859-3711
FAX 650-326-8916
Home Page: www.srifcu.org

Steve Bowles, President

Articles discuss the activities of SRI International Chemical Industries Centers.

4634 Chemical Industry Monitoring
Cyrus J Lawrence
1290 Avenue of the Americas
New York, NY 10006
Don Pattison, Editor

Prices and technological developments in the industry.

4635 Chemical Product News
US Dept. of Commerce, Business & Defense Service
200 Constitution Ave Nw
Washington, DC 20210-0001

202-693-5000
FAX 202-219-8822
Home Page: www.dol.gov

Hilda L Solis, CEO

Offers information about chemical products and related issues.

4636 Chemical Regulation Reporter
Bureau of National Affairs
1801 S Bell St
Arlington, VA 22202-4501

703-341-3000
800-372-1033
FAX 202-452-4084
E-Mail: customercare@bna.com
Home Page: www.bnabooks.com

Paul N Wojcik, Chairman

A notification and reference service consisting of six binders that comprehensively covers federal chemical regulations.
Cost: $1103.00
Frequency: Weekly
Founded in 1929

4637 Chemical and Engineering News
American Chemical Society
1155 16th St Nw
Suite 600
Washington, DC 20036-4892

202-872-4600
800-227-5558
FAX 202-872-4615
E-Mail: service@acs.org
Home Page: www.acs.org

Madeleine Jacobs, CEO

Covers news relating to chemical engineering and technology.
Frequency: Weekly
Circulation: 137,664
ISSN: 0009-2347
Founded in 1876

4638 Chemweek's Business Daily
Chemical Week/Access Intelligence
110 William St
Suite 11
New York, NY 10038-3910

212-621-4900
FAX 212-621-4800
E-Mail: ltattum@chemweek.com
Home Page: www.chemweek.com

John Rockwell, VP
Joe Minnella, Global Sales Manager

Daily electronic newsletter covering the latest chemical industry business and financial news, including markets, pricing, regulatory and security issues, research, technologies and new services.
Cost: $1049.00
Frequency: Daily
Founded in 2002
Printed in 4 colors

4639 Chlor-Alkali Marketwire
Chemical Week/Access Intelligence

110 William St
Suite 11
New York, NY 10038-3910

212-621-4900
FAX 212-621-4800
E-Mail: ltattum@chemweek.com
Home Page: www.chemweek.com

John Rockwell, VP
Joe Mennella, Global Sales Director

Weekly electronic newsletter covering chlor-al-kali market sector, including market trends in supply and demand, pricing fluctuations, production rates in caristic soda and chlorine. Also covers vinyls, soda ash and related derivatives
Cost: $1699.00
Frequency: Weekly
Founded in 2002
Printed in 4 colors

4640 Chlorine Institute Newsletter

Chlorine Institute
1300 Wilson Blvd
Arlington, VA 22209-2323

703-741-5760
FAX 703-894-4130
E-Mail: aonna@cl2.com
Home Page: www.chlorineinstitute.org

Arthur Dungan, President

Articles featuring safe handling of chlorine and caustic materials.
5 Pages
Printed in 2 colors on matte stock

4641 Clinical & Forensic Toxicology News

1850 K St NW
Suite 625
Washington, DC 20006-2215

202-857-0717
800-892-1400
FAX 202-887-5093
Home Page: www.aacc.org
Social Media: *Facebook, Twitter, LinkedIn, YouTube*

Greg rd Miller, President
Nancy Sasavage, Ph.D., Editor
Robert Dofour, Treasury

Online only newsletter provides practical and timely information on the clinical, forensic, technical, and regulatory issues faced by toxicology laboratories.

4642 Clinical Laboratory Strategies

1850 K St NW
Suite 625
Washington, DC 20006-2215

202-857-0717
800-892-1400
FAX 202-887-5093
Home Page: www.aacc.org
Social Media: *Facebook, Twitter, LinkedIn, YouTube*

Richard Flaherty, VP
Penelope Jones, Director

Online newsletter for laboratory directors and managers gives strategic information on how to better manage the changes faced in jobs every day.

4643 Composites and Adhesives Newsletter

T/C Press
223 S Detroit Street
PO Box 36006
Los Angeles, CA 90036

323-938-7023
FAX 323-938-6923
E-Mail: tcpress@msn.com

Mark Albert, Editor-In-Chief
Sherry Baranek, Senior Editor
Tom Beard, Senior VP
Lori Beckman, Managing Editor

News about composites and adhesives industry. Accepts very limited and selective advertising.
Cost: $190.00
20 Pages
Frequency: Quarterly
Circulation: 300
ISSN: 0888-1227
Founded in 1984

4644 Electronic Chemicals News

Chemical Week Associates
2 Grand Central Tower
140 E. 45th St., 40th Floor
New York, NY 10017

212-884-9528
FAX 212-884-9514
E-Mail: lyn.tattum@ihs.com
Home Page: www.chemweek.com

Lyn Tattum, Publisher & Director
Natasha Alperowicz, Executive Editor

Written for and about the chemicals industry and contains industry developments, environmental news, new products, and financial and corporate briefs.
Cost: $699.00

4645 Government Affairs Update

American Association for Clinical Chemistry
1850 K St NW
Suite 625
Washington, DC 20006-2215

202-857-0717
800-892-1400
FAX 202-887-5093
Home Page: www.ashrae.org
Social Media: *Facebook, Twitter, LinkedIn, YouTube*

Richard Flaherty, VP
Penelope Jones, Director

Online government affairs newsletter presents a comprehensive summary of legislative and government news that affect clinical labs and manufacturers.

4646 ILTA Newsletter

Independent Liquid Terminals Association
1444 I St Nw
Suite 400
Washington, DC 20005-6538

202-842-9200
FAX 202-326-8660
E-Mail: info@ilta.org
Home Page: www.ilta.org

E David Doane, President

International trade association representing bulk liquid terminal companies that store commercial liquids in aboveground storage tanks and transfer products to and from oceangoing tank ships, tank barges, pipelines, tank trucks, and tank rail cars.
Frequency: Monthly
Circulation: 1200
Founded in 1974
Printed in 2 colors on matte stock

4647 Inside R&D

John Wiley & Sons
111 River St
Hoboken, NJ 07030-5790

201-748-6000
FAX 201-748-6088
E-Mail: info@wiley.com
Home Page: www.wiley.com

William J Pesce, CEO

Weekly service offering information about current research and development, concentrating on new and significant developments that create new products/markets in the near-term and

this are valuable to a company's bottom line.
Cost: $790.00
6 Pages
Frequency: Weekly
Founded in 1807
Mailing list available for rent

4648 Langmuir: QTL Biosystems

American Chemical Society
1322 Pouseo de Peralta
Santa Fe, NM 87501

505-989-1907
FAX 505-989-1979
E-Mail: service@acs.org
Home Page: www.pubs.acs.org

David Whitten PhD, Editor

Edited for an audience involved with high-vacuum surface chemistry and spectroscopy, heterogeneous catalysis, all aspects of interface chemistry involving fluid interfaces and disperse systems.
Frequency: BiWeekly
Circulation: 1,200

4649 North American Catalysis Society Newsletter

PO Box 80262
Wilmington, DE 19880-262

302-695-2488
FAX 302-695-8347
E-Mail: michael.b.damore@usa.dupont.com
Home Page: www.nacatsoc.org

Michael B D Amore, Editor
John N Armor, President
Gary McVicker, VP

Fosters an interest in heterogeneous and homogeneous catalysis. Organizes national meetings. Members are chemists and chemical engineers engaged in the study and use of reactions involving catalysts.
Cost: $45.00
38448 Pages
Frequency: Monthly
Founded in 1956
Mailing list available for rent: 3,500 names at $160 per M

4650 Pine Chemicals Association Newsletter

3350 Riverwood Parkway SE
Suite 1900
Atlanta, GA 30339

770-984-5340
FAX 404-994-6267
E-Mail: wjones@pinechemicals.org
Home Page: www.pinechemicals.org

Walter L Jones, President/COO
Gary Reed, Chairman/Board of Directors

An association of producers, processors and consumers of pine chemicals. Promotes innovative, safe and environmentally responsible practices to assure a reliable supply of high quality products.
Frequency: Quarterly

4651 SOCMA Newsletter

Synthetic Organic Chemical Manufacturers Assn
1850 M St Nw
Suite 700
Washington, DC 20036-5803

202-721-4100
FAX 202-296-8120
E-Mail: info@socma.com
Home Page: www.socma.com

Joseph Acker, President
Vivian Diko, Executive Assistant & CEO
Liesa Brown,
Editor/Marketing/Communications

Offers information on the organic chemical industry.
10 Pages
Frequency: Bi-monthly
Founded in 1921

Magazines & Journals

4652 AATCC Review Journal
PO Box 12215
Research Triangle Park, NC 27709-2215

919-549-8141
800-360-5380
FAX 919-549-8933
E-Mail: danielsj@aatcc.org
Home Page: www.aatcc.org
Social Media: *Facebook, Twitter, LinkedIn*

John Daniels, Executive VP
Debra Hibbard, Executive Assistant
Charles E Gavin, Treasurer
Chris Shaw, Advertising Sales

Covers fibers to finished products, and chemical synthesis to retail practices.
3000 Members

4653 AICHE Journal
American Institute of Chemical Engineers
3 Park Ave
New York, NY 10016-5991

212-591-7338
800-242-4363
FAX 212-591-8888
E-Mail: CustomerService@aiche.org
Home Page: www.aiche.org
Social Media: *Facebook, Twitter, LinkedIn*

June Wispelwey, Executive Director
Steve Smith, Publications Director
Bette Lawler, Director of Operations
Neil Yeoman, Treasurer

Serves as a journal emcompassing data and results of the latest information in significant research and trends in the field.
Cost: $1250.00
Frequency: Monthly
ISSN: 0001-1541
Founded in 1908

4654 Accounts of Chemical Research
American Chemical Society
1155 16th St NW
Suite 600
Washington, DC 20036-4892

202-872-4600
800-227-5558
FAX 202-872-4615
E-Mail: service@acs.org
Home Page: www.acs.org

Madeleine Jacobs, CEO

Chemical research and statistical information.
Cost: $526.00
Frequency: Monthly
Circulation: 159,000
Founded in 1968

4655 Advanced Coatings and Surface Technology
605 3rd Avenue
9th Floor
New York, NY 10158

212-850-6824
FAX 212-850-8643

4656 American Laboratory
International Scientific Communications

395 Oyster Pint Blvd.
#321
South San Francisco, CA 94080

650-243-5600
E-Mail: info@americanlaboratory.com
Home Page: www.americanlaboratory.com

Brian Howard, Editor-In-Chief
Robert G Sweeny, Publisher
Donna Frankel, Direcetor Of Editorial
Susan Messinger, Managing Editor

American Laboratory serves industry, university, government, independent and foundation research laboratories.
50 Pages
Frequency: Monthly
Circulation: 91611
ISSN: 0044-7749
Founded in 1969
Printed in 4 colors on glossy stock

4657 An Energy Efficient Solution
Alliance for Responsible Atmoshperic Policy
2111 Wilson Blvd
Suite 850
Arlington, VA 22201-3001

703-243-0344
FAX 703-243-2874
E-Mail: info@arap.org
Home Page: www.arap.org

David Stirpe, Executive Director

4658 Asia Pacific Chemicals
Reed Chemical Publications
360 Park Avenue South
10th Floor
New York, NY 10010

713-525-2613
888-525-3255
E-Mail: jlucas@chemexpo.com
Home Page: www.reedchemicals.com

Stanley F Reed
Bernard Petersen, Sales Manager
Karen Yanard, Sales Executive
Alan Taylor, Editor

4659 Asian Chemical News
Reed Chemical Publications
360 Park Avenue South
10th Floor
New York, NY 10010

212-791-4208
888-525-3255
E-Mail: csc@icis.com
Home Page: www.reedchemicals.com

Stanley F Reed
Bernard Petersen, Sales Manager
Karen Yanard, Sales Executive
Alan Taylor, Editor

4660 CPI Purchasing
Reed Business Information
2000 Clearwater Dr
Oak Brook, IL 60523-8809

630-574-0825
FAX 630-288-8781
E-Mail: k.doyle@reedbusiness.com
Home Page: www.reedbusiness.com

Jeff Greisch, President
Kathy Doyle, Publisher

Trade magazine for purchasing professionals in the chemical/process industry. Accepts advertising.
Cost: $74.95
100 Pages
Circulation: 95078
Founded in 1983

4661 Cereal Chemistry
American Association of Cereal Chemists

3340 Pilot Knob Rd
Eagan, MN 55121-2055

651-454-7250
FAX 651-454-0766
E-Mail: akohn@scisoc.org
Home Page: www.mbaa.com

Mary Ellen Camire, President
Bernie Bruinsma, Chair of Board
Laura Hansen, Treasurer

Cereal chemistry explores raw materials, processes and products utulizing cereal.
Cost: $79.00
Frequency: Bi-Monthly
ISSN: 0009-0352

4662 Chemical Engineering
Chemical Week Associates
2 Grand Central Tower
140 East 45th Street,40th Floor
New York, NY 10017

212-884-9528
FAX 212-884-9514
E-Mail: ltattum@chemweek.com
Home Page: www.chemweek.com

Lyn Tattum, Publisher/Director
Robert Westervelt, Editor-In-Chief

Highlights include a calendar of related trade shows, new products listings, operations and maintenance techniques and marketing services ideas.
Cost: $59.00
Frequency: Monthly
Circulation: 69000
ISSN: 0009-2460
Founded in 1902
Printed in 4 colors on glossy stock

4663 Chemical Engineering Progress
American Institute of Chemical Engineers
3 Park Ave
New York, NY 10016-5991

203-702-7660
800-242-4363
FAX 203-775-5177
E-Mail: CustomerService@aiche.org
Home Page: www.aiche.org

June Wispelwey, Executive Director
Marty Clancy, Director Membership/Cust. Service

Offers updated information for chemical engineers.
Cost: $245.00
Frequency: Quarterly
Founded in 1908

4664 Chemical Equipment
Reed Business Information
301 Gibraltar Drive
PO Box 650
Morris Plains, NJ 07950-650

973-920-7000
FAX 973-539-3476
E-Mail: privacymanager@reedbusiness.com
Home Page: www.reedbusiness.com

Bud Ramsey, Publisher
Geoffery Bridgman, Editor
Gerard Van de Aast, CEO/President

Chemical Equipment is for engineers, plant management personnel, maintenance engineering and others concerned with design, building, engineering, operating and maintaining chemical process plants.
Frequency: Monthly
Circulation: 106032
Founded in 1959

4665 Chemical Equipment Literature Review
Reed Business Information

St 600
Rockaway
New Jersey, NJ 07866

973-920-7000
800-222-0289
FAX 973-920-7531
E-Mail: plundy@reedbusiness.com
Home Page: www.chemicalequipment.com

Geoff Bridgman, Editor
Gail Kirberger, Circulation Manager
Patrick Lundy, Publisher

Covers reviews of new catalogs and brochures
on products for the chemical industry.
8 Pages
Frequency: Monthly
Circulation: 106038
Founded in 1985

4666 Chemical Heritage
Chemical Heritage Foundation
315 Chestnut St
Philadelphia, PA 19106-2793

215-925-2222
FAX 215-925-1954
E-Mail: info@chemheritage.org
Home Page: www.chemheritage.org

Michal Meyer, Editor

Dedicated to sharing the story chemistry and
related sciences, technologies, and industries.
48 Pages
Circulation: 25000
ISSN: 0736-4555

4667 Chemical Intelligencer
Springer Verlag
233 Spring St
Suite 6
New York, NY 10013-1578

212-460-1500
800-777-4643
FAX 212-460-1575
E-Mail: serviceny@springer.com
Home Page: www.springer.com

William Curtis, President

Written for the scientist interested in the history and culture of chemistry. Includes articles
and essays that develop and comment on the
current directions and concerns in chemistry,
new discoveries and experiments as well as
present trends and opportunities in chemistry,
philosophy and education.
Cost: $79.00
Frequency: Quarterly
Circulation: 1,000

4668 Chemical Management Review
Reed Chemical Publications
2 Wall St
26th Floor, Suite 13
New York, NY 10005-2044

212-732-3200
FAX 212-791-4311
E-Mail:
helga.tilton@chemicalmarketreporter.com
Home Page: www.reedchemicals.com

Stanley F Reed
Helga Tilton, Editor
Keith Jones, CEO/President
Jane Burgess, Marketing

Provides information for senior managers in
the chemical industry and other industrial mar-
kets.
Cost: $195.00
Frequency: Monthly
Founded in 1871
Printed in 4 colors on glossy stock

4669 Chemical Market Reporter
Schnell Publishing Company

2 Rector St
26th Floor
New York, NY 10006-1819

212-791-4267
FAX 212-791-4321
E-Mail: editor@chemexpo.com
Home Page: www.chemexpo.com

James Hannan, Publisher
Helga Tilton, Editor in Chief

Regular issue highlights include news of the
week, coverage of pertinent industry trade
shows/meetings, a review of new materials, and
periodic insight reports on segments of the industry.
Cost: $109.00
Frequency: Weekly
Circulation: 14714

4670 Chemical Processing
Putman Media
555 W Pierce Rd
Suite 301
Itasca, IL 60143-2626

630-467-1300
FAX 630-467-0197
E-Mail: chemicalprocessing@putman.net
Home Page: www.putman.net

Mark Rosenzweig, Editor-in-Chief
Amanda Joshi, Managing Editor

Carries technical overview and case history ar-
ticles presented in a problem-solving environ-
ment geared to operations, engineering and
R&D management. Topics include instrumenta-
tion, pumping, corrosion, heat transfer, mixing
and energy conservation. Accepts advertising.
60 Pages
Frequency: Monthly
Circulation: 55000
ISSN: 0009-2630
Founded in 1938
Printed in 4 colors

4671 Chemical Times & Trends
Allen Press
900 17th St NW
Washington, DC 20006-2106

202-872-8110
FAX 202-872-8114
E-Mail: info@cspa.org
Home Page: www.cspa.org

Christopher Cathcart, President
Keith Fulk, Vice President & Controller

Editorial focus emphasizes trends in legisla-
tion, industry events, packaging topics, and
marketing concepts.
Cost: $27.00
Frequency: Quarterly
Circulation: 7000
Founded in 1935

4672 Chemist
American Institute of Chemists
315 Chestnut St
Suite 420
Philadelphia, PA 19106-2702

215-873-8224
FAX 215-925-1954
E-Mail: info@theaic.org
Home Page: www.theaic.org

Davidah Manuta, President
Ray Mcafel, President-Elect
Jerry d Jasinski, Chair

Topics of professional, economic, social and
legislative interest to individual chemists or
chemical engineers.
Cost: $35.00
32 Pages
Frequency: Quarterly
Circulation: 5000
Founded in 1923

4673 Chemistry Research in Technology
American Chemical Society
1155 16th St NW
Suite 600
Washington, DC 20036-4892

202-872-4600
800-227-5558
FAX 202-872-4615
E-Mail: service@acs.org
Home Page: www.acs.org

Madeleine Jacobs, CEO/Executive Director
Elizabeth Zubritsky, Manager

Information and research summaries of the lat-
est in the chemical industry.
Cost: $49.00
Frequency: 1 Year 3 Issues
Founded in 1876

4674 Clinical Chemistry
1850 K St NW
Suite 625
Washington, DC 20006-2215

202-857-0717
800-892-1400
FAX 202-887-5093
Home Page: www.aacc.org
*Social Media: Facebook, Twitter, LinkedIn,
YouTube*

Nadar Rifai, Editor-In-Chief
Tom Annesley, Deputy Editor
James Boyd, Deputy Editor

The leading forum for peer-reviewed, original
research on innovative practices in today's clinical laboratory.

4675 Clinical Laboratory News
1850 K St NW
Suite 625
Washington, DC 20006-2215

202-857-0717
800-892-1400
FAX 202-887-5093
Home Page: www.aacc.org
*Social Media: Facebook, Twitter, LinkedIn,
YouTube*

Robert Christenson, President
Dennis Dietzen, Director
Elizabeth Frank, Secretary

News magazine that is the authoritative source
for timely analysis of issues and trends affecting clinical laboratorians and clinical
laboratories.
Founded in 1948

4676 Coatings World
Rodman Publishing
70 Hilltop Rd
3rd Floor, Suite 3000
Ramsey, NJ 07446-1150

201-825-2552
FAX 201-825-0553
E-Mail: info@rodpub.com
Home Page: www.nutraceuticalsworld.com

Rodman Zilenziger Jr, President
Matt Montgomery, VP

Cutting edge technical information and the
most advanced and pertinent management and
distribution techniques.
Frequency: 10 issues per y
Circulation: 17000
Founded in 1964

4677 Combustion and Flame
Combustion Institute
5001 Baum Blvd.
Suite 635
Pittsburgh, PA 15213-1851

412-687-1366
FAX 412-687-0340

E-Mail: office@combustioninstitute.org
Home Page: www.combustioninstitute.org

Barbara Waronek, Executive Administrator
Prof. Katherine Kohs-Hosinghaus, President
Derek Dunn-Rankin, Treasurer

A monthly publication that focuses on combustion phenomena and related topics.
6000 Members
Frequency: Monthly
Founded in 1954

4678 Compoundings Magazine
Independent Lubricant Manufacturers
Association
651 S Washington Street
Alexandria, VA 22314

703-684-5574
FAX 703-836-8503
E-Mail: ilma@ilma.org
Home Page: www.ilma.org

Tom Osborne, Editor
Martha Jolkovski, Director Publications &
Advertising
Carla Mangone, Managing Editor

Association and marketing news, meetings and programs, as well as employment and business opportunities to the US and international independent lubricant industry.
Cost: $150.00
Frequency: Monthly
Circulation: 2050
ISSN: 1042-508X
Founded in 1948
Printed in 4 colors on glossy stock

4679 Energy Process
American Institute of Chemical Engineers
3 Park Ave
New York, NY 10016-5991

212-591-7338
800-242-4363
FAX 212-591-8888
Home Page: www.aiche.org

John Sofranko, Executive Director

Offers updated information for chemical engineers.
Cost: $20.00
Frequency: Quarterly

4680 European Chemical News
Reed Chemical Publications
Wall St
26th Floor, Suite 13
New York, NY 10005-2044

212-732-3200
FAX 212-791-4311
E-Mail: jonathan.sismey@icis.com
Home Page: www.europeanchemicalnews.com

Stanley F Reed
Simon Platt, Director
Christopher Flook, Managing Director
Cost: $711.00
Frequency: Weekly
Circulation: 14112

4681 European Journal of Clinical Chemistry and Clinical Biochemistry
Walter De Gruyter
200 Saw Mill Road
Hawthorne, NY 1052

Home Page: journalseek.net/

Water De Gruyler, Editor

Up-to-date information on the chemistry industry.
Frequency: Monthly

4682 HAPPI Household and Personal Products Industry
Rodman Publishing

70 Hilltop Rd
3rd Floor
Ramsey, NJ 07446-1150

201-825-2552
FAX 201-825-0553
E-Mail: info@rodpub.com
Home Page: www.nutraceuticalsworld.com

Rodman Zilenziger Jr, President
Matt Montgomery, VP

Highlights current developments, marketing, production, formulations, technical innovations, packaging, and management problems. Includes in-depth news on developments abroad as well as in the United States.
Cost: $52.00
Frequency: Monthly
Circulation: 140000
Founded in 1964

4683 I&EC Research
American Chemical Society
1155 16th St NW
Suite 600
Washington, DC 20036-4892

202-872-4600
800-227-5558
FAX 202-872-4615
E-Mail: service@acs.org
Home Page: www.acs.org

Madeleine Jacobs, CEO/Executive Director

Offers information and statistical updates for chemists.
Circulation: 4600
Founded in 1876

4684 IHS Chemical Week
2 Grand Central Tower
140 E 45th St., 40th Fl.
New York, NY 10017

212-884-9528
FAX 212-884-9514
Home Page: www.chemweek.com
Social Media: *Facebook, Twitter, LinkedIn, YouTube*

Lyn Tattum, Publisher
Robert Westervelt, Editor-in-chief

News and analysis from the chemical, petrochemical and specialty chemical industries.

4685 Industrial & Engineering Chemistry Research
American Chemical Society
1155 16th St NW
Suite 600
Washington, DC 20036-4892

202-872-4600
800-227-5558
FAX 202-872-4615
E-Mail: help@acs.org
Home Page: www.acs.org

Madeleine Jacobs, CEO/Executive Director
Judith Benham, Chair
Elizabeth Zubritsky, Manager

Features fundamental research, design methods, process design and development, product research and development for chemists and chemical engineers.
Circulation: 4600
Founded in 1876

4686 Inform
American Oil Chemists' Society
2710 S Boulder
Urbana, IL 61802-6996

217-359-2344
FAX 217-351-8091
E-Mail: keine@aocs.org
Home Page: www.aocs.org

Lori Stewart, Publications Director
Kimmy Farris, Production Editor

Kethy Heine, Managing Editor
Patrick Donnelly, CEO

A member benefit that provides international news on fats, oils, surfactants, detergents, and related materials.
Cost: $175.00
100 Pages
Frequency: Monthly
Circulation: 4500
ISSN: 0897-8026
Founded in 1990
Printed in 4 colors on glossy stock

4687 International Laboratory
International Scientific Communications
PO Box 870
Shelton, CT 06484-0870

203-926-9300
FAX 203-926-9310
E-Mail: webmaster@iscpubs.com
Home Page: www.iscpubs.com/

Brian Howard, Publisher
Robert G Sweeney, Publisher

International Laboratory serves the industry, universities, government, independent and foundation research laboratories.
50 Pages
Circulation: 50036
ISSN: 0010-2164
Founded in 1971
Printed in 4 colors on glossy stock

4688 International Laboratory Pacific Rim Edition
International Scientific Communications
PO Box 870
Shelton, CT 06484-0870

203-926-9300
FAX 203-926-9310
E-Mail: webmaster@iscpubs.com
Home Page: www.iscpubs.com

Brian Howard, Publisher
Robert G Sweeney, Publisher

Edited for chemists and biologists throughout Far East Asia and Australia who have a professional interest in various aspects of modern laboratory practice and basic research.
40 Pages
Founded in 1986

4689 Journal of AOAC International
AOAC International
481 N Frederick Ave
Suite 500
Gaithersburg, MD 20877-2450

301-924-7078
800-379-2622
FAX 301-924-7089
E-Mail: aoac@aoac.org
Home Page: www.aoac.org

James Bradford, Executive Director

Publishes fully refereed contributed papers in the fields of chemical and biological analysis: on original research on new techniques and applications, collaborative studies, authentic data of composition, studies leading to method development, meeting symposia, newly adopted AOAC approved methods and invited reviews.
Cost: $98.00

4690 Journal of Analytical Toxicology
Preston Publications
6600 W Touhy Ave
PO Box 48312
Niles, IL 60714-4516

847-647-2900
FAX 847-647-1155

E-Mail: circulation@jatox.com
Home Page: www.prestonpub.com

Tinsley Preston, Owner
Dr. Bruce A. Goldberger, Editor
Maria Tamacho, Circulation Manager

An international publication for toxicologists, pathologists, analytical chemists, researchers, educators and others. Dedicated to the isolation, indentification, and quantification of potentially toxic substances. Emphasis is on the practical applications for use in clinical, forensic, industrial, and other toxicology laboratories, drug abuse testing, therapeutic drug monitoring, and environmental pollution. Includes new products and litrature, meetings and short courses.
Cost: $475.00
Frequency: 8 issues per ye
Circulation: 1148
Founded in 1977
Mailing list available for rent: 9939 names at $125 per M

4691 Journal of Biological Chemistry
9650 Rockville Pike
Suite 300
Bethesda, MD 20814-3999

301-530-7150
FAX 301-634-7126
E-Mail: publicaffairs@asbmb.org
Home Page: www.asbmb.org

Herbert Taber, Editor
Barbara Gordon, Executive Director

Features research papers on biochemistry and molecular biology and other articles of interest to the professional.
Frequency: TriAnnual

4692 Journal of Chemical Education
Division of Chemical Education
Department of Chemistry
University of Georgia
Athens, GA 30602-2556

706-542-6559
FAX 706-542-9454
E-Mail: norbert-pienta@jce.acs.org
Home Page: www.pubs.acs.orgorg
Social Media: Facebook, Twitter

Norbert J Oienta, Editor-in-Chief
Renee S. Cole, Associate Editor

Provides information about and examples of teaching techniques for classroom and laboratory, curricular innovations, chemistry content, and chemical education research.
Cost: $45.00
136 Pages
Frequency: Monthly
ISSN: 0021-9584
Founded in 1924
Printed in on glossy stock

4693 Journal of Chemical Information & Computer Sciences
American Chemical Society
1155 16th St NW
Suite 600
Washington, DC 20036-4892

202-872-4600
800-227-5558
FAX 202-872-4615
E-Mail: service@acs.org
Home Page: www.acs.org

Madeleine Jacobs, CEO/Executive Director
George A. Milne, Editor

Offers the latest technological information and news directed at the chemical industry.
Cost: $27.00
Frequency: Bi-Monthly

4694 Journal of Chemical Physics
American Institute of Physics

2 Huntington Quadrangle
Suite 101
Melville, NY 11747-4502

516-576-2200
FAX 516-349-7669
E-Mail: jcp@aip.org
Home Page: www.aip.org

H. Frederick Dylia, Executive Director/CEO
Darlene Walters, Senior VP
John Haynes, VP Publishing

Targets both chemists and physicists involved in research and applications of chemical physics technology.
Frequency: Weekly
Circulation: 5,000

4695 Journal of Chemical and Engineering Data
American Chemical Society
180 Fitzpatrick Hall
Univerity of Notre Dame
Notre Dame, IN 46556

574-631-1149
FAX 516-349-9704
E-Mail: squarles@aip.org
Home Page: www.aip.org

Joan F. Brennecke, Ph.D., Editor
Marc Brodsky, CEO

Offers the latest updates and new information in the chemical industry.
Cost: $458.00
Frequency: Weekly
Circulation: 5000
Founded in 1931

4696 Journal of Chromatographic Science
Preston Publications
6600 W Touhy Ave
Niles, IL 60714-4516

847-647-2900
FAX 847-647-1155
E-Mail: tpreston@prestonpub.com
Home Page: www.prestonpub.com

Tinsley Preston, Owner
Kevin Bailey, Managing Editor
Janice Gordon, Director Marketing

An international publication for scientists, analytical chemists, researchers, educators, and other allied to the field. Provides in depth information about analytical techniques, applications, sample preparation methods, systems problem solving, etc. Articles cover more practical information on all types of separations—gas, liquid, thin layer, supercritical fluid, electrophoresis, spectrometry, hyphenated methods, etc. any other single source. Also problem solving/troubleshooting answers.
Cost: $405.00
Frequency: Monthly
Circulation: 1000
Founded in 1961

4697 Journal of Colloid & Interface Science
Academic Press
525 B St
Suite 1900
San Diego, CA 92101-4401

619-235-6336
800-321-5068
FAX 619-699-6280
Home Page: www.aceparking.com

D.T. Wasan, Editor-in-Chief
Claudia Romas, Publisher

Presents chemical and physiochemical aspects of theory and practice of colloids.
Cost: $883.00
Frequency: Monthly
Circulation: 2000
Founded in 1885

4698 Journal of Medicinal Chemistry
American Chemical Society
1155 16th St NW
Suite 600
Washington, DC 20036-4892

202-872-4600
800-227-5558
FAX 202-872-4615
E-Mail: service@acs.org
Home Page: www.acs.org

Madeleine Jacobs, CEO/Executive Director

Information on the chemistry industry, dealing with aspects directly pertaining to the medical profession.
Founded in 1876

4699 Journal of Organic Chemistry
American Chemical Society
1155 16th St NW
Washington, DC 20036-4892

202-872-4600
800-227-5558
FAX 202-872-4615
E-Mail: service@acs.org
Home Page: www.acs.org

Madeleine Jacobs, CEO/Executive Director

Areas emphasized are the multiple facets of organic reactions, natural products, studies of mechanism, theoretical organic chemistry and the various aspects of spectroscopy related to organic chemistry.
Cost: $1260.00
Frequency: BiWeekly
Circulation: 8,500

4700 Journal of Physical Chemistry
American Chemical Society
GA Institute of Technology
Boggs Building
Atlanta, GA 30332

404-894-0293
800-227-5558
FAX 404-894-0294
E-Mail: jphyschm@chemistry.gatech
Home Page: www.pubs.acs.org

Mostafa A El-Sayed, Editor

Reports on both experimental and theoretical research dealing with the fundamental aspects of physical chemistry and chemical physics.
Frequency: Weekly
Circulation: 3774

4701 Journal of Society of Cosmetic Chemists
Society of Cosmetic Chemists
120 Wall St
Suite 2400
New York, NY 10005-4088

212-668-1500
FAX 212-668-1504
E-Mail: societycoschem@worldnet.att.net
Home Page: www.scconline.org

Theresa Cesario, Administrator
Mindy Goldstein, Journal Editor
Doreen Scelso, Publication Coordinator

Features highlight new products, processing techniques, safety issues, and pharmacological features.
Cost: $200.00
Circulation: 4200
Founded in 1945

4702 Journal of Surfactants and Detergents
AOCS Press

12024 Vista Parke Drive
PO Box 200135
Austin, TX 78720-0135

512-331-2441
FAX 512-331-2387
E-Mail: mfcox@cvcnet.com

Michael F Cox, Editor-in-Chief

Reports on the development and performance of surfactants in all areas, from household detergents to industrial uses, as well as on the development and manufacture of other detergent ingredients and their formulation into finished products.
Cost: $85.00
Frequency: Quarterly
Circulation: 1,500

4703 Journal of the American Chemical Society

American Chemical Society
1155 16th St NW
Suite 600
Washington, DC 20036-4892

202-872-4600
800-227-5558
FAX 202-872-4615
E-Mail: service@acs.org
Home Page: www.acs.org

Madeleine Jacobs, CEO/Esecutive Director

Association news, member information and chemical industry information.
Cost: $125.00
Frequency: Weekly

4704 Journal of the American Leather Chemists Association

American Leather Chemists Association
1314 50th Street
Suite 103
Lubbock, TX 79412

806-744-1798
FAX 806-744-1785
E-Mail: alca@leatherchemists.org
Home Page: www.leatherchemists.org

Carol Adcock, Executive Secretary
Cost: $175.00
Frequency: Monthly
Circulation: 500

4705 Journal of the Electrochemical Society

Electrochemical Society
65 S Main St
Building D
Pennington, NJ 08534-2839

609-737-1902
FAX 609-737-2743
E-Mail: ecs@electrochem.org
Home Page: www.electrochem.org

Roque J. Calvo, Executive Director
Annie Goedkoop, Publications Director
Paul B. Cooper, Editorial Manager

Leader in the field of solid-state and electrochemical science and technology. This peer-reviewed journal publishes an average of 450 pages of 70 articles each month. Articles are posted online, with a monthly paper edition following electronic publication. The ECS membership benefits package includes access to the electronic edition of this journal.
450 Pages
Frequency: Monthly
ISSN: 0013-4651

4706 LCGC North America

Advanstar Communications

Woodbridge Corporate Plaza
485 Route 1 S, Building F
Iselin, NJ 08830

732-225-9500
FAX 732-225-0211
E-Mail: lcgcedit@lcgcmag.com
Home Page: www.lcgcmag.com/lcgc/
Social Media: Facebook

David Esola, VP/General Manager
Michael Tessalone, Group Publisher
Tria Deibert, Marketing Director

Includes product and literature reports along with meeting and seminar listings.
Cost: $67.00
100 Pages
Frequency: Monthly
Circulation: 56000
Founded in 1987
Mailing list available for rent: 47,543 names at $155 per M
Printed in 4 colors on glossy stock

4707 Laboratorio y Analisis

Keller International Publishing Corporation
150 Great Neck Rd
Suite 400
Great Neck, NY 11021-3309

516-829-9210
FAX 516-829-9306
Home Page: www.supplychainbrain.com

Terry Beirne, Publisher
Bryan DeLuca, Editor
Jerry Keller, President
Mary Chavez, Director of Sales

4708 Lipids

American Oil Chemists' Society
2710 S Boulder
Urbana, IL 61802-6996

217-359-2344
FAX 217-351-8091
E-Mail: general@aocs.org
Home Page: www.aocs.org

Jody Schonfeld, Publications Director
Pam Landman, Journals Coordinator
Kimmy Farris, Production Editor
Lori Stewart, Books and Publications
Jenna Tatar, Customer Service

Scientific journal features full-length original research articles, short communications, methods papers and review articles on timely topics. All papers are meticulously peer-reviewed and edited by some of the foremost experts in their respective fields.
Cost: $461.00
Frequency: Monthly
Circulation: 2400
Founded in 1966

4709 Nucleus

American Chemical Society — Northeast
12 Corcoran Ave.
Burlington, MA 01803

800-872-2054
800-872-2054
FAX 508-653-6329
E-Mail: webmaster@nesacs.org
Home Page: www.nesacs.org

Vincent J Gale, Editor
Amy Tapper, Secretary
Anna Singer, Administrative Secretary
Liming Shao, Chair

Content includes local meeting announcements; news of members of the Northeastern Section, American Chemical Society; historical articles; book reviews; calender of events covering all chemistry disciplines in the area. No Company or product information is published. Advertising is accepted.
Frequency: Monthly
Circulation: 7500

Founded in 1888
Printed in 2 colors on matte stock

4710 PaintSquare

PaintSquare
2100 Wharton Street
Suite 310
Pittsburgh, PA 15203

412-431-8300
800-837-8303
FAX 412-431-5428
E-Mail: webmaster@paintsquare.com
Home Page: www.paintsquare.com
Social Media: Facebook, Twitter

Harold Hower, Publisher

Mission is to make PaintSquare a viable and useful tool to make your job easier and more efficient.
Founded in 2002

4711 Performance Chemicals Europe

Reed Chemical Publications
Quadrant House, The Quadrant
Sutton, Surrey, UK SM2 5AS

212-732-3200
+44 20 8652 3335
FAX 212-791-4311
FAX +44 20 8652 3375
E-Mail: csc@icis.com
Home Page: www.performancechemicals.com

Stanley F Reed
Neil Sinclair, Director
Simon Platt, Director
Christopher Flook, Managing Director
Cost: $711.00

4712 PetroChemical News

William F Bland Co.
709 Turmeric Ln
Durham, NC 27713-3103

919-544-1717
FAX 919-544-1999
E-Mail: pcn@petrochemical-news.com
Home Page: www.petrochemical-news.com

Susan Kensil, Editor
Michelle Zard, Circulation Director

Covers new plants and projects, awards of contracts, mergers and acquisitions, current technology, and related government actions.
Cost: $807.00
Frequency: Weekly
Founded in 1963

4713 Pine Chemicals Review

Kriedt Enterprises
3803 Cleveland Ave.
New Orleans, LA 70119

504-482-3914
FAX 504-482-4205
E-Mail: info@pinechemicalsreview.com
Home Page: www.pinechemicalsreview.com

Romney Richard, Publisher
Charley Richard, Editor

Pine Chemicals Review is the only trade journal covering pine and pulp chemicals within the naval stores industry. It is directed to producers and processors of pine gum and wood naval stores; pulp chemicals and pine derivative chemicals for the adhesives, coatings, printing ink, paper chemicals, flavor and fragrance.
Cost: $110.00
24 Pages
Frequency: Monthly
Circulation: 300
ISSN: 0164-4580
Founded in 1890
Printed in 4 colors on glossy stock

4714 Polyurethane Professional Development Program
Center for the Polyurethanes Industry
1300 Wilson Blvd
Suite 990
Arlington, VA 22209-2307

703-841-0012
FAX 703-841-0525
Home Page: www.polyurethane.org
Social Media: *Facebook, Twitter*

Calvin Dooley, President
Frequency: Yearly

4715 Powder and Bulk Engineering
CSC Publishing
1155 Northland Dr
St Paul, MN 55120-1288

651-287-5600
FAX 651-287-5650
Home Page: www.cscpublishinginc.com

Richard R Cress, Publisher
Terry O'Neill, Editor
Katherine Davich, Senior Editor

Featured editorial includes technical articles, case histories, test centers, product news and literature, and industry news items.
Frequency: Monthly
Circulation: 35379
Founded in 1986

4716 Powder/Bulk Solids
Reed Business Information
301 Gibralter Drive
Box 650
Morris Plains, NJ 07950

973-920-7000
FAX 973-539-3476
E-Mail: scrow@reedbusiness.com
Home Page: www.reedbusiness.com

Mark Kelsey, CEO

Equipment and technological news for dry particulates processors.
Cost: $74.95
Frequency: Monthly
Circulation: 45,070
ISSN: 8740-6653
Founded in 1993

4717 Proceedings of The Combustion Institute
Combustion Institute
5001 Baum Blvd.
Suite 635
Pittsburgh, PA 15213-1851

412-687-1366
FAX 412-687-0340
E-Mail: office@combustioninstitute.org
Home Page: www.combustioninstitute.org

Barbara Waronek, Executive Administrator
Prof. Katharina Kohse-Hoinghaus, President
Marcus Alden, VP
Derek Dunn-Rankin, Treasurer

Contains forefront contributions in fundamentals and applications of combustion science.
6000 Members
Frequency: Biennially
Founded in 1954

4718 Processing
Putman Media Company
555 W Pierce Rd
Suite 301
Itasca, IL 60143-2626

630-467-1300
FAX 630-467-0197

E-Mail: webmaster@putman.net
Home Page: www.putman.net

John Cappelletti, CEO
Mike Bacidore, Editor-in-Chief
Tonia Becker, Publisher

Product areas covered include mechanical and pneumatic conveying, material handling, packaging, and storage. Each issue includes a specific editorial spotlight, product showcase and new literature section.
Frequency: Monthly
Circulation: 95035
ISSN: 0896-8659
Founded in 1972
Printed in 4 colors

4719 Quimica Latinoamericana
Reed Chemical Publications
2 Wall St
26th Floor, Suite 13
New York, NY 10005-2044

212-732-3200
888-525-3255
FAX 212-791-4311
E-Mail: cnihelp@cnionline.com
Home Page:
www.quimicalatinoamericana.com/

Stanley F Reed
Christopher Flook, Publisher
Neil Sinclair, Managing Editor
Jeff Evans, CEO/President
Jing Huang, Project Manager

Publication of Latin American petrochemicals.

4720 Soap/Cosmetics/Chemical Specialties
Cygnus Publishing
445 Broad Hollow Road
Suite 21
Melville, NY 11747-3601

631-845-2700
800-308-6397
FAX 631-845-2798
E-Mail: soap@erols.com
Home Page: www.cygnuspub.com

Anita Hipius Shaw, Editor-in-Chief
Paul Bonaiuto, CFO
Kathy Scott, Director of Public Relations
John French, CEO

Includes tips on general management, purchasing, as well as new products and market trends, personal care, industrial and institutional markets, especially as they affect chemical, packing and equipment suppliers and their R and D professionals.
Cost: $30.00
Frequency: Monthly
Circulation: 6,491

4721 Spray Technology & Marketing
Industry Publications
3621 Hill Rd
Parsippany, NJ 07054-1001

973-331-9545
FAX 973-331-9547
E-Mail: info@spraytechnology.com
Home Page: www.spraytechnology.com

Cynthia Hundley, Publisher
Michael L. SanGiovanni, Executive Editor
Shirleen Dorman, Editor

Features include articles on marketers, chemical and fragrance manufacturers and components manufacturers.
Frequency: Monthly
Circulation: 6,491
ISSN: 1055-2340
Founded in 1954
Mailing list available for rent
Printed in 4 colors on glossy stock

4722 Sulfuric Acid Today
PO Box 3502
Covington, LA 70434

985-893-9692
FAX 985-893-8693
E-Mail: h2s04today.com
Home Page: www.h2so4today.comm

Earl B Heard, Publisher

Editorial covers industry news, engineering, technology and upcoming events.
Cost: $39.00
Frequency: SemiAnnual
Circulation: 5,000

4723 Today's Chemist at Work
American Chemical Society
1155 16th St NW
Washington, DC 20036-4892

202-872-4600
800-227-5558
FAX 202-872-4615
E-Mail: service@acs.org
Home Page: www.acs.org

Madeleine Jacobs, CEO/Executive Director
William F Carroll, VP

Covers reports on materials, new products, chemical education, analytical chemistry and instrumentation.
Cost: $18.00
Frequency: Monthly
Circulation: 120000
Founded in 1876

Trade Shows

4724 AACC International Annual Meeting
3340 Pilot Knob Road
St. Paul, MN 55121-2055

651-454-7250
800-328-7560
FAX 651-454-0766
E-Mail: aacc@scisoc.org
Home Page: www.aaccnet.org
Social Media: *Facebook, Twitter, LinkedIn*

Betty Ford, Meetings Director
Rhonda Wilkie, Meetings Coordinator
Deborah Rogers, Chair
David Hahn, President
Steven C. Nelson, Executive Vice President

Formerly the American Association of Cereal Chemists, the AACC meeting offers the chance to come together, network with peers, discuss critical issues in the science and discover the methods of others.
1200 Attendees
Frequency: October

4725 ACOS Annual Meeting & Expo
American Oil Chemists' Society
2710 S Boulder
Urbana, IL 61802-6996

217-693-4813
FAX 217-351-8091
E-Mail: meetings@aocs.org
Home Page: www.aocs.org

Greg Hatfield, General Chairperson
Doreen Berning, Registration
Jeff Newman, Meeting Management/Logistics

The premier global science and business forum on fats, oils, surfactants, lipids and related materials. Includes oral and poster presentations, short courses, and exhibit, and networking with more than 1,600 colleagues from 60 countries.
2000 Attendees
Frequency: Annual/April-May

4726 ACS Mid-Atlantic Regional Meeting
American Chemical Society
1155 Sixteenth Street, NW
Washington, DC 20036

202-872-4600
800-227-5558
FAX 989-835-8356
E-Mail: service@acs.org
Home Page: www.acs.org

Madeleine Jacobs, CEO/Executive Director

Attend poster sessions, symposia and workshops to experience the most exciting and cutting-edge research in the field of chemistry.
1M Attendees
Frequency: Annual/Spring

4727 ACS Spring & Fall National Meeting & Expos
American Chemical Society
1155 Sixteenth Street NW
Washington, DC 20036

202-872-4600
800-227-5558
FAX 202-776-8044
E-Mail: conf_vendorrel@acs.org
Home Page: www.acs.org

Madeleine Jacobs, CEO/Executive Director

Symposia, poster sessions, and workshops around cutting-edge chemistry research.
1.2M Attendees
Frequency: Biennial

4728 ALCA Annual Meeting
American Leather Chemists Association
1314 50th Street
Suite 103
Lubbock, TX 79412

806-744-1798
FAX 806-744-1785
E-Mail: alca@leatherchemists.org
Home Page: www.leatherchemists.org

Carol Adcock, Executive Secretary
100 Attendees

4729 AOAC International Annual Meeting & Expo
AOAC International
481 North Frederick Avenue
Suite 500
Gaithersburg, MD 20877-2417

301-924-7077
800-379-2622
FAX 301-924-7089
E-Mail: aoac@aoac.org
Home Page: www.aoac.org
Social Media: *Facebook, LinkedIn*

Lauren Chelf, Director, Meetings & Exposition

The meeting offers a diverse program of symposia, workshops, and poster and scientific sessions. Specific educational tracks are offered for analytical chemists, microbiologists, laboratory managers, and other laboratory personnel.
Frequency: August

4730 ASBC Annual Meeting
American Society of Brewing Chemists
3340 Pilot Knob Road
Saint Paul, MN 55121

651-454-7250
800-328-7560
FAX 651-454-0766
Home Page: www.meeting.asbcnet.org
Social Media: *Facebook, Twitter*

Charles F. Strachan, President
Steven Nelson, Executive Officer

Karen Cummings, Director of Publications
A. Hope, VP Operations
300 Attendees
Frequency: June/Non-Members Fee
Founded in 1934

4731 Agricultural Retailers Association Convention and Expo
Agricultural Retailers Association
1156 15th Street
Suite 500
Washington, DC 20005

202-457-0825
800-844-4900
FAX 314-567-6808
E-Mail: kelly@aradc.org
Home Page: www.aradc.org

Daren Coppock, President/CEO
Richard Gupton, Sr. VP, Public Policy
Michelle Hummel, VP
Marketing/Communications

Annual show of 120 manufacturers, suppliers and distributors of agricultural chemicals and fertilizers. Seminar, conference and banquet.
1200 Attendees
Frequency: Annual
Founded in 1993

4732 American Assn of Textile Chemists & Colorists International Conference
American Assn of Textile Chemists & Colorists
PO Box 12215
Research Triangle Park, NC 27709-2215

919-549-8141
800-360-5380
FAX 919-549-8933
E-Mail: danielsj@aatcc.org
Home Page: www.aatcc.org

John Daniels, Executive VP
Debra Hibbard, Executive Assistant
Charles E Gavin, Treasurer

Colorants and chemical finishes for the textile trade are on display.
Frequency: Annual

4733 American Chemical Society: Southeastern Regional Conference & Exhibition
American Chemical Society
1155 16th Street NW
Washington, DC 20036

202-872-4600
800-227-5558
FAX 202-872-4615
E-Mail: service@acs.org
Home Page: www.acs.org

Madeleine Jacobs, CEO/Executive Director

Booths featuring exhibits of the chemicals industry.
Frequency: Annual

4734 American College of Toxicology Annual Meeting
9650 Rockville Pike
Bethesda, MD 20814

301-634-7840
FAX 301-634-7852
E-Mail: clemire@actox.org
Home Page: www.actox.org

Carol Lemire, Executive Director
Eve Gamzu Kagan, Asst. Executive Director

Education courses and scientific symposia, exhibits of contract laboratories, toxicology supplies and equipment and science journal publishing companies.
500 Attendees
Frequency: November

4735 American Institute Chemical Engineers Petrochemical Refining Expo
3 Park Avenue
New York, NY 10016-4363

212-591-8100
800-242-4363
FAX 212-591-8888
Home Page: www.aiche.org
Social Media: *Facebook, Twitter, LinkedIn*

Marie Stewart, Director

A marketplace for materials used in processing chemicals.
20M Attendees
Frequency: April

4736 American Society Biochemistry and Molecular Biology Expo
American Society of Biochem & Molecular Biology
9650 Rockville Pike
Bethesda, MD 20814-3996

301-634-7145
FAX 301-881-2080
E-Mail: asbmb@asbmb.org
Home Page: www.asbmb.org

600 booths of products used in biomedical research.
8M Attendees

4737 Annual Green Chemistry & Engineering Conference
ACS Green Chemistry Institute
1155 16th Street NW
Washington, DC 20036

202-872-6102
800-227-5558
FAX 202-872-4615
E-Mail: gci@acs.org
Home Page: www.GCandE.org

Speakers, sessions, education, exhibits.
Frequency: Annual

4738 CPMA Conference
Color Pigments Manufacturers Association
300 N Washington St
Suite 105
Alexandria, VA 22314-2530

703-684-4044
FAX 703-684-1795
E-Mail: cpma@cpma.com
Home Page: www.pigments.org

J Lawrence Robinson, President

Brings together pigments manufacturers their suppliers and users, and others with an interest in color pigments including regulators, consultants, and exhibitors.
Frequency: Annual

4739 Chem Show: Chemical Process Industries Exposition
International Exposition Company
15 Franklin Street
Westport, CT 06880-5903

203-221-9232
FAX 203-221-9260
E-Mail: info@chemshow.com
Home Page: www.chemshow.com

Mark Stevens, VP
Jeff Stevens, Sales VP
Kelley Stevens, Sales Manager

Bringing together in one place major manufacturers of equipment, systems and services for the CPI. Product categories include; process equipment, fluid handling equipment and systems, solids handling equipment and sytems, engineered materials, instruments and controls,

environmental and safety equipment and systems and services.
7481 Attendees
Frequency: Biennial/Oct
Founded in 1915

4740 Chem-Distribution
PennWell Publishing Company
1421 S Sheridan Road
Tulsa, OK 74112-6619

918-835-3161
800-331-4463
FAX 918-831-9834
E-Mail: headquarters@pennwell.com
Home Page: www.pennwell.com

Bill Pryor, CEO/President
Junior Isles, Publisher/Editor

Exhibits of technology for the distribution, transfer and storage of chemicals and petrochemicals.

4741 Chem-Safe
PennWell Conferences and Exhibitions
1421 S Sheridan Road
Tulsa, OK 74112-6619

918-835-3161
800-331-4463
FAX 918-831-9834
E-Mail: headquarters@pennwell.com
Home Page: www.pennwell.com

Bill Pryor, CEO/President
Junior Isles, Publisher/Editor

Exhibits of environmental, safety and health technology for the chemical and process industries.

4742 Chlorine Institute Annual Meeting & Trade Show
Chlorine Institute
1300 Wilson Blvd
Arlington, VA 22209-2323

703-741-5760
FAX 703-894-4130
E-Mail: aonna@cl2.com
Home Page: www.chlorineinstitute.org

Arthur Dungan, President
Frequency: Annual/Spring

4743 Conchem Exhibition and Conference
Reed Exhibition Companies
255 Washington Street
Newton, MA 02458-1637

617-584-4900
FAX 617-630-2222

Elizabeth Hitchcock, International Sales

The international event featuring specialty additives and chemicals for the building industry.
Frequency: November

4744 Consumer Specialty Products Association
Chemical Specialties Products Association
900 17th Street NW
Suite 300
Washington, DC 20006

202-872-8110
FAX 202-872-8114
E-Mail: info@cspa.org
Home Page: www.cspa.org

Christopher Cathcart, President

Nonprofit organization trade show for the many companies involved in the formulation, manufacture, testing and marketing of chemical specialty products. 100 booths.
2M Attendees

4745 Eastern Analystical Symposium & Exposition
Eastern Analytical Symposium, Inc

PO Box 633
Montchanin, DE 19710-0633

610-485-4633
FAX 610-485-9467
E-Mail: easinfo@aol.com
Home Page: www.eas.org

Sheree Gold, Exposition Director

The world's leading community for analytcal chemists seeking education and career advancement. Technical programs, speakers, and the expo. 240 booths.
6M Attendees
Frequency: Annual

4746 Electrochemical Society Meetings
Electrochemical Society
65 S Main St
Building D
Pennington, NJ 08534-2827

609-737-1902
FAX 609-737-2743
E-Mail: meetings@electrochem.org
Home Page: www.electrochem.org

Roque J Calvo, Executive Director
Colleen Keepser, Executive Administrator
Mary Yess, Deputy Executive Director
Corey Eberhart, Global Sales Director
Karen Baliff Ornstein, Marketing Manager

Providing a forum for exchanging information on the latest scientific and technical developments in the fields of electrochemical and solid-state science and technology. ECS meetings bring together scientists, engineers, and researchers from academia, industry, and government laboratories to share results and discuss issues on related topics through a variety of formats, such as oral presentations, poster sessions, panel discussions, and tutorial sessions.
8000 Members
Frequency: Biannual/Spring & Fall
Founded in 1902

4747 Federation of Spectroscopy Societies
13 N Cliffe Drive
Wilmington, DE 19809-1623

302-656-0771

Dr. Edward Brame Jr, Show Manager

120 booths of analytical chemistry.
2M Attendees
Frequency: October

4748 GlobalChem Conference and Exhibition
1850 M St NW
Suite 700
Washington, DC 20036-5810

202-721-4100
FAX 202-296-8120
E-Mail: info@socma.com
Home Page: www.socma.com

Larry Sloan, President/CEO
Alicia Massey, Senior Manager

Provides information and interaction with experts on the U.S. Toxic Substances Control Act, emerging issues and trends in the product stewardship arena and equivalent international regulations.
6 Members
Founded in 1985

4749 ILTA Storage Tank & Bulk Liquid Terminal Int'l Operating Conf. & Trade Show
Independent Liquid Terminals Association
1005 North Glebe Road
Suite 600
Arlington, VA 22201

703-875-2011
FAX 703-875-2018

E-Mail: info@ilta.org
Home Page: www.ilta.org

E David Doane, President
Melinda Whitney, Director/Government Affairs
Renita Gross, Director of Mtgs/Info. Services

Containing 202 booths and 161 exhibits.
2,700 Attendees
Frequency: June

4750 IUPAC World Polymer Congress
2 Davidson Hall
Blacksburg, VA 24061-0001

540-231-7257
FAX 540-231-3971
E-Mail: adhesoc@vt.edu
Home Page: www.adhesionsociety.org

Lynn Penn, President
Paul J Clark, Treasurer
Esther Brann, Manager

Enabling technologies for a safe, sustainable, healthy world.
400 Members
Founded in 1978

4751 InformexUSA
1850 M St NW
Suite 700
Washington, DC 20036-5810

202-721-4100
FAX 202-296-8120
E-Mail: info@socma.com
Home Page: www.socma.com

Jill Aker, President

Serving businesses across a broad range of end-use markets such as pharmaceuticals, biopharmaceuticals, agrochemicals, adhesives, electronics, paints, and plastics. Utilizing an advisory committee, made up of industry executives and decision makers from across markets to help us make decisions that come directly from the chemical industry.
6 Members
Founded in 1985

4752 International Conference on the Methods and Applications
American Nuclear Society
555 N Kensington Ave
La Grange Park, IL 60526-5592

708-352-6611
800-323-3044
FAX 708-352-0499
E-Mail: advertising@ans.org
Home Page: www.ans.org
Social Media: *Facebook, Twitter, LinkedIn*

Stephen Kuczynski, General Chair
Sedatel Goluoglu, Program Chair
Mikey Brady Raap, Treasurer

Of Radioanalytical Chemistry
10500 Members
Founded in 1954

4753 International Thermal Spray Conference & Exposition
ASM International
9639 Kinsman Road
Materials Park, OH 44073

440-338-5151
800-338-5152
FAX 440-338-4634
E-Mail: natalie.nemec@asminternational.org
Home Page: www.asminternational.org

Natalie Neme, Event Manager
Kelly Thomas, Exposition Account Manager

Global annual event attracting professional interested in thermal spray technology focusing on advances in HVOF, plasma and detonation gun, flame spray and wire arc spray processes,

performance of coatings, and future trends. 150 exhibitors.
1000 Attendees
Frequency: Annual/May

4754 Optimizing Your Lab Automation: Lessons from the Front Line
1850 K St NW
Suite 625
Washington, DC 20006-2215

202-857-0717
800-892-1400
FAX 202-887-5093
Home Page: www.aacc.org
Social Media: *Facebook, Twitter, LinkedIn, YouTube*

Robert Christenson, President
Steven Wong, President-Elect
Patricia Jones, Director

The premiere event for clinical laboratorians, industry representatives, and health care executives to network and get ahead.

4755 PCA International Conference
Pine Chemicals Associations, Inc
3350 Riverwood Parkway SE
Suite 1900
Atlanta, GA 30339

770-984-5340
FAX 770-984-5341
E-Mail: wjones@pinechemicals.org
Home Page: www.pinechemicals.org

Walter L Jones, President/COO
Gary Reed, Chairman/Board of Directors
200 Attendees
Frequency: September

4756 Powder Bulk Solids Conference and Expo
Reed Business Information
2000 Clearwater Drive
Oak Brook, IL 60523

630-740-0825
Home Page: www.reedbusiness.com

Angela Piermartini, Show Manager
1,300 booths.
11M Attendees
Frequency: May

4757 Spray Foam Conference & EXPO
Spray Polyurethane Foam Alliance
4400 Fair Lakes Court
Suite 105
Fairfax, VA 22033

800-523-6154
FAX 703-222-5816
E-Mail: info@sprayfoam.org
Home Page: www.sprayfoam.org

Sig Hall, President
Robert Duke, Vice President
Peter Davis, Secretary/Treasurer

Training and accreditation programs, general and breakout sessions, awards, networking receptions, and the exhibit hall.
Frequency: Annual/February
Founded in 1987

4758 TRADEWORX
Chemical Specialties Products Association
900 17th Street NW
Suite 300
Washington, DC 20006

202-872-8110
FAX 202-872-8114
E-Mail: info@cspa.org
Home Page: www.cspa.org

Christopher Cathcart, President

Not-for-profit organization composed of many companies involved in the formulation, manu-

facture, testing and marketing of chemical specialty products.
2M Attendees
Frequency: May

Directories & Databases

4759 Adhesives Digest
International Plastics Selector/DATA Business Pub.
15 Inverness Way E
#6510
Englewood, CO 80112-5710

303-904-0407

A who's who directory of services and supplies to the industry.
Cost: $180.00
Frequency: Biennial

4760 Advanced Coatings and Surface Technology
John Wiley & Sons
111 River St
Hoboken, NJ 07030-5790

201-748-6000
FAX 201-748-6088
E-Mail: info@wiley.com
Home Page: www.wiley.com

William J Pesce, Chief Executive Officer

Offers information on coatings and surface technology, covering breakthroughs in traditional coating processes, chemical vapor deposition and ion beam methods.
Frequency: Full-text

4761 American Coke & Coal Chemicals Institute Directory and By-Laws
1140 Connecticut Ave NW
Suite 705
Washington, DC 20036-4011

202-452-7177
FAX 202-496-9702
E-Mail: information@accci.org
Home Page: www.recycle-steel.org

Chip Foley, VP
Charles Stewart, Chairman

Represents merchant oven coke producers, integrated coke producers, tar distillers, sales agents, and industry suppliers.
75 Pages
Founded in 1944

4762 American Laboratory Buyers Guide
International Scientific Communications
PO Box 870
Shelton, CT 06484-0870

203-926-9300
FAX 203-926-9310
E-Mail: webmaster@iscpubs.com
Home Page: www.iscpubs.com

Brian Howard, Editor
Robert G Sweeny, Publisher

Manufacturers of and dealers in scientifi instruments, equipment, apparatus, and chemicals worldwide.
Cost: $25.00
Frequency: Annual

4763 Available Chemicals Directory
MDL Information Systems
3100 Central Expressway
Santa Clara, CA 05051-6608

408-764-2000
800-635-0064
FAX 408-748-0175

E-Mail: info@mdli.com
Home Page: www.mdli.com

Magnetic tape, covers approximately 240,000 commercially available chemicals, including organic, and inorganic chemicals.
Frequency: Semiannual

4764 CEH On-Line
SRI International
333 Ravenswood Ave
Menlo Park, CA 94025-3493

650-859-3711
FAX 650-326-8916
Home Page: www.srifcu.org

Steve Bowles, President

Database containing economic data for more than 1300 major commodity and specialty chemical products.
Frequency: Full-text

4765 CERCLIS Database of Hazardous Waste Sites
Environmental Protection Agency
Ariel Rios Building
1200 Pennsylvania Avenue NW
Washington, DC 20460

202-272-0167
E-Mail: r9.info@epa.gov
Home Page: www.epa.gov

Bob Zachariasiewicz, Acting Director
Shushona Hyson, Contact
Curt Spalding, Regional

Stands for Comprehensive Environmental Response, Compensation, and Liability Information System. This database contains information on more than 36,000 releases of hazardous substances reported to the US Environmental Protection Agency.
Frequency: Directory

4766 CHEMEST
Technical Database Services
62 W 39th Street
Rm 704
New York, NY 10018

212-245-0384
FAX 212-556-0036

Mildred Green, Principal

This database contains information for estimating the properties of pharmaceuticals and chemicals of environmental concern.
Frequency: Properties

4767 CLAIMS/Comprehensive Data Base
IFI/Plenum Data Corporation
PO Box 1148
Madison, CT 06443

203-779-5301
FAX 203-583-4521
E-Mail: info@ificlaims.com

Harry M Allcock, VP

This database contains enhanced indexing of the US chemical and chemically related patents included in the CLAIMS/UNITERM database.

4768 Chem Source USA
Chemical Sources International
PO Box 1824
Clemson, SC 29633

864-646-7840
FAX 864-642-6168
E-Mail: information@chemsources.com
Home Page: www.chemsources.com

Mike Desing, Editor

Book containing information on where to obtain chemicals in the US and Canada.
Cost: $495.00
1700 Pages
Frequency: Annual January

Circulation: 10000
Founded in 1958

4769 Chem Sources International
PO Box 1824
Clemson, SC 29633-1824

864-646-7840
800-222-4531
FAX 864-646-6168
E-Mail: csinfo@chemsources.com
Home Page: www.chemsources.com

Mike Desing, Editor
Dale Krohn, Owner

The most comprehensive directory ever compiled on the world's chemical industry. Includes the products of more than 8,000 chemical firms spanning 128 countries.
Cost: $750.00
Frequency: Biennial
Founded in 1958

4770 Chemcyclopedia
American Chemical Society
676 East Swedesford Road
Suite 202
Wayne, PA 19087-1612

610-964-8061
FAX 610-964-8061
E-Mail: carroll@acs.org
Home Page: www.acs.org
Social Media: 1

Madeleine Jacobs, Executive Director/CEO
Ken Carroll, Publisher

List of over 900 chemical manufacturers in the US.
Cost: $60.00
Frequency: Annual

4771 Chemical Abstracts
American Chemical Society
1155 16th St NW
Suite 600
Washington, DC 20036-4892

202-872-4600
800-227-5558
FAX 202-872-4615
E-Mail: service@acs.org
Home Page: www.acs.org

Madeleine Jacobs, CEO

Newsletter covering this branch of the American Chemical Society.
Frequency: Monthly

4772 Chemical Exposure and Human Health
McFarland & Company Publishers
PO Box 611
Jefferson, NC 28640-0611

336-246-4460
800-253-2187
FAX 336-246-5018
E-Mail: info@mcfarlandpub.com
Home Page: www.mcfarlandpub.com

Cynthia Wilson, Editor

A list of organizations concerned with the effects of chemical exposure. Government exposure standards on over 300 chemicals.
Cost: $55.00
ISBN: 0-899508-10-3

4773 Chemical Regulations and Guidelines System
Network Management CRC Systems
11242 Waples Mill Road
Fairfax, VA 22030-6079

703-219-3865

This database contains citations, with abstracts, to US government statutes and federal guidelines.

4774 Chemical Week: Financial Survey of the 300 Largest Companies in the US
Chemical Week Associates
110 William St
New York, NY 10038-3910

212-621-4900
FAX 212-621-4800
Home Page: www.chemweek.com

John Rockwell, Vice President

Offers information on over 300 chemical process companies in the United States.
Cost: $8.00
7 Pages
Frequency: Annual
Circulation: 50,615

4775 DRI Chemical
DRI/McGraw-Hill
24 Hartwell Ave
Lexington, MA 02421-3103

781-860-6060
FAX 781-860-6002
E-Mail: support@construction.com
Home Page: www.construction.com

Keith Fox, President
Linda Brennan, VP Operations
Bob Stuono, Senior VP And General Manager

The coverage of this database encompasses the chemical industry in the United States, including imports and exports, inventories, production, sales, shipments and uses.

4776 DRI Chemical Forecast
DRI/McGraw-Hill
24 Hartwell Ave
Lexington, MA 02421-3103

781-860-6060
FAX 781-860-6002
E-Mail: support@construction.com
Home Page: www.construction.com

Keith Fox, President

This time series contains over 700 quarterly forecasts on US supply and demand for more than 120 chemical products.

4777 Directory of Bulk Liquid Terminal and Storage Facilities
Independent Liquid Terminals Association
1005 North Glebe Road
Arlington, VA 22201

703-875-2011
FAX 703-875-2018
E-Mail: info@ilta.org
Home Page: www.ilta.org

E David Doane, President
Melinda Whitney, Director/Executive VP

Published annually in April.
Cost: $95.00

4778 Directory of Chemical Producers: East Asia
SRI Consulting/IHS Global
333 Ravenswood Ave
Menlo Park, CA 94025-3493

650-859-3711
FAX 650-326-8916
Home Page: www.srifcu.org

Steve Bowles, President

Over 2,000 companies producing over 14,000 chemicals in 2,600 plant locations in Indonesia, Japan, Korea, Taiwan and the Philippines.
Cost: $1800.00
800 Pages
Frequency: Annual

4779 Directory of Chemical Producers: U.S.
SRI Consulting/IHS Global

333 Ravenswood Ave
Menlo Park, CA 94025-3493

650-859-3711
FAX 650-326-8916
Home Page: www.srifcu.org

Steve Bowles, President

Over 1,500 United States basic chemical producers manufacturing almost 10,000 chemicals in commercial quantities at 4,500 plant locations. Providing comprehensive, accurate and timely coverage of the international chemical industry since 1961.
Cost: $1460.00
1100 Pages
Frequency: Annual

4780 Directory of Chemical Producers: Western Europe
SRI Consulting/IHS Global
333 Ravenswood Ave
Menlo Park, CA 94025-3493

650-859-3711
FAX 650-326-8916
Home Page: www.srifcu.org

Steve Bowles, President

Covered are over 2,500 western European chemical producers, chemicals and plant locations.
Cost: $1930.00
Frequency: Annual
Circulation: 2,100

4781 Directory of Custom Chemical Manufacturers
Delphi Marketing Services
400 E 89th Street
Apartment 2J
New York, NY 10128-6728
Newman Giragosian, Editor

A list of over 280 custom chemical manufacturers.
Cost: $295.00
220 Pages

4782 Directory of Suppliers of Services
Independent Liquid Terminals Association
1005 North Glebe Road
Arlington, VA 22201

703-875-2011
FAX 703-875-2018
E-Mail: info@ilta.org
Home Page: www.ilta.org

E David Doane, President
Melinda Whitney, Director/Executive VP
Cost: $25.00

4783 Environmental Fate Data Bases
Syracuse Research Corporation
6225 Running Ridge Rd
North Syracuse, NY 13212-2510

315-452-8000
800-724-0451
FAX 315-452-8100

Cheryl Wolfe, President

This database, consisting of 4 interrelated files of information on the fate of organic chemicals. The files include information in physical/chemical properties, degradation and transport, and monitoring for 16,000 chemicals.

4784 Environmental Industry Yearbook and The Gallery
Environmental Economics
1026 Irving Street
Philadelphia, PA 19107-6707

215-877-2063
FAX 215-440-0116

More than 80 publicly traded companies, plus Fortune 500 firms that have an impact on envi-

375

ronmental concerns.
Cost: $75.00
250 Pages
Frequency: SemiAnnual

4785 Fine Chemicals Database
Chemron
PO Box 2299
Paso Robles, CA 93447

210-340-8121
800-423-1148
FAX 210-340-8123

This large database provides supplier information for more than 27,000 chemical products available from over 50 manufacturers and distributors in North America.
Frequency: Directory

4786 Index to Chemical Regulations
Bureau of National Affairs
1801 S Bell St
Arlington, VA 22202-4501

703-341-3000
800-372-1033
FAX 800-253-0332
E-Mail: customercare@bna.com
Home Page: www.bnabooks.com

Paul N Wojcik, Chairman
Gregory C McCaffery, President

A one-binder index containing more than 80,000 citations by chemical name to the Code of Federal Regulations and the Federal Register.
Cost: $988.00
Frequency: Monthly

4787 Information Officers of Member Companies
Chemical Manufacturers Association
1300 Wilson Boulevard
Arlington, VA 22209-2307

703-741-5502
FAX 703-741-6807

Thomas J Gilroy, Associate Media Director
About 180 companies.
Frequency: Biennial

4788 International Chemical Regulatory Monitoring System
Ariel Research Corporation
4320 East West Highway
Suite 440
Bethesda, MD 20814-3319

301-951-2500
FAX 301-986-1681
Home Page: www.3ecompany.com

John Wyatt, CEO

This database contains references to regulations and precautionary data on more than 100,000 chemical substances.
Frequency: Full-text

4789 Kirk-Othmer Encyclopedia of Chemical Technology Online
John Wiley & Sons
111 River St
Hoboken, NJ 07030-5790

201-748-6000
800-825-7550
FAX 201-748-6088
E-Mail: info@wiley.com
Home Page: www.wiley.com

Warren J Baker, President
Richard M Hochhauser, CEO

This comprehensive database offers complete text, citations, tables and abstracts of all 1,200 chapters in the 25-volume Encyclopedia of the same name. With no concurrent usage restriction, you can call up information covering the

entire chemical industry and allied fields any time with a click of your mouse from the library, office or laboratory.

4790 McCutcheons Functional Materials
McCutcheons Division
P.O.Box 2249
New Preston Marble Dale, CT 06777-0249

201-652-2655
FAX 201-652-3419
E-Mail: mcinfo@gomc.com
Home Page: www.gomc.com

Michael Allured, Publisher

List of materials commonly used in conjunction with surfactants such as enzymes, lubricants, waxes, corrosion inhibitors, and other chemicals produced worldwide.
Cost: $40.00
Frequency: Monthly
Founded in 1921

4791 Multilingual Thesaurus of Geosciences
Information Today
143 Old Marlton Pike
Medford, NJ 08055-8750

609-654-6266
800-300-9868
FAX 609-654-4309
E-Mail: custserv@infotoday.com
Home Page: www.infotoday.com

Thomas H Hogan, President
Roger R Bilboul, Chairman Of The Board

Represents the state of the art use of geoscience terminology by information centers around the world.
Cost: $99.00
654 Pages
ISBN: 1-573870-09-9

4792 OPIS/STALSBY Electric Power Industry Directory
OPIS/STALSBY
1255 Highway 70
Suite 32-N
Lakewood, NJ 08701

732-901-8800
877-210-4287
FAX 732-901-9632
Home Page: www.opisnet.com

Karen England, Senior Editor
Karen Reng, Marketing Manager
Christine Kaniuk, Production/Advertising Coordinator

Provides detailed listings of over 1,200 companies and more than 2,700 personnel of the electric power industry. Company categories include producer, marketer, trader, broker, transmission, investor-owned, municipal, rural/co-op/fed/local government and independent. Personnel listings include sales/marketing, supply/purchasing, operations/transmissions, finance/treasury. Company listings include address, direct telephone, fax numbers and e-mails. CD-ROM $495.
Cost: $141.00
Frequency: 2 per year
Circulation: 625
Printed in 4 colors

4793 OPIS/STALSBY Petrochemicals Directory
OPIS/STALSBY
3349 State Route 138
Unit D
Wall Township, NJ 07719-9671

732-730-2500
877-210-4287

FAX 732-280-0542
Home Page: www.ucg.com

Ben Brockwell, Manager
Karen Reng, Marketing Manager
Christine Kaniuk, Production/Advertising Coordinator
Bruce Levenson, Co-Founder

Provides detailed listings of over 2,100 companies and more than 7,000 personnel covering all segments of the petrochemical gas industry, including manufacturing, trading and distributing of petrochemicals. Company listings include addresses, telephone, fax, TLX, personal phone/fax numbers, cell phones and home addresses, area of responsibility and job titles. Five separate indices are provided for complete cross-referencing. CD-ROM $995.
Cost: $175.00
Frequency: 2 per year
Circulation: 425
Printed in 4 colors

4794 OPIS/STALSBY Petroleum Supply Americas Directory
OPIS/STALSBY
1255 Highway 70
Suite 32-N
Lakewood, NJ 08701

732-901-8800
877-210-4287
FAX 732-901-9632
Home Page: www.opisnet.com

Karen England, Senior Editor
Karen Reng, Marketing Manager
Christine Kaniuk, Production/Advertising Coordinator

Helps traders, marketers and suppliers of crude oil, refined products and gas liquids to access detailed information on over 2,500 companies and 10,000 personnel in North, Central and South America. Company listings include company address, telephone, fax, TLX, personal phone/fax numbers, car phones, home addresses, area of responsibility and job title. Four separate indices are provided for complete cross-referencing. CD-ROM $995.
Cost: $235.00
Frequency: 2 per year
Circulation: 2,045
Printed in 4 colors

4795 OPIS/STALSBY Petroleum Supply Europe Directory
OPIS/STALSBY
1255 Highway 70
Suite 32-N
Lakewood, NJ 08701

732-901-8800
877-210-4287
FAX 732-901-9632
Home Page: www.opisnet.com

Karen England, Senior Editor
Karen Reng, Marketing Manager
Christine Kaniuk, Production/Advertising Coordinator

Helps traders, marketers and suppliers of crude oil, refined products and gas liquids to access detailed information on over 1,500 companies and 6,600 personnel in Europe, Eastern Europe, Africa and the Middle East. Listings include company address, telephone, fax, TLX, personal phone/fax numbers, car phones, home addresses, area of responsibility and job titles. Four separate indices are provided for complete cross-referencing. CD-OM $995.
Cost: $190.00
Frequency: 2 per year
Circulation: 425
Printed in 4 colors

4796 OPIS/STALSBY Petroleum Terminal Encyclopedia
OPIS/STALSBY
1255 Highway 70
Suite 32-N
Lakewood, NJ 08701

732-901-8800
877-210-4287
FAX 732-901-9632
Home Page: www.opisnet.com

Karen England, Senior Editor
Karen Reng, Marketing Manager
Christine Kaniuk, Production/Advertising Coordinator

Provides detailed listings of over 2,800 petroleum terminals. Information includes pipeline and rail interconnections and truck facilities for each terminal; berth, waterway and docking information for marine terminals; details on both public and private terminals for market analysis and exchange planning. Three separate indices are provided for complete cross-referencing. CD-ROM $995.
Cost: $245.00
Frequency: 2 per year
Circulation: 825
Printed in 4 colors

4797 OPIS/STALSBY Who's Who in Natural Gas
OPIS/STALSBY
1255 Highway 70
Suite 32-N
Lakewood, NJ 08701

732-901-8800
877-210-4287
FAX 732-901-9632
Home Page: www.opisnet.com

Karen England, Senior Editor
Karen Reng, Marketing Manager
Christine Kaniuk, Production/Advertising Coordinator

Provides detailed listings of over 2,600 companies and more than 11,000 personnel covering all segments of the natural gas industry, including producers, processors, marketers, traders, transporters, major buyers, LDCs, brokers, gas storage, regulatory, etc. Company listings include addresses, telephone, fax, TLX, personal phone/fax numbers, car phones and home addresses, area of responsibility and job titles. Four separate indices are provided for complete cross-referencing. CD-ROM $995.
Cost: $200.00
Frequency: 2 per year
Circulation: 950
Printed in 4 colors

4798 Purchasing/CPI Edition: Chemicals Yellow Pages
Reed Business Information
2000 Clearwater Dr
Oak Brook, IL 60523-8809

630-574-0825
FAX 630-288-8781
Home Page: www.reedbusiness.com

Jeff Greisch, President

Manufacturers and distributors of 10,000 chemicals and raw materials; manufacturers and distributors of containers and packaging.
Cost: $85.00
Frequency: Annual

4799 Refining & Gas Processing
Midwest Publishing Company
PO Box 4468
Suite E
Tulsa, OK 74159-0468

918-583-9999
800-829-2002
FAX 918-587-9349

E-Mail: info@midwestdirectories.com
Home Page: www.midwestpub.com

Will L Hammack, Owner

Over 5,200 refineries, gas processing plants, engineering contractors, equipment manufacturers and supply companies.
Cost: $145.00
Frequency: Annual, May
Founded in 1943

4800 Regulated Chemical Directory
Kluwer Academic Publishers
101 Philip Drive
Norwellk, MA 02061

617-871-6600
FAX 617-871-6528
E-Mail: kluwer@wkap.com
Home Page: www.hcirn.com

List of major federal and selected state and international regulatory and advisory sources of information regarding chemicals in the US, Canada, Australia, Germany and Israel.
Cost: $375.00
Frequency: Annual, January

4801 STN Easy
Chemical Abstracts Service
PO Box 3012
Columbus, OH 43210-0012

614-473-3600
800-848-6538
FAX 614-447-3713
E-Mail: help@cas.org
Home Page: www.cas.org

Easy web acccess to scientific research and patents. STN Easy provides access to more than 60 databases covering all types of sci/tech information including chemistry, life sciences, buisiness, MSDS, math/computer science, engineering, medicine, pharmaceuticals, general science, food and agriculture, and regulatory information.

4802 Soap/Cosmetics/Chemical Specialties: Blue Book Issue
Cygnus Publishing
445 Broad Hollow Road
Suite 21
Melville, NY 11747-3601

631-845-2700
FAX 631-845-2723
Home Page: www.cygnuspub.com

Anita Shaw, Editor-in-Chief
Shelley Colwell, CFO
Paul Bonaiuto, CFO
Kathy Scott, Director of Public Relations

Sources of raw materials, equipment and services for the chemical, soap and cosmetics industries. Includes a list of trade associations.
Cost: $15.00
Frequency: Annual, April
Circulation: 19,000

Industry Web Sites

4803 http://gold.greyhouse.com
G.O.L.D Grey House OnLine Databases
Grey House Publishing's online database platform, GOLD, offers Quick Search, Keyword Search and Expert Search for most business sectors including chemical and agriculture markets. The GOLD platform makes finding the information you need quick and easy - whether you're a novice searcher or an experienced database user. All of Grey House's directory products are be available for subscription on the GOLD platform.

4804 www.aaccnet.org
American Association of Cereal Chemists
Nonprofit international organization of nearly 4,000 members who are specialists in the use of cereal grains in foods. AACC has been an innovative leader in gathering and disseminating scientific and technical information to professionals in the grain based foods industry worldwide for over 85 years.

4805 www.accci.org
American Coke & Coal Chemicals Institute Directory
For merchant oven coke producers, integrated coke producers, tar distillers, sales agents, and industry suppliers.

4806 www.actox.org
American College of Toxicology
Multidisciplinary society composed of professionals having a common interest in toxicology. Our mission is to educate and lead professionals in industry, government and related areas of toxicology by actively promoting the exchange of information and perspectives on the current status of safety assesment and the application of new developments in toxicology.

4807 www.aiche.org
American Institute of Chemical Engineers
Professional association of more than 50,000 members, providing leadership in advancing the chemical engineering profession. Members develop processes and design and operate manufacturing plants, as well as research the safe and environmentally sound manufacture, use and disposal of chemical products.

4808 www.americanchemistry.com
American Chemistry Council
Committed to improved environmental, health and safety performance through responsible care, common sense advocacy designed to address major public policy issues, health and environmental research and product testing.

4809 www.aoac.org
Association of Official Analytical Communities
Calender, publications and training courses. AOAC serves as the primary resource for timely knowledge exchange, networking and high quality laboratory information for its members.

4810 www.aocs.org
American Oil Chemists Society
Encourages advancement of technology and research in fats, oils and other associated substances.

4811 www.asms.org
American Society for Mass Spectrometry
Formed to disseminate knowledge of mass spectrometry and allied topics. Members come from academic, industrial and governmental laboratories. Their interests include advancement of techniques and instrumentation in mass specrometry, as well as fundamental research in chemistry, geology, biological sciences and physics.

4812 www.chemheritage.org
Chemical Heritage Foundation
An independent, nonprofit organization, CHF maintains major collections of instruments, fine art, photographs, papers, and books. We host conferences and lectures, support research, offer fellowships, and produce educational materials.

4813 www.chemistry.org
American Chemical Society

Encourages advancement in all branches of chemistry. There are 34 ACS divisions and 188 local sections.

4814 www.chemtrec.org
American Chemistry Council

Serves as a referral service for non-emergency health and safety information, maintains library and speakers bureaus. Offers 24 hour emergency communication service center for hazardous materials, material data sheets, lending library, audio-visual training programs.

4815 www.coatingstech.org
Federation of Societies for Coatings Technology

Provides technical education and professional development to its members and to the global industry through its multi-national constituent societies and collectively as a federation.

4816 www.combustioninstitute.org
Combustion Institute

A non-profit, educational, scientific society whose purpose is to promote and disseminate research combustion science.

4817 www.csma.org
Chemical Specialties Manufacturers Association

For companies involved in the formulation, manufacture, testing and marketing of chemical specialty products.

4818 www.cspa.org
Consumer Specialty Products Association

Nonprofit organization composed of many companies involved in the formulation, manufacture, testing and marketing of chemical specialty products. Our line includes disinfectants that kill germs in homes, hospitals and restaurants, candles that eliminate odors, pest management products for home and garden, cleaning products and much more.

4819 www.dupont.com/nacs
DuPont Experimental Station

For chemists and chemical engineers engaged in the study and use of reactions involving catalysts. Publishes a newsletter

4820 www.electrochem.org
Electrochemical Society

The society is an international nonprofit, educational organization concerned with phenomena relating to electrochemical and solid state science and technology. Members are individual scientists and engineers, as well as corporations and laboratories.

4821 www.fibersource.com
American Fiber Manufacturers Association

Trade association for US companies that manufacture synthetic and cellulostic fibers. The industry employs 30,000 people and produces over 9 billion pounds of fiber in the US. The association maintains close ties to other manufactured fiber trade associations worldwide.

4822 www.greyhouse.com
Grey House Publishing

Authoritative reference directories for most business sectors incluidng chemical and agricultural markets. Users can search the online databases with varied search criteria allowing for custom searches by product category, geographic area, sales volume, keyword, subject and more. Full Grey House catalog and online ordering also available.

4823 www.ilta.org
Independent Liquid Terminals Association

Representing bulk liquid terminal companies that store commercial liquids in aboveground storage tanks and transfer products to and from oceangoing tanks ships, tank barges, pipelines, tank trucks, and tank rail cars.

4824 www.ioza.org
International Ozone Assn-Pan American Group Branch

Not for profit educational association which performs its information sharing functions through sponsorship of international symposia, seminars, publications, and the development of personal relationships among ozone specialists throughout the world.

4825 www.leatherchemists.org
American Leather Chemists Association

Publishes the Journal of the American Leather Chemists Association where original research reports are published along with abstracts of foreign articles. A four-day technical meeting is held annually. Promotes the advancement of the knowledge of science and engineering in their application to the problems facing the leather and leather products industries.

4826 www.methanol.org
American Methanol Institute

Our mission is to expand markets for the use of methanol as a chemical commodity building block, a hydrogen carrier for fuel cell applications, and an alternative fuel. AMI was formed in 1989, during the height of the Clean Air Act debate, and worked to help create the highly successful reformulated gasoline program.

4827 www.mti-link.org
Materials Tech. Institute of the Chemical Process

MTI provides leadership in materials technology for chemical processing to improve reliability, profitability and safety.

4828 www.nacatsoc.org
North American Catalysis Society

Fosters an interest in heterogeneous and homogeneous catalysis. Organizes national meetings. Members are chemists and chemical engineers engaged in the study and use of reactions involving catalysts. Publishes a newsletter.

4829 www.pemanet.org
Process Equipment Manufacturers' Association

Organized in 1960, we represent more than 40 companies in the process equipment field. Member companies serve the liquid-solids separation, food processing, pulp and paper, waste water treatment industry and others.

4830 www.pestworld.org
National Pest Control Association

For over 65 years, the NPMA has represented the interests of its members and the structural pest control industry. Through the efforts of NPMA, the pest control industry is stronger, more professional, and more unified. Guiding its members and industry through legislative and regulatory initiatives on the federal and state levels, the creation of verifiable training, the changing technologies used by the industry, and public and media relations, NPMA has been a clear, positive voice.

4831 www.pfa.org
Polyurethane Foam Association

Educating customers and other groups about flexible polyurethane foam and to promote its use in manufactured and indutrial products. This includes providing facts on environmental, health and safety issues related to polyurethane foam to the memebership of PFA,

polyurethane foam users, regulatory officials, business leaders and the media.

4832 www.pigments.org
Color Pigments Manufacturers Association

An industry trade association representing color pigment companies in Canada, Mexico and the US. Represents small, medium, and large color pigments manufacturers accounting for 95% of the production of color pigments in North America

4833 www.pima.org
Polyisocyanurate Insulation Manufacturers Assn

National association that advances the use of polyisocyanurate (polyiso) insulation. Polyiso is one of the nation's most widely used and cost-effective insulation products. PIMA's membership consiosts of manufacturers as well as suppliers to the industry.

4834 www.pinechemicals.org
Pine Chemicals Association

Association of producers, processors and consumers of pine chemicals. The PCA promotes innovative, safe and environmentally responsible practices to assure a reliable supply of high quality products.

4835 www.powdercoating.org
Powder Coating Institute

Founded in 1981 as a nonprofit organization, PCI works to advance the utilization of powder coating as an economical, non-polluting and high quality finish for industrial and consumer products.

4836 www.scisoc.org/asbc
American Society of Brewing Chemists

News, information, member directory and publications.

4837 www.simaflavor.org
Flavor & Extract Manufacturers Assn of the US

Locates suppliers and manufacturers of rare chemicals and oils used in the flavor and fragrance industry.

4838 www.socma.com
Synthetic Organic Chemical Manufacturers Assn

Trade association serving the specialty batch and custom chemical industry since 1921. Its more than 320 member companies have more than 2,000 manufacturing sites and 100,000 employees. SOCMA members encompass every segment of the industry - and manufacture 50,000 products annually that are valued at $60 billion dollars.

4839 www.toxicology.org
Society of Toxicology

Members are scientists concerned with the effects of chemicals on man and the environment. Promotes the aquisition and utilization of knowledge in toxicology, aids in the protection of public health and facilitates disiplines. The society has a strong commitment to education in toxicology and to the recruitment of students and new members into the profession.

Associations

4840 **American Cleaning Institute**
1331 L St NW
Suite 650
Washington, DC 20005

202-347-2900
FAX 202-347-4110
E-Mail: Info@CleaningInstitute.org
Home Page: www.cleaninginstitute.org
Social Media: *Facebook, Twitter, LinkedIn, RSS Feed, SchoolTube, YouTube*

Ernie Rosenberg, President & CEO
Helen Benz, CFO
Sandra Andrade, Program Coordinator, Meetings
Leonardo Bellisario, Govt. Affairs Coordinator
Melissa Bernardo, Manager of Sustainability Programs

Nonprofit trade association representing manufacturers of household, industrial and institutional cleaning products; their ingredients and finished packaging. Dedicated to advancing public understanding of the safety and benefits of cleaning products and protecting the ability of its members to formulate products that best meet consumer needs.
100+ Members
Founded in 1926
Mailing list available for rent

4841 **Association for Linen Management**
138 N Keeneland Dr.
Suite D
Richmond, KY 40475

859-624-0177
800-669-0863
FAX 859-624-3580
Home Page: www.almnet.org
Social Media: *Facebook, Twitter, Pinterest*

Randy Wendland, President
Cindy Molko, SVP
Graham Skinner, VP
Richard Bott, Chief Financial Officer
Shane Woodson, Secretary

Association for the advancement of professional development in the laundry institute.
Founded in 1939

4842 **Building Service Contractors Association International**
330 N. Wabash Ave.
Suite 2000
Chicago, IL 60611

312-321-5167
800-368-3414
FAX 312-673-6735
E-Mail: info@bscai.org
Home Page: www.bscai.org
Social Media: *LinkedIn*

Chris Mundschenk, EVP/ CEO
Paul Greenland, President
Jim Harris, Jr. Treasurer
Tom Kruse, Vice President
Michael Diamond, Director

Trade association for companies offering security, maintenance and cleaning services. The international membership now represents over 10% of the association's professional membership.
Cost: $30.00
2500 Members
Founded in 1965
Mailing list available for rentat $75 per M

4843 **Chlorine Free Products Association**
1304 S Main St
Algonquin, IL 60102-2757

847-658-6104
FAX 847-658-3152
E-Mail: info@chlorinefreeproducts.org
Home Page: www.chlorinefreeproducts.org

Archie Beaton, Executive Director
Richard Albert, Technical Staff Manager
Dr. Kevin Lyons, Chief Procurement Officer
Frank Perkowski, President, Business Development
Jane Bloodworth, Business Manager

A nonprofit association that's primary purpose is to promote total chlorine free policies, programs and technologies throughtout the world.

4844 **Cleaning Equipment Trade Association**
PO Box 270908
Oklahoma City, OK 73137-0908

704-635-7362
800-441-0111
FAX 651-982-0030
E-Mail: info@ceta.org
Home Page: www.ceta.org

Linda Chappell, President
Curtis Brarber, Senior Vice President
Aaron Auger, Vice President
Kyle Notch, Secretary
Chad Rasmussen, Treasurer

International nonprofit reade association made up of manufacturers, distributors, and suppliers who coordinate their efforts to promote public awareness, professionalism, industry wide safety standards, and education for the advancement of the powered cleaning equipment industry.
300 Members
Founded in 1996

4845 **Cleaning Management Institute**
125 Wolf Road Suite 112
Albany, NY 12205

800-225-4772
FAX 847-982-1012
E-Mail: brant@issa.com
Home Page: www.cminstitute.net
Social Media: *Facebook, RSS*

Maicah Ogburn, Director
Pat Harrington, Administrative Manager
Brant Insero, Training Sales Specialist
Matt Moberg, Training Development

CMI provides education, training and career improvement opportunities for building cleaning and maintenance professionals.
1000 Members
Founded in 1964

4846 **Coin Laundry Association**
1 S. 660 Midwest Rd.
Suite 205
Oakbrook Terrace, IL 60181

630-953-7920
800-570-5629
FAX 630-953-7925
E-Mail: info@coinlaundry.org
Home Page: www.coinlaundry.org
Social Media: *Facebook, Twitter, LinkedIn, YouTube, Google+*

Brian Wallace, President & CEO
Craig Krichner, Chairman
Jeff Gardner, Chair Elect
Michael Sokolowski, EVP
James Whitmore, Vice-Chairman

Association for self-service laundry and dry cleaning industry.
2700+ Members
Founded in 1960

4847 **Environmental Management Association**
Vickie Lewis, EMA President
38575 Mallast
Harrison Township, MI 48045

313-875-9450
866-999-4EMA
FAX 586-463-8075
E-Mail: emadirector@gmail.com
Home Page: www.emaweb.org
Social Media: *Facebook, LinkedIn*

Nancy Kapral, EMA Director
Vickie Lewis, President
Karen Terry-Johnson, VP & Membership Chair

Association for manufacturers, suppliers and distributors of sanitation maintenance supplies, products, services.
11 Members
Founded in 1994

4848 **Halogenated Solvents Industry Alliance**
3033 Wilson Boulevard
Suite 700
Arlington, VA 22201

703-875-0683
FAX 703-875-0675
E-Mail: info@hsia.org
Home Page: www.hsia.org

Steve Risotto, Executive Director

Represents manufacturers of perchloroetheylene and related solvents.

4849 **ISSA**
3300 Dundee Road
Northbrook, IL 60062

847-982-0800
800-225-4772
FAX 847-982-1012
E-Mail: info@issa.com
Home Page: www.issa.com
Social Media: *Facebook, Twitter, LinkedIn*

John Barrett, Executive Director
Alan R Tomblin, President
John Swigart, Secretary
John Barrett, Treasurer

The worldwide cleaning industry association.
5700+ Members
Founded in 1923

4850 **International Drycleaners Congress**
9016 Oak Branch Dr.
Apex, NC 27502

919-363-5062
FAX 919-387-8326
Home Page: www.idcnews.org

Manfred Wentz, Executive Director
Nobuyasu Igarashi, President

International organization for cleaners.
Founded in 1959

4851 **International Kitchen Exhaust Cleaning Association**
100 N. 20th St.
Suite 400
Philadelphia, PA 19103

215-320-3876
FAX 215-564-2175
E-Mail: information@ikeca.org
Home Page: www.ikeca.org
Social Media: *Facebook, Twitter, LinkedIn, YouTube*

Kathy Slomer, President
Randall Rauth, President-Elect
Anne Levine, Secretary
Jesse Getz, Treasurer
Jack Grace, Immediate Past President

Promotes fire safety in restaurants through stringent standards and practices for contrac-

tors engaged in kitchen exhaust cleaning. Conducts a variety of educational programs, and works with influential code setting bodies such as the National Fire Protection Association to improve existing codes and regulations.
Founded in 1989

4852 International Maintenance Institute

PO Box 751896
Houston, TX 77275

281-481-0869
FAX 281-481-8337
E-Mail: iminst@swbell.net
Home Page: www.imionline.org
Social Media: *Facebook, Twitter, LinkedIn*

George Masterson, Chairman
Gerard Goudreau, President
Joyce Rhoden, Executive Secretary
Edward Stedman, Secretary
Kevin O'Rourke, Treasurer

Focuses on plant workers and vendors who have products tailored to the maintenance industry. The philosophy of the organization is to professionalize the maintenance function by helping maintenance managers to work smarter through the exchange of ideas and education.
2.5M Members
Founded in 1960

4853 Laundry and Dry Cleaning International

14700 Sweitzer Lane
Laurel, MD 20707

301-622-1900
800-638-2627
FAX 240-295-0685
E-Mail: techline@ifi.org
Home Page: www.ifi.org

Patrick Jones, Manager

Sponsors and supports The League of Voter Education Political Action Committee.

4854 Multi-Housing Laundry Association

1500 Sunday Drive
Suite 102
Raleigh, NC 27607-5151

919-861-5579
800-380-3652
FAX 919-787-4916
E-Mail: nshore@mla-online.com
Home Page: www.mla-online.com
Social Media: *Facebook, Twitter, LinkedIn*

David Feild, Executive Director
Penny DePas CAE, Asst Exec Director/Conference Mgr

Furnishes information on tax and business development and promotes high business standards. Annual meetings held in June.
15M Members
Founded in 1959

4855 National Association of Diaper Services

994 Old Eagle School Rd
Suite 1019
Wayne, PA 19087-1802

610-971-4850
FAX 610-971-4859
E-Mail: nads@diapernet.org
Home Page: www.diapernet.org

John Shiffert, Executive Director

The international professional trade association for the diaper service industry.
Founded in 1938

4856 National Association of Institutional Linen Management

2130 Lexington Road
Richmond, KY 40475-7923

800-669-0863
FAX 859-624-3580
Home Page: www.nailm.org

Jim Thacker, Executive Director

Seeks improvement of laundry technology. Conducts formal schools.
1.4M Members
Founded in 1959

4857 National Cleaners Association

252 W 29th St
New York, NY 10001

212-967-3002
800-888-1622
FAX 212-967-2240
E-Mail: info@nca-i.com
Home Page: www.nca-i.com
Social Media: *Facebook, LinkedIn, Pinterest*

Debra Kravet, President
Nora Nealis, Executive Director
Simon Bai, Member Services Staff
Clint Lee, Member Services Staff
Vivian Benn, Office Staff

Professional trade association dedicated to the welfare of well groomed consumers and the professional cleaners who serve them. Elected officials, government angencies, consumer groups, fashion designers and major media outlets have recognized and responded to NCA's activities, reports and tradition of excellence.
4000 Members
Founded in 1946

4858 North East Fabricare Association

P.O.Box 920
Pelham, NH 03076

603-635-0322
800-442-6848
FAX 781-942-7393
E-Mail: peteblke@aol.com
Home Page: www.nefabricare.com

Robert Joel, Vice-President
John Dallas, President
Yaahkov Cohn, Treasurer
John Dallas, Secretary

Serves cleaners in the New England, New Jersey and New York with information and news about the fabricare industry.
Founded in 1992

4859 Power Washers of North America

PO Box 270634
Saint Paul, MN 55127

800-393-7962
800-393-7962
FAX 651-213-0369
E-Mail: pwnahq@pwna.org
Home Page: www.pwna.org

Eric Clark, President
Tom Bickett, Treasurer
John Nearon, VP
Charlie Arnold, Secretary
Jackie Gavett, Executive Dir.

Developing and communicating high standards in ethical business practices, environmental awareness and safety through continuing education and active representation of the membership. PWNA educated and trained contractors raise the level of professionalism and value to their customers.
550 Members
Founded in 1992
Mailing list available for rent: 500 names

4860 Restoration Industry Association

2025 M Street, NW
Suite 800
Rockville, MD 20852

202-367-1180
800-272-7012
FAX 202-367-2180
E-Mail: info@restorationindustry.org
Home Page: www.restorationindustry.org
Social Media: *Facebook, Twitter, LinkedIn*

Scott Stamper, President
Chuck Violand, First Vice President
Mark Springer, Vice President
Jack A White, Secretary
Larry Holder, Treasurer

A trade association for cleaning and restoration professionals worldwide, and the foremost authority, trainer and educator in the industry.
1100 Members
Founded in 1946

4861 Rocky Mountain Fabricare Association

2110 65th Ave.
Greely, CO 80634

970-330-0124
866-964-RFMA
FAX 303-458-0002
E-Mail: info@rmfa.org
Home Page: www.rmfa.org
Social Media: *Facebook*

Colleen Mulhern, Executive Director
Brad Ewing, Secretary/Treasurer
Jim Nixon, President

Enhancing the image and viability of the fabricare industry through education and development of the skills, talents and professionalism of its membership. Serves cleaners in Colorado, Utah and Wyoming.
900 Members

4862 South Eastern Fabricare Association

14700 Sweitzer Lane
Laurel, MD 20707

877-707-7332
877-707-7332
FAX 912-355-3155
E-Mail: peter@sefa.org
Home Page: www.sefa.org

Tim Morrow, President
Mark Watkins, VP-Alabama
Julia Campbell, Secretary
Wash Respress, Chairman
Russ Ballard, VP- South Carolina

Trade association that represents its members who have an interest in the dry cleaning and laundry industry.
900+ Members
Founded in 1972
Mailing list available for rent

4863 Southwest Drycleaners Association

5750 Balcones Dr.
Suite 201
Austin, TX 78731

512-873-8195
FAX 512-873-7423
E-Mail: de.sda@sbcglobal.net
Home Page: www.sda-dryclean.com
Social Media: *Facebook, Twitter*

Andrew Stanley, Executive Director
Michael E. Nesbit, CED, President
Douglas Johnson,CGCP, 1st Vice President
Amin Bata, CPD, 2nd Vice President
Jeff Schwarz, Sergeant at Arms

Serves cleaners in Louisiana, Mississippi, Missouri, Kansas, Arkansa, New Mexico, Oklahoma and Texas.

4864 Sponge and Chamois Institute
10024 Office Center Ave.
Suite 203
St. Louis, MO 63128

314-842-2230
FAX 314-842-3999
E-Mail: scwaters@swbell.net
Home Page: www.chamoisinstitute.org

Jules Schwimmer, Executive Secretary

Members are dealers and suppliers of natural sponges and chamois leather.
Founded in 1933

4865 Uniform and Textile Service Association
12587 Fair Lakes Cir
Fairfax, VA 22033-3822

703-247-2600
800-486-6745
FAX 703-841-4750
E-Mail: info@utsa.com
Home Page: www.utsa.com

David Hobson, President
Jennifer Kellar, Executive Coordinator
Larry Patton, Director Plant Operations
Deborah Hodges, Director Finance/Administration

Represents textile supply and service companies. Represents 95% of the annual sales generated by the uniform service industry and 65% of the annual sales generated by the linen supply industry. UTSA members provide, clean, and maintain reusable textile products, such as uniforms, sheets, table linen, shop and print towels, floor mats, mops and other items to thousands of businesses.
100 Members
Founded in 1933

Newsletters

4866 Bulletin
Neighborhood Cleaners Association
252 W 29th St
New York, NY 10001-5271

212-967-3002
FAX 212-967-2240
E-Mail: ncaiclean@aol.com
Home Page: www.nca-i.com

Debra Kravet, President

Technical info for the dry cleaning industry. Government regulation compliance.
Frequency: Bi-Monthly

4867 Coin Laundry Association: Journal
Coin Laundry Association
1315 Butterfield Road
Suite 212
Downers Grove, IL 60515-5602

630-963-5547
FAX 630-963-5864
E-Mail: info@coinlaundry.org
Home Page: www.coinlaundry.org

Clay Pederson, Chairman
Brian Wallace, President
Bob Nieman, Editor
Laurie Moore, Circulation Manager
Bill Gilbert, Marketing Manager

Committed to offering coin-op owners the information necessary to become and remain competitive in today's changing market.
4 Pages
Frequency: Monthly
Founded in 1960

4868 Fabricare News
Drycleaning & Laundrey Institute International
14700 Sweitzer lane
Laurel, MD 20707

301-622-1900
800-638-2627
FAX 240-295-4200
E-Mail: techline@dlionline.org
Home Page: www.dlionline.org
Social Media: *Facebook*

David MacHesny, President
Charlie Smith, Chair
Mary Scalco, CEO

Information of interest to dry cleaners and launderers.
8 Pages
Frequency: Monthly
Circulation: 5000
Founded in 1883

4869 Maytag Commercial Newsletter
Whirlpool Corporation
553 Benson Road
Benton Harbor, MI 49022-2692

269-923-5000
800-344-1274
Home Page: www.maytag.com

Mike Klosterman, Publisher
Debbie White, Executive Director

Self-service laundry industry news.
8 Pages
Frequency: BiWeekly

4870 Reclaimer
South Eastern Fabricare Association
7373 Hodgson Memorial Dr
Building 3, Suite C
Savannah, GA 31406-1595

912-355-3364
877-707-7332
FAX 912-355-3155
E-Mail: barry@sefa.org
Home Page: www.sefa.org

Billy Stewart, President
Ron McLamb, VP

A monthly newsletter dedicated to the service of the drycleaning industry.
Cost: $5.00
Frequency: Monthly
Circulation: 2200

Magazines & Journals

4871 American Coin-Op
Crain Communications Inc
360 N Michigan Ave
Suite 7
Chicago, IL 60601-3800

312-649-5200
FAX 312-649-7937
E-Mail: info@crain.com
Home Page: www.crain.com

Keith Crain, CEO

Offers operators, manufacturers and suppliers in-depth coverage of the latest industry trends, new products, energy-saving methods and management strategies.
Frequency: Monthly
Circulation: 17622
Mailing list available for rent

4872 American Drycleaner
Crain Communications Inc

360 N Michigan Ave
Suite 7
Chicago, IL 60601-3800

312-649-5200
FAX 312-649-7937
E-Mail: info@crain.com
Home Page: www.crain.com

Keith Crain, CEO

Brings news, expert advice and indepth features to drycleaning businesses and suppliers nationwide every month. Stories focus on management, equipment and operations to help owners build their skills and profits.
Frequency: Monthly
Circulation: 24217

4873 American Laundry News
Crain Communications Inc
360 N Michigan Ave
Suite 7
Chicago, IL 60601-3800

312-649-5200
FAX 312-649-7937
E-Mail: info@crain.com
Home Page: www.crain.com

Keith Crain, CEO

Focuses on the widely varied issues facing the industry: productivity, technology, labor, workplace safety, the environment and more.
Frequency: Monthly
Circulation: 15350
Founded in 1974

4874 American Window Cleaner Magazine
12 Twelve Publishing Corporation
750-B NW Broad Street
Southern Pines, NC 28387

910-693-2644
FAX 910-246-1681
E-Mail: info@awcmag.com
Home Page: www.awcmag.com

Norman J Finegold, President

Information on new products, add-on businesses, association and convention news and safety.
Frequency: 6x/Year
Circulation: 8000

4875 Broom Brush & Mop
Rankin Publishing Company
204 E Main St
PO Box 130
Arcola, IL 61910-1416

217-268-0130
FAX 217-268-4815
E-Mail: DRankin125@aol.com
Home Page: www.ragsmag.com

Don Rankin, Owner
Harrell Kerkhoff, Editor
Ron White, Associate Editor

Reports on import and export totals as well as updates on new products and trade show coverage, also industry trends and market conditions.
Cost: $25.00
Frequency: Monthly
Circulation: 1,700
Founded in 1912

4876 Brushware
Brushware
750-B NW Broad St
Southern Pines, NC 28387

910-693-2644
FAX 910-246-1681
E-Mail: editors@brushwaremag.com
Home Page: www.brushwaremag.com/

Karen Grinter, Publisher
Norman J Finegold, President

Information on products that apply materials, clean and polish surfaces, covers also industry

news, products, methods and trends, market reports, profiles and interviews.
Cost: $45.00
Circulation: 2000
Founded in 1898

4877 Cleaner
COLE Publishing
1720 Maple Lake Dam Road
PO Box 220
Three Lakes, WI 54562

715-546-3346
800-257-7222
FAX 715-546-3786
Home Page: www.cleaner.com

Ted Roulphe, Editor
Geoff Bruss, CEO

The latest tools and equipment promoting safety and efficiency, employment and environmental concerns, as well as industry profiles.
Cost: $15.00
Frequency: Monthly
Circulation: 24000
Founded in 1979

4878 Cleaner Times
Advantage Publishing Company
1000 Nix Rd
Little Rock, AR 72211-3235

866-828-9267
800-525-7038
FAX 501-280-9233
E-Mail: advpub@adpub.com
Home Page: www.adpub.com

Charlene Yarbrough, Publisher
Gerry Plus, Circulation Manager
Jim McMurry, Editor

Application, information, and productivity for persons engaged in the manufacturing, distribution, or the use of high pressure water systems and accessories. The emphasis is on safety, regulatory, which affect the industry as well as cleaning applications.
Cost: $36.00
72 Pages
Frequency: Monthly
Circulation: 25,000
ISSN: 1073-9602
Founded in 1989
Printed in 4 colors on glossy stock

4879 Cleanfax Magazine
National Trade Publications
19 British Amer. Blvd. West
Latham, NY 12110-2197

518-783-1281
FAX 518-783-1386
E-Mail: webmaster@cleanfax.com
Home Page: www.cleanfax.com

Micah Ogburn, Publisher
Jeff Cross, Senio Editor
Barry Lovette, General Manager

Information on carpet cleaning, water and fire damage restoration, industry news and updates.
80 Pages
Frequency: Monthly
Circulation: 20,000
Founded in 1981
Printed in 4 colors on glossy stock

4880 Cleaning & Restoration Magazine
Restoration Industry Association
9810 Patuxent Woods Dr
Suite K
Columbia, MD 21046-1595

443-878-1000
800-272-7012
FAX 443-878-1010

E-Mail: info@restorationindustry.org
Home Page: www.restorationindustry.org

Donald E Manger, Executive Director
Patricia L Harman, Communications Director

Trade journal covering fire and water damage restoration, rug and textile cleaning, indoor air quality and business issues.
Frequency: Monthly
Circulation: 6000

4881 Commercial Floor Care
Business News Publishing Company
22801 Ventura Blvd
Suite 115
Woodland Hills, CA 91364-1230

818-224-8035
800-835-4398
FAX 818-224-8042
E-Mail: stoufferj@bnpmedia.com
Home Page: www.bnpmedia.com

Phil Johnson, Publisher
Jeffrey Stouffer, Editor
Amy Levin, Production Manager
Jim Michaelson, Associate Publisher

Dedicated to floor care in the commercial environment.
40 Pages
Frequency: Monthly
Circulation: 26700
Founded in 1926
Printed in 4 colors on glossy stock

4882 Fabricare
Drycleaning & Laundry Institute
International
14700 Sweitzer Lane
Laurel, MD 20707

301-622-1900
800-638-2627
FAX 240-295-0685
E-Mail: techline@dlif.org
Home Page: www.dlifi.org

Charlie Smith, Chairman
Jan Barlow, President
Dave MacHesny, President-Elect

The central publication of the International Fabricare Institute. This publication provides information, knowledge and education about drycleaning and laundry issues, the industry, as a whole, and the association.
8 Pages
Frequency: Monthly
Circulation: 8,000
Founded in 1883

4883 ICS Cleaning Specialist
Business News Publishing Company
2401 West Big Beaver Road
Troy, MI 48054

818-224-8035
800-835-4398
FAX 818-224-8042
Home Page: www.bnpmedia.com

Phil Johnson, Publisher
Evan Kessler, Publisher
Eric Fish, Editor
Amy Levin, Production Manager
Jim Michaelson, Associate Publisher

For carpet cleaning, restoration and floor care service providers.
68 Pages
ISSN: 1522-4708
Founded in 1928
Printed in on glossy stock

4884 Industrial Launderer Magazine
Uniform & Textile Service Association

1501 Lee Hwy.kes Cir
Suite 304
Arlington, VA 22209

703-247-2600
800-486-6745
FAX 703-841-4750

George Harrinton Jr, President

The authoritative source for information for the uniform and textile service industry. It provides practical guidance and assistance for businesses that rent, lease or sell uniforms and other textiles including linen supply.
Cost: $100.00
Frequency: Monthly
Circulation: 6000

4885 International Fabricare Institute
12251 Tech Rd
Silver Spring, MD 20904-1901

301-622-1900
800-638-2627
FAX 301-236-9320
E-Mail: techline@ifi.org
Home Page: www.ifi.org

William E Fisher, Publisher

The association of Professional Dry Cleaners, wetcleaners, and launderers. With its education, research, testing and professional training, IFI offers solutions that help member businesses provide expert garment care.
Founded in 1883

4886 Journal of the Coin Laundering and Drycleaning Industry
Coin Laundry Association
1315 Butterfield Road
Suite 212
Downers Grove, IL 60515-5602

630-963-5547
800-570-5629
FAX 630-963-5864
E-Mail: info@coinlaundry.org
Home Page: www.coinlaundry.org

Brian Wallace, President
Clay Pederson, Chairman

The official voice of the coin laundry and drycleaning industry. It's the most cost effective way to reach over 28,000 small business entrepreneurs. Besides industry specific items these owners operate over 38,000 company vehicles, utilize business management materials and more. Accepts advertising.
52 Pages
Frequency: Monthly

4887 Maintenance Sales News
Rankin Publishing Company
204 E Main St
PO Box 130
Arcola, IL 61910-0130

217-268-4959
800-598-8083
FAX 217-268-4815
E-Mail: drankin125@aol.com
Home Page: www.ragsmag.com

Don Rankin, Owner
Linda Rankin, Co-Publisher
Harrell Kerkhoff, Editor
Rick Mullen, Editor

Information on selling techniques, business management, training, merchandise, and seminars.
Circulation: 18,000

4888 Maintenance Solutions
Trade Press Publishing Corporation
2100 W Florist Avenue
Milwaukee, WI 53209

414-228-7701
FAX 414-228-1134

E-Mail: contact@facilitiesnet.com
Home Page: www.facilitiesnet.com

Dick Yake, Editoridal Director
Dan Hounsell, Editor
Brad Ehlert, VP Publisher
Robert Geissler, Publisher
Stephen Bolte, Publisher

How to articles and features designed to alleviate reader problems as well as new product information and applications.
Cost: $45.00
42 Pages
Frequency: Monthly
Circulation: 35000
ISSN: 1072-3560
Founded in 1993

4889 Maintenance Supplies
Cygnus Publishing
3 Huntington Quadrangle
Suite 301N
Melville, NY 11747-3601

631-845-2700
800-308-6397
FAX 720-945-2798
E-Mail: Rich.DiPaolo@cygnuspub.com
Home Page: www.cygnusb2b.com

Tracy Rossi, Publisher
Paul Mackler, President
Rich Di Paolo, Editor
Kathy Scott, Director of Public Relations
Elise Schafer, Assistant Editor

Case histories and general industry news, also supply distributors, new methods and equipment in the field.
Cost: $66.00
Frequency: Monthly
Circulation: 16,500
Founded in 1966

4890 National Association of Institutional Linen Management News Magazine
2161 Lexington Rd
Suite 2
Richmond, KY 40475-7952

859-624-0177
800-669-0863
FAX 859-624-3580
Home Page: www.nlmnet.org

Linda Fairbanks, Executive Director
Randy Wendland, Corporate Director

Offers information for cleaners of fine fabrics.
Frequency: Monthly

4891 Sanitary Maintenance
Trade Press Publishing Corporation
2100 W Florist Avenue
Milwaukee, WI 53201-3799

414-228-7701
FAX 414-228-1134
E-Mail: info@tradepress.com
Home Page: www.tradepress.com

Dick Yake, Editorial Director
Brian Terry, Publisher
Pat Foran, Editor
Robert Wisniewski, CEO

Business management, inventory control and product trends, also includes industrial paper products, cleaning chemicals, safety supplies, janitorial supplies and packaging products.
58 Pages
Frequency: Monthly
Circulation: 16052
ISSN: 0036-4436
Founded in 1943

4892 Services Magazine
Building Service Contractors Association Int'l

401 N Michigan Avenue
22nd Floor
Chicago, IL 60611

312-321-5167
800-368-3414
FAX 312-673-6735
E-Mail: info@bscai.org
Home Page: www.bscai.org

Oliver Yandle, Executive VP/CEO
Karen Lawver, Director Membership Services

The Building Service Contractors Association International is the trade association serving the facility services industry through education, leadership, and representatiion.
Cost: $30.00
56 Pages
Frequency: Monthly
Circulation: 20064
ISSN: 0279-0548
Founded in 1981
Mailing list available for rent: 20000 names

4893 Textile Rental Magazine
Textile Rental Services Association
1800 Diagonal Rd
Suite 200
Alexandria, VA 22314-2842

703-519-0029
877-770-9274
FAX 703-519-0026
E-Mail: trsa@trsa.org
Home Page: www.trsa.org

Roger Cocivera, President/CEO
Jack Morgan, Editor
Steven Biller, Editorial Director
Packed with valuable tips and ideas.
Frequency: Monthly

4894 Water Conditioning & Purification Magazine
Publicom, Incorporated
2800 E. Ft. Lowell Road
Tucson, AZ 85716

520-323-6144
FAX 520-323-7412
E-Mail: info@wcponline.com
Home Page: www.wcponline.com

Kurt C. Peterson, Publisher
Sharon Peterson, Business Manager
Denise Roberts, Executive Editor

Water Conditioning & Purification Magazine(WC&P) has been the premier source for news, technical artticles and water science features sine 1959. We are committed to the water treatment industry. Our pro bono participation includes event and activity sponsorship, committe members, task force cahiras and association leadership.

Trade Shows

4895 Association of Specialists in Cleaning & Restoration Convention
Restoration Industry Association
9810 Patuxent Woods Drive
Suite K
Columbia, MD 21046-1595

443-878-1000
800-272-7012
FAX 443-878-1010
E-Mail: info@restorationindustry.org
Home Page: www.restorationindustry.org

Donald E Manger, Executive Director
Patricia L Harman, Communications Director

Annual convention and exhibits of carpet, upholstery and draperies cleaning and restoration

equipment, duct cleaning supplies and services, 100+ booths.
600 Attendees
Frequency: Annual
Founded in 1945

4896 Building Service Contractors Association International Trade Show
401 N Michigan Avenue
22nd Floor
Chicago, IL 60611

312-321-5167
800-368-3414
FAX 312-673-6735
E-Mail: info@bscai.org
Home Page: www.bscai.org

Oliver Yandle, Executive VP/CEO
Karen Lawver, Director Membership Services

Containing 400 booths and 185 exhibits.
2000 Attendees
Frequency: March/April
Founded in 1965

4897 Clean Show
Riddle & Associates
1874 Piedmont Road
Suite 360
Atlanta, GA 30305

404-876-1988
FAX 404-876-5121
E-Mail: info@cleanshow.com
Home Page: www.cleanshow.com

John Riddle, Manager
Ann Howell, Communications

World's largest exposition for laundry, drycleaning and textile services industry featuring working equipment and educational program. Draws international attendance.
17000 Attendees
Frequency: Biennial, Odd Years
Founded in 1977

4898 Educational Congress for Laundering & Drycleaning
Coin Laundry Association
1315 Butterfield Road
Suite 212
Downers Grove, IL 60515-5602

630-963-5547
800-570-5629
FAX 630-963-5864
E-Mail: info@coinlaundry.org
Home Page: www.coinlaundry.org

Brian Wallace, President
Clay Pederson, Chairman

Two thousand one hundred booths of equipment and products for the cleaning industry. Service schools and other events planned.
22M Attendees
Frequency: July

4899 National Educational Exposition and Conference
Environmental Management Association
Fishbones In Greektown
400 Monroe Street
Detroit, MI 48226-3333

Annual show of 15 manufacturers, suppliers and distributors of sanitation maintenance supplies, products, services.
150 Attendees

4900 Power Clean
Cleaning Equipment Trade Association
P0 Box 1710
Indian Trail, NC 28079

704-635-7362
800-441-0111

FAX 704-635-7363
Home Page: www.ceta.org

Troy Tranquill, President
Karl Loeffelholz, Manager

Annual show of 100 manufacturers and suppliers of cleaning equipment, high pressure washers and related component accessories and products.
1200 Attendees
Frequency: October, Dallas

4901 Southern Drycleaners Show
South Eastern Fabricare Association
PO Box 912
Cumming, GA 30028

877-707-7332
FAX 770-998-1441
Home Page: www.sefa.org

Joel Deutsch, Manager

Trade show for the drycleaning industry with 120 exhibitors and 250 booths.
2500 Attendees
Frequency: August

4902 Tex Care
National Cleaners Association
252 W 29th Street
New York, NY 10001

212-967-3002
FAX 212-967-2240
E-Mail: ncaiclean@aol.com
Home Page: www.nca-i.com

Joseph Hallak, President
Ted Aveni, First Vice President

Containing 350 exhibits of interest to member cleaners.
5000+ Attendees
Frequency: April

Directories & Databases

4903 Carpet Cleaners Institute of the Northwest Membership Roster
147 SE 102nd Avenue
Portland, OR 97216-2703

503-253-9091
805-261-8222
FAX 503-253-9172
E-Mail: info@ccinw.org
Home Page: www.ccinw.org

Over 330 member companies involved in the carpet cleaning industry in Washington, Oregon, and Montana, USA and Alberta and British Columbia, Canada.
Frequency: Annual

4904 Cleaning and Maintenance Management: Buyer's Guide Directory Issue
National Trade Publications
13 Century Hill Drive
Latham, NY 12110-2197

518-783-1281
FAX 518-783-1386
Home Page: cmmonline.com

Alice J Savino, Group Publisher
Chris Sanford, Executive Editor

Over 500 manufacturers are profiled that supply equipment used in building maintenance and housekeeping.
Cost: $42.00
84 Pages
Frequency: Annual
Circulation: 42000
ISSN: 1051-5720
Founded in 1966
Mailing list available for rent: 42M names at

$125 per M
Printed in 4 colors on glossy stock

4905 Coin Laundry Association of Suppliers
Coin Laundry Association
1315 Butterfield Road
Downers Grove, IL 60515

630-963-5547
800-570-5629
FAX 630-963-5864
E-Mail: info@coinlaundry.org
Home Page: www.coinlaundry.org

Brian Wallace, President
Clay Pederson, Chairman
Bob Nieman, Editor
Kathy Sherman, Director Administration
Sue Lally, Director Membership

Lists over 500 manufacturers and suppliers of products and services to the coin and dry cleaning laundry industries.
2700+ Pages
Founded in 1960

4906 Inside Textile Service - Directories
Uniform & Textile Service Association
12587 Fair Lakes Cir
Fairfax, VA 22033-3822

703-247-2600
800-486-6745
FAX 703-841-4750
E-Mail: info@utsa.com
Home Page: www.utsa.com

David Hobson, President
Jennifer Kellar, Executive Coordinator

The uniform and textile service industry's most comprehensive guide to US textile service companies. Includes contact data for UTSA's membership, and for hundreds of other textile service companies as well. Contains listings of all UTSA affiliated suppliers with catalog-like data on their products and services. Free to members.
Circulation: 3,000

4907 Textile Rental Services Association Roster
Textile Rental Services Association
1800 Diagonal Rd
Suite 200
Alexandria, VA 22314-2842

703-519-0029
FAX 703-519-0026
E-Mail: trsa@trsa.org
Home Page: www.trsa.org

Roger Cocivera, President
Scott Mallan, Finance Manager
Michael Wilson, Director Government Affairs
Jack Morgan, Editor

Offers a list of over 1,800 companies that supply linen, uniforms and other textile products to other industries.
1300 Pages
Founded in 1913

Industry Web Sites

4908 http://gold.greyhouse.com
G.O.L.D Grey House OnLine Databases

Grey House Publishing's online database platform, GOLD, offers Quick Search, Keyword Search and Expert Search for most business sectors inlcuding the cleaning and laundry markets. Finding the information you need quick and easy - whether you're a novice searcher or an experienced database user. All of Grey House's directory products are available for subscription on the GOLD platform.

4909 www.ascr.org
Assn of Specialists in Cleaning and Restoration

For professionals involved in the cleaning and restoration of interior textiles and structures, including air handling systems.

4910 www.bscai.org
Building Service Contractors Association Int'l

For companies offering security, maintenance and cleaning services.

4911 www.ceta.org
Cleaning Equipment Trade Association

For manufacturers and suppliers of cleaning equipment, high pressure washers and related component accessories and products.

4912 www.cminstitute.net
Cleaning Management Institute

CMI provides education, training and career improvement opportunities for building cleaning and maintenance professionals.

4913 www.coinlaundry.org
Coin Laundry Association

For self-service laundry and dry cleaning industry. CLA is a not for profit trade association representing the 30,000 coin laundry owners in the US and the world.

4914 www.greyhouse.com
Grey House Publishing

Authoritative reference directories for most business sectors including cleaning and laundry markets. Users can search the online databases with varied search criteria allowing for custom searches by product category, geographic area, sales volume, keyword, subject and more. Full Grey House catalog and online ordering also available.

4915 www.ifi.org
International Fabricare Institute

With its education, research, testing and professional training, IFI offers solutions that help member businesses provide expert garment care.

4916 www.ikeca.org
International Kitchen Exhaust Cleaning Association

Education for members about safety, cleaning techniques and many other areas. Since its inception, IKECA, a not for profit trade association, has established stringent standards and practices for contractors engaged in kitchen exhaust clening, conducted a variety of educational programs, and worked with influential code setting bodies such as the National Fire Protection Association to improve existing codes and regulations.

4917 www.imionline.org
International Maintenance Institute

Focuses on plant workers and vendors who have products tailored to the maintenance industry. The philosophy of the organization is to professionalize the maintenace functiuon by helping maintenace managers to work smarter through the exchange of ideas and function.

4918 www.jriddle.com
Riddle & Associates

For the laundering, drycleaning and textile care industry - from single-owner coin-operated laundry and drycleaning establishments to giant industrial and institutional laundries. Our management capabilities work for any type of trade show - large or small. Our experience with heavy utility shows, and shows with highly technical requirements, gives us an expertise in these areas that is difficult to find.

4919 www.nailm.org
National Assn of Insurance Litigation Management

National educational and research group concerned primarily with the advancement of the art of manageing litigated claims.

4920 www.natclo.com
National Clothesline

News of interest to drycleaners. Links to regional and state associations, calendar of events.

4921 www.nca-i.com
Neighborhood Cleaners Association

Professional trade association dedicated to the welfare of well-groomed consumers and the professional cleaners and suppliers who serve them. for over 50 years, NCA has been at the vanguard of education, research and information distribution concerning garment and household fabric care. Elected officials, goverment agencies, consumer groups, fashion designers and major media outlets have recognized and responded to NCA's activities, reports and tradition of excellence.

4922 www.pwna.org
Power Washers of North America

Developing and communicating the highest standards in ethical business practices, environmental awareness and safety through continuing education and active representation of the membership. PWNA educated and trained contractors raise the level of professionalism and value to their customers.

4923 www.rmfa.org
Rocky Mountain Fabricare Association

Enhancing the image and viability of the fabricare industry through education and development of the skills, talents, and professionalism of its membership.

4924 www.sdahq.org
Soap and Detergent Association

Nonprofit tade association representing over 100 North American manufacturers of household, industrial and institutional cleaning products; their ingredients and finished packaging. Established in 1926, SDA is dedicated to advancing public understanding of the safety and benefits of cleaning products and protecting the ability of its members to formulate products that best meet consumer needs.

4925 www.sefa.org
South Eastern Fabricare Association

Trade association that represents its members who have an interest in the dry cleaning and laundry industry. The not for profit asscoiation provides value through education, research, legislative representation, industry specific information programs, products and services.

4926 www.uniforminfo.com
Uniform & Textile Service Association

Uniform companies provide more than just corporate apparel programs. Companies on this site offer a wide variety of products and services that will not only ensure that your unique corporate identity is conveyed consistently, but will help your workplace run more smoothly.

4927 www.utsa.com
Uniform & Textile Service Association

One stop place for important industry and UTSA news. It has complete information on upcoming events and activities, including online meeting brochures and secure online registration. Each department at UTSA has its own page where you will find information about committees, projects, regulations, and links to dozens of other pertinent sites such as the Clean Show or government sites.

Associations

4928 Accuracy in Media
4350 East West Highway
Suite 555
Bethesda, MD 20814

202-364-4401
800-787-4567
FAX 202-364-4098
E-Mail: info@aim.org
Home Page: www.aim.org
Social Media: *Facebook, Twitter, LinkedIn, YouTube*

Don Irvine, Chairman
Deborah Lambert, Director of Special Projects
Roger Aronoff, Editor
Cliff Kincaid, Dir. AIM Center

Accuracy in Media is a non-profit, grassroots citizens watchdog of the news media that critiques botched and bungled news stories and sets the record straight on important issues that have received slanted coverage.
3500 Members
Founded in 1969

4929 Advanced Television Systems Committee
1776 K Street NW
8th Floor
Washington, DC 20006-2304

202-872-9160
FAX 202-872-9161
E-Mail: atsc@atsc.org
Home Page: www.atsc.org
Social Media: *Facebook, Twitter*

Mark Richer, President
Jerry Whitaker, Vice President
Lindsay Shelton Gross, Director, Communications
Daro Bruno, Office Manager

ATSC is an international, non-profit organzation developing voluntary standards for digital television.

4930 Agricultural Comm. Excellence in Ag., Natural Resources and Life Sciences
University of Florida
59 College Road
Taylor Hall
Durham, NH 03824

855-657-9544
FAX 603-862-1585
E-Mail: ace.info@unh.edu
Home Page: www.aceweb.org
Social Media: *Facebook, LinkedIn, YouTube, Pinterest, RSS*

Brad Beckman, President
Suzanne Steel, VP
Steve Miller, President-elect
Bob Furbee, Retirees Director
Holly Young, Executive Director

Members are writers, editors, broadcasters and communicators who are involved in the dissemination of agricultural, food sciences and natural resource information in land-grant colleges, federal and state agencies, international agencies and other private communications work.
700+ Members
Founded in 1970

4931 Alliance for Telecommunication Industry Solutions
1200 G St NW
Suite 500
Washington, DC 20005

202-628-6380
FAX 202-393-5453
E-Mail: membership@atis.org
Home Page: www.atis.org
Social Media: *Twitter*

Susan Miller, President/CEO
Andrew White, VP of Technology & Standards
Lauren Layman, VP of Marketing & Public Relations
Kris Rinne, Chairman
Bill Klein, VP Finance/Operations

Membership organization that provides the tools necessary for the industry to identify standards, guidelines and operating procedures that make the inoperability of existing and emerging telecommunications products and services possible.
1400 Members
Founded in 1983

4932 Alliance for Telecommunications Industry Solutions
1200 G Street, NW
Suite 500
Washington, DC 20005

202-628-6380
Home Page: www.atis.org
Social Media: *Twitter, LinkedIn*

Susan Miller, President & CEO
Thomas Goode, General Counsel
Lauren Layman, VP, Marketing and Public Relations
Andrew White, VP, Technology and Standards

A standards organization that develops technical and operational standards and solutions for the ICT industry.

4933 American Communication Association
College of Business Administration
The University of Northern Iowa
1227 W 27th Street
Cedar Falls, IA 50614-0125

209-667-3374
E-Mail: pdecaro@csustan.edu
Home Page: www.americancomm.org

Dr. Phillip J. Auter, Executive Director
Prof. Jim Parker, President
Vernon Humphrey, CFO
Myrene Augustin Magabo, Secretary
Dr. John Malalala, CIO

Founded for the purposes of fostering research and scholarship in all areas of human communication behavior, promoting and improving excellence in the pedagogy of communication, providing a voice in communication law and policy, providing evaluation and certification services for academic programs in communication study.
Founded in 1993

4934 American Public Communications Council
3213 Duke Street
Suite 806
Alexandria, VA 22314

703-739-1322
FAX 703-739-1324
E-Mail: APCC@apcc.net
Home Page: www.apcc.net

Willard R. Nichols, President
Deborah Sterman, CFO
Helly Shareefy, Office Manager
Dan Collins, Corporate Counsel
Evelyn Bruggeman, Account Manager

Formed to promote and address, at the FCC and on Capitol Hill, the legal and regulatory issues facing payphone service providers.
1200 Members
Founded in 1988

4935 Armed Forces Broadcasters Association
Po Box 447
Sun City, CA 92586-0447

951-672-7299
FAX 951-679-5484
E-Mail: webmaster@afbanational.org
Home Page: www.afbanational.org

Mary Carnes, President

Enhances comaraderie among former, present, and future members of the military broadcasting community; provides employment search assistance.
600 Members
Founded in 1982

4936 Armed Forces Communications & Electronics Association
4400 Fair Lakes Ct
Fairfax, VA 22033-3899

703-631-6100
800-336-4583
FAX 703-631-6169
Home Page: www.afcea.org
Social Media: *Facebook, Twitter, LinkedIn, YouTube, Flickr*

Kent Schneider, President/CEO
Nancy Temple, International Secretary
James L. Griggs, Jr., VP, CIO & CTO
Linda Gooden, Chairman
Patrick Miorin, EVP, CFO & International Treasurer

A non-profit membership association serving the military, government, industry, and academia as an ethical forum for advancing professional knowledge and relationships in the fields of communications, IT, intelligence, and global security.
31000 Members
Founded in 1946

4937 AscdiNatd
131 NW First Avenue
Delray Beach, FL 33444

561-266-9016
FAX 561-431-6302
Home Page: www.ascdi.com
Social Media: *Facebook, Twitter, LinkedIn, YouTube*

Rob Neumeyer, Board Member
Jerry Roberts, Board Member
Todd A. Bone, Board Member
Thomas Weltin, Board Member
Scott Fluty, Board Member

An international trade association made up of companies who providetechnology solutions, technical support, and value added services to the business community.

4938 Association Media & Publishing
12100 Sunset Hills Road
Suite 130
Reston, VA 20190

703-234-4063
FAX 703-435-4390
E-Mail: info@associationmediaandpublishing.org
Home Page: associationmediaandpublishing.org
Social Media: *Facebook, Twitter, LinkedIn*

Erin Pressley, President, BOD
Angel Alvarez-Mapp, Vice President, BOD
Kim Howard, CAE, Immediate Past President
Leslie McGee, Treasurer
John Falcioni, Assistant Treasurer

Serves the needs of association publishers, communications professionals and the media they create.
Founded in 1963

4939 Association for Business Communication
181 Turner St, NW
Blacksburg, VA 24061

540-231-8460
FAX 646-349-5297
E-Mail: abcoffice@businesscommunication.org
Home Page: businesscommunication.org
Social Media: *Facebook, Twitter*

Kathy Rentz, First VP
Peter W. Cardon, Second VP
Nancy Schullery, President
Jim Dubinsky, Executive Dir.
Marilyn Buerkens, Office Manager

International organization commited to fostering excellence in business communication scholarship, research, education, and practice.
72 Members
Founded in 1935

4940 Association for Conservation Information
Division of Fish Game and Wildlife
Po Box 400
Trenton, NJ 08625-0400

609-984-0837
FAX 609-984-1414
Home Page: www.aci-net.org
Social Media: *Facebook*

Micah Holmes, President
Robin Cahoon, Vice-President
Kim Nix, Secretary
Judy Stokes Weber, Treasurer
Rachel Bradley, Board Member

Works to upgrade the quality of all forms of communication in and among agencies devoted to the protection and management of natural resources and wildlife.
110 Members
Founded in 1984

4941 Association for Educational Communications and Technology
320 W. 8th St.
Suite 101
Bloomington, IN 47404-3745

812-335-7675
877-677-2328
FAX 812-335-7678
E-Mail: aect@aect.org
Home Page: www.aect.org
Social Media: *Facebook, Twitter*

Phillip Harris, Executive Director
Larry Vernon, Electronic Services
Robert Maribe Branch, President

For audiovisual and instructional materials specialists, educational technologists, audiovisual and television production personnel, school media specialists.
2200 Members
Founded in 1923
Mailing list available for rentat $159 per M

4942 Association for Information Systems
Po Box 2712
Atlanta, GA 30301-2712

404-651-0348
FAX 404-651-4938
E-Mail: WebMaster@ALSNe.org
Home Page: www.aisnet.org
Social Media: *Facebook, Twitter, LinkedIn*

Pete Tinsley, Executive Director
Jane Fedorowicz, President
Mary C. Jones, Secretary
Matthew Nelson, Treasurer
Richard Baskerville, VP of Communications

AIS members are academics with interest in information systems and related fields.
4300 Members
Founded in 1994

4943 Association for Information and Image Management
1100 Wayne Avenue
Suite 1100
Silver Spring, MD 20910

301-587-8202
800-477-2446
E-Mail: aiim@aiim.org
Home Page: www.aiim.org
Social Media: *Facebook, Twitter, LinkedIn, YouTube, Google+, RSS*

Paul Engel, Board Chair
Anthony Peleska, Vice Chair
Timothy Elmore, Immediate Past Chair
Daniel Antion, Treasurer
Mark Patrick, Executive Committee Member At Large

A nonprofit membership organization that provides education, marketresearch, certification, and standards for information professionals.

4944 Association for Interactive Marketing
1430 Broadway Avenue
8th Floor
New York, NY 10018

888-337-0008
FAX 212-391-9233
E-Mail: info@interactivehq.org
Home Page: www.interactivehq.org

Kevin Noonan, Executive Director

AIM is a non-profit trade association for interactive marketers and service providers.

4945 Association for Multi-Media International
PO Box 1897
Lawrence, KS 66044

866-393-4264
FAX 785-843-1274
E-Mail: hq@ami.org

Vanessa Reilly, Executive Director

The professional objectives of the AMI are to promote the safety and advancement of medical illustration and allied fields of visual communication, and to promote understanding and cooperation with the medical profession and related health science professions.
1M Members
Founded in 1974

4946 Association for Postal Commerce
1800 Diagonal Rd.
Suite 320
Alexandria, VA 22314-2862

703-524-0096
FAX 703-997-2414
Home Page: www.postcom.org

Gene Del Polito, President

National organization representing those who use, or who support, the use of mail as a medium for communication and commerce. Publishes a weekly newsletter covering postal policy and operational issues.
231 Members
Founded in 1947

4947 Association for Service Managers International
11031 Via Frontera
Suite A
San Diego, CA 92127

239-275-7887
800-333-9786
FAX 239-275-0794
E-Mail: info@afsmi.org
Home Page: www.afsmi.org

J.B. Wood, President
Thomas Lah, Executive Director

A global organization dedicated to furthering the knowledge, understanding, and career development of executives, managers and professionals in the high technology service industry.
3000+ Members
Founded in 1975

4948 Association for Women in Communications
3337 Duke Street
Alexandria, VA 22314

703-370-7436
FAX 703-342-4311
Home Page: www.womcom.org
Social Media: *Facebook, Twitter, LinkedIn, YouTube, Google+*

Mitzie Zerr, Chair
Missy Kruse, Vice Chair
Pat Meads, Treasurer
Judy Arent-Morency, Immediate Past Chair
Lisa Angle, Secretary

An American professional organization for women in the communications industry.
Founded in 1909

4949 Association of Alternative Newsmedia
116 Cass Street
Traverse City, MI 49684ÿ

703-470-2996
FAX 866-619-9755
E-Mail: web@aan.org
Home Page: www.altweeklies.com
Social Media: *Facebook, Twitter, RSS, Google+*

Blair Barna, President
Chuck Strouse, Vice President
Ellen Meany, Treasurer
Tiffany Shackelford, Executive Director
Jason Zaragoza, Deputy Director

A trade association of alternative weekly newspapers in North America.
Founded in 1978

4950 Association of Cable Communicators
9259 Old Keene Mill Road
Suite #202
Burke, VA 22015

703-372-2215
800-210-3396
FAX 703-782-0153
E-Mail: services@cablecommunicators.org
Home Page: www.cablecommunicators.org
Social Media: *Facebook, Twitter, LinkedIn*

Catherine Frymark, President
Catherine Frymark, Secretary
Steven R. Jones, Executive Dir.
Annie Howell, EVP, Communications
Catherine Frymark, Communications

ACC is the only national, professional organization specifically addressing the issues, needs and interests of the cable industry's communications and public affairs professionals.
Founded in 1985

4951 Association of Federal Communications Consulting Engineers
PO Box 19333
Washington, DC 20036

941-329-6000
FAX 703-591-0115
Home Page: www.afcce.org
Social Media: *Facebook, Twitter, LinkedIn*

Eric Wandel, President
Bob Weller, VP
David Layer, Secretary
Ronald Chase, Treasurer
David Snavely, Immediate Past President

An organization of professional engineering consultants serving the telecommunications industry.
250 Members
Founded in 1948

4952 Association of Information Technology Professionals

1120 Route 73
Suite 200
Mount Laurel, NJ 08054-5113

856-380-6910
800-224-9371
FAX 856-439-0525
E-Mail: aitp_hq@aitp.org
Home Page: www.aitp.org
Social Media: *Twitter, LinkedIn*

Barbara Viola, President
Julian Wade, EVP/President Elect
Christine Leja, Treasurer
John Council, Secretary
Michael Welch, Immediate Past President

A professional association that focuses on information technology education for business professionals.
Founded in 1951

4953 Association of Medical Illustrators

201 E. Main St.
Suite 1405
Lexington, KY 40507

866-393-4264
FAX 859-514-9166
E-Mail: hq@ami.org
Home Page: www.ami.org
Social Media: *RSS Feed*

Scott Weldon, Treasurer
Emily Shaw, Secretary
David Cheney, Chairman
Melanie Bowzer, Account Executive
Mark Schornak, President

An international organization of media professionals who promote, produce and utilize a wide range of presentation media.
1M Members
Founded in 1944

4954 Association of Professional Communication Consultants

211 E 28th st
Tulsa, OK 74114-3329

918-743-4793
FAX 918-745-0932
Home Page: www.consultingsuccess.org
Social Media: *LinkedIn*

Reva Daniel, Association Manager
Lee Johns, Treasurer

Professional community of communication consultants where members can increase their knowledge, grow their business and achieve high standards of professional practice. Services include professional development workshops, online newsletter and referral database and active listserve discussions.
200 Members
Founded in 1982

4955 Association of Schools of Journalism & Mass Communications

234 Outlet Pointe Boulevard
Columbia, SC 29210-5667

803-798-0271
FAX 803-772-3509
E-Mail: aejmchq@aol.com
Home Page: www.asjmc.org

Brad Rawlins, President
Jan Slater, President Elect
Maryanne Reed, Vice-President
Ann Brill, Past President

Mary Jean Land, Executive Committee Representative

Promotes excellence in journalism and mass communication education. Non-profit, educational association composed of some 190 JMC programs at the college level. Eight international journalism and communication schools have joined the association in recent years.
202 Members
Founded in 1917

4956 Association of Teachers of Technical Writing

Department Of Linguistics And Technical Comm.
1155 Union Circle #305298
Denton, TX 76203-5017

940-565-4458
E-Mail: sims@unt.edu
Home Page: www.attw.org
Social Media: *Facebook, Twitter, LinkedIn*

Michelle Eble, President
Angela Haas, Vice-President
Brenda Sims, Secretary
Stuart Blythe, Treasurer
Huiling Ding, Member at Large

Provides communication among teachers of technical writing and develops technical communications as an academic discipline.
600 Members
Founded in 1973

4957 Association of Women in Communications

3337 Duke Street
Alexandria, VA 22314

703-370-7436
FAX 703-342-4311
E-Mail: info@womcom.org, members@womcom.org
Home Page: www.womcom.org
Social Media: *Facebook, Twitter, LinkedIn, Youtube*

Mitzie Zerr, Chair
Missy Kruse, Vice Chair
Pat Meads, Treasurer
Lisa Angle, Secretary
Judy Arent-Morency, Immediate Past President

Professional organization that champions the advancement of women across all communications disciplines by recognizing excellence, promoting leadership and positioning its members at the forefront of the evolving communications era. Hosts an internal, bi-annual meeting.
3500 Members
Founded in 1909
Mailing list available for rent

4958 BioCommunications Association

220 Southwind Lane
Hillsborough, NC 27278

919-245-0906
E-Mail: office@bca.org
Home Page: www.bca.org
Social Media: *Facebook, Twitter, LinkedIn, YouTube*

Connie Johansen, RBP, President
Susanne Loomis, Vice President
James Koepfler, FBCA, Treasurer/Secretary
Susanne Loomis, FBCA, Immediate Past President
Karen M. Hensley, Director of Communication

An international association of photographers and media professionals who create and use quality images in visual communications for teaching, documentation and presentations in the life sciences and medicine.
Founded in 1931

4959 Business Information Technology Network

414 Locust Street
Suite 203
Burlington, ON L7S 1T7

E-Mail: info@bitnet.ca
Home Page: www.bitnet.ca
Social Media: *Facebook, Twitter, LinkedIn, YouTube*

Ron Durkin, President
Steve Rieck, Vice President
Paul Walker, Treasurer
Kathryn Rogers, Secretary

An association of individuals, business and organizations with a common interest in the practical and innovative use and development of technology.
Founded in 1992

4960 Cable in the Classroom

25 Massachussetts Ave NW
Suite 100
Washington, DC 20001

202-222-2335
FAX 202-222-2336
E-Mail: webmaster@ncta.com
Home Page: www.ciconline.org
Social Media: *Facebook, Twitter, LinkedIn*

Frank Gallagher, Executive Director
Helen Chamberlin, Deputy Executive Director
Kat Stewart, Director, Strategic Initiatives
Beverly Hicks, Assistant Director

Promotes the visionary, sensible, responsible and effective use of cable's broadband technology, services, and content in teaching and learning. CIC also advocates digtial citizenship and supports the complimentary provision, by cable industry companies, of broadband and multichannel video services and educational content to the nation's schools.
Founded in 1992

4961 CanWest Media Sales

121 Bloor Street East
Suite 1500
Toronto, ON M4W 3M5

416-967-1174
FAX 416-967-1285
E-Mail: info@shawmedia.ca
Home Page: www.shawmedia.ca

Barbara Williams, Executive Vice President
Christine Shipton, SVP/Chief Creative Officer
Troy Reeb, SVP, Global News & Station Ops
Dervla Kelly, VP, Marketing and Comm

Televison and newspaper advertising, marketing, and sales company.

4962 Center for Communication

110 East 23rd Street
Suite 900
New York, NY 10010

216-686-5005
FAX 212-504-2632
E-Mail: info@cencom.org
Home Page: www.cencom.org
Social Media: *Facebook, Twitter, Youtube*

David Barrett, Chairman
Tim Armstrong, CEO & chairman
Catherine Williams, Executice Dir.
Alaina Bendi, VP Membership/Business Development
Kate Stanley, Program Dir.

Exposes young people to the issues, the ethics, the people, and the creative product that defines the media business. Offers students interested in media careers a unique opportunity to learn about the world of communications.

4963 Center for International Media Assistance

1025 F Street NW
Suite 800
Washington, DC 20004

202-378-9700
FAX 202-378-9407
E-Mail: CIMA@ned.org
Home Page: cima.ned.org
Social Media: *Facebook, Twitter*

Mark Nelson, Senior Director
Don Podesta, Manager and Editor
Valerie Popper, Assist Program & Officer
Rosemary D'Amour, Associate Editor
Paul Rothman, Assistant Partnerships Officer

Provides information, builds networks, conducts research, and highlights the role media play in the creation and development of sustainable democracies.
Founded in 1977

4964 Center for Media Literacy

22837 Pacific Coast Highway
#472
Malibu, CA 90265

310-804-3985
E-Mail: cml@medialit.org
Home Page: www.medialit.org
Social Media: *YouTube*

Elizabeth Thoman CHM, Founder
Tessa Jolls, President, CEO
Beth Thornton, Communications

An educational organization that provides leadership, public education, professional development and educational resources nationally and internationally.
Founded in 1977

4965 Communication Media Management Association

Home Page: www.cmma.org
Social Media: *Facebook, Twitter, LinkedIn, RSS*

Gregg Moss, President
Gregg Moss, President-Elect
Gerry Harris, Vice President
Thomas M. Densmore, Treasurer
Susan Kehoe, Secretary

Provides professional development and networking opportunities for communications media managers.
Founded in 1946

4966 CompTIA

3500 Lacey Road
Suite 100
Downers Grove, IL 60515

630-678-8300
866-678-8300
FAX 630-678-8384
E-Mail: techvoice@comptia.org
Home Page: www.comptia.org
Social Media: *Facebook, Twitter, LinkedIn, Google+, YouTube, Pinterest*

Todd Thibodeaux, President/ Chief Executive Officer
Nancy Hammervik, Senior VP, Industry Relations
Kelly Ricker, SVP, Events and Education
David Sommer, Chief Financial Officer
Randy Gross, Chief Information Officer

A nonprofit trade association created by representatives of five microcomputer leaderships and is a provider of professional certifications for theinformation technology (IT) industry.

4967 Computer and Communications Industry Association

900 17th Street, NW
Suite 1100
Washington, DC 20006

202-783-0070
FAX 202-783-0534
Home Page: www.ccianet.org
Social Media: *Facebook, Twitter, RSS*

Edward Black, President, CEO
Daniel Johnson, Vice President & General Counsel
Catherine Sloan, VP, Government Relations
Matthew Schruers, Vice President, Law & Policy
Dan O'Connor, Vice President, Public Policy

Association of computer product vendors and communications firms lobbying for free trade and open markets.

4968 Consolidated Tape Association

C/O New York Stock Exchange
11 Wall Street, 21st Floor
New York, NY 10005

212-656-2052
FAX 212-656-5848
E-Mail: phussey@nyse.com

Patricia Hussey, Administrator

Members are stock exchanges and the National Association of Securities Dealers. CTA melds the reporting of transactions from the various stock exchanges.
9 Members
Founded in 1974

4969 Consortium for School Networking

1025 Vermont Ave NW
Suite 1010
Washington, DC 20005-3599

202-861-2676
866-267-8747
FAX 202-393-2011
E-Mail: info@cosn.org
Home Page: www.cosn.org
Social Media: *Facebook, Twitter, LinkedIn*

Randy Wilhelm, CEO & Co-Founder
Michael Jamerson, Chair
Tom Ryan, Treasurer
Donna Williamson, Secretary
Walter l. Fox, Executive Director

Promotes the development and use of internet and information technologies for K-12 learning. Members are school districts, states, nonprofits and commercial organizations, all of whom share the goal of promoting the state of the art in computer networking technologies in schools.
450 Members
Founded in 1992

4970 Cooperative Communicators Association

174 Crestview Dr
Bellefonte, PA 16823-8516

877-326-5994
FAX 814-355-2452
E-Mail: CCA@communicators.coop
Home Page: www.communicators.coop
Social Media: *Facebook, Twitter, YouTube, Flickr*

Marian McLemore, President
Marian Douglas, Director
Nickie Sabo, Treasurer
Marian Douglas, Secretary
Chandra Allen, Director

A teaching and news tool for the Cooperative Communicators Association, CCA consists communicators, editors, photographers, graphics, designers, public relations specialists

who work for cooperatives in 35 states, Canada and Poland.
350 Members
Founded in 1953

4971 Council of Communication Management

65 Enterprise
Aliso Viejo, CA 92656

866-463-6226
FAX 949-715-6931
E-Mail: info@thecommunicationexchange.org
Home Page: www.ccmconnection.com
Social Media: *Facebook, Twitter, LinkedIn*

Becky Healy, President
Jeff Kosiorek, VP
Kerrin Nally, Secretary
Barry Mike, Past President
Hannah Bauer, Director

Provides a network through which managers, consultants and educators, who work at the policy level in organizational communication can help one another advance the practice of communication in business.
270 Members
Founded in 1955

4972 Council of Science Editors

10200 W 44th Ave.
Suite 304
Wheat Ridge, CO 80033

720-881-6046
FAX 703-435-4390
E-Mail: CSE@CouncilScienceEditors.org
Home Page: www.councilscienceeditors.org
Social Media: *Facebook, Twitter, LinkedIn*

Angela Cochran, President
Barbara Gomez, Executive Vice President
Patricia K Baskin, President-Elect
Sarah Tegen, VP
Tim Cross, Past President

Membership consists of individuals concerned with writing, editing and publishing in the life sciences and related fields.
1200 Members
Founded in 1957

4973 Digital Media Association (DiMA)

1050 17th St., NW
Suite 220
Washington, DC 20036

202-639-9509
E-Mail: info@digmedia.org
Home Page: www.digmedia.org

Lee Knife, Executive Director
Greg Barnes, General Counsel
Ann Brown, Communications Consultant
Aileen Atkins, SVP/General Counsel
Bill Way, VP/ General Counsel

National trade organization devoted primarily to the online audio and video industries, and more generally to commercially innovative digital media opportunities.

4974 Drug Information Association

800 Enterprise Road
Suite 200
Horsham, PA 19044-3595

215-442-6100
FAX 215-442-6199
E-Mail: DIA@diahome.org
Home Page: www.diahome.org
Social Media: *Facebook, Twitter, LinkedIn, YouTube, Weibo, Digg, Reddit*

Sandra A Milligan, MD, JD, President
John Roberts, Treasurer
Barbara Lopez Kunz, Global Chief Executive
Bayard Gardineer, CPA, CFO
Elizabeth Lincoln, MA, Worldwide Dir., HR

Provides a neutral global forum for the exchange and dissemination of information on the

discovery, development, evaluation and utilization of medicines and related health care technologies. Through these activities the DIA provides development opportunities for its members.
20000 Members
Founded in 1964

4975 EDUCAUSE
1150 18th St NW
Suite 900
Washington, DC 20036

202-872-4200
FAX 202-872-4318
E-Mail: info@educause.edu
Home Page: www.educause.edu
Social Media: *Facebook, Twitter, LinkedIn, Flickr*

Mark Luker, VP

EDUCAUSE is a nonprofit association whose mission is to advance higher education by promoting the intelligent use of information technology.
17M Members
Founded in 1962

4976 Eastern Communication Association
600 Forbes Ave
340 College Hall
Pittsburgh, PA 15282

E-Mail: info@ecasite.org
Home Page: www.ecasite.org
Social Media: *Facebook, Twitter*

J. Kanan Sawyer, President
Jason S. Wrench, Vice President
Benjamin R Bates, First Vice President Elect
Thomas R. Flynn, Immediate Past President
Ronald C. Arnett, Executive Director

A professional organization of scholars, teachers, and students of Communcation Studies.
Founded in 1910

4977 Electronic Retailing Association
607 14th St., NW
Suite 530
Washington, DC 20005

703-841-1751
800-987-6462
FAX 425-977-1036
E-Mail: webadmin@retailing.org
Home Page: www.retailing.org
Social Media: *Facebook, Twitter, LinkedIn, YouTube, Flickr*

Julie Coons, President & CEO
Kevin S. Kelly, CFO & COO
Bill McClellan, VP, Govt Affairs
Dave Martin, VP, Marketing & Content
Cecilia Mason, Accounting Manager

To foster growth, development and acceptance of the rapidly growing direct response industry worldwide for the companies who use the power of electronic media to sell goods and services to the public.
Founded in 1991
Mailing list available for rent

4978 Enterprise Wireless Alliance (EWA)
2121 Cooperative Way
Suite 225
Herndon, VA 20171

703-528-5115
800-482-8282
FAX 703-524-1074
E-Mail:
customerservice@enterprisewireless.org
Home Page: www.enterprisewireless.org

Mark Crosby, President/CEO
Andre Cote, Senior VP
Ila Dudley, EVP, Spectrum Solutions
Ron Franklin, Customer Service Manager
Karen Fouchie, Accounting Manager

Formerly ITA and AMTA, works to preserve spectrum rights and assets for enterprise wireless customers.
1200 Members
Founded in 1953

4979 Forest Industries Telecommunications
1565 Oak St
Eugene, OR 97401

541-485-8441
FAX 541-485-7556
E-Mail: license@landmobile.com
Home Page: www.landmobile.com
Social Media: *Facebook, Twitter*

Kevin Mc Carthy, President

Organized to assist the forest industry in radio matters before the FCC.
600 Members
Founded in 1947

4980 Forestry Conservation Commuications Association
122 Baltimore St.
Gettysburg, PA 17325

717-398-0815
844-458-0298
FAX 717-778-4237
E-Mail:
ralph.haller@frequencycoordination.org
Home Page: www.fcca-usa.org

Chief Paul M. Leary, President
Roy Mott, VP
John McIntosh, Secretary/Treasurer
Matt Hogan, Executive Dir.
Michelle Fink, National Frequency Coordinator

Certified by the FCC as the radio frequency coordinator for the Forestry Conservation Radio Service.
200 Members
Founded in 1944

4981 Foundation for American Communications
44 Avenue Road South
Suite 1200
Arlington, VA 22203

703-276-0100
FAX 703-525-8277
E-Mail: info@facsnet.org
Home Page: www.facsnet.org

John E Cox, CEO, President
Peter C McCarthy, Senior VP, COO
Paul Davis, Senior VP, Programs
Randy Reddick, Director
Christina Gardner, VP, Operations

A national non-profit educational organization with the mission of improving the quality of information reaching the public through the news.
Mailing list available for rent

4982 Freedom Information Center
133 Neff Annex University of Missouri
Columbia, MO 65211

573-882-4856
FAX 573-884-6204
E-Mail: edwardsm@missouri.edu
Home Page: web.missouri.edu/~foiwww/
Social Media: *Facebook, Twitter*

Barbara A Petersen, President
Peter Scheer, VP
Katherine Garner, Secretary
Mal Leary, Treasurer

Maintains files documenting actions by government, media and society affecting the flow and content of information. Call or write for assistance with researching media topics or instruction in using access laws.
Founded in 1989

4983 Fulfillment Services Association of America
3030 Malmo Drive
Arlington Heights, IL 60005-4728

847-364-1222
FAX 847-364-1268

Frederick J Herzog, Executive VP

Formerly Association of Publishing and fulfillment services.
1450 Members
Founded in 1986

4984 Geospatial Information & Technology Association
1360 University Ave. West
Suite 455
St. Paul, MN 55104-4086

E-Mail: president@gita.org
Home Page: www.gita.org
Social Media: *Facebook, Twitter, LinkedIn, YouTube*

Mark Limbruner, President
Talbot J Brooks, Immediate Past President
Matthew Thomas, President Elect
Eric Hoogenraad, Secretary
Elizabeth Bialek, P.E., Treasurer

A nonprofit educational association dedicated to promoting the use and benefits of geospatial information technologies.

4985 Health Industry Business Communications Council
2525 E Arizona Biltmore Circle
Suite 127
Phoenix, AZ 85016

602-381-1091
FAX 602-381-1093
E-Mail: info@hibcc.org
Home Page: www.hibcc.org

Robert A Hankin PhD, President & CEO
DuWayne Schlittenhard, Chair
Patrick DeGrace, Immediate Past Chair
Greg Stivers, At Large

An industry-sponsored nonprofit council organized by major health care associations to develop a standard for data transfer using uniform bar code labeling, and later as the focal point for many other electronic data interchange standards.
12000 Members
Founded in 1984

4986 IEEE Communications Society

Home Page: www.comsoc.org
Social Media: *Facebook, Twitter, LinkedIn, Tumblr, Instagram, Pinterest*

Sergio Benedetto, President
Vijay Bhargava, Past President
Stan Moyer, Treasurer
Hikmet Sari, Vice President - Conferences
Susan Brooks, Executive Director

A diverse group of industry professionals with a common interest inadvancing all communications technologies.
Founded in 1952

4987 InfoComm International
11242 Waples Mill Road
Suite 200
Fairfax, VA 22030

703-273-7200
FAX 800-659-7469
Home Page: www.infocomm.org
Social Media: *Facebook, Twitter, LinkedIn, Google+, YouTube, Flickr*

Johanne Belanger, CPA, CA, LSC Chair
Matt Emerson, CTS, President
Craig Janssen, President-Elect
Gary Hall, CTS-D, CTS-I, Treasurer, Secretary

David Labuskes, CTS, RCDD, Executive Director, CEO

Educating, training, and certifying the communications industry.

4988 Information Resources Group

Ste A
2721 Industrial Dr
Jefferson City, MO 65109

573-632-6IRG
877-600- IRG
FAX 877-295-7989
E-Mail: webmaster@irginc.net
Home Page: www.irginc.net
Social Media: *Facebook, Twitter, LinkedIn*

Shyam Goel, President

A national organization that offers MIS and corporate professionals at over 150,000 companies throughout the United States.
1M Members

4989 Information Systems Consultants

4131 Idlevale Drive
Tucker, GA 30084

770-491-1500
800-832-7767

Nonprofit organization of small businesses and individuals providing consulting services to all industries and government.
350 Members
Founded in 1986

4990 Information Systems Management Benchmarking Consortium

Houston, TX

281-440-5044
Home Page: ismbc.org
Social Media: *Facebook, Twitter*

An international resource for business process research and metrics.
Founded in 1992

4991 Information Technology Industry Council

1101 K St., NW
Suite 610
Washington, DC 20005

202-737-8888
FAX 202-638-4922
E-Mail: info@itic.org
Home Page: www.itic.org
Social Media: *Facebook, Twitter, Google+, RSS, YouTube, Blog*

Dean C. Garfield, President, CEO
Andy Halataei, SVP, Government Affairs
John Neuffer, SVP, Global Policy
Rick Goss, SVP, Environment and Sustainability
A.R. Trey Hodgkins, SVP, Public Sector

A Washington, D.C.-based trade association that represents companies from the information and communications technology (ICT) industry.
Founded in 1916

4992 Instructional Telecommunications Council

426 C St., NE
Washington, DC 20002-5839

202-293-3110
FAX 651-450-3679
E-Mail: cullins@itcnetwork.org, cmeredith@itcnet
Home Page: www.itcnetwork.org

Anne Johnson, Chair
Christine Mullins, Executive Director
Carol Spalding, Ed.D., Treasurer
Mickey Slimp, Executive Director
Loraine Schmitt, Chair-Elect

Members are educators and organizations involved in higher education instructional telecommunications and distance learning
500 Members
Founded in 1977

4993 Interactive Multimedia and Collaborative Communications Association

PO Box 756
Syosset, NY 11797-0756

516-818-8184
FAX 516-922-2170
Home Page: www.imcca.org
Social Media: *Facebook, LinkedIn, RSS Feed*

Carol Zelkin, Executive Director
Rick Snyder, Chairperson
Anne Hardwick, Treasurer
Ken Scaturro, Vice chairperson
David J. Danto, Dir., Emerging Technology

Provides a clearinghouse for the exchange of information between users, researchers, and providers in the field of teleconferencing.
1000 Members
Founded in 1998

4994 International Academy of Television Arts a nd Sciences

25 West 52nd Street
New York, NY 10019

212-489-6969
FAX 212-489-1946
E-Mail: iemmys@iemmys.tv
Home Page: www.iemmys.tv
Social Media: *Facebook, Twitter, YouTube*

Fred Cohen, Chairman
Larry Gershman, Vice Chairman
Bruce Paisner, President & CEO
Simon Sutton, Secretary
Rainer Siek, Nominating Committee Chairman

Member based organization comprised of leading media and entertainment figures from over 50 countries and 500 companies from all sectors of television including internet, mobile and technology.
Founded in 1969

4995 International Association of Audio Informa tion Services

1090 Don Mills Road
P.O. Box 847
Lawrence, KS 66044

416-422-4222
800-280-5325
FAX 416-422-1622
E-Mail: info@iaais.org
Home Page: www.iaais.org

Stuart Holland, President
Lori Kessinger, Chairperson
Marjorie Williams, 1st Vice President
Mark Dewitt, Awards Committee Chair
Lori Kesinger, Co-Chair

Encourages and supports the establishment and maintenance of audio information services that provide access to printed information for individuals who cannot read conventional print because of blindness or any other visual, physical, or learning disability.
Founded in 1977

4996 International Association of Audio Visual Communicators

The Cindy Competitions
57 West Palo Verde Avenue
PO Box 270779
Flower Mound, TX 75027-0779

469-464-4180
FAX 469-464-4170
E-Mail: sheemonw@cindys.com
Home Page: www.cindys.com

Social Media: *Facebook, Twitter, LinkedIn, YouTube*

Sheemon Wolfe, Contact

Members are audio-visual professionals using the media of film, video, slides, filmstrips, multi-image and interactive media to communicate information
5200 Members
Founded in 1959

4997 International Association of Business Communicators

601 Montgomery St.
Suite 1900
San Francisco, CA 94111

415-544-4700
800-776-4222
FAX 415-544-4747
E-Mail: service_centre@iabc.com
Home Page: www.iabc.com
Social Media: *Twitter, LinkedIn*

Michael Ambjorn, Chair
Dianne Lynn Chase, Vice Chair
Carlos Fulcher, Executive Dir.
Mari Pavia, Dir., HR Administration
Aaron Heinrich, Dir. Of Communications

International knowledge network for professionals engaged in stategic business communication management.
13,00 Members
Founded in 1970

4998 International Association of Information Technology Asset Managers

4848 Munson St. NW
Canton, OH 44718ÿ

330-628-3012
877-942-4826
FAX 330-628-3289
E-Mail: info@iaitam.org
Home Page: www.iaitam.org
Social Media: *Facebook, Twitter, LinkedIn, YouTube*

Barbara Rembiesa, President, Founder, CEO

The professional association for individuals and organizations involved in any aspect of IT Asset Management ("ITAM"), Software Asset Management ("SAM"), Hardware Asset Management, and the lifecycle processes supporting IT Asset Management in organizations of every size and industry across the globe.
Founded in 2002

4999 International Communication Association

1500 21st Street, NWÿ
PO Box 418950
Washington, DC 20036ÿ

202-955-1444
FAX 202-955-1448
E-Mail: icahdq@icahdq.org
Home Page: www.icahdq.org
Social Media: *Facebook, Twitter, LinkedIn, Tumblr, Pinterest*

Amy B Jordan, President
Peng Hwa Ang, President Elect
Peter Vorderer, Past President
Michael L. Haley, Executive Director
Sam Luna, Member Services Director

An academic association for scholars interested in the study, teaching, and application of all aspects of human and mediated communication.
Founded in 1950

5000 International Communications Association
1500 21st St NW
Washington, DC 20036

202-955-1444
FAX 202-955-1448
E-Mail: icahdq@icahdq.org
Home Page: www.icahdq.org
Social Media: *Facebook, Twitter, LinkedIn, Tumblr, Pinterest*

Amy B Jordan, President
Peng Hwa Ang, President-Elect
Paula M Gardner, President-Elect-Select
Peter Vorderer, Immediate Past President
Francois Heinderyckx, Past President

International association for scholars interested in the study, teaching and application of all aspects of human mediated communication. ICA began as a small association of US reseachers and has matured into a international association with members in 65 countries.
3400+ Members
Founded in 1950

5001 International Communications Industry Association
11242 Waples Mill Road
Suite 200
Fairfax, VA 22030

703-273-7200
800-659-7469
FAX 703-278-8082
E-Mail: customerservice@infocomm.org
Home Page: www.infocomm.org
Social Media: *Facebook, Twitter, LinkedIn, Flickr, YouTube, SlideShare*

Johanne Belanger, CPA, CA, LSC Chair
Greg Jeffreys, Chair
Matt Emerson, President
Gary Hall, Secretary-Treasurer
David J. Labuskes, Executive Director

Centers on the technologies, products and systems for visual display, audio reproduction, video and audio production, interfacing and signal distribution, lighting, control systems, interactive display and audio presentation systems, remote video and web conferencing.

5002 International Digital Enterprise Alliance
1600 Duke St.
Suite 420
Alexandria, VA 22314

703-837-1070
FAX 703-837-1072
E-Mail: info@idealliance.org
Home Page: www.idealliance.org
Social Media: *Facebook, Twitter, LinkedIn*

Joe Duncan, Chairman
Marriott Winchester, Vice Chair
David J. Steinhardt, President & CEO
Frank Balser, VP of operations & Managing Dir.
Steve Bonoff, EVP

IDEAlliance programs and activities enable its members to strengthen their staff skills, participate in the development of standards, influence the development of tools and technologies, develop strategies and partnerships to deploy technology solutions, and position themselves as industry leaders.
200 Members
Founded in 1966

5003 International Documentary Association
3470 Wilshire Blvd.
Los Angeles, CA 90010

213-232-1660
FAX 213-232-1669

E-Mail: michael@documentary.org
Home Page: www.documentary.org
Social Media: *Facebook, Twitter, LinkedIn, YouTube*

Michael Lumpkin, Executive Director
Jon Curry, Office Manager
Cindy Chyr, Development

A nonprofit membership organization dedicated to supporting the efforts of nonfiction film and video makers throughout the United States and the world; promoting the documentary form; and expanding opportunities for the production, distribution, and exhibition of documentary.
2800+ Members
Founded in 1982
Mailing list available for rent: 2800 names at $250 per M

5004 International Interactive Communications Society
180 West 8th Ave
Suite 300
Eugene, OR 97401-2916

541-302-3777
FAX 541-302-3778
E-Mail: worldhq@iics.org
Home Page: www.iste.org
Social Media: *Facebook, Twitter, LinkedIn, YouTube*

Kecia Ray, EdD, Chair
Matt ÿ Harris, EdD, Chair-Elect
Mia Williams, PhDÿ, Secretary
Mila Thomas Fuller, Ed.D., Treasurer
Laurie Conzemius, At-Large Representative

Association of communications industry professionals dedicated to the advancement of interactive technologies. Provides a forum to share ideas, applications and techniques for effective use of interactive media.
3000 Members
Founded in 1983
Mailing list available for rent: 8000 names

5005 International Regional Magazine Association
38 Burgess Ave.
Toronto, ON M4E 1W7

416-705-6884
FAX 888-806-1533
E-Mail: us002848@mindspring.com
Home Page: www.regionalmagazines.org

Chris Amundson, President
Penny Caldwell, VP
Shawn Dalton, Director
Joan Henderson, Director
Matt Holliday, Treasurer

IRMA provides a forum for regional magazine publishers to exchange ideas with the view to improving their respective publications.
250-3 Members
Founded in 1960

5006 International Society for Technology in Education
180 W 8th Avenue
Suite 300
Eugene, OR 97401-2916

541-302-3777
800-336-5191
FAX 541-302-3778
E-Mail: iste@iste.org
Home Page: www.iste.org
Social Media: *Facebook, Twitter, LinkedIn, YouTube, Pinterest*

Kecia Ray, EdD, Chair
Matt ÿ Harris, EdD, Chair-Elect
Mia Williams, PhDÿ, Secretary
Mila Thomas Fuller, Ed.D., Treasurer
Laurie Conzemius, At-Large Representative

A large nonprofit organization serving the technology-using educator.
10000 Members
Founded in 1979

5007 International Society of Business
7159 Navajo Road
San Diego, CA 92119-1606

619-687-3450

Audio and videotape professionals.
Founded in 1983

5008 Internet Society
1775 Wiehle Ave
Suite 201
Reston, VA 20190-5108

703-439-2120
FAX 703-326-9881
E-Mail: isoc@isoc.org
Home Page: www.isoc.org
Social Media: *Facebook, Twitter, LinkedIn, YouTube, Google+*

Terry Weigler, Manager
Gregory Kapfer, CFO
Nicole Armstrong, Sr. Events Manager
Jane Coffin, Dir.,Development Strategy

Members are technologists, developers, educators, researchers, government representatives, business people and other with an interest in internet technologies and applications.
20000 Members
Founded in 1992

5009 Land Mobile Communications Council
2121 Cooperative Way
Suite 225
Herndon, VA 20171

703-528-5114
FAX 703-524-1074
E-Mail: mark.crosby@enterprisewireless.org
Home Page: www.lmcce.org

Gregory Kunkle, President
Ralph Haller, VP
Mark Crosby, Secretary

A nonprofit association of organizations representing land mobile radio carriers and manufacturers equipment; LMCC membership represents diverse telecommunications sectors such as public safety, industrial/land transportation, private radio, specialized mobile radion and critical infrastructure.
Founded in 1967

5010 Local Media Association
116 Cass Street
Traverse City, MI 49684

888-486-2466
FAX 231-932-2985
E-Mail: hq@localmedia.org
Home Page: www.localmedia.org
Social Media: *Facebook, Twitter, LinkedIn, Tumblr, Instagram, Google+*

Gordon Borrell, Board Chairman
Suzanne Schlicht, First Vice Chairman
Matt Coen, Second Vice Chairman
Mark Poss, Treasurer
Robert Brown, Secretary

A nonprofit, professional trade association specifically serving the local media industry.

5011 Media Alliance
1904 Franklin St
Suite 818
Oakland, CA 94612

510-684-6853
FAX 510-238-8557
E-Mail: information@media-alliance.org

Home Page: www.media-alliance.org
Social Media: *Facebook, Twitter*

Tracy Rosenberg, Executive Director
Eloise Rose Lee, Program Director

A nonprofit training and resource center for media workers, community organizations and political activists.
Founded in 1976

5012 Media Communications Association-Internati onal
PO Box 5135
Madison, WI 53705-0135

888-899-MCAI
FAX 888-862-8150
E-Mail: loiswei@aol.com
Home Page: www.mca-i.org
Social Media: *Facebook, Twitter, LinkedIn, Google+*

Jim Dufek, President
Brian Page, President-Elect
Art Kirsch, Treasurer
Liz De Nesnera, Secretary
Brian President, Past President

Global community that provides its members opportunities for networking, learning and career advancement. Members work in video, film, collaborative communication, distance learning, web design and creation, and all forms of interactive visual communication, along with associated crafts; serving businesses, nonprofit organizations, the government, educational institutions, the medical field, and electronic media. Chapters are throughout the US, with affiliates in Asia and Europe.
Founded in 1970

5013 Media Institute
2300 Clarendon Blvd
Suite 602
Arlington, VA 22201

703-243-5700
FAX 703-243-8808
E-Mail: info@mediainstitute.org
Home Page: www.mediainstitute.org
Social Media: *Twitter, RSS Feed, You Tube*

Patrick Maines, President
Richard T. Kaplar, Vice President
Susanna Coto, Director, Public Events
Wendy Wood, Webmaster

Non-profit research foundation specializing in communications policy isssues.
Founded in 1979

5014 Media Research Center
1900 Campus Commons Drive
Suite 600
Reston, VA 20191

571-267-3500
800-672-1423
FAX 571-375-0099
Home Page: www.mrc.org
Social Media: *Facebook, Twitter*

A politically conservative content analysis organization.
Founded in 1987

5015 Media Research Directors Association
Ogilvy and Mather
309 W 49th Street
New York, NY 10019-7316

212-375-5502
Home Page: www.mrda.org

Provides support for research and maintains library.

5016 Minority Media and Telecommunications Coun cil
3636 16th Street NW
Suite B 366
Washington, DC 20010

202-332-0500
FAX 202-332-0503
E-Mail: info@mmtconline.org
Home Page: www.mmtconline.org
Social Media: *Twitter*

Hon Julia L Johnson, Chairperson
Hon Deborah Taylor Tate, Vice Chair
David Honig, President
Ari Fitzgerald, Secretary
Ronald Johnson, Treasurer

National non-profit organization dedicated to promoting and oreserving equal opportunity and civil rights in the mass media, telecommunications and broadband industries, and closing the digital divide.

5017 NTCA-The Rural Broadband Association
4121 Wilson Boulevard
Suite 1000
Arlington, VA 22203

703-351-2000
FAX 703-351-2001
Home Page: www.ntca.org

Shirley A. Bloomfield, CEO
Michael L. Viands, CFO
James M Dauby, President
Doug Boone, Vice President
William P Hegmann, Secretary/Treasurer

A nonprofit association representing small and rural telephone cooperatives and commercial companies.

5018 National Association for Media Literacy Education
10 Laurel Hill Drive
Cherry Hill, NJ 8003

888-775-2652
Home Page: namle.net
Social Media: *Facebook, Twitter, Google+, Flickr, RSS*

David W Brown, President
Erin Reilly, 1st Vice President
Tony Streit, Treasurer
Joanne Parsont, Secretary
Lynda Bergsma, PhD, Past President

A national membership organization dedicated to media literacy as abasic life skill for the 21st century.
Founded in 1997

5019 National Association for Multi-Ethnicity in Communications
50 Broad Street
Suite 1801
New York, NY 10004

212-594-5985
FAX 212-594-8391
E-Mail: info@namic.com
Home Page: www.namic.com
Social Media: *Facebook, Twitter, LinkedIn, Instagram*

Eglon E Simons, President/CEO
James Jones, VP Programs
Michelle L Rice, Chair
Mark DePietro, Treasurer
Jamie J. Rodriguez, Secretary

Works for diversity in the telecommunications industry.
2000 Members
Founded in 1980

5020 National Association of Air Medical Communication Specialists
Po Box 19240
Topeka, KS 66619

877-396-2227
FAX 866-827-2296
E-Mail: info@naacs.org
Home Page: www.naacs.org
Social Media: *Facebook, Twitter, LinkedIn*

Steve Goff, President
Chris Forncrook, President-Elect
Mac Snead, Treasurer
Charles W Sheppard, MD, FACEP, At- Large Board Members
Garet Hickman, At- Large Board Members

Professional organization whose mission is to represent the air medical communications specialist on a national level through education, standardization and recognition.
200 Members

5021 National Association of Broadcasters
1771 N Street NW
Washington, DC 20036

202-429-5300
E-Mail: nab@nab.org
Home Page: www.nab.org
Social Media: *Facebook, Twitter, LinkedIn, YouTube*

Gordon H. Smith, President, CEO

A trade association, workers union, and lobby group representing the interests of for-profit, over-the-air radio and television broadcasters in theUnited States.

5022 National Association of Communication Centers
Home Page: commcenters.org
Social Media: *Facebook*

Marlina Davidson, Chair
Bonnie Wentzel, Vice Chair
Anand Rao, Vice Chair Elect
Russell Carpenter, Past Chair
Brandi Quesenberry, Secretary

An organization devoted to the support of communication centers on college and university campuses across the country.

5023 National Association of Hispanic Publications
529 14th St, NW.
Suite 923
Washington, DC 20045

202-662-7250
FAX 703-610-9005
E-Mail: info@nahp.org
Home Page: www.nahp.org
Social Media: *Facebook, Twitter*

Martha Mantoya, President
Angela Angulo, Vice President
Robert D Bush, Secretary
Ivan Cruz, Treasurer
Eddie Escobedo Jr., Vice Chair

Founded in the belief that the most effective way to reach the more than 29 million Hispanic Americans in the country is through their own language.
234 Members
Founded in 1982

5024 National Association of Independent Writers and Editors
P.O. Box 549
Ashland, VA 23005

804-767-5961
Home Page: naiwe.com
Social Media: *Facebook, Twitter*

Janice Campbell, Director

A professional association for writers and editors, providing individual member websites and other benefits.
Founded in 2007

5025 National Association of Media Women

601 Pennsylvania Avenue NW
South Building, Suite 900
Washington, DC 20004

800-556-2926
FAX 202-403-3788
E-Mail: national@nawbo.org
Home Page: www.nawbo.org
Social Media: *Facebook, Twitter, LinkedIn, Google+, YouTube*

Crystal Arredondo, Chair
Kathy Warnick, Secretary/ Treasurer
Teresa Meares, Treasurer
Darla Beggs, Immediate Past Chair
Jeanette Armbrust, Director

Sponsors studies, research and seminars to find solutions to problems and create opportunities for women. Presents annual awards.
300 Members
Founded in 1975

5026 National Association of State Technology Directors

PO Box 11910
Lexington, KY 40578-1910

859-244-8186
FAX 859-244-8001
Home Page: www.nastd.org

Jack Ries, President
Mark McCord, Executive Dir.
Pam Johnson, Meetings & Member Services Manager
Paul Czarnecki, Comm. & Research Specialist

Concerned with providing a forum for the exchange of ideas and practices and the development of a unified position on matters of national telecommunications policy and regulatory issues.
1000 Members
Founded in 1978

5027 National Association of Telecommunications Officers and Advisors

3213 Duke St.
Suite 695
Alexandria, VA 22314

703-519-8035
FAX 703-997-7080
E-Mail: info@natoa.org
Home Page: www.natoa.org
Social Media: *Facebook, Twitter, LinkedIn, RSS*

Jodie Miller, Chair
Catherine Rice, Co-Chair
Tony Perez, President
Steve Traylor, Executive Director
Tonya Rideout, Deputy Director

A national association that represents the communications and interests of local governments, and those who advise local governments.
800 Members
Founded in 1980

5028 National Cable & Telecommunications Association

25 Massachusetts Avenue, NW
Suite 100
Washington, DC 20001ÿ

202-222-2300
FAX 202-222-2514
E-Mail: info@ncta.com

Home Page: www.ncta.com
Social Media: *Facebook, Twitter, LinkedIn*

Michael Powell, President, CEO
Bruce Carnes, SVP, Finance & Administration
William Check, SVP, Science & Technology
Barbara York, SVP, Industry Affairs
Rick Chessen, SVP, Law & Regulatory Policy

Trade association for U.S. cable industry.

5029 National Cable and Telecommunications

25 Massachusetts Ave Nw
Suite 100
Washington, DC 20001-1434

202-222-2300
FAX 202-222-2514
E-Mail: webmaster@ncta.com
Home Page: www.ncta.com
Social Media: *Facebook, Twitter, LinkedIn*

Micheal Powell, President & CEO
Brian Dietz, Vice President, Communications
James M. Assey, Executive Vice President
K. Dane Snowden, Chief of Staff
Jill Luckett, Senior Vice President
3189 Members
Founded in 1948

5030 National Captioning Institute

3725 Concorde Parkway
Suite 100
Chantilly, VA 20151

703-917-7600
FAX 703-917-9853
E-Mail: info@ncicap.org
Home Page: www.ncicap.org
Social Media: *Facebook, Twitter, LinkedIn*

Gene Chao, Chairman
Drake Smith, Chief Technology Officer
Jill Toschi, Vice President for Operations
Juan Mario Agudelo, Director, Sales & Marketing
Beth Nubbe, Director, Administration

Non-profit organization whose primary purposes are to deliver effective captioning services and encourage, develop and fund the continuing development of captioning, subtitling, and other media access services for the benefit of peopl who require additional access to the auditory and visual information.
Founded in 1979

5031 National Communication Association

1765 N Street NW
Washington, DC 20036

202-464-4622
FAX 202-464-4600
E-Mail: inbox@natcom.org
Home Page: www.natcom.org
Social Media: *Facebook, Twitter, YouTube, Blog*

Kim Griffin, CPAÿ, CFO
Nancy Kidd, Ph.D.ÿ, Executive Director
Mark Fernandoÿ, Chief of Staff
Trevor Parry-Giles, Ph.D., Dir., Academic & Prof. Affairs
Michelle Randallÿ, Dir., Conventions and Meetings

A not-for-profit membership-based scholarly society.
Founded in 1914

5032 National Communications Association

1765 N Street NW
Washington, DC 20036

202-464-4622
FAX 202-464-4600
E-Mail: inbox@natcom.org
Home Page: www.natcom.org

Social Media: *Facebook, Twitter, YouTube, NCA Blog*

Nancy Kidd, Ph.D., Executive Director
Mark Fernando, Chief Of Staff
Kim Griffin, CPA, CFO
Wendy Fernando, Dir. Of Publications
Andy G. Riskind, Dir. Of Public Affairs

The NCA is the most dynamic and responsive of the communication-related organizations. It has achieved this prominence by serving the needs of departmental administrators in the communication arts and sciences.
7700 Members
Founded in 1914
Mailing list available for rent

5033 National Council of Writing Program Administrators

Department of English
Miami University
Oxford, OH 45056

513-529-5221
FAX 513-529-1392
Home Page: www.wpacouncil.org
Social Media: *Facebook, Twitter, LinkedIn*

John Tassoni, Chair
Susan Miller-Cochran, President
Dominic DelliCarpini, Vice President
Rita Malenczyk, Immediate Past President

National organization that fosters professional development, communication and community among college and university writing progrma administrators and other interested faculty.
700 Members
Founded in 1975

5034 National Federation Abstracting & Information Services

801 Compass Way
Suite 201
Annapolis, MD 21401

443-221-2980
FAX 443-221-2981
E-Mail: nfais@nfais.org
Home Page: www.nfais.org
Social Media: *Facebook, Twitter, LinkedIn*

Mary Sauer-Games, President
Chris McCue, Past President
Chris Burghardt, President-Elect
Peter Simon, Treasurer
Lynn Willis, Secretary

Serves those groups that aggregate, organize, and facilitate access to information. To improve member capabilities and contribute to their ongoing success. Provides opportunities for education, advocacy, and a forum to address common interests.
60 Members
Founded in 1958
Printed in on matte stock

5035 National Newspaper Association

P.O. Box 7540
Columbia, MO 65205-7540

573-777-4980
FAX 573-777-4985
E-Mail: tonda@nna.org
Home Page: nnaweb.org
Social Media: *Facebook, Twitter, RSS*

John Edgecombe Jr., President
Chip Hutcheson, Vice President
Robert M. Williams Jr.ÿ, Immediate Past President
Tonda Rush, Chief Executive Officer
Carol Pierce, Managing Director

An association representing community newspapers, publishers, and editors. Lists resources, events, membership benefits, and jobs.
Founded in 1885

5036 National Newspaper Publishers Association

1816 12th Street, NW
Washington, DC 20009

202-588-8764
FAX 202-588-8960
E-Mail: admin@nnpa.org
Home Page: nnpa.org
Social Media: *Facebook, Twitter, Google+*

Cloves C. Campbell, Chair
Mollie F. Belt, 1st Vice Chair
John B. Smith, Srÿ, 2nd Vice Chair
Lenora Alexander, Treasurer
Natalie Cole, Secretary

A trade association composed of more than 200 black newspapers in the United States and the Virgin Islands. It also created an electronic news service which enables newspapers to provide real time news and information to its national constituency.

5037 National Speakers Association

1500 S Priest Dr
Tempe, AZ 85281-6203

480-968-2552
FAX 480-968-0911
E-Mail: memberservices@NSAspeaker.org
Home Page: www.nsaspeaker.org
Social Media: *Facebook, Twitter, Google+, YouTube, Instagram*

Stacy Tetschner, CAE, FASAE, CEO
William Peterson, MBA, Director Of Finance
Michelle Reynolds, Director of Member Experiences
Christie Turley, Director of Marketing, Consultant
Barbara Parus, Director of Publications

The leading organization for experts who speak professionally. NSA's members include experts in a variety of industries and disciplines, who reach audiences as trainers, educators, humorists, motivators, consultants, authors and more. NSA provides resources and education designed to advance the skills, integrity, and value of its members and speaking profession. NSA the voice of the speaking profession.
3500 Members
Founded in 1973
Mailing list available for rent: 3200 names

5038 National Telemedia Council

1922 University Avenue
Madison, WI 53726

608-218-1182
FAX 608-218-1183
E-Mail: ntelemedia@aol.com
Home Page: www.nationaltelemediacouncil.org

Marieli Rowe, Director

Promotes media literacy through workshops and telemediun.
Founded in 1953

5039 National Translator Association

5611 Kendall Court
Suite 2
Arvada, CO 80002

303-378-8209
FAX 303-465-4067
E-Mail: stcl@comcast.net
Home Page:
www.nationaltranslatorassociation.org

Byron St. Clair, President
Arnold Cruze, Vice President
Alan Greager, Secretary/Treasurer

Dedicated to the preservation of free over-the-air TV in all geographical areas. It works to improve the technology of rebroadcast translators and regulatory climate which governs them. It continuously promotes the concept of universal free over-the-air TV

and reprsents the ineterests of translator operators before the FCC and other government agencies such as the Forest Service and the Bureau of Land Management. Membership is open to all individuals and organizations that are interested.
Founded in 1967

5040 National Writers Association

Home Page: www.nationalwriters.com

A nonprofit organization that provides education and an ethical resource for writers at all levels of experience. It also awards scholarships and provides no or low cost workshops and seminars.

5041 Networking Institute

PO Box 650037
West Newton, MA 02465-1928

617-965-3340
FAX 617-965-2341
E-Mail: info@netage.com
Home Page: www.netage.com

Jessica Lipnack, Owner
Jeffrey Stamps, Co-Founder
Carrie Kuempel, Director Training
Rich Carpenter, Strategy Advisor

Promotes networks to help people work together. Offers consulting services, educational workshops and seminars. To order: The Age of the Network and The TeamNet Factor call Oliver Wright productions at 800-343-0625.
Founded in 1982

5042 New America Media Ethnic Media Association

209 9th St.
Suite 200
San Francisco, CA 94103

415-503-4170
E-Mail:
communications@newamericamedia.org
Home Page: newamericamedia.org

Sandy Close, Executive Editor & Director

An association for the promotion of ethnic media organizations.
Founded in 1996

5043 Newspaper Association Managers

32 Dunham Road
Beverly, MA

978-338-2555
Home Page: nammanagers.com

Lisa Hills, President
Layne Bruce, Vice President
Greg Sherrill, Immediate Past President
George White, Secretary
Tom Newton, Director

An organization of executives representing newspaper associations in the United States and Canada.

5044 Newspaper Association of America

4401 Wilson Blvd
Suite 900
Arlington, VA 22203-4195

571-366-1000
FAX 571-366-1195
E-Mail: joan.mills@naa.org
Home Page: www.naa.org
Social Media: *Facebook, Twitter, LinkedIn, Google+, YouTube*

Donna Barrett, Chairman
Stephen P Hills, Vice Chairman
Tony W Hunter, Secretary
Michael J. Klingensmith, Treasurer
Robert J Dickey, Past Chairman

Focuses on the major issues that affect today's newspaper industry public policy and legal matters, advertising revenue growth and audi-

ence development across the medium's broad portfolio of products and digital platforms.
2000 Members
Founded in 1992

5045 North American Serials Interest Group

1902 Ridge Rd
West Seneca, NY 14224-3312

E-Mail: info@nasig.org
Home Page: www.nasig.org

Joyce Tenney, President
Steve Kelley, Vice President/President-Elect
Shana McDanold, Secretary
Jennifer Arnold, Treasurer
Beverly Geckle, Treasurer-Elect

An independent organization taht promotes communication and sharing of ideas among all members of the serials information chain, anyone working with or concerned about serial publications.
1200 Members
Founded in 1985

5046 Organization for the Promotion and Advance of Small Telecommunications Co.

21 Dupont Cir NW
Suite 700
Washington, DC 20036-1109

202-833-2775
FAX 202-659-4619
E-Mail: membership@ncta.org
Home Page: www.opastco.org

John Rose, President
Corey Watkins, Network Administrator

Protects the interests of small, rural, independent commercial telephone companies and cooperatives that have less than 50,000 access lines.
675 Members
Founded in 1963

5047 PCIA- The Wireless Industry Association

500 Montgomery Street
Suite 500
Alexandria, VA 22314

703-971-7100
800-759-0300
FAX 703-836-1608
E-Mail: andrewd@pcia.com
Home Page: www.pcia.com
Social Media: *Facebook, Twitter, LinkedIn*

Thomas A. Murray, Chairman
Steven Marshall, Vice Chairman
David E Weisman, Treasurer
Jonathan S. Adelstein, President & CEO
Tim House, Vice President, External Relations

Represents companies that develop, own, manage and operate towers, commercial rooftops and other facilities for the provision of all types of wireless, broadcasting and telecommunications services.
3000 Members
Founded in 1949

5048 Paley Center for Media

25 West 52nd Street
New York, NY 10019

212-621-6800
FAX 212-621-6600
E-Mail: coman@paleycenter.org
Home Page: www.paleycenter.org
Social Media: *Facebook, Twitter, YouTube, Google+, Hulu*

Maureen J Reidy, President, CEO
John Lanaway, Interim CFO
Maxim Thorne, Executive Vice President
Diane Lewis, Vice President, Public Affairs
Maureen J. Reidy, Chief Marketing Officer

Leads the discussion about the cultural, creative, and social significance of television, radio, and emerging platforms for the professional community and media-interested public.

5049 Personal Achievement Institute

1 Speaking Success Road
Box 6543
Kingman, AZ 86402-6543

928-753-5315
800-321-1225
FAX 928-753-7554
Home Page: www.speakingsuccess.com

Burt Dubin, President

Education that provides advice and business strategies for both novices and experts in mastering the field of professional speaking. Free monthly newsletter is accessible through Website.
Founded in 1978
Printed in one color on matte stock

5050 Portable Computer and Communications Association

PO Box 680
Hood River, OR 97031

541-490-5140
FAX 413-410-8447
E-Mail: pcca@pcca.org
Home Page: www.pcca.org

Gloria Kowalski, Director
Peter Rysavy, Executive Director

Represents firms, organizations, and individuals interested in moblie communications.
65 Members

5051 Public Relations Society of America

33 Maiden Ln.
11th Fl.
New York, NY 10038

212-460-1400
Home Page: www.prsa.org
Social Media: *Facebook, Twitter, LinkedIn, Pinterest, Tumblr*

Kathy Barbour, Chair
Mark W. McClennan, Chair-Elect
Jane Dvorak, Treasurer
Marisa Vallbona, Secretary

The PRSA is the foremost professional development and standards and ethics body in the public relations industry.
22000 Members
Founded in 1947

5052 Railway Systems Suppliers

13133 Professional Drive
Suite 100
Jacksonville, FL 32225

904-379-3366
FAX 904-379-3941
E-Mail: rssi@rssi.org
Home Page: www.rssi.org

John Paljug, President
N. Michael Choat, Executive Vice President
Walter Winzen, First Vice President
Franklin Brown, Second Vice President

A trade association serving the communication and signal segment of the rail transportation industry. Primary activity is to organize and manage a trade show for its members to exhibit their products and services.
260 Members
Founded in 1966

5053 Real Estate Information Professionals Association

2501 Aerial Center Parkway
Suite 103
Morrisville, NC 27560

919-459-2070
801-999-1212
FAX 919-459-2075
Home Page: www.reipa.org

Sarah Gillian, Executive Director

Supports professional information providers in the real estate industry.
110 Members
Founded in 1995

5054 Religious Communication Association

Department of Communication
University of Texas at Tyler
3007 North Ben Wilson
Victoria, TX 77901

903-566-7093
FAX 903-566-7287
E-Mail: wardm@uhv.edu
Home Page: www.relcomm.org

Kristen Lynn Majocha, President
Mark A. E. Williams, Immediate Past President
Denise P Ferguson, First Vice President
Mark Allan Steiner, Second Vice President
Janie Harden Fritz, Executive Director

An academic society of individuals interested in the study of all aspects of public religious communication, members include teachers, students, clergy, broadcasters and other scholars and professionals.
210 Members
Founded in 1973

5055 Republican Communications Association

PO Box 550
Washington, DC 20515

E-Mail: RCA@mail.house.gov
Home Page: www.rcaweb.org
Social Media: *Facebook, Twitter, Google+*

Lisa Boot, President
Neal Patel, Vice President
Shea Snider, Treasurer
Michael Tadeo, Social Director
Justin LaFranco, Social Director

Sponsors professional development and networking programs. Conducts seminars, briefings, and tours.
165 Members
Founded in 1970

5056 Satellite Broadcasting and Communications Association

1100 17th Street NW
Suite 1150
Washington, DC 20036-4557

202-349-3620
800-541-5981
FAX 202-349-3621
E-Mail: info@sbca.org
Home Page: www.sbca.com
Social Media: *Facebook, Twitter, LinkedIn, YouTube*

Jeffrey Blum, Chairman
Andrew Reinsdorf, Vice Chairman
Joseph Widoff, Executive Director
Benjamin Rowan, Education Manager
Lisa Volpe McCabe, Director Public Policy and Outreach

The national trade organization representing all segments of the satellite industry. It is committed to expanding the utilization of satellite technology for the broadcast delivery of video,

audio, data, music, voice, interactive and broadband services.
100 Members
Founded in 1986

5057 Society for Technical Communication

9401 Lee Hwy
Suite 300
Fairfax, VA 22031-1803

703-522-4114
FAX 703-522-2075
E-Mail: stc@stc.org
Home Page: www.stc.org

Bernard Aschwanden, President
Jane Wilson, Treasurer
Adriane Hunt, Vice President
Alyssa Fox, Secretary
Chris Lyons, Executive Director

Seeks to advance the theory and practice of technical communication in all media. Presents awards and sponsors high school writing contests.
19000 Members
Founded in 1953
Mailing list available for rent: 9000 names at $120 per M

5058 Society of Satellite Professionals International

250 Park Avenue
7th Floor
New York, NY 10177

212-809-5199
FAX 212-825-0075
E-Mail: rbell@sspi.org
Home Page: www.sspi.org
Social Media: *Facebook, Twitter, LinkedIn, YouTube*

Chris Stott, Chairman & CEO
Bryan McGuirk, COO
Dawn Harms, VP, Business Development
Tony Rayner, Chief Operating Officer

Members are individuals in the fields of businesss, education, entertainment, media, science and industry who share common interests in satellite technology.
1700 Members
Founded in 1983

5059 Society of Telecommunications Consultants

13275 State Highway 89
PO Box 70
Old Station, CA 96071

530-335-7313
800-782-7670
FAX 530-335-7360
E-Mail: stchdq@stcconsultants.org
Home Page: www.stcconsultants.org
Social Media: *Facebook, Twitter, Pinterest*

J. R Simmons, President
Elizabeth K English, Executive Vice President
Molly Zraik, Senior Vice President

The STC is an international organization of independent telecommunications and information technology consultants who serve clients in business and government
180 Members
Founded in 1976

5060 Telecommunications Benchmarking International Group

4606 Fm 1960 Rd W
Suite 250
Houston, TX 77069-4617

281-440-5044
888-739-8244
FAX 281-440-6677

E-Mail: tbig@benchmarkingnetwork.com
Home Page: www.benchmarkingnetwork.com

Mark Czarnecki, President

An association of contact center professionals within telecommunications companies dedicated to providing members with an opportunity to identify, document and establish best practices through benchmakring to increase value, effiencies, and profits.
3500+ Members
Founded in 1976

5061 Telecommunications Industry Association (TIA)
1320 N. Courthouse Rd
Suite 200
Arlington, VA 22201-3834

703-907-7700
FAX 703-907-7727
E-Mail: gseiffert@tiaonline.org
Home Page: www.tiaonline.org

Thomas Stanton, Chair
Susan Schramm, Vice Chair
Jennifer Pentecost Sims, Treasurer
Grant Seiffert, President
Danielle Coffey, Vice President Government Affairs

The Telecommunications Industry Association/TIA represents providers of communications and information technology products and services for the global marketplace through its core competencies in standards development, domestic and international advocacy, as well as market development and trade promotion programs.

5062 The Association of Business Information and Media Companies
675 Third Avenue
Suite 2200
New York, NY 10017-5704

212-661-6360
FAX 212-370-0736
E-Mail: info@abmmail.com
Home Page: www.abmassociation.com
Social Media: *Facebook, Twitter, LinkedIn, WordPress, YouTube*

Doug Manoni, Chair
Doug Manoni, Vice Chair
Edward Keating, Treasurer
Ethan Eisner, Past Chair
Marion Minor, Secretary

An association that focuses on the integrated business-to-business media model—which includes print publications, events, digital media and business information.
Founded in 1906

5063 The Center for Media and Public Affairs
933 N. Kenmore St.
Suite 405
Arlington, VA 22201

571-319-0029
FAX 571-319-0029
E-Mail: rieckd@cmpa.com
Home Page: www.cmpa.com
Social Media: *Facebook, Twitter*

Truman Anderson, Chairman of the Board
Dr. Robert Lichter, Founder, President
Nell Minow, Treasurer & Secretary of the Board
Donald Rieck, Executive Director
Dan Amundson, Research Director

A nonpartisan, nonprofit research organization in Washington, D.C.,conducting scientific studies of the news and entertainment media.
Founded in 1985

5064 The Energy Telecommunications and Electrical Association
5005 W Royal Lane
Suite 116
Irving, TX 75063

972-929-3169
888-503-8700
FAX 972-915-6040
Home Page: www.entelec.org
Social Media: *Twitter, LinkedIn*

William Gage, President
John Lapham, First Vice President
Jerry O Roberts, Second Vice President
Russel W Treat, Third Vice President
Richard Nation, Secretary-Treasurer

A user association focusing on communications and control technologies used by petroleum, natural gas, pipeline and electric utility companies.
Founded in 1928

5065 The International Foundation for Information Technology
P. O. Box 907
Summit, NJ 07901-2508

Home Page: www.if4it.com
Social Media: *Facebook, Twitter, LinkedIn, Google+*

A global industry best practices association that promotes the interests and career development of practitioners, educators, and students who wish to extend their knowledge and understanding of IT operations, management, and leadership.

5066 Toastmasters International
23182 Arroyo Vista
Rancho Santa Margarita
Mission Viejo, CA 92688-2620

949-858-8255
949-835-1300
FAX 949-858-1207
E-Mail: newsletters@toastmasters.org
Home Page: www.toastmasters.org
Social Media: *Facebook, Twitter*

Jim Kokocki, DTM, International President
Mike Storkey, DTM, International President-Elect
Balraj Arunasalam, DTM, First Vice President
Lark Doley, DTM, Second Vice President
Mohammed Murad, DTM, Immediate Past Intl. President

Publishes educational articles on the subjects of communication and leadership. Topics include language, listening, humor, self-improvement, goal setting, success and logical thinking.
19500 Members
Founded in 1924

5067 United States Internet Service Providers
700 12th St NW
Suite 700 E
Washington, DC 20005-4052

202-904-2351
E-Mail: kdean@usispa.org
Home Page: www.usispa.org

John Albertine, President

Will serve both as the ISP community's representative during policy debates and as a forum in which members can share information and develop best practices for handling specific legal matters.
7 Members
Founded in 1991

5068 United States Telecom Association
607 14th Street, NW
Suite 400
Washington, DC 20005

202-326-7300
FAX 202-315-3603
Home Page: www.ustelecom.org
Social Media: *Facebook, Twitter, LinkedIn, YouTube*

Robert A Hunt, Chairman of the Board
Walter B. McCormick, Jr., President, CEO
Mark Kulish, SVP, Administration, CFO
Alan J. Roth, Senior Executive Vice President
Anne Veigle, SVP, Communications

A trade association that represents telecommunications-related businesses based in the United States.

5069 United Telecom Council
1129 20th Street
Suite 350
Washington, DC 20036

202-872-0030
FAX 202-872-1331
E-Mail: bill.moroney@utc.org
Home Page: www.utc.org
Social Media: *Facebook, Twitter, LinkedIn*

Connie Darshak, President/CEO
Kathleen Fitzpatrick, VP and General Counsel
Brett Kilbourne, Vice President, Government
Mike Oldak, Vice President, Strategy
Karnel Thomas, Vice President - Member & Industry

Represents organizations using telecommunications in their operations before various federal and state legislative and regulatory agencies, particularly the FCC
1500 Members
Founded in 1948

5070 Utility Communicaotrs International
150 Mark Trai
Sandy Springs, GA 30328

970-368-2021
FAX 512-864-7203
E-Mail: info@utilitycommunicators.com
Home Page: www.utilitycommunicators.com
Social Media: *Facebook, Twitter, LinkedIn*

Brian Phillips, President
Jeff Rogers, Vice President
Jennifer Moffatt, Treasurer
Jerry Cargile, Board
Eunice Tanjuaquio Bray, Board

International organization comprimsed of advertising, public relations and marketing professionals from electric, gas and water utlities, energy companies, telephone companies, advertising and public relations agencies, and suppliers who communicate for and about the utility and energy industries.
400 Members
Founded in 1922

5071 Wikibon
5 Mount Royal Ave.
Suite 280
Marlborough, MA 1752

774-463-3400
FAX 774-463-3405
Home Page: wikibon.org
Social Media: *Facebook, Twitter, LinkedIn, Blog*

A professional community solving technology and business problems through an open source sharing of free advisory knowledge.
Founded in 2007

Newsletters

5072 Wireless Communications Association International
1333 H St NW
Suite 700 W
Washington, DC 20005-4754

202-452-7823
FAX 202-452-0041
E-Mail: president@wcai.com
Home Page: www.wcai.com
Social Media: *Facebook, Twitter, LinkedIn*

Fred Campbell, President

The non-profit trade and professional association for the Wireless Broadband industry. Mission is to advance the interests of the wireless carriers that provide high-speed data, internet, voice and video services on broadband spectrum through land-based systems using reception/transmit devices in all broadband spectrum bands.
250 Members
Founded in 1987

5073 Wireless Dealers Association
9746 Tappenbeck Dr
Houston, TX 77055-4102

713-467-0077
800-624-6918
E-Mail: contact@wirelessindustry.com
Home Page: www.wirelessindustry.com

Robert Hutchinson, President

Business association made up of cellular and wireless communications agents, dealers, resellers, carriers, manufacturers, distributors and importers.
2500 Members
Founded in 1986

5074 Women in Cable and Telecommunications
2000 K Street, NW
Suite 350
Washington, DC 20006

202-827-4794
FAX 202-450-5596
E-Mail: membership@wict.org
Home Page: www.wict.org
Social Media: *Facebook, Twitter, YouTube*

Maria E. Brennan, CAE, President & CEO
Mary Meduski, Immediate Past Chair
Gail Mackinnon, Treasurer
Michelle Rice, Governance Chair
Parthavi Das, Chief of Staff

Provides opportunitites for leadership, networking, and advocacy in the industry.
4600 Members
Founded in 1979

5075 World Teleport Association
250 Park Avenue
Suite 14B
New York, NY 10177

646-291-6166
FAX 212-825-0075
E-Mail: icf@intelligentcommunity.org
Home Page: www.intelligentcommunity.org
Social Media: *Facebook, Twitter, YouTube*

Robert Bell, Executive Director

Promotes the understanding, development, and use of eleports as a means to achieve economic, political and social progress locally, regionally and worldwide.
606 Members
Founded in 1985

Newsletters

5076 411 Newsletter
United Communications Group
11300 Rockville Pike
Suite 1100
Rockville, MD 20852-3030

301-287-2700
FAX 301-816-8945
E-Mail: webmaster@ucg.com
Home Page: www.ucg.com

Benny Dicecca, President
Business newsletter for professionals in the communications industry.
Cost: $339.00
Founded in 1977

5077 ATTW Bulletin
Association of Teachers of Technical Writing
Department of Linguistics and Technical Comm
1155 Union Circle #305298
Denton, TX 76203-5017

940-565-4458
E-Mail: sims@unt.edu
Home Page: www.attw.org

Barbara Sims, Executive Secretary

Publishes news about members, the association, and the profession as well as bibliographic resources for teachers, teaching techniques, suggested assignments, implications of current research for the classroom, opinions on professional issues, notices and highlights of conferences, calls for papers and proposals, job announcements, and other information that will interest new and experienced teachers in undergraduate or graduate curricula.
Frequency: Semi-Annual

5078 Advertising & Newspaper Media
Newspaper Association of America
4401 Wilson Blvd
Suite 900
Arlington, VA 22203-4195

571-366-1000
FAX 571-366-1195
E-Mail: joan.mills@naa.org
Home Page: www.naa.org

Reggie Hall, Senior VP

Electronic newsletters delivers retail, national and classified advertising ideas plus updates on your most important customers. If your job responsibilities include any type advertising revenue you need to be a subscriber.
Frequency: Monthly

5079 Bandwidth Minutes and IP Transport Markets Will Capacity Traders Succeed?
Probe Research
3 Wing Drive
Suite 240
Cedar Knolls, NJ 07927-1000

973-285-1500
FAX 973-285-1519
Home Page: www.proberesearch.com

We look into capacity exchanges and determine how they add value, whter participants will find exchanges useful, what are the presequisites for a robust capacity market, what are the risk to telcos if they use exchanges, and what do the exchanges need to do in order to increase trading volume.

5080 Bandwidth Pricing Trends
Probe Research
3 Wing Drive
Suite 240
Cedar Knolls, NJ 07927-1000

973-285-1500
FAX 973-285-1519
Home Page: www.proberesearch.com

Provides an analysis of the trends in capacity pricing and the expected effects on demand. It provides a view of the drivers that determine what the bandwidth cost will be on a particular route. Also looks at how these determinants have contributes to the level of price erosion each of the routes analyzed.

5081 Big Ideas Newsletter
Newspaper Association of America
4401 Wilson Blvd
Suite 900
Arlington, VA 22203-4195

571-366-1000
FAX 571-366-1195
E-Mail: joan.mills@naa.org
Home Page: www.naa.org

Reggie Hall, Senior VP

Designed especially for smaller market newspapers, featuring ways to increase revenues, cut costs or otherwise improve your newspaper.
Frequency: Bi-Monthly

5082 Brandwidth Supply and Demand Analysis WIT IP Traffic Demand Update
Probe Research
3 Wing Drive
Suite 240
Cedar Knolls, NJ 07927-1000

973-285-1500
FAX 973-285-1519
Home Page: www.proberesearch.com

Provides an analysis of the bandwidth supply and demand on number of interregional routes. Describes methodology of building up the bandwidth supply and demand picture on these routes. Analyzes what the supply and demand balance is on these routes. Concludes what the business ramifications are for ISPs and backbone providers, banks and vendors.

5083 Broadband Wireless
Probe Research
3 Wing Drive
Suite 240
Cedar Knolls, NJ 07927-1000

973-285-1500
FAX 973-285-1519
Home Page: www.proberesearch.com

In this bulletin, we take a look into is going on with terrestrial fixed wireless last mile solutions in the MMDS, LMDS spectrums. LMDS is emerging as the next platform for CLECs. However, these CLECs will be entering the market at the end of a long line of competitors in many cities.

5084 Business Publisher
JK Publishing
3105 N Newhall Street
Milwaukee, WI 53211

414-332-1625
FAX 414-332-0916

John Kenney, Editor
Jean O'Brien, Circulation Manager

Offers information and full coverage of the magazine and business/trade publishing industry.
Cost: $335.00
8 Pages
Frequency: BiWeekly

5085 CMA Newsletter
College Media Advisers
University
#300
Memphis, TN 38152

512-471-5084
FAX 901-678-4798
Home Page: www.collegemedia.org

Ken Rosenauer, Publisher

Provides news and information to those who advise/supervise college media run by students (i.e. newspapers, magazines, yearbooks, radios, and TV stations).
Cost: $60.00
6 Pages
Circulation: 750
Founded in 1954

5086 Cantu's Newsletter
Cantu's Comedy Newsletter
PO Box 210495
San Francisco, CA 94121

415-668-2402
E-Mail: info1@HumorMall.com
Home Page: www.humormall.com

John Cantu, Publisher

Articles of interest to public speakers, writers, comedians, comedy writers.
Cost: $29.95
Circulation: 3000
Founded in 1999

5087 Chamber Executive
American Chambers of Congress Exec
Communications
4875 Eisenhower Ave
Suite 250
Alexandria, VA 22304-4850

703-998-0072
FAX 703-212-9512
E-Mail: webmaster@acce.org
Home Page: www.acce.org

Mick Flemming, Manager

Newsletter aimed at management level communications professionals.
Cost: $99.00
12 Pages
Founded in 1914
Mailing list available for rent
Printed in 4 colors on matte stock

5088 Circulation Update E-Newsletter
Newspaper Association of America
4401 Wilson Blvd
Suite 900
Arlington, VA 22203-4195

571-366-1000
FAX 571-366-1195
E-Mail: joan.mills@naa.org
Home Page: www.naa.org
Social Media: *Facebook, Twitter*

Reggie Hall, Senior VP

Focused on newspaper executives with responsibility for marketing their newspapers to readers. You will find a balance of recent headline stories, consumer marketing research, information about your retailers, and regulatory information blended with success stories and resources to help you in your mission of building circulation and readership.
Frequency: Weekly

5089 Classified Communications Newsletter
PO Box 4242
Prescott, AZ 86302

520-778-6788
E-Mail: classa@northlink.com

Agnes Franz, Publisher

Information and ad-writing tips for small budget advertisers. Both display and word classifieds addressed. Will also review books on advertising and marketing.
Cost: $35.00
8 Pages
Frequency: Monthly
Circulation: 2000
Founded in 1989
Printed in 2 colors on glossy stock

5090 Communication Briefings
Briefings Publishing Group
1101 King St
Suite 110
Alexandria, VA 22314-2944

703-548-3800
FAX 703-684-2136
Home Page: www.combriefings.com

William G Dugan, Group Publisher
Susan Marshall, Executive Editor
Lois Willingham, Marketing Manager
Charles Blakeney, Owner

This newsletter provides subscribers with communications ideas and techniques to use to persuade clients, and motivate employees.
Cost: $79.00
8 Pages
Frequency: Monthly
Circulation: 55000
Founded in 1981

5091 Communications Business Daily
Warren Communications News
2115 Ward Ct Nw
Washington, DC 20037-1209

202-872-9200
800-771-9202
FAX 202-318-8350
E-Mail: info@warren-news.com
Home Page: www.warren-news.com

Brig Easley, Manager
Daniel Warren, President/Editor
Founded in 1945

5092 Communications Concepts
Communication Concepts
508 Mill Stone Dr
Beavercreek, OH 45434-5840

937-426-8600
FAX 937-429-3811
E-Mail: cci.dayton@pobox.com
Home Page:
www.communication-concepts.com

Rodger L Southworth, President

Ideas and methods for professional communications.

5093 DBS Report
Kagan World Media
1 Lower Ragsdale Dr
Building One, Suite 130
Monterey, CA 93940-5749

831-624-1536
800-307-2529
FAX 831-625-3225
E-Mail: info@kagan.com
Home Page: www.kagan.com

Tim Baskerville, President
Cost: $1045.00
Frequency: Monthly
Founded in 1969

5094 Daily Deal
Vicki King
105 Madison Avenue
New York, NY 10016

212-313-9200
888-667-3325

E-Mail: customerservice@thedeal.com
Home Page: www.thedeal.com

Mickey Hernandez, Advertising Sales
Elena Freed, Marketing

Reports and analyzes all the aspects of the booming, high stakes world of the deal economy. Areas of coverage include mergers and aquisitions, private equity, venture capital and bankruptcies.
Cost: $498.00
26 Pages
Frequency: Daily
Circulation: 40893
Founded in 1999

5095 EHS News Briefs
Newspaper Association of America
4401 Wilson Blvd
Suite 900
Arlington, VA 22203-4195

571-366-1000
FAX 571-366-1195
E-Mail: joan.mills@naa.org
Home Page: www.naa.org

Reggie Hall, Senior VP

These news briefs spotlight what is happening in Congress, the Administration, Courts and around the industry.
Frequency: Weekly

5096 Emerging Media Report
Knight MediaCom International
2400 Kettner Boulevard
Suite 237
San Diego, CA 92101

619-338-9885
FAX 619-338-9886
E-Mail: knightsmedia@hotmail.com
Home Page: www.knightmedia.com

Covers VR, TV, CD, PC, and entertainment marketing.
Founded in 1978

5097 Fusion Magazine
Newspaper Association of America
4401 Wilson Blvd
Suite 900
Arlington, VA 22203-4195

571-366-1000
FAX 571-366-1195
E-Mail: joan.mills@naa.org
Home Page: www.naa.org

Reggie Hall, Senior VP

This newsletter focuses on the business of diversity within the newspaper industry. In it you will find new strategies for making diversity work in advertising, news and editorial, circulation, marketing, production, human resources and the business office.
Frequency: Quarterly

5098 Growing Audience E-Newsletter
Newspaper Association of America
4401 Wilson Blvd
Suite 900
Arlington, VA 22203-4195

571-366-1000
FAX 571-366-1195
E-Mail: joan.mills@naa.org
Home Page: www.naa.org

Reggie Hall, Senior VP

This newsletter provides an unparalleled array of information to keep you informed on the most current newspaper readership issues, experiments, results, ideas, successes and failures.
Frequency: Weekly

5099 Information Broker
Burwell Enterprises

5619 Plumtree Drive
Dallas, TX 75252

972-331-1951
FAX 972-733-1951
Home Page: www.burwellinc.com

Helen Burwell, Publisher
Jeanne Paulino, Marketing Director

Covers fee-based information services for practitioners and users of information services. Accepts advertising.
Cost: $40.00
12 Pages
Frequency: Bi-Monthly
Circulation: 500
Printed in one color on matte stock

5100 Intercom
Society for Technical Communication
9401 Lee Hwy
Suite 300
Fairfax, VA 22031-1803

703-522-4114
FAX 703-522-2075
E-Mail: stc@stc.org
Home Page: www.stc.org

Susan Burton, Executive Director
Anita Dosik, Publications Director
Maurice P. Martin, Editor
Antoinette DeSalvo, Marketing Coordinator
Suzanna Laurent, President

A monthly magazine offering Society members with information and articles on communication industry trends and activities.
Cost: $95.00
Circulation: 20000
Founded in 1957
Mailing list available for rent: 1000 names at $120 per M

5101 Labor & Employment Law Letter
Newspaper Association of America
4401 Wilson Blvd
Suite 900
Arlington, VA 22203-4195

571-366-1000
FAX 571-366-1195
E-Mail: joan.mills@naa.org
Home Page: www.naa.org

Reggie Hall, Senior VP

This newsletter offers readers information on critical employment issues facing the newspaper industry.
Frequency: Bi-Monthly

5102 Lifestyle Media-Relations Reporter
InfoCom Group
5900 Hollis Street
Suite L
Emeryville, CA 94608

510-596-9300
800-959-1059
Home Page: www.infocomgroup.com

This newsletter offers information on media placement in lifestyle and consumer media.
Cost: $369.00
Frequency: Monthly
Founded in 1980

5103 MAPNetter
Architecture Technology Corporation
9977 Valley View Rd
Suite 300
Eden Prairie, MN 55344-3586

952-829-5864
FAX 952-829-5871
E-Mail: info@atcorp.com
Home Page: www.atcorp.com
Social Media: Facebook

Kenneth Thurber, President

Monthly newsletter covering important developments in the field of factory communication systems.
Cost: $432.00
12 Pages
Frequency: Monthly
Founded in 1981

5104 MRC Cyberalert
Media Research Center
325 S Patrick St
Alexandria, VA 22314-3501

703-683-9733
800-672-1423
FAX 703-683-9736
E-Mail: mrc@mediaresearch.org
Home Page: www.mrc.org
Social Media: Facebook

Brent Bozell, CEO

A news-daily report which documents and exposes liberal media bias. MRC is the nation's leading media watchdog.
Cost: $29.00
Frequency: Monthly
Circulation: 13000
Founded in 1987

5105 Marketing Library Services
Information Today
143 Old Marlton Pike
Medford, NJ 08055-8750

609-654-6266
800-300-9868
FAX 609-654-4309
E-Mail: custserv@infotoday.com
Home Page: www.infotoday.com

Thomas H Hogan, President
Roger R Bilboul, Chairman of the Board

Provides information professional in all types of libraries with specfic ideas for marketing their services.
Cost: $79.95
Frequency: Bi Monthly
ISSN: 0896-3908

5106 Marketing New Media
Kagan World Media
1 Lower Ragsdale Dr
Building One, Suite 130
Monterey, CA 93940-5749

831-624-1536
800-307-2529
FAX 831-625-3225
E-Mail: info@kagan.com
Home Page: www.kagan.com

Tim Baskerville, President
Tom Johnson, Marketing Manager

News of the Marketing New Media. Three month trial available.
Cost: $795.00
Frequency: Monthly
Founded in 1878

5107 Media Access
WGBH Educational Foundation
PO Box 200
Boston, MA 02134-1008

617-300-2000
FAX 617-300-1032
E-Mail: feedback@wgbh.org
Home Page: www.wgbh.org

Jonathan Abbott, President
Russell Peotter, Owner
Mary Cotton, Owner

Includes information on NCAM's research and development projects, which strive to make media and technology accessible to disabled populations.
2 Pages
Circulation: 15000

Founded in 1951
Printed in 2 colors on matte stock

5108 Media File
Media Alliance
1904 Franklin St
Suite 500
Oakland, CA 94612-2926

510-832-9000
FAX 510-238-8557
Home Page: www.media-alliance.org

Tracy Rosenberg, Executive Director
Eloise Rose Lee, Program Director

Information about media and media workers.
8 Pages
Frequency: Quarterly

5109 Media Law Reporter
Bureau of National Affairs
1801 S Bell St
Arlington, VA 22202-4501

703-341-3000
800-372-1033
FAX 800-253-0332
E-Mail: customercare@bna.com
Home Page: www.bnabooks.com

Paul N Wojcik, CEO

A weekly reference service containing the full-text of federal and state court decisions and selected agency rulings affecting newspapers, magazines, radio, television, film and other media.
Cost: $1856.00
Frequency: Weekly
ISSN: 0148-1045
Founded in 1929

5110 Media Mergers & Acquisitions
Kagan World Media
1 Lower Ragsdale Dr
Building One, Suite 130
Monterey, CA 93940-5749

831-624-1536
800-307-2529
FAX 831-625-3225
E-Mail: info@kagan.com
Home Page: www.kagan.com

Tim Baskerville, President
Tom Johnson, Marketing Manager

Where it all comes together. Exclusive scorecard of deals done by media companies. Dollar amounts, multiples paid, trends captured in succinct summaries of complex transactions. Three month trial available.
Cost: $795.00
Frequency: Monthly
Founded in 1969

5111 Media Sports Business
Kagan World Media
1 Lower Ragsdale Dr
Building One, Suite 130
Monterey, CA 93940-5749

831-624-1536
FAX 831-625-3225
E-Mail: info@kagan.com
Home Page: www.kagan.com

Tim Baskerville, President
Tom Johnson, Marketing Manager
Cost: $945.00
Frequency: Monthly
Founded in 1969

5112 Motion Picture Investor
Kagan World Media
1 Lower Ragsdale Dr
Building One, Suite 130
Monterey, CA 93940-5749

831-624-1536
800-307-2529

FAX 831-625-3225
E-Mail: info@kagan.com
Home Page: www.kagan.com

Tim Baskerville, President
Tom Johnson, Marketing Manager
Cost: $845.00
Frequency: Monthly
Founded in 1969

5113 NAMIC E-Newsletter
Natl Assoc for Multi-Ethnicity in
Communications
320 West 37th Street
8th Floor
New York, NY 10018

212-594-5985
FAX 212-594-8391
E-Mail: info@namic.com
Home Page: www.namic.com
Social Media: *Facebook, Twitter*

Kathy A Johnson, President
James Jones, VP Programs

For members only, provides timely and useful
national and local information about industry-related issues, trends and events
Frequency: Bi-Monthly

5114 NFAIS e-Notes
National Federation Abstracting & Info
Services
1518 Walnut St
Suite 1004
Philadelphia, PA 19102

215-893-1561
FAX 215-893-1564
E-Mail: nfais@nfais.org
Home Page: www.nfais.org
Social Media: *Facebook, Twitter, LinkedIn*

Bonnie Lawlor, Executive Director
Jill O'Neil, Director Communications

Membership organization for all organizations
that create, aggregate or provide ease of access
to credible information.
80 Members
Frequency: Monthly
Founded in 1958

5115 Newspaper Investor
Kagan World Media
1 Lower Ragsdale Dr
Building One, Suite 130
Monterey, CA 93940-5749

831-624-1536
800-307-2529
FAX 831-625-3225
E-Mail: info@kagan.com
Home Page: www.kagan.com

Tim Baskerville, President
Tom Johnson, Marketing Manager
Cost: $845.00
Frequency: Monthly
Founded in 1969

**5116 Online Publishing Update
E-Newsletter**
Newspaper Association of America
4401 Wilson Blvd
Suite 900
Arlington, VA 22203-4195

571-366-1000
FAX 571-366-1195
E-Mail: joan.mills@naa.org
Home Page: www.naa.org

Reggie Hall, Senior VP

A round-up of news, research, industry trends,
best practices and more, focusing on items of
interest to newspaper and digital media executives. Online Publishing Update e-newsletter is

published every Monday, Wednesday and
Friday.
Frequency: 3x/Weekly

5117 Pacific Dialogue
Robert Miko
33 Ferry Ct
Stratford, CT 06615

203-378-2803
E-Mail: bmiko@pacificdialogue.com
Home Page: www.pacificdialogue.com

Robert Miko, Publisher

Corporate communications of the Pacific Re-
gion.
Cost: $196.00
4 Pages
Frequency: Weekly
Circulation: 1,000

5118 Party Line
Party Line Publishing Company
35 Sutton Place
New York, NY 10022-2464

212-755-3487
FAX 212-755-4859
Home Page: www.partylinepublishing.com

Morton Yarmon, Publisher
Betty Yarmon, Editor
Betty Yarmon, Marketing

Weekly media placement newsletter with
up-to-date news of the media for public rela-
tions executives in all aspects of business, hos-
pitals, publishers and associations.
Cost: $200.00
Frequency: Weekly
Circulation: 2000
Founded in 1960
Mailing list available for rentat $100 per M
Printed in 2 colors on matte stock

5119 Pay TV Newsletter
Kagan World Media
126 Clock Tower Place
Carmel, CA 93923-8746

831-624-1536
FAX 831-625-3225
E-Mail: info@kagan.com
Home Page: www.kagan.com

George Niesen, Editor
Tom Johnson, Marketing Manager
Cost: $845.00
Frequency: Monthly

5120 SIGNAL Connections
4400 Fairfax Lakes Court
Fairfax, VA 22033

703-631-6100
800-336-4583
FAX 703-631-6169
E-Mail: promo@afcea.org
Home Page: www.afcea.org
Social Media: *Facebook, Twitter, LinkedIn*

Richard K Ackerman, Editor in Chief

Bridges the gap between issues of SIGNAL by
providing additional news and feature articles
about the industry and the Association.
Frequency: Monthly

5121 Satellite Week
Warren Communications News
2115 Ward Ct Nw
Washington, DC 20037-1209

202-872-9200
800-771-9202
FAX 202-318-8350
E-Mail: info@warren-news.com
Home Page: www.warren-news.com

Brig Easley, Manager
Daniel Warren, President/Editor
Founded in 1945

5122 Smaller Market E-Newsletter
Newspaper Association of America
4401 Wilson Blvd
Suite 900
Arlington, VA 22203-4195

571-366-1000
FAX 571-366-1195
E-Mail: joan.mills@naa.org
Home Page: www.naa.org
Social Media: *Facebook, Twitter*

Reggie Hall, Senior VP

Stay ahead of industry news and trends with
the latest reports outlining how to improve
your smaller market newspaper. Also receive a
synopsis on new NAA products and services
and how they can benefit smaller market
newspapers.
Frequency: Monthly

5123 Speech Technology Magazine
2628 Wilhite Court
Suite 100
Lexington, KY 40503

859-278-2223
877-993-9767
FAX 859-278-7364
Home Page: www.speechtechmag.com/

John Kelly, Publisher & Editor
Sheila Willison, Circulation Director
Stephanie Owens, Associate Editor
Devon Taylor, Magazine Sales
Kerrie Porath, Sales Coordinator

Divided into four sections: applications, technology, new products, and a special focus section. Authors from the field contribute their
expertise to this trade magazine.
73 Pages
Frequency: Fortnightly
Circulation: 25000
Founded in 1996

5124 Telecom A.M.
Warren Communications News
2115 Ward Ct Nw
Washington, DC 20037-1209

202-872-9200
800-771-9202
FAX 202-318-8350
E-Mail: info@warren-news.com
Home Page: www.warren-news.com

Brig Easley, Manager
Daniel Warren, President/Editor
Founded in 1945

**5125 Telemarketing Update: The
Regulations and the Impact**
Newspaper Association of America
4401 Wilson Blvd
Suite 900
Arlington, VA 22203-4195

571-366-1000
FAX 571-366-1195
E-Mail: joan.mills@naa.org
Home Page: www.naa.org
Social Media: *Twitter*

Reggie Hall, Senior VP

Perspective on the Federal Telemarketing Regulations and an explanation of how newspapers
are being impacted by the changes. What's
working and what's not and what the Federal
Government has in store for newspapers.

5126 Television A.M.
Warren Communications News
2115 Ward Ct Nw
Washington, DC 20037-1209

202-872-9200
800-771-9202
FAX 202-318-8350

E-Mail: info@warren-news.com
Home Page: www.warren-news.com

Brig Easley, Manager
Daniel Warren, President/Editor
Founded in 1945

5127 The RCA News
Grove City College
Attn: Daniel Brown
100 Campus Drive, Box 3014
Grove City, PA 16127

724-458-3793
E-Mail: dsbrown@gcc.edu
Home Page: www.americanrhetoric.com/rca

Daniel S Brown, Newsletter Editor
Ken Danielson, Executive Secretary
Janie Harden Fritz, President

A newsletter for the academic society of individuals interested in the study of all aspects of
public religious communication, members include teachers, students, clergy, broadcasters
and other scholars and professionals.
210 Members
Founded in 1973

5128 Washington Internet Daily
Warren Communications News
2115 Ward Ct Nw
Washington, DC 20037-1209

202-872-9200
800-771-9202
FAX 202-318-8350
E-Mail: info@warren-news.com
Home Page: www.warren-news.com

Brig Easley, Manager
Daniel Warren, President/Editor
Founded in 1945

Magazines & Journals

5129 15 Minutes Magazine.Com
7334 173rd Street
Fresh Meadows, NY 11366-1428

718-969-0404
FAX 718-591-3660
E-Mail: editor@15minutesmagazine.com
Home Page: www.15minutesmagazine.com

Tim Boxer, Editor/Publisher
Nina Boxer, Associate Editor
Bernie Ilson, PR Consultant
Stanley Donen, Founder
Michael Fredo, Owner

Monthly magazine online covering society ben-
efits, with reviews of arts and entertainment,
travel and new products. Targets 715,000 read-
ers in affluent market
Cost: $50.00
Frequency: Monthly
Circulation: 4,45,000
Founded in 1999
Printed in 4 colors

5130 AV Video and Multimedia Producer
Knowledge Industry Publications
701 Westchester Ave
Suite 101W
West Harrison, NY 10604-3077

914-328-9157
FAX 914-328-9093
Home Page: www.kipinet.com/av_mmp/

Ollie Bieniemy, Publisher

Covers product development, graphics and animation, software and equipment, and industry
news for readers involved in professional production, multimedia production, and presenta-

tion technology.
Cost: $53.00
Frequency: Monthly
Circulation: 100,000

5131 Archive Magazine
Luerzer's Archive Inc
410 Park Avenue
Suite 1530
New York, NY 10022-9441

212-941-2496
FAX 212-941-5490
E-Mail: office@showcase.com
Home Page: www.lurzersarchive.net
Social Media: *Twitter, LinkedIn*

Walter Lurzer, Editor

Read by advertising agency executives in 35
countries, archive presents tv commercials and
print ads that are currently running around the
world.
Frequency: 6x a year
Circulation: 40000

5132 Business Communications Review
BCR Enterprises
3025 Highland Pkwy
Suite 200
Downers Grove, IL 60515-5668

630-986-1432
800-227-1234
FAX 630-323-5324
E-Mail: bcrsubscriptions@cmp.com
Home Page: www.bcr.com

Offers a complete package of the latest information for persons associated with the communications industry.
Cost: $46.00
80 Pages
Frequency: Monthly

5133 Communication World
Int'l Association of Business
Communicators
601 Montgomery Street
Suite 1900
San Francisco, CA 94111

415-544-4700
FAX 415-544-4747
E-Mail: cwmagazine@iabc.com
Home Page: www.iabc.com

Natasha Nicholson, Executive Editor
Sue Khodarahmi, Managing Editor
Sue Cavallaro, Production Editor

Covers the leatest in communication research,
technology and trends through in-depth reports
and insightful interviews.
Cost: $150.00
Frequency: Bi-Monthly
Circulation: 13,000
ISSN: 0744-7612
Founded in 1982
Printed in on matte stock

5134 Communications ASP
Technology Marketing Corporation
1 Technology Plz
Norwalk, CT 06854-1936

203-852-6800
800-243-6002
FAX 203-853-2845
E-Mail: tmc@tmcnet.com
Home Page: www.tmcnet.com

Rich Tehrani, CEO

Communication solution magazine.
Cost: $2000.00
Frequency: Monthly
Founded in 1972

5135 Communications Arts
Coyne & Blanchard

110 Constitution Dr
Menlo Park, CA 94025-1107

650-326-6040
800-688-1971
FAX 650-326-1648
E-Mail: ca@commarts.com
Home Page: www.commarts.com

Patrick Coyne, Publisher/Editor

The leading professional journal in the US on
graphic arts, commercial photography, illustra-
tion and interactive design. Features profile in-
dividuals, studios, and agencies with examples
of their work. Accepts advertising.
Cost: $53.00
140 Pages
Frequency: 1 Year 8 Issues
Circulation: 74,834
ISSN: 0010-3519
Founded in 1959
Printed in on glossy stock

5136 Communications Daily
Warren Publishing
2115 Ward Ct NW
Washington, DC 20037-1209

202-872-9200
800-771-9202
FAX 202-318-8350
E-Mail: info@warren-news.com
Home Page: www.warren-news.com

Brig Easley, Manager
Daniel Warren, President/Editor

Covers the entire spectrum of the telephone,
data communications, broadcasting, cable TV,
electronic information distribution, cellulars,
PCS and satellite.
Cost: $4295.00
Frequency: Daily
Founded in 1945

5137 Computers in Libraries
Information Today
143 Old Marlton Pike
Medford, NJ 08055-8750

609-654-6266
800-300-9868
FAX 609-654-4309
E-Mail: custserv@infotoday.com
Home Page: www.infotoday.com

Thomas H Hogan, President
Roger R Bilboul, Chairman of the Board

Coverage of news and issues in the field of library information technology. Focuses on practical applications of technology in community,
school, academic and special libraries. Includes
discussions of the impact of emerging computer technologies on library systems and services and on the library community itself.
Cost: $99.95
Frequency: 10 issues/yr
Mailing list available for rent: 4M names
Printed in 4 colors on glossy stock

5138 Digital Magic
PennWell Publishing Company
10 Tara Boulevard
5th Floor
Nashua, NH 03062-2800

603-891-0123
FAX 603-891-0539
Home Page: www.digitalmagicmag.com

Dennis Allen, Publisher

Insights on new technology trends and techniques, covers the latest in hardware and software products to keep digital effects
professional competitive and up to date.
Cost: $19.95
Frequency: Bi-Monthly
Circulation: 30,000

5139 Documentary
International Documentary Association
1201 W 5th St
Suite M270
Los Angeles, CA 90017-1476

213-534-3600
FAX 213-534-3610
E-Mail: michael@documentary.org
Home Page: www.documentary.org

Michael Lumpkin, Executive Director
Jon Curry, Office Manager
Cindy Chyr, Development

Offers essential information and keeps readers on track with the industry.
Cost: $45.00
Frequency: Quarterly

5140 Extra!
Fairness & Accuracy in Publishing
112 W 27th Street
New York, NY 10001

212-633-6700
FAX 212-727-7668
E-Mail: fair@fair.org
Home Page: www.fair.org

Deborah Thomas, Publisher
Jeff Cohen, Founder

Progressive media criticism.
Cost: $21.00
Frequency: Bi-monthly
Circulation: 21800
Founded in 1987

5141 Folio: Magazine for Magazine Management
Red 7 Media, LLC
10 Norden Place
Norwalk, CT 06855

203-854-6730
FAX 203-854-6735
E-Mail: tsilber@red7media.com
Home Page: www.foliomag.com

Stefanie Botelho, Associate Editor
Kerry Smith, President/CEO
Dan Trombetto, Group Creative Director
Tony Silber, General Manager
John Ellertson, Director Advertising Sales Manager

Written for the people who run the nation's magazines. Offers authoritative intelligence on the magazine market to enable industry professionals to navigate the widening range of strategic options. Every issue delivers features on the people and technologies that are transforming the magazine business, along with useful columns and departments, thought-provoking analysis and tactical advice for building successful magazines.
Cost: $96.00
Frequency: Monthly
Circulation: 11550
Founded in 1971

5142 Government Video
Miller Freeman Publications
810 7th Ave
27th Fl, Suite 4
New York, NY 10019-5818

212-636-2700
FAX 212-636-2750
E-Mail: sedorusa@optonline.net
Home Page: www.governmentvideo.com

Gary Rhodes, International Sales Manager

Articles on audio, video production and technologies, training and presentation, multimedia, video conferencing, and medical and scientific applications.
Frequency: Monthly
Circulation: 18,000

5143 IEEE Wireless Communications
IEEE Communications Society
3 Park Ave
17th Floor
New York, NY 10016-5997

212-705-8920
FAX 212-705-8999
E-Mail: publications@comsoc.org
Home Page: www.ieee.org

Laura Book, Manager
Jack Howell, Executive Director

An interdisciplinary bimonthly magazine, covers technical and policy issues relating to personal, location-independent communications in all media and at all protocol layers.
Frequency: Bi-Monthly

5144 Information Week
UBM LLC
600 Community Drive
Manhasset, NY 11030

516-562-5000
FAX 516-562-5036
E-Mail: rpreston@techweb.com
Home Page: www.informationweek.com

Rob Preston, VP/Editor In Chief
Laurianne McLaughlin, Editor In Chief
Fritz Nelson, VP/Editorial Director

Delivers breaking news, blogs, high-impact image galleries, proprietary research as well as analysis on IT trends, a whitepaper library, video reports and interactive tools, al i a 24/7 environment.
Circulation: 440,000

5145 International Communications Association
1500 21st St NW
Washington, DC 20036-1000

202-955-1444
FAX 202-955-1448
E-Mail: publications@icahdq.org
Home Page: www.icahdq.org

M Haley, Executive Director
Wolfgang Donfback, Administrative Assistant
Colleen Brady, Administrative Assistant
James Danowski, Secretary

Bi-monthly newsletter that supports all students and professionals in the international communications industry.
Cost: $30.00
Circulation: 3500
Founded in 1950
Printed in on matte stock

5146 Journal of Applied Communications
Agricultural Communicators in Education
University of Florida
PO Box 110810
Gainesville, FL 32611

352-392-9588
FAX 352-392-8583
E-Mail: ace@ifas.ufl.edu
Home Page: www.aceweb.org/jac/jac.html

Amanda Aubuchon, Managing Editor
Mark Tucker, Executive Editor

A peer-reviewed professional journal which accepts original contributions about communications, research, innovations and other pertinent information. The Journal is provided to all members, libraries and other interested people.
Cost: $75.00
Frequency: Quarterly
Circulation: 700
ISSN: 1051-0834
Founded in 1990

5147 Journal of Open Computing
Association for Communication
Administration

1765 N Street NW
Washington, DC 20036

202-464-4622
FAX 202-464-4600
Home Page: www.natcom.org

5148 Journal of the Association of Information Systems
Case Western Reserve University
PO Box 2712
Atlanta, GA 30301-2712

404-413-7440
FAX 404-413-7443
E-Mail: publications@aisnet.org
Home Page: www.aisnet.org

Doug Vogel, President

Publishes the highest quality scholarship in the field of information systems. Covers all aspects of Information Systems and Information Technology. Publishes rigorously developed and forward looking conceptual and empirical contributions.Encourages multidisciplinary and nontraditional approaches.
Frequency: Quarterly

5149 Journal of the Relgious Communication Association
Department of Communication & Rhetorical Studies
340 College Hall
600 Forbes Ave
Pittsburgh, PA 15282

E-Mail: owner@americanrhetoric.com
Home Page: www.americanrhetoric.com/rca

Kathleen Edelmayer, President
Matthew Melton, VP

The JCR addresses the concerns of the religious communicator and the communication scholar and includes reviews of current publications in the field of religious communication. The journal is semi-annual and is included with membership.
Circulation: 675

5150 MAIL: Journal of Communication Distribution
Gold Key Box 2425
Milford, PA 18337

607-746-7600
FAX 607-746-2750
E-Mail: mailmagazine@msn.com
Home Page: www.mailomg.com

Offers updated information on electronic mail and mail messaging systems.
Cost: $6.00
105 Pages
Frequency: Monthly

5151 Managing Media Relations in a Crisis
NACHA: The Electronic Payments Association
13450 Sunrise Valley Drive
Suite 100
Herndon, VA 20171

703-561-1100
FAX 703-787-0996
E-Mail: info@nacha.org
Home Page: www.nacha.org

Janet O Estep, CEO
Marcie Haitema, Chairperson

Designed to assist your organization to develop, test and execute a crisis communication plan. With this guide, you will understand how to address issues, whom to call and in what order to alert them, which vendors you can count on to help and how to develop a means to track the crisis as it grows or abates.
Cost: $30.00

5152 Media Studies Journal
Columbia University, Freedom Forum
Media Center
2960 Broadway
New York, NY 10027-6902

212-854-1754
FAX 212-678-4817
Home Page: www.columbia.edu

Lee C Bollinger, President

Aimed at scholars, practitioners and commentators. Offers information on mass communications issues involving the media and the public at large.
Cost: $20.00
Frequency: Quarterly
Circulation: 9000
Founded in 1754

5153 Novedades USA
Echo Media
900 Circle 75 Pkwy SE
Suite 1600
Atlanta, GA 30339-6014

770-955-3346
E-Mail: sales@echo-media.com
Home Page: www.echo-media.com

Michael Puffer, CEO
Stacey Reece, VP
Frequency: Weekly
Circulation: 100,000
Founded in 1986
Printed in 4 colors on newsprint stock

5154 Presstime Magazine
Newspaper Association of America
4401 Wilson Blvd
Suite 900
Arlington, VA 22203-4195

571-366-1000
FAX 571-366-1195
E-Mail: joan.mills@naa.org
Home Page: www.naa.org
Social Media: *Twitter*

Reggie Hall, Senior VP

The flagship publication reaches top executives across all departments with information about the issues that affect newspaper operations today and in the future.
Frequency: Monthly
Mailing list available for rent

5155 Professional Journal: Sbusiness Publication
AFSM International
11031 Via Frontera
Suite A
San Diego, CA 92127-1709

858-673-3055
800-333-9786
FAX 239-275-0794
E-Mail: info@afsmi.org
Home Page: www.afsmi.org

JB Wood, President
Thomas Lah, Executive Director

A global organization dedicated to furthering the knowledge, understanding, and career development of executives, managers, and professionals in the high-technology services and support industry as well as to provide leadership and direction that helps our individual and corporate members expand their capabilities to meet the growing complexities and challenges of the industry. Sbusiness publication is distributed bi-monthly serving international decision makers.
Cost: $ 95.00
114 Pages
Circulation: 10000
ISSN: 1049-2135
Founded in 1975
Printed in 4 colors on matte stock

5156 Publishers Weekly
PO Box 51593
Harlan, IA 51593

800-278-2991
FAX 712-733-8019
E-Mail: pwycustserv@cdsfulfillment.com
Home Page: www.publishersweekly.com
Social Media: *Facebook, Twitter*

Jim Milliot, Co-Editorial Director
Michael Coffey, Co-Editorial Director
Diane Roback, Children's Book Editor
Louisa Ermelino, Reviews Director
Calvin Reid, News Editor

PW is the international journal of book publishing and bookselling including business news, reviews and bestseller lists targeted at publishers, booksellers, librarians and literary agents.
Frequency: Weekly
Founded in 1872

5157 Red Herring: The Business of Technology
Red Herring
1900 Alameda De Las Pulgas
Suite 1
San Mateo, CA 94403-1222

650-428-2900
FAX 650-428-2901
E-Mail: info@redherring.com
Home Page: www.redherring.com

Alex Vieux, Publisher
Christopher Alden, Editorial Director
Joel Dreyfuss, Editor-in-Chief

Offers information on new and rising companies, as well as current industrial technology issues and topics.
Frequency: Weekly
Circulation: 45000
Founded in 1993

5158 Replication News
Miller Freeman Publications
810 7th Ave
27th Fl, Suite 4
New York, NY 10019-5818

212-636-2700
FAX 212-636-2750
E-Mail: sedorusa@optonline.net
Home Page: www.governmentvideo.com
Social Media: *Facebook, Twitter*

Gary Rhodes, International Sales Manager

Information on electronic and recording media through news coverage and analysis to provide executives with the market for strategic business planning.
Frequency: Monthly
Circulation: 16,490
Mailing list available for rent

5159 SIGNAL Magazine
4400 Fair Lakes Court
Fairfax, VA 22033-3899

703-631-6100
800-336-4583
FAX 703-631-6133
E-Mail: promo@afcea.org
Home Page: www.afcea.org
Social Media: *Facebook, Twitter, LinkedIn*

Robert K Ackerman, Editor in Chief

International news magazine serving the critical information needs of government, military and industry professionals active in the fields of command, control, communications, computers, intelligence, surveillance and reconnaissance (C4ISR); information security, research and development; electronics; and homeland security.
Frequency: Monthly
Circulation: 90000

5160 Signal Magazine
Armed Forces Communications &
Electronics Assoc
4400 Fair Lakes Court
Fairfax, VA 22033-3899

703-631-6100
800-336-4583
FAX 703-631-6405
E-Mail: service@afcea.org
Home Page: www.afcea.org
Social Media: *Facebook, Twitter, LinkedIn*

Kent Schneider, President/CEO
Becky Nolan, Executive VP
John A Dubia, Executive VP

5161 Speaker Magazine
National Speakers Association
1500 S Priest Dr
Tempe, AZ 85281-6203

480-968-2552
FAX 480-968-0911
E-Mail: andrea@nsaspeaker.org
Home Page: www.nsaspeaker.org

Ronald Culberson, President

Trends, issues and perspectives about and for the professional speaking industry.
Cost: $49.00
Frequency: 10x/Year

5162 TV Guide
United Video Satellite Group
1211 Avenue of the Americas
4th Floor
New York, NY 10036-8701

212-852-7500
FAX 212-852-4914

Richard Porter, Publisher

Focuses on all aspects of network, cable and pay television programming and how it affects and reflects their audience.
Cost: $39.88
Frequency: Weekly
Circulation: 13mm

5163 TV Technology
IMAS Publishing
PO Box 1214
Falls Church, VA 22041

703-998-7600
FAX 703-998-2966
E-Mail: webmaster@imaspub.com
Home Page: www.tvtechnology.com

Steven Dana, President
Tom Butts, Editor
Eric Trabb, Publisher
Kwentin Keenan, Circulation Manager
Bob Moses, Executive Director

News of a technical nature covering topics ranging from regulatory developments through maintenance and new products.
Cost: $39.95
Frequency: Fortnightly
Circulation: 37,000
Founded in 1978

5164 Tech Trenda
Association for Educational Comm and
Technology
1800 N Stonelake Drive
Suite 2
Bloomington, IN 47404

812-335-7675
FAX 812-335-7678
Home Page: www.aect.org

Mark Childress, President
Cost: $125.00
Frequency: Bi-Monthly
Circulation: 3500

5165 Television International Magazine
Television International Magazine
PO Box 2473
Universal City, CA 91610-8471

323-462-1099
FAX 702-939-4725
E-Mail: tvi@smart90.com
Home Page: www.tvimagazine.com

Josie Cory, Publisher
Mark Soval, Advertising Director

News and information regarding the television industry, includes the who's who of the business; geared toward the executives and professionals of the industry.
Cost: $129.00
Frequency: Monthly
Circulation: 16000
Founded in 1956
Printed in 4 colors on glossy stock

5166 xchange
Virgo Publishing LLC
3300 N Central Ave
Suite 300
Phoenix, AZ 85012-2532

480-675-9925
FAX 480-990-0819
E-Mail: mikes@vpico.com
Home Page: www.vpico.com
Social Media: *Twitter, LinkedIn*

Jenny Bolton, President

Provides in-depth, executive-level news and analysis regarding strategy, technology and regulation to help communications service providers create new revenue, lower costs and achieve sustainable business models.
Cost: $75.00
Frequency: Monthly
Circulation: 35,003
Founded in 1986

Trade Shows

5167 AFCEA TechNet International
Armed Forces Communications and
Electronics Assn
4400 Fair Lakes Court
Fairfax, VA 22033-3899

703-631-6200
800-564-4220
FAX 703-654-6931
E-Mail: technetinternational@jspargo.com
Home Page: www.afcea.org
Social Media: *Facebook, Twitter, LinkedIn*

Paul doCarmo, Sales Manager
Connie Shaw, Sales Manager

This event draws commanders and staff from every branch of the military, including warfighting integration organizations charged with the most critical responsibilities of synthesizing military power on land, at sea, and in the air.
7500 Attendees
Frequency: June

5168 AM&AA Summer Conference
Alliance of Merger and Acquisition
Advisors
150 North Michigan Avenue
Suite 2700
Chicago, IL 60601

877-844-2535
FAX 312-729-9800
E-Mail: aemerson@amaaonline.org
Home Page: www.amaaonline.org

Ainsley Emerson, Director

Premier international organization serving the educational and resource needs of the middle market and M&A profession.
Frequency: Annual

5169 ATTW Conference
Association of Teachers of Technical
Writing
Department of Linguistics and Technical
Comm
1155 Union Circle #305298
Denton, TX 76203-5017

940-565-4458
E-Mail: sims@unt.edu
Home Page: www.attw.org

Bill Davidson, President
Brenda Sims, Secretary
600 Members
Frequency: Annual/April
Founded in 1973
Mailing list available for rent

5170 American Public Communications
Council Conference & Expo
American Public Communications Council
625 Slaters Lane
Suite 104
Alexandria, VA 22314

703-739-1322
FAX 703-739-1324
Home Page: www.apcc.net

Willard Nichols, President
Michael Bright, Director

Conference, luncheon and 100 exhibits of public communications equipment and information including, pay phones, internet, atm, multimedia and more. Discussions include lobbying, the political climate, legal regulatory and legislative updates.
Founded in 1988

5171 Association for Business
Communication Annual Symposium
Po Box 6143
Nacogdoches, TX 75962-0001

936-468-6280
FAX 646-468-6281
E-Mail: abcjohnson@sfasu.edu
Home Page: www.businesscommunication.org

Nancy Schullery, President

Workshop and displays from textbook publishers, speech and business writing, technical publications and corporate communication.
400 Attendees
Founded in 1935

5172 DISA Customer Partnership AFCEA
Technology Showcase
Armed Forces Communications and
Electronics Assn
4400 Fair Lakes Court
Fairfax, VA 22033

703-631-6200
800-564-4220
FAX 703-654-6931
E-Mail: disaexhibits@jspargo.com
Home Page: www.afcea.org
Social Media: *Facebook, Twitter, LinkedIn*

Paul doCarmo, Assistant Director/Exhibit Sales
Connie Shaw, Exhibit Sales Account Manager

This conference facilitates a continuing interface with customers and strategic partners by allowing attendees to benefit from the perspective of DoD (Department of Defense) and industry speakers. It offers information sessions that provide a forum for questions, concerns and problem resolution.
1200 Attendees
Frequency: April-May

5173 Entelec Conference & Expo
Energy Telecommunications and Electrical
Assoc
5005 W Royal Lane
Suite 116
Irving, TX 75063

972-929-3169
888-503-8700
FAX 972-915-6040
E-Mail: info@entelec.org
Home Page: www.entelec.org

Michael Burt, President
James Coulter, VP

To bring together communications and control technology professionals from the petroleum, natural gas, pipeline, and electric utility companies for three days of quality training, seminars, exhibits and networking.
Frequency: Annual/May

5174 Graphic Communications Conference
of the Int'l Brotherhood of Teamsters
1900 L Street NW
Washington, DC 20036

202-462-1400
FAX 202-721-0600
E-Mail: webmessenger@gciu.org
Home Page: www.gciu.org

James Hoff, President
Robert Lacey, Secretary/Treasurer

Combines three independent shows: Printing XPO, Type-X, and Art-X and gives you a complete overview of the most recently introduced technologies and the newest information in the field of graphic arts.
15000 Members
Founded in 1983

5175 LandWarNet Conference
Armed Forces Communications and
Electronics Assn
4400 Fair Lakes Court
Fairfax, VA 22033

703-631-6200
800-564-4220
FAX 703-654-6931
E-Mail: landwarnet@jspargo.com
Home Page: www.afcea.org
Social Media: *Facebook, Twitter, LinkedIn*

Nathan Wills, Account Manager

Thousands of key communications/information technology buyers and influencers attend the conference every year. This is an opportunity to network with the best and develop crucial relationships with some of the Army's most influential decision-makers.
3700 Attendees
Frequency: August

5176 MILCOM
Armed Forces Communications and
Electronics Assn
4400 Fair Lakes Court
Fairfax, VA 22033

703-631-6200
800-564-4220
FAX 703-654-6931
E-Mail: milcom@jspargo.com
Home Page: www.afcea.org
Social Media: *Facebook, Twitter, LinkedIn*

Paul doCarmo, Assistant Director/Exhibit Sales
Connie Shaw, Exhibit Sales Account Manager

For over 20 years, MILCOM has been the premier international conference for military communications, with over 3,000 attendees every year. It attracts decision-makers from government, military, academia and industry, including heads of multi-national forces from around the globe, all who contribute key tech-

nologies decisions and investments for their agency.
3000 Attendees
Frequency: October

5177 Mailcom
The Art & Science of Mail Communications
Po Box 7045
Philadelphia, PA 19149

732-280-8865
FAX 732-280-7854
E-Mail: ljhumphries@msn.com
Home Page: www.mailcom.org

Lance Humphries, Managing Director

Learn how business communications can become strategic corporate tools
9000 Attendees
Frequency: Oct Las Vegas
Mailing list available for rent

5178 NAA Annual Convention
Newspaper Association of America
4401 Wilson Boulevard
Suite 900
Vienna, VA 22203-1867

571-366-1000
FAX 571-366-1195
E-Mail: joan.mills@naa.org
Home Page: www.naa.org

James Moroney, President
Donna Barret, Treasurer

This event will welcome industry executives from across the country and is the opportunity for senior level newspaper professionals to learn, share ideas and network. The agenda will showcase the strategies and tactics necessary to address the key issues of revenue, audience, digital and infrastructure.
Frequency: Annual
Mailing list available for rent

5179 NAMIC Conference
Natl Assoc for Multi-Ethnicity in Communications
320 West 37th Street
8th Floor
New York, NY 10018

212-594-5985
FAX 212-594-8391
E-Mail: info@namic.com
Home Page: www.namic.com
Social Media: *Facebook, Twitter, LinkedIn*

Kathy A Johnson, President
James Jones, VP Programs

Educational forum focused on leadership development, corporate diversity and inclusion, digital media and multi-ethnic content and programming. Content emphasizes diversity as a strategic business imperative
700 Attendees
Frequency: Annual

5180 NFAIS Annual Conference
National Federation Abstracting & Info Services
1518 Walnut St
Suite 1004
Philadelphia, PA 19102

215-893-1561
FAX 215-893-1564
E-Mail: nfais@nfais.org
Home Page: www.nfais.org

Bonnie Lawlor, Executive Director
Jill O'Neil, Director Communications
300 Attendees
Frequency: February/March

5181 NSA Convention
National Speakers Association

1500 S Priest Dr
Tempe, AZ 85281-6203

480-968-2552
FAX 480-968-0911
E-Mail: andrea@nsaspeaker.org
Home Page: www.nsaspeaker.org

Ronald Culberson, President
1500 Attendees
Frequency: Annual

5182 National Hispanic Market Trade Show and Media Expo (Se Habla Espanol)
Hispanic Business
425 Pine Avenue
Santa Barbara, CA 93117-3709

805-964-4554
FAX 805-964-5539
E-Mail: info@hispanstar.com
Home Page: www.hispanstar.com
Social Media: *Facebook, Twitter, LinkedIn*

John Pasini, Cfo/Coo

Annual show of 100 exhibitors of market/research, media, advertising, public relations, information services and recruitment.
1500 Attendees

5183 PRSA International Conference
Public Relations Society of America
33 Maiden Ln.
11th Fl.
New York, NY 10038

212-460-1400
Social Media: *Facebook, Twitter, LinkedIn, Reddit, Tumblr*

Kathy Barbour, Chair

Actionable best practices are the focus of this annual event.

5184 Toastmasters Trade Show
Toastmasters International
PO Box 9052
Mission Viejo, CA 92690-9052

949-858-8255
949-835-1300
FAX 949-858-1207
E-Mail: newsletters@toastmasters.org
Home Page: www.toastmasters.org

Focuses on communication in general and public speaking in particular. Topics include language, listening, humor, self improvement, goal setting, success and logical thinking.
2M Attendees
Frequency: August

Directories & Databases

5185 ACCE Communications Council Directory
4875 Eisenhower Ave
Suite 250
Alexandria, VA 22304-4850

703-998-0072
FAX 703-212-9512
E-Mail: webmaster@acce.org
Home Page: www.acce.org
Social Media: *Facebook, Twitter, LinkedIn*

Michael Flemming, President

Offers member information on the council activities.
Frequency: Annual+
Founded in 1914

5186 Adweek Directory
Prometheus Global Media

770 Broadway
New York, NY 10003-9595

212-493-4100
FAX 646-654-5368
Home Page: www.prometheusgm.com

Richard D. Beckman, CEO
Jame A. Finkelstein, Chairman
Madeline Krakowsky, Vice President Circulation
Tracy Brater, Executive Director Creative Service

Adweek Directories Online is where you will find searchable databases with comprehensive information on ad agencies, brand marketers and multicultural media.
Frequency: Annual
Circulation: 800
Founded in 1981

5187 American Showcase Illustration
Luerzer's Archive Inc
Ste 1530
410 Park Ave
New York, NY 10022-9441

212-941-2496
FAX 212-941-5490
E-Mail: office@showcase.com
Home Page: www.lurzersarchive.net

Walter Lurzer, Editor

Illustrators and graphic designers.
Mailing list available for rent

5188 Association for Educational Communications and Technology Membership Directory
Association for Educational Comm and Technology
1800 N Stonelake Drive
Suite 2
Bloomington, IN 47404

812-335-7675
FAX 812-335-7678
Home Page: www.aect.org

Mark Childress, President
Mary Beth Jordan, Secretary/Treasurer

5,000 audiovisual and instructional materials specialists, educational technologists, audiovisual and television production personnel, school media specialists
Frequency: Annual

5189 Bacon's Newspaper & Magazine Directories
Cision U.S., Inc.
322 South Michigan Avenue
Suite 900
Chicago, IL 60604

312-263-0070
866-639-5087
E-Mail: info.us@cision.com
Home Page: us.cision.com

Joe Bernardo, President & CEO
Heidi Sullivan, VP & Publisher
Valerie Lopez, Research Director
Jessica White, Research Director
Rachel Farrell, Research Manager

Two volume set listing all daily and community newspapers, magazines and newsletters, news service and syndicates, syndicated columnists, complete editorial staff listings of each publication provided, covers U.S., Canada, Mexico, and Carribean.
Cost: $350.00
4,700 Pages
Frequency: Annual
ISSN: 1088-9639
Founded in 1951
Printed in one color on matte stock

5190 Bacon's Radio/TV/Cable Directory
Cision U.S., Inc.
332 South Michigan Avenue
Suite 900
Chicago, IL 60604

312-263-0070
866-639-5087
E-Mail: info.us@cision.com
Home Page: www.us.cision.com

Joe Bernardo, President & CEO
Heidi Sullivan, VP & Publisher
Valerie López, Research Director
Jessica White, Research Director
Rachel Farrell, Research Manager

Includes comprehensive coverage for contact and programming information for more than 3,500 television networks, cable networks, television syndicators, television stations, and cable systems in the United States and Canada.
Cost: $350.00
Frequency: Annual
ISSN: 1088-9639
Printed in one color on matte stock

5191 Burrelle's Media Directory
BurrellesLuce
75 E Northfield Rd
Livingston, NJ 07039-4532

973-992-6600
800-631-1160
FAX 973-992-7675
Home Page: www.burrellesluce.com
Social Media: *Facebook, Twitter, LinkedIn*

Robert C Waggoner, CEO

Approximately 60,000 media listings in North America. Listings cover newspapers, magazines (trades and consumer), broadcast, and internet outlets.
Cost: $795.00
Frequency: Annual

5192 Corporate Yellow Book
Leadership Directories
104 5th Ave
New York, NY 10011-6901

212-627-4140
FAX 212-645-0931
E-Mail: corporate@leadershipdirectories.com
Home Page: www.leadershipdirectories.com

David Hurvitz, CEO

Contact information for over 48,000 executives at over 1,000 companies and 6,000 subsidiaries and divisions, and more than 9,000 board members and their outside affiliations.
Cost: $360.00
1,400 Pages
Frequency: Quarterly
ISSN: 1058-2908
Founded in 1986
Mailing list available for rent: 50,000 names at $105 per M

5193 Film & Video Finder
Information Today
143 Old Marlton Pike
Medford, NJ 08055-8750

609-654-6266
800-300-9868
FAX 609-654-4309
E-Mail: custserv@infotoday.com
Home Page: www.infotoday.com

Thomas H Hogan, President
Roger R Bilboul, Chairman Of The Board

Contains information on 130,000 films and videos. The most comprehensive reference available to educational films and videos. A three volume hardbound set.
Cost: $295.00
6434 Pages
Frequency: Annual
ISBN: 0-937548-29-4

5194 Gale Database of Publications and Broadcast Media
Gale/Cengage Learning
PO Box 09187
Detroit, MI 48209-0187

248-699-4253
800-877-4253
FAX 248-699-8049
E-Mail: gale.galeord@cengage.com
Home Page: www.gale.com
Social Media: *Facebook, Twitter, LinkedIn*

Patrick C Sommers, President

This media directory contains thousands of listings for radio and television stations and cable companies.
Founded in 2008

5195 Gale's Ready Reference Shelf
Gale/Cengage Learning
PO Box 09187
Detroit, MI 48209-0187

248-699-4253
800-877-4253
FAX 248-699-8049
E-Mail: gale.galeord@cengage.com
Home Page: www.gale.com
Social Media: *Facebook, Twitter, LinkedIn*

Patrick C Sommers, President

Gale's Ready Reference Shelf allows you to search the entire database of integrated content at one time and the data updates are automatic allowing the user to access the latest information available.

5196 Gebbie Press All-in-One Directory
Gebbie Press
PO Box 1000
New Paltz, NY 12561-0017

845-255-7560
FAX 845-256-1239
Home Page: www.gebbieinc.com

Mark Gebbie, Editor/Publisher

TV and radio stations, daily and weekly newspapers, consumer and trade magazines, black and Hispanic media, news syndicates, networks, AP/UPI bureaus. Compact spiral bound 6x9 inches.
Cost: $140.00
500 Pages
Frequency: Also on Disk
Founded in 1970

5197 Hudson's Washington News Media Contacts Directory
Grey House Publishing
4919 Route 22
PO Box 56
Amenia, NY 12501

518-789-8700
800-562-2139
FAX 845-373-6390
E-Mail: books@greyhouse.com
Home Page: www.greyhouse.com
Social Media: *Facebook, Twitter*

Leslie Mackenzie, Publisher
Richard Gottlieb, President

A comprehensive guide to the entire Washington, D.C. press corps, broken down into categories.
Cost: $289.00
350 Pages
ISBN: 1-592378-53-6
Printed in one color on matte stock

5198 Hudson's Washington News Media Contacts - Online Database
Grey House Publishing

4919 Route 22
PO Box 56
Amenia, NY 12501

518-789-8700
800-562-2139
FAX 845-373-6390
E-Mail: gold@greyhouse.com
Home Page: www.gold.greyhouse.com
Social Media: *Facebook, Twitter*

Leslie Mackenzie, Publisher
Richard Gottlieb, President

With 100% verification of data, Hudson's is the most accurate, most up-to-date source for media contacts in our nation's capital. With the largest concentration of news media in the world, having access to Washington's news media will get your message heard by these key media outlets.

5199 Journalism and Mass Communication Directory
AEJMC
234 Outlet Pointe Boulevard
Suite A
Columbia, SC 29210-5667

803-798-0271
FAX 803-772-3509
E-Mail: aejmchq@aol.com
Home Page: www.aejmc.org
Social Media: *Facebook, Twitter, LinkedIn*

Kyo Hum, President

Over 3,000 professionals, academics and graduate students; more than 400 journalism and mass communications schools and departments in four-year colleges and universities, including 200 members of the Association of Schools of Journalism and Mass Communication.
Cost: $25.00
Frequency: Annual
Circulation: 5000
Founded in 1983
Mailing list available for rent

5200 Kagan Media Index
Kagan World Media
126 Clock Tower Place
Carmel, CA 93923-8746

831-624-1536
FAX 831-625-3225
E-Mail: info@kagan.com
Home Page: www.kagan.com

George Niesen, Editor
Tom Johnson, Marketing Manager

The most comprehensive collection of media industry databases found anywhere. Current estimates of industry growth for a dozen different media businesses, shown on a 145-line spreadsheet, projected forward and updated monthly. Three month trial available.
Cost: $795.00
Frequency: Monthly

5201 M Street Radio Directory
M Street Corporation
81 Main Street, Suite 2
PO Box 442
Littleten, NH 03561

603-444-5720
800-248-4242
FAX 603-444-2872
E-Mail: info@insideradio.com
Home Page: ww.mstreet.net

Cathy Devine, Research Director
Kelli Grisez, Operations Manager
Frank Saxe, Senior Editor

Approximately 14,000 AM and FM radio stations in the US and Canada.
Cost: $79.00
Frequency: Annual
Printed in on matte stock

5202 News Media Directories
PO Box 316
Mount Dora, FL 32757

352-589-9020
800-749-6399
FAX 866-586-7020
Home Page: www.newsmediadirectories.com

Dean Highberger, Editor

Directory for lists, daily papers, new services, magazines, weekly papers, special publications and radio stations. We have directories covering eight states , Alabama, Florida, Georgia, Mississippi, North Carolina, Ohio, South Carolina and Tennessee. Also, we have a condensed southeast edition. Listings include address, phone, fax, e-mail, and key associates.
Frequency: Annual

5203 News Media Yellow Book
Leadership Directories
104 5th Ave
New York, NY 10011-6901

212-627-4140
FAX 212-645-0931
E-Mail: newsmedia@leadershipdirectories.com
Home Page: www.leadershipdirectories.com
Social Media: *Facebook, Twitter*

David Hurvitz, CEO
James M Petrie, Associate Publisher

Contact information for over 39,000 journalists at over 2,500 new services, networks, newspapers, television, radio stations, as well as independent journalists and syndicated columnists.
Cost: $325.00
1,200 Pages
Frequency: Quarterly
ISSN: 1071-8931
Founded in 1989
Mailing list available for rent: 32,000 names at $125 per M

5204 O'Dwyer's Directory of Public Relations Firms
JR O'Dwyer Company
271 Madison Ave
Suite 600
New York, NY 10016-1013

212-679-2461
FAX 212-683-2750
E-Mail: jack@odwyerpr.com
Home Page: www.odwyerpr.com

Jack O'Dwyer, Publisher
Kevin McCauley, Editor
Sharlene Spingler, Associate Publisher

Exclusive ranking of public relations firms and lists more than 1,700 firms in the US and 55 countries.
Cost: $125.00
400 Pages
Frequency: Annual
Founded in 1968

5205 Pocket Media Guide
Media Distribution Services
307 W 36th St
Department P
New York, NY 10018-6519

212-279-4800
800-637-3282
FAX 212-643-0576
Home Page: www.mdsconnect.com

Dan Cantelmo, President

Designed to fit easily into a wallet, the palm size guide includes names and addresses, with phone numbers, of more than 700 major print and media in North America, plus a calendar, annual media statistics, and a publicity primer.
40 Pages
Frequency: Annual

5206 Power Media Selects
Broadcast Interview Source
2233 Wisconsin Ave NW
Suite 301
Washington, DC 20007-4132

202-333-5000
800-932-7266
FAX 202-342-5411
Home Page: www.expertclick.com

Mitchell Davis, Owner
Alan Caruba, Production Manager

Approximately 3,000 media contacts throughout the US, including newswire services, syndicates, syndicated columnists, national newspapers, magazines, radio and television talk shows, etc.
Cost: $166.50
Frequency: Annual

5207 Sound & Communications
Testa Communications
25 Willowdale Avenue
Port Washington, NY 11050-3779

516-767-2500
FAX 516-767-9335

David Silverman, Editor
Bob Beoder, Advertising Manager

The systems magazine for contractors and consultants who design, specify, sell, and install audio and display systems. Installation profiles, news, business and product updates, incisive theory and applications reporting.
Cost: $15.00
Frequency: Monthly
Circulation: 23,000
Founded in 1955

Industry Web Sites

5208 http://gold.greyhouse.com
G.O.L.D Grey House OnLine Databases

Grey House Publishing's online database platform, GOLD, offers Quick Search, Keyword Search and Expert Search for most business markets including broadcasting, communications and media markets. The GOLD platform makes finding the information you need quick and easy - whether you're a novice searcher or an experienced database user. All of Grey House's directory products are available for subscription on the GOLD platform.

5209 www.acce.org
American Chamber of Commerce Executives

National organization uniquely serving individuals involved in the management of chambers of all sizes. Chamber executives and their staffs can capitalize on a wealth of information, leadership, skill development, management techniques and innovative program offerings. Also works diligently to upgrade the economic status and professional standing of those active in the chamber field.

5210 www.adweek.com
Adweek

Leading decision makers in the advertising and marketing field go to Adweek.com every day for breaking news, insight, buzz, opinion, analysis, research and classifieds. The resources of all six regional editions of Adweek, as well as the national edition of Brandweek are combined with the knowledge of our editors and the multimedia-interactive capabilities of the Web to deliver vital information quickly and effectively to our target audience.

5211 www.aim.org
Accuracy in Media

Nonprofit, grassroots citizens watchdog of the news media that critiques botched and bungled news stories and sets the record straight on important issues that have recieved slanted coverage.

5212 www.americomm.org
American Communication Association

Founded for the purposes of fostering research and scholarship in all areas of human communication behavior, promoting and improving excellence in the pedagogy of communication, providing a voice in communication law and policy, and providing evaluation and certification services for academic programs in communication study.

5213 www.amta.org
Antenna Measurement Techniques Association

Nonprofit professional organization, open to individuals with an interest in antenna measurements. Areas of interest include: measurement facilities, unique or innovative measurement techniques, test instrumentation and systems, RCS measurements, compact range design and evaluation, near-field techniques and their applications, and the practical aspects of measurement problems problems and their solutions.

5214 www.apcc.net
American Public Communications Council

APCC proudly offers offers a wide array of services to the public communications industry, from Perspectives magazine to our annual trade show to our involvement in legal and regulatory issues. This site is a place for the public to find out about our industry and for our members to learn of legal and regulatory developments, to become aware of APCC programs events, and to have a forum for discussion.

5215 www.apco911.org
Association of Public-Safety Communications

The world's oldest and largest professional organization dedicated to the enhancement of public safety communications and to serving its more than 15,000 members, the people who use public safety communications systems and services.

5216 www.attw.org
Association of Teachers of Technical Writing

Provides communication among teachers of technical writing and develops technical communications as an academic discipline.

5217 www.bowker.com
Reed Reference Publishing RR Bowker

Offers, in four separate volumes, syndicates, newspapers, radio and television stations, feature writers, photographers, illustrators and internal house organs.

5218 www.consultingsuccess.org
Assn of Professional Communication Consultants

Professional community where communication consultants increase their knowledge, grow their business, achieve high standards of professional practice. APCC's mission is to support members as they help clients reach their goals through better communication.

5219 www.digmedia.org
Digital Media Association

National trade organization devoted primarily to the online audio and video industries, and more generally to commercially innovative digital media opportunities.

5220 www.drudgereport.com

Links to international news sources and columnists.

5221 www.entelec.org
Energy Telecommunications and Electrical Assoc

A user association focusing on communications and control technologies used by petroleum, natural gas, pipeline and electric utility companies.

5222 www.greyhouse.com
Grey House Publishing

Authoritative reference directories for most business sectors including broadcasting, communications and meida markets. Users can search the online databases with varied search criteria allowing for custom searches by product category, geographic area, sales volume, keyword, subject and more. Full Grey House catalog and online ordering also available.

5223 www.iaais.org
Int'l Association of Audio Information Services

Formerly the National Association of Radio Reading Services, we are an organization of services that provide audio access to information for people who are print disabled. People served are blind, visually impared, learning disabled or physically disabled.

5224 www.iabc.com
Int'l Association of Business Communications

International knowledge network for professionals engaged in strategic business communication management. IABC links communicators in a global network that inspires, establishes and supports the highest professional standards.

5225 www.icahdq.org
International Communications Association

International association for scholars interested in the study, teaching and application of all aspects of human mediated communication.

5226 www.iics.org
International Interactive Communication Society

For communications industry professionals dedicated to the advancement of interactive technologies. Provides a forum to share ideas, applications amd techniques for effective use of interactive media.

5227 www.iste.org
International Society for Technology in Education

Nonprofit professional organization with a worldwide membership of leaders and potential leaders in educational technology.

5228 www.kagan.com
Kagan World Media

For those interested in investments in radio and TV stations and publicly held companies.

5229 www.kausfiles.com
Kausfiles

Site for journalists and media specialists.

5230 www.liberty.uc.wlu.edu
Journalism Resources

Lists of newspapers, film resources, jobs and internships and political advocacy groups.

5231 www.missouri.edu/~foiwww
Affiliation of University of Missouri

Maintains files documenting actions by government, media and society affecting the flow and content of information. Call or write for assistance with researching media topics or instruction in using access laws.

5232 www.netage.com
Networking Institute

Promotes networks to help people work together. Offers consulting services, educational workshops and seminars.

5233 www.nfais.org
National Federation Absrtacting & Info Services

Serves those groups that aggregate, organize, and facilitate access to information. To improve member capabilities and contribute to their ongoing success. Provides opportunities for education, advocacy, and a forum to address common interests.

5234 www.nsaspeaker.org
National Speakers Association

The leading organization for experts who speak professionally. NSA's 4000 members include experts in a variety of industries and disciplines, who reach audiences as trainers, educators, humorists, motivators, consultants, authors and more. NSA provides resources and education designed to advance the skills, integrity, and value of its members and speaking profession. NSA the voice of the speaking profession.

5235 www.postcom.org
Association for Postal Commerce

National Organization representing those who use, or support the use, of mail as a medium for communication and commerce. Postcom publishes a weekly newsletter covering postal policy and operational issues.

5236 www.poynter.org
Poynter Online

Poynter Institute is dedicated to teaching and inspiring journalists and media leaders. Promotes excellence and integrity in the practice of craft and in the practical leadership of successful businesses.

5237 www.regionalmagazines.org
International Regional Magazine Association

Promotes the interests of international and regional magazine professionals.

5238 www.retailing.org
Electronics Retailing Association

For infomercial producers, marketers, product developers, broadcasters and other industries serving the infomercial market.

5239 www.speakingsuccess.com
Personal Achievement Institute

5240 www.theabc.org
Association for Business Communication

International organization commited to fostering excellence in business communication scholarship, research, education, and practice.

5241 www.toastmasters.org
Toastmasters International

Publishes educational articles on the subjects of communication and leadership. Topics include language, listening, humor, self-improvement, goal setting, success and logical thinking.

5242 www.wgbh.org
WGBH Educational Foundation

WGBH productions are seen and heard on stations around the country.

409

Associations

5243 AIM Global

One Landmark North, 20399 Route 19
Suite 203
Cranberry Township, PA 16066

724-934-4470
FAX 724-742-4476
E-Mail: info@aimglobal.org
Home Page: www.aimglobal.org
Social Media: *Facebook, Twitter, LinkedIn, Pinterest*

Chuck Evanhoe, Chairperson
Mary Lou Bosco, COO
Diana Bowser, Manager, Finance and Administration

International trade association representing automatic identification and mobility technology solution providers.
900+ Members
Founded in 1972

5244 ARMA International

11880 College Blvd
7th Floor
Overland Park, KS 66210

913-341-3808
800-422-2762
FAX 913-341-3742
E-Mail: headquarters@armaintl.org
Home Page: www.arma.org
Social Media: *Facebook, Twitter, LinkedIn*

Julie J. Colgan, CRM, President
Brenda Prowse, CRM, Treasurer
Fred Pulzello, CRM, President-Elect
Komal Gulich, CRM, Chair / Immediate Past President

A not-for-profit professional association and the authority on managing records and information.
11000 Members
Founded in 1955

5245 Alpha Micro Users Society

210 N Iris Avenue
Rialto, CA 92376-5727

909-874-6214
FAX 909-874-2143
E-Mail: info@amus.org
Home Page: www.amus.org

Jeff Kreider, President

An organization supported by members to promote the uses of computers manufactured by Alpha Micro Products of Irvine, California. This basic purpose has expanded, over the years, from merely a focal point for the exchange of technical information on its use and versatility, to promotion of products (Software and Hardware) from Alpha Micro and various third party organizations having an interest in users of Alpha Micro computers.
125 Members
Founded in 1978

5246 American Association for Artificial Intelligence

2275 East Bayshore Road
Suite 160
Palo Alto, CA 94303

650-328-3123
FAX 650-321-4457
E-Mail: info@aaai.org
Home Page: www.aaai.org

Alan Mackworth, President
Ted Senator, Treasurer/Secretary

Nonprofit society devoted to advancing the scientific understanding of the mechanisims un-

derlying thought and intelligent behavior and their embodiment in machines.
6000 Members
Founded in 1979
Mailing list available for rent

5247 American Council for Technology

3040 Williams Dr
Suite 610
Fairfax, VA 22031-4618

703-208-4800
FAX 703-208-4805
E-Mail: act-iac@actgov.org
Home Page: www.actgov.org
Social Media: *Facebook, Twitter, LinkedIn, YouTube*

Ken Allen, Executive Director
Don Arnold, Director
April Davis, Director Of Member Service
Jim Beaupre, Director, ACT-IAC Academy
Don Becker, Associate Director, Communications

A non-profit educational organization established to assist government in acquiring and using information technology, resources effectively and efficiently. Working with all levels of the government, ACT provides education, programming, and networking opportunities that enhance and advance the government IT profession.
50000 Members
Founded in 1978

5248 American Medical Informatics Association

4720 Montgomery Lane
Suite 500
Bethesda, MD 20814-6052

301-657-1291
FAX 301-657-1296
E-Mail: mail@mail.amia.org
Home Page: www.amia.org
Social Media: *Facebook, Twitter, LinkedIn, YouTube, Flickr*

Kevin M. Fickenscher, MD, CPE,, AMIA President and CEO
Sara Ward, Executive Assistant
Karen Greenwood, Executive Vice President & COO
Ross D. Martin, MD, MHA, Vice President Corporate Relations
Jeffrey Williamson, M.Ed, Vice President, Education

Support all those involved with commercial and scientific medical informatics software and hardware, supplies and services. Hosts annual trade show.
3200 Members
Founded in 1990
Mailing list available for rent: 2000 names

5249 American Society for Information Science and Technology

8555 16th Street
Suite 850
Silver Spring, MD 20910

301-495-0900
FAX 301-495-0810
E-Mail: asis@asis.org
Home Page: www.asist.org
Social Media: *Facebook, Twitter, LinkedIn*

Andrew Dillon, President
Vicki Gregory, Treasurer
Richard Hills, Executive Director
William Senn, Chapter Assembly Director
Naresh Agarwal, Deputy Chapter Assembly Director

ASIS&T has been the society for information professionals leading the search for new and

better theories, techniques, and technologies to improve access to information.
4000 Members
Founded in 1937

5250 American Society for Precision Engineering

PO Box 10826
Raleigh, NC 27605-0826

919-839-8444
FAX 919-839-8039
E-Mail: webmaster@aspe.net
Home Page: www.aspe.net

Alexander H. Slocum, President
John S. Taylor, Vice President
Thomas A. Dow, Executive Director
Ilka Lee, Publications and Office Manager
Wendy Shearon, Meetings & Membership Manager

Members are from academia, industry and government, and include professionals in engineering, materials science, physics, chemistry, mathematics and computer science. Multidisciplinary professional and technical society concerned with precision engineering research and development, design and manufacturing of high accuracy components and systems.
Founded in 1985

5251 Armed Forces Communications & Electronics Association (AFCEA)

4400 Fair Lakes Ct
Fairfax, VA 22033-3899

703-631-1397
800-336-4583
FAX 703-631-4693
E-Mail: service@afcea.org
Home Page: www.afcea.org
Social Media: *Facebook, Twitter, LinkedIn, Google+, YouTube*

Kent Schneider, President/CEO
Becky Nolan, Executive VP
John A Dubia, Executive VP

A non-profit membership association serving the military, government, industry, and academia as an ethical forum for advancing professional knowledge and relationships in the fields of communications, IT, intelligence, and global security.
31000 Members
Founded in 1946

5252 Association for Computing Machinery

2 Penn Plz
Suite 701
New York, NY 10121-0799

212-868-5716
800-342-6626
FAX 212-944-1318
E-Mail: acmhelp@acm.org
Home Page: www.acm.org
Social Media: *Facebook, Twitter, LinkedIn, YouTube*

John R White, Executive Director/CEO
Patricia Ryan, Deputy Exec Director Operations/COO
Wayne Graves, Director of Information Systems
Russell Harris, Director of Financial Services

Association for advancing the skills of information technology professionals and for interpreting the impact of information technology on society.
80000 Members
Founded in 1947

5253 Association for Educational Communication and Technology
320 W. 8th St
Suite 101
Bloomington, IN 47404

812-335-7675
877-677-AECT
FAX 812-335-7678
E-Mail: aect@aect.org
Home Page: www.aect.org
Social Media: *Facebook, Twitter*

Robert Maribe Branch, President
Kay Persichitte, President-Elect
Michael Grant, Executive Secretary
Stephen Harmon, Past President

A professional association of thousands of educators and others whose activities are directed towards improving instruction through technology.
Founded in 1923

5254 Association for Information and Image Management International
1100 Wayne Avenue
Suite 1100
Silver Spring, MD 20910

301-587-8202
800-477-2446
FAX 301-587-2711
E-Mail: aiim@aiim.org
Home Page: www.aiim.org
Social Media: *Facebook, Twitter, LinkedIn, YouTube*

John F. Mancini, President and CEO
Felicia Dillard, CFO
Atle Skjekkeland, Chief Operating Officer
Peggy Winton, Vice President and CMO
Georgina Clelland, Director, Events

Global authority on enterprise content management (ECM). ECM Technologies are used to create, capture, customize, deliver, and manage information to support business process.
Founded in 1943

5255 Association for Services Management International
11031 Via Frontera
Suite A
San Diego, CA 92127

239-275-7887
800-333-9786
FAX 239-275-0794
E-Mail: info@afsmi.org
Home Page: www.afsmi.org

JB Wood, President
Thomas Lah, Executive Director

Provides the knowledge, fellowship and career connections that customer services and support managers for technology based products and solutions needed for professional and career development.
Cost: $375.00
Frequency: Membership Fee
Founded in 1975

5256 Association for the Advancement of Computing in Education
P.O. Box 719
Waynesville, NC 28786

828-246-9558
FAX 828-246-9557
E-Mail: info@aace.org
Home Page: www.aace.org
Social Media: *Facebook*

Dr Gary H Marks, Executive Director

An international, educational and professional nonprofit organization dedicated to the advancement of the knowledge, theory and qual-

ity of learning and teaching at all levels with information technology.
Founded in 1981

5257 Association of Information Technology Professionals
1120 Route 73
Suite 200
Mount Laurel, NJ 08054-5113

856-380-6910
800-224-9371
FAX 856-439-0525
E-Mail: aitp_hq@aitp.org
Home Page: www.aitp.org
Social Media: *Twitter, LinkedIn*

Barbara Viola, President
Julian Wade, Executive Vice-President
Christine Leja, Treasurer
John Council, Secretary
Michael Welch, Immediate Past President

Comprised of career minded individuals who seek to expand their potential employers, employees, managers, programmers, and many others. The organization seeks to provide avenues for all their members to be teachers as well as students and to make contacts with other members in the IS field, all in an effort to become more marketable in rapidly changing, technological careers.
Founded in 1951

5258 Business Software Alliance
20 F Street, NW
Suite 800
Washington, DC 20001

202-872-5500
FAX 202-872-5501
E-Mail: info@bsa.org
Home Page: www.bsa.org
Social Media: *Facebook, Twitter, LinkedIn, YouTube*

Victoria A. Espinel, President and CEO
Jodie L. Kelley, General Counsel and SVP
Matthew Reid, Senior Vice President
Scott Van Hove, CFO and Vice President

An organization dedicated to promoting a safe and legal digital world. BSA educates consumers on software management and copyright protection, cyber security, trade, e-commerce and other internet related issues.
Founded in 1988

5259 Business Technology Association
12411 Wornall Rd
Suite 200
Kansas City, MO 64145-1212

816-941-3100
800-826-6159
FAX 816-941-2829
E-Mail: info@bta.org
Home Page: www.bta.org
Social Media: *Facebook, Twitter, LinkedIn*

Dave Quint, President
Brent Hoskins, Executive Director
Valerie Briseno, Marketing Manager
Elizabeth Marvel, Associate Editor
Brian Smith, Membership Sales Representative

Serving independent dealers, value-added resellers, systems integrators, manufacturers and distributors in the business equipment and systems industry. BTA helps its members profit through a wide variety of services, including free legal advice and guidance; business benchmarking studies and reports; information on the latest news, trends, and products in the industry.
Founded in 1926

5260 CEMA: Computer Event Marketing Association
1512 Weiskopf Loop
Round Rock, TX 78664-6128

512-310-8330
FAX 512-682-0555
E-Mail: info@cemaonline.com
Home Page: www.cemaonline.com
Social Media: *Facebook, Twitter, LinkedIn*

Kimberley Gishler, President & CEO
Chris Meyer, Vice President
Heather Shatz, Treasurer
Ashley Muntan, Secretary
Kimberley Gishler, Executive Director

Serving marketing professionals in the high technology industry. CEMA has grown to represent the interest of marketing communications professionals in the information technology industry.
500 Members
Frequency: $275-$775 Membership Fee
Founded in 1990

5261 Carnegie Mellon University: Information Networking Institute
4616 Henry Street
Pittsburgh, PA 15213

412-268-7195
FAX 412-268-7196
E-Mail: ini@cmu.edu
Home Page: www.ini.cmu.edu
Social Media: *Facebook, Twitter, LinkedIn, YouTube, Google+*

Dena Haritos-Tsamitis, Director
Terri Weinberg, Administrative Assistant
Tracey Bragg, Business & Enrollment Manager
Sean O'Leary, Manager

Established as the nation's first research and education center devoted to Information Networking. INI focuses on professional degree programs that combine technologies, economics, and policies of global communication networks and information security.
300 Members
Founded in 1989

5262 CompTIA
3500 Lacey Road
Suite 100
Downers Grove, IL 60515

630-678-8300
866-835-8020
FAX 630-678-8384
E-Mail: info@comptia.org
Home Page: www.comptia.org
Social Media: *Facebook, Twitter, LinkedIn, YouTube, Flickr*

MJ Shoer, Chairman
Frank Vitagliano, Vice Chair
Todd Thibodeaux, President and CEO
Nancy Hammervik, Senior Vice President, Industry
David Sommer, Chief Financial Officer

CompTIA is a trade association representing the international technology community. Its goal is to provide a unified voice, global advocacy and leadership, and to advance industry growth through standards, professional competence, education and business solutions.
20000 Members
Founded in 1984

5263 Computer Assisted Language Instruction Consortium
Texas State University
214 Centennial Hall
San Marcos, TX 78666

512-245-1417
FAX 512-245-9089
E-Mail: info@calico.org

Home Page: www.calico.org
Social Media: *Twitter*

Robert Fischer, Executive Director
Esther Horn, Manager

A professional organization involved in language teaching and technology.
780 Members
Founded in 1983

5264 Computer Security Institute

350 Hudson Street
Suite 300
New York, NY 10014

415-947-6320
FAX 415-905-2218
E-Mail: csi@ubm.com
Home Page: www.gocsi.com
Social Media: *Facebook, Twitter, LinkedIn*

Robert Richardson, Director
Nancy Baer, Marketing Manager
Mary Griffin, Membership Director
Fran Timmerman, Operations Manager

The world's leading membership organization specifically dedicated to serving and training the information, computer and network security professional.
Cost: $224.00
Frequency: Membership Fee
Founded in 1974

5265 Computerized Medical Imaging

National Biomedical Research Foundation
37th and O Streets, N.W
Washington, DC 20057

202-687-0100
FAX 202-687-1662
E-Mail: ledley@nbrf.georgetown.edu
Home Page: www.georgetown.edu
Social Media: *Facebook, Twitter, LinkedIn, YouTube, Flickr*

Blaire V Mossman, Chief Administrator
Dr. John J. DeGioia, Ph.D, President
William J Doyle, Chair
Thomas Parkes, S.J, Vice Chair

Formerly the Computerized Radiology Society. A source for the exchange of information concerning the medical use of computerized tomography in radiological diagnosis.
Founded in 1798

5266 Computing Research Association

1828 L Street
Suite 800
Washington, DC 20036-4632

202-234-2111
FAX 202-667-1066
E-Mail: info@cra.org
Home Page: www.cra.org
Social Media: *Facebook, Twitter, YouTube*

J Strother Moore, Chair, Board of Directors
Ronald Brachman, Treasurer
Laura M. Haas, Vice Chair, Board of Directors
Susan B. Davidson, Chair, Board of Directors
Andrew Bernat, Executive Director

Our mission is to seek to strengthen research and advanced education in computing and allied fields.
200 Members
Founded in 1972

5267 Data Interchange Standards Association (DISA)

7600 Leesburg Pike
Suite 430
Falls Church, VA 22043-2004

703-970-4480
888-363-2334
FAX 703-970-4488
E-Mail: info@disa.org

Home Page: www.disa.org
Social Media: *Twitter, LinkedIn*

Jerry C. Connors, President
Jim Taylor, Chair
Stephanie Fetzer, Vice Chair
Jim Leach, Treasurer
Jonathan Lyon, Secretary

Nonprofit home for the development of cross-country electronic business interchange standards.
350+ Members
Founded in 1986

5268 Data Management Association

One State Street Plaza
27th Floor
New York, NY 10004

414-607-0979
FAX 262-546-0794
E-Mail: help@sourcemedia.com
Home Page:
www.information-management.com
Social Media: *Facebook, Twitter, LinkedIn, Google+*

Tony Carrini, Director of Business Development
Peggy Schecter, Publisher
David Weldon, Editorial-in-Chief
Eric Kavanagh, DM Radio Host

A vendor independent professional organization dedicated to the advancement of data asset management concepts.
Founded in 1986

5269 Electronics Industries Alliance

2500 Wilson Boulevard
Arlington, VA 22201

703-907-7500
FAX 703-907-7602
Home Page: www.eia.org

Dave McCurdy, President/CEO
Charles L Robinson, COO
James Shiring, Secretary/Treasurer

A national trade organization that includes a full spectrum of U.S. manufacturers. The alliance is a partnership of electronic and high-tech associations and companies whose mission is promoting the market development and competitiveness of the U.S. high-tech industry through domestic and international policy efforts.
1300 Members
Founded in 1952

5270 Enterprise Computing Solutions

26024 Acero
Mission Viejo, CA 92691-2768

949-609-1980
FAX 949-609-1981
E-Mail: cbulter@thinkecs.com
Home Page: www.thinkecs.com

David Buttler, President
Cheryl Butler, CFO
John Foley, CTO

A leading provider of IT infrastructure solutions for Fortune 500 and mid-tier companies throughout California. ECS builds sophisticated IT infrastructure solutions for mission-critical applications, provides enterprise storage solutions that ensure data protection and business continuity, and delivers state-of-the-art server solutions for optimal computing capacity.
500 Members
Founded in 1995

5271 Independent Computer Consultants Association (ICCA)

11131 S Towne Sq
Suite F
St Louis, MO 63123-7817

314-892-1675
FAX 314-487-1345
E-Mail: execdirector@icca.org
Home Page: www.icca.org

Joyce Burkard, Executive Director

Provides professional development opportunities and business support programs for independent computer consultants. Chapters are in many major metropolitan areas representing consulting firms nationwide.
1000 Members
Founded in 1977

5272 Information Resources Management Association

701 E Chocolate Ave
Suite 200
Hershey, PA 17033-1240

717-533-8845
FAX 717-533-8661
E-Mail: member@irma-international.org
Home Page: www.irma-international.org

Jan Travers, Executive Director
Sherif Kamel, Communications Director

An international professional organization dedicated to advancing the concepts and practices of information resources management in modern organizations. The primary objective of IRMA is to assist organizations and professionals in enhancing the overall knowledge and understanding of effective information resources management in the early 21st century and beyond.
Mailing list available for rent

5273 Information Systems Audit & Control Association (ISACA)

3701 Algonquin Rd
Suite 1010
Rolling Meadows, IL 60008-3124

847-253-1545
FAX 847-253-1443
E-Mail: news@isaca.org
Home Page: www.isaca.org
Social Media: *Facebook, Twitter, LinkedIn*

Susan Caldwell, CEO

With members in more than 160 countries, ISACA is a recognized worldwide leader in IT governance, control, security and assurance. Sponsors international conferences, publishes the thw ISACA Journal and develops international information systems auditing and control standards.
75000 Members
Founded in 1967

5274 Information Technology Management Institute

PO Box 890
Merrifield, VA 22116

703-208-9610
FAX 703-208-9604
E-Mail: info@itm-inst.com
Home Page: www.itm-inst.com

Dr. Diane Murphy, CEO/Founder

Association for information technology organizations primarily in the US.
90 Members
Founded in 1996

5275 Institute of Electrical & Electronics Engineers Computer Society
2001 L Street N.W.
Suite 700
Washington, DC 20036-4928

202-371-0101
FAX 202-728-9614
E-Mail: help@computer.org
Home Page: www.computer.org
Social Media: *Facebook, Twitter, LinkedIn, YouTube, Google+*

Angela R Burgess, Executive Director
Anne Marie Kelly, Director, Governance
Chris Jensen, Director of Marketing and Sales
Ray Kahn, Director of Information Technology
John G. Miller, Director of Finance and Accounting

Supports all those involved in use and design of multimedia hardware, software and systems in industry, business, academia and the arts.
10000 Members
Founded in 1946

5276 International Association for Computer Systems Security
6 Swarthmore Lane
Dix Hills, NY 11746-4829

631-499-1616
FAX 631-462-9178
E-Mail: iacssjalex@aol.com
Home Page: www.iacss.com

Robert J Wilk, President/Founder

Offers a testing program and upholds professional ethics. Supports education through workshops and sponsors lectures.
Founded in 1981

5277 International Association of Knowledge Engineers
973 Russell Avenue
Gaithersburg, MD 20879-3292

301-948-5390
FAX 301-926-4243
Home Page: www.iake.org

Milton White, Owner
Julie Walker-Lowe, Executive Director

An international association of computer professionals concerned with designing reasoning machines and computer systems to receive, organize and maintain human knowledge.
Founded in 1987

5278 International Society for Technology in Education
180 W 8th Avenue
Eugene, OR 97401-2916

541-302-3777
800-336-5191
FAX 541-302-3778
E-Mail: iste@iste.org
Home Page: www.iste.org
Social Media: *Facebook, Twitter, LinkedIn, YouTube, Pinterest*

Kekia Ray, EdD, Chair
Mila Thomas Fuller, Ed.D, Treasurer
Mia Williams, PhDy, Secretary
Brian Lewis, M.A., CAE, Chief Executive Officer
Jessica Medaille, Chief Membership Officer

A large nonprofit organization serving the technology-using educator.

5279 International Technology Law Association/ ITechLaw
7918 Jones Branch Drive
Suite 300
McLean, VA 01880-6200

703-506-2895
FAX 703-579-4366

E-Mail: memberservices@itechlaw.org
Home Page: www.itechlaw.org
Social Media: *Facebook, Twitter, LinkedIn*

Jenna Karadbil, President
Susan Barty, Vice President
Robert Weiss, Treasurer
Christian Frank, Secretary
Charles Morgan, Assistant Secretary

Computer Law Association changed its identity to ITechLaw to better reflect its global activities and expanded focus. Providing benefit to the worldwide community of information technology law professionals.
2000 Members
Founded in 1971

5280 Internet Alliance
1615 L Street NW
Suite 1100
Washington, DC 20036-5624

202-861-2407
E-Mail: tammy@internetalliance.org
Home Page: www.internetalliance.org

Kris Larsen, Manager
Kaye Caldwell, California Policy Director

Formerly the Interactive Services Association, the Alliance has been the only consisted voice representint internet companies in the 50 states. We have a proven track record of blocking or mitigating privacy and anti-spam legislation, and a high level of expertise in the Internet state tax area.
Founded in 1999

5281 NaSPA: Association for Corporate Computing Technical Professionals
NaSPA
7044 S 13th Street
Oak Creek
Milwaukee, WI 53154

414-908-4945
FAX 414-768-8001
E-Mail: j.tucker@naspa.com
Home Page: www.naspa.com
Social Media: *LinkedIn*

Scott Sherer, Chairman
Leo Wrobel, President / Director
Sharon Wrobel, Director / Secretary / Treasurer
Radi Shourbaji, VP of Marketing
Edward J. Krueger, Director of Membership Services

Our mission is to serve the means to enhance the status and promote the advancement of all network and systems professionals; nurture member's technical and managerial knowledge and skills and many more.
50000 Members
Founded in 1986

5282 National Association of Computer Consultant Businesses
1420 King St
Suite 610
Alexandria, VA 22314-2750

703-838-2050
FAX 703-838-3610
E-Mail: staff@naccb.org
Home Page: www.naccb.org
Social Media: *Facebook, Twitter, LinkedIn*

Susan Thaden, Chair
Chris Walters, President
Jim Carteris, Vice-President
Tom Nunn, Treasurer
Mark Roberts, Chief Executive Officer

Members are companies providing technical support services to clients such as programming, systems analysis and software/hardware engineering.
300 Members
Founded in 1987

5283 National BDPA
9500 Arena Dr.
Suite 106
Largo, MD 20774

301-584-3135
FAX 301-560-8300
E-Mail: info@bdpa.org
Home Page: www.bdpa.org
Social Media: *Facebook, Twitter, LinkedIn*

Earl Pace, Founder
Pamela Mathews, President
Mike Williams, Vice President

Association for the professional advancement of African Americans and other minorities in information technology and related STEM industries.
Founded in 1975

5284 Online Audiovisual Catalogers
Minnesota State University
Memorial Library 3097
PO Box 8419
Mankota, MN 56002-2645

507-892-2147
FAX 904-620-2719
E-Mail: gerhart@u.washington.edu
Home Page: www.olacinc.org
Social Media: *RSS*

Stacie A Traill, President
Annie Glerum, Vice President/Presidnet Elect
Jennifer Eustis, Secretary
Autumn Faulkner, Treasurer/Membership Coordinator
Marcy A. Strong, Newsletter Editor

To establish and maintain a group that could speak for catalogers of audiovisual materials. Provides a means for exchange of information, continuing education, and communication among catalogers of audiovisual materials and with the Library of Congress. Maintaining a voice with the bibliographic utilities that speak for catalogers of audiovisual materials, works toward common understanding of AV cataloging practices and standards.
Founded in 1980

5285 Open Applications Group
PO Box 4897
Marietta, GA 30061-4897

404-402-1962
FAX 801-740-0100
E-Mail: inquiry@oagi.org
Home Page: www.openapplications.org

David M Connelly, CEO
Mike Rowell, Chief Architect
Ralph Hertlein, VP, Operations
Jim Wilson, Chemical Industry Architect
Michelle Rascoe, Business Manager

A not-for-profit open standards group building process-based XML standards for both B2B and A2A integration.
Founded in 1994

5286 Optical Society of America
2010 Massachusetts Ave Nw
Washington, DC 20036-1023

202-223-8130
FAX 202-223-1096
E-Mail: info@osa.org
Home Page: www.osa.org
Social Media: *Facebook, Twitter, LinkedIn, YouTube*

Philip Russell, President
Eric Mazur, Vice President
Georges Bayz, Treasurer
Elizabeth A. Rogan, Chief Executive Officer
Philip Russell, President

The Optical Society of America (OSA) was organized to increase and diffuse the knowledge of optics, pure and applied; to promote the

common interests of investigators of optical problems, of designers and of users of optical apparatus of all kinds; and to encourage cooperation among them. The purposes of the Society are scientific, technical and educational.
Cost: $95.00
15000 Members
Frequency: Membership Fee
Founded in 1916

5287 Personal Computer Memory Card International Association
2635 N 1st St
Suite 218
San Jose, CA 95134-2048

408-433-2273
FAX 408-433-9558
E-Mail: office@pcmcia.org
Home Page: www.pcmcia.org
Social Media: *Facebook*

Patrick Maher, Executive Director
Ken Stufflebeam, President
Brian Ikeya, Secretary
Jim Koser, Treasurer

Created to establish standards for Integrated Circuit cards and to promote interchangeability among mobile computers where ruggedness, low power, and small size were critical.
200+ Members
Founded in 1989

5288 Polar Microsystems
Po Box 403
Huntingdon Valley, PA 19006

215-676-1590
FAX 215-676-1596
E-Mail: polar@netaxs.com
Home Page: www.polarmicro.com

Doug C Baer, Senior Systems Engineer

Provides consulting services that enable our clients to advance their businesses through full utilization of the Apple Macintosh hardware and software platform.

5289 Portable Computer and Communications Association
PO Box 680
Hood River, OR 97031

541-490-5140
FAX 413-410-8447
E-Mail: pcca@pcca.org
Home Page: www.pcca.org

Peter Rysavy, Executive Director

Represents firms, organizations and individuals interested in mobile communications. PCCA publishes information, standards, software and other materials.
Cost: $100.00
75 Members
Frequency: Individual Membership Fee
Founded in 1992

5290 Society For Modeling Simulation International
2598 Fortune Way
Suite I
Vista, CA 92081

858-277-3888
FAX 858-277-3930
E-Mail: scs@scs.org
Home Page: www.scs.org
Social Media: *Facebook, LinkedIn*

Lin Zhang, President
Bjorn Johansson, Treasurer
Oletha Darensburg, Executive Director
Vicki Pate, Publications Manager & Editor
Aleah Hockridge, Conferences Director

The only technical Society dedicated to advancing the use of modeling & simulation to solve real-world problems. SCS is the principal technical society devoted to the advancement of simulation and allied computer arts in all fields.
Cost: $55.00
Frequency: Regular Membership Dues
Founded in 1952

5291 Society for Imaging Science and Technology
7003 Kilworh Lane
Springfield, VA 22151-4088

703-642-9090
FAX 703-642-9094
E-Mail: info@imaging.org
Home Page: www.imaging.org

Geoff J Woolfe, President
Steven J Simske, Executive VP
Scott Silence, Treasurer
Ingeborg Tastl, Secretary
Suzanne E. Grinnan, Executive Director

Our goal is to keep members aware of the latest scientific and technological developments in the field of imaging through conferences, journals and other publications. We focus on imaging in all its aspects, with particular emphasis on silver halide, digital printing, electronic imaging, photofinishing, image preservation, image assessment, pre-press technologies and hybrid imaging systems.
2000+ Members
Founded in 1947

5292 Society for Information Display
1475 S Bascom Ave
Campbell, CA 95008-4006

408-879-3901
FAX 408-879-3833
E-Mail: office@sid.org
Home Page: www.sid.org
Social Media: *Facebook, Twitter, LinkedIn, YouTube*

Amal Ghosh, President
Helge Seetzen, Treasurer
Takatoshi Tsujimura, Secretary
Dave Eccles, VP-Americas
Bao Ping Wang, VP -Asia

Representing the international and local display communities. Offers opportunites to network, recieve information and publications and news about trade shows.
6000 Members
Founded in 1962

5293 Society for Materials Engineers and Scientists
3440 E University Drive
Phoenix, AZ 85034

602-470-5700
FAX 602-437-8497
E-Mail: general.inquiries@asm.com
Home Page: www.asm.com
Social Media: *Twitter*

Chuck D del Prado, President and CEO
Peter A.M Van Bommel, Member of the Management Board
Per Ove Hansson, General Manager Thermal Products
Tominori Yoshida, General Manager Plasma Products
Fokko LeutScher, Vice President of Front-end Global

A leading supplier of semiconductor process equipment in both front and back end markets. The Company possesses a strong technological base, state-of-the-art manufacturing facilities, a competent and qualified workforce and a highly trained, strategically distributed support network.
Founded in 1968

5294 Society of Manufacturing Engineers International
1 SME Drive
Po Box 930
Dearborn, MI 48121

313-425-3000
800-733-4763
FAX 313-425-3401
E-Mail: service@sme.org
Home Page: www.sme.org
Social Media: *Facebook, Twitter, LinkedIn, YouTube, Google+*

Wayne F Frost, CMfgE, President
Jeffrey M Krause, CEO
Wayne F. Frost, CMfgE, Vice President
Dean L. Bartles, PhD, FSME, Secretary/Treasurer
Nancy S. Berg, Executive Director/General Manager

An association that provides information on various automated and computerized systems.
33 Members
Founded in 1932

5295 Software Engineering Institute
4500 Fifth Avenue
Pittsburgh, PA 15213-2612

412-268-5800
FAX 412-268-5758
E-Mail: customer-relations@sei.cmu.edu
Home Page: www.sei.cmu.edu
Social Media: *Facebook, Twitter, LinkedIn, YouTube*

Paul D Nielsen, CEO
Clyde Chittister, Chief Operating Officer

A federally funded research and development center sponsored by the U.S. Department of Defense through the Office of the Under Secretary of Defense for Acquisition, Technology, and Logistics. Supports all those engineers involved in the software industry.

5296 Software Management Network
55 Madison Avenue
STE400
Morristown, CA 07960

973-285-3264
FAX 973-538-0503
E-Mail: jmgolub@softwaremanagement.com
Home Page: www.softwaremanagement.com

Nicholas Zvegintzov, President/Chief Technical Officer
Judith Marx Golub, VP/CFO

A publishing, consulting, and training group that serves professional software teams responsible for working, installed software systems. Its unique mission is to make available the most effective resources for managing active software.
Founded in 1996

5297 Uni Forum Association
PO Box 3177
Annapolis, MD 21403

410-715-9500
800-333-8649
FAX 240-465-0207
E-Mail: afedder@uniforum.org
Home Page: www.uniforum.org

Alan Fedder, President
Deborah Murray, VP
John Lehmann, Board Member
Phil Hughes, Board Member
Paul Wolotsky, Board Member

Professional association for end users, developers and vendors. Promotes and exchanges information about the practices and benefits of open technologies and related hardware, software, applications and standards.
Founded in 1981

5298 Vmebus International Trade Association
9100 Paseo del Vita
Oklahoma City, OK 73131

480-837-7486
E-Mail: info@vita.com
Home Page: www.vita.com
Social Media: *Facebook, Twitter, LinkedIn*

Jerry Gipper, Executive Director
Jing Kwok, Technical Director
Ray Alderman, Chairman of the Board

Association for manufacturers of microcomputer boards, hardware, software, military products, controllers, bus interfaces and other accessories compatible with VMEbus architecture.
Cost: $2500.00
150 Members
Frequency: Regular Membership Fee
Founded in 1981

Newsletters

5299 AAR Newsletter
School of Information Technology & Engineering
University of Ottawa
800 King Edward Avenue
Ottawa, Canada

613-562-5738
FAX 613-562-5664
E-Mail: pieper@mcs.anl.gov
Home Page: www-unix.mcs.anl.gov

Gail W Pieper, Editor
Mary Dzielski, Secretary
Janet Werner, Executive Secretary

Represents research notes and problem sets, discusses software advances and announces conferences and workshops.
Frequency: Quarterly

5300 ADAIC News
Ada Information Clearinghouse
201 ILR Extension Building
Cornell University
Ithaca, NY 14853-3901

607-255-2763
800-949-4232
E-Mail: northeastada@cornell.edu
Home Page: www.northeastada.org

Susan Carlson, Publisher
Lorrie Fessenden, Administrative Assistant

Information on Ada-an internationally standardized, general purpose computer language used in a variety of applications includes news of the Ada community.
Circulation: 20,000
Founded in 2001

5301 AEC Automation Newsletter
Technology Automation Services
PO Box 3593
Englewood, CO 80155-3593

303-770-1728
FAX 303-770-3660
Home Page: www.aecnews.com

Jeff Rowe, Editor
David Weisberg, Circulation Director
Randall S Newton, Editor-In-Chief
W Bradley Holtz, Group Publisher
Joel N Orr, Senior Editor

Reports on computer hardware and software issues relevant to architectural design, civil engineering, structural design, process plant design and geographic information management. Includes articles on software developments, new computer hardware, business issues, operating

systems, application software, networking and technology developments.
Cost: $235.00
16 Pages
Frequency: Monthly
Founded in 1977
Printed in one color on matte stock

5302 AI Interactions
Academy of International Business
Michigan State University
7 Eppley Center
East Lansing, MI 48824-1121

517-432-4336
FAX 517-432-1009
E-Mail: ciber@msu.edu
Home Page: aib.msu.edu

G Tomas M Hult, Executive Secretary
Tunga Kiyak, Managing Director
Irem Kiyak, Treasurer

Calls for papers, meeting notices and membership news of interest to professors of international business around the world.
Circulation: 3000
Mailing list available for rent: 3000 names at $250 per M

5303 AIM Connections
AIM Global
125 Warrendale Bayne Rd
Suite 100
Warrendale, PA 15086-7570

724-934-4470
FAX 724-934-4495
E-Mail: info@aimglobal.org
Home Page: www.aimglobal.org

Mary Lou Bosco, President
Linda Young, Business Development Director

E-newsletter focused on automatic identification and mobile computing for a broad audience. Each issue contains analysis and news about the industry with a focus on what's happeneing in the market today.
900+ Members
Founded in 1972
Mailing list available for rent

5304 Acronyms
Computer Laboratory Michigan State University
40F Computer Ctr
East Lansing, MI 48824-1042

517-355-3600
FAX 517-355-5176

Linda Dunn, Publisher

A listing of procedures, policies, hardware and software for computer users.
Frequency: Quarterly

5305 Advanced Office Technologies Report
DataTrends Publications
Po Box 4460
Leesburg, VA 20177-8541

703-779-0574
800-766-8130
FAX 703-779-2267
E-Mail: info@stemcellresearchnews.com
Home Page: www.stemcellresearchnews.com

Paul G Ochs, Owner

Offers information on products, technological breakthroughs and industry developments in office automation technology.
Frequency: Full-text

5306 Alpha Forum
Pinnacle Publishing

316 N Michigan Avenue
Suite 300
Chicago, IL 60601

312-272-2401
800-493-4867
FAX 312-960-4106
E-Mail: pinpub@ragan.com
Home Page: www.pinpub.com

Brent Smith, Publisher
David Stevenson, Editor

Technical newsletter for application developers and users. Hands-on articles with specific usage and programming techniques, tips and product updates.
16 Pages
Frequency: Monthly
Circulation: 8000
Founded in 1990
Mailing list available for rent
Printed in 2 colors on matte stock

5307 Applications Software
Thomson Media
1 State St
27th Floor
New York, NY 10004-1481

212-825-8445
FAX 212-843-9600

James Malkin, President/CEO
William Johnson, CFO

General business management and word processing, reference services, custom services and CD-ROM services.
Frequency: Monthly

5308 Artificial Intelligence Letter
Kluwer Academic Publishers
101 Philip Drive
Norwell, MA 02061-1677

781-871-6600
FAX 781-871-6528

Masoud Yazdani, Publisher

Provides a forum for the work of researchers and application developers from artificial intelligence, cognitive science and related disciplines.
Circulation: 625

5309 Bits and Bytes Review
Bits and Bytes Computer Resources
623 Iowa Ave
Whitefish, MT 59937-2336

406-862-7280
800-361-7280
FAX 406-862-1124
E-Mail: Info@bitsbytescomputer.com
Home Page: www.bitsbytescomputer.com

John J Hughes, Owner

Resources and products for the academic field.
Cost: $56.90
Frequency: Monthly

5310 Branch Automation News
Phillips Publishing
7811 Montrose Road
Potomac, MD 20854

301-340-2100
E-Mail: feedback@healthydirections.com
Home Page: www.healthydirections.com

Strategies for planning, implementing and managing bank technology.
Cost: $495.00
Circulation: 1000
Founded in 1974
Mailing list available for rent: 30342 names at $125 per M
Printed in 2 colors on matte stock

5311 Business Computer Report
Guidera Publishing Corporation

3 Myrtle Bank Road
Hilton Head Island, SC 29926-1809
Lawrence C Oakley, Editor

Hands-on review of business related software, as well as hardware, primarily for the PC world (as opposed to the MAC World). Readers are primarily owners of small to medium-sized businesses.
Cost: $95.00
8 Pages
Frequency: Monthly
Circulation: 125,000
Printed in one color on matte stock

5312 Business Software News

110 N Bell Avenue
Suite 300
Shawnee, OK 74801-6967

405-275-3100
FAX 405-275-3101
Home Page: www.cpatechadvisers.com

Shari Bodger, Publisher
Melody Wrinkle, Editor
Shari Bodger, Marketing Manager

Offers updated information on computer software, marketing and technology news. Columnists address networks, sales and management with every issue including independent, comparative software reviews.
Cost: $40.00
8 Pages
Circulation: 1000
Founded in 1991
Printed in 4 colors on matte stock

5313 C/C & Users Journal

Miller Freeman Publications
2800 Campus Drive
San Mateo, CA 94403

650-513-4300
800-365-1364
FAX 650-513-4601
E-Mail: cuj@neodata.com
Home Page: www.cuj.com

Peter Westerman, Publisher
Jon Erickson, Editorial Director
Jessica Marty, Director of Marketing
Amy Stephens, Managing Editor

Information for intermediate and advanced C and C++ programmers. Includes programming techniques, tutorials and software reviews.
Cost: $29.95
Frequency: Monthly
Circulation: 39,048
Founded in 1988

5314 C/Net News.Com

CNET
100 Pine St
Suite 1775
San Francisco, CA 94111-5127

415-409-8900
FAX 415-395-9254
Home Page: www.ccolaw.com

Therese Cannata, Partner
John Morris, Editor
Christina Koukkos, Managing Editor

Provides information for high end audiences in the market for tech news, including the IS community, the technology business itself and the financial community.
Frequency: Daily
Founded in 1992

5315 COM-AND: Computer Audit News & Developments

Management Advisory Services & Publications

PO Box 81151
Wellesley Hills, MA 02481-0001

781-235-2895
FAX 781-235-5446
E-Mail: info@masp.com
Home Page: www.masp.com

New standards and practices. Tutorials on impact of EDP on audit and control matters. Practical coverage of technical EDP developments for auditors and internal controls specialists.
Cost: $70.00
8 Pages
Founded in 1972
Mailing list available for rent
Printed in 2 colors on matte stock

5316 COMDEX Show Daily

Key 3 Media Group
795 Folsom Street
6th Floor
San Francisco, CA 94107-1243

415-905-2300
FAX 415-905-2329
Home Page: www.medialiveinternational.com

Sean Cassidy, Marketing Manager
Robert Priest-Heck, President/CEO

Tabloid newspaper of computer related exhibits.
Frequency: Daily
Circulation: 3445

5317 CPA Technology Advisor

Harcourt Brace Professional Publishing
9720 Carroll Centre Rd
Suite 1900
San Diego, CA 92126-4551

858-271-7390
800-831-7799
Home Page: www.hbpp.com

Bruce Ta, Owner
Frank Peterson, Editor

Concise unbiased recommendations on hardware and software for CPA's.
Cost: $19.00

5318 Client/Server Economics Letter

Computer Economics
2082 Business Center Drive
Suite 240
Irvine, CA 92612

949-831-8700
FAX 949-442-7688
Home Page: www.computereconomics.com

Frank Scavo, President
Dan Husiak, VP

Economic look at the client/server revolution. Provides critical economic data on costs and risks of client/server computing, backed up with research and presentation-quality graphs and tables. Provides the information you need to make sound business decisions.
Cost: $395.00
Frequency: Daily
Founded in 1978

5319 Comp-U-Fax Computer Trends Newsletter

Microcomputers Software and Consulting
28 S 12th Avenue
Mount Vernon, NY 10550-2913
Bob James, Publisher

Corporate information resource newsletter.

5320 Computer Aided Design Report

CAD/CAM Publishing
7100 N Broadway
Suite 2-P
Denver, CO 80221

303-482-2813
FAX 303-484-3610

E-Mail: info@cadcamnet.com
Home Page: www.cadcamnet.com

Randall Newton, Editor

Uses of computers by engineers in the manufacturing trades.
Cost: $195.00

5321 Computer Architecture

IEEE Computer Society
1730 Massachusetts Avenue NW
Washington, DC 20036-1992

202-371-1013
FAX 202-728-9614

Henry Ayling, Publisher
Lee Blue, Production Manager

Current trends in computer networks, hardware description languages, performance.
Circulation: 2303

5322 Computer Business

Round Table Association SAB
5340 W 57th Street
Los Angeles, CA 90056-1339

310-649-2846

A Hassan, Publisher/Editor
J Hassan, Circulation Manager

Best computer/communications articles of previous month, briefly abstracted.
Cost: $20.00

5323 Computer Economics Report

Computer Economics
2082 Business Center Drive
Suite 240
Irvine, CA 92612

949-831-8700
FAX 949-442-7688
Home Page: www.computereconomics.com

Frank Scavo, President
Dan Husiak, VP

Written from an end-user perspective, this monthly newsletter provides analyses of new IBM technologies, plus acquisition and financial management strategies. Regular features include cost comparisons, price/performance analysis, new product forecasts, and evaluations of acquisition techniques for medium and large computer systems.
Cost: $595.00
Frequency: Monthly
Founded in 1978

5324 Computer Industry Report

International Data Corporation
5 Speen Street
Framingham, MA 01701

508-872-8200
E-Mail: leads@idc.com
Home Page: www.idc.com/

Kirk Campbell, President/CEO

Research and analysis of the computer processing industry.
Founded in 1964

5325 Computer Integrated Manufacture and Engineering

Lionheart Publishing
2555 Cumberland Pkwy Se
Suite 299
Atlanta, GA 30339-3921

770-432-2551
FAX 770-432-6969

Explores cutting edge developments in manufacturing systems operation management.
Circulation: 24,000

5326 Computer Modeling and Simulation in Engineering

Sage Science Press

2455 Teller Rd
Newbury Park, CA 91320-2234

805-499-9774
800-818-7243
FAX 805-499-0871
E-Mail: info@sagepub.com
Home Page: www.sagepub.com

Blaise R Simqu, CEO/President

Publishes application-oriented papers that utilize computer modeling and simulation techniques to understand and resolve industrial problems or processes that are of immediate and contemporary interest.
Frequency: Monthly

5327 Computer Protocols
Worldwide Videotex
PO Box 3273
Boynton Beach, FL 33424-3273

561-738-2276
E-Mail: markedit@juno.com
Home Page: www.wvpubs.com

Mark Wright, Editor/President
Linda Dera, Marketing Manager
Linda Dera, Circulation Manager

Covers news and developments of bridges, gateway and LAN. Coverage also provided on the development of internal protocols.
Cost: $165.00
Frequency: Monthly
Circulation: 30000
Founded in 1981

5328 Computer Reseller News
CMP Publications
One Jericho Plaza
Jericho, NY 11753-1680

516-562-5000
FAX 516-562-7243
E-Mail: shadowram@mcimail.com
Home Page: www.crn.com

John Russell, Publisher
Computer news for resellers and distributors.

5329 Computer and Communications Buyer
Technology News of America Company
PO Box 20008
New York, NY 10025-1510

212-222-1123
E-Mail: subs@eintelligence.com
Home Page: www.eintelligence.com

Annotated statistical reports on capital equipment. $450.00 outside of United States.
Cost: $395.00
8 Pages
Frequency: Monthly
ISSN: 1042-4296
Founded in 1984
Mailing list available for rent

5330 Computer and Computer Management News and Developments
Management Advisory Services & Publications
PO Box 81151
Wellesley Hills, MA 02481-0001

781-235-2895
FAX 781-235-5446
E-Mail: info@masp.com
Home Page: www.masp.com

Newsletter aimed at the management level of the computer industry.

5331 Computers & Security
Elsevier Science

6277 Sea Harbor Drive
Orlando, FL 32887

407-345-4020
877-839-7126
FAX 407-363-1354
E-Mail: usjcs@elsevier.com
Home Page: www.elsevier.com

Andrew Fletcher, Publisher
E Schultz, CEO/President
Ann Dudley, Circulation Manager
Carl Lampert, Editor

International newsletter for the management of computer and information security.
Circulation: 1500

5332 Computers & Structures
Elsevier Science
PO Box 945
New York, NY 10010-945

212-989-5800
888-437-4636
FAX 212-633-3680
E-Mail: usinfo@sciencedirect.com
Home Page: www.sciencedirect.com

Keith Lambert, Publisher/Editor

Analyzes the many relationships between computer technology and the different fields of engineering.
Circulation: 1500
Founded in 1962

5333 Computers, Foodservice and You
Mike Pappas
Po Box 338
Raton, NM 87740-0338

575-445-9811
FAX 575-445-3080

Mike Pappas, Owner

A newsletter focusing on computers for the hospitality industry.
Cost: $119.00
16 Pages
Frequency: Bi-Monthly
Circulation: 450
Printed in one color on matte stock

5334 DM Direct
220 Regency Court
Suite 210
Brookfield, WI 53045

262-784-0444
FAX 262-782-9489
Home Page: www.dmreview.com

Tony Carrini, Associate Publisher

In this e-mail newsletter you will find articles, online columnists, news and industry events exclusive to you, the online reader. Our goal is to ensure that DM Direct provides the information you need to compete in the business intelligence, data warehousing and analytics marketplace.

5335 DP Budget
Computer Economics
2082 Business Center Drive
Suite 240
Irvine, CA 92612

949-831-8700
FAX 949-442-7688
Home Page: www.computereconomics.com

Frank Scavo, President
Dan Husiak, VP

Report analyzing DP expenses, salary issues and acquisition costs. Focuses on increasing productivity and improving the return on your DP investment.
Cost: $495.00
Frequency: Monthly

5336 DPFN
Directory & Database Publishers Forum & Network
352 Seventh Avenue
New York, NY 10001-546

212-643-5458
845-358-8034
E-Mail: gstone@ptmcomm.com
Home Page: www.dpfn.com

Barry Lee, Membership Chair
Jeff Fandl, President

Contains events, seminar information, publishers story, industry snapshots, and news pertaining to the industry. Members are large and small directory publishers, vendors to the trade and consultants. Provides networking opportunities and exposure to industry experts through their meetings and workshops.
Founded in 1990
Printed in on matte stock

5337 Data Channels
Phillips Publishing
7811 Montrose Road
Potomac, MD 20854

301-340-2100
E-Mail: feedback@healthydirections.com
Home Page: www.healthydirections.com

Source of intelligence for executives making data communications decisions. Accepts advertising.
Cost: $397.00
9 Pages

5338 Data Security Management
Auerbach Publications
535 5th Avenue
Room 806
New York, NY 10017-3610

800-737-8034
Home Page: www.auerbach-publications.com

Rich O'Hanley, Editor

Technical and management information for security managers, networks and systems administrators and data center managers.
Cost: $495.00
Frequency: Bi-Monthly
Circulation: 1,500
ISSN: 1096-7907
Printed in on matte stock

5339 Dental Computer Newsletter
Andent
1000 N Avenue
Waukegan, IL 60085

847-223-5077
E-Mail: info@andent.net
Home Page: www.andent.net

For and by an international group of Dentists, Physicians and allied health professionals interested in computers. Emphasis is on the practical use of all brands of computers for the professional office.
Cost: $25.00
Frequency: Quarterly
Circulation: 3100

5340 Digital Directions Report
Computer Economics
2082 Business Center Drive
Suite 240
Irvine, CA 92612

949-831-8700
FAX 949-442-7688
Home Page: www.computereconomics.com

Frank Scavo, President

Provides details on the financial ramifications of future DEC products. The information is critical for decision makers involved with cost-control, strategy planning and new product

analysis.
Cost: $525.00
Frequency: Monthly

5341 Directory of Top Computer Executives
Applied Computer Research
Po Box 41730
Phoenix, AZ 85080

602-216-9100
800-234-2227
FAX 602-548-4800
E-Mail: tara@topitexecs.com
Home Page: www.acrhq.com

Computer performance and management.
Cost: $370.00
Circulation: 1000
ISSN: 0193-9920
Founded in 1972
Printed in one color on matte stock

5342 Document Imaging Report
Corry Publishing
5539 Peach Street
Erie, PA 16509

814-380-0025
FAX 814-864-2037
E-Mail: corrypub@corrypub.com
Home Page: www.corrypub.com

john Coiston, Publisher
Terry Peterson, CEO
Micole Hykes, Editor
Karrie Boocious, Marketing
Melinda Fadden, Circulation Manager

Timely and actionable information on electronic imaging applications, products and user implementation.
Frequency: Monthly
Circulation: 43000

5343 Dvorak Developments
Freelance Communications
PO Box 666
Ridgway, CO 81432

970-626-2255

Randy Cassingham, Publisher

Promotes the use of the Dvorak keyboard for typewriters and computers. Dvorak is more ergonomic than the common Qwerty keyboard. Accepts advertising.
8 Pages

5344 E-News
Patricia Seybold Group
Po Box 240565
Boston, MA 02129

617-742-5200
800-826-2424
FAX 617-742-1028
E-Mail: feedback@psgroup.com
Home Page: www.psgroup.com

Patricia Seybold, Founder/CEO

E-mail newsletter includes perspectives on the e-commerce industry, research and upcoming events.

5345 EDI News
Phillips Publishing
7811 Montrose Road
Potomac, MD 20854

301-340-2100
E-Mail: feedback@healthydirections.com
Home Page: www.healthydirections.com

Electronic data interchange marketplace information.
Cost: $397.00
9 Pages

5346 Education Technology News
Business Publishers

2222 Sedwick Dr
Suite 101
Durham, NC 27713

800-223-8720
FAX 800-508-2592
E-Mail: custserv@bpinews.com
Home Page: www.bpinews.com

Information on educational hardware and software, trends in computer-aided teaching and computer uses in the classroom.
Cost: $217.00
Circulation: 500
Founded in 1963

5347 Electronic Education Report
Simba Information
60 Long Ridge Rd
Suite 300
Stamford, CT 06902-1841

203-325-8193
888-297-4622
FAX 203-325-8915
E-Mail: info@simbanet.com
Home Page: www.simbanet.com

Linda Kopp, Publisher

News and analysis from a business perspective on software, multimedia/CD-ROM, videodisc, distance learning, Internet/online services and educational videocassettes.
Cost: $625.00
Founded in 1989

5348 Electronic Marketing News
Software Assistance International
PO Box 750
Morris Plains, NJ 07950-0750

973-644-0022
FAX 973-539-3253

George Papov, Editor

Supplier of electronic catalogs to business and industries.
Circulation: 6,000

5349 End-User Computing Management
Auerbach Publications
535 5th Avenue
Room 806
New York, NY 10017-3610

800-737-8034
FAX 212-297-9176

Kim Hovan Kelly, Publisher

Technical and mangement information.
Cost: $495.00
Frequency: BiWeekly
Circulation: 1,000

5350 Federal Computer Week
101Communications
3141 Fairview Park Drive
#777
Falls Church, VA 22042-4507

703-876-5100
FAX 703-876-5126
Home Page: www.fcw.com

Anne Armstrong, Publisher
Jeff Calore, General Manager

The Federal Computer Week provides practical news, analysis and insight on how to buy, build and manage technology in government.
Circulation: 93000

5351 Forestry Computer Applications
Michaelsen's Micro Magic Publishers
PO Box 7332
Fredericksburg, VA 22404-7332
Nancy Michaelsen, Publisher

Offers news and information on computers and electronics used in the forestry services industry, including manufacturing, building, con-

struction and architecture.
Cost: $29.95

5352 Frontline
Computer Security Institute
600 Harrison Street
San Francisco, CA 94107

415-947-6320
FAX 818-487-4550
Home Page: www.gocsi.com

Robert Richardson, Editorial Director
Chris Keating, Director

This quarterly newsletter is to improve the security practices of your entire organization to increase end-user awareness of critical security topics pertaining to them.
Cost: $1860.00
4 Pages
Frequency: Annual Subscription

5353 GCN Tech Edition
Post Newsweek Tech Media
10 G St Ne
Suite 500
Washington, DC 20002-4228

202-772-2500
866-447-6864
FAX 202-772-2511
E-Mail: editorial@gcn.com
Home Page: www.gcn.com

David Greene, President
Tom Temin, Editor-in-Chief
Kirstin Crane, Marketing Manager
Bar Blaskowsky, Circulation Manager

Evaluates performance, cost and applications of hardware, software, peripheral and communication products available to government agencies and businesses.
Cost: $95.00
Circulation: 87500
Founded in 1998
Printed in on glossy stock

5354 Government Computer News
Reed Business Information
2000 Clearwater Dr
Oak Brook, IL 60523-8809

630-574-0825
FAX 630-288-8781
Home Page: www.reedbusiness.com

Jeff Greisch, President

The national newspaper of government computing.
Cost: $53.00
55 Pages
Frequency: Monthly
Founded in 1982

5355 Graphic Communications Today
IDEA Alliance
1421 Prince Street
Suite 230
Alexandria, VA 22314-2805

703-837-1070
FAX 703-837-1072
Home Page: www.idealliance.org

Alan Kotok, Editor
David Steinhardt, CEO

Electronic commerce, direct marketing, printing and paper aspects, and graphics updates.
Frequency: Daily
Circulation: 200
Founded in 1966

5356 HIS Insider
United Communications Group

11300 Rockville Pike
Street 1100
Rockville, MD 20852-3030

301-287-2700
FAX 301-816-8945
E-Mail: webmaster@ucg.com
Home Page: www.ucg.com

Benny Dicecca, President

News and reports on new hospital and clinical information system technologies, upcoming vendor merger acquisitions, analyses of telecommunicaiton systems used in health care.
Cost: $427.00
Frequency: Weekly
Founded in 1977

5357 IN SYNC Magazine
Agate Publishing
21 West 26th Street
New York, NY 10010

847-475-4457
E-Mail: seibold@agatepublishing.com
Home Page: www.agatepublishing.com

Doug Seibold

News and how-to for distributed and cooperative applications. Particularly how to link multiple computer systems to gain best advantage from each.
Cost: $8.00
Circulation: 1000

5358 IS Budget
Computer Economics
2082 Business Center
Dr. Ste 240
Irvine, CA 92612

949-831-8700
FAX 949-442-7688
Home Page: www.computereconomics.com

Frank Scavo, President
Dan Husiak, VP

Tackles today's toughest IS budgeting issues head-on with exhaustively researched line-item cost comparisons by type of industry, installation size, company revenue and type of expenditure. Regular features include MIS spending comparisons, analyses of budgeting issues and inside information on vendor discounts.
Cost: $495.00
Frequency: Monthly
Founded in 1978

5359 Independent Computer Consultants Newsletter
Independent Computer Consultants Association
11131 S Towne Sq
Suite F
St Louis, MO 63123-7817

314-892-1675
FAX 314-487-1345
E-Mail: execdirector@icca.org
Home Page: www.icca.org

Joyce Burkard, Executive Director

Promotes professional standards in the industry. Conducts educational programs and maintains local chapters in many major cities. Available to members only.
Circulation: 1000
Founded in 1976
Mailing list available for rent: 1200 names at $500 per M
Printed in 2 colors

5360 Inside the Internet
Cobb Group
115 6th Ave
Dayton, KY 41074-1111

859-291-1146
800-733-2040

FAX 859-655-2482
E-Mail: tomherman@cobbinc.com
Home Page: www.cobbinc.com

Tom Herman, President
Adam Browning, Production Manager

Practical advice and instructions for Internet users.

5361 Intelligence: The Future of Computing
Intelligence
PO Box 20008
New York, NY 10025-1510

212-222-1123
800-638-7257
Home Page: www.eintelligence.com

Edward Rosenfeld, Editor/Publisher

Provides coverage of advanced computing: neutral networks, AI, genetic algorithms, fuzzy systems, wavelets, et. al., and the Net, the Web, Nanotechnologies quanteum, molecular and DNA computing.
Cost: $395.00
8 Pages
Frequency: Monthly
ISSN: 1042-4296
Founded in 1984
Printed in one color on matte stock

5362 International Spectrum
International Spectrum Magazine & Conferences
8956 Fox Drive
Suite 102
Thornton, CO 80260

720-259-1356
FAX 603-250-0664
E-Mail: nathan@intl-spectrum.com
Home Page: www.intl-spectrum.com

Nathan Rector, President
Monica Giobbi, Manager
Clif Oliver, Editor

Trade magazine for PICK/UNIX/DOS computer industry which covers hardware, software and peripherals. Company produces major trade show held annually in Southern California and regional exhibitions and conferences across the country.
88 Pages
Frequency: 6 issues/Yr
Circulation: 50,000
Founded in 1982
Mailing list available for rent: 80M names
Printed in 4 colors on glossy stock

5363 Managing Human Resource Information Systems
Institute of Management and Administration
1 Washington Park
Suite 1300
Newark, NJ 07102

212-244-0360
FAX 973-622-0595
Home Page: www.ioma.com

Covers management issues critical to building and maintaining state-of-the-art HRIS software, hardware, and Internet/intranet activities. It is intended to help control costs of HRIS, make better use of new technologies, migrate HRIS from mainframe, mini, and client/server systems.
Cost: $259.00
Frequency: Monthly
Circulation: 180000
Founded in 1982

5364 Micro Publishing
Cygnus Publishing

445 Broad Hollow Road
Melville, NY 11747

631-845-2700
800-308-6397
FAX 631-845-2798
Home Page: www.cygnuspub.com

James Cavuoto, Publisher
Nancy Whelan, Advertising/Sales
Kenneth Spears, Production
Mark Erikson, Circulation Manager
Paul Bonaiuto, CFO

A newsletter for hardware and software vendors that examines the micro-based publishing systems market, including workstation publishing, printers, scanners, networks, technology and data-based publishing, production methods and page layout software. The editorials consists of microcomputer publishing product reviews, notes, and trend analysis, and new product announcements.
Cost: $295.00
10 Pages
Frequency: Monthly
Printed in on matte stock

5365 Network Economics Letter
Computer Economics
5841 Edison Place
Carlsbad, CA 92008-6500

760-438-8100
800-326-8100
FAX 760-431-1126
Home Page: www.computereconomics.com

Bruno Bassi, Publisher
Don Trevillian, Editor

Provides an executive overview for MIS and network professionals who are involved in network strategic planning and implementation. It covers such topics as comparative analysis of hardware and software systems, cost of ownership studies, analysis of emerging protocols and standards and cost-saving opportunities.
Cost: $395.00
Frequency: Monthly

5366 OSINetter Newsletter
Architecture Technology Corporation
9977 Valley View Rd
Suite 300
Eden Prairie, MN 55344-3586

952-829-5864
FAX 952-829-5871
E-Mail: info@atcorp.com
Home Page: www.atcorp.com

Noel Schmidt, Executive VP

Covers products and company activity in the area of open systems interconnection.
Cost: $50.00
Founded in 1955

5367 Official Memory News
Phillips Publishing
7811 Montrose Road
Potomac, MD 20854

301-340-2100
E-Mail: feedback@healthydirections.com
Home Page: www.healthydirections.com

Provides the latest news and analysis on OSI standards developments. Accepts advertising.
Cost: $497.00
9 Pages
Founded in 1974

5368 Open Systems Economics Letter
Computer Economics

2082 Business Center Drive
Suite 240
Irvine, CA 92612

949-831-8700
FAX 949-442-7688
Home Page: www.computereconomics.com/

Dan Husiak, Vo
Frank Scavo, President

Addresses the critical economic issues associated with the worldwide transformation to open systems. In a concise, monthly format, this report provides the information that you must have to successfully adopt an open systems strategy, manage your transition to open standards, and protect your corporate investment in new technology.
Cost: $395.00
Frequency: Monthly

5369 Optical Memory News
Phillips Publishing
7811 Montrose Road
Potomac, MD 20854

301-340-2100
E-Mail: feedback@healthydirections.com
Home Page: www.healthydirections.com

Provides the latest news and analysis on the optical storage marketplace from vendor perspective. Accepts advertising.
Cost: $397.00
9 Pages
Frequency: BiWeekly
Printed in one color on matte stock

5370 Product Data Management Report
CAD/CAM Publishing
7100 N Broadway
Suite 2-P
Denver, CO 80221

303-482-2813
FAX 303-484-3610
E-Mail: info@cadcamnet.com
Home Page: www.cadcamnet.com

Randall Newton, Editor

Devoted to product data management software and systems that are used by major manufacturing firms to store, control, and distribute CAD and other engineering data.
Cost: $345.00

5371 Public and Policy
American Public Human Services Association
1133 19th St NW
Suite 400
Washington, DC 20036

202-682-0100
FAX 202-204-0071
Home Page: www.aphsa.org

Tracy Wareing, Executive Director
Frequency: Bimonthly

5372 Rapid Prototyping Report
CAD/CAM Publishing
2880 Stone Trail Dr
Bethesda, MD 20817-4556

240-425-4004
FAX 301-365-4586
E-Mail: info@cadcamnet.com
Home Page: www.cadcamnet.com

Geoff Smith-Moritz, Editor
L Wolf, Production Manager

Gives in-depth objective appraisals of strengths and weaknesses of rapid prototyping technology. Includes applications on how RP technology is used in the industry.
Cost: $295.00
Frequency: Monthly

5373 Report on IBM
DataTrends Publications
Po Box 4460
Leesburg, VA 20177-8541

703-779-0574
FAX 703-779-2267
Home Page: www.stemcellresearchnews.com

Paul G Ochs, Owner

For information technology professionals.
Cost: $495.00
Founded in 1983

5374 Retail Price Week
Personal Technology Research
63 Fountain Street
#400
Framingham, MA 01702-6262

508-875-5858

Casey Dworkin, Publisher

Product-specific advertising and pricing data on microcomputer software, perhipherals and desktop retail commodities.
Frequency: Weekly
Circulation: 300

5375 Semiconductor Economics Report
Relayer Group
8232 E Buckskin Trail
Scottsdale, AZ 85255-2132
Howard Dicken, Publisher

Economics in the microelectronics industry.

5376 Small Business Systems
Charles Moore Associates
277 Alexander Street
Suite 410
Rochester, NY 14607

585-325-5242
FAX 585-325-5242

Charles Moore, Editor
Nancy Hannigan, Circulation Manager

Case histories which apply computers to solve small business problems.

5377 Softletter
Mercury Group
990 Washington Street
Suite 308 S
Dedham, MA 02026

781-518-8600
860-663-0552
FAX 301-816-8945
E-Mail: customer@softletter.com
Home Page: www.softletter.com

Merrill R Chapman, Publisher
Gail Wertheimer, Editor
Rick Chapman, Marketing Manager
Ruth Greenfield, Director

Trends in the microcomputer software industry.
Cost: $596.00
Frequency: Fortnightly
ISSN: 0882-3499
Founded in 1983
Printed in 2 colors

5378 Softrader
Amerasia Group
PO Box 53114
Indianapolis, IN 46253-0114
Ben Yanto, Publisher

Shareware public domain programs guide. Accepts advertising.
16 Pages
Frequency: BiWeekly

5379 Software Economics Letter
Computer Economics

5841 Edison Place
Carlsbad, CA 92008-6500

760-438-8100
800-326-8100
FAX 760-431-1126
Home Page: www.computereconomics.com

Bruno Bassi, Publisher
Don Trevillian, Editor

Devoted to management and cost control of software investments. Provides the corporate user and information systems communities with a concise analysis of software issues. Profiles the latest trends in software and software licensing and includes analysis of vendor policies and practices.
Cost: $395.00
Frequency: Daily

5380 Step-By-Step Electronic Design
Dynamic Graphics
6000 N Forest Park Drive
Peoria, IL 61614-3592

309-688-8851
FAX 309-688-6579
Home Page: www.dgusa.com

Tom Biederbeck, Editor
Kris Elwell, Publisher
Alan Meckler, CEO/President
Mike Demilt, Marketing
Marcy Slane, Manager

For electronic designers, illustrators and prepress professionals, how-to articles with step-by-step techniques.
Cost: $36.00
Circulation: 24000
Founded in 1995

5381 System Development
Applied Computer Research
PO Box 41730
Phoenix, AZ 85080

602-216-9100
800-234-2227
FAX 602-548-4800
E-Mail: tara@topitexecs.com
Home Page: www.acrhq.com

Philip Howard, Publisher
Allen Howard, CEO
Tara Saenz, Circulation Manager

Improvement ideas and techniques for software development.
Cost: $630.00
12 Pages
Frequency: Bi-annually
Founded in 1971
Mailing list available for rent: 20M names at $105 per M
Printed in one color on matte stock

5382 Systems Reengineering Economics Letter
Computer Economics
2082 Business Center Drive
Suite 240
Irvine, CA 92612

949-831-8700
FAX 949-442-7688
Home Page: www.computereconomics.com

Frank Scavo, President
Dan Husiak, VP

Economic look at the re-engineering explosion, delivering critical information on the methods, costs and risks of systems and business process re-engineering. Updates on the analyses, data, opinions, and case studies you need to make sound business decisions and capitalize on your re-engineering process.
Cost: $395.00
Frequency: Daily
Founded in 1978

5383 TechTarget
TechTarget
117 Kendrick St
Suite 800
Needham Heights, MA 02494-2728

781-657-1000
888-274-4111
FAX 781-657-1100
E-Mail: info@techtarget.com
Home Page: www.techtarget.com

Greg Strakosch, CEO
Don Hawk, President
Lisa Johnson, VP Marketing
Catherine Engelke, Director Public Relations

IBM iSeries focused media. The IBM e-Server iSeries (formerly the AS/400) is considered to be the world's most often used multi-user business computer. The installed base worldwide is huge and will get bigger, fueled by incresed Web development. The iSeries come with an integrated Web application server and all the tools needed to build internet, intranet, extranet, and e-commerce sites quickly and will figure promenently into IT strategy and implementation for years to come.
Frequency: Monthly
Founded in 1999

5384 Technology Advertising & Branding Report
Simba Information
60 Long Ridge Rd
Suite 300
Stamford, CT 06902-1841

203-325-8193
888-297-4622
FAX 203-325-8915
E-Mail: info@simbanet.com
Home Page: www.simbanet.com

Linda Kopp, Publisher

Offers news, statistics and analysis of advertising strategies in the technology industry. Provides competitive information on the advertising and marketing activities of computer hardware and software companies. Helps computer publishers target advertising sales by reporting the plans of computer advertisers. Shows computer advertisers how to get best buys.
Cost: $549.00
8 Pages

5385 Techweek
Metro States Media
1156 Aster Avenue
#B
Sunnyvale, CA 94086-6810

408-249-8300
FAX 408-249-0727
Home Page: www.techweek.com

John Leggett, Publisher

Provides articles for the local high technology industry programmers. Includes information about the internet, finances, job market, and new products for technology professionals.
Frequency: BiWeekly
Circulation: 100,000

5386 TidBITS
TidBITS
50 Hickory Road
Ithaca, NY 14850

E-Mail: ace@tidbits.com
Home Page: www.tidbits.com

Adam Engst, Publisher
Tonya Engst, Managing Editor
Jeff Carlson, Managing Editor

Online newsletter and web site, devoted to the person behind the most personal of personal computers, the Macintosh. TidBITS relates events and products to real life uses and concerns. New TidBITS issues go out every Monday night; breaking news and important updates appear on the web site more frequently.
Frequency: Weekly
Circulation: 150000
Founded in 1990

5387 Wireless LAN
Information Gatekeepers
1340 Soldiers Field Rd
Suite 3
Brighton, MA 02135-1000

617-782-5033
800-323-1088
FAX 617-782-5735
E-Mail: info@igigroup.com
Home Page: www.igigroup.com

Paul Polishuk, CEO
Cathey Mallen, Production Manager
Brian Mark, Newsletter Managing Editor
Bev Wilson, Managing Editor
Yesim Taskor, Controller

LAN technological trends and market opportunities.
Cost: $695.00
Frequency: Monthly
Founded in 1977

5388 Work Process Improvement Today
Recognition Technologies Users Association
75 Federal Street
Suite 901
Boston, MA 02110-1413

617-426-1167
800-99 -2974
FAX 617-521-8675
E-Mail: kguarino@tawpi.org
Home Page: www.tawpi.org

Dan Bllida, Editor
Debra Sanderson, Publisher
Frank Moran, Owner

Accepts advertising.
Cost: $60.00
Circulation: 10000

5389 iACTion Newsletter
American Council for Technology
3040 Williams Dr
Suite 610
Fairfax, VA 22031-4618

703-208-4800
FAX 703-208-4805
E-Mail: act-iac@actgov.org
Home Page: www.actgov.org

Ken Allen, Executive Director
Frequency: Monthly

Magazines & Journals

5390 2600 Magazine
PO Box 752
Middle Island, NY 11953

631-751-2600
FAX 631-474-2677
E-Mail: webmaster@2600.com
Home Page: www.2600.com/.

Emanuel Golstein, Editor

Written for computer hackers.
Cost: $20.00
Frequency: Quarterly
Founded in 1984

5391 ACM QUEUE
1515 Broadway
17th Floor
New York, NY 10036-5701

212-869-7440
800-342-6626
FAX 212-302-5826
E-Mail: acmhelp@acm.org
Home Page: www.acm.org

Mark Mandelbaum, Director Publication
John R White, Associate Director
Robert Okajima, Associate Director
Alain Chesnais, Founder
Liliana Cintron, Administrative Assistant

Published by the Association for Computing Machinery.
Circulation: 25000
Founded in 1947

5392 AFSM International Professional Journal and High-Technology Service Mgmt.
AFSM International
11031 Via Frontera
Suite A
San Diego, CA 92127-1709

858-673-3055
800-333-9786
FAX 239-275-0794
E-Mail: info@afsmi.org
Home Page: www.afsmi.org

John Shoenewald, Executive Director
Jb Wood, President/Ceo

For trade association members.
Cost: $150.00
86 Pages
Frequency: Monthly
Circulation: 20000
Founded in 1975
Printed in 4 colors on glossy stock

5393 AI Expert
Miller Freeman Publications
2655 Seely Avenue
San Jose, CA 95134

408-943-1234
FAX 408-943-0513

Regina Star Ridley, Editor

Practical applications of artificial intelligence in any field.
Cost: $37.00
42 Pages
Frequency: Monthly
Founded in 1986

5394 AI Magazine
American Association for Artificial Intelligence
445 Burgess Drive
Menlo Park, CA 94025-3442

650-328-3123
FAX 650-321-4457
Home Page: www.aimagazine.org

David Leake, Editor
David M Hamilton, Managing Editor
Michael Wellman, Book Review Editor
Carol McKenna Hamilton, Executive Director, AAAI
Alanna Spencer, Director

Quarterly issued magazine, available through AAAI membership. AI Magazine features articles regarding research in the field of artificial intelligence.
128 Pages
Frequency: Quarterly
Circulation: 7000
ISSN: 0738-4602
Founded in 1980
Printed in on matte stock

5395 ASR News

Voice Information Associates
P.O.Box 2861
Acton, MA 01720-6861

978-266-1966
FAX 978-263-3461
Home Page: www.asrnews.com

Walt Tetschner, Publisher and Editor

Developments in products, marketing, technology, and investments in the automatic speech recognition industry.
Cost: $345.00
Frequency: Monthly
Founded in 1990

5396 Advanced Imaging

Cygnus Publishing
3 Huntington Quadrangle
Suite 301N
Melville, NY 11747-3601

631-845-2700
800-308-6397
FAX 631-845-2736
E-Mail: info@advancedimaging.com
Home Page: www.advancedimagingmag.com

Dave Brambert, Publisher
Larry Adams, Editor-in-Chief
Paul Mackler, CEO

The only international magazine specifically designed to meet the needs of professionals using all forms of electronic imaging technologies. Offering monthly coverage of imaging application solutions for medical/diagnostic, industrial machine vision, government/security, and scientific imaging markets.
Frequency: Monthly
Circulation: 44009
Founded in 1966

5397 Aixpert

IBM Corporation
1133 Westchester Avenue
White Plains
New York, NY 10604-3406

914-423-3000
FAX 866-722-9226
Home Page: www.ibm.com

George Noren, Editor-in-Chief

Provides timely up-to-date technical material to help developers plot, develop, and enhance applications for IBM AIX products.
Frequency: Quarterly
Circulation: 10,000

5398 Aldus Magazine

Aldus Corporation
801 N 34th Street
Seattle, WA 98103-8882
Carla Noble, Publisher
Harry Edwards, Editor

Supports and educates graphics professionals using ALDUS software. Covers tips, tricks and how-to pointers for maximizing PageMaker, Freehand, PhotoStyler and Persuasion. Also covers trends in electronic publishing.
Cost: $ 24.00
68 Pages
Frequency: 8 per year
Circulation: 220,000
Founded in 1989

5399 Algorithmica

Springer Verlag
233 Spring St
New York, NY 10013-1578

212-460-1500
FAX 212-460-1575

E-Mail: service@springer-ny.com
Home Page: www.springer-ny.com

William Curtis, President
D T Lee, Managing Editor
Rubin Wang, Managing Editor

Provides an in-depth look into distributed computing, parellel processing, automated design, and software tools.
Cost: $1008.00
Frequency: Quarterly
Circulation: 1000
Founded in 1855

5400 Analysis Solutions

ConnectPress
2530 Camino Entrada
Santa Fe, NM 87505-4807

505-474-5000
FAX 505-474-5001
Home Page: www.analysismag.com

Carolyn Mascarenas, Publisher

Design analysis and optimization for ANSYS technology users. Covers engineering simulation, acousitc analysis, model meshing, new products and case studies.
Cost: $90.00
Frequency: Quarterly
Circulation: 27,575

5401 Application Development Trends

600 Worcester Road
Suite 301
Framingham, MA 01702

508-875-6644
FAX 508-875-6622
Home Page: www.adtmag.com

Sheryl Katz, Publisher
Michael Alexander, Editorial-in-Chief
Tracy S. Cook, Marketing Director
Christina Schaller, Managing Editor

The number one information source on today's key application development options delivering a high powered, management-oriented editorial that covers the application development industry in greater depth and breadth than any other publication.
Frequency: Monthly
Circulation: 45000
Founded in 1998

5402 Applied Computing Technologies

9041 Executive Park Dr
Suite 222
Knoxville, TN 37923-4603

865-675-0508
FAX 865-694-9096

Peyman Dehkordi, Owner

5403 Applied Optics

Optical Society of America
2010 Massachusetts Ave Nw
Washington, DC 20036-1023

202-223-8130
FAX 202-223-1096
E-Mail: info@osa.org
Home Page: www.osa.org

Elizabeth Rogan, Executive Director

5404 Automatic ID News

Advanstar Communications
641 Lexington Ave
8th Floor
New York, NY 10022-4503

212-951-6600
FAX 212-951-6793
E-Mail: info@advanstar.com
Home Page: www.advanstar.com

Joseph Loggia, CEO

Information for decision-makers in all industries seeking definitive information about automatic data collection technology. The technology includes optical, magnetic, radio frequency and voice recognition systems and peripherals.
Frequency: Monthly
ISSN: 0890-9768

5405 BAM Publications

BAM Publications
3470 Buskirk Avenue
Pleasant Hill, CA 94523-4340

925-932-5900

Dennis Erokan, Editor

Provides regionally focused product and channel news to computer products and services.
Cost: $120.00
60 Pages
Frequency: Monthly
Founded in 1988

5406 Better Channel

ABCD: The Microcomputer Industry Association
450 E 22nd Street
Suite 230
Lombard, IL 60148-6158

630-268-1818
FAX 630-268-1384

John Venator, Executive VP

A professional magazine that is exclusively dedicated to representing and serving all segments of the microcomputer industry. Accepts advertising.
Cost: $150.00
32 Pages
Frequency: Monthly

5407 CADALYST

Advanstar Communications
641 Lexington Ave
8th Floor
New York, NY 10022-4503

212-951-6600
FAX 212-951-6793
E-Mail: info@advanstar.com
Home Page: www.advanstar.com

Joseph Loggia, CEO

Expert coverage of the latest developments in auto CAD systems, their products and the various CAD applications.
Cost: $4.00
Frequency: Monthly
Circulation: 70000

5408 CALICO Journal

Texas State University
214 Centennial Hall
San Marcos, TX 78666

512-245-1417
FAX 512-245-9089
E-Mail: info@calico.org
Home Page: www.calico.org

Robert Fischer, Editor

Devoted to the dissemination of information concerning the application of technology to language teaching and language learning. The CALICO Journal is fully refereed and publishes articles, research studies, reports, software reviews, and professional news and announcements.
Cost: $85.00
Frequency: 3x/Year
Circulation: 800
ISSN: 0742-7778

5409 CASE Strategies

Cutter Information Corporation

37 Broadway
Suite 1
Arlington, MA 02474-5500

781-648-1950
FAX 781-648-1950
Home Page: www.cutter.com

Verna Allee, Senior Consultant

Implementation strategies, reviews and case studies in areas of computer-aided systems engineering.
Cost: $295.00

5410 CBT Solutions
SB Communications
183 Whiting Street
#15
Hingham, MA 02043-3845

781-749-2151
E-Mail: cbstol@ziplink.net
Home Page: www.cbtsolutions.com

Steve Blumberg, Publisher

Featured editorials include advanced technology in the past and future, interactive web programs, new methods to access and control information, and personal profiles.
Frequency: Bi-Monthly
Circulation: 15,000

5411 CD-ROM Enduser
Disc Company
6609 Rosecroft Pl
Falls Church, VA 22043-1828
Linda Helgerson, Editor

For people who use CD-ROM applications.
Cost: $3.00
Frequency: Monthly
Founded in 1989

5412 CD-ROM Librarian
Mecklermedia Corporation
20 Ketchum Street
Westport, CT 06880-5808

203-226-6967
FAX 203-454-5840

Alan Meckler, Editor

A periodical intended for the library professional.
Cost: $80.00
Frequency: Monthly
Founded in 1986

5413 CHANCE: New Directions for Statistics and Computing
Springer Verlag
233 Spring St
New York, NY 10013-1578

212-460-1500
FAX 212-460-1575
E-Mail: service@springer-ny.com
Home Page: www.springer-ny.com

William Curtis, President
John E Rolph, Editor
Derk Haank, CEO
Peter Hendriks, President of Marketing
Rubin Wang, Managing Editor

Covers both statistics and computing. Designed for everyone who has an interest in the analysis of data. The informal style highlights and encourages sound statistical practice.
Cost: $7.00
Frequency: Monthly
Circulation: 4500
Founded in 1842

5414 CRN
UBM LLC

550 Cochituate Road
First Floor-West Wing, Suite 5
Framingham, MA 01701

508-416-1100
E-Mail: kelley.damore@ec.ubm.com
Home Page: www.crn.com

Kelley Damore, VP/Editorial Director
Steven Burke, Editor
Jane O'Brien, Managing Editor

Delivers strategic information and useful business tools that Solution Providers and other Channel professionals
Cost: $89.00
Frequency: BiWeekly
Circulation: 95,072

5415 Cadence
Miller Freeman Publications
2655 Seely Avenue
San Jose, CA 95134

408-468-8603
FAX 408-468-1902
E-Mail: info@gartner.com
Home Page: www.gartner.com

Johanna Kleppe, Publisher
Kathleen Maher, Managing Editor
Michael Fister, CEO
Tom McCall, Senior Director Public Relations
Michael Bingle, Director

For users of Autocad - a construction/architecture program.
Cost: $6.00
Circulation: 72664

5416 Catalyst
Western Center for Microcomputers
1259 El Camino Real
#275
Menlo Park, CA 94025

650-855-8064
Home Page:
www.home.earthlink.net/~thecatalyst/index.html

Sue Swezey, Editor
Robert Scott, Chief Information Officer

Reporting on both the increasing sophistication of technology and the increasing complexity special education. We've covered the profound changes in the lives of children and adults with special needs as they have benefited from computer use, as well as on the obstacles confronting them and those who serve them.
Cost: $18.00
Frequency: Quarterly

5417 Christian Computing
PO Box 319
Belton, MO 64012-0319

800-456-1868
FAX 800-456-1868
E-Mail: steve@ccmag.com
Home Page: www.ccmag.com

Steve Hewitt, Editor-in-Chief
Frequency: Monthly
Founded in 1989

5418 CircuiTree
Business News Publishing Company
1050 IL Route 83
Suite 200
Bensenville, IL 60106-1096

630-377-5909
Home Page: circuitree.com

Katie Rotella, Manager
Tom Esposito, Group Publisher
Darryl Seland, Associate Publisher/

Karl Dietz, Technical Editor
Cost: $64.00
Frequency: Monthly
Circulation: 12000
Founded in 1926

5419 Civic.com
FCW Government Technology Group
3141 Fairview Park Drive
Suite 777
Falls Church, VA 22042-4507

FAX 703-876-5126
Home Page: www.fcw.com

Edith Holmes, President
Steve Vito, Publisher
Agnes Vanek, Circulation Director
Margo Dunn, Production Manager
Anne Armstrong, Editor

A print magazine and electronic companion designed for volume IT buyers, chief information officers and IT planners in state and local government.

5420 CleanRooms Magazine
PennWell Publishing Company
98 Spit Brook Rd
Suite 100
Nashua, NH 03062-5737

603-891-0123
FAX 603-891-9294
E-Mail: johnh@pennwell.com
Home Page: www.pennwell.com

Christine Shaw, VP
James Enos, Publisher
Angela Godwin, Managing Editor
Steve Smith, News Editor
Bob Johnson, National Sales Manager

Serves the contamination control and ultrapure materials and process industries. Written for readers in the microelectronics, pharmaceutical, biotech, health care, food processing and other user industries. Provides technology and business news and new product listings.
Cost: $97.00
Frequency: Monthly
Circulation: 35031
Founded in 1987

5421 Com-SAC, Computer Security, Auditing & Controls
Management Advisory Services & Publications
PO Box 81151
Wellesley Hills, MA 02481-0001

781-235-2895
FAX 781-235-5446
E-Mail: info@masp.com
Home Page: www.masp.com

A quarterly journal of in-depth tutorials in computer security, auditing and the most comprehensive digest service of all publications in computer security and controls.
Cost: $98.00
Frequency: Quarterly
Founded in 1973

5422 Common Knowledge
230 W Monroe St
Suite 220
Chicago, IL 60606-4802

312-416-3656
800-777-6734
FAX 312-201-9588
E-Mail: info@knowledgenetworks.com
Home Page: www.knowledgenetworks.com

Kris Neeley, Publisher

Features interviews with industry experts, case studies, tutorials, the latest industry news and overviews of management concerns.
Frequency: Quarterly
Circulation: 15,000

5423 Communications of the ACM
Association for Computing Machinery
2 Penn Plz
Suite 701
New York, NY 10121-0799

212-868-5716
800-342-6626
FAX 212-944-1318
E-Mail: acmhelp@acm.org
Home Page: www.acm.org

Jerry Ashton, President
John R White, CEO
Edward Grossman, Publisher
Diane Crawford, Executive Editor
Brian Hebert, Marketing/Communications Manager

Technical magazine covering developments in computer science for professional scientific and business dp, systems programming, database techniques and more.
Cost: $17.00
Frequency: Monthly
Circulation: 82,867
Founded in 1947

5424 CompactPCI Systems
CompactPCI Systems
13253 La Montana
Dr 207
Fountain Hills, AZ 85268-5328

480-967-5581
FAX 480-837-6466
Home Page: www.compactpci-systems.com

Mike Hopper, Publisher
Joe Pavlat, Editor

Features application success stories that demonstrate how and where CompactPCI technology has provided solutions.
Circulation: 20000

5425 Component Development Strategies
Cutter Information Corporation
37 Broadway
Suite 1
Arlington, MA 02474-5500

781-648-1950
800-964-5118
FAX 781-648-1950
E-Mail: press@cutter.com
Home Page: www.cutter.com

Karen Coburn, President and CEO
Tom Welsh, Senior Consultant
Hillel Glazer, Senior Consultant
Ron Blitstein, Director

Editorial content covers the latest information and technology on object-oriented programming, databases, and analysis and design.
Cost: $2400.00
Frequency: Monthly
Founded in 1991

5426 CompuServe Magazine
5000 Arlington Centre Blvd
Columbus, OH 43220-5439

614-326-1002
800-848-8199
Home Page:
webcenters.netscape.compuserve.com/menu/

Offers updated and statistical information for computer professionals.

5427 Computer
IEEE Computer Society
10662 Los Vaqueros Circle
P. O. Box 3014
Los Alamitos, CA 90720-1314

714-821-8380
800-272-6657
FAX 714-821-4010

E-Mail: volunteer.services@computer.org
Home Page: www.computer.org/

Matt Loeb, Publisher
Doris L. Carver, Editor in Chief
Bill Schilit, Associate Editor
Judi Prow, Managing Editor
Jim Sanders, Senior Editor

Information on late breaking news, business trends, and a variety of technology specific departments.
Cost: $63.00
Frequency: Monthly
Circulation: 84340
Founded in 1988

5428 Computer Business Review
ComputerWire
245 5th Avenue
4th Floor
New York, NY 10016

212-770-0409
FAX 212-686-2626
E-Mail: info@computerwire.com
Home Page: www.computerwire.com/cbr

Jake Sharp, Publisher
Micheal Danzon, CEO
Jason Stamper, Editor

Company profiles, computer market coverage and technology trends and news for investors and professionals in the computer, communications and microelectronics industries.
Cost: $195.00
Frequency: Monthly
Circulation: 20450
Founded in 1984

5429 Computer Buyer's Guide & Handbook
Bedford Communications
1410 Broadway
21st Floor
New York, NY 10018-5008

212-807-8220
FAX 212-807-1098
Home Page: www.techworthy.com

Ed Brown, Owner
A guide to buying peripherals and software, as well as general advice and news on the world of computing.
Cost: $36.00
128 Pages
Frequency: Monthly
Circulation: 50000
Founded in 1981

5430 Computer Design
PennWell Publishing Company
10 Tara Boulevard
5th Floor
Nashua, NH 03062-2800

603-891-0123
FAX 603-891-0514
Home Page: www.computer-design.com

John Carroll, Group Publisher

Each issue contains in-depth articles and timely features written by experienced senior editors who concentrate on the critical technologies, components and tools needed to design microprocessor and computer based OEM products and systems.
Frequency: Monthly
Circulation: 105,028

5431 Computer Graphics Review
Primedia
Po Box 12901
Shawnee Mission, KS 66282-2901

913-341-1300
FAX 913-514-6895

E-Mail: inquiries@primediabusiness.com *uirie*
Home Page: www.penton.com

Eric Jacobson, Senior VP

To identify and interpret significant technological and business developments.
Cost: $48.00
120 Pages
Frequency: Monthly
Founded in 1986

5432 Computer Graphics World
PennWell Publishing Company
98 Spit Brook Rd
Nashua, NH 03062-5737

603-891-0123
800-225-0556
FAX 603-891-9294
E-Mail: phil@pennwell.com
Home Page: www.pennwell.com

Christine Shaw, VP
Jenny Donelan, Managing Editor

Covers specific applications of computer graphics, written by users and vendors of equipment and services to the industry. The magazine of 3D computer graphics for engineering and animation professionals.
Frequency: Monthly
Founded in 1978
Printed in 4 colors on glossy stock

5433 Computer Industry Almanac
304 W White Oak
Arlington Heights, IL 60005

847-758-3687
FAX 847-758-3686
E-Mail: ej@c-i-a.com
Home Page: www.c-i-a.com

Egil Juliussen, President

Annual reference book for and about the computer industry. The Almanac has ranking and awards of products, people and companies. Includes salary information, market forecasts, technology trends and directories of companies, publications, market research firms, associations and trade shows.
Cost: $45.00
Frequency: Annual

5434 Computer Journal
Oxford University Press
2001 Evans Rd
Cary, NC 27513-2010

919-677-0977
800-852-7323
FAX 919-677-2673
Home Page:
www3.oup.co.uk/computer_journal/

F Leroy, Editorial Assistant:
F Murtagh, Editor-in-Chief
Julie Gribben, Special Sales Manager

Provides information on web sites, personal computers, hardware, software and online uses.
Cost: $920.00
Circulation: 18000

5435 Computer Language
600 Harrison Street
6th Floor
San Francisco, CA 94107

415-947-6000
FAX 415-941-6055

Computer news and information.

5436 Computer Link Magazine
Millennium Publishing

100 Mobile Dr
Suite 1
Rochester, NY 14616-2145

585-797-4399
E-Mail: info@computerlinkmag.com
Home Page: www.techny.com

Justin Ziemniak, Editor-in-Chief

Website reviews, employment opportunities, and women's involvement in the technology age. Includes reports on the Western New York computer market.
Cost: $20.00
Frequency: Monthly
Circulation: 20000

5437 Computer Manager

Story Communications
116 N Camp Street
Seguin, TX 78155-5600

830-303-3328
FAX 830-372-3011
E-Mail: story@storycomm.com
Home Page: www.compumgr.com

James M Story, Publisher
K Wiemann, Circulation Manager

Information to help corporate end users purchase computers and communications equipment easily.
Frequency: Quarterly
Circulation: 50000

5438 Computer Price Guide

Computer Merchants
22 Saw Mill River Road
Hawthorne, NY 10532-1533

914-347-0290
FAX 914-347-0292

Svend Hartmann, Publisher

Market trends and developments, prices on used IBM computer equipment.
Cost: $70.00
Frequency: Quarterly
Circulation: 3500

5439 Computer Security Journal

Computer Security Institute
600 Harrison Street
San Francisco, CA 94107

415-947-6320
866-271-8529
FAX 415-947-6023
Home Page: www.gocsi.com

Russell Kay, Publisher
Chris Keating, Director
Robert Richardson, Editorial Director
Nancy Baer, Marketing Manager

Keeps you informed with comprehensive, practical articles, case studies, reviews and commentaries written by knowledgeable computer security professionals.
Cost: $25.00
Frequency: Quarterly
Circulation: 3000
Founded in 1974

5440 Computer Security, Auditing and Controls (COM-SAC)

Management Advisory Services & Publications
PO Box 81151
Wellesley Hills, MA 02481-0001

781-235-2895
FAX 781-235-5446
E-Mail: info@masp.com
Home Page: www.masp.com

Indepth tutorials in computer security and auditing and the most comprehensive digest service of all publications in computer security, auditing and internal controls. Security hard-

ware-software news.
Cost: $98.00
Frequency: Quarterly
ISSN: 0738-4262
Founded in 1973
Printed in on glossy stock

5441 Computer Shopper

Segal Company
1 Battery Park Plz
New York, NY 10004-1487

212-858-1000
FAX 212-251-5490
E-Mail: info@segalco.com

Glenn E Siegel

A buyer's guide of sorts, listing the latest information and equipment for the world of computers.

5442 Computer Survival Journal

Enterprise Publishing
Po Box 328
Blair, NE 68008-0328

402-426-2121
FAX 402-426-2227
E-Mail: mrhoades@enterprisepub.com
Home Page: www.enterprisepub.com

Mark Rhoades, President
Dave Smith, Production Manager
Tracy Prettyman, Business Manager

Reviews and features on all areas of computer, office and home products (hardware and software). Also includes information on cellular phones, TV's and appliances, home electronics and television.
Cost: $250.00
50 Pages

5443 Computer Technology Review

West World Productions
420 N Camden Dr
Beverly Hills, CA 90210-4507

310-276-9500
888-889-3130
FAX 310-276-9874
E-Mail: sinan@kanatsiz.com
Home Page: www.wwpi.com

Yuri R Spiro, Publisher

Computer Technology Review is an all-inclusive tabloid that covers the full spectrum of new and emerging technologies vital to systems integrators, high-end VARS, and OEM.
Cost: $10.00
60 Pages
Frequency: Monthly
Circulation: 64044
ISSN: 0278-9647
Founded in 1981
Printed in 4 colors on matte stock

5444 Computer User Magazine

Key Professional Media
220 S 6th St
Suite 500
Minneapolis, MN 55402-4501

612-339-7571
800-788-0204
FAX 612-333-5806
E-Mail: info@computeruser.com
Home Page: www.computeruser.com

Nat Opperman, President
Elizabeth Milllard, Associate Publisher

For small to medium-size business professionals and computer owners, ComputerUser is published in 13 markets nationally.
Cost: $14.00
60 Pages
Frequency: Monthly
Circulation: 64000
Founded in 1981
Printed in 4 colors on newsprint stock

5445 Computer World/Focus

PO Box 9171
Framingham, MA 01701-9171
Joe Maglitta, Feature Editor

A comprehensive magazine offering information on the computer industry.

5446 Computer-Aided Engineering

Penton Media
1300 E 9th St
Cleveland, OH 44114-1503

216-696-7000
FAX 216-696-6662
E-Mail: caenetmaster@penton.com
Home Page: www.penton.com

Jane Cooper, Marketing

Applications, news, trends and products for CAD/CAM technology as applied in manufacturing, electronics, architectural and construction industries.
Cost: $50.00
Frequency: Monthly
Circulation: 56,062

5447 Computers User

220 S 6th Street
Suite 500
Minneapolis, MN 55042

612-339-7571
E-Mail: info@computeruser.com
Home Page: www.computeruser.com

David Needle, Editor
Matt Kusilek, Publisher

End user computer magazine for business and professional users of PC and Macintosh computers, software and peripherals.
Cost: $24.99
Frequency: Monthly

5448 Computers and Biomedical Research

Academic Press
1901 E South Campus Drive
Suite 1195
Salt Lake City, UT 84112-9359

801-581-6461
FAX 801-585-5414
Home Page: www.aoce.utah.edu

T Allan Pryor, Editor
Liz McCoy, Executive Assistant
Brynn Roundy, Executive Secretary

Information on application of computer technology in biomedical research for medical professionals. Evaluates and discusses various techniques. Accompanied by photographs, charts, graphs and figures.
Cost: $325.00
Frequency: 6 per year
Circulation: 1,425

5449 Computers in the Schools

Taylor & Francis Group LLC
325 Chestnut St
Suite 800
Philadelphia, PA 19106-2614

215-625-8900
800-354-1420
FAX 215-625-2940
E-Mail: haworthorders@taylorandfrancis.com
Home Page: www.taylorandfrancis.com

Kevin Bradley, President

Articles emphasize the practical aspect of any application but also tie theory to practice, relate present accomplishments to past efforts and future trends, identify conclusions and their implications and discuss the theoretical and philosophical basis for the application.
Frequency: Quarterly

5450 Computertalk

Computertalk Associates

425

492 Norristown Road
Suite 160
Blue Bell, PA 19422

610-825-7686
FAX 610-825-7641
E-Mail: wal@computertalk.com
Home Page: www.computertalk.com

William A Lockwood Jr, President
Maggie L Lockwood, Director of Publications

Profiles on various sytems available for pharmacists purchasing and using computers.
Cost: $50.00
Frequency: Monthly
Circulation: 32,000
Founded in 1980
Printed in 4 colors on glossy stock

5451 Computerworld
CW Publishing
One Speen Street
PO Box 9171
Framingham, MA 01701-4653

508-879-0700
800-343-6474
FAX 508-626-2705
E-Mail: editor@computerworld.com
Home Page: www.computerworld.com

Mitch Betts, Executive Editor
Don Tennant, VP/Editor in Chief
Matt Sweeney, CEO

For computer professionals who evaluate and implement information systems.
Cost: $99.99
170 Pages
Circulation: 170000
Founded in 1967

5452 Computing Surveys
Association for Computing Machinery
One Astor Place
1515 Broadway
New York, NY 10036-5701

212-869-7440
800-342-6626
FAX 212-302-5826
E-Mail: acmhelp@acm.org
Home Page: www.acm.org

Mark Mandelbaum, Director Publication
John R. White, CEO
Gul Agha, Editor in Chief
Robert Okajima, Associate Director
Alain Chesnais, Founder

Carefully planned and presented introductions to complex issues, supported by exhaustive and comprehensive notations on the relevant literature.
Cost: $170.00
Frequency: Quarterly
Founded in 1947

5453 Computing in Science & Engineering
American Institute of Physics
2 Huntington Quad
Melville, NY 11747-4502

516-576-2200
FAX 516-349-7669
Home Page: www.aip.org

Darlene Walters, Senior VP
Angela Burgess, Publisher
Georgann Carter, Marketing Manager

Computer science's interdisciplinary juncture with physics, astronomy and engineering.
Cost: $55.00

5454 Control Solutions
PennWell Publishing Company
1421 S Sheridan Rd
Tulsa, OK 74112-6619

918-831-9421
800-331-4463

FAX 918-831-9476
Home Page: www.pennwell.com

Robert Biolchini, President
Ron Kuhfeld, Editor-in-Chief

Represents control technology for engineers and engineering manage4ment.

5455 Cryptosystems Journal
Cryptosystems Journal
485 Middle Holland Road
Holland, PA 18966-2870
Tony Patti, Publisher/Editor

Unique international journal devoted to implementation of cryptographic systems on IBM-PC's and compatibles.

5456 Cyber Defense Magazine
PO Box 71748
Phoenix, AZ 85050

480-990-0407
866-487-6652
FAX 480-990-7306
Home Page: www.cyberdefensemag.com

John Riccio, Publisher
Curt Blakeney, Editor

Computer/Network security magazine.
Cost: $31.00
64 Pages
Frequency: 12 issues
Circulation: 64,000
Founded in 2003
Printed in 4 colors on glossy stock

5457 DBMS-Database Management Systems
Miller Freeman Publications
2655 Seely Avenue
San Jose, CA 95134

408-943-1234
FAX 408-943-0513

Phillip Chapnick, Publisher
David Kohman, Editor

Covers the database and database applications marketplace.
Circulation: 69,029

5458 DG Review
Data Base Publications
9390 Research Blvd
Suite 300
Austin, TX 78759-7374

512-418-9590
FAX 512-418-8165
Home Page: www.bancvue.com

Gabe Krajicek, CEO
Gloria Trent, Editor

For Data General and compatible computer users.
Cost: $48.00
64 Pages
Frequency: Monthly
Founded in 1981

5459 DM Review
Powell Publishing Company
16655 W Bluemound Rd
Suite 201
Brookfield, WI 53005-5935

262-780-0202
FAX 414-771-8058
Home Page: www.b-eye-network.com

Ron Powell, Owner
Val Latzke, Editor
Jean Schauer, Editor in Chief
Mary Jo Nott, Executive Editor

Provides a wealth of knowledge through columns by top industry experts, data warehouse success stories, timely and informative articles,

third-party product reviews, and executive interviews.
Frequency: Monthly
Circulation: 75012
Founded in 1994

5460 DSP Engineering
13253 La Montana Dr
Suite 207
Fountains Hills, AZ 85268

480-967-5581
FAX 480-837-6466
Home Page: wwwdspengineering.com

Rosemary Kristoff, VP
Phyllis Thompson, Circulation Manager
Patrick Hopper, VP Marketing
Mike Hopper, Publisher

5461 Data Bus
AM Publications
PO Box 20044
Saint Petersburg, FL 33742

727-577-5500
FAX 727-576-0622
E-Mail: ampubs@aol.com

Al Martino, Publisher/Editor

Contains new product reviews, trade literature and personnel announcements.
Frequency: Monthly
Circulation: 24000

5462 Data Communications
McGraw Hill
PO Box 182604
Columbus, OH 43272

614-866-5769
FAX 614-759-3759
E-Mail: customer.service@mcgraw-hill.com
Home Page: www.mcgraw-hill.com

Kevin Harold, Publisher
Steve Weiss, Production Manager

Networking magazine edited for the technical managers responsible for the implementation and integration of computer information networks.
Cost: $5.00
Circulation: 112,941

5463 Data Sources
Ziff Davis Publishing Company
28 E 28th St
New York, NY 10016-7940

212-503-5772
E-Mail: info@ziffdavis.com
Home Page: www.ziffdavis.com

Steve Weitzner, CEO
Leo Greisman, General Counsel
Stephen Hicks, General Counsel
Steve Horowitz, COO
Cost: $240.00
Frequency: Monthly
Circulation: 700000
Founded in 1981

5464 Data Storage
PennWell Publishing Company
PO 91372
Calabasas, CA 91372

818-348-1240
FAX 818-348-1742
Home Page: www.datastorage.com

Becky Adams, Publisher
David Simpson, Editor
Kevin Komiega, Senior Editor

Features news and information on all types of systems such as magnetic disk drives, media and magnetic tape drives, CD-ROM, optical,

magneto-optical, holographic and nonvolatile semiconductor storage devices.
Frequency: Monthly
Circulation: 15,140

5465 Data to Knowledge
Business Rule Solutions
2476 Bolsover Street
#488
Houston, TX 77005-2518

713-681-1651
FAX 604-681-7223
E-Mail: datatoknow@brsolutions.com
Home Page: www.brcommunity.com

Gladys S W Lam, Publisher
Ronald G Ross, Executive Editor
Keri Anderson Healy, Editor
Marie Yang, Director, Marketing & Business Dev
John Hall, Technology Review Editor

Provides analysis, news and tutorials for data management professionals, data administrators, DBA's and other involved in the planning, design and construction of large-scale information systems.
Circulation: 4603
Founded in 1973

5466 Database Searcher
Mecklermedia Corporation
11 Ferry Lane W
Westport, CT 06880-5808
Alan Meckler, Editor

Covers online and micro-computer techniques.
Cost: $95.00
Frequency: Monthly
Founded in 1985

5467 Datamation
Reed Business Information
2000 Clearwater Dr
Oak Brook, IL 60523-8809

630-574-0825
FAX 630-288-8781
Home Page: www.reedbusiness.com

Jeff Greisch, President
William Semich, Editor-in-Chief

The magazine that interprets products, events and technologies for computer professionals in large companies worldwide.
Cost: $4.00
Circulation: 189,101

5468 Design Automation
Miller Freeman Publications
2655 Seely Avenue
San Jose, CA 95134

408-943-1234
FAX 408-943-0513

Lindsey Vereen, Editor

Targeted to computer design engineers.
Frequency: Monthly

5469 Designfax
NP Communications, LLC
2500 Tamiami Trail N
Nokomis, FL 34275

941-966-9521
FAX 941-966-2590
E-Mail: mfoley@nelsonpub.com
Home Page: www.designfax.net

Mike Foley, Editor
John W Holmes, National Sales Manager

eMagazine whose primary content focuses on the latest exciting applications and products for Electrical/Electronic, Mechanical, Motion Control, Fluid Power, and Materials engineering, including articles on powerful software pro-

grams that serve as a primary engineering tool.
Cost: $54.00
Frequency: Weekly
Circulation: 128,000
Founded in 1979
Printed in 4 colors on glossy stock

5470 Desktop Engineering
Helmers Publishing
174 Concord Street
PO Box 874
Peterborough, NH 03458

603-924-9631
FAX 603-924-4004
E-Mail: jgooch@deskeng.com
Home Page: www.deskeng.com

Brian Vaillancourt, Publisher
Anthony J Lockwood, Editorial Director
Bill Fahy, Circulation Director
Carol Laughner, Marketing Director

Magazine providing design solutions from concept throughout manufacture, focuses on hardware, software, and technologies for hands-on design engineers and engineering management in the manufacturing solutions throughout extensive product reviews, comparisons, technology updates, real-world application stories, news, product resource guides, and new product reports.
60 Pages
Frequency: Monthly
Circulation: 63000
ISSN: 1085-0422
Founded in 1995
Printed in 4 colors on glossy stock

5471 Distributed Computing Monitor
Patricia Seybold Group
Po Box 240565
Boston, MA 02129

617-742-5200
800-826-2424
FAX 617-742-1028
E-Mail: feedback@psgroup.com
Home Page: www.psgroup.com

Patricia Seybold, Founder/CEO

The editors give advanced technologists and strategic technology architects the technical details and business perspective necessary to sell upper management on how, why and when to implement the leading edge.
Frequency: Monthly
Founded in 1978

5472 Distributing Computing
DC Corporation
236 W 26th Street
#7SW
New York, NY 10001-6736

212-446-9330
Home Page: www.distributedcomputing.com

Hal Avery, Publisher

Editorial includes case studies of applications, technical, management, organizational, and cultural techniques.
Frequency: Monthly
Circulation: 40000

5473 E-doc
Association for Information and Image Management
1100 Wayne Avenue
Suite 1100
Silver Spring, MD 20910-5603

301-587-8202
800-477-2446
FAX 301-587-2711

E-Mail: aiim@aiim.org
Home Page: www.aiim.org

Jan Andersson, Chair
Robert Zagami, Vice Chair
Peggy Winton, Marketing Director

Association magazine on electronic document management.
Circulation: 40000
Founded in 1943

5474 EServer Magazine
IBM Corporation
220 S 6th Street
Suite 500
Minneapolis, MN 55402

612-339-7571
FAX 612-336-9220
Home Page: www.eservercomputing.com

Doug Rock, Editor/Publisher
Mari Adamson-Bray, Marketing Manager
Kelly McManus, Production Manager

New products and services, technological information, and related topics that benefit the decision makers in the optimization and management of these systems are included.
80 Pages
Frequency: Monthly
Circulation: 45000
ISSN: 1074-7082
Founded in 1993
Printed in 4 colors on glossy stock

5475 Educational Technology
Educational Technology Publications
700 Palisade Avenue
PO Box 1564
Englewood Cliffs, NJ 07632-564

201-871-4007
800-952-2665
FAX 201-871-4009
E-Mail: edtecpubs@aol.com
Home Page: www.bookstoread.com/etp

Lawrence Lipsitz, Publisher/Editor

Systematic design of software and applications, and their impact on the educational community worldwide. Emphasis on computer-based instruction, the Internet, multimedia, electronic performance support, television and videoconferencing.
Cost: $139.00
Frequency: Bi-annually
ISSN: 0013-1962
Founded in 1960
Printed in on glossy stock

5476 Educational Technology Research and Development
Association for Educational Comm and Technology
1800 N Stonelake Drive
Suite 2
Bloomington, IN 47404

812-335-7675
FAX 812-335-7678
Home Page: www.aect.org

Mary Herring, President
Mary Beth Jordan, Secretary/Treasurer

Communcations, technology and instructional development news.
Cost: $75.00
Frequency: Quarterly
Founded in 1923

5477 Educational Technology Review
AACE International
PO Box 3728
Norfolk, VA 23514

757-623-7588
FAX 703-977-8760

E-Mail: info@aace.org
Home Page: www.aace.org

Gary H Marks, Editor

Promotes the use of information technology in education. New products including software, hardware and related materials.
Cost: $38.00
Founded in 1981

5478 Electronic Design
Penton Media
1300 E 9th St
Suite 310
Cleveland, OH 44114-1503

216-696-7000
FAX 216-696-6662
E-Mail: information@penton.com
Home Page: www.penton.com

Jane Cooper, Marketing
David B Nussbaum, CEO

Celebrating 50 years of innovation, this authoritative magazine provides leading-edge technical information to electronic and engineering managers around the world.
Cost: $105.00
Circulation: 145000
Founded in 1890

5479 Embedded Systems Programming
Miller Freeman Publications
600 Harrison Street
6th Floor
San Francisco, CA 94107

415-947-6000
FAX 415-947-6055
Home Page: www.mfi.com

Frequency: Monthly
Circulation: 45,000
Founded in 1986

5480 Enterprise Management Issues
AFCOM
742 E Chapman Ave
Orange, CA 92866-1644

714-997-7966
FAX 714-997-9743
E-Mail: afcom@afcom.com
Home Page: www.afcomchicago.com

Jill Eckhaus, President

Content includes an in-depth cover story and features on current developments and the impact of advancing technology. Regular departments are devoted to automation issues and data processing news.
Frequency: Bi-Monthly
Circulation: 4,000

5481 European Sources and News
SSC Group
3126 Woodley Road NW
Washington, DC 20008-3448

202-232-0822
FAX 202-337-5354
Home Page: www.euroreseller.com

Robert Snyder, Publisher
Steve Solomon, Editor

Provides European resellers, VAR, systems integrators and OEM with information on product sources and reseller management strategies.
Circulation: 49000

5482 Federal Computer Week
FCW Government Technology Group
3141 Fairview Park Drive
Suite 777
Falls Church, VA 22042-4507

703-876-5100
866-293-3194

FAX 703-876-5126
Home Page: www.fcw.com

Jeffrey Calore, General Manager, Sales & Marketing
Anne Armstrong, Publisher
John Zyskowski, Senior Editor

The markets leading newspaper for influential users and volume buyers of federal information technology.
Cost: $100.00
48 Pages
Frequency: Weekly
Circulation: 100000
Founded in 1987

5483 Foghorn
FOG Publications
PO Box 1030
Dixon, CA 95620-1030
Gale Rhoades, Editor

For users of 16 and 32 bit systems.
Cost: $30.00
64 Pages
Frequency: Monthly
Founded in 1985

5484 GEOWorld
Bel-Av Communications
359 Galahad Road
Bolingbrook, IL 60440-2108

E-Mail: tdanielson@geoplace.com
Home Page: www.geoplace.com

Jo Treadwell, VP/Group Publisher
Todd Danielson, Editor

Offers a wealth of knowledge through features, news and commentary covering the geospatial industry. Covers local and federal government, emergency management, infrastructure, natural resource management, industry trends and onnovations and much more.
Cost: $72.00
Frequency: Monthly
Circulation: 25,000

5485 Game Developer Magazine
Think Services
600 Harrison Street
6th Floor
San Francisco, CA 94107

Home Page: www.gdmag.com

Simon Carless, Publisher
Brandon Sheffield, Editor-In-Chief
Jeffrey Fleming, Production Editor

Written specifically for creators of entertainment software, provides technical and industry information to professional game developers. Features articles written by professional game developers on cutting-edge game development techniques in the areas of graphics and AI programming, audio design and engineering, art and animation.
Cost: $49.95
Frequency: Monthly
Circulation: 35,000
Founded in 1971

5486 Genealogical Computing
Ancestry
360 W 4800 N
Provo, UT 84604-5675

801-705-7000
800-262-3787
FAX 801-705-7001
Home Page: www.myfamily.com

Timothy P Sullivan, CEO
Elizabeth Kelley Kerstens, Managing Editor
Jennifer Browning, Senior Editor

For readers who use computers and technology to organize and enhance their research into ac-

counts of ancestries and descent.
Cost: $25.00
Frequency: Quarterly

5487 Gilder Technology Report
Gilder Publishing
291 Main St
Suite A
Great Barringto, MA 01230-1608

413-644-2100
FAX 413-644-2123
E-Mail: info@gilder.com
Home Page: www.gildertech.com

George Gilder, Editor in Chief

Focuses on the ascendence of the telecoms and the centrality of the Internet.
Cost: $195.00
Frequency: Monthly
Founded in 1995

5488 Global Technology Business
Global Technology Business Publishing
1157 San Antonio Road
Mountain View, CA 94043

650-934-2300
FAX 650-934-2306
Home Page: www.gtbusiness.com

Alex Vieux, Publisher
Laurence Scott, Editor
Bob Beauchamp, CEO

Emphasizes the business aspects of the global computer and communications industries through corporate strategies, financial performance, technological directions.
Frequency: Monthly
Circulation: 45000

5489 Global Techventures Report
Miller Freeman Publications
2655 Seely Avenue
San Jose, CA 95134

408-943-1234
FAX 408-943-0513

Annie Feldman, Publisher

Editorial content profiles vital capital investments and start-up companies, and addresses a variety of legislation, security and communication issues as they relate to today's technology.
Frequency: SemiMonthly

5490 Government Best Buys
FCW Government Technology Group
3141 Fairview Park Drive
Suite 777
Falls Church, VA 22042-4507

703-876-5100
866-293-3194
FAX 703-876-5126
Home Page: www.fcw.com

Edith Holmes, President
John Stein Monroe, Editor-in-Chief
Christopher J. Dorobek, Executive Editor

Covers the hardware and software products available to government buyers on agency contracts and the General Services Administration schedule.
Founded in 1987

5491 Hard Copy Observer
Lyra Research
320 Nevada Street 1st Floor
PO Box 9143
Newtonville, MA 02640-9143

617-454-2600
FAX 617-454-2601
Home Page: www.lyra.com

Charles LeCompte, President
Ann Priede, Director of Marketing
Carolyn ODonnell, Director of Marketing

News on the latest products, market news, supplies, end-user reponse and product testing for the computer printer industry.
Cost: $617.00
80 Pages
Frequency: Monthly
Founded in 1991

5492 Heller Report on Educational Technology Markets
Nelson B Heller & Associates
810 S Alfred Street
#1
Alexandria, VA 22314

303-209-9410
FAX 303-209-9444
E-Mail: info@hellerreports.com
Home Page: www.hellerreports.com

Anne Wujcik, Publisher/Managing Editor

Information on the marketing of technology and telecommunications equipment to educators at all levels.
Cost: $395.00
Frequency: Monthly
Circulation: 1,100

5493 Home Networking News
111 Spleen
Suite 200
Framingham, MA 01701-2000

508-663-1500
FAX 508-663-1599
E-Mail: kmoyes@ehpub.com
Home Page: www.ehpub.com

Kenneth Moyes, CEO/Publisher
Cindy Tazis, Editor
Elizabeth Cruze, Marketing Manager
Christine Ayers, Circulation Manager
Cost: $14.95
Frequency: Monthly
Circulation: 100000
Founded in 1994

5494 IEEE Computational Science & Engineering
IEEE Computer Society
PO Box 3014
Los Alamitos, CA 90720-1314

714-821-8380
FAX 714-821-4010
E-Mail: mloeb@computer.org
Home Page: computer.org

Matt Loeb, Publisher
Scott Andresen, Editor
Monette Velasco, Production Manager
Paul Croll, Treasurer
David Grier, VP Publications

Developments in computation and algorithms, high-performance evaulation, and visualization techniques in the computational science field.
Cost: $98.00
Frequency: Quarterly
Circulation: 5713
Founded in 1946

5495 IEEE Computer
IEEE Computer Society
10662 Los Vaqueros Circle
PO Box 3014
Los Alamitos, CA 90720-1314

714-218-8380
800-272-6657
FAX 714-821-4010
E-Mail: aburgess@computer.org
Home Page: www.computer.org

Angela Burgess, Executive Director
Marilyn Potes, Managing Editor
Rakesh Gupta, Editor in Chief
Paul Croll, Treasurer
David Grier, VP Publications

Examines a wide range of computer-related technologies. Written and refereed by experts, it features articles on the latest developments in computer technology, applications and research in the computer field.
Cost: $37.00
Circulation: 85930
Founded in 1946

5496 IEEE Computer Graphics and Applications
IEEE Computer Society
10662 Los Vaqueros Circle
PO Box 3014
Los Alamitos, CA 90720-1314

714-821-8380
800-272-6657
FAX 714-821-4010
E-Mail: help@computer.org
Home Page: www.computer.org/

Angela Burgess, Executive Director
Sandy Brown, Marketing Director
Robin Baldwin, Managing Editor
Christine Kelly, Staff Editor
Tammi Titsworth, Staff Editor

Focuses on the design and use of computer graphics and systems. Addresses topics such as solid modeling, animation, CAD/CAM, tools for rendering graphics and graphics in medicine, science and business.
Cost: $70.00
Circulation: 10028
Founded in 1946

5497 IEEE Computer Society of Computing Software Magazine
Po Box 3014
Los Alamitos, CA 90720-1314

714-821-8380
FAX 714-821-4010
E-Mail: volunteer.services@computer.org
Home Page: www.computer.org

Angela Burgess, Executive Director
Warren Harrison, Treasurer
Paul Croll, Treasurer
David Grier, VP Publications

Offers information on the latest software programs for computer professionals.
Circulation: 10000
Founded in 1945

5498 IEEE Expert
IEEE Computer Society
10662 Los Vaqueros Circle
PO Box 3014
Los Alamitos, CA 90720

714-821-8380
800-272-6657
FAX 714-821-4010
E-Mail: volunteer.services@computer.org
Home Page: www.computer.org

Crystal Shif, Managing Editor
Angela Burgess, Executive Director
Matthew Bertholf, Advertising Manager
Sandy Brown, Senior Business Development Manager
Paul Croll, Treasurer

Accepts advertising.
Cost: $58.00
Circulation: 3,463
Founded in 1986

5499 IEEE Intelligent Systems
IEEE Computer Society
10662 Los Vaqueros Circle
PO Box 3014
Los Alamitos, CA 90720-1314

714-821-8380
800-272-6657
FAX 714-821-4010

E-Mail: volunteer.services@computer.org
Home Page: www.computer.org

Angela Burgess, Executive Director
Paul Croll, Treasurer
Doris L Carver, Editor-in-Chief
David Grier, VP Publications

Features emphasize advanced research that is ready to be used in the real world. Departments include interviews, books and product reviews, opinion pieces, and conference calendars.
Cost: $47.00
Circulation: 15355
Founded in 1946

5500 IEEE Network
Institute of Electrical & Electronics Engineers
3 Park Ave
17th Floor
New York, NY 10016-5997

212-419-7900
FAX 212-752-4929
E-Mail: society-info@ieee.org
Home Page: www.ieee.org

Daniel J Senese, CEO
Dr. Warren Gifford, Editor

Technical magazine serving both users and designers of multimedia hardware, software and systems in industry, business, academia and the arts.
Circulation: 14388
Founded in 1871

5501 IEEE Transactions on Computers
IEEE Computer Society
10662 Los Vaqueros Circle
PO Box 3014
Los Alamitos, CA 90720

714-821-8380
FAX 714-821-4010
E-Mail: help@computer.org
Home Page: www.computer.org

Jean-Luc Gaudidt, Editor-in-Chief
Angela Burgess, Treasurer
Paul Croll, Treasurer
David Grier, VP Publications

Includes technical research reports and papers on the theory, design and applications of computer systems.
Cost: $72.00
Frequency: Monthly
Circulation: 8000
Founded in 1979

5502 ISACA Journal
Information Systems Audit & Control Association
3701 Algonquin Rd
Suite 1010
Rolling Meadows, IL 60008-3124

847-253-1545
FAX 847-253-1443
E-Mail: publication@isaca.org
Home Page: www.isaca.org

Susan Caldwell, CEO

Provides professional development information to those spearheading IT governance and those involved with information systems audit, control and security
Cost: $75.00
Circulation: 35000
Founded in 1969
Printed in 4 colors

5503 ISR: Intelligent Systems Report
Lionheart Publishing
2555 Cumberland Pkwy SE
Suite 299
Atlanta, GA 30339-3921

770-432-2551
FAX 770-432-6969

E-Mail: llewellyn@lionhrtpub.com
Home Page: www.lionhrtpub.com

John Llewellyn, Publisher
Marvin Diamond, Advertising Sales Manager

Provides an in-depth look into the integration and application of advanced decision support technologies including artificial intelligence, speech recognition, neural networks, fuzzy logic, expert systems, multimedia and virtual reality, and artificial life.
Frequency: Monthly

5504 Imaging World
American Business Media
1300 Virginia Drive
Suite 400
Fort Washington, PA 19034-3297

215-643-8000
FAX 215-643-8159
Home Page: www.boucher1.com

Robert Boucher Jr, President/CEO
Dan Marsh, Publisher, Eyecare Business
Stephanie De Long, Editor-in-Chief, Eyecare

Serves the needs of vendors wishing to reach the North American market for electronic imaging and document-based information management and workflow.
Frequency: Monthly
Circulation: 75000
Founded in 1997

5505 InTech Computing Magazine
ISA Services
67 Alexander Drive
PO Box 12277
Research Triangle Park, NC 27709

919-549-8411
FAX 919-549-8288
E-Mail: info@isa.org
Home Page: www.isa.org

Gregory Hale, Editor
Richard T Simpson, Publisher

Key source of information on automating manufacturing processes.
Cost: $45.00
Frequency: Monthly
Founded in 1945
Printed in 4 colors on glossy stock

5506 Info Log Magazine
BBS Press Service

785-286-4272
FAX 239-992-4862

Alan Bechtold, Editor

A comprehensive magazine offering the latest information on aspects of the computer industry.
Frequency: Monthly
Founded in 1982

5507 Information Display
Ste 114
1475 S Bascom Ave
Campbell, CA 95008-0628

408-977-1013
FAX 408-977-1531
E-Mail: office@sid.org
Home Page: www.sid.org

Ken Werner, Editor
Jenny Needham, Circulation Manager
Shigeo Nikoshiba, CEO/President

A magazine published by the Society for Information Display.
Cost: $55.00
Frequency: Monthly
Circulation: 12000
Founded in 1964

5508 Information Management Magazine
ARMA International

11880 College Blvd
Suite 450
Overland Park, KS 66215

913-341-3808
800-422-2762
FAX 913-341-3742
E-Mail: hq@arma.org
Home Page: www.arma.org

Marilyn Bier, Executive Director
Jody Becker, Associate Editor

The leading source of information on topics and issues central to the management of records and information worldwide. Each issue features insightful articles written by experts in the management of records and information.
Cost: $115.00
Frequency: Bi-monthly
Circulation: 11000
ISSN: 1535-2897
Mailing list available for rent: 9000 names
Printed in 4 colors on glossy stock

5509 Information Systems Management
Auerbach Publications
3701 Algonquin Road
Suite 1010
Rolling Meadows, IL 60008

847-253-1545
FAX 847-253-1443
E-Mail: publication@isaca.org
Home Page: www.isaca.org

Debra Cutts, Marketing
Jen Blader, Editorial
Susan Caldwell, CEO

Coverage includes information technology developments and business applications, financial issues, IS staff development, and relationships with business management.
Cost: $75.00
Frequency: Bi-monthly
Circulation: 40,000
ISSN: 1058-0530
Founded in 1969

5510 Information World Review
143 Old Marlton Pike
Medford, NJ 08055-8750

609-654-7777
FAX 609-654-4309

Offers a full overview of the computer industry overseas.

5511 InformationWEEK
CMP Publications
600 Community Dr
Manhasset, NY 11030-3810

516-562-5000
FAX 516-562-5036
E-Mail: llally@cmp.com
Home Page: www.cmp.com

Stephanie Stahl, Editor-in-Chief
Mike Friedenberg, Publisher

For information systems management.
Frequency: Weekly
Circulation: 440,000
Founded in 1985

5512 Infostor
PennWell Publishing Company
98 Spit Brook Rd
Nashua, NH 03062-5737

603-891-0123
FAX 603-891-9294
E-Mail: mark@pennwell.com
Home Page: www.pennwell.com

Christine Shaw, VP
Jill Davis, Marketing Communications

News and information for enterprise storage professionals.
Cost: $120.00
Frequency: Monthly
Circulation: 38000
Founded in 1997

5513 Infoworld Magazine
Infoworld
501 Second Street
San Francisco, CA 94107

847-291-5217
E-Mail: feedback@infoworld.com
Home Page: www.infoworld.com/

Bob Ostrow, President/Publisher
Paul Calento, VP Marketing
Kevin McKean, Chairman
Steve Fox, Editor-in-Chief
Kathy Badertscher, Executive Managing Editor

Offers information for computer professionals.
Frequency: Weekly

5514 Inside DPMA
Data Processing Management Association
505 Busse Highway
Park Ridge, IL 60068-3143

847-825-0880
FAX 847-825-1693

Paul Zuziak, Editor

A monthly newspaper for the DPMA and the information management profession. Accepts advertising.
Cost: $16.00
Frequency: Monthly
Founded in 1988

5515 Inside Technology Training
Ziff Davis Publishing Company
500 Unicorn Park Drive
Woburn, MA 01801

781-938-2600
E-Mail: editor@itrain.com
Home Page: www.itrain.com/

Nancy J Weingarten, Publisher

Targets management level executives, technology trainers, information technology training managers, CIO's and independent training consultants. Includes reports on new software, new media and new career paths. Also features designed to help training managers create and successfully implement strategy training and reskilling programs that anyone on any level can use.
Frequency: 10 per year
Circulation: 40,000

5516 Inside Visual Basic
ZD Journals
500 Canal View Boulevard
Rochester, NY 14623-2800

585-407-7301
FAX 585-240-7760
Home Page: www.zdjournals.com

Jon Pyles, Publisher

Authors discuss subjects covering the building and creating of external objects, as well as topics surrounding class development. The publication informs readers of Visual Basic online resources, and addresses real world questions reagrding controls written in the program, uses of the status bar and extending functions capabilities.
Frequency: Monthly

5517 Integrated System Design
Verecom Group

954 San Rafael Avenue
Mountain View, CA 94043-1926

650-988-9677
Home Page: www.isdmag.com

James Uhl, Publisher
Richard Wallace, VP

Articles are written by designers who explain unique methods for solving design challenges. Publication supplies information on design methodologies and the use of tools and semiconductor capabilities.
Frequency: Monthly
Circulation: 58082

5518 Intelligent Enterprise

Miller Freeman Publications
411 Boral Avenue
#100
San Mateo, CA 94402-3522

650-573-3210
FAX 650-655-4350
Home Page: www.intelligententerprise.com

David Kalman, Publisher

Each issue provides detailed analyses of the products, trends and strategies that help accelerate the creation of the enterprise's information infrastructure. Topics include: business intelligence; enterprise resource planning; knowledge management; transaction processing and performance monitoring; applications and systems management.
Frequency: 18 per year
Circulation: 103,000

5519 Interactions

Association for Computing Machinery
2 Penn Plz
Suite 701
New York, NY 10121-0799

212-868-5716
800-342-6626
FAX 212-944-1318
E-Mail: acmhelp@acm.org
Home Page: www.acm.org

Mark Mandelbaum, Director Publication
Jonathan Arnowitz, Editors in Chief

Editorial content covers business, design, methods and tools, book previews, conference previews and current events pertaining to designers, developers and researchers.
Founded in 1947

5520 International Journal of IT Standards and Standardization Research

Information Resources Management Association
701 E Chocolate Ave
Suite 200
Hershey, PA 17033-1240

717-533-8879
FAX 717-533-8661
E-Mail: members@irma-international.org
Home Page: www.irma-international.org

Jan Travers, Executive Director
Koichi Asatani, Associate Editors
Carl Cargill, Associate Editor
Tineke Egyedi, Associate Editor
Richard Hawkins, Associate Editor

An authoritative source and information outlet for the diverse community of IT standards researchers, publishing research findings with the goal of advancing knowledge and research in all aspects of IT standards and standardization in modern organizations.
Cost: $115.00
Frequency: Semi-Annual
ISSN: 1539-3062

5521 International Journal of Information and Communication Technology Education

Information Resources Management Association
701 E Chocolate Ave
Suite 200
Hershey, PA 17033-1240

717-533-8879
FAX 717-533-8861
E-Mail: member@irma-international.org
Home Page: www.irma-international.org

Jan Travers, Executive Director
Tonya Barrier, Associate Editor
Dencho Batanov, Associate Editor
David Carbonara, Associate Editor
Martin Crossland, Associate Editor

Includes new applications of technology for teaching and learning, and document those practices that contribute irrefutable verification of information technology education as a discipline.
Cost: $115.00
Frequency: Quarterly
ISSN: 1550-1876
Printed in

5522 Interpersonal Computing and Technology Journal

Association for Educational Comm and Technology
1800 N Stonelake Drive
Suite 2
Bloomington, IN 47404

812-335-7675
FAX 812-335-7678
Home Page: www.aect.org

Mary Herring, President
Mary Beth Jordan, Secretary/Treasurer

The focus is on computer-mediated communication, and the pedagogical issues surrounding the use of computers and technology in educational settings.
Frequency: 2-4 times a year

5523 Iris Universe: Magazine of Visual Computing

Silicon Graphics
1500 Crittenden Lane
Mountain View, CA 94043

650-960-1980
800-800-7441
FAX 650-932-6102
Home Page: www.sgi.com

Warren C Pratt, CEO/President
Gaye Graves, Features Editor
Anne Marie Gambelin, Publisher
Dominic Martinelli, Chief Information Officer

Written to appeal to all users of computer visualization, from the most technically oriented to the novice. Devoted to cutting edge techniques and technology used and presents the best in new products available.
Frequency: Quarterly
Founded in 1981

5524 Journal of American Society for Information Science

John Wiley & Sons
111 River St
Hoboken, NJ 07030-5790

201-748-6000
FAX 201-748-6088
E-Mail: info@wiley.com
Home Page: www.wiley.com

William J Pesce, CEO
Richard M Hochhauser, CEO

Communications, management, applications, economics, and other news of interest in the science field.
Cost: $95.00
72 Pages
Frequency: Bi-Monthly

5525 Journal of Imaging Science and Technology

Society for Imaging Science & Technology
7003 Kilworh Lane
Springfield, VA 22151-4088

703-642-9090
FAX 703-642-9094
E-Mail: info@imaging.org
Home Page: www.imaging.org

George T.C. Chin, Editor
Donna Smith, Managing Editor

Provides the imaging community documentation of a broad range of research, development, and applications in imaging. The selection of papers reflects the role of IS&T as the window on imaging, promoting communication and understanding across the boundaries of the many disciplines involved in modern imaging.
Cost: $95.00
Circulation: 2000
ISSN: 1062-3701
Founded in 1947

5526 Journal of Interactive Learning Research

AACE International
1 Morton Drive
Suite 500
Charlottesville, VA 22903

434-977-5029
FAX 434-977-5431
E-Mail: info@aace.org
Home Page: www.aace.org

John Self, Editor

Reports on the research, developments, applications, and integration of intelligent computer technologies in education.
Frequency: Quarterly
Circulation: 3M

5527 Journal of Object-Oriented Programming

SIGS Publications
9121 Oakdale Avenue
Chatsworth, CA 91311

818-734-1520
FAX 818-734-1522
Home Page: www.101com.com

Richard S Weiner, Editor
Mike Valenti, Executive Vice President

Provides an international forum for research, developments, applications, and new products in the field.
Circulation: 3,50,000
Founded in 1998

5528 KM World

Information Today
143 Old Marlton Pike
Medford, NJ 08055-8750

609-654-6266
800-300-9868
FAX 609-654-4309
E-Mail: custserv@infotoday.com
Home Page: www.infotoday.com

Thomas H Hogan, President
Roger R Bilboul, Chairman of the Board

Serves the knowledge management industry by offering components and processes, including success stories, designed to improve business.
Cost: $23.95
Mailing list available for rent: 4M names
Printed in 4 colors on glossy stock

5529 LAN Magazine
Miller Freeman Publications
600 Harrison Street
6th Fl
San Francisco, CA 94107

415-947-6000
FAX 415-947-6055
Home Page: www.mfi.com

Covers Local Area Networks.
Cost: $20.00
180 Pages
Frequency: Monthly
Founded in 1986

5530 Law Office Computing
James Publishing
PO Box 25202
Santa Ana, CA 92799-5202

714-755-5450
FAX 714-751-5508
E-Mail: jamessale@jamespublishig.com
Home Page: www.jamespublishing.com

Jamie Tyo, Managing Editor
Amanda Flatten, Editor & Publisher
Jim Pawell, Marketing and Circulation

Legal software reviews, productivity enhancing
tips and resources to improve law office automation.
Cost: $39.00
Founded in 1981

**5531 Learning and Leading with
Technology**
International Society for Technology in
Education
180 W 8th Avenue
Eugene, OR 97401-2916

541-302-3777
800-336-5191
FAX 541-302-3778
E-Mail: iste@iste.org
Home Page: www.iste.org

Don Knezek, CEO
Leslie Conery, Deputy CEO

Authors and teachers include school and state
administrators, classroom and lab teachers, tech
coordinators, and teachers educators. Most are
involved in tech-purcashing decisions for their
school and district. Every issue of L&L includes: a feature subject of broad appeal, articles about using tech in specific subject areas,
lesson plans, reproducible worksheets, professional development advice, and referral to sup-
plementary information on the L&L web site at
www.iste.org.
Cost: $89.00
Circulation: 17000
ISSN: 1082-5754
Founded in 1989

5532 Library Software Review
Sage Publications
Vanderbilt University
419 21st Avenue S
Nashville, TN 37240-0001

615-343-6094
FAX 615-343-8834
E-Mail: info@sagepub.com
Home Page: www.sagepub.com

Marshall Breeding, Editor

Provides the library professional with information necessary to make intelligent software
evaluation, procurement, integration and installation decisions. Issues review software and
software books and periodicals.
Cost: $52.00
Frequency: Quarterly
Circulation: 1M

5533 Link-Up Digital
Information Today

143 Old Marlton Pike
Medford, NJ 08055-8750

609-654-6266
800-300-9868
FAX 609-654-4309
E-Mail: custserv@infotoday.com
Home Page: www.infotoday.com

Thomas H Hogan, President
Roger R Bilboul, Chairman Of The Board

A web-only product featuring articles, reviews
and more for users and producers of electronic
information products and services.
Mailing list available for rent: 4M names
Printed in 4 colors on glossy stock

5534 MD Computing
Springer Verlag
175 5th Ave
New York, NY 10010-7703

212-477-8200
FAX 212-473-6272
Home Page: www.mdcomputing.com

Nhora Cortes-Comerer, Executive Editor
Kelley Suttenfield, Assistant Editor

Provides comprehensive and up-to-date information about the various segments of medical
and healthcare informatics, such as clinical
computing, health care information and delivery systems, telemedicine, radiology, and many
others.
Cost: $69.00
74 Pages
Frequency: Bi-Monthly
Circulation: 19,771
ISSN: 0724-6811
Printed in 4 colors on glossy stock

5535 MacWeek
MacWorld Communications
501 2nd St
San Francisco, CA 94107-1496

415-243-0505
FAX 415-442-0766

Mike Kisseberth, CEO
David Ezequelle, Publisher
Rick Lepage, President

Covers Apple's Macintosh computers. Accepts
advertising.
Cost: $99.00
72 Pages
Frequency: 44 per year
Founded in 1987

5536 MacWorld Magazine
Mac Publishing
501 2nd St
San Francisco, CA 94107-1496

415-243-0505
FAX 415-442-0766
E-Mail: letters@macworld.com
Home Page: www.macworld.com

Mike Kisseberth, CEO
Dan Miller, Executive Editor
Scholle Sawyer McFarland, Senior Editor
Dan Frakes, Senior Writer

The ultimate resource for Mac professionals
and savvy Mac users. Each issue is packed with
practical how-tos, in-depth features, the latest
troubleshooting tips and tricks, industry news,
future trends and more.
Cost: $19.97
Frequency: Year Subscription

5537 Marketing Computers
V&U

770 Broadway
F18
New York, NY 10003-9595

646-654-5000
FAX 646-654-5374
Home Page: www.marketingcomputers.com

Donna Tapellini, Editor
Tony DiCamillo, Publisher

Edited for advertising and marketing executives in the high-tech industries. The publication covers interpretive news, timely big
picture features, departments and analysis by
staff editors and industry experts.
Cost: $149.00
100 Pages
Frequency: Weekly
Circulation: 15484

5538 Mobile Office
4845 West 111th Street
Alsip, IL 60658

708-636-5400
FAX 708-636-8637
E-Mail: sales@mobileofficeinc.com
Home Page: mobileofficeinc.com

Jeff Hecox, Editor

Office equipment, computer technology and information.

5539 Motion System Distributor
Penton Media
1300 E 9th St
Cleveland, OH 44114-1503

216-696-7000
FAX 216-696-6662
E-Mail: information@penton.com
Home Page: www.penton.com

Jane Cooper, Marketing
David B. Nussbaum, CEO
Larry Berardinis, Editor

Provides selling and technical information to
individuals and distributors, specializing in
power transmission, motion control and fluid
products.
Frequency: Monthly
Circulation: 54000
Founded in 1892

5540 NCR Connection
Publications & Communications
505 Cypress Creek Road
Suite B
Cedar Park, TX 78613

512-250-9023
FAX 512-331-3900

Mary Wilson, Editor

For users of NCR computer systems.
Cost: $92.00
32 Pages
Frequency: Monthly
Founded in 1983

5541 NEWS 3X/400
Duke Communications International
221 E 29th Street
Loveland, CO 80538-2769

970-634-4700
FAX 970-667-2321

Tim Fixmer, Publisher
Trish Faubion, Editor

Leading technical journal for IBM Systems.
Cost: $119.00
220 Pages
Frequency: 16 per year
Circulation: 31,000
Founded in 1982

5542 Network Support Magazine
Technical Enterprises

7044 S 13th Street
Oak Creek, WI 53154-1429

414-768-8000
FAX 414-768-8001
E-Mail: customercare@naspa.com
Home Page: www.naspa.com

Denise Rockhill, Publisher/Advertising Sales
Rachael Zimmerman, Editor
Matthew Jossart, Art Director

The most comprehensive how to publication in the industry. Orientedtoward professionals involved with a myriad of computing technologies and discusses the topic of importance in mainframe, host based and network oriented environments.
Cost: $5.00
68 Pages
Frequency: Monthly
Circulation: 50,000
Founded in 1987

5543 Network World
Network World
118 Turnpike Road
Southborough, MA 01772-9108

508-756-6400
800-622-1108
FAX 508-460-1192
Home Page: www.networkworld.com

Evilee T Ebb, CEO/Publisher
John Gallant, CFO
Dylan Smith, CFO

For network IS professionals with direct responsibility for planning and managing their companies network computing environment.
Cost: $129.00
100 Pages
Frequency: Weekly
Circulation: 170,000
Founded in 1986

5544 Newmedia Age
HyperMedia Communications
PO Box 299
Brooklin, ME 04616

207-359-6573
800-935-0040
FAX 207-359-9809
E-Mail: support@hypernet.com

Ben Calica, Editor

Covers new products and technology trends in audio and video computing.
Cost: $24.00
Frequency: Quarterly
Circulation: 40,000

5545 OfficeWorld News
366 Ramtown Greenville Road
Howell, NJ 07731-2789

732-785-5976
FAX 732-785-1347

William Urban, Publisher
Kim Chandlee McCabe, Editor-in-Chief

Provides a diverse population of business products resellers the news and information to best serve the needs of small, mid and large business customers. Provides insight into partnering with their peers in this diverse marketplace.
Frequency: Monthly
Circulation: 31,500
Printed in 4 colors on glossy stock

5546 PC Arcade
Softdisk Publishing
606 Common Street
Shreveport, LA 71101-3437

318-218-8718
FAX 318-221-8870

Al Vekovius, President
Ronda Farries, Circulation Director

Publisher of software subscriptions for DOS, Windows and Macintosh computers.
Cost: $19.95
Frequency: Monthly
Founded in 1990

5547 PC Sources
Ziff Davis Publishing Company
500 Unicorn Park Drive
Woburn, MA 01801

781-938-2600
FAX 781-938-2626
E-Mail: info@ziffdavis.com
Home Page: www.ziffdavis.com

Peter McKie, Editor
Robert F Callahan, CEO
Michael J Miller, Editor-in-chief
Stephen Hicks, General Counsel

Serves experienced PC users.
Cost: $149.75
Frequency: Monthly
Founded in 1985

5548 PC Systems and Support
Technical Enterprises
7044 S 13th Street
Oak Creek, WI 53154

414-325-3366
FAX 414-768-8001

Scott Sherer, President
Amy Birschbach, Editor

Offers solutions with tutorials on hardware and software implementation/upgrade techniques, workstation customization, integration and optimization. The how-to material presented each month guides those professionals in evaluating, selecting, acquiring, implementing, and supporting PC distributed resources. Presents in-depth technical information that can be applied at work.

5549 PC Techniques
Coriolis Group
14455 N Hyden Road
Suite 220
Scottsdale, AZ 85260

480-483-0192

Keith Weiskamp, Publisher
Jeff Duntemann, Editor

Covers information on a wide variety of computer systems and language technology.
Cost: $22.00
104 Pages
Frequency: Bi-Monthly
Founded in 1990

5550 Pen Computing Magazine
Aeon Publishing Group
PO Box 408
Plainview, NY 11803-0408

Home Page: www.pencomputing.com

Conrad H Blickenstorfer, Editor-in-Chief
Howard Borgen, Publisher
Wayne Laslo, Advertising Manager

In-depth coverage of pen technology, wireless communications and mobile computing.
Cost: $18.00
Frequency: Monthly
Circulation: 79515
Founded in 1993

5551 Physicians & Computers
Moorhead Publications
600 S Waukegan Road
#200
Lake Forest, IL 60045-2672

847-615-8333
Home Page: www.physicians-computers.com

Tom Moorhead, Publisher

Provides physicians with information on computer advances helpful in the private practice of medicine. Practice management, current medical and nonmedical software, computer diagnostics, etc.
Cost: $50.00
Frequency: Monthly

5552 Powerbuilding Developer's Journal
SYS-CON Publications
135 Chestnut Ridge Rd
Montvale, NJ 07645-1152

201-782-9600
800-513-7111
FAX 201-782-9601
Home Page: www.powerbuilderjournal.com

Fuat Kircaali, Publisher

Covers provide an advanced look at Powerbuilder techniques, new products, reader feedback and interaction, and training in the Powerbuilder language.
Frequency: Monthly
Circulation: 20000

5553 Precision Engineering Journal
Elsevier Science Publishing
6277 Sea Harbor Drive
Orlando, FL 32887-4800

407-345-4020
877-839-7126
FAX 407-363-1354
E-Mail: usjcs@elsevier.com
Home Page: www.elsevier.com /www.aspe.net

W T Estler, Editor-in-Chief
D G Chetwynd, Editor
T. Moriwaki, Co-Editor
Bill Godfrey, Chief Information Officer

Provides an integrated approach to all subjects related to the development, design, manufacture, and application of high-precision machines, systems, and components. International news, reviews, conference reports, informed comment, and a calendar of forthcoming events complete the spectrum of coverage designed to keep readers abreast with a fast-moving technology.
Cost: $1014.00
ISSN: 0141-6359
Founded in 1979

5554 Processor
Peed Corporation
PO Box 85518
Lincoln, NE 68501-5518

402-479-2141
800-819-9014
FAX 402-479-2120
E-Mail: feedback@processor.com
Home Page: www.processor.com

Susy Miller, Publisher
Rhonda Peed, CEO

Information on computer products and services.
Cost: $26.00
84 Pages
Frequency: Weekly
Founded in 1978

5555 Products for Document Management
Acron Publishing
1306 Gaskins Road
Richmond, VA 23233-4919

804-754-2101
FAX 804-754-1534

Irwin Posner, Publisher

News and reviews of latest technology and applications for document management world, including hardware, software, supplies and services.
Frequency: Quarterly
Circulation: 10.963

5556 Pure Java Developer's Journal
ZD Journals
500 Canal View Boulevard
Rochester, NY 14623-2800

585-407-7301
FAX 585-240-7760
E-Mail: purejavadj@zdjournals.com
Home Page: www.elementkjournal.com

Jon Pyles, Publisher

Offers tips for Java developers and answers
questions regarding serving side and the aspects of BeanInfo, writing, and mathematical
equations
Frequency: Monthly

5557 RIS/Retail Info Systems News
Edgell Communications
4 Middlebury Boulevard
Randolph, NJ 07869-4221

973-252-0100
FAX 973-252-9020
Home Page: www.risnews.com

Andrew Gaffney, Publisher
Jeff Zabe, Circualtion Manager
Gabriele A. Edgell, CEO
Gerald C Ryerson, President

Updates on the latest development in retail
management technologies with articles that focus on the application of managerial and
hi-tech advancements.
Frequency: Monthly
Founded in 1984
Printed in 4 colors on glossy stock

5558 RTC
RTC Group
27312 Calle Arroyo
San Juan Capistrano, CA 92675-2768

949-443-4400
FAX 949-489-8502
E-Mail: johnr@rtcgroup.com
Home Page: www.rtcgroup.com

John Reardo, Publisher

Provides information to answer real life ques-
tions about the open systems computer market.
Also news, product updates, tech updates and
standard tracking.
Frequency: Monthly
Circulation: 29,500

5559 Real Time Graphics
Computer Graphic Systems Development
Corporation
2483 Old Middlefield Way
#140
Mountain View, CA 94043-2330

650-903-4920
FAX 650-967-5252
Home Page: www.cgsd.com

Roy Latham, Owner

In-depth information on the technology of real
time graphics, VR, simulations and coverage of
industry news.
Cost: $205.00
Frequency: Monthly
Circulation: 1M

5560 Real-Time Engineering
Micrology PBT
2618 S Shannon
Tempe, AZ 85282-2936

480-967-5581
FAX 480-968-3446
E-Mail: micrology@aol.com
Home Page: www.realtime-engineering.com

John Black, Editor-in-Chief

Focuses on software and operating systems.
Frequency: Quarterly
Circulation: 10,000

**5561 Red Herring: The Business of
Technology**
Red Herring Communications
1550 Bryant St
Suite 450
San Francisco, CA 94103-4832

415-486-2819
FAX 415-865-2280
E-Mail: info@redherring.com
Home Page: www.redherring.com

**5562 Report on Healthcare Information
Management**
Aspen Publishers
1101 King Street
#444
Alexandria, VA 22314

703-683-4100
FAX 703-739-6517
Home Page: www.healthcarenet.com

Mike Brown, Publisher
H. Stephen Lieber, CEO/President
Timothy B Clark, Marketing & Business Dev

System development, clinical information systems, cost-effective clinical integration, data
collection, network security and confidentiality
for the health care industry.
Cost: $358.00
Frequency: Monthly

5563 Retail Systems Alert
Retail Systems Alert Group
377 Elliot Street
PO Box 332
Newton Upper Falls, MA 02464

617-527-4626
FAX 617-527-8102
Home Page: www.retailsystems.com

Tom Friedman, President
Hideo Funamoto, Contributing Editor

Provides updated information on automation
news and trends, including decision systems,
information systems implementation, in-store
merchandise management, and case studies of
retailers.
Cost: $295.00
8 Pages
Frequency: Monthly
Founded in 1988

5564 Retail Systems Reseller
Edgell Communications
4 Middlebury Boulevard
Suite 1
Randolph, NJ 07869-1111

973-252-0100
FAX 973-252-9020
Home Page: www.edgellcommunications.com

michael Kachmar, Publisher
Joe Skorupa, Editor-in-Chief
Gabriele Edgell, CEO
Gerald C. Ryerson, President
John Chiego, Vice President

Offers information to retailers, dealers, systems
integraters, VARs, VADs, etc., on retail tech-
nology for small to mid-size retailers.
Cost: $190.00
Frequency: Monthly
Founded in 1984

5565 RetailTech
Progressive Grocer Associates
23 Old King's Highway South
Darien, CT 06820-4538

646-654-7561
FAX 203-656-3800

E-Mail: info@progressivegrocer.com
Home Page: www.progressivegrocer.com

John Failla, Publisher
Jenny McTaggart, Senior Editor
Stephen Dowdell, Editor-in-Chief
Joseph Tarnowski, Tech Editor, Equipment &
Design

Editoral content covers software, computer peripherals, communications, electronic retailing,
point-of-sale systems, networking, data warehousing, logistics/distribution systems, and the
Internet.
Cost: $99.00
Frequency: Monthly

5566 Robot Explorer
Appropriate Solutions
85 Grove Street
PO Box 458
Peterborough, NH 03458

603-924-6079
FAX 603-924-8668
E-Mail: asi@appropriatesolutions.com
Home Page: www.appropriatesolutions.com

Raymond Cote, Editor

Targets the world of non-industrial robots.
From eight-legged walking machines exploring
Antarctic volcanoes, to microscopic nano-ma-
chines, Robot Explorer provides practical con-
struction details and fascinating reviews of
current technology.
Cost: $14.95
Circulation: 500

5567 SCO Magazine
600 Community Drive
Manhasset, NY 11030-3847

516-562-5836
FAX 516-562-5466

H Newton Barrett, Publisher

5568 SIGNAL Magazine
4400 Fair Lakes Center
Fairfax, VA 22033-3899

703-631-6100
800-336-4583
FAX 703-631-6169
E-Mail: bmowery@afcea.org
Home Page: www.afcea.org

Beverly Mowery, Associate Publisher
Robert K Ackerman, Editor-in-Chief

A news magazine targeted to serve the critical
information needs of government, military and
industry professionals active in the fields of
command, control, communications, computers, intelligence, surveillance and reconnaissance, or C4ISR; information security; research
and development; electronics; and homeland
security.
Cost: $56.00
Frequency: Monthly/Year Subscription
Mailing list available for rent

5569 SQL Forum Online
Informant Communications Group
10519 E Stockton Boulevard
Suite 100
Elk Grove, CA 95624-9703

916-863-3700
FAX 916-379-0610
Home Page: www.informant.com

Forrest Freeman, Owner
Tom Bondur, Publisher

Written for data-base professionals to share and
exchange ideas. Has papers and articles that are
filled with answers to common data-base questions.
Frequency: Monthly

5570 Sawtooth News
Sawtooth Technologies
1500 Skokie Boulevard
Suite 510
Northbrook, IL 60062

847-239-7300
FAX 847-239-7301
E-Mail: info@sawtooth.com
Home Page: www.sawtooth.com

Nicole Garneau, Editor

Articles on computer aided telephone interviewing, computer interviewing, conjoint analysis, and other advanced research techniques.
Founded in 1995

5571 Scan Tech News
Reed Business Information
2000 Clearwater Dr
Oak Brook, IL 60523-8809

630-574-0825
FAX 630-288-8781
Home Page: www.reedbusiness.com

Jeff Greisch, President

Updates in trends in ADC technology and standards, the latest news from leading industry events, and product developments that streamline the flow of essential information in industrial settings.
Frequency: Monthly
Circulation: 82M

5572 Scan: Data Capture Report
Corry Publishing
5905 Beacon Hill Lane
Erie, PA 16509

814-380-0025
FAX 814-864-2037
E-Mail: rickm@scandcr.com
Home Page: www.rmgenterprises.com/

Larry Roberts, CEO and Publisher
(Jon) Rick Morgan, President and Editor

Developments in bar code scanning, biometric identification, electronic commerce and areas of automatic data capture.
Cost: $597.00
Frequency: Fortnightly
Founded in 1996

5573 Scientific Computing & Automation
Reed Business Information
2000 Clearwater Dr
Oak Brook, IL 60523-8809

630-574-0825
FAX 630-288-8781
E-Mail: mlally@cahners.com
Home Page: www.reedbusiness.com

Jeff Greisch, President

Provides the scientists working in industrial/analytical labs, clinical labs, life science labs and electronics R&D labs with information on developments in computing and automation technology for the laboratory.
Cost: $60.00
Frequency: Monthly
Circulation: 50,059

5574 Scientific Computing & Instrumentation
Reed Business Information
45 E 85th St
4th Floor
New York, NY 10028-0957

212-772-8300
FAX 630-288-8686
E-Mail: subsmail@reedbusiness.com
Home Page: www.scimag.com

Lawrence S Reed
Suzanne Tracy, Editor in Chief

5575 Semiconductor Magazine
Semiconductor Equipment & Materials International
3081 Zanker Road
San Jose, CA 95134

408-943-6900
FAX 408-428-9600
E-Mail: semihq@semi.org
Home Page: www.semi.org

T Buehler, Editor-in-Chief
Chris Bucholtz, Editor
Marie Claussell, Circulation Manager
Barbara Wietzel, Marketing Manager

Covers the technical and business information needs of inportant worldwide semiconductor manufacturers, including captive manufacturers, merchant manufacturers, research and development laboratories, equipment suppliers, government/military installations and consortiums.
Cost: $125.00
Frequency: Monthly
Founded in 1980

5576 Sensors Magazine
Advanstar Communications
275 Grove Street
Suite 2-130
Newton, MA 02466

603-924-5400
FAX 603-924-5401
Home Page: www.sensormag.com

Barbara Goode, Group Editorial Director
Stephanie Henkel, Executive Editor
Jill Thiry, Group Publishing Director

Source among design and production engineers of information on sensor technologies and products, and topic integral to sensor-based systems and applications. Provides practical and in-depth yet accessible information on sensor operation, design, application, and implementation within systems. Covers the effective use of state-of-the-art resources and tools that enable readers to get the maximum benefit from their use of sensors.
Frequency: Monthly
Circulation: 66676
Founded in 1999

5577 Serverworld Magazine
Publications & Communications
11675 Jollyville Rd
Suite 150
Austin, TX 78759

512-250-9023
800-678-9724
FAX 512-331-3900
E-Mail: pci@pcinews.com
Home Page: www.pcinews.com

David Wohlbrueck, Editor
Gary Pittman, CEO/President
Bill Lifland, VP Operations

Dedicated to Hewlett-Packard computing.
Cost: $45.00
60 Pages
Frequency: Monthly
Founded in 1979

5578 Simulation
Simulation Councils
PO Box 17900
San Diego, CA 92177-7900

858-277-3888
FAX 858-277-3930
E-Mail: info@scs.org
Home Page: www.scs.org

William Gallagher, Publisher
Richard Fujimoto, Editor-in-Chief
Steve Branch, Executive Director

Information on computer simulation including, applications, methodologies and techniques of computer simulation.
Cost: $195.00
Frequency: Monthly
Circulation: 3800
Founded in 1952

5579 Small Business Advisor: Software News
Software News Publishing Company
110 N Bell Avenue
Suite 300
Shawnee, OK 74801-6967

405-275-3100
800-456-0864
FAX 405-275-3101
Home Page: www.cpatechadvisor.com

Sharie Dodgen, Publisher
Melody Wrinkle, Manager
Isaac OBannon, Manager
Thomson Reuters, Executive Editor

Published for advisers to small businesses and for software installers for small businesses.
Cost: $48.00
Circulation: 50000
Founded in 1991

5580 Smart Reseller
Ziff Davis Publishing Company
500 Unicorn Park Drive
Woburn, MA 01801-4874

781-938-2600
FAX 781-938-2626
Home Page: www.smartreseller.com

Sloan Seymour, Publisher

Identifies the most lucrative new business opportunities and details how to profitably take advantage of them. In-depth business management strategies and trusted new technology solutions-based reviews.
Frequency: SemiMonthly
Circulation: 60M

5581 Software Development
Miller Freeman Publications
2655 Seely Avenue
San Jose, CA 95134

408-943-1234
800-227-4675
FAX 408-943-0513

Veronica Costanza, Publisher
Nicole Freeman, Editor
Laura Merling, Executive Director

For corporate developers and technical managers involved in the development of software applications within the industries.
Circulation: 73297

5582 Software Digest
National Software Testing Laboratories
670 Sentry Pkwy
2nd Floor
Blue Bell, PA 19422-2325

610-832-8400
FAX 610-941-9952
E-Mail: info@nstl.com
Home Page: www.nstl.com

Lowrenie Goldstein, Publisher
Andrew Froning, Editor

Independent and comparative ratings on IBM PC software. All categories tested free of bias. No advertising is accepted.
Frequency: Monthly
Founded in 1983

5583 Solid Solutions
ConnectPress

551 W Cordova Road
Suite 701
Santa Fe, NM 87505-4100

505-474-5000
FAX 505-474-5001
E-Mail: info@solidprofessor.com
Home Page: www.solidmag.com

Dale Bennie, Publisher

Covers the latest market developments and tracks the growth of SolidWorks software in the CAD/CAM/CAE market. Reviews of workstations, 3D printers, and Windows NT graphic accelerators.
Cost: $99.00
Frequency: Monthly

5584 Solutions Integrator

International Data Group
3 Post Office Sq
4th Floor
Boston, MA 02109-3939

617-423-9030
FAX 617-423-0240
Home Page: www.solutionsintegrator.com

Bob Carrigan, CEO
Joel Shore, Editor-In-Chief

Provides accessment of technology, IT buying practices and plans, business strategies and vendor technology roadmaps.
Circulation: 90000

5585 Speech Recognition Update

CI Publishing
PO Box 570730
Tarzana, CA 91357-730

818-708-0962
888-632-7419
FAX 818-345-2980
E-Mail: info@tmaa.com
Home Page: www.tmaa.com

William S Meisel, President
Bill Meisel, Editor

News and analysis of speech recognition markets, companies and technologies.
Cost: $195.00
Frequency: Monthly
Founded in 1993

5586 Storage Management Solutions

West World Productions
420 N Camden Dr
Beverly Hills, CA 90210-4507

310-276-9500
FAX 310-276-9874
Home Page: www.wwpi.com

Yuri R Spiro, Publisher/CEO
Steve Schone, Circulation Manager

Articles on tutorials, case studies, lab tests and new products that offer solutions to issues of data accessibility, availablity and protection and network storage.
Cost: $10.00
72 Pages
Frequency: Monthly
Circulation: 64044
ISSN: 1097-5152
Founded in 1995
Printed in 4 colors on glossy stock

5587 Studio City

Resource Central
4126 Pennsylvania Avenue
Suite 3
Kansas City, MO 64111-3018

Tom Weishaar, President

Information on using the multimedia package Hyper Studio, mailed on 3.5 inch disk, 6 times a year. Available in Macintosh and Apple II versions.
Frequency: Bi-Monthly

5588 Sun Observer

Publications & Communications
11675 Jollyville Rd
Suite 150
Austin, TX 78759

512-250-9023
800-678-9724
FAX 512-331-3900
E-Mail: pci@pcinews.com
Home Page: www.pcinews.com

Gary Pittman, CEO/President
Robert Martin, Editor

Journal of news and information devoted to the users of Sun Microsystems.
Cost: $14.95
80 Pages
Founded in 1980

5589 Supply Chain Systems Magazine

Helmers Publishing
174 Concord Street
P O Box 874
Peterborough, NH 03458-1291

603-924-9631
FAX 603-924-7408
Home Page: www.scs-mag.com

David Andrewso, Publisher/Editorial
Bill Fahy, Circulation Director
Paul Quinn, Editor/Senior Writer

Educates its readers about the benefits and bast practices of supply chain management in manufacturing and service industries. We educate our readers about how e-business, Enterprises Resource Planning, asset management, data capture, warehouse management and management can be integrated to create effective and efficient supply chain systems.
60 Pages
Frequency: Weekly
Circulation: 53000
Founded in 1979
Printed in 4 colors on glossy stock

5590 Synapps

Synergis Technologies
472 California Rd
Quakertown, PA 18951-2463

215-643-6620
FAX 215-536-9249
E-Mail: marketingsupport@synergis.com
Home Page: www.synergis.com

Barbara White, VP

Information for professional management of AutoCAD systems and includes application articles.
Frequency: Quarterly
Circulation: 25000

5591 Sys Admin

CMP Media
4601 West 6th Street
Suite B
Lawrence, KS 66046

785-841-1631
FAX 785-841-2047
E-Mail: samag@neodata.com
Home Page: www.sysadminmag.com

Edwin Rothrock, Publisher
Amber Ankerholz, Editor
Gary Marshall, President
Bob Cucciniello, Marketing
Deirdre Blake, Managing Editor

SYS ADMIN serves the Unix and Linux system administration market.
Cost: $43.00
100 Pages
Frequency: Monthly
Circulation: 29121
Founded in 1992
Printed in on glossy stock

5592 Systematic Magazine

American Payroll Association
711 Navarro Street
Suite 100
San Antonio, TX 78205-1710

210-226-4600
FAX 210-226-4027
Home Page: www.americanpayroll.org

Daniel J Maddux, Publisher

Covers new systems and implementation, the latest technology and its relation to human resources, payroll and accounting for CFOs, MIS department heads and top management in companies that use information technology for communication.
Frequency: Quarterly
Circulation: 14M

5593 Systems Development Management

Auerbach Publications
535 5th Avenue
Room 806
New York, NY 10017-3610

800-737-8034
FAX 212-297-9176
Home Page: www.auerbach-publications.com

Rich O'Hamley, Publisher
Janet Butler, Editor

Technical and managerial information on systems development.
Cost: $495.00
Frequency: Bi-Monthly
Circulation: 1,000
ISSN: 1096-7893
Printed in on matte stock

5594 Systems Integration

Reed Business Information
360 Park Ave S
New York, NY 10010-1737

646-746-6400
FAX 646-756-7583
E-Mail: slebris@reedbusiness.com
Home Page: www.reedbusiness.com

John Poulin, CEO
Thomas Temin, Editor
James Reed, Owner
Jim Casella, CEO

Covers trade and developments for mini-micro based computer systems.
Cost: $75.00
Frequency: Monthly
Founded in 1968

5595 TAAR: The Automated Agency Report

Automation Management Group
4964 Sundance Square
Boulder, CO 80301-3739

303-581-0525
Home Page: www.taan.com

Rick Morgan, Editor

Covers trends, developments and news, reviews new and current technology, and offers ideas and profiles on the productivity benefits.
Cost: $175.00
Frequency: Monthly

5596 Tech Week

1156 Aster Avenue
Suite B
Sunnyvale, CA 94086

408-249-8300
FAX 408-249-0727

5597 Techlinks
3350 Riverwood Parkway
Suite 1900
Atlanta, GA 30339

678-627-8157
FAX 678-627-8159

5598 Technical Services Quarterly
Taylor & Francis Group LLC
325 Chestnut St
Suite 800
Philadelphia, PA 19106-2614

215-625-8900
800-354-1420
FAX 215-625-2940
E-Mail: haworthorders@taylorandfrancis.com
Home Page: www.taylorandfrancis.com

Kevin Bradley, President

This journal publishes up to the minute information that technical services professionals and paraprofessionals need in order to successfully negotiate changes in the field and take full advantage of automated systems that ultimately make collections more accessible to users.
Frequency: Quarterly

5599 Technical Support Magazine
Technical Enterprises
7044 S 13th Street
Oak Creek, WI 53154

414-908-4945
FAX 414-768-8001
E-Mail: customercare@naspa.com
Home Page: www.naspa.com

Rachael Zimmerman, Editor
Denise Rockhill, President

Provides tips and techniques for MVS, VM and VSE mainframe operating systems and NT environments. It also examines security and system performance, product installation experiences and a host of other related enterprise concerns.
68 Pages
Frequency: Monthly
Circulation: 50,000
Founded in 1986
Printed in 4 colors on glossy stock

5600 Technical Training
American Society for Training & Development
1640 King St
Box 1443
Alexandria, VA 22314-2743

703-683-8100
FAX 703-683-8103
E-Mail: customercare@astd.org
Home Page: www.astd.org

Tony Bingham, President

Industry trends, technologies and techniques within computer, manufacturing, telecommunications and government industries.
Cost: $59.00
Frequency: Bi-Monthly
Circulation: 11M

5601 Technology & Learning
Tech & Learning
1111 Bayhill Drive
Suite 125
San Bruno, CA 94066

650-238-0260
FAX 650-238-0263
E-Mail: techlearning@nbmedia.com
Home Page: www.techlearning.com

Allison Knapp, Publisher
Kevin Hogan, Editorial Director
Christine Weiser, Managing Editor

Serves the K-12 education community with practical resources and expert strategies for transforming education through integration of digital technologies. Often used as a professional development tool to help educators across the board get up to speed with the newest technologies and products in order to best prepare students for the global digital workforce.
Frequency: Monthly
Circulation: 81000
Founded in 1971
Printed in on glossy stock

5602 Technology and Practice Guide
ABA Publishing
321 N Clark St
Chicago, IL 60654-7598

312-988-5000
800-285-2221
FAX 312-988-5280
E-Mail: askaba@abanet.org
Home Page: www.abanet.org

Tommy H Wells Jr, President

Helps law professionals of general practice in making decisions about legal information management and technology.
Cost: $18.00
Frequency: SemiAnnual
Circulation: 13,477

5603 Techscan: The Managers Guide to Technology
Richmond Research
266 W 37th St
PO Box 537
New York, NY 10018-6609

212-594-9795
E-Mail: techscan@pipeline.com

Larry Richmond, President

Information and insights on how various new technologies, products and design techniques are used to solve business problems.
Cost: $87.50
Frequency: Monthly
Circulation: 2,500

5604 Text Technology: The Journal of Computer Text Processing
McMaster University
1280 Main Street W
Hamilton, On 0

905-525-9140
FAX 905-577-6930
E-Mail: buckleyj@mcmaster.ca
Home Page: texttechnology.mcmaster.ca

Joanne Buckley, Editor
Edie Rasmussen, Editor

Tips, techniques and programs for TEXT, Icon, Macintosh and other software and word-processing programs, desktop publishing and Internet as they apply to educational applications.
Cost: $45.00
Frequency: Quarterly
Circulation: 800

5605 Trends in Computing
Scientific American
415 Madison Ave
New York, NY 10017-7934

212-451-8200
800-333-1199
FAX 212-832-2998
E-Mail: webmaster@sciam.com
Home Page: www.sciam.com

Gretchen G Teichgraeber, CEO
Elias Arnett, Owner

Targets computer managers and professionals.
Cost: $24.97
Frequency: Annual+
Founded in 1845

5606 Unicenter TNG Advisor
Advisor Media
P.O.Box 503350
San Diego, CA 92150-3350

858-278-5600
FAX 858-278-0300
Home Page: www.advisor.com

John Hawkins, CEO

Advice on TNG programs and equipment, covers end to end management in support of multi-platform infrastructure, integration of management functions and open extensibility.
Cost: $39.00
Frequency: Monthly
Circulation: 35000

5607 Unisys World/Network Computing News
Publications & Communications
505 Cypress Creek Road
Suite B
Cedar Park, TX 78613-1868

512-250-9023
FAX 512-331-3900

Larry Storer, Editor

Dedicated to the users and OEMs of convergent technologies products.
Cost: $48.00
24 Pages
Frequency: Monthly
Founded in 1983

5608 Varindustry Products
VIPublishing
30506 Palos Verdes Drive W
Rancho Palos Verdes, CA 90275-4471
Kenneth Allen, Editor

Focuses on new products and services.
Frequency: Monthly
Founded in 1990

5609 Vision Systems Design
PennWell Publishing Company
98 Spit Brook Rd
5th Floor
Nashua, NH 03062-5737

603-891-0123
FAX 603-891-9294
E-Mail: cholton@pennwell.com
Home Page: www.pennwell.com

Christine Shaw, VP
Andrew Wilson, Editor
Bonnie Heines, Managing Editor

Each issue discusses the development of leading edge industrial, scientific, medical, military, and aerospace machine vision applications.
Cost: $85.00
Frequency: Monthly
Circulation: 32000
Founded in 1910
Mailing list available for rent
Printed in 4 colors

5610 Visual Basic Programmer's Journal
Fawcette Technical Publications
2600 S El Camino Real
Suite 300
San Mateo, CA 94403-2381

650-378-7100
800-848-5523
FAX 650-853-0230
Home Page: www.fawcette.com/vsm/

James Fawcette, President
Tina Fontenot, Marketing

Karin Becker, Associate Publisher
Karen Koenen, Sr. Circulation Director

Provides technical news on how to increase productivity and process applications more efficiently.
Cost: $71.40
Frequency: Monthly
Circulation: 109874
Founded in 1990

5611 WINDOWS Magazine
CMP Publications
600 Community Dr
Manhasset, NY 11030-3810

516-562-5000
FAX 516-562-5995

Scott Wolfe, Publisher

Offers the latest information and updates for the WINDOWS user.

5612 Wall Street Computer Review
Miller Freeman Publications
1199 S Belt Line Rd
Suite 100
Coppell, TX 75019-4666

972-906-6500
FAX 972-419-7825

Elizabeth Katz, Publisher
Pavan Sahgal, Editor

For financial and investment professionals and individual investors.
Cost: $5.00
Circulation: 34,000

5613 Waters
Waters Information Services
270 Lafayette St
Suite 700
New York, NY 10012-3311

212-925-6990
FAX 212-925-7585
E-Mail: jkotz@riskwaters.com
Home Page: www.watersinfo.com

Andrew Delaeny, Editor-in-Chief
Phil Albinus, Editor
John Waters, CEO
Farrell McManus, Advertising Manager

Articles on technology applications leading strategic business success, career enhancements and workplace changes.
Cost: $240.00
Frequency: Monthly
Circulation: 20000
Founded in 1993

5614 Windows & Dot Net
Duke Communications International
221 E 29th Street
Loveland, CO 80538

970-663-4700
800-621-1544
FAX 970-667-2321
E-Mail:
CorporateCustomerService@penton.com
Home Page: www.penton.com

Bart Taylor, Group Publisher
Kim Paulsen, Publisher
David B. Nussbaum, CEO
Cost: $49.95
Frequency: Monthly
Circulation: 100000
Founded in 1982

5615 Windows Developer's Journal
600 Harrison Street
San Francisco, CA 94107

415-947-6000
FAX 415-947-6027
Home Page: www.wdj.com

John Dorsey, Editor in Chief
Kerry Gates, Publisher
Holly Vessichelli, Director of Marketing
Deirdre Blake, Managing Editor

Publication for professional Windows developers.
Founded in 1990

5616 Windows NT Magazine
Duke Communications International
221 E 29th Street
PO Box 447
Loveland, CO 80539-447

970-663-4700
800-621-1544
FAX 970-203-2996
Home Page: www.winntmag.com

Mark Smith, Publisher
Karen Forster, Manager
John Savill, Manager

Serves technical decision makers using the Windows NT application, and related systems.
Cost: $49.95
Frequency: Monthly
Circulation: 75000

5617 Windows/DOS Developer's Journal
R&D Associates
6701 W 121st Street
Suite 310
Overland Park, KS 66209

913-491-0345
FAX 785-841-2624
Home Page: www.rndassociates.com

Ron Burk, Editor

Information for professional Windows and DOS programmers.
Cost: $29.00
Frequency: Monthly
Circulation: 22000
Founded in 1996

5618 Windowspro Magazine
Ziff Davis Publishing Company
500 Unicorn Park Drive
Woburn, MA 01801

781-938-2600
FAX 781-938-2626
Home Page: www.windowspro.com

Jason Young, Publisher
Jacquelyn Gavron, Editor-in-Chief

Serves technology-experts responsible for Windows NT based support. Includes technologies, products, solutions, and how-to instructions.
Frequency: Monthly
Circulation: 150,000

5619 Wired
Wired News
520 3rd St
1st Floor
San Francisco, CA 94107-6805

415-276-8400
800-769-4733
FAX 415-276-8500
E-Mail: info@wired.com
Home Page: www.wired.com

Evan Hansen, Editor-in-Chief
Jeremy Barna, Production Manager
Alison Macondray, General Manager
Drew Schutte, Publisher

Focuses on people and ideas behind digital technology.
Frequency: Monthly
Circulation: 305097

5620 Workstation News
Data Base Publications
9390 Research Blvd
Suite 300
Austin, TX 78759-7374

512-418-9590
FAX 512-418-8165
Home Page: www.bancvue.com

Gabe Krajicek, CEO

Aimed at workstation users and volume buyers.
Frequency: Monthly
Founded in 1990

Trade Shows

5621 AAAI National Conference
American Association for Artificial Intelligence
445 Burgess Drive
Menlo Park, CA 94025-3442

650-328-3123
800-968-1738
FAX 650-321-4457
Home Page: www.aaai.org

Keri Vasser Harvey, Senior Conference Coordinator
Corina Anzaldo, Conference Coordinator

The conference provides a forum for a broad range of topics, including knowledge representation and automated reasoning, planning, machine learning and data mining, autonomous agents, robotics and machine perception, probabilistic inference, constraint satisfaction, search and game playing, natural language processing, neural networks, multi-agent systems, computational game theory and cognitive modeling.
1.2M Attendees
Frequency: July
Founded in 1980

5622 ACT Management of Change Conference
American Council for Technology
3040 Williams Drive
Suite 610
Fairfax, VA 22031

703-208-4800
FAX 703-208-4805
E-Mail: act-iac@actgov.org
Home Page: www.actgov.org

Kelly Olsen, Conference Director

For government and industry executives who are interested in unleashing the tremendous innovation potential of their organizations. It will explore the processes and effects of creative ideas, experiments and ventures that hold the promise of a better and safer America.
Frequency: June

5623 AIA Business Conference
Automated Imaging Association
900 Victors Way
Suite 140
Ann Arbor, MI 48108

734-994-6088
800-994-6099
FAX 734-994-3338
E-Mail: jburnstein@robotics.org
Home Page: www.machinevisiononline.org

Jeff Burnstein, Executive Director

The annual AIA Business Conference has become the machine vision industry's most important networking event. The Conference gathers top industry executives to do business with their peers and hear presentations on issues affecting the global economy in general and the machine vision industry specifically.
300+ Attendees
Frequency: February

5624   AIIM Annual Expo Conference & Exposition
Association for Information and Image Management
1100 Wayne Avenue
Suite 1100
Silver Spring, MD 20910

301-587-8202
800-477-2446
FAX 301-587-2711
E-Mail: aiim@aiim.org
Home Page: www.aiim.org

Jan Andersson, Chair
Robert Zagami, Vice Chair

The largest enterprise content & document management conference and exposition showcasing the technologies and solutions that provide intelligence behind information. For more than 50 years, this annual event attracts business professionals and executive management seeking the latest technologies.
Frequency: May

5625   AIM Expo
AIM Global
125 Warrendale Bayne Rd
Suite 100
Warrendale, PA 15086-7570

724-934-4470
FAX 724-934-4495
E-Mail: info@aimglobal.org
Home Page: www.aimglobal.org

Mary Lou Bosco, President
Linda Young, Business Development Director
900+ Members
Founded in 1972

5626   AMIA Annual Symposium
American Medical Informatics Association
4915 St Elmo Avenue
Suite 401
Bethesda, MD 20814

301-657-1291
FAX 301-657-1296
E-Mail: mail@amia.org
Home Page: www.amia.org

Charles P Friedman, Meeting Chairman
Karen Greenwood, Executive Vice President

Features an outstanding program of scientific papers, posters, tutorials and other educational events that provide information about cutting-edge work in medical informatics.
2000 Attendees
Frequency: Annual/October
Founded in 1977

5627   ARMA International Conference & Expo
ARMA International
11880 College Blvd
Suite 450
Overland Park, KS 66215

913-341-3808
800-422-2762
FAX 913-341-3742
E-Mail: hq@arma.org
Home Page: www.arma.org/conference

Carol Jorgenson, Meetings/Education Coordinator
Wanda Wilson, Senior Manager, Conferences
Elizabeth Zlitni, Exposition Manager

Conference, seminar, workshop, banquet, award ceremony and 175 exhibits of micrographics, optical disk, automated document storage and retrieval systems and more technology of interest to information professionals.
3500 Attendees
Frequency: Annual
Founded in 1956

5628   ASIS&T Annual Meeting
American Society for Information Science & Techn.
1320 Fenwick Lane
Suite 510
Silver Spring, MD 20910

301-495-0900
FAX 301-495-0810
E-Mail: asis@asis.org
Home Page: www.asis.org

Richard B Hill, Executive Director
Nancy Roderer, President

Focus on the diversity of perspectives and insights from all those participating in the information science and technology community, as they generate innovative ideas, define theoretical concepts or work out the nuts and bolts of implementing well-tested ideas in new ways and in new settings.
Frequency: Annual/Oct-Nov

5629   ASPE Annual Meeting
American Society for Precision Engineering
PO Box 10826
Raleigh, NC 27605-0826

919-839-8444
FAX 919-839-8039
Home Page: www.aspe.net

Erika Deutsch Layne, Meetings Manager
Thomas A Dow, Chairman

Offering the latest in precision engineering research through presentations from national and international speakers. Participants in the Annual Meeting have the opportunity to exchange ideas with internationally renowned experts in the field.
Frequency: Annual/Oct-Nov

5630   AWWA Annual Conference and Exposition
American Water Works Association
6666 W Quincy Avenue
Denver, CO 80235

303-794-7711
800-926-7337
FAX 303-347-0804
E-Mail: info@montana-awwa.org
Home Page: www.awwa.org

Nilaksh Kothari, President
Jack W. Hoffbuhr, Executive Director

The source of knowledge and information for water professionals who work to improve the quality and supply of drinking water in North America and beyond. You'll learn from industry experts in the field, hear about cutting edge research and exceptional best practices, and have the opportunity to ask questions, seek advice, and interact with other water professionals regarding both universal topics and items specifically focused to meet your needs.
Frequency: Annual/June

5631   AWWA Information Management & Technology Conference
American Water Works Association
6666 W Quincy Avenue
Denver, CO 80235

303-794-7711
800-926-7337
FAX 303-347-0804

E-Mail: info@montana-awwa.org
Home Page: www.awwa.org

Nilaksh Kothari, President
Jack W. Hoffbuhr, Executive Director

This event is North America's premier conference in the area of water supply information management technology and applications for the water and wastewater industry.
Frequency: March

5632   Association For Services Management World Conference Expo
AFSM International
11031 Via Frontera
Suite A
San Diego, CA 92127

239-275-7887
800-333-9786
FAX 239-275-0794
E-Mail: info@afsmi.org
Home Page: www.afsmi.org

John Schoenewald, Executive Director
Jb Wood, President/Ceo

World's largest gathering of executives in the services and support industry.
Frequency: October

5633   Association of College Unions International Conference
Association of College Unions International
120 W 7th Street
One City Centre, Suite 200
Bloomington, IN 47404-3925

812-245-2284
FAX 812-245-6710
E-Mail: acui@acui.org
Home Page: www.acui.org

Rich Steele, President
Marsha Herman-Betzen, Executive Director

Educational programs, speakers, and exhibits and the opportunity for attendees to connect and network.
Frequency: April
Founded in 1914

5634   Autodesk Expo
AEC Systems International/Penton Media
1300 E 9th Street
Cleveland, OH 44114

800-451-1196
FAX 610-280-7106
E-Mail: sales@acesystems.com
Home Page: www.acesystems.com

Philip McKay, Manager

Highlights AutoCAD and related products from Autodesk and third party developers. 500 exhibits.
20M Attendees
Frequency: May

5635   BDPA Annual Conference and Career Fair
National BDPA
9500 Arena Dr.
Suite 106
Largo, MD 20774

301-584-3135
FAX 301-560-8300
E-Mail: info@bdpa.org
Home Page: www.bdpa.org

Earl Pace, Founder
Pamela Mathews, President

5636   Bentley MicroStation Mail
AEC Systems International/Penton Media
1300 E 9th Street
Cleveland, OH 44114

800-451-1196
FAX 610-280-7106

439

E-Mail: sales@acesystems.com
Home Page: www.acesystems.com

Philip McKay, Manager

Showcases a comprehensive line-up of intergrated design, facility management and GIS solutions built around MicroStation software. 500 exhibits.
20M Attendees
Frequency: May

5637 CALICO Annual Conference
Computer Assisted Language Instruction Consortium
Southwest Texas State University
116 Centennial Hall
San Marcos, TX 78666

512-245-1417
FAX 512-245-8298
E-Mail: info@calico.org
Home Page: www.calico.org

Robert Fischer, Executive Director
Esther Horn, Manager

Providing a forum for discussions of state-of-the-art educational technology and its applications to the more effective teaching and learning of languages. The symposia accommodate workshops, papers, demonstrations, panels, and special interest groups for participants at all levels of expertise.
450 Attendees
Frequency: May

5638 CLA World Computer and Internet Law Congress Conference
Computer Law Association
3028 Javier Road
Suite 402
Fairfax, VA 22031

703-560-7747
FAX 703-207-7028
Home Page: www.cla.org

Barbara Fieser, Executive Director

This conference will provide you with proven strategies and best practices that will enable you to effectively address your existing clients' IT-related challenges and problems and seek out clients whom you can assist with knowledge you will gain from the conference.
2000+ Attendees
Frequency: May

5639 CSI Annual Computer Securtiy Conference & Exhibition
CMP Media/Computer Security Institute Services
600 Community Drive
Manhasset, NY 11030

516-562-5000
866-271-8529
FAX 818-487-4550
E-Mail: jstevens@cmp.com
Home Page: www.cmp.com

Jennifer Stevens, Conference Manager
Kimber Heald, Registration Manager
Annette Campo, Manager

The exhibition features 150 security vendors, from the industry leaders to the up-and-coming, displaying the latest security technologies.
950 Attendees
Frequency: November

5640 CUMREC
Educause
4772 Walnut Street
Suite 206
Boulder, CO 80301-2538

303-449-4430
FAX 303-440-0461

E-Mail: info@educause.edu
Home Page: www.educause.edu

Beverly Williams, Director of Conference Activities
Lisa Gesner, Assistant Director of Marketing

Higher education administrative technology conference. The purpose of CUMREC is to provide a forum for higher education professionals to share their expertise and experiences with computer systems in our ever changing world of technology. The CUMREC annual conference, founded in 1956, is devoted to promoting the understanding and use of information technology in higher education.
3M Attendees
Frequency: May
Founded in 1956

5641 Comdex Spring and Fall Shows
MediaLive International
795 Folsom Street
6th Floor
San Francisco, CA 94107-1243

415-905-2300
FAX 415-905-2FAX
Home Page: www.medialiveinternational.com

Eric Faurot, VP
Marco Pardi, Exhibit Sales

COMDEX is the global marketplace for the IT industry. Buyers and sellers from around the world converge to learn how best to use technology to solve their business challenges and remain competitive. COMDEX is where hardware manufacturers, software vendors and service providers launch new products, where thought-leaders discuss industry trends, and where the media reports on the latest in the IT industry and considers its future.
100M+ Attendees
Frequency: November

5642 CompTIA Annual Breakaway Conference
CompTIA
1815 S Meyers Road
Suite 300
Oakbrook Terrace, IL 60181-5228

630-678-8300
FAX 630-678-8384
E-Mail: breakaway@comptia.org
Home Page: www.comptia.org

John A Venator, President/CEO
Karen Lukasik, VP Operations
Laurel Chivari, VP Marketing & Communications
Rachel Fabro, Public Relations Specialist
Robert Kramer, VP Public Policy

The annual CompTIA Breakaway conference is the computing industry's premier partnering event. The conference focuses on business-building solutions, networking forums, and the latest industry trends and technologies.
Frequency: Annual/August

5643 Design Automation Conference
Design Automation
5405 Spine Road
Suite 102
Boulder, CO 80301

303-530-4333
FAX 303-530-4334
E-Mail: feedback@dac.com
Home Page: www.dac.com

Kevin Lepine, Co-President
Lee Wood, Co-President
Nannette Jordan, Registration Coordinator

The premier Electronic Design Automation (EDA) and silicon solution event. DAC features over 50 technical sessions covering the latest in design methodologies and EDA tool developments, and an Exhibition and Demo

Suite area with over 250 of the leading EDA, silicon, and IP Providers.
11M+ Attendees
Frequency: June

5644 ESRI Southwest Users Group Conference
Southwest Users Group
18727 Nadal Street
Canyon Country, CA 91351

E-Mail: admin@swug2009.com
Home Page: www.swuggis.org

Interface with ESRI users to learn about the latest technologies and discuss ESRI software-related topics.
Frequency: Annual

5645 Embedded Systems Conference
CMP Media Headquarters
600 Community Drive
Manhasset, NY 11030

516-562-5000
E-Mail: cfahlen@cmp.com
Home Page: www.esconline.com

Christian Fahlen, Senior Conference Manager
Ardis Gough, Conference Manager
Kara Pistochini, Conference Assistant
Annette Campo, Manager

The only conference to focus on the art and science of microcomptroller and microprocessor based development, covering the needs of real-time software engineers.
2.7M Attendees
Frequency: September
Mailing list available for rent

5646 FOSE
Post Newsweek Tech Media
10 G Street NE
Suite 500
Washington, DC 20002-4228

202-772-2500
800-791-FOSE
FAX 202-772-2511
Home Page: www.ntpshow.com

Lauri Nichols, Trade Show Operations Manager
Melanie Woodfolk, Show Marketing Manager
David Greene, President

Largest information technology exposition serving the government marketplace.
4000 Attendees
Frequency: April

5647 Graph Expo & Convention
Graphic Arts Show Company
1899 Preston White Drive
Reston, VA 20191

703-264-7200
FAX 703-620-9187
E-Mail: info@gasc.org
Home Page: www.gasc.org

Kelly Kilga, Conference/Show Operations Director
Lilly Kinney, Conference Manager

The largest, most comprehensive prepress, printing, converting and digital equipment trade show and conference in the Americas.
40000 Attendees
Frequency: October

5648 Graphics of the Americas
Printing Association of Florida
6275 Hazeltine National Drive
Orlando, FL 32822

407-240-8009
800-331-0461

FAX 407-240-8333
Home Page: www.pafgraf.org

Anne Gaither, Convention Director
Michael H Streibig, Staff Executive

We are the second largest Graphic Arts and
Converting show in America. We give you two
vital markets — southeast US and Latin America: Mexico, South America, Central America
and the Caribbean. Our 28 year track record reflects our success with both exhibitors and
show visitors.
20000 Attendees
Frequency: Feb

**5649 Healthcare Information and
Management Systems Society
Conference**
Healthcare Information and Management
Systems
230 E Ohio
Suite 500
Chicago, IL 60611-3269

312-664-4467
FAX 312-664-6143
E-Mail: kmalone@himss.org
Home Page: www.himss.org

Karen Malone, Director of Meetings
John Daniels, Vice President

An opportunity to learn the latest industry intelligence, find solutions to your most pressing
professional challenges, and network with your
peers. Pre-conference workshops and education
session, see industry newsmakers, explore the
latest technologies in more than 600 exhibits
and earn continuing education credit and
certification.
20000 Attendees
Frequency: February

**5650 IAAP International Convention and
Education Forum**
Int'l Association of Administrative
Professionals
10502 NW Ambassador Drive
Kansas City, MO 16415

816-891-6600
FAX 816-891-9118
E-Mail: tgoodall@iaap-hq.org
Home Page: www.iaap-hq.org

Inge Hafkemeyer,
Convention/Meetings/Exhibit Manager
Don Bretthauer, Executive Director

An opportunity to showcase your product or
service to this important audience. Office Expo
exhibitors include major office product manufacturers, publishers, software vendors, staffing
firms, gift suppliers, paper companies, and
many more.
2000 Attendees
Frequency: July

**5651 IAPP Privacy and Data Security
Academy Expo**
Internet Alliance
1111 19th Street NW
Suite 1180
Washington, DC 20035-5782

202-284-4380
FAX 202-955-8081
E-Mail: info@internetalliance.org
Home Page: www.internetalliance.org

Emily T Hackett, Executive Director
Katy Caldwell, California Policy Director

The conference will showcase the latest thinking on important privacy issues in healthcare,
financial services, technology and marketing.
Attendees will gain a deeper understanding of

strategies and tools required to meet today's
privacy challenges.
1000 Attendees
Frequency: October
Founded in 1981

5652 IEEE SoutheastCon
IEEE Meeting & Conference Management
(MCM)
445 Hoes Lane
Piscataway, NJ 08854

732-562-3878
800-678-4333
FAX 732-971-1203
E-Mail: conference-services@ieee.org
Home Page: www.ieee.org

A student conference, technical conference, and
business meeting.
800 Attendees
Frequency: Annual

5653 IRMA Annual Conference
Information Resources Management
Association
701 E Chocolate Avenue
Suite 200
Hershey, PA 17033

717-533-8879
FAX 717-533-8661
E-Mail: member@irma-international.org
Home Page: www.irma-international.org

Mehdi Khosrow-Pour PhD, President
Sherif Kamel PhD, Communications Director
Gerald Grant PhD, IRMA Doctoral Symposium
Director
Lech Janczewski PhD, IRMA World
Representative Director
Paul Chalekian, IRMA United States
Representative

Provides forums for researchers and practitioners to share leading-edge knowledge in the
global resource information management area.
Various seminars, conventions and conferences, and other training programs are offered
by IRMA throughout the year.
Frequency: May

**5654 IS&T/SPIE Annual Symposium
Electronic Imaging**
International Society for Optical
Engineering
1000 20th Street
PO Box 10
Bellingham, WA 98227-6705

360-763-3290
FAX 360-647-1445
E-Mail: customerservice@spie.org
Home Page: www.spie.org

Giordano B Beretta, Director
Robert L Stevenson, Co-Director
Eugene Arthurs, Executive Director
Amy Nelson, Manager

Electronic Imaging's top-notch technical program gathers the world's prominent experts to
discuss and push the forefront of imaging technology and it's applications.
1200 Attendees
Frequency: Annual/January

5655 ISACA International Conference
Information Systems Audit & Control
Association
3701 Algonquin Road
Suite 1010
Rolling Meadows, IL 60008

847-253-1545
FAX 847-253-1443
E-Mail: conference@isaca.org
Home Page: www.isaca.org

Sandy Arens, Registration

The International Conference has long been re-
cognised throughout the world for providing
in-depth coverage of the leading-edge technical
and managerial issues facing IT governance,
control, security and assurance professionals.
Frequency: June

5656 Industrial Virtual Reality
Reed Exhibitions
US Consumer Show Division
225 Wyman Street
Waltham, MA 02451

781-622-8616
FAX 781-622-8042
E-Mail: inquiry@sport.reedexpo.com
Home Page: www.reedexpo.com

Elizabeth Hitchcock, International Sales

The first trade show focusing on industrial applications of virtual reality and tele-existence.
Frequency: June

5657 Information Technology Week
Information Week/CMP Media
600 Community Drive
Manhasset, NY 11030

516-562-5000
FAX 516-562-5036
E-Mail: lmonvign@cmp.com
Home Page: www.informationweek.com

Lisa Monvigner, Events Associate Director
Stephanie Iannuzzi, Sr. Marketing Manager
Michael Friedenberg, Publisher

A forum for computer technicians and profes-
sionals.
Frequency: May
Mailing list available for rent

**5658 International Conference on Methods
for Surveying Hard-To-Reach
Populations**
American Association for Public Opinion
Research
111 Deer Lake Road
Suite 100
Deerfield, IL 60015

847-205-2651
FAX 847-480-9282
E-Mail: aapor-info@goamp.com
Home Page: www.aapor.org
Social Media: *Facebook, Twitter, LinkedIn*

Paul Lavrakas, President
Rob Santos, VP/President-Elect
Scott Keeter, Secretary-Treasurer

The conference will address both the statistical
and survey design aspects of including hard to
reach groups. Researchers will report findings
from censuses and surveys and other research
related to the identification, definition, measurement, and methodologies for surveying and
enumerating undercounted populations.
850 Attendees
Frequency: Annual
*Mailing list available for rent: 1000 names at
$400 per M*

**5659 International Conference on Software
Engineering**
Software Engineering Institute
Carnegie Mellon University
Pittsburgh, PA 15213-3890

412-687-7700
FAX 412-268-6257
E-Mail: customer-relations@sei.cmu.edu
Home Page: www.sei.cmu.edu

Paul Nielsen, CEO
Clyde Chittister, COO
Douglas Schmidt, Deputy Dir Research

ICSE is the premier software engineering conference, providing a forum for researchers,
practitioners and educators to present and dis-

cuss the most recent innovations, trends, experiences, and concerns in the field of software engineering.
800 Attendees
Frequency: May

5660 International Consumer Electronics Show (C ES)

Consumer Electronics Association
Las Vegas Hotel & Casino
3000 S. Paradise Road
Las Vegas, NV 89109

866-539-8430
Home Page: www.cesweb.org

Tara Dunion, Event Director
Kristen Peifer, Event Manager
Leah Arnold, Exhibitor Coordinator

The largest annual consumer technology tradeshow offering a wealth of opportunity for your business.
140M Attendees
Frequency: Annual/January

5661 International Spectrum MultiValue Conference & Exhibition

International Spectrum
715 J Street
Suite 301
San Diego, CA 92101-2478

619-515-9930
FAX 619-515-9933
E-Mail: editor@intl-spectrum.com
Home Page: www.intl-spectrum.com

Monica Giobbi, President
Gus Giobbi, Chairman

A conference and exhibition showcasing MultiValue products and services.
6M Attendees
Frequency: March

5662 Interop Conference

Interop
C/O MediaLive International
795 Folsom Street, 6th Floor
San Francisco, CA 94107-1243

415-905-2300
FAX 415-905-2FAX
E-Mail: jennifer.sioteco@mlii.com
Home Page: www.interop.com

Jennifer Sioteco, Sr. Operations Manager
Lenny Heymann, General Manager

Provides you an overview of the robust conference offerings, workshops and tutorials, and special programs.
60000 Attendees

5663 Java One Conference

Sun Microsystems
4150 Network Circle
Santa Clara, CA 95054

650-960-1300
866-382-7151
Home Page: www.java.sun.com

Jonathan Schwartz, President/CEO
Anil Gadre, Chief Executive Officer

Gain knowledge and Java technology education directly from Sun Microsystems, Inc. and other industry leaders. Get expert advice on solving the most common Java challenges. Benefit from four full days of content. Choose from hundreds of technical sessions and test drive real-world Java technology solutions.
5000 Attendees
Frequency: June

5664 MacWorld Conference & Expo

MacWorld 2010

PO Box 3221
Boston, MA 02241

805-290-1341
800-645-EXPO
FAX 805-654-1676
E-Mail: macworld2010@rcsreg.com
Home Page: www.macworldexpo.com

Annual show with hundreds of exhibitors of Mac equipment, supplies and services. Provides education, networking and thought leadership that professionals and consumers alike need to get the most from their technology investment.
65000 Attendees
Frequency: Annual

5665 Marketechnics

Food Marketing Institute
2345 Crystal Drive
Suite 800
Arlington, VA 22202

202-452-8444
FAX 202-429-4519
Home Page: www.fmi.org

Tim Hammonds, CEO

Provides a once-a-year opportunity to hear, see and discuss new technologies and their impact on the supply chain, store operations and marketing/merchandising strategies.
7000 Attendees
Frequency: Jan-Feb

5666 NACCB Annual Conference

National Association of Computer Consultants
1420 King Street
Suite 610
Alexandria, VA 22314

703-838-2050
FAX 703-838-3610
E-Mail: susan@naccb.org
Home Page: www.naccb.org

Susan Donohoe, Director of Programs/Public Policy
Beth Berman, Program & Administrative Coord.

The only educational, networking, and leadership event exclusively for the IT Services Industry. The NACCB conference provides a platform where IT services firms connect to address issues and solutions most affecting business today.
Frequency: Annual/November
Founded in 1988

5667 National Ergonomics Conference and Exposition

Continental Exhibitions
370 Lexington Avenue
Suite 1407
New York, NY 10017-6503

212-370-5005
FAX 212-370-5699
E-Mail: information@ergoexpo.com
Home Page: www.ergoexpo.com

Larry L Elyea, Executive Program Director
Pedro Caceres, Senior VP of Operations

The NECE maximizes your time and effort by providing direct contact with industry leaders that comprise our speaker faculty, direct contact with leading providers of ergonomics products and services, and direct contact with your peers at networking receptions during the exposition.
Frequency: Nov-Dec

5668 Object World Conference

Object Management Group/IDG
Management

111 Speen Street
PO Box 9107
Framingham, MA 01701-9514

800-225-4698
FAX 508-872-8237
Home Page: www.omg.com

Mary DeCristoforo, Conference Director
David Elliott, Exhibit Sales Manager

An annual conference sponsored by the Object Management Group and IDG Management Group to advance object-oriented technology in commercial software development. The event features tutorials and conference sessions.
6.5M Attendees
Frequency: October

5669 Optical Fiber Communications Conference

Optical Society of America
2010 Massachusetts Avenue NW
Washington, DC 20036

202-238-8130
FAX 202-416-6140
E-Mail: info@ofcconference.org
Home Page: www.ofcnfoec.org

Colleen Morrison, Media Relations Director
Melissa Russell, Exhibit Sales Director
Colleen Morrison, Media Relations Manager
Angela Stark, Director Communications

Provides leading edge, peer reviewed educational programming along with a high powered, commerce driven exhibition. This unique combination attracts the field's most progressive professionals and exhibiting companies.
13111 Attendees
Frequency: March
Founded in 1916

5670 PCB Design Conference West

UP Media Group
2400 Lake Park Dr Se
Suite 440
Smyrna, GA 30080-7695

678-589-8800
FAX 678-589-8850
E-Mail: askarbek@upmediagroup.com
Home Page: www.pcbwest.com

Alyson Skarbek, Show Operations Manager
Andy Shaughnessy, Conference Chairperson
Brooke Anglin, Exhibit Sales Manager

The first and only conference 100% dedicated to the needs of the PCB designer.
750 Attendees
Frequency: March

5671 PIMA Leadership Conference

Paper Industry Management Association
4700 W Lake Avenue
Glenview, IL 60025-1485

847-375-6860
877-527-5973
FAX 732-460-7333
E-Mail: info@pimaweb.org
Home Page: www.pima-online.org

Carol Waugh, Meetings Manager
Julie Weir, Account Manager
Mary Cornell, Account Manager

Three-day conference to bring together IT and process control professionals from around the world to share their knowledge of information technology in the pulp and paper industry and to promote systems applications. The only IT conference planned for and by IT professionals.
500 Attendees
Frequency: Annual/June

5672 Pacific Telecommunications Council Conference: PTC Conference

Pacific Telecommunications Council

2454 S Beretania Street
3rd Floor
Honolulu, HI 96826-1596

808-941-3789
FAX 808-944-4874
E-Mail: snakama@ptc.org
Home Page: www.ptc.org

Sharon Nakama, Conference Director
Dolores Fung, Conference/Seminar
Coordinator
Claudine Naruse, Conference/Seminar
Coordinator
Justin Riel, Conference/Seminar Assistant

Provides an opportunity to learn and to analyze
current issues. Registrants from the ranks of senior corporate officers and management, experts from law and consulting firms, noted
analysts and scholars, and technical experts
provide a wide diversity of ideas.
1500 Attendees
Frequency: January

**5673 SC: High Performance Networking &
Computing**
Hall-Erickson
98 E Naperville Road
Westmont, IL 60559

630-639-9185
FAX 630-434-1216
Home Page: www.sc-conference.org

William Kramer, Conference General Chair
Barbara Horner-Miller, Conference Deputy
Chair

The world's leading conference on high performance computing, networking and storage.
Representatives from many technical communities together to exchange ideas, celebrate past
successes and plan for the future.
6000 Attendees
Frequency: Annual/November
Founded in 1988

**5674 SCSC: Summer Simulation
Multiconference**
Society for Modeling and Simulation
International
PO Box 17900
San Diego, CA 92177-7900

858-277-3888
FAX 858-277-3930
E-Mail: scs@scs.org
Home Page: www.scs.org

Steve Branch, Executive Director
Mark Yen, Event Coordinator

Focusing on Innovative Technologies for Simulation this year. Modeling and Simulation is a
very critical area for supporting Research and
Development as well as competitiveness worldwide; new technologies are enabling new use
of M&S and increasing its impact in new areas;
SCSC provides an international forum for presenting the state of the art in the international
simulation community.
600 Attendees
Frequency: July

**5675 SID International Symposium,
Seminar and Exhibition**
Society for Information Display
610 S 2nd Street
San Jose, CA 95112

408-977-1013
FAX 408-977-1531
E-Mail: office@sid.org
Home Page: www.sid.org

Mark Goldfab, Conference Coordinator
Bill Klein, Symposium Coordinator
Kate Dickie, Exhibition/Sponsorship Sales
Mgr.
Danielle Rocco, Exhibition/Sponsorship

Coordinator
Jenny Needham, Manager

The premier international gathering of scientists, engineers, manufacturers and users in the
electronic display industry. The event provides
access to a wide range of technology and applications from high-definition flat-panel displays
using both emissive and liquid-crystal technology to the latest in OLED displays and
large-area projection-display systems.
6000 Attendees
Frequency: May
Founded in 1962

5676 SIGGRAPH Conference
Association for Computing Machinery
2 Penn Plaza
Suite 701
New York, NY 10121-0701

212-626-0500
800-342-6626
FAX 212-944-1318
E-Mail: acmhelp@acm.org
Home Page: www.siggraph.org

Dino Schweitzer, Conference Chief Staff
Executive
James Mohler, Conference Chairperson

The annual conference and its year round initiatives provide unique crossroads for a diverse
community of researchers, developers, creators,
educators and practitioners. Our continuing
mission is to be the premier annual conference
on leading edge theory and practice of computer graphics and interactive techniques, inspiring progress through education, excellence,
and interaction.
50000 Attendees
Frequency: July-August

**5677 SMC: Spring Simulation
Multiconference**
Society for Modeling and Simulation
International
PO Box 17900
San Diego, CA 92177-7900

858-277-3888
FAX 858-277-3930
E-Mail: sbranch@scs.org
Home Page: www.scs.org

Drew Hamilton, Conference General Chair
Steve Branch, Executive Director

Bringing together eight symposia and providing a forum for academia, industry, business
and government covering a wide variety of disciplines and domains that utilize modeling and
simulation to present their work in a unique
setting.
400 Attendees
Frequency: April

5678 Seybold Seminars
MediaLive International
795 Folsom Street
6th Floor
San Francisco, CA 94107-1243

415-905-2300
FAX 415-905-2FAX
Home Page: www.medialiveinternational.com

Jackie Rees, Program Director
Cynthia Wood, Conference Content Director

Four focused conferences; Chicago, New York,
San Francisco, that will deliver new solutions,
emerging technologies and real world examples
of businesses that have successfully implemented new digital publishing workflow and
content management strategies.
21000 Attendees
Frequency: Sept, Oct, Nov

5679 TAWPI Annual Forum & Exposition
Association for Work Process Improvement

185 Devonshire Street
Suite M102
Boston, MA 02110-1407

617-426-1167
800-998-2974
FAX 617-521-8675
E-Mail: info@tawpi.org
Home Page: www.tawpi.org

Sandra Savage, Conference Planner
Jenny Star, Director Business Development
Tonya Gregoire, Director Business
Development

Leading event for technology and management
professionals in data capture, mail, imaging,
payment/remittance, document and forms
processing.
1500 Attendees
Frequency: July

5680 TechNet International
Armed Forces Communications and
Electronics Assn
4400 Fair Lakes Court
Fairfax, VA 22033

703-631-6100
800-336-4583
FAX 703-631-6405
Home Page: www.afcea.org

Kent Schneider, President/CEO
Becky Nolan, Executive VP
John A Dubia, Executive VP

An annual event representing top government,
industry and military professionals in the fields
of communications, electronics, intelligence,
information systems, imaging and multi-media.
Frequency: Annual/June

**5681 UNITE Golden Opportunities Annual
Technology Conference**
UNITE
21523 Harper Avenue
St Clair Shores, MI 48080-2209

586-443-6901
FAX 586-443-6902
E-Mail: cathmurphy39@hotmail.com
Home Page: www.unite.org

Catherine Murphy, Conference Chair
George Gray, Conference Vice Chair

Held in mid October. Development and use of
information technology. Pre-registration for
full conference attendees: $1,095; daily atten-
dees: $740.
Frequency: October

5682 Usenix Annual Technical Conference
Usenix
2560 9th Street
Suite 215
Berkeley, CA 94710-2573

510-528-8649
FAX 510-548-5738
E-Mail: conference@usenix.org
Home Page: www.usenix.org

Jennifer Joost, Conference Manager
Devon Shaw, Administrative Assistant
Andrew Gustafson, Administrative Assistant
Dan Klein, Director
John Arrasjid, Secretary

A 5 day training running alongside a 3 day conference program filled with the latest research,
security breakthroughs, sessions devoted to
Linux and open source software and practical
approaches to the puzzles and problems you
wrestle with.
3M Attendees
Frequency: June

5683 Vue/Point Conference
Graphic Arts Show Company

1899 Preston White Drive
Reston, VA 20191

703-264-7200
FAX 703-620-9187
E-Mail: info@gasc.org
Home Page: www.gasc.org

Kelly Kilga, Conference/Show Operations
Director
Lilly Kinney, Administrative Assistant
Erin Omwake, Administrative Assistant
Deborah Vieder, Director of Communications

The only interactive, peer-to-peer conference
event in the graphic communications industry.
Frequency: April

**5684 WMC: Western Simulation
Multiconference**
Society for Modeling and Simulation
International
PO Box 17900
San Diego, CA 92177-7900

858-277-3888
FAX 858-277-3930
E-Mail: sbranch@scs.org
Home Page: www.scs.org

Steve Branch, Executive Director
Mark Yen, Events & Publications Coordinator

15 booths of technical and scientific papers.
300+ Attendees
Frequency: January

5685 Westec Exposition
Society of Manufacturing Engineers
One SME Drive
Dearborn, MI 48121

313-425-3000
800-733-4763
FAX 408-428-9600
E-Mail: service@sme.org
Home Page: www.sme.org

Ana Christiansen, Exposition Marketing
Leslie Schade, Exhibitor Services

The West Coast's definitive manufacturing
event, showcasing crucial breakthroughs in machine tools, production methods, materials and
management strategies. More than 450
exhibitors.
1500 Attendees
Frequency: Annual

5686 Western Conference & Exposition
Armed Forces Communications and
Electronics Assn
4400 Fair Lakes Court
Fairfax, VA 22033

703-631-1397
FAX 703-818-9177
E-Mail: gmcgovern@afcea.org
Home Page: www.afcea.org

Gina McGovern, Patron/Sponsor Director
Kim Couranz, Senior Vice President
Booz Hamilton, Senior Vice President

Largest event on the West Coast for communications, electronics, intelligence, information
systems, imaging, military weapon systems,
aviation, shipbuilding, and more. Featuring the
people you need to hear from, the products and
services you need to do your job, and the critical issues of today and tomorrow.
7000 Attendees
Frequency: January

Directories & Databases

**5687 ACM-SIGGRAPH Computer
Graphics Education Directory**
Association for Computing Machinery

1515 Broadway
17th Floor
New York, NY 10036-8901

212-869-7440
800-342-6626
FAX 212-944-1318
E-Mail: acmhelp@acm.org
Home Page: www.acm.org

Lynn D'Addesio-Kraus, Production Manager
Roma Simon, Associate Director
Robert Okajima, Associate Director
Alain Chesnais, Founder
Liliana Cintron, Administrative Assistant

Compiled to create a unified site where educators, students, and others can find information
about computer graphics educational programs,
computer graphics curriculum, computer
graphics text.
Cost: $20.00
0 Pages
Frequency: Biennial

5688 ARMA International's Buyers Guide
ARMA International
11880 College Blvd
Suite 450
Overland Park, KS 66215

913-341-3808
800-422-2762
FAX 913-341-3742
E-Mail: hq@arma.org
Home Page: www.arma.org/conference

75-100 companies listed. Free.

5689 AV Market Place
Information Today
143 Old Marlton Pike
Medford, NJ 08055-8750

609-654-6266
800-300-9868
FAX 609-654-4309
E-Mail: custserv@infotoday.com
Home Page: www.infotoday.com

Thomas H Hogan, President
Roger R Bilboul, Chairman Of The Board

The complete business directory of audio, audio visual, computer systems, film, video, and
programming with industry yellow pages. The
only guide needed to find more than 7,500
companies that create, apply or distribute AV
equipment and services for business, education,
science, and government.
Cost: $199.95
1700 Pages
Frequency: February
ISBN: 1-573871-87-7

5690 CD-ROM Databases
Worldwide Videotex
PO Box 3273
Boyton Beach, FL 33424

561-738-2276
E-Mail: markedit@juno.com
Home Page: www.wvpubs.com

Contains information on currently marketed databases available on CD-ROM.
Frequency: Directory

5691 CD-ROMs in Print
Thomson Gale
PO Box 09187
Detroit, MI 48209-0187

248-699-4253
800-877-4253
FAX 248-699-8049
Home Page: www.galegroup.com

Patrick C Sommers, President
Rich Foley, Account Manager
Judy Roberts, Account Manager
Maria Moffre, Product Manager

International guide to CD-ROM, Cdi, 3Do,
Mmcd, Cd32, Multimedia, Laserdisc and Elec-
tronic Products.
Cost: $205.00
Circulation: 13,000
ISBN: 0-787671-33-9

5692 Computer Database
Information Access Company
362 Lakeside Drive
Foster City, CA 94404-1171

650-378-5200
800-227-8431
FAX 650-378-5368
Home Page: www.iacnet.com

Robert Howells, President

Comprehensive database offering over 500,000
citations, with abstracts, to literature from over
150 trade journals, industry newsletters and
platform-specific publications covering the
computer, telecommunications and electronics
industries.

5693 Computer Industry Almanac
Computer Industry Almanac
304 W White Oak
Arlington Heights, IL 60005-3201

847-758-3687
FAX 847-758-3686
E-Mail: ej@c-i-a.com
Home Page: www.c-i-a.com

Egil Juliussen, Editor
Karen Petska-Juliussen, Editor

A reference book about the computer industry.
Cost: $63.00
800 Pages
Frequency: Annual
ISBN: 0-942107-08-X

**5694 Computer Industry Market
Intelligence System**
Hart-Hanks Market Intelligence
9980 Huennekens St
Suite 100
San Diego, CA 92121-2917

858-625-4800
FAX 858-452-6857
Home Page: www.hartehanksmi.com

Terry Olson, CEO
Randy Ilas, Product Management Director

Database of more than 250,000 business locations with mainframe, mini or micro computer
systems.

5695 Computer Review
Computer Review
19 Pleasant St
Gloucester, MA 01930-5937

978-283-2100
E-Mail: info@computerreview.com
Home Page: www.computerreview.com

George Luhowy, Owner

Your personal business tool for mining the
Knowledge economy. This is a well organized
hardcopy directory with a daily online monitor.
It shows you what's happening in 12,000 com-
panies from 77 technology sectors.
Cost: $495.00
750 Pages
Frequency: Annual
ISBN: 0-914730-02-9
ISSN: 0093-416X

5696 DACS Annotated Bibliography
Data & Analysis Center for Software
775 Daedalian Drive
Rome, NY 13441-4909

315-334-4905
800-214-7921
FAX 315-334-4964

E-Mail: cust-liasn@dacs.dtic.mil
Home Page: www.iac.dtic.mil/dacs

Thomas McGibbon, Director

Offers citations on over 9,000 technical reports, articles, papers and books concerned with software development and engineering.
Cost: $60.00
400 Pages

5697 DIALOG Publications
Dialog, Thomas Business
11000 Regency Parkway
Suite 10
Cary, NC 27511

919-462-8600
800-3DI-ALOG
FAX 919-468-9890
Home Page: www.dialog.com

Mike Eastwood, VP Finance & Administration
Al Zink, VP Human Resources
Roy Martin, CEO

Offers descriptions of DIALOG system and database publications that are available for purchase.

5698 DP Directory
525 Goodale Hill Rd
Glastonbury, CT 06033-4022

860-659-1065
E-Mail: al@dpdirectory.com
Home Page: www.dpdirectory.com

Al Harberg, President

Offers mailing lists for the computer trade as well as information on the value and uses of press releases for marketers.

5699 Datapro Directory of Microcomputer Hardware
S. Karger Publishers
26 W Avon Road
PO Box 529
Farmington, CT 06085

860-675-7834
800-828-5479
FAX 860-675-7302
E-Mail: karger@snet.net
Home Page: www.libri.ch

Martin Buess, Managing Director
Andrea Murdoch, CEO
Monika Augstburger, Account Manager
Marianne Dill, Manager Customer Service

Offers valuable information on over 1,500 manufacturers of microcomputers and peripheral equipment.
Cost: $675.00
1000 Pages
Frequency: Monthly
ISSN: 1074-3308

5700 Directory of Computer and High Technology Grants
Research Grant Guides
PO Box 1214
Loxahatchee, FL 33470-1214

561-795-6129

Richard M Eckstein, Author

Offers information on over 750 foundations and corporations that award grants to nonprofit organizations for computers, computer training and software.
Cost: $52.50
200 Pages
Frequency: Biennial
ISBN: 0-945078-07-2

5701 Directory of Library Automation Software, Systems and Services
Information Today

143 Old Marlton Pike
Medford, NJ 08055-8750

609-654-6266
800-300-9868
FAX 609-654-4309
E-Mail: custserv@infotoday.com
Home Page: www.infotoday.com

Thomas H Hogan, President
Roger R Bilboul, Chairman Of The Board

Recognized as the primary reference source for software packages used in automating libraries. This entirely new expanded 2004-2005 edition provides detailed descriptions of hundreds of currently available microcomputer, minicomputer, and mainframe software packages and services.
Cost: $89.00
351 Pages
Frequency: Bi-Annually
Founded in 1983

5702 Directory of Simulation Software
Society for Modeling and Simulation International
4838 Ronson Ct
PO Box 17900
San Diego, CA 92177-7900

858-277-3888
FAX 858-277-3930
E-Mail: info@scs.org
Home Page: www.scs.org

Amy Shapiro, Publications Manager & Editor
Steve Branch, Executive Director

About 200 simulation software packages and their suppliers.
Cost: $40.00
Frequency: Annual
Circulation: 2,000
Mailing list available for rent

5703 Directory of Top Computer Executives
Applied Computer Research
PO Box 41730
Phoenix, AZ 85080

602-216-9100
800-234-2227
FAX 602-548-4800
E-Mail: tara@topitexecs.com
Home Page: www.acrhq.com

Contains the names of more than 52,000 of the most influential information technology managers in the US and Canada. Entepreneurs and corporate executives have used this data base to build successful businesses for over 30 years.
Cost: $245.00
Frequency: Semi-Annual
Founded in 1972

5704 Directory of US Government Software for Mainframes and Microcomputers
US National Technical Information Service
5285 Port Royal Road
Springfield, VA 22161

703-605-6000
800-553-6847
FAX 703-605-6900
E-Mail: info@ntis.gov
Home Page: www.ntis.gov

Patrik Ekstr"m, Business Development Manager
Reuel Avila, Managing Director

Contains descriptions of some 550 mainframe and microcomputer programs made available from more than 100 federal agencies, or their contractors since 1984. The directory is an essential reference tool for users who wish to tap

the wealth of U.S. Government software.
Cost: $65.00
174 Pages
Frequency: Annual
ISBN: 0-934213-37-2

5705 Electronic Imaging an Image Processing: An Assessment of Technology & Products
Richard K Mill & Associates
5880 Live Oak Parkway
Suite 270
Norcross, GA 30093-1707

770-416-0006
FAX 770-416-0052

Richard K Miller, Editor/President
Kelli D Washington, Editor-in-Chief

List of producers and suppliers of electronic imaging computer software and hardware.
Cost: $485.00
ISBN: 0-896711-12-9

5706 Guide to Free Films, Flimstrips and Slides
Educators Progress Service
214 Center St
Randolph, WI 53956-1497

920-326-3126
888-951-4469
FAX 920-326-3127
E-Mail: questions@freeteachingaids.com
Home Page: www.freeteachingaids.com

Kathy Nehmer, President

Offers sources for films, filmstrips, slide sets, audiotapes and videotapes.
Cost: $37.95
135 Pages
Frequency: Annual
ISBN: 0-877083-51-7

5707 Hoover's Guide to Computer Companies
Hoover's
5800 Airport Blvd
Austin, TX 78752-3826

512-374-1187
800-486-8666
FAX 512-374-4501
E-Mail: customersupport@hoovers.com
Home Page: www.hoovers.com

David Mather, President
Paul Pellman, Executive VP Marketing/Products

250 of the largest public and private computer industry companies in in-depth profiles.
Cost: $34.95
737 Pages
Frequency: Annual
ISBN: 1-878753-80-0

5708 IT Computer Economics Report Journal
Computer Economics
2082 Business Center Drive
Suite 240
Irvine, CA 92612

949-831-8700
FAX 949-442-7688
Home Page: www.computereconomics.com

Frank Scavo, President
Dan Husiak, VP

Provides decision makers throughout the world with timely insights into the management of information systems.
Frequency: Monthly
Founded in 1978

5709 Index to AV Producers & Distributors 10th Edition
Information Today

143 Old Marlton Pike
Medford, NJ 08055-8750

609-654-6266
800-300-9868
FAX 609-654-4309
E-Mail: custserv@infotoday.com
Home Page: www.infotoday.com

Thomas H Hogan, President
Roger R Bilboul, Chairman Of The Board

Contains over 23,500 producers and distributors of AV materials of all kinds. This handy softbound volume is an indispensible tool for buyers of audiovisual materials of all kinds.
Cost: $89.00
626 Pages
ISBN: 0-937548-30-8

5710 Internet & Personal Computing Abstracts Journal
Information Today
143 Old Marlton Pike
Medford, NJ 08055-8750

609-654-6266
800-300-9868
FAX 609-654-4309
E-Mail: custserv@infotoday.com
Home Page: www.infotoday.com

Thomas H Hogan, President
Roger R Bilboul, Chairman Of The Board

This comprehensive database contains over 150,000 citations, with abstracts to reviews of commentaries on the use and applications of microcomputers and software packages.
Cost: $235.00
Frequency: Quarterly
Circulation: 10,000
Founded in 1980

5711 Inventor's Desktop Companion: A Guide to Successfully Marketing Ideas
Visible Ink Press/Gale Research
PO Box 09187
Detroit, MI 48209-0187

248-699-4253
800-877-GALE
FAX 248-699-8049

Patrick C Sommers, President

Offers information on agencies and organizations of interest to inventors, including regional and national associations, university innovation research centers and business incubators for the computer and desktop industries.
Cost: $24.95
470 Pages

5712 Micro Publishing Report's Directory of Desktop Publishing Suppliers
Cygnus Publishing
PO Box 803
Fort Atkinson, WI 53538-0803

920-000-1111
800-547-7377
FAX 920-563-1699
E-Mail: rich.reiff@cygnuspub.com
Home Page: www.cygnusb2b.com

John French, CEO
Tom Martin, Director of Public Relations
Kathy Scott, Director of Public Relations
Paul Bonaiuto, CFO

Offers valuable information on over 200 suppliers of microcomputer systems for desktop publishing.
Cost: $35.00
30 Pages
Frequency: Annual

5713 Microcomputer Market Place
Random House

202 E 50th St
New York, NY 10022

212-572-6120

Offers information on manufacturers and suppliers of computer equipment and accessories.
Cost: $29.95
795 Pages

5714 Microprocessor Integrated Circuits
DATA Digest
321 Inverness Drive South
Englewood, CO 80112

303-790-0600
800-525-7052
Home Page: www.ihs.com

Jerre Stead, Chair/CEO
Michael Armstrong, Director

Offers a list of over 185 manufacturers and distributors of microprocessor integrated circuits.
Cost: $205.00
Frequency: SemiAnnual

5715 Microsoft Applications and Systems Forums
Microsoft Corporation
1 Microsoft Way
Redmond, WA 98052-8300

425-882-8080
800-426-9400
FAX 425-936-7329
Home Page: www.microsoft.com

Steve Ballmer, CEO

This database provides an exchange of information and tips on Microsoft computer systems for participants.

5716 Modern Machine Shop's Handbook for Metalworkingi Industries on CD-ROM
Gardner Publications
6915 Valley Ln
Cincinnati, OH 45244-3153

513-527-8800
800-950-8020
FAX 513-527-8801
Home Page: www.gardnerweb.com

Rick Kline Sr, CEO
John Campos, Manager
Brian Wertheimer, Account Manager
Eddie Kania, Sales Manager

Provides a balanced blend of traditional and modern topics. In addition to containing a wide range of reference tables covering all aspects of machining, composition of materials, and dimensions of tooling and machine components.
Cost: $55.00
2368 Pages
ISBN: 1-569903-55-7
Founded in 2002

5717 National Directory of Bulletin Board Systems
Penton Media
1300 E 9th St
Suite 316
Cleveland, OH 44114-1503

216-696-7000
FAX 216-696-6662
E-Mail: information@penton.com
Home Page: www.penton.com

Jane Cooper, Marketing

Computer bulletin board systems that display notices of special events or new products are profiled.
Cost: $45.00
400 Pages
Frequency: Annual

5718 NetWire
Novell
165 Nantasket Beach Avenue
Hull, MA 02045

78- 9-5 17
800-453-2167
FAX 781-925-6545
E-Mail: john@netwire.com
Home Page: netwire.com

This database concentrates on Novell computer software and hardware information.

5719 Online Networks, Databases & Bulletin Boards on Assistive Technology
ERIC Document Reproduction Service
7420 Fullerton Road
Suite 110
Springfield, VA 22153-2852

703-440-1400
800-443-ERIC
FAX 703-440-1408

Directory of electronic networks that focus on technology-related services.

5720 Orion Blue Book: Computer
Orion Research Corporation
14555 N Scottsdale Rd
Suite 330
Scottsdale, AZ 85254-3487

480-951-1114
800-844-0759
FAX 480-951-1117
E-Mail: orion@orionbluebook.com
Home Page: www.orionbluebook.com

Roger Rohrs, Owner

63,053 products listed from 1970's to present. Over 1,000 manufacturers listed.
695 Pages
Frequency: Annual
Founded in 1985

5721 PC-Link
America Online
8619 Westwood Center Drive
Suite 200
Vienna, VA 22182-2238

Home Page: pclink.com.eg

Provides access to a variety of databases and computer services of interest to users of IBM and compatible computers running MS-DOS.
Frequency: Directory

5722 ParaTechnology Directory of Systems and Network Integrators
ParaTechnology
1215 120th Ave NE
Suite 101
Bellevue, WA 98005-2135

425-453-0676
800-377-2021
FAX 425-453-0338
Home Page: www.eside.org

One thousand computer system and network integrators in North America.
Cost: $495.00
Frequency: Annual

5723 Personal Computing Directory
Resources
PO Box 1067
Cambridge, MA 02238-1067

Directory of services and supplies to the industry.
Cost: $29.95
Frequency: Annual

5724 Pocket Guides to the Internet: Telnetting
Information Today
143 Old Marlton Pike
Medford, NJ 08055-8750

609-654-6266
800-300-9868
FAX 609-654-4309
E-Mail: custserv@infotoday.com
Home Page: www.infotoday.com

Thomas H Hogan, President
Roger R Bilboul, Chairman Of The Board
Logon information and resources available via telnetting.
Cost: $9.95

5725 Q-Link
America Online
8619 Westwood Center Drive
Suite 200
Vienna, VA 22182-2238

800-227-6364
FAX 540-265-2135

Anne Botsford
This database consists of several files of general interest news and information for users of Commodore computers.
Frequency: Full-text

5726 Shareware Magazine: PC SIG's Encyclopedia of Shareware Section
Shareware Magazine
1030 E Duane Avenue
Suite D
Sunnyvale, CA 94086-2624

408-733-8900

Offers a variety of software programs for the IBM PC and its compatibles.
Cost: $19.95
Frequency: Bi-Monthly

5727 SoftBase
Information Resources
PO Box 8120
Berkeley, CA 94707-8120

510-525-6220
FAX 510-525-1568
Home Page: www.searchsoftbase.com

Ruth K Koolish, Editor
It produces software products, services and companies abstracted from more than 200 business, computer, technical, trade and consumer publications.
Frequency: Monthly

5728 Software Encyclopedia
R R Bowker LLC
630 Central Ave
New Providence, NJ 07974-1506

908-286-0288
888-269-5372
FAX 908-464-3553
E-Mail: info@bowker.com
Home Page: www.bowker.com

R R Bowker
A comprehensive easy to navigate guide filled with detailed information on microcomputer software. Listings of over 44,600 software programs from 4,646 publishers and distributors are fully annotated to facilitate research and acquisition.
Frequency: 2 Volume set
ISBN: 0-835249-69-0

5729 Software Engineering Bibliography
Kaman Sciences Corporation

258 Genesse Street
Utica, NY 13502

315-732-1955
Home Page: www.dacs.com

Citation for over 15,000 technical reports, articles, theses, papers and books concerned with software technology.
Cost: $30.00
Frequency: Annual

5730 Software Life Cycle Tools Directory
Data & Analysis Center for Software
PO Box 1400
Rome, NY 13442-1400

315-334-4905
800-214-7921
FAX 315-334-4964
E-Mail: cust-liasn@dacs.dtic.mil
Home Page: www.iac.dtic.mil/dacs

Offers sources of more than 400 software packages for software engineering and maintenance.
Cost: $40.00
500 Pages

5731 Telecom Internet Directory
Information Gatekeepers Group
1340 Soldiers Field Rd
Suite 302
Brighton, MA 02135-1000

617-782-5033
800-323-1088
FAX 617-782-5735
E-Mail: info@igigroup.com
Home Page: www.igigroup.com

Paul Polishuk, CEO
Bev Wilson, Controller
Yesim Taskor, Controller
Developed to help find information in telecommunications efficiently and timely manner. A wide range of researchers, market analysts, information specialists, librarians and others will find the directory useful in finding information about telecommunications on the Internet.
Cost: $195.00

5732 Top 100 Service Companies
Coordinated Service
20A Court Street
Groton, MA 01450-4217

978-448-2472

100 of the largest US based independent computer service companies.

5733 UNISYS World Software Directory
Publications & Communications
Cypress Creek Road
Suite B
Cedar Park, TX 78613

512-250-9023

Offers valuable information on suppliers of computer software packages compatible with UNISYS Corporation computer systems.
140 Pages
Frequency: SemiAnnual
Circulation: 650

5734 Uplink Directory
Virginia A Ostendorf
PO Box 2896
Littleton, CO 80161-2896

303-797-3131

Directory of services and supplies to the industry.

5735 User's Directory of Computer Networks
Digital Press

129 Parker Street
Maynard, MA 01754-2199

978-493-1770

Offers a list of hosts, site contacts and administrative domains.
Cost: $35.95
630 Pages

Industry Web Sites

5736 http://gold.greyhouse.com
G.O.L.D Grey House OnLine Databases
Grey House Publishing's online database platform, GOLD, offers its Quick Search, Keyword Search and Expert Search for most business sectors including comuputer and data processing markets. The GOLD platform makes finding the information you need quick and easy - whether you're a novice searcher or an experienced database user. All of Grey House's directory products are available for subscription on the GOLD platform.

5737 www.4w.com
Information Analytics
Dedicated to the non-profit professional development of information systems managers, directors and analysts.

5738 www.aaai.org
American Association for Artificial Intelligence
A scientific society devoted to advancing the scientific understanding of the mechanisms underlying thought and intelligent behavior and their embodiment in machines.

5739 www.aace.org
Assn for the Advancement of Computing in Education
Promotes the use of computers and the internet in educational settings.

5740 www.adweek.com
Adweek
Leading decision makers in the advertising and marketing field go to Adweek.com every day for breaking news, insight, buzz, opinion, analysis, research and classifieds. The resources of all six regional editions of Adweek, as well as the national edition of Brandweek are combined with the knowledge of our online editors and the multimedia-interactive capabilities of the web to deliver vital information quickly and effectively to our target audience.

5741 www.afsmi.org
Association for Services Management International
Provides the knowledge, fellowship and career connections that customer services and support managers for technology based products and solutions needed for professional and career development.

5742 www.aiim.org
Association for Information and Image Management
The leading international organization focused on helping users to understand the challenges associated with managing documents, content, and business processes.

5743 www.aimglobal.org
AIM Global
International trade association representing automatic identification and mobility technology solution providers.

5744 www.aitp.org

Association of Information Technology Professional

Comprised of career minded individuals who seek to expand their potential employers, employees, managers, programmers and many others. This organization seeks to provide avenues for all their members to be teachers as well as students and to make contacts with other members in the IS field, all in an effort to become more marketable in rapidly changing technological careers.

5745 www.apple.com

Apple

Official web site for Apple; Macintosh computers and software.

5746 www.asm.com

Society for Materials Engineers and Scientists

A leading supplier of semiconductor process equipment in both front and back end markets. The Company possesses a strong technological base, state-of-the-art manufacturing facilities, a competent and qualified workforce and a highly trained, strategically distributed support network.

5747 www.bsa.org

Business Software Alliance

An organization dedicated to promoting a safe and legal digital world. BSA educates consumers on software management and copyright protection, cyber security, trade, e-commerce and other internet related issues.

5748 www.bta.org

Business Technology Association

Serving independent dealers, value added resellers, system integrators, manufacturers and distributors in the business equipment and system industry. BTA helps its members profit through a wide variety of services, including free legal advice and guidance; business benchmarking studies and reports; information on the latest news, trends, and products in the industry.

5749 www.calico.org

Computer Assisted Language Instruction Consortium

For language teachers, linguists, courseware developers and governments who are interested in teaching languages with the use of computer assisted instruction.

5750 www.comptia.org

CompTIA

Representing the international technology community. The goal is to provide a unified voice, global advocacy and leadership and to advance industry growth through standards, professional competence, education and business solutions.

5751 www.devx.net

DevX

The leading provider of technical and services that enable corporate application development teams to efficiently conquer development challenges and keep projects moving.

5752 www.disa.org

Data Interchange Standards Association

Many industries are looking to develop and implement eXtensible Markup Language (XML) specifications to eliminate paperwork, improve data accuracy, increase productivity, and reduce operating costs. This effort requires technical and administrative support. DISA can help.

5753 www.greyhouse.com

Grey House Publishing

Authoritative reference directories for most business sectors including computer and data processing markets. Users can search the online databases with varied search criteria allowing for custom searches by product category, geographic area, sales volume, keyword, subject and more. Full Grey House catalog and online ordering also available.

5754 www.guide.sbanetweb.com

Guide to Computer Vendors

Planning and project management involved in the installation and implementation of client server accounting systems. We provide consulting assitance to a wide range of services such modeling agencies, publishing firms as well as manufacturing and distributors.

5755 www.icca.org

Independent Computer Consultants Association

Represents a wide variety of information technology consultants who provide consulting, implementation, support, training, strategic planning, and business analysis services.

5756 www.internet.com

Internet.Com/Mecklermedia

A leading source of global Internet news, and analyses. To learn about Internet.com's latest activities

5757 www.intl-spectrum.com

International Spectrum

The independent source of information for users and vendors of IBM's UniVerse and UniData; jBASE International's jBASE; Northgate information Solutions Reality; ONgroup's ONware; Raining Data's D3, mvBASE and mvEnterprise; Revelation Software's Opensight and VIA Systems UniVision Databases.

5758 www.ioma.com

IOMA

Supports managers involved in building and maintaining state-of-the-art HRIS software, hardware, and Internet/intranet activities. Publishes newsletter.

5759 www.irga.com

International Reprographic Association

Provides a framework for the exchange of information and support for the reprographic industry. The IRgA continues to be the only independent association serving the reprographics industry and the AEC community.

5760 www.iste.org

International Society for Technology in Education

A worldwide membership of leaders and potential leaders in educational technology. We are dedicated to providing leadership and service to improve teaching and learning by advancing the effective use of technology in K-12 education and teacher education. We provide our members with information, networking opportunities, and guidance as they face the challenge of incorporating computers, the Internet, and other new technologies into their schools.

5761 www.openapplications.org

Open Applications Group

A open standards group building process-based XML standards for both B2B and A2A integration.

5762 www.pcca.org

Portable Computer and Communications Association

A forum for disparate industries to meet, learn about each other, and collaborate on the interaction of the multiple technologies involved in wireless solutions.

5763 www.polarmicro.com

Polar Microsystems

Provides consulting services that enable our clients to advance their businesses through full utilization of the Apple Macintosh hardware and software platform.

5764 www.sei.cmu.edu

Software Engineering Institute

Works closely with defense and government organizations, industry, and academia to continually improve software-intensive systems.

5765 www.sme.org

Automated Systems Technical Group/SME

This group harnesses the power of information technology for advancing product development and design, manufacturing automation, enterprise integration, and communication throughout the product life cycle and supply chain.

5766 www.spie.org

International Society for Optical Engineering

Serves the international technical community as the premier provider of education, information, and resources covering optics, photonics, and their applications.

5767 www.thinkecs.com

Enterprise Computing Solutions

A leading provider of IT infrastructure solutions for Fortune 500 and mid-tier companies throughout California. ECS builds sophisticated IT infrastructure solutions for mission critical applications, provides enterprise storage solutions that ensure data protection and business continuity and delivers state of the art server solutions for optimal computing capacity.

5768 www.unf.edu/library

University of North Florida, Carpenter Library

For catalogers of audiovisual materials and electronic resources. Provides information exchange, continuing education, and works toward a common understanding of practices and standards.

5769 www.vita.com

VMEbus International Trade Association

For manufacturers of microcomputer boards, hardware, software, military products, controllers, bus interfaces and other accessories compatible with VMEbus architecture. VITA is an incorporated, nonprofit organization of vendors and users having a common market interest.

5770 www.webdeveloper.com

Mecklermedia/Internet.Com

Information on maintaining and growing business web sites and intranets.

5771 www1.hp.com

Hewlett Packard /Compaq

The official Web site for the Compaq PCs.

Associations

5772 Aesthetics' International Association
310 E. Interstate 30
Suite B107
Garland, TX 75043

972-203-8530
877-968-7539
FAX 972-962-1480
Home Page: www.aestheticsassociation.com

Patricia Strunk, President
Michelle D'Allaird, Vice President
Michelle D'Allaird, VP, Director of Education
Saundra S. Brown, VP, Director of Operations
Melissa Lawrence, Membership Director

The association for the advancement of education and public awareness on aesthetics. Paramedical aesthetics and body spa therapy. Professionals from the medical, paramedical and beauty industries working together for the most advanced techniques for the patients and clients.
Founded in 1972

5773 Allied Beauty Association (ABA)
145 Traders Blvd. E.
Suites 26&27
Mississauga, ON IL4Z3L3

800-268-6644
FAX 905-568-1581
E-Mail: abashows@abacanada.com
Home Page: abacanada.com
Social Media: *Facebook, Twitter, LinkedIn*

Marc Speir, Executive Director

Manufacturers and distributors of the professional beauty industry that serve Canada.
Founded in 1957

5774 American Association for Esthetics Education
310 E. Interstate 30
Suite B107
Garland, TX 75043

312-321-6809
877-968-7539
Home Page: www.aestheticsassociation.com
Social Media: *Facebook, Twitter, YouTube*

Patricia Strunk, President
Michelle D'Allaird, Vice President
Michelle D'Allaird, VP, Director of Education
Melissa Lawrence, Membership Director

Provides access to educational experts, methods for increasing profits, and infomation on the latest products and techniques.
Cost: $105.00
Founded in 1972

5775 American Association of Cosmetology Schools
9927 E. Bell Road
Suite 110
Scottsdale, AZ 85260

480-810-0431
800-831-1086
FAX 480-905-0993
E-Mail: jim@beautyschools.org
Home Page: www.beautyschools.org
Social Media: *Facebook, Twitter, LinkedIn, YouTube*

Jim Cox, Executive Director
Lisa Zarda, General Manager
Sandra Bruce, Director
Lynelle Lynch, Secretary
Frank Trieu, Treasurer

Association open to all privately owned cosmetology schools.
1100 Members
Founded in 1924

5776 American Beauty Association
4330 Gaines Ranch Loop
Austin, TX 78735

512-872-2830
800-868-4265
FAX 312-245-1080
E-Mail: support@beautyassociation.org
Home Page: beautyassociation.org
Social Media: *Facebook, Twitter, YouTtbe, Google+, Instagram, P*

Pablo Arellano Jr., President
Myriam Clifford, VP
Bruce Selan, First VP
Lydia Sarfati, Second VP
George Schaeffer, Secretary

ABA members are manufacturers, manufacturer reps and consultants in the professional beauty industry. Associate members are made up of trade publications, distributors and salons. The ABA's mission is to expand, serve and protect the interests of the professional beauty industry.
200 Members
Founded in 1985

5777 American Cosmetics Manufacturers Association
1050 17th St. NW
Suite 600
Washington, DC 20036-4702

202-441-7500
E-Mail: info@acma.us
Home Page: www.acma.us
Social Media: *Facebook, Twitter, YouTube, Google+*

An association to support the export of American-made cosmetics and personal care products.

5778 American Hair Loss Association
23679 Calabasas Road
#682
Calabasas, CA 91301-1502

E-Mail: membership@americanhairloss.org
Home Page: www.americanhairloss.org

The American Hair Loss Association is the only national, non-profit membership organization dedicated to educating the public, healthcare professionals, main stream media and legislators about the emotionaally devastating disease of hair loss (alopecia). Committed to the prevention and treatment of hair loss, the ALHA is dedicated to supporting research that will ultimately treat and cure thoses who suffer from this silent epidemic.

5779 American Hair Loss Council
30 South Main
Shenandoah, PA 17976

412-765-3666
FAX 412-765-3669
E-Mail: info@ahlc.org
Home Page: www.ahlc.org
Social Media: *Facebook, Twitter, LinkedIn*

Susan Kettering, Executive Director

The nation's only, unbiased, not for profit agency, dedicated to sorting through this information, discovering what works and what doesn't,a nd presenting our findings to the consumer.

5780 American Health & Beauty Aids Institute
PO Box 19510
Chicago, IL 60619-0510

708-633-6328
FAX 708-633-6329

Home Page: www.ahbai.org
Social Media: *Facebook, Twitter*

Joe Dudley, Senior President
Jory Luste, President
Nathaniel Bronner, Jr. Executive VP

AHBAI reresents leading, African American-owned companies manufacturing ethnic hair care and beauty products. Members serve African Americans through employment, scholarships and education.

5781 American Society of Hair Restoration Surgery
225 W. Wacker Drive
Suite 650
Chicago, IL 60606

312-981-6760
FAX 312-981-6787
E-Mail: info@cosmeticsurgery.org
Home Page: www.cosmeticsurgery.org
Social Media: *Facebook, Twitter, LinkedIn*

Michael J Will, MD, DDS, FAC, President
Robert A Shumway, MD, FACS,
President-Elect
Joe Niamtu, III, DMD, Secretary
Robert H Burke, MD, DDS, FACS, Treasurer
Jane Petro, MD, Immediate Past President

Comprised of physicians specializing in hair loss, dedicated to promulgating the highest standards of medical practice and medical ethics. Provides continuing education to physicians specializing in hair transplant surgery and gives the public the latest information on medical and surgical treatments for hair loss.
1600 Members

5782 American Society of Perfumers
PO Box 1256
Piscataway, NJ 08855-1256

201-500-6101
FAX 877-732-0090
E-Mail: info@perfumers.org
Home Page: www.perfumers.org
Social Media: *Facebook, Twitter, LinkedIn, Pinterest*

Christopherÿ Diienno, President
Roger Howell, Vice-President
John Gamba, Treasurer
James Krivda, Secretary
Linda Chinery, Director

Nonprofit organization fosters and encourages the art and science of perfumery in the US while promoting professional exchange and a high standard of professional conduct within the fragrance industry. The ASP holds yearly symposiums in the New York City area where leading members of the fragrance industry are invited to speak and present information on all aspects of the industry.
Founded in 1947

5783 Association Accredited Cosmetology Schools
5201 Leesburg Pike
Falls Church, VA 22041-3244
Ronald Smith, Publisher

Association for those concerned with cosmetology.
6 Members

5784 B-cause
PO Box 4814
Poughkeepsie, NY 12601

845-431-6670
Home Page: www.bcause.org
Social Media: *Facebook*

Rudy Sprogis, Founder/President

Non-profit organization that advances charitable causes for salon owners and beauty industry professionals.
Founded in 2000

5785 BOBSA
PO Box 25173
San Francisco, CA 94128

650-863-3491
FAX 858-712-1934
Home Page: bobsaone.org
Social Media: *Facebook, Twitter, LinkedIn*

Sam Ennon, President

Representing beauty store operators in the ethnic health and beauty-care industry.

5786 Chain Drug Marketing Association
43157 W Nine Mile Road
PO Box 995
Novi, MI 48376-0995

248-449-9300
FAX 248-449-9396
E-Mail: support@chaindrug.com
Home Page: www.chaindrug.com
Social Media: *Facebook, Twitter, LinkedIn, YouTube, Pinterest*

Jack Walker, Chairman
Jim Devine, President
Jim Salley, Treasurer
Judy Aspinall, Secretary

Members are regional drug chains from across North ASmerica Association markets over 800 products under the name Quality Choice to its members.
101 Members
Founded in 1926

5787 Consumer Healthcare Products Association
1625 Eye Street, NW
Suite 600
Washington, DC 20006-2105

202-429-9260
FAX 202-223-6835
E-Mail: eassey@chpa-info.org
Home Page: www.chpa-info.org
Social Media: *Twitter, YouTube, Pinterest*

Paul L. Sturman, Chair
Scott Melville, President/CEO
John F. Gay, Vice President, Government Affairs
Tiffany Currie, Controller
Susan M DiBartolo, Manager, IT, Database & Website

Promotes industry growth through consumer understanding, appreciation, and acceptance of responsible self-care in America's health care system by developing and sustaining a climate that provides consumers with convenient access to safe and effective nonprescription medicines and other self-care products marketed without undue restrictions.
Founded in 1881

5788 Cosmetic Executive Women
159 West 25th Street
8th Floor
New York, NY 10001

212-685-5955
646-929-8000
FAX 212-685-3334
E-Mail: ksweeney@cew.org
Home Page: www.cew.org
Social Media: *Facebook, Twitter, LinkedIn, YouTube*

Carlotta Jacobson, President
Kelly McPhilliamy, Treasurer
Jill Scalamandre, Chairwoman
Barbara Kotlikoff, Vice Chairwomen
Heidi Manheimer, Vice Chairwomen

To advance the professional growth and leadership development of women in the beauty industry.
4000 Members
Founded in 1954

5789 Cosmetic Industry Buyers and Suppliers
36 Lakeville Road
New Hyde Park, NY 11040

516-775-0220
FAX 516-328-9789
E-Mail: cibsmail@cibsonline.com
Home Page: www.cibsonline.com
Social Media: *LinkedIn*

Rafael Cruz, President
Jo_anne Greco, Vice President
Myoschi. T Oriol, Treasurer
Nick LoPrinzi, Director
Laura Carey, Director

Members are individuals providing and obtaining essential oils, chemicals, packaging and other goods for the cosmetic industry.
800 Members
Founded in 1948

5790 Cosmetologists Chicago
440 S. LaSalle Street
Suite 2325
Chicago, IL 60611-4255

312-321-6809
800-648-2505
FAX 312-673-6612
E-Mail: info@americasbeautyshow.com
Home Page:
www.chicagomidwestbeautyshow.com
Social Media: *Facebook, Twitter, YouTube, Pinterest*

Denise Provenzano, President
Larry Silvestri, First VP
Robert Passage, Second Vice President
Karen Gordon, Secretary
Joseph Cartagena, Immediate Past President

A beauty voice and presenter of cosmetology shows.

5791 Cosmetology Advancement Foundation
PO Box 811
FDR Station
New York, NY 10150

212-750-2412
FAX 212-593-0862
E-Mail: nalcopr@aol.com
Home Page: cosmetology.org

Norma A. Lee, Executive Director

Members represent the professional beauty industry's varied constituencies: cosmetologists, salon owners, cosmetology schools, distributors, manufacturers, associations and professional publications. CAF works through the All-Industry Summit to identify issues that affect the future growth and development of the industry.

5792 Drug, Chemical & Associated Technologies Association
One Union St
Suite 208
Robbinsville, NJ 08691-3162

609-208-1888
800-640-3228
FAX 609-208-0599
E-Mail: mtimony@dcat.org
Home Page: www.dcat.org

George Svokos, Executive Director
Laura Kuhen, Project Coordinator
Lyra Myers, Finance Officer
Dr. Folker Ruchatz, First Vice President
Jeanne Motola, Administrative Assistent

The premier business development association whose membership is comprised of companies that manufacture, distribute or provide services to the pharamceutical, chemical, nutritional and related industries.
Founded in 1890

5793 Esthetics Manufacturers and Distributors Alliance
401 N Michigan Avenue
Chicago, IL 60611

312-215-5120
800-868-4265
FAX 312-245-1080

Paul Dykstra, Executive Director
Paul Scott Premo, President
Charles Mizelle, VP
Mark Lees, Chairman
Julianne Bendel, Manager

A member of the American Beauty Association, whose members are manufacturers of specific products related to the professional beauty industry. EMDA is dedicated to meeting the needs of skin care and body care manufacturers and distributors and the salons they service. The mission of the American Beauty Association and all of its sub-groups is to expand, serve and protect the interests of the professional beauty industry.
40 Members
Founded in 1993

5794 Fragrance Foundation
621 2nd Avenue
2nd Floor
New York, NY 10016

212-725-2755
FAX 646-786-3260
E-Mail: info@fragrance.org
Home Page: www.fragrance.org
Social Media: *Facebook, Twitter, LinkedIn, YouTube*

Elizabeth Mushmanno, President
Marc Blaison, Executive VP

Nonprofit, educational arm of the international fragrance industry. Devotes its energies to creating an atmosphere of understanding and appreciation of the benefits and pleasures of fragrance in all its many forms.
160 Members
Founded in 1949

5795 Fragrance Materials Association of the US
1620 I St NW
Suite 925
Washington, DC 20006-4076

202-293-5800
FAX 202-463-8998
Home Page: www.fmafragrance.org
Social Media: *Facebook, Twitter*

Glenn Roberts, Executive Director
Daniel J Carey, VP
Robert Bedoukian, Secretary
Stephen A Block, Treasurer
90 Members
Founded in 1927

5796 Fragrance Research Fund
621 2nd Avenue
2nd Floor
New York, NY 10016

212-725-2755
FAX 646-786-3260
E-Mail: info@fragrance.org
Home Page: www.fragrance.org/
Social Media: *Facebook, Twitter, YouTube*

Elizabeth Mushmanno, President
Marc Blaison, Executive VP
Theresa Molnar, Executive Director
Amy Rubins, Special Projects and Events
Lilia Nicoletti, Director of Office Operations

Offers financial support for doctors and clinical researchers. Bestows awards.
Founded in 1949

5797 Handmade Cosmetic Alliance
Home Page:
www.handmadecosmeticalliance.org
Advocating for state and federal legislation that
supports the growing handmade cosmetics and
soap industry.
Founded in 2007

**5798 Independent Cosmetic Manufacturers
and Distributors**
21925 Field Parkway
Suite 205
Deer Park, IL 60010

847-991-4499
800-334-2623
FAX 847-991-8161
E-Mail: info@icmad.org
Home Page: www.icmad.org
Social Media: *Facebook, Twitter, LinkedIn*

Pam Busiek, President/CEO
Sheila Sebor, VP Operations
Vance Seaton, Executive Assistant
Stan Katz, Chairman Emeritus
Karen Acker, Director

Represents cosmetic manufacturers, distributors and suppliers to industry. Mission: to represent, educate and foster the growth and
profitability of entrepreneurial companies in
the cosmetic and personal care industries
worldwide.
540 Members
Founded in 1974

5799 Indoor Tanning Association (ITA)
2025 M St, NW
Suite 800
Washington, DC 20036

888-377-0477
FAX 202-367-2142
Home Page: www.theita.com
Social Media: *Facebook, Twitter, LinkedIn*

Dan Humiston, President
John Overstreet, Executive Director
Dan Humiston, President
Karen Bentlage, Public Relations

Represents indoor tanning manufacturers, distributors, facility owners and members from
other support industries.
1000+ Members
Founded in 1999

5800 International Aloe Science Council
8630 Fenton Street
Suite 918
Silver Spring, MD 20910-3818

734-476-9690
FAX 301-588-1174
Home Page: www.iasc.org

Steven Dentali, President
Jasen Lavoie, President-Elect
Charlie Metcalfe, Treasurer
Walt Jones, Director
Roger Poore, Chairman

Explores the use of aloe in cosmetic industries,
hair products, herb preparations,
pharmaceuticals and drinks.
300 Members
Founded in 1981

**5801 International Association of Color
Manufacturers**
1101 17th Street NW
Suite 700
Washington, DC 20036

202-293-5800
FAX 202-463-8998
E-Mail: info@iacmcolor.org

Home Page: www.iacmcolor.org
Social Media: *LinkedIn*

Glenn Roberts, Executive Director
David R. Carpenter, President & Treasurer
Rohit Tibrewala, Secretary

Actively represents the interests of the regulated color industry by demonstrating the safety
of color additives and promotes the industry's
economic growth by participating in new color
approvals, regulatory and legislative issues that
affect the industry worldwide.
15 Members
Founded in 1972

**5802 International Fragrance Association
North America**
1655 Fort Myer Dr.
Suite 875
Arlington, VA 22209

571-317-1500
FAX 571-312-8033
E-Mail: info@ifrana.org
Home Page: ifrana.org
Social Media: *Facebook, Twitter, Pinterest*

Jennifer Abril, President
Megan Ekstrom, Director, Government Affairs
Suzanne Hartigan, Director, Sci. Pol'y & Reg.
Affairs

Part of the International Fragrance Association
network, IFRA North America advocates for
the interests of companies in the fragrance
manufacturing and fragrance materials supply
trades.
60 Members
Founded in 2011

**5803 International Perfume Bottle
Association**
PO Box 1299
Paradise, CA 95967

E-Mail: paradise@sunset.net
Home Page: www.perfumebottles.org
Social Media: *Facebook*

Jeffrey Sanfilippo, President
Teri Wirth, Vice President
Lillie Gold, Membership Secretary
Steven Shulman, Treasurer
Madeleine Winkelmann, Recording Secretary

Worldwide non-profit organization of people
who collect and deal in the variety of perfume
containers.
Cost: $45.00
2000+ Members
Founded in 1988

5804 International SPA Association
2365 Harrodsburg Road
Suite A325
Lexington, KY 40504

859-226-4326
888-651-4772
FAX 859-226-4445
E-Mail: ispa@ispastaff.com
Home Page: www.experienceispa.com
Social Media: *Facebook, Twitter, LinkedIn,
YouTube*

Michael Tompkins, Chair
Ella Stimpson, Vice Chair
Jennifer Wayland-Smith, Vice Chairman
Todd Shaw, Secretary/ Treasurer

International community of spa professionals,
product manufacturers and service providers.
Cost: $530.00
Founded in 1990

**5805 International SalonSpa Business
Network**
4712 E 2nd St
#445
Belmont Shore, CA 90803

562-453-3995
FAX 866-444-5139
Home Page: salonspanetwork.org
Social Media: *Facebook, Twitter, Google+*

Rhoda Olsen, President
Eric Bakkan, Vice President
Pat Neville, Vice President
Larry Walt, Treasurer
Charles Penzone, Secretary

The association strives to unify the industry
and drive it to become more politically active.
Members share information, conduct
roundtables and help each other recruit, train
and retain their staffs.
60+ Members

5806 Nail Manufacturers Council
Professional Beauty Association
15825 N. 71st Street
Suite 100
Scottsdale, AZ 85254-1521

480-281-0424
800-468-2274
FAX 480-905-0708
E-Mail: info@probeauty.org
Home Page: www.probeauty.org/nmc
Social Media: *Facebook, Twitter, LinkedIn,
YouTube, Pinterest*

Reuben Carranza, Chair
Scott Buchanan, Chairman
Bruce Selan, Treasurer

The NMC comprises the leading manufacturers
of nail care products sold to, and used in, professional salons. Members cooperate with the
association to assure the dissemination of education, training, and technical information concerning nail care products. The NMC has been
active in working with international, federal,
and state bodies to maintain high professional
standards and ensure the safety of industry professionals and their customers, as well as the
communities they serve.
50 Members
Founded in 1990

**5807 National Accrediting Commission of
Cosmetology Arts &
Sciences(NACCAS)**
4401 Ford Avenue
Suite 1300
Arlington, VA 22302

703-600-7600
FAX 703-379-2200
E-Mail: naccas@naccas.org
Home Page: naccas.org

Tony Mirando, Executive Director
Eddie Broomfield, Assistant to Executive
Director

To accredit post-secondary cosmetology
schools and programs.
1050 Members

**5808 National Beauty Culturists' League
(NBCL)**
25 Logan Circle N.W.
Washington, DC 20005

202-332-2695
FAX 202-332-0940
E-Mail: mercedestoregano@hotmail.com
Home Page: www.nbcl.info

Dr. Katie B. Catalon, President

Continuing education and higher learning degree program that serves as a unifying force

and a catalyst for professionalism, excellence and growth of the beauty industry.
Founded in 1940

5809 National Coalition of Estheticians Manufacturers/Distributors Assns.

484 Spring Avenue
Ridgewood, NJ 07450-4624

201-670-4100
FAX 201-670-4265
E-Mail: nceaorg@aol.com
Home Page: www.ncea.tv

Susanne S Warfield, Executive Director

Represents and promotes the esthetic and related professions industry by sharing information, building consensus and providing a unified voice on behalf of the industry.
7000+ Members
Founded in 2000

5810 National Cosmetology Association

15825 N. 71st Street
#100
Scottsdale, AZ 85254-1521

480-281-0424
800-468-2274
FAX 480-905-0708
Home Page: www.probeauty.org
Social Media: *Facebook, Twitter, LinkedIn, YouTube, Pinterest, Instagram*

Reuben Carranza, Chair
Beth Hickey, Vice Chair
Steve Sleeper, Executive Director
Rachel Molepske, Manager of Leadership Operations
Eric Z Horn, CMP, Associate Executive Director

Nationwide community of salon professionals, connected by a common passion for learning, growing and raising the professionalism of the entire salon industry. As a group we have a storng voice in our communities, our industry and with our government because ithe NCA is for everyone in the professional salon industry. Members have access to education, fashion events, community service and inurance — all the tools needed to build your career.
30000 Members

5811 National Interstate Council of State Boards of Cosmetology

7622 Briarwood Cir
Little Rock, AR 72205-4811

501-227-8262
FAX 501-227-8212
E-Mail: dnorton@nictesting.org
Home Page: www.nictesting.org

Kay Kendrick, President
Betty Leake, Vice President
Wayne Kindle, Secretary/ Treasurer

Merger of National Council of State Boards of Cosmetology and Interstate Council of State Boards of Cosmetology. Persons commissioned by the state governments to administer cosmetology laws and examine applicants for cosmetology licenses.
3200 Members
Founded in 1950

5812 National Latino Cosmetology Association NLCA

7925 W Russell Rd
PO Box 401044
Las Vegas, NV 89140

702-448-5020
877-658-3801
FAX 702-448-8993
E-Mail: marketing@nlcamerican.org

Home Page: nlcamerican.org
Social Media: *Facebook, Twitter, Pinterest*

Julie Zepeda, President/ CEO
Gustavo Castillo, Executive Producer
Mark Sejvar, Marketing Manager

Unites beauty professionals, including salon/spa owners, licensed cosmetologists, barbers, estheticians, nail technicians, students, distributors and manufacturers representing the interests of the beauty industry on a global level.
Founded in 2006

5813 Personal Care Products Council

1620 L Street
Suite 1200
Washington, DC 20036-4702

202-331-1770
FAX 202-331-1969
Home Page: www.personalcarecouncil.org
Social Media: *Facebook, Twitter, LinkedIn, YouTube*

Pamela Bailey, President
Mark Pollak, VP
Cheryl Mason, Secretary

The leading national trade association representing the global cosmetic and personal care products industry. Member companies manufacture, distribute, and supply the vast majority of finished personal care products marketed in the U.S.
600 Members
Founded in 1894

5814 Professional Beauty Association

15825 N 71st Street
Suite 100
Scottsdale, AZ 85254

480-281-0424
800-468-2274
FAX 480-905-0708
Home Page: www.probeauty.org
Social Media: *Facebook, Twitter, LinkedIn, YouTube*

Scott Buchanan, Chair
Reuben Carranza, Vice Chair
Bruce Selan, Treasurer

A non-profit trade association that represents the interests of the professional beauty industry from manufacturers and distributors to salons and spas. Offers business tools, education, advocacy, networking and more to improve individual businesses and the industry as a whole.

5815 Professional Beauty Foundation

13034 Saticoy Avenue
N Hollywood, CA 91605

800-211-4872
Home Page: www.probeautyfederation.org

A nonprofit organization made up of professional beauty organizations dedicated to promote and protect the professional beauty industry as it relates to government laws and regulation.

5816 RIFM: Research Institute for Fragrance Materials

50 Tice Boulevard
Woodcliff Lake, NJ 07677

201-689-8089
FAX 201-689-8090
E-Mail: rifm@rifm.org
Home Page: www.rifm.org
Social Media: *Facebook, Twitter, LinkedIn, Pinterest*

Sean G. Traynor, Ph.D, President (Chair)
Robert H. Bedoukian, Ph.D, President (Vice Chair)
David C. Shipman, Group Vice President (Treasurer)

Steven Hicks, Secretary
Michael Carlos, President (Fragrance Division)

Evaluates and distributes scientific data on the safety of fragrance raw materials found in cosmetics, perfumes, shampoos, acndles, air fresheners and other personal products, to encourage uniform safety standards. Membership is open to all companies that manufacture , sell, distribute or engage in business related to the fragrance industry for at least one year.
Founded in 1966

5817 Regulatory Affairs Professionals Society

5635 Fishers Lane
Suite 550
Rockville, MD 20852-3048

301-770-2920
FAX 301-841-7956
E-Mail: raps@raps.org
Home Page: www.raps.org
Social Media: *Facebook, Twitter, LinkedIn, YouTube, Google+, Flickr*

Rainer Voelksen, Chairman of the Board
Martha A Brumfield, PhD, President
Todd Chermak, RPh, PhD, President-Elect
Salma Michor, Secretary/ Treasurer
Don Boyer, BSc, RAC, FRAPS, Director

The foremost worldwide member organization creating and upholding standards of ethica, credentialing and education for the regulatory affairs profession within the health product sector.
10000 Members
Founded in 1976

5818 Scent Marketing Institute

7 Fox Meadow Road
New York, NY 10583

646-236-4606
FAX 914-470-2416
E-Mail: info@scentmarketing.org
Home Page: www.scentmarketing.org
Social Media: *Facebook, Twitter, LinkedIn, YouTube*

Harald H Vogt, Founder/Chief Marketer
Avery Gilbert PhD, Chief Scientist

Provides networking, educational and marketing support to our member companies and supplies information about scent marketing to the press, marketing, advertising and branding agencies and brand owners.
Founded in 2004

5819 Sense of Smell Institute

621 2nd Avenue
2nd Floor
New York, NY 10016

212-725-2755
FAX 646-786-3260
E-Mail: info@fragrance.org
Home Page: www.senseofsmell.org
Social Media: *Facebook, Twitter*

Elizabeth Mushmanno, President

Provides information resources to the public, members of the media, corporate and academic sectors. Also sponsors and conducts educational and public outreach programs to increase awareness of the important role the sense of smell plays in our lives.
Founded in 1949

5820 Society of Clinical and Medical Hair Removal

2424 American Lane
Madison, WI 53704-3102

608-443-2470
FAX 608-443-2474
E-Mail: homeoffice@scmhr.org

Home Page: www.scmhr.org
Social Media: *Facebook, Twitter, Google+*

William A. Moore, President
Fadia Hoyek, Executive Vice President
Carol Crowley, Vice President
Lisa Birket, Treasurer
Denise MacIsaace, Secretary

An international non profit organization with members in the United States, Canada, Australia, Japan and beyond. Supports all methods of hair removal and is dedicated to the research of new technology that will keep its members at the pinnacle of thier professsion, offering safe, effective hair removal to their clients.
600 Members
Founded in 1985

5821 Society of Cosmetic Chemists
120 Wall St
Suite 2400
New York, NY 10005-4088

212-668-1500
FAX 212-668-1504
E-Mail: scc@scconline.org
Home Page: www.scconline.org
Social Media: *Facebook, Twitter, LinkedIn*

Guy Padulo, President
Dawn Burke, Vice President
Peter Tsolis, Treasurer
Dawn Burke-Colvin, Secretary
Dawn Thiel Glase, Secretary

Dedicated to the advancement of cosmetic science, the Society strives to increase and disseminate scientific information through meetings and publications. By promoting research in cosmetic science and industry, and by setting high ethical, professional and educational standards, we reach our goal of improving the qualifacations of cosmetic scientists.
4000 Members
Founded in 1945

5822 The Day Spa Association
2863 Hedberg Drive
Union City, NJ 07087

877-851-8998
FAX 855-344-8990
Home Page: dayspaassociation.com
Social Media: *Facebook, Google+*

Allan Share, President & Executive Director

Open to day spas, spa salons, individuals working in the spa industry and companies supplying products and services to the industry. Its aim is to unify and support the spa industry.
900 Members

5823 Women in Flavor & Fragrance Commerce
3301 State Route 66
Suite 205
Neptune, NJ 07753-2705

732-922-0500
FAX 732-922-0560
E-Mail: info@wffc.org
Home Page: www.wffc.org
Social Media: *Facebook, LinkedIn*

Amy Marks-Mcgee, President
Kay Murano, Ph.D., Vice President
Bea Hornedo, Secretary
Erica Lermond Mcdonnell, Treasurer

This organization was borne out of a recognized need for a networking, education and support system for women in our industry. Providing a center of education, camaraderie, support, and networking.
300 Members
Founded in 1982

Newsletters

5824 American Society of Perfumers Newsletter
PO Box 1551
West Caldwell, NJ 07004

201-991-0040
FAX 201-991-0073
E-Mail: info@perfumers.org
Home Page: www.perfumers.org
Social Media: *Twitter*

Marvel Fields, President

Information on upcoming events, industry news, fragrance related issues and special articles.
Founded in 1947

5825 FDC Reports: Rose Sheet
FDC Reports
5550 Friendship Boulevard
Suite 1
Chevy Chase, MD 20815-7256

301-657-9830
800-332-2181
FAX 301-664-7238
Home Page: www.fdcreports.com

Brooke Mcmanus, Editor
Susan Easton, Publisher
Mike Squires, President
Shaun Smith, Marketing
Nicole Tesschamts, Circulation Manager

For executives in the cosmetics, toiletries, fragrances and skin care industries. Provides, coverage of the regulatory and legal environment for cosmetics, major scientific developments and testing methods product marketing news, new product launches; promotions and advertising, retail weekly trademark listings, mergers and acquisitions and developments in the European community.
Cost: $1050.00
Frequency: Weekly
ISSN: 0279-1110
Founded in 1939

5826 Perfume Bottle Quarterly
PO Box 1299
Paradise, CA 95967

E-Mail: paradise@sunset.net
Home Page: www.perfumebottles.org

Ed Lefkowith, President
Anne Conrad, Publications Chair

Features association news bottle photos, people, literature reviews, trade events, and classified ads. Providing a tremendous resource of knowledge about our field, PBQ is essential to staying current on information, events, and people of the field.
24 Pages
Frequency: Quarterly
Founded in 1997
Printed in 4 colors

5827 Society of Cosmetic Chemists Newsletter
Society of Cosmetic Chemists
120 Wall St
Suite 2400
New York, NY 10005-4088

212-668-1500
FAX 212-668-1504
E-Mail: scc@scconline.org
Home Page: www.scconline.org

Randy Wickett, Ph.D, President
Joseph Dallal, Vice President
Guy Padulo, Vice President-Elect

Dawn Burke-Colvin, Secretary
Tony O'Lenick, Treasurer

Issued once a month providing up-to-date information about activities within the SCC and contemporary issues in international arbitration and mediation.
3600 Members
Founded in 1945

5828 WFFC Newsletter
Women in Flavor & Fragrance Commerce
3301 State Route 66
Suite 205
Neptune, NJ 07753-2705

732-922-0500
FAX 732-922-0560
E-Mail: info@wffc.org
Home Page: www.wffc.org

Joanne Kennedy, President
Celine Roche, Vice President
Kathryn Bardsley, Secretary
Anne Marie Api, Treasurer

This organization was borne out of a recognized need for a networking, education and support system for women in our industry. Providing a center of education, camaraderie, support, and networking.
300 Members
Founded in 1982

Magazines & Journals

5829 Beauty Fashion
Ledes Group
286 Madison Ave
Suite 200
New York, NY 10017-6407

212-840-8800
FAX 212-840-7246
Home Page: www.beautyfashion.com

John Ledes, Owner
Michelle Krell Kydd, Marketing

The authoritative magazine in the field of cosmetics, toiletries, fragrances and personal care.
Cost: $25.00
131 Pages
Frequency: Monthly
Circulation: 18672
ISSN: 0005-7487
Printed in 4 colors on glossy stock

5830 Beauty Fashion: Body/Bath/Sun Issue
Beauty Fashion
16 E 40th Street
New York, NY 10016

212-328-6789
FAX 212-840-7246
Home Page: www.beautyfashion.com
Social Media: *Facebook*

Offers listings of body/bath and sun products as well as manufacturers and US distributors.
Cost: $25.00
Frequency: Annual
Circulation: 17,000

5831 Beauty Fashion: CTFA Convention Issue
Beauty Fashion
16 E 40th Street
New York, NY 10016

212-328-6789
FAX 212-840-7246
Home Page: www.beautyfashion.com

Offers various suppliers of goods and services to the cosmetics industry manufacturers represented at Cosmetic, Toiletry and Fragrance As-

sociation convention.
Cost: $25.00
Frequency: Annual
Circulation: 17,000

5832 Beauty Fashion: Cosmetics Issue
Beauty Fashion
16 E 40th Street
New York, NY 10016

212-328-6789
FAX 212-840-7246
Home Page: www.beautyfashion.com

Offers listings of color cosmetics products for women as well as manufacturers and US distributors.
Cost: $25.00
Frequency: Annual
Circulation: 17,000

5833 Beauty Fashion: Women's Fragrance Issue
Beauty Fashion
16 E 40th Street
New York, NY 10016-5101

212-328-6789
FAX 212-840-7246
Home Page: www.beautyfashion.com/

Michelle Kre Kydd, Marketing
Veronica Kelly, Circulation Manager
Adelaide Farah, Editor

Offers listings of women's fragrance products including perfumes, eau de toilettes, and colognes as well as manufacturers and US distributors.
Cost: $25.00
Frequency: Monthly
Circulation: 17000

5834 Beauty Fashion: Women's Treatment Issue
Beauty Fashion
Ste 700
286 Madison Ave
New York, NY 10017-6407

212-840-8800
FAX 212-840-7246
Home Page: www.beautyfashion.com/

Adelaide Farah, Group Editorial Director
Veronica Kelly, Subscription
Michelle Krell Kydd, Marketing

Offers listings of products and manufacturers and US distributors of cosmetics called treatment products.
Cost: $25.00
Frequency: Monthly

5835 Beauty Forum NAILPRO
Creative Age Publications
7628 Densmore Ave
Van Nuys, CA 91406-2042

818-782-7560
800-442-5667
FAX 818-782-7450
E-Mail: dayspa@creativeage.com
Home Page: www.creativeage.com

Linda Lewis, Editor
Linda Kossoff, Marketing Manager

NAILPRO for a number of markets in Europe.
Cost: $22.00
Frequency: Monthly
Founded in 1971

5836 Beauty Inc.
Fairchild Publications
7 W 34th St
New York, NY 10001-8100

212-630-3880
800-289-0273
FAX 212-630-3868

E-Mail: customerservice@fairchildpub.com
Home Page: www.fairchildpub.com

Mary Berner, President
Jenny B. Fine, Editor-in-Chief
Sarah Murphy, Publisher

The ONLY resource for the global beauty supply chain-from the suppliers and manufacturers who develop the products to the retailers who influence purchase. Packed with immediate actionable information and inspiration.
Cost: $ 60.00
Frequency: Monthly
Circulation: 40056

5837 Beauty Packaging
Rodman Publishing
70 Hilltop Rd
3rd Floor
Ramsey, NJ 07446-1150

201-825-2552
FAX 201-825-0553
E-Mail: info@rodpub.com
Home Page: www.nutraceuticalsworld.com

Rodman Zilenziger Jr, President
Matt Montgomery, VP

Covering all types of packaging. Beauty Packaging is published for executives involved in the personal care, cosmetic and fragrance industry.
Cost: $40.00
Circulation: 17387
Founded in 1965

5838 Beauty Store Business
Creative Age Publications
7628 Densmore Ave
Van Nuys, CA 91406-2042

818-782-7560
800-442-5667
FAX 818-782-7450
E-Mail: dayspa@creativeage.com
Home Page: www.creativeage.com

Linda Lewis, Editor
Linda Kossoff, Marketing Manager

Products, news and trends for open-line and professional beauty stores and distributors.
Cost: $22.00
Frequency: Monthly
Founded in 1971

5839 Cosmetic Ingredient Review
1101 17th St NW
Suite 310
Washington, DC 20036-4720

202-331-0651
FAX 202-331-0088
E-Mail: cirinfo@cir-safety.org
Home Page: www.cir-safety.org

Alan Andersen, Executive Director
Wilma F. Bergfeld, Chairman

Assesses the safety of ingredients used in cosmetics in an unbiased manner and publishes the result in open, peer written literature.
Cost: $100.00
Frequency: Annual+
Founded in 1976

5840 Cosmetic World
Ledes Group
286 Madison Ave
Suite 200
New York, NY 10017-6407

212-840-8800
FAX 212-840-7246
Home Page: www.cosmeticworld.com

John Ledes, Owner
Dorene Kaplan, Managing Editor

Current industry events, legislation, management changes and corporate activities, as well as marketing developments and financial analy-

sis.
Cost: $175.00
Frequency: Weekly
Circulation: 5397

5841 Cosmetics & Toiletries
Allured Publishing Corporation
336 Gundersen Dr
Suite A
Carol Stream, IL 60188-2403

630-653-2155
FAX 630-653-2192
E-Mail: customerservice@allured.com
Home Page: www.allured.com

Janet Ludwig, President
Linda Knott, Director Of Operations

This magazine presents a full range of products covering the international cosmetic technology field - including the magazine, a tradeshow, conferences, books and extensive Web sites. The magazine brings the most current technologies in formulating, research, regulations and new ingredients. It also delivers for you a devoted readership base of cosmetic chemists and scientists around the world.
Cost: $98.00
110 Pages
Frequency: Monthly
Circulation: 15,000
ISSN: 0361-4387
Printed in 4 colors on glossy stock

5842 DaySpa Magazine
Creative Age Publications
7628 Densmore Ave
Van Nuys, CA 91406-2042

818-782-7560
800-442-5667
FAX 818-782-7450
E-Mail: dayspa@creativeage.com
Home Page: www.creativeage.com

Linda Lewis, Editor
Linda Kossoff, Marketing Manager

Powerful ideas to build your spa business.
Cost: $22.00
Frequency: Monthly
Founded in 1971

5843 Delicious Living
New Hope Natural Media
1401 Pearl St
Suite 200
Boulder, CO 80302-5346

303-939-8440
FAX 303-939-9886
E-Mail: info@newhope.com
Home Page: www.newhope.com
Social Media: *Facebook, Twitter*

Fred Linder, President
Pamela Emanoil, Advertising Manager

A trusted health and wellness resource for more than 25 years.
Cost: $12.99
Frequency: Monthly

5844 Dermascope Magazine
Aesthetics International Association
2611 N Belt Line Rd
Suite 101
Mesquite, TX 75182-9301

972-203-8530
800-961-3777
FAX 972-226-2339
Home Page: www.dermascope.com

William Strunk, Publisher
Rachel Valma, Circulation Director
Casey Fore, Editor

The official publication for the advancement of education and public awareness. Variety of articles on skin care, makeup, body spa therapy and paramedical articles where medical and

beauty specialists interact.
Cost: $45.00
Frequency: Monthly
Circulation: 80000
Founded in 1972

5845 Global Cosmetic Industry

Allured Publishing Corporation
336 Gundelsen Drive
Suite A
Carol Stream, IL 60188-2755

630-653-2155
FAX 630-597-0118
Home Page: www.gcimagazine.com

Jeff Falk, Editor in Chief
Kim Jednachowski, Sales/Account Manager

The business information resource for marketers, brand managers, manufacturers and executives in the global beauty industry. Industry professionals look to GCI for the strategies, trends, analyses and market data that translate into brand impact.
Circulation: 36,500

5846 Happi

Rodman Publishing
70 Hilltop Rd
3rd Floor
Ramsey, NJ 07446-1150

201-825-2552
FAX 201-825-0553
E-Mail: info@rodpub.com
Home Page: www.nutraceuticalsworld.com

Rodman Zilenziger Jr, President
Matt Montgomery, VP

Serves the manufacturers and fillers of cosmetics, toiletries, fragrances, pharmaceuticals, detergents and chemical specialties inclusing household cleaning products and others product lines allied to the field.
Founded in 1964

5847 Health Products Business

Cygnus Publishing
2 Huntington Quad
Suite 301n
Melville, NY 11747-4618

631-845-2700
FAX 631-845-2723
E-Mail: feedback@magazines.com
Home Page: www.healthproducts.com

Susanne Alberto, Editor/Features
Bruce Leftakels, Publisher

This is a trade magazine that covers news and trends in the natural health products industry vitamins, herbs, dietary supplements and other products. Publishes annual raw materials directory and purchasing guide. Target audience, natural products retail store owners, buyers and managers. Qualified subscription only.
Founded in 1996

5848 Inside Cosmeceuticals

Virgo Publishing LLC
3300 N Central Ave
Suite 300
Phoenix, AZ 85012-2532

480-675-9925
FAX 480-990-0819
E-Mail: peggyj@vpico.com
Home Page: www.vpico.com

Jenny Bolton, President

An online information source exploring emerging product trends and scientific research designed to support the growth and development of the cosmeceuticals market. Visited by manufacturers, marketers and formulators of healthy and innovative cosmetics and personal care products.
Mailing list available for rent: 17000+ names at $var per M

5849 Inspire

Creative Age Publications
7628 Densmore Ave
Van Nuys, CA 91406-2042

818-782-7560
800-442-5667
FAX 818-782-7450
E-Mail: dayspa@creativeage.com
Home Page: www.creativeage.com

Linda Lewis, Editor
Linda Kossoff, Marketing Manager

America's most popular line of hairstyling books.
Cost: $22.00
Frequency: Monthly
Founded in 1971

5850 Journal of Essential Oil Research/JEOR

Allured Publishing Corporation
336 Gundersen Dr
Suite A
Carol Stream, IL 60188-2403

630-653-2155
FAX 630-653-2192
E-Mail: customerservice@allured.com
Home Page: www.allured.com

Janet Ludwig, President
Linda Knott, Director Of Operations

Forum for the publication of essential oil research and analysis.
Cost: $660.00
Frequency: 6x/Year

5851 Launchpad

Creative Age Publications
7628 Densmore Ave
Van Nuys, CA 91406-2042

818-782-7560
800-442-5667
FAX 818-782-7450
E-Mail: dayspa@creativeage.com
Home Page: www.creativeage.com

Linda Lewis, Editor
Linda Kossoff, Marketing Manager

News and features about new products for hair, nails, makeup, skincare and tools for beauty professionals.
Cost: $22.00
Frequency: Monthly
Founded in 1971

5852 LiveSpa Magazine

International Spa Association
2365 Harrodsburg Road
Suite A325
Lexington, KY 40504

888-651-4772
FAX 859-226-4445
E-Mail: ispa@ispastaff.com
Home Page: www.experienceispa.com
Social Media: Facebook, Twitter

Lynne Walker McNees, President
Deborah Waldvogel, Chairman
Jennifer Wayland-Smith, Vice Chairman
Ella Stimpson, Secretary/ Treasurer

ISPA's consumer magazine, explores a variety of fascinating and useful spa topics and answer spa-goer questions. Insights coming straight from the experts, LiveSpa provides consumers with the practical information they need to better embrace this important aspect of their overall wellness routine. (Also available in digital format)
Cost: $530.00

5853 MedEsthetics

Creative Age Publications

7628 Densmore Ave
Van Nuys, CA 91406-2042

818-782-7560
800-442-5667
FAX 818-782-7450
E-Mail: dayspa@creativeage.com
Home Page: www.creativeage.com

Linda Lewis, Editor
Linda Kossoff, Marketing Manager

News, features and education about noninvasive cosmetic therapies, trends, products and equipment for medical professionals and spa owners/managers in the U.S.
Cost: $22.00
Frequency: Monthly
Founded in 1971

5854 NAILPRO

Creative Age Publications
7628 Densmore Ave
Van Nuys, CA 91406-2042

818-782-7560
800-442-5667
FAX 818-782-7450
E-Mail: dayspa@creativeage.com
Home Page: www.creativeage.com

Linda Lewis, Editor
Linda Kossoff, Marketing Manager

The magazine for nail professionals.
Cost: $22.00
Frequency: Monthly
Founded in 1971

5855 Nails Magazine

Bobit Business Media
3520 Challenger St
Torrance, CA 90503

310-533-2400
FAX 310-533-2507
Home Page: www.nailsmag.com

Dedicated to the success of nail professionals.
Cost: $34.50
Frequency: Bi-Monthly
Circulation: 4,500

5856 Perfume 2000 Magazine

Nathalie Publishing Corp
444 Brickell Avenue
Suite 510
Miami, FL 33131

305-669-4602
FAX 305-669-6116
Home Page: www.perfume2000.com

Bernard Pommier, Circulation Manager
Joseph P Quick, Publisher

Provides an inside look at the American and international prefume industry.
Cost: $18.00
Frequency: Bi-Monthly
ISSN: 1081-7220

5857 Perfumer & Flavorist

Allured Publishing Corporation
336 Gundersen Dr
Suite A
Carol Stream, IL 60188-2403

630-653-2155
FAX 630-653-2192
E-Mail: customerservice@allured.com
Home Page: www.allured.com

Janet Ludwig, President
Linda Knott, Director Of Operations

Helps readers to analyze global trends, discover new ingredients and innovations, and keep up-to-date with industry news and analysis.
Cost: $135.00
Frequency: 8 Issues + 3 Bonus Issues

5858 Proud Magazine
PO Box 19510
Chicago, IL 60619-0510

708-633-6328
FAX 708-633-6329
Home Page: www.ahbai.org

Joe Dudley, Senior President
Jory Luste, President
Nathaniel Bronner, Jr. Executive VP

AHBAI reresents leading, African American-owned companies manufacturing ethnic hair care and beauty products. Members serve African Americans through employment, scholarships and education.

5859 Pulse Magazine
International Spa Association
2365 Harrodsburg Road
Suite A325
Lexington, KY 40504

888-651-4772
FAX 859-226-4445
E-Mail: ispa@ispastaff.com
Home Page: www.experienceispa.com
Social Media: *Facebook, Twitter*

Lynne Walker McNees, President
Deborah Waldvogel, Chairman
Jennifer Wayland-Smith, Vice Chairman
Ella Stimpson, Secretary/ Treasurer

The magazine for the spa professional. An in-depth look at the latest spa industry trends or tips on balancing your personal and professional life. At Pulse, our goal is to be a source for spa business solutions as well as a medium for personal exploration.
Cost: $530.00

5860 Rite Aid Be Healthy & Beautiful
Drug Store News Consumer Health Publications
425 Park Ave
New York, NY 10022-3526

212-756-5220
800-766-6999
FAX 212-756-5250
E-Mail: jtanzola@lf.com
Home Page: www.drugstorenews.com

Lebhar Friedman, Publisher

Provides health and beauty tips to millions of women who visit Rite Aid stores.
Frequency: Quarterly
Circulation: 450,000
Founded in 2002

5861 SalonOvation Magazine
Milady Publishing Company
5 Southside Dr
Clifton Park, NY 12065-3870

518-280-9500
800-998-1498
FAX 518-373-6200
E-Mail: esales@thomsonlearning.com
Home Page: www.delmarlearning.com

Shannon Melldady, Owner
Donna Lewis, Executive Marketing Director
Ron Schlosser, President/CEO

Dedicated to furthering the education of new and established beauty professionals, available by paid subscription to cosmetology students, and practicing massage therapists, cosmetologists, nail technicians, barber-stylists and estheticians.
Cost: $20.00
Frequency: Monthly
Circulation: 80000
Founded in 1945

5862 Scent Marketing Digest
7 Fox Meadow Road
Scarsdale, NY 10583

646-236-4606
FAX 914-470-2416
E-Mail: info@scentmarketing.org
Home Page: www.scentmarketing.org

Harald H Vogt, Founder/Chief Marketer
Avery Gilbert PhD, Chief Scientist

The essential blog for Scent Marketing resources, industry experts, scent developers and scent solution providers.

5863 The Colorist
Creative Age Publications
7628 Densmore Ave
Van Nuys, CA 91406-2042

818-782-7560
800-442-5667
FAX 818-782-7450
E-Mail: dayspa@creativeage.com
Home Page: www.creativeage.com

Linda Lewis, Editor
Linda Kossoff, Marketing Manager

The latest in haircolor trends, techniques, products and fashion.
Cost: $22.00
Frequency: Monthly
Founded in 1971

5864 The Link
30 South Main
Shenandoah, PA 17976

412-765-3666
FAX 412-765-3669
E-Mail: info@ahlc.org
Home Page: www.ahlc.org

Susan Kettering, Executive Director

The voice of the American Hair Loss Council.

5865 WWD Beauty Biz
Fairchild Publications
7 W 34th St
New York, NY 10001-8100

212-630-3880
800-289-0273
FAX 212-630-3868
E-Mail: customerservice@fairchildpub.com
Home Page: www.fairchildpub.com

Mary Berner, President
Jenny B. Fine, Editor-in-Chief
Sarah Murphy, Publisher

The premier guide to the beauty industry. Provides in-depth coverage and analysis on all aspects of the industry, including trends, brands, retailers, and personalities driving both the general comsumer and insider sides of the business.
Cost: $60.00
Frequency: Monthly
Circulation: 40056

Trade Shows

5866 AACS Annual Convention
9927 E. Bell Road
Suite 110
Scottsdale, AZ 85260

480-810-0431
800-831-1086
FAX 480-905-0993
E-Mail: jim@beautyschools.org
Home Page: www.beautyschools.org
Social Media: *Facebook, Twitter*

Jim Cox, Executive Director
Lisa Zarda, General Manager

Association open to all privately owned cosmetology schools.
1100 Members
Founded in 1924

5867 AACS Annual Convention & Expo
American Association of Cosmetology Schools
9927 E. Bell Road
Suite 110
Scottsdale, AZ 85260

480-281-0431
800-831-1086
FAX 480-905-0993
E-Mail: jim@beautyschools.org
Home Page: www.beautyschools.org

Jim Cox, Executive Director
Lisa Zarda, General Manager

An opportunity to bring your professional team together to lead your school into the future. Education tracks, ckasses, social events, and the expo hall complete the experience.
Frequency: Annual/Fall

5868 AHBAI Mid-Year Conference
American Health & Beauty Aids Institute
PO Box 19510
Chicago, IL 60619-0510

708-633-6328
FAX 708-633-6329
Home Page: www.ahbai.org

Joe Dudley, Senior President
Jory Luste, President
Nathaniel Bronner, Jr. Executive VP

AHBAI reresents leading, African American-owned companies manufacturing ethnic hair care and beauty products. Members serve African Americans through employment, scholarships and education.

5869 Aesthetics' and Spa World Conference
Aesthetics' International Association
2611 N Belt Line Road
Suite 140
Sunnyvale, TX 75182

972-038-8530
800-961-3777
Home Page: www.dermascope.com/aia

Networking, workshops, classes, exhibitors and more for the aesthetics' and spa professionals.
2000 Attendees

5870 America's Beauty Show
America's Beauty Show
401 N Michigan Avenue
Chicago, IL 60611

312-321-6809
800-648-2505
FAX 312-321-0575
E-Mail: info@americasbeautyshow.com
Home Page: www.americasbeautyshow.com

Pat Dwyer, Tradeshow Logistics Manager
Ingrid Qualls, Tradeshow Sr Coordinator

Evaluate new products, meet with distributors, continuing education classes on the show floor, and purchase product.
Frequency: Annual/March

5871 America's Expo for Skin Care & Spa
Allured Publishing Corporation
336 Gundersen Drive
Suite A
Carol Stream, IL 60188-2403

630-653-2155
FAX 630-653-2192
E-Mail: customerservice@allured.com
Home Page: www.allured.com

Janet Ludwig, President
Linda Knott, Director of Operations

Interactive exhibition focuses on professional skin care and spa services. Showcases the newest products, services and technologies from industry manufacturers and suppliers.
Frequency: May

5872 American Society of Perfumers Annual Symposium
PO Box 1551
West Caldwell, NJ 07004

201-991-0040
FAX 201-991-0073
E-Mail: info@perfumers.org
Home Page: www.perfumers.org
Social Media: *Twitter*

Marvel Fields, President

All about Perfumery with special guest perfumers speaking about creativity and honors to those who help build our industry.
Founded in 1947

5873 Annual Scientific Meeting and Technology Showcase
Society of Cosmetic Chemists
120 Wall St
Suite 2400
New York, NY 10005-4088

212-668-1500
FAX 212-668-1504
E-Mail: scc@scconline.org
Home Page: www.scconline.org

Randy Wickett, Ph.D, President
Joseph Dallal, Vice President
Guy Padulo, Vice President-Elect
Dawn Burke-Colvin, Secretary
Tony O'Lenick, Treasurer

Furthering the interest and recognition of cosmetic scientists.
3600 Members
Founded in 1945

5874 Annual Scientific Seminar
Society of Cosmetic Chemists
120 Wall St
Suite 2400
New York, NY 10005-4088

212-668-1500
FAX 212-668-1504
E-Mail: scc@scconline.org
Home Page: www.scconline.org

Randy Wickett, Ph.D, President
Joseph Dallal, Vice President
Guy Padulo, Vice President-Elect
Dawn Burke-Colvin, Secretary
Tony O'Lenick, Treasurer

Providing information and forums for the exchange of ideas and new developments in cosmetic research and technology.
3600 Members
Founded in 1945

5875 Association of Image Consultants Annual Convention & Exhibitor Showcase
Association of Image Consultants International
910 Charles Street
Fredericksburg, VA 22401

540-370-0311
800-383-8831
FAX 540-370-0015
Home Page: www.aici.org

Conference and industry related exhibits.
250 Attendees
Founded in 1991

5876 Beacon
Professional Beauty Association

15825 N. 71st Street
Suite 100
Scottsdale, AZ 85254

480-281-0424
800-468-2274
FAX 480-905-0708
E-Mail: info@probeauty.org
Home Page: www.probeauty.org/nmc

Max Wexler, Chair
Scott Buchanan, Vice Chair
Bruce Selan, Treasurer

Beacon is held annually to provide the nation's top cosmetology students with the guidance to achieve maximum career success. Beacon students attend the most celebrated industry events during PBA Beauty Week, and benefit from specially designed educational sessions to help them embark on a successful career path.
50 Members
Founded in 1989

5877 Beauty Exposition USA
Beauty Expo USA
10725 Midwest Industrial Blvd
Saint Louis, MO 63132

314-426-6333
FAX 314-426-6335
E-Mail: btexpo@yahoo.com
Home Page: www.beautyexpousa.com

Leon Beatty, Owner
Ann Park, Marketing Director

Hair and beauty supply trade show with a mission of connecting buyers and exhibitors for concentrated business exchanges. Training for retailers in product knowledge and display methods.
2,000 Attendees
Frequency: Annual/Winter

5878 Beauty Supply Show: West Coast
West Coast Beauty Supply
5001 Industrial Way
Benicia, CA 94510

707-484-4800
800-233-3141
FAX 707-748-4623
E-Mail: info@westcoastbeauty.com
Home Page: www.westcoastbeauty.com

Jennifer Coleman, Director
Wayne Clark, President
Jane West, Principal

200 booths of the newest and the best beauty products for the individual and business.
15M Attendees
Frequency: March

5879 CDMA Education & Trade Show
Chain Drug Marketing Association
43157 W Nine Mile Road
PO Box 995
Novi, MI 48376-0995

248-499-9300
FAX 248-449-9396
Home Page: www.chaindrug.com
Social Media: *Facebook, Twitter, LinkedIn*

James Devine, President
Judy Aspinall, VP
John Devine, VP of Store

Hundreds of exhibitors and thousands of buyers from regional chains, regional wholesalers, and independent pharmacies.
Frequency: Annual
Founded in 1926

5880 CEA Annual Convention
Cosmetology Educators of America

9927 E. Bell Road
Suite 110
Scottsdale, AZ 85260

480-810-0431
800-831-1086
FAX 480-905-0993
E-Mail: jim@beautyschools.org
Home Page: www.beautyschools.org
Social Media: *Facebook, Twitter*

Jim Cox, Executive Director
Lisa Zarda, General Manager
Chris Cox, Member services Manager

Association open to all privately owned cosmetology schools.
1100 Members
Founded in 1924

5881 CHPA Annual Executive Conference
Consumer Health Care Products Association
900 19th St NW
Suite 700
Washington, DC 20006-2105

202-429-9260
FAX 202-223-6835
E-Mail: eassey@chpa-info.org
Home Page: www.chpa-info.org

Scott Melville, President and CEO
Katie Bernard, State Legislative Analyst
Roman Blazauskas, VP
Chelsea Crutti, Associate Director, State Gov

Join top healthcare executives from across the nation and participate in high-level education sessions focused on the industry's rapidly shifting environment.

5882 Capitol Hill Visits
Professional Beauty Association
15825 N. 71st Street
Suite 100
Scottsdale, AZ 85254

480-281-0424
800-468-2274
FAX 480-905-0708
E-Mail: info@probeauty.org
Home Page: www.probeauty.org/nmc

Max Wexler, Chair
Scott Buchanan, Vice Chair
Bruce Selan, Treasurer

PBA takes Capitol Hill by storm each year. Armed with talking points about issues such as tip-tax reform, association health plans and more, members meet with their Congressional representatives.
50 Members
Founded in 1989

5883 Circle of Champions
Premiere Show Group
444 Brickell Avenue
Suite 510
Miami, FL 33131

305-669-4602
FAX 305-669-6116
E-Mail: magazine@perfume2000.com
Home Page: www.perfume2000.com

Bernard Pommier, Circulation Manager
Joseph P Quick, Publisher

Rewarding the best of the perfume industry.
Frequency: Bi-Monthly

5884 Cosmetic Science Symposium & Expo
Personal Care Products Council
1101 17th Street NW
Suite 300
Washington, DC 20036-4702

202-331-1770
FAX 202-331-1969
Home Page: www.personalcarecouncil.org

Social Media: *Facebook, Twitter, LinkedIn, YouTube*

Pamela Bailey, President
Mark Pollak, VP
Cheryl Mason, Secretary

Attracts industry leaders and decision-makers and offers personal care products industry staff one-stop shopping for information about Microbiology, Quality Assurance, Safety, and Environmental. The Science Symposium is a great opportunity to learn from the experts and meet colleagues and friends in the industry. Also features the Cosmetic Science Expo.
525 Members
Founded in 1894

5885 Cosmoprof North America
Professional Beauty Association
15825 N 71st Street
Suite 100
Scottsdale, AZ 85254

800-468-2274
FAX 480-905-0708
E-Mail: Cpnainfo@probeauty.org
Home Page: www.cosmoprofnorthamerica.com
Social Media: *Facebook, Twitter, LinkedIn*

Jen Ingalls, Trade Show Manager
Nathan Miner, Sales Manager
Melissa Coe, Registration Manager
Bonnie Bonadeo, Director Education

Best in hair,cosmetics,packagin and style. Attracted 25,000 professionals from 32 countries with 760 exhibitors.
10M Attendees
Frequency: July
Founded in 2002

5886 DCAT Western Education Conference
Drug, Chemical & Associated Technologies
1 Washington Boulevard
Suite 7
Robbinsville, NJ 08691

609-448-1000
800-640-3228
FAX 609-448-1944
E-Mail: brooke@dcat.org
Home Page: www.dcat.org

Brooke DiGiuseppe, Meeting Services
Margaret Timony, Executive Director

Gain important insights into issues and trends that will affect the future of the nutrition and health industry. Participate in discussion on key business issues with industry experts.

5887 Elements Showcase
Skylight West
500 West 36th Street
New York, NY 10018

E-Mail: info@elements-showcase.com
Home Page: www.elements-showcase.com
Social Media: *Facebook, Twitter, LinkedIn, YouTube*

Showcasing diverse range of cosmetic products. Get to know the latest product range and services that will be displayed by leading and well known companies from every corner of the world.

5888 Emerging Issues Conference
Personal Care Products Council
1101 17th Street NW
Suite 300
Washington, DC 20036-4702

202-331-1770
FAX 202-331-1969
Home Page: www.personalcarecouncil.org
Social Media: *Facebook, Twitter, LinkedIn, YouTube*

Pamela Bailey, President
Mark Pollak, VP
Cheryl Mason, Secretary

Regulations being considered in California have an impact on every manufacturer and consumer in the United States. Water, waste, air, packaging, ingredients, recycling, new technology, whatever the issue, the discussions often begin in this state. The Council will host an annual Emerging Issues Conference focusing on the many challenges we see on the horizon for our industry.
525 Members
Founded in 1894

5889 Engredea
New Hope Natural Media
1401 Pearl St
Suite 200
Boulder, CO 80302-5346

303-939-8440
FAX 303-939-9886
E-Mail: info@newhope.com
Home Page: www.newhope.com
Social Media: *Facebook, Twitter*

Fred Linder, President
Pamela Emanoil, Advertising Manager

Encompassing the world of ingredients, Engredea brings together the community of leading suppliers and manufacturers to source new ingredients, packaging, technologies, equipment, and services. Cultivating innovation for tomorrow's best-selling products across food/ beverage, dietary supplement and nutricosmetic categories by offering exhibits, formulation demos, networking events and education opportunities for the industry.
Frequency: Monthly

5890 Extracts: Essentials for Spa, Home, & Travel
George Little Management
10 Bank Street
Suite 1200
White Plains, NY 10606

914-486-6070
800-292-4560
FAX 914-948-6289
E-Mail: laura_woodward@glmshows.com
Home Page:
www.extractsny.com/www.glmshows.com

Rita Malek, Show Manager
Laura Anne Woodward, Show Coordinator
George Little II, President
Paula Bertolotti, Sales Manager

EX-TRACTS: Essentials for Spa, Home and Travel is co-located with the International Hotel/Motel Restaurant Show® (IH/MRS). Presenting the finest Apparel & Accessories, Aromatherapy Products & Candles, Baby and Cildren's Spa Products, Bathrobes and Loungewear, Business Services, Cosmetics, Cosmeceuticals, Home Environment Products, Essential Oils, Frangrances, Home Spa Electrics, Massage/Reflexology, Men's Spa Products, Music & Recordings.
10000 Attendees
Frequency: Nov
Founded in 1997

5891 Extracts: New Discoveries in Beauty and Wellness
George Little Management
10 Bank Street
Suite 1200
White Plains, NY 10606

914-486-6070
800-292-4560
FAX 914-948-6289
E-Mail: laura_woodward@glmshows.com
Home Page: www.extractsny.com

Rita Malek, Show Manager
Laura Anne Woodward, Show Coordinator
George Little II, President
Paula Bertolotti, Sales Manager

EXTRACTS® at the NYIGF is a unique, high-quality environment, showcasing the most innovative personal care and wellness products for the gift industry: aromatherapy, bath & bodycare, cosmetics, beauty accessories, candles, home fragrances, massage oils, music & recordings, natural/organic products, perfumes, potpourri and skincare.
43M Attendees
Frequency: Jan/Aug
Founded in 1997

5892 Face & Body Spa & Healthy Aging
Allured Publishing
444 Brickell Avenue
Suite 510
Miami, FL 33131

305-669-4602
FAX 305-669-6116
E-Mail: magazine@perfume2000.com
Home Page: www.perfume2000.com

Bernard Pommier, Circulation Manager
Joseph P Quick, Publisher

Spa professionals gather at Face & Body for practical business solutions, trend information and the latest offerings and insights from leading industry suppliers.
Frequency: Bi-Monthly
ISSN: 1081-7220

5893 Face & Body Spa Conference & Expo
Allured Business Media
336 Gundersen Drive
Suite A
Carol Stream, IL 60188-2403

630-653-2155
FAX 630-653-2192
E-Mail: fbmw@allured.com
Home Page: www.faceandbody.com
Social Media: *Facebook*

Maureen Nolimal, Account Executive
Sandy Chapin, Group Show Director
Mary Richter, Event Coordinator
Andrew Blood, Exhibits Coordinator

Skin care professionals gather at the Face & Body Midwest for practical business solutions, education, treatments, trends, products and equipment, as well as the latest offerings and insights from leading industry suppliers.
Frequency: Annual

5894 General Merchandise/Health and Beauty Care Conference
Food Marketing Institute
2345 Crystal Drive
Suite 800
Arlington, VA 22202-2709

202-452-8444
FAX 202-429-4519
E-Mail: fmi@fmi.org
Home Page: www.fmi.org
Social Media: *Facebook, Twitter, LinkedIn, you Tube*

Don McWhirter, Owner

Annual show of 150 exhibitors of health and beauty care products.
3000 Attendees

5895 HAIRCOLOR USA
International Beauty Show Group
757 Thrid Ave
5th Floor
New York, NY 10017

212-895-8200
FAX 212-895-8209
Home Page: www.beautyshows.com
Social Media: *Facebook, Twitter, YouTube*

Mike Boyce, Show Manager
Rick Rosalina, Operations
Nicole Peck, Media partnerships

0
1500 Attendees
Frequency: June

5896 Health & Beauty America

HBA
350 Hudson St
Ste 300
New York, NY 10014

609-759-4700
FAX 347-962-3889
E-Mail: jgonzalez@cmprinceton.com
Home Page: www.hbaexpo.com
Social Media: *Facebook, Twitter, LinkedIn*

Jack Gonzalez, Director Health/Beauty Events
Caitlin Carragee, Sales Coordinator

America's largest industry-specific educational conference and exposition for cosmetics, toiletries, fragances and personal care.
16500 Attendees

5897 ICMAD Annual Meeting

Independent Cosmetic Manufacturers & Distributors
444 Brickell Avenue
Suite 510
Miami, FL 33131

305-669-4602
FAX 305-669-6116
E-Mail: magazine@perfume2000.com
Home Page: www.perfume2000.com

Bernard Pommier, Circulation Manager
Joseph P Quick, Publisher

Information about programs and services available to help companies succeed in the beauty and personal care industries.
ISSN: 1081-7220

5898 ISPA Conference & Expo

International Spa Association
2365 Harrodsburg Road
Suite A325
Lexington, KY 40504

888-651-4772
FAX 859-226-4445
E-Mail: ispa@ispastaff.com
Home Page: www.experienceispa.com
Social Media: *Facebook, Twitter, LinkedIn, YouTube*

Lynne Walker McNees, President
Deborah Waldvogel, Chairman
Jennifer Wayland-Smith, Vice Chairman
Ella Stimpson, Secretary/ Treasurer

The largest ISPA event of the year for spa professionals. The expectation of Conference attendees is to provide spa owners, directors, managers and suppliers with cutting edge tips on where the industry is headed and how to ensure that business is sustainable. Also brings together the leading suppliers in the industry to network with spa decision makers.

5899 ISSE Long Beach

Professional Beauty Association
15825 N. 71st Street
Suite 100
Scottsdale, AZ 85254

480-281-0424
800-468-2274
FAX 480-905-0708
E-Mail: info@probeauty.org
Home Page: www.probeauty.org/nmc

Max Wexler, Chair
Scott Buchanan, Vice Chair
Bruce Selan, Treasurer

The International Salon and Spa Expo is the biggest cash-and-carry beauty show on the West Coast. ISSE Long Beach delivers valuable technical education, quality manufacturers on the exhibit floor and a professionals-only atmosphere.
50 Members
Founded in 1989

5900 ISSE Midwest

Professional Beauty Association
15825 N. 71st Street
Suite 100
Scottsdale, AZ 85254

480-281-0424
800-468-2274
FAX 480-905-0708
E-Mail: info@probeauty.org
Home Page: www.probeauty.org/nmc

Max Wexler, Chair
Scott Buchanan, Vice Chair
Bruce Selan, Treasurer

The International Salon and Spa Expo is the biggest cash-and-carry beauty show. ISSE delivers valuable technical education, quality manufacturers on the exhibit floor and a professionals-only atmosphere.
50 Members
Founded in 1989

5901 Intercoiffure America-Canada

Creative Age Publications
7628 Densmore Ave
Van Nuys, CA 91406-2042

818-782-7560
800-442-5667
FAX 818-782-7450
E-Mail: dayspa@creativeage.com
Home Page: www.creativeage.com

Deborah Carver, President and CEO
Mindy Rosiejka, VP and COO
Barbara Shepherd, Circulation Director

Creative Age Publications is the association management firm for Intercoiffure America-Canada, the premier organization for salon owners.
Frequency: Monthly
Founded in 1971

5902 International Beauty Show

International Beauty Show Group
757 Third Avenue
5th Floor
New York, NY 10017

212-895-8200
800-736-7170
FAX 212-895-8209
Home Page: www.ibsnewyork.com
Social Media: *Facebook, Twitter, LinkedIn, YouTube*

Deborah Carver, Founder
Rick Rosalina, Operations

Annual exposition of hair and skin care products manufacturers and beauty technicians. Held in New York city.
75000 Attendees
Frequency: March

5903 International Congress of Esthetics & Spa

310 E. Interstate 30
Suite B107
Garland, TX 75043

972-203-8530
877-968-7539
FAX 972-962-1480
E-Mail: AIAtheKey@aol.com
Home Page: www.aestheticsassociation.com

Deborah Carver, Founder
Michelle D'Allaird, VP, Director of Education
Melissa Guillette, Director of Operations

The association for the advancement of education and public awareness on aesthetics. Paramedical aesthetics and body spa therapy. Professionals from the medical, paramedical and beauty industries working together for the most advanced techniques for the patients and clients.
Founded in 1972

5904 International Perfume Bottle Association Annual Convention

PO Box 1299
Paradise, CA 95967

E-Mail: paradise@sunset.net
Home Page: www.perfumebottles.org
Social Media: *Facebook*

Deborah Carver, Founder
Walter Jones, Vice President
Peggy Tichenor, Membership Secretary
Janet Ziffer, Treasurer
Barbara W. Miller, Recording Secretary

The most exciting event in perfume bottle collecting. A three-day extravaganza featuring the world's premiere exhibition and sale with the field's leading dealers featuring thousands of bottles and an internationally recognized auction. The convention draws together collectors and dealers from around the world.
2000+ Members

5905 Medical Device Submission & Compliance Strategies for the U.S. Market

5635 Fishers Lane
Suite 550
Rockville, MD 20852-3048

301-770-2920
FAX 301-770-2924
E-Mail: raps@raps.org
Home Page: www.raps.org
Social Media: *Facebook, Twitter, LinkedIn, YouTube*

Susan E. James, Chairman of the Board
Cecilia Kimberlin, President
Paul Brooks, President-elect
Leigh M. Vaughan, Secretary/ Treasurer
Linda Bowen, Director

Featuring an expert panel of industry professionals and US Food and Drug Administration (FDA) regulators, this RAPS workshop will provide critical information on navigating the medical device submission process and creating compliance strategies for products for the US market.
10000 Members
Founded in 1976

5906 Mid American Beauty Classic

Premiere Show Group
444 Brickell Avenue
Suite 510
Miami, FL 33131

305-669-4602
FAX 305-669-6116
E-Mail: magazine@perfume2000.com
Home Page: www.perfume2000.com

Bernard Pommier, Circulation Manager
Joseph P Quick, Publisher

Beauty trade show for members of the professional beauty industry. Hair Show, Nail Show, Skincare Show.
Frequency: Bi-Monthly
ISSN: 1081-7220

5907 NAHA

Professional Beauty Association
15825 N. 71st Street
Suite 100
Scottsdale, AZ 85254

480-281-0424
800-468-2274
FAX 480-905-0708

E-Mail: info@probeauty.org
Home Page: www.probeauty.org/nmc

Max Wexler, Chair
Scott Buchanan, Vice Chair
Bruce Selan, Treasurer

The North American Hairstyling Awards (NAHA) is the most prestigious photographic beauty competition in North America, celebrating the artistry and skill of the professional salon industry. Individuals are recognized in 13 categories of excellence, including the Student Hairstylist of the Year, during a star-studded Awards Ceremony.
50 Members
Founded in 1989

5908 NAILPRO Competitions
Creative Age Publications
7628 Densmore Ave
Van Nuys, CA 91406-2042

818-782-7560
800-442-5667
FAX 818-782-7450
E-Mail: dayspa@creativeage.com
Home Page: www.creativeage.com

Deborah Carver, President and CEO
Mindy Rosiejka, VP and COO
Barbara Shepherd, Circulation Director

Nail artists from all over the world compete at trade shows all over the U.S. for a chance to be the best and win the coveted annual NAILPRO Cup.
Frequency: Monthly
Founded in 1971

5909 NAILPRO Nail Institute
Creative Age Publications
7628 Densmore Ave
Van Nuys, CA 91406-2042

818-782-7560
800-442-5667
FAX 818-782-7450
E-Mail: dayspa@creativeage.com
Home Page: www.creativeage.com

Deborah Carver, President and CEO
Mindy Rosiejka, VP and COO
Barbara Shepherd, Circulation Director

Practical marketing education helps nail professionals build their businesses.
Frequency: Monthly
Founded in 1971

5910 NAILPRO Sacramento
Creative Age Publications
7628 Densmore Ave
Van Nuys, CA 91406-2042

818-782-7560
800-442-5667
FAX 818-782-7450
E-Mail: dayspa@creativeage.com
Home Page: www.creativeage.com

Deborah Carver, President and CEO
Mindy Rosiejka, VP and COO
Barbara Shepherd, Circulation Director

The industry's hottest nails-only trade show spotlights new products and innovative techniques for nail technicians from top manufacturers.
Frequency: Monthly
Founded in 1971

5911 NBCL Annual Convention
National Beauty Culturalists' League
25 Logan Circle NW
Washington, DC 20005-3725

202-332-2695
FAX 202-332-0940

E-Mail: nbcl@bellsouth.net
Home Page: www.nbcl.org

Dr. Katie B Catalon, President
Dr. William Lindsay, Executive Manager

One hundred booths of beauty industry associates, manufacturing companies and other businesses.
Frequency: July

5912 NBJ Summit
New Hope Natural Media
1401 Pearl St
Suite 200
Boulder, CO 80302-5346

303-939-8440
FAX 303-939-9886
E-Mail: info@newhope.com
Home Page: www.newhope.com
Social Media: *Facebook, Twitter*

Fred Linder, President
Pamela Emanoil, Advertising Manager

The premier leadership event for progressive nutrition industry CEOs, investors and thought leaders. It has provided unparalleled education and a tremendous venue for thoughtful leaders to establish strategic relationships and grow the potential of their businesses.
Frequency: Monthly

5913 Natural Products Association MarketPlace
New Hope Natural Media
1401 Pearl St
Suite 200
Boulder, CO 80302-5346

303-939-8440
FAX 303-939-9886
E-Mail: info@newhope.com
Home Page: www.newhope.com
Social Media: *Facebook, Twitter*

Fred Linder, President
Pamela Emanoil, Advertising Manager

An intimate trade show for the natural and healthy products industries. Topics cover advocacy, retail training and trends, standards and industry regulation, marketing, sustainability, and other relevant, timely topics direct from industry experts and business leaders.
Frequency: Monthly

5914 Natural Products Expo
New Hope Natural Media
1401 Pearl St
Suite 200
Boulder, CO 80302-5346

303-939-8440
FAX 303-939-9886
E-Mail: info@newhope.com
Home Page: www.newhope.com
Social Media: *Facebook, Twitter*

Fred Linder, President
Pamela Emanoil, Advertising Manager

Where new products turn into record profits. Join in an experience with exhibits from different companies showcasing the newest products in natural and specialty foods, organic, health and beauty, natural living, supplements and pet products.
Frequency: Monthly

5915 Nutracon
New Hope Natural Media
1401 Pearl St
Suite 200
Boulder, CO 80302-5346

303-939-8440
FAX 303-939-9886

E-Mail: info@newhope.com
Home Page: www.newhope.com

Fred Linder, President
Pamela Emanoil, Advertising Manager

The premier education and networking conference for the health and nutrition industry. Provides relevant insights for innovation based on science and technology, case studies and market intelligence. Gain an understanding of the impact of next generation ingredients, emerging markets, consumer trend data and regulatory constraints.
Frequency: Monthly

5916 PBA Beauty Week
Professional Beauty Association
15825 N. 71st Street
Suite 100
Scottsdale, AZ 85254

480-281-0424
800-468-2274
FAX 480-905-0708
E-Mail: info@probeauty.org
Home Page: www.probeauty.org/nmc

Max Wexler, Chair
Scott Buchanan, Vice Chair
Bruce Selan, Treasurer

PBA Beauty Week is North America's largest, most inclusive beauty event, offering unlimited networking, education, and professional growth opportunities to all sectors of the beauty industry. This week of beauty also features the North American Hairstyling Awards, Best Practice Club, City of Hope and Beacon. PBA Beauty Week is produced by the Professional Beauty Association in cooperation with Cosmoprof North America.
50 Members
Founded in 1989

5917 PBA Symposium
Professional Beauty Association
15825 N. 71st Street
Suite 100
Scottsdale, AZ 85254

480-281-0424
800-468-2274
FAX 480-905-0708
E-Mail: info@probeauty.org
Home Page: www.probeauty.org/nmc

Max Wexler, Chair
Scott Buchanan, Vice Chair
Bruce Selan, Treasurer

PBA Symposium provides the upper-level business education, unlimited networking and powerful industry research. Held annually during PBA Beauty Week, this three-day educational summit will inspire and educate salon owners and licensed professionals to take their businesses and careers, as well as the entire industry, to the next level.
50 Members
Founded in 1989

5918 Paperboard Packaging Council Annual Convention
Independent Cosmetic Manufacturers & Distributors
444 Brickell Avenue
Suite 510
Miami, FL 33131

305-669-4602
FAX 305-669-6116
E-Mail: magazine@perfume2000.com
Home Page: www.perfume2000.com

Bernard Pommier, Circulation Manager
Joseph P Quick, Publisher

Industry leaders specializing in sustainability, the economy, and education will come together

to impart their knowledge, experience, and business predictions.
Frequency: Bi-Monthly
ISSN: 1081-7220

5919 Perfumers Choice Awards
The American Society of Perfumers
444 Brickell Avenue
Suite 510
Miami, FL 33131

305-669-4602
FAX 305-669-6116
E-Mail: magazine@perfume2000.com
Home Page: www.perfume2000.com

Bernard Pommier, Circulation Manager
Joseph P Quick, Publisher

Excellence in fragrance creation takes center stage.
Frequency: Bi-Monthly
ISSN: 1081-7220

5920 Personal Care Products Council Annual Meeting
Personal Care Products Council
1101 17th Street NW
Suite 300
Washington, DC 20036-4702

202-331-1770
FAX 202-331-1969
Home Page: www.personalcarecouncil.org
Social Media: *Facebook*

Round-tables, R&D, business strategy, and learning panels, along with companies with exhibits of supplies and raw materials for the cosmetic industry.
Frequency: Annual

5921 Personal Care Products Council Legal & Regulatory Conference
Personal Care Products Council
1101 17th Street NW
Suite 300
Washington, DC 20036-4702

202-331-1770
FAX 202-331-1969
Home Page: www.personalcarecouncil.org
Social Media: *Facebook, Twitter, LinkedIn, YouTube*

Pamela Bailey, President
Mark Pollak, VP
Cheryl Mason, Secretary

The premier annual meeting for industry general counsel and legal staff, regulatory affairs staff, and outside counsel representing member companies. Held each year exclusively for Council members.
525 Members
Founded in 1894

5922 Professional Beauty Association Annual Convention
Professional Beauty Association
15825 N 71st Street
Suite 100
Scottsdale, AZ 85254

480-281-0424
800-468-2274
FAX 480-905-0708
E-Mail: cpna@probeauty.org
Home Page: www.probeauty.org

Steven Sleeper, Executive Director
Eric Z Horn, Director Sales/Show Manager

Annual show of 700 exhibitors of industry related equipment, supplies and services.
10M Attendees

5923 Proud Lady Beauty Show
PO Box 19510
Chicago, IL 60619-0510

708-633-6328
FAX 708-633-6329
E-Mail: ahbail@sbcglobal.net
Home Page: www.ahbai.org

Clyde Hammond, Senior President
Jory Luste, President
Nathaniel Bronner, Jr. Executive VP

The Beauty Professionals Marketplace
Founded in 1981

5924 RAPS Executive Development Program at the Kellogg School of Management
5635 Fishers Lane
Suite 550
Rockville, MD 20852-3048

301-770-2920
FAX 301-770-2924
E-Mail: raps@raps.org
Home Page: www.raps.org
Social Media: *Facebook, Twitter, LinkedIn, YouTube*

Susan E. James, Chairman of the Board
Cecilia Kimberlin, President
Paul Brooks, President-elect
Leigh M. Vaughan, Secretary/ Treasurer
Linda Bowen, Director

Strong business skills are essential to your success and the ability of your company to survive in a volatile and competitive regulatory environment. This program brings the opportunity to cultivate your business management skills through vigorous discussions with some of the world's best business professors in an intimate learning environment.
10000 Members
Founded in 1976

5925 RAPS; The Regulatory Convergence
5635 Fishers Lane
Suite 550
Rockville, MD 20852-3048

301-770-2920
FAX 301-770-2924
E-Mail: raps@raps.org
Home Page: www.raps.org
Social Media: *Facebook, Twitter, LinkedIn, YouTube*

Susan E. James, Chairman of the Board
Cecilia Kimberlin, President
Paul Brooks, President-elect
Leigh M. Vaughan, Secretary/ Treasurer
Linda Bowen, Director

Delivers the knowledge, competence development and resources you need to design effective solutions to complex challenges, seize opportunities and lead.
10000 Members
Founded in 1976

5926 Salon Focus
Advantsar Communications
641 Lexington Avenue
8th Floor
New York, NY 10022

212-951-6600
FAX 212-951-6793
E-Mail: info@advanstar.com
Home Page: www.advanstar.com

Joseph Loggia, CEO
Thomas Ehardt, EVP and CFO
Chris Demoulin, EVP

Educational and exhibiting forum for the Southwest professional salon industry. 140 booths.
6.5M Attendees
Frequency: November

5927 Scent World Expo
7 Fox Meadow Road
Scarsdale, NY 10583

646-236-4606
FAX 914-470-2416
E-Mail: info@scentmarketing.org
Home Page: www.scentmarketing.org

Harald H Vogt, Founder/Chief Marketer
Avery Gilbert PhD, Chief Scientist

Learn about the latest scent technology, fragrance trends and success stories. Members of the scent marketing industry, executives from marketing and branding firms as well as consumer goods companies, hotels/ cruise ships, cosmetic companies and other end users of scent. A wonderful lineup of speakers, with top researchers, creative marketing & branding gurus, innovative perfumers and dynamic scent professionals. Take your business to the next level.

5928 Spring Management and Financial Aid Conference
9927 E. Bell Road
Suite 110
Scottsdale, AZ 85260

480-810-0431
800-831-1086
FAX 480-905-0993
E-Mail: jim@beautyschools.org
Home Page: www.beautyschools.org
Social Media: *Facebook, Twitter*

Jim Cox, Executive Director
Lisa Zarda, General Manager
Chris Cox, Member services Manager

Association open to all privately owned cosmetology schools.
1100 Members
Founded in 1924

5929 Techniques
New Dimensions Advertising
47 W Main Street
Mechanicsburg, PA 17055-6262

717-697-4181
800-845-4694
FAX 717-790-9441

Triennial show of 25 exhibitors of cosmetics and accessories.
1500 Attendees

5930 The Makeup Show
E-Mail:

Focuses on and celebrates the art of makeup and networking. Strengthening the working capability and build a professional network for all the people from the makeup artistry community.

5931 Welcome to Our World
Professional Beauty Association
15825 N. 71st Street
Suite 100
Scottsdale, AZ 85254

480-281-0424
800-468-2274
FAX 480-905-0708
E-Mail: info@probeauty.org
Home Page: www.probeauty.org/nmc

Max Wexler, Chair
Scott Buchanan, Vice Chair
Bruce Selan, Treasurer

The professional beauty industry invites Congress for its annual makeover each year. While Congress enjoys the beauty services, members push legislative issues important to the industry.
50 Members
Founded in 1989

5932 West Coast Spring Style and Beauty Show

West Coast Beauty Supply
5001 Industrial Way
Benicia, CA 94510

707-484-4800
800-233-3141
FAX 707-748-4623
E-Mail: info@westcoastbeauty.com
Home Page: www.westcoastbeauty.com

Paul Eggert, Show Director
Wayne Clark, President
John Golliher, Manager
200 booths.
15M Attendees
Frequency: March

5933 World International Nail and Beauty Association

1221 N Lake View Ave
Anaheim, CA 92807

714-779-9892
800-541-9838
FAX 714-779-9971
E-Mail: dkellenberger@inmnails.com

David Kellenberger

Represents industry, promotes effective use of products, sponsors competition and bestows awards. Also offers world championship competitions for nails, hair and makeup.
13000 Members
Founded in 1981

Directories & Databases

5934 Beauty Fashion: Men's Issue

Beauty Fashion
16 E 40th Street
New York, NY 10016

212-328-6789
0
FAX 212-840-7246
Home Page: www.beautyfashion.com
Social Media: *Facebook*

Debra Davis, Advertising Director
Adelaide Farah, Editorial Director

Offers listings of men's fragrances, toiletries and related products as well as manufacturers and US distributors.
Cost: $25.00
Frequency: Annual
Circulation: 17,000

5935 Complete Directory of Cosmetic Specialties

Sutton Family Communications & Publishing Company
920 State Route 54 East
Elmitch, KY 42343

270-276-9500
E-Mail: jlsutton@apex.net

Theresa Sutton, Editor
Lee Sutton, General Manager

Print-out from database of wholesalers, manufacturers, distributors, importers and close-out houses. Database is updated daily to guarantee the most current and up-to-date sources available.
Cost: $39.50
100+ Pages

5936 Complete Directory of Personal Care Items

Sutton Family Communications & Publishing Company

920 State Route 54 East
Elmitch, KY 42343

270-276-9500
E-Mail: jlsutton@apex.net

Theresa Sutton, Editor
Lee Sutton, General Manager

Print-out from database of wholesalers, manufacturers, distributors, importers and close-out houses. Database is updated daily to guarantee the most current and up-to-date sources available.
Cost: $39.50
100+ Pages

5937 Cosmetics & Toiletries: Cosmetic Bench Reference

Allured Publishing Corporation
336 Gundersen Dr
Suite A
Carol Stream, IL 60188-2403

630-653-2155
FAX 630-653-2192
E-Mail: customerservice@allured.com
Home Page: www.allured.com

Janet Ludwig, President
Linda Knott, Director Of Operations

Offers a full list of cosmetics ingredient suppliers.
Cost: $95.00
Frequency: Biennial

5938 Cosmetics & Toiletries: Who's Who in R&D Directory Issue

Allured Publishing Corporation
336 Gundersen Dr
Suite A
Carol Stream, IL 60188-2403

630-653-2155
FAX 630-653-2192
E-Mail: customerservice@allured.com
Home Page: www.allured.com

Janet Ludwig, President
Linda Knott, Director Of Operations

Offers a list of cosmetic manufacturers and consultants for product development, legal, safety and regulatory assistance.
Cost: $25.00
Frequency: Annual
Circulation: 3,200

5939 Fragrance Foundation Reference Guide

Fragrance Foundation
545 5th Ave
Suite 900
New York, NY 10017-3636

212-779-9058
FAX 212-779-9058
E-Mail: info@fragrance.org
Home Page: www.fragrance.org

Terry Molnar, Executive Director
Mary Lapsansky, VP

Over 1100 fragrances are listed that are available in the US, with dates of introduction and description, alphabetically indexed with company name, address and phone number.
Cost: $60.00
112 Pages
Frequency: Annual

5940 Fragrance and Olfactory Dictionary

Fragrance Foundation
545 5th Ave
Suite 900
New York, NY 10017-3636

212-779-9058
FAX 212-779-9058

E-Mail: info@fragrance.org
Home Page: www.fragrance.org

Terry Molnar, Executive Director
Mary Lapsansky, VP

Definitions of ingredients, techniques, language of fragrance and olfactory references.
Cost: $7.00
32 Pages

5941 Passion

Milady Publishing Company
5 Southside Dr
Clifton Park, NY 12065-3870

518-280-9500
800-998-1498
FAX 518-373-6200
E-Mail: esales@thomsonlearning.com
Home Page: www.delmarlearning.com
Social Media: *Twitter*

Shannon Melldady, Owner
Donna Lewis, Executive Marketing Director
Ron Schlosser, President/CEO

A Salon Professionals Handbook for Building a Successful Business
Cost: $20.00
Frequency: Monthly
Circulation: 80000
Founded in 1945

5942 Perfume 2000

Perfume 2000
444 Brickell Avenue
Suite 510
Miami, FL 33131

305-374-6849
FAX 305-374-6850
E-Mail: ana@perfume2000.com
Home Page: www.perfume2000.com

Ana Murias, Public Relations

Comprehensive database; services encourage industry networking and integration.

5943 RIFM Database of Fragrance & Flavor Materials

50 Tice Boulevard
Woodcliff Lake, NJ 07677

201-689-8089
FAX 201-689-8090
E-Mail: rifm@rifm.org
Home Page: www.rifm.org/nd

A comprehensive source offering safety evaluations and toxicology data on more than 4,500 fragrance and flavor materials. Operated in full cooperation with Flavor & Extracts Manufacturing Association (FEMA).
Founded in 1966

5944 Who's Who: Membership Directory of the Cosmetic, Toiletry & Fragrance Assn

Personal Care Products Council
1101 17th Street NW
Suite 300
Washington, DC 20036-4702

202-331-1770
FAX 202-331-1969
Home Page: www.personalcarecouncil.org

Gwen Hal111, Director Publications/Comm
Pamela Bailey, President

About 500 member companies of the cosmetics industry.
Cost: $75.00
Frequency: Annual, June

Industry Web Sites

5945 http://gold.greyhouse.com
G.O.L.D Grey House OnLine Databases
Grey House Publishing's online database platform, GOLD, offers Quick Search, Keyword Search and Expert Search for most business sectors including beauty, cosmetics, perfumes and personal care markets. The GOLD platform makes finding the information you need quick and easy - whether you're a novice searcher or an experienced database user. All of Grey House's directory products are available for subscription on the GOLD platform.

5946 www.abbies.org
American Beauty Association
Works to expand, serve and protect the interests of the professional beauty industry.

5947 www.ahbai.org
American Health and Beauty Aids Institute
Trade association representing leading Black-owned companies manufacturing ethnic hair care and beauty products that feature the Proud Lady symbol. Members serve Black America through employment, scholarships and education of consumers on recycling their dollars into the Black community.

5948 www.bbsi.org
Beauty and Barber Supply Institute
Our members are wholesaler-distributors, manufacturers and manufacturers' representatives from around the world. Our mission is to maximize the potential of the salon industry.

5949 www.beautyworks.com/aia
Aestheticis International Association
For the advancement of education and public awareness on aesthetics. Paramedical aesthetics and body spa therapy. Professionals from the medical, paramedical and beauty industries working together for the most advanced techniques for the patients and clients.

5950 www.cew.org
Cosmetic Executive Women
Nonprofit trade organization of approximately 1,500 executives in the beauty, cosmetics, fragrance and related industries. Based in New York City, CEW has associated organizations in France and the United Kingdom. As a leading trade organization in the beauty industry, CEW helps develop the career contacts, knowledge and skills of its members so that they may advance on both professional and personal levels.

5951 www.cosmeticindex.com
CosmeticIndex.Com

Home Page: www.cosmeticindex.com

Online source for cosmetics, resources and services.

5952 www.cosmeticsinfo.org
Personal Care Products Council
1620 L St. NW
Suite 1200
Washington, DC 20036

202-331-1770
FAX 202-331-1969
Social Media: *Facebook, Twitter*

Lezlee Westine, President & CEO
Thia Breen, Chair
Information about safety, testing and regulation of cosmetics and personal care products. Sponsored by the Personal Care Products Council.

5953 www.greyhouse.com
Grey House Publishing
Authoritative reference directories for most business segments incluidng beauty, cosmetic, perfume and personal care markets. Users can search the online databases with varied search criteria allowing for custom searches by product category, geographic area, sales volume, keyword, subject and more. Full Grey House catalog and online ordering also available.

5954 www.iacmcolor.org
International Association of Color Manufacturers
Actively represents the interests of the regulated color industry by demonstrating the safety of color additives and to promote the industry's economic growth by participating in new color approvals, regulatory and legislative issues that affect the industry worldwide.

5955 www.iasc.org
International Aloe Science Council
Nonprofit trade organization for the Aloe Vera Industry world-wide. Its membership includes Aloe growers, processors, finished goods manufacturers, marketing companies, insurance companies, equipment suppliers, printers, sales organizations, physicians, scientists and researchers.

5956 www.icmad.org
Independent Cosmetic Manufacturers & Distributors
Information on government consumers and the media. Provides group programs for product liability.

5957 www.inmnails.com
World International Nail and Beauty Association
Promotes effective use of products, sponsors competition and bestows awards. Also offers world championship competitions for nails, hair and makeup.

5958 www.isnow.com
Cosmetologists Chicago
Voice of the salon industry. For over eight decades, we have been a beauty authority and presenter of the Chicago Midwest Beauty Show. We are stylists, estheticians, color technicians, salon owners, educators and nail technicians.

5959 www.perfumers.org
American Society of Perfumers
Nonprofit organization fostering and encouraging the art and science of perfumery in the US while promoting professional exchange and a high standard of professional conduct within the fragrance industry. The ASP holds symposiums in the New York City area where leading members of the fragrence community are invited to speak and present information on all aspects of the industry.

5960 www.personalcarecouncil.org
Personal Care Products Council
Provides a complete range of services that support the personal care products industry's needs and interests in the scientific, legal, regulatory, legislative and international fields. CTFA strives to ensure that the personal care products industry has the freedom to pursue creative product development and compete in a fair and responsible marketplace.

5961 www.salonprofessionals.org
National Cosmetology Association
Nationwide community of 30,000 salon professionals, connected by a common passion for learning, growing and raising the professionalim of the entire salon industry. As a group, we have a strong voice in our communities, our industry and with our government because the NCA is for everyone in the professional community. Members have access to education, fashion events, community service and insurance — all the tools needed to build your career.

Associations

5962 ACA International
Association of Credit and Collection Professionals
PO Box 390106
Minneapolis, MN 55439-0106

952-926-6547
FAX 952-926-1624
E-Mail: aca@acainternational.org
Home Page: www.acainternational.org
Social Media: *Facebook, Twitter, LinkedIn, YouTube*

Lucia Lebens, director

International trade organization of credit and collection professionals providing a variety of accounts receivable management services to over 1,000,000 credit grantors.
5300 Members
Founded in 1995
Mailing list available for rent

5963 Advertising Media Credit Executives Association
PO Box 433
Louisville, KY 40201

502-582-4327
FAX 502-582-4330
E-Mail: amcea@amcea.org
Home Page: www.amcea.org
Social Media: *Facebook*

Norman Taylor, President
Kimberly Archibald Russell, VP
Newt Collins, Secretary - Treasurer
Vickie Bolinger, Immediate Past President
Sandra Lawson, Directors

A non-profit organization that exists to serve the media credit manager. Directed and managed by professionals just like you, media credit managers who volunteer for various projects to benefit the industry and our association.
Founded in 1953

5964 Affordable Housing Tax Credit Coalition
1090 K Street NW
12th Floor
Washington, DC 20006

202-661-7698
FAX 202-661-2299
E-Mail: info@taxcreditcoalition.org
Home Page: www.taxcreditcoalition.org
Social Media: *Facebook, Twitter, LinkedIn, YouTube*

Jeff Whiting, Chairman
Todd Crow, President
Tony Alfieri, First VP
Joseph Hagan, President Emeritus
Michael Novogradac, VP

Plays a major role in assuring the conitinuance of the low income housing tax credit, with the primary goal of achieving permanent extension of the low income housing tax credit program.
105 Members
Founded in 1988

5965 American Bankruptcy Institute
66 Canal Center Plaza
Suite 600
Alexandria, VA 22314-1546

703-739-0800
FAX 703-739-1060
E-Mail: info@abiworld.org
Home Page: www.abiworld.org
Social Media: *Facebook, Twitter, LinkedIn, YouTube*

Samuel Gerdano, Executive Director
Felicia S Turner, Deputy Executive Director

Patricia A Redmond, Chairman
James Patrick Shea, President
Brian L Shaw, Immediate Past President

Multidisiplinary, nonpartisan organization dedicated to research and education on matters related to insovency. Engaged in numerous educational and research activities as well as the production of a number of publications both for the insolvency practitioner and the public.
11700 Members
Founded in 1982

5966 American Financial Services Association
919 18th Street NW
Suite 300
Washington, DC 20006-5517

202-296-5544
E-Mail: info@afsamail.org
Home Page: www.afsaonline.org
Social Media: *Facebook, Twitter, LinkedIn, Google+*

Chris Steinebert, President/CEO
Gary L. Phillips, Chairman
Nathan D. Benson, Member
Dietmar W. Exler, VP

A national trade association for market funded providers of financial services to consumers and small businesses.
400 Members
Founded in 1916

5967 American Recovery Association
5525 N MacArthur Boulevard
Suite 135
Irving, TX 75038

972-755-4755
FAX 972-870-5755
E-Mail:
homeoffice@americanrecoveryassn.org
Home Page: www.repo.org
Social Media: *Facebook, LinkedIn, Google+*

Jerry Wilson, President
David Handschin, VP
Bennett Deese, Secretary/Treasurer

Approximately 500 offices around the US, Canada and Germany, providing repossesion services around the world.
280 Members
Founded in 1965

5968 BCCA
550 W Frontage Rd
Suite 3600
Northfield, IL 60093-1243

847-881-8757
FAX 847-784-8059
E-Mail: info@bccacredit.com
Home Page: www.bccacredit.com
Social Media: *Facebook, Twitter, LinkedIn*

Mary Collin, CEO
Jamie Smith, Director of Operations
Cindy Laser, Sales/Membership

BCCA is the media industry's credit association that functions as a central clearing house for credit information on advertisers, agencies and buying services, both locally and nationally. Also provides an Electronic Media Credit Application (EMCAPP.com) to members that helps streamline the application process. One app in one location!
600 Members
Founded in 1972

5969 Broadcast Cable Credit Association
550 W Frontage Rd
Suite 3600
Northfield, IL 60093-1243

847-881-8757
FAX 847-784-8059

E-Mail: info@bccacredit.com
Home Page: www.bccacredit.com
Social Media: *Facebook, Twitter, LinkedIn*

Mary Collin, CEO
Cheryl Ingram, Chairman
Dalton Lee, Secretary
John Drain, SVP, Finance

Subsidiary of the Media Financial Management Association. BCCA provides industry specific credit reports on individual agencies, advertisers or buying services both national and local. These reports may be obtained upon request online and by phone or fax. Its mission is to provide tools and services that will allow members to perform their functions to the best of their abilities, and help them achieve a profitable bottom line.
600 Members
Founded in 1972

5970 Business Products Credit Association
P.O. Box 5003
St. Paul, MS 55101-7003

651-998-9609
E-Mail: info@bcpa.org
Home Page: www.bcpa.org
Social Media: *Facebook, Twitter, LinkedIn*

Heidi Piche, President
Sandra Sandra, Secretary
Matt Shillerstrom, Treasurer
Marie Strawser, Program Director
Bob Kunzer, Information Director

Credit Trade Association for manufacturers and wholesalers.
Founded in 1875

5971 CDC Consumer Debt Counseling
831 W. Morse Blvd.
Winter Park, FL 32789

314-647-9006
800-820-9232
FAX 407-599-5954
Home Page: www.consumerdebtcounselors.org

Philip Johnston, President
Melissa Towel, Advisor
Janice Diaz, Customer Care

Nonprofit provider of quality, face-to-face and telephone budget and debt counseling education.
Founded in 1998

5972 Capital Markets Credit Analysts Society
25 N Broadway
Tarrytown, NY 10591

914-332-0040
FAX 914-332-1541
E-Mail: cmcas@cmcas.org
Home Page: www.cmcas.org
Social Media: *Facebook*

Stuart Plesser, President
Kelly Byrne, Account Manager
Bikas Tomkoria, Treasurer
Claudia Calderon, Secretary

A professional society whose membership consists primarily of managers and analysts in credit risk departments that directly support their employers' capital market activities.
500 Members
Founded in 1989
Mailing list available for rent

5973 Coalition of Higher Education Assistance Organizations
1101 Vermont Ave NW
Suite 400
Washington, DC 20005-3586

202-289-3910
FAX 202-371-0197

E-Mail: hwadsworth@wpllc.net
Home Page: www.coheao.com

Maria Livolsi, President
Carl Perry, VP
Lori Hartung, Treasurer
Tom Schmidt, Secretary

Focus is on legislative and regulatory advocacy for Federal Perkins and other campus based student loan programs.
365 Members
Founded in 1981

5974 Commercial Finance Association

370 7th Ave. Ste. 1801
7 Penn Plz
New York, NY 10001-3979

212-792-9390
FAX 212-564-6053
E-Mail: info@cfa.com
Home Page: www.cfa.com
Social Media: *Facebook, Twitter, LinkedIn, YouTube*

Patrick Trammell, President
D. Michael Monk, Vice President - Finance
Andrea Petro, First Vice President
Robert Trojan, CEO
David Grende, VP

Trade group of the asset-based, financial services industry, with members throughout the US, Canada and around the world. Members include the asset-based lending arms of domestic and foreign commercial banks, small and large independent finance companies, floor plan financing organizations, factoring organizations and financing subsidiaries of major industrial corporations. CFA membership is by organization, not by individual.
Founded in 1944

5975 Commercial Mortgage Securities Association

20 Broad St
7th Floor
New York, NY 10005

212-509-1844
FAX 646-884-7569
E-Mail: info@crefc.org
Home Page: www.crefc.org
Social Media: *Facebook, Twitter, LinkedIn*

Stephen Renna, CEO
Ed DeAngelo, VP
Michael Flood, VP

International trade organization for the commercial real estate capital markets. Also represents and promotes an orderly and ethical global institutional secondary market for the sale of commercial mortgage loans and equity investments.
309 Members
Founded in 1994

5976 Consumer Credit Industry Association

6300 Powers Ferry Road
Suite 600-286
Atlanta, GA 30339

678-858-4001
E-Mail: webmaster@cciaonline.com
Home Page: www.cciaonline.com

Tom Keepers, Executive VP
John Euwema, VP Legislative Regulatory Counsel
Stephanie Neal, Director of Member Services

To preserve, promote and enhance the availability, utility and integrity of insurance and related products and services delivered in connection with financial transactions.
140 Members
Founded in 1951

5977 Consumer Credit Insurance Association

6300 Powers Ferry Road
Suite 600-286
Atlanta, GA 30339

678-858-4001
FAX 312-939-8287
E-Mail: webmaster@cciaonline.com
Home Page: www.cciaonline.com

Jim Pangburn, President
Dick Williams, Chairman
Michelle Dicks, General Counsel

To preserve, promote and enhance the availability, utility and integrity of insurance and related products and services delivered in connection with financial transactions.
140 Members
Founded in 1951

5978 Credit Union National Association

601 Penn Ave
NW South Building, Suite 600
Washington, DC 20004-2601

202-628-5777
800-356-9655
FAX 202-638-7734
Home Page: www.cuna.org
Social Media: *Facebook, Twitter, YouTube*

Susan Newton, Executive Director
Pat Sowick, VP
Richard Dines, Senior State and League Affairs
Alicia Valencia Erb, League Relations
Shellee Mitchell, Executive Assistant

The premier trade association in the financial services arena. Supports, protects, unifies and advances the credit union movement.

5979 FCIB

Finance, Credit, International Business Assoc.
8840 Columbia 100 Pkwy
Columbia, MD 21045-2158

410-423-1840
888-256-3242
FAX 410-740-5574
E-Mail: fcib_info@fcibglobal.com
Home Page: www.fcibglobal.com
Social Media: *Twitter, LinkedIn*

Marta Chacon-Martinez, Director
Mike Mino, CCE, Chairman
Ron Shepherd, Director, Membership & Business

FCIB enjoys an international reputation as the premier Assocation of executives in finance, credit and international business, providing critical export credit and collections insight, practical advice and intelligence to companies of all sizes - from Fortune 500 multi-nationals to medium and small private companies. With international credit management and trade finance professionals in 55 countries around the world, FCIB offers unique networking and educational opportunities
1200 Members
Founded in 1919

5980 Farm Credit

7951 East Maplewood Ave.
Suite 200
Greenwood Village, CO 80111

E-Mail: ask@farmcredit.com
Home Page: www.farmcreditnetwork.com
Social Media: *Facebook, Twitter, YouTube, Pinterest, Instagram*

Todd Van Hoose, President & CEO
Curtis Hancock, Chairman

Farm Credit member organizations provide credit to farmers, ranchers and rural communities for agriculture and infrastructure projects.
Founded in 1916

5981 International Association of Commercial Collectors

4040 W 70th Street
Minneapolis, MN 55435

952-925-0760
800-859-9526
FAX 952-926-1624
E-Mail: iacc@commercialcollector.com
Home Page: www.commercialcollector.com
Social Media: *LinkedIn*

Tom Brenan, President
Greg Cohen, Vice President
Paul Eisenberg, Treasurer
Lee Vandenheuvel, Immediate Past President
Marc Bressler, Director

International trade association comprised of collection specialists and commercial attorneys, with members throughout the US and 20 international countries. IACC's mission is to promote the commercial collection profession by providing IACC members with the resources to excel in the industry.
350 Members
Founded in 1970

5982 International Energy Credit Association

1120 Route 73
Suite 200
Mt. Laurel, NJ 08054

856-380-6854
FAX 856-439-0525
E-Mail: mbiordi@ahint.com
Home Page: www.ieca.net
Social Media: *Facebook, Twitter, LinkedIn, RSS*

Gary Nicholson, EVP
Michele Biordi, Executive Director
Zachary Starbird, President
James Hawkins, First Vice President
Amanda Kenly, Past President

The oldest international industry credit association in the United States. Membership includes companies located in the Uited States, Canada, most Western European countries, Mexico, South America and Asia.
700 Members
Founded in 1923

5983 Jewelers Board of Trade

95 Jefferson Blvd
Warwick, RI 02888-1046

401-467-0055
FAX 401-467-1199
E-Mail: jbtinfo@jewelersboard.com
Home Page: www.jewelersboard.com
Social Media: *Twitter*

Dione Kenyen, President

A not for profit jewelry trade association whose primary function is to compile and disseminate accurate and reliable credit information among its members as to the financial standing, credit history and background of dealers of jewelry and related products.
3200 Members
Founded in 1884

5984 Mortgage Bankers Association

1919 M Street NW
5th floor
Washington, DC 20036

202-557-2700
800-793-6222
E-Mail: membership@mortgagebankers.org
Home Page: www.mba.org
Social Media: *Facebook, Twitter, LinkedIn, YouTube*

David H Stevens, President and CEO
Marcia Davies, COO
Michael Fratantoni, Chief Economist/ SVP

Bill Killmer, SVP, Legislative & Pol. Affairs
Thomas T. Kim, SVP, Commercial/Multifamily

Representing the real estate finance industry, MBA serves its membership by representing their legislative and regulatory interests before the US Congress and federal agencies; by meeting their educational needs through programs and a range of periodicals and publications; and by supporting their business interests with a variety of research initiatives and other products and services.
2900 Members
Founded in 1918

5985 NACUSO
PMB 3419 Via Lido
#135
Newport Beach, CA 92663

949-645-5296
888-462-2870
FAX 949-645-5297
E-Mail: info@nacuso.org
Home Page: www.nacuso.org

Jack Antonini, President/CEO
Mark Zook, Chairman
Mike Atkins, Secretary
400 Members
Founded in 1984

5986 National Association of Consumer Credit
PO Box 20871
Columbus, OH 43220-871

614-326-1165
FAX 614-326-1162
E-Mail: nacca2007@sbcglobal.net
Home Page: www.naccaonline.org

Joe Mulberry, President
Mike Larsen, First VP
Brian Landis, Second VP
Carri Grube-Lybarker, Secretary/treasurer

Improving the supervision of consumer credit agencies; facilitating the administration of laws governing these agencies by providing a forum for the exchange of information, ideas and experiences among public officials having supervision of such agencies and changes with the administration of such laws; facilitating intercommunication among its members and developing standard information collection concerning consumer credit agencies in each state.
55 Members
Founded in 1935

5987 National Association of Credit Management
8840 Columbia 100 Pkwy
Columbia, MD 21045-2100

410-740-5560
FAX 410-740-5574
E-Mail: robins@nacm.org
Home Page: www.nacm.org
Social Media: *Facebook, Twitter, LinkedIn, Pinterest, RSS*

Rocky Thomas, CCE, Chairperson
Gary Gaudette, CCE, ICCE, Chairman/elect
Kevin Quinn, Director
Jay Snyder, CCE, ICCE, Director

NACM and its network of affiliated associations are the leading resource for credit and financial management information and education, delivering products and services which improve the management of business credit and accounts receivable. Our collective voice has influenced legislative results concerning commercial business and trade credit to our nation's policy makers for more than 100 years, and continues to play an active part in legislative issues pertaining to business credit.
18000 Members
Founded in 1896

5988 National Association of Credit Union Service Organizations
PMB 3419 Via Lido
Suite 135
Newport Beach, CA 92663

949-645-5296
888-462-2870
FAX 949-645-5297
E-Mail: info@nacuso.org
Home Page: www.nacuso.org

Jack Antonini, President/CEO
Mark Zook, Chairman
Mike Atkins, Secretary

Leading professional trade association for credit unions and CUSO's seeking to provide a full aray of services, such as mortgages, business lending and business lending depository services, trust services, investments and insurance to their members and non members alike.
412 Members
Founded in 1984

5989 National Association of Federal Credit Unions
3138 10th St N
Arlington, VA 22201-2160

703-522-4770
800-336-4644
FAX 703-524-1082
E-Mail: lcorbin@nafcu.org
Home Page: www.nafcu.org
Social Media: *Facebook, Twitter, LinkedIn, YouTube*

Fred Becker, President
Alicia Hosmer, VP, Marketing
Ed Templeton, Chair/Director-at-Large
Richard L Harris, Vice Chair/Region V Director
Jeanne Kucey, Treasurer

A respected and influential trade association that exclusively represents the interest of federal credit unions before the federal government and the public.
804 Members
Founded in 1967

5990 National Association of State Credit Union Supervisors
1655 Fort Myer Dr
Suite 300
Arlington, VA 22209-3108

703-528-8351
800-728-7927
FAX 703-528-3248
E-Mail: offices@nascus.org
Home Page: www.nascus.org
Social Media: *Twitter*

Lucy Ito, President/CEO
Tammy Gentilini, State Programs Coordinator
Patrick Keefe, Vice President, Communications
Steve Pleger, Chairman
Mary Ellen O'Neill, Chairman-Elect

State chartered credit unions and state credit union supervisors.
900 Members
Founded in 1965

5991 National Chemical Credit Association
500 Seneca Street
Suite 400
Buffalo, NY 14209-1963

716-887-9527
844-937-3268
FAX 716-878-0479
E-Mail: robert.gagliardi@abc-amega.com
Home Page: www.ncca1.org
Social Media: *Twitter, LinkedIn, YouTube, Google+*

Glenn Lifrieri, Executive Board Chair

Members are major producers of basic chemicals and allied products.
100 Members
Founded in 1938

5992 National Council of Postal Credit Unions
PO Box 160
Del Mar, CA 92014-0160

858-792-3883
FAX 858-792-3884
E-Mail: ncpcu@ncpcu.org
Home Page: www.ncpcu.org

Kevin A Yaeger, Chairman
Rebecca Cuddy, Vice Chair
Sidney Parfait, Treasurer
Neil Crean, Secretary

Organized to represent the special interests of postal credit unions.
160 Members
Founded in 1984

5993 National Credit Reporting Association
701 E. Irving Park Rd
Suite 306
Roselle, IL 60712

630-539-1525
FAX 630-539-1526
E-Mail: tclemans@ncrainc.org
Home Page: www.ncrainc.org
Social Media: *Facebook, Twitter, LinkedIn*

Terry W Clemans, Executive Director
Jan Gerber, Office & Members Services Manager

Purpose is to promote the general welfare of its members. Also provides leadership in education, legislation, ethics and enhanced vendor's relation
150 Members
Founded in 1992

5994 National Credit Union Administration
1775 Duke St
Alexandria, VA 22314-6115

703-518-6300
800-755-1030
FAX 703-518-6539
E-Mail: consumerassistance@ncua.gov
Home Page: www.ncua.gov
Social Media: *Facebook, Twitter, YouTube*

Debbie Matz, Chairman

Governed by a three member board appointed by the President and confirmed by the US Senate, this independent federal agency charters and supervises federal credit unions. NCUA, with the backing of the full faith and credit of the US government, operates the National Credit Union Share Insurance Fund, insuring the savings of 80 million account holders in all federal credit unions and many state chartered credit unions.
82M Members
Founded in 1970

5995 National Federation of Community Development Credit Unions
39 Broadway
Suite 2140
New York, NY 10006-3063

212-809-1850
800-437-8711
FAX 212-809-3274
E-Mail: info@cdcu.coop
Home Page: www.cdcu.coop
Social Media: *Facebook, Twitter, LinkedIn*

Cathie Mahon, President/CEO
Eben Sheaffer, CFO/Chief Investment Officer
Pablo DeFilippi, CUDE, VP, Membership & BD
Pamela Owens, CUDE, Vice President, Programs

Ysemny (Nachi) Abood, Technical Assistance Specialist

Serve and represent financial cooperatives in low income communities. Members are community based credit unions. Provides training and management support to CDCU's and asists groups in organizing new credit unions.
200 Members
Founded in 1974

5996 National Foundation for Credit Counseling

2000 M Street NW
Suite 505
Washington, DC 20036

202-677-4300
800-338-2227
Home Page: www.nfcc.org
Social Media: *Facebook, Twitter, YouTube*

Susan C Keating, CEO
Paul Weiss, Chief Of Staff/CFO
Lydia Sermons-Ward, Senior VP Marketing

Sets the standard for quality credit counseling, debt reduction services and education for financial wellness.
1200 Members

5997 National Installment Lenders Association

PO Box 65615
Washington, DC 20035

Home Page: nilaonline.org
Social Media: *Facebook, Twitter, YouTube*

An organization formed to educate people about the advantages of installment loans as sources of consumer credit over credit cards, payday loans and other financial products.
Founded in 2008

5998 National Rural Lenders Association

2402 E 44th Place
Tulsa, OK 74105

918-430-3956
FAX 918-550-8293
Home Page: nrla-usda.org

Stephen Van Sickle, Chairman
Greg O'Donnell, Executive Director

The NRLA is an advocate for United States Department of Agriculture lending programs to support rural development.

5999 New York Media Credit Group

500 Seneca Street
Suite 400
Buffalo, NY 14209

716-887-9547
844-937-3268
FAX 716-878-0479
E-Mail: robert.gagliardi@abc-amega.com
Home Page: www.ny-media.com
Social Media: *Twitter, LinkedIn, YouTube, Google+*

Glenn Lifrieri, Executive Board Chair

One of the most active credit association for media credit professionals today. Many of the members are from major media including cable television, sports and news cable TV, and radio.
Founded in 1938

6000 Risk Management Association

One Liberty Place
1801 Market St
Suite 300
Philadelphia, PA 19103-1613

215-446-4000
800-677-7621
FAX 215-446-4101
E-Mail: customers@rmahq.org

Home Page: www.rmahq.org
Social Media: *Facebook, Twitter, LinkedIn*

Dwight Overturf, CFO
William F Githens, President/CEO
Maurice H Hartigan II, President/CEO
Reid Adamson, Senior VP
William S Aichele, President/CEO

Champions risk management while also monitoring emerging trends. Our strong relationship with members and regulators helps us develop new risk management techniques, innovative products and education and training programs geared to risk management professionals at different stages of their careers.
3000 Members
Founded in 1914

Newsletters

6001 AHTCC News

Affordable Housing Tax Credit Coalition
401 9th Street NW
Suite 900
Washington, DC 20004

202-585-8162
FAX 202-585-8080
E-Mail: info@taxcreditcoalition.org
Home Page: www.taxcreditcoalition.org

Joseph Hagan, President
Frequency: Monthly

6002 ARA News & Views

American Recovery Association
5525 N MacArthur Boulevard
Suite 135
Irving, TX 75038

972-755-4755
FAX 972-870-5755
E-Mail: homeoffice@americanrecoveryassn.org
Home Page: www.repo.org/

Mary Jane Hogan, President
Paul Hallock

Provides news, information and coverage of the recovery industry. Free to members only in print. Available to all others online
28 Pages
Frequency: Quarterly
Founded in 1965

6003 Bankcard Barometer

RAM Research Group
320 E 72nd St
Suite 9C
New York, NY 10021

212-724-7535
FAX 212-208-4384
E-Mail: info@investmentTechnologies.com
Home Page: www.investmenttechnologies.com

Brian Rom, Owner
Robert B McKinley, Publisher

Reports on the pricing and performance of US bank credit card portfolios. Trendline charts follow deliquency, charge-offs, attrition, payment rates, bankruptcy rates, fraud losses, interest yield, operating expenses, net interest margin and return on assets.
Cost: $1295.00
40 Pages
Frequency: Monthly
Founded in 1986
Printed in 4 colors

6004 Bankcard Dispatch

RAM Research Group

999 Vanderbilt Beach Road
2nd Floor
Naples, FL 34108

239-325-5300
E-Mail: staff@ramresearch.com
Home Page: www.cardweb.com

Robert B McKinley, Editor

Covers the entire payment card industry as it affects the US market. Comprehensive periodical is prepared for payment card executives.
Cost: $1295.00
40 Pages
Frequency: Monthly
Printed in 4 colors

6005 Bankcard Update

RAM Research Group
999 Vanderbilt Beach Road
2nd Floor
Naples, FL 34108

239-325-5300
E-Mail: staff@ramresearch.com
Home Page: www.cardweb.com

Robert B McKinley, Editor/chairman

Updated printed report and CD-ROM on quarterly statistics of the top US issuers. Covers hundreds of portfolios comprising more than 95 percent of the US market. Subscription includes both the printed version and CD-ROM.
Cost: $ 1295.00
40 Pages
Frequency: Monthly
Founded in 1986
Printed in 4 colors

6006 Capitol Watch

National Association of Credit Unions
3138 10th St N
Arlington, VA 22201-2149

703-522-4770
800-336-4644
FAX 703-524-1082
Home Page: www.nafcu.org
Social Media: *Facebook, Twitter, YouTube*

Fred Becker, President
Alicia Hosmer, VP, Marketing

This members only electronic format newsletter is NAFCU's monthly communication for credit unions with assets of $50 million or less.

6007 Collection Agency Report

First Detroit Corporation
30033 Paul Ct
Warren, MI 48092-1805

586-573-0045
800-366-5995
FAX 586-573-9219
E-Mail: ascace@firstdetroit.com
Home Page: www.firstdetroit.com

Albert Scace, President
Patricia Herrick, Marketing Manager
Patricia Herrick, Circulation Manager

Provides financially oriented news on the collection agency and bad debt buying industries worldwide.
Cost: $420.00
8 Pages
Frequency: Monthly
ISSN: 1052-4029
Founded in 1988
Mailing list available for rentat $110 per M

6008 Communicator

Consumer Data Industry Association
1090 Vermont Ave Nw
Suite 200
Washington, DC 20005-4964

202-371-0910
FAX 202-371-0134

E-Mail: cdia@cdiaonline.org
Home Page: www.cdiaonline.org

Norm Magnuson, VP
Alicia Payne, Contact

Comprehensive online news about the consumer reporting industry, legislation, member news and schedule of industry events. Members only benefit.
16 Pages
Frequency: Monthly
Circulation: 3000
Founded in 1906

6009 Consumer Bankruptcy News
LRP Publications
Po Box 24668
West Palm Beach, FL 33416-4668

561-622-6520
800-341-7874
FAX 561-622-2423
E-Mail: custserv@lrp.com
Home Page: www.lrp.com

Kenneth Kahn, President

Keeps readers up-to-date on the latest news and cases involving consumer bankruptcy. A must-have for every bankruptcy professional.
Cost: $290.00
Mailing list available for rent
Printed in 2 colors on matte stock

6010 Covering Credit Newsletter
Covering Credit
13 Calle Larspur
Rancho Santa Margarita, CA 92688

949-460-7609
FAX 949-460-7609
E-Mail: newsletter@coveringcredit.com
Home Page: www.coveringcredit.com
Social Media: *Facebook, LinkedIn*

Michael C Dennis, Communications Advisor
Steve Kozack, Financial Consultant

Intended for business professionals dealing with credit risk management and/or commercial debt collection and their advsiors. Free and online.
Frequency: Monthly
Founded in 1989

6011 Credit Union News Watch
Credit Union National Association
601 Penn Ave
NW South Building, Suite 600
Washington, DC 20004

202-628-5777
800-356-9655
FAX 202-638-7729
Home Page: www.cuna.org
Social Media: *Facebook, Twitter*

Susan Newton, Executive Director
Pat Sowick, VP
Richard Dines, Senior State and League Affairs Dir
Alicia Valencia Erb, League Relations
Shellee Mitchell, Executive Assistant

Offers news and reports on credit and lending services.
Cost: $50.00
Frequency: Weekly
Founded in 1970

6012 Credit Union Report
Callahan & Associates
1001 Connecticut Ave Nw
Suite 1001
Washington, DC 20036-5523

202-223-3920
800-446-7453
FAX 202-223-1311

E-Mail: pubs@creditunions.com
Home Page: www.callahan.com

Nader Moghaddam, President/CEO

Keeps an eye on the future, providing stategic vision for every level of credit union management. Each issue includes leading-edge ideas from the industry's top consultants and CEO's, as well as financial trend analysis to help credit unions operate more effectively. Available in print and electronic formats.
Cost: $149.00
Frequency: Monthly

6013 Credit Union Times
33-41 Newark Street
2nd Floor
Hoboken, NJ 07030

201-526-1230
800-543-0874
FAX 201-526-1260
E-Mail: subscriptions@cutimes.com
Home Page: www.cutimes.com
Social Media: *Facebook, Twitter, LinkedIn*

Sarah Snell Cooke, Editor in Chief
Sarah Snell Cooke, Publisher/Editor in Chief
Donald Shoultz, Managing Editor

Reports on marketing, regulation, technology and developing trends.
Cost: $120.00
Frequency: Weekly
Circulation: 9337
Printed in 4 colors on matte stock

6014 Inside MBS & ABS
Inside Mortgage Finance Publishers
7910 Woodmont Ave
Suite 1000
Bethesda, MD 20814-7019

301-951-1240
FAX 301-656-1709
E-Mail: service@imfpubs.com
Home Page: www.imfpubs.com
Social Media: *Twitter, LinkedIn, YouTube*

Guy Cecala, Owner
John Bancroft, Managing Editor

If you're involved in issuing, underwriting, investing, research, rating or trading mortgage-backed securities and asset-backed securities, this publication is for you.
Cost: $1699.00
Founded in 1984

6015 Jumbo Rate News
Bauer Financial
2655 S Le Jeune Rd
Suite 1A
Coral Gables, FL 33134-5827

305-445-9500
800-388-6686
FAX 305-445-6775
E-Mail: customerservice@bauerfinancial.com
Home Page: www.bauerfinancial.com

Karen L Dorway, President/CEO

Each issue contains over 1,000 separate Jumbo CD rates in seven categories from over 200 creditworthy banks and thrifts nationwide. Includes star ratings, wire transfer fees, deposit requirements and financial highlights for each institution.
Cost: $4150.00
Frequency: Weekly
Founded in 1986
Printed in 2 colors on matte stock

6016 MBA Newslink
Mortgage Bankers Association
1717 Rhode Island Avenue NW
Suite 400
Washington, DC 20036

202-557-2700
E-Mail: mbsnewslink@mortgagebankers.org

Home Page: www.mortgagebankers.org
Social Media: *Facebook, Twitter, LinkedIn, YouTube*

David H Stevens, President/CEO
Marcia Davies, Chief of Staff/SVP

Learn the latest residential, commercial, and multifamily real estate finance news. Hear what's happening at MBA, read special features that provide vital facts and insight into industry trends, news from Washington, DC and more.
Cost: $69.95
Frequency: Daily
Circulation: 54,000

6017 NACM E-News
National Association of Credit Management
8840 Columbia 100 Pkwy
Columbia, MD 21045-2100

410-740-5560
FAX 410-740-5574
E-Mail: robins@nacm,org
Home Page: www.nacm.org
Social Media: *Facebook, Twitter, LinkedIn*

Toni Drake, Chairperson
Chris Meyers, Chairman Elect
Kevin Quinn, Director
Jay Snyder, Director

News items of interest to credit and business professionals. Free online.

6018 National Mortgage News
Thomson Financial Publishing
1 State St
27th Floor
New York, NY 10004-1481

212-803-8333
800-221-1809
FAX 800-235-5552
E-Mail: custserv@thomsonmedia.com
Home Page: www.nationalmortgagenews.com
Social Media: *Facebook, Twitter, LinkedIn*

Timothy Murphy, Group Publisher

Mortgage information, legislation and news.
Cost: $228.00
Frequency: Weekly
Printed in 2 colors on newsprint stock

6019 Newsbreak
First Entertainment Credit Union
PO Box 100
Hollywood, CA 90078

323-851-3673
888-800-3328
FAX 323-874-1397
E-Mail: mail@firstent.org
Home Page: www.firstent.org
Social Media: *Facebook, Twitter, You tube*

Charles A Bruen, President/CEO

Provides industry, resources and investment news and information for the First Entertainment Credit Union member. Free online.
Frequency: Quarterly

6020 SNL Daily ThriftWatch
SNL Financial
212 7th Street NE
Charlottesville, VA 22902

434-977-1600
866-296-3743
FAX 434-977-4466
E-Mail: CustMerDept@snl.com
Home Page: www.snl.com

Mike Chin, President

Provides the information that thrift executives and investors require to stay on top of the in-

dustry. Available in print and electronic formats.
5 Pages
Frequency: Daily
Founded in 1987

6021 Scope
International Association of Commercial Collectors
4040 W 70th St
Minneapolis, MN 55435-4104

952-925-0760
800-859-9526
FAX 952-926-1624
E-Mail: iacc@commercialcollector.com
Home Page: www.commercialcollector.com
Social Media: *LinkedIn*

Johon Yursha, President
Tammy Schoenberg, Executive Director
Jessica Hartman, Director
Sara Bobrowski, IACC Coordinator
Randy Frazee, Board Treasurer

Provides updates on developments in the industry, important legislative and legal issues, and IACC events and resources. Free to members only.
350 Members
Frequency: Monthly
Circulation: 350
Founded in 1970
Printed in on glossy stock

6022 Trade Vendor Quarterly
Blakeley & Blakeley
2 Park Plaza
Suite 400
Irvine, CA 92614

949-260-0611
FAX 949-260-0613
E-Mail: administrator@vendorland.com
Home Page: www.vendorlaw.com

Scott Blakey, Esq.

Highlights developments in commercial, creditors' rights, e-commerce and bankruptcy law of interest to the credit and financial professional. Free online.
Frequency: Quarterly

Magazines & Journals

6023 Affordable Housing Finance
Hanley Wood
300 Montgomery Street
Suite 1060
San Francisco, CA 94104

415-315-1241
FAX 415-315-1248
E-Mail: ahf@omeda.com
Home Page: www.housingfinance.com
Social Media: *Facebook, Twitter*

John McManus, Editorial Director
Jerry Ascierto, Editor in Chief

Offers practical information on obtaining debt and equality financing from federal, state, and local governments as well as private resources. In-depth coverage on the federal low-income housing tax credit program, tax-exempt bond financing, corporate tax credit investigation.
Cost: $83.00
88 Pages
Frequency: Monthly
Circulation: 9000
Founded in 1993
Printed in 4 colors on glossy stock

6024 American Bankruptcy Institute Journal
American Bankruptcy Institute

44 Canal Center Plz
Suite 404
Alexandria, VA 22314-1546

703-739-0800
FAX 703-739-1060
E-Mail: Support@abiworld.org
Home Page: www.abiworld.org
Social Media: *Facebook, Twitter, LinkedIn*

James Markus, President
Patricia Redmond, President-elect
Margaret Howard, VP Research
Brian Shaw, VP Membership

Benefit to ABI members. Written by experts in the insolvency community, the Journal addresses timely issues involving consumer bankruptcy, the intersection of state laws and the Bankrupcy Code, valuation, turnaround managagement concerns, recent legislative developments, the US trustee system and more. Available in print or online.
Cost: $225.00
Frequency: 1 Year 10 Issue
Circulation: 10500
Founded in 1982
Printed in 5 colors on matte stock

6025 Apartment Finance Today Magazine
Hanley Wood LLC
One Thomas Circle, NW
Suite 600
Washington, DC 20005

202-452-0800
FAX 202-785-1974
Home Page: www.hanleywood.com

Peter Goldston, CEO
Frank Anton, Vice Chairman

Provides in-depth and unbiased reporting and insightful analysis for owners, developers and asset managers
80 Pages
ISSN: 1097-4059
Founded in 1995
Printed in 4 colors on glossy stock

6026 Business Credit Magazine
National Association of Credit Management
8840 Columbia 100 Pkwy
Columbia, MD 21045-2100

410-740-5560
FAX 410-740-5574
E-Mail: robins@nacm.org
Home Page: www.nacm.org
Social Media: *Facebook, Twitter, LinkedIn*

Toni Drake, Chairperson
Chris Meyers, Chairman/elect
Kevin Quinn, Director
Jay Snyder, Director

Serves those responsible for extending business and trade credit and overseeing risk management for their companies. Keeps individuals up-to-date on cutting-edge trends and important legislative, bankruptcy, business ethics, trade finance, asset protection, benchmarking and scoring issues.
Frequency: 9x/Year
Circulation: 22000

6027 Card Technology
Thomson Financial Publishing
Thomson Reuters
3 Times Square
New York, NY 10036

646-223-4000
E-Mail: general.info@thomsonreuters.com
Home Page: www.tfn.com

Thomas H Glocer, Chief Executive Officer

Store-value cards, optical-memory cards, biometrics, cards on the Internet, cards for electronic data storage, and devices used with these cards in banking, government, telecommunica-

tions, transportation and education.
Cost: $ 98.00
Frequency: Monthly
Circulation: 25000
Founded in 1961
Printed in 4 colors on glossy stock

6028 Collections & Credit Risk
Thomson Financial Publishing
1 State St
27th Floor
New York, NY 10004-1481

212-803-8200
800-221-1809
FAX 800-843-9600
E-Mail: custserv@sourcemedia.com
Home Page: www.creditcollectionsworld.com

Darren Waggoner, Chief Editor
Melissa Buonos, National Sales Manager

Focuses on news and trends of strategic and competitive importance to collections and credit policy executives. Covers the credit risk industry's growth, diversification and technology in both commercial and consumer credit.
Cost: $98.00
66 Pages
Frequency: Monthly
Circulation: 25000
Founded in 1996

6029 Commercial Collection Guidelines for Credit Grantors
International Association of Commercial Collectors
4040 W 70th St
Minneapolis, MN 55435-4104

952-925-0760
800-859-9526
FAX 952-926-1624
E-Mail: iacc@commercialcollector.com
Home Page: www.commercialcollector.com
Social Media: *LinkedIn*

John Yursha, President
Tammy M. Schoenberg, Executive Director
Jessica Hartman, Director
Sara Bobrowski, IACC Coordinator
Randy Frazee, Board Treasurer

Helps to assist commercial account credit managers and their staffs in evaluating receivables and collecting accounts. Topics include internal credit control, credit granting and collecting and professional commercial collection service.
Cost: $70.00
350 Members
Frequency: Monthly
Founded in 1970

6030 Commercial Mortgage Insight
Zackin Publications
PO Box 2180
Waterbury, CT 06722-2180

203-755-0158
800-325-6745
FAX 203-262-4680
E-Mail: info@cmi-online.com
Home Page: www.cmi-online.com
Social Media: *Facebook, Twitter*

Paul Zackin, Publisher
Phil Hall, Editor
Christina Stanevich, Marketing

For desicion making executives in commercial mortgage banking and brokerage firms, commercial banks and community/savings institutions. Provides professionals with timely and comprehensive market news, trends and know-how needed to make informed decisions and choices.
Cost: $48.00
32 Pages
Frequency: Monthly
Circulation: 18000
ISSN: 1095-0729

Founded in 1997
Printed in 4 colors

6031 Credit & Financial Management Review
Credit Research Foundation
1812 Baltimore Blvd
Suite H
Westminster, MD 21157

443-821-3000
FAX 443-821-3627
E-Mail: lylew@crfonline.org
Home Page: www.crfonline.org

Lyle Wallis, President

Referred journal that publishes original material concerned with all aspects of credit, accounts receivable and customer financial relationships. It is devoted to the improvement and further development of the theory and practice of credit management.
Cost: $80.00
56 Pages
Frequency: Quarterly
Circulation: 3000
Printed in 2 colors

6032 Credit Card Management
Thomson Financial Publishing
Thomas Reuters
3 Times Square
New York, NY 10036

646-223-4000
800-782-5555
FAX 646-223-8593
E-Mail: generial.info@thomsonreuters.com
Home Page: www.tfn.com

Thomas H Glocer, Chief Executive Officer

Information on the major developments in the credit card industry.
Cost: $98.00
74 Pages
Frequency: Monthly
Circulation: 19000
Printed in 4 colors on glossy stock

6033 Credit Professional
Credit Professionals International
10726 Manchester Rd
Suite B
St Louis, MO 63122-1320

314-821-9393
FAX 314-821-7171
E-Mail: creditpro@creditprofessionals.org
Home Page: www.creditprofessionals.org

Sue Heusing, President
Rhonda McKinney, VP
Charlotte Rancilio, Editor

A bi-annual magazine published by Credit Professionals International.
Cost: $15.00
Frequency: Bi-annually
Circulation: 550
Founded in 1989

6034 Credit Union Magazine
Credit Union National Association
601 Penn Ave
NW South Building, Suite 600
Washington, DC 20004

202-628-5777
800-356-9655
FAX 202-638-7729
E-Mail: webservices@cuna.org
Home Page: www.cuna.org
Social Media: *Facebook, Twitter*

Daniel A Mica, CEO
Tom Dorety, Vice Chairman
Kathy Kuehn, Manager Periodicals

The role and operations of modern credit unions.
Cost: $50.00
100 Pages
Frequency: Monthly
Circulation: 34401
ISSN: 0011-1066
Printed in 4 colors on glossy stock

6035 Federal Credit Union Magazine
National Association of Federal Credit Unions
3138 10th St N
Arlington, VA 22201-2149

703-522-4770
800-336-4644
FAX 703-524-1082
E-Mail: fbecker@nafcu.org
Home Page: www.nafcu.org
Social Media: *Facebook, Twitter, YouTube*

Fred Becker, President
Alicia Hosmer, VP, Marketing

Written for CEO's, senior staff and volunteers of Federal Credit Unions. Offers legislative and regulatory news, as well as technology and operational issues. Call for rates.
50 Pages
Circulation: 1500
ISSN: 1043-7789
Founded in 1967
Printed in 4 colors on glossy stock

6036 News and Views
Advertising Media Credit Executives Association
8840 Columbia 100 Parkway
Columbia, MD 21045-2158

410-992-7609
FAX 410-740-5574
E-Mail: amcea@amcea.org
Home Page: www.amcea.org

Sheila Wroten, President
Mary Younger, VP
Vickie Bolinger, Director

Our magazine reports on current trends and legal issues while offering tips on customer service, time management and collections.
Frequency: Quarterly
Founded in 1953

Trade Shows

6037 AMCEA Conference
Advertising Media Credit Executives Association
8840 Columbia 100 Parkway
Columbia, MD 21045-2158

410-992-7609
FAX 410-740-5574
E-Mail: amcea@amcea.org
Home Page: www.amcea.org

Sheila Wroten, President
Kimberly Riley, VP
Vickie Bolinger, Director

The conference encompasses four days and is a networking extravaganza. Top attorneys discuss bankruptcy and legal issues. We invite advertising agencies to discuss network buying and liability problems.
Frequency: Annual

6038 Credit Union Executive Society Annual Convention: CUES
5510 Research Park Drive
Madison, WI 53711-5377

608-712-2664
800-252-2664
FAX 608-271-2303

E-Mail: cues@cues.org
Home Page: www.cues.org
Social Media: *Facebook, Twitter, LinkedIn*

Fred Johnson, CEO/President

Offers a rainbow of marketing and technology topics, as well as a supplier showcase, geared toward board members.
Frequency: June
Founded in 1962

6039 Credit Union National Association Governmental Affairs Conference
Credit Union National Association
601 Penn Ave
NW South Building, Suite 600
Washington, DC 20004

202-628-5777
800-356-9655
FAX 202-638-7729
Home Page: www.cuna.org
Social Media: *Facebook, Twitter*

Susan Newton, Executive Director
Pat Sowick, VP
Richard Dines, Senior State and League Affairs Dir
Alicia Valencia Erb, League Relations
Shellee Mitchell, Executive Assistant

Annual conference held in Washington, DC, with a focus on legislative issues impacting credit unions.
Frequency: February

6040 Credit Union National Association Future Forum
601 Penn Ave
NW South Building, Suite 600
Washington, DC 20004

202-628-5777
800-356-9655
FAX 202-638-7729
Home Page: www.cuna.org
Social Media: *Facebook, Twitter*

Susan Newton, Executive Director
Pat Sowick, VP
Richard Dines, Senior State and League Affairs Dir
Alicia Valencia Erb, League Relations
Shellee Mitchell, Executive Assistant

Convention and annual general meeting with exhibit hall, educational sessions, and other events.
Frequency: September

6041 Defense Credit Union's Annual Conference
Defense Credit Union Council
601 Pennsylvania Avenue NW
South Building, Suite 600
Washington, DC 20004

202-638-3950
FAX 202-638-3410
E-Mail: admin@dcuc.org
Home Page: www.dcuc.org

Conference and exhibits of equipment, supplies and services for credit unions that serve Department of Defense personnel with problems peculiar to military installations and personnel.
200 Attendees
Frequency: August

6042 Education Credit Union Council Annual Conference
Education Credit Union Council
PO Box 7558
Spanish Fort, AL 36577-7558

251-626-3399
FAX 251-626-3565
E-Mail: l.webster@ecuc.org
Home Page: www.ecuc.org

Lorraine B Zerfas, Executive Director

Any CEOs, directors, committee members and top management active in the operations of any credit union that serves the educational community who want to achieve professional excellence should attend. Interact with peers from across the US serving the fields of education, introduce executive staff and managers to credit union ideas and philosophy on a national level and discuss issues important to your credit union in the coming year.
Frequency: February

6043 Finance, Credit & International Business Global Conference
Finance, Credit & International Business
8840 Columbia 100 Parkway
Columbia, MD 21045-2158

410-423-1840
888-256-3242
FAX 410-423-1845
E-Mail: fcib_info@fciglobal.com
Home Page: www.fcibglobal.com
Social Media: *Twitter, LinkedIn*

Annual gathering of international credit and finance professionals draws upon the combined expertise of financial executives from all regions of the world to provide attendees with practical insight for managing in a rapidly evolving international environment.
Frequency: November

6044 Fleet/Lease Remarketing
S&A Conferences Group
Westview At Weston
301 Cascade Pointe Lane
Cary, NC 27513

800-608-7500
FAX 919-674-6027
Home Page: www.autoremarketing.com
Social Media: *Facebook, Twitter, LinkedIn*

Ron Smith, President

Executive conference focused on remarketing strategies for manufacturer, bank, finance, commercial and rental fleet/lease vehicles.
Frequency: February

6045 International Association of Commercial Collectors Annual Convention
4040 W 70th Street
Minneapolis, MN 55435

952-925-0760
800-859-9526
FAX 952-926-1624
E-Mail: iacc@commercialcollector.com
Home Page: www.commercialcollector.com
Social Media: *LinkedIn*

John Yursha, President
Tammy M. Schoenberg, Executive Director

International trade association comprised of more than 230 collection specialists and 140 commercial attorneys, with members throughout the US and 20 international countries. IACC's mission is to promote the commercial collection profession by providing IACC members with the resources to excel in the industry.
350 Members
Frequency: January
Founded in 1970

6046 Legal Issues & Regulatory Compliance Conference
Mortgage Bankers Association
1717 Rhode Island Avenue NW
Suite 400
Washington, DC 20036

202-557-2700
E-Mail: meetings@mortgagebankers.org
Home Page: www.mortgagebankers.org

Social Media: *Facebook, Twitter, LinkedIn, YouTube*

David H Stevens, President/CEO
Marcia Davies, Chief of Staff/SVP

Learn about all the legal and regulatory developments facing the industry.
Frequency: Annual/May

6047 NFCC Leaders Conference
National Foundation for Credit Counseling
2000M Street NW
Suite 505
Washington, DC 20036

202-677-4300
800-388-2227
Home Page: www.nfcc.org
Social Media: *Facebook, Twitter, YouTube*

Susan C Keating, President/CEO
Paul Weiss, CFO/ Chief Of Staff
William Binzel, Chief Counsel

Three-day conference to discuss credit counceling industry practices, trends and issues.
300 Attendees
Frequency: Annual/Fall
Founded in 1965

6048 NRLA Annual Conference
National Rural Lenders Association
2402 E 44th Place
Tulsa, OK 74105

918-430-3956
FAX 918-550-8293
E-Mail: media@nrla-usda.org
Home Page: nrla-usda.org

Greg O'Donnell, Executive Director

Hear from, and interact with, policy makers.
Frequency: Annual
Founded in 2015

6049 National Association of Credit Management: Annual Credit Congress
National Association of Credit Management
8840 Columbia 100 Parkway
Columbia, MD 21045

410-740-5560
FAX 410-740-5574
E-Mail: robins@nacm.org
Home Page: www.nacm.org
Social Media: *Facebook, Twitter, LinkedIn*

Toni Drake, Chairperson
Chris Meyers, Chairman/elect
Kevin Quinn, Director
Jay Snyder, Director

The event for the business credit and financial professional offering relevant, timely educational offerings, including industry specific programs, over 100 specialized service providers on the expo floor, showcasing the latest products and services, countless networking and relationship-building events to facilitate the sharing of knowlege and expertise.
18000 Members
2000 Attendees
Frequency: May/June

6050 National Fraud Issues Conference
Mortgage Bankers Association
1717 Rhode Island Avenue NW
Suite 400
Washington, DC 20036

202-557-2700
E-Mail: meetings@mortgagebankers.org
Home Page: www.mortgagebankers.org
Social Media: *Facebook, Twitter, LinkedIn, YouTube*

David H Stevens, President/CEO
Marcia Davies, Chief of Staff/SVP

The forum where industry professionals can learn about the issues related to the growing incidence and complexity of mortgage fraud.
Frequency: Annual/March

6051 National Mortgage Servicing Conference & Expo
Mortgage Bankers Association
1717 Rhode Island Avenue NW
Suite 400
Washington, DC 20036

202-557-2700
E-Mail: meetings@mortgagebankers.org
Home Page: www.mortgagebankers.org
Social Media: *Facebook, Twitter, LinkedIn, YouTube*

David H Stevens, President/CEO
Marcia Davies, Chief of Staff/SVP

Provides the opportunity to reach key servicing executives from residential mortgage companies and showcase the product offerings, network with key decision makers, and obtain qualified leads that can help reach goals.
Frequency: Annual/February

6052 National Policy Conference
Mortgage Bankers Association
1717 Rhode Island Avenue NW
Suite 400
Washington, DC 20036

202-557-2700
E-Mail: meetings@mortgagebankers.org
Home Page: www.mortgagebankers.org
Social Media: *Facebook, Twitter, LinkedIn, YouTube*

David H Stevens, President/CEO
Marcia Davies, Chief of Staff/SVP

Brings together key officials, cabinet members and special guest speakers to address these critical issues.
Frequency: Annual/March

6053 National Technology in Mortgage Banking Conference
Mortgage Bankers Association
1717 Rhode Island Avenue NW
Suite 400
Washington, DC 20036

202-557-2700
E-Mail: meetings@mortgagebankers.org
Home Page: www.mortgagebankers.org
Social Media: *Facebook, Twitter, LinkedIn, YouTube*

David H Stevens, President/CEO
Marcia Davies, Chief of Staff/SVP

Forum to learn about the newest industry solutions and how they can increase your company's competitive edge. The conference focuses on relevant topics, including legal / regulatory updates, eMortgages, investor reporting changes and technology advances such as mobile computing.
Frequency: Annual/March

6054 Risk Management Conference
Risk Management Association
1801 Market Street
Suite 300
Philadelphia, PA 19103-1628

215-446-4000
800-677-7621
FAX 215-446-4100
E-Mail: customers@rmahq.org
Home Page: www.rmahq.org

William F Githens, President/CEO
Kathleen M Beans, Public Relations Manager

Educates and helps risk management professionals develop new techniques and learn about new innovative products at different stages of

their careers. Mailing list available for exhibitors and sponsors only.
800 Attendees
Frequency: October

Directories & Databases

6055 AMCEA Member Handbook & Roster
Advertising Media Credit Executives Association
8840 Columbia 100 Parkway
Columbia, MD 21045-2158

410-992-7609
FAX 410-740-5574
E-Mail: amcea@amcea.org
Home Page: www.amcea.org

Sheila Wroten, President
Kimberly Riley, VP
Vickie Bolinger, Director

Inside you will find direct telephone numbers to every credit manager in our association along with numbers for credit references and fax inquiries. We also include their e-mail addresses and computer hardware and software information.

6056 American Recovery Association Directory
American Recovery Association
5525 N MacArthur Boulevard
Suite 135
Irving, TX 75038

972-755-4755
FAX 972-870-5755
E-Mail: homeoffice@americanrecoveryassn.org
Home Page: www.repo.org

Mary Jane Hogan, President
Tom Crosby, Secretary/Treasurer

Contain's listings of ARA's members, offices and services. Available in hardcopy and electronic formats.
308 Pages
Frequency: Annual
Founded in 1965

6057 Banksearch Book
Sheshunoff Information Services
2801 Via Fortuna
Suite 600
Austin, TX 78746-7970

512-472-4000
800-477-1772
E-Mail: editorialqueries.sis@thomsonmedia.com
Home Page: www.smslp.com

Gabrielle Sheshunoff, CEO

Offers information on savings and loans, savings banks and credit unions with assets over 10 million. Customized for your institutution type: bank thrift, bank holding company or credit union. You buy only the data you want — by state, region or nation.
Cost: $295.00
Frequency: Annual

6058 Business Products Credit Association
BCPA
607 Westridge Drive
O'Fallon, MO 63366

636-924-5775
FAX 636-754-0567
E-Mail: service@bpca.org
Home Page: www.bpca.org

BPCA has a database of over 400,000 companies and their payment histories. This is available to members over the Internet.

6059 Callahan's Credit Union Directory
Callahan & Associates
1001 Connecticut Ave NW
Suite 1001
Washington, DC 20036-5523

202-223-3920
800-446-7453
FAX 202-223-1311
Home Page: www.callahan.com

Sean Hession, CEO
Charles Filson, Chairman
Jay Johnson, EVP
Alix Patterson, COO

This directory turns raw data into research, giving you the tools you need to keep up with the credit union industry. Access all the credit union information found in the print edition through the Online Edition on this website. In a special Users Area only for purchasers of the print edition, you can access updated finacials four times a year, conduct searches on key information and save those search results to return to over and over again. Real time updates directly from our database.
Cost: $135.00
Frequency: Annual

6060 Collection Agency Directory
First Detroit Corporation
PO Box 5025
Warren, MI 48090-5025

586-573-0045
800-366-5995
FAX 586-573-9219
E-Mail: ascace@firstdetroit.com
Home Page: www.firstdetroit.com

Albert W Scace, Publisher

Offers information and statistics on nearly 900 collection agencies throught the world.
Cost: $347.00
301 Pages
Frequency: Annual, Paperback
ISSN: 1058-983X
Founded in 1991
Mailing list available for rent: 11,000 names at $150 per M
Printed in one color on matte stock

6061 Credit
American Financial Services Association
919 18th Street NW
Suite 300
Washington, DC 20006-5517

202-296-5544
E-Mail: sharrison@afsamail.org
Home Page: www.afsaonline.org
Social Media: *Twitter*

Chris Steinebert, President/CEO

Focuses on breaking developments on legislative and regulatory issues on the federal and state levels, as well as consumer education initiatives, industry news, news inside AFSA and information on meetings and conferences. Free online access.
1500 Pages
Frequency: Bi-Monthly

6062 Credit Card and Check Fraud: A Stop-Loss Manual
Fraud & Theft Information Bureau
9770 S. Military Trail
Suite 380
Boynton Beach, FL 33436

561-737-8700
FAX 561-737-5800
E-Mail: sales@fraudandtheftinfo.com
Home Page: www.fraudandtheftinfo.com

Larry Schwartz, Founder and Director
Pearl Sax, Founder and Director

The Fraud And Theft Information Bureau is the leading consultant on credit card and check fraud control and loss prevention — and the publisher of related manuals and fraud-blocker data bases
Cost: $199.95
300 Pages
Founded in 1982

6063 Credit Union Cooperatives
Callahan & Associates
1001 Connecticut Ave NW
10th Floor
Washington, DC 20036-5523

202-223-3920
800-446-7453
FAX 202-223-1311
Home Page: www.callahan.com

Sean Hession, CEO
Charles Filson, Chairman
Jay Johnson, EVP
Alix Patterson, COO

Your source for information on credit union service organizations (CUSOs) and other cooperative providers to the credit industry. The directory has up-to-date contact names, addresses and phone numbers for more than 700 CUSOs and their associated credit unions. Use this publication to compare services offered by CUSOs or if you're looking to start or expand an existing CUSO.
Cost: $165.00

6064 Credit Union Directory
National Credit Union Administration
1775 Duke St
Suite 4206
Alexandria, VA 22314-6115

703-518-6300
800-755-1030
FAX 703-518-6539
E-Mail: consumerassistance@ncua.gov
Home Page: www.ncua.gov
Social Media: *Facebook, Twitter, YouTube*

Debbie Matz, Chairman

Federal credit and state-chartered credit unions are the focal point of this directory. Free online.
Frequency: Annual

6065 Credit Union Financial Yearbook
Callahan & Associates
1001 Connecticut Ave NW
Washington, DC 20036-5523

202-223-3920
800-446-7453
FAX 202-223-1311
Home Page: www.callahan.com

Sean Hession, CEO
Charles Filson, Chairman
Jay Johnson, EVP
Alix Patterson, COO

Each quarter Callahan publishes a comprehensive study on the state of the industry that includes detailed financials for all credit unions over $50 million. The third quarter edition is published in 3 volumes based on asset size. Fourth quarter edition is based on total assets for the year. Asset sizes considered are $50 to $100 million, $100 - $250 million and over $250 million.
Cost: $565.00
Frequency: Complete Year Price

6066 Defense Credit Union Directory
Defense Credit Union Council
601 Pennsylvania Ave NW
Suite 600
Washington, DC 20004-2601

202-638-3950
FAX 202-638-3410

E-Mail: admin@dcuc.org
Home Page: www.dcuc.org

Roland Arteata, President

Listing of about 360 credit unions with membership consisting wholly or partly of the military and civilian personnel of the United States and worldwide.
Cost: $150.00
60 Pages
Frequency: Biennial
Founded in 1963

6067 Directory of Venture Capital & Private Equity Firms - Online Database
Grey House Publishing
4919 Route 22
PO Box 56
Amenia, NY 12501

518-789-8700
800-562-2139
FAX 845-373-6390
E-Mail: gold@greyhouse.com
Home Page: http://gold.greyhouse.com
Social Media: Facebook, Twitter

Leslie Mackenzie, Publisher
Richard Gottlieb, Editor

Packed with need-to-know information, this database offers immediate access to 2,300 VC firms, over 10,000 managing partners, and over 11,500 VC investments.
Frequency: Annual

6068 Directory of Venture Capital and Private Equity Firms
Grey House Publishing
4919 Route 22
PO Box 56
Amenia, NY 12501

518-789-8700
800-562-2139
FAX 845-373-6390
E-Mail: books@greyhouse.com
Home Page: www.greyhouse.com
Social Media: Facebook, Twitter

Richard Gottlieb, President
Leslie Mackenzie, Publisher

Offers access to over 2,300 domestic and international venture capital and private equity firms, with detailed contact information and extensive data on investment and funds.
Cost: $685.00
1200 Pages
Frequency: Annual
ISBN: 1-592372-72-4

6069 Dun's Credit Guide
Dun & Bradstreet Information Service
103 John F Kennedy Pkwy
Short Hills, NJ 07078-2708

973-921-5500
800-234-3867
FAX 908-665-5803
Home Page: www.dnb.com
Social Media: Facebook, Twitter, LinkedIn, YouTube

Sara Mathew, CEO
James Fernandez, EVP and COO

Providing a dollar-specific credit guideline on manufacturers, wholesalers and retailers, this database is updated continuously for the interested business person.

6070 National Credit Union Administration Directory
National Credit Union Administration

1775 Duke St
Suite 4206
Alexandria, VA 22314-6115

703-518-6300
FAX 703-518-6539
E-Mail: ociomail@ncua.gov
Home Page: www.ncua.gov

Debbie Matz, Chairman

Directory of credit unions governed by a three member board appointed by the President and confirmed by the US Senate, by the independent federal agency that charters and supervises federal credit unions. NCUA, with the backing of the full faith and credit of the US government, operates the National Credit Union Share Insurance Fund, insuring the savings of 80 million account holders in all federal credit unions and many state chartered credit unions.

6071 Thomson Credit Union Directory
4709 Golf Road
Skokie, IL 60076-1231

847-676-9600
800-321-3373
FAX 847-933-8101
E-Mail: custserv@accuitysolutions.com
Home Page: www.accuitysolutions.com

Hugh Johnes IV, President and CEO
Kerry Hewson, EVP
Jay Ryan, Head of Sales

Semi-annual directory that includes valuable industry statistics, a quick telephone lookup index of all credit unions and a resource guide featuring vendors within the credit union marketplace. Includes over 12,500 major credit unions and 5,500 branches, with asset rankings, membership totals and more. Published in partnership with the Credit Union National Association.
Cost: $199.00
Frequency: January/July
ISBN: 1-563103-24-9

6072 Who's Who in Credit and Financial
New York Credit and Financial Management Assn
520 8th Avenue
New York, NY 10018-6507

212-695-4807

Directory of services and supplies to the industry.

6073 World Council of Credit Unions Directory
World Council of Credit Unions
5710 Mineral Point Road
Madison, WI 53705

608-395-2000
FAX 608-395-2001
E-Mail: mail@woccu.org
Home Page: www.woccu.org

Pepi Dougherty, Executive
Mike Muckian, Marketing & Communications

Lists over 100 World Council of Credit Union leaders and member organizations in each of seven confederations. African, Asian, Australian, Canadian, Caribbean, Latin-American and the United States.

Industry Web Sites

6074 http://gold.greyhouse.com
G.O.L.D Grey House OnLine Databases
Grey House Publishing's online database platform, GOLD, offers Quick Search, Keyword Search and Expert Search for most business sectors including banking, credid and lending service markets. The GOLD platform makes

finding the information you need quick and easy - whether you're a novice searcher or an experienced database user. All of Grey House's directory products are available for subscription on the GOLD platform.

6075 www.aacul.org
American Association of Credit Union Leagues
Voluntary membership association for credit union leagues that are members of the Credit Union National Association. AACUL provides representation, products, services and programs to its members.

6076 www.abiworld.org
American Bankruptcy Institute
ABI is the largest multi-diciplinary, non-partisan organization dedicated to research and education on matters related to insolvency. The ABI membership provides a forum for the exchange of ideas and information. ABI is engaged in numerous educational and research activities, as well as the production of a number of publications both for the insolvency practitioner and the public.

6077 www.afsaonline.com
American Financial Services Association
National trade association for market funded providers of financial services to consumers and small businesses. These providers offer an array of finacial services, including unsecured personal loans, automobile loans, home equity loans and credit cards through specialized bank institutions.

6078 www.amcea.org
Advertising Media Credit Executives Association
Improving the professionalism, principles, understanding and techniques of media credit management by encouraging the exchange of ideas, methods and procedures within the membership. Providing additional education and training in the business fundamentals of media credit and credit policies and in the related areas of finance, accounting, law and economics for the purpose of enhancing the career development of members.

6079 www.bccacredit.com
Broadcast Cable Credit Association
Subsidiary of the Broadcast Cable Financial Management Association. BCCA provides industry specific credit reports on individual agencies, advertisers, or buying services (national and local).

6080 www.bpca.org
Business Products Credit Association
Nonprofit trade association for credit personnel of manufacturers, wholesalers and factors. The national credit group consists of discount stores, superstores, commercial stationers, printing and publications, business machines, computer peripherals and software, plus mass merchandisers. In addition, BPCA has groups on school supply, janitorial/sanitary supplies, fine pens/promotional products.

6081 www.cdiaonline.org
Consumer Data Industry Association
Trade association representing consumer information companies that provide fraud prevention and risk management products, credit and mortgage reports, tenant and employment screening services, check fraud and verifacation services and collection services. Sets industry standards and provides education for it's members. Provides educational materials for consumers regarding their credit rights and how consumer credit reporting agencies can better serve their needs.

6082 www.cfa.com

Commercial Finance Association

Trade group of the asset-based financial services industry, with members throughout the US, Canada and around the world. Members include the asset-based lending arms of domestic and foreign commercial banks, small and large independent finance companies, floor plan financing organizations, factoring organizations and financing subsidiaries of major industrial corporations.

6083 www.collector.com

American Collectors Association

International trade organization of credit and collection professionals that provides a variety of accounts recievable management services.

6084 www.commercialcollector.com

International Association of Commercial Collectors

International trade association comprised of more than 230 collection specialists and 140 commercial attorneys, with members throughout the US and 20 international countries. IACC's mission is to promote the commercial collection profession by providing IACC members with the resources to excel in the industry.

6085 www.creditunions.com

Callahan & Associates

National credit union research and consulting firm specializing in financial publications and analysis software, strategic planning and investment management.

6086 www.crfonline.org

Credit Research Foundation

Independent, member run organization, consisting of a dynamic community of like minded business professionals with a vested interest in improving and fostering the field of business credit — more specifically, the practices and technologies of business credit.

6087 www.cues.org

Credit Union Executives Society

For credit union executives, we serve to advance the professional development of CEOs, senior management and directors.

6088 www.cuna.org

Credit Union National Association

The premier trade association in the financial services arena. Supports, protects, unifies and advances the credit union movement.

6089 www.ecuc.org

Education Credit Union Council

Dedicated to providing educational and networking opportunities to credit unions who serve educational communities, industry teachers, administrators, students, support staff and others in the educational community.

6090 www.electran.org

Electronic Transaction Association

International trade association serving the needs of organizations offering transaction processing products and services.

6091 www.fcibglobal.com

FCIB

Provider of products and services to many small, medium and large size exporters as well as major multinational corporations in 30 countries around the world.

6092 www.firstent.org

First Entertainment Credit Union

Nonprofit institution serves as the financial resource for the entertainment community to more than 700 entertainment based companies.

6093 www.fraudandtheftinfo.com

Fraud & Theft Information Bureau

Provides problem solving, crime prevention, money saving manuals and fraud blocker databases.

6094 www.greyhouse.com

Grey House Publishing

Authoritative reference directories for most business sectors including banking, credit and lending service markets. Users can search the online databases with varied search criteria allowing for custom searches by product category, geographic area, sales volume, keyword, subject and more. Full Grey House catalog and online ordering also available.

6095 www.mbaa.org

Mortgage Bankers Association of America

Representing the real estate finance industry, MBA serves its membership by representing their legislative and regulatory interests before the US Congress and federal agencies; by meeting their educational needs through programs and a range of periodicals and publications; and by supporting their business interests with a variety of research initiatives and other products and services.

6096 www.nacm.org

National Association of Credit Management

Promotes honest and fair dealings in credit transactions, fosters and encourages research in the field of credit.

6097 www.ncua.gov

National Credit Union Administration

Governed by a three-member board appointed by the President and confirmed by the US Senate, this is the independent federal agency that charters and supervises the nation's federal credit unions.

6098 www.nfcc.org

National Foundation for Credit Counceling

National nonprofit credit counseling oranization with 1,200 offices helping 1.5 million households annually. Identify NFCC members (Consumer Credit Counseling Service CCCS) by the NFCC member seal representing high standards, free and low-cost confidential services.

6099 www.repo.org

American Recovery Association

Approximately 500 offices throughout the US, Canada and Germany, providing repossesion services around the world.

6100 www.rmahg.org

Risk Management Association

Financial services association that champions best practices in risk management, monitors emerging trends, develops new risk management techniques, innovative products, and education and training programs geared to risk management professionals.

Associations

6101 ATM Industry Association

Home Page: www.atmia.com
Social Media: *Facebook, Twitter, LinkedIn, YouTube*

Mike Lee, Chief Executive Officer
Sharon Lane, Global Director, Finance
Dana Benson, Dir., Conferences & Sponsorships
Amanda Hardy, Marketing Director, Europe
David Tente, Executive Director, USA

Alliance promoting the proliferation of automated teller machines, ATMs and cash.
5000 Members
Founded in 1997

6102 Advanced Network & Services

2600 South Road
Suite 44-193
Poughkeepsie, NY 12601

845-795-2090
FAX 845-795-2180
E-Mail: contact@advanced.org
Home Page: www.advanced.org
Social Media: *Facebook, Twitter, LinkedIn*

William Howle, Chairman of the Board
Allan Weis, Founder/President/Managing Director
Kristin Mortensen, Secretary/Treasurer

A nonprofit corporation dedicated to advancing education by accelerating the use of computer networking applications and technology.
Mailing list available for rent

6103 American e-Commerce Association

Home Page: www.aeaus.com

Computer training, e-commerce education, membership, recognition, endorsement, and evaluation services.

6104 Armed Forces Communications and Electronics Association (AFCEA)

4400 Fair Lakes Court
Fairfax, VA 22033-3899

703-631-6100
800-336-4583
FAX 703-631-6169
Home Page: www.afcea.org
Social Media: *Facebook, Twitter, LinkedIn, Google+, Flickr, YouTube*

Linda Gooden, Chair of the Board of Directors
Brig Gen John Meincke, Vice Chair, B.O.D.
LtGen Robert M. Shea, President, CEO
Pat Miorin, CPA, EVP, CFO, Int. Treasurer
Mike Warlick, Vice President, Defense Operations

A nonprofit international organization that serves its members by providing a forum for the ethical exchange of information and is dedicated to increasing knowledge through the exploration of issues relevant to information technology, communication, and electronics for the defense, homeland security and intelligence communities.

6105 Business Software Alliance

20 F Street, NW
Suite 800
Washington, DC 20001

202-872-5500
FAX 202-872-5501
E-Mail: info@bsa.org
Home Page: www.bsa.org
Social Media: *Facebook, Twitter, LinkedIn, YouTube, RSS*

Steven Dietz, Chair
Bruce Sewell, Vice Chair

Bradford Smith, Secretary
Scott Taylor, Treasurer

An organization dedicated to promoting a safe and legal digital world. BSA educates consumers on software management and copyright protection, cyber security, trade, e-commerce and other internet related issues.
Founded in 1988

6106 Center for Internet Security

31 Tech Valley Drive
Suite 2
East Greenbush, NY 12061

518-266-3460
FAX 518-283-3216
E-Mail: contact@cisecurity.org
Home Page: www.cisecurity.org
Social Media: *Facebook, Twitter, LinkedIn, Blog, YouTube*

John M Giiligan, Chairman
Jack Arthur, Treasurer
Deirdre O' Callaghan, Chief Counsel and Secretary
Jane Holl Lute, CEO
Steven J Spano, President and CEO

A nonprofit organization that provides products and resources that help partners achieve security goals through expert guidance and cost-effective solutions.

6107 CompTIA

3500 Lacey Road
Suite 100
Downers Grove, IL 60515

630-678-8300
866-835-8020
FAX 630-678-8384
E-Mail: techvoice@comptia.org
Home Page: www.comptia.org
Social Media: *Facebook, Twitter, LinkedIn, Pinterest, Google+, YouTube*

Todd Thibodeaux, President, CEO
Charles Eaton, CEO, Educational Foundation
Ann Batko, SVP, Marketing
Kelly Ricker, SVP, Events and Education
David Sommer, Chief Financial Officer

A nonprofit trade association created by representatives of five microcomputer leaderships and is a provider of professional certifications for theinformation technology (IT) industry.

6108 Council on CyberSecurity

1700 North Moore Street
Suite 2100
Arlington, VA 22209

703-600-1935
E-Mail: info@counciloncybersecurity.org
Home Page: www.cisecurity.org
Social Media: *Facebook, Twitter, LinkedIn*

John M Giiligan, Chairman
Jack Arthur, Treasurer
Deirdre O' Callaghan, Chief Counsel and Secretary
Jane Holl Lute, CEO
Steven J Spano, President and CEO

Organization that mobilizes a broad community of stakeholders to identify, validate, promote and sustain the adoption of cybersecurity best practice.

6109 Cyber Security Research Alliance

401 Edgewater Place
Suite 600
Wakefield, MA 1880

781-876-8860
E-Mail: aobrien@cybersecurityresearch.org
Home Page: www.cybersecurityresearch.org

Julian Warrick, Interim President
Steven Kester, Treasurer
Claire Vishik, Secretary

A nonprofit organization founded by industry stakeholders as a forum develop R & D strategy to address grand challenges in cyber security, and to facilitate public-private partnerships that define a more focused, coordinated, and concerted approach to cyber security research and development.

6110 Cyber, Space, & Intelligence Association

703-855-3917
E-Mail: richcoleman1@gmail.com
Home Page: cyberspaceintel.org

Richard Coleman, Chairman, President and Founder
Tidal W. (Ty) McCoy, Senior Executive
Timothy J. Evans, Senior Advisor
Founded in 2011

6111 Cybersecurity Association

127 Segre Place
Santa Cruz, CA 95060

831-426-9827
E-Mail: paul.hoffman@cybersecurity.org
Home Page: www.cybersecurity.org

Organization focused on testing the security capabilities and performance of firewalls, intrusion prevention systems and other similar security equipment.

6112 High Technology Crime Investigation Association

3288 Goldstone Drive
Roseville, CA 95747

916-408-1751
FAX 916-384-2232
E-Mail: info@htcia.org
Home Page: www.htcia.org
Social Media: *Facebook, Twitter, LinkedIn*

Carol Hutchings, Executive Director
Jimmy Garcia, Public Relations
Elisa Hutchings, Membership Inquiries

A nonprofit professional organization devoted to the prevention, investigation, and prosecution of crimes involving advanced technologies.
Founded in 1984

6113 ISACA

3701 Algonquin Road
Suite 1010
Rolling Meadows, IL 60008

847-253-1545
FAX 847-253-1443
Home Page: www.isaca.org
Social Media: *Facebook, Twitter, LinkedIn, Google+*

A nonprofit, independent association that advocates for professionals involved in information security, assurance, risk management and governance.
Founded in 1969

6114 Information Systems Security Association

12100 Sunset Hills Road
Suite 130
Reston, VA 20190

866-349-5818
703-234-4077
FAX 703-435-4390
Home Page: www.issa.org
Social Media: *Facebook, Twitter, LinkedIn*

Ira Winkler, President
Andrea C. Hoy, Vice President
Kevin D. Spease, Treasurer/CFO
Bill Danigelis, Secretary
Anne Rogers, Director

A nonprofit, international professional organization of informationsecurity professionals and practitioners.

6115 InfraGard

E-Mail: infragardmembership@leo.gov
Home Page: www.infragard.org
Social Media: *RSS*

A nonprofit organization serving as a public-private partnership between U.S. businesses and the Federal Bureau of Investigation.

6116 Institute for Security, Technology, and Society

7 Maynard Street
Sudikoff Laboratory
Hanover, NH 03755ÿ

603-646-0700
FAX 603-646-1672
E-Mail: info.ists@dartmouth.edu
Home Page: www.ists.dartmouth.edu
Social Media: *Facebook, Twitter, Flickr, YouTube, iTunes*

Organization dedicated to pursuing research and education to advance information security and privacy throughout society.
Founded in 2000

6117 Intelligence and National Security Alliance

Ballston Metro Center Office Towers
901 North Stuart Street, Suite 205
Arlington, VA 22203

703-224-4672
FAX 703-224-4681
Home Page: www.insaonline.org
Social Media: *Facebook, Twitter, LinkedIn, Google+, Flickr, YouTube*

John Negroponte, Chairman of the Board
Joseph R. DeTrani, President
Charles E. Allen,
SeniorÿIntelligenceÿAdvisorÿ
Chuck Alsup, Vice Presidentÿof Policy
Robert Joseph, Senior NationalÿSecurity Advisor

A nonprofit, non-partisan, public-private organization that works to promote and recognize the highest standards within the national security and intelligence communities. Members include current and former high-ranking intelligence, military and government agency leaders, analysts, and experts from industry and academia.
Founded in 1979

6118 Internet Merchants Association

E-Mail: info@imamerchants.org
Home Page: www.imamerchants.org
Social Media: *Facebook*

Fred Neff, President
Scott Cole, Vice-President
Doyle Carver, Secretary
Andy Sollofe, Treasurer

Develops, promotes, and protects the economic vitality of internet merchants through a positive business environment and fosters a climate in whichcommerce, industry, and technology will flourish.

6119 Internet Security Alliance

703-907-7090
E-Mail: admin@isalliance.orgÿ
Home Page: www.isalliance.org

Tim McKnight, Board Chairman
Jeff Brown, Board Vice Chairman
Gary McAlum, Board Second Vice Chairman
Larry Clinton, President, CEO
Julie Taylor, Board Member

A nonprofit organization that acts as a forum for information sharing and leadership on information security, and it lobbies for corporate securityinterests.

6120 National Cyber Security Alliance

Home Page: www.staysafeonline.org
Social Media: *Facebook, Twitter, LinkedIn, Google+, YouTube*

Jacqueline Beauchere, Board President
Michael Kaiser, Executive Director
Tiffany Barrett, Director
Kara Wright, Director of Digital Strategy
Betty Hallman, Director, Development

A nonprofit, public-private partnership working with the Departmentof Homeland Security (DHS), private sector sponsors, and nonprofit collaboratorsto promote cyber security awareness for home users, small and medium size businesses, and primary and secondary education.

6121 National Cyber-Forensics & Training Alliance

2000 Technology Drive
Suite 450
Pittsburgh, PA 15219

412-802-8000
FAX 412-802-8510
E-Mail: info@ncfta.net
Home Page: www.ncfta.net

A nonprofit corporation focused on identifying, mitigating, and neutralizing cyber crime threats through strategic alliances and partnerships with Subject Matter Experts (SME) in the public, private, and academic sectors.

6122 National CyberWatch Center

301 Largo Road
Largo, MD 20774

E-Mail: tkepner@nationalcyberwatch.org
Home Page: www.nationalcyberwatch.org
Social Media: *Facebook, Twitter, LinkedIn, YouTube*

Anita Shelton, Administrative Associate
Bob Spear, Senior Advisor
Casey W O'Brien, Executive Director
Costis Toregas, Director, Business Development

An organization of higher education institutions, public and private schools, businesses, and government agencies focused on collaborative efforts to advance cybersecurity education and strengthen the national cybersecurity workforce.

6123 National Cybersecurity and Communications Integration Center

245 Murray Lane SW
Building 410
Washington, DC 20598

888-282-0870
E-Mail: info@us-cert.gov
Home Page: www.us-cert.gov/nccic
Social Media: *Twitter, RSS*

Serves as a central location where a diverse set of partners involved in cybersecurity and communications protection coordinate and synchronize their efforts. Partners include other government agencies, the private sector, and international entities.

6124 National Initiative for Cybersecurity Careers and Studies

E-Mail: NICCS@hq.dhs.gov
Home Page: niccs.us-cert.gov

Robin Williams, Chief

A national resource for cybersecurity awareness, education, careers, and training.

Newsletters

6125 ATM Industry Association Global Newsletter

Home Page:
www.atmia.com/media/atmia-global-newsletter
Social Media: *Facebook, LinkedIn, YouTube*

Mike Lee, Chief Executive Officer
Sharon Lane, Global Director, Financeÿ
Dana Benson, Dir., Conferences & Sponsorships
Amanda Hardy, Marketing Director, Europe
David Tente, Executive Director, USA

Alliance promoting the proliferation of automated teller machines, ATMs and cash.
5000 Members
Founded in 1997

6126 Center for Internet Security

31 Tech Valley Drive
Suite 2
East Greenbush, NY 12061

518-266-3460
FAX 518-283-3216
E-Mail: contact@cisecurity.org
Home Page: msisac.cisecurity.org/newsletters
Social Media: *Facebook, Twitter, LinkedIn, Blog, YouTube*

William F. Pelgrin, President, CEO
Thomas Duffy, SVP, Operations and Services
Laura Iwan, SVP, Programs
Julie Evans, Chief Operating Officer
Al Szesnat, Chief Financial Officer

A nonprofit organization that provides products and resources that help partners achieve security goals through expert guidance and cost-effective solutions.

6127 Dot.COM

Business Communications Company
25 Van Zant Street
Suite 13
Norwalk, CT 06855-1713

203-853-4266
FAX 203-853-0348
E-Mail: sales@bccresearch.com
Home Page: www.bccresearch.com

Louis Naturman, Publisher
C Toenne, Editor

Updates readers on the commercial use of the Internet and related platforms.
Cost: $38.00

6128 E-Healthcare Market Reporter

Health Resources Publishing
1913 Atlantic Ave
Suite 200
Manasquan, NJ 08736-1067

732-292-1100
888-843-6242
FAX 732-292-1111
E-Mail: info@themcic.com
Home Page: www.healthresourcesonline.com

Robert K Jenkins, Publisher
Judith Granel, Marketing
John Russel, Editor
Brett Powell, Regional Director
Alice Burron, Director

A bi-monthly covering strategies, new products, innovation, privacy issue, business solutions, service available, vendor news and comparative for implementing sales and marketing on the internet.
Cost: $397.00
Frequency: Fortnightly
ISSN: 1098-5654
Founded in 1988

6129 Internet Alliance Cyberbrief
Internet Alliance
1615 L Street NW
Suite 1100
Washington, DC 20036-5624

202-861-2407
E-Mail: tammy@internetalliance.org
Home Page: www.internetalliance.org

Tammy Cota, Executive Director

Coverage of public policy changes in government, enhancing consumer satisfaction in interactive services, and education.
Frequency: Weekly

6130 Internet Business
Information Gatekeepers
1340 Soldiers Field Rd
Suite 3
Brighton, MA 02135-1000

617-782-5033
800-323-1088
FAX 617-782-5735
E-Mail: info@igigroup.com
Home Page: www.igigroup.com

Paul Polishuk, CEO
Hui Pan, Chief Analyst, Editor in Chief
Bev Wilson, Managing Editor

Covers the rapid developments in the industry.
Cost: $695.00
Frequency: Monthly

6131 Internet World
Mecklermedia Corporation
20 Ketchum Street
Westport, CT 06880

212-260-0758
FAX 203-454-5840
E-Mail: bbesch@mecklermedia.com

Bill Besch, Publisher

Internet industry news, product reviews and technical reports, with an emphasis on Internet technology, hardware, management and security.
Cost: $160.00
Frequency: Weekly
Circulation: 98,947

6132 Mealey's Litigation Report: Cyber Tech & E -Commerce
LexisNexis Mealey's
555 W 5th Avenue
Los Angeles, CA 90013

213-627-1130
E-Mail: mealeyinfo@lexisnexis.com
Home Page: www.lexisnexis.com/mealeys

Tom Hagy, VP/General Manager
Maureen McGuire, Editorial Director
Mark Rogers, Editor

The Report covers disputes arising from e-commerce. The report tracks emerging legal issues, including: Internet security, data destruction and/or alteration, defamation on the Web, software errors, hardware failure, electronic theft, e-mail trespass, online privacy, government action, shareholder lawsuits, Internet jurisdiction issues, file sharing (copyright) disputes and much more.
Cost: $999.00
100 Pages
Frequency: Monthly
Founded in 1999

6133 Online Reporter
G2 Computer Intelligence
PO Box 7
Glen Head, NY 11545-1616

516-759-7025
FAX 516-759-7028

E-Mail: news@g2news.com
Home Page: www.g2news.com

Maureen O'Gara, Publisher

Information on recent developments on the Internet through news briefs and a section called Chat Room. Includes information on e-commerce, Java and network security.
Cost: $695.00
Frequency: Weekly

6134 Privacy Journal
PO Box 28577
Providence, RI 02908

401-274-7861
FAX 401-274-4747
E-Mail: orders@privacyjournal.net
Home Page: www.privacyjournal.net

Robert Ellis Smith, Publisher

An independent monthly on privacy in a computer age.
Cost: $65.00
Frequency: Monthly
ISSN: 0145-7659
Founded in 1974
Printed in one color

6135 The CyberSkeptic's Guide to Internet Research
Information Today
143 Old Marlton Pike
Medford, NJ 08055-8750

609-654-6266
800-300-9868
FAX 609-654-4309
E-Mail: custserv@infotoday.com
Home Page: www.infotoday.com

Thomas H Hogan, President
Roger R Bilboul, Chairman Of The Board

A monthly subscription newsletter in print, that explores and evaluates free and low cost Web sites and search strategies to help you use the Internet and stay up to date.
Cost: $164.95
ISSN: 1085-2417

Magazines & Journals

6136 Active Server Developer's Journal
ZD Journals
500 Canal View Boulevard
Rochester, NY 14623-2800

585-407-7301
FAX 585-214-2387
E-Mail: asp@zdjournals.com
Home Page: www.asdj.com

Jon Pyles, Publisher
Taggard Andrews

Addresses such issues as database publishing, creating hack-proof files and getting the most out of server-side components. Special sections focus on client-side solutions, covering the basics and taking an in-depth look at more detailed techniques.
Cost: $149.00
Frequency: Monthly

6137 Electronic Commerce Advisor
Thomson Reuters
195 Broadway # 4
New York, NY 10007-3124

646-822-2000
800-231-1860
FAX 646-822-2800
E-Mail: trta.lei-support@thomsonreuters.com
Home Page: www.ria.thomsonreuters.com

Elaine Yadlon, Plant Manager
Thomas H Glocer, CEO & Director

Robert D Daleo, Chief Financial Officer
Kelli Crane, Senior Vice President & CIO

Offers the latest in electronic commerce covering what's available and how to select and employ the best technology without costly trial-and-error mistakes. Information on EDI, e-mail, fax gateways, Internet, encryption, VANs, procurement cards, imaging, voice response, remote computing and other related information.
Cost: $155.00
Circulation: 4500
Founded in 1940

6138 ISACA
3701 Algonquin Road
Suite 1010
Rolling Meadows, IL 60008ÿ

847-253-1545
FAX 847-253-1443
Home Page:
www.isaca.org/journal/pages/default.aspx
Social Media: *Facebook, Twitter, LinkedIn*

A nonprofit, independent association that advocates for professionals involved in information security, assurance, risk management and governance.
Founded in 1969

6139 Information Security
International Computer Security Association
117 Kendrick Street
Suite 800
Needham, MA 02494

781-657-1000
FAX 781-657-1100
E-Mail: lwalsh@infosecuritymag.com
Home Page: www.infosecuritymag.com

Andrew Briney, VP
Lawrence Walsh, Editor
Michael S Mimoso, Senior Editor
Gabrielle DeRussy, Advertising Sales
Susan Rastellini Smith, Product Management

Articles and analysis of information-security issues such as media, entwork and virus protection, internet security and encryption reports.
Cost: $100.00
Frequency: Monthly
Circulation: 60000
Founded in 1999

6140 Information Systems Security
Auerbach Publications
2494 Bayshore Boulevard
Suite 201
Dunedin, FL 34698

703-891-6781
800-737-8034
FAX 703-891-0782
E-Mail: institute@isc2.org
Home Page: www.isc2.org
Social Media: *Facebook, Twitter, YouTube*

David Shearer, COO
Debra Taylor, CFO
John Colley, Chairman
Debra Taylor, Chief Financial Officer
Hord Tipton, Executive Director

Facts and experience, expert opinion on directions in security, public policy, computer crime and ethics related to the information security field.
Cost: $175.00
Circulation: 1500
Founded in 2003

6141 Internet Security Alliance
703-907-7090
E-Mail: admin@isalliance.orgÿ

Home Page:
www.isalliance.org/isa-publications

Tim McKnight, Board Chairman
Jeff Brown, Board Vice Chairman
Gary McAlum, Board Second Vice Chairman
Larry Clinton, President, CEO
Julie Taylor, Board Member

A nonprofit organization that acts as a forum for information sharing and leadership on information security, and it lobbies for corporate securityinterests.

Trade Shows

6142 ATM Industry Association

Home Page: www.atmia.com/conferences/usa
Social Media: *Facebook, LinkedIn, YouTube*

Mike Lee, Chief Executive Officer
Sharon Lane, Global Director, Financeÿ
Dana Benson, Dir., Conferences & Sponsorships
Amanda Hardy, Marketing Director, Europe
David Tente, Executive Director, USA

Alliance promoting the proliferation of automated teller machines, ATMs and cash.
5000 Members
Founded in 1997

6143 CompTIA

3500 Lacey Road
Suite 100
Downers Grove, IL 60515

630-678-8300
FAX 630-678-8384
E-Mail: techvoice@comptia.org
Home Page: www.comptia.org/events
Social Media: *Facebook, Twitter, LinkedIn, Pinterest, Google+, YouTube*

Todd Thibodeaux, President, CEO
Charles Eaton, CEO, Educational Foundation
Ann Batko, SVP, Marketing
Kelly Ricker, SVP, Events and Education
David Sommer, Chief Financial Officer

A nonprofit trade association created by representatives of five microcomputer leaderships and is a provider of professional certifications for theinformation technology (IT) industry.

6144 Cyber Security Summit

Home Page: www.cybersecuritysummit.org
Social Media: *Facebook, Twitter, LinkedIn*

Andrew Borene, Esq., Chair

Because of the scope of cyber threats, the Summit endeavors to bring together all stakeholders - industry, government and academia - to improve cyber security.
Frequency: Annual
Founded in 2011

6145 DMD New York Conference & Expo
Direct Marketing Conferences
20 Academy Street
Norwalk, CT 06850-4032

203-854-9166
800-969-6566
E-Mail: connecticut@dmdays.com
Home Page: www.dmdays.com

Direct Marketing Days New York offers new ideas in media, creative, database, eCommerce and technology. Hundreds of exhibits showcase the newest technologies, products and services. Over 85 sessions and 25 consultation centers led by A level speakers. Network with top-level executives.
Frequency: Annual/June

6146 GovSec
National Trade Productions

313 S Patrick Street
Alexandria, VA 22314

703-838-8500
FAX 703-836-4486
Home Page: www.govsecinfo.com

Denise Medved, General Manager

Provides a full spectrum of security solutions for federal, state, and local governments tasked with developing comprehensive strategies that address physical security, information security and cyber security needs. Educational programs held in conjunction with displays of a wide variety of security products and services designed specifically for government users.
Frequency: Annual/May

Directories & Databases

6147 ATM Industry Association

Home Page:
www.atmia.com/directory-of-atm-services
Social Media: *Facebook, LinkedIn, YouTube*

Mike Lee, Chief Executive Officer
Sharon Lane, Global Director, Financeÿ
Dana Benson, Dir., Conferences & Sponsorships
Amanda Hardy, Marketing Director, Europe
David Tente, Executive Director, USA

Alliance promoting the proliferation of automated teller machines, ATMs and cash.
5000 Members
Founded in 1997

Industry Web Sites

6148 www.bsa.org
Business Software Alliance

An organization dedicated to promoting a safe and legal digital world. BSA educates consumers on software management and copyright protection, cyber security, trade, e-commerce and other internet related issues.

6149 www.cisecurity.org
Center for Internet Security

Helps organizations around the world effectively manage the risks related to internet security.

6150 www.nga.org/cms/statecyber
National Governors Association
Hall of the States
444 N Capitol St., Suite 267
Washington, DC 20001-1512

202-624-5300
FAX 202-624-5313
Home Page: www.nga.org
Social Media: *Facebook, Twitter*

Gov. Gary Herbert, Utah, Chair
Gov. Terry McAuliffe, Virginia

Tools and resources to help states improve their cybersecurity policies and practices. Provided by the National Governors Association.

Associations

6151 Advertising Mail Marketing Association

Advertising Mail Marketing Association
1333 F Street NW
Suite 710
Washington, DC 20004-1108

202-347-0055
FAX 202-347-0789
E-Mail: chadr@amma.org
Home Page: www.amma.org
Social Media: *Facebook, Twitter, LinkedIn*

Gene A DelPolito, Publisher
Chad W Robbins, Editor

For those who use mail for fundraising or business purposes.
Founded in 1947

6152 American Marketing Association

311 S Wacker Dr
Suite 5800
Chicago, IL 60606-6629

312-542-9000
800-262-1150
FAX 312-542-9001
Home Page: www.marketingpower.com
Social Media: *Facebook, Twitter, LinkedIn, YouTube, Pinterest, Google+*

Rob Malcolm, Chairperson
Valarie Zeithaml?, Chairperson-elect
Mary Garrett, Vice President
Finance/Secretary?
Ric Sweeney, Immediate Past Chairperson

A professional association for individuals and organizations involved in the practice, teaching and study of marketing worldwide.
40000 Members
Founded in 1953

6153 American Teleservices Association

3815 River Crossing Parkway
Suite 20
Indianapolis, IN 46240

317-816-9336
877-779-3974
FAX 317-218-0323
E-Mail: contact@ataconnect.org
Home Page: www.ataconnect.org

Tim Searcy, CEO

Represents the call centers, trainers, consultants and equipment suppliers that initiate, facilitate and generate telephone, Internet and e-mail sales, service and support.
240 Members

6154 Art Directors Club

106 W 29th St
New York, NY 10001-5301

212-643-1440
FAX 212-643-4266
E-Mail: info@adcglobal.org
Home Page: www.adcglobal.org
Social Media: *Facebook, Twitter, LinkedIn, Pinterest*

Ami Brophy, CEO
Jon Kamen, VP
Vickie Peslak, Second VP
Thomas Mueller, Secretary
Myrna Davis, Executive Director

An international nonprofit organization of leading creatives in advertising, graphic design, interactive media, broadcast design, typography, packaging, environmental design, photography, illustration and related disciplines.
1200 Members
Founded in 1920
Mailing list available for rent

6155 Association of Direct Marketing Agencies

Cohn & Wells
350 Hudson Street
New York, NY 10014-4504

212-192-2278
FAX 212-302-6714
E-Mail: jwpgroup@aol.com
Home Page: www.cyberdirect.com/ADMA

John A Greco Jr, President/CEO

Members are direct response advertising agencies.
100 Members

6156 Association of Hispanic Advertising Agencies

8280 Willow Oaks Corporate Drive
Suite 600
Fairfax, VA 22031

703-745-5531
E-Mail: info@ahaa.org
Home Page: www.ahaa.org
Social Media: *Facebook, Twitter, LinkedIn, YouTube, Storify*

Aldo Quevedo, Chair
Horacio Gavilan, Executive Director
Fulvia Lee, Program Manager
Gabriela Alcantara-Diaz, Treasurer
Carlos Santiago, Secretary

Trade organization for promoting the Hispanic marketing and advertising industry.
Founded in 1996

6157 Association of Teleservices International

222 South Westmonte Drive
Suite 101
Altamonte Springs, FL 32714

866-896-ATSI
FAX 407-774-6440
E-Mail: admin@atsi.org
Home Page: atsi.org
Social Media: *Facebook, Twitter, LinkedIn*

Jeff Zindel, President
Doug Robbins, Vice President
Josue Leon, VP- Secretary
JoAnn Fussell, VP- Treasurer
Gary Edwards, Director

An international trade association established by and for entrepreneurs in the TeleServices business. It provides a wide variety of services to businesses, governmental agencies, local emergency respondents and the general public.
35000 Members
Founded in 1942

6158 Business Marketing Association: Atlanta

13 Corporate Square
Suite 100
Atlanta, GA 30329

404-641-9417
800-664-4262
FAX 312-822-0054
E-Mail: info@bmaatlanta.com
Home Page: www.bmaatlanta.com
Social Media: *Facebook, Twitter*

Ed King, President-Elect
John Wiley, Marketing & Public Relations
Barry Mirkin, Development & Research
Stacey Krizan,
Membership/Education/Certification
Joe Noonan, Programs Co-Chair

The Atlanta chapter of the BMA includes marketing executives from a variety of industries and backgrounds including research, advertising, promotions, events, Web development, printing and more. The BMA offers an information-packed Web site, online skills-building, marketing certification programs, and industry

surveys and papers. In addition, members have the opportunity to interact with peers at seminars, participate in chapter training programs and the BMA Annual Conference.

6159 Business Marketing Association: Boston

246 Hampshire Street
Cambridge, MA 02130

617-418-4000
800-664-4262
FAX 312-822-0054
E-Mail: info@thebmaboston.com
Home Page: www.thebmaboston.com/

Michael Lewis, President
Will Robinson, VP Public Relations
Matthew Mamet, VP Internet Marketing
Larry Perreault, VP Finance
Chris Perkett, VP Programming

BMA Boston helps members improve their ability to manage business-to-business marketing and communications for greater productivity and profitability by providing unique access to information, ideas, and the experience of peers. The BMA offers an information-packed Website, online skills-building, marketing certification programs, and industry surveys and papers. In addition, members have the opportunity to interact with peers at seminars, chapter training programs and the BMA Annual Conference.

6160 Cable & Telecommunications Association for Marketing

120 Waterfront Street
Suite 200
National Harbor, MD 20745

301-485-8900
FAX 301-560-4964
E-Mail: info@ctam.com
Home Page: www.ctam.com
Social Media: *Facebook, Twitter, LinkedIn, YouTube*

Mark Greatrex, Chair
Jamia Bigalow, Vice Chairman
Bob Benya, President/ CEO
Todd Esenwein, Director of Business Services
Zell Murphy, SVP Finance & Administration

Provides marketing knowledge and industry scale to help its membersmanage the future and drive business results. Also provides consumer research, an interactive executive innovation series, conferences and awards.

6161 Color Marketing Group

1908 Mount Vernon Avenue
Alexandria, VA 22301

703-329-8500
FAX 703-535-3190
E-Mail: sgriffis@colormarketing.org
Home Page: www.colormarketing.org
Social Media: *Facebook, Twitter, LinkedIn, Google+, Pinterest*

John West, CMG, President
Heather Beland, CMG, Vice President Marketing
Geraldine Chmiel, Secretary
Art Schmehling, Treasurer
Sharon Griffis, Executive Director

A nonprofit international association of color designers involved in the use of color as it applies to the profitable marketing of goods and services.
1300 Members
Founded in 1962

6162 Digital Analytics Association
401 Edgewater Place
Suite 600
Wakefield, WA 1880

781-876-8933
FAX 781-224-1239
Home Page:
www.digitalanalyticsassociation.org
Social Media: *Facebook, Twitter, LinkedIn, Google+*

Casey Carey, President
Eric Feinberg, Vice President
Steve Petitpas, Vice President-Marketing
Mike Levin, Executive Director
Jacki Conn, Education Manager

A global organization of practitioners, corporations, vendors, marketing and public relations agencies, consultants, academics, and more involved in the growing digital analytics industry.
Founded in 2004

6163 Digital Concepts for Business
PO Box 745
Suite 102
Crystal Lake, IL 60039-0745

815-575-0089
FAX 847-458-5134
E-Mail: info@dcfb.com
Home Page: www.dcfb.com
Social Media: *Facebook, Twitter, LinkedIn, Google+, Pinterest*

Mary Owens, Owner

Provides services to companies throughout the US and is dedicated to providing high-quality business communcations solutions using the latest hardware and software for both PC and Macintosh.
Founded in 1996

6164 Direct International
1501 3rd Avenue
New York, NY 10028-2101

212-861-4188
FAX 212-986-3757

Alfred Goodloe, President

Offers publications and services for the international direct marketing executive.

6165 Direct Marketing Association
1120 Avenue of the Americas
New York, NY 10036-6700

212-768-7277
FAX 212-302-6714
Home Page: thedma.org
Social Media: *Facebook, Twitter, LinkedIn*

Thomas J. Benton, Chief Executive Officer
Bob Greco, SVP of Operations, Finance & Events
Peggy Hudson, SVP, Government Affairs
Linsay Hutter, SVP, Communications
Xenia Boone, JD, SVP, General Counsel

Advances and protects responsible data-driven marketing.

6166 Direct Selling Association
1667 K St NW
Suite 1100
Washington, DC 20006-1660

202-452-8866
FAX 202-452-9010
E-Mail: info@dsa.org
Home Page: www.wfdsa.org
Social Media: *Facebook, Twitter, RSS*

Neil H Offen, President
Douglas L DeVos, Vice Chairman
Neil H Offen, President
John A Addison Jr, Director
Mark Bosworth, Director

National trade of the leading firms that manufacture and distribute goods and services sold directly to consumers. Members of the association are copanies including many well-known brand names. The association's mission is to protect, serve and promote the effectiveness of member companies and the independent business people they represent.
Founded in 1978

6167 Direct-to-Direct Marketing Association Council for Hispanic Marketing
Direct Marketing Association
1120 Avenue of the Americas
New York, NY 10036-6700

212-768-7277
FAX 212-768-6714
Home Page: thedma.org

Allison Longley, Manager

Provides education, information and networking opportunities for direct marketing professionals targeting the Hispanic market.
120 Members
Founded in 1992

6168 EMarketing Association
40 Blue Ridge Dr
Charlestown, RI 02813

800-496-2950
FAX 408-884-2461
E-Mail: admin@emarketingassociation.com
Home Page: www.emarketingassociation.com
Social Media: *Facebook, Twitter, LinkedIn*

Robert Fleming, President
Todd Daum, VP
John Hastings, VP
Linda Jaffe, VP

An international association of emarketing professionals. Members include government, companies, professionals and students involved with the emarketing arena.

6169 Internet Marketing Association
10 Mar Del Rey
San Clemente, CA 92673

949-443-9300
FAX 949-443-2215
E-Mail: info@imanetwork.org
Home Page: imanetwork.org
Social Media: *Facebook, Twitter, LinkedIn, YouTube, RSS, Google+*

Sinan Kanatsiz, CIM, Chairman/ Founder
Matthew Langie, Vice Chairman, Education
Rachel Reenders, CIM, Executive Director
David Steinberg, CIM, VP of Business Alliances
Vince Walden, Finance Director

A professional organization that has gained more than 900,000 members in fields including sales, marketing, business ownership, programming and creative development. It provides a platform where proven Internet marketing strategies are demonstrated and shared to increase members value to their organizations.
90000 Members
Founded in 2001

6170 Life Insurance Direct Marketing Association
3227 S. Cherokee Lane
Suite 1320
Woodstock, GA 30188

770-516-0207
866-890-LEAD
E-Mail: info@lidma.org
Home Page: lidma.org
Social Media: *Facebook, Twitter, LinkedIn*

Pat Wedeking, Chair
Byron Udell, President
Patrick M Bowen, CLU, VP, Senior Account

Manager
Staci Birk, Director
Cynthia Farrow, Secretary/ Treasurer

A nonprofit organization dedicated specifically to supporting businesses and professionals active in direct sales of term life insurance products to consumers.

6171 Mail Advertising Service Association
1800 Diagonal Road
Suite 320
Alexandria, VA 22314-2862

703-836-9200
FAX 703-548-8204
E-Mail: webmaster@epicomm.org
Home Page: www.mfsanet.org
Social Media: *Facebook, Twitter, LinkedIn, YouTube, Pinterest, Google+*

Ken Garner, President and CEO
Tom Saggiomo, Vice Chairman
John Rafner, Second Vice Chairman
Wayne Marshall, Treasurer

Supports all those involved in the mailing, addressing, and inserting industries.
Founded in 2014

6172 Mailing & Fulfillment Service Association
One Meadowlands Plaza
Suite 1511
East Rutherford, NJ 07073

201-634-9600
FAX 703-548-8204
E-Mail: webmaster@epicomm.org
Home Page: www.mfsanet.org
Social Media: *Facebook, Twitter, LinkedIn, YouTube, Pinterest, Google+*

Ken Garner, President
Bill Stevenson, Director Marketing

The national trade association for the mailing and fulfillment services industry.
Founded in 2014

6173 Midwest Direct Marketing Association
P.O. Box 75
Suite S256
Andover, MN 55304

763-607-2943
FAX 763-753-2240
E-Mail: office@mdma.org
Home Page: www.mdma.org

Ed Harrington, Manager
Ben DuBois, Director

Dedicated to the advancement of professional and ethical practice of direct response marketing by members throughout the Upper Midwest.
600 Members
Founded in 1960

6174 Mobile Marketing Association
41 E 11th St
11th floor
New York, NY 10003

646-257-4515
E-Mail: northamerica@mmaglobal.com
Home Page: www.mmaglobal.com
Social Media: *Facebook, Twitter, LinkedIn, Google+*

John Costello, President
Jack Philbins, Co-Founder, President and CEO
Carolyyn Everson, VP, Global Marketing

A global nonprofit trade association comprised of more than 800 member companies that strive to accelerate the transformation and innovation of marketing through mobile, driving business growth with closer and stronger consumerengagement.
800 Members

6175 Mobile Marketing Research Association
216 W. Jackson Blvd.
Suite 625
Chicago, IL 60606

312-252-2502
Home Page: www.mmra-global.org
Social Media: *Facebook, Twitter, LinkedIn, Pinterest*

Rebecca West, President
Rick West, Vice President
Mark Michelson, Executive Director
Sheila Gidley, Director of Operations
Jan Willem Smulders, Treasurer

A global trade association dedicated to the promotion and development of professional standards and ethics for conducting marketing research on mobile devices.
Founded in 2011

6176 Multi-Level Marketing International Association
119 Stanford Ct
Irvine, CA 92612

949-854-0484
E-Mail: info@mlmia.com
Home Page: www.mlmia.com
Social Media: *Facebook, Twitter*

Doris Wood, President Emeritus
Carrol Leclerc, President, Canada
Tom Leffler, VP of Support Board
Michael L. Sheffield, Co-Founder
Linda Bruno, Secretary

A nonprofit professional trade organization representing all sectors of the networking marketing industry on a worldwide basis.

6177 North American Farmers' Direct Marketing Association
62 White Loaf Road
Southampton, MA 1073

FAX 413-233-4285
E-Mail: Charlie @ Whiteloafridge.com
Home Page: www.farmersinspired.com
Social Media: *Facebook, Twitter, Pinterest, YouTube*

Cynthia Chiles, President/ Chair
Charlie Touchette, Executive Director
Becky Walters, VP of Membership
Ben Beaver, VP of Education
Mike Dunn, Treasurer/ Finance Team Chair

A membership association that advances the prosperity of its members and the farm direct marketing industry through networking, participation, education, and innovation.

6178 Professional Association of Customer Engagement
8500 Keystone Crossing
Suite 480
Indianapolis, IN 46240

317-816-9336
E-Mail: tom.chandler@paceassociation.com
Home Page: www.paceassociation.com
Social Media: *Facebook, Twitter, LinkedIn, YouTube, RSS*

Michael Rauscher, Chair
Barbra Merwin, Vice Chairman
Tom Rocca, Chief Executive Officer
Susan Burt, Finance Director
Angie Brown, Operations Director

A nonprofit trade organization dedicated exclusively to the advancement of companies that utilize contact centers as an integral channel of operations.

6179 Society of Publication Designers
27 Union Square West
Suite 207
New York, NY 10003

212-223-3332
FAX 212-223-5880
E-Mail: mail@spd.org
Home Page: www.spd.org
Social Media: *RSS*

Tim Leong, President
David Curcurito, Vice President
Allyson Torrisi, Vice President
Keisha Dean, Executive Director
Leah Bailey, Treasurer

An organization dedicated to promoting and encouraging excellence in editorial design. Members include art directors, designers, photo editors, editors, and graphics professionals.
Founded in 1965

Newsletters

6180 Business Owner
Mailing & Fulfillment Service Association
1421 Prince Street
Suite 410
Alexandria, VA 22314-2806

703-836-9200
FAX 703-548-8204
E-Mail: mfsa-mail@mfsanet.org
Home Page: www.mfsanet.org

David L Perkins Jr, Editor
Developed specifically to communicate with owners and CEOs on issues unique to them. You'll receive a wealth of knowledge on growing your business, tax issues, insurance, estate planning, management, finance and much more.
Frequency: Bi-Monthly

6181 Career News Update
American Marketing Association
311 S Wacker Dr
Suite 5800
Chicago, IL 60606-6629

312-542-9000
800-262-1150
FAX 312-542-9001
Home Page: www.marketingpower.com

Dennis Dunlap, CEO

You'll receive the latest career and hiring advice as well as useful job resources and employment listings.
Frequency: Monthly

6182 Daily News E-Mail (3D)
Direct Marketing Association
1120 Avenue of the Americas
New York, NY 10036-6700

212-768-7277
FAX 212-302-6714
E-Mail: customerservice@the-dma.org
Home Page: www.the-dma.org

Lawrence M Kimmel, CEO

Delivers the essential news, research, hot trends, and technological developments from the nations leading newspapers, trade publications, and the government all in an easy-to-read, time-saving format

6183 Direct Response
Direct Marketing Center
21171 S. Western Ave
Suite 260
Torrance, CA 90501

310-212-5727
FAX 310-212-5773

E-Mail: cdmg@cdmginc.com
Home Page: www.directmarketingcenter.net

Craig Huey, President/Publisher
Kent Komae, Editor
Direct marketing information.
Cost: $79.00
Frequency: Monthly

6184 Direct Selling Association International Bulletin
World Federation of Direct Selling Associations
1667 K St Nw
Suite 1100
Washington, DC 20006-1660

202-452-8866
FAX 202-452-9010
E-Mail: info@wfdsa.org
Home Page: www.wfdsa.org

Neil H Offen, President
Association activities, legislation affecting direct selling and trends.
Circulation: 1200

6185 Direction
Direct Marketing Consultants
705 Franklin Tpke
Allendale, NJ 07401-1637

201-327-9213

Hugh P Curley, Publisher

How to' information on motivating buying decisions via more creative use of direct mail, sales promotion, newsletters, and other marketing tools.
Cost: $40.00
Circulation: 3800

6186 Empoyment Points
Mailing & Fulfillment Service Association
1421 Prince Street
Suite 410
Alexandria, VA 22314-2806

703-836-9200
FAX 703-548-8204
E-Mail: mfsa-mail@mfsanet.org
Home Page: www.mfsanet.org

The content is written for business owners and operators who want to stay informed about current employment issues. The editorial is targeted on human resource issues and employment practices in the mailing and fulfillment services industry.
Frequency: 4x/Year
Circulation: 2000

6187 Fred Goss' What's Working in Direct Marketing
United Communications Group
11300 Rockville Pike
Street 1100
Rockville, MD 20852-3030

301-287-2700
FAX 301-816-8945
E-Mail: webmaster@ucg.com
Home Page: www.ucg.com/

Benny Dicecca, President
Direct response marketing-all forms.
Cost: $242.00
Founded in 1977

6188 Friday Report
Hoke Communications
224 7th Street
Garden City, NY 11530-5771

516-746-6700
800-229-6700
FAX 516-294-8141

E-Mail: dmmagazine@aol.com
Home Page: www.directmarketingmag.com

Henry R Hoke, Publisher
Joseph D Gatti, Editor
Stuart W Boysen, President
Edson Georges, Mailing Systems Manager

Weekly newsletter of direct marketing.
Cost: $165.00
8 Pages
Frequency: Weekly
Founded in 1951

6189 General Encouragement, Motivation and Inspirational Handbook
Economics Press
12 Daniel Road
Fairfield, NJ 07004-2565

973-227-1224
FAX 973-227-3558
E-Mail: info@epinc.com
Home Page: www.epinc.com

Allan Yahalen, President
Rob Gilbert, Editor
Cost: $20.00
24 Pages
Frequency: Monthly
Circulation: 200000
Mailing list available for rent: 200,000 names
Printed in 4 colors on matte stock

6190 Inside Mail Order
Mellinger Company
PO Box 956
Santa Clarita, CA 91380-9056

661-259-2303
FAX 805-257-4840
E-Mail: mell@tradezone.com
Home Page: www.tradezone.com

BL Mellinger III, Publisher

A newsletter offering the latest information to businesses on marketing and advertising through direct mail.

6191 Mail Order Digest & Washington Newsletter
National Mail Order Association
2807 Polk St Ne
Minneapolis, MN 55418-2954

612-788-1673
FAX 612-788-1147
E-Mail: editor@nmoa.org
Home Page: www.nmoa.org

John Schulte, President
J Bradley, Editor
Paul Muchnick, Founder Director

Contains information of interest to small to midsize mail marketers including new products available, money saving techniques, industry contacts, help for beginners, new concepts for mail order selling, and postal changes and regulations.
Cost: $99.00
Frequency: Monthly
Circulation: 7000
Founded in 1972

6192 Marketing Academics Newsletter
American Marketing Association
311 S Wacker Dr
Suite 5800
Chicago, IL 60606-6629

312-542-9000
800-262-1150
FAX 312-542-9001
Home Page: www.marketingpower.com

Dennis Dunlap, CEO

This newsletter provides news and information that affect and inform this important constituency. It reviews Academic Council activities,

profiles Academic SIGS and highlights upcoming events.

6193 Marketing Matters Newsletter
American Marketing Association
311 S Wacker Dr
Suite 5800
Chicago, IL 60606-6629

312-542-9000
800-262-1150
FAX 312-542-9001
Home Page: www.marketingpower.com

Dennis Dunlap, CEO

This e-newsletter updates readers on the latest happenings in the marketing profession through news briefs, indepth features and interviews.
Frequency: 2x/Monthly

6194 Marketing Power Newsletter
American Marketing Association
311 S Wacker Dr
Suite 5800
Chicago, IL 60606-6629

312-542-9000
800-262-1150
FAX 312-542-9001
Home Page: www.marketingpower.com

Dennis Dunlap, CEO

This update of the latest news, research and trends in the marketing industry and allied fields.
Frequency: Weekly

6195 Marketing Researchers Newsletter
American Marketing Association
311 S Wacker Dr
Suite 5800
Chicago, IL 60606-6629

312-542-9000
800-262-1150
FAX 312-542-9001
Home Page: www.marketingpower.com

Dennis Dunlap, CEO

This e-newsletter provides members with content designed to educate and inform researchers or any member interested in marketing research topics.

6196 Marketing Through Leaders Newsletter
American Marketing Association
311 S Wacker Dr
Suite 5800
Chicago, IL 60606-6629

312-542-9000
800-262-1150
FAX 312-542-9001
Home Page: www.marketingpower.com

Dennis Dunlap, CEO

These articles focus on the issues and concepts that shape marketing today and tomorrow.
Frequency: Monthly

6197 Memo to Mailers
US Postal Service
475 Lenfant Plz Sw
Room 10523
Washington, DC 20260-1805

202-268-2900
800-275-8777
FAX 202-268-6436
E-Mail: mmailers@usps.com
Home Page: www.usps.com

Robert F Gardner, Manager

Carries information and news about the Postal Service as well as value added information about using the mail effectively and efficiently.

Also offers information to mail center managers on ways to cut costs.
8 Pages
Frequency: Daily
Circulation: 100000

6198 Nonprofit Mailers Foundation
125 Michigan Avenue NE
#239
Washington, DC 20017-1004

202-628-4380

Esther Huggins, Manager

Promotes welfare of groups using nonprofit mail rates for communications and fundraising.
600 Pages
Founded in 1982

6199 PD&D Direct Mail List
Chilton Way
Radnor, PA 19089-0001

973-920-7782
FAX 973-607-5492
E-Mail:
newslettermaterials@advantagemedia.com

Tom Lynch, Group Publisher
Christina Schmidt, Publisher
Don Grennan, Director of Marketing
Jeff Reinke, Editorial Director
David Mantey, Editor

This list is a proven response vehicle for product promotion, seminar announcements and trade show promotions.

6200 PostScripts
Mailing & Fulfillment Service Association
1421 Prince Street
Suite 410
Alexandria, VA 22314-2806

703-836-9200
FAX 703-548-8204
E-Mail: mfsa-mail@mfsanet.org
Home Page: www.mfsanet.org

Leo Raymond, Editor

Each issue of PostScripts highlights a theme relevant to mailing or fulfillment operations, such as production management or information technology.
Frequency: 18x/Year
Circulation: 2800

6201 Postal Points
Mailing & Fulfillment Service Association
1421 Prince Street
Suite 410
Alexandria, VA 22314-2806

703-836-9200
FAX 703-548-8204
E-Mail: mfsa-mail@mfsanet.org
Home Page: www.mfsanet.org

Leo Raymond, Editor

Deals exclusively with current and pending postal and delivery issues. Here you will find the facts and analysis of developing postal issues.
Frequency: 18x/Year

6202 Target Market News
Target Market News
228 S Wabash Ave
Suite 210
Chicago, IL 60604-2383

312-408-1867
FAX 312-408-1867
E-Mail: info@targetmarketnews.com
Home Page: www.targetmarketnews.com

Ken Smikle, President
Hallie Mummert, Editor

News and developments in the areas of black consumer marketing and black-oriented media.
Cost: $40.00
12 Pages
Frequency: Monthly
Founded in 1988

6203 TeleResponse
InfoCision Management
325 Springside Dr
Akron, OH 44333-4504

330-668-1400
FAX 330-668-1401
Home Page: www.infocision.com

Carl Albright, CEO

Specializes in making outbound sales calls for the infomercial, catalog and direct marketing industries.

6204 Telephone Selling Report
Business By Phone
13254 Stevens Street
Omaha, NE 68137-1728

402-455-1111
800-326-7721
FAX 402-896-3353
E-Mail: arts@businessbyphone.com
Home Page: www.businessbyphone.com

Art Sobczak, Production Manager

For businesses that use the phone to prospect, service and sell. How-to information on getting through screens; creating interest-grabbing openings; closes that work; overcoming tough objections; and beating call reluctance. Accepts advertising inserts.
Cost: $109.00
8 Pages
Frequency: Monthly
Mailing list available for rent: 2M names
Printed in 2 colors

6205 Venture Views & News
Venture Communications
60 Madison Ave
New York, NY 10010-1600

212-447-5247
FAX 212-576-1129
E-Mail: sales@ven.com
Home Page: www.venturedirect.com

Rachel Krasny, Editor
Richard Baumer, CEO/President
Neal Mandel, Group Division Sales Manager
Michael Platt, Founder

News and practical advice in the field of direct response marketing.
Frequency: Weekly
Founded in 1983

6206 What's Working in DM and Fulfillment
United Communications Group
11300 Rockville Pike
Suite 1100
Rockville, MD 20852-3030

301-816-8950
800-929-4824
FAX 301-816-8945
E-Mail: webmaster@ucg.com
Home Page: www.ucg.com/

Barbara W Kaplowitz, Publisher
Monica Brown, Circulation Manager

Tested tips, tactics and techniques for direct marketers in all industries, news, legislative updates and winning (and losing) DM ideas including hard costs and how to's.
Cost: $242.00
8 Pages
Founded in 1977
Mailing list available for rent at $125 per M
Printed in 2 colors on matte stock

Magazines & Journals

6207 BtoB Magazine
Ad Age Group/ Division of Crain Communications
711 3rd Ave
New York, NY 10017-4014

212-210-0785
FAX 212-210-0200
E-Mail: info@crain.com
Home Page: www.crain.com

Norm Feldman, Manager

Dedicated to integrated business to business marketing. Every page is packed with substance news, reports, technologies, benchmarks, best practices served up by the most knowledgeable journalists.
Frequency: Monthly
Circulation: 45000

6208 Chief Marketer
Penton Media, Inc.
249 W 17th Street
New York, NY 10011

212-204-4200
Home Page: www.penton.com
Social Media: *Facebook, Twitter, LinkedIn*

Tyler T. Zachehm, Co-CEO
Anup Bagaria, Co-CEO
Nicola Allais, EVP & CFO
Jasmine Alexander, SVP & CIO

Chief Marketer provides fresh, multi-disciplined approaches to direct marketing, events, advertising research, and promotional marketing.
Frequency: Monthly
Founded in 1976

6209 Customer Interface
Advanstar Communications
6200 Canoga Avenue
2nd Floor
Woodland Hills, CA 91367

818-593-5000
FAX 818-593-5020
E-Mail: info@advanstar.com
Home Page: www.advanstar.com

Joseph Loggia, President
Chris DeMoulin, VP
Susannah George, Marketing Director

Magazine for decision-makers actively involved in planning, managing or operating a business call center.
Cost: $39.00
104 Pages
Circulation: 50000
Founded in 1992

6210 Dateline: DMA
Direct Marketing Association
11 W 42nd Street
New York, NY 10036-8002

212-391-9683
FAX 212-768-4546

Offers comprehensive information on the Direct Marketing Association, trends in the industry, technological advances and more for the marketing and advertising professional.

6211 Direct
Chief Marketer

249 W 17th Street
New York, NY 10011

212-204-4200
Home Page: www.chiefmarketer.com
Social Media: *Facebook, Twitter, LinkedIn*

Beth Negus Viveiros, Managing Editor
Brian Quinton, Executive Editor
Patricia Odell, Managing Editor
Richard Levey, Senior Writer
Larry Riggs, Senior Editor

Information Resource for Direct Marketers.
Frequency: Monthly
Founded in 1976

6212 Direct Marketing News
Haymarket Media, Inc.
114 W 26th St.
4th Fl.
New York, NY 10001

646-638-6000
Home Page: www.dmnews.com

Lee Maniscalco, Chairman & CEO
Ginger Conlon, Editor-in-Chief

Valuable information on the newest trends in direct marketing, catalog statistics and advertising information for persons working in the direct mail industry.
Cost: $148.00
Frequency: Monthly
ISSN: 1187-7111
Founded in 1979

6213 Journal of Direct Marketing
John Wiley & Sons
111 River St
Hoboken, NJ 07030-5790

201-748-6000
800-825-7550
FAX 201-748-6088
E-Mail: info@wiley.com
Home Page: www.wiley.com

William J Pesce, CEO
Richard M Hochhauser, CEO

Publication featuring research articles from some of the best minds in the field of direct marketing. Offers creative ideas for marketing products, analysis of what works, pioneering research from the nation's top universities, articles from other direct marketing publications and special reports on overseas direct marketing.
Cost: $1000.00
Frequency: Quarterly
Founded in 1807

6214 Journal of International Marketing
American Marketing Association
311 S Wacker Dr
Suite 5800
Chicago, IL 60606-6629

312-542-9000
800-262-1150
FAX 312-542-9001
Home Page: www.marketingpower.com

Dennis Dunlap, CEO

Presents scholarly and managerially relevant articles on international marketing.

6215 Journal of Marketing
American Marketing Association
311 S Wacker Dr
Suite 5800
Chicago, IL 60606-6629

312-542-9000
800-262-1150
FAX 312-542-9001
Home Page: www.marketingpower.com

Dennis Dunlap, CEO

The premier broad based scholarly journal of the marketing discipline that focuses on substantive issues in marketing and marketing management.

6216   Journal of Marketing Research
American Marketing Association
311 S Wacker Dr
Suite 5800
Chicago, IL 60606-6629

312-542-9000
800-262-1150
FAX 312-542-9001
Home Page: www.marketingpower.com

Dennis Dunlap, CEO

Covers a wide range of marketing research concepts, methods and applications. You'll read about new techniques, contributions to knowledge based on experimental methods and developments in related fields that have a bearing on marketing research.

6217   Journal of Public Policy & Marketing
American Marketing Association
311 S Wacker Dr
Suite 5800
Chicago, IL 60606-6629

312-542-9000
800-262-1150
FAX 312-542-9001
Home Page: www.marketingpower.com

Dennis Dunlap, CEO

Each issue features a wide ranging forum for the research, findings and discussion of marketing subjects related to business and government.

6218   Marketing Health Services
American Marketing Association
311 S Wacker Dr
Suite 5800
Chicago, IL 60606-6629

312-542-9000
800-262-1150
FAX 312-542-9001
Home Page: www.marketingpower.com

Dennis Dunlap, CEO

Specifically aimed at senior level healthcare marketers and managers, offers targeted information, practical strategies and thought provoking commentary to help achieve your goals and shape your vision.
Frequency: Quarterly

6219   Marketing Management
American Marketing Association
311 S Wacker Dr
Suite 5800
Chicago, IL 60606-6629

312-542-9000
800-262-1150
FAX 312-542-9001
Home Page: www.marketingpower.com

Dennis Dunlap, CEO

Focuses on strategic marketing issues that marketing managers face every day.
Frequency: 6x/Year

6220   Marketing News
American Marketing Association
311 S Wacker Dr
Suite 5800
Chicago, IL 60606-6629

312-542-9000
800-262-1150
FAX 312-542-9001
Home Page: www.marketingpower.com

Dennis Dunlap, CEO

Covers the industry's basics, the core concepts around which winning programs are built.

6221   Marketing Research
American Marketing Association
311 S Wacker Dr
Suite 5800
Chicago, IL 60606-6629

312-542-9000
800-262-1150
FAX 312-542-9001
Home Page: www.marketingpower.com

Dennis Dunlap, CEO

Researchers and managers count on this quarterly resource to help stay on top of current methodologies and issues, management concerns and the latest books and software.
40000 Members
Frequency: Quarterly

6222   Multichannel Merchant
Chief Marketer
249 W 17th Street
New York, NY 10011

212-204-4200
Home Page: www.chiefmarketer.com
Social Media: *Facebook, Twitter, LinkedIn*

Beth Negus Viveiros, Managing Editor
Brian Quinton, Executive Editor
Patricia Odell, Managing Editor
Richard Levey, Senior Writer
Larry Riggs, Senior Editor

Exclusively serves online merchants and catalog companies, as well as retailers, manufacturers and wholesale/distributors.
Frequency: Monthly
Founded in 1976

6223   Operations & Fulfillment
Primedia
Po Box 12901
Shawnee Mission, KS 66282-2901

913-341-1300
800-775-3777
FAX 913-514-6895
E-Mail: rramaswami@primediabusiness.com
Home Page: www.penton.com

Eric Jacobson, Senior VP
Glenn Laudenslager, Marketing Manager
Leslie Bacon, Publisher
Leonard Roberto, Circulation Manager
John French, President

Provides executives information they can't get anywhere else and reach executives and managers with purchasing authority in all areas of operations management. Information on direct to customer fulfillment..
Cost: $36.00
Frequency: Monthly
Founded in 1905

6224   Politically Direct
Direct Marketing Association
1120 Avenue of the Americas
New York, NY 10036-6700

212-768-7277
FAX 212-302-6714
E-Mail: customerservice@the-dma.org
Home Page: www.the-dma.org

Lawrence M Kimmel, CEO

Published both in print and digital, this newsletter on DMA advocacy efforts keeps DMA members informed and involved in the politics and policies that impact them today and ahead of the curve on developments that will affect them tomorrow.
Frequency: Quarterly

6225   Promo
Chief Marketer

249 W 17th Street
New York, NY 10011

212-204-4200
Home Page: www.chiefmarketer.com
Social Media: *Facebook, Twitter, LinkedIn*

Beth Negus Viveiros, Managing Editor
Brian Quinton, Executive Editor
Patricia Odell, Managing Editor
Richard Levey, Senior Writer
Larry Riggs, Senior Editor

Promo Magazine covers the Promotions and the Promotional Marketing Industry.
Frequency: Monthly
Founded in 1976

6226   Target
North American Publishing Company
1500 Spring Garden St
Suite 1200
Philadelphia, PA 19130-4094

215-238-5300
FAX 215-238-5342
E-Mail: editor.tm@napco.com
Home Page: www.targetmarketingmag.com

Ned S Borowsky, CEO
Peggy Hatch, Publisher
Lois Boyle, President

This monthly magazine is the authoritative information source for direct marketers with hands-on, how-to-do-it, ideas you can take to the bank.
Cost: $24.95
Frequency: Monthly
Circulation: 35000
Founded in 1977
Mailing list available for rent
Printed in 4 colors on glossy stock

6227   Telemarketing Magazine
Technology Marketing Corporation
1 Technology Plz
Norwalk, CT 06854-1936

203-852-6800
800-243-6002
FAX 203-853-2845
E-Mail: tmc@tmcnet.com
Home Page: www.tmcnet.com

Rich Tehrani, CEO
Linda Driscoll, Editor/VP
Rich Tehrani, President/Editor-in-Chief

Serves telemarketing, marketing, customer service, sales and telecommunications professionals. Features legislative updates, new product and service releases, techniques and beginner information.
Cost: $49.00
Frequency: Monthly
Founded in 1972

Trade Shows

6228   &Then
Direct Marketing Association
1120 Avenue of the Americas
New York, NY 10036-6700

212-768-7277
FAX 212-302-6714
Home Page: thedma.org/events

The Direct Marketing Association's annual event.
Frequency: Annual

6229   Annual Conference and Mailing Fulfillment Expo
Mailing & Fulfillment Service Association

1421 Prince Street
Suite 410
Alexandria, VA 22314-2806

703-836-9200
FAX 703-548-8204
E-Mail: mfsa-mail@mfsanet.org
Home Page: www.mfsanet.org

Ken Garner, President
Jennifer Root, Director
Bill Stevenson, Director Marketing

Quality educational sessions, industry specific exhibit hall, networking and more.
Frequency: Annual

6230 Annual Conference for Catalog and Multichannel Merchants
PRISM Business Exhibitions
11 River Bend Drive South
Stamford, CT 06907

203-358-9900
800-927-5007
FAX 203-358-5816
E-Mail: registration@prismb2b.com
Home Page: www.accmshow.com

Ed Berkowitz, Sales Director
Angela Eastin, Group Show Director

Co-presented by the Direct Marketing Association and Multichannel Merchant Magazine, ACCM offers the latest advances, technology and information and solutions for cataloger, retailers and multichannel merchants.
Frequency: May

6231 Business-to-Business Database Marketing Conference
Interlect Events
11 Riverbend Drive S
Stamford, CT 06907

203-852-4200
Home Page:
http://www.importexporthelp.com/b2b-lists.htm

Robin Altman, Contact

The only database marketing conference that is focused exclusively on business-to-business marketing database strategies and tactics. 40 tabletop exhibits.
500 Attendees
Frequency: Fall

6232 DMA Annual Conference & Exhibition
Direct Marketing Association
1120 Avenue of Americas
New York, NY 10036-6700

212-768-7277
FAX 212-302-6714
E-Mail: dmaconferences@the-dma.org
Home Page: www.the-dma.org

Lawrence M Kimmel, CEO
Julie A Hogan, SVP Conferences/Events

Brings together thousands of practitioners and experts from the entire marketing continuum to discuss solutions and best practices to achieve optimal channel mix and integration that lead to measurable results and increase real-time customer engagement.
12000 Attendees
Frequency: October

6233 DMD New York Conference & Expo
Direct Marketing Conferences
20 Academy Street
Norwalk, CT 06850-4032

203-854-9166
800-969-6566

E-Mail: connecticut@dmdays.com
Home Page: www.dmdays.com

Direct Marketing Days New York offers new ideas in media, creative, database, eCommerce and technology. Hundreds of exhibits showcase the newest technologies, products and services. Over 85 sessions and 25 consultation centers led by A level speakers. Network with top-level executives.
Frequency: Annual/June

6234 Email Evolution Conference
Direct Marketing Association
1120 Avenue of Americas
New York, NY 10036-6700

212-768-7277
FAX 212-302-6714
E-Mail: dmaconferences@the-dma.org
Home Page: www.the-dma.org

Julie A Hogan, SVP Conference/Events
Lawrence M Kimmel, CEO

Focuses on the ever-changing and evolving world of email marketing, providing attendees with the best ways to capitalize on the high ROI this low-cost communication tool can provide both on its own, and integrated with social, search, mobile, video and other email enhancers.
10M Attendees
Frequency: Annual/February

6235 ICSB Annual World Conference
International Council for Small Business
2201 G Street NW
Suite 315
Washington, DC 20052

202-944-0704
FAX 202-994-4930
E-Mail: icsb@gwu.edu
Home Page: www.icsb.org

David Smallbone, President
Don B. Bradley, III, President-Elect
Rita Grant, VP/Finance/Control
Ayman El Tarabishy, Executive Director
Michael Battaglia, Operations Manager

Annual business conference attended by entrepreneurs, policy makers, business service providers and researchers.
2000+ Members
Founded in 1956

6236 Internet Telephony Conference & EXPO (East or West)
Technology Marketing Corporation (TMCnet)
One Technology Plaza
Norwalk, CT 06854

203-852-6800
800-243-6002
FAX 203-853-2845
E-Mail: tmc@tmcnet.com
Home Page: www.tmcnet.com

Frank Coppola, Conference Team
Lorna Lyle, Conference Team
Tim Zaccagnini, Conference Team
Kevin Lake, Exhibit Sales
Natasha Barbera, Operations Contact

The world's foremost forum on IP and VoIP, and all things telephony: workshops, training courses, focused tracks, and exhibitors.
Frequency: East/West - Winter/Fall

6237 MFSA Mailing and Fulfillment Expo
Mailing & Fulfillment Service Association
1421 Prince Street
Suite 100
Alexandria, VA 22314-2805

703-369-9200
800-333-6272
FAX 703-548-8204

E-Mail: wecasey@mfsanet.org
Home Page: www.mfsanet.org

Eric Casey, Manager
David Weaver, President

Annual exposition of suppliers to mailing and fulfillment companies. Containing 60 booths and 50 exhibits.
250 Attendees
Frequency: June
Mailing list available for rent

6238 MFSA Midwinter Executive Conference
Mailing & Fulfillment Service Association
1421 Prince Street
Suite 410
Alexandria, VA 22314-2806

703-836-9200
FAX 703-548-8204
E-Mail: mfsa-mail@mfsanet.org
Home Page: www.mfsanet.org

Ken Garner, President
Jennifer Root, Director
Bill Stevenson, Director Marketing

Will address financial operations and business valuation, marketing your own company, the changing world of postal regulations, technology in fulfillment, building a sales team, being strong in digital printing and the landscape of employment law.

6239 Mailer Strategies Conference
Mailing & Fulfillment Service Association
1421 Prince Street
Suite 410
Alexandria, VA 22314-2806

703-836-9200
FAX 703-548-8204
E-Mail: mfsa-mail@mfsanet.org
Home Page: www.mfsanet.org

Ken Garner, President
Jennifer Root, Director
Bill Stevenson, Director Marketing

This conference will focus solely on postal issues that are important to your operations.

6240 Marketing in the Millennium
Florida Direct Marketing Association
8851 NW 10th Pl
Plantation, FL 33322-5007

954-472-6374
800-520-FDMA
FAX 954-472-8165
E-Mail: fdma@juno.org
Home Page: www.fdma.org

Beth Kaufman, Manager

Yearly exhibit of legislative updates and more for members of the direct marketing industry.
Frequency: February
Founded in 1999

6241 NCDM Conference
Direct Marketing Association
1120 Avenue of Americas
New York, NY 10036-6700

212-768-7277
FAX 212-302-6714
E-Mail: dmaconferences@the-dma.org
Home Page: www.the-dma.org

Julie A Hogan, SVP Conference/Events
Lawrence M Kimmel, CEO

Presents industry experts and hard-hitting case studies from a variety of verticles, such as financial services, retail, automotive, publishing, non-profit and many more, who will share the latest strategies and methodologies in gathering, analyzinf, leveraging and protecting the

most valuable business asset-the customer
database.
10M Attendees
Frequency: Annual/December

6242 National Catalog Operations Forum
Primedia
9800 Metcalf Avenue
Overland Park, KS 66212

913-341-1300
FAX 913-967-1898
Home Page: www.primediabusiness.com

Robin Altman, Contact

The only major national conference devoted
exclusively to the sharing of vital catalog operations information. This conference is dedicated to the crucial background of the catalog
business, and brings operations management
together to meet and learn; 140 booths.
1.2M+ Attendees
Frequency: April/May

**6243 National Conference on Operations &
Fulfillment (NCOF)**
Direct Marketing Association
1120 Avenue of Americas
New York, NY 10036-6700

212-768-7277
FAX 212-302-6714
E-Mail: dmaconferences@the-dma.org
Home Page: www.the-dma.org

Julie A Hogan, SVP Conference/Events
Lawrence M Kimmel, CEO

Focuses on innovative solutions for the warehouse, distribution, operations, and ecommerce
needs in the ever-changing world of operations
and fulfillment.
10M Attendees
Frequency: Annual/April

6244 New York Nonprofit Conference
Direct Marketing Association
1120 Avenue of Americas
New York, NY 10036-6700

212-768-7277
FAX 212-302-6714
E-Mail: dmaconferences@the-dma.org
Home Page: www.the-dma.org

Julie Hogan, SVP Conference/Events

Discover which acknowledgement programs
work best and why, increase revenue with
membership options-as well as traditional fundraising appeals, learn how the Internet and
e-mail campaigns can improve fundraising,
lower costs and increase advocacy.
10M Attendees

Directories & Databases

6245 Adweek Directory
Prometheus Global Media
770 Broadway
New York, NY 10003-9595

212-493-4100
FAX 646-654-5368
Home Page: www.prometheusgm.com

Richard D. Beckman, CEO
James A. Finkelstein, Chairman
Madeline Krakowsky, Vice President
Circulation
Tracy Brater, Executive Director Creative
Service

Adweek Directories Online is where you will
find searchable databases with comprehensive

information on ad agencies, brand marketers
and multicultural media.
Frequency: Annual
Circulation: 800
Founded in 1981

6246 Annual Guide to Telemarketing
Marketing Logistics
1460 Cloverdale Avenue
Highland Park, IL 60035-2817

847-831-1575

Arnold Fishman, Editor

About 400 telemarketing services bureaus in
the United States.
Cost: $475.00
Frequency: Irregular

6247 Art Directors Annual
Art Directors Club
106 W 29th St
New York, NY 10001-5301

212-643-1440
FAX 212-643-4266
E-Mail: info@adcglobal.org
Home Page: www.adcglobal.org

Ami Brophy, CEO
Myrna Davis, Executive Director

Innovative advertising, design, publishing,
photography, illustration, film, video, and interactive media.
Cost: $65.00
520 Members
Circulation: 7,000
Mailing list available for rent

6248 Associations Yellow Book
Leadership Directories
104 5th Ave
New York, NY 10011-6901

212-627-4140
FAX 212-645-0931
E-Mail:
associations@leadershipdirectories.com
Home Page: www.leadershipdirectories.com

David Hurvitz, CEO
James M Petrie, Associate Publisher

Contact information for over 41,000 officers
and board members at 1,000 trade and profes-
sional associations, coalitions, PACs, and foun-
dations.
Cost: $245.00
1,300 Pages
Frequency: SemiAnnual
ISSN: 1054-4070
Founded in 1991
*Mailing list available for rent: 37,000 names at
$125 per M*

6249 Catalog Success
North American Publishing Company
4001 S Business Park Avenue
Marshfield, WI 54449-9027

715-387-3400
FAX 715-486-4185
E-Mail: daniel.gust@donnelleymarketing.com
Home Page: www.catalogsuccess.com

Putting marketing management to the test.
Frequency: Monthly
ISSN: 1524-2307
Printed in 4 colors

6250 Corporate Yellow Book
Leadership Directories
104 5th Ave
New York, NY 10011-6901

212-627-4140
FAX 212-645-0931
E-Mail: corporate@leadershipdirectories.com
Home Page: www.leadershipdirectories.com

David Hurvitz, CEO

Contact information for over 48,000 executives
at over 1,000 companies and more than 9,000
board members and their outside affiliations.
Cost: $360.00
1,400 Pages
Frequency: Quarterly
ISSN: 1058-2098
Founded in 1986
*Mailing list available for rent: 50,000 names at
$105 per M*

6251 Customer Interaction Solutions
Technology Marketing Corporation
1 Technology Plz
Norwalk, CT 06854-1936

203-852-6800
800-243-6002
FAX 203-853-2845
Home Page: www.tmcnet.com

Rich Tehrani, CEO
Tracy Schelmetic, Editor

Over 1100 domestic and foreign suppliers of
equipment products and services to the tele-
communications/telemarketing industry.
Cost: $25.00
Frequency: Annual/December/89 Pages
Founded in 1982
*Mailing list available for rent: 63,000 names at
$25 per M*

6252 D&B Million Dollar Database
Dun & Bradstreet Information Service
3 Sylvan Way
Parsippany, NJ 07054-3822

973-605-6000
800-526-0651
FAX 973-605-9630

160,000 public and private businesses with either a net worth of 500,000 or more, 250
emplyees at that location or 25,000,000 or
more in sales volume.

**6253 D&B Million Dollar Database:
International**
Dun & Bradstreet Information Service
3 Sylvan Way
Parsippany, NJ 07054-3822

973-605-6000
800-526-0651
FAX 973-605-9630

50,000 top corporations, utilities, transportation companies, bank and trust companies,
stock brolers, mutual and stock insurance companies, wholesalers, retailers, and domestic
susidiaries of foreign corporations.

6254 Direct Mail Service
Information Resource Group
50495 Corporate Drive
Suite 112
Shelby Township, MI 48315-3132

586-726-6237

This database offers over 1,000,000 MIS and
corporate professionals at over 150,000 companies throughout the United States.
Cost: $150.00

6255 Direct Selling World Directory
World Federation of Direct Selling
Association

1776 K St NW
Suite 600
Washington, DC 20006-2304

202-546-5330
FAX 202-463-4569
Home Page: www.dsa.org

Over 50 direct selling associations and over 1,000 associated member companies are offered in this comprehensive directory.
90 Pages
Frequency: Annual

6256 Directory of Mail Order Catalogs
Grey House Publishing
4919 Route 22
PO Box 56
Amenia, NY 12501

518-789-8700
800-562-2139
FAX 845-373-6390
E-Mail: books@greyhouse.com
Home Page: www.greyhouse.com
Social Media: *Facebook, Twitter*

Leslie Mackenzie, Publisher
Richard Gottlieb, Editor

The premier source of information on the mail order catalog industry. Covers over 13,000 consumer and business catalog companies with 44 different product chapters from Animals to Toys and Games.
Cost: $395.00
1900 Pages
Frequency: Annual
ISBN: 1-592373-96-8
Founded in 1981

6257 Directory of Mail Order Catalogs - Online Database
Grey House Publishing
4919 Route 22
PO Box 56
Amenia, NY 12501

518-789-8700
800-562-2139
FAX 845-373-6390
E-Mail: gold@greyhouse.com
Home Page: http://gold.greyhouse.com
Social Media: *Facebook, Twitter*

Leslie Mackenzie, Publisher
Richard Gottlieb, Editor

Reach over 10,000 consumer catalog companies in one easy-to-use source with The Directory of Mail Order Catalogs - Online Database. Filled with business-building detail, each company profile gives you the information you need to access that organization quickly and easily. Listings provide key contacts, sales volume, employee size, printing information, circulation, list data, product descriptions and much more.
Frequency: Annual
Founded in 1981

6258 Directory of Major Mailers
North American Publishing Company
1500 Spring Garden St
Suite 1200
Philadelphia, PA 19130-4094

215-238-5300
FAX 215-238-5342

Ned S Borowsky, CEO

Offers over 7,500 major direct mailers and the key players with their names, addresses, phones and fax numbers, executive contacts, types of business, and the size of the house file. The Directory also contains actual reproductions of these mailings - letters, envelopes, order cards, brochures, etc. You'll see what was mailed,

what worked and what didn't.
Cost: $395.00
Frequency: Annual
Founded in 1994
Mailing list available for rent
Printed in one color on matte stock

6259 International Job Finder: Where the Jobs are Worldwide
Planning/Communications
7215 Oak Ave
River Forest, IL 60305-1935

708-366-5200
888-366-5200
FAX 708-366-5280
E-Mail: dl@planningcommunications.com
Home Page:
www.planningcommunications.com

Daniel Lauber, President

Describes in detail over 1,200 print and online sources of jobs outside the USA; newsletters, magazines, directories, web sites, online job databases, resume banks, email job alerts, and salary surveys.
Cost: $19.95
384 Pages
Frequency: Every 4 Years
Circulation: 8,000
ISBN: 1-884587-10-0
Founded in 2002
Printed in one color on matte stock

6260 Nonprofit Sector Yellow Book
Leadership Directories
104 5th Ave
New York, NY 10011-6901

212-627-4140
FAX 212-645-0931
E-Mail: info@leadershipdirectories.com
Home Page: www.leadershipdirectories.com

David Hurvitz, CEO
James M Petrie, Associate Publisher

Contact information for over 51,000 nonprofit executives and trustees at over 1,300 nonprofit organizations, including foundations, colleges and universities, museums, performing arts group and centers, medical institutions, library systems, preparatory schools, and charitable service organizations.
Cost: $245.00
1,200 Pages
Frequency: SemiAnnual
ISSN: 1520-9148
Founded in 1999
Mailing list available for rent: 45,000 names at $125 per M

6261 Nonprofits Job Finder: Where the Jobs are in Charities and Nonprofits
Planning/Communications
7215 Oak Ave
River Forest, IL 60305-1935

708-366-5200
888-366-5200
FAX 708-366-5280
E-Mail: dl@planningcommunications.com
Home Page:
www.planningcommunications.com

Daniel Lauber, President

Describes in detail over 1,500 sources of jobs in the nonprofit sectors job database online, resume banks, email job alerts, directories, salary surveys, newsletters, and magazines.
Cost: $17.95
300 Pages
Circulation: 6,000
ISBN: 1-884587-06-2
Founded in 2005
Printed in one color on matte stock

6262 Who's Who: MASA Buyer's Guide to Blue Ribbon Mailing Services
Mailing & Fulfillment Service Association
1421 Prince Street
Suite 410
Alexandria, VA 22314-2806

703-836-9200
FAX 703-548-8204
E-Mail: mfsa-mail@mfsanet.org
Home Page: www.mfsanet.org

Ken Garner, President
Bill Stevenson, Director Marketing

Offers a detailed listing of suppliers of equipment, products and services to the direct mail industry, most containing a description of the specific products they provide.
Frequency: Annual

6263 Yellow Pages & Directory Report
Simba Information
11200 Rockville Pike
Suite 504
Rockville, MD 20852

240-747-3096
877-352-2021
FAX 340-747-3004
E-Mail: dgoddard@imslocalsearch.com
Home Page:
www.yellowpagesanddirectoryreport.com
Social Media: *Facebook, Twitter, LinkedIn*

David Goddard, EVP/Senior Analyst/Editor
Kyle Kroll, President

Covers directory publishing, advertising, printing and releases from national yellow pages accounts.
Cost: $695.00

Industry Web Sites

6264 http://gold.greyhouse.com
G.O.L.D Grey House OnLine Databases

Grey House Publishing's online database platform, GOLD, offers Quick Search, Keyword Search and Expert Search for most business sectors including direct marketing and public relations markets. The GOLD platform makes finding the information you need quick and easy - whether you're a novice searcher or an experienced database user. All of Grey House's directory products are available for subscription on the GOLD platform.

6265 www.adweek.com
Adweek

Leading decision makers in the advertising and marketing field go to Adweek.com everyday for breaking news, insight, buzz, opinion, analysis, research and classifieds. The resources of all six regional editions of Adweek, as well as the national edition of Brandweek are combined with the knowledge of our online editors and the multimedia-interactive capabilities of the web to deliver vital information quickly and effectively to our target audience.

6266 www.amma.org
Advertising Mail Marketing Association

Represents the interests of those who use mail for fundraising or business purposes.

6267 www.ataconnect.org
American Teleservices Association

Represents the call centers, trainers, consultants and equipment suppliers that initiate, facilitate and generate telephone, Internet and e-mail sales, service and support.

6268 www.cadm.org
Chicago Association of Direct Marketing

Promotes the interests of Chicago's direct marketing professionals. Fosters member development through business, educational and social opportunities and provides a high-quality forum for the exchange of ideas by direct marketing professionals.

6269 www.cyberdirect.com/ADMA
Cohn & Wells

Members are direct response advertising agencies.

6270 www.dmad.org
Direct Marketing Association of Detroit

Not for profit organization dedicated to providing networking and educational opportunities to a dynamic group of direct marketing professionals. It is the premier resource for direct response marketing information, and is committed to recognizing outstanding direct marketing achievements in the Detroit area.

6271 www.dmnews.com
Haymarket Media, Inc.
114 W 26th St.
4th Fl.
New York, NY 10001

646-638-6000

Ginger Conlon, Editor-in-Chief
Al Urbanski, Senior Editor
Natasha Smith, Senior Editor

Direct Marketing News covers the latest trends, proven strategies and essential technologies.

6272 www.dsa.org
Direct Selling Association

National trade association of the leading firms that manufacture and distribute goods and services sold directly to consumers. More than 150 companies are members of the association, including many well-known brand names. The association's mission is to protect, serve and promote the effectiveness of member companies and the independent business people they represent.

6273 www.fraudandtheftinfo.com
Fraud & Theft Information Bureau

Provides problem solving, crime prevention, money saving manuals and fraud blocker databases.

6274 www.greyhouse.com
Grey House Publishing

Authoritative reference directories for most business sectors including direct marketing and public relations markets. Users can search the online databases with varied search criteria allowing for custom searches by product category, geographic area, sales volume, keyword, subject and more. Full Grey House catalog and online ordering also available.

6275 www.ims-lists.com/links
IMS Direct Marketing Links
Professional associations links.

6276 www.marketingpower.com
American Marketing Association

A professional association for individuals and organizations involved in the practice, teaching and study of marketing worldwide.

6277 www.mdma.org
Midwest Direct Marketing Association

Advancing the professional and ethical practice of direct response marketing by members throughout the Upper Midwest. The MDMA seeks to accomplish this by sponsoring educational and professional networking events to share and encourage the best practices in

telemarketing, direct mail and online marketing techniques and strategies.

6278 www.mfsanet.org
Mailing & Fulfillment Service Association

The national trade association for the mailing and fulfillment services industry.

6279 www.nedma.com
New England Direct Marketing Association

6280 www.nmoa.org
National Mail Order Association

Offers the strongest and lowest cost means for people to come together for the purpose of conducting business and creating sales. Small to medium sized organizations come for education, information, ideas, resources and new contacts.

6281 www.the-dma.org
Direct Marketing Association

Trade association in the direct marketing field with more than 3,500 member companies from the United States and 54 foreign nations. Included are catalogers, direct marketers from consumer to business-to-business, publishers, retail stores as well as service industries that support them.

Associations

6282 Academy of Managed Care Pharmacy
100 N Pitt St
Suite 400
Alexandria, VA 22314-3141

703-683-8416
800-827-2627
FAX 703-683-8417
E-Mail: sandres@amcp.org
Home Page: www.amcp.org
Social Media: *Facebook, Twitter, LinkedIn*

Judy Cahill, Executive Director
Elaine Manieri, Director
Cathryn A Carroll, PhD, Treasurer

Promotes the development and application of appropriate and accessible medication therapy. Represents professional pharmacists and associates practicing in managed care settings.
4800 Members
Founded in 1989
Mailing list available for rent

6283 Academy of Managed Care Pharmacy (AMCP)
100 North Pitt Street
Suite 400
Alexandria, VA 22314

703-683-8416
800-827-2627
FAX 703-683-8417
E-Mail: memberservices@amcp.org
Home Page: www.amcp.org
Social Media: *Facebook, Twitter, LinkedIn*

Dana Davis McCormick, President
Raulo S Frear, President Elect
Kim A. Caldwell, Past President
Stanley E. Ferrell, Director
H Eric Cannon, Treasurer
6000 Members

6284 Accreditation Council for Pharmacy Education
135 S. LaSalle Street
Suite 4100
Chicago, IL 60603-4810

312-664-3575
FAX 312-664-4652
E-Mail: info@acpe-accredit.org
Home Page: www.acpe-accredit.org
Social Media: *Facebook*

Janet Cline, Chair
Tian Merren Owens, Vice Chair
Stephanie F. Gardner, President
Bruce Canaday, Vice President
Michael A. Mone, Secretary/Treasurer

A nonprofit accreditation national agency.
Founded in 1932

6285 American Association of Colleges of Pharmacy
1727 King St
Alexandria, VA 22314-2700

703-739-2330
FAX 703-836-8982
E-Mail: mail@aacp.org
Home Page: www.aacp.org
Social Media: *Facebook, Twitter, LinkedIn, YouTube*

Lucinda Maine, Executive VP
Kenneth W Miller, Senior VP
Daniel J Cassidy, COO

National organization representing the interests of pharmaceutical education and educators. Comprising all 111 US pharmacy colleges and schools including more than 5,000 faculty, 50,000 students enrolled in professional programs and 4,000 individuals pursuing graduate

study. AACP is committed to excellence in pharmaceutical education.
3670 Members
Founded in 1900
Mailing list available for rent

6286 American Association of Pharmaceutical Scientists
2107 Wilson Blvd
Suite 700
Arlington, VA 22201-3042

703-243-2800
FAX 703-243-9650
E-Mail: aaps@aaps.org
Home Page: www.aaps.org
Social Media: *Facebook, Twitter, LinkedIn, YouTube*

Gene Fiese, President
Patrick Deluca, President Elect
Peter Inchauteguiz, Director Marketing
James Greif, Communcations Specialist
Maureen Downs, Director of Finance

Aims to advance science through the open exchange of scientific knowledge, serve as an information resource and contribute to human health through pharmaceutical research and development.
11000 Members
Founded in 1986
Mailing list available for rent

6287 American Association of Pharmacy Technicians (AAPT)
PO Box 1447
Greensboro, NC 27402

336-333-9356
877-368-4771
FAX 336-333-9068
E-Mail: aapt@pharmacytechnician.com
Home Page: www.pharmacytechnician.com
Social Media: *Facebook, Twitter*

Judy Neville, BS, CPhT, President
Susan Jeffery, VP
Danalynne Young, BS, CPhT, Secretary
Bobbie Craddock, CPhT, Treasurer

Provides leadership and represents the interests of its members to the public as well as health care organizations. Promotes safe efficacious and cost effective dispensing, distribution and use of medications. Provides continuing education programs and services to help technicians update their skills and keep pace with changes in pharmacy services. Promotes pharmacy technicians as an integral part of the patient care team.
850 Members
Founded in 1979

6288 American Association of Pharmacy Technicia
P.O. Box 1447
Greensboro, NC 27402

336-333-9356
877-368-4771
FAX 336-333-9068
E-Mail: aapt@pharmacytechnician.com
Home Page: www.pharmacytechnician.com
Social Media: *Facebook, Twitter*

Judy Neville, BS, CPhT, President
Judy Neville, Vice President
Ann Barlow Oberg, Immediate Past President
Danalynne Young, BS, CPhT, Secretary
Bobbie Craddock, Treasurer
Founded in 1979

6289 American Chemical Society
1155 16th St Nw
Washington, DC 20036-4892

202-872-4600
800-333-9511
FAX 202-872-4615

E-Mail: service@acs.org
Home Page: www.acs.org
Social Media: *Facebook, Twitter, LinkedIn, Google+*

Madeleine Jacobs, CEO
Diane Grob Schmidt, President
John Crum, Executive Director
Thomas R Gilbert, Director

Supports scientists and other professionals working in the field of drug discovery. Publishes monthly magazine.
159K Members
Founded in 1876

6290 American Clinical Laboratory Association
1100 New York Ave Nw
Suite 880
Washington, DC 20005-6172

202-637-9466
FAX 202-637-2050
E-Mail: info@clinical-labs.org
Home Page: www.acla.com
Social Media: *Facebook, Twitter, RSS*

Alan Mertz, President
Julie Khani, SVP
Francesca Fierro O'Reilly, Vice President Government Affairs
Thomas Sparkman, Vice President Government Affairs
Peter M Kazon, Legal Counsel

Members are clinical laboratories licensed and regulated under medicare and the interstate laboratory program.
Founded in 1971

6291 American College of Apothecaries
2830 Summer Oaks Dr
Bartlett, TN 38134-3811

901-383-8119
FAX 901-383-8882
E-Mail: aca@acainfo.org
Home Page: www.acainfo.org

D C Huffman, Executive VP
Jeffrey Denton, President
Randall S Myers, VP

Disseminates and translates knowledge, research data and recent developments in professional pharmacy practice for the benefit of pharmacists, pharmacy students and the public. This is achieved through regular distribution of periodicals, development of major publications and continuing education courses on clinical and administrative topics and conducting educational conferences.
1M Members
Founded in 1940

6292 American College of Clinical Pharmacology
21750 Red Rum Drive
Suite 137
Ashburn, VA 20147

571-291-3493
FAX 571-918-4167
E-Mail: Info@ACCP1.org
Home Page: www.accp1.org
Social Media: *Facebook, LinkedIn*

Lisa Von Moltke, President
Krista K Levy, Executive Director
Keri J Sperry, Director of Education
Erica Serow, Manager of meetings

A national organization of clinical pharmacology healthcare professionals who seek to advance clinical pharmacology.
Founded in 1969

6293 American College of Clinical Pharmacy

13000 W. 87th Street Parkway
Suite 650
Lenexa, KS 66215-4530

913-492-3311
FAX 913-492-0088
E-Mail: accp@accp.com
Home Page: www.accp.com

Michael S Maddux, Pharm.D., FCCP, Executive Director

Professional and scientific society that provides leadership, education, advocacy and resources enabling clinical pharmacists to achieve excellence in practice and research. Membership is composed of practitioners, scientists, educators, administrators, students, residents, fellows and others committed to excellence in clinical pharmacy and patient pharmacotherapy.
Founded in 1979

6294 American College of Medical Quality

5272 River Road
Suite 630
Bethesda, MD 20816

301-718-6516
800-924-2149
FAX 301-656-0989
E-Mail: acmq@acmq.org
Home Page: www.acmq.org
Social Media: *Facebook, LinkedIn*

Prathibha Varkey, President
Mark Lyles, MD, MBA, FACMQ, President-Elect
Donald E Casey, Jr MD, MPH, VP

The mission of the American College of Medical Quality is to provide leadership and education in healthcare quality management.
900 Members
Founded in 1972

6295 American Council on Pharmaceutical Education

20 N Clark Street
Suite 2500
Chicago, IL 60602

312-664-3575
FAX 312-664-4652

Robert Buchman, Executive Director

Promotes the education of pharmaceutical medicine.

6296 American Institute of the History of Pharmacy

777 Highland Ave
Madison, WI 53705-2222

608-262-5378
FAX 608-262-3397
E-Mail: Institute@aihp.org
Home Page: www.pharmacy.wisc.edu/aihp
Social Media: *Facebook, LinkedIn*

Dr. Gregory Higby, Executive Director
Dr. Elaine C Stroud, Assistant Director
Beth D Fisher, Assoc. Dir. Curatorial Affairs
Joseph Gabriel, Ph.D., Historian
William Zellmer, President

Non-profit national organization devoted to advancing knowledge and understanding of the place of pharmacy in history. Contributes to the understanding of the development of civilization by fostering the creation, preservation, and dissemination of knowledge concerning the history and related humanistic aspects of the pharmaceutical field.
900 Members
Founded in 1941

6297 American Pharmacists Association

2215 Constitution Ave NW
Washington, DC 20037-2985

202-628-4410
800-237-2742
FAX 202-783-2351
E-Mail: infocenter@aphanet.org
Home Page: www.pharmacist.com
Social Media: *Facebook, Twitter, LinkedIn, YouTube, RSS*

Thomas E Menighan, CEO
Elizabeth Keyes, Chief Operating Officer
Joseph J Janela, CFO

It is the largest association of pharmacists in the United States, whose mission is to provide information, education, and advocacy to empower its members to improve medication use and advance patient care.
60000 Members
Founded in 1852

6298 American Public Health Association

800 I Street NW
Washington, DC 20001-3710

202-777-2742
FAX 202-777-2534
E-Mail: coments@apha.org
Home Page: www.apha.org
Social Media: *Facebook, Twitter*

Jay M Bernhardt, Vice Chair
Gene Lutz, President
Georges Benjamin, Executive Director
Jose F Cordero, Member Services
Louise A Anderson, Director Operations

Brings together researchers, health service providers, administrators, teachers and other health workers in a unique, multidisciplinary environment of professional exchange, study and action in the effort to prevent disease and promote health.
50000 Members
Founded in 1872

6299 American Society for Automation in Pharmacy

492 Norristown Road
Suite 160
Blue Bell, PA 19422

610-825-7783
FAX 610-825-7641
Home Page: www.asapnet.org

Tammy Devine, President
Tim Tannert, R.Ph, Vice President
Chuck Welch, Secretary/Treasurer

Assists its members in advancing the application of computer technology in the pharmacist's role as care giver, in the efficient operation of a pharmacy and promoting standards, legislation and guidelines.
350 Members
Founded in 1988

6300 American Society for Clinical Pharmacology and Therapeutics

528 N Washington St
Alexandria, VA 22314

703-836-6981
E-Mail: info@ascpt.org
Home Page: www.ascpt.org
Social Media: *Facebook, Twitter, LinkedIn, Google+*

Mario L Rocci, Jr., PhD, President
Julie A Johnson, PharmD, President Elect
Russ B. Altman, Immediate Past President
Gregory L. Kearns, Secretary/Treasurer
Sharon J. Swan, Chief Executive Officer

Focuses on improving the understanding and use of existing drug therapies and developing safe and more effective treatments for the future.
2200 Members
Founded in 1900

6301 American Society for Parenteral & Enteral Nutrition

8630 Fenton Street
Suite 412
Silver Spring, MD 20910

301-587-6315
800-727-4567
FAX 301-587-2365
E-Mail: aspen@nutr.org
Home Page: www.nutritioncare.org
Social Media: *Facebook, Twitter, LinkedIn, YouTube*

Marion F Winkler, President
Vincent W Vanek, VP
Robin Kriegel, CAE, Executive Director
Joanne Kieffer, Director Finance

Promotes professional communication among and within professional disciplines in the broad field of clinical nutrition including parenteral and enteral nutrition (tube feeding) through national and regional meetings, local seminars, scientific, clinical and educational exhibits and publications.
6000 Members
Founded in 1979

6302 American Society for Pharmacy Law

3085 Stevenson Drive
Suite 200
Springfield, IL 62703

217-529-6948
FAX 217-529-9120
E-Mail: info@aspl.org
Home Page: www.aspl.org
Social Media: *LinkedIn*

Laura Carpenter, President
Brian Guthrie, Director
Janet Bascom, Member Services Director
Nathela Chatara, CAE, Executive Director
Jim Boyd, Treasurer

An organization of pharmacists and lawyers who are interested in the law as it applies to the pharmacy industry.
Founded in 1974

6303 American Society of Consultant Pharmacists

1321 Duke St
Alexandria, VA 22314-3563

703-739-1300
800-355-2727
FAX 703-739-1321
E-Mail: info@ascp.com
Home Page: www.ascp.com
Social Media: *Facebook, Twitter, LinkedIn, YouTube*

Frank Grosso, RPh?, Executive Director and CEO
Phylliss M Moret, Associate Executive Director/COO
Linda Williams, Director Communications/Marketing
Claudia Schlosberg, Director, Policy/Advocacy
Trish D'Antonio, Director, Education

The international professional association that provides leadership, education, advocacy and resources to advance the practice of senior care pharmacy.
6500+ Members
Founded in 1969

6304 American Society of Consultant Pharmacists Foundation
1321 Duke Street
Alexandria, VA 22314-3563

703-739-1300
800-355-2727
FAX 703-739-1500
E-Mail: info@ascpfoundation.org
Home Page: www.ascpfoundation.org

Nancy L Losben, Chairman
Frank Grosso, Executive Director
Jan Allen, Treasurer
Carla McSpadden, Board of Trustees
Ross W. Brickley, Board of Trustees

A charitable organization affiliated with the American Society of Consultant Pharmacists. It sponsors research, administers programs, holds traineeships in pharmacy practice, and performs other educational and outreach functions.
Founded in 1982

6305 American Society of Health-System Pharmacists
7272 Wisconsin Ave
Bethesda, MD 20814-4861

301-657-3000
866-279-0681
FAX 301-664-8877
Home Page: www.ashp.org
Social Media: *Facebook, Twitter, LinkedIn, YouTube*

John A Armitstead, President
Paul W Abramowitz, EVP/CEO

An association that brings together health-system pharmacists who practice in hospitals, health maintenance organizations, long-term care facilities, home care, and other components of health care systems. ASHSP has a long history of medication error prevention efforts and believe the mission of pharmacists is to help people make the best use of medicines.
31M Members
Founded in 1942
Mailing list available for rent

6306 American Society of Pharmacognosy

E-Mail: j.porter@usciences.edu
Home Page: www.pharmacognosy.us/
Social Media: *Facebook, Twitter, LinkedIn, RSS*

Brad Moore, Chair
Phil Crews, President
Ed Kennelly, Vice President
William J. Keller, Secretary
Jim McAlpine, Treasurer

A scientific society that promotes the growth and development of pharmacognosy through presentation of research achievements and publication of meritous research.
1100 Members
Founded in 1959

6307 Aspirin Foundation of America
529 14th St NW
Suite 807
Washington, DC 20045-1801

202-393-0000
800-432-3247
FAX 202-737-8406
E-Mail: info@aspirin.org
Home Page: www.aspirin.org

A non-profit educational foundation with a membership of companies engaged in the manufacture, preparation, compounding or processing of aspirin and aspirin products. AFA serves as a central source of information on the health benefits of aspirin and aspirin products, when used as directed.
Founded in 1981

6308 Association of Clinical Research Professionals
99 Canal Center Plaza
Suite 200
Alexandria, VA 22314

703-254-8100
FAX 703-254-8101
E-Mail: office@acrpnet.org
Home Page: www.acrpnet.org
Social Media: *Facebook, Twitter, LinkedIn, YouTube*

Norbert Clemens, MD, PhD, CPI, Chair, Board of Trustees
Thomas L Adams, CAE, President/CEO
James Thomasell, Director Finance

The Academy of Clinical Research Professionals and the Academy of Pharmaceutical Physician and Investigators are affiliates of ACRP. The Academy asministers non-physician certification programs and governmental affairs activities. APPI represents all physician members of ACRP.
21000 Members
Founded in 1976

6309 Board of Pharmacy Specialties
2215 Constitution Avenue NW
Washington, DC 20037-2985

202-429-7591
FAX 202-429-6304
Home Page: www.bpsweb.org
Social Media: *Facebook, Twitter, YouTube*

Sharon M Durfee, Chair
William Evans, Chair Elect

A post-licensure certification agency that improves patient care bypromoting the recognition and value of specialized training, knowledge, and skills in pharmacy and specialty board certification of pharmacists.
Founded in 1973

6310 College of Psychiatric and Neurologic Pharmacists
8055 O Street
Suite S113
Lincoln, NE 68510

402-476-1677
FAX 888-551-7617
E-Mail: info@cpnp.org
Home Page: www.cpnp.org
Social Media: *Facebook, Twitter, LinkedIn, YouTube, Google+*

Ray Love, President
Christopher Thomas, President-Elect
Steven Burghart, Past President
Jennifer Zacher, PharmD, BCPP, Secretary
Robert Haight, PharmD, BCPP, Treasurer

Organization that advances the reach and practice of neuropsychiatric pharmacists.
Founded in 1998

6311 Drug Information Association
800 Enterprise Road
Suite 200
Horsham, PA 19044-3595

215-442-6100
FAX 215-442-6199
E-Mail: dia@diahome.org
Home Page: www.diaglobal.org
Social Media: *Facebook, Twitter, LinkedIn*

Paul Pomerantz BA MBA, Worldwide Executive Director
Lisa Zoks BA, Worldwide Dir Met/Communications

Provides a neutral global forum for the exchange and dissemination of information on the discovery, development, evaluation and utilization of medicines and related health care technologies. Through these activities the DIA

provides development opportunities for its members.
20000 Members
Founded in 1964

6312 Drug, Chemical & Associated Technologies Association
One Union St
Suite 208
Robbinsville, NJ 8691

609-208-1888
800-640-3228
FAX 609-208-0599
Home Page: www.dcat.org
Social Media: *Facebook, LinkedIn*

George Svokos, President
Folker Ruchatz, First Vice President
Milton Boyer, Second Vice President
Margaret M. Timony, Executive Director
David Beattie, Director

A nonprofit, member-supported business development association for the global pharmaceutical manufacturing industry.
Founded in 1890

6313 Drug, Chemical & Associated Technologies
One Union St
Suite 208
Robbinsville, NJ 08691-3162

609-208-1888
FAX 609-448-1944
Home Page: www.dcat.org

Margaret Timony, Executive Director
James K Martin, Senior Vice President
Bob Kanuga, Vice President

The premier business development association whose membership is comprised of companies that manufacture, distribute or provide services to the pharamceutical, chemical, nutritional and related industries.
Founded in 1890

6314 Federation of Pharmacy Networks
30131 Town Center Drive
Suite 100
Laguna Niguel, CA 92677

949-495-5257
FAX 949-495-1258
E-Mail: info@fpn.org
Home Page: www.fpn.org

Don Anderson, President
Tom Scono, Vice President
Carol Carlson, CEO
Cathi Clark, Secretary
Curtis Woods, Treasurer

An organization of independent pharmacy group purchasing organizations established for the purpose of providing a forum for its members to exchangeideas that promote, advance and ensure the future of independent pharmacy.

6315 Food & Drug Law Institute
1155 15th Street NW
Siute 910
Washington, DC 20005-2706

202-371-1420
800-956-6293
FAX 202-371-0649
E-Mail: comments@fdli.org
Home Page: www.fdli.org
Social Media: *Facebook, LinkedIn*

Amy Comstock Rick, JD, President & CEO
Iris V. Stratton CPA, VP Finance & Administration
Michael Sprott, Membership Manager

A nonprofit, educational organization dedicated to improving the understanding of the laws, regulations, and policies affecting health care technologies, food and cosmetics. FDLI is neu-

tral, nonpartisan and does not lobby or advocate positions on any issue.
550+ Members
Founded in 1949

6316 Food and Drug Administration
10903 New Hampshire Avenue
Silver Spring, MD 20993

888-463-6332
Home Page: www.fda.gov
Social Media: *Facebook, Twitter, YouTube, Flickr*

Margaret A Hamburg, Commissioner of Food and Drugs
Walter S Harris, Deputy Commissioner for Operations
James Tyler, Chief Financial Officer
Denise Esposito, Chief of Staff
Mitch Zeller, Director

A federal agency of the United States Department of Health and Human Services that is responsible for protecting and promoting public health through the regulation and supervision of food safety, tobacco products, dietary supplements, prescription and over-the counter medications, vaccines, animal foods, veterinary products, etc.

6317 Generic Pharmaceutical Association
777 Sixth Street, NW
Suite 510
Washington, DC 20001

202-249-7100
FAX 202-249-7105
E-Mail: info@gphaonline.org
Home Page: www.gphaonline.org
Social Media: *Facebook, Twitter, LinkedIn, Google+, YouTube*

Chester Davis, Jr, President
David Gaugh, R.Ph, Senior Vice President
Doug Boothe, Secretary/Treasurer

Represents the manufacturers and distributors of finished generic pharmaceutical products, manufacturers and distributors of bulk active pharmaceutical chemicals, and suppliers of other goods and services to the generic pharmaceutical industry.

6318 Healthcare Distribution Management Association
901 N Glebe Rd
Suite 1000
Arlington, VA 22203-1853

703-787-0000
FAX 703-812-5282
Home Page: www.healthcaredistribution.org
Social Media: *Twitter, LinkedIn*

Ted Scherr, President/CEO
Nancy E Hanagan, Executive VP/COO
Susan Mirvis, Senior VP Marketing/Communications

An organization representing all major constituents of healthcare product distribution management.

6319 Hematology/Oncology Pharmacy Association
8735 W. Higgins Road
Suite 300
Chicago, IL 60631

877-467-2791
E-Mail: board@hoparx.org
Home Page: www.hoparx.org

John Kuhn, Chair
Barry Goldspiel, Vice Chair
Scott Soefge, President
Helen Marshall, Secretary
Jolynn Sessions, Treasurer

A nonprofit professional organization created to help oncology and hematology.
Founded in 1995

6320 IAGIM
4901 Midtown Lane PBG
Florida 33418

561-376-2224
E-Mail: info@iagim.org
Home Page: www.iagim.org

Publishes generic pharmaceutical journals and technical handbooks.

6321 Independent Pharmacy Cooperative
1550 Columbus St
Sun Prairie, WI 53590-3901

608-825-9556
800-755-1531
FAX 608-825-1535
E-Mail: member.services@ipcrx.com
Home Page: www.ipcrx.com

Don Anderson, CEO
Gary Helgerson, COO
Chuck Benjamin, CFO

Provides member pharmacies with the lowest possible contract pricing on quality products and services.
4500 Members
Founded in 1984

6322 Institute for Safe Medication Practices
200 Lakeside Drive
Suite 200
Horsham, PA 19044

215-947-7797
FAX 215-914-1492
Home Page: www.ismp.org
Social Media: *Facebook, Twitter*

Michael R Cohen, RPh, MS, ScD, President
Mark J Cziraky, PharmD, Executive Vice President
Judy Smetzer, Vice President
Susan F. Paparella, Vice President
Russell H. Jenkins, Medical Director

A nonprofit organization devoted entirely to medication error prevention and safe medication use.
Founded in 1975

6323 International Pharmaceutical Excipients Council of the Americas
3138 N. 10th Street
Suite 500
Arlington, VA 22201

571-814-3449
FAX 703-525-5157
E-Mail: ipecamer@ipecamericas.org
Home Page: www.ipecamericas.org

Kimberly Beals, Executive Director
Tammy Kramer, Office Manager
Valeria Stewart, Training Coordinator
Linda A. Herzog, Technical & Membership Operations

Members are companies with an interest in the otherwise inert chemicals used as vehicles for medicines. IPEC is a federation of three independent regional associations headquartered in the US. and Japan. Each association focuses its attention on the applicable laws, regulations, science and business practices of its region to accomplish its members goals.
300 Members
Founded in 1991

6324 International Pharmaceutical Federation
2517 JP The Hague
The Netherlands

170-302-1970
FAX 170-302-1999
Home Page: www.fip.org
Social Media: *Facebook, Twitter, LinkedIn*

Luc Besancon, Chief Executive Officer
Rachel Van Kesteren, Executive Secretary
Paula Cohen, Secretary
Carola Van der Hoeff, Chief Operating Officer
Lin-Nam Wang, Communication Manager

An international federation of national organizations that represent pharmacists and pharmaceutical scientists.
Founded in 1912

6325 International Society for Pharmacoepidemiology
5272 River Road
Suite 630
Bethesda, MD 20816

301-718-6500
FAX 301-656-0989
E-Mail: ISPE@paimgmt.com
Home Page: www.pharmacoepi.org
Social Media: *Facebook, LinkedIn, YouTube*

Sonia Hernandez-Diaz, FISPE, President
Kiyoshi Kubota, FISPE, President Elect
Alison Bourke, Vice-President Finance
Mark H. Epstein, Executive Secretary
Andrew Jerdonek, Account Manager

A nonprofit international professional membership organization dedicated to advancing the health of the public by providing a forum for the open exchange of scientific information and for the development of policy, education, and advocacy for pharmacoepidemiology, pharmacovigilance, drug use research, outcomes research, comparative effectiveness research, and therapeutic risk management.

6326 International Society for Pharmaceutical Engineering (ISPE)
600 N. Westshore Blvd
Suite 900
Tampa, FL 33609

813-960-2105
FAX 813-264-2816
E-Mail: ask@ispe.org
Home Page: www.ispe.org
Social Media: *Facebook, Twitter, LinkedIn, Myspace, YouTube*

John Bournas, President & CEO
Victoria Smoke, CFO
Kindra Bess, Director, Event Operations
Gloria Hall, Editor & Director of Publications
Karleen Kos, VP of Member Relations

Global society for technical professionals in pharmaceutical manufacturing and drug development sectors.
2000 Members
Founded in 1980

6327 Joint Commission on the Accreditation of Healthcare Organizations
601 13th Street, NW
Suite 560
Washington, DC 20005

630-792-5800
FAX 630-792-5005
Home Page: www.jointcommission.org
Social Media: *Facebook, Twitter, LinkedIn, YouTube, Google+*

Mark R Chassin, President
Anne Marie Benedicto, Executive Vice President
Ann Jacobson, Executive Director

Amy Panagopoulos, Senior Director
Anita Giuntoli, Director

A nonprofit organization that accredits and certifies more than 20,500 health care organizations and programs in the United States.
Founded in 1951

6328 Lambda Kappa Sigma (International Professional Pharmacy Fraternity)

P.O. Box 570
Muskego, WI 53150-0570

800-LKS-1913
FAX 262-679-4558
E-Mail: ExecutiveDirector@lks.org
Home Page: www.lks.org
Social Media: *Facebook, Twitter*

Jenny Brandt, President
Patti Lozano, Vice President
Joan Rogala, Executive Director
Kim Hancock, Secretary
Sandy Mullen, Treasurer

An international professional pharmacy fraternity open to undergraduate and graduate pharmacy students and participating pharmacists. It also provides lifelong opportunities for women in pharmacy.
25000 Members
Founded in 1913

6329 National Alliance of State Pharmacy Associations

2530 Professional Road
Suite 202
Richmond, VA 23235

804-285-4431
804-612-6555
E-Mail: rsnead@naspa.us
Home Page: www.naspa.us
Social Media: *Facebook, Twitter, LinkedIn*

Mike Larkin Kansas, President
Pat Epple Pennsylvania, President-Elect
Joni Cover Nebraska, 1st Vice President
Jon Roth, 2nd Vice President
Louise Jones Alabama, Secretary/Treasurer

Promotes leadership, sharing, learning, and policy exchange among state pharmacy associations and pharmacy leaders nationwide, and provides education and advocacy to support pharmacists, patients, and communities working together to improve public health.
Founded in 1927

6330 National Alliance of State Pharmacy

2530 Professional Rd
Suite 202
Richmond, VA 23235-3217

804-285-4431
FAX 804-285-4227
E-Mail: becky@naspa.us
Home Page: www.naspa.us
Social Media: *Twitter*

Rebecca Snead, Executive Director
Joni Cover Nebraska, First VP
400 Members
Founded in 1927

6331 National Association of Boards of Pharmacy

1600 Feehanville Dr
Mount Prospect, IL 60056

847-698-6227
800-774-6227
FAX 847-391-4502
E-Mail: custserv@nabp.net
Home Page: www.nabp.net
Social Media: *RSS*

Joseph L Adams, RPh, Chairperson
Edward G McGinley, MBA, RPh, President
Jeanne D Waggener, RPh, Treasurer

Serves all American boards of pharmacy in matters of interstate reciprocity of licensure and licensing as well as other matters of mutual concern.
Founded in 1904

6332 National Association of Chain Drug Stores

413 N Lee Street
PO Box 1417-D49
Alexandria, VA 22313-1480

703-549-3001
FAX 703-836-4869
Home Page: www.nacds.org
Social Media: *Facebook, Twitter, LinkedIn, YouTube*

Randy Edeker, Chairman
Martin Otto, Vice Chairman
Craig L Fuller, President/CEO
Mark Griffin, Director
David Bernauer, Treasurer

Association for manufacturers or suppliers of chain drug store equipment, supplies and services.
210 Members
Founded in 1933

6333 National Community Pharmacists Association

100 Daingerfield Road
Alexandria, VA 22314

703-683-8200
800-544-7447
FAX 703-683-3619
E-Mail: info@ncpanet.com
Home Page: www.ncpanet.org
Social Media: *Facebook, Twitter, Google+, YouTube*

Bradley Arthur, President
Bruce Roberts RPh, Executive VP/CEO

Represents pharmacy owners, managers and employees of nearly 25,000 independent community pharmacies across the US.
60000 Members
Founded in 1898

6334 National Council for Prescription Drug Programs

9240 E Raintree Dr
Scottsdale, AZ 85260-7518

480-477-1000
FAX 480-767-1042
E-Mail: info@ncpdp.org
Home Page: www.ncpdp.org

Lee Ann Stember, President
Dennis Kitterman, Director Marketing Communications
Phillip D Scott, SVP Sales/Marketing
Joanne Longie, VP Operations

Members are computer companies, drug manufacturers, drug store chains, drug wholesalers, insurers, mail order prescription drug companies, pharmaceutical claim processors, prescription drug providers, software vendors, service organizations, government agencies and others with a interest in drug program administration standardization.
1350 Members
Founded in 1977

6335 National Institute for Pharmacist Care Outcomes

100 Daingerfield Road
Alexandria, VA 22314

703-683-8200
FAX 703-683-3619
E-Mail: kathryn.kuhn@ncpanet.org

Home Page: www.ncpanet.org
Social Media: *Facebook, Twitter, Google+*

Kathryn Kuhn, Executive Director, NIPCO Programs
Eleanor Nespica, Coordinator, NIPCO Programs
Mike Clark, Manager
Bradley Arthur, President

The national accrediting organization for pharmacist care education and training programs leading to the pharmacist care diplomate credential. A leading authority in helping community pharmacists develop new market niches in disease management and wellness.

6336 National Pharmaceutical Alliance

427 King Street
Suite 222
Alexandria, VA 22314

703-836-8816
FAX 919-469-5858
Home Page: www.npa.org

Cristina Sizemore, Executive Director
Deborah Kline, Manager Communications

Represents the interests of small pharmaceutical companies and allied industries.
Founded in 1993

6337 National Pharmaceutical Association

107 Kilmayne Drive
Suite C
Cary, NC 27511

877-215-2091
FAX 919-469-5858
E-Mail: npha@npha.net
Home Page: www.npha.net
Social Media: *Facebook, Twitter*

Dr. Carleton Maxwell, President
Erica Hanesworth, President Elect
Cornetta Levi, Immediate Past-President
Gayle Tuckett, Secretary
Joseph T. Lee, Treasurer

A nationwide, professional organization of pharmacists.
Founded in 1950

6338 National Pharmaceutical Council

1717 Pennsylvania Ave., NW
Suite 800
Washington, DC 20006

703-620-6390
FAX 202-827-0314
E-Mail: info@npcnow.com
Home Page: www.npcnow.org
Social Media: *Facebook, Twitter, LinkedIn, YouTube*

Daniel Leonard, President
Pat Adams, VP Business Operations
Gary Persinger, VP Health Care Systems
Richard Levy, VP Scientific
Jeffery Warren, Senior Advisor

Represents major, research-intensive, pharmaceutical companies. Conducts national and state studies, holds educational forums and generates publications for consumer and for health care cost containment programs.
31 Members
Founded in 1953

6339 National Pharmacy Purchasing Association

4747 Morena Blvd
Suite 340
San Diego, CA 92117-3468

858-581-6373
888-544-6772
FAX 858-581-6372
E-Mail: info@pharmacypurchasing.com

Home Page: www.pharmacypurchasing.com
Social Media: *Facebook, Twitter*

Dale J Kroll, President & CEO
Francine Morgano, Vice President
Michael Thomas, Event & Editorial Assistant
Debby Flannery, Advisory Board
Deb Harden, Advisory Board

An association that promotes the profession of pharmacy purchasing and offers educational opportunities for pharmacy buyers. Members include pharmacy buyers and managers from private, nonprofit, or government-run institutional facilities that work to promote the profession of pharmacy purchasing and offerseducational opportunities for pharmacy buyers.
Founded in 1991

6340 National Pharmacy Technician Association
PO BOX 683148
Houston, TX 77268

888-247-8700
FAX 888-247-8706
E-Mail: mikej@pharmacytechnician.org
Home Page: www.pharmacytechnician.org
Social Media: *Facebook, Twitter, LinkedIn, YouTube, RSS*

Mike Johnston, Chairman
Robin Luke, President
Wendy Meigs, Board Member
Carol Reyes, Board Member
Rhonda Wilson, Board Member

The world's largest professional organization established specifically for pharmacy technicians.
Founded in 1999

6341 New York State Council of Health-Systems Pharmacists
210 Washington Ave
Albany, NY 12203

518-456-8819
518-456-8819
FAX 518-456-9319
E-Mail: nyschpweb@nyschp.org
Home Page: www.nyschp.org
Social Media: *Facebook, Twitter, LinkedIn*

Stephanie Seyse, President
Joseph Pinto, President Elect
Monica Mehta, Vice President
Shaun C. Flynn, Executive Director
Philip Manning, Treasurer

Provides leadership and resources to promote quality pharmaceuticalservices directed at appropriate medication therapy and positive patient outcomes.
2200 Members

6342 Pan American Health Organization
525 Twenty-third Street, N.W.
Washington, DC 20037

202-974-3000
FAX 202-974-3663
Home Page: www.paho.org
Social Media: *Facebook, Twitter, LinkedIn, YouTube, Flickr, RSS*

The world's oldest international public health agency that providestechnical cooperation and mobilizes partnerships to improve health and quality of life in the countries of the Americas.
Founded in 1902

6343 Parenteral Drug Association
3 Bethesda Metro Center
Suite 1500
Bethesda, MD 20814

301-860-0293
FAX 301-986-0296
E-Mail: info@pda.org

Home Page: www.pda.org
Social Media: *Twitter, LinkedIn, YouTube*

Vince R Anicetti, Chairman
Richard Jahnson, President and CEO
Wanda Neal-Ballard, Director Programs/Meetings
Lance K Hoboy, MBA, VP Finance
Matthew Clark, Director Marketing

A non-profit international association of scientists involved in the development, manufacture, quality control and regulation of pharmaceuticals/biopharmaceuticals and related products. The association also provides educational opportunities for government and university sectors that have a vocational interest in pharmaceutical/biopharmaceutical sciences and technology.
10500 Members
Founded in 1946

6344 Pediatric Pharmacy Advocacy Group
5865 Ridgeway Center Parkway
Suite 300
Memphis, TN 38120-4014

901-820-4434
FAX 901-767-0704
E-Mail: membership@ppag.org
Home Page: www.ppag.org
Social Media: *Facebook, Twitter, LinkedIn*

Jared Cash, PharmD, President
Lisa Lubsch, PharmD, President-Elect
Kimberly Novak, PharmD, Secretary
Jeffrey Low, Treasurer
Matthew R. Helms, Executive Director

A nonprofit organization that strives to improve the health of children.
800 Members
Founded in 1990

6345 Pennsylvania Pharmacists Association
508 North Third Street
Harrisburg, PA 17101

717-234-6151
E-Mail: ppa@papharmacists.com
Home Page: www.papharmacists.com
Social Media: *Facebook, Twitter, LinkedIn, YouTube, Flickr*

Donna Hazel, President
Eric Pusey, President-Elect
Nicholas Leon, First Vice President
Nicholas Leon, Second Vice President
Eric Esterbrook, Immediate Past President

A professional membership society of registered pharmacists, student pharmacists, pharmacy technicans, and others who reside, work, attend college,or are interested in pharmacy in Pennsylvania.
Founded in 1878

6346 Pharmaceutical Care Management Association
325 7th St. NW
9th Fl.
Washington, DC 20004

202-756-5700
FAX 202-756-5708
Home Page: www.pcmanet.org
Social Media: *Facebook, Twitter*

Mark Merritt, President & CEO
Brenda Palmer, Chief Financial Officer
Brian McCarthy, Chief Operating Officer

National association of pharmacy benefit managers.
Founded in 2009

6347 Pharmaceutical Outsourcing Management Association
8865 W Okeechobee Boulevard
Suite 202
West Palm Beach, FL 33411

561-795-5503
FAX 561-795-5503
Home Page: www.pomasite.com

Shannon Brome-Ward, President
Linda Wauk, VP
Charles Calvert, Treasurer
Fran Grote, Secretary

Established as a forum to exchange ideas and experiences about outsourcing in the pharmaceutical industry.
Founded in 1995

6348 Pharmaceutical Research and Manufacturers of America
950 F Street, NW
Suite 300
Washington, DC 20004

202-835-3400
E-Mail: newsroom@phrma.org
Home Page: www.phrma.org
Social Media: *Facebook, Twitter, YouTube, Flickr, Google+*

Kenneth C Frazier, Chairman
George A Scangos, Chairman Elect
Jack Bailey, President
Joaquin Duato, Treasurer

Mission is to conduct effective advocacy for public policies that encourage discovery of important new medicines for patients by pharmaceutical/biotechnology research companies.
Founded in 1958

6349 Pharmacy Benefit Management Institute, Inc .
2901 N Dallas Pkwy
Ste 420
Plano, TX 75093

480-730-0814
FAX 480-222-4229
E-Mail: jlutz@pbmi.com
Home Page: www.pbmi.com
Social Media: *LinkedIn*

Jane Lutz, Executive Director
Kathleen Fairman, Vice President
Linda DeChant, Director of Sales
Julie Blackman, Marketing Manager
Shelly Carey, Research Director

Pharmacy benefit management education, research, and consulting.

6350 Pharmacy Technician Certification Board
2215 Constitution Avenue NW
Suite 101
Washington, DC 20037

800-363-8012
FAX 202-888-1699
E-Mail: contact@ptcb.org
Home Page: www.ptcb.org
Social Media: *Facebook, Twitter*

Paul Abramowitz, Chair
Paul Abramowitz, Vice Chair
Thomas Menighan, Executive Vice President
Everett B. McAllister, Executive Director & CEO
Larry Wagenknecht, Treasurer

Develops, maintains, promotes, and administers a nationally accredited certification and recertification program for pharmacy technicians to enablethe most effective support of pharmacists to advance patient safety.
Founded in 1995

6351 Pinoy Pharmacy

Home Page: www.pinoypharmacy.com
Social Media: *Facebook, Twitter*

An online community for Filipino pharmacy
professionals around the world.

6352 Professional Compounding Centers of America

9901 South Wilcrest Drive
Houston, TX 77099

281-933-6948
800-331-2498
FAX 281-933-6627
E-Mail: customerservice@pccarx.com
Home Page: www.pccarx.com
Social Media: *Facebook, Twitter, LinkedIn, YouTube, Flickr*

Provides independent pharmacists with a complete support system forcompounding unique dosage forms.
3900 Members
Founded in 1981

6353 Regulatory Affairs Professionals Society

5635 Fishers Lane
Suite 550
Rockville, MA 20852

301-770-2920
FAX 301-770-2924
E-Mail: raps@raps.org
Home Page: www.raps.org
Social Media: *Facebook, Twitter, LinkedIn, YouTube, Google+, Flickr*

Donald A Middlebrook, Chairman
Rainer Voelksen, President
Martha A. Brumfield, President Elect
Salma Michor, Secretary/Treasurer
Gautam Maitra, Director

The largest global organization of and for those involved with the regulation of healthcare and related products, including medical devices, pharmaceuticals, biologics and nutritional products.
Founded in 1976

6354 Roundtable of Toxicology Consultants

P.O. Box 98224
Raleigh, NC 27624

E-Mail: toxconsultants@earthlink.net
Home Page: www.toxconsultants.com

Jane Allen, President
Joann Schuh, President Elect
Dave Hobson, Past President
Lori Dostal, Secretary
Merrill Osheroff, Treasurer

An organization of independently practicing toxicologists dedicatedto solving the problems for clients.
Founded in 1986

6355 Society for Laboratory Automation and Screening

100 Illinois Street
Ste. 242
St. Charles, IL 60174

630-256-7527
877-990-7527
E-Mail: slas@slas.org
Home Page: www.slas.org
Social Media: *Facebook, Twitter, LinkedIn, YouTube*

Dean Ho, Ph.D., President
Richard Eglen, Ph.D., Vice President
Alastair Binnie, Director
Michele A Cleary, Ph.D., Secretary
Mike Snowden, Ph.D., Treasurer

A global community of more than 18,000 scientists from academia, government and industry collectively focused on leveraging the power of technologyto achieve scientific objectives.
18000 Members
Founded in 2009

6356 Society of Critical Care Medicine

500 Midway Drive
Mount Prospect, IL 60056

847-827-6869
FAX 847-827-6886
E-Mail: info@sccm.org
Home Page: www.sccm.org
Social Media: *Twitter, Google+*

J. Christopher Farmer, President
David J Martin, Chief Executive Officer
Dorothy Suwanski, Executive Assistant
Ellen Turney, Human Resources Manager
Karen Boman, Business Analyst

The largest multiprofessional organization dedicated to ensuring excellence and consistency in the practice of critical care.

6357 Southeastern Society of Health-System Pharmacists

Home Page: www.smshp.org
Social Media: *Facebook, Twitter*

A regional association representing pharmacists and related personnel associated with organized health-care settings.

6358 Student National Pharmaceutical Association

PO Box 761388ÿ
San Antonio, TX 78245

210-383-7381
FAX 210-579-1059
E-Mail: contactsnpha@snpha.org
Home Page: www.snpha.org
Social Media: *Facebook, Twitter, YouTube, Instagram*

Joshua Blackwell, PharmD, Executive Chairman
Jessie Nai Hwang, President
Gevorg Martirosyan, President Elect
Dr. Carmita Coleman, Executive Director
Kyle Brown, Vice President

An educational service association of pharmacy students who are concerned about pharmacy and healthcare related issues, and the poor minority representation in pharmacy and other health-related professions.
Founded in 1972

Newsletters

6359 AACP News

American Association of Colleges of Pharmacy
1727 King St
Suite 210
Alexandria, VA 22314-2700

703-739-2330
FAX 703-836-8982
Home Page: www.aacp.org

Lucinda Maine, Executive VP
Kenneth W Miller, Senior VP
Daniel J Cassidy, COO

Activities and issues in pharmacy education. 12 pages, free to members. Published since 1874.
Cost: $35.00
Frequency: Monthly
Circulation: 300
Founded in 1900
Mailing list available for rent: 300 names
Printed in on newsprint stock

6360 ACCP Report

American College of Clinical Pharmacy
13000 W. 87th St Parkway
Lenexa, KS 66215-4530

913-492-3311
FAX 913-492-0088
E-Mail: accp@accp.com
Home Page: www.accp.com

George Puiges, Publisher
Bruce Mueller, Editor
Micheal Maddux, Executive Director
Jon Poynter, Project Manager, Membership
Kimma Sheldon, Medical Editor

The American College of Clinical Pharmacy (ACCP) is a professional and scientific society that provides leadership, education, advocacy, and resources enabling clinical pharmacists to achieve excellence in practice and research.
Cost: $45.00
Frequency: Monthly
Circulation: 12000

6361 Alternative Medicine Alert

American Health Consultants
3525 Piedmont Rd Ne
Building Six, Suite 400
Atlanta, GA 30305-1578

404-467-4243
800-688-2421
FAX 404-262-7837
Home Page: www.ahcpub.com

Jeff Mac Donald, CEO

Reports on studies of herbs in medicine, reactions in relation to different herbs. Studies that are out and those being done.
Cost: $299.00
Frequency: Monthly
Mailing list available for rent
Printed in 4 colors on matte stock

6362 Annals of Pharmacotherapy

Harvey Whitney Books Company
8044 Montgomery Road
PO Box 42696
Cincinnati, OH 45242-0696

513-793-3555
877-742-7631
FAX 513-793-3600
E-Mail: customer-services@theannals.com
Home Page: www.theannals.com

Tina Whitney, Finance Executive
Eugene Sorkin, Associate Editor
Harvey Whitney, CEO
Greg Johnson, Marketing
Ann Brandwieve, Circulation Manager

For 38 years this independent peer reviewed journal has been dedicated to the advancement of pharmacotherapy. Article categories include; original research, comprehensive reviews, case reports, editorials, and letters. special article features include new drug evaluations, therapeutic controversies, recent theraputic advances, international reports, continuing education articles, and more.
Cost: $158.00
Frequency: Monthly
Circulation: 50000
ISSN: 1060-0280
Founded in 1967
Printed in 4 colors on glossy stock

6363 Chapter News

American College of Cardiology
76 S State Street
Concord, NH 03301-3520

603-228-1231
FAX 603-228-2118
E-Mail: assnrhc@aol.com

Walter Perry, Executive Director

Newsletter for cardiovascular specialists in Maine, New Hampshire and Vermont.
Frequency: Quarterly
Mailing list available for rent

6364 Clin-Alert-Newsletter
Technomic Publishing Company
300 S Riverside Plz
Suite 1200
Chicago, IL 60606-6637

312-876-0004
FAX 312-876-1158
E-Mail: foodinfo@technomic.com
Home Page: www.technomic.com

Ronald Paul, President
Darren Tristano, Executive Vice President
Neil Stern, Senior Partner

This unique adverse drug reaction/interaction reporting service presents-in newsletter format-a summary of adverse clinical events, collected from 103 key medical and research journals from around the world. Approximately 360 abstracts per year.
Cost: $155.00
8 Pages
Frequency: Semimonthly
ISSN: 0069-4770
Printed in 2 colors

6365 Clinical Investigator News
CTB International Publishing
PO Box 218
Maplewood, NJ 07040-218

973-966-0997
FAX 973-966-0242
E-Mail: info@ctbintl.com
Home Page: www.ctbintl.com

FG Racioppi, Marketing Director
William Robison, Circulation Manager

Alerts independent investigators to existing or emerging opportunities to participate in clinical trials of drugs and maintain a steady flow of studies. Covers preclinical development through Phase II/III, approvals and post-marketing surveillance (PMS) studies.
Cost: $647.00
48 Pages
Frequency: Monthly
Founded in 1980
Mailing list available for rent
Printed in one color on newsprint stock

6366 Clinical Trials Monitor
CTB International Publishing
PO Box 218
Maplewood, NJ 07040-218

973-966-0997
FAX 973-379-0242
E-Mail: info@ctbintl.com
Home Page: www.ctbintl.com

Oykue Brogna, Publisher
Christopher Brogna, Editor

Tracks clinical trials planned, underway, completed or abandoned. Lists the drug, the company, the indication, phase or stage, principal investigator, where and when trials will be held, enrollment plans and proposed end points. Reports results at meetings, and in journals.
Cost: $1197.00
64 Pages
Frequency: Monthly
Founded in 1985
Printed in one color on newsprint stock

6367 Consumer Pharmacist
Elba Medical Foundation

PO Box 494
Metairie, LA 70004

504-889-7070
FAX 504-889-7060

John DiMaggio, Publisher
Drug information newsletter.
Cost: $30.00
Frequency: Monthly

6368 DIA Newsletter
Drug Information Association
800 Enterprise Rd
Suite 200
Horsham, PA 19044-3595

215-442-6100
FAX 215-442-6199
E-Mail: dia@diahome.org
Home Page: www.diahome.org
Social Media: *Facebook, Twitter, LinkedIn, YouTube*

Ling Su, President
John Roberts, Treasurer
Paul Pomerantz,MBA, Worldwide Executive Director

Association activities, technical developments, supplying, and production of drugs.
Cost: $40.00
20 Pages
Frequency: Monthly
Founded in 1964

6369 Diagnostics Intelligence
CTB International Publishing
PO Box 218
Maplewood, NJ 07040-218

973-966-0997
FAX 973-966-0242
E-Mail: info@ctbintl.com
Home Page: www.ctbintl.com

Oyque Brogna, CEO/President
F Racioppi, Marketing Director

Covers the latest in research, development, new product language, regulatory affairs, patents, litigations, opportunities and finance in the invitro diagnostics business.
Cost: $578.00
20 Pages
Frequency: Monthly
Mailing list available for rent
Printed in one color on newsprint stock

6370 Drug Development Pipeline
CTB International Publishing
PO Box 218
Maplewood, NJ 07040

973-966-0997
FAX 973-966-0242
E-Mail: info@ctbintl.com
Home Page: www.ctbintl.com/

FG Racioppi, Marketing Director
Chris Brogna, President
Laszlo Novak, Editor

Newsletter that summarizes the changes in the drug development plans of US and Canadian pharmaceutical companies. Each issue will alert the reader to more than 120 products that are moving through the pipeline.
Cost: $198.00
Frequency: Monthly
Founded in 1982
Mailing list available for rent
Printed in one color on newsprint stock

6371 Emerging Pharmaceuticals
CTB International Publishing
PO Box 218
Maplewood, NJ 07040-218

973-966-0997
FAX 973-966-0242

E-Mail: info@ctbintl.com
Home Page: www.ctbintl.com

FG Racioppi, Marketing Director

Covers the earliest stage of drug development, from discovery through preclinical trials. Alerts readers to news and insights about novel compounds, innovative screening methods and candidates for the R&D pipeline.
Cost: $542.00
14 Pages
Frequency: Monthly
Mailing list available for rent
Printed in one color on newsprint stock

6372 FDC Reports: Gold Sheet
FDC Reports
5550 Friendship Boulevard
Suite 1
Chevy Chase, MD 20815-7278

301-657-9830
800-332-2181
FAX 301-656-3094
E-Mail: fdc.customer.service@elsevier.com
Home Page: www.fdcreports.com

Bill Paulson, Editor
Michael Magoulias, VP Sales/Marketing
Mike Squires, CEO/President
William Paulson, Executive Editor

A specialized publication which focuses each month on important changes in FDA's policies for regulating good manufacturing practices for pharmaceutical companies and their suppliers. Since 1967, this publication has provided quality control officials with the latest useful information on state-of-the-art production and quality control techniques.
Cost: $595.00
Frequency: Monthly
ISSN: 1530-6194
Founded in 1939
Mailing list available for rent
Printed in 2 colors on matte stock

6373 FDC Reports: Green Sheet
FDC Reports
5550 Friendship Boulevard
Suite 1
Chevy Chase, MD 20815-7256

301-657-9830
FAX 301-656-3094
Home Page: www.fdcreports.com

Mike Squires, President
Michael Koppenhoffer, Editor

For nearly 40 years The Green Sheet has been an independent source of news and information on the pharmacy profession and the pharmaceutical distribution system. This four-page publication provides pharmacists, wholesalers, drugstore managers and trade relations executives with concise coverage of: professional policy; national and state pharmacy association activities; reimbursement issues; new drug introductions and pharmaceutical pricing and deals.
Cost: $65.00
4 Pages
Frequency: Weekly
Founded in 1939

6374 FDC Reports: Pink Sheet
FDC Reports
5550 Friendship Boulevard
Suite 1
Chevy Chase, MD 20815-7256

301-657-9830
800-332-2181
FAX 301-656-3094
E-Mail: PinkEditor@elsevier.com
Home Page: www.fdcreports.com

Wallace Werble Jr, Publisher
Janet Coleman, Editor
Mike Squires, CEO/President

Shawn Smith, Marketing
Emily Brainard, Circulation Manager

Provides in-depth weekly news and analysis about developments affecting the prescription medicines. The publication closely tracks regulatory policies and actions by FDA, FTC, HCFA, Congress, the courts and other key federal and state agencies with jurisdiction over the drug industry. Regular coverage areas include: NDA and Generic Drug approvals, FDA recalls and seizures, mergers, the R&D pipeline, biotechnology start-ups and new product activity.
Cost: $1580.00
35 Pages
Frequency: Weekly
ISSN: 1068-5324
Founded in 1939

6375 FDC Reports: Tan Sheet
FDC Reports
5550 Friendship Boulevard
Suite 1
Chevy Chase, MD 20815-7256

301-657-9830
FAX 301-656-3094
E-Mail: FDC.Customer.Service@Elsevier.com
Home Page: www.fdcreports.com

Mike Squires, CEO/President
Ramsey Baghdadi, Editor
Michael Magoulias, Marketing Manager
Emily Brainard, Circulation Manager

Provides in-depth coverage of nonprescription pharmaceuticals and dietary supplement/nutritionals. Spectrum of coverage includes: regulatory activities of FTC, CPSC and FDA, including monograph and non-monograph decisions, enforcement actions, advisory committee reviews and approvals; Congressional hearings and legislation; business and marketing news such as Rx-to-OTC switches, product development and new product introductions; FDA recalls and seizures and regular listing of product trademarks
Cost: $1285.00
Frequency: Weekly
ISSN: 1068-5316
Founded in 1939

6376 FDLI Prospectus
Food & Drug Law Institute
1155 15th Street NW
Suite 800
Washington, DC 20005

202-371-1420
800-956-6293
FAX 202-371-0649
E-Mail: comments@fdli.org
Home Page: www.fdli.org

Michael D. Levin-Epstein, Vice President, Publications
Abby C. Foster, Managing Editor

weekly e-newsletter
Frequency: Weekly

6377 Food and Drug Letter
FDAnews
300 N Washington St
Suite 200
Falls Church, VA 22046-3441

703-538-7600
888-838-5578
FAX 703-538-7676
E-Mail: customerservice@fdanews.com
Home Page: www.fdanews.com

Cynthia Carter, President
Michael Miven, Editor
Maritva Lizama, Marketing
J T Hrontith, Sales Director

Provides reliable, in-depth analysis of how FDA's regulations and procedures will affect your current decisions and long-term plans and

gives you in-depth interpretation to tell you why FDA is making or proposing revisions.
Cost: $1095.00
8 Pages
Frequency: Annual+

6378 Health News Daily
FDC Reports
5550 Friendship Boulevard
Suite 1
Chevy Chase, MD 20815-7256

301-657-9830
800-332-2181
FAX 301-656-3094
Home Page: www.healthnewsdaily.com

Jim Chicca, Editor
Mike Squires, Executive Director

Provides up-to-the-minute coverage on a broad spectrum of health care issues including pharmaceuticals, medical devices and diagnostics, biomedical research, federal health policy and legislation, Medicare-Medicaid, technology reimbursement and cost-containment. Special emphasis is placed on federal regulatory and legislative developments. Published each business day, the publication draws on the expertise of more than 40 F-D-C reports editors and reporters.
Cost: $ 1480.00
Frequency: Daily
Founded in 1939

6379 International Pharmaceutical Regulatory Monitor
Omniprint
9700 Philadelphia Ct
Lanham, MD 20706-4405

301-731-7000
800-345-2611
FAX 301-731-7001
Home Page: www.omniprint.net

Ken Kaufman, President
Stephen Brown, VP

Comprehensive reports on the world's drug and biotechnology regulations for testing and marketing; provides actual regulatory documents (English texts).
Cost: $595.00
60 Pages
Frequency: Monthly
ISSN: 0888-6393
Founded in 1973
Mailing list available for rent
Printed in 2 colors on matte stock

6380 Mealey's Emerging Drugs & Devices
LexisNexis Mealey's
555 W 5th Avenue
Los Angeles, CA 90013

213-627-1130
E-Mail: mealeyinfo@lexisnexis.com
Home Page: www.lexisnexis.com/mealeys

Tom Hagy, VP/General Manager
Maureen McGuire, Editorial Director
Tom Moylan, Editor

The report covers cases involving a variety of prescription drug vaccines, implants and devices. Duract, Parlodel, Accutane, fen-phen, Rezulin, Propulsid, dietary supplements and blood products are among the topics tracked. Medical devices covered include heart catheters, breast implants, heart valves, intraocular lenses, jaw implants, joint replacements, latex gloves, pacemakers, pedicle screws, penile implants, and surgical lasers.
Cost: $1249.00
100 Pages
Frequency: Semi-Monthly
Founded in 1996

6381 Mealey's Litigation Report: Baycol
LexisNexis Mealey's

555 W 5th Avenue
Los Angeles, CA 90013

213-627-1130
E-Mail: mealeyinfo@lexisnexis.com
Home Page: www.lexisnexis.com/mealeys

Tom Hagy, VP/General Manager
Maureen McGuire, Editorial Director
Dylan McGuire, Editor

This report tracks the litigation surrounding Baycol and other statin-based anti-cholesterol drug cases. Since the voluntary withdrawl of Bayer's Baycol and Lipobay brand cerivastatin anti-cholesterol drugs, numerous complaints have been filed. The report will cover hard-to-find filings, new complaints, class actions, MDL developments, trial updates and more.
Cost: $950.00
100 Pages
Frequency: Monthly
Founded in 2002

6382 Mealey's Litigation Report: Fen-Phen/Redux
LexisNexis Mealey's
555 W 5th Avenue
Los Angeles, CA 90013

213-627-1130
E-Mail: mealeyinfo@lexisnexis.com
Home Page: www.lexisnexis.com/mealeys

Tom Hagy, VP/General Manager
Maureen McGuire, Editorial Director
Michael Lefkowitz, Editor

The report provides detailed coverage of the litigation surrounding fen-phen, Redux and other diet drugs. The report covers new filings, class actions, MDL proceedings, trials, settlements, rulings, medical studies, FDA activity and more.
Cost: $995.00
100 Pages
Frequency: Monthly
Founded in 1997

6383 NABP Newsletter
National Association of Boards of Pharmacy
700 Busse Highway
Park Ridge, IL 60068

847-698-6227
800-774-6227
FAX 847-698-0124
E-Mail: custserv@nabp.net
Home Page: www.nabp.net

Malcom Broussard, Chairperson
Michael Burlson, President
Joseph Adams, Treasurer

Provides coverage of issues important to those who practice pharmacy and those who regulate that practice. Information about NABP's competency assessment and licensure transfer programs, news about the boards of pharmacy, and articles that impact the practice and regulation of pharmacy appear in each issue.
Cost: $35.00
Frequency: 10 Per Year

6384 NCPA Newsletter
National Community Pharmacists Association
100 Daingerfield Road
Alexandria, VA 22314

703-683-8200
800-544-7447
FAX 703-683-3619
E-Mail: info@ncpanet.com
Home Page: www.ncpanet.org

Mike Conlan, VP Publications
Chris Linville, Managing Editor

Stay up-to-date on the latest developments in legislation, federal regulation, pharmacy news, and other important events with the NCPA

Newsletter. Independent pharmacists get the information they need to understand the policies, politics, and government actions that affect independent pharmacy practice. Annual subscription is included in NCPA memership dues.
Cost: $50.00

6385 Nation's Health
American Public Health Association
800 I Street NW
Washington, DC 20001-3710

202-777-2742
FAX 202-777-2534
E-Mail: membership.mail@apha.org
Home Page: www.apha.org
Social Media: *Facebook, Twitter, LinkedIn, YouTube, Blogs*

Georges C Benjamin, Executive Director
Mazin Abdelgader, Publication Services
Michele Late, Executive Editor

For the latest news on public health, public health professionals, legislators and decision-makers. This newsletter is part of APHA membership.
Cost: $50.00
Frequency: 10 Per Year

6386 PDA Letter
Parenteral Drug Association
1894 Preston White Drive
Reston, VA 20191-5433

703-620-6390
FAX 703-476-0904
E-Mail: info@npcnow.org
Home Page: www.npcnow.org

Walter L Morris, III, Senior Editor

Designed to keep members informed of the latest information in the regulatory arena along with scientific happenings within the Association and the industry. It also contains details on upcoming PDA events, as well as worldwide Chapter activities.
Frequency: Monthly
Founded in 1949

6387 Pharmaceutical & Med Packaging News
Canon Communications
11444 W Olympic Blvd
Suite 900
Los Angeles, CA 90064-1555

310-445-4200
FAX 310-445-4299
E-Mail: feedback@cancom.com
Home Page: www.cancom.com

Klaus Weinmann, CEO
Rudolf Hotter, COO
Frequency: Monthly
Founded in 1992

6388 Pharmaceutical News Daily
CTB International Publishing
PO Box 218
Maplewood, NJ 07040

973-966-0997
FAX 973-966-0242
E-Mail: info@ctbintl.com
Home Page: www.ctbintl.com

Kris Brogina, CEO/President
Kistine Yanicek, Editor
Oykue Brogina, Publisher
T Tseng, Circulation Manager

This daily electronic newsletter updates the highly competitive pharmaceutical and biotechnology industries. Delivered by e-mail.
Cost: $279.00
Frequency: Daily
Founded in 1984
Mailing list available for rent
Printed in one color on newsprint stock

6389 Pharmacist's Letter
Therapeutic Research
3120 W March Lane
PO Box 8190
Stockton, CA 95208-190

209-472-2240
FAX 209-472-2249
Home Page: www.pletter.com

Jeff Jellin, Publisher

A newsletter to pharmacists offering coverage of drug development, production, distribution, legislation, safety and other issues concerning the industry.
Cost: $85.00
ISSN: 0883-0371

6390 Pharmacy Practice News
McMahon Group
545 W 45th St
8th Floor
New York, NY 10036-3409

646-557-0966
FAX 646-957-7230
E-Mail: davidb@mcmahonmed.com
Home Page: www.strategiesinmedicine.com

Raymond Mc Mahon, CEO
Van Velle, President
David Bronstein, Editor-in-Chief
Marsha Radebaugh, Circulation Manager
Michelle McMohan, Creative Director

Created to inform hospital pharmacists of the latest news on drugs, nutrition, research and trends in the pharmaceutical industry.
Cost: $60.00
Frequency: Monthly
Circulation: 45460
Founded in 1972

6391 Pharmacy Student
APLA
2215 Constitution Avenue NW
Washington, DC 20037-2977

202-429-7576

Rick Harding, Publisher

Practical information to help pharmacy students grow.
Cost: $35.00
Frequency: Monthly
Circulation: 100000

6392 Pharmacy Today
American Pharmacists Association
2215 Constitution Avenue NW
Washington, DC 20037-2977

202-429-7557
800-237-2742
FAX 202-783-2351
E-Mail: pt@aphanet.org
Home Page: www.pharmacists.org

Frank Bennicasa, Publisher
L Michael Posey, Editor
Carli Richard, Managing Editor

Offering readers profiles of practices that employ unique MTM techniques to effectively serve their patients. Readers can use these profiles as models to develop and improve their own MTM practice, increase patient adherence, and build patient loyalty.
Cost: $200.00
Frequency: Monthly
ISSN: 1042-0991
Founded in 1962

6393 Prescriber's Letter
Therapeutic Research

PO Box 8190
Stockton, CA 95208

209-472-2240
FAX 209-472-2249
Home Page: www.pletter.com

Jeff Jellin PharmD, Publisher

A newsletter to pharmacists offering coverage of drug development, production, distribution, legislation, safety and other issues concerning the industry.
Cost: $85.00
ISSN: 1073-7219

6394 Preventive Medicine Update
HealthComm International
5800 Soundview Drive
PO Box 1729
Gig Harbor, WA 98335-2000

253-858-3315
800-843-9660
FAX 253-851-9749

Jeffrey Bland, CEO/Contact

6395 Psoriasis Resource
National Psoriasis Foundation
6600 Sw 92nd Ave
Suite 300
Portland, OR 97223-7195

503-244-7404
800-723-9166
FAX 503-245-0626
E-Mail: getinfo@npfusa.org
Home Page: www.psoriasis.org

Pam Field, CEO
Bill Taggart, Managing Editor
Gail Zimmerman, CEO

A newsletter published for members of the National Psoriasis Foundation. Highlights interesting articles on psoriasis products and medications andother health related topics. Contains advertisements for psoriasis-related products and services.
16 Pages
Circulation: 40000
Mailing list available for rent: 28000 names
Printed in 2 colors on matte stock

6396 Results Newsletter
American Clinical Laboratory Association
1100 New York Ave Nw
Suite 725
Washington, DC 20005-6172

202-637-9466
FAX 202-637-2050
E-Mail: info@clinical-labs.org
Home Page: www.clinical-labs.org

Alan Mertz, President
Frequency: Monthly
Mailing list available for rent

6397 Rx Ipsa Loquitur
American Society for Pharmacy Law
1224 Centre West Dr
Suite 400
Springfield, IL 62704-2184

217-698-6163
FAX 217-698-6164
Home Page: www.aspl.org

Michael Monson, Owner
Francis B Palumbo, Director
Pamela Tolson CAE, Executive Director
William Fassett, Treasurer

Featuring recent court decisions, legislative and regulatory news, and other current pharmacy law news and articles.
Frequency: Bi-Monthly

6398 Washington Drug Letter
FDAnews

300 N Washington St
Suite 200
Falls Church, VA 22046-3441

703-538-7600
888-838-5578
FAX 703-538-7676
E-Mail: customerservice@fdanews.com
Home Page: www.fdanews.com

Cynthia Carter, President
Maritza Lizama, Marketing Director

Summaries of FDA regulatory changes and key legislation that affects prescription and over the counter drugs. Each weekly issue brings you up-to-date on pre approval and post approval issues that directly impact your operation.
Cost: $897.00
Frequency: Weekly

Magazines & Journals

6399 AAPS Newsmagazine

American Association of Pharmaceutical Scientists
2107 Wilson Blvd
Suite 700
Arlington, VA 22201-3042

703-243-2800
FAX 703-243-9054
E-Mail: aaps@aaps.org
Home Page: www.aaps.org

John Lisack, Executive Director
Karol Shadle, Associate Director
Maria Nadeau, Member Groups Manager
Me'Gesha Portlock, Administrative Assistant

Exclusive to AAPS members. Features expanded coverage of the industry, complete with expert information on marketplace trends, regulatory matters, and career opportunities.
Mailing list available for rent

6400 AAPS Online Buyers Guide

American Association of Pharmaceutical Scientists
2107 Wilson Blvd
Suite 700
Arlington, VA 22201-3042

703-243-2800
FAX 703-243-9054
E-Mail: aaps@aaps.org
Home Page: www.aaps.org

John Lisack, Executive Director
Karol Shadle, Associate Director
Maria Nadeau, Member Groups Manager
Me'Gesha Portlock, Administrative Assistant

comprehensive sourcebook you need as a pharmaceutical scientist. Research the more than 500 companies providing the products and service you need. You can browse the entire Online Buyers Guide or you can refine your search by Company Name, Region, Business Category, or Keyword.
Mailing list available for rent

6401 AAPS PharmSciTech Journal

American Association of Pharmaceutical Scientists
2107 Wilson Blvd
Suite 700
Arlington, VA 22201-3042

703-243-2800
FAX 703-243-9054
E-Mail: aaps@aaps.org
Home Page: www.aaps.org

John Lisack, Executive Director
Karol Shadle, Associate Director
Maria Nadeau, Member Groups Manager
Me'Gesha Portlock, Administrative Assistant

An online-only journal published and owned by the American Association of Pharmaceutical Scientists. The journal's mission is to disseminate scientific and technical information on drug product design, development, evaluation and processing to the global pharmaceutical research community, taking full advantage of web-based publishing by presenting innovative text with 3-D graphics, interactive figures and databases, video and audio files.
ISSN: 1530-9932
Mailing list available for rent

6402 America's Pharmacist

National Community Pharmacists Association
100 Daingerfield Road
Alexandria, VA 22314

703-683-8200
800-544-7447
FAX 703-683-3619
E-Mail: info@ncpanet.com
Home Page: www.ncpanet.org

Mike Conlan, VP Publications/Editor
Chris Linville, Managing Editor

This informative magazine gives 25,000 independent pharmacists insight into current issues that affect independent pharmacy and NCPA's activities to address those issues. Also, it serves the readers by including monthly articles on clinical topics, a continuing education series for pharmacists who want to earn CE credit, information on how to manage finances, and proven tips on better marketing, as well as profiles of NCPA members from across the country. Annual subscription included in dues.
Cost: $50.00
Frequency: Monthly

6403 American Institute of the History of Pharmacy

777 Highland Ave
Madison, WI 53705-2222

608-262-5378
FAX 608-262-3397
E-Mail: aihp@aihp.org
Home Page: www.aihp.org/

Dr. Gregory Higby, Executive Director
Dr. Elaine Stroud, Assistant Director
Beth Fisher, Assoc. Dir. Curatorial Affairs

Articles on pharmaceutical history and usage.
Cost: $50.00
200 Pages
Frequency: Quarterly
Circulation: 1200
Founded in 1960
Printed in on glossy stock

6404 American Journal of Health-System Pharmacy

American Society of Health-System Pharmacists
7272 Wisconsin Ave
Bethesda, MD 20814-4861

301-657-3000
866-279-0681
FAX 301-664-8877
E-Mail: ajhp@ashp.org
Home Page: www.ashp.org
Social Media: *Facebook, Twitter, LinkedIn, YouTube*

Kathryn Shultz, President
Paul Abramowitz, CEO
Philip Schneider, Treasurer

The journal for pharmacists practicing in all area's of acute care, ambulatory care, home care, long term care, HMO's, PPO's, and PBM's.
Cost: $165.00
54 Pages
Frequency: Bi-Weekly
Circulation: 42,000

ISSN: 1079-2082
Printed in 2 colors on glossy stock

6405 American Journal of Medical Quality

American College of Medical Quality
4334 Montgomery Ave
Suite B
Bethesda, MD 20814-4415

301-913-9149
800-924-2149
FAX 301-913-9142
E-Mail: acmq@acmq.org
Home Page: www.acmq.org

Bridget Brodie, Manager
Frequency: Bi-Monthly

6406 American Journal of Pharmaceutical Education

American Association of Colleges of Pharmacy
1727 King St
Alexandria, VA 22314-2700

703-739-2330
FAX 703-836-8982
Home Page: www.aacp.org

Lucinda Maine, Executive VP
Kenneth W Miller, Senior VP
Daniel J Cassidy, COO

Official publication of the American Association of Colleges of Pharmacy. Dedicated to all those with interest in professional, graduate, and postgraduate pharmaceutical education. Its purpose is to documnet and advance pharmaceutical education in the United States and Internationally. Features original research articles, editorials, reports on the state of pharmaceutical education, descriptions of teaching innovations, and book reviews.
Cost: $65.00
120 Pages
Frequency: Quarterly
Circulation: 3200
ISSN: 0002-9459
Founded in 1937
Printed in one color on matte stock

6407 American Journal of Public Health

American Public Health Association
800 I Street NW
Washington, DC 20001-3710

202-777-2742
FAX 202-777-2534
Home Page: www.apha.org
Social Media: *Facebook, Twitter, LinkedIn, YouTube, Blogs*

Mary E Northridge PhD, Editor-in-Chief

Provides in-depth information in the field of public health. Research and program evaluations are accompanied by authoritative editorials, throught-provoking commentary, and timely health policy analysis.
Cost: $419.00
120 Pages
Frequency: Monthly
Founded in 1990

6408 BioPharm

Advantstar Communications
6200 Canoga Avenue
2nd Floor
Woodland Hills, CA 91367

818-593-5000
FAX 818-593-5020
Home Page: biopharminternational.com

Joseph Loggia, President
Chris DeMoulin, VP
Susannah George, Marketing Director

Publication taking a practical approach to the technology and business of developing and manufacturing biotechnology-derived pharmaceutical products. Regular topics include pro-

cess development, downstream processing, facilities design, emerging technologies and regulatory compliance.
Cost: $64.00
Frequency: Monthly
Circulation: 29,200
ISSN: 1040-8304
Founded in 1987

6409 Chain Drug Review
Racher Press
220 5th Avenue
New York, NY 10001

212-213-6000
FAX 212-725-3961
E-Mail: info@racherpress.com
Home Page: www.racherpress.com

Kevin Burke, VP/Group Advertising
Jeff Woldt, VP/Editorial Director
David Pinto, Editor

Chain Drug Review serves the chain drug industry.
Cost: $185.00
Frequency: Bi-weekly
Circulation: 54000
Founded in 1978
Printed in 4 colors on glossy stock

6410 Chemistry
American Chemical Society
1155 16th St Nw
Washington, DC 20036-4892

202-872-4600
800-227-5558
FAX 202-872-4615
E-Mail: help@acs.org
Home Page: www.acs.org

Madeleine Jacobs, CEO
Judith L Benham, Board Chair

Published for members, student affiliates, and those interested in learning more about the chemical sciences and the American Chemical Society.

6411 CleanRooms Magazine
PennWell Publishing Company
98 Spit Brook Rd
Suite 100
Nashua, NH 03062-5737

603-891-0123
FAX 603-891-9294
E-Mail: georgem@pennwell.com
Home Page: www.pennwell.com

Christine Shaw, VP
James Enos, Publisher
Bob Johnson, Sales & Marketing Manager

Serves the contamination control and ultrapure materials and process industries. Written for readers in the microelectronics, pharmaceutical, biotech, health care, food processing and other user industries. Provides technology and business news and new product listings.
Cost: $97.00
Frequency: Monthly
Circulation: 35031
Founded in 1987

6412 Community Pharmacist
ELF Publications
5285 W Louisiana Ave
Lakewood, CO 80232-5976

303-975-0075
800-922-8513
FAX 303-975-0132
E-Mail: mcasey@elfpublications.com
Home Page: www.elfpublications.com

Judy Lane, Owner
Ronald R Quam, Editor/Publisher

Pharmacy trade journal that meets the professional educational needs of today's practitioner
Cost: $12.00
40 Pages
ISSN: 1096-9179
Founded in 1972
Printed in 4 colors on glossy stock

6413 Contract Pharma
Rodman Publishing
70 Hilltop Rd
3rd Floor
Ramsey, NJ 07446-1150

201-825-2552
FAX 201-825-0553
E-Mail: info@rodpub.com
Home Page: www.nutraceuticalsworld.com

Rodman Zilenziger Jr, President
Matt Montgomery, VP

A global publication providing most up-to-date news, outsourcing information, business trends, commentary, and viewpoints to the Pharmaceutical and Biopharmaceutical outsourcing industry.
Frequency: Monthly
Circulation: 20026
Founded in 1999

6414 DIA Global Forum
Drug Information Association
800 Enterprise Road
Suite 200
Horsham, PA 19044-3595

215-442-6100
FAX 215-442-6199
E-Mail: dia@diahome.org
Home Page: www.diahome.org

Paul Pomerantz BA MBA, Worldwide
Executive Director
Lisa Zoks BA, Worldwide Dir
Mktg/Communications

Presents important news from DIA conferences and workshops, reports of the Board of Directors and the regional advisory councils that directly impact DIA members, as well as practical tips, regulatory and global updates, upcoming DIA events, program notes, and more.
Frequency: Bi-Monthly
Circulation: 20000
ISSN: 1944-1991
Printed in 4 colors

6415 DVM News
Advanstar Communications
8033 Flint St
Lenexa, KS 66214-3335

913-492-4300
800-255-6864
FAX 913-492-4157
E-Mail: dverdon@advanstar.com
Home Page: www.dvm360.com

Rebecca Turner Chapman, VP

Information from veterinary medicine covering news, features, practice management and new products and services.
Cost: $4.00
Frequency: Monthly
ISSN: 0012-7337
Founded in 1987

6416 Drug Information Journal
Drug Information Association
800 Enterprise Road
Suite 200
Horsham, PA 19044-3595

215-442-6100
FAX 215-442-6199
E-Mail: dia@diahome.org
Home Page: www.diahome.org

Paul Pomerantz BA MBA, Worldwide
Executive Director

Lisa Zoks BA, Worldwide Dir
Mktg/Communications

Purpose is to disseminate information on manual and automated drug research, development, and information systems; to foster communication between educational, research, industrial and governmental personnel engaged in drug information activities; and to provide a forum for the development of improved methods of presenting research data generated from chemical, toxicologic, pharmacologic, and clinical studies.
Frequency: Bi-Monthly
Circulation: 20000
ISSN: 0092-8615
Founded in 1964

6417 Drug Store News
Lebhar-Friedman
425 Park Ave
New York, NY 10022-3526

212-756-5088
FAX 212-838-9487
E-Mail: editor@drugstorenews.com
Home Page: www.drugstorenews.com

Heather Martin, Manager
J Rodger Friedman, CEO

Publication consists of merchandising trends and pharmacy developments. Provides extensive coverage of every major segment of chain drug retailing and combination stores.
Cost: $119.00
Circulation: 45000
Founded in 1925

6418 Drug Topics
Medical Economics Publishing
5 Paragon Dr
Montvale, NJ 07645-1791

973-944-7777
FAX 973-944-7778
E-Mail: drug.topics@Medec.com
Home Page: www.drugtopics.com

Jim Granto, Publisher
Heather Schlosser, National Account Manager

Information on the distributing and dispensing drug trade.
Cost: $61.00
Printed in 4 colors on glossy stock

6419 Food & Drug Packaging
Stagnito Publishing Group
155 Pfingston Road
Suite 205
Deerfield, IL 60015

847-205-5660
FAX 847-205-5680
E-Mail: gvansomeren@stagnito.com
Home Page: www.fdp.com
Social Media: *Facebook, Twitter, LinkedIn, you tube*

Lisa McTigue Pierce, Editor-in-Chief
Blayne Long, Senior Marketing Manager
Geneine Van Someren, Circulation Manager
Vince Miconi, Advertising Production Manager
George Misko, Regional Sales Manager

Food and Drug Packaging serves industries engaged in packaging food, beverages, pharmaceuticals, cosmetics and consulting/engineering firms.
Frequency: Monthly
Circulation: 75140
Founded in 1959

6420 Food and Drug Law Journal
Food & Drug Law Institute
1155 15th Street NW
Suite 800
Washington, DC 20005

202-371-1420
800-956-6293

FAX 202-371-0649
E-Mail: comments@fdli.org
Home Page: www.fdli.org

Michael D. Levin-Epstein, Vice President, Publications
Abby C. Foster, Managing Editor

Award-winning journal offering scholarly, in-depth, analytical articles, providing insight into action of the FDA, FTC, and USDA, how the courts interpret these actions, and the reaction of the industry.
Cost: $379.00
Frequency: Quarterly
ISSN: 1064-590x

6421 Formulary
Advanstar Communications
6200 Canoga Avenue
2nd Floor
Woodland Hills, CA 91367

818-593-5000
FAX 818-593-5020
E-Mail: info@advanstar.com
Home Page: www.advanstar.com

Joseph Loggia, President
Chris DeMoulintein, VP
Susannah George, Marketing Director

Peer-reviewed publication providing drug information for physicians, pharmacists, and other health care professionals who influence the selection and use of drugs in hospitals, HMO's, and other managed care settings.
Cost: $61.00
Frequency: Monthly
Circulation: 51402
ISSN: 1082-801X
Founded in 1992
Mailing list available for rent

6422 HealthCare Distributor
ELF Publications
5285 W Louisiana Ave
Lakewood, CO 80232-5976

303-975-0075
800-922-8513
FAX 303-975-0132
E-Mail: elfpub@qwest.net
Home Page: www.elfpublications.com

Judy Lane, Owner
Ronald R Quam, Editor/Publisher
Chuck Austin, Senior Editor
Jerry Lester, Director of Sales

Multi-market publication devoted to the issues and opportunities facing the wholesale drug, chain drug, medical/surgical and home care products distribution industries
Cost: $12.00
80 Pages
Frequency: Bi-annually
Circulation: 12000
ISSN: 1096-9160
Founded in 1972
Printed in 4 colors on glossy stock

6423 Hospital Pharmacy
Facts and Comparisons
111 Westport Plz
Suite 300
St Louis, MO 63146-3011

314-216-2100
800-223-0554
FAX 314-878-5563
E-Mail: service@drugfacts.com
Home Page: www.factsandcomparisons.com

John Pins, VP

Provides pharmacists with peer-reviewed articles and monthly features covering clinical and administrative areas such as drug use, drug distribution systems in hospitals and health-systems, automation, medication errors and adverse events, Joint Commission drug-related

material and current FDA drug information.
Cost: $124.95
Frequency: Monthly
ISSN: 0018-5787
Founded in 1965

6424 Inform
American Oil Chemists' Society
2710 S Boulder
Urbana, IL 61802-6996

217-359-2344
FAX 217-351-8091
E-Mail: kheine@aocs.org
Home Page: www.aocs.org
Social Media: *Facebook, Twitter, LinkedIn, Blog*

Jody Schonfeld, Publications Director
Kimmy Farris, Production Editor
Kathy Heine, Managing Editor

Member benefit pmagazine providing international news on fats, oils, surfactants, detergents, and related materials.
Cost: $175.00
462 Pages
Frequency: Monthly
Circulation: 3700
ISSN: 0897-8026
Founded in 1909
Printed in on glossy stock

6425 International Pharmaceutical Abstracts
American Society of Health-System Pharmacists
7272 Wisconsin Ave
Bethesda, MD 20814-4861

301-657-3000
866-279-0681
FAX 301-664-8877
E-Mail: ipa@ashp.org
Home Page: www.ashp.org

Mark Woods, President

These reports offering the latest in the development of drugs overseas, clinical use, cosmetics and, alternative and herbal medicine. Reports on pharmacy practice are also included.
Cost: $240.00
Frequency: Monthly
Circulation: 31,000
ISSN: 0020-8264
Founded in 1936

6426 Journal of Managed Care Pharmacy
Academy of Managed Care Pharmacy
100 N Pitt St
Suite 400
Alexandria, VA 22314-3141

703-683-8416
800-827-2627
FAX 703-683-8417
E-Mail: sandres@amcp.org
Home Page: www.amcp.org
Social Media: *Facebook, Twitter, LinkedIn*

Douglas Burgoyne, President
Robert Gregory, Treasurer

Features articles on trends and recent developments in managed care pharmacy, updates from pharmacy educators about the inclusion of managed care topics in cirricula and news and information about the academy and it's activities.
Cost: $60.00
Frequency: Bi-Monthly

6427 Journal of Parenteral and Enteral Nutrition
Amer. Society for Parenteral & Enteral Nutrition

8630 Fenton Street
Suite 412
Silver Spring, MD 20910-3803

301-587-6315
800-727-4567
FAX 301-587-2365
E-Mail: jpen@nutr.org
Home Page: www.nutritioncare.org
Social Media: *Facebook, Twitter*

Is the premier scientific journal of nutrition and metabolic support. It publishes original, peer-reviewd studies that define the cutting edge of basic and clinical research in the field. It explores the science of optimizing the care of patients receiving enteral or IV therapies. This is included as benefits of membership in AS-PEN.
Cost: $90.00
Frequency: Fortnightly
Circulation: 7800
ISSN: 0148-6071
Founded in 1977

6428 Journal of Pharmaceutical Innovation
Int'l Society for Pharmaceutical Engineering
3109 W Dr Martin Luther King Jr Boulevard
Suite 250
Tampa, FL 33607

813-960-2105
FAX 813-264-2816
E-Mail: ask@ispe.org
Home Page: www.ispe.org

Gloria N Hall, Editor & Director of Publications
Lynda Goldbach, Publications Manager
Amy Lecceardone, Publications Coordinator
Valerie Adams, Advertising Sales Coordinator
Frequency: 4/Year
Circulation: 2000

6429 Journal of Pharmaceutical Marketing and Management
Taylor & Francis Group LLC
325 Chestnut St
Suite 800
Philadelphia, PA 19106-2614

215-625-8900
800-354-1420
FAX 215-625-2940
E-Mail: haworthorders@taylorandfrancis.com
Home Page: www.taylorandfrancis.com

Kevin Bradley, President

The journal maintains a vigorous policy of publishing quality research reports of interest to individuals involved in the manufacturing, wholesale, institutional, retail, regulatory, organizational and academic components of the pharmaceutical industry.
Frequency: Quarterly

6430 Journal of Pharmaceutical Sciences
Wiley InterScience
350 Main St
Malden, MA 02148-5089

781-388-8250
800-835-6770
FAX 781-388-8210
E-Mail: cs-journals@wiley.com
Home Page: www.wiley.com

Amy Yodaniss, VP
Julie Fisher, Assistant Editor
Roger Hall, VP
Laurie Beagell, Circulation Manager

A comprehensive look at the world of drugs and pharmaceuticals.
Frequency: Monthly
Circulation: 225

6431 Journal of Pharmacy Practice
Technomic Publishing Company

PO Box 3535
Lancaster, PA 17601

717-291-5609
800-233-9936
FAX 717-295-4538
E-Mail: aflannery@techpub.com
Home Page: www.techpub.com

Amy Flannery, Marketing

The journal provides useful, timely reports on the most challenging issues of pharmacy today and anticipates the unique demands of this rapidly changing field. Each issue's single-topic format and thoughtful, readable analysis gives a better grasp of difficult problems and provides immediately useful information.
Cost: $210.00
80 Pages
ISSN: 0897-1900
Printed in 2 colors on matte stock

6432 Journal of Pharmacy Technology
Harvey Whitney Books Company
PO Box 42696
Cincinnati, OH 45242-696

513-793-3555
877-742-7631
FAX 513-793-3600
E-Mail: customerserv@jpharmtechnol.com
Home Page: www.jpharmtechnol.com

Harvey Whitney, Publisher/Editor
Eugene Sorkin, Associate Editorial
Ann Brandewiede, Circulation Manager

Latest information on drugs, for health professionals. Topics covered include new drug profiles, education and training, legal dilemmas, drug distribution, products and equipment and continuing education.
Cost: $122.00
Circulation: 1000
ISSN: 8755-1225

6433 Journal of Surfactants and Detergents
American Oil Chemists' Society
2710 S Boulder
Urbana, IL 61802-6996

217-359-2344
FAX 217-351-8091
E-Mail: general@aocs.org
Home Page: www.aocs.org
Social Media: *Facebook, Twitter, LinkedIn, Blog*

Jody Schonfeld, Publications Director
Pam Landman, Journals Coordinator
Kimmy Farris, Production Editor

Dedicated to the practical and theoretical aspects of oleochemical and petrochemical surfactants, soaps and detergents. This growing scientific journal publishes peer-reviewed research papers, and reviews related to surfactants and detergents technologies.
Cost: $457.00
Frequency: Quarterly
Founded in 1998

6434 Journal of the American Oil Chemists' Society
American Oil Chemists' Society
2710 S Boulder
Urbana, IL 61802-6966

217-359-2344
FAX 217-351-8091
E-Mail: general@aocs.org
Home Page: www.aocs.org
Social Media: *Facebook, Twitter, LinkedIn, Blog*

Jodey Schonfeld, Publications Director
Pam Landman, Journals Coordinator
Kimmy Farris, Production Editor

The leading source for technical papers related to the fats and oils industries. A peer-reviewed journal devoted to fundamental and practical research, production, processing, packaging and distribution in the growing field of fats, oils, proteins and other related substances.
Cost: $619.00
Frequency: Monthly
Founded in 1947

6435 Journal of the American Pharmacists Association
American Pharmacists Association
2215 Constitution Ave NW
Washington, DC 20037-2985

202-628-4410
800-237-2742
FAX 202-783-2351
Home Page: www.pharmacist.com
Social Media: *Facebook, Twitter, YouTube*

L Michael Posey, Editor
L Douglas Reid, Editor-In-Chief

The official peer-reviewed journal of APhA, provides information on pharmaceutical care, drug therapy, diseases and other health issues, trends in pharmacy practice and therapeutics, informed opinion, and original research.
ISSN: 1544-3191

6436 Lipids
American Oil Chemists' Society
2710 S Boulder
Urbana, IL 61802-6996

217-359-2344
FAX 217-351-8091
E-Mail: general@aocs.org
Home Page: www.aocs.org
Social Media: *Facebook, Twitter, LinkedIn, Blog*

Jody Schonfeld, Publications Director
Pam Landman, Journals Coordinator
Kimmy Farris, Production Editor

Scientific journal features full-length original research articles, short communications, methods papers and review articles on timely topics. All papers are meticulously peer-reviewed and edited by some of the foremost experts in their respective fields.
Cost: $461.00
Frequency: Monthly
Founded in 1966

6437 MPMN: Medical Product Manufacturing News
UBM Canon
2901 28th St
Ste. 100
Santa Monica, CA 90045

310-445-4200
FAX 310-445-4299
E-Mail: john.bethune@cancom.com
Home Page: www.devicelink.com
Social Media: *Twitter*

Shana Leonard, Editor in Chief
Bob Michaels, Managing Editor

A product tabloid magazine that provides information on the new products and services available to medical device manufacturers.
Frequency: 10x/yr

6438 Med Ad News
Canon Communicaitons Pharmaceutical Media Group
828A Newtown Yardley Road
Newtown, PA 18940

215-944-9800
FAX 215-867-0053
E-Mail: sandra.baker@cancom.com
Home Page: www.pharmalive.com

Christiane Truelove, Editor

Provides extensive coverage and incisive analyses of issues, events, trends and strategies shaping pharmaceutical business, marketing and sales.
Frequency: Monthly

6439 Modern Drug Discovery
American Chemical Society
1155 16th St Nw
16th Street NW
Washington, DC 20036-4892

202-872-4600
800-227-5558
FAX 202-872-4615
E-Mail: service@acs.org
Home Page: www.acs.org

Madeleine Jacobs, CEO/Executive Director

Reports matters of interest to scientists and other professionals working in the field of drug discovery.
Frequency: Monthly

6440 Monitor
Association of Clinical Research Professionals
1012 14th Street NW
Suite 108
Washington, DC 20006

202-737-8100
FAX 202-737-8101
E-Mail: acrp@associationhq.com
Home Page: www.acrpnet.org

Sharada Gilkey, Editor-in-Chief

Features peer-reviewed articles, columns, and home study.
Frequency: Quarterly

6441 Nutrition in Clinical Practice
Amer. Society for Parenteral & Enteral Nutrition
8630 Fenton Street
Suite 412
Silver Spring, MD 20910

301-587-6315
800-727-4567
FAX 301-587-2365
E-Mail: aspen@nutr.org
Home Page: www.nutritioncare.org
Social Media: *Facebook, Twitter*

Bridget Hollick, Managing Editor

This compliments the Journal of Parenteral and Enteral Nutrition with practical information and advice. It provides peer-reviewed clinical studies, reviews, techniques and procedures, teaching cases, clinical observations, and nutrition news. Included as benefits of membership is ASPEN.
Cost: $45.00
Frequency: Bi-Monthly
ISSN: 0884-5336

6442 PDA Journal of Pharmaceutical Science and Technology
Parenteral Drug Association
1894 Preston White Drive
Reston, VA 20191-5433

703-620-6390
FAX 703-476-0904
E-Mail: infoQnpcnow.com
Home Page: www.npcnow.org

Lee Kirsch, Editor

One of the most relevant and outstanding peer-reviewed scientific and technical papers in the pharmaceutical/biopharmaceutical industry. The Journal is distributed to members as a membership benefit.
Frequency: Bi-Monthly

6443 Pharmaceutical & Medical Packaging News
Canon Communications

11444 W Olympic Blvd
Suite 900
Los Angeles, CA 90064-1555

310-445-4200
FAX 310-445-4299
E-Mail: feedback@cancom.com
Home Page: www.pmpnews.com

Charlie McCurdy, President
Daphne Allen, Editor
Justine Hamilton, Marketing Director
Peter Manfre, Account Executive

Information and news on events, new technology, industry trends, regulatory matters, and health care trade associations for professionals involved in the pharmaceutical and medical product packaging industry.
Cost: $150.00
Frequency: Monthly
Circulation: 20,000
ISSN: 1081-5481
Founded in 1978

6444 Pharmaceutical Engineering

Int'l Society for Pharmaceutical Engineering
3109 W Dr Martin Luther King Jr Boulevard
Suite 250
Tampa, FL 33607

813-960-2105
FAX 813-264-2816
E-Mail: ask@ispe.org
Home Page: www.ispe.org

Gloria N Hall, Editor & Director of Publications
Lynda Goldbach, Publications Manager
Amy Lecceardone, Publications Coordinator
Valerie Adams, Advertising Sales Coordinator

Journal is published bi-monthly for members only and is considered by ISPE members to be the number one member benefit. Feature articles provide practical application and specification information on the design, construction, supervision and maintenance of process equipment, plant systems, instrumentation and facilities.
Frequency: Bi-monthly
Circulation: 2000

6445 Pharmaceutical Executive

Advanstar Communications
131 W 1st St
Duluth, MN 55802-2065

218-740-7200
800-598-6008
FAX 218-723-9537
E-Mail: info@advanstar.com
Home Page: www.advanstar.com

Kent Akervik, Manager
Kim Brown, Production Manager

Publication designed to meet the diverse management and marketing needs of professionals in the pharmaceutical industry worldwide. Editorial provides useful information on marketing, sales and promotion, as well as legal and regulatory issues.
Cost: $70.00
Frequency: Monthly
Circulation: 16237
ISSN: 0279-6570
Founded in 1987
Mailing list available for rent

6446 Pharmaceutical Formulation & Quality

Carpe Diem Communications
208 Floral Vale Boulevard
Yardley, PA 19067

215-860-7800
FAX 215-860-7900

E-Mail: pharmaeditor@carpediemcomm.com
Home Page: www.pharmaquality.com

Rachel Burley, Publisher
Lisa Dionne, Editorial Director
Paul Juestrich, Creative Director
Karen Devlin, Production Manager

A dynamic magazine written to keep the pharmaceutical and related industries informed about the very latest technologies, techniques and regulations affecting product development and formulation. PFQ's coverage extends throughout the full product lifecycle, from initial development through clinical trials and scale up top manufacturing, focusing on current issues in the competitive business of producing pharmaceuticals and biopharmaceuticals.
Cost: $90.00
100 Pages
Circulation: 20000
ISSN: 1092-7514
Founded in 1998
Mailing list available for rent: 20000 names at $185 per M
Printed in 4 colors on glossy stock

6447 Pharmaceutical Processing

Reed Business Information
100 Enterprise drive
Suite 600
Rockaway, NJ 07866-912

973-920-7000
800-222-0289
FAX 973-920-7531
Home Page: www.reedbusiness.com

Tim Canny, Publisher
Mike Auerbach, Editor
R Reed, Owner

Contents include news on new products/equipment/services, case history and application articles focusing on equipment, instrumentation, process systems, packaging, validation and outsourcing services offered to the pharmaceutical marketplace.
Frequency: Monthly
Circulation: 31075
Founded in 1984

6448 Pharmaceutical Research

Plenum Publishing Corporation
233 Spring St
New York, NY 10013-1522

212-242-1490
FAX 212-807-1047
E-Mail: info@plenum.com
Home Page: www.plenum.com

Wolfgang Sadee, Editor

Research reports and summaries of the latest in development of certain drugs and pharmaceuticals.
Cost: $49.95
Frequency: Monthly
Founded in 1998

6449 Pharmaceutical Technology Magazine

Advanstar Communications
485 Route One South
Building F, First Floor
Iselin, NJ 08830

732-596-0276
FAX 732-596-0005
E-Mail: mtracey@advanstar.com
Home Page: www.pharmtech.com

Mike Tracey, Publisher
Douglas McCormick, Editor in Chief
Paul Milazzo, Director of Sales
Tria Deibert, Marketing Director

Provides authoritative and timely information covering all aspects of conventional and biotech pharmaceutical manufacturing including: applied research and development, drug

delivery, solid dosage, manufacturing machinery and equipment, information technologies, contract services, biotechnology trends, and regulatory issues.
Frequency: Monthly
Circulation: 33691
Founded in 1987

6450 Pharmacy Times

Romaine Pierson Publishers
666 Plainsboro Rd
Plainsboro, NJ 08536

609-716-7777
FAX 609-716-4747
E-Mail: cms@skainfo.com
Home Page: www.pharmacytimes.com
Social Media: Facebook, Twitter, LinkedIn, YouTube

Emilie McCardell, Editor-In-Chief
Cam Bishop, CEO
James Granato, Publisher
James Marshal, Production Director
Margaret P. Roeske, Associate Editor

News, analysis and trends in the pharmaceutical business.
Cost: $65.00
Frequency: Monthly
Circulation: 174,104
Founded in 1897

6451 Pharmacy West

Western Communications
Po Box 6020
Bend, OR 97708-6020

541-382-1811
FAX 541-385-5802

Gordon Black, President

Distributed to pharmacies in the thirteen western states.
Cost: $18.00
Frequency: Monthly

6452 Profile of Pharmacy Faculty

American Association of Colleges of Pharmacy
1727 King St
Alexandria, VA 22314-2700

703-739-2330
FAX 703-836-8982
Home Page: www.aacp.org

Lucinda Maine, Executive VP
Kenneth W Miller, Senior VP
Daniel J Cassidy, COO

Provides statistics describing faculty at U.S. colleges and schools of pharmacy including a summary of the demographics, teaching discipline, rank, highest degree earned, tenure status, type of appointment, and salary of over 3,000 full time faculty members. Updated annually.
Cost: $25.00

6453 Scrip Magazine

1775 Broadway
Suite 511
New York, NY 10019

212-262-8230
FAX 212-262-8234
E-Mail: chonour@ThetaReports.com

An in-depth view of the issues and challenges facing all sectors of the pharmaceutical industry worldwide. Analytical features are written by pharmaceutical experts and opinion leaders as well as specialist journalists.
Frequency: Monthly

6454 The Consultant Pharmacist

American Society of Consultant Pharmacists

1321 Duke St
Suite 120
Alexandria, VA 22314-3563

703-739-1300
800-355-2727
FAX 703-739-1321
E-Mail: info@ascp.com
Home Page: www.ascp.com
Social Media: *Facebook, Twitter, LinkedIn, YouTube, Blogs*

Patti Thompson, Production Manager
Marlene Bloom, Editor
Debbie Furman, Circulation

Official peer reviewed journal of the American Society of Consultant Pharmacists. Editorial deals with geriatric pharmacotherapy.
Cost: $50.00
6m Members
76 Pages
Circulation: 13000
Founded in 1982
Printed in 4 colors on glossy stock

6455 Update Magazine
Food & Drug Law Institute
1155 15th Street NW
Suite 800
Washington, DC 20005

202-371-1420
800-956-6293
FAX 202-371-0649
E-Mail: comments@fdli.org
Home Page: www.fdli.org
Social Media: *Facebook, Twitter, LinkedIn*

Michael D. Levin-Epstein, Vice President, Publications
Erin M Jones, Membership and Marketing
Susan C Winckler, President & CEO

Update brings you the latest news from FDLI and the industry, featuring viewpoints on trends, artilces on topics of regulatory concern, changes at the FDA, news about FDLI activities, and recurring columns about current events in the industry. Free to individuals within FDLI member organizations.
Cost: $100.00
Frequency: Bimonthly

Trade Shows

6456 AACP Annual Meeting and Seminars
American Association of Colleges of Pharmacy
1727 King Street
Alexandria, VA 22314

703-739-2330
FAX 703-836-8982
Home Page: www.aacp.org

Lucinda L Maine, Executive VP
Kenneth W Miller, Senior VP
Daniel J Cassidy, COO

A chance to learn and exchange ideas on pharmacy education and recent innovations in health care.
Frequency: July

6457 AACP Institute
American Association of Colleges of Pharmacy
1727 King Street
Alexandria, VA 22314

703-739-2330
FAX 703-836-8982
Home Page: www.aacp.org

Lucinda L Maine, Executive VP
Kenneth W Miller, Senior VP
Daniel J Cassidy, COO
Frequency: May

6458 AAPS Annual Meeting & Expo
American AssociationOf Pharmaceutical Scientists
2107 Wilson Boulevard
Suite 700
Arlington, VA 22201-3042

703-243-2800
FAX 703-243-9650
E-Mail: aaps@aaps.org
Home Page: www.aaps.org

John Lisack, Executive Director
Maureen Downs, Director Finance

925 booths of raw materials, supplies and equipment, research and contract service labs, computer software, packaging and more.
Frequency: Annual November
Mailing list available for rent

6459 AAPT Annual Convention
American Association of Pharmacy Technicians
PO Box 1447
Greensboro, NC 27402

877-368-4771
FAX 336-333-9068
E-Mail: aapt@pharmacytechnician.com
Home Page: www.pharmacytechnician.com

Sandra Covington, President
Susan Jeffery, VP

Education programs and services to help technicians update their skills to keep pace with changes in the pharmacy services.
Frequency: August

6460 ACLA Annual Meeting
American Clinical Laboratory Association
1250 H Street NW
Suite 880
Washington, DC 20005

202-637-9466
FAX 202-637-2050
E-Mail: info@clinical-labs.org
Home Page: www.clinical-labs.org

Aan Mertz, President
JoAnne Glisson, VP
Jason DuBois, VP of Govt. Relations
Francesca O'Reilly, VP of Govt. Affairs

Dedicated to providing the latest information for clinical laboratories.
Frequency: January
Founded in 1971

6461 ACMP Conference
Academy of Managed Care Pharmacy
100 N Pitt Street
Suite 400
Alexandria, VA 22314-3134

703-683-8416
800-827-2627
FAX 703-683-8417
E-Mail: sadres@amcp.org
Home Page: www.amcp.org
Social Media: *Facebook, Twitter, LinkedIn*

Aimee O'Conner, Assistant Director

Offers an exciting lineup of speakers, workshops, and topical sessions designed to meet the challenges of today's pharmacist practicing in a dynamic and constantly evolving managed care environment.
Frequency: October

6462 APHA Annual Meeting & Exposition
American Public Health Association
800 I Street NW
Washington, DC 20001-3710

202-777-2742
FAX 202-777-2534

E-Mail: diane.lentini@apha.org
Home Page: www.apha.org

Diane Lentini, Meetings Manager
Gene Lutz, President
Georges C Benjamin, Executive Director
Jose F Cordero, Member
Louise A Anderson, Director Operations

The premier platform to share successes and failures, discover exceptional best practices and learn from expert colleagues and the latest reasearch in the field.
13000 Attendees
Frequency: November

6463 ASHP Summer Meeting
American Society of Health-System Pharmacists
7272 Wisconsin Avenue
Bethesda, MD 20814-4836

301-657-3000
866-279-0681
FAX 301-664-8857
E-Mail: info@ascp.com
Home Page: www.ascp.com

Janet A Silvester R.Ph.,MBA, President

Offers a variety of programming, and delivers expertise on subject areas that are crucial to advancing a professional practice. Series programming, learning communities, and updates on hot topics, combined with exhibits and a variety of networking opportunities.
Frequency: June

6464 ASPL Developments in Pharmacy Law Seminar
American Society for Pharmacy Law
1224 Centre W
Suite 400B
Springfield, IL 62704

217-391-0219
FAX 217-793-0041
Home Page: www.aspi.org

Melissa Madigan, President
Francis B Paulumbo, Director
Pamela Tolson, CAE, Executive Director
William Fassett, Treasurer

An annual highlight with nationally renowned speakers and panelists discussing issues pertaining to pharmacy law. This seminar has evolved into an excellent educational opportunity for practicing pharmacists, attorneys, and academicians with the opportunity to gain both pharmacy and legal continuing education credits.
Frequency: Annual

6465 Academy of Pharmaceutical Research and Science Convention
American Pharmaceutical Association
2215 Constitution Avenue NW
Washington, DC 20037

202-429-7524
800-237-2742
FAX 202-628-0443
Home Page: www.aphanet.org

Windy K Christner, Meetings/Expositions

Main exhibits, pharmaceutical equipment supplies and services.
Frequency: Annual

6466 American Association of College Pharmacies
1727 King Street
Alexandria, VA 22314

703-739-2330
FAX 703-836-8982
Home Page: www.aacp.org

Lucinda L Maine, Executive VP
Kenneth W Miller, Senior VP
Daniel J Cassidy, COO

Educational association representing pharmacy scientists, educators and administrators.
2.3M Attendees
Frequency: July

6467 American College of Medical Quality Annual Meeting

American College of Medical Quality
4334 Montgomery Avenue
Suite B
Bethesda, MD 20814

301-913-9149
800-924-2149
FAX 301-656-0989
E-Mail: acmq@aol.com
Home Page: www.acmq.org
Social Media: *Facebook, Twitter, LinkedIn*

Alan Krumholz, MD, President
James D. Cross, President-elect
Andrew Jerdonek, Executive Director
Donald Casey, Jr MD, Treasurer

Annual show and 10-20 exhibits of computer hardware and software, pharmaceuticals, medical publications and related equipment, supplies and services.
150 Attendees
Founded in 1973

6468 American Pharmacists Annual Meeting & Expo

American Pharmacists Association
2215 Constitution Avenue, NW
Washington, DC 20037

202-429-7593
800-237-2742
FAX 203-737-3211
E-Mail: lmace@aphanet.org
Home Page: www.aphameeting.org

Laura Larson, Exposition & Exchange Information
Todd McDonald, Meeting Schedule Information
Lindsey Mace, General Conference Assistant
Kristen Binaso, Sponsorship Coordinator
Stacy Berkowitz, Educational Coordinator

The APhA Annual Meeting and Exposition provides information on the latest trends and best practices in pharmacy, while providing attendees the opportunity to share experiences and ideas with 7,000 pharmacy professionals from every practice setting; chain, independent, hospital, federal, long-term care, nuclear, and more.
Frequency: Annual/Spring

6469 Annual NCPA Convention & Trade Exposition

National Community Pharmacists Associations
100 Daingerfield Road
Alexandria, VA 22314

703-683-8200
800-544-7447
FAX 703-683-3619
E-Mail: info@ncpanet.com
Home Page: www.ncpanet.org

Litsa Deck, Director Convention/Trade Expos

Workshops and education programs pretaining to Pharmacy industry.
Frequency: October
Mailing list available for rent

6470 Annual North American Conference and European Annual Conference

Association of Clinical Research Professionals
1012 14th Street NW
Suite 108
Washington, DC 20006

202-737-8100
FAX 202-737-8101

E-Mail: acrp@associationhq.com
Home Page: www.acrpnet.org

Robin Newman, Vice Chair
Thomas L Adams, CAE, President/CEO
Larry J Medley, CAE, Director Finance
Alan Armstrong, Director Marketing/COO

The world's leading conferences for clinical research professionals, presenting diverse educational opportunities and face-to-face interactions with industry experts.
Frequency: April, September

6471 DCAT Western Education Conference

Drug, Chemical & Associated Technologies
1 Washington Boulevard
Suite 7
Robbinsville, NJ 08691

609-448-1000
800-640-3228
FAX 609-448-1944
E-Mail: info@dcat.org
Home Page: www.dcat.org
Social Media: *Facebook, LinkedIn*

Brooke DiGiuseppe, Meeting Services
Margaret Timony, Senior Manager
Jacklyn Vitelli, Deputy Executive Director
Jeanne Motola, Administrative Assistant

Gain important insights into issues and trends that will affect the future of the nutrition and health industry. Participate in discussion on key business issues with industry experts.
Frequency: April

6472 DIA Annual Meeting

Drug Information Association
800 Enterprise Road
Suite 200
Horsham, PA 19044-3595

215-442-6100
FAX 215-442-6199
E-Mail: dia@diahome.org
Home Page: www.diahome.org

Paul Pomerantz BA MBA, Worldwide Executive Director
Lisa Zoks BA, Worldwide Dir Mktg/Communications

6473 Distribution & Logistics Conference

National Association of Chain Drug Stores
413 N Lee Street
PO Box 1417 D-49
Alexandria, VA 22313-1480

703-549-3001
FAX 703-836-4869
Home Page: www.nacds.org
Social Media: *Facebook, Twitter, LinkedIn, YouTube*

Greg Wasson, Chairman
Bob Narveson, Vice Chairman
John Standley, Treasurer

This unique conference explores and evaluates current systems and emerging technologies, and helps retailers and suppliers forge stronger links through supply chain management. The exhibit hall allows leading industry consultants and vendors to demonstrate their products and services.
Frequency: March

6474 Distribution Management Conference & Expo

Healthcare Distribution Management Association
900 N Glebe Road
Suite 1000
Arlington, VA 22203

703-787-0000
FAX 703-935-3200

E-Mail: lburke@hdmanet.org
Home Page: www.healthcaredistribution.org

John Grey, President and CEO
Ann Bittman, EVP and COO
Patrick Kelly, SVP

Provides the latest information on the most important topics affecting healthcare distribution.
Frequency: June

6475 FDLI & FDA Annual Conference

Food and Drug Law Institute
1155 15th Street NW
Suite 800
Washington, DC 20005

202-371-1420
800-956-6293
FAX 202-371-0649
E-Mail: comments@fdli.org
Home Page: www.fdli.org

Susan C. Winckler, President & CEO
Iris V. Stratton CPA, VP Finance & Administration
Michael Sprott, Membership Manager

Bringing together high-ranking officials from the food and drug industry together with top executives.
550+ Members
Founded in 1949

6476 HDMA Annual Meeting

Healthcare Distribution Management Association
900 N Glebe Road
Suite 1000
Arlington, VA 22203

703-787-0000
FAX 703-935-3200
E-Mail: lburke@hdmanet.org
Home Page: www.healthcaredistribution.org

John Grey, President and CEO
Ann Bittman, EVP and COO
Patrick Kelly, SVP

Provides a unique opportunity for senior-level retailer and supplier member executives to interact and discuss strategic issues.
Frequency: October

6477 IPC Annual Meeting

Independent Pharmacy Cooperative
1550 Columbus Street
Sun Prairie, WI 53590

608-259-9556
800-755-1531
FAX 800-274-5525
E-Mail: staff@ipcrx.com
Home Page: www.ipcrx.com

Mike Flint, President/CEO
Gary Helgerson, COO
Chuck Benjamin, CFO

A venue to provide independent pharmacies vital information to maximize their store's profitability
Frequency: July

6478 ISPE Annual Meeting

Int'l Society for Pharmaceutical Engineering
3109 W Dr. Martin Luther King Jr Boulevard
Suite 250
Tampa, FL 33607

813-960-2105
FAX 813-264-2816
E-Mail: ask@ispe.org
Home Page: www.ispe.org

Education and training on topics pretaining to the pharmaceutical manufacturing industry.
Frequency: Annual

6479 Midyear Industry & Technology Issues Conference
American Society for Automation in Pharmacy
492 Norristown Road
Suite 160
Blue Bell, PA 19422

610-825-7783
FAX 310-825-7641
Home Page: www.asapnet.org

WA Lockwood, Executive Director

Learn about the industry and technology issues facing the pharmacy market today.
Frequency: June

6480 NABP's Annual Meeting
National Association of Boards of Pharmacy
700 Busse Highway
Park Ridge, IL 60068

847-698-6227
800-774-6227
FAX 847-698-0124
E-Mail: custserv@nabp.net
Home Page: www.nabp.net

Carmen A Catizone, Executive Director/Secretary

Building regulatory foundation for patients safety.
Frequency: May

6481 NABP's Fall Educational Conference
National Association of Boards of Pharmacy
700 Busse Highway
Park Ridge, IL 60068

847-698-6227
800-774-6227
FAX 847-698-0124
E-Mail: custserv@nabp.net
Home Page: www.nabp.net

Malcom Broussard, Chairperson
Michael Burlson, President
Joseph Adams, Treasurer
Frequency: December

6482 NACDS Annual Meeting
National Association of Chain Drug Stores
413 N Lee Street
Alexandria, VA 22314

703-549-3001
FAX 703-836-4869
Home Page: www.nacds.org

Jodi Witmer, Executive Director
Terry Arth, VP Meetings/International Programs
Larry Lotridge, VP Conference Exhibits

This meeting provides a stage to meet and discuss strategic issues with key trading partners: Strategic Exchange Appointments in which to do business, participants and sponsors from dozens of relevant companies.
1M Attendees
Frequency: April

6483 NCPA Annual Conference on National Legislation and Government Affairs
National Community Pharmacists Associations
100 Daingerfield Road
Alexandria, VA 22314

703-683-8200
800-544-7447
FAX 703-683-3619
E-Mail: info@ncpanet.com
Home Page: www.ncpanet.org

Litsa Deck, Director Convention/Trade Expos

An opportunity to be an insider to discuss community pharmacy issues on Capitol Hill with the people that can make things happen. It will enhance your understanding of the political process and the many legislative issues that will have a dramatic impact on the way you deliver health care in the coming years.
Frequency: April

6484 NCPA Annual Meeting
National Council of State Pharmacy Association
5501 Patterson Avenue
Suite 200
Richmond, VA 23226

804-285-4145
FAX 804-285-4227
E-Mail: becky@ncspae.org
Home Page: www.ncspae.org

Rebecca P Snead, Executive Vice President
Brad Hall, Executive Director

Offers cutting-edge training for professionals from every facet of the pharmacy industry. Learn the latest about prescription drugs, natural products, and over-the-counter remedies. Discover new products and services from the industry's leading manufacturers, and gain knowledge and insights to better aid patients and advance your career.
Frequency: October

6485 NCPDP's Annual Conference
National Council for Prescription Drug Programs
9240 E Raintree Drive
Scottsdale, AZ 85260-7518

480-477-1000
FAX 480-767-1042
E-Mail: ncpdp@ncpdp.org
Home Page: www.ncpdp.org

Beth Fagan, Meeting Planning
Lee Ann Stember, President

Topic will be Building New Technologies. Offers educational sessions, a trade show, kenote speakers and more.
Frequency: March

6486 National Clinical Issues Forum: Metabolic Syndrome
American Pharmaceutical Association Foundation
2215 Constitution Avenue NW
Washington, DC 20037

202-297-7524
800-237-APHA
FAX 202-429-6300
E-Mail: info@aphafoundation.org
Home Page: www.aphafoundation.org

Carol Bugdalski-Stutrud, Director
Carl Emswiller, Director
Hazel Pipkin, VP
Marie Michnich, Director Health Policy Program
Michael Stewart, Director Public Relations

To provide an opportunity for the exchange of information between leading clinical pharmacists from across the U.S. who are providing innovative patient care services for people afflicted with the co-morbidities of diabetes, hypertension and hyperlipidemia.
Frequency: May

6487 National Community Pharmacists Association Convention and Exhibition
National Community Pharmacists Association
100 Daingerfield Road
Alexandria, VA 22314-2833

703-683-8200
800-544-7447
FAX 703-683-3619

E-Mail: info@ncpanet.com
Home Page: www.ncpanet.org

Litsa Deck, Director Convention/Meetings
Faith James, Coordinator Convention/Meetings
Deleisa Johnson, VP Public Relations

Annual show of 450 exhibitors of pharmaceutical and related equipment, supplies and services.
Frequency: October, Florida

6488 National Conference on Advances in Perinatal and Pediatric Nutrition
Amer. Society for Parenteral & Enteral Nutrition
8630 Fenton Street
Suite 412
Silver Spring, MD 20910

301-587-6315
800-727-4567
FAX 301-587-2365
E-Mail: aspen@nutr.org
Home Page: www.nutritioncare.org
Social Media: *Facebook, Twitter*

Marion F Winkler, President
Vincent W Vanek, VP
Robin Kriegel, CAE, Executive Director
Joanne Kieffer, Director Finance

The purpose of the conference is to increase knowledge and awareness of the nutritional requirements of these special need patients. Has been planned for dieticians, nurses, obstetricians, neonatologiests, pediatricians, pediatric gastroenterologists, pharmacists, and other health care professionals involved in the care of high risk pregnant mothers, premature infants, and pediatric patients.
Frequency: July

6489 PCMA Annual Meeting
Pharmaceutical Care Management Association
325 7th St. NW
9th Fl.
Washington, DC 20004

202-756-5700
FAX 202-756-5708
Home Page: www.pcmanet.org
Social Media: *Facebook, Twitter*

Mark Merritt, President & CEO

The industry's annual event for decision makers.
Frequency: Annual
Founded in 2009

6490 RX Expo: An Educational Forum and Buying Show
National Community Pharmacists Association
100 Daingerfield Road
Alexandria, VA 22314-2833

703-683-8200
800-544-7447
FAX 703-683-3619
E-Mail: info@ncpanet.org
Home Page: www.ncpanet.org

Stephen Giroux PD, President
Bruce Roberts RPh, Executive VP/CEO

Annual show and exhibits of general gifts, sundries and seasonal items, over the counter products, health and beauty aids, electronic products, prescription drug products, personal care products, home health care products, IV products and related products.
1700 Attendees

6491 Senior Care Pharmacy: ASCP's Annual Meeting
American Society of Consultant Pharmacists

1321 Duke Street
Alexandria, VA 22314-3563

703-739-1300
800-355-2727
FAX 703-739-1321
E-Mail: info@ascp.com
Home Page: www.ascp.com

Jackie Hajji, Director Meetings/Conventions

Annual meeting of 300 exhibitors of
pharmaceuticals, drug distribution systems,
packaging equipment, computers, durable medical equipment and medical supplies.
2000 Attendees
Frequency: November
Founded in 1969

**6492 The Consultant Pharmacist
Conference and Exhibition**
American Society of Consultant Pharmacists
1321 Duke St
Suite 120
Alexandria, VA 22314-3563

703-739-1300
800-355-2727
FAX 703-739-1321
E-Mail: info@ascp.com
Home Page: www.ascp.com
Social Media: *Facebook, Twitter, LinkedIn,
YouTube, Blogs*

Patti Thompson, Production Manager
Marlene Bloom, Editor
Debbie Furman, Circulation

Learn the most up-to-date clinical, business,
and regulatory information; discover the latest
pharmacy and health information technologies;
and establish the professional contacts that are
critical for today's consultant and senior care
pharmacy practitioners, managers, and business
owners.
6m Members
1200 Attendees
Founded in 1982

6493 USP Annual Scientific Meeting
United States Pharmacopeial Convention
12601 Twinbrook Parkway
Rockville, MD 20852-1790

301-810-0667
800-227-8772
FAX 301-816-8148
E-Mail: support@usp.org
Home Page: www.usp.org

Anju K Malhotra, Manager
Conferences/Meetings
Roger Williams, Executive Director

Open to the public and serves as an interactive
forum where USP and its stakeholders can discuss new direction and standards that affect the
pharmaceutical industry. The meeting provides
attendees an opportunity to better understand
the scope of USP's scientific work and provide
input on key standards-setting issues.
Frequency: September

**6494 Western Section Meeting of the
Triological Society**
Triological Society
555 N 30th Street
Omaha, NE 68131-2136

402-346-5500
FAX 402-346-5300
E-Mail: info@triological.org
Home Page: www.triological.org

I Kaufman Arenberg, MD, Executive Director

Annual show of 30 exhibitors of medical services and supplies related to Otolaryngology.
152 Attendees
Frequency: May

Directories & Databases

6495 American Drug Index
Lippincott Williams & Wilkins
16522 Hunters Green Pkwy
PO Box 1600
Hagerstown, MD 21740

301-223-2300
800-638-3030
FAX 301-223-2400
Home Page: www.lww.com
Social Media: *Facebook, Twitter*

Norman Billups, Editor
Shirley Billups, Editor

Contains more than 22,000 entries. Practical
features include: alphabetically listed drug
names, extensive cross-indexing, complete information on the distributor's brand name,
manufacturer, generic and/or chemical names,
chemical strength and much more useful information. Electronic version available.
Cost: $69.95
1088 Pages
Frequency: Annual, Hardcover
ISBN: 1-574391-33-X

6496 Annual Meeting & Showcase
Academy of Managed Care Pharmacy
100 N Pitt St
Suite 400
Alexandria, VA 22314-3141

703-683-8416
800-827-2627
FAX 703-683-8417
E-Mail: sandres@amcp.org
Home Page: www.amcp.org
Social Media: *Facebook, Twitter, LinkedIn*

Douglas Burgoyne, President
Robert Gregory, Treasurer

Nationally reowned keynote speakers, new research presentations, achievement awards,
competitions and Board inaugurations fill the
agenda for managed care pharmacy's premier
event.
Frequency: April

6497 CSO Directory
Drug Information Association
800 Enterprise Road
Suite 200
Horsham, PA 19044-3595

215-442-6100
FAX 215-442-6199
E-Mail: dia@diahome.org
Home Page: www.diahome.org

Paul Pomerantz BA MBA, Worldwide
Executive Director
Lisa Zoks BA, Worlwide Dir
Mktg/Communications

One of the industry's most respected and comprehensive reference guides, compiles company
descriptions and contact information from hundreds of companies that provide services for
every phase of the clinical trial and drug
development process.

**6498 DCAT Digest and Directory of
Membership**
Drug, Chemical & Associated Technologies
1 Washington Blvd
Suite 7
Robbinsville, NJ 08691-3162

609-448-1000
800-640-3228
FAX 609-448-1944
E-Mail: info@dcat.org

Home Page: www.dcat.org
Social Media: *Facebook, LinkedIn*

Margaret Timony, Executive Director
Lynda M Doyle, Senior Manager
Jacklyn Vitelli, Deputy Executive Director
Jeanne Motola, Administrative Assistant

Keeping members in touch with their colleagues throughout the industry.

6499 DIOGENES
FOI Services
704 Quince Orchard Rd
Gaithersburg, MD 20878-1700

301-975-9400
FAX 301-975-0702
E-Mail: infofoi@foiservices.com
Home Page: www.foiservices.com

John Carey, President
Marlene Bobka, Vice President of Services

This comprehensive database contains citations
to more than 1 million unpublished US Food
and Drug Administration regulatory documents
covering prescription and over-the-counter
drugs.
Founded in 1975

6500 DRUGDEX System
Thompson Micromedex
6200 South Syracuse Way
Suite 300
Greenwood Village, CO 80111-4740

303-679-9500
800-525-9083
FAX 303-486-6464
Home Page: www.micromedex.com
Social Media: *Facebook*

This comprehensive database covers all aspects
of drugs and their use, including investiga-
tional, FDA-approved, and OTC preparations.
Frequency: Full-text

6501 DataStat
NDCHealth
3975 Research Park Drive
Ann Arbor, MI 48108

734-994-0540
800-225-5632
FAX 734-663-9084
E-Mail: mweindorf@datastat.com
Home Page: www.datastat.com

Marielle Weindorf, Senior Research Director
Ellen Johnson
Randolph Hutto, EVP Business Development
Charles W Miller, EVP Corporate Initiatives

This comprehensive database offers descriptions of drug interactions at the ingredient level
for individual drugs and therapeutic classes of
drugs.
Frequency: Full-text
Founded in 1967

6502 Directory of Hospital Personnel
Grey House Publishing
4919 Route 22
PO Box 56
Amenia, NY 12501

518-789-8700
800-562-2139
FAX 845-373-6390
E-Mail: books@greyhouse.com
Home Page: www.greyhouse.com
Social Media: *Facebook, Twitter*

Richard Gottlieb, President
Leslie Mackenzie, Publisher

A Who's Who of the hospital universe that
makes it easy to get in touch with over 10,000
key decision makers. Comprehensive data includes listing of US hospitals, detailed contact
information, number of physicians and employees, teaching affiliations, accreditation and

much more.
Cost: $325.00
2300 Pages
ISBN: 1-592372-86-4
Founded in 1981

6503 Directory of Hospital Personnel - Online Database
Grey House Publishing
4919 Route 22
PO Box 56
Amenia, NY 12501

518-789-8700
800-562-2139
FAX 845-373-6390
E-Mail: gold@greyhouse.com
Home Page: http://gold.greyhouse.com
Social Media: *Facebook, Twitter*

Richard Gottlieb, President
Leslie Mackenzie, Publisher

The DHP Online Database is the best resource you can have at your fingertips when researching or marketing a product or service to the hospital market. A 'Who's Who' of the hospital universe, this database puts you in touch with over 140,000 key decision-makers at 5,800 hospitals nationwide.
Founded in 1981

6504 Drug Store and HBC Chains
Chain Store Guide
3922 Coconut Palm Dr
Tampa, FL 33619-1389

813-627-6700
800-778-9794
FAX 813-627-7094
E-Mail: info@csgis.com
Home Page: www.csgis.com

Mike Jarvis, Publisher
Chris Leedy, Advertising Sales

Tap into the lucrative drug industry with profiles on more than 1,700 US and Canadian companies operating two or more retail drug stores, deep discount stores, health and beauty care (HBC) stores, cosmetic stores or vitamin stores that have industry sales of at least $250,000. This powerful database empowers you to sell and market your products successfully by reaching more than 8,300 key decision makers.
Cost: $335.00

6505 Drug and Cosmetic Industry Catalog
Advanstar Communications
One Park Avenue
New York, NY 10016

212-797-7631
FAX 212-951-6793
E-Mail: info@advanstar.com
Home Page: www.advanstar.com

Eric Lisman, Executive VP

Over 1,000 manufacturers and suppliers of packaging equipment, private formulas and raw materials used in the drug and cosmetics industries are profiled.
Cost: $25.00
270 Pages
Frequency: Annual
Circulation: 4,000
Mailing list available for rent

6506 FDC Reports: The NDA Pipeline
FDC Reports
5550 Friendship Boulevard
Suite 1
Chevy Chase, MD 20815-7278

301-657-9830
FAX 301-664-7238

E-Mail: fdc.customer.service@elsevier.com
Home Page: www.fdcreports.com

Karl Uhlendo, Executive Editor
Mike Squires, President

The NDA Pipeline is a searchable database available through the Web that contains up-to-date coverage of over 900 companies and more than 7,00 approval records. The NDA Pipeline tracks drug and biological product research, clinical trials and approvals. It also includes a comprehensive listing of products in research, descriptions of phases of development and licensing information and linked articles from The Pink Sheet and other FDC Reports publications.
900 Pages
Frequency: Annual
ISSN: 7012-8630
Founded in 1939

6507 GAMP Good Practice Guide
Int'l Society for Pharmaceutical Engineering
3109 W Dr. Martin Luther King Jr Boulevard
Suite 250
Tampa, FL 33607

813-960-2105
FAX 813-264-2816
E-Mail: ask@ispe.org
Home Page: www.ispe.org

Provides new comprehensive guidance on meeting current regulatory expectations for compliant electronic records and signatures, which includes the need for record integrity, security, and availability throughout the required retention period. This is achieved by well documented, validated systems, and the application of appropriate operational controls.

6508 ISPE Good Practice Guide
Int'l Society for Pharmaceutical Engineering
3109 W Dr. Martin Luther King Jr Boulevard
Suite 250
Tampa, FL 33607

813-960-2105
FAX 813-264-2816
E-Mail: ask@ispe.org
Home Page: www.ispe.org

Provides a standard methodology for use in testing the containment efficiency of solids handling systems used in the pharmaceutical industry under closely defined conditions. It covers the main factors that affect the test results for specific contained solids handling systems, including material handled, room environment, air quality, ventilation and operator technique.

6509 Ident-A-Drug Reference
Therapeutic Research
3120 W March Lane
PO Box 8190
Stockton, CA 95219-0190

209-472-2240
FAX 209-472-2249
Home Page: www.pletter.com

Jeff Jellin, PharmD, Editor

It gives you all the drug identification information found on this web site for more than 30,000 entries.
Cost: $85.00
704 Pages
ISBN: 0-967613-65-5

6510 InVitro Diagnostics Industry Directory
CTB International Publishing
PO Box 218
Maplewood, NJ 07040-0218

973-966-0997
FAX 973-966-0242

E-Mail: info@ctbintl.com
Home Page: www.ctbintl.com

Lists address, phone and fax number of invitro diagnostics companies, suppliers, regulatory agencies, professional societies and trade associations worldwide and contains over 2,300 entries worldwide-more than 1,200 contact names.
Cost: $277.00
ISBN: 1-887566-17-1
Printed in one color on matte stock

6511 International Pharmaceutical Abstracts Database
Thomson Scientific
1500 Spring Garden St
Philadelphia, PA 19130-4067

215-386-0100
800-336-4474
FAX 215-386-2911
E-Mail: ts.info.na@thomson.com
Home Page: www.thomson.com

Robert C Cullen, President/CEO
Craig Soderstrom, VP Office of CEO
Kristen McCarthy, VP Marketing/Communications
James Smith, Chief Operating Officer

These reports offering the latest in the development of drugs overseas, clinical and inventigotional use, cosmetics and, alternative and herbal medicine. Reports on pharmacy practice are also included.
ISSN: 0020-8264

6512 NABP Manual
National Association of Boards of Pharmacy
700 Busse Highway
Park Ridge, IL 60068

847-698-6227
800-774-6227
FAX 847-698-0124
E-Mail: custserv@nabp.net
Home Page: www.nabp.net

Malcom Broussard, Chairperson
Michael Burlson, President
Joseph Adams, Treasurer

Developed to be read in conjunction with state laws. It presents general information essential to all board of pharmacy members, and serves as a valuable reference for new board members. The manual is ideal for compiling and cross-referencing amendments and other records.
Cost: $25.00

6513 Natural Medicines Comprehensive Database
Therapeutic Research
PO Box 8190
Stockton, CA 95208-0190

209-472-2240
FAX 209-472-2249
Home Page: www.pletter.com

Jeff Jellin, PharmD, Editor

Provides you with monographs on each natural ingredient plus updated helpful charts and tables.
Cost: $85.00
2000 Pages
ISBN: 0-967613-68-X

6514 Pharma Industry Directory
CTB International Publishing
PO Box 218
Maplewood, NJ 07040

973-966-0997
FAX 973-966-0242

E-Mail: info@ctbintl.com
Home Page: www.ctbintl.com

This is divided into 4 sections. The first section contains a complete alphabetical listing of the names, addresses, and phone and fax numbers of over 1,300 companies. The other sections are alphabetical listings of the companies with tables identifying them as to the fields they are involved in. The last section is a business index.
Cost: $250.00
ISBN: 1-887566-21-X
Printed in one color on matte stock

6515 Pharmaceutical News Index

UMI/Data Courier
620 S 3rd Street
Suite 400
Louisville, KY 40202-2475

502-583-4111
800-626-2823
FAX 502-589-5572

Contains the latest US and international information about pharmaceutial, cosmetics, medical devices, and related health industries.

6516 Physicians' Desk Reference

Thomson Medical Economics
5 Paragon Drive
Montvale, NJ 07645-1742

201-358-7500
800-442-6657
FAX 201-573-8999
E-Mail: PDRbookstore@medec.com
Home Page: www.pdr.net

Thomas Eck, Marketing Manager

Physicians have turned to PDR for the latest word in prescription drugs for 57 years. Today, it is considered the standard prescription drug reference and can be found in virtually every phyician's office, hospital and pharmacy in the US.
Cost: $92.95
3,000 Pages
Frequency: Hardcover

6517 Roster of Faculty and Professional Staff

American Association of Colleges of Pharmacy
1727 King St
Suite 210
Alexandria, VA 22314-2700

703-739-2330
FAX 703-836-8982
Home Page: www.aacp.org

Lucinda Maine, Executive VP
Kenneth W Miller, Senior VP
Daniel J Cassidy, COO

A directory of more than 5,000 full and part-time pharmacy faculty members including mailing and e-mail addresses, phone and fax numbers, degrees, and disciplines. Also included is valuable information about AACP such as officers, committee members, staff, and addresses and phone numbers for affiliated associations and corporations. $10 AACP Member.
Cost: $100.00
Frequency: November
Mailing list available for rent

Industry Web Sites

6518 http://gold.greyhouse.com
G.O.L.D Grey House OnLine Databases
Grey House Publishing's online database platform, GOLD, offers Quick Search, Keyword Search and Expert Search for most business sectors including drug, pharmaceutical and healthcare markets. The GOLD platform makes finding the information you need quick and easy - whether you're a novice searcher or an experienced database user. All of Grey House's directory products are available for subscription on the GOLD platform.

6519 www.aacp.org
American Association of Colleges of Pharmacy
National organization representing the interests of pharmaceutical education and educators. Comprising all 83 US pharmacy colleges and schools including more than 4,000 faculty, 36,000 student enrolled in professional programs and 3,600 individuals pursuing graduate study, AACP is committed to excellence in pharmaceutical education.

6520 www.aaps.org
American Association of Pharmaceutical Scientists
Aims to advance science through the open exchange of scientific knowledge, serve as an information resource and contribute to human health through pharmaceutical reseach and development.

6521 www.accp.com
American College of Clinical Pharmacy
Professional and scientific society that provides leadership, education, advocacy and resources enabling clinical pharmacists to achieve excellence in practice and research.

6522 www.acrpnet.org
Association of Clinical Research Professionals
Provides global leadership for the clinical research profession by promoting and advancing the highest ethical standards and practices.

6523 www.aihp.org
American Instiute of the History of Pharmacy
Supplies information regarding pharmaceutical history and usage.

6524 www.apha.org
American Public Health Association
Brings together researchers, health service providers, administrators, teachers and other health workers in a unique, multidisciplinary environment of professional exchange, study and action on the effort to prevent disease and promote health.

6525 www.asapnet.org
American Society for Automation in Pharmacy
Is to assist its members in advancing the application of computer technology in the pharmacists role as caregiver and in the efficient operation and management of a pharmacy.

6526 www.ashp.org
American Society of Health-System Pharmacy
An association that brings together health-system pharmacists and addresses their concerns.

6527 www.aspl.org
American Society for Pharmacy Law
An organization of pharmacists and lawyers who are interested in the law as it applies to the pharmacy industry.

6528 www.diahome.org
Drug Information Association
Association for those interested in technical developments, supply, and production of drugs.

Exchanges and disseminates information by continuing to provide a neutral forum, respecting and welcoming all participants and offering quality driven programming.

6529 www.fdli.org
Food and Drug Law Institute
Nonprofit educational organization dedicated to improving the understanding of the laws, regulations and policies affecting the food, drug, medical device and biologics industries. A neutral, non-partisan organization that does not lobby.

6530 www.greyhouse.com
Grey House Publishing
Authoritative reference directories for most business sectors including drug, pharmaceutical and healthcare markets. Users can search the online databases with varied search criteria allowing for custom searches by product category, geographic area, sales volume, keyword, subject and more. Full Grey House catalog and online ordering also available.

6531 www.ipecamericas.org
International Pharmaceutical Excipients Council
Members are companies with an interest in the otherwise inert chemicals used as vehicles for medicines. Federation of three independent regional industry associations headquartered in the US. Each association focuses its attention on the applicable law, regulations, science and business practices of its region. The three associations work together on excipient safety and public health issues, in connection with international trade matters, and to achieve harmonization of regulatory standards.

6532 www.ncpanet.org
National Community Pharmacists Association
Represents independent pharmacists, provides support for undergraduate pharmacy education.

6533 www.npa.org
National Pharmaceutical Alliance
Represents the interests of small pharmaceutical companies and allied industries.

6534 www.nutritioncare.org
American Soc. for Parenteral & Enteral Nutrition
Strives to be a conduit amoung those interested in Nutrition Support.

6535 www.pda.org
Parenteral Drug Association
Members are makers of parenteral (injectable) drugs and other pharmaceuticals, as well as suppliers, academia and regulatory bodies. Our mission is to advance the pharmaceutical and biopharmaceutical technology internationally by promoting scientifically sound and practical technical information and education for industry and regulatory issues.

6536 www.pdr.net
Thomson Medical Economics
Physicians have turned to PDR for the latest word on prescription drugs for 57 years. Today it is considered the standard prescription drug reference and can be found in virtually every phyician's office, hospital and pharmacy in the US.

6537 www.pharmacist.com
American Pharmacists Association
APhA was the first established national professional society of pharmacists, founded in 1852 as the American Pharamceutical Assocation. It is the largest assocation of pharamcists in the

US, whose mission is to provide information, education, and advocacy to empower its members to improve medication use and advance patient care.

6538 www.pharmacytechnician.com
American Association of Pharmacy Technicians

Provides leadership and represents the interests of its members to the public as well as healthcare organizations. Promotes the safe, effectacious, and cost effective dispensing distribution and use of medications. Provides continuing education programs and services to help technicians update their skills to keep pace with changes in pharmacy services.

6539 www.thompson.com
Thompson Scientific and Healthcare

Professionals in business, government, law and academia have reliedon us for the most authoritative, timely and practical guidance available.

6540 www.usp.org
United States Pharmacopeia

Helps to ensure that consumers recieve quality medicines by establishing state-of-the-art standards that pharmaceutical manufacturers must meet. We provide standards for more than 3,800 medicines, dietary supplements and other health care products.

Associations

6541 Advanced Network & Services
1225 Eye Street, NW
Suite 550
Washington, DC 20005

845-795-2090
FAX 845-795-2180
E-Mail: contact@advanced.org
Home Page: consumerbankers.com
Social Media: *Facebook, Twitter, LinkedIn*

Wiiliam Howle, Chair
Ross Elect, Chair Elect
Timothy Wennes, Past Chair

A nonprofit corporation dedicated to advancing
education by accelerating the use of computer
networking applications and technology.
Mailing list available for rent

6542 Advertising Specialty Institute
4800 Street Rd
Langhorne, PA 19053-6698

215-953-4000
800-546-1350
FAX 215-953-3045
E-Mail: customerservice@asicentral.com
Home Page: www.asicentral.com
Social Media: *Facebook, Twitter, LinkedIn,
YouTube, Instagram, Pinterest*

Timothy M Andrews, CEO
Susanne Curry, SVP Marketing

Advertising Specialty Institute provides distributors, suppliers and decorators in the advertising specialty industry with catalogs,
information directories, newsletters, magazines, web sites and databases, and offers interactive e-commerce, marketing and selling
tools.
26000 Members
Founded in 1950

6543 Alliance for Public Technology
919 18th St NW
Suite 900
Washington, DC 20006-5512

480-624-2500
FAX 202-263-2960
Home Page: www.apt.org

Sylvia Rosenthal, Executive Director
Matthew Bennett, Policy Director

A nonprofit membership organization based in
Washington, DC.

**6544 American Public Communications
Council**
3213 Duke Street
Suite 806
Alexandria, VA 22314

703-739-1322
800-868-2722
FAX 703-739-1324
E-Mail: apcc@apcc.net
Home Page: www.apcc.net

Mason Harris, State Assistant Director
Troy Lee, Additional Director
Michael Bright, At-Large Director
Donald Goens, At-Large Director

Aims to protect and expand domestic and foreign markets for public communications and
provide business opportunities for members.
Founded in 1988

**6545 American Registry for Internet
Numbers**
3635 Concorde Parkway
Suite 200
Chantilly, VA 20151-1130

703-227-9840
FAX 703-227-0676
E-Mail: hostmaster@arin.net
Home Page: www.arin.net

John Curran, President
Paul Andersen, Treasurer
Timothy Denton, Secretary

Manage the internet numbering resources for
North America focused completely on serving
our members and the Internet community at
large.

6546 American e-Commerce Association

Home Page: www.aeaus.com

Computer training, e-commerce education,
membership, recognition, endorsement, and
evaluation services.

**6547 Association for the Advancement of
Computing in Education**
P.O. Box 719
Waynesville, NC 28786

757-623-7588
FAX 828-246-9557
E-Mail: info@aace.org
Home Page: www.aace.org

International, educational and professional
nonprofit organization dedicated to the advancement of the knowledge, theory and quality of learning and teaching at all levels with
information technology. Encourages scholarly
inquiry related to information technology and
research results through publications, conferences, societies and chapters plus
inter-organizational projects.
Founded in 1981

6548 Association of Internet Researchers
910 W. Van Buren St.
Suite 142
Chicago, IL 60607-3523

Home Page: www.aoir.org
Social Media: *Facebook, Twitter*

Lori Kendall, President
Jennifer Stromer-Galley, Vice-President
Michael Zimmer, Treasurer
Andrew Herman, Secretary

A learned society dedicated to the advancement
of the transdisciplinary field of Internet Studies.

**6549 Business Marketing Association:
Boston**
246 Hampshire Street
Cambridge, MA 02130

617-418-4000
800-664-4262
FAX 312-822-0054
E-Mail: info@thebmaboston.com
Home Page: www.thebmaboston.com/

Michael Lewis, President
Will Robinson, VP Public Relations
Matthew Mamet, VP Internet Marketing
Larry Perreault, VP Finance
Chris Perkett, VP Programming

BMA Boston helps members improve their
ability to manage business-to-business marketing and communications for greater productivity and profitability by providing unique access
to information, ideas, and the experience of
peers. The BMA offers an information-packed
Website, online skills-building, marketing certification programs, and industry surveys and
papers. In addition, members have the opportu-

nity to interact with peers at seminars, chapter
training programs and the BMA Annual
Conference.

6550 Business Software Alliance
20 F Street, NW
Suite 800
Washington, DC 20001

202-872-5500
FAX 202-872-5501
E-Mail: info@bsa.org
Home Page: www.bsa.org
Social Media: *Facebook, Twitter, LinkedIn,
YouTube, RSS*

Steven Dietz, Chair
Bruce Sewell, Vice Chair
Bradford Smith, Secretary
Scott Taylor, Treasurer

An organization dedicated to promoting a safe
and legal digital world. BSA educates consumers on software management and copyright protection, cyber security, trade, e-commerce and
other internet related issues.
Founded in 1988

6551 CTIA-The Wireless Association
1400 16th Street, NW
Suite 600
Washington, DC 20036

202-785-0081
Home Page: www.ctia.org̈
Social Media: *Facebook, Twitter, LinkedIn*

Meredith Attwell Baker, President/ CEO
Michael Altschul, Sr. VP, General Counsel
Scott Bergmann, Vice President, Regulatory
Affairs
Heather Blanchard, Director, Internet
Development
Rocco Carlitti, VP, Finance & Administration

An industry trade group that represents the international wireless telecommunications
industry.

**6552 Consumer Electronics Association
(CEA)**
1919 S Eads Street
Arlington, VA 22202

703-907-7600
866-858-1555
FAX 703-907-7675
E-Mail: communications@ce.org
Home Page: www.ce.org
Social Media: *Facebook, Twitter, LinkedIn,
Flickr, Google+*

Gary Shapiro, President/CEO
Daniel Pidgeon, Chairman
Peter Lesser, Industry Executive Advisor
Jason Oxman, VP Communications
Jenny Pareti, Public Policy Director

Consumer Electronics Association (CEA) provides valuable and innovative member-only resources including: exclusive information and
unparalleled market research, networking opportunities with business advocates and leaders, up-to-date educational programs and
technical training, exposure in extensive promotional programs, and representation from the
voice of the industry.
2000 Members

6553 EMarketing Association
40 Blue Ridge Dr
Charlestown, RI 02813

401-315-2194
FAX 408-884-2461
E-Mail: service@emarketingassociation.com
Home Page: www.emarketingassociation.com
Social Media: *Facebook, Twitter, LinkedIn*

Robert Fleming, President
Todd Daum, VP

John Hastings, VP
Linda Jaffe, VP

An international association of emarketing professionals. Members include government, companies, professionals and students involved with the emarketing arena.

6554 Electronic Retailing Association

607 14th Street, NW
Suite 530
Washington, DC 20005

703-841-1751
800-987-6462
FAX 425-977-1036
E-Mail: webadmin@retailing.org
Home Page: www.retailing.org
Social Media: *Facebook, Twitter, LinkedIn, Flickr, YouTube*

Julie Coons, CEO
Christopher Hearing, Treasurer
Babak Azad, Member of the Board

To foster growth, development and acceptance of the rapidly growing direct response industry worldwide for the companies who use the power of electronic media to sell goods and services to the public.

6555 Hispanic Chamber of E-Commerce

750 B St
Ste. 3308
San Diego, CA 92101

858-768-2483
FAX 858-456-5238
E-Mail: info@hiscec.com
Home Page: www.hiscec.com
Social Media: *Facebook, YouTube*

Tayde Aburto, Founder
Claudia Garcia, Founder/Chief Education Officer
Lisa Maino, Founder & CEO
German M Bravo, Founder/Chief Technology Officer
Rodrigo Gomez, Founder/Market Intelligence

The Hispanic Chamber of E-Commerce is a B2B membership-based national business association focused on providing tools and solutions to members to increase their presence online.
200 Members
Founded in 2008

6556 Information Systems Security Association

12100 Sunset Hills Road.
Suite 130
Reston, VA 20190

703-234-4077
866-349-5818
FAX 703-435-4390
Home Page: www.issa.org
Social Media: *Facebook, Twitter, LinkedIn, YouTube, Google+*

Andrea C. Hoy, CISM, CISSP, MBA, President
Justin White, Vice President
Anne Rogers, Secretary/ Director of Operations
Pamela Fusco, Treasurer/ Chief Financial Officer
Frances Alexander, Director

A nonprofit, international professional organization of information security professionals and practitioners.

6557 International Society for Technology in Education

180 W 8th Avenue
Eugene, OR 97401-2916

541-302-3777
800-336-5191
FAX 541-302-3778
E-Mail: iste@iste.org
Home Page: www.iste.org

Social Media: *Facebook, Twitter, LinkedIn, YouTube, Pinterest*

Kecia Ray, EdD, Chair
Matt Harris, EdD, Chair-Elect
Mia Wiiliams, PhD, Secretary
Mila Thomsa Fuller, Ed.D, Treasurer

A large nonprofit organization serving the technology-using educator.
12M Members
Founded in 1979

6558 Internet Marketing Association

10 Mar Del Rey San
Clemente, CA 92673

949-443-9300
FAX 949-443-2215
E-Mail: info@imanetwork.org
Home Page: www.imanetwork.orgÿ
Social Media: *Twitter, LinkedIn*

Rachel Reenders, CIM Account Executive
Sinan Kanatsiz, CIM, Chairman and Founder
Matthew Langie, CIM, Vice Chairman of Education
Jeff Marcoux, Director
David Krauss, Director

A professional internet marketing group that provides educational resources on effective internet marketing strategies to business professionals.

6559 Internet Merchants Association

E-Mail: info@imamerchants.org
Home Page: www.imamerchants.org
Social Media: *Facebook*

Fred Neff, President
Scott Cole, Vice-President
Doyle Carver, Secretary
Andy Sollofe, Treasurer

Develops, promotes, and protects the economic vitality of internet merchants through a positive business environment and fosters a climate in whichcommerce, industry, and technology will flourish.

6560 Internet Society

1775 Wiehle Ave
Suite 201
Reston, VA 20190-5158

703-439-2120
FAX 703-326-9881
E-Mail: isoc@isoc.org
Home Page: www.isoc.org

Kathryn Brown, President/ CEO
Gregory Kapfer, CFO

Technologists, developers, educators, researchers, government representatives, and business people.
16000 Members
Founded in 1992

6561 Internet Societyÿ

1775 Wiehle Avenue
Suite 201
Reston, VA 20190-5108

703-439-2120
E-Mail: isoc@isoc.org
Home Page: www.internetsociety.org
Social Media: *Facebook, Twitter, LinkedIn*

Kathryn Brown, President/ CEO
Ms. Nicole Armstrong, Senior Events Manager
Howard Baggott, Senior Events Manager
Brenda Boggs, Senior Drupal Developer
Andre Copelin, Chief of Staff

An international, nonprofit organization that provides leadership in Internet related standards, education, and policy.
Founded in 1992

6562 National E-Commerce Association

PO Box 2825
Peoria, AZ 85380

Home Page: www.ecommerceassoc.com

The National E-Commerce Association provides an ear and a voice for the E-Commerce industry at the local, state and federal level. In addition to this, we have and will continue to negotiate the most aggressive pricing on goods and services for our members.
Founded in 1980

6563 NetSuite Ecommerce

2955 Campus Drive
Suite 100
San Mateo, CA 94403-2511

650-627-1000
877-638-7848
FAX 650-627-1001
E-Mail: info@netsuite.com
Home Page: www.netsuite.com
Social Media: *Facebook, Twitter, LinkedIn, YouTube*

Evan Goldberg, Co-Founder/Chief Technology Officer
Zach Nelson, CEO
Jim McGeever, President/COO
Ron Gill, Chief Financial Officer
Fred Studer, Chief Marketing Officer

NetSuite E-commerce provides you with the tools you need to drive growth in your e-commerce channel and streamline and automate your business operations.
10000 Members
Founded in 1998

6564 The Entertainment Software Association

575 7th Street, NW
Suite 300
Washington, DC 20004

E-Mail: esa@theESA.com
Home Page: www.theesa.com
Social Media: *Facebook, Twitter*

Michael D. Gallagher, President/ CEO

A U.S. association exclusively dedicated to serving the business and public affairs needs of companies that publish computer and video games for video game consoles, handheld devices, personal computers, and the Internet.

6565 US Internet Industry Association

PO Box 302
Luray, VA 22835

540-742-1928
Home Page: www.usiia-net.org

Dennis C. Hayes, Chairman
David P. McClure, President/ CEO
Michael McKeehan, Chair Public Policy
Christian Dawson, Chair, Web Hosting Council
Stephen B. May, Chief Technology Officer

A nonprofit North American trade association for Internet commerce, content and connectivity.
Founded in 1994

6566 Uniform Code Council

Princeton Pike Corporate Center
1009 Lenox Drive Suite 202
Lawrenceville, NJ 08648

609-620-0200
FAX 609-620-1200
Home Page: www.gs1us.org
Social Media: *Facebook, Twitter, LinkedIn*

Robert W Carpenter, President/CEO
Laura DiSciullo, SVP, Solutions
Gayle (Jones) Reilich, SVP, Customer Engagement
Yegneswaran Kumar, SVP/CFO
Siobhan O'Bara, SVP, Industry Engagement

Barcodes, eCommerce and data synchronization, to EPC/RFID and business process automation standards.
Frequency: Members 280,000
Founded in 1974

6567 Women in eCommerce
PO Box 550856
Fort Lauderdale, FL 33355-0856

954-625-6606
877-947-3337
E-Mail: heidi@wecai.org
Home Page: www.wecai.org
Social Media: *Facebook, Twitter, LinkedIn*

Suzannah Richards, President
Rosana Santos, President Elect
Ellen Sue Burton, VP/Logistics & Hospitality
Racheli Smilovitz, VP/Professional Development
Dalila J. Grohowski, VP/Membership Development

The original business and social networking community for social and professional networking and business development for successful women who want to take their businesses to a new level offline and online. We offer tools, resources and networking opportunities to build a strong foundation for future growth and expansion.
Founded in 2001

6568 eCommerce Merchants Trade Association
917-388-1698
E-Mail: membersupport@ecmta.org
Home Page: www.ecmta.org

Brandon Dupsky, Managing Director
Jonathan Garriss, Executive Director

eCommerce Merchants is a trade association founded by a group of online retailers who realized that by working together they could enjoy the premium services and discounted pricing normally available to very large companies.
Founded in 2005

6569 eMarketing Association
40 Blue Ridge Dr
Suite 129
Charlestown, RI 02813

800-496-2950
FAX 408-884-2461
E-Mail: service@eMarketingAssociation.com
Home Page: www.emarketingassociation.com
Social Media: *Facebook, Twitter, LinkedIn*

Chris Baggott, CEO
Bert DuMars, C-Founder/CEO
Murray Gaylord, VP/Marketing
Jeff Hilmire, President
Simms Jenkins, Founder & Principal

The eMA provides marketing resources, services, research, certifications, educational programs and events to its members and the marketing community. The eMA works with a number of organizations, companies and governments on issues related to e-commerce, multi-channel marketing and legislative issues.~
Founded in 1997

Newsletters

6570 APT News
Alliance for Public Technology

919 18th St Nw
Suite 1000
Washington, DC 20006-5512

202-263-2970
FAX 202-263-2960
Home Page: www.apt.org

Sylvia Rosenthal, Executive Director
Frequency: Bi-Monthly

6571 Dot.COM
Business Communications Company
25 Van Zant Street
Suite 13
Norwalk, CT 06855-1713

203-853-4266
FAX 203-853-0348
E-Mail: sales@bccresearch.com
Home Page: www.bccresearch.com

Louis Naturman, Publisher
C Toenne, Editor

Updates readers on the commercial use of the Internet and related platforms.
Cost: $38.00

6572 E-Healthcare Market Reporter
Health Resources Publishing
1913 Atlantic Ave
Suite 200
Manasquan, NJ 08736-1067

732-292-1100
888-843-6242
FAX 732-292-1111
E-Mail: info@themcic.com
Home Page: www.healthresourcesonline.com

Robert K Jenkins, Publisher
Judith Granel, Marketing
John Russel, Editor
Brett Powell, Regional Director
Alice Burron, Director

A bi-monthly covering strategies, new products, innovation, privacy issue, business solutions, service available, vendor news and comparative for implementing sales and marketing on the internet.
Cost: $397.00
Frequency: Fortnightly
ISSN: 1098-5654
Founded in 1988

6573 E-News
Patricia Seybold Group
Po Box 240565
Boston, MA 02129

617-742-5200
800-826-2424
FAX 617-742-1028
E-Mail: feedback@psgroup.com
Home Page: www.psgroup.com

Patricia Seybold, Founder/CEO

E-mail newsletter includes perspectives on the e-commerce industry, research and upcoming events.

6574 Ecommerce @lert
ZD Journals
500 Canal View Boulevard
Rochester, NY 14623-2800

585-407-7301
FAX 585-214-2387
E-Mail: eca@zd.com
Home Page: www.ecommercealert.com
Social Media: *Facebook, Twitter, LinkedIn*

Bob Artner, Managing Editor

Explores the emerging digital and online technology used in sales management, as well as the companies in the forefront of this change.
Cost: $495.00

6575 Electronic Commerce News
Phillips Publishing

PO Box 60037
Potomac, MD 20859

301-208-6787
FAX 301-424-2098
E-Mail: htreat@phillips.com
Home Page: www.ectoday.com

Heather Treat, Publisher
Stuart Zipper, Editor
Diane Schwartz, Publisher
Laurie Hofmann, Director of Marketing

Provides business strategies for the extended enterprise with the latest technological development and opportunities.
Cost: $597.00
Frequency: Weekly

6576 Higher Education Technology News
Business Publishers
2222 Sedwick Dr
Suite 101
Durham, NC 27713

800-223-8720
FAX 800-508-2592
E-Mail: custserv@bpinews.com
Home Page: www.bpinews.com

Provides timely, independent coverage of the issues surrounding technology in a higher educational setting. Offers news from federal and state government, the business world and others educators.
Cost: $307.00
8 Pages
Founded in 1963

6577 International Cyber Centers
Probe Research
3 Wing Drive
Suite 240
Cedar Knolls, NJ 07927-1000

973-285-1500
FAX 973-285-1519
E-Mail: probe@proberesearch.com
Home Page: www.proberesearch.com

Strategic positioning and product portfolios of major domestic and international carriers in collocation, Web hosting, applications hosting, e-commerce, IP-centric data, managed services and other value added offerings. Examines the global square footage race in building or upgrading what are variously known as Internet centers, data centers or cyber centers worldwide. Profiles of several key players are included in the bulletin issue.

6578 Internet Alliance Cyberbrief
Internet Alliance
1615 L Street NW
Suite 1100
Washington, DC 20036-5624

202-861-2407
E-Mail: tammy@internetalliance.org
Home Page: www.internetalliance.org

Tammy Cota, Executive Director

Coverage of public policy changes in government, enhancing consumer satisfaction in interactive services, and education.
Frequency: Weekly

6579 Internet Business
Information Gatekeepers
1340 Soldiers Field Rd
Suite 3
Brighton, MA 02135-1000

617-782-5033
800-323-1088
FAX 617-782-5735

E-Mail: info@igigroup.com
Home Page: www.igigroup.com

Paul Polishuk, CEO
Hui Pan, Chief Analyst, Editor in Chief
Bev Wilson, Managing Editor

Covers the rapid developments in the industry.
Cost: $695.00
Frequency: Monthly

6580 Internet Business Advantage
ZD Journals
500 Canal View Boulevard
Rochester, NY 14623-2800

585-407-7301
FAX 585-214-2387
E-Mail: iba@zdjournals.com
Home Page: www.zdjournals.com

Bob Artner, Editor-in-Chief

Keeps readers up-to-date of technological advances and new services available on the Internet. Reviews new products and provides tips on businss applications.
Cost: $295.00

6581 Internet Media Investor
Kagan World Media
126 Clock Tower Place
Carmel, CA 93923-8746

831-624-1536
800-307-2529
FAX 831-625-3225
E-Mail: info@kagan.com
Home Page: www.kagan.com
Social Media: Facebook, Twitter, LinkedIn, YouTube

George Niesen, Editor
Tom Johnson, Marketing Manager

Follows public stocks and private deals, analyzes publicly held interactive multimedia companies, tracks key industry subgroups through Kagan stock averages that relate companies by product lines, projects growth of new TV and data networks, programming and technology. Provides economic modeling of new corporate ventures and interprets announcements and events. Three month trial is available.
Cost: $1095.00
Frequency: Monthly
Founded in 1969

6582 Internet World
Mecklermedia Corporation
20 Ketchum Street
Westport, CT 06880

212-260-0758
FAX 203-454-5840
E-Mail: bbesch@mecklermedia.com

Bill Besch, Publisher

Internet industry news, product reviews and technical reports, with an emphasis on Internet technology, hardware, management and security.
Cost: $160.00
Frequency: Weekly
Circulation: 98,947

6583 Internetweek
CMP Media
600 Community Drive
Manhasset, NY 11030-3847

516-562-5000
FAX 516-562-5554
E-Mail: mazzara@cmp.com
Home Page: www.internetweek.com

Mike Azzara, Publisher

News and coverage of the latest trends in electronic commerce and intranet application platforms, the effects of high technology on daily production, changing regulations and operating standards, the best tools and practices, and re-

lated business and financial news.
Cost: $143.00
Frequency: Weekly
Circulation: 161264

6584 Manufacturing Automation
Vital Information Publications
754 Caravel Lane
Foster City, CA 94404-1712

650-345-7018
Home Page: www.sensauto.com

Peter Adrian, Owner
Gary Kuba, Marketing Director

Provides market research data and vital information about key products, applications, and technologies for a wide range of industrial automation segments, such as CAD/CAM, supply chain management, e-Commerce solutions, enterprise resource planning, automation software, manufacturing technology, industrial controls, and manufacturing systems.

6585 Mass Storage News
Corry Publishing
2840 W 21st Street
Erie, PA 16506

814-838-0025
FAX 814-838-0035
E-Mail: terryp@corrypub.com
Home Page: www.corrypub.com

Terry Peterson, Publisher

News on optical disk based imaging and storage systems, new products, technical developments and industry developments.
Cost: $597.00
Frequency: BiWeekly
Circulation: 1,500

6586 Mealey's Litigation Report: Class Actions
LexisNexis Mealey's
555 W 5th Avenue
Los Angeles, CA 90013

213-627-1130
E-Mail: mealeyinfo@lexisnexis.com
Home Page: www.lexisnexis.com/mealeys

Tom Hagy, VP/General Manager
Maureen McGuire, Editorial Director
David Elreth, Editor

This report will provide in-depth coverage of class action litigation involving mass torts and beyond - including consumer law, employment law, securities litigation and e-commerce disputes. Get the latest on: hard-to-find filings, notice plans, fairness hearings, class certification rulings, settlements, trial news and verdicts, attorney fee news, appeals, breaking news stories, new complaints, Supreme Court battles, and much more.
Cost: $1195.00
100 Pages
Frequency: Semi-Monthly
Founded in 1997

6587 Mealey's Litigation Report: Cyber Tech & E -Commerce
LexisNexis Mealey's
555 W 5th Avenue
Los Angeles, CA 90013

213-627-1130
E-Mail: mealeyinfo@lexisnexis.com
Home Page: www.lexisnexis.com/mealeys

Tom Hagy, VP/General Manager
Maureen McGuire, Editorial Director
Mark Rogers, Editor

The Report covers disputes arising from e-commerce. The report tracks emerging legal issues, including: Internet security, data destruction and/or alteration, defamation on the Web, software errors, hardware failure, electronic theft,

e-mail trespass, online privacy, government action, shareholder lawsuits, Internet jurisdiction issues, file sharing (copyright) disputes and much more.
Cost: $999.00
100 Pages
Frequency: Monthly
Founded in 1999

6588 Mobile Internet
Information Gatekeepers
1340 Soldiers Field Rd
Suite 3
Brighton, MA 02135-1000

617-782-5033
800-323-1088
FAX 617-782-5735
E-Mail: info@igigroup.com
Home Page: www.igigroup.com

Paul Polishuk, CEO
Hui Pan, Chief Analyst, Editor in Chief
Bev Wilson, Managing Editor

Covers worldwide developments in 3G wireless networks, with an emphasis on the worldwide PCS/GSM/CDMA markets.
Cost: $695.00
Frequency: Monthly
Founded in 1977

6589 Multimedia & Internet Training Newsletter
Brandon Hall Resources
690 W Fremont Ave
#9C
Sunnyvale, CA 94087-4200

408-736-2335
E-Mail: editor@brandon-hall.com
Home Page: www.brandon-hall.com
Social Media: Facebook, Twitter, LinkedIn

Mike Cooke, CEO
Rachel Ashkin, COO
Michael Rochelle, CSO

The latest in multimedia news, virtual clasroom reports, insight into web-based training, and technology tutorial. Job bank listings, upcoming events, seminars, and tips and techniques.
Cost: $189.00
Frequency: Monthly
Circulation: 900

6590 Online & CD-ROM Review
Information Today
1308 W Main
University of Illinois
Urbana, IL 61801

217-333-1074
800-248-8466
FAX 217-762-3956
E-Mail: custserv@infotoday.com
Home Page: www.infotoday.com/

Martha Williams, Editor
Thomas H Hogan, CEO/President
Heather Rudolph, Marketing
Inge Coffey, Circulation Manager

Covers the use and management of online and CD-ROM services, the training and education of online and CD-ROM users, creation and marketing of databases, and new development in search aids.
Cost: $115.00
Frequency: Monthly
Circulation: 4745

6591 Online Libraries & Microcomputers
Information Intelligence
PO Box 31098
Phoenix, AZ 31098

602-996-2283
Home Page: www.infointelligence.com

George Machovec, Managing Editor

Examines new library online and automation applications with reviews of new software and hardware, industry news and trends, and upcoming related events.
Cost: $62.50
9 Pages
Frequency: 10 per year
ISSN: 0737-7770
Founded in 1983

6592 Online Newsletter

Information Intelligence
PO Box 31098
Phoenix, AZ 85046-1098

602-996-2283
E-Mail: news@infointelligence.com
Home Page: wwww.infointelligence.com

Richard S Huleatt, Editor

Covers all aspects of online and CD-ROM developments throughout the world. Regular feature sections include news and events, mergers and acquisitions, people in the news, telecommunications, and networks. Editoral reflects product development and its impact on users, and provides listings of upcoming events related to this industry.
Cost: $62.50
9 Pages
Frequency: 10 per year
ISSN: 0194-0694
Founded in 1983

6593 Online Reporter

G2 Computer Intelligence
PO Box 7
Glen Head, NY 11545-1616

516-759-7025
FAX 516-759-7028
E-Mail: news@g2news.com
Home Page: www.g2news.com

Maureen O'Gara, Publisher

Information on recent developments on the Internet through news briefs and a section called Chat Room. Includes information on e-commerce, Java and network security.
Cost: $695.00
Frequency: Weekly

6594 Privacy Journal

PO Box 28577
Providence, RI 02908

401-274-7861
FAX 401-274-4747
E-Mail: orders@privacyjournal.net
Home Page: www.privacyjournal.net

Robert Ellis Smith, Publisher

An independent monthly on privacy in a computer age.
Cost: $65.00
Frequency: Monthly
ISSN: 0145-7659
Founded in 1974
Printed in one color

6595 Report on Electronic Commerce

Telecommunications Reports International
1333 H Street NW
#100 E
Washington, DC 20005-4707

202-842-3022
FAX 202-842-1875
Home Page: www.tr.com

Jerry Ashworth, Editor
Brian Hammond, Managing Editor

Provides insiths on the latest developments in EDI, EFT, EBT, digital cash, home shopping and baking, value-added networks, and transaction processing. Offers articles, analysis and case studies regarding financial and business

transaction over the Internet.
Cost: $745.00
Frequency: BiWeekly

6596 Sysop News and Cyberworld Report

BBS Press Service
5610 SW 10th Avenue
Topeka, KS 66604-2104

785-286-4272
FAX 785-271-0192
E-Mail: alanbenchtold@sysop.com
Home Page: www.sysop.com

Alan R Bechtold, Publisher
Debbie Boos, Owner

Online industry news and updates, Web site reviews, event announcements, Web design basics, Internet-based applicaitons, business solutions and various technical articles of interest.
Cost: $59.95
Frequency: Weekly
Circulation: 18M

6597 TechTarget

TechTarget
117 Kendrick St
Suite 800
Needham Heights, MA 02494-2728

781-657-1000
888-274-4111
FAX 781-657-1100
E-Mail: info@techtarget.com
Home Page: www.techtarget.com

Greg Strakosch, CEO
Don Hawk, President
Lisa Johnson, VP Marketing
Catherine Engelke, Direector Public Relations

IBM iSeries focused media. The IBM e-Server iSeries (formerly the AS/400) is considered to be the world's most often used multi-user business computer. The installed base worldwide is huge and will get bigger, fueled by incresed Web development. The iSeries comes with an integrated Web application server and all the tools needed to build internet, intranet, extranet, and e-commerce sites quickly and will figure prominently into IT strategy and implementation for years to come.
Frequency: Monthly
Founded in 1999

6598 The CyberSkeptic's Guide to Internet Research

Information Today
143 Old Marlton Pike
Medford, NJ 08055-8750

609-654-6266
800-300-9868
FAX 609-654-4309
E-Mail: custserv@infotoday.com
Home Page: www.infotoday.com

Thomas H Hogan, President
Roger R Bilboul, Chairman Of The Board

A monthly subscription newsletter in print, that explores and evaluates free and low cost Web sites and search strategies to help you use the Internet and stay up to date.
Cost: $164.95
ISSN: 1085-2417

6599 Trade Vendor Quarterly

Blakeley & Blakeley
2 Park Plaza
Suite 400
Irvine, CA 92614

949-260-0611
FAX 949-260-0613
E-Mail: administrator@vendorland.com
Home Page: www.vendorlaw.com

Scott Blakey, Esq.

Highlights developments in commercial, creditors' rights, e-commerce and bankruptcy law of interest to the credit and financial professional. Free online.
Frequency: Quarterly

6600 Web Review

Miller Freeman Publications
600 Harrison Street
San Francisco, CA 94107

650-573-3210

Veronica Costanza, Publisher

Timely and practical information on the practice of Internet development as well as news on the latest techniques and technologies.
Frequency: BiWeekly
Circulation: 12M

6601 Webdeveloper.com

Mecklermedia Corporation
23 Old Kings Hwy S
Darien, CT 06820-4541

203-662-2800
FAX 203-655-4686
E-Mail: info@WebMediaBrands.com
Home Page: www.webmediabrands.com

Alan M Meckler, CEO
Mike Demiot, Marketing Manager

Product reviews, practical techniques, codes, tools and tips for Internet professionals who design, develop and maintain Web sites and Internet services.
Frequency: Daily

6602 West Side Leader/Green Leader

Leader Publications
3075 Smith Rd
Suite 204
Akron, OH 44333-4454

330-665-0909
888-945-9595
FAX 330-665-9590
E-Mail: webmaster@akron.com
Home Page: www.akron.com

Kathryn Core, Editor
Kathleen Collins, Managing Editor
Maria Lindsay, Assistant Editor

Weekly newspapers.
Cost: $10.00
Circulation: 53000

Magazines & Journals

6603 Active Server Developer's Journal

ZD Journals
500 Canal View Boulevard
Rochester, NY 14623-2800

585-407-7301
FAX 585-214-2387
E-Mail: asp@zdjournals.com
Home Page: www.asdj.com

Jon Pyles, Publisher
Taggard Andrews

Addresses such issues as database publishing, creating hack-proof files and getting the most out of server-side components. Special sections focus on client-side solutions, covering the basics and taking an in-depth look at more detailed techniques.
Cost: $149.00
Frequency: Monthly

6604 Bio & Software and Internet Report

Mary Ann Liebert

140 Huguenot St # 3
3rd Floor
New Rochelle, NY 10801-5215

914-740-2100
FAX 914-740-2101
E-Mail: info@liebertpub.com
Home Page: www.liebertpub.com
Social Media: *Facebook, Twitter, LinkedIn*

Mary A Liebert, Owner
Gerry Elman, Editor-in-Chief
Robert A Bohrer, Executive Editor
Judith Gunn Bronson, Managing Editor

News and reviews of all areas of scientific
computing, including software, hardware and
network products.
Cost: $1554.00
ISSN: 1527-9162
Founded in 1980

6605 Boardwatch Magazine
Penton Media
1300 E 9th St # 316
Cleveland, OH 44114-1503

216-696-7000
FAX 216-696-6662
E-Mail: rgoldner@boardwatch.com
Home Page: www.penton.com

Jane Cooper, Marketing
David Icopf, Editorial Director

Editorial coverage for communications service
providers.
Cost: $72.00
Frequency: Monthly
Circulation: 50,000
ISSN: 1054-2760
Founded in 1987
*Mailing list available for rent: 50,000 names at
$250 per M*

6606 BtoB Magazine
Ad Age Group/ Division of Crain
Communications
711 3rd Ave
New York, NY 10017-4014

212-210-0785
FAX 212-210-0200
E-Mail: info@crain.com
Home Page: www.crain.com

Norm Feldman, Manager

Dedicated to integrated business to business
marketing. Every page is packed with substance news, reports, technologies,
benchmarks, best practices served up by the
most knowledgeable journalists.
Frequency: Monthly
Circulation: 45000

6607 Card Technology
Thomson Financial Publishing
1 State St
27th Floor
New York, NY 10004-1481

212-825-8445
800-221-1809
FAX 212-843-9622
E-Mail: custserv@thomsonmedia.com
Home Page: www.cardtechnology.com

Daniel Wolfe, Editor in Chief
Austin Kilgore, Managing Editor
Ed McKinley, Independent Sales Organizations
Hope Lerman, National Sales Manager

Store-value cards, optical-memory cards,
biometrics, cards on the Internet, cards for electronic data storage, and devices used with these
cards in banking, government, telecommunications, transportation and education.
Cost: $ 98.00
Frequency: Monthly
Circulation: 25000
Printed in 4 colors on glossy stock

**6608 Computer & Online Industry
Litigation Reporter**
Andrews Publications
175 Strafford Avenue
Building 4, Suite 140
Wayne, PA 19087-3331

610-225-0510
800-345-1101
FAX 610-225-0501
Home Page: www.andrewspub.com

John Backe, Publisher

Editorial covers telecommuncations and the
Internet for attorneys and professionals in the
legal field.
Cost: $850.00

6609 Computer Gaming World
Ziff Davis Publishing Company
101 2nd St # 900
8th Floor
San Francisco, CA 94105-3650

415-547-8000
FAX 415-547-8777
E-Mail: info@ziffdavis.com
Home Page: www.ziffdavis.com

Dale Strang, Manager
Matt Leone, Editor
Paul Fusco, Sales Director
Bobby Markowitz, Marketing Director
Stephen Hicks, General Counsel

Reviews commercially available and on-line
games. Features interviews with game design-
ers, as well as strategy tips, contests and news.
Cost: $98.88
Frequency: Monthly
Circulation: 212783

6610 Computer Journal
Las Vegas Computer Journal
2232 S Nellis Boulevard
#169
Las Vegas, NV 89104-6213

702-270-4656
FAX 702-432-6204
E-Mail: info@internetsurfer.com
Home Page: www.internetsurfer.com

Johanna Nezhoda, Publisher

Spotlights Web news, site reviews, interface
tools and commentary on the changing face of
computing.
Cost: $24.95
Frequency: Monthly
Circulation: 25M

6611 Computer Music Journal
MIT Press
3 Cambridge Ctr # 23
Cambridge, MA 02142-1613

617-499-3200
FAX 617-621-0856
E-Mail: journals-orders@mit.edu
Home Page: www.adoptaboat.org

Miguel Suarez, Manager
Keeril Makan, Managing Editor

Tutorials and research articles, news and reviews of computer music systems, hardware
and software for music sound, digital audio,
signal processing and multimedia.
Cost: $82.00
120 Pages
Frequency: Quarterly
Circulation: 5000
Founded in 1926

**6612 Computer Service & Repair
Magazine**
Searle Publishing Company

5511 Morning Glory Ln
#210-110
Littleton, CO 80123-2701

303-730-3006
810-797-8708
FAX 303-797-0276
E-Mail: csr@searlepub.com
Home Page: www.independentcable.com

Robert Searle, Publisher
Roderick Robles, Associate Publisher

Information on the maintenance and repair of
computer systems. Reviews new products and
technology.

6613 Corporate Help Desk Solutions
Gartner Group
Po Box 10212
Stamford, CT 06904-2212

203-964-0096
FAX 203-316-6488
E-Mail: help@gartner.com
Home Page: www.gartner.com
Social Media: *Facebook, Twitter, LinkedIn*

Jean Hall, CEO
Gene Hall, CEO/President
David Godfrey, Marketing/Circulation
Robin Kranich, SVP Human Resources

Key technologies, management practices and
techniques for the most cost-effective help desk
solutions.
Cost: $395.00
Frequency: Monthly
Founded in 1979

6614 Customer Interaction Solutions
Technology Marketing Corporation
1 Technology Plz
Norwalk, CT 06854-1936

203-852-6800
800-243-6002
FAX 203-853-2845
E-Mail: tmc@tmcnet.com
Home Page: www.tmcnet.com

Rich Tehrani, CEO
Tracey Schelmetic, Managing Editor
Erik D Lounsbury, Editorial Director

Magazine devoted to teleservices and e-services outsourcing, marketing and consumer
management issues.
Frequency: Monthly
Founded in 1982

6615 Customer Interface
Advanstar Communications
6200 Canoga Avenue
2nd Floor
Woodland Hills, CA 91367

818-593-5000
FAX 818-593-5020
E-Mail: info@advanstar.com
Home Page: www.advanstar.com

Joseph Loggia, President
Chris DeMoulin, VP
Susannah George, Marketing Director

Business management resource for senior and
mid-level decision makers who are responsible
for call centers, customer contact and customer
service initiatives. We are stewards for the industry as we prepare it for continued transformation and growth.
Circulation: 50,000
Founded in 1988

6616 CyberDealer
Meister Publishing Company
37733 Euclid Ave
Willoughby, OH 44094-5992

440-942-2000
800-572-7740

FAX 440-975-3447
Home Page: www.meisternet.com

Gary Fitzgerald, President

Helps agricultural dealerships better manage their operations.
Frequency: 6 per year

6617 Desktop Video Communications
BCR Enterprises
950 York Road
#203
Hinsdale, IL 60521-8609

630-789-6700
FAX 630-323-5324
Home Page: www.bcr.com

Fred Knight, Publisher/Editor-in-Chief

Useful information for communications and informations systems managers, line managers, system developers and integrators, value-added resellers, and software vendors.
Frequency: Bi-Monthly
Circulation: 30M

6618 Digital Travel
Jupiter Communications Company
627 Broadway
2nd Floor
New York, NY 10012-2612

212-533-8885
FAX 212-780-6075
Home Page: www.jup.com

Eva Papoutsakis, Editor
Marla Kammer, Managing Director
Ellen Daley, Managing Director
Charles Rutstein, Chief Operating Officer

Editorial includes the latest information and technology in agencies, airlines, lodging, ticketing, mapping, Web advertising, transaction processing, revenue models, demographics, and full-service sites.
Cost: $595.00
Frequency: Monthly

6619 E-Business Advisor
Advisor Media
P.O.Box 503350
San Diego, CA 92150-3350

858-278-5600
800-336-6060
FAX 858-278-0300
E-Mail: pr@advisor.com
Home Page: www.e-businessadvisor.com

John L Hawkins, Editorial Director
Jane Falla, Senior Editor
Brian Dunning, Technical Editor

E-Business Advisor is the monthly magazine presenting the best innovation, strategies, and practices for e-business leaders. It is an independent guide for the team of business and technical managers within an enterprise responsible for strategic innovation, planning, design, implementation, and management of e-business and e-commerce solutions.
Cost: $49.00
68 Pages
Circulation: 60000
ISSN: 1098-8912
Founded in 1983
Mailing list available for rent: 60000 names at $175 per M

6620 E-Content
Information Today
143 Old Marlton Pike
Medford, NJ 08055-8750

609-654-6266
800-300-9868
FAX 609-654-4309

E-Mail: custserv@infotoday.com
Home Page: www.infotoday.com

Thomas H Hogan, President
Roger R Bilboul, Chairman Of The Board

Delivers essential research, reporting, news and analysis of content related issues. It is essential reading for executive and professionals involved in content creation, management, acquisition, organization and distribution in both commercial and enterprise environments.
Cost: $115.00
Frequency: 10 issues/yr
Mailing list available for rent: 4M names
Printed in 4 colors on glossy stock

6621 ESchool News
IAQ Publications
7920 Norfolk Ave # 900
Suite 900
Bethesda, MD 20814-2539

301-913-0115
FAX 301-913-0119
E-Mail: gdowney@eschoolnews.com
Home Page: www.eschoolnews.com

Robert Morrow, Owner

Guide to buying and updating classroom technology for K-12 educators. Product information listings, industry updates and related reports. Covers grant writing and funding, as well as government legislation regarding education.
Cost: $90.00

6622 Electronic Commerce Advisor
Thomson Reuters
195 Broadway # 4
New York, NY 10007-3124

646-822-2000
800-231-1860
FAX 646-822-2800
E-Mail: trta.lei-support@thomsonreuters.com
Home Page: www.ria.thomsonreuters.com

Elaine Yadlon, Plant Manager
Thomas H Glocer, CEO & Director
Robert D Daleo, Chief Financial Officer
Kelli Crane, Senior Vice President & CIO

Offers the latest in electronic commerce covering what's available and how to select and employ the best technology without costly trial-and-error mistakes. Information on EDI, e-mail, fax gateways, Internet, encryption, VANs, procurement cards, imaging, voice response, remote computing and other related information.
Cost: $155.00
Circulation: 4500
Founded in 1940

6623 Electronic Mail & Messaging Systems
Business Research Publications
1333 H Street NW
Suite 100 East
Washington, DC 20005-4707

202-364-6473
800-822-6338
FAX 202-842-1875

Rod Kuckro, Editor-in-Chief

Exclusive biweekly intelligence technology applications, products and market trends in electronic mail, computer fax, wireless messaging and the Internet.
Cost: $595.00
Frequency: BiWeekly

6624 Electronic Publishing
PennWell Publishing Company
98 Spit Brook Rd # LI-1
Nashua, NH 03062-5737

603-891-0123
FAX 603-891-9294

E-Mail: genepri@pennwell.com
Home Page: www.pennwell.com

Christine Shaw, VP
Keith V. Hevenor, Editor

For those who communicate in print, including service bureaus, printers, prepress houses and desktop publishers, it provides latest products, news and related developments.
Cost: $59.00
Frequency: Monthly
Circulation: 68441
Founded in 1910

6625 Electronic Retailer Magazine
Electronic Retailing Association
2000 14th St N # 300
Suite 300
Arlington, VA 22201-2573

703-841-1751
800-987-6462
FAX 703-841-1860
E-Mail: contact@retailing.org
Home Page: www.retailing.org

Julie Coons, CEO
Vitisia Paynich, Editor-in-Chief
Tom Dellner, Executive Editor

Delivers news updates, exclusives, industry research, educational features and in-depth coverage of issues relating to government affairs, legal aspects, concepts and products, production, media-buying as well as all back end services.
Frequency: Monthly
Circulation: 21000

6626 Emediaweekly
Mac Publishing
501 2nd St
San Francisco, CA 94107-1496

415-243-0505
800-288-6848
FAX 415-442-0766
E-Mail: sitehelp@macworld.com
Home Page: www.macworld.com
Social Media: *Facebook, Twitter, YouTube*

Mike Kisseberth, CEO

Covers the creation, technologies, applications and hardware for the publishing spectrum, including print, Web, multimedia, CD and digital video. Emphasis on hardware and software products, along with analysis, reviews, and buyer's guides.
Cost: $125.00
Frequency: Weekly

6627 Explore the Net with Internet Explorer
ZD Journals
500 Canal View Boulevard
Rochester, NY 14623-2800

585-407-7301
FAX 585-214-2386
E-Mail: etn_editor@zdjournals.com
Home Page: www.zdjournals.com

Joelle Martin, Publisher

Informs readers of new features and how they may be used; covering such concepts as browser upgrades, compatibility issues, authoring tools and connection utilities. Regular departments showcase the 'site of the month,' in addition to reviewing other sites that have attractive interfaces and are valauble resources.
Cost: $49.00
Frequency: Monthly

6628 Ezine - WECommerce News
Women in eCommerce

PO Box 550856
Fort Lauderdale, FL 33355-0856

954-625-6606
877-947-3337
E-Mail: heidi@wecai.org
Home Page: www.wecai.org

Suzannah Richards, President
Rosana Santos, President Elect
Ellen Sue Burton, VP/Logistics & Hospitality
Racheli Smilovitz, VP/Professional
Development
Dalila J. Grohowski, VP/Membership
Development

Helping women do business on the web.
Founded in 2001

6629 GEOWorld
Bel-Av Communciations
359 Galahad Rd
Bolingbrook, IL 60440-2108

E-Mail: tdanielson@geoplace.com
Home Page: www.geoplace.com

Jo Treadwell, VP/Group Publisher
Todd Danielson, Editor

Offers a wealth of knowledge through festures, news and commentary covering the geospatial industry. Covers local and federal government, emergency management, infrastructure, natural resource management, industry trends and innovations and more.
Cost: $72.00
Frequency: Monthly
Circulation: 25000

6630 Genealogical Computing
Ancestry
360 W 4800 N
Provo, UT 84604-5675

801-705-7000
800-262-3787
FAX 801-705-7001
E-Mail: pr@myfamilyinc.com
Home Page: www.myfamily.com
Social Media: *Facebook, Twitter*

Timothy P Sullivan, CEO
Matthew Wright, Contributing Editor
David C Moon, CEO
Mary-Kay Evans, Director, Public Relations

For readers who use computers and technology to organize and enhance their research into accounts of ancestries and descent.
Cost: $25.00
Frequency: Quarterly

6631 Geospatial Solutions
Advanstar Communications
201 Sandpointe Ave # 600
Suite 500
Santa Ana, CA 92707-8700

714-513-8400
FAX 714-513-8680
Home Page: www.geospatial-solutions.com

Mike Weldon, Plant Manager

Practical applications of geographic information systems and technologies for planning, developing, preserving, analyzing and managing environments.
Frequency: Monthly
Circulation: 30000
Founded in 1987

6632 Harlow Report: Geographic Information Systems
Advanced Information Management Group
905 Thistledown Lane
Birmingham, AL 35244-3361

334-982-9203
E-Mail: chris@geoint.com
Home Page: www.theharlowreport.com/

Chris Harlow, Publisher/Editor

Key management issues and new software highlights, service providers and users for the geographic information systems industry.
Cost: $190.00
Frequency: Monthly
Founded in 1982

6633 Heller Report on Internet Strategies for Education Markets
Nelson B Heller & Associates
9933 Lawler Avenue
#502
Skokie, IL 60077-3708

800-525-5811
877-435-5373
FAX 303-209-9444
E-Mail: info@hellerreports.com
Home Page: www.hellerreports.com
Social Media: *Facebook, Twitter*

Nelson B Heller, President/Publisher
Emily Garner, Sales/Marketing Director

Covers Internet hardware, software and services for educational use. Discusses the funding and deadlines relevant to the products and services offered through the Internet.
Cost: $397.00
12 Pages
Frequency: Monthly
Circulation: 500
Founded in 1981
Printed in 2 colors

6634 IEEE Internet Computing
IEEE Computer Society
PO Box 3014
Los Alamitos, CA 90720-1314

714-821-8380
800-272-6657
FAX 714-821-4010
E-Mail: volunteer.services@computer.org
Home Page: www.computer.org/internet
Social Media: *Facebook, Twitter, LinkedIn, YouTube*

Angela Burges, Executive Director
Davis Hennage, CEO/President
Steve Woods, Production Manager
Sandy Brown, Marketing
Steve Woods, Production Manager

Provides a technology roadmap for high-end users and application developers, as well as a venue for standards, case histories, and new ideas. Essays, interview, and roundtable discussions address the Internet's impact on engineering practice. Describes Internet tools, technologies, and application-oriented research.
Cost: $28.00
Frequency: Quarterly
Circulation: 11265
Founded in 1946

6635 IT Cost Management Strategies
Computer Economics
2082 Business Center Dr
Suite 240
Irvine, CA 92612

949-831-8700
FAX 949-442-7688
Home Page: www.computereconomics.com

Frank Scavo, President
Dan Husiak, VP

Covers budgeting, financial news, computer programming, marketing and management for management information systems directors as a planning assistant.
Frequency: Monthly
Founded in 1978

6636 ITS World
Advanstar Communications

859 Willamette Street
Eugene, OR 97401-2918

541-431-0026
FAX 541-344-3514
Home Page: www.itsworld.com

Phillip Arndt, Publisher

Articles on industry news, current issues that affect Intelligent Transportation Systems, practical advice, applications, new and existing technology, and new product information.
Cost: $35.00
Frequency: 9 per year
Circulation: 15,124

6637 Information Display
Palisades Institute for Research Services
2 Shadybrook Lane
Norwalk, CT 06854

203-853-7069
FAX 203-855-9769
E-Mail: office@sid.org
Home Page: www.sid.org

Kenneth I Werner, Editor
Shigeol Mikoshiba, President/CEO

State-of-the-art developments in electronic, electromechanical and hardcopy display equipment; input and output technologies; storage media; human factors and display standards; entrepreneurship, marketing and management; and manufacturing.
Cost: $36.00
Frequency: Monthly
Circulation: 11000
Founded in 1962
Printed in 4 colors

6638 Information Retrieval & Library Automation
Lomond Publications
PO Box 88
Mount Airy, MD 21771-0088

202-362-1361
FAX 202-362-6156

Thomas Hattery, Publisher

New technology, products and equipment that improve information systems and library services, for science, social, social science, law, medicine, academic institutions and the public.
Cost: $75.00
Frequency: Monthly

6639 Information Security
International Computer Security Association
117 Kendrick Street
Suite 800
Needham, MA 02494

781-657-1000
FAX 781-657-1100
E-Mail: lwalsh@infosecuritymag.com
Home Page: www.infosecuritymag.com

Andrew Briney, VP
Lawrence Walsh, Editor
Michael S Mimoso, Senior Editor
Gabrielle DeRussy, Advertising Sales
Susan Rastellini Smith, Product Management

Articles and analysis of information-security issues such as media, entwork and virus protection, internet security and encryption reports.
Cost: $100.00
Frequency: Monthly
Circulation: 60000
Founded in 1999

6640 Information Systems Security
Auerbach Publications
2494 Bayshore Boulevard
Suite 201
Dunedin, FL 34698

703-891-6781
800-737-8034

FAX 703-891-0782
E-Mail: institute@isc2.org
Home Page: www.isc2.org
Social Media: *Facebook, Twitter, YouTube*

David Shearer, COO
Debra Taylor, CFO
John Colley, Chairman
Debra Taylor, Chief Financial Officer
Hord Tipton, Executive Director

Facts and experience, expert opinion on directions in security, public policy, computer crime and ethics related to the information security field.
Cost: $175.00
Circulation: 1500
Founded in 2003

6641 Inside the Internet
ZD Journals
500 Canal View Boulevard
Rochester, NY 14623-2800

585-407-7301
FAX 585-214-2387
E-Mail: int@zdjournals.com
Home Page: www.zdjournals.com

Joelle Martin, Publisher

Information and hands-on instruction for applications along with some pictorial explanation.
Cost: $49.00
Frequency: Monthly

6642 Internet & Intranet Business and Technology Report
Computer Technology Research Corporation
6 N Atlantic Wharf
Charleston, SC 29401-2115

843-766-5293
FAX 843-853-7210
Home Page: www.ctrcorp.com

Edward Wagner, Publisher

Reports on international news, historical profiles of the impact of various applications, and developing standards and regulations. Topics covered include domain registration, Webcasting and the market for Internet e-mail.
Cost: $390.00
Frequency: Monthly

6643 Internet Business
Ziff Davis Publishing Company
28 E 28th St
New York, NY 10016-7940

212-503-5772
E-Mail: steven_thompson@zd.com

Steve Weitzner, CEO
Adam Gordon, VP

Provides in-depth information and analysis on Internet products, techniques and tools, based on comparative lab testing and real world experience. Feature articles address technology segments that optimize an Internet strategy such as firewalls, authoring tools, etc., and how-to columns look at technical issues surrounding Web site development.
Cost: $24.99
Frequency: Monthly

6644 Internet Business Strategies
Gartner Group
Po Box 10212
Stamford, CT 06904-2212

203-964-0096
FAX 203-316-6488
E-Mail: info@gartner.com
Home Page: www.gartner.com
Social Media: *Facebook, Twitter, LinkedIn*

Jean Hall, CEO
Eugene Hall, CEO
David Godfrey, Senior Vice President

John Gardner, President
Robin Kranich, SVP Human Resources

Helps readers make informed decisions about how to use the Internet to deploy electronic commerce and interactive initiatives.
Cost: $395.00
Frequency: Weekly
Circulation: 10,000
Founded in 1993

6645 Internet Reference Service Quarterly
Taylor & Francis
325 Chestnut Street
Suite 800
Philadelphia, PA 19106

800-354-1420
FAX 215-625-2940
Home Page: www.tandf.co.uk

Brenda Reeb, Editor

Designed to function as a comprehensive information source librarians can turn to and count on for keeping up-to-date on emerging technological innovations, while emphasizing theoretical, research, and practical applications of Internet-related information services, sources and resources.
Cost: $82.00
Frequency: Quarterly
Circulation: 3000
ISSN: 1087-5301
Founded in 1978

6646 Internet Shopper
Mecklermedia Corporation
20 Ketchum Street
Westport, CT 06880-5908

203-662-2800
FAX 203-454-5840
Home Page: www.internetshopper.com

Susan Leiterstein, Publisher

Edited for consumers who purchas products and services direct from Interet Web sites. Covers online malls, computers and electronics, stocks, books, home furnishings, music and more. Reviews the best sites within their categoreis and includes tips on how to conduct safe and effective online transactions.
Frequency: Daily

6647 Internet Telephony
Technology Marketing Corporation
1 Technology Plz
Norwalk, CT 06854-1936

203-852-6800
800-243-6002
FAX 203-853-2845
E-Mail: tmc@tmcnet.com
Home Page: www.tmcnet.com

Rich Tehrani, CEO
Richard Tehrani, President/Group Publisher
Shirley A. Russo, Circulation Director

News and departments focus on providing readers with information they need to learn about and purchase the equipment, software and services necessary for Internet telephony, through the convergence of voice, video, fax and data.
Frequency: Monthly
Circulation: 28024
Founded in 1972

6648 Internet World
Mecklermedia Corporation
20 Ketchum Street
Westport, CT 06880-5908

203-226-6967
FAX 203-454-5840

Corey Friedman, Publisher
Michael Neubarth, Editor

For noncommercial and commercial uses of Internet and the National Research and Educa-

tion Network.
Cost: $5.00
Circulation: 256883
Founded in 1971

6649 Journal of Electronic Imaging
International Society for Optical Engineering
1000 20th Street
Bellingham, WA 98225-10

360-676-3290
FAX 360-647-1445
E-Mail: customerservice@spie.org
Home Page: www.spie.org

Kristin Lewotsky, Executive Editor
Winn Hardin, Senior Editor
Michael Brownell, Contributing Editors
Amy Nelson, Manager

Timely information about evolving imaging technologies, including image acquistions, image data storage, image data display, image visualization, image processing, image data communciations, hard copy output and multimedia systems.
Cost: $135.00
Frequency: Quarterly
Circulation: 1500
Founded in 1992

6650 Journal of Internet Law
Apen Publishers
400 Hamilton Avenue
Palo Alto, CA 94301-1809

650-328-6561
FAX 650-327-3699
E-Mail: mailops@gcfw.com
Home Page: www.gcfw.com

Mark F Radcliffe, Editor-in-Chief

Discusses strategies utilized by top intellectual property, computer law and information technology industry experts.
Frequency: Monthly

6651 Journal of Research on Computing in Education
International Society for Technology in Education
180 W 8th Avenue
Eugene, OR 97401-2916

541-302-3777
800-336-5191
FAX 541-302-3778
E-Mail: iste@iste.org
Home Page: www.iste.org

Don Knezek, CEO
Leslie Conery, Deputy CEO

Covers computer research and developments relating to all levels of education. Articles define the state of current and future use of technology in education.
Cost: $79.00
Frequency: Quarterly
Circulation: 4500
Founded in 1989
Mailing list available for rent

6652 Journal of Technology in Human Services
Taylor & Francis
325 Chestnut Street
Suite 800
Philadelphia, PA 19106

800-354-1420
FAX 215-625-2940
Home Page: www.tandf.co.uk

Dick Schoech PhD, Editor

Explores the potentials of computer and telecommunications technologies in mental health, developmental disability, welfare, ad-

dictions, education, and other human services.
Cost: $120.00
Frequency: Quarterly
ISSN: 1522-8835
Founded in 1978
Mailing list available for rent
Printed in one color on matte stock

6653 KM World
Information Today
18 Bayview Street
PO Box 1358
Camden, ME 04843-1358

207-236-8524
FAX 207-236-6452
E-Mail: webmaster@kmworld.com
Home Page: www.kmworld.com
Social Media: *Facebook, Twitter, LinkedIn*

Hugh McKellar, Editor in Chief
Sandra Haimila, Managing Editor
Michael V Zarrello, Advertising Director
Andy Moore, Publisher
David Panara, Sales Manager

Serves content, document and knowledge of
management market to help improve business
performance.
Circulation: 56000

6654 MacTech
Xplain Corporation
PO Box 5200
Westlake Village, CA 91359-5200

805-494-9797
FAX 805-494-9798
E-Mail: custservice@mactech.com
Home Page: www.mactech.com
Social Media: *Twitter*

Neil Ticktin, Publisher
Dave Mark, Executive Editor
Edward Marczak, Executive Editor
David Allen, Production Manager

Provides web developers and network administrators with the most technically advanced information for them to combat the needs of the industry. How to articles, technically oriented product reviews with a Mac focus.
Cost: $19.95
Frequency: Monthly
ISBN: 3-212874-88-7
ISSN: 1067-8360
Founded in 1984
Printed in on glossy stock

6655 On the Internet
Rickard Group
1775 Wiehle Ave
Suite 201
Reston, Va 20190-5108

703-439-2120
E-Mail: editor@isoc.org
Home Page: www.isoc.org
Social Media: *Facebook, Twitter, LinkedIn, YouTube*

Wendy Rickard Bollentin, Publisher

Internet information for technologists, developers, educators, researchers, government representatives, and business people.
Cost: $22.00
Frequency: Bi-Monthly
Circulation: 9M

6656 Optical Technology 21st Century
Frames Data
PO Box 2141
Skokie, Il 60077

800-739-7555
847-763-9532
E-Mail: customerservice@framesdata.com
Home Page: www.framesdata.com

Skip Johnson, President
Hunter Noell, Business Development Manager

Movement of product electronically; computerization of office functions, lab work, testing procedures and equipment; information on the Internet, optical Web sites, and onlines services.
Cost: $299.00
Frequency: Quarterly
Circulation: 19M

6657 PCAI
Knowledge Technology
PO Box 30130
Phoenix, AZ 85046

602-971-1869
FAX 602-971-2321
E-Mail: info@pcai.com
Home Page: www.pcai.com/pcai

Terry Hengl, Publisher
Daniel W Rasmus, Editorial Advisor
Don Barker, Senior Editor
Robin Okun, VP of Marketing

Information necessary to help managers, programmers, executives and other professionals understand the unfolding realm of artificial intelligence and intelligent applications.
Cost: $24.00
Founded in 1987

6658 PDN's Pix
VNU Business Media
30 E 23rd St # 5
New York, NY 10010-4442

212-673-1100
FAX 212-673-7074
E-Mail: bmcomm@vnuinc.com
Home Page: www.vnu.com

Penny Vane, Owner
Rob Ruijter, CFO

Covers the world of electronic digital imaging to help readers use new imaging technology and the Web, digital meda, image capture and transfer.
Cost: $19.94
Circulation: 51753
Founded in 1964

6659 Virus Bulletin
Virus Bulletin
590 Danbury Road
Ridgefield, CT 06877-2722

203-438-7714
FAX 203-431-8165

Richard Ford, Editor
Victoria Lammer, Production Manager

An international journal addressing computer viruses, Trojan horses and other malicious programs. Emphasis is placed on providing technical and procedural countermeasures for businesses using computers.
Cost: $35.00

6660 WWWiz Magazine
WWWiz Corporation
8840 Warner Avenue
Suite 200
Fountain Valley, CA 92708

714-848-9600
FAX 714-375-2493
E-Mail: wiz@wwwiz.com
Home Page: www.wwwiz.com

Don Hamilton, Editor-in-Chief
Vivian Hamilton, Managing Editor

WWWiz is a publication focused on the internet with content aimed entrepenuers and business professionals. We interview people who have found success in internet business along with articles pertaining to legal issues, marketing, technology, travel, and other special

interest areas.
Cost: $28.00
Frequency: Monthly
Circulation: 120000
Founded in 1995

6661 Wall Street & Technology
Miller Freeman Publications
11 West 19th Street
New York, NY 10011

212-780-0400
FAX 212-600-3045
E-Mail: mfrieden@cmp.com
Home Page: www.wallstreetandtech.com

Michael Friedenberg, Group Publisher
Richard Rosenblatt, CEO/President
Kerry Massaro, Editor-in-Chief
Anne Marie Miller, Senior VP/Sales & Marketing

Editoral emphasis on the automation of brokerage houses and money management firms.
Frequency: Monthly
Circulation: 21226

6662 Web Builder
Fawcette Technical Publications
2600 S El Camino Real # 300
Suite 300
San Mateo, CA 94403-2381

650-378-7100
800-848-5523
FAX 650-853-0230
E-Mail: customerservice@fawcette.com
Home Page: www.ftponline.com

James Fawcette, President
Karen Koenen, Sr. Circulation Director
John Sutton, Executive VP
Susan Ogren, Marketing Manager
Henry Allain, President

Highly technical, code-sensitive articles that cover all that goes into designing interfaces for sophisticated Internet/Intranet applications. Features a case-study approach to finding out who is using which Web sites and how.
Cost: $32.96
Frequency: Monthly

6663 Web Content Report
Lawrence Ragan Communications
316 N Michigan Ave # 400
Suite 400
Chicago, IL 60601-3773

312-960-4100
800-493-4867
FAX 312-960-4106
E-Mail: cservice@ragan.com
Home Page: www.ragan.com

Jim Ylisela, Publisher
Mark Ragan, CEO/President
Kasia Chalko, Marketing Director Events
Frank Bleers, Marketing Director Publisher

Outlines ways to attract visitors to a Web site, and be able to then monitor and evaluate the traffic on the home page. New developments in Web technology, how products can be sold on sites, budgeting matters and communicaiton with management.
Cost: $269.00
Frequency: Monthly
Founded in 1996
Printed in 2 colors on matte stock

6664 Web Guide Monthly
H&S Media
430 Oak Grove Street
Suite 100
Minneapolis, MN 55403-3234

612-990-3203
FAX 612-879-1082

E-Mail: wdorn@webguidemag.com
Home Page: www.webguidemag.com

Dan Beaver, Publisher

Examines and evaluates useful tools that merge the Internet with everyday life, at work and at home. Sites are sorted into categories, and are referenced in an index.
Cost: $34.95
Frequency: Monthly
Circulation: 120M

6665 Web Techniques
Miller Freeman Publications
411 Borel Avenue
#100
San Mateo, CA 94402-3516

650-573-3210
FAX 650-655-4250
E-Mail: editors@web-techniques.com
Home Page: www.webtechniques.com

Manny Sawit, Publisher
Deirdre Blake, Managing Editor

Latest information, tips and techniques to Web site developers. Contains information on new products and the latest information about the ever-changing world of Web development.
Cost: $34.95
Frequency: Monthly
Circulation: 100M

6666 Webserver Online Magazine
Computer Publishing Group
1340 Centre Street
Newton Centre, MA 02459-2499

617-641-9101
FAX 617-641-9102
E-Mail: editor@cpg.com
Home Page: www.cpg.com

S Henry Sacks, CEO/President
Doug Pryor, Editorial Director
Carol Flanagan, Marketing Manager
Tina Jackson, Circulation Manager
S Sacks, Publisher

Source for information Web professionals who need to get the most ot of their Web development and deployment efforts. Technology and industry news, systems and network adminstration issues, the latest in Web tools, and a guide to new products, services and resources.
Frequency: Monthly
Founded in 1989

6667 WirelessWeek.com
PO Box 266008
Highlands Ranch, CO 80163-6008

303-470-4800
FAX 303-470-4892
E-Mail: subsmail@reedbusiness.com
Home Page: www.wirelessweek.com

Gerard Van de Aast, CEO
Debby Denton, Publisher
Rhonda Wickham, Editor -in- Chief
Glenn Comar, Marketing Director

Trade Shows

6668 American Public Communications Council Conference & Expo
625 Slaters Lane
Suite 104
Alexandria, VA 22314

703-739-1322
FAX 703-739-1324

E-Mail: apcc@apcc.net
Home Page: www.apcc.net

Wilard Nichols, President
Deborah Sterman, CFO
Dan Collins, Corporate Counsel

Conference, luncheon and 100 exhibits of public communications equipment and information including, pay phones, internet, atm, multimedia and more.
Founded in 1988

6669 DMD New York Conference & Expo
Direct Marketing Conferences
20 Academy Street
Norwalk, CT 06850-4032

203-854-9166
800-969-6566
E-Mail: connecticut@dmdays.com
Home Page: www.dmdays.com

Direct Marketing Days New York offers new ideas in media, creative, database, eCommerce and technology. Hundreds of exhibits showcase the newest technologies, products and services. Over 85 sessions and 25 consultation centers led by A level speakers. Network with top-level executives.
Frequency: Annual/June

6670 E-Sports & Business Services Show at the Super Show
Communications & Show Management
1450 NE 123rd Street
North Miami, FL 33161

305-893-8771
FAX 305-893-8783
Home Page: www.bizbash.com
Social Media: *Facebook*

David Adler, CEO and Founder
Richard Aaron, President
Chad Kaydo

Retailers, distributors, wholesalers, importers/exporters and other buyers of sports related products come for 10,000 exhibits of sports apparel, footwear, accessories and e-commerce products and services.
100k Attendees
Frequency: January

6671 EcomXpo
Wordwide Business Research
535 5th Ave
8th Floor
New York, Ny 10017

888-482-6012
FAX 646-200-7535
E-Mail: info@ecomxpo.com
Home Page: www.ecomxpo.com

Rick Worden, Chairman and CEO
Steve Goldring, Managing Director

An educationally focused, online virtual trade show designed specifically for search, affiliate and interactive marketers.
Frequency: July

6672 How To Make A Living On-line
Women in eCommerce
PO Box 550856
Fort Lauderdale, FL 33355-0856

954-625-6606
877-947-3337
E-Mail: heidi@wecai.org
Home Page:
www.wecai.org/3909/how-to-make-a-living-online/

Suzannah Richards, President
Rosana Santos, President Elect
Ellen Sue Burton, VP/Logistics & Hospitality
Racheli Smilovitz, VP/Professional Development

Racheli Smilovitz, VP/Professional Development

An action packed, content-rich luncheon on the topic of internet marketing.
Founded in 2001

6673 Info Today Conference
Information Today
143 Old Marlton Pike
Medford, NJ 08055-8758

609-654-6266
800-300-9868
FAX 609-654-4309
E-Mail: custserv@infotoday.com
Home Page: www.infotoday.com

Thomas H Hogan, Publisher/President
Roger R Bilboul, Chairman Of The Board

Users of online information services, electronic databases and the Internet. 200 booths.
6M Attendees
Frequency: May
Founded in 1980
Mailing list available for rent: 5000 names

6674 International Consumer Electronics Show (C ES)
Las Vegas Hotel & Casino
3000 S. Paradise Road
Las Vegas, NV 89109

866-539-8430
Home Page: www.ceweb.org
Social Media: *Facebook, Twitter, LinkedIn*

Gary Shapiro, President/CEO
Pat Lavelle, Chairman
Peter Lesser, Industry Executive Advisor
Jason Oxman, VP Communications
Jenny Pareti, Public Policy Director

The CES reaches across global markets, connects the industry and enables consumer electronics to grow and thrive. International CES is owned and prroduced by the Consumer Electronics Association (CEA).
2000 Members
Frequency: January

6675 Internet Communications Exposition
IDG Expositions
1400 Providence Highway
Norwood, MA 02062

508-879-6700

6676 National Conference on Operations & Fulfillment (NCOF)
Direct Marketing Association
1120 Avenue of Americas
New York, NY 10036-6700

212-768-7277
FAX 211-302-6714
E-Mail: dmaconferences@the-dma.org
Home Page: www.the-dma.org

Julie A Hogan, SVP Conference/Events
Lawrence M Kimmel, CEO

Focuses on innovative solutions for the warehouse, distribution, operations, and ecommerce needs in the ever-changing world of operations and fulfillment.
10M Attendees

6677 Sporting Goods Manufacturers Markets
1150 17th Street NW
8th Floor
Washington, DC 20036-1604

202-775-1762
FAX 202-296-7462

E-Mail: info@sgma.com
Home Page: www.sgma.com

Tom Cove, President/CEO
Gregg Harrlety, VP
Kalinda Mathis, Director Marketing

Retailers, distributors, wholesalers, importers/exporters and other buyers of sports related products come for 10,000 exhibits of sports apparel, footwear, accessories and e-commerce products and services.
80000 Attendees
Frequency: Biannual/Spring/Fall

6678   SuiteWorld User Conference
NetSuite Ecommerce
2955 Campus Drive
Suite 100
San Mateo, CA 94403-2511

650-627-1000
FAX 650-627-1001
E-Mail: info@netsuite.com
Home Page: www.netsuite.com

Evan Goldberg, Co-Founder/Chief Technology Officer
Zach Nelson, President & CEO

SuiteWorld provides customers, users and partners with the opportunity to gain insights, inspiration and hands-on training to run your business smarter and faster on NetSuite.
10000 Members
Founded in 1998

6679   VoIP 2.0
Technology Marketing Corporation
One Technology Plaza
Norwalk, CT 06854

203-852-6800
800-243-6002
FAX 203-853-2845
Home Page: www.itexpo.com

Frequency: October, San Diego

6680   eM Conference
91 Point Judith Road
Suite 129
Narragansett, RI 02882

800-496-2950
FAX 408-884-2461
E-Mail: service@eMarketingAssociation.com
Home Page: www.emarketingassociation.com

Chris Baggott, CEO
Bert DuMars, C-Founder/CEO
Murray Gaylord, VP/Marketing
Jeff Hilmire, President
Simms Jenkins, Founder & Principal

The Power of eMarketing Conference offers an unparalleled experience in best practices, case histories and processes for social, email and search marketing.
Frequency: Annual/April
Founded in 1997

Directories & Databases

6681   Adweek Directory
Prometheus Global Media
770 Broadway
New York, NY 10003-9595

212-493-4100
FAX 646-654-5368
Home Page: www.prometheusgm.com

Richard D. Beckman, CEO
James A. Finkelstein, Chairman
Madeline Krakowsky, Vice President Chairman
Tracy Brater, Executive Director Creative Service

Adweek Directories Online is where you will find searchable databases with comprehensive information on ad agencies, brand marketers and multicultural media.
Frequency: Annual
Circulation: 800
Founded in 1981

6682   America Online
8619 Westwood Center Drive
Suite 200
Vienna, VA 22182-2238

800-227-6364
FAX 540-265-2135

Jack Daggitt, Director
Anne Botsford

This multi-faceted information service provides complete access to a variety of databases and computer services of interest to users of Macintosh and Apple II computers. Databases included in this systems range from Computing & Software to Lifestyles & Interests.
Frequency: Full-text

6683   Boardwatch Magazine Directory of Internet Service Providers
Penton Media
1300 E 9th St # 316
Cleveland, OH 44114-1503

216-696-7000
FAX 216-696-6662
E-Mail: rgolden@boardwatch.com
Home Page: www.penton.com

Jane Cooper, Marketing
Bill McCarthy, Editorial Director

Reviews various Internet providers and lists different programs available through their individual companies who operate in the US and Canada.
Cost: $72.00
Frequency: Monthly
Circulation: 70,000

6684   Fulltext Sources Online
Information Today
143 Old Marlton Pike
Medford, NJ 08055-8750

609-654-6266
800-300-9868
FAX 609-654-4309
E-Mail: custserv@infotoday.com
Home Page: www.infotoday.com

Thomas H Hogan, President
Roger R Bilboul, Chairman Of The Board

A directory of periodicals accessible online in full text through 28 aggregator products. Lists over 22,000 newspapers, journals, newsletters, newswires, and transcripts.
Cost: $145.00
Frequency: Biannually Jan & July
ISBN: 1-573872-23-7

6685   Global Business Directory
Women in eCommerce
PO Box 550856
Fort Lauderdale, FL 33355-0856

954-625-6606
877-947-3337
E-Mail: heidi@wecai.org
Home Page: www.wecai.org

Suzannah Richards, President
Rosana Santos, President Elect
Ellen Sue Burton, VP/Logistics & Hospitality
Racheli Smilovitz, VP/Professional Development
Racheli Smilovitz, VP/Professional Development

30 member institutions; also lists free resources, global network and internet resources.
Founded in 2001

6686   IQ Directory Adweek
Prometheus Global Media
770 Broadway
New York, NY 10003-9595

212-493-4100
FAX 646-654-5368
Home Page: www.prometheusgm.com

Richard D. Beckman, CEO
James A. Finkelstein, Chairman
Madeine Krakowsky, Vice President Circulation
Tracy Brater, Executive Director Creative Service

Profile of companies at the leading edge of digital marketing, has the specifics you'll need to investigate, launch and/or expand your digital presence. Profiles over 2,200 interactive agencies, web developers, brand marketers, online media, CD-ROM developers, POP/Kiosk designers and multimedia creative companies
Founded in 1981

6687   Internet Blue Pages
Information Today
143 Old Marlton Pike
Medford, NJ 08055-8750

609-654-6266
800-300-9868
FAX 609-654-4309
E-Mail: custserv@infotoday.com
Home Page: www.infotoday.com

Thomas H Hogan, President
Roger R Bilboul, Chairman Of The Board

The Guide to Federal Government Web Sites is the leading guide to federal government information on the web. Includes over 1,800 annotated agency listings, arranged in the US Government Manual style to help you find the information you need.
Cost: $34.95
464 Pages
ISBN: 0-910965-43-9

6688   Key Guide to Electronic Resources: Language and Literature
Information Today
143 Old Marlton Pike
Medford, NJ 08055-8750

609-654-6266
800-300-9868
FAX 609-654-4309
E-Mail: custserv@infotoday.com
Home Page: www.infotoday.com

Thomas H Hogan, President
Roger R Bilboul, Chairman Of The Board

Part of the ongoing topic related series of reference guides is an evaluative directory of electronic reference sources in the fields of language and literature.
Cost: $39.50
120 Pages
ISBN: 1-573870-20-x

6689   On-Line Networks, Databases & Bulletin Boards on Assistive Technology
ERIC Document Reproduction Service
7420 Fullerton Road
Suite 110
Springfield, VA 22153-2852

703-440-1400
800-443-ERIC
FAX 703-440-1408

Directory of electronic networks that focus on technology-related services.

6690   Professional Trade Association Membership
Local Hispanic Chamber of Commerce

1424 K Street NW
Suite 401
Washington, DC 20005

202-715-0494
E-Mail: membership@ushcc.com
Home Page: www.ushcc.com

Javier Palomarez, President & CEO
DeVere Kutscher, Chief of Staff & VP of Strategy

The USHCC is a not-for-profit (501(c)6) organization founded in 1979 to foster Hispanic economic development and to create sustainable prosperity for the benefit of American society.
Founded in 1979

6691 Trade Show News Network

Tarsus Group plc
16985 W Bluemound Road
Suite 210
Brookfield, WI 53005

262-782-1900
FAX 603-372-5894
E-Mail: rwimberly@tsnn.com
Home Page: www.tsnn.com

Rachel Wimberly, Editor-in-Chief
John Rice, Sales & Business Development
Arlene Shows, Marketing Manager

The world's leading online resource for the trade show, exhibition and event industry since 1996. TSNN.com owns and operates the most widely consulted event database on the internet, containing data about more than 19,500 trade shows, exhibitions, public events and conferences.
13900 Members
Frequency: Bi-Monthly
Founded in 1196

Industry Web Sites

6692 http://gold.greyhouse.com
G.O.L.D Grey House OnLine Databases

Grey House Publishing's online database platform, GOLD, offers Quick Search, Keyword Search and Expert Search for most business sectors including e-commerce and internet markets. The GOLD platform makes finding the information you need quick and easy - whether you're a novice searcher or an experienced database user. All of Grey House's directory products are available for subscription on the GOLD platform.

6693 www.aace.org
Association for the Advancement of Computing in Ed

Promotes the use of computers and the internet in educational settings.

6694 www.adsl.com/adsl_forum.html

Information about ADSL, Asymmetric Digital Subscriber Line, a system that provides high-speed Internet connections

6695 www.apcc.net
American Public Communications Council

APCC Proudly offers a wide array of services to the public communications industry, from Perspectives magazine to our annual trade show to our involvement in legal and regulatory issues. This site is a place for the public to find out about our industry and for our members to learn of legal and regulatory developments, to become aware of APCC programs and events and to have a forum for discussion.

6696 www.bsa.org
Business Software Alliance

An organization dedicated to promoting a safe and legal digital world. BSA educates consumers on software management and copyright protection, cyber security, trade, e-commerce and other internet related issues.

6697 www.cabledatacomnews.com/cmic.htm
Cable modems

6698 www.computercpa.com
Accountant's Home Page

Provides information on general accounting for manufacturing, contstruction, service, not-for-profit, e-commerce and more.

6699 www.conferences.calendar.com/

Academic conferences, symposia, courses and workshops.

6700 www.dititalmx.com/wires/

Integrated Services Digital Network

6701 www.greyhouse.com
Grey House Publishing

Authoritative reference directories for most business sectors incluidng e-commerce and internet markets. Users can search the online databases with varied search criteria allowing for custom searches by product category, geographic area, sales volume, keyword, subject and more. Full Grey House catalog and online ordering also available.

6702 www.hayes.com/prodinfo/adsl/intro.html

Information about ADSl, Asymmetric Digital Subscriber Line, a system that provides high-speed Internet connections

6703 www.internets.com
Internets.com

Searchable database and related industry links.

6704 www.iste.org
International Society for Technology in Education

Nonprofit professional organization with a worldwide membership of leaders and potential leaders in educational technology.

6705 www.sdl.com/en/wcm/
eMarketing Association

SDL Tridion R5, the core product, provides complete Web content management and content delivery capabilities, focusing on ease-of-use for all content contributors, site managers and power users.

6706 www.shop.com
Altura International

CatalogCity.com is a powerful and flexible e-commerce technology. This site includes recognized brand names such as Blair, Bombay, Chef's Catalog, Fisher-Price, Gump's by Mail, Hammacher Schlemmer, Ross-Simmons, The Sharper Image, and many more.

6707 www.spie.org
International Society for Optical Engineering

Serves the international technical community as the premier provider of education, information, and resources covering optics, photonics, and their applications.

6708 www.wecommercenews.com
Women in eCommerce

A qualified audience of women looking for e-commerce solutions, information and tolls to run their online endeavors.

Associations

6709 American Automatic Control Council
3640 Col Glenn Hwy
Dayton, OH 45435

937-775-5062
FAX 937-775-3936
E-Mail: pmisra@cs.wright.edu
Home Page: www.a2c2.org

Tariq Samad, President
Glenn Y Masada, President-elect
Linda Bushnell, Treasurer
B.Wayne Bequette, Secretary

Supports all those involved in the manufacturer and distribution of automatic controls. Hosts annual trade show.

6710 Association for High Technology Distributors
N19 W24400 Riverwood Drive
Waukesha, WI 53188

262-696-3645
800-488-4845
E-Mail: ahtd@ahtd.org
Home Page: www.ahtd.org
Social Media: *Twitter, LinkedIn*

Thomas Swenton, President
Bryan Roeesler, Executive Director
Brian Lepsis, VP
John Pirner, Secretary/Program Chair
Paul Burk, Treasurer

Works to increase productivity and profitability of high technology automation solutions, providers and manufacturers.
250 Members
Founded in 1985

6711 Association of Edison Illuminating Companies
600 18th Street N
PO Box 2641
Birmingham, AL 35291

205-257-2530
FAX 205-257-2540
E-Mail: aeicdir@bellsouth.net
Home Page: www.aeic.org

Terry H Waters, Executive Director/Secretary
Len Holland, Manager AEIC Services
Becky Neel, Administrative Assistant
Cindy McLeod, Administrative Assistant

Association of electric utilities concerned with generating, transmitting and distributing electricity. This organization supplies information and support to the industry.
165 Members
Founded in 1885

6712 Bioelectromagnetics Society
2412 Cobblestone Way
Frederick, MD 21702-2626

301-663-4252
FAX 301-694-4948
E-Mail: office@bems.org
Home Page: www.bems.org
Social Media: *Facebook, Twitter*

Gloria Parsley, Executive Director
Richard Nuccitelli, VP
Jonna Wilen, Secretary

Nonprofit organization and international resource for excellence in scientific research, knowledge and understanding of the interaction of electromagnetic fields with biological systems. Members are biological and physical scientists, physicians and engineers interested in the interactions of nonionizing radiation with biological systems.
400 Members
Founded in 1978

6713 Contract Services Association of America
1000 Wilson Boulevard
Suite 1800
Arlington, VA 22209

703-243-2020
FAX 703-243-3601
E-Mail: info@csa-dc.org
Home Page: www.csa-dc.org

Barry Cullen, President
Colleen Preston, Senior VP

Represents the government services contracting industry. Membership ranges from small businesses and corporations servicing federal and state government in numerous capacities. CSA acts to foster the effective implementation of the government's policy of reliance on the private sector for support services. Largest DOD association of service contractors.
650 Members
Founded in 1965

6714 EOS/ESD Association, Inc. (DBA ESD Association)
Electrostatic Discharge Association
7900 Turin Road
Building 3
Rome, NY 13440-2069

315-339-6937
FAX 315-339-6793
E-Mail: info@esda.org
Home Page: www.esda.org
Social Media: *Facebook, Twitter, LinkedIn*

Terry Welsher, President
Gianluca Boselli, Sr. VP
Ginger Hansel, VP
Lisa Pimpinella, Director of Operations

EOS/ESD Association is a professional voluntary association dedicated to advancing the theory and practice of electrical overstress and electrostatice avoidance. The Association expands EOS/ESD awareness through atandards development, educational programs, local chapters, publications, tutorials, certification and symposia.
Cost: $60.00
2000+ Members
Frequency: Bi-Monthly
Founded in 1982

6715 Edison Electric Institute
701 Pennsylvania Avenue NW
Washington, DC 20004-2696

202-508-5000
FAX 202-508-5360
E-Mail: feedback@eei.org
Home Page: www.eei.org
Social Media: *Facebook, Twitter, YouTube*

Thomas R Kuhn, President
David Owens, Executive VP
Brian Wolff, Senior VP, External Affairs

The association of U.S. Shareholder-owned electric companies.
180 Members
Founded in 1933

6716 Electric Association
40 Shuman Blvd
Suite 247
Naperville, IL 60563-8446

630-305-3050
FAX 630-305-3056
E-Mail: cspaeth@eachicago.org
Home Page: www.eachicago.org
Social Media: *Facebook, LinkedIn*

Mark Gibson, President
Rick Jamerson, Vice President
Steven Anixter, Treasurer
Thomas Scherzer, Secretary

Provides members of the electrical industry of Chicagoland and their employees with formal educational opportunities, professional development, information exchange, and member services.
Founded in 1926

6717 Electric Power Research Institute
3420 Hillview Avenue
Palo Alto, CA 94304

650-855-2121
800-313-3774
FAX 650-855-2954
E-Mail: askepri@epri.com
Home Page: www.epri.com
Social Media: *Facebook, Twitter, LinkedIn, YouTube, Flikr*

Gil C Quiniones, Chairman
Michael W Howard, President/CEO

Nonprofit, energy research consortium for the benefit of utility members, their customers and society. Mission is to provide science and technology-based solutions of indispensable value to our global energy customers by managing a far-reaching program of scientific research, technology development and product implementation.
660 Members
Founded in 1973

6718 Electrical Apparatus Service Association
1331 Baur Boulevard
St Louis, MO 63132-1903

314-993-2220
FAX 314-993-1269
E-Mail: easainfo@easa.com
Home Page: www.easa.com
Social Media: *Facebook, Twitter, LinkedIn, YouTube*

Mike Dupuis, Chair
Linda J Raynes CAE, President/CEO
Richard Tutka, Finance Manager

An international trade organization of electro-mechanical sales and service firms in 58 countries. Provides members with a means of keeping up to date on materials, equipment, and state of the art technology.
2100 Members
Founded in 1937
Mailing list available for rent

6719 Electrical Association
One Energy Center
40 Shuman Boulevard, Suite 247
Naperville, IL 60563

630-305-3050
FAX 630-305-3056
E-Mail: cspaeth@eachicago.org
Home Page: www.eachicago.org
Social Media: *Facebook, LinkedIn*

Mark Gibson, President
Rick Jamerson, Vice President
Steven Anixter, Treasurer
Thomas Scherzer, Secretary

Provides members of the electrical industry of Chicagoland and their employees with formal educational opportunities, professional development, information exchange and member services

6720 Electrical Equipment Representatives Association
638 W 39th Street
Kansas City, MO 64111

816-561-5323
800-728-2272
FAX 816-561-1991

E-Mail: info@eera.org
Home Page: www.eera.org

Kier Cooper, President
Rob Rigsby, President Elect
Jennifer Tibbetts, VP
Bobby Cox, Secretary
Doug Softy, Treasurer

Provides technically competent, hands-on, local representation for companies providing products and services to the electric power industry.

6721 Electrical Generating Systems Association

1650 S Dixie Hwy
Suite 400
Boca Raton, FL 33432-7461

561-750-5575
FAX 561-395-8557
Home Page: www.egsa.org
Social Media: *Facebook*

Ed Murphy, President
Charlie Habic, VP
David Brown, Secretary/Treasurer

A trade association made up of companies in the USA and around the world that design, manufacture, sell, distribute, rent, specify, service and use on site power equipment.
600 Members
Founded in 1965

6722 Electrical Safety Foundation International

1300 N 17th Street
Suite 900
Arlington, VA 22209

703-841-3229
FAX 703-841-3329
E-Mail: info@esfi.org
Home Page: www.esfi.org
Social Media: *Facebook, Twitter, LinkedIn, YouTube*

Stephen Sokolow, Chairman
John Engel, Vice Chairman
Kevin Cosgriff, Treasurer
Patrick Davin, Secretary

The mission of the Electrical Safety Foundation International (ESFI) is to advocate electrical safety in the home and in the workplace in order to reduce electrically-related fatalities, injuries and property loss.
Founded in 1994

6723 Electrochemical Society

65 S Main St
Building D
Pennington, NJ 08534-2827

609-737-1902
FAX 609-737-2743
E-Mail: ecs@electrochem.org
Home Page: www.electrochem.org
Social Media: *Facebook, Twitter, LinkedIn*

Roque J. Calvo, Executive Director/CEO
Dinia Agarwala, Graphic Designer
Marcelle Austin, Board Relations Specialist
Rob Gerth, Director, Mktg. & Digital Eng.
Annie Goedkoop, Director of Publications Production

Members are electrochemists and professionals in related industries.
8000 Members
Founded in 1902

6724 Electronic Industries Association

2214 rock Hill Rd
Suite 170
Herndon, VA 20170

571-323-0294
FAX 571-323-0245

Home Page: www.eia.org
Social Media: *LinkedIn, YouTube*

Ronald L Turner, Chairman
Mike Kennedy, Vice Chairman
Dave McCurdy, President
Charles Robinson, Chief Operating Officer
James Shiring, Secretary/Treasurer

Is a national trade organization that includes the full spectrum of U.S. manufacturers.
1300 Members

6725 Electronic Technicians Association

5 Depot St
Greencastle, IN 46135-8024

765-653-8262
800-288-3824
FAX 765-653-4287
E-Mail: eta@eta-i.org
Home Page: www.eta-i.org
Social Media: *Facebook, Twitter, LinkedIn, YouTube, Google+*

Fred Weiss, Chairman
John Baldwin, Vice Chairman
Joseph LaGanga, Secretary
Ira Wiesenfeld, Treasurer
William Brinker, Communications Division Chair

Association for electronics technicians worldwide offering over 70 certifications.
5000 Members
Founded in 1978

6726 IPC: Association Connecting Electronics

3000 Lakeside Dr
Suite 309 S
Bannockburn, IL 60015-1249

847-615-7100
FAX 847-615-7105
E-Mail: webmaster@ipc.org
Home Page: www.ipc.org
Social Media: *Facebook, Twitter, LinkedIn, YouTube, Google+, RSS*

John W. Mitchell, President & CEO
Tom Sandman, CFO
Dave Bergman, VP, International Relations
John Hassleman, VP, Government Relation
Sanjay Huprikar, VP, Member Success

A trade association for the printed circuit boards and electronics assembly industries, offering programs and resources to board manufacturers and electronic assemblers, designers, industry suppliers and original equipment manufacturers.
2700 Members
Founded in 1957

6727 Independent Electrical Contractors Association

4401 Ford Ave
Suite 1100
Alexandria, VA 22302-1464

703-549-7351
800-456-4324
FAX 703-549-7448
E-Mail: info@ieci.org
Home Page: www.ieci.org
Social Media: *Facebook, Twitter, LinkedIn, YouTube, Instagram, Flickr*

Thayer Long, Executive Vice President/CEO
Vernice Howard, CFO
Alicia Johnson, Office Manager
Bruna Patio, Staff Accountant

The mission of IEC is to create success among independent electrical contractors by developing a professional workforce, communicating clearly with government, promoting ethical business practices, and providing leadership for the electrical industry.
73000 Members
Founded in 1957

6728 Institute of Electrical and Electronics Engineers

3 Park Ave.
17th Fl.
New York, NY 10016-5997

212-419-7900
FAX 212-752-4929
Home Page: www.ieee.org
Social Media: *Facebook, Twitter, LinkedIn, YouTube, Google+*

Howard E. Michel, President & CEO
E. James Prendergast, Executive Director

Supports all those involved in the field of electrical engineering. Publishes newsletter and hosts trade show.
430K Members
Founded in 1963

6729 Institute of Electrical/Electronic

3 Park Ave
17th Floor
New York, NY 10016-5997

732-562-3878
FAX 732-562-6046
E-Mail: ieee-mce@ieee.org
Home Page: www.ieee.org
Social Media: *Facebook, Twitter, LinkedIn, YouTube, Google+*

Moshe Kam, President and CEO
Roger Pollard, Director and Secretary
Dr Mohamed El-Hawary, Director/Secretary
365K Members
Founded in 1963

6730 Instrumentation and Measurement Society

3 Park Ave
17th Floor
New York, NY 10016-5997

212-419-7900
FAX 732-981-0225
E-Mail: webmaster@ieee.org
Home Page: www.ieee-ims.org
Social Media: *Twitter, LinkedIn*

Reza Zoughi, President
Ruth A. Dyer, Executive VP
Dario Petri VP Finance Committee
Dr Mohamed El-Hawary, Director/Secretary

A subsidiary of the Institute of Electrical and Electronics Engineers. Provides support to scientists and technicians who design and develop electrical and electronic measuring instruments and equipment.
36000 Members
Founded in 1980

6731 Instrumentation, Systems, and Automation Society

67 Alexander Drive
Box 12277
Research Triangle Park, NC 27709

919-549-8411
FAX 919-549-8288
E-Mail: info@isa.org
Home Page: www.isa.org
Social Media: *Facebook, Twitter, LinkedIn, YouTube, Flickr*

Ken Baker, President
Patrick Gouhin, Executive Director
Debbie Eby, Executive Assistant
Leo Staples, Treasurer

Nonprofit, educational organization connecting people and ideas in automation. The Society fosters advancement in the theory, design, manufacture, and use of sensors, instruments, computers, and systems for automation in a wide variety of applications.
33000 Members
Founded in 1945

6732 International Brotherhood of Electrical Workers
900 7th St. NW
Washington, DC 20001

202-833-7000
FAX 202-728-7676
Home Page: www.ibew.org
Social Media: *Facebook, Twitter, YouTube, Flickr, Vimeo*

Lonnie R. Stephenson, President
Salvatore J. Chilia, Secretary/Treasurer

Among the largest unions in the AFL-CIO, the IBEW represents electrical workers in many fields, from railroads to telecommunications.

6733 International Electrical Testing Association
3050 Old Centre Ave.
Suite 102
Portage, MI 49024

269-488-6382
888-300-6382
FAX 269-488-6383
E-Mail: neta@netaworld.org
Home Page: www.netaworld.org
Social Media: *Facebook, LinkedIn, YouTube*

Melissa Richard, Finance and Business Manager
Jayne Tanz, Executive Director
Ron Widup, 1st VP
Lynn Hamrick, Secretary
John White, Treasurer

Defines the standards by which electrical equipment is deemed safe and reliable. Creates specifications, procedures, testing and requirements for commissioning new equipment and testing the reliability and performance of existing equipment.
2000 Members
Founded in 1972

6734 International Institute of Connector and Interconnection
3000 Lakeside Drive
Bannockburn, IL 60015

E-Mail: info@iicit.org
Home Page: www.iicit.org

Dale Reed, Content Editor

Dedicated to the spread of technological information throughout the industry. In a time of global competition, success depends on communicating technological breakthroughs, innovations and changes in specifications to engineers, designers, specifiers, consultants and other professionals using your product or services.
2640 Members
Founded in 1958

6735 International League of Electrical Associations
P.O. Box 24
Mumford, NY 14511

585-538-6350
FAX 585-538-6166
E-Mail: inco@ileaweb.org
Home Page: www.ileaweb.org
Social Media: *LinkedIn*

Chris Price, President
Robert Morris, VP
Kirstie Steves, Secretary
Barbette Cejalvo, Treasurer

An organization of professional electric association and electric league managers from more than thirty US and seven Canadian cities.
Founded in 1936

6736 International Magnetics Association
Eight South Michigan Avenue
Suite 1000
Chicago, IL 60603-3310

312-456-5590
FAX 312-580-0165
E-Mail: ima@gss.net
Home Page: www.intl-magnetics.org

August Sisco, Chair
Lowell Bosley, President
George Orenchak, Secretary/Treasurer

Is the worldwide trade association representing manufacturers of magnetic materials, distributors and fabricators, suppliers to the magnetics industry and others with an interest in magnetics.
35 Members
Founded in 1959

6737 International Microwave Power Institute
PO Box 1140
Mechanicsville, VA 23111-5007

804-559-6667
FAX 804-559-4087
E-Mail: info@impi.org
Home Page: www.impi.org
Social Media: *Facebook, Twitter*

Molly Poisant, President
Ben Wilson, Vice President
Dorin Bolder, Secretary
Amy Lawson, Treasurer

To be the global organization that provides a forum for the exchange of information on all aspects of microwave and RF heating technologies.
Founded in 1966

6738 Laser Institute of America
13501 Ingenuity Dr
Suite 128
Orlando, FL 32826-3009

407-380-1553
800-345-2737
FAX 407-380-5588
E-Mail: lia@lia.org
Home Page: www.lia.org
Social Media: *Facebook, Twitter, LinkedIn, Google+*

Robert Thomas, President
Stephen Capp, Treasurer
Paul Denny, Secretary

The Laser Institute of America is the professional membership society dedicated to fostering lasers, laser applications and safety worldwide.
1200 Members
Founded in 1968

6739 Laser and Electro-Optic Manufacturers
123 Kent Road
Pacifica, CA 94044-3923

650-738-1492
FAX 650-738-1769
E-Mail: info@leoma.com
Home Page: www.leoma.com

John Ambroseo, President
Breck Hitz, Executive Director
Lynn Strickland, Treasurer
Brian Lula, Secretary

Is the trade association for North American manufacturers of lasers and associated electro-optics equipment.
Founded in 1986

6740 National Association of Electrical Distributors
1181 Corporate Lake Drive
St. Louis, MO 63132

314-991-9000
888-791-2512
FAX 314-991-3060
E-Mail: memberservices@naed.org
Home Page: www.naed.org
Social Media: *Facebook, Twitter, LinkedIn, YouTube*

Tom Naber, President
Michelle McNamara, VP/Executive Director
Sheila Logan, Office & Executive Manager

Supports manufacturers and distributors of electrical components, supplies and equipment. Publishes directory.
Founded in 1997

6741 National Electrical Contractors
3 Bethesda Metro Ctr
Suite 1100
Bethesda, MD 20814-5372

301-657-3110
FAX 301-215-4500
E-Mail: beth.margulies@necanet.org
Home Page: www.necanet.org
Social Media: *Facebook, Twitter, LinkedIn, YouTube*

John M Grau, CEO
Geary Higgins, VP, Labor Relations
Dan Walter, Vice President and COO
Beth Ellis, Executive Director

Represents a segment of the construction market comprised of over 70,000 electrical contracting firms.
65000 Members
Founded in 1901

6742 National Electrical Manufacturers Representatives Association
28 Deer Street
Suite 302
Portsmouth, NH 03801

914-524-8650
800-446-3672
FAX 603-319-1667
E-Mail: nemra@nemra.org
Home Page: www.nemra.org
Social Media: *Twitter, LinkedIn*

Kenneth Hooper, President
Kirsty Stebbins, Manager of Marketing
Sue Todd, Office Manager

Promotes the function of the independent manufacturer's representative as the most effective way to market electrical products. Increases the income of the rep's firm employees and sales staff by increasing the value of the rep firm to owners and customers. Offers educational opportunities that help representatives strengthen the management, technical and professional capabilities of their firms. Promotes communication between independent electrical representatives and manufacturing partners.

6743 National Electronics Service Dealers Association
3000-A Landers St,
Fort Worth, TX 76107

817-921-9061
800-797-9197
FAX 817-921-3741
E-Mail: info@nesda.com
Home Page: www.nesda.com
Social Media: *Facebook*

Ben Fowler, President
Jerrell Helms, Vice President
Wayne Markman, Secretary
George Weiss, Treasurer

Trade association supporting professionals within the electronics business who repair appliances, consumer electronic equipment and computers.
8 Members
Founded in 1950

6744 National Rural Electric Cooperative Association

4301 Wilson Blvd
Suite 1
Arlington, VA 22203-1860

703-907-5500
FAX 703-907-5526
Home Page: www.nreca.org
Social Media: *Twitter*

Glenn English, CEO

Organized specifically to overcome World War II shortages of electric construction materials, to obtain insurance coverage for newly constructed rural electric cooperatives, and to mitigate wholesale power problems. Since those early days, NRECA has been an advocate for consumer owned cooperatives on energy and operational issues as well as rural community and economic development.
1000 Members
Founded in 1942

6745 National Systems Contractors Association

3950 River Ridge Drive NE
Cedar Rapids, IA 52402

319-366-6722
800-446-6722
FAX 319-366-4164
E-Mail: nsca@nsca.org
Home Page: www.nsca.org
Social Media: *Facebook, Twitter, LinkedIn, YouTube*

Michael Hester, President
Ray Bailey, Vice President
Josh Shanahan, Treasurer
David Ferlino, Secretary
Chuck Wilson, Executive Director

Represents the commercial electronic systems industry. Serves as an advocate for all those who work within the low-voltage industry, including systems contractors/integrators, product manufacturers, consultants, sales representatives and a growing number of architects, specifying engineers and others.
2800 Members
Founded in 1980

6746 North American Electric Reliability Corporation

3353 Peachtree Road, N.E
Suite 600 North Tower
Atlanta, GA 30326

404-446-2560
E-Mail: info@nerc.com
Home Page: www.nerc.com

Gerry W. Cauley, President/CEO
Mark Rossi, SVP/Chief Reliability Officer
Marcus H. Sachs, SVP/Chief Security Officer
Charles A. Berardesco, SVP/General Counsel/Corp Secretary
Michael Walker, SVP/CFO/CAO/Treasurer

Principal organization for coordinating and promoting North America's electrical supplies, demands and reliability issues.
11 Members
Founded in 1968

6747 North Central Electrical League

2901 Metro Dr
Suite 203
Bloomington, MN 55425-8699

952-854-4405
800-925-4985

FAX 952-854-7076
E-Mail: dale@ncel.org
Home Page: www.ncel.org
Social Media: *Facebook, Twitter, LinkedIn, Flickr*

Dan Paulson, Chair
Ed Studniski, Vice Chair
Dale Yohnke, Executive Director
Nikki Borgen, Manager - Membership Engagement
Eryka Pluff, Coordinator - Member Benefits

Trade association representing all segments of the electrical industry in the Upper Midwest.
1500 Members
Founded in 1936

6748 Power Sources Manufacturers Association

PO Box 418
Mendham, NJ 07945-0418

973-543-9660
FAX 973-543-6207
E-Mail: power@psma.com
Home Page: www.psma.com
Social Media: *LinkedIn*

Ernie Parker, Chairman
Eric Persson, President
Stephen Oliver, VP
Michel Grenon, Secretary/Treasurer

The PSMA is a not-for-profit organization incorporated in the state of California. The purpose of the Association shall be to enhance the stature and reputation of its members and their products, improve their knowledge of technological and other developments related to power sources, and to educate the entire electronics industry, plus academia, as well as government and industry agencies as to the importance of, and relevant applications for, all types of power sources and conversion devices.
155 Members
Founded in 1985

6749 Relay and Switch Industry Association

2500 Wilson Boulevard
Arlington, VA 22201

703-907-8024
FAX 703-875-8908
E-Mail: narm@ecaus.org
Home Page: www.ec-central.org/RSIA

Robert Willis, President
James Kaplan, Chairman and CEO

Represents the electronics industry sector comprised of companies that manufacturer, produce or market relay and switch technologies and products.
Founded in 1947

6750 SMMA: The Motor & Motion Association

PO Box P182
South Dartmouth, MA 02748

508-979-5935
FAX 508-979-5845
E-Mail: info@smma.org
Home Page: www.smma.org

Paul Murphy, President
Matt French, Vice President
Steve Herrmann, Secretary/Treasurer

Trade association for the electric motor and motion control industry in North America. The voice of the motor and motion industry providing a forum for education, communication, research and networking.
120 Members
Founded in 1975

6751 Semiconductor Equipment and Materials International

3081 Zanker Road
San Jose, CA 95134

408-943-6900
FAX 408-428-9600
E-Mail: semihq@semi.org
Home Page: www.semi.org
Social Media: *Twitter, LinkedIn*

Yong Han Lee, Chairman
Tetsuo Tsuneishi, Vice Chairman
Mary G. Puma, Secretary/Treasurer
Denny McGuirk, President/CEO
Laith Altimime, President, SEMI Europe

Global industry association serving the manufacturing supply chains for the microelectronic, display and photovoltaic industries.
2300 Members
Founded in 1970

6752 Semiconductor Industry Association

1101 K Street NW
Suite 450
Washington, DC 20005

202-446-1700
866-756-0715
FAX 202-216-9745
E-Mail: mailbox@sia-online.org
Home Page: www.sia-online.org
Social Media: *Facebook, Twitter*

John Neuffer, President/CEO
Latoya Arnold, Executive Assistant/Office Manager
Jimmy Goodrich, Vice President, Global Policy
Joe Pasetti, Director, Government Affairs
Dan Rosso, Communications Manager

Trade association representing the US microchip industry. Provides a forum for working collectively to enhance the competitiveness of the US chip industry.
70 Members
Founded in 1977

6753 Society of Manufacturing Engineers

1 SME Drive
Dearborn, MI 48128

313-425-3000
800-733-4763
FAX 313-425-3400
E-Mail: service@sme.org
Home Page: www.sme.org
Social Media: *Facebook, Twitter, LinkedIn, YouTube, Google+, RSS*

Wayne F. Frost, CMfgE, President
Jeffrey M. Krause, Chief Executive Officer
Kathleen Borgula, Human Resources
Erica Ciupak, Information Technology
Debbie Clark, Governance

Supports all those engineers involved in electrical manufacturing. Hosts trade show.
25K Members
Founded in 1932

6754 Surface Mount Technology Association

5200 Willson Rd
Suite 215
Edina, MN 55424-1316

952-920-7682
FAX 952-926-1819
E-Mail: joann@smta.org
Home Page: www.smta.org
Social Media: *Facebook, Twitter, LinkedIn, YouTube, Google+*

Bill Barthel, President
Eileen Hibbler, VP of Membership
Raiyomand Aspandiar, Ph.D., VP Technical Programs
Michelle Ogihara, VP Communications
Richard Henrick, Secretary

Network of professionals building skills, sharing practical experience and developing solutions in electronic assembly technologies and related business operations.
3200 Members
Founded in 1984

6755 U.S. Department of Energy
1000 Independence Ave. SW
Washington, DC 20585

202-586-5000
FAX 202-586-4403
Home Page: www.energy.gov
Social Media: *Facebook, Twitter*

Dr. Ernest Moniz, Secretary of Energy
Dr. Elizabeth Sherwood-Randall, Deputy
Secretary of Energy

The Energy Department is responsible for the transformation of the nation's energy system through the application of the latest science and technology solutions.

Newsletters

6756 Advanced Battery Technology
Seven Mountains Scientific
913 Tressler Street
PO Box 650
Boalsburg, PA 16827

814-466-6559
FAX 814-466-2777
E-Mail: jo@7ms.com
Home Page: www.7ms.com

E Thomas Chesworth, Technical Editor
Josephine Chesworth, Managing Editor

The oldest, most widely read international newsletter reporting on battery technology, marketing and industry events including new products and financial news. Accepts advertising. Print and online versions available.
Cost: $ 180.00
Circulation: 1000
Printed in 4 colors on matte stock

6757 Cleanroom Markets Newsletter
McIlvaine Company
191 Waukegan Rd
Suite 208
Northfield, IL 60093-2743

847-784-0012
FAX 847-784-0061
E-Mail: editor@mcilvainecompany.com
Home Page: www.mcilvainecompany.com

Robert McIlvaine, Owner
Robert McIvaine, President
Marilyn McIlvaine, EVP

Information on clean rooms markets worldwide.
Cost: $460.00
8 Pages
Frequency: Monthly
Printed in on newsprint stock

6758 Cleanroom Technology Newsletter
McIlvaine Company
191 Waukegan Rd
Suite 208
Northfield, IL 60093-2743

847-784-0012
FAX 847-784-0061
Home Page: www.mcilvainecompany.com

Robert McIlvaine, Owner
Robert McIvaine, President
Marilyn McIlvaine, EVP

Information on clean room technology.

6759 Continuous Improvement
James Publishing

PO Box 25202
Santa Ana, CA 92799-5202

714-755-5450
800-394-2626
FAX 714-751-2709
E-Mail:
customer-service@jamespublishing.com
Home Page: www.jamespublishing.com

Jim Pawell, Founder and President
Stephen Sicillan, Editor

Tutorial and news on new quality assurance technologies and ISO 9000, QS 9000 and ISO 14000.
Cost: $20.00
Circulation: 2000

6760 Currents
Electrical Apparatus Service Association
1331 Baur Boulevard
Saint Louis, MO 63131-1903

314-993-2220
FAX 314-993-1269
E-Mail: easinfo@easa.com
Home Page: www.easa.com

Kevin Toor, Chairman
William Gray, Vice Chairman
Kenneth Gralow, Secretary Treasurer

Provides information on EASA's programs, seminars, technical articles and industry trends and events. Members receive a copy each month.
Frequency: Monthly
Circulation: 2000+

6761 Display Technology News
Business Communications Company
49 Walnut Park
Building 2
Wellesley, MA 02481

781-489-7301
866-285-7215
FAX 781-253-3933
E-Mail: sales@bccresearch.com
Home Page: www.bccresearch.com
Social Media: *Facebook, Twitter*

Greg Lindberg, Chairman and CEO
Bridgett Hurley, CMO
Kevin Fitzgerald, Editorial Director
Sharon Blank, Sales Director
Mark McCarthy, Operations Director

Market reports and technology updates of topics such as news materials, news applications, patents, technology transfer, processing and equipment.
Cost: $500.00
Frequency: Monthly
Founded in 1971

6762 Document Imaging Report
Corry Publications
5340 Fryling Road
Knowledge Park, Suite 300
Erie, PA 16510

814-897-9000
FAX 814-899-5583
E-Mail: corrypub@corrypub.com
Home Page: www.corrypub.com

Nicole Hykes, Editor
John Toiston, Publisher
Carry Procious, Marketing
Mindy Sadden, Circulation Manager

Presents the most timely and actionable information on electronic imaging applications, products and user implementation.
Frequency: Monthly
Circulation: 50

6763 EA Extra
Electrical Association of Philadelphia

527 Plymouth Road
Suite 408
Plymouth Meeeting, PA 19462-1641

610-825-1600
FAX 610-825-1603
E-Mail: electric@eap.org
Home Page: www.eap.org
Social Media: *Facebook, Twitter, YouTube*

Kevin Lane, President
Joe Henry, Vice President
Kim Schneider, Treasurer
Kenneth Hull, Secretary

Carries information on industry trends, events, educational and business opportunities, economic briefings, member happening, mergers, and member benefit updates.
450 Members
Founded in 1917

6764 Electrical Connection
Electrical Association of Rochester
PO Box 20219
Rochester, NY 14602-0219

585-538-6350
FAX 585-538-6166
E-Mail: info@peawny.com
Home Page: www.eawny.com

Joe Lengen, President
Bonnie Curran, First VP
Coreg Merrill, Secretary/Treasurer
Kirstie Steves, Executive Director

Contains information on upcoming events, recaps past events, a message from the President, the current calendar and much more.
Frequency: Quarterly
Founded in 1924

6765 Electrical Product News
Business Marketing & Publishing
PO Box 7457
Wilton, CT 06897

203-834-9959
E-Mail: info@epnweb.com
Home Page: www.epnweb.com
Social Media: *Facebook*

George Young, Editor/Publisher

Accepts advertising.
Cost: $39.50
20 Pages
Frequency: Monthly
Circulation: 3500
Printed in 2 colors on newsprint stock

6766 Electro Manufacturing
Worldwide Videotex
PO Box 3273
Boynton Beach, FL 33424-3273

561-738-2276
E-Mail: markedit@juno.com
Home Page: www.wvpubs.com

Computer and electronic technologies used to help improve manufacturing efficiency.
Cost: $165.00

6767 Executive Newsline
Electric Power Research Institute
PO Box 10412
Palo Alto, CA 94303-0813

650-855-2000
800-313-3774
FAX 650-855-2954
E-Mail: askepri@epri.com
Home Page: www.epri.com
Social Media: *Facebook, Twitter, LinkedIn, YouTube, Flikr*

Steven R Specker, CEO
Jackie Turner, Communications Manager
Don Kintner, Communications Manager
Rick Langley, Director

Contains brief highlights of EPRI science and technology developments and announcements of interest to utility executives.

6768 Global Electronics
Pacific Studies Center
222B View Street
Mountain View, CA 94041-1344

650-969-1545
FAX 650-961-9818

Leonard Siegel, Editor

News items detailing the industry throughout the world and the social, environmental and military implications of production and application.
Cost: $1.00
Circulation: 400

6769 IEEE Transactions on Applied Superconductivity
IEEE Instrumentation and Measurement Society
67 Alexander Drive
PO Box 12277
Research Triangle Park, NC 27709

919-549-8411
FAX 919-549-8288
E-Mail: info@isa.org
Home Page: www.isa.org
Social Media: *Facebook, Twitter, LinkedIn*

Ken Baker, President
Patrick Gouhin, Executive Director
Jerry Clemons, Department VP
Leo Staples, Treasurer

Concentrates on materials and their applications to electronics and power systems where superconductivity is central to the work.

6770 IEEE Transactions on Mobile Computing
IEEE Instrumentation and Measurement Society
67 Alexander Drive
PO Box 12277
Research Triangle Park, NC 27709

919-549-8411
FAX 919-549-8288
E-Mail: info@isa.org
Home Page: www.isa.org
Social Media: *Facebook, Twitter, LinkedIn*

Ken Baker, President
Patrick Gouhin, Executive Director
Jerry Clemons, Department VP
Leo Staples, Treasurer

Research papers are presented in this publication dealing with mobile computing, wireless networks, reliability, quality assurance, distributed systems architecture and high-level protocols.
Frequency: Quarterly

6771 IFAC Newsletter
American Automatic Control Council
3640 Col Glenn Hwy
Dayton, OH 45435

937-775-5062
FAX 937-775-3936
E-Mail: pmisra@cs.wright.edu
Home Page: www.a2c2.org

John Watkins, Editor

It contains up-to-date information about forthcoming IFAC events as well as brief announcements of other IFAC related activities. It is sent free of charge to NMO's, IFAC Affiliates and libraries.
Frequency: Bi-Monthly

6772 Inside FERC
McGraw Hill

PO Box 182604
Columbus, OH 43272

720-485-5000
877-833-5524
FAX 614-759-3749
E-Mail: customer.service@mcgraw-hill.com
Home Page: www.mcgraw-hill.com
Social Media: *Facebook, Twitter, LinkedIn, YouTube*

Harold McGraw, President and CEO
Jack Callahan, Executive VP/CFO
John Berisford, EVP, Human Resources

Provides coverage of the Federal Energy Regulatory Commission's activities and federal regulations.
Cost: $975.00
14 Pages
Frequency: Monthly
Founded in 1884

6773 Inside NRC
McGraw Hill
PO Box 182604
Columbus, OH 43272

614-304-4000
877-833-5524
FAX 614-759-3749
E-Mail: customer.service@mcgraw-hill.com
Home Page: www.mcgraw-hill.com
Social Media: *Facebook, Twitter, LinkedIn, YouTube*

Harold McGraw, President and CEO
Jack Callahan, Executive VP/CFO
John Berisford, EVP, Human Resources

Focuses exclusively on the US Nuclear Regulatory Commission.
Cost: $1310.00
13 Pages
Founded in 1800

6774 SMT Trends
New Insights
303 Vallejo Street
Crockett, CA 94525-1237

510-787-2273
FAX 415-389-8671

Michael New, Publisher/Editor

Marketing and business news for the surface mount industry. Covers component and packaging trends, CAD, CAE, pick and place, robotics and test inspection.
Printed in one color on matte stock

6775 SMTA News
Surface Mount Technology Association
5200 Wilson Road
Suite 215
Minneapolis, MN 55424

952-920-7682
FAX 952-926-1819
E-Mail: joann@smta.org
Home Page: www.smta.org

Dan Baldwin, President
Marie Cole, VP Tech Programs
Kola Akinade, Secretary
Hal Hendrickson, Treasurer

6776 Seven Mountain Scientific
PO Box 650
Boalsburg, PA 16827-651

814-466-6559
FAX 814-466-2777
E-Mail: abt@7ms.com
Home Page: www.7ms.com

E Thomas Chesworth, President

Industry news in battery and fuel cell technology, marketing and industry events including new products, electric vehicle, R&D and envi-

ronmental news.
Cost: $180.00
ISSN: 0001-8627
Founded in 1965

6777 Tech Notes
National Technical Information Service
5301 Shawnee Rd
Alexandria, VA 22312

703-605-6000
FAX 703-605-6900
E-Mail: info@ntis.gov
Home Page: www.ntis.gov
Social Media: *Facebook, Twitter*

Bruce Borzino, Director
Patrik Ekstrom, Business Development Manager
Reuel Avila, Managing Director

Describes new processes, equipment, materials and techniques developed by Federal laboratories.
Cost: $8.00

6778 Threshold Newsletter
Electrostatic Discharge Association
7900 Turin Road
Building 3
Rome, NY 13440-2069

315-339-6937
FAX 315-339-6793
E-Mail: info@esda.org
Home Page: www.esda.org
Social Media: *Facebook, LinkedIn, YouTube*

Donn Bellmore, President
Leo G. Henry, Sr. VP
Terry Welsher, VP
Lisa Pimpinella, Director of Operations
Donn Pritchard, Treasurer

Benefits of ESD membership include a subscription to the Threshold Newsletter in addition to other Association activities and programs such as educational tutorials and seminars; the EOS/ESD Symposium; participation in local chapters; discounts on Association standards and other publications; extensive networking; membership roster, and participation in standards development.
2000+ Members
Founded in 1982

6779 Transformers for Electronic Circuits
Power Sources Manufacturers Association
PO Box 418
Mendham, NJ 07945-0418

973-543-9660
FAX 973-543-6207
E-Mail: power@psma.com
Home Page: www.psma.com

Dusty Becker, Chairman
Carl Blake, President
Jim Marinos, VP
Michel Grenon, Secretary/Treasurer

It is a complete, one-stop guide to transformer and inductor design and applications for everyone who designs, builds, or uses power magnetics components. Combines analysis and synthesis, and all theory is related to the solution of real world problems.
Cost: $100.00
155 Members
Founded in 1985

6780 Update
Power Sources Manufacturers Association
PO Box 418
Mendham, NJ 07945-0418

973-543-9660
FAX 973-543-6207
E-Mail: power@psma.com

Home Page: www.psma.com
Social Media: *LinkedIn*

Dusty Becker, Chairman
Carl Blake, President
Jim Marinos, VP
Michel Grenon, Secretary/Treasurer

PSMA Update is published and distributed via e-mail quarterly by the Power Sources Manufacturers Association.
Frequency: Quarterly
Circulation: 2700

6781   Vision
Society of Manufacturing Engineers
1 SME Drive
PO Box 930
Dearborn, MI 48128

313-425-3000
800-733-4763
FAX 313-425-3400
E-Mail: service@sme.org
Home Page: www.sme.org

Paul Bradley, President
Mark Tomlinson, Executive Director/CEO

The newsletter highlights the latest developments in the machine vision industry including applications, techniques and methods.
Cost: $85.00
Frequency: Quarterly
Circulation: 1100
ISSN: 1544-3531

6782   Wafer News Confidential
PennWell Publishing Company
98 Spit Brook Rd
Suite L1-1
Nashua, NH 03062-5737

603-891-0123
800-225-0556
FAX 603-891-9294
E-Mail: ATD@PennWell.com
Home Page: www.pennwell.com

Christine Shaw, VP
Barbara Pennwell, CEO/President

Provides semiconductor equipment industry executives with information on developments, trends, news and market insights.
Cost: $15.00
Frequency: Monthly
Founded in 1910

Magazines & Journals

6783   Bioelectromagnetics Journal
John Wiley & Sons
2412 Cobblestone Way
Frederick, MD 21702-3519

301-663-4252
FAX 301-694-4948
E-Mail: office@bems.org
Home Page: www.bems.org

James Lin, Editor in Chief
Carmela Marino, Associate Editor
Andrei Pakhomov, Associate Editor

It is a peer-reviewed, internationally circulated scientific journal that specializes in reporting original data on biological effect and applications of electromagnetic fields that range in frequency from zero hertz static fields) to the terahertz undulations of visible light.
Frequency: 6x yearly

6784   Contact
1000 McKee Street
Batavia, IL 60510-1682

630-879-6000
FAX 630-879-0867

Steve Wilcox, Editor

Application of electric motor controls to electrically operated machinery and equipment.
Circulation: 4,000

6785   Control Solutions
PennWell Publishing Company
1421 S Sheridan Rd
Tulsa, OK 74112-6619

918-835-3161
800-331-4463
FAX 918-831-9497
E-Mail: Headquarters@PennWell.com
Home Page: www.pennwell.com

Robert Biolchini, President
Ron Kuhfeld, Editor-in-Chief
Frequency: Monthly

6786   Diesel & Gas Turbine Worldwide
Diesel & Gas Turbine Publications
20855 Watertown Rd
Suite 220
Waukesha, WI 53186-1873

262-754-4100
FAX 262-754-4175
Home Page: www.dieselspec.com

Michael Osenga, President
Lynne Diefenbach, Advertising Manager

Concentrates its editorial on the design, packaging, operation and maintenance of medium and high output diesel, natural gas and gas turbine engine systems used in the electrical power generation, cogeneration, oil and gas, marine propulsion and railroad markets throughout the world.
Cost: $65.00
Frequency: 10x yearly
Circulation: 22,000
Founded in 1969

6787   ECN Magazine
Reed Business Information
360 Park Ave S
4th Floor
New York, NY 10010-1737

646-746-6400
FAX 646-756-7583
E-Mail: submail@reedbusiness.com
Home Page: www.reedbusiness.com

John Poulin, CEO
Aimee Kalnoskas, Editor
Steve Wirth, Publisher Director
James Reed, Owner

Provides product solutions for designed engineers in the electronics industry.
Cost: $96.19
Frequency: Monthly

6788   EE Product News
Penton Media
1166 Avenue of the Americas/10th Fl
New York, NY 10036

212-204-4200
E-Mail:
CorporateCustomerService@penton.com
Home Page: www.penton.com

David Kieselstien, CEO
Nicola Allais, CFO
Jasmine Alexander, CIO

Source of information on new products necessary to successfully design, assemble and test

prototypes of commercial, industrial, military and aerospace electronic products.
Frequency: Monthly
Circulation: 111968
Founded in 1892

6789   EE: Evaluation Engineering
Nelson Publishing
2500 Tamiami Trl N
Nokomis, FL 34275-3476

941-966-9521
800-226-6113
FAX 941-966-2590
E-Mail: pmilo@evaluationengineering.com
Home Page: www.healthmgttech.com
Social Media: *Facebook, Twitter*

Kristine Russel, President
Phil Colpas, Managing Editor

Magazine devoted exclusively to companies that test, evaluate, design and manufacture electronic products and equipment.
Cost: $43.00
84 Pages
Frequency: Monthly
Founded in 1962
Mailing list available for rent: 65,000 names
Printed in 4 colors on glossy stock

6790   ElectriCITY
Electric Association
40 Shuman Boulevard
Suite 247
Naperville, IL 60563

630-305-3050
FAX 630-305-3056
E-Mail: cspaeth@eachicago.org
Home Page: www.eachicago.org

Mark Gibson, President
Rick Jamerson, Vice President
Steven Anixter, Treasurer
Thomas Scherzer, Secretary
Founded in 1925

6791   ElectriCITY Magazine
Electric Association
40 Shuman Boulevard
Suite 247
Naperville, IL 60563-8446

630-305-3050
FAX 630-305-3056
E-Mail: admin@eachicago.org
Home Page: www.eachicago.org
Social Media: *Facebook, LinkedIn*

Mark Gibson, President
Rick Jamerson, Vice President
Steven Anixter, Treasurer
Thomas Scherzer, Secretary
Bob Porter, Secretary

Corporate news, timely articles, career announcements, product line changes, industry-dates calendars, career placement services, and government legislation updates; circulation across the Midwest.
Frequency: Quarterly

6792   Electric Co-op Today
National Rural Electric Cooperative Association
4301 Wilson Blvd
Suite 1
Arlington, VA 22203-1860

703-907-5500
FAX 703-907-5526
Home Page: www.nreca.org
Social Media: *Twitter*

Glenn English, CEO

Devoted to accurate, critical coverage of electric cooperative developments and electric cooperative industry news, unavailable in any other publication. The only weekly publication covering electric cooperative industry news,

legislation and regulation, and community and economic development. Each issue highlights what you need to know to understand key industry issues clearly, quickly, and easily.
Cost: $40.00
Frequency: Weekly
Founded in 1994

6793 Electric Light & Power
PennWell Publishing Company
1421 S Sheridan Rd
Tulsa, OK 74112-6619

918-835-3161
800-331-4463
FAX 918-831-9497
E-Mail: Headquarters@PennWell.com
Home Page: www.pennwell.com

Serves the North American Electric Utility Industry including electric power generation, delivery, and information technology operations in investor-owned electric utilities.
Frequency: Monthly
ISSN: 0013-4120
Founded in 1902

6794 Electric Perspectives
Edison Electric Institute
701 Pennsylvania Avenue NW
Washington, DC 20004-2696

202-508-5000
FAX 202-508-5360
E-Mail: feedback@eei.org
Home Page: www.eei.org
Social Media: *Facebook, Twitter, YouTube*

Thomas R Kuhn, President
David Owens, Executive VP Business Operations
Brian Wolff, Senior VP, External Affairs
Written and edited specifically for management-level employees at shareholder-owned electric utilities.
Frequency: Bi-Monthly
Circulation: 15,000
ISSN: 0364-474X

6795 Electrical Apparatus
Barks Publications
400 N Michigan Ave
Suite 900
Chicago, IL 60611-4164

312-321-9440
FAX 312-321-1288
E-Mail: info@barks.com
Home Page: www.barks.com

Horace Barks, Owner
Elsie Dickson, Associate Publisher
Horace Barks, CEO
Joseph Hoff, Manager

Serves the electromechanical and electronic maintenance and application industries, including manufacturing plants, institutional facilities and service companies.
Cost: $45.00
Frequency: Monthly
Circulation: 15500
Founded in 1969

6796 Electrical Construction & Maintenance
Primedia
1166 Avenue of the Americas/10th Fl
New York, NY 10036

212-204-4200
E-Mail: CorporateCustomerService@penton.com
Home Page: www.penton.com

David Kieselstien, CEO
Nicola Allais, CFO
Jasmine Alexander, CIO

Owners and company officials, engineers, electrical personnel, electrical inspectors, architects

and designers, purchasing and other related personnel.
Circulation: 104344

6797 Electrical Contractor Magazine
National Electrical Contractors Association
3 Bethesda Metro Ctr
Suite 1100
Bethesda, MD 20814-5372

301-657-3110
FAX 301-215-4500
E-Mail: beth.margulies@necanet.org
Home Page: www.necanet.org
Social Media: *Facebook, Twitter, LinkedIn, YouTube*

John M Grau, CEO
Dan Walter, VP and COO
Michael Thompson, Secretary/Treasurer

The magazine has been the complete information source for electrical construction professionals. Its goal is to serve all participants in the power and integrated building systems industries. It delivers the latest information in the areas of power, communications and controls in both high voltage and low voltage applications to electrical contractors who compete in residential, commercial, industrial and institutional market segments of the construction arena.
Circulation: 85,000
Founded in 1939

6798 Electrical Distributor Magazine
National Association of Electrical Distributors
1181 Croporate Lake Drive
St Louis, MO 63132

314-991-9000
888-791-2512
FAX 314-991-3060
E-Mail: info@naed.org
Home Page: www.naed.org
Social Media: *Facebook, Twitter, YouTube*

Robert Reynolds, Chairman
Tom Naber, President and CEO

An informative, insightful publication that offers electrical distributors the latest information affecting their business. Subscriptions are free to NAED members.

6799 Electrical Wholesaling
Primedia
1166 Avenue of the Americas/10th Fl
New York, NY 10036

212-204-4200
E-Mail: CorporateCustomerService@penton.com
Home Page: www.penton.com

David Kieselstien, CEO
Nicola Allais, CFO
Jasmine Alexander, CIO

Offers information on manufacturers, suppliers, prices and marketing of electrical products.
Cost: $25.00
Frequency: Monthly
Circulation: 22,500
Founded in 1905

6800 Electricity Today
1885 Clements Road
Unit 218
Pickering, Canada, ON L1W-3V4

905-686-1040
FAX 905-686-1078
E-Mail: carol@electricityforum.com
Home Page: www.electricty-today.com

Randy Hurst, Publisher

Electricity Today is a leading electrical transmission and distribution magazine distributed free of charge to North American T&D electric utility engineering, construction and mainte-

nance personnel, and high voltage T&D consulting engineers.

6801 Electronic Design
Penton Media
1166 Avenue of the Americas/10th Fl
New York, NY 10036

212-204-4200
E-Mail: CorporateCustomerService@penton.com
Home Page: www.penton.com

David Kieselstien, CEO
Nicola Allais, CFO
Jasmine Alexander, CIO

Celebrating 50 years of innovation, this authoritative source provides leading-edge information to electronic and engineering managers around the world.

6802 Fringe Ware Review
Fringe Ware
PO Box 49921
Austin, TX 78765-4858

512-444-2393

Paco Nathan, Co-Founder
Don Lebkowsky, Co-Founder
Monte McCarter, Art Director
Tiffany Lee Brown, Assistant Editor

Stories and review on electronic products made by smaller producers.
Cost: $4.00
Founded in 1992

6803 High Tech News
Electronic Technicians Association International
5 Depot St
Greencastle, IN 46135-8024

765-653-8262
800-288-3824
FAX 765-653-4287
E-Mail: eta@eta-i.org
Home Page: www.eta-i.org
Social Media: *Facebook, Twitter, LinkedIn*

Teresa Maher, CSS, President
Cindy Reed, Financial Director
Richard Glass, CETsr, CEO Emeritus

Exclusive bi-monthly publication of ETA International, and a subscription is included with each individual membership. Each issue features information on the changing electronics industry: specialty techniques & technology, trends, qualification opportunities and educational advice.
4500 Members
Frequency: Bi-Monthly
Circulation: 10000
Founded in 1978

6804 IEEE Instrumentation and Measurement Magazine
IEEE Instrumentation and Measurement Society
67 Alexander Drive
PO Box 12277
Research Triangle Park, NC 27709

919-549-8411
FAX 919-549-8288
E-Mail: info@isa.org
Home Page: www.isa.org
Social Media: *Facebook, Twitter, LinkedIn*

Kim Fowler, Editor-in-Chief

This publication is included in member dues, it contains applications-oriented articles and news nominations, awards, highlights of conferences, Technical Committee news, book reviews, tutorials and contributions from the membership.
Frequency: Quarterly

6805 IEEE Sensors Journal
IEEE Instrumentation and Measurement Society
67 Alexander Drive
PO Box 12277
Research Triangle Park, NC 27709

919-549-8411
FAX 919-549-8288
E-Mail: info@isa.org
Home Page: www.isa.org
Social Media: *Facebook, Twitter, LinkedIn*

Ken Baker, President
Patrick Gouhin, Executive Director
Jerry Clemons, Department VP
Leo Staples, Treasurer

Specializes in the theory, design, fabrication, manufacturing and applications of devices for sensing and transducing physical, chemical and biological phenomena.
Frequency: Bi-Monthly

6806 IEEE Transactions on Intelligent Transportation Systems
IEEE Instrumentation and Measurement Society
67 Alexander Drive
PO Box 12277
Research Triangle Park, NC 27709

919-549-8411
FAX 919-549-8288
E-Mail: info@isa.org
Home Page: www.isa.org
Social Media: *Facebook, Twitter, LinkedIn*

Ken Baker, President
Patrick Gouhin, Executive Director
Jerry Clemons, Department VP
Leo Staples, Treasurer

This journal contains basic and applied research to expand the knowledge base on transportation for improved design, management and control of future transportation systems.
Frequency: Quarterly

6807 IEEE Transactions on Nanotechnology
IEEE Instrumentation and Measurement Society
67 Alexander Drive
PO Box 12277
Research Triangle Park, NC 27709

919-549-8411
FAX 919-549-8288
E-Mail: info@isa.org
Home Page: www.isa.org
Social Media: *Facebook, Twitter, LinkedIn*

Ken Baker, President
Patrick Gouhin, Executive Director
Jerry Clemons, Department VP
Leo Staples, Treasurer

The journal is devoted to the dissemination of new results and discussions related to understanding the physical basis and engineering applications of phenomena at the nanoscale level.
Frequency: Quarterly

6808 Industrial Laser Solutions
PennWell Publishing Company
98 Spit Brook Rd
Nashua, NH 03062-5737

603-891-0123
80- 2-5 05
FAX 603-891-9294
Home Page: www.pennwell.com

Christine Shaw, VP
David Belforte, Editor

For all industries that use industrial lasers.
Cost: $260.00
45 Pages
Frequency: Monthly
Circulation: 10,000

ISSN: 1523-4266
Founded in 1986

6809 Industrial Market Place
Wineberg Publications
7842 Lincoln Avenue
Skokie, IL 60077

847-676-1900
800-323-1818
FAX 847-676-0063
E-Mail: info@industrialmktpl.com
Home Page: www.industrialmktpl.com

Eliot Wineberg, President
Jackie Bitensky, Editor

Has advertisements on machinery, industrial and plant equipment, services and industrial auctions in each issue.
Cost: $175.00
60 Pages
Frequency: Bi-Monthly
Circulation: 14,000
Founded in 1951
Printed in 4 colors on glossy stock

6810 Interface Magazine
Electrochemical Society
65 S Main St
Building D
Pennington, NJ 08534-2827

609-737-1902
FAX 609-737-2743
E-Mail: ecs@electrochem.org
Home Page: www.electrochem.org

Christine Garzon, President
Tetsuya Osaka, Sr. VP
Harikila Deligianni, Secretary
Christina Bock, Treasurer

Is an authoritative accessible publication for those in the field of solid-state and electrochemical science and technology which contains technical articles about the latest developments in the field, and presents news and information about and for members of ECS.
Cost: $40.00
Frequency: Quarterly
Circulation: 9000
ISSN: 1064-8208
Founded in 1902
Printed in 4 colors

6811 Journal of Laser Applications
Laser Institute of America
13501 Ingenuity Dr
Suite 128
Orlando, FL 32826-3009

407-380-1553
800-345-2737
FAX 407-380-5588
E-Mail: lia@lia.org
Home Page: www.lia.org
Social Media: *Facebook, Twitter, LinkedIn*

Klaus Loeffler, President
Stephen Capp, Treasurer
Robert Thomas, Secretary

The official journal of the Laser Institute of America and serves as the major international forum for exchanging ideas and information in disciplines that apply laser technology. Internationally known editors, reviewers, and columnists deliver the latest results of their research worldwide, dealing with the diverse, practical applications of photonic technology.
Cost: $410.00

6812 Journal of Lightwave Technology
IEEE Instrumentation and Measurement Society

67 Alexander Drive
PO Box 12277
Research Triangle Park, NC 27709

919-549-8411
FAX 919-549-8288
E-Mail: info@isa.org
Home Page: www.isa.org
Social Media: *Facebook, Twitter, LinkedIn*

Ken Baker, President
Patrick Gouhin, Executive Director
Jerry Clemons, Department VP
Leo Staples, Treasurer

The Journal is concerned with research, applications and methods used in all aspects of lightwave technology and fiber optics.
Frequency: Monthly

6813 Journal of Microwave Power and Electromagnetic Energy
International Microwave Power Institute
PO Box 1140
Mechanicsville, VA 23111-5007

804-559-6667
FAX 804-559-4087
E-Mail: info@impi.org
Home Page: www.impi.org

Bob Schiffmann, President
Ben Wilson, Vice President
Dorin Bolder, Secretary
Amy Lawson, Treasurer

The quarterly, technical journal of the Institute published by the Industrial, Scientific, Medical and Instrumentation (ISMI) section. Designed for the information needs of professionals specializing in the research and design of industrial and bio-medical applications, the Journal exemplifies the highest standards of scientific and technical information on the theory and application of electromagnetic power.
Cost: $250.00
Frequency: Quarterly

6814 Journal of the Electrochemical Society
Electrochemical Society
65 S Main St
Building D
Pennington, NJ 08534-2827

609-737-1902
FAX 609-737-2743
E-Mail: ecs@electrochem.org
Home Page: www.electrochem.org

Roque J Calvo, President

This peer reviewed journal publishes 60 articles each month. Articles are posted online, with a monthly paper edition following electronic publication. The ECS membership benefits package includes access to the electronic edition of this journal. Free with membership.
Cost: $110.00
Frequency: Monthly
Circulation: 8300
ISSN: 0013-4651
Founded in 1902

6815 LIA Today
Laser Institute of America
13501 Ingenuity Dr
Suite 128
Orlando, FL 32826-3009

407-380-1553
800-345-2737
FAX 407-380-5588
E-Mail: lia@lia.org
Home Page: www.lia.org
Social Media: *Facebook, Twitter, LinkedIn*

Klaus Loeffler, President
Stephen Capp, Treasurer
Robert Thomas, Secretary

Includes articles on the latest industry news to keep members and other laser professionals current on important issues that impact the laser community. Readers of LIA TODAY consist of production managers, supervisors, safety professionals, researchers, end-users, laser physicians and nurses.
Frequency: Bi-Monthly
Circulation: 5000

6816 Laser Tech Briefs
Associated Business Publications International
317 Madison Avenue
New York, NY 10017

212-490-3999
FAX 212-986-7864
Home Page: www.abpi.net

Domenic Mucchetti, CEO
Josheph Pramberger, President
Luke Schnirring, Executive VP

For purchasers of laser/optical products.
Circulation: 40,000

6817 Lighting Dimensions
Primedia Business
249 W 17th St
New York, NY 10011-5382

212-206-1894
800-827-3322
FAX 212-514-3719
Home Page: www.lightingdimensions.com
Social Media: *Facebook, Twitter*

Doug MacDonald, Group Publisher
David Johnson, Associate Publisher
Marian Sandberg-Dierson, Editor
Ellen Lampert-Greaux, Consulting Editor
Jennifer Hirst, Art Director

Trade publication for lighting professionals in film, theatre, television, concerts, clubs, themed environments, architectural, commercial, and industrial lighting. Sponsors of the LDI Trade Show and the Broadway Lighting Master Classes.
Cost: $34.97
Frequency: Monthly
Circulation: 14,177
Founded in 1989

6818 Market Trends
Electronic Industries Association
2500 Wilson Boulevard
Arlington, VA 22201-3834

703-907-7500
FAX 703-907-7767

Statistical information and marketing trends in the electronics industry.
Cost: $195.00
Frequency: Monthly

6819 Motion Control
ISA Services
P.O. Box 787
Williamsport, PA 17703

570-567-1982
800-791-8699
FAX 570-320-2079
E-Mail:
briefingsweborders@publishersserviceasso
Home Page: www.douglaspublications.com

Janine Nunes, Editor
Edward Mueller, Publisher

Information for those who design and maintain motion control systems.
56 Pages
Frequency: Monthly
Circulation: 16,490
ISSN: 1058-4644
Founded in 1985
Printed in 4 colors on glossy stock

6820 NETA World
International Electrical Testing Association
Po Box 687
Morrison, CO 80465-0687

303-697-8441
888-300-6382
FAX 303-697-8431
E-Mail: neta@netaworld.org
Home Page: www.netaworld.org
Social Media: *Facebook, YouTube*

Mose Ramieh, President
David Huffman, First VP
Ron Widup, Second VP
John White, Treasurer
Walter Cleary, Secretary

Features articles of interest to electrical testing and maintenance companies, consultants, engineers, architects, and plant personnel directly involved in electrical testing and maintenance. Free with membership.
Frequency: Quarterly

6821 Power Conversion & Intelligent Motion
Primedia
1166 Avenue of the Americas/10th Fl
New York, NY 10036

212-204-4200
E-Mail:
CorporateCustomerService@penton.com
Home Page: www.penton.com

David Kieselstien, CEO
Nicola Allais, CFO
Jasmine Alexander, CIO

Directed to engineers, designers and manufacturers of power electronic and electronic motion control components, subsystems and systems. Feature articles interpret trends and innovation in these subjects.
Circulation: 31,113

6822 Power Engineering International
PennWell Publishing Company
1421 S Sheridan Rd
Tulsa, OK 74112-6619

918-831-9421
800-331-4463
FAX 918-831-9476
E-Mail: headquarters@pennwell.com
Home Page: www.pennwell.com

Robert Biolchini, President

Serves the global electric power generation and transmission industry.
Frequency: Monthly
Circulation: 34000
ISSN: 1069-4994
Founded in 1896

6823 Powerline Magazine
Electrical Generating Systems Association
1650 S Dixie Hwy
Suite 500
Boca Raton, FL 33432-7461

561-750-5575
FAX 561-395-8557
Home Page: www.egsa.org
Social Media: *Facebook*

Debra Laurentis, President
Edward Murphy, VP
Bob Hafich, Secretary/Treasurer

Focuses on the entire on-site power generation industry.
Cost: $5.00
Frequency: Bi-Monthly

6824 ProService Magazine
National Electronics Service Dealers Association

3608 Pershing Ave
Fort Worth, TX 76107-4527

817-921-9061
800-797-9197
FAX 817-921-3741
E-Mail: webmaster@nesda.com
Home Page: www.nesda.com
Social Media: *Facebook*

Ben Fowler, President
Jerrell Helms, Vice President
Wayne Markman, Secretary
George Weiss, Treasurer

Published for members of NESDA/ISCET.
24 Pages
Frequency: Bi-Monthly

6825 Process Heating
Business News Publishing Company
155 Pfingsten Road
Suite 205
Deerfield, IL 60015

847-405-4000
FAX 248-502-1001
E-Mail: PHeditors@bnpmedia.com
Home Page: www.process-heating.com
Social Media: *Facebook, Twitter*

Anne Armel, Publisher
Linda Becker, Associate Publisher & Editor
Beth McClelland, Production Manager

Magazine covers heat processing at temperatures up to 1000 degrees F at end user and OEM plants in 9 industries. Follow us at twitter.com/ProcessHeating,
www.facebook.com/ProcessHeating
Circulation: 25000
Founded in 1994

6826 RE Magazine
National Rural Electric Cooperative Association
4301 Wilson Blvd
Suite 1
Arlington, VA 22203-1860

703-907-5500
FAX 703-907-5526
Home Page: www.nreca.org
Social Media: *Twitter*

Glenn English, CEO

Editorial content covers utility operations, deployment of the latest industry products and services; a showcase of new products, services, and catalogs; online resources; safety; member(customer) services; business and management trends; marketing tools; community and economic development; local leaders and rural issues; co-op personnel news; and politics and regulatory policies impacting electric co-ops.
Cost: $43.00
Frequency: Monthly
Founded in 1942

6827 Rural Electrification
National Rural Electric Cooperative Association
4301 Wilson Blvd
Arlington, VA 22203-1860

703-907-5500
FAX 703-907-5526
Home Page: www.nreca.org
Social Media: *Twitter*

Glenn English, CEO

Serves people involved in the rural electric cooperative industry including generation and transmission cooperatives, distribution systems and public utility district members of NRECA; electric equipment manufacturers; US Congress, state and federal regulatory agencies and commissions; and others allied to the field.
Cost: $85.00
Frequency: Monthly
Founded in 1942

6828 Service Contractor Magazine
Contract Services Association of America
1000 Wilson Boulevard
Suite 1800
Arlington, VA 22209

703-243-2020
FAX 703-243-3601
E-Mail: info@csa-dc.org
Home Page: www.csa-dc.org

Barry Cullen, President
Colleen Preston, Senior VP

Focuses on industry developments, regulatory and legislative issues, and any issues encountered in the process of competing for and securing contracts, such as changes in the acquisitions or procurement process. It tailors its content exclusively to government contractors.
Frequency: Bi-Annual

6829 Standard for Certification of Electrical Testing Technicians
International Electrical Testing Association
Po Box 687
Morrison, CO 80465-0687

303-697-8441
888-300-6382
FAX 303-697-8431
E-Mail: neta@netaworld.org
Home Page: www.netaworld.org
Social Media: *Facebook, YouTube*

Mose Ramieh, President
David Huffman, First VP
Ron Widup, Second VP
John White, Treasurer
Walter Cleary, Secretary

Specifying requisite levels of training, experience, and education for the evaluator of electrical power equipment is an important test procedure itself. The requirements parallel those of the National Skill Standards Board in Washington, DC, which promulgates for various occupations.
Cost: $55.00
36 Pages

6830 Standard for Electrical Maintenance Testing of Dry-Type Transformers
International Electrical Testing Assocaition
Po Box 687
Morrison, CO 80465-0687

303-697-8441
888-300-6382
FAX 303-697-8431
E-Mail: neta@netaworld.org
Home Page: www.netaworld.org
Social Media: *Facebook, YouTube*

Mose Ramieh, President
David Huffman, First VP
Ron Widup, Second VP
John White, Treasurer
Walter Cleary, Secretary

This Standard has been an individual section within the NETA document entitled Maintenance Testing Specifications for Electrical Power Distribution Equipment and Systems since 1975. The Maintenance Testing Specifications along with NETA's Acceptance Testing Specifications have long been in general use by organizations and individuals involved with testing of electrical apparatus.
Cost: $55.00
18 Pages

6831 Standard for Electrical Maintenance Testin g of Liquid-Filled Transformers
International Electrical Testing Association

PO Box 687
Morrison, CO 80465-0687

303-697-8441
888-300-6382
FAX 303-697-8431
E-Mail: neta@netaworld.org
Home Page: www.netaworld.org
Social Media: *Facebook, YouTube*

Mose Ramieh, President
David Huffman, First VP
Ron Widup, Second VP
John White, Treasurer
Walter Cleary, Secretary

The Standard has been an individual section within the NETA document entitled Maintenance Testing Specifications for Electrical Power Distribution Equipment and Systems since 1975. The Maintenance Testing Specifications along with NETA's Acceptance Testing Specifications have long been in general use by organizations and individuals involved with testing of electrical apparatus.
Cost: $55.00
21 Pages

Trade Shows

6832 AHTD Trade Show
Association for High Technology Distributors
N19 W24400 Riverwood Drive
Waukesha, WI 53188

262-696-3645
800-488-4845
E-Mail: ahtd@ahtd.org
Home Page: www.ahtd.org
Social Media: *Twitter, LinkedIn*

Neil Montogomery, President
John Pirner, Vice President
Thomas Swenton, Secretary
Brian Lepsis, Treasurer

Works to increase productivity and profitability of high technology automation solutions, providers and manufacturers.
250 Members
Frequency: Annual/September
Founded in 1985

6833 American Control Conference
American Automatic Control Council
2145 Sheridan Road
Evanston, IL 60208-3118

847-491-8175
FAX 847-491-4455
E-Mail: aacc@ece.northwestern.edu
Home Page: www.a2c2.org

R. Russell Reinehart, President
Tariq Samad, President-elect
Jordan Berg, Treasurer
B.Wayne Bequette, Secretary

Covers a broad range of topics relevant to the theory and practice of control and automation, including robotics, manufacturing, guidance and control, power systems, process control, identification and estimation, signal processing, modeling and advanced simulation.
800 Attendees
Frequency: Annual/June

6834 Annual Connector & Interconnection Technology Symposium and Trade Show
International Institute of Connector and Intercon
PO Box 20002
Sarasota, FL 34276

941-929-1806
800-854-4248

FAX 941-929-1807
E-Mail: info@iicit.org
Home Page: www.iicit.org

Dale Reed, Content Editor

Offers the opportunity to meet with other connector/interconnection industry users and vendors to learn about the latest advances in interconnection technology in the areas of radio frequency interconnection, quality, high speed connectors, personal computer interconnections, automotive Interconnections, materials, finishes, and platings, test methods, automation, surface mount technology, fiber optics, spaceflight connector technology, and medical applications.

6835 Annual Legislative & Regulatory Roundtable
Electronic Industries Association
2214 rock Hill Rd
Suite 170
Herndon, VA 20170

571-323-0294
FAX 571-323-0245
Home Page: www.eia.org
Social Media: *LinkedIn, YouTube*

Gail Tannenbaum, CMP, Manager Meetings

Panel topics in the past have included Broadband, Tax, Trade, Environment, Defense, Space, and the Congressional Leadership Agenda.
Frequency: Annual/August

6836 Applied Power Electronics Conference & Exposition (APEC)
Power Sources Manufacturers Association
PO Box 418
Mendham, NJ 07945-0418

973-543-9660
FAX 973-543-6207
E-Mail: power@psma.com
Home Page: www.psma.com
Social Media: *LinkedIn*

Dusty Becker, Chairman
Carol Blake, President
Jim Marinos, VP
Michel Grenon, Secretary/Treasurer

APEC continues the long-standing tradition of addressing issues of immediate and long-term interest to the practicing power electronics engineer.
1000 Attendees

6837 Bioelectromagnetics - Stun Gun Mini Symposium
Bioelectromagnetics Society
2412 Cobblestone Way
Frederick, MD 21702-3519

301-663-4252
FAX 301-694-4948
E-Mail: office@bems.org
Home Page: www.bems.org

David Black, President
Gloria Parsley, Executive Director

The focus of this symposium will be the technology, physiology and potential adverse side effects of the use of electronic weapons or stun guns, which are rapidly being deployed in military and police use.
Frequency: Annual/June

6838 Bioelectromagnetics - U.S. Air Force Workshop
Bioelectromagnetics Society
2412 Cobblestone Way
Frederick, MD 21702-3519

301-663-4252
FAX 301-694-4948

E-Mail: office@bems.org
Home Page: www.bems.org

David Black, President
Gloria Parsley, Executive Director

Will focus on the use of molecular biology to identify changes in genes and proteins that may lead to physiological, pathological, or behavioral events.
Frequency: Annual/June

6839 Bioelectromagnetics Society Meeting
Bioelectromagnetics Society
2412 Cobblestone Way
Frederick, MD 21702-3519

301-663-4252
FAX 301-694-4948
E-Mail: office@bems.org
Home Page: www.bems.org

David Black, President
Gloria Parsley, Executive Director
Richard Nuccitelli, VP

This is a joint meeting of The Bioelectromagnetics Society and The European BioElectromagnetics Association. Topics will be: Electric Fields, Human Studies, Exposure Assessment, Dosimetry, In Vitro ELF, Epidemiology, Unique EMF Signals, Medical applications, Mechanisms, Electromagnetic Therapy.
400 Attendees
Frequency: Annual/June

6840 CSA Winter Meeting
Contract Services Association of America
1000 Wilson Boulevard
Suite 1800
Arlington, VA 22209

703-243-2020
FAX 703-243-3601
E-Mail: info@csa-dc.org
Home Page: www.csa-dc.org

Barry Cullen, President
Colleen Preston, Senior VP

This one day workshop is a free flowing exchange of information with real time interaction and information exchange.
Frequency: Annual/January

6841 Coherence and Electromagnetic Fields in Biological Systems
Bioelectromagnetics Society
2412 Cobblestone Way
Frederick, MD 21702-3519

301-663-4252
FAX 301-694-4948
E-Mail: office@bems.org
Home Page: www.bems.org

David Black, President
Gloria Parsley, Executive Director
Richard Nuccitelli, VP

Highlights of the symposium organized by the Institute of Radio Engineering and Electronics, the Academy of Sciences of the Czech Republic and others are expected to include biophysical principles of coherence, role of endogenous EMF in the organization of biological systems, biophysical mechanisms of interaction of biological systems with EMF and more.
Frequency: Annual/July

6842 Consulting Electrical Engineers(CEE) Technical Forum & Table-Top
Electric Association
One Energy Center,40 Shuman Boulevard
Suite 247
Naperville, IL 60563

630-305-3050
FAX 630-305-3056
E-Mail: admin@eachicago.org

Home Page: www.eachicago.org
Social Media: *Facebook, LinkedIn*

Mark Gibson, President
Rick Jamerson, VP
Steven Anixter, Treasurer
Thomas Scherzer, Secretary

This event will feature a free technical forum for engineers, specifiers, and designers on Short Circuit analysis, Coordination, and Arc Flash Hazard analysis using conventional and computerized methods. The Table Top tradeshow will feature 45 vendors and their latest technology.
Frequency: Annual/May

6843 EASA Annual Convention
Electrical Apparatus Services Association
1331 Baur Boulevard
Saint Louis, MO 63131-1903

314-993-2220
FAX 314-993-1269
E-Mail: easainfo@easa.com
Home Page: www.easa.com

Linda Raynes, President/CEO
Anne Vogel, Executive Secretary

Provides members with a means of keeping up to date on materials, equipment, and state-of-the-art technology. 100+ exhibitor booths.
2500 Attendees
Frequency: Annual/June
Mailing list available for rent

6844 EDS: Where the Electronics Industry Connects
Electronics Distributions Show Corporation
2214 Rock Hill Road
Suite 170
Herndon, VA 20170

312-648-1140
FAX 312-648-4282
E-Mail: eds@edsconnects.com
Home Page: www.edsconnects.com
Social Media: *LinkedIn*

Gretchen Oie-Weghorst, Director
Gerald M Newman, Executive VP

Attendees are manufacturers of electronic components who sell their products through electronics distributors. Provides networking and meeting opportunities, and opens doors to new business. Hundreds of exhibits, thousands of attendees.
6M Attendees
Frequency: Annual/May
Founded in 1937

6845 EEI Annual Convention/Expo
Edison Electric Institute
701 Pennsylvania Avenue NW
Washington, DC 20004-2696

202-508-5000
FAX 202-508-5360
E-Mail: feedback@eei.org
Home Page: www.eei.org
Social Media: *Facebook, Twitter, YouTube*

Thomas Kuhn, President
David Owens, Executive VP Business Operations
Brian Wolff, Senior VP, External Affairs
1000 Attendees
Frequency: Annual/June

6846 EEI Financial Conference
Edison Electric Institute
701 Pennsylvania Avenue NW
Washington, DC 20004-2696

202-508-5000
FAX 202-508-5335
E-Mail: feedback@eei.org

Home Page: www.eei.org
Social Media: *Facebook, Twitter, YouTube*

Thomas Kuhn, President
David Owens, Executive VP Business Operations
Brian Wolff, Senior VP, External Affairs

Provides a unique forum for exchange of ideas and experience; and to give you insight into emerging critical issues.
Frequency: Annual/November

6847 EERA Annual Meeting
Electrical Equipment Representation
638 W 39th Street
Kansas City, MO 64111

816-561-5323
800-728-2272
FAX 816-561-1249
E-Mail: info2005@eera.org
Home Page: www.eera.org

Vince Brown III, President
Brad Cahoon, President Elect
Don Shirk, VP
Kier Cooper, Secretary
Rob Rigsby, Treasurer
Frequency: Annual/April

6848 EGSA Annual Spring Convention
Electrical Generating Systems Association
1650 S Dixie Highway
Suite 500
Boca Raton, FL 33432

561-750-5575
FAX 561-398-8557
Home Page: www.egsa.org
Social Media: *Facebook*

Cara Clark, Director Conventions/Meetings
Bob Breese, Director of Education

Offers educational sessions covering a broad range of issues effecting the on-site power industry.
Frequency: Annual/March

6849 EIA's Congressional Technology Forum
Electronic Industries Association
2214 rock Hill Rd
Suite 170
Herndon, VA 20170

571-323-0294
FAX 571-323-0245
Home Page: www.eia.org
Social Media: *LinkedIn, YouTube*

Gail Tannenbaum, CMP, Manager Meetings

Discusses the issues most relevant for the electronics and high-tech industries.
Frequency: Annual/October

6850 Electri...FYI
Electrical Association of Rochester
PO Box 20219
Rochester, NY 14602-0219

585-538-6350
FAX 585-538-6166
E-Mail: info@earoch.com
Home Page: www.eawny.com

Ed Langschwager, President
Joe Lengen, First VP
Rich Monroe, Secretary/Treasurer
Kirstie Steves, Executive Director

Upstate Electrical Show. 120+ exhibitors. Free entry.
2000 Attendees
Frequency: Tri-Annual

6851 Electric West Conference
PRIMEDIA Business Exhibitions

11 River Bend Drive S
PO Box 4232
Stamford, CT 06907-0232

203-358-9900
FAX 203-358-5816
Home Page: www.primediaevents.com

David Small, Show Director
Tara Keating-Magee, Show Coordinator

Educational sessions attract electrical professionals from contracting companies, industrial plants, consulting engineering firms, datacom installers and electricians. Presentations focus on such topics as power quality, lighting, the NEC, project management, claims management and fiber optics. Also provides in-depth coverage of National Electrical Code changes that directly impact the work of electrical professionals. 250 Exhibitors.
6000 Attendees
Frequency: Annual/March

6852 Energy - Exhibit Promotions Plus
US Department of Energy/US Dept. of Defense/GSA
11620 Vixens Path
Ellicott City, MD 21042

301-596-3028
FAX 410-997-0764
Home Page: www.energy2003.ee.doe.gov

Harve Horowitz, President
Kevin Horowitz, Senior Association Manager

Energy is an exclusive Federal Grant sponsored annual educational forum and exhibition.
1000+ Attendees
Frequency: Annual/August

6853 Fall Technical and Marketing Conference
Electrical Generating Systems Association
1650 S Dixie Highway
Suite 500
Boca Raton, FL 33432

561-750-5575
FAX 561-395-8557
Home Page: www.egsa.org
Social Media: *Facebook*

Cara Clark, Director Conventions/Meetings
Bob Breese, Director of Education

Will focus on technical presentations and marketing efforts.
Frequency: Annual/September

6854 IETA Annual Technical Conference
International Electrical Testing Association
106 Stone Street
Morrison, CO 80465

303-697-8441
888-300-6382
FAX 303-697-8431
E-Mail: neta@netaworld.org
Home Page: www.netaworld.org
Social Media: *Facebook, YouTube*

Mose Ramieh, President
David Huffman, First VP
Ron Widup, Second VP
John White, Treasurer
Walter Cleary, Secretary

Targets the electrical testing industry.
Frequency: Annual/March

6855 IFAC World Congress
American Automatic Control Council
3640 Col Glenn Hwy
Dayton, OH 45435

937-775-5062
FAX 937-775-3936
E-Mail: pmisra@cs.wright.edu
Home Page: www.a2c2.org

R. Russell Reinehart, President
Tariq Samad, President-elect

Jordan Berg, Treasurer
B.Wayne Bequette, Secretary

You will have the opportunity to take part in the wide spectrum of categories for technical presentations, including plenary lectures, survey papers, regular papers of both lecture and poster session types, panel discussions and case studies.
Frequency: Annual/July

6856 ILEA Annual Conference
International League of Electrical Association
12165 West Center Road
Suite 59
Omaha, NE 68144

402-330-7227
FAX 402-330-7283
E-Mail: info@ileaweb.org
Home Page: www.ileaweb.org
Social Media: *LinkedIn*

Monique DeBoer, President
Chris Price, VP
Kirstie Steves, Secretary
Barbette Cejalvo, Treasurer

Provides a venue through which information and ideas exchanged and by encouraging all members to attend and share ideas.
Frequency: Annual/July

6857 IMA Spring Meeting
International Magnetics Association
8 S Michigan Avenue
Suite 1000
Chicago, IL 60603-3310

312-456-5590
FAX 312-580-0165
Home Page: www.intl-magnetics.org

August Sisco, Chair
Lowell Bosleyeo, President
George Orenchak, Secretary/Treasurer

Promote the worldwide growth, development, and use of magnetic materials through: collection and dissemination of global trade statistics, publication of industry standards and user and industry education.
Frequency: Annual/May

6858 IMAPS International Symposium on Microelectronics
International Microelectronics & Packaging Society
611 2nd Street NE
Washington, DC 20002

202-548-4001
888-464-6277
FAX 202-548-6115
E-Mail: imaps@imaps.org
Home Page: http://www.imaps.org

Michael O'Donoghue, Executive Director
Ann Bell, Manager Marketing/Communications

Symposium for the microelectronics and electronics packaging industries. Features a powerful technical program, progressive professional development courses and many forums to share the latest developments in microelectronics. Comprehensive exhibition of materials and equipment for the industry.
3000 Attendees
Frequency: Annual/September

6859 IMPI Annual Symposium
International Microwave Power Institute
PO Box 1140
Mechanicsville, VA 23111

804-596-6667
FAX 804-559-4087
E-Mail: info@impi.org
Home Page: www.impi.org

Bob Schiffman, President
Ben Wilson, Vice President

Dorin Bolder, Secretary
Amy Lawson, Treasurer

Brings together researchers from across the globe to share the latest findings related to non-communications uses of microwave energy.
Frequency: Annual/June

6860 IPC Printed Circuits Expo
IPC: Association Connecting Electronics
3000 Lakeside Drive
Suite 309 S
Bannockburn, IL 60015

847-615-7100
FAX 847-615-7105
Home Page: www.ipc.org
Social Media: *Facebook, Twitter, LinkedIn, YouTube*

Robert Ferguson, Chairman
Stephen Pudles, Vice Chairman
Don Schroeder, Secretary/Treasurer

Meet with everyone who designs, manufactures, and assembles printed circuit boards and electronics assemblies.
Frequency: Annual/February

6861 ISA Expo
ISA
67 Alexander Drive
Box 12277
Research Triangle Park, NC 27709

919-549-8411
FAX 919-549-8288
E-Mail: info@isa.org
Home Page: www.isa.org
Social Media: *Facebook, Twitter, LinkedIn*

Tracey Berrett-Noble, Event Manager
Rodney Jones, Conference Coordinator
Cyrus Taft, Program Chair
Dale Lee, Director Convention Services
Tracey Berrett, Manager Convention Services

Features the latest and most extensive products and services exhibition, a strategically relevant technical conference, and a prominent continuing education and training program. With practitioners from over 70 countries. Offers the most complete automation and control experience in today's marketplace.
15000 Attendees
Frequency: Annual/October

6862 ISA Fugitive Emissions LDAR Symposium and Training
Instrumentation, Systems, and Automation Society
67 Alexander Drive
Box 12277
Research Triangle Park, NC 27709

919-549-8411
FAX 919-549-8288
E-Mail: info@isa.org
Home Page: www.isa.org
Social Media: *Facebook, Twitter, LinkedIn*

Dale Lee, Director Convention Services
Tracey Berrett, Manager Convention Services

Covers topics including, but not limited to leak detection repair methods and fugitive emissions management systems. Industry experts in leak detection and repair will discuss implementations and improvements in LDAR programs in plant facilities.
Frequency: Annual/May

6863 Innovation in Power Generation Measurement & Control Conference
Instrumentation, Systems, and Automation Society

67 Alexander Drive
Box 12277
Research Triangle Park, NC 27709

919-549-8411
FAX 919-549-8288
E-Mail: info@isa.org
Home Page: www.isa.org
Social Media: *Facebook, Twitter, LinkedIn*

Denny Younie, Conference General Chair
Rodney Jones, Conference Coordinator
Cyrus Taft, Program Chair
Dale Lee, Director Convention Services
Tracey Berrett, Manager Convention Services

Dedicated to instrumentation and control in the fossil and nuclear power generation industry. This year's conference includes approximately 50 technical papers presented in 8 sessions over two and a half days, a vendor exhibition area, 5 training courses, several ISA committee meetings, and the EPRI I&C Interest Group meeting and a Sunday evening welcome reception.
Frequency: Annual/June

6864 International Conference and Exhibition on Device Packaging

International Microelectronics & Packaging Society
611 2nd Street NE
Washington, DC 20002

202-548-4001
888-464-6277
FAX 202-548-6115
E-Mail: imaps@imaps.org
Home Page: www.imaps.org

Jim Drehle, President
Michael O'Donoghue, Executive Director
Steve Capp, Treasurer
Lawrence J Rexing, Secretary

Will provide a comprehensive technical program addressing the challenges of applications, and the latest developments in packaging for emerging devices, circuits, MEMS, sensors as well as materials and processes.
Frequency: Annual/March

6865 International Congress Applications of Lasers and Electro-Optics

Laser Institute of America
13501 Ingenuity Drive
Suite 128
Orlando, FL 32826-3204

407-380-1553
800-345-2737
FAX 407-380-5588
E-Mail: icaleo@laserinstitute.org
Home Page: www.laserinstitute.org
Social Media: *Facebook, Twitter, LinkedIn*

Klaus Loeffler, President
Yongfeng Lu, President Elect
Stephen Capp, Treasurer
Robert Thomas, Secretary

Provides an international forum for the exchange of technical information between the people in the industrial, government and academic communities who apply laser/electro-optic technologies and the scientists, engineers and technicians engaged in developing these technologies. Accepts advertising.
5M Attendees
Frequency: Annual/October

6866 International Instrumentation Symposium

Instrumentation, Systems, and Automation Society
67 Alexander Drive
Box 12277
Research Triangle Park, NC 27709

919-549-8411
FAX 919-549-8288

E-Mail: info@isa.org
Home Page: www.isa.org
Social Media: *Facebook, Twitter, LinkedIn*

Denny Younie, Conference General Chair
Rodney Jones, Conference Coordinator
Cyrus Taft, Program Chair
Dale Lee, Director Convention Services
Tracey Berrett, Manager Convention Services

Provides an outstanding opportunity to gain valuable technical information and training in the traditional areas of measurements/sensors, instrumentation systems, data and advanced system/sensor technology as well as innovative papers in many other state of the art areas.
Frequency: Annual/May

6867 International Laser Safety Conference

Laser Institute of America
13501 Ingenuity Drive
Suite 128
Orlando, FL 32826

407-380-1553
800-345-2737
FAX 407-380-5588
E-Mail: lia@laserinstitute.org
Home Page: www.laserinstitute.org
Social Media: *Facebook, Twitter, LinkedIn*

Klaus Loeffler, President
Yongfeng Lu, President Elect
Stephen Capp, Treasurer
Robert Thomas, Secretary

A comprehensive four-day conference covering all aspects of laser safety practice and hazard control. Technical sessions and workshops will address developments in regulatory, mandatory and voluntary safety standards for laser products and laser use.
Frequency: Annual/March

6868 International Symposium on Bioenergetics and Bioelectrochemistry

Bioelectromagnetics Society
2412 Cobblestone Way
Frederick, MD 21702-3519

301-663-4252
FAX 301-694-4948
E-Mail: office@bems.org
Home Page: www.bems.org

David Black, President
Gloria Parsley, Executive Director
Richard Nuccitelli, VP
Phil Chadwick, Treasurer
Jonna Wilen, Secretary

Covers analytical chemistry.
Frequency: Annual/June

6869 Joint Conference on Decision and Control & European Control Conference

American Automatic Control Council
3640 Col Glenn Hwy
Dayton, OH 45435

937-775-5062
FAX 937-775-3936
E-Mail: pmisra@cs.wright.edu
Home Page: www.a2c2.org

R. Russell Reinehart, President
Tariq Samad, President-elect
Jordan Berg, Treasurer
B. Wayne Bequette, Secretary

Dedicated to the advancement of the theory and practice of systems and control. It brings together an international community of experts to discuss the state-of-the-art, new research results, perspectives of future developments, and innovative applications relevant to decision making, control, automation, and related areas.
Frequency: Annual/December

6870 Laser Institute of America

Laser Institute of America

13501 Ingenuity Drive
Suite 128
Orlando, FL 32826

407-380-1553
FAX 407-380-5588
E-Mail: lia@lia.org
Home Page: www.lia.org
Social Media: *Facebook, Twitter, LinkedIn*

Klaus Loeffler, President
Stephen Capp, Treasurer
Robert Thomas, Secretary

Devoted to the field of laser applications and laser safety in both medical and industrial fields.

6871 Magnetism Conference: Institute of Electrical/Electronics Engineers

Courtesy Associates
2000 L Street NW
Suite 710
Washington, DC 20036

202-331-2000
FAX 202-331-0111
E-Mail: magnetism@courtesyassoc.com
Home Page: www.magnetism.org

Paul Crowell, Chair
Yumi Ljiri, Treasurer
Brian Maranville, Publicity

Conference brings together scientists and engineers interested in recent developments in all branches of fundamental and applied magnetism. Emphasis is placed on experimental and theoretical research in magnetism, the properties and synthesis of new magnetic materials and advances in magnetic technology. Program consists of invited and contributed papers.
1.1M Attendees
Frequency: Annual/October

6872 Meeting of the Electrochemical Society

Appliance Manufacturer
65 South Main Street
Building D
Pennington, NJ 08534

609-737-1902
FAX 609-737-2743
E-Mail: ecs@electrochem.org
Home Page: www.electrochem.org

Christine Garzon, President
Tetsuya Osaka, Sr. VP
Harikila Deligianni, Secretary
Christina Bock, Treasurer

Has become the leading society for solid-state and electrochemical science and technology. ECS has 8000 scientists and engineers in over 75 countries worldwide who hold individual membership, as well as roughly 100 corporations and laboratories who hold corporate membership.
Frequency: Annual/May
Founded in 1902

6873 Mid-Atlantic Electrical Exposition

S&L Productions
1916 Crain Highway S
Suite 16
Glen Burnie, MD 21061-5572

410-863-1180
888-532-3669
FAX 410-863-1187
E-Mail: slprod@erois.com

Triennial show and 150 exhibits with 200 booths of electrical supplies, hardware and services.
3000 Attendees
Frequency: Annual/October
Founded in 2000

6874 NAED Annual Meeting
National Association of Electrical Distributors
1181 Corporate Lake Drive
St Louis, MO 63132

314-991-9000
888-791-2512
FAX 314-991-3060
E-Mail: info@naed.org
Home Page: www.naed.org
Social Media: *Facebook, Twitter*

Tom Naber, President and CEO
Michelle McNamara, Senior VP

The only event to bring the entire industry together in the same place at the same time. In addition to offering strong topical and informational programming, the NAED Annual Meeting provides distributors access to the top management of more than 225 electrical product suppliers.

6875 NECA
National Electrical Contractors Association
3 Bethesda Metro Center
Suite 1100
Bethesda, MD 20814

301-657-3110
FAX 301-215-4500
E-Mail: beth.margulies@necanet.org
Home Page: www.necanet.org
Social Media: *Facebook, Twitter, LinkedIn, YouTube*

Russell Alessi, President
John Grau, CEO
Dan Walter, VP and COO
Michael Thompson, Secretary/Treasurer

Brings the largest manufacturers, utilities, contractors, engineers, consultants, plant engineers, and distributors from all over North America and 31 foreign countries.
8000 Attendees
Frequency: Annual/September

6876 NEMA Annual Meeting
National Electrical Manufacturers Association
1300 North 17th Street
Suite 1752
Rosslyn, VA 22209

703-841-3200
FAX 703-841-5900
Home Page: www.nema.org
Social Media: *Facebook, Twitter, LinkedIn, You tube*

Evan Gaddis, President

Provides a forum for the standardization of electrical equipment, enabling consumers to select from a range of safe, effective and compatible electrical products.
Frequency: Annual/November
Founded in 1926

6877 NEMRA Annual Conference
Nat'l Electrical Mfgs Representatives Association
28 Deer Street
Suite 302
Portsmouth, NH 03801

914-524-8650
800-446-3672
FAX 603-319-1667
E-Mail: nemra@nemra.org
Home Page: www.nemra.org
Social Media: *Twitter, LinkedIn*

Mark Gibson, Chairman
Greg reynolds, Chairman Elect
Greg Baker, Secretary/Treasurer

Provides a forum for the standardization of electrical equipment, enabling consumers to se-

lect from a range of safe, effective, and compatible electrical products.
Frequency: Annual/March

6878 NORTHCON
Electronic Conventions
8110 Airport Boulevard
Los Angeles, CA 90045-3119

800-877-2668
FAX 310-641-5117

Donna Ybarra, Show Manager
400 booths featuring exhibits of components and microelectronics instrumentation.
6057 Attendees
Frequency: Annual/October

6879 NOx Emissions & Source Monitoring Technical Conference and Training
Instrumentation, Systems, and Automation Society
67 Alexander Drive
Box 12277
Research Triangle Park, NC 27709

919-549-8411
FAX 919-549-8288
E-Mail: info@isa.org
Home Page: www.isa.org
Social Media: *Facebook, Twitter, LinkedIn*

Denny Younie, Conference General Chair
Rodney Jones, Conference Coordinator
Cyrus Taft, Program Chair
Dale Lee, Director Convention Services
Tracey Berrett, Manager Convention Services

Will present experiences with the measurement and control of low level NOx emissions, new concepts for NOx reduction techniques, and innovative monitoring systems. Presenters will participate in Q&A sessions, panel discussions, and be accessible throughout the two days to answer your questions.
Frequency: Annual/August

6880 NRECA's Annual Meeting
National Rural Electric Cooperative Association
4301 Wilson Boulevard
Suite 1
Arlington, VA 22203-1860

703-907-5500
FAX 703-907-5514
Home Page: www.nrcea.coop

Glenn L English, CEO

The national service organization dedicated to representing the national interests of cooperative electric utilities and the consumers they serve. An advocate for consumer-owned cooperatives on energy and operational issues as well as rural community and economic development.
Frequency: Annual/February
Founded in 1942

6881 NSCA Systems Integration Expo
National Systems Contractors Assocaition
3950 River Ridge Drive NE
Cedar Rapids, IA 52402

319-366-6722
800-446-6722
FAX 319-366-4164
E-Mail: nsca@nsca.org
Home Page: www.nsca.org
Social Media: *Facebook, Twitter, LinkedIn, YouTube*

Injolf de Jonh, President
Kelley McCarthy, Vice President
Michael Hester, Treasurer
Ron Bailey, Secretary

Dedicated to building connections between the people, knowledge and new ideas of the commercial electronic systems industry. A leading not-for-profit association representing the com-

mercial electronic systems industry. A powerful advocate of all who work within the low-voltage industry, including systems contractors/integrators, product manufacturers, consultants, sales representatives, a growing number of architects, engineers and others. 600 exhibitors
11000 Attendees
Frequency: Annual/March

6882 National Electrical Equipment Show
Reed Exhibition Companies
255 Washington Street
Suite 275
Newton, MA 02458-1649

617-584-4900
FAX 617-630-2222

Mike Rusbridge, Chairman/CEO

Serves the electrical and electronic industries.
7.5M Attendees
Frequency: Annual/March

6883 National Electrical Wire Processing Technology Expo
Expo Productions
510 Hartbrook Drive
Hartland, WI 53029

262-367-5500
800-367-5520
FAX 262-367-9956
E-Mail: cheryl@epishows.com
Home Page: www.electricalwireshow.com
Social Media: *Facebook*

Cheryl L Luck, Sales Manager
Jay Partington, Show Manager

Only trade show tailored expressly to the electrical wire cable processing industry.
2000 Attendees
Frequency: Annual/May

6884 National Lighting Fair
Dallas Market Center
2100 N Stemmons Freeway
Suite 1000
Dallas, TX 75207-3009

214-556-6100
FAX 214-655-6100

Charlie Sullivan, Executive Director
Cindy Morris, Chief Operating Officer

250 booths.
5M Attendees
Frequency: Annual/February

6885 National Professional Service Convention
National Electronics Service Dealers Association
3608 Pershing Avenue
Fort Worth, TX 76107

817-921-9061
FAX 817-921-3741
E-Mail: npsc@nesda.com
Home Page: www.nesda.com
Social Media: *Facebook*

PAtricia Bohon, Trade Show Manager

Annual show of 55 manufactures, suppliers and distributor of electronics, receivers, recorders, and supplies, software, telecommunications equipment, computers, videocassette recorders, parts and accessories, business forms, warranty companies and magazines/associations. Containing 100 booths and 70 exhibits.
950 Attendees
Frequency: Annual/July
Founded in 1964

6886 Pacific International Conference on Applications of Lasers and Optics
Laser Institute of America

13501 Ingenuity Drive
Suite 128
Orlando, FL 32826

407-380-1553
FAX 407-380-5588
E-Mail: lia@laserinstitute.org
Home Page: www.laserinstitute.org
Social Media: *Facebook, Twitter, LinkedIn*

Milan Brandt, Conference General Chair

Will focus on growth and application of lasers
and optics in the Pacific region.
Frequency: Annual/April

6887 Power-Gen International Trade Show
Electrical Generating Systems Association
1650 S Dixie Highway
Suite 500
Boca Raton, FL 33432

561-750-5575
FAX 561-395-8557
Home Page: www.egsa.org

Cara Clark, Director Conventions/Meetings
Bob Breese, Director of Education

This is a special section of a larger show where
we concentrate booths of firms that make, sell,
and distribute on-site power products.
Frequency: Annual/December

**6888 Product Safety and Liability
Conference**
National Electrical Manufacturers
Association
1300 North 17th Street
Suite 1752
Rosslyn, VA 22209

703-841-3200
FAX 703-841-5900
Home Page: www.nema.org
Social Media: *Facebook, Twitter, LinkedIn,
YouTube*

Evan Gaddis, President
Tom Hixon, Vice President

Provides a forum for the standardization of
electrical equipment, enabling consumers to select from a range of safe, effective and compatible electrical products.
Frequency: Annual/September

**6889 Reliability and Maintenance
Symposium**
Consulting Services
1768 Lark Lane
Cherry Hill, NJ 08003-3215

856-428-2342
FAX 856-616-9315
E-Mail: vrmonshaw@ieee.org
Home Page: www.rams.org

V R Monshaw, Administrator
Raymond Sears, Treasurer
Patrick Dallosta, Secretary, Treasurer

The symposium offers the opportunity to explore and learn more about this and other related R&M subjects. 50 booths.
1M Attendees
Frequency: Annual/January

6890 Rocky Mountain Electronics Expo
Conference and Management Specialists
138 Garfield St
Denver, CO 80206-5517

303-568-8028
FAX 303-799-0678

Karen Hone, Executive Director

Annual show and exhibits of products and services related to the hi-tech electronics industry.

6891 SESHA Annual Symposium
Semiconductor Environmental, Safety &
Health Assn

1313 Dolly Madison Boulevard
Suite 402
McLean, VA 22101

703-790-1745
FAX 703-790-2672
E-Mail: sesha@burkinc.com
Home Page: seshaonline.org

John D Cox, President
Brett Burk, Co-Founder
Glenn Tom, Co-Founder

For individuals employed within the electronics and related high technology industries with
an interest in environmental, health and safety
issues.
1235 Attendees
Frequency: Annual/May
Founded in 1978

6892 SMMA: Fall Technical Conference
SMMA: The Motor & Motion Association
PO Box P182
South Dartmouth, MA 02748

508-979-5935
FAX 508-979-5845
E-Mail: info@smma.org
Home Page: www.smma.org

Elizabeth B Chambers, Executive Director
William Chambers, Operations Director

Provide members and prospective members the
opportunity to interact with industry colleagues. Attendees learn about industry trends
and technologies, identify new supplier partners and network with other motor and drives
professionals.
120 Attendees
Frequency: Annual/November

**6893 SMMA: Spring Management
Conference**
SMMA: The Motor & Motion Association
PO Box P182
S Dartmouth, MA 02748

508-979-5935
FAX 508-979-5845
E-Mail: info@smma.org
Home Page: www.smma.org

Elizabeth B Chambers, Executive Director
William Chambers, Operations Director

Provide members and prospective members the
opportunity to interact with industry colleagues. Attendees learn about industry trends
and technologies, identify new supplier partners and network with other motor and drives
professionals.
80 Attendees
Frequency: Annual/May

6894 SMTA International
Surface Mount Technology Association
5200 Wilson Road
Suite 215
Minneapolis, MN 55424

952-920-7682
FAX 952-926-1819
E-Mail: joann@smta.org
Home Page: www.smta.org

Dan Baldwin, President
Marie Cole, VP Technical Programs
Kola Akinade, Secretary
Hal Hendrickson, Treasurer

A network of professionals who build skills,
share practical experience and develop solutions in electronics assembly technologies and
related business operations.
1200 Attendees
Frequency: Annual/October

6895 SOUTHCON
Electronic Conventions

12340 Rosecrans Avenue
Suite 100
Manhattan Beach, CA 90266

310-524-4100
800-877-2668
FAX 310-643-7328
Home Page: www.southcon.org

Donna Ybarra, Show Manager

Companies attending represent a major
cross-section of the electronics industry including consumer, computer, medical, automotive
and others. Offers conference sessions,
in-depth technical sessions, product demonstrations and exhibits by vendors.
10M Attendees
Frequency: Annual/March

6896 TechAdvantage Conference
National Rural Electric Cooperative
Association
4301 Wilson Boulevard
Suite 1
Arlington, VA 2203-1860

703-907-5500
FAX 703-907-5514

Glenn L English, CEO

The only utility industry trade show exclusively for electric cooperative network management; engineering and operations; information
services and technology; and purchasing
employees.

6897 Upper Midwest Electrical Expo
North Central Electrical League
2901 Metro Drive
Suite 203
Bloomington, MN 55425

952-854-4405
800-925-4985
FAX 952-854-7076
E-Mail: dale@ncel.org
Home Page: www.ncel.org

Jeff Keljik, Chair
Chuck Healy, Vice Chair
Dan Paulson, Treasurer
Dale Yohnke, Secretary

Unites our electrical industry by providing vital
industry commerce, educational discussion forums and offering various outlets for peer interaction. NCEL is the bridge between industry
sectors and our electrical industry joins together to develop, expand and to protect all
stakeholder interests in our Upper MIdwest
Electrical Industry.
10213 Attendees
Frequency: Every 2 Years

6898 eastec Exposition
Society of Manufacturing Engineers
Deerborn, MI 48128

313-425-3000
800-763-4763
Home Page: www.sme.org

500 booths of new technologies in equipment,
materials and products used in the manufacture
of semiconductors and flat panel displays.
8M Attendees
Frequency: Annual/October

Directories & Databases

**6899 Buyer's Guide and Member Services
Directory**
Diesel & Gas Turbine Publications

1650 S Dixie Highway
Suite 500
Boca Raton, FL 33432

561-750-5575
FAX 561-395-8557
Home Page: www.egsa.org

Donald M Ferreira, Director Publications
George Rowley, Director of Education

It is the ultimate gen-set industry buyer's guide, because the members are listed in one or more of 23 different product categories. Each member's listing also shows whether they sell, rent, and/or service equipment.
Cost: $6.00
Frequency: Annual

6900 Circuits Assembly: Buyers' Guide Issue

Miller Freeman Publications
600 Harrison Street
Suite 400
San Francisco, CA 94107-1391

FAX 415-905-2239

Ron Daniels, Editor-in-Chief

List of suppliers of products and services to the surface mount industry; representatives and distributors.
Cost: $7.00
Frequency: Annual, November
Circulation: 40,500

6901 Compressor Tech Two

Diesel & Gas Turbine Publications
20855 Watertown Rd
Suite 220
Waukesha, WI 53186-1873

262-754-4100
FAX 262-832-5075
Home Page: www.dieselspec.com

Michael Osenga, President
Phil Burnside, Editor-in-Chief
Brent Haight, Managing Editor
Kara Kane, Advertising Manager
Sheila Lizdas, Circulation Manager

Covers the operation, application and design of gas compression systems, as used in the gas gathering, transportation, storage, processing and related industries worldwide. Featured are new products, new technologies and interesting new applications related to gas compression systems and components.
Cost: $45.00
Frequency: 6 per year
Circulation: 13,000
Founded in 1996

6902 Diesel Progress: International Edition

Diesel & Gas Turbine Publications
20855 Watertown Rd
Suite 220
Waukesha, WI 53186-1873

262-754-4100
FAX 262-832-5075
Home Page: www.dieselspec.com

Michael Osenga, President
Michael J Brezonick, Editor-in-Chief
Katie Evans, Advertising Sales Manager

Covers the design of engine-powered equipment manufactured outside of North America. This includes various types of mobile on-and-off-highway equipment including construction, mining, forestry, agricultural and turf maintenance vehicles, trucks and buses; specialty vehicles; pleasure boats; and generator, pump and compressor set manufacturers. Editorial focus is on new products and technology for these markets.
Cost: $40.00
Frequency: 6 per year
Circulation: 12,000

ISSN: 1091-3696
Founded in 1981

6903 Diesel Progress: North American Edition

Diesel & Gas Turbine Publications
20855 Watertown Rd
Suite 220
Waukesha, WI 53186-1873

262-754-4100
FAX 262-832-5075
Home Page: www.dieselspec.com

Michael Osenga, President
Patricia May, Advertising Sales Manager

Published for those concerned with the design, distribution and service of equipment powered by diesel, gasoline, or alternatively fueled engines. This includes all types of mobile on-and-off-highway equipment and stationary equipment. Markets covered include: construction, mining, forestry, agricultural and turf maintenance equipment; trucks and buses; pleasure boats; and generator, pump and compressor sets. Editorial focus is on new products and technology for these markets.
Cost: $75.00
Frequency: Monthly
Circulation: 30,000
ISSN: 1091-370X
Founded in 1935

6904 Directory of Electrical Wholesale Distributors

Penton
249 W. 17th Street
New York, NY 10011

212-204-4200
Home Page: www.penton.com

Sharon Reynolds, CEO

Features a full search and download capabilities, you can easily assess your current distributor network and look for new distributors for your products. Search by MSA market, location square footage, employee count and many other critical variables. The handy main house and branch cross-reference brings the ever-changing electrical distribution market into focus. Using the simple search functions, you can build and download highly targeted lists in just seconds.
Frequency: Cd-Rom

6905 EASA Yearbook

Electrical Apparatus Services Association
1331 Baur Boulevard
Saint Louis, MO 63131-1903

314-993-2220
FAX 314-993-1269
E-Mail: easainfo@easa.com
Home Page: www.easa.com

Kevin Toor, Chairman
William Gray, Vice Chairman
Kenneth Gralow, Secretary/Treasurer
Cost: $100.00
267 Pages
Mailing list available for rent

6906 Electrical Construction Materials Directory

Underwriters Laboratories
2600 N.W. Lake Rd
Camas, WA 98607

877-854-3577
FAX 360-817-6278
E-Mail: cec@us.ul.com
Home Page: www.UL.com

Keith E Williams, CEO
John Drengenberg, Manager Consumer Affairs

Offers information on companies that have qualified to use the UL listing mark or classification marking with products that have been

found to be in compliance with UL regulations.
Cost: $40.00
912 Pages
Frequency: Annual
Printed in on glossy stock

6907 Electrical Distributor

National Association of Electrical Distributors
1181 Corporate Lake Drive
St. Louis, MO 63132

314-991-9000
888-791-2512
FAX 314-991-3060
E-Mail: info@naed.org
Home Page: www.naed.org

Robert Reynolds, Chair
Clarence Martin, Chair Elect

List of manufacturers and distributors of electrical components, supplies and equipment.
Cost: $295.00
Frequency: Biennial
Circulation: 3,500

6908 Electrical Equipment Representatives Association Membership Directory

Electrical Equipment Representatives Association
638 W 39th Street
Kansas City, MO 64111

816-561-5323
800-728-2272
FAX 816-561-1249
Home Page: www.eera.org

Scott Whitehead, President
Vince Brown, President Elect
Brad Cahoon, Vice-President
Don Shirk, Secretary
Kier Cooper, Treasurer

More than 105 manufacturers representatives of electrical equipment companies.
Frequency: Annual, October
Founded in 1948

6909 Engineers Relay Handbook

Relay and Switch Industry Association
2500 Wilson Boulevard
Arlington, VA 22201

703-907-8025
FAX 703-875-8908
E-Mail: narm@ecaus.org
Home Page: www.ec-central.org/RSIA

Dave Baicjaome, Chairman
Jeffrey Boyce, Director Business Development
Rodd Ruland, Director Business Development
Steve Lane, General Manager

In summary, special effort has been made by the editors to cover specification parameters in sufficient detail to provide systems and product design engineers with all the information they need to obtain the correct types of relays for their applications.
Cost: $60.00
Frequency: Annual

6910 Global Sourcing Guide

Diesel & Gas Turbine Publications
20855 Watertown Rd
Suite 220
Waukesha, WI 53186-1873

262-754-4100
FAX 262-832-5075
Home Page: www.dieselspec.com

Michael Osenga, President
Michael J Mercer, Managing Editor
Kara Kane, Publication Manager
Christa Stern, Production Manager
Sheila Lizdas, Circulation Manager

The Global Sourcing Guide is one of the premier references and purchasing guides for the power systems and components industry. Cov-

ering products and systems used across the mobile and stationary engine-powered equipment industries, this guide incorporates information in a wide range of classifications.
Cost: $110.00
Frequency: Annual
Founded in 1935

6911 High-Performance Composites Directory
Ray Publishing
PO Box 992
Morrison, CO 80465-0992

303-467-1776
FAX 303-467-1777
Home Page: www.compositesworld.com

Judith Hazen, Publisher
Mike Mussleman, Managing Editor

The publisher of High-Performance Composites and Composites Technology magazines and well as the Sourcebook Industry directory and special design and application guides.
60 Pages
Founded in 1993
Printed in 4 colors on glossy stock

6912 Indoor Electrical Safety Check Booklet
Electrical Safety Foundation International
1300 N 17th Street
Suite 1847
Rosslyn, VA 22209

703-413-3209
FAX 703-841-3329
E-Mail: info@esfi.org
Home Page: www.electrical-safety.org

Grant J Carter, Chair
David Tallman, Vice Chair
Michael Clendenin, Executive Director
Barbara R Guthrie, Secretary

Instructions on running an electrical safety audit of your home and at the same time learn about electrical inspections, circuit maps, power audits, and potential electrical hazards and safety tips from your circuit breaker or fuse panel to your outlets, power cords and extension cords, light bulbs, space heaters, ground fault circuit interrupters (GFCIs), arc fault circuit interrupters (AFCIs), batteries, and much more.

6913 NEMA Database
National Electrical Manufacturers Association
1300 17th St N
Suite 1752
Rosslyn, VA 22209-3806

703-841-3200
FAX 703-841-5900
Home Page: www.nema.org

Evan R Gaddis, CEO
Tom Hixon, VP

This database offers time series on orders, shipments and unfilled orders for 6 major segments of the electrical manufacturing industry.

6914 National Electrical Manufacturers Representatives Association Locator
National Electrical Manufacturers Rep Assoc
28 Deer Street
Suite 302
Portsmouth, NH 03801

914-524-8650
800-446-3672
FAX 603-319-1667

E-Mail: nemra@nemra.org
Home Page: www.nemra.org

Michael Gorin, Chairman
Mark Gibson, Chair Elect
Greg Reynolds, Secretary/Treasurer

Approximately 1,000 electrical manufacturers representative companies.
Cost: $200.00
Frequency: Annual

6915 National Electronic Distributors Association Membership Directory
National Electronic Distributors Association
1111 Alderman Dr
Suite 400
Alpharetta, GA 30005-4175

678-393-9990
FAX 678-393-9998
Home Page: www.nedassoc.org

Brian McNally, President
Michael Knight, President Elect
Robin Gray, Executive VP

Approximately 300 member distributors and 180 member manufacturers of electronics products, plus 1,100 branch offices.

6916 On-Site Power Generation: A Reference Book
Electrical Generating Systems Association
1650 S Dixie Hwy
Suite 400
Boca Raton, FL 33432-7461

561-750-5575
FAX 561-395-8557
Home Page: www.egsa.org

Jalane Kellough, Executive Director
George Rowley, Director of Education

This book contains the most complete and up-to-date technical information covering on-site electrical power generation.
Cost: $95.00
600 Pages

6917 Outdoor Electrical Safety Check Booklet
Electrical Safety Foundation International
1300 N 17th Street
Suite 1847
Rosslyn, VA 22209

703-413-3209
FAX 703-841-3329
E-Mail: info@esfi.org
Home Page: www.electrical-safety.org

Grant J Carter, Chair
David Tallman, Vice Chair
Michael Clendenin, Executive Director
Barbara R Guthrie, Secretary

Use this handy booklet to learn about available electrical safety devices, and the safety rules related to hot tubs, spas and pools, extension cords, electrical lawn and garden products, battery operated products and power tool safety.

6918 Product and Supplier Information
Electrical Generating Systems Association
1650 S Dixie Hwy
Suite 400
Boca Raton, FL 33432-7461

561-750-5575
FAX 561-395-8557
Home Page: www.egsa.org

Jalane Kellough, Executive Director
George Rowley, Director of Education

EGSA publishes a new Buyer's Guide and Member Services Directory listing every member.

6919 SMMA: Directory
SMMA: Small Motors & Motion Association

PO Box P182
S Dartmouth, MA 02748

508-979-5935
FAX 508-979-5845
E-Mail: info@smma.org
Home Page: www.smma.org

Elizabeth Chambers, Executive Director
William Chambers, Operations Director

Manufacturers, suppliers and users of fractional and subfractional horsepower electric motors.
Founded in 1975

6920 Transmission and Distribution: Specifiers and Buyers Guide Issue
Penton
249 W. 17th Street
New York, NY 10011

212-204-4200
E-Mail: CorporateCustomerService@penton.com
Home Page: www.penton.com

Sharon Rowlands, CEO

List of manufacturers and distributors of equipment for electric power transmission and distribution.
Cost: $20.00
Frequency: Annual, September
Circulation: 49,000

6921 Wholesale Source Directory of Electrical Products, Supplies & Accessories
Sutton Family Communications & Publishing Company
155 Sutton Lane
Fordsville, KY 42343

270-740-0870
E-Mail: jlsutton@apex.net
Home Page: www.fleamarketeer.net

Theresa Sutton, Editor
Lee Sutton, General Manager

Listings include names, addresses, phone/fax numbers and product descriptions for wholesale distributors, importers, manufacturers, close-out houses and liquidators. Every item needed to become an electrical contractor, open an electrical store or sell this type of merchandise in a hardware store, flea market or other market. Daily updated laser printed copy. Price includes shipping and handling.
Cost: $57.20
100+ Pages
Founded in 1977

Industry Web Sites

6922 http://gold.greyhouse.com
G.O.L.D Grey House OnLine Databases

Grey House Publishing's online database platform, GOLD, offers Quick Search, Keyword Search and Expert Search for most business sectors including electrical markets. The GOLD platform makes finding the information you need quick and easy - whether you're a novice searcher or an experienced database user. All of Grey House's directory products are available for subscription on the GOLD platform.

6923 www.7ms.com
Seven Mountains Scientific

Industry news in battery technology, marketing and industry events including new products, electric vehicles, R&D and environmental news.

6924 www.ahtd.org
Association for High Technology
Distributors

Works to increase productivity and profitability
of high technology automation solutions, providers and manufacturers.

6925 www.bioelectromagnetics.org
Bioelectromagnetics Society

International resource for excellence in scientific research, knowledge and understanding of
the interaction of electromagnetic fields with
biological systems. Members of the society are
biological and physical scientists, physicians
and engineers interested in the interactions of
nonionizing radiation with biological systems.

6926 www.construction.com
McGraw-Hill Construction

McGraw-Hill Construction (MHC), part of The
McGraw-Hill Companies, connects people and
projects across the design and construction industry, serving owners, architects, engineers,
general contractors, subcontractors, building
product manufacturers, suppliers, dealers, distributors and adjacent markets.

6927 www.csa-dc.org
Contract Services Association of America

Represents the government services contracting
industry in Washington, DC. Members range
from small businesses to large corporations servicing federal and state government in numerous capacities. CSA acts to foster effective
implementation of the government's policy of
reliance on the private sector for support
services.

6928 www.eachicago.org
Electric Association

Its purpose is to serve as the umbrella organization for the various electrical disciplines in the
Chicagoland area.

6929 www.easa.com
Electrical Apparatus Service Association

An international trade organization of electro-
mechanical sales and service firms in 58 countries. Provides members with a means of
keeping up to date on materials, equipment,
and state-of-the-art technology

6930 www.ec-central.org/RSIA
Relay and Switch Industry Association

The purpose and aims shall be to encourage the
advancement of the art and science of making
and using those switching devices generally
known as relays; to promote and further interest of relay manufacturers consistent with the
best interest of relay users; to create a spirit of
mutual esteem, respect and recognition among
members, and between the members and their
customers and suppliers.

6931 www.eei.org
Edison Electric Institute

Advocates public policy, expands market opportunities and provides strategic business information for the shareholder-owned electric
utility industry. Find out more about EEI's
members, upcoming meetings, career opportunities and products and services.

6932 www.eera.org
Electrical Equipment Representatives
Association

Sales agents for manufacturers of electrical
equipment used by utilities. Mission is to advance the quality and increase effectiveness of
manufacturer's representatives in the electrical
equipment industry.

6933 www.electric-find.com
Electric Find

A directory/search engine for the electrical construction industry. Search results have been
screened by electrical professionals.

6934 www.electrochem.org
Electrochemical Society

The society is an international nonprofit, educational organization concerned with phenomena relating to electrochemical and solid state
science and technology. Members are individual scientists and engineers, as well as
corporations and laboratories.

6935 www.epri.com
Electric Power Research Institute

Research relating to the production, transmission, distribution and utilization of electric
power.

6936 www.esda.org
Electrostatic Discharge Association

Dedicated to advancing the theory and practice
of electrostatic discharge avoidance.

6937 www.ewh.ieee.org
Instrumentation and Measurement Society

A subsidiary of the Institute of Electrical and
Electronics Engineers. Provides support to scientists and technicians who design and develop
electrical and electronic measuring instruments
and equipment.

6938 www.greyhouse.com
Grey House Publishing

Authoritative reference directories for most
business sectors incluidng electrical markets.
Users can search the online databases with varied search criteria allowing for custom searches
by product category, geographic area, sales volume, keyword, subject and more. Full Grey
House catalog and online ordering also
available.

6939 www.icea.net
Insulated Cable Engineers Association

Professional organization dedicated to developing cable standards for the electric power, control and telecommunications industries.
Ensures safe, economical and efficient cable
systems utilizing proven state-of-the-art materials and concepts. ICEA documents are of interest to cable manufacturers, architects and
engineers, utility and manufacturing plant personnel, telecommunication engineers,
consultants and OEMs.

6940 www.imaps.org
International Microelectronics & Packaging
Society

Dedicated to the advancement and growth of
the use of microelectronics and electronic packaging through public and professional education, dissemination of information by means of
symposia, workshops and conferences and promotion of the Society's portfolio of
technologies.

6941 www.impi.org
International Microwave Power Institute

IMPI's members include scientists, researchers,
lab technicians, product developers, marketing
managers and a variety of other professionals
in the microwave industry. The Institute serves
the information needs of all specialists working
with dielectric (microwave and RF) heating
sytems, and was expanded in 1977 to meet the
information needs relating to consumer
microwave ovens and related products.

6942 www.ipc.org
IPC: Association Connecting Electronics

Works to develop standards in circuit board assembly equipment. Brings together all players
in the electronic interconnection industry, including designers, board manufacturers, assembly companies, suppliers and original
equipment manufacturers. Offers workshops,
conferences, meetings and online
communications.

6943 www.ncel.org
North Central Electrical League

Trade association representing all segments of
the electrical industry in the Upper Midwest.

6944 www.necanet.org
National Electrical Contractors Association

Represents a segment of the construction market comprised of over 70,000 electrical firms.

6945 www.nerc.com
North American Electric Reliability Council

Voluntary organization promoting bulk electric
system reliability and security.

6946 www.netaworld.org
International Electrical Testing Association

Defines the standards by which electrical
equipment is deemed safe and reliable. Creates
specifications, procedures, testing and requirements for commissioning new equipment and
testing the reliability and performance of
existing equipment.

6947 www.nsca.org
National Systems Contractors Association

Not-for-profit association representing the
commercial electronic systems industry. Serves
as an advocate for all those who work within
the low-voltage industry including systems
contractors/integrators, product manufacturers,
consultants, sales representatives and a growing number of architects, specifying engineers
and others.

6948 www.platts.com
Electrical World

The latest trends in utility engineering and IT,
equipment and services, best business practices
and critical industry thinking. For managers,
engineers and technicians who plan, design,
build, maintain and upgrade electric T&D systems around the world.

6949 www.psma.com
Power Sources Manufacturers Association

Worldwide membership consists of manufacturers of power sources and conversion equipment. Nonprofit association strives to integrate
the resources of the power sources industry to
more effectively and profitably serve the needs
of the power sources users, providers and
PSMA members. Educates the electronics industry and others on the relevant applications
for power sources and conversion devices.

6950 www.semi.org
Semiconductor Equipment & Materials
International

Strengthens the performance of member companies through lobbying, promotion, education
and statistical research.

6951 www.seshaonline.org
Semiconductor Environmental, Safety &
Health Assn

Members are individuals employed within the
electronics and related high technology industries with an interest in environmental, health
and safety issues.

6952 www.sia-online.org
Semiconductor Industry Association

Trade association representing the US microchip industry.

6953 www.smma.org
SMMA: Small Motors & Motion Association

Trade association for the electric motor and motion control industry in Northern America. The voice of the motor and motion industry providing a forum for education, communication, research and networking.

6954 www.smta.org
Surface Mount Technology Association

A network of professionals building skills, sharing practical experience and developing solutions in electronic assembly technologies and related business operations.

6955 www.sweets.construction.com
McGraw Hill Construction

In depth product information that lets you find, compare, select, specify and make purchase decisions in the industrial product marketplace.

Associations

6956 AG Electronic Association
10 S Riverside Plaza
Suite 1220
Chicago, IL 60606-3710

312-321-1470
FAX 312-321-1480
E-Mail: age@agelectronicsassn.org
Home Page: www.agelectronicsassn.org

Darrin Dollinger, Marketing Manager

Identifies, develops & or facilitates appropriate action aimed at furthering the compatibility & interchangeability of electronics and information systems used in agriculture.

6957 AVS Science & Technology Society
125 Maiden Ln
15th Floor
New York, NY 10038

212-248-0200
FAX 212-248-0245
E-Mail: ricky@avs.org
Home Page: www.avs.org
Social Media: *Facebook, Twitter, LinkedIn*

Ivan G. Petrov, President
Gregory J. Exarhos, Treasurer
Yvonne Towse, Managing Director
Joseph E Greene, Clerk/Secretary
Peter Burke, Financial Administrator

Supports all those involved with all aspects of science and technology through research, education, new products, publications and conferences.
5500 Members
Founded in 1953

6958 Aircraft Electronics Association
3570 Ne Ralph Powell Rd
Lees Summit, MO 64064-2360

816-347-8400
FAX 816-347-8405
E-Mail: info@aea.net
Home Page: www.aea.net
Social Media: *Facebook, Twitter, LinkedIn, Flickr, YouTube*

Paula Derks, President
Debra McFarland, Executive Vice President
Mike Adamson, VP, Member Programs & Education
Linda Adams, VP, Member Services
Aaron Ward, Director of Information Services

AEA represents aviation businesses, including repair stations that specialize in maintenance, repair and installation of avionics and electronic systems in general aviation aircraft.
1250 Members
Founded in 1957
Mailing list available for rent

6959 American Electronics Association
5201 Great America Parkway
Santa Clara, CA 95054

408-987-4200
800-284-4232
FAX 408-987-4298
E-Mail: csc@aeanet.org
Home Page: www.aeanet.org

John V Harker, Chairman
William T Archey, President/CEO
Samuel J Block, VP/Controller
Tim Bennett, COO/EVP

Works to foster a healthy business climate by providing services education and research programs.
3500 Members
Founded in 1943

6960 American Association of Electronic Reporters and Transcribers
P.O. Box 9826
Wilmington, DE 19809

302-765-3510
800-233-5306
FAX 302-241-2177
E-Mail: sherry@aaert.org
Home Page: www.aaert.org
Social Media: *Facebook, Twitter, LinkedIn*

Buchanan Buck Ewing, President
Steve Townsend, Vice President
Richard Russell, Treasurer
Geoffrey Hunt, Secretary
Michael F. Tannen, CSEP, Executive Director

A national professional association that deals with the electronic court reporting.

6961 Armed Forces Communications and Electronics Association (AFCEA)
4400 Fair Lakes Ct
Fairfax, VA 22033-3899

703-631-6100
800-336-4583
FAX 703-631-6169
Home Page: www.afcea.org
Social Media: *Facebook, Twitter, LinkedIn, Flickr, YouTube, Google+, Slid*

LtGen Robert M. Shea, USMC (Ret.), President
LTG John R. Wood, USA (Ret.), Executive VP
Pat Miorin, CPA, EVP/CFO/Treasurer
James L. Griggs Jr., VP/CIO/CTO
Tina Jordan, VP, Region and Chapter Outreach

A non-profit membership association serving the military, government, industry, and academia as an ethical forum for advancing professional knowledge and relationships in the fields of communications, IT, intelligence, and global security.
30000 Members
Founded in 1946

6962 Association for Electronics Manufacturing
1 SME Drive
PO Box 930
Dearborn, MI 48121

313-425-3000
800-733-4763
FAX 313-425-3400
E-Mail: service@sme.org
Home Page: www.sme.org
Social Media: *Facebook, Twitter, LinkedIn, YouTube, Google+*

Wayne F. Frost, CMfgE, President
Jeffrey M. Krause, Chief Executive Officer
Kathleen Borgula, Human Resources
Erica Ciupak, Information Technology
Debbie Clark, Governance

Represents the electrical manufacturers.
3.6M Members
Founded in 1932

6963 Association of Progressive Rental Organizations
1540 Robinhood Trail
Austin, TX 78703-2624

512-794-0095
800-204-2776
FAX 512-794-0097
E-Mail: cferguson@rtohq.org
Home Page: www.rtohq.org
Social Media: *Facebook, Twitter, YouTube, Flickr*

Bill Keese, Executive Director
Gary Ferriman, President
Jonathan Rose, Secretary
Gopal Reddy, First Vice President
Mark Connelly, Second Vice President

Members include television, appliance and furniture dealers who rent merchandise with an option to purchase.
2000 Members
Founded in 1980

6964 Consumer Electronics Association (CEA)
1919 S Eads Street
Arlington, VA 22202

703-907-7600
866-858-1555
FAX 703-907-7675
E-Mail: communications@ce.org
Home Page: www.ce.org
Social Media: *Facebook, Twitter, LinkedIn, Flickr, Google+*

Gary Shapiro, President/CEO
Daniel Pidgeon, Chairman
Patrick Lavelle, Industry Executive Advisor
David Hagan, Vice Chair
Glenda MacMullin, Treasurer

Consumer Electronics Association (CEA) provides valuable and innovative member-only resources including: exclusive information and unparalleled market research, networking opportunities with business advocates and leaders, up-to-date educational programs and technical training, exposure in extensive promotional programs, and representation from the voice of the industry.
2000 Members

6965 Consumer Electronics Forum
CompuServe Information Service
5000 Arlington Center Boulevard
Columbus, OH 43220

614-457-8600
800-848-8199

Offers valuable information on electronic consumer products, including audio, video and satellite systems and radar detectors.

6966 Custom Electronic Design & Installation Association
7150 Winton Drive
Suite 300
Indianapolis, IN 46268

317-328-4336
800-669-5329
FAX 317-735-4012
E-Mail: info@cedia.org
Home Page: www.cedia.org
Social Media: *Facebook, Twitter, YouTube*

Larry Pexton, Chairman
Dennis Erskine, Vice Chairman
Federico Bausone, Immediate Past Chairman
Richard Millson, Secretary
David Humphries, Treasurer

A global authority in the home technology industry that provides access to industry-leading education, certification, research, and consumer awareness.
3500 Members

6967 Electrical Apparatus Service Association
1331 Baur Blvd.
St. Louis, MO 63132

314-993-2220
FAX 314-993-1269
E-Mail: easainfo@easa.com
Home Page: www.easa.com
Social Media: *Facebook, Twitter, LinkedIn, YouTube*

Linda J. Raynes, CAE, President & CEO
Anne Vogel, Executive Secretary
Richard Tutka, Finance Manager
Randy D. Joslin, Communications Manager
Tyler Voss, Membership Specialist

An international trade organization of more than 1,900 electromechanical sales and service firms in 62 countries that provides members with a meansof keeping up to date on materials, equipment, and state-of-the-art technology.

6968 Electronic Components Industry Association

1111 Alderman Drive
Suite 400
Alpharetta, GA 30005

678-393-9990
FAX 678-393-9998
E-Mail: jwood@ecianow.org
Home Page: www.ecianow.org
Social Media: *Facebook, Twitter, LinkedIn, YouTube*

Blair Haas, Chair
Ed Smith, Chair Elect
John Denslinger, President and CEO
Victor Meijers, VP, Marketing & Comm.
Barney Martin, VP, Industry Practices

Organization made up of electronic component manufacturers, their manufacturer representatives and authorized distributors that provides resources and opportunities for members to improve their business performance while enhancing the industry's overall capacity for growth and profitability.

6969 Electronic Industries Alliance

2500 Wilson Boulevard
Arlington, VA 22201-3834

703-907-7500
FAX 703-907-7500
Home Page: www.eia.org

Ronald L Turner, Chairman
Mike Kennedy, Vice Chairman
Dave McCurdy, President/CEO
Neal McDonald, Senior Coordinator
James Shiring, Secretary/Treasurer

Trade organization representing the entire spectrum of manufacturers and consumer manufacturers involved in electronic products.
1.5M Members
Founded in 1924

6970 Electronic Retailing Association

607 14th Street, NW
Suite 530
Washington, DC 20005

703-841-1751
800-987-6462
FAX 425-977-1036
E-Mail: webadmin@retailing.org
Home Page: www.retailing.org
Social Media: *Facebook, Twitter, LinkedIn, YouTube, Flickr*

Julie Coons, CEO
Cecilia Mason, Accounting Manager
Bill McClellan, Vice President, Government Affairs
Dave Martin, VP, Marketing and Content
Vi Paynich, Content Manager

The trade association that represents the leaders of direct response: members who maximize revenues through electronic retailing on television, online and on radio. ERA strives to protect the regulatory and legislative climate of direct response while ensuring a favorable landscape that enhances e-retailers' ability to bring quality products and services to the consumer.
Founded in 1990

6971 Electronic Security Association

6333 North State Highway 161
Suite 350
Irving, TX 75038

972-807-6800
888-447-1689

FAX 972-807-6883
Home Page: www.esaweb.orgÿ
Social Media: *Facebook, Twitter, LinkedIn*

Marshall Marinace, President
Dee Ann Harn, Vice President
Merlin Guilbeau, Executive Director
Jon Sargent, Secretary
Steve Paley, Treasurer

A nonprofit trade association that represents, promotes, and enhances the growth and professional development of the electronic life safety, security, and integrated sytems industry.
Founded in 1948

6972 Electronic Transactions Association

1101 16th Street NW
Suite 402
Washington, DC 20036

202-828-2635
800-695-5509
FAX 202-828-2639
E-Mail: meghan.cieslak@electran.org
Home Page: www.electran.org
Social Media: *Facebook, LinkedIn, YouTube, Flickr*

Debra Rossi, President
Jeff Rosenblatt, Treasurer
Mary Albert, Director of Regulatory Affairs
Jeff Sloan, Secretary
Grant Carlson, Government Affairs Coordinator

ETA is the international trade association serving the needs of organizations offering transaction processing products/services.
400M Members
Founded in 1990

6973 Electronics Representatives Association

300 W Adams St
Suite 617
Chicago, IL 60606-5109

312-419-1432
800-776-7377
FAX 312-419-1660
E-Mail: info@era.org
Home Page: www.era.org

Paul C. Nielsen, CPMR, Chairman
Dan Parks, CPMR, President
David Norris, SVP, Fiscal & Legal
Chuck Tanzola, CPMR, SVP, Industry
John O'Brien, CPMR, SVP, Membership

Provides services and benefits to electronic industry manufacturers and manufacturers' representatives.
Cost: $48.00
450 Members
Founded in 1935

6974 Electronics Technicians Association International

5 Depot Street
Greencastle, IN 46135

765-653-8262
800-288-3824
FAX 765-653-4287
E-Mail: eta@eta-i.org
Home Page: www.eta-i.org
Social Media: *Facebook, Twitter, LinkedIn, YouTube, Google+*

Teresa Maher, CSS, President
Bryan Allen, CSM, CSS, Vice President
Richard Glass, CETsr, CEO Emeritus
Delores Andrews, Staff Support
Emily Hatfield, Research & Development

Association for electronic technicians worldwide offering over 70 certifications.
4500 Members
Founded in 1978

6975 ElectronicÿTransactionÿAssociationÿ

1101 16th Street NW
#402
Washington, DC 20036

202-828-2635
800-695-5509
E-Mail: meghan.cieslak@electran.org
Home Page: www.electran.orgÿ
Social Media: *Facebook, LinkedIn, YouTube, Flickr*

Debra Rossi, President
Jeff Rosenblatt, Treasurer
Mary Albert, Director of Regulatory Affairs
Jeff Sloan, Secretary
Grant Carlson, Government Affairs Coordinator

International trade association for the payment processing industry.
Founded in 1990

6976 Federated Rural Electric

77100 US Highway 71
PO Box 69
Jackson, MN 56143-0069

507-728-8366
800-321-3520
FAX 507-728-8366
E-Mail: info@federatedrea.coop
Home Page: www.federatedrea.coop

David A. Hansen, President
Dave Meschke, Vice-President
Darvin Voss, Secretary
Bruce Brockmann, Director
Glenn Dicks, Director

A distribution electric utility.
Founded in 1935

6977 IEEE Photonics Society

445 Hoes Lane
Piscataway, NJ 08855-1331

732-562-3926
FAX 732-562-8434
E-Mail: C.Jannuzzi@ieee.org
Home Page: www.photonicssociety.org

Dalma Novak, President
Paul Juodawlkis, VP Membership
Catrina Coleman, VP Publications
Christopher Jannuzzi, Executive Director
Douglas Razzano, Associate Executive Director

A leading professional network of 7,000+ members that provide access to technical information.
Founded in 1965

6978 IEEE Power Electronics Society

E-Mail: m.p.kelly@ieee.org
Home Page: www.ieee-pels.org
Social Media: *Twitter, LinkedIn*

Philip Krein, History Chair
Michael P. Kelly, Executive Director
Donna Florek, Tech Community Program Specialist
Michael Markowycz, Tech Community Program Specialist
Jo-Ellen Snyder, Tech Community Program Specialist

A society of the Institute of Electrical and Electronics (IEEE) that focuses on the developmnet of power electronics technology.
7000 Members

6979 IPC Associationÿ

3000 Lakeside Drive
105 N
Bannockburn, IL 60015

847-615-7100
FAX 847-615-7105
E-Mail: answers@ipc.org
Home Page: www.ipc.org

Social Media: *Facebook, Twitter, LinkedIn, YouTube, Google+, RSS*

Marc Peo, Chairman
Joseph Joe O'Neil, Vice Chairman
John W. Mitchell, President/ CEO
Mikel H. Williams, Secretary/ Treasurer
Stephen Steve Pudles, Immediate Past Chairman

A trade association that standardizes the assembly and production requirements of electronic equipment and assemblies.

6980 IPC: Association Connecting Electronics

3000 Lakeside Drive
105 N
Bannockburn, IL 60015

847-615-7100
FAX 847-615-7105
E-Mail: webmaster@ipc.org
Home Page: www.ipc.org
Social Media: *Facebook, Twitter, LinkedIn, YouTube, Google+, RSS*

Marc Peo, Chairman
Joseph Joe O'Neil, Vice Chairman
John W. Mitchell, President/ CEO
Mikel H. Williams, Secretary/ Treasurer
Jennifer Sandahl, Controller

A trade association for the printed circuit boards and electronics assembly industries, offering programs and resources to board manufacturers and electronic assemblers, designers, industry suppliers and original equipment manufacturers.
2000 Members
Founded in 1957

6981 Independent Distributors of Electronics Association

116 Helen Highway
#2900
Cleveland, GA 30528

714-670-0200
FAX 714-670-0201
E-Mail: info@IDofEA.org
Home Page: www.idofea.orgy
Social Media: *Facebook, Twitter, LinkedIn*

Paul Romano, President
Dan Ellsworth, Vice President
Homey Shorooghi, Secretary/ Treasurer
Brian Wilson, Executive Board member
Jason Jowers, Executive Board member

A global trade association comprised of organizations for independent distributors to find relevant information and to participate in advancing industry ethics, ensuring customer satisfaction, establishing standards, and promoting education.

6982 Independent Electrical Contractors

4401 Ford Avenue
Suite 1100
Alexandria, VA 22302

703-549-7351
800-456-4324
FAX 703-549-7448
E-Mail: info@ieci.org
Home Page: www.ieci.org
Social Media: *Facebook, Twitter, LinkedIn, YouTube, Flickr, Instagram*

Mark Gillespie, National President
Bruce Seilhammer, National Senior Vice President
Thayer Long, Executive Vice President/CEO
Vernice Howard, Chief Financial Officer
Bruna Patio, Staff Accountant

A national trade association for merit shop electrical and systems contractors.
Founded in 1957

6983 Instrumentation & Measurement Society

Home Page: www.ieee-ims.org
Social Media: *Facebook, Twitter, LinkedIn*

Reza Zoughi, President
Ruth A Dyer, Executive VP
Dario Petri, VP Finance
Alessandra Flammini, VP Conferences
Mark Yeary, VP Publications

A professional society of the IEEE whose field of interest is the science, technology, and application of instrumentation and measurement.

6984 Instrumentation and Measurement Society

799 N Beverly Glen
Los Angeles, CA 90077

310-446-8280
FAX 732-981-0225
E-Mail: bob.myers@ieee.org
Home Page: www.ewh.ieee.org

Robert Myers, Executive Director
Lee Myers, Assistant Director
Robert Rassa, President
Barry Oakes, VP Finance

A subsidiary of the Institute of Electrical and Electronics Engineers. Provides support to scientists and technicians who design and develop electrical and electronic measuring instruments and equipment.
6500+ Members
Founded in 1950

6985 International Electrical Testing Association

3050 Old Centre Ave.,
Suite 102
Portage, MI 49024

269-488-6382
FAX 269-488-6383
E-Mail: mrichard@netaworld.org
Home Page: www.netaworld.org
Social Media: *Facebook, LinkedIn, YouTube*

Dave Huffman, President
Ron Widup, 1st Vice President
Jim Cialdea, 2nd Vice President
Jayne Tanz, Executive Director
Melissa Richard, Finance and Business Manager

Establishes standards, publishes specifications, accredits independent, third-party, electrical testing companies, certifies test technicians, and promotes the services of association members.

6986 International Federation of Air Traffic Safety Electronics Associations

E-Mail: info@ifatsea.org
Home Page: www.ifatsea.org

Daniel Boulet, President
Theodore Kiritsis, Vice-President

Federation represents the interests of air traffic safety electronics personnel.
50 Members
Founded in 1972

6987 International Microelectronics and Electronic Packaging

611 2nd Street NE
Washington, DC 20002

202-548-4001
888-464-6277
FAX 919-287-2339
E-Mail: imaps@imaps.org
Home Page: www.imaps.org

Michael O'Donoghue, Executive Director
Jennifer Davis, Office Assistant
Brian Schieman, Director Information Technology

Ann Bell, Manager Marketing/Communications
Brianne Lamm, Membership & Events Manager

Promotes interaction among technologies of ceramics, thin and thick films, semiconductor packaging, surface mount technology, multichip modules, semiconductor devices and monolithic circuits. Dedicated to the advancement and growth of the use of microelectronics and electronic packaging through education. Disseminates information through symposia, workshops and conferences.
11000 Members
Founded in 1967

6988 International SEMATECH

257 Fuller Road
Albany, NY 12203

518-437-8686
FAX 512-356-3135
E-Mail: rcollier@sunypoly.edu
Home Page: www.sunycnse.com

Alain Kaloyeros, Founding President/CEO
Walter Gerald Barber, President/Chief Admin Officer
Scott Bateman, CFO
Patricia Bucklin, Vice President for Administration
Richard Collier, Director for Student Affairs

A global consortium of leading semiconductor manufacturers who engage in cooperative precompetitive efforts to improve semiconductor manufacturing technology through the support of their members.
Founded in 2004

6989 International Society of Certified Electronic Technicians

3000-A Landers St.,
Fort Worth, TX 76107-5642

817-921-9101
800-946-0201
FAX 817-921-3741
E-Mail: info@iscet.org
Home Page: www.iscet.org

Pete Founding PresidentCEO, President
Daniel Champion, Vice President
Mack Blakely, Executive Director
Rich Reid, Secretary
John Wilkins, Treasurer

Helps train, prepare, and test technicians in the electronics and appliance service industry.
Founded in 1965

6990 International Society of Certified Electronic Technicians

3000-A Landers St.,
Fort Worth, TX 76107-5642

817-921-9101
800-946-0201
FAX 817-921-3741
E-Mail: info@iscet.org
Home Page: www.iscet.org

Pete Rattigan, President
Daniel Champion, Vice President
Mack Blakely, Executive Director
Rich Reid, Secretary
John Wilkins, Treasurer

Seeks to provide awareness of and services to certified electronics technicians. Provides educational materials in electronics training to schools, technical institutes and junior colleges. Offers certification programs for electronics technicians in associate and journeyman levels.
46000 Members
Founded in 1965

6991 Minerals, Metals & Materials Society
184 Thorn Hill Road
Warrendale, PA 15086-7514

724-776-9000
800-759-4867
FAX 724-776-3770
E-Mail: webmaster@tms.org
Home Page: www.tms.org
Social Media: *Facebook, LinkedIn, YouTube*

James Robinson, Executive Director
Adrianne Carolla, Deputy Executive Director
Nancy Lesko, Executive & Board Administrator
Marleen Schrader, Accounting & HR Specialist
Paul Zappas, Information Technology Manager
Supports all those in the minerals, metals and materials industries with education, publications, trade shows and conferences.
Founded in 1971

6992 Mobile Electronics Retailers Associationÿ
85 Flagship Drive
Suite F
North Andover, MA 1845

800-949-6372
E-Mail: info@merausa.org
Home Page: www.merausa.org

Mike Anderson, Chairman
Chris Cook, President
Mike Bartells, Advisory Board
Tony Dehnke, Advisory Board
Joe Forcella, Advisory Board
Focuses on education and networking opportunities designed to advance the professionalism and profitability of the mobile electronics industry.
Founded in 1992

6993 National Association of Relay Manufacturers
2500 Wilson Boulevard
Arlington, VA 22201

703-907-8025
FAX 703-875-8908
E-Mail: narm@ecaus.org
Home Page: www.ec-central.org/NARM

Dave Bauchaine, Chairman
Jeffrey Boyce, President
NARM is a trade association for the electro-mechanical relay and associated switching devices industry. An affiliate of Electronic Industries Alliance.
32 Members
Founded in 1947

6994 National Electrical Manufacturers Association
1300 North 17th Street
Suite 900
Arlington, VI 22209

703-841-3200
Home Page: www.nema.org
Social Media: *Facebook, Twitter, LinkedIn, YouTube, Google+, Instagram*

Donald J. Hendler, Chairman
Maryrose Sylvester, Vice Chairman
Kevin J. Cosgriff, President
Donald R. Leavens, PhD., Vice President and Chief Economist
John Caskey, Assistant VP, Operations
Develops standards for the electrical manufacturing industry.
Founded in 1926

6995 National Electronic Distributors Association
2211 South 47th Street
Suite 400
Phoenix, AZ 85034

678-393-9990
800-408-8353
FAX 678-393-9998
E-Mail: customer.care@avnet.com
Home Page: avnetexpress.avnet.com
Social Media: *Facebook, Twitter, LinkedIn, YouTube*

Ed Smith, President
Rick Hamada, CEO
Debbie Conyers, Director Marketing
Barney Martin, VP Industry Practices
Conducts research and offers educational programs for wholesale distributors of electronic components.
Founded in 1921
Mailing list available for rent

6996 National Electronics Service Dealers Association
3608 Pershing Ave
Fort Worth, TX 76107-4527

817-921-9061
800-797-9197
FAX 817-921-3741
E-Mail: info@nesda.com
Home Page: www.nesda.com

Mack Blakely, Executive Director
Sheila Fredrickson, Dir Communications/Info Technology
Patricia Bohon, Membership & Trade Show Coordinator
James Keesler, Associate Editor/Graphic Designer
Margaret Vazquez, Bookkeeper/Administrative Assistant
A national trade association for professionals in the business of repairing consumer electronics equipment, appliances, and computers. NESDA has an e-mail group of members and manufacturers that communicate daily for information sharing. NESDA also has an annual convention and trade show.
600 Members
Founded in 1950

6997 National Marine Electronics Association
692 Ritchie Highway
Suite 104
Severna Park, MD 21146

410-975-9425
FAX 410-975-9450
E-Mail: info@nmea.org
Home Page: www.nmea.org
Social Media: *Facebook*

Johnny Lindstrom, Chairman
Mike Spyros, Vice Chairman
Mark Reedenauer, President & Executive Director
Michael S. Quarders, Treasurer
Jules Rutstein, Secretary
Is the unifying force behind the entire marine electronics industry, bringing together all aspects of the industry for the betterment of all in our business.
400 Members
Founded in 1957

6998 National Rural Electric Cooperative Association
4301 Wilson Blvd.
Arlington, VA 22203

703-907-5500
Home Page: www.nreca.coop

Social Media: *Facebook, Twitter, LinkedIn, YouTube*

Jo Ann Emerson, Chief Executive Officer
Kirk Johnson, SVP of Government Relations
Peter Baxter, SVP
Marc Breslaw, Executive Director
Jeffrey Connor, Chief of Staff and COO
An organization that represents the interests of over 900 electric cooperatives in the United States to various legislatures.
Founded in 1933

6999 Optical Society of America
2010 Massachusetts Ave Nw
Washington, DC 20036-1023

202-223-8130
FAX 202-223-1096
E-Mail: info@osa.org
Home Page: www.osa.org
Social Media: *Facebook, Twitter, LinkedIn, YouTube*

Philip Russell, President
Eric Mazur, Vice President
Elizabeth A. Rogan, Chief Executive Officer
Sean Bagshaw, COO/CIO
Tracy Schario, Chief External Relations Officer
The Optical Society of America (OSA) was organized to increase and diffuse the knowledge of optics, pure and applied; to promote the common interests of investigators of optical problems, of designers and of users of optical apparatus of all kinds; and to encourage cooperation among them. The purposes of the Society are scientific, technical and educational.
15000 Members
Founded in 1916

7000 Power Electronics Society
799 N Beverly Glen
Los Angeles, CA 90077

310-446-8280
FAX 310-446-8390
E-Mail: bob.myers@ieee.org
Home Page: www.pels.org

Michael P. Kelly, Executive Director
Donna Florek, Program Specialist
Michael Markowycz, Program Specialist
Jo-Ellen Snyder, Tech Community Program Specialist
Grant Pitel, Volunteer PELS Webmaster
A subsidiary of the Institute of Electrical & Electronics Engineers. Supports professionals working in the field of power electronics technology.
5000 Members
Founded in 1987

7001 Power Sources Manufacturers Association
PO Box 418
Mendham, NJ 07945-0418

973-543-9660
FAX 973-543-6207
E-Mail: power@psma.com
Home Page: www.psma.com
Social Media: *LinkedIn*

Ernie Parker, Chairman
Eric Persson, President
Stephen Oliver, VP
Michel Grenon, Secretary/ Treasurer
The PSMA is a not-for-profit organization incorporated in the state of California. The purpose of the Association shall be to enhance the stature and reputation of its members and their products, improve their knowledge of technological and other developments related to power sources, and to educate the entire electronics industry, plus academia, as well as government and industry agencies as to the

importance of, and relevant applications for, all types of power sources and conversion devices.
155 Members
Founded in 1985

7002 SPIE
1000 20th St.
Bellingham, WA 98225-6705

360-676-3290
888-504-8171
FAX 360-647-1445
E-Mail: CustomerService@SPIE.org
Home Page: www.spie.orgÿ
Social Media: *Facebook, Twitter, LinkedIn, RSS, YouTube, Blogspot*

Dr. H. Philip Stahl, President
Mr. William Arnold, Immediate Past President
Prof Toyohiko Yatagai, President Elect
Dr. Robert A Lieberman, Vice President
Brian Lula, Secretary/ Treasurer

A nonprofit international professional society for optics and photonics technology.
Founded in 1955

7003 Semiconductor Environmental, Safety & Health Association
1313 Dolly Madison Boulevard
Suite 420
McLean, VA 22101

703-790-1745
FAX 703-790-2672
E-Mail: sesha@burkinc.com
Home Page: www.seshaonline.org

Hilary Matthews, President
Raymond McDaid, Secretary
Brian Sherin, Treasurer
Karl Albrecht, Secretary

Members are individuals employed within the electronics and related high technology industries with an interest in environmental, health and safety issues.
1500 Members
Founded in 1978

7004 Semiconductor Equipment and Materials International
3081 Zanker Road
San Jose, CA 95134

408-943-6900
FAX 408-428-9600
E-Mail: semihq@semi.org
Home Page: www.semi.org

Yong Han Lee, Chairman
Tetsuo Tsuneishi, Vice Chairman
Denny McGuirk, President/CEO
Richard Salsman, CFO/VP, Operations
Peter Gillespie, Chief Marketing Officer

An international trade association representing firms supplying equipment, materials and services to the semiconductor industry. Strengthens the performance of members through promotion, lobbying, education and statistical research.
2300 Members
Founded in 1970

7005 Semiconductor Industry Association
1101 K Street NW
Suite 450
Washington, CA 20005

202-446-1700
866-756-0715
FAX 202-216-9745
E-Mail: mailbox@sia-online.org
Home Page: www.sia-online.org

John Neuffer, President and CEO
Jimmy Goodrich, Vice President, Global Policy
Mike Williams, Chief Financial Officer
Joe Pasetti, Director, Government Affairs
Dan Rosso, Communications Manager

Trade association representing the US microchip industry. Provides a forum for working collectively to enhance the competitiveness of the US chip industry.
70 Members
Founded in 1977

7006 Society of Manufacturing Engineers
1 SME Drive
PO Box 930
Dearborn, MI 48128

313-425-3000
800-733-4763
FAX 313-425-3400
E-Mail: service@sme.org
Home Page: www.sme.org
Social Media: *Facebook, Twitter, LinkedIn, Google+, RSS*

Wayne F. Frost, President
Jeffrey M. Krause, Chief Executive Officer
Kathleen Borgula, Human Resources
Erica Ciupak, Information Technology
Julie Duff, Finance

Supports all engineers in electronics manufacturing. Publishes quarterly newsletter.
70M Members
Founded in 1932

7007 Surface Mount Technology Association
5200 Willson Rd
Suite 215
Minneapolis, MN 55424-1316

952-920-7682
FAX 952-926-1819
E-Mail: joann@smta.org
Home Page: www.smta.org
Social Media: *Facebook, Twitter, LinkedIn*

Bill Barthel, President
JoAnn Stromberg, Executive Administrator
Eileen Hibbler, VP Membership
Raiyomand Aspandiar, Ph.D., VP Technical Programs
Debbie Carboni, VP Expos

Network of professionals building skills, sharing practical experience and developing solutions in electronic assembly technologies and related business operations.
3200 Members
Founded in 1984

7008 Tobacco Vapor Electronic Cigarette Association
1005 Union Center Dr.
Suite F
Alpharetta, GA 30004

888-998-8322
E-Mail: info@tveca.com
Home Page: www.tveca.com
Social Media: *Facebook, Twitter, LinkedIn, Google+*

Ray Story, CEO
Keith Nelson, US Chief Political Officer
Thomas R. Kiklas, CFO
Chrissy Keheley, Secretary
Christopher Fowler, CTO/Web Development

A nonprofit organization dedicated to create a sensible and responsible electronic cigarette market by providing the media, legislative bodies, andconsumers with education, communication, and research.

7009 Universal Association of Computer and Electronics Engineers
42 Broadway
Suite 12-217
New York, NY 10004

212-901-3781
FAX 212-901-3786

E-Mail: support@uacee.org
Home Page: www.uacee.org

A registered nonprofit society to promote research.

7010 Video Electronics Standards Association
1754 Technology Dr.
Suite 238
San Jose, CA 95110

408-982-3850
FAX 408-669-0976
E-Mail: moderator@vesa.org
Home Page: www.vesa.org
Social Media: *Twitter, YouTube*

Alan Kobayashi, Chairman
Syed Athar Hussain, Vice Chairman
Richard Hubbard, Secretary/ Treasurer
Bill Lempesis, Executive Director
Joan White, Membership Services Manager

An international nonprofit corporation standards body for computer graphics.

7011 Wheatland Rural Electric Association
P. O. Box 1209
Wheatland, WY 82201

307-322-2125
800-344-3351
FAX 307-322-5340
Home Page: www.wheatlandrea.com
Social Media: *Facebook*

Robert Brockman, President
Bill Teter, Vice-President
Britt Wilson, Secretary/ Treasurer
Sandra Hranchak, Director
Jack Finnerty, Director

Home power usage calculations, product and new service information,and youth scholarships.
Founded in 1936

Newsletters

7012 AEA Monthly News
American Electronics Association
5201 Great America Parkway
Santa Clara, CA 95054

408-987-4200
800-284-4232
FAX 408-987-4298
Home Page: www.aeanet.org

John V Harker, Chairman
William T Archey, President/CEO
Samuel J Block, VP/Controller
Tim Bennett, COO/EVP

AEA Advancing the Business of Technology, Access to Investors, State, Federal & International Lobbying, Insurance Services, Government Procurement, Business Networking, Foreign Market Access, Select Business Services, Executive Education.
Frequency: Monthly

7013 AEA by the Bay
American Electronics Association
5201 Great America Parkway
Santa Clara, CA 95054

408-987-4200
800-284-4232
FAX 408-987-4298
Home Page: www.aeanet.org

John V Harker, Chairman
William T Archey, President/CEO
Samuel J Block, VP/Controller
Tim Bennett, COO/EVP

Newsletter for the AEA Bay Area Council.
Frequency: Monthly

7014 AEA's Californica Monday Morning Report

American Electronics Association
5201 Great America Parkway
Santa Clara, CA 95054

408-987-4200
800-284-4232
FAX 408-987-4298
Home Page: www.aeanet.org

John V Harker, Chairman
William T Archey, President/CEO
Samuel J Block, VP/Controller
Tim Bennett, COO/EVP

A weekly report of what is going on in Californica policy relating to the high-tech industry, and how to change it.
Frequency: Weekly

7015 American Electronics Association Impact

American Electronics Association
5201 Great America Parkway
Santa Clara, CA 95054-1122

408-987-4200
FAX 408-970-8565
Home Page: www.aeanet.org

William Archey, President

Representing the electronics software and information technology industries. Covers business and management issues for electronics executives.
Frequency: Monthly
Circulation: 25000
Founded in 1945

7016 Consumer Electronic and Appliance News

Kasmar Publications
41905 Boardwalk
Suite L
Palm Desert, CA 92221

800-253-9992
800-253-9992
FAX 760-723-2876
Home Page: www.kasmarpub.com

Donald Martin, Editor

Home entertainment, consumer electronics and major appliances.
28 Pages
Founded in 1970

7017 Currents

Electrical Apparatus Service Association
1331 Baur Boulevard
Saint Louis, MO 63132-1903

314-993-2220
FAX 314-993-1269
E-Mail: easainfo@easa.com
Home Page: www.easa.com
Social Media: *Facebook, Twitter, LinkedIn*

Linda J Raynes, President/CEO
Dale Shuter, Meetings/Expositions Manager

EASA is a trade association recognized internationally as the leader in the electrical and mechanical apparatus sales, service and repair industry.
Frequency: Monthly
Circulation: 2000+
Founded in 1933

7018 Electronic Advertising Marketplace Report

Simba Information
PO Box 4234
Stamford, CT 06907-0234

203-258-8193
FAX 203-358-5825

E-Mail: simbainfo@simbanet.com
Home Page: www.simbanet.com

Linda Kopp, Editor
Donna Devall, Marketing Director
Joyce Brigish, Circulation Manager

Provides news, analysis and opinion for the emerging business of electronic advertising and shopping and commerce. Discover how publishers, telephone companies, distributors, and retailers are now using information technologies to build the information infrastructure that will reach new customers and match buyers with sellers. Covers electronic marketing, new electronic classified and transactional services, the role of the Internet, electronic yellow pages, etc.
Cost: $499.00
Frequency: BiWeekly

7019 Electronic Education Report

Simba Information
PO Box 4234
Stamford, CT 06907-0234

203-258-8193
FAX 203-358-5825
E-Mail: simbainfo@simbanet.com
Home Page: www.simbanet.com

Megan St. John, Manager
Patrick Quinn, Editor

Provides information on the multi-billion dollar market for electronic instructional materials. Includes company rankings, financial profiles, sales and distrbution trends, funding and adoptions, enrollment and demographics, trademark and copyright issues, strategic alliances and mergers.
Cost: $445.00
Frequency: BiWeekly

7020 Electronic Imaging Report

Phillips Publishing
7811 Montrose Road
Potomac, MD 20854

301-340-2100
E-Mail: feedback@healthydirections.com
Home Page: www.healthydirections.com

Written for top-level executives interested in learning how imaging technology can streamline their operations, cut their overhead costs and boost their competitiveness. Accepts advertising.
Cost: $397.00
9 Pages
Frequency: BiWeekly

7021 Electronic Information Report

Simba Information
PO Box 4234
Stamford, CT 06907-234

203-258-8193
FAX 203-358-5825
E-Mail: simbainfo@simbanet.com
Home Page: www.simbanet.com

Linda Kopp, Editor
Charlie Friscia, Marketing Director

The original information industry newsletter. Every week, this report monitors, analyzes, and reports on trends and developments in information services. It covers new storage and distribution media, databases, electronic publishing, value-added fax, online, multimedia and voice services. Readers will receive up-to-the-minute news written from a product, financial and marketing viewpoint.
Cost: $685.00
Frequency: 46 Issues Per Y
Founded in 1989

7022 Electronic Materials Technology News

Business Communications Company

25 Van Zant Street
Suite 13
Norwalk, CT 06855-1713

203-853-4266
FAX 203-853-0348
E-Mail: sales@bccresearch.com
Home Page: www.bccresearch.com

Louis Naturman, President
Marc Favrean, Editor
Alan Hall, Editorial Director
Thomas Abraham, VP Research
Marc Favreau, VP Development

Reports on electronic materials and processes, patents, companies involved, trends and business opportunities.
Cost: $35.00
Founded in 1971

7023 Electronics Manufacturing Engineering

Society of Manufacturing Engineers
1 SME Drive
PO Box 930
Dearborn, MI 48128

313-425-3000
800-733-4763
FAX 313-425-3400
E-Mail: service@sme.org
Home Page: www.sme.org

Mark Tomlinson, Executive Director/General Manager
Greg Sheremet, Publisher
Bob Harris, Director Finance

Covers various aspects of electronics manufacturing.
Cost: $60.00
8 Pages
Frequency: Quarterly
Circulation: 2147
Mailing list available for rent: 18190 names at $95 per M
Printed in 2 colors on matte stock

7024 IEEE All-Society Periodicals Package(ASPP)

Power Electronics Society
799 N Beverly Glen
Los Angeles, CA 90077

310-446-8280
FAX 310-446-8390
E-Mail: bob.myers@ieee.org
Home Page: www.pels.org

Jerry Hudgins, President
Robert Myers, Executive Director
Steven Leeb, Treasurer
Ronald Harley, VP Operations

Provides access to our core collection of engineering, electronics, and computer science periodicals.

7025 ISCET Update

Int'l Society of Certified Electronics Technicians
3608 Pershing Ave
Fort Worth, TX 76107-4527

817-921-9101
800-946-0201
FAX 817-921-3741
E-Mail: info@iscet.org
Home Page: www.iset.org

Ed Clingman, Administrator
Sheila Fred, Editor
Brian Gibbson, Circulation Manager

News and information for the electronics community.
Frequency: Monthly
Circulation: 1300

7026 Integrated Circuit Manufacturing Synopsis
Semiconductor Equipment & Materials
International
3081 Zanker Road
San Jose, CA 95134

408-943-6900
FAX 408-428-9600
E-Mail: semihq@semi.org
Home Page: www.semi.org

Maggie Hershey, Manager
Anne Miller, Author
Victoria Hadfield, Executive VP/President, N America

An illustrated booklet that provides an excellent introduction to the semiconductor industry and makes a great handout for new employee orientation or as a resource for industry suppliers. It is easy to understand and free of technical terminology.
Cost: $15.75
35 Pages

7027 Manufacturing Market Insider
JBT Communications
PO Box 782
Needham Heights, MA 02494-0006

781-444-2154
FAX 781-455-8409
Home Page: www.mtgmkt.com

John B Tuck, Publisher/Editor
Ann Connors, Circulation Manager

Specializes in contract manufacturing of electronics. Includes acquisitions, expansions, financial results and contract awards announced by contract manufacturers of electronics.
Cost: $420.00
8 Pages
Frequency: Monthly
ISSN: 1072-8651
Founded in 1991
Printed in one color on matte stock

7028 Military & Aerospace Electronics
PennWell Publishing Company
98 Spit Brook Rd
Suite L1-1
Nashua, NH 03062-5737

603-891-0123
FAX 603-891-9294
E-Mail: ATD@PennWell.com
Home Page: www.pennwell.com

Christine Shaw, VP
Tobias Naegele, Editor

Engineering newspaper written exclusively for military-aeronautical electronic systems designers, buyers and project managers.
Cost: $10.00
Frequency: Monthly
Circulation: 48,100
Founded in 1910

7029 Optics & Photonics News (OPN)
Optical Society of America
2010 Massachusetts Ave Nw
Washington, DC 20036-1023

202-223-8130
FAX 202-223-1096
E-Mail: info@osa.org
Home Page: www.osa.org

Elizabeth Rogan, Executive Director

Optics & Photonics/OPN is a monthly magazine that keeps members up to date on technical innovations, industry news, OSA activities and much more. OPN promotes the generation application, archiving and worldwide dissemination of knowledge in optics and photonics.
Frequency: Monthly
Circulation: 17000
Mailing list available for rent

7030 SITE
American Electronics Association
5201 Great America Parkway
Santa Clara, CA 95054

408-987-4200
800-284-4232
FAX 408-987-4298
Home Page: www.aeanet.org

John V Harker, Chairman
William T Archey, President/CEO
Samuel J Block, VP/Controller
Tim Bennett, COO/EVP

Brings High-Tech HR professionals important information about compensation and benefits, employment law, relevant legislation, education and training.
Frequency: Bi-Monthly

7031 SouthWest Technology Report
Communications
PO Box 23899
Tempe, AZ 85285-3899

480-345-1118
FAX 480-345-1119

Walter J Schuch, Publisher

Focused on business and technology news related to high tech and electronics companies and organizations based in the Southwestern United States.
Cost: $69.00
8 Pages
Frequency: Monthly
Printed in one color on matte stock

7032 Technician Association News
Electronic Technicians Association
International
5 Depot St
Greencastle, IN 46135-8024

765-653-8262
800-288-3824
FAX 765-653-4287
E-Mail: eta@eta-i.org
Home Page: www.eta-i.org

Dick Glass, President
Brianna Pinson, Office Manager

A professional and trade journal servicing electronic technicians nationwide. Lists new certified electronics technicians, technical repair services, upcoming seminars and satellite training sessions.
Frequency: Monthly
ISSN: 1092-9592
Founded in 1978
Printed in 2 colors

7033 Technology News Today
American Electronics Association
5201 Great America Parkway
Santa Clara, CA 95054

408-987-4200
800-284-4232
FAX 408-987-4298
Home Page: www.aeanet.org

John V Harker, Chairman
William T Archey, President/CEO
Samuel J Block, VP/Controller
Tim Bennett, COO/EVP
Melissa La vigna, Contact

Aims to benefit investors with exclusive information on high-tech industry trends available only through AEA's extensive research, legislative monitoring and high-leveled networking capabilities.
Frequency: Quarterly

7034 Twice: This Week in Consumer Electronics
Reed Business Information

360 Park Ave S
15th Floor
New York, NY 10010-1737

646-746-6400
800-826-6270
FAX 646-756-7583
E-Mail: mgrand@reedbusiness.com
Home Page: www.reedbusiness.com

John Poulin, CEO
Jeff Greisch, Editor/CEO/President
Stephen F Smith, Editor-in-Chief
James Reed, Owner
Patricia Kennedy, Production Manager

Features include industry news, statistics, financial reports and new product trends and announcements.
Cost: $94.90
Frequency: Monthly
Circulation: 41000

Magazines & Journals

7035 Advancing Microelectronics
ISHM-Microelectronics Society
611 2nd street NE
Washington Dc, DC 20002

202-548-4001
888-464-6277
FAX 202-548-6115
E-Mail: imaps@imaps.org
Home Page: www.imaps.org

For the Microelectronics Society.
Circulation: 4010

7036 Applied Microwave & Wireless
Noble Publishing Corporation
1334 Meridian Rd
Thomasville, GA 31792

229-377-0587
FAX 229-377-0589
E-Mail: randy@noblepub.com
Home Page: www.noblepub.com

Joseph White, Publisher
Randy W Rhea, CEO

Edited for the RF and microwave professional.
Cost: $30.00
Frequency: Monthly
Circulation: 26287
ISSN: 1075-0207
Founded in 1994

7037 AudioXpress
Audio Amateur Publications
PO Box 876
Peterborough, NH 03458

603-924-9464
888-924-9465
FAX 603-924-9467
E-Mail: editorial@audioxpress.com
Home Page: www.audioxpress.com

Edward Dell, Publisher

Focuses on the developments in sound production and enhancements in audio equipment and contains information on the construction of new and modification of existing audio equipment. Projects include schematics, parts lists and instructions necessary for completion aimed at electronic engineers and hobbyists.
Cost: $34.95
72 Pages
Frequency: Monthly
Circulation: 11000
ISSN: 1548-6028
Founded in 2001
Printed in 4 colors on glossy stock

7038 Avionics News Magazine
Aircraft Electronics Association

3570 Ne Ralph Powell Rd
Lees Summit, MO 64064-2360

816-347-8400
FAX 816-478-3100
E-Mail: info@aea.net
Home Page: www.aea.net

Paula Derks, President
Tracy Lykins, Editor
Linda Adams, Managing Editor

This publication is the voice of the general aviation electronics industry. It is recognized as one of the leading publications for the latest information in avionics technology. Subscriptions are complimentary within North America, however, subscribers must be employed within the aviation industry to receive the magazine.
Cost: $132.00
Frequency: Monthly
Mailing list available for rent

7039 Channel Magazine
Semiconductor Equipment & Materials International
3081 Zanker Road
San Jose, CA 95134-4080

408-943-6900
FAX 408-428-9600
E-Mail: semihq@semi.org
Home Page: www.semi.org

Karen Savala, Publisher
Steve Buehler, Editor

A forum for equipment and material suppliers committed to the environment, health and safety as a Global Care member.
Founded in 1970

7040 Circuits Assembly
Circuit Assembly
18 Thomas Street
Irvine, CA 92618-2777

949-855-7887
FAX 949-855-4298
E-Mail: sales@circuitassembly.com
Home Page: www.circuitassembly.com

Laura Brown Sims, Associate Publisher

Devoted to the global electronics assembly industry.
Frequency: Monthly

7041 CleanRooms Magazine
PennWell Publishing Company
98 Spit Brook Rd
Nashua, NH 03062-5737

603-891-0123
800-225-0556
FAX 603-891-9294
E-Mail: jhaystead@pennwell.com
Home Page: www.pennwell.com

Christine Shaw, VP
Angela Godwin, Managing Editor
Heidi Barns, Circulation Manager
Lisa Bergevin, Marketing
James Enos, Publisher

Serves the contamination control and ultrapure materials and process industries. Written for readers in the microelectronics, pharmaceutical, biotech, health care, food processing and other user industries. Provides technology and business news and new product listings.
Frequency: Monthly
Circulation: 35031
Founded in 1987

7042 CommVerge
Reed Business Information

2000 Clearwater Dr
Oak Brook, IL 60523-8809

630-574-0825
FAX 630-288-8781
Home Page: www.reedbusiness.com

Jeff Greisch, President

The world leading publisher and information provider. Provides a range of communication and information channels, magazines, exhibitions, directories, online media, marketing services across five continents. Prestige brands in leading positions in key business sectors we deliver unrivalled access to business professionals across a diverse range of industries.

7043 Computer Business Review
ComputerWire
150 Post Street
#520
San Francisco, CA 94108-4707

415-274-8290
FAX 415-274-8281
E-Mail: cbred@computerwire.com
Home Page: www.computerwire.com/cbr

Tim Langford, Publisher

Company profiles, computer market coverage and technology trends and news for investors and professionals in the computer, communications and microelectronics industries.
Cost: $195.00
Frequency: Monthly
Circulation: 23M

7044 Computer-Aided Engineering
Penton Media
1300 E 9th St
Cleveland, OH 44114-1503

216-696-7000
FAX 216-696-6662
E-Mail: caenetmaster@penton.com
Home Page: www.penton.com

Jane Cooper, Marketing

Applications, news, trends and products for CAD/CAM technology as applied in manufacturing, electronics, architectural and construction industries.
Cost: $50.00
Frequency: Monthly
Circulation: 56,062

7045 Consumer Electronics Vision
Consumer Electronics Association (CEA)
1919 S Eads Street
Arlington, VA 22202

703-907-7600
866-858-1555
FAX 703-907-7675
E-Mail: cea@ce.org
Home Page: www.ce.org

Cindy Stevens, Publications Director
Jason Oxman, VP Communications
Jenny Pareti, Public Policy Director
Gary Shapiro, President/CEO
Pat Lavelle, Chairman

Provides the latest information on industry standards, public policy, market research, CEA events and training opportunities. Is the premier source of information for the top management of more than 1,000 US corporations that design, develop, manufacture and distribute audio, video, mobile electronics, wireless and landline communications, IT, multimedia, accessory products and related services sold through consumer channels.
Frequency: Monthly
Circulation: 1000
Founded in 1844

7046 Control Solutions
PennWell Publishing Company

1421 S Sheridan Rd
Tulsa, OK 74112-6619

918-831-9421
800-331-4463
FAX 918-831-9476
E-Mail: headquarters@pennwell.com
Home Page: www.pennwell.com

Robert Biolchini, President
Ron Kuhfeld, Editor-in-Chief
Frequency: Monthly
Founded in 1910

7047 Dealerscope
North American Publishing Company
1500 Spring Garden St
Suite 1200
Philadelphia, PA 19130-4094

215-238-5300
800-627-2689
FAX 215-238-5342
E-Mail: webmaster@napco.com
Home Page: www.napco.com

Ned S Borowsky, CEO
Rhoda Dixon, Circulation Manager
Eric Schwartz, President/Publishing Dir

Dedicated to delivering peer-based knowledge and experience, Dealerscope is the ultimate vehicle for presenting product and service solutions to the consumer.
Frequency: Monthly
Founded in 1958

7048 ECN Magazine
Reed Business Information
360 Park Ave S
4th Floor
New York, NY 10010-1737

646-746-6400
FAX 646-756-7583
E-Mail: subsmail@reedbusiness.com
Home Page: www.reedbusiness.com

John Poulin, CEO
James Reed, Owner

Provides product solutions for designed engineers in the electronics industry.
Circulation: 117923
Founded in 1957

7049 EDN Asia
Reed Business Information
45 E 85th St
4th Floor
New York, NY 10028-0957

212-772-8300
FAX 630-288-8686
E-Mail: mike.pan@rbi-asia.com
Home Page: www.edn.com/

Lawrence S Reed
Mike Pan, Editor
Robin Peter Lange, Managing Editor
Raymond Wong, Publishing Director
Chen Wai Chun, Publisher

A source for all the design features, technology trends, design ideas, hands-on applications and product updates.
Frequency: Monthly
Circulation: 30000
Founded in 1990

7050 EDN China
Reed Business Information
45 E 85th St
4th Floor
New York, NY 10028-0957

212-772-8300
FAX 630-288-8686
E-Mail: john.dodge@reedbusiness.com
Home Page: www.edninteractive.com

Lawrence S Reed
William Zhang, Publisher Director

John Mu, Executive Editor
Stephen D. Moylan, President

A source for design, development, & applications information foe electronics engineers & managers.
Frequency: Monthly
Circulation: 30018
Founded in 1946

7051 EDN Europe
Reed Business Information
45 E 85th St
4th Floor
New York, NY 10028-0957

212-772-8300
FAX 630-288-8686
E-Mail: gprophet@reedbusiness.com
Home Page: www.edninteractive.com

Lawrence S Reed
Martin Savery, Publisher
Graham Prophet, Editor

A focused product specific to, and unique in, its own region, that draws on a unique international network of editorial expertise. EDN serves design engineers, providing exactly the information they need to conceive and create tomorrow's electronic products.
Circulation: 35,024

7052 EE Product News
Penton Media
1300 E 9th St
Cleveland, OH 44114-1503

216-696-7000
FAX 216-696-6662
E-Mail: information@penton.com
Home Page: www.penton.com

Jane Cooper, Marketing
David B. Nussbaum, CEO

Source of information in new products necessary to successfully design, assemble and test prototypes of commerical, industrial, military and aerospace electronic products.
Frequency: Monthly
Circulation: 111968
Founded in 1892

7053 EE: Evaluation Engineering
Nelson Publishing
2500 Tamiami Trl N
Nokomis, FL 34275-3476

941-966-9521
800-226-6113
FAX 941-966-2590
E-Mail: pmilo@evaluationengineering.com
Home Page: www.healthmgttech.com

A Verner Nelson, Owner
Michael Hughes, Sales

Magazine devoted exclusively to companies that test, evaluate, design and manufacture electronic products and equipment.
Cost: $43.00
84 Pages
Frequency: Monthly
Founded in 1962
Mailing list available for rent: 65,000 names
Printed in 4 colors on glossy stock

7054 Electromagnetic News Report
Seven Mountains Scientific
913 Tressler Street
PO Box 650
Boalsburg, PA 16827

814-466-6559
FAX 814-466-2777
E-Mail: enr@7ms.com
Home Page: www.7ms.com

Josephine Chesworth, Managing Editor
E Thomas Chesworth, Technical Editor
Patrick D. Elliott, Production Manager

Offers industry news and technical articles of interest to readers as well as a calendar of events, product news and EMI publications.
Cost: $90.00
40 Pages
Circulation: 1000
ISSN: 0270-4935
Founded in 1972
Printed in 4 colors on matte stock

7055 Electronic Business
Reed Business Information
5525 Sierra Rd
Building N
San Jose, CA 95132-3421

408-926-6340
FAX 408-345-4400
E-Mail: subsmail@reedbusiness.com
Home Page: www.reedbusiness.com

Donald Reed, Owner
Kathleen Doler, Editor-in-Chief
James A Casella, CEO
Shahrokh Rad, Owner
Salina Le Bris, Corporate Communications/PR
Frequency: Monthly
Circulation: 65732
Founded in 1975

7056 Electronic Components
Global Sources
7341 Washington Avenue
Suite C
Whittier, CA 90602

562-945-4612
FAX 562-945-4192
E-Mail: mktgserv@globalsources.com
Home Page: www.globalsources.com

Anna Maria Anguiano, Account Manager
Mark Sanderson, Publisher
Dan Katz, Managing Director
Cost: $75.00
Frequency: Monthly
Founded in 1971

7057 Electronic Design
Penton Media
1300 E 9th St
Cleveland, OH 44114-1503

216-696-7000
FAX 216-696-6662
E-Mail: information@penton.com
Home Page: www.penton.com

Jane Cooper, Marketing
Mark David, Editor in Chief
Janet Connors, Marketing

Celebrating 50 years of innovation, this authoritative source provides leading-edge technical information to electronic and engineering managers around the world.
Frequency: Monthly
Circulation: 145000
Founded in 1892

7058 Electronic Packaging & Production
Reed Business Information
1350 E Touhy Avenue
Des Plaines, IL 60018

630-320-7000
FAX 630-288-8686
E-Mail: epp@cahners.com
Home Page: www.cahners.com

Vicky Steen, Publisher
Michael Sweeney, Editorial Director

Edited for engineers and managers who are involved in packaging designed, printed circuit board fabrication and assembly, and production testing of electronic circuits, systems, products and equipment.

7059 Electronic Products
Hearst Business Communications

645 Stewart Ave
Garden City, NY 11530-4769

516-227-1300
FAX 516-227-1342
E-Mail: ralphr@electronicproducts.com
Home Page: www.elecprod2.com

Todd Christenson, Publisher
Gail Meyer, Production Manager
R Pell, Editor-in-Chief

News about developments in electronic components and equipment.
Frequency: Monthly
Circulation: 123767
Founded in 1958
Mailing list available for rent: 123767 names
Printed in 4 colors on glossy stock

7060 Electronic Products Magazine

Home Page: www.electronicproducts.com

Electronic products and product technology news from an engineering standpoint.

7061 Electronics Manufacturing Engineering
Society of Manufacturing Engineers
1 SME Drive
PO Box 930
Dearborn, MI 48128

313-425-3000
800-733-4763
FAX 313-425-3400
E-Mail: service@sme.org
Home Page: www.sme.org

Mark Tomlinson, Executive Director/General Manager
Greg Sheremet, Publisher
Bob Harris, Director Finance

For manufacturing engineers and managers involved with electronics manufacturing.
Circulation: 3,300

7062 High Density Interconnect
CMP Media
600 Community Drive
Manhasset, NY 11030

516-562-5000
FAX 415-947-6090
Home Page: www.cmp.com

7063 High Tech News
Electronic Technicians Association International
5 Depot St
Greencastle, IN 46135-8024

765-653-8262
800-288-3824
FAX 765-653-4287
E-Mail: eta@eta-i.org
Home Page: www.eta-i.org
Social Media: *Facebook, Twitter, LinkedIn*

Teresa Maher, CSS, President
Chrissy Baker, Marketing Coordinator
Richard Glass, CETsr, CEO Emeritus

Exclusive bi-monthly publication of ETA International, and a subscription is included with each individual membership. Each issue features information on the changing electronics industry: specialty techniques & technology, trends, qualification opportunities and educational advice.
4500 Members
Frequency: Bi-Monthly
Circulation: 10000
Founded in 1978

7064 IEEE Control Systems Magazine
IEEE Control Systems Society (CSS)

445 Hoes Lane
PO Box 1331
Piscataway, NJ 08854-1331

732-981-0060
FAX 732-981-1721
E-Mail: society-info@ieee.org
Home Page: www.ieee.org

Dennis S Bernstein, Editor
Susan Schneiderman, Business Development
Manager

Focuses on applications of technical knowledge
and concentrates on industrial implementations,
design tools, technology review, control education and applied research. Geared towards readers with many different responsibilities
including applied research, device design,
product development and design including
software and semiconductor components.
Cost: $210.00
Founded in 1973
Mailing list available for rent

**7065 Journal of Microelectronics &
Electronic Packaging**
International Microelectronics & Electronic
Pack.
611 2nd Street NE
Washington, DC 20002

202-548-4001
888-464-6277
FAX 202-548-6115
E-Mail: imaps@imaps.org
Home Page: www.imaps.org

Fred D Barlow III PhD, Editor-in-Chief

**7066 Journal of Microelectronics and
Electronic Packaging**
International Microelectronics & Electronics
611 2nd Street NE
Washington, DC 20002

202-548-4001
888-464-6277
FAX 202-548-6115
E-Mail: impas@imaps.org
Home Page: www.imaps.org

Michael O'Donoghue, Executive Director
Rick Mohn, Operations Manager
Brian Schieman, Director Information
Technology
Ann Bell, Manager Marketing/Communications

Dedicated to publishing peer-reviewed papers
in microelectronics, multichip module technologies, electronic packaging, electronic materials, surface mount and other related
technologies, interconnections, RF and micro-
waves, wireless communications, manufacturing, design, test, and reliability.
Cost: $35.00

**7067 Journal of Microwave Power and
Electromagnetic Energy**
International Microwave Power Institute
PO Box 1140
Mechanicsville, VA 23111-5007

804-559-6667
FAX 804-559-4087
E-Mail: info@impi.org
Home Page: www.impi.org
Social Media: *Facebook, Twitter*

Molly Poisant, Executive Director

The quarterly, technical journal of the Institute
published by the Industrial, Scientific, Medical
and Instrumentation (ISMI) section. Designed
for the information needs of professionals specializing in the research and design of industrial and bio-medical applications, the Journal
exemplifies the highest standards of scientific
and technical information on the theory and ap-

plication of electromagnetic power.
Cost: $250.00
Frequency: Quarterly

7068 Laser Focus World
PennWell Publishing Company
98 Spit Brook Rd
Nashua, NH 03062-5737

603-891-0123
FAX 603-891-9294
E-Mail: allisono@pennwell.com
Home Page: www.pennwell.com

Christine Shaw, Publisher
Carol Settino, Managing Editor

The world of optoelectronics.
Cost: $150.00
173 Pages
Frequency: Monthly
Circulation: 70004
Founded in 1965
Printed in 4 colors on glossy stock

**7069 Modeling Power Devices and Model
Validation**
Power Sources Manufacturers Association
PO Box 418
Mendham, NJ 07945-0418

973-543-9660
FAX 973-543-6207
E-Mail: power@psma.com
Home Page: www.psma.com

Dusty Becker, Chairman
Carl Blake, President
Jim Marinos, VP

This report consists of two parts, one devoted
to modeling, and the other, model validation.
The first article in the report reviews commonly used device models used in circuit simulations, and applies these to simulation
designed power converters and rectifiers. The
second article establishes processes by which
the features and accuracy of a model are determined by simulating the results of test circuits
containing power devices and comparing these
results with the results of actual measurements
Cost: $20.00
155 Members
Founded in 1985

7070 Optics Letters
Optical Society of America
2010 Massachusetts Ave Nw
Washington, DC 20036-1023

202-223-8130
FAX 202-223-1096
E-Mail: info@osa.org
Home Page: www.osa.org

Elizabeth Rogan, Executive Director

Offers rapid dissemination of new results in all
areas of optics with short, original, peer-reviewed communications. Optics Letters covers
the latest research in optical science, including
atmospheric optics, quantum electronics, Fou-
rier optics, integrated optics, and fiber optics.
Frequency: 24 issues per year
ISSN: 0146-9592

**7071 Power Conversion & Intelligent
Motion**
Primedia
Po Box 12901
Shawnee Mission, KS 66282-2901

913-341-1300
FAX 913-514-6895
Home Page: www.penton.com

Eric Jacobson, Senior VP
Sam Davis, Editor

Directed to engineers, designers and manufacturers of power electronic and electronic motion control components, subsystems and

systems. Feature articles interpret trends and
innovation in these subjects.
Circulation: 31,113

7072 Power Electronics Technology
Penton Media, Inc
249 W 17th Street
New York, NY 10011

212-204-4200
E-Mail: bill.baumann@penton.com
Home Page: www.powerelectronics.com

Bill Baumann, Group Publisher
Sam Davis, Editor-in-Chief

Formerly PCIM Power Electronic Systems, de-
livers timely information to professionals in the
power electronic industry.
Frequency: Monthly
Circulation: 36,000
Founded in 1975

7073 Printed Circuit Fabrication
CMP Media
600 Community Drive
Manhasset, NY 11030

516-562-5000
FAX 415-947-6090

7074 ProService
Int'l Society of Certified Electronics
Technicians
3608 Pershing Ave
Fort Worth, TX 76107-4527

817-921-9101
800-946-0201
FAX 817-921-3741
E-Mail: info@iscet.org
Home Page: www.iset.org

Ed Clingman, Administrator
Shiela Fredrickson, Publisher

A bi-monthly magazine published by the International Society of Certified Electronics Technicians.
24 Pages
Founded in 1965

7075 ProService Magazine
National Electronics Service Dealers
Association
3608 Pershing Ave
Fort Worth, TX 76107-4527

817-921-9061
800-797-9197
FAX 817-921-3741
E-Mail: webmaster@nesda.com
Home Page: www.nesda.com

Brian Gibson, President
Don Cressin, VP
Mack Blakely, Executive Director
Fred Paradis, CSM, Treasurer
Wayne Markman, Secretary

For members of NESDA/ISCET, and a printed
magazine is mailed to the membership address
on file in April and August.
Frequency: Bi-Monthly

7076 RTOHQ: The Magazine
Association of Progressive Rental
Merchandise
1540 Robinhood Trail
Austin, TX 78703-2624

512-794-0095
800-204-APRO
FAX 512-794-0097

E-Mail: cferguson@rtohq.org
Home Page: www.rtohq.org

Bill Keese, Executive Director
John C Cleek, President
Bill Kelly, Secretary
Frequency: Bi-Monthly
Circulation: 11000

7077 Representor Magazine
Electronics Representatives Association
300 W Adams St
Suite 617
Chicago, IL 60606-5109

312-527-3050
800-776-7377
FAX 312-527-3783
E-Mail: info@era.org
Home Page: www.era.org

Tom Shanahan, Executive VP
Bob Walsh, President

Devoted to fulfilling the management, informational, educational and communications needs of representatives and manufacturers in the electronics industry.
Cost: $15.00
450 Members
Frequency: Quarterly
Founded in 1935

7078 Review of the Electronic and Industrial Distribution Industries
National Electronic Distributors Association
1111 Alderman Dr
Suite 400
Alpharetta, GA 30005-4175

678-393-9990
FAX 678-393-9998
E-Mail: admin@nedassoc.org
Home Page: www.nedassoc.org

Robin B Gray Jr, Executive VP
Debbie Conyers, Director Marketing
Barney Martin, VP Industry Practices

Contains academic articles on topics pertinent to our members' business. Leading electronic and industrial distribution academicians provides the content. Offers insightful articles aimed at improving industry practices. $12.00 per volume or $20.00 for an annual subscription.
Cost: $20.00
Frequency: Bi-Annually

7079 SIGNAL Magazine
Armed Forces Communications and
Electronics Assn
4400 Fair Lakes Ct
Fairfax, VA 22033-3899

703-631-1397
800-336-4583
FAX 703-631-4693
Home Page: www.afcea.org

Kent Schneider, President/CEO
Becky Nolan, Executive VP
John A Dubia, Executive VP

Is a international news magazine serving the critical information needs of government, military and industry professionals active in the fields of command, control, communications, computers, intelligence, surveillance and reconnaissance (C4ISR); information security; research and development; electronics; and homeland security.
Frequency: Monthly

7080 Sensors Magazine
Questex Media
275 Grove St
Suite 2-130
Auburndale, MA 02466-2275

617-219-8300
888-552-4346

FAX 617-219-8310
E-Mail: jmcmahon@questex.com
Home Page: www.questex.com

Kerry C Gumas, CEO
Stephanie Henkel, Executive Editor

Source among design and production engineers of information on sensor technologies and products, and topic integral to sensor-based systems and applications. Provides practical and in-depth yet accessible information on sensor operation, design, application, and implementation within systems. Covers the effective use of state-of-the-art resources and tools that enable readers to get the maximum benefit from their use of sensors.
Cost: $99.00
Frequency: Monthly
Circulation: 75000
Founded in 1984

7081 Tech Briefs
Associated Business Publications
International
1466 Broadway
Suite. 910
New York, NY 10036-7309

212-490-3999
FAX 212-986-7864
E-Mail: alfredo@abpi.net
Home Page: www.techbriefs.com

Dominic Mucchetti, CEO
Hugh Dowling, Circualtion Manager
Linda Bell, Chief Editor

Serves design engineers, managers and scientists in the industries of electronics, industrial equipment, computers, communications, bio-medical, transportation/automotive, power and energy, materials, chemicals and many more related fields.
Cost: $75.00
Frequency: Monthly
Founded in 1958

7082 Test & Measurement World
Reed Business Information
275 Washington St
Suite 275
Newton, MA 02458-1611

617-964-3030
FAX 617-558-4470
E-Mail: tmswales@cahners.com
Home Page: www.designnews.com

Rick Nelson, Chief Editor
Deborah M Sargent, Managing Editor
Russ Pratt, Publisher

The magazine on test, measurement and inspection in the electronics industry
Frequency: Monthly
Circulation: 65000
Founded in 1981
Mailing list available for rent

7083 The Minerals, Metals & Materials Society/ Journal of Electronic Materials
Minerals, Metals & Materials Society
184 Thorn Hill Road
Warrendale, PA 15086-7528

724-776-9000
800-759-4867
FAX 724-776-3770
Home Page: www.tms.org

Suzanne Mohney, Editor-In-Chief

Reports on the science and technology of electronic materials, while examining new applications for semiconductors, magnetic alloys, insulators, optical and display materials.
Cost: $131.00
11000 Members
Frequency: Monthly
Circulation: 1400

ISSN: 0361-5235
Founded in 1957
Printed in 2 colors on glossy stock

7084 Wideband
Advanstar Communications
641 Lexington Ave
8th Floor
New York, NY 10022-4503

212-951-6600
FAX 212-951-6793
E-Mail: info@advanstar.com
Home Page: www.advanstar.com

Joseph Loggia, CEO

Covers accessories, equipment, services, products, and an anlysis of major market trends, industry news, statistics, new products, and personnel changes are featured in every issue.
Frequency: SemiMonthly
Circulation: 26,000

Trade Shows

7085 AEA Annual Convention & Trade Show
Aircraft Electronics Association
4217 S Hocker
Independence, MO 64055

816-373-6565
FAX 816-478-3100
E-Mail: info@aea.net
Home Page: www.aea.net

Paula Derks, President
Debra McFarland, VP
Tracy Lykins, Director Communications
Mark Gibson, Administration/Meeting
Management

Annual show of 131 exhibitors of industry related equipment and supplies.
1500 Attendees
Frequency: Annual
Founded in 1957

7086 AFCEA Sponsored Conferences/Symposia
Armed Forces Communications and
Electronics Assn
4400 Fair Lakes Court
Fairfax, VA 22033-3899

703-631-6100
800-336-4583
FAX 703-631-6405
Home Page: www.afcea.org

Kent Schneider, President/CEO
Becky Nolan, Executive VP
John A Dubia, Executive VP

Offers problem solving and networking opportunities through exhibits, technical panels, and featured speakers. Decision-makers from around the world attend AFCEA conferences for hands-on demonstrations, question-and-answer sessions and system solutions.

7087 AFCEA TechNet Asia-Pacific
Armed Forces Communications and
Electronics Assn
4400 Fair Lakes Court
Fairfax, VA 22033-3899

703-631-6200
800-654-4220
FAX 703-654-6931
E-Mail: technet@jspargo.com
Home Page: www.afcea.org

Paul doCarmo, Assistant Director/Exhibit Sales
Connie Shaw, Exhibit Sales Account Manager

Military, government and industry communications and electronics professionals gather to see

exhibits of communications and electronics equipment, supplies and services. Seminar, conference, dinner and luncheon. Co-sponsored by AFCEA International and AFCEA Hawaii.
2000 Attendees
Frequency: Nov 7-9
Founded in 1985

7088 AFCEA TechNet International
Armed Forces Communications and Electronics Assn
4400 Fair Lakes Court
Fairfax, VA 22033-3899

703-631-6200
800-564-4220
FAX 703-654-6931
E-Mail: technetinternational@jspargo.com
Home Page: www.afcea.org

Paul doCarmo, Sales Manager
Connie Shaw, Sales Manager

This event draws commanders and staff from every branch of the military, including warfighting integration organizations charged with the most critical responsibilities of synthesizing military power on land, at sea, and in the air.
7500 Attendees
Frequency: June

7089 AFCEA/USNI West Conference & Exposition
Armed Forces Communications and Electronics Assn
4400 Fair Lakes Court
Fairfax, VA 22033

703-631-6200
800-564-4220
FAX 703-654-6931
E-Mail: west@jspargo.org
Home Page: www.afcea.org

Paul doCarmo, Assistant Direct/Exhibit Sales
Connie Shaw, Exhibit Sales Account Manager

Over 350 of the industry's most recognized defense and technology organizations showcase their technology products and services to top decision-makers from the US Pacific Fleet, Naval Station San Diego, Space & Warfare Command, Naval Base Coronado, Camp Pendleton Marine Corps Base and many other west coast military and government facilities.
6000 Attendees
Frequency: January
Founded in 1980

7090 APRO Rent-To-Own Convention & Trade Show
1504 Robin Hood Trail
Austin, TX 78703

512-794-0095
800-204-APRO
FAX 512-794-0097
E-Mail: cmay@aprovision.org
Home Page: www.rtohq.org

Shannon Strunkec, President
John C Cleek, First VP
Jeannie Hutchison, Program Coordinator
Bill Keese, Manager

Seminar, reception and tours, plus 280 exhibits of products and services of interest to rent to own dealers: stereos, televisions, furniture, fabric protection and more.
1400 Attendees
Frequency: Annual

7091 ASM/TMS Spring Symposium
Minerals, Metals & Materials Society
184 Thorn Hill Road
Warrendale, PA 15086-7514

724-776-9000
FAX 724-776-3770

E-Mail: foundation@tms.org
Home Page: www.tms.org

Tresa Pollock, President
Brajendra Mishra, VP
Alexander Scott, Executive Director
John Parsey, Financial Planning Officer
Marc DeGraef, Director Information Technology

This symposium, organized by the local chapters of TMS and ASM, will focus on materials for extreme environments, with sessions on materials characterization in three dimensions, structural materials for high temperature, materials for space applications, and materials by design.
Frequency: May

7092 ATE and Instrumentation West
Miller Freeman Publications
600 Harrison Street
Suite 400
San Francisco, CA 94107-1391

415-905-2354
FAX 415-905-2232

Steve Schulderfrei, Trade Show Director
Geared to the test and measurement of electronics.
5.8M Attendees
Frequency: January

7093 AVS Annual Symposium & Exhibition
AVS Science & Technology Society
125 Maiden Lane
15th Floor
New York, NY 10038

212-248-0200
FAX 212-248-0245
Home Page: www.avs.org

Christie R Marrian, President
John Coburn, Treasurer
Joseph E Greene, Clerk/Secretary
Yvonne Towse, Executive Director

Promotes communication, dissemination of knowledge, recommended practices, research, and education in the use of vacuum and other controlled environments to develop new materials, process technology, devices, and related understanding of material properties for the betterment of humanity.
Frequency: Annual/February

7094 AVS International Symposium and Exhibition
AVS Science & Technology Society
120 Wall Street
32nd Floor
New York, NY 10005-3993

212-248-0200
FAX 212-248-0245
E-Mail: angela@avs.org
Home Page: www.avs.org

Christie R Marrian, President
John Coburn, Office Manager
Nancy Schultheis, Office Manager
Joseph E Greene, Clerk/Secretary
Yvonne Towse, Executive Director

This conference has been developed to address cutting edge issues associated with vacuum science and technology in both the research and manufacturing communities. The equipment exhibition is one of the largest in the world and provides an excellent opportunity to view the latest products and services offered by over 200 participating companies.
3000 Attendees

7095 All-Service Convention
Electronic Technicians Association International

5 Depot Street
Greencastle, IN 46135

765-653-4301
800-288-3824
FAX 765-653-4287
E-Mail: eta@eta-i.org
Home Page: www.eta-i.org

Teresa Maher, President
Chrissy Baker, Marketing Coordinator

Appliances and electronic service products and services. Third party administrators. Certification exams and study materials. Tools and test equipment. Containing 40 booths and 50 exhibits.

7096 Annual Legislative & Regulatory Roundtable
Electronic Industries Alliance
2500 Wilson Boulevard
Arlington, VA 22201-3834

703-907-7500
703-907-7500
Home Page: www.eia.org

Gail Tannenbaum, CMP, Manager Meetings/Industry Relations
Frequency: Annual/August

7097 Asia Card Technology Exhibition
Reed Exhibition Companies
383 Main Avenue Suite 3
PO Box 6059
Norwalk, CT 06851

203-840-4800
FAX 203-840-9628

Emily Hackett, Executive Director
Peter DiLeo, Marketing Director
Deborah Luongo, Conference Manager

Trade professionals see exhibits on computers and electronics.
Frequency: Annual

7098 Assembly Northeast Exhibition
Reed Exhibition Companies
383 Main Avenue Suite 3
PO Box 6059
Norwalk, CT 06851

203-840-4800
FAX 203-840-9628

Emily Hackett, Executive Director
Peter DiLeo, Marketing Director
Deborah Luongo, Conference Manager
Gregg Vautrin, CEO

Assembly industry equipment, supplies and services for engineers and managers from electronic and automated assembly operations.
1365 Attendees
Frequency: Annual
Founded in 1999

7099 Assembly Technology Exposition
Reed Exhibition Companies
383 Main Avenue Suite 3
PO Box 6059
Norwalk, CT 06851

203-840-4800
800-267-3796
FAX 203-840-9686
Home Page: www.atexpo.com

Emily Hackett, Executive Director
Peter DiLeo, Marketing Director
Deborah Luongo, Conference Manager

525 exhibitors with robotics, vision systems, electronics and production machinery of interest to engineers and managers from automated assembly plants.
14000 Attendees
Frequency: Annual
Founded in 1979

7100 Assembly West Exhibition
Reed Exhibition Companies
383 Main Avenue Suite 3
PO Box 6059
Norwalk, CT 06851

203-840-4800
FAX 203-840-9628

Emily Hackett, Executive Director
Peter DiLeo, Marketing Director
Deborah Luongo, Conference Manager
Gregg Vautrin, CEO

Assembly industry equipment, supplies and
services for engineers and managers from electronic and automated assembly operations.
3000 Attendees
Frequency: Annual

**7101 Automated Manufacturing
Exposition: New England**
TEC
2001 Assembly Street
Suite 204
Columbia, SC 29201

803-779-7123
Home Page: www.amexpo.com/newengland

Tony Smith, Founder
Rafael Pastor, Chairman/CEO
Richard Carr, President/Vice Chairman
Jerry Schneider, Chief Financial Officer

In addition to the exhibits, the conference will
feature seminars that focus on topics such as
continuous improvement and lean
manufacturing.

7102 CEA Industry Forum
Consumer Electronics Association (CEA)
1919 S Eads Street
Arlington, VA 22202

703-907-7600
866-858-1555
FAX 703-907-7675
E-Mail: cea@ce.org
Home Page: www.ce.org/Events/default.asp

Gary Shapiro, President/CEO
Pat Lavelle, Chairman
Peter Lesser, Industry Executive Advisor
Jason Oxman, VP Communications
Jenny Pareti, Public Policy Director

The CEA Industry Forum is a conference designed to inform and connect leaders in the CE
industry. The CEA Industry Forum offers a
chance to network with the industry's top executives and decision-makers from retailer, manufacturer and service provider companies. It
provides needed information on the industry's
hottest topics and offers a voice in the direction
of the CE industry on future policies, standards
and industry initiatives.
Frequency: October

**7103 CEA Winter Technology & Standards
Forum**
Consumer Electronics Association (CEA)
1919 S Eads Street
Arlington, VA 22202

703-907-7600
866-858-1555
FAX 703-907-7675
E-Mail: cea@ce.org
Home Page: www.ce.org/Events/default.asp

Gary Shapiro, President/CEO
Pat Lavelle, Chairman
Peter Lesser, Industry Executive Advisor
Jason Oxman, VP Communications
Jenny Pareti, Public Policy Director

Attendees can focus on the development of
emerging industry standards, contribute their
company's viewpoints, and gain networking
opportunities. Interface with industry technical

leaders as they consider, develop, and finalize
crucial CE standards.
Frequency: March, Florida

7104 CEO Summit
Consumer Electronics Association (CEA)
1919 S Eads Street
Arlington, VA 22202

703-907-7600
866-858-1555
FAX 703-907-7675
E-Mail: cea@ce.org
Home Page: www.ce.org/Events/default.asp

Gary Shapiro, President/CEO
Pat Lavelle, Chairman
Peter Lesser, Industry Executive Advisor
Jason Oxman, VP Communications
Jenny Pareti, Public Policy Director

Presents a rare opportunity to network in a
qualified, executive-only environment, to
gather insight helpful to your business and to
focus on the issues most critical to the industry.
Frequency: June

7105 CLEO/QELS Conference
Optical Society of America
2010 Massachusetts Avenue NW
Washington, DC 20036-1012

202-223-8130
FAX 202-223-1096
E-Mail: info@osa.org
Home Page: www.osa.org

Elizabeth A Rogan, Executive Director

Is a unique conference that gathers
distringuished leaders to discuss the latest research in the fields of optics and photonics.
The conference includes application-focused
forums, educational sessions and an applications-oriented exhibit.
Frequency: May

7106 COM Conference of Metallurgists
Minerals, Metals & Materials Society
184 Thorn Hill Road
Warrendale, PA 15086-7514

724-776-9000
FAX 724-776-3770
E-Mail: foundation@tms.org
Home Page: www.tms.org

Tresa Polloc, President
Brajendra Mishra, VP
Alexander Scott, Executive Director
John Parsey, Financial Planning Officer
Marc DeGraef, Director Information
Technology

Topic: Challenges for the Metals and Materials
Industry. This conference will feature symposia
on computational analysis in hydrometallurgy;
nickel and cobalt; pipelines for the 21st century; materials degradation: innovation, inspection, control, and rehabilitation; light metals;
fuel cell and hydrogen technologies; recruitment and early career development programs;
and the treatment of gold ores.
Frequency: August

**7107 CONNECTIONS - The Digital Living
Conference and Showcase**
Parks Associates
5310 Harvest Hill Road
Suite 235, Lock Box 162
Dallas, TX 75230-5805

972-490-1113
800-727-5711
E-Mail: info@parksassociates.com
Home Page: www.connectionsconference.com

Tricia Parks, Founder and CEO
Stuart Sikes, President
Farhan Abid, Research Analyst
Bill Ablondi, Director, Home Systems

Research
John Barrett, Director of Research

This conference attracts over 500 executives
focused on innovative consumer technology solutions. The unique conference and showcase
highlights consumer and industry research from
Parks Associates, showcases key players and
new technologies, and delivers insight and recommendations for new business models and
opportunities in digital media/content, mobile
applications and services, connected consumer
electronics, broadband and value-added
services, and home systems.
Frequency: Annual
Founded in 1986
Mailing list available for rent

**7108 Ceramic Interconnect and Ceramic
Microsystems**
International Microelectronics & Electronics
611 2nd Street
Washington, DC 20002

202-548-4001
888-464-6277
FAX 202-548-6115
E-Mail: imaps@imaps.org
Home Page: www.imaps.org

Michael O'Donoghue, Executive Director
Rick Mohn, Operations Manager
Brian Schieman, Director Information
Technology
Ann Bell, Manager Marketing/Communications
Frequency: April

7109 DistribuTech Conference
PennWell Conferences and Exhibitions
350 Post Oak Blouevard
Suite 205
Houston, TX 77056

713-621-8833
FAX 713-963-6284
Home Page: www.pennwell.com

Bob Biolchini, CEO

Is the leading automation and information technology conference and exhibition in the utility
industry; and provides the best resources, tools
and networking opportunities relating to electric utility automation and control systems, IT,
T&D engineering, power and delivery equipment, and water utility technology.
3000 Attendees
Frequency: January

7110 EASA Conference
Electrical Apparatus Service Association
1331 Baur Boulevard
Saint Louis, MO 63132-1903

314-993-2220
FAX 314-993-1269
E-Mail: easainfo@easa.com
Home Page: www.easa.com
Social Media: *Facebook, Twitter, LinkedIn*

Linda J Raynes, President/CEO
Dale Shuter, Meetings/Expositions Manager

EASA is a trade association recognized internationally as the leader in the electrical and mechanical apparatus sales, service and repair
industry.
2000+ Attendees
Frequency: Annual, June
Founded in 1933

**7111 EIA's Congressional Technology
Forum**
Electronic Industries Alliance

2500 Wilson Boulevard
Arlington, VA 22201-3834

703-907-7500
FAX 703-907-7500
Home Page: www.eia.org

Gail Tannenbaum, CMP, Manager
Meetings/Industry Relations
Frequency: October

7112 EOS/ESD Symposium & Exhibits
Electrostatic Discharge Association
7900 Turin Road
Building 3
Rome, NY 13440-2069

315-339-6937
FAX 315-339-6793
E-Mail: info@esda.org
Home Page: www.esda.org
Social Media: *Facebook, LinkedIn*

Donn Bellmore, President
Leo G. Henry, Sr. VP
Terry Welsher, VP
Lisa Pimpinella, Director of Operations
Donn Pritchard, Treasurer

International technical forum on electrical
overstress and electrostatic discharge that features research, technology, and solutions to increase understanding, enhance quality and
reliability, reduce and control costs, and improve yields and productivity.
2000+ Members
1M Attendees
Frequency: September
Founded in 1982

7113 ETA Annual Meeting and Expo
Electronic Transactions Association
1101 16th Street NW
Suite 402
Washington, DC 20036

202-828-2635
800-695-5509
FAX 202-828-2639
Home Page: www.electran.org

Jennifer Leo, Meetings Manager
Kurt Strawhecker, Managing Director
Steve Carnevale, Senior Vice President

Featuring valuable networking opportunities,
outstanding speakers and educational seminars.
Frequency: April, Las Vegas

7114 ETA Expo Network
Electronic Transactions Association
1101 16th Street NW
Suite 402
Washington, DC 20036

202-828-2635
800-695-5509
FAX 202-828-2639
Home Page: www.electran.org

Jennifer Leo, Meetings Manager
Kurt Strawhecker, Managing Director
Steve Carnevale, Senior Vice President

Offers conference events that focus specifically
on delivering need to know education to ISOs
and sales agents. ETA created these meetings to
increase educational and business development
opportunities for the industry. These affordable
and easily accessible conferences are the ideal
opportunity to increase your knowledge and
meet new business partners.

7115 East Coast Video Show
Expocon Management Associates

363 Reef Road
PO Box 915
Fairfield, CT 06430-0915

203-882-1300
FAX 203-256-4730
Diane Stone, Show Director
8000 Attendees

**7116 Electronic Distribution Show and
Conference**
Electronic Distribution Show Corporation
222 S Riverside Plaza
Suite 2160
Chicago, IL 60606-6160

312-648-1140
FAX 312-648-4282
E-Mail: eds@edsc.org
Home Page: www.edsc.org

Gretchen Oie-Weghorst, Show Manager
Gretchen Oie, Manager

Annual conference and exhibits of 500 manufacturers of electronic components who sell
through distribution. Containing 700 booiths
and 500 exhibits.
10M Attendees
Frequency: May

7117 Electronic Imaging East
Miller Freeman Publications
600 Harrison Street
Suite 400
San Francisco, CA 94107-1391

415-905-2354
FAX 415-905-2232

Stephen Schuldenfrei, Trade Show Director
300 booths consisting of electrical equipment
and services.
5.3M Attendees
Frequency: October

7118 Electronic Imaging West
Miller Freeman Publications
600 Harrison Street
Suite 400
San Francisco, CA 94107-1391

415-905-2534
FAX 415-905-2232

Stephen Schuldenfrei, Trade Show Director
Exhibits of equipment, supplies and services
for the computer and electronics industries.
3M Attendees

7119 Electronic Materials Conference
Minerals, Metals & Materials Society
184 Thorn Hill Road
Warrendale, PA 15086-7514

724-776-9000
FAX 724-776-3770
E-Mail: foundation@tms.org
Home Page: www.tms.org

Tresa Pollock, President
Brajendra Mishra, VP
Alexander Scott, Executive Director
John Parsey, Financial Planning Officer
Marc DeGraef, Director Information
Technology

This conference will provide a forum for topics
of current interest and significance related to
the preparation and characterization of electronic materials. Individuals actively engaged
or interested in electronic materials research
and development are encouraged to submit an
abstract or attend the meeting. A technological
exhibition will also be held.
Frequency: June

**7120 Electronic West: Annual Western
Electrical Exposition Conference**
Continental Exhibitions

370 Lexington Avenue
Suite 1401
New York, NY 10017

212-370-5005
FAX 212-370-5699
10000 Attendees

7121 Embedded Systems Conference - West
Miller Freeman Publications
600 Harrison Street
Suite 400
San Francisco, CA 94107

415-905-2354
FAX 415-905-2220
Home Page: www.esconline.com

Lisa Ostrom, Electronics Show Director
Christian Fahlen, CEO

This is an ideal forum to learn relevant new
skills, and about the latest technologies and
products; to network with industry experts,
vendors and your peers; and to discover an exhibits floor featuring leading companies
showcasing cutting edge products.
13000 Attendees
Frequency: March

**7122 Executive Leadership Forum &
Board of Governors Meeting**
Electronic Industries Alliance
2500 Wilson Boulevard
Arlington, VA 22201-3834

703-907-7500
FAX 703-907-7500
Home Page: www.eia.org

Gail Tannenbaum, CMP, Manager
Meetings/Industry Relations
Frequency: February, California

7123 IMPI Annual Symposium
International Microwave Power Institute
7076 Drinkard Way
PO Box 1140
Mechanicsville, VA 23111

804-596-6667
FAX 804-559-4087
E-Mail: info@impi.org
Home Page: www.impi.org
Social Media: *Facebook, Twitter*

Bob Schiffmann, President
Ben Wilson, VP
dorin Boldor, Secretary
Amy Lawson, Treasurer
Juan Aguilar, Editor in Chief

Brings together researchers from across the
globe to share the latest findings related to
non-communications uses of microwave
energy.
Frequency: Annual/June

7124 IS&T/SPIE's Electronic Imaging
International Society for Optical
Engineering
1000 20th Street
PO Box 10
Bellingham, WA 98227-0010

360-763-3290
FAX 360-647-1445
E-Mail: meetinginfo@spie.org
Home Page: www.spie.org

Electronic Imaging's top-notch technical program gathers the world's most prominent experts to discuss and push the forefront of
imaging technology and it's applications.
1200 Attendees
Frequency: Annual/January

**7125 Industry Wide Service and Retail
Convention**
Electronic Technicians Association
International

5 Depot Street
Greencastle, IN 46135

765-653-4301
800-288-3824
FAX 765-653-4287
E-Mail: eta@eta-i.org
Home Page: www.eta-i.org

Teresa Maher, President
Brianna Pinson, Office Manager

Three groups united to offer the largest schedule of business management and technical seminars and trade show for educators, servicers and retailers. Thirty booths.
200 Attendees
Frequency: February

7126 International CES
Consumer Electronics Association
1919 S Eads Street
Arlington, VA 22202

703-907-7600
866-858-1555
FAX 703-907-7675
E-Mail: cesreg@ce.org
Home Page: www.cesweb.org

Gary Shapiro, President/CEO
Randy Fry, Chairman
Glenda MacMullin, Treasurer
Karen Chupka, Secretary

Join fellow CEA members and prominent consumer electronics industry leaders at the Las Vegas Convention and World Trade Center for the largest show in the industry. Educates the masses and unites manufacturers, retailers and market movers in addition to offering a glimpse into the digital future.

7127 International Conference on Trends in Welding Research
Minerals, Metals & Materials Society
184 Thorn Hill Road
Warrendale, PA 15086-7514

724-776-9000
FAX 724-776-3770
E-Mail: foundation@tms.org
Home Page: www.tms.org

Tresa Pollock, President
Brajendra Mishra, VP
Alexander Scott, Executive Director
John Parsey, Financial Planning Officer
Marc DeGraef, Director Information Technology

This conference will feature five days of technically intensive programming focusing on both fundamental and applied topics related to welding and joining. Top researchers from industry, government, and academia will present the latest in experimental and modeling developments.
Frequency: May

7128 International Consumer Electronics Show (C ES)
Las Vegas Hotel & Casino
3000 S. Paradise Road
Las Vegas, NV 89109

866-539-8430
Home Page: www.ceweb.org
Social Media: *Facebook, Twitter, LinkedIn*

Gary Shapiro, President/CEO
Pat Lavelle, Chairman
Peter Lesser, Industry Executive Advisor
Jason Oxman, VP Communications
Jenny Pareti, Public Policy Director

The CES reaches across global markets, connects the industry and enables consumer electronics to grow and thrive. International CES is

owned and prroduced by the Consumer Electronics Association (CEA).
2000 Members
Frequency: January

7129 International Symposium for Testing & Failure Analysis
ASM International
9639 Kinsman Road
Materials Park, OH 44073

440-338-5151
800-336-5152
FAX 440-338-4634
E-Mail: kim.schaefer@asminternational.org
Home Page: www.asminternational.org

Kim Schaefer, Event Manager
Kelly Thomas, Exposition Account Manager

Annual event focusing on microelectronic and elcetronic device failure analysis, techniques, EOS/ESD testing and descretes aimed at failure analysis engineers and managers, technisians and new failure analysis engineers. 200 exhibitors.
1100 Attendees
Frequency: Annual/November

7130 Materials, Science & Technology
Minerals, Metals & Materials Society
184 Thorn Hill Road
Warrendale, PA 15086-7514

724-776-9000
FAX 724-776-3770
E-Mail: foundaton@tms.org
Home Page: www.tms.org

Tresa Pollock, President
Brajendra Mishra, VP
Alexander Scott, Executive Director
John Parsey, Financial Planning Officer
Marc DeGraef, Director Information Technology

Offers a materials science and applied technology event unlike any other.
Frequency: September

7131 NCSLI Workshop & Symposium
NCSL
1800 30th Street
Suite 305 B
Boulder, CO 80301

303-440-3339
FAX 303-440-3384
E-Mail: info@ncsli.org
Home Page: www.ncsli.org

Harry J Moody, President
William T Pound, Executive Director

Will provide a forum to discuss the impact of these advances have had on metrology, as well as other related issues. Please join us as we reflect on how far and fast metrology has progressed over the past quarter of a century and to discuss its future needs and directions.
1200 Attendees
Frequency: August, Washington

7132 NEDA Executive Conference
National Electronic Distributors Association
1111 Alderman Drive
Suite 400
Alpharetta, GA 30005-4175

678-393-9990
FAX 678-393-9998
E-Mail: admin@nedassoc.org
Home Page: www.nedassoc.org

Francis Flynn Jr, President
Robin B Gray Jr, Executive VP
Debbie Conyers, Director Marketing
Barney Martin, VP Industry Practices
Frequency: November

7133 NMEA Convention & Expo
National Marine Electronics Association

Seven Riggs Avenue
Severna Park, MD 21146

410-975-9425
FAX 410-975-9450
E-Mail: info@nmea.org
Home Page: www.nmea.org

Mark Young, Chairman
Jules Rutstein, Vice Chairman
Beth Kahr, Executive Director
Michael Cerchiaro, Treasurer
Christopher Harley, Secretary
Frequency: October

7134 NPSC Meeting
National Electronics Service Dealers Association
3608 Pershing Avenue
Fort Worth, TX 76107-4527

817-921-9061
800-797-9197
FAX 817-921-3741
E-Mail: webmaster@nesda.com
Home Page: www.nesda.com

Brian Gibson, President
Don Cressin, VP
Mack Blakely, Executive Director
Fred Paradis, CSM, Treasurer
Wayne Markman, Secretary

Featuring Training, Sponsored Meal Events, Meetings, and Opportunities to Network with other service professionals as well as key service industry representatives.
Frequency: July

7135 Northwest Electronics Technology Conference
Electronic Conventions Management
8110 Airport Boulevard
Los Angeles, CA 90045-3119

310-215-3976
800-877-2668
FAX 310-641-5117
E-Mail: northcon@ieee.org
Home Page: www.northcon.org

James Lipman, PhD, Conference Director
Sue Kingston, Trade Show Manager

Offers a concentrated technical conference with complimenting exhibits. It provides a venue where those involved with the design, production and marketing of electronics-related products can converge in a real time, interactive atmosphere.
7000 Attendees
Frequency: May

7136 OEMBoston
Canon Communications
11444 W Olympic Boulevard
Suite 900
Los Angeles, CA 90064-1549

310-445-4200
FAX 310-445-4299
Home Page: www.oemboston,com

William F Cobert, President/CEO
Diane O'Conner, Trade Show Director
Dan Cutrone, Show Marketing Director

The creation of two seperate shows, OEM Electronics and OEMed, the OEMBoston is accessible to thousands of electronics and medical OEMs, who can benefit from the combination of the two shows. The different product classification found at this show include Contract Manufacturing, Electronics Components, Component Fabrication, Production/Assembly Equipment, Packaging Equipment & Supplies, Tubing and more. Held at the Bayside Expo Center in Boston, Massachusetts.
1604 Attendees
Frequency: September

7137 OFC/NFOEC Conference
Optical Society of America
2010 Massachusetts Avenue NW
Washington, DC 20036-1012

202-223-8130
FAX 202-223-1096
E-Mail: info@osa.org
Home Page: www.osa.org

Elizabeth A Rogan, Executive Director

With more than 750 presentations focused on the industry's hottest topics, FTTx and ROADMs at the top of the list, the conference again established itself as the leading technical conference for optical communications. OFC/NFOEC is the show to present new product and corporate announcements.
15000 Attendees
Frequency: March
Founded in 1916

7138 OSA Technical Conference
Optical Society of America
2010 Massachusetts Avenue NW
Washington, DC 20036-1012

202-223-8130
FAX 202-223-1096
E-Mail: info@osa.org
Home Page: www.osa.org

Elizabeth A Rogan, Executive Director

Connect with the most accomplished international scientists, researchers, engineers and business leaders as they shape the future of optics, photonics, and laser science.
Frequency: October

7139 PhAST Conference
Optical Society of America
2010 Massachusetts Avenue NW
Washington, DC 20036-1012

202-223-8130
FAX 202-223-1096
E-Mail: info@osa.org
Home Page: www.osa.org

Elizabeth A Rogan, Executive Director

Will feature previews of new application areas, access to industry innovators and discussions of the engineering ideas behind new products.
Frequency: May

7140 SEMI Expo CIS
Semiconductor Equipment & Materials International
3081 Zanker Road
San Jose, CA 95134

408-943-6900
FAX 408-428-9600
E-Mail: semihq@semi.org
Home Page: www.semi.org

Scott Smith, Public Relations Manager

Will highlight CIS as a region with huge potential and a new developing market for the world semiconductor equipment and materials manufacturers.
Frequency: September

7141 SESHA Annual Symposium
Semiconductor Environmental, Safety & Health Assn
1313 Dolly Madison Boulevard
Suite 402
McLean, VA 22101

703-790-1745
FAX 703-790-2672
E-Mail: sesha@burkinc.com
Home Page: seshaonline.org

Bernie First, President
Brett Burk, Co-Founder
Glenn Tom, Co-Founder
Brian Sherin, Treasurer
Karl Albrecht, Secretary

For individuals employed within the electronics and related high technology industries with an interest in environmental, health and safety issues.
1235 Attendees
Frequency: May
Founded in 1978

7142 SOUTHCON
Electronic Conventions
12340 Rosecrans Avenue
Suite 100
Manhattan Beach, CA 90266

310-524-4100
800-877-2668
FAX 310-643-7328
Home Page: www.southcon.org

Susan Kingston, Show Manager

Companies attending represent a major cross-section of the electronics industry including consumer, computer, medical, automotive and others. Offers conference sessions, in-depth technical sessions, product demonstrations and exhibits by vendors.
10M Attendees
Frequency: March

7143 Semiconductor
Semiconductor Equipment & Materials International
3081 Zankeer Road
San Jose, CA 95134

408-943-6900
FAX 408-428-9600
E-Mail: semihq@semi.org
Home Page: www.semi.org

Scott Smith, Public Relations Manager

The future of the European Semiconductor Industry.
Frequency: June

7144 Service & Retail Convention
Electronic Technicians Association International
5 Depot Street
Greencastle, IN 46135

765-653-4301
800-288-3824
FAX 765-653-4287
E-Mail: eta@eta-i.org
Home Page: www.eta-i.org

Teresa Maher, President
Brianna Pinson, Office Manager

7145 Southeastern Technology Week
TEC
2001 Assembly Street
Suite 204
Columbia, SC 29201

803-779-7123
FAX 803-772-9964
Home Page: www.teconline.com

7146 Strategic Leadership and Networking Forum
Electronic Transactions Association
1101 16th Street NW
Suite 402
Washington, DC 20036

202-828-2635
800-695-5509
FAX 202-828-2639
Home Page: www.electran.org

Jennifer Leo, Meetings Manager
Kurt Strawhecker, Managing Director
Steve Carnevale, Senior Vice President

A unique event designed to help executives thrive in the new payments industry. The Forum goes far beyond fundamental education to

tackle the strategic, big-picture issues that today's payment executives and CEOs deal with each day. ETA takes a distinct approach to executive education and has adopted interactive formats conducive to peer-to-peer learning and business-to-business networking.

7147 Strategic Materials Conference
Semiconductor Equipment & Materials International
3081 Zanker Road
San Jose, CA 95134

408-943-7805
FAX 408-428-9600
E-Mail: amorais@semi.org
Home Page: www.semi.org

Anna Morais, Conference Contact

Hear about new business models, emerging players, green requirements and the the diverse partnerships in the semiconductor materials sector; the latest market trends, forecasts, best-practices, and discussions.
12000 Attendees
Frequency: May, Singapore

7148 Summer Technology & Standards Forum
Consumer Electronics Association (CEA)
1919 S Eads Street
Arlington, VA 22202

703-907-7600
866-858-1555
FAX 703-907-7675
E-Mail: cea@ce.org
Home Page: www.ce.org/Events/default.asp

Gary Shapiro, President/CEO
Pat Lavelle, Chairman
Peter Lesser, Industry Executive Advisor
Jason Oxman, VP Communications
Jenny Pareti, Public Policy Director

Focus on development of emerging industry standard, contribute your company's viewpoint, and gain networking opportunities. Take advantage of valuable opportunities to interface with industry technical leaders as they consider, develop, and finalize, crucial CE standards.
Frequency: July

7149 TABES Technical Business Exhibition & Symposium
Huntsville Association of Technical Societies
3414 Governors Dr SW
PO Box 1964
Huntsville, AL 35805

256-882-1234
FAX 205-837-4275
Home Page: www.hats.org/society

J Tardy, Manager
John Young, Treasurer

Brings new business into the community.
10000 Attendees
Founded in 1969

7150 Tech Advantage Exposition
National Rural Electric Cooperative Association
4301 Wilson Blouevard
Arlington, VA 22203

703-907-5500
FAX 703-907-5528
Home Page: www.nreca.org

Gary Pfann, Conference Contact
Barbara Christiana, Expo Contact
11000 Attendees

7151 westec Exposition
Society of Manufacturing Engineers

One SME Drive
Dearborn, MI 48121

313-425-3000
800-733-4763
FAX 408-428-9600
E-Mail: service@sme.org
Home Page: www.sme.org

Ana Christiansen, Exposition Marketing
Leslie Schade, Exhibitor Services

The West Coast's definitive manufacturing
event, showcasing crucial breakthroughs in machine tools, production methods, materials and
management strategies. More than 450
exhibitors.
1500 Attendees
Frequency: Annual

Directories & Databases

7152 Antenna Book
Electronic Technicians Association
International
5 Depot St
Greencastle, IN 46135-8024

765-653-8262
800-288-3824
FAX 765-653-4287
E-Mail: eta@eta-i.org
Home Page: www.eta-i.org

Dick Glass, President
Brianna Pinson, Office Manager

Written by professional technicians who have
worked closely with antennas, this two book
series is the ultimate study guide for technicians seeking certification through ETA-I's
Video Distribution, Certified Satellite Installer
and TVRO programs. It can also serve as study
materials for electronics classes, employee
training, or as a quick reference guide your
whole shop can use. Includes shipping & handling.
Cost: $33.00
ISBN: 1-891749-14-5
Printed in on matte stock

7153 Battery Report
Power Sources Manufacturers Association
PO Box 418
Mendham, NJ 07945-0418

973-543-9660
FAX 973-543-6207
E-Mail: power@psma.com
Home Page: www.psma.com

Dusty Becker, Chairman
Carl Blake, President
Jim Marinos, VP

Is a comprehensive report describing the
state-of-the-art, current problems and R&D
needs for numerous battery systems. The report
also includes battery global market trends, status of electric/hybrid vehicle battery development and UN requirements for shipping
lithium.
Cost: $125.00
155 Members
Founded in 1985

7154 ERA Rep Locator
Electronics Representatives Association
444 N Michigan Avenue
Suite 1960
Chicago, IL 60611

312-527-3050
800-776-7377
FAX 312-527-3783

E-Mail: info@era.org
Home Page: www.era.org

Mark Motsinger, Chairman
Dave Rossi, Vice Chairman
Mike Kunz, President
Raymond J Hall, EVP/CEO
William R Warfield, Director
Finance/Operations

Manufacturers match your products and territories with qualified, professional representatievs
firms. The Locator lists ERA member companies with informtion on size of firm, territories
covered, type of products represented and customer bases.
Cost: $90.00
Frequency: Annually

**7155 Electronic Buyers News: Specialized
and Local/Regional Directory**
CMP Publications
600 Community Dr
Manhasset, NY 11030-3810

516-562-5000
FAX 516-562-5123

Hailey McKeefry, Editor

List of about 325 distributors of electronic
products and supplies operating on less than
national scale, or offering only one or a few
produst nationwide.

**7156 Electronic Buyers News: Top 50
Distributors Issue**
CMP Publications
600 Community Dr
Manhasset, NY 11030-3810

516-562-5000
FAX 516-562-5123

David Gabel, Editor

List of electronic distributors ranked by annual
gross sales.

7157 Electronic Distribution Directory
Electronic Distribution Show Corporation
222 S Riverside Plz
Suite 2160
Chicago, IL 60606-6112

312-648-1140
FAX 312-648-4282
E-Mail: eds@edsc.org
Home Page: www.edsconnects.com

Gretchen Oie, Manager

**7158 Electronic Industries Association:
Trade Directory and Membership List**
Electronic Industries Alliance
2500 Wilson Boulevard
Arlington, VA 22201-3834

703-907-7500
FAX 703-907-7501
Home Page: www.eia.org

Dave McCurdy, President/CEO
Charles L Robinson, Chief Operating Officer

More than 1,200 member companies in the
electronic manufacturing industry.
Frequency: Annual

**7159 Electronic Materials & Process
Handbook**
International Microelectronics & Electronics
611 2nd Street NE
Washington, DC 20002

202-548-4001
888-464-6277
FAX 202-548-6115
E-Mail: imaps@imaps.org
Home Page: www.imaps.org

Charles A Harper, Editor
Ronald M Sampson, Editor

Offers guidance on insulations, conductors, and
semiconductor materials, defines critical manufacturing parameters, and shows how these parameters can be combined to create successful
electronic devices.
Cost: $80.00
ISBN: 0-070542-99-6

7160 Electronic Representatives Directory
Harris Publishing Company
360 B Street
Idaho Falls, ID 83402-1938

208-524-4217
FAX 208-522-5241
E-Mail:
customerservice@harrispublishing.com
Home Page: www.harrispublishing.com

Directory of services and supplies to the indus-
try.
Cost: $25.00
320 Pages
Frequency: Annual
Circulation: 7,500

**7161 Electronics Manufacturers Directory
on Diskette**
Harris InfoSource International
2057 E Aurora Rd
Twinsburg, OH 44087-1938

330-425-4481
800-888-5900
FAX 330-487-5368
Home Page: www.harrisinfo.com

David Wilkof, VP

Diskette. Covers approximately 1,000,000
manufacturers of electronic equipment and
products.
Cost: $329.00
Frequency: Annual

**7162 North American Directory of
Contract Electronic Manufacturers**
Miller Freeman Publications
600 Harrison Street
Suite 400
San Francisco, CA 94107-1391

FAX 415-905-2239
Home Page: www.cassembly.com

Kimberly Cassidy, Editor

Over 1,350 electronics manufacturers facilities
in the United States, Canada, and Mexico.
Cost: $295.00
Frequency: Annual

7163 ProService Directory and Yearbook
National Electronics Service Dealers
Association
3608 Pershing Ave
Fort Worth, TX 76107-4527

817-921-9061
800-797-9197
FAX 817-921-3741
E-Mail: webmaster@nesda.com
Home Page: www.nesda.com

Clyde Nabors, Publisher
Wallace Harrison, Editor
Mary Margaret Merill, Production Manager

The yearbook is an annual resource listing for
servicers. This directory is sent each January to
current members.
Frequency: Annual

**7164 Product Source Guide for Electronic
Devices**
Reed Business Information
275 Washington St
Newton, MA 02458-1611

617-964-3030
FAX 617-558-4470

E-Mail: sales@eb-mag.com
Home Page: www.designnews.com

Donald Swanson, Editor

List of over 4,000 manufacturers and suppliers of equipment and materials used in the production, testing, and packaging of electronic devices and systems.
Cost: $25.00
Frequency: Annual

7165 Source Book
Armed Forces Communications and
Electronics Assn
4400 Fair Lakes Ct
Suite 100
Fairfax, VA 22033-3899

703-631-1397
800-336-4583
FAX 703-631-4693
Home Page: www.afcea.org

Kent Schneider, President/CEO
Becky Nolan, Executive VP
John A Dubia, Executive VP

The Source Book published in the January issue, contains the company profiles and contacts of AFCEA's corporate members. It is the who's who of C$ISR and homeland secuity organizations. The annual Security Directory, published in the February issue, focuses on security solutions and the organizations that provide them.
31000 Members
Founded in 1946

7166 Who's Who in Electronics Buyer's Guide
Harris Publishing Company
360 B Street
Idaho Falls, ID 83402-1938

208-524-4217
FAX 208-522-5241
E-Mail:
customerservice@harrispublishing.com
Home Page: www.harrispublishing.com

A list of over 15,000 manufacturers and distributors of electronics products in five regional volumes.
Cost: $65.00
Frequency: Annual
Circulation: 60,000

Industry Web Sites

7167 http://gold.greyhouse.com
G.O.L.D Grey House OnLine Databases

Grey House Publishing's online database platform, GOLD, offers Quick Search, Keyword Search and Expert Search for most business sectors including electronics markets. The GOLD platform makes finding the information you need quick and easy - whether you're a novice searcher or an experienced database user. All of Grey House's directory products are available for subscription on the GOLD platform.

7168 www.afcea.org
Armed Forces Communications and
Electronics Assn

An association that represents the professional communications, electronics, intelligence and information systems community.

7169 www.aprovision.org
Association of Progressive Rental
Organizations

Members include television, appliance and furniture dealers who rent merchandise with an option to purchase.

7170 www.era.org
Electronics Representatives Association

Provides services and benefits to electronic industry manufacturers representatives.

7171 www.eta-i.org
Electronic Technicians Association
International

A worldwide professional association founded by electronics technicians and servicing dealers.

7172 www.ewh.ieee.org
Instrumentation and Measurement Society

A subsidiary of the Institute of Electrical and Electronics Engineers. Provides support to scientists and technicians who design and develop electrical and electronic measuring instruments and equipment.

7173 www.greyhouse.com
Grey House Publishing

Authoritative reference directories for most business sectors including electronic markets. Users can search the online databases with varied search criteria allowing for custom searches by product category, geographic area, sales volume, keyword, subject and more. Full Grey House catalog and online ordering also available.

7174 www.imaps.org
International Microelectronics & Packaging
Society

Dedicated to the advancement and growth of the use of microelectronics and electronic packaging through public and professional education, dissemination of information by means of symposia, workshops and conferences and promotion of the Society's portfolio of technologies.

7175 www.ipc.org
IPC-Association Connecting Electronics
Industries

Works to develop standards in circuit board assembly equipment. Brings together all players in the electronic interconnection industry, including designers, board manufacturers, assembly companies, suppliers and original equipment manufacturers. Offers workshops, conferences, meetings and online communications.

7176 www.iscet.org
Int'l Society of Certified Electronics
Technicians

Designed to measure the degree of theoretical knowledge and technical proficiency of practicing technicians.

7177 www.nesda.com
National Electronics Service Dealers
Association

A national trade association for professionals in the business repairing consumer electronics equipment, appliances, and computers. NESDA has an e-mail group of over 600 members and manufacturers that communicate daily for information sharing. NESDA also has an annual convention and trade show.

7178 www.nmea.org
National Marine Electronics Association

The unifying force behind the entire marine electronics industry, bringing together all aspects of the industry for the betterment of all in the business.

7179 www.psma.com
Power Sources Manufacturers Association

Worldwide membership consists of manufacturers of power sources and conversion equip-

ment. Nonprofit association strives to integrate the resources of the power sources industry to more effectively and profitably serve the needs of the power sources users, providers and PSMA members. Educates the electronics industry and others on the relevant applications for power sources and conversion devices.

7180 www.semi.org
Semiconductor Equipment & Materials
International

Strengthens the performance of member companies through lobbying, promotion, education and statistical research.

7181 www.seshaonline.org
Semiconductor Environmental, Safety &
Health Assn

Members are individuals employed within the electronics and related high technology industries with an interest in environmental, health and safety issues.

7182 www.sia-online.org
Semiconductor Industry Association

Trade association representing the US microchip industry.

7183 www.sme.org
Society of Manufacturing Engineers
Represents the electrical manufacturers.

7184 www.smta.org
Surface Mount Technology Association

A network of professionals building skills, sharing practical experience and developing solutions in electronic assembly technologies and related business operations.

Associations

7185 ASM International/Materials Information Society
9639 Kinsman Rd
Materials Park, OH 44073-0002

440-338-5151
800-336-5152
FAX 440-338-4634
E-Mail:
memberservicecenter@asminternational.org
Home Page: www.asminternational.org
Social Media: *Facebook, Twitter, LinkedIn*

Dr. Sunniva R. Collins, FASM, President
Jon D. Tirpak, P.E., FASM, Vice-President
Craig D. Clauser, P.E., Treasurer
Managing Director, Terry F. Mosier

The society for materials engineers and scientists, a worldwide network dedicated to advancing industry, technology and applications of metals and materials.
35000 Members
Founded in 1913

7186 ASME/International Gas Turbine Institute
Three Park Avenue
New York, NY 10016-5990

973-882-1170
800-843-2763
E-Mail: infocentral@asme.org
Home Page: www.asme.org

Julio Guerrero, President
Thomas G. Loughlin, Executive Director
James W. Coaker, Secretary/Treasurer
David Soukup, Managing Director Operations
William Garofalo, Assistant Treasurer

Supports all those involved with engineering and energy technology.
12500 Members
Founded in 1958

7187 ASTM International
100 Barr Harbor Drive
PO Box C700
W Conshohocken, PA 19428-2959

610-832-9500
FAX 610-832-9555
E-Mail: service@astm.org
Home Page: www.astm.org
Social Media: *Facebook, Twitter, LinkedIn, RSS, Youtube*

Ronald J. Ebelhar, Chairman
D. Thomas Marsh, Vice Chairman
James A. Thomas, President

Not-for-profit organization that provides a global forum for the development and publication of voluntary consensus standards for materials, products, systems and services. Members are users, producers, consumers and representatives of academia and government. Formerly known as the American Society for Testing and Materials.
30000 Members
Founded in 1898

7188 AVS Science & Technology Society
125 Maiden Ln
15th Floor
New York, NY 10038-4714

212-248-0200
FAX 212-248-0245
E-Mail: ricky@avs.org
Home Page: www.avs.org

Ricky Baldeo, Office Services Coordinator
Peter Burke, Financial Administrator
Angela Klink, Member Services Administrator
Jeannette DeGennaro, Exhibition & Sales

Manager
Yvonne Towse, Managing Director

AVS is a resource for scientists, engineers, industrialists, students and educators.
6000 Members
Founded in 1963

7189 Abrasive Engineering Society
144 Moore Rd
Butler, PA 16001-1312

724-282-6210
FAX 724-234-2376
E-Mail: aes@abrasiveengineering.com
Home Page: www.abrasiveengineering.com

Doug Haynes, President
Ted Giese, Executive Director

Dedicated to promoting technical information about abrasives minerals and their uses including abrasives grains and products such as grinding wheels, coated abrasives and thousands of other related tools and products that serve manufacturing and the consumer.
500 Members
Founded in 1957

7190 Accreditation Board for Engineering and Technology
415 North Charles Street
Suite 1050
Baltimore, MD 21201

410-347-7700
FAX 410-625-2238
E-Mail: info@abet.org
Home Page: www.abet.org

Michael Milligan, Executive Director, CEO
Joe Sussman, PhD, F.ASME, Chief Accreditation Officer, CIO
Lance Hoboy, MBA, CAE, CFO/COO
Danielle Baron, Senior Director
Rochelle Williams, PhD, Director, Programs and Events

Accreditation of engineering, technology and applied science educational programs.
31 Members
Founded in 1932

7191 Acoustical Society of America
2 Huntington Quad
Suite 1N01
Melville, NY 11747-4505

516-576-2360
FAX 516-576-2377
E-Mail: asa@aip.org
Home Page: acousticalsociety.org

Christy K. Holland, President
Lily M. Wang, VP
Susan E. Fox, Executive Director
James F. Lynch, Editor-in-Chief
Christopher J. Struck, Standards Director

Supports all those involved with the acoustics industry.
7000 Members
Founded in 1929

7192 Adhesive & Sealant Council
7101 Wisconsin Ave
Suite 990
Bethesda, MD 20814-4805

301-986-9700
FAX 301-986-9795
E-Mail: data@ascouncil.org
Home Page: www.ascouncil.org
Social Media: *Twitter, LinkedIn, RSS*

Matt Croson, President
Kate Zando, Director, Finance and Admin.
Malinda Armstrong, Director, Meetings & Expositions
Mark Collatz, Director, Government Relations
Steve Duren, Senior Director, Member Services

A North American trade association dedicated to representing the adhesive and sealant industry. ASC is bound by the collective efforts of its members, and strives to improve the industry operating environment and strengthen its member companies.
124 Members
Founded in 1958

7193 Air & Waste Management Association
420 Fort Duquesne Blvd.
Pittsburgh, PA 15222-1435

412-232-3444
800-270-3444
FAX 412-232-3450
E-Mail: info@awma.org
Home Page: www.awma.org
Social Media: *Facebook, Twitter, LinkedIn*

Dallas Baker, President
Stephanie Glyptis, Executive Director
Carrie Hartz, Conferences & Events Planner
Gloria Henning, Education Programs Coordinator
Nancy Bernheisel, Publications Coordinator

Professional organization that provides training, information, and networking opportunities to environmental professionals.

7194 Alpha Pi Muÿ
3005 Lancaster Drive
Blacksburg, VA 24060

540-553-2043
E-Mail: office@alphapimu.com
Home Page: www.alphapimu.com

Dr. Wafik H Iskander, President
Sarah Lam, Executive Vice President
Dr. C. Patrick Koelling, Executive Director
Dr. Wafik H Iskander, Vice President
Dr. S. Balachandran, Treasurer

An honor society for Industrial and Systems Engineering students.
Founded in 1949

7195 American Academy of Environmental Engineers
130 Holiday Ct
Suite 100
Annapolis, MD 21401-7003

410-266-3311
FAX 410-266-7653
E-Mail: info@aaee.net
Home Page: www.aaee.net
Social Media: *Facebook, LinkedIn*

Joseph Cavaretta, CAE, Executive Director
Brian P Flynn, P.E., BGEE, President
Dr. Cecil Lue-Hing, Past President
Joyce Dowen, Executive Assistant
Yolanda Moulden, Production Manager

Periodical for environmental engineers and environmental engineer professionals, as well as environmental engineering services
2500 Members
Founded in 1955

7196 American Association of Engineering Societies
1801 Alexander Bell Drive
Reston, VA 20191

202-296-2237
888-400-2237
FAX 202-296-1151
E-Mail: dbateson@aaes.org
Home Page: www.aaes.org

Dr. James L. Melsa, Chairman
Alyse Stofer, Vice Chair
Wendy Cowan, CAE, Executive Director/Secretary
Mark W. Woodson, P.E., Treasurer

Association for national, U.S. organizations concerned with engineering and related fields.
14 Members
Founded in 1979

7197 American Automatic Control Council
Northwestern University
3640 Col Glenn Highway
Dayton, OH 45435

937-775-5062
FAX 937-775-3936
E-Mail: pmisra@cs.wright.edu
Home Page: www.a2c2.org

Tariq Samad, President
Linda Bushnell, Treasurer
B. Wayne Bequette, Secretary
Pradeep Misra, Secretary

Supports industry of automatic controls producers.
1M Members
Founded in 1960

7198 American Council of Engineering Companies
1015 15th St
8th floor NW
Washington, DC 20005-2605

202-347-7474
FAX 202-898-0068
E-Mail: acec@acec.org
Home Page: www.acec.org
Social Media: *Facebook, Twitter, Pinterest*

Ralph W. Christie, Chairman
Harvey M. Floyd, Senior Vice Chair and Treasurer
David A. Raymond, President and CEO
Mary Ann Emely, VP, Operations & Membership
Steven Hall, Vice President, Government Affairs

Membership includes US firms engaged in a range of engineering works. Mission is to contribute to the nation's prosperity through advancing the interests of member firms.
55000 Members
Founded in 1905

7199 American Crystallographic Association
Ellicott Station
PO Box 96
Buffalo, NY 14205-0096

716-898-8690
FAX 716-898-8695
E-Mail: aca@hwi.buffalo.edu
Home Page: www.amercrystalassn.org
Social Media: *Twitter*

Christopher Cahill, President
Tom Terwilliger, Vice President
William L. Duax, Chief Executive Officer
S.N. Rao, Chief Financial Officer
Kristina Vitale, Membership Secretary

Supports all those involved with hardware, software, and x-ray equipment for the crystal industry.
2200 Members
Founded in 1949

7200 American Design Drafting Association
105 East Main Street
Newbern, TE 38059

731-627-0802
FAX 731-627-9321
E-Mail: okparker@adda.org
Home Page: www.adda.org
Social Media: *Facebook, Twitter, LinkedIn, Google+*

Rick Frymyer, Chairman
Richard Button, Governor

Alex Devereux, Vice President
Olen K Parker, Executive Director
Donna Brenton, Administrative Manager

An individual membership society for the design drafting community across all industries.
Founded in 1948

7201 American Engineering Association, Inc.
533 Waterside Blvd.
Monroe Township, NJ 08831

201-664-6954
E-Mail: aea@aea.org
Home Page: www.aea.org

Richard F. Tax, President
Charles Fischer, Vice President
Jenny Blackford, Marketing Director
Laurie Johnson, Office Assistant

As a national nonprofit professional association the AEA is a voice for engineers. The AEA, Inc. is dedicated to the enhancement of the engineering profession and U.S. Engineering capabilities. AEA is a strong advocate for providing opportunities for US engineers and is involved in issues of utilization, skill enhancement, loss of jobs, offshore manufacturing, layoffs, and many others that affect the lives and professional welfare of our engineers.
Founded in 1979

7202 American Helicopter Society
2701 Prosperity Avenue
Suite 210
Fairfax, VA 22031

703-684-6777
855-247-4685
FAX 703-739-9279
E-Mail: staff@vtol.org
Home Page: www.vtol.org
Social Media: *Facebook, Twitter, LinkedIn, YouTube, RSS*

Mick Maurer, Chair
Leanne Caret, President
Mike Hirschberg, Executive Director
Kay Yosua Brackins, Deputy Executive Director
David Renzi, Director

The professional society for the advancement of vertical flight technology and its useful application throughout the world.
Founded in 1943

7203 American Indian Science and Engineering Society
2305 Renard SE
Suite 200
Albuquerque, NM 87106

505-765-1052
FAX 505-765-5608
Home Page: www.aises.org
Social Media: *Facebook, Twitter, LinkedIn, YouTube, Instagram*

Richard Stephens, Chair
Dr. Twyla Baker-Demaray, Vice-Chair
Marlene Watson, Secretary
Dr. James May, Treasurer
Sarah Echohawk, Chief Executive Officer

A nonprofit professional association with the goal of increasing American Indian and Alaskan Native representation in the fields of engineering, science, and other related technology disciplines.
3500 Members
Founded in 1977

7204 American Institute of Chemical Engineers
120 Wall Street
FL 23
New York, NY 10005-4020

203-702-7660
800-242-4363
FAX 203-775-5177
E-Mail: xpress@aiche.org
Home Page: www.aiche.org
Social Media: *Facebook, Twitter, LinkedIn, YouTube, Flickr, Slideshare*

Maria Burka, President
Kimberly Ogden, Secretary
Andre Da Costa, Treasurer
June Wispelwey, Executive Director

Professional association providing leadership in advancing the chemical engineering profession. Members are those who develop processes and design and operate manufacturing plants, as well as researchers who assure the safe and environmentally sound manufacture, use and disposal of chemical products.
50000 Members
Founded in 1908

7205 American Institute of Physics
1 Physics Ellipse
College Park, MD 20740-3841

301-209-3100
FAX 301-209-0843
E-Mail: dylla@aip.org
Home Page: www.aip.org

Louis J. Lanzerotti, Chair
Robert G. W. Brown, Chief Executive Officer
Gigi Swartz, Chief Financial Officer
Margaret Wiley, Senior Executive Secretary
Liz Dart Caron, Senior Director

Presents original research in high performance polymer science and technology. Primarily applications-driven, with a major focus on the molecular structure/processability/property relationship with regard to the specified applications.
1931 Members
Founded in 1931

7206 American Iron and Steel Institute
25 Massachusetts Avenue, NW
Suite 800
Washington, DC 20001

202-452-7100
Home Page: www.steel.org
Social Media: *Facebook, Twitter, YouTube*

Chuck Schmitt, Chairman
John Ferriola, Vice Chairman
Kevin M. Dempsey, SVP, Public Policy, General Counsel
David E Bell, VP, Finance and Administration
Lisa Harrison, SVP, Communications

Steel information for consumers, engineers, and other professionals.
125 Members
Founded in 1855

7207 American Nuclear Society
555 N Kensington Ave
La Grange Park, IL 60526-5592

708-352-6611
800-323-3044
FAX 708-352-0499
Home Page: www.ans.org
Social Media: *Facebook, Twitter, LinkedIn*

Eugene S. Grecheck, President
Andrew C. Klein, Vice President
Robert C. Fine, JD, CAE, Executive Director
Staci B. Levy, CPA, Director, Finance
Tari Marshall, Department Director

Serves its members in their efforts to develop and safely apply nuclear science and technol-

ogy for public benefit through knowledge exchange, professional development, and enhanced public understanding.
Founded in 1954

7208 American Oil Chemists Society

2710 S. Boulder
Urbana, IL 61802

217-359-2344
FAX 217-351-8091
E-Mail: general@aocs.org
Home Page: www.aocs.org
Social Media: *Facebook, Twitter, LinkedIn, Blogger*

M. Trautmann, President
B. Hendrix, VP
Patrick J. Donnelly, Chief Executive Officer
Jamie Lourash, Data Services Coordinator
Jeffry L. Newman, Senior Director, Programs

A global forum to promote the exchange of ideas, information, and experience, to enhance personal excellence, and to provide high standards of quality among those with a professional interest in the science and technology of fats, oil, surfactants, and related materials.
5400+ Members
Founded in 1909

7209 American Oil Chemists' Society (AOCS)

2710 S Boulder Drive
PO Box 17190
Urbana, IL 61803-6996

217-359-2344
FAX 217-351-8091
E-Mail: general@aocs.org
Home Page: www.aocs.org
Social Media: *Facebook, Twitter, LinkedIn, Blogger*

M. Trautmann, President
B. Hendrix, VP
Patrick J. Donnelly, Chief Executive Officer
Jamie Lourash, Data Services Coordinator
Jeffry L. Newman, Senior Director, Programs

AOCS is a global scientific society open to all individuals and corporations who are interested in fats, oils, surfactants, detergents and related materials. AOCS is a trusted source of information for its members and thousands of non-members from more than 90 countries worldwide.

4500 Members
Founded in 1909
Mailing list available for rent

7210 American Society for Engineering Education

1818 N St NW
Suite 600
Washington, DC 20036-2476

202-331-3500
FAX 202-265-8504
E-Mail: prism@asee.org
Home Page: www.asee.org

Norman Fortenberry, Executive Director
Joe Dillon, Managing Director, Finance/CFO
Keith Mounts, Chief Information Officer (CIO)
Ashok Agrawal, Managing Director
Patti Greenawalt, Managing Director, Member Services

Supports all those educators in the engineering technology fields.
12000 Members
Founded in 1893

7211 American Society for Precision Engineering

PO Box 10826
Raleigh, NC 27605-0826

919-839-8444
FAX 919-839-8039
Home Page: www.aspe.net

Byron R. Knapp, President
Robert D. Grejda, Vice President
Thomas A. Dow, ASPE Executive Director
Ilka Lee, Publications and Office Manager
Wendy Shearon, Meetings & Membership Manager

Members are from academia, industry and government, and include professionals in engineering, materials science, physics, chemistry, mathematics and computer science. Multidisciplinary professional and technical society concerned with precision engineering research and development, design and manufacturing of high accuracy components and systems. Member and nonmember rates for annual meetings, spring and summer topical meetings, books and video tapes. Membership is $65 regular, $30 student.
Founded in 1986

7212 American Society for Quality

600 N Plankinton Avenue
PO Box 3005
Milwaukee, WI 53201-3005

414-272-8575
800-248-1946
FAX 414-272-1734
E-Mail: help@asq.org
Home Page: www.asq.org
Social Media: *Facebook, Twitter, LinkedIn, YouTube, Google+*

Cecilia L. Kimberlin, Chair
Bill Troy, Chief Executive Officer
Eric Hayler, Treasurer
Sue Campbell, Executive Assistant

ASQ's mission is to facilitate continuous improvement and increase customer satisfaction. Promotes quality principles, concepts and technologies. Provides information, contacts and opportunities to make things better in the workplace, in communities and in people's lives.
100M Members
Founded in 1946

7213 American Society for the Geoprofessional Business Association (ASFE)

1300 Piccard Dr.
LL14
Rockville, MD 20850

301-565-2733
FAX 301-589-2017
E-Mail: info@geoprofessional.org
Home Page: www.asfe.org
Social Media: *Facebook, Twitter, LinkedIn, YouTube, RSS*

Gordon M. MathesonE, President
Joel G. Carson, Executive Director
Sara Menase, Program Manager
Barb Nappy, Director of Events
Charles L. Head, P.E., P.G., Secretary/Treasurer

Not-for-profit trade association. Supports all employees of engineering companies.
300 Members
Founded in 1969

7214 American Society of Agricultural and Biological Engineers

2950 Niles Rd
St Joseph, MI 49085-8607

269-429-0300
800-371-2723
FAX 269-429-3852

E-Mail: hq@asabe.org
Home Page: www.asabe.org

Mary Leigh Wolfe, President
Darrin Drollinger, Executive Director
Joann McQuone, Executive Assistant
Mark Zielke, Senior Director
Dolores Landeck, Director of Public Affairs

Holds annual meetings and conferences and publishes journals related to agricultural engineering, biological engineering and food process engineering.
8500 Members
Founded in 1907

7215 American Society of Certified Engineering

PO Box 1348
Flowery Branch, GA 30542

770-967-9173
FAX 770-967-8049
Home Page: www.ascet.org

Russell E Freier, Chairman
Leo Saenz, CET, President
Kurt Schuler, Secretary/Treasurer

Strives to obtain recognition of engineering technicians as essential to the engineering scientific team. Provides a forum for discussion of employment issues and improvement of the professional status of engineering technicians.
2000 Members
Founded in 1964

7216 American Society of Civil Engineers

1801 Alexander Bell Dr
Reston, VA 20191-4382

703-295-6300
800-548-2723
FAX 703-295-6222
E-Mail: cybrarian@asce.org
Home Page: www.asce.org/
Social Media: *Facebook, Twitter, LinkedIn, YouTube, Google+*

Robert D. Stevens, President
Dennis D. Truax, Ph.D., P.E., Treasurer
Randall M. Perkinson, P.E., Assistant Treasurer
Thomas W. Smith III, ENV SP, CAE, Secretary

Professional association of engineers and scientists working in civil and structural engineering, applied mechanics and engineering science, aeronautics and astronautics.
Founded in 1852

7217 American Society of Gas Engineers

PO Box 66
Artesia, CA 90702

562-455-9417
E-Mail: asgecge@aol.com
Home Page: www.asge-national.org

Mike O'Donnell, President
Ray Maddock, Vice President
Chad Johnson, Treasurer
Jerry Moore, Executive Director

Supports all engineers in the gas industry.
250 Members
Founded in 1954

7218 American Society of Heating, Refrigerating , and Air Conditioning Engineers

1791 Tullie Circle, N.E.
Atlanta, GA 30329

404-636-8400
800-527-4723
FAX 404-321-5478
E-Mail: ashrae@ashrae.org
Home Page: www.ashrae.org
Social Media: *Facebook, Twitter, YouTube*

T. David Underwood, President
Walid Chakroun, Ph.D., P.E., Vice President
Patricia T. Graef, P.E., Vice President

James K. Vallort, Vice President
Jeff H. Littleton, Secretary

Global society that focuses on building systems, energy efficiency, indoor air quality, refrigeration, and sustainability.

7219 American Society of Heating, Refrigeration & Air-Conditioning Engineers

1791 Tullie Cir Ne
Atlanta, GA 30329-2398

404-636-8400
800-527-4723
FAX 404-321-5478
E-Mail: ashrae@ashrae.org
Home Page: www.ashrae.org

T. David Underwood, President
Walid Chakroun, Ph.D., P.E., Vice President
Patricia T. Graef, P.E., Vice President
James K. Vallort, Vice President
Jeff H. Littleton, Secretary

An international organization that fulfills its mission of advancing heating, ventilation, air conditioning and refrigeration to serve humanity and promote a sustainable world through research, standards writing, publishing and continuing education.
55000 Members
Founded in 1894

7220 American Society of Mechanical Engineers

Three Park Ave
New York, NY 10016-5902

973-882-1170
800-843-2763
FAX 202-429-9417
E-Mail: infocentral@asme.org
Home Page: www.asme.org

Mark Goldsmith, President
Webb Marner, Secretary/Treasurer

To promote and enhance the technical competency and professional well-being of the members, and through quality programs and activities in mechanical engineering, better enable its practitioners to contribute to the well being of human kind
12000 Members
Founded in 1880

7221 American Society of Naval Engineers

1452 Duke Street
Alexandria, VA 22314-3458

703-836-6727
FAX 703-836-7491
E-Mail: asnehq@navalengineers.org
Home Page: www.navalengineers.org

Anthony W. Lengerich, USN, President
Mr. Mike D'Amato, Vice President
Dr. William H. Luebke, Vice President
VADM Paul E. Sullivan, USN (Ret.), Vice President
Dr. Leigh McCue, Executive Dir/Secretary/Treasurer

Naval engineering includes all arts construction and sciences as applied in research, development design, construction, operation, maintenance, and logistic support of: surface/sub-surface ships and marine craft.
Founded in 1888

7222 American Society of Petroleum Operations Engineers

301 East Culpeper Street
Culpeper, VA 22701

703-768-4159
800-918-8962
Home Page: www.aspoe.org

Social Media: *Facebook, Twitter, LinkedIn, YouTube, Google+, Instagram, P*

John B Stanley, President
Gerald Holton, VP
Harry Lyon, Executive VP
Coles Marsh, Treasurer
Cheryl George, Secretary

Works to stimulate interest from the academic world in the qualifications necessary to become a Petroleum Operations Engineer.
Founded in 1976

7223 American Society of Plumbing Engineers

6400 Shafer Ct.
Suite 350
Rosemont, IL 60018-4914

847-296-0002
FAX 773-695-9007
E-Mail: info@aspe.org
Home Page: www.aspe.org

Mitch Clemente, CPD, President
Billy Smith, FASPE Executive Director / CEO
Donald Thurner, Director of Finance & Admin.
Stacey A. Kidd, Director of Membership & Meetings
Richard Albrecht, Director of Information Technology

Supports all those engineers in the plumbing industry.
7500 Members
Founded in 1964

7224 American Society of Safety Engineers

520 N. Northwest Hwy
Park Ridge, IL 60068

847-699-2929
FAX 847-768-3434
E-Mail: customerservice@asse.org
Home Page: www.asse.org

Michael Belcher, CSP, President
James D. Smith, M.S., CSP, Senior VP
Stephanie A. Helgerman, CSP, VP of Finance
Fred J. Fortman, Secretary and Executive Director

The oldest and largest professional safety organization. Its members manage, supervise and consult son safety, health, and environmental issues in industry, insurance, government and education.
30000 Members
Founded in 1911

7225 American Society of Sanitary Engineering

18927 Hickory Creek Drive
Suite 220
Mokena, IL 60448

708-995-3019
FAX 708-479-6139
Home Page: www.asse-plumbing.org

Douglas A. Marian, President
Dana Colombo, Vice President
Scott Hamilton, Executive Director
Conrad Jahrling, Staff Engineering Supervisor
Benjamin Ryan, Communications Editor

Members are from all segments of the plumbing industry, including contractors, engineers, inspectors, journeymen, apprentices and others who are involved in various segments of the industry. Provides information, an opportunity to exchange ideas, solve problems and offers a forum where all sides can express their views.
300 Members

7226 American Water Works Association

6666 W. Quincy Ave.
Denver, CO 80235

303-794-7711
800-926-7337

FAX 303-347-0804
Home Page: www.awwa.org
Social Media: *Facebook, Twitter, LinkedIn, YouTube*

David B. LaFrance, Chief Executive Officer
Paula I. MacIlwaine, Deputy Chief Executive Officer
Kevin Mann, Chief Financial Officer
Kevin Turntine, Chief Information Officer
Susan Franceschi, Chief Membership Officer

An international nonprofit scientific and educational association founded to improve water quality and supply.
50000 Members
Founded in 1881

7227 Applied Technology Council

201 Redwood Shores Parkway
Suite 240
Redwood City, CA 94065

650-595-1542
FAX 650-593-2320
E-Mail: atc@atcouncil.org
Home Page: www.atcouncil.org

James A. Amundson, President
Victoria Arbitrio, Vice President
William Staehlin, Secretary/Treasurer
Jon A. Heintz, Executive Director
Scott D. Schiff, Director of Projects

Nonprofit, tax-exempt corporation established through the efforts of the Structural Engineers Association of California. ATC's mission is to develop and promote state-of-the-art, user-friendly, engineering resources and applications for use in mitigating the effects of natural and other hazards on the built environment.
300 Members
Founded in 1973

7228 Association for Computing Machinery

2 Penn Plaza
Suite 701
New York, NY 10121-0701

212-626-0500
800 342-6626
FAX 212-944-1318
E-Mail: acmhelp@acm.org
Home Page: www.acm.org
Social Media: *Facebook, Twitter, LinkedIn, YouTube, Google+*

Alexander L Wolf, President
Vicki L. Hanson, Vice President
John R. White, Executive Director and CEO
Erik R Altman, Secretary/Treasurer
Erik R Altman, Secretary/Treasurer

A U.S.-based international learned society for computing.

7229 Association for Facilities Engineering

8200 Greensboro Drive
Suite 400
McLean, VA 22102

571-395-8777
FAX 571-766-2142
E-Mail: Info@AFE.org
Home Page: www.afe.org

Dennis M Hydrick, President
Wayne P. Saya Sr., CPE, Executive Director
Scott Klahne, Director, Government Liaison
Gabriella Rosales, Manager, Professional Development
Charlie Clunk, Administrative Assistant

Provides education, certification, technical information and other relevant information for plant and facility engineering operations and maintenance professionals worldwide.
5000 Members
Founded in 1954

7230 Association for Iron & Steel Technology (AIST)

186 Thorn Hill Rd
Warrendale, PA 15086-7528

724-814-3000
FAX 724-814-3001
E-Mail: memberservices@aist.org
Home Page: www.aist.org
Social Media: *Facebook, Twitter, LinkedIn, YouTube*

George J. Koenig, President
Wendell L. Carter, First Vice President
Randy C. Skagen, Second Vice President
Joseph Dzierzawski, Treasurer
Ronald E. Ashburn, Secretary

The Association for Iron & Steel Technology (AIST) is an international technical association representing iron and steel producers, their allied suppliers and related academia. The association is dedicated to advancing the technical development, production, processing and application of iron and steel.
13800 Members
Founded in 2004

7231 Association for the Advancement of Cost Engineering

1265 Suncrest Towne Centre Drive
Suite 100
Morgantown, WV 26505-1876

304-296-8444
800-858-2678
FAX 304-291-5728
E-Mail: info@aacei.org
Home Page: www.aacei.org
Social Media: *Facebook, Twitter, LinkedIn*

Ms Julie K Owen, President
Charity A. Golden, MBA CIA CCT, Executive Director
Penny Whoolery, Manager, Certification
Jennie Amos, Director
Amanda Bliss, Certification Administrator

Leading-edge society for cost estimators, cost engineers, schedulers project managers, and project control specialists.
7000 Members
Founded in 1956

7232 Association of Building Officials and Code Administrators

500 New Jersey Ave
6th Floor
Washington, DC 20001-2070

202-370-1800
888-422-7233
FAX 202-783-2348
E-Mail: webmaster@iccsafe.org
Home Page: www.iccsafe.org
Social Media: *Facebook, Twitter, LinkedIn*

Alex Olszowy III, President
M. Dwayne Garriss, Vice President
Jay Elbettar, P.E., CBO, Secretary/Treasurer
Dominic Sims, CEO
John Belcik, COO/CFO

An independent nonprofit organization which conducts a voluntary program of evaluation of both traditional and innovative building materials, products and systems for compliance with BOCA National Codes.
14000 Members
Founded in 1994

7233 Association of Energy Engineers

3168 Mercer University Drive
Suite 420
Atlanta, GA 30341

770-447-5083
FAX 770-446-3969

E-Mail: info@aeecenter.org
Home Page: www.aeecenter.org

Dr. Scott Dunning, President
Albert Thumann, P.E., C.E.M., Executive Director
Bill Younger, Secretary
Paul Goodman, Treasurer
Angie Quarles, Assistant to the Executive Director

Membership organization of professionals and certification programs in the fields of energy efficiency, utility deregulation, facility management, plant engineering and environmental compliance. Offers seminars, conferences, books to critical buyer-seller, networking trade shows, job listings and certification programs.
8000+ Members
Founded in 1977

7234 Association of Engineering Geologists

1100-H Brandywine Blvd.
Suite 575
Zanesville, OH 43701

303-757-2926
844-331-7867
FAX 720-230-4846
E-Mail: aeg@aegweb.org
Home Page: www.aegweb.org

Paul Santi, President
Dale Andrews, Vice President
Kathy Troost, Treasurer
Kevin Richards, Secretary

Meets the professional needs of geologists who are applying their scientific training and experience to the broad field of civil and environmental engineering. Mission is to provide leadership in the development and application of geologic principles and knowledge to serve engineering, environmental and public needs.
3000 Members
Founded in 1957
Mailing list available for rent: 3000 names at $100 per M

7235 Association of State Dam Safety Officials

239 S. Limestone
Lexington, KY 40508

859-550-2788
E-Mail: info@damsafety.org
Home Page: www.damsafety.org
Social Media: *Facebook, Twitter, LinkedIn, YouTube*

Jim Pawloski, President
Jon Garton, Secretary
Roger Adams, P.E., Secretary
Jon Garton, Secretary
Dusty Myers, Treasurer

Provides outreach programs and a forum for the exchange of information to advance and improve the safety of dams.
Founded in 1983

7236 Audio Engineering Societyÿ

551 Fifth Ave.
Suite 1225
New York, NY 10176

212-661-8528
FAX 212-682-0477
Home Page: www.aes.org
Social Media: *Facebook, Twitter, LinkedIn, YouTube, Google+*

Andres Mayo, President
Michael Fleming, VP, Central Region, USA/Canada
David W Scheirman, VP, Western Region, USA/Canada
Ron Streicher, Secretary
Garry Margolis, Treasurer

Worldwide professional association for professionals and students involved in the audio industry.

7237 Biomedical Engineering Society

8201 Corporate Dr
Suite 1125
Landover, MD 20785-2224

301-459-1999
877-871-2637
FAX 301-459-2444
E-Mail: info@bmes.org
Home Page: www.bmes.org
Social Media: *Facebook, Twitter, LinkedIn*

Richard T. Hart, PhD, President
Edward L. Schilling, III, Executive Director
Doug Beizer, Communications Director
Michele Surricchio Ciapa, Education Director
Terry Young, BMES Career Connections Director

Supports all those involved in the biomedical engineering industry.
3800 Members
Founded in 1968

7238 Carnegie Mellon University: Information Networking Institute

Carnegie Mellon University
Electrical & Computer Engineering Department
4616 Henry Street
Pittsburgh, PA 15213

412-268-7195
FAX 412-268-7196
E-Mail: ini@cmu.edu
Home Page: www.ini.cmu.edu
Social Media: *Facebook, Twitter, LinkedIn, YouTube, Instagram, Google+, F*

Dr. Dena Haritos Tsamitis, Director
Mike Niederberger, Business/Finance Administrator
Donald Shields, Director Development
Dean Haritos Tsamitis, Director Information Networking
Sean O'Leary, Manager

Focusing on professional degrees programs combining economics, technologies and global communication networks - information security policies.
Founded in 1989

7239 Cold Regions Research and Engineering Laboratory

US Army Corps of Engineers
72 Lyme Road
Hanover, NH 03755-1290

603-646-4100
FAX 603-646-4278
E-Mail: info@crrel.usace.army.mil
Home Page: www.crrel.usace.army.mil/welcome

James L Wuebben, PE, Director
Dr Mary Albert, Research Mechanical Engineer

The mission of this Laboratory is to understand the characteristics of the cold regions of the world and to apply this knowledge to make it easier for people to live and work in those regions. For example, CRREL engineers have conducted a long-term program on the correct design of roofs in heavy snowfall areas.

7240 Cold-Formed Steel Engineers Institute

25 Massachusetts Avenue, N.W.
Suite 800
Washington, DC 20001

202-263-4488
866-465-4732
FAX 202-452-1039

E-Mail: info@cfsei.org
Home Page: www.cfsei.org

Jennifer Zabik, P.E., S.E., Chairman
Robert Warr, P.E, Vice Chairman
Jennifer Zabik, Vice Chairman

Produces safe and efficient designs for commercial and residential structures with cold-formed steel.
Founded in 1849

7241 Construction Financial Management Association
100 Village Blvd.
Suite 200
Princeton, NJ 8540

609-452-8000
888-421-9996
FAX 609-452-0474
E-Mail: info@cfma.org
Home Page: www.cfma.org
Social Media: *Facebook, Twitter, LinkedIn, YouTube*

Stuart Binstock, President/ CEO
Brian Summers, VP, Content Strategy & Education
Ariel Sanchirico, Director, Online Learning
Erica O'Grady, CAE, Vice President, Operations
Robert Rubin, CPA, Vice President, Finance & Admin

Support and networking for construction financial professionals within the United States.
Founded in 1981

7242 Construction Management Association of America
7926 Jones Branch Drive
Suite 800
McLean, VA 22102-3303

703-356-2622
FAX 703-356-6388
E-Mail: info@cmaanet.org
Home Page: www.cmaanet.org
Social Media: *Facebook, Twitter, LinkedIn, YouTube*

Rebecca Jones, Chair
Sandy Hamby, AIA, CCM, Vice Chair
Tim Murchison, JD, CCM, Vice Chair
Brian Ott, CCM, Vice Chair
Tim Murchison, JD, CCM, Vice Chair

A nonprofit and non-governmental professional association serving the construction management industry.
11000 Members
Founded in 1982

7243 Construction Owners Association of America
5000 Austell Powder Springs Road
Suite 217
Austell, GA 30106

770-433-0820
800-994-2622
FAX 404-577-3551
E-Mail: coaa@coaa.org
Home Page: www.coaa.org
Social Media: *Facebook, Twitter, LinkedIn*

Kevin Lewis, President
Dean McCormick, Vice President
Lisa DeGolyer, Chief Executive, Conferences & Edu
Valerie Delaney, Chief Executive, Finance & Ops
Donna Heavener, Director

A national organization of public and private owners who manage facilities development and capital improvement projects.

7244 CorrConnect
530 University Ave
Palo Alto, CA 94301

E-Mail: contact@mvesystems.com
Home Page: www.corrconnect.com

Joshua Bane, Project Manager

An online resource center for training modules on corrosion.
Founded in 2007

7245 Council of Engineer and Scientific Specialty Board
PO Box 1448
Annapolis, MD 21401-1448

410-266-3766
FAX 410-721-1746
E-Mail: wanderson@cesb.org
Home Page: www.cesb.org

William C Anderson PE DEE, Executive Director

Accredits engineering, science and technology certification programs from professional to technician certificates.
Founded in 1990
Mailing list available for rent

7246 Electric Power Research Institute
3420 Hillview Avenue
Palo Alto, CA 94304

650-855-2121
800-313-3774
E-Mail: orders@epri.com
Home Page: www.epri.com
Social Media: *Facebook, Twitter, LinkedIn, YouTube*

Gil C Quiniones, Chair
Pat K. Vincent-Collawn, Vice Chair
Michael W Howard, President/ Chief Executive Officer
Tom Alley, Vice President, Generation
Pamela J. Keefe, SVP, CFO and Treasurer

A nonprofit organization that conducts research on issues related to the electric power industry in the USA.
Founded in 1965

7247 Engineering Workforce Commission
1801 Alexander Bell Drive
Reston, VA 20191

202-296-2237
888-400-2237
FAX 202-296-1151
E-Mail: dbateson@aaes.org
Home Page: www.ewc-online.org

Dan Batson, Director

AAES's Engineering Workforce Commission monitors engineering job stats that help universities, corporations, and government set salary, hiring, enrollment, and degree trends in the marketplace. It publishes three major surveys per year that are regarded as the most accurate, objective and timely reports about the engineering workforce: Degrees, Enrollments, and Salaries.
35 Members
Founded in 1950

7248 Environmental Information Association
6935 Wisconsin Ave
Suite 306
Chevy Chase, MD 20815-6112

301-961-4999
888-343-4342
FAX 301-961-3094
E-Mail: info@eia-usa.org
Home Page: www.eia-usa.org

Kevin Cannan, President
Steve Fulford, Vice President

Brent Kynoch, Managing Director
Kim Goodman, Membership and Marketing Manager
Kelly Rutt, Development and Comm. Manager

Nonprofit organization dedicated to providing environmental information to individuals, members and industry. Disseminates information on the abatement of asbestos and lead-based paint, indoor air quality, safety and health issues, analytical issues and environmental site assessments.

7249 Ergosyst Associates
4840 W 15th Street
Suite 1012
Lawrence, KS 66049

785-842-7334
FAX 785-842-7348

John Burch, Publisher

Association for those interested in economics/human factors.

7250 Eta Kappa Nu
445 Hoes Lane
Piscataway, NJ 08854

732-465-5846
800-406-2590
E-Mail: info@hkn.org
Home Page: hkn.org

Evelyn Hirt, President
S.K. Ramesh, President-Elect
Ronald Jensen, Treasurer

Eta Kappa Nu (HKN) is the electrical and computer engineering honor society of the Institute of Electrical and Electronics Engineers (IEEE).
Founded in 1904

7251 Federation of Materials Societies
910 17th St NW
Suite 800
Washington, DC 20006-2606

202-296-9282
FAX 202-833-3014
E-Mail: betsyhou@ix.netcom.com
Home Page: www.materialsocieties.org

Betsy Houston, Executive Director
Petr Vanysek, President

Promotes cooperation among societies concerned with the understanding, development and application of materials and processes.
700K Members
Founded in 1972

7252 ICC Evaluation Service
3060 Saturn Street
Suite 100
Whittier, CA 92821

562-699-0541
800-423-6587
FAX 562-695-4694
E-Mail: es@icc-es.org
Home Page: www.iccsafe.org
Social Media: *Facebook, Twitter, LinkedIn*

Alex Olszowy III, President
M. Dwayne Garriss, Vice President
Jay Elbettar, P.E., CBO, Secretary/Treasurer
Dominic Sims, CEO
John Belcik, COO/CFO

An independent, nonprofit organization that conducts a voluntary program of evaluation of both traditional and innovative building materials, products and systems for compliance with the three major model codes in the United States.
Founded in 2003

7253 Illuminating Engineering Society of North America

120 Wall Street
17th Floor
New York, NY 10005

212-248-5000
FAX 212-248-5018
E-Mail: ies@ies.org
Home Page: www.ies.org

Clayton Gordon, Marketing Manager
Nicole DeGirolamo, Executive Assistant
Samuel Fontanez, Senior Art Director
Robert Horner, Director of Public Policy
Samantha Schwirck, Senior Associate Editor, LD+A

To advance knowledge and disseminate information for the improvement of the lighted environment to the benefit of society. Publishes a monthly magazine; Lighting Design & Applications.
7000 Members
Founded in 1906

7254 Industrial Designers Society of America

555 Grove St.
Suite 200
Herndon, VA 20170

703-707-6000
FAX 703-787-8501
E-Mail: idsa@idsa.org
Home Page: www.idsa.org
Social Media: *Facebook, Twitter, LinkedIn, Pinterest, Vimeo Flickr*

John Barratt, Chairman
Daniel Martinage, CAE, Executive Director
Karen Berube, Senior Creative Director
Lisa Brenner, CPA, Director of Finance & Accounting
Jordan Fleger, Member Relations Coordinator

The IDSA is the world's oldest, largest, member-driven society for product design, industrial design, interaction designs, human factors, ergonomics, design research, design management, university design and related fields.

7255 Industrial Fabrics Association International

1801 County Road B W
Roseville, MN 55113-4061

651-222-2508
800-225-4324
FAX 651-631-9334
E-Mail: generalinfo@ifai.com
Home Page: www.ifai.com
Social Media: *Facebook, Twitter, LinkedIn, YouTube*

Stephen Warner, CEO
JoAnne Ferris, Marketing Director

A not-for-profit trade association whose member companies represent the international specialty fabrics marketplace, who facilitates the development, application and promotion of products manufactures by the diverse membership.
2000 Members

7256 Industrial Research Institute

2200 Clarendon Boulevard
Suite 1102
Arlington, VA 22201

703-647-2580
FAX 703-647-2581
Home Page: www.iriweb.org

Tom Kavassalis, Chairman
Edward Bernstein, President
Ana Escobar, Associate, Executive & Publications
Lee Green, Vice President, Knowledge

Creation
Pamela R. Hanner, Manager, Web & IT

The mission is to enhance the effectiveness of technological innovation industry.
200 Members
Founded in 1938

7257 Institute of Biological Engineeringÿ

3493 Lansdowne Drive
Suite 2
Lexington, KE 40517

859-977-7450
FAX 859-271-0607
E-Mail: info@ibe.org
Home Page: www.ibe.org
Social Media: *Facebook, LinkedIn*

Jeong Yeol Yoon, President
Prem Parajuli, Secretary
Melanie Correll, Treasurer

A nonprofit professional organization which encourages inquiry and interest in the field of biological engineering.

7258 Institute of Industrial Engineers

3577 Parkway Lane
Suite 200
Norcross, GA 30092

770-449-0460
800-494-0460
FAX 770-441-3295
E-Mail: cs@iienet.org
Home Page: www.iienet.org
Social Media: *Facebook, Twitter, LinkedIn, YouTube, Google+*

Don Greene, CEO
Donna Calvert, COO
Nancy LaJoice, Director of Membership
Pam Patterson, Membership Administrator
Elaine Schwartz, Membership Administrator

Supports all industrial engineers with training, education, publications, conferences, etc.
15000 Members
Founded in 1948

7259 Institute of Noise Control Engineering

12100 Sunset Hills Rd.
Suite 130
Reston, VA 20190

703-234-4073
FAX 703-435-4390
E-Mail: ibo@inceusa.org
Home Page: www.inceusa.org

Gordon Ebbitt, President
Joseph M. Cuschieri, Executive Director
George C. Maling, Jr., Managing Director Emeritus
Deane Jaeger, Treasurer
Karl B. Washburn, Secretary

Supports those involved with hearing protection, modal analysis, and signal processing.
1200 Members

7260 Institute of Transportation Engineers

1627 Eye Street, NW
Suite 600
Washington, DC 20006

202-785-0060
FAX 202-785-0609
E-Mail: ite_staff@ite.org
Home Page: www.ite.org
Social Media: *Facebook, Twitter, LinkedIn, YouTube, Instagram, Google+*

W. Hibbett Neel, International President
John J Kennedy, International Vice President
Zaki Mustafa, Immediate Past President
Colleen L Hill-Stramsak, International Director
Dean J Kaiser, International Director

An international educational and scientific association of transportation professionals who

are responsible for meeting mobility and safety needs.
13199 Members
Founded in 1930

7261 Instrument Society of America

67 T.W. Alexander Drive
PO Box 12277
Research Triangle Park, NC 27709

919-549-8411
FAX 919-549-8288
E-Mail: info@isa.org
Home Page: www.isa.org
Social Media: *Facebook, Twitter, LinkedIn, YouTube, Flickr, Google+*

Richard W. Roop, President
Michelle Anderson, Human Resources Manager
Eugenia Bell, Production Coordinator
Patrick J Gouhin, Executive Director/CEO
James W Keaveney, Treasurer

A nonprofit technical society for engineers, technicians, businesspeople, educators and students who work, study or are interested in industrial automation and pursuits related to it, such as instrumentation.
30000 Members
Founded in 1945

7262 Instrumentation and Measurement Society

799 N Beverly Glen
Los Angeles, CA 90077

310-446-8280
FAX 732-981-0225
E-Mail: bob.myers@ieee.org
Home Page: http://sites.ieee.org/

Michael P. Kelly, Executive Director
Donna Florek, Program Specialist
Michael Markowycz, Program Specialist
Jo-Ellen Snyder, Tech Community Program Specialist
Grant Pitel, Volunteer PELS Webmaster

A subsidiary of the Institute of Electrical and Electronics Engineers. Provides support to scientists and technicians who design and develop electrical and electronic measuring instruments and equipment.
6500 Members
Founded in 1950

7263 Insulated Cable Engineers Association

PO Box 2694
Alpharetta, GA 30023

770-830-0369
E-Mail: info@icea.net
Home Page: www.icea.net

Lauri J Hiivala, President
Webmaster

Professional organization dedicated to developing cable standards for the electric power, control and telecommunications industries. Ensures safe, economical and efficient cable systems utilizing proven, state-of-the-art materials and concepts. ICEA documents are of interest to cable manufacturers, architects and engineers, utility and manufacturing plant personnel, telecommunication engineers, consultants and OEMs.
Founded in 1925

7264 International Association for Radio, Telec ommunications and Electromagnets

600 N. PLANKINTON AVE
Suite 301
Milwaukee, WI 53201

888-722-2440
888-722-2440
FAX 414-765-8661

E-Mail: info@exemplarglobal.org
Home Page: www.narte.org
Social Media: *Facebook, Twitter, LinkedIn, YouTube, Google+*

Peter Holtmann, President & Chief Executive Officer
Sal Agnello, General Manager, iNARTE

A worldwide, nonprofit, professional association which certifies qualified engineers and technicians in the fields of Telecommunications, Electromagnetic Compatibility/Interference (EMC/EMI), Product Safety (PS), Electrostatic Discharge control (ESD) and Wireless Systems Installation.

7265 International Facility Management Association

800 Gessner Rd.
Ste. 900
Houston, TX 77024-4257

713-623-4362
FAX 713-623-6124
E-Mail: ifma@ifma.org
Home Page: www.ifma.org
Social Media: *Facebook, Twitter, LinkedIn, YouTube, Flickr, RSS*

Michael D. Feldman, FMP, CM, Chair
Maureen Ehrenberg, FRICS, CRE, First Vice Chair
Tony Keane, CAE, President/CEO
John Perry, Chief Operating Officer
Aaron Clark, Vice President, Corporate Services

International association for facility management professionals.
22659 Members
Founded in 1978

7266 International Reprographic Association

401 N Michigan Avenue
Chicago, IL 60611

708-218-7755
FAX 312-527-6705
E-Mail: ed.avis@irga.com
Home Page: www.irga.com
Social Media: *LinkedIn*

Tony Militano, President
Steve Andrikut, Vendor Director
Ed Avis, Managing Director
Michael Shaw, Director
Joe Williamson, Director

Represents entrepreneurial businesses serving the wide-format imaging needs of graphic arts, architectural, engineering, manufacturing, corporate, legal, retail, and POP industries.
Founded in 1927

7267 International Society Weighing/Measurement

13017 Wisteria Drive
#341
Germantown, MD 20874

240-753-4397
FAX 866-285-3512
E-Mail: staff@iswm.org
Home Page: www.iswm.org

James Baxter, President
Jerry Finnegan, Vice President
Jamie Notter, Executive Director

Supports all those involved in the weighing and measurement industry.

7268 International Society for Optical Engineering

1000 20th Street
P O Box 10
Bellingham, WA 98225-6705

360-676-3290
888-504-8171

FAX 360-647-1445
E-Mail: spie@spie.org
Home Page: www.spie.org/
Social Media: *Facebook, Twitter, LinkedIn, RSS, YouTube, Blogspot*

Katerina Svanberg, President
William Arnold, Vice President
Brian Lula, Ssecretary/Treasurer
Eugene Arthurs, CEO

Serves the international, technical community as the premier provider of education, information, and resources covering optics, photonics, and their applications.
16000 Members
Founded in 1955

7269 Investigative Engineers Association

10001 W Oakland Park Blvd.
Suite 301
Sunrise, FL 33351

954-530-0715
844-217-6975
FAX 954-537-4942
E-Mail: jhogge@ienga.net
Home Page: www.ienga.net
Social Media: *Facebook, Twitter, LinkedIn*

Lewis W Ernest, Advisor
James R Hogge, CEO
Tom Hogge, President
Nancy Pashkoff, Marketing Director
Tammy Lane, National Director

Consists of independent forensic engineering firms nationwide and abroad.

7270 Materials Research Society

506 Keystone Dr
Warrendale, PA 15086-7573

724-779-3003
FAX 724-779-8313
E-Mail: info@mrs.org
Home Page: www.mrs.org

Oliver Kraft, President
Kristi S. Anseth, Vice President
Sean J. Hearne, Secretary
Michael R. Fitzsimmons, Treasurer
Todd M. Osman, Executive Director

The Materials Research Society is a not-for-profit organization that brings together scientists, engineers and research managers from industry, government, academia and research laboratories to share findings in the research and development of new materials of technological importance. The Materials Research Society promotes communication for the advancement of interdisciplinary materials research to improve the quality of life.
16000 Members
Founded in 1973

7271 NACE International

1440 S Creek Drive
Houston, TX 77084-4906

281-228-6200
800-797-6223
FAX 281-228-6300
E-Mail: firstservice@nace.org
Home Page: www.nace.org
Social Media: *Facebook, Twitter, LinkedIn, YouTube, Google+, Instagram*

Jim Feather, President
A. I. Sandy Williamson, Vice President
D. Terry Greenfield, Treasurer
Bob Chalker, CEO

Advances the knowledge of corrosion engineering and science in all major industries through education, certification, standards, publications, and public awareness.
21000 Members
Founded in 1943

7272 National Academy of Engineering

500 5th Street NW
Washington, DC 20001

202-334-3200
FAX 202-334-2290
Home Page: www.nae.edu
Social Media: *Twitter, LinkedIn, YouTube*

C. D. Mote, Jr., President
Alton D. Romig, Jr., Executive Officer
Mary Lee Berger-Hughes, Membership Director
Joan Zaorski, Director of Finance
Randy Atkins, Senior Program Officer

Promotes public understanding of the role that engineering plays in the technical fields. Sponsors programs aimed at meeting national needs in the field. Encourages research.
2000 Members
Founded in 1964

7273 National Association of Fire Equipment Distributors

180 N. Wabash Avenue
Suite 401
Chicago, IL 60601

312-461-9600
FAX 312-461-0777
E-Mail: dharris@nafed.org
Home Page: www.nafed.org
Social Media: *LinkedIn, YouTube*

Ed Hugill, President
Danny Harris, Executive Director/CEO
Norbert Makowka, Vice President, Technical
Tamara Matthews, Communications Manager
Socorro Garcia, Office Manager

Improves the economic environment, business performance, and technical competence in the fire protection industry.
Founded in 1963

7274 National Association of Minority Engineers

701 West Stadium Ave.
Suite 130
West Lafayette, IN 47907

765-494-4936
FAX 407-629-2502
E-Mail: namepa@namepa.org
Home Page: www.namepa.org

Virginia Booth Womack, President and Executive Director
Darryl A. Dickerson, Treasurer
Alaine M. Allen, Secretary
Jahi Sauk Simbai, Treasurer
Ivan Favila, Secretary

Provides a communication network among college-level administrators of minority engineering programs.
575 Members

7275 National Board of Boiler and Pressure Vessel Inspectors

1055 Crupper Ave
Columbus, OH 43229-1108

614-888-8320
FAX 614-888-0750
E-Mail: information@nationalboard.org
Home Page: www.nationalboard.org

Don Tanner, Executive Director
Connie Homer, Senior Executive Secretary

Membership is composed of chief boiler inspectors of states, major US cities and Canadian provinces having boiler laws.
55 Members
Founded in 1919

7276 National Council of Examiners for Engineering and Surveying
280 Seneca Creek Road
Seneca, SC 29678

864-654-6824
800-250-3196
FAX 864-654-6033
Home Page: www.ncees.org
Social Media: *Facebook, Twitter, LinkedIn, YouTube, RSS, Google+*

Michael Conzett, P.E., President
Jerry Carter, Chief Executive Officer
Davy McDowell, P.E., Chief Operating Officer
Tim Miller, P.E., Director of Exam Services
Donna Moss, SHRM-CP, PHR, Director of Human Resources

Promotes uniform standards of registration and coordinates interstate registration of engineers and surveyors.
68 Members
Founded in 1920

7277 National Electrical Contractors Association
3 Bethesda Metro Center
Suite 1100
Bethesda, MD 20814

301-657-3110
FAX 301-215-4500
Home Page: www.necanet.org
Social Media: *Facebook, Twitter, LinkedIn, YouTube, Flickr*

John M Grau, Chief Executive Officer
Daniel G Walter, Vice President & COO
Beth Ellis, Exe. Dir., Convention/Exposition
Michael Johnston, Executive Director
Bill Triplett, Executive Director

A trade association in the United States that represents the electrical industry.
Founded in 1901

7278 National Environmental Balancing Bureau
8575 Grovemont Cir
Gaithersburg, MD 20877-4121

301-977-3698
866-497-4447
FAX 301-977-9589
E-Mail: karen@nebb.org
Home Page: www.nebb.org

Jean-Paul Le Blanc, President
Glenn Fellman, Executive Vice President
Tiffany J. Suite, Operations Manager
Sheila Simms, Manager of Certifications
Leonard Maiani, Technical Director

NEBB is an international certification association for firms that deliver high performance building systems. Members perform testing, adjusting and balancing (TAB) of heating, ventilating and air-conditioning systems, commission and retro-commission building systems commissioning, execute sound and vibration testing, and test and certify lab fume hoods and electronic and bio clean rooms. NEBB holds the highest standards in certification.
Founded in 1971

7279 National Fire Protection Association
1 Batterymarch Park
Quincy, MA 02169-7471

617-770-3000
800-844-6058
FAX 617-770-0700
Home Page: www.nfpa.org
Social Media: *Facebook, Twitter, LinkedIn, YouTube, Flickr, Google+*

Ernest J Grant, Chair
Randolph W Tucker, First Vice Chair
Jim Pauley, President/ CEO
Julie Lynch, Vice President, Talent & Culture

Bruce H. Mullen, Executive Vice President and CFO

Publishes fire and building safety standards including the NationalElectrical Code.
Founded in 1896

7280 National Institute for Certification in Technologies
1420 King St
Alexandria, VA 22314-2750

703-548-1518
888-476-4238
FAX 703-682-2756
E-Mail: certify@nicet.org
Home Page: www.nicet.org
Social Media: *Facebook, LinkedIn*

Greg Cagle, SET, Chair
Thomas J. Frericks, Jr., CT, Vice-Chair
Michael A. Clark, Chief Operating Executive
Regina L. Stevenson, Director, Administrative Services
Gloria Mathson, Manager, General Services

Issues certification to engineering technicians and technologists who voluntarily apply for certification and satisfy competency criteria through examinations and verification of work experience.
113K Members
Founded in 1961

7281 National Society of Black Engineers
205 Daingerfield Road
Alexandria, VA 22314

703-549-2207
FAX 703-683-5312
E-Mail: info@nsbe.org
Home Page: www.nsbe.org
Social Media: *Facebook, Twitter, LinkedIn, Pinterest, Google+*

Neville Green, National Chair
Candice M Dixon, Vice Chairperson
Justin Brown, National Parliamentarian
Jennifer Jasper, National Secretary
Carl Mack, Executive Director

Supports all black technical professionals involved in the manufacturing engineering industry.
15000 Members
Founded in 1971

7282 National Society of Professional Engineers
1420 King St
Alexandria, VA 22314-2794

703-684-2800
FAX 703-836-4875
Home Page: www.nspe.org
Social Media: *Facebook, Twitter, LinkedIn*

Tim Austin, P.E., F.NSPE, President
Thomas C. Roberts, P.E., F.NSPE, Vice President
Julia M. Harrod, P.E., F.NSPE, Treasurer
Mark Golden, FASAE, CAE, Executive Director and Secretary

The mission of the Society is to promote the ethical, competent and licensed practice of engineering and to enhance the professional, social and economic well-being of its members.
60000 Members
Founded in 1934

7283 North American Die Casting Association
3250 N. Arlington Heights Rd
Ste 101
Arlington Heights, IL 60004

847-279-0001
FAX 847-279-0002

E-Mail: nadca@diecasting.org
Home Page: www.diecasting.org

Daniel Twarog, President

The organization serves as the voice of the industry, promoting growth and enhancing member's ability to compete domestically in the global marketplace.
3700 Members
Founded in 1989

7284 North American Manufacturing Research Institute
1 SME Drive
Dearborn, MI 48128

313-425-3000
800-733-4763
FAX 313-425-3400
E-Mail: service@sme.org
Home Page: www.sme.org
Social Media: *Facebook, Twitter, LinkedIn, Google+, RSS*

Wayne F. Frost, President
Jeffrey M. Krause, Chief Executive Officer
Kathleen Borgula, Human Resources
Erica Ciupak, Information Technology
Julie Duff, Finance

Members are engaged in manufacturing, research and technology development.
180 Members
Founded in 1973

7285 Order Of The Engineer
PO Box 25473
Scottsdale, AZ 85255-0107

866-364-7464
FAX 480-585-6418
E-Mail: orderofeng@gmail.com
Home Page: www.order-of-the-engineer.org

Paula Ostaff, Executive Director

An association for graduate and professional engineers in the United States that emphasizes pride and responsibility in the engineering profession.

7286 Pi Tau Sigma
Home Page: www.pitausigma.net

Dr. Mun Young Choi, President
Dr. Gloria J Wiens, Eastern Region Vice-President
Dr. Alex Moutsoglou, National Secretary-Treasurer
Dr. Chris Wilson, Central Region Vice-President
Dr. Darryl James, Western Region Vice-President

An International Mechanical Engineering Honor Society.
Founded in 1947

7287 Professional Engineers in Private Practice
1420 King Street
Alexandria, VA 22314-2750

703-684-2800
FAX 703-836-4875
Home Page: www.nspe.org
Social Media: *Facebook, Twitter, LinkedIn*

Terrance N Glunt, Chair
Larry L Britt, PE, Chair-Elect
Steve M Theno, PE, Secretary

Addresses the concerns of individual engineers in private practice, primarily working in design for construction. Offers resources, standard contracts, newsletters and management guidance in the forms of videos, books, and newsletters.
24M Members
Founded in 1956

7288 Railway Engineering: Maintenance Suppliers Association
500 New Jersey Ave. NW
Suite 400
Washington, DC 20001

202-715-2921
FAX 202-204-5753
E-Mail: info@remsa.org
Home Page: www.remsa.org

Trent Marshall, President
Bruce R. Wise, Vice President
Alan D. Reynolds, Secretary/Treasurer
David Tennent, Executive Director, REMSA
C. David Soule, CEM, Director of Trade Shows, REMSA

Members are distributors and manufacturers of railway machinery supplies and services.
225 Members
Founded in 1965

7289 Refrigeration Service Engineers Society
1911 Rohlwing Road
Suite A
Rolling Meadows, IL 60008-1397

847-297-6464
800-297-5660
FAX 847-297-5038
E-Mail: general@rses.org
Home Page: www.rses.org
Social Media: *Facebook, Twitter, LinkedIn, RSS*

Harlan Krepcik, CMS, RCT, Intl President
Michael J. Thompson, CMS, Intl Vice President
Nick Reggi, CMS, RCT, Intl Secretary/Treasurer
Roger M. Hensley, CMS, RCT, Board Chairman
Steve Wright, Sr., CMS, RCT, International Sergeant at Arms

A leading education, training and certification association for heating, ventilation, air conditioning and refrigeration professionals. RSES credentials include the SM/CM/CMS exam series as well as one of the largest EPA Section 608 certification programs in the industry.
15231 Members
Founded in 1933

7290 Reliability Engineering and Management Institute
1077 N Highland
Tucson, AZ 85721

520-626-8324
FAX 520-621-8191
E-Mail: dimitri@u.arizona.edu
Home Page: www.u.arizona.edu

Michele Norin, VP for IT/CIO
Christian Schreiber, Chief Information Security Officer
Derek Masseth, Deputy Chief Info Officer/CTO
Thomas C Bourgeois, Executive Director
Kay Stevens Beasock, Director, Communications/Marketing

Supports all engineers and managers who deal with the issue of Reliability Engineering. Provides publications, training, education, new techniques and product forums and two annual conference.
Founded in 1963
Mailing list available for rent: 44000 names

7291 Research Council on Structural Connections
Sargent & Lundy

55 E Monroe Street
Chicago, IL 60603-5780

312-269-2000
FAX 312-269-3681
E-Mail: rshaw@steelstructures.com
Home Page: www.boltcouncil.org

Ray Tide, Chairman Executive Committee
Geoff Kulak, Vice Chairman
Charles Carter, Chairman Membership/Funding
Emile Troup, Secretary/Treasurer

Researches the effects of stress on bolted and riveted joints for its member companies and institutions.
45 Members
Founded in 1946

7292 Robotics Industries Association
900 Victors Way
Suite 140
Ann Arbor, MI 48108

734-994-6088
FAX 734-994-3338
E-Mail: webmaster@robotics.org
Home Page: www.robotics.org
Social Media: *Facebook, Twitter, LinkedIn, Google+*

Stuart Shepherd, Chairperson
Jeff Burnstein, President
Dana Whalls, Vice President
Bob Doyle, Director of Communications
Alex Shikany, Director, Market Analysis

Trade group organized specifically to serve the robotics industry. Member companies include leading robot manufacturers, users, system integrators, component suppliers, research groups and consulting firms. Trade show is held every two years.
250+ Members
Founded in 1974

7293 Science and Technology Society
125 Maiden Ln
15th Floor
New York, NY 10038

212-248-0200
FAX 212-248-0245
E-Mail: ricky@avs.org
Home Page: www.avs.org

Christie R Marrian, President
John Coburn, Treasurer
Joseph E Greene, Clerk/Secretary

Supports all those in the vacuum industry, especially scientists and engineers.
6000 Members
Founded in 1953

7294 Sigma Phi Delta
438 Smithfield Street
East Liverpool, OH 43920-1723

330-385-5287
E-Mail: webmaster@sigphi.org
Home Page: www.sigphi.org
Social Media: *Facebook, Twitter, LinkedIn*

Alixandre R. Minden PE, PMP, Grand President
Eric J. Pew, Grand VP
Tyler S Condon, Treasurer
Joshua J. Lester, Director of Alumni Relations
Erik N. Schultz, Director of Chapter Development

A professional and social fraternity in engineering.
7200 Members
Founded in 1924

7295 Society for Experimental Mechanics
7 School St
Bethel, CT 06801-1855

203-790-6373
FAX 203-790-4472

E-Mail: sem@sem1.com
Home Page: www.sem.org
Social Media: *Facebook, Twitter, YouTube*

Peter Ifgu, President
Emmanuel Gdoutos, Vice President
Jon Rogers, Treasurer
Tom Proulx, Executive Director

Supports all those involved with general experimental mechanics and the measurement of stresses and strains in metals and other materials.
Founded in 1943

7296 Society for the Advancement of Material and Process Engineering
1161 Parkview Drive
Suite 200
Covina, CA 91724-3759

626-331-0616
800-562-7360
FAX 626-332-8929
E-Mail: sampe@sampe.org
Home Page: www.sampe.org
Social Media: *Facebook, Twitter, LinkedIn*

Gregg Balko, Executive Director
Mike Keilty, Controller
Dr Scott Beckwith, Technical Director

An international professional member society, provides information on new materials and processing technology either via technical forums, journal publications, or books in which professionals in this field can exchange ideas and air their views.
Founded in 1944

7297 Society of Allied Weight Engineers
5734 E. Lucia Walk
Long Beach, CA 90803-4015

562-596-2873
FAX 562-596-2874
E-Mail: exdirector@sawe.org
Home Page: www.sawe.org

Anthony Primozich, President
Robert Hundl, Executive VP
Rick Watkins, Senior VP
Jerry L. Pierson, VP Training
Ronald Fox, Executive Director

Consists of engineers in the aerospace, shipbuilding, land vehicles, offshore and allied industries.
800 Members
Founded in 1941

7298 Society of American Military Engineers
607 Prince St
Alexandria, VA 22314-3117

703-549-3800
800-336-3097
FAX 703-684-0231
E-Mail: webmanager@same.org
Home Page: www.same.org

Jane C. Penny, President
Col. Kurt Ubbelohde, F.SAME, Vice President
Gen. Joseph Schroedel, P.E.,, Executive Director
Desyre, Jones, Senior Operations & Admin Manager
Belle Febbraro, Program Manager

Brings together professional engineers and those in engineering related fields to improve and increase the engineering capabilities of the nation and to exchange and advance the knowledge of engineering technologies, applications and practices.
20000 Members
Founded in 1920

7299 Society of Automotive Engineers
1200 G St., NW
Suite 800
Washington, DC 20005

202-463-7318
FAX 202-463-7319
Home Page: www.sae.org
Social Media: *Facebook, Twitter, LinkedIn, Google+*

Frank Menchaca, Chief Product Officer
Dana M Pless, Chief Financial Officer
David L Schutt, Chief Executive Officer
George Bradley, Esq., General Counsel
Sandra L. Dillner, Director of Human Resources

Advances mobility in land, sea, air, and space.
Founded in 1905

7300 Society of Broadcast Engineers
9102 North Meridian Street
Suite 150
Indianapolis, IN 46260

317-846-9000
Home Page: www.sbe.org
Social Media: *Facebook, Twitter, LinkedIn, YouTube, Blogger*

Jerry Massey, President
James E. Leifer, CPBE, Vice President
John Poray, CAE, Executive Director
Megan Clappe, Certification Director
Debbie Hennessey, Sustaining Member Manager

A professional organization for engineers in broadcast radio and television.
5500 Members

7301 Society of Fire Protection Engineers
9711 Washingtonian Blvd
Suite 380
Gaithersburg, MD 20878

301-718-2910
FAX 240-328-6225
E-Mail: foundation@sfpe.org
Home Page: www.sfpe.org
Social Media: *Facebook, Twitter, LinkedIn, YouTube, RSS*

Michael Madden, P.E., FSFPE, President
Milosh Puchovsky, P.E., FSFPE, President Elect
Jack Poole, P.E., FSFPE, Secretary-Treasurer
Nicole Testa Boston, CAE, Ex-Officio
David Barber, Director

The largest professional society for fire safety engineers.
4500 Members
Founded in 1971

7302 Society of Hispanic Professional Engineers
323-725-3970
703-373-7930
E-Mail: shpenational@shpe.org
Home Page: national.shpe.org
Social Media: *Facebook, Twitter, LinkedIn, YouTube, Instagram*

Barry Cordero, Chair
Miguel Alemany, Vice Chair
Yuliana Porras Mendoza, Secretary
Ernesto Felix, Treasurer
Rodrigo T. Garcia, President

A national organization of professional engineers to serve as rolemodels in the Hispanic community.
Founded in 1974

7303 Society of Manufacturing Engineers
1 SME Drive
Dearborn, MI 48128

313-425-3000
800-733-4763

FAX 313-425-3400
E-Mail: service@sme.org
Home Page: www.sme.org
Social Media: *Facebook, Twitter, LinkedIn, Google +, RSS, YouTube*

Wayne F. Frost, President
Jeffery M. Krause, Chief Executive Officer
Dean L. Bartles, PhD, FSME, President-Elect
Sandra L. Bouckley, Vice President
Thomas R. Kurfess, PhD, FSME, PE, Treasurer

Professional society dedicated to advancing scientific knowledge in the field of manufacturing and to applying its resources for researching, writing, publishing and disseminating information.
70M Members
Founded in 1932

7304 Society of Naval Architects and Marine Engineers
99 Canal Center Plaza
Suite 310
Alexandria, VA 22314

703-997-6701
FAX 703-997-6702
Home Page: www.sname.org

Erik Seither, Executive Director
Jodi Lane, Executive Administrative
Mike Hall, Director Of Membership
Carole Herzog, Membership Coordinator
Susan Evans Grove, Director Of Content

A global professional society that provides a forum for the advancement of the engineering profession as applied to the marine field.
8500 Members
Founded in 1893

7305 Society of Petroleum Engineers
222 Palisades Creek Dr.
Richardson, TX 75080

972-952-9393
800-456-6863
FAX 972-952-9435
E-Mail: spedal@spe.org
Home Page: www.spe.org
Social Media: *Facebook, Twitter, LinkedIn, Instagram, YouTube*

Helge Hove Haldorsan Statoil, President
Roland Moreau, Vice President, Finance
Dan Hill, Director For Academia
David Curry, Technical Director
Trey Shaffer, Technical Director

To provide the means for collection, dissemination and exchange of technical information concerning the development of oil and gas resources, subsurface fluid flow and production of other materials through well bores for the public benefit.
64000 Members
Founded in 1957

7306 Society of Rheology
American Institute of Physics
2 Huntington Quadrangle
Suite 1N01
Meville, NY 11747-4502

516-576-2471
FAX 516-576-2223
E-Mail: rheology@aip.org
Home Page: www.rheology.org

Greg McKenna, President
Gareth H. McKinley, Vice President
Albert Co, Secretary
Montgomery T. Shaw, Treasurer
Ralph H. Colby, Editor

Composed of physicists, chemists, biologists, engineers, and mathematicians interested in advancing and applying rheology, which is defined as the science of deformation and flow of matter.
1700 Members

7307 Society of Tribologists and Lubrication Engineers
840 Busse Hwy
Park Ridge, IL 60068-2376

847-825-5536
FAX 847-825-1456
E-Mail: information@stle.org
Home Page: www.stle.org

Dr. Martin N. Webster, President
Dr. Eli Erdemir, Vice President
Mr. Michael Anderson, Secretary
Mr. Greg Croce, Treasurer
Mr. James Arner, Director

Strives to advance the science of lubrication tribology and related arts and sciences. Sponsors courses and an annual meeting.
4400 Members
Founded in 1960

7308 Society of Women Engineers
203 N La Salle Street
Suite 1675
Chicago, IL 60601

877-793-4636
E-Mail: hq@swe.org
Home Page: societyofwomenengineers.swe.org
Social Media: *Facebook, Twitter, LinkedIn, YouTube, Instagram, Google+*

Colleen M. Layman, President
Jessica Rannow, President Elect
Stephanie Loete, Secretary
Cindy Hoover, Treasurer
Mary Perkinson, Director Of Advocacy

An organization that stimulates women to achieve full potential in careers as engineers.

7309 Tau Beta Pi Association
PO Box 2697
Knoxville, TN 37901-2697

865-546-4578
FAX 865-546-4579
Home Page: www.tbp.org
Social Media: *Facebook, Twitter, WordPress*

Joseph P. Blackford, President
Norman Pih, Vice President
Curtis D. Gomulinski, Exec. Dir./ Sec-Treasurer & Editor
James D. Froula, Secretary-Treasurer Emeritus
Susan L. R. Holl, Councillor

The National Engineering honor society recognizes engineering students of superior scholarship and exemplary character and practitioners of engineering. The organization includes 230 collegiate chapters and 16 alumnus chapters.
525K Members
Founded in 1885

7310 The American Association for Wind Engineers
1415 Blue Spruce Drive
Suite 3
Fort Collins, CO 80524

970-498-2334
FAX 970-221-3124
E-Mail: aawe@aawe.org
Home Page: www.aawe.org

Dr. Partha Sarkar, President
Dr. Greg Kopp, President Elect
Dr. Steve C. S. Cai, Secretary/Treasurer
Dr. David O Prevatt, Board of Directors
Dr. Anne Cope, Board of Directors

A nonprofit professional organization that promotes and disseminates technical information in the research community.
Founded in 1995

7311 The American Society For Nondestructive Testing
1711 Arlingate Lane
Columbus, OH 43228-0518

614-274-6003
800-222-2768
FAX 614-274-6899
E-Mail: pwhite@asnt.org
Home Page: www.asnt.org
Social Media: *Facebook, Twitter, LinkedIn, YouTube*

Amy Bereson, Executive Director
Michelle Thomas, Executive Dir. Admin. Assistant
Heather Cowles, Senior Manager
Pat White, Membership Coordinator
Debbie Segor, Sections Coordinator

A technical society for nondestructive testing professionals.
Founded in 1941

7312 The Associated General Contractors of America
2300 Wilson Blvd.
Suite 300
Arlington, VA 22201

703-548-3118
800-242-1767
FAX 703-837-5405
E-Mail: info@agc.org
Home Page: www.agc.org
Social Media: *Facebook, Twitter, LinkedIn*

Charles L. Greco, President
Art Daniel, Senior Vice President
Mark Knight, Vice President
Joseph Stella, Treasurer
Stephen E. Sandherr, Executive Director

Trade association for the construction industry.
26000 Members

7313 The Order of the Engineer, Inc.
PO Box 25473
Scottsdale, AZ 85255-0107

866-364-7464
FAX 480-585-6418
Home Page: www.order-of-the-engineer.org

Kenneth McGowan, Chair
Paula Ostaff, Executive Director

Association for graduate and professional engineers emphasizing pride and responsibility.
Founded in 1970

7314 Theta Tau
1011 San Jacinto
Suite 205
Austin, TX 78701

512-482-1904
800-264-1904
FAX 512-472-4820
E-Mail: central.office@thetatau.org
Home Page: www.thetatau.org
Social Media: *Facebook, Twitter, LinkedIn*

Michael Livingston, Grand Regent
Justin Wisemen, Grand Vice Regent
Rachael Stensrud, Grand Scribe
J. Matthew Clark, Grand Treasurer

A professional fraternity in engineering. Founded at the University of Minnesota. Purpose of the fraternity is to develop and maintain a high standard of professional interest among its members, and to unite them in a strong bond of fraternal fellowship.
30000 Members
Founded in 1904

7315 TheÿTire Society
810 E. 10th St.
Lawrence, KS 66044

785-865-9403
800-627-0326

FAX 785-843-6153
E-Mail: tst@allenpress.com
Home Page: www.tiresociety.org

Saied Taheri, President
Randy Jenniges, Vice President
Ric Mousseau, Past President
Michell Hoo Fatt, Secretary
Rusty Adams, Treasurer

A professional engineering society that increases and disseminates knowledge as it pertains to the science and technology of tires.

7316 United Engineering Foundation
16 Copper Penny Road
Flemington, NJ 08822-5540

E-Mail: engfnd@aol.com
Home Page: www.uefoundation.org

Ian Sadler, President
Patrick J. Natale, Executive Director

Supports research in engineering science and seeks to advance the profession of engineering.
19 Members
Founded in 1904

7317 United Engineering Trustees
16 Copper Penny Road
Flemington, NJ 08822-5540

E-Mail: engfnd@aol.com
Home Page: www.uefoundation.org

Ian Sadler, President
Patrick J. Natale, Executive Director

Aims to advance engineering arts and sciences.
Founded in 1904

Newsletters

7318 AEG News
Association of Engineering Geologists
PO Box 460518
Denver, CO 80246

303-757-2926
FAX 303-757-2969
E-Mail: aeg@aegweb.org
Home Page: www.aegweb.org

Dave Bieber, President
Darrel Schmitz, President-Elect/VP
Becky Roland, Chief Staff Executive
Terry West, Treasurer
Dorian Kuper, Secretary

Includes reports of committee activities, section news, and other news items of interest to the profession.
Frequency: Quarterly

7319 AIP History Newsletter
American Institute of Physics
1 Physics Ellipse
College Park, MD 20740-3841

301-209-3100
FAX 301-209-0843
E-Mail: dylla@aip.org
Home Page: www.aip.org

Marc Brodsky, CEO
Margaret Wiley, Senior Executive Secretary
Benjamin Snavely, AIP Corporate Secretary
Melissa Poleski, Assistant To Corporate Secretary

Our Newsletter reports on work in the history of physics (and allied fields such as astronomy and geophysics), carried out at the American Institute of Physics and elsewhere. It includes lists of recent publications in the history of modern physics, and reports on papers deposited in archives worldwide.

7320 ASFE Newslog
ASFE/The Geoprofessional Business Association
8811 Colesville Rd
Suite G106
Silver Spring, MD 20910-4343

301-565-2733
FAX 301-589-2017
E-Mail: info@asfe.org
Home Page: www.asfe.org

David Gaboury, President

Information on geo professional, environmental, and civil engineering firms. Past issues are available through the online store. Electronic copies are always free to members.

7321 ASGE Newsletter
American Society of Gas Engineers
PO Box 66
Artesia, CA 90702

562-455-9417
E-Mail: asgecge@aol.com
Home Page: www.asge-national.org

Nancy Wilson, President
Sham Kassab, VP
Susan McCarthy, Treasurer
Jerry Moore, Executive Director

Keeps members current on events and issues facing the Gas Appliance Industry. Features articles that address new technologies and trends.

7322 ASTM International Business Link
ASTM International
PO Box C700
W Conshohocken, PA 19428-0700

610-832-9500
FAX 610-832-9555
E-Mail: service@astm.org
Home Page: www.astm.org

James A Thomas, President

Provides information on the topics connecting the business and technical communities.
Frequency: Semi-Annual

7323 Access ASTM International
ASTM International
PO Box C700
W Conshohocken, PA 19428-0700

610-832-9500
FAX 610-832-9555
E-Mail: service@astm.org
Home Page: www.astm.org

James A Thomas, President
John Pace, Manager
Jeff Adkins, Manager
Fran Dougherty, Administrative Assistant

Periodic update for ASTM's global customers.
Frequency: Semi-Annual

7324 American Automatic Control Council Newsletter
AACC Secretariat
2145 Sheridan Road
Evanston, IL 60208-3118

847-491-8175
FAX 847-491-4455
E-Mail: aacc@ece.northwestern.edu
Home Page: www.a2c2.org

Bonnie Heck, Publisher
William Levine, President
A Ulsoy, Vice-President

Automatic control council information.
4 Pages
Frequency: Quarterly
Founded in 1961

7325 BMES Bulletin
Biomedical Engineering Society

8401 Corporate Dr
Suite 140
Hyattsville, MD 20785-2263

301-459-1999
FAX 301-459-2444
E-Mail: info@bmes.org
Home Page: www.bmes.org

Barbara Dunlevy, Executive Director
Heather Comstock, Meeting Manager

The Bulletin presents bioengineering science
articles, student chapter news, Society and public policy announcements, employment opportunities, and a calendar of conference and
events. It is also a forum for member opinions
through editorials and letters.
Cost: $30.00
Frequency: Monthly
Circulation: 3500
Founded in 1969
Printed in 2 colors on matte stock

7326 Bulletin of Tau Beta Pi
Tau Beta Pi Association
PO Box 2697
Knoxville, TN 37901-2697

865-546-4578
FAX 865-546-4579
Home Page: www.tbp.org

R E Hawks, Editor

The purpose of The Bulletin is to disseminate
news and information about Tau Beta Pi of special interest to the collegiate chapters. It is an
important vehicle for the annual repetition of
instructions from the Executive Council and
national headquarters to the chapters on election and initiation procedures and for the exchange of chapter project ideas and experience.
Frequency: 3x Annually
Founded in 1925

7327 Catalyst Newsletter
Adhesive & Sealant Council
7101 Wisconsin Ave
Suite 990
Bethesda, MD 20814-4805

301-986-9700
FAX 301-986-9795
E-Mail: info@ascouncil.org
Home Page: www.ascouncil.org

Matt Croson, President

**7328 Computer Integrated Manufacture
and Engineering**
Lionheart Publishing
506 Roswell St Se
Suite 220
Marietta, GA 30060-4101

770-422-3139
FAX 770-432-6969
E-Mail: lpi@lionhrtpub.com
Home Page: www.lionhrtpub.com/

Marvin Diamond, Advertising Sales Manager

Explores cutting edge developments in manufacturing systems operation management.
Circulation: 24000

7329 Cross Connection Protection Devices
American Society of Sanitary Engineering
901 Canterbury Rd
Suite A
Westlake, OH 44145-1480

440-835-3040
FAX 440-835-3488
Home Page: www.asse-plumbing.org

James Bickford, President
Donald Summers, First VP
John Flader, Treasurer

Summary of backflow conditions and method
of eliminating or minimizing their possible

dangers.
Cost: $15.00

7330 Echoes Newsletter
Acoustical Society of America
2 Huntington Quad
Suite 1N01
Melville, NY 11747-4505

516-576-2360
FAX 516-576-2377
E-Mail: asa@aip.org
Home Page: www.asa.aip.org

Charles E Schmid, President

Covers current and topical happenings of general interest and features articles about current
research and personalities. Distributed free to
members.
Frequency: Quarterly

**7331 Engineering Department
Management and Administration
Report**
Institute of Management and Administration
3 Bethesda Metro Center
Suite 250
Bethesda, MD 20814

703-341-3500
FAX 800-253-0332
Home Page: www.ioma.com

Focuses on improving efficiency and productivity.
Cost: $245.00
16 Pages
Frequency: Monthly

7332 Engineering Times
National Society of Professional Engineers
1420 King St
Alexandria, VA 22314-2794

703-684-2800
FAX 703-836-4875
E-Mail: webmaster@nspe.org
Home Page: www.nspe.org

Larry Jacobson, Executive Director/Secretary
Robert Grey, President

Reports on issues affecting the engineering
profession; featured monthly series on ethics.
Free to members.
Cost: $30.00
24 Pages

7333 High-Tech Materials Alert
Technical Insights
605 3rd Avenue
New York, NY 10158

212-850-6824
800-245-6217
FAX 212-850-8643

Kenneth Kovaly, Publisher

Opportunities in advanced materials.
Cost: $867.00
12 Pages

**7334 Hufact Quarterly: A Current
Awareness Resource**
Ergosyst Associates
123 W 8th Street
Suite 210
Lawrence, KS 66044-2687

FAX 785-842-7348

John Burch, Publisher

Covers economics/human factors.
Cost: $100.00

7335 IE News: Ergonomics
Institute of Industrial Engineers

3577 Parkway Lane
Suite 200
Norcross, GA 30092

770-449-0460
800-494-0460
FAX 770-441-3295
E-Mail: cs@iienet.org
Home Page: www.iienet.org

Don Greene, CEO
Donna Calvert, COO

Newsletter for Ergonomics Division.
4 Pages
Frequency: Quarterly
Founded in 1948

**7336 IE News: Facilities Planning and
Design**
Institute of Industrial Engineers
25 Technology Pkwy S
Suite 150
Norcross, GA 30092-2946

770-449-0461
FAX 770-263-8532

Dona Brown, Publisher

Accepts advertising.
4 Pages

7337 IE News: Operations Research
Institute of Industrial Engineers
25 Technology Pkwy S
Suite 150
Norcross, GA 30092-2946

770-449-0461
FAX 770-263-8532

Dona Brown, Publisher

News for industrial engineers. Accepts advertising.
4 Pages

**7338 IE News: Quality Control and
Reliability Engineering**
Institute of Industrial Engineers
25 Technology Pkwy S
Suite 150
Norcross, GA 30092-2946

770-449-0461
FAX 770-263-8532

Dona Brown, Publisher

Association news.
4 Pages

7339 Innovators Digest
InfoTeam
PO Box 15640
Plantation, FL 33318-5640

954-473-9560
FAX 954-473-0544

Merton Allen, Editor

A multidisciplinary publication covering developments in science, engineering, products, markets, business development, manufacturing and
other technological developments having industrial or commercial significance.
Frequency: Bi-Annual

7340 Instrumentation Newsletter
National Instruments
6504 Bridge Point Parkway
Austin, TX 78730-5017

512-389-9119
888-280-7645
FAX 512-794-8411

E-Mail: info@natinst.com
Home Page: www.natinst.com

Gail Folkins, Managing Editor
John Graff, Vice President of Sales
James Truchard, President
Frequency: Quarterly
Circulation: 150000
Founded in 1976

7341 Last Word

American Council of Engineering
Companies
1015 15th St
8th Floor NW
Washington, DC 20005-2605

202-347-7474
FAX 202-898-0068
E-Mail: acec@acec.org
Home Page: www.acec.org
Social Media: *Facebook, Twitter*

Dave Raymond, President
Ann Randstapter, Editor
Sheila Mahoutchian, Marketing Manager
Mary Jaffe, Director, Publications
Alan Crockett, Director, Public Relations

Independent private practice engineering companies.
Cost: $90.00
2 Pages
Frequency: Monthly
Circulation: 5800
Founded in 1905
Printed in on glossy stock

7342 Leadership and Management in Engineering

American Society of Civil Engineers
1801 Alexander Bell Dr
Suite 100
Reston, VA 20191-4382

703-295-6300
800-548-2723
FAX 703-295-6222
E-Mail: cybrarian@asce.org
Home Page: www.afce.org

D Wayne Klotz, President

A cutting-edge periodical focusing on the art and practice of management and leadership in the civil engineering community.
Frequency: Quarterly

7343 Licensure Exchange

National Council of Examiners for
Engineering
280 Seneca Creek Road
PO Box 1686
Clemson, SC 29633

864-654-6824
800-250-3196
FAX 864-654-6033
Home Page: www.ncees.org

Keri Anderson, Editor
Ashley Cheney, Treasurer
David Widmer, Treasurer
Theodore Sack, Vice President

Provides information, opinion, and ideas regarding the licensure of engineers and land surveyors.
Frequency: Bi-Monthly

7344 Nuclear News

American Nuclear Society
555 N Kensington Ave
La Grange Park, IL 60526-5592

708-352-6611
FAX 708-352-0499
Home Page: www.ans.org

Jack Tuohy, Executive Director

Covers the latest developments in the nuclear field, a large part of which concerns nuclear en-

ergy - in particular, the 104 operating U.S. nuclear power plants, and another 334 operating elsewhere around the globe.
Cost: $365.00
Frequency: Monthly
Founded in 2005

7345 Plumbing Systems & Design

American Society Of Plumbing Engineers
2980 S River Rd
Des Plaines, IL 60018-4203

773-693-2773
FAX 773-695-9007
E-Mail: info@psdmagazine.org
Home Page: www.psdmagazine.org/

Tom Govedarica, Executive Publisher
Gretchen Pienta, Managing Editor
Maria Barriga, Circulation Manager
Jill Dirksen, Technical Director
David Ropinski, Graphic Designer

Industry leading technical publication with ASPE news and features. Free to ASPE members and subscribers.
Cost: $150.00
Circulation: 25500
Printed in 4 colors on glossy stock

7346 Power

McGraw Hill
PO Box 182604
Columbus, OH 43272-1095

720-485-5000
877-833-5524
FAX 614-759-3749
Home Page: www.mcgraw-hill.com

Harold McGraw, Chairman and President
Jack Callahan, Executive VP

Published for engineers who design, construct, operate and maintain power operating facilities in cogeneration and independent power plants in electric utilities. Accepts advertising.
Cost: $50.00
Frequency: Monthly
Founded in 1888

7347 Rheology Bulletin

Society of Rheology
2 Huntington Quadrangle
Suite 1N01
Meville, NY 11747-4502

516-576-2471
FAX 516-576-2223
E-Mail: rheology@aip.org
Home Page: www.rheology.org

Faith Morrison, President
Jeffrey Giacomin, Vice President
Albert Co, Secretary
Montgomery Shaw, Treasurer

To inform members of the Society affairs and matters of general interest to rheologists.
Frequency: 2x yearly

7348 Robotics Today

Society of Manufacturing Engineers
1 Sme Drive
Dearborn, MI 48128

313-425-3000
800-733-4763
FAX 343-425-3400
E-Mail: service@sme.org
Home Page: www.sme.org

Paul Bradley, President
Mark Tomlinson, CEO and Executive Director
Dennis Bray, Vice President
Michael Molner, Secretary/Treasurer

Reports on robotics used in manufacturing.
Cost: $60.00
8 Pages
Frequency: Quarterly
Mailing list available for rentat $95 per M
Printed in 2 colors on matte stock

7349 SAWE Technical Papers

Society of Allied Weight Engineers
5734 E. Lucia Walk
Long Beach, CA 90803-4015

562-596-2873
FAX 562-596-2874
E-Mail: exdirector@sawe.org
Home Page: www.sawe.org

Patrick Brown, President
Jeffrey Cerro, Executive VP
Ronald Fox, Executive Director

The Technical Paper Index.
Frequency: Every 3 Years

7350 Systems

Institute of Industrial Engineers
25 Technology Pkwy S
Suite 150
Norcross, GA 30092-2946

770-449-0461
FAX 770-263-8532

SL Browder, Publisher

Newsletter for IIE's society.
4 Pages
Frequency: Quarterly

7351 The AOCS Newsletter

American Oil Chemists' Society
2710 S Boulder Drive
P.O. Box 17190
Urbana, IL 61803-6996

217-359-2344
FAX 217-351-8091
E-Mail: general@aocs.org
Home Page: www.aocs.org
Social Media: *Facebook, Twitter, LinkedIn*

Gloria Cook, Senior Director, Finance
Jeffry L. Newman, Senior Director, Programs

The AOCS Newsletter is sent electronically each month to approximately 4,200 AOCS members and 10,000 other related industry professionals. It contains the latest AOCS news, including discounted offers, upcoming meeting information and registration details, AOCS press releases, and technical services updates.
4500 Members
Frequency: Annual/April-May
Founded in 1909

7352 Tribology Letters

Kluwer Academic/Plenum Publishers
840 Busse Highway
Park Ridge, IL 60068-2376

847-825-5536
FAX 847-825-1456
E-Mail: information@stle.org
Home Page: www.stle.org

Karl Phipps, Associate Managing Editor

Devoted to the development of the science of Tribology and to its applications. It also serves as the depository for new information on the mechanical properties of surfaces.
Frequency: 95x Yearly

7353 Velocitus Officers Newsletter

Theta Tau
815 Brazos
Suite 710
Austin, TX 78701

512-482-1904
800-264-1904
FAX 512-472-4820
E-Mail: central.office@thetatau.org
Home Page: www.thetatau.org

Michael T Abraham, Executive Director
Dana Wortman, Grand Treasurer
Brandon J Satterwhite, Western Regional
Director
Matthew Clark, Treasurer

Available by request via email or calling our 800 number.

Magazines & Journals

7354 AFE Facilities Engineering Journal
Association for Facilities Engineering
8160 Corporate Park Drive
#125
Cincinnati, OH 45242-3309

513-489-2473
FAX 513-247-7422
E-Mail: Info@AFE.org
Home Page: www.afe.org

Gabriella Jacobs, Communications Manager
Bob Kruhm, Advertising Manager
Patrick Janszen, Art Director
Michael Ireland, Executive Director

Information on maintenance management, energy conservation, safety and security, computerized maintenance management systems, environmental compliance, telecommunications and related issues.
Cost: $225.00
Frequency: Monthly
Circulation: 6000
ISSN: 1088-5900
Founded in 1956
Mailing list available for rent: 10000 names at $100 per M
Printed in 4 colors on glossy stock

7355 ASEE Prism
American Society for Engineering Education
1818 N St NW
#600
Washington, DC 20036-2476

202-331-3500
FAX 202-265-8504
E-Mail: pubsinfo@asee.org
Home Page: www.asee.org

Frank L Huband, Executive Director
Mary Dalheim, Editor
Sherra E. Kerns, President

Geared towards educators in the engineering technology fields.
Frequency: Monthly
Circulation: 12000
Founded in 1893

7356 ASME News
American Society of Mechanical Engineers
3 Park Ave
New York, NY 10016-5902

212-591-7000
800-843-2763
FAX 212-591-8676
E-Mail: infocentral@asme.org
Home Page: www.asme.org

Virgil R Carter, CEO
John G Falcioni, Managing Director
David Soukup, Managing Director

News, profiles and more from the American Society of mechanical engineers.
Cost: $125.00
Frequency: Monthly
Circulation: 125000
Founded in 1880
Printed in 4 colors on matte stock

7357 ASTM Standardization News
ASTM International
100 Barr Harbor Drive
PO Box C700
W Conshohocken, PA 19428-2959

610-832-9500
610-832-9500

FAX 610-832-9555
E-Mail: service@astm.org
Home Page: www.astm.org

James A Thomas, President
Jeff Grove, Vice President

The official magazine of ASTM International, SATM Standardization news reports events in materials research and standardization.
Cost: $18.00
88 Pages
Frequency: Monthly
Circulation: 35000
Founded in 1898

7358 Advanced Materials & Processes
ASM International
9639 Kinsman Rd
Materials Park, OH 44073

440-338-5151
800-336-5152
FAX 440-338-4634
Home Page: www.asminternational.org

Ed Kubel, Senior Editor
Julie Kalista, Editor
Joanne Miller, Production Manager

AM&P, the monthly technical magazine from ASM International, is designed to keep readers aware of leading-edge developments and trends in engineering materials - metals and alloys, engineering polymers, advanced ceramics, and composites - and the methods used to select, process, fabricate, test, and characterize them.
36000 Members
Frequency: Monthly
Circulation: 32M
Founded in 1977

7359 Aerospace Engineering
400 Commonwealth Drive
Warrendale, PA 15096-1

724-776-4841
FAX 724-776-9765
Home Page: www.sae.org

JE Robertson PE, President
Robert E Spitzer, VP Aerospace
Raymond Morris, Executive Vice President
Richard Schaum, VP Automotive
Andrew Brown, Treasurer

Serves the international aerospace design and manufacturing field which consists of producers of airliners, helicopters, spacecraft, missiles, and power plants, propulsion systems, avionics, electronic/electrical systems, parts and components.
Cost: $75.00
Circulation: 28440
Founded in 1905

7360 American Consulting Engineer
American Council of Engineering Companies
1015 15th St
8th Floor NW
Washington, DC 20005-2605

202-347-7474
FAX 202-898-0068
E-Mail: acec@acec.org
Home Page: www.acec.org
Social Media: *Facebook, Twitter*

David A Raymond, President

American Consulting Engineer serves engineers and surveyors who are employed by Consulting Engineering Firms, Architectural & Engineering Firms, and Surveying Firms.
Cost: $45.00
42 Pages
Frequency: Monthly
Circulation: 15841
ISSN: 1050-2203
Founded in 1905
Printed in 4 colors on glossy stock

7361 Annals of Biomedical Engineering
Biomedical Engineering Society
8201 Corporate Dr
Suite 1125
Landover, MD 20785-2224

301-459-1999
877-871-2637
FAX 301-459-1999
E-Mail: info@bmes.org
Home Page: www.bmes.org

Edward L. Schilling, Executive Director
Barbara Colburn, Membership Director
Heather Comstock, Meeting Manager

Presents original research in the following areas: tissue and cellular engineering and biotechnology; biomaterials and biological interfaces; biological signal processing and instrumentation; biomechanics, rheology, and molecular motion; dynamical, regulatory, and integrative biology; transport phenomena, systems analysis and electrophysiology; imaging.
Frequency: Monthly

7362 Automotive Engineering International
Society of Automotive Engineers
400 Commonwealth Dr
Warrendale, PA 15086-7511

724-776-4841
877-606-7323
FAX 724-776-5760
E-Mail: magazines@sae.org
Home Page: www.saesections.org

Richard O Schaum, President
Kevin Jost, Editor
J Robertson, President

For engineers involved in the auto design industry.
Cost: $120.00
125 Pages
Frequency: Monthly
Circulation: 124451
Founded in 1905

7363 Biomedical Engineering Society
8401 Corporate Dr
Suite 140
Hyattsville, MD 20785-2263

301-459-1999
FAX 301-459-2444
E-Mail: info@bmes.org
Home Page: www.bmes.org

Barbara Dunlevy, Executive Director
Heather Comstock, Meeting Manager

Of interest to those in the biomedical engineering field. To promote the increase of biomedical engineering knowledge and its utilization.
Cost: $175.00
Frequency: Monthly
Founded in 1968
Printed in 8 colors on matte stock

7364 Bridge
National Academy of Engineering
500 5th Street NW
Washington, DC 20001

202-334-3200
FAX 202-334-2290
Home Page: www.nae.edu

Charles M. Vest, President
Laura Mersky, Senior Executive Assistant

Solicited articles only. News related to the organization
Frequency: Quarterly
Circulation: 6500
Founded in 1954

7365 CET Magazine
American Society of Certified Engineering

PO Box 1348
Flowery Branch, GA 30542-0023

770-967-9173
FAX 770-967-8049
Home Page: www.ascet.org

Russell E Freier, Chairman
Leo Saenz, CET, President
Kurt Schuler, Secretary/Treasurer

It contains technical, educational, notices of
upcoming events, employment opportunities,
legislative and informational articles. Also included are national, regional and local society
news, reports and activities.
32 Pages
Frequency: Bi-Monthly
Founded in 1964
Printed in one color

7366 Chemical & Engineering News
American Chemical Society
1155 16th St Nw
Suite 600
Washington, DC 20036-4892

202-872-4600
800-227-5558
FAX 202-872-4615
E-Mail: service@acs.org
Home Page: www.acs.org

Madeleine Jacobs, CEO

Professional magazine which covers all areas
of interest to the chemical community, including business, science and government.
Frequency: Weekly
Founded in 1934

7367 Civil Engineering
American Society of Civil Engineers
1801 Alexander Bell Dr
Reston, VA 20191-4382

703-295-6300
800-548-2723
703-295-6300
FAX 703-295-6222
E-Mail: member@asce.org
Home Page: www.asce.org

D Wayne Klotz, President
Virginia Fairweather, Editor-in-Chief
Anne Powell, Editor

Comprised of news, information and updates
for the civil engineering industry.
Cost: $180.00
Frequency: Monthly
Circulation: 107,000
Founded in 1855
Printed in 4 colors

7368 Clientship
American Council of Engineering
Companies
1015 15th St
8th Floor NW
Washington, DC 20005-2605

202-347-7474
FAX 202-898-0068
E-Mail: acec@acec.org
Home Page: www.acec.org
Social Media: *Facebook, Twitter*

Dave Raymond, President
Frequency: Monthly

7369 Community Matters
Accreditation Board for Engineering &
Technology
111 Market Place
Suite 1050
Baltimore, MD 21202-4012

410-347-7700
FAX 410-625-2238

E-Mail: info@abet.org
Home Page: www.abet.org

Phillip E. Borrowman, President
Larry A. Kaye, President-Elect/VP
Frequency: Monthly
Founded in 1932

7370 Composites Technology
Ray Publishing
P.O.Box 992
Morrison, CO 80465-0992

303-467-1776
FAX 303-467-1777
Home Page: www.raypubs.com

Judith Ray Hazen, Publisher/Editor
Michael Musselman, Managing Editor
Donna K. Dawson, Senior Editor
Susan Rush, Copy Editor
Dirk Weed, Global Sales Manager

To provide comprehensive coverage of the
composites industry by focusing on the design,
engineering, manufacture and performance of
products made from this type of material. Particular attention is given to the transfer of technology from traditional end-use markets into
high-volume commercial and industrial arenas.
Cost: $15.00
44 Pages
Circulation: 24000
ISSN: 1083-4117
Founded in 1993
Printed in 4 colors on glossy stock

7371 Composites in Manufacturing
Society of Manufacturing Engineers
1 SME Drive
PO Box 930
Dearborn, MI 48121

313-425-3000
800-733-4763
FAX 313-425-3400
E-Mail: service@sme.org
Home Page: www.sme.org

Mark Tomlinson, Executive Director/General
Manager
Greg Sheremet, Publisher
Bob Harris, Director Finance

Covers various aspects of composite materials
used in manufacturing.
Frequency: Bi-Annual
Circulation: 20000
Founded in 1932
*Mailing list available for rent: 13727 names at
$95 per M*

7372 Computer-Aided Engineering
Penton Media
249 W. 17th Street
New York, NY 10011

216-696-7000
FAX 216-696-6662
E-Mail: information@penton.com
Home Page: www.penton.com

Sharon Rowlands, CEO

Database applications in design and manufacturing.
Cost: $50.00
96 Pages
Founded in 1982

7373 Computing in Science & Engineering
American Institute of Physics
2 Huntington Quad
Suite 1N01
Melville, NY 11747-4502

516-576-2200
FAX 516-349-7669
Home Page: www.aip.org

Darlene Walters, Senior VP
Angela Dombroski, CEO
Randolph Nanna, Publisher

Computer science's interdisciplinary juncture
with physics, astronomy and engineering.
Cost: $42.00
Frequency: Monthly
Founded in 1931

7374 Consulting-Specifying Engineer
Reed Business Information
360 Park Avenue South
New York, NY 10010

646-746-6400
877-422-4637
FAX 630-288-8781
E-Mail: e-letters@reedbusiness.com
Home Page: www.reedbusiness.com

Jeff Greisch, President
Jim Crockett, Chief Editor
Scott Siddens, Senior Editor

Serves engineering management and engineer-
ing personnel who perform mechanical and/or
electrical engineering activities.
100 Pages
Frequency: Monthly
Circulation: 46,157
ISSN: 0892-5046
Founded in 1958
Printed in 4 colors on glossy stock

7375 Control Solutions
PennWell Publishing Company
1421 S Sheridan Rd
Tulsa, OK 74112-6619

918-831-9421
800-331-4463
FAX 918-831-9476
Home Page: www.pennwell.com

Robert Biolchini, President
Ron Kuhfeld, Editor-in-Chief

A highly diversified, business-to-business media company providing authoritative print and
online publications, conferences and exhibitions, research, databases, online exchanges
and information products to strategic global
markets.
Founded in 1910

7376 Corrosion Journal
NACE International
1440 S Creek Dr
Houston, TX 77084-4906

281-492-0535
FAX 281-228-6300
Home Page: www.nace.org

Angela Jarrell, Managing Editor
Suzanne Moreno, Editorial Assistant

Recognized internationally as the world's lead-
ing research journal devoted exclusively to fur-
thering corrosion science and engineering
Cost: $150.00
Frequency: Monthly
Circulation: 7800

7377 Cost Engineering Journal
AACE International
1265 Suncrest Towne Centre Drive
Morgantown, WV 26501-1876

304-296-8444
800-858-2678
FAX 304-291-5728
E-Mail: info@aacei.org
Home Page: www.aacei.org

Michael R. Nosbisch, President
Marlene Hyde, President-Elect

International journal of cost estimation,
cost/schedule control, and project management
read by cost professionals around the world to
get the most up-to-date information about the
profession.
Frequency: Monthly

7378 Cutting Tool Engineering
CTE Publications
40 Skokie Blvd
Suite 395
Northbrook, IL 60062-1698

847-498-9100
FAX 847-559-4444
E-Mail: alanr@jwr.com
Home Page: www.ctemag.com

John W Roberts, CEO
Don Nelson, CEO
Alan Rooks, Director

Serves manufacturing plants in the metal working industries.
Cost: $65.00
72 Pages
Frequency: Monthly
Circulation: 34871
ISSN: 0011-4189
Founded in 1955
Printed in 4 colors on glossy stock

7379 Design News
Reed Business Information
225 Wyman St
Waltham, MA 02451-1216

781-734-8000
FAX 781-290-3178
Home Page: www.reedbusiness.com

Mark Finklestein, President
Karen Auguston Field, CFO
Stuart Whayman, CFO
Tracey Farina, Marketing,
Reck Allis, Circulation Manager

A magazine devoted exclusively to engineering design.
Frequency: Monthly
Circulation: 170114
Founded in 1958
Printed in 4 colors on glossy stock

7380 EE: Evaluation Engineering
Nelson Publishing
2500 Tamiami Trl N
Nokomis, FL 34275-3476

941-966-9521
800-226-6113
FAX 941-966-2590
Home Page: www.healthmgttech.com

Kristine Russel, President
Phil Colpas, Managing Editor

Magazine devoted exclusively to companies that test, evaluate, design and manufacture electronic products and equipment.
Cost: $43.00
84 Pages
Frequency: Monthly
Circulation: 80000
Founded in 1962
Mailing list available for rent: 65,000 names
Printed in 4 colors on glossy stock

7381 Energy Engineering Journal
The Fairmont Press, Association of Energy Engineer
4025 Pleasantdale Road
Suite 420
Atlanta, GA 30340

770-447-5083
FAX 770-446-3969
E-Mail: info@aeecenter.org
Home Page: www.aeecenter.org

Jennifer Vendola, Accountant
Ruth Whitlock, Executive Admin

Engineering solutions to cost efficiency problems and mechanical contractors who design, specify, install, maintain, and purchase non-residential heating, ventilating, air conditioning

and refrigeration equipment and components.
Cost: $160.00
Circulation: 8000

7382 Energy Services Marketing Institute News
Association of Energy Engineers
4025 Pleasantdale Rd
Suite 420
Atlanta, GA 30340-4264

770-447-5083
FAX 770-446-3969
E-Mail: info@aeecenter.org
Home Page: www.aeecenter.org

Eric A. Woodroof, President
Gary Hogsett, President-Elect
Paul Goodman, Treasurer
Laurie Wiegand-Jackson, Secretary

Subjects addressed include IPMVP Management and Verification Standard; Performance Contracting; Energy Project Financing and Energy Procurement.
Frequency: 3x Yearly

7383 Engineering Automation Report
Technology Automation Services
PO Box 3593
Englewood, CO 80155-3593

303-689-9099
FAX 303-770-3660
Home Page: www.eareport.com/eareport

David Weisberg, Publisher
Steve Weisberg, Editor
Dave White, President

Internet/intranet technologies for use in engineering design are covered along with software news.
Cost: $235.00
Frequency: Monthly

7384 Engineering News Record
McGraw Hill
2 Penn Plaza
9th Floor
New York, NY 10121-2298

212-904-3507
FAX 212-904-2820
E-Mail: scott_lewis@mcgraw-hill.com
Home Page: www.enr.com

Richard Korman, Managing Senior Editor
Ilan Kapla, Senior Manager
Keith Wallace, Production Editor

Provides the news, analysis, commentary and data that construction industry professionals need to do their jobs more effectively. ENR is the national news magazine for the construction industry.
Cost: $82.00
Frequency: Weekly
Circulation: 60000
Founded in 1874

7385 Engineering and Mining Journal
Primedia Business
29 N Wacker Drive
10th Floor
Chicago, IL 60606-2802

312-726-2802
FAX 312-726-2574
E-Mail: pjohnson@mining-media.com
Home Page: www.mining-media.com

Peter Johnson, Publisher
Steve Fiscor, Managing Editor
Russ Carter, Managing Editor
Victor Matteucci, National Sales Manager

Serves the field of mining including exploration, development, milling, smelting, refining of metals and nonmetallics.
Cost: $79.00
Circulation: 20589
Founded in 1989

Mailing list available for rent
Printed in 4 colors

7386 Engineering in Medicine and Biology
445 Hoes Lane
Piscataway, NJ 08854-1331

732-981-0060
800-678-4333
FAX 732-981-1721
E-Mail: customer-service@ieee.org
Home Page: www.spectrum.ieee.org/ieeemedia

DesirTe de Myer, Managing Editor
John Enderle, Editor
Susan Schneiderman, Business Development

Focuses on up-to-date biomedical engineering applications for engineers who are at the forefront of electrotechnology innovation.
Cost: $300.00
Circulation: 7983
ISSN: 0739-5175
Founded in 1988

7387 Environmental Engineer
American Academy of Environmental Engineers
130 Holiday Ct
Suite 100
Annapolis, MD 21401-7003

410-266-3311
FAX 410-266-7653
Home Page: www.aaee.net

Joseph Cavarretta, Executive Director
J. Sammi Olmo, Manager

Articles dealing with environmental engineering practice issues and history.
Cost: $20.00
Frequency: Quarterly
Circulation: 12000
Founded in 1955
Mailing list available for rent

7388 Environmental and Engineering Geosciences
Association of Engineering Geologists
PO Box 460518
Denver, CO 80246

303-757-2926
FAX 303-757-2969
E-Mail: aeg@aegweb.org
Home Page: www.aegweb.org

Dave Bieber, President
Darrel Schmitz, President-Elect/VP
Becky Roland, Chief Staff Executive
Terry West, Treasurer
Dorian Kuper, Secretary

Presents reviewed technical papers and discussions and book reviews related to the general field of engineering geology.
Frequency: Quarterly

7389 Experimental Mechanics
Society for Experimental Mechanics
2455 Teller Road
Thousand Oaks, CA 91320-1855

800-818-7243
FAX 805-499-0871
E-Mail: info@sagepub.com
Home Page: www.sagepub.com

Thomas W Proulx, Publisher
N R Sottos, Editor
Hugh Bruck, Associate Tech Editor

Concentrates on advanced research and development. EM is the archival publication of the Society and is recognized as one of the many journals in engineering mechanics. Members receive free electronic access.
Cost: $767.04
Frequency: Quarterly
Circulation: 4500
Founded in 1965

7390 Experimental Techniques
Society for Experimental Mechanics
7 School St
Bethel, CT 06801-1855

203-790-6373
FAX 203-790-4472
E-Mail: sem@sem1.com
Home Page: www.sem.org

Kathy Ramsey, Manager
Thomas Proulx, Execetive Director

Focused on the techniques utilized in experimental mechanics. ET includes Society news, peer-reviewed technical articles and notes, new product information and much more. All members receive a printed copy of the journal and free electronic access.
Cost: $145.00
48 Pages
Circulation: 4000
Founded in 1943
Printed in 4 colors on glossy stock

7391 Exponent
Iowa Engineering Society
100 Court Ave
#102
Des Moines, IA 50309-2257

515-284-7055
FAX 515-284-7301
E-Mail: ies@iaengr.org
Home Page: www.iaengr.org

David Scott, Executive Director
Brian E Roth, President

Supplies the Iowa engineering society members with vital information on issues and activities such as state legislation, education, ethics.
Cost: $6.00
26 Pages
Frequency: Quarterly
Circulation: 1000

7392 Facilities Engineering Journal
Association for Facilities Engineering
8160 Corporate Park Drive
Suite 125
Cincinnati, OH 45242

513-489-2473
FAX 513-247-7422
E-Mail: Info@AFE.org
Home Page: www.afe.org

Gabriella Jacobs, Editor/Communications Manager

Provides you with practical, in-depth information on the key issues you face on the job every day.

7393 Fiberoptic Product News
Reed Business Information
100 Enterprise Drive
Suite 600
Rockaway, NJ 07866-912

973-920-7000
FAX 973-920-7534
Home Page: www.fpnmag.com

Steve Wirth, VP/Group Publisher
Diane Himes, Editor
Kim Potts, Managing Editor
Ernest Worthman, Technical Editorial Director
R Reed, Owner

Edited for designers, engineers, researchers and management personnel who design, install and the buy the products and services that make up the fiberoptic marketplace.
Frequency: Monthly
Circulation: 35000
Founded in 1986
Printed in 4 colors on glossy stock

7394 Fusion Science and Technology
American Nuclear Society

555 N Kensington Ave
La Grange Park, IL 60526-5592

708-352-6611
FAX 708-352-0499
Home Page: www.ans.org

Jack Tuohy, Executive Director
E James Reinsch, President-Elect/VP
Harry Bradley, Executive Director
William F Naughton, Treasurer

Is the source of information on fusion plasma physics and plasma engineering, fusion plasma enabling science and technology, fusion nuclear technology and material science, fusion applications, fusion design and system studies.
Cost: $1425.00
Frequency: 8x Yearly
Founded in 2005

7395 Geotechnical Fabrics Report
Industrial Fabrics Association International
1801 County Road B W
Roseville, MN 55113-4061

651-222-2508
800-225-4324
FAX 651-631-9334
E-Mail: generalinfo@ifai.com
Home Page: www.ifai.com

Stephen Warner, CEO
Chris Kelsey, Editor
Susan.B Smeed, Assistant Circulation Manager
Miller Weldmaster, Director
JoAnne Ferris, Director of Marketing

Peer reviewed technical journal for civil engineers using geosynthetics in road construction, erosion control, hazardous waste, drainage, containment and reinforcement.
Cost: $49.00
Circulation: 16000
ISSN: 0882-4983
Founded in 1982
Printed in 4 colors on glossy stock

7396 Geotechnical Testing Journal
ASTM International
PO Box C700
W Conshohocken, PA 19428-0700

610-832-9500
FAX 610-832-9555
E-Mail: service@astm.org
Home Page: www.astm.org

James A Thomas, President
Jeff Adkins, Manager
Fran Dougherty, Administrative Assistant

Provides a high quality publication that informs the profession of new developments in soil and rock testing and related fields; provides a forum for the exchange of information, particularly that which leads to the development of new test procedures; and to stimulate active participation of the profession in the work of ASTM International Committee D18 on Soil and Rock and related information.
Cost: $229.00
Frequency: Bi-Monthly

7397 Global Design News
Reed Business Information
360 Park Avenue South
New York, NY 10010

646-746-6400
877-422-4637
FAX 630-288-8781
E-Mail: e-letters@reedbusiness.com
Home Page: www.reedbusiness.com

Jeff Greisch, President
Jim Crockett, Chief Editor
Scott Siddens, Senior Editor

Publication includes articles that cover the key product areas necessary for product development; reports on new technologies in the OEM industries, developments in the field of engi-

neering design; and regular features on European product listings, technique and system updates.
Circulation: 30173
Founded in 1958

7398 Heat Transfer Engineering
Taylor & Francis Group Ltd
2 Park Square
Milton Park
Abingdon Oxford UK OX14 4RN

4.40207E+12
FAX 4.40207E+12
Home Page: www.tandf.com.uk

James Edward, Publisher
Afshin Ghajar, Editor-in-Chief
Jack Taylor, Owner

Information on refereed papers of original work, state-of-the-art reviews, articles on new developments in equipment and practices and news items on people and companies in the field.

7399 Hispanic Engineer & Information Technology
Career Communications Group
729 E Pratt St
Suite 504
Baltimore, MD 21202-3302

410-244-7101
FAX 410-752-1837
E-Mail: eaddison@ccgmag.com
Home Page: www.ccgmag.com

Jean Hamilton, Chief Financial Officer
Vishal Thakkar, Director of Marketing
Diane Jones, Director of Marketing
Christy Flemming, Director

Devoted to science and technology and to promoting opportunities in those fields for Hispanic Americans.
Cost: $13.00
56 Pages
ISSN: 1088-3452
Founded in 1982
Printed in 4 colors on glossy stock

7400 Hydraulics & Pneumatics
Penton Media
249 W. 17th Street
New York, NY 10011

212-204-4200
FAX 216-696-6662
E-Mail: hp@penton.com
Home Page: www.penton.com

Sharon Rowlands, CEO
Nicola Allais, Executive VP

Issues highlight the application of new hydraulic and pneumatic components, new equipment research and listings, new design and literature innovations in fluid power and motion control systems.
Cost: $65.00
Frequency: Monthly
Circulation: 49,878
Founded in 1892

7401 ID International Design
F&W Publications
38 E 29th St
Floor 3
New York, NY 10016-7911

212-447-1400
FAX 212-447-5231
E-Mail: idedit@fwpubs.com
Home Page: www.printmag.com

Joyce Rutter Kaye, VP
Julie Lasky, Editor - in - chief
Nicole Martin, Circualtion Manager
Barbara Schmitz, VP

The issues include news and features on computers, new technologies, case studies, design

management, materials, aesthetics, new components and design trends. They also cover new sources, a calendar of events, personnel news, book reviews and products.
Cost: $30.00
Circulation: 19852
Founded in 1954

7402 IIE Solutions
Institute of Industrial Engineers
3577 Parkway Lane
Suite 200
Norcross, GA 30092

770-449-0460
800-494-0460
FAX 770-441-3295
E-Mail: cs@iienet.org
Home Page: www.iienet.org

Don Greene, CEO
Donna Calvert, Chief Operating Officer

Listings, literature and news for executive engineers.
Cost: $66.00
Frequency: Monthly
Circulation: 26276
Founded in 1948

7403 InTents
Industrial Fabrics Association International
1801 Country Road BW
Roseville, MN 55113

651-222-2508
800-225-4324
FAX 651-631-9334
E-Mail: jrwallace@ifai.com
Home Page: www.ifai.com

Peter F. McKernan, Chairman
Kevin Yonce, Vice Chairman

Promotes the use of tents and accessories to the special-event and general rental industries.
Cost: $39.00
Frequency: Bi-Monthly
Circulation: 12,000

7404 Industrial Equipment News
TCC Media Group
90 W Aftan Avenue
#117
Yardley, PA 19067

267-519-1705
800-733-1127
E-Mail: todd@ien.com
Home Page: www.ienonline.com/

Todd Baker, President

Serves the industrial field including manufacturing, mining, utilities, construction, transportation,governmental establishments, and educational services.
Frequency: Monthly
Circulation: 205000
ISSN: 0019-8258
Founded in 1933

7405 Inform
American Oil Chemists' Society
2710 S Boulder Drive
P.O. Box 17190
Urbana, IL 61803-6996

217-359-2344
FAX 217-351-8091
E-Mail: general@aocs.org
Home Page: www.aocs.org
Social Media: *Facebook, Twitter, LinkedIn*

Gloria Cook, Senior Director, Finance & Operatio
Jeffry L. Newman, Senior Director, Programs

Inform magazine is an AOCS member benefit providing international news on fats, oils, surfactants, detergents, and related materials.
4500 Members
Frequency: Annual/April-May
Founded in 1909

7406 Innovation
Industrial Designers Society of America
45195 Business Court
Suite 250
Dulles, VA 20166-6717

703-707-6000
FAX 703-787-8501
E-Mail: idsa@idsa.org
Home Page: www.idsa.org

Clive Roux, CEO
Annette Butler, Executive Assistant
Kaycee Childress, Marketing
Roxann Henze, Press, Media & Public Relations

IDSA is the world's oldest, largest, member-driven society for product design, industrial design, interaction design, human factors, ergonomics, design research, design management, universal design and related design fields. IDSA publishes Innovation, a quarterly on design. IDSA's charitable arm, the Design Foundation, supports the dissemination of undergraduate scholarships annually to further industrial design education.
Cost: $50.00
Frequency: Quarterly
Circulation: 3500
Founded in 1965

7407 Interface Magazine
Electrochemical Society
65 S Main St
Building D
Pennington, NJ 08534-2827

609-737-1902
FAX 609-737-2743
E-Mail: interface@electrochem.org
Home Page: www.electrochem.org

Roque J Calvo, Executive Director
Mary E. Yess, Deputy Executive Director

Editorial material contains news, reviews, advertisements and articles on technical matters in the fields of electrochemical and solid state science and technology.
Cost: $61.97
Frequency: Quarterly
Circulation: 8000
Founded in 1902

7408 International Dredging Review
PO Box 1487
Fort Collins, CO 80522-1487

970-416-1903
FAX 970-416-1878
E-Mail: editor@dredgemag.com
Home Page: www.dredgemag.com

Judith Powers, Publisher/Editor
Leonard F Cors, Business Manager
Nelson Spencer, Business Manager
Julia Leach, Production Manager

Targeted to dredging company executives, project managers and dredge crew members, suppliers and service people such as pump manufacturers, hydrographic surveyors, consulting engineers, etc.
Cost: $85.00
Circulation: 3300
ISSN: 0737-8181
Founded in 1981
Mailing list available for rent
Printed in 4 colors on glossy stock

7409 Iron & Steel Technology
Association for Iron & Steel Technolgy (AIST)

186 Thorn Hill Rd
Warrendale, PA 15086-7528

724-814-3000
FAX 724-814-3001
E-Mail: memberservices@aist.org
Home Page: www.aist.org
Social Media: *Facebook, Twitter, LinkedIn*

Ron Ashburn, Executive Director
Lori Wharrey, Board Administrator
Chris McKelvey, Assistant Board Administrator

The official monthly publication of AIST, this is the premier technical journal for metallurgical, engineering, operating and maintenance personnel in the global iron and steel industry.
Cost: $20.00
Frequency: Monthly
Circulation: 9500

7410 JSME International Journal
American Society of Mechanical Engineers
3 Park Ave
New York, NY 10016-5902

212-591-7000
800-843-2763
FAX 212-591-8676
E-Mail: infocentral@asme.org
Home Page: www.asme.org

Victoria Rockwell, President
Marc Goldsmith, President-Elect
David Soukup, Managing Director Operations

Provides advanced scientific and technological information for the mechanical engineering industry to facilitate the international exchange and transfer of technology.
Cost: $200.00
Frequency: Monthly

7411 Journal of Applied Mechanics
American Society of Mechanical Engineers
3 Park Ave
New York, NY 10016-5902

212-591-7000
800-843-2763
FAX 212-591-8676
E-Mail: infocentral@asme.org
Home Page: www.asme.org

Victoria Rockwell, President
Marc Goldsmith, President-Elect

To serve as a vehicle for the communication of original research results of permanent interest in all branches of mechanics.
Cost: $60.00
Frequency: Bi-Monthly
ISSN: 0021-8936

7412 Journal of Biomechanical Engineering
American Society of Mechanical Engineers
3 Park Ave
New York, NY 10016-5902

212-591-7000
800-843-2763
FAX 212-591-8676
E-Mail: infocentral@asme.org
Home Page: www.asme.org

Victoria Rockwell, President
Marc Goldsmith, President-Elect

Reports research results involving the application of mechanical engineering and knowledge, skills and principles to the conception, design, development, analysis, and operation of biomechanical systems, including; artificial organs and prostheses; bioinstrumentation and measurements; bio-heat transfer; biomaterials; biomechanics; bioprocess engineering; cellular mechanics; design and control of biological systems, and physiological systems.
Frequency: Bi-Monthly
ISSN: 0148-0731

7413 Journal of Construction Engineering and Management
American Society of Civil Engineers
1801 Alexander Bell Dr
Reston, VA 20191-4382

703-295-6300
800-548-2723
FAX 703-295-6222
E-Mail: cybrarian@asce.org
Home Page: www.afce.org

D Wayne Klotz, President

Quality papers that aim to advance the science of construction engineering, to harmonize construction practices with design theories, and to further education and research in construction engineering and management.

7414 Journal of Engineering Education
American Society for Engineering Education
1818 N St NW
Suite 600
Washington, DC 20036-2476

202-331-3500
FAX 202-265-8504
E-Mail: pubsinfo@asee.org
Home Page: www.asee.org

Frank L Huband, Executive Director

It serves as an archival record of scholarly research in engineering education.
Frequency: Quarterly
ISSN: 1069-4730

7415 Journal of Engineering for Industry
American Society of Mechanical Engineers
3 Park Ave
New York, NY 10016-5902

212-591-7000
800-843-2763
FAX 212-591-8676
E-Mail: infocentral@asme.org
Home Page: www.asme.org

Virgil R Carter, CEO
David Soukup, Managing Director
William T Cousins, President

Covers interfaces of mechanical engineering.
Frequency: Quarterly
Circulation: 2162
Founded in 1880

7416 Journal of Forensic Sciences
ASTM International
PO Box C700
W Conshohocken, PA 19428-0700

610-832-9500
FAX 610-832-9555
E-Mail: service@astm.org
Home Page: www.astm.org

James A Thomas, President
Jeff Adkins, Manager
Fran Dougherty, Administrative Assistant

Is the official publication of the American Academy of Forensic Sciences (AAFS). It is devoted to the publication of original investigations, observations, scholarly inquiries, and reviews in the various branches of the forensic sciences.
Cost: $249.00
Frequency: Bi-Monthly

7417 Journal of Management in Engineering
American Society of Civil Engineers
1801 Alexander Bell Dr
Reston, VA 20191-4382

703-295-6300
800-548-2723
FAX 703-295-6222

E-Mail: cybrarian@asce.org
Home Page: www.afce.org

D Wayne Klotz, President

Examines contemporary issues associated with leadership and management for the twenty-first century civil engineer.

7418 Journal of Materials Engineering and Performance
ASM International
9639 Kinsman Road
Materials Park, OH 44073-0002

440-338-5151
800-336-5152
FAX 440-338-4634
Home Page: www.asminternational.org

Jeane Deatherage, Administrator
Charles Hayes, Executive Director
Virginia Shirk, Executive Assistant

Peer-reviewed journal that publishes contributions on all aspects of materials selection, design, characterization, processing and performance testing. The journal for solving day-to-day engineering challenges - especially those involving components for larger systems.
Cost: $1965.00
Frequency: Bi-Monthly
Circulation: 305
Founded in 1992

7419 Journal of Petroleum Technology
Society of Petroleum Engineers
PO Box 833836
Richardson, TX 75083-3836

972-529-9300
800-456-6863
FAX 972-952-9435
E-Mail: spedal@spe.org
Home Page: www.spe.org

Giovanni Paccaloni, President
Bill Cobb, VP Finance
John E Bethancourt, Director Management/Information
Ian Gorman, Director Production/Operations
Niki Bradbury, Managing Director

A suite of peer-reviewed, discipline-centered journals; books written by the industry's most honored professionals; and an online, 35,000-paper library.
Cost: $15.00
Frequency: Monthly

7420 Journal of Phase Equilibria
ASM International
9639 Kinsman Rd
Materials Park, OH 44072

440-338-5151
800-336-5152
FAX 440-338-4634
Home Page: www.asminternational.org

Jeane Deatherage, Administrator
Charles Hayes, Executive Director
Virginia Shirk, Executive Assistant

Peer-reviewed journal that contains basic and applied research results, evaluated phase diagrams, a survey of current literature, and comments or other material pertinent to the previous three areas. The aim is to provide a broad spectrum of information concerning phase equilibria for the materials community.
Cost: $1965.00
Frequency: Bi-Monthly
Circulation: 305

7421 Journal of Process Control
Butterworth Heinemann

313 Washington Street
Suite 302
Newton, MA 02458-1626

617-928-5460
FAX 617-928-5494

JD Perkins, Editor
T McAvoy, Regional Editor

Covers the application of control theory, operations research, computer science and engineering principles to the solution of process control problems.

7422 Journal of Quality Technology
American Society for Quality
600 N Plankinton Avenue
PO Box 3005
Milwaukee, WI 53201-3005

414-272-8575
800-248-1946
FAX 414-272-1734
E-Mail: help@asq.org
Home Page: www.asq.org

Roberto M Saco, President
Mike Adams, Director
Erica Gumieny, Sales
Fay Spano, Communications/Media Relations

Published by the American Society for Quality, the JQT is a quarterly, peer-reviewed journal that focuses on the subject of quality control and the related areas of reliability and similar disciplines.
Cost: $30.00
100M Members
Frequency: Quarterly
Founded in 1946

7423 Journal of Rheology
Society of Rheology
2 Huntington Quadrangle
Suite 1N01
Meville, NY 11747-4502

516-576-2471
FAX 516-576-2223
E-Mail: rheology@aip.org
Home Page: www.rheology.org

Faith A. Morrison, President
A. Jeffrey Giacomin, Vice President
Frequency: Bi-Monthly

7424 Journal of Surfactants and Detergents (JSD)
American Oil Chemists' Society
2710 S Boulder Drive
P.O. Box 17190
Urbana, IL 61803-6996

217-359-2344
FAX 217-351-8091
E-Mail: general@aocs.org
Home Page: www.aocs.org
Social Media: *Facebook, Twitter, LinkedIn*

Gloria Cook, Senior Director, Finance
Jeffry L. Newman, Senior Director, Programs

Since 1998, JSD has remained dedicated to the practical and theoretical aspects of oleochemical and petrochemical surfactants, soaps and detergents. This growing quarterly scientific journal publishes peer-reviewed research papers, and reviews related to surfactants and detergents technologies.
4500 Members
Frequency: Annual/April-May
Founded in 1909

7425 Journal of Testing and Evaluation
ASTM International
PO Box C700
W Conshohocken, PA 19428-0700

610-832-9500
FAX 610-832-9555

E-Mail: service@astm.org
Home Page: www.astm.org

James A Thomas, President
Jeff Adkins, Manager
Fran Dougherty, Administrative Assistant

Provides a multidisciplinary forum for applied sciences and engineering.
Cost: $249.00
Frequency: Bi-Monthly

7426 Journal of Thermal Spray Technology
ASM International
9639 Kinsman Rd
Materials Park, OH 44072-9603

440-338-5151
800-336-5152
FAX 440-338-4634
Home Page: www.asminternational.org

Jeane Deatherage, Administrator
Charles Hayes, Executive Director
Virginia Shirk, Executive Assistant

Peer-reviewed journal which publishes contributions on all aspects, fundamental and practical, of thermal spray science, including processes, feedstock manufacture, testing and characterization. As the primary vehicle for thermal spray information transfer, its mission is to synergize the rapidly advancing thermal spray industry and related industries by presenting research and development efforts leading to advancements in implementable engineering applications of the technology.
Cost: $1577.00
Frequency: Bi-Monthly
Circulation: 680
Founded in 1952

7427 Journal of the Acoustical Society of America
Acoustical Society of America
2 Huntington Quad
Suite 1N01
Melville, NY 11747-4505

516-576-2360
FAX 516-576-2377
E-Mail: asa@aip.org
Home Page: www.asa.aip.org

Charles E Schmid, President

Distributed free to members.
Cost: $1545.00
7000 Pages
Frequency: Monthly

7428 Journal of the American Oil Chemists' Society (JAOCS)
American Oil Chemists' Society
2710 S Boulder Drive
P.O. Box 17190
Urbana, IL 61803-6996

217-359-2344
FAX 217-351-8091
E-Mail: general@aocs.org
Home Page: www.aocs.org
Social Media: *Facebook, Twitter, LinkedIn*

Gloria Cook, Senior Director, Finance
Jeffry L. Newman, Senior Director, Programs

Since 1947, the Journal of the American Oil Chemists' Society has been the leading source for technical papers related to the fats and oils industries. JAOCS is a monthly, peer-reviewed journal devoted to fundamental and practical research, production, processing, packaging and distribution in the growing field of fats, oils, proteins and other related substances.
4500 Members
Frequency: Annual/April-May
Founded in 1909

7429 Journal of the Electrochemical Society
Electrochemical Society

65 S Main St
Building D
Pennington, NJ 08534-2827

609-737-1902
FAX 609-737-2743
E-Mail: ecs@electrochem.org
Home Page: www.electrochem.org

Roque J Calvo, Executive Director
Mary E. Yess, Deputy Executive Director
Roque Calvo, Manager

Contains technical papers covering basic research and technology.
Cost: $63.00
Circulation: 8300
Founded in 1902

7430 LD&A
Illuminating Engineering Society of North America
120 Wall Street
17th Floor
New York, NY 10005

212-248-5000
FAX 212-248-5017
E-Mail: ies@ies.org
Home Page: www.ies.org

Denis Lavoie, President
Chip Israel, Vice President

A magazine for professionals involved in the art, science, study, manufacture, teaching and implementation of lighting. LD&A is designed to enhance and improve the practice of lighting. Free to members.
Cost: $44.00
Frequency: Monthly
Circulation: 7000
ISSN: 0360-6325
Mailing list available for rent: 8000 names

7431 LEUKOS, The Journal Of IES
Illuminating Engineering Society of North America
120 Wall Street
17th Floor
New York, NY 10005

212-248-5000
FAX 212-248-5017
E-Mail: ies@ies.org
Home Page: www.ies.org

Denis Lavoie, President
Chip Israel, Vice President

LEUKOS serves members of the IES, the lighting community, and the public. The journal contains international technical developments of current interest and lasting importance relating to illuminating engineering and lighting design. Free to members, online.
Cost: $250.00
Frequency: Quarterly
ISSN: 1550-2729
Mailing list available for rent: 8000 names

7432 Lighting Design & Application
Illuminating Engineering Society of North America
120 Wall St
17th Floor
New York, NY 10005-4001

212-248-5000
FAX 212-248-5017
E-Mail: iesna@iesna.org
Home Page: www.ies.org

Denis Lavoie, President
Chip Israel, Vice President

Is a magazine for professionals involved in the art, science, study, manufacture, teaching and implementation of lighting. LD+A is designed to enhance and improve the practice of lighting. Every issue of LD+A includes feature articles on design projects, technical articles on the science of illumination, new product develop-

ments, industry trends, news of the Illuminating Engineering Society and vital information about the illuminating profession.
Cost: $32.00
Frequency: Monthly
Circulation: 8000
ISSN: 0360-6325

7433 Lipids
American Oil Chemists' Society
2710 S Boulder Drive
P.O. Box 17190
Urbana, IL 61803-6996

217-359-2344
FAX 217-351-8091
E-Mail: general@aocs.org
Home Page: www.aocs.org
Social Media: *Facebook, Twitter, LinkedIn*

Gloria Cook, Senior Director, Finance
Jeffry L. Newman, Senior Director, Programs

Introduced in 1966, Lipids is a premier journal published in the lipid field today. This monthly scientific journal features full-length original research articles, short communications, methods papers and review articles on timely topics. All papers are meticulously peer-reviewed and edited by some of the foremost experts in their respective fields.
4500 Members
Frequency: Annual/April-May
Founded in 1909

7434 Low Temperature Physics
200 Huntington Quadrangle
Suite 1N01
Melville, NY 11747-4502

516-516-2270
FAX 516-349-9704

7435 Machine Design
1300 E 9 Street
Cleveland, OH 44114-2518

216-696-7000
847-763-9670
FAX 216-696-0177
E-Mail: mdeditor@penton.com
Home Page: www.machinedesign.com

Leland Teschler, Editor
Ken Korane, Managing Editor
Bobbie Macy, Circulation Manager

The only magazine for applied technology for design engineering edited for design engineers and engineering managers. It covers new products and design practices in the fields of mechanical, electromechanical, electronics, motion control and process engineering.
Circulation: 180000
Founded in 1929

7436 Maintenance Solutions
Trade Press Publishing Corporation
2100 W Florist Avenue
Milwaukee, WI 53209

414-228-7701
FAX 414-228-1134
E-Mail: contact@facilitiesnet.com
Home Page: www.facilitiesnet.com/

Dick Yake, Editorial Director
Dan Hounsell, Editor
Brad R. Ehlert, VP
Brian Terry, Publisher
Renee Gryzkewicz, Associate Editor

How to articles and features designed to alleviate reader problems as well as new product information and applications.
Cost: $45.00
42 Pages
Frequency: Monthly
Circulation: 35000

ISSN: 1072-3560
Founded in 1993

7437 Maintenance Technology
Applied Technology Publications
1300 S Grove Ave
Suite 105
Barrington, IL 60010-5246

847-382-8100
FAX 847-304-8603
Home Page: www.mt-online.com

Jane Alexander, Editor-in-Chief
Rick Carter, Executive Editor
Randy Buttstadt, Director of Creative Services

Maintenance Technology magazine serves the
business and technical information needs of
managers and engineers responsible for assuring availability of plant equipment and systems. It provides readers with articles on
advanced technologies, strategies, tools, and
services for the life-cycle management of
capital assets.
Frequency: Monthly
Circulation: 50,827
Mailing list available for rent: 35,263 names at
$$15 per M

7438 Marine Fabricator
Industrial Fabrics Association International
1801 County Road B W
Roseville, MN 55113-4061

651-222-2508
800-225-4324
FAX 651-631-9334
E-Mail: generalinfo@ifai.com
Home Page: www.ifai.com

Peter F. McKernan, Chairman
Kevin Yonce, Vice Chairman

Educates and informs 5,000 marine shop pro-
fessionals and also provides reportage that re-
flects the innovations and trends of the
industry.
Cost: $34.00
Frequency: Bi-Monthly

7439 Material Handling Business
Penton Media
249 W. 17th Street
New York, NY 10011

212-204-4200
FAX 216-696-6662
E-Mail: information@penton.com
Home Page: www.penton.com

Sharon Rowlands, CEO
Nicola Allais, Executive VP
Antoinette Sanchez Perkins, Circulation
Manager

Journal written for design engineering manag-
ers, system integrates, material handling dis-
tributors and manufacturing sales executives.
86 Pages
Circulation: 92836
Founded in 1892
Printed in 4 colors on glossy stock

7440 Materials Performance
NACE International
1440 S Creek Dr
Houston, TX 77084-4906

281-492-0535
800-797-6223
FAX 281-228-6300
E-Mail: stephanie.garner@nace.org
Home Page: www.nace.org

Oliver Moghissi, President
Kevin Garrity, Vice President

Provides current news and features, practical
data, and information on new products and ser-
vices in the corrosion industry.
Frequency: Monthly
Circulation: 22000
Founded in 1943

7441 Materials at High Temperatures
Butterworth Heinemann
313 Washington Street
Newton, MA 02458-1626

617-928-5460
FAX 781-933-6333
T Suzuki, Co-Editor
TB Gibbons, Co-Editor

Serves the needs of those developing and using
materials for high temperature applications in
the power, chemical, engine, processing and
furnace industries.

7442 Measurements and Control News
Measurements and Data Corporation
100 Wallace Avenue
Suite 100
Sarasota, FL 34237

941-954-8405
FAX 941-366-5743

Ken Kemski, Editor-in-Chief
Kristine Burmester, Associate Editor

Serves engineers, technichians, scientists, and
other professionals involved in the recommen-
dation and specification, of instuments and de-
vices for measurement, inspection, testing,
analysis, computing, and control.
Frequency: Bi-Monthly

7443 Medical Equipment Designer
Adams Business Media
6001 Cuchran Road
Suite 300
Cleveland, OH 44139

216-249-9444
FAX 440-248-0187
Home Page: www.medicaldesigner.com

Terry Person, Publisher
Steve Wafalosky, Publisher

Published for the design function as it relates
specifically to medical manufacturing and de-
sign of materials, components and complete
systems.
1004 Pages
Frequency: Bi-Monthly
Circulation: 15,000
Founded in 1985
Printed in 4 colors on glossy stock

7444 Medical Physics
2 Huntington Quadrangle
Suite 1N01
Melville, NY 11747

516-576-2200
FAX 516-576-2481
Home Page: www.aip.org

Bill Hendee, Editor
Founded in 1931

7445 Microwave and RF
Penton Media
45 Eisenhower Drive
5th Floor
Paramus, NJ 07652

201-452-2400
800-829-9028
FAX 201-845-2493
Home Page: www.mwrf.com

Jack Browne, Publisher/Editor
Dawn Prior, Editorial Assistant

Dedicated to educating senior level design en-
gineers, engineering managers, both domestic
and foreign, who work all types of microwave

systems, subsystems and components.
Cost: $81.00
Frequency: Monthly
Circulation: 47000
Founded in 1967
Mailing list available for rent
Printed in on glossy stock

7446 Modern Materials Handling
Reed Business Information
275 Washington St
Newton, MA 02458-1611

617-964-3030
FAX 617-630-3925
E-Mail: support@designnews.com
Home Page: www.designnews.com

Peter Boniface, Publisher
Raymond Kulwiec, Editor
James A Casella, CEO
Jason Cassidy, VP
Greg Flores, Senior Vice President

The magazine for managers and engineers re-
sponsible for handling materials and managing
inventories in manufacturing, warehousing and
distribution.
Frequency: 14x Yearly
Founded in 1977
Printed in 4 colors on glossy stock

7447 Motion Control
ISA Services
Po Box 12277
Resrch Trngle P, NC 27709-2277

919-549-8411
FAX 919-549-8288
E-Mail: info@isa.org
Home Page: www.isa.org

Pat Gouhin, Executive Director

Information for those who design and maintain
motion control systems.
Cost: $54.00
56 Pages
Circulation: 41000
ISSN: 1058-4644
Founded in 1945
Printed in 4 colors on glossy stock

7448 Motion System Distributor
Penton Media
249 W. 17th Street
New York, NY 10011

212-204-4200
800-249-9365
FAX 216-696-6662
E-Mail: information@penton.com
Home Page: www.penton.com

Sharon Rowlands, CEO
Nicola Allais, Executive VP
Larry Berardinis, Editor

Provides selling and technical information to
individuals and distributors specializing in
power transmission, motion control and fluid
products.
Cost: $65.00
Frequency: Monthly
Circulation: 54,000
Founded in 1892

7449 NSBE Magazine
National Society of Black Engineers
1454 Duke Street
Alexandria, VA 22314-3403

703-549-2207
FAX 703-683-5312
E-Mail: office@nsbe.org
Home Page: www.nsbe.org

Pamela D Sharif, Publisher
Carl Mack, Manager
George Bowman, Manager

Coverage of all aspects of manufacturing engi-
neering, geared towards black technical profes-

sionals.
Cost: $30.00
Circulation: 100000
Printed in 4 colors on glossy stock

7450 Naval Engineers Journal
American Society of Naval Engineers
1452 Duke Street
Alexandria, VA 22314-3458

703-836-6727
FAX 703-836-7491
E-Mail: asnehq@navalengineers.org
Home Page: www.navalengineers.org

Susan King, Editor

It contains technical papers authored by professionals engaged in naval and related engineering fields. Its high quality content is sought by those with an interest in topics of importance to the advancement of naval engineering.
Frequency: Quarterly

7451 New Equipment Digest
Penton Media
1300 E 9th St
Cleveland, OH 44114-1503

216-696-7000
FAX 216-696-1752
E-Mail: information@penton.com
Home Page: www.penton.com

Sharon Rowlands, CEO
Dave Madonia, Publisher
Robert.F King, Editor
Nicola Allais, Executive VP & CEO

New Equipment Digest serves the general industrial field which includes manufacturing, processing, engineering services, construction, transportation, mining, public utilities, wholesale distributors, educational services, libraries and governmental establishments.
Cost: $65.00
Frequency: Monthly
Circulation: 206006
Founded in 1936

7452 Noise Control Engineering Journal
Institute of Noise Control Engineering
62 Timberline Drive, Arlington Branch
PO Box 3206
Poughkeepsie, NY 12603-0206

845-462-4006
FAX 845-463-0201
Home Page: www.ince.org

Alan Marsh, Editor

Includes articles on hearing protection, modal analysis, and signal processing. Information is refereed, authoritative, and technical.
Cost: $110.00
Frequency: Bi-Monthly
Circulation: 2,000
ISSN: 0736-2501

7453 Noise/News International
Institute of Noise Control Engineering
9100 Purdue Road
Suite 200
Indianapolis, IN 46268

317-735-4063
E-Mail: ibo@inceusa.org
Home Page: www.inceusa.org

James K Thompson, President
Rich Peppin, Advertising/Expo Manager

Contains not only news items but also feature articles on a wide variety of topics of broad interest in noise control engineering.
Cost: $60.00
Frequency: Quarterly
ISSN: 1021-643X

7454 Nuclear Science and Engineering
American Nuclear Society

555 N Kensington Ave
La Grange Park, IL 60526-5592

708-352-6611
FAX 708-352-0499
Home Page: www.ans.org

Jack Tuohy, Executive Director
E James Reinsch, President-Elect/VP
Harry Bradley, Executive Director
William F Naughton, Treasurer

The journal is widely recognized as an outstanding source of information on research in all scientific areas related to the peaceful use of nuclear energy and radiation. Technical papers, notes, critical reviews, and computer code abstracts are presented.
Cost: $1200.00
Frequency: 9x Yearly
Founded in 1956

7455 Nuclear Technology
American Nuclear Society
555 N Kensington Ave
La Grange Park, IL 60526-5592

708-352-6611
FAX 708-352-0499
Home Page: www.ans.org

Jack Tuohy, Executive Director
E James Reinsch, President-Elect/VP
Harry Bradley, Executive Director
William F Naughton, Treasurer

Leading international publication reporting on new information in all areas of the practical application of nuclear science. Topics include all aspects of reactor technology: operations, safety materials, instrumentation, fuel, and waste management. Also covered are medical uses, radiation detection, production of radiation, health physics, and computer applications.
Cost: $1315.00
Frequency: Monthly
Founded in 2005

7456 Off-Highway Engineering
SAE
400 Commonwealth Dr
Warrendale, PA 15086-7511

724-776-4841
FAX 724-776-5760
Home Page: www.saesections.org

Richard O Schaum, President
Mark Davies, Editor-In-Chief

Off-Highway Engineering serves the international off highway design and manufacturing field which consists of producers of construction, lawn and garden, agricultural equipment, and industrial vehicles. Also served are makers of engines and parts and components and others allied to the field.
Cost: $70.00
66 Pages
Circulation: 16308
ISSN: 1074-6919
Founded in 1905
Printed in 4 colors on glossy stock

7457 Optics and Spectroscopy
Optical Society of America
2010 Massachusetts Ave Nw
Washington, DC 20036-1023

202-223-8130
FAX 202-223-1096
E-Mail: info@osa.org
Home Page: www.osa.org

Elizabeth Rogan, Executive Director
Elizabeth Nolan, Chief Publishing Officer

Optics and Spectroscopy covers such topics as multiphoton spectroscopy, phase conjugation, holography, scattering, and quantum electronics.
Frequency: Monthly
Founded in 1916

7458 PM Engineer
Business News Publishing Company
2401 W Big Beaver Road
Suite 700
Troy, MI 48084

248-362-3700
Home Page: www.bnpmedia.com

Katie Rotella, Manager

Provides technical sheets, manufacturer product brochures, news features and analysis of useful industry information on the engineering and design of plumbing, piping, hydronics, cooling/heating, and fire protection/sprinkler systems. Free to trade engineers.
Cost: $64.00
80 Pages
Frequency: Monthly
Circulation: 25000
Founded in 1970
Printed in 4 colors on glossy stock

7459 PT Design
Penton Media
1300 E 9th St
Cleveland, OH 44114-1503

216-696-7000
FAX 216-696-1752
E-Mail: information@penton.com
Home Page: www.penton.com

Sharon Rowlands, CEO
David Madonia, Publisher

Blends state-of-the-art motion system designs with traditional electrical and mechanical technology for the system designer. Also features articles on new products and technology, industry trends and application ideas.
Cost: $65.00
Frequency: Monthly
Circulation: 54000
Founded in 1892

7460 PT Distributor
Reed Business Information
2000 Clearwater Dr
Oak Brook, IL 60523-8809

630-288-8000
FAX 630-288-8781
Home Page: www.reedbusiness.com

Mark Kelsey, Global CEO
Jeff DeBalko, President, Media Division

provides information on selling techniques, fiscal and personnel management, purchasing, improving profits, training, and inventory and warehousing control.
Cost: $30.00
Frequency: Bi-Monthly
Circulation: 10,000

7461 Pharmaceutical Engineering
Int'l Society for Pharmaceutical Engineering
600 N Westshore Blvd.
Suite 900
Tampa, FL 33609

813-960-2105
FAX 813-264-2816
E-Mail: ask@ispe.org
Home Page: www.ispe.org

Charles DiMarco, Director of Marketing
Danielle Hould, Communications Manager
Angie Brumley, Publications Coordinator
Valerie Adams, Advertising Sales Coordinator

Journal is published bi-monthly for members only and is considered by ISPE members to be the number one member benefit. Feature articles provide practical application and specification information on the design, construction, supervision and maintenance of process equipment, plant systems, instrumentation and facilities.
Circulation: 13138

7462 Plant Engineering
Reed Business Information
8878 Barrons Blvd
Littleton, CO 80129-2345

303-470-4000
800-446-6551
FAX 303-470-4691
E-Mail: submail@reedbusiness.com
Home Page: www.reedbusiness.com

Tim Myers, Executive
Bobbie Wisniewski, Advertising Production
Manager
Rick Ellis, Circulation Manager
Rick Dunn, Editor
Jim Silvestri, Managing Editor

Provides a constant reminder of engineering
products and services and helps keep your
company at the top of your customers' minds.
Frequency: Monthly
Circulation: 100034
Founded in 1947

7463 Plant Services
Putman Media
555 W Pierce Rd
Suite 301
Itasca, IL 60143-2626

630-467-1301
800-984-7644
FAX 630-467-0197
Home Page: www.putman.net

John Cappelletti, CEO
Mike Bacidore, Editor-in-Chief
Mike Brenner, Group Publisher
Keith Larson, VP Content

The newsletters reach a monthly world wide
audience of more than 150,000 professionals
responsible for optimizing the productivity and
insuring the reliability of manufacturing plants,
facilities and utilities in North America and
across the globe.
Cost: $96.00
Frequency: Monthly
Circulation: 80100
ISSN: 0199-8013
Founded in 1938
Mailing list available for rent: 10,000 names
Printed in 4 colors on glossy stock

7464 Plastics Engineering
Society of Plastics Engineers
13 Church Hill Rd
Newtown, CT 06470

203-775-0471
FAX 203-775-8490
E-Mail: info@4spe.org
Home Page: www.4spe.org

Susan Oderwald, Executive Director

A communication to SPE's global audience of
plastics professionals about current developments in the industry, technology, and activities
of the Society.
Frequency: Monthly

7465 Plumbing Engineer
Delta Communications
1167 W Bluemound Road
Wauwatosa, WI 53226

262-542-8820
FAX 262-542-9111
E-Mail: delta@deltacommunications.com
Home Page: www.deltacommunications.com

Edwin Scott, Editor

Offers news and updates to plumbing engineers
and manufacturers.
Cost: $35.00
Frequency: Monthly
Founded in 1973

7466 Plumbing Standard Magazine
American Society of Sanitary Engineering

901 Canterbury Rd
Suite A
Cleveland, OH 44145-1480

440-835-3040
FAX 440-835-3488
Home Page: www.asse-plumbing.org

Ken Van Wagnen, Manager
Donald Summers, First VP
Steve Silber, Second VP
Scott Hamilton, Third VP
Shannon Corcoran, Executive Director

This magazine includes technical articles, current information on codes, standards, and other
developments in the plumbing industry and related fields. Free with membership.
Cost: $12.00
Frequency: Quarterly

7467 Powder Diffraction
International Center for Diffraction Data
12 Campus Boulevard
Newton Square, PA 19073-3200

610-325-9814
FAX 610-325-9823
E-Mail: info@icdd.com
Home Page: www.icdd.com

Timothy Fawcett, Executive Director
Cathyann Colaiezzi, Managing Editor
Theresa Kahmer, Publication Manager

A quarterly journal devoted to the use of the
powder method for material characterization is
available on annual subscription. The journal
focus is on materials. Characterization employing x-ray powder diffraction and related techniques.
Cost: $90.00
Frequency: Quarterly
Founded in 1941

7468 Powder and Bulk Engineering
CSC Publishing
1155 Northland Dr
St Paul, MN 55120-1288

651-287-5600
FAX 651-287-5650
Home Page: www.cscpublishinginc.com

Richard R Cress, Publisher
Terry O'Neill, Editor

Featured editorial includes technical articles,
case histories, test centers, product news and
literature, and industry news items.
Cost: $100.00
Frequency: Monthly

7469 Power Engineering International
PennWell Publishing Company
1421 S Sheridan Rd
Tulsa, OK 74112-6619

918-835-3161
800-331-4463
FAX 918-831-9497
E-Mail: candiced@pennwell.com
Home Page: www.pennwell.com

Robert Biolchini, President
Brian Schimmoller, Managing Editor

Serves the global electric power generation and
transmission industry.
Cost: $180.00
Frequency: Monthly
ISSN: 1069-4994
Founded in 1896

7470 Precision Engineering
Elsevier Science
PO Box 10826
Raleigh, NC 27605-0826

919-839-8444
FAX 919-839-8039
Home Page: www.aspe.net

W T Estler, Editor-in-Chief

Is the foremost international journal devoted to
the study of ultra-high precision engineering
and metrology.

7471 Printed Circuit Design
CMP Media
240 West 35th Street
New York, NY 10001

516-562-5000
FAX 415-947-6090
Home Page: www.cmp.com

David Levin, CEO

7472 Process Heating
Business News Publishing Company
155 Pfingsten Road
Suite 205
Deerfield, IL 60015

847-405-4000
FAX 248-502-1001
E-Mail: PHeditors@bnpmedia.com
Home Page: www.process-heating.com
Social Media: *Facebook, Twitter*

Anne Armel, Publisher
Linda Becker, Associate Publisher & Editor
Beth McClelland, Production Manager

Magazine covers heat processing at temperatures up to 1000 degrees F at end user and
OEM plants in 9 industries. Follow us at twit-
ter.com/ProcessHeating,
www.facebook.com/ProcessHeating
Circulation: 25000
Founded in 1994

7473 Processing
Putman Media
PO Box 698
Birmingham, AL 35243

888-431-2877
FAX 205-408-3797
E-Mail: webmaster@grandviewmedia.com
Home Page: www.grandviewmedia.com

Dennis Van Milligen, Editor in Chief
Mike Wasson, Publisher

Offers information on printing, publishing and
processing. Information is given on the latest
technology in these and other desktop industries.
Cost: $15.00
53 Pages
Frequency: Monthly
Founded in 1960

7474 Product Design and Development
Reed Business Information
301 Gibraltar Drive
Box 650
Morris Plains, NJ 07950

973-292-5100
FAX 630-288-8686
Home Page: www.reedbusiness.com

Stuart Whayman, CFO

**7475 Product Development Best Practices
Report**
Management Roundtable
92 Crescent St
Waltham, MA 02453-4315

781-891-8080
FAX 781-398-1889
Home Page: www.pharmcentric.com

Stewart Maws, Owner

The goal of this publication is to help firms
market, manufacture and design better products
at a lower rate.
Cost: $219.00
Frequency: Monthly

7476 Professional Safety Journal
American Society of Safety Engineering

1800 E Oakton Street
Des Plaines, IL 60018

847-699-2929
FAX 847-768-3434
E-Mail: customerservice@asse.org
Home Page: www.asse.org
Social Media: *Facebook, Twitter, LinkedIn*

Fred Fortman, Executive Director
Bruce Sufranski, Finance/Controller Director
Diane Hurns, Manager Public Relations
Department
Sally Madden, Human Resources Manager

The American Society of Safety Engineers
(ASSE) is the oldest professional safety society
committed to protecting people, property and
the environment. ASSE has more than 32,000
occupational safety, health and environmental
(SH&E) professional members who manage,
supervise, research and consult on safety,
health, transportation and the environment in
all industries, government, labor and education.
34000 Members
Frequency: Monthly
Circulation: 40,000
Founded in 1911

7477 Quality Engineering

American Society for Quality
600 N Plankinton Avenue
PO Box 3005
Milwaukee, WI 53201-3005

414-272-8575
800-248-1946
FAX 414-272-1734
E-Mail: help@asq.org
Home Page: www.asq.org

Roberto M Saco, President
Paul E Borawski, CEO
Erica Gumieny, Sales
Fay Spano, Communications/Media Relations

Co-published with Taylor and Francis, this
journal is for professional practitioners and researchers whose goal is quality engineering improvements and solutions.
Cost: $34.75
100M Members
Frequency: Quarterly/Members Price
Founded in 1946

7478 Quality Management Journal

American Society for Quality
600 N Plankinton Avenue
PO Box 3005
Milwaukee, WI 53201-3005

414-272-8575
800-248-1946
FAX 414-272-1734
E-Mail: help@asq.org
Home Page: www.asq.org

Roberto M Saco, President
Paul E Borawski, CEO
Erica Gumieny, Sales
Fay Spano, Communications/Media Relations

Published by the American Society for Quality,
the QMT is a quarterly, peer-reviewed journal
that focuses on the subject of quality management practice and provides a discussion forum
for both practitioners and academics in the area
of research.
Cost: $50.00
100M Members
Frequency: Quarterly
Founded in 1946

7479 Quality Progress

American Society for Quality
600 N Plankinton Avenue
PO Box 3005
Milwaukee, WI 53201-3005

414-272-8575
800-248-1946

FAX 414-272-1734
E-Mail: help@asq.org
Home Page: www.asq.org

Roberto M Saco, President
Paul E Borawski, CEO
Erica Gumieny, Sales
Fay Spano, Communications/Media Relations

Published by the American Society for Quality,
the QP is a peer-reviewed journal that focuses
on the subject of quality control, discussing the
usage and implementation of quality principles
including the subject areas of organizational
behavior, knowledge management and process
improvement.
Cost: $55.00
100M Members
Founded in 1946

7480 RSES Journal

Refrigeration Service Engineers Society
1666 Rand Rd
Des Plaines, IL 60016-3552

847-297-6464
800-297-5660
FAX 847-297-5038
E-Mail: general@rses.org
Home Page: www.rses.org
Social Media: *Facebook, Twitter, LinkedIn*

Robert Sherman, President
Lawrence Donaldson, Vice President
Wes Maxfield, Secretary Treasurer

Providing quality technical content in digital
and printed forms that can be applied on the
job site.
Frequency: Monthly
Circulation: 15231

7481 Radwaste Solutions

American Nuclear Society
555 N Kensington Ave
La Grange Park, IL 60526-5592

708-352-6611
FAX 708-352-0499
Home Page: www.asn.org

Jack Tuohy, Executive Director
E James Reinsch, President-Elect/VP
Harry Bradley, Executive Director
William F Naughton, Treasurer
Cal Poly, Vice President

Containing articles that discuss practical approaches and solutions to everyday problems
and issues in all fields of radioactive waste
management and environmental restoration.
Cost: $455.00
Frequency: Bi-Monhtly
Founded in 2005

7482 Reliability Engineering and Management Proceedings

7340 N La Oesta Ave
Tucson, AZ 85704-3119

520-621-6120
FAX 520-621-8191
E-Mail: dimitri@u.arizona.edu
Home Page: www.u.arizona.edu

Dimitri B Kececioglu, Owner

Proceedings where over 15 leading corpora-
tions present their latest techniques in this
field.
Cost: $50.00
Frequency: Annual+
Circulation: 50
Founded in 1963
*Mailing list available for rent: 43000 names at
$152 per M*

7483 Repro Report

International Reprographic Association

401 N Michigan Avenue
Chicago, IL 60611

312-245-1026
FAX 312-527-6705
E-Mail: info@irga.com
Home Page: www.irga.com

Bryan Thomas, President
Dan Stephens, Executive Director
Steve Bova, Executive Director
Ben Barclay, Director of Operations

Articles on blueprint service companies, engi-
neering equipment manufacturers and suppli-
ers.
Cost: $150.00
Circulation: 1000
Founded in 1927

7484 Research-Technology Management

Industrial Research Institute
2300 Clarendon Boulevard
Suite 400
Arlington, VA 22201-3331

703-647-2580
FAX 703-647-2581
E-Mail: information@iriweb.org
Home Page: www.iriweb.org

Martha Collins, Chairman
Daniel Abramowicz, Chairman-Elect
Edward Bernstein, President
James Euchner, Editor-in-Chief
Maryanne Gobble, Managing Editor

As the official journal of IRI, Research-Tech-
nology Management, is the bi-monthly, peer-reviewed journal, providing authoritative,
practitioner-oriented articles for technology
leaders.
200 Members
Frequency: 6x Yearly
Circulation: 1800
ISSN: 0895-6308
Founded in 1938

7485 Resource

American Society of Agricultural Engineers
2950 Niles Rd
St Joseph, MI 49085-8607

269-429-0300
800-371-2723
FAX 269-429-3852
E-Mail: hq@asabe.org
Home Page: www.asabe.org

Ronald McAllister, President
Donna Hull, Publication Director

Accepts advertising.
Cost: $75.00
Circulation: 9000
ISSN: 1076-3333
Founded in 1907
Printed in on matte stock

7486 Review of Scientific Instruments

American Institute of Physics
2 Huntington Quadrangle
Melville, NY 11747-4502

516-576-2200
FAX 516-349-7669
E-Mail: rsi@aip.org
Home Page: www.aip.org

Darlene Walters, Senior VP
Douglas LaFrenier, Marketing Director

Presents original articles on new principles, de-
vices and techniques in scientific instrumenta-
tion.
Cost: $90.00
Frequency: Monthly
Circulation: 3100
Founded in 1931

7487 Robotics and Computer-Intergrated Manufacturing

Elsevier Science

PO Box 945
New York, NY 10159

212-895-5800
FAX 212-633-3680
E-Mail: usinfo-f@elsevier.com
Home Page: www.elsevier.com

Nam P Sata, Editor
A. Sharon, Chief Executive Officer
Bill Godfrey, Chief Information Officer
David Clark, Senior Vice President

Contains original papers on theoretical, applied and experimental robotics and computer-integrated manufacturing, with emphasis on flexible manufacturing systems.
Cost: $1156.00
Circulation: 2500
Founded in 1880

7488 SAMPE Journal
Society for the Advancement of Material & Process
1161 Park View Drive
Suite 200
Covina, CA 91724-3751

626-331-0616
800-562-7360
FAX 626-332-8929
E-Mail: sampeibo@sampe.org
Home Page: www.sampe.org
Social Media: Facebook, LinkedIn

Dr Scott Beckwith, Technical Editor
Jennifer Stephens, Production Manager
Patty Hunt, Advertising Rep

An informative and acclaimed publication provides a steady stream of technical articles, industry and international technical news, product and new literature announcements, book reviews, technical events calendars, and local SAMPE information. This publication is mailed complimentary to all SAMPE members.
Cost: $82.00
Frequency: Bi-Monthly

7489 SAWE Weight Engineers Handbook
Society of Allied Weight Engineers
5734 E. Lucia Walk
Long Beach, CA 90803-4015

562-596-2873
FAX 562-596-2874
E-Mail: exdirector@sawe.org
Home Page: www.sawe.org

Patrick Brown, President
Jeffery Cerro, Executive VP
Ronald Fox, Executive Director
Robert Ridenour, VP Publications
Clint Bower, Executive VP

Contains technical information on materials, engineering formulas as well as other reference materials.
Cost: $100.00
348 Pages
Frequency: Periodic

7490 SPE Drilling & Completion
Society of Petroleum Engineers
PO Box 833836
Richardson, TX 75083-3836

972-529-9300
800-456-6863
FAX 972-952-9435
E-Mail: spedal@spe.org
Home Page: www.spe.org

Giovanni Paccaloni, President
Bill Cobb, VP Finance
John E Bethancourt, Director Management/Information
Ian Gorman, Director Production/Operations
Niki Bradbury, Managing Director

Features papers covering bit technology, completions, drilling fluids and operations, equipment and instrumentation, perforation and sand

control, simulations tubulars, well control, and work over well construction related topics.
Cost: $30.00
Frequency: Quarterly

7491 SPE Journal
Society of Petroleum Engineers
PO Box 833836
Richardson, TX 75083-3836

972-529-9300
800-456-6863
FAX 972-952-9435
E-Mail: spedal@spe.org
Home Page: www.spe.org

Giovanni Paccaloni, President
Bill Cobb, VP Finance
John E Bethancourt, Director Management/Inforamtion
Ian Gorman, Director Production/Operations
Niki Bradbury, Managing Director

Includes full length technical papers covering all aspects of petroleum technology. SPE Journal covers the theories and emerging concepts that will become the new technologies of tomorrow.
Cost: $60.00
Frequency: Quarterly

7492 SPE Production & Facilities
Society of Petroleum Engineers
PO Box 833836
Richardson, TX 75083-3836

972-529-9300
800-456-6863
FAX 972-952-9435
E-Mail: spedal@spe.org
Home Page: www.spe.org

Giovanni Paccaloni, President
Bill Cobb, VP Finance
John E Bethancourt, Director Management/Information
Ian Gorman, Director Production/Operations
Niki Bradbury, Managing Director

It includes papers on artificial lift, chemical treatments, design and operation of surface facilities and downhole equipment, formation damage control, fracturing, gas production and storage, offshore operations, production logging and optimization systems, sand control, separation and processing, and work over-production improvement.
Cost: $30.00
Frequency: Quarterly

7493 SPE Reservoir Evaluation & Engineering
Society of Petroleum Engineers
PO Box 833836
Richardson, TX 75083-3836

972-529-9300
800-456-6863
FAX 972-952-9435
E-Mail: spedal@spe.org
Home Page: www.spe.org

Giovanni Paccaloni, President
Bill Cobb, VP Finance
John E Bethancourt, Director Management/Information
Ian Gorman, Director Production/Operations
Niki Bradbury, Managing Director

The journal covers a wide range of topics, including the following: Reservoir Engineering.
Cost: $40.00
Frequency: Bi-Monthly

7494 Sea Technology Magazine
Compass Publications, Inc.

1501 Wilson Blvd
Suite 1001
Arlington, VA 22209-2403

703-524-3136
FAX 703-841-0852
E-Mail: seatechads@sea-technology.com
Home Page: www.sea-technology.com
Social Media: Facebook, Twitter

Amos Bussmann, President/Publisher
Joy Carter, Circulation Manager
Meghan Ventura, Managing Editor

Worldwide information leader for marine/offshore business, science and engineering. Read in more than 110 countries by management, engineers, scientists and technical personnel working in industry, government and education.
Cost: $40.00
Frequency: Monthly
Circulation: 16304
ISSN: 0093-3651
Founded in 1960
Mailing list available for rentat $80 per M
Printed in 4 colors

7495 Software Quality Professional
American Society for Quality
600 N Plankinton Avenue
PO Box 3005
Milwaukee, WI 53201-3005

414-272-8575
800-248-1946
FAX 414-272-1734
E-Mail: help@asq.org
Home Page: www.asq.org

Roberto M Saco, President
Paul E Borawski, CEO
Erica Gumieny, Sales
Fay Spano, Communications/Media Relations

Published by the American Society for Quality, the SQP is a quarterly, peer-reviewed journal for software development professionals that focuses on the subject of quality practice principles in the implementation of software and the development of software systems.
Cost: $45.00
100M Members
Frequency: Quarterly
Founded in 1946

7496 TEST Engineering & Management
Mattingley Publishing Company
3756 Grand Ave
#205
Oakland, CA 94610-1545

510-839-0909
FAX 510-839-2950
Home Page: www.mattingley-publ.com

Eve Mattingley, Owner
Nora Archambeau, Advertising Sales Manager

Includes mechanical testing, environmental simulation, and related technologies in industry, government, testing labs, and universities.
Cost: $45,00
Frequency: Monthly
Circulation: 9500
ISSN: 0193-4120
Founded in 1959
Printed in 4 colors on glossy stock

7497 The Bent
Tau Beta Pi Association
PO Box 2697
Knoxville, TN 37901-2697

865-546-4578
800-250-3196
FAX 865-546-4579
Home Page: www.tbp.org
Social Media: Facebook

James D Froula, Executive Director/Editor
Dr. Larry Simonson, President

The official publication of the Tau Beta Pi Association - the engineering honor society and the world's largest engineering organization.
Cost: $10.00
Frequency: Quarterly
Circulation: 87000
ISSN: 0005-884x

7498 The Bridge
IEEE-Eta Kappa Nu
445 Hoes Lane
Piscataway, NJ 08854

732-465-5846
800-406-2590
E-Mail: info@hkn.org
Home Page:
www.ieee.org/education_careers/education/ieee_hkn/bridge

Steve Watkins, Editor-in-Chief
Nancy Ostin, Managing Editor

The award-winning digital magazine of the IEEE-HKN.
Frequency: 3x/year

7499 Tribology & Lubrication Technology
Society of Tribologists & Lubrication
840 Busse Hwy
Park Ridge, IL 60068-2376

847-825-5536
FAX 847-825-1456
E-Mail: information@stle.org
Home Page: www.stle.org

Ed Salek, Executive Director
Karl Phipps, Associate Editor
Dr Neil Canter, Contributing Editor

Technical magazine that serves an audience of interdisciplinary professionals from industry, academic institutions and government. Included in this group are scientists, engineers, corporate leaders, researchers and product developers, plant managers and maintenance professionals, sales and marketing people and more.
Frequency: Monthly
Circulation: 7,000

7500 Tribology Transaction
Society of Tribologists & Lubrication
840 Busse Hwy
Park Ridge, IL 60068-2376

847-825-5536
FAX 847-825-1456
E-Mail: information@stle.org
Home Page: www.stle.org

Ed Salek, Executive Director

Provides you with new and useful reports and analysis of every aspect of tribology and lubrication presented by renowned authors from around the globe. Available online as well.
Frequency: Quarterly

7501 US Black Engineer & Information Technology
Career Communications Group
729 E Pratt St
Suite 504
Baltimore, MD 21202-3302

410-244-7101
FAX 410-752-1837
E-Mail: customer_service@ccgmag.com
Home Page: www.ccgmag.com

Jean Hamilton, Chief Financial Officer
Lango Deen, Technology Editor
Antonio Watson, VP Sales
Guy Madison, Publisher
Diane Jones, Director of Marketing

Devoted to engineering, science, and technology and to promoting opportunities in those fields for Black Americans.
Cost: $26.00
84 Pages
Frequency: Quarterly
Circulation: 100,000
ISSN: 1088-3444
Printed in 4 colors on glossy stock

7502 VXI Journal
30233 Jefferson Avenue
Saint Clair Shores, MI 48282

586-415-6500
FAX 586-415-4882

Magazine is geared towards test engineers who are using or considering VXI bus systems and equipment.
Frequency: Quarterly
Circulation: 8000

7503 Way Ahead Magazine
Society of Petroleum Engineers
PO Box 833836
Richardson, TX 75083-3836

972-529-9300
800-456-6863
FAX 972-952-9435
E-Mail: spedal@spe.org
Home Page: www.spe.org

Giovanni Paccaloni, President
Bill Cobb, VP Finance
John E Bethancourt, Director
Management/Information
Ian Gorman, Director Production/Operations
Niki Bradbury, Managing Director

Designed for and written by young professionals in the oil and gas industry. In it, you will find items of particular interest to the younger members of our industry, including articles on the current state of the job market, how to improve communication skills, and what SPE young professionals are doing will be.
Frequency: 3x Yearly

7504 Weighing & Measurement
Key Markets Publishing Company
4729 Charles Street
PO Box 5867
Rockford, IL 61125-0867

815-636-7739

David M Mathieu, Publisher

Articles on new products, industry news, previews and reviews of events, and technical approaches to measurement.
Frequency: Bi-Monthly
Circulation: 12,000

7505 Wireless Design & Development
Reed Business Information
301 Gibraltar Drive
PO Box 650
Morris Plains, NJ 07950-0650

973-292-5100
FAX 973-292-0783
Home Page: www.wirelessdesignmag.com

Wayne Curtis, Group Publisher
Kim Stokes, Editor

Edited for wireless component and system design engineers in the commercial RF and microwave market.
Frequency: Monthly

Trade Shows

7506 AACE Annual Meeting
Association of Cost Engineering
1265 Suncrest Towne Centre Drive
Morgantown, WV 26505-1876

304-296-8444
800-858-2678
FAX 304-291-5728
E-Mail: info@aacei.org
Home Page: www.aacei.org

Jennie Amos, Marketing/Meetings Manager

See and hear outstanding technical presentations, panel discussions, workshops, tours, and guest speakers
Frequency: Annual/June

7507 ACA Annual Meeting & Exhibition
American Crystallographic Association
Ellicott Station
PO Box 96
Buffalo, NY 14205-0096

716-898-8690
FAX 716-898-8695
E-Mail: aca@hwi.buffalo.edu
Home Page: www.AmerCrystalAssn.org

Thomas Koetzle, President
George Philip, Vice President

75 manufacturers exhibits of commercial hardware and software, and x-ray equipment. In addition to the exhibition, take advantage of workshops, and scientific and poster sessions.
1000 Attendees
Frequency: Annual
Founded in 1955

7508 AEE Globacon
Association of Energy Engineers
4025 Pleasantdale Road
Suite 420
Atlanta, GA 30340

770-447-5083
FAX 770-446-3969
E-Mail: ashley@aeecenter.org
Home Page: www.aeecenter.org

Ashley Clark, Exhibits Manager
Patricia Ardavin, Conference Registration Director
Michelle Oxner, Conference Speakers Director
Lauren Lake, Event & Marketing Director
Bill Kent, Sponsorship Programs

Decision makers from business, industry and government coming together to seek integrated solutions to assure secure and affordable power supplies, effective management practices of both energy and overall operations costs, and exploring new technologies. The multi-track conference offer opportunity to learn about innovative and cost-conscious strategies, compare energy supply options, network, and workshops. Expo includes the Northeast Green Showcase by Energy Star.
8.2M Attendees
Mailing list available for rent

7509 AHR Expo
Refrigeration Service Engineers Society
1666 Rand Road
Des Plaines, IL 60016-3552

847-297-6464
800-297-5660
E-Mail: webmaster@rses.org
Home Page: www.rses.org

Robert Sherman, Intl President
Lawrence Donaldson, Intl Vice President

Attracts thousands of attendees from all facets of the industry, including contractors, engineers, dealers, distributors, wholesalers, OEM's, architects and builders, industrial plant operators, facility owners and managers, agents and reps.
Frequency: Annual/January

7510 AISTech Conference & Exposition
Association for Iron & Steel Technology

186 Thorn Hill Rd
Warrendale, PA 15086-7528

724-814-3000
FAX 724-814-3001
E-Mail: info@aist.org
Home Page: www.aist.org

Ronald E Ashburn, Executive Director
Brian Bliss, Technology Programs Manager
Karen Hickey, Publications Manager/Editor
Mark Didiano, Finance & Administration Manager
Stacy Varmecky, Membership Services Manager

Featuring technologies from across the globe, allowing steel producers to compete in today's global market. Submit technical papers for presentation at the event. 300 exhibitors. Registration starts at $425.
7000 Attendees
Frequency: Annual/Spring

7511 AMSE International Manufacturing Science & Engineering Conference
American Society of Mechanical Engineers
Three Park Avenue
New York, NY 10016-5990

973-882-1167
800-843-2763
E-Mail: infocentral@asme.org
Home Page: www.asme.org

Victoria Rockwell, President
The MSEC highlights cutting edge manufacturing research in technical paper, poster and panel sessions.
3200 Attendees
Frequency: Annual/Fall
Mailing list available for rentat $125 per M

7512 ANS Annual Meeting
American Nuclear Society
555 North Kensington Avenue
La Grange Park, IL 60526

708-352-6611
FAX 708-352-0499
Home Page: www.ans.org

Dr Lawrence Papay, General Chair
Dr Atambir Rao, Technical Program Chair
Harry Bradley, Executive Director
Frequency: Annual/June

7513 AOCS Annual Meeting & Expo
American Oil Chemists Society
2710 S Boulder
Urbana, IL 61802-6996

217-359-2344
FAX 217-351-8091
E-Mail: general@aocs.org
Home Page: www.aocs.org

Joy McClaugherty, Conference Contact
Jodey Schonfeld, Publications
Frequency: Annual/April-May

7514 APPA Annual Conference & Exposition
Association of Higher Education Facilities
1643 Prince Street
Alexandria, VA 22314-2818

703-684-1446
FAX 703-549-2772
E-Mail: katy@appa.org
Home Page: www.appa.org

E. Lander Medlin, Executive VP
Anita Dosik, Publications Manager
Ted Weidner, CAPPA Event Contact

Discussions and programs centered around today's educational facilities professionals: gain insight on current trends and conditions, identify challenges and solutions being implemented by industry experts, CEU and

networking opportunities, and the innovative showcase of exhibitors.
Frequency: Annual

7515 ASA Annual Meeting & Noise-Con
Acoustical Society of America
2 Huntington Quadrable
Suite 1NO1
Melville, NY 11747

516-576-2360
FAX 516-576-2377
E-Mail: asa@aip.org
Home Page: asa.aip.org

Charles E Schmid, Executive Director
Elaine Moran, ASA Office Manager
Mardi Hastings, President
700 Attendees
Frequency: Annual/Spring

7516 ASA: Drive Systems-Control Units-Automation
Stygar Associates
1202 Allanson Road
Mundelein, IL 60060

847-566-4566
FAX 847-566-4580
E-Mail: estygariii@aol.com
Home Page: www.stygarassociates.com

376 exhibitors of hydraulic and pneumatic elements, compressed air systems, automation components, openloop and measuring controls.
40000 Attendees
Frequency: Biennial

7517 ASCE Annual Civil Engineering Conference & Exposition
American Society of Civil Engineers
1801 Alexander Bell Drive
Reston, VA 20191-4400

703-295-6000
800-548-2723
FAX 703-295-6144
E-Mail: conf@asce.org
Home Page: www.asce.org

Mark Geiger, Sr Coor, Exhibits & Meeting Svcs
Heather Doughlin, Sr Mgr, Conferences & Meeting Svcs
Kathy Caldwell, President
175 exhibits of industry related products and services, seminars, workshops and banquet plus continuing education classes.
3000 Attendees
Frequency: Annual/Fall
Founded in 1879

7518 ASCE Annual Meeting
American Society of Certified Engineering
PO Box 1348
Flowery Branch, GA 30542-0023

770-967-9173
FAX 770-967-8049
Home Page: www.ascet.org

Russell E Freier, Chairman
Leo Saenz, CET, President
Kurt Schuler, Secretary/Treasurer
Frequency: Annual/June

7519 ASCE's Annual Civil Engineers Conference
American Society of Civil Engineers
1801 Alexander Bell Drive
Reston, VA 20191-4400

703-295-6000
800-548-2723
FAX 703-295-6144
Home Page: www.asce.org

Phil Gaughan, President
Focus on the challenges faced by companies and agencies already implementing the next

generation of infrastructure in Water (e.g. dams, desalination, and recycling) and Transportation (e.g. seaports, rail, and roads). 100 booths.
24M Attendees
Frequency: Annual/October

7520 ASEE Annual Conference & Exposition
American Society for Engineering Education
1818 N Street NW
Suite 600
Washington, DC 20036-2476

202-331-3500
FAX 202-265-8504
E-Mail: pubsinfo@asee.org
Home Page: www.asee.org

Patti Greenawalt, Director Meetings/Conventions
Frank Huband, Executive Director
Frequency: Annual/June

7521 ASFE Fall Meeting
ASFE/The Geoprofessional Business Association
8811 Colesville Road
Suite G106
Silver Springs, MD 20910

301-565-2733
FAX 301-589-2017
E-Mail: info@asfe.org
Home Page: www.asfe.org

John P Bachner, Executive VP
David Gaboury, President
Frequency: Annual/Fall

7522 ASFE Spring Meeting
ASFE/The Geoprofessional Business Association
8811 Colesville Road
Suite G106
Silver Springs, MD 20910

301-565-2733
FAX 301-589-2017
E-Mail: info@asfe.org
Home Page: www.asfe.org

John P Bachner, Executive VP
David Gaboury, President
Frequency: Annual/Spring

7523 ASFE Winter Leadership Conference
ASFE/The Geoprofessional Business Association
8811 Colesville Road
Suite G106
Silver Springs, MD 20910

301-565-2733
FAX 301-589-2017
E-Mail: info@asfe.org
Home Page: www.asfe.org

John Bachner, Executive VP
David Gaboury, President
Frequency: Annual/January

7524 ASGE National Conference
American Society of Gas Engineers
PO Box 66
Artesia, CA 90702

562-455-9417
E-Mail: asgecge@aol.com
Home Page: www.asge-national.org

Nancy Wilson, President
Sham Kassab, VP
Jerry Moore, Executive Director

Where members meet to discuss the most current events and issues facing the Gas Appliance industry. Allows individuals to learn about new

technology and to network with other Gas Industry Professionals.
Frequency: Annual

7525 ASM Heat Treating Society Conference & Exposition
ASM International/Materials Information
9639 Kinsman Road
Materials Park, OH 44073

440-338-5151
800-336-5152
FAX 440-338-4634
E-Mail: pamela.kleinman@asminternational.org
Home Page: www.asminternational.org

Pamela Kleinma, Senior Manager, Events
Kellye Thomas, Exposition Account Manager
Dr. Mark Smith, President

Conference and exhibits of heat treating equipment and supplies plus information of interest to metallurgists, manufacturing, research and design technical professionals. 300 exhibitors.
3500 Attendees
Frequency: Bi-Annual
Founded in 1974

7526 ASM Materials Science & Technology (MS&T)
ASM International
9639 Kinsman Road
Materials Park, OH 44073-0002

440-338-5151
800-336-5152
FAX 440-338-4634
E-Mail: pamela.kleinman@asminternational.org
Home Page: www.asminternational.org

Pamela Kleinman, Senior Manager, Events
Kelly Thomas, Exposition Account Manager
Dr. Mark Smith, President

Annual event focusing on testing, analysis, characterization and research of materials such as engineered materials, high performance metals, powdered metals, metal forming, surface modification, welding and joining. 350 exhibitors.
4,000 Attendees
Frequency: Annual/October
Founded in 2005

7527 ASME Annual Meeting
American Society of Mechanical Engineers
Three Park Avenue
New York, NY 10016

973-882-1170
800-843-2763
FAX 212-591-7856
E-Mail: infocentral@asme.org
Home Page: www.asme.org

Melissa Torres, Meetings Manager
Mary Jakubowski, Meetings Manager
Marc Goldsmith, President
Frequency: Annual/June

7528 ASME Gas Turbine Users Symposium (GTUS)
American Society of Mechanical Engineers/IGTI
6525 The Corners Pkwy
Suite 115
Norcross, GA 30092

404-847-0072
FAX 404-847-0151
E-Mail: igtiprogram@asme.org
Home Page: www.asme.org/igti

Smita Solanki, Coordinator, IGTI Conferences
Kristen Barranger, Manager, IGTI Conferences & Expos
Michael Ireland, Managing Director

A show focused on the role gas turbines will play in meeting the nation's future energy de-

mands, provides the information related to gas turbine operations, maintenance, advances, and design.
2000 Attendees
Frequency: Annual

7529 ASNT Fall Conference & Quality Testing Show
American Society for Nondestructive Testing
1711 Arlingate Lane
PO Box 28518
Columbus, OH 43228-0518

614-274-6003
800-222-2768
FAX 614-274-6899
Home Page: www.asnt.org

Michael O'Toole, Sernior Manager, Conferences
Jacquie Guinta, Meeting Coordinator
Ruth Staat, Exhibit/Event Supervisor

Seminar, conference and 150 exhibits of nondestructive testing equipment, services, supplies and laboratory representatives. Holds a smaller conference in the spring.
3000 Attendees
Frequency: Annual/Fall

7530 ASPE Technical Symposium
American Society of Plumbing Engineers
8614 Catalpa Avenue
Suite 1007
Chicago, IL 60656-1116

773-693-2773
FAX 773-695-9007
E-Mail: info@aspe.org
Home Page: www.aspe.org

Pat Delaney, Convention/Symposium Information
Stan Wolson, Executive Director

For professional plumbing engineers, designers and contractors to improve their skills, learn original design concepts and make important networking contacts to help them stay abreast of current trends, codes and technologies.
Frequency: Annual/October

7531 ASPE's Annual Meeting
American Society for Precision Engineering
PO Box 10826
Raleigh, NC 27605-0826

919-839-8444
FAX 919-839-8039
Home Page: www.aspe.net

Erika Deutsch-Layne, Meetings Manager

Offers the latest in precision engineering research through presentations from national and international.
Frequency: Annual/October

7532 ATCE
Society of Petroleum Engineers
PO Box 833836
Richardson, TX 75083-3836

972-529-9300
800-456-6863
FAX 972-952-9435
E-Mail: spedal@spe.org
Home Page: www.spe.org

Giovanni Paccaloni, President
Bill Cobb, VP Finance
John E Bethancourt, Director Management/Information
Ian Gorman, Director Production/Operations
Niki Bradbury, Managing Director
40482 Attendees
Frequency: Annual/October

7533 AVS International Symposium & Exhibition
American Vacuum Society

125 Maiden Lane
15th Floor
New York, NY 10038

212-248-0200
FAX 212-248-0245
E-Mail: jeannette@avs.org
Home Page: www.avs.org

Jeannette DeGennaro, Exhibition & Sales Coordinator
Angela Klink, Membership Services Coordinator
Heather Korff, Events/Office Coordinator AVS West
Yvonne Towse, Managing Director
Angus Rockett, President

The Symposium and Exhibition has been developed to address cutting-edge issues associated with the vacuum science and technology in both the research and manufacturing communities. It offers a week long forum for exchange, topical conferences, courses, training, career workshops and networking. Over 200 booths of the latest products and services around vacuum science and technology.
3000 Attendees
Frequency: Annual

7534 AVS International Symposium and Exhibition
AVS Science & Technology Society
120 Wall Street
32nd Floor
New York, NY 10005-3993

212-248-0200
FAX 212-248-0245
E-Mail: david_aspnes@avs.org
Home Page: www.avs.org

David E Aspnes, President
Christie R Marrian, President-Elect
John Coburn, Treasurer
Joseph J Greene, Clerk/Secretary
Yvonne Towse, Executive Director

This has been developed to address cutting-edge issues associated with vacuum science and technology in both the research and manufacturing communities. The Symposium is a week long forum for science and technology exchange featuring papers from technical divisions and technology groups, and topical conferences on emerging technologies.
3000 Attendees
Founded in 1953

7535 AVS New Mexico Chapter Annual Symposium Short Courses/Vendor Show
AVS Science & Technology Society
120 Wall Street
32nd Floor
New York, NY 10005-3993

212-248-0200
FAX 212-248-0245
E-Mail: david_aspnes@avs.org
Home Page: www.avs.org

David E Aspnes, President
Christie R Marrian, President-Elect
John Coburn, Treasurer
Joseph J Greene, Clerk/Secretary
Yvonne Towse, Executive Director
Frequency: Annual/May

7536 Adhesion Society Annual Meeting
Adhesion Society
2 Davidson Hall-0201
Blacksburg, VA 24061

540-231-7257
FAX 540-231-3971

E-Mail: adhesoc@vt.edu
Home Page: www.adhesionsociety.org

Ken Shull, Program Chair
Leonardo Lopez, Exhibition Chair
Esther Brann, Office Manager

Engineers, chemists, biologists, mathematicians, physicists, physicians and dentists visit exhibits relating to the study of adhesion's role in coatings, composite materials, the function of biological tissues, and the performance of bonded structures.
400 Attendees
Frequency: Annual/February

7537 Adhesive & Sealant Fall Convention

Adhesive & Sealant Council
7101 Wisconsin Avenue
Suite 990
Bethesda, MD 20814

301-986-9700
FAX 301-986-9795
E-Mail: info@ascouncil.org
Home Page: www.ascouncil.org

Malinda Armstrong, Senior Manager Conventions/Meetings
Matt Croson, President
400 Attendees
Frequency: Annual/October

7538 AeroMat Conference and Exposition

ASM International
9639 Kinsman Road
Materials Park, OH 44073-0002

440-338-5151
800-336-5152
FAX 440-338-4634
Home Page: www.asminternational.org

Kim Schaefer, Event Manager
Kelly Thomas, Exposition Account Manager
Mark F Smith, President
Stanley Theobald, Managing Director

Conference for Aerospace Materials Engineers, Structural Engineers and Designers. The annual event focuses on affordable structures and low-cost manufacturing, titanium alloy technology, advanced intermetallics and refractory metal alloys, materials and processes for space applications, aging systems, high strength steel, NDT evaluation, light alloy technology, welding and joining, and engineering technology. 150 exhibitors.
1500 Attendees
Frequency: Annual/June
Founded in 1984

7539 Airlines Engineering Committee

Aeronautical Radio
2551 Riva Road
Annapolis, MD 21401-7435

410-266-4000
FAX 410-266-4040

Daniel Martinec, Director Avionics

Commercial airline and other transport aircraft avionics engineers.
800 Attendees
Frequency: October

7540 American Society for Engineering Education Conference and Exposition

American Society for Engineering Education
1818 N State Street
Suite 600
Washington, DC 20036

202-331-3500
FAX 202-265-8504
E-Mail: conferences@asee.org
Home Page: www.asee.org

Patti Greenawalt, Director Conventions/Meetings

Jennifer Atkinson, Meetings Assistant
Kathi J Springer, Manager Exhibits/Sponsorships
Frank Huband, Executive Director

Annual conference of 150 publishers, manufacturers, producers, suppliers, designers of scientific instrumentation and distributors. Exhibits include publications, engineering supplies and equipment, computers, software and research companies all products and services related to engineering education.
1700 Attendees
Frequency: Annual/June

7541 American Society of Plumbing Engineers Meeting

American Society of Plumbing Engineers
2980 S River Road
Des Plaines, IL 60018

847-296-0002
FAX 773-695-9007
E-Mail: info@aspe.org
Home Page: www.aspe.org

Cliff Reis, Managing Director of Education
Jim Kendzel, Executive Director

Biennial meeting and exhibits for the plumbing engineering industry. 600 booths.
7000 Attendees
Founded in 1964

7542 American Society of Safety Engineers Professional Development Conference

American Society of Safety Engineers
1800 E Oakton Street
Des Plaines, IL 60018

847-699-2929
FAX 847-768-3434
E-Mail: customerservice@asse.org
Home Page: www.asse.org

Terri Norris, President
James Smith, Vice President/ Finance
Diane Hurns, Manager Public Relations Department

Annual conference and expo of 250 manufacturers and suppliers of safety equipment and health products.
3500 Attendees
Frequency: Annual/June

7543 Annual Applied Reliability Engineering and Product Assurance

The University of Arizona
Aerospace and Mechanical Engineering Department
Building 119, PO Box 210119
Tucson, AZ 85721-0119

520-215-5511
FAX 520-621-8191
E-Mail: dimitri@u.arizona.edu
Home Page: www.u.arizona.edu/~dimitri

Dimitri B Kececioglu PE, Professor Aerospace/Mechanical Eng.
Frequency: Annual/July

7544 Annual Canadian Conference on Intelligent Systems

Robotics Industris Association
900 Victors Way
PO Box 3724
Ann Arbor, MI 48106

734-994-6088
FAX 734-994-3338
E-Mail: webmaster@robotics.org
Home Page: www.robotics.org

Don Vincent, Executive VP
Brian Huse, Director Marketing/PR
Jim Adams, Manager of Public Relations
Sharon Adams, Accounting Manager

Canada's leading showcase of research excellence and breakthroughs in robotics and intelli-

gent systems, featuring technology displays, demonstrations, presentations and workshops.
Frequency: Annual/June

7545 Annual Lean Management Solutions Conference

Institute of Industrial Engineers
3577 Parkway Lane
Suite 200
Norcross, GA 30092

770-449-0460
800-494-0460
FAX 770-441-3295
E-Mail: cs@iienet.org
Home Page: www.iienet.org

Gregg Griffith, Marketing Director
Don Greene, CEO

Will enable you to significantly improve performance, reduce costs, and increase customer satisfaction. With over 60 presentations and new tracks in MRO, Food Processing, Aviation, Healthcare, and Product Design, you will find what you need.
Frequency: Annual/December

7546 Annual Lean Six Sigma Conference

American Society for Quality
600 N Plankinton Avenue
PO Box 3005
Milwaukee, WI 53201-3005

414-272-8575
800-248-1946
FAX 414-272-1734
E-Mail: help@asq.org
Home Page: www.asq.org

Paul Borawski, CEO
James Rooney, Chair
Erica Gumieny, Sales
Fay Spano, Communications/Media Relations

An exclusive two-day briefing and networking event designed by and for the top practitioners in the Six Sigma community.
100M Members
Frequency: Annual/February
Founded in 1946

7547 Annual Meeting of the Society of Rheology

Socieety of Rheology
2 Huntington Quadrangle
Suite 1N01
Meville, NY 11747-4502

516-576-2471
FAX 516-576-2223
E-Mail: rheology@aip.org
Home Page: www.rheology.org

A. Jeffrey Giacomin, VP
Faith Morrison, President
Frequency: Annual/October

7548 Annual Physical Electronics Conference

AVS Science & Technology Society
120 Wall Street
32nd Floor
New York, NY 10005-3993

212-248-0200
FAX 212-248-0245
E-Mail: david_aspnes@avs.org
Home Page: www.avs.org

David E Aspnes, President
Christie R Marrian, President-Elect
John Coburn, Treasurer
Joseph J Greene, Clerk/Secretary
Nancy Schultheis, Office Manager

Will provide a forum for the dissemination and discussion of new research results in the physics and chemistry of surfaces and interfaces. The conference will continue to emphasize fundamental science in materials systems, includ-

ing metals, semiconductors, insulators and biomaterials.
Frequency: Annual/June

7549 Annual Quality Audit Conference
American Society for Quality
600 N Plankinton Avenue
PO Box 3005
Milwaukee, WI 53201-3005

414-272-8575
800-248-1946
FAX 414-272-1734
E-Mail: help@asq.org
Home Page: www.asq.org

Paul Borawski, President
James Rooney, Chair

Topics of interest include: new innovating audit/process approaches, value added involvement, corporate expectations, corporate/social responsibility, auditing in the overall corporate scheme.
100M Members
Frequency: Annual/October
Founded in 1946

7550 Annual RSES Conference & Expo
Refrigeration Service Engineers Society
1666 Rand Road
Des Plaines, IL 60016-3552

847-297-6464
800-297-5660
E-Mail: webmaster@rses.org
Home Page: www.rses.org

Robert Sherman, Intl President
Lawrence Donaldson, Intl Vice President
Frequency: Annual/September

7551 Annual Service Quality Conference
American Society for Quality
600 N Plankinton Avenue
PO Box 3005
Milwaukee, WI 53201-3005

414-272-8575
800-248-1946
FAX 414-272-1734
E-Mail: help@asq.org
Home Page: www.asq.org

James Rooney, President
Paul E Borawski, CEO
Erica Gumieny, Sales
Fay Spano, Communications/Media Relations

The sessions we plan will help you to navigate through unpredictable consumer behavior and increasing competition to build a strong foundation for reaching superior levels of quality service.
100M Members
Frequency: Annual/September
Founded in 1946

7552 Annual Simulation Solutions Conference
Institute of Industrial Engineers
3577 Parkway Lane
Suite 200
Norcross, GA 30092

770-449-0460
800-494-0460
FAX 770-441-3295
E-Mail: cs@iienet.org
Home Page: www.iienet.org

Greg Griffith, Marketing Director
Don Greene, CEO

You will have a rich menu of over forty presentations by successful practitioners of simulation in transportation and military applications; management strategies; manufacturing; lean scheduling and operations; healthcare; simulation skills; supply chain, material handling, and

distribution; and service and business processes.
Frequency: Annual/May

7553 Annual World Conference on Quality and Improvement
American Society for Quality
600 N Plankinton Avenue
PO Box 3005
Milwaukee, WI 53201-3005

414-272-8575
800-248-1946
FAX 414-272-1734
E-Mail: help@asq.org
Home Page: www.asq.org

James Rooney, President
Paul E Borawski, CEO
Erica Gumieny, Sales
Fay Spano, Communications/Media Relations

Conference focuses on quality and improvement with more than 2,000 exhibits and attendees. Keynote speakers and sessions discuss quality tools, techniques and methodologies. Provides the opportunity for members to meet and network with colleagues in the industry.
100M Members
Frequency: Annual/May
Founded in 1946

7554 Atlantic Design & Manufacturing
Canon Communications
11444 W Olympic Boulevard
Suite 900
Los Angeles, CA 90064-1549

310-445-4200
FAX 310-445-4299
Home Page: www.cancom.com

Diane O'Conner, Trade Show Director
Dan Cutrone, Show Marketing Manager

Serves the East Coast's dynamic design, process, and manufacturing marketplace. This exposition, recently acquired by Canon Communications, is now co-located with Medical Design and Manufacturing East. Product classifications include: Coatings and Finishes, Composites, Computer Aided Design/Computer Aided Manufacturing, Electrical/Electronic, Electric Optical Components and Equipment, Engineered Safety Products, Engineering Management and Tools, Fasteners, Fluid Media, Fluid Power and Control.
Frequency: Annual/May

7555 Atomic Layer Deposition
AVS Science & Technology Society
120 Wall Street
32nd Street
New York, NY 10005-3993

212-248-0200
FAX 212-248-0245
E-Mail: david_aspnes@avs.org
Home Page: www.avs.org

David E Aspnes, President
Christie R Marrian, President-Elect
John Coburn, Treasurer
Joseph J Greene, Clerk/Secretary
Nancy Schultheis, Office Manager

Conference will be a three-day meeting, dedicated to the science and technology of atomic layer controlled deposition of thin films, in particular atomic layer deposition.
Frequency: Annual/August

7556 BMES Annual Fall Meeting
Biomedical Engineering Society
8201 Corporate Drive
Suite 1125
Landover, MD 20785-2224

301-459-1999
877-871-BMES
FAX 301-459-2444

E-Mail: info@bmes.org
Home Page: www.bmes.org

Richard Waugh, President
Edward Schilling, Executive Director
Debra Tucker, Meetings Director
Frequency: Annual/September

7557 Design Part Show
Job Shop Company
16 Waterbury Road
Prospect, CT 06712-1215

800-317-0474
Home Page: www.jobshoptechnology.com

Gerald Schmidt, President
Jennifer Bryda, Production Manager

The show is designed to attract the highest caliber engineers and buyers from your major DEM product manufacturers.
2000 Attendees
Frequency: Annual/April
Founded in 1999

7558 ESTECH, IEST's Annual Technical Meeting and Exposition
American Institute of Physics
One Physics Ellispe
College Park, MD 20740-3843

301-209-3100
E-Mail: dylla@aip.org
Home Page: www.aip.org

H. Frederick Dylia, Executive Director/CEO
John Haynes, Vice President Publishing
Benjamin Snavely, AIP Corporate Secretary
Melissa Poleski, Assistant To Corporate Secretary

Will feature a cutting-edge technical program, hot-topic tutorials, must attend Working Group meetings, and a state-of-the-art exposition.
Frequency: Annual/May

7559 Earth and Space
American Society of Civil Engineers
1801 Alexander Bell Drive
Reston, VA 20191

703-295-6000
800-548-2723
FAX 703-295-6222
E-Mail: webmaster@asce.org
Home Page: www.asce.org

Patricia Galloway, President
Lawrence Roth, Deputy Executive Director
Patrick Natale, Secretary/Treasurer

You will be among experts from a variety of disciplines and have ample, enjoyable opportunities to discuss exploration, engineering, construction, and operations in challenging environments on Planet Earth, in Space, and on other planetary bodies such as the Moon and Mars.
Frequency: Annual/March

7560 Electric West
PRIMEDIA Business Exhibitions
11 River Bend Drive S
PO Box 4949
Stamford, CT 06907-0949

203-358-9900
FAX 203-358-5816
Home Page: www.primediaevents.com

Liza Wylie, Show Director
Mandy Ferreira-Nunez, Operations Manager

Educational sessions attract electrical professionals from contracting companies, industrial plants, consulting engineering firms, datacom installers and electricians. Presentations focus on such topics as power quality, lighting, the NEC, project management, claims management and fiber optics. Also provides in-depth coverage of National Electrical Code changes that

directly impact the work of electrical professionals.
Frequency: Annual/March

7561 European Symposium of the Protein Society
American Institute of Physics
One Physics Ellipse
College Park, MD 20740-3843

301-209-3100
E-Mail: dylla@aip.org
Home Page: www.aip.org

H. Frederick Dylla, Executive Director/CEO
John Haynes, Vice President Publishing
Benjamin Snavely, AIP Corporate Secretary
Melissa Poleski, Assistant To Corporate Secretary

The meeting features sessions on nanotechnology, biosensors and proteins as materials, proteomics, protein networks and systems biology. membrane proteins and diseases, protein folding and diseases, protein flexibility, and molecular recognition.
Frequency: Annual/May

7562 Finishing Expo
Society of Manufacturing Engineers
1 SME Drive
PO Box 930
Dearborn, MI 48121

313-425-3000
800-733-4763
FAX 313-425-3400
E-Mail: service@sme.org
Home Page: www.sme.org

Mark Tomlinson, Executive Director/General Manager
Paul Bradley, President
Bob Harris, Director Finance

The conference will include workshops, tutorials, and technical sessions. 200 booths.
25M Attendees

7563 General Convention
Sigma Phi Delta
438 Smithfield Street
East Liverpool, OH 43920-1723

330-385-5287
E-Mail: webmaster@sigphi.org
Home Page: www.sigphi.org

Derek R Troy, Grand President
Alixandre R Minden, Grand VP
Steven A Weiss, Communications Director
Edward A Hurst, Treasurer
Levon Haig Barsoumian, Executive Secretary

Includes a tentative schedule of business sessions, symposiums and events.
Frequency: Annual/July

7564 GeoFlorida
Geo-Institute, American Society of Civil Engineers
1801 Alexander Bell Drive
Reston, VA 20191-4400

703-295-6350
FAX 703-295-6351
E-Mail: stacey.gardiner@tggroup.com
Home Page: content.geoinstitute.org

Stacey Gardiner, Conference Director
Greory DiLoreto, President- Elect
Mark Rusnica, Deputy Executive Director

The annual geo-conference of the Geo-Institute of ASCE. Presents developments in geotechnical engineering analysis, modeling and design; opportunities to share knowledge, learn about innovations and emerging technologies; panel discussions, technical sessions, lectures, short courses, workshops and student competition; and an extensive exhibit hall.
Frequency: Annual

7565 Geoline Expo
Association of Engineering Geologists
PO Box 460518
Denver, CO 80246

303-757-2926
FAX 720-230-4846
E-Mail: aeg@aegweb.org
Home Page: www.aegweb.org

Becky Roland, Chief Staff Executive

The symposium will cover three major topics. Session 1 Field investigations: Strategy, Organization, Methods, and Uncertainties, Session 2 Inserting the Structure in its Environment, Session 3 Construction, Monitoring, Evolution and Maintenance.
400 Attendees
Frequency: Annual/December

7566 GlobalCon Conference & Expo
Association of Energy Engineers
4025 Pleasantdale Rd
Suite 420
Atlanta, GA 30340-4264

770-447-5083
FAX 770-446-3969
E-Mail: info@aeecenter.org
Home Page: www.aeecenter.org
Social Media: *Facebook, Twitter, LinkedIn, YouTube*

Eric A. Woodroof, President
Gary Hogsett, President Elect
Bill Younger, Secretary
Paul Goodman, C.P.A., Treasurer

Designed specifically to facilitate those seeking to expand their knowledge of fast-moving developments in the energy field, explore promising new technologies, compare energy supply options, and learn about innovative and cost-conscious project implementation strategies.
8.2M Members
Founded in 1977

7567 Government Affairs Briefing
North American Die Casting Association
241 Holbrook Drive
Wheeling, IL 60090-5809

847-279-0001
FAX 847-279-0002
E-Mail: twarog@diecasting.org
Home Page: www.diecasting.org

Daniel Twarog, President

Will provide you with important information in the following informative sessions, state of US manufacturing, trade and global competition, metalcasting research programs, health care & other worker issues, new air standards & other environmental issues.
Frequency: Annual/June

7568 IDSA National Conference
Industrial Designers Society of America
45195 Business Court
Suite 250
Sterling, VA 20166-6717

703-707-6000
FAX 703-787-8501
E-Mail: idsa@idsa.org
Home Page: www.idsa.org

Clive Roux, CEO
Bob Swartz, Executive Director
Kaycee Childress, Marketing
Roxann Henze, Press, Media & Public Relations

IDSA is the world's oldest, largest, member-driven society for product design, industrial design, interaction design, human factors, ergonomics, design research, design management, universal design and related design fields. IDSA organizes the renowned Interna-

tional Design Excellence Award competition annually; hosts the International Design Conference and five regional conferences each year.
800 Attendees
Frequency: Annual/August

7569 IES Annual Meeting
Illuminating Engineering Society of North America
120 Wall Street
17th Floor
New York, NY 10005

212-248-5000
FAX 212-248-5018
E-Mail: ies@ies.org
Home Page: www.ies.org

William Hanley, Executive VP
Marianne Conrad, Director Member Services
400 Attendees
Frequency: Annual

7570 IFAI Annual Expo
Industrial Fabrics Association International
1801 Country Road BW
Roseville, MN 55113

651-222-2508
800-225-4324
FAX 651-631-9334
E-Mail: generalinfo@ifai.com
Home Page: www.ifai.com

Todd Lindemann, VP Conference Manger
Stephen Warner, President

A trade event in the Americas for the technical textiles and specialty fabrics industry.
Frequency: Annual/September

7571 IFAI Outlook
Industrial Fabrics Association International
1801 Country Road BW
Roseville, MN 55113

651-222-2508
800-225-4324
FAX 651-631-9334
E-Mail: generalinfo@ifai.com
Home Page: www.usifi.com

Todd Lindemann, VP Conference Manger
Stephen Warner, President

Will bring industry leaders together to discuss important issues and challenges faced by the United States textile industry.
Frequency: Annual/May

7572 IIE Annual Conference
Institute of Industrial Engineers
3577 Parkway Lane
Suite 200
Norcross, GA 30092

770-449-0460
800-494-0460
FAX 770-441-3295
E-Mail: cs@iienet.org
Home Page: www.iienet.org

Greg Griffith, Marketing Director
Don Greene, CEO

With over 600 content filled presentations and expert speakers, it is the productivity event of the year. Discover the latest tools, techniques and solutions from top professionals in the field. Network with peers, decision makers, and leaders during the conference.
1,100 Attendees
Frequency: Annual/May

7573 IPTC
Society of Petroleum Engineers
PO Box 833836
Richardson, TX 75083-3836

972-529-9300
800-456-6863

FAX 972-952-9435
E-Mail: spedal@spe.org
Home Page: www.spe.org

Giovanni Paccaloni, President
Bill Cobbs, VP Finance
John E Berthancourt, Director
Management/Information
Ian Gorman, Director Production/Operations
Niki Bradbury, Managing Director

The theme for the conference is Sustaining
World Growth - Technology and People. A new
meeting brought to you by four leading industry societies (AAPG, EAGE, SEG, and SPE).
Natural gas will be a major focus of this
meeting.
Frequency: Annual/November

7574 IRI Annual Meeting
Industrial Research Institute
2200 Clarendon Boulevard
Suite 1102
Arlington, VA 22201

703-647-2580
FAX 703-647-2581
Home Page: www.iriweb.org

Robert Kumpf, Chairman
Ryan Dirkx, Chairman-Elect
Edward Bernstein, President
Frequency: Annual/May

**7575 IRgA Annual Convention and Trade
Show**
International Reprographic Association
401 N Michigan Avenue
Chicago, IL 60611

312-673-4805
FAX 312-321-5150
E-Mail: info@irga.com
Home Page: www.irga.com

Robert Roperti, President
Dan Mulrooney, VP
Steve Bova, Executive Director

You will gain first hand knowledge and experience from technical sessions presented by experts in their field, access to the latest products
and services available to enhance your company's performance at the trade show, re-estab-
lish contacts and connections as you interact
with peers to find out how they are handling
the latest challenges.
Frequency: Annual/May

7576 ISWM Annual Conference & Expo
International Society of Weighing &
Measurement
1801 Alexander Bell Avenue
Reston, VA 20191

703-295-6350
FAX 703-295-6351
E-Mail: staff@iswm.org
Home Page: content.geoinstitute.org

Kate Fitzgerald CMP, Director of Meetings

150 booths; presentations from industry leaders; workshops, panels, and discussions.
1.8M Attendees

**7577 International Code Council Annual
Conference**
BOCA Evaluation Services
500 New Jersey Avenue
6th Fl
Washington, DC 20001-2070

888-422-7233
FAX 202-783-2348
E-Mail: webmaster@iccsafe.org
Home Page: www.iccsafe.org

James Brothers, President
William Dupler, Vice President

The conference features the Final Action Hearings, the Education Program, the Annual Busi-

ness Meeting, the International Code Council
Expo and networking opportunities with your
peers in the building safety and fire prevention
fields.
Frequency: Annual/September

**7578 International Conference on
Construction
Engineering/Management**
American Society for Civil Engineers
1801 Alexander Bell Drive
Reston, VA 20191

703-295-6000
800-548-2723
FAX 703-295-6222
E-Mail: webmaster@asce.org
Home Page: www.asce.org

Patricia Galloway, President
Lawrence Roth, Deputy Executive Director
Patrick Natale, Secretary/Treasurer
Frequency: Annual/October

**7579 International Conference on
Deburring and Surface Finishing**
Abrasive Engineering Society
144 Moore Road
Butler, PA 16001

724-282-6210
FAX 724-234-2376
E-Mail: aes@abrasiveengineering.com
Home Page: www.abrasiveengineering.com

Doug Haynes, President
Ted Giese, Executive Director

The program, which is part of series of international conferences, is scheduled for June. This
conference will include a Technical Exhibition
and Tours. A special course on deburring and
surface finishing will be taught following the
conference.
Frequency: Annual/June

**7580 International Conference on
Metallurgical Coatings and Thin
Films**
AVS Science & Technology Society
120 Wall Street
32nd Floor
New York, NY 10005-3993

212-248-0200
FAX 212-248-0245
E-Mail: david_aspnes@avs.org
Home Page: www.avs.com

David E Aspnes, President
Christie R Marrian, President-Elect
John Coburn, Treasurer
Joseph J Greene, Clerk/Secretary
Steve Sukman, Executive Vice President

Internationally recognized as a vibrant technical conference that integrates fundamentals and
applied research focused on thin film deposition, characterization, and advanced surface
modification techniques leading-edge
technology.
Frequency: Annual/May

**7581 International Symposium for Testing
& Failure Analysis**
ASM International
9639 Kinsman Road
Materials Park, OH 44073

440-338-5151
800-336-5152
FAX 440-338-4634
Home Page: www.asminternational.org

Jaime Creighton, Event Manager
Kelly Thomas, Exposition Account Manager

Annual event focusing on microelectronic and
electronic device failure analysis, techniques,
EOS/ESD testing and desecrates aimed at failure analysis engineers and managers, techni-

cians and new failure analysis engineers. 200
exhibitors.
1100 Attendees
Frequency: Annual/November

**7582 International Symposium on
Advances in Abrasives Technology**
Abrasive Engineering Society
141 Moore Road
Butler, PA 16001

724-826-6210
FAX 742-234-2376
E-Mail: aes@abrasiveengineering.com
Home Page: www.abrasiveengineering.com

Doug Haynes, President
Ted Giese, Executive Director

Jointly sponsored by the International Committee for Abrasives Technology and the Japan Society for Abrasive Technology, which has
conducted eight international conferences on
abrasives technologies. Topics including abrasive machining, finishing, assessment of grinding performance, machine tools and systems,
coolant and other topics.
Frequency: Annual/November

**7583 International Thermal Spray
Conference & Exposition**
ASM International
9639 Kinsman Road
Materials Park, OH 44073

440-338-5151
800-336-5152
FAX 440-338-4634
E-Mail: natalie.nemec@asminternational.org
Home Page: www.asminternational.org

Pamela Kleinman, Event Manager
Kelly Thomas, Exposition Account Manager

Global annual event attracting professional interested in thermal spray technology focusing
on advances in HVOF, plasma and detonation
gun, flame spray and wire arc spray processes,
performance of coatings, and future trends. 150
exhibitors.
1000 Attendees
Frequency: Annual/May

**7584 International Workshop on Deep
Inelastic Scattering - DIS05**
American Institute of Physics
One Physics Ellipse
College Park, MD 20740-3843

301-209-3100
E-Mail: dylla@aip.org
Home Page: www.aip.org

H. Frederick Dylla, Executive Director/CEO
Benjamin Snavely, Senior Executive Secretary
Benjamin Snavely, AIP Corporate Secretary
Melissa Poleski, Assistant to Corporate
Secretary

The aim of these workshops is to review the
progress in the field of DIS and QCD and to
discuss and lay the groundwork for the future.
DIS 2005 will bring together about 250
experimentalists and theorists. The workshop
format will involve plenary sessions with review talks and parallel working group sessions
with shorter contributions.
Frequency: Annual/April

**7585 LIGHTFAIR International Trade
Show**
Illuminating Engineering Society of North
America
120 Wall Street
17th Floor
New York, NY 10005

212-248-5000
FAX 212-248-5018

E-Mail: ies@ies.org
Home Page: www.ies.org

William Hanley, Executive VP
Marianne Conrad, Director Member Services
Denis Lavoie, President
23000 Attendees
Frequency: Annual

7586 MCAA Annual Conference
Mechanical Contractors Association of
America
1385 Piccard Drive
Rockville, MD 20850-4340

301-869-5800
FAX 301-990-9690
Home Page: www.mcaa.org

Lonnie Coleman, MCAA President

Containing 100 booths and 95 exhibits. Education sessions, leadership and keynote presentations, exhibitions.

**7587 MIACON Construction, Mining &
Waste Management Show**
Finocchiaro Enterprises
2921 Coral Way
Miami, FL 33145

305-441-2865
FAX 305-529-9217
Home Page: www.miacon.com

Michael Finocchiaro, President
Jose Garcia, VP
Justine Finocchiaro, Chief Operations

Annual show of 650 manufacturers, suppliers, distributors and exporters of equipment, machinery, supplies and services for the construction, mining and waste managment industries. There will be 600 booths.
10M Attendees
Frequency: Annual/October
Founded in 1994

**7588 Meeting of the Acoustical Society of
America**
Acoustical Society of America
2 Huntington Quandrangle
Suite 1N01
Melville, NY 11747-4502

516-576-2360
FAX 516-576-2377
E-Mail: asa@aip.org
Home Page: www.asa.aip.org

William A Kuperman, President
William A Yost, President-Elect
Mark F Hamilton, VP
Donna L Neff, VP Elect
Charles E Schmid, Executive Director
Frequency: Annual/May

7589 Metalcasting Congress
North American Die Casting Association
241 Holbrook Drive
Wheeling, IL 60090-5809

847-279-0001
FAX 847-279-0002
E-Mail: twarog@diecasting.org
Home Page: www.diecasting.org

Daniel Twarog, President

With the wide range of opportunities for technology transfer, it promises to be the industry's premier show. The American Foundry Society and the North American Die Casting Association are joining together.
Frequency: Annual/April

7590 Mid-Atlantic Job Shop Show
Edward Publishing

16 Waterbury Road
Prospect, CT 06712-1215

203-758-6658
FAX 203-758-4476
Home Page: www.jobshoptechnology.com

Jennifer Bryda, Production Manager

The show is designed to attract the highest caliber engineers and buyers from your major DEM product manufacturers. There will be 260 exhibitors and booths.
2500 Attendees
Frequency: Annual/May
Founded in 1999

**7591 NACE International Annual
Conference & Expo (CORROSION)**
NACE International
1440 S Creek Drive
Houston, TX 77084-4906

281-228-6200
800-797-6223
FAX 281-228-6300
E-Mail: firstservice@nace.org
Home Page: www.nace.org

Oliver Moghissi, President
Bob Chalker, Executive Director

World's largest conference dedicated to Corrosion control and prevention
5000 Attendees
Frequency: Annual

7592 NADCA Sales Training
North American Die Casting Association
241 Holbrook Drive
Wheeling, IL 60090-5809

847-279-0001
FAX 847-279-0002
E-Mail: twarog@diecasting.org
Home Page: www.diecasting.org

Daniel Twarog, President

NADCA will be providing a one day seminar to address the challenges we face in today's marketplace.
Frequency: Annual/June

7593 NSPE Annual Convention and Expo
National Society of Professional Engineers
1420 King Street
Alexandria, VA 22314-2794

703-684-2800
888-285-2853
FAX 703-836-4875
E-Mail: webmaster@nspe.org
Home Page: www.nspe.org

Katrina Robinson, Marketing Manager

The National Society of Professional Engineers is the only engineering society that represents individual engineering professionals and licensed engineers across all disciplines. Founded in 1934, NSPE serves some 60,000 members and the public through 53 state and territorial societies and more than 500 chapters nationally and internationally. The conference brings together the decision makers of engineering companies and business owners nationwide to network and discuss issues of importance.
700 Attendees
Frequency: Annual/July
Mailing list available for rent: 50,000+ names at $130 per M

**7594 National Industrial Automation,
Integration & Control Show**
Reed Exhibition Companies
383 Main Avenue Suite 3
PO Box 6059
Norwalk, CT 06851-1543

203-840-4800
FAX 203-840-5805

E-Mail: inquiry@reedexpo.com
Home Page: www.reedexpo.com

Peter DiLeo, Marketing Director
Mike Rusbridge, CEO
Domonic Shine, Chief Information Officer

Annual show of 200 exhibitors of chemical engineering and processing, electronics, machinery equipment, supplies and services.
19M Attendees

**7595 National Quality Education
Conference**
American Society for Quality
600 N Plankinton Avenue
PO Box 3005
Milwaukee, WI 53201-3005

414-272-8575
800-248-1946
FAX 414-272-1734
E-Mail: help@asq.org
Home Page: www.asq.org

James Rooney, Chair
Paul E Borawski, CEO
Erica Gumieny, Sales
Fay Spano, Communications/Media Relations

Provides teachers, administrators, and support personnel opportunities to examine continuous improvement principles used in education. It provides resources and best practices to help you address requirements of No Child Left Behind, while helping you increase student achievement and improve overall performance.
100M Members
Frequency: Annual/November
Founded in 1946

**7596 Northern American Material
Handling Show & Forum**
Appliance Manufacturer
5900 Harper Road
Suite 105
Solon, OH 44139-1935

440-349-3060
800-345-1815
FAX 440-498-9121
E-Mail: cmiller@mhia.org
Home Page: www.mhia.com

Carol Miller, Senior Director Marketing
Frequency: Bi-Annual

**7597 Northwest Plant Engineering &
Maintenance Show and Conference
(NWPE)**
Cygnus Expositions
3167 Skyway Court
Fremont, CA 94539

510-543-3131
FAX 510-354-3159
E-Mail: showinfo@proshows.com
Home Page: proshows.com

Erin Sparks, Marketing Manager
Paul Bonaiuto, CFO
Kathy Scott, Director of Public Relations

Annual show of 233 exhibitors of low-tech cleaning systems, high-tech computerized maintenance management systems, diagnostic problem software, indoor air quality controllers and related products and services.
5000 Attendees
Frequency: Annual/May

**7598 Nuclear and Emerging Technologies
for Space**
555 N Kensington Ave
La Grange Park, IL 60526-5592

708-352-6611
800-323-3044
FAX 708-352-0499
E-Mail: advertising@ans.org

Home Page: www.ans.org
Social Media: *Facebook, Twitter, LinkedIn*

Jack Tuohy, Executive Director
James S Tulenko, VP
William F Naughton, Treasurer

Positive collaborative environment and series of discussion forums and technical showcasing.
10500 Members
Founded in 1954

7599 OTC Expo
Society of Petroleum Engineers
PO Box 833836
Richardson, TX 75083-3836

972-529-9300
800-456-6863
FAX 972-952-9435
E-Mail: spedal@spe.org
Home Page: www.spe.org

Giovanni Paccaloni, President
Bill Cobbs, VP Finance
John E Bethancourt, Director Management/Information
Ian Gorman, Director Production/Operations
Niki Bradbury, Managing Director
51300 Attendees

7600 Pacific Design & Manufacturing
Canon Communications
11444 W Olympic Boulevard
Suite 900
Los Angeles, CA 90064-1549

310-445-4200
FAX 310-445-4299
Home Page: www.pacdesignshow.com

Diane O'Conner, Trade Show Director
Dan Cutrone, Show Marketing Manager

The Pacific Design Engineering show is the most comprehensive event serving the West Coast's design, process and manufacturing marketplace. Product classifications include Coatings & Finishes, Composites, Computer Aided Design/Computer Aided Manufacturing, Electrical/Electronic, ElectroOptical Components & Equipment, Engineered Safety products, Engineering Management & Tools and more. Held at the Anaheim Convention Center in Anaheim, California.
35970 Attendees
Frequency: Annual/January

7601 Plant & Facilities Expo (PFE)
Association of Energy Engineers
4025 Pleasantdale Road
Suite 420
Atlanta, GA 30340

770-447-5083
FAX 770-446-3969
E-Mail: info@aeecenter.org
Home Page: www.aeecenter.org

Ruth Whitlock, Executive Director
Jennifer Vendola, Accountant

Seek solutions for plant and facility needs. Vendors have an opportunity to meet prospective customers, reacquaint themselves with existing customers, and network with other vendors.
5000 Attendees
Frequency: October

7602 ProMat
Material Handling Industry of America
8720 Red Oak Blvd
Suite 201
Charlotte, NC 28217

704-676-1190
800-345-1815
FAX 704-676-1199
Home Page: www.mhia.org

Tom Carbott, Exhibiting Information
Terri Heisey, Educational Conference & Seminar

You can compare the latest solutions essential to the productivity of your manufacturing, warehousing, and distribution operations. The material handling & logistics solutions you discover at ProMat will help you differentiate your product, improve customer service and increase overall corporate profitability. 700 exhibits.
Frequency: Annual

7603 Professional Development Conference & Exposition
1800 E Oakton Street
Des Plaines, IL 60018

847-699-2929
FAX 847-768-3434
E-Mail: customerservice@asse.org
Home Page: www.asse.org
Social Media: *Facebook, Twitter, LinkedIn*

Fred Fortman, Executive Director
Bruce Sufranski, Finance/Controller Director
Diane Hurns, Manager Public Relations Department
Sally Madden, Human Resources Manager

The American Society of Safety Engineers (ASSE) is the oldest professional safety society committed to protecting people, property and the environment. ASSE has more than 32,000 occupational safety, health and environmental (SH&E) professional members who manage, supervise, research and consult on safety, health, transportation and the environment in all industries, government, labor and education.
34000 Members
4,000 Attendees
Founded in 1911

7604 REMSA and AREMA Meeting
Railway Engineering: Maintenance Supplies Assn
500 New Jersey Avenue
Suite 400
Washington, DC 20001

202-715-2921
FAX 202-204-5753
E-Mail: home@remsa.org
Home Page: www.remsa.org

Philip Hoffman, President
John Fox, VP
David Soule, Executive Director
Ronald C Olds, Secretary/Treasurer

Holding the exhibits and technical conference simultaneously in Louisville give added benefit to REMSA members.
Frequency: Annual/September

7605 REMSA and NRC: Synergy in Action
Railway Engineering: Maintenance Supplies Assn
500 New Jersey Avenue
Suite 400
Washington, DC 20001

202-715-2921
FAX 202-204-5753
E-Mail: home@remsa.org
Home Page: www.remsa.org

Philip Hoffman, President
John Fox, VP
David Soule, Executive Director
Ronald C Olds, Secretary/Treasurer

Members and other industry suppliers discuss their products, services and equipment with attendees representing a broad spectrum of railroaders: transits, short lines, commuter and

Class I railroads. There were 56 exhibiting companies.
Frequency: Annual/January

7606 RSES Annual Conference and HVAC Technology Expo
Refrigeration Service Engineers Society
1666 Rand Road
Des Plaines, IL 60016-3552

847-297-6464
800-297-5660
E-Mail: general@rses.org
Home Page: www.rses.org
Social Media: *Facebook, Twitter, LinkedIn*

Lawrence Donaldson, Intl. Executive Vice President
Josh Flaim, Operations Manager
Jean Birch, Conference & Seminar Manager

80 booths consisting primarily of products and services.

7607 RoboBusiness Conference and Exposition
American Institute of Physics
One Physics Ellipse
College Park, MD 20740-3843

301-209-3100
E-Mail: dylla@aip.org
Home Page: www.aip.org

H. Frederick Dylla, Executive Director/CEO
John Haynes, Vice President Publishing
Benjamin Snavely, AIP Corporate Secretary
Melissa Poleski, Assistant To Corporate Secretary

Focuses on the business development and technical issues involved with the commercial application of mobile robotics and intelligent systems technology to develop entirely new markets and product categories, open additional lines of business and enhance existing product lines.
Frequency: Annual/May

7608 SAFETY Expo
American Society of Safety Engineers
1800 E Oakton Street
Des Plaines, IL 60018

847-699-2929
FAX 847-768-3434
E-Mail: info@asse.org
Home Page: www.asse.org

Terri Norris, President
Kathy Seabrook, Senior Vice President
Diane Hurns, Manager Public Relations Department

A full 3-day conference featuring more than 200 sessions, an exposition with 300 exhibitors, special pre- and post-conference seminars, conference proceedings on CD, numerous networking events and more.
Frequency: Annual/July

7609 SAMPE Tech Conference
Society for the Advancement of Material & Process
1161 Park View Drive
Suite 200
Covina, CA 91724-3751

626-331-0616
800-562-7360
FAX 626-332-8929
E-Mail: sampeibo@sampe.org
Home Page: www.sampe.org
Social Media: *Facebook, LinkedIn*

Gregg Balko, Executive Director
Rosemary Loggia, Conference/Exhibits Manager
Priscilla Heredia, Conference/Symposia Assistant Mgr

Known for its excellent conference programs. Featuring expert speakers and industry insiders, the information take-away from this event is invaluable to M&P professionals.
Frequency: Annual/October

7610 SME Annual Meeting
Society of Manufacturing Engineers
1 SME Drive
PO Box 930
Dearborn, MI 48121

313-425-3000
800-733-4763
FAX 313-425-3400
E-Mail: service@sme.org
Home Page: www.sme.org

Mark Tomlinson, Executive Director/General Manager
Greg Sheremet, Publisher
Bob Harris, Director Finance

Bringing together hundreds of SME members to interact and exchange ideas with their fellow practitioners. This yearly forum offers technical training, special sessions for members, and a celebration of the best that manufacturing has to offer through our International Honor Awards Banquet.
Frequency: Annual/June

7611 STL Annual Meeting
Society of Tribologists & Lubrication
840 Busse Highway
Park Ridge, IL 60068-2376

847-825-5536
FAX 847-825-1456
E-Mail: information@stle.org
Home Page: www.stle.org

Merle Hedland, Meetings Manager
Expect more than 300 technical and practical presentations will be selected for the Calgary program.
Frequency: Annual/May

7612 Street & Area Lighting Conference
Illuminating Engineering Society of North America
120 Wall Street
17th Floor
New York, NY 10005

212-248-5000
FAX 212-248-5018
E-Mail: ies@ies.org
Home Page: www.ies.org

William Hanley, Executive VP
Valerie Landers, Director Member Services
500 Attendees
Frequency: Annual

7613 TBP Annual Convention
Tau Beta Pi Association
PO Box 2697
Knoxville, TN 37904-2697

865-546-4578
FAX 865-546-4579
Home Page: www.tbp.org
Social Media: *Facebook, LinkedIn*

James D Froula, Executive Director
Larry Simonson, President
James Froula, Executive Director

A convention at which members conduct the official business of the Association, network with engineers from around the country, and participate in a recruiting fair.
500+ Attendees

7614 Texoma Regional Education & Training Conference
Society of American Military Engineers

607 Prince Street
Alexandria, VA 22314-3117

703-549-3800
800-336-3097
FAX 703-684-0231
E-Mail: webmanager@same.org
Home Page: www.same.org

Dr Robert D Wolff, Executive Director
Ann McLeod, Director of Meetings
Jenni Ford, CPA, Director Finance/Accounting

Will provide opportunities to attend SAME sponsored sessions as well as TSPE sponsored training sessions. This diversity of training venues is intended to provide the attendee with exposure to a wide variety of topics and will provide a beneficial learning experience.
Frequency: Annual/June

7615 Total Product Development
American Supplier Institute
17333 Federal Drive
Suite 220
Allen Park, MI 48101-3614

313-336-8877
800-462-4500
FAX 313-336-3187
Home Page: www.amsup.com

Dr Genichi Taguchi, Executive Director

Annual show and exhibits relating to the encouragement of change in US industry through development and implementation of advanced manufacturing and engineering technologies.
200 Attendees

7616 UNYVAC's Co-Sponsored Symposium
AVS Science & Technology Society
120 Wall Street
32nd Floor
New York, NY 10005-3993

212-248-0200
FAX 212-248-0245
E-Mail: david_aspnes@avs.org
Home Page: www.avs.org

David E Aspnes, President
Christie R Marrian, President-Elect
John Coburn, Treasurer
Joseph J Greene, Clerk/Secretary
Nancy Schultheis, Office Manager

Topic: Functional Coatings and Surface Engineering. Will provide a forum for training and discussion of the physics and chemistry of functional coatings and surfaces.
Frequency: Bi-Annual

7617 West Coast Energy Management Congress EMC
Association of Energy Engineers
4025 Pleasantdale Road
Suite 420
Atlanta, GA 30340

770-447-5083
FAX 770-446-3969
E-Mail: info@aeecenter.org
Home Page: www.aeecenter.org

Jennifer Vendola, Accountant
Ruth Whitlock, Executive Admin

Specifically for business, industrial and institutional energy users. It brings together the top experts in all areas of the field to help you set a clear, optimum path to both energy cost control and energy supply security.
Frequency: Annual/June

7618 Winter Meeting and Nuclear Technology Expo
American Nuclear Society

555 North Kensington Avenue
La Grange Park, IL 60526

708-352-6611
FAX 708-352-0499
Home Page: www.ans.org

Thomas A Christopher, General Co-Chair
Michael Wallac, General Co-Chair

Topic: Talk About Nuclear Differently: A Good Story Untold.
Frequency: Annual/November

7619 World Energy Engineering Congress
Association of Energy Engineers
4025 Pleasantdale Road
Suite 420
Atlanta, GA 30340

770-447-5083
FAX 770-446-3969
E-Mail: info@aeecenter.org
Home Page: www.aeecenter.org

Jennifer Vendola, Accountant
Ruth Whitlock, Executive Admin

A comprehensive forum where participants can fully assess the big picture and see exactly how the economic and market forces, new technologies, regulatory developments and industry trends all merge to shape their critical decisions on their organizations' energy and economic future.
Frequency: Annual/September

Directories & Databases

7620 AEG Annual Directory
Association of Engineering Geologists
300 S Jackson Street, Suite 100
PO Box 460518
Denver, CO 80246

303-757-2926
FAX 303-757-2969
E-Mail: webeditor@aegweb.org
Home Page: www.aegweb.org

Dave Bieber, President
Darrel Schmitz, President-Elect/VP
Becky Roland, Chief Staff Executive
Terry West, Treasurer
Dorian Kuper, Secretary

Contains member and Association information.

7621 ANS Buyers Guide
American Nuclear Society
555 N Kensington Ave
La Grange Park, IL 60526-5592

708-352-6611
FAX 708-352-0499
Home Page: www.ans.org

Jack Tuohy, Executive Director
E James Reinsch, President-Elect/VP
Harry Bradley, Executive Director
William F Naughton, Treasurer

Buyer's Guide Directory lists approximately 1150 suppliers of products and services to the nuclear industry. This comprehensive listing contains approximately 500 categories representing the wide range of nuclear components and services available today.
Cost: $110.00
Frequency: Annual
Founded in 2005

7622 ASME Database
American Society of Mechnical Engineers
3 Park Ave
Suite 21
New York, NY 10016-5990

212-591-7000
800-843-2763

FAX 212-591-7674
E-Mail: infocentral@asme.org
Home Page: www.asme.org

Victoria Rockwell, President
Warren Leonard, Managing Director Operations
Virgil Carter, Executive Director

Provides proven direct mail buyers and selection options that enable you to customize lists to achieve your objective.

7623 AWWA Buyer's Guide
American Water Works Association
6666 W Quincy Ave
Denver, CO 80235-3098

303-794-7711
800-926-7337
FAX 303-347-0804
Home Page: www.awwa.org

Jerry Stevens, President
David LaFrance, Executive Director

The official resource guide to water industry products and services.

7624 Advanced Energy Design Guide for Small Office Buildings
Illuminating Engineering Society of North America
120 Wall St
17th Floor
New York, NY 10005-4001

212-248-5000
FAX 212-248-5017
E-Mail: ies@ies.org
Home Page: www.ies.org

William Hanley, Executive VP
Valerie Landers, Director Member Services

Provides a sensible approach by including practical products and readily-available, off-the-shelf technology. The Guide offers you all the tools you need to create an energy-efficient building where the owners will see a 30 percent energy savings compared to buildings that only meet the minimum requirements of Standard 90.1.
Cost: $47.00
390 Pages
Founded in 2004

7625 American Association of Cost Engineers Membership Directory
Association for Total Cost Management
209 Prairie Avenue
#100
Morgantown, WV 26501-5949

FAX 304-291-5728

Andy Dowd, Executive Director

Member directory.
Cost: $35.00
100 Pages
Frequency: Annual

7626 American Society for Engineering Education Membership Directory
1818 N St NW
Suite 600
Washington, DC 20036-2476

202-331-3500
FAX 202-265-8504
E-Mail: f.huband@asee.org
Home Page: www.asee.org

Frank L Huband, Executive Director

Offers information on over 10,000 colleges and university engineering professors and personnel, practicing engineers and industry executives who are members of the ASEE.
200 Pages
Frequency: Annual
Circulation: 10,000

7627 American Society of Civil Engineers Official Register
1801 Alexander Bell Dr
Suite 100
Reston, VA 20191-4382

703-295-6300
800-548-2723
FAX 703-295-6222
E-Mail: conf@asce.org
Home Page: http://www.asce.org

D Wayne Klotz, President

Provides ready access to governing documents, statistics, and general information about ASCE for leadership, members, and staff.
Cost: $24.00
640 Pages
Frequency: Annual
ISBN: 0-784407-73-8
Founded in 2005

7628 BMES Membership Directory
Biomedical Engineering Society
8201 Corporate Dr
Suite 1125
Landover, MD 20785-2224

301-459-1999
888-871-BMES
FAX 301-459-2444
E-Mail: info@bmes.org
Home Page: www.bmes.org

Richard Waugh, President
Debra Tucker, Meeting Manager
Edward Schilling, Executive Director

A directory listing members' names, mailing addresses, telephone numbers, e-mail addresses, areas of specialization, as well as indexes of professional interest and geographic location.
Frequency: Annual

7629 Basics of Code Division Multiple Access (CDMA)
International Society for Optical Engineering
PO Box 10
Bellingham, WA 98227-0010

360-676-3290
FAX 360-647-1445
E-Mail: customerservice@spie.org
Home Page: www.spie.org

Raghuveer Rao, Editor
Sohail Dianat, President
Amy Nelson, Manager

This text, aimed at the reader with a basic background in electrical or optical engineering, covers CDMA fundamentals: from the basics of the communication process and digital data transmission, to the concepts of code division multiplexing, direct sequence spreading, diversity techniques, the near-far effect, and the IS-95 CDMA standard form.
Cost: $35.00
120 Pages
ISBN: 0-819458-69-4

7630 CED Directory of Engineering and Engineering Technology Programs
Mississippi State University
PO Box 6046
Mississippi State, MS 39762-6046

662-258-8122
FAX 662-325-8733

Mike Mathews, Editor

Over 150 colleges and universities with cooperative education programs in engineering and engineering technology are listed.
Cost: $50.00
250 Pages
Frequency: Biennial

7631 CRC Press
2000 NW Corporate Boulevard
Boca Raton, FL 33431

561-994-0555
800-272-7737
FAX 772-998-0876
E-Mail: techsupport@crcpress.com
Home Page: www.crcpress.com

Eleanor Riemer, Publisher
Emmett Dages, CEO

Publisher in science, medicine, environmental science, forensic, engineering, business, technology, mathematics, and statistics. Our food science and nutrition books and our journal, Critical Reviews in Food and Nutrition, are well established and respected publications in the food science industry.

7632 CSA Engineering
Cambridge Scientific Abstracts
7200 Wisconsin Ave
Suite 601
Bethesda, MD 20814-4890

301-961-6700
FAX 301-961-6790
E-Mail: service@csa.com
Home Page: www.csa.com

Andrew M Snyder, President
Martin Nowicki, Editor, Engineering

This database offers information on more than 500,000 citations, with abstracts, to international periodical and other research literature covering all fields of engineering and science.
Cost: $945.00
Frequency: Monthly

7633 Coolant Filtration-Additional Technologies
Society of Tribologists & Lubrication
840 Busse Hwy
Park Ridge, IL 60068-2376

847-825-5536
FAX 847-825-1456
E-Mail: information@stle.org
Home Page: www.stle.org

Ed Salek, Executive Director

The text covers coolant cleaning and handling for metalworking operations where coolants are used as part of the process. The publication also provides the latest thinking on specific metalworking applications with some comprehensive guidelines. 76 illustrations.
Cost: $56.00
223 Pages

7634 Design-Build Project Delivery (ACEC)
American Council of Engineering Companies
1015 15th St
8th Floor NW
Washington, DC 20005-2605

202-347-7474
FAX 202-898-0068
E-Mail: acec@acec.org
Home Page: www.acec.org
Social Media: *Facebook, Twitter*

Dave Raymond, President
Howard Messner, Executive Director

Guide for firms considering design/build projects. Analyzes risks, steps and milestones necessary for successful completion of design/build projects.

7635 Directory of Accredited Engineering & Technology Certification Programs
Council of Engineer and Scientific Specialty Board

PO Box 1448
Annapolis, MD 21404-1488

410-266-3766
FAX 410-721-1746
E-Mail: academy@aaee.net
Home Page: www.cesb.org

Ronald Council, Owner
William C Anderson PE DEE, Executive Director

Provides a description of existing programs for persons interested in being certified and for those seeking an objective assessment of an expert's capability and competence.

7636 Directory of Engineering Document Sources
Global Engineering Documents
15 Inverness Way E
Englewood, CO 80112-5710

303-900-0600
800-854-7179
FAX 303-397-2740
E-Mail: CustomerCare@ihs.com
Home Page: www.global.ihs.com

Charles Picasso, CEO

Offers over 10,000 document initialisms and acronyms for governmental, military and industry specifications and related publications.
Cost: $145.00
274 Pages
Frequency: Annual

7637 Directory of Engineers in Private Practice
National Society of Professional Engineers
1420 King St
Suite 500
Alexandria, VA 22314-2794

703-684-2800
FAX 703-836-4875
E-Mail: webmaster@nspe.org
Home Page: www.nspe.org

Larry Jacobson, Executive Director

Consulting engineering firms and individuals who are members of the Society's Professional Engineers in Private Practice division.
Cost: $85.00
260 Pages
Frequency: Annual

7638 Directory of Iron and Steel Plants
186 Thorn Hill Rd
Warrendale, PA 15086-7528

724-814-3000
FAX 724-814-3001
E-Mail: memberservices@aist.org
Home Page: www.aist.org

Ronald E Ashburn, Executive Director
William A Albaugh, Technology Programs Manager
Joann Cantrell, Publications Manager/Editor
Mark Didiano, Finance & Administration Manager
Stacy Varmecky, Membership Communications Manager

The Directory lists more than 2,000 companies and 17,500 individuals. Featuring data on essentially ever steel producer in the USA, Canada and Mexico, including names and titles of executive, engineering, maintenance and operating personnel. Also includes an alpha listing of all major equipment, product and service providers to the international iron and steel industry, and a listing of associations affiliated with the industry, with complete geo-indexing. Softbound book with CD.
Cost: $95.00
ISBN: 1-935117-00-1

7639 EI Page One
Engineering Information
1 Castle Point Ter
Hoboken, NJ 07030-5906

201-356-6800
800-221-1044
FAX 201-356-6801
E-Mail: eicustomersupport@elsevier.com
Home Page: www.ei.org

This database contains a table of contents listing citations to more than 350,000 journal articles and conference papers and proceedings in all fields of engineering.

7640 ENR: Top International Design Firms Issue
McGraw Hill
1221 Avenue of the Americas
47th Floor
New York, NY 10020-1095

212-512-2000
FAX 212-512-3840
E-Mail: webmaster@mcgraw-hill.com
Home Page: www.mcgraw-hill.com

Harold W McGraw III, CEO

Offers a list of over 200 design firms competing outside their own national borders who received largest dollar volumes in foreign contracts.
Cost: $270.00
Frequency: Annual
Circulation: 900,000

7641 Energy Engineering: Directory of Software for Energy Managers and Engineers
Fairmont Press
700 Indian Trail Lilburn Rd NW
Lilburn, GA 30047-6862

770-925-9388
FAX 770-381-9865
Home Page: www.fairmontpress.com

Brian Douglas, President

Directory of services and supplies to the industry.
Cost: $15.00
Circulation: 8,500
ISSN: 0199-8895

7642 Manufacturer and Repair Directory
National Board of Boiler & Pressure Vessel
1055 Crupper Ave
Columbus, OH 43229-1108

614-888-0750
FAX 614-888-0750
E-Mail: information@nationalboard.org
Home Page: www.nationalboard.org

Don Tanner, Manager
Connie Homer, Senior Executive Secretary

Manufacturers of boilers, pressure vessels, or other pressure-retaining items who are authorized to register these items with the National Board, Repair organizations holding National Board certificates of authorization for use of either the R, VR, or NR stamps.

7643 Mechanical Contractor Directory Marketing
Mechanical Contractors Association America
1385 Piccard Dr
Rockville, MD 20850-4329

301-869-5800
FAX 301-990-9690
E-Mail: webmaster@mcaa.org
Home Page: www.mcaa.org

John Gentille, Executive VP
John Gentille, Executive VP

7644 Plumbing Directory
American Society of Sanitary Engineering
901 Canterbury Rd
Suite A
Cleveland, OH 44145-1480

440-835-3040
FAX 440-835-3488
Home Page: www.asse-plumbing.org

Ken Van Wagnen, Manager
Sara Marxen, Compliance Coordinator
Steven Hazzard, Staff Engineer

Contains more than 4,000 plumbing words and terms, abbreviations, cross references, helpful charts and illustrations, solar energy terms. A great teaching tool for plumbing and related fields.
Cost: $21.00

7645 Research, Training, Test, and Production Reactor Directory
American Nuclear Society
555 N Kensington Ave
La Grange Park, IL 60526-5592

708-352-6611
FAX 708-352-0499
Home Page: www.asn.org

Jack Tuohy, Executive Director
E James Reinsch, President-Elect/VP
Harry Bradley, Executive Director
William F Naughton, Treasurer
Cal Poly, Vice President

This comprehensive directory includes administrative, operational, and technical data for all nonpower reactors in the United States.
Cost: $400.00
876 Pages
ISBN: 0-894485-12-1
Founded in 1988

7646 Tau Beta Pi Information Book
Tau Beta Pi Association
PO Box 2697
Knoxville, TN 37901-2697

865-546-4578
FAX 865-546-4579
Home Page: www.tbp.org
Social Media: *Facebook, LinkedIn*

Larry Simonson, President
Solange Dao, VP
Curtis D. Gomulinski, Executive Director/Treasurer

The book also serves as a reference to membership and alumni giving statistics as well as names of past and present officers, fellows, scholars, and other award winners.
Frequency: Yearly

7647 US Abrasives Industry Directory
Abrasive Engineering Society
144 Moore Rd
Butler, PA 16001-1312

724-282-6210
FAX 724-234-2376
E-Mail: aes@abrasiveengineering.com
Home Page: www.abrasiveengineering.com

Ted Giese, Owner

Though the scene for industrial abrasive manufacturers has changed significantly over the last decade, the US continues as one of the world's largest manufacturers of abrasive products developing new abrasive grains and products that set international standards for quality and performance.

7648 Wage & Benefit Survey
North American Die Casting Association
241 Holbrook Drive
Wheeling, IL 60090-5809

847-279-0001
FAX 847-279-0002

E-Mail: twarog@diecasting.org
Home Page: www.diecasting.org

Daniel Twarog, President

This survey provides a comprehensive look at 13 different job classifications of hourly wage earners, how they are compensated, what benefits they receive and how practices vary by company size and location.
Cost: $200.00
42 Pages
Founded in 2004

7649 Who's Who in Environmental Engineering
American Academy of Environmental Engineers
130 Holiday Ct
Suite 100
Annapolis, MD 21401-7003

410-266-3311
FAX 410-266-7653
E-Mail: info@aaee.net
Home Page: www.aaee.net

Brian P. Flynn, President
Pasquale S. Canzano, Vice President
Joseph S. Cavarretta, Executive Director
Howard B. LaFever, Treasurer

A recognized reference for industry, consultants, recruiters, attorneys and health professionals who need to identify and locate experts in the environmental engineering profession.
Frequency: Annual
Mailing list available for rent

7650 World Directory of Nuclear Utility Management
American Nuclear Society
555 N Kensington Ave
La Grange Park, IL 60526-5592

708-352-6611
FAX 708-352-0499
Home Page: www.ans.org

Jack Tuohy, Executive Director
E James Reinsch, President-Elect/VP
Harry Bradley, Executive Director
William F Naughton, Treasurer

Is a handy desk reference listing key personnel at nuclear utility headquarters and nuclear plant sites, including plant managers, maintenance superintendents, radwaste managers, contacts for purchasing and public relations, and more.
Cost: $850.00
249 Pages
Founded in 2005

Industry Web Sites

7651 http://gold.greyhouse.com
G.O.L.D Grey House OnLine Databases
Grey House Publishing's online database platform, GOLD, offers Quick Search, Keyword Search and Expert Search for most business sectorc incluidng engineering markets. The GOLD platform makes finding the information you need quick and easy - whether you're a novice searcher or an experienced database user. All of Grey House's directory products are available for subscription on the GOLD platform.

7652 www.aacei.org
Association for Advancement of Cost Engineering
Individuals interested in applying scientific principals to the solution of problems.

7653 www.aaee.net
American Academy of Environmental Engineers
Improves the standards of environmental engineering. Certifies those with the special knowledge of environmental engineering and supplies a list of certified engineers to the public. Publishes reference books and other matters of interest for the profession.

7654 www.aaee.org
American Association for Employment in Education
Provides information and other resources to assist colleges and universities in the employment of education.

7655 www.aaes.org
American Association of Engineering Societies
A multidisciplinary organization dedicated to advancing the knowledge, understanding and practice of engineering in the public interest.

7656 www.abet.org
Accreditation Board for Engineering and Technology
Accreditation of engineering, technology and applied science educational programs.

7657 www.abrasiveengineering.org
Abrasive Engineering Society
Dedicated to promoting technical information about abrasives minerals and their uses including abrasives grains and products such as grinding wheels, coated abrasives and thousands of other related tools and products that serve manufacturing and the consumer.

7658 www.acec.org
American Council of Engineering
Membership includes more than 5,800 US firms engaged in a range of engineering works. Mission is to contribute to the nation's prosperity through advancement of the business interests of member firms.

7659 www.acesystems.com
AEC Systems International/Penton Media
Focuses on Internet/Intranet for the design, engineering and construction industries.

7660 www.aea.org
American Engineering Association, Inc.
Dedicated to the enhancement of the engineering profession and U.S. Engineering capabilities.

7661 www.aeecenter.org
Association of Energy Engineers
Source of information on the field of energy efficiency, utility deregulation, plant engineering, facility management and environmental compliance. Membership includes more than 8,000 professionals and certification programs. Offers seminars, conferences, job listings and certification programs.

7662 www.aegweb.org
Association of Engineering Geologists
Meets the professional needs of geologists who are applying their scientific training and experience to the broad field of civil and environmental engineering. Mission is to provide leadership in the development and application of geologic principles and knowledge to serve engineering, environmental and public needs.

7663 www.aes.org
Audio Engineering Society
Professional society devoted to audio technology. Membership includes leading engineers, scientists and other authorities in the field. Serves its members, the industry and the public by stimulating and facilitating advances in the constantly changing field of audio.

7664 www.aiche.org
American Institute of Chemical Engineers
Professional association of more than 50,000 members, providing leadership in advancing the chemical engineering profession. Members are those who develop processes and design and operate manufacturing plants, as well as researchers who assure the safe and environmentally sound manufacture, use and disposal of chemical products.

7665 www.akropolis.net
Akropolis
Directory of architects, engineers, designers, construction professionals and others in related fields. Web portal to showcase modules and applications developed by our company.

7666 www.aocs.org
American Oil Chemists Society
Largest international society focused on the science and technology of fats, oils, lipids, and related substances.

7667 www.ascet.org
American Society of Certified Engineering
Strives to obtain recognition of engineering technicians as essential to the engineering scientific team. Provides a forum for discussion of employment issues and improvement of the professional status of engineering technicians.

7668 www.asem.org
American Society for Engineering Management
Strives to promote the profession of engineering management as well as assisting its members in developing and improving their skills as practicing managers of engineering and technology. Members are from academic, field, industrial and governmental organizations.

7669 www.asfe.org
ASFE
Not-for-profit trade association. Helps geoprofessional, environmental and civil engineering firms profit through professionalism.

7670 www.asnt.org
American Society for Nondestructive Testing
Helps create a safer world by serving the nondestructive testing professions and promoting NDT technologies through publishing, certification, research and conferencing.

7671 www.aspe.net
American Society for Precision Engineering
Technical society emphasizing research, design, development, manufacture and measurement of high accuracy components and systems. Members come from the fields of engineering, materials science, physics, chemistry, mathematics and computer science, and work in industry, academia and national labs.

7672 www.asq.org
American Society for Quality
ASQ's mission is to facilitate continuous improvement and increase customer satisfaction. Promotes quality principles concepts and technologies. Provides information, contacts and opportunities to make things better in the workplace, in communities and in people's lives.

7673 www.asse-plumbing.org
American Society of Sanitary Engineering
Members are from all segments of the plumbing industry, including contractors, engineers, inspectors, journeymen, apprentices and others involved in the industry. Provides information, the opportunity to exchange ideas, solve prob-

lems and offers forum where all sides can express their views.

7674 www.astm.org
ASTM International

Not-for-profit organization providing a global forum for development and publication of voluntary consensus standards for materials, products, systems and services. Over 30,000 members from 100 nations include producers, users, consumers and representatives of academia and government. Formerly known as the American Society for Testing and Materials.

7675 www.atcouncil.org
Applied Technology Council

A nonprofit, tax-exempt corporation established through the efforts of the Structural Engineers Association of California. ATC's mission is to develop and promote state-of-the-art, user-friendly engineering resources and applications for use in mitigating the effects of natural and other hazards on the built environment.

7676 www.construction.com
McGraw-Hill Construction

McGraw-Hill Construction (MHC), part of The McGraw-Hill Companies, connects people and projects across the design and construction industry, serving owners, architects, engineers, general contractors, subcontractors, building product manufacturers, suppliers, dealers, distributors and adjacent markets.

7677 www.eia-usa.org
Environmental Information Association

Nonprofit organization dedicated to providing environmental information to individuals, members and the industry. Disseminates information on the abatement of asbestos and lead-based paint, indoor air quality, safety and health issues, analytical issues and environmental site assessments.

7678 www.electrochem.org
Electrochemical Society

The society is an international nonprofit, educational organization concerned with phenomena relating to electrochemical and solid state science and technology. Members are individual scientists and engineers, as well as corporations and laboratories.

7679 www.ewh.ieee.org
Instrumentation and Measurement Society

A subsidiary of the Institute of Electrical and Electronics Engineers. Provides support to scientists and technicians who design and develop electrical and electronic measuring instruments and equipment.

7680 www.greyhouse.com
Grey House Publishing

Authoritative reference directories for most business sectors incluidng engineering markets. Users can search the online databases with varied search criteria allowing for custom searches by product category, geographic area, sales volume, keyword, subject and more. Full Grey House catalog and online ordering also available.

7681 www.icc-es.org
ICC Evaluation Service

An independent, nonprofit organization that conducts a voluntary program of evaluation of both traditional and innovative building materials, products and systems for compliance with the three major model codes in the United States.

7682 www.iccsafe.org
International Code Council

Nonprofit membership association with more than 16,000 members who span the building community, from code enforcement officials to materials manufacturers. Dedicated to preserving the public health, safety and welfare in the built environment through the effective use and enforcement of model codes.

7683 www.icea.net
Insulated Cable Engineers Association

Professional organization dedicated to developing cable standards for the electric power, control and telecommunications industries. Ensures safe, economical and efficient cable systems utilizing proven state-of-the-art materials and concepts. ICEA documents are of interest to cable manufacturers, architects and engineers, utility and manufacturing plant personnel, telecommunication engineers, consultants and OEMs.

7684 www.iienet.org
Institute of Industrial Engineers

Founded in Columbus, Ohio as the American Institute of Industrial Engineers.

7685 www.irga.com
International Reprographic Association

Represents entrepreneurial businesses serving the wide-format imaging needs of graphic arts, architectural, engineering, manufacturing, corporate, legal, retail, and POP industries.

7686 www.manufacturing.net
Manufacturing Marketplace

Manufacturing industry news and resources for the engineering, design, purchasing, logistics and distribution professional.

7687 www.materialsocieties.org
Federation of Materials Societies

Promotes cooperation among societies concerned with the understanding, development and application of materials and processes.

7688 www.mt-online.com
Applied Technology Publications

MT-online.com is the premier source of capacity assurance and best practice solutions for manufacturing, process and service operations worldwide. Online home of Maintenance Technology magazie, the dynamic MT-online.com portal serves the critical technical, business and professional-development needs of engineers, managers and technicians from across all industrial, institutional and commercial sectors.

7689 www.nace.org
National Association of Corrosion Engineers

Conducts research on corrosion control. Sponsors short courses annually at universities.

7690 www.nationalboard.org
National Board of Boiler & Pressure Vessel Inspec.

Membership is composed of chief boiler inspectors of states, major US cities and Canadian provinces having boiler laws.

7691 www.naval.org
American Society of Naval Engineers

Includes all arts construction and sciences as applied in research, development design, construction, operation, maintenance, and logistic support of surface/sub-surface ships and marine craft.

7692 www.ncees.org
Natl Council of Examiners for Engineering & Survey

Promotes uniform standards of registration and to coordinate interstate registration of engineers and surveyors.

7693 www.nspe.org
National Society of Professional Engineers

The mission of the Society is to promote the ethical, competent and licensed practice of engineering and to enhance the professional, social and economic well-being of its members.

7694 www.remsa.org
Railway Engineering-Maintenance Suppliers Assn

Members are distributors and manufacturers of railway track machinery supplies and services.

7695 www.reta.com
Refrigerating Engineers & Technicians Association

Seeks to upgrade the skills and knowledge of experienced members. Offers home-study courses on refrigeration and air conditioning.

7696 www.rses.org
Refrigeration Service Engineers Society

RSES is the leading training and education association for heating, ventilation, air conditioning and refrigeration professionals. It is a non-profit organization of 25,000 members in 421 chapters in the US and Canada, as well as affiliate organizations in other countries.

7697 www.same.org
Society of American Military Engineers

Brings together professional engineers and those in engineering-related fields to improve and increase the engineering capabilities of the nation, and to exchange and advance the knowledge of engineering technologies, applications, and practices.

7698 www.sawe.org
Society of Allied Weight Engineers

Consists of engineers in the aerospace industry.

7699 www.sme.org
Society of Manufacturing Engineers

Members are engaged in manufacturing, research and technology development.

7700 www.spe.org
Society of Petroleum Engineers

To provide the means for collection, dissemination and exchange of technical information concerning the development of oil and gas resources, subsurface fluid flow and production of other materials through well bores for the public benefit. To provide opportunities through its programs for interested individuals to maintain and upgrade their individual technical competence in the aforementioned areas for the public benefit.

7701 www.steelnews.com
Association for Iron and Steel Technology (AIST)

SteelNews.com is a publication created by the Association for Iron and Steel Technology (AIST) for the steel community. The site features daily updates of the latest global headlines.

7702 www.sweets.construction.com
McGraw Hill Construction

In depth product information that lets you find, compare, select, specify and make purchase decisions in the industrial product marketplace.

7703 www.tbp.org
Tau Beta Pi Association

The National Engineering honor society recognizes engineering students of superior scholarship and exemplary character and practitioners of engineering. Founded in 1885, the world's largest engineering organization includes 218 collegiate chapters and 220 alumnus chapters.

7704 www.thetatau.org
Theta Tau
A professional fraternity in engineering. Founded at the Univerity of Minnesota. Purpose of the fraternity is to develop and maintain a high standard of professional interest among its members, and to unite them in a strong bond of fraternal fellowship.

7705 www.u.arizona.edu/n aimitril
Reliability Engineering and Management Institute
This is an annual conference on Reliability Engineering and Management of all types of products. Over 15 leading corporations present their latest techniques in this field, and the proceedings thereof are published.

7706 www.uefoundation.org
United Engineering Foundation
Aims to advance engineering arts and sciences.

7707 www.usace.army.mil
US Army Corps of Engineers
Information on flood control, environmental protection, disaster response, military construction and support of others through the sharing of engineering expertise with other agencies, state and local governments, academia and foreign nations.

Associations

7708 ASFE/The Geoprofessional Business Association
8811 Colesville Rd
Suite G106
Silver Springs, MD 20910-4343

301-565-2733
FAX 301-589-2017
E-Mail: info@geoprofessional.org
Home Page: www.geoprofessional.org
Social Media: *Facebook, Twitter, LinkedIn, YouYube, RSS*

Gordon M. Matheson, President
Laura R. Reinbold, P.E., President-Elect
John P. Bachner, Executive Vice President
Charles L. Head, P.E., P.G., Secretary/Treasurer
Joel G. Carson, Executive Director

Not-for-profit trade association. Supports all employes of engineering companies.
300 Members
Founded in 1969

7709 Academy for Educational Development
1825 Connecticut Ave Nw
Washington, DC 20009-5728

202-884-8978
FAX 202-884-8997
E-Mail: rjohn@aed.org
Home Page:
www.pciaonline.org/academy-educational-deve lopment-aed
Social Media: *Facebook, Twitter, YouTube*

Edward W. Russell, Chairman of the Board
Roberta N. Clarke, Vice Chairman of the Board
Rebecca Logan, President and CEO

A nonprofit organization working globally to improve education, health, civil society and economic development-the foundation of thriving societies.
Founded in 1961

7710 Adirondack Council
103 Hand Ave, Suite 3
PO Box D-2
Elizabethtown, NY 12932-0640

877-873-2240
FAX 518-873-6675
E-Mail: info@adirondackcouncil.org
Home Page: www.adirondackcouncil.org
Social Media: *Facebook, Twitter, YouTube, Flickr*

Robert K. Kafin, Chair
Lee Keet, Vice-Chair
Meredith Prime, Vice-Chair
Curt R. Welling, Treasurer
Virginia M. Lawrence, Secretary

Research, education and advocacy to protect the natural character and communities of the Adirondack Park. Also publishes an annual State of Park Report and quarterly newsletters.
Founded in 1975
Mailing list available for rent

7711 African American Environmentalist Association
1629 K Street, NW
Suite 300
Washington, DC 20006

443-569-5102
E-Mail:
africanamericanenvironmentalist@msn.com
Home Page: aaenvironment.Blogspot.com
Social Media: *Facebook, Twitter, LinkedIn, YouTube, RSS*

Norris McDonald, President
Derry Bigby, Vice President

Dedicated to providing energy and environmental information and educating the African American community.

7712 Agricultural Research Institute
1034 Miner Farm Road
PO Box 90
Chazy, NY 12921

518-846-7121
FAX 518-846-8445
Home Page: www.whminer.com
Social Media: *Facebook, Google +*

Richard J. Grant Ph.D, President
Kirk E. Beattie, Vice President
Rachel Dutil, Secretary
Joseph C. Burke Ph.D, Trustees
Richard Eakins, Trustees

Institutions concerned with environmental issues, pest control, agricultural meteorology, biotechnology, food irradiation, agricultural policy, research and development, food safety, technology transfer and remote sensing.
125 Members

7713 Air & Waste Management Association
420 Fort Duquesne Boulevard
One Gateway Center, 3rd Floor
Pittsburgh, PA 15222-1435

412-232-3444
800-270-3444
FAX 412-232-3450
E-Mail: info@awma.org
Home Page: www.awma.org
Social Media: *Facebook, Twitter, LinkedIn*

Dallas Baker, President
Brad Waldron, QEP, CHMM, President Elect
Michael Miller, Immediate Past President
Nancy Meilahn Fowler, Treasurer
Stephanie Glyptis, Secretary/ Executive Director

Supports all those involved with the environment, specifically the air and waste management industry. Publishes a magazine.
9000 Members
Founded in 1907

7714 Air Pollution Control Association
420 Fort Duquesne Boulevard
One Gateway Center, 3rd Floor
Pittsburgh, PA 15222-1435

412-232-3444
800-270-3444
FAX 412-232-3450
E-Mail: info@awma.org
Home Page: www.awma.org
Social Media: *Facebook, Twitter, LinkedIn*

Dallas Baker, President
Brad Waldron, QEP, CHMM, President Elect
Michael Miller, Immediate Past President
Nancy Meilahn Fowler, Treasurer
Stephanie Glyptis, Secretary/ Executive Director

Association for the environment and conservation industry.
9000 Members
Founded in 1907

7715 Alliance for Bio-Integrity
54 North Park Street
Fairfield, IA 52556

206-888-4852
E-Mail: info@biointegrity.org
Home Page: www.biointegrity.org

Steven M Druker, Executive Director

A nonprofit organization dedicated to the advancement of human and environmental health through sustainable and safe technologies.

7716 Alliance to Save Energy
1850 M Street, NW
Suite 610
Washington, DC 20036

202-857-0666
Home Page: www.ase.org
Social Media: *Facebook, Twitter, LinkedIn, RSS, Google+, Flickr, YouTube*

Sen Jeanne Shaheen, Honorary Chair
Jane Palmieri, Co-Chair
Sen Chris Coons, Honorary Vice Chair
Sen. Rob Portman, Honorary Vice Chair
Sen-Susan Collins, Honorary Board Member

Promotes energy efficiency to achieve a healthier economy, a cleaner environment, and greater energy security.

7717 America the Beautiful Fund
P.O. Box 6007
Indianapolis, IN 46206-6007

202-638-1649
800-421-4225
FAX 888-421-4351
E-Mail: katie@america-the-beautiful.org
Home Page: www.americanfunds.com

Nanine Bilski, President
Kathleen Rehicaldt, Program Director
Daniel Schneider, Secretary

Groups and private citizens that improve the quality of the environment.
1M Members
Founded in 1965

7718 American Association for Aerosol Research (AAAR)
12100 Sunset Hills Road
Suite 130
Reston, VA 20190

703-437-4377
800-485-3106
FAX 856-439-0525
E-Mail: info@aaar.org
Home Page: www.aaar.org

Jay Turner, President
Sheryl Ehrman, Vice President
Allen Robinson, Vice President Elect
Linsey Marr, Treasurer
Suresh Dhaniyala, Secretary

AAAR is a nonprofit professional organization for scientists and engineers who wish to promote and communicate technical advances in the field of aerosol research. The Association fosters the exchange of information among members and with other disciplines through conferences, symposia and publication of a professional journal. Committed to the development of aerosol and its application to important social issues, AAAR offers an international forum for education, communication and networking.
1000 Members
Founded in 1982

7719 American Bird Conservancy
4249 Loudoun Ave.
P.O. Box 249
The Plains, VA 20198-2237

540-253-5780
888-247-3624
FAX 540-253-5782
Home Page: www.abcbirds.org

Warren F. Cooke, Chair
V Richard Eales, Treasurer & Vice Chair
William H. Leighty, Vice Chair
William F. Sheehan, Vice Chair
George H. Fenwick, President

A nonprofit membership organization dedicated to the conservation of wild birds and their habitats in the Americas.
Founded in 1980

7720 **American Council on Science and Health**

1995 Broadway
Suite 202
New York, NY 10023-5882

212-362-7044
866-905-2694
FAX 212-362-4919
E-Mail: acsh@acsh.org
Home Page: www.acsh.org
Social Media: *Facebook, Twitter, YouTube*

Hank Campbell, President
Cheryl Martin, Director Of Development
Dr. Gilbert Ross, M.D., Medical Director
Ruth Kava Ph.D, Senior Nutrition Fellow
Lila Abassi M.D., Director Of Medicine

A consumer education organization providing the public with scientifically accurate evaluations of food, chemicals, the environment and health.
Founded in 1978

7721 **American Farmland Trust**

1150 Connecticut Avenue
Suite 600
The Plains, VA 20036

800-431-1499
FAX 202-659-8339
E-Mail: halthouse@farmland.org
Home Page: www.farmland.org
Social Media: *Facebook, Twitter, LinkedIn, Pinterest*

Barton H. Thompson, Jr., Chair
John Hardin Jr., Vice Chair
William Cohan, Treasurer
Ralph Grossi, Interim President
Susan Sink, VP, Dev. & Ext. Affair

An organization that protects farmland and ranch land in the UnitedStates, promotes environmentally sound farming practices and keeps farmers on the land.
Founded in 1980

7722 **American Fisheries Society**

5410 Grosvenor Ln
Suite 110
Bethesda, MD 20814-2199

301-897-8616
FAX 301-897-8096
E-Mail: sjohnston@fisheries.org
Home Page: www.fisheries.org
Social Media: *Facebook, Twitter, vimeo, flickr*

Bob Hughes, President
Donna L. Parrish, President-Elect
Ronald J. Essig, First Vice President
Joe Margraf, Second Vice President
John Boreman, Past President

Supports all those involved in the fishing industry, specifically environmental issues that the profession addresses.
8500 Members
Founded in 1870

7723 **American Forests**

1220 L Street NW
Suite 750
Washington, DC 20005

202-737-1944
E-Mail: info@americanforests.org
Home Page: www.americanforests.org
Social Media: *Facebook, Twitter*

Ann Nichols, Chair
Bruce Lisman, Vice Chair
Roderick DeArment, Treasurer
Scott Steen, President & CEO
Peter Hutchins, Vice President/ COO

The oldest national nonprofit conservation organization in the U.S.that advocates for the protection and expansion of forests.
Founded in 1990

7724 **American Institute of Hydrology**

1230 Lincoln Drive
Carbondale, IL 62901

618-453-7809
E-Mail: aih@engr.siu.edu
Home Page: www.aihydrology.org

Dr. Mustafa M. Aral, President
Dr. Rao S. Govindaraju, President-Elect
Dr. John L. Nieber, VP For Academic Affairs
John W. Balay, VP For Institute Development
Ed A. Baquerizo, VP For International Affairs

Registers and certifies hydrologists and hydrogeologists, provides a forum to discuss national and international issues, and provides educational courses.
1000 Members
Founded in 1981

7725 **American Nuclear Society**

555 N Kensington Ave
La Grange Park, IL 60526-5592

708-352-6611
800-323-3044
FAX 708-352-0499
E-Mail: advertising@ans.org
Home Page: www.ans.org
Social Media: *Facebook, Twitter, LinkedIn*

Eugene S. Grecheck, President
Andrew C. Klein, Vice President/President-Elect
Steven A. Arndt, Treasurer
Michaele C. Brady Raap, Immediate Past President
Robert C. Fine, JD, CAE, Executive Director

Supports all those involved in the fields of radioactive waste management, removal, handling, disposal, treatment, cleanup and environmental restoration.
10500 Members
Founded in 1954

7726 **American Phytopathological Society**

3340 Pilot Knob Road
Saint Paul, MN 55121-2097

651-454-7250
800-328-7560
FAX 651-454-0766
E-Mail: aps@scisoc.org
Home Page: www.apsnet.org
Social Media: *Facebook, Twitter, LinkedIn, Pinterest*

Sally A. Miller, President
Timothy D. Murray, President-Elect
Mary E. Palm, Vice President
Steven A. Slack, Treasurer
David M. Gadoury, Internal Communications Officer

Scientific organization that studies plant diseases and their control.
4500 Members
Founded in 1908

7727 **American Public Works Association**

2345 Grand Blvd
Suite 700
Kansas City, MO 64108-2625

816-472-6100
800-848-2792
FAX 816-472-1610
Home Page: www.apwa.net
Social Media: *Facebook, Twitter, YouTube*

Mr. Brian R. Usher, PWLF, President
Mr.Ronald J. Calkins, PE, PWLF, President Elect
Richard F. Stinson, Director, Region I
Mr. Harry L. Weed, II, PWLF, Director, Region II
William Barney Mills, Jr., Director, Region III

International educational and professional association of public agencies, private sector companies, and individuals dedicated to providing high quality public works, goods and services. APWA provides a forum brings important public works-related topics to public attention in local, state, and federal areas. Mailing list for members only.
Cost: $100.00
26000 Members
Founded in 1937

7728 **American Shore and Beach Preservation Association**

5460 Beaujolais Lane
Fort Myers, FL 33919

239-489-2616
FAX 239-362-9771
E-Mail: managing@asbpa.org
Home Page: www.asbpa.org
Social Media: *Facebook, Twitter*

Anthony P. Pratt, Acting President
Russell Boudreau, Vice President
Nicole Elko Ph.D, Vice President
Phillip Roehrs, Vice President
Brad Pickel, Treasurer

Federal, state and local government agencies and individuals interested in conservation, development and restoration of beaches and shorefronts.
1M Members
Founded in 1926

7729 **American Society for Environmental History**

UW Interdisciplinary Arts and Sciences Program
1900 Commerce Street
Tacoma, WA 98402

206-343-0226
FAX 206-343-0249
E-Mail: info.aseh@gmail.com
Home Page: www.aseh.net

Kathleen Brosnan, President
Graeme Wynn, Vice President/ President Elect
Jay Tylor, Secretary
Mark Madison, Treasurer
Emily Greenwald, Executive Committee

ASEH members are techers and researchers with an interest in human ecology and environmental history.
1200 Members
Founded in 1976

7730 **American Society for Photogammetry and Remote Sensing (ASPRS)**

5410 Grosvenor Lane
Suite 210
Bethesda, MD 20814-2160

301-493-0290
FAX 301-493-0208
E-Mail: asprs@asprs.org
Home Page: www.asprs.org
Social Media: *Facebook, Twitter*

Dr. E. Lynn Usery, President
Dr. Charles K. Toth, CP, President-Elect
Ms. Rebecca A. Morton, CP, Vice President
Dr. A. Stewart Walker, CP, Immediate Past President
Mr. Gregory Brunner, National Director

Supports all those involved in mapping, photogrammetry, environmental management, remote sensing, geographic infromation, and natural resources.
6000 Members
Founded in 1934

7731 **American Society of Agronomy**

5585 Guilford Rd.
Madison, WI 53711-1086

608-273-8080
FAX 608-273-2021
E-Mail: headquarters@sciencesocieties.org

Home Page: www.agronomy.org
Social Media: *Facebook, Twitter, LinkedIn*

Newell Kitchen, President
Kenneth Barbarick, President-Elect

Supports educators and scientists interested in the impacts of environmental perturbations on the biological and physical sciences.
10000 Members
Founded in 1907

7732 American Society of Mining and Reclamation
American Society of Mining and Reclamation
1305 Weathervane,
Champaign, IL 61821

217-333-9489
217-493-7847
FAX 859-335-6529
E-Mail: rdarmody@illinois.edu
Home Page: www.asmr.us
Social Media: *Facebook*

Eddie Bearden, President
Bruce Buchanan, President Elect
Richard Barnhisel, Executive Secretary

Dissemination of technical information relating to the reclamation of lands disturbed by mineral extraction. Members yearly issue is paid out of proceeding. Membership dues $50 regular $10 students.
500 Members
Founded in 1983

7733 American Society of Safety Engineers
520 N. Northwest Hwy
Park Ridge, IL 60068

847-699-2929
FAX 847-768-3434
E-Mail: info@asse.org
Home Page: www.asse.org
Social Media: *Facebook, Twitter, LinkedIn, Instagram*

Michael Belcher, CSP, President
Thomas F. Cecich, CSP, CIHÿ, President-Elect
James Smith, M.S., CSP, Senior Vice President
Fred J. Fortman, Jr., Secretary and Executive Director
Stephanie A. Helgerman, CSP, Vice President, Finance

The oldest and largest professional safety organization. Its members manage, supervise and consult on safety, health, and environmental issues in industry, insurance, government and education.
30000 Members
Founded in 1911

7734 Animal Protection and Rescue League
302 Washington St.
#404
San Diego, CA 92103

858-999-2343
E-Mail: info@aprl.org
Home Page: www.aprl.org
Social Media: *Facebook, Twitter, YouTube*

A nonprofit organization that influences animal protection legislation, conducts rescues of abused factory farmed animals and educates people abouthumane eating.
Founded in 2003

7735 Aquatic Plant Management Society
7922 NW
71st Street
Gainesville, FL 32653

FAX 601-634-5502
E-Mail: dpetty@ndrsite.com

Home Page: www.apms.org
Social Media: *Facebook, LinkedIn*

Rob Richardson, President
John Madsen, President-Elect
John Rodgers, Vice-President
Jeremy Slade, Treasurer
Jeff Schardt, Secretary

An international organization of scientists, educators, students, commercial pesticide applicators, administrators, and concerned individuals interested in the management and study of aquatic plants.
Founded in 1961

7736 Association for Environmental Health and Sciences (AEHS) Foundation, Inc.
150 Fearing Street
Amherst, MA 01002

413-549-5170
FAX 413-549-0579
Home Page: www.aehsfoundation.org

Paul T Kostecki, PhD, Executive Director
Brenna Lockwood, Managing Director
Sierra Pelletier, Program Assistant
Ed Calabrese, Editor-In-Chief
Denise Leonard, Managing Editor

AEHS Foundation is a multi-disciplinary association providing a forum for individual professionals concerned with soil protection and cleanup. Fields represented include chemistry, geology, hydrogeology, law, engineering, modeling, toxicology, regulatory science, public health and public policy.
600 Members
Founded in 1989

7737 Association for Population/Family Planning Libraries & Information Conference
Family Health International Library
PO Box 13950
Research Triangle Park, NC 27709

919-447-7040
Home Page: www.aplici.org

Yan Fu, President
Alli Buehler, Vice-President
Jill Leonard, Treasurer
Liz Nugent, Recording Secretary
Debra Dickson, Past President

Offers support for all those involved in issues concerning population and family planning, including publications, training and conferences.
Frequency: Annual

7738 Association of Engineering Geologists
1100-H Brandywine Blvd.
Zanesville, OH 43701

303-757-2926
844-331-7867
FAX 740-452-2552
E-Mail: aeg@aegweb.org
Home Page: www.aegweb.org
Social Media: *Facebook, Twitter*

Paul Santi, President
Dale Andrews, Vice President/ President Elect
Kathy Troost, Treasurer
Kevin Richard, Secretary
Ken Fergason, Past President

Meets the professional needs of geologists who are applying their scientific training and experience to the broad field of civil and environmental engineering. Mission is to provide leadership in the development and application of geologic principles and knowledge to serve engineering, environmental and public needs.
3000 Members
Founded in 1957
Mailing list available for rent: 3000 names at $100 per M

7739 Association of Environmental Engineering and Science Professors
1211 Connecticut Ave NW,
Suite 650
Washington, DC 20036

202-640-6591
FAX 217-355-9232
E-Mail: bschorr@aeesp.org
Home Page: www.aeesp.org

Gregory W. Characklis, President
Peter J. Vikesland, President-Elect
Linda K. Weavers, Vice President
Ching Hua Huang, Secretary
Andrea Ferro, Treasurer

Individuals working or teaching in the field of environmental engineering, including water quality and treatment, air quality, air pollution control and solid and hazardous waste management.
700 Members
Founded in 1963

7740 Association of Environmental and Resource Economists
13006 Peaceful Terrace
Silver Spring, MD 20904

202-559-8998
FAX 202-559-8998
E-Mail: info@aere.org
Home Page: www.aere.org

W.L (Vic) Adamowicz, President
Dr. Richard G. Newell, Vice President
Prof. Sarah West, Secretary
Dr. Dallas Burtraw, Treasurer
Prof. Elena G. Irwin, Board Of Director

AERE serves as an information resource for economists involved in natural resources policy planning and research. It was estabilshed as a way to exchange ideas, stimulate research, and promote graducate research in environmental economics.
900 Members
Founded in 1979

7741 Association of Fish & Wildlife Agencies
1100 First Street NE
Suite 825
Washington, DC 20002

202-838-3474
FAX 202-350-9869
E-Mail: info@fishwildlife.org
Home Page: www.fishwildlife.org
Social Media: *Facebook, Twitter*

Ron Regan, Executive Director
Dave Chanda, President
Nick Wiley, Vice President
Carol Bambrey, Association Council
Glenn Normandeau, Secretary/Treasurer

The organization that represents all of North America's fish and wildlife agencies that promotes sound management and conservation, and speaks with a unified voice on important fish and wildlife issues.
Founded in 1902

7742 Association of State Floodplain Managers
575 D'Onofrio Drive
Suite 200
Madison, WI 53719

608-828-3000
FAX 608-828-6319
E-Mail: Larry@floods.org
Home Page: www.floods.org
Social Media: *Facebook, Twitter, Google+*

Larry Larson, Director Emeritus
Maria Cox Lamm, Vice Chair
Leslie Durham, Secretary

Karen McHugh, Treasurer
Ingrid Danler, Deputy Director

Promotes common interest in flood damage abatement, supports environmental protection for floodplain areas, provides education on floodplain management practices and policy and urges incorporating multi-objective management approaches to solve local flooding problems.
6500 Members
Founded in 1977

7743 Association of Zoos and Aquariums

8403 Colesville Rd
Suite 710
Silver Spring, MD 20910-6331

301-562-0777
FAX 301-562-0888
E-Mail: membership@aza.org
Home Page: www.aza.org
Social Media: *Facebook, Twitter*

Dennis E Pate, Executive Director & CEO
Steve Burns, Chair-Elect
Dennis W. Kelly, Vice-Chair
Jim Breheny, Director
Lynn Clements, Director

A nonprofit organization dedicated to the advancement of accredited zoos and aquariums in the areas of animal care, wildlife conservation, education and science.
200 Members
Founded in 1924

7744 Center for Biological Diversity

P.O. Box 710ÿ
Tucson, AZ 85702-0710

520-623-5252
866-357-3349
FAX 520-623-9797
E-Mail: center@biologicaldiversity.org
Home Page: www.biologicaldiversity.org
Social Media: *Facebook, Twitter, YouTube, Instagram*

Marcey Olajos, Board Chair
Stephanie Zill, Treasurer
Robin Silver, Secretary
Paula Simmonds, Director, Development
Mike Stark, Communications Director

National U.S. group using science, law, and creative media to protect the lands, waters, and climate that species need to survive.

7745 Center for Environmental Philosophy

1155 Union Circleÿ
#310980
Denton, TX 76203-5017

940-565-2727
FAX 940-565-4439
E-Mail: cep@unt.edu
Home Page: www.cep.unt.edu

Graduate program in environmental ethics at the University of NorthTexas.

7746 Center for Food Safety

660 Pennsylvania Ave, SE
#302
Washington, DC 20003

202-547-9359
FAX 202-547-9429
E-Mail: office@centerforfoodsafety.org
Home Page: www.centerforfoodsafety.org
Social Media: *Facebook, Twitter, Pinterest, YouTube*

Andrew Kimbrell, Executive Director
Rebecca Spector, West Coast Director
Adam Keats, Senior Attorney
Cristina Stella, Staff Attorney
Amy Van Saun, Legal Fellow

A U.S. environmental, nonprofit organization based in Washington, D.C.

7747 Center for a Livable Future

Johns Hopkins Bloomberg School of Public Health
615 N Wolfe St., W7010
Baltimore, MD 21205-2179

410-502-7578
FAX 410-502-7579
E-Mail: clf@jhsph.edu
Home Page:
www.jhsph.edu/research/centers-and-institutes
Social Media: *Facebook, Twitter, YouTube*

Robert Lawrence, Director
Polly Walker, Senior Fellow
Shawn McKenzie, Associate Director

Research and programs for a secure, equitable and resilient food system.

7748 Center for a New American Dream

POÿBoxÿ797
Charlottesville, VA 22902

301-891-3683
E-Mail: newdream@newdream.org
Home Page: www.newdream.org
Social Media: *Facebook, Twitter, YouTube, Pinterest*

Wendy Philleo, Executive Director
Sarah Baird, Dir., Outreach & Comm.
Guinevere Higgins, Dir., Development
Edna Rienzi, Program Coordinator
Lisa Mastny, Sr. Editor & Dir. - Publications

A nonprofit organization that helps Americans reduce and shift their consumption to improve quality of life, protect the environment, and promote social justice.
Founded in 1997

7749 Citizens Campaign for the Environment

225-A Main Street
Farmingdale, NY 11735

516-390-7150
FAX 516-390-7160
E-Mail: farmingdale@citizenscampaign.org
Home Page: www.citizenscampaign.org
Social Media: *Facebook, Twitter, YouTube, RSS, Blog*

Adrienne Esposito, Executive Director
Brian Smith, Associate Exe. Dir.
Mary Ellen Dour, Education & Financial Director
Sarah Eckel, Policy Director
Jacob McCaffery, Outreach Dir.

Works to protect the environment and public health with the supportof members in New York and Connecticut.
Founded in 1985

7750 Citizens' Climate Lobbyÿ

1330 Orange Ave
#300
Coronado, CA 92118

619-437-7142
E-Mail: ccl@citizensclimatelobby.org
Home Page: citizensclimatelobby.org
Social Media: *Facebook, Twitter, Instagram, YouTube, Google+*

Marshall Saunders, Founder/ President
Mark Reynolds, Executive Director
Steve Valk, Communications Director
Amy Bennett, Director, Operations
Danny Richter, Legislative Director

An international grassroots environmental group that trains and supports volunteers to build relationships with their Members of Congress in order to influence climate policy.

7751 Coastal Conservation Association

6919 Portwest Dr
Suite 100
Houston, TX 77024-8049

713-626-4234
800-201-FISH
FAX 713-626-5852
E-Mail: ccantl@joincca.org
Home Page: www.joincca.org
Social Media: *Facebook, Twitter, RSS*

Degraaf Adams, Executive Board, Texas
Bill Bird, Executive Board, Florida
Stan Brogdon, Executive Board, Washington
Robert Donlin, Executive Board, South Carolina
Jim Flannery, Executive Board , Maryland

Seeks to advance protection and conservation of all marine life. Conducts seminars and bestows awards.
85000 Members
Founded in 1977

7752 Committee for a Constructive Tomorrow

P.O. Box 65722
Washington, DC 20035

202-429-2737
Home Page: www.cfact.org
Social Media: *Facebook, Twitter, RSS, YouTube*

David Rothbard, President/ Co-Founder
Craig Rucker, Executive Director, Co-Founder
Marc Morano, Director of Communications
Duggan Flanakin, Director of Policy Research
Christina Wilson Norman, Development Officer

A conservative Washington, D.C.-based nonprofit organization that promotes a positive voice on environment and development issues.

7753 Community Alliance with Family Farmers

PO Box 363
Davis, CA 95617-363

530-756-8518
FAX 530-756-7857
E-Mail: info@caff.org
Home Page: www.caff.org
Social Media: *Facebook, Twitter, YouTube*

Rich Collins, Board Chair
Carol Presley, Vice Chair
Judith Redmond, Secretary
Vicki Williams, Treasurer
Diane Del Signore, Executive Director

Non-profit organization that advocates for California's family farmers and sustainable agriculture. Strives to build on shared values around food and agriculture, and work together in practical, on-the-ground programs. Parterships create locally based economic vitality, improved human and environmental health, and long-term sustainability of family farms.
Cost: $47.95

7754 Conservation Education Association

Department of Conservation
PO Box 180
Jefferson City, MO 65102-0180

573-751-4115
FAX 573-751-4467
Home Page: www.conservation.state.mo.us

John Hoskins, Director
Lorna Domke, Outreach/Education
Tom Cwyner, Editor

Focuses on conservation and the importance of protecting the environment.
Founded in 1937

7755 Conservation Fund
1655 N. Fort Myer Drive
Suite 1300
Arlington, VA 22209-3199

703-525-6300
FAX 703-525-4610
E-Mail: webmaster@conservationfund.org
Home Page: www.conservationfund.org
Social Media: *Facebook, Twitter, LinkedIn, YouTube*

J. Rutherford Seydel II, Chairman
R. Michael Leonard, Vice Chairman
Lawrence A. Selzer, President and CEO
Richard L. Erdmann, Executive VP and General Counsel
David K. Phillips, Jr., Treasurer, Executive VP & CFO

Works with private and public agencies and organizations to protect wildlife habitats, historic sites and parks.
Founded in 1985

7756 Conservation International
2011 Crystal Dr
Suite 500
Arlington, VA 22202-3787

703-341-2400
800-429-5660
E-Mail: community@conservation.org
Home Page: www.conservation.org
Social Media: *Facebook, Twitter, YouTube, Instagram, RSS*

Peter Seligmann, Chairman of the Board & CEO
Rob Walton, Chairman Of Executive Committee
Harrison Ford, Vice Chair
Andr, Esteves, Vice Chair
Dawn Arnall, Board Member

Mission is to conserve the Earth's living heritage-our global biodiversity-and to demonstrate that human societies are able to live harmoniously with nature.
60M Members
Founded in 1987

7757 Conservation Law Foundation
62 Summer Street
Boston, MA 02110-1016

617-350-0990
E-Mail: e-info@clf.org
Home Page: www.clf.org
Social Media: *Facebook, Twitter, LinkedIn, RSS, Instagram, Pinterest, Goo*

Sara Molyneaux, Chair
Gordan Hall III, Vice Chair
Peter Nessen, Vice Chair
Eugene H. Clapp, Treasurer
Bradley Campbell, President

An environmental advocacy organization based in New England that advocates on behalf of the region's environment and its communities.
Founded in 1966

7758 Conservation Treaty Support Fund
3705 Cardiff Road
Chevy Chase, MD 20815

301-654-3150
800-654-3150
FAX 301-652-6390
E-Mail: ctsf@conservationtreaty.org
Home Page: www.conservationtreaty.org

George A Furness Jr, President
Frederick E. Morris
John C. Goldsmith

Promotes awareness, understanding and support of conservation treaties and their goals. Through the International Endangered Species Treaty, the Wetlands Convention, and other conservation agreements, more than 150 na-

tions are committed to work together to preserve the wildlife and habitats that are our shared natural heritage.
Founded in 1986

7759 Conservation and Preservation Charities of America
1100 Larkspur Landing Circle
Suite 340
Larkspur, CA 94939

800-626-6685
Home Page: www.conservenow.org

Patrick Mcguire, President

CPCA is a consortium of environmental stewardship organizations. CPCA acts as a central focus for charitable giving dedicated to the protection of the natural habitat and historic treasures. Sponsors workplace giving campaigns in support of its member organizations.

7760 Defenders of Wildlifeÿ
1130 17th Street, NW
Washington, DC 20036

202-682-9400
800-385-9712
E-Mail: defenders@mail.defenders.org
Home Page: www.defenders.org
Social Media: *Facebook, Twitter, RSS, YouTube, Flickr*

Winsome Dunn McIntosh, Chair
Susan Wallace, Vice Chair
Mark Caylor, Treasurer
Caroline Gabel, Secretary
Jamie Rappaport Clark, President, CEO

A nonprofit conservation organization based in the United States that protects all animals and plants native to North America in their natural communities.
Founded in 1947

7761 Earth Island Institute
2150 Allston Way
Suite 460
Berkeley, CA 94704-1375

510-859-9100
FAX 510-859-9091
E-Mail: arch@earthisland.org
Home Page: www.earthisland.org
Social Media: *Facebook, Twitter, YouTube*

Michael Mitrani, President
Martha Davis, Vice President
Kenneth Brower, Vice President
Jennifer Snyder, Secretary
Alex Giedt, Treasurer

Seeks to prevent destruction of environment and sponsors fund drives and activist projects to protect wildlife.
33M Members
Founded in 1985

7762 Earth Policy Institute
1350 Connecticut Avenue NW
Suite 403
Washington, DC 20036

202-496-9290
FAX 202-496-9325
E-Mail: epi@earthpolicy.org
Home Page: www.earth-policy.org
Social Media: *Facebook, Twitter, RSS*

Judith Gradwohl, Chairman
Lester R. Brown, Founder, President
Reah JaniseÿKauffman, Co-Founder, VP
Janet Larsen, Director of Research
J. Matthew Roney, Research Associate

An independent nonprofit environmental organization based in Washington D.C. in the United States.
Founded in 2001

7763 Earth Regeneration Society
1442A Walnut Street
#57
Berkeley, CA 94709-1405

510-527-9716
FAX 510-559-8410
E-Mail: alden@earthregenerationsociety.org
Home Page: www.earthregenerationsociety.org

Alden Bryant, President
Cynthia Johnson, Secretary
Glen A. Frendel, Executive Director
Alden Bryant, Acting Treasurer
Dolores Huerta, Board Of Director

Organized to develop and study scientific and practical solutions to environmental issues.

7764 Earth Society Foundation
238 East 58th Street
Suite 2400
New York, NY 10022

212-832-3659
800-3EA-THDA
E-Mail: earthsociety1@hotmail.com
Home Page: www.earthsocietyfoundation.org
Social Media: *Facebook*

Helen Garland, Chairperson
Thomas C. Dowd, President
Tom Dowd, VP

News of interest in environmental and sociological issues. Purpose is to promote Earth Day and the Earth Trustee agenda; Every individual and institution should seek choices in ecology, economics, and ethics that will eliminate pollution, poverty, and violence.

7765 Earth's Birthday Project
PO Box 1536
Santa Fe, MN 87504-1536

505-986-6040
800-698-4438
FAX 505-984-9176
E-Mail: info@earthsbirthday.org
Home Page: www.earthsbirthday.org
Social Media: *Facebook, Twitter*

Albert Scharfÿ, President
Richard Murray, Treasurer
Mary Hofstedt, Secretary
Clifford Ross, Executive Director
Alia Munn, Operations Director

A U.S. based educational nonprofit organization that inspires wonder, learning, and care of the natural world in children, teachers, and parents.
Founded in 1989

7766 Earthjustice
50 California St.
Suite 500
San Francisco, CA 94111

800-584-6460
FAX 415-217-2040
E-Mail: headquarters@earthjustice.org
Home Page: earthjustice.org
Social Media: *Facebook, Twitter*

Trip Van Noppen, President
Drew Caputo, VP, Litig.,
Lands/Wildlife/Oceans
Abigail Dillen, VP, Litigation, Climate & Energy
Lisa Garcia, VP, Litigation, Healthy Communities
Martin Hayden, VP, Litigation, Policy/Legislation

Non-profit environmental law organization.
Founded in 1971

7767 Ecological and Toxicological Association of Dyes

Stadthausgasse 18
4051 Basel
Switzerland

616-909-966
FAX 616-914-278
Home Page: www.etad.com

Jill Aker, President

Represents the interests of manufacturers and formulators of dyes in the region with regard to environmental and health hazards in the manufacture, processing, shipment, use and disposal of thier products.
Founded in 1974

7768 Energy & Environmental Research Center

University of North Dakota
15 N 23rd St., Stop 9018
Grand Forks, ND 58202-9018

701-777-5000
FAX 701-777-5181
Social Media: *Facebook, Twitter, LinkedIn, Google+, YouTube, Flickr*

Thomas A. Erickson, Director
John A. Harju, Ass. Dir., Strategic Relationships
Erin M. O'Leary, Ass. Dir., Business & Operations
Edward N. Steadman, Ass. Dir., Research
Michael J. Holmes, Dep. Ass. Dir., Research

The EERC conducts research on fossil, renewable and altenative fuels, as well as pollution prevention and environmental cleanup.
Founded in 1951

7769 Energy Action Coalition

Home Page: www.energyactioncoalition.org
Social Media: *Facebook, Twitter, RSS, Flickr, YouTube, Vimeo*

Lydia Avila, Executive Director
Kristina Banks, Operations Coordinator
Sean Estelle, National Divestment Campaigner
Tina Johnson, Sr. Dir of Env. Justice & Programs
Kendall Mackey, National Tar Sands Organizer

A North American nonprofit organization made up of 50 partner organizations in the U.S. and Canada that runs campaigns to build the youth and student clean energy movement and advocate for changes on local, state, national, andinternational levels in North America.

7770 Environmental & Energy Study Institute

1112 16th Street, NW
Suite 300
Washington, DC 20036

202-628-1400
FAX 202-204-5244
E-Mail: alaporte@eesi.org.
Home Page: www.eesi.org
Social Media: *Facebook, Twitter, YouTube, Google+*

Jared Blum, Board Chair
Shelley Fidler, Board Secretary/Treasurer
Richard L. Ottinger, Board Chair Emeritus
Quincalee Brown, Executive Director
Frances S. Buchholzer, Director

A non-profit organization dedicated to promoting environmentally sustainable societies.
Founded in 1984

7771 Environmental Alliance for Senior Involvement

PO Box 250
Milford, CT 06460

203-779-0024
FAX 203-779-0025
E-Mail: easi@easi.org
Home Page: www.easi.org

Thomas Benjamin, President
Roy Geiger, VP Administration
Peggy Knight, VP Programs

Engaging senior volunteers to use their experience in the restoration and maintenance of environmentally sound environments. International network.
Founded in 1990

7772 Environmental Assessment Association

PO Box 879
Palm Springs, CA 92263

877-743-6806
877-810-5643
FAX 760-327-5631
E-Mail: info@eaa-assoc.org
Home Page: www.eaa-assoc.org
Social Media: *LinkedIn*

Bill C. Merrell Ph.D , CEI, National Education Director

Supports all those involved in environmental assessment, including training and education, publications, conferences and research resources.

7773 Environmental Bankers Association

1827 Powers Ferry Rd.
Building 14, Suite 100
Atlanta, GA 30339

678-619-5045
800-966-7475
FAX 678-229-2777
E-Mail: eba@envirobank.org
Home Page: www.envirobank.org

Sharon Valverde, President
Georgina Dannatt, Vice President
Richard Belyea, Secretary
David Lambert, Treasurer
Julie Kilgore, Affiliate Chair

EBA voting members are banks, trust companies, credit unions, savings and loan associations, and other financial services organizations with an interest in environmental risk management and related issues. Active participants are bankers from Trust or Credit offices with responsibility for environmental liability, and financial services officers with environmental interests. Affiliate members are from law firms, consulting and insurance organizations.
Founded in 1994

7774 Environmental Business Association

126 State Street
3rd Floor
Albany, NY 12207-1637

518-432-6400
FAX 518-432-1383
Home Page: www.eba-nys.org

John L. Cusack, President
Linda R. Shaw, Vice President
Martha M. Holstein, Secretary
Ronald J. Beruta, Treasurer
Robert Hall, Director

EBA members represent all segments of the environmental industry—consultants, labaoratories, remediation companies, disposal firms, recyclers and technology innovators. EBA facilitates arrangements and information exchange among members to develop business opportunities. Services include sponsoring

seminars, monthly meetings, industry trends, changes in technology and legislation.
Founded in 1989

7775 Environmental Compliance Institute

165 Sherwood Ave
Farmingdale, NY 11735

631-414-7757
866-670-5366
FAX 631-843-6331
E-Mail: pbany@c2g.us
Home Page: www.c2g.us

Attorneys and corporations interested in environmental law and federal regulations governing waste disposal and other matters related to the environment.

7776 Environmental Council of the States(ECOS)

50 F Street NW
Suite 350
Washington, DC 20001

202-266-4920
FAX 202-266-4937
E-Mail: ecos@ecos.org
Home Page: www.ecos.org

Martha Rudolf, President
John Linc Stine, Vice President
Elizabeth Dieck, Secretary-Treasurer
John Stine, Committe Chair, Air
Sara Parker Pauley, Committe Chair, Water

Improving the capability of State environmental agencies and their leaders to protect and improve human health and the environment of the United States of America.

7777 Environmental Design Research Association

1760 Old Meadow Road
Suite 500
McLean, VA 22102

703-506-2895
FAX 703-506-3266
E-Mail: edra@telepath.com
Home Page: www.edra.org
Social Media: *Facebook, Twitter, LinkedIn*

Gowri Betrabet Gulwadi, Chair
Lynne Manzo, Chair-Elect
Paula Horrigan, Secretary
Shauna Mallory-Hill, Treasurer
Rula Awwad-Rafferty, Ex- Officio

Is to advance the art and science of environmental design research, to improve understanding of the interrelationships between people and their built and natural surroundings, and to help create environments responsive to human needs. EDRA members are designers and other professionals with an interest in environmental design research.
700 Members
Founded in 1968

7778 Environmental Industry Association

4301 Connecticut Ave Nw
Suite 300
Washington, DC 20008-2304

202-244-4700
800-424-2869
FAX 202-966-4824
E-Mail: wa@envasns.org
Home Page: www.envasns.org
Social Media: *Facebook*

Bruce Parker, President

Supports all those involved with technology of recycling, resource recovery and sanitary landfills. Publishes magazine.

7779 Environmental Information Association
6935 Wisconsin Ave
Suite 306
Chevy Chase, MD 20815-6112

301-961-4999
888-343-4342
FAX 301-961-3094
E-Mail: info@eia-usa.org
Home Page: www.eia-usa.org

Kevin Cannan, President
Chris Gates, President Elect
Steve Fulford, Vice President
Robert De Malo, Secretary
Kyle Burroughs, Treasurer

Nonprofit organization dedicated to providing environmental information to individuals, members and industry. Disseminates information on the abatement of asbestos and lead-based paint, indoor air quality, safety and health issues, analytical issues and environmental site assessments.

7780 Environmental Law Institute
1730 M Street NW
Suite 700
Washington, DC 20036-4919

202-939-3800
800-433-5120
FAX 202-939-3868
E-Mail: law@eli.org
Home Page: www.eli.org
Social Media: *Facebook, Twitter, LinkedIn*

Scott Fulton, President
Scott Schang, Executive Vice President
Martin Dickinson, VP Development
John V. Pendergrass, Acting VP, Research & Policy
Loretta Reinersmann, VP, Finance & Administration

Supports all those involved in environmental issues from a legal perspective, fostering the exchange of ideas and solutions for pressing environmental issues.

7781 Environmental Mutagen Society
1821 Michael Faraday Drive
Suite 300
Reston, VA 20190

703-438-8220
FAX 703-438-3113
E-Mail: emshq@ems-us.org
Home Page: www.emgs-us.org

Suzanne M. Morris, President
Bevin P. Engelward, Vice President
Barbara L. Parsons, Secretary
Barbara S. Shane, Treasurer
Marguerite Leishman, Executive Director

Members are scientists of diverse backgrounds and varied interests working in the field of molecular genetics and mutagenesis, whether in academia, industry or government. Focus is to encourage the study mutagens in the human environment particularly as they affect public health.
1500 Members
Founded in 1969

7782 Environmental and Energy Study Instituteÿ
1112 16th Street, NW
Suite 300
Washington, DC 20036

202-628-1400
FAX 202-204-5244
E-Mail: alaporte@eesi.org
Home Page: www.eesi.org

Social Media: *Facebook, Twitter, YouTube, Google+*

Jared Blum, Board Chair
Richard L. Ottinger, Chaise-Emeritus
Shelley Fidler, Board Secretary/Treasurer
Quincalee Brown, Executive Director
Frances S. Buchholzer, Director

Educating Congress on energy efficiency and renewable energy; advancing innovative policy solutions.
Founded in 1984

7783 Federation of Environmental Technologists
W175 N11081 Stonewood Dr.
Ste 203
Germantown, WI 53022-4771

262-437-1700
FAX 262-437-1702
E-Mail: info@fetinc.org
Home Page: www.fetinc.org
Social Media: *Facebook, LinkedIn*

Dan Brady, Board Chair
Mark Steinberg, President
Dave Seitz, Vice President
Anthony Montemurro, Treasurer
Jeffrey Nettesheim, Secretary

FET assists members in interpretation of and compliance with environmental regulations.
700 Members
Founded in 1981

7784 Floodplain Management Association
PO Box 712080
Santee, CA 92072-2080

760-936-3676
FAX 619-749-9524
E-Mail: admin@floodplain.org
Home Page: www.floodplain.org
Social Media: *Facebook, LinkedIn, YouTube*

Mark Seits, Chair
Maria Lorenzo Lee, Vice Chair
John Powderly, Secretary
George Booth, Treasurer
Andrew Trelease, Director

A nonprofit educational association established to promote the reduction of flood losses and to encourage the protection and enhancement of nautral floodplain values through the use of effective wetland management strategies and engineering technolgies.
Founded in 1990

7785 Forest History Society
701 William Vickers Ave
Durham, NC 27701-3162

919-682-9319
FAX 919-682-2349
E-Mail: recluse2@duke.edu
Home Page: www.foresthistory.org
Social Media: *Facebook, Twitter, LinkedIn, Flickr*

Hayes Brown, Chairman
Kent Gilges, Co-Vice Chairman
Chris Zinkhan, Co-Vice Chairman
Henry I. Barclay III, Treasurer
Steven Anderson, Secretary & President

Nonprofit, educational institution that explores the history of the environment, forestry and conservation.
2000 Members
Founded in 1946

7786 Forestry, Conservation Communications Association
122 Baltimore Street
Gettysburg, PA 17325

717-778-4237
844-458-0298
FAX 717-398-0815

E-Mail: david.steinour@frequencycoordination.org
Home Page: www.fcca.info

Chief Paul M. Leary (ret.), President
Roy Mott, Vice President
John McIntosh, Secretary/Treasurer
Ralph Haller, Executive Director
Janet Muncy, Financial Assistant

Association for manufacturers or suppliers of forestry and conservation communications equipment, systems and procedures.

7787 Friends of the Earth USA
1100 15th St. NW
11th Fl.
Washington, DC 20005

202-783-7400
877-843-8687
FAX 202-783-0444
Home Page: www.foe.org
Social Media: *Facebook, Twitter, LinkedIn, Instagram, Pinterest, Flickr*

Erich Pica, President

Global organization of environmental activists.

7788 Friends of the Trees Society
PO Box 165
Hot Springs, MT 59845

406-741-5809
E-Mail: friendsofthetrees@yahoo.com
Home Page: www.friendsofthetrees.net

Michael Pilarski, Founder & Director

Nonprofit organization helping tree lovers worldwide.
Founded in 1978

7789 GREENGUARD Environmental Institute
2211 Newmarket Parkway
Suite 110
Marietta, GA 30067

888-485-4733
FAX 770-980-0072
E-Mail: environment@ul.com
Home Page: www.greenguard.org

An industry-independent organization that aims to protect human health and improve quality of life by enhancing indoor air quality and reducing people's exposure to chemicals and other pollutants.

7790 Global Water Policy Project
E-Mail: info@globalwaterpolicy.org
Home Page: www.globalwaterpolicy.org

Promotes the preservation and sustainable use of Earth's fresh water through research, writing, outreach, and public speaking.

7791 Great Lakes United
4380 Main St
Amherst, NY 14226-3592

716-886-0142
FAX 716-204-9521
E-Mail: glu@glu.org
Home Page: www.glu.org

Catherine Gillespie, President
Julie O'Leary, VP
Robert Miller, Treasurer

An international, environmental coaltion working to preserve and protect the Great Lakes and St. Lawrence River. Memberships are as follows: $100 organizational members, $25 organizational members w/bugdets below $15,000, $25 individuals, and $50 family members.
1.1M Members
Founded in 1982

7792 Green Zionist Alliance
PO Box 1176
Long Beach, NY 11561

347-559-4492
E-Mail: info@aytzim.org
Home Page: www.aytzim.org

Rabbi Michael Cohen, Co-founder
David Krantz, Board of Director
Susan Levine, Board of Director
Netta Schmeidler, Board of Director
Pesach Stadlin, Board of Director

A North America-based nonprofit organization
that works to educate and mobilize people
around the world for Israel's environment, to
protect Israel's environment and support its environmental movement.
Founded in 2001

7793 Greenpeace USA
702 H St NW
Suite 300
Washington, DC 20001-3876

202-462-1177
800-722-6995
FAX 202-462-4507
E-Mail: goa@wdc.greenpeace.org
Home Page: www.greenpeaceusa.org
Social Media: *Facebook, Twitter, YouTube*

John Passacantando, CEO
Ellen McPeake, COO

Leading independent campaigning organization
that uses non-violent direct action and creative
communication to expose global environmental
problems and to promote solutions that are essential to a green and peaceful future.
2.5M Members
Founded in 1971

7794 Honor The Earth
PO Box 63
607 Main Ave,
Callaway, MN 56521

218-375-3200
E-Mail: info@honorearth.org
Home Page: www.honorearth.org
Social Media: *Facebook, Twitter*

A nonprofit organization founded to raise
awareness and financial support for Indigenous
environmental justice.
Founded in 1993

**7795 Institute for Energy and
Environmental Research**
6935 Laurel Ave,
Suite 201
Takoma Park, MD 20912ÿ

301-270-5500
FAX 301-270-3029
E-Mail: info@ieer.org
Home Page: ieer.org
Social Media: *Facebook, Twitter, RSS*

Arjun Makhijani, President, Senior Engineer
Sadaf Rassoul Cameron, Vice President
David Close, Ph.D., Treasurer, Secretary
Annie Makhijani, Project Scientist
Christina Mills, Staff Scientist

Focuses on the environmental safety of nuclear
weapons production, ozone layer depletion, and
other issues relating to energy.
Founded in 1987

7796 Institute for Environmental Auditing
City Office Park
Tritton Road
Lincoln LNS7AS

152-254-0069
FAX 152-254-0090
E-Mail: info@iema.net

Home Page: www.iema.net
Social Media: *Twitter, LinkedIn, Google+*

Dr Diana Montgomery FIEMA, Chairman
Richard Powell OBE, Executive Director
Tim Balcon, Chief Executive
Martin Baxter FIEMA, CEnv, Executive
Director Policy
Dave Stanley. FIEMA, Cenv, Director

A professional organization of environmental
auditors.
100 Members

**7797 Institute for World Resource
Research**
PO Box 50303
Palo Alto, CA 94303-0303

630-910-1551
FAX 202-729-7610
Home Page: www.globalwarming.net

BJ Jefferson, Advertising/Sales

Supports those involved in all phases of developments in forestry and reforestation of northern nations including the US, Canada, Russia,
Sweden, Finland, Norway, China, Japan and
others. Its goal is to increase the worldwide understanding of the ecological and economic
roles of the northern forest regions of the
world.

**7798 Institute of Environmental Sciences
and Technology**
2340 South Arlington Heights Road
Suite 620
Arlington, IL 60005-4510

847-981-0100
FAX 847-981-4130
E-Mail: information@iest.org
Home Page: www.iest.org
Social Media: *Facebook, Twitter, LinkedIn*

Shawn Windley, President
Wei Sun, President-Elect
Kevin Stultz, Fiscal Vice President
Gordon Ely, Technical Vice President
Rick Meyer, Education Vice President

Is an international professional society that
serves members and the industries they represent through education and the development of
recommended practices and standards.
1600 Members
Founded in 1953

7799 Institute of Gas Technology
1700 S Mount Prospect Rd
Des Plaines, IL 60018-1804

847-768-0500
FAX 847-768-0501
E-Mail: publicrelations@gastechnology.org
Home Page: www.gastechnology.org
Social Media: *Twitter, LinkedIn, YouTube*

David Carroll, President & CEO
Ronald Snedic, Vice President/ Corporate
Devel.
Jim Ingold, Vice President, Finance
Edward Johnston, VP, Research Operations
Paul Armstrong, Director

Supports all those involved in the gas industry
worldwide, including energy industry production, consumption, reserves, imports and
prices.

**7800 Institute of Scrap Recycling
Industries**
1615 L St NW
Suite 600
Washington, DC 20036-5664

202-662-8500
FAX 202-626-0900
E-Mail: isri@isri.org
Home Page: www.isri.org

Social Media: *Facebook, Twitter, LinkedIn,
Instagram*

Doug Kramer, Chairman
Mark Lewon, Chair Elect
Brian Shine, Vice Chair
Gary Champlin, Secretary Treasurer
Robin K. Wiener, President

Supports all those involved in the scrap processing and recycling industry.
165 Members
1987 Attendees

**7801 International Association for Food
Protection**
6200 Aurora Ave
Suite 200W
Des Moines, IA 50322-2864

515-276-3344
800-369-6337
FAX 515-276-8655
E-Mail: info@foodprotection.org
Home Page: www.foodprotection.org
Social Media: *Facebook, Twitter, LinkedIn*

Alejandro S. Mazzotta, President
Linda J. Harris, President-Elect
Mickey Parish, Vice President
Tim Jackson, Secretary
David W. Tharp, Executive Director

Nonprofit, educational association of food protection professionals. The association is dedicated to the education and service of its
members, specifically, as well as industry
personnel.
3400 Members
Founded in 1911

**7802 International Association of Wildland
Fire**
1418 Washburn Street
Missoula, MT 59801

406-531-8264
888-440-4293
E-Mail: iawf@iawfonline.org
Home Page: www.iawfonline.org
Social Media: *Facebook, Twitter, LinkedIn*

Tom Zimmerman, President
Alan Goodwin, Vice President
David Moore, Treasurer
Kathy Clay, Secretary
Timothy Brown, Board Member

IWAF members are academics and professionals with an interest in wildland fires.
800 Members
Founded in 1990

**7803 International Council on
Nanotechnology - ICON**

214-494-2071
Home Page: icon.rice.edu

Vicki Colvin, Executive Director
Kristen Kulinowski, Director

A portal for information about the environmental, health, and safety aspects of
nanotechnology.

7804 International Ecotourism Society
427 North Tatnall Street
Wilmington, DE 19801-2230

202-506-5033
FAX 202-789-7279
E-Mail: info@ecotourism.org
Home Page: www.ecotourism.org
Social Media: *Facebook, Twitter, YouTube*

Kelly Bricker, Chair
Tony Charters, Vice Chair
Neal Inamdar, Director Finance/Administration

Society members include park managers, tour
operators, conservation professionals, and oth-

ers with an interest in the development of ecology-centered tourism.
900 Members
Founded in 1990

7805 **International Lead Zinc Research Organization**
1822 NC Highway 54 East
Suite 120
Durham, NC 27713

919-361-4647
FAX 919-361-1957
E-Mail: rputnam@ilzro.org
Home Page: www.ilzro.org

Stephen Wilkinson, President
Frank Goodwin, VP Materials Sciences
Scott Mooneyham, Treasurer
Rob Putnam, Director Communications

ILZRO members are miners and refiners of lead and zinc. Trade association of the lead and zinc industry worldwide. Focus on research and development to detect new uses for the metals and refine existing uses.
Founded in 1958

7806 **International Society for Ecological Economics**
15 River Street
#204
Boston, MA 02108

703-790-1745
FAX 703-790-2672
E-Mail: secretariat@ecoeco.org
Home Page: http://www.isecoeco.org/
Social Media: *Facebook, Twitter, LinkedIn, Google+, Pinterest*

Dr. Marina Fischer-Kowalski, President
Sabine O'Hara, President-Elect
Anne Carter Aitken, Treasurer
Bina Agarwal, Past President
Rashid Hassan, Board of Director

Members are researchers, academics, and other professionals who study the impact of economic models and policies on the environment.
750 Members
Founded in 1989

7807 **Isaak Walton League**
707 Conservation Lane
Gaithersburg, MD 20878

301-548-0150
800-453-5463
FAX 301-548-0146
E-Mail: info@iwla.org
Home Page: www.iwla.org
Social Media: *Facebook, Twitter, LinkedIn, Google+, Pinterest*

Jodi Arndt Labs, Chair
Shawn Gallagher, President
Jeff Deschamps, Vice President
Jim Storer, Secretary
Walter Lynn Jr., Treasurer

Protects America's outdoors through education, community-based conservation, and promoting outdoor recreation.
37000 Members
Founded in 1922

7808 **Keep America Beautiful**
1010 Washington Boulevard
Stamford, CT 6901

203-659-3000
FAX 203-659-3001
E-Mail: info@kab.org
Home Page: www.kab.org
Social Media: *Facebook, Twitter, Tumblr, YouTube, Pinterest*

Howard Ungerleider, Chairman
Tom Waldeck, Treasurer
Thomas H. Tamoney, Jr., Secretary

Shannon Reiter, President
Gregory H. Ray, Senior Vice President
Nonprofit organization that builds and sustains vibrant communities.
Founded in 1953

7809 **League of Conservation Votersÿ**
1920 L Street, NW
Suite 800
Washington, DC 20036

202-785-8683
FAX 202-835-0491
E-Mail: seth_stein@lcv.org.
Home Page: www.lcv.org
Social Media: *Facebook, Twitter, YouTube, Flickr*

Carol Browner, Chair
Sherwood Boehlert, Vice Chair
Trip Van Noppen, Treasurer
Carrie Clark, Secretary
Gene Karpinski, President

A political advocacy organization that advocates for sound environmental policies and elects pro-environmental candidates who will adopt and implement such policies.

7810 **Marine Technology Society**
1100 H St., Nw
Suite LL-100
Washington, DC 20005

202-717-8705
FAX 202-347-4302
E-Mail: membership@mtsociety.org
Home Page: www.mtsociety.org
Social Media: *Facebook, Twitter, LinkedIn, YouTube*

Ray Toll, President
Donna Kocak, President-Elect
Andy Clark, VP of Industry and Technology
Liesl Hotaling, VP of Education and Research
Justin Manley, VP of Gov. & Public Affairs

Addresses coastal zone management, marine, mineral and energy resources, marine environmental protection, and ocean engineering issues.
2M Members
Founded in 1963

7811 **Midwest for Environmental Science and Public Policy**
1845 N Farwell Avenue
Suite 100
Milwaukee, WI 53202

414-271-7280
FAX 414-273-7293
Home Page: www.mcespp.org

Patrice Ann Morrow, Chair
Jeffery A Foran, President/CEO

For citizens concerned with environmental protection.

7812 **NORA: Association of Responsible Recyclers**
7250 Heritage Village Plaza,
Suite 201
Gainesville, VA 20155

703-753-4277
FAX 703-753-2445
E-Mail: sparker@noranews.org
Home Page: www.noranews.org

Bill Hinton, President
Chris Bergstrom, Executive Vice President
Roy Schumacher, Vice President
Brandon Velek, Past President
Ellie Bruce, Board Of Director

Is a trade association representing the interests of companies in the United States engaged in the safe recycling of used oil, antifreeze, waste water and oil filters.
Founded in 1984

7813 **National Association for Environmental Management**
1612 K St NW
1002
Washington, DC 20006-2830

202-986-6616
800-391-6236
FAX 202-530-4408
E-Mail: programs@naem.org
Home Page: www.naem.org
Social Media: *Facebook, Twitter, LinkedIn*

Rick Taylor, President
Kris Morico, 1st Vice President
Mark Hause, 2nd Vice President
Alan Leibowitz, Treasurer
Stephen Evanoff, Ex-Officio Member - Past President

Dedicated to advancing the profession of environmental management and supports the professional corporate and facility environmental manager.
1000+ Members
Founded in 1990

7814 **National Association for PET Containers**
7310 Turfway Road
Suite 550
Florence, KY 41042

859-372-6635
FAX 707-935-1998
E-Mail: n4mayshun@napcor.com
Home Page: www.napcor.com
Social Media: *Facebook*

Rick Moore, Executive Director
Resa Dimino, Director Of Public Policy
Kate Eagles, Project Director

National association for the PET plastic industry. Promotes the use of PET plastic packaging and facilitates the recycling of PET containers.
Frequency: Bi-Monthly
Founded in 1987

7815 **National Association of Environmental Professionals**
PO Box 460
Collingswood, NJ 08108

856-283-7816
FAX 856-210-1619
E-Mail: naep@bowermanagementservices.com
Home Page: www.naep.org
Social Media: *Facebook, LinkedIn*

Brock Hoegh, CEPÿ, President
David Dickson, Vice President
Courtney Arena, Treasurer
Kristin Bennett, Secretary
Harold Draper,ÿD.Sc., CEPÿ, Immediate Past President

Our mission is to be the interdisciplinary organization dedicated to developing the highest standards of ethics and proficiency in the environmental professions. Our members are public and private sector professionals who promote excellence in decision-making in light of the environmental, social, and economic impacts of those decisions.

7816 **National Association of Local Government Environmental Professionals**
1001 Connecticut Avenue
Suite 405
Washington, DC 20036-1532

202-337-4503
FAX 202-429-5290
E-Mail: nalgep@nalgep.org
Home Page: www.nalgep.org
Social Media: *Facebook*

Ellen Walkowiak, Chair
John Stufflebean, Vice Chair

Douglas MacCourt, Treasurer
Lee Ilan, Secretary
Chris Bird, Director

Is a national organization representing local government professionals responsible for environmental compliance and the development of local environmental policy. NALGEP brings together local environmental officials to share information on practices, conduct policy projects, promote environmental training and education, and communicate the view of local officials on national environmental issues.
150 Members
Founded in 1993

7817 National Audubon Society

225 Varick Street
New York, NY 10014

212-979-3000
E-Mail: webmaster@audubon.org
Home Page: www.audubon.org
Social Media: *Facebook, Twitter, YouTube*

Conserves and restores natural ecosystems, focusing on birds, other wildlife, and their habitats for the benefit of humanity and the earth's biological diversity.
50000 Members
Founded in 1992

7818 National Center for Appropriate Technology

3040 Continental Drive
Butte, MT 59702

406-494-4572
800-275-6228
FAX 406-494-2905
Home Page: www.ncat.org
Social Media: *Facebook, Twitter, LinkedIn, RSS, Pinterest*

Gene Brady, Chairman
Randall Chapman, Vice Chairman
Jeannie Jertson, Secretary
Brian Castelli, Treasurer
John Colgan, Commissioner

Their mission is to help people by championing small-scale, local, and sustainable solutions to reduce poverty, promote healthy communities, and protect natural resources.
Founded in 1976

7819 National Conference of Local Environmental Health Administrators

1010 South Third Street
Dayton, WA 99328

509-382-2181
FAX 360-382-2942
E-Mail: David_Riggs@co.columbia.wa.us
Home Page: www.ncleha.org

A professional association for supervisors, administrators and managers of environmental health programs in local agencies.

7820 National Council for Science and the Environment

1101 17th Street NW
Suite 250
Washington, DC 20036ÿ

202-530-5810
FAX 202-628-4311
E-Mail: NCSE@NCSEonline.org
Home Page: www.ncseonline.org
Social Media: *Facebook, Twitter, LinkedIn, YouTube, Flickr*

Peter Saundry, Ph.D., Executive Director
Andi Glashow, Director, Finance
Sudeep Vyapari, Ph.D., Associate Executive Director
Jessica Soule, Director, EnvironMentors
David Blockstein, Ph.D., Senior Scientist, Dr. Education

A U.S. based nonprofit organization that improves the scientific basis for environmental decision-making.

7821 National Environmental Balancing Bureau

8575 Grovemont Circle
Gaithersburg, MD 20877-4121

301-977-3698
866-497-4447
FAX 301-977-9589
E-Mail: karen@nebb.org
Home Page: www.nebb.org

Jean-Paul Le Blanc, President
Jim Kelleher,, President-Elect
Donald E. Hill, Vice President
Jim Whorton, Treasurer
James Huber, Past President

NEBB is an international certification assocaition for firms that deliver high performance building systems. Members perform testing, adjusting and balancing (TAB) of heating, ventilating and air-conditioning systems, commission and retro-commission building systems commissioning, execute sound and vibration testing, and test and certify lab fume hoods and electronic and bio clean rooms. NEBB holds the highest standards in certification.
Founded in 1971

7822 National Environmental Development Association

One Thomas Circle NW
10th Floor
Washington, DC 20006

202-332-2933
FAX 202-530-0659
Home Page: www.nedacap.org

Phil Clapp, President
Steve Hellem, Executive Director

NEDA members are companies and other organizations concerned with balancing environmental and economic interests to obtain both a clean environment and a strong economy.
Founded in 1973

7823 National Environmental, Safety and Health Training Association

2700 N. Central Avenue
Suite 900
Phoenix, AZ 85004-1147

602-956-6099
FAX 602-234-1867
E-Mail: neshta@neshta.org
Home Page: www.neshta.org
Social Media: *Facebook, Twitter, LinkedIn, Google+, Pinterest, Tumblr*

Myrtle I. Turner-Harris, President
Jeffery K. Dennis,ÿCET, CSP, CHMM, Vice President
Dave Owings,ÿCET, General Manager
Bruce V. Guiliani,ÿCET, CSP, Dir. Of Saftey Loss & Prevention
David L. Galt, Managing Editor for Safety

A non-profit educational society for environmental, safety, health and other technical training and adult education professionals. Mission is to promote trainer competency through trainer skills training, continuing education, voluntary certification, peer networking and the adoption of national and international training and trainer standards.
Founded in 1977

7824 National Institutes for Water Resources

47 Harkness Road
Pelham, MA 10002

413-253-5686
FAX 413-253-1309

E-Mail: tracy@uidaho.edu
Home Page: niwr.net

Jeffery Allen, President
Reagan Waskom, President-Elect
John Tracy, Secretary-Treasurer

NIWRD represents state and territorial Water Research Institutes and Centers in collective activities to implement the provisions of the Water Resources Act of 1984, and subsequesnt federal legislation. NIWR networks these separate institutes into a coordinated unit, represented by 8 regional groupings, and facilitates the response of the Water Research Institutes and its membership to other mutual concerns and interests in water resources.
54 Members
Founded in 1974

7825 National Parks Conservation Association

777 6th St. NW
Suite 700
Washington, DC 20001-3723

202-223-6722
800-628-7275
FAX 202-454-3333
E-Mail: npca@npca.org
Home Page: www.npca.org
Social Media: *Facebook, Twitter*

Theresa Pierno, President & CEO

Advocates for the preservation of America's national parks and historical sites.
Founded in 1919

7826 National Registry of Environmental Professionals

PO Box 2099
Glenview, IL 60025

847-724-6631
FAX 847-724-4223
E-Mail: nrep@nrep.org
Home Page: www.nrep.org
Social Media: *Facebook, Twitter, LinkedIn, YouTube*

Scott Spear, Executive Chairperson
Richard Young, PhD, REM, P, Executive Director
Edward C. Beck, PhD, REM, PE,, Director
Charles J. McAfee, REM, CEA,, Director
Marie Hunter , REM, Director

To promote legal and professional recognition of individuals possessing education, training and experience as environmental managers, engineers, technologists, scientists and technicians-and to consolidate that recognition in one centralized source-so that the public, government, employers and insurers can justify the importance and acceptance of such individuals to carry out operations and management of environmental activities.
17000 Members
Founded in 1983
Mailing list available for rent

7827 National Society of Environmental Consultants

PO Box 460
Collingswood, NJ 08108

856-283-7816
FAX 856-210-1619
E-Mail: naep@bowermanagementservices.com
Home Page: www.naep.org

Brock Hoegh, CEPÿ, President
David Dickson, Vice President
Courtney Arena, Treasurer
Kristin Bennett, Secretary
Harold Draper,ÿD.Sc., CEPÿ, Immediate Past President

Supports all activities of environmental consultants.

600 Members
Founded in 1992

7828 National Solid Wastes Management Association
4301 Connecticut Ave NW
Suite 300
Washington, DC 20008-2304

202-244-4700
800-424-2869
FAX 202-966-4824
E-Mail: wa@envasns.org
Home Page: www.wasterecycling.org
Social Media: *Facebook, Twitter, Google +*

Sharon H. Kneiss, President
Kevin Kraushaar, Esq., CAE, VP, Gov. Affairs & Chapters
Christopher Doherty, VP, Communications
Sheila R. Alkire, Director, Education
Tiffany Jones, Director, Certification

Supports all those involved in the environment industry, especially the handling, transportation and disposal of infectious wastes.

7829 National Wildlife Federation
PO Box 1583
Merrifield, VA 22116-1583

703-438-6000
800-822-9919
FAX 703-438-3570
Home Page: www.nwf.org
Social Media: *Facebook, Twitter, LinkedIn, YouTube*

Bruce Wallace, Chair
Paul Beaudette, Eastern Vice Chair
Clark Bullard, Central Vice Chair
Kent Salazar, Western Vice Chair
Brian Bashore, Director

Encourages management of natural resources. Gives financial aid to local groups and graduate studies. Conducts guided nature trail tours, produces programs and sponsors competitions.
4.5MM Members
Founded in 1936

7830 National Wildlife Refuge Associationÿ
1001 Connecticut Ave. NW
Suite 905
Washington, DC 20036

202-417-3803
E-Mail: nwra@refugeassociation.org
Home Page: refugeassociation.org
Social Media: *Facebook, Twitter, LinkedIn, RSS*

Rebecca Rubin, Chair
Donal O'Brien, Vice Chair
David Houghton, President
Anne Truslow, VP, Chief Operating Officer
Desiree Sorenson-Groves, VP, Government Affairs

An independent membership organization that works to conserve American wildlife.

7831 National Woodland Owners Association
374 Maple Ave E
Suite 310
Vienna, VA 22180-4718

703-255-2300
800-470-8733
E-Mail: argow@nwoa.net
Home Page: www.nationalforestry.net

Keith A Argow, President
Bert Udell, Executive Committee Chair
Gerald A Rose, Midwest Regional VP

Provides timely information about forestry and forest practices with news from Washington, DC and state capitals. Written for non-in-

dustrial land owners. Includes state landowner association news.
39M Members
Founded in 1983

7832 Native Forest Councilÿ
PO Box 2190
Eugene, OR 97402

541-688-2600
FAX 541-461-2156
E-Mail: info@forestcouncil.org
Home Page: forestcouncil.org
Social Media: *Facebook, Twitter, Vimeo, YouTube*

Bill Barton, Board of Director
Allan Branscomb, Board of Director
Calvin Hececta, Board of Director
Timothy Hermach, Board of Director
Timothy Moxley, Board of Director

Provides news and resources for the protection of publicly owned lands from logging, mining, grazing, drilling, and off-road vehicles.
Founded in 1987

7833 Natural Resources Defense Council
40 W 20th St
New York, NY 10011-4231

212-727-2700
FAX 212-727-1773
E-Mail: nrdcinfo@nrdc.org
Home Page: www.nrdc.org
Social Media: *Facebook, Twitter, YouTube, Tumblr, RSS*

Daniel R. Tishman, Chair
Frederick A.O. Schwarz Jr., Chair Emeritus
Wendy K. Neu, Vice Chair
Alan F. Horn, Vice Chair
Patricia Bauman, Vice Chair

Dedicated to the wise management of natural resources through research, public education and the development of effective public policies.
50000 Members
Founded in 1970

7834 Nature's Classroom
19 Harrington Rd.
Charlton, MA 1507

508-248-2741
800-433-8375
FAX 508-248-2745
E-Mail: info@naturesclassroom.org
Home Page: www.naturesclassroom.org
Social Media: *Facebook*

A nonprofit outdoor environmental education program.

7835 NatureServe
4600 N. Fairfax Dr.
7th Floor
Arlington, VA 22203

703-908-1800
FAX 703-229-1670
E-Mail: info@natureserve.org
Home Page: www.natureserve.org
Social Media: *Facebook, Twitter, LinkedIn, YouTube, Vimeo, Flickr, RSS*

Mary Klein, President/ CEO
Lori Scott, Chief Information Officer
Ravi Shankar, CFO/ COO
Leslie Honey, VP, Conservation Services
Don Kent, Director of Network Relations

A nonprofit organization that provides proprietary wildlife conservation-related data, tools, and services to private and government clients, partner organizations, and the public.
Founded in 1974

7836 Negative Population Growth
2861 Duke St.
Suite 36
Alexandria, VA 22314

703-370-9510
FAX 703-370-9514
Home Page: www.npg.org
Social Media: *Facebook, Twitter, LinkedIn, RSS, YouTube*

Donald Mann, President
Craig Lewis, Executive Vice President
Tracy Canada, Deputy Director
Dianeÿ Saco, Board of Director
Sharon Marks, Board of Director

A membership organization in the United States that works on overpopulation issues and advocates a gradual reduction in U.S. and world population.
Founded in 1972

7837 North American Association for Environmental Education
2000 P Street NW
Suite 540
Washington, DC 20036

202-419-0412
FAX 202-419-0415
E-Mail: info@naaee.org
Home Page: www.naaee.org
Social Media: *Facebook*

Jose Pepe Marcos-Iga, President
Judy Braus, Executive Director
Susan McGuire, Secretary
Mary Ford, Treasurer
Flisa Stevenson, At-Large Board Member

Purpose is to assist and support the work of individuals and groups engaged in environmental education, research and service.
1500 Members
Founded in 1971

7838 North American Chapter - International Society for Ecological Modelling
550 M Ritchie Highway
PMB 255
Severna Park, MD 21146

E-Mail: webmaster@isemna.org
Home Page: www.isemna.org

Sven E. Jorgensen, President
Tarzan Legovic, Secretary-General
David A. Mauriello, Treasurer
Brian D. Faith, President, North America
Guy Larocque,, Secretary, North America

Promotes the international exchange of general knowledge, ideas and scientific results in the area of the application of systems analysis and simulation to ecology, environmental science and natural resource management using mathematical and computer modelling of ecological systems.
150 Members
Founded in 1983

7839 North American Lake Management Society
PO Box 5443
Madison, WI 53705-443

608-233-2836
FAX 608-233-3186
E-Mail: info@nalms.org
Home Page: www.nalms.org
Social Media: *Facebook, LinkedIn, Flickr*

Reed Green, President
Julie Chambers, President-Elect
Sara Peel, Secretary
Mike Perry, Treasurer
Terry McNabb, CLM, Past President

Members are academics, lake managers and others interested in furthering the understand-

ing of lake ecology. The North American Lake Management Society's mission is to forge partnerships among citizens, scientists and professionals to foster the management and protection of lakes and reservoirs for today and tomorrow. Please call for rate information.
1700 Members
Founded in 1980

7840 Oceana
1350 Connecticut Ave.
5th Fl.
Washington, DC 20036

202-833-3900
FAX 202-833-2070
E-Mail: info@oceana.org
Home Page: oceana.org
Social Media: *Facebook, Twitter, Instagram, YouTube, Google+*

Andrew Sharpless, Chief Executive Officer
Simon Sidamon-Eristoff, Chair
Environmental organization focused solely on the protection and restoration of the world's oceans.
Founded in 2001

7841 Organic Seed Alliance
PO Box 772
Port Townsend, WA 98368-0772

360-385-7192
FAX 360-385-7455
E-Mail: info@seedalliance.org
Home Page: www.seedalliance.org
Social Media: *Facebook, Twitter*

Sebastian Aguilar, President
Atina Diffley, Vice President
Sean Schmidt, Secretary
Zea Sonnabend, Treasurer
Micaela Colley, Executive Director
Organic Seed Alliance suppports the ethical development and stewardship of the genetic resources of agricultural seed.
25M Members
Founded in 1975

7842 Plant Growth Regulation Society of America
Rhone-Poulenc, Ag Company
1018 Duke Street
Alexandria, VA 22314

703-836-4606
FAX 706-883-8215
E-Mail: dmancini@ashs.org
Home Page: www.pgrsa.org
Social Media: *Facebook, Twitter, RSS*

Dr. Carl Sams, President
Dr. Holly Little, 1st Vice President
Mr. Michael Rethwisch, 2nd Vice President
Dr. Tim Spann, Past President
Dr. Chris Gunter, Secretary
Functions as a nonprofit educational and scientific organization.
325 Members
Founded in 1973

7843 Rachel Carson Council
8600 Irvington Avenue
Bethesda, MD 20817

301-214-2400
E-Mail: office@rachelcarsoncouncil.org
Home Page: rachelcarsoncouncil.org
Social Media: *Twitter*

Diana Post, Executive Director
David B McGrath, Treasurer
Dr Diana Post, Secretary
Library and clearinghouse on pesticide toxicity, lower risk alternatives for pest control, and Rachel Carson. Produces publications and sponsors conventions/meetings on these topics, issues newsletter. Nonprofit.
Founded in 1965

7844 Rainforest Action Network (RAN)
425 Bush St.
Suite 300
San Francisco, CA 94108

415-398-4404
E-Mail: answers@ran.org
Home Page: www.ran.org
Social Media: *Facebook, Twitter, YouTube*

Noel R. Natividad, Chief Operating Officer
Lindsey Allen, Executive Director
Environmental organization focused on forest systems.

7845 Renewable Fuels Association
425 Third Street, SW
Suite 1150
Washington, DC 20024

202-289-3835
FAX 202-289-7519
E-Mail: info@ethanolrfa.org
Home Page: www.ethanolrfa.org
Social Media: *Facebook, Twitter, LinkedIn, YouTube, Google+, Instagram*

Randall Doyal,, Chairman
Mick Henderson, Vice Chairman
Jim Seurer, Treasurer
Bob Dinneen, President
Geoff Cooper, Senior Vice President
Members are companies and individuals involved in the production and use of ethanol.
55 Members
Founded in 1981

7846 Renewable Natural Resources Foundation
6010 Executive Boulevard
5th Floor
Bethesda, MD 20852-3827

301-493-9101
FAX 301-770-9104
E-Mail: info@rnrf.org
Home Page: www.rnrf.org
Social Media: *Facebook, Twitter*

Richard A. Engberg, Chairman
John E. Durrant, Vice-Chairman
Robert D. Day, Executive Director
Sarah Gerould, Director
Erik Hankin, Director
A consortium of professional and scientific societies whose members are concerned with the advancement of research, education, scientific practice and policy formulation for the conservation, replenishment and use of the earth's renewable natural resources.
14 Members
Founded in 1972

7847 Resource Policy Institute
1525 Selby Avenue
Ste. 304
Los Angeles, CA 90024-5796

310-470-9711
Home Page: www.bu.edu/hrpi

Dr Arthur Purcell, Director/Founder
Education, and consulting research group concerned with environmental policies, technologies, and management strategies..
Founded in 1975

7848 Safe Buildings Alliance
Metropolitan Square
655 15th Street NW
Suite 1200
Washington, DC 20005-5701

202-879-5120
FAX 202-638-2103
Home Page: sba.lfpc.org

Association of building products companies that formerly manufactured asbestos-containing

materials for building construction. Its main focus is to provide public information on issues relating to asbestos in building. SBA promotes a reasonable, safe response to the problem of asbestos in buildings, including the development of uniform, objective Federal and State standards for asbestos identification and abatement, nonremoval alternatives and the regulation of inspectors.
Founded in 1984

7849 Sagamore Institute of the Adirondacks Inc
Great Camp Sagamore
PO Box 40
Raquette Lake, NY 13436-0040

315-354-5311
FAX 315-354-5851
E-Mail: info@greatcampsagamore.org
Home Page: www.greatcampsagamore.org
Social Media: *Facebook, YouTube*

Garet Livermore, Executive Director
Bob Henisler, Superintendant
Dr. Jeffery Flagg, Program Director
Hannah Gibbons, Program Manager
Andrew Gillcrist, Director Of Family Programs
Non-profit 501c3 National Historic Landmark, former retreat of the Vanderbilts, offering educational programs on history, ecology and culture of the Adirondack Park.

7850 Sierra Club
85 Second St.
2nd Fl.
San Francisco, CA 94105

415-977-5500
FAX 415-977-5797
E-Mail: information@sierraclub.org
Home Page: www.sierraclub.org
Social Media: *Facebook, Twitter*

Michael Brune, Executive Director
Lou Barnes, Chief Financial Officer
Founded in 1892, the largest environmental organization in the United States campaigns for the protection of endangered species, habitat conservation, environmental protection and an end to the use of fossil fuels.
Founded in 1892

7851 Silicones Environmental Health and Safety
700 Second St., NE
Washington, DC 20002

202-249-7000
FAX 202-249-6100
E-Mail: sehsc@sehsc.com
Home Page: www.sehsc.com
Social Media: *Facebook, Twitter*

Calvin M. Dooley, President
Dell Perelman, Chief Of Staff & General Counsel
Raymond J. O'Bryan, Chief Financial Officer
Nacole B. Hinton, Managing Director
Anne Womack Kolton, VP Of Communications
A not-for-profit trade association comprised of North American silicone chemical producers and importers.
6 Members
Founded in 1971

7852 Society for Ecological Restoration International
1017 O Street NW
Washington, DC 20001

202-299-9518
FAX 270-626-5485
E-Mail: info@ser.org
Home Page: www.ser.org
Social Media: *Facebook, Twitter, LinkedIn*

Alan Unwin, Chair
Cara R. Nelson, Vice Chair

Stuart Allison, Secretary
Jim Hallet, Treasurer
James Aronson, Representative - At- Large

SER members are academics, scientists, environmental consultants, government agencies and others with an interest in ecological restoration.
2300 Members
Founded in 1988

7853 Society for Environmental Geochemistry and Health

4698 S Forrest Avenue
Springfield, MO 65810

417-851-1166
FAX 417-881-6920
E-Mail: DRBGWIXSON@aol.com
Home Page: www.segh.net

Dr Chaosheng Zhang, President
Dr Chaoshengÿ Zhang, European Chair
Kyoung-Woong Kim, Asia/Pacific Chair
Anthea Brown, Membership Secretary/Treasurer
Malcolm Brown, Secretary

Promotes a multi-disciplinary approach to research in fields of geochemistry and health to facilitate and expand communication among scientists within these disciplines and to advance knowledge in the area.
400 Members
Founded in 1971

7854 Society for Human Ecology

College of the Atlantic
105 Eden Street
Bar Harbor, ME 04609-0180

207-801-5630
FAX 207-288-3780
E-Mail: info@societyforhumanecology.org
Home Page: www.societyforhumanecology.org
Social Media: *Facebook, Twitter*

Rob Dyball, President
Lee Cerveny, Second Vice President
Chiho Watanabe, Third Vice President-International
Rob Lilieholm, Treasurer
Barbara Carter, Secretary

SHE members are academics, scientists, health professionals and others with an interest in studying the interrelationship of man's actions and his environment.
150 Members
Founded in 1981

7855 Society for Occupational and Environmental Health

111 North Bridge Road
#21-01 Peninsula Plaza
Singapore 179098

E-Mail: oehsadmin@gmail.com
Home Page: www.oehs.org.sg

Dr. Lee Lay Tin, President
Mr. Eric Ng, Vice President
Kam Wai Kuen, Honorary Secretary
Dr. Lucy Leong, Honorary Treasurer
Dr. Gregory Chan, Committee Members

Members include physicians, hygienists, economists, laboratory scientists, academicians, labor and industry representatives, or anyone interested in occupational and/or environmental health. Serves as a forum for the presentation of scientific data and the exchange of information among members; sponsors conferences and meetings which address specific problem areas and policy questions.
300 Members
Founded in 1972

7856 Society of Environmental Journalists

Po Box 2492
Jenkintown, PA 19046

215-884-8174
FAX 215-884-8175
E-Mail: sej@sej.org
Home Page: www.sej.org
Social Media: *Facebook, Twitter*

Jeff Burnside, President
Jennifer Bogo, 1st VP & Programs Chair
Kate Sheppard, 2nd VP & Membership Chair
Gloria Gonzalez, Treasurer
Bobby Magill, Secretary

To advance public understanding of environmental isues by improving the quality, accuracy, and visibility of environmental reporting.
Founded in 1990

7857 Society of Environmental Toxicology and Chemistry

229 South Baylen Street
2nd Floor
Pensacola, FL 32502

850-469-1500
FAX 888-296-4136
E-Mail: setac@setac.org
Home Page: www.setac.org
Social Media: *Facebook, Twitter, LinkedIn*

Paul van den Brink, President
Tim Canfield, Vice President
Fred Heimbach, Treasurer

Is a professional society established to promote the use of multidisciplinary approaches to solving problems of the impact of chemicals and technology on the environment. SETA members are professionals in the fields of chemistry, toxicology, biology, ecology, atmospheric sciences, health sciences, earth sciences, and environmental engineering.
4000 Members
Founded in 1979

7858 Society of Exploration Geophysicists

8801 South Yale
Suite 500
Tulsa, OK 74137-3575

918-497-5500
877-778-5463
FAX 918-497-5557
E-Mail: web@seg.org
Home Page: www.seg.org
Social Media: *Facebook, Twitter, LinkedIn*

Mary Fleming, Executive Director
Vladimir Grechka, Editor

The Society of Exploration Geophysicists/SEG is a not-for-profit organization that promotes the science of geophysics and the education of applied geophysicists. SEG fosters the expert and ethical practice of geophysics in the exploration and development of natural resources, in characterizing the near surface, and in mitigating earth hazards.
Founded in 1930

7859 Soil and Plant Analysis Council

347 North Shores Circle
Windsor, CO 80550

970-686-5702
E-Mail: rmiller@lamar.colostate.edu
Home Page: www.spcouncil.com

Rao Mylavarapu, President
Robert Mikkelsen, Vice President
Rigas Karamanos, Past President
Robert Miller, Secretary/Treasurer
Brad Joern, Individual Class Member

Supports all those involved in the analysis of soil and plants.

7860 Soil and Water Conservation Society

945 SW Ankeny Rd
Ankeny, IA 50023-9764

515-289-2331
800-843-7645
FAX 515-289-1227
E-Mail: swcs@swcs.org
Home Page: www.swcs.org
Social Media: *Facebook, Twitter, LinkedIn*

Mark Berkland, President
Jon Scholl, Vice-President
Mike Collins, Secretary
Susan Meadows, Treasurer
Wendi Goldsmith, NE Region Director

SWCS is a nonprofit scientific and educational organization that serves as an advocate for conservation professionals and for science-based conservation practice, programs, and policy.
5000+ Members
Founded in 1943

7861 Southeastern Association of Fish and Wildlife Agencies

27 Sylwood Place
Jackson, MS 39209

601-668-6916
FAX 850-893-6204
E-Mail: crayhopkins@bellsouth.netÿ
Home Page: www.seafwa.org

Bob Ziehmer, President
Gordon Myers, Vice President
Robert Barham, Secretary/Treasurer
Nick Wiley, Past President
Ed Carter, At Larger Executive Board Member

An organization whose members are the state agencies with primary responsibility for management and protection of the fish and wildlife resources in 16 states, Puerto Rico and the US Virgin Islands.
18 Members
Founded in 1947

7862 Steel Recycling Institute

680 Andersen Drive
Pittsburgh, PA 15220-2700

412-922-2772
800-876-7274
FAX 412-922-3213
Home Page: www.recycle-steel.org
Social Media: *Facebook, Twitter, YouTube, Google+*

William H Heenan Jr, President

Promotes steel recycling and works to forge a coalition of steelmakers, can manufacturers, legislators, government officials, solid waste managers, business and consumer groups.
Founded in 1988

7863 Student Conservation Association

4245 North Fairfax Drive
Suite 825
Arlington, VA 22203

703-524-2441
FAX 603-543-1828
E-Mail: jcota@thesca.org
Home Page: www.thesca.org
Social Media: *Facebook, Twitter, YouTube*

Jamie Berman Matyas, President and CEO
Karen Davis, SVP & Chief Advancement Officer
Aimee Dobrzeniecki, Chief Financial Officer
Barbara Gonzalez-McIntosh, Chief Counsel
Laura Herrin, Senior VP, Programs

To build the next generation of conservation leaders and inspire lifelong stewardship of our environment and communities by engaging young people in hands-on service to the land.
35000 Members
Founded in 1957

7864 Surfaces in Biomaterials Foundation
1000 Westgate Drive
Suite 252
St Paul, MN 55114-8679

651-290-6267
FAX 651-290-2266
E-Mail: memberservices@surfaces.org
Home Page: www.surfaces.org
Social Media: *Twitter, LinkedIn*

Dr. Aylvin A. Dias, President
Chander Chawla, President-Elect
Bill Theilacker, Vice President
Mark Smith PhD, Treasurer
Joe McGonigle, Secretary

Dedicated to exploring creative solutions to technical challenges at the BioInterface by fostering education and multidisciplinary cooperation among industrial, academic, clinical and regulatory communities.
250 Members

7865 Test Boring Association
181 Beagle Club Road
Washington, PA 15301

722- 22- 299
888-267-4647
FAX 724-228-2992
E-Mail: jrselvoski@testboringservices.com
Home Page: www.testboring.com

Patrizia Zita, Management Executive

Contractors engaged in test boring and core drilling.
Founded in 1941

7866 The African Wild Dog Conservancyÿ
208 N California Ave.
Silver City, NM 88061

E-Mail: lycaonpictus@awdconservancy.org
Home Page: www.awdconservancy.org

A nonprofit, non-governmental organization working with local communities, and national and international stakeholders to conserve the African wilddog through scientific research and education.
Founded in 2001

7867 The Center for International Environmental Law
1350 Connecticut Avenue NW
Suite #1100
Washington, DC 20036

202-785-8700
FAX 202-785-8701
E-Mail: info@ciel.org
Home Page: www.ciel.org
Social Media: *Facebook, Twitter, LinkedIn, RSS*

Carroll Muffett, President/ CEO
Jeffrey Wanha, Dir., Finance & Admin.
Marcos A. Orellana, Director, Human Rights
Cameron Aishton, Administrator
Kevin Parker, Development Directorÿ

Nonprofit organization that provides environmental legal services in international and comparative environmental law.

7868 The Indoor Air Institute
2548 Empire Grade
Santa Cruz, CA 95060

831-426-0148
FAX 831-426-6522
E-Mail: info@IndAir.org
Home Page: indair.org

Hal Levin, President
William Fisk, Vice President
William Nazaroff, Vice President

Supports all those involved with indoor air quality and climate with training, education, resource materials and an annual conference.

7869 The Marine Mammal Center
2000 Bunker Road
Fort Cronkhite
Sausalito, CA 94965-2619

415-289-7325
415-289-SEAL
E-Mail: info@tmmc.org
Home Page: www.marinemammalcenter.org
Social Media: *Facebook, Twitter, RSS, Pinterest, YouTube*

Marci Davis, Chief Financial Officer
Dr. Jeff Boehm, Executive Director
Nancy Sackson, Dir., Marketing & Development
Rachel Bergren, Education Director
Heather Groninger, Human Resources Director

A private, nonprofit U.S. organization established for the purpose of rescuing, rehabilitating, and releasing marine mammals who are injured, ill, or abandoned.
Founded in 1975

7870 The Nature Conservancy
4245 North Fairfax Drive
Suite 100
Arlington, VA 22203-1606

703-841-5300
800-628-6860
E-Mail: members@tnc.org
Home Page: www.nature.org
Social Media: *Facebook, Twitter, LinkedIn, Google+, Flickr*

Craig O. McCaw, Chairman
James E. Rogers, Vice Chair
Frank e. Loy, Secretary
Mark R. Tercek, President & CEO
Muneer A. Satter, Treasurer

The leading conservation organization working around the world to protect ecologically important lands and waters for nature and people. Addresses the most pressing conservation threats at the largest scale.
Founded in 1984

7871 The School for Field Studies
100 Cummings Center
Suite 534-G
Beverly, MA 1915

978-741-3567
800-989-4418
FAX 978-922-3835
E-Mail: jcramer@fieldstudies.org
Home Page: www.fieldstudies.org
Social Media: *Facebook, Twitter, LinkedIn, YouTube, Google+, Flickr*

Terry Andreas, Chairman Of Board
James A. Cramer, President
Leslie Granese, B.A, Vice President
Carrie Camp, B.S, Chief Finance Officer
Yizette Colon, M.B.A, Accounting Manager

Creates transformative study abroad experiences through field-basedlearning and research.
Founded in 1980

7872 The Wilderness Society
1615 M St NW
Washington, DC 20036-3258

202-833-2300
800-843-9453
FAX 202-429-3945
E-Mail: member@tws.org
Home Page: wilderness.org
Social Media: *Facebook, Twitter, LinkedIn, Pinterest, YouTube*

Jamie Williams, President
Thomas Tepper, VP, Finance & Administration
Melyssa Watson, Vice President, Conservation
Kitty Thomas, VP, Communications & Marketing
Ame Hellman, VP, Philanthropy

An American nonprofit organization that is dedicated to protecting wilderness areas as national public lands in the United States.
200M Members
Founded in 1935

7873 Union of Concerned Scientists
Two Brattle Sq.
Cambridge, MA 02138-3780

617-547-5552
FAX 617-864-9405
Home Page: www.ucsusa.org
Social Media: *Facebook, Twitter, Google+*

James J. McCarthyÿ, Chair
Peter A. Bradford, Vice Chair
James S. Hoyte, Treasurer
Thomas H. Stone, Secretary
Kenneth Kimmell, President

A nonprofit science advocacy organization based in the United States.

7874 United Association of Used Oil Services
318 Newman Road
Sebring, FL 33870-6702

941-655-3880
800-877-4356

Established to be an effective presence in dealing with regulations and to provide a network for those with an interest in the collection and proper disposition of used lubricating oils.
Founded in 1987

7875 Water Environment Federation
601 Wythe St
Alexandria, VA 22314-1994

703-684-2400
800-666-0206
FAX 703-684-2492
E-Mail: inquiry@wef.org
Home Page: www.wef.org
Social Media: *Facebook, Twitter*

Paul Bowen, President
Rick Warner, President-Elect
Jenny Hartfelder, Vice President
Ed McCormick, Immediate Past President
Ralph Exton, Treasurer

Supports those involved in issues that affect the international water environment.
79 Members
ISSN: 1044-9943
Founded in 1928

7876 Water Quality Association
4151 Naperville Rd
Lisle, IL 60532-3696

630-505-0160
FAX 630-505-9637
E-Mail: wqa@wqa.org
Home Page: www.wqa.org
Social Media: *Facebook, Twitter, YouTube*

David Westman, MBA, CAE, CPA, Interim Executive Director
Pauli Undesser, MWS, Deputy Executive Director
Ken G. Kabira, Associate Executive Director
Susan Barkach, Business Operations Director
Larry Deutsch, Marketing & Communications Director

An international, nonprofit trade association representing retail/dealers and manufacturer/suppliers in the point of use/entry water quality improvement industry. Membership benefits and services include technical and scientific information, educational seminars and home correspondence course books, professional certification and discount services.
2.5M Members
Founded in 1974

7877 Wilderness Society
1615 M St NW
Washington, DC 20036-3258

202-833-2300
800-843-9453
FAX 202-429-3945
E-Mail: member@tws.org
Home Page: www.wilderness.org
Social Media: *Facebook, Twitter, LinkedIn, Pinterest, YouTube*

Jamie Williams, President
Thomas Tepper, VP, Finance & Administration
Melyssa Watson, Vice President, Conservation
Kitty Thomas, VP, Communications & Marketing
Ame Hellman, VP, Philanthropy

Establishes the land ethic as a basic element of the American culture and educates people on the importance of wilderness preservation and land protection.
200M Members
Founded in 1935
Mailing list available for rent: 178000 names at $90 per M

7878 Wildlife Conservation Society
2300 Southern Boulevard
Bronx, NY 10460

718-220-5100
FAX 718-584-2625
E-Mail: membership@wcs.org
Home Page: www.wcs.org
Social Media: *Facebook, Twitter, YouTube, Google+, Instagram*

Ward W. Woods, Chair
Edith McBean, Vice Chair
Gordon B. Pattee, Vice Chair
Brian J. Heidtke, Treasurer
Andrew H. Tisch, Secretary

Supports all those involved in the conservation of wildlife, especially the most rare and endangered species.

7879 Wildlife Habitat Council
8737 Colesville Road
Suite 800
Silver Spring, MD 20910

301-588-8994
FAX 301-588-4629
E-Mail: whc@wildlifehc.org
Home Page: www.wildlifehc.org
Social Media: *Facebook, Twitter, LinkedIn, YouTube, Flickr*

Margaret O'Gorman, President
Josiane Bonneau, Sr. Director
Linda Duvall, Director, Finance & HR
Monica Keller, Director, Marketing & Comm.
Thelma Redick, Sr. Director

Supports corporate, government and conservation leaders from around the globe involved in environmental stewardship.
120+ Members
Founded in 1988

7880 Wildlife Management Institute
4426 VT Route 215N
Cabot, VT 05647

802-563-2087
FAX 802-563-2157
E-Mail: wmisw@together.net
Home Page: www.wildlifemanagementinstitute.org

Richard E McCabe, Executive VP
Scot J Williamson, VP
Carol J Peddicord, Finance Manager
Robert L Byrne, Wildlife Program Coordinator
Ronald R Helinski, Conservation Policy Specialist

Supports all those involved with the challenges of modern conservation.

7881 Wildlife Society
5410 Grosvenor Ln
Suite 200
Bethesda, MD 20814-2144

301-897-9770
FAX 301-530-2471
E-Mail: tws@wildlife.org
Home Page: www.wildlife.org
Social Media: *Facebook, Twitter, LinkedIn*

Michael Hutchins, Executive Director
Laura Bies, Director, Government Affairs
Jane Jorgensen, Office and Finance Manager
Yanin Walker, Operations Manager

Supports all those involved in wildlife conservation, including wildlife artists, environmental consultants, conservation groups, scientific associations and natural resource companies, industry groups and government agencies.
9000 Members
Founded in 1937

7882 Women's Council on Energy and the Environment
PO Box 33211
Washington, DC 20033-0211

202-997-4512
FAX 202-478-2098
Home Page: www.wcee.org
Social Media: *Facebook, Twitter, Pinterest*

Robin Cantor, President
Mary Brosnan-Sell, Vice President
Alice Grabowski, Secretary
Barbara Tyran, Treasurer
Joyce Chandran, Executive Director

Supports women involved in the environmental community with education, research, new trend information and several publications.

7883 World Research Foundation
PO Box 20828
Sedona, AZ 86341

928-284-3300
FAX 928-284-3530
E-Mail: info@wrf.org
Home Page: www.wrf.org
Social Media: *Facebook, Twitter, Google+*

Steven A Ross, President

A unique, international, health information network, so that people could be informed of all available treatments around the world, and so that they could have the freedom to choose, based on complete and in-depth information.
41000 Members
Founded in 1984

7884 World Resources Institute
10 G St NE
Suite 800
Washington, DC 20002-4252

202-729-7600
FAX 202-729-7686
E-Mail: front@wri.org
Home Page: wri.org
Social Media: *Facebook, Twitter, LinkedIn, YouTube, RSS*

James A. Harmon, Chairman
Harriet C. Babbitt, Vice Chair
Susan Tierney, Vice Chair
Afsaneh M. Beschloss, President & CEO
Frances Beinecke, Former President

Compiles information, conducts research, publishes the Environmental Almanac and more.
Founded in 1982

7885 World Society for the Protection of Animals
Nelson Tower Building
450 Seventh Avenue, 31st Floor
New York, NY 10123

646-783-2200
FAX 212-564-4250
E-Mail: info@worldanimalprotection.us.org
Home Page: www.worldanimalprotection.org
Social Media: *Facebook, Twitter, YouTube*

Robert S. Cummings, President
John Bowen, Secretary
Carter Luke, Treasurer

International animal protection news reports. Lobbies for effective animal welfare laws and provides educational material.
12 Members

7886 World Wildlife Fund
1250 24th Street, NW
Washington, DC 20037

800-963-0993
E-Mail: membership@wwfus.org
Home Page: www.worldwildlife.org
Social Media: *Facebook, Twitter, YouTube, Instagram, Google+*

Neville Isdell, Chair
Carter Roberts, President & CEO
Margaret Ackerley, Senior VP & general Counsel
Brad Ack, Senior VP, Oceans
Suzanne Apple, Senior VP, Pvt Sector Engagement

Supports all those involved in maintaining wildlife and their environment. Monitors human development, and seeks to influence public opinion and policy makers in favor of ecologically sound practices.
4M Members
Founded in 1961

7887 Worldwatch Institute
1400 16th Street NW
Suite 430
Washington, DC 20036

202-745-8092
FAX 202-478-2534
E-Mail: worldwatch@worldwatch.org
Home Page: www.worldwatch.org
Social Media: *Facebook, Twitter, LinkedIn, RSS, YouTube, Flickr*

Ed Groarky, Chair
Robert Charles Friese, Vice Chair
John Robbins, Treasurer
Nancy Hitzy, Secretary
Barbara Fallin, Dir., Finance & Administration

Analyzes interdisciplinary environmental data from around the world, providing information on how to build a sustainable society.
Founded in 1974

Newsletters

7888 AEESP Newsletter
2303 Naples Court
Champaign, IL 61822

217-398-6969
FAX 217-355-9232
Home Page: www.aeesp.org

Joanne Fetzner, Business Secretary

Official newsletter of the Association of Environmental Engineering and Science Professors. Topics cover the scope and diversity of challenges faced in environmental engineering and science.
Frequency: Quarterly

7889 AEG News
Association of Engineering Geologists
PO Box 460518
Denver, CO 80246-0518

303-757-2926
FAX 720-230-4846
E-Mail: aeg@aegweb.org
Home Page: www.aegweb.org
Social Media: *Facebook, Twitter*

Jennifer Bauer, President
Matthew B. Morris, Vice President/ President Elect
Gary Lice, Treasurer
Ken Fergason, Secretary

Connecting Professionals, Practice and the Public.
3000 Members
Founded in 1957
Mailing list available for rent: 3000 names at $100 per M

7890 AERE Newsletter
Association of Environmental and Resource
1616 P St Nw
Suite 400
Washington, DC 20036-1434

202-328-5157
FAX 202-939-3460
E-Mail: voigt@rff.org
Home Page: www.aere.org

Marilyn Voigt, Executive Secretary
Ralph Metts, President

Includes policy essays, meeting announcements, calls for papers, new publications, research reports, position announcements and other information of interest to AERE members and environmental economists in general.
Frequency: Semi-Annual

7891 AIH Bulletin
American Institute of Hydrology
1230 Lincold Drive
Carbondale, IL 62901

618-453-7809
E-Mail: aih@engr.siu.edu
Home Page: www.aihydrology.org

Cathy Lipsett, Owner
Cathryn Seaburn, Manager

Newsletter for the American Institute of Hydrology, providing information designed to improve professional skills and abilities of its members, the professional community and the public at large.
Frequency: Quarterly

7892 APLIC Communicator
Family Health International Library
PO Box 13950
Research Triangle Park, NC 27709

919-447-7040
Home Page: www.aplici.org

Claire Twose, President
Lori Rosman, Vice-President
Joann Donatiello, Treasurer

Read by population and reproductive health information specialists, librarians, and documentalists.
Frequency: Annual

7893 ASBPA Newsletter
American Shore & Beach Preservation Association
5460 Beaujolais ch Road
Fort Myers, FL 33919

239-489-2616
FAX 239-362-9771
E-Mail: exdir@asbpa.org

Home Page: www.asbpa.org
Social Media: *Facebook, Twitter*

Harry Simmons, President
Nicole Elko, Secretary
Brad Pickel, Treasurer
Kate Gooderham, Editor

Federal, state and local government agencies and individuals interested in conservation, development and restoration of beaches and shorefronts.
1M Members
Founded in 1926

7894 ASEH News
American Society for Environmental History
UW Interdisciplinary Arts and Sciences Program
1900 Commerce Street
Tacoma, WA 98402

206-343-0226
FAX 206-343-0249
E-Mail: director@aseh.net
Home Page: www.aseh.net

John McNeill, President
Gregg Mitman, Vice President/ President Elect
Ellen Stroud, Secretary
Mark Madison, Treasurer

Updated and timely information on current environmental issues and their historical background, as well as Society news and events.
1200 Members
Founded in 1976

7895 ASFE Newslog
ASFE/The Geoprofessional Business Association
8811 Colesville Rd
Suite G106
Silver Springs, MD 20910-4343

301-565-2733
FAX 301-589-2017
E-Mail: info@asfe.org
Home Page: www.asfe.org

John P Bachner, Executive VP

Information on geo professional, environmental, and civil engineering firms. Past issues are available through the online store. Electronic copies are always free to members.
Cost: $240.00
16 Pages
Frequency: 6/Year
Circulation: 5000

7896 ASMR Newsletter
American Society of Mining and Reclamation
3134 Montavesta Road
Lexington, KY 40502

859-335-6529
E-Mail: asmr@insightbb.com
Home Page: www.ca.uky.edu/assmr

Richard I Barnhisel, Executive Secretary

Promotes the advancement of basic and applied reclamation science.
Frequency: 10/year

7897 ATTRAnews
National Center for Appropriate Technology
3040 Continental Drive
PO Box 3838
Butte, MT 59702

406-494-4572
800-275-6228
FAX 406-494-2905
Home Page: www.ncat.org
Social Media: *Facebook, Twitter, LinkedIn*

Eugene Brady, Chairman
Kathleen Hadley, Executive Director

ATTRAnews brings you up to date on the latest developments in sustainable agriculture, what's

happening at the USDA and with Sustainable Agriculture Working Groups around the country. ATTRAnews features events and opportunities in sustainable agriculture, information on funding and financing, and it keeps you current on programs and policies that can affect your future.
Frequency: 6x/Year
Founded in 1976

7898 Advisor
Great Lakes Commission
2805 S Industrial Hwy
Suite 100
Ann Arbor, MI 48104-6791

734-971-9135
FAX 734-971-9150
Home Page: www.glc.org

Tim Eder, Executive Director
Cook Havtrkamp, Author

Covers economic and environmental issues of the Great Lakes region with a special focus on activities of the Great Lakes Commission.
12 Pages
Frequency: Quarterly
Founded in 1955
Printed in one color on matte stock

7899 Air Water Pollution Report's Environment Week
Business Publishers
8737 Colesville Road
Suite 1100
Silver Spring, MD 20910-3928

301-876-6300
800-274-6737
FAX 301-589-8493
E-Mail: custserv@bpinews.com
Home Page: www.bpinews.com

Leonard A Eiserer, Publisher
Beth Early, Operations Director
David Goeller, Editor

Provides a balanced, insightful update on the week's most important environmental news from Washington, D.C.
Cost: $595.00
Frequency: Weekly
Founded in 1963

7900 Annual Research Program Report
National Institutes for Water Resources

Home Page: niwr.net

Paul Joseph Godfrey, PhD, Executive Director

7901 Aquatic Plant News
Aquatic Plant Management Society
PO Box 821265
Vicksburg, MS 39182-1265

FAX 601-634-5502
E-Mail: dpetty@ndrsite.com
Home Page: www.apms.org
Social Media: *Facebook, LinkedIn*

Linda Nelson, President
Terry Goldsby, VP
Sherry Whitaker, Treasurer

Aquatic Plant News is produced 3 times each year, and is distributed primarily by email.
Frequency: 3x/Year
Founded in 1961

7902 Asbestos & Lead Abatement Report
Business Publishers
8737 Colesville Road
Suite 1100
Silver Spring, MD 20910-3928

301-876-6300
800-274-6737
FAX 301-589-8493

E-Mail: custserv@bpinews.com
Home Page: www.bpinews.com

Leonard Eiserer, Publisher

Contains articles on regulation compliance, environmental trends, and business opportunities.
Cost: $382.00
Frequency: Monthly
Founded in 1963

7903 BNA's Environmental Compliance Bulletin

Bureau of National Affairs
1801 S Bell St
Arlington, VA 22202-4501

703-341-3000
800-372-1033
FAX 800-253-0332
E-Mail: customercare@bna.com
Home Page: www.bnabooks.com

Paul N Wojcik, CEO
Gregory C McCaffery, President

Water and air pollution, waste management and regulatory updates, as well as a summary of selected regulatory actions and a list of key environmental compliance dates.
Cost: $649.00
Frequency: Annual+
Founded in 1929

7904 BankNotes

Environmental Bankers Association
510 King St
Suite 410
Alexandria, VA 22314-3212

703-549-0977
FAX 703-548-5945
E-Mail: eba@envirobank.org
Home Page: www.envirobank.org

Rick Ferguson, President
Sharon Valverde, Vice President
Scott Beckerman, Treasurer
Stephen Richardson, Secretary

Timely information on the EBA, read by bank and non-bank financial institutions, insurers, asset management firms and those who provide services to them. Covers environmental risk issues, risk management, development, and due diligence policies and procedures.
Frequency: Bi-Monthly

7905 Biosolids Technical Bulletin

Water Environment Federation
601 Wythe St
Alexandria, VA 22314-1994

800-666-0206
FAX 703-684-2492
Home Page: www.wef.org
Social Media: Facebook, Twitter

Matt Bond, President
Cordell Samuels, President-Elect
Sandra Ralston, Vice President
Chris Browning, Treasurer
Jeff Eger, Secretary and Executive Director

A must have for anyone involved in residuals and biosolids management. The latest treatment processes, odor management, beneficial use options, environmental management systems, or public outreach approaches.
79 Members
ISSN: 1044-9943
Founded in 1928

7906 Bulletins

World Research Foundation
41 Bell Rock Plz
Sedona, AZ 86351-8804

928-284-3300
FAX 928-284-3530

E-Mail: laverne@wrf.org
Home Page: www.wrf.org

Steven A Ross, President

Updates on recent research including topics involving health information pertinent to the World Research Foundation.
Frequency: Quarterly

7907 CCA Newsletter

Coastal Conservation Association
6919 Portwest Dr
Suite 100
Houston, TX 77024-8049

713-626-4234
800-201-FISH
FAX 713-626-5852
E-Mail: ccantl@joincca.org
Home Page: www.joincca.org
Social Media: Twitter

David Cummins, President

Contains timely updates from CCA state chapters and bulletins on developing fisheries issues.
85000 Members
Founded in 1977

7908 CCHEST Newsletter

Council on Certification of Health, Environmental
2301 W. Bradley Avenue
Champaign, IL 61821

217-359-9263
FAX 217-359-0055
E-Mail: cchest@cchest.org
Home Page: www.cchest.org
Social Media: Facebook, Twitter, LinkedIn

Margaret M. Carroll, President
Carl W. Heinlein, Vice President
Emory E. Knowles III, Treasurer

Keeps members up to date on events, OSHA news and the latest safety courses.
Frequency: Annual
Mailing list available for rent: 20,000 names

7909 Capitol Connect

Society of Chemical Manufacturers & Affiliates
1850 M St Nw
Suite 700
Washington, DC 20036-5803

202-721-4100
FAX 202-296-8120
E-Mail: info@socma.org
Home Page: www.socma.org

Larry Brotherton, Ph.D., Chair
Dave Hurder, Vice Chair
Davide DeCuir, Treasurer
J. Steel Hutchinson, Secretary

Government relations newsletter covering a range of environmental, safety, security, chemicals management and trade topics.
10 Pages
Frequency: Bi-Weekly

7910 ChemStewards

Society of Chemical Manufacturers & Affiliates
1850 M St Nw
Suite 700
Washington, DC 20036-5803

202-721-4100
FAX 202-296-8120
E-Mail: info@socma.org
Home Page: www.socma.org

Larry Brotherton, Ph.D., Chair
Dave Hurder, Vice Chair
Davide DeCuir, Treasurer
J. Steel Hutchinson, Secretary

e-Newsletter focusing on ChemStewards Training Opportunities, upcoming events, and the latest program news.
10 Pages
Frequency: Bi-Weekly

7911 Clean Water Report

CJE Associates
Silver Spring, MD 20910-3928

301-589-5103
800-274-6737
FAX 301-589-8493
E-Mail: custserv@bpinews.com
Home Page: www.bpinews.com

Follows the latest news from the EPA, Congress, the states, the courts, and private industry. A key information source for environmental professionals, covering the important issues of ground and drinking water, wastewater treatment, wetlands, drought, coastal protection, non-point source pollution, agrichemical contamination and more.
8 Pages

7912 Climate Change News

Environmental & Energy Study Institute
122 C Street NW
Suite 630
Washington, DC 20001

202-628-1400
FAX 202-628-1825
E-Mail: eesi@eesi.org
Home Page: www.eesi.org
Social Media: Facebook, Twitter, YouTube

Jared Blum, Board Chair
Shelley Fidler, Board Treasurer
Richard L. Ottinger, Board Chair Emeritus

Recounts the top climate science, business, and politics stories of the week and includes a list of upcoming events and pending federal legislation.
Founded in 1984

7913 Composting News

McEntee Media Corporation
9815 Hazelwood Ave
Strongsville, OH 44149-2305

440-238-6603
FAX 440-238-6712
E-Mail: ken@recycle.cc
Home Page: www.recycle.cc

Ken Mc Entee, Owner

The latest in composting, wood waste recycling and organics management in a monthly newsletter.
Cost: $83.00
Frequency: Monthly
Circulation: 2000
Founded in 1990

7914 Conservation Commission News

New Hampshire Association of Conservation Comm.
54 Portsmouth Street
Concord, NH 03301-5486

603-225-3431
FAX 603-228-0423

Marjory Swope, Publisher

Encourage conservation and appropriate use of New Hampshire's natural resources by providing assistance to New Hampshire's municipal conservation commissions and by facilitating communication among commissions and between commissions and other public and private agencies involved in conservation.
Cost: $5.00
8 Pages
Frequency: Quarterly
Circulation: 1,650
Printed in one color on matte stock

7915 Convention Proceedings
Society for Human Ecology
College of the Atlantic
105 Eden Street
Bar Harbor, ME 04609-0180

207-288-5015
FAX 207-288-3780
E-Mail: carter@ecology.coa.edu
Home Page: www.societyforhumanecology.org

Barbara Carter, Assistant to Executive Director

7916 Cosecha Mensual
National Center for Appropriate Technology
3040 Continental Drive
PO Box 3838
Butte, MT 59702

406-494-4572
800-275-6228
FAX 406-494-2905
Home Page: www.ncat.org
Social Media: *Facebook, Twitter, LinkedIn*

Eugene Brady, Chairman
Kathleen Hadley, Executive Director

NCAT's Spanish-language electronic newsletter on sustainable agriculture. Subscribers enjoy news items and reviews of
Spanish-language resources.
Frequency: Monthly
Founded in 1976

7917 Council on Women in Energy and Environmental Leadership Newsletter
Association of Energy Engineers
4025 Pleasantdale Rd
Suite 420
Atlanta, GA 30340-4264

770-447-5083
FAX 770-446-3969
E-Mail: info@aeecenter.org
Home Page: www.aeecenter.org
Social Media: *Facebook, Twitter, LinkedIn, YouTube*

Eric A. Woodroof, President
Gary Hogsett, President Elect
Bill Younger, Secretary
Paul Goodman, C.P.A., Treasurer

Addressing the high cost of energy, present and future sources of energy, and the impact of energy on the environment.
8.2M Members
Founded in 1977

7918 Daily Environment Report
Bureau of National Affairs
1801 S Bell St
Arlington, VA 22202-4501

703-341-3000
800-372-1033
FAX 800-253-0332
E-Mail: customercare@bna.com
Home Page: www.bnabooks.com

Paul N Wojcik, CEO
Gregory C McCaffery, President

A 40-page daily report providing comprehensive, in-depth coverage of national and international environmental news. Each issue contains summaries of the top news stories, articles, and in-brief items, and a journal of meetings, agency activities, hearings and legal proceedings. Coverage includes air and water pollution, hazardous substances, and hazardous waste, solid waste, oil spills, gas drilling, pollution prevention, impact statements and budget matters.
Cost: $ 3537.00
40 Pages
Frequency: Daily
ISSN: 1060-2976

7919 Digital Traveler
International Ecotourism Society

733 15th Street NW
Suite 1000
Washington, DC 20005

202-547-9203
FAX 202-387-7915
Home Page: www.ecotourism.org

Martha Honey, Executive Director
Amos Bien, Director International Programs
Neal Inamdar, Director Finance/Administration
Regular updates about TIES work and programs.
Frequency: Monthly

7920 E&P Environment
Pasha Publications
1616 N Fort Myer Dr
Suite 1000
Arlington, VA 22209-3107

703-528-1244
800-424-2908
FAX 703-528-1253
Home Page: www.newsletteraccess.com

Harry Baisden, Group Publisher
Jerry Grisham, Editor

Reports on environmental regulations, advances in technology and litigation aimed specifically at the exploration and production segments of the oil and gas industry.
Cost: $395.00

7921 E-Scrap News
Resource Recycling
PO Box 42270
Portland, OR 97242-270

503-233-1305
FAX 503-233-1356
E-Mail: info@resource-recycling.com
Home Page: www.resource-recycling.com

Jerry Powell, Publisher/Editor
Andrew Santosusso, Managing Editor
Betsy Loncar, Circulation Director

Monthly newsletter covering all aspects of recovering, recycling, and managing electronics scrap. Coverage includes market prices and trends, collection events, product stewardship developments and global trends.
Cost: $99.00
6 Pages
Frequency: Monthly
Circulation: 1000
ISSN: 1536-3856
Founded in 1983
Mailing list available for rent: 40,000 names at $100 per M
Printed in 2 colors on matte stock

7922 ECOMOD Newsletter
International Society for Ecological Modelling
University of California, Animal Sciences Dept
One Shields Avenue
Davis, CA 95616-8521

530-752-5362
FAX 530-752-0175
Home Page: www.isemna.org

Wolfgang Pittroff, Secretary-General

Information on conferences, workshops and symposia that promote the systems philosophy in ecological research and teaching. Members frequently contribute articles.
Frequency: Quarterly

7923 EH&S Software News Online
Donley Technology
PO Box 152
Colonial Beach, VA 22443-152

804-224-9427
800-201-1595

FAX 804-224-7958
Home Page: www.ehssoftwarenews.com

John Donley, Editor

Reports on news and upgraded software products, database, and on-line systems from commercial developers and government resources.
Cost: $125.00
Founded in 1988

7924 EMS Newsletter
Environmental Mutagen Society
1821 Michael Faraday Drive
Suite 300
Reston, VA 20190

703-438-8220
FAX 703-438-3113
E-Mail: emshq@ems-us.org
Home Page: www.ems-us.org

Kathleen Hill, Editor
Barbara Parsons, Editor
Cathy Klein, Editor

Current scientific research, policies, and guidelines for the causes and consequences of damage to the genome and epigenome.
Frequency: Bi-Annual

7925 Economic Opportunity Report
Business Publishers
2222 Sedwick Dr
Suite 101
Durham, NC 27713

800-223-8720
FAX 800-508-2592
E-Mail: custserv@bpinews.com
Home Page: www.bpinews.com

Antipoverty news coverage and analysis which gives insight into developments that affect social programs.
Cost: $383.00
Frequency: Weekly

7926 Environment Reporter
Bureau of National Affairs
1801 S Bell St
Arlington, VA 22202-4501

703-341-3000
800-372-1033
FAX 800-253-0332
E-Mail: customercare@bna.com
Home Page: www.bnabooks.com

Paul N Wojcik, CEO
Gregory C McCaffery, President

A weekly notification and reference service covering the full-spectrum of legislative, administrative, judicial, industrial and technological developments affecting pollution control and environmental protection.
Cost: $3776.00
Frequency: Weekly
ISSN: 0013-9211
Founded in 1929

7927 Environmental Design Research Association Newsletter
Environmental Design Research Association
PO Box 7146
Edmond, OK 73083-7146

405-330-4863
FAX 405-330-4150
E-Mail: edra@telepath.com
Home Page: www.edra.org

Janet Singer, Executive Director

Document collection includes pdfs of full papers that have appeared in the annual EDRA conference proceedings.
Frequency: Annual

7928 Environmental Engineers and Managers Institute Newsletter
Association of Energy Engineers

4025 Pleasantdale Rd
Suite 420
Atlanta, GA 30340-4264

770-447-5083
FAX 770-446-3969
E-Mail: info@aeecenter.org
Home Page: www.aeecenter.org
Social Media: *Facebook, Twitter, LinkedIn, YouTube*

Eric A. Woodroof, President
Gary Hogsett, President Elect
Bill Younger, Secretary
Paul Goodman, C.P.A., Treasurer

Keeps members ahead on trends, upcoming conferences, industry leaders, jobs, relevant publications and more.
8.2M Members
Founded in 1977

7929 Environmental Health Newsletter
International Lead Zinc Research Organization
2525 Meridian Parkway, Suite 100
PO Box 12036
Durham, NC 27713

919-361-4647
FAX 919-361-1957
Home Page: www.ilzro.org

Stephen Wilkinson, President
Frank Goodwin, VP Materials Sciences
Scott Mooneyham, Treasurer
Rob Putnam, Director Communications

Information on environmental health sciences, use of technology, rules, and public education.
Frequency: Quarterly

7930 Environmental Nutrition
52 Riverside Drive
Suite 15A
New York, NY 10024

212-362-0424
800-424-7887
FAX 212-362-2066
E-Mail: betty@environmentalnutrition.com
Home Page: www.environmentalnutrition.com

Betty Goldblatt, Publisher
Susan Male Smith, Editor

Monthly nutrition newsletter on nutrition and health. Written and edited by registered dietitians.
Cost: $24.00
Frequency: Monthly
Circulation: 50000
Founded in 1977
Printed in 2 colors on matte stock

7931 Environmental Policy Alert
Inside Washington Publishers
1919 S Eads St
Suite 201
Arlington, VA 22202-3028

703-418-3981
800-424-9068
FAX 703-416-8543
E-Mail: iwp@sprintmail.com
Home Page: www.iwpnews.com

Alan Sosenko, Owner

Adresses the legislative news and provides reports on the federal environmental policy process.
Cost: $560.00
Founded in 1980

7932 Environmental Problems & Remediation
InfoTeam

PO Box 15640
Plantation, FL 33318-5640

954-473-9560
FAX 954-473-0544
E-Mail: infoteamma@aol.com

Merton Allen, Editor

Concerned with environmental problems and effects, the methods and approaches for mitigation and remediation. Covers air pollution; surface and ground water pollution; wastewater; soil contamination; waste recycling; medical wastes; landfills and waste sites; stack gases; combustion and incineration; earth warming and more.

7933 Environmental Regulatory Advisor
JJ Keller
3003 W Breezewood Lane
Neenah, WI 54956-368

920-722-2848
800-327-6868
FAX 800-727-7516
E-Mail: sales@jjkeller.com
Home Page: www.jjkeller.com

Webb Shaw, Editor
Robert Keller, CEO

Covers developments at the EPA.
Founded in 1953

7934 Environotes Newsletter
Federation of Environmental Technologists
PO Box 624
Slinger, WI 53086-0624

414-540-0070
FAX 262-644-7106
E-Mail: info@fetinc.org
Home Page: www.fetinc.org

Triese Haase, Administrator

Educating and Developing Excellence in Environmental Professionals
Frequency: Monthly

7935 Facility Managers Institute Newsletter
Association of Energy Engineers
4025 Pleasantdale Rd
Suite 420
Atlanta, GA 30340-4264

770-447-5083
FAX 770-446-3969
E-Mail: info@aeecenter.org
Home Page: www.aeecenter.org
Social Media: *Facebook, Twitter, LinkedIn, YouTube*

Eric A. Woodroof, President
Gary Hogsett, President Elect
Bill Younger, Secretary
Paul Goodman, C.P.A., Treasurer

Online newsletter addresses subjects such as the Integrated Approach to plant management, security and safety issues, and overall facility management.
8.2M Members
Founded in 1977

7936 Fibre Market News
GIE Media
4012 Bridge Avenue
Cleveland, OH 44113-3320

216-961-4130
800-456-0707
FAX 216-961-0364

Richard Foster, Publisher
Daniel Sandoval, Editor

Covers the international paper recycling industry. Trends, markets, expansions, economics covered in an in-depth fashion. Also have

weekly fax update covering late-breaking news.
Cost: $115.00
16 Pages
Frequency: BiWeekly

7937 ForeFront
National Registry of Environmental Professionals
PO Box 2099
Glenview, IL 60025

847-724-6631
FAX 847-724-4223
E-Mail: nrep@nrep.org
Home Page: www.nrep.org
Social Media: *Facebook, Twitter, LinkedIn*

Richard A Young, PhD, Executive Director
Edward Beck, PhD, Senior Director
Carol Schellinger, Director
Christopher Young, Director of Operation
Marie Hunter, Director

Information on continuing education, certification, and recognition for the professionals who help understand and study the environment.
20000 Members
Frequency: Bi-Monthly
Founded in 1987

7938 Forest History Society
Forest History Society
701 William Vickers Ave
Durham, NC 27701-3162

919-682-9319
FAX 919-682-2349
E-Mail: recluce2@duke.edu
Home Page: www.foresthistory.org

Steven Anderson, President
R Scott Wallinger, Chairman
Yvan Hardy, Co-Vice Chairman
Mark Wilde, Co Vice-Chairman

Nonprofit educational institution that explores the history of the environment, forestry and conservation.

7939 From the Ground Up
Ecology Center
117 Division Street
Ann Arbor, MI 48104-1523

734-761-3186
FAX 734-663-2414
Home Page: www.ecocenter.org

Ted Sylvester, Editor
Mike Wallad, President
Michael Garfield, Director

Progressive environmental news from southeast Michigan.
Cost: $30.00
32 Pages
Frequency: Monthly
Circulation: 5000
Founded in 1970
Printed in 4 colors on newsprint stock

7940 GRAS Flavoring Substances 25
Flavor & Extract Manufacturers Association
1620 I Street NW
Suite 925
Washington, DC 20006

202-293-5800
FAX 202-462-8998
Home Page: www.femaflavor.org
Social Media: *YouTube, RSS Feed*

Ed R. Hays, Ph.D., President
George C. Robinson, III, President Elect
Mark Scott, Treasurer
Arthur Schick, VP & Secretary
John Cox, Executive Director

The 25th publication by the Expert Panel of the Flavor and Extract Manufacturers Association provides an update on recent progress in the consideration of flavoring ingredients generally

recognized as safe under the Food Additive Amendment.
123 Members
Frequency: Biennial
Founded in 1909

7941   Global Environmental Change Report
Aspen Publishers
76 Ninth Avenue
7th Floor
New York, NY 10011

212-771-0600
800-638-8437
Home Page: www.aspenpublishers.com

Mark Dorman, CEO
Gustavo Dobles, VP Operations

News and analysis of policy, science and industry developments in the areas of global warming and acid rain.
Cost: $447.00
Frequency: BiWeekly

7942   HazTECH News
Haztech News
14120 Huckleberry Lane
Silver Spring, MD 20906

301-871-3289
FAX 301-460-5859
E-Mail: HazTECH@ix.netcom.com

Cathy Dombrowski, Editor/Publisher

Describes technologies for hazardous waste management, site remediation, industrial wastewater treatment and VOC control.
Cost: $385.00
8 Pages
Frequency: Bi-Weekly
Printed in one color

7943   Hazardous Materials Intelligence Report
World Information Systems
PO Box 535
Cambridge, MA 02238-535

617-492-3312
FAX 617-492-3312
Home Page:
members.aol.com/socejp/hmir.html

Richard S Golob, Publisher
Roger B Wilson Jr, Editor

Provides news analysis on environmental business, hazardous materials, waste management, pollution prevention and control. Covers regulations, legislation and court decisions, new technology, contract opportunities and awards and conference notices.
Cost: $375.00
Frequency: Weekly
Circulation: 50000

7944   Hazardous Materials Transportation
Bureau of National Affairs
1801 S Bell St
Arlington, VA 22202-4501

703-341-3000
800-372-1033
E-Mail: customercare@bna.com
Home Page: www.bnabooks.com

Gregory C McCaffery, President
Paul N Wojcik, Chairman

A two-binder service containing the full-text of rules and regulations governing shipment of hazardous material by rail, air, ship, highway and pipeline, including DOT's Hazardous Materials Tables and EPA's rules for its hazardous waste tracking system.
Cost: $933.00
Frequency: Monthly

7945   Hazardous Waste Report
Aspen Publishers

7201 McKinney Cir
Frederick, MD 21704-8356

301-698-7100
800-638-8437
FAX 212-597-0335
Home Page: www.aspenpublishers.com

Paul Gibson, Publisher
Sally Almeria, Editor
Bruce Becker, CEO/President
Tom Ceodi, Marketing

Provides information on industry news.
Cost: $875.00
8 Pages
Founded in 1958

7946   Health Facts and Fears.com
American Council on Science and Health
1995 Broadway
2nd Floor
New York, NY 10023-5882

212-362-7044
FAX 212-362-4919
E-Mail: acsh@acsh.org
Home Page: www.acsh.org

Dr Elizabeth Whelan, President
Jeff Stier, Associate Director

Daily e-mail blast on the latest public health news and junk science scares.
Frequency: Weekly

7947   IES Quarterly Newsletter
International Ecotourism Society
733 15th Street NW
Suite 1000
Washington, DC 20005

202-547-9203
FAX 202-387-7915
Home Page: www.ecotourism.org

Martha Honey, Executive Director
Amos Bien, Director International Programs
Neal Inamdar, Director Finance/Administration

Offering information on advocacy uniting communities, conservation, and sustainable travel.
Frequency: Quarterly

7948   Industrial Health & Hazards Update
InfoTeam
PO Box 15640
Plantation, FL 33318-5640

954-473-9560
FAX 954-473-0544
E-Mail: infoteamma@aol.com

Merton Allen, Editor

Covers occupational safety, health, hazards, and disease, mitigatioin and control of hazardous situations; waste recycling and treatment; environmental pollution and control; product safety and liability; fires and explosions; plant and computer security,; air pollution; surface and ground water; wastewater; soil gases; combustion and incineration; earth warming; ozone layer depletion; electromagnetic radiation; toxic materials; and many other related topics.

7949   Infectious Wastes News
National Solid Wastes Management Association
4301 Connecticut Ave Nw
Suite 300
Washington, DC 20008-2304

202-966-4701
FAX 202-966-4818
E-Mail: wa@envasns.org
Home Page: www.envasns.org

Bruce Parker, President

A publication by the Environmental industry association geared toward providing readers with timely news and information about the

handling, transportation and disposal of infectious wastes.
Frequency: BiWeekly

7950   Integrated Environmental Assessment and Management
Society of Environmental Toxicology and Chemistry
1013 N 12th Ave
Pensacola, FL 32501-3306

850-437-1901
FAX 850-469-9778
E-Mail: rparrish@setac.org
Home Page: www.edwardjones.com

Rodney Parrish, Executive Director

Focuses on the application of science in environmental decision-making, regulation, and management, including aspects of policy and law, and the development of scientifically sound approaches to environmental problem solving.
Frequency: Quarterly

7951   Integrated Waste Management
1801 S Bell Street
Arlington, VA 22202

212-512-3916
800-372-1033
FAX 212-512-2723
Home Page: www.bna.com

Gregory C McCaffery, President
Paul N Wojcik, Chairman

Articles geared toward integration of solid waste management.
Cost: $745.00
8 Pages
Frequency: BiWeekly

7952   Interface Newsletter
Society for Environmental Geochemistry and Health
4698 S Forrest Avenue
Springfield, MO 65810

417-885-1166
FAX 417-881-6920
E-Mail: drbgwixson@wixson.com
Home Page: www.segh.net

Bobby Wixson, Director Membership

7953   International Environment Reporter
Bureau of National Affairs
1801 S Bell St
Arlington, VA 22202-4501

703-341-3000
800-372-1033
FAX 800-253-0332
E-Mail: customercare@bna.com
Home Page: www.bnabooks.com

Gregory C McCaffrey, President
Paul N Wojcik, Chairman

A four-binder information and reference service covering international environmental law and developing policy in the major industrial nations.
Cost: $2555.00

7954   Journal of Science and Sustainability
National Registry of Environmental Professionals
PO Box 2099
Glenview, IL 60025

847-724-6631
FAX 847-724-4223
E-Mail: nrep@nrep.org
Home Page: www.nrep.org
Social Media: *Facebook, Twitter, LinkedIn*

Richard A Young, PhD, Executive Director
Edward Beck, PhD, Senior Director
Carol Schellinger, Director

Christopher Young, Director of Operation
Marie Hunter, Director

Digital journal serving sustainability professionals worldwide.
20000 Members
Frequency: Semi-Annual
Circulation: 50,000
Founded in 1987

7955 **Marine Conservation News**
Center for Marine Conservation
2029 K Street
Washington, NW 20006

202-750-0574
800-519-1541
FAX 202-872-0619
Home Page: www.cmc-ocean.org

Rose Bierce, Publisher
Roger Rufe, President
Stephanie Drea, VP Commun
Matt Schatzle, VP Membership & Development
Wanda Cantrell, Manager

Updates members of CMC on the organization projects and activities.
24 Pages
Frequency: Quarterly
Circulation: 100000
Printed in 2 colors on matte stock

7956 **McCoy's Hazardous Waste Regulatory Update**
McCoy & Associates
25107 Genesee Trail Road
Suite 200
Golden, CO 80228-4173

303-526-2674
FAX 303-526-5471
E-Mail: info@mccoyseminars.com
Home Page:
www.mccoyseminars.com/contact.cfm

Offers a complete text of the federal hazardous waste regulations, summaries, interpretations and indexes.
Founded in 1983

7957 **McCoy's Regulatory Analysis Service**
McCoy & Associates
25107 Genesee Trail Road
Golden, CO 80401-5708

303-526-2674
FAX 303-526-5471
E-Mail: info@mccoyseminars.com
Home Page: www.mccoyseminars.com

Provides timely, in-depth analyses of hazardous waste regulations within 10 working days after their publication in the Federal Register.
Cost: $550.00
Founded in 1983

7958 **Mealey's Litigation Report: Insurance**
LexisNexis Mealey's
555 W 5th Avenue
Los Angeles, CA 90013

213-627-1130
E-Mail: mealeyinfo@lexisnexis.com
Home Page: www.lexisnexis.com/mealeys

Tom Hagy, VP/General Manager
Maureen McGuire, Editorial Director
Vivi Gorman, Editor
Shawn Rice, Co-Editor

The report tracks declaratory judgment actions regarding coverage for litigation arising from long-tail claims, including environmental contamination and latent damage and injury allegedly caused by asbestos, tox chemicals and fumes, lead, breast implants, medical devices, construction defects, and more. Key issues: allocation, occurrence, policy exclusion, choice of law, discovery, duty to defend, notice, trigger of coverage and known loss.
Founded in 1984

7959 **Montana Green Power Update**
National Center for Appropriate Technology
3040 Continental Drive
PO Box 3838
Butte, MT 59702

406-494-4572
800-275-6228
FAX 406-494-2905
Home Page: www.ncat.org
Social Media: *Facebook, Twitter, LinkedIn*

Eugene Brady, Chairman
Kathleen Hadley, Executive Director

This free monthly electronic newsletter contains the latest success stories in renewable energy development in the state of Montana, hot tips, information on financing and tax incentives, upcoming events, and links to stories from regional and national sources as featured on the Montana Green Power web site.
Frequency: Monthly
Founded in 1976

7960 **Motor Carrier Safety Report, HAZMAT Transp ortation Report**
J.J. Keller & Associates, Inc.
3003 Breezewood Lane
PO Box 368
Neenah, WI 54957-0368

920-722-2848
800-327-6868
FAX 800-727-7516
E-Mail: sales@jjkeller.com
Home Page: www.jjkeller.com

Stephanie Hallman, Business Development

The nation's leader in risk and regulatory management solutions, including printed publications, videos, and online training for workplace safety, hazardous materials, transportation, human resources, and environmental safety.
Cost: $90.00
12 Pages
Frequency: Monthly
ISSN: 1056-3164
Founded in 1953

7961 **NAESCO Newsletter**
National Association of Energy Service Companies
1615 M St NW
Suite 800
Washington, DC 20036-3213

202-822-0950
FAX 202-822-0955
E-Mail: info@naesco.org
Home Page: www.naesco.org

Terry E Singer, Executive Editor
Michael Hamilton, Marketing Manager
Mary Lee Berger-Hughes, Publisher

Targets energy service companies, electric and gas utilities amd other energy providers. Highlights industry news and features energy conservation.
Circulation: 200
Founded in 1985

7962 **NCAT Action**
National Center for Appropriate Technology
3040 Continental Drive
PO Box 3838
Butte, MT 59702

406-494-4572
800-275-6228
FAX 406-494-2905
Home Page: www.ncat.org
Social Media: *Facebook, Twitter, LinkedIn*

Eugene Brady, Chairman
Kathleen Hadley, Executive Director

Action is a quarterly newsletter featuring local solutions for a sustainable future. Each issue focuses on a different topic, providing information that will help you move toward a more sustainable lifesytle in your home and in your community. Action features thought-provoking commentary, informative news stories, and extensive resource lists compiled by NCAT's expert professional staff.
Frequency: Quarterly
Founded in 1976

7963 **NORA News**
NORA: an Association of Responsible Recyclers
5965 Amber Ridge Rd
Haymarket, VA 20169-2623

703-753-4277
FAX 703-753-2445
E-Mail: sparker@noranews.org
Home Page: www.noranews.org

Scott Parker, Executive Director

7964 **National Association of Conservation Districts**
National Association of Conservation Districts
509 Capitol Ct. NE
Washington, DC 20002-4937

202-547-6223
FAX 202-547-6450
Home Page: www.nacdnet.org

Krysta Harden, CEO
Bob Cordova, Second Vice President

Highlights forestry issues of importance to districts and to showcase district-related forestry projects and success stories. Funded through a cooperative agreement between NACD and the U.S. Forest Service.
Cost: $35.00
12 Pages
Frequency: Monthly
Circulation: 25000
Founded in 1937

7965 **Nature's Voice**
National Resources Defense Council
40 W 20th St
New York, NY 10011-4231

212-727-2700
FAX 212-727-1773
E-Mail: nrdcinfo@nrdc.org
Home Page: www.nrdc.org
Social Media: *Facebook, Twitter, YouTube*

Frances Beinecke, President
Daniel R. Tishman, Chair
Frederick A.O. Schwarz Jr., Chair Emeritus
Adam Albright, Vice Chair
Patricia Bauman, Vice Chair

Environmental news and activism, using law, science and the support of more than 1 million members and online activists to protect the plante's wildlife and wild places and to ensure a healthy environment for all living things.
50000 Members
Founded in 1970

7966 **Networker**
National Center for Appropriate Technology
3040 Continental Drive
PO Box 3838
Butte, MT 59702

406-494-4572
800-275-6228
FAX 406-494-2905
Home Page: www.ncat.org
Social Media: *Facebook, Twitter, LinkedIn*

Eugene Brady, Chairman
Kathleen Hadley, Executive Director

The newsletter is compiled by the LIHEAP Clearinghouse, and NCAT project. Stories

highlight state energy assistance program and low-income energy news.
Frequency: Quarterly
Founded in 1976

7967 News Flash
National Association of Local Government
1333 New Hampshire Ave Nw
Suite 400
Washington, DC 20036-1532

202-887-4107
FAX 202-393-2866
E-Mail: nalgep@spiegelmcd.com
Home Page: www.nalgep.org

Kenneth E Brown, Executive Director
David Dickson, Projects Manager

Brings together noteworthy funding opportunities, conferences, legislative tracking on climate change and highlights projects completed on the federal or local level.
Frequency: Bi-Weekly

7968 Noise Regulation Report
Business Publishers
2222 Sedwick Dr
Suite 101
Durham, NC 27713

800-223-8720
FAX 800-508-2592
E-Mail: custserv@bpinews.com
Home Page: www.bpinews.com

Exclusive coverage of airport, highway, occupational and open space noise, noise control and mitigation issues.
Cost: $511.00
10 Pages
Frequency: 12 per year
Printed in on matte stock

7969 Nuclear Monitor
Nuclear Information & Resource Services
1424 16th Street NW
Suite 404
Washington, DC 20036-2239

202-328-0002
FAX 202-462-2183
E-Mail: nirsnet@nirs.org
Home Page: www.nirs.org
Social Media: *Twitter, YouTube*

Michael Mariotte, Editor
Linda Gunder, Media Manager

NIRS and WISE merged the Nuclear Monitor and WISE News Communique into a new Nuclear Monitor. Now available as an international edition.
Cost: $250.00
12 Pages
Frequency: 18 issues per y
Circulation: 1200
Founded in 1978
Printed in one color on matte stock

7970 Nuclear Waste News
Business Publishers
2222 Sedwick Dr
Suite 101
Durham, NC 27713

800-223-8720
FAX 800-508-2592
E-Mail: custserv@bpinews.com
Home Page: www.bpinews.com

Worldwide coverage of the nuclear waste management industry including waste generation, packaging, transport, processing and disposal.
Cost: $697.00
10 Pages
Frequency: 25 per year
Mailing list available for rent
Printed in 2 colors on matte stock

7971 Outdoor News Bulletin
Wildlife Management Institute
4426 VT Route 215N
Cabot, VT 05647

802-563-2087
FAX 802-563-2157
E-Mail: wmisw@together.net
Home Page:
www.wildlifemanagementinstitute.org

Richard E McCabe, Executive VP
Scot J Williamson, VP
Carol J Peddicord, Finance Manager
Robert L Byrne, Wildlife Program Coordinator
Ronald R Helinski, Conservation Policy Specialist

Reports on select, significant issues, circumstances and other information that bear on the professional management of wildlife and related natural resources.

7972 RESTORE
Society for Ecological Restoration
1017 O Street NW
Washington, DC 20001

202-299-9518
FAX 270-626-5485
E-Mail: info@ser.org
Home Page: www.ser.org

Steve Whisenant, Chair
Cara R. Nelson, Vice Chair
Mary Travaglini, Treasurer
Alan Unwin, Secretary

Weekly e-bulletin. Contains articles of interest to people in the field of restoration ecology, and is an indispensable way to keep up with what's happening in the world of ecological restoration, rounding up all the latest, breaking news from around the world on a wide variety of restoration-related issues. Available in electronic form only.
Frequency: Semi-Annual

7973 Reclamation Matters
American Society of Mining and Reclamation
3134 Montevesta Road
Lexington, KY 40502-3548

859-351-9032
FAX 859-335-6529
E-Mail: asmr@insightbb.com
Home Page: www.asmr.us

Eddie Bearden, President
Bruce Buchanen, President Elect
Richard Barnhisel, Executive Secretary

Newsletter of the ASMR. Free to members or $10/year.
500 Members
Founded in 1983

7974 Recycling Markets
NV Business Publishers Corporation
43 Main St
Avon By the Sea, NJ 07717-1051

732-502-0500
FAX 732-502-9606
E-Mail: nvrecycle@aol.com
Home Page: www.nvpublications.com

Ted Vilardi, Owner
Anna Dutko, Managing Editor
Tom Vilardi, President/Publisher
Ted Vilardi Jr., Co-Publisher

Contains profiles on recycling mills, as well as large users and generators of recycled materials for the broker, dealers and processors of paper stock, scrap metal, plastics and glass.
Cost: $180.00
Frequency: Weekly
Circulation: 3315
Printed in 4 colors on newsprint stock

7975 Resource Conservation & Recovery Act: A Guide to Compliance
McCoy & Associates
13701 W Jewell Avenue
Suite 202
Lakewood, CO 80228-4173

303-870-0835
FAX 303-989-7917

Drew McCoy, Publisher
Deborah McCoy, President

Land disposal restrictions for hazardous waste.
300 Pages
Frequency: Annual

7976 Resource Development Newsletter
University of Tennessee
PO Box 1071
Knoxville, TN 37996-1071

865-974-1000
FAX 865-974-7448
E-Mail: rpdavis@utk.edu

Alan Barefield, Publisher

Community development information.
4 Pages
Frequency: Quarterly
Circulation: 2000
Founded in 1794
Printed in one color on matte stock

7977 Resource Recovery Report
PO Box 3356
Warrenton, VA 20188-1956

540-347-4500
800-627-8913
FAX 540-349-4540
E-Mail: rwill@coordgrp.com
Home Page: www.coordgrp.com

Richard Will, Production Manager

Covers all alternatives to landfills, i.e., recycling, energy recovery, composting in North America, Government, industry, associations, universities, etc. are included.
Cost: $227.00
12 Pages
Frequency: Monthly
Mailing list available for rent: 12M names
Printed in one color on matte stock

7978 SEG Extra
Society of Exploration Geophysicists
8801 South Yale
Suite 500
Tulsa, OK 74137-3575

918-497-5500
FAX 918-497-5557
E-Mail: web@seg.org
Home Page: www.seg.org
Social Media: *Facebook, Twitter, LinkedIn*

Mary Fleming, Executive Director
Vladimir Grechka, Editor

eNewsletter, delivering the most relevant, up-to-date information pertaining directly to SEG members and stakeholders.
Founded in 1930

7979 SEJournal
Society of Environmental Journalists
PO Box 2492
Jenkintown, PA 19046

215-884-8174
FAX 215-884-8175
Home Page: www.sej.org
Social Media: *Facebook, Twitter*

Carolyn Whetzel, President
Peter Fairley, 1st Vice Pres
Jeff Burnside, 2nd Vice Pres
Don Hopey, Treasurer

In-depth stories on hot topics on the environment beat.
Founded in 1990

7980 SOCMA Newsletter
Society of Chemical Manufacturers &
Affiliates
1850 M St Nw
Suite 700
Washington, DC 20036-5803

202-721-4100
FAX 202-296-8120
E-Mail: info@socma.org
Home Page: www.socma.org

Larry Brotherton, Ph.D., Chair
Dave Hurder, Vice Chair
Davide DeCuir, Treasurer
J. Steel Hutchinson, Secretary

Provides the specialty, batch and custom chemical industry with the latest regulatory, legislative and commerce news in a convenient newsletter exclusively compiled for members.
10 Pages
Frequency: Bi-Weekly

7981 Salt & Highway Deicing Newsletter
Salt Institute
700 N Fairfax St
Suite 600
Alexandria, VA 22314-2085

703-549-4648
FAX 703-548-2194
E-Mail: info@saltinstitute.org
Home Page: www.saltinstitute.org

Richard L Hanneman, President
Tammy Goodwin, Director
Mark OKeefe, Director of Communications

A quarterly e-newsletter published by the Salt Institute that focuses on highway uses of salt.
Frequency: Quarterly
Circulation: 77000
Founded in 1914
Printed in on glossy stock

7982 Salt and Trace Minerals Newsletter
Salt Institute
700 N Fairfax St
Suite 600
Alexandria, VA 22314-2085

703-549-4648
FAX 703-548-2194
E-Mail: info@saltinstitute.org
Home Page: www.saltinstitute.org

Richard L Hanneman, President

E-Newsletter containing information on animal nutrition.
Frequency: Quarterly
Circulation: 77000
Founded in 1914
Printed in on glossy stock

7983 SmartBrief
American Wind Energy Association
1501 M Street NW
Suite 1000
Washington, DC 20005

202-383-2500
FAX 202-383-2505
E-Mail: windmail@awea.org
Home Page: www.awea.org
Social Media: *Facebook, Twitter, YouTube*

Ned Hall, Chair
Thomas Carnahan, Chair-Elect
Gabriel Alonso, Secretary
Don Furman, Treasurer
Vic Abate, Past Chair

Delivers quickly digestible summaries of the day's wind energy-related stories from across the media, keeps readers informed about the in-

dustry, and allows readers to stay on top of what's being said about it.
2400 Members

7984 Society Update
American Society of Safety Engineers
1800 E Oakton Street
Des Plaines, IL 60018

847-699-2929
FAX 847-768-3434
E-Mail: customerservice@asse.org
Home Page: www.asse.org
Social Media: *Facebook*

Terrie S. Norris, President
Richard A. Pollock, President Elect
Kathy Seabrook, Senior Vice President
Fred J. Fortman, Jr., Secretary & Executive Director
James D. Smith, Vice President, Finance

Highlights the latest Society news, activities, upcoming events and notable member achievements.
30000 Members
Founded in 1911

7985 Society of Chemical Manufacturers & Affiliates Newsletter
1850 M St NW
Suite 700
Washington, DC 20036-5803

202-721-4100
FAX 202-296-8120
E-Mail: info@socma.org
Home Page: www.socma.org

Larry Brotherton, Ph.D., Chair
Dave Hurder, Vice Chair
Davide DeCuir, Treasurer
J. Steel Hutchinson, Secretary

Newsletter tailored to provide industry executives with the most up-to-date information on events hosted or sponsored by SOCMA.
10 Pages
Frequency: Bi-Weekly

7986 State Recycling Laws Update
Raymond Communications
5111 Berwin Road
Suite no#115
College Park, MD 20740

301-345-4237
FAX 301-345-4768
Home Page: www.raymond.com

Lorah utter, Editor
Bruce Popka, Vice President of Communications
Allyn Weet, Circulation Manager

Contains analysis and reports, provides coverage of recycling legislation affecting business, as well as the outlook on future legislation across the states and Canada. Also publishes special reports on related topics, for example, Transportation Packaging and the Environment.
Cost: $367.00
Frequency: Monthly
Circulation: 200
Founded in 1991

7987 Superfund Week
Pasha Publications
8737 Colesville Road
Suite 1100
Silver Spring, MD 20910-3928

301-589-5103
800-274-6737
FAX 301-589-8493
E-Mail: custserv@bpinews.com
Home Page: www.bpinews.com

Harry Baisden, Group Publisher
Michael Hopps, Editor

Reporting the most recent developments in Congress, the EPA, and other government offices affecting hazardous waste investigations and cleanups in the federal Superfund and RCRA programs. Contains progress reports on specific cleanup sites in federal and state programs.
Cost: $525.00
Frequency: Weekly
Founded in 1963

7988 SurFACTS in Biomaterials
Surfaces in Biomaterials Foundation
1000 Westgate Drive
Suite 252
St Paul, MN 55114-8679

651-290-7487
FAX 651-290-2266
E-Mail: memberservices@surfaces.org
Home Page: www.surfaces.org

Steven Goodman, Executive Editor
Janeyy Duntley, Managing Editor

Dedicated to exploring creative solutions to technical challenges at the BioInterface by fostering education and multidisciplinary cooperation among industrial, academic, clinical and regulatory communities.
Frequency: Bimonthly

7989 The Current
Women's Council on Energy and the Environment
PO Box 33211
Washington, DC 20033-0211

202-997-4512
FAX 202-478-2098
Home Page: www.wcee.org
Social Media: *Facebook, Twitter*

Ronke Luke, President
Mary Brosnan-Sell, Secretary
Robin Cantor, Vice President
Alice Grabowski, Treasurer
Joyce Chandran, Executive Director

Keeps members up to date on energy and environmental issues to foster the professional development.

7990 The Dirt
Land and Water
Po Box 1197
Fort Dodge, IA 50501-1197

515-576-3191
FAX 515-576-2606
Home Page: www.landandwater.com
Social Media: *Facebook*

Amy Dencklau, Publisher
Shanza Dencklau, Assistant Editor
Rasch M. Kenneth, President

eNewsletter including information relating to the erosion control and water management industry such as: feature stories, industry news, conferences, expert tips and video clips, new products and more. Striving to keep readers up-to-date on all current happenings and relevant information beyond the pages of Land and Water Magazine.
Cost: $20.00
72 Pages
Circulation: 20000
Founded in 1959
Mailing list available for rent: 20M names
Printed in 4 colors on glossy stock

7991 The Forest Timeline
Forest History Society
701 William Vickers Ave
Durham, NC 27701-3162

919-682-9319
FAX 919-682-2349
E-Mail: recluce2@duke.edu

Home Page: www.foresthistory.org
Social Media: *Facebook, Twitter*

L. Michael Kelly, Chairman
Robert Healy, Co-Vice Chairman
Mark Wilde, Co-Vice Chairman
Henry I. Barclay III, Treasurer
Steven Anderson, Secretary & President

E-newsletter to keep the public informed of
FHS news and activities.
2000 Members
Founded in 1946

7992 The Networker
National Center for Appropriate Technology
3040 Continental Drive
PO Box 3838
Butte, MT 59702

406-494-4572
800-275-6228
FAX 406-494-2905
Home Page: www.ncat.org
Social Media: *Facebook, Twitter, LinkedIn*

Gene Brady, Chairman
Randall Chapman, Vice Chairman
George Ortiz, Chairman Emeritus
Jeannie Jertson, Secretary
Brian Castelli, Treasurer

Compiled by the LIHEAP Clearinghouse, an
NCAT project. Stories highlight state energy
assistanc program and low-income energy
news.
Founded in 1976

7993 The Resource
National Association of Conservation
Districts
509 Capitol Ct. NE
Washington, DC 20002-4937

202-547-6223
FAX 202-547-6450
Home Page: www.nacdnet.org

Krysta Harden, CEO
Bob Cordova, Second Vice President

NACD's print publication provides in depth
coverage of the association's recent activities
and features columns by the NACD CEO and
President, in addition to guest and partnership
columns.
Cost: $35.00
12 Pages
Frequency: Monthly
Circulation: 25000
Founded in 1937

7994 The Soil Plant Analyst
Soil and Plant Analysis Council
347 North Shores Circle
Windsor, CO 80550

970-686-5702
E-Mail: rmiller@lamar.colostate.edu
Home Page: www.spcouncil.com/

Rigas Karamanos, President
Robert Miller, Secretary/Treasurer
Rao Mylavarapu, Vice President

Quarterly newsletter dedicated to the Agricul-
tural Laboratory Industry.
Cost: $80.00
Circulation: 250

7995 TipSheet
Society of Environmental Journalists
PO Box 2492
Jenkintown, PA 19046

215-884-8174
FAX 215-884-8175
Home Page: www.sej.org
Social Media: *Facebook, Twitter*

Carolyn Whetzel, President
Peter Fairley, 1st Vice Pres

Jeff Burnside, 2nd VP
Don Hopey, Treasurer

News tips to notify journalists of potential environmental stories and sources.
Founded in 1990

7996 WEF Highlights
Water Environment Federation
601 Wythe St
Alexandria, VA 22314-1994

800-666-0206
FAX 703-684-2492
Home Page: www.wef.org
Social Media: *Facebook, Twitter*

Matt Bond, President
Cordell Samuels, President-Elect
Sandra Ralston, Vice President
Chris Browning, Treasurer
Jeff Eger, Secretary and Executive Director

Covers current Federation activities, Member
Association news, and items of concern to the
water quality field.
79 Members
ISSN: 1044-9943
Founded in 1928

7997 Washington Environmental Protection Report
Callahan Publications
PO Box 1173
Mc Lean, VA 22101-1173

703-356-1925
FAX 703-356-9614
E-Mail: sue@newsletteraccess.com
Home Page: www.newsletteraccess.com

Vincent Callahan, Editor

Twice-monthly letter on contracting opportunities, legislation, research and development, and
rules and regulations for the nation's environmental programs. The war on pollution, in all
its forms, is coming to the forefront of federal
priorities and could be the answer to the many
economic problems facing America.
Cost: $190.00
8 Pages
Frequency: Bi-monthly
Founded in 1990
Printed in one color

7998 Waste Handling Equipment News
Lee Publications
6113 Strate Highway 5
PO Box 121
Palatine Bridge, NY 13428

518-673-3237
800-218-5586
FAX 518-673-2381
E-Mail: mstanley@leepub.com
Home Page: www.wastehandling.com

Fred Lee, Publisher
Matt Stanley, Sales Manager
Holly Rieser, Editor

Addresses equipment needs of owners and operating managers involved in construction demolition, asphalt/concrete recycling, wood
waste recycling, scrap metal recycling and
composting. Every issue features editorial on
new equipment, equipment adaptations, site
stories, and news focused on our targeted
segment of the recycling industry.
Frequency: Monthly
Circulation: 14000
Founded in 1993
Printed in on newsprint stock

7999 Waste News
Crain Communications

1155 Gratiot Ave.
Detroit, MI 48207-2997

313-446-6000
E-Mail: info@wastenews.com
Home Page: www.crain.com

Keith Crain, Chairman
Rance Crain, President
Mary Kay Crain, Treasurer/Assistant Secretary
Merrilee P. Crain, Secretary/Assistant Treasurer

Trade publication covering the solid waste in-
dustry.
Frequency: Bi-Weekly
Circulation: 52838
Founded in 1995

8000 Waste Recovery Report
Icon: Information Concepts
211 S 45th St
Philadelphia, PA 19104-2995

215-349-6500
FAX 215-349-6502
E-Mail: wasterec@aol.com
Home Page: www.wrr.icodat.com

Alan Krigman, Publisher/Editor

Contains information on waste-to-energy, recy-
cling, composting and other technologies.
Cost: $60.00
6 Pages
Frequency: Monthly
Circulation: 500
ISSN: 0889-0072
Founded in 1975

8001 Water Environment Laboratory Solutions
Water Environment Federation
601 Wythe St
Alexandria, VA 22314-1994

800-666-0206
FAX 703-684-2492
Home Page: www.wef.org
Social Media: *Facebook, Twitter*

Matt Bond, President
Cordell Samuels, President-Elect
Sandra Ralston, Vice President
Chris Browning, Treasurer
Jeff Eger, Secretary and Executive Director

Focuses on day-to-day concerns regarding
equipment use, sample tracking, and quality
control, as well as discussing certification issues, staff management approaches, and new
and revised analytical methods.
79 Members
ISSN: 1044-9943
Founded in 1928

8002 Water Environment Regulation Watch
Water Environment Federation
601 Wythe St
Alexandria, VA 22314-1994

800-666-0206
FAX 703-684-2492
Home Page: www.wef.org
Social Media: *Facebook, Twitter*

Matt Bond, President
Cordell Samuels, President-Elect
Sandra Ralston, Vice President
Chris Browning, Treasurer
Jeff Eger, Secretary and Executive Director

Monthly snapshot of Washington's water quality activities. Provides concise reports of related bills, regulations, legal decisions,
congressional hearings, and other federal government actions, following key issues from introduction to final determination.
79 Members
ISSN: 1044-9943
Founded in 1928

8003 Weather & Climate Report
Nautilus Press
1056 National Press Building
Washington, DC 20045-2001

202-347-6643

John R Botzum, Editor
Reports on federal actions which impact weather, climate research and global changes in climate.

8004 Weekly Harvest
National Center for Appropriate Technology
3040 Continental Drive
PO Box 3838
Butte, MT 59702

406-494-4572
800-275-6228
FAX 406-494-2905
Home Page: www.ncat.org
Social Media: *Facebook, Twitter, LinkedIn*

Eugene Brady, Chairman
Kathleen Hadley, Executive Director

This e-newsletter is a Web digest of sustainable agriculture news, resources, events and funding opportunities gleaned from the Internet and featured on the website.
Frequency: Weekly
Founded in 1976

8005 World Research News
World Research Foundation
41 Bell Rock Plz
Sedona, AZ 86351-8804

928-284-3300
FAX 928-284-3530
E-Mail: laverne@wrf.org
Home Page: www.wrf.org

LaVerne Boeckman, Co-Founder
Steven Ross, Co-Founder

Health information that is collected, categorized and disseminated in an independent and unbiased manner. Including allopathic medicine alongside complementary and alternative medicine... ancient and traditional techniques and healing therapies as well as the latest medical technology.
Frequency: Quarterly

8006 World Wildlife Fund: Focus
World Wildlife
PO Box 97180
Washington, DC 20090-7180

202-293-4800
FAX 202-293-9211
Home Page: www.worldwildlife.org

Kathryn S Fuller, CEO
Jennifer Seeger, Chief Financial Officer
Michael Bauer, Chief Financial Officer
Marcia Marsh, Chief Operating Officer

WWF projects are highlighted around the world in 450 national parks and nature reserves, with emphasis on coverage of programs and activities in the US.
8 Pages
Frequency: Monthly
Founded in 1960

8007 eNotes
National Association of Conservation Districts
509 Capitol Ct. NE
Washington, DC 20002-4937

202-547-6223
FAX 202-547-6450
Home Page: www.nacdnet.org

Krysta Harden, CEO
Bob Cordova, Second Vice President

NACD's weekly news briefs.
Cost: $35.00
12 Pages
Frequency: Monthly
Circulation: 25000
Founded in 1937

Magazines & Journals

8008 ACCA Insider
Air Conditioning Contractors of America
2800 Shirlington Rd
Suite 300
Arlington, VA 22206-3607

703-575-4477
E-Mail: info@acca.org
Home Page: www.acca.org
Social Media: *Facebook, Twitter, LinkedIn, YouTube*

Paul Stalknecht, President & CEO
Offering targeted news to ACCA members.

8009 ASNT Annual Fall Conference
American Society for Nondestructive Testing
1711 Arlingate Lane
PO Box 28518
Columbus, OH 43228

614-274-6003
800-222-2768
FAX 614-274-6899
Home Page: www.asnt.org

Tim Jones, Senior Manager, Publications
Wayne Holliday, Executive Director

Research, reviews and information of nondestructive testing materials. Provides members and subscribers the latest news and technical information concerning this industry.
Cost: $75.00
12000 Members
90 Pages
Frequency: Monthly
Circulation: 13000
ISSN: 0025-5327
Founded in 1942
Printed in 4 colors on glossy stock

8010 Aerosol Science and Technology (AS&T)
American Association for Aerosol Research
15000 Commerce Parkway
Suite C
Mount Laurel, NJ 08054

856-439-9080
FAX 856-439-0525
E-Mail: info@aaar.org
Home Page: www.aaar.org

Peter McMurry, Editor-In-Chief
Tami C Bond, Editor
Warren H Finlay, Editor

AS&T is the offficial journal of AAAR. It publishes the results of theoretical and experimental investigations into aerosol phenomena and closely related material as well as high-quality reports on fundamental and applied topics.
Cost: $1214.00

8011 Agronomy Journal
American Society of Agronomy
5585 Guilford Rd.
Madison, WI 53711-1086

608-273-8080
FAX 608-273-2021
E-Mail: headquarters@sciencesocieties.org
Home Page: www.agronomy.org
Social Media: *Facebook, Twitter, LinkedIn*

Newell Kitchen, President
Kenneth Barbarick, President-Elect

Journal of agriculture and natural resource sciences. Articles convey original research in soil science, crop science, agroclimatology, agronomic modeling, production agriculture, instrumentation, and more.
10000 Members
Founded in 1907

8012 American Environmental Laboratory
International Scientific Communications
30 Controls Drive
PO Box 870
Shelton, CT 06484-0870

203-926-9300
Home Page: www.iscpubs.com

Brian Howard, Editor
Robert G Sweeny, Publisher

Laboratory activities, new equipment, and analysis and collection of samples are the main topics.
Cost: $282.42
Frequency: Monthly
Circulation: 185000

8013 American Forests
Po Box 2000
Suite 800
Washington, DC 20013-2000

202-737-1944
FAX 202-955-4588
E-Mail: info@amfor.org
Home Page: www.americanforests.org

Deborah Gangloff, Executive Director

A publication that offers our members the best in conservation news. Articles include different perspectives on current environmental issues, stories on wildlife restoration projects, updates on forest management practices, and ways to engage the conservation movement in your community.
Cost: $25.00
Frequency: Quarterly
Founded in 1875

8014 American Waste Digest
Charles G Moody
226 King St
Pottstown, PA 19464-9105

610-326-9480
800-442-4215
FAX 610-326-9752
E-Mail: awd@americanwastedigest.com
Home Page: www.americanwastedigest.com

Carasue Moody, Publisher
Shannon Costa, Circulation Manager
J. Robert Tagert, Sales Manager

Provides reviews on new products, profiles on sucessful waste removal businesses, and provides discussion on legislation on municipal regulations on recycling.
Cost: $24.00
86 Pages
Frequency: Monthly
Circulation: 33000
Printed in 4 colors on glossy stock

8015 Archives of Environmental Health
Society for Occupational and Environmental Health
111 North Bridge Road #21-01
Peninsula Plaza
Singapore 179098

703-556-9222
FAX 703-556-8729
Home Page: www.oehs.org

Laura Degnon, Manager

Publishing new research based on the most rigorous methods and discussion to put this work in perspective for public health, public policy, and sustainability, the Archives addresses such topics of current concern as health significance

of chemical exposure, toxic waste, new and old energy technologies, industrial processes, and the environmental causation of disease.
Frequency: Bi-Monthly

8016 Bio-Mineral Times
Allen C Forter & Son
3450 W Central Avenue
#328
Toledo, OH 43606-1418

419-535-6374
FAX 419-535-7008
E-Mail: info@nviro.com
Home Page: www.nviro.com

Bonnie Hunter, Publisher
James McHugh, Chief Financial Officer

Issues focus on environmental legislation efforts, regulation compliance, and finding answers to the mechanics and practical applications of the distribution and management of biosolids derived products.
Frequency: Quarterly
Circulation: 25,000

8017 CONNECT Magazine
Association of Zoos and Aquariums
8403 Colesville Rd
Suite 710
Silver Spring, MD 20910-6331

301-562-0777
FAX 301-562-0888
Home Page: www.aza.org
Social Media: *Facebook, Twitter*

L. Patricia Simmons, Chair
Tom Schmid, Chair-Elect
Jackie Ogden, PhD, Vice-Chair

Window to the professional zoo and aquarium world. Magazine features fascinating stories that explore trends, educational initiatives, member achievements and conservation efforts.
200 Members
Founded in 1924

8018 CSA News
American Society of Agronomy
5585 Guilford Rd.
Madison, WI 53711-1086

608-273-8080
FAX 608-273-2021
E-Mail: headquarters@sciencesocieties.org
Home Page: www.agronomy.org
Social Media: *Facebook, Twitter, LinkedIn*

Newell Kitchen, President
Kenneth Barbarick, President-Elect

The official magazine for members of the American Society of Agronomy, Crop Science Society of America, and Soil Science Society of America.
10000 Members
Founded in 1907

8019 Crop Science
American Society of Agronomy
5585 Guilford Rd.
Madison, WI 53711-1086

608-273-8080
FAX 608-273-2021
E-Mail: headquarters@sciencesocieties.org
Home Page: www.agronomy.org
Social Media: *Facebook, Twitter, LinkedIn*

Newell Kitchen, President
Kenneth Barbarick, President-Elect

Publishes original research in crops and turfgrass science.
10000 Members
Founded in 1907

8020 Crops & Soils
American Society of Agronomy

5585 Guilford Rd.
Madison, WI 53711-1086

608-273-8080
FAX 608-273-2021
E-Mail: headquarters@sciencesocieties.org
Home Page: www.agronomy.org
Social Media: *Facebook, Twitter, LinkedIn*

Newell Kitchen, President
Kenneth Barbarick, President-Elect

The magazine for certified crop advisors, agronomists, and soil scientists, Focuses on solutions to the daily challenges facing those working in the field and features information on new technology and products, company strategies, CEU articles and quizzes, and regulatory and industry news.
10000 Members
Founded in 1907

8021 E/Environmental Magazine
28 Knight St
Norwalk, CT 06851-4719

203-854-5559
800-967-6572
FAX 203-866-0602
E-Mail: info@emagazine.com
Home Page: www.emagazine.com

Jim Motavalli, Editor
Karen Soucy, Associate Publisher
Doug Moss, Publisher & Executive Dir
Brita Belli, Director
Trudy Hodenfield, Operations Manager

Providing information about environmental issues and sharing ideas and resources so that readers can live more sustainable lives and connect with ongoing efforts for change. Covers everything environmental, from big issues like climate change, renewable energy and toxins and health, to the topics that directly impact our readers' daily lives; how to eat right and stay healthy, where to invest responsibly and how to save energy at home.
Cost: $19.95
Circulation: 185,000
Founded in 1988

8022 EI Digest: Hazardous Waste Marketplace
Environmental Information
PO Box 390266
Minneapolis, MN 55439

952-831-2473
FAX 952-831-6550
Home Page: www.envirobiz.com

Cary Perket, President

Focused on serving the market information needs of the commercial hazardous waste management sector. Included those involved in recycling and re-use, energy recovery, waste treatment, and waste disposal. Provides compilations and analysis of the commercial markets for hazardous waste energy recovery, fuel blending, incineration, landfill and solvent recovery. Also undertakes special reports on chemical distributors, RCRA metal recyclers and wastewater treatment.
ISSN: 1042-251X
Founded in 1983
Printed in 2 colors

8023 EM
Air & Waste Management Association
420 Fort Duquesne Boulevard
One Gateway Center, 3rd Floor
Pittsburgh, PA 15222-1435

412-652-2458
FAX 412-232-3450
E-Mail: info@awma.org

Home Page: www.awma.org
Social Media: *Facebook, Twitter, LinkedIn*

Jeffry Muffat, President
Merlyn L. Hough, President Elect
Mike Kelly, Secretary/ Executive Director
Amy Gilligan, Treasurer
Dallas Baker, Vice President

A&WMA's magazine for environmental managers, explores a range of issues affecting the industry with timely, provocative articles and regular columns written by leaders in the field. Keeps readers informed of coverage of regulatory changes, EPA research, new technologies, market analyses, environment, health, and safety issues, new products, professional development opportunities, and more.
9000 Members
Founded in 1907

8024 Earth First! Journal
PO Box 964
Lake Worth, FL 33460

561-320-3840
E-Mail: collective@earthfirstjournal.org
Home Page: earthfirstjournal.org
Social Media: *Facebook, Twitter, Google+, Reddit*

Quarterly voice of the radical environmental movement.
Frequency: Quarterly
Founded in 1979

8025 Earth Island Journal
2150 Allston Way
Suite 460
Berkeley, CA 94704-1375

510-859-9100
FAX 510-859-9091
E-Mail: arch@earthisland.org
Home Page: www.earthisland.org
Social Media: *Facebook, Twitter, YouTube*

Martha Davis, President
Kenneth Brower, Vice President
Michael Hathaway, Vice President
Jennifer Snyder, Secretary
Alex Giedt, Treasurer

Combines investigative journalism and thought-provoking essays that make the subtle but profound connections between the environment and other contemporary issues. The Journal's unique brand of environmental journalism is a key resource for anyone eager to help protect our shared planet.
33M Members
Founded in 1985

8026 Ecological Economics, The ISEE Journal
International Society for Ecological Economics
15 River Street
#204
Boston, MA 02108

703-790-1745
FAX 703-790-2672
E-Mail: secretariat@ecoeco.org
Home Page: www.ecoeco.org
Social Media: *Facebook, Twitter*

John Gowdy, President
Bina Agarwal, President-Elect
Anne Aitken, Managing Editor

Concerned with extending and integrating the study and management of ecology and economics. This integration is necessary because conceptual and professional isolation have led to economic and environmental policies which are mutually destructive rather than reinforcing in the long term.
750 Members
Founded in 1989

8027 Ecological Management & Restoration
Society for Ecological Restoration
International
1017 O Street NW
Washington, DC 20001

202-299-9518
FAX 270-626-5485
E-Mail: info@ser.org
Home Page: www.ser.org
Social Media: *Facebook*

Steve Whisenant, Chair
Cara R. Nelson, Vice Chair
Mary Travaglini, Treasurer
Alan Unwin, Secretary

Aims to bridge the gap between the ecologist's perspective and field manager's experience. Answers the growing need among land managers for reliable, relevant information and acknowledges the need for two-way communication in devising new hypotheses, sound experimentation, effective treatments and reliable monitoring.
2300 Members
Frequency: Quarterly
Founded in 1988

8028 Economics of Energy and Environmental Policy (EEEP)
International Association for Energy
Economics
28790 Chagrin Blvd
Suite 350
Cleveland, OH 44122-4642

216-464-5365
FAX 216-464-2737
E-Mail: iaee@iaee.org
Home Page: www.iaee.org
Social Media: *Facebook, LinkedIn*

Mine Yucel, President
Lars Bergman, President-Elect
David L. Williams, Executive Director

Policy oriented, focusing on all policy issues in the interface between energy and environmental economics. Provides a research-based, scholarly, yet easily read and accessible source of information on contemporary economic thinking and analysis of energy and environmental policy.
3400 Members
Founded in 1977

8029 Energy Engineering
Association of Energy Engineers
4025 Pleasantdale Rd
Suite 420
Atlanta, GA 30340-4264

770-447-5083
FAX 770-446-3969
E-Mail: info@aeecenter.org
Home Page: www.aeecenter.org

Albert Thumann, Executive Director
Ruth Whitlock, Executive Admin
Albert Thumann, Executive Director
Ruth Marie, Managing Editor

Engineering solutions to cost efficiency problems and mechanical contractors who design, specify, install, maintain, and purchase non-residential heating, ventilating, air conditioning and refrigeration equipment and components.
Circulation: 8000
Founded in 1976

8030 Environ: A Magazine for Ecologic Living and Health
Environ

1616 Seventeenth Street
Suite 468
Denver, CO 80202

303-285-5543
FAX 303-628-5597
Home Page: www.environcorp.com

Suzanne Randegger, Publisher/Editor
Ed Randegger, Co-Publisher/Ad Director
John Haasbeek, Senior Manager
Chris Keller, Managing Director

Designed to keep health and ecology conscious readers aware of circumstances hazardous to human health, and provide alternatives - practical, political, and global. Coverage of environmental legislation, ecologic food-growing practices and certification, geographically and climatically safe and hazardous locations, and a view of today's health problems with active solutions. Supported by screened advertisers.
Cost: $15.00
40 Pages
Frequency: Quarterly

8031 Environment
Helen Dwight Reid Educational Foundation
1319 18th Street NW
Washington, DC 20036-1802

202-296-6267
FAX 202-296-5149
E-Mail: brichman@heldref.org
Home Page: www.heldref.org

Douglas Kirkpatrick, Publisher
Barbara Richman, Editor
Fred Huber, Circulation Manager
Emily Tawlowski, Marketing Manager
Steve Hellem, Executive Director

Analyzes the problems, places, and people where environment and development come together, illuminating concerns from the local to the global. Articles and commentaries from researchers and practitioners who provide a broad range of international perspectives. Also features in-depth reviews of major policy reports, conferences, and environmental education initiatives, as well as guides to the best Web sites, journal articles, and books.
Cost: $51.00
Frequency: Monthly
Circulation: 11,408
Founded in 1956

8032 Environmental & Engineering Geoscience Journal
Association of Engineering Geologists
PO Box 460518
Denver, CO 80246-0518

303-757-2926
FAX 720-230-4846
E-Mail: aeg@aegweb.org
Home Page: www.aegweb.org
Social Media: *Facebook, Twitter*

Jennifer Bauer, President
Matthew B. Morris, Vice President/ President Elect
Gary Lice, Treasurer
Ken Fergason, Secretary

Publishes peer reviewed manuscripts that address issues relating to the interaction of people with hydrologic and geologic systems. Theoretical and applied contributions are appropriate, and the primary criteria for acceptance are scientific and technical merit.
3000 Members
Founded in 1957
Mailing list available for rent: 3000 names at $100 per M

8033 Environmental Business Journal
Environmental Business International

4452 Park Boulevard Suite 306
PO Box 371769
San Diego, CA 92116-1769

619-295-7685
FAX 619-295-5743
E-Mail: ebi@ebiusa.com
Home Page: www.ebiusa.com

Grant Ferrier, Publisher
Dan Johnson, Manager

An overview piece, segment analysis by country, profiles of domestic and foreign firms, financial data on listed environmental companies in the region, the latest developments on government initiatives and regulations, company news and projects are included in the features of this publications.
Cost: $495.00
Founded in 1988
Printed in 2 colors

8034 Environmental Communicator
North American Association for
Environmental
2000 P St NW
Suite 540
Washington, DC 20036-6921

202-419-0412
FAX 202-419-0415
E-Mail: email@naaee.org
Home Page: www.naaee.org

Brian Day, Executive Director

A publication of the North American Association for EE. Feature articles, association news, affiliate news, op-ed pieces, announcements on new EE resources, available jobs, and future events and opportunities.
Frequency: Bi-Monthly

8035 Environmental Engineering Science
Mary Ann Liebert
140 Huguenot St
New Rochelle, NY 10801-5215

914-740-2100
FAX 914-740-2101
E-Mail: info@liebertpub.com
Home Page: www.liebertpub.com

Mary A Liebert, Owner
Dumpnico Grosso, Editor-in-Chief
Stephanie Paul, Production Editor
Lisa Cohen, Associate Editors

Publishing studies of innovative solutions to problems in air, wter, and land contamination and waste disposal. Features application of environmental engineering and scientific discoveries, policy issues, environmental economics, and sustainable development.
Cost: $330.00
Frequency: Monthly
Circulation: 1800
ISSN: 1092-8758
Founded in 1980

8036 Environmental Forensics
AEHS Foundation Inc
150 Fearing Street
Amherst, MA 01002

413-549-5170
FAX 413-549-0579
Home Page: www.aehsfoundation.org

Paul T Kostecki, PhD, Executive Director

An international publication offering scientific studies that explore source, fate, transport and ecological effects of environmental contamination, with contamination being delineated in terms of chemical characterization, biological influence, responsible parties and legal consequences.
600 Members
Founded in 1989

8037 Environmental Geochemistry and Health
Society for Environmental Geochemistry and Health
4698 S Forrest Avenue
Springfield, MO 65810

417-885-1166
FAX 417-881-6920
Home Page: www.segh.net

Bobby Wixson, Director Membership

Publishes original research papers, short communications, reviews and topical special issues across the broad field of environmental geochemistry. Coverage includes papers that directly link health and the environment.
Frequency: Quarterly

8038 Environmental History (EH)
UW Interdisciplinary Arts and Sciences Program
1900 Commerce Street
Tacoma, WA 98402

206-343-0226
FAX 206-343-0249
E-Mail: director@aseh.net
Home Page: www.aseh.net

John McNeill, President
Gregg Mitman, Vice President/ President Elect
Ellen Stroud, Secretary
Mark Madison, Treasurer

The world's leading scholarly journal in environmental history. Brings together scholars, scientists, and practitioners from a wide array of disciplines to explore changing relationships between humans and the environment over time.
1200 Members
Founded in 1976

8039 Environmental Practice
National Association of Environmental Professional
PO Box 2086
Bowie, MD 20718-2086

888-251-9902
FAX 301-860-1141
Home Page: www.naep.org

John Perkins, Editor

Incorporates original research articles, news of issues and of the NAEP, and opinion pieces. Of interest to private consultants, academics, and professionals in federal, state, local, and tribal governments, as well as in corporations and non-governmental organizations. Reports on historic and contemporary environmental issues that help inform current practices.
Frequency: Quarterly

8040 Environmental Protection
Stevens Publishing Corporation
5151 Belt Line Rd
10th Floor
Dallas, TX 75254-7507

972-687-6700
FAX 972-687-6767
Home Page: www.eponline.com

Craig S Stevens, President
Dana Cornett, President/COO
Randy Dye, Publisher
Sherleen Mahoney, Editor
Margaret Perry, Circulation Director

The comprehensive online information resource for environmental professionals.
Circulation: 63000
Founded in 1925

8041 Environmental Science and Technology
American Chemical Society

1155 16th St Nw
Washington, DC 20036-4892

202-872-4600
800-227-5558
FAX 202-872-4615
E-Mail: service@acs.org
Home Page: www.acs.org

Madeleine Jacobs, CEO/Executive Director

Publishes news and research in diverse areas of environmental science and engineering.
Cost: $156.00
110 Pages
Frequency: Monthly
Circulation: 13000
Founded in 1966

8042 Environmental Times
Environmental Assessment Association
1224 N Nokomis NE
Alexandria, MN 56308

320-763-4320
E-Mail: info@eaa-assoc.org
Home Page: www.iami.org/eaa.html

Robert Johnson, Executive Director

This publications contents contain environment conferences and expos, industry trends, federal regulations related to the environment and industry assessments.
Cost: $19.95
24 Pages
Circulation: 7000
Founded in 1972
Printed in 4 colors on newsprint stock

8043 Environmental Toxicology and Chemistry
Society of Environmental Toxicology and Chemistry
1013 N 12th Ave
Pensacola, FL 32501-3306

850-437-1901
FAX 850-469-9778
E-Mail: rparrish@setac.org
Home Page: www.edwardjones.com

Chad Stacy, Manager

Dedicated to furthering scientific knowledge and disseminating information on environmental toxicology and chemistry, including the application of these sciences to risk management. Provides a forum for professionals in academia, business, and government.

8044 Environmental and Molecular Mutagenesis
Environmental Mutagen Society
1821 Michael Faraday Drive
Suite 300
Reston, VA 20190

703-438-8220
FAX 703-438-3113
E-Mail: emshq@ems-us.org
Home Page: www.ems-us.org

Publishes original research articles on environmental mutangenesis. Manuscripts published in the six general areas of mechanisms of mutagenesis, genomics, DNA damage, replication, recombination and repair, public health, and DNA technology.
Frequency: 8/year

8045 ExecutiveBrief
Synthetic Organic Chemical Manufacturers Assn
1850 M St Nw
Suite 700
Washington, DC 20036-5803

202-721-4100
FAX 202-296-8120

E-Mail: info@socma.org
Home Page: www.socma.org

Joseph Acker, President
Vivian Diko, Executive Assistant & CEO
Charlene Patterson, Editor

Provides quality content on software development, outsourcing, project and risk management.

8046 Fisheries
American Fisheries Society
5410 Grosvenor Ln
Suite 110
Bethesda, MD 20814-2199

301-897-8616
FAX 301-897-8096
Home Page: www.fisheries.org

Gus Rassam, Executive Director
Charles Moseley, Journals Manager

Peer reviewed articles that address contemporary issues and problems, techniques, philosophies and other areas of interest to the general fisheries profession. Monthly features include letters, meeting notices, book listings and reviews, environmental essays and organization profiles.
Cost: $76.00
50 Pages
Frequency: Monthly
Founded in 1870
Mailing list available for rent: 8500 names at $250 per M

8047 Forest History Today
Forest History Society
701 William Vickers Ave
Durham, NC 27701-3162

919-682-9319
FAX 919-682-2349
E-Mail: recluce2@duke.edu
Home Page: www.foresthistory.org
Social Media: *Facebook, Twitter*

L. Michael Kelly, Chairman
Robert Healy, Co-Vice Chairman
Mark Wilde, Co-Vice Chairman
Henry I. Barclay III, Treasurer
Steven Anderson, Secretary & President

Providing members of FHS with engaging writings in forest history and staying updated with current FHS activities.
2000 Members
Founded in 1946

8048 Fusion Science and Technology
American Nuclear Society
555 N Kensington Ave
La Grange Park, IL 60526-5592

708-352-6611
800-323-3044
FAX 708-352-0499
E-Mail: advertising@ans.org
Home Page: www.ans.org
Social Media: *Facebook, Twitter, LinkedIn*

Jack Tuohy, Executive Director
James S Tulenko, VP
William F Naughton, Treasurer

Information on fusion plasma physics and plasma engineering, fusion plasma enabling science and technology, fusion nuclear technology and material science, fusion applications, fusion design and system studies. Plasma and fusion energy physics, tokamak experiments, stellarators, next step burning plasma experiments, target fabrications and technology for inertial confinement fusion, inertial fusion science and applications, tritium science and technology, and more.
10500 Members
Founded in 1954

8049 Geophysics
Society of Exploration Geophysicists
8801 South Yale
Suite 500
Tulsa, OK 74137-3575

918-497-5500
FAX 918-497-5557
E-Mail: web@seg.org
Home Page: www.seg.org
Social Media: *Facebook, Twitter, LinkedIn*

Mary Fleming, Executive Director
Vladimir Grechka, Editor

An archival journal encompassing all aspects of research, exploration, and education in applied geophysics.
Founded in 1930

8050 Hauler
Hauler Magazine
166 S Main Street
PO Box 508
New Hope, PA 18938

800-220-6029
800-220-6029
FAX 215-862-3455
E-Mail: mag@thehauler.com
Home Page: www.thehauler.com

Thomas N Smith, Publisher/Editor
Barbara Gibney, Circulation Manager
Leslie T Smith, Marketing Director

Dedicated to the refuse and solid waste industry. It is the acknowledged leader in the new and used refuse truck and equipment marketplace, and now lists hundreds of new and used trash trucks, trailers, containers, services, plus parts and accessories from the best suppliers in the industry.
Cost: $12.00
Frequency: Monthly
Circulation: 18630
Founded in 1978

8051 Hazardous Management
Ecolog
1450 Don Mills Road
Don Mills, Ontario M3B-2X7

416-442-2292
888-702-1111
FAX 416-442-2204
Home Page: www.hazmatmag.com

Lynda Reilly, Publisher

The latest environmental regulations and programs as well as the evolving technology and equipment needed to achieve compliance.
Cost: $39.50
Frequency: Bi-Monthly
Circulation: 16,000
ISSN: 0843-9303
Founded in 1989
Mailing list available for rentat $250 per M
Printed in 4 colors on glossy stock

8052 Hazardous Waste Consultant
Aspen Publishers
8400 east cresent parkway
6 floor greenwood village
Lakewood, CO 80111

720-528-4270
800-638-8437
FAX 212-597-0335

A unique approach to hazardous waste issues. It is written by engineers and regulatory specialists who have an extensive background in the field and understand the problems that industry, consultants, and regulators face.
Cost: $475.00

8053 Human Ecology Review
Society for Human Ecology

College of the Atlantic
105 Eden Street
Bar Harbor, ME 04609-0180

207-288-5015
FAX 207-288-3780
E-Mail: carter@ecology.coa.edu
Home Page: www.societyforhumanecology.org

Barbara Carter, Assistant to Executive Director

Publishes peer-reviewed research and theory on the interaction between humans and the environment and other links between culture and nature, essays and applications relevant to human ecology, book reviews, and relevant commentary, announcements, and awards.
Frequency: Semi-Annual

8054 Human and Ecological Risk Assessment
AEHS Foundation Inc
150 Fearing Street
Amherst, MA 01002

413-549-5170
FAX 413-549-0579
Home Page: www.aehsfoundation.org

Paul T Kostecki, PhD, Executive Director

Devoted to providing a framework for professionals researching and assessing developments in both human and ecological risk assessment.
600 Members
Founded in 1989

8055 Hydrological Science and Technology
American Institute Of Hydrology
300 Village Green Circle
Suite 201
Smyrna, GA 30080

770-269-9388
Home Page: www.aihydro.org

Cathy Lipsett, Owner
Cathryn Seaburn, Manager

Peer-reviewed international journal covering research and practical studies on hydrological science, technology, water resources and related topics including water, air and soil pollution and hazardous waste issues. Communicating ideas, findings, methods, techniques and summaries of interesting projects or investigations in the area of hydrology.
Frequency: Quarterly

8056 IEEE Power and Energy Magazine
IEEE
PO Box 1331
Piscataway, NJ 08855

732-981-0061
FAX 732-981-9667
E-Mail: society-info@ieee.org
Home Page: www.ieee.org

Mel Olken, Editor
Susan Schneiderman, Business Development

Dedicated to disseminating information on all matters of interest to electric power engineers and other professionals involved in the electric power industry. Feature articles focus on advanced concepts, technologies, and practices associated with all aspects of electric power from a technical perspective in synergy with nontechnical areas such as business, environmental, and social concerns.
Cost: $260.00
82 Pages
Frequency: Monthly
Circulation: 23000
ISSN: 1540-7977
Founded in 2003
Mailing list available for rent
Printed in on glossy stock

8057 Identifying Business Risks & Opportunities
World Resources Institute
10 G St NE
Suite 800
Washington, DC 20002-4252

202-729-7600
FAX 202-729-7610
E-Mail: front@wri.org
Home Page: www.wcdassessment.org

Jonathan Lash, President

8058 Indoor Air Journal
The Indoor Air Institute
2548 Empire Grade
Santa Cruz, CA 95060

831-426-0148
FAX 831-426-6522
E-Mail: info@IndAir.org
Home Page: indair.org

Hal Levin, President
William Fisk, Vice President
William Nazaroff, Vice President

Providing a location for reporting original research results in the broad area defined by the indoor environment of non-industrial buildings. The results will provide the information to allow designers, builders, owners and operators to provide a healthy and comfortable environment for building occupants. Health effects, monitoring and modelling, source characterization, ventilation and other environmental control techniques, thermal comfort, and public policy.

8059 Indoor Environment Review
IAQ Publications
7920 Norfolk Ave
#900
Bethesda, MD 20814-2539

301-913-0115
FAX 301-913-0119
Home Page: www.eschoolnews.com

Robert Morrow, Owner

New technology, research and legislation concerning all indoor air and water quality issues.
Frequency: Monthly
Circulation: 10000

8060 Industrial Safety & Hygiene
Business News Publishing Company
2401 W. Big Beaver Road
Suite 700
Troy, MI 48084

847-763-9534
FAX 847-763-9538
E-Mail: ishn@halldata.com
Home Page: www.ishn.com

Randy Green, Publisher/ West Coast Manager
Dave Johnsen, Editor
Maureen Brady, Managing Editor/Project Editor
Vince Miconi, Production Manager
Lydia Stewart, Inside Sales/Classifides

A business-to-business trade publication targeted at key safety, health and industrial hygiene buying influencers at manufacturing facilities of all sizes. Designed for the busy professionals with early mail dates and short articles backed by dynamite graphics. Each issue is packed with vital editorial on OSHA and EPA regulations, ho-to features, safety and health management topics, and the latest product news. For safety and health managers at high-hazard worksites.

8061 Industrial Wastewater
Water Environment Federation

601 Wythe St
Alexandria, VA 22314-1994

800-666-0206
FAX 703-684-2492
Home Page: www.wef.org
Social Media: *Facebook, Twitter*

Matt Bond, President
Cordell Samuels, President-Elect
Sandra Ralston, Vice President
Chris Browning, Treasurer
Jeff Eger, Secretary and Executive Director

Discusses relevant regulatory and legal issues, provides examples of real-world treatment options, and offers suggestions on minimizing waste and preventing pollution.
79 Members
ISSN: 1044-9943
Founded in 1928

8062 Inside EPA

Inside Washington Publishers
1919 S Eads St
Arlington, VA 22202-3028

703-418-3981
800-424-9068
FAX 703-416-8543
E-Mail: support@iwpnews.com
Home Page: www.iwpnews.com

Alan Sosenko, Owner

Gives timely information on all facets of waste, water, air, and other environmental regulatory programs.
Frequency: Weekly
Founded in 1980

8063 Inside Waste

John Cupps Associates
2757 13th Street
Sacramento, CA 95818-2907

916-448-5272
FAX 916-448-7862

John A Cupps, Publisher/Editor

The waste trade spans a diverse range of activities, from waste collection to resource recovery to landfilling. The operating environment varies from state to state, between urban and rural areas, and even among different councils. Inside Waste brings this all together, covering all the news, projects, contracts and issues that matter to the waste trade.
Frequency: Monthly

8064 Integrated Environmenal Assessment and Management

SETAC
1013 N 12th Ave
Pensacola, FL 32501-3306

850-437-1901
FAX 850-469-9778
E-Mail: setac@setac.org
Home Page: www.setac.org
Social Media: *Facebook, Twitter, LinkedIn*

Paul van den Brink, President
Tim Canfield, Vice President
Fred Heimbach, Treasurer

Bridges the gap between scientific research and its application in environmental decision-making, regulation, and management.
4000 Members
Founded in 1979

8065 International Dredging Review

PO Box 1487
Fort Collins, CO 80522-1487

970-416-1903
FAX 970-416-1878

E-Mail: editor@dredgemag.com
Home Page: www.dredgemag.com

Judith Powers, Publisher
Julia Leach, Business Manager
Nelson Spencer, Business Manager

Targeted to dredging company executives, project managers and dredge crew members, suppliers and service people such as pump manufacturers, hydrographic surveyors, consulting engineers, etc.
Cost: $85.00
Frequency: Monthly
Circulation: 3300
ISSN: 0737-8181
Founded in 1967

8066 International Environmental Systems Update

CEEM
3975 University Drive
Suite 230
Fairfax, VA 22030-3223

703-437-9000
800-745-5565
FAX 703-437-9001
Home Page: www.qsuonline.com

Paul Scicchitano, Publisher
Suzanne Leonard, Senior Editor

Provides information covering the emerging environmental issues that affect business and industry around the globe including competitive advantages, global updates, strategies, management systems and company profiles.
Cost: $ 390.00
24 Pages
Frequency: Monthly
Circulation: 50000
ISSN: 1079-0837
Founded in 1994
Mailing list available for rent
Printed in 2 colors on matte stock.

8067 International Journal of Phytoremediation

AEHS Foundation Inc.
150 Fearing Street
Amherst, MA 01002

413-549-5170
888-540-2347
Home Page: www.aehsfoundation.org

Paul T Kostecki, PhD, Executive Director

Devoted to the publication of current laboratory and field research describing the use of plant systems to remediate contaminated environments. Designed to link professionals in the many environmental disciplines involved in the development, application, management, and regulation of emerging phytoremediation technologies.
600 Members
Frequency: Quarterly
Founded in 1989

8068 International Journal of Wildland Fire

International Association of Wildland Fire
4025 Fair Ridge Drive
Fairfax, VA 22033

785-423-1818
FAX 785-542-3511
E-Mail: sandy@iawfonline.org
Home Page: www.iawfonline.org
Social Media: *Facebook, Twitter*

Sacha Dick, Programs Manager
Mikel Robinson, Executive Director

Online journal publishing new and significant papers that advance basic and applied research concerning wildland fire. Aims to publish quality papers on a broad range of wildland fire issues, and has an international perspective, since

wildland fire plays a major social, economic, and ecological role around the globe.
Frequency: Quarterly

8069 Journal of Air & Waste Management Association

Air & Waste Management Association
1 Gateway Center
3rd Floor
Pittsburgh, PA 15222-1435

412-652-2458
800-270-3444
FAX 412-232-3450
E-Mail: info@awma.org
Home Page: www.awma.org
Social Media: *Facebook, Twitter, LinkedIn*

Andy Knopes, Production Manager/Editor
Richard Sherr, Execetive Director

Intended to serve those occupationally involved in air pollution control and waste management through the publication of timely and reliable information. Descriptions of contemporary advances in air quality and waste management science and technology for use in improving environmental protection.
Cost: $330.00
Frequency: Monthly
Circulation: 3500
ISSN: 1047-3289
Founded in 1907

8070 Journal of Environmental Economics and Management

Association of Environmental and Resource
1616 P St Nw
Suite 400
Washington, DC 20036-1434

202-328-5125
FAX 202-939-3460
E-Mail: info@aere.org
Home Page: www.aere.org

Devoted to the publication of theoretical and empirical papers concerned with the linkage between economic systems and environmental and natural resources systems. The top journal in natural resources and environmental economics, it concentrates on the management and/or social control of the economy in its relationship with the management and use of natural resources and the natural environment.
Frequency: Bi-Monthly

8071 Journal of Environmental Education

Heldref Publications
1319 18th St Nw
Washington, DC 20036-1802

202-296-6267
FAX 202-296-5149
E-Mail: jee@heldref.org
Home Page: www.heldref.org

James Denton, Executive Director
J. Heldref, Editor

Details how best to present environmental issues and how to evaluate programs already in place for primary through university level and adult students. Publishes material that advances the instruction, theory, methods, and practice of environmental education and communication. Subject areas include the sciences, social sciences, and humanities.
Cost: $58.00
Frequency: Quarterly
Circulation: 1250
Founded in 1970

8072 Journal of Environmental Engineering

American Society of Civil Engineers

1801 Alexander Bell Dr
Reston, VA 20191-4382

703-295-6300
800-548-2723
703-295-6300
FAX 703-295-6222
E-Mail: webmaster@asce.org
Home Page: www.asce.org

D Wayne Klotz, President
M. Kathy Banks, Editor

Emphasizes on the implementaion of effective and safe methods for handling, transporting, and treating waste materials.
Cost: $308.00
Frequency: Monthly
Circulation: 2,500
Founded in 1852

8073 Journal of Environmental Geochemistry and Health

Society for Environmental Geochemistry & Health
4698 S Forrest Avenue
Springfield, MO 65810

417-851-1166
FAX 417-881-6920
E-Mail: DRBGWIXSON@aol.com
Home Page: www.segh.net

Prof. Xiangdong Li, President
Prof. Andrew Hursthouse, European Chair
Kyoung-Woong Kim, Asia/Pacific Chair
Anthea Brown, Membership Secretary/
Treasurer
Malcolm Brown, Secretary

Publishes original research papers, research notes and reviews across the broad field of environmental geochemistry.
400 Members
Founded in 1971

8074 Journal of Environmental Health

National Environmental Health Association
720 S Colorado Blvd
Suite 970S
Denver, CO 80246-1926

303-756-9090
FAX 303-691-9490
E-Mail: staff@neha.org
Home Page: www.neha.org
Social Media: Facebook, Twitter, LinkedIn

Nelson Fabian, Executive Director
Julie Collins, Research
Kim Brandow, Marketing/Sales Manager
Larry Marcum, Managing Director
Bob Custard, Manager

A practical journal containing information on a variety of environmental health issues.
Cost: $90.00
5000 Members
70 Pages
Frequency: 10 per year
Circulation: 20,000
ISSN: 0022-0892
Founded in 1937
Printed in 4 colors on glossy stock

8075 Journal of Environmental Quality

American Society of Agronomy
5585 Guilford Rd.
Madison, WI 53711-1086

608-273-8080
FAX 608-273-2021
E-Mail: headquarters@sciencesocieties.org
Home Page: www.agronomy.org
Social Media: Facebook, Twitter, LinkedIn

Newell Kitchen, President
Kenneth Barbarick, President-Elect

Papers are grouped by subject matter and cover water, soil, and atmospheric research as it relates to agriculture and the environment.
10000 Members
Founded in 1907

8076 Journal of Food Protection

International Association for Food Protection
6200 Aurora Ave
Suite 200W
Des Moines, IA 50322-2864

515-276-3344
800-369-6337
FAX 515-276-8655
E-Mail: info@foodprotection.org
Home Page: www.foodprotection.org
Social Media: Facebook, Twitter, LinkedIn

Isabel Walls, President
Katherine M.J. Swanson, President-Elect
Don Schaffner, Vice President
Don Zink, Secretary
David W. Tharp, Executive Director

Each issue contains scientific research and authoritative review articles reporting on a variety of topics in food science pertaining to food safety and quality.
3400 Members
Founded in 1911

8077 Journal of Intelligent Material Systems and Structures

Sage Journals Online

Home Page: www.jim.sagepub.com

Dan Inman, Editor-In-Chief

An international peer reviewed journal that publishes the highest quality original research. JIMSS reports on the results of experimental or theoretical work on any aspect of intelligent materials systems and/or structures research also called smart structure, smart materials, active materials, adaptive structures and adaptive materials.
Cost: $995.00
80 Pages
Frequency: Monthly
ISSN: 1045-389X
Printed in 2 colors on matte stock

8078 Journal of Natural Resources & Life Sciences Education

American Society of Agronomy
5585 Guilford Rd.
Madison, WI 53711-1086

608-273-8080
FAX 608-273-2021
E-Mail: headquarters@sciencesocieties.org
Home Page: www.agronomy.org
Social Media: Facebook, Twitter, LinkedIn

Newell Kitchen, President
Kenneth Barbarick, President-Elect

Today's educators look here for the latest teaching ideas in the life sciences, natural resources, and agriculture.
10000 Members
Founded in 1907

8079 Journal of Plant Registrations

American Society of Agronomy
5585 Guilford Rd.
Madison, WI 53711-1086

608-273-8080
FAX 608-273-2021
E-Mail: headquarters@sciencesocieties.org
Home Page: www.agronomy.org
Social Media: Facebook, Twitter, LinkedIn

Newell Kitchen, President
Kenneth Barbarick, President-Elect

Publishes cultivar, germplasm, parental line, genetic stock, and mapping population registration manuscripts.
10000 Members
Founded in 1907

8080 Journal of Soil and Water Conservation

Soil and Water Conservation Society
945 SW Ankeny Rd
Ankeny, IA 50023-9764

515-289-2331
800-843-7645
FAX 515-289-1227
E-Mail: pubs@swcs.org
Home Page: www.swcs.org

Oksana Gieseman, Director of Publications

The JSWC is a multidisciplinary journal of natural resource conservation research, practice, policy, and perspectives. The journal has two sections: the A Section containing various departments and features and the Research Section containing peer-reviewed research papers.
Cost: $99.00
Frequency: Bimonthly
Circulation: 2000
ISSN: 0022-4561
Founded in 1945

8081 Journal of Wildlife Management

Wildlife Society
5410 Grosvenor Ln
Suite 200
Bethesda, MD 20814-2197

301-897-9770
FAX 301-530-2471
E-Mail: tws@wildlife.org
Home Page: www.wildlife.org
Social Media: Facebook, Twitter, LinkedIn

Michael Hutchins, Executive Director

One of the world's leading scientific journals covering wildlife science, management and conservation.
Founded in 1937

8082 Journal of the Air Pollution Control Association

Air Pollution Control Association
1 Gateway Center 3rd Floor
420 Fort Duquesne Blvd.
Pittsburgh, PA 15222-1435

412-232-3444
800-270-3444
FAX 412-232-3450
E-Mail: info@awma.org
Home Page: www.awma.org/
Social Media: Facebook, Twitter, LinkedIn

Tim Keener, Technical Editor-in-Chief
George Hidy, Co-Editor
Jeffrey Brook, Associate Editor

A comprehensive journal offering information to the environment and conservation industry.
Cost: $95.00
Frequency: Monthly
Circulation: 700
Founded in 1907

8083 Journal of the IEST

Institute of Environmental Sciences and Technology
5005 Newport Drive
Suite 506
Rolling Meadows, IL 60008-3841

847-255-1561
FAX 847-255-1699
Home Page: www.iest.org
Social Media: Facebook, Twitter, LinkedIn

Julie Kendrick, Executive Director
Robert Burrows, Director Communications Services

Corrie Roesslein, Director
Programs/Administration

The official publication of the IEST. Contains technical articles and reports on simulation, testing, modeling, control, current research, covering contamination control, environmental laboratory and field-testing and evaluation, reliability assessment and evaluation methods, and others. To support the pursuit of knowledge, the advancement of technology, and the creation of pathways of communication in the environmental sciences.
1600 Members
Founded in 1953

8084 Journal of the Institute of Environmental Sciences and Technology

Institute of Environmental Sciences and Technology
5005 Newport Drive
Suite 506
Rolling Meadows, IL 60008-3841

847-255-1561
FAX 847-255-1699
E-Mail: information@iest.org
Home Page: www.iest.org

Julie Kendrick, Executive Director
Robert Burrows, Director Communications Services
Corrie Roesslein, Director
Programs/Administration

Contains technical articles and reports on simulation, testing, modeling, control, current research, and the teaching of the enrionmental sciences and technologies. The content covers contamination control, environmental laboratory and field-testing and evaluation, reliability assessment and evaluation methods, environmental instrumentation and measurements, envrionmental effects, environmental and safety standards, computer applications, and many other topics.
Frequency: Annual

8085 Journal of the U.S. SJWP

Water Environment Federation
601 Wythe St
Alexandria, VA 22314-1994

800-666-0206
FAX 703-684-2492
Home Page: www.wef.org
Social Media: *Facebook, Twitter*

Matt Bond, President
Cordell Samuels, President-Elect
Sandra Ralston, Vice President
Chris Browning, Treasurer
Jeff Eger, Secretary and Executive Director

Electronic publication. Purpose is to share the fresh thinking of today's young scientists with the entire water quality community. In addition to the benefit of research exchange, students are mentored in scientific writing and publication.
79 Members
ISSN: 1044-9943
Founded in 1928

8086 Lake & Reservoir Management

North American Lake Management Society
PO Box 5443
Madison, WI 53705

608-233-2836
FAX 608-233-3186
E-Mail: info@nalms.org
Home Page: www.nalms.org
Social Media: *Facebook, LinkedIn, Flickr*

Bev Clark, President
Reesa Evans, Secretary

Publishes original studies relevant to lake and reservoir management. Papers address the man-

agement of lakes and reservoirs, their watersheds and tributaries, along with limnology and ecology needed for sound supervision of these systems.
Frequency: Quarterly

8087 LakeLine Magazine

North American Lake Management Society
PO Box 5443
Madison, WI 53705-443

608-233-2836
FAX 608-233-3186
E-Mail: info@nalms.org
Home Page: www.nalms.org

Bev Clark, President
Reesa Evans, Secretary
Linda Green, Treasurer

Contains news, commentary and articles on topics affecting lakes, reservoirs and watersheds. Organized around a theme, like control of invasive species or resolving recreational conflicts, each issue becomes a valued resource for lake users and advocates.
Frequency: Quarterly

8088 Land and Water Magazine

Land and Water
Po Box 1197
Fort Dodge, IA 50501-1197

515-576-3191
FAX 515-576-2606
Home Page: www.landandwater.com
Social Media: *Facebook*

Amy Dencklau, Publisher
Shanza Dencklau, Assistant Editor
Rasch M. Kenneth, President

Edited for contractors, engineers, architects, government officials and those working in the field of natural resource management and restoration from idea stage through project completion and maintenance.
Cost: $20.00
72 Pages
Circulation: 20000
Founded in 1959
Mailing list available for rent: 20M names
Printed in 4 colors on glossy stock

8089 MSW Management

Forester Communications
2946 De La Vina street
Santa Barbara, CA 93105

805-682-1300
FAX 805-682-0200
E-Mail: customerservice@forester.net
Home Page: www.foresterpress.com

Daniel Waldman, Publisher/President
John Trotti, Group Editor

Provides municipal solid waste professionals with general news on facility construction, financing, new equipment and revenue issues.
Cost: $94.95
Circulation: 25000
Founded in 1990

8090 Marine Technology Society Journal

Marine Technology Society
1100 H St., Nw
Suite LL-100
Washington, DC 20005

202-717-8705
FAX 202-347-4302
E-Mail: membership@mtsociety.org
Home Page: www.mtsociety.org
Social Media: *Facebook, Twitter, LinkedIn*

Jerry Boatman, President
Drew Michel, President-Elect
Jerry Wilson, VP of Industry and Technology
Jill Zande, VP of Education and Research
Justin Manley, VP of Gov. & Public Affairs

Publishes the highest caliber, peer-reviewed papers on subjects of interest to the society; marine technology, ocean science, marine policy and education. Dedicated to publishing timely special issues on emerging ocean community concers while also showcasing general interest and student-authored works.
2M Members
Founded in 1963

8091 Natural History Magazine

American Museum of Natural History
79th St & Central Park W
New York, NY 10024

212-769-5400
FAX 212-769-5009
E-Mail: communications@amnh.org
Home Page: www.library.amnh.org

Michael J Novacek, CEO
Victor W Fazio, Editor

Chronicled the major expeditions and research findings by curators at the American Museum of Natural History and at other natural history museums and science centers. Mission of this magazine is to promote public understanding and appreciation of nature and science.
Cost: $55.00

8092 Natural Resources & Environment

American Bar Association
321 N Clark St
Chicago, IL 60654-7598

312-988-5000
800-285-2221
FAX 312-988-5280
E-Mail: askaba@abanet.org
Home Page: www.abanet.org
Social Media: *Facebook, Twitter*

Lori Lyons, Staff Editor
Christine LeBel, Executive Editor

Practical magazine on the latest developments in the field of natural resources law for the ABA Section of Environment, Energy, and Resources.
Cost: $80.00
64 Pages
Frequency: Quarterly
ISSN: 0822-3812
Printed in 4 colors

8093 North American Elk: Ecology & Management

Wildlife Management Institute
1146 19th St NW
Suite 700
Washington, DC 20036-3727

202-973-7710
FAX 202-785-1348
Home Page:
www.wildlifemanagementinstitute.org

Dale E Toweill, Editor

8094 Northeast Sun

NE Sustainable Energy Association
50 Miles St
Greenfield, MA 01301-3255

413-774-6051
FAX 413-774-6053
E-Mail: nesea@nesea.org
Home Page: www.nesea.org

David Barclay, Executive Director
Paul Horowitz, Chairman

Includes articles by leading authorities on sustainable energy practices, energy efficiency and renewable energy.
Frequency: Quarterly
Circulation: 5000
Founded in 1974

8095 Nuclear News

American Nuclear Society

555 N Kensington Ave
La Grange Park, IL 60526-5592

708-352-6611
800-323-3044
FAX 708-352-0499
E-Mail: advertising@ans.org
Home Page: www.ans.org
Social Media: *Facebook, Twitter, LinkedIn*

Jack Tuohy, Executive Director
James S Tulenko, VP
William F Naughton, Treasurer

The flagship membership publication of the American Nuclear Society, the recognized credible advocate for advancing and promoting nuclear science and technology.
10500 Members
Founded in 1954

8096 Nuclear Science and Engineering

American Nuclear Society
555 N Kensington Ave
La Grange Park, IL 60526-5592

708-352-6611
800-323-3044
FAX 708-352-0499
E-Mail: advertising@ans.org
Home Page: www.ans.org
Social Media: *Facebook, Twitter, LinkedIn*

Jack Tuohy, Executive Director
James S Tulenko, VP
William F Naughton, Treasurer

The research journal of the American Nuclear Society, widel recognized as an outstanding source of information on research in all scientific areas related to the peaceful use of nuclear energy and radiation. Technical papers, notes, critical reviews, and computer code abstracts are presented.
10500 Members
Founded in 1954

8097 Nuclear Technology

American Nuclear Society
555 N Kensington Ave
La Grange Park, IL 60526-5592

708-352-6611
800-323-3044
FAX 708-352-0499
E-Mail: advertising@ans.org
Home Page: www.ans.org
Social Media: *Facebook, Twitter, LinkedIn*

Jack Tuohy, Executive Director
James S Tulenko, VP
William F Naughton, Treasurer

The leading international publication reporting on new information in all areas of the practical application of nuclear science. Topics include all aspects of reactor technology; operations, safety materials, instrumentation, fuel, and waste management. Also covered are medical uses, radiation detection, production of radiation, health physics, and computer applications.
10500 Members
Founded in 1954

8098 Occupational Health and Safety

Stevens Publishing Corporation
5151 Belt Line Rd
10th Floor
Dallas, TX 75254-7507

972-687-6700
FAX 972-687-6767
Home Page: www.ohsonline.com

Craig S Stevens, President
Dana Cornett, President/COO
Randy Dye, Publisher
Jerry Laws, Editor
Margaret Perry, Circulation Director

Practical advice on how to keep the workplace safe from hazards and in full compliance with ever-changing laws and regulations. Delivering

the most up-to-date info for professionals in the health, safety, industrial hygiene, environmental, security and fire protection fields with in-depth features, new product releases and more!
Circulation: 63000
Founded in 1925

8099 Oceana

1350 Connecticut Ave.
5th Fl.
Washington, DC 20036

202-833-3900
E-Mail: membership@oceana.org
Home Page: oceana.org/publications/magazine

Suzannah Evans, Interim Editor
Brianna Elliott, Online Content Editor

The magazine of Oceana, the largest environmental organization focused solely on ocean conservation.

8100 OnEarth

National Resources Defense Council
40 W 20th St
New York, NY 10011-4231

212-727-2700
FAX 212-727-1773
E-Mail: nrdcinfo@nrdc.org
Home Page: www.nrdc.org
Social Media: *Facebook, Twitter, YouTube*

Frances Beinecke, President
Daniel R. Tishman, Chair
Frederick A.O. Schwarz Jr., Chair Emeritus
Adam Albright, Vice Chair
Patricia Bauman, Vice Chair

Publication exploring the challenges that confront our world, the solutions that promise to heal it, and the way we can use those solutions to improve our homes, our health, our communities, and our future.
50000 Members
Founded in 1970

8101 Outdoor America

Isaak Walton League
707 Conservation Lane
Gaithersburg, MD 20878

301-548-0150
FAX 301-548-0146
E-Mail: general@iwla.org
Home Page: www.iwla.org

David Hoskins, Executive Director

Entertaining and educational articles about the conservation work of IWLA members. Also provides in-depth coverage of broader conservation issues such as national energy policy, urban sprawl, and wetland loss.
Cost: $36.00
Frequency: Quarterly
Circulation: 37000
ISSN: 0021-3314

8102 Photogrammetric Engineering & Remote Sensing (PE&RS)

ASPRS
5410 Grosvenor Lane
Suite 210
Bethesda, MD 20814-2160

301-493-0290
FAX 301-493-0208
E-Mail: asprs@asprs.org
Home Page: www.asprs.org
Social Media: *Facebook, Twitter*

Jaws Plasker, Exec. Director

The official journal for imaging and geospation information science and technology.
6000 Members
Founded in 1934

8103 Phytopathology

American Phytopatholgical Society

3340 Pilot Knob Road
Saint Paul, MN 55121-2097

651-454-7250
800-328-7560
FAX 651-454-0766
E-Mail: aps@scisoc.org
Home Page: www.apsnet.org

Greg Grahek, Director of Marketing

The premier international journal for publication of articles on fundamental research that advances understanding of the nature of plant diseases, the agents that cause them, their spread, the losses they cause, and measures that can be used to control them.
Frequency: Monthly
Circulation: 1200
ISSN: 0031-949X
Printed in 4 colors

8104 Plant Disease

American Phytopathlgical Society
3340 Pilot Know Road
Saint Paul, MN 55121-2097

651-454-7250
800-328-7560
FAX 651-454-0766
E-Mail: aps@scisoc.org
Home Page: www.apsnet.org

Greg Grahek, Director of Marketing

Leading international journal for rapid reporting of research on new diseases, epidemics, and methods of disease control. Covers basic and applied research, which focuses on practical aspects of disease diagnosis and treatment.The popular Disease Notes section contains brief and timely reports of new diseases, new disease outbreaks, new hosts, and pertinent new observations of plant diseases and pathogens worldwide.
Frequency: Monthly
Circulation: 1200
ISSN: 0191-2917

8105 Plastics Recycling Update

Resource Recycling
PO Box 42270
Portland, OR 97242-270

503-233-1305
FAX 503-233-1356
E-Mail: pru@resource-recycling.com
Home Page: www.resource-recycling.com

Jerry Powell, Publisher

The only magazine in North America focusing exclusively on polymer recovery efforts. A superb source for marketing recycling equipment and services and offers an excellent means of sourcing new suppliers of recovered plastics. The authority in plastic recycling market analysis, coverage of the latest legislation, industry news and views, and technical specs on the latest equipment.
Cost: $59.00
6 Pages
Frequency: Monthly
Circulation: 1000
ISSN: 1052-4908
Founded in 1981
Mailing list available for rent: 40,000 names at $100 per M
Printed in one color on matte stock

8106 Pollution Engineering

Business News Publishing Company
2401 W Big Beaver Rd
Suite 700
Troy, MI 48084-3333

248-362-3700
FAX 248-362-0317
E-Mail: Roy@PollutionEngineering.com

Home Page: www.bnpmedia.com
Social Media: *Facebook, Twitter*

Mitchell Henderson, CEO
Roy Bigham, Managing Editor
Seth Fisher, Products Editor

Providing must read information for today's
Engineers and Consulting Engineers in Pollution Control for; Air, Wastewater, and
Remediation Hazardous Solid Waste.
Up-to-date information on regulatory requirements, coverage of economic benefits of environmental control techniques, and up-to-date
information on innovative and cost-effective
environmental equipment, products, technology
and services.
Frequency: Monthly
ISSN: 0032-3640
Founded in 1969

8107 Pollution Equipment News

Rimbach Publishing
8650 Babcock Blvd
Suite 1
Pittsburgh, PA 15237-5010

412-364-5366
800-245-3182
FAX 412-369-9720
E-Mail: info@rimbach.com
Home Page: www.rimbach.com
Social Media: *Facebook, Twitter*

Norberta Rimbach, President
Karen Galante, Circulation Manager
Paul Henderson, VP of Sales and Marketing

Provides information to those responsible for
selecting products and services for air, water,
wastewater and hazardous waste pollution
abatement.
Frequency: Bi-Annually
Circulation: 91000
Founded in 1968

8108 Pollution Prevention Northwest

US EPA
Ariel Rios Building
1200 Pennsylvania Avenue NW
Washington, DC 20460

202-272-0167
Home Page: www.epa.gov

Bob Zachariasiewicz, Acting Director

Articles include recent information on source
reduction and sustainable technologies in industry, transportation, consumer, agriculture,
energy, and the international sector.
Frequency: Monthly
Circulation: 12000
Founded in 1970

8109 Popular Science

2 Park Ave
9th Floor
New York, NY 10016-5614

212-779-5000
FAX 212-986-2656
E-Mail: letters@popsci.com
Home Page: www.popsci.com

Greg Hano, Publisher
Robert Novick, General Manager

A leading source of science and technology
news, with insightful commentary on the new
innovations, and even scientific takes on the
hottest Hollywood stories.
Cost: $48.00
Frequency: Monthly
Founded in 1964

8110 Pumper

COLE Publishing
PO Box 220
Three Lakes, WI 54562-220

715-546-3346
FAX 715-546-3786

E-Mail: info@pumper.com
Home Page: www.pumper.com
Social Media: *Facebook, Twitter, YouTube*

Ted Rulseh, Editor
Jeff Bruss, President

Emphasis on companies, individuals and industry events while focusing on customer service,
environmental issues and employment trends.
Cost: $16.00
Frequency: Monthly
Circulation: 20,740
Founded in 1978

8111 Radwaste Solutions

American Nuclear Society
555 N Kensington Ave
La Grange Park, IL 60526-5592

708-352-6611
800-323-044
FAX 708-352-0499
E-Mail: advertising@ans.org
Home Page: www.ans.org/advertising

Jack Tuohy, Executive Director
Sarah Wells, Editor
Harry Bradley, Executive Director
Gloria Naurocki, Membership & Marketing
Mary Beth Gardner, Scientific Publications

The magazine of radioactive waste management and facility remediation. Serving the nuclear waste management and cleanup business
segments of the industry. Also included are articles on radwaste management programs and
practices outside the US, as well as guest editorials and letters to the editor, shorter
thought-pieces, and articles on recent academic/technical advances detailing their immediate or planned practical applications.
Cost: $455.00
Frequency: Fortnightly
Circulation: 2000
Founded in 1954
Printed in on matte stock

8112 Recharger Magazine

1050 E Flamingo Rd
Suite 237
Las Vegas, NV 89119-7427

702-438-5557
FAX 702-873-9671
E-Mail: info@rechargermag.com
Home Page: www.rechargermag.com
Social Media: *Facebook, Twitter*

Phyllis Gurgeview, Publisher
Amy Turner, Managing Editor
Brenda Potts, Circulation Manager
Becky Fenton, Manager
Amy Weiss, Director

Information on remanufacturing imaging supplies including articles that cover business and
marketing, technical updates, association and
industry news, and company profiles. Related
features focus on supply sales and equipment
service.
Cost: $45.00
250 Pages
Frequency: Monthly
Circulation: 8000
ISSN: 1053-7503
Printed in 4 colors

8113 Reclamation Matters

American Society of Mining and
Reclamation
3134 Montevesta Road
Lexington, KY 40502-3548

859-351-9032
FAX 859-335-6529
E-Mail: asmr@insightbb.com

Home Page: www.asmr.us
Social Media: *Facebook*

Eddie Bearden, President
Bruce Buchanan, President Elect
Richard Barnhisel, Executive Secretary

The official magazine of ASMR.
500 Members
Founded in 1983

8114 Recycling Laws International

Raymond Communications
P.O.Box 4311
Silver Spring, MD 20914-4311

301-345-4237
FAX 301-345-4768
E-Mail: circulation@raymond.com
Home Page: www.raymond.com

Lorah Utter, Editor
Allyn Sweet, Circulation Manager
Michele Raymond, President

Covers recycling, takeback, green labeling policy for business in 35 countries. Also contains
a country page document that is updated annually.
Cost: $485.00
200 Pages
Circulation: 150
Founded in 1991

8115 Recycling Product News

Baum Publications
2323 Boundary Road
#201
Vancouver, BC 0

604-291-9900
FAX 604-291-1906
E-Mail: webadmin@baumpub.com
Home Page: www.baumpub.com

Engelbert J Baum, Publisher
Keith Barker, Editor

Published for the recycling center operators
and other waste mangers, articles discuss technology and new products.
Circulation: 14000

8116 Recycling Today

GIE Media
4012 Bridge Avenue
Cleveland, OH 44113-3320

216-961-4130
800-456-0707
FAX 216-961-0364
E-Mail: info@recyclingtoday.com
Home Page: www.recyclingtoday.com/
Social Media: *Facebook, Twitter*

James R Keefe, Group Publisher
Brian Taylor, Editor
Richard Foster, CEO
Debbie Kean, Manager

Published for the secondary commodity processing/recycling market.
Cost: $30.00
Frequency: Monthly
Circulation: 15000

8117 Renewable Resources Journal

Renewable Natural Resources Foundation
5430 Grosvenor Ln
Suite 220
Bethesda, MD 20814-2193

301-493-9101
FAX 301-493-6148
E-Mail: info@rnrf.org
Home Page: www.rnrf.org

Robert D Day, Executive Director
Ryan M Colker, Programs Director
Chandru Krishna, Circulation

Provides information of general interest concerning public policy issues related to natural
resources management. Comprised of contrib-

uted and solicited articles on a wide range of natural resource issues, news items about RNRF's members, notices of significant meetings, editorials, and commentaries.
Cost: $25.00
32 Pages
Frequency: Quarterly
Circulation: 1800
ISSN: 0738-6532
Founded in 1975
Printed in 2 colors on matte stock

8118 Resource Recycling

Resource Recycling
PO Box 42270
Portland, OR 97242-270

503-233-1305
FAX 503-233-1356
E-Mail: info@resource-recycling.com
Home Page: www.resource-recycling.com

Jerry Powell, Editor/Publisher
Rick Downing, Graphic Designer
Suzette Ducharme, Graphic Designer
Mary Lynch, Executive Editor

The nation's leading recycling and composting magazine. This monthly journal focuses on efforts in the US and Canada to recover materials from homes and businesses for recycling. Accepts advertising.
Cost: $52.00
64 Pages
Frequency: Monthly
Circulation: 14000+
ISSN: 0744-4710
Founded in 1982
Printed in 4 colors on glossy stock

8119 Restoration Ecology

Blackwell Science
350 Main St
Malden, MA 02148-5089

781-388-8250
FAX 781-388-8210
E-Mail:
subscrip@bos.blackwellpublishing.com
Home Page: www.blackwellpublishing.com

Amy Yodaniss, VP
Richard Hobbs, Editor

Provides the most recent developments in the ecological and biological restoration field for both the fundamental and practical implications of restorations.
Cost: $200.00
Frequency: Quarterly
Circulation: 2000
Founded in 1897

8120 Restoration Ecology Journal

Society for Ecological Restoration International
1017 O Street NW
Washington, DC 20001

202-299-9518
FAX 270-626-5485
E-Mail: info@ser.org
Home Page: www.ser.org
Social Media: Facebook

Steve Whisenant, Chair
Cara R. Nelson, Vice Chair
Mary Travaglini, Treasurer
Alan Unwin, Secretary

Primary emphases are: research on restoration and ecological principles that help explain restoration processes, descriptions of techniques that the authors have pioneered and that are likely to be of use to other practicing restorationists, desriptions of setbacks and surprises encountered during restoration and the lessons learnt, analytical opinions, and reviews

of articles that summarize literature on specialized aspects of restoration.
2300 Members
Frequency: Bi-Monthly
Founded in 1988

8121 Review of Environmental Economics and Policy (REEP)

Association of Environmental and Resource Economis
13006 Peaceful Terrace
Silver Spring, MD 20904

202-559-8998
FAX 202-559-8998
E-Mail: info@aere.org
Home Page: www.aere.org

Catherine L. Kling, President
Sarah L. Stafford, Secretary
Juha Siikamaki, Treasurer
Wiktor L. Adamowicz, Vice President

Designed for broad appeal to economists and others in academia, government, the private sector, and the advocacy world who share a common interest in environmental and natural resource policy. Rather than focusing on technical and methodological aspects of research, articles will focus on the broad lessons that can be learned, for environmental and resource economics or for public policy, from broader lines of research.
900 Members
Founded in 1979

8122 Risk Policy Report

Inside Washington Publishers
1919 S Eads St
Suite 1400
Arlington, VA 22202-3028

703-418-3981
FAX 703-415-8543
E-Mail: support@iwpnews.com
Home Page: www.iwpnews.com

Alan Sosenko, Owner
David Clarke, Editor

Contains analysis, great perspectives, industry news, policymaking profiles and a calendar of events.
Cost: $295.00
Frequency: Monthly
Founded in 1980

8123 SETAC Globe

Society of Environmental Toxicology and Chemistry
1013 N 12th Ave
Pensacola, FL 32501-3306

850-437-1901
FAX 850-469-9778
E-Mail: rparrish@setac.org
Home Page: www.edwardjones.com

Chad Stacy, Manager
Greg Schifer, Manager

Stay up to date on the latest firm news, and learn about the companies followed with Edward Jones.
Frequency: Bi-Monthly

8124 SOLAR TODAY

American Solar Energy Society
4760 Walnut Street
Suite 106
Boulder, CO 80301-2843

303-443-3130
FAX 303-443-3212
E-Mail: ases@ases.org
Home Page: www.ases.org
Social Media: Facebook, Twitter, LinkedIn

David G. Hill, Chair
Bill Poulin, Treasurer
Jason Keyes, Secretary
Jeff Lyng, Immediate Past Chair

Trusted source for the latest technology, policy advances and analysis. Brings together ASES' professional members as contributors and readers, amid the community of ASES chapters nationwide, to publish industry-leading editorial.
ISSN: 1042-0630

8125 Science Magazine

American Assn for the Advancement of Science
1200 New York Avenue NW
Washington, DC 20005-3941

202-266-6721
FAX 202-371-9227
E-Mail: membership@aaas.org
Home Page: www.aaas.org
Social Media: Facebook, Twitter

Kathy Fishback, Publication Services Director

The world's leading outlet for scientific news, commentary, and cutting-edge research. Available online and in print, Science Magazine continues to publish the very best in scientific research, news, and opinion.

8126 Scrap Magazine

Institute of Scrap Recycling Industries
1615 L St NW
Suite 600
Washington, DC 20036-5664

202-662-8500
FAX 202-626-0900
E-Mail: isri@isri.org
Home Page: www.isri.org

John Sacco, Chairman
Jerry I. Simms, Chair Elect
Douglas Kramer, Vice Chair
Mark R. Lewon, Secretary Treasurer

Providing practical and useful information to scrap professionals through articles and columns that will increase the profitability of their businesses. The editorial content is designed to stimulate- to help scrap professionals manage all aspects of their businesses more successfully.
165 Members
1987 Attendees

8127 Security Products

Stevens Publishing Corporation
5151 Belt Line Rd
10th Floor
Dallas, TX 75254-7507

972-687-6700
FAX 972-687-6767
Home Page: www.secprodonline.com

Craig S Stevens, President
Dana Cornett, President/COO
Randy Dye, Publisher
Ralph Jensen, Editor-In-Chief
Margaret Perry, Circulation Director

Leading new product and technology resource for security dealers, integrators and end users seeking comprehensive product-related information.
Circulation: 63000
Founded in 1925

8128 Shore & Beach

American Shore and Beach Preservation Association
5460 Beaujolais Lane
Fort Myers, FL 33919

239-489-2616
FAX 239-362-9771
E-Mail: exdir@asbpa.org
Home Page: www.asbpa.org
Social Media: Facebook, Twitter

Harry Simmons, President
Kate Gooderham, Executive Director
Lesley Ewing, Editor

Beth Sciaudone, Managing Editor
Ken Gooderham, Production

Information and articles regarding management of shores and beaches.
1M Members
Founded in 1926

8129 Sierra
85 Second St.
2nd Fl.
San Francisco, CA 94105-3459

E-Mail: sierra.magazine@sierraclub.org
Home Page: www.sierraclub.org/sierra
Social Media: *Facebook, Twitter, Pinterest, Instagram*

Jason Mark, Editor-in-Chief
Tracy Cox, Art Director

The official magazine of the Sierra Club.
Cost: $3.95
Frequency: Bimonthly
Circulation: 1000000
ISSN: 0161-7362

8130 Soil Science Society of America Journal
American Society of Agronomy
5585 Guilford Rd.
Madison, WI 53711-1086

608-273-8080
FAX 608-273-2021
E-Mail: headquarters@sciencesocieties.org
Home Page: www.agronomy.org
Social Media: *Facebook, Twitter, LinkedIn*

Newell Kitchen, President
Kenneth Barbarick, President-Elect

Publishes basic and applied soil research in agricultural, forest, wetlands, urban settings and more.
10000 Members
Founded in 1907

8131 Soil Survey Horizons
American Society of Agronomy
5585 Guilford Rd.
Madison, WI 53711-1086

608-273-8080
FAX 608-273-2021
E-Mail: headquarters@sciencesocieties.org
Home Page: www.agronomy.org
Social Media: *Facebook, Twitter, LinkedIn*

Newell Kitchen, President
Kenneth Barbarick, President-Elect

Informs and entertains with research updates, soil problems and solutions, history of soil survey, and personal essays from the lives of soil scientists in the field.
10000 Members
Founded in 1907

8132 Soil and Sediment Contamination
AEHS Foundation Inc.
150 Fearing Street
Suite 21
Amherst, MA 01002

413-549-5170
888-540-2347
Home Page: www.aehs.com

Paul T Kostecki, PhD, Executive Director

Focuses on soil and sediment contamination from; sludges, petroleum, petrochemicals, chlorinated hydrocarbons, pesticides, and lead and other heavy metals. Offers detailed descriptions of all the latest and most efficient offsite and in situ remediation techniques, strategies for assessing health effects and hazards, and tips for dealing with everyday regulatory and legal issues. Assess, mitigate, and solve rural and urban soil contamination problems.
Frequency: Bi-Monthly

8133 Solid Waste & Recycling
Southam Environment Group
1450 Don Mills Road
Don Mills, ON 0

905-305-6155
888-702-1111
FAX 416-442-2026
E-Mail: bobrien@solidwastemag.com
Home Page: www.solidwastemag.com

Brad O'Brien, Publisher
Bibi Khan, Circualtion Manager
Guy Crittenden, Editor-in-Chief

Emphasizes municipal and commercial aspects of collection, handling, transportation, hauling, disposal and treatment of solid waste , including incineration, recycling and landfill technology.
Cost: $29.95
Frequency: Weekly
Circulation: 10000

8134 Solid Waste Report
Business Publishers
2222 Sedwick Dr
Suite 101
Durham, NC 27713

800-223-8720
FAX 800-508-2592
E-Mail: custserv@bpinews.com
Home Page: www.bpinews.com

Comprehensive news and analysis of legislation, regulation and litigation in solid waste management including resource recovery, recycling, collection and disposal. Regularly features international news, state updates and business trends.
Cost: $567.00
Founded in 1963

8135 TIDE
Coastal Conservation Association
6919 Portwest Dr
Suite 100
Houston, TX 77024-8049

713-626-4234
800-201-FISH
FAX 713-626-5852
E-Mail: ccantl@joincca.org
Home Page: www.joincca.org
Social Media: *Twitter*

David Cummins, President

The official magazine of the CCA.
85000 Members
Founded in 1977

8136 The Leading Edge
Society of Exploration Geophysicists
8801 South Yale
Suite 500
Tulsa, OK 74137-3575

918-497-5500
FAX 918-497-5557
E-Mail: web@seg.org
Home Page: www.seg.org
Social Media: *Facebook, Twitter, LinkedIn*

Mary Fleming, Executive Director
Vladimir Grechka, Editor

A gateway publication, introducing new geophysical theory, instrumentation, and established practices to scientists in a wide range of geoscience disciplines. Most material is presented in a semitechnical manner that minimizes mathematical theory and emphasizes practical application. Also serves as SEG's publication venue for official society business.

8137 The Plant Genome
American Society of Agronomy

5585 Guilford Rd.
Madison, WI 53711-1086

608-273-8080
FAX 608-273-2021
E-Mail: headquarters@sciencesocieties.org
Home Page: www.agronomy.org
Social Media: *Facebook, Twitter, LinkedIn*

Newell Kitchen, President
Kenneth Barbarick, President-Elect

Electronic journal providing leadership of the latest advances and breakthroughs in plant genomics research.
10000 Members
Founded in 1907

8138 Tree Farmer Magazine, the Guide to Sustaining America's Family Forests
American Forest Foundation
1111 19th St NW
Suite 780
Washington, DC 20036

202-463-2700
FAX 202-463-2785
E-Mail: info@forestfoundation.org
Home Page: www.forestfoundation.org

Tom Martin, President & CEO
Brigitte Johnson APR, Director Communications, Editor

The official magazine of ATFS, this periodical provides practical, how-to and hands-on information and techniques, and services to help private fore landowners to become better stewards, save money and time, and add to the enjoyment of their land.

8139 Vadose Zone Journal
American Society of Agronomy
5585 Guilford Rd.
Madison, WI 53711-1086

608-273-8080
FAX 608-273-2021
E-Mail: headquarters@sciencesocieties.org
Home Page: www.agronomy.org
Social Media: *Facebook, Twitter, LinkedIn*

Newell Kitchen, President
Kenneth Barbarick, President-Elect

Focuses on multidisciplinary research in the unsaturated zone appealing to a diverse group of scientists and engineers.
10000 Members
Founded in 1907

8140 Washington Environmental Compliance Update
M Lee Smith Publishers
PO Box 5094
Bentwood, TN 37024-5094

615-737-7517
800-274-6774

F Lee Smith, Publisher
Douglas S Little, Editor

Review of environmental laws.
Cost: $225.00
8 Pages
Frequency: Daily
Mailing list available for rent
Printed in 2 colors on matte stock

8141 Waste Age
Environmental Industry Association
4301 Connecticut Ave NW
#300
Washington, DC 20008-2304

202-966-4701
FAX 202-966-4818
E-Mail: contact@envasns.org

Home Page: www.envasns.org
Social Media: *Facebook, Twitter, YouTube*

Bruce Parker, President
Patricia-Ann Tom, Editor
Laura Magliola, Marketing Manager
Christine Hutcherson, Director Member Services
Alice Jacobsohn, Director Education

Contents focus on new system technologies, recycling, resource recovery and sanitary landfills with regular features on updates in the status of government regulations, new products, guides, company profiles, exclusive survey information, legislative implications and news.
Frequency: Monthly
Circulation: 38000

8142 Waste Age's Recycling Times
Environmental Industry Association
4301 Connecticut Ave NW
#300
Washington, DC 20008-2304

202-966-4701
FAX 202-966-4818
E-Mail: rct@envasns.org
Home Page: www.wasteage.com

Bruce Parker, President
Wendy Angel, Assistant Editor
Gregg Herring, Group Publisher

Features municipalities, recycling goals and rates, program innovations, waste habits, and new materials being recycled.
Cost: $99.00
Frequency: Monthly
Circulation: 5000

8143 Water & Wastes Digest
Scranton Gillette Communications
3030 W Salt Creek Lane
Suite 201
Arlington Heights, IL 60005-5025

847-391-1000
FAX 847-390-0408
E-Mail: nsimeonova@sgcmail.com
Home Page: www.scrantongillette.com
Social Media: *Facebook, Twitter, LinkedIn*

Neda Simeonova, Editorial Director
Caitlin Cunningham, Managing Editor

Serves readers in the water and/or wastewater industries. These people work for municipalities, in industry, or as engineers. They design, specify, buy, operate and maintain equipment, chemicals, software and wastewater treatment services.
Cost: $40.00
128 Pages
Frequency: Monthly
Circulation: 101000
ISSN: 0043-1181
Founded in 1961

8144 Water Environment & Technology (WE&T)
Water Environment Federation
601 Wythe St
Alexandria, VA 22314-1994

800-666-0206
FAX 703-684-2492
Home Page: www.wef.org
Social Media: *Facebook, Twitter*

Matt Bond, President
Cordell Samuels, President-Elect
Sandra Ralston, Vice President
Chris Browning, Treasurer
Jeff Eger, Secretary and Executive Director

Premier magazine for the water quality field. Provides information on what professionals demand; cutting-edge technologies, innovative

solutions, regulatory and legislative impacts, and professional development.
79 Members
ISSN: 1044-9943
Founded in 1928

8145 Water Environment Research (WER)
Water Environment Federation
601 Wythe St
Alexandria, VA 22314-1994

800-666-0206
FAX 703-684-2492
Home Page: www.wef.org
Social Media: *Facebook, Twitter*

Matt Bond, President
Cordell Samuels, President-Elect
Sandra Ralston, Vice President
Chris Browning, Treasurer
Jeff Eger, Secretary and Executive Director

Original, fundamental and applied research in all scientific and technical areas related to water quality, pollution contro, and management.
79 Members
ISSN: 1044-9943
Founded in 1928

8146 Water Quality Products
Scranton Gillette Communications
3030 W Salt Creek Lane
Suite 201
Arlington Heights, IL 60005

847-391-1000
FAX 847-390-0408
E-Mail: nsimeonova@sgcmail.com
Home Page: www.wqpmag.com
Social Media: *Facebook, Twitter*

Neda Simeonova, Editorial Director
Dennis Martyka, VP/Group Publisher
Kate Cline, Managing Editor

Provides balanced editorial content including developments in water conditioning, filtration and disinfection for residential, commercial and industrial systeme.
Cost: $40.00
68 Pages
Frequency: Monthly
Circulation: 19000
ISSN: 1092-0978
Founded in 1995

8147 Wildfire Magazine
International Association of Wildland Fire
4025 Fair Ridge Drive
Fairfax, VA 22033

785-423-1818
FAX 785-542-3511
E-Mail: sandy@iawfonline.org
Home Page: www.iawfonline.org

Sacha Dick, Programs Manager
Mikel Robinson, Executive Director

Addresses the needs of chiefs and wildland forestry managers by providing a unique international prospective. Each issue focuses on the demand of leaders responsible for managing and controlling wildland fires. Readers are the top decision makers and leaders who have influence over purchasing equipment, supplies and contracted services. Readership includes fire chiefs, governmental agencies, private sector professionals, consultants and contractors.
Frequency: Monthly

8148 Wildlife Conservation Magazine
2300 S Boulevard
Bronx, NY 10460

718-220-5121
800-786-8226
FAX 718-584-2625

E-Mail: magazine@wcs.org
Home Page: www.wildlifeconservation.org/

Debby Bahler, Editor
Diana Warren, Advertising Director
4teve Sanderson, President

A national nature and science magazine. Contains stunning photography, conservation news and special updates on endangered species. Learn how to help protect local wildlife, and the secrets of the world's rarest and most mysterious animals.
Cost: $19.95
96 Pages
Circulation: 150000
Founded in 1895

8149 World Resource Review
SUPCON International
International Headquarters 2W381
75th Street
Naperville, IL 60565-9245

630-910-1551
FAX 630-910-1561
E-Mail: syshen@megsinet.net
Home Page: www.globalwarming.net

Dr. Sinyan Shen, Production Manager

For business and government readers, provides expert worldwide reviews of global warming and extreme events in relation to the management of natural, mineral and material resources. Subjects include global warming impacts on agriculture, energy, and infrastructure, monitoring of changes in resources using remote sensing, actions of national and international bodies, global carbon budget, greenhouse budget and more.
Cost: $72.00
Frequency: Quarterly
Circulation: 12000
ISSN: 1042-8011

8150 World Wastes: The Independent Voice
Communication Channels
6151 Powers Ferry Road NW
Atlanta, GA 30339-2959

770-953-4805
FAX 770-618-0348

Bill Wolpin, Editor
Jerrold France, President Argus Business

Reaches individuals and firms engaged in the removal and disposal of solid wastes.
Cost: $48.00
Frequency: Monthly
Circulation: 36,000

8151 World Water
Water Environment Federation
601 Wythe St
Alexandria, VA 22314-1994

800-666-0206
FAX 703-684-2492
Home Page: www.wef.org
Social Media: *Facebook, Twitter*

Matt Bond, President
Cordell Samuels, President-Elect
Sandra Ralston, Vice President
Chris Browning, Treasurer
Jeff Eger, Secretary and Executive Director

International magazine for the water quality industry. Provides the most cutting-edge and helpful information on global water issues.
79 Members
ISSN: 1044-9943
Founded in 1928

8152 World Water Reuse & Desalination
Water Environment Federation

601 Wythe St
Alexandria, VA 22314-1994

800-666-0206
FAX 703-684-2492
Home Page: www.wef.org
Social Media: *Facebook, Twitter*

Matt Bond, President
Cordell Samuels, President-Elect
Sandra Ralston, Vice President
Chris Browning, Treasurer
Jeff Eger, Secretary and Executive Director

Becoming the global news and information resource for the water reuse and quality industries. Provides the most up-to-date and innovative information on all facets of global water reuse and desalination issues.
79 Members
ISSN: 1044-9943
Founded in 1928

Trade Shows

8153 AAAR Annual Conference
American Association for Aerosol Research
15000 Commerce Parkway
Suite C
Mount Laurel, NJ 08054

856-439-9080
877-777-6753
FAX 856-439-0525
E-Mail: info@aaar.org
Home Page: www.aaar.org

William Nazaroff, President
Barbara Turpin, Vice President
Barbara Wyslouzil, Vice President Elect
Murray Johnston, Treasurer
CY Wu, Secretary

Benefit from learning about the latest advances across the full frontier of aerosol science and technology. An excellent opportunity to renew old acquaintances and to meet new colleagues.
1000 Members
Founded in 1982

8154 AAAR Annual Meeting
American Association for Aerosol Research
15000 Commerce Parkway
Suite C
Mount Laurel, NJ 08054

856-439-9080
FAX 856-439-0525
E-Mail: dbright@ahint.com
Home Page: www.aaar.org

Lynn Russell, Program Chair
Melissa Baldwin, Executive Director

Exhibits related to aerosol research in areas including industrial process, air pollution, and industrial hygiene. Over 600 professionals attend.
600 Attendees
Frequency: Annual, October

8155 AAAS Annual Meeting
Renewable Natural Resources Foundation
5430 Grosvenor Ln
Bethesda, MD 20814-2193

301-493-9101
FAX 301-493-6148
E-Mail: info@rnrf.org
Home Page: www.rnrf.org

Howard N. Rosen, Chairman
Richard A. Engberg, Vice-Chairman
Robert D. Day, Executive Director

The most important general science venue for a growing segment of scientists and engineers.
14 Members
Founded in 1972

8156 ACCA Annual Meetings
Air Conditioning Contractors of America
2800 Shirlington Rd
Suite 300
Arlington, VA 22206

703-575-4477
E-Mail: info@acca.org
Home Page: www.acca.org
Social Media: *Facebook, Twitter, LinkedIn, YouTube*

Paul T Stalknecht, President & CEO

Where America's most successful HVACR, building services, and energy professionals come together to share, learn, and collaborate. Options for learning how to take your business to the next levels of profitability and success.
Frequency: February/March

8157 ACE Annual Conference
Air & Waste Management Association
420 Fort Duquesne Boulevard
One Gateway Center, 3rd Floor
Pittsburgh, PA 15222-1435

412-652-2458
FAX 412-232-3450
E-Mail: info@awma.org
Home Page: www.awma.org
Social Media: *Facebook, Twitter, LinkedIn*

Jeffry Muffat, President
Merlyn L. Hough, President Elect
Mike Kelly, Secretary/ Executive Director
Amy Gilligan, Treasurer
Dallas Baker, Vice President

Environmental professionals from around the world to the outstanding technical program, exhibits of the latest products and services, and networking and professional development opportunities.
9000 Members
Founded in 1907

8158 AEESP Annual Meeting
Association of Environmental Engineering and
2303 Naples Court
Champaign, IL 61822

217-398-6969
FAX 217-355-9232
E-Mail: joanne@aeesp.org
Home Page: www.aeesp.org

Joanne Fetzner, Business Secretary

With the Water Environment Federation
Frequency: Fall

8159 AERE Summer Conference
Association of Environmental and Resource
1616 P Street NW
Suite 600
Washington, DC 20036

202-328-5125
FAX 202-939-3460
E-Mail: voigt@rff.org
Home Page: www.aere.org

Marilyn Voigt, Executive Director

nonprofit international professional association for economists working on the environment and natural resources.
850 Members
350 Attendees
Frequency: January
Founded in 1979

8160 APLIC Annual Conference
Family Health International Library

PO Box 13950
Research Triangle Park, NC 27709

919-447-7040
Home Page: www.aplici.org

Claire Twose, President
Lori Rosman, Vice-President
Joann Donatiello, Treasurer

Focuses on current issues in communication, information, and resource technology and management.
Frequency: Annual

8161 APWA International Public Works Congress & Expo
American Public Works Association
2345 Grand Boulevard
Suite 700
Kansas City, MO 64108-2625

816-472-6100
800-848-2792
FAX 816-472-1610
E-Mail: ddancy@apwa.net
Home Page: www.apwa.net

Peter King, Executive Director
David Dancy, Director Of Marketing

Offers the benefit of a variety of educational sessions, depth of the exhibit program and endless opportunities for networking. The latest cutting-edge technologies, managerial techniques and regulatory trends designed to keep you focused on the right solutions at the right time.
6500 Attendees
Frequency: Annual/September
ISSN: 0092-4873
Founded in 1894

8162 ASAS Annual Meeting
American Society of Animal Science
1111 N Dunlap Avenue
Savoy, IL 61874

217-356-9050
FAX 217-398-4119
Home Page: www.asas.org

Paula Schultz, Meetings Coordinator
Lorena Nicholas, General Meeting Information
Kim Surles, Exhibits/Advertising
Jerry Baker, Executive Director

This meeting serves as an international forum to gather vital information for the future of the animal agriculture industry. A cutting-edge scientific program in food science, animal health, dairy production, beef nutrition, swine nutrition, reproduction, companion animals, and many other diverse interests.
3500 Attendees
Frequency: July/Non-Members Fee
Founded in 1908

8163 ASEH Annual Meeting
American Society for Environmental History
119 Pine Street
Suite 301
Seattle, WA 98101

206-343-0226
FAX 206-343-0249
Home Page: www.aseh.net

Lisa Mighetto, Acting Executive Director

Individuals and groups all over the world will attend to collaborate on ways to live better with nature, and to make a better world for all outside of traditional political structures and older models of environmentalism.
Frequency: Spring, Texas

8164 ASES National Solar Conference
American Solar Energy Society

4760 Walnut Street
Suite 106
Boulder, CO 80301-2843

303-443-3130
FAX 303-443-3212
E-Mail: ases@ases.org
Home Page: www.ases.org
Social Media: *Facebook, Twitter, LinkedIn*

David G. Hill, Chair
Bill Poulin, Treasurer
Jason Keyes, Secretary
Jeff Lyng, Immediate Past Chair

America's premier educational event for solar energy professionals. The conference introduces you to the leaders, innovators and technologies moving the industry forward.
ISSN: 1042-0630

8165 ASES National Solar Tour
American Solar Energy Society
4760 Walnut Street
Suite 106
Boulder, CO 80301-2843

303-443-3130
FAX 303-443-3212
E-Mail: ases@ases.org
Home Page: www.ases.org
Social Media: *Facebook, Twitter, LinkedIn*

David G. Hill, Chair
Bill Poulin, Treasurer
Jason Keyes, Secretary
Jeff Lyng, Immediate Past Chair

The largest grassroots solar event in history. Offers participants the opportunity to tour homes and buildings to see how neighbors are using solar energy, energy efficiency and other sustainable technologies to reduce their monthly utility bills and help tackle climate change.
ISSN: 1042-0630

8166 ASFE Fall Meeting
ASFE/The Geoprofessional Business Association
8811 Colesville Road
Suite G106
Silver Springs, MD 20910

301-565-2733
FAX 301-589-2017
E-Mail: info@asfe.org
Home Page: www.asfe.org

John P Bachner, Executive VP

Providing geotechnical, geologic, environmental, construction materials engineering and testing, and related professional services information and education.
Frequency: Annual/Fall

8167 ASFE Spring Meeting
ASFE
8811 Colesville Road
Suite G106
Silver Springs, MD 20910

301-565-2733
FAX 301-589-2017
E-Mail: info@asfe.org
Home Page: www.asfe.org

John P Bachner, Executive VP

Provides geotechnical, geologic, environmental, construction materials engineering and testing, and related professional services information and education.
Frequency: Annual/Spring

8168 ASFE Winter Leadership Conference
ASFE/The Geoprofessional Business Association

8811 Colesville Road
Suite G106
Silver Springs, MD 20910

301-565-2733
FAX 301-589-2014
E-Mail: info@asfe.org
Home Page: www.asfe.org

John Bachner, Executive VP

ASFE's leaders meet to finish priorities for the current year and determine the direction of ASFE for the coming year.
Frequency: Annual/January

8169 ASFPM Annual Conference
Association of State Floodplain Managers
2809 Fish Hatchery Road
Suite 204
Madison, WI 53713

608-274-0123
FAX 608-274-0696
E-Mail: memberhelp@floods.org
Home Page: www.floods.org

Larry Larson, Executive Director
Alison Stierli, Manager
Diane Brown, Manager

Focus on floodproofing techniques, materials, floodproofing and elevation contractors, current issues and programs, new federal tax impications and the various means of funding floodproofing projects. implications.
Frequency: Annual

8170 ASFPM Annual National Conference
Association of State Floodplain Managers
2809 Fish Hatchery Rd
Suite 204
Madison, WI 53713-5020

608-274-0123
FAX 608-274-0696
E-Mail: Larry@floods.org
Home Page: www.floods.org
Social Media: *Facebook*

Sally McConkey, Chair
William Nechamen, Vice Chair
Alan J. Giles, Secretary
John V. Crofts, Treasurer

The national conferences all community, state and federal floodplain managers plan to attend. Many of the most important consulting firms and product vendors associated with floodplain management attend.
6500 Members
Founded in 1977

8171 ASMA Annual Meeting
American Society of Mining and Reclamation
3134 Montevesta Road
Lexington, KY 40502-3548

859-351-9032
FAX 859-335-6529
E-Mail: asmr@insightbb.com
Home Page: www.asmr.us

Dennis Neuman, President
Richard Bamhisel, Executive Secretary

Approximately 30 exhibitors.
300 Attendees
Frequency: Annual

8172 ASMR Meeting & Conference
American Society of Mining and Reclamation
3134 Montavesta Road
Lexington, KY 40502

859-335-6529
E-Mail: asmr@insightbb.com
Home Page: www.ca.uky.edu/assmr

Richard I Barnhisel, Executive Secretary

Promoting the advancement of basic and applied reclamation science through research and technology transfer.
Frequency: June

8173 ASPRS Annual Conference
American Society for Photogammetry/Remote Sensing
5410 Grosvenor Lane
Suite 210
Bethesda, MD 20814-2160

301-493-0290
FAX 301-493-0208
E-Mail: asprs@asprs.org
Home Page: www.asprs.org

Dr. Carolyn J. Merry, Ph.D., President
Roberta Lenczowski, VP
Dr. Donald Laurer, Treasurer
James Plasker, Executive Director

One hundred exhibits of mapping, photogrammetry, environmental management, remote sensing, geographic information, natural resources and much more.
6000 Members
2000 Attendees
Founded in 1934

8174 AWEA Offshore Windpower Conference Exhibition
American Wind Energy Association
1501 M Street NW
Suite 1000
Washington, DC 20005

202-383-2500
FAX 202-383-2505
E-Mail: windmail@awea.org
Home Page: www.awea.org
Social Media: *Facebook, Twitter, YouTube*

Ned Hall, Chair
Thomas Carnahan, Chair-Elect
Gabriel Alonso, Secretary
Don Furman, Treasurer
Vic Abate, Past Chair

Brings together exhibitors and attendees from all over the world who are interested in becoming players in this new and highly promising market.
2400 Members

8175 Aerosol/ Atmospheric Optics: Visibility and Air Pollution
A&WMA
420 Fort Duquesne Boulevard
One Gateway Center, 3rd Floor
Pittsburgh, PA 15222-1435

412-652-2458
FAX 412-232-3450
E-Mail: info@awma.org
Home Page: www.awma.org
Social Media: *Facebook, Twitter, LinkedIn*

Jeffry Muffat, President
Merlyn L. Hough, President Elect
Mike Kelly, Secretary/ Executive Director
Amy Gilligan, Treasurer
Dallas Baker, Vice President

Provide a technical forum on advances in the scientific understanding of the effects of aerosols.
9000 Members
Founded in 1907

8176 Air Quality Measurement Methods and Technology
A&WMA
420 Fort Duquesne Boulevard
One Gateway Center, 3rd Floor
Pittsburgh, PA 15222-1435

412-652-2458
FAX 412-232-3450
E-Mail: info@awma.org

Home Page: www.awma.org
Social Media: *Facebook, Twitter, LinkedIn*

Jeffry Muffat, President
Merlyn L. Hough, President Elect
Mike Kelly, Secretary/ Executive Director
Amy Gilligan, Treasurer
Dallas Baker, Vice President

Explore advances in measurement technology, data quality assurance, and data uses.
9000 Members
Founded in 1907

8177   Air and Waste Management Association Annual Conference and Exhibition
Air and Waste Management Association
1 Gateway Center
3rd Floor
Pittsburgh, PA 15222-1435

412-652-2458
800-270-3444
FAX 412-232-3450
E-Mail: info@awma.org
Home Page: www.awma.org

Deborah Hilfman, Show Manager
Robert Greenbaum, Exhibit Manager

Environmental professionals from all sectors of the economy including colleges, universities, natural resource manufacturing and process industries, consultants, local state, provincial, regional and federal governments, construction, utilities industries. Over 300 exhibits of envirmomental control products.
6000 Attendees

8178   Alternative Clean Transportation Expo(ACT)
Society of Environmental Journalists
PO Box 2492
Jenkintown, PA 19046

215-884-8174
FAX 215-884-8175
Home Page: www.sej.org
Social Media: *Facebook, Twitter*

Carolyn Whetzel, President
Peter Fairley, 1st Vice Pres
Jeff Burnside, 2nd Vice Pres
Don Hopey, Treasurer

The largest alternative fuels and clean vehicle technologies show in North America.
Founded in 1990

8179   American Meteorological Society Annual Meeting
Renewable Natural Resources Foundation
5430 Grosvenor Ln
Bethesda, MD 20814-2193

301-493-9101
FAX 301-493-6148
E-Mail: info@rnrf.org
Home Page: www.rnrf.org

Howard N. Rosen, Chairman
Richard A. Engberg, Vice-Chairman
Robert D. Day, Executive Director

Technology in research and operations, how we got here and where we're going.
14 Members
Founded in 1972

8180   American Occupational Health Conference & Exhibits
Slack
4930 Del Ray Avenue
Bethesda, MD 20814

301-654-2055
FAX 301-654-5920
E-Mail: member@gastro.org
Home Page: www.gastro.org

Robert Greenberg, Executive Vp
Michael Stolar, Senior Vp

400 exhibits of pharmaceuticals, equipment, software and supplies for health professionals, offices and labs.
4500 Attendees

8181   American Society for Environmental History Annual Conference
Society of Environmental Journalists
PO Box 2492
Jenkintown, PA 19046

215-884-8174
FAX 215-884-8175
Home Page: www.sej.org
Social Media: *Facebook, Twitter*

Carolyn Whetzel, President
Peter Fairley, 1st Vice Pres
Jeff Burnside, 2nd VP
Don Hopey, Treasurer

Join for an intellectual and collegial journey, from the local to the global; ethics, environmentalism, and environmental history in an interdependent world.
Founded in 1990

8182   American Society of Safety Engineers Professional Development Conference
American Society of Safety Engineers
1800 E Oakton Street
Des Plaines, IL 60018

847-699-2929
FAX 847-768-3434
E-Mail: customerservice@asse.org
Home Page: www.asse.org

Fred Fortman, Executive Director
Jim Drzewiecki, Finance/Controller Director
Diane Hurns, Manager Public Relations Department

Annual conference and expo of 250 manufacturers and suppliers of safety equipment and health products.
3500 Attendees
Frequency: June

8183   American Water Resources Association Annual Water Resource Conference
Renewable Natural Resources Foundation
5430 Grosvenor Ln
Bethesda, MD 20814-2193

301-493-9101
FAX 301-493-6148
E-Mail: info@rnrf.org
Home Page: www.rnrf.org

Howard N. Rosen, Chairman
Richard A. Engberg, Vice-Chairman
Robert D. Day, Executive Director

Brings together a diverse group of water resource professionals from across the state. Presenting a unique opportunity for water resource practitioners from diverse disciplines to gether and interact together.
14 Members
Founded in 1972

8184   Annual EcoFarm Conference
Community Alliance with Family Farmers
PO Box 363
Davis, CA 95617-363

530-756-8518
FAX 530-756-7857
E-Mail: info@caff.org
Home Page: www.caff.org
Social Media: *Facebook, Twitter, YouTube*

Carol Presley, Board Chair
Pete Price, Vice President
Judith Redmond, Secretary
Vicki Williams, Treasurer

Oldest and largest ecological agricultural gathering in the West, meets every year to create, maintain, and promote healthy, safe, and just

food farming systems. Myriad opportunities for networking with colleagues, discovering the newest ecological agricultural delvelopment and techniques, and building skills for individuals and together as a community.

8185   Annual International Conference on Soil, Water, Energy, and Air
AEHS Foundation Inc
150 Fearing Street
Amherst, MA 01002

413-549-5170
FAX 413-549-0579
Home Page: www.aehsfoundation.org

Paul T Kostecki, PhD, Executive Director

Live equipment demonstrations augment the exhibition hall, bringing real world application to the technical theory presented in the sessions. An exciting opportunity for all those concerned with the challenge of developing creative, cost-effective assessments and solutions that can withstand the demands of regulatory requirements.
600 Members
Founded in 1989

8186   Annual International Conference on Soils, Sediments, Water and Energy
AEHS Foundation Inc
150 Fearing Street
Amherst, MA 01002

413-549-5170
FAX 413-549-0579
Home Page: www.aehsfoundation.org

Paul T Kostecki, PhD, Executive Director

Live equipment demonstrations augment the exhibition hall, bringing real world application to the technical theory presented in the sessions. An exciting opportunity for all those concerned with the challenge of developing creative, cost-effective assessments and solutions that can withstand the demands of regulatory requirements.
600 Members
Founded in 1989

8187   Annual National Ethanol Conference
Renewable Fuels Association
425 Third Street, SW
Suite 1150
Washington, DC 20024

202-289-3835
FAX 202-289-7519
E-Mail: info@ethanolrfa.org
Home Page: www.ethanolrfa.org
Social Media: *Facebook, Twitter*

Chuck Woodside, Chairman
Neill McKinstray, Vice Chairman
Randall Doyal, Treasurer
Walter Wendland, Secretary

Delivers accurate, timely information on marketing, legislative and regulatory issues facing the ethanol industry. Industry leaders and experts address accelerating innovation in technology, marketing, logistics and feedstocks for the production of advanced ethanol.
55 Members
Founded in 1981

8188   Annual Odors and Air Pollutants Conference
Water Environment Federation
601 Wythe St
Alexandria, VA 22314-1994

800-666-0206
FAX 703-684-2492
Home Page: www.wef.org
Social Media: *Facebook, Twitter*

Matt Bond, President
Cordell Samuels, President-Elect
Sandra Ralston, Vice President

Chris Browning, Treasurer
Jeff Eger, Secretary and Executive Director

Topics covered include: odor and emission
Control Systems, Biological odor control, innovative technologies, design of odor control systems, collection systems tunnel ventilation,
emission from biosolids, fate and odor
modeling, and many more.
79 Members
ISSN: 1044-9943
Founded in 1928

8189 Annual SWCS International Conference
Soil and Water Conservation Society
945 SW Ankeny Rd
Ankeny, IA 50023-9764

515-289-2331
800-843-7645
FAX 515-289-1227
E-Mail: swcs@swcs.org
Home Page: www.swcs.org

Bill Boyer, President
Dan Towery, Vice-President
Clark Gantzer, Secretary
Jerry Pearce, Treasurer

Considering Ecology, Economics and Ethics.
5000+ Members
Founded in 1943

8190 Aquatic Plant Management Society Annual Meeting
Aquatic Plant Management Society
PO Box 821265
Vicksburg, MS 39182-1265

FAX 601-634-2398
E-Mail: dpetty@ndrsite.com
Home Page: www.apms.org
Social Media: *Facebook, LinkedIn*

Linda Nelson, President
Terry Goldsby, VP
Sherry Whitaker, Treasurer
Jeff Schardt, Secretary
Greg Aguillard, Director

An international organization of educators, scientists, commercial pesticide applicators, administrators and individuals interested in
aquatic plant species and plant management.
Founded in 1961

8191 Biennial International Conference on Petroleum Geophysics
Society of Exploration Geophysicists
8801 South Yale
Suite 500
Tulsa, OK 74137-3575

918-497-5500
FAX 918-497-5557
E-Mail: web@seg.org
Home Page: www.seg.org
Social Media: *Facebook, Twitter, LinkedIn*

Mary Fleming, Executive Director
Vladimir Grechka, Editor

Continuing education courses, exhibitions and
networking.
Founded in 1930

8192 BioInterface
Surfaces in Biomaterials Foundation
1000 Westgate Drive
Suite 252
Saint Paul, MN 55114

651-290-6295
FAX 651-290-2266
E-Mail: memberservices@surfaces.org
Home Page: www.surfaces.org

Bill Monn, Executive Director
Larry Salvati, President

One of the best technical and most stimulating
conferences in the field of biomaterials science.

Connect, share and learn by relaxed contact
with fellow attendees. Be enriched by the science, and the high quality of interaction that is
fostered by the unique blend of industry, academic, regulatory and clinical attendees.
150 Attendees
Frequency: Annual/Fall

8193 CONTE Conference on Nuclear Training and Education
555 N Kensington Ave
La Grange Park, IL 60526-5592

708-352-6611
800-323-3044
FAX 708-352-0499
E-Mail: advertising@ans.org
Home Page: www.ans.org
Social Media: *Facebook, Twitter, LinkedIn*

Jack Tuohy, Executive Director
James S Tulenko, VP
William F Naughton, Treasurer

Topics of interest include knowledge retention,
industry training practices, workforce development, government support, partnerships with
colleges and universities, applications of technology to training, and training for next generation of nuclear plants.
10500 Members
Founded in 1954

8194 Coastal Summit
American Shore & Beach Preservation
Association
5460 Beaujolais Lane
Fort Myers, FL 33919

239-489-2616
FAX 239-362-9771
E-Mail: exdir@asbpa.org
Home Page: www.asbpa.org
Social Media: *Facebook, Twitter*

Harry Simmons, President
Nicole Elko, Secretary
Brad Pickel, Treasurer
Anthony Pratt, Chair

Federal, state and local government agencies
and individuals interested in conservation, development and restoration of beaches and
shorefronts.
1M Members
Founded in 1926

8195 Conference of the Brazilian Association for Aerosol Research
American Association for Aerosol Research
15000 Commerce Parkway
Suite C
Mount Laurel, NJ 08054

856-439-9080
877-777-6753
FAX 856-439-0525
E-Mail: info@aaar.org
Home Page: www.aaar.org

William Nazaroff, President
Barbara Turpin, Vice President
Barbara Wyslouzil, Vice President Elect
Murray Johnston, Treasurer
CY Wu, Secretary

Opportunity to meet with other aerosol scientists and learn the latest advances in all frontiers of aerosol science and technology. Meet
new colleagues, and network with academia,
government, and industry researchers.
1000 Members
Founded in 1982

8196 Conference on the Applications of Air Pollution Meteorology
A&WMA

420 Fort Duquesne Boulevard
One Gateway Center, 3rd Floor
Pittsburgh, PA 15222-1435

412-652-2458
FAX 412-232-3450
E-Mail: info@awma.org
Home Page: www.awma.org
Social Media: *Facebook, Twitter, LinkedIn*

Jeffry Muffat, President
Merlyn L. Hough, President Elect
Mike Kelly, Secretary/ Executive Director
Amy Gilligan, Treasurer
Dallas Baker, Vice President

Topics dealing with ALL aspects of air pollution meteorology ranging from the microscale
to the global scale and including field and laboratory measurements, instrumentation, theoretical studies, numerical modeling, evaluation
studies and applications. Also on transport and
dispersion modeling systems, urban meteorology and dispersion, and regional to global scale
transport and dispersion.
9000 Members
Founded in 1907

8197 Department of Defense Fire & Emergency Services Conference
International Association of Fire Chiefs
4025 Fair Ridge Dr
Fairfax, VA 22033-2868

703-273-0911
FAX 703-273-9363
Home Page: www.iafc.org
Social Media: *Facebook, LinkedIn*

Al H. Gillespie, President & Chairman of the
Board
Hank Clemmensen, First Vice President
William R. Metcalf, Second Vice President
Richard Carrizzo, Treasurer
Luther L. Fincher, Jr., Director-At-Large

Official conference for the military fire and
emergency service, including Army, DLA,
Navy, Marine Corp, Air Force and Coast Guard
fire service personnel.
12000 Members
Founded in 1873

8198 Downscaling Climate Models for Planning
A&WMA
420 Fort Duquesne Boulevard
One Gateway Center, 3rd Floor
Pittsburgh, PA 15222-1435

412-652-2458
FAX 412-232-3450
E-Mail: info@awma.org
Home Page: www.awma.org
Social Media: *Facebook, Twitter, LinkedIn*

Jeffry Muffat, President
Merlyn L. Hough, President Elect
Mike Kelly, Secretary/ Executive Director
Amy Gilligan, Treasurer
Dallas Baker, Vice President
9000 Members
Founded in 1907

8199 EBA Annual Meeting
Environmental Business Association
1150 Connecticut Avenue NW
9th Floor
Washington, DC 20036-4129

202-624-4363
FAX 202-828-4130
E-Mail: wbode@bode.com

William H Bode, President

Learn more about the research, development
and demonstration activities in fuel cells, hydrogen production delivery and storage
technologies.
Frequency: June

8200 EBA Semi-Annual Meeting
Environmental Bankers Association
510 King Street
Suite 410
Alexandria, VA 22314

703-549-0977
800-966-7475
FAX 703-548-5945
Home Page: www.environbank.org

D J Telego, Executive Co-Director

Network with peers in the bank and non-bank financial institutions, insurers, asset management firms and those who provide services to them. Learn more about environmental risk management, sustainable development, and due diligence policies and procedures in financial institutions.
Frequency: January, June

8201 ECOS Annual Meeting
Society of Environmental Journalists
PO Box 2492
Jenkintown, PA 19046

215-884-8174
FAX 215-884-8175
Home Page: www.sej.org
Social Media: *Facebook, Twitter*

Carolyn Whetzel, President
Peter Fairley, 1st Vice Pres
Jeff Burnside, 2nd Vice Pres
Don Hopey, Treasurer

Members of the Environmental Council of the States, the national association of state and territorial environmental agency leaders, will confer on matters of importance to the states such as air, water, waste, compliance, cross-media, and planning.
Founded in 1990

8202 EDRA Annual Meeting
Environmental Design Research Association
PO Box 7146
Edmond, OK 73083-7146

405-304-4863
FAX 403-330-4150
E-Mail: edra@telepath.com
Home Page: www.edra.org

Janet Singer, Executive Director

Providing information about the advancement and dissemination of environmental design research, improving understanding of the interrelationships between people, their built and natural surroundings, and creating environments responsive to human needs.
Frequency: Spring-Summer

8203 EHS Management Forum
National Assoc. for Environmental Management
1612 K St NW
Suite 1102
Washington, DC 20006-2830

202-986-6616
800-391-6236
FAX 202-530-4408
E-Mail: programs@naem.org
Home Page: www.naem.org
Social Media: *Facebook, Twitter, LinkedIn*

Kelvin Roth, President
Stephen Evanoff, 1st Vice President
Debbie Hammond, 2nd Vice President
Frank Macielak, Secretary and Treasurer

The largest annual gathering of EHS and sustainability decision-makers. Three days of interactive breakout sessions and keynote presentations, the Forum is the best opportunity for professional networking, benchmarking, and best-practice sharing available to EHS and sustainability practitioners today.
1000+ Members
Founded in 1990

8204 EIA's National Conference & Exposition
Environmental Information Association
6935 Wisconsin Ave
Suite 306
Chevy Chase, MD 20815-6112

301-961-4999
888-343-4342
FAX 301-961-3094
E-Mail: info@eia-usa.org
Home Page: www.eia-usa.org

Dana Hudson, President
Mike Schrum, President Elect
Kevin Cannan, Vice President
Joy Finch, Secretary
Chris Gates, Treasurer

Providing the environmental industry with the information needed to remain knowledgeable, responsible, and competitive in the environmental health and safety industry.

8205 EMS Annual Meeting
Environmental Mutagen Society
1821 Michael Faraday Drive
Suite 300
Reston, VA 20190

703-438-8220
FAX 703-438-3113
E-Mail: emshq@ems-us.org
Home Page: www.ems-us.org

Tonia Masson, Executive Director
Suzanne Morris, Secretary
Barbara Shane, Treasurer

Environmental Impacts on the Genome and Epigenome; Mechanisms and Risks.
Frequency: Spring

8206 EPRI-A&WMA Workshop on Future Air Quality Model Development Needs
American Association for Aerosol Research
15000 Commerce Parkway
Suite C
Mount Laurel, NJ 08054

856-439-9080
877-777-6753
FAX 856-439-0525
E-Mail: info@aaar.org
Home Page: www.aaar.org

William Nazaroff, President
Barbara Turpin, Vice President
Barbara Wyslouzil, Vice President Elect
Murray Johnston, Treasurer
CY Wu, Secretary

Designed to bring together researchers from academia, government and private institutions, industry, and other stakeholders to brainstorm on various air quality model development needs and to develop a comprehensive research agenda that can be used by the community to help guide research plans and to promote collaboration amongst researchers.
1000 Members
Founded in 1982

8207 ESTC Annual Convention
International Ecotourism Society
PO Box 96503 #34145
Washington, DC 20090-6503

202-506-5033
FAX 202-789-7279
E-Mail: info@ecotourism.org
Home Page: www.ecotourism.org
Social Media: *Facebook, Twitter, YouTube*

Kelly Bricker, Chair
Tony Charters, Vice Chair
Neal Inamdar, Director Finance/Administration

Highlighting global challenges and local opportunities, supporting sustainable development of tourism and promoting solutions that balance conservation, communities and sustainable travel.
900 Members
Founded in 1990

8208 ESTECH Annual Technical Meeting and Exposition of IEST
Institute of Environmental Sciences and Technology
5005 Newport Drive
Suite 506
Rolling Meadows, IL 60008-3841

847-255-1561
FAX 847-255-1699
Home Page: www.iest.org

Heather Dvorak, Marketing Associate

IEST's annual technical meeting and exposition presents the finest educational program with tutorials, technical sessions, and working group meeting, as well as displays in the tabletop exhibition for design, test and evaluation.
300 Attendees
Frequency: May

8209 ETAD Annual Meeting
Ecological and Toxicological Association of Dyes
1850 M Street NW
Suite 700
Washington, DC 20036

202-721-4154
FAX 202-296-8120
Home Page: www.etad.com

Dr C Tucker Helmes, Executive Director

Cooperate with ETAD member companies and value chain for the benefit of health and the environment. Learn more about environmental regulations.
Frequency: Spring

8210 Effective Cover Cropping in the Midwest
Soil and Water Conservation Society
945 SW Ankeny Rd
Ankeny, IA 50023-9764

515-289-2331
800-843-7645
FAX 515-289-1227
E-Mail: swcs@swcs.org
Home Page: www.swcs.org

Bill Boyer, President
Dan Towery, Vice-President
Clark Gantzer, Secretary
Jerry Pearce, Treasurer

Targeted to farmers and cover crop service providers. Provides a forum for farmers to exchange information, discuss opportunities for collaboration, and learn about new and successful practices related to cover crops. Goal of this conference is to get farmers together to learn how to effectively manage cover crops in a way that enhances soil quality, keeps nutrients in the fields, and increases the bottom line.
5000+ Members
Founded in 1943

8211 Enviro Expo
Industrial Shows Northeast
333 Trapelo Road
Belmont, MA 02478-1856

617-489-2302
800-543-5259

FAX 781-489-5534
Home Page: www.enviroexpo.com
Social Media: *Facebook, Twitter, LinkedIn*

Russ Ryan, President
Diane Fisher, Show Manager

A single stop responsible family-oriented event, designed to educate and entertain. Variety of products and services that specialize in; health & wellness, transportation, home & garden, renewable energy, and Eco fashions.
5,000 Attendees
Frequency: May
Founded in 1987

8212 Environmental Technology Expo
Association of Energy Engineers
4025 Pleasantdale Road
Suite 420
Atlanta, GA 30340

770-447-5083
FAX 770-446-3969
E-Mail: info@aeecenter.org
Home Page: www.aeecenter.org

Ruth Whitlock, Executive Admin
Jennifer Vendola, Accountant

Annual show and exhibits of air and water pollution contrasts, waste-to-energy services information, asbestos abatement and monitoring instruments and equipment.
Frequency: October

8213 Executive Edge
International Association of Fire Chiefs
4025 Fair Ridge Dr
Fairfax, VA 22033-2868

703-273-0911
FAX 703-273-9363
Home Page: www.iafc.org
Social Media: *Facebook, LinkedIn*

Al H. Gillespie, President & Chairman of the Board
Hank Clemmensen, First Vice President
William R. Metcalf, Second Vice President
Richard Carrizzo, Treasurer
Luther L. Fincher, Jr., Director-At-Large

Fire service experts take participants through an intensive program that teaches lessons not taught in any school. Executive leadership program is designed for newly appointed fire chiefs and those preparing to become fire chiefs.
12000 Members
Founded in 1873

8214 FET Annual Meeting
Federation of Environmental Technologists
PO Box 624
Slinger, WI 53086-0624

414-540-0070
FAX 262-644-7106
E-Mail: info@fetinc.org
Home Page: www.fetinc.org

Triese Haase, Administrator

Attend the program, visit the exhibitions and hear from keynote speakers on relevant environmental topics.
Frequency: March

8215 FET's Environment Annual Conference & Exhibition
Federation of Environmental Technologists
W175 N11081 Stonewood Dr.
Ste 203
Germantown, WI 53022-4771

262-437-1700
FAX 262-437-1702
E-Mail: info@fetinc.org
Home Page: www.fetinc.org

Dan Brady, Board Chair
Mark Steinberg, President

Dave Seitz, Vice President
Anthony Montemurro, Treasurer
Jeffrey Nettesheim, Secretary

Courses on Air Pollution Control, Emergency Preparedness and Business Continuity, Managing Contaminated Sediments and an Environmental, Health & Safety Primer.
700 Members
Founded in 1981

8216 Fish Wildlife Agencies Association Southeast
8005 Freshwater Farms Road
Tallahassee, FL 32309

850-893-1204
FAX 850-893-6204
E-Mail: seafwa@aol.com
Home Page: www.seafwa.org

Robert Brently, Executive Secretary

Fifteen booths.
1,000 Attendees
Frequency: October

8217 Forestry, Conservation Communications Association Annual Meeting
Forestry, Conservation Communications Association
Hall of the States
444 N Capitol
Washington, DC 20001

202-624-5416
FAX 202-751-9099

Joe Friend, Executive Director

Annual meeting and exhibits of forestry and conservation communications equipment, systems and procedures.

8218 Global Warming International Conference & Expo
SUPCON International
PO Box 5275
Woodridge, IL 60517-0275

630-910-1551
FAX 630-910-1561
E-Mail: syshen@megsinet.net
Home Page: www.globalwarming.net

Environmental and energy technology, global warming mitigation, journals, publications and software, greenhouse gas measurements, alternative vehicles and alternative energy. Containing 100 booths and exhibits.
2000 Attendees
Frequency: April Boston

8219 GlobalCon Conference & Expo
Association of Energy Engineers
4025 Pleasantdale Rd
Suite 420
Atlanta, GA 30340-4264

770-447-5083
FAX 770-446-3969
E-Mail: info@aeecenter.org
Home Page: www.aeecenter.org
Social Media: *Facebook, Twitter, LinkedIn, YouTube*

Eric A. Woodroof, President
Gary Hogsett, President Elect
Bill Younger, Secretary
Paul Goodman, C.P.A., Treasurer

Designed specifically to facilitate those seeking to expand their knowledge of fast-moving developments in the energy field, explore promising new technologies, compare energy supply options, and learn about innovative and cost-conscious project implementation strategies.
8.2M Members
Founded in 1977

8220 Green Industry Conference - GIC
Professional Lawncare Network, Inc (PLANET)
950 Herndon Parkway
Suite 450
Herndon, VA 20170

703-736-9666
800-395-2522
FAX 703-736-9668
E-Mail: info@gie-expo.com
Home Page:
www.landcarenetwork.or/cmc/gic.html

Held in conjunction with the GIE+EXPO, the conference offers leadership series, workshops, educational opportunities, events, and new member orientation.
Frequency: Annual

8221 Healthy Buildings Conference & Exhibition
The Indoor Air Institute
2548 Empire Grade
Santa Cruz, CA 95060

831-426-0148
FAX 831-426-6522
E-Mail: info@IndAir.org
Home Page: indair.org

Hal Levin, President
William Fisk, Vice President
William Nazaroff, Vice President

Issues addressed relate to indoor air quality and its impact on health. The main focus is on buildings as confined spaces where we spend around 90% of our life.

8222 Heating with Biomass;
Environmental & Energy Study Institute
122 C Street NW
Suite 630
Washington, DC 20001

202-628-1400
FAX 202-628-1825
E-Mail: eesi@eesi.org
Home Page: www.eesi.org
Social Media: *Facebook, Twitter, YouTube*

Jared Blum, Board Chair
Shelley Fidler, Board Treasurer
Richard L. Ottinger, Board Chair Emeritus

Win-Win for Households, Economic Development, Energy Security. Learn about how clean, renewable, efficient biomass heating can contribute to job creation, economic development, and energy security in communities across the country, as well as ways in which policies can help overcome some of the existing challenges and barriers to biomass use in the residential, commercial, and institutional sectors.
Founded in 1984

8223 HydroVision
HCI Publications
410 Archibald Street
Kansas City, MO 64111-3001

816-931-1311
FAX 816-931-2015
Home Page: www.hcipub.com

Leslie Eden, Manager

Focusing on asset management, civil works and dam safety, new development, ocean/ tidal/ stream power, operations and maintenance, policies and regulations, and water resources.
1,600 Attendees
Frequency: July-August

8224 IAWF Annual Meetings
International Association of Wildland Fire
4025 Fair Ridge Drive
Fairfax, VA 22033

785-423-1818
FAX 785-542-3511

E-Mail: sandy@iawfonline.org
Home Page: www.iawfonline.org
Social Media: *Facebook, Twitter*

Sacha Dick, Programs Manager
Mikel Robinson, Executive Director

Participants represent a wide range of organizations, disciplines, and countries. Conference program includes workshops, invited speakers, oral and poster presentations, panels, and vendor displays.

8225 IEST Annual Meeting
Institute of Environmental Sciences and Technology
5005 Newport Drive
Suite 506
Rolling Meadows, IL 60008-3841

847-255-1561
FAX 847-255-1699
E-Mail: information@iest.org
Home Page: www.iest.org

Julie Kendrick, Executive Director

Single source of contamination control knowledge for the industry. Participate in exceptional continuing education training courses and interactive working group meetings.
Frequency: Spring

8226 ILZRO Annual Meeting
International Lead Zinc Research Organization
2525 Meridian Parkway, Suite 100
PO Box 12036
Durham, NC 27713-2036

919-361-4647
FAX 919-361-1957
Home Page: www.ilzro.org

Stephen Wilkinson, President
Frank Goodwin, VP Materials Sciences
Scott Mooneyham, Treasurer
Rob Putnam, Director Communications

Focused on new technology and its role in managing risks in the production and use of lead, the drivers for health and environmental legislation and their likely future direction, trends, threats and opportunities in the global lead/zinc market, in particular those arising from the increasing desire for more low emission vehicles. Enabling delegates to meet a wide cross-section of key players in the lead producing and consuming countries.
Frequency: November

8227 ISEE Annual Meetings
International Society for Ecological Economics
1313 Dolley Madison Boulevard
Suite 402
McLean, VA 22101

703-790-1745
FAX 703-790-2672
Home Page: www.ecologicaleconomics.org
Social Media: *Facebook, Twitter, LinkedIn*

Heide Scheiter-Rohland, Director Membership

Provides an excellent opportunity for members to meet other ecological economists, test their ideas by presenting papers, and participate in the governance of the Society.
Frequency: Summer or Fall

8228 ISEMNA Annual Meeting
International Society for Ecological Modelling
University of California, Animal Sciences Dept
One Shields Avenue
Davis, CA 95616-8521

530-752-5362
FAX 530-752-0175

E-Mail: webmaster@isemna.org
Home Page: www.isemna.org

Wolfgang Pittroff, Secretary-General
David Mauriello, Treasurer

Providing a forum for scientists from around the world to exchange ideas, theories, concepts, methodologies, and results from ecological modelling that address these important issues.
Frequency: August

8229 IWA-WEF Wastewater Treatment Modelling Seminar
Water Environment Federation
601 Wythe St
Alexandria, VA 22314-1994

800-666-0206
FAX 703-684-2492
Home Page: www.wef.org
Social Media: *Facebook, Twitter*

Matt Bond, President
Cordell Samuels, President-Elect
Sandra Ralston, Vice President
Chris Browning, Treasurer
Jeff Eger, Secretary and Executive Director

With stricter effluent limits for nutrients and other contaminants, and concerns about plant efficiency, climate change, and emerging contaminants, there is a drive for new, more sophisticated application of modeling. Objective is to present recent findings and successful case studies with the aim of bringing together different approaches.
79 Members
ISSN: 1044-9943
Founded in 1928

8230 IWLA National Convention
Izaak Walton League
707 Conservation Lane
Gaithersburg, MD 20878

301-548-0150
800-453-5463
FAX 301-548-0146
E-Mail: general@iwla.org
Home Page: www.iwla.org
Social Media: *Facebook, Twitter*

Jim A. Madsen, President
Robert Chapman, Vice President
Marj Striegel, Secretary
Walter Lynn Jr., Treasurer

Explore how Izaak Walton League members can make a difference for the future of America's great rivers, and the people and wildlife that depend on them.
37000 Members
Founded in 1922

8231 Instructional Technology for Occupational Safety and Health Professionals
Nat. Environmental, Safety & Health Training Assoc
2700 N. Central Avenue
Suite 900
Phoenix, AZ 85004-1147

602-956-6099
FAX 602-956-6399
E-Mail: neshta@neshta.org
Home Page: www.neshta.org

Design, develop, deliver, evaluate and manage workplace safety and health training programs. Prepare and give a 15-minute presentation on a relevant workplace health and safety topic. The presentation will include skills and techniques learned in the course; however you will be encouraged to also bring materials that you are currently working on to use as a reference.
Founded in 1977

8232 Int'l Conference on Southern Hemisphere Meteorology & Oceanography
Renewable Natural Resources Foundation
5430 Grosvenor Ln
Bethesda, MD 20814-2193

301-493-9101
FAX 301-493-6148
E-Mail: info@rnrf.org
Home Page: www.rnrf.org

Howard N. Rosen, Chairman
Richard A. Engberg, Vice-Chairman
Robert D. Day, Executive Director

An interdisciplinary forum for presentations of our current state of knowledge, as well as motivating new research and applications within the variety of disciplines related to weather and climate of the ocean and atmosphere.
14 Members
Founded in 1972

8233 Inter-American Dialogue on Water Management
Water Environment Federation
601 Wythe St
Alexandria, VA 22314-1994

800-666-0206
FAX 703-684-2492
Home Page: www.wef.org
Social Media: *Facebook, Twitter*

Matt Bond, President
Cordell Samuels, President-Elect
Sandra Ralston, Vice President
Chris Browning, Treasurer
Jeff Eger, Secretary and Executive Director

The most prominent water encounter in the region. Gathering a wide myriad of sectors, government officials, national and international cooperation agency representatives, stakeholders, and practitioners in water management in the Americas. Address the need to evolve towards an inter-generation dialogue to embrace water management challenges beyond sectoral barriers that we have built in recent generations.
79 Members
ISSN: 1044-9943
Founded in 1928

8234 International Association for Energy Economics Conference
International Association for Energy Economics
28790 Chagrin Boulevard
Suite 350
Cleveland, OH 44122-4630

216-464-5365
FAX 216-464-2737
E-Mail: iaee@iaee.org
Home Page: www.iaee.org

David Williams, Executive Director
John Jimison, Managing Director

Semi-annual conference and exhibits relating to energy economics including publications, consultants, energy database software.
325 Attendees

8235 International Conference & Exhibition on Liquefied Natural Gas (LNG)
Institute of Gas Technology
1700 S Mount Prospect Rd
Des Plaines, IL 60018-1804

847-768-0664
FAX 847-768-0669
Home Page: www.gastechnology.org

Social Media: *Facebook, Twitter, LinkedIn, YouTube*

David Carroll, President & CEO
Ronald Snedic, Vice President/ Corporate Dev
Paul Chromek, General Counsel & Secretary

A landmark strategic, technical and commercial event for leaders, experts and committed professionals of the worldwide LNG Industry.

8236 International Conference On Air Quality- Science and Application
A&WMA
420 Fort Duquesne Boulevard
One Gateway Center, 3rd Floor
Pittsburgh, PA 15222-1435

412-652-2458
FAX 412-232-3450
E-Mail: info@awma.org
Home Page: www.awma.org
Social Media: *Facebook, Twitter, LinkedIn*

Jeffry Muffat, President
Merlyn L. Hough, President Elect
Mike Kelly, Secretary/ Executive Director
Amy Gilligan, Treasurer
Dallas Baker, Vice President

One of the most prominent forums for discussing the latest scientific developments, applications and implications for policy and other uses. An important feature it that it brings together scientists and other stakeholders from the air pollution, climate change, policy and health communities.
9000 Members
Founded in 1907

8237 International Conference on Facility Operations-Safeguards Interface
555 N Kensington Ave
La Grange Park, IL 60526-5592

708-352-6611
800-323-3044
FAX 708-352-0499
E-Mail: advertising@ans.org
Home Page: www.ans.org
Social Media: *Facebook, Twitter, LinkedIn*

Jack Tuohy, Executive Director
James S Tulenko, VP
William F Naughton, Treasurer

New methods, products, instructions and ideas for the nuclear science and technology safety field.
10500 Members
Founded in 1954

8238 International Conference on Ground Penetrating Rador GPR
Society of Exploration Geophysicists
8801 South Yale
Suite 500
Tulsa, OK 74137-3575

918-497-5500
FAX 918-497-5557
E-Mail: web@seg.org
Home Page: www.seg.org
Social Media: *Facebook, Twitter, LinkedIn*

Mary Fleming, Executive Director
Vladimir Grechka, Editor

Devoted to the development of ground penetrating radar. Presents the most recent technical information and case studies on ground penetrating radar for engineers, scientists, and end users.
Founded in 1930

8239 International Conference on Indoor Air Quality and Climate
International Academy of Indoor Air Sciences

343 Soquel Avenue
PMB 312
Santa Cruz, CA 95062

831-426-0148
FAX 831-426-6522
Home Page: www.indoorair2002.org

Multidisciplinary event involving participants from medicine, engineering, architecture and related fields. The conference will cover all aspects of Indoor Air Quality and Climate and the effects on human health, comfort and productivity. Cutting-edge research results will be presented, including ways to achieve an optimal indoor environment in a sustainable manner. Will address a variety of indoor environments, residential, office, school, industrial, commercial and transport.
Frequency: June-July

8240 International Hazardous Materials Response Teams Conference
International Association of Fire Chiefs
4025 Fair Ridge Drive
Fairfax, VA 22033

703-273-0911
FAX 703-273-9363

One of the largest gatherings of hazmat responders, facilitating new ideas. Dedicated exhibit hours and events, and indoor and outdoor exhibits.

8241 International High-Level Radioactive Waste Management
555 N Kensington Ave
La Grange Park, IL 60526-5592

708-352-6611
800-323-3044
FAX 708-352-0499
E-Mail: advertising@ans.org
Home Page: www.ans.org
Social Media: *Facebook, Twitter, LinkedIn*

Jack Tuohy, Executive Director
James S Tulenko, VP
William F Naughton, Treasurer

Subject coverage includes site characterization, analogue studies, geochemical studies, disruptive events, spent fuel and high-level-waste transportation, engineered barrier systems, design and testing, disposal containers, and waste form. Performance assessment and regulatory issues are also addressed.
10500 Members
Founded in 1954

8242 International Society for Environmental Epidemiology Meeting
American Association for Aerosol Research
15000 Commerce Parkway
Suite C
Mount Laurel, NJ 08054

856-439-9080
877-777-6753
FAX 856-439-0525
E-Mail: info@aaar.org
Home Page: www.aaar.org

William Nazaroff, President
Barbara Turpin, Vice President
Barbara Wyslouzil, Vice President Elect
Murray Johnston, Treasurer
CY Wu, Secretary

Discussion of problems unique to the study of health and the environment.
1000 Members
Founded in 1982

8243 International Symposium on Environmental Geochemistry
Society for Environmental Geochemistry & Health

4698 S Forrest Avenue
Springfield, MO 65810

417-851-1166
FAX 417-881-6920
E-Mail: DRBGWIXSON@aol.com
Home Page: www.segh.net

Prof. Xiangdong Li, President
Prof. Andrew Hursthouse, European Chair
Kyoung-Woong Kim, Asia/Pacific Chair
Anthea Brown, Membership Secretary/ Treasurer
Malcolm Brown, Secretary

Convey expertise in a range of scientific fields, such as geochemistry, biology, engineering, geology, hydrology, epidemiology, chemistry, medicine, nutrition and toxicology.
400 Members
Founded in 1971

8244 International Topical Meeting on Nuclear Plant Instrumentation
555 N Kensington Ave
La Grange Park, IL 60526-5592

708-352-6611
800-323-3044
FAX 708-352-0499
E-Mail: advertising@ans.org
Home Page: www.ans.org
Social Media: *Facebook, Twitter, LinkedIn*

Jack Tuohy, Executive Director
James S Tulenko, VP
William F Naughton, Treasurer

Control and Human Machine Interface Technologies
10500 Members
Founded in 1954

8245 International Workshop on Seismic Anisotropy
Society of Exploration Geophysicists
8801 South Yale
Suite 500
Tulsa, OK 74137-3575

918-497-5500
FAX 918-497-5557
E-Mail: web@seg.org
Home Page: www.seg.org
Social Media: *Facebook, Twitter, LinkedIn*

Mary Fleming, Executive Director
Vladimir Grechka, Editor

Cover both theoretical and applied aspects of seismic anisotropy in earth sciences. Focusing on applications of anisotropic models and methods in exploration & development of both conventional and unconventional Oil & Gas reservoirs, earthquake seismology, and reservoir monitoring using seismic anisotropy and microseismic.
Founded in 1930

8246 Joint International Conference PBC/ SEGH
Society for Environmental Geochemistry & Health
4698 S Forrest Avenue
Springfield, MO 65810

417-851-1166
FAX 417-881-6920
E-Mail: DRBGWIXSON@aol.com
Home Page: www.segh.net

Prof. Xiangdong Li, President
Prof. Andrew Hursthouse, European Chair
Kyoung-Woong Kim, Asia/Pacific Chair
Anthea Brown, Membership Secretary/ Treasurer
Malcolm Brown, Secretary

On behalf of the Pacific Basin Consortium and the Society for Environmental Geochemistry and Health (Asia/ Pacific region)
400 Members
Founded in 1971

8247 MEGA Symposium
A&WMA
420 Fort Duquesne Boulevard
One Gateway Center, 3rd Floor
Pittsburgh, PA 15222-1435

412-652-2458
FAX 412-232-3450
E-Mail: info@awma.org
Home Page: www.awma.org
Social Media: *Facebook, Twitter, LinkedIn*

Jeffry Muffat, President
Merlyn L. Hough, President Elect
Mike Kelly, Secretary/ Executive Director
Amy Gilligan, Treasurer
Dallas Baker, Vice President

Addresses issues related to power plant air emissions through the combined efforts of four key industry payers. Update seasoned professionals and provide an excellent learning experience for early career engineers.
9000 Members
Founded in 1907

8248 MTS TechSurge, Oceans in Action
Marine Technology Society
1100 H St., Nw
Suite LL-100
Washington, DC 20005

202-717-8705
FAX 202-347-4302
E-Mail: membership@mtsociety.org
Home Page: www.mtsociety.org
Social Media: *Facebook, Twitter, LinkedIn*

Jerry Boatman, President
Drew Michel, President-Elect
Jerry Wilson, VP of Industry and Technology
Jill Zande, VP of Education and Research
Justin Manley, VP of Gov. & Public Affairs

Learn how government agencies and universities are supporting both current and emerging oceanographic operations worldwide. Discover how marine science, technology, engineering, products and services come together to support real-world issues around the globe, including piracy, disaster monitoring and recovery, prediction and forecast of ocean properties, coastal restoration, hypoxia, harmful algal blooms, fisheries and much more.
2M Members
Founded in 1963

8249 Middle East Geosciences Conference & Exhibition
Society of Exploration Geophysicists
8801 South Yale
Suite 500
Tulsa, OK 74137-3575

918-497-5500
FAX 918-497-5557
E-Mail: web@seg.org
Home Page: www.seg.org
Social Media: *Facebook, Twitter, LinkedIn*

Mary Fleming, Executive Director
Vladimir Grechka, Editor
Founded in 1930

8250 NAAEE Annual Meeting
North American Association for Environmental
2000 P Street NW
Suite 540
Washington, DC 20036

202-419-0412
FAX 202-419-0415

E-Mail: email@naaee.org
Home Page: www.naaee.org

William H Dent, Jr, Executive Director
Barbara Eager, Conference Coordinator
Paul Werth, Owner

Concurrent sessions, plenary sessions and networking, as well as workshops, field experiences and special events.
Frequency: Fall

8251 NAEP Annual Meeting
National Association of Environmental Professional
PO Box 2086
Bowie, MD 20718-2086

301-860-1140
888-251-9902
FAX 301-860-1141
Home Page: www.naep.org

Sandi Worthman, Administrator

Learn unbiased information on environmental practices.
Frequency: Spring

8252 NALGEP Annual Meetings
National Association of Local Government
1333 New Hampshire Avenue NW
Washington, DC 20036

202-638-6254
FAX 202-393-2866
E-Mail: nalgep@spiegelmcd.com
Home Page: www.nalgep.org

Kenneth Brown, Executive Director
David Dickson, Project Manager

Discussion of congressional issues
Frequency: Regional Workshops

8253 NALMS Symposium
North American Lake Management Society
4513 Vernon Boulevard, Suite 100
PO Box 5443
Madison, WI 53705-443

608-233-2836
FAX 608-233-3186
E-Mail: nalms@nalms.org
Home Page: www.nalms.org

Bev Clark, President
Reesa Evans, Secretary
Linda Green, Treasurer

A collection of professional presentations, general workshops and non-stop discussions on managing lakes and reservoirs. Vendors are present with the latest lake management tools displayed. Scientific and environmental minds will offer a variety of relevant topical subject matter to be covered in breakout educational sessions, and networking opportunities will allow for collaboration with lake property association members and other interested parties.
1700 Members
Frequency: Annual/October
Founded in 1980

8254 NAPE
Society of Exploration Geophysicists
8801 South Yale
Suite 500
Tulsa, OK 74137-3575

918-497-5500
FAX 918-497-5557
Home Page: www.napeexpo.com
Social Media: *Facebook, Twitter, LinkedIn*

Mary Fleming, Executive Director
Vladimir Grechka, Editor

Provides a marketplace for the buying, selling and trading of oil and gas products and producing properties via exhibit booths. Brings prospects and producing properties, capital formation, services and technologies all to-

gether in one location, creating an environment to establish strategic alliances for doing business and initiating purchases and trades.
Founded in 1930

8255 NEHA Annual Educational Conference and Exhibition
National Environmental Health Association
720 S Colorado Boulevard
Suite 970-S
Denver, CO 80246-1925

303-756-9090
FAX 303-691-9490
E-Mail: staff@neha.org
Home Page: www.neha.org

Toni Roland, Conference Coordinator
Kim Brandow, Managing Director
Larry Marcum, Managing Director
Bob Custard, Manager
Jill Cruickshank, Communications Manager

The National Environmental Health Association (NEHA) is a unique organization representing all professionals in environmental health. NEHA offers credentials, publications, training, Journal of Environmental Health, and discounts for members. Each year NEHA conducts the Annual Educational Conference and Exhibition, this year it will be at the Minneapolis Hilton in Minneapolis, MN.
2000 Attendees
Frequency: June-July

8256 NEHA Annual Meeting
National Conference of Local Environmental Health
c/o NEHA, 720 S Colorado Boulevard
South Tower, Suite 970
Denver, CO 80246-1925

303-756-9090
FAX 303-691-9490
E-Mail: nfabian@neha.org
Home Page: http://www.neha.org

Nelson E Fabian, Executive Director

Held with the National Environmental Health Association.
Frequency: June

8257 NESHTA Annual Meetings
National Environmental, Safety and Health Training
PO Box 10321
Phoenix, AZ 85064-0321

602-956-6099
FAX 602-956-6399
E-Mail: info@neshta.org
Home Page: www.neshta.org

Charles L Richardson, Executive Director
Joan J Jennings, Manager Association Services
Suzanne Lanctot, Manager Certification/Membership

The network for academic, government, industrial, utility and consulting trainers and training managers responsible for protecting public health, workers, and our physical environment.
Frequency: June

8258 NGWA Ground Water Summit & GWPC Spring Meeting
Renewable Natural Resources Foundation
5430 Grosvenor Ln
Bethesda, MD 20814-2193

301-493-9101
FAX 301-493-6148
E-Mail: info@rnrf.org
Home Page: www.rnrf.org

Howard N. Rosen, Chairman
Richard A. Engberg, Vice-Chairman
Robert D. Day, Executive Director

Innovate and Integrate.
14 Members
Founded in 1972

8259   NIWR Annual Conference
National Institutes for Water Resources
47 Harkness Road
Pelham, MA 10002

413-253-5686
FAX 413-253-1309
E-Mail: tracy@uidaho.edu
Home Page: niwr.net

Jeffery Allen, President
Reagan Waskom, President-Elect
John Tracy, Secretary-Treasurer

Water Resource Institute directors and associate directors are invited to join for the annual meeting.
54 Members
Founded in 1974

8260   NORA Semi-Annual Meetings
NORA: Association of Responsible Recyclers
5965 Amber Ridge Road
Haymarket, VA 20169

703-753-4277
FAX 703-753-2445
E-Mail: sparker@noranews.org
Home Page: www.noranews.org

Scott D Parker, Executive Director
Jim Letteney, Vice President

The liquid recycling industry's premier networking and education event.
Frequency: May, November

8261   NREP Annual Meetings
National Registry of Environmental Professionals
PO Box 2099
Glenview, IL 60025

847-724-6631
FAX 847-724-4223
E-Mail: nrep@nrep.org
Home Page: www.nrep.org

Richard A Young, PhD, Executive Director

Certification preparatory workshops, technical papers and special seminars.
1000 Attendees
Frequency: Semi-Annual
Mailing list available for rent

8262   National Coastal Conference
American Shore and Beach Preservation Association
5460 Beaujolais Lane
Fort Myers, FL 33919

239-489-2616
FAX 239-362-9771
E-Mail: exdir@asbpa.org
Home Page: www.asbpa.org
Social Media: *Facebook, Twitter*

Harry Simmons, President
Kate Gooderham, Executive Director
Nicole Elko, Secretary
Russell Boudreau, VP
Brad Pickel, Treasurer

Federal, state and local coastal policy and legal issues, shoreline processes and coastal management, shoreline projects and global coastal issues are discussed.
1M Members
Founded in 1926

8263   National Environmental Balancing Bureau Meeting
National Environmental Balancing Bureau

8575 Grovemont Circle
Gaithersburg, MD 20877-4121

301-977-3698
FAX 301-977-9589

Michael Dolim, VP

Annual meeting and exhibits of testing and balancing equipment, supplies and services.

8264   National Fish & Wildlife Conservation Congress
Association of Fish & Wildlife Agencies
444 N Capitol St NW
Suite 725
Washington, DC 20001-1553

202-624-7890
FAX 202-624-7891
E-Mail: info@fishwildlife.org
Home Page: www.fishwildlife.org
Social Media: *Facebook, Twitter*

Jon Gassett, President
Jeff Vonk, Vice President
Dave Chanda, Secretary/ Treasurer
Curtis Taylor, Past President

Bring together leading fish and wildlife scientists, government leaders, federal, provincial, state and local fish and wildlife agencies, conservation organizations and anglers and hunters to participate in discussions and debates about the future of fish and wildlife resources in North America.
Founded in 1902

8265   National Flood Risk Management; Flood Risk Summit
Association of State Floodplain Managers
2809 Fish Hatchery Rd
Suite 204
Madison, WI 53713-5020

608-274-0123
FAX 608-274-0696
E-Mail: Larry@floods.org
Home Page: www.floods.org
Social Media: *Facebook*

Sally McConkey, Chair
William Nechamen, Vice Chair
Alan J. Giles, Secretary
John V. Crofts, Treasurer

Invitation-only. Soliciting feedback and providing updates to local, state, regional, and federal officials and the private sector on vital national policies currently under construction at the Federal level.
6500 Members
Founded in 1977

8266   National FloodProofing Conference and Exposition Levees and Beyond
Association of State Floodplain Managers
2809 Fish Hatchery Rd
Suite 204
Madison, WI 53713-5020

608-274-0123
FAX 608-274-0696
E-Mail: Larry@floods.org
Home Page: www.floods.org
Social Media: *Facebook*

Sally McConkey, Chair
William Nechamen, Vice Chair
Alan J. Giles, Secretary
John V. Crofts, Treasurer

Making Wise Choices Highlighting the various floodproofing methods, products, techniques, programs, funding sources, and issues that have developed. Showcasing the state-of-the-art in materials, services, equipment, accessories and techniques.
6500 Members
Founded in 1977

8267   National Planning Conference
Renewable Natural Resources Foundation
5430 Grosvenor Ln
Bethesda, MD 20814-2193

301-493-9101
FAX 301-493-6148
E-Mail: info@rnrf.org
Home Page: www.rnrf.org

Howard N. Rosen, Chairman
Richard A. Engberg, Vice-Chairman
Robert D. Day, Executive Director

Hosted by the American Planning Association.
14 Members
Founded in 1972

8268   National Quail Symposium
Wildlife Habitat Council
8737 Colesville Road
Suite 800
Silver Spring, MD 20910

301-588-8994
FAX 301-588-4629
E-Mail: whc@wildlifehc.org
Home Page: www.wildlifehc.org
Social Media: *Facebook, YouTube*

Greg Cekander, Chairman
Lawrence A Selzer, Vice Chairman
Kevin Butt, Secretary-Treasurer

Highlight the diversity in conservation of quails. Serve as an excellent venue to publish current research and advance quail conservation.
120+ Members
Founded in 1988

8269   National Real Estate Environmental Conference
National Society of Environmental Consultants
PO Box 12528
San Antonio, TX 78212-0528

210-225-2897
800-486-3676
FAX 956-225-8450

Annual conference and exhibits related to the environmentally responsible use of real estate.

8270   National Water Monitoring Conference
Renewable Natural Resources Foundation
5430 Grosvenor Ln
Bethesda, MD 20814-2193

301-493-9101
FAX 301-493-6148
E-Mail: info@rnrf.org
Home Page: www.rnrf.org

Howard N. Rosen, Chairman
Richard A. Engberg, Vice-Chairman
Robert D. Day, Executive Director

National forum provides an exceptional opportunity for federal, state, local, tribal, volunteer, academic, private, and other water stakeholders to exchange information and technology related to water monitoring, assessment, research, protection, restoration, and management, as well as to develop new skills and professional networks.
14 Members
Founded in 1972

8271 North American Environmental Field Conferences & Expositions
1230 Lincoln Drive
Carbondale, IL 62901

618-453-7809
E-Mail: aih@engr.siu.edu
Home Page: www.aihydrology.org

Emitt C. Witt, III, President
Marzi Sharfaei, Secretary
T. Allen J. Gookin, Treasurer

Interactive indoor workshops, presented by some of the world's foremost authorities in the field, discussing cutting-edge field-based technologies and methods for environmental site characterization, sampling monitoring and remediation. Hands-on interactive outdoor workshops and equipment demos featuring the latest environmental field methods and equipment.
1000 Members
Founded in 1981

8272 North American Wildlife and Natural Resources Conference
Wildlife Management Institute
1101 14th Street NW
Suite 801
Washington, DC 20005

202-371-1808
FAX 202-408-5059
Home Page:
www.wildlifemanagementinstitute.org

Meeting the challenges of modern conservation. Industry leaders dedicated to the conservation, enhancement and management of North America's wildlife and other natural resources.

8273 Ocean Sciences Meeting
Renewable Natural Resources Foundation
5430 Grosvenor Ln
Bethesda, MD 20814-2193

301-493-9101
FAX 301-493-6148
E-Mail: info@rnrf.org
Home Page: www.rnrf.org

Howard N. Rosen, Chairman
Richard A. Engberg, Vice-Chairman
Robert D. Day, Executive Director

Largest worldwide conference in the geophysical sciences, attracting Earth and space scientists, educators, students and policy makers. Meeting showcases current scientific theory focused on discoveries that will benefit humanity and ensure a sustainable future for our planet.
14 Members
Founded in 1972

8274 Oceans MTS/IEEE Conference
Marine Technology Society
1100 H St., Nw
Suite LL-100
Washington, DC 20005

202-717-8705
FAX 202-347-4302
E-Mail: membership@mtsociety.org
Home Page: www.mtsociety.org
Social Media: *Facebook, Twitter, LinkedIn*

Jerry Boatman, President
Drew Michel, President-Elect
Jerry Wilson, VP of Industry and Technology
Jill Zande, VP of Education and Research
Justin Manley, VP of Gov. & Public Affairs

The major international forum for scientists, engineers, and responsible ocean users to present the latest research results, ideas, developments, and applications in Oceanic Engineering and Marine Technology.
2M Members
Founded in 1963

8275 Offshore Technology Conference
Marine Technology Society
1100 H St., Nw
Suite LL-100
Washington, DC 20005

202-717-8705
FAX 202-347-4302
E-Mail: membership@mtsociety.org
Home Page: www.mtsociety.org
Social Media: *Facebook, Twitter, LinkedIn*

Jerry Boatman, President
Drew Michel, President-Elect
Jerry Wilson, VP of Industry and Technology
Jill Zande, VP of Education and Research
Justin Manley, VP of Gov. & Public Affairs

The world's foremost event for the development of offshore resources in the fields of drilling, exploration, production and environmental protection. A worldwide forum for the exchange of technical information vital to exploration and development of ocean resources.
2M Members
Founded in 1963

8276 Plant Growth Regulation Society of America Annual Conference
Rhone-Poulenc, Ag Company
1018 Duke Street
Alexandria, VA 22314

703-836-4606
FAX 706-883-8215
E-Mail: dmancini@ashs.org
Social Media: *Facebook, Twitter*

Dr Eric A Curry, President
Dr Louise Ferguson, VP
Dr Ed Stover, Secretary

Highlights the latest in basic and applied research in plant growth regulation including hormone binding, stress physiology and plant growth regulator application.
325 Members
Founded in 1973

8277 Residuals and Biosolids Conference
Water Environment Federation
601 Wythe St
Alexandria, VA 22314-1994

800-666-0206
FAX 703-684-2492
Home Page: www.wef.org
Social Media: *Facebook, Twitter*

Matt Bond, President
Cordell Samuels, President-Elect
Sandra Ralston, Vice President
Chris Browning, Treasurer
Jeff Eger, Secretary and Executive Director

Highlights beneficial reuse options, science, and technologies currently available to leverage biosolids as a valuable resource.
79 Members
ISSN: 1044-9943
Founded in 1928

8278 SEG Annual Meeting
Society of Exploration Geophysicists
PO Box 702740
Tulsa, OK 74170-2740

918-497-5500
FAX 918-497-5557
E-Mail: web@seg.org
Home Page: www.seg.org/index.shtml

Mary Fleming, Executive Director
Vladimir Grechka, Editor

The world's largest oil, energy and mineral exposition showcasing cutting-edge technology for use in exploration and associated industries. It is the premier venue for individuals to meet and discuss new geophysical technologies and their uses.
9300 Attendees
Frequency: October

8279 SEGH Annual Meetings
Society for Environmental Geochemistry and Health
4698 S Forrest Avenue
Springfield, MO 65810

417-885-1166
FAX 417-881-6920
Home Page: www.segh.net

Bobby Wixson, Director Membership

Environmental determinants of quality of life, including water resources, sediments and soil pollution and climate change, engineered solutions to hazardous waste including treatment of hazardous substances and regulatory solutions and approaches to hazardous substances, and all other environmental quality and human health issues.
Frequency: Summer-Fall

8280 SEJ Annual Meeting
Society of Environmental Journalists
PO Box 2492
Jenkintown, PA 19046

215-884-8174
FAX 215-884-8175
E-Mail: jletto@sej.org
Home Page: www.sej.org

Jay Letto, Annual Conference Coordinator

Organized by journalists for journalists who cover environment and related issues. Co-hosted by the University of Vermont and Vermont Law School.
Frequency: September

8281 SER Annual Meeting
Society for Ecological Restoration
285 West 18th Street #1
Tucson, AZ 85701

520-622-5485
FAX 520-622-5491
E-Mail: info@ser.org
Home Page: www.ser.org

Mary Kay C LeFevour, Executive Director
Jane Cripps, Membership
Julie St John, Communications
Dennis Martinez, Founder
Val Schaefer, Secretary

Provides members (and non-members) with the opportunity to exchange ideas and information, participate in activities such as workshops and field trips, reconnect with friends and colleagues, and make new acquaintances.
Frequency: Fall

8282 SER World Conference on Ecological Restoration
Society for Ecological Restoration
1017 O Street NW
Washington, DC 20001

202-299-9518
FAX 270-626-5485
E-Mail: info@ser.org
Home Page: www.ser.org

Steve Whisenant, Chair
Cara R. Nelson, Vice Chair
Mary Travaglini, Treasurer
Alan Unwin, Secretary

Provide members and non-members with the opportunity to exchange ideas and information, participate in activities such as workshops and field trips, reconnect with friends and colleagues, and make new acquaintances.
Frequency: Semi-Annual

8283 SETAC Annual Meeting
Society of Environmental Toxicology and
Chemistry
1010 N 12th Street
Pensacola, FL 32501-3367

850-469-1500
FAX 850-469-9778
E-Mail: rparrish@setac.org
Home Page: www.setac.org

Rodney Parrish, Executive Director
Greg Schifer, Manager

Information and collaboration on environmental toxicology and chemistry.
Frequency: Fall

8284 SHE Bi-Ennial Meetings
Society for Human Ecology
College of the Atlantic
105 Eden Street
Bar Harbor, ME 04609-0180

207-288-5015
FAX 207-288-3780
E-Mail: carter@ecology.coa.edu
Home Page: www.societyforhumanecology.org

Barbara Carter, Assistant to Executive Director

Brings together scholars and practitioners associated with the study and practice of human ecology because of the importance of the disciplines' philosophy and applications in developing mutually beneficial solutions for society and the environment. A platform for sharing knowledge on present status and approaches for sustainable development.

8285 SOCMA Annual Meeting
Synthetic Organic Chemical Manufacturers
Assn
1850 M Street NW
Suite 700
Washington, DC 20036

202-721-4100
FAX 202-296-8120
E-Mail: info@socma.com
Home Page: www.socma.com

Joseph Acker, President
Vivian Diko, Executive Assistant & CEO
Charlene Patterson, Director Human Resources

Industry leaders come together.
Frequency: Early Spring

8286 SOEH Annual Meeting
Society for Occupational and Environmental
Health
6728 Old McLean Village Drive
McLean, VA 22101

703-556-9222
FAX 703-556-8729
E-Mail: soeh@degnon.org
Home Page: www.soeh.org

George K Degnon, CAE, Executive Director

Topic will be international aspects of pesticide exposure and health, and key interest areas for presentations and posters will be; chronic health effects from pesticide exposure, agricultural worker surveillance and biomonitoring studies, good models of integrated pesticide management and involvement of community members, and much more.
Frequency: Spring

**8287 Science, Politics, and Policy:
Environmental Nexus**
National Association of Environmental
Professional
PO Box 460
Collingswood, NJ 08108

856-283-7816
FAX 856-210-1619
E-Mail: naep@bowermanagementservices.com

Home Page: www.naep.org
Social Media: *Facebook, LinkedIn*

Paul Looney, President
Harold Draper, Vice President
Joseph F. Musil Jr., Treasurer
Robert P. Morris Jr., Secretary

NEPA and Decision Making, program on what happens after NEPA documents are prepared, and how that information is useful to their preparation. Also a program on Advance Topics in Visual Resource Impact Assessment.

8288 SeminarFest
American Society of Safety Engineers
1800 E Oakton Street
Des Plaines, IL 60018

847-699-2929
FAX 847-768-3434
E-Mail: customerservice@asse.org
Home Page: www.asse.org
Social Media: *Facebook*

Terrie S. Norris, President
Richard A. Pollock, President Elect
Kathy Seabrook, Senior Vice President
Fred J. Fortman, Jr., Secretary & Executive
Director
James D. Smith, Vice President, Finance

Pass your ASP, CSP, OHST and CHST exams with confidence by taking our certification preparation workshops. Earn a certificate of completion in Safety Management & the Executive Program in Safety Management. Develop business acumen, leadership and training skills. Measure safety effectiveness and review safety management approaches. Also participate in technical and topical seminars.
30000 Members
Founded in 1911

**8289 Sino-European Symposium on
Environment and Health (SESH)**
Society for Environmental Geochemistry &
Health
4698 S Forrest Avenue
Springfield, MO 65810

417-851-1166
FAX 417-881-6920
E-Mail: DRBGWIXSON@aol.com
Home Page: www.segh.net

Prof. Xiangdong Li, President
Prof. Andrew Hursthouse, European Chair
Kyoung-Woong Kim, Asia/Pacific Chair
Anthea Brown, Membership Secretary/
Treasurer
Malcolm Brown, Secretary

Provides an opportunity for a direct communication between experts from China and the rest of the world.
400 Members
Founded in 1971

8290 Smart Energy Summit
Parks Associates
5310 Harvest Hill Road
Suite 235, Lock Box 162
Dallas, TX 75230-5805

972-490-1113
800-727-5711
E-Mail: info@parksassociates.com
Home Page: www.parksassociates.com

Tricia Parks, Founder and CEO
Stuart Sikes, President
Farhan Abid, Research Analyst
Bill Ablondi, Director, Home Systems
Research
John Barrett, Director of Research

Smart Energy Summit is an annual three-day event that examines the opportunities and technical business requirements inherent in the consumer programs and advanced systems and

services made possible by Smart Grids and Residential Energy Management solutions.
Frequency: Annual
Founded in 1986

**8291 Soil and Water Conservation Society
Annual International Conference**
Soil and Water Conservation Society
945 SW Ankeny Road
Ankeny, IA 50021-9764

515-289-2331
800-843-7645
FAX 515-289-1227
Home Page: www.swsc.org

Craig A Cox, Executive VP

Explores ways to improve the linkages among conservation science, policy and application at local, national, and international scales. The conference will provide participants an opportunity to teach skills, learn techniques, compare successes, and improve understanding.
1200 Attendees
Frequency: Annual

**8292 Spatial Cognition for Architectural
Design Symposium**
Environmental Design Research Association
1760 Old Meadow Road
Suite 500
McLean, VA 22102

703-506-2895
FAX 703-506-3266
E-Mail: edra@telepath.com
Home Page: www.edra.org
Social Media: *Facebook, Twitter, LinkedIn*

Nick Watkins, Chair
Mallika Bose, Chair-Elect
Vikki Chanse, Secretary
Shauna Mallory-Hill, Treasurer
Kate O'Donnell, Executive Director(ex-officio)

Addresses the theoretical and methodological achievements of the cognitive and computational disciplines in the domain of architectural design. A dialogue between scientists from design research and educational disciplines is sought with the aim to identify how such application of knowledge may provide real benefit for the theory and professional practice of architectural design.
700 Members
Founded in 1968

**8293 Sustainability in Public Works
Conference**
2345 Grand Blvd
Suite 700
Kansas City, MO 64108-2625

816-472-6100
800-848-2792
FAX 816-472-1610
Home Page: www.apwa.net
Social Media: *Facebook, Twitter, YouTube*

Diane M. Linderman, President
Elizabeth Treadway, President Elect
Richard F. Stinson, Director, Region I
Edward A. Gottko, Director, Region II
William Barney Mills, Jr., Director, Region III

International educational and professional association of public agencies, private sector companies, and individuals dedicated to providing high quality public works, goods and services. APWA provides a forum brings important public works-related topics to public attention in local, state, and federal areas. Mailing list for members only.
26000 Members
Founded in 1937

**8294 Sustainable Water Management
Conference**
Water Environment Federation

601 Wythe St
Alexandria, VA 22314-1994

800-666-0206
FAX 703-684-2492
Home Page: www.wef.org
Social Media: *Facebook, Twitter*

Matt Bond, President
Cordell Samuels, President-Elect
Sandra Ralston, Vice President
Chris Browning, Treasurer
Jeff Eger, Secretary and Executive Director

Will focus on large-scall sustainability issues related to water supply and management topics such as water conservation, urban planning and design, and sustainable utilities, infrastructure, and communities.
79 Members
ISSN: 1044-9943
Founded in 1928

8295 Take It Back
Raymond Communications
5111 Berwin Road
#115
College Park, MD 20740

301-345-4237
FAX 301-345-4768
Home Page: www.raymond.com

Michele Raymond, Publisher/Editor

The conference brings in the top recycling policy experts from around the world to brief customers. We also have practical sessions with case histories on such issues as packaging design, design for environment in electronics, and lifecycle issues.
150 Attendees
Frequency: March
Founded in 1996

8296 Teaming With Wildlife Fly-In Day
Association of Fish & Wildlife Agencies
444 N Capitol St NW
Suite 725
Washington, DC 20001-1553

202-624-7890
FAX 202-624-7891
E-Mail: info@fishwildlife.org
Home Page: www.fishwildlife.org
Social Media: *Facebook, Twitter*

Jon Gassett, President
Jeff Vonk, Vice President
Dave Chanda, Secretary/ Treasurer
Curtis Taylor, Past President

Join in supporting funding for the State & Tribal Wildlife Grants Program, the nation's CORE program for preventing fish and wildlife from becoming endangered in every state and territory.
Founded in 1902

8297 The Utility Management Conference
Water Environment Federation
601 Wythe St
Alexandria, VA 22314-1994

800-666-0206
FAX 703-684-2492
Home Page: www.wef.org
Social Media: *Facebook, Twitter*

Matt Bond, President
Cordell Samuels, President-Elect
Sandra Ralston, Vice President
Chris Browning, Treasurer
Jeff Eger, Secretary and Executive Director

Water and wastewater managers and professionals will gather to be part of the latest approaches, practices, and techniques in all aspects of utility management.
79 Members
ISSN: 1044-9943
Founded in 1928

8298 Thermal Treatment Technologies/ Hazardous Waste Combustors
A&WMA
420 Fort Duquesne Boulevard
One Gateway Center, 3rd Floor
Pittsburgh, PA 15222-1435

412-652-2458
FAX 412-232-3450
E-Mail: info@awma.org
Home Page: www.awma.org
Social Media: *Facebook, Twitter, LinkedIn*

Jeffry Muffat, President
Merlyn L. Hough, President Elect
Mike Kelly, Secretary/ Executive Director
Amy Gilligan, Treasurer
Dallas Baker, Vice President

Brings together industry experts from around the world to share experiences, lessons learned and new ideas on how to best operate thermal treatment facilities.
9000 Members
Founded in 1907

8299 Topical Meeting on the Technology of Fusion Energy (TOFE)
555 N Kensington Ave
La Grange Park, IL 60526-5592

708-352-6611
800-323-3044
FAX 708-352-0499
E-Mail: advertising@ans.org
Home Page: www.ans.org
Social Media: *Facebook, Twitter, LinkedIn*

Jack Tuohy, Executive Director
James S Tulenko, VP
William F Naughton, Treasurer

Providing a forum for sharing the exciting new progress that has been made in fusion research as well as presenting the future of national and worldwide fusion programs. Draws together scientists, engineers, and students from various countries.
10500 Members
Founded in 1954

8300 Underwater Intervention Conference
Marine Technology Society
1100 H St., Nw
Suite LL-100
Washington, DC 20005

202-717-8705
FAX 202-347-4302
E-Mail: membership@mtsociety.org
Home Page: www.mtsociety.org
Social Media: *Facebook, Twitter, LinkedIn*

Jerry Boatman, President
Drew Michel, President-Elect
Jerry Wilson, VP of Industry and Technology
Jill Zande, VP of Education and Research
Justin Manley, VP of Gov. & Public Affairs

The conference is of interest to a number of diverse marine industries, including offshore oil and gas, marine construction, shipwreck exploration, ocean mining and marine salvage. Presentation tracks include cable, remote intervention, commercial diving, and shipwreck salvage, among others.
2M Members
Founded in 1963

8301 Utility Working Conference and Vendor Technology Expo
555 N Kensington Ave
La Grange Park, IL 60526-5592

708-352-6611
800-323-3044
FAX 708-352-0499
E-Mail: advertising@ans.org

Home Page: www.ans.org
Social Media: *Facebook, Twitter, LinkedIn*

Jack Tuohy, Executive Director
James S Tulenko, VP
William F Naughton, Treasurer

Dedicated to identifying innovations in all areas of nuclear power plant operations. The functional area tracks/ sessions bring together professionals with different perspectives focusing on current issues and innovations.
10500 Members
Founded in 1954

8302 WINDPOWER Conference and Exhibition
American Wind Energy Association (AWEA)
1501 M Street NW
Suite 1000
Washington, DC 20005

202-383-2500
FAX 202-383-2505
E-Mail: windmail@awea.org
Home Page: www.windpowerexpo.org

Denise Bode, Chief Executive Officer
Pam Poisson, Chief Financial Officer
Britt Theismann, Chief Operating Officer
Rob Gramlich, Senior VP, Public Policy
Peter Kelley, VP, Public Affairs

The WINDPOWER Conference & Exhibition is produced by the American Wind Energy Association to provide a venue for the wind industry to network, do business, and solve problems. Recognized as one of the fastest-growing trade shows in the U.S., WINDPOWER includes nearly 1,400 exhibiting companies, thousands of qualified wind energy professionals, engaging educational information and unmatched networking opportunities and special events.
2500 Members
20000 Attendees
Frequency: Annual

8303 WSSA Annual Meeting
Weed Science Society of America
PO Box 7050
Lawrence, KS 66044

785-429-9622
800-627-0629
FAX 785-843-1274
Home Page: www.wssa.net

Rhonda Green, Registration Coordinator

Usually held during the first full week of February in the United States or Canada. These Meetings provide a venue for the exchange of research and educational ideas and for discussion and activity on society business.
1M Attendees
Frequency: February
Founded in 1956

8304 Waterpower XIII
HCI Publications
410 Archibald Street
Kansas City, MO 64111-3001

816-931-1311
FAX 816-931-2015
Home Page: www.hcipub.com

Leslie Eden, Manager

The conference offers industry professionals a forum in which to share new ideas and approaches to move hydropower forward as the world's leading source of renewable energy. Containing 120 booths.
1,000 Attendees
Frequency: July-August

8305 Wildlife Habitat Council Annual Symposium
Wildlife Habitat Council

8737 Colesville Road
Suite 800
Silver Spring, MD 20910

301-588-8994
FAX 301-588-4629
E-Mail: whc@wildlifehc.org
Home Page: www.wildlifehc.org

Bill Howard, President
Martha Gruelle, Program Manager
Linda Duvall, Accounting Manager
Tiffany Msonthi, Executive Assistant

The annual symposium brings together corporate, government and conservation leaders from around the globe for informative sessions, exhibits and field trips on environmental stewardship.
400 Attendees
Frequency: November

8306 Wildlife Society Annual Conference
Wildlife Society
5410 Grosvenor Lane
Suite 200
Bethesda, MD 20814-2144

301-897-9770
FAX 301-530-2471
E-Mail: tws@wildlife.org
Home Page: www.wildlife.org

Lisa Moll, Program Assistant/Membership

Hear from industry leaders to discuss new and evolving trends and innovations in wildlife management and conservation, learn about the latest research from original research and techniques presented by wildlife professionals, connect with colleagues at the largest gathering of wildlife professionals in North America.
1200 Attendees
Frequency: September
Founded in 1994

8307 Windpower Conference
American Wind Energy Association
1501 M Street NW
Suite 1000
Washington, DC 20005

202-383-2500
FAX 202-383-2505
E-Mail: windmail@awea.org
Home Page: www.awea.org
Social Media: *Facebook, Twitter, YouTube*

Ned Hall, Chair
Thomas Carnahan, Chair-Elect
Gabriel Alonso, Secretary
Don Furman, Treasurer
Vic Abate, Past Chair
2400 Members

8308 World Future Energy Summit
Society of Environmental Journalists
PO Box 2492
Jenkintown, PA 19046

215-884-8174
FAX 215-884-8175
Home Page: www.sej.org
Social Media: *Facebook, Twitter*

Carolyn Whetzel, President
Peter Fairley, 1st Vice Pres
Jeff Burnside, 2nd Vice Pres
Don Hopey, Treasurer

World leaders, international policy makers, industry leaders, investors, experts, academia, intellectuals and journalists to find practical and sustainable solutions for today's energy security, climate change challenges and the advancement of clean technology.
Founded in 1990

Directories & Databases

8309 A Guide to Internet Resources
American Assoc for the Advancement of Science
1200 New York Avenue NW
Washington, DC 20005-3941

202-266-6721
FAX 202-371-9227
E-Mail: membership@aaas.org
Home Page: www.aaas.org

Nathan E Bell, Editor

Free online document provides a starting point for finding internet resources. Topics include internet resources for math, science, health, english, software, grants, shareware, and much more.

8310 ACCA Membership Directory
Air Conditioning Contractors of America
2800 Shirlington Rd
Suite 300
Arlington, VA 22206-3607

703-575-4477
E-Mail: info@acca.org
Home Page: www.acca.org
Social Media: *Facebook, Twitter, LinkedIn, YouTube*

Paul Stalknecht, President & CEO

8311 ACSH Media Update
American Council on Science and Health
1995 Broadway
2nd Floor
New York, NY 10023-5882

212-362-7044
FAX 212-362-4919
E-Mail: acsh@acsh.org
Home Page: www.acsh.org

Elizabeth Whelan, President
Jeff Stier, Director of Publications
Alyssa Pelish, Director of Publications
Gilbert Ross, Executive Director
Frequency: Semi-Annual

8312 ASMR Membership Directory
American Society of Mining and Reclamation
3134 Montavesta Road
Lexington, KY 40502

859-335-6529
E-Mail: asmr@insightbb.com
Home Page: www.ca.uky.edu/assmr

Richard I Barnhisel, Executive Secretary
Frequency: Annual

8313 Aboveground Storage Tank Management and SPCC Guide
ABS Group
PO Box 846304
Dallas, TX 75284-6304

FAX 301-921-0264

8314 Acid Rain
Watts, Franklin
90 Sherman Turnpike
Danbury, CT 06816

203-797-3500
800-621-1115
FAX 203-797-3657

Lists over 4,000 citations, with abstracts, to the worldwide literature on the sources of acid rain and its effects on the environment.

8315 Alternative Energy Network Online
Environmental Information Networks
119 S Fairfax Street
Alexandria, VA 22314-3301

703-548-1202

Reports on news of all energy sources designed as alternatives to conventional fossil fuels, including wind, solar and alcohol fuels.
Frequency: Full-text

8316 American Recycling Market: Directory/Reference Manual
Recycling Data Management Corporation
PO Box 577
Ogdensburg, NY 13669-0577

315-785-9072

Offers information, in three volumes, encompassing over 15,000 recycling companies and centers.
Cost: $175.00
1000 Pages
Frequency: Annual
ISSN: 0885-2537

8317 Business and the Environment: A Resource Guide
Island Press
1718 Connecticut Ave NW
Suite 300
Washington, DC 20009-1148

202-232-7933
FAX 202-234-1328
E-Mail: info@islandpress.org
Home Page: www.islandpress.org

Chuck Savitt, President
Allison Pennell, Editor

List of approximately 185 business and environmental educators working to integrate environmental issues into management, research, education and practices.
Cost: $60.00

8318 Canadian Environmental Directory
Grey House Publishing
4919 Route 22
PO Box 56
Amenia, NY 12501

518-789-8700
800-562-2139
FAX 845-373-6390
E-Mail: books@greyhouse.com
Home Page: www.greyhouse.com
Social Media: *Facebook, Twitter*

Leslie Mackenzie, Publisher
Tannys Williams, Managing Editor

Canada's most complete national listing of environmental associations and organizations, government regulators and purchasing groups, product and service companies, special libraries, and more.
Cost: $315.00
900 Pages
ISBN: 1-592372-24-9
Founded in 1981

8319 Carcinogenicity Information Database of Environmental Substances
Technical Database Services
10 Columbus Circle
New York, NY 10019-1203

212-556-0001
FAX 212-556-0036

This database contains test results on the carcinogenic and mutagenic effects of approximately 1000 substances of environmental or health concerns.

8320 Conservation Directory
National Wildlife Federation
11100 Wildlife Center Dr
Reston, VA 20190-5362

703-438-6000
800-822-9919
FAX 703-438-3570
E-Mail: info@nwf.org
Home Page: www.nwf.org

Mark Van Putten, CEO

Federal agencies, national and international organizations and state government agencies.
Cost: $20.00
500 Pages
Frequency: Annual

8321 Department of Energy Annual Procurement and Financial Assistance Report
US Department of Energy
1000 Independence Ave SW
Washington, DC 20585-0001

202-586-5000
FAX 202-586-0573
Home Page: www.energy.gov

Mary Lein, Manager

Offers a list of universities, research centers and laboratories that represent the Department of Energy.
Frequency: Annual

8322 Directory of Environmental Websites: Online Micro Edition
US Environmental Directories
PO Box 65156
Saint Paul, MN 55165-0156

612-331-6050
Home Page:
www.geocities.com/usenvironmentaldirectories

Roger N McGrath, Publisher
John C Brainard, Editor

The Directory is a complete guide to the environmental movement on the Internet, provides a concise, practical listing of over 190 of the major Internet addresses of the Environmental Movement. A clear, understandable and comprehensive guide to national and international environmental organizations, directories, networks and services on the Internet.
Cost: $25.75
48 Pages
ISSN: 1096-3316
Founded in 1998

8323 Directory of International Periodicals & Newsletters on Built Environments
Division of Mineral Resources
PO Box 3667
Charlottesville, VA 22903-0667

434-951-6341
FAX 434-951-6365
Home Page: www.mme.state.va.us

Scott Richeson, Programs Director

More than 1,400 international periodicals and newsletters that cover architectural design and the building industry, and the aspects of the environment that deal with the industry are covered.
Cost: $6.00
29 Pages

8324 EDOCKET
Environmental Protection Agency
1200 Pennsylvania Avenue NW
Mail Code 3213A
Washington, DC 20460

202-260-2090
FAX 202-566-0545

E-Mail: r9.info@epa.gov
Home Page: www.epa.gov

An electronic public docket and on-line comment system designed to expand access to documents in EPA's major dockets.
Frequency: Full-text

8325 EH&S Compliance Auditing & Teaching Software Report
Donley Technology
PO Box 152
Colonial Beach, VA 22443-0152

804-224-9427
800-201-1595
FAX 804-224-7958
E-Mail: donleytech@donleytech.com
Home Page: www.donleytech.com

Elizabeth Donley, Editor

Profiles 25 software packages for achieving and maintaining compliance, including detailed product descriptions, tables comparing system features, and contact information.
Cost: $195.00
240 Pages
Frequency: Every 2 Years
ISBN: 1-891682-08-3
Founded in 1997
Printed in on matte stock

8326 EMS Membership Roster
Environmental Mutagen Society
1821 Michael Faraday Drive
Suite 300
Reston, VA 20190

703-438-8220
FAX 703-438-3113
E-Mail: emshq@ems-us.org
Home Page: www.ems-us.org

Tonia Masson, Executive Director
Suzanne Morris, Secretary
Barbara Shane, Treasurer
Frequency: Irregular

8327 Ecology Abstracts
Cambridge Scientific Abstracts
7200 Wisconsin Ave
Suite 601
Bethesda, MD 20814-4890

301-961-6700
800-843-7751
FAX 301-961-6790
E-Mail: service@csa.com
Home Page: www.csa.com

Andrew M Snyder, President
Theodore Caris, Publisher
Robert Hilton, Editor
Mark Furneaux, VP Marketing
Angela Hitti, Production Manager

This large database updated continuously, offers over 150,000 citations, with abstracts, to the worldwide literature available on ecology and the environment.
Cost: $945.00
Frequency: Monthly

8328 Education for the Earth: A Guide to Top Environmental Studies Programs
Peterson's Guides
202 Carnegie Center
#2123
Princeton, NJ 08540-6239

800-338-3282
FAX 609-869-4531

Colleges and universities that offer programs in environment and conservation are listed.
Cost: $10.95
192 Pages

8329 Educational Communications
Educational Communications

PO Box 351419
Los Angeles, CA 90035-9119

310-559-9160
FAX 310-559-9160
E-Mail: ECNP@aol.com
Home Page: www.ecoprojects.org

Nancy Pearlman, Editor/Executive Director

Directory of over 6,500 environmental organizations worldwide are the focus of this comprehensive directory. Over 400 1/2 hour television shows on the environment. Environmental directions - radio has over 1,500 interviews with ecological experts. Monthly newsletter, TV and radio series about ecological problems and solutions; promotion of ecotourem. Audo/video cassettes available.
Cost: $20.00
244 Pages
Frequency: Annual Paperback
Founded in 1957
Mailing list available for rent

8330 El Environmental Services Directory
Environmental Information Networks
7301 Ohms Lane
Suite 460
Eding, MN 55439

952-831-2473
FAX 952-831-6550
E-Mail: customerservice@envirobiz.com
Home Page: www.envirobiz.com

Cary Perket
James Rue, Secretary
Marshall Sanders, Manager
Bruce McGranahan, Director

Waste-handling facilities, transportation and spill response firms, laboratories and the broad scope of environmental services. Online versions are also available.
Cost: $1250.00
Frequency: Biennial
ISSN: 1053-475N
Founded in 1984

8331 Emergency Response Directory for Hazardous Materials Accidents
Odin Press
PO Box 536
New York, NY 10021-0011

212-605-0338

Pamela Lawrence, Editor

Over 1,000 federal, state and local governmental agencies, chemical manufacturers and transporters, hotlines and strike teams, burn care centers, civil defense and disaster centers and other organizations concerned with the containment and cleanup of chemical spills and other hazardous materials accidents.
Cost: $36.00
Frequency: Biennial

8332 Energy Statistics Spreadsheets
Institute of Gas Technology
1700 S Mount Prospect Rd
Des Plaines, IL 60018-1804

847-768-0664
FAX 847-768-0669
Home Page: www.gastechnology.org

Carol L Worster, Manager
Edward Johnston, Managing Director

The coverage of this database encompasses worldwide energy industry statistics, including production, consumption, reserves, imports and prices.

8333 Energy User News: Energy Technology Buyers Guide
Chilton Company

300 Park Ave
Suite 19
New York, NY 10022-7409

212-751-3596
FAX 212-443-7701
Home Page: www.chiltonfunds.com

Richard L Chilton Jr, Owner
Lisa Czachor, Director
Mary Morse, Senior Vice President

A list of about 1,500 manufacturers, dealers and distributors of energy conservation and used equipment.
Cost: $10.00
Frequency: Annual
Circulation: 40,000

8334 Environmental Bibliography
International Academy at Santa Barbara
5385 Hollister Avenue
#210
Santa Barbara, CA 93111

805-683-8889
FAX 805-965-6071
E-Mail: info@iasb.org
Home Page: www.iasb.org

Gloria Lindfield, Executive Assistant
Hilary Eastman, Manager
Tom Seidenstein, Chief Operating Officer

Over 615,000 citations are offered in this database, aimed at scientific, technical and popular periodical literature dealing with the environment.
Cost: $1750.00
ISSN: 1053-1440
Founded in 1972

8335 Environmental Cost Estimating Software Report
Donley Technology
PO Box 152
Colonial Beach, VA 22443-0152

804-224-9427
800-201-1595
FAX 804-224-7958
E-Mail: donleytech@donleytech.com
Home Page: www.donleytech.com

Elizabeth Donley, Editor
John Donley, Editor

Profiles 20 software packages for estimating the cost of environmental projects, including detailed product descriptions, tables comparing system features, and contact information.
Cost: $195.00
162 Pages
ISBN: 1-891682-05-9
Founded in 1996
Printed in on matte stock

8336 Environmental Health & Safety Dictionary
ABS Group
PO Box 846304
Dallas, TX 75284-6304

FAX 301-921-0264

Lydia Simpson, Manager

8337 Environmental Law Handbook
ABS Group
PO Box 846304
Dallas, TX 75284-6304

FAX 301-921-0264

8338 Environmental Protection Agency Headquarters Telephone Directory
Environmental Protection Agency

1200 Pennsylvania Avenue NW
Pittsburgh, PA 15250-7954

412-442-4000
FAX 202-512-2250
Home Page:
www.epa.gov/customerservice/phonebook

Ken Bowman, Executive Director

Directory of services and supplies to the industry.
Cost: $15.00
400 Pages

8339 Environmental Resource Handbook
Grey House Publishing
4919 Route 22
PO Box 56
Amenia, NY 12501

518-789-8700
800-562-2139
FAX 845-373-6390
E-Mail: books@greyhouse.com
Home Page: www.greyhouse.com
Social Media: Facebook, Twitter

Leslie Mackenzie, Publisher
Richard Gottlieb, Editor

The most up-to-date and comprehensive source for Environmental Resources and Statistics. Included is contact information for resource listings in addition to statistics and rankings on hundreds of important topics such as recycling, air and water quality, climate, toxic chemicals and more.
Cost: $155.00
1200 Pages
ISBN: 1-592371-95-7
Founded in 1981

8340 Environmental Resource Handbook - Online Database
Grey House Publishing
4919 Route 22
PO Box 56
Amenia, NY 12501

518-789-8700
800-562-2139
FAX 845-373-6390
E-Mail: gold@greyhouse.com
Home Page: http://gold.greyhouse.com
Social Media: Facebook, Twitter

Leslie Mackenzie, Publisher
Richard Gottlieb, Editor

With a subscription to Environmental Resource Handbook - Online Database, you'll have immediate access to over 7,000 associations, organizations & government agencies, awards & honors, conferences & trade shows, foundations & charities, national parks & wildlife refuges, research centers & educational programs, legal resources and much more.
Founded in 1981

8341 Environmental Statutes
Government Institutes
4 Research Place
Suite 200
Rockville, MD 20850-3226

301-921-2323
FAX 301-921-0264
Home Page: www.govinst.com

Two-volume set. Complete and exact text of the statues and amendments made by Congress concerning environmental law.
Cost: $125.00
1678 Pages
Frequency: Paperback
ISBN: 0-865879-33-8

8342 Fibre Market News: Paper Recycling Markets Directory
Recycling Media Group GIE Publishers

4012 Bridge Avenue
Cleveland, OH 44113-3320

216-961-4130
800-456-0707
FAX 216-961-0364
Home Page: www.giemedia.com

Dan Moreland, Executive Vice President

A list of over 2,000 dealers, brokers, packers and graders of paper stock in the United States and Canada.
Cost: $28.00
Frequency: Annual
Circulation: 3,000

8343 Floodplain Management: State & Local Programs
Association of State Floodplain Managers
2809 Fish Hatchery Rd
Suite 204
Fitchburg, WI 53713-5020

608-274-0123
FAX 608-274-0696
E-Mail: memberhelp@floods.org
Home Page: www.floods.org

Larry A Larson, Executive Director
Alison Stierli, Member Services Coordinator
Anita Larson, Member Services
Mark Riebau, Project Manager
Diane Brown, Manager

The most comprehensive source assembled to date, this report summarizes and analyzes various state and local programs and activities.
Cost: $25.00

8344 Geothermal Progress Monitor
Office of Geothermal Technologies EE-12
1000 Independence Avenue SW
Washington, DC 20585-0001

202-586-1361
FAX 202-586-8185

Allan J Jelacic, Director

Lists of operating, planned and under construction geothermal electric generating plants; geothermal articles and publications; federal and state government employees active in geothermal energy development.
Frequency: Annual

8345 Grey House Safety & Security Directory
Grey House Publishing
4919 Route 22
PO Box 56
Amenia, NY 12501

518-789-8700
800-562-2139
FAX 845-373-6390
E-Mail: books@greyhouse.com
Home Page: www.greyhouse.com
Social Media: Facebook, Twitter

Leslie Mackenzie, Publisher
Richard Gottlieb, Editor
Kristen Thatcher, Production Manager

Comprehensive guide to the safety and security industry, including articles, checklists, OSHA regulations and product listings. Focuses on creating and maintaing a safe and secure enviroment, and dealing specifically with hazardous materials, noise and vibration, workplace preparation and maintenance, electrical and lighting safety, fire and rescue and more.
Cost: $165.00
1600 Pages
ISBN: 1-592373-75-5
Founded in 1981

8346 Handling Dyes Safely - A Guide for the Protection of Workers Handling Dyes
ETAD North America

1850 M St NW
Suite 700
Washington, DC 20036-5810

202-721-4100
FAX 202-296-8120
Home Page: www.etad.com

Jill Aker, President

8347 Hazardous Materials Guide
JJ Keller
PO Box 368
Neenah, WI 54957-0368

920-722-2848
800-327-6868
FAX 800-727-7516
E-Mail: contactus@jjkeller.com
Home Page: www.jjkeller.com

Webb Shaw, Editor

A complete reference guide of hazardous materials regulations.

8348 Hazardous Materials Information Resource System
One Church Street
Suite 200
Rockville, MD 20850

301-577-1842
FAX 301-738-2330

CAPT Michael J. Macinski, Commanding Officer
CAPT Robert W. Farr, Executive Officer
HMCM Robert E. Searles, II, Command Master Chief

The Hazardous Materials Information Resource System is a Department of Defense (DOD) automated system developed and maintained by the Defense Logistics Agency. HMIRS is the central repository for Material Safety Data Sheets (MSDS) for the United States Government military services and civil agencies.

8349 Hazardous Waste Guide
JJ Keller
PO Box 368
Neenah, WI 54957-0368

920-722-2848
800-327-6868
FAX 800-727-7516
E-Mail: contactus@jjkeller.com
Home Page: www.jjkeller.com

Webb Shaw, Editor

Contains word-for-word regulations.

8350 Hydro Review: Industry Sourcebook Issue
HCI Publications
410 Archibald St
Kansas City, MO 64111-3288

816-931-1311
FAX 816-931-2015
E-Mail: hci@aol.com
Home Page: www.hcipub.com

Leslie Eden, President

List of over 800 manufacturers and suppliers of products and services to the hydroelectric industry in the US and Canada.
Cost: $20.00
180 Pages
Frequency: Annual December
Circulation: 5000
Founded in 1984
Printed in 4 colors on glossy stock

8351 IES Membership Directory
International Ecotourism Society

733 15th Street NW
Suite 1000
Washington, DC 20005

202-547-9203
FAX 202-387-7915
Home Page: www.ecotourism.org

Martha Honey, Executive Director
Amos Bien, Director International Programs
Neal Inamdar, Director Finance/Administration
Frequency: Annual

8352 International Directory of Human Ecologists
Society for Human Ecology
College of the Atlantic
105 Eden Street
Bar Harbor, ME 04609-0180

207-288-5015
FAX 207-288-3780
E-Mail: carter@ecology.coa.edu
Home Page: www.societyforhumanecology.org

Barbara Carter, Assistant to Executive Director
Frequency: Irregular

8353 LEXIS Environmental Law Library
Mead Data Central
9443 Springboro Pike
Dayton, OH 45401

888-223-6337
FAX 518-487-3584
Home Page: www.lexis-nexis.com

Andrew Prozes, CEO
Rebecca Schmitt, Chief Financial Officer

This database contains decisions related to environmental law from the Supreme Court and other legislative bodies.
Frequency: Full-text

8354 NIWR Member Directory
National Institutes for Water Resources
47 Harkness Road
Pelham, MA 10002

413-253-5686
FAX 413-253-1309
E-Mail: godfrey@tei.umass.edu
Home Page: snr.unl.edu/NIWR

Paul Joseph Godfrey, PhD, Executive Director

8355 National Directory of Conservation Land Trusts
Land Trust Alliance
1319 F Street NW
Suite 501
Washington, DC 20004-1106

202-638-4725
FAX 202-638-4730
E-Mail: info@lta.org
Home Page: www.lta.org

More than 1,200 nonprofit land conservation organizations at the local and regional levels are profiled.
Cost: $12.00
210 Pages
Frequency: Biennial

8356 National Environmental Data Referral Service
US National Environmental Data Referral Service
1825 Connecticut Avenue NW
Washington, DC 20235-0003

202-606-4089

More than 22,200 data resources that have available data on climatology and meteorology, ecology and pollution, geography, geophysics and geology, hydrology and limnology, oceanography and transmissions from remote sensing satellites.
Frequency: Quarterly

8357 National Organic Directory
Community Alliance with Family Farmers
PO Box 363
Davis, CA 95617-0363

530-756-8518
800-892-3832
FAX 530-756-7857
E-Mail: info@caff.org
Home Page: www.caff.org

Wriiten for all sectors of the booming organic food and fiber industry. Offers international listing with full contact information and extensive, cross-referenced index - Also provides regulatory updates, essays by industry leaders and other ressources.
Cost: $47.95
324 Pages
Frequency: Annual
Circulation: 2,500
ISBN: 1-891894-04-8
Founded in 1983

8358 POWER
US Department of Energy
Forrestal Building
5H - 021
Washington, DC 20585-0001

202-646-5095
FAX 202-586-1605
Home Page: www.eren.doe.gov

Timothy Unruh, Program Manager

A large database offering information on all forms of energy, including fossil, nuclear, solar, geothermal and electrical.

8359 Pollution Abstracts
Cambridge Scientific Abstracts
7200 Wisconsin Ave
Suite 601
Bethesda, MD 20814-4890

301-961-6700
FAX 301-961-6790
E-Mail: service@csa.com
Home Page: www.csa.com

Andrew M Snyder, President
Ted Caris, Publisher
Evelyn Beck, Editor
Mark Furneaux, VP Marketing
Angela Hitti, Production Manager

This database offers information on environmental pollution research and related engineering studies.
Cost: $985.00
Frequency: Monthly

8360 Public Citizen Organizations
Public Citizen
215 Pennsylvania Ave SE
Suite 3
Washington, DC 20003-1188

202-544-4985
FAX 202-547-7392
E-Mail: cmep@citizen.org

Bob Ritter, Manager
Patricia Lovera, Organizer
Ronald Taylor, Manager

We provide many publications regarding nuclear safety, nuclear waste, water, food, and energy deregulation.
Frequency: Annual

8361 RIFM/FEMA Fragrance and Flavor Database
Flavor & Extract Manufacturers Association
1620 I Street NW
Suite 925
Washington, DC 20006

202-293-5800
FAX 202-462-8998

Home Page: www.femaflavor.org
Social Media: *YouTube, RSS Feed*

Ed R. Hays, Ph.D., President
George C. Robinson, III, President Elect
Mark Scott, Treasurer
Arthur Schick, VP & Secretary
John Cox, Executive Director

The Database currently contains over 50,000 references and more than 103,000 human health and environmental studies.
Frequency: Annual
Founded in 1909

8362 Recycling Today: Recycling Products & Services Buyers Guide
Recycling Today GIE Publishers
4012 Bridge Avenue
Cleveland, OH 44113-3320

216-961-4130
FAX 216-961-0364
Home Page: http://www.recyclingtoday.com

Richard Foster, President
James Keefe, Publisher
Mark Phillips, Editor
Rosalie Slusher, Circulation Director
Jami Childs, Production Manager

Directory of services and supplies to the industry.
Cost: $19.95
Frequency: Annual
Circulation: 22,000

8363 Using Multiobjective Management to Reduce Flood Losses in Your Watershed
Association of State Floodplain Managers
2809 Fish Hatchery Rd
Suite 204
Fitchburg, WI 53713-5020

608-274-0123
FAX 608-274-0696
E-Mail: memberhelp@floods.org
Home Page: www.floods.org

Larry A Larson, Executive Director
Alison Stierli, Manager
Diane Brown, Manager

Introduction to multiobjective management and planning process that helps a community select suitable flood loss reduction measures.
Cost: $15.00

8364 Waste Manifest Software Report
Donley Technology
PO Box 152
Colonial Beach, VA 22443-0152

804-224-9427
800-201-1595
FAX 804-224-7958
E-Mail: donleytech@donleytech.com
Home Page: www.donleytech.com

Elizabeth Donley, Editor

Profiles 30 software packages for solid and hazardous waste management, including detailed product descriptions, tables comparing system features, and contact information.
Cost: $97.50
118 Pages
ISBN: 1-891682-01-6
Founded in 1996
Printed in on matte stock

8365 Water Environment and Technology Buyers Guide/Yearbook
Water Environment Federation
601 Wythe St
Alexandria, VA 22314-1994

703-684-2400
800-666-0206
FAX 703-684-2492

E-Mail: confinfo@wef.org
Home Page: www.wef.org

Bill Bertera, Executive Director

Offers listings of the Water Environment Federation and consultant members.
Cost: $28.00
Frequency: Annual
ISSN: 1044-9943

8366 Weather America
Grey House Publishing
4919 Route 22
PO Box 56
Amenia, NY 12501

518-789-8700
800-562-2139
FAX 845-373-6390
E-Mail: books@greyhouse.com
Home Page: www.greyhouse.com
Social Media: *Facebook, Twitter*

Leslie Mackenzie, Publisher
Richard Gottlieb, Editor

Provides extensive climatological data for over 4,000 places throughout the United States - states, counties, cities, and towns. Included are rankings across the US for precipitation, snowfall, fog, humidity, wind speed and more.
Cost: $175.00
2020 Pages
ISBN: 1-891482-29-7
Founded in 1981

8367 Who's Who in Training
National Environmental, Safety and Health Training
5320 N 16th Street
Suite 114
Phoenix, AZ 85016-3241

602-956-6099
FAX 602-956-6399
E-Mail: info@neshta.org
Home Page: www.neshta.org

Charles L Richardson, Executive Director
Joan J Jennings, Manager Association Services
Suzanne Lanctot, Manager Certification/Membership
Frequency: Annual

8368 Wilderness Preservation: A Reference Handbook
ABC-CLIO
PO Box 1911
Santa Barbara, CA 93116-1911

805-705-9339

Offers a list of agencies and organizations concerned with wilderness preservation.

8369 World Directory of Environmental Organizations
California Institute of Public Affairs
PO Box 189040
Sacramento, CA 95818-9040

916-442-2472
FAX 916-442-2478
Home Page: www.interenvironment.org

Over 2,500 governmental, intergovernmental and United Nations organizations are covered.
Cost: $47.00
232 Pages

8370 Your Resource Guide to Environmental Organizations
Smiling Dolphin Press
4 Segura
Irvine, CA 92612-1726

Information is offered, in three separate sections, on non-governmental organizations, federal agencies and state agencies that address

environmental concerns.
Cost: $15.95
514 Pages

Industry Web Sites

8371 The Environmental Literacy Council
1625 K St. NW
Suite 1020
Washington, DC 20006

202-296-0390
FAX 202-822-0991
Home Page: enviroliteracy.org
Social Media: *Facebook, LinkedIn*

Roger A. Sedjo, Chairman
Kathleen Berry, President

The Council provides resources on environmental topics for teachers and students.

8372 http://gold.greyhouse.com
G.O.L.D Grey House OnLine Databases
Grey House Publishing's online database platform, GOLD, offers Quick Search, Keyword Search and Expert Search for most business sectors including environment and conservation markets. The GOLD platform makes finding the information you need quick and easy - whether you're a novice searcher or an experienced database user. All of Grey House's directory products are available for subscription on the GOLD platform.

8373 www.adirondackcouncil.org
Adirondack Council

Research, education and advocacy to protect the natural character and communities of the Adirondack Park. Also publishes an annual State of Park Report and quarterly newsletters.

8374 www.aeecenter.org
Association of Energy Engineers

Source of information on the field of energy efficiency, utility deregulation, plant engineering, facility management and environmental compliance. Membership includes more than 8,000 professionals and certification programs. Offers seminars, conferences, job listings and certification programs.

8375 www.aga.org
American Gas Association

Association for the natural gas industry.

8376 www.america-the-beautiful-fund.org
America the Beautiful Fund

Groups and private citizens that improve the quality of the environment.

8377 www.apwa.net
American Public Works Association

The American Public Works Association is an international educational and professional association of public agencies, private sector companies, and individuals dedicated to providing high quality public works goods and services. APWA provides a forum in which public works professionals competency, increase the performance of their agencies and companies, and bring important public works-related topics to public attention in local, state, and federal areas. Mailing list for members only.

8378 www.asbpa.org
American Shore and Beach Preservation Association

Federal, state and local government agencies and individuals interested in conservation, development and restoration of beaches and shorefronts.

8379 www.ases.org
American Solar Energy Society
Individuals and professionals working in the field of solar energy and conservation.

8380 www.asfe.org
ASFE
Not-for-profit trade association. Helps geoprofessional, environmental and civil engineering firms profit through professionalism.

8381 www.audbon.org
National Audubon Society
Conserves and restores natural ecosystems, focusing on birds, other wildlife, and thier habitats for the benefit of humanity and the earth's biological diversity.

8382 www.bisoncentral.com
National Bison Association
The National Bison Association was formed to promote the production, marketing, and preservation of bison.

8383 www.blr.com
Business & Legal Reports
Provides essential tools for safety and environmental compliance and training needs

8384 www.cbemw.org
Citizens for a Better Environment
For citizens concerned with environmental protection. Maintains library.

8385 www.cnie.org/nle
National Library for the Environment
Environment-related information: daily environment and congressional news, upcoming conferences, education resources and congressional research reports.

8386 www.conservation.state.mo.us
Department of Conservation
Focuses on conservation and the importance of protecting the environment.

8387 www.conservationfund.org
Conservation Fund
Works with private and public agencies and organizations to protect wildlife habitats, historic sites and parks.

8388 www.conservationtreaty.org
Conservation Treaty Support Fund
Promotes awareness, understanding and support of conservation treaties and their goals.

8389 www.construction.com
McGraw-Hill Construction
McGraw-Hill Construction (MHC), part of The McGraw-Hill Companies, connects people and projects across the design and construction industry, serving owners, architects, engineers, general contractors, subcontractors, building product manufacturers, suppliers, dealers, distributors and adjacent markets.

8390 www.earthisland.org/ei
Earth Island Institute
Seeks to prevent destruction of environment and sponsors fund drives and activist projects to protect wildlife.

8391 www.earthsite.org
Earth Society Foundation
News of interest in environmental and sociological issues. Purpose is to promote Earth Day and the Earth Trustee agenda.

8392 www.eia-usa.org
Environmental Information Association

Nonprofit organization dedicated to providing environmental information to individuals, members and the industry. Disseminates information on the abatement of asbestos and lead-based paint, indoor air quality, safety and health issues, analytical issues and environmental site assessments.

8393 www.epa.gov
US Environmental Protection Agency

8394 www.ethenolrfa.org
Renewable Fuels Association
Members are companies and individuals involved in the production and use of ethanol.

8395 www.femaflavor.org
Flavor & Extract Manufacturers Assn of the US
1620 I Street NW
Suite 925
Washington, DC 210006

202-293-5800
FAX 202-463-8998

Ed R. Hayes, President
George C. Robinson III, President Elect
Mark Scott, Treasurer
Arthur Schick, Vice President & Secretary

FEMA is comprised of flavor manufacturers, flavor users, flavor ingredient suppliers, and others with an interest in the U.S. flavor industry. FEMA works with legislators and regulators to assure that the needs of members and consuemr are continuously addressed and is committed to assuring a substantial supply of safe flavoring substances.

8396 www.floods.org
Association of State Floodplain Managers
Promotes common interest in flood damage abatement, supports environmental protection for floodplain areas, provides education on floodplain management practices and policy, and urges incorporating multi-objective management approaches to solve local flooding problems.

8397 www.greyhouse.com
Grey House Publishing
Authoritative reference directories for most business sectors including environment and conservation markets. Users can search the online databases with varied search criteria allowing for custom searches by product category, geographic area, sales volume, keyword, subject and more. Full Grey House catalog and online ordering also available.

8398 www.ia-usa.org
National BioEnergy Industries Association

8399 www.iaee.org
International Association for Energy Economics
Association for those involved in energy economics including publications, consultants, energy database software.

8400 www.iaia.org
International Association for Impact Assessment
IAIA provides a forum for the exchange of the ideas and experiences to stimulate innovation in assessing, managing and mitigating the consequences of development.

8401 www.iwla.org
Isaak Walton League
Conducts research and education on river ecosystems and healthy fisheries.

8402 www.joincca.org
Coastal Conservation Association

Seeks to advance protection and conservation of all marine life. Conducts seminars and bestows awards.

8403 www.lib.duke.edu/forest/
Forest History Society
Non-profit educational institution that explores the history of the environment, forestry, and conservation.

8404 www.members.aol.com/rccouncil
Rachael Carson Council
Seeks to promote awareness of the problems of environmental contamination and by serving as an information clearing house on chemical contaminates, especially pesticides.

8405 www.mtsociety.org
Marine Technology Society
Addresses coastal zone management, marine mineral and energy resources, marine environmental protection, and ocean engineering issues.

8406 www.nacdnet.org
National Association of Conservation Districts
Association for those interested in the environment.

8407 www.naem.org
National Association for Environmental Management
Dedicated to advancing the profession of environmental management and supports the professional corporate and facility environmental manager.

8408 www.nalms.org
North American Lake Management Society
Members are academics, lake managers and others interested in furthering the understanding of lake ecology.

8409 www.napcor.com
National Association for Pet Container Resources
National trade association which promotes the recycling of food containers made from PET plastic (containers with recycle code #1).

8410 www.nationalwoodlands.org
National Woodland Owners Association
Provides timely information about forestry and forest practices with news from washington,Dc and state capitals, written for non-industrial land owners. Includes state landowner association news.

8411 www.ncat.org
National Center for Appropriate Technology
A resource center for information and expertise on methods of promoting conservation and energy self sufficiency. The term, appropriate technology, is defined as a small-scale, environmentally sound, low-cost, locally based approach to problems with an emphasis on self help.

8412 www.neha.org
National Environmental Health Association
Association for suppliers of environmental educational materials.

8413 www.noaa.gov
National Oceanic and Atmospheric Administration
National weather forecasts, statistics, searchable databases, agency directory and links to related agencies and sites.

8414 www.pollutiononline.com
Pollution Online

For vendors and professionals in pollution equipment and control industries. News, product information, links to related web sites and business information.

8415 www.purezone.com
PureZone

Devoted to indoor air quality. Discussion forum moderated by industry experts on topics such as sensors and transducers technology.

8416 www.recycle-steel.srs
Steel Recycling Institute

Promotes steel recycling and works to forge a coalition of steelmakers, can manufacturers, legislators, government officials, solid waste managers, business and consumer groups.

8417 www.rnrf.org
Renewable Natural Resources Foundation

A consortium of professional and scientific societies whose members are concerned with the advancement of research, education, scientific practice and policy formulation for the conservation, replenishment and use of the earth's renewable natural resources.

8418 www.sca-inc.org
Student Conservation Association

8419 www.socma.com
Silicone Health Council

Coordinates health, environmental and safety programs. Conveys scientifically sound information about silicones.

8420 www.sweets.construction.com
McGraw Hill Construction

In depth product information that lets you find, compare, select, specify and make purchase decisions in the industrial product marketplace.

8421 www.techknow.org
TechKnow

Lists environmentally friendly remediation and ozone-depleting substance management resources.

8422 www.terrassa.pnl.gov:2080/hydrology
Hydrology Web

Lists of related internet resource lists.

8423 www.usace.army.mil
US Army Corps of Engineers

Information on flood control, environmental protection, disaster response, military construction and support of others through the sharing of engineering expertise with other agencies, state and local governments, academia and foreign nations.

8424 www.woodlandowners.org
National Woodland Owners Association

Provides timely information about forestry and forest practices with news from washington,Dc and state capitals. written for non-industrial land owners. Includes state landowner association news.

8425 www.wqa.org
Water Quality Association

An international nonprofit trade association representing retail/dealers and manufacturer/suppliers in the point of use/entry water quality improvement industry. Membership benefits and services include technical and scientific information, educational seminars, and home correspondence course books, professional certification and discount services.

Associations

8426 AMC Institute
700 N Fairfax Street
Suite 510
Alexandria, VA 22314

571-527-3108
FAX 571-527-3105
E-Mail: info@amcinstitute.org
Home Page: www.amcinstitute.org

Charles T. Hall Jr., Board Chair
Greg Schultz, Chair-Elect
Deidre Gish-Panjada, MBA, Immediate Past
Chair
Fred Stringfellow, CAE, Treasurer
Lori B. Gordon, Secretary

AMCs are professional service firms that provide executive, administrative, and financial management; strategic counsel planning; membership development; public affairs and lobbying; education and professional development; statistical research; meetings management; and marketing and communication services.
175 Members
Founded in 2006

8427 American Business Media
675 Third Avenue
Suite 2200
New York, NY 10017-5704

212-661-6360
FAX 212-370-0736
E-Mail: info@abmmail.com
Home Page: www.siia.net
Social Media: *Facebook, Twitter, LinkedIn*

Doug Manoni, Chair
Marion Minor, Secretary
Edward Keating, Treasurer
Ethan Eisner, Immediate Past Chair
Ty Bobit, Board Member

An association for business-to-business information providers, including producers of print publications, Web sites, trade shows and other media.
200+ Members
Founded in 1906

8428 American Society of Association Executives
1575 I St NW
Washington, DC 20005-1103

202-371-0940
888-950-2723
Flickr
FAX 202-371-8315
E-Mail: service@asaenet.org
Home Page: www.asaenet.org
Social Media: *Facebook*

Abe Eshkenazi, Chairman
Scott D. Wiley , FASAE, CAEÿ, Chair-Elect
Susan K. Neely , CAE, Immediate Past
President
Matthew R. Shay, CAE, Secretary/Treasurer
Lori M. Anderson, CAE, Board Member

ASAE is the premier source of learning, knowledge and future-oriented research for the association and nonprofit profession, and provides resources, education, ideas and advocacy to enhance the power and performance of the association and nonprofit community.
21M Members
Founded in 1920

8429 Association of Collegiate Conference and Special Events
Colorado State University

S. College Avenue
Suite 3B
Fort Collins, CO 80525

970-449-4960
FAX 970-449-4965
E-Mail: info@acced-i.org
Home Page: www.acced-i.colostate.edu
Social Media: *Facebook, Twitter, LinkedIn*

Trish Carlson, President
Lisa Beringer Salazar, CCEP, President-Elect
Daniel L. Dykstra, Immediate Past President
Jim Hodges, Treasurer
Mary Kay Baker, CCEP, Director

Members are college and university conference and special events directors, professionals and others who design, market and coordinate conferences and special events.
1400 Members
Founded in 1980

8430 Association of International Meeting Planners
2547 Monroe Street
Dearborn, MI 48124-3013

313-563-0360
FAX 972-702-3070

Meeting planners.
40 Members
Founded in 1986

8431 Association of Science-Technology Centers
818 Connecticut Avenue, NW
7th Floor
Washington, DC 20006-2734

202-783-7200
FAX 202-783-7207
E-Mail: info@astc.org
Home Page: www.astc.org
Social Media: *Facebook, Twitter, LinkedIn*

Chevy Humphrey, Chair
Linda Conlon, Chair-Elect
Joanna Haas, Secretary
David Chesebrough, Treasurer
Kate Bennett, Director

Organization of science centers and museums dedicated to futhering the public understanding of science among increasingly diverse audiences. Encourages excellence and innovation in informal science learning by serving and linking its members worldwide and advancing their common goals.
550 Members
Founded in 1973

8432 CEMA
1512 Weiskopf Loop
Round Rock, TX 78664-6128

512-310-8330
FAX 510-682-0555
E-Mail: ebrunke@cemaonline.com
Home Page: www.cemaonline.com

Erika Brunke, Executive Director
Olga Rosenbrook, Member Services
Alexia Henrie, Secretary
Trinette R Cunningham, Executive Staff

Professionals from the event, trade show and marketing communications industry. Striving to be the definitive resource for event marketing professionals in the information technology industry.
250 Members
Founded in 1990

8433 Center for Exhibition Industry Research
12700 Park Central Dr
Suite 750
Dallas, TX 75251-1526

972-687-9242
FAX 972-692-6020
E-Mail: info@ceir.com
Home Page: www.ceir.org
Social Media: *Facebook, LinkedIn*

Britton Jones, Chair
Aaron Bludworth, Vice Chair
Dennis Slater, immediate Past Chair
Steve Moster, Secretary/Treasurer
David Audrain, Director

The Center for Exhibition Industry Research is an apolitical, nonprofit orgnization with the dual mission of producing research that supports the unique features and value of exhibitors; then, using that research and other tools to promote the image and growth of the exhibition industry

8434 Connected International Meeting
9200 Bayard Place
Fairfax, VA 22032

512-684-0889
FAX 267-390-5193
E-Mail: susan2@cimpa.org
Home Page: www.cimpa.org

Andrea Sigler, President/CEO

Members are conference and convention planners with a certificate in convention management. Specializes in planning meetings events, incentives, using the internet.
8000 Members
Founded in 1982

8435 Convention Industry Council
700 N Fairfax Street
Alexandria, VA 22314

571-527-3116
FAX 571-527-3105
E-Mail: cichq@conventionindustry.org
Home Page: www.conventionindustry.org
Social Media: *Facebook, Twitter, LinkedIn, YouTube*

David Dubois, CMP, CAE, Chair
Bonnie Fedchock, CAE, Vice Chair
Bob Gilbert, CHME CHBA, Immediate Past
Chair
Vicki Hawarden, CMP, Board Member
At-Large
Kimberly Miles, CMP, Board Member
At-Large

An organization that represents individuals as well as 15,000 firms and properties involved in the meetings, conventions and exhibitions industries.
98000 Members
Founded in 1949

8436 Convention Liaison Council
10200 W 44th Avenue
Suite 310
Wheat Ridge, CO 80033-2840

303-420-2902
FAX 303-422-8894
E-Mail: clc@resourcenter.com
Home Page: www.clc.org

Francine Butler, Executive VP

Members are associations which are directly involved in the convention, exposition, trade show and meeting industry.

8437 Display Distributors Association
Modern Display

424 S 700 E
Salt Lake City, UT 84102-2864

801-355-7427
FAX 801-521-3040

Members are distributors of display equipment.
16 Members
Founded in 1950

8438 Event Service Professionals Association

191 Clarksville Road
Princeton Junction, NJ 08550

609-799-3712
FAX 609-799-7032
E-Mail: info@espaonline.org
Home Page: www.espaonline.org
Social Media: *Facebook, Twitter, LinkedIn*

Denise I. Suttle,CMP, President
Madonna Carr, CMP, President-Elect
Paul Ruby, CMP, 1st Vice President
Kathy Denkenberger, 2nd Vice President
Amy Cabe, Treasurer

Dedicated to elevating the event and convention service profession and to preparing members, through education and networking, for their pivotal role in innovating and successful event execution.
400 Members
Founded in 1988

8439 Exhibit Designers & Producers Association

10 Norden Place
Norwalk, CT 06855

203-852-5698
FAX 203-854-6735
E-Mail: jprovost@edpa.com
Home Page: www.edpa.com

Robert Campbell, President
Kelli Glasser, VP, Finance & Administration
Gwen Hill, VP, Education
Donna Shultz, VP, Member Services
Dave Flory, VP, Member Development

Internationally recognized, national trade association with corporate members from 18 countries that are engaged in the design, manufacture, transport, installation and service of displays and exhibits primarily for the trade show industry. EDPA's purpose is to champion the prosperity of member businesses.
400+ Members
Founded in 1956

8440 Exhibit and Event Marketers Association

2214 NW 5th St.
Bend, OR 97701

541-317-8768
FAX 541-317-8749
E-Mail: tsea@tsea.org
Home Page: www.tsea.org

Amanda Helgemoe, President
Michael Mulry, Vice President
Glenda Brundgardt, Treasurer
Chris Griffin, Secretary
Jim Wurm, Executive Director

Supports marketing and management professionals.

8441 Exposition Service Contractors Association

5068 West Plano Parkway
Suite 300
Plano, TX 75093

972-447-8212
877-792-3722

FAX 972-447-8209
Home Page: www.esca.org

Jay Atherton, President
Lenny Servedio, President-Elect
Julia Smith, Vice President
Richard P. Curran, Secretary/Treasurer
Bruce Nable, Immediate Past President

Annual guide to exposition service is distributed annually and lists safety regulations and building rules in major US convention centers.
120 Members
Founded in 1970

8442 Healthcare Convention & Exhibitors Association

1100 Johnson Ferry Rd NE
Suite 300
Atlanta, GA 30342-1733

678-298-1183
FAX 404-385-5595
E-Mail: hcea@kellencompany.com
Home Page: www.hcea.org
Social Media: *Facebook, Twitter, LinkedIn*

Christine Farmer, President
Don Schmid, MBA, CME/H, President-Elect
Kyle Wood, Vice President
Sue Huff, Secretary/Treasurer
Diane Benson, CTSM, Immediate Past President

Trade association of organizations involved in health care exhibiting or providing services to health care conventions, exhibitions, and/or meetings.
600 Members
Founded in 1930

8443 Hospitality Sales & Marketing Association International

7918 Jones Branch Drive
Suite 300
McLean, VA 22102

703-506-3280
FAX 703-506-3266
E-Mail: info@hsmai.org
Home Page: www.hsmai.org
Social Media: *Facebook, Twitter, LinkedIn, Google+*

Rob Torres, Chair
Jeff Senior, Chair-Elect
Marina MacDonald, Vice Chair
Mark Thompson, CHBA, CHSE, Secretary/Treasurer
Barb Bowden, CRDE, Immediate Past Chairman

The hospitality industry's source for knowledge, community, and recognition for leaders committed to professional development, sales growth, revenue optimization, marketing and branding.
7000 Members
Founded in 1927

8444 International Association for Exhibition Management

12700 Park Central Dr
Suite 308
Dallas, TX 75251-1313

972-458-8002
FAX 972-458-8119
E-Mail: info@iaee.com
Home Page: www.iaee.com
Social Media: *Facebook, Twitter, LinkedIn, YouTube*

Megan Tanel, CEM, Chairperson
Julia Smith, CEM, CTA, Chair-Elect
Daniel McKinnon, CEM, Secretary/Treasurer
Jonathan Skip Cox, Immediate Past Chairperson
Vicki Bedi, Director

Members are managers of shows, exhibits and expositions; associate members are industry suppliers.
3500 Members
Founded in 1928

8445 International Association for Modular Exhibitry

155 W Street
Suite 3
Wilmington, MA 01887-3064

978-988-1200

Irving Sacks, Executive Director

Members are companies that promote the use of modular exhibits for trade shows and museums.
47 Members
Founded in 1987

8446 International Association of Exhibitions and Events

12700 Park Central Dr.
Suite 308
Dallas, TX 75251

972-458-8002
FAX 972-458-8119
E-Mail: info@iaee.com
Home Page: www.iaee.com
Social Media: *Facebook, Twitter, LinkedIn, YouTube*

Megan Tanel, Chairperson
Daniel McKinnon, Secretary/Treasurer

Represents the interests of both those who produce trade shows and exhibitions, and those who provide the exhibition industry with products and services.
9000 Members
Founded in 1928

8447 International Association of Assembly Management

635 Fritz Dr
Suite 100
Coppell, TX 75019-4462

972-906-7441
800-935-4226
FAX 972-906-7418
E-Mail: mike.meyers@iaam.org
Home Page: www.iaam.org

Dexter King, Executive Director
Robyn Williams, First Vice President

Members are managers of auditoriums, arenas, convention centers, stadiums and performing arts centers.
400 Members
Founded in 1924

8448 International Association of Conference Centers

35 East Wacker Drive
Suite 850
Chicago, IL 60601

312-224-2580
FAX 312-644-8557
E-Mail: info@iacconline.org
Home Page: http://www.iacconline.org/
Social Media: *Facebook, Twitter, LinkedIn*

Alex Cabañas, President
Rachael Bartlett, Vice President, UK
TJ Fimmano, Vice President, USA
Sean Anderson, Director
Lotta Boman, Director

Facilities-based organization which advances the understanding and awareness of conference centers as distinct within the training, education, hospitality and travel fields.
377 Members
Founded in 1981

8449   International Association of Fairs and Expositions

3043 E Cairo
PO Box 985
Springfield, MO 65802

417-862-5771
800-516-0313
FAX 417-862-0156
E-Mail: iafe@fairsandexpos.com
Home Page: www.fairsandexpos.com
Social Media: *Facebook, Twitter, YouTube*

John Sykes, CFE, Chair
Kent Hojem, CFE, 1st Vice Chair
Becky Brashear, CFE, 2nd Vice Chair
Jim Tucker, President
John Hanschen, Director at large

The International Association of Fairs and Expositions (IAFE) is a voluntary, non-profit corporation whose members provide services and products that promote the overall development and improvement of fairs, shows, expositions, and allied fields.
Founded in 1885

8450   International Congress and Convention Association

PO Box 6833
Freehold, NJ 07728-6833

732-851-6603
FAX 732-851-6584
E-Mail: n.america@iccaworld.org
Home Page: www.iccaworld.com

Martin Sirk, Chief Executive Officer
Joanne H. Joham, Regional Director, North America

Representing events specialists in more than 90 countries.
1000+ Members
Founded in 1963

8451   International Festivals and Events Association

2603 W Eastover Ter
Boise, ID 83706-2800

208-433-0950
FAX 208-433-9812
E-Mail: nia@ifea.com
Home Page: www.ifea.com

Cindy Lerick, Chair
Guy LaFlamme, Chair-Elect
James L. Holt, CFEE, Immediate Past Chair
William O'Toole, CFEE, Secretary
Michael Berry, CFEE, President & CEO

A voluntary association of events, event producers, event suppliers, and related professionals and organizations whose common purpose is the production and presentation of festivals, events, and civic and private celebrations.
2000 Members
Founded in 1956

8452   International Laser Display Association

7062 Edgeworth Drive
Orlando, FL 32819

407-797-7654
FAX 503-344-3770
E-Mail: mail@laserist.org
Home Page: www.laserist.org

Christine Jenkin, President
Abdulwahab Baghdadi, 3rd Dimension EvenTech
Brian Gonzalez, Individual Member

ILDA members are individuals involved in the laser entertainment and display industry.
Founded in 1986

8453   International Special Events Society

330 M Wabash Ave.
Suite 2000
Chicago, IL 60611-4267

312-321-6853
800-688-4737
FAX 312-673-6953
E-Mail: info@ises.com
Home Page: www.ises.com

Jodi Collen, CSEP, President
Judy Brillhart, President-Elect
Ingrid Nagy, CSEP, Treasurer
Sara Hunt, CSEP, Secretary
Kevin White, CSEP, Immediate Past President

Professionals in over a dozen countries representing special event producers, caterers, decorators, florists, destination management companies, rental companies, special effects experts, tent suppliers, audio-visual technicians, party and convention coordinators, ballon artists, educators, journalists, hotel sales managers, specialty entertainers, convention center managers and more.
4000 Members
Founded in 1987

8454   Meeting Professionals International

3030 LBJ Fwy
Suite 1700
Dallas, TX 75234-2759

972-702-3000
FAX 972-702-3065
E-Mail: feedback@mpiweb.org
Home Page: www.mpiweb.org
Social Media: *Facebook, Twitter, LinkedIn*

Paul Van DeVenter, President & CEO
Michael Woody, Chief Operating Officer
Daniel Gilmartin, Chief Financial Officer
Darren Temple, Chief Business Dev Officer

MPI members manage meetings and related activities for association, corporations, and educational institutions, or provide goods and services to the meetings industry.
1900 Members
Founded in 1972

8455   National Association for Campus Activities

13 Harbison Way
Columbia, SC 29212

803-732-6222
800-845-2338
FAX 803-749-1047
E-Mail: info@naca.org
Home Page: www.naca.org
Social Media: *Facebook, Twitter, Instagram, YouTtube, Pinterest*

Steve Westbrook, Director Student Affairs
Alan Davis, Executive Director
Gordon Schell, Manager/Member Services
Dawn Thomas, Director/Educational/Events
Erin Wilson, Manager Communications

Largest collegiate organization for campus activities. Purpose is to assist in marketing entertainment services to educational institutions and providing student leadership development programs and services.
1100 Members
Founded in 1960

8456   National Association of Agricultural Fair Agencies

MI State Department of Agriculture
PO box 40627
Nashville, TN 37204

615-837-5081
FAX 517-373-9146
Home Page: www.nasda.org

Director Greg Ibach, President
Comm. Michael Strain, 1st Vice President

Comm. Steven Reviczky, 2nd Vice President
Director Jeff Witte, Secretary-Treasurer
Scott Enright, Past President

U.S. and Canadian representatives of state/provincial agencies that are responsible for the support of education and agricultural fairs.
Founded in 1966

8457   National Association of Consumer Shows

147 Se 102nd Ave
Portland, OR 97216-2703

503-253-0832
800-728-6227
FAX 503-253-9172
E-Mail: info@publicshows.com
Home Page: www.publicshows.com
Social Media: *Facebook, Twitter*

Mark Adams, President
Marc McIntosh, Treasurer
Mark Concilla, Secretary
Carolyn Alt, Director
Jim Fricke, Director

Nonprofit organization dedicated to furthering the interests of consumer show producers and suppliers.
265 Members
Founded in 1987

8458   National Association of Display Industries

4651 Sheridan Street
Suite 200
Hollywood, FL 33021

954-893-7300
FAX 954-893-7500
E-Mail: nadi@nadi-global.com
Home Page: www.nadi-global.com

Klein Merriman, Executive Director
Tracy Dillon, Director Communications

Sponsors seminars and annual contests. Conducts research programs and maintains placement services.
400 Members
Founded in 1937

8459   National Association of Professional Organizers

1120 Route 73
Suite 200
Mount Laurel, NJ 08054-2212

856-380-6828
FAX 856-439-0525
E-Mail: napo@napo.net
Home Page: www.napo.net
Social Media: *Facebook, Twitter, Pinterest, Flickr, YouTube*

Ellen Faye , CPO, COC, President
Susie Hayman, Secretary
Lisa Mark , CPO, Treasurer
Danielle Liu, MPA, CPO, Director
Elizabeth Dodson, Corp Associate Members Director

Members are time, productivity and organization management consultants.
1800 Members
Founded in 1985

8460   National Catholic Educational Exhibitors

2621 Dryden Road
Suite 300
Dayton, OH 45439

937-293-1415
888-555-8512
FAX 937-293-1310
E-Mail: cynpleg@aol.com
Home Page: www.nceeonline.org

Peter Li, Executive Director

A group for companies that provide products or services for Catholoc education.
500 Members
Founded in 1950

8461 National Coalition of Black Meeting Planners
700N Fairfax Street
Suite 510
Alexandria, VA 22314

571-527-3110
FAX 301-860-0500
E-Mail: info@ncbmp.org
Home Page: www.ncbmp.com

Ana Aponte-Curtis, Chair
Kevin J. Johnson, President
JoAnn S. Brown, Vice President
Stephanie Marshall, CMP, Secretary
Myron L. Hardiman, Treasurer

Nonprofit organization dedicated to the training needs of African American meeting planners.
Founded in 1983

8462 North American Farm Show Council
590 Woody Hayes Drive
Room 232
Columbus, OH 43210

614-292-4278
FAX 614-292-9448
E-Mail: gamble.19@osu.edu
Home Page: www.farmshowcouncil.org

Chip Blalock, President
Chuck Gamble, Secretary-Treasurer
David Zimmerman, 1st Vice President
Matt Jungmann, 2nd Vice President
Dennis Alford, Immediate Past-President

Strives to improve the value of its member shows through education, communication and evaluation. The overall goal is to provide the beest possible marketing showcase for exhibitors for agricultural equipment and related products to the farmer/rancher/producer customer.
37 Members
Founded in 1972

8463 Professional Convention Management Association
35 East Wacker Drive
Suite 500
Chicago, IL 60601-2105

312-423-7262
877-827-7262
FAX 312-423-7222
E-Mail: communications@pcma.org
Home Page: www.pcma.org
Social Media: *Facebook, Twitter, LinkedIn*

Ray Kopcinski, CMP, Chair
William Reed , FASAE, CMP, Chair-Elect
Mary Pat Heftman, Secretary-Treasurer
Christopher Wehking, CMP, Immediate Past Chair
Martin Balogh, Director

PCMA delivers superior and innovative education, to promote the value of professional convention management.
6100 Members
Founded in 1957

8464 Professional Show Managers Association
41 Applewood Lane
Avon, CT 06001

860-677-0094
FAX 860-286-0787
E-Mail: info@rdpgroup.com

Home Page: www.psmashows.org
Social Media: *Facebook, LinkedIn*

Dordy Fontinel, President
Christine Palmer, Vice President
Frank Gaglio, Secretary/Treasurer
Nancy Johnson, Immediate Past President
Bart Caple, Director
Founded in 1987

8465 Religious Conference Management Assocation
7702 Woodland Drive
Suite 120
Indianapolis, IN 46278

317-632-1888
FAX 317-632-7909
E-Mail: rcma@rcmaweb.org
Home Page: www.rcmaweb.org
Social Media: *Facebook, LinkedIn, YouTube*

Harry R. Schmidt, Executive Director/CEO
DeanDean Jones, Director of Conferenec & Events
Judy Valenta, Special Projects Cooordinator
Debbie Hochstetler, Director of Finance

Provides members with a wealth of resources designed specifically to enhance their professionalism and overall effectiveness as religious leaders.
3200 Members
Founded in 1972

8466 Society of Government Meeting Professionals
PO Box 321025
Alexandria, VA 22320

703-549-0892
FAX 703-549-0708
E-Mail: headquarters@sgmp.org
Home Page: www.sgmp.org
Social Media: *LinkedIn, YouTube*

Maggie McGowan, CGMP, CMP, President
Michelle Milligan, First Vice President
James Lynton, CGMP, 2nd Vice President
Brett Sterenson, Treasurer
Maurine Hill, Secretary

Trade association for government meeting planners and exhibitors.
3100 Members
Founded in 1981

8467 Society of Independent Show Organizers
2601 Ocean Park Blvd
Suite 200
Santa Monica, CA 90405-5250

310-450-8831
877-937-7476
FAX 310-450-9305
Home Page: www.shomex.com
Social Media: *Facebook, Twitter, LinkedIn*

David Audrain, Chairman
Rick McConnell, Vice Chair
Charles McCurdy, Treasurer
Tony Calanca, Secretary
Lewis R. Shomer, Executive Director
200 Members
Founded in 1990

8468 Visitor Studies Association
2885 Sanford Ave SW
Suite 18100
Grandville, MI 49418

740-872-0566
FAX 301-637-3312
E-Mail: info@visitorstudies.org
Home Page: www.visitorstudies.org
Social Media: *Facebook, Twitter, LinkedIn*

Joe Heimlich, President
Kimberly Kiehl, President-elect
Dave Ucko, Vice President, Organizational Dev

Bob Breck, Vice President, Outreach
Jessica Luke, Vice President, Professional Dev

Members are professionals at various institutions interested in studying audience experiences at museums, zoos, parks, etc. Promotes research in visitor participation and application of such research to programming and policy.
365 Members
Founded in 1990

Newsletters

8469 ACOMmodate
Association for Convention Operations Management
191 Clarksville Road
Princeton Junction, NJ 08550

609-799-3712
FAX 609-799-7032
E-Mail: info@acomonline.org
Home Page: www.acomonline.org

Lynn McCullough, Executive Director

Includes news, networking ideas, and articles of professional interest.
Frequency: Quarterly

8470 Affiliate Connection
International Festivals and Events Association
2603 W Eastover Ter
Boise, ID 83706-2800

208-433-0950
FAX 208-433-9812
E-Mail: craig@ifea.com
Home Page: www.ifea.com

Steven Schmader, President
Nia Forster, VP/Marketing
Craig Sarton, Director

The IFEA newsletter provides information and news 24 hours a day, 7 days a week, keeping members, suppliers and affiliates up-to-date and current.
2000 Members
Frequency: Monthly
Founded in 1956

8471 Annual Conference Abstracts
Visitor Studies Association
8175-A Sheridan Boulevard
Suite 362
Arvada, CO 80003-1928

303-467-2200
FAX 303-467-0064
E-Mail: info@visitorstudies.org
Home Page: www.visitorstudies.org

Alan Friedman, President
Ellen Cox, Treasurer
Jessica Luke, Treasurer
Frequency: Annual

8472 Aviso
American Association of Museums
1575 Eye Street NW
Suite 400
Washington, DC 20005-1113

202-289-1818
FAX 202-289-6578
E-Mail: membership@aam-us.org
Home Page: www.aam-us.org

Ford Bell, President
Kim Igone, VP Policy & Program

Reports on musuems in the news, federal legislation affecting museums, upcoming seminars and workshops, fedel grant deadlines and AAM activities and services.
Frequency: Monthly
Mailing list available for rent

8473 CEMA Communicator
Computer Event Marketing Association
1512 Weiskopf Loop
Round Rock, TX 78664-6128

512-310-8330
FAX 978-443-4715
Home Page: www.cemaonline.com

Mitch Ahiers, President
Newsletter posted directly on the Internet.
Frequency: Monthly
Founded in 1990

8474 ESCA Voice Newsletter
Exhibition Services and Contractors
Association
2260 Corporate Circle
Suite 400
Henderson, NV 80914

702-319-9561
877-792-3722
FAX 702-450-7732
E-Mail: askus@esca.org
Home Page: www.esca.org

Susan L Schwartz, Director Communications
Cynthia Kelly, Accounting Manager
Frequency: Quarterly

8475 Exhibition Perspectives
American Academy of Equine Art
c/o Kentucky Horse Park
4089 Iron Works Parkway
Lexington, KY 40511

859-281-6031
FAX 859-281-6043
Home Page: www.aaea.net

Julie Buchanan, Director
Frequency: Annual

8476 HCEA Edge
Healthcare Convention & Exhibitors
Association
5775 Peachtree Dnwdy Rd
Building G, Suite 500
Atlanta, GA 30342-1556

404-252-3663
FAX 404-252-0774
E-Mail: hcea@kellencompany.com
Home Page: www.hcea.org

Eric Allen, Executive Vice President

News and events of the trade association of
over 600 organizations involved in healthcare
exhibiting or providing services to healthcare
conventions, exhibitions and/or meetings.
Frequency: Monthly, Members Only

8477 IEG Endorsement Insider
IEG
640 N La Salle Dr
Suite 600
Chicago, IL 60654-3186

312-944-1727
800-834-4850
FAX 312-944-1897
E-Mail: valuationservices@sponsorship.com
Home Page: www.sponsorship.com

Lesa Ukman, CEO
John Ukman, Publisher

A newsletter covering the use of sports and entertainment personalities for endorsements, appearances and other marketing purposes.
Cost: $295.00
Frequency: Monthly

8478 IEG Sponsorship Report
IEG

640 N La Salle Dr
Suite 600
Chicago, IL 60654-3186

312-944-1727
800-834-4850
FAX 312-944-1897
E-Mail: ieg@sponsorship.com
Home Page: www.sponsorship.com

Lesa Ukman, CEO
John Ukman, Publisher
Bart Zautcke, CEO
Brad Smith, Marketing

Newsletter on sports, arts, event, entertainment
and cause marketing.
Cost: $415.00
8 Pages
Frequency: Biweekly
Circulation: 15000
Founded in 1982

8479 NAAFA Newsletter
National Association of Agricultural Fair
Agencies
MI State Department of Agriculture
PO Box 30017
Lansing, MI 48909

517-373-9766
FAX 517-373-9146

Carol Carlson, Secretary/Treasurer
Frequency: Annual

8480 NAFSC Brochure
North American Farm Show Council
590 Woody Hayes Drive
Columbus, OH 43210-6131

614-292-4278
FAX 614-292-9448
E-Mail: gamble19@osu.edu
Home Page: www.farmshows.org

Dennis Alford, First VP
Chuck Gamble, Secretary-Treasurer

The North American Farm Show Council
strives to improve the value of its member
shows through education, communication and
evaluation. The goal of the Council is to provide the best possible marketing showcase for
the exhibitors of agricultural equipment &
related products.
Frequency: Bi-Ennial
Founded in 1972

8481 NCEE News
National Catholic Educational Exhibitors
2621 Dryden Road
Suite 300
Dayton, OH 45439

937-293-1415
888-555-8512
FAX 937-293-1310
E-Mail: cynpleg@aol.com
Home Page: www.nceeonline.org

Peter Li, Executive Director

A regular newsletter for the exclusive use of
NCEE members. Each issue brings messages
from the NCEE president and the NCEA Convention and Exposition Director; market and
association updates, and the Exhibition
Planning Calendar

8482 Newsbytes
Meeting Professionals International
3030 Lbj Fwy
Suite 1700
Dallas, TX 75234-2759

972-702-3000
FAX 972-702-3070
E-Mail: feedback@mpiweb.org
Home Page: www.mpiweb.org

Bruce Mac Millan, President
Frequency: Weekly

8483 Newsletter
American Academy of Equine Art
c/o Kentucky Horse Park
4089 Iron Works Parkway
Lexington, KY 40511

859-281-6031
FAX 859-281-6043
Home Page: www.aaea.net

Julie Buchanan, Director
Frequency: Semi-Annual

8484 Workshop Brochure
American Academy of Equine Art
c/o Kentucky Horse Park
4089 Iron Works Parkway
Lexington, KY 40511

859-281-6031
FAX 859-281-6043
Home Page: www.aaea.net

Julie Buchanan, Director
Frequency: Annual

Magazines & Journals

8485 American Speaker
Briefings Publishing Group
1101 King St
Suite 110
Alexandria, VA 22314-2944

703-548-3800
800-722-9221
FAX 703-684-2136
Home Page: www.briefings.com

Aram Bakshian Jr, Editor-in-Chief
Alan Douglas, President

An updateable loose leaf product geared to am-
ateur and polished public speakers. The prod-
uct has tips on speaking, model speeches, and
filler material for all speaking needs.
Cost: $395.00
Frequency: Monthly
Founded in 1992
Mailing list available for rent: 14000 names at
$125 per M
Printed in 2 colors on matte stock

8486 Association Conventions & Facilities
Coastal Communications Corporation
2700 N Military Trail
Suite 120
Boca Raton, FL 33431

561-989-0600
FAX 561-989-9509
E-Mail: ccceditor@att.net
Home Page: www.themeetingmagazines.com

Harvey Grotsky, Publisher/Editor-In-Chief
Susan Wycoff Fell, Managing Editor
Susan Gregg, Managing Editor

Edited for association meeting planners with
the responsibility for staging and planning
meetings, conferences and conventions, for site
selection, specifying accommodations and
transportation. Issues provide in-depth focus on
sites and transportation, current legislation,
seminar and training oprtions, budget and cost
controls, and destination reports.
Cost: $60.00
Frequency: BiMonthly
Circulation: 20,500
ISSN: 2162-8831
Founded in 2008

8487 Association Meetings
Primedia

Po Box 12901
Shawnee Mission, KS 66282-2901

913-341-1300
FAX 913-514-6895
E-Mail: bblair@primediabusiness.com
Home Page: www.penton.com

Eric Jacobson, Senior VP
Larry Keltto, Editor

Directed to association executive directors and meeting planners with the objective of aiding the planning, site selection, and organization of meetings and conventions.
Cost: $223.65
Circulation: 20065
Printed in 4 colors

8488 Convene Magazine

Professional Convention Management Association
2301 S Lake Shore Dr
Suite 1001
Chicago, IL 60616-1419

312-423-7262
877-827-7262
FAX 312-423-7222
E-Mail: communications@pcma.org
Home Page: www.pcma.org

Deborah Sexton, President/CEO
Kati S Quigley CMP, Chairman of Board
Barry L Smith, Chair Board of Trustees

The leading meetings industry trade publication for education content and timely, relevant information from the Professional Convention Management Association
Frequency: Monthly
Circulation: 35000

8489 Convention South

2001 W First Street
2001 West First Street
Gulf Shores, AL 36542

251-968-5300
FAX 251-968-4532
E-Mail: info@conventionsouth.com
Home Page: www.conventionsouth.com

J Talty O'Connor, Editor/Publisher
Kristen S McIntosh, VP/Executive Editor
Pamela Redden, Marketing Services Manager
Suzanne Kellams, Manager, Circulation Development

For planners of meetings, conferences, seminars and similar events that are held in the South
Frequency: Monthly
Circulation: 18000
ISSN: 1074-0627
Founded in 1983
Printed in 4 colors on glossy stock

8490 Corporate & Incentive Travel

Coastal Communications Corporation
2700 N Military Trail
Suite 120
Boca Raton, FL 33431

561-989-0600
FAX 561-989-9509
E-Mail: ccceditor1@att.net
Home Page: www.themeetingmagazines.com

Harvey Grotsky, Publisher/Editor-In-Chief
Susan Wyckoff Fell, Managing Editor
Susan Gregg, Managing Editor

The magazine for corporate meetings and incentive travel planners. In-depth editorial focus on site selection, accommodations and transportation, current legislation, conference, seminar and training facilities, budget and cost controls, and destination reports. Regular features highlight industry news and develop-

ments, trends and personalities, meeting values, facilities, and destinations.
Frequency: Monthly
Circulation: 40,000
Founded in 1983

8491 Corporate Meetings & Incentives

Primedia
Po Box 12901
Shawnee Mission, KS 66282-2901

913-341-1300
FAX 913-514-6895
E-Mail: bbair@primediabusiness.com
Home Page: www.penton.com

Eric Jacobson, Senior VP
Melissa Fromento, Publisher

Senior executives guide to decision-making.
138 Pages
Frequency: Monthly
Circulation: 34246
Founded in 1980
Printed in 4 colors on glossy stock

8492 ESCA Extra Magazine

Exhibition Services and Contractors Association
2260 Corporate Circle
Suite 400
Henderson, NV 80914

702-319-9561
877-792-3722
FAX 702-450-7732
E-Mail: askus@esca.org
Home Page: www.esca.org

Susan L Schwartz, CEM, Executive Director
Heather Geldner, Accounting Manager
Cynthia Kelly, Accounting Manager
Frequency: Monthly

8493 EXPO Magazine

Expo Magazine
7015 College Blvd
Overland Park, KS 66211-1579

913-469-1185
800-444-4388
FAX 913-469-0806
E-Mail: expo@halldata.com
Home Page: www.expoweb.com

Cam Bishop, President
Donna Sanford, Publisher
Danica Tormohlen, Editor-in-Chief

Magazine for exposition managment.
Cost: $48.00
134 Pages
Circulation: 7500
ISSN: 1046-3925
Founded in 1989
Printed in 4 colors on glossy stock

8494 Event Solutions

Virgo Publishing LLC
3300 N Central Ave
Suite 300
Phoenix, AZ 85012-2532

480-675-9925
FAX 480-990-0819
E-Mail: mikes@vpico.com
Home Page: www.vpico.com

Jenny Bolton, President

Topics featured include decor, themes, high tech support, indoor facility equipment, food and beverage ideas, special effects, new products, and financial issues and regulations. Provides corporate, product and even profiles with suggestions from experts in the field.
Cost: $45.00
Frequency: Monthly
Circulation: 25,000

8495 Events World

International Special Events Society:
Indiana
401 North Michigan Avenue
Chicago, IL 60611-4267

312-321-6853
800-688-4737
FAX 312-673-6953
E-Mail: info@ises.com
Home Page: www.ises.com

Kevin Hacke, Executive Director
Kristin Prine, Operations Director

Editorial contents include practical information on each of the seven disciplines, news on promotions, job banks, people in the industry, ISES activities and events, technology trends, and global vision information about environmental, legal and political issues relating to the special events industry.
Frequency: Monthly
Circulation: 20000
Founded in 1987

8496 Exhibit Builder

Exhibit Builder
22900 Ventura Boulevard #245
PO Box 4144
Woodland Hills, CA 91365

818-225-0100
800-356-4451
FAX 818-225-0138
Home Page: www.exhibitbuilder.net

Jill Brookman, CEO/President
Judy Pomerantz, Managing Editor
Jollen Ryan, Circulation Manager
Scott Gray, Editors

Devoted to the business and technical interest of the designers and fabricators of exhibits for trade shows, museums and point of purchase displays, includes application articles, new products, and new technology for creating booths.
Cost: $40.00
72 Pages
Frequency: Annual+
Circulation: 15000
ISSN: 0887-6878
Founded in 1983
Printed in 4 colors on glossy stock

8497 Exhibit Marketing Magazine

Eaton Hall Publishing
256 Columbia Turnpike
Florham Park, NJ 07932-1231

973-514-5900
800-746-9646
FAX 973-514-5977
E-Mail: info@eatonhall.com
Home Page: www.eatonhall.com

Scott Goldman, Publisher

Eaton Hall is a publishing and trade show firm which specializes in bringing buyers and sellers together.
Cost: $5.00
52 Pages
Frequency: Quarterly
Circulation: 31000
Founded in 1990
Printed in 4 colors on glossy stock

8498 Exhibitor

Exhibitor Magazine Group
Po Box 368
Suite 745
Rochester, MN 55903-0368

507-289-6556
888-235-6155
FAX 507-289-5253

E-Mail: webmaster@exhibitoronline.com
Home Page: www.exhibitoronline.com

Lee Knight, Owner
John Pavek, VP Publishing
Cara Schulz, National Sales Manager
Nicole Brudos Ferrara, Managing Editor
Whitney Archibald, Editor

The magazine for trade show and event marketing management.
Cost: $78.00
122 Pages
Frequency: Monthly
Circulation: 30000
ISSN: 0739-6821
Founded in 1982
Printed in 4 colors on glossy stock

8499 Facilities & Destinations
Bedrock Communications
650 1st Ave
7th Floor
New York, NY 10016-3240

212-532-7088
FAX 212-213-6382
E-Mail: mikecaffin@aol.com
Home Page: www.facilitiesonline.com

Stella Johnson, Senior Executive Editor
Timothy Herrick, Director

Serves the association meeting industry defined as finance, banking, health, education,religious, trade, labor, fraternal, manufacturing, civic, social, professional, government/military, association management companies, independent meeting planners, destination management companies, trade show/event production companies and other groups who use the facilities industry for meetings, conferences, exhibitions, trade shows and conventions.
45 Pages
Circulation: 34000+
Founded in 1988

8500 Facilities & Event Management
Bedrock Communications
650 1st Ave
7th Floor
New York, NY 10016-3240

212-532-7088
FAX 212-213-6382
E-Mail: mikecaffin@aol.com
Home Page: www.facilitiesonline.com/

Michael Caffin, Managing Editor
Glen O'Grady, Director
Timothy Herrick, Director

Editorial articles solve problems based on industry facts and statistics and coverage encompasses various segments of the facilities industry, including: convention centers, exhibition halls, hotel/conference centers, civic centers, arenas, stadiums, arts centers, etc. Monthly features detail facility business activity and provide coverage of the products and services available. Subscription, $48.00
Cost: $4.95
52 Pages
Frequency: Monthly
Circulation: 30000
ISSN: 1524-0258

8501 Fairs and Expositions
International Association of Fairs & Expositions
3043 E Cairo
PO Box 985
Springfield, MO 65802

417-862-5771
800-516-0313
FAX 417-862-0156

E-Mail: iafe@fairsandexpos.ocm
Home Page: www.fairsandexpos.com

Jim Tucker, President
Steve Siever, Director
Max Willis, Editor

The source of information for fair trends, innovative ideas and association activities.
Frequency: 10/year
Founded in 1885

8502 Feed and Grain
Cygnus Business Media
1233 Janesville Avenue
Fort Atkinson, WI 53538

920-563-6388
FAX 920-563-1702
Home Page: www.feedandgrain.com

Arlette Sambs, Publisher
Jackie Roembke, Editor

Committed to providing targeted editorial that addresses the specific needs of its readers. Subscribers consist of feed manufacturers, integrated livestock operators, pet food manufacturers, soybean processors, builders, designers and millwrights, as well as businesses such as rice mills, country and terminal elevators, flour mills, breweries and distilleries.
Cost: $48.00
Frequency: Bi-Monthly
Circulation: 15700
Founded in 1966
Mailing list available for rent: 16,505 names at $100 per M
Printed in 4 colors on glossy stock

8503 IE - Business of International Events Magazine
International Festivals and Events Association
2603 W Eastover Ter
Boise, ID 83706-2800

208-433-0950
FAX 208-433-9812
E-Mail: craig@ifea.com
Home Page: www.ifea.com

Steven Schmader, President
Nia Forster, VP/Marketing
Craig Sarton, Director

IFEA'S quarterly magazine that provides members with the latest news and features focusing on current trends and topics, events, resources and more.
2000 Members
Founded in 1956

8504 Inside Events
Trio Communications
8899 Beverly Boulevard
#408
Los Angeles, CA 90048-2431

310-888-8566
FAX 310-888-1866

Elisabeth Familian, Publisher

Articles include area listings of sites and vendors for any type of gathering. Profiles the creative ideas of industry professionals.
Frequency: Quarterly
Circulation: 20,000

8505 Insurance & Financial Meetings Management
Coastal Communications Corporation
2700 N Military Trail
Suite 120
Boca Raton, FL 33431-6394

561-989-0600
FAX 561-989-9509

E-Mail: ccceditor@att.net
Home Page: www.themeetingmagazines.com

Harvey Grotsky, Publisher/Editor-In-Chief
Susan Wyckoff Fell, Managing Editor
Susan Gregg, Managing Editor

The executive source for planning meetings and incentives for the financial and insurance sectors. With regular features and special focus on site selection, destinations, industry-related studies and activities, motivational and incentive programs, program and event planning.
Frequency: Monthly
Circulation: 40,000
Founded in 1983

8506 Insurance Conference Planner
Primedia
Po Box 12901
Shawnee Mission, KS 66282-2901

913-341-1300
866-505-7173
FAX 913-514-6895
Home Page: www.penton.com

Eric Jacobson, Senior VP
Melissa Fromento, Publisher

Meeting and incentive strategies for the financial services industry.
148 Pages
Frequency: Monthly
Circulation: 8005
Founded in 1965
Printed in 4 colors on glossy stock

8507 Laserist
International Laser Display Association
7062 Edgeworth Drive
Orlando, FL 32819

407-797-7654
FAX 503-344-3770
E-Mail: president@laserist.org
Home Page: www.laserist.org

Tim Walsh, President
Patrick Murphy, Executive Director

Providing the latest news about the art and technology of laser displays
Frequency: Quarterly
Founded in 1986

8508 Medical Meetings
Primedia
11 Riverbend Dr S
Stamford, CT 06907-2524

203-316-8178
FAX 203-358-5812
Home Page: www.meetingsnet.com

Betsy Bair, Editor Director
Melissa Framento, Publisher

International guide for health care and meeting planners.
106 Pages
Frequency: Monthly
Circulation: 10,823
Founded in 1973
Printed in 4 colors on glossy stock

8509 Meeting Professionals
Meeting Professionals International
3030 LBJ Fwy
Suite 1700
Dallas, TX 75234-2759

972-702-3000
FAX 972-702-3070
E-Mail: feedback@mpiweb.org
Home Page: www.mpiweb.org

Bruce MacMillan, President
Eric Rozenberg CMP,CMM, Vice Chairman Administration

Furthers the professional development and education of all those who participate in the meet-

ings industry.
Cost: $99.00
Frequency: Monthly
Circulation: 28,000
Founded in 1972

8510 Meetings & Conventions
Reed Business Information
500 Plaza Drive
Secaucus, NJ 07094

201-021-1960
FAX 201-902-2053
E-Mail: lcioffi@ntmllc.com
Home Page: www.meetings-conventions.com

Bernard Lynch, Associate Editor
Lori Cioffi, Editor in Chief
Loren G. Edelstein, Executive Editor
Allen Sheinman, Managing Editor
Lisa Grimaldi, Senior Editor

Serves the corporate and independent travel and meeting planner with features on meeting facilities, hotels/airports/car rental, incentive travel options, trade show coverage, entertainment/leisure options and industry news.
Cost: $70.00
Frequency: Monthly
Circulation: 70013
Founded in 1965

8511 Meetings Industry
Dunn Enterprises
513 Commerce Dr
Upper Marlboro, MD 20774-7434

301-249-4600
FAX 301-249-9100
Home Page: www.jtdunn.com

Barbara Cox, Owner
Robert Lantang, Graphic Designer

Profiles meetings sites and accomodations for meetings of all sizes. Includes personnel appointments of other meeting planners.
Circulation: 35000

8512 Programming Magazine
National Association for Campus Activities
13 Harbison Way
Columbia, SC 29212-3401

803-732-6222
800-845-2338
FAX 803-749-1047
E-Mail: info@naca.org
Home Page: www.naca.org

Glenn Farr, Editor
Erin Wilson, Circulation

Features cover facilities and financial management, promotions, and student development to help plan a wide range of events.
Cost: $70.00
Circulation: 4300
Founded in 1960

8513 Religious Conference Manager
Religious Conference Management Association
7702 Woodland Drive
Suite 120
Indianapolis, IN 46228-6150

317-632-1888
FAX 317-632-7909
E-Mail: rcma@rcmaweb.org
Home Page: www.rcmaweb.org

Eric Allen, Executive Director

Presents timely information for the meeting professional. Content focuses on current trends and features educational articles and news within this specialized field.
Frequency: Bi-Monthly

8514 Resorts, Hotels, Meetings & Incentives
Publishing Group

PO Box 318
Trumbull, CT 06611-0318

860-279-0149

John Mortimer, Publisher

Editorial contents include in-depth articles on industry trends, budgeting, planning tips, and profiles of the top meeting facilities in the world.
Frequency: Monthly
Circulation: 58,601

8515 Special Events Magazine
Primedia Publication
17383 W Sunset Blvd
Suite A220
Pacific Plsds, CA 90272-4187

310-230-7160
800-543-4116
FAX 310-230-7168
E-Mail: lhurley@specialevents.com
Home Page: www.specialevents.com

Lisa Hurley, Editor
Lisa Perrin, President, Chief Executive Officer
Wanda McKnight, Sales Manager

Resource for event professionals who design and produce special events (including social, corporate and public events) in hotels, resorts, banquet facilities and other venues.
Cost: $48.43
Frequency: Monthly
Circulation: 2000+
Founded in 1982

8516 Tradeshow & Exhibit Manager
Goldstein & Associates
2117 Highland Avenue
Louisville, KY 40204

502-548-3188
FAX 502-742-8749
Home Page: www.goldsteinandassociates.com

Steve Goldstein, Publisher

Featured articles focus on the issues, trends and products of interest connected to the tradeshow industry. Topics include security, boothmanship, legislation and shipping.
Cost: $80.00
Circulation: 14600

8517 Tradeshow Week
Reed Business Information
5700 Wilshire Boulevard
Suite 120
Los Angeles, CA 90036-5804

323-576-6600
FAX 323-965-2407
Home Page: www.tradeshowweek.com

Amy Lacey, Marketing Director
Adam Schaffer, Publisher
Michael Hart, Editor-in-Chief
Carlos Lopez, Production Director
Heidi Genoist, Senior Associate Editor

For corporate exhibit managers, independent show managers, special event and meeting planners, association show managers and industry suppliers. Focuses on changing trends, new ideas and issues shaping the exposition industry in the US/Canada and abroad. Each issue contains a national and international show calendar.
Cost: $439.00
Frequency: Weekly
Circulation: 2394
Founded in 1971
Printed in 4 colors on matte stock

8518 Visitor Studies Today
Visitor Studies Association

8175-A Sheridan Boulevard
Suite 362
Arvada, CO 80003-1928

303-467-2200
FAX 303-467-0064
E-Mail: info@visitorstudies.org
Home Page: www.visitorstudies.org

Alan Friedman, President
Ellen Cox, Treasurer
Jessica Luke, Treasurer
Frequency: 3/year

Trade Shows

8519 AAEA Annual Meetings
American Academy of Equine Art
c/o Kentucky Horse Park
4089 Iron Works Parkway
Lexington, KY 40511

859-281-6031
FAX 859-281-6043
Home Page: www.aaea.net

Shelley Hunter, Executive Director
Julie Buchanan, President
Frequency: April, September

8520 AAM Annual Meeting & MuseumExpo
American Alliance of Museums
2451 Crystal Dr.
Suite 1005
Arlington, VA 22202

202-289-1818
FAX 202-289-6578
E-Mail: membership@aam-us.org
Home Page: www.aam-us.org

Andrea Streat, Director, Meetings & Events

The largest gathering of museum professionals in the world.
Frequency: Annual/May

8521 ASTC Annual Conference & Exhibit Hall
Association of Science/Technology Centers
1025 Vermont Avenue NW
Suite 500
Washington, DC 20005-6310

202-783-7200
FAX 202-783-7207
E-Mail: conference@astc.org
Home Page: www.astc.org

Cindy Kong, Director, Meetings & Conferences
Wendy Pollock, Dir, Research, Pubs, Exhibitions
Sheryl Thorpe, Manager, Conference & Exhibit Hall

Provides science center professionals from across the world a forum to exchange ideas and discuss the field's leading issues. With over 100 conference sessions, participants are challenged to explore ways of making science centers more essential to their communities.
1500 Attendees
Founded in 1973

8522 Affordable Meetings Exposition and Conference
George Little Management
10 Bank Street
Suite 1200
White Plains, NY 10606-1954

914-486-6070
800-272-7469
FAX 914-948-6180

E-Mail: customer_relations@glmshows.com
Home Page: www.glmshows.com

Susan Sloan, Show Manager
George Little II, President

Focuses on the needs of meeting planners from all types and sizes of organizations who are responsible for producing successful yet cost effective meetings. 430 booths.
3M Attendees
Frequency: September

8523 Association of Collegiate Conference & Events Directors Conference

Assn of Collegiate Conference & Events Directors
1301 S College Avenue
Fort Collins, CO 80523-8037

877-502-2233
FAX 970-491-0667
E-Mail: acced@colostate.edu
Home Page: acced-i.colostate.edu

Deborah Blom, Executive Director
Monica Nesbit Schultz, Marketing/Sales Manager

Workshop, conference, banquet and luncheon plus exhibits of conference and special event planning supplies, equipment and service information.
1300 Attendees
Frequency: March
Founded in 1980

8524 Business to Business Exposition

Trade Shows West
2880 S Main
Suite 110
Salt Lake City, UT 84115

801-485-0176
FAX 801-485-0241

16000 Attendees

8525 Conventions and Expositions

American Society of Association Executives
1575 I Street NW
Washington, DC 20005-1105

202-262-2723
FAX 202-626-8825

Judy Comeaux, Advertising
John Young, Production

Exposition planners trade show; 500-700 booths.
2-5M Attendees
Frequency: March

8526 ESC Semi-Annual Meetings

Exhibition Services and Contractors Association
2260 Corporate Circle
Suite 400
Henderson, NV 80914

702-319-9561
877-792-3722
FAX 702-450-7732
E-Mail: askus@esca.org
Home Page: www.esca.org

Susan L Schwartz, CEM, Executive Director
Heather Geldner, Accounting Manager
Cynthia Kelly, Accounting Manager

December Meeting with International Association for Exposition Management and Summer Educational Conference.
Frequency: December, Summer

8527 ESCA's Summer Educational Conference

Exhibition Services & Contractors Association

2340 E Trinity Mills Road
Suite 100
Carrollton, TX 75006

469-574-0698
877-792-ESCA
FAX 469-574-0697
Home Page: www.esca.org

Designed to give attendees the opportunity to advance their knowledge and to have an impact on the shape of the exhibition industry's future, as well as to network. Three session tracks, interactive forums and roundtables, speakers, and exhibits.
Frequency: Annual

8528 ESPA Annual Conference

Event Service Professionals Association
191 Clarksville Road
Princeton Junction, NJ 08550

609-799-3712
FAX 609-799-7032
E-Mail: info@espaonline.org
Home Page: www.acomonline.org
Social Media: *Facebook, Twitter, LinkedIn*

Lynn McCullough, Executive Director
Diane Galante, Meeting Planner
Elizabeth Roe, Association Coordinator
Meghan Higgins, Public Relations Manager

Conference geared specifically to the event and convention services industry.
Frequency: Annual

8529 Exhibit Ideas Show

Exhibit Builder
1600 Golf Road
Suite 550
Rolling Meadows, IL 60008-4273

800-638-6396
FAX 847-280-0771

Russ Eisenhardt, Show Manager
Jill Brookman, Publisher

Marketplace for products, services and technologies for exhibit builders and buyers. Elements included in trade show, museum and point of purchase booth construction are displayed, as are portable, modular and custom exhibit systems. 700 booths.
20M Attendees
Frequency: April

8530 Exhibit Industry Conference & Exposition

Trade Show Exhibitors Association
McCormick Place, 2301 S Lake Shore Drive
Suite 1005
Chicago, IL 60616

312-842-8732
FAX 312-842-8744
E-Mail: tsea@tsea.org
Home Page: www.tsea.org

Stephen Schuldenfrei, President
Emily Burger, Sales Manager
Frequency: July

8531 Exhibitor Conference

Exhibitor Magazine Group
98 E Naperville Road
Westmont, IL 60559

630-434-7779
800-752-6312
FAX 630-434-1216
E-Mail: exhibitorshow@heiexpo.com
Home Page: www.exhibitorshow.com

Carol Fojtik, Managing Director/Sr VP

Conference program combined with exhibit hall featuring latest products and resources shaping the future of exhibiting and corporate event programs. Anyone responsible for planning, managing or implementing trade show or corporate event marketing functions should at-

tend. Conference is held annually in Las Vegas, NV.
5M Attendees
Frequency: March
Founded in 1989

8532 HCEA Annual Meeting

Healthcare Convention & Exhibitors Association
1100 Johnson Ferry Rd NE
Suite 300
Atlanta, GA 30342-1733

404-252-3663
FAX 404-252-0774
E-Mail: hcea@kellencompany.com
Home Page: www.hcea.org

Eric Allen, Executive Vice President
Jackie Beaulieu, Associate Director

Cost varies; approximately 50 booths; 800 attendees.
200 Attendees
Frequency: Annual

8533 HCEA Marketing Summit

Healthcare Convention & Exhibitors Association
1100 Johnson Ferry Rd NE
Suite 300
Atlanta, GA 30342-1733

404-252-3663
FAX 404-252-0774
E-Mail: hcea@kellencompany.com
Home Page: www.hcea.org

Eric Allen, Executive Vice President
Jackie Beaulieu, Associate Director

Cost varies; no exhibits; 200-250 attendees.
200 Attendees
Frequency: Annual

8534 IAAM Annual Conference & Trade Show

International Association of Assembly Managers
635 Fritz Drive
Suite 100
Coppell, TX 75019-4442

972-906-7441
800-935-4226
FAX 972-906-7418
E-Mail: kristie.todd@iaam.org
Home Page: www.iaam.org

Kristie Todd, Membership & Exposition Coordinator
JoAnn Ramsey, Exhibition Manager

Members are managers of auditoriums, arenas, convention centers, stadiums and performing arts centers, coming together for education and networking opportunities, expert speakers, and exhibits.
3000 Attendees
Frequency: Annual/
Founded in 1925
Mailing list available for rent: 2800 names at $300 per M

8535 IAEE Expo! Expo!

International Assn of Exhibitions and Events
12700 Park Central Drive
Suite 308
Dallas, TX 75251

972-458-8002
FAX 972-458-8119
E-Mail: news@iaee.com
Home Page: www.iaee.com

Annual show of 250 exhibitors of conventions and visitor bureaus, hotels, travel airlines, car rental, shippers, insurance, computer hardware and software, service contractors, printing products, specialty advertisement products,

photography equipment and audio-visual equipment.
2500 Attendees
Frequency: Annual/December
Founded in 1928

8536 IAEM Semi-Annual Meetings
International Association for Exhibition Mgmt
8111 LBJ Freeway, Suite 750
PO Box 802425
Dallas, TX 75251-1313

972-458-8002
FAX 972-458-8119
E-Mail: iaem@iaem.org
Home Page: www.iaem.org

Steven G Hacker, CAE, President
Cathy Breden, CAE CMP, SVP
Susan Brower, Director
Marketing/Communications

Annual show of 250 exhibitors of conventions and visitor bureaus, hotels, travel airlines, car rental, shippers, insurance, computer hardware and software, service contractors, printing products, specialty advertisement products, photography equipment and audio-visual equipment.
2200 Attendees
Frequency: June, December

8537 IAFE Annual Meeting
International Association of Fairs & Expositions
3043 E Cairo
PO Box 985
Springfield, MO 65802

417-862-5771
800-516-0313
FAX 417-862-0156
E-Mail: iafe@fairsandexpos.com
Home Page: www.fairsandexpos.com

Jim Tucker, President
Steve Siever, Director

Many branch divisions of the IAFE within the United States and Canada have their own annual meetings where members can meet, have access to resources, programs and workshops.
5000 Attendees
Frequency: Fall, Neveda
Founded in 1885

8538 IBTM America
800-417-8646
203-840-5636
E-Mail: ibtmamerica@reedexpo.com
Home Page: www.ibtmamerica.com
Social Media: *Facebook, Twitter, LinkedIn, Instagram, Pinterest, YouTube*

Jaime McAuley, Event Director

IBTM's 8 global and regional events are showcases for the meetings and events industry.

8539 IFEA Annual Convention and Expo
International Festivals and Events Associations
2603 W Eastover Terrace
Boise, ID 83706

208-433-0950
FAX 208-433-9812
E-Mail: shauna@ifea.com
Home Page: www.ifea.com

Steve Wood Schmader, President
Nia Forster, VP/Marketing
Shauna Spencer, Director

Unites hundreds of the world's leading festivals and events, suppliers, media, sponsors and related industry professionals to share information on every aspect of event production

through in-depth workshops, round-table discussions and networking.
2000 Members
800 Attendees
Frequency: Fall
Founded in 1956

8540 ILDA Conference
International Laser Display Association
7062 Edgeworth Drive
Orlando, FL 32819

407-797-7654
FAX 503-344-3770
E-Mail: president@laserist.org
Home Page: www.laserist.org

Tim Walsh, President
Patrick Murphy, Executive Director

One of the world's largest exhibitions of entertainment technology. Features international exhibitors from the fields of lighting, lasers, audio, video and staging.
70000 Attendees
Founded in 1986

8541 International Technology Meetings & Incentives Conference
Techno-Savvy Meeting Professional
9200 Bayard Place
Fairfax, VA 22032-2103

703-978-6287
FAX 703-978-5524
E-Mail: cimpa@cimpa.org
Home Page: www.cimpa.org

Andrea Sigler, President

Containing 100 booths and 100 exhibits.
Frequency: November

8542 MPI Semi-Annual Meetings
Meeting Professionals International
3030 LBJ Freeway
Suite 1700
Dallas, TX 75234

972-023-3000
FAX 972-702-3070
E-Mail: feedback@mpiweb.org
Home Page: www.mpiweb.org

Colin C Rorrie, Jr PhD CAE, President/CEO
Frequency: Summer, Winter

8543 NAAFA Semi-Annual Meetings
National Association of Agricultural Fair Agencies
MI State Department of Agriculture
PO Box 30017
Lansing, MI 48909

517-373-9766
FAX 517-373-9146

Carol Carlson, Secretary/Treasurer
Frequency: Summer, Winter

8544 NAFSC Annual Meeting
North American Farm Show Council
590 Woody Hayes Drive
Columbus, OH 43210-6131

614-292-4278
FAX 614-292-9448
E-Mail: gamble19@osu.edu
Home Page: www.farmshows.org

Dennis Alford, First VP
Chuck Gamble, Secretary/Treasurer
Frequency: May
Founded in 1972

8545 NCEE Annual Meeting
National Catholic Educational Exhibitors
2621 Dryden Road
Suite 300
Dayton, OH 45439

937-293-1415
888-555-8512

FAX 937-293-1310
E-Mail: bthomas@peterli.com

Bret Thomas, Executive Director

In conjunction with the National Catholic Educational Association.
Frequency: March

8546 PCMA Annual Meeting
Professional Convention Management Association
2301 S Lake Shore Dr
Suite 1001
Chicago, IL 60616-1419

312-423-7262
877-827-7262
FAX 312-423-7222
E-Mail: communications@pcma.org
Home Page: www.pcma.org

Deborah Sexton, President/CEO
Kati S Quigley CMP, Chairman of Board
Barry L Smith, Chair Board of Trustees
3000 Members

8547 RCMA Conference & Exposition
Religious Conference Management Association
7702 Woodland Drive
Suite 120
Indianapolis, IN 46228-6150

317-632-1888
FAX 317-632-7909
E-Mail: rcma@rcmaweb.org
Home Page: www.rcmaweb.org

Eric Allen, Executive Director
Frequency: Annual

8548 The Special Event Annual Conference & Exhibition
Special Event Magazine
PO Box 8987
Malibu, CA 90265-8987

708-486-0731
866-486-0731
FAX 310-317-0264
E-Mail: registration@penton.com
Home Page: www.specialevents.com

Sharon Morabito, Group Show Director
Tara Melingonis, Conference Manager
Kim Romano, Special Events Manager
Wanda McKnight, Sales Manager
Dacia Coppola, Show Coordinator

Brings together those in the special events industry for new product displays, education, networking and learning. 275 booths.
3M Attendees
Frequency: Annual/January

8549 VSA Annual Meeting
Visitor Studies Association
8175-A Sheridan Boulevard
Suite 362
Arvada, CO 80003-1928

303-467-2200
FAX 303-467-0064
E-Mail: info@visitorstudies.org
Home Page: www.visitorstudies.org

Alan Friedman, President
Ellen Cox, Treasurer
Jessica Luke, Treasurer
Frequency: Summer

Directories & Databases

8550 Association Management: Convention Bureau and Convention Hall Issue
American Society of Association Executives

1575 Eye St NW
Washington, DC 20005-1103

202-626-2700
FAX 202-371-8825
E-Mail: publicpolicy@asaenet.org
Home Page: www.asaenet.org

A list of halls, centers, auditoriums, arenas and
visitors bureaus in the United States and Canada.
Cost: $4.00
Circulation: 20,000

**8551 Audarena International Guide &
Facility Buyers Guide**
VNU Business Publications
49 Music Sq W
4th Floor
Nashville, TN 37203-3213

615-321-4251
FAX 615-320-0454
E-Mail: Research@billboard.com
Home Page: www.billboard.com

Ken Schlager, Executive Editor
Mitch Tebo, Directory Marketing Director
George Van, President
Monica Herrera, Manager
Bill Werde, Director
Cost: $99.00
310 Pages
Frequency: October

**8552 CEMA Member Directory and
Meeting Planner**
Computer Event Marketing Association
1512 Weiskopf Loop
Round Rock, TX 78664-6128

512-310-8330
FAX 510-682-0555
Home Page: www.cemaonline.com

Erika Brunke, Executive Director
Olga Rosenbrook, Member Services

All event managers and primary IA members.
500 Pages
Founded in 1990

8553 Constitution and Membership Roster
National Association of Agricultural Fair
Agencies
MI State Department of Agriculture
PO Box 30017
Lansing, MI 48909

517-373-9766
FAX 517-373-9146

Carol Carlson, Secretary/Treasurer
Frequency: Annual

**8554 Corporate and Incentive Travel:
Official**
2700 N Military Trl
Suite 120
Boca Raton, FL 33431-6394

561-989-0600
FAX 561-989-9509
Home Page: www.corporate-inc-travel.com

Harvey Grotsky, President

**8555 HCEA Directory of Healthcare
Meetings and Conventions**
Healthcare Convention & Exhibitors
Association
5775 Peachtree Dnwdy Rd
Building G, Suite 500
Atlanta, GA 30342-1556

404-252-3663
FAX 404-252-0774
E-Mail: hcea@kellencompany.com
Home Page: www.hcea.org

Eric Allen, Executive Director
Carol Wilson, Director Meetings

Information on 6,000 health care meetings,
available to members only.
500 Pages
Founded in 1930

8556 IAFE Directory
International Association of Fairs &
Expositions
3043 E Cairo
PO Box 985
Springfield, MO 65802

417-862-5771
800-516-0313
FAX 417-862-0156
E-Mail: iafe@fairsandexpos.com
Home Page: www.fairsandexpos.com

Jim Tucker, President
Steve Siever, Director

A annual reference guide giving members access to their associate members' products, services, and business activities.
1300 Members
Frequency: Annual
Founded in 1885

8557 IEG Sponsorship Sourcebook
IEG
640 N La Salle Dr
Suite 450
Chicago, IL 60654-3186

312-944-1727
800-834-4850
FAX 312-944-1897
E-Mail: ieg@sponsorship.com
Home Page: www.sponsorship.com

Lesa Ukman, CEO
John Ukman, Publisher
Alicia Fidler, Product Manager

A directory of sponsors, properties, agencies
and suppliers from th most active sponsors to
the hottest sponsorship opportunities. Contains
the critical data you need to make smart sponsorship connections.
Cost: $299.00
468 Pages
Frequency: Annual
ISBN: 0-944807-43-7
Printed in on glossy stock

8558 MPI Membership Directory
Meeting Professionals International
3030 Lbj Fwy
Suite 1700
Dallas, TX 75234-2759

972-702-3000
FAX 972-702-3070
E-Mail: feedback@mpiweb.org
Home Page: www.mpiweb.org

Bruce Mac Millan, President
Frequency: Annual

**8559 Meetings and Conventions: Gavel
International Directory Issue**
Reed Travel Group
500 Plaza Dr
Suite C
Secaucus, NJ 07094-3619

201-902-1800
FAX 207-319-1628

Alina Dalmau, Editor
Lori Cioffi, Manager

Lists over 4,000 convention halls and hotels in
the United States, suitable for meetings.
Cost: $35.00
Frequency: Annual
Circulation: 80,000

8560 NCEE Membership Directory
National Catholic Educational Exhibitors

2621 Dryden Road
Suite 300
Dayton, OH 45439

937-293-1415
888-555-8512
FAX 937-293-1310
E-Mail: bthomas@peterli.com

Bret Thomas, Executive Director
Frequency: Annual

**8561 Nationwide Directory of Corporate
Meeting Planners**
Reed Reference Publishing RR Bowker
121 Chanlon Road
New Providence, NJ 07974-1541

908-665-2834
FAX 908-464-3553
E-Mail: info@bowker.com
Home Page: www.bowker

Offers valuable information on over 12,000
corporations that hold regular, off-site meetings
arranged by over 18,000 corporate meeting
planners.
Cost: $297.00
1140 Pages
Frequency: Annual

8562 Official Meeting Facilities Guide
Reed Travel Group
500 Plaza Dr
Suite C
Secaucus, NJ 07094-3619

201-902-1800
FAX 201-902-2053

Virginia Nonneman, Editor
Lori Cioffi, Manager

One thousand national and international meet-
ing facilities, primarily hotels in the US.
Cost: $45.00
Frequency: SemiAnnual
Circulation: 18,500

8563 Protocol
Protocol Directory
101 W 12th St
Suite PH-H
New York, NY 10011-8142

212-633-6934
FAX 212-633-6934
E-Mail:
noemail@councilofprotocolexecutives.org
Home Page:
www.councilofprotocolexecutives.org

Edna Greenbaum, Editor

Approximately 4,000 suppliers of products and
services used by planners of executive meet-
ings, special events and other entertainment.
Cost: $60.00
Frequency: 1 issue
Founded in 1989
Printed in on matte stock

**8564 Sports Market Place Directory -
Online Database**
Grey House Publishing
4919 Route 22
PO Box 56
Amenia, NY 12501

518-789-8700
800-562-2139
FAX 845-373-6390
E-Mail: gold@greyhouse.com
Home Page: http://gold.greyhouse.com
Social Media: *Facebook, Twitter*

Leslie Mackenzie, Publisher
Richard Gottlieb, Editor

For over 20 years, this comprehensive,
up-to-date directory provides current key information about the people, organizations and
events involving the sports industry including,

contact information and key executives for single sports organizations, multi-sport organizations, media, sponsors, college sports, manufacturers, trade shows and more.
Founded in 1981

8565 Trade Show Exhibitors Association: Membership Directory
Trade Show Exhibitors Association
2301 S Lake Shore Dr
Suite 1005
Chicago, IL 60616-1419

312-842-8732
FAX 541-317-8749
E-Mail: tsea@tsea.org
Home Page: www.tsea.org

Steve Schuldenfrei, President
Emily Burger, Sales Manager

About 1,900 members of the Trade Show Exhibitors Association.
Cost: $55.00
Frequency: Annual February

8566 Trade Show News Network
Tarsus Group plc
16985 W Bluemound Road
Suite 210
Brookfield, WI 53005

262-782-1900
FAX 603-372-5894
E-Mail: rwimberly@tsnn.com
Home Page: www.tsnn.com

Rachel Wimberly, Editor-in-Chief
John Rice, Sales & Business Development
Arlene Shows, Marketing Manager

The world's leading online resource for the trade show, exhibition and event industry since 1996. TSNN.com owns and operates the most widely consulted event database on the internet, containing data about more than 19,500 trade shows, exhibitions, public events and conferences.
13900 Members
Frequency: Bi-Monthly
Founded in 1196

8567 TradeShow & Exhibit Manager's Buyer's Guide
2117 Highland Avenue
Louisville, KY 40204

502-548-3188
FAX 502-742-8749
Home Page: www.goldsteinandassociates.com

Steve Goldstein, Publisher

Over 1,000 suppliers of products and services to the trade show industry are profiled.
Cost: $60.00
150 Pages
Frequency: Annual
Circulation: 12,000

8568 Tradeshow Week Exhibit Manager
Goldstein & Associates
2117 Highland Avenue
Louisville, KY 40204

502-548-3188
FAX 502-742-8749
Home Page: www.goldsteinandassociates.com

Steve Goldstein, Publisher

For exhibit managers.
Cost: $80.00
Frequency: Bi-Monthly
Founded in 1983

8569 Tradeshow Week's Tradeshow Services Directory
Business Information Publication

5700 Wilshire Blvd
Suite 120
Los Angeles, CA 90036-7209

323-549-4100
FAX 323-965-2407
Home Page: www.tradeshowweek.com

Tina George-Reyes, Editor
Adam Schaffer, Publisher

Offers information on designers, builders, carriers and decorators involved in tradeshow and convention industries.
Cost: $95.00
300 Pages
Frequency: Annual

8570 VSA Membership Directory
Visitor Studies Association
8175-A Sheridan Boulevard
Suite 362
Arvada, CO 80003-1928

303-467-2200
FAX 303-467-0064
E-Mail: info@visitorstudies.org
Home Page: www.visitorstudies.org

Alan Friedman, President
Ellen Cox, Treasurer
Jessica Luke, Treasurer
Frequency: Annual

8571 Who's Who in Exposition Management
International Assn for Exhibition Management
PO Box 802425
Dallas, TX 75380-2425

972-216-1511
FAX 972-458-8119

Over 1,500 show manager members and 1,500 associate members.
Cost: $225.00
Frequency: Annual June

8572 Worldwide Tradeshow Schedule
1700 K Street NW
Suite 403
Washington, DC 20006-3810

202-463-4088

Over 110 international trade fairs are listed in all major industrial sectors.
10 Pages

Industry Web Sites

8573 http://gold.greyhouse.com
G.O.L.D Grey House OnLine Databases

Grey House Publishing's online database platform, GOLD, offers Quick Search, Keyword Search and Expert Search for most business sectors including exhibit and meeting planning markets. The GOLD platform makes finding the information you need quick and easy - whether you're a novice searcher or an experienced database user. All of Grey House's directory products are available for subscription on the GOLD platform.

8574 www.aacei.org
Association for Advancement of Cost Engineering

Association for Advancement of Cost Engineering provides its members with the resources they need to enhance their performance and ensure continued grouth and success. Serves cost management professionals: cost management and engineers, project managers, planners and schedulers, estimators and bidders, and value engineers.

8575 www.acced-i.colostate.edu
Colorado State University

Members are college and university conference and special events directors, profesionals and others who design, market and coordinate conferences and special events.

8576 www.acmenet.org
Association for Convention Marketing Executives

Annual meetings for marketing and sales executives.

8577 www.acomonline.org
Association for Convention Operations Management

Dedicated to advancing the practice of convention services management in the meetings industry, and to preparing CSM professionals for their critical role in the growth and success of their organizations.

8578 www.cimpa.org
Connected Int'l Meeting Professionals Association

Members are conference and convention planners with a certificate in convention management. Specializes in planning meetings events, incentives, using the internet.

8579 www.clc.org
Convention Liaison Council

Members are associations which are directly involved in the convention, exposition, trade show and meeting industry.

8580 www.edpa.com
Exhibit Designers & Producers Association

Exhibit Designers and Producers Association is an internationally recognized national trade association with more than 370 corporate members from 18 countries that are engaged in the design, manufacture, transport, installation and service of display and exhibits primarily for the trade show industry

8581 www.edsc.org
Electronic Distribution Show Corporation

Attendees are manufacturers of electronic components who sell their products through electronics distributors.

8582 www.esca.org
Exposition Service Contractors Association

Guide to exposition service is distributed annually and lists safety regulations and building rules in major US convention centers.

8583 www.greyhouse.com
Grey House Publishing

Authoritative reference directories for most business sectors including exhibit and meeting planning markets. Users can search the online databases with varied search criteria allowing for custom searches by product category, geographic area, sales volume, keyword, subject and more. Full Grey House catalog and online ordering also available.

8584 www.hcea.org
Healthcare Convention & Exhibitors Association

Trade association of over 700 organizations involved in health care exhibiting or providing services to health care conventions, exhibitions and/or meetings.

8585 www.iaam.org
International Association of Assembly Managers

Members are managers of auditoriums, arenas, convention centers, stadiums and performing arts centers.

8586 www.iacc.online.org
International Association of Conference Centers
A facilities-based organization which advances the understanding and awareness of conference centers as distinct within the training, education, hospitality and travel fields.

8587 www.iaem.org
Int'l Association for Exposition Management
Members are managers of shows, exhibits and expositions; associate members are industry suppliers.

8588 www.moderndisplay.com
Modern Display
Members are distributors of display equipment.

8589 www.mpiweb.org
Meeting Planners International
Meeting industry professionals who plan and/or manage meetings, trade shows and conferences for corporations, educational institutions and associations.

8590 www.naca.org
National Association for Campus Activities
Largest collegiate organization for campus activities.

8591 www.nceeonline.org
National Catholic Educational Exhibitors
A group for companies that provide products or services for Catholoc education.

8592 www.pcma.org
Professional Convention Management Association
Features emphasize solutions of practical and logistical problems concerning business travel, the hospitality/hotel industry, and related event planning topics

8593 www.publicshows.com
National Association of Consumer Shows
Non-profit organization dedicated to furthering the interests of consumer show producers and suppliers.

8594 www.rcmaweb.org
Religious Conference Management Association
Provides members with a wealth of resources designed specifically to enhance their professionalism and overall effectiveness as religious leaders.

8595 www.sgmp.org
Society of Government Meeting Planners
Trade association for government meeting planners and exhibitors.

8596 www.tsea.org
Trade Show Exhibitors Association
Provides knowledge to marketing and management professionals.

Associations

8597 ACA International
Association of Credit and Collection
Professionals
4040W 70th Street
Minneapolis, MN 55435

952-926-6547
FAX 952-926-1624
E-Mail: aca@acainternational.org
Home Page: www.acainternational.org
Social Media: *Facebook, Twitter, LinkedIn,
YouTube, The Hub*

Mark Neeb, President

International trade organization of over 5,300
credit and collection professionals providing a
variety of accounts receivable management services to over 1,000,000 credit grantors.

**8598 About US Association for Financial
Counseling and Planning Education**
1940 Duke Street
Suite 200
Alexandria, VA 22314

703-684-4484
FAX 703-684-4485
E-Mail: rwiggins@afcpe.org
Home Page: www.afcpe.org
Social Media: *Facebook, Twitter, LinkedIn*

Michael Gutter, President
Barry Wilkinson, Past President
Jinhee Kim, President-Elect
Brenda Vaughn, Secretary
Leslie Green-Pimentel, Treasurer

AFCPE is a non-profit professional organization created to promote the education and training of the professional in financial
management.
810 Members
Founded in 1983

**8599 Alliance of Merger & Acquisition
Advisors**
222 North LaSalle Avenue
Suite 300
Chicago, IL 60601

312-856-9590
877-844-2535
FAX 312-729-9800
E-Mail: info@amaaonline.org
Home Page: www.amaaonline.com
Social Media: *Facebook, Twitter, LinkedIn,
Google+*

Michael Nall, CM&AA, CGMA, Founder and
Managing Director
Diane Niederman, VP Business Development
Amie Schneider, Director of Operations
Dylan Whitcher, CM&AA, Business
Development Manager
Maxie Gallegos, Social Media & Marketing
Specialist

AM&AA is the premier International Organization serving the educational and resource needs
of the middle market M&A profession.
Founded in 1998

**8600 Alliance of Merger and Acquisition
Advisors**
222 North LaSalle Avenue
Suite 300
Chicago, IL 60601

312-856-9590
877-844-2535
FAX 312-729-9800
E-Mail: info@amaaonline.org
Home Page: www.amaaonline.com

Social Media: *Facebook, Twitter, LinkedIn,
Google+*

Michael Nall, CM&AA, CGMA, Founder and
Managing Director
Diane Niederman, VP Business Development
Amie Schneider, Director of Operations
Dylan Whitcher, CM&AA, Business
Development Manager
Maxie Gallegos, Social Media & Marketing
Specialist

A national organization serving the educational
and resource needs of the M&A profession.
200 Members
Founded in 1999

8601 Allied Financial Adjusters Conference
956 S. Bartlett Road
Suite 321
Bartlett, IL 60103

800-843-1232
FAX 888-949-8520
E-Mail: alliedfinanceadjusters@gmail.com
Home Page: www.alliedfinanceadjusters.com
Social Media: *Facebook, LinkedIn, YouTube*

George Badeen, President
Jamie Hernandez, First Vice President
James Osselburn, Second Vice President
Elisa Schmid, Executive Secretary
Bryan Finn, Treasurer

Membership is composed of professsional liquidators, repossessors and skip tracers. Membership fee varies with size of populations of
the city served.
200 Members
Founded in 1936

**8602 American Association of Individual
Investors**
625 N Michigan Ave
Suite 1900
Chicago, IL 60611-3151

312-280-0170
800-428-2244
FAX 312-280-9883
E-Mail: members@aaii.com
Home Page: www.aaii.com

James B Cloonan, Ph.D., CEO

An independent, nonprofit corporation formed
in 1978 for the purpose of assisting individuals
in becoming effective managers of their own
assets through programs of education, information and research.
13000 Members
Founded in 1978

**8603 American Association of Residential
Mortgage Regulators**
1025 Thomas Jefferson Street NW
Suite 500 East
Washington, DC 20007

202-521-3999
FAX 202-833-3636
E-Mail: efreundel@aarmr.org
Home Page: www.aarmr.org

Cindy Begin, President
Charlie Fields, Vice President
Don DeBastiani, Treasurer
Louisa Broudy, Secretary
David A. Saunders, Executive Director

Members are state employees responsible for
administration or residential mortgage oversight. Primary members include model legislation and best practics.
100 Members
Founded in 1989

8604 American Bankers Association
1120 Connecticut Avenue NW
Washington, DC 20036-3902

202-663-5000
800-226-5377
FAX 202-828-4540
E-Mail: custserv@aba.com
Home Page: www.aba.com
Social Media: *Facebook, Twitter, LinkedIn,
YouTube, Google+, Instagram*

John A. Ikard, Chairman
R. Daniel Blanton, Chairman-Elect
Dorothy A. Savarese, Vice Chairman
G. William Beale, Treasurer
Frank Keeting, President and CEO

Brings together all categories of banking institutions to best represent the interests of this
rapidly changing industry. It's membership —
which includes community, regional and
money center banks and holding companies, as
well as savings associations, trust companies
and savings banks, makes ABA one of the largest banking trade associations in the country.
Founded in 1875

8605 American Bankruptcy Institute
66 Canal Center Plaza
Suite 600
Alexandria, VA 22314-1546

703-739-0800
FAX 703-739-1060
E-Mail: support@abiworld.org
Home Page: www.abiworld.org
Social Media: *Facebook, Twitter, LinkedIn,
Flickr*

Patricia A. Redmond, Chairman
James Patrick Shea, President
Brian L. Shaw, Immediate Past President
Jeffrey N. Pomerantz, President Elect
Douglas E. Deutsch, Vice President-Research /
Grants

Multidisiplinary, nonpartisan organization dedicated to research and education on matters related to insovency. Engaged in numerous
educational and research activities as well as
the production of a number of publications
both for the insolvency practitioner and the
public.
11700 Members
Founded in 1982

8606 American Benefits Council
1501 M St. NW
Suite 600
Washington, DC 20005

202-289-6700
FAX 202-289-4582
E-Mail: info@abcstaff.orf
Home Page: www.americanbenefitscouncil.org

James A. Klein, President
Lynn D. Dudley, SVP, Global Retirement &
Comp. Pol.
Katy Spangler, SVP, Health Policy

On behalf of its members - benefit plan sponsors or service providers - advocates for employer-sponsored benefit programs in
Washington.

8607 American Cash Flow Association
255 S Orange Avenue
#600
Orlando, FL 32801

407-206-6523
800-253-1294
E-Mail: info@americancashflow.com
Home Page: www.acfa.org

Fred Rewey, President

8608 American Council of Life Insurance
101 Constitution Ave NW
Suite 700
Washington, DC 20001-2133

202-624-2000
877-674-4659
E-Mail: contact@acli.com
Home Page: www.acli.com
Social Media: *Facebook, Twitter, YouTube*

Dirk Kempthorne, President & Chief Executive Officer
Larry Burton, CEO
Brian Waidmann, Chief of Staff
Gary E. Hughes, Executive Vice President
David C. Turner, Executive Vice President

Works to advance the interests of the life insurance industry and to provide effective government relations. Conducts investment and social research programs.
631 Members
Founded in 1976

8609 American Education Finance Association
8365 S Armadillo Trail
Evergreen, CO 80439

303-674-0857
FAX 303-670-8986
Home Page: www.aefa.cc

Ed Steinbecher, Executive Director

AEFA encourages communications among groups and individuals in the education finance field, including academicians, researchers, policy makers and practitioners. Serving as a forum for a broad range of issues and concerns, AEFA concerns include traditional school finance concepts, issues of public policy, and teaching school finance.
650 Members
Founded in 1975
Mailing list available for rent

8610 American Finance Association
350 Main Street
Malden, MA 02148

781-388-8599
800-835-6770
FAX 781-388-8232
E-Mail: cs-membership@wiley.com
Home Page: www.afajof.org
Social Media: *Facebook, Twitter*

Patrick Bolton, President
Campbell R. Harvey, President Elect
David Scharfstein, Vice President
James (Jim) Schallheim, Executive Secretary and Treasurer
Kenneth J. Singleton, Editor of the Journal of Finance

Seeks to improve public understanding of financial problems and to provide for exchange of ideas.
11500 Members
Founded in 1939

8611 American Financial Services Association
919 18th Street NW
Suite 300
Washington, DC 20006-5517

202-296-5544
E-Mail: info@afsamail.org
Home Page: www.afsaonline.org
Social Media: *Facebook, Twitter, LinkedIn, Google+*

Andrew Stuart, Chair
Nathan D. Benson, Chair-Elect
Gary Phillips, Immediate Past Chair
Chris Stinebert, President & CEO
Jeffery D. Adams, Executive Vice President

The American Financial Services Association is the national trade association for market funded providers of financial services to consumers and small business. These providers offer an array of financial services, including unsecured personal loans, automotive loans, home equity loans and credit cards through specialized bank institutions
400 Members
Founded in 1916

8612 American Society of Appraisers
11107 Sunset Hills Rd
Suite 310
Reston, VA 20190

703-478-2228
800-272-8258
FAX 703-742-8471
E-Mail: asainfo@appraisers.org
Home Page: www.appraisers.org
Social Media: *Facebook, Twitter, YouTube*

Linda B. Trugman, ASA, International President
Susan Golashovsky, ASA, International Vice President
Sharon A. Desfor, ASA, International Secretary/Treasurer
Gary L. Smith, ASA, MGA, International Past President
Gary Snowdon, ASA, Region 1 Governor

Professional association of appraisers of all kinds.
6500 Members
Founded in 1936

8613 American Society of Military Comptrollers
415 N Alfred St
Alexandria, VA 22314-2269

703-549-0360
800-462-5637
FAX 703-549-3181
Home Page: www.asmconline.org
Social Media: *Facebook, Twitter, LinkedIn*

Mr. Craig Bennett, President
Gretchen Anderson, Vice President
Mr. Mike Ramsey, Vice President
Mr. Richard Voigt, Vice President
Ann-Cecile M. McDermott, Vice President

ASMC is the successor to the Society of Military Accountants and Statisticians.
18000 Members
Founded in 1948

8614 American Trucking Associations
950 North Glebe Road
Suite 210
Arlington, VA 22203-4181

703-838-1700
E-Mail: nafc@trucking.org
Home Page: www.truckline.com
Social Media: *Facebook, Twitter, YouTube*

Pat Thomas, Chairman
Kevin Burch, First Vice Chairman
David Manning, Second Vice Chairman
Bill Graves, President & CEO
John M. Smith, Secretary

ATA's mission is to serve and represent the trucking industry with a single, united voice to influence policies beneficial to the industry; promote safety on America's highways; improve the industry's image, efficiency, and competitiveness; educate the public about the critical role trucking plays in the economy
1000 Members
Founded in 1933

8615 Association for Financial Professionals
4520 East West Hwy
Suite 750
Bethesda, MD 20814-3319

301-907-2862
FAX 301-907-2864
E-Mail: customerservice@afponline.org
Home Page: www.afponline.org
Social Media: *Facebook, Twitter, LinkedIn, YouTube*

Anthony Scaglione, CTP, Chairman
Roberta Eiseman, CTP, Vice Chairman
Jeff Johnson, CTP, CPA, Vice Chairman
Ann Anthony, CTP, Board of Director
Terry Crawford, CTP, Board of Director

Association of 12,000 financial professionals. Please call for our publication listings or visit us online.
14000 Members
Founded in 1979

8616 Association for Financial Technology
10813 Pleasant Valley Road
Frazeysburg, OH 43822

614-895-1208
FAX 614-895-3466
E-Mail: aft@aftweb.com
Home Page: www.aftweb.com
Social Media: *Twitter, LinkedIn*

Wade Arnold, President
Russ Bernthal, Immediate Past President & Scholars
Xan Kasprzak, Vice President & Program Committee
James R. Bannister, Executive Director
Susan Hurley, Managing Director

Trade association for companies providing services to the financial industry. Our members provide systems, applications and outsourcing services to 90% of America's banks. Vendors of computer hardware, software and ancilliary products and services are also welcome.
52 Members
Founded in 1975

8617 Association for Management Information in Financial Services
14247 Saffron Circle
Carmel, IN 46032

317-815-5857
FAX 317-815-5877
E-Mail: ami2@amifs.org
Home Page: www.amifs.org
Social Media: *LinkedIn*

Jefferson Nathasingh, President
Robert McDonald, EVP
Meg Foster, Treasurer
Andy Streiff, Immediate Past President
Kevin W. Link, Executive Director

The Association for Management Information in Financial Services is the preeminent organization for management information professionals in the financial services industry.
300 Members
Founded in 1980

8618 Association for the Advancement of Cost Engineering
1265 Suncrest Towne Centre Drive
Morgantown, WV 26505-1876

304-296-8444
FAX 304-291-5728
E-Mail: info@aacei.org
Home Page: www.aacei.org
Social Media: *Twitter, LinkedIn*

Ms Julie K. Owen, CCP, PSP, President
Mr John C. Livengood, President-Elect
Mr James E. Krebs, PE, CCP, VP - Administration

Mr. Joseph W. Wallwork. PE, CCP,CFCC, VP - Finance
Dr. Dan Melamed CCP, EVP, VP -TEC

The leading-edge professional society for cost estimators, cost engineers, schedulers project managers, and project control specialists.
7000 Members
Founded in 1956

8619 Association of Commercial Finance Attorneys

Kennedy Covington Lobdell & Hickman, LLP
214 N Tryon St
22nd Floor
Charlotte, NC 28202-2367

704-350-7721
E-Mail: acfa@acfalaw.org
Home Page: www.acfalaw.org

Alison Manzer, President
R. Marshall Grodner, Vice President
Janet Nadile, Vice President
Paul Ricotta, Treasurer
Kenneth Lewis, Secretary

ACF members are attorneys specializing in commercial finance and bankruptcy law, ACFA provides continuing education and publishes material relevant to the field for its members.
350 Members
Founded in 1958

8620 Association of Finance and Insurance Professionals

4104 Felps Drive
Suite H
Colleyville, TX 76034-5868

817-428-2434
FAX 817-428-2534
E-Mail: info@afip.com
Home Page: www.afip.com
Social Media: *Facebook, Twitter, LinkedIn*

Deb Hankins, Manager
Linda J Robertson, Senior Vice President

A nonprofit educational foundation that serves the needs of in-dealership finance and insurance personnel for the automobile, RV, commercial truck and equipment, motorcycle, and motorized sports industries while assisting the lenders, vendors and independent general agents who support the F&I function.
Founded in 1989
Mailing list available for rent

8621 Association of Government Accountants

2208 Mount Vernon Avenue
Alexandria, VA 22301-1314

703-684-6931
800-AGA-7211
FAX 703-548-9367
E-Mail: agacgfm@agacgfm.org
Home Page: www.agacgfm.org
Social Media: *LinkedIn*

Ann M. Ebberts, MS, PMP, Chief Executive Officer
John E. Homan, MBA, CGFM, 2015-2016 National President
Cristina Barbudo, MS, CPA, Director of Finance
Katya Silver, Director of Professionals
Maryann Malesardi, Director of Communications/Journal

AGA is an educational association dedicated to enhancing public financial management by serving the professional interests of governmental managers and public accounting firms.
15000 Members
Founded in 1950

8622 Association of Mortgage Professionals

2701 W. 15th Street
Suite 536
Plano, TX 75075

972-758-1151
FAX 530-484-2906
E-Mail: membership@namb.org
Home Page: www.namb.org
Social Media: *Facebook, Twitter, LinkedIn, YouTube*

John Councilman, CMC, CRMS, President
Rocke Andrews, CMC, CRMS, President-Elect
Fred Kreger, CMC, Vice President
Rick Bettencourt,CRMS, Secretary
Andy W. Harris ,CRMS, Treasurer

The only national trade association representing the mortgage broker industry. Promotes the industry through programs and services such as education, professional certification and government affairs representation.
25000 Members
Founded in 1973

8623 BCCA

550 W Frontage Rd
Suite 3600
Northfield, IL 60093-1243

847-881-8757
FAX 847-784-8059
E-Mail: info@bccacredit.com
Home Page: www.bccacredit.com
Social Media: *LinkedIn*

Ralph Bender , CFO, Chairman
Timothy Mulvaney, Vice Chair
Mary M. Collins, President & CEO
Robert Damon, Secretary
Cindy Pekrul, Treasurer

BCCA is the media industry's credit association that functions as a central clearing house for credit information on advertisers, agencies and buying services, both locally and nationally. Also provides an Electronic Media Credit Application (EMCAPP.com) to members that helps streamline the application process. One app in one location
600 Members
Founded in 1972

8624 Bond Market Foundation

360 Madison Avenue
New York, NY 10017-7111

646-637-9067
FAX 646-637-9120

Micah Green

The Bond Market Foundation is a charitable and educational not for profit (501-c-3) association. The Foundation develops and enhances the public's access to quality saving and investor education in addition to providing credible non-proprietary research capacity and expert discussion on public issues relevant to the bond markets. The Bond Market Foundation is partner to the Securities Industry and Financial Markets Association (SIFMA).

8625 Broadcast Cable Credit Association

550 W Frontage Rd
Suite 3600
Northfield, IL 60093-1243

847-881-8757
FAX 847-784-8059
E-Mail: info@bccacredit.com
Home Page: www.bccacredit.com
Social Media: *Twitter, LinkedIn*

Ralph Bender , CFO, Chairman
Timothy Mulvaney, Vice Chair
Mary M. Collins, President & CEO
Robert Damon, Secretary
Cindy Pekrul, Treasurer

Subsidiary of the Media Financial Management Association. BCCA provides credit information, education, and netwroking opportunities which enables members to efficiently manage credit risk and increase profitability.
600 Members
Founded in 1972

8626 CFA Institute

560 Ray C. Hunt Drive
PO Box 3668
Charlottesville, VA 22903

434-951-5499
800-247-8132
FAX 434-951-5262
E-Mail: info@cfainstitute.org
Home Page: www.cfainstitute.org
Social Media: *Facebook, Twitter, LinkedIn, YouTube, Google+, Instagram*

Beth Hamilton- Keen, CFA, Chair, Board of Governors
Frederic P. Lebel, CFA, Vice Chair
Aaron Low, CFA, Immediate Past Chair
Paul Smith, CFA, President & CEO
John L. Bowman , CFA, Managing Director

CFA Institute is the global, non-profit professional association that administers the Chartered Financial Analyst curriculum and examination program worldwide and sets voluntary, ethics-based professional and performance-reporting standards for the investment industry.
70000 Members
Founded in 1990

8627 CRE Finance Council

20 Broad St
7th Ffloor
New York, NY 10005

FAX 646-884-7569
E-Mail: info@crefc.org
Home Page: www.crefc.org
Social Media: *Facebook, Twitter, LinkedIn*

Gregory Michaud, Chairman
Matthew Borstein, Chairman-Elect
Nik Chillar, Membership Committee Chair
Daniel E. Bober, Treasurer
Stephen M. Renna, President & CEO

International trade organization for the commercial real estate capital markets. Also represents and promotes an orderly ans ethical global institutional secondary market for the sale of commercial mortgage loans and equity investments.
309 Members
Founded in 1994

8628 Coalition of Higher Education Assistance Organizations

1101 Vermont Ave NW
Suite 400
Washington, DC 20005-3586

202-289-3910
FAX 202-371-0197
E-Mail: hwadsworth@wpllc.net
Home Page: www.coheao.com

Maria Livolsi, President
Carl Perry, Vice President
Tom Schmidt, Secretary
Lori Hartung, Treasurer
Robert Perrin, Past President

Focus is on legislative and regulatory advocacy for Federal Perkins and other campus based student loan programs.
365 Members
Founded in 1981

8629 Commercial Finance Association

370 7th Avenue
Suite 1801
New York, NY 10001

212-792-9390
FAX 212-564-6053
E-Mail: info@cfa.com
Home Page: www.cfa.com
Social Media: *Facebook, Twitter, LinkedIn, YouTube*

Michael Coiley, Chairman of the Board
Patrick Trammel, President
Andrea Petro, First Vice President
D. Michael Monk, Vice President - Finance
David Grende, Vice President

Trade group of the asset based financial services industry, with members throughout the US, Canada and around the world. Members include the asset based lending arms of domestic and foreign commercial banks, small and large independent finance companies, floor plan financing organizations, factoring organizations and financing subsidiaries of major industrial corporations. CFA membership is by organization, not by individual.
300 Members
Founded in 1944

8630 Defense Credit Union Council

601 Pennsylvania Ave NW
South Building, Suite 600
Washington, DC 20004-2601

202-638-3950
FAX 202-638-3410
E-Mail: admin@dcuc.org
Home Page: www.dcuc.org
Social Media: *Facebook, Twitter*

Denise Floyd, Chairman & At Large Representative
Gordon A. Simmons, 1st Vice Chair
Frank Padak, 2nd Vice Chair
Michael Kloiber, Secretary & Air Force Rep.
Craig Chamberlin, Treasurer & Marine Corps Rep

Organizations of credit unions whose membership consists wholly or in part of personnel of the US Department of Defense, both military and civilians.
14 m Members
Founded in 1963

8631 EMTA - Emerging Markets Trade Association

360 Madison Avenue
17th Floor
New York, NY 10017

646-289-5410
FAX 646-289-5429
E-Mail: awerner@emta.org
Home Page: www.emta.org

Mark L. Coombs, Co-Chair
Robert H. Milam, J.P, Co-Chair
Brian Weinstein, Vice Chair
Alberto Agrest, Vice Chair
Marcel Naime, Vice Chair

EMTA is the principal trade group for the Emerging Markets trading and investment community and is dedicated to promoting the orderly development of fair, efficient, and transparent trading markets for Emerging Markets into the global capital markets.
Founded in 1990

8632 Emerging Markets Private Equity Association

1077 30th St. NW
Suite 100
Washington, DC 20007

202-333-8171
E-Mail: support@empea.org

Home Page: empea.org
Social Media: *Facebook, Twitter, LinkedIn*

Robert W. van Zwieten, President & CEO
Shannon Stroud, VP, Programs & Business Development
Randy Mitchell, VP, Strategic Engagement
Ann Marie Plubell, VP, Regulatory Affairs

A nonprofit organization that supports private equity investors in emerging markets with data and market intelligence.

8633 Evangelical Council for Financial Accountability

440 W Jubal Early Dr
Auite 100
Winchester, VA 22601-6319

540-535-0103
800-323-9473
FAX 540-535-0533
E-Mail: info@ecfa.org
Home Page: www.ecfa.org
Social Media: *Facebook, Twitter, LinkedIn, YouTube*

Michael Little, Chair
Michael Batts, Vice Chair
Kenneth Larson, Secretary
Richard A. Alvis, Treasurer
Thomas Addington, Board Member

Helps organizations earn the public's trust through developing and maintaining standards of accountability that convey ethical practices.
1500 Members
Founded in 1979

8634 FSC/DISC Tax Association

3 Bethesda Metro Center
Suite 250
Bethesda, MD 20814-5377

703-341-3500
800-372-1033
FAX 914-328-5757
E-Mail: blawhelp@bna.com
Home Page: www.bna.com
Social Media: *Facebook, Twitter*

Michele Harris, Principal
Joan Fisher, Vice President
Sri Rajan, Manager

The only organization operating on a national level devoted to educational interests of companies that have set up a foreign sales corporation.
300 Members
Founded in 1982

8635 Financial & Security Products Association (FSPA)

1024 Mebane Oaks Road
Suite 273
Mebane, NC 27302

919-648-0664
800-843-6082
FAX 919-648-0670
E-Mail: info@fspa1.com
Home Page: www.fspa1.com

Linda Abell, Chairman
L. A. Smith, President
Gene Polito, Vice President
Kevin Callahan, Secretary/Treasurer
Joe Petchulat, Director

Independent dealers, manufacturers and associates whose outstanding products and services give financial institutions a crucial edge in performance, efficiency and economy.
Founded in 1973

8636 Financial Executives International

1250 Headquarters Plaza
West Tower, 7th Floor
Morristown, NJ 07960

973-765-1000
FAX 973-765-1018
E-Mail: membership@financialexecutives.org
Home Page: www.financialexecutives.org
Social Media: *Facebook, Twitter, LinkedIn, YouTube, Google+*

Taylor Hawes, Sr., Chair
Donald Robillard, Jr., Vice Chair
Gregory Ulferts, National Secretary
Ann Flatz, National Treasurer
Marie N. Hollein, CTP, President and CEO

A professional organization of individuals performing the duties of CFO, Controller, Treasurer or VP of Finance. Has an annual budget of $6.5 million.
15M Members
Founded in 1931

8637 Financial Management Association International

University of South Florida
4202 E Fowler Ave
BSN 3331
Tampa, FL 33620-5500

813-974-2084
FAX 813-974-3318
E-Mail: fma@coba.usf.edu
Home Page: www.fma.org

Jay R. Ritter, President
David Denis, President-Elect
Brad Barber, Vice President- Program
John Graham, Vice President- Elect
Andrea J. Heuson, Treasurer

The mission of the FMA is to broaden the common interests between academicians and practitioners, provide opportunities for professional interaction between and among academicians, practitioners and students, promote the development and understanding of basic and applied research and of sound financial practices, and to enhance the quality of financial education in finance.
3000 Members
Founded in 1970

8638 Financial Managers Society

1 North LaSalle Street
Suite 3100
Chicago, IL 60602-4003

312-578-1300
800-275-4367
FAX 312-578-1308
E-Mail: info@fmsinc.org
Home Page: www.fmsinc.org/cms

Sydney K. Garmong, Chairman
John Westwood, Vice Chairman
Alan Renfroe, Immediate Past President
Dick Yingst, President
Darrell E. Blocker, Director- At- Large

Is the only individual membership society exclusively serving the technical and professional needs of today's bank, thrift and credit union financial officers.
1600 Members
Founded in 1948

8639 Financial Markets Association

333 Second Street NE
#104
Washington, DC 20002

202-547-6327
E-Mail: dp-fma@starpower.org
Home Page: www.fmaweb.org

Peter Wadkins, President
Geoffrey Gowey, Vice President
Robert J Tum-Suden, Treasurer
Carlene Crnkovich, Secretary

A world-class organization of Foreign Exchange, Money Market, and Derivative traders, salespersons, brokers, vendors, and corporate participants organized for the purpose of education, promotion, fellowship, and advancement of the wholesale market within the United States.
300 Members
Founded in 1958

8640 Financial Planning Association

7535 E. Hampden Avenue
Suite 600
Denver, CO 80231

303-759-4900
800-322-4237
FAX 303-759-0749
E-Mail: info@onefpa.org
Home Page: www.plannersearch.org
Social Media: *Facebook, Twitter, LinkedIn*

Marv Tuttle, Executive Director
Ian McKenzie, Managing Director/Publishing
Lauren Schadle CAE, Associate Executive Director/COO

FPA is the professional membership association that represents the financial planning community.
29000 Members
Founded in 2000

8641 Financial Services Technology Consortium

600 13th Street NW
Suite 400
Washington, DC 20005

202-289-4322
FAX 202-628-2558
E-Mail: bits@fsround.org
Home Page: www.bits.org
Social Media:

Christopher F. Feeney, President
Nancy Guglielmo, Vice President
Andrew Kennedy, Senior Program Manager
Josh Magri, Regulatory Counsel
Denise Miller, Executive & Comm. Assistant

Association of leading North American-based financial institutions, technology vendors, independent research organizations and government agencies. Goal is to promote interoperable, open-standard technologies that provide critical infrastructures for the finacial services industry.
Founded in 1993

8642 Financial Services Roundtable

600 13th Street NW
Suite 400
Washington, DC 20005

202-289-4322
FAX 202-628-2558
E-Mail: info@fsroundtable.org
Home Page: www.fsroundtable.org
Social Media: *Twitter, LinkedIn, YouTube*

Frederick H Waddel, Chairman
Ajaypal S. Banga, Chairman-Elect
Larry Zimpleman, Immediate Past Chairman
Kessel Stelling, Treasurer
Richard K. Davis, Director

Mission is to be the premier executive forum for the leaders of the financial services industry; to provide powerful legislative and regulatory advocacy; to enhance the industry's public reputation; and led by BITS, to promote best practices and a strong infrastrucutre in technology.
Founded in 1993

8643 Financial Services Technology Consortium

600 13th Street NW
Suite 400
Washington, DC 20005

202-289-4322
FAX 202-628-2558
E-Mail: bits@fsround.org
Home Page: www.bits.org

Christopher F. Feeney, President
Nancy Guglielmo, Vice President
Andrew Kennedy, Senior Program Manager
Josh Magri, Regulatory Counsel
Denise Miller, Executive & Comm. Assistant

FSTC sponsors product testing, development programs, and other projects to ensure the continued viability of new technologies in the financial sector.
Founded in 1993

8644 Financial Services Technology Network

411 Borel Ave
Ste 620
San Mateo, CA 94402

312-782-4951
FAX 312-580-0165
E-Mail: fstn@gss.net
Home Page: www.fsnweb.com
Social Media: *Facebook, Twitter, LinkedIn*

Kathleen Luleasile, Executive Director
Dale Smith, President
Kathy Johnson, Secretary/Treasurer

8645 Financial Women International

1027 W Roselawn Avenue
Roseville, MN 55113

651-487-7632
866-807-6081
FAX 651-489-1322
E-Mail: info@fwi.org
Home Page: www.fwi.org

Melissa Curzon, President
Cindy Hass, VP
Carleen DeSisto, Secretary

FWI is dedicated to developing leaders, accelerating careers, and generating results for professionals in the banking and financial services industry.
1000 Members
Founded in 1921

8646 Fraud & Theft Information Bureau

9770 S Military Trail
Suite 380
Boynton Beach, FL 33436

561-737-8700
FAX 561-737-5800
E-Mail: sales@fraudandtheftinfo.com
Home Page: www.fraudandtheft.com

Larry Schwartz, Founder/Director
Pearl Sax, Founder/Director

A leading consultant on credit card and check fraud control and loss prevention, and the publisher of related manuals and fraud-blocker data bases.
Founded in 1982

8647 Futures Industry Association

2001 Pennsylvania Ave NW
Suite 600
Washington, DC 20006-1823

202-446-5460
FAX 202-296-3184
E-Mail: info@fia.org
Home Page: www.fia.org

Social Media: *Facebook, Twitter, LinkedIn, Flickr*

Gerald Corcoran, Chairman & CEO
M. Clark Hutchison, Treasurer
Emily Portney, Secretary
Craig Abruzzo, Managing Director
Antoine Babule, Managing Director

Representative of all organizations that have an interest in the futures market.
180 Members
Founded in 1955

8648 Global Association of Risk Professionals

111 Town Square Place
14th Floor
Jersey City, NJ 07310-2778

201-719-7210
FAX 201-222-5022
E-Mail: Memberservices@garp.com
Home Page: www.garp.com
Social Media: *Facebook, Twitter, LinkedIn, Google+, YouTube*

William Martin, Chairman
Jacques Longerstaey, Chairman Compensation Committee
Dr. Ren, Stulz, Chairman Governance Committee
Victor Ng, Chairman Adult & Risk Committee
Richard Apostolik, President & CEO

GARP's international membership includes a varity of professionals from the finance industry who share a common interest in financial risk management practice and research.
52330 Members
Founded in 2000

8649 Government Finance Officers Association

203 N La Salle St
Suite 2700
Chicago, IL 60601-1216

312-977-9700
FAX 312-977-4806
E-Mail: inquiry@gfoa.org
Home Page: www.gfoa.org
Social Media: *Facebook, Twitter, LinkedIn, YouTube*

Heather A. Johnston, President
Marc Gonzales, President-Elect
Bob Eichem, Past President
Robert Bishop, Director Of Finance
Lori A. Economy-Scholler, Chief Financial Officer

The purpose of the Government Finance Officers Association is to enhance and promote the professional management of governments for the public benefit by identifying and developing financial policies and practices and promoting them through education, training and leadership.
17300 Members
Founded in 1906

8650 Healthcare Billing and Management Association

2025 M Street NW
Suite 800
Washington, DC 20036

877-640-4262
FAX 202-367-2177
E-Mail: info@hbma.org
Home Page: www.hbma.org
Social Media: *Facebook, Twitter, LinkedIn, YouTube*

Andre Williams, Executive Director
Zoe Fuller, Operations & Administration
Caroline Fabacher, Program Coordinator
Ellie Hurley, Event Services
David Merli, Advertising/ Sales

Members are companies providing third-party medical billing services.
500 Members
Founded in 1993
Mailing list available for rent

8651 Healthcare Financial Management Association

3 Westbrook Corporate Center
Suite 600
Westchester, IL 60154

708-531-9600
800-252-4362
FAX 708-531-0032
E-Mail: webmaster@hfma.org
Home Page: www.hfma.org
Social Media: *Facebook, Twitter, LinkedIn, YouTube*

Joseph J. Fifer, FHFMA, CPA, CEO & President
Edwin P. Czopek, FHFMA, CPA, CA, Senior Vice President
Susan Brenkus, Vice President, Human Resources
Richard L Gundling, Vice President, Healthcare
Tod Nelson, Vice President, Education

Brings perspective and clarity to the industry's complex issues for the purpose of preparing our members to succeed. Through our programs, publications and partnerships we enhance the capabilities that strengthen not only individual careers, but also the organizations from which our members come.
40000 Members

8652 Initiatives of Change, USA

2201 West Broad Street
Suite 200
Richmond, VA 23220-2022

804-305- 176
FAX 804-358-1769
E-Mail: support@web.iofc.org
Home Page: www.us.iofc.org
Social Media: *Facebook, Twitter*

H. Alexander Wise, Chairman
Patrick T. Mcnamara, Executive Vice Chairman
William S. Elliott, Executive Director
Valerie Lemmie, Treasurer
Anjum A. Ali, Secretary

Is the national voice for lenders and investors engaged in the reverse mortgage business.
Founded in 1997
Mailing list available for rent

8653 Institute for Divorce Financial Analysts

2224 Sedwick Road
Suite 102
Durham, NC 27713

989-631-3605
800-875-1760
FAX 919-287-2952
E-Mail: info@institutedfa.com
Home Page: www.institutedfa.com
Social Media: *Twitter, LinkedIn*

The Institute for Divorce Financial Analysts (IDFAT) is the premier national organization dedicated to the certification, education and promotion of the use of financial professionals in the divorce arena.
Founded in 1993

8654 Institute of Internal Auditors

247 Maitland Ave
Altamonte Springs, FL 32701-4201

407-937-1111
FAX 407-937-1101
E-Mail: customerrelations@theiia.org

Home Page: www.theiia.org
Social Media: *Facebook, Twitter, LinkedIn*

Lawrence J. Harrington, Chairman of the Board
J. Michael Joyce Jr. CIA , CRMA, Chairman of North American Board
Richard F. Chambers, CIA, CGAP, C, President and CEO

Independent, objective assurance and consulting activity designed to add value to an organization's operations. It helps an organization accomplish its objectives by bringing a systematic, disciplined approach to evaluate and improve the effectiveness of risk management, control and governance processes. Representation from more than 100 countries.
10000 Members
Founded in 1941

8655 Institute of International Finance

1333 H St NW
Suite 800 E
Washington, DC 20005-4770

202-857-3600
FAX 202-775-1430
E-Mail: info@iif.com
Home Page: www.iif.com
Social Media: *Facebook, YouTube*

Douglas J. Flint, Chairman
Roberto E Setubal, Vice Chairman
Walter Kielholz, Vice Chairman
Marcus Wallenberg, Vice Chairman and Treasurer
Timothy D. Adams, President and CEO

Members are primarily international, commercial banks that focus on middle-income countries by communicating with the debtor countries, international financial institutions and regulatory agencies in order to improve the process of international lending.
450 Members
Founded in 1983

8656 Institute of Management & Administration

3 Bethesda Metro Center
Suite 250
Bethesda, MD 20814-5377

800-372-1033
703-341-3500
FAX 800-253-0332
E-Mail: blawhelp@bna.com
Home Page: www.ioma.com
Social Media: *Facebook, Twitter, YouTube*

Gregory C. McCaffery, President & CEO
Sue Martin, Chief Operating Officer
Paul Albergo, Bureau Chief
Joe Breda, Executive Vice President - Product
Daniel M. Fine, Executive Vice President- Strategy

An independent source of exclusive business management information for experienced senior and middle management professionals.

8657 Institute of Management Accountants

10 Paragon Drive
Suite 1
Montvale, NJ 07645-1760

201-573-9000
800-638-4427
FAX 201-474-1600
E-Mail: ima@imanet.org
Home Page: www.imanet.org
Social Media: *Facebook, Twitter, LinkedIn, YouTube*

Benjamin R. Mulling CMA, CPA, CITP, Chair
Joseph A. Vincent CMA, Chair- Emeritus
Marc P. Palker CMA, Chair- Elect
Jeffrey C Thomson, President & CEO
Atul Kumar Agarwal, Director

To provide a dynamic forum for management accounting and finance professionals to de-

velop and advance their careers through certification, research and practice development, education, networking, and the advocacy of the highest ethical and professional practices.
65000 Members
Founded in 1919

8658 Institutional Shareholder Services

101 Federal St.
Suite 2105
Boston, MA 02110

646-680-6350
FAX 301-556-0491
Home Page: www.issgovernance.com

Gary Retelny, President & CEO
Stephen Harvey, Chief Revenue Officer
Nancy Adler, Head of Marketing
Chris Cernich, Deputy Director Of Global Research
Mark Brockway, Head of the ISS Corporate Services

Leading provider of independent and impartial research on coporations and their shareholders.
500 Members
Founded in 1972

8659 Interactive & Newsmedia Financial

MFM, 550 W. Frontage Road
Ste. 3600
Northfield, IL 60093

847-716-7000
FAX 847-716-7004
E-Mail: info@mediafinance.org
Home Page: www.infe.org
Social Media: *Twitter, LinkedIn*

Mary M. Collins, President & CEO
Chad Richardsonŷ, Chairman
Dalton A. Lee, Vice Chairman
Jamie L. Smith, MFM/BCCA Director of Operations
Arcelia Pimentel, MFM Membership Manager & Sales

Focuses on newspaper financial management, with members representing most North American newpaper companies, as well as many offshore. INFE's activities include publishing, conferences, workshops, industry surveys and studies, and offers members networking opportunities.
1200 Members
Founded in 1961

8660 International Association of Financial Engineers

555 Eight Avenue
Suite 1902
New York, NY 10018

646-736-0705
FAX 646-417-6378
E-Mail: main@iafe.org
Home Page: www.iaqf.org

David Jaffe, Executive Director

The IAFE is a not-for-profit, professional society dedicated to fostering the profession of quantitative finance by providing platforms to discuss cutting-edge and pivotal issues in the field. Its composed of individual academic and practioners from banks, broker dealers, hedge funds, pension funds, asset managers, technology firms, regulators, accounting, consulting and law firms and universities worldwide.
Founded in 1992

8661 International Association of Purchasing

45 Woodside W
Patchogue, NY 11772

631-654-2384
FAX 516-475-2754

A professional organization dedicated to the advancement of world trade. Membership is

open to buyers, purchasing managers, executives and all individuals that may be involved or have an interest in the important function of buying goods and services on the global market. A nonprofit organization.
1600 Members
Founded in 1985

8662 International Society of Financiers

64 Brookside Drive
Hendersonville, NC 28792-9207

828-698-7805
FAX 828-698-7806
Home Page: www.insofin.com

Ronald I Gershen, Chairman/President

A professional society of brokers, consultants, investors and corporate lenders active in financial projects and transactions. ISF provides an exclusive and confidential forum for member-to-member exchange and business networking.
300 Members
Founded in 1979

8663 International Swaps and Derivatives Association

360 Madison Ave
16th Floor
New York, NY 10017

212-901-6000
FAX 212-901-6001
E-Mail: isda@isda.org
Home Page: www.isda.org

Eric Litvack, Chairman
Richard Prager, Vice Chairman
Keith Bailey, Secretary
Dianeÿ Genova, Treasurer
Yasunobu Arima, Director

Represents firms, primarily financial institutions, corporations and government entities who deal in privately-negoiated derivatives, as well as firms who provide services to such institutions. ISDA's mission is to encourage the productive development of interest rate, currency, commodity, and equity swaps as financial products.
Founded in 1985

8664 International Union of Housing Finance

Rue Jacques de Lalaing 28
B-1040 Brussels
Belgium

322-231-0371
FAX 322-230-8245
E-Mail: info@housingfinance.org
Home Page: www.houisngfinance.org

Dale Bottom, Secretary General

Disseminates information in housing finance policies and techniques worldwide.
107 Members
Founded in 1914

8665 Investment Company Institute

1401 H St NW
Suite 1200
Washington, DC 20005

202-326-5800
E-Mail: webmaster@ici.org
Home Page: www.ici.org
Social Media: *Facebook, Twitter, LinkedIn, vimeo.com*

F.William McNabb III, Chairman
Gregory E. Johnson, Vice Chairman
Paul Schott Stevens, President & CEO
Peter H Gallary, Chief Operating Officer
Donald C Auerbach, Chief Government Affairs Officer

Acts to represent members in matters of legislation, taxation, regulation, economic research

and marketing and public information regarding investments and mutual funds.
9400+ Members
Founded in 1940

8666 Investment Recovery Association

638 W 39th Street
Kansas City, MO 64111

816-561-5323
800-728-2272
FAX 816-561-1991
E-Mail: jmale@swassn.com
Home Page: www.invrecovery.org

Barry Street, President
Sean Byro, Senior Vice President
Kelly May, Secretary
Todd Thompson, Treasurer
Paul Hoffman, Director

Helps fulfill an important role by bringing people together from disparate industries...all focused on sharing best IR practices and improving the knowledge and skills necessary to properly perform the wide-ranging responsibilities required of investment recovery practitioners.

8667 Latin American Private Equity and Venture Capital Association

589 Eighth Ave.
18th Fl.
New York, NY 10018

646-315-6735
Home Page: lavca.org
Social Media: *Twitter, LinkedIn*

Cate Ambrose, President & Executive Director
Ivonne Cuello, Director, Bus. Dev. & Strategy

A nonprofit organization that supports the growth of the private equity and venture capital industry in Latin America.
170+ Members

8668 Media Financial Management Association

550 W. Frontage Road
Suite 3600
Northfield, IL 60093

847-716-7000
FAX 847-716-7004
E-Mail: info@mediafinance.org
Home Page: www.mediafinance.org
Social Media: *Twitter, LinkedIn*

Mary M. Collins, President & CEO
Chad Richardsonÿ, Chairman
Dalton A. Lee, Vice Chairman
Jamie L. Smith, MFM/BCCA Director of Operations
Arcelia Pimentel, MFM Membership Manager & Sales

Professional society of more than 1,300 of media's top financial, MIS Credit and HR executives, plus associates in auditing, data processing, software development, law, tax and credit and collections.
1200 Members
Founded in 1961

8669 Mortgage Bankers Association of America

1919 M Street NW
5th Floor
Washington, DC 20036

202-557-2700
800-793-6222
E-Mail: membership@mortgagebankers.org
Home Page: www.mortgagebankers.org

David H Stevens, President & CEO
Marcia Davies, Chief Operating Officer
Michael Fratantoni, Chief Economist. Enior VP
Peter J. Grace, Senior Vice President
Bill Kilmer, Senior Vice President

Association for all state and local MBA officers.
2200 Members

8670 Mutual Fund Education Alliance

100 NW Englewood Rd
Suite 130
Kansas City, MO 64118-4076

816-454-9422
FAX 816-454-9322
E-Mail: mfea@mfea.com
Home Page: www.mfea.com
Social Media: *Facebook, Twitter*

Michelle Smith, Executive Director

Conducts public education and public relation activities in an effort to acquaint investors, industry organizations and government agencies with direct market funds.
Founded in 1971

8671 Mutual Fund Investors Association

85 Wells Avenue
Suite 109
Newton, MA 02459

617-321-2200
800-492-6868
FAX 61 -32 -221
E-Mail: info@adviserinvestments.com
Home Page: www.kobren.com

Daniel P Weiner, Chair & CEO
David Thorne, President
James H. Lowell, Chief Investment Officer
Chris Keith, Senior Vice President
Jeffrey DeMaso, Director Of Research

Association for those interested in information and rates for mutual funds, investments, stocks and bonds.
Founded in 1994

8672 NACHA - Electronic Payments Association

2550 Wasser Terrace
Suite 400
Herndon, VA 20171

703-561-1100
FAX 703-787-0996
E-Mail: abuse@nacha.org.
Home Page: www.nacha.org
Social Media: *Facebook, Twitter, LinkedIn*

Janet O Estep, CEO
Deb Evans-Doyle, Sr Director Conference Marketing
Julie Hedlund, Sr Director Electronic Commerce
Michael Herd, Director Public Relations

NACHA is a trade association that forms the cooperative foundation for the automated clearing house (ACH) payments system through a network of 21 ACH associations nationwide. It also provides marketing and educational members through direct memberships and a network of regional payment associations.
Founded in 1974

8673 Nat'l Institute of Pension Administrators

330 N Wabash Ave
Suite 2000
Chicago, IL 60611-7621

800-999-6472
800-999-6272
FAX 312-673-6609
E-Mail: nipa@nipa.org
Home Page: www.nipa.org
Social Media: *LinkedIn*

Patrick M. Shelton, President
Michelle Marsh, President Elect and CFO
Joseph Burt, Chief financial Officer
Robert Chin, Director
Ralph DelSesto, Director

The Institute is responsible for the formation
Of professional standards, an ongoing education program consisting of workshops and
home study courses, and awards of the APA
and the APR designations by examination and
experience.
1000 Members
Founded in 1983

8674 National Aircraft Finance Association

PO Box 1570
Edgewater, MD 21037

410-571-1740
FAX 410-571-1780
E-Mail: info@nafa.aero
Home Page: www.nafa.aero
Social Media: *Facebook, Twitter, LinkedIn*

David Jarvis, President
Chris Miller, Vice President
Ford Von Weise, Vice President
Karen Griggs, Executive Director
Anthony Kioussis, Secretary

A non-profit corporation dedicated to promoting the general welfare of individual and organization providing aircraft financing and loans
secured by aircraft; to improve the industry's
service to the public; to work with government
agencies to foster a greater understanding of
our member's needs.
95 Members
Founded in 1969

8675 National Association of Affordable Housing Lenders

1667 K St NW
Suite 210
Washington, DC 20006

202-293-9850
FAX 202-293-9852
E-Mail: naahl@naahl.org
Home Page: www.naahl.org

Buzz Roberts, President & CEO
Paul Haaland, Chief Operating Officer
Sara Olson, Administrative Assistant

Is the only association devoted to increasing
private capital lending and investment in low
and moderate income communities.
800 Members
Founded in 1977

8676 National Association of Bankruptcy Trustees

One Windsor Cove
Suite 305
Columbia, SC 29223

803-252-5646
800-445-8629
FAX 803-765-0860
E-Mail: info@nabt.com
Home Page: www.nabt.com

Richard D. Nelson, President
Dwayne Murray, President Elect
Ronald R. Peterson, Vice President
Brian L. Budsberg, Treasurer
Raymond J. Obuchowski, Secretary

The majority of the members of the NABT are
Chapter 7 trustees who primarily liquidate nonexempt assets for the benefit of creditors.
1200 Members
Founded in 1982

8677 National Association of Certified Valuators and Analysts

5217 South State Street
Suite 400
Salt Lake City, UT 84107

801-486-0600
800-677-2009
FAX 801-486-7500

E-Mail: nacva1@nacva.com
Home Page: www.nacva.com

Pamela Bailey, Executive Advisory Board
Melissa Bizyak, Executive Advisory Board
Parnell Black, Executive Advisory Board
Rod Burket, Executive Advisory Board
Mark Hanson, Executive Advisory Board

Global, professional association that supports
the business valuation and litigation consulting
disciplines within the CPA and professional
communities. Along with its training and certification programs, NACVA offers a range of
support services, reference materials, software,
and customized databases to enhance the professional capabilities and capacities of its
members.
6500 Members
Founded in 1990

8678 National Association of Corporate Treasurers

12100 Sunset Hills Road
Suite 130
Reston, VA 20190-3221

703-437-4377
FAX 703-435-4390
E-Mail: nact@nact.org
Home Page: www.nact.org
Social Media: *LinkedIn*

Ramon Yi, Chairman
Mary Dean Hall, President
Joseph C. Sullivan, Vice-President
Ruud Roggekamp, Secretary/Treasurer
Thomas C. Deas, Immediate Past Chairman

Members are corporate chief financial officers,
treasurers or assistant treasurers.
825 Members
Founded in 1982

8679 National Association of Development Companies

1725 Desales St NW
Suite 504
Washington, DC 20036

202-349-0070
FAX 202-349-0071
E-Mail: info@nadco.org
Home Page: www.nadco.org
Social Media: *Facebook, Twitter, Stumbleupon*

Sally Robertson, Chairman
Mary Mansfield, Vice Chair
Randy Griffin, Treasurer
Pat MacKrell, Secretary
Barbara Vohryxek, President & CEO

Provides long term, fixed asset financing to
small businesses.
135 Members
Founded in 1981

8680 National Association of Division Order Analysts

PO Box 2300
Less Summit, MO 64063

972-715-4489
E-Mail: administrator@nadoa.org
Home Page: www.nadoa.org
Social Media: *Facebook, Twitter, LinkedIn*

Jason Lucas, President
Mary Sons, Vice President
Nancy Cemino, CDOA, 2nd Vice President
Angela Korthauer, Treasurer
Kim Henderson, CDOA, Corresponding
Secretary

Division order analysts are petroleum and gas
company employees or independent consultants
responsible for royalty working interest and
overiding royalty payments. Offers a certification program providing education, training and
testing for qualified applicants desiring to at-

tain Certified Divison Order Analyst
credentials.
900 Members
Frequency: 4
Founded in 1974

8681 National Association of Equipment Leasing Brokers

100 North 20th Steet
Suite 400
Philadelphia, PA 19103

800-996-2352
FAX 215-564-2175
E-Mail: info@naelb.org
Home Page: www.naelb.org
Social Media: *Facebook, Twitter, LinkedIn, YouTube*

Joe Casey, Executive Director
Laura Huestis, Associate Director

Broker-oriented association.
500 Members
Founded in 1990

8682 National Association of Federal Credit Unions

3138 10th St N
Arlington, VA 22201-2149

703-522-4770
800-336-4644
FAX 703-524-1082
E-Mail: msc@nafcu.org.
Home Page: www.nafcu.org
Social Media: *Facebook, Twitter*

B. Dan Berger, President
Anthony W. Demangone, Vice President
Carolyn Sable, Executive Assistant
Leann Obermeir, Executive Assistant
Martin Breland, Region II Director

Trade association exclusively represents the interests of federal credit unions before the federal government and the public. Provides
members with representation, information, education and assistance to meet the challenges
that cooperative financial institutions face in
today's economic environment. Stands as a national forum for the federal credit union community where new ideas, issues, concerns and
trends can be identified, discussed and
resolved.
Founded in 1967

8683 National Association of Independent Public Finance Advisors

19900 MacArthur Boulevard
Suite 1100
Irvine, CA 92612

630-896-1292
844-770-6262
FAX 209-633-6265
E-Mail: rhoban@naipfa.com
Home Page: www.naipfa.com

Jeanine Rogers Caruso, President
Terri Heaton, Vice President
Bruce A. Kimmel, CIPFA, Secretary
Micheal Sudsina, CIPFA, Treasurer
Shelly Aronson,CIPFA, Director at large

A professional organization limited to firms
that specialize in providing financial advice on
bond sales and financial planning on public
projects of public agencies. Promotes the common interests of independent advisory firm
members.
48 Members
Founded in 1989

8684 National Association of Investors Corporation
711 W 13mile Road
Suite 900
Madison Heights, MI 48071

248-654-3047
877-275-6242
FAX 248-583-4880
E-Mail: webmaster@betterinvesting.org
Home Page: www.betterinvesting.org
Social Media: *Facebook, Twitter*

Roger H Ganser, Chairman
Kamie Zaracki, CEO
Stephen Sanborn, Treasurer
Gary Ball, Director
Robert Brooker, Director

Strives to counsel and teach investing techniques and sound investment procedures to interested people.
23000 Members
Founded in 1951

8685 National Association of Local Housing Finance Agencies
2025 M St NW
Suite 800
Washington, DC 20036

202-367-1197
FAX 202-367-2197
E-Mail: info@nalhfa.org
Home Page: www.nalhfa.org

Ron Williams, President
W.D Morris, Vice President
Vivian Benjamin, Treasurer
Tom Cummings, Secretary
Kurt Creager, Director

The National Association of Local Housing Finance Agencies, founded in 1982, is the national association of professionals working to finance affordable housing in the broader community development context at the local level. As a non-profit association, NALHFA is an advocate before Congress and federal agencies on legislative and regulatory issues affecting affordable housing and provides technical assistance and educational opportunities to its members and the public.
Founded in 1982

8686 National Association of Personal Financial Advisors
8700 W. Bryn Mawr Avenue
Suite 700 N
Chicago, IL 60631

847-483-5400
888-333-6659
FAX 847-483-5415
E-Mail: info@napfa.org
Home Page: www.napfa.org

Geoffrey Brown, CEO
Mardi Lee, Assistant to CEO
Bevin Callan, Member Services Senior Manager
Laura J Maddalone, Controller

Members are financial planners who are compensated only by fees. NAPFA members are prohibited from receiving any type of product-related compensation, such as sales commissions. Members do not sell products nor do they direct sales to parties with whom they have financial interests.
2400 Members
Founded in 1983

8687 National Association of Publicly Traded Partnerships
1200 19th Street, NW
Suite 700
Washington, DC 20036

202-973-2400
800-621-8390
FAX 202-973-2401
E-Mail: inquiries@navigant.com
Home Page: www.navigantconsulting.com
Social Media: *LinkedIn, YouTube*

William M Goodyear, Chairman And CEO
Thomas A. Glidehaus, Director
Cynthia A. Glassman, Phd, Director
Julie M. Howard, Director & Navigant CEO
Stephan A. James, Director

A trade association representing publicly traded limited partnerships (and publicly traded LLCs taxed partnerships) and those who work with them.
Founded in 1983
Mailing list available for rent

8688 National Association of Review Appraisers & Mortgage Underwriters
810 N Farrell Drive
Palm Springs, CA 92262

760-327-5284
877-743-6805
FAX 760-327-5631
E-Mail: support@assoc-hdqts.org
Home Page: www.naramu.org
Social Media: *LinkedIn*

Jerry M. Green, Owner
Gary R. Vermaat, President
Robert e. Runyan, Vice President

Association for professionals who review real estate appraisals and underwrite real estate mortgages. The association offers the CRA, Certified Review Appraiser and RMU, Registered Mortgage Underwriter, professional designation.
2852 Members
Founded in 1975
Mailing list available for rent: 3500 names at $75 per M

8689 National Association of Sales Professionals
555 Friendly Street
Bloomfield Hills, MI 48341

480-596-6634
866-365-1520
FAX 248-254-6757
E-Mail: info@nasp.com
Home Page: www.nasp.com
Social Media: *Facebook, Twitter, LinkedIn*

Rod Hairston, CEO & Chairman
Idris Grant, President and COO
Tonia Revere, Director
Sabine Grant, Vice President
Amanda Ritz, Membership, director & advisor

Members are companies who purchase structured settlements, lottery annuities, and similar periodic payment plans from their beneficiaries.
Founded in 1991

8690 National Association of State Budget Officers
444 N Capitol St NW
Suite 642
Washington, DC 20001

202-624-5382
FAX 202-624-7745
E-Mail: spattison@nasbo.org
Home Page: www.nasbo.org
Social Media: *Facebook, Twitter, LinkedIn*

Scott D. Pattison, Executive Director
Stacy Mazer, Senior Staff Associate

Brian Sigritz, Director of State Fiscal Studies
Michael Streepey, Fiscal Policy Analyst
Kathryn Vesey White, Director, Member Relations

Membership limited to three budget officers per state. Affiliated with the National Governors Association.
160 Members
Founded in 1945

8691 National Association of Tax Professionals
PO Box 8002
Appleton, WI 54912-8002

800-558-3402
800-558-3402
FAX 800-747-0001
E-Mail: natp@natptax.com
Home Page: www.natptax.com

Jo Ann Schoen, EA, President
Jean Millerchip,EA,CPF, Vice-President
Gerard F. Cannito CPA,CPF, Treasurer
Praticia(Ann) Mcneer EA, Secretary
Dorothy Atchison, EA, Director

The National Association of Tax Professionals (NATP) is a nonprofit professional association founded in 1979 and is committed to excellence in the tax profession. Our national headquarters is located in Appleton, Wisconsin and employs 42 professionals and 25 instructors. NATP was formed to serve professionals who work in all areas of tax practice and has more than 19,500 members nationwide.
24000 Members
Founded in 1979

8692 National Association of Trade Exchanges
926 easterm Avenue
Malden, MA 02148

617-763-3311
E-Mail: bartertrainer@aol.com
Home Page: www.natebarter.com
Social Media: *Facebook, LinkedIn*

Anne Weiser, President
Ric Zampatti, Vice President
Rolf Wilkin, Director
Maurya Lane, Director
Kim Ames, Secretary

NATE offers their members additional benefits such national and regional meetings and accreditation opportunities.
80 Members
Founded in 1984

8693 National Automotive Finance Association
7037 Ridge Road
Suite 300
Hanover, MD 21076-1343

410-712-4036
800-463-8955
FAX 410-712-4038
E-Mail: inquire@nafassociation.com
Home Page: www.nafassociation.com
Social Media: *LinkedIn*

Steve Hall, Chairman
Mark Floyd, President
Scot Seagrave, Vice President
Ian Anderson, Vice President
Gary Schultz, Secretary

NAF Association serves companies and professionals in the non-prime auto lending industry.
85 Members
Founded in 1996

8694 National Bankers Association
1513 P St Nw
Washington, DC 20005

202-588-5432
FAX 202-588-5443

E-Mail: eholliday@nationalbankers.org
Home Page: www.nationalbankers.org

Preston Pinkett III, Chairman
B. Doyle Mitchell, Immediate Past Chairman
Michael A. Grant, President
Cynthia N. Day, Secretary
Neill S. Wright, Treasurer

Association for banks owned or controlled by
minority group persons or women.
15000 Members
Founded in 1927

**8695 National Community Capital
Association**
Public Ledger Building, 620 Chestnut Street
Suite 572
Philadelphia, PA 19106

215-923-4754
FAX 215-923-4755
E-Mail: info@opportunityfinance.net
Home Page: www.ofn.org
Social Media: *Facebook, Twitter, LinkedIn,
www.vimeo.com*

Trinita Logue, Chair President
Eric Belsky, Executive Director
John Berdes, President/CEO
Keith Bisson, Program Management &
Development
Lori Chatman, Vice Chair

Provides support for nonprofit, revolving loan
funds that lend capital and offer technical assistance in distressed and disenfranchised
communities.
52 Members
Founded in 1986

8696 National Credit Union Administration
1775 Duke St
Alexandria, VA 22314-6115

703-518-6300
FAX 703-518-6539
E-Mail: ociomail@ncua.gov
Home Page: www.ncua.gov

Michael Fryzel, Manager

Governed by a three member board appointed
by the President and confirmed by the US Senate, this independent federal agency charters
and supervises federal credit unions. NCUA,
with the backing of the full faith and credit of
the US government, operates the National
Credit Union Share Insurance Fund, insuring
the savings of 80 million account holders in all
federal credit unions and many state chartered
credit unions.

**8697 National Defined Contribution
Council**
307 Waverley Oaks Rd.
Waltham, MA 02452

781-693-7500
FAX 866-904-9666
Home Page: www.zoominfo.com
Social Media: *Facebook, Twitter, LinkedIn*

Yonaton Stern, CEO & Chief Scientist
Eugenia Gillan, Vice President of Engineering
Steve Hill, Chief Financial Officer
Hila Nir, Vice President of Production Mgt.
Philip Garlick, VP, Corporate Development

NDCC is dedicated to the promotion and protection of the defined contribution industry and
the public it serves. The Council specifically
addresses the legislative needs of the defined
contribution industry's plan service providers.
300 Members
Founded in 1995

**8698 National Federation of Municipal
Analysts**
PO Box 14893
Pittsburgh, PA 15234

412-341-4898
FAX 412-341-4894
E-Mail: lgood@nfma.org
Home Page: www.nfma.org
Social Media: *Twitter, LinkedIn*

Jeffery Burger, Chairman
Susan Dushock, Vice Chairman
Jennifer Johnston, Treasurer
Lisa Washburn, Secretary
Lisa Good, Executive Director

Promotes the profession of municipal credit analysts through educational programs, industry,
communications and related programming.
1000 Members
Founded in 1997

8699 National Finance Adjusters
PO Box 2652
Glenville, NY 12325

623-516-1018
FAX 410-728-2528
E-Mail: info@nfacoop.com
Home Page: www.nfacoop.com

Burton Greenwood Jr, Secretary/Treasurer
Jack S Barnes, Executive Director

Members are collateral recovery specialists.

8700 National Futures Association
300 S. Riverside Plaza
#1800
Chicago, IL 60606-6615

312-781-1300
FAX 312-781-1467
E-Mail: information@nfa.futures.org
Home Page: www.nfa.futures.org

Christopher K. Hehmeyer, Chairman
Michael C. Dawley, Vice Chair
Leo Melamed, Chaise & CEO
Scott A. Cordes, President
Gerald F. Corcoran, Chief Executive Officer

Association for corporations and firms that are
registered with the Commodity Futures Trading
Commission.

**8701 National Home Equity Mortgage
Association**
42484 Bellagio Drive
Bermuda Dunes, CA 92203

760-772-5806
Home Page: www.nhema.org

Jeffrey Zeltzer, Principal

Mission is to promote the growth and recognition of the home equity lending industry.
300 Members
Founded in 1974

**8702 National Institute of Pension
Administrators**
330 N Wabash Ave
Suite 2000
Chicago, IL 60611-7621

800-999-6472
FAX 312-673-6609
E-Mail: nipa@nipa.org
Home Page: www.nipa.org
Social Media: *LinkedIn*

Patrick M. Shelton, GBA, President
Michelle Marsh, QKA, President Elect and
CFO
Joseph Burt, Chief Financial Officer
Darren Holsy, Executive Committee
Member-at-Large
Laura Rudzinski, Executive Director

The mission is to enhance professionalism in
the retirement plan industry
1000 Members
Founded in 1983

**8703 National Investment Company
Service Association**
8400 Westpark Drive
2nd Floor
McLean, VA 22102

508-485-1500
FAX 508-488-1560
E-Mail: info@nicsa.org
Home Page: www.nicsa.org
Social Media: *Facebook, Twitter, LinkedIn,
Google+*

George Batejan, Chairman
Dan Houlihan, Vice Chairman
Barry Benjamin, Treasurer
Steve Avera, Co-Chair
Jim Fitzpatrick, President

NICSA works to facilitate and promote leadership and innovation within the operations sector of the mutual fund industry.
10000 Members
Founded in 1962

8704 National Pawnbrokers Association
891 Keller parkway
Suite 220
Keller, TX 76248

817-337-8830
FAX 817-337-8875
E-Mail: info@nationalpawnbrokers.org
Home Page: www.nationalpawnbrokers.org
Social Media: *Facebook, Twitter, Youtube*

Larry Nuckols, President
Tim Collier, Vice President
Robert Anderson, Treasurer
Kathleen barbee, Secretary
Edward Bean, Director

NPA was founded to unite all pawnbrokers in
their common efforts to improve the image of
the industry, educate the public, adn disseminate professional information and assistance.
2000 Members
Founded in 1987

8705 National Vehicle Leasing Association
N83 W13410 leon road
Menomonee Falls, WI 53051

414-533-3300
800-225-6852
FAX 410-712-4038
E-Mail: info@nvla.org
Home Page: www.nvla.org
Social Media: *LinkedIn*

Ben Carfrae, CVLE, Past President
PJ McMahon, CVLE, President/Treasurer
Terry L. Bowlder, 1st Vice president
David Blassingame, 2nd Vice President
Scott Crawford, CVLE, Director

Fosters education, publishing, conferences, legal services, advancement and industry relations certification.
500 Members
Founded in 1968

8706 National Venture Capital Association
25 Massachusetts Avenue NW
Suite 730
Washington, DC 20001

202-864-5920
FAX 202-864-5930
E-Mail: info@nvca.org
Home Page: www.nvca.org
Social Media: *Facebook, Twitter, LinkedIn,
Youtube*

Jon Callaghan, Chairman
Venky Ganesan, Chair-Elect
Scott Kupar, Treasurer

John Backus, Secretary
Maria Cirino, At Large
National trade association that represents venture capital firms. Activities include advocacy, professional development, networking and research.
450 Members
Founded in 1973

8707 Neighborhood Reinvestment Corporation
5111 North Scottsdale Road
Suite 201
Scottsdale, AZ 85250

800-808-3372
FAX 480-994-4456
E-Mail: sales@federalregister.com
Home Page: www.federalregister.com

Supplies training, grants, developmental assistance, and a range of other technical services designed to help the local partnerships achieve substantially self-reliant neighborhoods. The goal is to improve a neighborhood's housing and physical conditions, build a positive community image, and establish a healthy real estate market and a core of neighbors capable of managing the continued health of their neighborhood.
Founded in 1978

8708 Partnership for Philanthropic Planning
233 McCrea St
Suite 300
Indianapolis, IN 46225

317-269-6274
FAX 317-269-6268
E-Mail: info@pppnet.org
Home Page: www.pppnet.org
Social Media: *Facebook, Twitter, LinkedIn, YouTube, flickr*

Gregory Sharkey, Chair
Melanie Norton, Chair-elect
Alexandra Brovey, Treasurer
Thomas H. Armstrong, Secretary
Michael Kenyon, President and CEO

Members are professionals involved in the process of planning and cultivating charitable gifts.
11500 Members
Founded in 1988

8709 RMA - Risk Management Association
1801 Market Street
Suite 300
Philadelphia, PA 19103-1628

215-446-4137
800-677-7621
FAX 215-446-4100
E-Mail: customers@rmahq.org
Home Page: www.rmahq.org

J Tol Broome Jr, Chairman
Helga Houston, Vice Chairman
Nancy J. Foster, Immediate Past Chair
William F Githens, President & CEO
H. Lynn Harton, Director

Seeks to improve the risk management capabilities and principles of commercial lending and credit functions, loan administration and asset management in commercial banks and other financial industries.
17500 Members
Founded in 1914

8710 Retirement Industry Trust Association
4251 Pasadena Circle
Sarasota, FL 34233

941-724-0900
FAX 301-577-6476

E-Mail: MMohr@ritauus.org
Home Page: www.ritaus.org

Mary L. Mohr, Executive Director

8711 Securities Industry and Financial Markets Association (SIFMA)
1101 New York Ave NW
8th Floor
Washington, DC 20005

202-962-7300
FAX 202-962-7305
E-Mail: webmaster@sifma.org
Home Page: www.sifma.org
Social Media: *Twitter, LinkedIn, Youtube, Google+*

William A. Johnstone, Chairman
John F.W Rogers, Chair-elect
Timothy C. Scheve, Vice Chair
Gerad McGraw, Treasurer
Kenneth E Bentson Jr, President & CEO

SIFMA's mission is to champion policies and practices that benefit investors and issuers, expand and perfect global capital markets, and foster the development of new products and services. SIFMA provides an enhanced member network of access and forward-looking services, as well as premiere educational resources for the professionals within the industry and the investors whom they serve.

8712 Security Traders Association
1115 Broadway
Suite 1110
New York, NY 10010

646-699-5996
FAX 212-321-3449
E-Mail: sta@securitytraders.org
Home Page: www.securitytraders.org
Social Media: *Facebook, Twitter, LinkedIn, Instagram*

Rory O'Kane, Chairman
Jim Toes, President & CEO
John Russell, Vice Chairman
Jon Schneider, Treasurer
Doug Clark, Secretary

Members involved in the securities industry.
7000 Members
Founded in 1934

8713 Small Business Investor Alliance
1100 H Street NW
Suite 1200
Washington, DC 20005

202-628-5055
FAX 202-628-5080
E-Mail: info@sbia.org
Home Page: www.sbia.org
Social Media: *Twitter, LinkedIn*

Mike Blackburn, Chairman
JD White, Chair-Elect
Jeri Harman, Vice Chairman
Carolyn Galiette, Secretary
Brett Palmer, President

Trade association representing federally licensed venture capital firms and small private equity firms.
400 Members
Founded in 1958

8714 Society for Information Management
1120 Royte73
Ste 200
Mount Laurel, NJ 08054-5113

800-387-9746
800-387-9746
FAX 856-439-0525
E-Mail: sim@simnet.org
Home Page: www.simnet.org

Social Media: *Facebook, Twitter, LinkedIn, www.multiview.com*

Eric Gorham, Chairman
Kevin More, Vice Chairman
Caren Shiozaki, Treasurer/Secretary
Jim Knight, Chair Emeritus
Kevin Sauer, Director, Chapter Representative

SIM was formed to enhance international recognition of information as a basic organizational resource and to promote the effective utilization and management of this resource towards the improvement of management performance. It attempts to enhance communications between IS executives and the senior executives responsible for management of the business enterprise.
3000 Members
Founded in 1969

8715 Society of Financial Examiners
12100 Sunset Hills Rd
Suite 130
Reston, VA 20190-3221

703-234-4140
800-787-7633
FAX 888-436-8686
E-Mail: sofe@sofe.org
Home Page: www.sofe.org
Social Media: *Facebook, LinkedIn*

L Brackett, Executive Director
Judy Estus, Administrator
Annete Knief, President
James Katman, Treasurer
Mark Murphy, Secretary

Is a professional society for examiners of insurance companies, banks, savings and loans, and credit unions.
1600 Members
Founded in 1973

8716 Society of Quantitative Analysts
1450 Western avenue
Suite 101
Albany, NY 12203

518-694-3157
800-918-7930
E-Mail: sqa@sqa-us.org
Home Page: www.sqa-us.org
Social Media: *Facebook, LinkedIn*

Peg DioRio, President
Inna Okounkova, Vice President
Kennith N. Hightower, Secretary
Randy O' Toole, Treasurer
Indrani De, CFA PRM, Past President

SQA is concerned with the application of new and innovative techniques for finance, with particular emphasis on the use of quantitative techniques in investment management.
350 Members
Founded in 1989

8717 Stable Value Investment Association
1025 Connecticut Avenue NW
Suite 1000
Washington, DC 20036

202-580-7620
800-327-2270
FAX 202-580-7621
E-Mail: info@StableValue.org
Home Page: www.stablevalue.org
Social Media: *Twitter, LinkedIn*

Marc Magnoli, Chair

Members are firms and individuals with a professional interest in savings for retirement.
Founded in 1990

8718 State Debt Management Networking
2760 Research Park Drive
Lexington, KY 40511

859-244-8175
FAX 859-244-8053

E-Mail: nast@csg.org
Home Page: www.sdmn.org

Hon. Manju Ganeriwala, Chair
Steve Wisloski, Vice-chair
Laura Lockwood-Mccall, Director, Debt Management
Ellen Evans, Deputy Treasurer Debt Management
Robert L. Watson, Assistant Director

SDMN members are state officials concerned with the insurance or management of state debt. The purpose is to enhance debt management practices through training, development of educational materials, and data collection and dissemination
50 Members
Founded in 1991

8719 State Risk and Insurance Management Association
PO Box 13777
Austin, TX 78711

304-766-2646
E-Mail: robert.a.fisher@wv.gov
Home Page: www.strima.org

Robert Fischer, President

STRIMA members are state government risk and insurance managers.
50 Members
Founded in 1974

8720 Tax Executives Institute
1200 G St NW
Suite 300
Washington, DC 20005

202-638-5601
FAX 202-638-5607
Home Page: www.tei.org

Timothy Mc Cormally, Executive Director
Deborah K Gaffney, Director Conference Planning
Deborah C Giesey, Director Administration

A professional organization of corporate tax executives. Membership is open to corporate officers and employees chargesd with administering their company's tax affairs.
7000 Members
Founded in 1944

8721 The Fiduciary & Investment Risk Management Association
P.O.Box 507
Stockbridge, GA 30281-0507

678-565-6211
FAX 678-565-8788
E-Mail: info@thefirma.org
Home Page: www.thefirma.org
Social Media: *Facebook, Twitter, LinkedIn*

Bruce K Goldberg, CTA, CPA, President
Jennifer De Vries, CTA, Vice President
David Jonke CTA, CPA, Secretary
John L. Clark, Director
Daniele G Nicotra, Director-Compliance

Members are audit and compliance professionals.
820 Members
Founded in 1989

8722 The Resource Centre for Religious Institutes
8824 Cameron Street
Silver Spring, MD 20910

301-589-8143
FAX 301-589-2897
E-Mail: trcri@trcri.org
Home Page: www.trcri.org
Social Media: *Facebook, Twitter, www.blogspot.com*

Fr. Thomas Carkhuff, OSC, President
Sr. Lynn McKenzie, OSB, Vice-President

Daniel J. Ward, OSB, JCL, JD, Executive Director
Sr. Margaret Ma Cosgrove, BVM, Treasurer
Sr. Margaret Perron, RJM, Secretary

The leading resource and provider of education, services, and information to meet the current and emerging stewardship needs of all religious institutes throughout the Unted States.
Founded in 1981

8723 Urban Homesteading Assistance Board
120 Wall St
20th Floor
New York, NY 10005

212-479-3300
FAX 212-344-6457
E-Mail: webmaster@uhab.org
Home Page: www.uhab.org
Social Media: *Facebook, Twitter, Youtube*

Andrew Reicher, Executive Director
Anya Irons, Director Of Operations
Charles Laven, President
Janice Lancaster, Office Manager
Julie Harris, Director

The oldest provider of technical assistance to homesteading and sweat equity groups in the country. Promotes homesteading as an important component of comprehensive self-help housing programs. Provides technical assistance and training in self-help housing rehabilitation and managment to low income tenants, cooperative shareholders and homesteaders.
8 Members
Founded in 1973

8724 Wall Street Technology Association
620 Shrewsbury Ave
Suite C
Tinton Falls, NJ 07701

732-530-8808
FAX 732-530-0020
E-Mail: info@wsta.org
Home Page: www.wsta.org
Social Media: *Facebook, Twitter, LinkedIn*

John Killeen, President
Chris Randazzo, 1st Vice President
Joseph Weitekamp, 2nd Vice President
Ronald F. Ries, Treasurer
Michael Maffattone, Secretary

Nonprofit educational organization that focuses on technologies, operational approaches, and business issues for the global financial community.
2600+ Members
Founded in 1967

8725 Wall Street Technology Association (WSTA)
620 Shrewsbury Ave
Suite C
Tinton Falls, NJ 07701

732-530-8808
FAX 732-530-0020
E-Mail: info@wsta.org
Home Page: www.wsta.org
Social Media: *Facebook, Twitter, LinkedIn*

John Killeen, President
Chris Randazzo, 1st Vice President
Joseph Weitekamp, 2nd Vice President
Ronald F. Ries, Treasurer
Michael Maffattone, Secretary

Nonprofit educational organization that focuses on technologies, operational approaches, and business issues for the global financial community.
2800+ Members
Founded in 1967

8726 Washington Municipal Treasurers Associaion
2601 Fourth Avenue
Suite 800
Seattle, WA 98121-1280

206-625-1300
E-Mail: hstewart@mrsc.org
Home Page: www.wmta-online.com

Stpehanie McKanzie, President
Elizabeth Alba, President-Elect
Philip Steffan, Secretary
Gwen Pilo, Treasurer
Cheryl Grant, Director

Mission is to promote the profession of municipal treasurers through education, mutual support, professional recognition, and legislative advocacy.
Founded in Was

Newsletters

8727 AARMR Newsletter
American Association of Residential Mortgage
1025 Thomas Jefferson Street NW
Suite 500 East
Washington, DC 20007

202-521-3999
FAX 202-833-3636
E-Mail: efreundel@aarmr.org
Home Page: www.aarmr.org

David A Saunders, Executive Director
Erika Freundel, Manager Of Member Services
Frequency: Quarterly

8728 AEFA Newsletter
American Education Finance Association
8365 S Armadillo Trail
Evergreen, CO 80439

303-674-0857
FAX 303-670-8986
Home Page: www.aefa.cc

Ed Steinbacher, Executive Director
Frequency: Quarterly

8729 AFCPE Newsletter
Association for Financial Counseling and Planning
2112 Arlington Avenue
Suite H
Upper Arlington, OH 43221

614-485-9650
FAX 614-485-9621
Home Page: www.afcpe.org

Sharon Burns, PhD, Executive Director
Frequency: Quarterly

8730 AMI Bulletin
Assn for Management Information in Financial Svcs
14247 Saffron Circle
Carmel, IN 46032

317-518-5857
FAX 317-518-5877
E-Mail: ami2@amifs.org
Home Page: www.amifs.org

Adam Schabes, President

News, calendars, events, and industry articles.
Frequency: Quarterly

8731 Airline Financial News
PBI Media

1201 Seven Locks Road
Suite 300
Potomac, MD 20854-2931

301-354-1400
800-777-5006
FAX 301-309-3847
Home Page: www.aviationtoday.com

Richard Koulbanis, Publisher

Provides information for CEO's financial directors, operations managers, engine aircraft manufacturers and suppliers on financial, market development, buying, leasing and aircraft transactions.
Cost: $697.00
Frequency: Weekly
Circulation: 1850

8732 Annual Statement Studies
RMA - Risk Management Association
6147 Ridge Ave
Suite 2300
Philadelphia, PA 19128-2627

215-482-3222
800-677-7621
FAX 215-446-4101
E-Mail: customers@rmahq.org
Home Page: www.rmahq.org

Angelo Roma, Owner
William F Githens, Director Member Relations
Dwight Overturf, CFO/Information Technology Officer
Florence J Wetzel, COO/Administrative Officer
John Rumm, Executive Director
Frequency: Annual

8733 Asset-Backed Alert
Harrison Scott Publications
5 Marine View Plz
Suite 301
Hoboken, NJ 07030-5722

201-386-1491
FAX 201-659-4141
E-Mail: info@hspnews.com
Home Page: www.hspnews.com

Andy Albert, Owner
Tom Ferris, Editor
Daniel Cowles, CEO/President
Barbara Bannace, Marketing
Joan Tassie, Operations Director

A weekly newsletter on the securitization of consumer and corporate receivables.
Cost: $2297.00
10 Pages
Frequency: Weekly
Circulation: 2178
ISSN: 1520-3700
Founded in 1988
Printed in 4 colors on matte stock

8734 BNA Pension & Benefits Reporter
Bureau of National Affairs
1801 S Bell St
Arlington, VA 22202-4501

703-341-3000
800-372-1033
FAX 800-253-0332
E-Mail: customercare@bna.com
Home Page: www.bnabooks.com

Gregory C McCaffrey, President
Paul N Wojcik, Chairman

Covers latest pension developments stemming from the passage of ERISA and its amendments, plus pension and welfare benefit regulations, standards, enforcement actions, court decisions, legislative and administrative actions, agency options, and employee benefit trust fund requirements.
Cost: $1448.00
Frequency: Weekly
Founded in 1929
Printed in on matte stock

8735 Back-Office Bulletin
United Communications Group
Two Washingtonian Center
9737 Washingtonian Blvd Suite 100
Gaithersburg, MD 20878-7364

301-287-2700
FAX 301-287-2039
Home Page: www.ucg.com

Daniel Brown, Publisher

For financial operations professionals.
Founded in 1970

8736 Bandwidth Investor
Kagan World Media
1 Lower Ragsdale Dr
Building 1, Suite 130
Monterey, CA 93940-5749

831-624-1536
FAX 831-625-3225
E-Mail: info@kagan.com
Home Page: www.kagan.com

Tim Baskerville, President/CEO
Harvey Kraft, Circulation/Marketing Manager
Cost: $1195.00
Frequency: Monthly
Founded in 1969

8737 Bank 13D Dictionary
SNL Securities
PO Box 2124
Charlottesvle, VA 22902-2124

434-977-1600
FAX 434-977-4466
E-Mail: isales@snl.com
Home Page: www.snl.com

Todd Davenport, Editor
Reid Nagle, Chief Operating Officer
Nick Cafferillo, Chief Operating Officer
Adam Hall, Managing Director

For banks, thrifts, investors, investment bankers, law firms, consultants and regulatory agencies. Contains all active 13D filings and related filings for every public traded bank in the country, including those which trade on the 'pink sheets.'
Frequency: Quarterly
Founded in 1987

8738 Benefax
SNL Securities
PO Box 2124
Charlottesvle, VA 22902-2124

434-977-1600
FAX 434-977-4466
E-Mail: isales@snl.com
Home Page: www.snl.com

Keith Davis, Editor
Reid Nagle, Chief Operating Officer
Nick Cafferillo, Chief Operating Officer
Adam Hall, Managing Director

For bank and thrift executives. Contains only summaries of available information.
1 Pages
Frequency: Monthly
Founded in 1987

8739 Bondweek
Institutional Investor
225 Park Ave S
7th Floor
New York, NY 10003-1605

212-224-3300
FAX 212-224-3197
E-Mail: iieditor@institutionalinvestor.com
Home Page: www.institutionalinvestor.com

Christopher Brown, CEO
Erik Kolk, Publisher
Deirdre Brennan, Managing Editor
Nick Ferris, Group Marketing Director

Coverage of stocks, bonds and investments for the financial professional and consumer, information includes rates.
Cost: $2245.00
Frequency: 51 issues per y
Founded in 1967

8740 Broadcast Banker/Broker
Kagan World Media
1 Lower Ragsdale Dr
Building One,Suite 130
Monterey, CA 93940-5749

831-624-1536
800-307-2529
FAX 831-625-3225
E-Mail: info@kagan.com
Home Page: www.kagan.com

Tim Baskerville, President
Tom Johnson, Marketing Manager

A readers guide to equity deals and debt financing for radio and TV Station buying and selling analyzed. Key details on station trades with critical yardsticks of value. Three month trial is available.
Cost: $925.00
Frequency: Monthly

8741 Broadcast Investor
Kagan World Media
126 Clock Tower Place
Carmel, CA 93923-8746

831-624-1536
FAX 831-624-5882
E-Mail: info@kagan.com
Home Page: www.kagan.com

George Niesen, Editor
Tom Johnson, Marketing Manager

The newsletter on investments in radio and TV stations and publicly held companies. Comprehensive analysis of cash flow multiples and trends that impact value. Three month trial available.
Cost: $895.00
Frequency: Monthly

8742 Broker Magazine
Thomson Media
1 State St
27th Floor
New York, NY 10004-1481

212-825-8445
800-221-1809
FAX 800-235-5552
Home Page: www.sourcemedia.com

Timothy Murphy, Publisher
James Malkin, Director of Sales
Melissa Sefic, Director of Sales

Features on training, motivation, technology, legislation and marketing
Frequency: Monthly
Circulation: 750000

8743 Budget Processors in the States
National Association of State Budge Officers
444 N Capitol St NW
Suite 642
Washington, DC 20001-1512

202-624-5382
FAX 202-624-7745
E-Mail: spattison@nasbo.org
Home Page: www.nasbo.org

Frequency: Bi-Ennial

8744 Bull & Bear Financial Report
PO Bo 917179
Longwood, FL 32791

954-781-3455
800-336-2855

FAX 954-781-5865
Home Page: www.thebullandbear.com

David J Robinson, Publisher/Editor

Dozens of original articles by leading investment pros with investment information on precious metals, commodities, mutual funds, currencies, economic trends and monetary survival.
Circulation: 55000

8745 Bulletin Newsletter

EMTA - Trade Association for the Emerging Markets
360 Madison Avenue
17th Floor
New York, NY 10017

646-289-5410
FAX 646-289-5429
E-Mail: awerner@emta.org
Home Page: www.emta.org

Michael M Chamberlin, Executive Director
Aviva Werner, General Counsel
Jonathan Murno, Managing Director
Suzette Ortiz, Office Manager
Monika Forbes, Administrative Assistant
Frequency: Quarterly

8746 CFMA Building Profits

Construction Financial Management Association
29 Emmons Drive
Princeton, NJ 08540

609-452-8000
FAX 609-452-0474
E-Mail: pwristen@cfma.org
Home Page: www.cfma.org

Paula Wristen, Editor
Sarah Patt, Sales/Advertising Director
William Schwab, President

The leading source of education and information about financial management within the construction industry. The only magazine dedicated to helping financial managers in the construction business find practical solutions to emerging issues in the industry. Accepts advertising.
32 Pages
Circulation: 6500

8747 CIPFA Newsletter

National Association of Independent Public Finance
PO Box 304
Montgomery, IL 60538-0304

630-896-1292
800-624-7321
FAX 209-633-6265
E-Mail: rhoban@naipfa.com
Home Page: www.naipfa.com

Roseanne M Hoban, Executive Director
Frequency: Quarterly

8748 CRA/HMDA Update

Inside Mortgage Finance Publishers
7910 Woodmont Ave
Suite 1000
Bethesda, MD 20814-7019

301-951-1240
FAX 301-656-1709
E-Mail: service@imfpubs.com
Home Page: www.imfpubs.com

Guy Cecala, Owner
John Lewis, President

Complete coverage of Community Reinvestment Act and Home Mortgage Disclosure Act developments and other affordable housing and community development issues.
Cost: $395.00
Frequency: Monthly
Circulation: 450

8749 Cable Program Investor

Kagan World Media
126 Clock Tower Place
Carmel, CA 93923-8746

831-624-1536
FAX 831-624-5882
E-Mail: info@kagan.com
Home Page: www.kagan.com

George Niesen, Editor
Tom Johnson, Marketing Manager

Covers the economics of basic cable programming networks. Numbers, perspective unavailable from any other source. Programmers applaud its accuracy. Three month trial available.
Cost: $845.00
Frequency: Monthly

8750 Cable TV Finance

Kagan World Media
126 Clock Tower Place
Carmel, CA 93923-8746

831-624-1536
800-307-2529
FAX 831-624-5882
E-Mail: info@kagan.com
Home Page: www.kagan.com

George Niesen, Editor
Tom Johnson, Marketing Manager
Tim Baskerville, CEO/President

Cable's financial bible. Analyzes sources of funding for cable TV. Selling and buying of cable systems. Financing strategies and trends. Exclusive surveys of capital sources. Three month trial available.
Cost: $995.00
Frequency: Monthly
Founded in 1969

8751 Cable TV Investor

Kagan World Media
1 Lower Ragsdale Dr
Building One, Suite 130
Monterey, CA 93940-5749

831-624-1536
800-307-2529
FAX 831-625-3225
E-Mail: info@kagan.com
Home Page: www.kagan.com

Tim Baskerville, President
Tom Johnson, Marketing Manager

Readers road map to cable stock trends. Chart service tracking stock price movements of 37 publicly held cable TV companies. Each graph shows two years of stock price activity. Three month trial available.
Cost: $945.00
Frequency: Monthly

8752 Card News

Phillips Publishing
7811 Montrose Road
Potomac, MD 20854

301-340-2100
E-Mail: feedback@healthydirections.com
Home Page: www.healthydirections.com

Covering the financial card marketplace.

8753 Client Information Bulletin

WPI Communications
55 Morris Ave
Suite 300
Springfield, NJ 07081-1422

973-467-8700
FAX 973-467-0368
E-Mail: info@wpicomm.com
Home Page: www.wpicomm.com

Steve Klinghoffer, Owner
Marilyn Lang, Chairman

Bulletin for lawyers and CPAs to distribute to clients to keep them informed on tax matters. This original publication which has been helping accountants build their practices since 1952, has been redesigned. Covers important new tax developments, general business principals, financial planning, estate planning and other related topics.

8754 Collection Agency Report

First Detroit Corporation
PO Box 5025
Warren, MI 48090-5025

586-573-0045
800-366-5995
FAX 586-573-9219
E-Mail: info@firstdetroit.com
Home Page: www.firstdetroit.com

Albert Scace, President
Petricia Herrick, Marketing Manager

Provides financially oriented news on the collection agency and bad debt buying industries worldwide.
Cost: $289.00
8 Pages
Frequency: Monthly
ISSN: 1052-4029
Mailing list available for rent; 5000 names at $110 per M

8755 Commercial Mortgage Alert

Harrison Scott Publications
5 Marine View Plz
Suite 301
Hoboken, NJ 07030-5722

201-386-1491
FAX 201-659-4141
E-Mail: info@hspnews.com
Home Page: www.hspnews.com

Andy Albert, Owner
Tom Ferris, Director
Michelle Lebowitz, Director

A weekly newsletter on the securitization of consumer and corporate receivables.
Cost: $1497.00
10 Pages
Frequency: Weekly
Circulation: 500
ISSN: 1520-3700
Printed in 4 colors on matte stock

8756 Conference Executive Summaries

Society for Information Management
401 N Michigan Avenue
Chicago, IL 60611

312-215-5190
FAX 312-245-1081
Home Page: www.simnet.org

Jim Luisi, Executive Director
Frequency: Semi-Annual

8757 Conversion Candidates List

SNL Securities
PO Box 2124
Charlottesvle, VA 22902-2124

434-977-1600
FAX 434-977-4466
E-Mail: isales@snl.com
Home Page: www.snl.com

Chris Smith, Editor
Reid Nagle, Chief Operating Officer
Nick Cafferillo, Chief Operating Officer
Adam Hall, Managing Director

For thrift executives, individual investors and institutional investors. Lists mutual thrifts that are in a position to convert to stock ownership by offering shares for sale.
Frequency: Monthly
Founded in 1987

8758 Conversion Watch
SNL Securities
PO Box 2124
Charlottesvle, VA 22902-2124

434-977-1600
FAX 434-977-4466
E-Mail: isales@snl.com
Home Page: www.snl.com

Chris Smith, Editor
Nick Cafferillo, Chief Operating Officer
Adam Hall, Managing Director

Delivered via fax whenever new activity is announced, including rumored, pending, announced and completed activity. Provides relevant data from conversion-related filings, including eligible record dates, offering size, Pro Formas, opening and closing dates for the subscription, asset size, net worth and rating of the thrift.
Cost: $1200.00
5 Pages
Frequency: Annual+
Founded in 1987

8759 Cost Control News
Siefer Consultants
PO Box 1384
Storm Lake, IA 50588-1384

712-732-7340
FAX 712-732-7906
E-Mail: info@siefer.com
Home Page: www.siefer.com/

Dan Siefer, Publisher

Cost cutting opportunities for financial institutions.
Cost: $297.00
8 Pages
Founded in 1981

8760 Credit Collections News
SourceMedia
550 W Van Buren
Suite 1100
Chicago, IL 60607-6680

312-913-1334
FAX 312-913-1340
Home Page: www.sourcemedia.com

John Stewart, Publisher
Melissa Sefic, Director of Sales

Analysis of the global economy, current industry trends and policies, as well as problems commonly encountered in credit collections.
Frequency: Monthly

8761 Credit Union Journal
SourceMedia
224 Datura Street
Suite 615
West Palm Beach, FL 33401

561-832-2929
FAX 561-832-2939
Home Page: www.cujournal.com

Frank J Dierkmann, Publisher/Editor
Tim O'Hara, Co-Publisher

JournalScan to review recent credit union developments, industry news articles, an agenda of upcoming meetings, deadlines and events and Washington Watch covering the latest news in Washington DC.
Frequency: Weekly
Circulation: 5300

8762 Credit Union Management
Credit Union Executives Society
PO Box 14167
Madison, WI 53714-167

608-271-2664
800-252-2664
FAX 608-271-2303

E-Mail: cues@cues.org
Home Page: www.cues.org

Mary Arnold, Publisher
Theresa Sweeney, Editor
Fred Johnson, CEO/President
Cost: $93.00
Frequency: Monthly
Printed in 4 colors on glossy stock

8763 Credit and Collection Manager's Letter
Bureau of Business Practice
76 Ninth Avenue
7th Floor
New York, NY 10011

212-771-0600
FAX 212-771-0885
Home Page: www.aspenpublishers.com
Social Media: *Facebook, Twitter, LinkedIn*

Mark Dorman, CEO
Gustavo Dobles, VP Operations

Hands-on information for improving the credit and collection departments in both commercial and consumer markets.
Frequency: SemiMonthly
Circulation: 9380

8764 Daily Tax Report
Bureau of National Affairs
1801 S Bell St
Arlington, VA 22202-4501

703-341-3000
800-372-1033
FAX 800-253-0332
E-Mail: customercare@bna.com
Home Page: www.bnabooks.com

Paul N Wojcik, CEO

A daily tax notification service that covers legislative, regulatory, judicial and policy developments on a national basis, designed to give tax professionals rapid notification and comprehensive coverage of those developments.
Cost: $3215.00
Frequency: Daily
ISSN: 0092-6884

8765 Debit Card News
SourceMedia
224 Datura Street
Suite 615
West Palm Beach, FL 33401

561-832-2929
FAX 561-832-2939
Home Page: www.cujournal.com

Don Davis, Editor

Marketing, pricing, different card applications, smart cards, point-of-sale and other electronic banking activities.
Frequency: SemiMonthly

8766 Declined Contribution Market Insights
National Defined Contribution Council
9101 E Kenyon
Suite 300
Denver, CO 80237-0467

303-770-5353
FAX 303-770-1812
Home Page: www.ndcconline.org

Al Brust, Executive VP
Frequency: Annual

8767 Equipment Leasing & Finance
Equipment Leasing And Finance Association
1825 K Street NW
Suite 900
Washington, DC 20006

202-238-3400
FAX 202-238-3401

E-Mail: EL&F@elfaonline.org
Home Page: www.elfaonline.org

Amy Vogt, Managing Editor

As the flagship publication of the Equipment Leasing and Finance Association, Equipment Leasing & Finance is the trusted leader, bringing readers unrivaled coverage of the people, trends and issues that have an impact on the $628 billion equipment finance industry. Information of funding sources, portfolio management, sales and marketing strategy, large ticket leasing, transportation leasing, the computer leasing market, remarketing equipment, and the role of the equipment manager.
Frequency: 6x/Year
Circulation: 10000
Founded in 1961
Printed in 4 colors on glossy stock

8768 Executive Brief
Society for Information Management
401 N Michigan Avenue
Chicago, IL 60611

312-215-5190
FAX 312-245-1081
Home Page: www.simnet.org

Jim Luisi, Executive Director
Frequency: Quarterly

8769 Executive Compensation Review for Commercial Banks
SNL Securities
PO Box 2124
Charlottesvle, VA 22902-2124

434-977-1600
FAX 434-977-4466
Home Page: www.snlnet.com

Keith Davis, Editor
Nick Cafferillo, Chief Operating Officer
Reid Nagle, Publisher
Mark Outlaw, Advertising Director
Adam Hall, Managing Director

For banks, regulatory agencies and executive recruiters. Includes detailed compensation and benefit information for the top 5 officers of all publicly traded banks, thrifts, REITs and insurance companies.
550 Pages
Frequency: Annual
Founded in 1988

8770 Executive Compensation Review for Insurance Companies
SNL Securities
PO Box 2124
Charlottesvle, VA 22902-2124

434-977-1600
FAX 434-977-4466
Home Page: www.snlnet.com

Keith Davis, Editor
Nick Cafferillo, Chief Operating Officer
Reid Nagle, Publisher
Mark Outlaw, Advertising Director
Pat LaBua, Subscription Manager

For insurance companies, investment analysts, service providers to the insurance industry and regulators. Includes detailed compensation and benefit information for the top 5 officers of all publicly traded banks, thrifts, REITs and insurance companies.
200 Pages
Frequency: Annual
Founded in 1997

8771 Executive Compensation Review for REITs
SNL Securities
PO Box 2124
Charlottesvle, VA 22902-2124

434-977-1600
FAX 434-977-4466

E-Mail: isales@snl.com
Home Page: www.snl.com

Keith Davis, Editor
Chandler Spears, Chief Operating Officer
Nick Cafferillo, Chief Operating Officer
Adam Hall, Managing Director

For REITs, REIT service providers, investment companies, executive recruiters and regulators. Annual data digests that include detailed compensation and benefit information for the top 5 officers of all publicly traded banks, thrifts, REITs and insurance companies.
Cost: $495.00
Frequency: Monthly
Founded in 1987

8772 Executive Compensation Review for Thrift Institutions
SNL Securities
PO Box 2124
Charlottesvle, VA 22902-2124

434-977-1600
FAX 434-977-4466
E-Mail: isales@snl.com
Home Page: www.snl.com

Keith Davis, Editor
Nick Cafferillo, Chief Operating Officer
Adam Hall, Managing Director

For thrifts, regulatory agencies and executive recruiters. Annual data digests that include detailed compensation and benefit information for the top 5 officers of all publicly traded banks, thrifts, REITs and insurance companies.
Cost: $495.00
Frequency: Monthly
Founded in 1987

8773 Export Finance Letter
International Business Affairs Corporation
5523 Brite Dr
#346
Bethesda, MD 20817-6304

301-907-8647
FAX 301-907-8650
E-Mail: editor@exportsourcebook.com
Home Page: www.exportsourcebook.com

Richard Barovick, Owner

A report on government and private resources in US Export & Import Finance, Payments and Risk Management.
Founded in 1979

8774 FEI Briefing
Financial Executives Institute
200 Campus Drive
PO Box 674
Forham Park, NJ 07932

973-360-0177
FAX 973-765-1023
Home Page: www.fei.org

P Norman Roy, Publisher
Christopher Allen, Editor
Colleen Sayther Cunningham, CEO/President
Christopher Allen, Marketing
Lucinda Arsenio, Secretary

Up-to-date news for treasurers and controllers of large corporations.
Circulation: 14000
Founded in 1931

8775 FSR Newsletter
Financial Services Roundtable
1001 Pennsylvania Ave Nw
Suite 500 S
Washington, DC 20004-2508

202-628-2455
FAX 202-289-1903

E-Mail: info@fsround.org
Home Page: www.fsround.org

Steve Bartlett, CEO
Frequency: Monthly

8776 Federal Securities Act
Matthew Bender and Company
744 Broad St
Newark, NJ 07102-3885

973-820-2000
800-227-9597
FAX 937-865-1284
E-Mail: info.in@lexisnexis.com
Home Page: www.lexisnexis.com

Kent Frankstone, Manager
Rebecca Schmitt, Chief Financial Officer

A comprehensive, up-to-date treatise on the Securities Act of 1933 and all amendments thereto, as well as the application of the Trust Indenture Act of 1939.

8777 Fee Income Report
Siefer Consultants
PO Box 1384
Storm Lake, IA 50588-1384

712-732-7340
FAX 712-732-7906
E-Mail: info@siefer.com
Home Page: www.siefer.com

Dan Siefer, Publisher

Fee income news and opportunities for financial institutions.
Cost: $297.00
8 Pages
Frequency: Monthly
Founded in 1981

8778 Fidelity Insight
Mutual Fund Investors Association
20 William St
Suite 200
Wellesley, MA 02481-4138

781-235-1560
800-586-4727
Home Page: www.kobren.com

Eric Kobren, President
Chris Keith, Senior Vice President
Todd Peters, Senior Vice President

Offers information and rates for mutual funds, investments, stocks and bonds.
Cost: $127.00
8 Pages
Frequency: Monthly
Founded in 1985

8779 Finance Company Weekly
SNL Securities
PO Box 2124
Charlottesvle, VA 22902-2124

434-977-1600
FAX 434-977-4466
E-Mail: isales@snl.com
Home Page: www.snl.com

David Meadors, Editor
Nick Cafferillo, Chief Operating Officer
Adam Hall, Managing Director

Weekly news on publicly and privately traded finance companies. Includes consumer, commercial, credit card companies, pawn shops and leasing companies. Summarizes recent industry earnings announcement, trends, registration statements and performance rankings.
Cost: $396.00
10 Pages
Frequency: Weekly
Founded in 1987

8780 Financial Management Association International (FMA)
University of South Florida

4202 E Fowler Ave
Tampa, FL 33620-9951

813-974-2011
FAX 813-974-5530
E-Mail: fma@coba.usf.edu OR info@fma.org
Home Page: www.usf.edu

Judy L Genshaft, President
William Christie, Financial Management Editor
Keith M Howe, Journal of Applied Finance Editor
James Schallheim, FMA Survey Synthesis Series Editor
John Finnerty, Editor FMA Online

Financial books, textbooks, databases, newspapers, research services, software and related products and services.
Frequency: Quarterly
Founded in 1970

8781 Financial Managers Update
Financial Managers Society
100 W Monroe
Suite 810
Chicago, IL 60603

312-578-1300
800-275-4367
FAX 312-578-1308
E-Mail: info@fmsinc.com
Home Page: www.fmsinc.org/cms

Dick Yingst, President/CEO
Jennifer Vimarco, Professional Development Director
Jennifer Doak, Director of Marketing

The latest accounting and regulatory information related to financial institutions, as well as news and trends. Includes a regulatory check list.
8 Pages
Circulation: 1400
Mailing list available for rent
Printed in one color

8782 Financial NetNews
Institutional Investor
488 Madison Ave
15th Floor
New York, NY 10022-5701

212-303-3100
800-115-9196
FAX 212-224-3491
E-Mail: iieditor@institutionalinvestor.com
Home Page: www.institutionalinvestor.com

Dahlia Weinman, Publisher
Deirdre Brennan, Editor
Nick Ferris, Marketing Manager
Chris Brown, CEO/President

Businesses and their Web sites, providing up-to-date information on networkings and assessment of industry trends and mistakes.
Frequency: Weekly

8783 Financial News
Financial News Corporation
PO Box 1769
Jacksonville, FL 32201-1769

904-356-2466
FAX 904-353-2628
E-Mail: editorial@jaxdailyrecord.com
Home Page: www.jaxdailyrecord.com

James F Bailey Jr, Publisher
Angie Campbell, Business Manager
Karen Mathis, Managing Editor

Business and legal information for financial institutions.
Cost: $89.00
Frequency: Daily

8784 Financial Planning Advisory
WPI Communications

55 Morris Ave
Suite 300
Springfield, NJ 07081-1422

973-467-8700
800-323-4995
FAX 973-467-0368
E-Mail: info@wpicomm.com
Home Page: www.wpicomm.com

Steve Klinghoffer, Owner
Marilyn Lang, Chairman

Offers institutions and businesses information
on financial planning and campaigns.
Founded in 1952

8785 Financial Services
8180 Corporate Park Drive
Suite 305
Cincinnati, OH 45242-3309

513-591-0149
FAX 513-527-3141

Linda Niesz, Publisher

National and regional news for members.
Cost: $7.00
6 Pages
Frequency: Monthly

8786 Financial Services Daily
SNL Securities
PO Box 2124
Charlottesvle, VA 22902-2124

434-977-1600
FAX 434-977-4466
E-Mail: isales@snl.com
Home Page: www.snl.com

David Meadors, Editor
Nick Cafferillo, Chief Operating Officer
Adam Hall, Managing Director

Daily fax of news headlines on finance companies, mortgage banks, investment advisors and
brokers/dealers, plus divident and earnings announcements, stock highlights and index values, registration statements and ownership
filings.
6 Pages
Frequency: Daily
Founded in 1987

8787 Financial Services M&A Insider
SNL Securities
PO Box 2124
Charlottesvle, VA 22902-2124

434-977-1600
FAX 434-977-4466
E-Mail: isales@snl.com
Home Page: www.snl.com

L Vencil, Editor
Reid Nagle, Chief Operating Officer
Nick Cafferillo, Chief Operating Officer
Adam Hall, Managing Director

Fax newsletter featuring in-depth articles and
the latest financial information on financial services M&A activity. Covers mortgage banks,
finance companies, investment advisors and
broker/dealers. Analyzes industry trends and
specific market and ownership changes to identify potential consolidation activity.
Cost: $695.00
10 Pages
Frequency: Monthly
Founded in 1987

8788 Financial Women Today
Financial Women International
1027 W Roselawn Avenue
Roseville, MN 55113

651-487-7632
866-807-6081
FAX 651-489-1322

E-Mail: info@fwi.org
Home Page: www.fwi.org

Melissa Curzon, President
Cindy Hass, VP
Carleen DeSisto, Secretary

Covers financial services industry trends, as
well as women's issues and association news.
1000 Members
Circulation: 10,000
Founded in 1921

8789 First Friday
ASCU
PO Box 5488
Madison, WI 53705-0488

608-238-2646
FAX 608-238-2646

C Barle, Publisher

Market research and statistics.
Cost: $35.00
6 Pages
Frequency: Monthly
Founded in 1973
Mailing list available for rent: 11,000 names at
$60 per M
Printed in on matte stock

8790 Fiscal Survey of the States
National Association of State Budget
Officers
444 N Capitol St Nw
Suite 642
Washington, DC 20001-1556

202-624-8020
FAX 202-624-7745
E-Mail: spattison@nasbo.org
Home Page: www.nasbo.org

Scott Pattison, Executive Director
Frequency: Semi-Annual

8791 Focus on Accountability
Evangelical Council for Financial
Accountability
440 W Jubal Early Dr
Suite 130
Winchester, VA 22601

540-535-0103
800-323-9473
FAX 540-535-0533
E-Mail: info@ecfa.org
Home Page: www.ecfa.org

Dan Busby, President
Frequency: Quarterly
Circulation: 30000

8792 Forecaster
Forecaster Publishing Company
19623 Ventura Blvd
Tarzana, CA 91356-2918

818-345-4421
FAX 818-345-0468

John Kamin, Owner
Brian Kamin, CEO/President

Analyzes lucrative speculations in unusual ar-
eas. Researches gold, silver, coins, gems, prop-
erty, antiques, interest rates, business cycles,
economic advice, tax strategies, wine, guns,
collector cars and more.
Cost: $180.00
8 Pages
Frequency: Weekly
ISSN: 0095-294X
Founded in 1962
Mailing list available for rentat $170 per M
Printed in 2 colors on matte stock

8793 Fund Directions
Financial Communications Company

225 Park Avenue S
New York, NY 10003

212-953-3500
800-715-9195
FAX 212-224-3699
E-Mail: customerservice@iinews.com
Home Page: www.funddirections.com

Colin Minnihan, Publisher
Wendy Connett, Executive Editor
Amy Cohen, Managing Editor
Kevin Francella, Plant Manager
Kim Lemmonds, Marketing Director

Trends in the rapidly changing fund environment and analysis of key issues in fund governance.
Frequency: Monthly
Circulation: 2500

8794 Futures Market Alert
Robbins Trading Company
8700 W Bryn Mawr Ave
Seventh Floor, S Tower
Chicago, IL 60631-3530

773-380-9700
800-453-4444
FAX 773-380-9701
E-Mail: info@robbinstrading.com
Home Page: www.rabjohnsnef.com

Reginold Rabjohns, Partner

Covers futures trading.

8795 Genomics Investing
Asset Alternatives
170 Linden Street
Wellesley, MA 02482

781-304-1400
FAX 781-304-1440
Home Page: www.assetnews.com

Tom Salemi, Senior Editor
Brian Gormley, Editor
Lisa Hughes, Circulation Manager
Barbara Bissonnette, VP Marketing/Sales

The genomics market offers a wealth of public
and pivate investment opportunities. Genomics
Investing helps you determine which are likely
to be winners by identifying the most attractive
companies and industry sub-sectors, and uncovering hot trends in genomics investing. Every monthly issue puts you intouch with the
investment analysts, mutual fund managers,
venture capitalists, and industry executives
who are shaping the marketplace.
Cost: $1195.00
Frequency: Monthly
Printed in on matte stock

8796 Global Money Management
Institutional Investor
225 Park Ave S
7th Floor
New York, NY 10003-1605

212-224-3300
800-543-4444
FAX 212-224-3197
E-Mail: iieditor@institutionalinvestor.com
Home Page: www.institutionalinvestor.com

Christopher Brown, President/CEO
Deirdre Brennan, Managing Editor
Stuart Wise, Senior Editor
Nick t Ferris, Group Marketing Director

Money management news. Accepts advertising.
Cost: $11.95
Frequency: Fortnightly
Founded in 1967

8797 Gold Newsletter
Blanchard and Company

2400 Jefferson Hwy
Suite 600
New Orleans, LA 70121-3838

504-835-0029
800-877-8847
FAX 504-837-4884
E-Mail: gnlmail@jeffersoncompanies.com
Home Page: www.neworleansconference.com

James Blanchard, President
Brien Lundin, CEO

Offers information and news for the financial community on stocks, bonds and investment opportunities.
Cost: $198.00
Frequency: Monthly
Founded in 1971

8798 Government Affairs Bulletin
Financial Services Roundtable
1001 Pennsylvania Ave Nw
Suite 500 S
Washington, DC 20004-2508

202-628-2455
FAX 202-289-1903
E-Mail: info@fsround.org
Home Page: www.fsround.org

Steve Bartlett, CEO
Frequency: Monthly

8799 Government Finance Officers Association Newsletter
Government Finance Officers Association
203 N La Salle St
Suite 2700
Chicago, IL 60601-1216

312-977-9700
FAX 312-977-4806
E-Mail: inquiry@gfoa.org
Home Page: www.gfoa.org

Jeffrey L Esser, Executive Director
Karen Utterback, Editor/Research & Consulting
Rebecca Russum, Senior Editor Technical Services
Barbara Mollo, Director Operations & Marketing
John Jurkash, CFO/Financial Administration

The purpose of the Government Finance Officers Association is to enhance and promote the professional management of governments for the public benefit by identifying and developing financial policies and practices and promoting them through education, training and leadership. Membership includes a twice-monthly newsletter in addition to specialty newsletters on cash management, accounting, auditing, and financial reporting.
17300 Pages
Founded in 1906

8800 HBMA Newsletter
Healthcare Billing and Management Association
1540 South Coast Highway
Suite 203
Laguna Beach, CA 92651

877-640-4262
Home Page: http://www.hbma.org

Bradley Lund, Executive Director
Paul Myers, Director of Education
Frequency: Monthly

8801 HFMA's Leadership E-Newsletter
Healthcare Financial Management Association
Two Westbrook Corporate Center
Suite 700
Westchester, IL 60154-5700

708-319-9600
800-252-4362

FAX 708-531-0032
Home Page: www.hfma.org/leadership

Robert Fromberg, Editor-in-Chief
Maggie Van Dyke, Product Manager & Editor
Chris Burke, Advertising Manager
Kurt Belisle, Sponsorhip Manager

Showcases examples of how leading healthcare organizations are driving down costs, enhancing quality, and collaborating across disciplines and care sites. The initiative highlightes innovative providers. Subscription includes a twice-yearly print publication, monthly e-newsletter, webcasts, and exclusive invites.
Frequency: Monthly
Circulation: 32900

8802 HFMA's The Business of Caring
Healthcare Financial Management Association
Two Westbrook Corporate Center
Suite 700
Westchester, IL 60154-5700

708-319-9600
800-252-4362
FAX 708-531-0032
Home Page: www.hfma.org/boc

Robert Fromberg, Editor-in-Chief
Maggie Van Dyke, Product Manager & Editor
Chris Burke, Advertising Manager
Kurt Belisle, Sponsorhip Manager

Helps nurse managers navigate the business side of health care to become successful hospital leaders. Topics discussed include: budgeting, workforce management, cost containment, and IT implementation. Available Free Online.
Frequency: Quarterly

8803 Hedge Fund Alert
Harrison Scott Publications
5 Marine View Plz
Suite 301
Hoboken, NJ 07030-5722

201-386-1491
FAX 201-659-4141
E-Mail: info@hspnews.com
Home Page: www.hspnews.com

Andy Albert, Owner
Tom Ferris, Editor
Howard Kapiloff, Managing Editor
Barbara Eannace, Advertising Director
Michelle Lebowitz, Director

A weekly newsletter on the securitization of consumer and corporate receivables.
Cost: $2097.00
10 Pages
Frequency: Weekly
Circulation: 500
ISSN: 1520-3700
Printed in 4 colors on matte stock

8804 High Yield Report
American Banker-Bond Buyer
1 State St
27th Floor
New York, NY 10004-1561

212-803-8450
800-367-3989
FAX 212-843-9624
Home Page: www.sourcemedia.com

Jim Malkin, CEO
Mario DiUbaldi, Director of Sales
Melissa Sefic, Director of Sales

The only financial publication dealing exclusively with high yield corporate debt and distressed bank debt.
Cost: $795.00
Frequency: Weekly
Circulation: 350

8805 Housing Finance Report
National Assn. of Local Housing Finance Agencies
2025 M St Nw
Suite 800
Washington, DC 20036-2422

202-367-1197
FAX 202-367-2197
Home Page: www.noca.org

Greg Brown, Editor
Karen Thompson, Production Manager

This newsletter covers major developments in housing finance in the Congress, federal agencies and private sector. It also gives highlights new and innovative activities of ALHFA members.
Circulation: 450
Founded in 1982

8806 IBC's Money Fund Report
IBC Financial Data
1 Research Dr
Westborough, MA 01581-3922

508-616-5567
FAX 508-616-5511
E-Mail: info@imoneynet.com
Home Page: www.imoneynet.com/

Kenneth Bohlin, Publisher
Peter Crane, Editor
Randy Wood, CEO
Claudia Missert, marketin

Compiles yield, average maturity and portfolio data for each money fund along with summary information for more than a dozen categories.
Cost: $3125.00
Frequency: Weekly
Circulation: 200
Founded in 1975
Printed in 2 colors on matte stock

8807 IE News: Financial Services
Institute of Industrial Engineers
25 Technology Pkwy S
Suite 150
Norcross, GA 30092-2946

770-449-0461
FAX 770-263-8532

Offers full coverage of the financial community pertaining to engineering and industrial corporations.

8808 IHS Haystack Standard Standards
Information Handling Services
15 Inverness Way E
Englewood, CO 80112-5710

303-790-0600
800-525-7052
FAX 303-754-3940
Home Page: www.ihs.com

Jerre L Stead, CEO
Michael Armstrong, Director
Frequency: Daily

8809 IPO Reporter
Securities Data Publishing
1290 6th Avenue
36th Floor
New York, NY 10104-0101

212-765-5311
FAX 212-957-0420

Ted Weissberg, Group Publisher

Reliable news, data and analysis. Provides the most comprehensive coverage available, including a detailed calendar of upcoming deals; new IPOs filled with the SEC; valuation information; comaparison data; company name and locationas well as names of underwriters, auditors and counsels.
Frequency: Weekly

8810 IRA Reporter
Universal Pensions
PO Box 979
Brainerd, MN 56401-0979

218-855-0565
800-346-3860
FAX 218-829-4814

Thomas G Anderson, President
Jennifer M Norquist, Editor
Discusses IRS rulings, regulations, legislation and other industry news and trends relating to IRA's.
Cost: $115.00
8 Pages
Frequency: Monthly
Printed in on glossy stock

8811 ISDA Newsletter
International Swaps and Derivatives Association
360 Madison Ave
16th Floor
New York, NY 10017-7126

212-901-6000
FAX 212-901-6001
E-Mail: isda@isda.org
Home Page: www.isda.org

Robert Pickel, CEO
Ruth Ainslie, Director Communications
Corrine Gerasley, Director Administration
Frequency: 5/year

8812 Inside Mortgage Technology
Inside Mortgage Finance Publishers
7910 Woodmont Ave
Suite 1000
Bethesda, MD 20814-7019

301-951-1240
FAX 301-656-1709
E-Mail: service@imfpubs.com
Home Page:
http://www.insidemortgagefinance.com

Guy Cecala, Owner
Francis Solomon, President

Focuses on the evolving technology developments that are changing the mortgage business. Covers internet strategies, what's new and whats working, automated systems and e-commerce businesses.
Cost: $556.00
13 Pages
ISSN: 1093-4049

8813 Insurance M&A Newsletter
SNL Securities
One SNL Plaza
PO Box 2124
Charlottesville, VA 22902

434-977-1600
FAX 434-977-4466
E-Mail: subscriptions@snl.com
Home Page: www.snl.com

L Todd Vencil, Editor
Reid Nagle, Chief Executive Officer
Nick Cafferillo, Chief Operating Officer
Adam Hall, Managing Director

For investment bankers, analysts, insurance investors, insurance company executives and insurance regulators. Features in-depth articles and the latest financial information on insurance mergers and acquisitions activity.
Cost: $998.00
15 Pages
Frequency: Fortnightly
Founded in 1987

8814 Interactive Mobile Investor
Kagan World Media

126 Clock Tower Place
Carmel, CA 93923-8746

831-624-1536
FAX 831-625-3225
E-Mail: info@kagan.com
Home Page: www.kagan.com

George Niesen, Editor
Tom Johnson, Marketing Manager
Cost: $945.00
Frequency: Monthly

8815 Interactive TV Investor
Kagan World Media
126 Clock Tower Place
Carmel, CA 93923-8746

831-624-1536
FAX 831-625-3225
E-Mail: info@kagan.com
Home Page: www.kagan.com

George Niesen, Editor
Tom Johnson, Marketing Manager
Cost: $895.00
Frequency: Monthly

8816 International Financier Newsletter
International Society of Financiers
PO Box 398
Naples, NC 28760

828-698-7805
FAX 828-698-7806
Home Page: www.insofin.com

Ronald I Gershen, Chairman/President
Frequency: Monthly

8817 International Securitization & Structured Finance
WorldTrade Executive
2250 Main Street Suite 100
PO Box 761
Concord, MA 01742-761

978-287-0301
FAX 978-287-0302
E-Mail: info@wtexec.com
Home Page: www.wtexec.com

Jill McKenna, Production Manager
Gary Brown, CEO
Scott stutbar, Editor
John Margel, Marketing
Heather Margel, Circulation Manager

A twice monthly report devoted exclusively to asset-backed securities in international markets. Covers all aspects of international asset-backed securitization, including innovative product trends, issuer considerations, regulatory matters, and tax and accounting considerations. Examines what is working in emerging markets and spotlights unique US transactions.
Cost: $1333.00

8818 International Wealth Success
PO Box 1866
Merrick, NY 11566

516-378-3922
800-323-0548
FAX 516-766-5919

Tyler G Hicks, Publisher

Monthly newsletter giving sources and techniques for financing a variety of small businesses - import-export, mail order, real estate, home-based activities, etc. Gives specific, hands-on methods for beginners to start and own a successful business of their own.
Cost: $24.00
16 Pages
Frequency: Monthly
Mailing list available for rent: 100 M names at $75 per M
Printed in 2 colors on matte stock

8819 Internet Media Investor
Kagan World Media
126 Clock Tower Place
Carmel, CA 93923-8746

831-624-1536
FAX 831-625-3225
E-Mail: info@kagan.com
Home Page: www.kagan.com

George Niesen, Editor
Tom Johnson, Marketing Manager
Cost: $945.00
Frequency: Monthly

8820 Investing in Crisis
KCI Communications
1750 Old Meadow Road
Suite 301
McLean, VA 22102

703-905-8000
800-832-2330
FAX 703-905-8100
E-Mail: service@kci-com.com
Home Page: www.2.kci-com.com

Allie Ash Jr, Publisher

Offers information on investments, low-risk bonds, stocks and campaigns for businesses in times of economic survival.
Cost: $195.00
80 Pages

8821 Investment Dealers' Digest
Thomson Financial Publishing
195 Broadway
Suite 4
New York, NY 10007-3124

646-822-2000
FAX 646-822-2800
Home Page: www.thomson.com

Elaine Yadlon, Plant Manager
James Smith, Chief Operating Officer

Corporation financing, market conditions, financial techniques and organizational strategies.
Frequency: Weekly
Circulation: 6255

8822 Investment News
Crain Communications Inc
711 3rd Ave
Suite 3
New York, NY 10017-9214

212-210-0171
FAX 212-210-0237
E-Mail: info@crain.com
Home Page: www.investmentnews.com

Rance Crain, President

Provides news vital to their businesses, including news affecting their clients investments and reports about the growing financial advisory industry and the companies that serve it.
Frequency: Weekly
Circulation: 61000
Founded in 1916

8823 Investment Quality Trends
IQ Trends
2888 Loker Avenue East
Suite 116
Carlsbad, CA 92010

866-927-5250
FAX 866-927-5251
E-Mail: info@iqtrends.com
Home Page: www.iqtrends.com

Michael Minney, Publisher
Kelley Wright, Managing Editor
Geraldine Weiss, Publisher Emeritus

Investment newsletter specializing in high-quality, divident-paying blue chip stocks,

macro-economics, and market outlook.
Cost: $310.00
12 Pages
Frequency: Bi-monthly
Founded in 1966

8824 Investment Recovery Association
638 W 39th Street
Kansas City, MO 64111

816-561-5323
800-728-2272
FAX 816-561-1991
E-Mail: ira@invrecovery.org
Home Page: www.invrecovery.org

David Rupert CMIR, President
Al Kidney CMIR, VP

Helps fulfill an important role by bringing people together from disparate industries...all focused on sharing best IR practices and improving the knowledge and skills necessary to properly perform the wide-ranging responsibilities required of investment recovery practitioners.
Cost: $300.00
16 Pages
Frequency: Monthly
Circulation: 900

8825 Investor Relations Newsletter
Kennedy Information
1 Pheonix Mill Lane
Floor 3
Petersborough, NH 03458

603-924-1006
800-531-0007
E-Mail: bookstore@kennedyinfo.com
Home Page: www.kennedyinfo.com

Gerald Murray, Editor

Provides practical, hands on strategy and tactics for the investor relations professional.
Cost: $295.00
Frequency: Monthly
ISSN: 1535-5802
Founded in 1970

8826 John Bollinger's Capital Growth Letter
Bollinger Capital Management
Po Box 3358
Manhattan Beach, CA 90266-1358

310-798-8855
800-888-8400
FAX 310-798-8858
E-Mail: bbands@bollingerbands.com
Home Page: www.bollingerbands.com

John Bollinger, Owner

Covers stocks, bonds, precious metals, commodities, the dollar and the international markets. Utilizes a technically driven asset allocation approach and investment recommendations. A free twice-a-week hotline is available to all subscribers. Online or by mail.
Cost: $300.00
12 Pages
Frequency: Monthly
Circulation: 500
Founded in 1980
Printed in 2 colors

8827 John Bollinger's Group Power
Bollinger Capital Management
Po Box 3358
Manhattan Beach, CA 90266-1358

310-798-8855
800-888-8400
FAX 310-798-8855
E-Mail: BBands@BollingerBands.com
Home Page: www.bollingerbands.com

John Bollinger, Owner
Dorit Kehr, Contact

Electronic daily newsletter available everyday via email or on Bollinger's home page. Provides group analysis using a group structure, provides a wide array of marketing statistics designed to assist the investor in making market timing and investment decisions.
Frequency: Daily

8828 Jumbo Rate News
Bauer Financial
Gables International Plaza
PO Box 143520
Coral Gables, FL 33114

800-388-6686
FAX 800-230-9569
E-Mail: customerservice@bauerfinancial.com
Home Page: www.bauerfinancial.com

Karen L Dorway, President/CEO
Caroline Jervey, Editor

Each issue contains over 1,000 separate Jumbo CD rates in seven categories from over 200 creditworthy banks and thrifts nationwide. Includes star ratings, wire transfer fees, deposit requirements and financial highlights for each institution.
Cost: $445.00
Frequency: Weekly
Founded in 1983
Printed in 2 colors on matte stock

8829 Kagan Media Investor
Kagan World Media
126 Clock Tower Place
Carmel, CA 93923-8746

831-624-1536
800-307-2529
FAX 831-625-3225
E-Mail: info@kagan.com
Home Page: www.kagan.com

George Niesen, Editor
Tom Johnson, Marketing Manager
Robin Flynn, Senior VP

News of the Kagan Media Investor. Three month trial available.
Cost: $1195.00
Frequency: Monthly
Founded in 1969

8830 Kagan Media Money
Kagan World Media
1 Lower Ragsdale Dr
Bldg 1 Suite 130
Monterey, CA 93940-5749

831-624-1536
FAX 831-625-3225
E-Mail: info@kagan.com
Home Page: www.kagan.com

George Niesen, Editor
Harvey Kraft, Marketing Manager
Tim Baskerville, CEO
Harvey Kraft, Circulation Manager
Sandy Borthwick, Communications Manager

Analysts dissect deals, anticipate trends, project revenues, track financings and value the debt and equity of hundreds of privately held and publicly traded advertising, broadcasting, cable TV, digital TV, home video, Internet media, motion picture, newspaper, pay TV, professional sports and wireless telecommunications companies in the US and abroad.
Cost: $1245.00
Frequency: Monthly
Founded in 1969

8831 Kagan Music Investor
Kagan World Media
126 Clock Tower Place
Carmel, CA 93923-8746

831-624-1536
FAX 831-625-3225

E-Mail: info@kagan.com
Home Page: www.kagan.com

George Niesen, Editor
Tom Johnson, Marketing Manager

News and analysis for investors in the music industry.
Cost: $945.00
Frequency: Monthly

8832 Kiplinger Tax Letter
Kiplinger Washington Editors
1729 H St Nw
Washington, DC 20006-3924

202-887-6400
800-544-0155
FAX 202-778-8976
E-Mail: sub.services@kiplinger.com
Home Page: www.kiplinger.com

Knight Kiplinger, VP
Steven D Ivins, Editor

Biweekly tax letter for investors, business owners and managers. Covers current developments in Congress, IRS and the courts.
Cost: $54.00
4 Pages
Circulation: 125000
Mailing list available for rent
Printed in one color

8833 Latin American Finance & Capital Markets
WorldTrade Executive
PO Box 761
Concord, MA 01742-0761

978-287-0301
FAX 978-287-0302
E-Mail: info@wtexec.com
Home Page: www.wtexec.com

Alison French, Production Manager

An action-oriented report on treasury management, tax, legal, accounting and other operational issues that impact doing business in Latin America. Provides an independent assessment of local capital markets.
Cost: $595.00
Frequency: Twice monthly

8834 Limelight eNewsletter
Wall Street Teechnology Association
521 Newman Springs Road
Suite 12
Lincroft, NJ 07738

732-530-8808
FAX 732-530-0020
E-Mail: info@wsta.org
Home Page: www.wsta.org

Phyllis Lampell, Executive Director
JoAnn Cooper, Executive Director
Frequency: Monthly
Circulation: 14000

8835 Long Term Investing
Concept Publishing
5202 Humphreys Road
Lake Park, GA 31636

229-257-0367
FAX 229-219-1097
Home Page: www.newconceptspublishing.com

Jim Dovan, Publisher
David Coleman, Editor
Madris Gutierrez, Editor-in-Chief
Andrea DePasture, Senior Editor

Offers full coverage of long term stocks, bonds and investments.
Cost: $98.00
12 Pages
Frequency: Monthly
Circulation: 600
Founded in 1998
Printed in one color on matte stock

8836 MAR/Hedge
Managed Account Reports
1250 Broadway
26th Floor
New York, NY 10001

212-213-6202
800-638-2525
FAX 212-213-1870
E-Mail: subs@marhedge.com
Home Page: www.marhedge.com

Greg Newton, Publisher
Randall Devere, Editor-in-Chief
Lisa McErlane, Director of Marketing
Gary Lynch, President/Publisher

The first newsletter to cover the field of hedge funds in its entirety with industry news, in-depth articles and reviews of hedge fund managers and fund of funds and rankings of these managers and fund of funds.
Cost: $1195.00
16 Pages
Frequency: Monthly
Circulation: 300
Founded in 1994
Printed in 2 colors on matte stock

8837 Managing 401(k) Plans
Institute of Management and Administration
1 Washington Park
Suite 1300
Newark, NJ 07102

212-244-0360
FAX 973-622-0595
Home Page: www.ioma.com

The definitive resource for HR and Financial Department managers looking to run the best plan for their company.
Cost: $429.00

8838 Managing Credit, Receivable & Collections
Institute of Management and Administration
1 Washington Park
Suite 1300
Newark, NJ 07102

212-244-0360
FAX 973-622-0595
Home Page: www.ioma.com

Accelerate receivables and learn what technology and techniques are working best.
Cost: $269.00
Frequency: Monthly

8839 Media Mergers & Acquisitions
Kagan World Media
126 Clock Tower Place
Carmel, CA 93923-8746

831-624-1536
FAX 831-624-5882
E-Mail: info@kagan.com
Home Page: www.kagan.com

George Niesen, Editor
Tom Johnson, Marketing Manager

Where it all comes together. Exclusive scorecard of deals done by media companies. Dollar amounts, multiples paid, trends captured in succinct summaries of complex transactions. Three month trial available.
Cost: $795.00
Frequency: Monthly

8840 Merger Strategy Report
SNL Securities
PO Box 2124
Charlottesvle, VA 22902-2124

434-977-1600
FAX 434-977-4466
Home Page: www.snlnet.com

Erik Winthrow, Editor
John Minor, Editor

Reid Nagle, Publisher
Mark Outlaw, Advertising Director
Nick Cafferillo, Chief Operating Officer

For bank and thrift executives, with a regional M&A recap; list of deals; ranking of advisors and lawyers.
5 Pages
Frequency: Quarterly
Founded in 1995

8841 Mergers & Acquisitions Executive Compensation Review
SNL Securities
One SNL Plaza
PO Box 2124
Charlottesvle, VA 22902-2124

434-977-1600
FAX 434-977-4466
E-Mail: isales@snl.com
Home Page: www.snl.com

John Minor, Editor
Michael Spears, Advertising
Mike Scott, Mergers/Acquisitions
Nick Cafferillo, Chief Operating Officer
Adam Hall, Managing Director

For banks, thrifts, investment banks, law firms that advise on mergers, executives at banks expecting to merge and personnel and compensation specialists. Provides compensation information on the executives of banks that have entered into agreements to be acquired.
Cost: $495.00
10 Pages
Frequency: Monthly
Founded in 1987

8842 Micro Ticker Report
Waters Information Services
PO Box 2248
Binghamton, NY 13902-2248

607-770-8535
FAX 607-723-7151

Dennis Waters, Publisher
Andrew Delaney, Editor

Covers the financial quotation industry.

8843 Money Management Letter
Institutional Investor
225 Park Ave S
12th Floor
New York, NY 10003-1605

212-224-3300
FAX 212-224-3197
E-Mail: iieditor@institutionalinvestor.com
Home Page: www.institutionalinvestor.com

Christopher Brown, CEO
Tom Lamont, Editor

This newsletter offers businesses information on investments, stocks, bonds, low-risk campaigns and financial planning opportunities.

8844 Mortgaged Backed Securities Letter
American Banker-Bond Buyer
1 State St
26th Floor
New York, NY 10004-1483

212-803-8350
FAX 212-843-9600
Home Page: www.securitiesindustry.com

John Del Mauro, VP
Tom Steinert-Threlkeld, Director

Provides coverage of structured finance and includes comprehensive listings of asset backed securities.
Frequency: Weekly
Circulation: 4200

8845 Motion Picture Investor
Kagan World Media

126 Clock Tower Place
Carmel, CA 93923-8746

831-624-1536
FAX 831-625-3225
E-Mail: info@kagan.com
Home Page: www.kagan.com/

George Niesen, Editor
Tom Johnson, Marketing Manager
Cost: $845.00
Frequency: Monthly
Founded in 1969

8846 NACHA Operating Rules & Guidelines
NACHA: The Electronic Payments Association
13450 Sunrise Valley Drive
Suite 100
Herndon, VA 20171

703-561-1100
FAX 703-787-0996
E-Mail: info@nacha.org
Home Page: www.nacha.org

Janet O Estep, CEO
Marcie Haitema, Chairperson

Reflects the results of the Rules Simplification initiative. PReviously organized around major topics, the simplified Rules framework is structured around the rights and responsibilities of participants in the ACH Network.
Cost: $78.00
Frequency: Annual

8847 NADOA Newsletter
National Association of Division Order Analysts
2805 Oak Trail Court
Suite 6312
Arlington, TX 76016

972-715-4489
E-Mail: administrator@nadoa.org
Home Page: www.nadoa.org

Lynn S McCord, Administrator
Frequency: Bi-Monthly

8848 NALHFA Newsletter
National Association of Local Housing Finance
2025 M St Nw
Suite 800
Washington, DC 20036-2422

202-367-1197
FAX 202-367-2197
E-Mail: john_murphy@nalhfa.org
Home Page: www.noca.org

John C Murphy, Executive Director
Scott Lynch, Association Manager
Kim McKinon, Coordinator Membership
Frequency: Bi-Monthly

8849 NAPFA Newslink
National Association of Personal Financial Advisor
3250 N Arlington Heights Road
Suite 109
Arlington Heights, IL 60004

847-483-5400
800-366-2732
FAX 847-483-5415
E-Mail: info@napfa.org
Home Page: www.napfa.org

Ellen Turf, CEO
Margery Wasserman, Director Conference
Frequency: Quarterly

8850 NASDAQ Subscriber Bulletin
National Association of Securities Dealers

1212newyork anenue
suite950
Washington, DC 20005-1516

202-371-5535
FAX 202-371-5536

Margo Porter, Publisher
Richard DeLouise, Editor
Pamela Anderson, Executive

Developments in the NASDAQ market.

8851 NATRI Newsletter

National Association for Treasurers of
Religious
8824 Cameron Street
Silver Springs, MD 20910

301-587-7776
FAX 301-589-2897
Home Page: www.natri.org

Laura Reicks, Publisher
Lorelle Elcock, Associate Director Finance
Frequency: Bi-Monthly

8852 NICSA News

National Investment Company Service
Association
36 Washington Street
Suite 70
Wellesley Hills, MA 02481

781-416-7200
FAX 781-416-7065
E-Mail: info@nicsa.org
Home Page: www.nicsa.org

Barbara V Weidlich, President
Keith Dropkin, Director Operations
Doris Jaimes, Registrar
Sheila Kobaly, Events Manager
Chris Ludent, IT Manager
Frequency: Quarterly

8853 National Mortgage News

Thomson Financial Publishing
1 State St
27th Floor
New York, NY 10004-1481

212-825-8445
800-235-5552
FAX 212-292-5216
Home Page: www.nationalmortgagenews.com/

Timothy Murphy, Group Publisher
Mark Fogarty, Editorial Director
Paul Muolo, M&A/Data Editor
Timothy Reifschneider, Advertising Director
Jose Thomas, Manager

Mortgage information, legislation and news.
Cost: $228.00
Frequency: Weekly
Circulation: 5000
Printed in 2 colors on newsprint stock

8854 Network Newsletter

Society for Information Management
401 N Michigan Avenue
Chicago, IL 60611

312-215-5190
FAX 312-245-1081
Home Page: www.simnet.org

Jim Luisi, Executive Director
Frequency: Bi-Monthly

8855 Newspaper Investor

Kagan World Media
1 Lower Ragsdale Dr
Building One, Suite 130
Monterey, CA 93940-5749

831-624-1536
831-625-3225
FAX 831-625-3225

E-Mail: info@kagan.com
Home Page: www.kagan.com

Tim Baskerville, President
Tom Johnson, Marketing Manager
Cost: $845.00
Frequency: Monthly
Founded in 1969

8856 OTC Chart Manual

Standard & Poor's Corporation
55 Water St
New York, NY 10041-0003

212-438-1000
FAX 212-438-0299
Home Page: www.standardandpoors.com

Deven Sharma, President

Charts on over 800 OTC stocks.

8857 Origination News

4709 Golf Road
Skokie, IL 60076

847-676-9600
800-321-3373
FAX 847-933-8101
E-Mail: custserv@accuitysolutions.com
Home Page: www.accuitysolutions.com

Timothy Murphy, Group Publisher
Mark Fogarty, Editorial Director
Jose Thomas, Manager
Malcolm Taylor, Managing Director

Information for mortgage industry executives
on mortgage brokers, mortgage bankers and
mortgage executives in commercial banks, savings banks, savings and loan associations and
credit unions.
Cost: $78.00
Frequency: Monthly

8858 Pawnbroker News

National Pawnbrokers Association
P.O.Box 508
Keller, TX 76244-0508

817-491-4554
FAX 817-491-8770
E-Mail: info@NationalPawnbrokers.org
Home Page: www.nationalpawnbrokers.org

Bob Benedict, CAE, Executive Director
Emmett Murphy, Director
Teresa Congleton, Administrative Assistant
Frequency: 8/year

8859 Pink Comparison Report

SNL Securities
PO Box 2124
Charlottesvle, VA 22902-2124

434-977-1600
FAX 434-977-4466
Home Page: www.snlnet.com

Maria Moyer, Editor
Reid Nagle, Publisher
Mark LaBua, Subscription Manager
Mark Outlaw, Advertising Director
Nick Cafferillo, Chief Operating Officer

For CEOs, CFOs and IRCs of banks. Compares
a subscribing bank or thrift's consolidated financial and market performance to other banks
and thrifts chosen by the subscriber and banks
and thrifts of similar asset size and location.
40 Pages
Frequency: Quarterly

8860 Private Equity Week

Securities Data Publishing
40 W 57th St
New York, NY 10019-4001

212-484-4701
FAX 212-956-0112
Home Page: www.sdponline.com

Jennifer Reed, Editor-in-Chief
Edward Cortese, Marketing Executive

News of the past week and forecast of the
weeks to come for investors.
Cost: $780.00
Frequency: Weekly

8861 Private Placement Letter

Securities Data Publishing
1290 6th Avenue
36th Floor
New York, NY 10104-101

212-765-5311
FAX 212-957-0420
E-Mail: custserv@sourcemedia.com
Home Page: www.privateplacementletter.com/

John Toth, Publisher
Ronald Cooper, Editor-in-Chief
Lauren Klopacs, Marketing Manager
Mark Cialdella, Circulation Manager
David Harkey, Advertising Manager

Highly sophisticated information on the debt
private placement market including senior and
mezzanine level debt.
Cost: $1395.00

8862 Proceedings of the National Conference on Planned Giving

National Committee on Planned Giving
233 S McCrea St
Suite 400
Indianapolis, IN 46225-1068

317-269-6274
FAX 317-269-6276
Home Page: www.ncpg.org

Tanya Howe Johnson, President
Sandra Kerr, Director Government Education
Barbara Owens, Director Membership
Kathryn J Ramsey, Director Meetings
Kurt Reusze, Manager Education/Technology
Frequency: Annual

8863 Quality Performance Report

Managed Account Reports
220 5th Avenue
19th Floor
New York, NY 10001-7708

212-213-6202
800-638-2525
FAX 212-213-6273
Home Page: www.marhedge.com

Randall Devere, Editor-in-Chief
Lois Peltz, Editor
Gary Lynch, President
Lisa McErlane, Marketing

The pre-eminent source of qualitative and
quantitative information on global managed derivatives. Delivers in-depth analysis on the performance of the trading advisors in MAR's
qualified database. Now covering over 500
trading advisors and programs.
Cost: $299.00
Frequency: Quarterly
Circulation: 400
Founded in 1913
Printed in 2 colors on matte stock

8864 REIT Daily Fax

SNL Securities
One SNL Plaza
PO Box 2124
Charlottesvle, VA 22902-2124

434-977-1600
FAX 434-293-0407
E-Mail: isales@snl.com
Home Page: www.snl.com

Amy Woolard, Editor
Nick Cafferillo, Chief Operating Officer
Alan Zimmerman, Publisher
Pat LaBua, Customer Service Director
Adam Hall, Managing Director

Newsletter designed specifically for REIT industry professionals and investors. Features im-

portant industry events, condensed news stories, recent capital offerings and the latest market information.
4 Pages
Frequency: Daily
Founded in 1987

8865 REIT Performance Graph
SNL Securities
One SNL Plaza
PO Box 2124
Charlottesvle, VA 22902-2124

434-977-1600
FAX 434-977-4466
E-Mail: subscriptions@snl.com
Home Page: www.snl.com

Steve Arnold, Vice Chairman, CFO
Chandler Spears, Editor
Keven Lindemann, Real Estate
Gregg Amonette, General Media
Nick Cafferillo, Chief Operating Officer

For publicly traded REITs and REIT service providers. Compares the investment performance of a publicly traded REIT to a specific SNL index or to a selected peer group and the appropriate broad multi-industry index. Covers a 5-year period or the period beginning with the IPO date.
Cost: $399.00
1 Pages
Founded in 1987

8866 Real Estate Alert
Harrison Scott Publications
5 Marine View Plz
#301
Hoboken, NJ 07030-5722

201-386-1491
FAX 201-659-4141
E-Mail: info@hspnews.com
Home Page: www.hspnews.com

Andy Albert, Owner
Bob Mura, Editor
Barbara Eannaci, Marketing Manager
Michelle Lebowitz, Director

Information on investment opportunities in institutional grade commercial real estate, includes sales acquisitions and personnel changes.
Cost: $1597.00
Frequency: Weekly
Circulation: 650
Founded in 1989

8867 Real Estate Finance Today
Mortgage Bankers Association of America
1919 Pennsylvania Avenue NW
Washington, DC 20006-3404

202-557-2700
E-Mail: info@mortgagebankers.org
Home Page: www.mortgagebankers.org

Information on anticipating industry trends, regulatory changes, economic outlook, federal and state legislation and trends in the secondary mortgage industry.
Cost: $100.00
Frequency: Monthly
Circulation: 1500
Founded in 1939

8868 Real-Estate Alert
Harrison Scott Publications
5 Marine View Plz
Suite 301
Hoboken, NJ 07030-5722

201-386-1491
FAX 201-659-4141

E-Mail: info@hspnews.com
Home Page: www.hspnews.com

Andy Albert, Owner
Tom Ferris, Director
Michelle Lebowitz, Director

A weekly newsletter on the securitization of consumer and corporate receivables.
Cost: $1497.00
10 Pages
Frequency: Weekly
Circulation: 600
ISSN: 1520-3700
Printed in 4 colors on matte stock

8869 Reducing Benefits Costs
Institute of Management and Administration
1 Washington Park
Suite 1300
Newark, NJ 07102

212-244-0360
FAX 973-622-0595
Home Page: www.ioma.com

Provides information on controlling benefit costs.
Cost: $245.00
16 Pages
Frequency: Monthly

8870 Regional Economic Digest
Federal Reserve Bank of Kansas City
925 Grand Avenue
Kansas City, MO 64198-0001

816-881-2970
800-333-1010
FAX 816-881-2569
Home Page: http://ideas.repec.org

Thomas Davis, Publisher
Bob Regan, Editor

A review of financial and economic conditions in the Tenth District. Includes articles of regional interest, statistics on District commercial banks and the area economy and results of a survey of agricultural credit conditions.
32 Pages

8871 Regulatory Risk Monitor
United Communications Group
11300 Rockville Pike
Street 1100
Rockville, MD 20852-3030

301-287-2700
FAX 301-816-8945
E-Mail: webmaster@ucg.com
Home Page: www.ucg.com

Benny Dicecca, President

Updates banking officials, credit union, compliance officers, attorneys and auditors with current independent news and guidance.
Founded in 1970

8872 Report on Financial Analysis, Planning & Reporting
Institute of Management and Administration
1 Washington Park
Suite 1300
Newark, NJ 07102

212-244-0360
FAX 973-622-0595
Home Page: www.ioma.com

FARP regularly covers performance measurements effective use of new FASB, IRS and SEC financial and accounting requirements for all industries, shows managers the best way to evaluate business opportunities, how to read and evaluate capital budgets, earbug reports and analysts see the big picture through the use of new financial tools such as Economic Value Assets and Shareholder Valuations models.
Cost: $269.00
Frequency: Monthly

8873 Retirement Plans Bulletin
Universal Pensions
PO Box 979
Brainerd, MN 56401

218-855-0565
800-346-3860
FAX 218-829-4814

Thomas G Anderson, President
Jennifer M Norquist, Editor

Digests IRS technical jargon on IRA's and qualified plans and translates it into understandable articles and advice for financial organizations.
Cost: $89.00
10 Pages
Frequency: Monthly
Printed in 2 colors on glossy stock

8874 SNL Bank M&A DataSource
SNL Securities
One SNL Plaza
PO Box 2124
Charlottesvle, VA 22902-2124

434-977-1600
FAX 434-977-4466
E-Mail: subscriptions@snl.com
Home Page: www.snl.com

John Minor, Publisher
Eric Hoffer, Editor
John McCune, Banks/Thrifts Manager
Michael Spears, Advertising
Nick Cafferillo, Chief Operating Officer

For investment bankers, investment companies, banks, thrifts, consultants and broker/dealers. Includes all merger and acquisition activity involving a bank or thrift as a buyer or seller.
Founded in 1987

8875 SNL Branch Migration DataSource
SNL Securities
PO Box 2124
Charlottesvle, VA 22902-2124

434-977-1600
FAX 434-977-4466
Home Page: www.snlnet.com

Melissa Hobson, Editor
John Minor, Editor
Reid Nagle, Publisher
Mark Outlaw, Advertising Director
Nick Cafferillo, Chief Operating Officer

For investment bankers, investment companies, banks, thrifts, consultants and regulatory agencies. Re-assigns bank and thrift branch deposits to account for all M&A activity that has occurred since the last regulatory release.
Frequency: Annual
Founded in 1991

8876 SNL Corporate Performance Graphs for Banks
SNL Securities
One SNL Plaza
PO Box 2124
Charlottesvle, VA 22902-2124

434-977-1600
FAX 434-977-4466
E-Mail: subscriptions@snl.com
Home Page: www.snl.com

Will Wick, Editor
James Record, Editor
John McCune, Banks/Thrifts Manager
Michael Spears, Advertising
Nick Cafferillo, Chief Operating Officer

For publicly traded banks, law firms, accountants and consulting firms. Includes a 5-year comparison of an institution's stock to both a selected peer group index and a broad multi-industry index.
1 Pages
Founded in 1987

8877 SNL Financial DataSource
SNL Securities
One SNL Plaza
PO Box 2124
Charlottesvle, VA 22902-2124

434-977-1600
FAX 434-977-4466
E-Mail: subscriptions@snl.com
Home Page: www.snl.com

Steve Tomasi, Editor
Steve Ferguson, Editor
Edward Metz, Financial
Michael Spears, Advertising
Nick Cafferillo, Chief Operating Officer

For investment bankers, investment companies,
banks, thrifts, institutional investors, consultants and broker/dealers. Available in six separate interactive modules that contain data for
equity research, industry trend analysis, peer
group comparisons and identification of investment and acquisition opportunities.
Founded in 1987

**8878 SNL Mutual Thrift Conversion
Investors Kit**
SNL Securities
One SNL Plaza
PO Box 2124
Charlottesvle, VA 22902-2124

434-977-1600
FAX 434-977-4466
E-Mail: subscriptions@snl.com
Home Page: www.snl.com

Chris Smith, Editor
Reid Nagle, Publisher
John McCune, Banks/Thrifts Manager
Michael Spears, Advertising
Nick Cafferillo, Chief Operating Officer

For thrift executives, individual investors and
institutional investors. Contains a set of articles
explaining the mechanics of mutual-to-stock
conversion and the 'how-to' of investing, reviewing profitability of conversion investments
and outlining regulatory issues that affect conversions.
Cost: $495.00
100 Pages
Frequency: Monthly
Founded in 1987

8879 SNL Pink Quarterly
SNL Securities
PO Box 2124
Charlottesvle, VA 22902-2124

434-977-1600
FAX 434-977-4466
Home Page: www.snlnet.com

Maria Moyer, Editor
Reid Nagle, Publisher
Mark Outlaw, Advertising Director
Pat LaBua, Subscription Manager
Nick Cafferillo, Chief Operating Officer

For investment companies, banks and thrifts,
broker/dealers and individual investors. Contains detailed financial and market information
on all banks and thrifts traded on the OTC bulletin boards and by market makers, as well as
in-depth analysis of this sector.
240 Pages
Frequency: Quarterly
Founded in 1995

**8880 SNL Securities Thrift Performance
Graph**
SNL Financial

PO Box 2124
Charlottesvle, VA 22902-2124

434-977-1600
FAX 434-977-4466
Home Page: www.snlnet.com

Reid Nagle, Publisher
John Racine, Editor
Mark Outlaw, Advertising Director
Pat Labua, Subscription Manager
Jeff Sternberg, Production Editor

SNL Securities is a research and publishing
company that focuses on banks, thrifts, REITs
insurance companies, and specialized, financial
service companies. Founded in 1987, SNL securities has become the authority for information on financial institutions.

**8881 SNL Securities Bank Comparison
Report**
SNL Securities
PO Box 2124
Charlottesvle, VA 22902-2124

434-977-1600
FAX 434-977-4466
Home Page: www.snlnet.com

Mona Thompson, Editor
Dan Oakey, Editor
Keith Davis, Editor
Reid Nagle, Publisher
Nick Cafferillo, Chief Operating Officer

For CEOs, CFOs and IRCs of banks. Compares
a subscribing bank's consolidated financial and
market performance to that of banks and thrifts
of similar asset size and location.
40 Pages
Frequency: Quarterly
Founded in 1987

**8882 SNL Securities Thrift Comparison
Report**
SNL Securities
PO Box 2124
Charlottesvle, VA 22902-2124

434-977-1600
FAX 434-977-4466
Home Page: www.snlnet.com

Dave Spence, Editor
Reid Nagle, Publisher
Mark Outlaw, Advertising Director
Pat LaBua, Subscripton Manager
Nick Cafferillo, Chief Operating Officer

Report for CEOs, CFOs and IRCs of thrifts and
major corporate stockholders. Illustrates and
compares a subscribing thrift's consolidated financial and market performance to thrifts of
similar asset size and location.
40 Pages
Frequency: Quarterly
Founded in 1988

8883 Secured Leader
Commercial Finance Association
Ste 1801
7 Penn Plz
New York, NY 10001-3979

212-594-3490
FAX 212-564-6053
E-Mail: info@cfa.com
Home Page: www.cfa.com

Bruce H Jones, Executive Director
Theodore Kompa, President

Only publication devoted exclusively to the asset-based financial services industry. Editorial
matter is directed toward practitioners of asset-based financing. Accepts advertising.
Cost: $56.00
76 Pages
Circulation: 5000
Founded in 1944

8884 Securities Industry News
Source Media
1 State St
27th floor
New York, NY 10004-1561

212-803-8200
800-221-1809
FAX 212-843-9608
E-Mail: custserv@sourcemedia.com
Home Page: www.sourcemedia.com

James M Malkin, CEO
Michael Eggebrecht, Managing Editor
Edward Hanasik, Marketing Director
Omar Asmar, Art Director
David Greenough, VP/Business Technology
Group

Securities Industry News is a weekly newspaper in the global securities and financial markets that delivers original, time-critical news
and analysis to senior decision-makers in
charge of operations, technology, processing
services, and compliance in the global securities and financial markets.
Cost: $575.00
Frequency: 42 Issues Annually

8885 Securities Week
McGraw Hill
PO Box 182604
Columbus, OH 43272

614-304-4000
877-833-5524
FAX 614-759-3759
E-Mail: customer.service@mcgraw-hill.com
Home Page: www.mcgraw-hill.com

Michael Ocrant, Managing Editor
Harold McGraw, CEO

Information on firms and exchanges strategy
plans, new hires, events and issues, as well as
legislation and legal rulings impacting the securities industry.
Frequency: Weekly
Founded in 1884

8886 Seller/Service Update
Inside Mortgage Finance Publishers
7910 Woodmont Ave
Suite 1000
Bethesda, MD 20814-7019

301-951-1240
FAX 301-656-1709
E-Mail: service@imfpubs.com
Home Page: www.imfpubs.com

Guy Cecala, Owner
John Bancroft, Managing Editor
Mary Lou Probka, Director of Marketing
Mary Lou Probka, Director of Circulation

Complete coverage of underwriting and servic-
ing, changes occurring in the mortgage market.
Focuses on Fannie Mae, Freddie Mac, HUD,
FHA, VA, private mortgage insurers and pri-
vate conduits.
Cost: $395.00
Frequency: Monthly
Circulation: 500
Founded in 1984

8887 Shareholder Satisfaction Survey
National Investment Company Service
36 Washington Avenue
Suite 70
Wellesley Hills, MA 02481

781-416-7200
FAX 781-416-7065
E-Mail: info@nicsa.org
Home Page: www.nicsa.org

Barbara V Weidlich, President
Keith Dropkin, Director Operations
Doris Jaimes, Registrar

Sheila Kobaly, Events Manager
Chris Ludent, IT Manager
Frequency: Annual

8888 Special Stock Report
Wall Street Transcript
67 Wall Street
9th Floor
New York, NY 10005-3701

212-952-7400
800-246-7673
FAX 212-668-9842
E-Mail: twsteditor@twst.com
Home Page: www.twst.com

Andrew Pickup, President/CEO
Doug Estadt, Online Editor
Andrew Pickup, Publisher
Jason Flatt, Marketing
Monthly stock pick based on research, interviews, and data contained in the wall st. transcript.
Cost: $399.00
Frequency: Monthly
Circulation: 7274
Founded in 1963

8889 Specialty Lender
SNL Securities
PO Box 2124
Charlottesvle, VA 22902-2124

434-977-1600
FAX 434-977-4466
Home Page: www.snlnet.com

Dave Meadors, Editor
Jim Allen, Editor
L Todd Vencil, Editor
Reid Nagle, Publisher
Nick Cafferillo, Chief Operating Officer
For executives of specialty lending companies, banks and thrifts which have specialty lending operations, heads of captive finance companies, investors, investment bankers and equity analysts. Provides news, analysis and financial and market information about specialty lenders, focusing on credit management and access to capital.
40 Pages
Frequency: Monthly
Founded in 1996

8890 Specialty Lender Performance Graph
SNL Securities
PO Box 2124
Charlottesvle, VA 22902-2124

434-977-1600
FAX 434-977-4466
Home Page: www.snlnet.com

David Meadors, Editor
Reid Nagle, Publisher
Mark Outlaw, Advertising Director
Pat LaBua, Subscription Manager
Nick Cafferillo, Chief Operating Officer
For publicly traded specialty lenders and specialty lender service providers. Compares the investment performance of a specialty lender to a specific SNL index or to a selected peer group and the appropriate broad multi-industry index. Covers a 5-year period or the period beginning with the IPO date.
Frequency: By request
Founded in 1997

8891 Streaming Media Investor
Kagan World Media
126 Clock Tower Place
Carmel, CA 93923-8746

831-624-1536
FAX 831-624-5882

E-Mail: info@kagan.com
Home Page: www.kagan.com

George Niesen, Editor
Tom Johnson, Marketing Manager
News of the Streaming Media Investor. Three month trial available.
Cost: $895.00
Frequency: Monthly

8892 TV Program Investor
Kagan World Media
126 Clock Tower Place
Carmel, CA 93923-8746

831-624-1536
800-307-2529
FAX 831-625-3225
E-Mail: info@kagan.com
Home Page: www.kagan.com

George Niesen, Editor
Harvy Kraft, Marketing Manager
Tim Baerville, CEO/President
Robert Naylor, Circulation Manager
Cost: $895.00
Frequency: Monthly
Founded in 1969

8893 Tax Management Compensation Planning
1250 23rd Street NW
Washington, DC 20037-1164

202-337-7240
800-223-7270
FAX 202-496-6013

David McFarland, President
Glenn Davis, Managing Editor
Nearly 40 portfolios, each focusing on specific tax, labor and other aspects of qualified and non-qualified retirement plans, employee welfare benefit plans, executive compensation, employment taxes and accounting for deferred compensation. Offers practitioner-authored articles, analysis of recent developments and decisions, and insightful comments from leading practitioners on the latest planning strategies.
Cost: $837.00
Frequency: Monthly

8894 Taxpractice
Tax Analysts
6830 North
Fairfax Drive
Arlington, VA 22213-1001

703-533-4400
800-955-2444
FAX 703-533-4444
E-Mail: webmaster@tax.org
Home Page: www.tax.org

Thomas F Field, Publisher
Jill Biden, Vice President
Contains comprehensive coverage of IRS rulings, court decisions, tax law changes and other topics of interest.
Cost: $749.00
Frequency: Weekly
Circulation: 2200
Founded in 1970

8895 TheStreet Ratings, Inc.
14 Wall Street
15th Floor
New York, NY 10005

212-321-5000
800-289-9222
FAX 212-321-5016
E-Mail: letters@thestreet.com
Home Page: www.thestreet.com

Dave Kansas, Editor-in-Chief
Information on what is happening on Wall Street, along with mutual fund and economic news, stock quotes, market summaries, and

analyses of key indicators.
Cost: $69.95
Frequency: Daily

8896 Thrift 13D Dictionary
SNL Securities
PO Box 2124
Charlottesvle, VA 22902-2124

434-977-1600
FAX 434-977-4466
Home Page: www.snlnet.com

Todd L Davenport, Editor
Reid Nagle, Publisher
Mark Outlaw, Advertising Director
Pat LaBua, Subscription Manager
Nick Cafferillo, Chief Operating Officer
Contains all active 13D filings and related filings for every publicly traded bank in the country, including those which trade on the pink sheets.
250 Pages
Frequency: Quarterly

8897 Thrift Performance Graph
SNL Securities
One SNL Plaza
PO Box 2124
Charlottesvle, VA 22902-2124

434-977-1600
FAX 434-977-4466
E-Mail: subscriptions@snl.com
Home Page: www.snl.com

Will Wick, Editor
James Record, Editor
John McCune, Banks/Thrifts Manager
Michael Spears, Advertising
Nick Cafferillo, Chief Operating Officer
Compares investment performance of a publicly traded Thrift company to a specific SNL index or to a selected peer group and the appropriate broad multi-industry index. Graph covers a 5-year period or the period beginning with the IPO date. For publicly traded thrifts, law firms, accountants and consulting firms.
1 Pages
Founded in 1987

8898 Trading Technology Week
Waters Information Services
270 Lafayette St
Suite 700
New York, NY 10012-3311

212-925-6990
FAX 212-925-7585
E-Mail: eugene.grygo@incisivemedia.com
Home Page: www.dealingwithtechnology.com

Tim Weller, CEO
Eugene Grygo, Editor
Adrian Goulbourn, Publisher
Lillian Lopez, Production Manager
Melissa Jao, Business Development Manager
Information covering the latest applications, platforms and strategies in trading room systems and proprietary execution.
Cost: $2025.00
Frequency: Weekly
Founded in 2000

8899 Transactions
AACE International
209 Prairie Ave
Suite 100
Morgantown, WV 26501-5934

304-296-8444
800-858-2678
FAX 304-291-5728
E-Mail: info@aacei.org
Home Page: www.aacei.org

Andrew Dowd, Executive Director
Megan McCulla, Asst Manager

Jenny Alms, Marketing Manager
Cost: $65.00
Frequency: Monthly
Circulation: 5000
Founded in 1956

8900 Turning Points
Concept Publishing
PO Box 500
York, NY 14592-500

800-836-4575
800-836-4575
FAX 585-243-3148
E-Mail: publishing@conceptpub.com
Home Page: www.conceptpub.com

Jim Dovan, Publisher
David Coleman, Editor
Economic news.
Cost: $198.00
2 Pages
Circulation: 600
Founded in 1974
Printed in one color on matte stock

8901 VOD Investor
Kagan World Media
126 Clock Tower Place
Carmel, CA 93923-8746

831-624-1536
800-307-2529
FAX 831-625-3225
E-Mail: info@kagan.com
Home Page: www.kagan.com

George Niesen, Editor
Tom Johnson, Marketing Manager
Robin Flynn, Senior VP

News of the VOD Investor. Three month trial available.
Cost: $1045.00
Frequency: Monthly
Founded in 1969

8902 Venture Capital & Health Care
Asset Alternatives
170 Linden Street
Wellesley, MA 02482-7919

781-304-1400
FAX 781-304-1440
Home Page: www.assetnews.com

Tom Salemi, Senior Editor
Lisa Hughes, Circulation Manager

Explores the business of health care investing in the trillion dollar health care market. Provides insight into the deals, deal makers, and portfolio companies in all sectors of health care, including services, biotechnology, medical devices, and 'infomedics.'
Cost: $795.00
Frequency: Monthly

8903 Venture Capital Information Technology
Asset Alternatives
170 Linden Street
Wellesley, MA 02482-7919

781-304-1400
FAX 781-304-1440
E-Mail: info@PrivateEquityAnalyst.com
Home Page: www.assetnews.com

Lisa Hughes, Circulation Manager
Barbara Bissonnette, Vice President Marketing/Sales

Delivers information an insight into the fast-moving world of venture investing in technology. Every month, it brings readers the IT deals, fund formations, exits, and personnel news at the venture firms and corporate venturing groups they need to stay abreast of venture investing in IT.
Cost: $795.00
Frequency: Monthly

8904 Video Investor
Kagan World Media
126 Clock Tower Place
Carmel, CA 93923-8746

831-624-1536
FAX 831-624-5882
E-Mail: info@kagan.com
Home Page: www.kagan.com

George Niesen, Editor
Tom Johnson, Marketing Manager

Authoritative look inside the business of renting and selling video cassettes. Exclusive estimates of retail and wholesale transactions and inventories. Tracking movies into the home. Three month trial is available.
Cost: $ 795.00
Frequency: Monthly

8905 Wall Street Technology Association Enewsletter
620 Shrewsbury Ave
Suite C2
Tinton Falls, NJ 07701

732-530-8808
FAX 732-530-0020
E-Mail: info@wsta.org
Home Page: www.wsta.org
Social Media: *Facebook, Twitter, LinkedIn*

John Killeen, President
Phyllis Lampell, Executive Director
JoAnn Cooper, Executive Director

Nonprofit educational organization that focuses on technologies, operational approaches, and business issues for the global financial community.
2000+ Members
Frequency: Monthly
Circulation: 14000+
Founded in 1967

8906 Water Investment Newsletter
US Water News
230 Main St
Halstead, KS 67056-1913

316-835-2222
800-251-0046
FAX 316-835-2223
Home Page: www.uswaternews.com

Thomas Bell, Owner
Toni Young, Chairman

News, features and profiles of shareholder owned water supply and treatment companies. General news on water-related investment opportunities with stock portfolio.
Cost: $140.00
8 Pages
Frequency: Monthly
ISSN: 1049-443X
Printed in one color on matte stock

8907 Wireless Market Stats
Kagan World Media
1 Lower Ragsdale Dr
Building One, Suite 130
Monterey, CA 93940-5749

831-624-1536
800-307-2529
FAX 831-625-3225
E-Mail: info@kagan.com
Home Page: www.kagan.com

Tim Baskerville, President
Tom Johnson, Marketing Manager

News of the Wireless Market Stats. Three month trial available.
Cost: $1095.00
Frequency: Monthly
Founded in 1969

8908 Wireless Telecom Investor
Kagan World Media

1 Lower Ragsdale Dr
Bldg 1, Suite 130
Monterey, CA 93940-5749

831-624-1536
800-307-2529
FAX 831-625-3225
E-Mail: info@kagan.com
Home Page: www.kagan.com

Tim Baskerville, President
Harvey Kraft, Director of Marketing
George Niesen, Editor
Robert Naylor, Circulation Manager
Sandie Borthwick, Publisher

Exclusive analysis of private and public values of wireless telecommunications companies, including cellular telephone, ESMR and PCS. Exclusive databases of subscribers, market penetrations, market potential, industry growth. Catching super-fast growth in a capsule. Three month trial available.
Cost: $1095.00
Frequency: Monthly
Founded in 1970

8909 Wireless/Private Cable Investor
Kagan World Media
126 Clock Tower Place
Carmel, CA 93923-8746

831-624-1536
FAX 831-624-5882
E-Mail: info@kagan.com
Home Page: www.kagan.com

George Niesen, Editor
Tom Johnson, Marketing Manager

The original bible of the wireless cable, multipoint distribution pay TV industry. Published continuously since 1972, this newsletter is the window on cable competition. Three month trial available.

Magazines & Journals

8910 AAII Journal
American Association of Individual Investors
625 N Michigan Avenue
Chicago, IL 60611

312-280-0170
800-428-2244
FAX 312-280-9883
E-Mail: members@aaii.com
Home Page: www.aaii.com

James Cloonan, Chairman
James Cloonan, Founder

Journal focusing on personal finance, specifically investing in stocks and mutual funds and portfolio management.
Cost: $29.00
40 Pages
Circulation: 170000
ISSN: 0192-3315
Founded in 1978

8911 AG Lender
Food 360/Vance Media
10901 W 84th Ter
Lenexa, KS 66214-1631

913-438-5721
800-808-2623
FAX 913-438-0697
E-Mail: rkeller@vancepublishing.com
Home Page: www.vancepublishing.com

Cliff Becker, VP

AG Lender magazine reaches key agricultural financial leaders with editorial material geared to their business success.
Frequency: Monthly
Circulation: 1700
Founded in 1923

8912 AGA Today
Association of Government Accountants
2208 Mount Vernon Ave
Alexandria, VA 22301-1314

703-562-0900
800-242-7211
FAX 703-548-9367
E-Mail: agacgfm@agacgfm.org
Home Page: www.agacgfm.org

Relmond Van Daniker, Executive Director

This publication acts as a clearinghouse for current government financial management information.
Frequency: Bi-Weekly
Circulation: 12,000

8913 Accounting and Business Review World
Scientific Publishing Company
1060 Main Street
River Edge, NJ 07661-2013

201-487-9655
FAX 201-487-9656

Ed Yang Hoong Pang

Aims to provide a forum for the publication of accounting and business research papers which are of interest to educators, students and practitioners.
Cost: $60.00

8914 Affiliate Forum
NACHA: Electronic Payments Association
13665 Dulles Technology Dr
Suite 300
Herndon, VA 20171-4607

703-561-1100
FAX 703-787-0996
E-Mail: info@nacha.org
Home Page: www.nacha.org

Janet O Estep, CEO

8915 Alert
Defense Credit Union Council
601 Pennsylvania Ave NW
South Building, Suite 600
Washington, DC 20004-2601

202-638-3950
FAX 202-638-3410
Home Page: www.dcuc.org

Roland Arteata, President
Frequency: Monthly

8916 American Cash Flow Journal
American Cash Flow Association
255 S Orange Avenue
#600
Orlando, FL 32801

407-206-6523
800-253-1294
E-Mail: info@americancashflow.com
Home Page: www.acfa.org

Fred Rewey, President

Issues cover factoring accounts receivable and dealing with privately held mortgages, along with thirty income streams. Offering updates on the legal and regulatory aspects of handling debt instruments and reports on new technology.
Frequency: Monthly
Circulation: 25,000

8917 Annual Institute Journal
National Association of Division Order Analysts
2805 Oak Trail Court
Suite 6312
Arlington, TX 76016

972-715-4489
E-Mail: administrator@nadoa.org
Home Page: www.nadoa.org

Lynn S McCord, Administrator
Frequency: Annual

8918 Armed Forces Comptroller
American Society of Military Comptrollers
415 N Alfred St
Alexandria, VA 22314-2269

703-549-0360
800-462-5637
FAX 703-549-3181
Home Page: www.asmconline.org

Robert Hale, Executive Director
Frequency: Quarterly

8919 Asset Management
ASMC
170 Avenue at the Common
PO Box 7930
Shrewsbury, NJ 07702-4803

732-389-8700
FAX 732-389-8701
Home Page: www.djassetmanagement.com

Barry Vinocur, Publisher

Departments include a mutual fund snapshot, a variable annuity databank, asset allocation, a journal watch and much more. Also offering topical features of interest to industry professionals.
Frequency: Bi-Monthly
Circulation: 30,000

8920 Asset Protection: Offshore Tax Reports
Offshore Press
4500 W 72nd Ter
Shawnee Mission, KS 66208-2824

913-362-9667
FAX 913-432-7174
E-Mail: jacobs@offshorepress.com
Home Page: www.offshorepress.com

Vernon K Jacobs, President
Cost: $120.00
Frequency: Weekly
Founded in 1981

8921 Barter News
PO Box 3024
Mission Viejo, CA 92690-1024

949-831-0607
FAX 949-831-9378
E-Mail: bmeyer@barternews.com
Home Page: www.barternews.com

Bob Meyer, Publisher/Editor
Michael Mercier, VP
Fredrick Fuest, COO
Julia Homer, CFO

Industry news is covered including listings of CEO's and CFO's and editorials. An in-depth look into the changes and evolution of barter, and shows how-to profitability use barter to increase the bottom line.
Cost: $40.00
96 Pages
Frequency: Quarterly
Circulation: 30,000
Founded in 1980
Printed in 4 colors on glossy stock

8922 Business Credit
National Association of Credit Management

8840 Columbia 100 Pkwy
Columbia, MD 21045-2100

410-740-5560
FAX 410-740-5574
E-Mail: robins@nacm.org
Home Page: www.nacm.org

Robin Schauseil, President
Jim Vanghel, Vice President

For professionals responsible for extending credit and collecting receivables. Topics include business law, lein law, technology, credit management, collections, deductions, fraud, credit risk, credit scoring, outsourcing, information services, trade finance and more.
Cost: $54.00
72 Pages
Circulation: 32000
Founded in 1896
Printed in 4 colors on matte stock

8923 Business Finance
Duke Communications International
221 E 29th Street
PO Box 3438
Loveland, CO 80539-3438

970-634-4700
FAX 970-593-1050
E-Mail: info@businessfinancemag.com
Home Page: www.businessfinancemag.com

David Blansfield, Publisher
Laurie Brannen, Editor-in-Chief
Meg Waters, Managing Editor
Matthew Weiner, Associate Publisher
Bruce Lynn, Managing Partner

Articles cover a broad range of topics from accounting to the Internet, from benchmarking to best practices, and cost management to career management.
Frequency: Monthly
Circulation: 50000

8924 CEIR - Quarterly National Economic Reports
National Association of Certified Valuation
1111 Brickyard Road
Suite 200
Salt Lake City, UT 84106-5401

303-698-1883
800-677-2009
E-Mail: sherril@nacva.com
Home Page: www.navca.com

Pamela R Bailey, Executive Director
Parnell Black, MBA CPA CVA, CEO
Roberto Castro, Director Business Development
Dean Dinas, Director Economic Research
Brien K Jones, General Manager Conferences
Frequency: Quarterly

8925 CMBA World
Commerical Mortgage Securities Association
30 Broad St
28th Floor
New York, NY 10004-4119

212-509-1844
FAX 212-509-1895
E-Mail: info1@cmbs.org
Home Page: www.cmbs.org

Dottie Cunningham, CEO
Frequency: Quarterly

8926 Capitol Comment
National Association of Mortgage Brokers
8201 Greensboro Drive
Suite 300
McLean, VA 22102

703-610-9009
FAX 703-610-9005

E-Mail: rdeloach@namb.org
Home Page: www.namb.org
Frequency: Monthly

8927 Collections & Credit Risk
Thomson Financial Publishing
1 State St
27th Floor
New York, NY 10004-1481

212-825-8445
800-221-1809
FAX 212-803-1592
Home Page: www.creditcollectionsworld.com

Sharon Rowlands, President/CEO
Louis Eccleston, Marketing Director
Catherine Ladwig, Editor
Darren Waggoner, Executive Editor
Jose Thomas, Manager

Focuses on news and trends of strategic and competitive importance to collections and credit policy executives. Covers the credit risk industry's growth, diversification and technology in both commercial and consumer credit.
Cost: $98.00
66 Pages
Frequency: Monthly
Circulation: 25000
ISSN: 1093-1260
Founded in 1961
Printed in 4 colors on glossy stock

8928 Collector Magazine
ACA International
PO Box 390106
Minneapolis, MN 55439-106

952-926-6547
FAX 952-926-1624
E-Mail: aca@acainternational.org
Home Page: www.acainternational.org

Timothy Dressen, Editor/Director Comm
Gary Rippentrop, CEO
Anne Rosso, Associate Editor

Brings you vital, up to the minute information on industry trends, regulations and legislation each month.
Cost: $70.00
Frequency: Monthly
Circulation: 6000
Founded in 1939

8929 Commercial Mortgage Insight
Zackin Publications
PO Box 2180
Waterbury, CT 06722-2180

203-755-0158
800-325-6745
FAX 203-755-3480
E-Mail: info@cmi-online.com
Home Page: www.cmi-online.com

Joe Caton, Editor
Paul Zackin, Publisher
June Han, Marketing

For desicion making executives in commercial mortgage banking and brokerage firms, commercial banks and community/savings institutions. Provides professionals with timely and comprehensive market news, trends and know-how needed to make informed decisions and choices.
Cost: $48.00
32 Pages
Frequency: Monthly
Circulation: 18000
ISSN: 1095-0729
Founded in 1969
Printed in 4 colors

8930 Computerized Investing
American Association of Individual Investors

625 N Michigan Avenue
Chicago, IL 60611

312-280-0170
800-428-2244
FAX 312-280-9883
E-Mail: mambers@aaii.com
Home Page: www.aaii.com

James Cloonan, Chairman

Offers information on computed investing, stocks and bonds.
Cost: $40.00
Founded in 1978

8931 Consumer Finance Law Quarterly Report
Conference on Consumer Finance Law
Oklahoma City University School of Law
2501 N Blackwelder
Oklahoma City, OK 73106

405-208-5363
FAX 405-208-5089
E-Mail: ccflqr@lec.okcu.edu
Home Page: www.ccfonline.org

Alvin C Harrell, Executive Director
Frequency: Quarterly

8932 Contingency Planning & Management
Witter Publishing Corporation
84 Park Avenue
Flemington, NJ 08822

908-788-0343
FAX 908-788-3782
Home Page: www.WitterPublishing.com

Steve Biggers, Publisher
Andy Hagg, Editor
Andrew Witter, President

Serves the fields of financial/banking, manufacturing industrial, transportation, utilities, telecommunications, health care, government, insurance and other allied fields.
Founded in 1996

8933 Controller's Quarterly
Institute of Management Accountants
10 Paragon Dr
Suite 1
Montvale, NJ 07645-1774

201-573-9000
800-638-4427
FAX 201-474-1600
E-Mail: ima@imanet.org
Home Page: www.imanet.org

Paul Sharman, President
Sandra Richtermeyer, Chair
Frequency: Monthly

8934 Corporate Controller
Thomson Reuters
195 Broadway
New York, NY 10007-3124

646-822-2000
800-231-1860
FAX 646-822-2800
E-Mail: trta.lei-support@thomsonreuters.com
Home Page: www.ria.thomsonreuters.com

Elaine Yadlon, Plant Manager
Thomas H Glocer, CEO & Director
Robert D Daleo, Chief Financial Officer
Kelli Crane, Senior Vice President & CIO

Includes health care costs, cash management, executive compensation and environmental insurance as well as regular columns on tax planning, technology advances, and innovative business trends.
Frequency: Bi-Monthly
Circulation: 3500

8935 Corporate Risk Management
Oster Communications

219 Main St
Cedar Falls, IA 50613-2742

319-277-1271
FAX 319-277-7481

Merrill Oster, President

Written for financial decision makers.
48 Pages
Frequency: Monthly
Founded in 1989

8936 Cost Engineering Journal
AACE International
209 Prairie Avenue
Suite 100
Morgantown, WV 26501-5934

304-296-8444
800-858-2678
FAX 304-291-5728
E-Mail: info@aacei.org
Home Page: www.aacei.org

Marvin Gelhausen, Managing Editor
Noah Kinderknecht, Editor

International journal of cost estimation, cost/schedule control, and project management read by cost professionals around the world to get the most up-to-date information about the profession.
Frequency: Monthly

8937 Cost Management Update
Institute of Management Accountants
10 Paragon Dr
Suite 1
Montvale, NJ 07645-1774

201-573-9000
800-638-4427
FAX 201-474-1600
E-Mail: ima@imanet.org
Home Page: www.imanet.org

Paul Sharman, President
Sandra Richtermeyer, Chair
Frequency: Monthly

8938 Credit Card Management
Thomson Financial Publishing
1 State St
27th Floor
New York, NY 10004-1481

212-825-8445
800-535-8403
FAX 800-235-5552
E-Mail: custserv@sourcemedia.com
Home Page: www.cardforum.com

James Daly, Editor
Sharon Rowlands, President/CEO
Louis Eccleston, Marketing Director
Jose Thomas, Manager

Information on the major developments in the credit card industry.
Cost: $98.00
74 Pages
Frequency: Monthly
Circulation: 19000
Founded in 1962
Printed in 4 colors on glossy stock

8939 Credit Scoring
Credit Research Foundation
8840 Columbia 100 Pkwy
Suite 100
Columbia, MD 21045-2100

410-740-5499
FAX 410-740-4620
E-Mail: crf_info@crfonline.org
Home Page: www.crfonline.org

Terry Callahan, President
Michael Durant, Vice-Chairman

8940 Credit Union Executive Journal
Credit Union National Association

Po Box 431
Madison, WI 53701-0431

608-231-4000
800-356-9655
FAX 608-231-1869
E-Mail: dorothy@cuna.org
Home Page: www.cuna.org

Daniel A Mica, CEO

Techniques and concepts available in management, finance, marketing, lending, human resources and technology for credit unions.
Cost: $202.00
Circulation: 2400
Founded in 1930

8941 Credit Union Magazine
Credit Union National Association
5710 Mineral Point Road
Madison, WI 53705-4454

800-356-9655
FAX 608-231-4263
E-Mail: dorothy@cuna.org
Home Page: www.cuna.org

Daniel A Mica, CEO
Tom Dorety, Vice Chairman
Bill Merrick, Managing Editor

The role and operations of modern credit unions.
Cost: $50.00
100 Pages
Frequency: Monthly
Circulation: 32776
ISSN: 0011-1066
Founded in 1981
Printed in 4 colors on glossy stock

8942 Credit Union Technology
Credit Union Technology
110-64 Queens Boulevard
#106
Forest Hills, NY 11375-6347

718-793-9400
FAX 718-793-9414
Home Page: www.cutmag.com

Andrew Mallon, Publisher

Information on improving customer service through technological advances.
Cost: $36.00
24 Pages
Frequency: Bi-Monthly
Circulation: 6000
ISSN: 1054-7304
Founded in 1991
Printed in 4 colors on glossy stock

8943 Credit and Collection Survey
Broadcast Cable Credit Association
550 W Frontage Rd
Suite 3600
Northfield, IL 60093-1243

847-881-8757
FAX 847-784-8059
E-Mail: info@bccacredit.com
Home Page: www.bccacredit.com

Mary Collin, CEO
Jamie Smith, Director of Operations
Rachelle Brooks, BCCA Sales
Frequency: Bi-Ennial

8944 DC Advocate
National Defined Contribution Council
9101 E Kenyon
Suite 300
Denver, CO 80237-0467

303-770-5353
FAX 303-770-1812
Home Page: www.ndcconline.org

Al Brust, Executive VP
Frequency: Quarterly

8945 Disclosure Record
Newsfeatures
8511 249th Street
Jamaica, NY 11426-2105
Jack Lotto, Editor

Full texts of corporate and financial news reports.
Cost: $50.00
8 Pages
Frequency: Monthly
Founded in 1973

8946 Economic Outlook
America's Community Bankers
900 19th Street NW
Suite 400
Washington, DC 20006

202-857-3100
888-872-0275
FAX 202-296-8716
E-Mail: info@acbankers.org
Home Page:
www.americascommunitybankers.com

Nancy Feig, Editor
Debra Cope, Publisher
Diane Casey-Landry, President/CEO

A first rate resource for strategically countering the hanging economic winds of the financial world.
Cost: $315.00
4 Pages
Frequency: Monthly
Founded in 1992

8947 Electronics Payment Journal
NACHA: Electronic Payments Association
13665 Dulles Technology Dr
Suite 300
Herndon, VA 20171-4607

703-561-1100
FAX 703-787-0996
E-Mail: info@nacha.org
Home Page: www.nacha.org

Janet O Estep, CEO
Deb Evans-Doyle, Senior Director Conference Mktg
Julie Hedlund, Senior Director Electronic Commerce
Michael Herd, Director Public Relations
Priscilla Holland, AAP, Senior Director Corporate Pymts

8948 Estate Planning Review
2700 Lake Cook Road
Riverwoods, IL 60015-3867

847-267-7000
800-224-8299
FAX 800-224-8299
Home Page: www.support.cch.com

Robert Becker, President and CEO
Cost: $275.00
Frequency: Monthly
Founded in 1913

8949 Examiner
Society of Financial Examiners
174 Grace Blvd
Altamonte Spgs, FL 32714-3210

407-682-4930
800-787-7633
FAX 407-382-3175
Home Page: www.sofe.org

Pauline Keyes, Owner
Stephen J Szypula, Financial Administrator
Frequency: Quarterly

8950 F & I Management Technology
Association of Finance and Insurance
Professionals

4112 Southwood E
Colleyville, TX 76034

817-428-2434
FAX 817-428-2534
Home Page: www.afip.com

David N Robertson, Executive Director

8951 Federal Credit Union Magazine
National Association of Federal Credit Unions
3138 10th St N
Arlington, VA 22201-2160

703-522-4770
800-336-4644
FAX 703-524-1082
E-Mail: fbecker@nafcu.org
Home Page: www.nafcu.org

Fred Becker, President

Written for CEO's, senior staff and volunteers of Federal Credit Unions. Offers legislative and regulatory news, as well as technology and operational issues. Call for rates.
50 Pages
Circulation: 1500
ISSN: 1043-7789
Founded in 1967
Printed in 4 colors on glossy stock

8952 Financial Analysts Journal
CFA Institure
Po Box 3668
Charlottesville, VA 22903-0668

434-951-5499
800-247-8132
FAX 434-951-5262
E-Mail: info@cfainstitute.org
Home Page: www.cfainstitute.org

John Rogers, CEO
Rodney N Sullivan, Associate Editor

To advance the knowledge and understanding of the practice of investment management through the publication of high-quality, practitioner-relevant research
Founded in 1945

8953 Financial Executive
Financial Executives International
200 Campus Dr
Suite 8
Florham Park, NJ 07932-1007

973-236-0177
800-336-0773
FAX 973-765-1018
Home Page: www.financialexecutives.com

Jim Abel, President
Ellen Heffes, Managing Editor
Colleen S Cunningham, President
Maria O'Grady, Marketing Manager

Addresses accounting and treasury subjects, as well as overall strategies in corporate financial mangement.
Cost: $74.39
72 Pages
Frequency: Monthly
Circulation: 16500
ISSN: 0895-4186
Founded in 1931
Printed in 4 colors on glossy stock

8954 Financial Management Journal
Financial Management Association
International
4202 E Fowler Ave
BSN 3331
Tampa, FL 33620-9951

813-974-2084
FAX 813-974-3318

E-Mail: info@fma.org
Home Page: www.fma.org

Jack S Rader, Executive Director
Jeffrey Coles, Advisory Editor
John Graham, Advisory Editor
Michael Lemmon, Advisory Editor
Jay Ritter, Advisory Editor

Financial Management serves both academicians and practitioners who are concerned with the financial management of non-financial businesses, financial institutions, and public and private not-for-profit organizations. The journal serves the profession by publishing significant new scholarly research in finance that is of the highest quality.
Frequency: Quarterly

8955 Financial Manager
Broadcast Cable Financial Management
Association
550 W Frontage Rd
Suite 3600
Northfield, IL 60093-1243

847-716-7000
FAX 847-784-8059
E-Mail: info@bccacredit.com
Home Page: www.bcfm.com

Mary Collins, President
Jamie Smith, Director of Operations
Rachelle Brooks, BCCA Sales

A bi-monthly magazine published by the Broadcast Cable Financial Management Association.
Cost: $69.00
36 Pages
Circulation: 300
Mailing list available for rent: 1100 names at $495 per M

8956 Financial Manager/Credit Topics
Broadcast Cable Credit Association
550 W Frontage Rd
Suite 3600
Northfield, IL 60093-1243

847-881-8757
FAX 847-784-8059
E-Mail: info@bccacredit.com
Home Page: www.bccacredit.com

Mary Collin, CEO
Jamie Smith, Director of Operations
Rachelle Brooks, BCCA Sales
Frequency: Bi-Monthly

8957 Financial Planning & Counseling Journal
Association for Financial Counseling and
Planning
2112 Arlington Avenue
Suite H
Upper Arlington, OH 43221

614-485-9650
FAX 614-485-9621
Home Page: www.afcpe.org

Sharon Burns, PhD, Executive Director
Frequency: Semi-Annual

8958 Financial Planning Digest
Harcourt Brace Professional Publishing
6277 Sea Harbor Drive
Orlando, FL 32887

407-345-2000
FAX 407-345-3016
Home Page: www.harcourt.com

Angelita Streeter, Editor
Paul Amidei, Managing Editor

Estate, retirement, insurance planning tips and strategies, practice management insight, book reviews and legislation updates.
Cost: $99.00
Frequency: Monthly

8959 Financial Review Magazine
NFR Communications
4948 Washburn Avenue S
Minneapolis, MN 55410

612-929-8110
FAX 612-929-8146
Home Page: www.nfrcom.com

Tom Bengtson, Editor
Jackie Hilgert, Production Manager

Trade publication covering the commercial banking industry in the upper midwest. Designed for the decision-maker in the bank.
Frequency: 25 per year

8960 Financial Services Quarterly
SNL Securities
One SNL Plaza
PO Box 2124
Charlottesvle, VA 22902-2124

434-977-1600
FAX 434-977-4466
E-Mail: subscriptions@snl.com
Home Page: www.snl.com

Pam Askea, Editor
Dan Oakey, Editor
Michael Spears, Advertising
Edward Metz, Financial Services
Nick Cafferillo, Chief Operating Officer

Comprehensive reference guide available on finance companies, mortgage banks, investment advisors and securities brokers/dealers. In-depth company profiles and financial data on these publicly traded companies and summary financials on thousands of non-public financial services companies.
Cost: $696.00
400 Pages
Frequency: Quarterly
Founded in 1987

8961 Financier
Bank Administration Institute
1 N Franklin St
Chicago, IL 60606-3598

312-553-4600
FAX 312-683-2373
E-Mail: info@bai.org
Home Page: www.bai.org

Deborah Bianucci, CEO
Willard Rappleye Jr, Executive Vice President
Ann Barcroft, Executive Vice President
Anne Matsumoto, Managing Director

Forum of ideas for the private sector.
Cost: $5.00
Circulation: 32,000

8962 Forbes Global
Forbes Media LLC.
60 5th Ave
New York, NY 10011-8868

212-620-2200
FAX 212-620-1857
E-Mail: readers@forbes.com
Home Page: www.forbes.com

Malcolm S Forbes Jr, CEO
Bruce Rogers, VP Marketing
Paul Maidment, Executive Director
Michael Smith Maidment, VP, GM Operations

A magazine giving detailed information about business and finance.
Frequency: Monthly

8963 Forbes Magazine
Forbes Media LLC.
60 5th Ave
11th Floor
New York, NY 10011-8868

212-620-2200
FAX 212-620-1857

E-Mail: customerservice@forbes.com
Home Page: www.forbes.com

Malcolm S Forbes Jr, CEO
Bruce Rogers, VP Marketing
Paul Maidment, Executive Director
Micheal Smith Maidment, VP, GM Operations

A magazine giving detailed information about business and finance.
Cost: $4.95
304 Pages
Founded in 1917

8964 Futures Industry
Futures Industry Association
2001 Pennsylvania Ave NW
#600
Washington, DC 20006-1823

202-223-1528
FAX 202-296-3184
E-Mail: info@futuresindustry.org
Home Page: www.futuresindustry.org

John Damgard, President/CEO
Erin Kairys, Manager
Will Acworth, Editor
Roselia Marmolejos, Administrative Assistant

Front and back office operations, marketing, research, money management, regulatory and brokerage issues from a domestic and international perspective.
Circulation: 15000
Founded in 1955

8965 Futures Magazine
Oster Communications
219 Main St
Suite 6
Cedar Falls, IA 50613-2742

319-277-1271
FAX 319-277-7481
Home Page: www.futuresmag.com

Merrill Oster, President
Ginger Szala, Publisher

News, analysis, and strategies for futures, options and derivatives traders. Descriptions include annual sourcebook directory of exchange, contract, company and product information.
Cost: $39.00
Frequency: Monthly
Circulation: 60000
Founded in 1972

8966 Global Custodian
Asset International
125 Greenwich Avenue
Greenwich, CT 06830

203-295-5015
FAX 203-629-5024
E-Mail: office@assetpub.com
Home Page: www.globalcustodian.com

Dominic Hobson, Editor-in-Chief
Charles Ruffel, Executive Editor
Meredith Hughes, Publisher
Alix Hughes, Sales Director

An in-depth perspective on the business of international investing, custody and clearing, and directory-type data on industry participants and trends. Provides investment professionals with an analysis of the strength and weaknessed of the players and systems that underlie international investing.
Cost: $185.00
Circulation: 30,488
Founded in 1989

8967 Global Finance
7 E 20th St.
New York, NY 10003

Home Page: www.gfmag.com
Social Media: *Facebook, Twitter, LinkedIn*

Joseph Giarraputo, Publisher & Editorial
Director

The magazine offers analysis, articles and data
to help corporate leaders, bankers and investors
make decisions.
Frequency: Monthly
Circulation: 50,050
Founded in 1987

8968 Global Investment Magazine
Global Investment Technology
820 2nd Ave
4th Floor
New York, NY 10017-4504

212-370-3700
FAX 212-370-4606
E-Mail: info@globalinv.com
Home Page: www.globalinv.com

Micheal Horton, Publisher
Pierre-Yves Sacchi, Managing Director

Portfolio management, trading and global asset
services, and a wide range of issues pertaining
to institutional portfolio management strategies
and decision making in the US and cross-bor-
der markets.
Frequency: Quarterly
Circulation: 15000

8969 Global Investment Technology
Global Investment Technology
820 2nd Ave
4th Floor
New York, NY 10017-4504

212-370-3700
FAX 212-370-4606
E-Mail: info@globalinv.com
Home Page: www.globalinv.com

Micheal Horton, Publisher
Pavan Sehgal, Managing Director
Pierre-Yves Sacchi, Managing Director

The strategic business interests of top-level de-
cision makers as well as their operations and
systems professionals.
Cost: $695.00
Circulation: 1800
Founded in 1990

8970 Healthcare Financial Management
2 Westbrook Corporate Ctr #700
Westchester, IL 60154-5723

708-531-9614
FAX 708-531-0032
Home Page: www.hfma.org

Richard L Clarke, President

8971 IBIS Review
Charles D Spencer
250 S Wacker Drive
#600
Chicago, IL 60606-5800

312-993-7900
FAX 312-993-7910
E-Mail: ibisnet@mindspring.com
Home Page: www.ibisnews.com

Charles D Spencer, Publisher
Celia Cruz, Owner

For the individual responsible for the compensation and benefits of employees working
abroad. Topics include pensions and
profit-sharing plans, stock purchase and savings plans, death and disability benefits, health
care coverage, termination indemnities, execu-

tive renumeration plans, investments, and
expatriate plans.
Frequency: Monthly
Circulation: 1500

8972 IMA Focus
Institute of Management Accountants
10 Paragon Dr
Suite 1
Montvale, NJ 07645-1774

201-573-9000
800-638-4427
FAX 201-474-1600
E-Mail: ima@imanet.org
Home Page: www.imanet.org

Paul Sharman, President
Frequency: Bi-Monthly

8973 INSIGHT
Society of Financial Examiners
174 Grace Blvd
Altamonte Spgs, FL 32714-3210

407-682-4930
800-787-7633
FAX 407-682-3175
Home Page: www.sofe.org

Pauline Keyes, Owner
Stephen J Szypula, Financial Administrator
Frequency: Monthly

8974 ISM Info Edge
Institute for Supply Management
2055 E Centennial Circle
PO Box 22160
Tempe, AZ 85285-2160

480-752-6276
800-888-6276
FAX 480-752-7890
E-Mail: infocenter@ism.ws
Home Page: www.ism.ws

Paul Novak, CPM, CEO
Holly LaCroix Johnson, Senior Vice President
Deborah Webber, SVP
Jean McHale, Manager
Frequency: Quarterly

8975 Inside Mortgage Finance
Inside Mortgage Finance Publishers
7910 Woodmont Ave
Suite 1010
Bethesda, MD 20814-7019

301-951-1240
FAX 301-656-1709
E-Mail: service@imfpubs.com
Home Page:
http://www.insidemortgagefinance.com

Industry news and related trade literature. Includes extensive market data, from rankings of
top originators to the leading private mortgage
insurers.
Cost: $889.00
12 Pages
ISSN: 8756-0003
Founded in 1984
Printed in 2 colors on matte stock

8976 Inside Mortgage Update
Inside Mortgage Finance Publishers
7910 Woodmont Ave
Suite 1010
Bethesda, MD 20814-7019

301-951-1240
FAX 301-656-1709
E-Mail: service@imfpubs.com
Home Page:
http://www.insidemortgagefinance.com

Guy Cecala, Owner
John Bancroft, President

Covers this dynamic market of lending to borrowers with less than perfect credit with news,

analysis and truly useful market intelligence.
Cost: $659.00
14 Pages
Circulation: 1000
ISSN: 1093-4030
Founded in 1996
Printed in 2 colors on matte stock

8977 Inside Supply Management
Insitute for Supply Management
2055 E Centennial Circle
PO Box 22160
Tempe, AZ 85285-2160

480-752-6276
800-888-6276
FAX 480-752-7890
E-Mail: infocenter@ism.ws
Home Page: www.ism.ws

Paul Novak, CPM, CEO
Holly LaCroix Johnson, Senior Vice President
Deborah Webber, SVP
Jean McHale, Manager
Frequency: Monthly

8978 Institute of Management &
Administration Newsletter
Institute of Management and Administration
1 Washington Park
Suite 1300
Newark, NJ 07102

212-244-0360
FAX 973-622-0595
Home Page: www.ioma.com

Information for those involved in international
sales. Regular monthly features,

8979 Institutional Investor
225 Park Ave. S
New York, NY 10003

212-224-3300
E-Mail: info@institutionalinvestor.com
Home Page: www.institutionalinvestor.com
Social Media: *Facebook, Twitter, LinkedIn,*
Google+, StockTwits

Diane Alfano, Chairman
David E. Antin, Chief Executive Officer
Allison Adams, Publisher

Authoritative financial news for institutional
investors.

8980 Insurance & Financial Meetings
Managment
Coastal Communications Corporation
2700 N Military Trail
Suite 120
Boca Raton, FL 33431

561-989-0600
FAX 561-989-9509
E-Mail: ccceditor@att.net
Home Page: www.themeetingmagazines.com

Harvey Grotsky, Publisher/Editor-In-Chief
Susan Wycoff Fell, Managing Editor
Susan Gregg, Managing Editor

The executive source for planning meetings
and incentives for the financial and insurance
sectors. With regular features and special focus
on site selection, destinations, industry-related
studies and activities, motivational and incentive programs, program and event planning.
Frequency: Monthly
Circulation: 40,000
Founded in 1983

8981 International Journal of Supply
Chain Management
Institute for Supply Management
New York, NY 10007-31

2055 E Centennial Circle
PO Box 22160
Tempe, AZ 85285-2160

480-752-6276
800-888-6276
FAX 480-752-7890
E-Mail: infocenter@ism.ws
Home Page: www.ism.ws

Paul Nocak, CPM, CEO
Holly LaCroix Johnson, Senior Vice President
Deborah Webber, SVP
Jean McHale, Manager
Frequency: Quarterly

8982 Investor Relations Business
Securities Data Publishing
40 W 57th St
New York, NY 10019-4001

212-484-4701
FAX 212-956-0112
E-Mail: sdp@tfn.com

Matthew Greco, Editor
Edward Cortese, Marketing Executive

News updates, career opportunities and personnel announcements for CEO's, CFO's, treasurers and directors of corporations.
Cost: $415.00
Frequency: Bi-Monthly

8983 Journal of Applied Finance
Financial Management Association
International
4202 E Fowler Ave
BSN 3331
Tampa, FL 33620-9951

813-974-2084
FAX 813-974-3318
E-Mail: info@fma.org
Home Page: www.fma.org

Jack S Rader, Executive Director
Ali Fatemi, Editor
Reena Aggarwal, Associate Editor
James S Ang, Associate Editor
Robert F Bruner, Associate Editor

Launched in 2001, JAF publishes easy-to-read pieces that focus on financial practice and education - a standard reference for those seeking knowledge on the new developments in applied finance.
Frequency: Bi-Annual

8984 Journal of Asset Protection
Thomson Reuters
195 Broadway
New York, NY 10007-3124

646-822-2000
800-231-1860
FAX 646-822-2800
E-Mail: trta.lei-support@thomsonreuters.com
Home Page: www.ria.thomsonreuters.com

Elaine Yadlon, Plant Manager
Thomas H Glocer, CEO & Director
Robert D Daleo, Chief Financial Officer
Kelli Crane, Senior Vice President & CIO

Information on shielding personal and business assets from creditors, third party attachments and government claims.
Cost: $195.00
Frequency: Bi-Monthly
Circulation: 2,000

8985 Journal of Cost Management
Thomson Reuters
195 Broadway
New York, NY 10007-3124

646-822-2000
800-231-1860
FAX 646-822-2800

E-Mail: trta.lei-support@thomsonreuters.com
Home Page: www.ria.thomsonreuters.com

Elaine Yadlon, Plant Manager
Thomas H Glocer, CEO & Director
Robert D Daleo, Chief Financial Officer
Kelli Crane, Senior Vice President & CIO

Information on cost management techniques and manufacturing technology. Provides essays and or research papers by professionals and educators.
Cost: $210.00
Frequency: Monthly
Circulation: 5000
Founded in 1940

8986 Journal of Education Finance
American Education Finance Association
5249 Cape Leyte Drive
Sarasota, FL 34242-1805

941-349-7580

Information and news to educational organizations on financial investing and prospecting.
150 Pages
Frequency: Quarterly
Circulation: 700
Founded in 1978

8987 Journal of Finance
American Finance Association
Haas School of Business
Berkley, CA 94720-1900

510-642-2397
FAX 510-525-6246
E-Mail: pyle@haas.berkley.edu
Home Page: www.afajof.org

Robert F Stambaugh, Editor
Anat R Admati, Associate Editors
Wendy Washburn, Editorial Assistant
David H Pyle, Business Manager

Covers theory and practice in the field of finance.
Frequency: Bi-Monthly
Circulation: 10000+
Founded in 1939

8988 Journal of Financial Planning
4100 E Mississippi Avenue
Suite 400
Denver, CO 80246

303-759-4900
800-322-4237
FAX 303-759-0749
E-Mail: journal@fpanet.org
Home Page: www.fpanet.org

Marvin W Tuttle CAE, Executive
Director/CEO
Ian McKenzie, Managing Director/Publishing

A comprehensive financial publication offering information and news on financial planning, investing and prospecting.
Cost: $90.00
Frequency: Monthly
Circulation: 50,000
Founded in 1979

8989 Journal of Fixed Income
Institutional Investor
488 Madison Ave
16th Floor
New York, NY 10022-5701

212-303-3100
800-945-2034
FAX 212-224-3491
E-Mail: iieditor@institutionalinvestor.com
Home Page: www.institutionalinvestor.com/

Allison Adams, Publisher
Brian Bruce, Editor
Anne O'Brien, Marketing

Reporting on analysis of theories and ideas involving fixed income.
Cost: $370.00
Frequency: Quarterly
Circulation: 2500
Founded in 1967

8990 Journal of Gift Planning
National Committee on Planned Giving
233 S McCrea St
Suite 400
Indianapolis, IN 46225-1068

317-269-6274
FAX 317-269-6276
Home Page: www.ncpg.org

Tanya Howe Johnson, President
Sandra Kerr, Director Government Education
Barbara Owens, Director Membership Manager
Kathryn J Ramsey, Director Meetings
Kurt Reusze, Manager Education/Technology
Frequency: Quarterly

**8991 Journal of Government Financial
Management**
Association of Government Accountants
2208 Mount Vernon Ave
Alexandria, VA 22301-1314

703-562-0900
800-242-7211
FAX 703-548-9367
E-Mail: agacgfm@agacgfm.org
Home Page: www.agacgfm.org

Relmond Van Daniker, Executive Director

Provides valuable information for governmental decision makers. Examines budgeting, accounting, auditing and date process developments.
Frequency: Quarterly
Circulation: 14,769

**8992 Journal of Healthcare Administrative
Management**
American Association of Healthcare
Administrative
11240 Waples Mill Rd
Suite 200
Fairfax, VA 22030-6078

703-934-0164
FAX 703-359-7562
E-Mail: moayad@aaham.org
Home Page: www.aaham.org

Sharon Geller, Executive Director
Linda Sheaffer, Chair
Frequency: Quarterly

8993 Journal of Investing
Institutional Investor
1900 Preston Road
#267-310
Plano, TX 75093-5175

214-495-9533
FAX 212-224-3491
E-Mail: info@iijournals.com
Home Page: www.iijournals.com

Brian Bruce, Editor-in-Chief
Allison Adams, Publisher
Anne O'Brien, Director of Marketing

Features equity investments, fixed income investing, security valuation and related investment vehicles.
Cost: $360.00
Frequency: Quarterly
Circulation: 2500
Founded in 1967

8994 Journal of Mutual Fund Services
Securities Data Publishing

600 Atlantic Avenue
Boston, MA 02210-2211

617-723-6400
FAX 617-624-7200
Home Page: www.dalbar.com

Ken Heath, Publisher
Kathleen Whalen, Managing Director

Focuses on backroom operations of the mutual fund industry, with directories featuring transfer assets, fund accountants, custodians, attorneys and other service personnel.
Cost: $795.00
Frequency: 8 per year

8995 Journal of Performance Management
Assn for Management Information in Financial Svcs
14247 Saffron Circle
Carmel, IN 46032

317-815-5857
FAX 317-815-5877
E-Mail: ami2@amifs.org
Home Page: www.amifs.org

Adam Schabes, President
Cost: $200.00
Frequency: 3/year
Circulation: 350

8996 Journal of Portfolio Management
Institutional Investor
488 Madison Ave
16th Floor
New York, NY 10022-5701

212-303-3100
800-437-9997
FAX 212-224-3491
E-Mail: iieditor@institutionalinvestor.com
Home Page: www.institutionalinvestor.com/

Allison Adams, Publisher
Peter Bernstein, Editor
Anne O'Brien, Marketing Manager

Ideas and concepts in the practice and theory of portfolio management.
Cost: $430.00
Frequency: Quarterly
Circulation: 5000
Founded in 1975

8997 Journal of Taxation
Thomson Reuters
195 Broadway
New York, NY 10007-3124

646-822-2000
800-231-1860
FAX 646-822-2800
E-Mail: trta.lei-support@thomsonreuters.com
Home Page: www.ria.thomsonreuters.com

Elaine Yadlon, Plant Manager
Thomas H Glocer, CEO & Director
Robert D Daleo, Chief Financial Officer
Kelli Crane, Senior Vice President & CIO

Information on tax developments and trends, revenue rulings, court decisions and legislative and administrative actions of significance to the sophisticated tax professional.
Cost: $315.00
Frequency: Monthly
Circulation: 12000
ISSN: 0022-4863
Founded in 1984
Printed in on glossy stock

8998 Legislative Currents
American Association of Healthcare Administrative
11240 Waples Mill Rd
Suite 200
Fairfax, VA 22030-6078

703-934-0164
FAX 703-359-7562

E-Mail: moayad@aaham.org
Home Page: www.aaham.org

Sharon Geller, Executive Director
Linda Sheaffer, Chair
Frequency: Bi-Monthly

8999 MS Quarterly Journal
Society for Information Management
401 N Michigan Avenue
Chicago, IL 60611

312-215-5190
FAX 312-245-1081
Home Page: www.simnet.org

Jim Luisi, Executive Director
Frequency: Quarterly

9000 Management and Technology
Association of Finance and Insurance Professionals
412 Southwood E
Colleyville, TX 76034

817-428-2434
FAX 817-428-2534
Home Page: www.afip.com

David N Robertson, Executive Director

9001 Market Survey
International Swaps and Derivatives Association
360 Madison Ave
16th Floor
New York, NY 10017-7126

212-901-6000
FAX 212-901-6001
E-Mail: isda@isda.org
Home Page: www.isda.org

Robert Pickel, CEO
Ruth Ainslie, Director Communications
Corrine Greasley, Director Administration
Frequency: Semi-Annual

9002 Money
1271 Avenue of the Americas
32nd Floor
New York, NY 10020-1300

212-759-4094
FAX 212-522-0773

9003 Mortgage Originator
Pfingsten Publishing
3990 Oldtown Avenue
Suite A203
San Diego, CA 92110

619-223-9989
800-995-2090
FAX 619-223-9943
Home Page: www.mortgageoriginator.com

Chuck Hirsch, Publisher
David Robinson, Editor
Andy Strasser, Marketing Manager
Sue Burns, Circulation Director

Information on sales and marketing issues, correspondent management, retail mortgage, bankers and wholesale originators.
Cost: $58.00
Circulation: 19,500
ISSN: 1070-5708
Founded in 1998
Printed in 4 colors on glossy stock

9004 Mortgage Servicing News
Thomson Financial Publishing
1 State St
27th floor
New York, NY 10004-1481

212-825-8445
800-221-1809

FAX 212-292-5216
Home Page: www.mortgageservicingnews.com

Timothy Murphy, Publisher
Mark Fogarty, Editorial Director
Robert Cullen, CEO

Information on cross serving techniques, legislative decisions, management strategies, and professional profiles.
Cost: $98.00
Frequency: Monthly
Circulation: 20000

9005 NABTalk
National Association of Bankruptcy Trustees
One Windsor Cove
Suite 305
Columbia, SC 29233

803-252-5646
800-445-8629
FAX 803-765-0860
E-Mail: info@nabt.com
Home Page: www.nabt.com

Carol H Webber, Executive Director
Frequency: Quarterly

9006 NAPFA Advisor Magazine
National Association of Personal Financial Advisor
3250 N Arlington Heights Road
Suite 109
Arlington Heights, IL 60004

847-483-5400
800-366-2732
FAX 847-483-5415
E-Mail: info@napfa.org
Home Page: www.napfa.org

Ellen Turf, CEO
Margery Wasserman, Director Conferences
Frequency: Monthly

9007 NATE Update
National Association of Trade Exchange
8836 Tyler Road
Mentor, OH 44060

440-205-5378
FAX 440-205-5379
Home Page: www.nate.org

Thomas H McDowell, Executive Director

9008 Natinal Pawnbroker Magazine
National Pawnbrokers Association
P.O.Box 508
Keller, TX 76244-0508

817-491-4554
FAX 817-481-8770
E-Mail: info@NationalPawnbrokers.org
Home Page: www.nationalpawnbrokers.org

Bob Benedict, CAE, Executive Director
Emmett Murphy, Director
Teresa Congleton, Administrative Assistant
Frequency: Quarterly

9009 National Association of Investors Corporation
Po Box 220
Royal Oak, MI 48068-0220

248-583-6242
887-ASK-NAIC
FAX 248-583-4880

Kathleen Zaracki, CEO
Adam Ritt, Editor

Articles on counseling and teaching investing techniques. Magazine is included with membership.
100 Pages
Frequency: Monthly
Circulation: 250,000
Founded in 1951
Printed in 4 colors on glossy stock

9010 National Mortgage Broker

National Association of Mortgage Brokers
23425 N 39th Drive
104-193
Glendale, AZ 85310

623-516-2723
FAX 623-516-7738
Home Page: www.namb.org

Jon Ruzan, Publisher/Editorial Director
Mollie Regan, Editor
Michael Nizankiewicz, Executive Vice
President/CEO

Information on the National Association of
mortgage brokers including regulatory activi-
ties, education and certification, and building
consumer awareness.
Cost: $59.95
Frequency: Monthly
Circulation: 7500
Founded in 1973

9011 Nelson's World's Best Money Managers

Nelson Publishing
2500 Tamiami Trl N
Nokomis, FL 34275-3476

941-966-9521
FAX 941-966-2590
E-Mail: webmaster@nelsonpub.com
Home Page: www.healthmgttech.com

A Verner Nelson, Owner
George G Lindsey, COO
Kevin T Black, VP Database

A special quarterly report extracted from the
Nelson Investment Manager Database which
ranks the top investment managers by performance results in each of 200 categories.
Cost: $245.00
200 Pages
Frequency: Quarterly

9012 Newspaper Financial Executive Journal

Interactive & Newsmedia Financial
Executives
14237 Bookcliff Court
Suite 200
Purcellville, VA 20132

703-421-4060
FAX 703-421-4068
Home Page: www.infe.org

Jeff Hood, President

Trade publication for financial management of
newspapers. More than 800 members.
Frequency: Weekly
Circulation: 1000
Founded in 1947

9013 OCC Quarterly Journal

Comptroller of the Currency
250 E St Sw
250 E Street SW
Washington, DC 20219-0001

202-874-5000
800-613-6743
FAX 202-874-4490
E-Mail: Webmaster@occ.treas.gov
Home Page: www.occ.treas.gov

John C Dugan, CEO
Nancy K Jones, Administrative Assistant
Ruth Montgomery, Administrative Assistant
Teri Pote, Program Manager

Significant actions and policies of the Office of
Comptroller of the Currency, the agency that
regulates national banks. Legal interpretations,
merger decisions, speeches and testimony and
statistical and structural data on national banks

are included.
Cost: $100.00
132 Pages
Frequency: Quarterly
Circulation: 6500
Founded in 1863

9014 Pensions & Investments

Crain Communications
360 N Michigan Ave
Chicago, IL 60601-3800

312-649-5200
FAX 312-649-7937
E-Mail: info@crain.com
Home Page: www.crain.com

Keith Crain, CEO

Delivers critical financial news to executives
responsible for the investment of large institutional assets such as pension funds, endowments and foundations.
Frequency: Monthly
Circulation: 52000

9015 Plan Horizons

National Institute of Pension Administrators
401 N Michigan Avenue
Suite 2200
Chicago, IL 60611-4267

800-999-6472
E-Mail: nipa@nipa.org
Home Page: www.nipa.org

Laura J Rudzinski, Executive Director
Frequency: Quarterly

9016 Private Equity Analyst

Asset Alternatives
888 Worcester Street
3rd Floor
Wellesley, MA 02482

781-304-1400
800-257-2947
FAX 781-304-1440
E-Mail:
CustomerService@PrivateEquityAnalyst.com
Home Page: www.assetnews.com

David Toll, Managing Editor
Lisa Hughes, Circulation Manager

Insider contacts and timely reports on the latest
in venture capital, mezzanine, LBO and turn
around financing. Original research and
in-depth feature articles helps you understand
critical trends and issues in the market.
Cost: $1495.00
Frequency: Monthly

9017 Professional Collector

Pohly & Partners
27 Melcher Street
2nd Floor
Boston, MA 02210

617-451-1700
FAX 617-338-7767
Home Page: www.pohlypartners.com

Karen English, Editor
Piania Pohly, CEO/President
Annie Swearingven, Marketing Manager

Information on the latest technology, legisla-
tion and other issues affecting the debt collec-
tions industry.
Cost: $24.95
Frequency: Quarterly
Circulation: 148000
Printed in 4 colors

9018 Purchasing

Reed Business Information
225 Wyman St
Waltham, MA 02451-1216

781-734-8000
800-446-6551

FAX 781-290-3201
E-Mail: submail@reedbusiness.com
Home Page: www.reedbusiness.com

Mark Finklestein, President
Kathy Doyle, CFO
Stuart Whayman, CFO

Information for purchasing personnel in indus-
try.
Frequency: bi-monthly
Circulation: 95,078
Founded in 1915
Printed in 4 colors on glossy stock

9019 REIT Securities Monthly

SNL Securities
PO Box 2124
Charlottesvle, VA 22902-2124

434-977-1600
FAX 434-977-4466
Home Page: www.snlnet.com

Eden Rood, Editor
Reid Naglews, Chief Operating Officer
Nick Cafferillo, Chief Operating Officer
Adam Hall, Managing Director

Features sector analysis and interviews with industry leaders, as well as coverage of REIT investing and capital raising. The source for
REIT and real estate investors, analysts and
executives.
50 Pages
Frequency: Monthly

9020 RMA Journal

RMA - Risk Management Association
6147 Ridge Ave
Suite 2300
Philadelphia, PA 19128-2627

215-482-3222
800-677-7621
FAX 215-446-4101
E-Mail: customers@rmahq.org
Home Page: www.rmahq.org

Angelo Roma, Owner
William F Githens, Director Member Relations
Dwightce J Overturf, CFO/Information
Technology Officer
Florence J Wetzel, COO/Administrative Officer
Dom DiBernardi, Associate Director
Frequency: Monthly

9021 Regional Review

Federal Reserve Bank of Boston
600 Atlantic Ave
Boston, MA 02210-2204

617-973-3397
800-248-0168
FAX 617-973-4292
E-Mail: boston.library@bos.frb.org
Home Page: www.bos.frb.org

Joyce Hannan, Manager
Cathy E Minehan, President/CEO
Jane Katz, Editor

Reliable and balanced discussions of economic
issues. It is addressed to the opinion leaders of
New England's business and government
community.
Frequency: Quarterly
Circulation: 21000
Founded in 1913

9022 Registered Representative

Primedia
Po Box 12901
Shawnee Mission, KS 66282-2901

913-341-1300
866-505-7173
FAX 913-514-6895
E-Mail: rgcs@pbsub.com
Home Page: www.penton.com

Eric Jacobson, Senior VP
Rich Santos, Group Publisher

Magazine for retail stockbrokers that presents highly focused career-oriented editorials. Accepts advertising.
Cost: $59.00
Frequency: Monthly
Circulation: 108067
Founded in 1976
Printed in 4 colors on glossy stock

9023 Report on Business
Institute for Supply Management
2055 E Centennial Circle
PO Box 22160
Tempe, AZ 85285-2160

480-752-6276
800-888-6276
FAX 480-752-7890
E-Mail: infocenter@ism.ws
Home Page: www.ism.ws

Paul Novak, CFM, CEO
Holly LaCroix Johnson, Senior Vice President
Deborah Webber, SVP
Jean McHale, Manager
Frequency: Monthly

9024 Research
Financial Communications Company
PO Box 7588
San Francisco, CA 94120

415-621-0220
FAX 415-621-0735
Home Page: www.researchmag.com

Robert Tyndall, Publisher
Bill Nieder, Managing Director
Joseph Geraci, Managing Director

Corporate profiles, investment information, and reports on building and keeping client base.
Cost: $35.00
Frequency: Monthly
Circulation: 65,227

9025 Responsible Owner
Institute for Responsible Housing
Preservation
401 9th St NW
Suite 900
Washington, DC 20004-2145

202-585-8000
FAX 202-457-5355
E-Mail: info@housingpreservation.org

Kathryn Holmes, VP
Frequency: Monthly

9026 Reverse Mortgage Advisor
National Reverse Mortgage Lenders
Association
1625 Massachusetts Ave Nw
Suite 601
Washington, DC 20036-2212

202-939-1780
FAX 202-265-4435
Home Page: www.afjs.org

Peter H Bell, Executive Director
Glenn Petherick, Director Communications
Frequency: Quarterly

9027 Secondary Marketing Executive
LDJ Corporation
PO Box 2180
Waterbury, CT 06722-2330

203-755-0158
800-325-6745
FAX 203-755-3480
E-Mail: info@sme-online.com
Home Page: www.sme-online.com

Paul Zackin, Publisher
Mike Kling, Editor
June Han, Marketing

Delivers news, analysis and how-to advice to people involved in the buying and selling of

mortgage loans and servicing rights nationwide.
Cost: $48.00
44 Pages
Frequency: Monthly
Circulation: 21000
Founded in 1986

9028 Secured Lender
Commercial Finance Association
Ste 1801
7 Penn Plz
New York, NY 10001-3979

212-594-3490
FAX 212-564-6053
E-Mail: info@cfa.com
Home Page: www.cfa.com

Bruce H Jones, Executive Director
Theodore Kompa, President
Eileen M. Wubbe, Assistant Editor
Edward R. Fallon, Editorial Consultant
Linda C. Mohr, Production Manager

Provides in-depth reporting on federal and state legislation affecting the industry, legal notes on a wide range of issues, a full caladar year of industry workshops, meetings and seminars, personnel shifts, industry news and reviews of publications covering the industry. Discouted subscription rates for members.
Cost: $56.00
Frequency: 6 issues per ye
Circulation: 27000
Founded in 1944
Printed in 4 colors on glossy stock

9029 Small Business Update
Institute of Management Accountants
10 Paragon Dr
Suite 1
Montvale, NJ 07645-1774

201-573-9000
800-638-4427
FAX 201-474-1600
E-Mail: ima@imanet.org
Home Page: www.imanet.org

Paul Sharman, President
Frequency: Monthly

9030 Stable Times
Stable Value Investment Association
2121 K St Nw
Suite 800
Washington, DC 20037-1801

202-261-6530
800-327-2270
FAX 202-261-6527
E-Mail: info@StableValue.org
Home Page: www.stablevalue.org

Andrew Cohen, Editor
Frequency: Quarterly

9031 Strategic Finance
Institute of Management Accountants
10 Paragon Dr
Suite 1
Montvale, NJ 07645-1774

201-573-9000
800-638-4427
FAX 201-474-1600
E-Mail: ima@imanet.org
Home Page: www.imanet.org

Paul Sharman, President
Frederick Schea, Chair-Emeritus
Sandra Richtermeyer, Chair-Elect
Jeffrey Thomson, President & CEO

IMA's award winning magazine that provides the latest information about practices and trends in finance, accounting, and information management that will impact members and

their jobs.
Cost: $195.00
Frequency: Monthly
Printed in 4 colors on glossy stock

9032 Tax Executive
Tax Executives Institute
1200 G St NW
Suite 300
Washington, DC 20005-3833

202-638-5601
FAX 202-638-5607
Home Page: www.tei.org

Timothy Mc Cormally, Executive Director
Deborah K Gaffney, Director Conference Planning
Deborah C Giesey, Director Administration
Karina Horesky, Coordinator Membership
Fred F Murray, General Counsel
Frequency: Bi-Monthly

9033 Tax Lawyer
American Bar Association Section of Taxation
321 N Clark St
Chicago, IL 60654-7598

312-988-5000
800-285-2221
FAX 312-988-6281
E-Mail: askaba@abanet.org
Home Page: www.abanet.org

Louis A. Mezzullo, Editor-in-Chief
William H. Lyons, Managing Editor

Journal of scholarly articles written by highly respected tax attorneys and professors. It provides key reports by Section committees and task forces, and student notes and comments on timely topics.
Frequency: Quarterly

9034 Taxes: the Tax Magazine
CCH
2700 Lake Cook Rd
Riverwoods, IL 60015-3867

847-940-4600
800-835-5224
FAX 773-866-3095
E-Mail: taxes@cch.com
Home Page: www.cch.com

Mike Sabbatis, President
Douglas M Winterrose, Vice President & CFO
Jim Bryant, EVP Software Products

Information on legal, accounting and economic aspects of federal and state taxes.
Cost: $245.00
Frequency: Monthly
Circulation: 10000
Founded in 1913

9035 The Wall Street Journal

Home Page: www.wsj.com
Social Media: *Facebook, Twitter, LinkedIn, Google+, YouTube*

Gerard Baker, Editor-in-Chief

International English-language business newspaper.
Circulation: 2.4m
ISSN: 0099-9660
Founded in 1889

9036 ThriftInvestor
SNL Securities
One SNL Plaza
PO Box 2124
Charlottesvle, VA 22902

434-977-1600
FAX 434-977-4466

E-Mail: isales@snl.com
Home Page: www.snl.com

Mark Saunders, Editor
Pat LaBua, Customer Service
Michael Spears, Advertising Director
Nick Cafferillo, Chief Operating Officer
Adam Hall, Managing Director

Timely articles by industry experts on topics such as conversions, investment opportunities and government regulations. Source for important financial news, investor filings, conversion data and current financial and market information on all publicly traded thrifts.
Cost: $495.00
80 Pages
Frequency: Monthly
Founded in 1987

9037   Ticker Magazine
Wall Street Teechnology Association
521 Newman Springs Road
Suite 12
Lincroft, NJ 07738

732-530-8808
FAX 732-530-0020
E-Mail: info@wsta.org
Home Page: www.wsta.org

JoAnn Cooper, Managing Editor

Features articles that provide practical suggestions for technology professionals in the financial community, evaluate costs and benefits of alternate technologies, and disseminate news about the association
Frequency: Quarterly
Circulation: 14000

9038   Trader's World Magazine
Halliker's
2508 W Grayrock St
Springfield, MO 65810-2165

417-882-9697
FAX 417-886-5180
E-Mail: publisher@tradersworld.com
Home Page: www.tradersworld.com

Lawrence Jacobs, Owner

Information on stock indexes, techniques of trading, exchange activities and current developments.
Cost: $19.95
64 Pages
Frequency: Quarterly
Circulation: 12000
ISSN: 1045-7690
Founded in 1989
Printed in 4 colors on glossy stock

9039   Traders Magazine
Securities Data Publishing
40 W 57th St
11th Floor
New York, NY 10019-4001

212-484-4701
FAX 212-956-0112

Ken Heath, Publisher
Edward Cortese, Marketing Executive

Focuses on industry news, market and regulatory trends and the firms and individuals who shape the equities market.
Frequency: Monthly
Circulation: 6,000

9040   Trusts and Estates
PRIMEDIA Intertec-Marketing &
Professional Service
Po Box 12901
Shawnee Mission, KS 66282-2901

913-341-1300
FAX 913-514-6895

E-Mail: treddy@primediabusiness.com
Home Page: www.penton.com

Eric Jacobson, Senior VP
Rorie Sherman, Editor in Chief
Thrupthi Reddy, Editor
Rich Santos, Group Publisher

Features updates on trust department operations, estates and life insurance, wills, federal tax notes and current literature.
Cost: $199.00
Frequency: Monthly
Circulation: 14730
Founded in 1886

9041   Value Examiner
National Association of Certified Valuation
1111 Brickyard Road
Suite 200
Salt Lake City, UT 84106-5401

801-486-0600
800-677-2009
FAX 801-486-7500
E-Mail: nacva1@nacva.com
Home Page: www.nacva.com

Parnell Black, CEO
Frequency: Bi-Monthly

9042   Venture Capital Journal
Securities Data Publishing
40 W 57th St
New York, NY 10019-4001

212-484-4701
FAX 212-956-0112
E-Mail: sdp@tfn.com

Merry Logan, Associate Publisher
Edward Cortese, Marketing Executive

Provides information on recent issues, monitors current companies and looks at companies who have recently gone public.
Cost: $1025.00
Frequency: Monthly
Circulation: 1500

9043   Wall Street Computer Review
Miller Freeman Publications
1199 S Belt Line Rd
Suite 100
Coppell, TX 75019-4666

972-906-6500
FAX 972-419-7825

Elizabeth Katz, Publisher
Pavan Sahgal, Editor

For financial and investment professionals and individual investors.
Cost: $5.00
Circulation: 34,000

9044   Washington Alert
Institute for Responsible Housing
Preservation
401 9th St NW
Suite 900
Washington, DC 20004-2145

202-585-8000
FAX 202-457-5355
E-Mail: info@housingpreservation.org
Home Page: www.nixonpeabody.com

Kathryn Holmes, VP
Brian Moynihan, Communications Manager
Frequency: Irregular

9045   Washington Update
National Association of Affordable Housing
Lenders
1667 K St NW
Suite 905
Washington, DC 20006-1612

202-293-9850
FAX 202-293-9852

E-Mail: naahl@naahl.org
Home Page: www.naahl.org

Judy Kennedy, President
Frequency: Monthly

Trade Shows

9046   AACE Annual Meeting
AACE International
209 Prairie Avenue
Suite 100
Morgantown, WV 26501-5934

304-296-8444
800-858-2678
FAX 304-291-5728
E-Mail: info@aacei.org
Home Page: www.aacei.org

Andrew S Dowd Jr, Executive Director
Jennie Amos la, Marketing/Meetings Manager
Frequency: June

9047   AAHAM Annual Meeting
American Association of Healthcare
Administrative
11240 Waples Mill Road
Suite 200
Fairfax, VA 22030

703-281-4043
FAX 703-359-7562
E-Mail: moayad@aaham.org
Home Page: www.aaham.org

Robert Debiase, National President
Linda Sheaffer, Chair
Frequency: October

9048   AARMR Annual Meeting
American Association of Residential
Mortgage
1255 23rd Street NW
Suite 200
Washington, DC 20037

202-521-3999
FAX 202-883-3636
Home Page: www.aarmr.org

Christopher Murphy, Executive Director
Frequency: Fall

**9049   ABA Annual Convention, Business
Expo & Director' Forum**
American Bankers Association
1120 Connecticut Avenue NW
Washington, DC 20036

202-635-5000
800-BAN-KERS
E-Mail: custserv@aba.com
Home Page: www.aba.com

Gail Kolakowski, VP Bus Development &
Show Manager

Event for CEOs, presidents and other C-level executives from financial services firms across the nation, offering a products and services showcases, lanches and announcements, sessions focused on strategies and tactics for success, regulatory updates, effective leadership, and more.
Frequency: Annual

**9050   ACA Annual International
Convention & Exposition**
American Credit Association International
PO Box 390106
Minneapolis, MN 55439

952-926-6547
FAX 952-926-1624

E-Mail: aca@acainternational.org
Home Page: www.acainternational.com

Gary D Rippentorp CAE, CEO
Cathy Berg, Director Meetings

Annual international convention and exposition for credit and collection professionals.
Frequency: July

9051 AEFA Annual Meeting
American Education Finance Association
8365 S Armadillo Trail
Evergreen, CO 80439

303-674-0857
FAX 303-670-8986
Home Page: www.aefa.cc

Ed Steinbecher, Executive Director
Frequency: March

9052 AGA Annual Meeting
Association of Government Accountants
2208 Mount Vernon Avenue
Alexandria, VA 22301

703-684-6931
800-242-7211
FAX 703-548-9367
Home Page: www.agacgfm.org

Relmond P Van Daniker, Executive Director
Marie S Force, Director Communications
Susan Fritzlen, Deputy Exeucutive Director
Brian Watkins, Manager
Pamella Shaw, Accounting Manager
Frequency: July

9053 AMIFS Annual Meeting
Association for Management Information
3895 Fairfax Court
Atlanta, GA 30339

770-444-3557
FAX 770-444-9084
E-Mail: webmaster@amifs.org
Home Page: www.amifs.org

Kevin Link, Executive Director
Frequency: May

9054 AMIFS Annual Profitability & Performance Measurement Conference
Assn for Management Information in Financial Svcs
14247 Saffron Circle
Carmel, IN 46032

317-815-5857
FAX 317-815-5877
E-Mail: ami2@amifs.org
Home Page: www.amifs.org

Charles Stockton, Chairman Conference/EVP
Jane Blake, Conference Committee
Kevin W Link, Executive Director

3-day conference consisting of one day of workshops, and two days of educational sessions. 10 exhibitors.
Frequency: April

9055 ASMC Annual Meeting
American Society of Military Comptrollers
415 N Alfred Street
Alexandria, VA 22314-4650

703-549-0360
800-462-5637
FAX 703-549-3181
Home Page: www.asmconline.org

James F McCall, Executive Director
Frequency: May

9056 American Bankers Association Annual Convention & Banking Industry Forum
American Bankers Association

1120 Connecticut Avenue NW
Washington, DC 20036-3902

202-635-5000
FAX 202-663-5210
Home Page: http://www.aba.com

Edward Yingling, President/CEO

Annual convention and 200 exhibitors of systems and products for the banking industry.
5000 Attendees

9057 American Bankers Association National Agricultural Bankers Conference
1120 Connecticut Avenue NW
Washington, DC 20036-3902

800-226-5377
E-Mail: custserv@aba.com
Home Page: www.aba.com

Edward Yingling, President/CEO
Diane M Casey-Landry, COO/Senior Executive VP
1M Attendees
Frequency: Novembe

9058 American Bankers Association: Bank Operations & Technology Conference
American Bankers Association
1120 Connecticut Avenue NW
Washington, DC 20036-3902

202-635-5000
FAX 202-663-5210

Edward Yingling, President/CEO
Diane M Casey-Landry, COO/Senior Executive VP

Designed to address hot topics for bank operations professinals, covers critical issues and provides insights into the practical applications of bank technology
2600 Attendees
Frequency: April

9059 American Bankers Association: National Bank Card Conference
American Bankers Association
1120 Connecticut Avenue NW
Washington, DC 20036-3902

202-635-5000
FAX 202-663-5210
Home Page: http://www.aba.com

Edward Yingling

9060 Appraisers Association of America National Conference
Appraisers Association of America
386 Park Avenue S
Suite 2000
New York, NY 10016-8804

212-889-5404
FAX 212-889-5503
E-Mail: twniem@appraisersassoc.org
Home Page: www.appraisersassoc.org

Beth Weingast, President

Exhibits of interest to appraisers, workshops, and presentations.

9061 Association for Financial Professionals Annual Conference
Association for Financial Professionals
4520 East West Highway
Suite 750
Bethesda, MD 20814

301-907-2862
FAX 301-907-2864
E-Mail: AFP@AFPonline.org
Home Page: www.AFPonline.org

Loren Starr, Chairman
James Gilligan, Vice Chairman
Karen E Ball, Marketing Director

Workshop and 642 exhibits of lockboxes, check processing systems, computers, investments, pensions, foreign exchange, consulting, mergers, aquistions and more information of interest to finacial professionals.
6000 Attendees
Frequency: November
Founded in 1979

9062 BCCA Annual Meeting
Broadcast Cable Credit Association
550 Frontage Road
Suite 3600
Northfield, IL 60093

847-881-8757
FAX 847-784-8059
E-Mail: info@bccacredit.com
Home Page: www.bccacredit.com

Mary Collins, President/CEO
Jamie Smith, Director of Operations
Rachelle Brooks, BCCA Sales
Frequency: May

9063 CCFL Semi-Annual Meetings
Conference on Consumer Finance Law
Oklahoma City University School of Law
2501 N Blackwelder
Oklahoma City, OK 73106

405-521-5363
FAX 405-521-5089
E-Mail: ccflqr@lec.okcu.edu
Home Page: www.theccfl.com

Alvin C Harrell, Executive Director

Held with American Bar Association.
Frequency: Spring, Summer

9064 CDFA Annual Meeting
Council of Development Finance Agencies
301 NW 63rd Avenue
Suite 500
Oklahoma City, OK 73116

405-848-6059
FAX 405-842-3299
E-Mail: info@cdfa.net
Home Page: www.cdfa.net

Stan Provus, Training Director
Don Conkle, Manager
Frequency: Fall

9065 CDVCA Annual Conference
Community Development Venture Capital Alliance
330 Seventh Avenue
19th Floor
New York, NY 10001

212-594-6747
FAX 212-594-6717
E-Mail: info@cdvca.org
Home Page: www.cdvca.org

Kerwin Tesdell, President
Gary Brooks, Managing Director

Attended by management of social venture capital funds; those thinking of starting funds; investors in social venture capital funds; economic development professionals; banking and investment professionals; foundation representatives and policy makers and government professionals.
Frequency: March

9066 CFA Institute Annual Conference
CFA Institute
560 Ray C Hunt Drive
Charlottesville, VA

434-951-5499
800-247-8132
FAX 434-951-5262
E-Mail: info@cfainstitute.org
Home Page: www.cfainstitute.org

Jeffrey Diermeier, President/CEO

709

Provides an unparalleled look at the trends and investment issues critical to success in today's global marketplace
Frequency: April

9067 CIFA Semi-Annual Meetings
Council of Infrastructure Financing
Authorities
805 15th Street NW
Suite 500
Washington, DC 20005

202-371-9694
FAX 202-371-6601
Home Page: www.cifanet.org

Richard T Farrell, Executive Director
Richard T Farrell, Executive Director
Letitia Chambers, Owner

Legislative Conference, Spring & Workshop, Fall

9068 CMSA Annual Meeting
Commercial Mortgage Securities
Association
30 Broad Street
28th Floor
New York, NY 10004

212-509-1844
FAX 212-509-1895
E-Mail: info1@cmbs.org
Home Page: www.cmbs.org

Dottie Cunningham, CEO
Frequency: Winter

9069 CORFAC Semi-Annual Meetings
Corporate Facility Advisors
2000 N 15th Street
Suite 101
Arlington, VA 22201

703-528-3500
FAX 703-528-0113
E-Mail: info@corfac.com
Home Page: www.corfac.com

Thomas P Bennett, Executive Director
Bill Hawkins, Treasurer
Robert Tillsley, Secretary
Frequency: February, September

9070 CRF Annual Meeting
Credit Research Foundation
8840 Columbia Parkway
Suite 100
Columbia, MD 21045-2117

410-740-5499
FAX 410-740-4620
E-Mail: crf_info@crfonline.org
Home Page: www.crfonline.org

Alex Behm, Chairman
Michael Durant, Vice-Chairman
Frequency: May

9071 California Accounting & Business Show
Flagg Management
353 Lexington Avenue
New York, NY 10016

212-286-0333
FAX 212-286-0086
E-Mail: flaggmgmnt@msn.com
Home Page: www.flaggmgmt.com

Russell Flagg, President

150 exhibitors of investment management systems, databases, real-time and on-line systems. Global and US markets, Windows, PC and client/server systems. New income opportunities for CPAs in California with the change to commissionable financial services. The show is free; the conference is $40 per day and offers CPE sessions. Sponsored by the California CPA Education Foundation.
Frequency: Annual

9072 Credit Union Executives Expo
Credit Union Executives Society
Po Box 14167
Madison, WI 53708-0167

608-712-2664
800-252-2664
FAX 608-271-2303
E-Mail: fred@cues.org
Home Page: www.cues.org

Fred Johnson, President/CEO

Expo is held in conjunction with CUES Marketing, Operations and Technology Conference, where the top marketers and operations professionals in the industry gather.
500 Attendees
Frequency: May
Founded in 1962

9073 DCUC Annual Meeting
Defense Credit Union Council
601 Pennsylvania Avenue NW
South Building, Suite 600
Washington, DC 20004-2601

202-638-3950
FAX 202-638-3410
Home Page: www.dcuc.org

Frequency: August

9074 EMTA Annual Meeting
EMTA - Trade Association for the Emerging
Markets
360 Madison Avenue
18th Floor
New York, NY 10017

646-637-9100
FAX 646-637-9128
E-Mail: awerner@emta.org
Home Page: www.emta.org

Michael M Chamberlin, President
Aviva Werner, Managing Director
Jonathan Murno, Managing Director
Suzette Ortiz, Office Manager
Monika Forbes, Administrative Assistant
Frequency: December

9075 FMS Annual Meeting
Financial Managers Society
100 W Monroe Street
Suite 810
Chicago, IL 60603-1959

312-781-1300
800-275-4367
FAX 312-578-1308
E-Mail: diane@fmsinc.org
Home Page: www.fmsinc.org

Richard A Yingst, President/CEO
Jennifer Doak, Director Marketing
Diane Walter, VP/Director Professional Dev
Frequency: June

9076 FPA Annual Meeting
Financial Planning Association
4100 E Mississippi Avenue
Suite 400
Denver, CO 80246

303-759-4900
800-322-4237
FAX 303-759-0749
E-Mail: info@fpanet.org
Home Page: www.fpanet.org

Martin W Tuttle CAE, Executive Director/CEO
Ian McKenzie, Managing Director Publishing
Frequency: Fall

9077 FPA Experience: The Annual Conference of the Financial Planning Community
Financial Planning Association

7535 East Hampden Avenue
Suite 600
Denver, CO 80231

303-759-4900
800-322-4237
FAX 303-759-0749
Home Page: www.fpaannualconference.org
Social Media: *Facebook, Twitter, LinkedIn, FPA Connect*

The event provides networking and professional development opportunities, as well as exhibits.
24000 Members
3000 Attendees
Frequency: Annual/Fall
Founded in 2000

9078 FSR Semi-Annual Meetings
Financial Services Roundtable
1001 Pennsylvania Avenue NW
Suite 500 S
Washington, DC 20004

202-289-4322
FAX 202-628-2507
E-Mail: info@fsround.org
Home Page: www.fsround.org

Steve Bartlett, President/CEO
Frequency: Spring, Fall

9079 FSTC Annual Meeting
Financial Services Technology
44 Wall Street
12th Floor
New York, NY 10005

212-711-1400
FAX 646-349-3629
E-Mail: fstcadmin@fstc.org
Home Page: www.fstc.org

Zachary Tumin, Executive Director
Frequency: Spring

9080 Fiduciary and Risk Management Association Annual Meeting
Fiduciary and Risk Management
Association
PO Box 48297
Athens, GA 30604

706-354-0083
FAX 706-353-3994
E-Mail: info@thefirma.org
Home Page: www.thefirma.org

Hale Mast, Executive Director
Deborah A Austin, VP

To educate, support and promote risk management professionals and improve the effectiveness of risk management for the fiduciary and investment service industry.
Frequency: Spring

9081 FinEXPO
Miller Freeman Publications
1975 W El Camino Real
Suite 307
Mountain View, CA 94040-2218

FAX 650-966-8934

Sixty exhibitors of full range of systems, software, service and solutions that financial and information system decision makers need to meet the challenges of today and the future.
2000 Attendees

9082 Financial Management Association International Annual Meeting
University of South Florida
College of Business Administration/BSN 3331
4202 E Fowler Avenue
Tampa, FL 33620-5500

813-974-2084
FAX 813-974-3318

E-Mail: fma@coba.usf.edu OR info@fma.org
Home Page: www.fma.org/

Jonathan Karpoff, President Director
Jacqueline Garner, Vice President Financial
Education
Rawley Thomas, VP Practitioner Services
Kenneth Eades, Vice President Global Services
Anthony Saunders, Vice President Annual
Meeting

Annual meeting and exhibits of financial management related equipment, supplies and services.
Frequency: October

9083 Financial Women International Annual Conference
Financial Women International
1027 W Roselawn Avenue
Roseville, MN 55113

651-487-7632
866-807-6081
FAX 651-489-1322
E-Mail: info@fwi.org
Home Page: www.fwi.org

Melissa Curzon, President
Cindy Hass, VP
Carleen DeSisto, Secretary
Frequency: September

9084 HBMA Annual Meeting
Healthcare Billing and Management
Association
1540 South Coast Highway
Suite 203
Laguna Beach, CA 92651

877-640-4262
Home Page: http://www.hbma.org

Bradley Lund, Executive Director
Paul Myers, Director of Education
Frequency: March

9085 HMFA's ANI: The Healthcare Finance Conference
Healthcare Finance Management
Association
100 W Monroe Street
Suite 1001
Chicago, IL 60603

312-541-0567
FAX 312-541-0573
Home Page: www.hfma.org/events/ani

Access to education programs, speaker sessions and hundreds of vendors, as well as networking and best practices sharing opportunities.

9086 HMFA's Virtual Healthcare Finance Conference & Career Fair
Healthcare Finance Management
Association
100 W Monroe Street
Suite 1001
Chicago, IL 60603

312-541-0567
FAX 312-541-0573
E-Mail: virtualhcfc@hfma.org
Home Page: www.hfma.org

Access live education programs and on-demand sessions from your office. Keynote speakers and presenters, and a virtual exhibit hall and career fair.

9087 IMA Annual Meeting
Institute of Management Accountants
10 Paragon Drive
Suite 1
Montvale, NJ 07645-1718

201-573-9000
800-638-4427
FAX 201-474-1600

E-Mail: ima@imanet.org
Home Page: www.imanet.org

John Brausch, Chair
Frederick Schea, Chair-Emeritus
Sandra Richtermeyer, Chair-Elect
Jeffrey Thomson, President & CEO
1500 Attendees
Frequency: July

9088 IRHP Meeting/Conference
Institute for Responsible Housing
Preservation
401 Ninth Street NW
Suite 900
Washington, DC 20004

202-858-8000
FAX 202-585-8080
E-Mail: info@housingpreservation.org
Home Page: www.housingpreservation.org

Linda D Kirk, Executive Director
Frequency: January

9089 ISM Annual Meeting
Institute for Supply Management
2055 E Centennial Circle
PO Box 22160
Tempe, AZ 85285-2160

480-752-6276
800-888-6276
FAX 480-752-7890
E-Mail: infocenter@ism.ws
Home Page: www.ism.ws

Paul Novak, CPM, CEO
Holly LaCroix Johnson, Senior Vice President
Deborah Webber, SVP
Jean McHale, Manager
3000 Attendees
Frequency: May

9090 NAAHL Annual Meetings
National Association of Affordable Housing
Lenders
1300 Connecticut Avenue NW
Suite 905
Washington, DC 20036

202-293-9850
FAX 202-293-9852
E-Mail: naahl@naahl.org

Judith A Kennedy, President/CEO
Frequency: Winter, Spring

9091 NABT Semi-Annual Meetings
National Association of Bankruptcy
Trustees
One Windsor Cove
Suite 305
Columbia, SC 29233

803-252-5646
800-445-8629
FAX 803-765-0860
E-Mail: info@nabt.com
Home Page: www.nabt.com

Carol H Webster, Executive Director
Frequency: August

9092 NACM's Credit Congress and Exposition
National Association of Credit Management
8840 Columbia 100 Parkway
Columbia, MD 21045-2282

410-740-5560
FAX 410-740-5574
E-Mail: robins@nacm.org
Home Page: www.nacm.org

Jim Vanghel, Vice President
Robin Schauseil, President

Annual exhibits of relevance to credit and financial executives.
2500 Attendees
Frequency: June

9093 NACVA Annual Consultants' Conference
Nat'l Association of Certified Valuation
Analysts
1111 Brickyard Road
Suite 200
Salt Lake City, UT 84106-5401

801-486-0600
800-677-2009
FAX 801-486-7500
E-Mail: nacva1@nacva.com
Home Page: www.nacva.com

Parnell Black, CEO
750 Attendees
Frequency: June

9094 NADOA Annual Meeting
National Association of Division Order
Analyst
2805 Oak Trail Court
Suite 6312
Arlington, TX 76016

972-715-4489
E-Mail: administrator@nadoa.org
Home Page: www.nadoa.org

Lynn S McCord, Administrator
Frequency: September

9095 NAELB Annual Meeting
National Association of Equipment Leasing
Brokers
304 W Liberty Street
Suite 201
Louisville, KY 40202

800-996-2352
Home Page: www.naelb.org

Carol Davis, Administrator
Frequency: May

9096 NAFC Annual Meeting
National Accounting and Finance Council
2200 Mill Road
Alexandria, VA 22314

703-838-1915
E-Mail: nafc@trucking.org
Home Page: www.truckline.com

David Hershey, Executive Director
500 Attendees
Frequency: June

9097 NAFCU Annual Conference and Exhibition
National Association of Federal Credit
Unions
3138 10th Street N
Suite 300
Arlington, VA 22201-2149

703-224-4770
800-336-4644
FAX 703-524-1082
Home Page: http://www.nafcu.org

Jerome Bruce, Exhibits/Advertising Manager
Fred Becker, President

Annual show of 150 manufacturers and suppliers of complete range of financial products and services. 175 booths.

9098 NALHFA Semi-Annual Meetings
National Association of Local Housing
Finance
2025 M Street NW
Suite 800
Washington, DC 20036-3309

202-367-1197
FAX 202-367-2197

E-Mail: john_murphy@nalhfa.org
Home Page: www.nalhfa.org

John C Murphy, Executive Director
Scott Lynch, Association Manager
Kim McKinon, Coordinator Membership
Frequency: Spring, Fall

9099 NAMB Annual Meeting
National Association of Mortgage Brokers
8201 Greensboro Drive
Suite 300
McLean, VA 22102

703-610-9009
FAX 703-610-9005
E-Mail: rdeloach@namb.org
Home Page: www.namb.org

Michael J Nizankiewicz, PhD CAE, Executive VP/CEO
Roy DeLoach, Executive Vice President
Rebecca Dopkin, VP Meetings
Frequency: June

9100 NAPFA Annual Meeting
National Association of Personal Financial Advisor
3250 N Arlington Heights Road
Suite 109
Arlington Heights, IL 60004

847-483-5400
800-366-2732
FAX 847-483-5415
E-Mail: info@napfa.org
Home Page: www.napfa.org

Ellen Turf, CEO
Margery Wasserman, Director Conferences
800 Attendees
Frequency: May

9101 NAPTP Meeting/Conference
Nat'l Assoc of Publicly Traded Partnerships
805 15th Street NW
Suite 500
Washington, DC 20005

202-973-4515
FAX 202-973-3101
Home Page: www.ptpcoalition.org

Mary Lyman, Executive Director
Frequency: February

9102 NASBO Annual Meeting
National Association of State Budget Officers
444 North Capitol Street NW
Suite 642
Washington, DC 20001

202-624-5382
FAX 202-624-7745
E-Mail: spattison@nasbo.org
Home Page: www.nasbo.org

Scott Pattison, Executive Director
Lauren Cummings, Manager Member Relations
Frequency: Summer

9103 NATP National Conference & Expo
National Association of Tax Professionals
PO Box 8002
Appleton, WI 54912

920-749-1040
800-558-3402
FAX 800-747-0001
E-Mail: natp@natptax.com
Home Page: www.natptax.com

Annual conference and exhibits of computer hardware, tax accounting and planning software, tax research information, tax forms, one-write accounting, financial planning information, office products and business equipment.
Frequency: Annual

9104 NATRI National Conference
National Association for Treasurers of Religious
8824 Cameron Street
Silver Springs, MD 20910

301-587-7776
FAX 301-589-2897
E-Mail: natri@natri.org
Home Page: www.natri.org

Barbara Matteson, Executive Director
Helen Burke, Associate Director
Frequency: November

9105 NCPG Annual Meeting
National Committee on Planned Giving
233 McCre Street
Suite 400
Indianapolis, IN 46225-1030

317-269-6274
FAX 317-269-6276
Home Page: www.ncpg.org

Tanya Howe Johnson, President/CEO
Sandra Kerr, Director Government Education
Barbara Owens, Director Membership/Manager HR
Kathryn J Ramsey, Director Meetings
Kurt Reusze, Manager Education/Technology
1700 Attendees

9106 NDCC Semi-Annual Meetings
National Defined Contribution Council
9101 E Kenyon
Suite 300
Denver, CO 80237-0467

303-770-5353
FAX 303-770-1812
Home Page: www.ndcconline.org

Al Brust, Executive VP
Frequency: Spring, Fall

9107 NICSA Annual Meeting
National Investment Company Service Association
36 Washingtn Street
Suite 70
Wessesley Hills, MA 02481

781-416-7200
FAX 781-416-7065
E-Mail: info@nisca.org
Home Page: www.nisca.org

Barbara V Weidlich, President
Keith Dropkin, Director Operations
Doris Jaimes, Registrar
Sheila Kobaly, Events Manager
Chris Ludent, IT Manager
Frequency: February

9108 NIPA Semi-Annual Meetings
National Institute of Pension Administrators
401 N Michigan Avenue
Suite 2200
Chicago, IL 60611-4267

800-999-6472
E-Mail: nipa@nipa.org
Home Page: www.nipa.org

Laura J Rudzinski, Executive Director
Frequency: Winter, Spring

9109 NPA Annual Meeting
National Pawnbrokers Association
PO Box 1040
Roanoke, TX 76262

817-491-4554
FAX 817-491-8770

E-Mail: info@NationalPawnbrokers.org
Home Page: www.nationalpawnbrokers.org

Bob Benedict, CAE, Executive Director
Emmett Murphy, Director
Teresa Congleton, Administrative Assistant
1000 Attendees
Frequency: Summer

9110 National Association of Review Appraisers & Mortgage Underwriters Convention
National Assn of Review Appraisers/Mortgage Under.
1224 N Nokomis NE
Alexandria, MN 56308

320-763-7626
FAX 320-763-9290
E-Mail: nara@iami.org
Home Page: www.iami.org

Robert G Johnson, Executive Director

Annual convention of real estate related information and services. Containing 50-75 booths, as well as environmental, home inspection, and construction inspection.
450 Attendees
Frequency: October
Founded in 1962
Mailing list available for rent: 2500 names at $75 per M

9111 Payments
NACHA: Electronic Payments Association
13450 Sunrise Valley Drive
Suite 100
Herndon, VA 20171

703-561-1100
FAX 703-787-0996
E-Mail: info@nacha.org
Home Page: www.nacha.org

Marcie Haitema, Chairperson
Janet O Estep, CEO

The premier source for payments professionals from across industries and around the globe to get the most vital and actionable information needed to help address the myraid of issues and opportunities in today's rapidly changing environment.
1000 Attendees
Frequency: Annual/April-May

9112 Private Equity Analyst Conference
Asset Alternatives
170 Linden Street
2nd Floor
Wellesley, MA 02482-7919

781-304-1400
FAX 781-304-1440
Home Page: www.assetnews.com

Lisa Hughs, Production Manager

The industry's premiere gathering of more than 1000 institutional investors, venture capitalists, buyout specialists, deal originators, and senior and mezzanine lenders. Three specialized tracks focus on institutional, venture capital, and LBO investing.

9113 Private Equity Analyst Global Investing Conference
Asset Alternatives
170 Linden Street
2nd Floor
Wellesley, MA 02482-7919

781-235-4565
FAX 781-304-1440
Home Page: www.assetalt.com

Lisa Hughs, Production Manager

Hundreds of institutional investors, private equity managers, and deal sources to debate the merits of funds of funds and regional funds for investing in Western and Eastern Europe, Latin America, Asia, the Middle East, and elsewhere.

9114 Risk Management Association's Annual Conference
Risk Management Association
1801 Market St
Suite 300
Philadelphia, PA 19103-1628

215-446-4000
800-677-7621
FAX 215-446-4100
E-Mail: customers@rmahq.org
Home Page: www.rmahq.org

Kevin Blakely, President/CEO
Sonny Lyles, Vice Chair

Educates and helps risk management professionals develop new techniques and learn about new innovative products at different stages of their careers.
800 Attendees
Frequency: September/October

9115 SFE Annual Meeting
Society of Financial Examiners
174 Grace Boulevard
Altamonte Springs, FL 32714

407-682-4930
800-787-7633
FAX 407-682-3175
Home Page: www.sofe.org

Paula Keyes, Executive Director
Stephen J Szypula, Financial Administrator
500 Attendees

9116 SIM Annual Meeting
Society for Information Management
401 N Michigan Avenue
Chicago, IL

312-215-5190
FAX 312-245-1081
Home Page: www.simnet.org

Jim Luisi, Executive Director
Frequency: Fall

9117 SQA Annual Meeting
Society of Quantitative Analysts
25 North Broadway
Tarry Town, NY 10591

914-332-0040
FAX 914-332-1541
E-Mail: cmcas@cmcas.org
Home Page: www.cmcas.org

Stuart Ganes, President
Frequency: May

9118 STA's Annual Conference & Business Meeting
Security Traders Association
777 Post Road
Suite 200
Darien, CT 06820

203-202-7680
FAX 203-202-7681
E-Mail: traders@securitytraders.org
Home Page: www.securitytraders.org

John C Giesea, President & CEO

Keynote speakers, discussions on trading issues, regulatory updates, exchange topics, and exhibits.
1700 Attendees
Frequency: Annual

9119 Securities Industry and Financial Markets Association (SIFMA) Annual Meeting
1101 New York Avenue NW
8th Floor
Washington, DC 20005

202-962-7300
FAX 202-962-7305
Home Page: www.sifma.org

T Timothy Ryan Jr, President/CEO
Randy Snook, Senior Managing Director/EVP
Donald D Kittell, CFO

The Securities Industry and Financial Markets Association/SIFMA Annual Meeting and Conference program addresses a variety of topics that may include competitiveness of the U.S. capital markets, global exchange consolidation, regulatory and legal initiatives, and trends in the fixed-income and capital markets.

9120 Southern Finance Association
University of Florida
Mowry Road, Building 116
PO Box 110811
Gainesville, FL 32611-0811

352-392-5930
FAX 352-392-7902
Home Page: www.aceweb.org

Dr. Robert Radcliffe, Show Manager

Twenty five ooths.
1.4M Attendees
Frequency: November

9121 Success Forum
International Association for Financial Planning
2 Concourse Parkway NE
Suite 800
Atlanta, GA 30328-5588

770-351-9600
800-945-IAFP
FAX 770-668-7758

J Patrick Tinley, CEO

Annual show and exhibits of financial services equipment, supplies and services.
2500 Attendees

9122 TEI Annual Meeting
Tax Executives Institute
1200 G Street NW
Suite 300
Washington, DC 20005-3814

202-638-5601
FAX 202-638-5607
E-Mail: dgaffney@tei.org
Home Page: www.tei.org

Timothy J McNormally, Executive Director
Deborah K Gaffney, Director Conference Planning
Deborah C Giesey, Director Administration
Karina Horesky, Coordinator Membership
Fred F Murray, General Counsel/Dir Tax Affairs
Frequency: April

9123 Venture Capital & Health Care Conference
Asset Alternatives
170 Linden Street
2nd Floor
Wellesley, MA 02482-7919

781-235-4565
FAX 781-304-1440
Home Page: www.assetalt.com

Lisa Hughs, Production Manager

This annual gathering of top investors, deal sources, entrepreneurs, Wall Street analysts, and senior health care executives explores the

latest trends in health care services, devices, and medical information systems.
Circulation: 0

Directories & Databases

9124 AACE Directory
Assoc. for the Advancement of Cost Engineering
209 Prairie Ave
Suite 100
Morgantown, WV 26501-5934

304-296-8444
800-858-2678
FAX 304-291-5728
E-Mail: info@aacei.org
Home Page: www.aacei.org

Andrew Dowd, Executive Director
Megan McCulla, Asst Manager
Charla Miller, Staff Director Education
Carol S Rogers, Manager Finance
Frequency: Annual

9125 AEFA Membership Directory
American Education Finance Association
8365 S Armadillo Trail
Evergreen, CO 80439

303-674-0857
FAX 303-670-8986
Home Page: www.afea.cc

Ed Steinbecher, Executive Director
Frequency: Annual

9126 ALERT
AuTex Systems
11 Farnsworth Street
Boston, MA 02210-1210

617-345-2000

A database offering all available information on securities and securities trading information.

9127 ATLAS
Technical Data
11 Farnsworth Street
Boston, MA 02210-1210

617-345-2000

Contains a variety of financial data and analyses of 7 major government bond markets.

9128 All-Quotes
545 Madison Avenue
Suite 1400
New York, NY 10022-4219

FAX 212-425-6895

Offers real-time and delayed quotes, and price and volume history for about 100,000 stocks, options and commodities.

9129 Almanac of Business and Industrial Financial Ratios
Pearson Education
1 Lake St
Upper Saddle Rv, NJ 07458-1813

201-236-7000
800-947-7700
FAX 201-236-7696
Home Page: www.prenhall.com

Will Ethridge, President

Profiles corporate performance in two analytical tables for a variety of industries.
Cost: $69.95
Frequency: Annual

9130 American Banker On-Line
American Banker-Bond Buyer

1 State St
27th Floor
New York, NY 10004-1561

212-803-8450
207-581-3042
FAX 207-581-3015
Home Page: www.sourcemedia.com

Jim Malkin, CEO
Mario DiUbaldi, Publisher
Phil Roosevelt, Editor
Carole Lambert, Sales/Marketing Director
Stacy Weinstein, Production Director

World wide web edition of daily financial services newspaper. Journal available.

9131 American Financial Directory
4709 Golf Road
Skokie, IL 60076

847-676-9600
800-321-3373
FAX 847-933-8101
E-Mail: custserv@accuitysolutions.com
Home Page: www.accuitysolutions.com

Marideth Johnson, Manager,
Marketing/Communications
Malcolm Taylor, Managing Director
Cost: $523.00
Frequency: January/July
Circulation: 41300
ISBN: 1-563103-47-8

9132 American Society of Appraisers Directory
American Society of Appraisers
11107 Sunset Hills Rd
Suite 310
Reston, VA 20190

703-478-2228
800-272-8258
FAX 703-742-8471
E-Mail: asainfo@appraisers.org
Home Page: www.appraisers.org
Social Media: *Facebook, Twitter, LinkedIn, YouTube*

Jane Grimm, Executive VP
Susan Fischer, Governance Manager
Jack Washbourn, President

Directory of association members who are accredited appraisers.
Cost: $12.50
5000 Members
Circulation: 8,000
Founded in 1936
Mailing list available for rent: 5,000 names at $200 per M

9133 American Stock Exchange Fact Book
Publications Department
86 Trinity Pl
New York, NY 10006-1817

212-308-0046
FAX 212-306-2160

Neal Wolkoff, CEO

Lists addresses, telephone and fax numbers and ticker symbols of every listed company. Historical statistics and all-time trading records for equities, with a list of every stock option, index option and derivative security traded on the American Stock Exchange.
Cost: $20.00
Frequency: Annual
Circulation: 10,000
Founded in 1994

9134 American Stock Exchange Guide
CCH
2700 Lake Cook Rd
Riverwoods, IL 60015-3867

847-940-4600
800-835-5224

FAX 773-866-3095
Home Page: www.cch.com

Mike Sabbatis, President
Douglas M Winterrose, Vice President & CFO
Jim Bryant, EVP Software Products

Volume 1 lists a directory of officials, members, organizations and securities; Volume 2 lists by-laws and rules of the exchange.
Cost: $570.00

9135 Asia Pacific Securities Handbook
Reference Press
6448 E Highway 290
Suite E104
Austin, TX 78723-1041

512-331-1815
FAX 512-374-4501

Dan Capper, President

Offers stock information on the exchanges in Australia, Bangladesh, China, Hong Kong, India, Indonesia, Japan, Malaysia, Nepal, New Zealand, Pakistan, Taiwan, Sri Lanka, and Thailand.
Cost: $99.95
250 Pages
Founded in 1993

9136 Bank Mergers & Acquisitions Yearbook
SNL Securities
PO Box 2124
Charlottesvle, VA 22902-2124

434-977-1600
FAX 434-977-4466
Home Page: www.snlnet.com

John Minor, Editor
Nick Cafferillo, Chief Operating Officer
Christie Atkinson, Editor
Reid Nagle, Publisher
Mark Outlaw, Advertising Director

For bank and thrift CEOs, CFOs, investment banks, merger and acquisition advisors, law firms, accounting firms and individual investors. Covers all bank and thrift merger activity from the previous year, state-by-state reviews of all private sector whole-bank and whole-thrift transactions, branch sales, merger conversions and government-assisted transactions announced in that year.
150 Pages
Frequency: Annual
Founded in 1994

9137 Bank Securities Monthly
SNL Securities
212 7th Street NE
Charlottesville, VA 22902

434-977-1600
FAX 434-977-4466
E-Mail: subscriptions@snlnet.com
Home Page: www.snlnet.com

Mike Chinn, President
Steve Tomasi, Editor
Reid Nagle, Publisher
Mark Outlaw, Senior Vice President

Provides current financial, market and merger information on publicly traded banks. News highlights of the past month and comprehensive industry articles addressing topics such as bank investment opportunities, capital structure and earnings prospects.
70 Pages
Frequency: Monthly

9138 Bloomberg Business News
499 Park Ave
New York, NY 10022-1240

212-893-5555
FAX 212-369-5966
Home Page: www.bloomberg.com

Kim Bang, Manager
Matthew Winkler, Editor

A 24-hour global news service available exclusively on The Bloomberg. All stories are fully integrated into The Bloomberg's newsminder which instantly alerts you to developments in all stock and bond markets.

9139 Bloomberg Financial Markets Commodities News
PO Box 888
Princeton, NJ 08542-0888

609-279-3000
FAX 609-279-2028

Michael Bloomberg, Publisher
Matthew Winkler, Editor
Beth Mazzeo, Global Products

A leading multimedia distributor of news, information, data and analysis, providing information on everything from capital markets and airline schedules to employment opportunities and luxury goods.
Cost: $795.00
Frequency: Monthly

9140 Bond Buyer's Municipal Marketplace
Thomson Financial Publishing
4709 Golf Road
6th Floor
Skokie, IL 60076-1231

847-778-8037

James L Nowell, Editor

Offers information on firms and personnel in the municipal bond industry, including municipal bond dealers, chief finance officers of municipalities which issue bonds, and attorneys specializing in the field of municipal finance.
Cost: $185.00
937 Pages
Frequency: Semiannual

9141 Bonds Data Base
ADP Data Services
42 Broadway
Suite 1730
New York, NY 10004-1617

212-406-2820

This database, update daily, contains historical prices and trading volumes for more than 33,000 corporate, government and agency bonds.

9142 Bowser Directory of Small Stocks
Bowser Report
PO Box 6278
Newport News, VA 23606-0278

757-877-5979
FAX 757-595-0622
E-Mail: Ministocks@aol.com
Home Page: www.thebowsersreport.com

Cindy Bowser, Editor

Lists 14 fields of information on over 700 low-priced stocks.
Cost: $89.00
35 Pages
Frequency: Monthly
ISSN: 1053-0908

9143 Bridge Information System
717 Office Parkway
Saint Louis, MO 63141-7115

314-567-8100
800-325-3282
FAX 314-432-5391

Tony Bridge, Manager

This large database contains real-time, last sale and quote data on all listed and unlisted stocks, options, futures and foreign securities.

9144 Bull and Bear's Directory of Investment Advisory Newsletters
Bull & Bear Financial Report
PO Box 917179
Longwood, FL 32791-7179

407-682-6170
Home Page: www.thebullandbear.com

David J Robinson, President

Advice from investment advisory newsletters on various investment areas, small-cap stocks, global and domestic stock markets, mutual funds, precious metals and economy.
Cost: $29.00
48 Pages
Frequency: Annual
Circulation: 55,000
Founded in 1974

9145 Business and Financial News Media
Larriston Communications
PO Box 20229
New York, NY 10025-1518

310-871-0563

Sheila Gordon, Editor

Lists over 300 daily newspapers with at least 50,000 in circulation and a business or finance correspondent; television stations and all-news radio stations in the largest 40 markets.
Cost: $89.00
175 Pages
Frequency: Annual

9146 CDA/Wiesenberger Investment Companies Service
CDA Investment
1355 Piccard Drive
Suite 200
Rockville, MD 20850-4300
Jay Nadler, Editor

Lists 5,000 open and closed mutual funds, unit trusts and investment companies listing policies and objectives, history, and statistical information of the company.
1500 Pages
Frequency: Annual

9147 CIN: Corporation Index System
Office of Applications & Reports Services
450 5th Street NW
Washington, DC 20001-2739

202-942-0020

David Weiss, Manager

Lists 1,580 active companies registered under the Investment Company Act of 1940. Information is extend to include related underwriters and advisers and 800 number.
Cost: $90.00
Frequency: Monthly

9148 CISCO
CISCO
170 W Tasman Dr
San Jose, CA 95134-1706

408-526-4000
805-553-6387
FAX 408-853-3683

E-Mail: dljones@cisco-futures.com
Home Page: www.cisco-futures.com

Frank A Calderoni, Executive VP

Contains technical analyses and prices of commodities futures, and currencies.

9149 CUSIP Master Directory
Standard & Poor's Corporation
55 Water St
New York, NY 10041-0003

212-438-1000
FAX 212-438-0299

Deven Sharma, President

Official listings of numbers and descriptions for more than 1,500,000 stocks, bonds and warrants of 100,000 issuers, including corporations and municipalities of the United States and Canada.
Cost: $1900.00
Frequency: Annual

9150 Commodity Futures Trading Commission Geographic Directory
Three Lafayette Centre
1155 21st Street NW
Washington, DC 20581

202-418-5000
FAX 202-418-5521
E-Mail: opa@cftc.org
Home Page: www.cftc.org

Offers information on corporations and firms that are registered with the Commodity Futures Trading Commission.
Cost: $25.00

9151 Corporate Finance Sourcebook
National Register Publishing
430 Mountain Ave.
Suite 400
New Providence, NJ 07974

800-473-7020
FAX 908-673-1189
E-Mail: NRPeditorial@marquiswhoswho.com
Home Page: www.financesourcebook.com

Contains a variety of information on the financial services industry. Listings include securities research analysts, major private lenders, mergers and acquisitions, commercial finance firms, pension managers and leasing companies.
Cost: $425.00
1600 Pages
Frequency: Annual

9152 Corporate Venturing Directory & Yearbook
Asset Alternatives
170 Linden Street
Wellesley, MA 02482

781-304-1400
FAX 781-304-1440
Home Page: www.corporateventuring.com

Dave Barry, Senior Editor
Barbara Bissonnette, VP Marketink/Sales

Features the most comprehensive data ever essembled on corporations participating in venture-backet deals, and the young companies they're financing.
Cost: $495.00
Frequency: Annual
Printed in on matte stock

9153 Cost Engineers Notebook
AACE International
209 Prairie Ave
Suite 100
Morgantown, WV 26501-5934

304-296-8444
800-858-2678
FAX 304-291-5728

E-Mail: info@aacei.org
Home Page: www.aacei.org

Andrew Dowd, Executive Director
Megan McCulla, Asst Manager
Charla Miller, Staff Director Education
Carol S Rogers, Manager Finance
Frequency: Irregular

9154 Credit Decisioning Study
Credit Research Foundation
8840 Columbia Pkwy
Suite 100
Columbia, MD 21045-2100

410-740-5499
FAX 410-740-4620
E-Mail: crf_info@crfonline.org
Home Page: www.crfonline.org

Terry Callahan, President
Michael Durant, Vice-Chairman

9155 Current Market Snapshot
CompuServe Information Service
5000 Arlington Centre Blvd
Columbus, OH 43220-5439

614-326-1002
800-848-8199

Offers information on up-to-date stock prices foreign currency data, and general market statistics.

9156 DIAL/DATA
Track Data Corporation
95 Rockwell Pl
Brooklyn, NY 11217-1105

718-522-7373
FAX 718-260-4324
E-Mail: info@trackdata.com
Home Page: www.trackdata.com

Martin Kaye, CEO
Stan Stern, Senior Vice President

This database contains current and historical data on securities, options and commodities.

9157 DRI Commodities
DRI/McGraw-Hill
11000 Regency Parkway
Suite 400
Cary, NC 27511

919-462-8600
FAX 919-468-9890
Home Page: www.profound.com

This database contains more than 51,000 daily time series of price and trading data for major commodities traded on makrets in the US, Canada, London and Singapore.

9158 DRI Transportation
DRI/McGraw-Hill
11000 Regency Parkway
Suite 400
Cary, NC 27511

919-462-8600
FAX 919-468-9890
Home Page: www.profound.com

This large database contains over 15,000 weekly, monthly, and annual time series on commodity traffic by mode, carrier operations and financial data.

9159 DRI US Bonds
DRI/McGraw-Hill
11000 Regency Parkway
Suite 400
Cary, NC 27511

919-462-8600
FAX 919-468-9890
Home Page: www.profound.com

This financial database contains daily time series of current and historical prices, yields and

715

fundamental financial information for more than 60,000 dealer-priced debt issues.

9160 Daily Foreign Exchange Analysis & Updates
Technical Data
11 Farnsworth Street
Boston, MA 02210-1210

617-345-2000

This database offers daily reports from major world financial centers including, currency forecasts, analysis of the US bond and money markets, currency reports and the trends of the New York foreign exchange market.
Frequency: Full-text

9161 Dick Davis Digest
Dick Davis Publishing
P.O.Box 2049
Salem, MA 01970-6249

954-733-3996
FAX 954-733-8559
E-Mail: editorial@dickdavis.com
Home Page: www.dickdavis.com

Steven Halpern, Publisher/Editor
Lorianne Kiesl, Marketing Director
Donald Hanrahan, Owner

The digest excerpts over 400 newsletters and the research reports from leading Wall Street analysts and compiles this information into a 12 page compendium of what leading financial advisors currently recommend.
Cost: $165.00
Frequency: BiWeekly

9162 Directory of Alternative Investment Programs
Asset Alternatives
170 Linden Street
2nd Floor
Wellesley, MA 02482-7919

781-304-1400
FAX 781-304-1440
Home Page: www.assetnews.com

David Toll, Managing Editor

The private equity programs of more than 500 leading pension funds, endowments and other institutions, plus their advisors.
Cost: $595.00

9163 Directory of Buyout Financing Sources
Securities Data Publishing
40 W 57th St
New York, NY 10019-4001

212-484-4701
FAX 212-956-0112
E-Mail: sdp@tfn.com
Home Page: www.sdponline.com

Ted Weissberg, Editor-in-Chief
Deborah Chieglis, Advertising Manager
Edward Cortese, Marketing Executive

Over 700 sources of financing, including senior lenders, equity and mezzanine providers in the United States and international avenues, with detailed information on industry, geographic and invetment size preferances and recent activity for each firm.

9164 Directory of Defense Credit Union
Defense Credit Union Council
601 Pennsylvania Ave NW
Suite 600
Washington, DC 20004-2601

202-638-3950
FAX 202-638-3410
E-Mail: dcucl@cuna.org
Home Page: www.dcuc.org

Roland Arteata, President
Frequency: Bi-Ennial

9165 Directory of Manufacturers' Sales
Manufacturers' Agents National Association
PO Box 3467
Laguna Hills, CA 92654-3467

949-859-4040
FAX 949-855-2973
Home Page: www.manaonline.org

Joseph Miller, President
Susan Strouse, Secretary, Treasurer
Alane LaPlante, Director

Association for independent agents and firms representing manufacturers and other businesses in specified territories on a commission basis, including consultants and associate member firms interested in the manufacturer/agency method of marketing.
Cost: $129.00
Frequency: Annual
Circulation: 25,000

9166 Directory of Mastercard and Visa Credit Cards
Todd Publications
PO Box 635
Nyack, NY 10960-0635

845-358-6213
FAX 845-358-1059
E-Mail: toodpub@aol.com
Home Page: toddpublications.com

Barry Klein, Editor

Offers information on 500 credit cards from 200 banks across the country.
Cost: $50.00
1000 Pages
Frequency: Biennial
Circulation: 5,000
Founded in 1994
Mailing list available for rent: 200 names at $50 per M

9167 Directory of Mutual Funds
Investment Company Institute
100 F Street
Washington, DC 20549

202-942-8088

Sue Duncan, Editor
Cost: $5.00
247 Pages
Frequency: Annual

9168 Directory of Venture Capital & Private Equity Firms - Online Database
Grey House Publishing
4919 Route 22
PO Box 56
Amenia, NY 12501

518-789-8700
800-562-2139
FAX 845-373-6390
E-Mail: gold@greyhouse.com
Home Page: http://gold.greyhouse.com
Social Media: *Facebook, Twitter*

Leslie Mackenzie, Publisher
Richard Gottlieb, Editor

Packed with need-to-know information, this database offers immediate access to 2,300 VC firms, over 10,000 managing partners, and over 11,500 VC investments.
Frequency: Annual

9169 Directory of Venture Capital and Private Equity Firms
Grey House Publishing
4919 Route 22
PO Box 56
Amenia, NY 12501

518-789-8700
800-562-2139
FAX 845-373-6390

E-Mail: books@greyhouse.com
Home Page: www.greyhouse.com
Social Media: *Facebook, Twitter*

Leslie Mackenzie, Publisher
Richard Gottlieb, Editor

Offers access to over 2,300 domestic and international venture capital and private equity firms, including detailed contact information and extensive data on investments and funds.
Cost: $685.00
1200 Pages
Frequency: Annual
ISBN: 1-592372-72-4

9170 Dow Jones Business and Finance Report
Dow Jones & Company
PO Box 300
Princeton, NJ 08543-0300

609-520-4000
Home Page: http://www.dowjones.com

This large database offers financial news and information on developments in business and industry, domestic and international economies, and the stock market.
Frequency: Full-text

9171 Dow Jones Futures and Index Quotes
Dow Jones & Company
PO Box 300
Princeton, NJ 08543-0300

609-520-4000

This database, updated continuously, offers current and historical stock quotations for more than 80 contracts from major North American stock exchanges.

9172 Dow Jones Text Library
Dow Jones & Company
PO Box 300
Princeton, NJ 08543-0300

609-520-4000
Home Page: http://www.dowjones.com

This large database offers business and financial news covering more than 6,000 US companies, 700 Canadian companies and 50 industries.
Frequency: Full-text

9173 E-Z Telephone Directory of Brokers and Banks
106 7th Street
Garden City, NY 11530-5796

516-294-0350
FAX 516-294-0356

MJ Gentile, Editor

Security brokers, banks, and financial organizations in the New York area are listed in this directory.
Cost: $90.00
200 Pages
Frequency: SemiAnnual
Circulation: 10,000
Printed in on matte stock

9174 ECFA Member List
Evangelical Council for Financial Accountability
440 W Jubal Early Dr
Suite 130
Winchester, VA 22601

540-535-0103
800-323-9473
FAX 540-535-0533
E-Mail: dan@ecfa.org
Home Page: www.ecfa.org

Dan Busby, President
Frequency: Annual

9175 EMARKET
International Financial Corporation
1818 H St NW
Washington, DC 20433-0001

202-473-1000
FAX 202-974-4384
Home Page: www.ifc.org

Robert Zoellich, President

This database offers over 1,000 weekly, annual and monthly time series on company stocks from over 18 developing countries.

9176 Evans Economics Analysis and Commentary
Evans Economics
1660 L Street NW
Suite 207
Washington, DC 20036-5603

This database reports on changes in economic activity to all major financial markets. Over 20 files are listed that provide the forecasts and reports on the effect of economic variables on debt and equity markets.
Frequency: Full-text

9177 Financial Ratios for Manufacturing Corporations Database
US Department of Commerce
Herbert Rm 4885
Washington, DC 20230-0001

202-690-7650
FAX 202-482-0325
Home Page: www.access.gpo.gov

Pam Nacci

This database provides 20 quarterly seasonally adjusted financial and operating ratios for selected two- and three-digit SIC groups in the manufacturing sector.
Cost: $85.00
Frequency: Series

9178 Financial Services Canada
Grey House Publishing
4919 Route 22
PO Box 56
Amenia, NY 12501

518-789-8700
800-562-2139
FAX 845-373-6390
E-Mail: books@greyhouse.com
Home Page: www.greyhouse.com
Social Media: Facebook, Twitter

Leslie Mackenzie, Publisher
Richard Gottlieb, Editor

With over 18,000 organizations and hard-to-find business information, Financial Services Canada is the most up-to-date source for names and contact information of industry professionals, senior executives, portfolio managers, financial advisors, agency bureaucrats and elected representatives.
Cost: $325.00
900 Pages
ISBN: 1-592372-78-3
Founded in 1981

9179 Financial Yellow Book
Leadership Directories
104 5th Ave
New York, NY 10011-6901

212-627-4140
FAX 212-645-0931
E-Mail: financial@leadershipdirectories.com
Home Page: www.leadershipdirectories.com

David Hurvitz, CEO
James M Petrie, Associate Publisher

Contact information for over 26,000 executives at public and private financial institutions, and over 5,000 board members and their outside affiliations.
Cost: $245.00
900 Pages
Frequency: Semiannual
ISSN: 1058-2878
Founded in 1987
Mailing list available for rent: 20,000 names at $95 per M

9180 Financing Your Business in Eastern Europe
WorldTrade Executive
PO Box 761
Concord, MA 01742-0761

978-287-0301
FAX 978-287-0302
E-Mail: info@wtexec.com
Home Page: www.wtexec.com

Alison French, Production Manager

Provides reliable information on financing sources, including local and international banks, capital markets, venture capital funds, and government sources
Cost: $135.00

9181 FirstList
Vision Quest Publishing
37308 12th Street
Phoenix, AZ 86086

928-451-4445
E-Mail: mergers@firstlist.com
Home Page: http://www.firstlist.com

A Robert Weicherding, President

Information is offered in this directory covering companies that are candidates for merger or acquisition, buyers seeking acquisitions, sources of financinf, equity or debt financing and joint venture and licensing opportunities. Also available on-line and the Internet.
Cost: $350.00
120 Pages
Frequency: 8 per year

9182 Ford Data Base
Ford Investor Services
11722 Sorrento Valley Rd
Suite 1
San Diego, CA 92121-1021

858-755-1327
FAX 858-455-6316
E-Mail: info@fordequity.com
Home Page: www.fordequity.com

Tim Alward, President

This database offers 80 financial data items for each of 2,000 leading common stocks.

9183 Futures Magazine Sourcebook
Oster Communications
5081 Olympic Boulevard
Erlanger, KT 41018

319-277-1271
E-Mail: gszala@futuresmag.com
Home Page: www.futuresmag.com

Ginger Szala, Group Publisher/Editorial Director
Daniel P Collins, Managing Editor
Christine Birkner, Associate Editor

This issue deals with exchanges in futures and options contracts, including commodities, foreign currencies, stock indexes and international financial coverage.
Cost: $22.00
130 Pages
Frequency: Annual
Circulation: 60,000

9184 Galante's Venture Capital & Private Equity Directory
Asset Alternatives

170 Linden Street
Wellesley, MA 02482-7919

781-304-1400
FAX 781-304-1440
Home Page: www.assetnews.com

David Toll, Managing Editor

Complete investment criteria of venture capital, buyout, and mezzanine firms into one complete reference.

9185 Hulbert Guide to Financial Newsletters
Dearborn Financial Publishing
155 Wacker Avenue
Chicago, IL 60606

312-836-4400

Matt Schiff, Owner
Kathleen A Welton, VP

Lists over 100 financial newsletters offering descriptions and evaluation of model portfolios.
Cost: $27.95
574 Pages
Frequency: Biennial

9186 IBC/Donoghue's Money Fund Report/ Electronic
290 Eliot Street
#9104
Ashland, MA 01721-2351

This valuable database offers information and analyses of trends and developments in the money market mutual funds industry.
Frequency: Full-text

9187 IBC/Donoghue's Mutual Funds Almanac
290 Eliot Street
#9104
Ashland, MA 01721-2351
Ann V Needle, Editor

Over 2,400 load and no load mutual funds, including equity, bond and municipal funds.
Cost: $39.95
Circulation: 25,000

9188 Insider Trading Monitor Database
CDA Investment
3265 Meridian Parkway
Suite 130
Fort Lauderdale, FL 33331-3506

954-384-1500

More than 12,500 companies and all insider security transactions reported to the US Securities and Exchange Commission, FDIC, Toronto Stock Exchange and OTS.
Frequency: Daily

9189 Insiders' Chronicle
CDA Investment
3265 Meridian Parkway
Suite 130
Fort Lauderdale, FL 33331-3506

954-384-1500

Robert Gabele, Editor

Publicly held companies in whose securities there has been significant buying or selling by executive officers, directors, and those who hold 10% or more of its shares.
15 Pages

9190 International Financial Statistics
International Monetary Fund
700 19th St NW
Washington, DC 20431-0002

202-623-7000
FAX 202-623-4661

E-Mail: publications@imf.org
Home Page: www.imf.org

Masood Ahmed, VP
Kathleen Tilmans, Secretary
Olivier Blanchard, Secretary
Christine Lagarde, Managing Director

Offers informaiton on more than 23,000 annual, quarterly and monthly time series of economic and dinancial statistics on over 200 countries.

9191   International Investor's Directory
Asset International
125 Greenwich Avenue
Suite 5
Greenwich, CT 06830-5512

203-629-5015
FAX 203-629-5024

Eric Laursen, Editor

Directory of services and supplies to the industry.
Cost: $235.00
735 Pages
Frequency: Annual

9192   Investment Blue Book
Securities Investigations
PO Box 888
Woodstock, NY 12498-0888

845-679-2300

Lists over 6,000 brokers and dealers in tax shelter plans; 2,000 sponsors of tax shelter products and suppliers of service to the industry and mutual funds information.
Cost: $145.00
350 Pages
Frequency: Irregular
Circulation: 10,000

9193   Investment Recovery Association Directory
Investment Recovery Association
5800 Foxridge Drive
Suite 115
Mission, KS 66202-2338

913-624-4597
FAX 913-262-0174

Jane Male, Editor

Directory of services and supplies to the industry.
Cost: $250.00
Frequency: Annual
Circulation: 400

9194   Investor Relations Resource Guide
National Investor Relations Institute
8045 Leesburg Pike
Suite 600
Vienna, VA 22182

571-633-0532
FAX 703-506-3571
E-Mail: info@niri.org
Home Page: www.niri.org

Melissa Jones, Editor
Ariel Finno, Director Research

Lists about 110 investment counseling firms, 50 financial investment associations and 40 financial investment service firms such as publishers of magazines and newsletters.
Cost: $50.00
83 Pages
Frequency: Annual

9195   Japanese Investment in the Midwest
Japan-America Society of Greater Cincinnati

441 Vine Street
Cincinnati, OH 45202-2821

513-579-3114
FAX 513-579-3101
Home Page: www.patent-pros.com

Jack Adams, Executive Director

A list of more than 400 Japanese manufacturing firms in the states of Illinois, Indiana, Kentucky, Michigan, Ohio, and Tennessee.
Cost: $40.00
30 Pages
Frequency: Annual

9196   Lipper Marketplace
Lipper, A Thomson Reuters Company
3 Times Square
New York, NY 10036

646-223-4000
800-782-5555
E-Mail: salesinquiries@thomsonreuters.com
Home Page: www.lippermarketplace.com

James C Smith, Chief Executive Officer
Stephane Bello, Chief Financial Officer
David W Craig, President, Finance
Robert D Daleo, Vice Chairman
Susan Taylor Martin, President, Reuters Media

This powerful web-based solution opens the door to highly targeted prospects by putting the tools to identify your market at your fingertips. Designed with the input of institutional investment professionals, MarketPlace not only helps you qualify your prospects, it also gives you the cutting-edge competitive intelligence you need to transform your prospects into clients.

9197   Loan Broker: Annual Directory
Ben Campbell, Publisher
917 S Park Street
Owosso, MI 48867-4422

Lists approximately 800 loan brokers, private funding sources and business financing services operating in the continental United States.
Cost: $59.95
Frequency: Annual
Circulation: 3,000

9198   MJK Commodities Database
MJK Associates
1289 S Park Victoria Drive
Suite 205
Milpitas, CA 95035-6974

FAX 408-941-3404

Offers information on United States and Canadian commodities; internatinal monetary markets; futures indexes and stock index futures.

9199   Mentor Support Group Directory
National Association of Certified Valuation
1111 Brickyard Road
Suite 200
Salt Lake City, UT 84106-5401

801-486-0600
800-677-2009
FAX 801-486-7500
E-Mail: nacva1@nacva.com
Home Page: www.nacva.com

Parnell Black, CEO
Frequency: Annual

9200   Merger & Acquisition Sourcebook Edition
Quality Services Company
5290 Overpass Road
Suite 126
Santa Barbara, CA 93111-3009

805-964-7841
FAX 805-964-1073

Walter Jurek, Editor
Nancy Rothlein, Production Manager

Contains complete information on the previous years' merger and acquisitions actuary.
Cost: $350.00

9201   Merger Yearbook
Securities Data Publishing
40 W 57th St
11th Floor
New York, NY 10019-4001

212-484-4701
FAX 212-956-0112
E-Mail: sdp@tfn.com
Home Page: www.sdponline.com

Ted Weissberg, Editor-in-Chief
Deborah Chieglis, Advertising Manager
Edward Cortese, Marketing Executive

Information on tens of thousands of announces and completed deals plus charts giving awards information on industry rankings and transactions.

9202   Merger and Corporate Transactions Database
Securities Data Publishing
1180 Raymond Boulevard
Suite 5
Newark, NJ 07102-4107

This database contains more than 85,000 records on transactions involving mergers, acquisitions, divestitures leveraged buyouts and stock repurchases.
Frequency: Full-text

9203   Mergers & Acquisitions Yearbook
American Banker-Bond Buyer
1 State St
27th Floor
New York, NY 10004-1561

212-803-8450
800-367-3989
FAX 212-843-9624
Home Page: www.sourcemedia.com

Jim Malkin, CEO
Mario DiUbaldi, Publisher
Phil Roosevelt, Editor
Carole Lambert, Sales/Marketing Director
Stacy Weinstein, Production Director

Annual yearbook detailing all bank merger and acquisition activity for the previous year. Includes sale price, financial and legal advisors and governmental information.
Cost: $175.00
Frequency: Annual

9204   Mergers and Acquisitions Handbook
National Association of Division Order Analysts
2805 Oak Trail Court
Suite 6312
Arlington, TX 76016

972-715-4489
E-Mail: administrator@nadoa.org
Home Page: www.nadoa.org

Lynn S McCord, Administrator
Frequency: Annual

9205   Money Market Directory of Pension Funds and their Investment Managers
Money Market Directories
PO Box 1608
Charlottesville, VA 22902-1608

434-977-1450
800-446-2810
FAX 434-979-9962
Home Page: www.mmdaccess.com

Tom Lupo, Manager
John Martin, Production Manager
Dennis Thurston, Publications

Over 44,000 tax-exempt funds with over $1,000,000 in assets, and about 1,800 invest-

ment management services including bank trust departments and insurance companies, each handling at least $25,000,000 in tax-exempt funds.
Cost: $1150.00
2000 Pages
Frequency: Annual January
Circulation: 8,500
ISBN: 0-939712-31-8
ISSN: 0736-6051
Founded in 1970

9206 Money Source Book
Business Information Network
15851 Dallas Parkway
Suite 600
Dallas, TX 75248

972-982-8686

Over 1,500 traditional and non-traditional sources of business capital with an emphasis on the south-central United States.
Cost: $24.95
200 Pages
Frequency: Annual
Circulation: 20,000

9207 MoneyData
Technical Data
11 Farnsworth Street
Boston, MA 02210-1210

617-345-2000

This database offers a full line of information on money markets.

9208 MoneyWatch
McCarthy, Crisanti & Maffei
71 Broadway
New York, NY 10006-2601

212-675-5880
FAX 212-509-7389

This database offers valuable information on the money market, including economic indicators.
Frequency: Full-text

9209 Morningstar
Morningstar
225 W Washington Street
Chicago, IL 60602

312-384-4000
FAX 312-696-6001
E-Mail: productinfo@morningstar.com
Home Page: www.morningstar.com

Joe Mansueto, Chairman & CEO
Chris Boruff, President, Software Division
Peng Chen, President, Global Investment Div.
Bevin Desmond, President, International Operations
Scott Cooley, Chief Financial Officer

Morningstar provides data on approximately 330,000 investment offerings, including stocks, mutual funds, and similar vehicles, along with real-time global market data on more than 5 million equities, indexes, futures, options, commodities, and precious metals, in addition to foreign exchange and Treasury markets. Morningstar also offers investment management services and has more than $167 billion in assets under advisement and management.

9210 Mutual Fund Encyclopedia
Dearborn Financial Publishing
155 Wacker Drive
Chicago, IL 60606

312-836-4400

Gerald W Perritt, Author

Directory of services and supplies to the industry.
Cost: $35.95
600 Pages
Frequency: Annual

9211 Mutual Fund/Municipal Bond
Interactive Data Corporation
10 Post Office Sq
39th Floor
Boston, MA 02109-4695

617-428-1600
E-Mail: info@interactivedata.com
Home Page: www.interactivedata.com

James Murawski, Manager

This database contains over 3,000 time series of price data for municipal bonds held in the portfolios of selected mutual funds.

9212 NADOA Directory
National Association of Division Order Analysts
2805 Oak Trail Court
Suite 6312
Arlington, TX 76016

972-715-4489
E-Mail: administrator@nadoa.org
Home Page: www.nadoa.org

Lynn S McCord, Administrator
Frequency: Annual

9213 NALHFA Membership Directory
National Associatin of Local Housing Finance
2025 M St NW
Suite 800
Washington, DC 20036-2422

202-367-1197
FAX 202-367-2197
E-Mail: john_murphy@nalhfa.org
Home Page: www.noca.org

John C Murphy, Executive Director
Scott Lynch, Association Manager
Kim McKinon, Coordinator Membership
Frequency: Annual

9214 NASBO Newsletter
National Association of State Budget Officers
444 N Capitol St NW
Suite 642
Washington, DC 20001-1556

202-624-8020
FAX 202-624-7745
E-Mail: spattison@nasbo.org
Home Page: www.nasbo.org

Scott Pattison, Executive Director
Lauren Cummings, Manager Member Relations

9215 NASD Manual
CCH
2700 Lake Cook Rd
Riverwoods, IL 60015-3867

847-940-4600
800-835-5224
FAX 773-866-3095
Home Page: www.cch.com

Mike Sabbatis, President
Douglas M Winterrose, Vice President & CFO
Jim Bryant, EVP Software Products
Officials, members, by-laws and rules of NASD.
Founded in 1913

9216 NATRI Membership Directory
National Association for Treasurers of Religious

8824 Cameron Street
Silver Springs, MD 20910

301-587-7776
FAX 301-589-2897
Home Page: www.natri.org

Laura Reicks, Executive Director
Lorelle Elcock, Associate Director Finance
Frequency: Annual

9217 National Bankers Association: Roster of Minority Banking Institutions
National Bankers Association
1513 P St NW
Washington, DC 20005-1909

202-588-5432
FAX 202-588-5443
E-Mail: webmaster@nationalbankers.org
Home Page: www.nationalbankers.org

Michael Grant, President
Floyd Weekes, Chairman

About 140 banks owned or controlled by minority group persons or women.
Cost: $5.00
Frequency: Annual October

9218 National Credit Union Administration Directory
National Credit Union Administration
1775 Duke St
Suite 4206
Alexandria, VA 22314-6115

703-518-6300
FAX 703-518-6539
E-Mail: ociomail@ncua.gov
Home Page: www.ncua.gov

Michael Fryzel, Chairman
Sarah Vega, Executive Director

Directory of credit unions governed by a three member board appointed by the President and confirmed by the US Senate, by the independent federal agency that charters and supervises federal credit unions. NCUA, with the backing of the full faith and credit of the US government, operates the National Credit Union Share Insurance Fund, insuring the savings of 80 million account holders in all federal credit unions and many state chartered credit unions.

9219 National Directory of Investment Newsletters
GPS
PO Box 372
Morrisville, PA 19067-8372

215-295-8700
Home Page:
www.investmentnewsletterdirectory.com

George T Scilieber, Editor

Lists over 800 newsletters dealing with investments and financial planning and their publishers.
Cost: $49.95
60 Pages
Frequency: Biennial

9220 North American Financial Institutions Directory
4709 Golf Road
Skokie, IL 60076

847-676-9600
800-321-3373
FAX 847-933-8101
E-Mail: custserv@accuitysolutions.com
Home Page: www.accuitysolutions.com

Marideth Johnson, Manager, Marketing/Communications
Malcolm Taylor, Managing Director
Cost: $460.00
Circulation: 31850

9221 PC Bridge
Bridge Information Systems
717 Office Parkway
Saint Louis, MO 63141-7115

314-567-8100
FAX 314-432-5391

Tony Bridge, Manager

This database delivers real-time market information, monitoring up to 100 symbols per page on 10 available pages.

9222 Pacific Stock Exchange Guide
CCH
2700 Lake Cook Rd
Riverwoods, IL 60015-3867

847-940-4600
800-835-5224
FAX 773-866-3095
Home Page: www.cch.com

Mike Sabbatis, President
Douglas M Winterrose, Vice President & CFO
Jim Bryant, EVP Software Products

Lists officials, members, member organizations; by-laws and rules of the Pacific Stock Exchange.
Cost: $405.00

9223 Pensions & Investments: Investment Managers
Crain Communications
711 3rd Ave
New York, NY 10017-4014

212-210-0785
FAX 212-210-0465
E-Mail: jmurphy@crain.com

Norm Feldman, Manager
Chris Battaglia, Publisher

List of over 1,050 banks, insurance companies, investment advisors and other investment management organizations.
Cost: $40.00
Frequency: Annual May
Circulation: 41,000

9224 Pensions & Investments: Master Trust, Custody and Global Custody Banks
Crain Communications
711 3rd Ave
New York, NY 10017-4014

212-210-0785
FAX 212-210-0465
E-Mail: jmurphy@crain.com

Norm Feldman, Manager
Chris Battaglia, Publisher

List of banks with master trust/master custodial assets and global custody assets.
Cost: $10.00
Frequency: Annual October
Circulation: 41,000

9225 Philadelphia Stock Exchange Guide
CCH
2700 Lake Cook Rd
Riverwoods, IL 60015-3867

847-940-4600
800-835-5224
FAX 773-866-3095
Home Page: www.cch.com

Mike Sabbatis, President
Douglas M Winterrose, Vice President & CFO
Jim Bryant, EVP Software Products

Lists officials, members, member organizations, securities, by-laws and rules of the Exchange.
Cost: $350.00
Frequency: Monthly

9226 Pratt's Guide to Private Equity & Venture Capital Sources
Thomson Reuters
3 Times Square
New York, NY 10036

646-223-4431
800-782-5555
E-Mail: rpp.americas@thomsonreuters.com
Home Page: www.thomsonreuters.com

James C Smith, Chief Executive Officer
Stephane Bello, Chief Financial Officer
David W Craig, President, Finance
Robert D Daleo, Vice Chairman
Susan Taylor Martin, President, Reuters Media

This is the definitive reference source to actively investing private equity and venture capital firms operating around the world. Pratt's Guide is available in both hard copy and online format - the latter being continually updated with new fund-raising data, new investment and exit data and new contact information.

9227 Professional Investor Report
Dow Jones & Company
PO Box 300
Princeton, NJ 08543-0300

609-520-4000

Offers information on unusual stock trading activity taking place on the New York and American stock exchanges and the National Market System portion of the OTC market.

9228 Quarterly Financial Report
GE Information Services
401 N Washington Street
Rockville, MD 20850-1707

301-388-8284
FAX 301-294-5501

Cathy Ge, Owner

This unique database offers information on financial estimates for US enterprises within 31 industry classifications.

9229 RSP Funding for Nursing Students and Nurses
Reference Service Press
5000 Windplay Dr
Suite 4
El Dorado Hills, CA 95762-9319

916-939-9620
FAX 916-939-9626
E-Mail: info@rspfunding.com
Home Page: www.rspfunding.com

Gail Schlachter, Owner
R David Weber, Manager
Martin Sklar, Manager

You can find out about the more than 600 scholarships, fellowships, loans, loan repayment programs, forgivable loans, grants, awards, prizes and interships set aside specifically to support study, research, creative activities, past accomplishments, future projects, professional development and traineeships. This is more than twice the number of nursing related funding programs covered in any other source.
Cost: $30.00
210 Pages
Frequency: Biennial
ISBN: 1-588410-95-1
Founded in 1998

9230 Registry of Financial Planning Practitioners
International Association for Financial Planning

1580 W. El Camino Real
Suite 10
Mountain View, CA 94040

877-794-9511
650-390-6400
FAX 650-989-2131
E-Mail: customer.service@trademarkia.com
Home Page: www.trademarkia.com

J Patrick Tinley, CEO
Alexander Esq, Owner

Directory of services and supplies to the industry.
80 Pages
Frequency: Annual

9231 Research Reports
National Committee on Planned Giving
233 S McCrea St
Suite 400
Indianapolis, IN 46225-1068

317-269-6274
FAX 317-269-6276
Home Page: www.ncpg.org

Tanya Howe Johnson, President
Sandra Kerr, Director Government Education
Barbara Owens, Director Membership/Manager HR
Kathryn J Ramsey, Director Meetings
Kurt Reusze, Manager Education/Technology
Frequency: Irregular

9232 Roster of Minority Financial Institutions
US Department of the Treasury
401 14th Street SW
Room 523C
Washington, DC 20024-2106

202-874-5740
FAX 202-874-6907

Robert Jones, Editor

About 170 commercial, minority-owned and controlled financial institutions participating in the Department of the Treasury's Minority Bank Deposit program.
Frequency: Biennial

9233 S&P MarketScope Database
Standard & Poor's Corporation
55 Water St
New York, NY 10041-0003

212-438-1000
FAX 212-438-0299

Deven Sharma, President

Over 5,000 companies are listed in the Reference Section of Standard and Poors database offering names, addresses, background information and current and historical financial information.

9234 Secondary Marketing Executive Directory of Mortgage Technology
LDJ Corporation
P.O.Box 2180
Waterbury, CT 06722-2180

203-755-0158
FAX 203-755-3480

David Zackin, Publisher
John Florian, Editor

A who's who directory of technology products and services to the real estate finance industry.
Cost: $5.00
Frequency: Annual
Circulation: 21,000

9235 Service Directory
National Association for Treasurers of Religious

8824 Cameron Street
Silver Springs, MD 20910

301-587-7776
FAX 301-589-2897
Home Page: www.natri.org

Laura Reicks, Executive Director
Lorelle Elcock, Associate Director Finance
Frequency: Annual

9236 Sheshunoff Bank & S&L Quarterly
Sheshunoff Information Services
2801 Via Fortuna
Suite 600
Austin, TX 78746-7970

512-472-4000
800-477-1772
FAX 512-305-6575
E-Mail: sales@smslp.com
Home Page: www.smslp.com

Gabrielle Sheshunoff, CEO

Overview of the financial health of the banking
industry and of every bank and S&L in the nation. Information includes CAMEL, fachois,
asset quality, earnings, and rotation.
Cost: $543.00
Frequency: Quarterly

**9237 Sheshunoff Banking Organization
Quarterly**
Sheshunoff Information Services
2801 Via Fortuna
Suite 600
Austin, TX 78746-7970

512-472-4000
800-456-2340
FAX 512-305-6575
E-Mail: gsheshunoff@smslp.com
Home Page: www.smslp.com

Gabrielle Sheshunoff, CEO

Offers ownership structure for all bank holding
companies and overview and ratings for bank
holding companies and their brinking subs.
Cost: $499.00
Frequency: Quarterly

**9238 Small Business Investment Company
Directory and Handbook**
International Wealth Success
PO Box 186
Merrick, NY 11566-0186

516-766-5850
800-323-0548
FAX 516-766-5919
E-Mail: admin@iwsmoney.com
Home Page: www.iwsmoney.com
Social Media: *Facebook, LinkedIn*

Tyler G Hicks, President

Lists more than 400 small business investment
companies that invest in small businesses to
help them prosper. Also gives tips on financial
management in business.
Cost: $20.00
135 Pages
Frequency: Annual
ISBN: 1-561503-12-6
Founded in 1975

9239 Speakers Bureau Directory
National Association of Certified Valuation
1111 Brickyard Road
Suite 200
Salt Lake City, UT 84106-5401

801-486-0600
800-677-2009
FAX 801-486-7500
E-Mail: nacva1@nacva.com
Home Page: www.nacva.com

Parnell Black, CEO
Frequency: Annual

**9240 Standard & Poor's Directory of Bond
Agents**
Standard & Poor's Corporation
55 Water St
New York, NY 10041-0003

212-438-1000
FAX 212-438-0299

Deven Sharma, President

A list of paying agents, registrars, co-registrars
and conversion agents for 30,000 corporate and
municipal bonds are included.
Cost: $1250.00

**9241 Standard & Poor's Security Dealers
of North America**
Standard & Poor's Financial Services, LLC
401 East Market Street
PO Box 1608
Charlottesville, VA 22902

434-977-1450
800-446-2810
FAX 434-979-9962
Home Page: www.mmdwebaccess.com

Deven Sharma, President

The most comprehensive guide to brokerage
and investment banking firms in the US and
Canada. The directory contains all the facts you
need for conveniently locating firms and facilitating transactions.
Cost: $498.00
Frequency: 2x/Year

9242 State Expenditure Report
National Association of State Budget
Officers
444 N Capitol St NW
Suite 642
Washington, DC 20001-1556

202-624-8020
FAX 202-624-7745
E-Mail: spattison@nasbo.org
Home Page: www.nasbo.org

Scott Pattison, Executive Director
Lauren Cummings, Manager Member Relations
Frequency: Annual

9243 TA Guide & Checklist
National Investment Company Service
Association
36 Washington Street
Suite 70
Wellesley Hills, MA 02481

781-416-7200
FAX 781-416-7065
E-Mail: info@nisca.org
Home Page: www.nisca.org

Barbara V Weidlich, President
Keith Dropkin, Director Operations
Doris Jaimes, Registrar
Sheila Kobaly, Events Manager
Chris Ludent, IT Manager
Frequency: Annual

9244 TRW Trade Payment Guide
TRW Business Credit Services
500 City Pkwy W
Orange, CA 92868-2913

714-385-7000
800-344-0603
FAX 714-938-2586

Approximately 2,500,000 credit active business
locations.
Frequency: Quarterly

9245 Tax Directory
Tax Analysts

6830 N Fairfax Drive
Arlington, VA 22213-1001

703-533-4400
800-955-3444
FAX 703-533-4664
E-Mail: taxdir@tax.org
Home Page: www.tax.org

Amie Chant, Editor
Thomas F Field, Vice President
Jill Biden, Vice President

A reference tool that provides users with com-
prehensive listings of federal, state and private
sector tax professionals. Now in three sections
- Government Officials, Corporate Tax Manag-
ers and International Officials.
Cost: $ 399.00
960 Pages
Frequency: Quarterly
Circulation: 2,000
ISSN: 0888-1243

9246 Tax Free Trade Zones of the World
Matthew Bender and Company
11 Penn Plz
Suite 5101
New York, NY 10001-2006

212-000-1111

Eric Blood, Data Processing

Covers over 450 free trade zones, transit zones,
free perimeters and free ports. The emphasis is
placed on tax advantages of each.
Cost: $280.00
1000 Pages

9247 Technical Resources Handbook
National Association of Certified Valuation
1111 Brickyard Road
Suite 200
Salt Lake City, UT 84106-5401

801-486-0600
800-677-2009
FAX 801-486-7500
E-Mail: nacva1@nacva.com
Home Page: www.nacva.com

Parnell Black, CEO
Frequency: Annual

**9248 TheStreet Ratings Guide to Bond &
Money Market Mutual Funds**
Grey House Publishing
4919 Route 22
PO Box 56
Amenia, NY 12501

518-789-8700
800-562-2139
FAX 845-373-6390
E-Mail: books@greyhouse.com
Home Page: www.greyhouse.com
Social Media: *Facebook, Twitter*

Leslie Mackenzie, Publisher
Richard Gottlieb, Editor

Each quarterly edition provides ratings and
analyses of more than 4,200 fixed income
funds, more than any other publication, including corporate bond funds, municipal bond
funds, mortgage security funds, money market
funds, global bond funds, and government
bond funds.
Cost: $249.00
600 Pages
Frequency: Quarterly
Founded in 1981

**9249 TheStreet Ratings Guide to Common
Stocks**
Grey House Publishing

4919 Route 22
PO Box 56
Amenia, NY 12501

518-789-8700
800-562-2139
FAX 845-373-6390
E-Mail: books@greyhouse.com
Home Page: www.greyhouse.com
Social Media: *Facebook, Twitter*

Leslie Mackenzie, Publisher
Richard Gottlieb, Editor

Each quarterly edition provides reliable insight into the risk-adjusted performance of over 7,500 common stocks listed on the NYSE, AMEX, and NASDAQ, more than any other publication. This user-friendly guide offers step-by-step guidance for users to find out which type of stocks are best for them, and quickly and easily points the user to the best performing stocks in that category.
Cost: $249.00
600 Pages
Frequency: Quarterly
Founded in 1981

9250 TheStreet Ratings Guide to Exchange-Traded Funds
Grey House Publishing
4919 Route 22
PO Box 56
Amenia, NY 12501

518-789-8700
800-562-2139
FAX 845-373-6390
E-Mail: books@greyhouse.com
Home Page: www.greyhouse.com
Social Media: *Facebook, Twitter*

Leslie Mackenzie, Publisher
Richard Gottlieb, Editor

The intuitive, consumer-friendly ratings allow investors to instantly identify those funds that have historically done well and those that have under-performed the market. Identifies top-performing exchange-traded funds based on risk category, type of fund, and overall risk-adjusted performance.
Cost: $249.00
600 Pages
Frequency: Quarterly
Founded in 1981

9251 TheStreet Ratings Guide to Stock Mutual Funds
Grey House Publishing
4919 Route 22
PO Box 56
Amenia, NY 12501

518-789-8700
800-562-2139
FAX 845-373-6390
E-Mail: books@greyhouse.com
Home Page: www.greyhouse.com
Social Media: *Facebook, Twitter*

Leslie Mackenzie, Publisher
Richard Gottlieb, Editor

Offers ratings and analyses on more than 8,000 equity mutual funds, including growth funds, index funds, balanced funds and sector or international funds - more than any other publication.
Cost: $249.00
600 Pages
Frequency: Quarterly
Founded in 1981

9252 TheStreet Ratings Ultimate Guided Tour of Stock Investing
Grey House Publishing

4919 Route 22
PO Box 56
Amenia, NY 12501

518-789-8700
800-562-2139
FAX 845-373-6390
E-Mail: books@greyhouse.com
Home Page: www.greyhouse.com
Social Media: *Facebook, Twitter*

Leslie Mackenzie, Publisher
Richard Gottlieb, Editor

This user-friendly guide provides a step-by-step introduction to stock investing designed for the beginning to intermediate investor. Starting with the basics of stock investing and ending with an evaluation of the user's risk tolerance and the identification of the types of stocks that best match their needs, this easy-to-navigate guide pulls together all of the information necessary to educate the consumer on how to get the best start in investing.
Cost: $249.00
600 Pages
Frequency: Quarterly
Founded in 1981

9253 Top Mortgage Market Players Directory
Inside Mortgage Finance Publishers
7910 Woodmont Ave
Suite 1000
Bethesda, MD 20814-7019

301-951-1240
FAX 301-656-1709
E-Mail: service@imfpubs.com
Home Page: www.imfpubs.com

Guy Cecala, Owner
John Bancroft, Managing Editor
Didi Parks, Marketing/Advertising

Listing of over 4,500 residential mortgage lenders.
Cost: $375.00
Frequency: Annual

9254 Trading Volume Survey
EMTA - Trade Association for the Emerging Markets
360 Madison Avenue
18th Floor
New York, NY 10017

646-637-9100
FAX 646-637-9128
E-Mail: awerner@emta.org
Home Page: www.emta.org

Michael M Chamberlin, Executive Director
Aviva Werner, Managing Director
Jonathan Murno, Managing Director
Suzette Ortiz, Office Manager
Monika Forbes, Administrative Assistant
Frequency: Quarterly

9255 Trusts & Estates: Directory of Trust Institutions Issue
Primedia
PO Box 12901
Shawnee Mission, KS 66282-2901

913-341-1300
FAX 913-514-6895
Home Page: www.penton.com

Eric Jacobson, Senior VP

Offers a list of about 5,000 trust departments in the United States and Canadian banks.
Cost: $82.00
Frequency: Annual January
Circulation: 12,200

9256 Valuation Compilation
National Association of Certified Valuation

1111 Brickyard Road
Suite 200
Salt Lake City, UT 84106-5401

801-486-0600
800-677-2009
FAX 801-486-7500
E-Mail: nacva1@nacva.com
Home Page: www.nacva.com

Parnell Black, CEO
Frequency: Bi-Ennial

9257 Venture Capital: Where to Find it
National Association of Small Business Investment
1199 N Fairfax Street
Suite 200
Alexandria, VA 22314-1437

703-549-2100

Jeanette D Smith, Editor

Directory of services and supplies to the industry.
Frequency: Annual

9258 Weiss Ratings Consumer Box Set
Grey House Publishing
4919 Route 22
PO Box 56
Amenia, NY 12501

518-789-8700
800-562-2139
FAX 845-373-6390
E-Mail: books@greyhouse.com
Home Page: www.greyhouse.com
Social Media: *Facebook, Twitter*

Leslie Mackenzie, Publisher
Richard Gottlieb, Editor

Each guide in the Weiss Ratings Consumer Box Set is packed with accurate, unbiased information, including helpful, step-by-step Worksheets & Planners. The set consists of Consumer Guides to Variable Annuities, Elder Care Choices, Medicare Supplement Insurance, Medicare Prescription Drug Coverage, Homeowners Insurance, Automobile Insurance, Long-Term Care Insurance, and Term Life Insurance.
Cost: $249.00
600 Pages
Frequency: Quarterly
Founded in 1981

9259 Weiss Ratings Guide to Banks & Thrifts
Grey House Publishing
4919 Route 22
PO Box 56
Amenia, NY 12501

518-789-8700
800-562-2139
FAX 845-373-6390
E-Mail: books@greyhouse.com
Home Page: www.greyhouse.com
Social Media: *Facebook, Twitter*

Leslie Mackenzie, Publisher
Richard Gottlieb, Editor

Offers accurate, intuitive safety ratings your patrons can trust; supporting ratios and analyses that show an institution's strong & weak points; identification of the Weiss Recommended Companies with branches in your area and more.
Cost: $249.00
600 Pages
Frequency: Quarterly
Founded in 1981

9260 Weiss Ratings Guide to Credit Unions
Grey House Publishing

4919 Route 22
PO Box 56
Amenia, NY 12501

518-789-8700
800-562-2139
FAX 845-373-6390
E-Mail: books@greyhouse.com
Home Page: www.greyhouse.com
Social Media: *Facebook, Twitter*

Leslie Mackenzie, Publisher
Richard Gottlieb, Editor

This new reference tool provides accurate financial strength ratings of the 7,800 credit unions in the United States.
Cost: $249.00
600 Pages
Frequency: Quarterly
Founded in 1981

9261 Weiss Ratings Guide to Health Insurers
Grey House Publishing
4919 Route 22
PO Box 56
Amenia, NY 12501

518-789-8700
800-562-2139
FAX 845-373-6390
E-Mail: books@greyhouse.com
Home Page: www.greyhouse.com
Social Media: *Facebook, Twitter*

Leslie Mackenzie, Publisher
Richard Gottlieb, Editor

Weiss Ratings Guide to Health Insurers is the first and only source to cover the financial stability of the nation's health care system, rating the financial safety of more than 6,000 health maintenance organizations (HMOs) and all of the Blue Cross Blue Shield plans - updated quarterly to ensure the most accurate, up-to-date informations.
Cost: $249.00
600 Pages
Frequency: Quarterly
Founded in 1981

9262 Weiss Ratings Guide to Life & Annuity Insurers
Grey House Publishing
4919 Route 22
PO Box 56
Amenia, NY 12501

518-789-8700
800-562-2139
FAX 845-373-6390
E-Mail: books@greyhouse.com
Home Page: www.greyhouse.com
Social Media: *Facebook, Twitter*

Leslie Mackenzie, Publisher
Richard Gottlieb, Edtior

Each easy-to-use edition provides independent, unbiased ratings on the financial strength of 1,000 life and annuity insurers, including companies providing life insurance, annuities, guaranteed investment contracts (GICs) and other pension products.
Cost: $249.00
600 Pages
Frequency: Quarterly
Founded in 1981

9263 Weiss Ratings Guide to Property & Casualty Insurers
Grey House Publishing
4919 Route 22
PO Box 56
Amenia, NY 12501

518-789-8700
800-562-2139
FAX 845-373-6390
E-Mail: books@greyhouse.com

Home Page: www.greyhouse.com
Social Media: *Facebook, Twitter*

Leslie Mackenzie, Publisher
Richard Gottlieb, Editor

Updated quarterly, this publication is the only resource that provides independent, unbiased ratings and analyses on the 2,400 insurers offering auto & homeowners, business, worker's compensation, product liability, medical malpractice and other professional liability insurance in the United States.
Cost: $249.00
600 Pages
Frequency: Quarterly
Founded in 1981

9264 Who's Who in Economic Development Directory
International Economic Development Council (IEDC)
734 15th St NW
Suite 900
Washington, DC 20005-1013

202-223-7800
FAX 202-223-4745
Home Page: www.iedconline.org

Jeffrey Finkle, CEO
Jon Roberts, Managing Director
Jackie Gibson, Project Manager
Charles Stein, Founder

A listing of over 2,500 Council members and other certified individuals. Directory is limited to international coverage.
200 Pages
Frequency: Annual

9265 Who's Who in Venture Capital
Grey House Publishing
4919 Route 22
PO Box 56
Amenia, NY 12501

518-789-8700
800-562-2139
FAX 845-373-6390
E-Mail: books@greyhouse.com
Home Page: www.greyhouse.com
Social Media: *Facebook, Twitter*

Leslie Mackenzie, Publisher
Richard Gottlieb, Editor

Provides immediate access to nearly 10,000 principals, partners and managing directors heading the world's Venture Capital and Private Equity firms. The listings contain comprehensive profile information including partner and firm names, titles, education, professional background, directorships and full contact information.
Cost: $295.00
643 Pages
Founded in 1981

9266 World Emerging Stock Markets
Probus Publishing Company
1333 Burbridge Parkway
Burbridge, IL 60521

Directories of stock markets in Central and South America, Middle East and Europe.
Cost: $59.95

9267 Yearbook of Education Finance
American Education Finance Association
8365 S Armadillo Trail
Evergreen, CO 80439

303-674-0857
FAX 303-670-8986
Home Page: www.aefa.cc

Ed Steinbecher, Executive Director

Information and updates for educational institutions and organizations regarding financial investing, prospecting and fundraising.
Frequency: Annual

Industry Web Sites

9268 http://gold.greyhouse.com
G.O.L.D Grey House OnLine Databases
Grey House Publishing's online database platform, GOLD, offers Quick Search, Keyword Search and Expert Search for most business sectors including financial services and banking markets. The GOLD platform makes finding the information you need quick and easy - whether you're a novice searcher or an experienced database user. All of Grey House's directory products are available for subscription on the GOLD platform.

9269 www.aacei.org
Association for Advancement of Cost Engineering
Association for those interested in the financial aspects of engineering all aspects of cost management.

9270 www.aaii.com
American Association of Individual Investors
An independent nonprofit corporation formed in 1978 for the purpose of assisting individuals in becoming effective managers of their own assets through programs of education, information and research.

9271 www.abiworld.org
American Bankruptcy Institute
Provides a multi-disiplinary, non-partisan organization dedicated to research and education on matters related to insolvency. Provides a forum for the exchange of ideas and information. ABI is engaged in numerous educational and research activities, as well as the production of a number of publications both for the insolvency practitioner and the public.

9272 www.acainternational.org
ACA International
Formerly know as the American Collectors Association, is the association of credit and collection professionals. Founded in 1939, it has over 5,300 members, including third party collection agencies, attorneys, credit grantors and vendor affiliates. Headquartered in Minneapolis, ACA serves members in the US and Canada plus 58 other countries worldwide.

9273 www.aefa.org
American Education Finance Association
Encourages communications among groups and individuals in education financial fields.

9274 www.afponline.org
Association for Financial Professionals
Association of 12,000 financial professionals.

9275 www.afsaonline.com
American Financial Services Association
National trade association for market funded providers of financial services to consumers and small businesses. These providers offer an array of finacial services, including unsecured personal loans, automobile loans, home equity loans and credit cards through specialized bank institutions.

9276 www.agacgfm.org
Association of Government Accountants
AGA is an educational association dedicated to enhancing public financial management by serving the professional interests of governmental managers and public accounting firms.

723

9277 www.appraisalinstitute.org
Appraisal Institute

Promotes a code of ethics and uniform standards of the real estate appraisal practice. Publishes periodicals, books and appraisal-related materials, and sponsors courses and seminars.

9278 www.appraisers.org
American Society of Appraisers

Professional association of appraisers of all kinds.

9279 www.bcfm.com
Broadcast Cable Financial Management Association

Professional association for TV, radio and cable CEOs, bueinss managers, HR, MIS controllers and financial personnel, as well as associate members in legal, audit and related fields.

9280 www.bma.net.org
Bank Marketing Association

Association for suppliers of industry related products and services.

9281 www.communitycapital.org
National Community Capital Association

Provides support for non-profit revolving loan funds that lend capital and offer technical assistance in distressed and disenfranchised communities.

9282 www.dbcams.com
FCSI Industry Web Sites

A resource for the financial industry, including stock exchanges, news, pricing services, research, information and more.

9283 www.ecfa.org
Evangelical Council for Financial Accountability

Helps Christ-centered organizations earn the public's trust through developing and maintaining standards of accountability that convey God-honoring ethical practices.

9284 www.federalregister.com
Neighborhood Reinvestment Corporation

Supplies training, grants, developmental assistance, and a range of other technical services designed to help the local partnerships achieve substantially self-reliant neighborhoods. The goal is to improve a neighborhood's housing and physical conditions, build a positive community image, and establish a healthy real estate market and a core of neighbors capable of managing the continued health of their neighborhood.

9285 www.fei.org
Financial Executives International

A professional organization of individuals performing the duties of C.F.O., Controller, Treasurer or Vice President of Finance.

9286 www.financialratingsseries.com
Grey House Publishing

Financial Ratings Series Online combines the strength of Weiss Ratings and TheStreet Ratings to offer the library community with a single source for financial strength ratings and financial planning tools covering Banks, Insurers, Mutual Funds and Stocks. This powerful database will provide the accurate, independent information consumers need to make informed decisions about their financial planning.

9287 www.fma.org
Financial Management Association

Strives to facilitate exchanges of ideas among persons in financial management.

9288 www.fmsinc.com
Financial Managers Society

Provides technical information and education to financial officers in banks, thrifts and credit unions.

9289 www.globalpurchasing.org
International Association of Purchasing Managers

A professional organization dedicated to the advancement of world trade, membership is open to buyers, purchasing managers, executives and all individuals that may be involved or have an interest in the important function of buying goods and services on the global market. A NON-PROFIT organization..

9290 www.greenwood.com
Greenwood Publishing Group

Business and professional publishing; academic books in Business, Finance, Business Law, and Applied Economics management.

9291 www.greyhouse.com
Grey House Publishing

Authoritative reference directories for most business sectors including financial services and banking markets. Users can search the online databases with varied search criteria allowing for custom searches by product category, geographic area, sales volume, keyword, subject and more. Full Grey House catalog and online ordering also available.

9292 www.houisingfinance.org
Int'l Union of Housing Finance Institutions
Disseminates information in housing finance policies and techniques worldwide.

9293 www.iami.org
National Association of Review Appraisers

Association for professionals who review real estate appraisals and underwrite real estate mortgagers. The association offers the CRA, Certified Review Appraiser and RMU, Registered Mortgage Underwriter, professional designation.

9294 www.ici.org
Investment Company Institute

Acts to represent members in matters of legislation, taxation, regulation, economic research and marketing and public information regarding investments and mutual funds.

9295 www.investavenue.com
Invest Avenue

Online magazine featuring articles from leading professionals in the finaical world, current news and analysis. Newsletter can be e-mailed on request.

9296 www.invrecovery.org
Investment Recovery Association

Association for manufacturers of services and supplies to the industry.

9297 www.irrc.org
Investor Responsibility Research Center

Acts to publish reports and analyses of social issues and public policy affecting corporation and investors.

9298 www.kobren.com
Mutual Fund Investors Association

Association for those interested in information and rates for mutual funds, investments, stocks and bonds.

9299 www.marketresearch.com
Research Reports

Search financial services reports from over 350 sources. Updated daily.

9300 www.mfea.com
Mutual Fund Education Alliance

Conducts public education and public relation activities in an effort to acquaint industry, organizations and government agencies with direct market funds.

9301 www.mortgagepress.com
National Mortgage Professional

Information on new products, industry news, personnel announcements and calendar of events.

9302 www.nact.org
National Association of Corporate Treasurers

Members are corporate chief financial officers, treasurers or assistant treasurers.

9303 www.nadco.org
National Association of Development Companies

Provides long-term fixed asset financing to small businesses.

9304 www.nafa-us.org
National Aircraft Finance Association

Members are lending institutions involved in aircraft financing.

9305 www.nafcunet.org
National Association of Federal Credit Unions

Association for manufacturers and suppliers of complete range of financial products and services.

9306 www.nasbic.org
Nat'l Assn of Small Business Investment Companies

Trade Association representing federally licensed ventures capital firms, Email, and business investment companies.

9307 www.natptax.com
National Association of Tax Professionals

The National Association of Tax Professionals (NATP) is a nonprofit association dedicated to excellence in taxation and related financial services. NATP was formed to serve professionals who work in all areas of tax practice. Members include Enrolled Agents, Certified Public Accountants, individual practitioners, accountants, attorneys, and financial planners.

9308 www.nchffa.com
National Council of Health Facilities Finance

To serve the common interests and enhance the effectiveness of member Authorities through communication, education and advocacy.

9309 www.nfa.future.org
National Futures Association

Association for corporations and firms that are registered with the Commodity Futures Trading Commission.

9310 www.nfa.org
National Finance Adjusters

Serves collateral recovery specialists.

9311 www.nfma.org
National Federation of Municipal Analysts

Promotes the profession of municipal credit analysts through educational programs, industry, communications and related programming.

9312 www.nibesa.com
National Independent Bank Equipment & Systems Assn

Association of financial security equipment nationwide. Annual convention and showcase and monthly newsletter.

9313 **www.nipa.org**
National Institute of Pension Administrators
Enhancing professionalism in the retirement plan industry through education.

9314 **www.nvca.org**
National Venture Capital Association
Corporations, corporate financiers and private individuals who invest private capital in young companies on a professional basis.

9315 **www.nvla.org**
National Vehicle Leasing Association
Fosters education, publishing, conferences, legal services, advancement and industry relations certification.

9316 **www.plunkettresearch.com/finance/index.htm**
Plunkett Research
Free section of company web site provides a synopsis of trends in the finacial industry and a glossary of terms.

9317 **www.securitytraders.org**
Security Traders Association
Serves the securities industry.

9318 **www.snl.com**
SNL Securities
News articles on banks and thrifts, insurance and other financial services. Also features vital company information.

9319 **www.theiia.org**
Institute of Internal Auditors
International organization composed of internal auditors, corporate executives and board members. Contact and current development information.

9320 **www.thestreet.com**
TheStreet Ratings, Inc.
Publisher of ratings guides.

9321 **www.uhab.org**
Urban Homesteading Assistance Board
Information on affordable housing and self reliance. Activities include advocacy, organizing, classroom and on-site training, direct technical assistance, development consulting, development and sponsorship of new co-ops and services to member co-ops that include bookkeeping, insurance, legal services, bulk purchasing, newsletters and IT services.

9322 **www.wsta.org**
Wall Street Technology Association
White papers on the latest in technology for IT professionals working in the finacial field. Resource guide for industry products and services and information on seminars and conferences included.

Associations

9323 American Albacore Fishing Association
4364 Bonita Rd., Box 311
Bonita, CA 91902

619-941-2307
FAX 619-863-5046
E-Mail: nataliewebster@americanalbacore.com
Home Page: americanalbacore.com

Tim Thomas, President
Carl Nish, Vice President
Jack Vantress, Treasurer
Jack Webster, Secretary

A nonprofit representing commercial pole and line vessels that advocates for a sustainable tuna fishery.

9324 American Crappie Association
125 Ruth Avenue
Benton, KY 42025

270-395-4204
FAX 270-395-4381
E-Mail: office@crappieusa.com
Home Page: www.crappieusa.com
Social Media: *Facebook*

Darrell VanVactor, President
Charles Rogers, VP
Larry Crecelius, Public Relations Director
Jim Perry, Secretary/Treasurer
Dan Wagoner, Member

For all crappie anglers, from weekend fishermen to tournament pros. Influencing national manufacturers to produce more and better crappie fishing products, establishing a voice and lobby for crappie anglers everywhere and elevating the sport of crappie fishing to its rightful place in the limelight.
Cost: $20.00
Frequency: Individual Membership

9325 American Fisheries Society
5410 Grosvenor Ln
Suite 110
Bethesda, MD 20814

301-897-8616
FAX 301-897-8096
E-Mail: sjohnston@fisheries.org
Home Page: www.fisheries.org
Social Media: *Facebook, Twitter, vimeo, flickr*

Bob Hughes, President
Donna L. Parrish, President-Elect
Ronald J. Essig, First Vice President
Joe Margraf, Second Vice President
John Boreman, Past President

AFS promotes scientific research and enlightened management of resources for optimum use and enjoyment by the public. It also encourages a comprehensive education for fisheries scientists and continuing on-the-job training
Cost: $100.00
8500 Members
Frequency: Membership Fee
Founded in 1870
Mailing list available for rent: 8500 names

9326 American Fly Fishing Trade Association
321 East Main St.
Suite 300
Bozeman, MO 59715

406-522-1556
FAX 406-522-1557
Home Page: www.affta.com
Social Media: *Facebook*

Ben Bulis, President
Tucker Ladd, Chairman

A sole trade organization for the fly fishing industry. The mission is to promote the sustained growth of the fly fishing industry.
400 Members
Founded in 2003
Mailing list available for rent

9327 American Institute of Fishery Research Biologists
205 Blades Road
Havelock, NC 28532

Home Page: www.aifrb.org
Social Media: *Facebook, Twitter, LinkedIn, Stumbleupon, www.digg.com*

Tom Keegan, President
Allen Shimada, Treasurer
Barbara Warkentine, Secretary
Sarah Fox, Executive Editor
Linda Jones, Past President

A professional organization founded to promote conservation and proper utilization of fishery resources through application of fishery science and related sciences.
1000 Members
Founded in 1956

9328 American Littoral Society
18 Hartshorne Drive
Suite #1
Highlands, NJ 07732

732-291-0055
FAX 732-291-3551
E-Mail: driepe@nyc.rr.com
Home Page: www.littoralsociety.org
Social Media: *Facebook, Twitter, Stumbleupon*

Tim Dillingham, Executive Director
Kathleen Gasienica, President
Peter Hetzler, Vice President
Gregory Quirk, Treasurer
Sameul Huber, Secretary

Dedicated to the environmental well-being of coastal habitat.
5000+ Members
Frequency: Membership Fee: $30-$35
Founded in 1961
Mailing list available for rent

9329 American Shrimp Processors Association
PO Box 4867
EIN #72-6029637
Biloxi, MS 39535

857-445-4165
FAX 228-385-2565
E-Mail: info@fundraise.com
Home Page: www.fundraise.com
Social Media: *Facebook, Twitter*

Nate Drouin, CEO
Kurt Schneider, Chief Operating Officer
Kevin Bedell, Chief Technical Officer
Ivan Sifrim, UX Developer
Nick Alekhine, Developer

A non-profit trade organization designed to represent U.S. shrimp processors in all aspects of business. Allowing processors and related industries to work together to foster a business and technological climate in which its members can prosper while providing the highest quality product to its customers.
Founded in 1964

9330 American Sportfishing Association
1001 North Fairfax St.
Suite 501
Alexandria, VA 22314

703-519-9691
FAX 703-519-1872
E-Mail: info@asafishing.org

Home Page: www.asafishing.org
Social Media: *Facebook, Twitter*

Mike Nussman, President & CEO
Scott Gudes, VP, Government Affairs
Diane Carpenter, VP, Operations & CFO
Glenn Hughes, VP, Industry Relations
Jill Calabria, Membership Director

The Association advocates for fish, anglers and the sportfishing industry.
Founded in 1933

9331 Association of Fish and Wildlife Agencies
1100 First Street NE
Suite 825
Washington, DC 20002

202-838-3474
FAX 202-350-9869
E-Mail: info@fishwildlife.org
Home Page: www.fishwildlife.org
Social Media: *Facebook, Twitter*

Ron Regan, Executive Director
Dave Chanda, President
Nick Wiley, Vice President
Carol Bambrey, Association Council
Glenn Normandeau, Secretary/Treasurer

The organization that represents all of North America's fish and wildlife agencies that promotes sound management ans conservation, and speaks with a unified voice on important fish and wildlife issues.
Founded in 1902

9332 Association of Smoked Fish Processors
c/o Shuster Labs
85 John Road
Canton, MA 02120

781-821-2200
800-444-8705
FAX 781-821-9266
E-Mail: info@shusterlabs.com
Home Page: www.shusterlabs.com

Members are food processors with an interest in smoked fish.
Founded in 1963

9333 Association of Zoos and Aquariums
8403 Colesville Rd
Suite 710
Silver Spring, MD 20910-3314

301-562-0777
FAX 301-562-0888
E-Mail: membership@aza.org
Home Page: www.aza.org
Social Media: *Facebook, Twitter*

Dennis E. Pate, Executive Director & CEO
Steve Burns, Chair-Elect
Dennis W. Kelly, Vice-Chair
Jim Breheny, Director
Lynn Clements, Director

A nonprofit organization dedicated to the advancement of accredited zoos and aquariums in the areas of animal care, wildlife conservation, education and science.
200 Members
Founded in 1924

9334 At-Sea Processors Association
4039 21st Ave W
Suite 400
Seattle, WA 98199

206-285-5139
FAX 206-285-1841
E-Mail: jgilmore@atsea.org
Home Page: www.atsea.org

Stephanie Madsen, Executive Director
Paul MacGregor, General Counsel
Jim Gilmore, Public Affairs Director
Ed Richardson, PhD., Resource Economist

Melinda Madson Schmidt, Program
Coordinator

A trade association representing seven
copmanies that own and operate 19 U.S. flag
cathcer/processor vessels that participate principally in the Alaska pollack fishery and west
coast Pacific whiting fishery.
Cost: $500.00
7 Members
Frequency: Membership Fees Vary
Founded in 1985

**9335 Atlantic States Marine Fisheries
Commission**
1050 N. Highland St.
Suite 200 A-N
Arlington, VA 22201

703-842-0740
FAX 703-842-0741
E-Mail: info@asmfc.org
Home Page: www.asmfc.org
Social Media: *Facebook, Twitter*

Dr. Louis B. Daniel III, Chair
Douglas E Grout, Vice Chair
John M.R Bull, Commissioner
Laura C. Leach, Director
Cecelia Butler, Human Resources
Administrator

The commission was formed by the fifteen Atlantic coast states. It serves as a deliberative
body, coordinating the conservation and management of the states shared near shore fishery
resources.
45 Members
Founded in 1942

9336 Bass Anglers Sportsman Society
3500 Blue Lake Drive
Suite 330
Birmingham, AL 35243

334-272-9530
877-227-7872
FAX 334-279-7148
E-Mail:
bassmaster@emailcustomerservice.com
Home Page: www.bassmaster.com
Social Media: *Facebook, Twitter*

Dean Kassel, President
Chris Horton, Associate Director

A service organization for bass fishermen. It
protecs and preserves the fishing environment,
reports on the newest products and techniques,
and provides an arena for professional and amateur fishing competitions.
Cost: $14.95
600M Members
Frequency: Annual Membership Fee
Founded in 1972

9337 Blue Water Fishermen's Association
PO Box 779
Forked River, NJ 08731-0779

609-891-8672
FAX 732-279-4522
E-Mail: bwfa@usa.net
Home Page: www.bwfa-usa.org
Social Media: *Facebook, Twitter, LinkedIn,
Stumbleupon*

Nelson R Beideman, Executive Director

Non-profit organization of companies and individuals representing fishermen, Captains, vessel owners, docks, dealers, suppliers and
related service businesses.
Founded in 1990

**9338 California Fisheries & Seafood
Institute**
1521 I St
Sacramento, CA 95814

916-441-5560
FAX 916-446-1063

E-Mail: Info@calseafood.net
Home Page: www.calseafood.net

Kevin Joyce, President
Dave Rudie, 1st Vice President
Steve Foltz, Treasurer
Sal Balestrieri, Vice President-Legislative
Kathleen Halson, Vice President-Promotion

Regional trade organization representing members of the consumer seafood supply industry.
130+ Members
Founded in 1954

9339 California Salmon Council
PO Box 2255
Folsom, CA 95763-2255

916-933-7050
FAX 916-933-7055
E-Mail: info@calkingsalmon.org
Home Page: www.calkingsalmon.org

Greg Ambiel, Chairman
Bill Dawson, Vice-Chairman

Represents the marketing interests of California's commercial salmon fishermen. It creates
consumer awareness and demand for California
King Salmon.
Founded in 1989

9340 Catfish Farmers of America
1100 Highway 82 E
Suite 202
Indianola, MS 38751

662-887-2699
FAX 662-887-6857
Home Page: www.catfishfarmersofamerica.com
Social Media: *Facebook, Twitter*

Hugh Warren, President

Represents the largest aquaculture industry in
the United States. Represents the interests of
farm-raised catfish industry of farmers, processors, feed mills, researchers and supplier industries.
Cost: $40.00
Frequency: Membership Fee
Founded in 1968

9341 FishAmerica Foundation
1001 North Fairfax St.
Suite 501
Alexandria, VA 22314

703-519-9691
FAX 703-519-1872
E-Mail: fafgrants@asafishing.org
Home Page: www.fishamerica.org
Social Media: *Facebook, Twitter, Youtube*

Gregg Walner, Chairman
Dave Bulthuis, Vice Chairman
Donn Schaible, Secretary
Jim Hubbard, Treasurer
Jeff Marble, Immediate Past President

The sportfishing industry's trade association,
committed to looking out for the interests of
the entire sportfishing community.
650+ Members
Founded in 1962

9342 Fishermen's Marketing Association
1585 Heartwood Drive
Suite E
McKinleyville, CA 95519

707-840-0182
FAX 707-840-0539
E-Mail: fma@trawl.org
Home Page: www.trawl.org

Peter Leipzig, Executive Director

Represents commercial groundfish and shrimp
fishermen from San Pedro, California to
Bellingham, Washington. The mission is to engage in activities which promote stable prices

and an orderly flow of wholesome seafood to
the consumer
60 Members
Founded in 1952

9343 Fishing Vessel Owners Association
4005 20th Ave W
Room 232
Seattle, WA 98199

206-284-4720
FAX 206-283-3341
Home Page: www.fvoa.org

Per Odegaard, President
Paul Clampitt, Vice-President
John Crowley, Secretary/Treasurer
Robert D. Alverson, Manager
Miachel Offerman, Trustee

Trade association of longline vessel operators
which promotes safety at sea, habitat-friendly
gear with minimum bycatch and ensures competitive pricing.
Founded in 1914

9344 Garden State Seafood Association
212 W State St
Trenton, NJ 08608

609-898-1100
FAX 609-898-6070
E-Mail:
gregdidomenico@gardenstateseafood.org
Home Page: www.gardenstateseafood.org
Social Media: *Facebook, Twitter*

Ernie Panacek, President
Jeffrey Reichel, Vice-President
Greg DiDomenico, Executive Director
Rick Marks, Washington D.C. Representative
Scot Mackey, Trenton Representative

Dedicated to assure that New Jersey's marine
resources are managed responsibly and are able
to be enjoyed by anglers and seafood consumers for generations.
Founded in 1999

9345 Great Lakes Fishery Commission
2100 Commonwealth Blvd
Suite 100
Ann Arbor, MI 48105

734-662-3209
FAX 734-741-2010
E-Mail: info@glfc.org
Home Page: www.glfc.int
Social Media: *Facebook, Twitter*

Michael Hansen, Chairman
Dale Burkett, Director
Steve Domeracki, Manager
Robert (Bob) Lambe, Executive Secretary
Ted Treska, Information Manager

The commission has two major responsibilities;
to develop coordinated programs of research on
the Great Lakes and to formulate and implement a program to eradicate or minimize sea
lamprey populations in the Great Lakes.
Founded in 1955
Mailing list available for rent

**9346 Gulf and Caribbean Fisheries
Institute (GCFI)**
2796 Overseas Highway
Suite 119
Marathon, FL 33050

305-289-2330
FAX 305-289-2334
E-Mail: bob.glazer@gcfi.org
Home Page: www.gcfi.org
Social Media: *Facebook*

Gracia Garcia-Moliner, Chairman
Nancy Brown-Peterson, Vice Chair
LeRoy Cresswel, Executive Secretary
Mel Goodwin, PhD, Treasurer
Bob Glazer, Executive Director

Provides information exchange among governmental, non-governmental, academic and commerical users of marine resources in the Gulf and Carribean Region
950 Members
Founded in 1947

9347 Gulf of Mexico Fishery Management Council

2203 N Lois Avenue
Suite 1100
Tampa, FL 33607

813-348-1630
888-833-1844
FAX 813-348-1711
E-Mail: gulfcouncil@gulfcouncil.org
Home Page: www.gulfcouncil.org
Social Media: *Facebook*

Doug Gregory, Executive Director
Carrie Simons, Deputy Executive Director
Charlene Ponce, Public Information Officer
Cathy Readinger, Administrative Officer
Beth Hager, Financial Assistant

The council preserves fishery plans which are designed to manage fishery resources from where state waters end out to the 200 mile limit of the Gulf of Mexico.
Founded in 1976

9348 ICFA-USA

Home Page:
internationalcarpfishingassociation.com

David Moore, ICFA USA Representative

The International Carp Fishing Association promotes carp angling worldwide.
Founded in 2004

9349 International Institute of Fisheries Economics and Trade

Dept of Agricultural & Resource Economic
Oregon State University
Corvallis, OR 97331-3601

541-737-1416
FAX 541-737-2563
E-Mail: iifet@oregonstate.edu
Home Page: www.oregonstate.edu/dept/iifet

Ann L Shriver, Executive Director
Dr. Rebecca Metzner, President
Dr. Ralph Townsend, President-Elect
Kara Keenan, Assistant

An international group of economists, government managers, private industry members, and others interested in the exchange of research and information on marine resource issues. Founded to promote interaction and exchange between people from all countries and professional disciplines about marine resource economics and trade issues.
Founded in 1982

9350 National Fisheries Institute

7918 Jones Branch Dr
Suite 700
Mc Lean, VA 22102-3319

703-752-8890
FAX 703-752-7583
E-Mail: admin@SIRFonline.org
Home Page: www.sirfonline.org
Social Media: *Facebook, Twitter, LinkedIn*

Russ Mentzer, Chairman
Eric Bloom, Director
Jim Bonnvie, Director
Pete Cardone, Director
Dan DiDonato, Director

Members are farmers, food processors and food distributors with an interest in aquaculture.
Founded in 1964

9351 National Seafood Educators

PO Box 93
Shamokawa, WA 98647

206-546-6410
FAX 206-546-6411
E-Mail: Information@SeafoodEducators.com
Home Page: www.seafoodeducators.com

Evie Hansen, Founder

The goal is to educate and inform the public about the many health benefits of a seafood diet. National Seafood Educators has also consulted with many seafood retail businesses on how to sell, store and prepare wholesome seafood.
Founded in 1977

9352 National Shellfisheries Association

c/o US EPA, Atlantic Ecology Division
27 Tazewell Drive
Narragansett, RI 02880

631-653-6327
FAX 631-653-6327
E-Mail: webmaster@shellfish.org
Home Page: www.shellfish.org

Karolyn Mueller Hansen, President
Steven M. Allen, President-Elect
Shirley Baker, Vice-President
Lisa Milke, Secretary
John Scarpa, Treasurer

An international organization of scientists, management officials and members of industry, all deeply concerned with the biology, ecology, production, economics and management of shellfish resources-clams, oysters, mussels, scallops, snails, shrimp, lobsters, crabs, among many other species of commercial importance.
Cost: $85.00
1000 Members
Frequency: Membership Fee
Founded in 1908

9353 North Carolina Fisheries Association

PO Box 335
Bayboro, NC 28515-0335

252-745-0225
FAX 252-745-0258
E-Mail: peggy@ncfish.org
Home Page: www.ncfish.org

Brent Fulcher, Chairman
Karolyn Mueller Hansen, President
Leslie Daniel, Treasurer
Peggy C. Page, Accounting Manager
Lauren Morris, Membership and Operations Manager

Non-profit trade organization created to facilitate the promotion of North Carolina families, heritage and seafood through accessible data about the commercial fishing industry. NCFA lobbies Local, State, and Federal legislators and engages in a wide scope of public awareness projects.
Founded in 1952

9354 Pacific Coast Federation of Fishermen's Association

Building 991, Marine Drive, Crissy Field
PO Box 29370
San Francisco, CA 94129-0370

415-561-5080
FAX 415-561-5464
E-Mail: fish1ifr@aol.com
Home Page: www.pcffa.org

Zeke Grader, Executive Director
David Bitts, President
Vivian Helliwell, Watershed Conservation Director
Glen Spain, Northwest Regional Director
Mitch Farro, Fishey Enhancement Director

Commercial fishermen's organizations from California to Alaska. Works to prevent and improve the resources of the commercial fishing industry, protect rivers from herbicide and pesticide applications that may threaten salmon populations, maintain activity within the industry, regain local control over fisheries management.
22 Members
Founded in 1976

9355 Pacific Seafood Processors Association

1900 West Emerson Place
Suite 205
Seattle, WA 98119

206-281-1667
FAX 206-283-2387
E-Mail: info@pspafish.net
Home Page: www.pspafish.net

Glenn Reed, President
Nancy Diaz, Administrative Assistant

Trade association to foster a better public understanding of the seafood industry and its value to the regional and national economies.
25 Members
Founded in 1914

9356 Recreational Fishing Alliance

Po Box 3080
New Gretna, NJ 08224

609-404-1060
888-564-6732
FAX 609-294-3812
Home Page: www.joinrfa.org

Jim Donofrio, Executive Director
John DePersenaire, Researcher
Jim Martin, West Coast Regional Director
Gary Caputi, Corporate Relations Director

An organization that supports and fights back against federal government state legislatures impose unreasonable restrictions on our ability to enjoy recreational fishing.
Frequency: $35/Membership

9357 Southeastern Fisheries Association

1118-B Thomasville Rd.
Tallahassee, FL 32303

850-224-0612
FAX 850-222-3663
Home Page: www.seafoodsustainability.us

Bob Jones, Executive Director

To defend, preserve and enhance the commercial fishing industry in the southeastern United States for present participants as well as future generations through all legal means.
Founded in 1952

9358 The International Game Fish Association

300 Gulf Stream Way
3rd Fl.
Dania Beach, FL 33004

954-927-2628
FAX 954-924-4299
Home Page: www.igfa.org

Rob Kramer, President
Michael J. Myatt, Chief Operating Officer

A nonprofit organization that advocates for a sustainable game fishing industry.

9359 West Coast Seafood Processors Association

1618 SW 1st Ave
Suite 318
Portland, OR 97201

503-227-5076
FAX 503-296-2824

E-Mail: rod.wcseafood@gmail.com
Home Page: www.wcspa.com

Rod Moore, Executive Director
Susan Chambers, Deputy Director
Kim Lowman, Executive Assistant

Serves the needs of the shore-based seafood processors in California, Oregon and Washington, helping them to face and survive economic, environmental and regulatory challenges.
13 Members

9360 Women's Fisheries Network
2442 NW Market Street
#243
Seattle, WA 98107

206-789-1987
FAX 206-789-1987
Home Page: www.fis.com/wfn

Nancy Munro, President

Men and women dedicated to education of issues confronting the fishing and seafood industry.
2000 Members
Founded in 1993

Newsletters

9361 American Sportfishing
American Sportfishing Association
1001 North Fairfax Street
Suite 501
Alexandria, VA 22314

703-519-9691
FAX 703-519-1872
E-Mail: info@asafishing.org
Home Page: www.asafishing.org
Social Media: *Facebook*

Mike Nussman, President/CEO
Joyce Anderson-Logan, Executive Assistant
Gordon Robertson, Vice President
Diane Carpenter, Chief Financial Officer

Provides a broader view of the activities of ASA and our partners. Includes information about industry news, events, perspectives and trends that affect the sportfishing community.
Frequency: Bi-Monthly

9362 Aquaculture North America
Capamara Communications
815 1st Ave
#301
Seattle, WA 98104

250-474-3982
800-936-2266
FAX 250-478-3979
E-Mail: jeremy@capamara.com
Home Page: www.naqua.com

Peter Chetteburgh, Editor-in-Chief
Jeremy Thain, Sales Manager
James Lewis, Production Department

Follows the trends, issues, people and events that have set the pace for the fastest growing agribusiness sector on the continent. Coverage is relevant to all finfish and shellfish species grown in North America plus special reports from other regions around the world.
Cost: $27.95
Frequency: Bi-monthly
Circulation: 4000
Founded in 1985

9363 Briefs
American Institute of Fishery Research Biologists

205 Blades Road
Havelock, NC 28532

Home Page: www.aifrb.org

John Butler, Editor
John Merriner, Production Editor

It is intended to communicate the professional activities and accomplishments of the Institute, its District, and Members; the results of research; the effects of management; unusual biological events; matters affecting the profession; political problems and other matters of importance to the fishery community.
Frequency: Bi-Monthly

9364 Commercial Fisheries News
Compass Publications
Deer Isle, ME

800-989-5253
FAX 207-348-1059
E-Mail: comfish@fish-news.com
Home Page: www.fish-news.com

Richard W Martin, Publisher
Susan Jones, Editor

Provides the latest waterfront news along with coverage of the state and federal rules and regulations affecting the harvest of all the region's major species. Regular features include lobster and fish market reports, a safety column, new boats, the enforcement report, and the popular and effective classifieds section.
Cost: $21.95
72 Pages
Frequency: Monthly
Circulation: 9223
ISSN: 0273-6713
Founded in 1978
Printed in 4 colors on n stock

9365 Crow's Nest
Casamar Group/Holdings
8082 Firethorn Lane
Las Vegas, NV 89123

702-792-6868
FAX 702-792-6668
E-Mail: casamarholdings@casamarintl.com
Home Page:
www.casamarintl.com/CrowsNest/CrowsNest.html

Malu Marigomen, Executive Director

An in-depth report on the status of the Tuna Industry
Frequency: Monthly

9366 Currents
Women's Fisheries Network
2422 NW Market Square
Seattle, WA 98107

206-789-1987
FAX 206-789-1987
Home Page: www.fis.com/wfn

Debbie Slotivg, Editor
Ron Gawith, Owner

Features current topics in fisheries, members'activities, upcoming events and chapter reports.
Frequency: Monthly

9367 Fish Farming News
Compass Publications
Deer Isle, ME

800-989-5253
FAX 207-348-1059
E-Mail: comfish@fish-news.com
Home Page: www.fish-news.com

Richard W Martin, Publisher
Susan Jones, Editor

The business newspaper for the U.S. aquaculture industry. Readers are aquaculture professionals who are directly or indirectly involved in the business of growing fish and sea-

food products. Encompassing all major farm raised species (finfish, shellfish and aquatic plants) both marine (saltwater) and fresh water aquaculture.
Cost: $21.95
72 Pages
Frequency: Monthly
Circulation: 9223
ISSN: 0273-6713
Founded in 1978
Printed in 4 colors on n stock

9368 Fishermen's News
PCFFA
Building 991, Marine Drive
PO Box 29370
San Francisco, CA 94129-0370

415-561-5080
FAX 415-561-5464
E-Mail: fish1ifr@aol.com
Home Page: www.pcffa.org

Zeke Grader, Executive Director
Chuck Wise, President

Oldest publication in the west coast commercial fishing industry. Deals with resource protection and policy issues of great importance to the fishing industry, as well as with critical Congressional issues which affect us all.
22 Members
Founded in 1976

9369 IIFET Newsletter
International Institute of Fisheries Economics
Dept of Agricultural & Resource Economic
Oregon State University
Corvallis, OR 97331-3601

541-737-1439
FAX 541-737-2563
E-Mail: iifet@oregonstate.edu
Home Page: www.oregonstate.edu/dept/iifet

Provides conference listings, news items, and information on new publications and the activities of members.
20 Pages
Frequency: Semi-Annual
ISSN: 1048-9509

9370 Littorally Speaking
American Littoral Society Northeast Chapter
28 W 9th Rd
Broad Channel, NY 11693-1112

718-318-9344
FAX 718-318-9345
E-Mail: driepe@nyc.rr.com
Home Page: www.alsnyc.org

Don Riepe, Executive Director

A digest of environmental concerns

9371 Makin' Waves Quarterly Newsletter
Recreational Fishing Alliance
PO Box 3080
New Gretna, NJ 08224

609-404-1060
888-564-6732
FAX 609-294-3812
Home Page: www.joinrfa.org

James Donofrio, Executive Director
Gary Caputi, Corporate Relations Director
Courtney Howell Thompson, Marketing Coordinator/PR

This RFA paper has proven that fish and fishermen are not the only variables in the equation of fisheries management.
Frequency: $35/Membership

9372 NSA Newsletter
National Shellfisheries Association

c/o US EPA, Atlantic Ecology Division
27 Tazewell Drive
Narragansett, RI 02880

401-782-3155
FAX 401-782-3030
E-Mail: news@shellfish.org
Home Page: www.shellfish.org

Dr Evan Ward, Editor

Current issues and concerns in shellfish research and in the shellfish industry, including details regarding upcoming meetings, employment listings, and gossip items for our Metamorphoses column.

9373 National Shellfisheries Association Quarterly Newsletter
National Shellfisheries Association
C/O US EPA, Atlantic Ecology Division
27 Tazewell Drive
Narragansett, RI 02880

631-653-6327
FAX 631-653-6327
Home Page: www.shellfish.org

R. LeRoy Creswell, President
Christopher V. Davis, President-Elect
George E. Flimlin, VP & Program Chair
Marta Gomez-Chiarri, Secretary

An informative newsletter for the shellfish industry, shellfish managers and shellfish researchers.
Cost: $85.00
1000 Members
Frequency: Membership Fee
Founded in 1908

9374 PSPA Update
Pacific Seafood Processors Association
1900 W Emerson Pl
Suite 205
Seattle, WA 98119-1649

206-281-1667
FAX 206-283-2387
E-Mail: info@pspafish.net
Home Page: www.pspafish.net

Glenn Reed, President

Daily news update for major seafood processing companies with operations in Alaska and Washington.
25 Members
Founded in 1914

9375 Tradewinds
North Carolina Fisheries Association
PO Box 12303
New Bern, NC 28561

252-633-2288
FAX 252-633-9616
E-Mail: peggy@ncfish.org
Home Page: www.ncfish.org

Sean McKeon, President
Peggy C Page, Bookkeeper

Members only newspaper, which includes special bulletins regarding legislative issues and various articles concerning fisheries issues.
24 Pages
Frequency: Bi-Monthly

9376 Wheel Watch
Fishing Vessel Owners Association
4005 20th Ave W
Room 232, West Wall Bldg
Seattle, WA 98199-1273

206-284-4720
FAX 206-283-3341
Home Page: www.fvoa.org

Robert D. Alverson, Manager
Carol M. Batteen, Executive Assistant

Brings you up-to-date with regards to action of the Halibut Commission, North Pacific Council, Pacific Council, and market information.
Frequency: Quarterly

Magazines & Journals

9377 Aquaculture North America
Capamara Communications
PO Box 1409
Arden, NC 28704

250-474-3982
877-687-0011
FAX 250-478-3979
Home Page: aquaculturenorthamerica.com

Gregory J Gallagher, Editor/Publisher
Rebekah Craig, Circulation Manager
Brenda Jo McManama, Advertising/Sales

Earning the respect of aquaculture industry professionals throughout the world who hold its trade publications in high regard.
Cost: $24.00
96 Pages
Frequency: Annually/Summer
Circulation: 5000
ISSN: 0199-1388
Founded in 1968

9378 Atlantic Fisherman
Advocate Media Publishing
181 Brown's Point Road
Nova Scotia B0K-1H0

902-485-1990
800-236-9526
FAX 902-485-6353
Home Page: www.atlanticfisherman.com
Social Media: *Twitter*

Susan Purdy, Publications Manager

Provides news for the commercial fisherman in the four Atlantic provinces of Canada. Includes prespectives from the unions, the government and the fishermen themselves.
Cost: $16.00
Frequency: Monthly
Circulation: 9950

9379 Bass Times
Bass Anglers Sportsman Society
3500 Blue Lake Drive
Suite 330
Birmingham, AL 35243

334-272-9530
877-227-7872
FAX 334-279-7148
Home Page: www.bassmaster.com
Social Media: *Facebook, Twitter*

Dean Kassel, President
Chris Horton, Associate Director

Each issue includes; detailed, in-depth tips & techniques, bass biology, conservation news, BASS Federation Nation news, Bassmaster Tournament Trail coverage, and Legislation coverage.
Cost: $14.95
600M Members
Frequency: Annual Membership Fee
Founded in 1972

9380 Catfish Journal
Catfish Farmers of America
6311 Ridgewood Road
Suite W404
Jackson, MS 39211

601-977-9559
FAX 601-977-9632
E-Mail: info@catfishinstitute.com

Home Page: www.uscatfish.com
Social Media: *Facebook, Twitter*

Mike McCall, Editor
Sandra Goff, Production Manager

News on catfish production, processing, feed manufacturing and research.
Frequency: Monthly

9381 Connect Magazine
American Zoo and Aquarium Association
8403 Colesville Rd
Suite 710
Silver Spring, MD 20910-6331

301-562-0777
FAX 301-562-0888
Home Page: www.aza.org

Jim Maddy, Executive Director
Kris Vehrs, Executive Director
Muri Dueppen, Marketing

For the professional zoo and aquarium world. This magazine features fascinating stories that explore trends, educational initiatives, member achievements and conservation efforts.
200 Members
Frequency: Monthly
Circulation: 6000

9382 Esox Angler
Esox Angler
PO Box 895
Hayward, WI 54843

715-638-2311
E-Mail: info@esoxangler.com
Home Page: www.esoxangler.com

Jack Burns, Senior Editor
Rob Kimm, Editor

A muskie and pike magazine for the world's muskie and pike anglers. Articles focusing on proven techniques and new ideas from top name anglers, as well as regular guys who are catching lots of fish.

9383 Fish Sniffer
3201 Eastwood Road
Sacramento, CA 95821

916-685-2245
FAX 916-685-1498
E-Mail: danielbacher@fishsniffer.com
Home Page: www.fishsniffer.com
Social Media: *Facebook*

Dan Bacher, Editor
Cal Kellogg, Associate Editor

Current fishing reports, weather conditions, fishing news, photos, boats for sale, what and where to fish and much more.
Cost: $29.00
Frequency: Bi-Weekly

9384 Fisheries
American Fisheries Society
5410 Grosvenor Ln
Suite 110
Bethesda, MD 20814-2199

301-897-8616
FAX 301-897-8096
Home Page: www.fisheries.org
Social Media: *Facebook, Twitter*

Gus Rassam, Executive Director
Myra Merritt, Office Administrator

Peer reviewed articles that address contemporary issues and problems, techniques, philosophies and other areas of interest to the general fisheries profession. Monthly features include letters, meeting notices, book listings and reviews, environmental essays and organization profiles.
Cost: $106.00
50 Pages
Frequency: Monthly
Circulation: 9800

Founded in 1870
Mailing list available for rent: 8500 names at $250 per M

9385 Fishermen's News

Philips Publishing Group
2201 W Commodore Way
Seattle, WA 98199-1298

206-284-8285
FAX 206-284-0391
E-Mail: circulation@rhppublishing.com
Home Page: www.pacmar.com

Peter Philips, Publisher
Lisa Albers, Editor
Maggie Cheung, Circulatiom Manager

Covers commercial fishing activity, market trends, gear and boat building news, political news and financial matters related to the industry.
Founded in 1945

9386 Fly Fisherman

InterMedia Outdoors Inc
PO Box 420235
Palm Coast, FL 32142-0235

212-852-6600
Home Page: www.flyfisherman.com
Social Media: *Facebook, Twitter*

Jeff Paro, President

From the deepest bass ponds, wildest rivers or abundant saltwater flats, America's fishing sportsmen rely on this magazine to provide them with the newest techniques, tools and tips whenever and wherever they need this information.
Cost: $19.95
Frequency: Annually
Founded in 1969

9387 IAFWA Proceedings

International Association of Fish and Wildlife
444 N Capitol St NW
Suite 725
Washington, DC 20001-1553

202-638-7999
FAX 202-638-7291
E-Mail: info@iafwa.org
Home Page: www.statenet.com

Wayne Muhlstein, VP
Eric Schwaab, Resource Director

Reports on the business transacted by the Association at its March meeting held in conjunction with the North American Wildlife and Natural Resources Conference and at its September annual conference.

9388 In-Fisherman

InterMedia Outdoors Inc
PO Box 420235
Palm Coast, FL 420235

218-829-1648
E-Mail: ross.purnell@imoutdoors.com
Home Page: www.in-fisherman.com
Social Media: *Facebook, Twitter*

Ross Purnell, Editor

Written for the avid freshwater angler. In each issue, you'll find detailed instructions and demonstrations on catching, cleaning, and eating your favorite species of fish, and reports on the latest scientific studies concerning fish and habitat conservation.
Cost: $12.00
Frequency: 8x/year
Founded in 1975

9389 Island Fisherman

610 Azalea Place
Campbell River
BC Canada V9W 7H2

250-923-0939
E-Mail: ifmm@shaw.ca
Home Page:
www.islandfishermanmagazine.com

Larry E Stefanyk, Founder/Publisher
Bob Jones, Editor

Covering the west coast of British Columbia from the Queen Charlottes to Victoria on Vancouver Island. Covering saltwater and freshwater fishing with how to and where to tips to help you find the big one or just experience what the west coast of British Columbia has to offer.
Cost: $40.00
Frequency: Monthly
Founded in 2001

9390 Journal of Aquatic Animal Health

American Fisheries Society
5410 Grosvenor Ln
Suite 110
Bethesda, MD 20814-2199

301-897-8616
FAX 301-897-8096
Home Page: www.fisheries.org
Social Media: *Facebook, Twitter*

Bill Fisher, President
John Boreman, President-Elect
Bob Hughes, First Vice President
Donna Parrish, Second Vice President

International journal publishing original research on diseases affecting aquatic life, including effects, treatments and prevention.
Cost: $100.00
8500 Members
Frequency: Membership Fee
Founded in 1870

9391 Marine and Coastal Fisheries: Dynamics, Management, and Ecosystem Science

American Fisheries Society
5410 Grosvenor Ln
Suite 110
Bethesda, MD 20814-2199

301-897-8616
FAX 301-897-8096
Home Page: www.fisheries.org
Social Media: *Facebook, Twitter*

Bill Fisher, President
John Boreman, President-Elect
Bob Hughes, First Vice President
Donna Parrish, Second Vice President

Online publication focusing on marine, coastal, and estuarine fisheries.
Cost: $100.00
8500 Members
Frequency: Membership Fee
Founded in 1870

9392 Marlin

World Publications
460 N Orlando Avenue
Suite 200
Winter Park, FL 32789

407-628-4802
FAX 407-628-7061
Home Page:
www.marlinmag.com/www.worldpub.net

Dave Ferrell, Editor
Glen Hughes, Group Publisher
Terry Snow, Owner

The bible for big-game fishermen. It is written for the most affluent anglers who need to know what is happening around the world regarding offshore fishing. It is the who's who of the sport, written in the voice of the sportfisherman, one-on-one to a peer, as a member of this elite fraternity. Marlin magazine will continue to be the No. 1 buy in big-game fishing by delivering the best targeted edit to the wealthiest boat-owning saltwater fishermen in the world.
Cost: $24.95
Frequency: 8x/year
Circulation: 40,000

9393 National Fisherman

Diversified Business Communications
Po Box 7437
Portland, ME 04112-7437

207-842-5600
FAX 207-842-5503
E-Mail: editor@nationalfisherman.com
Home Page: www.nationalfisherman.com
Social Media: *Facebook, Twitter*

Nancy Hasselback, President/CEO
Lincoln Bedrosian, Senior Editor

Regional coverage of boats, fishing gear, environmental developments, technology, new products, and fishery resource information
Cost: $19.95
Frequency: Monthly
Circulation: 38,000
Founded in 1903

9394 North American Journal of Aquaculture

American Fisheries Society
5410 Grosvenor Ln
Suite 110
Bethesda, MD 20814-2199

301-897-8616
FAX 301-897-8096
Home Page: www.fisheries.org
Social Media: *Facebook, Twitter*

Gus Rassam, Executive Director
Myra Merritt, Office Administrator

Publishes research in all areas of fish culture.
Cost: $38.00
Frequency: Quarterly
ISSN: 1548-8454

9395 North American Journal of Fisheries Management

American Fisheries Society
5410 Grosvenor Ln
Suite 110
Bethesda, MD 20814-2199

301-897-8616
FAX 301-897-8096
Home Page: www.fisheries.org
Social Media: *Facebook, Twitter*

Bill Fisher, President
John Boreman, President-Elect
Bob Hughes, First Vice President
Donna Parrish, Second Vice President

Promotes communication among managers. Published with a focus on maintenance, enhancement, and allocation of resources.
Cost: $100.00
8500 Members
Frequency: Membership Fee
Founded in 1870

9396 Outdoor Journal

American Crappie Association
125 Ruth Avenue
Benton, KY 42025

270-395-4204
FAX 270-395-4381
E-Mail: office@crappieusa.com
Home Page: www.crappieusa.com

Darrell VanVactor, President
Larry Crecelius, Public Relations Director

Features news and updates on memberships, events, tournaments, and more for crappie anglers from amateurs to professionals.
Frequency: Annually
Circulation: 60000

9397 Pacific Fishing
Pacific Fishing
1000 Andover Park E
Seattle, WA 98188-7632

206-324-5644
FAX 206-324-8939
Home Page: www.pacificfishing.com

Michael Daigle, Owner
Jon Holland, Editor
Duane Brady, es & Marketing Manager

Serving owners and operators of commercial fishing boats throughout the world's most productive ocean, from Alaska to the tropical Pacific. Our readers also include crew members, processors, fisheries managers, suppliers, seafood brokers and distributors, educators, and others who want serious information about the business of hauling up food from the Pacific.
Cost: $15.00
Frequency: Monthly
Circulation: 7160
Founded in 1980

9398 SaltWater
Time, Inc.
2 Park Avenue
New York, NY 10016

212-221-1212
FAX 212-779-5999
E-Mail: editor@saltwatersportsman.com
Home Page: www.saltwatersportsman.com

David DiBenedetto, Editor
Gerald Bethge, Executive Editor
Jason Y Wood, Managing Editor
Karl Anderson, Senior Editor

A publication on salt-water sport fishing. Each monthly issue contains exciting feature stories, columns, award-winning color photos covering both big- and small-game fishing, the newest techniques, tackle, boats and equipment, and the latest developments in conservation and fishery management.
Founded in 1939

9399 Saltwater Sportsman
World Publications
460 N Orlando Avenue
Suite 200
Winter Park, FL 32789

407-628-4802
FAX 407-628-7061
Home Page:
www.marlinmag.com/www.worldpub.net
Social Media: *Facebook, Twitter*

Dave Ferrell, Editor
Glen Hughes, Group Publisher
Terry Snow, Owner

Designed for serious recreational salt water fishermen who demand the most accurate and detailed information available on inshore and offshore fishing from boats. Articles cover the entire spectrum of boat and tackle rigging, tactics and methods for catching game fish, travel, boat and equipment reviews, U.S. regional/ local coverage, and fisheries management and conservation.
Cost: $24.95
Frequency: 8x/year
Circulation: 40,000

9400 Sea Technology Magazine
Compass Publications, Inc.

1501 Wilson Blvd
Suite 1001
Arlington, VA 22209-2403

703-524-3136
FAX 703-841-0852
E-Mail: oceanbiz@sea-technology.com
Home Page: www.sea-technology.com
Social Media: *Twitter*

Amos Bussmann, President/Publisher
Joy Carter, Circulation Manager
Meghan Ventura, Managing Editor

Worldwide information leader for marine/offshore business, science and engineering. Read in more than 110 countries by management, engineers, scientists and technical personnel working in industry, government and education.
Cost: $40.00
Frequency: Monthly
Circulation: 16304
ISSN: 0093-3651
Founded in 1960
Mailing list available for rentat $80 per M
Printed in 4 colors

9401 Seafood Business
Diversified Business Communications
121 Free Street
PO Box 7438
Portland, ME 04112-7437

207-842-5542
E-Mail: mlarkin@divcom.com
Home Page: www.seafoodbusiness.com
Social Media: *Facebook, Twitter, LinkedIn*

Mary Larkin, Publisher
Fiona Robinson, Associate Publisher, Editor
James Wright, Associate Editor
Melissa Wood, Assistant Editor

Focuses on the business of buying and selling seafood and provides seafood buyers with the tools and analysis they need to make educated safood buying decisions.
Frequency: Monthly
Circulation: 15,000
Founded in 1982

9402 Sport Fishing
World Publications
460 N Orlando Avenue
Winter Park, FL 32789

407-628-4802
FAX 407-628-7061
E-Mail: editor@sportfishingmag.com
Home Page: www.sportfishingmag.com
Social Media: *Facebook, Twitter*

Glenn Hughes, Group Publisher
Bruce Miller, Circulation VP
Terry Snow, Owner

Written for the passionate angler who must have in-depth, cutting-edge information on the latest techniques, the hottest locations and the newest equipment to maximize his day on the water, Sport Fishing magazine is the source for saltwater fishing information.
Cost: $19.97
Frequency: 10x/year
Circulation: 150,000
Founded in 2001

9403 The Fisherman
326 12th Street
1st Floor
New Westminster, BC V3M-4H6

604-669-5569
FAX 604-688-1142
E-Mail: fisherman@ufawu.org
Home Page: www.thefisherman.ca
Social Media: *Facebook, Twitter, YouTube*

Sean Griffin, Editor
Suzanne Thomson, Advertising Manager

Covering saltwater and freshwater fishing from Maine through Delaware Bay. Local fishing reports.
Frequency: Monthly
Circulation: 8000

9404 Transactions of the American Fisheries Society
American Fisheries Society
5410 Grosvenor Ln
Suite 110
Bethesda, MD 20814-2199

301-897-8616
FAX 301-897-8096
Home Page: www.fisheries.org

Gus Rassam, Executive Director
Myra Merritt, Office Administrator

The Society's highly regarded international journal of fisheries science features results of basic and applied research in genetics, physiology, biology, ecology, population dynamics, economics, health, culture, and other topics germane to marine and freshwater finfish and shellfish and their respective fisheries and environments
Cost: $43.00
Frequency: Bi-Monthly
ISSN: 0002-8487
Founded in 1872

Trade Shows

9405 ASA Sportfishing Summit
American Sportfishing Association
225 Reinekers Lane
Suite 420
Alexandria, VA 22314

703-519-9691
FAX 703-519-1872
E-Mail: info@asafishing.org
Home Page: www.asafishing.org

Mary Jane Williamson, Communications Director
Amy Yohanes, Administrative Services Manager

Membership meeting and premier networking event. From special sessions, to busiess workshops to association committee meeting, the Summit provides a wide-range of opportunities to gain information on the most relevant issues facing the sportfishing industry.
Frequency: October

9406 ASA/Eastern Fishing & Outdoor Exposition
American Sportfishing Association
1001 North Fairfax Street
Suite 501
Alexandria, VA 22314

703-519-9691
FAX 703-519-1872
E-Mail: info@asafishing.org
Home Page: www.asafishing.org
Social Media: *Facebook*

Mike Nussman, President/CEO
Joyce Anderson-Logan, Executive Assistant
Gordon Robertson, Vice President
Diane Carpenter, Chief Financial Officer

The finest sportsmen's expos on the East Coast. The best outdoor gear, accessories and resources for fishing, boating, hunting, adventure and travel are available at these shows. The only sport shows where 100 percent of the proceeds go to safeguarding and promoting the enduring social, economic and conservation values of America's outdoor heritage.
Frequency: Bi-Monthly

9407 AZA Regional Conference
American Zoo and Aquarium Association
8403 Colesville Road
Suite 710
Silver Spring, MD 20910-3314

301-562-0777
FAX 301-562-0888
Home Page: www.aza.org

Jim Maddy, President
Kris Vehrs, Executive Director
Jill Nicoll, Marketing

Exhibits, workshops and discussions about the industry.
200 Members
Founded in 1924

9408 Annual Fish Baron's Ball
North Carolina Fisheries Association
PO Box 12303
New Bern, NC 28561

252-745-0225
FAX 252-633-9616
E-Mail: peggy@ncfish.org
Home Page: www.ncfish.org

Billy Carl Tillett, Chairman
Sherrill Styron, Vice Chairman
Sean McKeon, President
Janice Smith, Treasurer

Attendees getting together for an evening of great seafood and fun, and participate in the silent auction. Program proceeds go toward Association-related activities.
Founded in 1952

9409 CFA Fish Farming Trade Show
Catfish Farmers of America
1100 Highway 82 E
Suite 202
Indianola, MS 38751

662-887-2699
FAX 662-887-6857
Home Page: www.catfishfarmersamerica.org

America's largest fish farming equipment expo.
Frequency: February

9410 Catfish Farmers of America Annual Convention & Research Symposium
Catfish Farmers of America
1100 Highway 82 E
Suite 202
Indianola, MS 38751-2251
662-887-2699
FAX 662-887-6857
Home Page: www.catfishfarmersofamerica.org

Hugh Warren, President

Opportunity to launch new products, meet new buyers, learn emerging trends and access the North American seafood market.
Frequency: Membership Fee
Founded in 1968

9411 Eastern Fishing & Outdoor Expo
Eastern Fishing & Outdoor Expositions
PO Box 4720
Portsmouth, NH 00380

603-431-4315
FAX 603-431-1971
E-Mail: info@sportshows.com
Home Page: www.sportshows.com

Paul Fuller, President/Show Director
Judy L Chapman, Assistant Show Director

Partnership with American Sportfishing Association. Exhibitors representing the entire spectrum of saltwater sportfishing. This includes inshore to offshore, light tackle to big-game tackle, and everything in between. Fishermen will see and touch the latest from major tackle manufacturers and buy the latest tackle from local retailers at special show prices.

9412 Fish Expo Workboat Atlantic
National Fisherman/Diversified Bus. Communications
121 Free Street
PO Box 7437
Portland, ME 04112

207-425-5608
FAX 207-842-5509
E-Mail: fewa@divcom.com
Home Page: www.fishexpoatlantic.com

Bob Callahan, Show Director
Heather Palmeter, Show Coordinator

Newest products and technology, attend free seminars and workshops, talk to technical experts, and find the best deals on equipment and gear.
6,000 Attendees
Frequency: April

9413 Fly-Fishing Retailer World Trade Expo
VNU Expositions/Business Media
770 Broadway
New York, NY 10003

646-545-5100
Home Page: www.fly-fishing-retailer.com/www.vnubusinessmedia.com

Andy Tompkins, Show Director
Peter Devin, Group Show Director

Where brands are launched, innovations are unveiled and connections are made. Designed for the specialty fly-fishing industry, Fly-Fishing Retailer World Trade Expo connects a targeted audience to conduct business in a professional yet friendly atmosphere.
Frequency: August
Founded in 1998

9414 IAFWA Annual Meeting
International Association of Fish and Wildlife
444 North Capitol Street NW
Suite 725
Washington, DC 20001

202-624-7890
FAX 202-624-7891
Home Page: www.fishwildlife.org

Gary T Myers, Executive Director
Cindy Delaney, Meetings Coordinator
Wayne Muhlstein, VP

Providing many opportunities to hear from our nation's wildlife conservation leaders, partners, and management experts. The meeting is our response to the need for national consensus on state-by-state fish and wildlife management issues.
250 Attendees
Frequency: September

9415 ICAST
American Sportfishing Association
225 Reinekers Lane
Suite 420
Alexandria, VA 22314

703-519-9691
FAX 703-519-1872
E-Mail: mdelvalle@asafishing.org
Home Page: www.asafishing.org

Maria del Valle, ICAST Director
Kenneth Andres, ICAST Associate

The sportfishing industry's largest trade event is a major catalyst for sales and a terrific networking opportunity for the sportfishing community.

9416 IIFET Biennial International Conference
IIFET

Dept of Agricultural & Resource Economic
Oregon State University
Corvallis, OR 97331-3601

541-737-1416
FAX 541-737-2563
E-Mail: iifet@oregonstate.edu
Home Page: www.oregonstate.edu/dept/iifet

Ann L Shriver, Executive Director
Dr. Rebecca Metzner, President
Dr. Ralph Townsend, President-Elect

An important forum for members and others to learn about important research developments in seafood trade, aquaculture, and fisheries management issues. Attended by fisheries social scientists, managers, and industry members from all of the world's fishing areas. Provides participants with unparalleled opportunities to interact with the world's foremost fisheries economists in both formal and informal settings. Learn more about fishing and aquaculture activities across the globe.
Founded in 1982

9417 IPHC Annual Meeting
Pacific Seafood Processors Association
1900 West Emerson Place
Suite 205
Seattle, WA 98119-1649

206-281-1667
FAX 206-283-2387
E-Mail: nancy@pspafish.net
Home Page: www.pspafish.net

Glenn Reed, President

Annual members meeting to discuss catch limits each year.
25 Members
Founded in 1914

9418 International Boston Seafood Show
Diversified Business Communications
PO Box 7437
Portland, ME 04112-7437

207-842-5504
FAX 207-842-5505
E-Mail: customerservice@divcom.com
Home Page: www.bostonseafood.com

Diane Vassar, Promotions Director
David Lowell, President

This event attracts top-tier buyers and sellers of seafood. You will find exhibit categories representing every aspect of seafood including; seafood, seafood equipment, services and organizations and seafood packaging.
20M Attendees
Frequency: March/Silver Pkg $250

9419 International Convention of Allied Sportfishing Trades (ICAST)
American Sportfishing Association
1001 North Fairfax Street
Suite 501
Alexandria, VA 22314

703-519-9691
FAX 703-519-1872
E-Mail: info@asafishing.org
Home Page: www.asafishing.org
Social Media: Facebook

Mike Nussman, President/CEO
Joyce Anderson-Logan, Executive Assistant
Gordon Robertson, Vice President
Diane Carpenter, Chief Financial Officer

World's largest sportfishing trade show, representing the cornerstone of the sportfishing industry, driving sportfishing companies' product sales year round and is the showcase for the latest innovations in gear and accessories.
Frequency: Bi-Monthly

9420 International Fly Tackle Dealer Show
American Fly Fishing Trade Association

901 Front St.
Suite B-125
Louisville, CO 80027

303-604-6132
FAX 303-604-6162
Home Page: www.affta.com

Randi Swisher, President
Gary Berlin, Business Manager
Jim Klug, Chairman

The largest international gathering of fly fishing manufacturers, retailers, sales reps, media and fly fishing organizations in the world. Best venue to meet with the industry, people, products, innovations, emerging trends and the leading brand presentations, latest gear, equipment, waders, fly like, tippet and accessories for the upcoming season.
400 Members
Founded in 2003

9421 International West Coast Seafood Show

Diversified Business Communications
PO Box 7437
Portland, ME 04112-7437

207-842-5500
FAX 207-842-5503
E-Mail: mlarkin@divcom.com
Home Page: www.westcoastseafood.com

Mary Larkin, VP Seafood Expositions

A total resource for seafood industry leaders; showcases the latest seafood products and equipment from the US, Pacific Rim and beyond.
Frequency: October
Founded in 1996

9422 NSA Annual Meeting

National Shellfisheries Association
c/o US EPA, Atlantic Ecology Division
27 Tazewell Drive
Narragansett, RI 02880

401-782-3155
FAX 401-782-3030
E-Mail: news@shellfish.org
Home Page: www.shellfish.org

Dr Lou D'Abramo, President
Christopher Davis, Treasurer

A time and place to interact with other associations and industry people.
Frequency: Spring

9423 National River Rally

American Sportfishing Association
225 Reinekers Ln
Suite 420
Alexandria, VA 22314-2875

703-519-9691
FAX 703-519-1872
E-Mail: info@asafishing.org
Home Page: www.fishamerica.org

Mike Nussman, President/CEO
Diane Carpenter, CFO
Gordon Robertson, Vice President

The premier national event to come together to learn, inspire and celebrate the passionate work of all things rivers and watersheds. Trainings, field trips and a deeply moving River Heroes awards banquet honoring incredible River leaders.
650+ Members
Founded in 1962

9424 Pacific Marine Expo

Diversified Business Communications
121 Free Street
PO Box 7437
Portland, ME 04112

207-425-5608
FAX 207-842-5509

E-Mail: pme@divcom.com
Home Page: www.pacificmarineexpo.com

Bob Callahan, Show Director
Heather Palmeter, Show Coordinator

A trade show dedicated to the pacific maritime industry that provides a gathering of marine products and services. With nearly 500 manufacturers and distributors showcasing the latest technologies and thousands of products for all commercial vessels, tugs, barges, boat building, marine construction, passenger vessels, seafood processing plants and more, PME is the best source for all marine business needs.
6,000 Attendees
Frequency: November

9425 Seafood Processing America

Catfish Farmers of America
1100 Highway 82 E
Suite 202
Indianola, MS 38751-2251

662-887-2699
FAX 662-887-6857
Home Page: www.catfishfarmersofamerica.org

Hugh Warren, President

Opportunity to launch new products, meet new buyers, learn emerging trends and access the North American seafood market.
Frequency: Membership Fee
Founded in 1968

9426 Sportfishing Summit

American Sportfishing Association
1001 North Fairfax Street
Suite 501
Alexandria, VA 22314

703-519-9691
FAX 703-519-1872
E-Mail: info@asafishing.org
Home Page: www.asafishing.org
Social Media: *Facebook*

Mike Nussman, President/CEO
Joyce Anderson-Logan, Executive Assistant
Gordon Robertson, Vice President
Diane Carpenter, Chief Financial Officer

Where industry leaders met to discuss the issues impacting recreational fishing.
Frequency: Bi-Monthly

Directories & Databases

9427 AZA Membership Directory

American Zoo and Aquarium Association
8403 Colesville Rd
Suite 710
Silver Spring, MD 20910-3314

301-562-0777
FAX 301-562-0888
E-Mail: membership@aza.org
Home Page: www.aza.org
Social Media: *Facebook, Twitter*

L. Patricia Simmons, Chair
Tom Schmid, Chair-Elect
Jackie Ogden, Ph.D, Vice-Chair

Accredited institutions, professional affiliates, professional fellows, commercial members, related facilities and conservation partners receive one complimentary copy as a membership benefit.
Cost: $50.00
200 Members
Frequency: Annual
Founded in 1924

9428 Angling America Database

PO Box 22567
Alexandria, VA 22304

E-Mail: info@anglingamerica.com
Home Page: www.anglingamerica.com

Stephen Aaron, Director
Austin Ducworth, Director

The most searchable database for fishing charters and guides across America.

9429 Commercial Marine Directory & Fish Farmers Phone Book/ Directory

Compass Publications
Deer Isle, ME

800-989-5253
FAX 207-348-1059
E-Mail: comfish@fish-news.com
Home Page: www.fish-news.com

Richard W Martin, Publisher
Susan Jones, Editor

Go-to-reference tools for commercial fishermen and fish farmers. Comprehensive listing of suppliers providing essential goods and services and convenient industry yellow pages.
Cost: $21.95
72 Pages
Frequency: Monthly
Circulation: 9223
ISSN: 0273-6713
Founded in 1978
Printed in 4 colors on n stock

9430 IIFET Membership Directory

International Institute of Fisheries Economics
Dept of Agricultural & Resource Economic
Oregon State University
Corvallis, OR 97331-3601

541-737-1416
FAX 541-737-2563
E-Mail: iifet@oregonstate.edu
Home Page: www.orst.edu/dept/iifet
Social Media: *Facebook, Twitter, LinkedIn, YouTube, Flickr*

Ann L Shriver, Executive Director
Kara Kennan, Assistant Executive Director

This handbook lists all members with complete contact information, including an e-mail directory, plus areas of interest. Regular updates are provided with the newsletter.
Frequency: Biennial

9431 Who's Who in the Fish Industry

Urner Barry Publications
PO Box 389
Toms River, NJ 08754-0389

732-240-5330
800-932-0617
FAX 732-341-0891
E-Mail: sales@urnerbarry.com
Home Page: www.urnerbarry.com

Jay Bailey, Sales Manager
Janice Brown, Advertising Manager

The source for buying and selling contacts in the North American Seafood Industry. This 2006-2007 edition is fully updated and verified, boasting over 6,000 listings of seafood companies in the US and Canada. The directory boasts detailed information about each company listed such as products handled, contact names, product forms, product origin, sales volume, company website and much more.
Cost: $199.00
800 Pages
Frequency: Annual
ISSN: 0270-1600
Founded in 1979

Industry Web Sites

9432 http://gold.greyhouse.com
G.O.L.D Grey House OnLine Databases
Grey House Publishing's online database platform, GOLD, offers Quick Search, Keyword Search and Expert Search for most business sectors including fishing and food markets. The GOLD platform makes finding the information you need quick and easy - whether you're a novice searcher or an experienced database user. All of Grey House's directory products are available for subscription on the GOLD platform.

9433 www.asafishing.org
American Sportfishing Association
Manufacturers and importers of fishing tackle and allied products. Promotes fishing for children and adults. Compiles statistics. Sponsors National Fishing Week.

9434 www.fish307.com/links.htm
This site provides links to Lake George Regional Web Sites, Fishing Charters, International Web Sites related to fishing.

9435 www.fishhoo.com
Fishhoo search Index for Fishermen. The internet's best fishing resources. There are 2991 links to choose from and translate to: French, German and Spanish.

9436 www.greyhouse.com
Grey House Publishing
Authoritative reference directories for most businee sectors including fishing and food markets. Users can search the online databases with varied search criteria allowing for custom searches by product category, geographic area, sales volume, keyword, subject and more. Full Grey House catalog and online ordering also available.

9437 www.internets.com/sfishing.htm
Fishing Databases Search Engines.

9438 www.nauticalworld.com
Dedicated to bringing all related web sites within easy access to watersports enthusiasts. This search engine has been designed to locate advertiser's information within Nautical World but will also offer access to other watersport related web sites as well. Offers sections on marine electronics and hardware, sailing, boats, dock supplies, fishing accessories, diving accessories, industry news, watersports, weather forecasting and more.

9439 www.nfi.org
National Fishing Institute
Promotes the shipping and production of fishery products in international trade.

9440 www.ospafish.net
Pacific Seafood Processors Association
Trade association for the onshore processors in Oregon, Washington and Alaska.

9441 www.pcffa.org
Pacific Coast Federation of Fishermen's Assoc
Commercial fishermen's organizations from California to Alaska. Works to prevent and improve the resources of the commercial fishing industry, protect rivers from herbicide and pesticide applications that may threaten salmon populations, maintain activity within the industry, regain local control over fisheries management.

9442 www.web.mit.edu/seagrant/www/wfn.html
Women's Fisheries Network
Men and women dedicated to education of issues confronting the fishing and seafood industry. Conducts educational programs.

Associations

9443 AACC International
3340 Pilot Knob Road
St. Paul, MN 55121

651-454-7250
800-328-7560
FAX 651-454-0766
E-Mail: aacc@scisoc.org
Home Page: www.aaccnet.org
Social Media: *Facebook, Twitter, LinkedIn*

Jan A. Delcour, Chair
Gerad Downey, President
Lydia Tooker Midness, President-Elect
Dave L. Braun, Treasurer
Jon M Faubian, Director

Formerly the American Association of Cereal Chemists, a non-profit organization of members who are specialists in the use of cereal grains in foods.
Founded in 1915

9444 ASI Food Safety Consultants
7625 Page Avenue
St. Louis, MO 63133

314-725-2555
800-477-0778
FAX 314-727-2563
E-Mail: info@asifood.com
Home Page: www.asifood.com
Social Media: *Facebook, Twitter, LinkedIn*

Tom Huge, President
Gary Huge, Vice President
Jane Griffith, Technical Director
Jeff Capell, GMP, Technical Director
Jeanette Huge, Director

A full service provider of food safety audits, GMP audits, seminars and HACCP setups, as well as HACCP verification. Thoroughly addresses every vital concern of your valuable facility including food safety, pest control, employee practices and facility conditions.
Founded in 1930

9445 Academy of Nutrition and Dietics
120 S Riverside Plaza
Suite 2000
Chicago, IL 60606-6995

312-899-0040
800-877-1600
E-Mail: info@eatright.org
Home Page: www.eatright.org
Social Media: *Facebook, Twitter, LinkedIn, Pinterest, Youtube*

The American Dieteric Association is the World's largest organization of food and nutrition professionals. ADA is committed to improving the nation's health and advancing the profession of dietetics through research, education and advocacy.
75000 Members
Founded in 1917
Mailing list available for rent

9446 Agribusiness Council
P.O Box 5565
Washington, DC 20016

202-296-4563
FAX 202-887-9178
E-Mail: info@agribusinesscouncil.org
Home Page: www.agribusinesscouncil.org

Lyndon B. Jhonson, President

Organization dedicated to strengthening US agro-industrial competitiveness through programs which highlight international trade and development potentials as well as broad issues which encompass several individual agribusiness sectors and require a food systems approach.
Founded in 1967

9447 Agricultural & Applied Economics Association
555 E. Wells St.
Suite 1100
Milwaukee, WI 53202

414-918-3190
FAX 414-276-3349
E-Mail: Info@aaea.org
Home Page: www.aaea.org
Social Media: *Facebook, Twitter, LinkedIn*

Jill McClusky, President
Jayson Lusk, President-Elect
Michael Boland, Director
Hayley Chouinard, Director
Keith H. Koble, Director

A not-for-profit association serving the professional interests of members working in agricultural and broadly related fields of applied economics. Will be the leading organization for professional advancement in, knowledge about agricultural, development, environmental, food and consumer, natural resource, regional, rural, and associated areas of applied economics and business.
Cost: $150.00
4M Members
Frequency: Regular Membership Fee
Founded in 1910

9448 Agricultural Education National HQ
National FFA Organization
6060 FFA Drive
PO Box 68960
Indianapolis, IN 46268-0960

317-802-6060
888-332-2668
E-Mail: orders@ffa.org
Home Page: www.ffa.org
Social Media: *Facebook, Twitter*

Dr. Steve A. Brown, National FFA Advisor, Board Chair
Sherene R. Donaldson, National FFA Executive Secretary
Nancy J. Trivette, National FFA Organization Treasurer
W. Dwight Armstrong, CEO
Josh Bledose, Chief Operating Officer

Headquarters of the National FFA Organization, the organization's mission is to prepare students for successful careers and a lifetime of informed choices in the global agriculture, food, fiber and natural resources systems.
507M Members
Founded in 1928

9449 Agricultural Retailers Association
1156 15th St NW
Suite 500
Washington, DC 20005

202-457-0825
800-844-4900
FAX 202-457-0864
E-Mail: ara@aradc.org
Home Page: www.aradc.org
Social Media: *Facebook, Twitter*

Darren Coppock, President & CEO
Richard Gupton, Senior Vice President
Donnie Taylor, Vice President
Brian Reuwee, Director of Comm. and Marketing
David McKnight, Director of Member services

Nonprofit trade organization representing the interests of retailers across the United States on legislative and regulatory issues on Capitol Hill.
1200 Members
Frequency: Membership Dues Vary
Founded in 1993

9450 Allied Purchasing
PO Box 1249
Mason City, IA 50402-1249

800-247-5956
FAX 800-635-3775
E-Mail: kbamrick@alliedpurchasing.com
Home Page: www.alliedpurchasing.com
Social Media: *Facebook, LinkedIn*

Brian Janssen, President/CFO
Steve Husome, Executive Vice President
Kari Mondt, Senior Account Manager
Nicole Reisdorfer, Senior Account Manager
Kim Bamrick, Account Manager

A member owned not-for-profit buying organization established to negotiate favorable purchasing programs in part because we offer quantity purchases and prompt payment to suppliers. Purchases equipment, supplies, ingredients, and services for, dairy, soft drink, bottled water, water treatment and brewery industries.
Cost: $50.00
1200 Members
Frequency: Membership: 1 Share Stock
Founded in 1937

9451 Allied Trades of the Baking Industry
c/o Cereal Food Processors
2001 Shawnee Mission Parkway
Mission Woods, KS 66205

913-890-6300
E-Mail: t.miller@cerealfood.com
Home Page: www.atbi.org

Rick McGrath, President
Tom McCurry, First Vice President
John Hellman, Second Vice President
Tom McCurry, Secretary/Treasurer

An organization which exists to serve the grain-based food industry through cooperation between a large cross-section of suppliers to the wholesale manufacturers that each day provide our country with bread, rolls, cereals, cakes, cookies, crackers, tortillas and any number of other items that incorporate grains as their base. Values the relationships which have been built between the supplier and the manufacturer over the nearly 90 years since its inception.
Cost: $50.00
Frequency: Annual Dues
Founded in 1920

9452 Aluminum Foil Container Manufacturers Association
10 Vecilla Lane
Hot Springs Village, AR 71909

440-781-5819
FAX 440-247-9053
E-Mail: info@afcma.org
Home Page: www.afcma.org

Coke Williams, Executive Secretary

Represents leading manufacturers of aluminum foil containers in the United States and Canada. The Association has worked to promote aluminum foil as a superior packaging material since the beginning.
13 Members
Founded in 1955

9453 American Agricultural Law Association
American Agricultural Economics Association
PO Box 5861
Columbia, SC 29250

803-728-3200
FAX 360-423-2287
E-Mail: ellenberg@aglaw-assn.org
Home Page: www.aglaw-assn.org

Jesse J. Richardson Jr, President
Anne 'Beth' Crocker, President-elect

Kristy Thomason Ellenberg JD, Executive Director
Justin Schneider, Director
Amber Miller, Director

The only national professional organization focusing on the legal needs of the agricultural community. Crossing traditional barriers, it offers an independent forum for investigation of innovative and workable solutions to complex agricultural law problems. This role has taken on greater importance in the midst of the current international and environmental issues reshaping agriculture and the impending technological advances which promise equally dramatic changes.
600 Members
Founded in 1980

9454 American Angus Association

3201 Frederick Ave
St Joseph, MO 64506

816-383-5100
FAX 816-233-9703
E-Mail: angus@angus.org
Home Page: www.angus.org
Social Media: *Facebook, Twitter*

Steve Olson, President
Jim Sitz, Vice President
Richard Wilson, Interim CEO
Richard Wilson, Chief Financial Officer
Chris Stallo, Vice President of Operations

To provide programs, services, technology and leadership to enhance the genetics of the Angus breed, broaden its influence within the beef industry, and expand the market for superior tasting, high-quality Angus beef worldwide. Achieve Angus excellence through information, increase beef demand with Angus equity, identify and implement relevant technologies, optimize resources, and create opportunities.
Cost: $80.00
30+M Members
Frequency: Membership Fees Vary
Founded in 1883

9455 American Association of Candy Technologist

711 W Water St.
PO Box 266
Princeton, WI 54968

920-295-6959
FAX 920-295-6843
E-Mail: aactinfo@gomc.com
Home Page: www.aactcandy.org
Social Media: *LinkedIn*

Judy Cooley, President
Adam Lechter, First Vice President
Mike Gordon, Second Vice President
Lynn Wieland, Secretary
Mike Allured, Treasurer

A premier professional group of individual technologists, operations personnel, educators, students, business staff and others dedicated to the advancement of the confectionery industry.
Cost: $60.00
Frequency: Membership Fee
Founded in 1947

9456 American Association of Crop Insurers

1 Massachusetts Ave NW
Suite 800
Washington, DC 20001-1401

202-789-4100
FAX 202-408-7763
E-Mail: aaci@mwmlaw.com
Home Page: www.cropinsurers.com

Mike Mc Leod, Executive Director
David Graves, Manager/Secretary
Jahi Sauk Simbai

AACI is widely recognized on Capitol Hill as the leading source of crop insurance information and advice on legislative and administrative proposals. AACI is a member of a coalition of groups in Washington working together to improve the risk management options for America's farmers.
15 Members
Frequency: Membership Fee

9457 American Association of Grain Inspection and Weighing Agencies

PO Box 26426
Kansas City, MO 64196

816-569-4020
FAX 816-221-8189
E-Mail: info@aagiwa.org
Home Page: www.aagiwa.org

David Ayers, President
Tom Dahl, Vice President
David Reeder, Secretary/ Treasurer

Established to provide a liaison between the Federal Grain Inspection Service and designated agencies.
50 Members
Founded in 1964

9458 American Association of Meat Processors

One Meating Place
Elizabethtown, PA 17022

717-367-1168
FAX 717-367-9096
E-Mail: aamp@aamp.com
Home Page: www.aamp.com
Social Media: *Facebook, Twitter, YouTube, Google+*

Erica Hering, President
Louis Muench, 1st Vice President
Marty Manion, CAE, Executive Director
Diana Dietz, Communications Manager
Jane Frey, Accounting & Finances, Dues Billing

Membership consists of small to medium sized meat, poultry and food businesses including, slaughterers, processors, wholesalers, home food service businesses, deli and catering operators and suppliers to the industry. AAMP is affiliated with 32 state, regional and provincial associations.
1400 Members
Founded in 1939

9459 American Association of Nutritional Consultants

220 Parker St.
Warsaw, IN 46580

574-269-6165
888-828-2262
FAX 574-268-2120
E-Mail: registrar@aanc.net
Home Page: www.aanc.net
Social Media: *Facebook, Twitter, Pinterest*

Wendell Whitman, Owner

Promotes ethical standards in the field of nutrition consultants, and those who hold bachelor's degrees in the health related fields.
Cost: $60.00
Frequency: Annual Membership Fee
Founded in 1985

9460 American Bakers Association

1300 I St NW
Suite 700 West
Washington, DC 20005

202-789-0300
FAX 202-898-1164
E-Mail: info@americanbakers.org
Home Page: www.americanbakers.org

Social Media: *Twitter, LinkedIn, Youtube, Stationerswidows*

Rich Scalise, Chairman of the Board
Fred Penny, First Vice Chairman
Bradley K. Alexander, Second Vice Chairman
Robb MacKie, President & CEO
Lee Sanders, Secretary

A long and dedicated history of representing the interests of the wholesale baking industry before the U.S. Congress, federal agencies, state legislatures and agencies, and international regulatory authorities.
300 Members
Frequency: Membership Dues Vary
Founded in 1897

9461 American Beekeeping Federation

3525 Piedmont Rd
Bldg 5 Suite 300
Atlanta, GA 30305

404-760-2875
FAX 404-240-0998
E-Mail: info@abfnet.org
Home Page: www.abfnet.org

George Hansen, President
Tim Tucker, Vice President
Regina Robuck, Executive Director
Valerie Lake, Membership Coordinator
Tara Zeravsky, CMP, Senior Conference Planner

A national organization that continually works in the interest of all beekeepers, large or small, and those associated with the industry to ensure the future of the honey bee. Members share a common interest to work toward better education and information for all segments of the industry in the hope of increasing chances for survival in today's competitive world.
Cost: $35.00
1200 Members
Frequency: Membership Fees Vary
Founded in 1943

9462 American Berkshire Association

2637 Yeager Road
West Lafayette, IN 47906

765-497-3618
FAX 765-497-2959
E-Mail: berkshire@nationalswine.com
Home Page: www.americanberkshire.com
Social Media: *Facebook*

Lorraine Hoffman, President
John Baker, Vice President
Merrill Smith, Secretary
Steve Brown, Treasurer

The official national registry for the Berkshire breed of pigs. The ABA promotes the Berkshire breed of hogs, and maintains breed purity through registration of purebred Berkshires. Dedicated Berkshire breeders focus on delivering the superior meat quality that drives the popularity of Berkshire pork among discerning culinary experts.
300+ Members
Founded in 1998

9463 American Beverage Association

1101 Sixteenth Street NW
Washington, DC 20036

202-463-6732
FAX 202-659-5349
E-Mail: info@ameribev.org
Home Page: www.ameribev.org
Social Media: *Facebook, Twitter, YouTUBE*

Rodger L. Collins, Chair
Jeffrey Honickman, Vice Chair
Susan Neely, President
Mark Hammond, Chief Financial Officer
Ralph D. Crowley Jr., Treasurer

The national voice for the non-alcoholic refreshment beverage industry, providing a neu-

tral forum in which members convene to discuss common issues while maintaining their tradition of spirited competition in the American marketplace. Also serving as liaison between the industry, government and the public, and providing a unified voice in legislative and regulatory matters.
Founded in 1919

9464 American Beverage Licensees Association
5101 River Rd
Suite 108
Bethesda, MD 20816-1560

301-656-1494
FAX 301-656-7539
E-Mail: info@ablusa.org
Home Page: www.ablusa.org
Social Media: *Facebook, Twitter, RSS*

Warren Scheidt, President
Terry Harvath, Vice President
John D. Bodnovich, Executive Director
Susan Day Duffy, Director of Trade Relations & Ops
Jessica Anders, Manager, Comm. & PR

An association representing off-premise licensees in the open or license states and on-premise proprietors in markets across the nation. ABL was created after the merger of the National Association of Beverage Retailers (NABR) and the National Licensed Beverage Association (NLBA).
17000 Members
Founded in 2002

9465 American Brahman Breeders Association
3003 S Loop W
Suite 520
Houston, TX 77054

713-349-0854
FAX 713-349-9795
E-Mail: abba@brahman.org
Home Page: www.brahman.org
Social Media: *Facebook, Twitter, YouTube, Instagram*

J. D. Sartwelle, Jr., President
George Kempfer, Vice President
Chris Shivers, Executive Vice President
Armelinda Ibarra, Recording Secretary/Office Manager
Teresa Dominguez, Administrative Assistant

American Brahman is a beef crossbreeding organization that plays a big role in the United States and beyond.
Founded in 1924

9466 American Center for Wine, Food & the Arts
500 First Street
Napa, CA 94559

707-259-1600
888-512-6742
FAX 707-257-8601
E-Mail: info@copia.org
Home Page: www.copia.org

Arthur Jacobus, President
Kurt Nystrom, COO
Larry Tsai, Chief Marketing Officer

A non-profit discovery center whose mission is to explore and celebrate the cultural significance of wine, food and the arts.

9467 American Cheese Society
2696 S. Colorado Blvd
Suite 570
Denver, CO 80222-5954

720-328-2788
FAX 720-328-2786
E-Mail: info@cheesesociety.org
Home Page: www.cheesesociety.org

Social Media: *Facebook, Twitter, LinkedIn, YouTube*

Peggy Smith, Chair
Dick Roe, President
Jeff Jirik, Vice President
Nora Weiser, Executive Director
Jane Bauer, Education & Outreach Manager

The Society's membership includes farmstead, artisanal and specialty cheesemakers; academicians and enthusiasts; marketing and distribution specialists; food writers and cookbook authors and specialty foods retailers from the United States, Canada and Europe.
800 Members
Founded in 1983

9468 American Council on Science and Health
1995 Broadway
Suite 202
New York, NY 10023-5882

212-362-7044
866-905-2694
FAX 212-362-4919
E-Mail: acsh@acsh.org
Home Page: www.acsh.org
Social Media: *Facebook, Twitter, Youtube*

Nigel Bark, M.D., Chairman
Hank Campbell, President
Josh Bloom, Director of Chemical Science
Gilbert Ross, Senior Director
Josh Bloom, Ph.D., Director

A consumer education organization providing the public with scientifically accurate evaluations of food, chemicals, the environment and health.
Founded in 1978

9469 American Culinary Federation
180 Center Place Way
St Augustine, FL 32095

904-824-4468
800-624-9458
FAX 904-940-0741
E-Mail: acf@acfchefs.net
Home Page: www.acfchefs.org
Social Media: *Facebook, Twitter, Flickr, RSS*

Thomas J. Macrina, President
Heidi Cramb, Executive Director
Amy Thomason, Administrative Project Manager
Jayme Booth, Project Coordinator
Jennifer Manley, Director of Marketing and Comm.

A professional, not-for-profit organization for chefs and cooks. The principal goal of the founding chefs remains true to ACF today to promote the professional image of American chefs worldwide through education among culinarians at all levels, from apprentices to the most accomplished certified master chefs.
19000 Members
Founded in 1929

9470 American Dairy Association Mideast
5950 Sharon Woods Blvd
Columbus, OH 43229

614-890-1800
800-292-MILK
FAX 614-890-1636
E-Mail: info@drink-milk.com
Home Page: www.drink-milk.com
Social Media: *Facebook, Twitter, Youtube, Pinterest*

Scott Higgins, CEO
Jenny Hubble, Vice President of Communication

We represent dairy farmers and serve as the local affiliate for the American Dairy Association and the National Dairy Council. We work closely with Dairy Management Inc. and the

Milk Processors Education Program to extend national dairy promotion programs to the local level.
3800 Members
Founded in 1915

9471 American Dairy Council
Interstate Place II
100 Elwood Davis Road
North Syracuse, NY 13212

315-472-9143
FAX 315-472-0506
E-Mail: dairyinfo@adadc.com
Home Page: www.adadc.com
Social Media: *Facebook, Twitter, YouTube, Instagram*

Richard Naczi, Director

To economically benefit diary farmers by encouraging the consumption of milk and diary products through advertising, education and promotion, to reach consumers with product benefits and advantages.
Founded in 1915
Mailing list available for rent

9472 American Dairy Products Institute
126 N. Addison Avenue
Elmhurst, IL 60126

630-530-8700
FAX 630-530-8707
E-Mail: info@adpi.org
Home Page: www.adpi.org

Doug Wilke, President
Jerry O'Dea, Vice President
David Thomas, Chief Executive Officer
Dan Meyer, Director of Technical Services
Beth Holcomb, Director of Member Communications

An association for manufactured dairy products, including dry milks, whey, lactose, evaporated and condensed milk. ADPI's main purpose is to effectively communicate the many positive attributes and benefits of our members' products. Additionally, we serve our membership by offering the most current industry information available and by collaborating with dairy associations to represent members' interests before state and federal regulatory agencies.
150 Members
Founded in 1986

9473 American Dairy Science Association
1800 S. Oak Street
Suite 100
Champaign, IL 61820-6974

217-356-5146
FAX 217-398-4119
E-Mail: adsa@assochq.org
Home Page: www.adsa.org/foundation.asp

Susan Duncan, President
Lou Armentano, Vice President
Peter Studney, Executive Director
Vicki Paden, Administrative Assistant
Cara Tharp, Executive Assistant/Event Coor.

Organization of professional researchers. Publishes journals and holds annual member meetings.
4000 Members
Founded in 1896

9474 American Dry Bean Boardÿ

Home Page: www.americanbean.org

Health benefits of beans, bean salad recipes, healthy bean soup recipes, and bean facts.

9475 American Egg Board

1460 Renaissance Drive - Ste 301
PO Box 738
Park Ridge, IL 60068

847-296-7043
FAX 847-296-7007
E-Mail: aeb@aeb.org
Home Page: www.aeb.org
Social Media: *Twitter*

Joanne Ivy, CEO
Elisa Maloberti, Consumer Information
Coordinator

U.S. egg producer's link to the consumer in
communicating the value of the incredible egg.
As the egg industry's promotion arm, AEB's
foremost challenge is to convince the American
public that the egg is still one of nature's most
nearly perfect foods. AEB's basic task is to improve the demand for shell eggs, egg products,
as well as spent fowl throughout the United
States.
300 Members
Founded in 1976

9476 American Emu Association

510 W Madison Street
Suite 2
Ottawa, IL 61350

541-332-0675
E-Mail: info@aea-emu.org
Home Page: www.aea-emu.org
Social Media: *Facebook*

Tony Citrhyn, President
Terry Turner, Vice President
Joylene Reavis, Secretary
Susan Wright, Treasurer
Richard Merrow, Parliamentarian

A national, member driven, non-profit agricultural association dedicated to the emu industry.
AEA promotes public awareness of emu products, fosters research and publishes a
bi-monthly newsletter and several industry brochures. Represents an alternative agricultural
industry, dominated by the small farmer, who is
committed to humane and environmentally positive practices that produce high quality, beneficial products.
Cost: $100.00
1,700 Members
Frequency: Membership Fee
Founded in 1989

9477 American Farm Bureau Federation

600 Maryland Ave SW
Suite 1000W
Washington, DC 20024

202-484-3600
FAX 202-484-3604
E-Mail: webmaster@fb.org
Home Page: www.fb.org
Social Media: *Facebook, Twitter, YouTube,
Google+, RSS, Pintere*

Bob Stallman, President
Julie Anna Potts, Executive VP & Treasurer
Lynne Finnerty, Director
Jean Bennis, Executive Assistant

An independent, non-governmental, voluntary
organization governed by and representing
farm and ranch families united for the purpose
of analyzing their problems and formulating
action to achieve educational improvement,
economic opportunity and social advancement
and, thereby, to promote the national well-being. The voice of agricultural producers at all
levels.
3MM Members
Founded in 1919
Mailing list available for rent

**9478 American Forage and Grassland
Council**

PO Box 867
Berea, KY 40403

800-944-2342
FAX 859-623-8694
E-Mail: info@afgc.org
Home Page: www.afgc.org
Social Media: *Facebook, Twitter, YouTube*

Gary Wilson, President
Mark Kennedy, Vice President
Robert Shoemaker, Senior Vice President
Tom Keene, Secretary/Treasurer

An international organization with the primary
objective to promote the profitable production
and sustainable utilization of quality forage and
grasslands.
Cost: $30.00
3,000 Members
Frequency: Annual Dues
Mailing list available for rent: 2400+ names

9479 American Frozen Food Institute

2000 Corporate Ridge, Blvd.
Suite 1000
McLean, VA 22102

703-821-0770
FAX 703-821-1350
E-Mail: info@affi.com
Home Page: www.affi.com

Joseph Clayton, Interim President
Kraig R. Naasz, CEO
Kathleen R. Greco, Chief Administrative
Officer
Tom Kearney, Chief Financial Officer
Karim Kadrie, Director of Finance

AFFI is the national trade association the promotes and represents the interests of all segments of the frozen food industry.
500 Members
Founded in 1942

9480 American Guernsey Association

1224 Alton Darby Creek Road
Suite G
Columbus, OH 43228

614-864-2409
FAX 614-864-5614
E-Mail: info@usguernsey.com
Home Page: www.usguernsey.com
Social Media: *Facebook*

David Trotter, President & District 2
Duane Schuler, 1st Vice President & District 4
David Coon, 2nd Vice President & District 1
Brian Schnebly, Executive Secretary
Deb Hoffman, Office Manager

Promotes programs and services to the dairy industry.
36 Members
Founded in 1877

9481 American Herb Association

PO Box 1673
Nevada City, CA 95959

530-265-9552
FAX 530-274-3140
Home Page: www.ahaherb.com

Kathi Keville, Director
Robert Brucia, Co-Director
Marion Wyckoff, Secretary

An association of Medical Herbalists. Member-
ship is open to anyone interested in herbs and
includes the AHA Quarterly. The goals of the
AHA are to promote the understanding, accep-
tance and ecological use of herbs.
Cost: $20.00
Frequency: Membership Fee
Founded in 1981

**9482 American Herbal Products
Association**

8630 Fenton St
Suite 918
Silver Spring, MD 20910

301-588-1171
FAX 301-588-1174
E-Mail: ahpa@ahpa.org
Home Page: www.ahpa.org

Graham Rigby, Chair
Michael McGuffin, President
Maged Sharaf, Chief Science Officer
Merle Zimmermann, PhD, Chief Information
Analyst
Monica Kendrick, Office and Finance
Administrator

The national trade association which represents
manufacturers, importers and distributors of
herbs and herbal products. AHPA seeks
self-regulation, establishment of standards and
rules of ethical conduct, member enrichment
and public outreach.
Cost: $1000.00
300 Members
Frequency: Membership Fees Vary
Founded in 1983

9483 American Hereford Association

PO Box 014059
Kansas City, MO 64101

816-842-3757
FAX 816-842-6931
E-Mail: aha@hereford.org
Home Page: www.hereford.org
Social Media: *Facebook*

Craig Huffhines, Executive VP
Jack Ward, Chief Operating Officer
Leslie Mathews, Chief Financial Officer
Angie Stump Denton, Director of
Communications
Stacy Sanders, Director of Records Department

Association for people in the Hereford cattle
industry.
8M Members
Founded in 1986

**9484 American Honey Producers
Association**

PO Box 435
Mendon, UT 84325

281-900-9740
FAX 403-463-2583
E-Mail: cassie@AHPAnet.com
Home Page: www.americanhoneyproducers.org

Randy Verhoek, President
Darren Cox, VP
Cassie Cox, Executive Secretary
Kelvin Adee, Treasurer

Represents the interests of major US honey
producers and pollinators.
Cost: $150.00
700 Members
Frequency: Membership Fees Vary
Founded in 1969

**9485 American Institute for Cancer
Research**

1759 R Street, NW
Washington, DC 20009

202-328-7744
800-843-8114
FAX 202-328-7226
E-Mail: aicrweb@aicr.org
Home Page: www.aicr.org
Social Media: *Facebook, Twitter, Pinterest*

Melvin Hutson, Chairman
Lawrence Pratt, Vice Chairman
Marilyn Gentry, President
Kelly B. Browning, Chief Executive Officer
Susan Pepper, Secretary/Treasurer

First organization to focus research on the link between diet and cancer and translating the results into practical information for the public. AICR helps people make choices that reduce their chances of developing cancer.
Founded in 1982

9486 American Institute of Baking

1213 Bakers Way
PO Box 3999
Manhattan, KS 66505-3999

785-537-4750
800-633-5137
FAX 785-537-1493
E-Mail: sales@aibonline.org
Home Page: www.aibonline.org
Social Media: *Facebook, Twitter, LinkedIn*

Andre Biane, President/ CEO
Tom Ogle, Chief Financial Officer
Maureen Olewnik, SVP, Food Safety Services
Susan Hancock, VP, Innovation & PD
Brian Strouts, Vice President, Baking

A nonprofit corporation founded by the North American wholesale andretail baking industries as a technology transfer center for bakers and food processors.
Founded in 1919

9487 American Institute of Food Distribution

10 Mountain View Road
Suite S125
Upper Saddle River, NJ 07458

201-791-5570
FAX 201-791-5222
E-Mail: questions@foodinstitute.com
Home Page: www.foodinstitute.com
Social Media: *Facebook, Twitter, LinkedIn*

Dean Erstad, Chairman
Brian Todd, President/CEO
Donna L. George, President and COO
Susan T. Borra, Senior Vice President
Peter R. Lavoy, Former President & CEO

The best source for timely, current, and relevant information about the food industry. A nonprofit organization for providing information on the hottest topics and latest trends, reports and studies, and industry analysts to answer member inquiries.
Cost: $725.00
2700 Members
Frequency: Annual Membership Fee
Founded in 1928

9488 American Institute of Wine & Food

26384 Carmel Rancho Lane
Suite 200E
Carmel, CA 93923

831-250-7595
800-274-2493
FAX 831-250-7641
E-Mail: info@aiwf.org
Home Page: www.aiwf.org
Social Media: *Facebook*

Frank Giaimo, National Chair
Mary Chamberlin, National Vice Chair
Drew Jaglom, National Secretary
George Linn, National Treasurer
Shannon Madison, Executive Committee Member

The American Institute of Wine & Food is one of the few national organizations with the unique combination membership of dedicated wine and food enthusiasts and professionals. Wine and food enthusiasts get to meet and learn from reowned chefs, winemakers, authors, culinary historians, and food producers, while industry professionals have the opportunity to know and understand their core consum-

ers
Cost: $75.00
6000+ Members
Frequency: Memberships Vary
Founded in 1981

9489 American International Charolais Association

11700 NW Plaza Circle
Kansas City, MO 64153

816-464-5977
FAX 816-464-5759
E-Mail: north@charolaisusa.com
Home Page: www.charolaisusa.com

Larry Lehman, President
Bill Nottke, Vice President
Robb Creasey, Treasurer
John Chism, Secretary
J. Neil Orth, Executive VP

The official registry of Charolais and Charbray cattle in the United States.
2,900 Members

9490 American Jersey Cattle Association

6486 E Main Street
Reynoldsburg, OH 43068-2362

614-861-3636
FAX 614-861-8040
Home Page: www.usjersey.com
Social Media: *Facebook, Twitter*

Neal Smith, Executive Secretary & CEO
Whittney Smith, Administrative Assistant
Vickie White, Treasurer and Office Manager
Cindy Watson, Assistant to the Treasurer

They improve and promote the Jersey cattle breed.
Founded in 1868

9491 American Livestock Conservancy

33 Hillsboro St
PO Box 477
Pittsboro, NC 27312

919-542-5704
FAX 919-545-0022
E-Mail: albc@albc-usa.org
Home Page: www.livestockconservancy.org
Social Media: *Facebook, Blogger, Youtube*

Charles R Bassett, Executive Director
Don T Schrider, Communications Director
Jeannette Beranger, Research/Technical Program Manager
Anneke Jakes, Breed Registry Manager

Ensuring the future of agriculture through genetic conservation and the promotion of endangered breeds of livestock and poultry. A non profit membership organization working to protect over 180 breeds of livestock and poultry from extinction.
Cost: $30.00
Frequency: Membership Fee
ISSN: 1064-1599
Founded in 1977

9492 American Meat Institute

1150 Connecticut Ave NW
12th Floor
Washington, DC 20036

202-587-4200
FAX 202-587-4300
Home Page: www.meatami.com
Social Media: *Facebook, Twitter, LinkedIn*

Barry Carpenter, President & CEO
Ron Nunnery, Chief Financial Officer
Eric Mittenthal, Vice President, Public Affairs
Scott Goltry, Vice President, Regulatory Affairs
Susan Backus, Executive Director

AMI keeps its fingers on the pulse of legislation, regulation and media activity that impacts the meat and poultry industry and provides rapid updates and analyses to its members to

help them stay informed. Also conducts scientific research through its Foundation designed to help meat and poultry companies improve their plants and their products.
300 Members
Frequency: Membership Fees Vary
Founded in 1906

9493 American Meat Science Association

201 W Springfield Ave
Suite 1202
Champaign, IL 61820

217-356-5370
800-517-AMSA
FAX 888-205-5834
FAX 217-356-5370
E-Mail: information@meatscience.org
Home Page: www.meatscience.org
Social Media: *Facebook, Twitter, LinkedIn, Vimeo*

Bucky Gwartney, Ph.D., President
Steve Campano, Treasurer
Betsy L. Booren, Chair
Thomas Powell, Executive Director
Casey B. Frye, Treasurer

AMSA fosters community and professional development among individuals who create and apply science to efficiently provide safe and high quality meat.

9494 American Mushroom Institute

1284 Gap Newport Pike
Suite 800
Avondale, PA 19311

610-268-7483
FAX 610-268-8015
E-Mail: ami@mwmlaw.com
Home Page: www.americanmushroom.org

Joseph G. Poppiti, Chairman
Don Needham, Chairman Elect
Curtis Jurgensmeyer, Vice Chair/ Treasurer
Stephen Anania, Secretary
Laura Phelps, President

This organization is comprised of mushroom growers, associate businesses and suppliers who represent growers and coordinate industry research.
Founded in 1955

9495 American Oil Chemists' Society

2710 S. Boulder
Urbana, IL 61802-6996

217-359-2344
FAX 217-351-8091
E-Mail: general@aocs.org
Home Page: www.aocs.org
Social Media: *Facebook, Twitter, LinkedIn, Blogger*

M. Trautmann, President
B. Hendrix, Vice President
N. Widlak, Secretary
D. Bibus, Treasurer
P. Donnelly, Chief Executive Officer

Largest international society focused on the science and technology of fats, oils, lipids and related substances.
Cost: $10.00
5400 Members
Frequency: Membership Dues Vary
Founded in 1909

9496 American Ostrich Association

PO Box 166
Ranger, TX 75158

972-968-8546
FAX 936-333-6142
E-Mail: aoa@ostriches.org
Home Page: www.ostriches.org

Joel Brust, President
Boyd Clark, Vice President

Sharon Birmingham, Secretary/ Treasurer
Carol Garnett, Director at large

Organization that provides leadership for the ostrich industry and its future through the promotion of ostrich products.
Cost: $150.00
Frequency: Membership Fee
Founded in 1988

9497 American Peanut Council
1500 King St
Suite 301
Alexandria, VA 22314

703-838-9500
FAX 703-838-9508
E-Mail: info@peanutsusa.com
Home Page: www.peanutsusa.com
Social Media: *Facebook, Twitter*

Patrick Archer, President

The council was formed through a merger of the National Peanut Council and the National Peanut Council of America. Serving as a forum for all segments of the peanut industry to discuss issues which impact the production, utilization and marketing of peanuts and peanut products worldwide.
Founded in 1997

9498 American Peanut Research and Education Society
2360 Rainwater Road
UGA/NESPAL Building
Tifton, GA 31793

229-329-2949
FAX 229-386-7371
E-Mail: kim.cutchins@apresinc.com
Home Page: www.aprensic.org

Naveen Puppala, President
Kimberly J. Cutchins, Executive Officer
Kimberly J. Cutchins, Executive Officer
Jeffrey Pope, Board Representative
Howard Valentine, Director of Science & Technology

The purpose of this Society is to instruct and educate the public on the properties, production, and use of the peanut through the organization and promotion of public discussion groups, forums, lectures, and other programs or presentations to the interested public.
Cost: $80.00
550 Members
Frequency: Organizational Fee: $100
Founded in 1968

9499 American Pie Council
PO Box 368
Lake Forest, IL 60045

Home Page: www.piecouncil.org
Social Media: *Facebook, Twitter, Pinterest, YouTube*

The Pie Council is dedicated to preserving America's pie heritage.

9500 American Pomological Society
102 Tyson Building
University Park, PA 16802

814-863-6163
FAX 814-237-3407
E-Mail: aps@psu.edu
Home Page: www.americanpomological.org

Peter Hirst, President
Michele Warmund, 1st Vice-President
Marvin Pritts, 2nd Vice-President
Richard Marini, Secretary
Robert Crassweller, Treasurer/ Business Manager

The oldest fruit organization in North America, to foster the science and practice of fruit grow-

ing and variety development.
Cost: $40.00
1000 Members
Frequency: Annual Membership Fee
Founded in 1848

9501 American Poultry Association
PO Box 306
Burgettstown, PA 15021

724-729-3459
E-Mail: AmPoultryAssoc@yahoo.com
Home Page: www.amerpoultryassn.com

Dave Anderson, President
John Monaco, Vice President
Pat Horstman, Secretary/Treasurer
Dave Anderson, Director at large

The mission of the association is to promote and protect the standard bred poultry industry in all its phases. To encourage and protect poultry shows as being the show window of the industry, an education for both breeders and the public and a means of interesting young future breeders.
Cost: $25.00
Frequency: Annual Membership

9502 American Seafood Institute
25 Fairway Circle
Hope Valley, RI 02832

401-491-9017
FAX 401-491-9024
Home Page: www.americanseafood.org

Colleen Coyne, Director

9503 American Seed Trade Association
1701 Duke Street
Suite 275
Alexandria, VA 22314

703-837-8140
FAX 703-837-9365
E-Mail: infi@amseed.org
Home Page: www.amseed.com
Social Media: *Facebook, Twitter, Youtube, Googleplus*

Andy Lavigna, President & CEO
Bernice Slutsky, Senior Vice President
Jane Demarchi, Vice President
Rick Dunkle, Senior Director
Michelle Kohn, Director

Producers of seeds for planting purposes. Consists of companies involved in seed production and distribution, plant breeding and related industries in North America.
850 Members
Frequency: Membership Fees Vary
Founded in 1883

9504 American Sheep Industry Association
9785 Maroon Circle
Suite 360
Englewood, CO 80112

303-771-3500
FAX 303-771-8200
E-Mail: eatlamb@wildblue.net
Home Page: www.sheepusa.org
Social Media: *Facebook, Twitter*

Burton Pfliger, President
Mike Corn, Vice President
Peter Orwick, Executive Director
Rita Kourlis Samuelson, Director of Wool Marketing
Paul Rodgers, Deputy Director of Policy

A federation of state associations dedicated to the welfare and profitability of the sheep industry.
8000+ Members
Founded in 1865

9505 American Shrimp Processors Association
PO Box 4867
EIN #72-6029637
Biloxi, MS 39535

228-806-9600
FAX 228-385-2565
E-Mail: director@americanshrimp.com
Home Page: www.americanshrimp.com
Social Media: *Facebook, Twitter, Pinterest, YouTube, Instagram*

Andrew Blanchard, President
Jonathan McLendon, Vice President
Scott Young, Secretary/Treasurer
Ivan Sifrim, UX Developer
Nick Alekhine, Developer

A non-profit trade organization designed to represent U.S. shrimp processors in all aspects of business. Allowing processors and related industries to work together to foster a business and technological climate in which its members can prosper while providing the highest quality product to its customers.
Founded in 1964

9506 American Society for Enology and Viticulture
PO Box 1855
Davis, CA 95617-1855

530-753-3142
FAX 530-753-3318
E-Mail: society@asev.org
Home Page: www.asev.org
Social Media: *Twitter, LinkedIn*

Mark Greenspan, President
Nichola Hall, First Vice President
Dr. James Harbertson, Second Vice President
Tom Collins, Secretary/ Treasurer
Linda Bisson, AJEV Science Editor

A tax exempt professional society dedicated to the interests of enologists, viticulturists, and others in the fields of wine and grape research and production throughout the world.
2400+ Members
Founded in 1950

9507 American Society for Horticultural Science
1018 Duke Street
Alexandria, VA 22314

703-836-4606
FAX 703-836-2024
E-Mail: webmaster@ashs.org
Home Page: www.ashs.org
Social Media: *Facebook, Twitter, LinkedIn, Pinterest*

Michael A. Arnold, Chair
Curt Rom, President
John Dole, President-elect
Cynthia McKenney, Education Division Vice President
Angela Davis, Industry Division Vice President

A cornerstone of research and education in horticulture and an agent for active promotion of horticultural science.
2500+ Members
Frequency: Membership Fees Vary
ISSN: 0018-5345
Founded in 1903

9508 American Society for Parenteral and Enteral Nutrition
8630 Fenton Street
Suite 412
Silver Spring, MD 20910

301-587-6315
FAX 301-587-2365
E-Mail: aspen@nutritioncare.org
Home Page: www.nutritioncare.org

Social Media: *Facebook, Twitter, LinkedIn, YouTube*

Gordon Sacks, President
Charlene W. Compher, President-Elect
M. Molly McMahon, Vice President
Phil Ayers, Secretary/Treasurer
Albert Barrocas, Director

Advancing the science and practice of clinical nutrition and metabolism. An interdisciplinary organization whose members are involved in the provision of clinical nutrition therapies, including parenteral and enteral nutrition.
6400+ Members
Founded in 1976

9509 American Society of Agricultural Consultants

605 Columbus Ave South
New Prague, MN 56071

952-758-5811
FAX 952-758-5813
E-Mail: asac@gandgcomm.com
Home Page: www.agconsultants.org
Social Media: *Facebook, Twitter, LinkedIn, YouTube*

Russell Morgan, CAC, Principal
Norman Brown, President-Elect
Den Gardner, Executive Vice President
Kristy Mach, Associate
Roy Ferguson, Director

An association representing the full range of agricultural consultants which serves as an information, resource, and networking base for its members.
181 Members
Founded in 1963

9510 American Society of Agronomy

5585 Guilford Road
Madison, WI 53711-5801

608-273-8080
FAX 608-273-2021
E-Mail: membership@agronomy.org
Home Page: www.agronomy.org
Social Media: *Facebook, Twitter, LinkedIn*

Jean L. Steiner, President
David B. Mengel, President-elect
Ellen G.M. Bergfeld, Chief Executive Officer
Wes Meixelsperger, Chief Financial Officer
Sara Uttech, Senior Manager

Society members are dedicated to the conservation and wise use of natural resources to produce food, feed, and fiber crops while maintaining and improving the environment. Membership is tax deductible. ASA is seen as a progressive, scientific society.
11000 Members
Founded in 1907

9511 American Society of Animal Science

PO Box 7410
Champaign, IL 61826-7410

217-356-9050
FAX 217-568-6070
E-Mail: asas@asas.org
Home Page: www.asas.org
Social Media: *Facebook, Twitter, Youtube*

Dr. Michael L. Looper, President
Dr. Debora Hamernik, President-Elect
Dr. Todd A. Armstrong, Foundation Trustee Chair
Dr. James Sartin, Editor-in-chief
Dr. Phillip S. Miller, Recording Secretary

A professional organization for animal scientists designed to help members provide effective leadership through research, extension, teaching and service for the dynamic and rapidly changing livestock and meat industries.
5000+ Members
ISSN: 0021-8812
Founded in 1908

9512 American Society of Baking

7809 N Chestnut Avenue
Kansas City, MO 64119

800-713-0462
FAX 888-315-2612
E-Mail: info@asbe.org
Home Page: www.asbe.org
Social Media: *Facebook, Twitter, LinkedIn*

Ramon Rivera, Chairman
Mario Somoza, 1st Vice Chairman
Wendi Ebbing, 2nd Vice Chairman
Bill Zimmerman, 3rd Vice Chairman
Teresa Ruder, Secretary/ Treasurer

Formerly known as the American Society of Bakery Engineers, a professional society comprised of members in either engaged in, involved with, or interested in wholesale or large scale bakery production. The purpose is to promoted the advancement of baking science technology through the exchange of information and interaction among baking industry professionals.
Cost: $135.00
2900 Members
Frequency: Membership Fee
Founded in 1924

9513 American Society of Brewing Chemists

3340 Pilot Knob Rd
St. Paul, MN 55121

651-454-7250
FAX 651-454-0766
E-Mail: asbc@scisoc.org
Home Page: www.asbcnet.org
Social Media: *Facebook, Twitter, LinkedIn*

Christina Schoenberger, President
Christine S. White, President-Elect
Chris D. Powell, Vice President
Robert Christiansen, Secretary
Kelly A. Tretter, Treasurer-Elect

ASBC is dedicated to ensuring the highest quality, consistency and safety of malt-based beverages and their ingredients. Analytical, scientific process control methods, problem solving on industry-wide issues, scientific support to evaluate raw materials for optimum performance, and professional development opportunities.
Cost: $233.00
750+ Members
Frequency: Membership Fee
Founded in 1934

9514 American Society of Farm Managers and Rural Appraisers

950 S Cherry St
Suite 508
Denver, CO 80246-2664

303-758-3513
FAX 303-758-0190
E-Mail: hevans@asfmra.org
Home Page: www.asfmra.org
Social Media: *Facebook, Twitter, LinkedIn*

Fred L. Hepler, President
Merrill E. Swanson, President-Elect
Michael J. Krause, First Vice President
LeeAnn E. Moss, Academic Vice President
Jake Minton, District II Vice President

Protects and promotes the interest of members before government, regulatory bodies, and other organizations, enhances member opportunities for professional development and interation with peers, improves ethics, standards and quality of service offered by members, promotes awareness and confidence, and recruits and maintains a highly qualified, professional membership.
Cost: $175.00
Frequency: Membership Fees Vary
Founded in 1929

9515 American Society of Sugar Cane Technologists

LSU AgCenter
Sturgis Hall #128
Baton Rouge, LA 70803

225-578-6930
FAX 225-578-1403
E-Mail: assct@assct.org
Home Page: www.assct.org

Bruce McManus, President, Florida
Wallace Millet, President, Louisiana

With branches in Florida and Louisiana, the Society is dedicated to the study and advancement of the cane sugar industry in the United States.

9516 American Soybean Association

12125 Woodcrest Executive Drive
Suite 100
Saint Louis, MO 63141-5009

314-576-1770
800-688-7692
FAX 314-576-2786
E-Mail: membership@soy.org
Home Page: www.soygrowers.com
Social Media: *Facebook, Twitter, Youtube, Feedburner*

Wade Cowan, President
Ray Gaesser, Chairman
Richard Wilkins, 1st Vice President
Ron Moore, Secretary
Davie Stephens, Treasurer

A primary focus of the American Association is policy development and implementation and to improve US soybean farmer profitability.
21000 Members
Founded in 1920

9517 American Spice Trade Association

1101 17th St NW
Suite 700
Washington, DC 20036

202-331-2460
FAX 202-463-8998
E-Mail: info@astaspice.org
Home Page: www.astaspice.org

Greg Lightfood, President
Vinayak Narin, Vice President/ Secretary
Matt Meilander, Treasurer
Frank Collette, Associate Group Director
Cheryl Deem, Executive Director

ASTA, The voice of the US spice industry, works to ensure the supply of clean, safe spice, shape public policy on behalf of the global industry and advance the business interests of its members.
Frequency: Membership Dues Vary
Founded in 1907

9518 American Sugar Alliance

2111 Wilson Blvd
Suite 600
Arlington, VA 22201

703-351-5055
FAX 703-351-6698
E-Mail: info@sugaralliance.org
Home Page: www.sugaralliance.org
Social Media: *Facebook, Twitter, YouTube, Pinterest*

Don Phillips, Trade Adviser
Vickie Rideout Meyer, Executive Director
Jack Roney, Dir, Economics & Policy Analysis
Phillip W. Hayes, Director of Media Relations
Laura Gouge, Special Projects Coordinator

The American Sugar Aliance is a national coalition of sugarcane and sugarbett farmers, processors, refiners, suppliers, workers and others

dedicated to preserving a strong domestic sugar industry.
Frequency: Membership Fee
Founded in 1983

9519 American Sugar Beet Growers Association
1156 15th St NW
Suite 1101
Washington, DC 20005

202-833-2398
FAX 240-235-4291
E-Mail: info@americansugarbeet.org
Home Page: www.americansugarbeet.org
Social Media: *Facebook*

John Snyder, President
Ruthann Geib, Vice President
Luther Markwart, Executive Vice President
Galen Lee, Vice President
Mark Olson, Treasurer

The purpose of the organization is to unite sugarbeet growers in the United States and promote the common interest of state and regional beet grower associations, which include legislative and international representation and public relations.
10000 Members

9520 American Sugar Cane League
PO Drawer 938
206 E Bayou Rd.
Thibodaux, LA 70301

985-448-3707
FAX 985-448-3722
Home Page: www.amscl.org
Social Media: *Facebook, Twitter, LinkedIn, YouTube, Pinterest*

Michael Melancon, President
James H. Simon, General Manager

A Louisiana nonprofit involved in research, promotion and education in support of the state's sugar industry.
Founded in 1922

9521 American Veal Association
2900 NE Brooktree Lane
Suite 200
Gladstone, MO 64119

816-556-3169
E-Mail: info@americanveal.com
Home Page: www.americanveal.com
Social Media: *Facebook, Twitter, Digg, Stumbleupon,Reddit*

Jurian Bartelse, President
Dr. Adnan Aydin, Vice President
Chris Landwehr, Treasurer
Dale Bakke, Secretary

Provides information on veal production practices, industry facts, a tour of a modern veal barn and educational materials. Promoting the American veal industry, and encouraging communications and distributing information pertinent to the veal industry.
1300 Members
Founded in 1984

9522 American Wholesale Marketers Association
11311 Sunset Hills Road
Reston, VA 20190

703-208-3358
800-482-2962
FAX 703-573-5738
E-Mail: info@cdaweb.net
Home Page: www.cdaweb.net
Social Media: *Facebook, Twitter*

Scott Ramminger, President & CEO
Robert Pignato, IOM, Senior Vice President & COO
Anne Holloway, Vice President Government Affairs

Jane Berzan, Vice President of Strategy
Bob Gatty, Vice President, Communications

International trade organization working on behalf of convenience distributors in the U.S. Associate members include manufacturers, brokers, retailers and others allied to the convenience product industry. Typical products purchased and sold by convenience distributors include candy, tobacco, snacks, beverages, health and beauty care items, general merchandise, foodservice and groceries.
530 Members
Frequency: Membership Dues
Founded in 1942

9523 American Wine Society
PO Box 279
Englewood, OH 45322

888-297-9070
E-Mail:
executivedirector@americanwinesociety.or
Home Page: www.americanwinesociety.org
Social Media: *Facebook, Twitter, LinkedIn*

Willis L. Parker, President
Jane M. Duralia, Vice President
John W. Hames, Executive Director
Samuel D. Streiff, Treasurer

The oldest and largest consumer based wine education organization in North America. A non-profit, educational, consumer-oriented organization for those interested in learning more about all aspects of wine.
Cost: $52.00
5000 Members
Frequency: Membership Dues Vary
Founded in 1967

9524 Animal Agriculture Alliance
2101 Wilson Blvd
Suite 916-B
Arlington, VA 22201

703-562-5160
FAX 703-524-1921
E-Mail: info@animalagalliance.org
Home Page: www.animalagalliance.org
Social Media: *Facebook, Twitter*

Kay Johnson Smith, President & CEO
Morgan Hawley, Executive Assistant to President
Hannah Thompson, Communications Director
Shakera Daley, Administrative Assistant
Casey Whitaker, Communications Coordinator

The animal Agriculture Alliance is a 501 (c)(3) education foundation. The alliance's mission is to support and promote animal agricultural practices that provide for farm animal well-being through sound science and public education.
3000 Members
Founded in 1987

9525 Apple Processors Association
1701 K Street, NW
Suite 650
Washington, DC 20006

202-785-6715
FAX 202-331-4212
E-Mail: pweller@agriwashington.org
Home Page: www.appleprocessors.org
Social Media: *Facebook*

Andrea Ball, President
Paul S. Weller Jr., EVP Communications
Elizabeth Johnson, VP, Food & Nutrition Policy
Jacquie Ball, Director of Administration

A national association of companies that manufacture quality apple products from whole apples. Members are either apple grower/processor cooperatives, or proprietary firms.
25 Members
Founded in 1987

9526 Apple Products Research & Education Council
1100 Johnson Ferry Road
Suite 300
Atlanta, GA 30342

404-252-3663
FAX 404-252-0774
E-Mail: info@appleproducts.org
Home Page: www.appleproducts.org

Formerly known as The Processed Apples Institute. We are producers of processed apple products; suppliers of equipment, packaging or ingredients to the industry and brokers and concentrate manufacturers.
80 Members
Founded in 1951

9527 Association for Dressings & Sauces
1100 Johnson Ferry Road
Suite 300
Atlanta, GA 30342

678-298-1181
FAX 404-252-0774
E-Mail: ads@kellencompany.com
Home Page: www.dressings-sauces.org
Social Media: *Facebook, Twitter, YouTube, Pinterest*

Pam Chumley, President
Jeannie Milewski, Executive Director
Jacque Knight, Membership/Administration Manager

This association is comprised of manufacturers of mayonnaise, salad dressings and condiment sauces, as well as industry suppliers. Its purpose is to serve the best interests of industry members, its customers, and consumers of its products.
184 Members
Founded in 1926
Mailing list available for rent

9528 Association for Packaging and Processing Technologies
Packaging Machinery Manufacturers Institute
11911 Freedom Drive
Suite 600
Reston, VA 20190

703-243-8555
888-275-7664
FAX 703-243-8556
E-Mail: pmmiwebhelp@pmmi.org
Home Page: www.pmmi.org
Social Media: *Facebook, Twitter, LinkedIn, YouTube*

Charles D. Yuska, President
Katie Bergmann, Senior Vice President
Corinne G Mulligan, Executive Assistant
Caroline Abromavage, Director, Operations
Monjur Alam, Data Analyst

Members manufacture packaging and packaging-related converting machinery in the United States and Canada. PMMI's vision is to be the leading global resource for packaging. Its mission is to improve and promote members' abilities to meet the needs of their customers.
500+ Members
Founded in 1933

9529 Association of American Feed Control Officials
Purdue University
1800 S. Oak Street
Suite 100
Champaign, IL 61820-6974

217-356-4221
FAX 217-398-4119
E-Mail: aafco@aafco.org

Home Page: www.aafco.org
Social Media: *Facebook*

Tim Darden, President
Doug Lueders, President-Elect
Ali Kashani, Secretary/Treasurer
Mark LeBlanc, Sr. Director
Richard Teneyck, Sr. Director

A voluntary membership association of local, state and federal agencies charged by law to regulate the sale and distribution of animal feeds and animal drug remedies.
54 Members
Founded in 1909

9530 Association of American Seed Control Officials
Utah Department of Agriculture and Food
350 N Redwood Road
PO Box 146500
Salt Lake City, UT 84114-6500

801-538-7182
FAX 801-538-7189
E-Mail: walshm@purdue.edu
Home Page: www.seedcontrol.org

Jim Drews, President
Johnny Zook, 1st Vice President
Greg Stordahl, 2nd Vice President
Greg Helmbrecht, Treasurer
John Heaton, Secretary

The AASCO's purpose is to promote and establish basic requirements of a state seed law which shall serve as guidelines for member states, to promote and foster uniformity of procedures and policies by member states, to exchange problems and solutions or ideas and suggestions, to coordinate action and cooperate, and to impress and create a sense of mutual understanding between members and other organizations that are concerned with orderly legal merchandising of high quality seed.
Founded in 1949

9531 Association of Correctional Food Service Affiliates
PO Box 10065
Burbank, CA 91510

818-843-6608
FAX 818-843-7423
E-Mail: philip.atkinson@co.hennepin.mn.us
Home Page: www.acfsa.org
Social Media: *Facebook, Twitter, Shutterfly*

Laurie Maurino, President
Timothy Thielman, Vice President
Carlos Salazar Jr., Vice President
Elect/Treasurer
Linda Mills, RDN, FADA, Secretary
Jon Nichols, Executive Director

An international non-profit organization dedicated to the professional growth of our many nation's correctional foodservice employees. Association members are foodservice professionals employed in correctional facilities and agencies within federal, state and municipal prison/jail systems. Members are employed within government and commercially operated facilities within the United States, Canada, and an expanding international market.
Cost: $50.00
1300 Members
Frequency: Dues up to $150
Founded in 1969

9532 Association of Food Industries
3301 State Route 66
Building C, Suite 205
Neptune, NJ 07753

732-922-3008
FAX 732-922-3590
E-Mail: info@afius.org

Home Page: www.afius.org
Social Media: *Facebook*

Fred Mortati, Chair
Stephen O'Mara, 1st Vice Chair
James Libby, 2nd Vice Chair
John Sessler, Treasurer
Joe Fragola, Secretary

Promotes free trade and commerce in the food industry. Offers information and education on customs and usage of trade in the food markets and represents member interests in government.
Cost: $1040.00
800 Members
Frequency: Membership Dues Vary
Founded in 1906

9533 Association of Food and Drug Officials
2550 Kingston Rd
Suite 311
York, PA 17402

717-757-2888
FAX 717-650-3650
E-Mail: afdo@afdo.org
Home Page: www.afdo.org
Social Media: *Twitter*

Stephen Stich, President
Stan Stromberg, President-elect
Steven Mandernach, Vice-President
Steven Moris, Secretary/Treasurer
Joseph Corby, Executive Director

Promotes the enforcement of laws and regulations at all levels of government. Fosters understanding and cooperation between industry and regulators. Develops model laws and regulations and seeks their adoption.
800 Members
Frequency: Membership Dues Vary
Founded in 1896

9534 Association of Fruit and Vegetable Inspection
PO Box 588
Williamston, NC 27892

252-792-1672
FAX 252-792-4787
E-Mail: ronnie.wynn@ncagr.gov
Home Page: www.afvisa.org

Jack Dantzler, President
Russell Beamsley, Vice President
Carrie Porterfield, Second Vice President
Dennis Clary, Treasurer
Laura Thomas, Secretary

An organization of shipping point inspection programs that advocates for more uniformity between states.
Founded in 1986

9535 Association of Seafood Importers
Empress International
10 Harbor Park Drive
Port Washington, NY 11050-4681

516-621-5900
800-645-6244
FAX 516-621-8318

Burt C Faure
Membership is comprised of seafood importers focusing on problems facing the industry.

9536 Association of Smoked Fish Processors
85 John Road
Canton, MA 02021

781-821-2200
800-444-8705
FAX 781-821-9266
E-Mail: info@shusterlabs.com
Home: www.shusterlabs.com

This association provides technical consulation and services to the smoked fish and seafood in-

dustry. Services include recall manuals, plant audits, product evaluations, process evaluation, process evaluation, microbiological testing, analytical testing. HACCP plan development and plan ventilation.

9537 At-Sea Processors Association
4039 21st Ave W
Suite 400
Seattle, WA 98199

206-285-5139
FAX 206-285-1841
Home Page: www.atsea.org

Stephanie Madsen, Executive Director
Paul MacGregor, General Counsel
Jim Gilmore, Public Affairs Director

A trade association representing seven copmanies that own and operate 19 U.S. flag cathcer/processor vessels that participate principally in the Alaska pollack fishery and west coast Pacific whiting fishery.
Cost: $500.00
7 Members
Frequency: Membership Varies
Founded in 1985

9538 Bakery Equipment Manufacturers and Allieds (BEMA)
10740 Nall Avenue
Suite 230
Overland Park, KS 66211

913-338-1300
FAX 913-338-1327
E-Mail: info@bema.org
Home Page: www.bema.org
Social Media: *Facebook, Twitter*

KERWIN BROWN, President & CEO
Terry Bartsch, Chairman
Allen Wright, 1st Vice Chairman
Don Osborne, 2nd Vice Chairman
Paul Lattan, 3rd Vice Chairman

Through the exchange of information, active involvement on committees and participation in educational seminars, BEMA members are continually able to increase the efficiency and sophistication of their equipment while keeping design in adherence with Baking Industry Standarts Committee (BISSC) codes. Continually improving the efficiency of production and establishing sanitation standards.
208 Members
Frequency: Annual Membership Dues
Founded in 1918

9539 Baking Industry Sanitation Standards Committee
PO Box 3999
Manhattan, KS 66505-3999

866-342-4772
785-537-4750
FAX 785-537-1493
E-Mail: bissc@bissc.org
Home Page: www.bissc.org

James Munyon, President
Jon Anderson, Board Member

Develops and promotes sanitation standards for the design and construction of bakery equipment. Offers certification and third party verification programs for the member companies whose equipment conforms to the BISSC standards.
125 Members
Founded in 1949

9540 Beef Industry Food Safety Council
Attn: Deb Cole
9110 E. Nichols Ave
Centennial, CO 80112

303-850-3320
FAX 303-770-6921

E-Mail: dcole@beef.org
Home Page: www.bifsco.org

Deborah Cole, Administrative Coordinator
Gary Voogt, President
Forrest Roberts, CEO
Luisa Munsee, Treasurer
Bill Donald, VP

BIFSCo brings together representatives from all segments of the beef industry to develop industry-wide, science-based strategies to solve the problem of food borne pathogens.

9541 Beef and Lamb New Zealand
PO Box 121
Wellington, NZ 6140

644-473-9150
800-233-352
FAX 644-474-0800
E-Mail: enquiries@beeflambnz.com
Home Page: www.beeflambnz.com
Social Media: *Facebook, Twitter, LinkedIn, Youtube, Pinterest*

Dr. Scott Champion, Chief Executive Officer
Cros Spooner, Chief Operating Officer
Andrew Morrison, Director
Anne Munro, Director
Kirsten Bryant, Director

Funded by livestock producers through levies on all beef, sheep and goats slaughtered and on all wool sold. This income is used primarily to market New Zealand wool and meat worldwide, to maintain and extend trade access for New Zealand wool and meat, to provide solutions that will help improve New Zealand farm returns, and to provide technology to the wool industry.

9542 Beer Institute
Beer Institute
440 First Street NW
Suite 350
Washington, DC 20001

202-737-2337
800-379-2739
FAX 202-737-7004
E-Mail: info@beerinstitute.org
Home Page: www.beerinstitute.org
Social Media: *Facebook, Twitter*

James A. McGreevy III, President & CEO
Sandra Castro, Manager, Administration
Joy Dubost, Senior Director
Denise A. Dunckel, Vice President, Public Affairs
Susan Haney, Vice President of Operations

The national trade association for the brewing industry. Representing both big and small brewers as well as importers and industry suppliers.
Founded in 1986

9543 Beet Sugar Development Foundation
800 Grant Street
Suite 300
Denver, CO 80203

303-832-4460
FAX 303-832-4468
E-Mail: Tom@bsdf-assbt.org
Home Page: www.bsdf-assbt.org

J.W. Schorr, President
T.D. Knudsen, First Vice President
J. Dean, Second VP
T.K. Schwartz, Executive Vice President/Secretary
Aimee Dokes, Administrative Assistant

Association specializing in beet sugar research and the advertisement of seed companies.
Cost: $100.00
13 Members
Frequency: Membership Fee/Max. $450

9544 Biodynamic Farming & Gardening Association
1661 N Water Streetÿ
Suite 307
Milwaukeeÿ, WI 53202

262-649-9212
FAX 262-649-9213
E-Mail: info@biodynamics.com
Home Page: www.biodynamics.com
Social Media: *Facebook*

Robert Karp, Executive Director
Thea Maria Calson, Director of Programs
Jessica St. John, Director of Operations
Rebecca Briggs, Communications Coordinator
Ken Keffer, Program Assistant

A non-profit, membership organization open to the public with a purpose to foster knowledge of the practices and principles of the biodynamic method of agriculture, horticulture, and forestry in the North American continent and to advance the applications of this method through educational activities such as research, lectures, conferences; publishing literature on the biodynamic methods, and supporting consultation and extension services to farmers, gardeners, and foresters.
Cost: $45.00
Frequency: 6 per year
Circulation: 1000+
Founded in 1938

9545 Biscuit & Cracker Manufacturers' Association
6325 Woodside Court
Suite 125
Columbia, MD 21046

443-545-1645
FAX 410-290-8585
E-Mail: dvanlaar@thebcma.org
Home Page: www.thebcma.org
Social Media: *Facebook, Twitter, Googel+*

Dave Van Laar, President
Vanessa Vial, Comm. & eLearning Manager
Kathy Kinter Phelps, Member & Edu. Services Mgr
Todd Wallin, Treasurer
Kathy Kinter Phelps, Secretary

An international trade organization representing the entire spectrum of companies in the manufacturing of cookies and crackers and suppliers to theindustry.
Founded in 1901

9546 Blue Diamond Growers
1701 C Street
Sacramento, CA 95811

916-442-0771
800-987-2329
FAX 916-446-8461
E-Mail: feedback@bdgrowers.com
Home Page: www.bluediamondgrowers.com
Social Media: *Facebook, Twitter, Youtube, Pinterest*

Dan Cummings, Chairman of the Board
Dale Van Groningen, Vice Chairman
Mark Jansen, President & CEO
Don Yee, Director-at-large
Mel Machado, Director, Member relations

The world's largest tree nut processing and marketing company. Building markets and creating new products, uses, and opportunities for members.

9547 Board of Trade of Wholesale Seafood
7 Dey Street
Room 801
New York, NY 10007-3223

212-732-4340
FAX 212-732-6644

Home Page: www.aboutseafood.com
Social Media: *Facebook, Twitter, Googelplus*

Albert Altesnan, President/Administrator

Credit exchange and collection agency for wholesale seafood merchants and producers, in the US and Canada.
Founded in 1931

9548 Bread Bakers Guild of America
670 West Napa Street
Suite B
Sonoma, CA 95476

707-935-1468
FAX 707-935-1672
E-Mail: info@bbga.org
Home Page: www.bbga.org
Social Media: *Facebook, Twitter*

Jeff Yankellow, Board Chair
Phyllis Enloe, Board Vice Chair
Neale Creamer, Treasurer
Cathy Wayne, Director of Operations
Jill Valavanis, Administrative Assistant

Well known in the baking community as the go-to educational resource for substantive, accurate information on the craft of making bread. The definitive resource on all aspects of artisan baking in America, supporting and fostering the growth of the artisan baking community. Defining and upholding the highest professional standarts, and celebrating the craft and the passion of the artisan baker.
1300 Members
Founded in 1993

9549 Brewers Association
1327 Spruce Street
Boulder, CO 80302

303-447-0816
888-822-6273
FAX 303-447-2825
E-Mail: info@brewersassociation.org
Home Page: www.homebrewersassociation.org
Social Media: *Facebook, Twitter*

Sam Calagione, Chair
Gary Fish, Vice Chair
Mark Edelson, Treasurer/Secretary
Katie Brown, Finance Assistant
Tom Clark, Finance Director

The goal of the BA is to promote and protect small and independent American brewers, their craft beers and the community of brewing enthusiasts.
43000 Members
Founded in 1978

9550 Brown Swiss Association
800 Pleasant St
Beloit, WI 53511-5456

608-365-4474
FAX 608-365-5577
E-Mail: info@brownswissusa.com
Home Page: www.brownswissusa.com
Social Media: *Facebook*

Lee Barber, President
Tome Portner, Vice President
David Wallace, Executive Secretary
David Gunter, Director
Annissa Jones, Bookkeeper

Membership is comprised of key dairy industry leaders and dairy producers who are on the cutting edge of the world's latest agricultural technology.
800 Members
Founded in 1880

9551 Brown Swiss Cattle Breeder's Association
800 Pleasant Street
Beloit, WI 53511

608-365-4474
FAX 608-365-5577

E-Mail: info@brownswissusa.com
Home Page: www.brownswissusa.com
Social Media: *Facebook*

Lee Barber, President
Tom Portner, Vice President
David Wallace, Exec. Secretary
David Gunter, Director
Annissa Jones, Bookkeeper

Registers about 10,000 animals per year and promotes and expands the Brown Swiss breed with programs that assist the membership and industry to compete favorably in the market place.
800 Members
Founded in 1880

9552 CCFMA Annual Convention
Conference Caterers & Food Manufacturers Assoc.
1205 Spartan Drive
Madison Heights, MI 48071

248-982-5379
E-Mail: ccfma@ymail.com
Home Page: www.mobilecaterers.com

See the changes in the industry, learn tools to help business succeed and grow, and network with peers.
Frequency: Annual/October
Founded in 1964

9553 Calaveras Winegrape Alliance
P.O. Box 2492
Murphys, CA

209-728-9467
866-806-9463
E-Mail: calaveraswines@att.net
Home Page: www.calaveraswines.org
Social Media: *Facebook, Twitter, Pinterest*

Dedicated to increasing the awareness of all wines produced in Calaveras County and/or produced from Calaveras grapes.

9554 California Walnuts
101 Parkshore Dr.
Ste. 2503
Folsom, CA 95630

916-932-7070
FAX 916-932-7071
E-Mail: info@walnuts.org
Home Page: www.walnuts.org
Social Media: *Facebook, Twitter, YouTube, Pinterest*

Dennis A. Balint, Executive Director

Established to represent walnut growers and handlers. The board promotes usage of walnuts in the U.S. through publicity, product promotions and production research and education programs.
Founded in 1948
Mailing list available for rent

9555 Calorie Control Council
2611 Winslow Dr Ne
Atlanta, GA 30305-3777

678-608-3200
FAX 404-252-0774
E-Mail: webmaster@caloriecontrol.org
Home Page: www.caloriecontrol.org

An international non-profit association representing the low-calorie food and beverage industry. The Council seeks to provide an effective channel of communication among its members, the public and government officials, and to assure that scientific, medical and other pertinent research and information is developed and made available to all interested parties.
60 Members
Founded in 1966

9556 Can Manufacturers Institute
1730 Rhode Island Ave NW
Suite 1000
Washington, DC 20036

202-232-4677
FAX 202-232-5756
Home Page: www.cancentral.com
Social Media: *Facebook, Twitter, LinkedIn*

Robert Budway, President

Serves as the voice of the metal can making industry, providing a forum for members to advocate common industry problems to legislative and regulatory agencies whose activities impact the metal can market, to address issues of common concern, and to promote cost-effectively the benefits of the can to protect and grow the market.
35 Members
Founded in 1939

9557 Canned Foods
PO Box 5258
Madison, WI 53705-0000

608-231-2250
FAX 608-231-6952
E-Mail: webmaster@cannedveggies.org
Home Page: www.cannedveggies.org

Gene Kroupa, Executive Director

An educational and promotional organization of vegetable canners whose goals are to raise the awareness of consumer and food service buyers regarding canned vegetables.
80 Members
Founded in 1977

9558 Canola Council of Canada
167 Lombard Avenue Suite 400
Winnipeg, Manitoba
Canada R3B 0T6

204-982-2100
866-834-4378
FAX 204-942-1841
E-Mail: admin@canola-council.org
Home Page: www.canola-council.org

Patti Miller, President
Jim Everson, Vice President, Gov Relations
Bruce Jowett, Vice President, Market Development
Curtis Rempel, Vice President, Crop Production
Cari Mell, Comptroller

Representing canola growers, input suppliers, researchers, processors and marketers of canola and its products.

9559 Cape Cod Cranberry Growers Association
1 Carver Square Boulevard
PO Box 97
Carver, MA 02330

508-866-7878
FAX 508-866-4220
E-Mail: info@cranberries.org
Home Page: www.cranberries.org

Brad Morse, President
Gary Garretson, 1st Vice President
Keith Mann, 2nd Vice President
Carolyn DeMoranville, Secretary/ Treasurer
Brian Wick, Executive Director

Established to standardize the measure with which cranberries are sold, the CCCGA is one of the country's oldest farmers' organizations. Giving growers both a single voice and a collective strength in promoting the cranberry industry, and working to ensure that cranberry farming can survive urbanization and the open space and clean water, vital to growing, will be preserved.
Founded in 1888

9560 Carneros Wine Alliance
PO Box 189
Vineburg, CA 95487

707-812-1919
E-Mail: info@carneros.com
Home Page: www.carneros.com
Social Media: *Facebook, Twitter*

Anne Moller-Racke, Chair
Heidi Soldinger, Vice Chair
T. J. Evans, Treasurer
Alison Crowe, Board of Director
Carla Bosco, Secretary

A nonprofit association of wineries and grape-owners in the Carneros American Viticultural Area (AVA).

9561 Center for Food Safety & Applied Nutrition
5100 Paint Branch Parkway
College Park, MD 20740

888-723-3366
E-Mail: consumer@fda.gov
Home Page: www.cfsan.fda.gov

Provides services to consumers, domestic and foreign industry and other outside groups regarding field programs; agency administrative tasks; scientific analysis and support; and policy, planning and handling of critical issues related to food and cosmetics.

9562 Cheese Importers Association of America
204 E Street NE
Washington, DC 20002

202-547-0899
FAX 202-547-6348
E-Mail: info@theciaa.org
Home Page: www.theciaa.org

Thomas Gellert, President
Dominique Delugeau, First Vice President
Ken Olsson, 2nd Vice President
Philip Marfuggi, Treasurer
Daniel Schnyder, Secretary

Helps facilitate the efficient import of dairy products from around thw world into the United States. The CIAA endeavors to support dairy trade, within the context of compliance with international trade agreements and all applicable US regulations, and maintains active contacts with government officials worldwide in order to further the objectives of the organization and its members.
150 Members
Founded in 1942

9563 Cherry Marketing Institute
12800 Escanaba Drive
Suite A
Dewitt, MI 48820

925-838-5454
FAX 925-838-2311
E-Mail: info@choosecherries.com
Home Page: www.choosecherries.com
Social Media: *Facebook, Twitter*

Philip Korson II, President
Fred Tubbs, Chairman
Chris Dunkel, Manager

Association representing the cherry industry. Provides promotional material to food service operators, brokers, retailers and manufacturers.
Founded in 1988
Mailing list available for rent

9564 Chocolate Manufacturers Association
1101 30th Street NW
Suite 200
Washington, DC 20007

202-534-1440
FAX 202-337-0637

E-Mail: info@candyUSA.com
Home Page: www.thestoryofchocolate.com

Dennis Whalen, Chairman
Louise Hilsen, Vice Chairman
Alison Bodor, Executive Vice President
Susan S. Smith, SVP, Communications
Liz Clark, VP Government Affairs

The trade group for manufacturers and distributors of cocoa and chocolate products in the United States. The association was founded to fund and administer research, promote chocolate to the general public and serve as an advocate of the industry before Congress and government agencies.
9 Members
Founded in 1884

9565 Citrus Industry Magazine
5053 NW Hwy 225-A
Ocala, FL 34482

352-671-1909
FAX 888-957-2226
E-Mail: CitrusIndustry@SoutheastAgNet.com
Home Page: www.citrusindustry.net
Social Media: *Facebook*

Ernie Ness, Editor

Association for citrus grower organizations and other trade associations within the industry.
Founded in 1920
Mailing list available for rent

9566 Coca-Cola Bottlers Association
3282 Northside Parkway
Suite 200
Atlanta, GA 30327

404-872-2258
FAX 404-872-2869
E-Mail: ccba.atl@gmail.com
Home Page: www.ccbanet.com

Hank Flint, President
M. Trevor Messinger, Vice President
Mark Francouer, Treasurer
Ann Burton, CFO
John Gould, Executive Director & CEO

Assisting members in reducing costs and improving efficiency, the Association acts as a servicing arm and agent on behalf of participating Bottlers to meet their needs in numerous areas, including procurement, employee benefits, insurance programs and retirement plans. Also serves as a primary mechanism for fostering the exchange of ideas and information within the Coca-Cola system.
Founded in 1913

9567 Coffee, Sugar and Cocoa Exchange
New York Board of Trade
1 N End Avenue
New York, NY 10282-1101

212-748-4000
FAX 212-748-4039
Home Page: www.csce.com

Acts as a financial exchange where futures and options are traded, the CSCE provides hedging and investing, opportunities in the coffee, sugar, cocoa and dairy markets.

9568 Colombia Coffee Federation
140 E 57th Street
New York, NY 10022

212-421-8300
FAX 212-758-3816
E-Mail: judyb@juynvald.com
Home Page:
www.cafedecolombia.com/en/familia

John Boden, Manager
Founded in 1964

9569 Commercial Food Equipment Service Association
3605 Centre Circle
Fort Mill, SC 29715

336-346-4700
FAX 336-346-4745
E-Mail: asidders@cfesa.com
Home Page: www.cfesa.com
Social Media: *Facebook, LinkedIn, MySpace, YouTube*

Paul Toukatly, President
John Schwindt, Vice President
Gary Potvin, Vice President
Wayne Stoutner, Treasurer
David Hahn, Secretary

The trade association of professional service and parts distributors. Helps members meet the challenges of the industry and ensure customer satisfaction.
450 Members
Founded in 1963
Mailing list available for rent

9570 Communicating for America
112 E Lincoln Avenue
Fergus Falls, MN 56537

218-739-3241
800-432-3276
FAX 218-739-3832
E-Mail: memberbenefits@cainc.org
Home Page:
www.communicatingforamerica.org

Milt Smedsrud, Chairman
Patty Strickland, President & COO
Wayne Nelson, President
Stephen Rufer, Vice President & General Counsel
Roger Gussiaas, Vice President

Strives to promote health, well-being and advancement of people in agriculture and agribusiness.
40M Members
Founded in 1972

9571 Communication and Agricultural Education
Oklahoma State University
301 Umberger Hall
Manhattan, KS 66506

785-532-5804
FAX 785-532-5633
E-Mail: commdept@ksu.edu
Home Page: www.communications.ksu.edu
Social Media: *Facebook, Twitter, Youtube, Foursquare*

Beth Holz, President
Wyatt Betchel, First VP
Megan Brouk, Second VP
Amanda Spoo, Secretary
Brittney Machado, Treasurer

The Mission of National ACT is to build relationships among agricultural communication professionals and college students and faculty, to provide professional and academic development for members and to promote agriculture through communications efforts.
Founded in 1970

9572 Composite Can and Tube Institute
50 S Pickett Street
Suite 110
Alexandria, VA 22304-7206

703-823-7234
FAX 703-823-7237
E-Mail: ccti@cctiwdc.org
Home Page: www.cctiwdc.org

Kristine Garland, Executive VP
Janine Marczak, Associate Manager, Events
Wayne Vance, Association Counsel

CCTI is an international nonprofit trade association representing the interests of manufacturers of composite paperboard cans, containers, canisters, tubes, cores, edgeboard and related or similar composite products and suppliers to those manufacturers of such items as paper, machinery, adhesives, labels and other services and materials.
Founded in 1933

9573 Concord Grape Association
1 Cliffstar Avenue
Dunkirk, NY 14048

716-366-6100
E-Mail: info@concordgrape.org
Home Page: www.concordgrape.org

Pam Chumley, Executive Director
Linda Whitley, Contact

The Concord Grape Association represents processors of Concord grapes and manufacturers of products derived from them. The organization operates as the Concord Grape Section under the umbrella of the Juice Products Association (JPA), which represents the juice and juice products industry in the U.S. and overseas. Members handle more than the majority of the Concord grapes processed annually in the United States.
Founded in 1956

9574 Consultants Association for the Natural Products Industry (CANI)
PO Box 4014
Clovis, CA 93613

559-325-7192
FAX 559-325-7195
E-Mail: info@cani-consultants.org
Home Page: www.cani-consultants.org
Social Media: *LinkedIn*

Karena K. Dillon, President
Robert Forbes, Vice President
Ginni Garner, Treasurer
Sheldon Baker, Director
Kathy Francis, SECRETARY

Committed to working individually and collectively, to enhance the growth and integrity of the natural products industry by providing professional expertise and objective counsel to our clients. These specialized services contribute to the prosperity and values of the individual business as well as the industry as a whole.
Founded in 1991

9575 Convenience Caterers & Food Manufacturers Association
1205 Spartan Drive
Madison Heights, MI 48071

248-982-5379
E-Mail: ccfma@ymail.com
Home Page: www.mobilecaterers.com

Dedicated to the best interests of the growing industrial catering industry and to a commitment of excellence in service to catering truck operators, the food service industry, and the public. An international association representing food service professionals who are anxious to improve mobile catering operations.
Founded in 1964

9576 Cookware Manufacturers Association
PO Box 531335
Birmingham, AL 35253-1335

205-592-0389
FAX 205-599-5598
E-Mail: hrushing@usit.net
Home Page: www.cookware.org

Jay Zilinskas, President
Gene Karlson, VP
Hugh J Rushing, Executive VP

Represents manufactures of cookware and bakeware in the US and Canada. Publishes con-

sumer guides to cookware and engineering standards for industry.
21 Members
Founded in 1922

9577 Corn Refiners Association
1701 Pennsylvania Avenue N.W.
Suite 950
Washington, DC 20006

202-331-1634
FAX 202-331-2054
E-Mail: comments@corn.org
Home Page: www.corn.org
Social Media: *Facebook, Twitter, Stumbleupon, Digg*

Audrae Erickson, President
Shannon Weiner, Executive Assistant
Bob Adams, Director Public Affairs
Pat Saks, Assistant Director

Supports carbohydrate research programs through grants to colleges, government laboratories and private research centers.
8 Members
Founded in 1913

9578 Council for Agricultural Science and Technology
4420 West Lincoln Way
Ames, IA 50014-3447

515-292-2125
FAX 515-292-4512
E-Mail: cast@cast-science.org
Home Page: www.cast-science.org
Social Media: *Facebook, Twitter, LinkedIn, YouTube, Schooltube*

David Songstad, President
Mark Armfelt, President-Elect
Kent G. Schescke, Executive Vice President
Dan Gingerich, Treasurer
Melissa Sly, Director of Council Operations

Assembles, interprets and communicates science based information regionally, nationally and internationally on food, fiber, agriculture, natural resources, and related societal and environmental issues.
2000+ Members
Founded in 1972

9579 Council for Responsible Nutrition
1828 L St NW
Suite 510
Washington, DC 20036-5114

202-204-7700
FAX 202-204-7701
E-Mail: webmaster@crnusa.org
Home Page: www.crnusa.org
Social Media: *Twitter, Googleplus*

Steve Mister, President & CEO
Judy Blatman, Senior Vice President
Mike Greene, Vice President, Gov Relations
James C. Griffiths, Vice President, Scientific
Andrea Wong, Ph.D., Vice President, Science

The leading trade association representing dietary supplement manufacturers and ingredient suppliers. Member companies manufacture popular national brands as well as the store brands marketed by major supermarkets, drug store and discount chains. All members also agree to adhere to voluntary guidelines for manufacturing, marketing and CRN's Code of Ethics.
70 Members
Founded in 1973

9580 Council of Supply Chain Management Professionals
333 E Butterfield Rd
Suite 140
Lombard, IL 60148

630-574-0985
FAX 630-574-0989

E-Mail: cscmpadmin@cscmp.org
Home Page: www.cscmp.org
Social Media: *Facebook, Twitter, LinkedIn, YouTube*

Heather Sheehan, Chair
Theodore Stank, Chair-Elect
Kevin Smith, Vice Chair
Mary Long, Secretary & Treasurer

CSCMP's mission is to lead the evolving supply chain management profession by developing, advancing, and disseminating supply chain knowledge and research.
10000 Members
Founded in 1963

9581 Crop Insurance and Reinsurance Bureau
440 First St NW
Suite 500
Washington, DC 20001

202-544-0067
FAX 202-330-5255
E-Mail: mtorrey@cropinsurance.org
Home Page: www.cropinsurance.org

Sheri Bane, Chairwoman
Ron Rutledge, Vice-Chairman
Mike Torrey, Executive Vice President
Tara Smith, Federal Affairs Vice President
Zane Vaughn, Treasurer

National trade association made up of insurance providers and related organizations that provide a variety of insurance products for our nation's farmers.
Founded in 1964

9582 Crop Life America
1156 15th St NW
Washington, DC 20005

202-296-1585
FAX 202-463-0474
E-Mail: info@croplifeamerica.org
Home Page: www.croplifeamerica.org
Social Media: *Facebook, Twitter, LinkedIn, YouTube*

Jay Vroom, President
William Kuckuck, Executive VP & COO
Dr. Barbara Glenn, Senior Vice President
Rachel Lattimore, Senior Vice President
Doug Nelson, Senior Advisor

A trade association of manufacturers and distributors of agriculture crop protection and pest control products.
74 Members
Founded in 1933

9583 Crop Science Society of America
5585 Guilford Rd.
Madison, WI 53711-5801

608-273-8080
FAX 608-273-2021
E-Mail: membership@sciencesocieties.org
Home Page: www.crops.org
Social Media: *Facebook, Twitter, LinkedIn*

Roch E. Gaussoin, President
Michael A. Grusak, President-Elect
Ellen G.M. Bergfeld, CEO

Dedicated to the conservation and wise use of natural resources to produce food, feed, and fiber crops while maintaining and improving the environment. Continuously evolving and modifying it's educational offerings to support the changing needs of its members.
5000+ Members
Founded in 1956

9584 Dairy Farmers of America
10220 N Ambassador Dr
Kansas City, MO 64153

816-801-6455
888-332-6455
FAX 816-801-6456

E-Mail: webmail@dfamilk.com
Home Page: www.dfamilk.com
Social Media: *Facebook, Twitter, LinkedIn, YouTube*

Rick Smith, President & CEO
John McDaniel, Senior Vice President
Alex Bachelor, Senior Vice President
Randy McGinnis, Senior Vice President & COO
David Meyer, Senior Vice President, Finance

A milk marketing cooperative and dairy food processor dedicated to delivering value to members through secure markets, competitive pricing and increasing value throughout the entire diary chain.
Founded in 1998

9585 Dairy Management, Inc.
O'Hare International Center
10255 W Higgins Rd
Suite 900
Rosemont, IL 60018-5616

847-803-2000
800-853-2479
FAX 847-803-2077
Home Page: www.dairy.org

James Ahlem, Chair
Skip Hardie, Secretary
Thomas P. Gallagher, Chief Executive Officer
Barbara O'Brien, President
Mollie Waller, Chief Communication Officer

This association aims to provide the sale and consumption of milk and milk products in the US.
Founded in 1980

9586 Dairy and Food Industries Supply Association
1451 Dolley Madison Boulevard
McLean, VA 22101-3879

703-883-0515
FAX 703-761-4334

John Martin, President
Burce D'Agostino, Vice President
Mary O'Dea, Communications Manager

Trade association of almost 800 suppliers to the food, beverage, dairy, pharmaceutical and related sanitary processing industries.

9587 Diamond of California
1050 S Diamond Street
Stockton, CA 95205

209-467-6000
FAX 209-467-6788
Home Page: www.diamondnuts.com

Brian J. Discoll, President & CEO
Ray Silcock, Executive Vice President & CFO
Lloyd J. Jhonson, Executive Vice President
David Colo, Executive Vice President & COO
Stephen Kim, Senior Vice President

Walnut growers' association with Diamond guarantees a market for their crops and provides the company with high quality walnuts. Diamond provides information and resources to help growers to produce the best nuts in the world.
1900 Members
Founded in 1912

9588 Distillers Grains Technology Council
University of Louisville
3327 Elings Hall
Ames, IA 50011

515-294-4019
800-759-3448
FAX 502-852-1577
E-Mail: karosent@iastate.edu
Home Page: www.distillersgrains.org

Dr. Kurt Rosentrater, Executive Director/CEO

A non-profit organization that stresses the importance of utilization of distillers co-products in animal feeds. We address the production and product quality issues that are known to impact the market acceptability and production costs of these products.
7 Members
Founded in 1945

9589 Dr. Pepper Bottlers Association

PO Box 906
Rowlett, TX 75030-0906

972-475-7397
FAX 972-475-5290
Social Media: *Facebook, Twitter, Googleplus*

Bill Elmore Jr, President
James Lee, Vice President
Scott Chase, Secretary/ Director
Bill Yarbrough, Treasurer/ Director

Represents 430 bottlers for the Dr. Pepper Company.

9590 Drug, Chemical & Associated Technologies Association

One Union St.
Suite 208
Robbinsville, NJ 08691

609-208-1888
800-640-3228
FAX 609-208-0599
E-Mail: mtimony@dcat.org
Home Page: www.dcat.org

George Svokos, President
Dr. Folker Ruchatz, Sr. Vice President
Milton Boyer, 2nd Vice President
Christopher Rayfield, VP-Pharmaceutical Services Industry
David Beattie, VP-Biotechnology

The premier business development association whose membership is comprised of companies that manufacture, distribute or provide services to the pharamaceutical, chemical, nutritional and related industries.
Founded in 1890

9591 Eastern Frosted and Refrigerated Foods Association

17 Park St
Wanaque, NJ 07465

973-835-1710
FAX 973-835-1708
E-Mail: efra@efraweb.org
Home Page: www.efraweb.org

Hans Ketels, President
Paul Raguso, 1st Vice President
Ken Atkinson, 2nd Vice President
Jody Avallone, Director
Mike Ryan, Executive Director

Brings together all related segments of the frozen food industry; brokers, warehousing, manufacturers, transportation, distributors, packaging/labeling and retailers. Constantly gathering information for members from authoritative national and regional sources, other members, and publication editorials affecting the industry.
65 Members
Founded in 1937

9592 Eastern Perishable Products Association

61 Woodhollow Road
PO Box 478
Colts Neck, NJ 07722

973-831-4100
FAX 973-831-8100
Home Page: www.eppainc.org
Social Media: *Facebook*

Fred D'Agostino, President
Barry Kahn, Chairman

Robert Carley, Vice President
Stan Futoran, Vice President
Tom Tracy, Secretary

Regional association with national and international recognition. The EPPA keeps the industry current with the trends, new products, packaging, programs, changes and technical advances that are so dynamic in todays marketplace through projects, publications and activities.
130 Members

9593 Electric Foodservice Council

180 Raymond Court
PO Box 142156
Fayetteville, GA 30214

770-461-3870
FAX 770-461-7799
E-Mail: krhutchinson1@msn.com
Home Page: www.foodservicecouncil.org

Billy Griffis, President
Jim Wixson, Senior Vice President
Roshena Ham, Secretary
Mitzi Shanks, Treasurer

Unique organization designed to bring together utilities, equipment manufacturers, trade allies, and foodservice operators who are committed to the advancement of the foodservice industry.
Founded in 1987

9594 Farmer Direct Foods Inc.

511 Commercial
PO Box 326
Atchison, KS 66002

913-367-4422
800-372-4422
FAX 913-367-4443
E-Mail: orders@farmerdirectfoods.org
Home Page: www.farmerdirectfoods.com

Mark Fowler, President / Chief Executive Officer
Marcia Walters, Accounting Manager
Justin Howie, Plant Operations Manager

A producer owned cooperative marketing corporation formed in 1988 with the mission to develop white wheat markets for wheat producers.
125 Members
Founded in 1988

9595 Fermenters International Trade Association

PO Box 1373
Valrico, FL 33595

813-685-4261
FAX 813-681-5625
Home Page: www.hwbta.org
Social Media: *Facebook, Twitter*

Dee Roberson, Executive Director
Bill Metzger, Editor

Manufacturers, wholesalers, retailers, authors and editors having a commercial interest in the beer and wine trade. Offers publications to members only.
200+ Members
Founded in 1976

9596 Fertilizer Institute

425 Third Street, SW
Suite 950
Washington, DC 20024

202-962-0490
FAX 202-962-0577
E-Mail: information@tfi.org
Home Page: www.tfi.org
Social Media: *Facebook, Twitter, LinkedIn*

Chris Jahn, President
Pamela Guffain, Vice President, Member Services
Kathy Mathers, Vice President, Public affairs
Monica Conway, Executive Assistant to

President
Carol Dorrough, Director, Administration & Finance

Members include brokers, producers, importers, dealers and manufacturers of fertilizer and fertilizer-related equipment.
325 Members
Founded in 1969

9597 Fishermens Marketing Association

1585 Heartwood Drive
Suite E
McKinleyville, CA 95519

707-840-0182
FAX 707-840-0539
E-Mail: fma@trawl.org
Home Page: trawl.org

Peter Leipzig, Executive Director

An organization made up of fishermen which promotes stable prices and an orderly flow of wholesome seafood to the consumer.
Founded in 1952

9598 Flavor & Extract Manufacturers Association (FEMA)

1101 17th St NW
Suite 700
Washington, DC 20036

202-293-5800
FAX 202-463-8998
Home Page: www.femaflavor.org
Social Media: *YouTube, RSS Feed*

Kevin Renskers, President
Timothy Webster, President Elect
John Cavallo, Vice President & Secretary
John Cox, Executive Director
Gary Smith, Treasurer

Comprised of flavor manufacturers, flavor users, flavor ingredient suppliers, and others with an interest in the U.S. flavor industry. Working with legislators and regulators to assure that the needs of members and consumers are continuously addressed. FEMA is committed to assuring a substantial supply of safe flavoring substances.
123 Members
Founded in 1909

9599 Food & Nutrition Service

3101 Park Center Drive
Alexandria, VA 22302

703-305-2062
FAX 703-305-2312
Home Page: www.fns.usda.gov
Social Media: *Facebook, Twitter, Flickr, YouTube*

Audrey Rowe, Administrator
Kevin Concannon, Under Secretary
Dr. Janey Thronton, Deputy under Secretary
Telora Dean, Associate Administrator & COO
Rich Lucas, Deputy Administrator

Provides children and needy families better access to food and a more healthful diet through its food assistance programs and comprehensive nutrition education efforts. FNS also works to empower program participants with knowledge of the link between diet and health.
Founded in 1969
Mailing list available for rent

9600 Food Allergy Research & Education

7925 Jones Branch Dr.
Suite 1100
McLean, VA 22102

703-691-3179
800-924-4040
FAX 703-691-2713
E-Mail: faan@foodallergy.org
Home Page: www.foodallergy.org

Social Media: *Facebook, Twitter, Youtube, Flickr, Pinterest*

Janet Atwater, Chairman
Elliot S. Jaffe, Chairman Emeritus
Robert Nichols, Vice Chair
James R. Baker, Jr., Chief Executive Officer
Michael Lade, Treasurer

The only nonprofit organization in the United States devoted solelyto patient education for food allergies. Mission is to create public awareness about food allergies and anaphylaxis, to provide education, and to advance research on behalf of all those affected by food allergy.
Cost: $30.00
22000 Members
Frequency: 6 per year
Founded in 1991

9601 Food Distribution Research Society

PO Box 441110
Fort Washington, MD 20749-1110

301-292-1970
FAX 706-542-0739
E-Mail: Jonathan_baros@ncsu.edu
Home Page: www.fdrsinc.org

Dawn Thilmany, President
Kynda Curtis, President-Elect
Randall D. Little, Vice President Communication
Alba J. Collart, Vice President Education
Ronald L. Rainey, Vice President Logistics & Outreach

Food distribution research society encourages research, serves as an information clearinghouse and encourages implementation of research. The Society organizes conferences and meetings for industry, academic and government leaders within the food industry sector.
Founded in 1967

9602 Food Export Association of the Midwest USA

309 West Washington
Suite 600
Chicago, IL 60606

312-334-9200
FAX 312-334-9230
E-Mail: info@foodexportusa.org
Home Page: www.foodexportusa.org
Social Media: *Facebook*

Tim F Hamilton, Executive Director
Lauren Swartz, Deputy Director
John Belmont, Communications Manager
Suzanne Milshaw, International Marketing Program

A non-profit organization that promotes the export of food and agricultural products from the northeast region of the United States. The organization has been helping exporters of northeast food and agricultural products sell their products overseas since it was first organized.
Founded in 1973

9603 Food Industry Association Executives

664 Sandpiper Bay Dr., SW
Sunset Beach, NC 28468

910-575-3423
FAX 815-550-1731
E-Mail: bev@mgmt57.com
Home Page: www.fiae.net

Jamie Pfhul, Chairwoman
Ellie Taylor, Vice Chairwoman
Bev Lynch, President
Pat Davis, Vice President, State Government
Brian Jordan, Secretary/Treasurer

Sponsors meetings, activities, publications and services to advance the knowledge and professionalism of the food industry association exec-

utive, and serves as a vehicle for the advancement of the food industry's agenda.
125 Members
Founded in 1927

9604 Food Industry Suppliers Association

1207 Sunset Drive
Greensboro, NC 27408

336-274-6311
FAX 336-691-1839
E-Mail: stella@fisanet.org
Home Page: www.fisanet.org

Bob Morava, President
Brad Myers, Vice President
Joe Allman, Director
Chad Hawkins, Director
Andrew Mahoney, Director

Trade association dedicated to promoting distribution in serving high purity industries. Membership includes independent distributors and manufacturers who go to market through distribution. Members serve customers in food, beverage, personal care, pharmaceutical, Bio-Pharm and other high purity industries.
245 Members
Founded in 1968
Mailing list available for rent

9605 Food Information Service Center

21050 SW 93rd Lane Road
Dunnellon, FL 34431

352-489-8919
800-443-5820
FAX 352-489-8919
E-Mail: fcsgroup@artdc.net

James Allen Mixon, President

Publishes technical assistance manuals for operating congregate feeding food service programs. Reaches market through direct mail and publicity.
Founded in 1957

9606 Food Marketing Institute

2345 Crystal Drive
Suite 800
Arlington, VA 22202

202-452-8444
FAX 202-429-4519
Home Page: www.fmi.org
Social Media: *Facebook, Twitter, LinkedIn, YouTube*

Jerry Garland, Chair
Leslie G. Sarasin Esq., CAE, President & CEO
Rob Bartels, Vice-Chair
Russell T, Lund III, Vice-Chair
Joseph Sheridan, Vice-Chair

Food Marketing Institute (FMI) conducts programs in public affairs, food safety, research, education and industry relations on behalf of food retailers and wholesalers in the United States and around the world. FMI's U.S. members operate approximately 26,000 retail food stores and 14,000 pharmacies. Their combined annual sales volume of $680 billion represents three-quarters of all retail food store sales in the United States.
1500 Members
Founded in 1977
Mailing list available for rent

9607 Food Processing Suppliers Association

1451 Dolley Madison Blvd
Suite 101
Mc Lean, VA 22101-3850

703-761-2600
FAX 703-761-4334
E-Mail: info@fpsa.org
Home Page: www.fpsa.org
Social Media: *Facebook, Twitter, LinkedIn*

Gil Williams, Chairman, Vice Chair
David Seckman, President & CEO

Robyn Roche, CFO
Scott Gregory, Treasurer

FPSA members are organized in vertical industry councils which focus association programs on specific concerns and needs that are unique to that industry sector. Membership permits companies to participate in as many industry councils as appropriate at no additional cost.
510 Members
Founded in 2005

9608 Food Processors Suppliers Association

1451 Dolly Madison Boulevard
Suite 101
McLean, VA 22101-3850

703-761-2600
FAX 703-761-4334
E-Mail: info@fpsa.org
Home Page: www.fpsa.org
Social Media: *Facebook, Twitter, LinkedIn*

Gil Williams, Chairman, Vice Chair
David Seckman, President & CEO
Robyn Roche, CFO
Scott Gregory, Treasurer

MISA offers its members an opportunity to project a common and uniform stance on important industry issues, particularly in the regulatory and machinery safety and hygienic standards area.
500+ Members
Founded in 1983

9609 Foodservice & Packaging Institute

7700 Leesburg Pike
Suite 421
Falls Church, VA 22043

703-592-9889
FAX 703-592-9864
E-Mail: ldyer@fpi.org
Home Page: www.fpi.org
Social Media: *Facebook, Twitter, LinkedIn*

Lynn Dyer, President
Natha Dempsey, Vice President
Jennifer Goldman, Membership & Meetings Manager

A national association comprised of manufacturers and suppliers of single-use foodservice packaging products.
25 Members
Founded in 1933

9610 Foodservice Consultants Society International

PO Box 4961
Louisville, KY 40204

502-379-4122
FAX 519-856-0648
E-Mail: info@fcsi.org
Home Page: www.fcsi.org
Social Media: *Facebook, Twitter*

William Taunton, Chair
Wade Koehler, Executive Director
Kimberly Kissel, DIRECTOR OF EDUCATION
Mrs. Penny Price, DIRECTOR OF MEMBER SERVICES
James Petersen, SECRETARY/ TREASURER

Professional organization offering design and management consulting services, specialized in the foodservice and hospitality industry across the world.
Founded in 1955

9611 Foodservice Sales and Marketing Association

Grocery Manufactures Association
1801-J York Road
Suite 384
Lutherville, MD 21093

410-715-4084
800-617-1170

FAX 888-668-7496
E-Mail: info@fsmaonline.com
Home Page: www.fsmaonline.com
Social Media: *Facebook, Twitter, LinkedIn, Youtube*

Rick Abraham, President & CEO
Sharon Boyle, Vice President
Stuart Wolff, Chairman
Dan Cassidy, CEO of Key Imapct Sales
Jessica Muffoletto, Manager, Membership & Meetings

Advances the interests of the food, beverage and consumer products industry on key issues that effect the ability of brand manufacturers their products profitably and deliver superior value to the consumer.
250 Members
Founded in 2003

9612 Fresh Mushrooms - Nature's Hidden Treasure
2880 Zanker Road
Suite 203
San Jose, CA 95134

408-432-7210
FAX 408-432-7213
E-Mail: info@mushroomcouncil.org
Home Page: www.mushroomcouncil.org
Social Media: *Facebook, Twitter, YouTube, Pinterest, Google+, R*

Carla Blackwell-Mckinney, Vice Chair
Robert Crouch, Secretary

Plays an important role in the national promotion of fresh mushrooms through consumer public relations, foodservice communications and retail communications.
Founded in 1993
Mailing list available for rent

9613 Fresh Produce Association of the Americas
590 East Frontage Road
PO Box 848
Nogales, AZ 85621

520-287-2707
FAX 520-287-2948
E-Mail: info@freshfrommexico.com
Home Page: www.freshfrommexico.com

Alejandro Canelos, Chairman
Matt Mandel, Chairman Elect

Represents more than 125 member companies involved in growing, harvesting, marketing and importing of Mexican produce entering the US at Nogales, Arizona.
125 Members
Founded in 1944

9614 Fresh Produce and Floral Council
2400 E. Katella Ave.
Ste. 330
Anaheim, CA 92806

714-739-0177
FAX 714-739-0226
E-Mail: info@fpfc.org
Home Page: www.fpfc.org

Brad Martin, Chairman
Marvin Quebec, Chair Elect
Carissa Mace, President
Connie Stukenberg, Treasurer/Secretary
AMY WUN, MANAGER MEMBER PROGRAMS

Provides unique networking and business growth opportunities for professionals in the produce and floral industries in California. Members include growers, snippers, wholesalers, brokers, distributors and retailers of produce and/or floral items.
500 Members
Founded in 1965

9615 Frozen & Refrigerated Association of the North East
PO Box 6377
Wolcott, CT 06716-0377

203-597-7215
FAX 203-879-0594
E-Mail: frane@frane.org
Home Page: www.frane.org
Social Media: *Facebook*

Jim Wright, Chair
Donna Maglio, Executive Chair
Jason Adams, Director
Sal Marrocco, Vice-President
John Powers, Director

Non-profit regional trade association, representing the ever changing frozen and refrigerated industries throughout the Northeast. It remains one of the largest and most active associations in the United States and is affiliated with the National Frozen & Refrigerated Association (NFRA).
135 Members
Founded in 1955

9616 Future Food
101 Finsbury Pavement
London, UK EC2A 1RS

203-002-3002
FAX 203-003-3003
E-Mail: prteam@marcusevans.com
Home Page: www.marcusevans.com
Social Media: *Facebook, Twitter, LinkedIn, Googleplus,vimeo*

European events and publications for food industry.
Founded in 1983

9617 Ginseng Board of Wisconsin
668 Maratech Avenue
Suite E
Marathon, WI 54448

715-443-2444
FAX 715-443-2444
E-Mail: ginseng@ginsengboard.com
Home Page: www.ginsengboard.com

Joe Heil, President

Representing Wisconsin Ginseng producers as the worldwide leader of the American Ginseng industry, committed to the advertising, promotion and the sale of Wisconsin Ginseng, the purest ginseng in the world. Working to improve the health and wellness of consumers while suporting the sustainability of the industry and the rural economy associated with it.
Founded in 1986

9618 Glass Packaging Institute
1220 North Fillmore Street
Suite 400
Arlington, VA 22201

703-684-6359
FAX 703-546-0588
E-Mail: info@gpi.org
Home Page: www.gpi.org
Social Media: *Facebook, Twitter*

Andres Lopez, Chairman
Lynn M. Bragg, President
John Riordan, Director
Sanjay Gandhi, Director
John Gallo, Director

Represents the North American glass container industry. Through GPI, glass container manufacturers speak with one voice to advocate industry standards, promote sound environmental policies and educate packaging professionals. Member companies manufacture glass containers for food, beverage, cosmetic and many other products.
Founded in 1919

9619 Global Cold Chain Alliance
1500 King Street
Suite 201
Alexandria, VA 22314-2730

703-373-4300
FAX 703-373-4301
E-Mail: email@gcca.org
Home Page: www.gcca.org
Social Media: *Facebook, Twitter, LinkedIn*

Corey Rosenbuch, President & COO
Megan Costello, Vice President of Member & Industry
Rita Haley, Executive Assistant and Manager
Richard Tracy, Vice President
Tori Miller Liu, Director of Information Systems

The Global Cold Chain Alliance (GCCA) is committed to building and strengthening the temperature-controlled supply chain around the world. As part of that mission, GCCA provides specialized cold chain advisory services to government agencies, organizations, and associations through its core partner, the World Food Logistics Organization (WFLO)
900 Members
Frequency: Membership Dues Vary
Founded in 1891

9620 Glutamate Association: US
1010 Wiconsin Ave. NW
Ste. 350
Washington, DC 20007

202-384-1840
FAX 202-384-1850
E-Mail: info@watsongreenllc.com
Home Page: www.msgfacts.com
Social Media: *Facebook, Twitter, LinkedIn*

Lisa Watson, Executive Director

(TGA) ia an association of manufacturers,national marketers,and processed food users of glutamic acid and its salts, principally the flavor enhancer, monosodium glutamat (MSG). TGA seeks to povide an effective channel of communucation among its members, the public,the media,the scientific community, foof professionals and government officials about the use and safety of glutamates.
12 Members
Founded in 1977

9621 Golden Gold Chain Alliance
1500 King Street
Suite 201
Alexandria, VA 22314-2730

703-373-4300
FAX 703-373-4301
E-Mail: email@gcca.org
Home Page: www.gcca.org
Social Media: *Facebook, Twitter, LinkedIn*

Corey Rosenbuch, President & COO
Megan Costello, Vice President of Member & Industry
Rita Haley, Executive Assistant and Manager
Richard Tracy, Vice President
Tori Miller Liu, Director of Information Systems

The Global Cold Chain Alliance (GCCA) is committed to building and strengthening the temperature-controlled supply chain around the world. As part of that mission, GCCA provides specialized cold chain advisory services to government agencies, organizations, and associations through its core partner, the World Food Logistics Organization (WFLO)
900 Members
Founded in 1891

9622 Grocery Manufacturers Association
1350 Eye (I) Street NW
Suite 300
Washington, DC 20005

202-639-5900
FAX 202-639-5932
E-Mail: info@gmaonline.org
Home Page: www.gmaonline.org
Social Media: *Facebook, Twitter, RSS*

Advances the interests of the food, beverage and consumer products industry on key issues that affect the ability of brand manufacturers to market their products profitably and deliver superior value to the consumer.
Founded in 1908

9623 Hand in Hand Foundation
PO Box 67351
Scott's Valley, CA 95067

831-438-3736
FAX 831-535-6331
E-Mail: adoptions@handinhand.us
Home Page: www.handinhandfoundation.com

David Boschen, Director
Melissa Thomas, Case Worker
April Pao, Case Worker
Kristi VanPyken, Case Worker
Katie Garcia, Office Administrator

Not for profit that solicits food and donations for the needy.
Founded in 1971

9624 Hazelnut Council
424 2nd Avenue W
Seattle, WA 98119

206-270-4321
FAX 206-270-4656
E-Mail: info@hazelnutcouncil.org
Home Page: www.hazelnutcouncil.org

The Hazenut Council represents the world's leading hazelnut producers, importers and distributors.

9625 Healthy Water Association
PO Box 1417
Patterson, CA 95363

408-897-3023
FAX 408-897-3028
E-Mail: paulmason@mgwater.com
Home Page: www.mgwater.com/hwa.shtml

Paul Mason, President

Serves the bottled water industry.

9626 Herb Growing and Marketing Network
PO Box 245
Silver Spring, PA 17575-0245

717-393-3295
FAX 717-393-9261
E-Mail: herbworld@aol.com
Home Page: www.herbworld.com

Maureen Rogers, Director

The largest trade association for the herb industry.
Cost: $48.00
1000+ Members
Founded in 1990

9627 Herb Research Foundation
5589 Arapahoe Ave
Suite 205
Boulder, CO 80303

303-449-2265
FAX 303-449-7849
E-Mail: info@herbs.org
Home Page: www.herbs.org

Rob McCaleb, President

Provides scientific based and traditional information about use and safety of herbs for health.

Fee based hotline, information packs and literature are available to all.
Founded in 1983
Mailing list available for rent

9628 Herb Society of America
9019 Kirtland Chardon Rd
Kirtland, OH 44094

440-256-0514
FAX 440-256-0541
E-Mail: herbs@herbsociety.org
Home Page: www.herbsociety.org
Social Media: *YouTube, Wordpress*

Katrinka Morgan, Executive Director
Amy Rogers, Administrative Assistant
Robin Siktberg, Editor/Horticulturist
Brent DeWitt, Editor/Graphic Designer
Karen Frandanisa, Accountant

An organization that focuses on educating its members and the public on the cultivation of herbs and the study of their history and uses, both past and present.
Founded in 1933

9629 Holstein Association USA
1 Holstein Place
PO Box 808
Brattleboro, VT 05302-0808

802-254-4551
800-952-5200
FAX 802-254-8251
Home Page: www.holsteinusa.com
Social Media: *Facebook, Twitter, YouTube*

Glen E. Brown, President
Gordie Cook, Vice President
Barbara Casna, Treasurer
John M. Meyer, Executive Secretary
John S. Burket, Board of Directors

The world's largest dairy cattle breed organization offering information services to all dairy producers.
Founded in 1903

9630 Home Baking Association
10841 S Crossroads Drive
Suite 105
Parker, CO 80138

785-478-3283
FAX 785-478-3024
Home Page: www.homebaking.org
Social Media: *Facebook, Twitter, Flickr, Wordpress*

Kent Symms, President
Sam Garlow, First Vice President
Eric Wall, Second Vice President

Promoting home baking by providing educators tools and knowledge to perpetuate future generations of home bakers.
Founded in 1951
Mailing list available for rent

9631 Hospitality Link
866 SE 14th Terrace
Suite 128
Deerfield Beach, FL 33441

954-579-1802
FAX 954-421-1046
E-Mail: info@hospitalitylink.com
Home Page: www.hospitalitylink.com
Social Media: *LinkedIn*

Provides consulting for food technology.

9632 Hydroponic Society of America
PO Box 1183
El Cerrito, CA 94530

510-926-2908
Home Page: www.lisarein.com/hydroponics

Joseph O Brien, President

The scientific and educational arm of the hydroponic community. The H.S.A. is rooted in

science and physics, plant physiology and photo-biology and the other 16 disciplines required to understand the complexity of the science known as hydroponics. The H.S.A. separates the fiction from the fact, and the truth from the mythology.
Founded in 1976

9633 Independent Bakers Association
PO Box 3731
Washington, DC 20027-0231

202-333-8190
FAX 202-337-3809
E-Mail: independentbaker@yahoo.com
Home Page: www.independentbaker.net
Social Media: *Twitter, LinkedIn*

Ron Cardey, Chairman
Joe Davis, First Vice Chair
Scott Barth, Second Vice Chair
Brian Stevenson, Secretary
Heidi Brenner, Treasurer

National trade association of mostly family owned wholesale bakeries and allied industry trades. Protects the interests of independent wholesale bakers from antitrust and anti-competitive mergers and acquisitions; pressures Congress to support market-oriented farm commodity programs, seeking representation to consider federal labor, tax and environmental law.
400 Members
Founded in 1968

9634 Indian River Citrus League
7925 20th Street
Vero Beach, FL 32966

772-562-2728
FAX 772-562-2577
E-Mail: info@ircitrusleague.org
Home Page: ircitrusleague.org

Rusty Varn, Board of Director
Trey Smith, Board of Director
Scott Lambeth, Board of Director
Daniel R. Richey, Board of Director
Daniel Scott, Board of Directors

Organization of growers in the area. Newsletters, links and contactinformation.
Founded in 1807

9635 Institute of Food Science and Engineering
2650 North Young Avenue
Fayetteville, AR 72704

479-575-4040
FAX 479-575-2165
Home Page: www.uark.edu/depts/ifse

Steve Brooks, President & CEO
Dr. Jean Francois Meullent, Director
Dr. Donald Freeman, Advisory Board
Dr. Patti Landers, Advisory Board
Don McCaskill, Advisory Board

Serves as the primary entity in Arkansas for research, graduate education and extension to help ensure that; food supply is high quality, wholesome, safe and nutritious, value is added to raw agricultural products to enhance economic development of the state, region and nation, and the nutritional needs of society are understood, communicated and met.

9636 Institute of Food Technologists
525 W Van Buren
Suite 1000
Chicago, IL 60607

312-782-8424
800-438-3663
FAX 312-782-8348
E-Mail: info@ift.org
Home Page: www.ift.org

Social Media: *Facebook, Twitter, LinkedIn, Youtube*

Robert Gravani, Chairman
Colin Dennis, President
John Neil Coupland, President-Elect
Christie Tarantino, Executive Vice President
Robert Gravani, Treasurer

A nonprofit scientific society working in food science, food technology, and related professions in industry, academia and government.
18000 Members
Founded in 1939

9637 Institute of Food and Agricultural Sciences (IFAS)
University of Florida
PO Box 110180
Gainesville, FL 32611-0180

352-392-1971
Home Page: www.ifas.ufl.edu
Social Media: *Facebook, Twitter*

Ruth Borger, Assistant Vice President
Jenny Mooney, Manager

A federal-state-county partnership throughout Florida, dedicated to improving your life by developing and providing knowledge in agriculture, natural resources, and life sciences.
Founded in 1906

9638 Institute of Packaging Professionals
One Parkview Plaza
Suite 800
Oakbrook Terrace, IL 60181

630-544-5050
800-432-4085
FAX 630-544-5055
E-Mail: info@iopp.org
Home Page: www.iopp.org
Social Media: *Facebook, Twitter, LinkedIn, YouTube*

Jane Chase, Chair
Toby Wingfield, Treasurer
Dan Alexander, Vice Chair
Robert Meisner, EVP - Education & Certification
Suzanne Simmons, Executive VP-Membership

Information regarding the packaging industry internationally.

9639 Institute of Shortening & Edible Oils
1319 F Street NW
Suite 600
Washington, DC 20004

202-783-7960
FAX 202-393-1367
E-Mail: contactus@iseo.org
Home Page: www.iseo.org

Robert L. Collette, President
Diana L. Stare, Office Administrator

A trade association representing the refiners of edible fats and oils in the United States. Members represent approximately 90-95 percent of the edible fats and oils produced domestically that are used in baking and frying fats (shortening), cooking and salad oils, margarines, spreads, confections and toppings, and ingredients in a wide variety of foods.
Founded in 1936

9640 International Dairy-Deli-Bakery Association (IDDBA)
636 Science Drive
Madison, WI 53711-1073

608-310-5000
FAX 608-238-6330
E-Mail: iddba@iddba.orgÿ
Home Page: www.iddba.org

A nonprofit trade association providing education, training, and marketing resources for food

retailers, manufacturers, brokers, distributors, and other interested professionals.
Founded in 1964

9641 International Association for Color Manufacturers
1101 17th Street NW
Suite 700
Washington, DC 20036

202-293-5800
FAX 202-463-8998
E-Mail: info@iacmcolor.org
Home Page: www.iacmcolor.org
Social Media: *LinkedIn*

David R Carpenter, President & Treasurer
Rohit Tibrewala, President-Elect & Secretary
Bobby Gruber, Director
Philip Kaczmarski, Director
Sue Ann McAvoy, Director

The IACM is a trade association that represents the manufacturers and end-users of coloring substances that are used in foods. Members include producers and users of both certified and exempt colors.
Founded in 1972

9642 International Association of Culinary Professionals
1221 Avenue of the Americas
42nd Floor
New York, NY 10020

646-358-4957
866-358-4951
FAX 866-358-2524
E-Mail: info@iacp.com
Home Page: www.iacp.com
Social Media: *Facebook, Twitter, Youtube, Vimeo*

Martha Holmberg, Chief Executive Officer
Shani Phelan, Member Progams and Ops Manager
Margaret Bradley-Foley, Chair
Glenn Mack, Chair Elect
Kendra McMurray, CMP, Director, Conferences and Events

IACP connects culinary professionals with the people, places, and knowledge they need to succeed. IACP is a worldwide forum for the development and exchange of information, knowledge, and inspiration within the professional food and beverage community. This organization of creative and talented professionals is engaged in and committed to excellence in the food industry.
3000+ Members
Founded in 1978

9643 International Association of Ice Cream and Vendors
3601 East Joppa Road
Baltimore, MD 21234

410-931-8100
FAX 410-931-8111
E-Mail: info@iaicdv.org
Home Page: www.iaicdv.org
Social Media: *Facebook, Twitter, Stumbleupon, Gmail*

Hoss Rafaty, President
Taylor Dubord, Executive Director
Michelle Franklin, Vice President
Nick Nikbakht, Secretary-Treasurer

Members are manufacturers and distributors of ice cream novelties and street vendors.
Founded in 1969

9644 International Association of Milk Control Agencies
Department of Agriculture

Division of Dairy Industry Services
Albany, NY 12235-0001

518-457-3880
FAX 518-485-5816
E-Mail: charlie.huff@agmkt.state.ny.us
Home Page: www.nasda.org/cms

Charles Huff, Secretary/Treasurer

Founded to improve the effectiveness and uniformity of regulation among the economic regulatory agencies and to provide a forum for exchange of information.
Founded in 1935

9645 International Association of Operative Millers
12351 W. 96th Terrace
Suite 100
Lenexa, KS 66215

913-338-3377
FAX 913-338-3553
E-Mail: info@iaom.info
Home Page: www.iaom.info/about/
Social Media: *Facebook, Twitter, LinkedIn*

Roy Loepp, President
Brad Allen, Vice President
Melinda Farris, Executive Vice President
Stephen Doyle, Treasurer
Brad Beckwith, Director

An international organization, comprised of flour millers, cereal grain and seed processors and allied trades representatives and companies devoted to the advancement of technology in the flour milling, cereal grain processing industries.
1500 Members
Founded in 1896

9646 International Banana Society
1901 Pennsylvania Ave NW
Suite 1100
Washington, DC 20006-3412

202-303-3400
FAX 202-303-3433
E-Mail: info@eatmorebananas.com
Home Page: www.bananas.org
Social Media: *Facebook, LinkedIn, Youtube*

A trade organizatoin consisting of members engaged in teh business of importing bananas into the United States. Provides a forum for members to discuss common and technical issues pertaining to banana production, distribution, and marketing.
Founded in 1982

9647 International Beverage Dispensing Equipment Association
PO Box 248
Reisterstown, MD 21136

410-602-0616
877-404-2332
FAX 410-486-6799
E-Mail: ibdea@cornerstoneassoc.com
Home Page: www.ibdea.org
Social Media: *Facebook, LinkedIn, Youtube*

An international non-profit trade association representing companies that sell, lease, rent, manufacture and service beverage dispensing equipment and supplies. Members are companies that provide equipment, related products and services to restaurants, bars, taverns, hospitals, schools and other institutions.
250+ Members
Founded in 1971

9648 International Bottled Water Association

1700 Diagonal Rd
Suite 650
Alexandria, VA 22314

703-683-5213
800-928-3711
FAX 703-683-4074
E-Mail: info@bottledwater.org
Home Page: www.bottledwater.org
Social Media: *Facebook, Twitter, YouTube*

Bryan Shinn, Chairman
Joe Bell, Vice Chairman
Joseph Doss, President
Robert R. Hirst, Vice President
Shayron Barnes-Selby, Treasurer

The leading voice of the bottled water industry and serves to protect the interests of bottled water bottlers, distributors and suppliers.
Founded in 1958

9649 International Chewing Gum Association

1001 G Street NW
Suite 500 West
Washington, DC 20001

E-Mail: information@gumassociation.org
Home Page: www.gumassociation.org

Andy Pharoah, President

The leading voice of the chewing gum industry. ICGA continues to gain recognition and credibility among decision-makers across the globe.

9650 International Council on Hotel, Restaurant and Institutional Education

2810 N Parham Road
Suite 230
Richmond, VA 23294

804-346-4800
FAX 804-346-5009
E-Mail: info@chrie.org
Home Page: www.chrie.org
Social Media: *Facebook, Twitter, LinkedIn*

Maureen Brookes, President
Margaret Steiskal, Vice President
Kathy McCarty, Chief Executive Officer
Wanda Costen, Secretary
Stephanie Hein, Treasurer

A marketplace for facilitating exchanges of information, ideas, research, products and services related to education, training and resource development for the hospitality and tourism industry (food, lodging, recreation and travel services). Serving as the hospitality and tourism education network, striving to unite educators, industry executives and associations.
1400 Members
Founded in 1946

9651 International Dairy Foods Association

1250 H Street NW
Suite 900
Washington, DC 20005

202-737-4332
FAX 202-331-7820
E-Mail: membership@idfa.org
Home Page: www.idfa.org
Social Media: *Facebook, Twitter, YouTube, Blog, Smartbrief*

Patricia Stroup, Chair
Jeffery Kaneb, Vice Chair
Michael Walls, Secretary
Mike Reidy, Treasurer
Connie Tipton, President and CEO

Represents the nation's dairy manufacturing and marketing industries and their suppliers. IDFA is composed of three constituent organizations; Milk Industry Foundation, National Cheese Institute, and the International Ice Cream Association.
550 Members

9652 International Dairy-Deli-Bakery Association

636 Science Drive
PO Box 5528
Madison, WI 53705-0528

608-310-5000
FAX 608-238-6330
E-Mail: iddba@iddba.org
Home Page: www.iddbanet.org

William J. Klump, Chairman
David Leonhardi, Executive Vice Chairman
John Cheesman, Vice Chairman
Jewel Hunt, Treasurer

IDDBA members meet the challenges of today's business world by exchanging information and ideas, participating in educational programs and networking.
Founded in 1964

9653 International Flight Services Association

1100 Johnson Ferry Road
Suite 300
Atlanta, GA 30342

404-252-3663
FAX 404-252-0774
E-Mail: ifsa@kellencompany.com
Home Page: www.ifsanet.com
Social Media: *Facebook, Twitter, LinkedIn, YouTube*

David Loft, Chairperson
Pam Suder Smith, President
Jane Bernier -Tran, Vice President
Paul Platamone, Treasurer
Denise Poole, Secretary

Represents the $14 billion inflight and travel catering industry. Activities include annual conferences, trade shows, seminars and training events around the world.
400 Members
Founded in 1965

9654 International Food Additives Council

1100 Johnson Ferry Road
Suite 300
Atlanta, GA 30342

404-252-3663
FAX 404-252-0774
E-Mail: jrogers@kellencompany.com
Home Page: www.foodadditives.org

An international trade association of food additives manufacturers and businesses having interest in food additives.

9655 International Food Information Council Foundation

1100 Connecticut Ave NW
Suite 430
Washington, DC 20036

202-296-6540
FAX 202-296-6547
E-Mail: info@foodinsight.org
Home Page: www.foodinsight.org
Social Media: *Facebook, Twitter, LinkedIn*

David B. Schmidt, President & CEO
Geraldine McCann, COO
Marianne Smith Edge, Senior VP, Nutrition & Food Safety
Andy Benson, VP, International Relations
Kimberly Reed, President

Dedicated to the mission of effectively communicating science-based information on health, nutrition and food safety for the public good. Independent and non-profit, bringing together, working with, and providing information to consumers, health and nutrition professionals, educators, government officials, and food, beverage, and agricultural industry professionals.
33 Members
Founded in 1985

9656 International Food Processors Association

200 Daingerfield Road
Suite 100
Alexandria, VA 22314-2884

703-684-1080
FAX 703-548-6563

9657 International Food Service Brokers Association

1101 Pennsylvania Avenue
Washington, DC 20004

Home Page: www.foodbrokers.org

1500 Members
ISSN: 0884-7185
Founded in 1956

9658 International Food Service Editorial Council

7 Point Place
PO Box 491
Hyde Park, NY 12538

845-229-6973
FAX 845-229-6973
E-Mail: ifec@ifeconline.com
Home Page: www.ifeconline.com
Social Media: *Facebook, Twitter*

Sam Oches, President
Cathy Holley, Vice President
Bill Schreiber, Secretary
Rachel Tracy, Treasurer
Carol Lally, Executive Director

A networking association that fosters the open exchange of information and the building of productive working relationships among foodservice editor and publicist members. Conferences and other activities offer professional development as well as opportunities to make new contacts and gain hands-on-experience of the food cultures and personalities in cities where conferences are held.
265 Members
Founded in 1956

9659 International Food Service Executives Association

4955 Miller Street
Suite 107
Wheat Ridge, CO 80033

800-893-5499
E-Mail: ifseahqoffice@gmail.com
Home Page: www.ifsea.com
Social Media: *Facebook*

David Orosz, Chairman

Professional association with members from the food service and hospitality profession. IFSEA's mission is to enhance the careers of its members through food service certification, education seminars, networking, student mentorships and community service. Members inclued executive chefs, restaurant owners, catering directors, equipment manufacturers, food suppliers, military, professionals new to the industry and students.
3000 Members
Founded in 1901

9660 International FoodService Manufacturers Association

180 North Stetson Avenue
Suite 850
Chicago, IL 60601

312-540-4400
FAX 312-540-4401

E-Mail: ifma@ifmaworld.com
Home Page: www.ifmaworld.com
Social Media: *Facebook, LinkedIn, YouTube*

Richard Ferranti, Chairman
Joe Bybel, First Vice Chairman
Kevin Delahunt, Vice Chairman
Ben Shanley, Vice Chairman
Don Davis, Treasurer

Member companies of the IFMA can capitalize on opportunities, tackle challenges, as well as gain new customer contact and networking opportunities, education and training that helps company sales force build market share, and leadership roles in such initiatives as GS1.
650 Members
Founded in 1952

9661   International Foodservice Distributors Association
1410 Spring Hill Road
Suite 210
McLean, VA 22102

703-532-9400
FAX 703-538-4673
Home Page: www.ifdaonline.org
Social Media: *Twitter, LinkedIn*

Thomas A. Zatina, Chairman
James Crawford, Vice Chairman
Mark S. Allen, President & CEO
Jonathan Eisen, Senior Vice President
Andrew Mercier, Treasurer

Trade association comprised of food distribution companies that supply independent grocers and food service operations throughout the US, Canada and 19 other countries.
135 Members
Founded in 2003

9662   International Foodservice Distributors Ass
1410 Spring HIll Road
Suite 210
McLean, VA 22102

703-532-9400
FAX 703-538-4673
Home Page: www.ifdaonline.org
Social Media: *Twitter, LinkedIn*

Thomas A. Zatina, Chairman
James Crawford, Vice Chairman
Mark S. Allen, Jr., President/ CEO
Andy Mercier, Treasurer
Jonathan Eisen, SVP, Government Relations

9663   International Glutamate Technical Committee
5775 Peachtree Dunwoody Rd NE
Atlanta, GA 30342

404-252-3663
FAX 404-252-3663
E-Mail: info@aspartame.org
Home Page: www.aspartame.org

Andrew Ebert PhD, Chairman
Judy Rogers, Contact

Members are associations that are engaged in the manufacture, sale and commercial use of glutamates.
8 Members
Founded in 1965

9664   International HACCP Alliance
120 Rosenthal Center
2471 TAMU
College Station, TX 77843-2471

979-862-3643
FAX 979-862-3075
E-Mail: kharris@tamu.edu
Home Page: www.haccpalliance.org

Ranzell Nickelson, Chairman
Rosemary Mucklow, Vice Chairman
Robert Hibbert, Treasurer/ Secretary

Rafael Rivera, Past Chairman
Rena Pietrami, Board of Directors

Provides a uniform program to assure safer meat and poultry products.
Founded in 1994

9665   International Herb Association
PO Box 5667
Jacksonville, FL 32247-5667

904-399-3241
FAX 904-396-9467
Home Page: www.iherb.org

Matthias Reisen, President
Dianna Nance, Vice President
Karen O'Brien, Secretary
Marge Powell, Treasurer
Davy Dabney, Chairman

Supports herb businesses and educates the public.
Founded in 1986

9666   International Institute of Fisheries Economics & Trade
213 Ballard Hall
Corvallis, OR 97331-3601

541-737-2942
FAX 541-737-2563
E-Mail: osuweb@lists.orst.edu
Home Page: www.oregonstate.edu/dept/IIFET

Dr. Dan Holland, President
Dr. Claire Armstrong, President-elect
Ann L. Shriver, Executive Director
Kara Keenan, Assistant

Promotes discussion, research projects and sponsors educational courses. Publications available.
400 Members
Founded in 1982

9667   International Maple Syrup Institute
5072 Rock St. RR#4
Spencerville, ON K0E 1X0

613-658-2329
FAX 877-683-7241
E-Mail: agrofor@ripnet.com
Home Page: www.internationalmaplesyrupinstitute.com

Richard Norman, President
Yvon Poitras, Vice President
Steve Selby, Treasurer
Dave Chapeskie, Executive Director

Members are producers, processors, industry suppliers and others interested in promoting the industry.
15M Members
Founded in 1975

9668   International Natural Sausage Casing Association
12100 Sunset Hills Road
Suite 130
Reston, VA 20190

703-234-4112
FAX 703-435-4390
Home Page: www.insca.kdgp.me

David Blanga, Chairman
Elliot Simon, Vice Chairman
Michael Mayo, Treasurer

The only international association for the natural sausage casing industry. Members include producers, suppliers and brokers of natural casing products.
265+ Members
Founded in 1965

9669   International Olive Council
Principe de Vergara
154
Spain, MD 28002

491-590-3638
FAX 491-563-1263
E-Mail: iooc@internationaloliveoil.org
Home Page: www.internationaloliveoil.org

Jean Louis Barjol, Executive Director

The world's only international intergovernmental organization in the field of olive oil and table olives. The Council is a decisive player in contributing to the sustainable and responsible development of olive growing and serves as a world forum for discussing policymaking issues and tackling present and future challenges.
Founded in 1959

9670   International Organization of the Flavor Industry (IOFI)
Flavor & Extract Manufacturers Association
1101, 17th Street NW
Suite 700
Washington, DC 20036

202-293-5800
FAX 202-462-8998
Home Page: www.femaflavor.org

Kevin Renskers, President
Timothy Webster, President Elect
John Cavallo, Vice President & Secretary
John Cox, Executive Director
Gary Smith, Treasurer

FEMA staff monitors regulations that impact flavor and extracts all around the world.
Frequency: Annual
Founded in 1909
Mailing list available for rent

9671   International Packaged Ice Association
238 East Davis Blvd.
Suite 213
Tampa, FL 33606

813-258-1690
800-742-0627
FAX 919-251-2783
E-Mail: jane@packagedice.com
Home Page: www.packagedice.com

John Smibert, Chairman
Tommy Sedler, Vice Chairman/ Treasurer
Dann Ades, Secretary/ Assistant Treasurer
Mike Ringstaff, Conference Chairman
Bo Russell, Immediate Past Chairman

A trade association representing manufacturers and distributors of packaged ice and manufacturers of ice making equipment.
400 Members
Frequency: Call For Membership Info
Founded in 1917

9672   International Society of Beverage Technologists(ISBT)
14070 Proton Rd
Suite 100, LB 9
Dallas, TX 75244-3601

972-233-9107
FAX 972-490-4219
E-Mail: office@bevtech.org
Home Page: www.bevtech.org

Brian Stegmann, President
Cloeann Durham, 1st Vice President
Sieg Mueller, 2nd Vice President
Larry Hobbs, Executive Director
Jessica Anacker, Director

Enhance promotiee, development and dissemination of knowledge relating to art and science of beverage technology. Focus ares include beverage formulation, production, packaging and more. We provide forums, stimulate the uise of science in the industry, encourage and foster research.

9673 International Warehouse Logistics Association
2800 S River Rd
Suite 260
Des Plaines, IL 60018

847-813-4699
FAX 847-813-0115
E-Mail: email@iwla.com
Home Page: www.iwla.com

Rob Doyle, Chairman
Mark DeFabis, Vice Chairman
Steve DeHaan, President & CEO
Clifford Otto, Treasurer
Frank Anderson, Secretary

A trade association of warehouse logistics providers that helps members run high-quality, profitable businesses. IWLA focuses on the warehouse logistics business, providing ideas and information that make it easier for member companies to succeed.
Founded in 1891

9674 Interstate Professional Applicators Association
PO Box 1420
Milton, WA 98354-1420

253-922-9437
FAX 253-922-3788

Provides education and information for the professional horticultural applicator. Legislative work involves the states of Washington, Oregon, Idaho in the area of laws and regulations.

9675 Iowa Meat Processors Association
PO Box 334
Clarence, IA 52216

563-452-3329
FAX 563-452-2141
E-Mail: execdirector@iowameatprocessors.org
Home Page: www.iowameatprocessors.org

Tom Taylor, President
Merrill Angell, 1st Vice President
Dave Burma, 2nd Vice President
Jason Ludwig, 3rd Vice President
Marcia Richmann, Executive Directors

An organization comprised of beef, pork, wild game, and poultry processors and allied businesses from throughout the state of Iowa. Members include slaughterers, food service companies, packers, locker operators, butcher shops, ham manufacturers, smokehouse owners, wholesalers, custom operations, retail operations, and companies that supply goods and services to the meat industry.

9676 Islamic Food and Nutrition Council of America (IFANCA)
777 Busse Hwy
Park Ridge, IL 60068

847-993-0034
FAX 847-993-0038
E-Mail: m.masood@ifanca.org;
z.sadek@ifanca.org
Home Page: www.ifanca.org
Social Media: *Facebook, Twitter, LinkedIn, Youtube,stumbleupon,digg,frien*

Zeshan Sadek, Director International Services
Mujahid Masood, Ph.D., Senior Food Scientist

A non-profit Islamic organization dedicated to promote halel food and the institution of halel.
Founded in 1982

9677 Italian Trade Agency
Italian Trade Commission

33 E 67th St
New York, NY 10065-5949

212-980-1500
FAX 212-758-1050
E-Mail: newyork@ice.it
Home Page: www.italtrade.com

Pace Marisa, Executive Secretary
Augusta Smargiassi, Senior Deputy Trade Commissioner
Antonio Lucarelli, Senior Trade Commission

The Italian government agency entrusted with the promotion of trade, business opportunities and industrial cooperation between Italian and foreign companies. It supports the internationalisation of Italian firms and their consolidation in foreign markets.

9678 Italian Wine and Food Institute
One Grand Central Place
60 East 42nd St. Suite 2214
New York, NY 10165

212-867-4111
FAX 212-867-4114
E-Mail: iwfi@aol.com
Home Page:
www.italianwineandfoodinstitute.com

Lucio Caputo, President
Vincent Giampaolo, VP

Members are producers, distributors and marketers of Italian wines and foods.
Founded in 1983

9679 Juice Products Association
750 National Press Building
529 14th Street NW
Washington, DC 20045

202-785-3232
FAX 202-223-9741
E-Mail: jpa@kellencompany.com
Home Page: www.juiceproducts.org

Richard E Cristol, President
Carol Freysinger, Executive Director
Patricia Faison, Technical Director
Darrell McCook, Meetings Manager
Jim Wolters, Account Coordinator

The trade association for the fruit and juice products industry, including juice processors, packers, extractors, brokers as well as marketers of fruit juices and vegetable juices, juice beverages, fruit jams, jellies and preserves and similar products. JPA also represents juice industry suppliers and food testing laboratories and includes firms engaged in the trading of frozen concentrated orange juice futures and/or options on behalf of JPA processor members.
135 Members
Founded in 1957

9680 LaSalle Food Processing Association
108 S Broadway
PO Box 97
La Salle, MN 56056-0097

507-375-3408
FAX 507-642-3077

Pat Thiner, Manager

A meat packers trade association.

9681 Leafy Greens Council
PO Box 143
Waterport, NY 14571

716-517-0248
Home Page: www.leafy-greens.org

Ray Clark, Executive Director
Robert Strube, President

Purpose is to improve the marketing and increase consumption through national promotions, to educate consumers about the nutritional values of leafy greens through media campaigns, to represent member interests to government, and to provide networking opportunities for members. Members represent growers, shippers, brokers, terminal market operators, and suppliers.
117 Members
Founded in 1974

9682 Les Amis d'Escoffier Society of New York, Inc.
787 Ridgewood Road
Millburn, NJ 07041

212-414-5820
FAX 973-379-3117
Home Page: www.escoffier-society.com

Mark Arnao, President
George McNeill, First Vice President
Jay Jones, Secretary
Kurt Keller, TREASURER

Providing opportunitites for members' delight and edification and also generate gains in the perfection of the art of fine dining. Membership consists of chefs de cuisine, hotel executives, restaurateurs and business executives.
Founded in 1936

9683 Livestock Marketing Association
10510 NW Ambassador Drive
Kansas City, MO 64153

816-891-0502
800-821-2048
FAX 816-891-0552
E-Mail: lmainfo@lmaweb.com
Home Page: www.lmaweb.com
Social Media: *Facebook, Twitter*

Tim Starks, Chairman
Dan Harris, President
BRIAN GLICK, DIRECTOR
Mark Mackey, Chief Executive Officer
SHERI CRIST, INTERIM CHIEF FINANCIAL OFFICER

Committed to the support and protection of the local livestock auction markets. LMA is the voice for the auction markets on legislative and regulatory issues and in providing member services to maintain successful, viable marketing businesses and better service to all of the livestock producers who sell at auction.

9684 Machalek Communications, Inc.
Machalek Communications
12550 W Frontage Road
Suite 220
Burnsville, MN 55337

952-736-8000
800-846-5520
FAX 866-490-8834
E-Mail: info@machalek.com
Home Page: www.machalek.com
Social Media: *Facebook, LinkedIn*

Andrea McChalek, President/CEO
Deanna Morin, Vice Pres. of Business Development
Krista Gardner, Office Manager
Maria Palmer, Lead Graphic and Web Designer

Includes over 20 employees and publishes seven nationwide postcard advertising decks. Distributes more then 100 million postcards per year to over 800,000 qualified buyers. Company has furthermore evolved to include additional sales lead generation services including list rental, mail, and internet marketing.
25 Members
Founded in 1987
Mailing list available for rent

9685 Maraschino Cherry and Glace Fruit Processors
3301 State Route 66
Neptune, NJ 07753

732-922-3008

Richard Sullivan, Executive VP

9686 Master Brewers Association of the Americas
3340 Pilot Knob Rd.
St. Paul, MN 55121

651-454-7250
FAX 651-454-0766
E-Mail: mbaa@mbaa.com
Home Page: www.mbss.com
Social Media: *Facebook, Twitter, LinkedIn, Pinterest*

Amy Hope, Executive Vice President
Global association for the advancement of the brewing and allied industries.
3000 Members
Founded in 1887

9687 Material Handling Industry of America
8720 Red Oak Blvd
Suite 201
Charlotte, NC 28217-3996

704-676-1190
FAX 704-676-1199
E-Mail: dvarner@mhi.org
Home Page: www.mhi.org
Social Media: *Facebook, Twitter, LinkedIn, YouTube*

Dave Young, Executive Chairman
John Paxton, President
Gregg E. Goodner, Vice President
George Prest, CEO
Donna Varner, Executive Administrator

The complexity of managing supply chains that span continents and dominate markets demands strategies, equipment and systems that are agile, adaptable, and aligned. With product lifecycles shortening and worldwide competition increasing, success depends on effective material handling and logistics solutions for the global supply chain. Being able to deliver the right product to the right market at the right time.

9688 Meat & Livestock Australia
Level 1, 40 Mount Street
Locked Bag 991
North Sydney, NS 2060

294-639-333
FAX 294-639-393
E-Mail: info@mla.com.au
Home Page: www.mla.com.au
Social Media: *Facebook, Twitter, YouTube*

Michele Allan, Chairman
Richard Norton, Managing Director
Lucinda Corrigan, Director
Geoffrey Maynard, Director
John McKillop, Director

Providing marketing and research and development services to cattle, sheep and goat producer members and the broader red meat industry to help them meet community and consumer expectations. MLA is committed to fostering world leadership for the Australian red meat and livestock industry for creating opportunities for its stakeholders, the environment, red meat consumers and the community.
30000 Members
Founded in 1998

9689 Meat & Livestock Australia, North American Region
1401 K Street NW
Suite 602
Washington, DC 20005

202-521-2551
FAX 202-521-2699
E-Mail: info@mlana.com

Home Page: www.australian-meat.com
Social Media: *Facebook, Twitter, YouTube*

David Pietsch, Regional Manager, North America
Scott Hansen, Managing Director

Providing marketing and research and development services to cattle, sheep and goat producer members and the broader red meat industry to help them meet community and consumer expectations. MLA is committed to fostering world leadership for the Australian red meat and livestock industry for creating opportunities for its stakeholders, the environment, red meat consumers and the community.
30000 Members
Founded in 1998

9690 Meat Import Council of America
1901 Fort Myer Dr
Suite 1110
Arlington, VA 22209

703-522-1910
800-522-1910
FAX 703-524-6039
E-Mail: lauriebryant@micausa.org
Home Page: www.micausa.org

Kim Holzner, Chairman
David Rind, Vice Chairman
Donald E. Stewart, Treasurer
Laurie I. Bryant, Executive Director & Secretary

To foster the trade, commerce and interests of importers and exporters of fresh and/or frozen and/or cured and/or cooked and/or canned meats.
130 Members
Founded in 1962

9691 Meat Trade Institute
213 South Avenue East
Spencer Savings Bank Building
Cranford, NJ 07016

908-276-5111
FAX 212-279-4016
E-Mail: sflannagan@sprintmail.com
Home Page: www.spcnetwork.com/mti/

John J. Calcangno, President

A full-time fully-staffed trade association serving meat and poultry industries in the northeast. The Institute seeks to build and strengthen the relationships of its members with government, labor, and all other segments of the meat and poultry industry.

9692 Mid-Atlantic Canners Association
316 S Front Street
Hamburg, PA 19526

610-562-3061
FAX 610-562-0281

Robert Crosswell, Crosswell
D Seibert, VP Finance

Mid Atlantic Canners Association is a cooperative soft drink canning facility for the Coca-Cola system. All of the national Coca-Cola Company brands are canned, packaged and shipped by truck to various Coca-Cola franchised distributors located throughout the northeast United States.

9693 Mid-Atlantic Dairy Association
325 Chestnut St
Suite 600
Philadelphia, PA 19106

215-627-8800
FAX 215-627-8887
E-Mail: dairyspot@milk4u.org
Home Page: www.dairyspot.com
Social Media: *Facebook, Twitter, LinkedIn, Youtube, Pinterest, Googleplus*

Patty Purcell, CEO

Mid-Atlantic Dairy Association is one of 19 state and regional promotion organizations working under the umbrella of the United Dairy Industry Association. Working to bring a fully integrated national promotion program to the Mid-Atlantic region.
Mailing list available for rent

9694 Mid-States Meat Association
1335 Dublin Rd
Suite 10
Columbus, OH 43215-1000

614-459-5188
FAX 614-442-5516
E-Mail: kristin@ohiogrowers.org
Home Page: www.midstatesmeat.org

Kristin Mullins, Executive Director
100 Members

9695 Midwest Dairy Association
2015 Rice St
St Paul, MN 55113

651-488-0261
800-642-3895
FAX 651-488-0265
E-Mail: snewell@midwestdairy.com
Home Page: www.midwestdairy.com
Social Media: *Facebook, Twitter, Youtube, Pinterest*

Mike Kruger, CEO

Works on behalf of dairy farmers to increase dairy sales, foster innovation and inspire consumer confidence in dairy products and practices.
210M Members
Founded in 1940

9696 Midwest Food Processors Association
4600 American Pkwy
Suite 210
Madison, WI 53718-8334

608-255-9946
FAX 608-255-9838
E-Mail: info@mwfpa.org
Home Page: www.mwfpa.org
Social Media: *Facebook, Twitter, LinkedIn*

Nick George, President
Brian Elliot, Director of Communications
Robin Fanshaw, Manager
Brian Deschane, Director of Operations

Trade association that advocates on behalf of food processing companies and affiliated industries in Illinois, Minnesota, and Wisconsin. Influencing public policy and making the Midwest a great place for food processors to do business. Advocating, educating, communicating, and facilitating.
Founded in 1905

9697 Missouri Grocers Association
315 North Ken Avenue
Springfield, MO 65802

417-831-6667
FAX 417-831-3907
E-Mail: cmcmillian@missourigrocers.com
Home Page: www.missourigrocers.com
Social Media: *Facebook*

Erick Taylor, Chairman
John Porter, President
Mike Beal, Vice President
Chuck Murfin, III, Treasurer
Dan Shaul, State Director

Committed to the growth and profitability of its members by providing proactive state and federal legislative and regulatory representation, effective communication, beneficial member services, and education of industry innovations.

9698 Mushroom Council
2880 Zanker Road
Suite 203
San Jose, CA 95134

408-432-7210
FAX 408-432-7213
E-Mail: info@mushroomcouncil.org
Home Page: www.mushroomcouncil.org
Social Media: *Facebook, Twitter, YouTube, Pinterest, Google+, R*

Carla Blackwell-Mckinney, Vice Chair
Robert Crouch, Secretary

Plays an important role in the national promotion of fresh mushrooms through consumer public relations, foodservice communications and retail communications.
Founded in 1993

9699 National Advisory Group
19111 Detroit Road
Suite 201
Rocky River, OH 44116

440-250-1583
E-Mail: info@nagconvenience.com
Home Page: www.nag-net.com
Social Media: *Facebook*

Ben Jatlow, Chairman
Mary Banmiller, President

Mission is to provide industry retail leaders a peer-to-peer forum for the exchange of ideas to improve their business performance.
Founded in 1992

9700 National Agri-Marketing Association
11020 King Street
Suite 205
Overland Park, KS 66210

913-491-6500
FAX 913-491-6502
E-Mail: agrimktg@nama.org
Home Page: www.nama.org
Social Media: *Facebook, Twitter, LinkedIn, YouTube, Flickr*

Marvin Kokes, President
Matt Coniglio, 1st Vice President
Amy Bugg, Vice President
Amber Harrison, Vice President
Amy Bradford, Secretary/Treasurer

The nation's largest association for professionals in marketing and agribusiness.
Cost: $170.00
3500 Members
Frequency: Membership Dues
Founded in 1957

9701 National Agriculture Day
11020 King St
Suite 205
Overland Park, KS 66210

913-491-1895
FAX 913-491-6502
E-Mail: info@agday.org
Home Page: www.agday.org
Social Media: *Facebook, Twitter, YouTube, Flickr*

Curt Blades, Chair
Annette Degnan, Vice Chair
Lynn Henderson, Board of Director
Tres Bailey, Board of Director
Colin Woodall, Board of Director

An organization uniquely composed of leaders in the agriculture, food and fiber communities dedicated to increasing the public awareness of agriculture's vital role in our society.
Founded in 1973

9702 National Alcohol Beverage Control Association
4401 Ford Avenue
Suite 700
Alexandria, VA 22302-1433

703-578-4200
FAX 703-820-3551
E-Mail: nabca.info@nabca.org
Home Page: www.nabca.org
Social Media: *Facebook, Twitter, Youtube, Google*

Stephen Larson, Chairman
Stephanie O'Brien, Chairman-Elect
James M. Sgueo, President & CEO
Jeffrey R. Anderson, Board of Director
Andrew J. Deloney, Board of Director

It is the mission of the National Alcohol Beverage Control Association to support and benefit alcohol control systems by providing research, fostering relationships, and managing resources to address policy for the responsible sale and consumption of alcohol beverages. Members include control jurisdictions, supplier members and industry trade associations.
175 Members
Frequency: Membership Dues Vary
Founded in 1938

9703 National Association for the Specialty Food Trade
Home Page: www.specialtyfood.com
Social Media: *Facebook, Twitter, LinkedIn, YouTube, Pinterest*

Nonprofit business trade association established to foster trade, commerce, and interest in the specialty food industry.
Founded in 1952

9704 National Association of Agricultural Educators
University of Kentucky
300 Garrigus Building
Lexington, KY 40546-0215

859-257-2224
800-509-0204
FAX 859-323-3919
E-Mail: naae@uky.edu
Home Page: www.naae.org
Social Media: *Facebook, Twitter*

Charlie Sappington, President
Terry Rieckman, President-Elect
Jay Jackman, Executive Director
Alissa Smith, Associate Executive Director
Linda Berry, Staff Support Associate

A federation of 50 affiliated state vocational agricultural teacher associations. The mission is to provide agricultural education for the global community through visionary leadership, advocacy and service.
7600 Members
Founded in 1948

9705 National Association of Animal Breeders
PO Box 1033
Columbia, MO 65205

573-445-4406
FAX 573-446-2279
E-Mail: naab-css@naab-css.org
Home Page: www.naab-css.org

Charles Sattler, Chairman
Dr. Nate Zwald, Vice-Chairman
Gordon A. Doak, President
Gordon A. Doak, Secretary/Treasurer
Gordon A. Doak, Secretary/Treasurer

Unite those individuals and organizations engaged in the artificial insemination of cattle and other livestock into an affiliated federation operating under self-imposed standards of performance and to conduct and promote the mu-

tual interest and ideals of its members. Members are farmer co-ops and others interested in livestock improvement.
Founded in 1946

9706 National Association of Beverage Importers Inc.
529 14th St NW
Suite 1183
Washington, DC 20045

202-393-6224
FAX 202-393-6595
Home Page: www.bevimporters.org

John F. Beaudette, Chairman
Michael J. Rudy, Chairman of the Committee
Stacey M. Tank, Vice Chairman
William T. Earle, President
Marc P. Goodrich, Treasurer

Trade association representing US importers of alcohol beverages, representing the interests of importers of alcohol beverages on issues that have a principal impact on importers, and cooperating with other trade associations on issues that impact all alcohol beverages whether imported or domestic.
Founded in 1934

9707 National Association of Concessionaires
180 N. MICHIGAN AVENUE
Suite 2215
Chicago, IL 60601

312-236-3858
FAX 312-236-7809
E-Mail: info@naconline.org
Home Page: www.naconline.org
Social Media: *Facebook, LinkedIn*

John Evans Jr., Chairman
Jeff Scudillo, Presdient
Terry Conlon, President-Elect
Dan Borschke, Executive Vice President
Andrew Cretors, Treasurer

Trade association for the recreation and leisure-time food and beverage concessions industry. Providing members with information and services that maintain and enhance the standards of excellence and professionalism within the recreation and leisure time food, beverage and related services industry.
800 Members
Founded in 1944

9708 National Association of Convenience Stores
1600 Duke St
7th Floor
Alexandria, VA 22314

703-684-3600
800-684-3600
FAX 703-836-4564
E-Mail: nacs@nacsonline.com
Home Page: www.nacsonline.com
Social Media: *Facebook, Twitter, LinkedIn, YouTube*

Henry Armour, President & CEO
Lyle Beckwith, Sr. VP, Government Relations
Michael Davis, V.P., Member Services
Shirley Jaffe, V.P., Business Operations
Bob Hughes, V.P., Supplier Relations

Providing news, information and resources to the convenience and petroleum retail stores.
4000 Members
Founded in 1961

9709 National Association of Flavors and Food Ingredient Systems
3301 State Route 66
Building C, Suite 205
Neptune, NJ 07753

732-922-3218
FAX 732-922-3590

E-Mail: info@naffs.org
Home Page: www.naffs.org

Dave Adams, Chair
Christine Daley, President
Pia Henzi, President-Elect
Cynthia Astrack, Vice President
Chris Williams, Vice Presdient

A broad-based trade association of manufacturers, processors and suppliers of fruits, flavors, syrups, stabilizers, emulsifiers, colors, sweeteners, cocoa and related food ingredients. Its associate membership is open to all companies that provide products and services to the food industry.
120 Members
Founded in 1917

9710 National Association of Margarine Manufacturers

E-Mail: NAMM@kellencompany.com
Home Page: www.iheartbutterytaste.com
Social Media: *Facebook, Twitter, Pinterest*

Information and recipes about buttery soft spread margarines.

9711 National Association of Pizzeria Operators

909 S 8th Street
Suite 200
Louisville, KY 40203

502-736-9532
FAX 502-736-9502
E-Mail: dwyatt@pizzatoday.com
Home Page: www.napo.com
Social Media: *Facebook, Twitter, Youtube*

Joe Straughan, President
Mary Sullivan, Membership Coordinator

Mission is to create and foster a community of independent and small chain pizzeria operators and their industry suppliers where doing business with another is mutually beneficial.
1100+ Members
Founded in 1984
Mailing list available for rent: 25000 names

9712 National Association of State Departments of Agriculture

4350 North Fairfax Drive
Suite 910
Arlington, VA 22203

202-296-9680
FAX 703-880-0509
E-Mail: nasda@nasda.org
Home Page: www.nasda.org
Social Media: *Facebook, Twitter*

Greg Ibach, President
Michael Strain, 1st Vice President
Steven Reviczky, 2nd Vice President
Jeff Witte, Secretary/Treasurer
Chuck Ross, Director at large

Mission is to represent the state departments of agriculture in the development, implementation, and communication of sound public policy and programs which support and promote the American agricultural industry, while protecting consumers and the environment.
Founded in 1915

9713 National Association of Wheat Growers

415 Second Street NE
Suite 300
Washington, DC 20002-4993

202-547-7800
FAX 202-546-2638
E-Mail: wheatworld@wheatworld.org
Home Page: www.wheatworld.org
Social Media: *Facebook, Twitter, YouTube*

Wayne Hurst, President
Erik Younggren, 1st Vice President

Bing Von Bergen, 2nd Vice President
Paul Penner, Secretary/ Treasurer
Dana Peterson, CEO

A nonprofit partnership of US wheat growers who, by combining their strengths, voices and ideas, are working to ensure a better future for themselfves, their industry and the general public. Focusing on the policies of the US government that affect the livelihoods of US wheat producers.
Founded in 1950

9714 National Association of Wholesalers - Distributors

1325 G Street NW
Suite 1000
Washington, DC 20005-3100

202-872-0885
FAX 202-785-0586
E-Mail: naw@naw.org
Home Page: www.naw.org
Social Media: *Facebook, Twitter, YouTube*

Dirk Van Dongen, President
Jade West, Senior Vice President
James A. Anderson, Junior Vice President
Joy Goldman, Vice President-Administrative
Ron Schreibman, SVP-Strategic Direction

Representing the wholesale distributor industry. NAW is active in these areas: government relations and political action; research and education; and group purchasing. In addition the association operates the Wholesaler-Distributor Political Action Committee, the Distribution Research & Education Foundation, and the NAW Service Corporation.

9715 National Bar and Restaurant Association

307 W Jackson Avenue
Oxford, MS 38655

662-236-5510
FAX 202-331-2429
Home Page: www.bar-restaurant.com

Jennifer Robinson, COO
Laura Speakes, Financial Affairs VP

Founded by Nightclub and Bar magazine, the association's mission is to provide discounts, services and networking opportunities enabling restaurant, bar and hospitality professionals to increase revenues and profits through innovative promotions, marketing and management.
Founded in 1924

9716 National Barbecue Association

P.O. Box 9686
Naperville, IL 60567-9686

331-444-7347
888-909-2121
FAX 502-589-3602
E-Mail: info@nbbqa.org
Home Page: www.nbbqa.org
Social Media: *Facebook, Twitter, LinkedIn, Youtube*

Linda Orrison, President
Dave Raymond, President-Elect
Patrick Murty, Treasurer
Bonnie Gomez, Secretary
Jeff Allen, Executive Director

Mission is to provide the barbeque community with a visionary, beneficial, and responsive association. NBBQA's goals are to promote the art and enjoyment of barbecue, facilitate the effective networking of industry resources and to foster new business opportunities.
Founded in 1991

9717 National Beer Wholesalers Association

1101 King Street
Suite 600
Alexandria, VA 22314-2944

703-683-4300
FAX 703-683-8965
E-Mail: info@nbwa.org
Home Page: www.nbwa.org
Social Media: *Facebook, Twitter, YouTube, Flickr*

Greg LaMantia, Chair
Craig A Purser, President & CEO
Wendy Huerter, Executive Assistant
Patti Rouzie, VP Membership and Meetings
Kathleen Joyce, Communications Director

NBWA represents the interests of America's 2,850 independent, licensed beer distributors which service every congressional district and media market in the country.
Founded in 1938
Mailing list available for rent

9718 National Bison Association

8690 Wolff Ct
200
Westminster, CO 80031

303-292-2833
FAX 303-845-9081
E-Mail: david@bisoncentral.com
Home Page: www.bisoncentral.com
Social Media: *Facebook*

Bruce Anderson, President
Roy Liedtke, Vice-President
Jason Moore, Secretary/Treasurer
Dave Carter, Executive Director
Dick Gehring, Director at Large

Bringing together stakeholders to celebrate the heritage of American bison/buffalo, educating, and creating a sustainable future for our industry.
900 Members
Founded in 1975

9719 National Bulk Vendors Association

1202 East Maryland Avenue
Suite 1k
Phoenix, AZ 85014

888-628-2872
FAX 480-302-5108
E-Mail: admin@nbva.org
Home Page: www.nbva.org
Social Media: *Facebook*

Judi Heston, President
Shawn Dumphy, Vice President
Carl Morcate, Treasurer
John P. Winters, Secretary
George Wells, Membership Chair

A national, not-for-profit trade association comprised of the manufacturers, distributors and operators of bulk vending machines and products.
Founded in 1950

9720 National Cattlemen's Beef Association

9110 E. Nichols Ave.
#300
Centennial, CO 80112

303-694-0305
FAX 303-694-2851
E-Mail: customerservice@beef.org
Home Page: www.beef.org
Social Media: *Facebook, Twitter*

Forrest Roberts, CEO
John Queen III, President
Thad Larson, Director

Consumer focused, producer directed organization representing the largest segment of the nation's food and fiber industry.
28000 Members
Founded in 1898
Mailing list available for rent

9721 National Cherry Growers and Industries Foundation (NCGIF)
2667 Reed Road
Hood River, OR 97031

541-386-5761
FAX 541-386-3191
E-Mail: info@maraschinocherries.org
Home Page: maraschinocherries.org
Social Media: *Facebook, LinkedIn, YouTube, Pinterest*

B J Thurlby, President
Idell Dunn, Assessment Supervisor
Andrew Willis, Promotion Director
Cheryl Kroupa, Marketing Director

Formed for the purpose of having a unified effort from the processed cherry industry to lobby against excessive cherry imports. The foundation compiles and distributes to members a yearly statistical publication of information regarding cherry production, utilization, and sales, both import and export.
Founded in 1948

9722 National Coffee Association
45 Broadway
Suite 1140
New York, NY 10006

212-766-4007
FAX 212-766-5815
E-Mail: info@ncausa.org
Home Page: www.ncausa.org
Social Media: *Facebook, Twitter, LinkedIn*

Bruce Goldsmith, Chairman
John DeMuria, Vice Chairman
William (Bill) Murray, President & CEO
William M. Cortner, Secretary
Thrisha Andrews, Administrative Assistant

Established on the behalf of the coffee companies in the United States. Respond to external issues and represent the coffee industry before the legislative and executive branches of government.
200 Members
Founded in 1911

9723 National Confectioners Association
1101 30th Street NW
Suite 200
Washington, DC 20007

202-534-1440
FAX 202-337-0637
E-Mail: info@candyUSA.com
Home Page: www.candyusa.org
Social Media: *Facebook, Twitter, LinkedIn, YouTube, Pinterest, Instagram*

Peter W. Blommer, Chairman
Michael G. Rosenberg, Vice Chairman
John H. Downs, Jr., President
Martino Caretto, Vice President
John E. Brooks, Jr., Treasurer

Representing the entire confection industry, offering education and leadership in manufacturing, technical research, public relations, retailing practices, government relations, and statistical analyses.
Founded in 1884

9724 National Confectionery Sales Association
Spitfire House
3135 Berea Road
Cleveland, OH 44111

216-631-8200
FAX 216-631-8210

E-Mail: info@candyhalloffame.org
Home Page:
candyhalloffame.org/NCSA/contact.shtml
Social Media: *Facebook, Twitter*

Joe Muck, Chairman
John A. Leipold Jr., President
Russell Berg, Director
David Fleischer, Director
Anthony P. Cognetti, Treasurer

Dedicated to furthering positive growth and acceptance of confectionery and allied products by education, open and frank dialogue, and recognition of peers' notable accomplishments. The Associations' responsibility to principals, customers, members and the community is to represent their products and services professionally and ethically in all relationships.
375 Members
Founded in 1899

9725 National Conference of State Liquor Administrators
543 Long Hill Road
Gurnee, IL 60031

847-721-6410
E-Mail: pamsalario@cox.net
Home Page: www.ncsla.org

Jerry W. Waters, Sr, President
Matthew D. Botting, 1st Vice President
Richard Haymaker, 2nd Vice President
A. Keith Burt, 3rd Vice President
Pamela Frantz, Executive Director

Promoting the enactment of the most effective and equitable types of state alcoholic beverage control laws, to devise and promote the use of methods which provide the best enforcement of the particular alcoholic beverage control laws in each state, to work for the adoption of uniform laws, and to promote harmony with the federal government in its administration.

9726 National Conference on Interstate Milk Shipments
PO Box 108
Monticello, IL 61856

217-762-2656
E-Mail: ncims.bordson@gmail.com
Home Page: www.ncims.org

Dr. Stephen Beam, Chair
David E. Latten, Vice Chair
Marlena G. Bordson, Executive Secretary
Beth Briczinski, Board Member
Ken Anderson, Board Member

The goal is to assure the safest possible milk supply for all the people. The NCIMS is governed by an executive board comprised of representatives from state and local regulatory agencies from three geographical regions; FDA, USDA, industry and laboratories and academia.
Founded in 1940

9727 National Corn Growers Association
632 Cepi Drive
Chesterfield, MO 63005

636-733-9004
FAX 636-733-9005
E-Mail: corninfo@ncga.com
Home Page: www.ncga.com
Social Media: *Facebook, Twitter, Pinterest*

Brent Hostetler, Chair
Jessica Brown, CMP, Meetings Manager
Ellen Campen, Bookkeeper
Chris Novak, Chief Executive Officer
Kathy Baker, Executive Assistant

Mission is to create and increase opportunities for corn growers. The Association will continue to be the recognized leader working in cooperation with its suppliers and customers to maintain sustainability and to achieve new

business and profit opportunities for those it represents.
32300 Members
Founded in 1957
Mailing list available for rent

9728 National Council of Chain Restaurants
1101 New York Ave NW
Washington, DC 20005

202-783-7971
800-673-4692
FAX 202-737-2849
E-Mail: info@nrf.com
Home Page: www.nccr.net
Social Media: *Twitter*

KIP TINDELL, Chairman
MINDY F. GROSSMAN, Vice Chairman
MATTHEW R. SHAY, President & CEO
CARLEEN KOHUT, EVP , CEO
VICKI CANTRELL, SVP, COMMUNITIES AND EXECUTIVE DIRE

The leading trade association exclusively representing chain restaurant companies. Working to advance sound public policy that best serves the interests of restaurant businesses and the millions of people they employ.
Founded in 1965

9729 National Council of Farmer Cooperatives
50 F Street NW
Suite 900
Washington, DC 20001

202-626-8700
FAX 202-626-8722
Home Page: www.ncfc.org
Social Media: *Facebook, Twitter, Flickr*

Charles Conner, President/ CEO
Marlis Carson, SVP, Legal, Tax
Justin Darisse, Vice President, Communications
Lisa Van Doren, Vice President & Chief of Staff
Kevin Natz, Vice President

Regional and national farmer cooperatives.
Founded in 1929

9730 National Country Ham Association
PO Box 948
Conover, NC 28616

828-466-2760
800-820-4426
FAX 828-466-2770
E-Mail: eatham@countryham.org
Home Page: www.countryham.org

Allan Benton, President

Encourages promotion, development and improvement of the businesses of country ham carvers and encourages the use of country carved meats through co-operative methods of production, promotion, education and advertisement.
53 Members
Founded in 1992

9731 National Dairy Council
Interstate Place II
100 Elwood Davis Road
North Syracuse, NY 13212

315-472-9143
FAX 315-472-0506
E-Mail: ndc@dairyinformation.com
Home Page: www.nationaldairycouncil.org
Social Media: *Facebook, Twitter, Pinterest*

This association operates under the auspices of the United Dairy Industry Association. NDC provides timely, scientifically sound nutrition information to the media, physicians, dietitians,

nurses, educators, consumers and others concerned about fostering a healthier society.
Founded in 1915
Mailing list available for rent

9732 National Farmers Organization
528 Billy Sunday Road
Suite 100, P.O. Box 2508
Ames, IA 50010ÿ

800-247-2110
E-Mail: nfo@nfo.org
Home Page: www.nfo.org
Social Media: *Facebook, YouTube*

Paul Olson, President, Chairman
Paul Riniker, Vice President

Members represent a cross-section of both conventional and organic production—grain growers, cattle and hog producers and dairymen and women.

9733 National Farmers Unionÿ
20 F Street NW
Suite 300
Washington, DC 20001

202-554-1600
FAX 202-554-1654
Home Page: www.nfu.org
Social Media: *Facebook, Twitter, LinkedIn, YouTube, Flickr*

Roger Johnson, President
Jeff Knudson, Senior VP, Operations
Chandler Goule, SVP, Programs
Donn Teske, Vice President
Maria Miller, Executive Director

A national federation of state Farmers Union organizations in the United States.
Founded in 1902

9734 National Federation of Coffee Growers of Colombia
140 E 57th St
New York, NY 10022-2765

212-271-8802
Home Page: www.friendsofjuan.com

This organization is comprised of coffee growers from Colombia whose goal is to promote Colombian coffee in the US.

9735 National Frozen & Refrigerated Foods Association Inc.
4755 Linglestown Road Suite 300
PO Box 6069
Harrisburg, PA 17112

717-657-8601
FAX 717-657-9862
E-Mail: info@nfraweb.org
Home Page: www.nfraweb.org
Social Media: *Facebook, Twitter, LinkedIn*

H V Skip Shaw Jr, President/CEO
Jeff Rumachik, Executive Vice President/COO
Julie W. Henderson, Vice President of Communications
Jessica Kurtz, Vice President of Finance
Dayna Jackson, Director of Membership

NFRA is a non-profit trade association representing all segments of the frozen the frozen and refrigerated foods industry. Heaquartered in Harrisburg, PA, NFRA is the sponsor of March National Frozen Food Month, June Dairy Month, and the Summer Favorites Ice Cream novelties promotion as well as the October Cool Food for Kids educational outreach program. NFRA holds the annual National Frozen & Refrigerated Foods Convention in October.
400 Members
Founded in 1945

9736 National Frozen Dessert and Fast Food Association
9614 Tomstown Road
Waynesboro, PA 17268

800-535-7748

This association is made up of small, independent owners and operators of ice cream and fast food establishments.

9737 National Grape Growers Association
2 South Portage Street
Westfield, NY 14787

716-326-5200
FAX 716-326-5494
E-Mail: nationalinfo@welchs.com
Home Page: www.nationalgrape.com

Joseph C Falcone, President

More than just an organization of grape growers, stringent quality growing and harvesting standards, viticultural research, and aggressively funding new product development, manufacturing and marketing programs of Welch's.
Founded in 1897

9738 National Honey Board
11409 Business Park Circle
Suite 210
Firestone, CO 80504-9200

303-776-2337
FAX 303-776-1177
E-Mail: honey@nhb.org
Home Page: www.honey.com
Social Media: *Facebook, Twitter, YouTube, Pinterest, Google+, I*

Jill Clark, Chairperson
Mark Mammen, Vice Chairperson
Margaret Lombard, Chief Executive Officer
Eric S. Wenger, Secretary/Treasurer
Douglas Hauke, Producers

Conducts research, advertising and promotion programs to help maintain and expand domestic and foreign markets for honey.
Founded in 1987
Mailing list available for rent

9739 National Honey Packers & Dealers Association
3301 Route 66
Suite 205, Building C
Neptune, NJ 07753

732-922-3008
FAX 732-922-3590
E-Mail: info@nhpda.org
Home Page: www.nhpda.org

Bob Bauer, Executive Vice President

Comprised of US packers, importers and foreign exporters.

9740 National Hot Dog and Sausage Council
1150 Connecticut Avenue, NW
12th Floor
Washington, DC

202-587-4200
Home Page: www.hot-dog.org
Social Media: *Facebook, YouTube, Pinterest*

Janet Riley, President
Eric Mittenthal, Vice President, Public Affairs

Conducts scientific research to benefit hot dog and sausage manufacturers.
Founded in 1994

9741 National Hot Pepper Association
400 NW 20th Street
Fort Lauderdale, FL 33311-3818

954-565-4972
FAX 954-566-2208
E-Mail: pcppergal@mindspring.com

Networking among industry and private members. Education and information sharing.

9742 National Ice Cream Mix Association
2101 Wilson Blvd
Suite 400
Arlington, VA 22201

703-243-5630
FAX 703-841-9328
E-Mail: nicma@nmpf.org
Home Page: www.icecreammix.org

Joe Duscher, President
Pat Galloway, Vice President
Jamie Jonker, Vice President, Scientific Regs
Bob Kmetz, Treasurer
Tom Balmer, Executive Director

This group is made up of manufacturers of soft-serve ice cream, ice milk, shakes and other dessert mixes.
Founded in 1926

9743 National Ice Cream Retailers Association
1028 W Devon Avenue
Elk Grove Village, IL 60007

847-301-7500
866-303-5960
FAX 847-301-8402
E-Mail: info@nicra.org
Home Page: www.nicra.org
Social Media: *Facebook*

Carl Chaney, President, President Elect
Jim Oden, Vice President
Lynda Utterback, Executive Director
Jill Curran, Secretary/Treasurer

NICRA is a trade organization whose members are in the retail ice cream and frozen dessert business. NICRA will associate with similar associations dedicated to the same interests, facilitate communication and education that both newcomers and veterans in the industry desire to be successful.
500 Members
Founded in 1933
Mailing list available for rent

9744 National Mango Board
3101 Maguire Blvd
Suite 111
Orlando, FL 32803

407-629-7318
877-MAN-OS 1
Home Page: www.mango.org
Social Media: *Facebook, Twitter, Pinterest, YouTube*

Lucy Keith, Consumer Media
Susan Hughes, Foodservice
Kristine Concepcion, Mango Industry Contact
Katie Ola, Trade Media
Wendy McManus, Retail Contact

A national promotion and research organization which is supported by assessments from domestic and imported mangos.

9745 National Meat Canners Association
1150 Connecticut Avenue, NW
12th Floor
Washington, DC 20036

202-587-4200
FAX 202-587-4300
E-Mail: webmaster@meatami.com

761

Home Page: www.meatami.org
Social Media: *Facebook, Twitter, LinkedIn*

Nick Merigolli, Chairman
Greg Benedict, Vice-Chairman
Barry Carpenter, President & CEO
J. Michael Townsley, Treasurer
John Vatri, Secretary

AMI is the national trade association representing companies that process 70 percent of U.S. meat and their suppliers throughout America.

9746 National Milk Producers Federation

2101 Wilson Blvd
Suite 400
Arlington, VA 22201

703-243-6111
FAX 703-841-9328
E-Mail: info@nmpf.org
Home Page: www.nmpf.org
Social Media: *Facebook, Twitter, Flickr, YouTube*

Randy Mooney, Chairman
Ken Nobis, 1st Vice Chairman
Adrian Boer, 2nd Vice Chairman
Mike McCloskey, 3rd Vice Chairman
Pete Kappelman, Treasurer

Develops and carries out policies that advance the well being of dairy producers and the cooperatives they own. Provides a forum through which dairy farmers and their cooperatives formulate policy on national issues that affect milk production and marketing.
Founded in 1916
Mailing list available for rent

9747 National Oilseed Processors Association

1300 L St NW
Suite 1020
Washington, DC 20005

202-842-0463
FAX 202-842-9126
E-Mail: nopa@nopa.org
Home Page: www.nopa.org

Thomas A. Hammer, President
David J. Hovermale, Executive Vice President
David C. Ailor, Executive Vice President
Jeanne L. Seibert, Office Administrator

Represents firms engaged in the actual processing of oilseeds, and associate firms who are consumers of vegetable oil or oilseed meal, including some refiners and mixed feed manufacturers.
Founded in 1929

9748 National Onion Association

822 7th St
Suite 510
Greeley, CO 80631

970-353-5895
FAX 970-353-5897
Home Page: www.onions-usa.org
Social Media: *Twitter, Pinterest*

Shawn Hartley, President
John Rietveld, Vice President
Doug Stanley, 2nd Vice President
Wayne Mininger, Executive Vice President
Monna Canaday, Administrative Assistant

Represents interests of US onion producers. Informational lobbying and generic promotional headquarters for fresh dry bulb onion growers. Provides connections for networking and education exchange.
600 Members
Founded in 1913
Mailing list available for rent

9749 National Pasta Association

750 National Press Building
529 14th Street NW
Washington, DC 20045

202-591-2459
FAX 202-591-2445
E-Mail: info@ilovepasta.org
Home Page: www.ilovepasta.org

Greg Pearson, Chairman
Bastiaan DeZeeuw, Vice Chairman
Jim Meyer, Treasurer
Peter Bisaccia, Board Member
Randy Gilbertson, Board Member

To increase the consumption of pasta, to promote the development of sound public policy and, act as a center of knowledge for the industry.
Founded in 1904

9750 National Peanut Board

3350 Riverwood Parkway
Suite 1150
Atlanta, GA 30339

678-424-5750
866-825-7946
FAX 678-424-5751
E-Mail: peanuts@nationalpeanutboard.org
Home Page: www.nationalpeanutboard.org
Social Media: *Facebook, Twitter, Pinterest*

Bob H. White, Chairman
Monty Rast, Vice Chairman
Gayle White, Treasurer
Ed White, Secretary
Gregory Gill, Board Member

A farmer-funded national research, promotion and education check-off program. Through NPB, growers from across the United States come together to contribute to the research and promotion of USA-grown peanuts.

9751 National Pecan Shellers Association

1100 Johnson Ferry Road
Suite 300
Atlanta, GA 30342

678-298-1189
FAX 404-591-6811
E-Mail: npsa@kellencompany.com
Home Page: www.ilovepecans.org
Social Media: *Facebook, Twitter, Pinterest*

The NPSA is the trade association for the pecan shelling and processing industry. The association is dedicated to educating culinary and health professionals, food technologists, educators and the general public about the health benefits, nutritional value, variety of uses and all-around great taste of pecans.

9752 National Pork Board

1776 NW 114th St.
Des Moines, IA 50325

800-456-7675
E-Mail: info@pork.org
Home Page: www.pork.org

John Johnson, Chief Operating Officer

Uniting pork producers for the future of the pork industry.

9753 National Pork Producers Council

122 C Street NW
Suite 875
Washington, DC 20001

202-347-3600
FAX 202-347-5265
E-Mail: warnerd@nppc.org
Home Page: www.nppc.org
Social Media: *Facebook, Twitter, LinkedIn, Swinecast, Pinterest, Flickr*

Ron Prestage, President
John Weber, President-Elect
Ken Maschhoff, Vice President

Kent Bang, Board Member
Cory Bollum, Board Member

Conducts public-policy outreach on behalf of its 43 affiliated state associations, enhancing opportunities for the success of US pork producers and other industry stakeholders by establishing the US pork industry as a consistent and responsible supplier of high-quality pork to the domestic and world markets.

9754 National Potato Council

1300 L St NW
Suite 910
Washington, DC 20005

202-682-9456
FAX 202-682-0333
E-Mail: spudinfo@nationalpotatocouncil.org
Home Page: www.nationalpotatocouncil.org
Social Media: *Facebook, Twitter, Youtube*

DAN LAKE, President
JIM TIEDE, First Vice President
LARRY ALSUM, Vice President, Finance
DOMINIC LAJOIE, VP Environmental Affairs
Dwayne Weyers, Vice President, Growers

Represents US potato growers on federal legislative and regulatory issues.
6000 Members
Founded in 1948

9755 National Poultry & Food Distributors Association

2014 Osborne Road
Saint Marys, GA 31558

770-535-9901
FAX 770-535-7385
E-Mail: kkm@npfda.org
Home Page: www.npfda.org
Social Media: *Facebook, Twitter, LinkedIn*

Marc Miro, President
Ted Rueger, Vice President
Lee Wilson, Treasurer
Kristin McWhorter, Executive Director

To promote the poultry and food distributors, processors and allied industries by bringing them together and providing a forum to foster long term business relationships.
210 Members
Founded in 1967

9756 National Renderers Association

500 Montgomery Street
Suite 310
Alexandria, VA 22314

703-683-0155
FAX 571-970-2279
E-Mail: renderers@nationalrenderers.com
Home Page: www.nationalrenderers.org
Social Media: *Twitter*

Gerald F. Smith Jr., Chairman
Ross Hamilton, First Vice Chairman
Tim Guzek, Second Vice Chairman
Nancy Foster, President
Marty Covert, Convention Coordinator

Representing members' interests to regulatory and other governmental agencies, promoting the greater use of animal by-products and fostering the opening and expansion of trade between foreign buyers and North American exporters.
Founded in 1933

9757 National Restaurant Association Educational Foundation

2055 L. St. NW
Washington, DC 20036

202-315-4102
800-424-5156
E-Mail: wsafstrom@nraef.org

Home Page: www.nraef.org
Social Media: *Facebook, Twitter, Youtube*

Denise Marie Fugo, Chair
Mike Gibbons, Vice Chair
Dawn Sweeney, President & CEO
Rob Gifford, Executive Vice President
Michael Hickey, Treasurer

NRAEF is the philanthropic foundation of the National Restaurant Association. Committed to enhancing the restaurant industry's service to the public through education, community engagement and promotion of career opportunities.
Founded in 1987

9758 National Restaurant Association
2055 L. St. NW
Suite 700
Washington, DC 20036

202-331-5900
800-424-5156
FAX 202-331-2429
Home Page: www.restaurant.org
Social Media: *Facebook, Twitter, YouTube*

Jack Crawford, Chair
Joe Kadow, Vice Chair
Dawn Sweeney, President & CEO
Jeff Davis, Treasurer

Striving to help members build customer loyalty, find financial success and provide rewarding careers in foodservice.
60000 Members
Founded in 1919

9759 National Seafood Educators
PO Box 93
Skamokawa, WA 98647

206-546-6410
FAX 206-546-6411
E-Mail: information@seafoodeducators.com
Home Page: www.seafoodeducators.com

Evie Hansen, Founder

Goal is to educate and inform the public about the many health benefits of a seafood diet. Also has consulted with many seafood retail businesses on how to sell, store, and prepare wholesome seafood.
Founded in 1977

9760 National Seasoning Manufacturers Association Inc
8905 Maxwell Dr
Suite 200
Potomac, MD 20854

301-765-9675
FAX 301-299-7523
E-Mail: alsmeyerfood@isp.com

Dick Alsmeyer PhD, Executive Director

Food seasoning manufacturers, producers of meat curing compounds, flavors, supplies, services, and equipment used for the seasoning and preserving of food.
23 Members
Founded in 1972

9761 National Shellfisheries Association
National Marine Fisheries Service Laboratory
Oxford, MD 21654

631-653-6327
FAX 631-653-6327
E-Mail: webmaster@shellfish.org
Home Page: www.shellfish.org

Karolyn Mueller Hansen, President
Steven Allen, President-Elect
Shirley Baker, Vice President
Lisa Milke, Secretary
John Scarpa, Treasurer

Organization comprised of scientists, public health workers, shellfish producers and fishery administrators to promote and advance

shellfisheries research and the application of results to the shellfish industry.
1M Members
Founded in 1908

9762 National Society on Healthcare Foodservice
455 S. 4th Street
Suite 650
Louisville, KY 40202

888-528-9552
FAX 502-589-3602
E-Mail: info@healthcarefoodservice.org
Home Page: www.healthcarefoodservice.org
Social Media: *Facebook, Twitter, LinkedIn, YouTube*

Laura Watson, President
Lisette Coston, President-Elect
Jacqueline Sikoski, Secretary
Robert Darrah, Treasurer
Julie Jones, Treasurer-Elect

The only professional society dedicated to professionals and suppliers in the self-operated healthcare foodservice industry- those facilities who choose to keep their foodservice departments on staff, instead of outsourcing them to third-party contractors.

9763 National Sunflower Association
2401 46th Avenue SE
Suite 206
Mandan, ND 58554-4829

701-328-5100
888-718-7033
FAX 701-328-5101
E-Mail: larryk@sunflowernsa.com
Home Page: www.sunflowernsa.com
Social Media: *Facebook, YouTube*

John Sandbakken, Executive Director
Tina Mittlesteadt, Manager

A non-profit commodity organization working on problems and opportunities for the improvement of all members. Members include growers and the support industry.
20000 Members
Founded in 1981

9764 National Turkey Federation
1225 New York Avenue NW
Suite 400
Washington, DC 20005

202-898-0100
FAX 202-898-0203
E-Mail: info@turkeyfed.org
Home Page: www.eatturkey.com
Social Media: *Facebook, Twitter, Youtube, Pinterest*

John Burkel, Chairman
Gary Cooper, Vice Chairman
Joel Brandenberger, President
Damon Wells, Vice President
Jihad Douglas, Secretary-Treasurer

(NTF) is the national Advocate for all segments of the $8 billion turkey industry, providing services and conducting activities that increase demand for its members' products. The federation also protects and enhances its members' ability to effectively and profitably provide wholesome, high quality, nutritious turkey products.
264 Members
Founded in 1939

9765 National WIC Association
2001 S St NW
Suite 580
Washington, DC 20009

202-232-5492
FAX 202-387-5281
E-Mail: douglasg@nwica.org

Home Page: www.nwica.org
Social Media: *Facebook, Twitter, Pinterest*

Douglas Greenaway, President & CEO
Cecilia Richardson, Staff/Nutrition Program Director
DuWvaughn P. Francois, Office Manager
Robert A. Lee, Development Manager
Martelle Esposito, Government Affairs Manager

Members are geographic state, Native American state and local agency directors of the Special Supplement nutrition program for women, infants and children.
900 Members
Founded in 1983

9766 National Watermelon Promotion Board
1321 Sundial Point
Winter Springs, FL 32708

407-657-0261
877-599-9595
FAX 407-657-2213
E-Mail: info@watermelon.org
Home Page: www.watermelon.org
Social Media: *Facebook, Twitter, RSS, YouTube, Instagram*

Mark Arney, Executive Director
Rebekah Dossett, Director of Operationsÿ
Megan McKenna, Dir., Marketing
Stephanie Barlow, Director of Communications
Andrea Smith, Industry Affairs Manager

Increase consumer demand for fresh watermelon through promotion, research, and educational programs.
Founded in 1989

9767 National Yogurt Association
Washington, DC

703-245-7698
E-Mail: info@aboutyogurt.com
Home Page: aboutyogurt.com

Becky O'Grady, Co-Chairman
Gustavo Valle, Co-Chairman
Kraig R. Naasz, President

Non-profit representing the nation's yogurt manufacturers and marketers.

9768 Natural Marketing Institute
272 Ruth Road
Harleysville, PA 19438

215-513-7300
FAX 215-513-1713
E-Mail: Nancy.White@NMIsolutions.com
Home Page: www.NMIsolutions.com
Social Media: *Facebook, Twitter, LinkedIn*

Maryellen Molyneaux, President
George Ward, Vice President Strategic Consulting
John Devries, Vice President Strategic Consulting
Diane Ray, Vice President of Strategy
Kathryn Schulte, Director Project Management

NMI is an international strategic marketing consultancy specializing in health, wellness, sustainability and healthy aging with full-service consulting and market research services.
Founded in 1989

9769 Natural Products Association
1773 T Street, NW
Washington, DC 20009

202-223-0101
800-966-6632
FAX 202-223-0250
E-Mail: natural@NPAinfo.org
Home Page: www.npainfo.org

Social Media: *Facebook, Twitter, LinkedIn, Pinterest, Googleplus*

Jon Fiume, President Elect
Jain Drinkwalter, Chair
Roxanne Green, President
Daniel Fabricant, Executive Director & CEO
Mark LeDoux, Treasurer

The nation's largest and oldest non-profit organization dedicated to the natural products industry. NPA unites a diverse membership, from the smallest health food store to the largest dietary supplement manufacturer.
1900+ Members
Founded in 1936

9770 New York Apple Association

7645 Main Street
PO Box 350
Fishers, NY 14453-0350

585-924-2171
FAX 585-924-1629
Home Page: www.nyapplecountry.com
Social Media: *Facebook, Twitter*

Jim Allen, President
Julia Stewart, Communications
Molly Golden, Director of Marketing
Linda Quinn, Media Representative
Ellen Mykins, Accounting

The New York Apple Association is a non-profit trade association representing over 600 commercial apple growers in New York State. The apple industry produces about 25 million bushels each year at a value of approximately $137 million, making it one of the largest sectors in New York agriculture.
600 Members
Founded in 1950

9771 North American Association of Food Equipment Manufacturers

161 N Clark Street
Suite 2020
Chicago, IL 60601

312-821-0201
FAX 312-821-0202
E-Mail: info@nafem.org
Home Page: www.nafem.org
Social Media: *Facebook*

Michael L. Whiteley, President
Kevin Fink, President-Elect
Joseph Carlson, CFSP, Secretary/Treasurer
Deirdre Flynn, Executive Vice President
Genny Bertalmio, Office Manager

The North American Association of Food Equipment Manacturers (NAFEM) is a trade association of more than 625 foodservice equipment and supplies manufacturers that provide products for food preparation, cooking, storage and table service providers. NAFEM's biennial trade show attracts approximately 20,000 foodservice professionals and features more than 600 North American manufacturers.
625 Members

9772 North American Blueberry Council

80 Iron Point Circle
Suite 114
Folsom, CA 95630

916-983-2279
FAX 916-983-9370
E-Mail: info@nabcblues.org
Home Page: www.nabcblues.org

Bob Carini, President
Tom Bodtke, First Vice President
Tom Avinelis, Second Vice President
Art Galletta, Treasurer
Ken Patterson, Secretary

A non-profit association with the important role of acting as a voice for the highbush blueberry industry.
Founded in 1965

9773 North American Farm Show Council

590 Woody Hayes Drive
Columbus, OH 43210

614-292-4278
FAX 614-292-9448
E-Mail: gamble.19@osu.edu
Home Page: www.farmshows.org

Dennis Alford, President
Chip Blalock, 1st Vice President
David Zimmerman, 2nd Vice President
Chuck Gamble, Secretary/Treasurer

Strives to improve the value of its member shows through education, communication and evaluation. The overall goal is to provide the best possible marketing showcase for exhibitors of agricultural equipment and related products to the farmer/rancher/producer customer.
Founded in 1972

9774 North American Limousin Foundation

6 Inverness Court East
Suite 260
Englewood, CO 80112-5595

303-220-1693
FAX 303-220-1884
E-Mail: limousin@nalf.org
Home Page: www.nalf.org
Social Media: *Facebook, Twitter*

Chad Settje, President
Bret Begert, Vice President
Jim Bob Hendrickson, Secretary
Dexter Edwards, Treasurer
Mark Anderson, Executive Director

Register, promote and research on Limousin beef cattle.
4000 Members
Founded in 1968

9775 North American Meat Association

1150 Connecticut Avenue, NW
12th Floor
Washington, DC 20036

202-640-5333
800-368-3043
FAX 202-318-4078
E-Mail: info@meatassociation.com
Home Page: www.meatinstitute.org
Social Media: *Twitter, LinkedIn*

Mike Hesse, Co-Chairman
Brian Coelho, Co-President
Barry Carpenter, President & CEO
Phil Kimball, CAE, Executive Director
Sabrina Moore, Director, Meetings

Provides its members unique one-on-one assistance resolving regulatory issues. Mission is to be proactive and responsive in serving members both individually and collectively.
Founded in 2012

9776 North American Millers' Association

600 Maryland Ave SW
Suite 825 West
Washington, DC 20024

202-484-2200
FAX 202-488-7416
E-Mail: generalinfo@namamillers.org
Home Page: www.namamillers.org
Social Media: *Facebook*

Dan Dye, Chairman
Mark Kolkhorst, Vice Chairman
James A. McCarthy, President & CEO
James A. Bair, Vice President
Sherri Lehman, Director of Government Relations

Trade association representing the wheat, corn, oat and rye milling industry. NAMA members operate one hundred and seventy mills in thrirty-eight states and Canada. Their aggregate production of more than one hundred and sixty

million pounds per day is approximately ninety-five percent of the industry capacity in the U.S.
Founded in 1902

9777 North American Natural Casing Association

494 Eighth Avenue
Suite 805
New York, NY 10001

212-695-4980
FAX 212-695-7153
E-Mail: nanca18hq@yahoo.com
Home Page: www.nanca.org

Barbara Negron, President
Phil Schwartz, Vice President
Mike Wallace, Secretary
Eric Svendsen, Treasurer

To obtain legislation favorable to the industry's interests and prevent or change legistation deemed harmful at the local, state and federal levels, including protection from unfair trade practices by foreign countries, and working with member governments to ease trade. Also addresses common industry problems encountered by management in the production, distribution and financial function of the naturasl casing industry.

9778 North American Olive Oil Association

3301 Route 66
Suite 205, Building C
Neptune, NJ 07753

732-922-3008
FAX 732-922-3590
E-Mail: info@naooa.org
Home Page: www.naooa.org
Social Media: *Facebook, Twitter*

Eryn Balch, Executive Vice President

Committed to supplying North American consumers with quality products in a fair and competitive environment; to fostering a clear understanding of the different grades of olive oil; and to expounding the benefits of olive oil in nutrition, health, and the culinary arts.
Founded in 1989

9779 Northeast Fresh Foods Alliance

1189R N Main Street
Randolph, MA 02368

781-963-9726
FAX 781-963-5829

Brian Long, President
Bob Ogan, Executive VP
Chris Bruhn, First VP
Paul Sullivan, Secretary
Paul Palumbo, Treasurer
350 Members
Founded in 1979

9780 Northern Nut Growers Association, Inc.

Home Page: www.northernnutgrowers.org

Robert Stehli, President
Tim Ford, Vice President
Jeanne Romero-Severson, Treasurer
Tom Molnar, Secretary

The Association brings together people interested in growing nut trees, from amateurs to tree breeders.
Founded in 1910

9781 Northwest Cherry Briners Association Inc.

2667 Reed Rd
Hood River, OR 97031

E-Mail: director.orgcouncil@gmail.com
Home Page: www.orgcouncil.com

Carl Payne, VP Tech Services

Association of briners of sweet cherries in the northwestern US. The organization works to inform briners of regulatory decisions and current practices affecting brining operations.
8 Members
Founded in 1936

9782 Northwest Food Processors Association
8338 NE. Alderwood Road
Suite 160
Portland, OR 97220

503-327-2200
FAX 503-327-2201
E-Mail: info@nwfpa.org
Home Page: www.nwfpa.org
Social Media: *Facebook, Twitter, LinkedIn*

Kurt McKnight, Chair
Debbie Radie, Chair Elect
Steven Rowe, Vice Chair
David McGiverin, President
Greg Satrum, Director

NWFPA is an advocate for members interests and a resource for enhancing the food processing industry in Oregon, Washington and Idaho.
350 Members
Founded in 1914

9783 Northwest Meat Processors Association
2380 NW Roosevelt St
Portland, OR 97210-2323

503-226-2758
FAX 503-224-0947
E-Mail: haysmgmt@pipeline.com

Dennis Hays, Executive Director
250 Members
Founded in 1962

9784 Organic Alliance
Organic Alliance International
Asheville, NC 28804

828-337-6114
Home Page: www.organicalliance.org

An alliance of people, businesses and organizations working together to promote the goodness of organics and help to make it available to all.

9785 Organic Crop Improvement Association International (OCIA)
1340 North Cotner Boulevard
Lincoln, NR 68505-1838

402-477-2323
FAX 402-477-4325
E-Mail: info@ocia.org
Home Page: www.ocia.org

Jack Geiger, President
Susan Linkletter, 1st Vice President
Joel Koskan, 2nd Vice President
Demetria Stephens, Secretary
Jeff Kienast, Treasurer

An accredited world leader in the certified organic industry, provides certification, education and research services to thousands of organic farmers, processors and handlers from 20 countries in North, Central and South America and Asia.
3500 Members
Founded in 1985

9786 Organic Trade Association
28 Vernon St
Suite 413
Brattleboro, VT 05301

802-275-3800
FAX 802-275-3801
E-Mail: info@ota.com

Home Page: www.ota.com
Social Media: *Facebook, Twitter, LinkedIn*

Melissa Hughes, President
Kim Dietz, Vice President
Tony Bedard, Treasurer
Sarah Bird, Secretary
Laura Batcha, Chief Executive Officer

A business association for the organic industry in North America. OTA's mission is to encourage global sustainability through promoting and protecting the growth of diverse organic trade.
1400 Members
Founded in 1985
Mailing list available for rent

9787 Ozark Food Processors Association
2650 N Young Avenue
Fayetteville, AR 72704

479-575-4607
FAX 479-575-2165
E-Mail: ofpa@uark.edu
Home Page: ofpa.uark.edu

Jason Hayward, President
Andrea Dunigan, Vice President
Dr. Renee Threlfall, Secretary
Steve Crider, Board Member
Jared Brooks, Board Member

This association is comprised of regional food processors and national suppliers for the food service industry.
90 Members
Founded in 1906

9788 Pacific Coast Shellfish Growers Association
120 State Ave NE
#142
Olympia, WA 98501

360-754-2744
FAX 360-754-2743
E-Mail: pcsga@pcsga.net
Home Page: www.pcsga.net
Social Media: *Facebook, Flickr*

Margaret Pilaro Barrette, Executive Director
Connie Smith, Projects Manager
Mary Middleton, Executive Assistant

Members grow a wide variety of healthy, sustainable shellfish including oysters, clams, mussels, scallops and geoduck. PCSGA works on behalf of its members on a broad spectrum of issues, including environmental protection, shellfish safety, regulations, technology, and marketing.
Founded in 1930

9789 Paperboard Packaging Council
1350 Main Street
Suite 1508
Springfield, MA 01103-1670

413-686-9191
FAX 413-747-7777
E-Mail: paperboardpackaging@ppcnet.org
Home Page: www.ppcnet.org
Social Media: *Facebook, Twitter, LinkedIn, YouTube*

Kyle Eldred, Chair
Charles Johnson, Vice Chair
Ben Markens, President
Lou Kornet, Vice President
Steven Levkoff, Treasurer

Trade association serving converters and suppliers of all forms of paperboard packaging, including folding cartons, rigid boxes, paper cylinders, and laminated small flute containers.
Founded in 1929

9790 Peanut and Tree Nut Processors Association
PO Box 2660
Alexandria, VA 22301

301-365-2521
FAX 301-365-7705
Home Page: ptnpa.org

Brian Ezell, Chairman
JOEL PERKINS, Vice Chairman
Michael J. Valentine, Secretary/Treasurer
Jeannie Shaughnessy, Executive Director
Trish Schechtman, Project Manager

Representing the owners and operators of companies (large and small) who shell, process, salt and/or roast peanuts and tree nuts. In addition, our members also supply equipment and services that are critical to our industry.
Founded in 1939

9791 Pear Bureau Northwest
4382 SE International Way
Suite A
Milwaukie, OR 97222-4635

503-652-9720
FAX 503-652-9721
E-Mail: info@usapears.com
Home Page: www.usapears.com
Social Media: *Facebook, Twitter, LinkedIn, YouTube, Pinterest*

Kevin D. Moffitt, President & CEO
Linda Bailey, VP of Operations
Kathy Stephenson, Director Marketing Communications

A non-profit marketing organization that promotes, advertises and develops markets for fresh pears grown in Oregon and Washington. Through professional representatives in the U.S. and around the world, the Bureau coordinates activities designed to increase awareness and consumption of fresh USA Pears, facilitating research on behalf of the Northwest pear industry relative to consumer awareness and preferences, nutritional benefits and emerging global markets.
1600 Members
Founded in 1931

9792 Pickle Packers International Inc.
1101 17th Street NW
Suite 700
Washington, DC 20036

202-331-2465
FAX 202-463-8998
Home Page: www.ilovepickles.org
Social Media: *Facebook*

Sponsors research, represents industry before government agencies, produces educational materials, and provides superior networking opportunities to members. Members inlude processors, salters, green shippers, brokers, growers, seed companies, ingredient and equipment manufacturers, packaging suppliers, and those providing goods and services to the industry.
Founded in 1896

9793 Popcorn Board
330 N Wabash Avenue
Suite 2000
Chicago, IL 60611

312-644-6610
FAX 312-527-6783
E-Mail: info@popcorn.org
Home Page: www.popcorn.org
Social Media: *Facebook, Twitter, Blog*

A non-profit organization funded by US popcorn processors to raise awareness of popcorn as a versatile, whole-grain snack.
Founded in 1943

9794 Printing Industries of America
301 Brush Creek Road
Warrendale, PA 15086

412-741-6860
800-910-4283
FAX 412-741-2311
E-Mail: printing@printing.org
Home Page: www.printing.org
Social Media: *Facebook, Twitter, LinkedIn, Pinterest, Googleplus*

David A. Olberding, Chairman
Bradley L. Thompson II, 1st Vice Chairman
MR CURT KREISLER, 2nd Vice Chairman
Michael L. Wurst, Treasurer
BRYAN T. HALL, Secretary

Members are companies printing labels for food or consumer products.
40 Members
Founded in 1887

9795 Produce Marketing Association
1500 Casho Mill Road
PO Box 6036
Newark, DE 19711

302-738-7100
FAX 302-731-2409
E-Mail: solutionctr@pma.com
Home Page: www.pma.com
Social Media: *Facebook, Twitter, Flickr, YouTube, Xchange*

Cathy Burns, President
Bryan Silbermann, CEO
Tony Parassio, Chief Operating Officer
Yvonne Bull, CFO
Robert J. Whitaker, Ph.D., Chief Science & Technology Officer

Providing business solutions that strengthen and lead the global produce community, PMA has set the standard for quality events with the annual convention and continues to revolutionize one of the world's most vibrant industries.
100 Members
Founded in 1949

9796 Professional Farmers of America
6612 Chancellor Dr.
Cedar Falls, IA 50613

319-277-1278
800-772-0023
FAX 319-827-1792
E-Mail: editors@profarmer.com
Home Page: www.profarmer.com

Mike Walsten, VP
Merrill Oster, Executive Director
Rich Posson, Editor

Provides farmers with marketing strategies and market-trend data, as well as seminars and home study courses.
25M Members
Founded in 1972

9797 Quality Bakers of America Cooperative
1275 Glenlivet Drive
Suite 100
Allentown, PA 18106-3107

973-263-6970
FAX 973-263-0937
E-Mail: info@qba.com
Home Page: www.qba.com

Providing members with access to sources of appropriate services in order to maintain the highest product quality and sanitation standards.
Founded in 1922

9798 Quality Chekd Dairies
901 Warrenville Rd
Suite 405
Lisle, IL 60532

800-222-6455
FAX 630-717-1126
E-Mail: qchekd@qchekd.com
Home Page: www.qchekd.com

Peter Horvath, President
Mary DeMarco, Accounting & Admin Manager
Steve Drabek, Human Resource & Training Director
Laura Moehs, Training & Admin Coordinator
Chuck Yarris, Quality & Food Safety Director

A cooperative of dairy foods processors who use the Quality Checked trademark on their products and engage in group purchasing of ingredients and supplies.
Founded in 1944

9799 Raisin Administration Committee
2445 Capitol Street
Suite 200
Fresno, CA 93721-2236

559-225-0520
FAX 559-225-0652
E-Mail: info@raisins.org
Home Page: www.raisins.org

Gary Schulz, President
Debbie Powell, Sr. Vice President of Operations
Larry Blagg, Sr. Vice President of Marketing
Ron Degiuli, Vice President of Accounting

Administrative board of growers and packers of raisins.

9800 Red Angus Association of America
4201 N Interstate 35
Denton, TX 76207-3415

940-387-3502
FAX 888-829-6069
E-Mail: info@redangus.org
Home Page: www.redangus.org
Social Media: *Facebook*

Kim Ford, President
Twig Marston, CEO
Jeanene McCuistion, Accounting Director
Kevin Miller, 1st Vice President
Bob Morton, 2nd Vice President

Dedicated to providing its members with excellence and innovation in leadership, service, information and education. An association for breeders of Red Angus cattle.
2000 Members
Founded in 1954

9801 Refrigerated Foods Association
3823 Roswell Road
Suite 208
Marietta, GA 30062

678-426-8175
FAX 678-550-4504
E-Mail: info@refrigeratedfoods.org
Home Page: www.refrigeratedfoods.org

Steve Loehndorf, President
Wes Thaller, Vice President
Josh Knott, Secretary
Kenneth Funger, Treasurer
Megan Levin, Executive Director

An organization of manufacturers and suppliers of refrigerated prepared foods united by a common interest; to advance and safeguard the industry. Members include manufacturers and suppliers of wet salads, refrigerated entrees and side dishes, dips, desserts, soups, and ethnic foods, as well as companies engaged in business operations related to the refrigerated foods industry.
200+ Members
Founded in 1980

9802 Research and Development Associates for Military Food and Packaging Systems
16607 Blanco Rd
Suite 501
San Antonio, TX 78232

210-493-8024
FAX 210-493-8036
E-Mail: hqs@militaryfood.org
Home Page: www.militaryfood.org
Social Media: *Facebook*

Bill McCreary, Chairman
Daniel Weil, Vice Chairman
John Q. McNulty, Executive Director
Jan Cook, Director of Administration
Kimberly Addison Sanford, Marketing Events Coordinator

To provide the safest and highest food service to the US Armed Forces by linking industry, government and academics.
700 Members
Founded in 1946

9803 Retail Bakers of America
15941 Harlem Avenue
#347
Tinley Park, IL 60477

800-638-0924
FAX 800-638-0924
E-Mail: Info@retailbakersofamerica.org
Home Page: www.retailbankersofamerica.org
Social Media: *Facebook*

Richard Reinwald, Chairman
Paul Sapienza, Secretary
Dale A. Biles, Treasurer

Comprised of retail bakeries, allied suppliers and other industry members. The purpose is to offer our members knowledge and resources to enhance business operations through learning opportunities, shared best practices, networking and industry communication.
2000 Members
Founded in 1918

9804 Retail Confectioners International
2053 S. Waverly
Ste. C
Springfield, MO 65804

417-883-2775
800-545-5381
FAX 417-883-1108
E-Mail: info@retailconfectioners.org
Home Page: www.retailconfectioners.org
Social Media: *Facebook, Twitter, YouTube*

Brian Pelletier, President
Judith Hilliard McCarthy, 1st Vice President
Steve Vande Walle, 2nd Vice President
John Asher, III, 3rd Vice President
Angie Burlison, Secretary/Treasurer

Providing education, promotion and legislative services to our members who are manufacturing retailers of quality boxed chocolate and other confectionery products throughout the U.S., Canada and overseas.
600 Members
Founded in 1917

9805 Rocky Mountain Bean Dealers Association
PO Box 1285
Elizabeth, CO 80107

303-646-8883
FAX 720-306-2878
E-Mail: rmbean@revealmail.com

Vickie Root, Executive Director

This organization is dedicated to advancing the general interest of its members and the industry.

9806 Rocky Mountain Food Industry Association

PO Box 1083
Arvada, CO 80001-1083

303-830-7001
FAX 303-424-7114
Home Page: www.rmfia.org

Mary Lou Chapman, President/CEO

The trade organization for the Colorado and Wyoming grocery industry, representing retail grocers, convenience stores, and their wholesale suppliers. The association serves as a voice for its members with state legislatures, US Congress and the various governmental agencies that regulate the food industry.
500 Members
Founded in 1917

9807 Roundtable of Food Professionals

4363 Larwin Avenue
Cypress, CA 90630

714-562-5088
FAX 714-670-2965
E-Mail: info@rfporg.org
Home Page: www.rfporg.org

Barb Colucci, President
Jenny Rosoff, President-Emeritus
David Stennes, VP
Stephany Rosenthal, Membership Co-Chair

Provide opportunities for development and career expansion within the whole spectrum of the food industry.
50 Members
Founded in 2002

9808 Royal Crown Bottlers Association

515 Eline Ave
St Matthews, KY 40207-3655

502-896-0861
FAX 502-896-0861

Stephanie Garling, Executive Director

Represents franchised Royal Crown bottlers.
100 Members
Founded in 1964

9809 Salt Institute

700 N Fairfax St
Suite 600
Alexandria, VA 22314-2040

703-549-4648
FAX 703-548-2194
E-Mail: info@saltinstitute.org
Home Page: www.saltinstitute.org
Social Media: *Facebook, Twitter, YouTube*

Lori Roman, President
Morton Satin, Vice President
Jorge Amselle, Director of Communication
Wilfrid Nixon, VP Science and the Environment

A source of authoritative information about salt and its more than 14,000 known users. Provides public information and advocates on behalf of its members, including use of the website.
Founded in 1914

9810 Santa Gertrudis Breeders International

PO Box 1257
Kingsville, TX 78364

361-592-9357
FAX 361-592-8572
E-Mail: sgbi@sbcglobal.net
Home Page: www.santagertrudis.com
Social Media: *Facebook, Twitter, Googleplus*

Curtis Salter, President
Deanna Parker, Secretary/Treasurer
John E. Ford, Executive Director

The original American beef breed. Custom built for the range and market, these cattle have proven themselves worldwide to be a hardy and profitable breed from the mountains of Montana and Mexico to the tropics and deserts of Argentina and Australia. Worldwide, cattlemen are getting results using Santa Gertrudis genetics.
Founded in 1950

9811 School Nutrition Association

120 Waterfront St
Suite 300
National Harbor, MD 20745

301-686-3100
800-877-8822
FAX 301-686-3115
E-Mail: servicecenter@schoolnutrition.org
Home Page: www.schoolnutrition.org
Social Media: *Digg*

Jean Ronnei, President
Becky Domokos-Bays, President-Elect
Lynn Harvey, Vice President
Linda Eichenberger, Secretary/Treasurer
Patricia Montague, CEO

This is a national, nonprofit professional organization representing members who provide high quality, low-cost meals to students across the country.
55000 Members
Founded in 1946

9812 Sioux Honey Association

301 Lewis Boulevard
PO Box 388
Sioux City, IA 51101

712-258-0638
FAX 712-258-1332
Home Page: www.suebeehoney.com
Social Media: *Facebook, Twitter, Pinterest*

David Allibone, President/CEO

Established by five beekeepers so that they could market their honey at greater profit through sharing services and equipment, processing and packing facilities and complete marketing and sales organizations.
315 Members
Founded in 1921

9813 Small Farm Resource

Home Page: www.farminfo.org

Contains a wide variety of information useful to those with small farms and rural property.
Founded in 1995

9814 Snack Food Association

1600 Wilson Blvd
Suite 650
Arlington, VA 22209

703-836-4500
800-628-1334
FAX 703-836-8262
E-Mail: sfa@sfa.org
Home Page: www.sfa.org
Social Media: *Facebook, Twitter, LinkedIn, Youtube, Flickr*

Tom Dempsey, CEO
Liz Wells, Vice President, Meetings & Events
Paul Downey, Director of Finance and Admin
David Walsh, Director, Government Affairs
Meegan Smith, Director, Communications & Marketin

Representing snack manufacturers and suppliers worldwide. Serving as the voice for the snack industry before government, researches and compiles annual snack sales and consumer data, educates manufacturers on technological advances in equipment and raw ingredients and provides technical support to its members

through direct assistance, videos, seminars and publications.
800 Members
Founded in 1937

9815 Society for Laboratory Automatic and Screening

100 Illinois Street
Suite 242
St. Charles, IL 60174

630-256-7527
877-990-7527
FAX 630-741-7527
E-Mail: slas@slas.org
Home Page: www.slas.org
Social Media: *Facebook, Twitter, LinkedIn, YouTube*

Dean Ho, President
Richard Eglen, Vice President
Mike Snowden, Treasurer
Michele A. Cleary, Secretary
Alastair Binnie, Director

Supports research and discovery in pharmaceutical biotechnology and the agrichemical industry that utilize biomolecular screening procedures.
2000+ Members
Founded in 1994

9816 Society of Commercial Seed Technologists

653 Constitution Avenue NE
Washington, DC 200002

202-870-2412
FAX 607-273-1638
E-Mail: scst@seedtechnology.net
Home Page: www.seedtechnology.net

Barbara Cleave, President
David Stimpson, VP
Steve Beals, Director at Large
DaNell Jamieson, Director-at-Large
Heidi Jo Larson, Director-at-Large

A organization comprised of commercial, independent and government seed technologists. Developed over the years into a progressive organization that trains and provides accreditation of technologists, conducts research studies and proposes rule changes, and serves as an important resource to the seed industry.
Founded in 1922

9817 Southeast United Dairy Industry Association

5340 W Fayetteville Rd
Atlanta, GA 30349-5416

678-833-0580
800-343-4693
FAX 770-996-6925
E-Mail: info@sudiainc.com
Home Page: www.southeastdairy.org
Social Media: *Facebook, Twitter, YouTube, Pinterest*

Amanda Trice, Director of IR & Communications
Rebecca Egseiker, Assistant Director of Communication

Provides a wealth of information for milk and dairy consumers, media, school and health professionals and dairy farmers.
6000 Members
Founded in 1971
Mailing list available for rent

9818 Southeastern Dairy Foods Research Center

NCSU Department of Food Science
PO Box 7624
Raleigh, NC 27695

919-515-4197
FAX 919-513-0014
E-Mail: bernard_eckhardt@ncsu.edu

Home Page: fbns.ncsu.edu/
Social Media: *Facebook, Twitter, YouTube*

Chris Daubert, Department Head

One of six National Centers funded and managed by Dairy Management Incorporated. The mission is to conduct research to develop and apply new technologies for value-added processing of fluid milk and its components into dairy products and ingredients with improved safety, quality or expanded functionalities.
Founded in 1988

9819 Southern Peanut Farmers Federation
1025 Sugar Pike Way
Canton, GA 30115

770-751-6615
E-Mail: lpwagner@comcast.net
Home Page: www.southernpeanutfarmers.org

Formed to educate American consumers about the US peanut industry and its products.
Founded in 1998

9820 Southern Peanut Growers
1025 Sugar Pike Way
Canton, GA 30115

770-751-6615
E-Mail: lpwagner@comcast.net
Home Page: www.peanutbutterlovers.com
Social Media: *Facebook, Twitter, YouTube, Pinterest*

Leslie Wagner, Executive Director

A nonprofit trade association representing peanut farmers in Georgia, Alabama, Florida and Mississippi. Formed to educate American consumers about the US peanut industry and its products.
6000 Members
Founded in 1980
Mailing list available for rent

9821 Southern US Trade Association
701 Poydras Street
Suite 3845
New Orleans, LA 70139

504-568-5986
FAX 504-568-6010
E-Mail: susta@susta.org
Home Page: www.susta.org
Social Media: *Facebook*

Bernadette Wiltz, Executive Director
Danielle Viguerie, Marketing Director
Missie Lindsey, Marketing Coordinator
Tina Meshell, Office Manager
Troy Rosamond, Deputy Director & Financial Directo

A non-profit agricultural export trade development association comprised of the Departments of Agriculture of the 15 southern states and the Commonwealth of Puerto Rico.
Founded in 1973

9822 Soy Protein Council
1255 23rd Street NW
Washington, DC 20037

202-467-6610
FAX 202-833-3636
Home Page: www.spcouncil.org
Social Media: *Facebook, Twitter*

David A Saunders, Executive VP
Elroy Wolff, General Counsel

Primary purpose is to promote the growth and interests of the soy protein industry and broaden the acceptance of soy products as key components of the worldwide food system.
Founded in 1971

9823 Soyfoods Association of North America
1050 17th Street, NW
Suite 600
Washington, DC 20036

202-659-3520
E-Mail: info@soyfoods.org
Home Page: www.soyfoods.org
Social Media: *Facebook, Twitter, YouTube, Pinterest*

Kate Leavltt, President
Helen Kor, Vice President
Kate Leavitt, Treasurer
Nancy Chapman, Executive Director

A trusted advocate in providing information about the health benefits and nutritional advantages of soy consumption. Encouraging sustainability, integrity and growth of the soyfoods industry through members.
50+ Members
Founded in 1978

9824 Specialty Coffee Association of America
117 W. 4th St,
Suite 300
Santa Ana, CA 92701

562-624-4100
FAX 562-624-4101
E-Mail: info@scaa.org
Home Page: www.scaa.org
Social Media: *Facebook, Twitter, YouTube*

Tracy Allen, President
Ben Pitts, Vice President
Heather Perry, 2nd Vice President
Guy Burdett, Secretary/Treasurer
Colleen Anunu, Director

One of the primary functions is to set the industry's standards for growing, roasting and brewing. Members of the SCAA include coffee retailers, roasters, producers, exporters and importers, as well as manufacturers of coffee equipment and related products.
2500+ Members
Founded in 1982
Mailing list available for rent

9825 Specialty Food Association and Fancy Food Show
136 Madison Avenue
12th Floor
New York, NY 10016

646-878-0301
FAX 212-482-6459
Home Page: www.specialtyfood.com
Social Media: *Facebook, Twitter, LinkedIn, YouTube*

Mike Silver, Chair
Shawn McBride, Vice Chair
Ann Daw, President
Becky Renfro Borbolla, Treasurer
Matt Neilsen, Secretary

A business trade association to foster trade, commerce and interest in the specialty food industry. Composed of domestic and foreign manufacturers, importers, distributors, brokers, retailers, restaurateurs, caterers and others in the specialty foods business.
3000+ Members
Founded in 1952

9826 Sugar Association
1300 L Street NW
Suite 1001
Washington, DC 20005

202-785-1122
FAX 202-785-5019
E-Mail: sugar@sugar.org

Home Page: www.sugar.org
Social Media: *Facebook, Twitter, Pinterest*

Andrew Briscoe, President/CEO
P. Courtney Gaine, VP, Scientific Affairs
Cheryl Digges, VP Public Policy & Education
Lisa Swanson, Administrative Assistant

Promoting the consumption of sugar through sound scientific principles while maintaining an understanding of the benefits that sugar contributes to the quality of wholesome foods and beverages.
Founded in 1943

9827 Switzerland Cheese Association
704 Executive Blvd
Suite I
Valley Cottage, NY 10989-2010

845-268-2460
FAX 845-268-9991

Paul U Schilt, CEO

9828 Tea Association of the USA
362 Fifth Avenue
Suite 801
New York, NY 10001

212-986-9415
FAX 212-697-8658
E-Mail: info@teausa.com
Home Page: www.teausa.com
Social Media: *Facebook, Twitter*

Joe Simrany, President

Association of companies dedicated to the interests and growth of the US tea industry.
100 Members
Founded in 1899
Mailing list available for rent

9829 Tea Board of India
14 B.T.M. Sarani
Kolkata, KO 700001

332-235-1331
FAX 332-221-5715
Home Page: www.teaboard.gov.in

Santosh Sarangi, Chairman
A.K Das, Deputy Chairman
Sumita Lahiri, Personal Secretary to Chairman
A. Rajan, Secretary
Joydip Biswas, Deputy Director

This association promotes Indian tea and develops new markets for tea in the US and Canada.
Founded in 1953

9830 The American Dairy Association Indiana, Inc.
9360 Castlegate Drive
Indianapolis, IN 46256

317-842-3060
800-225-6455
FAX 317-842-3065
E-Mail: osza@winnersdrinkmilk.comy
Home Page: www.indianadairycouncil.org
Social Media: *Facebook, Twitter, LinkedIn, YouTube, Pinterest, Instagram*

Donald Gurtner, President
Paul Mills, Vice President
Steve Phares, Treasurer
Anita Schmitt, Secretary

A not-for-profit organization which promotes the sale and consumption of diary foods.
Founded in 1915

9831 The Biscuit & Cracker Manufacturers' Association
6325 Woodside Court
Suite 125
Columbia, MD 21046

443-545-1645
FAX 410-290-8585
E-Mail: info@thebcma.org

Home Page: www.thebema.org
Social Media: *Facebook, LinkedIn*

David Van Laar, President
Kathy Kinter Phelps, Membership & Education Manager
Vickie Clancy, Meetings Assistant
Dennis Loalbo, Technical Advisor
Blake Hutzley, Technical Advisor

International trade organization representing the entire spectrum of companies involved in the manufacturing of biscuits and crackers and the suppliers to the baking industry. Our mission is to bring unparalled educational training programs and networking opportunities to members of the cookie and cracker industry.
250 Members
Founded in 1901

9832   The Catfish Institute

6311 Ridgewood Road
Suite W404
Jackson, MS 39211

601-977-9559
FAX 662-887-6857
E-Mail: catfishinfo@uscatfish.com
Home Page: www.uscatfish.com
Social Media: *Facebook, Twitter, Youtube, Pinterest*

Butch Wilson, President
Roger Barlow, Executive Vice-President

Represents the largest aquaculture industry in the United States. Represents the interests of the farm-raised catfish industry of farmers, processors, feed mills, researchers, and supplier industries. Promotes the many healthy, great tasting uses for genuine U.S. Farm-Raised Catfish.
Cost: $40.00
Frequency: Membership Fees
Founded in 1986
Mailing list available for rent

9833   The Cranberry Institute

PO Box 497
Carver, MA 02330

508-866-1118
FAX 508-866-1199
E-Mail: cinews@cranberryinstitute.org
Home Page: www.cranberryinstitute.org

Kevin Hatton, Chairman
Bob Wilson, Vice Chairman
Steve Berlyn, Secretary/Treasurer

A nonprofit that supports cranberry growers and the cranberry industry.
Founded in 1951

9834   The Food and Beverage Association of America

111 East 14th Street
Suite 390
New York, NY 10003

212-344-8252
FAX 212-504-9536
E-Mail: office@fbassoc.com
Home Page: www.fbassoc.com
Social Media: *Facebook, LinkedIn, YouTube*

Steven V. Gattullo, President
Sean Cassidy, First Vice President
Gus Montesantos, Second Vice President
Guy Salisch, Secretary
Daniel Saalman, Treasurer

A nonprofit, philanthropic, trade organization for executives of the food and beverage industries of the New York metropolitan area.
Founded in 1956

9835   The Industry Council for Research on Packaging and the Environment

SoanePoint, 6-8 Market Place
Reading
Berkshire RG1 2EG

118-925-5991
FAX 202-833-3636
E-Mail: info@incpen.org
Home Page: www.incpen.org
Social Media: *Facebook, Twitter*

Steve Young, President

A research organization, which draws together an influential group of companies who share a vision of the future where all production, distribution, and consumption are sustainable. Aiming to ensure policies on packaging makes a positive contribution to sustainability, encourages the industry to minimize the environmental impact of packaging and continuously improve packaging, and explain the role of packaging in society.
Founded in 1974

9836   The National Chicken Council

1152 15th Street NW
Suite 430
Washington, DC 20005-2622

202-296-2622
FAX 202-293-4005
E-Mail: ncc@chickenusa.org
Home Page: www.nationalchickencouncil.org
Social Media: *Facebook, Twitter*

Michael J. Brown, President
Ashley Peterson, Senior Vice President
Mary M. Colville, VP of Government Affairs
Tom Super, Vice President of Communications
Margaret A. Ernst,, Senior Director

National, non-profit trade association representing the US chicken industry. Promoting and protecting the interests of the chicken industry and acts as the industry's voice before Congress and federal agencies. Members include chicken producer/processors, poultry distributors, and allied industry firms.
150+ Members
Founded in 1954

9837   The National Confectioners' Association

1101 30th Street, NW
Suite 200
Washington, DC 20007

202-534-1440
FAX 202-337-0637
E-Mail: info@CandyUSA.com
Home Page: www.candyusa.com
Social Media: *Facebook, Twitter, LinkedIn, Flickr, Pinterest, YouTube*

Robert M. Simpson, Jr., Chairman
Peter W. Blommer, Vice Chairman
John H. Downs, Jr., President/ CEO
Joseph Vittoria, Treasurer
Martino Caretto, Vice President

Advances, protects, and promotes the confectionery industry.
Founded in 1884

9838   The Peanut Institute

PO Box 70157
Albany, GA 31708-0157

229-888-0216
888-873-2688
FAX 229-888-5150
Home Page: www.peanut-institute.org
Social Media: *Facebook, Twitter, YouTube*

A nonprofit that supports nutrition research and advocates for the peanut's place in healthful lifestyles.

9839   Today's Market Prices

Home Page: www.todaymarket.com

A user friendly information center that provides within its market prices service, daily price information on more than 200 fruit, vegetables, and herbs from the most important wholesale markets of the USA, Canada, Mexico, and Europe.
Founded in 1996

9840   Tortilla Industry Association

1600 Wlison Blvd
Suite 650
Arlington, VA 22209

800-944-6099
FAX 800-944-6177
E-Mail: info@tortilla-info.com
Home Page: www.tortilla-info.com

Criss Cruz, Chairman
Jim Kabbani, Executive Director
Dana Beall, Secretary

Members include companies engaged in manufacturing tortillas and suppliers, food brokers and Mexican restaurant owners.
175 Members
Founded in 1886

9841   U.S. Meat Export Federationÿ

1855 Blake Street
Suite 200
Denver, CO 80202

303-623-6328
FAX 303-623-0297
E-Mail: migoe@usmef.org
Home Page: www.usmef.org
Social Media: *Facebook, Twitter, YouTube*

Leann Saunders, Chair
Roel Andriessen, Chair-elect
Bruce Schmoll, Vice Chair
Dennis Stiffler, Treasurer/ Secretary
Philip M. Seng, President, CEO

A nonprofit trade association working to create new opportunities and develop existing international markets for U.S. beef, pork, lamb, and veal.

9842   U.S. Poultry & Egg Associationÿ

1530 Cooledge Road
Tucker, GA 30084-7303

770-493-9401
FAX 770-493-9257
E-Mail: info@uspoultry.org
Home Page: www.uspoultry.org
Social Media: *Facebook, Twitter, LinkedIn, Google+, YouTube*

John Starkey, President
Charles Olentine, PhD, Executive Vice President
Gwen Venable, Vice President of Communications
Jason Rivera, Vice President, IT
Barbara Jenkins, Vice President - Education Programs

Represents producers and processors of broilers, turkeys, eggs and breeding stock, as well as allied companies.
Founded in 1947

9843   U.S. Wheat Associates

3103 10th Street, North
Suite 300
Arlington, VA 22201

202-463-0999
FAX 703-524-4399
E-Mail: info@uswheat.org
Home Page: www.uswheat.org
Social Media: *Facebook, Twitter, YouTube, Flickr*

Brian O'Toole, Chairman
Jason Scott, Vice Chairman

Roy Motter, Past Chairman
Alan Tracy, President
Mike Miller, Secretary-Treasurer

Supports the sale of wheat by offering education for overseas buyers, onsite training services, promotes trade policies, and consumer promotion.

9844 US Animal Health Association
4221 Mitchelle Ave.
Saint Joseph, MO 64507

816-671-1144
FAX 816-671-1201
E-Mail: usaha@usaha.org
Home Page: www.usaha.org
Social Media: *Facebook, Twitter*

Dr. Stephen Crawford, President
Dr. Bruce King, President-Elect
Dr. David Schmitt, First Vice President
Dr. Boyd Parr, Second Vice President
Mrs. Barbara Determan, 3rd Vice President

Seeks to prevent, control and eliminate livestock diseases.
1400 Members
Founded in 1897

9845 US Apple Association
8233 Old Courthouse Rd
Suite 200
Vienna, VA 22182

703-442-8850
FAX 703-790-0845
E-Mail: info@usapple.org
Home Page: www.usapple.org
Social Media: *Facebook, Twitter, Youtube*

Jim Bair, President & CEO
Diane Kurrle, Senior Vice President
Jessa Allen,
Director,Membership&Communicatons
Wendy Brannen, Director,Consumer Health
Niza Strike, Office manager

Providing all segments of the US apple industry the means to profitably produce and market apples and apple products. Committed to serving the entire US apple industry by representing the industry on national issues, increasing the demand for apples and apple products, and providing information on matters pertaining to the apple industry.
440 Members
Founded in 1970

9846 US Beet Sugar Association
1156 15th St NW
Suite 1019
Washington, DC 20005

202-296-4820
800-872-0127
FAX 202-331-2065
Home Page: www.beetsugar.org

James Johnson, President
Elin Peltz, VP
Claudia Tidwell, Director of Administration
Hillary Fabrico, Government Affairs Assistant
Cassie Bladow, Director of Government Affairs

Beet sugar processing companies make up the membership of this association.
Founded in 1911

9847 US Canola Association
600 Pennsylvania Ave SE
Suite 320
Washington, DC 20003

202-969-8113
FAX 202-969-7036
E-Mail: info@uscanola.com
Home Page: www.uscanola.com
Social Media: *Facebook, Twitter, YouTube*

Ryan Pederson, President
Jeff Scott, First VP
Robert Rynning, Second Vice President

Works to support and advance US canola production, marketing, processing and use through government and industry relations. Striving to develop and implement agricultural policies, promote efficient production of the crop, and develop markets for US canola products.
Founded in 1989

9848 US Grains Council
20 F Street, NW
Suite 600
Washington, DC 20001

202-789-0789
FAX 202-898-0522
E-Mail: grains@grains.org
Home Page: www.grains.org
Social Media: *Facebook, Twitter, Youtube, Flickr*

Alan Tiemann, Chairman
Chip Councell, Vice Chairman
Thomas Sleight, President & CEO
Debra Keller, Secretary/Treasurer
Jim Raben, At-Large Director

Develops export markets for US barley, corn, grain sorghum and related products. Members include producer organizations and agribusinesses with a common interest in developing export markets.
100 Members
Founded in 1960

9849 US Meat Export Federation
1855 Blake St
Suite 200
Denver, CO 80202

303-623-6328
FAX 303-623-0297
E-Mail: migoe@usmef.org
Home Page: www.usmef.org

Leann Saunders, Chair
Roel Andriessen, Chair-elect
Bruce Schmoll, Vice Chair
Dennis Stiffler, Treasurer/ Secretary
Philip M. Seng, President, CEO

A trade association working to create new opportunities and develop existing international markets for U.S. beef, pork, lamb and veal.
160 Members
Founded in 1996

9850 US Poultry & Egg Association
1530 Cooledge Rd
Tucker, GA 30084-7303

770-938-6915
FAX 770-493-9257
E-Mail: chanson@poultryegg.org
Home Page: www.poultryegg.org
Social Media: *Facebook*

Gary Cooper, Chairman
John Starkey, President
Carol 9anson, Executive Assistant

Representing the entire industry as an All Feather association. Membership includes producers and processors of broilers, turkeys, ducks, eggs, and breeding stock, as well as allied companies.
Cost: $300.00
600 Members
Frequency: Membership Dues
Founded in 1947

9851 USA Hops
PO Box 1207
301 W Prospect Place
Moxee, WA 98936

509-453-4749
FAX 509-457-8561
E-Mail: info@usahops.org
Home Page: www.usahops.org

Supports commercial hop producers in US Pacific Northwest.

9852 USA Rice Federation
2101 Wilson Boulevard
Suite 610
Arlington, VA 22201ÿÿ

703-236-2300
FAX 703-236-2301
E-Mail: riceinfo@usarice.com
Home Page: www.usarice.com
Social Media: *Facebook, Twitter, RSS, YouTube, Pinterest*

A national association representing producers, millers and allied businesses advancing the use and consumption of U.S. grown rice.

9853 United Agribusiness League
54 Corporate Park
Irvine, CA 92606

800-223-4590
FAX 949-975-1671
E-Mail: membership@unitedag.org
Home Page: www.unitedag.org
Social Media: *Facebook*

Brian Edmonds, Chairman
Anthony Vollering, Vice Chairman
A.J. Cisney, Treasurer
Les Graulich, Director
Jerry Pogorzelski, Director

Creating a community for agribusiness—networking and education.
Founded in 1983

9854 United Braford Breeders
Home Page: www.brafords.org

Organization that registers Braford cattle in the United States.

9855 United Egg Producers
1720 Windward Concourse
Alpharetta, GA 30005

770-360-9220
FAX 770-360-7058
Home Page: www.unitedegg.org
Social Media: *Facebook, Twitter*

Chad Gregory, President & CEO
David Inall, Senior Vice President
Sherry Shedd, Vice President of Finance
Oscar Garrison, Director of Food Safety
Derreck Nassar, Director of Operations

UEP is a Capper-Volstead cooperative of egg farmers from all across the United States and representing the ownership of all the nation's egg-laying hens.
Founded in 1968

9856 United Food and Commercial Workers International Union
1775 K St Nw
Washington, DC 20006

202-223-3111
FAX 202-466-1562
E-Mail: ssmith@ufcw.org
Home Page: www.ufcw.org
Social Media: *Facebook, Twitter, YouTube, Flickr*

Anthony Marc Perrone, President
Patrick J O'Neill, Secretary/Treasurer
Paul Meinema, Executive VP
Esther lopez, Executive VP
Wayne E. Hanley, Executive VP

UFCW is North America's neighborhood union, members standing together to improve the lives and livelihoods of workers, families and communities.
1.4 M Members
Founded in 1979

9857 United Fresh Produce Association

1901 Pennsylvania Ave NW
Suite 1100
Washington, DC 20006

202-303-3400
FAX 202-303-3433
E-Mail: united@unitedfresh.org
Home Page: www.unitedfresh.org
Social Media: *Facebook, Twitter, LinkedIn*

Brian W. Kocher, Chairman
Tony Freytag, Chairman-Elect
Lisa J. Strube, Secretary/Treasurer
Miriam Wolk, Vice President of Membership
Jeff Oberman, Vice President, Trade Relations

A trade association committed to driving the growth and success of produce companies ans their partners. Represents the interests of member companies throughout the global, fresh produce supply chain, including family-owned, private and publicly trade businesses as well as regional, national and international companies.
Founded in 1987

9858 United Soybean Board

16305 Swingley Ridge Rd
Suite 150
Chesterfield, MO 63017

636-530-1777
800-989-8721
FAX 636-530-1560
E-Mail: ydock@unitedsoybean.com
Home Page: www.unitedsoybean.org
Social Media: *Facebook, Twitter, YouTube*

Jim Stillman, Chairman
Jim Call, Vice Chair
John Becherer, CEO
Lewis Brainbridge, Secretary
Bob Haselwood, Treasurer

Mission is to ensure that US soy is of the highest quality and the most competitive in a global marketplace.
Founded in 1972
Mailing list available for rent

9859 United States Cane Sugar Refiners

1730 Rhode Island Ave NW
#608
Washington, DC 20036-3101

202-331-1458

Joseph Cox, President

9860 United States Potato Board

4949 S. Syracuse St.
#400
Denver, CO 80237

303-369-7783
FAX 303-369-7718
E-Mail: info@uspotatoes.com
Home Page: www.uspotatoes.com
Social Media: *Facebook, Twitter, LinkedIn, YouTube, Pinterest, Instagram*

Rob Davis, Chairman
Blair Richardson, President & CEO
Diana LeDoux, VP,Finance/Information Technology
David Fraser, VP, Industry Communciations
John Toaspern, Vice President, International

The nation's potato marketing organization. The central organizing force in implementing programs that will increase demand for potatoes, providing the ideas, information, tools and inspiration for the industry to unite in achieving common goals.
Founded in 1971

9861 United States Tuna Foundation

1101 17th St NW
Suite 609
Washington, DC 20036-4718

202-857-0610
Home Page: www.tunafacts.com

Desiree Filippone, Manager

Serves as an umbrella organization representing the various interests of the U.S. canned tuna industry. Representing the internationaln and domestic interests to federal and state regulations, to national legislation, to domestic marketing.
Founded in 1976

9862 Vegetarian Awareness Network/VEGANET

4041G Hadley Road,
Suite 101
South Plainfield, NJ 07080

908-769-1160
800-872-8343
FAX 908-769-1171
E-Mail: jasmineburroughs@wfcinc.com
Home Page: www.wholefoodsmagazine.com
Social Media: *Facebook, Twitter, LinkedIn*

Howard V. Wainer, President

Networks to promote healthful living, environmental healing, and respect for all life; to advance public awareness of the advantages of the increasingly popular vegetarian lifestyle; to enhance the visibility and accessibility of vegetarian products and services; and to facilitate the formation and expansion of local vegetarian organizations.
Founded in 1980

9863 Vegetarian Resource Group

PO Box 1463
Baltimore, MD 21203

410-366-8343
FAX 410-366-8804
E-Mail: vrg@vrg.org
Home Page: www.vrg.org
Social Media: *Facebook, Twitter*

Debra Wasserman, Director

An organization dedicated to educating the public on vegetarianism and the interrelated issues of health, nutrition, ecology, ethics, and world hunger.
15000 Members
Founded in 1982
Mailing list available for rent

9864 Vidalia Onion Committee

100 Vidalia Sweet Onion Drive
PO Box 1609
Vidalia, GA 30474

912-537-1918
FAX 912-537-2166
E-Mail: info@vidaliaonion.org
Home Page: www.vidaliaonion.org
Social Media: *Facebook, Twitter, YouTube, Pinterest*

Aries Haygood, Chairman
Michael E. Hively, Vice Chairman
Myrtle S. Jones, Secretary

Promote growth, distribution and awareness of this one of a kind crop.
225 Members
Founded in 1931

9865 Vinegar Institute

1100 Johnson Ferry Road
Suite 300
Atlanta, GA 30342

404-252-3663
FAX 404-252-0774
E-Mail: vidsmith@kellencompany.com

Home Page: www.versatilevinegar.org
Social Media: *Facebook*

Pamela A Chumley, President
Jeannie Milewski, Executive Director

Manufacturers and bottlers of vinegar and suppliers to the industry are the members of this association. Publications available only to members.
Founded in 1967

9866 Walnut Council

1007 N 725 W
West Lafayette, IN 47906-9431

765-583-3501
FAX 765-583-3512
E-Mail: walnutcouncil@walnutcouncil.org
Home Page: www.walnutcouncil.org

Jerry Van Sambeek, President
Dan Harris, Vice President
Liz Jackson, Executive Director
Bill Hoover, Treasurer
John Katzke, Quartermaster

Representing woodland owners, foresters, forest scientists and wood producing industry representatives. The purpose is to assist in the technical transfer of forest research to field applications, help build and maintain bettermarkets for wood products and nut crops.
1000 Members
Founded in 1970

9867 Western Dairy Association

12000 Washington
Suite 175
Thornton, CO 80241

303-451-7711
800-274-6455
FAX 303-451-0411
E-Mail: info@westerndairyassociation.org
Home Page: www.westerndairyassociation.org
Social Media: *Facebook, Twitter, YouTube*

Rick Podtburg, Chairman
Jim Webb, Vice-Chairman
Ron Shelton, Secretary
Tim Bernhardt, Treasurer
Cindy Haren, Chief Executive Officer

Leading dairy farmer members and the industry in a world class direction of partnerships and business resulting in economic viability, new innovations in dairy products and building stronger community commitment to dairy farms and dairy families.
Founded in 1936

9868 Western Growers Association

17620 Fitch Street
Irvine, CA 92614

949-863-1000
800-333-4942
FAX 949-863-9028
E-Mail: info@wga.com
Home Page: www.wga.com

Stephen J. Barnard, Chairman
Bruce C. Taylor, Senior Vice Chairman
Victor Smith, Vice Chairman
John S. Manfre, Secretary
Mark J. Teixeria, Treasurer

Association for growers, shippers, packers, brokers and distributors of fruits and vegetables in California and Arizona.
3000 Members
Founded in 1926

9869 Western U.S. Agricultural Trade Association

4601 NE 77th Ave
Suite 240
Vancouver, WA 98662

360-693-3373
FAX 360-693-3464

E-Mail: export@wusata.org
Home Page: www.wusata.org

Andy Anderson, Executive Directory
Janet Kenefsky, Deputy Director
Tricia Walker, FundMatch Manager
Betsy Green, Branded Coordinator
Robin Koss, Branded Coordinator

Exporting resource for agribusinesses based in the Western United States.
200 Members
Founded in 1980

9870 Western United States Agricultural Trade Association

4601 NE 77th Avenue
Suite 240
Vancouver, WA 98662

360-693-3373
FAX 360-693-3464
E-Mail: export@wusata.org
Home Page: www.wusata.org

Andy Anderson, Executive Director
Janet Kenefsky, Deputy Director
Tricia Walker, FundMatch Manager
Betsy Green, Branded Coordinator
Robin Koss, Branded Coordinator

This organization offers information and support to increase exports of US agricultural products.
200 Members
Founded in 1980

9871 Wheat Foods Council

51 Red Fox Lane
Unit D
Ridgway, CO 81432

970-626-9828
FAX 303-840-6877
E-Mail: wfc@wheatfoods.org
Home Page: www.wheatfoods.org
Social Media: *Facebook, Twitter*

Don Brown, Chair
Debi Rogers, Vice Chair
Tim O'Connor, President
Gayle Veum, Vice President
Reid Christopherson, Treasurer/Secretary

An industry-wide partnership dedicated to increasing wheat and other grain foods consumption through nutrition information, education, research and promotional programs.
Founded in 1972

9872 Wild Blueberry Association of North America

PO Box 100
Old Town, ME 04468

207-570-3535
FAX 207-581-3499
E-Mail: wildblueberries@gwi.net
Home Page: www.wildblueberries.com
Social Media: *Facebook, Twitter, Youtube, Pinterest, Googleplus*

Ragnar Kamp, President
Mike Collins, Marketing Manager

Represents processors and growers of wild blueberries in Eastern Canada and Maine. The Association is focused on the generic promotion of wild blueberries around the world. It offers promotional materials, joint buying, product development, assistance, seminars, newsletters, supplier lists and ongoing support to users of wild blueberries in all retail, manufacturing, food service and bakery trade segments.
Founded in 1981

9873 Wine & Spirits Wholesalers of America, Inc

805 15th Street NW
Suite 430
Washington, DC 20005

202-371-9792
FAX 202-789-2405
E-Mail: Info@wswa.org
Home Page: www.wswa.org
Social Media: *Facebook, Twitter, YouTube, RSS*

Craig Wolf, President and CEO
Jim Rowland, Senior VP, Government Affairs
Dawson Hobbs, Vice President, State Affairs
Reilly O Connor, Vice President, Government Affairs
Catherine McDaniel, Vice President, Government Affairs

Wine & Spirits Wholesalers of America, inc.(WSWA) is the national trade organization representing the wholesale tier of the wine and spirits industry. It is dedicated to advancing the interests and independence of wholesale distributors and brokers of wine and spirits.
450 Members
Founded in 1943

9874 Wine Appreciation Guild

360 Swift Ave
Unit 30-40
S San Francisco, CA 94080

650-866-3020
800-239-9463
FAX 650-866-3029
E-Mail: info@wineappreciation.com
Home Page: www.wineappreciation.com

James Mackey, Manager
Jason Simon, Manager
Jeff Szczesney, Contact
Hamlin Endicott, Contact
Amy Decker, Contact

Formed as the official successor in the distribution of wine accessories, and the publication and distribution of books and educational materials.
1500 Members
Founded in 1973

9875 Wine Institute

425 Market St
Suite 1000
San Francisco, CA 94105

415-512-0151
FAX 415-356-7569
E-Mail: info@wineinstitute.org
Home Page: www.wineinstitute.org

Robert Koch, President/CEO
Kaye Clement, Executive Assistant
Betty Easter, Receptionist
Steve Gross, VP State Relations
Nancy Light, VP Communications

Dedicated to initiating and advocating state, federal and international public policy to enhance the environment for the responsible consumption and enjoyment of wine.
887 Members
Founded in 1934

9876 Wine and Spirits Shippers Association

11800 Sunrise Valley Dr
Suite 332
Reston, VA 20191

703-860-2300
800-368-3167
FAX 703-860-2422
E-Mail: info@wssa.com
Home Page: www.wssa.com
Social Media: *Facebook, Twitter, LinkedIn*

V. James Andretta, Jr., Chairman Emeritus
Louis Healey, President
Howard Jacobs, Vice President

Alison Leavitt, Managing Director
Heather Randolph, Director of Operations

A non-profit shippers association composed of importers and exporters of beverages and allied products. Provides members, importers and exporters with efficient and economical ocean transportation and other logestic services.
400 Members
Founded in 1976

9877 Wine and Spirits Wholesalers of America, Inc.

805 15th Street, NW
Suite 430
Washington, DC 20036

202-371-9792
FAX 202-789-2405
E-Mail: Info@wswa.org
Home Page: www.wswa.org
Social Media: *Facebook, Twitter, YouTube, RSS*

Brien Fox, Chairman
Alan Dreeben, Immediate Past Chairman
Doug Epstein, Vice Chairman
Carmine Martignetti, Senior VP
Sydney Ross, Treasurer

National trade organization representing the wholesale branch of the wine and spirits industry.
450 Members
Founded in 1943

9878 Women in Flavor & Fragrance Commerce

Association of Food Industries
3301 Route 66
Suite 205, Building C
Neptune, NJ 07753

732-922-0500
FAX 732-922-0560
E-Mail: info@wffc.org
Home Page: www.wffc.org
Social Media: *Facebook, LinkedIn*

Amy Marks-Mcgee, President
Kay Bardsley-Murano, Vice President
BEA HORNEDO, Secretary
ERICA LERMOND MCDONNELL, Treasurer
Dolores Avezzano, Sales Manager

Provides a center of education, camaraderie, support and networking opportunities for women in our industry. Our membership encompasses women involved is sales, purchasing, customer service as well as technical and laboratory careers. WFFC has timely seminars as well as social and networking opportunities for our members and the industry as a whole.
300 Members
Founded in 1982

Newsletters

9879 AAMPlifier Bulletin

American Association of Meat Processors
One Meating Place
Elizabethtown, PA 17022

717-367-1168
FAX 717-367-9096
E-Mail: aamp@aamp.com
Home Page: www.aamp.com

Contains a wealth of information on industry trends, important national news, Association activities, and operational information to keep members fully informed about events affecting their business.
Frequency: Bi-Monthly
Founded in 1939

9880 ABF Newsletter
American Beekeeping Federation
3525 Piedmont Rd
Bldg 5 Suite 300
Atlanta, GA 30305-1509

404-760-2875
FAX 404-240-0998
E-Mail: info@abfnet.org
Home Page: www.abfnet.org

Robin Dahlen, President
David Mendes, VP

A member benefit published to inform members about ABF activities and happenings in the beekeeping industry.
Cost: $35.00
1200 Members
Frequency: Membership Fees Vary
Founded in 1943

9881 ABL Insider
American Beverage Licensees Association
5101 River Rd
Suite 108
Bethesda, MD 20816-1560

301-656-1494
FAX 301-656-7539
E-Mail: info@ablusa.org
Home Page: www.ablusa.org

Lyle Fitzsimmons, Editor

The voice of America's beer, wine & spirits retailers.
Frequency: Monthly

9882 ADPI Weekly Newsletter
American Dairy Products Institute
116 N York Street
Suite 200
Elmhurst, IL 60126

630-530-8700
FAX 630-530-8707
E-Mail: info@adpi.org
Home Page: www.adpi.org

Electronic communication of industry news, regulatory developments, and association matters.
Frequency: Weekly
Circulation: 1000

9883 AFFI Newsletter
American Frozen Food Institute
2000 Corporate Ridge
Suite 1000
McLean, VA 22102-7862

703-821-0770
FAX 703-821-1350
E-Mail: info@affi.com
Home Page: www.affi.com

Kraig R Naasz, President/CEO
Jason Bassett, Director Legislative Affairs
Chuck Fuqua, VP Communications
Robert L Garfield, SVP Public Policy/Intl Affairs
Frequency: Weekly

9884 AHA Quarterly
American Herb Association
PO Box 1673
Nevada City, CA 95959-1673

530-265-9552
FAX 530-274-3140
Home Page: www.ahaherb.com

Kathi Keville, Director
Robert Brucia, Co-Director
Marion Wyckoff, Secretary

Reports on the latest scientific studies, new herb, aromatherapy, cooking and gardening books, international herb news, legal and environmental issues, herb-related events and con-

ferences.
Cost: $20.00
20 Pages
Frequency: w/Membership
Founded in 1981

9885 AICR Newsletter
American Institute for Cancer Research
1759 R St NW
Washington, DC 20009-2570

202-328-7744
800-843-8114
FAX 202-328-7226
E-Mail: aicrweb@aicr.org
Home Page: www.aicr.org

Marilyn Gentry, President

Explains current cancer research, provides recipes and menu ideas for healthy eating, and offers practical advice to lower cancer risk.
Frequency: Quarterly
Circulation: 1.6MM
Founded in 1982

9886 ALBC News
American Livestock Breeds Conservancy
15 Hillsboro Street
PO Box 477
Pittsboro, NC 27312

919-542-5704
FAX 919-545-0022
E-Mail: albc@albc-usa.org
Home Page: www.albc-usa.org

Marjorie Bender, Prog. Coord./Research
Don Schrider, Communication Director
Charles Bassett, Executive Director
Angelique Thompson, Operations Manager
Jennifer Kendall, Communications Director

Breeders directory; annual conference; catalog of publications available.
Cost: $30.00
20 Pages
Circulation: 3000
ISSN: 1064-1599
Founded in 1977
Printed in one color on matte stock

9887 AMSA eNews
American Meat Science Association
2441 Village Green Pl
Champaign, IL 61822-7676

800-517-AMSA
FAX 888-205-5834
FAX 217-356-5370
E-Mail: information@meatscience.org
Home Page: www.meatscience.org

William Mikel, President
Scott J. Eilert, President Elect
Casey B. Frye, Treasurer

Published for all AMSA members every other week, including member news and meat science information updates.

9888 APIS
CITA International
3464 W Earll Drive
Suites E & F
Phoenix, AZ 85017

602-447-0480
FAX 602-447-0305
E-Mail: esam@citainternational.com
Home Page: www.citainternational.com

EM Morsy, Editor
PE Pederson, Advertising/Sales

The international bulletin for specialty livestock, pet animal and ag-chem product developments.
Frequency: Quarterly
Founded in 1988

9889 ASBC Newsletter
American Society of Brewing Chemists

3340 Pilot Knob Rd
Eagan, MN 55121-2055

651-454-7250
FAX 651-454-0766
E-Mail: asbc@scisoc.org
Home Page: www.asbcnet.org

Steven C Nelson, VP

Contains the annual meeting program, lists of ASBC committees and reports, and local section news.
Frequency: Quarterly
Circulation: 800+
Founded in 1934

9890 ASTA Advocate
American Spice Trade Association
2025 M St NW
Suite 800
Washington, DC 20036-2422

202-367-1127
FAX 202-367-2127
E-Mail: info@astaspice.org
Home Page: www.astaspice.org

Donna Tainter, President
Roger Clarke, Vice President/ Secretary
Gaspare Colletti, Treasurer
David Howe, Associate Group Director

Electronic newsletter designed to keep members informed about the spice industry, events impacting the industry and ASTA activities. ASTA Advocate is ASTA's regulatory newsletter.
Frequency: Membership Dues Vary
Founded in 1907

9891 Agri Times Northwest
Sterling Ag
PO Box 189
Pendleton, OR 97801

541-276-7845
FAX 541-276-7964
Home Page: www.agritimes.com/

Virgil Rupp, CEO/President
Sterling Allen, Publisher/Marketing Director

Regional agricultural newspaper.
Cost: $20.00
16 Pages
Circulation: 3700
Printed in 4 colors on newsprint stock

9892 Agri-Pulse
International Dairy Foods Association
1250 H Street NW
Suite 900
Washington, DC 20005

202-737-4332
FAX 202-331-7820
E-Mail: membership@idfa.org
Home Page: www.idfa.org
Social Media: *Facebook, Twitter, YouTube, Blog*

Connie Tipton, President & CEO
Mike Nosewicz, Chair
Brian Perry, Vice Chair
Jon Davis, Secretary
Ed Mullins, Treasurer

The latest information and news in agricultural information. Investigating several aspects of the food, fuel, feed and fiber industries, looking at the economic, statistical and financial trends and evaluate the changes impacting businesses.
550 Members
Frequency: Weekly

9893 Alcoholic Beverage Control Fast: From the State Capitals
Wakeman Walworth

PO Box 7376
Alexandria, VA 22307-7376

703-768-9600
FAX 703-768-9690
Home Page:
www.statecapitals.com/alcoholbev.html

Keyes Walworth, Publisher

Covers binge drinking laws, internet sales, advertising, taxes, bottle bills, Sunday sales laws, license regulation, drunk driving laws, under-age drinking, mini-bottles and other state laws affecting beer, liquor and wine distribution.
4 Pages
Frequency: Weekly
Founded in 1962
Printed in one color on matte stock

9894 Alcoholic Beverage Executives' Newsletter International
Patricia Kennedy
PO Box 3188
Omaha, NE 68103-1088

402-397-5514
FAX 402-397-3843

Patricia Kennedy, Editor

Current news of the wine, beer, and distilled spirits marketplace, and provides information and ideas for the marketing and advertising campaigns of these beverages.
Cost: $275.00
Frequency: Weekly
ISSN: 0889-3510

9895 American Agriculturist
Farm Progress Companies
255 38th Avenue
Suite P
St Charles, IL 60174-5410

630-462-2224
800-441-1410
E-Mail: jvogel@farmprogress.com
Home Page:
www.farmprogress.com/american-agriculturist/

John Vogel, Editor
Willie Vogt, Cororate Editorial Director
Dan Crummett, Executive Editor

Serves Northeast producers with information to help them maximize their productivity and profitability. Each issue is packed with information, ideas, news and analysis.
Cost: $29.65
Frequency: Monthly
Founded in 1842

9896 American Bakers Association Bulletin
American Bakers Association
1350 I Street NW
Suite 1290
Washington, DC 20005-3305

202-789-0300
FAX 202-898-1164
E-Mail: kkotche@americanbakers.org
Home Page: www.americanbakers.org

Kelly Kotche, Communications/Membership Manager
Paul Abenante, President/CEO

The association's newsletter that covers the conventions.
Frequency: Semi-Annual

9897 American Beekeeping Federation Newsletter
American Beekeeping Federation
3525 Piedmont Rd
Bldg 5 Suite 300
Atlanta, GA 30305-1509

404-760-2875
FAX 404-240-0998

E-Mail: info@abfnet.org
Home Page: www.abfnet.org

Raymond Payne, President
ABF-member benefit to inform members about ABF activities and happenings in the beekeeping industry.
24 Pages
Frequency: Bi-Monthly
Circulation: 1,200
Founded in 1943

9898 American Herb Association Quarterly Newsletter
American Herb Association
PO Box 1673
Nevada City, CA 95959-1673

530-265-9552
FAX 530-274-3140
Home Page: www.ahaherb.com

Kathi Keville, Director
Robert Brucia, Co-Director
Marion Wyckoff, Secretary

Updates and news on the herbal industry, such as; new scientific herbal and aromatherapy studies, plants interaction with ecology, reports on legal issues about herbs, a calendar of herbal and aromatherapy events, and a media report listing the herbal stories in the media.
Cost: $20.00
Frequency: Membership Fee
Founded in 1981

9899 American Institute of Baking Technical Bulletin
American Institute of Baking
PO Box 3999
Manhattan, KS 66505-3999

785-537-4750
866-342-4772
FAX 785-565-6060
E-Mail: bissc@bissc.org
Home Page: www.bissc.org

James Munyon, President

Developed to keep the baking and allied trades apprised of current trends in ingredients, products, equipment, processing, packaging, nutrition and research.
Frequency: Monthly

9900 American Meat Institute: Newsletter
American Meat Institute
1150 Connecticut Ave Nw
Suite 1200
Washington, DC 20036-4126

202-587-4200
FAX 202-587-4300
Home Page: www.meatami.com

J Patrick Boyle, CEO
Janet Riley, Editor
Ayoka Blandford, Marketing Manager

Subscription includes news of legislative and government regulations and actions relevant to the meat industry.
Frequency: Quarterly
Circulation: 3000
Founded in 1906

9901 American Society of Agricultural Consultants News
American Society of Agricultural Consultants
950 S Cherry Street
Suite 508
Denver, CO 80246-2664

303-758-3514
FAX 303-758-0190
Home Page: www.agconsultants.org

Deborah Wiig, Editor

Informs ASAC members of news regarding members, events, education and government issues.
8-12 Pages
Frequency: Quarterly
Circulation: 200
Founded in 1963
Printed in on newsprint stock

9902 American Soybean Association Newsletter
American Soybean Association
12125 Woodcrest Executive
Suite 100
Creve Coeur, MO 63141-5009

314-576-1770
800-688-7692
FAX 314-576-2786
E-Mail: bcallanan@soy.org
Home Page: www.soygrowers.com

Steve Censky, CEO
Neal Bredehoeft, President
Bob Metz, VP

Mission is to improve US soybean farmer profitability.
Frequency: Monthly
Founded in 1920
Printed in 4 colors on glossy stock

9903 Angus Beef Bulletin
American Angus Association
3201 Frederick Ave
St Joseph, MO 64506-2997

816-383-5100
FAX 816-233-9703
E-Mail: angus@angus.org
Home Page: www.angus.org
Social Media: *Facebook, Twitter*

Joe Hampton, Chair
Jarold Callahan, Vice Chair
Phil Trowbridge, Treasurer

To provide programs, services, technology and leadership to enhance the genetics of the Angus breed, broaden its influence within the beef industry, and expand the market for superior tasting, high-quality Angus beef worldwide. Achieve Angus excellence through information.
Cost: $80.00
30+M Members
Frequency: Membership Fees Vary
Founded in 1883

9904 Association of American Seed Control Officials Bulletin
Utah Department of Agriculture
801 Summit Crossing Place
Suite C
Gastonia, NC 28054

704-810-8877
FAX 704-853-4109
E-Mail: richard.payne2@usda.com
Home Page: www.seedcontrol.org

Ron Pence, President
John Heaton, Services Director
Brenda Ball, Second VP
Brenda Ball, Second VP
Greg Helmbrecht, Treasurer

Seed laws in the US and Canada.
Frequency: Annual

9905 Association of Food Industries Newsletter
Association of Food Industries
3301 State Route 66
Suite 205, Building C
Neptune, NJ 07753-2705

732-922-3008
FAX 732-922-3590

E-Mail: info@naooa.org
Home Page: www.naooa.org

Robert Bauer, President

Offers information & education on customs and usage of trade in the food industry and current events in the business.
Founded in 1906

9906 BEMA Newsletter
Bakery Equipment Manufacturers Association
10740 Nall Avenue
Suite 230
Overland Park, KS 66211

913-338-1300
FAX 913-338-1327
E-Mail: info@bema.org
Home Page: www.bema.org

Published by BEMA, to keep members informed about the latest baking and food industry news.
Frequency: Quarterly

9907 Bakers Band Together to Demand Relief-ABA Calls for March on Washington
American Bakers Association
1120 Connecticut Avenue NW
Washington, DC 200036

800-226-5377
Home Page: www.aba.com

Robb Mac Kie, President
Frequency: Monthly

9908 Beer Marketer's Insights Newsletter
Beer Marketer's Insights
49 E Maple Ave
Suffern, NY 10901-5507

845-624-2337
FAX 845-624-2340
Home Page: www.beerinsights.com

Benj Steinman, President

Reports on the competitive battle among brewers for a share of the beer market. Analyzes recent legislation and factors that affect the industry.
Frequency: Monthly

9909 Beer Perspectives
National Beer Wholesalers Association
1101 King Street
Suite 600
Alexandria, VA 22314-2965

703-683-4300
FAX 703-683-8965
E-Mail: info@nbwa.org
Home Page: www.nbwa.org
Social Media: *Facebook, Twitter*

Craig A Purser, President & CEO
Michael Johnson, EVP
Rebecca Spicer, VP Public Affairs/Chief
Paul Pisano, SVP Industry Affairs/Gen. Counsel

NBWA's newsletter reporting legislative, regulatory and industry news of importance to beer distributors.
Frequency: Bi-Weekly

9910 Beer Statistics News
Beer Marketer's Insights
49 E Maple Ave
Suffern, NY 10901-5507

845-624-2337
FAX 845-624-2340
Home Page: www.beerinsights.com

Benj Steinnan, CEO/President
Jerry Curley, Circulation Manager

Supplies data for major brewers' shipments in 39 reporting states.
Cost: $450.00
Frequency: Annual+

9911 Beverage Digest
Beverage Digest
PO Box 621
Bedford Hills, NY 10507-0621

914-244-0700
FAX 914-244-0774
E-Mail: order@beverage-digest.com
Home Page: www.beverage-digest.com

John Sicher, Editor/Publisher
Tom Fine, Managing Editor

Authoritative publication covering the non-alcoholic beverages industry.
Cost: $675.00
Frequency: 22 issues per y
Founded in 1982

9912 Beverage World Periscope
Keller International Publishing Corporation
150 Great Neck Rd
Suite 400
Great Neck, NY 11021-3309

516-829-9722
FAX 516-829-9306
Home Page: www.supplychainbrain.com

Terry Beirne, Publisher
Bryan DeLuca, Editor
Jerry Keller, President
Mary Chavez, Director of Sales

Analysis of developments as they occur in the beverage marketplace, presented in a tightly-written, four-color tabloid format, makes this a unique newsletter. This publication limits advertising to tabloid or standard pages.
Frequency: Monthly
Circulation: 33000
Founded in 1882

9913 Bottled Water Reporter
Bottled Water Association
1700 Diagonal Road
Suite 650
Alexandria, VA 22314-2844

703-683-5213
FAX 703-683-4074
E-Mail: mbusetti@bottledwater.org
Home Page: www.bottledwater.org

Sabrina Hicks, Editor

Trade news.

9914 Brewers Bulletin
PO Box 677
Thiensville, WI 53092

262-242-6105
FAX 262-242-5133
E-Mail: bulletindigest@milwpc.com

Thomas Volke, President

Brewing industry newspaper.
Cost: $53.00
Circulation: 550
Founded in 1907

9915 Brown Swiss Bulletin
Brown Swiss Cattle Breeder's Assoc of the USA
800 Pleasant St
Beloit, WI 53511-5456

608-365-4474
FAX 608-365-5577
E-Mail: info@brownswissusa.com
Home Page: www.brownswissusa.com

David Wallace, Executive Secretary
Charlotte Muenzenberg, Sup't of Records
Leonard Johnson, Genetic Programs/Show

Manager
Cost: $25.00
Frequency: Monthly
ISSN: 0007-2516

9916 Bu$Iness of Herbs
Herb Growing and Marketing Network
PO Box 245
Silver Spring, PA 17575-0245

717-393-3295
FAX 717-393-9261
E-Mail: herbworld@aol.com
Home Page: www.herbworld.com

Finds a wide variety of articles that will help with marketing, growing and genergal business issues. Has profiles of herb businesses and how they've created a business that allows them to support themselves with their passion.
Cost: $48.00
Frequency: Monthly

9917 Business of Herbs
Northwind Farm Publications
439 Ponderosa Way
Jemez Springs, NM 87025-8036

505-829-3448
FAX 505-829-3449
Home Page: www.herb-biz.com

David Oliver, Publisher
Paula Oliver, Editor

News of interest for herb growers and marketers. Covers all aspects of the herb industry and offers book reviews, events calendar, new products, business profiles, sources, resources, networking and more. Geared to small businesses.
Cost: $24.00
48 Pages
Frequency: Bi-Monthly
Circulation: 2,500
Printed in one color on matte stock

9918 CPA Connection Newsletter
Contract Packaging Association
1833 Centre Point Circle
Suite 123
Naperville, IL 60563-4848

630-544-5053
FAX 630-544-5055
E-Mail: info@contractpackaging.org
Home Page: www.contractpackaging.org

Joe Jaruszewski, President
Chris Nutley, Vice President
Vicky Smitley, Treasurer

Providing news that impacts the contract packaging industry.
155 Members
Founded in 1992

9919 Calorie Control Commentary
Calorie Control Council
2611 Winslow Dr Ne
Atlanta, GA 30305-3777

678-608-3200
FAX 404-252-0774
E-Mail: webmaster@caloriecontrol.org
Home Page: www.caloriecontrol.org

Timely information on low-calorie and reduced-fat foods and beverages, weight management, physical activity and healthy eating.
60 Members
Founded in 1966

9920 Cameron's Foodservice Marketing Reporter
Cameron's Publications
5423 Sheridan Drive
PO Box 676
Williamsville, NY 14231

519-586-8785
FAX 519-586-8816

E-Mail: mail@cameronpub.com
Home Page: www.cameronpub.com

Successful promotion and advertising case histories for the restaurant and hotel industry.

9921 Can Shipments Report
Can Manufacturers Institute
1730 Rhode Island Ave Nw
Suite 1000
Washington, DC 20036-3112

202-232-4677
FAX 202-232-5756
Home Page: www.cancentral.com

Robert Budway, President
Shawn Relly, Editor/Publisher

Provides a summary of the past year's accomplishments, as well as a look at the strategy to fulfill goals in the coming year.
Frequency: Annual
Founded in 1938

9922 Capitol Line-Up
American Association of Meat Processors
PO Box 269
Elizabethtown, PA 17022

717-367-1168
FAX 717-367-9096
E-Mail: aamp@aamp.com
Home Page: www.aamp.com

Tom K Inboden, President
Jon Frohling, First VP
Daniel T Weber, Second VP

Deals strictly with governmental affairs in the industry. Keeps AAMP members up to date with the latest news about government affairs from Congress and key agencies in Washington, as well as state legislatures and state regulatory bodies.
Frequency: 26x Yearly

9923 Catering Service Idea Newsletter
Prosperity & Profits Unlimited
PO Box 416
Denver, CO 80201

303-573-5564

A Doyle, Editor

Catering service business ideas and possibilities.

9924 Center of the Plate
American Culinary Federation
180 Center Place Way
St Augustine, FL 32095-8859

904-824-4468
800-624-9458
FAX 904-825-4758
E-Mail: acf@acfchefs.net
Home Page: www.acfchefs.org

Heidi Cramb, Executive Director
Kay Orde, Editor
Joachim Buchner, CEO
Michael Feierstein, Administrative Assistant
Bryan Hunt, Graphic Designer

Official membership newsletter of the American Culinary Federation.
Cost: $50.00
Frequency: Monthly
Circulation: 25,000
Founded in 1956

9925 Cereal Foods World
AACC International
3340 Pilot Knob Rd
Eagan, MN 55121-2055

651-454-7250
800-328-7560
FAX 651-454-0766

E-Mail: aacc@scisoc.org
Home Page: www.aaccnet.org

Steven Nelson, Publisher
Susan Kohn, Executive Editor
Amanda Aranowski, Managing Editor
Patti Ek, Production Manager

Covers grain-based food science, technology, and new product development. Includes articles that focus on advances in grain-based food science and the application of these advances to product development and food production practices.
Frequency: Bimonthly
ISSN: 0146-6283

9926 Champagne Wines Information Bureau
KCSA
800 2nd Avenue
5th Floor
New York, NY 10017-4709

212-682-6300
800-642-4267
FAX 212-697-0910
E-Mail: info@champagnes.com
Home Page: www.champagnes.com

Jean-Louis Carbonnier, Editor
Herbert L Corbin, President/CEO

Representative of Comite Interprofessionnel duVinde Champagne, Epernay, France.
4 Pages
Circulation: 10000
Printed in one color on matte stock

9927 Cheese Reporter
Cheese Reporter Publishing Company
2810 Crossroads Dr
Suite 3000
Madison, WI 53718-7972

608-246-8430
FAX 608-246-8431
E-Mail: info@cheesereporter.com
Home Page: www.cheesereporter.com

Dick Groves, Publisher/Editor
Kevin Thome, Marketing Director
Betty Mertes, Circulation Manager

Leading weekly publication serving manufacturers and marketers of cheese, butter, ice cream, yogurt and other fermented milk foods, whey and other dairy processors.
Cost: $150.00
16 Pages
Frequency: Weekly
Circulation: 2000
ISSN: 0009-2142
Founded in 1876
Printed in 4 colors on n stock

9928 Coffee Reporter
National Coffee Association
15 Maiden Ln
Suite 1405
New York, NY 10038-5113

212-766-4007
FAX 212-766-5815
E-Mail: info@ncausa.org
Home Page: www.ncausa.org

Robert F Nelson, President
Joseph F DeRupo, Communications/PR Director

Contains news of NCA activities and programs, new product development and market trends in both the U.S. and global coffee industry, regulatory action affecting the U.S. coffee industry and statistical data on ICO prices and U.S. retail prices. A single copy subscription is supplied free of charge to members, non-eligible parties for membership the cost is $40.00
Cost: $65.00
Frequency: Quarterly

9929 Coffee, Sugar and Cocoa Exchange Daily Market Report
New York Board of Trade
1 North End Avenue
New York, NY 10282-1101

212-748-4000
877-877-8890
FAX 212-748-4039
E-Mail: webmaster@nybot.com
Home Page: www.nybot.com

Leonel Fern ndez, President

Offers market reports on the stock market exchange covering foods and specific food investing.

9930 Communique
CHRIE
2810 N Parham Road
Suite 230
Richmond, VA 23294

804-346-4800
FAX 804-346-5009
E-Mail: info@chrie.org
Home Page: www.chrie.org
Social Media: *Facebook, Twitter, LinkedIn*

Susan Fournier, President
Josette Katz, Vice President
Chris Roberts, Secretary
John Drysdale, Treasurer
Kathy McCarty, CEO

Council on Hotel, Restaurant, and Institutional Educations informational newsletter.
Cost: $45.00
Frequency: Monthly

9931 Concessionworks Newsletter
National Association of Concessionaires
35 E Wacker Dr
Suite 1816
Chicago, IL 60601-2270

312-236-3858
FAX 312-236-7809
E-Mail: scross@naconline.org
Home Page: www.naconline.org

Charles A Winans, Executive Director

For members with updates on association happenings, feature articles, new member listings, product news and industry updates.
Founded in 1944

9932 Country World Newspaper
Echo Publishing Company
401 Church Street
PO Box 596
Sulphur Springs, TX 75483

903-885-8663
800-245-2149
FAX 903-885-8768
E-Mail: lori@countryworldnews.com
Home Page: www.countryworldnews.com

Scott Keys, Publisher
Lori Cope, Editor
Jim Horton, Advertising Manager

A newspaper offering agricultural information to farmers, ranchers, dairyfarmers, and agribusinesses.
Cost: $24.00
36 Pages
Frequency: Weekly
Circulation: 16200
Founded in 1981
Printed in 4 colors on newsprint stock

9933 Crop Protection Management
2892 Crescent Avenue
Eugene, OR 97408

541-343-5641
800-874-3276
FAX 541-686-0248

Jeff Powell, Publisher

This newsletter covers all aspects of crop management and protection, including pesticides, agricultural chemicals and legislation.
Frequency: 5 per year

9934 Daily Advocate
Thomson Newspapers
PO Box 220
Greenville, OH 45331-220

937-548-3151
FAX 937-548-3913
E-Mail: webmaster@dailyadvocate.com
Home Page: www.dailyadvocate.com

Gary Lamberg, Publisher
Bob Robinson, Editor
Ken Bowen, Circulation Manager
Ashley Fritz, Graphic Designer
Barb Wilson, Business Manager

Farming interests, grain, livestock. Sections on senior citizens, farmers, builders, religion, sports, as well as special sections on agriculture and home improvement.
Cost: $117.00
Frequency: Daily
Founded in 1883

9935 Dairy Council Digest
National Dairy Council
Interstate Place II
100 Elwood Davis Road
North Syracuse, NY 13212

315-472-9143
FAX 315-472-0506
E-Mail: ndc@dairyinformation.com
Home Page: www.nationaldairycouncil.org
Social Media: *Facebook, Twitter*

Provides a comprehensive review of research on topics ranging from the benefits of dairy foods in child nutrition, to dairy's potential protective role for metabolic syndrome and type 2 diabetes.
Frequency: Bi-Monthly
Founded in 1915

9936 Dairy Industry Newsletter
Eden Publishing Company
10255 W Higgins Road
Suite 900
Rosemont, IL 60018-4924

312-240-2880
Home Page: www.dairyindustrynewsletter.com

Resource serving all sectors of the dairy industry. Reports on commercial, trade, political and market information.
8 Pages
Frequency: 25x Yearly
Printed in 2 colors on glossy stock

9937 Dairy Market Report
American Butter Institute
2101 Wilson Boulevard
Suite 400
Arlington, VA 22201

703-243-5630
FAX 703-841-9328
E-Mail: AMiner@nmpf.org
Home Page: www.nmpf.org/ABI

Peter Vitaliano, Editor

9938 Dairy Profit Weekly
DairyBusiness Communications

6437 Collamer Road
East Syracuse, NY 13057-1031

315-703-7979
800-334-1904
FAX 315-703-7988
Home Page: www.dairybusiness.com

Dave Natzke, Editorial Director
Joel Hastings, Publisher
Eleanor Jacobs, Regional Editor

Latest information, tips, and trends.
Cost: $179.00
4 Pages
Frequency: Weekly
Circulation: 1700
Printed in 2 colors on newsprint stock

9939 Dairy-Deli-Bake Digest
International Dairy-Deli-Bakery Association
636 Science Drive
PO Box 5528
Madison, WI 53705-0528

608-310-5000
FAX 608-238-6330
E-Mail: IDDBA@iddba.org
Home Page: www.iddbanet.org

Carol Christison, Executive Director

Packed with practical how-to information to help readers run a successful business. Features new management trends, new products, reports, reviews, association news, features, and consumer attitudes and trends.
Frequency: Monthly
Founded in 1964

9940 Dairy-Deli-Bake Wrap-Up
International Dairy-Deli-Bakery Association
636 Science Drive
PO Box 5528
Madison, WI 53705-0528

608-310-5000
FAX 608-238-6330
E-Mail: IDDBA@iddba.org
Home Page: www.iddbanet.org

Carol Christison, Executive Director

Covers IDDBA's seminars, expositions, member news, awards, and programs and services.
Frequency: Quarterly
Founded in 1964

9941 Distributor News
Food Industry Suppliers Association
1207 Sunset Drive
Greensboro, NC 27408

336-274-6311
FAX 336-691-1839
E-Mail: stella@fisanet.org
Home Page: www.fisanet.org

David Brink, President
Bob Morava, Vice President

FISA's official newsletter, publishing industry happenings and business management information.
245 Members
Frequency: Quarterly
Founded in 1968

9942 Doane's Agricultural Report
Doane Agricultural Services
77 Westport Plz
Suite 250
St Louis, MO 63146-3121

314-569-2700
866-647-0918
FAX 314-569-1083
Home Page: www.doane.com

Dan Manternach, Editor

Provides information to US farmers and agricultural professionals. Doane keeps you up to date on factors affecting your farm program benefits and production costs too.
Frequency: Weekly

9943 FDRS Newsletter
Food Distribution Research Society
PO Box 441110
Fort Washington, MD 20749

301-292-1970
FAX 301-292-1787
E-Mail: Jonathan_baros@ncsu.edu
Home Page: fdrs.tamu.edu

John Park, President
Ron Rainey, President-Elect
Kellie Raper, Secretary/ Treasurer
Jennifer Dennis, Director
Stan Ernst, Director

Reports on Society events and happenings as well as related news from the industry and abroad.
Frequency: Quarterly

9944 FPA Update
Flexible Packaging Association
971 Corporate Blvd
Suite 403
Linthicum, MD 21090-2253

410-694-0800
FAX 410-694-0900
E-Mail: fpa@flexpack.org
Home Page: www.flexpack.org

Marla Donahue, President

Updating membership as well as the industry on FPA activities, events and accomplishments through the FPA Update, which is included within Flexible Packaging magazine.
Frequency: Monthly

9945 FSC Newsletter
Food Safety Consortium
110 Agriculture Building
University of Arkansas
Fayetteville, AR 72701

479-575-5647
FAX 479-575-7531
E-Mail: fsc@cavern.uark.edu
Home Page: www.fsconsortium.net

Dave Edmark, Communications Manager

A production of the three member schools of the consortium; University of Arkansas, Iowa State University and Kansas State University.
Frequency: Monthly
Founded in 1988

9946 FYI ASTA
American Spice Trade Association
2025 M St NW
Suite 800
Washington, DC 20036-2422

202-367-1127
FAX 202-367-2127
E-Mail: info@astaspice.org
Home Page: www.astaspice.org

Donna Tainter, President
Roger Clarke, Vice President/ Secretary
Gaspare Colletti, Treasurer
David Howe, Associate Group Director

Electronic newsletter designed to keep members informed about the spice industry, events impacting the industry and ASTA activities. The resource for members looking for information about ASTA, our programs and services.
Frequency: Membership Dues Vary
Founded in 1907

9947 Federal Focus
Natural Products Association

2112 E 4th St
Suite 200
Santa Ana, CA 92705-3816

714-460-7732
800-966-6632
FAX 714-460-7444
Home Page: www.npainfo.org
Social Media: *Facebook, Twitter, LinkedIn*

John F. Gay, Executive Director & CEO
Jeffrey Wright, President

Provides information and alerts from the federal and state agencies that affect the industry.
1900+ Members
Frequency: Monthly
Founded in 1936

9948 Fence Post
423 Main Street
Windsor, CO 80550-5129

970-686-5691
800-275-5646
FAX 970-686-5694
Home Page: www.thefencepost.com

Jim Eisberry, President
Gary Sweeney, Publisher
Luke Gonzales, Business Manager
Tom Vilsack, Secretary

Farming news and reports.
Cost: $39.00
Frequency: Weekly

9949 Food Allergy News
Food Allergy & Anaphlaxis Network
11781 Lee Jackson Mem Hwy
Suite 160
Fairfax, VA 22033-3309

703-691-3179
800-929-4040
FAX 703-691-2713
E-Mail: faan@foodallergy.org
Home Page: www.foodallergy.org

Anne Munoz-Furlong, President
Andreia Miller, Editor

Allergy newsletter with two pages of allergy-free recipes, coping strategies, research and studies.
Cost: $30.00
12 Pages
Circulation: 28000
ISSN: 1075-4318
Founded in 1991
Printed in 2 colors on glossy stock

9950 Food Industry Futures: A Strategy Service
CRS
PO Box 430
Fayetteville, NC 28302

910-486-9059
FAX 910-486-9058

Ian Cuthill, Publisher, Editor

Includes new developments concerning management or marketing practices, mergers and acquisitions, economics, trade policies, etc. It covers the industry from farm and retail stores, mostly in the US but also internationally. Accepts advertising.
Cost: $150.00
4 Pages

9951 Food Industry Newsletter
Newsletters
PO Box 342730
Bethesda, MD 20827-2730

301-469-8507
FAX 301-469-7271
E-Mail: foodltr@aol.com

Ellis Meredith, Publisher
Ray Marsili, Editor
Alice Corcoran, Circulation Manager

Concise, objective report for busy food executives, covering major food industry developments, including mergers and acquisitions, new trends and products, corporate and marketing strategies, etc. In addition to 22 regular issues a year, subscription also includes Special Food Marketing Reports on timely matters.
Cost: $245.00
Frequency: twice monthly except Aug.
Founded in 1972

9952 Food Insight
International Food Information Council
1100 Connecticut Ave Nw
Suite 430
Washington, DC 20036-4120

202-296-6540
FAX 202-296-6547
E-Mail: foodinfo@ific.org
Home Page: www.ific.org

Dave Schmidt, President
Nick Alexander, Associate Editor
Michael Hayes, Copy Editor
8 Pages
Frequency: 6 issues per ye
Circulation: 45000
Printed in 4 colors on glossy stock

9953 Food Institute Report
American Institute of Food Distribution
1 Broadway
2nd Floor
Elmwood Park, NJ 07407-1844

201-791-5570
FAX 201-791-5222
Home Page: www.foodinstitute.com

Brian Todd, President
Mike Slattery, Chairman
Michael Sansolo, Senior Vice President
Joe Crocker, Vice Chairman
Donna George, Treasurer

Membership includes a subscription to The Food Institute Report, an in-depth weekly digest that delivers insights on new products, crop markets, legislation, customer demographics, mergers, food industry statistics, competitors and market trends.
Frequency: Weekly
Circulation: 3000
Founded in 1928

9954 Food Merchants Advocate
New York State Food Merchant
130 Washington Ave
Albany, NY 12210-2220

518-463-0300
FAX 518-462-5474
Home Page: www.nyscar.org

Christopher Pellnat, Editor

A tabloid newspaper for food retailers.
Cost: $10.00
Frequency: Monthly

9955 Food Safety Professional
Carpe Diem
208 Floral Vale Boulevard
Yardley, PA 19067

215-860-7800
FAX 215-860-7900
Home Page: www.foodquality.com

Paul Juestrich, Production Manager
Ken Potuznik, Director
Lisa Dionne, Creative Director

The Food Safety Professional is a quarterly publication of The antional Registry of Food Safety Professionals. Practical hands on article and advice form the experts will keep you informed of the latest technique an technologies

in food safety.'
Cost: $20.00
Frequency: Quarterly
Circulation: 30,000

9956 Food Trade News
Best-Met Publishing
5537 Twin Knolls Rd
Suite 438
Columbia, MD 21045-3270

410-730-5013
FAX 410-740-4680
E-Mail: office@best-met.com
Home Page: www.best-met.com

Jeff Metzger, Publisher
Terri Maloney, Editor
Beth Pripstein, Office Manager
Cost: $63.00
Frequency: Monthly
Printed in one color on matte stock

9957 Food World Information Services
Best-Met Publishing Company
5537 Twin Knolls Rd
Suite 438
Columbia, MD 21045-3270

410-730-5013
FAX 410-740-4680
E-Mail: tmaloney@best-met.com
Home Page: www.best-met.com

Jeff Metzger, Publisher
Terri Maloney, Editor
Beth Pripstein, Office Manager
Richard J. Bestany, President

Provides market data for Baltimore, Washington, Central Pennsylvania and Philadelphia
Frequency: Monthly
Printed in on newsprint stock

9958 Food for Thought
D/FW Grocers Association
3044 Old Denton Rd
Suite 111, PMB 323
Carrollton, TX 75007

214-731-3132
800-791-6590
FAX 469-574-5252
E-Mail: info@dfwga.net
Home Page: www.dfwga.net

Offers information on grocery retailing and items of interest to members of the Grocers Association.
Frequency: Quarterly
Circulation: 1,000
Founded in 1947

9959 FoodTalk
Pike & Fischer
PO Box 25277
Alexandria, VA 22313

703-548-3146
FAX 703-548-3017
E-Mail: info@setantapublishing.com
Home Page: www.setantapublishing.com

Declan Couroy, Editor/Publisher

Sanitation tips for food workers.
Cost: $120.00
Frequency: Quarterly
Circulation: 5000
Founded in 1987
Printed in 2 colors on matte stock

9960 Friday Notes
Council for Agricultural Science and Technology
4420 West Lincold Way
Ames, IA 50014-3447

515-292-2125
FAX 515-292-4512

E-Mail: cast@cast-science.org
Home Page: www.cast-science.org

John Bonner, Executive VP
Lynette Allen, Assistant Editor

Electronic newsletter featuring lead articles on current topics being discussed in agriculture, congressional updates, and advance announcements of upcoming CAST publications and activities.
Frequency: 48x Yearly
Founded in 1972

9961 GRAS Flavoring Substances 25

Flavor & Extract Manufacturers Association
1620 I Street NW
Suite 925
Washington, DC 20006

202-293-5800
FAX 202-462-8998
Home Page: www.femaflavor.org
Social Media: YouTube, RSS Feed

Ed R. Hays, Ph.D., President
George C. Robinson, III, President Elect
Mark Scott, Treasurer
Arthur Schick, VP & Secretary
John Cox, Executive Director

The 25th publication by the Expert Panel of the Flavor and Extract Manufacturers Association provides an update on recent progress in the consideration of flavoring ingredients generally recognized as safe under the Food Additive Amendment.
Frequency: Biennial
Founded in 1909

9962 Global Food Marketer

Food Export USA
309 West Washington
Suite 600
Chicago, IL 60606

312-334-9200
FAX 312-334-9230
E-Mail: info@foodexportusa.org
Home Page: www.foodexportusa.org

Tim F Hamilton, Executive Director
Daleen D Richmond, Deputy Director

Newsletter for US exporters, containing useful articles, updates on overseas market conditions and trends, marketing tips, a column by a food export helpline counselor, and calendar of upcoming events.
Frequency: Bi-Monthly
Founded in 1973

9963 Gourmet News

Oser Communications Group
1877 N Kolb Road
Tuscon, AZ 85715

520-721-1300
Home Page: www.gourmetnews.com

Rocelle Aragon, Editor
Kate Seymour, Senior Associate Publisher

The authoritative voice, and publication of choice for thousands of professionals in the gourmet and specialty food business. Reports timely and trustworty stories about events, issues, trends and other happenings within the trade.
Cost: $65.00
Frequency: Monthly
Circulation: 23100
Founded in 1991

9964 Grayson Report

Grayson Associates

30728 Paseo Elegancia
San Juan Cpstrn, CA 92675-5426

949-487-9970
FAX 949-487-9975
Home Page: www.graysonassociates.com

Suzanne Grayson, President
Robert Grayson, Director

Marketing analysis of the packaged goods industry.
Founded in 1970

9965 Grocery Manufacturers of America:

Grocery Manufacturers Association of America
1350 I St Nw
Suite 300
Washington, DC 20005-3377

202-337-9400
FAX 202-639-5932
E-Mail: info@gmaonline.org
Home Page: www.gmabrands.com

Pamela G Bailey, CEO
Jeff Nedelman, VP Communications

Focuses on the productivity and public policy issues affecting our industry.
Founded in 1908

9966 Herd on the Hill

National Meat Association
1970 Broadway
Suite 825
Oakland, CA 94612

510-763-1533
FAX 510-763-6186
E-Mail: staff@nmaonline.org
Home Page: www.nmaonline.org

Robert Rebholtz, Chairman
Larry Vad, President
Marty Evanson, Vice President
Mike Hesse, Secretary
Brian Coelho, Treasurer

Provides up-to-date information on what's happening in Washington in relation to the meat and poultry industry.
600 Members
Frequency: Weekly
Founded in 1946

9967 Home Baking Association Newsletter

Home Baking Association
10841 S Crossroads Drive
Suite 105
Parker, CO 80135

785-478-3283
FAX 785-478-3024
Home Page: www.homebaking.org
Social Media: Facebook, Twitter, Flickr

Striving to bring a wide variety of educational materials that benefit the community of Bakers and Baking Educators worldwide. Newsletter includes the latest tips, recipes and baking resources.
Frequency: Monthly

9968 Hot Sheet

Fresh-Cut Produce Association
1600 Duke Street
Suite 440
Alexandria, VA 22314

530-756-8900
FAX 530-756-8901
Home Page: www.fresh-cuts.org

Jerry Gorny, President
Sean Handerhan, Marketing Director

A newsletter containing technical information, marketing news and exhibit information on the

produce trade. Serves over 500 members.
Cost: $35.00
Frequency: Monthly
Circulation: 23,000
Founded in 1987

9969 Hotel, Restaurant, Institutional Buyers Guide

Urner Barry Publications
PO Box 389
Toms River, NJ 08754

732-240-5330
800-932-0617
FAX 732-341-0891
E-Mail: help@urnerbarry.com
Home Page: www.urnerbarry.com/

Paul B Brown Jr, President
Sheila M Deane, Marketing Manager
Richard A. Brown, VP

Reports on perishable food prices, meat, seafood, fruits, vegetables and others compiled for the metropolitan New York, New Jersey and Connecticut markets.
Cost: $86.00
4 Pages
Frequency: Weekly
Circulation: 120
ISSN: 0270-4161
Founded in 1858

9970 Hotel, Restaurant, Institutional Meat Price Report

Urner Barry Publications
PO Box 389
Toms River, NJ 08754-2741

732-240-5330
800-932-0617
FAX 732-341-0891
E-Mail: help@urnerbarry.com
Home Page: www.urnerbarry.com

Paul B Brown Jr, President
Karen Mick, Circulation Director

Current meat and poultry pricing for the hotel, restaurant and institutional buyers.
Cost: $174.00
Frequency: Weekly
Circulation: 200
ISSN: 1067-3962
Founded in 1858

9971 IAFIS Global Food MegaTrends

International Assn of Food Industry Suppliers
1451 Dolley Madison Boulevard
Suite 101
McLean, VA 22101

703-761-2600
FAX 703-761-4334
E-Mail: info@fpsa.org
Home Page: www.fpsa.org

George Melnykovich, President
Andrew Drennan, VP

A quarterly bulletin covering international news and its effect on the food processing and packaging industries.

9972 IBDEA Report

International Beverage Dispensing Association
3837 Naylors Lane
Baltimore, MD 21208

410-602-0616
877-404-2332
FAX 410-486-6799
E-Mail: ibdea@cornerstoneassoc.com
Home Page: www.ibdea.org

Official newsletter of the International Beverage Dispensing Association, offering the latest news and technologies in the industry.
Frequency: Quarterly

9973 IDDBA & YOU
International Dairy-Deli-Bakery Association
636 Science Drive
PO Box 5528
Madison, WI 53705-0528

608-310-5000
FAX 608-238-6330
E-Mail: IDDBA@iddba.org
Home Page: www.iddbanet.org

Carol Christison, Executive Director

E-Newsletter designed for deli and bakery supermarket management and in-store staff teams. A fact-filled relevant resource on deli and bakery trends, timely sales data, merchandising ideas, training, new products, seminars, experts, news, and programs.
Frequency: Monthly
Founded in 1964

9974 IDDBA Legis-Letter
International Dairy-Deli-Bakery Association
636 Science Drive
PO Box 5528
Madison, WI 53705-0528

608-310-5000
FAX 608-238-6330
E-Mail: IDDBA@iddba.org
Home Page: www.iddbanet.org

Carol Christison, Executive Director

Formerly IDDA UPDATE, a membership benefit. Highlights recent legislative bills and reports, FDA activities, and topical issues such as state action on bst, NLEA, and HACCP.
Frequency: Monthly
Founded in 1964

9975 IFSEA Infusion
International Food Service Executives
4955 Miller Street
Suite 107
Wheat Ridge, CO 80033

800-893-5499
E-Mail: hq@ifsea.com
Home Page: www.ifsea.com
Social Media: *Facebook*

Barbara Sadler, Chairwoman
Fred Wright, Chair-Elect
David Orosz, Treasurer

Official newsletter of the IFSEA focusing on the happenings and news, as well as industry tips and recipes.
Frequency: Monthly

9976 INsight
Southern US Trade Association
701 Poydras St
Suite 3725
New Orleans, LA 70139-4596

504-568-5986
FAX 504-568-6010
E-Mail: susta@susta.org
Home Page: www.susta.org

Troy Rosamond, Financial Director
Bernadette Wiltz, Deputy Director

Providing the latest exporting information.
Frequency: Quarterly
Founded in 1973

9977 Ice Cream Reporter
Ice Cream Reporter
Hilton Terrace
Willsboro, NY 12996

518-963-4333
FAX 518-963-4999

Howard Waxman, Publisher/Editor

News for ice cream executives.
Cost: $395.00
Frequency: Monthly
Founded in 1987

9978 Independent Bakers Association Newsletter
Independent Bakers Association
Georgetown Station
PO Box 3731
Washington, DC 20027-0231

202-333-8190
FAX 202-337-3809
E-Mail: independentbaker@yahoo.com
Home Page: www.independentbaker.net

Updating Washington legislative and regulatory actions and analyzing pro-business positions impacting on wholesale baking, allied industry operations.
Frequency: Monthly

9979 Insight
Retailer's Bakery Association
14239 Park Central Drive
Laurel, MD 20707-5261

301-725-2149
800-638-0924
FAX 301-725-2187
E-Mail: Info@RBAnet.com
Home Page: www.rbanet.com

Bernard Reynolds, Publisher
Stewart Taylor, Convention Director
Katrina Cooley, Marketing & Communications Director

Member newsletter for baking industry professionals.
8 Pages
Frequency: Monthly
Founded in 1918
Printed in 2 colors on matte stock

9980 International Association of Food
1451 Dolley Madison Boulevard
Suite 101
McLean, VA 22101

703-761-2600
FAX 703-761-4334
E-Mail: info@fpsa.org
Home Page: www.fpsa.org

George Melnykovich, President
Andrew Drennan, VP

Dairy food and beverage industries, and related sanitary processing industries addressing the marketing and business information needs of the food supply channel.
Founded in 1983
Mailing list available for rent

9981 IoPP update
Institute of Packaging Professionals
Ste 123
1833 Centre Point Cir
Naperville, IL 60563-4848

630-544-5050
800-432-4085
FAX 630-544-5005
E-Mail: info@iopp.org
Home Page: www.iopp.org
Social Media: *Facebook, Twitter, LinkedIn, YouTube*

Edwin Landon, Executive Director
Patrick Farrey, General Manager
Stan Zelesnik, Director Education
Robert DePauw, Finance Manager
Kelly Staley, Member Services Manager

Emailed newsletter of the Institute of Packaging Professionals.
Frequency: Bi-Weekly

9982 Kane's Beverage Week
Whitaker Newsletters

313 S Avenue
#340
Fanwood, NJ 07023-1364

800-359-6049
FAX 908-889-6339

Joel Whitaker, Publisher

News on marketing, economic and regulatory factors affecting the alcohol beverage industry.
Cost: $499.00
6 Pages
Frequency: Quarterly
ISSN: 0882-2573

9983 Kashrus Magazine
Yeshiva Birkas Revuen
PO Box 204
Brooklyn, NY 11230

718-336-8544
FAX 718-336-8550
E-Mail: webmaster@kashrusmagazine.com
Home Page: www.kashrusmagazine.com

Rabbi Yosef Wikler, Editor
Vaad Hakashrut, Director
Rabbi Levin, Executive Director

Regular, complete update on Kosher food mislabelings, dairy/nondairy status, kosher supervision standards, newly certified products and food technology, travel and Jewish life.
Cost: $18.00
88 Pages
Circulation: 10000
Founded in 1980
Printed in 4 colors on glossy stock

9984 Kettle Talk
Retail Confectioners International
2053 S Waverly Ave
Suite 204
Springfield, MO 65804-2414

417-883-2775
800-545-5381
FAX 847-724-2719
E-Mail: info@retailconfectioners.org
Home Page: www.retailconfectioners.org

Terry Craft, President
Terry Hickling, Chairman of Marketing
Dan Malley, VP

Membership newsletter, including confection recipes. Also regional meetings.
Frequency: Monthly
Circulation: 550
Founded in 1917
Printed in on matte stock

9985 Kiplinger Agricultural Letter
Kiplinger Washington Editors
1729 H St Nw
Washington, DC 20006-3924

202-887-6400
800-544-0155
FAX 202-778-8976
E-Mail: sub.services@kiplinger.com
Home Page: www.kiplinger.com

Knight Kiplinger, VP
Kevin McCormally, Editorial Director
Fred Frailey, Editor
David Harrison, Manager

Forecasts and judgments on wages, income, food packaging, processing and marketing techniques.
Cost: $56.00
Founded in 1923

9986 Kitchen Times
Howard Wilson and Company
PO Box 290
Waukegan, IL 60079-0290

708-339-5111
800-245-7224

FAX 708-210-2069
Home Page: www.hwilson.com

Howard Wilson, Publisher/Editor

News on food and cooking.
Cost: $33.00
8 Pages
Frequency: Monthly
Founded in 1959

9987 Lean Trimmings
National Meat Association
1970 Broadway
Suite 825
Oakland, CA 94612-2299

510-763-1533
FAX 510-763-6186
E-Mail: staff@nmaonline.org
Home Page: www.nmaonline.org

Barry Carpenter, CEO
Jen Kempis, Operations Manager

Covers industry regulations, new technology
and export news, as well as labor issues and
business strategy.
Frequency: Weekly
Founded in 1946
Printed in one color on matte stock

9988 Legislative Onion Outlet
Legislative Onion Outlet
822 7th St
Suite 510
Greeley, CO 80631-3941

970-353-5895
FAX 970-353-5897
E-Mail: info@onions-usa.org
Home Page: www.onions-usa.org

Wayne Mininger, Executive VP
Tanya Fell, Public/Industry Relations

An annual bulletin published by the National
Onion Association.
Circulation: 600
Founded in 1913
Mailing list available for rent: 600 names

9989 Legislative Update
Independent Bakers Association
2 S Portage Street
Westfield, NY 14787

716-326-5200
E-Mail: nationalinfo@welchs.com
Home Page: www.nationalgrape.com

Nicholas Pyle, Manager

Updating Washington legislative and regulatory actions and analyzing pro-business positions impacting on wholesale baking, allied
industry operations.
Frequency: Monthly

9990 Link Newsletter
R&D Associates
16607 Blanco Road
Suite 1506
San Antonio, TX 78232-1940

210-493-8024
FAX 210-493-8036
E-Mail: hqs@militaryfood.org
Home Page: www.militaryfood.or

David Dee, Editor

Food packaging, food processing and
foodservice industry.
300 Pages
Frequency: Quarterly

9991 Loan Trimmings & Herd on the Hill
1970 Broadway Avenue
Suite 825
Oakland, CA 94612-2299

510-763-1533
FAX 510-763-6186

E-Mail: staff@amaonline.org
Home Page: www.nmaonline.org

Barry Carpenter, Executive Director
Jen Kempis, Associate Director
Frequency: Weekly
Circulation: 600

9992 Make It Tasty
Prosperity & Profits Unlimited
PO Box 416
Denver, CO 80201-0416

303-573-5564

AC Doyle, Publisher

Spice company blends food business newsletter
with salt-free, herb and spice blend recipes.
Founded in 1996

9993 Making a Difference
National FFA Organization
6060 FFA Drive
PO Box 68960
Indianapolis, IN 46268-0960

317-802-6060
888-332-2668
E-Mail: membership@ffa.org
Home Page: www.ffa.org

Steve A. Brown, National FFA Advisor
Marion D. Fletcher, National FFA Organization
Treasurer

Resource for Agriculture teachers. It features
news from FFA and Team Ag Ed, teaching resources, ideas, inspiration and more.
507M Members
Founded in 1928

9994 Market News
Meat & Livestock Australia
1401 K Street NW
Suite 602
Washington, DC 20005

202-521-2551
FAX 202-521-2699
E-Mail: info@mla.com.au
Home Page: www.mla.com.au
Social Media: *Facebook, Twitter, YouTube*

Don Heatley, Chairman
David Palmer, Managing Director
Bernie Bindon, Director
Chris Hudson, Director

eNewsletter presents the latest market news
from Australia and key international markets.
30000 Members
Frequency: Weekly
Founded in 1998

9995 Meat & Poultry
Meat Trade Institute
213 South Avenue East
Spencer Savings Bank Building
Cranford, NJ 07016

908-276-5111
FAX 212-279-4016
E-Mail: sflannagan@sprintmail.com
Home Page: www.spcnetwork.com/mti/

John Calcangno, President

A respected newsletter which keeps readers
abreast of membership information and all
news pertinent to Institute members. Available
online.
Frequency: Monthly

9996 Meat and Livestock Weekly
Meat & Livestock Australia
1401 K Street NW
Suite 602
Washington, DC 20005

202-521-2551
FAX 202-521-2699
E-Mail: info@mla.com.au

Home Page: www.mla.com.au
Social Media: *Facebook, Twitter, YouTube*

Don Heatley, Chairman
David Palmer, Managing Director
Bernie Bindon, Director
Chris Hudson, Director

eNewsletter providing the latest news, analysis
and trends for domestic and export markets, including information on buyer and competitor
activity and trends.
30000 Members
Frequency: Weekly
Founded in 1998

9997 More Beef from Pastures
Meat & Livestock Australia
1401 K Street NW
Suite 602
Washington, DC 20005

202-521-2551
FAX 202-521-2699
E-Mail: info@mla.com.au
Home Page: www.mla.com.au
Social Media: *Facebook, Twitter, YouTube*

Don Heatley, Chairman
David Palmer, Managing Director
Bernie Bindon, Director
Chris Hudson, Director

eNewsletter designed to keep readers
up-to-date with the latest developments in the
MLA More Beef from Pastures program.
30000 Members
Frequency: Quarterly
Founded in 1998

9998 NAFEM online
N. American Assn. of Food Equipment
Manufacturing
161 N Clark Street
Suite 2020
Chicago, IL 60601

312-821-0201
FAX 312-821-0202
E-Mail: info@nafem.org
Home Page: www.nafem.org

Steven R. Follett, President
Thomas R. Campion, President-Elect
Michael L. Whiteley, Secretary/Treasurer
Deirdre Flynn, Executive Vice President

The latest and greatest NAFEM and industry
news to all NAFEM members. e-Newsletter.
Frequency: Monthly

9999 NAMA Newsletter
North American Millers' Association
600 Maryland Ave SW
Suite 825 W
Washington, DC 20024

202-484-2200
FAX 202-488-7416
E-Mail: generalinfo@namamillers.org
Home Page: www.namamillers.org

Betsy Faga, President
James Bair, VP

Trade association representing the wheat, corn,
oat and rye milling industry. NAMA members
operate one hundred and seventy mills in
thrirty-eight states and Canada. Their aggregate
production of more than one hundred and sixty
million pounds per day is approximately
ninety-five percent of the industry capacity in
the U.S.
Frequency: Monthly
Circulation: 250

10000 NCA Annual Convention
National Coffee Association

15 Maiden Ln
Suite 1405
New York, NY 10038-5113

212-766-4007
FAX 212-766-5815
E-Mail: info@ncausa.org
Home Page: www.ncausa.org

Robert F Nelson, President
Steven M Wolfe, Membership/Marketing
Director

The coffee event of the year, industry executives from all over the world get together to learn from the most current educational sessions, see old friends and meet new ones.
Frequency: Annual/March
Founded in 1911

10001 NFRA Update
National Frozen & Refrigerated Foods
Association
4755 Linglestown Road Suite 300
PO Box 6069
Harrisburg, PA 17112

717-657-8601
FAX 717-657-9862
E-Mail: info@nfraweb.org
Home Page: www.nfraweb.org

H V Skip Shaw Jr, President/CEO
Jeff Romachik, Executive VP/COO
Marlene Barr, VP Membership

NFRA's main communication tool in keeping members informed of upcoming frozen and refrigerated food promotions and Association meetings and resources. Also covers local associations, members' personnel changes and member news such as the introduction of new products and facility expansions.
Frequency: Monthly
Circulation: 2300

10002 NICRA Bulletin
National Ice Cream Retailers Association
1028 W Devon Avenue
Elk Grove Village, IL 60007

847-301-7500
866-303-6960
FAX 847-301-8402
E-Mail: info@nicra.org
Home Page: www.nicra.org

Lynn Dudek, President
Dan Messer, VP

Information to assist you with Practical Advice on Daily Operations, Industry Trends, Tax Related Articles, Legislative Issues, Association News, Labeling Information, and more.
Frequency: Monthly
Circulation: 500

10003 NPA Fact of the Week
Natural Products Association
2112 E 4th St
Suite 200
Santa Ana, CA 92705-3816

714-460-7732
800-966-6632
FAX 714-460-7444
Home Page: www.npainfo.org
Social Media: *Facebook, Twitter, LinkedIn*

John F. Gay, Executive Director & CEO
Jeffrey Wright, President

Emailed to Congressional staffers who handle health issues for their representative or senator. Highlights the latest news, research and trends in dietary supplements and the natural products industry.
1900+ Members
Frequency: Weekly
Founded in 1936

10004 NPA NOW
Natural Products Association

2112 E 4th St
Suite 200
Santa Ana, CA 92705-3816

714-460-7732
800-966-6632
FAX 714-460-7444
Home Page: www.npainfo.org
Social Media: *Facebook, Twitter, LinkedIn*

John F. Gay, Executive Director & CEO
Jeffrey Wright, President

Provides members with important association and industry news on a timely basis.
1900+ Members
Frequency: 6x Yearly
Founded in 1936

10005 NPFDA NEWS
National Poultry & Food Distributors
2014 Osborne Road
Saint Marys, GA 31558

770-535-9901
FAX 770-535-7385
E-Mail: kkm@npfda.org
Home Page: www.npfda.org

Chris Sharp, President
Al Acunto, Vice President
Marc Miro, Treasurer
Kristin McWhorter, Executive Director

Brings the latest information about NPFDA members- featuring Member Spotlights, government regulations and upcoming industry events.
Frequency: Monthly
Founded in 1967

10006 NSA Newsletter
National Shellfisheries Association
National Marine Fisheries Service Laboratory
Oxford, MD 21654

631-653-6327
FAX 631-653-6327
E-Mail: webmaster@shellfish.org
Home Page: www.shellfish.org

R. LeRoy Creswell, President
Christopher V. Davis, President-Elect
George E. Flimlin, VP & Program Chair
Marta Gomez-Chiarri, Secretary
Sandra E. Shumway, Editor

Current issues and concerns in shellfish research and in the shellfish industry, including details regarding upcoming meetings, employment listings, and column.
1M Members
Frequency: Quarterly
Founded in 1908

10007 National Automatic Merchandising
National Automatic Merchandising
Association
20 N Wacker Dr
Suite 3500
Chicago, IL 60606-3102

312-346-0370
800-331-8816
FAX 312-704-4140
E-Mail: dmathews@vending.org
Home Page: www.vending.org

Richard Geerdes, President
Craig Hesch NCE, Senior Vice Chairman
Brad Ellis NCE, Vice Chairman

Serves food and refreshment, vending, contract foodservice management and office coffee service industries.
2500 Members
Founded in 1936

10008 National Conference on Interstate Milk Shipments
National Conference on Interstate Milk

123 Buena Vista Drive
Frankfort, KY 40601-8770

502-695-0253
FAX 502-695-0253
Home Page: www.ncims.org

Leon Townsend, Executive Secretary
Marlena Bordson, Chair
Founded in 1946

10009 National Fertilizer Solutions Association Newsletter
339 Consort Drive
Manchester, MO 63011-4439

636-256-6650
FAX 636-256-4901

Kelly O'Brien-Wray, Publisher
Fred Speckmann, Editor

Accepts advertising.
90 Pages

10010 National Honey Market News
US Department of Agriculture
21 N 1st Avenue
#224
Yakima, WA 98902-2663

509-575-2494
FAX 509-457-7132
E-Mail: FVInfo@ams.usda.gov
Home Page: www.ams.usda.gov/fv/mncs

Linda Verstrate, Publisher
Michael Jarvis, Director

Current honey market information and colony conditions in the US.
Cost: $24.00
10-12 Pages
Frequency: Monthly

10011 National Hot Pepper Association
400 NW 20th Street
Fort Lauderdale, FL 33311-3818

954-565-4972
FAX 954-566-2208
E-Mail: pcppergal@mindspring.com
Home Page: www.inter-linked.com/org/nhpa

Robert J Payton, Publisher
Betty Payton, Editor

Networking among industry and private members. Education and information sharing.
Cost: $20.00
28 Pages
Frequency: Quarterly
Printed in on matte stock

10012 National Nutritional Foods Association Today
National Nutritional Foods Association
2112 E 4th St
Suite 200
Santa Ana, CA 92705-3816

949-622-6272
800-966-6632
FAX 949-622-6266
Home Page: www.nnfa.org

Amanda Thomason, Editor/Publications
Manager
Paul Bennett, CEO/President

Nonprofit trade organization dedicated to protecting and advancing the natural products industry for both retailers and suppliers.
Cost: $48.00
Frequency: Monthly
Circulation: 8000
Founded in 1936

10013 National Onion Association Newsletter
National Onion Association

822 7th St
Suite 510
Greeley, CO 80631-3941

970-353-5895
FAX 970-353-5897
E-Mail: info@onions-usa.org
Home Page: www.onions-usa.org

Wayne Mininger, Executive VP
Kim Reddin, Public/Industry Relation

Newsletter published by and only for the National Onion Association.
Frequency: Monthly
Circulation: 600
Founded in 1913
Mailing list available for rent: 600 names

10014 National Seasoning Manufacturers Newsletter

National Seasoning Manufacturers
Association
2527 Mill Race Road
Frederick, MD 21701-6812

301-694-0419
FAX 301-299-7523
E-Mail: alsmeyerfood@isp.com

Dick Alsmeyer PhD, Executive Director
Frequency: Quarterly

10015 National Shellfisheries Association News

Long Island University/Southampton
College
Natural Sciences Division
Southampton, NY 11968

631-283-4000
FAX 631-287-8054

Sandra Shumway, Production Manager
Eric Lang, Owner

Newsletter focusing on information for public health workers, shellfish producers and fishery administrators.
Cost: $125.00
Circulation: 1000
Mailing list available for rent: 1M names
Printed in one color on matte stock

10016 National Young Farmer Educational News

National FFA Organization
PO Box 68960
6060 FFA Drive
Alexandria, VA 22309-160

317-802-6060
888-332-2668
FAX 800-366-6556
E-Mail: aboutffa@ffa.org
Home Page: www.ffa.org

Wayne Sprick, Publisher
Larry Case, CEO

Tabloid which receives articles and information from state associations as well as information from the National Association.
12 Pages
Founded in 1928

10017 Natural News Update

Natural Products Association
2112 E 4th St
Suite 200
Santa Ana, CA 92705-3816

714-460-7732
800-966-6632
FAX 714-460-7444
Home Page: www.npainfo.org
Social Media: *Facebook, Twitter, LinkedIn*

John F. Gay, Executive Director & CEO
Jeffrey Wright, President

A weekly news and information resource, offering the latest news, federal activity, association announcements and research.
1900+ Members
Frequency: Weekly
Founded in 1936

10018 Nebraska Alfalfa Dehydrators Bulletin

Nebraska Alfalfa Dehydrators Association
8810 Craig Dr
Shawnee Mission, KS 66212-2916

913-648-6800
FAX 913-648-2648
Home Page: www.nebada.org

Wanda L Cobb, Executive VP

Market Information on Alfalfa Pellets, Meal, Cubes, and Hay.
Frequency: Weekly
Founded in 1941

10019 News in a Nutshell

National Peanut Board
2839 Paces Ferry Road
Suite 210
Atlanta, GA 30339-5769

678-424-5750
866-825-7946
FAX 678-424-5751
E-Mail: peanuts@nationalpeanutboard.org
Home Page: www.nationalpeanutboard.org
Social Media: *Facebook, Twitter, YouTube, Flickr*

George Jeffcoat, Chairman
Cindy Belch, Vice Chairman
John Harrell, Secretary
Vic Jordan, Treasurer

e-Newlsetter from the National Peanut Board with news about everything peanut.
Frequency: Bi-Weekly

10020 No-Till Farmer

Lessiter Publications
PO Box 624
Brookfield, WI 53008-0624

262-782-4480
800-645-8455
FAX 262-782-1252
E-Mail: info@lesspub.com
Home Page: www.lesspub.com

Donna Schwierske, Manager
Frank Lessiter, Accounting Manager
Michael Storts, Accounting Manager

Management information for farmers interested in conservation tillage.
Cost: $37.95
16 Pages
Frequency: Monthly
Circulation: 5500
ISSN: 0091-9993
Founded in 1984
Mailing list available for rent: 5,000 names at $90m per M
Printed in 2 colors on glossy stock

10021 Organic Business News

Hotline Printing & Publishing
PO Box 161132
Atamonte Springs, FL 32716-1132

407-628-1377
FAX 407-628-9935
Home Page:
www.hotlineprinting.com/obn.html

Dennis Blank, Publisher/Editor
Christine Blank, Senior Editor

Leading industry publication that tracks the latest government actions, policy trends and financial development in development in the

organic food business.
Cost: $110.00
12 Pages
Printed in 2 colors

10022 Organic Trade Association Newsletter

Organic Trade Association
60 Wells Street
PO Box 547
Greenfield, MA 01302

413-774-7511
FAX 413-774-6432
E-Mail: info@ota.com
Home Page: www.ota.com

Christine Bushway, Executive Director/CEO
Linda Lutz, Membership Manager
Laura Batcha, Marketing/Public Relations
Director

Members are businesses involved in the organic agriculture and products industry. Seeks to promote the industry and establish production and marketing standards. Also publishes The Organic Page: North American Resource Directory

10023 Packer

Vance Publishing
400 Knightsbridge Parkway
Lincolnshire, IL 60069

847-634-2600
FAX 847-634-4379
E-Mail: info@vancepublishing.com
Home Page: www.vancepublishing.com

William C Vance, Chairman
Peggy Walker, President

News and information on fresh fruit and vegetable marketing.

10024 Pear Newsletter

Pear Bureau Northwest
4382 SE International Way
Suite A
Milwaukie, OR 97222-4627

503-652-9720
FAX 503-652-9721
E-Mail: info@usapears.com
Home Page: www.usapears.com

Kevin Moffitt, President/CEO
Cristie Mather, Communciations Manager
Frequency: Monthly

10025 Peterson Patriot

Peterson Patriot Printers-Publishers
202 Main Street
Peterson, IA 51047

712-295-7711
FAX 712-295-7711
E-Mail: patriot@iowatelecom.net

Roger Stoner, Publisher
Jane Stoner, Editor

Agricultural news.
Cost: $18.00
12 Pages
Frequency: Weekly
Circulation: 549

10026 Practical Gourmet

Linick Group
Gourmet Building 7 Putter Lane
PO Box 102
Middle Island, NY 11953-0102

631-924-3888
E-Mail: roger@practicalgourmet.com
Home Page: www.practicalgourmet.com

Gaylen Andrews, Publisher/Editor
Roger Dextor, VP/Director of PR
Barbara Deal, Marketing Manager
Andrew Linick, Manager
Bill Bruzy, Contributing Editor

Since 1982, the focus of this upscale monthly publication is on providing 'healthy dining trends for the affluent traveler' 45 plus; includes feature articles and in-depth interviews with award winning chefs, wineries/tastings, honoring 2-5 star restaurants with PG's Gold Taste Dining Awards, upscale hotels, properties, resorts, spas, cruises/yachting, airlines, ground operators, food festivals/contests, cooking schools and worldwide culinary events.
Cost: $48.00
36 Pages
Frequency: Monthly
Circulation: 210,000
Founded in 1975
Mailing list available for rent: 210 M names at $110 per M
Printed in 4 colors on glossy stock

10027 Produce Merchandiser

United Fresh Fruit & Vegetable Association
1901 Pennsylvania Ave Nw
Suite 1100
Washington, DC 20006-3412

202-862-4989
FAX 202-303-3433
E-Mail: united@uffva.org
Home Page: www.uffva.org

Thomas E Stenzel, CEO

Information on promotion and consumer issues.

10028 Product Alert

Marketing Intelligence Service
482 N Main St
Canandaigua, NY 14424-1049

585-374-6326
800-836-5710
FAX 585-374-5217
Home Page: www.productscan.com

Christine Dengler, Marketing/Sales Manager

A twice-monthly briefing on new packaged goods introduced in North America. Featuring product pictures and descriptions with indexing provided in two convenient formats. Also available in a twice monthly, international version.
Cost: $795.00
Frequency: Fortnightly

10029 RBA Newsbrief

Retail Bakers of America
202 Village Circle
Suite 1
Slidell, LA 70458

985-643-6504
800-638-0924
FAX 985-643-6929
E-Mail: Info@RBAnet.com
Home Page: www.rbanet.com
Social Media: *Facebook*

Felix Sherman, Sr., President
Kenneth Downey, Sr., 1st Vice President
Marlene Goetzeler, 2nd Vice President
Dale A. Biles, Treasurer
Susan Nicolais, CAE, Secretary

Distributed electronically to RBA members, containing articles gathered from an expansive list of sources.
2000 Members
Frequency: Weekly
Founded in 1918

10030 Regulatory Register

American Butter Institute
2101 Wilson Boulevard
Suite 400
Arlington, VA 22201

703-243-5630
FAX 703-841-9328

E-Mail: AMiner@nmpf.org
Home Page: www.nmpf.org/ABI

Randy Mooney, Chairman
Dave Fuhrmann, Secretary
Clyde Rutherford, 1st Vice Chairman
Cornell Kasbergen, 2nd Vice Chairman
Ken Nobis, Treasurer

A publication for dairy cooperatives and producers which details recent regulatory activity directly impacting the operation of their farms and manufacturing facilities. Highlights the following areas of regulatory affairs; animal health, food safety, nutrition, standards and labeling, and environment and energy.
31 Members
Founded in 1908

10031 Research Report for Foodservice

1 Bridge St
Irvington, NY 10533-1550

914-591-4297
E-Mail: info@restaurantchains.net
Home Page: www.restaurantchains.net

James Santo, President

Market research company that provides contact information for companies in the foodservice industry. Our two primary brands are RestaurantChains.net, a directory of company profiles and sales leads for US restaurant chains, and FoodserviceReport.com; a weekly bulletin on new US restaurant openings and changes of ownership.
3600 Members
Founded in 1996
Mailing list available for rent: 80000 names

10032 Restaurant Chain Growth

Research Report for Foodservice
1 Bridge St
Irvington, NY 10533-1550

914-591-4297
E-Mail: info@restaurantchains.net
Home Page: www.restaurantchains.net

James Santo, President

Providing the reader with proprietary information.
3600 Members
Frequency: Weekly
Founded in 1996
Mailing list available for rent: 80000 names

10033 Restaurants and Institutions

Reed Business Information
125 Park Avenue
23rd Floor
New York, NY 10017

212-309-8100
FAX 212-309-8187
Home Page: www.rimag.com

A magazine for restaurant professionals faced with fast-paced consumer demands, government regulations, health concerns and evolving food trends in a variety of market segments. R&I keeps these professionals informed and offers menu advice to prepare for new customers and business growth.

10034 Salad Special

Refrigerated Foods Association
2971 Flowers Rd S
Suite 266
Chamblee, GA 30341-5403

770-452-0660
FAX 770-455-3879
E-Mail: info@refrigeratedfoods.org
Home Page: www.refrigeratedfoods.org

Terry Dougherty, Executive Director

A newsletters covering technical and marketing aspects of the industry, including news of projects, conventions and expositions.
Frequency: Monthly
Founded in 1980

10035 Salt & Trace Mineral Newsletter

Salt Institute
700 N Fairfax St
Suite 600
Alexandria, VA 22314-2085

703-549-4648
FAX 703-548-2194
E-Mail: info@saltinstitute.org
Home Page: www.saltinstitute.org

Richard L Hanneman, President
Martina Moran, Director
Tammy Goodwin, Director
Mark OKeefe, Director of Communications

Information on animal nutrition.
Circulation: 3000
Founded in 1940
Printed in on glossy stock

10036 Seafood Price-Current

Urner Barry Publications
PO Box 389
Toms River, NJ 08754-389

732-240-5330
800-932-0617
FAX 732-341-0891
E-Mail: help@urnerbarry.com
Home Page: www.urnerbarry.com

Paul B Brown Jr, President
Karen Mick, Circulation Director

Spot market prices of the most widely traded fresh and frozen fin and shellfish items.
Cost: $383.00
8 Pages
Frequency: Weekly
Circulation: 1500
ISSN: 0270-4170
Founded in 1858

10037 Seafood Trend Newsletter

Seafood Trend
8227 Ashworth Ave N
Seattle, WA 98103-4434

206-523-2280
FAX 206-526-8719
E-Mail: seafoodtrend@aol.com

Ken Talley, Editor/Publisher

Provides information, statistics and economic facts and figures pertaining to the seafood market.
Cost: $235.00
4 Pages
Circulation: 400
ISSN: 1057-2708
Founded in 1984
Printed in 2 colors on matte stock

10038 Shelby Report of the Southeast

Shelby Publishing Company
517 Green St Nw
Gainesville, GA 30501-3300

770-534-8380
FAX 770-535-0110
E-Mail: shelbpub@bellsouth.net
Home Page: www.shelbypublishing.com

Ron Johnston, President
Chuck Gilmer, Editor
Carol Tomaseski, Circulation Manager
Ileen Bloch, VP Publishing

A newsletter offering information on the retail and wholesale food trade.
Cost: $36.00
Frequency: Monthly
Circulation: 25,201
Founded in 1966
Printed in on newsprint stock

10039 Shrimp News International
Aquaculture Digest
9450 Mira Mesa Boulevard
#B562
San Diego, CA 92126-4850

FAX 858-271-0324

Robert Rosenberry, Editor
Publishes reports and directories on the world's
shrimp industry.
Cost: $95.00
24 Pages
Frequency: Biweekly
Mailing list available for rent
Printed in one color on matte stock

10040 Signals Newsletter
Association for Communications Excellence
University of Florida
PO Box 110811
Gainesville, FL 32611-0811

FAX 352-392-8583
E-Mail: ace@ifas.ufl.edu
Home Page: www.aceweb.org

Features news of interest to members. Includes
articles with a professional development focus;
updates from special interest groups, states and
regions; announcements about upcoming workshops and conferences; and write-ups about
members' awards and accomplishments, job
changes and more.

10041 Soft Drink Letter
Whitaker Newsletters
313 S Avenue
#203
Fanwood, NJ 07023-1364

908-889-6336
800-359-6049
FAX 908-889-6339
E-Mail: bevnews@att.net
Home Page: www.att.net

Joel Whitaker, Editor
For managers and owners of bottling and soft
drink and water companies.
Cost: $349.00
Printed in one color

10042 Speedy Bee
Fore's Honey Farms
PO Box 998
Jesup, GA 31598

912-427-4018
FAX 912-427-8447

Troy Fore, Editor
Honey and beekeeping industry news.
Cost: $17.25
16 Pages
Frequency: Monthly
Circulation: 4000
ISSN: 0190-6798
Founded in 1972
Printed in on newsprint stock

10043 Spiceletter
American Spice Trade Association
2025 M St Nw
Suite 800
Washington, DC 20036-2422

202-367-1127
FAX 202-367-2127
Home Page: www.iamss.org

Cheryl Deem, Executive Director
Frequency: Bi-Monthly

**10044 Spirited Living: Dave Steadman's
Restaurant Scene**
5301 Towne Woods Rd
Coram, NY 11727-2808

631-736-0436
FAX 631-736-0436

Dave Steadman, Editor
Newsletter published biweekly except January,
July, and August.
Cost: $75.00

10045 Sunflower Week in Review
National Sunflower Association
2401 46th Avenue SE
Suite 206
Mandan, ND 58554-4829

701-328-5100
888-718-7033
FAX 701-328-5101
E-Mail: larryk@sunflowernsa.com
Home Page: www.sunflowernsa.com
Social Media: *Facebook, YouTube*

Larry Kleingartner, Executive Director
Provides the latest news regarding sunflower
information, conveniently summarized with
highlights and data to keep you informed.
Frequency: Weekly
Founded in 1981

10046 Supermarket News
Fairchild Publications
750 3rd Ave
New York, NY 10017-2703

212-630-4000
877-652-5295
FAX 212-630-3563
Home Page: www.fairchildpub.com

Mary G Berner, CEO
David Merrefield, VP, Editorial Director
David Orgel, Editor-in-Chief
Dan Bagan, Publishing Director
A weekly guide aimed at retailers, wholesalers,
manufacturers and others in the food industry.
Cost: $23.00
Frequency: Weekly
Circulation: 36346
Founded in 1892

10047 THE LINK
R & D Associates for Military Food &
Packaging
16607 Blanco Rd
Suite 501
San Antonio, TX 78232-1940

210-493-8024
FAX 210-493-8036
E-Mail: rda50@flash.net
Home Page: www.militaryfood.org

Barney Guarino, Chairman
Jim Merryman, Vice Chairman
Tim Zimmerman, President
Bill McCreary, Executive Vice President
Jim Fagan, Executive Director
Provides pertinent data available and will keep
readers informed of the activities of major gov-
ernment agencies.
Frequency: Quarterly
Founded in 1946

10048 TecAgri News
Clark Consulting International
PO Box 68
Park Ridge, IL 60068-0068

847-836-5100
FAX 847-792-7565
E-Mail: warren.clark@ccimarketing.com
Home Page: www.tecagrinews.com

Warren E Clark, President

News on new technology in agriculture reach-
ing large computerized family farmers.
Cost: $1200.00
Frequency: Weekly
Circulation: 100,000
Founded in 1986
*Mailing list available for rent: 2.1M names at
$250 per M*

10049 Technical E-News
Refrigerated Foods Association
1640 Powers Ferry Road
Bldg. 2, Suite 200A
Marietta, GA 30067

770-303-9905
FAX 770-303-9906
E-Mail: info@refrigeratedfoods.org
Home Page: www.refrigeratedfoods.org

Brian Edmonds, President
George Bradford, Vice President
Steve Loehndorf, Secretary
Wes Thaller, Treasurer
Contains the latest technical and regulatory
news affecting the industry.
200+ Members
Frequency: Bi-Monthly
Founded in 1980

10050 The Business Owner
Retail Bakers of America
202 Village Circle
Suite 1
Slidell, LA 70458

985-643-6504
800-638-0924
FAX 985-643-6929
E-Mail: Info@RBAnet.com
Home Page: www.rbanet.com
Social Media: *Facebook*

Felix Sherman, Sr., President
Kenneth Downey, Sr., 1st Vice President
Marlene Goetzeler, 2nd Vice President
Dale A. Biles, Treasurer
Susan Nicolais, CAE, Secretary
Publication delivering basic business advice
and know-how for today's small and mid-size
business proprietor. Each issue delivers knowledge in the areas of business strategy, profit
and cash flow maximization, risk reduction and
avoidance, insurance, sales and marketing,
advertising and branding.
2000 Members
Frequency: 6x Yearly
Founded in 1918

10051 The Business of Herbs
Herb Growing and Marketing Network
PO Box 245
Silver Spring, PA 17575-0245

FAX 717-393-9261
E-Mail: herbworld@aol.com
Home Page: www.herbnet.com,
www.herbworld.com

Maureena Rogers, Editor
Information on commercial cultivation of herbs
and marketing. Also regulatory information,
calender of events, business notes.
40 Pages
Frequency: Monthly
Circulation: 2,000
Founded in 1990

10052 The Coffee Reporter
National Coffee Association
45 Broadway
Suite 1140
New York, NY 10006

212-766-4007
FAX 212-766-5815
E-Mail: info@ncausa.org

785

Home Page: www.ncausa.org
Social Media: *Facebook, Twitter, LinkedIn*

Dub Hay, Chairman
John E. Boyle, Vice Chairman
Richard Emanuele, Secretary
Robert F. Nelson, President & CEO

National Coffee Association's official online
newsletter.
Frequency: Weekly

10053 The Culinary Insider

American Culinary Federation
180 Center Place Way
St Augustine, FL 32095-8859

904-824-4468
800-624-9458
FAX 904-825-4758
E-Mail: acf@acfchefs.net
Home Page: www.acfchefs.org
Social Media: *Facebook, Twitter*

Michael Ty, President
Thomas J. Macrina, Secretary
James Taylor, Treasurer

ACF's electronic newsletter featuring the latest
culinary news, events, continuing education opportunities and more.
19000 Members
Founded in 1929

10054 The Exchange

Agricultural & Applied Economics
Association
555 E. Wells St.
Suite 1100
Milwaukee, WI 53202-6600

414-918-3190
E-Mail: Info@aaea.org
Home Page: www.aaea.org

Robert P. King, President
Richard Sexton, President-Elect
Bruce A. Babcock, Director
Jayson Lusk, Director
Lori Lynch, Director

Bi-monthly electronic newsletter published by
AAEA for members only. The content of the
newsletter includes association announcements,
membership news, and updates from the profession.
Cost: $150.00
4M Members
Frequency: Regular Membership Fee
Founded in 1910

10055 Today's Grocer

Florida Grocer Publications
PO Box 430760
S Miami, FL 33243

305-661-0792
800-440-3067
FAX 305-661-6720
E-Mail: todaysgr@bellsouth.net
Home Page: www.todaysgrocer.com

Jack Nobles, Publisher
Dennis Kane, Editor

Provides the latest food industry news and
trends to Florida, Georgia, Alabama, Louisiana,
Mississippi and the Carolinas.
Cost: $29.00
24 Pages
Frequency: Monthly
Circulation: 19500
ISSN: 1529-4420
Founded in 1968
Printed in 4 colors on newsprint stock

10056 US Beer Market

Business Trend Analysts/Industry Reports

2171 Jericho Tpke
Suite 200
Commack, NY 11725-2937

631-462-5454
800-866-4648
FAX 631-462-1842
Home Page: www.bta-ler.com

Charles J Ritchie, Executive VP
Donna Priani, Marketing Director

Profiles markets for premium, superpremium,
popular and light beers.
Cost: $1495.00
Founded in 1978

10057 USA Rice Daily

USA Rice Federation
4301 N Fairfax Drive
Suite 425
Arlington, VA 22203

703-226-2300
FAX 703-236-2301
E-Mail: riceinfo@usarice.com
Home Page: www.usarice.com

Jamie Warshaw, Chairman

The latest news on issues and activities for the
U.S. rice industry.

10058 Uncorked

California Wine Club
2175 Goodyear Ave Suite 102
PO Box 3699
Ventura, CA 93006-3699

805-504-4330
800-777-4443
FAX 800-700-1599
E-Mail: info@cawineclub.com
Home Page: www.cawineclub.com

Bruce Boring, Publisher
Judy Reynolds, Editor

8 page newsletter that describes featured winery. It provides an upclose and personal look at
a small boutique California winery.
Circulation: 10000
Founded in 1990

10059 Update

National FFA Organization
6060 FFA Drive
PO Box 68960
Indianapolis, IN 46268-0960

317-802-6060
888-332-2668
E-Mail: membership@ffa.org
Home Page: www.ffa.org

Steve A. Brown, National FFA Advisor
Marion D. Fletcher, National FFA Organization
Treasurer

The National FFA's newsletter for State Staff
and Advisors. Find important news, information and program updates.
507M Members
Founded in 1928

10060 Urner Barry's Price-Current

Urner Barry Publications
PO Box 389
Toms River, NJ 08754-0389

732-240-5330
800-932-0617
FAX 732-341-0891
E-Mail: help@urnerbarry.com
Home Page: www.urnerbarry.com

Paul B Brown Jr, President
Sheila M Deane, Marketing Manager

Daily market price report serving the poultry
and egg industries.
Cost: $415.00
8 Pages
Frequency: Daily

Circulation: 3,000
ISSN: 0273-9992

10061 Urner Barry's Price-Current West Coast Edition

Urner Barry Publications
PO Box 389
Toms River, NJ 08754

732-240-5330
800-932-0617
FAX 732-341-0891
E-Mail: help@urnerbarry.com
Home Page: www.urnerbarry.com/

Paul Brown Jr, President
Sheila M Deane, Marketing Manager
Richard A. Brown, VP

Reports changes in price and market conditions
of poultry and eggs on the West Coast.
Cost: $444.00
8 Pages
Frequency: Daily
Circulation: 3000
ISSN: 0273-5016
Founded in 1858

10062 Urner Barry's Yellow Sheet

Urner Barry Publications
PO Box 389
Toms River, NJ 08754

732-240-5330
800-932-0617
FAX 732-341-0891
E-Mail: help@urnerbarry.com
Home Page: www.urnerbarry.com

Paul B Brown Jr, President
Richard A Brown, VP/Treasurer

Market price report of timely unbiased meat
quotes to help pinpoint the latest trading levels
of beef, pork, lamb, veal, meat by-products,
carcasses and boxed cuts.
Cost: $559.00
8 Pages
Frequency: Daily
Circulation: 1500
ISSN: 1066-8195
Founded in 1858

10063 Vegetarian Times

Active Interest Media
300 Continental Blvd
Suite 650
El Segundo, CA 90245-5067

310-356-4100
FAX 310-356-4110
E-Mail: editor@vegetariantimes.com
Home Page: www.amedia.com

Efrem Zymbalist III, CEO
John Robles, Marketing Manager

Inspiring everyone to eat healthier, live
greener, and be happier.
Cost: $19.95
Frequency: Monthly
Founded in 1999

10064 Vinotizie Italian Wine Newsletter

Italian Trade Commission
499 Park Ave
6th Floor
New York, NY 10022-1240

212-980-1500
FAX 212-758-1050
Home Page: www.italtrade.com/ice

Michelle Jones, Editor

This newsletter discusses developments in the
Italian wine industry and market, as well as re-
views of imported wines from Italy.
Frequency: Bi-Monthly

10065 WSSA Newsletter

Weed Science Society of America

P.O.Box 7065
Lawrence, KS 66044-7065

785-429-9622
800-627-0629
FAX 785-843-1274
E-Mail: wssa@allenpress.com
Home Page: www.wssa.net

David Shaw, Editor
Michael E Foley, Publications Director
Subscription is included in the annual dues.
Cost: $5.00
Frequency: Quarterly/Non-Member Fee

10066 Washington Association of Wine Grape Growers
PO Box 716
Cashmere, WA 98815

509-782-8234
FAX 509-782-1203
E-Mail: info@wawgg.org
Home Page: www.wawgg.org

Vicky Scharlau, Executive Director
Paul Champoux, Business Manager
Debbie Sands, Business Manager
Janet Heath, Office Manager
Julie Lindholm, Director

Guidance in research and education, and maintaining leadership in local, state and national wine grape issues.
Cost: $115.00
Founded in 1983

10067 Washington Report Newsletter
National Chicken Council
1015 15th Street NW
Suite 930
Washington, DC 20005-2622

202-081-1339
FAX 202-293-4005
E-Mail: ncc@chickenusa.org
Home Page: www.nationalchickencouncil.com

George Watts, President
William P Roenigk, Senior VP
Richard L Lobb, Communications Director
Margaret Ernst, Director Meetings/Membership Comm.

NCC's weekly, member's only newsletter provides information on current statistics, as well as information on economic, trade, and marketing developments, updates on regulatory, legislative, technology, and other industry issues and news
Frequency: Weekly
Circulation: 5000
Founded in 1954

10068 Webster Agricultural Letter
Webster Communications Corporation
1530 Key Blvd
Suite 401W
Arlington, VA 22209-1531

703-525-4512
FAX 703-852-3534
Home Page: www.agletter.com

James C Webster, Editor/CEO
Agricultural politics and policy issues.
Cost: $397.00
6 Pages
Frequency: Fortnightly
ISSN: 1073-4813
Founded in 1980
Printed in one color on matte stock

10069 Weekly Insiders Dairy & Egg Letter
Urner Barry Publications
PO Box 389
Toms River, NJ 08754

732-240-5330
800-932-0617
FAX 732-341-0891

E-Mail: help@urnerbarry.com
Home Page: www.urnerbarry.com

Paul B Brown Jr, President
Randy Pesciotta, Editor
Janice Brown, Advertising

Statistical newsletter of storage stocks of whole, liquid and dried eggs, slaughter and consumption figures and retail selling prices as well as critical data on butter, margarine and cheese.
Cost: $24.00
4 Pages
Frequency: Weekly
Circulation: 10000
ISSN: 0270-4153
Founded in 1858

10070 Weekly Insiders Poultry Report
Urner Barry Publications
PO Box 389
Toms River, NJ 08754-389

732-240-5330
800-932-0617
FAX 732-341-0891
E-Mail: help@urnerbarry.com
Home Page: www.urnerbarry.com

Paul B Brown Jr, President
Sheila M Deane, Marketing Manager

Statistical news of broiler eggs set and hatched, current chicken and fowl slaughter, storage holdings and competing red meat availability.
Cost: $190.00
4 Pages
Frequency: Weekly
Circulation: 230
ISSN: 0160-4910
Founded in 1858

10071 Weekly Insiders Turkey Report
Urner Barry Publications
PO Box 389
Toms River, NJ 08754-389

732-240-5330
800-932-0617
FAX 732-341-0891
E-Mail: help@urnerbarry.com
Home Page: www.urnerbarry.com

Paul B Brown Jr, President
Sheila M Deane, Marketing Manager
Richard A. Brown, VP Treasurer
Michael W. O'Shaughnessy, Secretary

Statistical report containing slaughter figures, consumption patterns, US Storage Stock Estimates and comparative weekly prices.
Cost: $173.00
4 Pages
Frequency: Weekly
Circulation: 230
ISSN: 0160-4910
Founded in 1858

10072 Weekly Livestock Reporter
Weekly Livestock
PO Box 7655
Fort Worth, TX 76111-0655

817-838-0106
FAX 817-831-3117
E-Mail: service@weeklylivestock.com
Home Page: www.weeklylivestock.com

Ted Gouldy, Publisher
Phil Stoll, Editor

Offers comprehensive weekly information for cattle farmers and livestock agricultural professionals.
Cost: $18.00
Frequency: Weekly
Circulation: 10000
Founded in 1897

10073 Weekly Weather and Crop Bulletin
NOAA/USDA Joint Agricultural Weather Facility
1400 Independence Ave SW
Washington, DC 20250

202-720-2791
E-Mail: jawfweb@oce.usda.gov
Home Page: www.noaa.gov

Robert Keeney, Administrator
David Miscus, Managing Editor

Provides a vital source of information on weather, climate and agricultural developments worldwide, along with detailed charts and tables of agrometeorological information that is appropriate for the season.
Frequency: Weekly
Circulation: 1500
Founded in 1807

10074 Western Hemisphere Agriculture and Trade Report
US Department of Agriculture
Room 112-A
US Department of Agriculture
Washington, DC 20250-3810

202-012-2000
FAX 202-690-4915
E-Mail: webmaster@usda.gov
Home Page: www.usda.gov

Miriam Stuart, Publisher
Abraham Lincoln, Chief Information Officer
Chris Smith, Chief Information Officer
Matt Paul, Director of Communications
Ramona Romero, General Counsel

Information on current and projected agricultural production and trade trends for North, Central, South America and the Caribbean. Includes information on trade agreements and blocks in the Hemisphere.
Founded in 1862

10075 What's News in Organic
Organic Trade Association
60 Wells Street
PO Box 547
Greenfield, MA 01302

413-774-7511
FAX 413-774-6432
E-Mail: info@ota.com
Home Page: www.ota.com
Social Media: *Facebook, Twitter, LinkedIn*

Matt McLean, President
Sarah Bird, Vice President
Todd Linsky, Secretary
Kristen Holt, Treasurer

Includes a feature focusing on a hot topic for the industry, a pertinent quotation, and a world of news section outlining brief news related to the industry. Electronic publication.
Frequency: Quarterly
Founded in 1985

10076 Wine on Line Food and Wine Review
Enterprise Publishing
PO Box 328
Blair, NE 68008-0328

402-426-2121
FAX 402-426-2227
E-Mail: mrhoades@enterprisepub.com
Home Page: www.enterprisepub.com

Mark Rhoades, President
Dave Smith, Production Manager
Tracy Prettyman, Business Manager

Reviews, feature articles and information on all areas of food and wine, including restaurants, hotels, trains and airlines. Accepts advertising.
Cost: $100.00
10 Pages
Frequency: Monthly

10077 fridayfeedback
Meat & Livestock Australia
1401 K Street NW
Suite 602
Washington, DC 20005

202-521-2551
FAX 202-521-2699
E-Mail: info@mla.com.au
Home Page: www.mla.com.au
Social Media: *Facebook, Twitter, YouTube*

Don Heatley, Chairman
David Palmer, Managing Director
Bernie Bindon, Director
Chris Hudson, Director

Providing a weekly wrap-up of market information, industry news and updates, and on-farm information including tools and calculators, and producer case studies.
30000 Members
Frequency: Weekly
Founded in 1998

Magazines & Journals

10078 ABF E-Buzz
American Beekeeping Federation
3525 Piedmont Rd
Bldg 5 Suite 300
Atlanta, GA 30305-1509

404-760-2875
FAX 404-240-0998
E-Mail: info@abfnet.org
Home Page: www.abfnet.org

Robin Dahlen, President
David Mendes, VP

A member benefit published electronically to inform members about ABF activities and happenings in the beekeeping industry.
Cost: $35.00
1200 Members
Frequency: Membership Fees Vary
Founded in 1943

10079 ABL Insider
American Beverage Licensees Association
5101 River Rd
Suite 108
Bethesda, MD 20816-1512

301-656-1494
FAX 301-656-7539
E-Mail: rogers@ablusa.org
Home Page: www.ablusa.org
Social Media: *Facebook, Twitter*

Chuck Ferrar, President
Ray Cox, Vice President
Harry Klock, Vice President
Victor Pittman, Vice President
Robert Sprenger, Vice President

A publication of the American Beverage Licensees, the voice of America's beer, wine, and spirits retailers.
17000 Members
Founded in 2002

10080 AHA Quarterly
American Herb Association
PO Box 1673
Nevada City, CA 9595-1673

530-265-9552
FAX 530-274-3140
Home Page: www.ahaherb.com

Kathi Keville, Editor/Director
Mindy Green, Associate Editor

Contains news bulletins, scientific studies, book reviews, research in the field and networking between members. Also offers directories of herb education and mail order sources of herbs.
Cost: $20.00
20 Pages
Frequency: Quarterly
Circulation: 1000
Founded in 1981
Printed in on matte stock

10081 ASMC Sales & Marketing Magazine
Association of Sales & Marketing
Companies
1010 Wisconsin Avenue NW, #900
9th Floor
Washington, DC 20007

202-337-9351
FAX 202-337-4508
E-Mail: info@asmc.org
Home Page: www.asmc.org

Jamie DeSimone, Dir, Marketing/Member
Services

Reports on the progress and change in the food broker profession.
Cost: $25.00
450 Pages
Frequency: Bi-Annual
ISSN: 0884-7185
Founded in 1904
Printed in 4 colors

10082 AWS Wine Journal
American Wine Society
PO Box 279
Englewood, OH 45322-0279

888-297-9070
FAX 937-529-7888
Home Page: www.americanwinesociety.org

John Hames, Executive Director

Contains articles on all aspects of wine appreciation, wine making, wine destinations, and wine & food. Articles provide a wide range of exciting stories and educational information.
Frequency: Quarterly
Founded in 1967

10083 AgProfessional Magazine
Agricultural Retailers Association
1156 15th St NW
Suite 500
Washington, DC 20005-1745

202-457-0825
800-844-4900
FAX 202-457-0864
Home Page: www.agprofessional.com
Social Media: *Twitter, YouTube*

Provides editorial and advertising for agronomic and business management solutions specifically to agricultural retailers/distributors, professional farm managers and crop consultants.
1200 Members
Frequency: Membership Dues Vary
Founded in 1993

10084 Agri Marketing Magazine
Henderson Communications LLC
1422 Elbridge Payne Rd
Suite 250
Chesterfield, MO 63017-8544

636-728-1428
FAX 636-777-4178
E-Mail: info@agrimarketing.com
Home Page: www.agrimarketing.com

Lynn Henderson, Owner

Covers the unique interests of corporate agribusiness executives, their marketing communications agencies, the agricultural media, ag trade associations and other ag related professionals.
Frequency: Monthly
Circulation: 8000
Founded in 1962

10085 Agribusiness Fieldman
Western Agricultural Publishing Company
4969 E Clinton Way
Suite 104
Fresno, CA 93727-1549

559-252-7000
888-382-9772
FAX 559-252-7387
E-Mail: westag@psnw.com
Home Page: www.westagpubco.com

Paul Baltimore, Publisher
Randy Bailey, Editor
Robert Fujimoto, Assistant Director

For the professional agricultural consultant, featuring the latest information on chemical regulation, pest control techniques and feature stories on PCA and PCO community.

10086 Agribusiness Fresh Fruit and Business News
Agribusiness Publications
PO Box 669
Sanger, CA 93657-669

559-875-4585
800-364-4894
FAX 559-875-4587
Home Page: www.agribusinesspublisher.com

John Van Nortwick, Publisher
Michelle Cox, Editor

Keeps subscribers abreast of business news for the fruit growing and producing industry.
Cost: $36.00
Frequency: Monthly
Circulation: 10000
Founded in 1980

10087 Airline Catering International
International Inflight Food Service
Association
5775 Peachtree-Dunwoody Road, Building G
Suite 500
Atlanta, GA 30342

404-252-3663
FAX 404-252-0774
E-Mail: ifsa@kellencompany.com
Home Page: www.ifsanet.com
Social Media: *Facebook, Twitter, LinkedIn, YouTube*

Sandra Pineau, President
Ken Samara, VP

A review of inflight catering and galley equipment. Provides expert coverage and analysis of next-generation galley technology through to the latest menu development trends and eco-friendly food packaging initiatives. Offers a fresh take on the fast-moving and specialized inflight catering market.
400 Members
Frequency: Bi-Annually
Founded in 1965

10088 Alaska Fisherman's Journal
Diversified Business Communications
PO Box 7437
Portland, ME 04112-7437

207-842-5600
FAX 207-842-5503
Home Page: www.divbusiness.com

Nancy Hasselback, CEO
Randy Le Shane, Production Manager
Mike Lodato, Publisher
Neil Casey, Advertising Coordinator
Stephanie Wendel, Audience Development
Manager

Primary publication serving the North Pacific commercial fishing fleet in the world's healthiest and most lucrative commercial fishing re-

gion.
Cost: $21.00
Frequency: Monthly
Circulation: 10,000
ISSN: 0164-8330

10089 Alimentos Balanceados Para Animales
WATT Publishing Company
122 S Wesley Ave
Mt Morris, IL 61054-1451

815-734-7937
FAX 815-734-4201
E-Mail: gill@wattmm.com
Home Page: www.wattnet.com

Clayton Gill, Editorial Director
James Watt, Owner

For feed industry professionals in Latin America.
Cost: $42.00
Circulation: 9471
ISSN: 0274-5571
Founded in 1917
Printed in 4 colors on glossy stock

10090 All About Beer
501 Washington St
Suite H
Durham, NC 27701-2169

919-530-8150
800-999-9718
FAX 919-530-8160
E-Mail: editor@allaboutbeer.com
Home Page: www.allaboutbeer.com

Julie Bradford, Publisher
Natalie Abernethy, Circulation Manager

Quality beers, breweries and restaurants.
Cost: $19.99

10091 Allied Tradesman
Allied Trades of the Baking Industry
2001 Shawnee Mission Pkwy
Mission Woods, KS 62205

707-935-0103
FAX 707-935-0174
Home Page: www.atbi.org

Gary Cain, President
Tim Miller, Secretary, Treasurer
Brad Hahn, Secretary, Treasurer
Matt Ungashick, Secretary
Bruce Criss, Vice President
Frequency: Monthly
Circulation: 500
Founded in 1920

10092 Almond Facts
Blue Diamond Growers
1802 C Street
PO Box 1768
Sacramento, CA 95811

916-442-0771
FAX 916-325-2880
E-Mail: feedback@bdgrowers.com
Home Page: www.bluediamond.com

Robert Donovan, CFO
Douglas D Youngdahl, CEO/President

The latest news affecting Blue Diamond and the almond industry with Almond Facts magazine. Service to Blue Diamond's grower-owners, also available online.
Cost: $25.00
Frequency: Bi-Monthly
Founded in 1910
Printed in 4 colors

10093 American Beefalo World Registry
30 Stevenson Road
#5
Laramie, WY 82070

307-745-3505
866-374-2297
FAX 307-745-3505
Home Page: www.abwr.org

Offers information for beef and cattle farmers.

10094 American Brewer
1049 B Street
PO Box 510
Hayward, CA 94543-510

510-886-7418
FAX 510-538-7644
E-Mail: info@ambrew.com
Home Page: www.ambrew.com

Bill Owens, Publisher
Greg Kitsock, Editor

A magazine covering the business of beer.
Cost: $50.00
Frequency: Quarterly
Founded in 1979

10095 American Fruit Grower
Meister Publishing Company
37733 Euclid Ave
Willoughby, OH 44094-5992

440-942-2000
800-572-7740
FAX 440-975-3447
E-Mail: afg.circ@meistermedia.com
Home Page: www.meisternet.com

Gary Fitzgerald, President
Joe Monahan, Group Publisher
Fran Mihalik, Circulation Manager

Specialized production and marketing information and industry-wide support for fruit growers.
Cost: $19.95
66 Pages
Frequency: Monthly
Circulation: 37,000
Founded in 1931

10096 American Journal of Enology and Viticulture
American Society for Enology and Vinticulture
1784 Picasso Avenue Suite D
PO Box 2160
Davis, CA 95617-2160

530-753-3142
FAX 530-753-3318
Home Page: www.ajevonline.org

Judith McKibben, Managing Editor

Full-length research papers, literature reviews, research notes and technical briefs on various aspects of enology and viticulture, including wine chemistry, sensory science, process engineering, wine quality assessments, microbiology, methods development, plant pathogenesis, diseases and pests of grape, rootstock and clonal evaluation, effect of field practices and grape genetics and breeding.
Frequency: Quarterly
Mailing list available for rent

10097 American Red Angus Magazine
Red Angus Association of America
4201 N Interstate 35
Denton, TX 76207-3415

940-387-3502
FAX 888-829-5573
E-Mail: info@redangus.org
Home Page: www.redangus.org
Social Media: Facebook

Joe Mushrush, President
Greg Comstock, CEO

The most comprehensive resource guide to the Red Angus breed. Keep informed about a breed that is focused on economic value, efficiency and quality.
2000 Members
Founded in 1954

10098 American Small Farm Magazine
560 Sunbury Rd
Suite 6
Delaware, OH 43015-8692

740-363-2395
FAX 740-369-9526
E-Mail: sales@smallfarm.com
Home Page: www.smallfarm.com

Marti Smith, Information
Andy Stevens, Editor

Published for the owner/operator of farms from five to three hundred acres. Focuses on production agriculture including alternative and sustainable farming ideas and technology, case studies, small farm lifestyle and tradition.
Cost: $18.00
ISSN: 1064-7473

10099 American Vegetable Grower
Meister Media Worldwide
37733 Euclid Ave
Willoughby, OH 44094-5992

440-942-2000
800-572-7740
FAX 440-975-3447
E-Mail: avg.circ@meistermedia.com
Home Page: www.meisternet.com

Gary Fitzgerald, President
Ken Hall, Communications Manager
Josep W Monahan, Publisher
Fran Mihalik, Circulation manager

Information source for commercial vegetable growers.
Cost: $19.95
Frequency: Monthly
Circulation: 34772
Founded in 1931

10100 American Wholesale Marketers Association/ Convenience Distribution
American Wholesale Marketers Association
2750 Prosperity Ave
Suite 530
Fairfax, VA 22031-4338

703-208-3358
800-482-2962
FAX 703-573-5738
E-Mail: info@awmanet.org
Home Page: www.awmanet.org;
www.conveniencedistributionmagazine.com

Scott Ramminger, Publisher Executive Editor
Joan Fay, Editor + Associate Publisher

A magazine specifically targeted toward convenience distributors. Our readers are involved in the purchase and sale of candy, tobacco, snacks, beverages, health and beauty care items, general merchandise, foodservice, groceries and more.
Cost: $36.00
Frequency: Monthly/Non-Members Fee
Circulation: 11,000
ISSN: 1083-9313
Printed in 4 colors on glossy stock

10101 Angus Journal
American Angus Association
3201 Frederick Ave
St Joseph, MO 64506-2997

816-383-5100
FAX 816-233-9703
E-Mail: angus@angus.org

Home Page: www.angus.org
Social Media: *Facebook, Twitter*

Joe Hampton, Chair
Jarold Callahan, Vice Chair
Phil Trowbridge, Treasurer

To provide programs, services, technology and leadership to enhance the genetics of the Angus breed, broaden its influence within the beef industry, and expand the market for superior tasting, high-quality Angus beef worldwide. Achieve Angus excellence through information.
Cost: $80.00
30+M Members
Frequency: Membership Fees Vary
Founded in 1883

10102 Applied Economic Perspectives and Policy
Agricultural & Applied Economics Association
555 E. Wells St.
Suite 1100
Milwaukee, WI 53202-6600

414-918-3190
E-Mail: Info@aaea.org
Home Page: www.aaea.org

Robert P. King, President
Richard Sexton, President-Elect
Bruce A. Babcock, Director
Jayson Lusk, Director
Lori Lynch, Director

Publishes articles that synthsize, integrate, and analyze areas of current applied economic research within the mission of the AAEA as well as stimulate linkages between sub-fields of agricultural and applied economics.
Cost: $ 150.00
4M Members
Frequency: Regular Membership Fee
Founded in 1910

10103 Applied Engineering in Agriculture
American Society of Agricultural Engineers
2950 Niles Rd
St Joseph, MI 49085-8607

269-429-0300
800-371-2723
FAX 269-429-3852
E-Mail: hq@asabe.org
Home Page: www.asabe.org

Mark D Zielke, CEO
Donna Hull, Pubilcation Director

Focus is on agricultural equipment, farm buildings, electrification, soil conservation, irrigation and food engineering.
26 Pages
Frequency: Monthly
Circulation: 9000
Founded in 1907

10104 Aquaculture Magazine
Achill River Corporation
PO Box 2329
Asheville, NC 28802-2329

828-687-0011
FAX 828-681-0601
E-Mail: info@aquaculturemag.com
Home Page: www.aquaculturemag.com

Gregory J Gallagher, Editor/Publisher
Doinita Cociovei, Circulation Manager
Joseth Strickland, Advertisement Manager

Focus emphasizes the production, processing, and marketing of aquatic organisms and plant life.
Founded in 1968

10105 Arbor Age
Green Media

1030 W Higgins Road
Suite 230
Park Ridge, IL 60068

847-720-5600
FAX 847-720-5601
Home Page: www.arborage.com

John Kmitta, Senior Editor

Targets arborists in the commercial, municipal and utility sectors. Content is provided by a wide range of green industry experts, including professional arborists, academicians, instructors, consultants, government bodies and research organizations.
43 Pages
Frequency: 9x Yearly
Circulation: 16,500
Founded in 1981
Printed in 4 colors on glossy stock

10106 Atlantic Control States Beverage Journal
Club & Tavern
3 12th Street
Wheeling, WV 26003-3276

304-232-7620
FAX 304-233-1236
Arnold Lazarus, Editor

A magazine for the alcoholic beverage industry. Serving bars, restaurants, clubs and industry personnel with West Virginia, Virginia, and North Carolina state editions. Includes states' liquor price lists.

10107 Automatic Merchandiser
Cygnus Business Media
1233 Janesville Avenue
Fort Atkinson, WI 53538

800-547-7377
E-Mail: gary.thom@vendingmarketwatch.com
Home Page: www.vendingmarketwatch.com

Gary Thom, Publisher

Serves the business management, marketing, technology and product information needs of its readers.
Cost: $66.00
84 Pages
Frequency: Monthly
Circulation: 14000
Founded in 1937
Mailing list available for rent: 16004 names at $150 per M
Printed in 4 colors on newsprint stock

10108 Bagel Bits
Independent Bakers Association
2 S Portage Street
Westfield, NY 14787

716-326-5200
E-Mail: nationalinfo@welchs.com
Home Page: www.nationalgrape.com

Nicholas Pyle, Manager
Founded in 1965

10109 Baker's Rack
Retail Bakers of America
202 Village Circle
Suite 1
Slidell, LA 70458

985-643-6504
800-638-0924
FAX 985-643-6929
E-Mail: Info@RBAnet.com
Home Page: www.rbanet.com
Social Media: *Facebook*

Felix Sherman, Sr., President
Kenneth Downey, Sr., 1st Vice President
Marlene Goetzeler, 2nd Vice President
Dale A. Biles, Treasurer
Susan Nicolais, CAE, Secretary

Reaching retail baking professionals and the baking industry as a whole. Articles are submitted from industry experts who understand the unique interests and needs of today's retail baker.
2000 Members
Frequency: Quarterly
Founded in 1918

10110 Bakery Production and Marketing
245 W 17th Street
1350 E Toughy Avenue
New York, NY 10011

212-414-1160
FAX 212-337-7198
Home Page: www.cahners.com

Doug Krumrei, Editor
Stuart Whayman, CFO

Dedicated to delivering sensible ideas for profitable baking with editorial that addresses solutions and opportunities found within retail, instore, food service and intermediate wholesale bakeries.
Cost: $70.00
Frequency: Monthly
Circulation: 31,000

10111 Baking Buyer
Sosland Publishing Company
4800 Main St
Suite 100
Kansas City, MO 64112-2513

816-756-1000
FAX 816-756-0494
E-Mail: web@sosland.com
Home Page: www.sosland.com

Gordon Davidson, President
John Unrein, Editor
Tarre Beach, Managing Editor

This publication offers information on state-of-the-art baked foods and ingredients.
Circulation: 31000
Founded in 1922

10112 Baking and Snack
Paul Lattan
4800 Main Street
Suite 100
Kansas City, MO 64112-2504

816-756-1000
FAX 816-756-0494
E-Mail: bbcservice@sosland.com
Home Page: www.bakingbusiness.com

Steve Barne, Editor
Laurie Gorton, Executive Editor

A magazine offering information on baking equipment and ingredients for the commercial baker.
Frequency: Monthly
Circulation: 12,494
Founded in 1922

10113 Bar & Beverage Business Magazine
Mercury Publications
1839 Inkster Boulevard
Winnipeg, Ma 0

204-954-2085
FAX 204-954-2057
E-Mail: webmaster@mercury.mb.ca
Home Page: www.mercury.mb.ca/

Frank Yeo, Publisher
Robert Thompson, National Account Manager
Kelly Gray, Editor
Angie Finnbogason, Circulation Manager
Carly Peters, Editorial Production Manager

The buying and selling of beverages, operator profiles, new products, product merchandising and trends.
Cost: $35.00
Frequency: Quarterly
Circulation: 16923

Founded in 1948
Mailing list available for rent

10114 Bartender Magazine

Foley Publishing Corporation
PO Box 157
Spring Lake, NJ 07762

732-449-4499
FAX 732-974-8289
E-Mail: barmag@aol.com
Home Page: www.bartender.com
Social Media: *Facebook, Twitter*

Raymond Foley, Publisher
Jaclyn Wilson Foley, Editor

Serves all full-service drinking establishments, including individual restaurants, hotels, motels, bars, taverns, lounges and all other full service on premise licenses.
76 Pages
Frequency: Quarterly
Circulation: 104000
Founded in 1979
Printed in 4 colors on glossy stock

10115 Bee Culture

AI Root Company
PO Box 706
Medina, OH 44258-0706

330-725-6677
800-289-7668
FAX 330-725-5624
E-Mail: weboptout@rootcandles.com
Home Page: www.rootcandles.com

John Root, President
Kathy Summers, Production Manager

Honey bees and their keeping for beginners and experienced apiculturists. Accepts advertising, press releases, new products, and book reviews.
Cost: $21.50
64 Pages
Circulation: 12000
ISSN: 1071-3190
Founded in 1863
Printed in 4 colors on matte stock

10116 Beer, Wine & Spirits Beverage Retailer

Oxford Publishing
Ste 1
1903b University Ave
Oxford, MS 38655-4150

662-236-5510
800-247-3881
FAX 662-236-5541
E-Mail: ncb@nightclub.com
Home Page: www.nightclub.com

Ed Meek, Publisher
Michael Harrelson, Editor
Jennifer Parsons, Marketing
Jennifer Robinson, COO
Adam Alson, Founder

Beverage Retailer serves retail establishments in the beer, wine and spirits industries, including liquor, package and wine stores and others allied to the field.
Cost: $30.00
52 Pages
Frequency: Monthly
Circulation: 19985
Founded in 1997
Printed in 4 colors on glossy stock

10117 Beverage Dynamics

The Beverage Information Group

17 High Street
2nd Floor
Norwalk, CT 06851

203-855-8499
E-Mail: lzimmerman@m2media360.com
Home Page: www.bevinfogroup.com

Liza Zimmerman, Editor-in-Chief
Jeremy Nedelka, Managing Editor

Provides a unique and essential communications link between suppliers and chain and independent retailers in the off-premise market (liquor stores, supermarkets, beverage outlets, etc)
Cost: $35.00
Frequency: Bi-Monthly
Founded in 1934

10118 Beverage Industry

Stagnito Communications
2401 W Big Beaver Road
Suite 700
Troy, MI 48084

847-763-9534
FAX 847-763-9538
E-Mail: bi@halldata.com
Home Page: www.bevindustry.com
Social Media: *Facebook, Twitter, LinkedIn*

Steve Pintarelli, Publisher
Jessica Jacobsen, Editor
Stephanie Cernivec, Managing Editor

Provides the most in-depth information about the beverage market including production, technology and distribution. The changing industry demands a change leader and BI fills that role by reporting behind the scenes of the gigantic 65 billion market.
Cost: $40.00
Frequency: Monthly
Circulation: 28000
Founded in 1946

10119 Beverage Journal

Michigan Licensed Beverage Association
920 N Fairview Ave
Lansing, MI 48912-3238

517-374-9611
877-292-2896
FAX 517-374-1165
E-Mail: info@mlba.org
Home Page: www.mlba.org

Lou Adado, CEO
Catherine Pavick, Executive Director

Offers information on the alcoholic beverage industry/retail sales
Cost: $52.00
Frequency: Monthly
ISSN: 1050-4427
Printed in on glossy stock

10120 Beverage Media

Beverage Media Group
152 Madison Avenue
Suite 600
New York, NY 10016

212-571-3232
FAX 212-571-4443
Home Page: www.bevnetwork.com

Journal offering information on the liquor, wine and beer trade. New products & promotions, industry news and current trends.
Cost: $119.00
Frequency: Monthly

10121 Beverage Network

4437 Concord Lane
Skokie, IL 60076-2605

617-497-0062
FAX 617-812-7740

E-Mail: sales@bevnet.com
Home Page: www.bevnet.com

Organization of beverage distributors dealing with specialty, nonalcoholic products.

10122 Beverage Retailer Magazine

Oxford Publishing
Ste 1
1903b University Ave
Oxford, MS 38655-4150

662-236-5510
800-247-3881
FAX 662-236-5541
E-Mail: br@beverage.retailer.com
Home Page: www.beverage-retailer.com

Ed Meek, Publisher
Brenda Owen, Editor
Ruth Ann Wolfe, Circualtion Manager

A magazine covering the off-premise market for retailers in the wine, beer and spirits business.
Cost: $30.00
Frequency: Monthly
Circulation: 25000
Founded in 1920
Printed in 4 colors on glossy stock

10123 Biodynamics

Biodynamic Farming & Gardening Association
PO Box 944
East Troy, WI 53120-0944

262-649-9212
E-Mail: info@biodynamics.com
Home Page: www.biodynamics.com
Social Media: *Facebook*

Charles Beedy, Contact

A membership publication providing a thoughtful collection of original articles centered on a theme of interest to the biodynamic community. Voices from the community, discussion of the biodynamic preparations, regional, national, and international news and updates, event overviews, book and film reviews, organizational updates, seasonal recipes, columns and more.
Cost: $45.00
Frequency: 6 per year
Circulation: 1000+

10124 Bison World Magazine

National Bison Association
8690 Wolff Ct
200
Westminster, CO 80234

303-292-2833
FAX 303-845-9081
E-Mail: david@bisoncentral.com
Home Page: www.bisoncentral.com

Jim Matheson, Assistant Director
Dave Carter, Executive Director

Featured articles and regular departments cover all aspects of raising bison and what's happening in this exciting industry. Available with all levels of membership with the association.
Frequency: Quarterly
Circulation: 1000

10125 Body, Mind & Spirit Magazine

PO Box 95
Dogsland, SK

306-356-4634
FAX 306-356-4634
Home Page:
www.saskworld.com/bodymindspirit

Jeni Mayer, Publisher
Adele Azar-Rucquoi, Contributing Writers
Frequency: Quarterly

10126 Bottled Water Reporter

International Bottled Water Association

1700 Diagonal Rd
Suite 650
Alexandria, VA 22314-2870

703-683-5213
817-719-6197
FAX 703-683-4074
E-Mail: ibwainfo@bottledwater.org
Home Page: www.bottledwater.org

Joseph Doss, Publisher/President

Covers IBWA events and programs while highlighting new technologies and equipment within the industry, taking notice of personnel changes and reporting on the latest industry statistical data. It also features useful articles on management, operations and marketing specific to the bottled water industry.
Cost: $50.00
74 Pages
Circulation: 2500
Founded in 1958
Printed in 4 colors on glossy stock

10127 Brahman Journal

American Brahman Breeders Association
915 12th Street
Suite 520
Houston, TX 77054

979-826-4347
FAX 979-826-2007
E-Mail: info@brahmanjournal.com
Home Page: www.brahmanjournal.com
Social Media: *Facebook*

Victoria Lambert, Editor
Brandy Barnes, Field Representative
Mandy Chambers, Assistant Editor

Provides timely, useful information about one of the largest, most dynamic and most influential breeds of beef cattle in the world. Each issue reports on American Brahman and International Brahman shows, American Brahman and international Brahman events, Brahman sales and Brahman history, as well as pertinent cattle industry news, technical articles and the latest research as it pertains to the Brahman Breed and its followers.
Cost: $25.00
Frequency: Monthly
Circulation: 7000
Founded in 1971

10128 Brandpackaging

Independent Publishing Company
P.O.Box 3116
Saint George, UT 84771-3116

435-656-1555
800-808-7449
FAX 435-656-1511
Home Page: www.independentpublishing.com

Josh Warburton, President/Publisher
Circulation: 5500
Founded in 1996

10129 Brewers Digest

Siebel Publishing Company
Business Office
PO Box 677
Thiensville, WI 53092-6026

915-877-3319
FAX 915-877-3319

Thomas Volke, Publisher
Dori Whitney, Editor

The gamut of operational, production, buying, engineering, and packaging issues affecting brewing companies and enterprises.
Cost: $20.00
70 Pages
Frequency: Monthly
Circulation: 3000
ISSN: 0006-971X
Founded in 1926
Printed in 4 colors on glossy stock

10130 Business of Herbs

Northwind Farm Publications
439 Ponderosa Way
Jemez Springs, NM 87025-8036

505-829-3448
FAX 505-829-3449
Home Page: www.herb-biz.com

Paula Oliver, Publisher
David Oliver, Editor

Primarily for herb businesses and those keenly interested in herbs and botanicals.
Cost: $4.00

10131 Calf News (Cattle Feeder Magazine)

1531 Kensington Boulevard
Garden City, KS 67846

620-276-7844
FAX 620-275-7333
E-Mail: steve@calfnews.com
Home Page: www.calfnews.com

Betty Jo Gigot, Editor & Publisher
Patti Wilson, Sales Manager
Larisa Willrett, Copy Editor/Circulation
Kathie Bedolli, Director

This magazine offers the latest information to cattle breeders and feeders.
Cost: $33.00
Circulation: 6,352
Founded in 1964

10132 Candy Industry

Stagnito Communications
155 Pfingsten Road
Suite 205
Deerfield, IL 60015

847-205-5660
FAX 847-205-5680
Home Page: www.stagnito.com

Harry Stagnito, President
Korry Stagnito, Publishing Director
Sue Ravenscraft, VP Circulation

Magazine serving chocolate and confectionary manufacturers.
Cost: $59.00
Frequency: Monthly
Founded in 1944
Printed in 4 colors on glossy stock

10133 Capital Press

Press Publishing Company
PO Box 2048
Salem, OR 97308-2048

503-364-4431
800-882-6789
FAX 503-370-4383
E-Mail: eshein@capitalpress.com
Home Page: www.capitalpress.com

Carl Sampson, Managing Editor
Elaine Shein, Editor/Publisher
Mike O'Brien, Circulation/General Manager

For the agricultural and forest community of the Pacific Northwest.
Cost: $44.00
60 Pages
Frequency: Weekly
Circulation: 37000
Founded in 1928
Printed in 4 colors on newsprint stock

10134 Carnetec

1415 N Dayton
Chicago, IL 60622

312-266-3311
FAX 312-266-3363
E-Mail: annica@meatingplace.com
Home Page: www.carnetec.com

Ryan Pfister, Product Manager

Spanish language magazine reaching executives in the Latin American meat and poultry

processing industry. Helps improve the manufacturing process, equipment, sanitation, safety and technology.

10135 Carrot Country

Columbia Publishing
8405 Ahtanum Rd
Yakima, WA 98903-9432

509-248-2452
800-900-2452
FAX 509-248-4056
Home Page: www.carrotcountry.com

Brent Clement, Editor/Publisher
Mike Stoker, Publisher

Includes information on carrot production, grower and shipper feature stories, carrot research, new varieties, market reports, spot reports on overseas production and marketing and other key issues and trends of interest to US and Canadian carrot growers.
Cost: $10.00
Frequency: Quarterly
Circulation: 2700
Founded in 1975
Printed in 4 colors on glossy stock

10136 Cereal Chemistry

AACC International
3340 Pilot Knob Rd
Eagan, MN 55121-2055

651-454-7250
800-328-7560
FAX 651-454-0766
Home Page: www.scientificsocieties.org

Steven Nelson, VP
Bernie Bruinsma, Chair of Board
Laura Hansen, Treasurer

The premier international archival journal in cereal science. No other journal surpasses it in the quantity and quality of juried, original research. Research presented explores raw materials, processes, products utilizing cereal, oilseeds, and pulses, as well as analytical procedures, technological tests and fundamental research in the cereals area.
Cost: $79.00
Frequency: Bi-Monthly
Circulation: 3539
Founded in 1915

10137 Cereal Foods World

AACC International
3340 Pilot Knob Rd
Eagan, MN 55121-2055

651-454-7250
800-328-7560
FAX 651-454-0766
Home Page: www.scientificsocieties.org

Steven Nelson, VP
Bernie Bruinsma, Chair of Board
Laura Hansen, Treasurer

A leading source of information on grain-based food science, technology, and new product development. Includes articles that focus on advances in grain-based food science and the application of these advances to product development and current food production practices.
Cost: $48.00
Frequency: Bi-Monthly
Circulation: 4500
ISSN: 0146-6283
Founded in 1956

10138 Cheers

Jobson Publishing Corporation

100 Avenue of the Americas
Suite 9
New York, NY 10013-1678

212-274-7000
FAX 212-431-0500
Home Page: www.jobson.com

Michael J Tansey, CEO

Every issue is designed to help on-premise operators enhance the profitability of their beverage operations.

10139 Cheese Market News

Quarne Publishing
PO Box 620244
Middleton, WI 53562

608-831-6002
FAX 608-831-1004
E-Mail: squarne@cheesemarketnews.com
Home Page: www.cheesemarketnews.com

Susan Quarne, Publisher
Kate Sander, Editorial Director

Weekly trade news for the nation's cheese and dairy/deli business
Cost: $105.00
16 Pages
Frequency: Weekly
Circulation: 2200
ISSN: 0891-1509
Founded in 1981
Mailing list available for rent: 2200 names at $500 per M
Printed in 4 colors on newsprint stock

10140 Chef

Talcott Communications Corporation
20 W Kinzie St
Suite 1200
Chicago, IL 60654-5827

312-849-2220
800-229-1967
FAX 312-849-2174
Home Page: www.talcott.com

Daniel Von Rabenau, Executive Director
Robert S Benes, Senior Editor

Information on food production and presentation, includes chef profiles, trend studies, marketing information and restaurant profiles.
Cost: $32.00
Circulation: 40,000
ISSN: 1087-061X
Founded in 1956
Printed in 4 colors on glossy stock

10141 Chemical and Pharmaceutical Press

C&P Press
90 william strret
5th Floor
New York, NY 10106-2899

212-326-6760
800-544-7377
FAX 646-733-6010
Home Page: www.cppress.com

Dr. Mary Conway, Executive Editor
Bron Zienkiewicz, Sales/Marketing
Sonia Tighe, Publisher

Supplies chemical information to professionals involved with the sale, application, storage or regulations of agricultural or ornamental and turf pesticides. Information is available in either reference book form or on computer disc. Complete product labels, MSDS's and indexes are included.
Founded in 1984

10142 Choices

Agricultural & Applied Economics Association

555 E Wells Street
Suite 1100
Milwaukee, WI 53202

414-918-3190
FAX 414-276-3349
E-Mail: info@aaea.org
Home Page: www.choicesmagazine.org

Walter J Armbruster, Editor
James Novak, Associate Editor

Provides current coverage regarding economic implications of food, farm, resource, or rural community issues directed toward a broad audience. Publishes thematic groupings of papers and individual papers.
Frequency: Quarterly
ISSN: 0886-5558
Founded in 1910
Printed in 4 colors on glossy stock

10143 Citograph

Western Agricultural Publishing Company
4969 E Clinton Way
#104
Fresno, CA 93727-1549

559-252-7000
FAX 559-252-7387
E-Mail: westag@psn.com
Home Page: www.westapub.com

Paul Baltimore, Publisher

The oldest continuous citrus-specific publication in the world. Stories centering on all aspects of citrus production from planting to harvest and all maintenance in between. Lemons, limes, oranges, avocados — all citrus is included.

10144 Citrus & Vegetable Magazine

Vance Publishing
400 Knightsbridge Parkway
Lincolnshire, IL 60069

847-634-2600
FAX 847-634-4379
E-Mail: info@vancepublishing.com
Home Page: www.vancepublishing.com

William C Vance, Chairman
Peggy Walker, President

Delivers profitable production and management strategies to commerical citrus and vegetable growers in Florida.
Cost: $45.00
Frequency: Monthly
Circulation: 12004

10145 CleanRooms Magazine

PennWell Publishing Company
98 Spit Brook Rd
Suite 100
Nashua, NH 03062-5737

603-891-0123
FAX 603-891-9294
E-Mail: info@pennwell.com
Home Page: www.pennwell.com

Christine Shaw, VP
James Enos, Publisher
Adam Japker, CEO

Serves the contamination control and ultrapure materials and process industries. Written for readers in the microelectronics, pharmaceutical, biotech, health care, food processing and other user industries. Provides technology and business news and new product listings.
Founded in 1987

10146 Communications in Soil Science and Plant Analysis

Marcel Dekker
270 Madison Avenue
New York, NY 10016

212-696-9000
800-228-1160

FAX 212-685-4540
Home Page: www.dekker.com

Harry A Mills, Editor
Marcel Dekker, President

All aspects of soil science and crop production in all climates.
Cost: $567.00
120 Pages
Circulation: 23500
ISSN: 0010-3624
Founded in 1963

10147 Concession Profession

National Association of Concessoinaires
35 East Wacker Drive
Suite 1816
Chicago, IL 60601-2270

312-236-3858
FAX 312-236-7809
E-Mail: info@naconline.org
Home Page: www.naconline.org
Social Media: Facebook, LinkedIn

Charles A Winans, Executive Director
Susan M Cross, Communications Director
Barbara Aslan, Membership Services Manager

The NAC member magazine devoted to the recreational and leisuretime food and beverage concessions industry, featuring news briefs, feature articles, association news and advertising opportunities.
800 Members
Founded in 1944

10148 Concession Professsion

National Association of Concessionaires
35 E Wacker Dr
Suite 1816
Chicago, IL 60601-2270

312-236-3858
FAX 312-236-7809
E-Mail: scross@NAConline.org
Home Page: www.naconline.org
Social Media: Facebook, LinkedIn

John Evans, Jr., President
Jeff Scudillo, President-Elect
Ron Krueger II, Board Chairman

Devoted to the recreational and leisuretime food and beverage concessions industry, featuring news briefs, feature articles, association news and advertising opportunities.
Frequency: Bi-Annual
Printed in 4 colors

10149 Convenience Store Decisions

Harbor Communications
19111 Detroit Road
Suite 201
Rocky River, OH 44116

440-250-1538
FAX 440-333-1892
Home Page: www.csdecisions.com

Jeff Donohoe, Owner
Jay Gordon, Editor

For buyers, directors, field managers, owners and executives in the convenience store business. Free to qualified subscribers.
180 Pages
Frequency: Monthly
Circulation: 40000+
Founded in 1892

10150 Cooking for Profit

CP Publishing
PO Box 267
Fond du Lac, WI 54936

920-923-3700
FAX 920-923-6805
E-Mail: comments@cookingforprofit.com
Home Page: www.cookingforprofit.com

Colleen Phalen, Editor-in-Chief/Publisher

Paid subscription trade magazine targeted to foodservice owners, managers and chefs. Each month features current trends in food preparation with step-by-step recipes and photographs; effective management techniques; and the latest in foodservice equipment — all written by industry experts. Also features in-depth profiles of a successful foodservice operation.
Cost: $26.00
28 Pages
Frequency: Monthly
Circulation: 75000
Founded in 1932
Printed in 4 colors on glossy stock

10151 Cooperative Grocer
361 East College Street
Iowa City, IA 52240-267

319-466-9029
FAX 866-600-4588
E-Mail: dave@cooperativegrocer.com
Home Page: cooperativegrocer.coop

Dave Gutknecht, Editor
Dan Nordley, Publisher
Don McLemore, CEO

Trade magazine by and for people working with consumer cooperative grocery stores.
Founded in 1999

10152 Cotton Farming
One Grower Publishing
5118 Park Avenue
Suite 111
Memphis, TN 38117-5710

901-767-4020
FAX 901-767-4026
E-Mail: throton@onegrower.com
Home Page: www.cottonfarming.com
Social Media: *Twitter, Flickr*

Lia Guthrie, Publisher/VP
Tommy Horton, Editor

Serving the industry, providing the latest news and technology information.
Frequency: Monthly
Founded in 1937

10153 Country Folks
Lee Publications
6113 State Highway 5
PO Box 121
Palatine Bridge, NY 13428-121

518-673-2269
800-218-5586
FAX 518-673-3245
E-Mail: subscriptions@leepub.com
Home Page: www.countryfolks.com

Frederick Lee, Publisher
Marjorie Struckle, Editor
Bruce Button, President
Janet Button, Marketing Manager
Tom Mahoney, Sales Manager

Agricultural news from national, state and local levels. Some features on farm and agricultural industry, rural interest, etc.
Cost: $12.00
75 Pages
Frequency: Weekly
Circulation: 27000

10154 Country Living
Arens Corporation
PO Box 69
Covington, OH 45318-0069

937-473-2020
FAX 937-473-2500
E-Mail: garyg@arenspub.com
Home Page: www.arenspub.com

Gary Godfrey, Publisher/President
Don Selanders, Sales Manager
Connie Didier, Circulation Manager

Current news and features devoted to the agricultural industry.
Cost: $1395.00
Frequency: Monthly
Circulation: 17500
Founded in 1950

10155 Country Woman
Reiman Publications
5400 S 60th St
Greendale, WI 53129-1404

414-423-0100
800-344-6913
FAX 414-423-1143
E-Mail: editors@countrywomanmagazine.com
Home Page:
www.countrywomanmagazine.com

Barbara Newton, President
Ann Kaiser, Editor

Offers recipes, stories, profiles and articles pertaining to the country woman.
Cost: $14.98
68 Pages
Founded in 1965

10156 Critical Reviews in Food and Nutrition
CRC Press
6000 Broken Sound Pkwy NW
Suite 300
Boca Raton, FL 33487-5704

561-994-0555
800-272-7737
FAX 561-989-9732
E-Mail: techsupport@crcpress.com
Home Page: www.crcpress.com

Emmett Dages, CEO
Susan Lee, Editor
Founded in 1913

10157 Culinary Trends
Culinary Trends Publications
6285 Spring St
Number 107
Long Beach, CA 90808

714-826-9188
FAX 714-826-0333
E-Mail: Editor@culinarytrends.net
Home Page: www.culinarytrends.net

Fred Mensigna, Publisher
Jean Hutchins, Director

Information for food and beverage managers along with managers of hotels and restaurants.
Cost: $21.00
Frequency: Quarterly
Circulation: 10000
Founded in 1993

10158 DDBC News
Dairy, Deli, Bakery Council of Southern California
PO Box 1872
Whittier, CA 90609

562-947-7016
FAX 562-947-7872
E-Mail: delicouncil@earthlink.net
Home Page: www.ddbcsc.com

Bob Dreffler, CEO
Dave Daniel, Editor
Susan Steele, Circulation Manager

Serves the deli, dairy, bakery and meat industry.
Cost: $25.00
Frequency: Monthly
Circulation: 5000
ISSN: 0011-7862
Founded in 1960
Printed in 4 colors on glossy stock

10159 DFA Leader
Dairy Farmers of America

10220 N Ambassador Dr
Kansas City, MO 64153-1367

816-801-6455
888-332-6455
FAX 816-801-6456
E-Mail: webmail@dfamilk.com
Home Page: www.dfamilk.com
Social Media: *Facebook, Twitter, LinkedIn, YouTube*

Randy Mooney, Chairman of the Board
George Mertens, Vice Chairman
Tom Croner, Secretary/Treasurer

Provides members with information about DFA and the dairy industry, along with features on members whose innovative ideas are worth emulating.
Frequency: Quarterly
Founded in 1998

10160 Dairy Foods Magazine
Business News Publishing
1050 IL Route 83
Suite 200
Bensenville, IL 60106-1096

630-377-5909
FAX 630-227-0527
Home Page: www.dairyfoods.com

Katie Rotella, Manager
David Phillips, Executive Editor
Marina Mayer, Executive Editor
Scott Wolters, Director
Barb Szatko, Regional Sales Manager

Dairy Foods serves the dairy industry by analyzing and reporting on technologies trends and issues and how they affest North America's processors of milk, cheese, frozen deserts and cultured products. Current issues and qualification forms for free subsciptions will be available to attendees. Dairy Foods is part of BNP Food Group.
Frequency: Weekly
Circulation: 20000
Founded in 1926
Printed in 4 colors on glossy stock

10161 Dairy Today
AgWeb
30 S 15th Street
Suite 900
Philadelphia, PA 19102-4826

215-557-8900
FAX 215-568-4436
E-Mail: jdickrell@farmjournal.com
Home Page: www.agweb.com

Bill Newham, Publisher
Jim Dickrell, Editor

A trusted source of dairy information for its subscriber base of US dairy producers.
Frequency: Monthly
Circulation: 65000
Founded in 1989

10162 Dairy, Food and Environmental Sanitation
International Association for Food Protection
6200 Aurora Ave
Suite 200W
Urbandale, IA 50322-2864

515-276-3344
800-369-6337
FAX 515-276-8655
E-Mail: info@foodprotection.org
Home Page: www.foodprotection.org

David W Tharp, Executive Director
Vickie Lewandowski, VP
Isabel Walls, Secretary

Published as the general membership publication by the International Association for Food Protection, each issue contains referred articles on applied research, applications of current

technology and general interest subjects for food safety professionals. Regular features include industry and association news, an industry related product section and a calendar of meetings, seminars and workshops.Updates of government regulations and sanitary design is also featured. All members receive DFES.
Cost: $227.00
Frequency: Monthly
Circulation: 3000
ISSN: 1043-3546
Mailing list available for rent: 3000+ names at $150 per M
Printed in 4 colors

10163 Dietitian's Edge
Rodman Publishing
70 Hilltop Rd
3rd Floor
Ramsey, NJ 07446-1150

201-825-2552
FAX 201-825-0553
E-Mail: info@rodpub.com
Home Page: www.nutraceuticalsworld.com

Rodman Zilenziger Jr, President
Matt Montgomery, VP

10164 Drovers Journal
Vance Publishing
400 Knightsbridge Parkway
Lincolnshire, IL 60069

847-634-2600
FAX 847-634-4379
E-Mail: info@vancepublishing.com
Home Page: www.vancepublishing.com

William C Vance, Chairman
Peggy Walker, President

Recognized as the beef industry leader for more than 30 years, valued for its management, production and marketing information.
Cost: $60.00
Frequency: Monthly
Circulation: 91715
Founded in 1937

10165 Eastern Milk Producer
Eastern Milk Producers Cooperative Association
PO Box 6966
Syracuse, NY 13217-6966

315-437-1225

Bob Stronach, Editor
Trish Stokes, Production Manager

Communicates to members of the association dairy issues, farm issues, association events and policy.
Cost: $13.00
20 Pages
Frequency: Monthly

10166 Egg Industry
WATT Publishing Company
303 N Main Street
Suite 500
Rockford, IL 61101

815-966-5400
FAX 815-966-6416
E-Mail: tokeefe@wattnet.net
Home Page: www.wattnet.com

James Watt, Chairman/CEO
Greg Watt, President/COO
Terrence O'Keefe, Editor

Reports on trends, production practices, processing, marketing and economics, and is regarded as the standard for information on current issues, personalities and emerging technology. A pivotal source of news, data and information for innovators and decision-makers in the buying centers of companies producing

eggs and further-processed products.
Cost: $36.00
Frequency: Monthly
Circulation: 1553
Founded in 1917

10167 El Restaurante Mexicano
Maiden Name Press
PO Box 2249
Oak Park, IL 60303

708-267-0023
E-Mail: kfurore@restmex.com
Home Page: www.restmex.com
Social Media: *Facebook*

A quarterly magazine featuring industry specific food news, features restaurant profiles and new product information for personnel of restaurants serving mexican/southwestern menu items nationwide.
Cost: $108.00
Circulation: 27000
ISSN: 1091-5885
Founded in 1997
Printed in 4 colors on glossy stock

10168 Europe Agriculture and Trade Report
USDA Economic Research Service
1800 M Street NW
Washington, DC 20036-5831

202-203-3935
800-999-6779
E-Mail: service@ers.usda.gov
Home Page: www.ers.usda.gov

Susan Offutt, Administrator
Leslee Lowstuter, Central Operations Staff Director
Thomas McDonald, Publishing/Communications
Suchada Langley, Global Agricultural Markets Branch
Ron Bianchi, Associate Director

An important resource for agribusiness and researchers.
Circulation: 2000

10169 Executive Guide to World Poultry Trends
WATT Publishing Company
303 N Main Street
Suite 500
Rockford, IL 61101

815-966-5400
FAX 815-966-6416
Home Page: www.wattnet.com

James Watt, Chairman/CEO
Greg Watt, President/COO
Jeff Swanson, Publishing Director

Packed with facts and figures that give a full overview of the world poultry market.
Frequency: Annual

10170 FEDA News & Views
Foodservice Equipment Distributors Association
2250 Point Boulevard
Suite 200
Elgin, IL 60123

224-293-6500
FAX 224-293-6505
E-Mail: feda@feda.com
Home Page: www.feda.com

Ray Herrick, EVP/Publisher/Editor-in-Chief
Stacy Ward, Editor

Keep updated with the latest issues within the dealer community. Well-read among the FEDA membership, and includes stories on dealers, letters to the editor on industry issues, the President's message, and other items of interes to

both dealers and manufacturer.
Cost: $160.00
Frequency: Bi-Monthly
Founded in 1933

10171 FFA New Horizons
National FFA Organization
6060 FFA Drive
Indianapolis, IN 46268

317-802-4235
800-772-0939
E-Mail: newhorizons@ffa.org
Home Page: www.ffanewhorizons.org

Jessy Yancey, Association Editor
Christina Carden, Associate Production Director
Julie Woodard, FFA Publications Manager

The official member magazine of the FFA is published bimonthly and mailed to more than 525,000 readers. Each issue contains information about agricultural education, career possibilities, chapter and individual accomplishments and news on FFA. Now available online.
100 Pages
ISSN: 1069-806x
Founded in 1928
Printed in 4 colors

10172 Fancy Foods & Culinary Products
Talcott Communications Corporation
20 W Kinzie St
12th Floor
Chicago, IL 60654-5827

312-849-2220
888-545-3676
FAX 312-849-2174
E-Mail: fancyfood@talcott.com
Home Page: www.talcott.com

Daniel Von Rabenau, Executive Director
Natalie Hamm Noblitt, Editor

Specialty food stores, department store specialty food departments, gift departments, confection stores, independent groceries and supermarket chains, gift basket retailers, cookware and kitchen stores, cooking school gift stores, cheese stores, coffee and tea stores brokers/represenatives/manufacturers/importers/wholesalers/distributors and others allied to the field.
Cost: $26.00
Frequency: Monthly
Circulation: 23,000
ISSN: 1521-5156
Founded in 1983

10173 Fastline Productions
PO Box 248
Buckner, KY 40010-0248

502-222-0146
800-626-6409
FAX 502-222-0615
E-Mail: custcare@fastline.com
Home Page: www.fastlinepub.com

William G Howard, President
Crysten Minzenberger, Marketing Director

Nationwide and regional picture buying guides for the farming industry.
Cost: $144.00
Frequency: Monthly
Founded in 1978

10174 Feedback
Meat & Livestock Australia
1401 K Street NW
Suite 602
Washington, DC 20005

202-521-2551
FAX 202-521-2699
E-Mail: info@mla.com.au

Home Page: www.mla.com.au
Social Media: *Facebook, Twitter, YouTube*

Don Heatley, Chairman
David Palmer, Managing Director
Bernie Bindon, Director
Chris Hudson, Director

The red meat and livestock industry journal, featuring on-farm updates and market information for the north, south-east and south-west areas of Australia.
30000 Members
Frequency: 9x Yearly
Founded in 1998

10175 Fine Foods Magazine

Griffin Publishing Group
201 Oak Street
Suite A
Pembroke, MA 02359

781-294-4700
FAX 781-829-0134
E-Mail: griffinbooks@earthlink.com
Home Page: www.griffenpublishing.com

Stephen Griffin, President

A magazine offering information on the Northeast specialty, ethnic and prepared foods business.
Frequency: Monthly

10176 Fisheries

American Fisheries Society
5410 Grosvenor Ln
Suite 110
Bethesda, MD 20814-2199

301-897-8616
FAX 301-897-8096
Home Page: www.fisheries.org

Gus Rassam, Executive Director
Myra Merritt, Office Administrator

Peer reviewed articles that address contemporary issues and problems, techniques, philosophies and other areas of interest to the general fisheries profession. Monthly features include letters, meeting notices, book listings and reviews, environmental essays and organization profiles.
Cost: $106.00
50 Pages
Frequency: Monthly
Circulation: 9800
Founded in 1870
Mailing list available for rent: 8500 names at $250 per M

10177 Food & Drug Packaging

Stagnito Communications
210 S 5th Street
Suite 202
Saint Charles, IL 60174

847-205-5660
FAX 630-377-1678
Home Page: www.fdp.com

Edwin Landon, Publisher
Vince Miconi, Advertising Production Manager
George Misko, Regional Sales Manager
Catherine Wynn, Sales Manager

Food and Drug Packaging serves industries engaged in packaging food, beverages, pharmaceuticals, cosmetics and consulting/engineering firms.
Frequency: Monthly
Circulation: 75140
Founded in 1959

10178 Food Aid Needs Assessment

US Department of Agriculture

200 Independence Ave SW
Washington, DC 20201-0007

202-690-7650
FAX 202-219-0942

Gene Mathia, Branch Chief

This annual report assesses the food situation in 60 developing countries. Most of the data are presented by region; crisis countries are covered individually.

10179 Food Arts Magazine

M Shanken Communications
387 Park Ave S
8th Floor
New York, NY 10016-8872

212-684-4224
FAX 212-684-5424
Home Page: www.cigaraficionado.com

Marvin Shanken, Publisher
Julie Mautner, President

A publication serving the fine food service industry is edited for restauranteurs, chefs, food and beverage directors and caterers.
Frequency: Monthly
Circulation: 50000
Founded in 1972
Printed in 4 colors on glossy stock

10180 Food Channel Trend Wire

Noble & Associates
2155 W Chesterfield Blvd
Springfield, MO 65807-8650

417-875-5000
800-545-4087
FAX 417-875-5051
Home Page: www.noble.net

Robert Noble, CEO

Designed to make the food industry professionals food trend experts. Encapsulates trend information from more than 125 food and consumer publications each month. Provides insights into emerging food trends.
Cost: $195.00
Circulation: 2000

10181 Food Distribution Research Society News

Silesia Companies
PO Box 441110
Fort Washington, MD 20749-1110

301-292-1970
FAX 706-542-0739
Home Page: www.fdrs.ag.utk.edu

John Strovinsky, Publisher
Wojciech Florkowski, Editor

Food distribution research society encourages research, serves as an information clearinghouse and encourages implementation of research. The Society organizes conferences, and meetings for industry, academic and government leaders within the food industry sector.
Cost: $65.00
16 Pages
Circulation: 150
Founded in 1960
Mailing list available for rent: 150 names

10182 Food Engineering

Business News Publishing Company
1050 IL Route 83
Suite 200
Bensenville, IL 60106-1096

630-377-5909
FAX 947-763-9538
Home Page: www.foodengineering.com
Social Media: *Facebook, Twitter*

Patrick Young, Publisher & District Sales Manager
Paul Kelly, District Sales Manager
Brian Gronowski, District Sales Manager

Wayne Wiggins Jr, District Sales Manager
Carolyn Dress, Inside & Online Sales Manager

A publication offering information on all facets of the food industry, from ingredients to food packaging and processing.
Cost: $64.00
Frequency: Monthly
Circulation: 15000
Founded in 1926

10183 Food Management

Penton Publishing Company
1300 E 9th St
Suite 1020
Cleveland, OH 44114-1514

216-861-0360
FAX 216-696-0836
E-Mail: information@penton.com
Home Page: www.food-management.com

Preston L Vice, CFO
Adrian Meredith, CFO
David Brodowski, General Manager
Denise Walde, Senior Production Manager

Combines the industry's most comprehensive circulation package with an editorial mix that emphasizes business management strategies and ideas, food trends and recipes and in-depth news analysis in a contemporary feature magazine.
90 Pages
Frequency: Monthly
Circulation: 47899
ISSN: 0091-018X
Founded in 1892
Printed in 4 colors on glossy stock

10184 Food Processing

555 W Pierce Road
Suite 301
Itasca, IL 60143

630-467-1300
FAX 630-467-1124
Home Page: www.foodprocessing.com

Lily Modjeski, Sales Manager
Patricia Donatiu, Circulation Manager
Dave Fusaro, Editor-in-Chief
Steve Slankis, Group Publisher
Anetta Gauthier, Production Manager

Information on food equipment, packaging material and other supplies and services.
Frequency: Monthly
Circulation: 65000
Founded in 1938

10185 Food Product Design

Virgo Publishing LLC
3300 N Central Ave
Suite 300
Phoenix, AZ 85012-2532

480-675-9925
FAX 480-990-0819
E-Mail: peggyj@vpico.com
Home Page: www.foodproductdesign.com

Jenny Bolton, President

Publication distributed to product development professionals and corporate management executives at food and beverage manufacturing and foodservice companies.
Circulation: 20000
Founded in 1986
Printed in on glossy stock

10186 Food Production/Management Magazine

CTI Publications
2823 Benson Mill Rd
Sparks Glencoe, MD 21152-9575

410-308-2080
FAX 410-308-2079
Home Page: www.ctipubs.com

Randy Gerstmyer, Publisher/Editor

Serves those in the canning, glasspacking, freezing and aseptic packaged food industries. Readers include corporate executives and staff personnel responsible for direction of management, operations, production, engineering, packaging, research and development. Accepts advertising.
Cost: $40.00
32 Pages
Frequency: Monthly
Circulation: 4482
ISSN: 0191-6181
Founded in 1878
Mailing list available for rent: 4500 names at $675 per M
Printed in 4 colors on glossy stock

10187 Food Protection Trends
International Association for Food Protection
6200 Aurora Ave
Suite 200W
Urbandale, IA 50322-2864

515-276-3344
800-369-6337
FAX 515-276-8655
E-Mail: info@foodprotection.org
Home Page: www.foodprotection.org

David W Tharp, Executive Director
Vickie Lewandowski, VP
Isabel Walls, Secretary

Each issue contains articles on applied research, applications of current technology and general interest subjects for food safety professionals. Regular features include industry and association news, and industy-related products section and a calendar of meetings, seminars and workshops. Updates of government regulations and sanitary design are also featured.
Cost: $227.00
Frequency: Monthly
Circulation: 9000
ISBN: 0-362028-X -
Founded in 1911
Mailing list available for rent
Printed in 4 colors on glossy stock

10188 Food Quality
Wiley-Blackwell
111 River Street
Hoboken, NJ 07030-5774

856-380-4117
800-322-9373
E-Mail: custsrvd@starrcorp.com
Home Page: www.foodquality.com

The established authority in the market as the science-based news magazinw focused on quality, assurance, safety, and security in the food and beverage industry.
Cost: $195.00
66 Pages
Frequency: Monthly
Circulation: 21000
ISSN: 1092-7514
Founded in 1994
Mailing list available for rent: 15,000 names at $195 per M
Printed in 4 colors on glossy stock

10189 Food Safety Magazine
Target Group
1945 W Mountain St
Glendale, CA 91201-1258

818-842-4777
FAX 818-769-2939
E-Mail: info@foodsafetymagazine.com
Home Page: www.foodsafetymagazine.com
Social Media: *Facebook, Twitter, LinkedIn*

Don Meeker, Owner/CEO
Andrea Karges, Circulation Manager
Barbara VanRenterghem, Editorial Director

Publicaton is for food safety and quality assurance/control professionals at food and beverage processors, food service companies and agri-food laboratories worldwide. These decision makers implement science-based food safety strategies and systems to prevent, control, test and verify that chemical, microbiological and physical hazards do not enter the food supply.
Cost: $19.00
Frequency: Monthly
Circulation: 20,000
Founded in 1980

10190 Food Service Equipment & Supplies Specialist
Reed Business Information
2000 Clearwater Dr
Oak Brook, IL 60523-8809

630-574-0825
FAX 630-288-8781
Home Page: www.reedbusiness.com

Jeff Greisch, President
Maureen Slocum, Publisher
Judy Erickson, Group Circulation Manager
Stuart Whayman, CFO

Magazine for professionals who specify, sell and distribute food service equipment, supplies and furnishings.
Cost: $69.95
Frequency: Monthly
Circulation: 22,740
Founded in 1948
Printed in 4 colors on glossy stock

10191 Food Technology
Institute of Food Technologists
525 W Van Buren
Suite 1000
Chicago, IL 60607-3842

312-782-8424
FAX 312-782-8348
E-Mail: info@ift.org
Home Page: www.ift.org

Bob Swientek, Editor-in-Chief

The leading publication addressing all facets of food science and technology. Its in-depth and balance coverage includes the latest research developments, industry news, consumer product innovations, and professional opportunities.
Cost: $190.00
Frequency: Monthly
Circulation: 18000
ISSN: 0015-6639

10192 Food Trade News
Best-Met Publishing
5537 Twin Knolls Rd
Suite 438
Columbia, MD 21045-3270

410-730-5013
FAX 410-740-4680
E-Mail: jmetzger@best-met.com
Home Page: www.best-met.com

Jeff Metzger, Publisher
Terri Maloney, Editor
Nina Weiland, VP
Beth Pripstein, Office Manager
Richard J Bestany, Advertising Director

A magazine aimed at the players in the food distribution industry.

10193 Food World
Best-Met Publishing Company
5537 Twin Knolls Rd
Suite 438
Columbia, MD 21045-3270

410-730-5013
FAX 410-740-4680

E-Mail: jmetzger@best-met.com
Home Page: www.best-met.com

Jeff Metzger, Publisher
Jeffrey W. Metzger, Publisher
Beth Pripstein, Office Manager
Richard J. Bestany, President

Regional food trade newspaper covering the Mid-Atlantic market
Frequency: Monthly
Printed in on newsprint stock

10194 FoodService and Hospitality
Kostuch Publications
Two City Place Drive
Suite 200 PMB 2004
Saint Louis ario, MO 63141-3P6

314-812-2565
FAX 314-835-0044
E-Mail: wgilchri@ix.netcom.com
Home Page: www.foodserviceworld.com

Mitch Kostuch, President
Rosanna Caira, Publisher/Editor
Wendy Gilchrist, Director Business Development
Phoebe Fung, Owner
Owen Knowlton, Director

Canada's only national specialty business magazine reaching owners,managers and buyers in all sections of the foodservice industry.
Cost: $50.00
Frequency: Monthly
Circulation: 25,000
Printed in on glossy stock

10195 FoodTalk
Pike & Fischer
PO Box 25277
Alexandria, VA 22313

703-548-3146
FAX 703-548-3017
E-Mail: info@setantapublishing.com
Home Page: www.setantapublishing.com

Declan Couroy, Editor/Publisher

Sanitation tips for food workers.
Cost: $120.00
Frequency: Quarterly
Circulation: 5000
Founded in 1987
Printed in 2 colors

10196 Foodservice Equipment & Supplies
Reed Europe
2000 Clearwter Drive
Oak Brook, IL 60523

630-320-7000
800-446-6551
FAX 630-288-8282
Home Page: www.fesmag.com

Maureen Slocum, Publisher
Mitchell Schechter, Editor-in-Chief

Edited for readers outside the US who are employed in firms that manufacture food and beverage products.
Frequency: Monthly
Founded in 1948

10197 For Fish Farmers
Mississippi Cooperative Extension Service
PO Box 9690
Mississippi State, MS 39762-9690

662-325-3174
FAX 601-857-2358

Martin W Bunson, Editor

A magazine offering information that addresses the concerns of fish farmers.
Frequency: Quarterly

10198 Fresh Cup Magazine
Fresh Cup Publishing Company

537 SE Ash Street Suite 300
PO Box 14827
Portland, OR 97293

503-236-2587
800-868-5866
FAX 503-236-3165
E-Mail: freshcup@freshcup.com
Home Page: www.freshcup.com

Ward Barbee, Publisher
Jan Weigel, President
Julie Beals, Marketing
Bill Berninger, Circulation Manager
Natalie Caceres, Marketing Coordinator
Cost: $60.00
80 Pages
Frequency: Monthly
Circulation: 15000
Founded in 1992
Printed in 4 colors on glossy stock

10199 Fresh Cut Magazine
Great American Publishing
75 Applewood Drive, Suite A
PO Box 128
Sparta, MI 49345

616-887-9008
FAX 616-887-2666
Home Page: www.freshcut.com

Matt McCallum, Publisher
Scott Christie, Managing Editor

The only publication covering all sectors of the
international value-added produce industry.
Growers, processors, retailers and foodservice
professionals all find information relating to
their day-to-day operations in the pages of
Fresh Cut magazine.
Cost: $15.00
40 Pages
Frequency: Monthly
ISSN: 1072-2831
Founded in 1993
Printed in 4 colors on glossy stock

10200 Frozen Food Digest, Inc.
271 Madison Ave
Suite 1402-A
New York, NY 10016-1014

212-557-8600
FAX 212-986-9868
E-Mail: saulbeckffdqffaol.com

Saul Beck, President/Hall of Fame Member
Cost: $45.00
Circulation: 16000
Founded in 1985

10201 Fruit Country
Clintron Publishing
PO Box 30998
Spokane, WA 99223-3016

509-248-2452
800-869-7923
FAX 509-458-3547
Home Page: www.agpowermag.com

Clintke Withers, Publisher
John M Dahlin, Editor
Tyson Graff, Circualtion Manager

Written for and about growers, their operations
and their needs. Stories on growers and shippers, developments and trends in the fruit industry, human interest stories and politics, new
products, chemicals and supplies, avant garde
management techniques, cultural practices and
tips on profitability. Advertising equipment and
services to the fruit industry and distribution
system.
Cost: $12.00
Frequency: Monthly
Circulation: 11500
Founded in 1976

10202 Futures Magazine
Futures Magazine
111 W Jackson Blvd
7th Floor
Chicago, IL 60604-4139

312-977-0999
FAX 312-846-4638
E-Mail: dcollins@futuresmag.com
Home Page: www.aip.com

Steve Lown, Manager
Daniel P Collins, Editor
Gabby Mouizerh, Production Manager
Steve Lown, Manager

Agriculture commodities charted by various
technical studies, plus analysis.
Cost: $39.00
24 Pages
Frequency: Monthly
Circulation: 60,000
Founded in 1972

10203 Game Bird Gazette
Allen Publishing
970 East
3300 South
Salt Lake City, UT 84106

801-485-1299
E-Mail: memberservices@gamebird.com
Home Page: www.gamebird.com

George Allen, Editor

All about keeping, breeding and raising pheas-
ants, quails, partridges, peacocks, doves, pi-
geons, waterfowl and gamebirds of all kinds.
Cost: $23.95
45 Pages
Frequency: Monthly
Founded in 1940

10204 Gourmet Retailer Magazine
3301 Ponce De Leon Blvd
Suite 300
Coral Gables, FL 33134-7273

305-273-0437
800-765-9797
FAX 305-446-2868
E-Mail: info@gourmetretailer.com
Home Page: www.gourmetretailer.com

Edward Loeb, Publisher
Michael Keighley, Editorial Director
Laura Everage, Managing Editor
Shari Levenson, Marketing Manager
Kathy Colwell, Advertising Production
Manager
Frequency: Monthly
Circulation: 25000
Founded in 1979

10205 Grape Grower
Western Agricultural Publishing Company
4969 E Clinton Way
#104
Fresno, CA 93727-1549

559-252-7000
888-382-9772
FAX 559-252-7387
E-Mail: westag@westagpubco.com
Home Page: www.westagpubco.com

Paul Baltimore, Publisher
Randy Bailey, Editor
Robert Fujimoto, Assistant Editor

The West's most widely read authority on the
cultivation of table grapes, raising grapes and
wine grapes. All aspects of production are covered with the most current university, government and private research.
Mailing list available for rent

10206 Greenhouse Product News
Scranton Gillette Communications

3030 W Salt Creek Lane
Suite 201
Arlington Heights, IL 60005-5025

847-391-1000
FAX 847-390-0408
E-Mail: bbellew@sgcmail.com
Home Page: www.gpnmag.com

Bob Bellew, VP/Group Publisher
Tim Hodson, Editorial Director
Jasmina Radjevic, Managing Editor

Features the industry's leading Buyer's Guide
directory, the PGR table and the bookstore are
just a few of the reasons the industry's buyers
keep coming back.
Cost: $30.00
Frequency: Monthly
Circulation: 19000
Mailing list available for rent: 19,000 names

10207 Griffin Report: Market Studies
Griffin Publishing Company
201 Oak Street
Pembroke, MA 02359

781-829-4700
FAX 781-829-0134
Home Page: www.griffinreport.com

Mike Berger, Editor
Kevin Griffin, Vice President
Karen Harty, Vice President
Julie Mignosa, Office Manager

This report offers statistics on the leading chain
and multi-store independent grocers in the
northeast.
Cost: $42.00
Frequency: Monthly
Founded in 1966
*Mailing list available for rent: 10,000 names at
$350 per M*
Printed in on newsprint stock

10208 Grocers Report
Super Markets Productions
PO Box 6124
San Rafael, CA 94903-124

415-479-0211
FAX 415-479-0211

Lori Abrams, CEO
JM Adlman, Publisher
Joan Adams, Circulation Manager

Offers information on the retail grocery indus-
try.
Cost: $10.00
Frequency: Quarterly
Circulation: 18000
Founded in 1978
Printed in 4 colors on glossy stock

10209 Growertalks Magazine
Ball Publishing
622 Town Road
PO Box 1660
West Chicago, IL 60186

630-231-3675
888-888-0013
FAX 630-231-5254
E-Mail: info@ballpublishing.com
Home Page: www.growertalks.com

Chris Beytes, Editor/Publisher
Jennifer Zurko, Associate Editor

Specializes in the publishing of horticulture in-
formation, primarily related to floriculture pro-
duction and marketing.
Frequency: Monthly
Circulation: 12000
Founded in 1937

10210 Growing for Market
Fairplain Publications

PO Box 3747
Lawrence, KS 66046

785-748-0605
800-307-8949
FAX 785-748-0609
E-Mail: growing4market@earthlink.net
Home Page: www.growingformarket.com

Lynn Byczynski, Editor/Publisher
Roger Yepsen, Author

A monthly periodical for small-scale farmers, market gardeners, and grower of vegetables, fruits, herbs and flowers. Offers news and ideas about organic production, pest control, tools and equipment and direct marketing.
Cost: $ 30.00
20 Pages
Frequency: Monthly
Circulation: 4000
ISSN: 1060-9296
Founded in 1992

10211 Guernsey Breeders' Journal
Purebred Publishing Inc
7616 Slate Ridge Blvd
Reynoldsburg, OH 43068-3126

614-575-4620
FAX 614-864-5614
E-Mail: khenson@usguernsey.com
Home Page: www.usguernsey.com

Katie Henson, Editor
The oldest dairy breed magazine published by a US breed organization. Contents range across current management trends, breeder stories and events withing the Guernsey industry in the US and worldwide.
Cost: $20.00
Frequency: 10x Yearly

10212 Health Products Business
Cygnus Publishing
445 Braod Hollow Road
Melville, NY 11747-3669

631-845-2700
800-308-6397
FAX 631-845-2723
E-Mail: micheal.schiavitz@cygnuspub.com
Home Page: www.healthproducts.com

Bruce Ceftakes, Publisher/Sales
Micheal Schiavetta, Editor
Christian Biscuiti, Assistant Editor

This is a trade magazine that covers news and trends in the natural health products industry including vitamins, herbs, dietary supplements and other products. Publishes annual raw materials directory and purchasing guide, as well as other speciality issues. Targets natural products retail store owners, buyers and managers. Qualified subscription only.
ISSN: 0149-9602

10213 Herb Quarterly
EGW Publishing Company
4075 Papazian Way
Suite 204
Fremont, CA 94538-4372

510-668-0268
FAX 510-668-0280
E-Mail: info@egw.com
Home Page: www.herbquarterly.com

Chris Slaughter, VP
Jennifer Barrett, Editor

Each issue introduces readers to new herbs and fascinating herbal lore; provides tips on hard to grow varieties and medicinals; showcases gardens from around the world; and tempts the palate with seasonal menus and tantalizing recipes built around herbs and edible flowers.
Cost: $19.97
68 Pages
Frequency: Quarterly
Circulation: 36753

Founded in 1978
Printed in 4 colors on matte stock

10214 Hereford World
American Hereford Association
PO Box 014059
Kansas City, MO 64101

816-842-3757
FAX 816-842-6931
E-Mail: aha@hereford.org
Home Page: www.hereford.org

Craig Huffhines, Executive VP

Trade magazine for breeders of registered Hereford cattle. Articles and columns provide in-depth information about the beef industry.
Frequency: Monthly
Circulation: 9500
Founded in 1742

10215 Honey Producer
American Honey Producers Association
PO Box 162
Power, MT 59468

406-463-2227
FAX 406-463-2583
E-Mail: beeguy4jensen@yahoo.com
Home Page: www.americanhoneyproducers.org

Lyle Johnston, Editor

Highlights current industry news, publishes submitted articles from the scientific community, informs of legal battles being fought in Washington,'DC, provides cmoplete AHPA convention schedules.
Cost: $20.00
Frequency: Quarterly
ISSN: 1091-3394

10216 Hospitality News Featuring Coffee Talk
PO Box 21027
Salem, OR 97307-1027

503-390-8343
800-685-1932
FAX 503-390-8344
E-Mail: eds@hospnews.com
Home Page: www.hospnews.com

Kerri R Goodman-Small, Publisher
Miles Small, Editor-in-Chief

Serves restaurants, lodges, health care facilities, schools, clubs,casinos, caterers, and culinary and beverage marketplaces nationally.
Circulation: 30000
ISSN: 1084-2551
Founded in 1988
Printed in on newsprint stock

10217 Hotline Magazine
International Food Service Executives
4955 Miller Street
Suite 107
Wheat Ridge, CO 80033

800-893-5499
E-Mail: hq@ifsea.com
Home Page: www.ifsea.com
Social Media: *Facebook*

Barbara Sadler, Chairwoman
Fred Wright, Chair-Elect
David Orosz, Treasurer

IFSEA's membership magazine that focuses on all things IFSEA and food service. Also available electronically.
Frequency: Bi-Annually

10218 IAFIS Reporter
International Assn of Food Industry Suppliers

1451 Dolley Madison Boulevard
Suite 101
McLean, VA 22101

703-761-2600
FAX 703-761-4334
E-Mail: info@fpsa.org
Home Page: www.fpsa.org

George Melnykovich, President
Andrew Drennan, VP

Happenings and trends in the food and dairy industry.
Founded in 1983

10219 IGA Grocergram
Pace Communications
PO Box 13607
Greensboro, NC 27415-3607

336-378-6065
FAX 336-275-2864
E-Mail: info@pacecommunications.com
Home Page: www.pacecommunications.com

Bonnie McElveen, CEO
Wes Isley, Chief Financial Officer
Leigh Klee, Chief Financial Officer
Ed Calfo, Executive Vice President

Edited for IGA retailers and wholesalers throughout the US. Focuses on training, merchandising, display, promotion, and advertising and marketing techniques. Also addresses financial and personnel management and innovations in store engineering and development.
Cost: $24.00
Frequency: Monthly

10220 Import Statistics
Association of Food Industries
3301 State Route 66
Suite 205, Building C
Neptune, NJ 07753-2705

732-922-3008
FAX 732-922-3590
E-Mail: info@afius.org
Home Page: www.naooa.org

Robert Bauer, President
Cost: $40.00
Frequency: Annual+
Circulation: 1200
Founded in 1906

10221 In Good Taste
Specialty Coffee Association of America
302 5th Avenue
5th Floor
New York, NY 10001

646-733-6000
800-544-7377
FAX 646-733-6010
Home Page: www.cppress.com

Ted R Lingle, Editor

This periodical offers business, promotional and educational advice in the areas of cultivation, processing, preparation and marketing of specialty coffee.
Frequency: Monthly

10222 Industria Alimenticia
Stagnito Communications
155 Pfingster Road
Suite 205
Deerfield, IL 60015

847-205-5660
FAX 847-205-5680
Home Page: www.stagnito.com

Harry Stagnito, President
Elsa Rico, Director/Editor
Mary Mazur, Circulation

Information source for Latin American food and beverage processors
Cost: $85.00
Printed in 4 colors on glossy stock

10223 Inform
American Oil Chemists' Society
2710 S. Boulder
PO Box 17190
Urbana, IL 61802-6996

217-359-2344
FAX 217-351-8091
E-Mail: general@aocs.org
Home Page: www.aocs.org
Social Media: *Facebook, Twitter*

E. Dumelin, President
D. Myers, Vice President
S. Erhan, Secretary
T. Kemper, Treasurer

The monthly business and scientific magazine of AOCS, providing international news on fats, oils, surfectants, detergents, and related materials.
Cost: $10.00
5400 Members
Frequency: Membership Dues Vary
Founded in 1909

10224 Insider Magazine
American Correctional Food Service Affiliates
210 N Glenoaks Blvd
Suite C
Burbank, CA 91502

818-843-6608
FAX 818-843-7423
Home Page: www.acfsa.org

Jon Nichols, Executive Director

Contains news pertaining to correctional foodservice activities of the Association and fellow members, as well as industry-specific educational articles.
56 Pages
Frequency: Quarterly
Circulation: 1500
Founded in 1969
Printed in 4 colors on glossy stock

10225 Institute of Food and Nutrition
HealthComm International
9770 44th Avenue
N.W. Suite 100
Gig Harbor, WA 98332

253-851-3943
800-692-9400
FAX 253-851-9749
E-Mail: info@metagenics.com
Home Page: www.metagenics.com

Jeffrey Bland, President/Chief Science Officer
Jeffrey Katke, Chairman of the Board/CEO
Carl Mickey Moore, Co-Chief Operating Officer
Janice Moore, Co-Chief Operating Officer
Matthew Tripp, VP of Research & Development
Founded in 1983

10226 Intermountain Retailer
Utah Food Industry Association
1578 W 1700 S
Suite 100
Salt Lake City, UT 84104-3489

801-973-9517
800-423-6636
FAX 801-972-8712
Home Page: www.utfood.com

James Olsen, President
Meik Rapp, Editor

This annual guide offers information on brokers in Utah that are serving the retail food industry.
Cost: $25.00
48 Pages
Frequency: Annual+
Circulation: 1200
Founded in 1896

10227 International Journal of Food Engineering
Reed Business Information
360 Park Ave S
New York, NY 10010-1737

646-746-6400
FAX 646-756-7583
E-Mail: corporatecommunications@reedbusiness.com
Home Page: www.reedbusiness.com

John Poulin, CEO
Peter Havens, Publisher
James Reed, Owner

Devoted to engineering disciplines related to processing foods. The areas of interest include heat, mass transfer and fluid flow in food processing; food microstructure development and characterization; application of artificial intelligence in food research; food biotechnology, and more.
Frequency: Annual
Circulation: 15,000

10228 International Product Alert
Marketing Intelligence Service
482 N Main St
Canandaigua, NY 14424-1049

585-374-6326
800-836-5710
FAX 585-374-5217
Home Page: www.productscan.com

Tom Vierhile, Executive Editor
Sherry Meeker-Barton, Editor-in-Chief

Reports the introduction of new food, beverage, health & beauty aides, household & pet products outside of North America. Reports include full product descriptions and selected illustrations of products and advertising backup.
Cost: $700.00

10229 Italian Cooking and Living
Italian Culinary Institute
302 5th Avenue
9th Floor
New York, NY 10001

212-899-9057
888-742-2373
FAX 212-889-3907
E-Mail: irene@italiancookingandliving.com
Home Page: www.italiancookingandliving.com

Paolo Villoresi, Publisher
Irene De Gasparis, Associate Publisher
Charles Pennino, Owner

American magazine devoted to Italian cuisine/culture/travel
Founded in 2001

10230 JAOCS
American Oil Chemists' Society
2710 S. Boulder
PO Box 17190
Urbana, IL 61802-6996

217-359-2344
FAX 217-351-8091
E-Mail: general@aocs.org
Home Page: www.aocs.org
Social Media: *Facebook, Twitter*

E. Dumelin, President
D. Myers, Vice President
S. Erhan, Secretary
T. Kemper, Treasurer

The leading source for technical papers related to the fats and oils industries. A peer-reviewed journal devoted to fundamental and practical research, production, processing, packaging and distribution in the growing field of fats,

oils, proteins and other related substances.
Cost: $10.00
5400 Members
Frequency: Membership Dues Vary
Founded in 1909

10231 Journal of Animal Science
American Society of Animal Science
2441 Village Green Pl
Champaign, IL 61822-7676

217-356-9050
FAX 217-398-4119
E-Mail: susanp@assochq.org
Home Page: www.asas.org

Meghan Wulster-Radcli, Executive Director
Susan Pollack, Managing Editor/Editorial Director

The official journal of the American Society of Animal Science, JAS publishes results of original research in Genetics, Growth and Physiology, Nutrition, Production, Products, and Special Topics. JAS consistently ranks in the top tier in the category of Agriculture, Dairy, and Animal Sciences
Frequency: Monthly
Circulation: 3500
ISSN: 0021-8812
Founded in 1908
Printed in on glossy stock

10232 Journal of Business Logistics
Council of Supply Chain Management Professionals
333 E Butterfield Rd
Suite 140
Lombard, IL 60148-5617

630-574-0985
FAX 630-574-0989
E-Mail: cscmpadmin@cscmp.org
Home Page: www.cscmp.org
Social Media: *Facebook, Twitter, LinkedIn, YouTube*

Rick Blasgen, President & CEO
Sue Paulson, Executive Assistant
Nancy Nix, Chair
Rick J. Jackson, Chair-Elect
Theodore Stank, Secretary & Treasurer

Provides a forum for the dissemination of original thoughts, research, and best practices within the logistics and supply chain arenas. Provides readers with new and helpful information, new supply chain management theory or techniques, research generalizations, creative views and sytheses of dispersed concepts, and articles in subject areas which have significant current impact on thought and practice in logistics and supply chain management.
10000 Members
Founded in 1963

10233 Journal of Child Nutrition & Management
School Nutrition Association
120 Waterfront St
Suite 300
National Harbor, MD 20745-1142

301-686-3100
800-877-8822
FAX 301-686-3115
E-Mail: servicecenter@schoolnutrition.org
Home Page: www.schoolnutrition.org

Helen Phillips, President
Sandy Ford, President-Elect
Leah Schmidt, Vice President
Beth Taylor, Secretary/Treasurer

Features up-to-date research articles on significant issues affecting child nutrition and school foodservice management. Provides timely and relevant insights into the many challenges and opportunities surrounding child nutrition programs. Information facilitates decision-making

and serves as evidence of how effective child nutrition programs are.
55000 Members
Frequency: Monthly
Founded in 1946

10234 Journal of Dairy Science
American Dairy Science Association
2441 Village Green Pl
Champaign, IL 61822-7676

217-356-5146
FAX 217-398-4119
E-Mail: adsa@assochq.org
Home Page: www.adsa.org

Michael Mangino, Senior Editor
Sharon Frick, Secretary
Diane Hekken, Secretary
Richard Pursley, Secretary, Treasurer

Research in dairy cattle production and dairy food products.
Cost: $110.00
Frequency: Monthly
Founded in 1990

10235 Journal of Environmental Quality
American Society of Agronomy
5585 Guilford Road
Madison, WI 53711-1086

608-273-8080
FAX 608-273-2021
E-Mail: headquarters@agronomy.org
Home Page: www.agronomy.org
Social Media: *Facebook, Twitter, LinkedIn*

Newell Kitchen, President
Kenneth Barbarick, President-Elect

Papers are grouped by subject matter and cover water, soil, and atmospheric research as it relates to agriculture and the environment.
11000 Members
Founded in 1907

10236 Journal of Food Distribution Research
Food Distribution Research Society
PO Box 441110
Fort Washington, MD 20749

301-292-1970
FAX 301-292-1787
E-Mail: Jonathan_baros@ncsu.edu
Home Page: fdrs.tamu.edu

John Park, President
Ron Rainey, President-Elect
Kellie Raper, Secretary/ Treasurer
Jennifer Dennis, Director
Stan Ernst, Director

Publishes articles that cover every aspect of our modern food system. JFDR is a peer reviewed journal published exlusively online.
Frequency: 3x Yearly

10237 Journal of Food Protection
International Association for Food Protection
6200 Aurora Ave
Suite 200W
Des Moines, IA 50322-2864

515-276-3344
800-369-6337
FAX 515-276-8655
E-Mail: info@foodprotection.org
Home Page: www.foodprotection.org
Social Media: *Facebook, Twitter, LinkedIn*

Isabel Walls, President
Katherine M.J. Swanson, President-Elect
Don Schaffner, Vice President
Don Zink, Secretary
David W. Tharp, Executive Director

Each issue contains scientific research and authoritative review articles reporting on a variety of topics in food science pertaining to food safety and quality.
3400 Members
Founded in 1911

10238 Journal of Food Science
Institute of Food Technologists
525 W Van Buren St
Suite 1000
Chicago, IL 60607-3842

312-782-8424
FAX 312-782-8348
E-Mail: info@ift.org
Home Page: www.ift.org

Barbara Byrd Keenan, Executive VP
Daryl B Lund, Editor-in-Chief

IFT's premier science journal, containing peer-reviewed reports of original research and critical reviews of all aspects of food science.
Frequency: 9x Yearly
Founded in 1936

10239 Journal of Foodservice Business Research
Taylor & Francis Group LLC
325 Chestnut St
Suite 800
Philadelphia, PA 19106-2614

215-625-8900
800-354-1420
FAX 215-625-2940
Home Page: www.taylorandfrancis.com

Kevin Bradley, President

Features articles from international experts in various disciplines, including management, marketing, finance, law, food technology, nutrition, psychology, information systems, anthropology, human resources, and more.
Frequency: Quarterly

10240 Journal of Hospitality & Tourism Research
CHRIE
2810 N Parham Road
Suite 230
Richmond, VA 23294

804-346-4800
FAX 804-346-5009
E-Mail: info@chrie.org
Home Page: www.chrie.org
Social Media: *Facebook, Twitter, LinkedIn*

Susan Fournier, President
Josette Katz, Vice President
Chris Roberts, Secretary
John Drysdale, Treasurer
Kathy McCarty, CEO

Offers high quality refereed articles which advance the knowledge base of the hospitality field. Articles on empirical research, theoretical developments and innovative methodologies are guided by an editor and a review board consisting of leading hospitality and tourism researchers.
Frequency: Quarterly

10241 Journal of Hospitality and Tourism Education
CHRIE
2810 N Parham Road
Suite 230
Richmond, VA 23294

804-346-4800
FAX 804-346-5009
E-Mail: info@chrie.org
Home Page: www.chrie.org
Social Media: *Facebook, Twitter, LinkedIn*

Susan Fournier, President
Josette Katz, Vice President
Chris Roberts, Secretary

John Drysdale, Treasurer
Kathy McCarty, CEO

A refereed, interdisciplinary quarterly magazine designed to serve the needs of all levels of hospitality and tourism education through the presentation of issues and opinions pertinent to the field.
Frequency: Quarterly

10242 Journal of Natural Resources & Life Sciences Education
American Society of Agronomy
5585 Guilford Road
Madison, WI 53711-1086

608-273-8080
FAX 608-273-2021
E-Mail: headquarters@agronomy.org
Home Page: www.agronomy.org
Social Media: *Facebook, Twitter, LinkedIn*

Newell Kitchen, President
Kenneth Barbarick, President-Elect

Today's educators look here for the latest teaching ideas in the life sciences, natural resources, and agriculture. Articles are written by and for educators in extension, universities, industry, administration, and grades k-12.
11000 Members
Founded in 1907

10243 Journal of Packaging
Institute of Packaging Professionals
Ste 123
1833 Centre Point Cir
Naperville, IL 60563-4848

630-544-5050
800-432-4085
FAX 630-544-5005
E-Mail: info@iopp.org
Home Page: www.iopp.org
Social Media: *Facebook, Twitter, LinkedIn, YouTube*

Edwin Landon, Executive Director
Patrick Farrey, General Manager
Stan Zelesnik, Director Education
Robert DePauw, Finance Manager
Kelly Staley, Member Services Manager

Serves the entire packaging community's educational needs. The Journal is a resource for professional analysis of all packaging issues. Available online only, it is a forum that covers issues in depth.
Frequency: Daily

10244 Journal of Plant Registrations
Crop Science Society of America
5585 Guilford Rd.
Madison, WI 53711-1086

608-273-8080
FAX 608-273-2021
Home Page: www.crops.org
Social Media: *Facebook, Twitter, LinkedIn*

Maria Gallo, President
Jeffrey Volenec, President-Elect
Ellen G.M. Bergfeld, CEO

Publishes cultivar, germplasm, parental line, genetic stock, and mapping population registration manuscripts.
4700 Members
Frequency: Monthly
Founded in 1955

10245 Journal of Shellfish Research
National Shellfisheries Association
National Marine Fisheries Service Laboratory
Oxford, MD 21654

631-653-6327
FAX 631-653-6327
E-Mail: webmaster@shellfish.org
Home Page: www.shellfish.org

R. LeRoy Creswell, President
Christopher V. Davis, President-Elect

George E. Flimlin, VP & Program Chair
Marta Gomez-Chiarri, Secretary
Sandra E. Shumway, Editor

The international journal promoting all aspects of shellfish research.
1M Members
Frequency: Monthly
Founded in 1908

10246 Journal of Sugar Beet Research

Beet Sugar Development Foundation
800 Grant Street
Suite 300
Denver, CO 80203

303-832-4460
FAX 303-832-4468
E-Mail: aa@bsdf-assbt.org
Home Page: www.bsdf-assbt.org

Fosters all phases of sugarbeet and beet sugar research, promotes the dissemination of relevant scientific knowledge, and strives to maintain high standards of ethics, and to cooperate with other organizations having objectives beneficial to the beet sugar industry.
Frequency: Quarterly
ISSN: 0899-1502

10247 Journal of Surfactants and Detergents (JSD)

American Oil Chemists' Society
2710 S. Boulder
PO Box 17190
Urbana, IL 61802-6996

217-359-2344
FAX 217-351-8091
E-Mail: general@aocs.org
Home Page: www.aocs.org
Social Media: *Facebook, Twitter*

E. Dumelin, President
D. Myers, Vice President
S. Erhan, Secretary
T. Kemper, Treasurer

A scientific journal dedicated to the practical and theoretical aspects of oleochemical and petrochemical surfectants, soaps, and detergents.
Cost: $10.00
5400 Members
Frequency: Membership Dues Vary
Founded in 1909

10248 Journal of the American Dietetic Association

Elsevier Health Publishing
1600 John F Kennedy Blvd
Suite 1800
Philadelphia, PA 19103-2398

215-239-3900
FAX 215-239-3990
E-Mail:
journal@eatright.org/elspcs@elsevier.com
Home Page: www.elsevier.com

Michael Hansen, CEO
Jason Swift, Editor
Ryan Lipscomb, Department Editor
Linda Van Horn, Editor-in-Chief

A premier source for the practice and science of food, nutrition, and dietetics. The Journal focuses on advancing professional knowledge across the range of research and practice issues such as: nutritional science, medical nutrition therapy, public health nutrition, food science and biotechnology, foodservice systems, leadership and management and dietetics education.
Cost: $229.00
Frequency: Monthly/Subscription
ISSN: 0002-8223

10249 Journal of the American Oil Chemists' Society

American Oil Chemists' Society

2710 S Boulder
Urbana, IL 61802-6996

217-359-2344
FAX 217-351-8091
E-Mail: general@aocs.org
Home Page: www.aocs.org

Jody Schonfeld, Publications Director
Pam Landman, Journals Coordinator
Kimmy Farris, Production Editor

The leading source for technical papers related to the fats and oils industries. A peer-reviewed journal devoted to fundamental and practical research, production, processing, packaging and distribution in the growing field of fats, oils, proteins and other related substances
Frequency: Monthly
Founded in 1947

10250 Journal of the American Pomological Society

103 Tyson Building
University Park, PA 16802-4200

814-863-6163
FAX 814-237-3407
E-Mail: bardenja@vt.edu
Home Page: www.americanpomological.org

Dr John Barden, Editor

The Journal contains refereed technical articles and a wide variety of applied articles relating to fruit varieties.
Frequency: Quarterly/Free to Members

10251 Journal of the American Society for Horticultural Science

American Society for Horticultural Science
113 S West St
Suite 200
Alexandria, VA 22314-2851

703-836-4606
FAX 703-836-2024
E-Mail: journal@ashs.org
Home Page: www.ashs.org

Michael Neff, Publisher/Executive Director
Katharine J Lewis, Managing Editor

A peer-reviewed publication of results of orginal research on horticultural plants and their products or directly related research areas. Its prime function is communication of mission-oriented, fundamental research to other researchers.
Cost: $55.00
Frequency: Bi-Monthly/Members Rate
ISSN: 0003-1062
Founded in 1903
Mailing list available for rent: 2500 names at $100 per M

10252 Journal of the Association of Food and Dru g Officials

Association of Food and Drug Officials
2550 Kingston Rd
Suite 311
York, PA 17402-3734

717-757-2888
FAX 717-755-8089
E-Mail: afdo@afdo.org
Home Page: www.afdo.org

Denise Rooney, Executive Director

News and the latest legislation for the Food and Drug Association.
Founded in 1937

10253 Kosher Today

1428 36th street
219
Brooklyn, NY 11218

718-854-4460
FAX 718-854-4474

E-Mail: info@koshertoday.com
Home Page: www.koshertoday.com/

Menachem Lubinsky, CEO
Bill Springer, Account Executive
Christine Salmon, Account Executive
Karyn Gilbert, Marketing Manager

Covers the kosher food industry.
28 Pages
Frequency: Weekly
Circulation: 20000
Founded in 1984
Printed in 4 colors on newsprint stock

10254 Lean Trimmings Prime

National Meat Association
1970 Broadway
Suite 825
Oakland, CA 94612

510-763-1533
FAX 510-763-6186
E-Mail: staff@nmaonline.org
Home Page: www.nmaonline.org

Robert Rebholtz, Chairman
Larry Vad, President
Marty Evanson, Vice President
Mike Hesse, Secretary
Brian Coelho, Treasurer

Brings a broad range of topics and essential association information to the membership and beyond.
600 Members
Frequency: Weekly
Founded in 1946

10255 Lipids

American Oil Chemists' Society
2710 S. Boulder
PO Box 17190
Urbana, IL 61802-6996

217-359-2344
FAX 217-351-8091
E-Mail: general@aocs.org
Home Page: www.aocs.org
Social Media: *Facebook, Twitter*

E. Dumelin, President
D. Myers, Vice President
S. Erhan, Secretary
T. Kemper, Treasurer

A premier journal in the lipid field, published monthly, featuring full-length original research articles, short communications, methods papers, and review articles on timely topics.
Cost: $10.00
5400 Members
Frequency: Membership Dues Vary
Founded in 1909

10256 Logistics Journal

Transportation Intermediaries Association
1625 Prince St
Suite 200
Alexandria, VA 22314-2883

703-299-5700
FAX 703-836-0123
E-Mail: info@tianet.org
Home Page: www.tianet.org

Robert Voltmann, President
Nancy King, Marketing Manager

Education and policy organization for North American transportation intermediaries. The only national association representing the interests of all third party transportation service providers. Members include logistics management firms, property brokers, perishable commodities brokers, freight forwarders, intermodal marketers and ocean and air forwarders.
Frequency: Monthly
Circulation: 1000
Founded in 1978

10257 Manufacturing Confectioner
MC Publishing
711 W Water Street
PO Box 266
Princeton, WI 54968

920-295-6969
FAX 920-295-6843
E-Mail: mcinfo@gomc.com
Home Page: www.gomc.com

Eric Schmoyer, President
Michael Allured, Publisher/Editor-in-Chief

The worldwide business, marketing and technology journal of the candy, chocolate, confectionery, cough drop, and sweet baked goods industry. Provides in-depth coverage of news, industry statistics, sales and marketing, ingredients, equipment and services.
Cost: $65.00
Frequency: Monthly
Founded in 1921

10258 Meat Marketing and Technology
Marketing & Technology Group
1415 N Dayton St
Suite 115
Chicago, IL 60642-7033

312-266-3311
FAX 312-266-3363
E-Mail: webinars@meatingplace.com
Home Page: www.meatingplace.com

Mark Lefens, Owner
Dan Allen, Editor-at-Large
Jim Goldberg, VP Sales/Marketing
John Gregerson, Editor
Deborah Silver, Managing Editor

Provides information on meat processing, retail, slaughtering and fabricating and rendering.
Cost: $40.00
Frequency: Monthly
Circulation: 20,009
Founded in 1993
Printed in 4 colors on glossy stock

10259 Meat Science
American Meat Science Association
2441 Village Green Pl
Champaign, IL 61822-7676

800-517-AMSA
FAX 888-205-5834
FAX 217-356-5370
E-Mail: information@meatscience.org
Home Page: www.meatscience.org

William Mikel, President
Scott J. Eilert, President Elect
Casey B. Frye, Treasurer

The official journal of AMSA. Peer-reviewed resource is the best way to stay current on the latest research in meat science across all meat products and in all aspects of meat production and processing. Available online or in print.

10260 Meat and Poultry
Sosland Publishing Company
4800 Main St
Suite 100
Kansas City, MO 64112-2513

816-756-1000
FAX 816-756-0494
E-Mail: web@sosland.com
Home Page: www.sosland.com

Gordon Davidson, President
Mark Sabo, President
Joel Crews, Editor

Serves meat, poultry and seafood processors, wholesalers-distributers, slaughterers, fabricators, cutters, meat buyers, and rendering and pet food manufacturers.
Cost: $42.00
Frequency: Monthly
Circulation: 21,000

Founded in 1955
Printed in 4 colors on glossy stock

10261 Midwest Food Service News
Pinnacle Publishing
316 N Michigan Avenue
Suite 300
Chicago, IL 60601

312-272-2401
800-493-4867
FAX 312-960-4106
E-Mail: pinpub@ragan.com
Home Page:
www.midwestfoodservicenews.com
Keith Hadley, Publisher
Joanne Cooper, Editor

Communicates directly and exclusively with restaurant and food service operations in Indiana, Kentucky, Michigan, Ohio, Pennsylvania and West Virginia.
52 Pages
Frequency: Bi-Monthly
Circulation: 40,000
Founded in 1982
Printed in 4 colors on newsprint stock

10262 Military Grocer
Downey Communications
4800 Montgomery Lane
Suite 710
Bethesda, MD 20814-3461

301-718-7600
FAX 301-718-7604

Richard T Carroll, Publisher
Loretta M Downey, CEO

Serves defense commissary employees worldwide.
Frequency: 5 per year
ISSN: 1058-8620
Printed in 4 colors on glossy stock

10263 Milk and Liquid Food Transporter
Glen Street Publications
W4652 Glen Street
Appletone, WI 54913

920-749-4880
FAX 920-749-4877
Home Page: www.glenstreet.com

Jane Plout, Publisher

Information for owners, operators and managers of companies that haul milk or other liquid foods in sanitary or food grade tankers. Publication covers maintenance, association news, state of the industry, business management, and activities of independent haulers.
16 Pages
Frequency: Monthly
Circulation: 4768
Founded in 1960
Printed in 4 colors on glossy stock

10264 Milling Journal
3065 Pershing Court
Decatur, IL 62526

217-877-9660
800-728-7511
FAX 217-877-6647
E-Mail: webmaster@grainnet.com
Home Page: www.grainnet.com

Jim Camillo, Editor
Mark Avery, Publisher
Kay Merryfield, Circulation Manager
Jody Sexton, Editorial Assistant
Deb Coontz, Sales Manager

Mailed to all active AOM members in the US, Canada, and internationally, including wheat flour/corn mills and corn/oilseed processors in US and Canada.
Frequency: Quarterly
Circulation: 1217

10265 Milling and Baking News
Sosland Publishing Company
4800 Main St
Suite 100
Kansas City, MO 64112-2513

816-756-1000
FAX 816-756-0494
E-Mail: web@sosland.com
Home Page: www.sosland.com

Gordon Davidson, President
Joshua Sosland, Editor
Neil N Sosland, Executive Editor
Eric Schroeder, Managing Editor
Jeff Gelski, Associate Editor

This magazine is aimed at baking, milling and food processing industries.
Cost: $52.00
Frequency: Monthly
Circulation: 4032

10266 Missouri Grocer
Missouri Grocers Association
315 North Ken Avenue
Springfield, MO 65802-6213

417-831-6667
FAX 417-831-3907
E-Mail: cmcmillian@missourigrocers.com
Home Page: www.missourigrocers.com
Social Media: *Facebook*

Erick Taylor, President
John Porter, Vice President
Mike Beal, Treasurer
Linda Ryan, Chairperson

Referred to as the pre-convention issue. Highlights the exhibitors, sponsors, awardees and events that will be taking place during the Annual Convention and Merchandising Show.

10267 Modern Baking
Penton Media
330 N Wabash
Suite 2300
Chicago, IL 60611

E-Mail: katie.martin@penton.com
Home Page: modern-baking.com

Jerry Rymont, VP Penton Food Group
Katie Martin, Chief Editor
Matt Reynolds, Group Managing Editor

Provides the latest product and service information to the $20 billion in-store and $14.9 billion retail baking and foodservice markets.
Cost: $75.00
112 Pages
Frequency: Monthly
Circulation: 27000
ISSN: 0897-6201
Founded in 1987
Mailing list available for rent: 27,000 names
Printed in 4 colors on glossy stock

10268 Modern Brewery Age
Business Journals
50 Day Street
S Norwalk, CT 06854-3100

203-853-6015
FAX 203-852-8175
E-Mail: pete@breweryage.com
Home Page: www.breweryage.com

Peter VK Reid, Editor
Britton Jones, President
Arthur Heilman, Circulation Manager

A magazine for the wholesale and brewing industry.
Cost: $95.00
Frequency: Quarterly
Founded in 1933

10269 Modern Brewery Age: Tabloid Edition
Business Journals

50 Day Street
#5550
Norwalk, CT 06854-3100

203-853-6015
FAX 203-852-8175

Peter VK Reid, Editor
Brewery industry tabloid.
Cost: $85.00
Frequency: Weekly

10270 Monthly Price Review
Urner Barry Publications
PO Box 389
Toms River, NJ 08754

732-240-5330
800-932-0617
FAX 732-341-0891
E-Mail: help@urnerbarry.com
Home Page: www.urnerbarry.com

Paul B Brown Jr, President
Karen Mick, Circulation Director

Lists price of eggs, turkeys, chickens, fowl,
butter, margarine, cheese and concentrated milk
products for the month and compares the
monthly average to the previous year.
Cost: $149.00
Frequency: Monthly
Circulation: 310
ISSN: 0566-3628
Founded in 1858

10271 Mushroom News
American Mushroom Institute
1284 Gap Newport Pike
Suite 2
Avondale, PA 19311-9503

610-268-7483
FAX 610-268-8015
E-Mail: mushroomnews@kennett.net
Home Page: www.americanmushroom.org

Sara Manning, Manager
Mark Wach, Chairman
Laura Phelps, President
Bill Barber, Publisher

For growers and scientists in mushroom pro-
duction.
Cost: $275.00
Frequency: Monthly
Founded in 1956

10272 NACS Magazine
National Association of Convenience Stores
1600 Duke St
Suite 700
Alexandria, VA 22314-3436

703-684-3600
FAX 703-836-4564
E-Mail: bmoyer@nacsonline.com
Home Page: www.nacsonline.com

Hank Armour, President
Ben Moyer, Advertising Manager

Delivered to all members, this magazine
reaches a majority of the convenience and petroleum marketing channel of trade.
Frequency: Monthly
Circulation: 27,632

10273 NAEDA Equipment Dealer
North American Equipment Dealers
Association
1195 Smizer Mill Rd
Fenton, MO 63026-3480

636-349-5000
FAX 636-349-5443
E-Mail: naeda@naeda.com
Home Page: www.naeda.com
Social Media: *Twitter, LinkedIn*

Paul Kindinger, President/CEO
Michael Williams, VP, Government
Relations/Treasurer

Terry Leath, Executive Assistant
Roger Gjellstad, First Vice Chair
Lester Killebrew, Chairman

Featuring articles about successful dealers, new
products, new technology, industry news, in-
surance loss control solutions and top manage-
ment tips.
Cost: $40.00
5000 Members
Frequency: Monthly
Circulation: 9,500
Founded in 1900
Printed in 4 colors on glossy stock

**10274 NWAC News: Thad Cochran National
Warmwater Aquaculture Center**
127 Experiment Station Road
Stoneville, MS 38776-197

662-686-3273
FAX 662-686-3320
E-Mail: javery@drec.msstate.edu
Home Page: www.msstate.edu/dept/tcnwac

Jimmy Avery, Editor
J Lee, CEO/President
Frequency: Monthly
Circulation: 1200
Founded in 1998
Printed in 3 colors on matte stock

10275 Nation's Restaurant News
Lebhar-Friedman
425 Park Ave
Suite 6
New York, NY 10022-3526

212-756-5088
FAX 212-838-9487
E-Mail: info@lf.com
Home Page: www.lf.com

Heather Martin, Manager
Michael Cardillo, VP Sales

Serves commercial and onsite food service and
lodging establishments including restaurants,
schools, universities, hospitals, nursing homes
and other health and welfare facilities, hotels
and motels with food service, government installations, clubs and other related firms.
Cost: $44.95
Circulation: 85999
Founded in 1925
*Mailing list available for rent: 100,000 names
at $100 per M*
Printed in 4 colors on matte stock

**10276 National Confectionery Sales
Association Annual Journal**
Teresa Tarantino
10225 Berea Road, Suite B
Cleveland, OH 44102

216-631-8200
FAX 216-631-8210
E-Mail: ttarantino@mail.propressinc.com
Home Page: www.candyhalloffame.com

Tony Rufrano, President
Steve Foster, Executive Director

Annual membership listing and biographies of
Candy Hall of Fame industees.
Cost: $25.00
76 Pages
Founded in 1997
Printed in 4 colors on matte stock

10277 National Culinary Review
American Culinary Federation
180 Center Place Way
St Augustine, FL 32095-8859

904-824-4468
800-624-9458
FAX 904-825-4758
E-Mail: acf@acfchefs.net
Home Page: www.acfchefs.org

Heidi Cramb, Executive Director

A monthly magazine that is circulated by paid
subscription. ACF members receive this publication as a benefit of membership in the American Culinary Federation. The National Culinary
Review contains chef-tested recipes, industry
news, and culinary techniques and is an educational resource for everyone interested in food
preparation.
Cost: $50.00
Frequency: 10x Yearly
Circulation: 25,000
Founded in 1932

10278 National Farmers Union News
National Farmers Union
11900 E Cornell Ave
Aurora, CO 80014-6201

303-368-7300
800-347-1961
FAX 303-368-1390
Home Page: www.nfu.org

David Frederickson, President
Rae Price, Publications Editor

A grass roots structure in which policy positions are initiated locally. The goal is to sustain
and strengthen family farm and ranch agriculture.
Cost: $30.00
Frequency: Monthly
Founded in 1902

10279 National Fisherman
Diversified Business Communications
PO Box 7437
Portland, ME 04112-7437

207-842-5600
FAX 207-842-5503
E-Mail: info@divcom.com
Home Page: www.divbusiness.com

Nancy Hasselback, President/CEO
Randy Le Shane, VP Operations
Nancy Gelette, VP Operations
Stephnie Wendel, Circulation Manager

The most widely read commercial fishing mag-
azine and the only commercial fishing publica-
tion providing national coverage and national
circulation.
Cost: $22.95
Frequency: Monthly
Circulation: 38000
ISSN: 0027-9250
Founded in 1949

**10280 National Food Processors Association
State Legislative Report**
National Food Processors Association
1350 Eye St NW
Suite 300
Washington, DC 20005-3377

202-393-0890
800-355-0983
FAX 202-639-5932
Home Page: www.nfpa-food.org

Cal Dooley, CEO
Lisa Weddig, Executive Director
Tammy Morgan, Contact
Frequency: Monthly
Circulation: 345
Founded in 1901

10281 National Grocer
National Grocers Association
1005 N Glebe Rd
Suite 250
Arlington, VA 22201-5758

703-516-0700
FAX 703-516-0115
Home Page: www.ngacampus.com

Thomas A Zaucha, President
Frank Dipasquale, Senior Vice President

Source of information on all aspects of the retail/wholesale grocery industry.
Cost: $5.00
Frequency: Quarterly
Circulation: 7000
Founded in 1992

10282 National Hog Farmer

7900 International Dr
Suite 300
Minneapolis, MN 55425-2562

952-851-4710
FAX 952-851-4601
Home Page: nationalhogfarmer.com/

Dale Miller, Editor
Tom Vilsack, Secretary
JoAnn DeSmet, Marketing
Robert Moraczewski, Senior Vice President

Offers production information for hog farming business managers.
Frequency: Monthly
Circulation: 84000
Founded in 1960
Mailing list available for rent: 84M names
Printed in 4 colors on glossy stock

10283 National Provisioner

Stagnito Communications
155 Pfingster Road
Suite 205
Deerfield, IL 60015

847-205-5660
FAX 847-205-5680
Home Page: www.nationalprovisioner.com

Ned Bardic, Publisher
Barbara Young, Editor
Tommy Howell, Marketing
Vito Laudati, Business Development Manager
Diana Rotman, Sales Manager

Magazine for meat, poultry, prepared food processors.
Cost: $85.00
Frequency: Monthly
Circulation: 25000
Founded in 1912

10284 Natural Foods Merchandiser

New Hope Natural Media
1401 Pearl St
Suite 200
Boulder, CO 80302-5346

303-939-8440
800-431-1255
FAX 303-939-9886
E-Mail: info@newhope.com
Home Page: www.newhope.com

Fred Linder, President
Marty Traynor, Editor
Lynne Brenner, Human Resources Executive

Natural Foods Merchandiser features a comprehensive overview of the industry, the latest reports on new ingredients and formulations, market news, new product releases and many other features specifically designed for the retailmarket. It offers the information and the products retailers require to succeed in the competitive natural products marketplace.
65 Pages
Frequency: Monthly
Circulation: 15,000
ISSN: 0164-335x
Founded in 1979
Printed in 4 colors on glossy stock

10285 Natural Products INSIDER

Virgo Publishing LLC

3300 N Central Ave
Suite 300
Phoenix, AZ 85012-2532

480-675-9925
FAX 480-990-0819
Home Page: www.naturalproductsinsider.com

Jenny Bolton, President

Official magazine for SupplySide. Provides timely information and news for marketers, manufacturers and formulators of dietary supplements, functional foods and personal care. The website also offers exclusive resources and offers, free weekly e-newsletters and a searchable news archive.
Mailing list available for rent: 15000+ names at $var per M

10286 Natural Products Marketplace

Virgo Publishing LLC
3300 N Central Ave
Suite 300
Phoenix, AZ 85012-2532

480-675-9925
FAX 480-990-0819
E-Mail: peggyj@vpico.com
Home Page: www.vpico.com

Jenny Bolton, President

Publication discussing the dietary supplement, food and personal care industries, focusing on the latest news, products and trend analysis to keep retailers informed and ahead of the competition.
Mailing list available for rent: 15000+ names at $var per M

10287 Nightclub & Bar Magazine

Oxford Publishing
Ste 1
1903b University Ave
Oxford, MS 38655-4150

662-236-5510
800-247-3881
FAX 662-236-5541
E-Mail: ed@oxpub.com
Home Page: www.nightclub.com

Ed Meek, Publisher
Taylor Rau, Editor
Jennifer Parsons, Marketing
Jennifer Robinson, CEO/President
Adam Alson, Founder

A monthly publication covering the nightclub and bar hospitality industry.
Cost: $30.00
Frequency: Monthly
Circulation: 30000
Printed in 4 colors on glossy stock

10288 North Africa and Middle East International Agricultural and Trade Report

US Department of Agriculture
1301 New York Avenue NW
#612
Washington, DC 20005-4701

202-219-0724
FAX 202-219-0942

Michael Kurrzig, Editor

Information on current and projected agriculture production and trade in North Africa and the Middle East. Reports include trade and production data and highlight US and European trade with the region.
Frequency: Annual

10289 North American Deer Farmers Magazine

North American Deer Farmers Association

104 S Lakeshore Dr
Lake City, MN 55041-1641

651-345-5600
FAX 651-345-5603
E-Mail: info@nadefa.org
Home Page: www.nadefa.org

Shawn Schafer, Executive Director
Dave McQuaig, First VP
Glenn Dice Jr, Second VP

National association of deer farming and ranching. Membership dues are $75-195 which include this quarterly magazine.
Frequency: Quarterly
Circulation: 1000
ISSN: 1084-0583
Founded in 1983
Mailing list available for rent
Printed in on glossy stock

10290 North American Journal of Aquaculture

American Fisheries Society
5410 Grosvenor Ln
Suite 110
Bethesda, MD 20814-2199

301-897-8616
FAX 301-897-8096
Home Page: www.fisheries.org

Gus Rassam, Executive Director
Myra Merritt, Office Administrator

Formerly published as The Progressive Fish-Culturist. The focus is on culture of all aquatic organisms that are of importance to North American culturists. Topics include, but are not limited to, nutrition and feeding, broodstock selection and spawning, drugs and chemicals, health and water quality, and testing new techniques and equipment for the management and rearing of aquatic species
Cost: $38.00
Frequency: Quarterly
ISSN: 1548-8454

10291 Northeast DairyBusiness

DairyBusiness Communications
6437 Collamer Road
East Syracuse, NY 13057-1031

315-703-7979
800-334-1904
FAX 315-703-7988
Home Page: www.dairybusiness.com

Eleanor Jacobs, Editor
Susan Harlow, Managing Editor

Business resource for successful milk producers. Devoted exclusively to the business and dairy management needs of milk producers in the 12 northeastern states.
Cost: $38.95
51 Pages
Frequency: Monthly
Circulation: 17,500
ISSN: 1523-7095
Founded in 1904
Printed in 4 colors on glossy stock

10292 Northwest Palate Magazine

Pacifica Publishing
PO Box 10860
Portland, OR 97296

503-224-6039
800-398-7842
FAX 503-222-5312
E-Mail: editorial@nwpalate.com
Home Page: http://www.northwestpalate.com

Cameron Nagel, Publisher/Editor
Angie Jabine, Owner
Ericka Burke, Owner

Regional magazine that focuses on food, wine and travel. Coverage includes restaurants, destinations and the wines of the Pacific North-

west states and British Columbia.
Cost: $15.00
56 Pages
Frequency: 6 issues per ye
Circulation: 45000
ISSN: 0892-8363
Founded in 1987
Printed in 4 colors on glossy stock

10293 Nut Grower

Western Agricultural Publishing Company
4969 E Clinton Way
Suite 104
Fresno, CA 93727-1549

559-252-7000
888-382-9772
FAX 559-252-7387
E-Mail: editorial@westgpubco.com
Home Page: www.westagpubco.com

Paul Baltimore, Publisher
Randy Bailey, Editor
Robert Fujimoto, Assistant Editor

Covers production topics, the latest in research
developments, and crop news on almonds, walnuts, pistachios, pecans and chestnuts.

10294 Nutraceuticals World

Rodman Publishing
70 Hilltop Rd
3rd Floor
Ramsey, NJ 07446-1150

201-825-2552
FAX 201-825-0553
E-Mail: info@rodpub.com
Home Page: www.nutraceuticalsworld.com

Rodman Zilenziger Jr, President
Matt Montgomery, VP

Articles about many aspects of the market,
from dietary supplements to functional foods to
nutritional beverages, and everything in
between.
Frequency: Monthly
Circulation: 12010

10295 Nutrition Action Healthletter

Center for Science in the Public Interest
1875 Connecticut Avenue NW
Suite 300
Washington, DC 20009

202-332-9110
FAX 202-265-4954
E-Mail: cspi@cspinet.org
Home Page: www.cspinet.org

Stephen B Schmidt, Editor-in-Chief
Chris Schmidt, Customer Service Manager
Michael Jacobson, Executive Director
Jamie Jonker, Director Regulatory Affairs

A magazine covering food and nutrition, the
food industry, and relevant government regula-
tions.
Cost: $32.00
16 Pages
Circulation: 800000
Founded in 1971
*Mailing list available for rent: 700,000 names
at $90 per M*
Printed in 4 colors on matte stock

10296 On-Campus Hospitality

Executive Business Media
825 Old Country Road
PO Box 1500
Westbury, NY 11590

516-334-3030
FAX 516-334-8959
E-Mail: ebm-mail@ebmpubs.com
Home Page: www.ebmpubs.com

Murry H Greenwald, President/Publisher
Paul Ragusa, Managing Editor

College and university food service operations
and outlets and related purchasing and adminis-

trative offices.
Cost: $30.00
Circulation: 9,445
ISSN: 0887-431X
Founded in 1979
Printed in 4 colors

10297 Onboard Services

International Publishing Company of
America
664 La Villa Dr
Miami Springs, FL 33166-6030

305-887-1700
800-525-2015
FAX 305-885-1923
Home Page: www.onboard-services.com

Alexander Morton, Owner
George Hulcher, Contributing Editor

Keeps airline, cruise ships, railroad, and terminal concessions management and purchasing
departments up-to-date on all phases of passenger services.
Cost: $25.00
24 Pages
ISSN: 0892-4236
Founded in 1968
Printed in 4 colors on glossy stock

10298 Organic WORLD

John Pappenheimer
3939 Leary Way NW
Seattle, WA 98107-5043

206-781-3347
FAX 206-632-7055

Covers the news of organic gardening.
Cost: $15.00
Frequency: Quarterly

10299 PMT Magazine

Packaging Machinery Manufacturers
Institute
11911 Freedom Drive
Suite 600
Reston, VA 20190

703-243-8555
888-275-7664
FAX 703-243-8556
E-Mail: pmmi@pmmi.org
Home Page: www.pmmi.org
Social Media: *Facebook, Twitter, LinkedIn,
YouTube*

Chuck Yuska, President

The only publication dedicated to the packaging machinery end user. The magazine features
articles on mechatronics, sustainability and the
packaging professional. Regular features bring
news about trends, automation solutions,
processing and more.
500+ Members

10300 Pacific Farmer-Stockman

999 West Riverside Avenue
PO Box 2160
Spokane, WA 99201-1006

509-595-5385
800-624-6618
FAX 509-459-3929
E-Mail: information@spokane.net
Home Page: www.nmv.pointshop.com

Barry Roach, Ad Director
Shaun Higgins, President
Colleen Striegel, Operations Manager
Mike Craigen, Marketing Executive

Offers farming news and information for farm-
ers and herdsmen located in the Pacific states.
Cost: $29.95
Frequency: Monthly

10301 Packer

Vance Publishing

400 Knightsbridge Parkway
Lincolnshire, IL 60069

847-634-2600
FAX 847-634-4379
E-Mail: info@vancepublishing.com
Home Page: www.vancepublishing.com

William C Vance, Chairman
Peggy Walker, President

Leading source of news and information on
fresh fruit and vegetable marketing.
Frequency: Weekly
Circulation: 12434
Founded in 1937
Printed in on glossy stock

10302 Peanut Farmer

Specialized Agricultural Publications
5808 Faringdon Place
Suite 200
Raleigh, NC 27609

919-872-5040
FAX 919-876-6531
E-Mail: publisher@peanutfarmer.com
Home Page: www.peanutfarmer.com

Dayton H Matlick, President
Mary Evans, Publisher
Mary Cornwall, Chief Copy Editor
Jeanne Sherman, Director of Circulation

Offers peanut farmers profitable methods of
raising, marketing and promoting peanuts, plus
key related issues.
Cost: $15.00
24 Pages
Frequency: Monthly
Circulation: 18500
Founded in 1965
Printed in 4 colors on glossy stock

10303 Peanut Grower

Vance Publishing
38 Peace Drive
Bronson, FL 32621

352-486-7006
FAX 352-486-7009
E-Mail: ahuber@svic.net
Home Page: www.peanutgrower.com

Amanda Huber, Editor
Lia Guthrie, Sales

Written for the largest 24,000 US peanut farmers. Covers disease, weed and insect control,
legislation, farm equipment, marketing and
new research.
Founded in 1937

10304 Peanut Science

American Peanut Research and Education
Society
Oklahoma State University
376 Ag Hall
Stillwater, OK 74078-6025

405-372-3052
FAX 405-624-6718
Home Page: www.peanutscience.com

Dr J Ronald Sholar, Executive Officer

A professional journal with current research re-
sults.
Cost: $9.00
Frequency: Bi-Annual
Founded in 1979

10305 Pig International

WATT Publishing Company
303 N Main Street
Suite 500
Rockford, IL 61101

815-966-5400
FAX 815-966-6416

E-Mail: rabbott@wattnet.net
Home Page: www.wattnet.com

James Watt, Chairman/CEO
Greg Watt, President/COO
Roger Abbott, Editor

Covers nutrition, animal health issues, feed procurement, and how producers can be profitable in the world pork market.
Cost: $50.00
Frequency: Monthly
Circulation: 17642
ISSN: 0191-8834
Founded in 1971
Printed in 4 colors on glossy stock

10306 Pizza Today

National Association of Pizzeria Operators
908 S 8th Street
Suite 200
Louisville, KY 40203

502-736-9500
800-489-8324
FAX 502-736-9502
E-Mail: plachapelle@pizzatoday.com
Home Page: www.pizzatoday.com
Social Media: *Facebook, Twitter*

Pete Lachapelle, Publisher/President
Jeremy White, Editor-in-Chief
Mandy Detwiler, Managing Editor
Pat Cravens, Editorial Coordinator

Up-to-date information on pizza restaurant management, pizza equipment for sale, a vendor directory and more.
130 Pages
Frequency: Monthly
Circulation: 47,000
Founded in 1983
Printed in 4 colors on glossy stock

10307 Pork

10901 W 84th Ter
Suite 200
Lenexa, KS 66214-1631

913-438-8700
800-255-5113
FAX 913-438-0695
E-Mail: info@vancepublishing.com
Home Page: www.vancepublishing.com

Cliff Becker, Publisher
Jane Messenger, Chief Financial Officer
Lori Eppel, Chief Financial Officer
Bill Raufer, Contributing Editor

A magazine specifically designed for the professional pork producer.
Cost: $59.88
Frequency: Monthly
Circulation: 21,464
Founded in 1981
Mailing list available for rent

10308 Potato Country

Columbia Publishing
8405 Ahtanum Rd
Yakima, WA 98903-9432

509-248-2452
800-900-2452
FAX 509-248-4056
Home Page: www.potatocountry.com

Brent Clement, Editor/Publisher
Mike Stoker, Publisher

Edited for potato growers and allied industry people throughout the Western fall-production states. Editorial material covers production, seed, disease forecast, equipment, fertilizer, irrigation, pest/weed management, crop reports and annual buyers guide.
Cost: $18.00
32 Pages
Circulation: 6300
ISSN: 0886-4780

Founded in 1975
Printed in 4 colors on glossy stock

10309 Potato Grower

Harris Publishing Company
360 B Street
Idaho Falls, ID 83402

208-524-4217
FAX 208-522-5241
Home Page: www.potatogrower.com

Jason Harris, Publisher
Gary Rawlings, Editor
Nancy Butler, Staff Writer
Rob Erickson, Marketing
Eula Endecott, Circulation

Current news on growing potatoes, market trends, technology.
Cost: $20.95
48 Pages
Frequency: Monthly
ISBN: m-mountai-n -w
Founded in 1965
Printed in 4 colors on glossy stock

10310 Poultry

Marketing and Technology Group
1415 N Dayton St
Suite 115
Chicago, IL 60642-7033

312-266-3311
FAX 312-266-3363
E-Mail: webinars@meatingplace.com
Home Page: www.meatingplace.com

Mark Lefens, Owner
Tom Cosgrove, Editor

Serves companies who deal with poultry slaughter, rendering or processing.
Frequency: Monthly
Circulation: 20,000
Founded in 1993
Printed in 4 colors on glossy stock

10311 Poultry Digest

WATT Publishing Company
122 S Wesley Ave
Mt Morris, IL 61054-1451

815-734-7937
FAX 815-734-4201
E-Mail: olentine@wattmm.com
Home Page: www.wattnet.com

James W Watt, President
Charles G Olentine Jr, PhD, Publisher

A magazine serving the production side of the entire poultry industry.
Founded in 1917

10312 Poultry International

WATT Publishing Company
303 N Main Street
Suite 500
Rockford, IL 61101

815-966-5400
FAX 815-966-6416
E-Mail: mclements@wattnet.net
Home Page: www.wattnet.com

James Watt, Chairman/CEO
Greg Watt, President/COO
Mark Clements, Editor

Viewed by commercial poultry integrators as the leading international source of news, data and information for their businesses. Serves commercial broiler, turkey, duck and egg producers.
Cost: $63.00
68 Pages
Frequency: Monthly
Circulation: 20000
ISSN: 0032-5767
Founded in 1962
Printed in 4 colors

10313 Poultry Times

Poultry & Egg News
PO Box 1338
Gainesville, GA 30503-1338

770-536-2476
FAX 770-532-4894
Home Page: www.poultrytimes.net
Social Media: *Facebook*

Cindy Wellborn, Manager
Chris Hill, CEO
Barbara L Olejnik, Associate Editor
Kyle Hatcher, National Sales Representative

The only newspaper in the poultry industry. Provides the most up to date news for the poultry industry.
Cost: $12.00
Frequency: 26 X a year
Circulation: 13000
ISSN: 0885-3371
Founded in 1954
Printed in on glossy stock

10314 Poultry USA

WATT Publishing Company
303 N Main Street
Suite 500
Rockford, IL 61101

815-966-5400
FAX 815-966-6416
Home Page: www.wattnet.com

James Watt, Chairman/CEO
Greg Watt, President/COO
Jeff Swanson, Publishing Director

Poultry USA serves individuals and firms engaged in the production, processing and marketing of broilers.
60 Pages
Frequency: Monthly
Circulation: 15,092
ISSN: 0007-2176
Founded in 1917
Printed in 4 colors on glossy stock

10315 Practical Winery & Vineyard

58 Paul Dr
Suite D
San Rafael, CA 94903-2054

415-479-5819
FAX 415-492-9325
E-Mail: Office@practicalwinery.com
Home Page: www.practicalwinery.com

Don Neel, Owner
Tina L Vierra, Associate Publisher

Journal of grape grown and wine production in North America.
Cost: $33.86
Frequency: 6 issues per ye
Circulation: 7,500
Founded in 1985

10316 Prepared Foods

Business News Publishing
2401 W Big Beaver Rd
Suite 700
Troy, MI 48084-3333

248-362-3700
FAX 248-362-0317
Home Page: www.bnpmedia.com

Mitchell Henderson, CEO
Kathy Travis, Art Director

About 600 food and beverage companies.
Cost: $95.00
109 Pages
Circulation: 70100
Founded in 1926
Printed in 4 colors on glossy stock

10317 Private Label Buyer

Stagnito Communications

155 Pfingsten Road
Suite 205
Deerfield, IL 60015

847-205-5660
FAX 847-205-5680
Home Page: www.stagnito.com

Steven T Lichtenstein, Publisher
Jill Bruss, Editor

Serves the private label industry, including re-
tailers, voluntaries, wholesalers, manufacturers
and others allied to the field.
Frequency: Monthly
Circulation: 30021
Founded in 1986

10318 Process Cooling & Equipment

BNP Publications
1050 IL Route 83
Suite 200
Bensenville, IL 60106-1096

630-377-5909
FAX 630-694-4002
E-Mail: GlennD@bnpmedia.com
Home Page: www.process-cooling.com

Katie Rotella, Manager
Doug Glenn, Publishing Director

Written for manufacturing engineers who use
cooling equipment, components, materials and
supplies. refrigerated engineers and technicians
assoc

10319 Prograzier

Meat & Livestock Australia
1401 K Street NW
Suite 602
Washington, DC 20005

202-521-2551
FAX 202-521-2699
E-Mail: info@mla.com.au
Home Page: www.mla.com.au
Social Media: *Facebook, Twitter, YouTube*

Don Heatley, Chairman
David Palmer, Managing Director
Bernie Bindon, Director
Chris Hudson, Director

Companion publication to feedback magazine.
Highlights how individual producers have
succesfully introduced best management practices into their farming enterprise and the benefits that have been achieved.
30000 Members
Frequency: Quarterly
Founded in 1998

10320 Progressive Farmer

2100 Lakeshore Drive
Birmingham, AL 35209-6721

205-877-6333
800-357-4466
FAX 205-877-6860
E-Mail: ProgressiveFarmer@timeinc.com
Home Page: www.progressivefarmer.com

Ed Dickinsen, Publisher
Jack Odle, Editor

Farming news with regional focus on the mid-
west, midsouth and southwest.
Cost: $84.00
106 Pages
Frequency: Monthly
Circulation: 610000
ISSN: 0033-0760

10321 Progressive Grocer's Marketing Guidebook

Trade Dimensions
770 Broadway
New York, NY 10003

847-763-9050
FAX 203-563-3131

E-Mail: info@progressivegrocer.com
Home Page: www.progressivegrocer.com

Jenny McTaggart, Senior Editor
Olivia Wilson, Publisher

Over 800 retailer chains and wholesalers in the
US and Canada. Also includes over 20,000 key
executives. Plus, over 1,700 speciality distributors including C-Store and smaller food store
wholesalers, food brokers, and candy, tobacco,
and media distributors.
Cost: $380.00
Founded in 1970

10322 QSR Magazine

101 Europa Drive
Suite 150
Chapel Hill, NC 27517

919-945-0705
FAX 919-945-0701
Home Page: www.qsrmagazine.com

Sam Oches, Editor
Eugene Drezner, National Sales Director
Webb Howell, President
Frequency: Monthly
Founded in 1997

10323 RCI Magazine

Retail Confectioners International
2053 S Waverly Ave
Suite 204
Springfield, MO 65804-2414

417-883-2775
800-545-5381
FAX 847-724-2719
E-Mail: info@retailconfectioners.org
Home Page: www.retailconfectioners.org

Evans Billington, Executive Director

Covers the retail confection industry.
Frequency: Monthly
Circulation: 800
Founded in 1917

10324 RF Design

131 E Main Street
Bellevue, OH 44811-1449

419- 48- 741
FAX 419-483-3617
Home Page: www.rfdesign.com/

David Morrison, Editor
Pete May, President

Comprehensive source of rural agricultural
news and information for farmers and the general public.
Frequency: Monthly
Founded in 2000

10325 Reciprocation

American Meat Science Association
2441 Village Green Pl
Champaign, IL 61822-7676

800-517-AMSA
FAX 888-205-5834
FAX 217-356-5370
E-Mail: information@meatscience.org
Home Page: www.meatscience.org

William Mikel, President
Scott J. Eilert, President Elect
Casey B. Frye, Treasurer

Published twice a year for all AMSA members,
this magazine features articles on current meat
science issues facing the industry.

10326 Refrigerated & Frozen Foods

Stagnito Communications

155 Pfingsten Road
Suite 205
Deerfield, IL 60015

847-205-5660
FAX 847-205-5680
Home Page: www.refrigeratedfrozenfood.com

Jeff Plaster, Publisher
Geneine Esquibel, Marketing Manager
Katie Gutierrez, Marketing Manager

Features on leading refrigerated and frozen
food processors. Current and future trends in
processing, packaging, new product development, food safety and logistics. Serves the
dairy, meat, vegetable, fruit, bakery, deli, ingredient, snack, ethnic and other food industry related organizations. Free to qualified
subscribers.
Cost: $65.00
64 Pages
Frequency: Monthly
Circulation: 20500
ISSN: 1061-6152
Founded in 1919
Printed in 4 colors on glossy stock

10327 Render

National Renderers Association
801 N Fairfax St
Suite 205
Alexandria, VA 22314-1776

703-683-0155
FAX 703-683-2626
Home Page: www.nationalrenderers.org

Thomas M Cook, President

Keeping members abreast of advancements and
trends taking place within the industry.
Frequency: Monthly

10328 Restaurant Business

National Council of Chain Restaurants
325 7th St NW
Suite 1100
Washington, DC 20004

202-783-7971
800-673-4692
FAX 202-737-2849
E-Mail: info@nrf.com
Home Page: www.nccr.net

Mike Starnes, Chairman
Rob Green, Executive Director
Scott Vinson, Vice President
Chip Kunde, Treasurer
Mary Schell, Secretary

The only publication that is all about and only
about the restaurant entrepreneur, serving regional and emerging chains, multi-concept operators and high-volume independents with
ideas to innovate and grow. Features include
growth strategies, innovations, the restaurant
life, and more.
Frequency: Monthly
Founded in 1965

10329 Restaurant Digest

Panagos Publishing
7913 Westpark Drive
Suite 305
McLean, VA 22102

703-917-6420
FAX 703-917-6408
Home Page: www.restaurantdigest.com

Bruce Panagos, Publisher

Developments and news of interest to owners,
managers, and operators of dining and entertainment establishments in the region.

10330 Restaurant Hospitality

Penton Media

1300 E 9th St
Suite 316
Cleveland, OH 44114-1503

216-696-7000
FAX 216-696-6662
E-Mail: information@penton.com
Home Page: www.penton.com

Jane Cooper, Marketing
Mike Sanson, Editor-in-Chief

A national trade publication that covers the full-service restaurant industry. It offers cover story features, an extensive food section with recipes, a multi-page news section and a variety of one page profiles on rising stars, equipment, food safety, beverages, design and more.
Cost: $70.00
130 Pages
Frequency: Monthly
Circulation: 117,721
ISSN: 0147-9989
Founded in 1892
Mailing list available for rentat $165 per M
Printed in 4 colors on glossy stock

10331 Restaurant Marketing
Oxford Publishing
Ste 1
1903b University Ave
Oxford, MS 38655-4150

662-236-5510
800-247-3881
FAX 662-236-5541
E-Mail: ed@oxpub.com
Home Page: www.nightclub.com

Ed Meek, Publisher
Taylor Rau, Editor
Jennifer Parsons, Marketing Director
Amy Dierks, VP Advertising
Michael Harrelson, Executive Editor

A trade magazine providing marketing information and promotional ideas for restaurant owners, hotel and casino operators and caterers.
Cost: $30.00
Frequency: Monthly
Circulation: 30000
Founded in 1985

10332 Restaurant Wine
Wine Profits
PO Box 222
Napa, CA 94559-222

707-224-4777
FAX 707-224-6740
Home Page: www.restaurantwine.com

Zelma Long, President
Ronn R Wiegand, Publisher
Sandy Flanders, Director of Marketing
Paul Grieco, Co-Owner

Information on the marketing of wine in restaurants, hotels and clubs, wine and food pairing ideas and review of wines.
Cost: $99.00
Circulation: 3000
ISSN: 1040-7030
Printed in 2 colors on matte stock

10333 Restaurants & Institutions
Reed Business Information
2000 Clearwater Dr
Oak Brook, IL 60523-8809

630-574-0825
800-446-6551
FAX 630-288-8781
Home Page: www.rimag.com

Jeff Greisch, President
Scott Hume, Managing Editor

For restaurant professionals faced with fast-paced consumer demands, government reg-

ulations, health concerns and evolving food trends in a variety of market segments.
Frequency: Monthly
Circulation: 154110
Founded in 1937
Printed in 4 colors on glossy stock

10334 Restaurants USA
National Restaurant Association
1200 17th St Nw
Washington, DC 20036-3006

202-331-5900
800-424-5156
FAX 202-331-2429
Home Page: www.restaurant.org

Dawn M Sweeney, CEO
Sarah Smith-Hamaker, Treasurer
Phil Hickey, Treasurer

A trade magazine offering information for restaurant owners and managers, including industry trends, operational pointers, management principles and association activities.
Cost: $125.00
48 Pages
Frequency: Monthly
Circulation: 44,000
Founded in 1980
Printed in 4 colors

10335 Rice Farming
Vance Publishing
5050 Poplar Avenue
Suite 200
Memphis, TN 38157-2099

901-767-4020
800-888-9784
FAX 901-767-4026
E-Mail: vlboyd@worldnet.att.net
Home Page: www.ricefarming.com

John Sowell, Publisher
Marci Deshores, Editor
Barbara Johnson, Manager

Profitable production strategies for commercial rice growers.
Founded in 1937

10336 Rice Journal
Specialized Agricultural Publications
3000 Highwoods Boulevard
Suite 300
Raleigh, NC 27604-1029

919-878-0540
FAX 919-876-6531
Home Page: www.ricejournal.com

Dayton H Matlick, President
Mary Evans, Publisher

Offers rice growers profitable methods of producing, marketing and promoting rice, plus key related issues.
Cost: $15.00
24 Pages
Frequency: Monthly January-July
Circulation: 11,600
Founded in 1897
Printed in 4 colors on glossy stock

10337 Ristorante|
1010 Lake St
Suite 604
Oak Park, IL 60301-1136

708-848-3200
FAX 708-445-9477
Home Page: www.ristorantemag.com

Joe Madden, Owner

10338 Rural Heritage
Allan Damerow

281 Dean Ridge Ln
Gainesboro, TN 38562-5039

931-268-0655
FAX 931-268-5884
E-Mail: info@ruralheritage.com
Home Page: www.ruralheritage.com

Gail Damerow, Owner
Allan Damerow, Publisher

Publication for people who farm and log with horses and other draft animals.
Cost: $28.00
100 Pages
ISSN: 0889-2970
Founded in 1976
Printed in 4 colors on glossy stock

10339 Rural Living
Michigan Farm Bureau
7373 W Saginaw Highway
PO Box 30960
Lansing, MI 48909-8460

517-237-7000
800-292-2680
FAX 517-323-6793
Home Page: www.michiganfarmbureau.com

Dennis Rudat, Editor
Sue Snyder, President
Brigette Leach, Director
Earl Butz, Secretary

Editorial emphasis on consumer food news, travel information and issue analysis.
24 Pages
Frequency: Quarterly

10340 S.O. Connected
National Society on Healthcare Foodservice
455 S. 4th Street
Suite 650
Louisville, KY 40202

888-528-9552
FAX 502-589-3602
E-Mail: info@healthcarefoodservice.org
Home Page: www.healthcarefoodservice.org
Social Media: *Facebook, LinkedIn, YouTube*

Patti Oliver, President
Beth Yesford, President-Elect
Laura Watson, Secretary
Randy Sparrow, Treasurer
Robert Darrah, Treasurer-Elect

An important resource for news and recognition.

10341 School Foodservice & Nutrition
School Nutrition Association
120 Waterfront St
Suite 300
Oxon Hill, MD 20745-1142

301-749-1481
800-877-8822
FAX 301-739-3915
E-Mail: servicecenter@schoolnutrition.org
Home Page: www.schoolnutrition.org

Mary Hill, Director
Dora Rivas SNS, President-Elect
Nancy Rice SNS, VP

This is the official publication of the School Nutrition Association which contains the latest information on a host of items that affect the successful operation of a school foodservice program.
Cost: $75.00
Frequency: Monthly
Circulation: 57,000

10342 School Nutrition Magazine
School Nutrition Association

120 Waterfront St
Suite 300
National Harbor, MD 20745-1142

301-686-3100
800-877-8822
FAX 301-686-3115
E-Mail: servicecenter@schoolnutrition.org
Home Page: www.schoolnutrition.org

Helen Phillips, President
Sandy Ford, President-Elect
Leah Schmidt, Vice President
Beth Taylor, Secretary/Treasurer

The latest information on a host of items that
affect the successful operation of a school
foodservice program.
55000 Members
Frequency: Monthly
Founded in 1946

10343 Science Matters

Natural Products Association
2112 E 4th St
Suite 200
Santa Ana, CA 92705-3816

714-460-7732
800-966-6632
FAX 714-460-7444
Home Page: www.npainfo.org
Social Media: *Facebook, Twitter, LinkedIn*

John F. Gay, Executive Director & CEO
Jeffrey Wright, President

Dedicated to providing timely information and
advancing the understanding of natural products from a scientific perspective.
1900+ Members
Frequency: Monthly
Founded in 1936

10344 Seafood Business

Diversified Business Communications
121 Free Street
PO Box 7437
Portland, ME 04112-7437

207-842-5500
FAX 207-842-5503
E-Mail: bspringer@divcom.com
Home Page: www.seafoodbusiness.com

Fiona Robinson, Editor
Bill Springer, Publisher
Nancy Hasselback, CEO
Linda Skinner, Managing Editor
Wendy Jalbert, Production Director

Current, comprehensive news on the rapidly
expanding seafood industry.
Frequency: Monthly
Circulation: 15,000
Founded in 1949

10345 Sheep!

145 Industrial Drive
Medford, WI 54451

715-785-7979
800-551-5691
FAX 715-785-7414
E-Mail: sheepmag@tds.net
Home Page: www.sheepmagazine.com

Dave Belanger, Publisher
Nathan Griffith, Editor

Explores a wide range of sheep-related topics
of interest to sheep growers and sheep product
marketers at all levels of experience.
Cost: $21.00
Frequency: 6x Yearly

10346 Shorthorn Country

Durham Management Company

5830 S 142nd St
Suite A
Omaha, NE 68137-2894

402-827-8003
FAX 402-827-8006
Home Page:
www.durhamstaffingsolutions.com

Machael Durham, President
Pat Cloutier, Production Manager

Magazine published for cattle producers who
breed and sell registered Shorthorn and Polled
Shorthorn cattle.
Cost: $24.00
Frequency: 11 per year
Circulation: 3,000
ISSN: 0149-9319

10347 Simply Seafood

Sea Fare Group
2360 W Commodore Way
Suite 210
Seattle, WA 98199

206-829-2323
FAX 206-789-0504
E-Mail: peter@seafare.com
Home Page: www.simplyseafood.com

Peter Redmayne, Editor

Articles on today's seafood, with cooking
ideas, tips & techniques and recipes for healthy
meal. Editor's Letter provides all the latest
news and insights on seafood products and
consumer issues as well as a Market Report
with each seasons best buys.
Frequency: Quarterly
Circulation: 131,257

10348 Sizzle

American Culinary Federation
180 Center Place Way
St Augustine, FL 32095-8859

904-824-4468
800-624-9458
FAX 904-825-4758
E-Mail: acf@acfchefs.net
Home Page: www.acfchefs.org
Social Media: *Facebook, Twitter*

Michael Ty, President
Thomas J. Macrina, Secretary
James Taylor, Treasurer

The American Culinary Federation quarterly
for students of cooking. The only magazine in
the United States exclusively targeting culinary,
baking, and pastry students. Includes articles
on emerging job markets, mentoring, continuing education, culinary trends and product application, as well as scholarship information
and culinary/ pastry techniques. Digital
publication.
19000 Members
Founded in 1929

10349 Snack Food & Wholesale Bakery

Stagnito Communications
155 Pfingster Road
Suite 205
Deerfield, IL 60015

847-205-5660
FAX 847-205-5680
Home Page: www.stagnito.com

Ron Bean, Publisher
Harry Stagnito, Publishing Director
Dan Malovany, Editor
Bernard Pacyniak, Editorial Director
Andy Hanacek, Managing Editor

Covers topics and products in the snack and
wholesale bakery market
Cost: $85.00
Frequency: Monthly
Circulation: 14,854
Founded in 1912
Printed in 4 colors on glossy stock

10350 Snack World

Snack Food Association
1233 Janesville Avenue
Fort Atkinson, WI 53538-2738

703-836-4500
800-547-7377
FAX 920-563-1702

Gloria Cosby, Publisher
Tracey McMahon, Editor

The official international publication of the
Snack Food Association covering trends in the
snack food industry, including new products
and services, industry news and supplier
services.
Frequency: 10 per year
Circulation: 14,000

10351 Southeastern Peanut Farmer

Southern Peanut Farmer's Federation
110 E 4th Street
PO Box 706
Tifton, GA 31794

229-386-3470
FAX 229-386-3501
E-Mail: info@gapeanuts.com
Home Page: www.gapeanuts.com/

Joy Carter, Editor

Offers information to peanut farmers.
Cost: $25.00
20 Pages
Frequency: 5x/Year
Circulation: 9000
ISSN: 0038-3694
Founded in 1961
Printed in 4 colors on glossy stock

10352 Southern Beverage Journal

14337 Sw 119th Ave
Miami, FL 33186-6006

305-233-7230
FAX 305-252-2580
E-Mail: info@bevmedia.com
Home Page: www.bevmedia.com

Sharon Mijares, Manager
William Slone, Publisher

A magazine for the alcoholic beverage industry.
Cost: $35.00
Frequency: Monthly
Circulation: 10000

10353 Soybean Digest

Primedia Business
7900 International Dr
Suite 300
Minneapolis, MN 55425-2562

952-851-9329
800-722-5334
FAX 952-851-4601
E-Mail:
CorporateCustomerService@penton.com
Home Page: www.penton.com

Robert Moraczewski, Executive VP
Ron Sorensen, Chairman
Kelly Conlin Conlin, President/CEO

Leading publication in the soybean market. Of-
fers in-depth coverage for wise management
decisions dealing with production of soybeans,
corn, wheat, sorghum and cotton.
Cost: $25.00
Frequency: Monthly
Circulation: 147000
Founded in 1940

10354 Soybean South
6263 Poplar Avenue
Suite 540
Memphis, TN 38119-4736

901-385-0595
FAX 901-767-4026

John Sowell, Publisher
Jeff Kehl, Circulation Director

Profitable prediction strategies for soybean farmers.
Frequency: 5 per year
Printed in 4 colors on glossy stock

10355 Specialty Food Magazine
National Association for the Specialty Food Trade
120 Wall St
27th Floor
New York, NY 10005-4011

212-482-6440
FAX 212-482-6459
Home Page: www.fancyfoodshows.com

Ann Daw, President

Provides comprehensive planning information for each Show and aggressive on-site bonus distribution, as well as the industry's most in-depth pre-Show, on-site, and post-Show coverage.
Cost: $30.00
Frequency: Monthly
Circulation: 30100
Founded in 1952

10356 Spudman Magazine
75 Applewood Drive
Sparta, MI 49435

616-887-9008
FAX 616-887-2666
Home Page: www.spudman.com

Matt McCallum, Publisher
Greg Brown, Managing Editor
Erica Bernard, Circulation Manager
Marnie Draper, Advertising Manager
Jill Peck, Creative Director

Information for potato farming and marketing.
Frequency: 9 issues per ye
Circulation: 15500
Founded in 1964

10357 StateWays
The Beverage Information Group
17 High St
2nd Floor
Norwalk, CT 06851

203-855-8499
E-Mail: lzimmerman@m2media360.com
Home Page: www.bevinfogroup.com

Liza Zimmerman, Editor-in-Chief
Jeremy Nedelka, Managing Editor

Written for commissioners, board members, headquarters personnel, and retail store managers responsible for buying beverage alcohol in the eighteen control states. Covered editorial product knowledge, market trends, store operations, merchandising, warehousing, computerization, administration, training and other topics.
Cost: $20.00
Frequency: Bi-Monthly
Circulation: 8500

10358 Stores Magazine
National Council of Chain Restaurants
325 7th St NW
Suite 1100
Washington, DC 20004

202-783-7971
800-673-4692
FAX 202-737-2849

E-Mail: info@nrf.com
Home Page: www.nccr.net

Mike Starnes, Chairman
Rob Green, Executive Director
Scott Vinson, Vice President
Chip Kunde, Treasurer
Mary Schell, Secretary

Offers an insider's view of the entire retail industry by featuring the latest trends, hottest ideas, current technologies and consumer attitudes.
Frequency: Monthly
Founded in 1965

10359 Sugar: The Sugar Producer Magazine
Idaho Golf Harris Publishing
520 Park Avenue
Idaho Falls, ID 83402

208-523-1500
800-638-0135
FAX 208-522-5241
E-Mail:
customerservice@harrispublishing.com
Home Page: www.sugarproducer.com

Jason Harris, Publisher
David FairBourn, Editor
Eula Endecott, Circulation Manager
Rob Erickson, Marketing Manager

Sugar beet industry information.
Cost: $15.95
Frequency: Monthly
Circulation: 16000
Founded in 1975

10360 Sunbelt Food Service
Shelby Publishing Company
517 Green St Nw
Gainesville, GA 30501-3300

770-534-8380
FAX 770-535-0110
E-Mail: shelbyfs@bellsouth.net
Home Page: www.shelbypublishing.com

Ron Johnston, President
Penny Smith, Account Manager

Sales and promotion of products and services sold through food service establishments across the sunbelt.
Cost: $36.00
Frequency: Monthly
Circulation: 30090
Founded in 1965
Printed in on newsprint stock

10361 Sunflower Magazine
National Sunflower Association
Ste 206
2401 46th Ave SE
Mandan, ND 58554-4829

701-328-5100
888-718-7033
FAX 701-328-5101
Home Page: www.sunflowernsa.com

Larry Kleingartner, Executive Director
John Sanbakken, Marketing Director

Magazine geared to sunflower products.
Cost: $9.00
Frequency: Monthly
Circulation: 29,300
Founded in 1981
Printed in 4 colors

10362 Sunflower and Grain Marketing Magazine
Sunflower World Publishers
3307 Northland Drive
Suite 130
Austin, TX 78731-4964

512-407-3434
FAX 512-323-5118

Ed Randall Allen

Offers news and information on the sunflower and grain industries.
Circulation: 15,000

10363 Supermarket News: Center Store
Penton Media Inc
249 W 17th St
Suite 6
New York, NY 10011-5390

212-204-4200
FAX 212-206-3622
E-Mail: julie.gallagher@penton.com
Home Page: www.penton.com

Sharon Rowlands, CEO
Jerry Rymont, Publisher

A nationally circulated weekly trade magazine for the food distribution industry.

10364 Supermarket News: Retail/Financial
Penton Media Inc
249 W 17th St
Suite 6
New York, NY 10011-5390

212-204-4200
FAX 212-206-3622
E-Mail: mark.hamstra@penton.com
Home Page: www.penton.com

Sharon Rowlands, CEO

A nationally circulated weekly trade magazine for the food distribution industry
Frequency: Monthly
Circulation: 36346
ISSN: 0039-5803
Founded in 1892

10365 Supermarket News: Technology & Logistics
Penton Media Inc
249 W 17th St
Suite 6
New York, NY 10011-5390

212-204-4200
FAX 212-206-3622
E-Mail: michael.garry@penton.com
Home Page: www.penton.com

Sharon Rowlands, CEO

A nationally circulated weekly trade magazine for the food distribution industry
Cost: $45.00
ISSN: 0039-5803
Founded in 1892

10366 Swine Practitioner
Vance Publishing
10901 W 84th Terrace
3 Pine Ridge Plaza
Lenexa, KS 66214-1649

913-438-8700
800-255-5113
FAX 913-438-0695
E-Mail: cbecker@vancepublishing.com
Home Page: www.vancepublishing.com

Jim Carlton, Editor
Cliff Becker, Group Publisher
William C Vance, Chairman

Offers technical information, primarily on swine health and related production areas, to veterinarians and related industry professionals.
Founded in 1937
Mailing list available for rent

10367 THE SUNFLOWER
National Sunflower Association
2401 46th Avenue SE
Suite 206
Mandan, ND 58554-4829

701-328-5100
888-718-7033
FAX 701-328-5101

E-Mail: larryk@sunflowernsa.com
Home Page: www.sunflowernsa.com
Social Media: *Facebook, YouTube*

Larry Kleingartner, Executive Director
Contains fresh, current and important articles on production strategies, ongoing research and market information.
Frequency: 6x Yearly
Founded in 1981

10368 Tea & Coffee Trade Journal
Lockwood Publications
26 Broadway
Floor 9M
New York, NY 10004-1704

212-391-2060
845-267-3489
FAX 212-391-2060
Home Page: www.lockwoodpublications.com

Robert Lockwood Sr, President

Premiere magazine for tea and coffee industry.
Cost: $49.00
Frequency: Monthly
Circulation: 12
Founded in 1901
Printed in 4 colors on glossy stock

10369 The County Agent
National Association of County Agricultural Agents
6584 W Duroc Road
Maroa, IL 61756

217-794-3700
FAX 217-794-5901
E-Mail: exec-dir@nacaa.com
Home Page: www.nacaa.com

Rick Gibson, President

Members receive professional improvement, news of association activities, shared education efforts from other states and reports from NACAA leadership and member states.
Frequency: Monthly
Circulation: 5000
Founded in 1916

10370 The New Brewer
Brewers Association
736 Pearl Street
Boulder, CO 80302

303-447-0816
888-822-6273
FAX 303-447-2825
E-Mail: webmaster@brewersassociation.org
Home Page: www.beertown.org
Social Media: *Facebook, Twitter*

Chris P. Frey, Chair
Jake Keeler, Vice Chair
Roxanne Westendorf, Secretary

Offers practical insights and advice for breweries of all sizes. Features on topics like brewing technology and problem solving, pub and restaurant management, and packaged beer sales and distribution. Also important industry news, sales charts and market share performance. The annual Industry Review tallies production for every craft brewery in America, producing both regional and national lists of the biggest players in every sector.
1900 Members
Founded in 1978

10371 TheConsultant
Food Service Consultants Society International
144 Parkedge Street
Rockwood, ON, Canada N0B 2K0

519-856-0783
FAX 519-856-0648

E-Mail: liz@fcsi.org
Home Page: www.fcsi.org

Liz Campbell, Editor

Professional publication for FCSI members and the food service industry.
Cost: $40.00
150 Pages
Frequency: Quarterly
Circulation: 4500
Printed in 4 colors on glossy stock

10372 Today's Grocers
Florida Grocer Publications
PO Box 430760
S Miami, FL 33246

305-661-0792
800-440-3067
FAX 305-661-6720

Jack Nobles, Publisher
Dennis Kane, Editor

Provides the latest food industry news and trends to Florida, Georgia, Alabama, Louisiana, Mississippi and the Carolinas.
Cost: $29.00
24 Pages
Frequency: Monthly
Circulation: 19,000
ISSN: 1529-4420
Founded in 1956
Printed in on newsprint stock

10373 Tomato Country
Columbia Publishing
8405 Ahtanum Rd
Yakima, WA 98903-9432

509-248-2452
800-900-2452
FAX 509-248-4056
Home Page: www.tomatomagazine.com

Brent Clement, Editor/Publisher
Mike Stoker, Publisher

Includes information on tomato production and marketing, grower and shipper feature stories, tomato research, from herbicide and pesticide studies to new varieties, market reports, feedback from major tomato meetings and conventions, along with other key issues and points of interest for US and Canada tomato growers.
Cost: $12.00
Frequency: Annually
Founded in 1993

10374 Trading Rules
National Oilseed Processors Association
1300 L St NW
Suite 1020
Washington, DC 20005-4168

202-842-0463
FAX 202-842-9126
E-Mail: nopa@nopa.org
Home Page: www.nopa.org

Kathy Pennington, Manager
David J Hovermale, Executive VP
Karri L Moore, Project Manager
Julia Kinnaird, Manager
Cost: $50.00
Founded in 1929

10375 Transactions of the American Fisheries Society
American Fisheries Society
5410 Grosvenor Ln
Suite 110
Bethesda, MD 20814-2199

301-897-8616
FAX 301-897-8096
Home Page: www.fisheries.org

Gus Rassam, Executive Director
Myra Merritt, Office Administrator

The Society's highly regarded international journal of fisheries science features results of basic and applied research in genetics, physiology, biology, ecology, population dynamics, economics, health, culture, and other topics germane to marine and freshwater finfish and shellfish and their respective fisheries and environments
Cost: $43.00
Frequency: Bi-Monthly
ISSN: 0002-8487
Founded in 1872

10376 Tree Fruit
Western Agricultural Publishing Company
4969 E Clinton Way
#104
Fresno, CA 93727-1546

559-252-7000
888-382-9772
FAX 559-252-7387
E-Mail: westag@westagpubco.com

Paul Baltimore, Publisher
Randy Bailey, Editor
Robert Fujimoto, Assistant Editor

For tree fruit growers in California.

10377 Truth About Organic Foods
Henderson Communications LLC
1422 Elbridge Payne Rd
Suite 250
Chesterfield, MO 63017-8544

636-728-1428
FAX 636-777-4178
E-Mail: info@agrimarketing.com
Home Page: www.agrimarketing.com

Lynn Henderson, Owner

This 231-page book provides a fair and balanced look from a scientific standpoint about the heritage, production and nutritive value of organic foods.

10378 US Beer Market: Impact Databank Review and Forecast
M Shanken Communications
387 Park Ave S
8th Floor
New York, NY 10016-8872

212-684-4224
FAX 212-684-5424
E-Mail: impact@mshanken.com
Home Page: www.cigaraficionado.com

Marvin Shanken, Publisher
Cost: $895.00
Frequency: Annual+
Founded in 1972

10379 US Fast Food and Multi-Unit Restaurants
Business Trend Analysts/Industry Reports
2171 Jericho Tpke
Suite 200
Commack, NY 11725-2937

631-462-5454
800-866-4648
FAX 631-462-1842
Home Page: www.businesstrendanalysts.com

Charles J Ritchie, Executive VP
Donna Priani, General Manager

This survey offers information on the fast food industry, including chains and franchises.
Cost: $1995.00
Founded in 1986

10380 US Liquor Industry
Business Trend Analysts/Industry Reports

2171 Jericho Tpke
Suite 200
Commack, NY 11725-2937

631-462-5454
FAX 631-462-1842
Home Page: www.businesstrendanalysts.com

Charles J Ritchie, Executive VP
Donna Priani, Marketing Director

A survey summarizing the past, current and future markets and trends in the liquor industry.
Cost: $1495.00
Founded in 1999

10381 US Market for Bakery Products
Business Trend Analysts/Industry Reports
2171 Jericho Tpke
Suite 200
Commack, NY 11725-2937

631-462-5454
800-866-4648
FAX 631-462-1842
Home Page: www.businesstrendanalysts.com/

Charles J Ritchie, Executive VP
Donna Priani, General Manager

Profiles markets for bread, rolls, cakes, pies, cookies, crackers, other sweets and pretzels; provides information on consumption patterns, distribution trends, pricing, new products, and advertising strategies.
Cost: $1495.00
Frequency: Annual+
Founded in 1978

10382 Valley Potato Grower
Ola Highway 2 E
East Grand Forks, MN 56721

218-773-7783
FAX 218-773-6227
E-Mail: communication@nppga.org
Home Page: www.rrvpotatoes.org

Duane W Maatz, President
Ted Kreis, Marketing

Information on potato farming.
Cost: $17.95
Frequency: Monthly
Founded in 1946

10383 Vegetable
US Department of Agriculture
PO Box 1258
Sacramento, CA 95812-1258

Home Page: www.usda.gov

Chris Smith, Chief Information Officer
Matt Paul, Director of Communications
Ramona Romero, General Counsel

Historic information relating to various types of vegetable crops.

10384 Vegetable Growers News
Great American Publishing
75 Applewood Drive Suite A
PO Box 128
Sparta, MI 49345-1531

616-887-9008
FAX 616-887-2666
Home Page: www.vegetablegrowersnews.com

Kimberly Warren, Managing Editor
Matt McCallum, Executive Publisher
Erica Bernard, Circulation Manager
Jill Peck, Creative Director
Greg Ryan, Graphic Designer

Market and marketing news.
Cost: $12.00
Frequency: Monthly
Circulation: 14000
Founded in 1970

10385 Vegetables
Western Agricultural Publishing Company

4969 E Clinton Way
#104
Fresno, CA 93727-1549

559-252-7000
888-382-9772
FAX 559-252-7387
E-Mail: editorial@westapubco.com

Paul Baltimore, Publisher
Randy Bailey, Editor
Robert Fujimoto, Assistant Editor

The definitive source for information on all aspects of western vegetable production.

10386 Vegetarian Journal
Vegetarian Resource Group
PO Box 1463
Baltimore, MD 21203

410-366-8343
FAX 410-366-8804
E-Mail: vrg@vrg.org
Home Page: www.vrg.org

Debra Wasserman, Director

The practical magazine for those interested in Vegetarian Health, Ecology, and Ethics.
Frequency: Quarterly
Circulation: 15000
Mailing list available for rent

10387 Veggie Life Magazine
EGW
4075 Papazian Way
Suite 204
Fremont, CA 94538-4372

510-668-0268
FAX 510-668-0280
E-Mail: info@egw.com
Home Page: www.veggielife.com

Chris Slaughter, VP
Shanna Masters, Editor

The modem voice on seasonal vegetarian cooking, optimum nutrition, and natural healing for today's health-conscious consumer features vauable tips techniques, recipes, and remedies from dietcians, herbalists, doctors and other health experts on new ways to prpare creative plant-based cuisine, implement diet programs, and use natural remedies for an improved and vibrant lifestyle.
Cost: $19.96
68 Pages
Frequency: Quarterly
Circulation: 80000
Founded in 1980

10388 Vending Times
Vending Times
1375 Broadway
6th Floor
New York, NY 10018

516-442-1850
FAX 516-442-1849
E-Mail: subscriptions@vendingtimes.net
Home Page: www.vendingtimes.com

Alicia Lavay-Kertes, President/Publisher
Nick Montano, VP/Executive Editor
Tim Sanford, Editor-in-Chief

Vending Times serves the automatic merchandising and coffee service industries. This includes music and game operations, vending operations, mobile catering operations, consultants and associations.
Cost: $40.00
Frequency: Monthly
Circulation: 16,000
Founded in 1962

10389 Vineyard and Winery Management
Vineyard & Winery Management

421 E Street
P.O. Box 14459
Santa Rosa, CA 95404

707-577-7700
800-535-5670
FAX 707-577-7705
Home Page: www.vwmmedia.com

Robert Merletti, CEO/Publisher
Jason Thomas, Business Manager
Tina Caputo, Editor-in-Chief
Ethan Simon, Director of Sales
Suzanne Webb, Marketing Director

Leading independent and award-winning wine trade magazine serving all of North America.
Cost: $37.00
100 Pages
Frequency: Bi-monthly
Circulation: 6900
ISSN: 1047-4951
Founded in 1975
Printed in 4 colors on glossy stock

10390 WATT Poultry Magazine
WATT Poultry USA
122 S Wesley Ave
Mt Morris, IL 61054-1451

815-734-7937
FAX 815-734-4201
E-Mail: watt@wattmm.com
Home Page: www.wattnet.com

James Watt, President
Charles Olentine, Publisher
Gary Thornton, Editor

Dedicated to supporting every phase of the turkey industry by providing information for decision-makers on breeding, production, management, processing and marketing.

10391 WD Hoard and Sons Company
Po Box 801
Fort Atkinson, WI 53538-0801

920-563-5551
FAX 920-563-7298
E-Mail: hoards@hoards.com
Home Page: www.hoards.com
Social Media: Facebook, Twitter

Brian V Knox, CEO
Gary L Vorpahl, Marketing Director

News aimed at the dairy farmer.
Cost: $18.00
Frequency: 20x/Year
Circulation: 63317
Founded in 1871
Printed in 4 colors on glossy stock

10392 Wallaces Farmer
Farm Progress Companies
255 38th Avenue
Suite P
St Charles, IL 60174-5410

630-462-2224
800-441-1410
E-Mail: rswoboda@farmprogress.com
Home Page: www.farmprogress.com

Rod Swoboda, Editor
Willie Vogt, Corporate Editorial Director
Frank Holdmeyer, Executive Editor

Serves Iowa farmers and ranchers with information to help them maximize their productivity and profitability. Each issue is packed with information, ideas, news and analysis.
Cost: $26.95
Frequency: Monthly
Founded in 1855

10393 Western Dairy Business
DairyBusiness Communications

6437 Collamer Road
East Syracuse, NY 13057-1031

315-703-7979
866-520-2880
FAX 315-703-7988
E-Mail: circ@dairybusiness.com
Home Page: www.dairybusiness.com

Ron Goble, Associate Publisher
Cecilia Parsons, Associate Editor
Scott A Smith, CEO

Business resource for successful milk producers. Covers 13 Western states. Provides information and news that is helpful in the daily operations of dairymen.
Cost: $38.95
67 Pages
Frequency: Monthly
Circulation: 14000
ISSN: 1528-4360
Founded in 1904
Printed in 4 colors on glossy stock

10394 Western Farm Press
Primedia
2104 Harvell Circle
Bellevue, NE 68005

913-341-1300
866-505-7173
FAX 913-967-1898
E-Mail: wfcs@pbsub.com
Home Page: www.westernfarmpress.com
Social Media: *Facebook, Twitter*

Robert Fraser, Managing Editor
Harry Cline, Editor
Greg Frey, Publisher
Darrah Parker, Marketing Director

Timely reliable information for western agriculture.
Circulation: 16,000
Founded in 1989

10395 Western Fruit Grower
Meister Media Worldwide
37733 Euclid Ave
Willoughby, OH 44094-5992

440-942-2000
800-572-7740
FAX 440-975-3447
E-Mail: afg.edit@meistermedia.com
Home Page: www.meisternet.com

Gary Fitzgerald, President
Brian Sparks, Editor
Terry Doak, Circulation Manager

Edited for commercial growers of deciduous crops and citrus fruit, nut grape crops in the Western US.
Cost: $20.00
66 Pages
Frequency: Monthly
Circulation: 36,000

10396 Western Grocery News
80 Willow Road
Menlo Park, CA 94025-3661

650-321-3600
800-227-7346
FAX 650-327-7537

Frequency: Bi-Monthly
Circulation: 9,187

10397 Western Growers & Shippers
Western Growers Association
PO Box 2130
Newport Beach, CA 92658-8944

949-863-1000
FAX 949-863-9028
Home Page: www.wga.com

Tom Nassif, President
Tim Linden, Editor

Listing over 3,000 growers, shippers, packers, brokers and distributors of fruits and vegetables in California and Arizona.
32 Pages
Frequency: Monthly
Circulation: 5000
ISSN: 0043-3799
Founded in 1926
Printed in 4 colors on glossy stock

10398 Western Livestock Journal
Crow Publications
7355 E Orchard Road
Suite 300
Greenwood Village, CO 80111

303-722-7600
800-850-2769
FAX 303-722-0155
E-Mail: editorial@wlj.net
Home Page: www.wlj.net

Pete Crow, Publisher

Offers its readers the best coverage of timely, necessary news and information that affects the livestock industry, particularly cattle.
Cost: $45.00
Frequency: Weekly
Founded in 1922

10399 Whole Foods Magazine
WFC
4041g Hadley Rd
Suite 101
South Plainfiel, NJ 07080-1120

908-769-1160
FAX 908-769-1171
E-Mail: info@wfcinc.com
Home Page: www.wfcinc.com
Social Media: *Facebook, Twitter, LinkedIn*

Howard Wainer, President
Kaylynn Ebner, Editor
Ronda Collins, Circulation Manager
Tim Person, Assistant Editor

Serves the natural/health products industry.
Cost: $70.00
Frequency: Monthly
Founded in 1979
Printed in on glossy stock

10400 Wine Advocate
Robert M Parker Jr
PO Box 311
Monkton, MD 21111

410-329-6477
FAX 410-357-4504
E-Mail: wineadvocate@erobertparker.com
Home Page: www.erobertparker.com

Robert M Parker Jr, Editor/CEO
Daniel Thomases, Partner

An independent magazine covering reviews of wine.
Cost: $60.00
64 Pages
Frequency: Bi-monthly
Circulation: 40000
Founded in 1978

10401 Wine World
Wine World Publishing
6433 Topanga Canyon Boulevard
#412
Canoga Park, CA 91303-2621
Dee Snidt, Editor

For the wine consumer and industry.
Cost: $16.00
48 Pages
Frequency: Monthly
Founded in 1971

10402 Wines & Vines
1800 Lincoln Ave
San Rafael, CA 94901-1298

415-453-9700
FAX 415-453-2517
E-Mail: info@winesandvines.com
Home Page: www.winesandvines.com

Chet Klingensmith, Publisher
Kendra Campbell, Director of Sales and Marketing
Tina Caputo, Editor
Jacques Brix, Vice President

Voice of the grape and wine industry.
Cost: $32.50
Frequency: Monthly
Circulation: 3200
Founded in 1919
Printed in 4 colors on matte stock

10403 Yankee Food Service
201 Oak Street
Suite A
Pembroke, MA 02359

781-829-4700
866-677-4700
FAX 781-829-0134
E-Mail: info@griffinpublishing.net
Home Page: www.griffinpublishing.net

Stephen M Griffin, President
Jack Walsh, Vice President
Karen Harty, Vice President
Julie Mignosa, Office Manager

Reports news and happenings of the food service industry in New England.
Cost: $47.00
48 Pages
Frequency: Monthly
Circulation: 22,111
Founded in 1970

Trade Shows

10404 A Year of Enchantment
Int'l Council on Hotel, Restaurant Institute Edu.
1200 17th Street NW
Washington, DC 20036-3006

202-467-6300
E-Mail: publications@chrie.org
Home Page: www.chrie.org

Susan Gould, Manager
Joseph Bradley, Treasurer

Containing over 70 booths and over 50 exhibits.
750 Attendees
Frequency: August
Founded in 1946

10405 AACC International Annual Meeting
3340 Pilot Knob Road
St. Paul, MN 55121-2055

651-454-7250
800-328-7560
FAX 651-454-0766
E-Mail: aacc@scisoc.org
Home Page: www.aaccnet.org
Social Media: *Facebook, Twitter, LinkedIn*

Betty Ford, Meetings Director
Rhonda Wilkie, Meetings Coordinator
Deborah Rogers, Chair
David Hahn, President
Steven C. Nelson, Executive Vice President

Formerly the American Association of Cereal Chemists, the AACC meeting offers the chance to come together, network with peers, discuss

critical issues in the science and discover the methods of others.
1200 Attendees
Frequency: October

10406 AACT Technical Conference
American Association of Candy Technologists
711 W. Water St.
PO Box 266
Princeton, WI 54968

920-295-6969
FAX 920-295-6843
E-Mail: aactinfo@gomc.com
Home Page: www.aactcandy.org

Bob Huzinec, President
Bill Dyer, First VP

Approximately 20 papers are presented to an audience of technologists in the sweet goods industry. These talks range from basics to innovations, provising the industry with practical information to help in understanding processes and ingredients used by their companies.
300 Attendees
Frequency: Annual/October

10407 AAEA Annual Meeting
American Agricultural Economics Association
1110 Buckeye Avenue
Ames, IA 50010-8063

515-233-9087
FAX 575-233-3101

Nancy Knight, Manager Meetings
Annual meeting and trade show of 25 exhibitors.
1700 Attendees

10408 AAW Annual Convention
American Agri-Women
2103 Zeandale Road
Manhattan, KS 66502

785-537-6171
FAX 785-537-9727
E-Mail: info@americanagriwomen.org
Home Page: www.americanagriwomen.org

Marcie Williams, President

Tradeshow consisting of products of interest to women in agriculture.
350 Attendees
Frequency: Annual/November

10409 ABI/ADPI Joint Annual Meeting
American Butter Institute
2101 Wilson Boulevard
Suite 400
Arlington, VA 22201

703-243-6111
FAX 703-841-9328
E-Mail: AMiner@nmpf.org
Home Page: www.butterinstitute.org

Jerome J Kozak, Executive Director
Chris Galen, Communications VP

This event is co-sponsored by The American Dairy Products Institute for manufacturers, marketers and suppliers of manufactured dairy products. 35 exhibitors.
700 Attendees
Frequency: Annual

10410 ACF National Convention
American Culinary Federation
180 Center Place Way
St Augustine, FL 32095-8859

904-824-4468
800-624-9458
FAX 904-825-4758
E-Mail: acf@acfchefs.net

Home Page: www.acfchefs.org
Social Media: *Facebook, Twitter*

Michael Ty, President
Thomas J. Macrina, Secretary
James Taylor, Treasurer

Learn the latest culinary trends during educational seminars and demonstrations and enjoy spectacular meal events. Competitions, exhibits and more.
19000 Members
Founded in 1929

10411 ACF National Convention & Trade Show
American Culinary Federation
180 Center Place Way
Saint Augustine, FL 32095

904-824-4468
800-624-9458
FAX 904-825-4758
E-Mail: acf@acfchefs.net
Home Page: www.acfchefs.org
Social Media: *Facebook, Twitter, Flickr*

Kevin Brune, Director, Events & Operations Mgmt
Jennifer Keith, Event & Sales Specialist
Claudia More, Events Management Coordinator

Two-hundred booths of products and foodstuffs for the food service industry. Seminars, workshops, cooking demos, more.
2000 Attendees
Frequency: Annual/July

10412 ACF Regional Conference
American Culinary Federation
180 Center Place Way
St Augustine, FL 32095-8859

904-824-4468
800-624-9458
FAX 904-825-4758
E-Mail: acf@acfchefs.net
Home Page: www.acfchefs.org
Social Media: *Facebook, Twitter*

Michael Ty, President
Thomas J. Macrina, Secretary
James Taylor, Treasurer

Catch up on the latest culinary trends and watch cooking demonstrations from expert chefs. This events series is a great way to earn continuing education hours and meet other professionals in the culinary industry.
19000 Members
Founded in 1929

10413 ACS Annual Conference and Competition
American Cheese Society
304 W Liberty Street
Suite 201
Louisville, KY 40202

502-583-3783
FAX 502-589-3602
E-Mail: mwilson@hqtrs.com
Home Page: www.cheesesociety.org

Marci Wilson, Executive Director
Carlos Scrivener, Manager

This Conference and Competition offers a unique opportunity to learn the latest about cheese in America and indulge your cheese fantasies by tasting more than 700 American artisan and specialty cheeses.
Frequency: Associate Fee

10414 ADPI/ABI Annual Conference
American Dairy Products Institute
126 N Addison St
Elmhurst, IL 60126

630-530-8700
FAX 630-530-8707

E-Mail: info@adpi.org
Home Page: www.adpi.org

Dale Kleber, CEO

Held in Chicago, this event attracts programs, the annual meeting, and the exhibition hall. Fifty exhibits of equipment and supplies for condensed milk, dry and evaporated milk and whey products, plus conference, seminar, workshop and banquet.
650 Attendees
Frequency: Annual/April

10415 AEA National Convention
American Emu Association
PO Box 2502
San Angelo, TX 76902

541-332-0675
E-Mail: info@aea-emu.org
Home Page: www.aea-emu.org

Charles Ramey, President
Martha Hendricks, VP

This convention provides a chance for the AEA Board of Directors (AEA-BOD) to meet, face to face, during the week prior to the actual convention. It is a place for members to gather to learn the latest information and research about the emu industry, see the latest new products and network with other emu growers from across the U.S. and around the world.
Frequency: July/Non-Member $230

10416 AFFI Frozen Food Convention
American Frozen Food Institute
2000 Corporate Ridge, Blvd.
Suite 1000
McLean, VA 22102-7862

703-821-0770
FAX 703-821-1350
E-Mail: info@affi.com
Home Page: www.affi.com

Kraig R Naasz, President/CEO
Thomas Bradshaw, Manager Legislative Affairs
Corey Henry, VP Communications
Robert L Garfield, SVP Public Policy/Intl Affairs

Learn more about the frozen food industry, network with peers, see new research, and get higher education.
500 Members
Founded in 1942

10417 AFFI-Con
American Frozen Food Institute
2000 Corporate Ridge Blvd
Suite 1000
McLean, VA 22102

703-821-0770
FAX 703-821-1350
E-Mail: info@affi.com
Home Page: www.affi.com

Mary Becton, Conference Director

Helping you make connections and helping you be better informed about industry issues.
1500 Attendees
Frequency: Annual/February

10418 AFS Annual Meeting
American Fisheries Society
5410 Grosvenor Lane
Bethesda, MD 20814

301-897-8616
FAX 301-897-8096
Home Page: www.fisheries.org
Social Media: *Facebook, Twitter, Flickr*

Gus Rassa,, Executive Director
Myra Merritt, Office Administrator

Held in conjunction with American Institute of Fishery Research Biologists. Explore the interrelation between fish, aquatic habitats and man;

highlight challenges facing aquatic resource professionals and the methods that have been employed to resolve conflicts between those that use or have an interest in our aquatic resources.
Frequency: Annual/September

10419 AMI International Meat, Poultry & Seafood Convention and Exposition
Convention Mangement Group
10472 Armstrong Street
Fairfax, VA 22031

703-934-4700
FAX 703-934-4899
Home Page: www.amiexpo.com
Social Media: *Facebook, Twitter, LinkedIn*

Anne Halal, Convention/Member Services VP
Anne Nuttall, Convention/Members Director
Katie Brannan, Convention/Members Sr. Manager

Sponsored by the American Meat Institute it features exhibits featuring the latest innovations in processing and packaging equipment, business and processing software systems, supplies, services and formulations.
25000 Attendees
Frequency: Annual/April

10420 AMSA Reciprocal Meat Conference
American Meat Science Association
2441 Village Green Place
Champaign, IL 61822

217-356-5370
800-517-AMSA
FAX 888-205-5834
FAX 217-356-5370
E-Mail: information@meatscience.org
Home Page: www.meatscience.org\rmc

Thomas Powell, Executive Director
Diedrea Mabry, Program Director
Kathy Ruff, Meetings & Member Svcs Director

RMC is the annual meeting for AMSA, featuring an interactive program tailored to bring attendees the very best and inspiring educational experience. Attendees are professionals in academia, government and industry, as well as students in the meat, food and animal science fields.
Frequency: Annual

10421 AOCS Annual Meeting & Exposition
American Oil Chemists' Society
2710 S Boulder
Urbana, IL 61802-6996

217-359-2344
FAX 217-359-8091
E-Mail: meetings@aocs.org
Home Page: www.aocs.org

Nurhan Dunford, General Chairperson
Mindy Cain, Meetings Specialist

The premier global science and business forum on fats, oils, surfactants, lipids, and related materials. Includes oral and poster presentations, short courses, and exhibit, and networking with more than 1,600 colleagues from 60 countries.
2000 Attendees
Frequency: Annual/April

10422 APA Annual Meeting
Apple Processors Association
1666 K Street NW
Suite 260
Washington, DC 20006

202-785-6710
FAX 202-331-4212
E-Mail: pweller@agriwashington.org
Home Page: www.appleprocessors.org

Paul S Weller Jr, President
Andrea Ball, Sr Director
Meetings/Administration

A three-day meeting which brings top industry and consumer experts together for a dialogue on timely issues. These include marketing tips, packaging trends, consumer research, and media reports and reaction to industry initiatives.
Frequency: Annual/June

10423 APS/CPS/MSA Annual Joint Meeting
American Phytopathological Society
3340 Pilot Knob Road
Saint Paul, MN 55121-2097

651-454-7250
800-328-7560
FAX 651-454-0766
E-Mail: aps@scisoc.org
Home Page: www.meeting.apsnet.org
Social Media: *Facebook, Twitter, LinkedIn, YouTube*

Betty Ford, Director of Meetings

Featuring over 18 state-of-the-art education sessions daily, over 700 poster presentations, one-of-a-kind preconvention tours and workshops and exhibits from leading suppliers.
Frequency: Annual/Summer

10424 ASA/CSSA/SSSA International Annual Meeting
American Society of Agronomy
677 S Segoe Road
Madison, WI 53711

608-273-8080
FAX 608-273-2021
Home Page: www.agronomy.org

Keith R Schlesinger, Meetings/Convention Director
Stacey Phelps, Exhibit/Meetings Assistant
Linda Nelson, Meetings Specialist
Ellen Bergfeld, Executive Vice President

Co-sponsored with Crop Science Society of America and with the Soil Science Society of America. This event is a unique convergence of the leading agronomy, crops, soils and environmental sciences professionals from around the world. A blend of technical sessions, poster sessions, social functions, career networking and exhibits draw a growing number of prominent professionals and students.
3,500 Attendees
Frequency: November
Founded in 1907

10425 ASABE Annual International Meeting
American Society of Agricultural & Biological Eng.
950 S Cherry Street
Suite 508
Denver, CO 80246-2664

303-759-5091
FAX 303-758-0190
E-Mail: chesser@asabe.org
Home Page: www.asabe.org

Michael Chesser, Meetings/Conference Director
Sharon McKnight, Meetings Support Staff

100 and more diverse technical sessions, 11 continuing professional development sessions, 5 technical tours, an industry exhibit hall and a keynote address from Dr. Lowell B. Catlett; this year's meeting is full of must attend events.
Frequency: July

10426 ASBC Annual Meeting
American Society of Brewing Chemists
3340 Pilot Knob Road
Saint Paul, MN 55121-2055

651-454-7250
FAX 651-454-0766

E-Mail: bford@scisoc.org
Home Page: www.meeting.asbcnet.org

Betty Ford, Meetings Director
Sue Casey, Meetings Coordinator
Steven Nelson, VP

Network with peers and learn about the latest technologies available to brewers.
300 Attendees
Frequency: Annual/June

10427 ASHS Annual Conference
American Society for Horticultural Science
1018 Duke Street
Alexandria, VA 22314

703-836-4606
FAX 703-836-2024
Home Page: www.ashs.org
Social Media: *Facebook*

Michael W Neff, Executive Director
Tracy Shawn, Assistant Executive Director

A place to meet with colleagues, talk with exhibitors and view over 400 posters.
1,200 Attendees
Frequency: Annual/July

10428 ASME Business Forum & Expo
Associaton of Sales and Marketing Companies
2100 Reston Parkway
Suite 400
Reston, VA 20191

703-758-7790
FAX 703-758-7787
E-Mail: info@asmc.org
Home Page: www.asmc.org

Julie Casson, Sales Manager

Seminar and 75 exhibits of food manufacturers, computer equipment and services, food product services, foreign trade, incentive displays, shelf space management and related information.
7000 Attendees
Frequency: Annual
Founded in 1985

10429 ASTA/CSTA Joint Annual Convention
American Seed Trade Association
225 Reinekers Lane
Suite 650
Alexandria, VA 22314-2875

703-837-8140
FAX 703-837-9365
Home Page: www.amseed.com

Jennifer Lord, Meetings Director
Jason Laney, Meetings Associate Director

Includes meetings of all divisions of ASTA and CSTA and several joint meetings of both organizations, exhibits, prominent keynote speakers relevant to both associations, sessions that include representatives discussing how seed moves through the pipelines of our industry to the end user and those whose roles affect the regulation and administration of the framework.
800 Attendees
Frequency: July/Fee $129-$799

10430 AWMA Real Deal Expo
American Wholesale Marketers Association
2750 Prosperity Avenue
Suite 530
Fairfax, VA 22031

703-208-3358
FAX 703-573-5738
E-Mail: info@awmanet.org
Home Page: www.awmanet.org

Marcia Barker, Public Affairs Manager
Nate Wills, Exhibit Information

The only trade show geared to convenience distributors. Exhibitors include purveyors of to-

bacco products, candy, beverages, snacks, foodservice, health and beauty care items, general merchandise, warehouse equipment, computer systems and much more.
2,500 Attendees
Frequency: Annual/February

10431 AWS National Conference

American Wine Society
PO Box 279
Englewood, OH 45322

888-297-9070
FAX 937-529-7888
Home Page: www.americanwinesociety.org

John Hames, Executive Director

The annual conference brings professional, serious amateurs and novices together to discover what is new in wine. Seminars and lectures on all aspects of wine appreciation, wine production, grape growing and cuisine. Attendees must be a member of the society.
Frequency: Annual/November

10432 Ag Progress Days

Penn State University Agricultural Sciences
420 Agricultural Administration Building
University Park, PA 16802

814-865-2081
FAX 814-865-1677
E-Mail: agprogressdays@psu.edu
Home Page: www.apd.cas.psu.edu

Bob Oberheim, Manager

Agricultural trade show focusing on the innovations and progress made in the agricultural industry.
50M Attendees
Frequency: Annual/August

10433 Agri News Farm Show

Agri News
18 1st Avenue SE
Rochester, MN 55904-3722

507-857-7707
800-633-1727
FAX 507-281-7474
E-Mail: rallen@agrinews.com
Home Page: www.agrinews.com

Rosie Allen, Advertising Manager
John Losness, President
Todd Heroff, Manager

Annual show of 160 exhibitors of farming equipment, supplies and services.
8000 Attendees
Frequency: March

10434 Agri-Marketing Conference

National Agri-Marketing Association
11020 King Street
Suite 205
Overland Park, KS 66210-1201

913-491-6500
FAX 913-491-6502
E-Mail: agrimktg@nama.org
Home Page: www.nama.org
Social Media: *Facebook, Twitter, LinkedIn, YouTube, Flickr*

Vicki Henrickson, President
Beth Burgy, President Elect
Paul Redhage, Secretary/Treasurer

Learn more about customer behaviors, market shares, and other top industry tips.
3500 Members
Frequency: Annual/April
Founded in 1957

10435 Agricultural Retailers Association Convention and Expo

Agricultural Retailers Association

1156 15th Street
Suite 500
Washington, DC 20005

202-457-0825
800-844-4900
FAX 314-567-6888
E-Mail: kellyaradc.org
Home Page: www.aradc.org

Daren Coppock, President/CEO
Richard Gupton, Sr. VP., Public Policy
Michelle Hummel, VP Marketing/Communications

Annual show of 120 manufacturers, suppliers and distributors of agricultural chemicals and fertilizers. Seminar, conference and banquet.
1200 Attendees
Frequency: December, St. Louis

10436 Agro-International Trade Fair for Agricultural Machinery & Equipment

Glahe International
PO Box 2460
Germantown, MD 20875-2460

301-515-0012
FAX 301-515-0016

Biennial show of agricultural machinery and equipment.

10437 All Candy Expo

National Confectioners Association
110 30th Street NW
Suite 200
Washington, DC 20007

202-534-1440
E-Mail: AllCandyExpo@CandyUSA.com
Home Page: allcandyexpo.com

Theresa Delaney, Expo/Membership Director
Daria Moore, Exhibits Manager

A trade show offering exhibits of confectionery industry supplies.
5000+ Attendees
Frequency: Annual/June

10438 All Things Organic Conference and Trade Show

Organic Trade Association
28 Vernon St.
Suite 413
Brattleboro, VT 05301

802-275-3800
FAX 802-275-3801
E-Mail: info@ota.com
Home Page: www.ota.com

Christine Bushway, Executive Director
Linda Lutz, Membership Manager
Laura Batcha, Marketing/Public Relations Director

Join OTA members, Board and staff for association business, member meetings, and social and networking events.
Frequency: Annual/June

10439 America's Supermarket Showcase

National Grocer's Association
1825 Samuel Morse Drive
Reston, VA 20190

703-437-5300
FAX 703-437-7768

Dan Rudt

350 exhibits of food and non food consumer goods and services, fixtures and equipment for supermarket operations. Workshop, conference, banquet, luncheon and tours.
5000 Attendees
Frequency: Annual
Founded in 1983

10440 American Bakery Expo

5 Executive Court
Suite 2
South Barrington, IL 60010

610-667-9600
FAX 610-667-1475
E-Mail: info@americanbakeryexpo.com
Home Page: www.americanbakeryexpo.com
Social Media: *Facebook, Twitter*

Mark Gedris, Membership Manager

Sponsored by Retail Bakers of America and New York/New Jersey Bakers Association. A trade show, creative decorating competition, bakery arts and cakes display, industry chats, tips and trends demonstrations and seminars.
8000 Attendees
Frequency: Annual/October

10441 American Beverage Licensees Annual Convention & Trade Show

American Beverage Licensees
5101 River Road
Suite 108
Bethesda, MD 20816-1560

301-656-1494
FAX 301-656-7539
Home Page: www.nabronline.org

Harry Wiles, Executive Director
Susan Day Pirieda, Office Manager

Annual show of 75 manufacturers, suppliers and distributors of alcoholic beverages.
700 Attendees
Frequency: March

10442 American Butter Institute Annual Conference

American Butter Institute
2101 Wilson Boulevard
Suite 400
Arlington, VA 22201

703-243-5630
FAX 703-841-9328
E-Mail: AMiner@nmpf.org
Home Page: www.butterinstitute.org

The annual conference and meeting is a joint project between the American Butter Institute and the American Diary Products Institute. Over 600 manufacturers, marketers and suppliers of butter and dairy products are represented at the convention which offers the opportunity to network with industry professionals.
Frequency: Annual/November

10443 American Convention of Meat Processors

American Association of Meat Processors
One Meating Place
Elizabethtown, PA 17022

717-367-1168
FAX 717-367-9096
E-Mail: aamp@aamp.com
Home Page: www.aamp.com

Tom K Inboden, President
Jon Frohling, First VP
Daniel T Weber, Second VP

Features a serious educational program for operators, sparkling entertainment, fun and fellowship...plus exhibits and displays by leading industry manufacturers and suppliers.
Frequency: Annual

10444 American Convention of Meat Processors & Suppliers' Exhibition

American Association of Meat Processors
One Meating Place
Elizabethtown, PA 17022

717-367-1168
FAX 717-367-9096

E-Mail: aamp@aamp.com
Home Page: www.aamp.com

Jon Frohling, President
Tim J. Haen, 1st Vice President
Kevin Western, 2nd Vice President
Gary Bardine, 3rd Vice President
Michael D. Sloan, Treasurer

Geared toward U.S., Canadian, and Foreign operators of small and very small firms in the meat, poultry & food business: packers, processors, wholesalers, HRI, retailers, caterers, deli operators, home food service dealers, and catalog marketers. Both members and non-members of the Association attend this event looking for a vast array of ideas, supplies, and services.
1400 Members
Founded in 1939

10445 American Correctional Food Service Association Conference
ACFSA
4248 Park Glen Road
Minneapolis, MN 55416-4758

952-928-4658
FAX 952-929-1318
E-Mail: webmaster@acfsa.org
Home Page: www.acfsa.org

Karen Wesloh, Executive Director
Hope Cook, Assistant Director Exhibits
Gloria Grove, Assistant Director Atendees

Annual exhibit of 200 exhibitors of food products, kitchen equipment, food processing equipment, dining facility equipment, tableware and related food service equipment.
450 Attendees
Frequency: August
Founded in 1999

10446 American Craft Beer Week
Brewers Association
736 Pearl Street
Boulder, CO 80302

303-447-0816
888-822-6273
FAX 303-447-2825
E-Mail: webmaster@brewersassociation.org
Home Page: www.beertown.org
Social Media: *Facebook, Twitter*

Chris P. Frey, Chair
Jake Keeler, Vice Chair
Roxanne Westendorf, Secretary

Celebrates craft brewers and craft beer culture in the US.
1900 Members
Founded in 1978

10447 American Cured Meat Championships, Cured Meat Competition
American Association of Meat Processors
One Meating Place
Elizabethtown, PA 17022

717-367-1168
FAX 717-367-9096
E-Mail: aamp@aamp.com
Home Page: www.aamp.com

Jon Frohling, President
Tim J. Haen, 1st Vice President
Kevin Western, 2nd Vice President
Gary Bardine, 3rd Vice President
Michael D. Sloan, Treasurer

This competition is the only national event of its kind in North America. Meat processors enter their products for evaluation by judges who are meat scientists and specialists in the meat industry. This evaluation provides information for product enhancement that could result in greater sales and business opportunities.
1400 Members
Founded in 1939

10448 American Farm Bureau Federation Annual Convention
600 Maryland Avenue SW
Suite 1000
Washington, DC 20024

202-406-3600
FAX 202-406-3602
E-Mail: bstallman@fb.org
Home Page: www.fb.org

Bob Stallman, President
Kathleen Early, Director
Julie Anna Potts, Secretary

Exhibits of farm equipment, chemical fertilizers and agricultural equipment and supplies.
6M Attendees
Frequency: Annual/January

10449 American Mushroom Institute
North American Mushroom Conference
1 Massachusetts Avenue, Suite 800
Washington, DC 20001

202-842-4344
FAX 202-408-7763

Laura Phelps, President

10450 American Peanut Research and Education Society Annual Meeting
American Peanut Research and Education Society
Oklahoma State University
376 Ag Hall
Stillwater, OK 74078

405-372-3052
FAX 405-624-6718
Home Page: www.apres.okstate.edu

Ron Sholar, Executive Officer

Annual meetings of the Society are held for the presentation of papers and/or discussion, and for the transaction of business. At least one general business session will be held during regular annual meetings at which reports from the executive officer and all standing committees will be given to such other matters as the Board of Directors may determine.
Frequency: Annual/July

10451 American Society for Enology and Vinticulture Annual Meeting
American Society for Enology and Vinticulture
PO Box 1855
Davis, CA 95617

530-753-3142
FAX 530-753-3318
E-Mail: society@asev.org
Home Page: www.asev.org

Bill Mead, Event/Tradeshow Coordinator

With technical sessions, research forums, symposia and a supplier shocasw.
Frequency: June
Founded in 1951
Mailing list available for rent

10452 American Spice Trade Association Annual Meeting
2025 M Street NW
Washington, DC 20036

202-367-1127
FAX 202-367-2127
E-Mail: info@astaspice.org
Home Page: www.astaspice.org

Cheryl Deem, Executive Director

10453 American Sugarbeet Growers Asscociation Annual Meeting
American SugarBeet

1156 15th Street NW
Suite 101
Washington, DC 20005-1704

202-833-2398
FAX 202-833-2962
E-Mail: RGeib@americansugarbeet.org
Home Page: www.americansugarbeet.org

Ruthann Geib, Meetings Director/VP
Luther Markwart, Executive VP
James Creek, Executive Assistant
Pam Alther, Office/Financial Manager

Attendees are primarily the officers and board members of these local associations and their spouses, as well as representatives of seed, chemical, and other supplier companies. The purpose of the Annual Meeting is to bring members up-to-date on legislative and international issues that affect the domestic sugar industry, and to determine future policy and strategies.
350 Attendees
Frequency: July/November
Founded in 1983

10454 American Wine Society
3006 Latta Road
Rochester, NY 14612-3298

585-225-7613
FAX 585-225-7613
E-Mail: angel910@aol.com
Home Page: americanwinesociety.com

Angel E Nardone, Executive Director

Twelve booths.
600 Attendees
Frequency: November
Founded in 1967

10455 Animal Transportation Association
PO Box 797095
Dallas, TX 75379-7095

FAX 214-769-2867

Cherie Derouin, Administrator
Sherry Lynne Boone, Administrative Assistant

An international association promoting the humane handling and transportation of animals.
10-15 booths.
150 Attendees
Frequency: Spring

10456 Annual Chicken Marketing Seminar
National Poultry & Food Distributors
2014 Osborne Road
Saint Marys, GA 31558

770-535-9901
FAX 770-535-7385
E-Mail: kkm@npfda.org
Home Page: www.npfda.org

Chris Sharp, President
Al Acunto, Vice President
Marc Miro, Treasurer
Kristin McWhorter, Executive Director

Features a very informative program, great networking opportunities, and golf. Learn new techniques for greater marketing success.
Frequency: Annual/July
Founded in 1967

10457 Annual Conference of the Food Distribution Research Society
Food Distribution Research Society
PO Box 441110
Fort Washington, MD 20749

301-292-1970
FAX 301-292-1787
E-Mail: Jonathan_baros@ncsu.edu
Home Page: fdrs.tamu.edu

John Park, President
Ron Rainey, President-Elect
Kellie Raper, Secretary/ Treasurer

Jennifer Dennis, Director
Stan Ernst, Director

Meeting the quality demands of food buyers. Discuss how the industry is meeting these specific aspects of quality demands, and how these factors impact trade success, how members of the food chain are incorporating them in food production and handling, and how sensory examination is incorporated into food quality assurance, design and product development.
Frequency: Annual/October

10458 Annual Food Manufacturing & Packaging Expo and Conference
The Foodservice Group, Inc
PO Box 681864
Marietta, GA 30068-0032

770-971-8116
FAX 770-971-1094
E-Mail: kreynolds@fsgroup.com
Home Page: www.fsgroup.com

Chris Bresler, President
Brad Johnson, Vice President
Bob Sheridan, Secretary
Bryan Lewis, Treasurer

This event attracts a diverse range of professionals including CEO's, plant managers, puchasing managers, production and quality assurance managers, engineers, and sales/marketing managers as well as mechanics on the production floor. See and experience the latest technology, systems and related information to improve business operations.
Frequency: Annual/January

10459 Annual Hotel, Motel and Restaurant Supply Show of the Southeast
Leisure Time Unlimited
PO Box 332
Myrtle Beach, SC 29577

843-448-9483
800-261-5991
FAX 843-626-1513
E-Mail: hmrss@sc.rr.com
Home Page: www.hmrsss.com
Social Media: *Facebook, Twitter*

Trade show for the hospitality industry.
23000 Attendees
Frequency: Annual/January

10460 Annual Meat Conference
American Meat Institute
1150 Connecticut Ave NW
12th Floor
Washington, DC 20036-4126

202-587-4200
FAX 202-587-4300
Home Page: www.meatami.com
Social Media: *Facebook, Twitter*

Dennis Vignieri, Chairman
Larry Odom, Vice Chairman
Nick Meriggioli, Treasurer
Greg Benedict, Secretary
J. Patrick Boyle, President & CEO

The educational format of this conference includes a variety of ways to explore the latest developments in meat retailing today. Gain tools, insights, inspiration and new ideas to differentiate unique products and services, fortify marketing ROI, increase sales, and build customer loyalty.
300 Members
Frequency: Membership Fees Vary
Founded in 1906

10461 Annual Sugar Outlook
1300 L Street NW
Suite 1001
Washington, DC 20005

202-785-1122
FAX 202-785-5019

E-Mail: sugar@sugar.org
Home Page: www.sugar.org
Social Media: *Facebook, Twitter*

Andrew Briscoe, President/CEO
Charles W Baker, Executive VP/Chief Science Officer
Melanie Miller, VP Public Relations
Cheryl Digges, VP Public Publicy & Education

To discuss sugar consumption and demand issues and initiatives.
Frequency: Annual/April

10462 Asia Food Processing & Packaging Technology Exhibition
Reed Exhibition Companies
383 Main Avenue
PO Box 6059
Norwalk, CT 06851

203-840-4800
FAX 203-840-9628

One hundred and seventy four exhibitors for an audience of manufacturers, packaging design and development professionals.
Frequency: Biennial

10463 Associated Food Dealers Annual Trade Show
Associated Food Dealers of Michigan
18470 W Ten Mile
Southfield, MI 48075

248-557-9600
FAX 248-557-9610
Home Page: www.afdom.org

Ginny Bennett, Show Manager
Frequency: September

10464 Association for Dressing and Sauces Annual Meeting
1100 Johnson Ferry Road
Atlanta, GA 30342

404-252-3663
FAX 404-252-0774
E-Mail: ads@kellencompany.com
Home Page: www.dressings-sauces.org
Social Media: *Facebook*

Pam Chumley, President
Jeannie Milewski, Executive Director
Jacque Knight, Membership/Administration Manager

Learn about the most up-to-date technologies and guidelines for packaging, food safety, emulsions and quality.
Frequency: Annual/October

10465 Association of College Unions International Conference
One City Centre, 120 W. 7th St.
Suite 200
Bloomington, IN 47404

812-245-2284
FAX 812-245-6710
E-Mail: acui@acui.org
Home Page: www.acui.org

Rich Steele, President
Marsha Herman-Betzen, Executive Director
Andrea Langeveld, Marketing

International conference with 100 exhibits of graphic supplies, recreation equipment, computer hardware & software, furnishings, entertainment and speaker bureau information, food service equipment, and more related information and supplies.
1000 Attendees
Frequency: Annual

10466 Atlantic Bakery Expo
Retail Bakers of America

202 Village Circle
Suite 1
Slidell, LA 70458

985-643-6504
800-638-0924
FAX 985-643-6929
E-Mail: Info@RBAnet.com
Home Page: www.rbanet.com
Social Media: *Facebook*

Felix Sherman, Sr., President
Kenneth Downey, Sr., 1st Vice President
Marlene Goetzeler, 2nd Vice President
Dale A. Biles, Treasurer
Susan Nicolais, CAE, Secretary

A complete educational program with demonstrations, seminars and hands-on classes to go along with a trade show floor packed with all the exhibitors.
2000 Members
Frequency: Annual
Founded in 1918

10467 Atlantic Coast Exposition: Showcasing the Vending and Food Service Industry
InfoMarketing
2501 Aerial Center Parkway
Suite 103
Morrisville, NC 27560

919-459-2070
FAX 919-459-2075
Home Page: www.atlanticcoastexpo.com
Social Media: *Facebook*

Sarah Gillian, Executive Director

This convention offers exhibits of vending machines, office coffee service products, commissary equipment, food and beverage products for the institututional market, as well as accountability systems and security devices.
3M Attendees
Frequency: Annual/May

10468 B&CMA Convention
Biscuit & Cracker Manufacturer's Association
6325 Woodside Court
Suite 125
Columbia, MD 21046

443-545-1645
FAX 410-290-8585
E-Mail: kkurowski@thebcma.org
Home Page: www.thebcma.org

Stacey Sharpless, President
Kerry Kurowski, Education/Meetings Manager

Provides members an invaluable opportunity to network with fellow executives.
Founded in 1901

10469 BIF Annual Meeting and Research Symposium
Red Angus Association of America
4201 N Interstate 35
Denton, TX 76207-3415

940-387-3502
FAX 888-829-5573
E-Mail: info@redangus.org
Home Page: www.redangus.org
Social Media: *Facebook*

Joe Mushrush, President
Greg Comstock, CEO

Seedstock and commercial cow-calf producers, university specialists and breed association leaders will gather to explore innovative technologies and management practices to improve beef production for the benefit of seedstock and commercial producers.
2000 Members
Founded in 1954

10470 BakingTech

American Society of Baking
PO Box 336
Swedesboro, NJ 08085

800-713-0462
FAX 888-315-2612
E-Mail: info@asbe.org
Home Page: www.asbe.org

Technical sessions, receptions, luncheons, meetings, speakers, and ceremonies with industry experts sharing their knowledge, ideas and experience.
Frequency: Annual/March

10471 Beer, Wine & Spirits Industry Trade Show

Indiana Association of Beverage
200 S Meridian Street
Suite 350
Indianapolis, IN 46225

317-684-7580
FAX 317-673-4210

Teresa Koch, Show Manager

Annual show of 125 exhibitors of alcohol beverage distillers brewers that are recognized primary sources in the state of Indiana as supplies for retailers.
2500 Attendees

10472 Beltwide Cotton Conference

National Cotton Council of America
7193 Goodlett Farms Parkway
Cordova, TN 38016

901-274-9030
FAX 901-725-0510
Home Page: www.cotton.org/beltwide/

Mark Lange, President/CEO
A. John Maguire, Senior Vice President

Offers a forum for agricultural professionals.
Frequency: Annual/January

10473 Big Iron Farm Show and Exhibition

Red River Valley Fair Association
PO Box 797
West Fargo, ND 58058-0797

701-282-2200
800-456-6408
FAX 701-282-6909
E-Mail: bryan@redrivervalleyfair.com
Home Page: www.bigironfarmshow.com

Bryan Schulz, Manager

Connects agricultural exhibitors and attendees who all come together for one purpose, to advance agriculture.
80M Attendees
Frequency: Annual/September

10474 Branding ID: Strategies to Drive Sales

Association of Sales & Marketing Companies
1010 Wisconsin Avenue NW #900
Washington, DC 20007

202-337-9351
FAX 202-337-4508
E-Mail: info@asmc.org

Mark Baum, President
Karen Connell, Executive VP
Rick Abraham, VP/COO Foodservice
Jamie DeSimone, Director Marketing/Member Services
Frequency: March

10475 CFESA Conference

Commercial Food Equipment Service Association

2216 W Meadowview Road
Suite 100
Greensboro, NC 27407

336-346-4700
FAX 336-346-4745
E-Mail: asidders@cfesa.com
Home Page: www.cfesa.com
Social Media: *Facebook, LinkedIn, MySpace, YouTube*

Scott Hester, President

Held twice yearly, members benefit from networking within the foodservice industry, viewing high quality presentations and speeches, visiting interactive workshops, and learning from group meetings to create awareness of new development.
450 Members
Frequency: Bi-Annual
Founded in 1963

10476 CMAA's World Conference on Club Management & Club Business Expo

Club Managers Association of America
1733 King Street
Alexandria, VA 22314

703-739-9500
FAX 703-739-0124
E-Mail: cmaa@cmaa.org
Home Page: www.cmaa.org

Guy Doria, Show Manager
Jim Singerling, Executive VP

Provides a variety of unique education opportunities that reflect the latest trends in the club industry.
5000 Attendees
Frequency: Annual/February

10477 California League of Food Processors Expo & Showcase of Processed Foods

980 Ninth Street
Sacramento, CA 95814

916-444-9260
FAX 916-444-2746
Home Page: www.clfp.com

Robert Graf, President/CEO
Ed Yates, Senior VP
Nora Basrai, Meetings/Members Services
Rob Neenan, Senior Vice President
Amy Alcorn, Marketing Manager

Information, networking and displays of processed food from apricots to zucchini in every package type imaginable.
Frequency: January
Founded in 1905

10478 Candy Hall of Fame

National Confectionery Sales Association
Spitfire House
3135 Berea Road
Cleveland, OH 44111

216-631-8200
FAX 216-631-8210
E-Mail: info@candyhalloffame.org
Home Page: www.candyhalloffame.com/NCSA
Social Media: *Facebook, Twitter*

Michael F. Gilmore, Chairman
Alastair Northway, President
Mark Antonucci, 1st Vice President
Joe Muck, 2nd Vice President
Morton B. Gleit, Treasurer

Recognizes the achievements of industry leaders drawn from across the world. Inductees are selected from numerous nominations of candy brokers, sales personnel, manufacturers, retail buyers, wholesalers, industry suppliers, retail confectioners and others allied to the industry.
375 Members
Founded in 1899

10479 CaterSource

PO Box 14776
Chicago, IL 60614

773-525-6800
800-932-3632
FAX 800-387-4744
E-Mail: info@catersource.com
Home Page: www.catersource.com

Micheal Roman, President
Jean Blackmer, Creative Director
Laurie Scheel, Advertising Director

10480 Cattle Industry Convention

Red Angus Association of America
4201 N Interstate 35
Denton, TX 76207-3415

940-387-3502
FAX 888-829-5573
E-Mail: info@redangus.org
Home Page: www.redangus.org
Social Media: *Facebook*

Joe Mushrush, President
Greg Comstock, CEO

The oldest and largest convention for the cattle business. The convention and trade show create a unique, fun environment for cattle industry members to come together to network, create policy for the industry and to have some fun.
2000 Members
Founded in 1954

10481 Chicken Marketing Seminar

National Chicken Council
1015 15th Street NW
Suite 930
Washington, DC 20005-2622

202-296-2622
FAX 202-293-4005
E-Mail: ncc@chickenusa.org
Home Page: www.nationalchickencouncil.org
Social Media: *Facebook*

Michael J. Brown, President
William P. Roenigk, Senior Vice President
Mary M. Colville, VP of Government Affairs
Dr. Ashley Peterson, VP of Science & Technology

Brings together poultry marketing and sales managers, distributors, supermarket and foodservice buyers, further processors, traders and brokers, and other executives working in the chicken industry. Informative general sessions, social networking events, and recreational opportunities.
Frequency: Annual/July
Founded in 1954

10482 Commodity Classic

American Soybean Association
12125 Woodcrest Executive Drive
Suite 100
Saint Louis, MO 63141-5009

314-576-1770
800-688-7692
FAX 314-576-2786
E-Mail: registration@commodityclassic.com
Home Page: www.commodityclassic.com

Meeting and exhibits of soybean industry related equipment and information.
4000 Attendees
Frequency: Annual/March

10483 Conference on New Food & Beverage Concepts Innovators

NorthStar Conferences
1211 Avenue of the Americas
New York, NY 10036

212-596-6006
FAX 212-596-6092

E-Mail: cservice@northstarconferences.com
Home Page: www.northstarconferences.com

Cheryl Callahan, Marketing Director

10484 Council of Food Processors Association Annual Convention

1401 New York Avenue NW
Suite 400
Washington, DC 20005-2124

202-471-1835
FAX 202-639-5932

John Cady, President
Barbara Arnwine, Executive Director

10485 Craft Brewers Conference and Brew Expo America

Brewers Association
736 Pearl Street
Boulder, CO 80302

303-447-0816
888-822-6273
FAX 303-447-2825
Home Page: www.craftbrewersconference.com

Charlie Papazian, President
Bob Pease, VP
Cindy Jones, Sales/Marketing Director

For professional brewers, CBC is the number one environment in North America for concentrated, affordable brewing education and idea sharing to improve brewery quality and performance.
2600 Attendees
Frequency: Annual/May

10486 Crop Life America & RISE Spring Conference

Crop Life America
1156 15th St NW
Washington, DC 20005-1752

202-296-1585
FAX 202-463-0474
E-Mail: webmaster@croplifeamerica.org
Home Page: www.croplifeamerica.org
Social Media: *Facebook, Twitter, LinkedIn, YouTube*

Jay Vroom, President
Rich Nolan, VP

Discuss the most up-to-date science and regulatory issues impacting the crop protection and specialty pesticide industries.
Frequency: Annual/April

10487 Crop Science Society of America Meeting and Exhibits

Crop Science Society of America
677 S Segoe Road
Madison, WI 53711-1048

608-273-8086
FAX 608-273-2021
E-Mail: tmoeller@agronomy.org
Home Page: www.crops.org

John Nicholiadis, Managing Editor
David M Kral, Associate Executive VP
Ellen Bergfeld, Executive VP

Annual exhibits of agricultural equipment, supplies and services.
Frequency: October

10488 Dairy-Deli-Bake Seminar & Expo

International Dairy-Deli-Bakery Association
636 Science Drive
Madison, WI 53711-1073

608-310-5000
FAX 608-238-6330
E-Mail: iddba@iddba.org
Home Page: www.iddba.org

Judy Valaskey, Membership Coordinator

The largest show in the world serving these categories. Also the most focused show be-

cause it only targets the serious buyers, merchandisers, and executives who have a shared passion for food.
7000 Attendees
Frequency: Annual/June

10489 Distribution Solutions Conference

International Foodservice Distributors Association
1410 Spring Hill Road
Suite 210
McLean, VA 22102-3035

703-532-9400
FAX 703-538-4673
Home Page: www.ifdaonline.org

Mark Allen, President & CEO
Jonathan Eisen, Senior VP/ Government Relations

Includes a robust operations agenda that incorporates warehouse and transportation issues, plus a powerful executive track, people issues in an HR track, and special sessions on convenience distribution and supply chain issues.
Frequency: Annual/October

10490 Dixie Classic Fair

City of Winston-Salem
PO Box 7525
Winston-Salem, NC 27109

336-727-2236
FAX 336-727-2236

David Sparks, Executive Director

10491 EMDA Industry Showcase

Equipment Marketing & Distribution Association
PO Box 1347
Iowa City, IA 52244

319-354-5156
FAX 319-354-5157
E-Mail: pat@emda.net
Home Page: www.emda.net

Patricia A Collins, Executive VP

Annual convention and 130 exhibits of equipments, supplies and services for wholesaler-distributor and independent manufacturer's representatives of shortline and specialty farm equipment, light industrial, lawn and garden, turf care equipment, eestate and park maintenance equipment.
600 Attendees
Frequency: Annual/November

10492 EastPack

Cannon Communications
11444 W Olympic Boulevard
Los Angeles, CA 90064-1549

323-755-7646
FAX 310-996-9499
Home Page: www.eastpackshow.com

10493 Eastern Perishable Products Association Trade Show

Eastern Perishable Products Association
17 Park Street
Wanaque, NJ 07465

973-831-4100
FAX 973-831-8100
Home Page: www.eppainc.org

Barry Kahn, President
Steve Migliara, Administrative Vice President

For the perishable food industry, including dairy, deli, bakery, seafood, food service, meat ect. Exhibitors are manufacturers and services of perishable food products. Attendees are buyers, executives, managers and supervisors of

supermarket chains, independents and specialty stores. 400 Booths
8M Attendees
Frequency: April
Founded in 1971

10494 El Foro

WATT Publishing Company
122 S Wesley Avenue
Mount Morris, IL 61054-1497

815-734-4171
FAX 815-734-7727
E-Mail: olentine@wattmm.com
Home Page: www.wattnet.com

James Watt, Owner

A trade show and technical symposium for the Latin American poultry, pig and feed industries. Containing 50 booths and 150 exhibits.
275 Attendees
Frequency: July

10495 Executive Conference

Association of Sales & Marketing Companies
1010 Wisconsin Avenue NW
#900
Washington, DC 20007

202-337-9351
FAX 202-337-4508
E-Mail: info@asmc.org

Mark Baum, President
Karen Connell, Executive VP
Rick Abraham, VP/COO Foodservice
Jamie DeSimone, Director Marketing/Member Services
Frequency: July

10496 Executive Leadership Forum

Snack Food Association
1600 Wilson Blvd
Suite 650
Arlington, VA 22209-2510

703-836-4500
800-628-1334
FAX 703-836-8262
E-Mail: sfa@sfa.org
Home Page: www.sfa.org

James A McCarthy, President/CEO

An invitation only event for CEO's and senior level executives in the international snack food industry.
800 Members
Frequency: Annual/September
Founded in 1937

10497 Expo Carnes

Consejo Mexicano de la Carne
Ave. Parque Fundidora
#505 Loc. 88, P.N. Col. Obrera
Monterrey N.L. Mexico

52(81)8369 6660
FAX 52(81)8369 6732
E-Mail: lsierra@apex.org.mx
Home Page: www.expocarnes.com

The every other year Meat Industry International Exposition and Convention that brings together meat suppliers, meat packers and other sectors of the meat industry, facilitating meat specialists from around the world to do business in Latin America. This event takes place in February 2011.
150 Members

10498 Expo of the Americas

EJ Krause & Associates

6550 Rock Spring Drive
Suite 500
Bethesda, MD 20817-1126

301-493-5500
FAX 301-493-5705
Home Page: www.ejkrause.com

Ned Krause, President

Annual show and exhibits of hotel and restaurant food and beverages.

10499 FEMA Annual Convention
FEMA
1620 I Street NW
Suite 925
Washington, DC 20006

202-293-5800
FAX 202-462-8998
Home Page: www.femaflavor.org
Social Media: *YouTube*

Ed R. Hays, Ph.D., President
George C. Robinson, III, President Elect
Mark Scott, Treasurer
Arthur Schick, VP & Secretary
John Cox, Executive Director

FEMA is comprised of flavor manufacturers, flavor users, flavor ingredient suppliers and others with an interest in the U.S. flavor industry.
Founded in 1909

10500 FEMA Winter Committee Meetings
FEMA
1620 I Street NW
Suite 925
Washington, DC 20006

202-293-5800
FAX 202-462-8998
Home Page: www.femaflavor.org
Social Media: *YouTube*

Ed R. Hays, Ph.D., President
George C. Robinson, III, President Elect
Mark Scott, Treasurer
Arthur Schick, VP & Secretary
John Cox, Executive Director

FEMA is comprised of flavor manufacturers, flavor users, flavor ingredient suppliers and others with an interest in the U.S. flavor industry.
Founded in 1909

10501 FFA National Agricultural Career Show
5632 Mount Vernon Memorial Highway
Alexandria, VA 22309-1502

888-332-2668
FAX 800-366-6556
E-Mail: jack-pitzer@ffa.org
Home Page: www.ffa.org

Jack Pitzer, Show Manager

Eight hundred and fifty booths encouraging high school youth to select careers in the agricultural industry.
45M Attendees
Frequency: November

10502 FIAE Annual Convention
Food Industry Association Executives
5657 W. 10770 North
Highland, UT 84003-2711

801-599-1095
FAX 815-550-1731
E-Mail: jolsen@fiae.net
Home Page: www.fiae.net

Jim Olsen, President

Format of the convention continues to provide valuable information and networking opportunities.
125 Members
Frequency: Annual/November
Founded in 1927

10503 FMI/AMI Annual Meat Conference
American Meat Institute
1150 Connecticut Avenue NW
Washington, DC 20036

202-587-4200
FAX 202-587-4223
Home Page: www.meatconference.com

Eric Zito, Manager, Convention & Member Svcs

400 booths for equipment, supplies and services to the meat-packaging industry.
12M Attendees
Frequency: Annual/Spring

10504 FPSA Annual Conference
Food Processing Suppliers Association
1451 Dolley Madison Blvd
Suite 101
Mc Lean, VA 22101-3850

703-761-2600
FAX 703-761-4334
E-Mail: info@fpsa.org
Home Page: www.fpsa.org
Social Media: *Facebook, Twitter, LinkedIn*

David Seckman, President
George Melnykovich, Senior Advisor
Robyn Roche, CFO

Where suppliers to the food and beverage industry connet and network. Ample opportunity is given to network with peers as participants expand their industry knowledge through educational business sessions and research roundtables.
510 Members
Frequency: Annual/November
Founded in 2005

10505 Farm Progress Show
Farm Progress Companies
255 38th Avenue
Suite P
St Charles, IL 60174-5410

630-462-2224
800-441-1410
E-Mail: drovner@farmprogress.com
Home Page: www.farmprogressshow.com
Social Media: *Facebook, Twitter*

Matt Jungmann, National Shows Manager

Annual farm show of 400 exhibitors representing various types of agricultural products and services for farmers and agribusiness, including small operations to top producers.
Frequency: Annual/August

10506 Farm Science Review
Ohio State University
590 Woody Hayes Drive
Agricultural Engr. Building- Rm 232
Columbus, OH 43210

614-292-3671
800-644-6377
FAX 614-292-9448
E-Mail: fendrick.1@osu.edu
Home Page: fsr.osu.edu
Social Media: *Facebook, Twitter, YouTube, Flickr*

Craig Fendrick, Manager

Annual show of 625 exhibitors of agricultural equipment, supplies and services.
140M Attendees
Frequency: Annual/September

10507 Farmfest
Farm Fairs

PO Box 731
Lake Crystal, MN 56055-0731

507-726-6863
800-347-5863
FAX 507-726-6750

Annual show of 450 manufacturers, suppliers and distributors of farm equipment and machinery, computers and software products, chemicals, seeds and crops, and techniques of planting, tillage and harvesting.
50M Attendees

10508 Fertilizer Outlook and Technology Conference
Fertilizer Institute
425 Third Street, SW
Suite 950
Washington, DC 20024

202-962-0490
FAX 202-962-0577
E-Mail: information@tfi.org
Home Page: www.tfi.org
Social Media: *Facebook, Twitter, LinkedIn*

Ford West, President

Geared towards industry members, financial analysts, business consultants, trade press representatives, agricultural retailers, agronomists, engineers and government economists. Key topics of discussion include new technology and issues that impact plant nutrition.
Frequency: Annual/November

10509 Fish Expo Workboat Northwest
National Fisherman Magazine
121 Free Street
PO Box 7437
Portland, ME 04112

207-842-5608
FAX 207-842-5509
E-Mail: cmmarketing@divcom.com
Home Page: www.fishexposeattle.com

Jane Bogual, Director

West Coast trade show attracting thousands of visitors from the fields of commercial fishing, workboat, port/harbor, boatbuilding, seafood processing, and other marine industries.
6,000 Attendees
Frequency: November

10510 Food & Nutrition Conference & Expo
American Dietetic Association
120 South Riverside Plaza
Suite 2000
Chicago, IL 60606

312-899-0040
800-877-1600
E-Mail: info@eatright.org
Home Page: www.eatright.org
Social Media: *Facebook, Twitter*

Katie Roski, Exhibits Manager

The premiere event for food and nutrition professionals. Features the latest nutrition science information, foodservice trends and access to the top experts.
Frequency: Annual/October

10511 Food Marketing Institute Conferences
2345 Crystal Drive
Suite 800
Arlington, VA 22202

202-452-8444
FAX 202-429-4519
E-Mail: fmi@fmi.org
Home Page: www.fmi.org

Laurel Kelly, Manager Education
Beth Watt, Contact
Tim Hammonds, CEO

Hosts shows that cover a number of different topics.

10512 Food Processing Suppliers Association Annual Conference

1451 Dolley Madison Boulevard
Suite 101
McLean, VA 22101

703-761-2600
FAX 703-761-4334
E-Mail: info@fpsa.org
Home Page: www.fpsa.org

George Melnykovich, President/CEO
Andrew Drennan, VP

Gain insights into the business of food processing and production.
Frequency: Annual/March

10513 Food Product Design

Virgo Publishing LLC
3300 N Central Avenue
Suite 300
Phoenix, AZ 85012

480-990-1101
FAX 480-675-8154
E-Mail: peggyj@vpico.com
Home Page: www.foodproductdesign.com

Peggy Jackson, Publishing Director

Publication distributed to product development professionals and corporate management executives at food and beverage manufacturing and foodservice companies.

10514 Food Safety Summit

ASI Food Safety Consultants
7625 Page Boulevard
St. Louis, MO 63133

314-725-2555
800-477-0778
FAX 314-727-2563
E-Mail: kristah@asifood.com
Home Page: www.asifood.com
Social Media: *Facebook, Twitter, LinkedIn*

Dr. W. Ernest McCullough, Vice President of Operations
Tom Huge, President, Food Safety Consultant
Gary Huge, VP, Food Safety Consultants

Provides useful food safety information and solutions to those responsible for assuring food safety across the food supply chain thereby keeping the food safety platform current and relevant for today and tomorrow.
Founded in 1930

10515 Food Safety Summit: Chicago

Eaton Hall Exhibitions
256 Columbia Turnpike
Florham Park, NJ 07932

973-514-5900
800-746-9646
FAX 973-514-5977
E-Mail: sgoldman@eatonhall.com
Home Page: www.foodsafetysummit.com

Scott Goldman, President
Michael Pesick, Exhibits/Sponsors
Amy Reimer, Registration

Food safety, quality assurance, microbiology and plant sanitation.
1500 Attendees
Frequency: October

10516 Food Safety Summit: Washington

Eaton Hall Exhibitions
256 Columbia Turnpike
Florham Park, NJ 07932

973-514-5900
800-746-9646
FAX 973-514-5977

E-Mail: sgoldman@eatonhall.com
Home Page: www.foodsafetysummit.com

Scott Goldman, President
Michael Pesick, Exhibits/Sponsors
Amy Reimer, Registration

Held in Washington DC. Food safety, quality assurance, microbiology and plant sanitation.
1500 Attendees
Frequency: March

10517 Food System Summit: Food Choices, Challenges and Realities

Crop Life America
1156 15th St NW
Washington, DC 20005-1752

202-296-1585
FAX 202-463-0474
E-Mail: webmaster@croplifeamerica.org
Home Page: www.croplifeamerica.org
Social Media: *Facebook, Twitter, LinkedIn, YouTube*

Jay Vroom, President
Rich Nolan, VP

Hosts speakers sharing a wide range of perspectives on key food and health issues focusing on four significant topic areas: food animal well-being, nutrition and health, food safety, and technology and innovation.
Frequency: Annual/October

10518 Food Tech

Glahe International
PO Box 6009
Sun City Center, FL 33571

813-633-6335
FAX 813-633-6355

Iye Boyd, President
Annual exhibits of food technology.

10519 Fresh Summit International Convention & Exposition

Produce Marketing Association
1500 Casho Mill Road
PO Box 6036
Newark, DE 19711

302-738-7100
FAX 302-731-2409
E-Mail: solutionctr@pma.com
Home Page: www.pma.com
Social Media: *Twitter, Flickr, YouTube, Xchange*

Bryan Silbermann, President & CEO
Lorna D. Christie, Vice President & COO
Duane Eaton, Senior VP, Administration
Yvonne Bull, CFO

Where participants throughout the global fresh produce and floral supply chains come together as a community to learn, network, build relationships and do business.
18500 Attendees
Frequency: Annual/October

10520 Global Minor Use Summit

Crop Life America
1156 15th St NW
Washington, DC 20005-1752

202-296-1585
FAX 202-463-0474
E-Mail: webmaster@croplifeamerica.org
Home Page: www.croplifeamerica.org
Social Media: *Facebook, Twitter, LinkedIn, YouTube*

Jay Vroom, President
Rich Nolan, VP

Brings regulators, growers, and representatives of the crop protection industry from around the world together to explore options and incentives for improving the availability of crop protection tools for production of minor crops.
Frequency: Annual/December

10521 Gourmet Products Show

George Little Management
577 Airport Boulevard
Suite 440
Burlingame, CA 94010

650-344-5171
800-272-SHOW
FAX 650-344-5270
Home Page: www.thegourmetshow.com

Susan Corwin, VP

Cookware, tabletop, gadgets, cutlery, specialtry electric appliances, home textiles, contemporary lifestyle, furnishings, garden and travel accessories, home storage items, personal care, coffee and teas and specialty foods. Contains 950 exhibitors. 2700 booths
9000 Attendees
Frequency: April

10522 Government Action Summit

American Frozen Food Institute
2000 Corporate Ridge Blvd.
Suite 1000
McLean, VA 22102-7844

703-821-0770
FAX 703-821-1350
E-Mail: info@affi.com
Home Page: www.affi.com

Kraig R. Naasz, President & CEO

National trade association representing the interests of the frozen food industry for more than 60 years. Its 540 corporate members account for more than 90 percent of the frozen food production in the US.
Frequency: Annual/September

10523 Government Affairs Conference

USA Rice Federation
4301 N Fairfax Drive
Suite 425
Arlington, VA 22203

703-226-2300
FAX 703-236-2301
E-Mail: riceinfo@usarice.com
Home Page: www.usarice.com

Jamie Warshaw, Chairman

Discuss issues and activities for the U.S. rice industry, legislation, training, and seminars.
Frequency: Annual

10524 Grape Grower Magazine Farm Show

Western Agricultural Publishing Company
4974 E Clinton Way
Suite 123
Fresno, CA 93727-1520

559-261-0396
FAX 559-252-7387

Phill Rhoads, Manager

Seminars, exhibits and prizes for grape growers. Containing 80 booths and exhibits.

10525 Great American Beer Festival

Brewers Association
736 Pearl Street
Boulder, CO 80302

303-447-0816
888-822-6273
FAX 303-447-2825
Home Page:
www.greatamericanbeerfestival.com
Social Media: *Facebook, Twitter*

Charlie Papazian, President
Bob Pease, VP
Cindy Jones, Sales/Marketing Director

Don't miss the largest gathering of beer enthusiasts.
Frequency: Annual/September

10526 GrowerExpo
Ball Publishing
PO Box 9
Batavia, IL 60510-0009

630-208-9080
800-456-5380
FAX 630-456-0132

John Martens, President

A trade show devoted to horticulture and floriculture production and marketing. 175 booths.
2M Attendees
Frequency: January

10527 HMAA Food & New Products Show
Pacific Expositions
1580 Makaola Street
Suite 1200
Honolulu, HI 92814

808-945-3594
FAX 808-946-6399

Pat Shine, General Sales Manager
Kimalar K Carroll, Show Director/Coordinator

This popular event, featuring the Food Show in
the arena and New Products Show in the exhibition hall, is the original new products expo.
Local and mainland exhibitors gather each year
to present electronic, household, recreational
and food products and service— often unvailed
for the first time in Hawaii.
96000 Attendees

10528 Hawkeye Farm Show
Midwest Shows
PO Box 737
Austin, MN 55912

507-437-7969
FAX 507-437-7752
E-Mail: salesfsu@farmshowsusa.com
Home Page: www.farmshowsusa.com

Penny Swank, Show Manager
18000 Attendees
Frequency: March

10529 Health & Nutrition Product Development Start to Finish
New Hope Natural Media
1401 Pearl Street
Suite 200
Boulder, CO 80302

303-998-9399
E-Mail: rdebarros@newhope.com

Rob DeBarros, Marketing Manager
Frequency: March, Anaheim

10530 Heart of America Hospitality Expo
Bartle Hall Convention & Entertainment Center
301 W 13th Street, Suite 100
Kansas City, MO 64105

816-513-5000
800-821-7060
FAX 816-513-5001
Home Page: www.kcconvention.com

Charles Hart II, President
Pat Bergaur, Regional Director

10531 Home Baking Association Annual Conference
10841 S Crossroads Drive
Suite 105
Parker, CO 80135

303-840-8787
FAX 303-840-6877
Home Page: www.homebaking.org

Sharon Davis, Show Manager

Learn the newest techniques and technologies
available to the home bakers of America!
Frequency: Annual

10532 Hospitality Food Service Expo
Reed Business Information
275 Washington Street
Boston, MA 02458

617-261-1166
FAX 630-288-8686
Home Page: www.reedbusiness.com

Patrick Paleno, Show Manager
Barry Reed Jr, CFO
Stuart Whayman, CFO

Four hundred booths featuring educational
seminars, culinary salon, and exhibits of products and services.
12M Attendees
Frequency: October

10533 Hydroponic Society of America
PO Box 6067
Concord, CA 94524-1067

FAX 510-232-2323

Gene Brisbon, Executive Director

Thirty five booths featuring the latest in hydroponic equipment.
500 Attendees
Frequency: April

10534 IACP Annual Conference
International Association of Culinary
Professional
1100 Johnson Ferry Road
Suite 300
Atlanta, GA 30342

404-252-3663
800-928-4227
FAX 404-252-0774
E-Mail: info@iacp.com
Home Page: www.iacp.com
Social Media: *Facebook, LinkedIn, Flickr*

Cynthia Nims, President
Doug Duda, VP & President-Elect
Julia Usher, Secretary/ Treasurer

Go behind the scenes with key industry players, getting access to the style-makers, tasting
the latest culinary trends.
3000+ Members
Frequency: Annual/March
Founded in 1978

10535 IAOM Conferences and Expos
International Association of Operative
Millers
10100 West 87th Street
Suite 306
Overland Park, KS 66212

913-338-3377
FAX 913-338-3553
E-Mail: info@iaom.info
Home Page: www.aomillers.org
Social Media: *Facebook, LinkedIn*

Bart Hahlweg, President
Joe Woodard, Executive VP
Aaron Black, Treasurer

Premier educational events for grain milling
and seed processing professionals. The annual
events gather milling and allied trade professionals from around the world for several days
of education, networking and fellowship.
Frequency: Annual/May
Founded in 1896

10536 IBA Messe Duesseldorf North America
150 N Michigan Avenue
Suite 2920
Chicago, IL 60601

312-621-5800
FAX 312-781-5188

E-Mail: info@mdna.com
Home Page: www.mdna.com

Frank Thorwirth, President
Pyon Klemon, Vice President
Eva Rowe, Vice President
Justin Kesselring, Project Manager
100 T Attendees
Frequency: October

10537 IBIE Bakery Expo
BEMA: Baking Industry Suppliers
Association
7101 College Boulevard
Suite 1505
Overland Park, KS 66210

913-338-1300
FAX 913-338-1327
E-Mail: info@bema.org
Home Page: www.ibie2007.org

Matt Zielsdorf, Convention Chairman

Co-sponsored with the American Bakers Association. event that offers complete equipment,
ingredient and supply solutions to serious baking professionals. Directors and managers from
every segment of the grain-based food industry
count on IBIE for the new technology, products, strategies and information they need to
stay competitive in all aspects of their
operation.
20000 Attendees
Frequency: October

10538 IBWA Convention & Trade Show International Bottled Water Assn
International Bottled Water Association
1700 Diagonal Road
Suite 650
Alexandria, VA 22314

703-683-5213
800-WAT-ER11
FAX 703-683-4074
E-Mail: ibwainfo@bottledwater.org
Home Page: www.bottledwater.org

Trade association representing the bottled water industry. IBWA's member companies produce and distribute 80 percent of the bottled
water sold in the US. Our membership includes
US and international bottlers, distributors and
suppliers.
3250 Attendees
Frequency: Annual/October

10539 IFDA Sales & Marketing Conference
International Foodservice Distributors
Association
1410 Spring Hill Road
Suite 210
McLean, VA 22102-3035

703-532-9400
FAX 703-538-4673
Home Page: www.ifdaonline.org

Mark Allen, President & CEO
Jonathan Eisen, Senior VP/ Government
Relations

Newest technologies and marketing ideas for
the foodservice distributors industry.
Frequency: Annual/July

10540 IFDA Supply Chain Connect
International Foodservice Distributors
Association
1410 Spring Hill Road
Suite 210
McLean, VA 22102-3035

703-532-9400
FAX 703-538-4673
Home Page: www.ifdaonline.org

Mark Allen, President & CEO
Jonathan Eisen, Senior VP/ Government
Relations

Designed to connect distributor and manufacturer counterparts involved in distributor inbound to help drive efficiencies.
Frequency: Annual/July

10541 IFEC Annual Conference
International Food Service Editorial Council
7 Point Place
PO Box 491
Hyde Park, NY 12538-491

845-229-6973
FAX 845-229-6973
E-Mail: ifec@ifeconline.com
Home Page: www.ifeconline.com
Social Media: *Facebook, Twitter*

Megan McKenna, President
Jeffrey Yarbrough, Vice President
Amelia Levin, Secretary
John Scroggins, Treasurer

Sessions with government and industry leaders, top chefs, and food tour hosts, gain new insights into the complex role that government plays in shaping America's diet, the growing impact that food environmentalism is having on foodservice, and the confluence of the two.
Frequency: Annual/November

10542 IFT Annual Meeting & Food Expo
Institute of Food Technologists
525 W Van Buren St
Suite 1000
Chicago, IL 60607-3842

312-782-8424
FAX 312-782-8348
Home Page: www.ift.org

Barbara Byrd Keenan, EVP
Marianne Gillette, President

Brings together the most repected food professionals in industry, government and academia.
20000 Attendees
Frequency: June

10543 IHA Educational Conference & Meeting of Members
International Herb Association
PO Box 5667
Jacksonville, FL 32247-5667

904-399-3241
FAX 904-396-9467
Home Page: www.iherb.org

Nancy Momsen, President
Kathryn Clayton, Vice President
Karen O'Brien, Secretary
Marge Powell, Treasurer

Conference offers tours, herb information and recipes, as well as leading industry news.
Frequency: Annual/July
Founded in 1986

10544 IMPA Convention & Trade Show
Iowa Meat Processors Association
PO Box 334
Clarence, IA 52216-0334

563-452-3329
FAX 563-452-2141
E-Mail: execdirector@iowameatprocessors.org
Home Page: www.iowameatprocessors.org

David L. Walter, President
Kent Stricker, 1st Vice President
Kevin Hastings, 2nd Vice President
Andy Thesing, 3rd Vice President

IMPA, leading the way in innovations, marketing, profits and adaptations. Also featuring a cured meat competition and product show.

10545 IS/LD Conference
1350 I Street NW
Suite 300
Washington, DC 20005

202-639-5900
FAX 202-639-5932
E-Mail: info@gmaonline.org
Home Page: www.gmabrands.com

Cindy Baker, Meetings/Conference Sr. Manager

A place where senior logistics and information technology executives from CPG manufacturers and leading retailers come together to study and seek solutions to the pressing issues affecting today's global supply chain.
Frequency: Annual/April

10546 IWLA Convention & Expo
International Warehouse Logistics Association
2800 S River Rd
Suite 260
Des Plaines, IL 60018-6003

847-813-4699
FAX 847-813-0115
E-Mail: email@iwla.com
Home Page: www.iwla.com

Joel Anderson, President & CEO
Linda Hothem, Chairman
Paul Verst, Treasurer
Tom Herche, Secretary

Promoting professional development and expose attendees to newer and better ways of doing business.
Founded in 1891

10547 Independent Bakers Association Annual Convention
Independent Bakers Association
Georgetown Station
PO Box 3731
Washington, DC 20027-0231

202-333-8190
FAX 202-337-3809
E-Mail: independentbaker@yahoo.com
Home Page: www.independentbaker.net

Enables bakers and allied industry representatives to tackle vital issues and develop strategies to enhance industry interests.
Frequency: Annual/June

10548 Institute of Food Technologists Annual Meeting & Food Expo
Institute of Food Technologists
525 W Van Buren
Suite 1000
Chicago, IL 60607-3814

312-782-8424
FAX 312-782-8348
E-Mail: info@ift.org
Home Page: www.ift.org

Roger Clemens, President
John Ruff, President-Elect
Bruce Stillings, Treasurer
Barbara Byrd Keenan, Executive VP

Technical exposition directed to the $302 billion food industry. Offering person-to-person marketplace and technical forum for suppliers of food ingredients. 2,400 booths.
24M Attendees
Frequency: Annual/June

10549 International Air Conditioning, Heating & Refrigerating Expo
ASHRAE
1791 Tullie Circle NE
Atlanta, GA 30329

404-636-8400
800-527-4723
FAX 404-321-5478

E-Mail: ashrae@ashrae.org
Home Page: www.ashrae.org

William A Harrison, President
Jeff H Littleton, Executive VP

The largest HVAC&R event in America featuring over 1,600 exhibiting companies. Held in conjunction with the ASHRAE Winter Meeting
30000 Attendees
Frequency: Annual/January

10550 International Assoc of Operative Millers Technical Conference/Trade Show
International Association of Operative Millers
10100 W 87th Street
Suite 306
Overland Park, KS 66212

913-338-3377
FAX 913-338-3553
E-Mail: info@iaom.info
Home Page: www.aomillers.org
Social Media: *Facebook, LinkedIn*

Joe Woodard, President
Aaron Black, Vice President
Joel Hoffa, Treasurer
Melinda Farris, Executive VP

Conference, banquet and over 100 exhibits of cereal milling equipment, ancillary equipment, supplies and information.
Frequency: Annual/May

10551 International Baking Industry Exposition
Retail Bakers of America
202 Village Circle
Suite 1
Slidell, LA 70458

985-643-6504
800-638-0924
FAX 985-643-6929
E-Mail: Info@RBAnet.com
Home Page: www.rbanet.com
Social Media: *Facebook*

Felix Sherman, Sr., President
Kenneth Downey, Sr., 1st Vice President
Marlene Goetzeler, 2nd Vice President
Dale A. Biles, Treasurer
Susan Nicolais, CAE, Secretary

Thousands of industry professionals unite for the world's largest, most comprehensive Baking Expo of the year. More than 700 exhibiting companies will showcase cutting-edge technologies, equipment and new products to help attendees from the grain-based foods industry strengthen their competitive position, uncover new opportunities and maximize profits.
2000 Members
Frequency: Annual/September
Founded in 1918

10552 International Beverage Industry Exposition
1101 16th Street NW
Washington, DC 20036-4803

202-857-4722

Lisa Feldman, Show Manager

450 booths.
16M Attendees
Frequency: October

10553 International Boston Seafood Show
National Fishermans Expositions
PO Box 7437
Portland, ME 04112-7437

207-842-5500
FAX 207-842-5505

Diane Vassar, Promotions Director
David Lowell, President

Nine hundred and seventy booths. Annual trade show for the seafood industry.
20M Attendees
Frequency: March

10554 International Dairy Foods Show

International Dairy Foods Association
1250 H St NW
Suite 900
Washington, DC 20005-5902

202-737-4332
FAX 202-331-7820
E-Mail: membership@idfa.org
Home Page: www.idfa.org

Constance Tipton, President
Neil Moran, Sr. VP,
Finance/Tradeshow/Admin.
Peggy Armstrong, VP, Communications
Diana Carmenates, VP, Meetings &
Educational Services
Cindy Cavallo, Director, Membership

The International Dairy Foods Association, the Milk Industry Foundation and the International Ice Cream Association work to represent the best interests of manufacturers, distributors and marketers of ice cream, frozen yogurt, frozen desserts, fluid milk, cultured dairy products, dips and other milk products.
Frequency: Annual

10555 International Exposition for Food Processors

Food Processing Machinery Association
1451 Dolly Madison Boulevard
Suite 200
McLean, VA 22101

703-761-2600
800-331-8816
FAX 703-548-6563
Home Page:
www.foodprocessingmachinery.com

Nancy Janssen, Show Manager

Show with more than 1,600 exhibitors, up-to-the-minute technology, fast-track educational sessions. Great source for solutions and networking with industry peers. Colocated with Pack Expo International. McCormick Place, Chicago, IL.
50M Attendees
Frequency: Annual/September

10556 International Food Processors Association Expo

200 Daingerfield Road
Suite 100
Alexandria, VA 22314-2884

703-299-5001
FAX 703-299-5100

George Melnykovich, Show Manager

Four hundred and twenty five booths of food processing and supplies.
16M Attendees
Frequency: January

10557 International Food Service Exposition

Florida Restaurant Association
230 S Adams Street
Tallahassee, FL 32301

850-224-2250
FAX 850-224-9213
Home Page: www.flra.com

Hosting the third largest food service show in the country with over 1,200 booths and over 23,000 qualified buyers and attendees.
22000 Attendees

10558 International Foodservice Distributors: Productivity Convention & Expo

201 Park Washington Court
Falls Church, VA 22046-4521

703-532-9400
FAX 703-538-4673
Home Page: www.ifdaonline.org

Mark Allen, President/CEO
Jonathan Eisen, Senior VP Of Government Relations

Workshops, assemblies, facility tours and an exposition are featured. Educational programming features many practitioners who sahre knowledge to be applied to various operations. Practical information for transportation, information technology, human resources and more.
Frequency: October
Founded in 2003

10559 International Fundraising Conference

Association of Fundraising Professionals
4300 Wilson Blvd.
Suite 300
Arlington, VA 22203

703-684-0410
800-666-3863
FAX 703-684-0540
Home Page: afpfc.com
Social Media: *Facebook, Twitter, LinkedIn, Instagram, YouTube*

Andrew Watt, President & CEO
Terry Rauh, Chief Operating Officer

Skills building and thought leaders in international fundraising and philanthropy.
Founded in 2006

10560 International Institute of Foods and Family Living Annual Meeting

225 W Ohio Street
Chicago, IL 60610-4198

312-527-3860
FAX 312-670-0824

Phyllis Favelman, President

10561 International Marketing Conference & Annual Membership Meeting

US Grains Council
1400 K St NW
Suite 1200
Washington, DC 20005-2449

202-789-0789
FAX 202-898-0522
E-Mail: grains@grains.org
Home Page: www.grains.org

Thomas C. Dorr, President/CEO
Wendell Shauman, Chairman
Don Fast, Vice Chairman
Julius Schaaf, Treasurer
Ron Gray, Secretary

Join Council members and guests to kick off this special meeting with a welcome reception. Great opportunity to network with industry colleagues, get acquainted with new Council members and talk with the Council's international directors and staff.
Frequency: Annual/February
Founded in 1960

10562 International Pizza Expo

MacFadden Protech
137 E Market Street
New Albany, IN 47150

812-949-0909
800-489-8324
FAX 812-949-1867

E-Mail: boakley@pizzatoday.com
Home Page: www.pizzaexpo.com

William T Oakley, Senior VP Expositions
Linda Keith, Manager
Patty Crone, Manager

One thousand booths featuring exhibits of equipment for pizza industry and restaurants.
6000 Attendees
Frequency: February/March

10563 International Poultry Expo

US Poultry & Egg Association/American Feed Assoc.
1530 Cooledge Road
Tucker, GA 30084-7303

770-493-9401
FAX 770-493-9257
E-Mail: colentine@poultryegg.org
Home Page:
www.internationalpoultryexposition.com
Social Media: *Facebook, Twitter, LinkedIn*

Charles Olentine, Executive VP
Pennie Stathes, Logistics Manager

A world large trade show for the poultry and feed sectors.
15000 Attendees
Frequency: January

10564 International Whey Conference

American Dairy Products Institute
126 N Addison St
Elmhurst, IL 60126

630-530-8700
FAX 630-530-8707
Home Page: www.iwc-2011.org

Dale Kleber, CEO

Offers an unparalleled opportunity to learn about the latest research, cutting-edge product innovations, technical developments and marketing strategies relating to this intriguing, value-added ingredient.
500 Attendees
Frequency: September

10565 Interpack

150 N Michigan Avenue
Suite 2920
Chicago, IL 60601

312-781-5180
FAX 312-781-5188
E-Mail: info@mdna.com
Home Page: www.mdna.com

Ryan Klemm, Senior Project Manager
Eva Rowe, Vice President
Justin Kesselring, Project Manager
Frequency: April

10566 JPA Annual Meeting

Juice Products Association
750 National Press Building
529 14th Street NW
Washington, DC 20045

202-785-3232
FAX 202-223-9741
E-Mail: jpa@kellencompany.com
Home Page: www.juiceproducts.org

Richard E Cristol, President
Carol Freysinger, Executive Director

Includes presentations of current interest, such as crop estimates and conditions, transportation and export problems, packaging and marketing concepts, advertising trends and government and regulatory reporting.
Frequency: Annual/Spring

10567 KFYR Radio Agri International Stock & Trade Show

KFYR Radio

PO Box 1658
Bismarck, ND 58502-1738

701-224-9393
800-472-2170
FAX 701-255-8155
E-Mail: mwall@clearchannel.com
Home Page: www.kfyr.com

Syd Stewart, General Manager
Michelle J Wall, Manager
Jim Lowe, Manager

Annual show of 250 exhibitors of agricultural equipment, supplies, livestock and services.
15000 Attendees
Frequency: February

10568 Keystone Farm Show
Lee Publications
PO Box 121
Palatine Bridge, NY 13428-0121

518-673-2269
FAX 518-673-2699
E-Mail: info@leepub.com
Home Page: www.leepub.com

Ken Maning, Show Manager
Tom Mahoney, Sales Manager

10569 MEATXPO
National Meat Association
1970 Broadway
Suite 825
Oakland, CA 94612

510-763-1533
FAX 510-763-6186
E-Mail: info@meatxpo.org
Home Page: www.meatxpo.org

Barry Carpenter, CEO
Jen Kempis, Operations Manager

Biennial suppliers' exposition that brings together consultants, equipment manufacturers and other professionals in the industry, to give a first-hand view of the newest industry equipment, packaging and related services.
Frequency: Annual/February
Founded in 1948

10570 MWR Expo
American Logistics Association
1133 15th Street NW
Suite 640
Washington, DC 20005-2708

202-466-2520
FAX 202-296-4419
E-Mail: membership@ala-national.org
Home Page: www.ala-national.org

Cologne Hunter, Meetings/Expo Director
Maurice Branch, Operations VP

A gathering of MWR professionals and brings together the many components of the Morale, Welfare and Recreation industry. The event features products and services that are sold to military and government agencies for use in community support activities on military installations throughout the world.
Frequency: Biennial/August
Founded in 1972

10571 Maraschino Cherry and Glace Fruit Processors Annual Convention
5 Ravine Drive
#776
Matawan, NJ 07747-3106

FAX 732-583-0798

Richard Sullivan, Executive VP
Frequency: April/May

10572 Marketechnics
Food Marketing Institute

800 Connecticut Avenue NW
Washington, DC 20006

202-220-0600
FAX 202-429-4519

Beth Watt, Contact
6000 Attendees

10573 Meat Industry Research Conference
American Meat Science Association
2441 Village Green Pl
Champaign, IL 61822-7676

800-517-AMSA
FAX 888-205-5834
FAX 217-356-5370
E-Mail: information@meatscience.org
Home Page: www.meatscience.org

William Mikel, President
Scott J. Eilert, President Elect
Casey B. Frye, Treasurer

Cosponsored by the American Meat Institute Foundation and the American Meat Science Association. A forum for presenting the latest research in terms of direct application for the meat industry.

10574 Mid-America Farm Show
Salina Area Chamber of Commerce
120 W Ash Street
PO Box 586
Salina, KS 67401

785-827-9301
FAX 785-827-9758
Home Page: www.salinakansas.org

Don Weiser, Show Manager

Annual show of 325 exhibitors of agricultural equipment, supplies and services, including irrigation equipment, fertilizer, farm implements, hybrid seed, agricultural chemicals, tractors, feed, farrowing crates and equipment, silos and bins, storage equipment and farm buildings.
13M Attendees
Frequency: Annual/March

10575 Mid-America Horticultural Trade Show
1000 N Rand Road
Suite 214
Wauconda, IL 60084-1188

847-526-2010
FAX 847-526-3993
E-Mail: mail@midam.org
Home Page: www.midam.org

Rand A Baldwin CAE, Managing Director
Suzanne Spohr, President
Jim Melka, Secretary

Mid-Am is the premier event featuring more than 650 leading suppliers offering countless products, equipment, and services for the horticulture industry. Mid-Am also offers a variety of educational seminars featuring the best and the brightest in the horticultural and business communities to help keep you informed of the latest trends.
Frequency: January

10576 Mid-America Resturant, Soft Serve & Pizza Exposition
Exhibition Productions
PO Box 81845
Wellesley, MA 02481

800-909-7469
FAX 617-431-2662

17000 Attendees

10577 Mid-Atlantic Food, Beverage & Lodging Expo
Restaurant Association of Maryland

6301 Hillside Court
Columbia, MD 21046

410-290-6800
800-874-1313
FAX 410-290-7898
E-Mail: dimbessi@marylandrestaurants.com
Home Page: www.midatlanticexpo.com

Dennis Imbessi, Director Expo/Membership Sales
Licia Spinelli, Director Marketing/Special Events
Valerie Maione, Owner

Annual Mid-Atlantic regional trade show of products and services for the restaurant and hospitality industry. Exhibitors include food manufacturers, equipment, beverages and services providers. Open to food service professionals, taking place annually during the month of September with 500 exhibitors and 600 booths.
15M Attendees
Frequency: Annual/October

10578 Midway USA Food Service and Hospitality Exposition
Kansas Restaurant and Hospitality Association
359 S Hydraulic Street
Wichita, KS 67211-1908

316-267-8383
FAX 316-267-8400

Dennis Carpenter, CEO

Annual show of 35 food service, beverage, suppliers.
6000 Attendees

10579 Midwest Expo: IL
Illinois Fertilizer & Chemical Association
130 W Dixie Highway
PO Box 186
Saint Anne, IL 60964-0186

815-939-1566
800-892-7122
FAX 815-427-6573

Jean Trobec, President

Annual show of 130 manufacturers, suppliers and distributors of agricultural chemical and fertilizer application equipment, supplies and services.
2500 Attendees
Frequency: August, Danville

10580 Midwest Farm Show
North Country Enterprises
5322 250th Street
Cadott, WI 54727

715-289-4632
E-Mail: nceinfo@yahoo.com
Home Page: www.northcoutnryentreprises.com

Steve Henry, President

Top farm show exhibiting dairy and Wisconsin's tillage equipment, feed and seed. 20 booths.
11M+ Attendees
Frequency: January
Founded in 1975

10581 Midwest Food Processors Association Convention/Trade Show
4600 American Pkwy
Suite 110
Madison, WI 53718-8334

608-255-9946
FAX 608-255-9838
E-Mail: info@mwfpa.org
Home Page: www.mwfpa.org

Nick George, President
Robin Fanshaw, Office Manager/Event Planner

Brian Elliott, Director of Communications
Bruce Jacobson, Chair

Processing industry members come together at
the convention to learn, network and gain insight to improve their company's course.
1M Attendees
Frequency: Annual/November
Founded in 1905

10582 Midwest Gourmet Exposition
Fairchild Urban Expositions
1395 S Marietta Parkway
Building 400, Suite 210
Marietta, GA 30067

678-901-1700
FAX 770-956-9644

Robert Collins, President

10583 Midwest Leadership Conference
Indiana Retail Grocers Association
115 W Washington Street
Suite 1364
Indianapolis, IN 46204

317-220-0033
FAX 317-231-7858

10584 Midwest Regional Grape & Wine Conference
Missouri Grape and Wine Board
1616 Missouri Boulevard
Jefferson City, MO 65109-0630

573-751-3374
800-392-WINE
FAX 573-751-2868
E-Mail: sue.berendzen@mda.mo.gov
Home Page: www.missouriwine.org
Social Media: *Facebook, Twitter, YouTube, Flickr*

Jim Anderson, Executive Director
Denise Kottwitz, Assistant

A major national conference for hundreds of
vintners, growers and wine industry executives
throughout the US Conference includes speakers, trade show, workshops and wine dinners.
Over 45 booths.
400+ Attendees
Frequency: Annual/February
Founded in 1985

10585 Midwestern Food Service and Equipment Exposition
Missouri Restaurant Association
9233 Ward Parkway
Suite 123
Kansas City, MO 64114

816-753-5222
FAX 816-753-6993
Home Page: www.morestaurants.org

Chad Treaster, President

Annual show of 200 suppliers of food service
and hospitality industries equipment, supplies
and services.
12M Attendees

10586 NAAB Annual Convention
National Association of Animal Breeders
PO Box 1033
Columbia, MO 65205

573-445-4406
FAX 573-446-2279
E-Mail: naab-css@naab-css.org
Home Page: www.naab-css.org

Gordon Doak, President
Jere Mitchell, Technical Director

A welcomer reception, election of directors,
consideration of Bylaw Amendments, resolu-

tions and other association business and a
award recognitions presentation.
Frequency: Annual/September

10587 NAAE Annual Convention
National Association of Agricultural
Educators
University of Kentucky
300 Garrigus Building
Lexington, KY 40546-215

859-257-2224
800-509-0204
FAX 859-323-3919
E-Mail: JJackman.NAAE@uky.edu
Home Page: www.naae.org

Wm Jay Jackman, Executive Director
Samantha Alvis, Associate Executive Director

Featuring a meet and greet, professional devel-
opment workshops, meetings, tours and a ca-
reer tech expo.
Frequency: Nov/Fees Vary
Founded in 1948
Mailing list available for rent

10588 NABCA Annual Conference
National Alcohol Beverage Control
Association
4401 Ford Avenue
Suite 700
Alexandria, VA 22302

703-784-4200
FAX 703-820-3551
E-Mail: jsgueo@nabca.org
Home Page: www.nabca.org
Social Media: *Facebook, Twitter*

James M Sgueo, President/CEO

An event to provides its members opportunities
to interact and conduct business. Featuring nationally known speakers, informative seminars,
interact workshops and suppliers and vendors
demonstrating their products.
Frequency: Annual

10589 NABR Tasting & Display Event Annual Convention
American Beverage Licensees
5101 River Road
Suite 108
Bethesda, MD 20816-1560

301-656-1494
FAX 301-656-7539
Home Page: www.nabronline.org

Harry Wiles, Executive Director
Shawn Ross, Office Manager

Offers exhibits on spirits, beer and wine industry supplies, equipment, bar accessories and
computers. The NABR Annual Convention is a
gathering of alcohol beverage retailers and proprietors for networking and educational opportunities. An exclusive trade display and tasting
event is held to promote brands and services of
use to retailers and proprietors. There are 25-75
booths.
500+ Attendees
Frequency: March

10590 NAC Annual Convention & Trade Show
35 E Wacker Drive
Suite 1816
Chicago, IL 60601-2103

312-236-3858
FAX 312-236-7809
Home Page: www.naconline.org
Social Media: *Facebook, LinkedIn*

John Evans Jr., President
Ron Krueger II, Board Chairman
Jeff Scudillo, President-Elect
Andrew Cretors, Treasurer

Bringing together the top food and beverage
concession leaders in the recreation and leisure-time industry at this annual event.
3M Attendees
Frequency: Annual/August
Founded in 1982

10591 NACD Annual Meeting
National Association of Conservation
Districts
509 Capitol Court NE
Washington, DC 20002-4937

202-547-6223
FAX 202-547-6450
Home Page: www.nacdnet.org
Social Media: *Facebook, Flickr*

Krysta Harden, CEO
Bob Cordova, Second Vice President

Discussions with agency leaders on priorities
for the coming years, training sessions, key
leaders in agricultural, conservation and wildlife discussing their perspectives on the future
Farm Bill, highlighted challenges and addressing areas of common interest.
Frequency: Annual/February
Founded in 1946

10592 NACS Show
National Association of Convenience Stores
1600 Duke Street
Alexandria, VA 22314

703-684-3600
FAX 703-836-4564
E-Mail: sromello@nacsonline.com
Home Page: www.nacsshow.com
Social Media: *Facebook, Twitter, LinkedIn, YouTube*

Sherri Romello, Conventions/Meeting Director
Bob Hughes, Expo/Advertising Director

Access thousands of new profit centers on the
expo floor, discover insights on issues facing
convenience and petroleum retailers in educational sessions and network with industry
peers.
24M Attendees
Frequency: Annual/October

10593 NAFEM Annual Meeting & Management Workshop
NAFEM
161 N Clark Street
Suite 2020
Chicago, IL 60601

312-821-0201
FAX 312-821-0202
E-Mail: info@nafem.org
Home Page: www.nafem.org

Steven R. Follett, President
Thomas R. Campion, President-Elect
Michael L. Whiteley, Secretary/Treasurer
Deirdre Flynn, Executive Vice President

Workshop geared toward CEOs, CFOs, COOs
and directors of member companies. Education
is offered on a wide range of topics designed to
inspire you personally and professionally.
Plenty of networking time with industry peers
is built in to encourage the exchange of ideas
and expertise.
625 Members
Frequency: Biennial/February

10594 NAFEM Show
North American Assoc of Food Equipment
Manufacture
161 N Clark Street
Suite 2020
Chicago, IL 60601

312-245-1054
FAX 312-821-0202

E-Mail: thenafemshow@nafem.org
Home Page: www.nafem.org

Deirdre Flynn, Executive VP

Attracts approximately 20,000 foodservice professionals and features 500+ exhibitors displaying products for food preparation, cooking, storage and table service.
Frequency: Biennial/February

10595 NAG Conference

National Convenience Store Advisory Group
3331 Street Road
Suite 410
Bensalem, PA 19020

215-245-4555
FAX 215-245-4060
E-Mail: jhowton@nag-net.com
Home Page: www.nag-net.com

Joseph Howton, Executive VP/COO

Promoting relationships, networking, and executable ideas and takeaways.
Frequency: Annual/September

10596 NAMA National Expo

National Automatic Merchandising Association
20 N Wacker Drive
Suite 3500
Chicago, IL 60606-3102

312-346-0370
800-331-8816
FAX 312-704-4140
E-Mail: dmathews@vending.org
Home Page: www.vending.org
Social Media: *Facebook, Twitter, YouTube*

Brad Ellis, Chairman
Mark Dieffenbach, Chairman-Elect
Pete Tullio, Vice Chairman
Dennis Hogan, Secretary/Treasurer

This event features an impressive array of the industry's newest products and hottest technology, educational sessions and unmatched networking opportunities.
5000+ Attendees
Frequency: Annual/October

10597 NAMP PROCESS EXPO

NAMP
1910 Association Drive
Reston, VA 20191-1545

703-758-1900
800-368-3043
FAX 703-758-8001
E-Mail: smoore@namp.com
Home Page: www.namp.com

Sabrina Moore, Accounting/Meeting Manager
Philip Kimball, Executive Director

Delivering the most valuable tradeshow experience to food industry suppliers and processors at the lowest possible cost.
250 Attendees
Frequency: Annual/November

10598 NAPO International Pizza Expo

National Association of Pizzeria Operators
908 S 8th Street
Suite 200
Louisville, KY 40203

502-736-9500
800-489-8324
FAX 502-736-9501
E-Mail: bmacintosh@pizzatoday.com
Home Page: www.pizzatoday.com

Bobbie MacIntosh, Booth/Sponsorship Sales Director

The trade show for the pizza industry that includes; pizzeria owners, operators, managers,

distributors and food brokers. Workshops, seminars and exhibits.
5400 Attendees
Frequency: March

10599 NASFT Fancy Food Shows

National Association for the Specialty Food Trade
136 Madison Avenue
12th Floor
New York, NY 10016

212-482-6440
FAX 212-482-6459
Home Page: www.fancyfoodshows.com
Social Media: *Facebook*

Dennis Deschaine, Chairman
Mike Silver, Vice Chairman
Shawn McBride, Treasurer
Becky Renfro Borbolla, Secretary

Held three times a year; winter, spring and summer time. Over 350 domestic exhibitors from around the country, presentations of exotic new specialty foods from all over the world, tastings, seminars and workshops. These shows are a chance to learn about each product first-hand and do business directly with the decision makers onsite.
30M Attendees
Frequency: 3x Yearly

10600 NBBQA Annual Convention

National Barbecue Association
455 S. 4th Street
Suite 650
Louisville, KY 40202

888-909-2121
FAX 502-589-3602
E-Mail: nbbqa@hqtrs.com
Home Page: www.nbbqa.org

Kell Phelps, President
Roy Slicker, President-Elect
Marc Farris, Treasurer
Bonnie Gomez, Secretary

Learn and network with a group of BBQ folks on how to better prepare and utilize grills, smokers, fuels, sauces, marinades, rubs and all the necessary utensils. Barbeque presentations, programming, demonstrations, contests, sampling and contacts and leads.
Frequency: Annual/February

10601 NBVA Annual Convention

National Bulk Vendors Association
1202 East Maryland Avenue
Suite 1K
Phoenix, AZ 85014

888-628-2872
Home Page: www.nbva.org
Social Media: *Facebook*

Bernie Schwarzli, President
Lauri Logue, Vice President
Steve Schnecher, Secretary
Andy Belsky, Treasurer & CPA

Each spring the leading manufacturers and suppliers of bulk vending machines and products display their merchandise. Featuring workshops and seminars to discuss current industry problems and interchange ideas.
530 Attendees
Frequency: Annual/Spring

10602 NBVA Conference

National Bulk Vendors Association
1202 East Maryland Avenue
Suite 1k
Phoenix, AZ 85014

888-628-2872
Home Page: www.nbva.org
Social Media: *Facebook*

Bernie Schwarzli, President
Lauri Logue, Vice President

Steve Schnecher, Secretary
Andy Belsky, Treasurer & CPA

Brings together suppliers, manufacturers, distributors and operators to see the newest products and innovations. Seminars are created to familiarize attendees with the latest bulk vending innovations and legal issues.
Frequency: Annual/April
Founded in 1950

10603 NBWA Annual Convention

National Beer Wholesalers Association
1101 King Street
Suite 600
Alexandria, VA 22314

703-683-4300
FAX 703-683-8965
E-Mail: info@nbwa.org
Home Page: www.nbwa.org
Social Media: *Facebook, Twitter*

Craig A Purser, President & CEO
Michael Johnson, EVP/Chief Advisory Officer
Rebecca Spicer, VP Public Affairs/Chief
Paul Pisano, SVP Industry Affairs & Gen. Counsel

Designed to provide valuable education programs and important networking opportunities for the beer industry. Featuring speakers and seminars on a number of topics of importance to beer distributors.
2500 Attendees
Frequency: Annual/Fall

10604 NBWA Legislative Conference

National Beer Wholesalers Association
1101 King Street
Suite 600
Alexandria, VA 22314-2944

703-683-4300
FAX 703-683-8965
E-Mail: info@nbwa.org
Home Page: www.nbwa.org
Social Media: *Facebook, Twitter, YouTube, Flickr*

Craig A Purser, President & CEO

Industry leaders meet in Washington, D.C. to discuss the industry's legislative goals and priorities with members of Congress and their staffs.
Frequency: Annual/April
Founded in 1938

10605 NBWA Trade Show

National Beer Wholesalers Association
1101 King Street
Suite 600
Alexandria, VA 22314-2944

703-683-4300
FAX 703-683-8965
E-Mail: info@nbwa.org
Home Page: www.nbwa.org
Social Media: *Facebook, Twitter, YouTube, Flickr*

Craig A Purser, President & CEO

Gives beer distributors an opportunity to interact with brewers and vendors and make valuable contacts for future business needs. Introduces distributors to new brewers as well as new products, innovative technologies and vendors who supply the materials needed to run their operations.
Frequency: Biennial
Founded in 1938

10606 NCA Annual Convention

National Coffee Association
45 Broadway
Suite 1140
New York, NY 10006

212-766-4007
FAX 212-766-5815

E-Mail: info@ncausa.org
Home Page: www.ncausa.org
Social Media: *Facebook, Twitter, LinkedIn*

Dub Hay, Chairman
John E. Boyle, Vice Chairman
Richard Emanuele, Secretary
Robert F. Nelson, President & CEO

Meet a worldwide mix of leadership in the industry in one location, get educational as well as social interaction that cannot be matched at any other convention.
Frequency: Annual/March

10607 NCA Coffee Summit
National Coffee Association
45 Broadway
Suite 1140
New York, NY 10006

212-766-4007
FAX 212-766-5815
E-Mail: info@ncausa.org
Home Page: www.ncausa.org
Social Media: *Facebook, Twitter, LinkedIn*

Dub Hay, Chairman
John E. Boyle, Vice Chairman
Richard Emanuele, Secretary
Robert F. Nelson, President & CEO

Bringing together industry knowledge and expertise, for the best available education, networking and product knowledge.
Frequency: Annual/March

10608 NCBA Annual Convention & Trade Show
National Cattlemen's Beef Association
9110 E Nichols Avenue
Suite 300
Centennial, CO 80112

303-694-0305
FAX 303-694-2851
E-Mail: dkaylor@beef.org
Home Page: www.beefusa.org
Social Media: *Facebook, Twitter*

Debbie Kaylor, Convention/Meetings Executive Dir.
Valerie Proni, Registration Manager
Kristin Torres, Trade Show Coordinator
Forest Roberts, CEO

The meeting features joint and individual meetings by five industry organizations. Over 250 companies will offer attendees a chance to see the latest products and services while networking with other cattle producers.
28000 Members
6000 Attendees
Frequency: Annual
Founded in 1898

10609 NCC's Annual Conference
National Chicken Council
1015 15th Street NW
Suite 930
Washington, DC 20005-2622

202-296-2622
FAX 202-293-4005
E-Mail: ncc@chickenusa.org
Home Page: www.nationalchickencouncil.org
Social Media: *Facebook*

Michael J. Brown, President
William P. Roenigk, Senior Vice President
Mary M. Colville, VP of Government Affairs
Dr. Ashley Peterson, VP of Science & Technology

Brings together senior executives from US chicken processing companies and allied industries to address current agricultural, public affiars, legislative, regulatory, political, economic, and world trade issues affecting the chicken industry.
Frequency: Annual/October
Founded in 1954

10610 NCIMS Conference
National Conference on Interstate Milk Shipments
585 County Farm Road
Monticello, IL 61856

217-762-2656
E-Mail: ncims.bordson@gmail.com
Home Page: www.ncims.org

Leon Townsend, Executive Secretary

Bringing together the people in the dairy industry to discuss laws that directly involve the dairy industry.
Frequency: Biennially/May
Founded in 1950

10611 NCPA's Annual Convention
National Cottonseed Products Association
866 Willow Tree Circle
Cordova, TN 38018-6376

901-682-0800
FAX 901-682-2856
E-Mail: info@cottonseed.com
Home Page: www.cottonseed.com
Social Media: *Twitter, Flickr, YouTube*

Ben Morgan, Executive VP & Secretary
Sandi Stine, Treasurer

Featuring a board of directors meeting, committee meeting, luncheons, and discussion on the latest trends in the industry.
Founded in 1897

10612 NCSLA Annual Conference
National Conference of State Liquor Administrators
C/O Massachusetts ABCC
239 Causeway Street, 1st Floor
Boston, MA 02114

617-727-3040
FAX 617-727-1510
E-Mail: cmarshall@tre.state.ma.us
Home Page: www.ncsla.org

Cheryl Marshall, Conference Coordinator

Provide opportunities for state-licensed administrators to meet and exchange ideas and information and to formulate uniform regulations, statue and laws affecting the sales of alcholic beverages.
Frequency: June/Fee Varies

10613 NICRA Annual Meeting
National Ice Cream Retailers Association
1028 W Devon Avenue
Elk Grove Village, IL 60007

847-301-7500
866-303-6960
FAX 847-301-8402
E-Mail: info@nicra.org
Home Page: www.nicra.org

Offers educational seminars, exhibits, networking and social opportunities
325 Attendees
Frequency: Annual/November
Founded in 1933

10614 NPFDA Annual Convention
National Poultry & Food Distributors
2014 Osborne Road
Saint Marys, GA 31558

770-535-9901
FAX 770-535-7385
E-Mail: kkm@npfda.org
Home Page: www.npfda.org

Chris Sharp, President
Al Acunto, Vice President
Marc Miro, Treasurer
Kristin McWhorter, Executive Director

Features the Poultry Suppliers Showcase and many opportunities to network with other industry representatives. Participating in this convention provides access to the latest indus-

try trends, presents ways to improve business operations, and increases number of industry contacts.
Frequency: Annual/January
Founded in 1967

10615 NW Food Manufacturing & Packaging Expo
Northwest Food Processors Association
9700 SW Capitol Highway
Suuite 250
Portland, OR 97219

503-327-2200
FAX 503-327-2201
E-Mail: nwfpa@nwfpa.org
Home Page: www.nwfpa.org

Teonna Embelton, Events Coordinator
Stephanie Kennedy, Events Consultant

Provides comprehensive programs encompassing topics ranging from food sciences and technologies to energy efficiencies.
Frequency: Jan Oregon

10616 NW Food Manufacturing and Packaging Expo
8338 NE. Alderwood Road
Suite 160
Portland, OR 97220

503-327-2200
FAX 503-327-2201
E-Mail: nwfpa@nwfpa.org
Home Page: www.nwfpa.org
Social Media: *Facebook, Twitter, LinkedIn*

David Zepponi, President
David C Klick, Cluster Outreach Executive
Craig Smith, VP
Connie Kirby, Scientific & Technical Director
Pam Barrow, Energy Affairs Manager

NWFPA is an advocate for members interests and a resource for enhancing the food processing industry in Oregon, Washington and Idaho.
350 Members
4000 Attendees
Founded in 1914

10617 NWA Annual Education and Networking Conference & Exhibits
National WIC Association
2001 S St NW
Suite 580
Washington, DC 20009-1165

202-232-5492
FAX 202-387-5281
Home Page: www.nwica.org
Social Media: *Facebook, Twitter*

Douglas Greenaway, President & CEO

Offers a terrific opportunity to learn new skills and to network with more than 1200 colleagues and peers, public health professionals, technical experts and nationally recognized speakers from a variety of fields who will engage participants during plenary and concurrent sessions.
900 Members
Frequency: Annual/May
Founded in 1983

10618 NWA Technology Conference
National WIC Association
2001 S St NW
Suite 580
Washington, DC 20009-1165

202-232-5492
FAX 202-387-5281
Home Page: www.nwica.org
Social Media: *Facebook, Twitter*

Douglas Greenaway, President & CEO

The future is now! Learn about the latest technologies available and used in all the WIC programs.
900 Members
Frequency: Annual/September
Founded in 1983

10619 NWA Washington Leadership Conference

National WIC Association
2001 S St NW
Suite 580
Washington, DC 20009-1165

202-232-5492
FAX 202-387-5281
Home Page: www.nwica.org
Social Media: *Facebook, Twitter*

Douglas Greenaway, President & CEO

The conference will provide a forum to discuss Federal initiatives affecting the health and nutritional wellbeing of WIC mothers and young children, WIC's role as a preventative public health nutrition program, as well as service delivery and the effective management of the Program.
900 Members
Frequency: Annual/March
Founded in 1983

10620 National Agri-Marketing Association Conference

National Agri-Marketing Association
11020 King Street
Suite 205
Overland Park, KS 66210-1201

913-491-6500
FAX 913-492-6502
E-Mail: agrimktg@nama.org
Home Page: www.nama.org
Social Media: *Facebook, Twitter, LinkedIn, YouTube, Flickr*

Stephanie Gable, National President
Vicki Henrickson, Vice President

Annual show of 60 exhibitors of marketing and communication suppliers, including trade publications, radio and television broadcast sales organizations, premium/incentive manufacturers, printers, marketing research firms and photographers.
1100 Attendees
Frequency: Annual

10621 National Agricultural Plastics Congress

American Society for Plasticulture
526 Brittany Drive
State College, PA 16803-1420

814-238-7045
FAX 814-238-7051
E-Mail: contact@plasticulture.org
Home Page: www.plasticulture.org

Patricia Heuser, Executive Director

Congress of research presentations, with exhibit area of equipment, supplies and services relating to greenhouse production and mulch film production of agricultural and horticultural crops.
225 Attendees
Frequency: September

10622 National Association Extension 4-H Agents Convention

University of Georgia
Hoke Smith Annex
Athens, GA 30602

706-542-3000
FAX 706-542-2115

Peggy Adkins, Show Manager

Fifty booths for young people, youth staff and volunteers involved in 4-H.
1.2M Attendees
Frequency: November

10623 National Association of College and University Food Services Convention

Michigan State University-Manly Miles Building
1405 S Harrison Road
Suite 305
East Lansing, MI 48823-5245

517-332-2494
FAX 517-332-8144
E-Mail: jspina@nacufs.org
Home Page: www.nacufs.org/nacufs

Joseph Spina, Executive Director
Donna Addy, Administrative Assistant
Nancy Lane, Director

Annual convention and exhibits of equipment, supplies and services for food preparation and service on college and university campuses.

10624 National Association of County Agricultural Agents Conference

National Association of County Agricultural Agents
Courthouse-Room 217
5th & Main Street
Ellensburg, WA 98926

FAX 509-627-74

Annual conference and exhibits for county agricultural agents and extension workers.

10625 National Association of Fruits, Flavors and Syrups Annual Convention

5 Ravine Drive
#776
Matawan, NJ 07747-3106

732-988-4800
FAX 732-583-0798

Bob Bauer, Director
Frequency: September

10626 National Chicken Council Conference

1015 15th Street NW
Suite 930
Washington, DC 20005-2622

202-296-2622
FAX 202-293-4005
Home Page: www.nationalchickencouncil.com

Michael J. Brown, President
William P. Roenigk, Senior VP

NCC's Annual Conference brings together senior executives from U.S. chicken processing companies and allied industries to address current agricultural, public affairs, legislative, regulatory, political, economic, and world trade issues affecting the chicken industry.
Frequency: Annual
Founded in 1954

10627 National Confectioners Association Education Exposition

National Confectioners Association
7900 Westpar Drive
Suite A-320
McLean, VA 22102

703-790-5750
FAX 730-790-5752

Linda Jamie, Finance Executive
600 Attendees

10628 National Confectioners Association Expo

8320 Old Courthouse Road
Suite 300
Vienna, VA 22182

703-790-5750
FAX 703-790-5752
E-Mail: info@candyusa.org
Home Page: www.allcandyexpo.com

Larry Graham, President
Libby Taylor, VP

Confectionery trade show featuring more chocolate, candy and gum than one can imagine. Held annually in June at Chicago's McCormick Place. 1200 booths.
15 M Attendees
Frequency: June

10629 National Conservation Association District Annual Convention

9150 W Jewell Avenue
Suite 113
Lakewood, CO 80232-6469

303-839-1852

Robert Raschke, Regional Representative

Eighty booths including companies who manufacture, service or who are otherwise involved with equipment used in agricultural production.
2M Attendees
Frequency: February

10630 National Convenience Store Advisory Group Convention

2063 Oak Street
Jacksonville, FL 32204

904-845-5989
FAX 904-387-3362
E-Mail: jhowton@nag-net.com
Home Page: www.nag-net.com

Joseph Howton, Executive VP/COO

One-hundred booths.
500 Attendees
Frequency: January

10631 National Corn Growers Association

1000 Executive Parkway Drive
Suite 105
Creve Cocur, MO 63141-6397

314-275-9915
FAX 314-275-7061

Peggy Findley, Director of Conventions

Five hundred and fifty booths of equipment, seed and chemicals.
4000 Attendees
Frequency: February

10632 National Country Ham Association Annual Meeting

PO Box 948
Conover, NC 28613

828-466-2760
800-820-4426
FAX 828-466-2770
E-Mail: eatham@countryham.org
Home Page: www.countryham.org

Candace Cansler, Executive Director

Providing an array of speakers, discussion topics and activities.
Frequency: Non-Members:$300

10633 National Farm Machinery Show and Championship Tractor Pull

Kentucky Fair and Exposition Center

PO Box 37130
Louisville, KY 40233

502-367-5000
FAX 502-367-5299
Home Page: www.farmmachineryshow.org

Harold Workman, Show Manager

Annual show of 800 plus exhibitors of agricultural products, equipment, supplies and services.
280M Attendees
Frequency: February

10634 National Food Processors Association Convention
National Food Processors Association
1350 I Street NW
Suite 300
Washington, DC 20005-3377
202-930-0890
FAX 202-639-5932

John Cady, President
Lisa Weddig, Executive Director

Annual convention and exhibits of equipment, supplies and services for food processing quality control measures, spoilage prevention, frozen food technology, sanitation techniques and waste treatment techniques.

10635 National Frozen and Refrigerated Foods Convention
National Frozen & Refrigerated Foods Association
4755 Linglestown Road Suite 300
PO Box 6069
Harrisburg, PA 17112

717-657-8601
FAX 717-657-9862
E-Mail: info@nfraweb.org
Home Page: www.nfraweb.org

Dayna Jackson, Admin Asst, Meetings/Member Service

The National Frozen and Refrigerated Foods Convention is an opportunity for you to meet with hundreds of frozen and refrigerated food decision-makers. This premier business event brings representatives from all segments of our industry together to conduct business and build relationships. it is structured around one-on-one business appointments, with ample opportunity to network.
1,200 Attendees
Frequency: Annual/October

10636 National Grange Annual Meeting
1616 H Street NW
Washington, DC 20006

202-628-3507
888-447-2643
FAX 503-622-0343
E-Mail: info@nationalgrange.org
Home Page: www.nationalgrange.org

William Steel, President
Jennifer Dugent, Secretary
Phil Prelli, Secretary
Judy Sherrod, National Secretary

Agricultural forum.
3M Attendees
Frequency: November

10637 National Grocers Association Annual Convenience & Supermarket Showcase
National Grocers Association
1825 Samuel Morse Drive
Reston, VA 22090

703-437-5300
FAX 703-437-7768

2800 Attendees

10638 National Homebrewers Conference and National Homebrew Competition
Brewers Association
736 Pearl Street
Boulder, CO 80302

303-447-0816
888-822-6273
FAX 303-447-2825
E-Mail: webmaster@brewersassociation.org
Home Page: www.beertown.org
Social Media: *Facebook, Twitter*

Chris P. Frey, Chair
Jake Keeler, Vice Chair
Roxanne Westendorf, Secretary

Education and fun combine for a great experience at the national conference for amateur brewers.
1900 Members
Founded in 1978

10639 National Ice Cream Retailers Association Annual Convention
1028 West Devon Avenue
Elk Grove Village, IL 60007

847-301-7500
866-303-6960
FAX 847-301-8402
E-Mail: info@nicra.org
Home Page: www.nicra.org

Dan Messer, President
David Zimmerman, President-Elect
Nanette Frey, Vice President
Carl Chaney, Secretary/Treasurer
Lynda Utterback, Executive Director

A major national convention for those in the retail ice ceam and frozen dessert business. Attendees are mostly independent operators/owners and vendors that sell to the retail/wholesale trade. Thirty-five to forty booths.
Frequency: Annual/November

10640 National Nutritional Foods Association
1773 T Street, NW
Washington, DC 20009

202-223-0101
800-966-6632
FAX 202-223-0250
E-Mail: natural@NPAinfo.org
Home Page: www.npainfo.org
Social Media: *Facebook, Twitter, LinkedIn*

John F. Gay, Executive Director & CEO
Jeffrey Wright, President

Six hundred booths including educational seminars and exhibits of health and natural foods.
7.5M Attendees
Frequency: Annual/June

10641 National Orange Show
PO Box 5749
San Bernardino, CA 92412-5749

909-888-6788
FAX 909-889-7666

Esther Armstrong, Executive Director
Brad Randall, Manager

Agricultural forum.
262M Attendees
Frequency: May

10642 National Pest Management Association Annual Eastern Conference
10460 North Street
Fairfax, VA 22030

703-352-6762
800-678-6722
FAX 703-352-3031

Home Page: www.npmapestworld.org
Social Media: *Facebook, Twitter*

Robert Lederer, Executive VP

Two hundred forty booths.
7000 Members
3500 Attendees
Frequency: Annual/October
Founded in 1933

10643 National Policy Conference
Crop Life America
1156 15th St NW
Washington, DC 20005-1752

202-296-1585
FAX 202-463-0474
E-Mail: webmaster@croplifeamerica.org
Home Page: www.croplifeamerica.org
Social Media: *Facebook, Twitter, LinkedIn, YouTube*

Jay Vroom, President
Rich Nolan, VP

Brings together leading experts, academics and politicos to engage in a debate on the development of the Farm Bill. How does Congress design a Farm Bill that addresses human, social, economic, research and environmental needs while taking into account farmers, consumers and the natural systems that give us the food and fiber we need to live?
Frequency: Annual/May

10644 National Potato Council's Annual Meeting
National Potato Council
5690 Dtc Boulevard
Greenwood Village, CO 80111-3232

303-773-9295
FAX 303-773-9296
E-Mail: npcspud@ix.netcom.com
Home Page: www.npcspod.com

Annual meeting and exhibits of potato growing equipment, supplies and services.

10645 National ProStart Invitational
NRAEF
175 W Jackson Boulevard
Suite 1500
Chicago, IL 60604-2814

312-715-1010
800-765-2122
FAX 312-583-9767
Home Page: www.nraef.org

Culinary and management competition attracts top high school ProStart students from around the country. Winning teams secure scholarships from the NRAEF and The Coca-Cola Company, along with colleges and universities.
Frequency: Annual/April
Founded in 1987

10646 National Restaurant Association Convention
National Restaurant Association
150 N Michigan Avenue
Suite 2000
Chicago, IL 60601

312-853-2525
FAX 312-853-2548

Mary Heftman, Senior VP
80000 Attendees
Frequency: May

10647 National Soft Drink Association Show
1101 16th Street NW
Suite 700
Washington, DC 20036-4877

202-463-6732
FAX 202-463-8178

Susan K Neely, President
Patricia M Vaughan, Secretary
Jim L Turner, Treasurer

Annual show of 300 members of soft drink
makers and their suppliers.
25M Attendees
Frequency: Annual Fall
Founded in 1919

**10648 National Turkey Federation Annual
Meeting**
National Turkey Federation
1225 New York Avenue NW
Suite 400
Washington, DC 20005-6404

202-898-0100
FAX 202-898-0203
E-Mail: info@turkeyfed.org
Home Page: www.eatturkey.com
Social Media: *Facebook, Twitter, YouTube*

Joel Brandenberger, President
Jennifer Zukowski, Meetings & Membership

Advocates for all segments of the US turkey industry, providing services and conducting activities that increase demand for its members'
products. The federation also protects and enhances its members' ability to effectively and
profitably provide wholesome, high quality,
nutritious turkey products.
Frequency: Annual

10649 National Watermelon Association
Annual Meeting
406 Railroad Street
Morven, GA 31638

229-775-2130
FAX 229-775-2344

Nacy Childers, Contact

**10650 National Wheat Growers Association
Convention**
415 2nd Street NE
Suite 300
Washington, DC 20002-4900

202-547-7800
FAX 202-546-2638
E-Mail: wheatworld@wheatworld.org
Home Page: www.wheatworld.org
Social Media: *Facebook, Twitter, YouTube*

Brett Blankenship, President
Jim Palmer, Chief Executive Officer

Major agri business exhibits including farm
equipment and services. 100 booths.
Frequency: Annual/January

10651 Natural Products Exposition East
New Hope Natural Media
1301 Spruce Street
Boulder, CO 80302

303-939-8440
FAX 303-939-9559

20000 Attendees

10652 Natural Products Exposition West
New Hope Communications
1301 Spruce Street
Boulder, CO 80302

303-939-8440
FAX 303-939-9559

31000 Attendees

**10653 New England Equipment Dealers
Association**
PO Box 895
Concord, NH 03302-0895

603-225-5510
FAX 603-225-5510

George M Becker, Managing Director

Annual convention and trade show held the
first weekend in December for farm, industrial
and outdoor equipment dealers in the six New
England states. 95 booths.
300 Attendees
Frequency: December

**10654 Nightclub & Bar Beverage Retailer
Beverage & Food Convention and
Trade Show**
Oxford Publishing
307 West Jackson Avenue
Oxford, MS 38655

662-236-5510
888-966-2727
FAX 662-513-3990
E-Mail: registration@oxpub.com
Home Page: www.nightclub.com

**10655 Nightclub & Bar/Beverage Retailer
Food & Beverage Trade Show**
Oxford Publishing
307 W Jackson Avenue
Oxford, MS 38655-2154

662-236-5510
888-966-2727
FAX 662-513-3990
E-Mail: jrobinson@oxpub.com
Home Page: www.nightclub.com

Jennifer Robinson, Show Manager
Adam Alson, Founder
Yosi Benvenisti, Owner

Fastest growing food, beverage and hospitality
show in the US. This show is for both on-premise and off-premise.
20M Attendees
Frequency: March/July/November

**10656 Nightclub and Bar/Beverage Retailer
Convention and Trade Show**
National Bar and Restaurant Association
307 Jackson Avenue W
Oxford, MS 38655

662-236-5510
800-247-3881
FAX 662-236-5541
Home Page: www.beverage-retailer.com

Jennifer Robinson, Senior VP
Hollis Green, Trade Show Director
Kaytee Hazlewood, VP Marketing

The industry's first national conference and
trade show devoted to business basics, promotions and marketing for liquor stores, nightclubs and bars. More than 2,500 exhibits.
38800 Attendees
Frequency: March

**10657 North American Deer Farmers
Association Annual Conference &
Exhibit**
North American Deer Farmers Association
104 S Lakeshore Drive
Lake City, MN 55041-1266

651-345-5600
FAX 651-345-5603
E-Mail: info@nadefa.org
Home Page: www.nadefa.org
Social Media: *Facebook*

Carolyn Laughlin, President
R.Ray Burdette, First VP
Will Ainsworth, Second VP

Bill Pittenger, Third VP
Dr. Hank Dimuzio, Treasurer

Annual show of more than 30 exhibitors of
deer farming equipment, supplies and services.
550+ Attendees
Frequency: Annual/Summer
Founded in 1984

**10658 North American Farm and Power
Show**
Tradexpos
811 W Oakland Avenue
PO Box 1067
Austin, MN 55912

507-437-4697
800-949-3976
FAX 507-437-8917
E-Mail: steve@tradexpos.com
Home Page: www.tradexpos.com

Steve Guenthner, Show Director

Agri-business farm show for the 5-state region.
Free admission and parking.
32M Attendees
Frequency: Annual/March

**10659 North American Fertilizer
Transportation Conference**
Fertilizer Institute
425 Third Street, SW
Suite 950
Washington, DC 20024

202-962-0490
FAX 202-962-0577
E-Mail: information@tfi.org
Home Page: www.tfi.org
Social Media: *Facebook, Twitter, LinkedIn*

Ford West, President

Provides an opportunity for shippers and carriers to discuss issues of concern and work to
reach mutually-beneficial solutions to logistical
problems.
Frequency: Annual/October

**10660 North American Olive Oil Association
Mid- Year Meeting**
North American Olive Oil Association
3301 Route 66
Suite 205, Building C
Neptune, NJ 07753

732-922-0500
FAX 732-922-3590
Home Page: www.aboutoliveoil.org

Bob Bauer, President

Olive growers and oil processors group for legislative advocacy and trade networking.

**10661 North American Specialty Coffee
Retailers' Expo**
PO Box 14827
Portland, OR 97293

503-236-2587
800-548-0551
FAX 503-236-3165
Home Page: www.nascore.net

Jan Weigel, Director
Founded in 1995

**10662 Northeast Food Service and Lodging
Expo and Conference**
Reed Exhibition Companies
383 Main Avenue
Norwalk, CT 06851

203-840-4800
FAX 203-840-4824

Linda Karpowich, Customer Service Manager

Annual show of 600 exhibitors of food services, operating equipment and services for the

hospitality and institutional foodservice industry.
29000 Attendees

10663 Northeast Pizza Expo

MacFadden Protech
137 E Market Street
New Albany, IN 47150

812-949-0909
800-489-8324
FAX 812-949-1867
E-Mail: lkeith@pizzatoday.com
Home Page: www.pizzaexpo.com

William T Oakley, Senior VP Expositions
Linda F Keith, Manager
Patty Crone, Manager

Manufacturers, food purveyors and service representatives from pizza or related industries.

10664 Northwest Agricultural Congress

4991 Drift Creek Rd SE
Sublimity, OR 97385-9764

503-769-8940
FAX 503-769-8946
Home Page: www.nwagshow.com

Jim Heater, Show Manager

Second largest agricultural show on the west coast. Show is produced by the Northwest Horticultural Congress which is a partnership between Oregon Horticultural Society, the Oregon Association of Nurseries and Northwest Nut Growers Association. Show held in conjunction with annual meetings and seminars by all three of the horticultural groups.
21000 Members

10665 Northwest Food Manufacturing & Packaging Association

Northwest Food Processors Association
6950 SW Hampton Street
Suite 340
Portland, OR 98223-8332

503-639-7676
FAX 503-639-7007
Home Page: www.nwpfa@nwpfa.org

Stephanie Green, Show Manager
Mindy Todd, Marketing Coordinator

Containing 450 booths.
3000 Attendees
Frequency: Janurary

10666 Nut Grower Magazine Farm Show

Western Agricultural Publishing Company
4974 E Clinton Way
Suite 123
Fresno, CA 93727-1520

559-261-0396
FAX 559-252-7387

Phill Rhoads, Manager

Productions seminars, guest speakers, prizes and exhibits for nut growers. Containing 80 booths and exhibits.

10667 OFPA Annual Convention and Exposition

Ozark Food Processors Association
2650 N Young Avenue
Fayetteville, AR 72704

479-575-4607
FAX 479-575-2165
E-Mail: ofpa@uark.edu
Home Page: ofpa.uark.edu

Cindy Stricklaw, President
Roure Threfall, Director

OFPA members and registered guests learn about new trends in the food industry during technical sessions and the exposition. The location for the 2012 meeting is Springfield, AR.
500 Attendees
Frequency: Annual/ April
Founded in 1906

10668 Oklahoma Restaurant Convention & Expo

Oklahoma Restaurant Association
3800 N Portland Avenue
Oklahoma City, OK 73112-2948

405-942-8181
800-375-8181
FAX 405-942-0541
Home Page: www.okrestaurants.com

Lori Culver, Convention Manager

Annual show of 450 manufacturers, suppliers and distributors. Exhibits of providers of food service and hospitality products, services and equipment. Held at the Myriad Convention Center in Oklahoma City, Oklahoma.
9M Attendees
Frequency: April
Founded in 1938

10669 PACK International Expo

Packaging Machinery Manufacturers Institute
4350 N Fairfax Drive
Suite 600
Arlington, VA 22203

703-243-8555
FAX 703-243-8556
E-Mail: expo@pmmi.org
Home Page: www.pei2006.packexpo.com

Jim Pittas, Trade Show VP
Dinah Sprouse, Trade Show Operations Director
Kim Beaulieu, Exhibitor Services Manager

Browse more than 2,000 packaging and processing exhibitors covering virtually the entire packaging supply chain. Network with others in the industry, attend specialized education sessions led by industry experts and evaluate the latest advances while experiencing hands on demonstrations of the latest technologies in the industry.
1600 Attendees
Frequency: Oct-Nov

10670 PACex International

Packaging, Food Process and Logistics Exhibition
2255 Sheppard Avenue E
Suite E330
Toronto Ontario M2J-4YI

416-490-7860
FAX 416-490-7844
Home Page: www.pacexinternational.com

Maria Tavares, Expositions Manager
15000 Attendees
Frequency: September-October

10671 PLMA Trade Show

Private Label Manufacturers Association
630 Third Avenue
New York, NY 10017-6506

212-972-3131
FAX 212-983-1382
E-Mail: info@plma.com
Home Page: www.plma.com

Brian Sharoff, President
Myra Rosen, VP
Tom Prendergast, Director, Research Services

The best place for private label networking.
3200+ Members
10000 Attendees
Frequency: Annual/November
Founded in 1979

10672 PMA Foodservice Conference & Exposition

Produce Marketing Association
1500 Casho Mill Road
Newark, DE 19711-3547

302-738-7100
FAX 302-731-2409
E-Mail: showmanagement@pma.com
Home Page: www.pma.com
Social Media: *Twitter, YouTube, Flickr*

Jamie Hillegas, Show Manager
Susan Eller, Trade Show Planner

Join the who's-who of chefs, menu developers, restaurant operators, grower-shippers, distributors and foodservice suppliers to see and sample the newest products and services, learn about the latest consumer trends and tastes, see old colleagues or make new contacts.
Frequency: Annual/July
Founded in 1981

10673 PMA Fresh Summit International Convention & Exposition

Produce Marketing Association
1500 Casho Mill Road
PO Box 6036
Newark, DE 19711-3547

302-387-7100
FAX 302-731-2409
E-Mail: showmanagement@pma.com
Home Page: www.pma.com/freshsummit
Social Media: *Facebook, Twitter, YouTube*

Don Harris, Summit Chairman
Jamie Hillegas, Show Manager
Susan Eller, Trade Show Planner
Sheli Parlier, Exhibits Sales Manager
Bryan Silbermann, President

An event that attracts buyers and suppliers from the produce and floral industries; from the retail and foodservice channels and from more than 70 counties.
17M Attendees
Frequency: Annual/October

10674 PTNPA Annual Convention

Peanut & Tree Nut Processors Association
PO Box 2660
Alexandria, VA 22301

301-365-2521
FAX 301-365-7705
E-Mail: ptnpa@mindspring.com
Home Page: www.ptnpa.org

General meeting sessions, keynote speakers, exhibitors from the industry.
400 Attendees
Frequency: Annual/January

10675 Pan-American International Livestock Exposition

State Fair of Texas
PO Box 150009
Dallas, TX 75315-0009

214-565-9931
FAX 214-421-8792
E-Mail: livestock@greatstatefair.com
Home Page: www.bigtex.com

Benny Clark, Director
Elvis Presley, Vice President

Annual show and exhibits of livestock, livestock equipment, agricultural technology and consumer products.
3.5M Attendees
Frequency: September/October

10676 Pickle Packers International Pickle Fair
1620 i St Nw
Suite 925
Washington, DC 20006-4035

202-312-2859
FAX 630-584-0759
E-Mail: staff@ppii.org

Richard Hentschell, Executive VP

Fifty booths, seminars and programs held in odd numbered years.
300+ Attendees
Frequency: October

10677 Poultry Supplier Showcase
National Poultry & Food Distributors
2014 Osborne Rd
Saint Marys, GA 31558

770-535-9901
877-845-1545
FAX 770-535-7385
E-Mail: info@npfda.org
Home Page: www.npfda.org

Chris Sharp, President
Al Acunto, Vice President
Marc Miro, Treasurer
Kristin McWhorter, Executive Director

Annual convention and poultry suppliers showcase. Three day convention and trade show.
900 Attendees
Frequency: Annual/January
Founded in 1967

10678 Pre-Harvest Food Safety Conference
North American Meat Processors
Association
1910 Association Drive
Reston, VA 20191-1500

703-758-1900
800-368-3043
FAX 703-758-8001
Home Page: www.namp.com

Philip Kimball, Executive Director
Sabrina Moore, Accounting/Meetings Manager
Ann Wells, Director Scientific Affairs
Jane Jacobs, Communications Director

Brings regulators and researchers together with experts from the poultry industry, and the allied industries that serve them, to discuss the known and unknown issues associated with the control of food borne pathogens in pre-harvest operations. Conference will be one of the most thorough explorations into the poultry pre-harvest arena that has ever been conducted.
Frequency: Annual/January

10679 Presidents Conference
International Foodservice Distributors
Association
1410 Spring Hill Road
Suite 210
McLean, VA 22102-3035

703-532-9400
FAX 703-538-4673
Home Page: www.ifdaonline.org

Mark Allen, President & CEO
Jonathan Eisen, Senior VP/ Government Relations

Gain breakthrough insights and take away high value solutions. Collaborate with fellow leaders in an information rich learning environment with plenty of networking opportunities. All-industry forum addressing issues impacting the foodservice supply chain.
Frequency: Annual/October

10680 Private Label Manufacturers Association Trade Show
630 Third Avenue
New York, NY 10017

212-972-3131
FAX 212-983-1382
E-Mail: info@plma.com
Home Page: www.plma.com

Brian Sharoff, President
Myra Rosen, Vice President

A private label trade show.
3200+ Members
Frequency: Annual/November
Founded in 1979

10681 ProMat
Material Handling Industry of America
8720 Red Oak Boulevard
Suite 201
Charlotte, NC 28217-3992

704-676-1190
FAX 704-676-1199
E-Mail: gbaer@mhia.org
Home Page: www.mhia.org

Greg Baer, Senior Sales Associate
Jennifer Breadling, Manager Of Communications

The premier showcase of material handling and logistics solutions in North America. The show is designed to offer productivity solutions and information by showcasing the products and services of over 700 leading material handling and logistics providers.
Frequency: Annual

10682 Process Expo
Food Processing Suppliers Association
1451 Dolley Madison Blvd
Suite 101
Mc Lean, VA 22101-3850

703-761-2600
FAX 703-761-4334
E-Mail: info@fpsa.org
Home Page: www.fpsa.org
Social Media: *Facebook, Twitter, LinkedIn*

David Seckman, President
George Melnykovich, Senior Advisor
Robyn Roche, CFO

Tradeshow where qualified buyers representing every market of the food industry meet face to face with suppliers showcasing the newest developments in processing technology. Exhibitors are able to demonstrate state-of-the-art food processing equipment in baking, beverage, dairy, fruit and vegetable, and meat/poultry industries.
510 Members
Frequency: Annual/November
Founded in 2005

10683 Produce Marketing Association
1500 Casho Mill Road
PO Box 6036
Newark, DE 19711-3547

302-738-7100
FAX 302-731-2409
E-Mail: bsilbermann@mail.pma.com
Home Page: www.pma.com

Bryan Silbermann, President
Dan Henderaon, Marketing

Largest convention and exposition for the fresh fruit, vegetable and floral industries. More than 12,000 people and 1,500 booths.
12M Attendees
Frequency: October

10684 Productivity Conference and Distribution/ Transportation Exposition
Food Distributors International

1410 Spring Hill Road
Suite 210
McLean, VA 22102

703-532-9400
FAX 703-538-4673
Home Page: www.ifdaonline.org

Mark S. Allen, President/CEO
Malcolm Sullivan, Jr., Chairman
Thomas Zatina, Vice Chairman
James Crawford, Treasurer

A conference exhibiting services and supplies geared toward the grocery industry. Containing 200 booths and 200 exhibits.
2400 Attendees
Frequency: Annual/October

10685 R&DA Annual Spring & Fall Meeting and Exhibition
R&D Associates
16607 Blanco Road
Suite 305
San Antonio, TX 78232-1940

210-682-4302
FAX 830-493-8036
E-Mail: jfagan@militaryfood.org

Jim Fagan, Meeting Coordinator

Hear presentations by key officials, network with decision makers, get updates on key issues and gain a competitive edge within the industry.
300 Attendees
Frequency: Apr/Oct/Non-Members: $1099

10686 RFA Annual Conference
Refrigerated Foods Association
1640 Powers Ferry Road
Bldg. 2, Suite 200A
Marietta, GA 30067

770-303-9905
FAX 770-303-9906
E-Mail: info@refrigeratedfoods.org
Home Page: www.refrigeratedfoods.org

Brian Edmonds, President
George Bradford, Vice President
Steve Loehndorf, Secretary
Wes Thaller, Treasurer

The RFA Conference is a great way to network and gain important new information affecting the industry, including technical innovations, sales and marketing tips, consumer trends, distribution solutions, new product and package development, and food safety issues.
200+ Members
Frequency: Annual/February
Founded in 1980

10687 RFA Annual Conference & Exhibition
Refrigerated Foods Association
2971 Flowers Road S
Suite 266
Atlanta, GA 30341-5403

770-452-0660
FAX 770-455-3879
E-Mail: info@refrigeratedfoods.org
Home Page: www.refrigeratedfoods.org

Brian Edmonds, President
George Bradford, Vice President
Steve Loehndorf, Secretary
Wes Thaller, Treasurer

Suppliers displaying the latest offerings in equipment, packaging, ingredients and services for the industry. A great way to network and gain important new information affecting the industry, including technical innovations, sales and marketing tips, consumer trends, distribution solutions, new product and packaging development and food safety issues.
Frequency: Annual/April

10688 Restaurants Rock
NRAEF

175 W Jackson Boulevard
Suite 1500
Chicago, IL 60604-2814

312-715-1010
800-765-2122
FAX 312-583-9767
Home Page: www.nraef.org

The only official party of the NRA Show, Restaurants Rock brings together the restaurant and hospitality industry in a night of networking and celebration.
Frequency: Annual/May
Founded in 1987

10689 Retail Confectioners International Annual Convention and Exposition

Retail Confectioners International
1807 Glenview Road
Suite 204
Glenview, IL 60025-2968

847-724-6120
FAX 847-724-2719

Van Billington, Director
Michelle May, Contact

Annual exhibition offering exhibits of confectionery equipment, supplies, finished products and packaging materials.
1.5M Attendees
Frequency: Annual

10690 SANA/USB Annual Soy Symposium

Soyfoods Association of North America
1001 Connecticut Avenue NW
Suite 1120
Washington, DC 20036

202-659-3520
E-Mail: info@soyfoods.org
Home Page: www.soyfoods.org

Nancy Chapman, Executive Director
Anne Chambers, Membership Coordinator

Co-sponsored with United Soybean Board, see the latest innovative designs and products from industry representatives.
Frequency: Apr/Non-Members:$995
Founded in 1978

10691 SAVOR, An American Craft Beer & Food Experience

Brewers Association
736 Pearl Street
Boulder, CO 80302

303-447-0816
888-822-6273
FAX 303-447-2825
E-Mail: webmaster@brewersassociation.org
Home Page: www.beertown.org
Social Media: *Facebook, Twitter*

Chris P. Frey, Chair
Jake Keeler, Vice Chair
Roxanne Westendorf, Secretary

The main beer and food pairing event in the US. Where beer enthusiasts and foodies can interact directly with some of the greatest brewers and brewery owners in the world.
1900 Members
Founded in 1978

10692 SBS Annual Conference & Exhibition

Society for Biomolecular Sciences
36 Tamarack Avenue
Suite 348
Danbury, CT 06811

203-788-8828
FAX 203-748-7557
E-Mail: email@sbsonline.org
Home Page: www.sbsonline.org

Agnes Amos, Exhibitions/Meetings Director
Marietta Manoni, Exhibitions/Meetings Manager

This event brings together leaders in the pharmaceutical, biotech and agrochemical industries from around the world. Highlighting the impact of screening and technology applications on drug discovery.
Frequency: Sept/Non-Members $1,445
Founded in 1995

10693 SCAA Annual Conference & Exhibition

Specialty Coffee Association of America
330 Golden Shore
Suite 50
Long Beach, CA 90802

562-624-4100
FAX 562-624-4101
E-Mail: coffee@scaa.org
Home Page: www.scaa.org

Ted Lingle, Executive Director
Scott Welker, Administrative Director

The country's premier coffee event, attracting coffee professionals from more than 40 countries. Attendees include coffee producers, exporters and importers, roasters, manufacturers, brew masters, and consumer enthusiasts.
8000 Attendees
Frequency: April/Non-Members:$585
Founded in 1982

10694 SCAA Annual Exposition

Specialty Coffee Association of America
330 Golden Shore
Suite 50
Long Beach, CA 90802-4246

562-624-4100
FAX 562-624-4101
E-Mail: info@scaa.org
Home Page: www.scaa.org
Social Media: *Facebook, Twitter, YouTube*

Ric Rhinehart, Executive Director
Tracy Ging, Deputy Executive Director
Ted Lingle, Senior Advisor

Roasters & retailers attend and have the opportunity to exhibit products on the show floor, network with industry's decision makers, and further their professional careers by participating in the SCAA's numerous lectures, labs or certification programs.
2500+ Members
Frequency: Annual/April
Founded in 1982

10695 SCST Annual Meeting

Society of Commerical Seed Technologists
101 E State Street
Suite 214
Ithaca, NY 14850

607-256-3313
FAX 607-256-3313
E-Mail: scst@twcny.rr.com
Home Page: www.seedtechnology.net

Anita Hall, Executive Director

A joint meeting with the Association of Official Seed Analysts and the Association of Official Seed Certifying Agencies. Workshops, Exhibits, speakers and more regarding the seed industry.
Frequency: June
Founded in 1922

10696 SEAFWA Annual Convention

Southeast Association of Fish & Wildlife Agencies
8005 Freshwater Farms Road
Tallahassee, FL 32309-9009

850-893-1204
FAX 850-893-6204
E-Mail: SEAFWA2006@dgif.virginia.gov

Home Page:
www.seafwa2006.org/www.seafwa.org

Robert M Brantly, Executive Secretary
Dianne Waller, Conference Coordinator

Providing a forum for presentation of information and exchange of ideas regarding the management and protection of fish and wildlife resources throughout the nation but emphasis on the southeast.
Frequency: Oct/Nov
Founded in 1947

10697 SFA's Legislative Summit

Snack Food Association
1600 Wilson Blvd
Suite 650
Arlington, VA 22209-2510

703-836-4500
800-628-1334
FAX 703-836-8262
E-Mail: sfa@sfa.org
Home Page: www.sfa.org

James A McCarthy, President/CEO

Discuss many of the most important legislative issues which will impact the snack food industry.
800 Members
Frequency: Annual/May
Founded in 1937

10698 SNAXPO

Snack Food Association
1600 Wilson Blvd
Suite 650
Arlington, VA 22209-2510

703-836-4500
800-628-1334
FAX 703-836-8262
E-Mail: sfa@sfa.org
Home Page: www.sfa.org

James A McCarthy, President/CEO

The world's largest, most comprehensive trade show devoted exclusively to the international snack food industry. Owners, executives and buyers from every segment of the industry around the globe come together for this premier event.
800 Members
Frequency: Annual/March
Founded in 1937

10699 SNAXPO: Snack Food Association

1600 Wilson Boulevard
Suite 650
Arlington, VA 22209-2510

703-836-4500
800-628-1334
FAX 703-836-8262
E-Mail: sfa@sfa.org
Home Page: www.sfa.org

Judi Barth, VP Marketing
Ann Wilkes, VP Communications
2000 Attendees
Frequency: February/March
Founded in 1938

10700 School Nutrition Association Annual National Conference

School Nutrition Association
120 Waterfront Street
Suite 300
National Harbor, MD 20745

301-686-3100
800-877-8822
FAX 301-686-3115
E-Mail: servicecenter@schoolnutrition.org
Home Page: www.schoolnutrition.org

Helen Phillips, President
Sandy Ford, President-Elect

Leah Schmidt, VP
Beth Taylor, Secretary/Treasurer

Learn, grow and exchange ideas with others committed to the healthful feeding of our children. With over 400 exhibitors and more than 90 quality education sessions, ANC gives you the opportunity to learn about the top trends and issues in school nutrition.
Frequency: Annual/July

10701 Southern Convenience Store & Petroleum Show
GA Ass'n of Convenience Stores/Petroleum Retailers
168 North Johnston Street
Suite 209
Dallas, GA 30132-4744

770-736-9723
877-294-1885
FAX 770-736-9725
E-Mail: jtudor@aol.com
Home Page: www.gacs.com
Social Media: *Facebook*

Jim Tudor, President
Angela Holland, Vice President

Targeted to reach key individuals in the convenience store and petroleum industry from throughout the South. Attendees will include board members and key representatives from the Georgia Association of Convenience Stores and will be open to retailers from throughout the southern US.
2000 Attendees
Frequency: Annual/October

10702 Southwest Foodservice Exposition
Texas Restaurant Association
PO Box 1429
Austin, TX 78767

512-472-8990
FAX 512-472-2777

31000 Attendees

10703 Special Event
Special Event Corporation
PO Box 8987
Malibu, CA 90265-8987

310-317-4522
FAX 310-317-9644

4300 Attendees

10704 Sunbelt Agricultural Exposition
PO Box 28
Tifton, GA 31793-0028

229-985-1968
FAX 229-387-7503
E-Mail: sunexpo@surfsouth.com

Dr. Edward White, Director

The latest agricultural technology in products and equipment plus harvesting and tillage demonstrations in the field. Largest farm show in North America, 4,000 booths.
Frequency: October

10705 Supermarket Industry Convention and Educational Exposition
Food Marketing Institute
2345 Crystal Drive
Suite 800
Arlington, VA 22202

202-452-8444
FAX 202-429-4519
Home Page: www.fmi.org
Social Media: *Facebook, Twitter, LinkedIn, YouTube*

Brian Tully, Show Manager
Matt Olmsted, Consumer Goods Exhibiting
Allyson Samuel, Technolgy and Packaging Exhibits
Carrie Anderson, Attending

Features over 1,500 exhibitors, over 30 educational workshops and unique pavilions as well as the presentation of the Food Marketing Institute's annual state of the industry research. Attended by a worldwide audience of professionals with an interest in the food distribution industry from CEOs through store level management.
36000 Attendees
Frequency: Annual/May

10706 SupplySide East
Virgo Publishing LLC
3300 N Central Avenue
Suite 300
Phoenix, AZ 85012

480-990-1101
FAX 480-675-8154
E-Mail: peggyj@vpico.com
Home Page: www.supplysideshow.com
Social Media: *Facebook, Twitter, LinkedIn*

Tradeshow that brings global dietary supplement, food and personal care companies together with healthy and innovative ingredient suppliers. Meadowlands Exposition Center, Secaucus New Jersey. More than 340 booths.
Frequency: Annual/May

10707 SupplySide West
Virgo Publishing LLC
3300 N Central Avenue
Suite 300
Phoenix, AZ 85012

480-990-1101
FAX 480-675-8154
E-Mail: peggyj@vpico.com
Home Page: www.supplysideshow.com

Tradeshow that brings global dietary supplement, food and personal care companies together with healthy and innovative ingredient supplier. More than 1100 booths.
Frequency: Annual/October

10708 TFI Fertilizer Marketing & Business Meeting
Fertilizer Institute
425 Third Street, SW
Suite 950
Washington, DC 20024

202-962-0490
FAX 202-962-0577
E-Mail: information@tfi.org
Home Page: www.tfi.org
Social Media: *Facebook, Twitter, LinkedIn*

Ford West, President

Brings together members from each sector of the fertilizer industry for two days of networking and conducting business leading up the the spring planting season.
Frequency: Annual/February

10709 TFI World Fertilizer Conference
Fertilizer Institute
425 Third Street, SW
Suite 950
Washington, DC 20024

202-962-0490
FAX 202-962-0577
E-Mail: information@tfi.org
Home Page: www.tfi.org
Social Media: *Facebook, Twitter, LinkedIn*

Ford West, President

Providing two days of networking and conducting business with industry leaders. Agenda includes two breakfast sessions with high profile speakers focusing on the global challenges facing the fertilizer industry.
Frequency: Annual/September

10710 The NAFEM Show
NAFEM

161 N Clark Street
Suite 2020
Chicago, IL 60601

312-821-0201
FAX 312-821-0202
E-Mail: info@nafem.org
Home Page: www.nafem.org

Steven R. Follett, President
Thomas R. Campion, President-Elect
Michael L. Whiteley, Secretary/Treasurer
Deirdre Flynn, Executive Vice President

Attracts foodservice professionals and features exhibitors displaying products for food preparation, cooking, storage and table service. Connecting buyers and sellers of foodservice equipment and supplies, The NAFEM Show provides a showcase for the hottest and coolest products available and features education sessions and social events with big-name entertainment.
625 Members
Frequency: Biennial/February

10711 The NGA Show
National Grocers Association
1005 N Glebe Rd
Suite 250
Arlington, VA 22201-5758

703-516-0700
FAX 703-516-0115
E-Mail: info@nationalgrocers.org
Home Page: www.nationalgrocers.org
Social Media: *Facebook, Twitter, LinkedIn, YouTube*

Peter J. Larkin, President & CEO
Charlie Bray, Executive VP & COO
Tom Wenning, Executive VP & General Counsel

Providing an unparalleled opportunity to network, learn, and advance business. Guaranted a convention experience that is informational, motivational, and enjoyable.
Frequency: Annual/February

10712 Top-to-Top Conference
Association of Sales & Marketing Companies
1010 Wisconsin Avenue NW
#900
Washington, DC 20007

202-337-9351
FAX 202-337-4508
E-Mail: info@asmc.org

Mark Baum, President
Karen Connell, Executive VP
Rick Abraham, VP/COO Foodservice
Jamie DeSimone, Director Marketing/Member Services
Frequency: February

10713 Top2Top
Grocery Manufactures Association
1801-J York Road
Suite 384
Lutherville, MD 21093

410-715-4084
800-617-1170
FAX 888-668-7496
E-Mail: info@fsmaonline.com
Home Page: www.fsmaonline.com
Social Media: *Facebook*

Rick Abraham, President & CEO
Sharon Boyle, Vice President
Jessica Muffoletto, Manager, Membership & Meetings

Learn, share, and be inspired. Network with industry peers and hear from extraordinary speakers.
250 Members
Founded in 1995

10714 Tortilla Industry Annual Convention and Trade Exposition

Tortilla Industry Association
1600 Wilson Blvd
Suite 650
Arlington, VA 22209

800-944-6099
FAX 800-944-6177
E-Mail: info@tortilla-info.com
Home Page: www.tortilla-info.com

Nathan W. Fisher, Chairman
Joseph F. Riley, Chairman-Elect
Nick Scheurer, 2nd Vice President
Sam Tamayo, Treasurer

A growing event for tortilla producers and suppliers that provides the only annual trade show featuring materials, equipment, and services exclusively for the Tortilla industry, plus business lectures to assist in improving your business and personal knowledge.
900 Attendees
Frequency: Annual/September

10715 Tree Fruit Expo

Western Agricultural Publishing Company
4974 E Clinton Way
Suite 123
Fresno, CA 93727-1520

559-261-0396
FAX 559-252-7387

Phill Rhoads, Manager

Productions seminars, dessert contest, guest speakers, prizes and exhibits for tree fruit growers. Containing 80 booths and exhibits.

10716 US Apple Association Annual Apple Crop Outlook & Marketing Conference

8233 Old Courthouse Road
Suite 200
Vienna, VA 22182

703-442-8850
FAX 703-790-0845
E-Mail: info@usapple.org
Home Page: www.usapple.org
Social Media: *Facebook, Twitter, YouTube*

Provides up to the minute apple market analysis and premier networking opportunities.
300+ Attendees
Frequency: Annual/April

10717 US Meat Export Federation

1050 17th Street
Suite 2200
Denver, CO 80265-2077

303-623-6328
FAX 303-623-0297
E-Mail: info@usmef.org
Home Page: www.usmef.org

Jackie Boubin, Director of Services
Phil Seng, President

A convention of meat packers, grain, cattle and hog producers, trade officials and agribusiness and a trade show offering exhibits of beef, pork, veal, lamb products and more for foreign buyers. Trade show in May, convention in November.
300 Attendees

10718 USA Rice Millers' Association Convention

USA Rice Millers Association/Federation
4301 N Fairfax Drive
Suite 425
Arlington, VA 22203-1616

703-226-2300
FAX 703-236-2301
E-Mail: riceinfo@usarice.com
Home Page:

www.usarice.com/industry/meetings/hotel_annual.html
Social Media: *Facebook, Twitter, YouTube*

Jeanette Davis, Convention Coordinator
Betsy Ward, President/CEO
Linda Sieh, Vice President Finance
Johnny Broussard, Legislative Affairs Director
Lauren Echols, Government Affairs Coordinator

Exhibits, seminars on the advances in products, technologies and services, keynote speakers from the industry. The convention is recognized as the annual gathering for the U.S. rice milling industry. It is an opportunity to strengthen business ties and make new connections.
Frequency: Annual/June
Founded in 1900

10719 Unified Wine and Grape Symposium

PO Box 1855
Davis, CA 95617-1855

530-753-3142
FAX 530-753-3318
E-Mail: info@unifiedsymposium.org
Home Page: unifiedsymposium.org

Bill Mead, Event/Tradeshow Coordinator

One of the industry's premier gatherings, presents a vital platform to focus on the issues shaping today, while interfacing the topics and trends shaping the future of grapegrowing and winemaking.
Frequency: Annual/January

10720 Unipro Food Service Companies Association

Unipro Food Service
PO Box 724945
Atlanta, GA 31139-1945

770-952-0871
FAX 770-952-0872

Donna Campbell, Show Manager
Roger Toomey, CEO

250 tables.
1.3M Attendees

10721 United Produce Show

United Fresh Fruit & Vegetable Association
1901 Pennsylvania Avenue NW
Suite 1100
Washington, DC 20006

202-303-3400
FAX 202-303-3433
E-Mail: united@unitedfresh.org
Home Page: www.uffva.org
Social Media: *Facebook, Twitter, YouTube*

Access to the best and newest products from the entire retail supply continuum, make new contacts, learn what your competition is bringing to the table and much more.
30M Attendees
Frequency: Annual/May

10722 Upper Midwest Hospitality Restaurant & Lodging Show

Corcoran Expositions
100 W. Monroe
Suite 1001
Chicago, IL 60603

312-541-0567
FAX 312-541-0573
Home Page: www.corcexpo.com

Tom Corcoran, President
33000 Attendees
Founded in 1990

10723 Vinegar Institute Annual Meeting

1100 Johnson Ferry Road
Suite 300
Atlanta, GA 30342

404-252-3663
FAX 404-252-0774
E-Mail: vi@kellencompany.com
Home Page: www.versatilevinegar.org

Pamela A Chumley, President
Jeannie Milewski, Executive Director

Presentations regarding possible health claims for vinegar, an economic update and a world wine and grape supply update. Other topics include from green to greenwashing; how food companies are succeeding (and failing) at market sustainability and best practices in energy & carbon management. Also numerous networking opportunities available for all attendees.
Frequency: Annual/March

10724 WFLO/IARW Annual Convention & Trade Show

World Food Logistics Organization
1500 King Street
Suite 201
Alexandria, VA 22314

703-373-4300
FAX 707-373-4301
E-Mail: mkalaski@iarw.org
Home Page: www.wflo.org

Megan Kalaski, Trade Show Coordinator
Lorien Onderdonk, Member Services Coordinator

offers a singular opportunity to present product and service information to the largest concentration of public refrigerated warehouse executives in the world.
Frequency: Annual/April

10725 WSWA Annual Convention

Wine and Spirits Wholesalers of America
805 15th Street NW
Suite 430
Washington, DC 20005

202-719-9792
FAX 202-789-2405
E-Mail: Kari.Mazanec@wswa.org
Home Page: www.wswa.org

Rae Ann Bevington, Convention Manager
Kari Mazanec, Exhibit Manager
Juanita Duggan, CEO

Get the latest information for wholesale wine distributors, exhibits and speakers from the industry.
Frequency: April-May
Founded in 1943

10726 WSWA Convention & Exposition

Wine and Spirits Wholesalers of America
805 15th Street NW
Suite 430
Washington, DC 20005

202-371-9792
FAX 202-789-2405
Home Page: www.wswa.org

Robert Harmelin, Chairman
Charles Merinoff, Vice Chairman
Douglas Hertz, Senior Vice President
Alan Dreeben, Vice President
Brien Fox, Secretary

Where distributors seek out new and exciting beverage products for US consumers, meet with existing portfolio partners and look for services to enhance internal operations. Providing the opportunities needed to introduce new

products or grow brands, products, or services in the US marketplace.
450 Members
Frequency: Annual/April
Founded in 1943

10727 WSWA Executive Committee Meeting
Wine and Spirits Wholesalers of America
805 15th Street NW
Suite 430
Washington, DC 20005

202-371-9792
FAX 202-789-2405
Home Page: www.wswa.org

Robert Harmelin, Chairman
Charles Merinoff, Vice Chairman
Douglas Hertz, Senior Vice President
Alan Dreeben, Vice President
Brien Fox, Secretary

The Executive Committee, Committee Chairs and Vice Chairs and past chairmen are invited to attend.
450 Members
Frequency: Annual/January
Founded in 1943

10728 Waldbaum International Food Nutrition Show
80 Town Line Road
Rocky Hill, CT 06067-1249

860-529-1416
FAX 860-721-6258

John Masterson, Manager

A wide variety of new and existing food products and services. 225 booths.
25M Attendees
Frequency: March

10729 Walnut Council Annual Meeting
Walnut Council
Wright Forestry Center
1011 N 725 West
West Lafayette, IN 47906-9431

765-583-3501
FAX 765-583-3512
E-Mail: walnutcouncil@walnutcouncil.org
Home Page: www.walnutcouncil.org

Liz Jackson, Exhibits Coordinator

Exhibits of equipment, supplies and services for walnut growing.
Frequency: Annual/July

10730 Washington Insight & Advocacy Conference
International Foodservice Distributors Association
1410 Spring Hill Road
Suite 210
McLean, VA 22102-3035

703-532-9400
FAX 703-538-4673
Home Page: www.ifdaonline.org

Mark Allen, President & CEO
Jonathan Eisen, Senior VP/ Government Relations

IFDA members from coast-to-coast converge on the capitol to gain insight from congressional leaders and federal regulators and let them know how their decisions affect the foodservice distribution idustry.
Frequency: Annual/April

10731 West Coast Seafood Show
Diversified Expositions
121 Free Street
Portland, ME 04112

207-842-5500
FAX 207-842-5505

E-Mail: food@divcom.com
Home Page: www.westcoastseafood.com

Karen Butland, Show Manager
Brian Perkins, Executive Director
Frequency: November

10732 Western Farm Show
Southwestern Association
638 W 39th Street
Kansas City, MO 64111

816-561-5323
800-728-2272
FAX 816-561-1991

Annual show of 700 manufacturers, suppliers and distributors of equipment, supplies and services relating to the agricultural industry.
35M Attendees
Frequency: February

10733 Western Food Industry Exposition
555 Capitol Mall
Suite 235
Sacramento, CA 95814-4557

FAX 703-876-0904
E-Mail: cga@cmgexpo.com

Keith Biersner, Account Executive

Retailers from 13 western states and suppliers from around the world. Relevant education sessions, vibrant exhibits and excellent social events are all designed to create the best form to enhance your companies bottom line. 400 booths.
3500 Attendees
Frequency: October
Founded in 1998

10734 Western Food Service and Hospitality Expo
California Restaurant Association
383 Main Avenue
PO Box 6059
Norwalk, CT 06851

203-840-5612
800-840-5612
FAX 203-840-9612
Home Page: www.westernfoodexpo.com

Chris Tatulli, Sales Manager
Steve Kalman, Industry VP

Showcases food products, food service equipment and allied services for the restaurant, food service and hospitality industries, as well as gourmet and prepared foods. Located on the West Coast, the show alternates annually between the Moscone Center in San Francisco and the LA Convention Center.
20M Attendees
Frequency: August

10735 Western Restaurant Show
California Restaurant Association
1011 10th St
Sacramento, CA 95814-3501

916-447-5793
FAX 213-384-1723

A trade show of food service equipment, supplies and services. 2,000 booths.
35M Attendees
Frequency: August

10736 Wine and Spirits Wholesalers of America
805 15th Street NW
Suite 430
Washington, DC 20005

202-371-9792
FAX 202-789-2405
E-Mail: wswa@wswa.org
Home Page: www.wswa.org

Craig Wolf, President/CEO
Megan McIntire, Director

Convention/Meetings
Karen Gravois, VP Public Relations/Communications

Suppliers of alcoholic beverages from around the world. 300 booths plus educational sessions.
3M Attendees
Frequency: April

10737 Wineries Unlimited
Vineyard & Winery Management
3883 Airway Drive
Suite 250
Santa Rosa, CA 95403

707-577-7700
FAX 707-577-7705
Home Page: www.wineriesunlimited.com
Social Media: *Facebook, Twitter*

The largest, longest running, and most powerful wine industry event in the eastern US.
2000 Attendees
Frequency: Annual/February

10738 Winter State Policy Conference
Wine and Spirits Wholesalers of America
805 15th Street NW
Suite 430
Washington, DC 20005

202-371-9792
FAX 202-789-2405
Home Page: www.wswa.org

Robert Harmelin, Chairman
Charles Merinoff, Vice Chairman
Douglas Hertz, Senior Vice President
Alan Dreeben, Vice President
Brien Fox, Secretary

Provides an opportunity for wholesaler state association leaders to discuss the political and legal issues facing wholesalers across the country.
450 Members
Frequency: Annual/December
Founded in 1943

10739 Wisconsin Restaurant Expo
Wisconsin Restaurant Association
2801 Fish Hatchery Road
Madison, WI 53703-3197

608-270-9950
800-589-3211
FAX 608-270-9960
E-Mail: dfaris@wirestaurant.org
Home Page: www.wirestaurant.org

Dawn Renz-Faris, Exposition Director
Carrie Douglas, Executive Assistant
Gail Parr, Executive Vice President

Comprehensive foodservice trade show featuring hundreds of exhibits, free educational seminars and exciting floor show events.
10000 Attendees
Frequency: March
Founded in 1933
Mailing list available for rent

10740 World Conference & Exhibition on Oil Seed and Vegetable Oil Utilization
American Oil Chemists Society
2710 S. Boulder
Urbana, IL 61802-6996

217-359-2344
FAX 217-351-8091
E-Mail: general@aocs.org
Home Page: www.aocs.org
Social Media: *Facebook, Twitter*

Sevim Erhan, Committee Chairperson

Attendees are interested in learning the latest information on currint and emerging technologies from all areas in oilseed and vegetable oil utilization.
Frequency: Annual/August

10741 World Dairy Expo
3310 Latham
Madison, WI 53713

608-224-6455
FAX 608-224-0300
E-Mail: wde@wdexpo.com
Home Page: www.worlddairyexpo.com

Tom McKittrick, Manager
Lisa Behnke, Marketing Manager
65M Attendees
Frequency: October, Annually
Founded in 1966

10742 World Pork Exposition
National Pork Producers Council
PO Box 10383
Des Moines, IA 50306-9960

515-788-8012
FAX 847-838-1941
E-Mail: wrigleyj@nppc.org
Home Page: www.worldpork.org

John Wrigley, General Manager
Alice Vinsand, Trade Show Manager

More than 450 companies show the newest
technology, information, products and services
for pork producers. Activities include breed
shows and sales, business district, environmental education center, pork product showcase,
big grill, pork 101, educational seminars and
activities.
40000 Attendees
Frequency: June

10743 World Wine Market
775 E Blithedale Avenue
#370
Mill Valley, CA 94941

415-383-1226
FAX 415-383-0858
E-Mail: sclarke@world-wine-market.com
Home Page: www.world-wine-market.com

Stephanie Clarke, VP Sales/Marketing

10744 World of Food and Fuel EXPO
Tennessee Grocers Association
1838 Elm Hill Pike
Suite 136
Nashville, TN 37210-3726

615-889-0136
800-238-8742
FAX 615-889-2877
Home Page: www.tngrocer.org

Jarron Springer, President
Cyndi Randle, Chairman
John Wampler, Treasurer
8000 Attendees
Frequency: April

10745 Worldwide Food Expo
Dairy and Food Industries Supply
Association
1451 Dolley Madison Boulevard
Suite 101
McLean, VA 22101

703-761-2600
FAX 703-761-4334
Home Page: www.worldwidefoodexpo.com

Trade show and education forum for the food,
dairy, beverage and technologically related industries, featuring equipment, services and ingredients that highlight new development and
technologies in processing and packaging.
350,000 square feet.
Frequency: Annual/October

Directories & Databases

10746 ACFSA Directory
American Correctional Food Service
Affiliates
210 N Glenoaks Blvd
Suite C
Burbank, CA 91502

818-843-6608
FAX 818-843-7423
Home Page: www.acfsa.org

Jon Nichols, Executive Director

Directory of ACFSA members and the services
provided by vender members.
Cost: $5.00
235 Pages
Frequency: Annually
Circulation: 1,500
Printed in 4 colors on glossy stock

10747 AGRICOLA
US National Agricultural Library
10301 Baltimore Ave
Room 13
Beltsville, MD 20705-2351

301-504-5755
FAX 301-504-5675
Home Page: www.nal.usda.gov

Gary K McCone, Associate Director

A database containing more than 3.2 million citations to journal literature, government reports, proceedings, books, periodicals, theses,
patents, audiovisuals, electronic information,
and other materials related to agriculture and
its allied sciences.

10748 ARI Network
330 E Kilbourn Ave
Suite 565
Milwaukee, WI 53202-3144

414-220-9100
800-558-9044
FAX 414-283-4357
Home Page: www.aris-corporation.com

Lawrence Shindell, Owner
John Kermath, Director

Offers current information on agricultural business, financial and weather information as well
as statistical information for farmers.

10749 Ag Ed Network
ARI Network Services
330 E Kilbourn Ave
Suite 565
Milwaukee, WI 53202-3144

414-220-9100
800-558-9044
FAX 414-283-4357
Home Page: www.aris-corporation.com

Lawrence Shindell, Owner
John Kermath, Director

Offers access to more than 1,500 educational
agriculture lessons covering farm business
management and farm production.
Frequency: Full-text

10750 AgriMarketing Services Guide
Henderson Communications LLC
1422 Elbridge Payne Rd
Suite 250
Chesterfield, MO 63017-8544

636-728-1428
FAX 636-777-4178
Home Page: www.agrimarketing.com

Lynn Henderson, Owner

AgriMarketing Services Guide is published
each December and is commonly referred to as
the Who's Who in the North American ag industry sector.
Frequency: Annual

**10751 Agribusiness Worldwide International
Buyer's Guide Issue**
Keller International Publishing Corporation
150 Great Neck Rd
Great Neck, NY 11021-3309

516-829-9722
FAX 516-829-9306
Home Page: www.supplychainbrain.com

Jerry Keller, President
Mary Chavez, Director of Sales

A list of companies that supply, manufacture or
distribute agricultural products and services.
Cost: $42.00
Frequency: Annual

**10752 Agricultural Research Institute:
Membership Directory**
Agricultural Research Institute
9650 Rockville Pike
Bethesda, MD 20814-3998

301-530-7122
FAX 301-530-7007

Richard A Herrett, Executive Director

One hundred and twenty-five member institutions; also lists study panels and committees interested in environmental issues, pest control,
agricultural meteorology, biotechnology, food
irradiation, agricultural policy, research and development, food safety, technology transfer and
remote sensing.
Cost: $50.00
Frequency: Annual

**10753 Airline, Ship & Catering: Onboard
Service Buyer's Guide & Directory**
International Publishing Company of
America
664 La Villa Dr
Miami Springs, FL 33166-6030

305-887-1700
FAX 305-885-1923

Alexander Morton, Owner

Offers information on over 6,000 airlines, rail-
roads, ship lines and terminal restaurants.
Cost: $125.00
Frequency: Annual
Circulation: 6,000

**10754 Almanac of Food Regulations and
Statistical Information**
Edward E Judge & Sons
PO Box 866
Westminster, MD 21158-0866

410-876-2052
800-729-5517
FAX 410-848-2034
Home Page: www.eejudge.com

Includes labeling law and FDA regulations,
HACCP requirements for seafood, FDA current
good manufacturing practice regulations,
USDA canning regulations, frozen food handling code, FDA standards of identity, quality
and fill of container, USDA quality grade standards, frozen fruit and vegetable pack statistics,
agricultural statistics, and census of manufacturing.
Cost: $71.00
824 Pages
Frequency: Annual
Circulation: 3,000
ISBN: 1-880821-19-2
Founded in 1916

10755 American Butter Institute: Membership Directory

American Butter Institute
2101 Wilson Boulevard
Suite 400
Arlington, VA 22201

703-243-5630
FAX 703-841-9328
Home Page: www.butterinstitute.org

Cindy Cazallo, Editor

This directory offers a comprehensive list of over 35 processors, distributors and packagers of butter in the US and suppliers to the industry. Members only.
Cost: $250.00
25 Pages
Frequency: Annual

10756 American Fruit Grower

Meister Media Worldwide
37733 Euclid Ave
Willoughby, OH 44094-5992

440-942-2000
800-572-7740
FAX 440-975-3447
E-Mail: jwmonahan@meistermedia.com
Home Page: www.meisternet.com

Gary Fitzgerald, President
Sue Stearns, Assistant Circulation Manager
JoAnne Mauer, Sales Assistant

Offers a list of manufacturers and distributors of equipment and supplies for the commercial fruit growing industry.
Cost: $19.95
66 Pages
Frequency: 10x
Circulation: 35,849
Founded in 1880

10757 American Meat Science Association Directory of Members

American Meat Science Association
2441 Village Green Pl
Champaign, IL 61822-7676

217-356-5370
800-517-AMSA
FAX 888-205-5834
FAX 217-356-5370
E-Mail: information@meatscience.org
Home Page: www.meatscience.org

Thomas Powell, Executive Director
Randy Huffman, President-Elect
Kathy Ruff, Meetings & Member Services Director

Directory for American Meat Science members only.
Cost: $20.00
230 Pages
Frequency: Biennial

10758 American Red Angus: Breeders Directory

Red Angus Association of America
4201 N Interstate 35
Denton, TX 76207-3415

940-387-3502
FAX 940-383-4036
E-Mail: info@redangus.org
Home Page: www.redangus.org
Social Media: *Facebook*

Judy Edwards, Manager
Betty Grimshaw, Association Admin Director
Clint Berry, Commercial Marketing Director

This directory is a list of over 1,800 breeders of Red Angus cattle.
Frequency: Annual
Circulation: 8,000

10759 American Society of Consulting Arborists: Membership Directory

American Society of Consulting Arborists
15245 Shady Grove Road
Rockville, MD 20850-3222

301-947-0483

Beth Palys, Executive Director
Steven Geist, President

About 270 persons specializing in the growth and care of urban shade and ornamental trees; includes expert witnesses and monetary appraisals.
Frequency: Annual March

10760 American Spice Trade Association Membership Roster

American Spice Trade Association
2025 M St NW
Suite 800
Washington, DC 20036-2422

202-367-1127
FAX 202-367-2127
Home Page: www.iamss.org

Cheryl Deem, Executive Director
Frequency: Annual

10761 Automatic Merchandiser Blue Book Buyer's Guide Issue

Cygnus Publishing
PO Box 803
Fort Atkinson, WI 53538-0803

920-000-1111
800-547-7377
FAX 920-563-1699
Home Page: www.cygnusb2b.com

John French, CEO
Kathy Scott, Director of Public Relations
Paul Bonaiuto, CFO

Thousands of suppliers are profiled that offer products, services and equipment to the merchandise vending, food service and office coffee service industries.
Cost: $35.00
Frequency: Annual

10762 BEMA Equipment & Suppliers Datebase

BEMA
10740 Nall Avenue
Suite 230
Overland Park, KS 66211

913-338-1300
FAX 913-338-1327
E-Mail: info@bema.org
Home Page: www.bema.org

Find the baking industry's leading suppliers.
220 Pages
Founded in 1918

10763 Bakery Materials and Methods

Elsevier Science
655 Avenue of the Americas
New York, NY 10010-5107

212-633-3800
FAX 212-633-3850
Home Page: www.elsevier.com

Young Suk Chi, Chairman
Bill Godfrey, Chief Information Officer
David Clark, Senior Vice President
Cost: $41.50
Founded in 1978

10764 Bakery Production and Marketing Buyers Guide Issue

Delta Communications

11617 W Bluemound Road
Wauwatosa, WI 53226

414-774-7270
FAX 414-777-7277
Home Page: delta@deltacommunications.com

Pat Reynolds, Editor

This publication offers a list of over 1,800 manufacturers of equipment, ingredients, and supplies for bakeries. Enteries offer company names, addresses, phones, faxes and name and title of contract.

10765 Bakery Production and Marketing Red Book Issue

Delta Communications
Ste 300
20900 Swenson Dr
Waukesha, WI 53186-4050

262-542-9111
FAX 262-542-8820
E-Mail: delta@deltacommunications.com
Home Page: www.deltacommunications.com

Offers a list of over 2,500 wholesale, multi-unit retail, grocery chain and co-op bakery companies and plants in the US and Canada that manufacture bread, cakes, cookies, crackers, pretzels, snack foods, and frozen bakery products.
Cost: $255.00
Frequency: Annual

10766 Baking Buyer Yearbook Issue

Sosland Publishing Company
4800 Main St
Suite 100
Kansas City, MO 64112-2513

816-756-1000
FAX 816-756-0494
E-Mail: web@sosland.com
Home Page: www.sosland.com

Gordon Davidson, President

Over 1,000 distributors and manufacturers of products and equipment for the baking industry are profiled in this comprehensive directory.
Cost: $75.00
Frequency: Annual

10767 Baking/Snack Directory and Buyer's Guide

Sosland Publishing Company
4800 Main St
Suite 100
Kansas City, MO 64112-2513

816-756-1000
FAX 816-756-0494
E-Mail: web@sosland.com
Home Page: www.sosland.com

Gordon Davidson, President

Wholesalers of bread and baked goods, as well as snacks and frozen dough are listed in this directory.
Cost: $90.00
Frequency: Annual
Circulation: 8,000

10768 Beef Sire Directory

American Breeders Service/Customer Service
PO Box 459
De Forest, WI 53532-0459

608-846-3721
FAX 608-846-6392
E-Mail: custserv_dept@absglobal.com
Home Page: www.absglobal.com

Ian Biggs, CEO

A directory listing beef cattle associations in the US and Canada.
Frequency: Annual

10769 Beverage Digest Fact Book

Beverage Digest
PO Box 621
Bedford Hills, NY 10507-0621

914-244-0700
FAX 914-244-0774
E-Mail: order@beverage-digest.com
Home Page: www.beverage-digest.com

John Sicher, Owner

This book is a complete portrait of the global non-alcoholic beverage business.

10770 Beverage Digest Soft Drink Atlas

Beverage Digest
PO Box 621
Bedford Hills, NY 10507-0621

914-244-0700
FAX 914-244-0774
E-Mail: order@beverage-digest.com
Home Page: www.beverage-digest.com

John Sicher, Owner

Book of US maps related to soft drink bottler territories. This book offers a geographic portrait of the US carbonated beverage bottling business.

10771 Beverage Marketing Directory

Beverage Marketing Corporation
2670 Commercial Ave
Mingo Junction, OH 43938-1613

740-598-4133
800-332-6222
FAX 740-598-3977
Home Page: www.beveragemarketing.com

Andrew Standardi III, Director of Operations
Kathy Smurthwaite, Editor

Publication is available in Print Copy (Price-$1,465), PDF Format (Price-$1,465), CD-ROM Format (For pricing, call number listed for details or visit website), and Online.
1196 Pages

10772 Biological & Agricultural Index

HW Wilson Company
950 Dr Martin L King Jr Blvd
Bronx, NY 10452-4297

718-588-8405
800-367-6770
FAX 718-590-1617
Home Page: www.hwwilson.com

Harold Regan, CEO
Kathleen McEvoy, Director of Public Relations

Provides fast access to core literature. In addition to citations to research and feature articles, users finding indexing of reports of symposia and conferences, and citations to current book reviews. Available on Web and disc.

10773 Blue Book Buyer's Guide

Food Processing Machinery Association
1451 Dolley Madison Blvd
Suite 101
McLean, VA 22101-3850

703-761-2600
FAX 703-761-4334
E-Mail: info@fpsa.org
Home Page: www.fpsa.org

A buyers guide offering information on over 500 member food and beverage industry firms. Entries are cross-referenced with both a product and commodity locator.
Cost: $50.00
200 Pages
Circulation: 30,000

10774 Blue Book: Fruit and Vegetable Credit and Marketing Service

Produce Reporter Company

845 E Geneva Rd
Carol Stream, IL 60188-3520

630-668-3500
FAX 630-668-0303
E-Mail: sales@bluebookprco.com
Home Page: www.bluebookprco.com

C James Carr, President

A directory offering information on over 15,000 produce growers, wholesalers, shippers and retailers in the US.
Cost: $575.00
1275 Pages
Frequency: Semiannual
Founded in 1901

10775 Bottled Water Market

MarketResearch.com
641 Avenue of the Americas
3rd Floor
New York, NY 10011

212-807-2629
800-298-6699
FAX 212-807-2676

The report provides descriptions and coverage of market size and growth, market comppsition, leading marketers, the competitive situation, new product trends, advertising and promotion, and more.
Cost: $2750.00
139 Pages

10776 Brand Directory

Vance Publishing
10901 W 84th Ter
Suite 200
Lenexa, KS 66214-1631

913-438-5721
800-255-5113
FAX 913-438-0697
E-Mail: info@vancepublishing.com
Home Page: www.vancepublishing.com

Cliff Becker, Vice President, Director
Dan Woods, Chief Financial Officer
Lori Eppel, Chief Financial Officer

A composite of major fresh fruit and vegetable brands and suppliers. It is divided into three sections and contains 66 commodities.
Cost: $10.00

10777 Brewers Digest: Buyers Guide and Brewery Directory

Ammark Publishing
4049 W Peterson Avenue
Chicago, IL 60646-6001

Lists all breweries in the Western Hemisphere, suppliers, associations and importers.
Cost: $30.00
Frequency: Annual
Circulation: 3,000

10778 Brewers Resource Directory

Brewers Association
736 Pearl Street
Boulder, CO 80302

303-447-0816
888-822-6273
FAX 303-447-2825
E-Mail: webmaster@brewerassociation.org
Home Page: www.beertown.org
Social Media: *Facebook, Twitter*

Various categories of listees are included that have a direct relation to the beer and liquor industry.
Mailing list available for rent

10779 Brown Swiss Cattle Breeders' Association Directory

Brown Swiss Cattle Breeders' Association

800 Pleasant St
Beloit, WI 53511-5456

608-365-4474
FAX 608-365-5577
E-Mail: info@brownswissusa.com
Home Page: www.brownswissusa.com

Roger Neitzel, Manager
David Kendall, Secretary

10780 CID Service

US Department of Agriculture
200 Independence Ave SW
Washington, DC 20201-0007

202-690-7650

This database contains 467 categories of information prepared by the US Department of Agriculture and its agencies.
Frequency: Full-text

10781 CRC Press

2000 NW Corporate Boulevard
Boca Raton, FL 33431

561-994-0555
800-272-7737
FAX 561-998-0876
E-Mail: techsupport@crcpress.com
Home Page: www.crcpress.com

Eleanor Riemer, Publisher
Emmett Dages, CEO

Publisher in science, medicine, environmental science, forensic, engineering, business, technology, mathematics, and statistics. Our food science and nutrition books and our journal, Critical Reviews in Food and Nutrition, are well established and respected publications in the food science industry.

10782 CRIS/USDA Database

Current Research Information System
1400 Independence Avenue SW
Suite 2270
Washington, DC 20250

202-690-0119
FAX 202-690-0634
E-Mail: cris@csrees.usda.gov
Home Page: cris.csrees.usda.gov

Ellen A Terpstra, CEO
Don Tilmon, Director

Offers over 35,000 ongoing and recently completed agricultural, food and nutrition and forestry research projects sponsored by the US Department of Agriculture.

10783 California League of Food Processors Annual Directory of Members

980 Ninth Street
Sacramento, CA 95814

916-444-9260
FAX 916-444-2746
Home Page: www.clfp.com

Robert Graf, President/CEO
Ed Yates, Senior VP
Nora Basrai, Meetings/Members Services
Rob Neenan, Senior Vice President
Amy Alcorn, Marketing Manager

Contains listings of all members, including plant locations and products produced. Over 800 industry leaders are listed.
200 Pages
Founded in 1905

10784 Candy Marketer: Candy, Snack and Tobacco Buyers' Guide

Stagnito Communications

155 Pfingster Road
Suite 205
Deerfield, IL 60015

847-205-5660
FAX 847-205-5680

Linda Stagnito, President

A publication that includes a list of suppliers to the confectionery, snack and tobacco products industries. Entries include company names, addresses, key personnel, warehouse locations and firms represented.
Cost: $25.00
Frequency: Annual

10785 Chain Restaurant Operators Directory

Chain Store Guide
3922 Coconut Palm Dr
Suite 300
Tampa, FL 33619-1389

813-627-6700
800-972-9202
FAX 813-627-7094
E-Mail: info@csgis.com
Home Page: www.csgis.com

Mike Jarvis, Publisher
Chris Leedy, Advertising Sales

Discover more than 5,600 listings and more than 26,000 unique personnel within the Restaurant Chain, Foodservice Management, and Hotel/Motel Operator markets in the U.S. and Canada. Each company must have at least $1 million in annual sales either system wide or industry and have two or more units/accounts.
Cost: $335.00
Frequency: Annual

10786 Cheese Market News: Annual

Quarne Publishing
PO 628254
Middleton, WI 53562

608-831-6002
FAX 608-831-1004
E-Mail: squarne@cheesemarketnews.com
Home Page: www.cheesemarketnews.com

Susan Quarne, Publisher

Comprehensive listings include the companies that manufacture the latest styles and varieties of cheese as well as the industry's key suppliers of cheese equipment, packaging equipment, materials and supplies and services.
Cost: $30.00
Frequency: Annual
Circulation: 3,000

10787 Citrus & Vegetable Magazine: Farm Equipment Directory Issue

Vance Publishing
10901 W 84th Ter
Suite 200
Lenexa, KS 66214-1631

913-438-5721
FAX 913-438-0697
E-Mail: info@vancepublishing.com
Home Page: www.vancepublishing.com

Cliff Becker, Vice President, Director
Lori Eppel, Chief Financial Officer

Offers information on a list of manufacturers of produce and citrus growing, handling, picking and packaging equipment.
Cost: $25.00
48 Pages
Frequency: Annual
Circulation: 12,000
ISSN: 0009-7586
Founded in 1938

10788 Coffee Anyone???

9616 Thunderbird Drive
Suite 215
San Ramon, CA 94583

925-829-4022
800-347-9687
FAX 925-829-4025
E-Mail: coffee@coffee-anyone.com
Home Page: http://www.coffeeanyone.com

This database contains descriptions of gourmet, regular, decaffenated and flavored coffees, including a chart summarizing the strength and taste of each coffee.

10789 Coffee, Sugar and Cocoa Exchange Guide

Commerce Clearing House
2700 Lake Cook Rd
Riverwoods, IL 60015-3867

847-940-4600
FAX 847-779-1535
E-Mail: mediahelp@cch.com
Home Page: www.cch.com

Mike Sabbatis, President

Offers information on member and member organizations of the Exchange.
Cost: $240.00
170 Pages
Frequency: Monthly

10790 Commercial Food Equipment Service Association Directory

Commercial Food Equipment Service Association
2216 W Meadowview Road
Suite 100
Greensboro, NC 27407

336-346-4700
FAX 336-346-4745
E-Mail: cstrickland@cfesa.com
Home Page: www.cfesa.com

Carla Strickland, Executive Director
Lauri Smith, Treasurer
Wayne Stoutner, Treasurer
David Hahn, Secretary

Independent food service companies that repair commercial food equipment.
Frequency: Annual

10791 Complete Directory of Concessions & Equipment

Sutton Family Communications & Publishing Company
920 State Route 54 East
Elmitch, KY 42343

270-276-9500
E-Mail: jlsutton@apex.net

Theresa Sutton, Editor
Lee Sutton, General Manager

Printout from database of wholesalers, manufacturers, distributors, importers and close-out houses; updated daily to guarantee the most current and up-to-date sources available.
Cost: $27.90
100+ Pages

10792 Complete Directory of Food Products

Sutton Family Communications & Publishing Company
920 State Route 54 East
Elmitch, KY 42343

270-276-9500
E-Mail: jlsutton@apex.net

Theresa Sutton, Editor
Lee Sutton, General Manager

Printout from database of wholesalers, manufacturers, distributors, importers and close-out houses. Database is updated daily to guarantee the most current and up-to-date sources avail-

able.
Cost: $27.90
100+ Pages

10793 Consumer's Guide to Fruits & Vegetables & Other Farm Fresh Products

Missouri Cooperative Extension Service
PO Box 29
Jefferson City, MO 65102-0029

573-681-5301
FAX 573-635-2314

David N Sasseville, Editor

A directory covering over 400 fruit and vegetable farm markets in Missouri.
124 Pages
Frequency: Annual

10794 Contemporary World Issues: Agricultural Crisis in America

ABC-CLIO
PO Box 1911
Santa Barbara, CA 93116-1911

805-705-9339
800-422-2546
FAX 805-685-9685

Barbara McEwan, Editor

List of agencies and organizations in the US concerned with agricultural issues.
Cost: $39.50

10795 Convenience Store Decisions Sales Tracking Study

Harbor Communications
19111 Detroit Road
Suite 201
Rocky River, OH 44116

440-250-1583
FAX 440-333-1892
Home Page: www.csdecisions.com

Joseph Howton, Executive VP/COO

Survey of convenience store chain buyers that tracks the effectiveness of supplier promotional programs. It reports on how manufacturers call on retail chains and how those chains are responding to suppliers' merchandising efforts.
Frequency: Annual

10796 Cookies Market

MarketResearch.com
641 Avenue of the Americas
3rd Floor
New York, NY 10011

212-807-2629
800-298-6699
FAX 212-807-2676

This report uncovers trends in its in-depth investigation of US retail sales of packaged and fresh-baked cookies. The analysis covers packaged cookie retail sales by distribution channel, marketer, and product line. The leading marketers are profiled in order to review growth-and-profit-oriented strategies. The data information is analyzed in order for users to uncover growing product lines, target key demographics, pinpoint distribution channel sales opportunities, and profitable strategies.
Cost: $2250.00
169 Pages

10797 Corn Annual

Corn Refiners Association

1701 Pennsylvania Ave NW
Suite 950
Washington, DC 20006-5806

202-331-1634
FAX 202-331-2054
Home Page: www.corn.org

Report featuring articles on the state of the industry. Includes statistical report on corn shipments, supply and consumption in the US and abroad.
Frequency: Annually
Circulation: 8,000

10798 Crop Protection Reference
C&P Press
565 5th Ave
5th Floor
New York, NY 10017-2413

212-587-8620
FAX 646-733-6010
Home Page: www.cppress.com

A single comprehensive source of up-to-date label information of crop protection products marketed in the US by basic manufacturers and formulators. Extensive product indexing helps to locate products by brand name, manufacturer, crop site, mode of action, disease, insect, week, product category, common name and tank mix.
Cost: $170.00
Frequency: Annual

10799 Culinary Collection Directory
International Association/Culinary Professionals
304 W Liberty Street
Suite 201
Louisville, KY 40202

502-587-7953
800-928-4227
FAX 502-589-3602
E-Mail: info@iacp.com
Home Page: www.iacp.com

Kerry Edwards, Sr Member Services Representative
Trina Gribbins, Manager

Teachers, cooking school owners, caterers, writers, chefs, media cooking personalities, editors, publishers, food stylists, food photographers, restauranteurs, leaders of major food corporations and vintners. Literally a who's who of the food world.

10800 Dairy Foods Market Guide
Delta Communications
455 N Cityfront Plaza Drive
Chicago, IL 60611-5503

312-836-2000
FAX 312-222-2026

A guide including a list of 1,600 manufacturers of dairy processing equipment and over 900 distributors of dairy processing equipment.
Cost: $99.00
Frequency: Annual

10801 Developing Successful New Products for Foodservice Markets
International Food Service Manufacturers
180 North Stetson Avenue
Suite 4400
Chicago, IL 60601-6766

312-540-4400
FAX 312-540-4401
E-Mail: ifma@ifmaworld.com
Home Page: www.ifmaworld.com
Social Media: *Facebook, LinkedIn, YouTube*

Larry Oberkfell, President & CEO
Jennifer Tarulis, CFO
Michael Hickey, Chairman

Mark Bendix, 1st Vice Chairman
Loren Kimura, Treasurer

Handbook on new product development offers sound advice on the critical success factors confronting new product managers. Up-to-date information on new products and practices and an expanded section on market research.
Cost: $ 495.00
Frequency: Annual

10802 Directory & Products Guide
Vineyard & Winery Services
PO Box 2358
Windsor, CA 95492

707-836-6820
800-535-5670
FAX 707-836-6825
Home Page: vwm-online.com

Jennifer Merietti, Sales/Marketing Manager
Dennis Black, General Manager
Suzanne Webb, Marketing Director

A must have reference book that belongs on the desk of every wine professional. Whether it's tracking down a particular vendor, shopping for the best deal on oak barrels or searching for out-of-state winery contacts, the DPG is a powerhouse of information. Over 2,300 supplier listings and 2,700 winery/vineyard listings, it is a reliable resource that saves time and money.
Cost: $95.00
450+ Pages
Frequency: Annually

10803 Directory of AFFI Member Companies
American Frozen Food Institute
2000 Corporate Ridge
Suite 1000
McLean, VA 22102-7862

703-821-0770
FAX 703-821-1350
E-Mail: info@affi.com
Home Page: www.knowitsyogurt.com

Robert L Garfield, President
Jason Bassett, Director Legislative Affairs
Chuck Fuqua, VP Communications
Cost: $100.00
Frequency: Annual
Circulation: 5000

10804 Directory of American Agriculture
Agricultural Resources & Communications
301 Broadway
Belvue, KS 66407

785-456-9705
FAX 785-456-1654
E-Mail: chris@agresources.com
Home Page: www.agresources.com

Christina Wilson, President

This directory lists over 7,000 state and national associations involved in providing products and services related to food and fiber industries, in 27 categories. There are categorical indexes as well. Includes guide to Washington, DC offices, USDA listings, and guide to ag commodity commissions. Available on CD for $99.
Cost: $64.95
350 Pages
ISSN: 0897-1919
Founded in 1988
Printed in on matte stock

10805 Directory of Convenience Stores
Trade Dimensions

45 Danbury Rd
Wilton, CT 06897-4445

203-563-3000
FAX 860-563-3131
Home Page: www.tradedimensions.com

Jennifer Gillbert, Editor
Lynda Guticulez, Managing Editor

The directory comprises nearly 1,500 detailed profiles on the companies you need to do business with. Extensive dependable information on the grocery industry's most volatile segment.
Cost: $245.00
Frequency: Annual

10806 Directory of Custom Food Processors and Formulators
Delphi Marketing Services
400 E 89th Street
Apartment 2J
New York, NY 10128-6728

Covers formulators and processors of custom food products.
Cost: $260.00
Frequency: Annual

10807 Directory of State Departments of Agriculture
US Department of Agriculture
200 Independence Ave SW
Room 3964
Washington, DC 20201-0007

202-690-7650
Home Page: www.usda.gov

Chris Smith, Chief Information Officer
Matt Paul, Director of Communications
Ramona Romero, General Counsel

Offer valuable information on all the state departments of agriculture, including their officials.
73 Pages
Frequency: Biennial

10808 Directory of the Canning, Freezing, Preserving Industries
Edward E Judge & Sons
PO Box 866
Westminster, MD 21158-0866

410-876-2052
FAX 410-848-2034
Home Page: www.eejudge.com

Daniel P Judge, Publisher

This directory offers extensive company profiles including over 10,000 managers, over 3,000 North American Food plants that are involved in canning, freezing and preserving fruits, vegetables, dinners, specialties and more. Published in standard edition, 768 pages, and special deluxe edition 1,408 pages.
Cost: $175.00
768 Pages
Frequency: Biennial
ISBN: 1-880821-20-6
Founded in 1966

10809 Diversified Business Communications
PO Box 7437
Portland, ME 04112-7437

207-842-5600
FAX 207-842-5503
Home Page: www.divbusiness.com

Nancy Hasselback, CEO
Nancy Gelette, VP Operations

A producer of international trade expositions for the seafood and commercial marine industries.

10810 EMDA Membership Directory
Equipment Marketing & Distribution Association

PO Box 1347
Iowa City, IA 52244-1347

319-354-5156
FAX 319-354-5157
E-Mail: pat@emda.net
Home Page: www.emda.net

Patricia A Collins, Executive VP

Annual directory of Association members, includes address, phone, fax, web, e-mail, territory covered (with map) product descriptions, key personnel and a descriptive paragraph.
Cost: $50.00

10811 Electronic Pesticide Reference: EPR II

C&P Press
New York, NY 10001

212-326-6760
FAX 646-733-6010
Home Page: www.cppress.com

Complete electronic reference to our 1,500 crop protection products; a full range of product information: full text labels and supplemental labels, full text MSDS's, product summaries, list of labeled tank mixes, worker protection information, DOT shipping information, SARA Title III reporting information. Search by brand name, manufacturer, common name crop, plant, site, weed, disease, insect plus much more. All versions of EPR II are provided on CD-ROM for windows.

10812 Essential Rendering

National Renderers Association
801 N Fairfax St
Suite 205
Alexandria, VA 22314-1776

703-683-0155
FAX 703-683-2626
Home Page: www.nationalrenderers.org

Thomas M Cook, President

An in-depth guide that covers the various aspects of rendering.
Frequency: Monthly

10813 Feed Additive Compendium

The Miller Publishing Company
12400 Whitewater Dr
Suite 160
Hopkins, MN 55343-4590

952-931-0211
FAX 952-938-1832
Home Page: www.feedcompendium.com

Sarah Muirhead, Publisher

Provides the latest information on which medicated additives can be used at what inclusion levels for what puposes. Also provides information on regulation, compliance and quality control, product specimen labels, and a directory of state and FDA contacts.
Cost: $52.00
Frequency: Weekly
Founded in 1931

10814 Food & Beverage Marketplace Directory

Grey House Publishing
4919 Route 22
PO Box 56
Amenia, NY 12501

518-789-8700
800-562-2139
FAX 845-373-6390
E-Mail: books@greyhouse.com
Home Page: www.greyhouse.com
Social Media: *Facebook, Twitter*

Richard Gottlieb, President
Leslie Mackenzie, Publisher

A three-volume set that is the most comprehensive resource in the food and beverage industry. Available in print, a subscription-based online database, as well as a mailing list and database formats.
Cost: $595.00
2000 Pages
Frequency: Annual

10815 Food & Beverage Marketplace: Online Database

Grey House Publishing
4919 Route 22
PO Box 56
Amenia, NY 12501

518-789-8700
800-562-2139
FAX 845-373-6390
E-Mail: gold@greyhouse.com
Home Page: http://gold.greyhouse.com
Social Media: *Facebook, Twitter*

Richard Gottlieb, President
Leslie Mackenzie, Publisher

This complete updated Food & Beverage Market Place: Online Database is the go-to source for the food and beverage industry. Anyone involved in the food and beverage industry needs this 'industry bible' and the important contacts to develop critical research data that can make for successful business growth.
Frequency: Annual
Founded in 1981

10816 Food Businesses: Snack Shops, Specialty Food Restaurants & Other Ideas

Prosperity & Profits Unlimited
PO Box 416
Denver, CO 80201

303-573-5564

A Doyle, Editor

Ideas and possibilities for food businesses, snack shops, restaurants.
Cost: $29.95
82 Pages
Circulation: 8000
ISBN: 0-911569-69-3
Founded in 1990
Printed in on matte stock

10817 Food Channel Database

Noble Communications
500 N Michigan Avenue
Chicago, IL 60611-3764

312-670-4470
FAX 312-670-7410

This database reports industry news and developments of interest to decision-makers in food processing, grocery, and c-store retailing distribution.

10818 Food Engineering Directory

Business News Publishing
3817 Timothy Lane
Bethlehem, PA 18020

610-317-6180
FAX 610-317-0378

George Misko

Hardbound reference book listing of all food and beverage companies with 20 or more employees throughout the US.
Cost: $395.00

10819 Food Master

BNP Media

45 Beacon St
Sommerville, MA 02143

617-660-1322
Home Page: www.foodmasterinc.com

Bob Iannaccone, Manager
Founded in 1947

10820 Food Processing Guide & Directory

555 W Pierce Road
Suite 301
Itasca, IL 60143

773-252-7891
FAX 630-467-1108

Lily Modjeski, Sales Manager

Presents advertising opportunities that will generate quality sales leads, increase market share, identify market opportunities and increase exposure through our website.
Frequency: Annual

10821 Food Production Management: Advertisers Buyers Guide Issue

CTI Publications
2823 Benson Mill Rd
Sparks Glencoe, MD 21152-9575

410-308-2080
FAX 410-308-2079
Home Page: www.ctipubs.com

W Randall Gerstmyer, Publisher
Cost: $15.00
48 Pages
Frequency: Annual
Circulation: 5,000
ISSN: 0191-6181
Founded in 1878

10822 Food Service Industry

MarketResearch.com
641 Avenue of the Americas
3rd Floor
New York, NY 10011

212-807-2629
800-298-6699
FAX 212-807-2676

The report analyzes sales and profit trends of full-service restaurants, limited-service restaurants, cafeterias, snack bars, in-plant contractors, caterers, mobile food services and drinking places.
Cost: $2250.00
240 Pages

10823 Food and Agricultural Export Directory

US Department of Agriculture
PO Box 2022
Washington, DC 20250-0001

202-690-7650
FAX 202-512-2250
Home Page: www.access.gpo.gov

Offers valuable information on federal and state agencies, trade associations and others willing to assist the US firms that wish to export food and agricultural products overseas.
100 Pages
Frequency: Annual

10824 Food, Beverages & Tobacco in US Industrial Outlook

Superintendent of Documents
US Government Printing Office
Washington, DC 20402-0001

FAX 202-512-2250

Contains industry reviews and forecasts; coverage includes bakery products.
Cost: $34.00
Frequency: Annual

10825 Food, Hunger, Agribusiness: A Directory of Resources

Third World Resources
218 E 21st Street
Oakland, CA 94606

510-533-7583
FAX 510-533-0923

Offers information on organizations and publishers of books and other materials on food, hunger and agribusiness overseas.
Cost: $12.95
160 Pages

10826 FoodService Distributors Database

Chain Store Guide
3922 Coconut Palm Dr
Suite 300
Tampa, FL 33619-1389

813-627-6700
800-778-9794
FAX 813-627-7094
E-Mail: info@csgis.com
Home Page: www.csgis.com

Mike Jarvis, Publisher
Shami Choon, Manager

Over 4,900 distributors of food, equipment and supplies to restaurants and institutions are reviewed in this directory for the food service industry. The names of more than 23,000 key executives are included, along with each company's distribution centers.
Cost: $335.00
800 Pages

10827 Foods ADLIBRA

Foods ADLIBRA Publications
9000 Plymouth Avenue N
Minneapolis, MN 55427-3870

763-764-4759
FAX 763-764-3166

Judith O'Connell, Editor

This database offers over 287,000 citations, with abstracts to journal literature on research and development in food technology and packaging. Seafood, food service, snacks and beverage monthly current awareness are also available.
Cost: $200.00
ISSN: 0146-9304

10828 Foodservice Yearbook International/Global Foodservice

150 Great Neck Road
Great Neck, NY 11021

516-829-9210
FAX 516-829-5414

10829 Foreign Countries and Plants Certified to Export Meat and Poultry to the US

US Department of Agriculture
Food Safety & Inspection Services
Washington, DC 20250-0001

202-690-7650
800-535-4555

A comprehensive list of over 1,000 meat and poultry plants in foreign countries.
150 Pages
Frequency: Annual

10830 Fortified Foods Market

MarketResearch.com

641 Avenue of the Americas
3rd Floor
New York, NY 10011

212-807-2629
800-298-6699
FAX 212-807-2676

This new study examines the regulatory environment, analyzes the growth and product trends shaping the fortified foods market and inspects the changing retail picture. It also unveils the marketing and promotional strategies of major players such as Kellogg's, General Mills, PepsiCo, Coca-Cola, Novartis, Heinz and many others. Finally, the study takes a look at differences and commonalities among consumers of fortified cereals, breads, juice drinks, baby foods and snacks.
Cost: $2750.00
234 Pages

10831 Frozen Dinners and Entrees

Leading Edge Reports/Industry Reports
2171 Jericho Turnpike
Suite 200
Commack, NY 11725-2937

631-462-5454
FAX 631-462-1842
E-Mail: bta@li.net
Home Page: www.businesstrendanalysts.com

Charles J Ritchie, Executive VP
Donna Priani, Marketing Director
Linda Sherman, Production Manager
Jennifer Wichert, Research Director

A product-by-product analysis of the markets for frozen dinners and entrees, including traditional as well as low-calorie and health oriented products.
Cost: $1995.00
170 Pages
Founded in 1996

10832 Getaways for Gourmets in the Northeast

Wood Pond Press
365 Ridgewood Rd
West Hartford, CT 06107-3517

860-521-0389
FAX 860-313-0185
Home Page: www.green-cuisine.com

Richard M Woodworth, Owner

Directory of services and supplies to the industry.
Cost: $14.95
514 Pages

10833 Gold Book: AAMP

American Association of Meat Processors
1 Meating Pl
Elizabethtown, PA 17022-2883

717-367-1168
FAX 717-367-9096
E-Mail: aamp@aamp.com
Home Page: www.aamp.com

Jay Wenther, Executive Director
Daniel W Flier, First VP
Jon Frohling, Second VP

Consists of AAMP members, including: honorary members, associates, operators/wholesalers, home food service companies, suppliers, distributors, allied and affiliated state/regional/provincial associations. A powerful source for meat business buyers seeking products/services.
Cost: $300.00
170 Pages
Frequency: Every 2 Years
Circulation: 2,000

10834 Grain & Milling Annual

Sosland Publishing Company

4800 Main St
Suite 100
Kansas City, MO 64112-2513

816-756-1000
FAX 816-756-0494
E-Mail: web@sosland.com
Home Page: www.sosland.com

Gordon Davidson, President

Offers a list of milling companies, mills, grain companies and cooperatives.
Cost: $90.00
Frequency: Annual
Circulation: 6,000

10835 Grain Journal

Country Journal Publishing Company
2490 N Water Street
Decatur, IL 62526-4251

217-877-9660
800-728-7511
FAX 217-877-6647
E-Mail: webmaster@grainnet.com
Home Page: www.grainnet.com

Mark Avery, Publisher
Ed Zdrojewski, Editor
Deb Coontz, Advertising Sales
Jeff Miller, Advertising Sales

Provides a list of over 700 equipment manufacturers, suppliers and system designers, as well as offering useful information on governmental agencies relevant to the grain industry.
Cost: $40.00
254 Pages
Frequency: Bi-Monthly
Circulation: 13,000
ISSN: 0274-7138
Founded in 1972
Mailing list available for rent: 10,000 names at $600 per M
Printed in 4 colors on glossy stock

10836 Great Lakes Vegetable Growers News

PO Box 128
Sparta, MI 49345-0128

616-887-9008
FAX 616-887-2666

Barry Brand, Editor

10837 Guernsey Breeders' Journal: Convention Directory Issue

Purebred Publishing Inc
7616 Slate Ridge Blvd
Reynoldsburg, OH 43068-3126

614-575-4620
FAX 614-864-5614
E-Mail: sjohnson@usguernsey.com
Home Page: www.usguernsey.com

Seth Johnson, Manager
Dale Jensen, President
Tom Ripley, VP

A convention directory offering a list of officers and national members of the American Guernsey Cattle Association.
Cost: $15.00
Frequency: Annual

10838 Guide to Poultry Associations

Poultry & Egg News
PO Box 1338
Gainesville, GA 30503-1338

770-536-2476
FAX 770-532-4894
E-Mail: ptedit@mindspring.com

Randall Smalladod, Publisher
Chris Hill, Editor

This directory offers information on national, regional and state poultry associations.
Cost: $25.00
24 Pages
Frequency: Annual
Circulation: 11,500

10839 Health and Natural Foods Market
MarketResearch.com
641 Avenue of the Americas
3rd Floor
New York, NY 10011

212-807-2629
800-298-6699
FAX 212-807-2676

The report covers six product categories: packaged groceries, bulk groceries, frozen, refrigerated, produce and other/miscellaneous. The major players in the market are profiled, including Gardenburger, Hain Food Group, Horizon Organic Dairy, Small Planet Foods and others. The report details which types of new products have been recently introduced and reports on consumer attitudes and behavior.
Cost: $2750.00
289 Pages

10840 Health and Natural Foods Market: Past Performance, Current Trends & More
Business Trend Analysts/Industry Reports
2171 Jericho Tpke
Suite 200
Commack, NY 11725-2937

631-462-5454
FAX 631-462-1842
Home Page: www.businesstrendanalysts.com

Charles J Ritchie, Executive VP
Vincent Seeno, Editor
Donna Priani, General Manager
Linda Holm, Production Manager

A statistical summary and analysis offering historical, current and projected sales data for the natural foods market.
Cost: $2195.00
335 Pages
Founded in 1986

10841 Herbal Green Pages
Herb Growing and Marketing Network
PO Box 245
Silver Spring, PA 17575-0245

FAX 717-393-9261
E-Mail: herbworld@aol.com
Home Page: www.herbnet.com

Maureen Rogers, Editor

This annual guide offers information on 5,000 companies involved in herbal marketing and growing.
Cost: $25.00
Frequency: Annual
Printed in one color on matte stock

10842 High Volume Independent Restaurants Database
Chain Store Guide
3922 Coconut Palm Dr
Suite 300
Tampa, FL 33619-1389

813-627-6700
800-778-9794
FAX 813-627-7094
E-Mail: info@csgis.com
Home Page: www.csgis.com

Mike Jarvis, Publisher
Shami Choon, Manager

Covers this growing niche through its nearly 5,900 listings featuring casual dining, family restaurants and fine dining establishments. Plus, access to over 15,000 key personnel

names puts you in contact with key decision makers.
Cost: $335.00
1,000 Pages
Frequency: Annual

10843 Hort Expo Northwest
Mt Adams Publishing and Design
14161 Fort Road
White Swan, WA 98552-9786

509-948-2706
800-554-0860
FAX 509-848-3896
Home Page: www.hortexponw.com

Vee Graves, Editor
Julie LaForge, Advertising Manager

Besides being mailed to it's family of subscribers it is also available complimentary at horticulture shows in the Northwest.
32 Pages
Frequency: Annually
Circulation: 11,000
Founded in 1989
Printed in 4 colors on glossy stock

10844 IGWB Buyer's Guide
BNP Media
PO Box 1080
Skokie, IL 60076-9785

847-763-9534
FAX 847-763-9538
E-Mail: igwb@halldata.com
Home Page: www.igwb.com

James Rutherford, Editor
Lynn Davidson, Marketing
Nikki Smith, Director

A comprehensive resource listing over 1000 gaming products and services suppliers.
Frequency: Annual
ISSN: 0 -

10845 Ice Cream and Frozen Desserts
Business Trend Analysts/Industry Reports
2171 Jericho Tpke
Commack, NY 11725-2937

631-462-5454
FAX 631-462-1842
E-Mail: bta@li.net
Home Page: www.businesstrendanalysts.com

Charles J Ritchie, Executive VP
Donna Priani, Marketing Director
Linda Sherman, Production Manager
Jennifer Wichert, Research Director

A survey of the ice cream and frozen dessert market, including low-calorie, low-fat and gourmet ice creams and frozen desserts.
Cost: $1295.00
Founded in 2000

10846 Illinois Beverage Guide
Indiana Beverage Life, Inc
7379 Fox Hollow Ridge
PO Box 5067
Zionsville, IN 46077

317-733-0527
FAX 317-733-0528
E-Mail: ibjzstew@indy.rr.com

Stewart Baxter, Publisher/Editor

10847 Impact International Directory: Leading Spirits, Wine and Beer Companies
M Shanken Communications
387 Park Ave S
8th Floor
New York, NY 10016-8872

212-684-4224
FAX 212-684-5424
Home Page: www.cigaraficionado.com

Marvin Shanken, Publisher

A directory offering information on the major players of the alcoholic beverage industry.
Cost: $295.00

10848 Impact Yearbook: Directory of the US Wine, Spirits & Beer Industry
M Shanken Communications
387 Park Ave S
8th Floor
New York, NY 10016-8872

212-684-4224
FAX 212-684-5424
Home Page: www.cigaraficionado.com

Marvin Shanken, Publisher

A directory offering information on the top 40 American distributors and profiles of companies.
Cost: $170.00
Frequency: Annual

10849 International Association of Food Industry Suppliers
1451 Dolley Madison Boulevard
Suite 101
McLean, VA 22101

703-761-2600
FAX 703-761-4334
E-Mail: info@fpsa.org
Home Page: www.fpsa.org

George Melnykovich, President/CEO

A directory offering information on member manufacturers and suppliers of equipment, ingredients and services to the food and dairy industry.
700 Pages
Founded in 1911

10850 International Dairy Foods Association: IDFA Membership Directory
IDFA Membership Directory
1250 H St NW
Suite 900
Washington, DC 20005-5902

202-737-4332
FAX 202-331-7820
E-Mail: membership@idfa.org
Home Page: www.idfa.org

Constance Tipton, President
Miriam Brown, Advisory Committee

The directory provides a complete listing of IDFA's members— over 500 companies— representing approximately 83 percent of all dairy foods processed in the US, as well as the industry's leading supplier companies. Information about locations, products and contacts is included.
Cost: $495.00
250 Pages

10851 International Directory of Refrigerated Warehouse & Distribution Centers
Int'l Association of Refrigerated Warehouses
1500 King Street
Suite 201
Alexandria, VA 22314

301-652-5674
FAX 703-373-4301
E-Mail: email@iarw.org
Home Page: www.iarw.org

Corey Rosenbusch, Vice President
Nikki Duncan, Programs Manager
Margot Dersal, Controller

A complete listing of public refrigerated warehouses available to the food industry.
Cost: $18.00

10852 International Green Front Report

Friends of the Trees
PO Box 1064
Tonasket, WA 98855-1064

FAX 509-485-2705
E-Mail: michael@friendsofthetrees.net

Michael Pilarski, Editor

Organizations and periodicals concerned with sustainable forestry and agriculture and related fields.
Cost: $7.00
Frequency: Irregular

10853 International Soil Tillage Research Organization

International Soil Tillage Research
1680 Madison Avenue
Wooster, OH 44691-4114

330-263-3700
FAX 330-263-3658

More than 750 individuals and institutions in 72 countries involved in the research or application of soil tillage and related subjects.
Cost: $100.00
Frequency: Semiannual

10854 Kosher Directory: Directory of Kosher Products & Services

Union of Orthodox Jewish Congregations of America
333 7th Avenue
18th Floor
New York, NY 10001-5004

212-563-4122
FAX 212-564-9058

Shelly Sharf, Editor

A directory covering over 10,000 consumer, institutional and industrial products and services.

10855 Landscape & Irrigation: Product Source Guide

Adams Business Media
Suite J
Cathedral City, CA 92234

760-322-9878
FAX 312-846-4638
Home Page: www.americanbusinessmedia.com

Leslee Adams, Owner

Offers information on suppliers, distributors and manufacturers serving the professional agriculture and landscaping community.
Cost: $6.00
Circulation: 37,000

10856 LifeWise Ingredients

350 Telser Rd
Lake Zurich, IL 60047-6701

847-550-8270
FAX 847-550-8272
E-Mail: info@lifewise1.com
Home Page: www.lifewise1.com

Millie Galey, Manager
Carol Bender, Manager
Richard Share, Owner

Manufacture industrial food ingredients.

10857 MISA Buyer's Guide on CD

Meat Industry Suppliers Alliance
1451 Dolly Madison Boulevard
McLean, VA 22101

703-761-2600
800-331-8816
FAX 703-548-6563
E-Mail: info@fpsa.org

Home Page:
www.foodprocessingmachinery.com

George O Melnkovich, PhD, President
Cheryl Clark, Director Member Services
Frequency: Annual

10858 Manufacturing Confectioner: Directory of Ingredients, Equipment & Packaging

Manufacturing Confectioner Publishing Company
P.O.Box 2249
New Preston Marble Dale, CT 06777-0249

201-652-2655
FAX 201-652-3419
E-Mail: mcinfo@gomc.com
Home Page: www.gomc.com

Kate Allured, Editor

Publication offers suppliers of machinery, equipment, raw materials, and supplies to the confectionery industry.
Cost: $25.00
Frequency: Annual

10859 Market for Nutraceutical Foods & Beverages

Frost & Sullivan Market Intelligence
2525 Charleston Road
Mountain View, CA 94043-1626

650-961-1000
FAX 650-961-5042

Analyzes the nutraceutical market and offers information on ongoing laboratory research and forecasts for this particular industry.
Cost: $1850.00

10860 Material Safety Data Sheet Reference

C&P Press
565 5th Ave
5th Floor
New York, NY 10017-2413

212-587-8620
FAX 646-733-6010
Home Page: www.cppress.com

Regulatory and product safety requirements. Contains full text MSDS's for products listed in the 1999 15th Edition Crop Protection Reference plus additional safety information such as DOT shipping information, SARA Title III regulations, Hazardous Chemical inventory reporting information plus much more.

10861 Meat Buyer's Guide

North American Meat Processors Association
1920 Association Dr
Suite 400
Reston, VA 20191-1500

703-758-8001
800-368-3043
FAX 703-758-8001
E-Mail: smoore@namp.com
Home Page: www.namp.com

Sabrina Moore, Accounting/Meeting Manager
Philip Kimball, Executive Director

A pictorial directory depicting the food service cuts of beef, lamb, pork, and veal, along with their corresponding IMPS numbers (Institutional Meat Purchase Specification) numbers, instituted by USDA. The Guide is used by chefs, meat processors, and purveyors, food service personnel in institutions, hotels and restaurants.

10862 Meat Price Book

Urner Barry Publications
PO Box 389
Toms River, NJ 08754-0389

732-240-5330
800-932-0617

FAX 732-341-0891
E-Mail: help@urnerbarry.com
Home Page: www.urnerbarry.com

Paul B Brown Jr, President
Sheila M Deane, Marketing Manager

Seven year price history of selected beef, lamb and veal cuts as quoted in Urner Barry's Yellow Sheet.
Cost: $95.00
Frequency: Annual
Circulation: 400

10863 Meat and Poultry Inspection Directory

US Department of Agriculture
Administration Building
Room 344
Washington, DC 20250-0001

202-690-7650
FAX 202-512-2250
Home Page: www.access.gpo.gov

Offers valuable information on all meat and poultry plants that ship meat interstate and therefore come under the US Department of Agriculture inspection.
Cost: $16.00
600 Pages
Frequency: Semiannual

10864 Membership Directory of the Retail Confectioners International

1807 Glenview Rd
Suite 104
Glenview, IL 60025-2961

847-657-7400
FAX 847-724-2719
Home Page: www.mdtechnical.com

Frequency: Annual

10865 Mid-Atlantic Retail Food Industry Buyers' Guide

Mid-Atlantic Food Dealers Services
19 Hamill Rd # E
Baltimore, MD 21210-1754

410-522-6924
FAX 410-377-7137

Robert Mead, Executive Director

Offers extensive coverage of retail food stores and suppliers to the food industry in the states of Delaware, Maryland, New Jersey, Virginia and Washington, DC.
Cost: $15.00
130 Pages
Frequency: Annual
Circulation: 5,000

10866 Missouri Grocers Association Annual Convention & Food Trade Show

Missouri Grocers Association
PO Box 10223
Springfield, MO 65808

417-831-6667
FAX 417-831-3907
Home Page: http://www.missourigrocers.com

1300 Pages

10867 NAMA Directory of Members

National Automatic Merchandising Association
20 N Wacker Dr
Suite 3500
Chicago, IL 60606-3102

312-346-0370
800-331-8816
FAX 312-704-4140

E-Mail: dmathews@vending.org
Home Page: www.vending.org

Richard Geerdes, President
Craig Hesch NCE, Senior Vice Chairman
Brad Ellis NCE, Vice Chairman

Listings of over 2,200 vending, coffee service and foodservice management firms that are NAMA members, including independent firms and branches of national operating companies. Listed by state and city, identifies products vending by each firm and other services provided. Includes listing of machine manufacturer and product supplier firms that are members as well as brokers and distributors and sustaining.
Cost: $25.00
Frequency: Annual
Founded in 1936

10868 NASDA Directory
National Association of State Dept of Agriculture
1156 15th St NW
Suite 1020
Washington, DC 20005-1711

202-296-9680
FAX 202-296-9686
E-Mail: nasda@patriot.net
Home Page: www.nasda.org

Stephen Haterius, Executive Director

Top agricultural officials in 50 states and four territories.
Cost: $100.00
Frequency: Annual

10869 National Agri-Marketing Association Directory
11020 King St
Suite 205
Overland Park, KS 66210-1201

913-491-6500
FAX 913-491-6502
E-Mail: agrimktg@nama.org
Home Page: www.nama.org

Jennifer Pickett, CEO
Vicki Henrickson, Vice President
Cost: $150.00
2500 Pages
Frequency: Annual Spring
Founded in 1956

10870 National Association of Specialty Food and Confection Brokers
11004 Wood Elves Way
Columbia, MD 21044-1085

410-969-3663
FAX 410-740-2958

Judi Epstein, Secretary

Lists members by state of residence and by states covered. Code of ethics and articles describing the function of a 'specialty' food broker in the marketplace.
86 Pages

10871 National Coffee Service Association: Membership Directory
8201 Greensboro Drive
Suite 300
McLean, VA 22102-3814

703-610-9000
800-221-3196
FAX 703-273-9011

A directory covering over 800 member operators and suppliers of office coffee service products.
Frequency: Annual

10872 National Meat Association: Membership Directory
1970 Broadway
Suite 825
Oakland, CA 94612-2299

510-763-1533
FAX 510-763-6186
E-Mail: staff@nmaonline.org
Home Page: www.nmaonline.org

Barry Carpenter, CEO
Jen Kempis, Associate Director

This annual guide offers information on over 250 meat packers, processors and jobbers in 19 western states.
100 Pages
Frequency: Annual

10873 National Organic Directory
Community Alliance with Family Farmers
PO Box 464
Davis, CA 95617-0464

916-786-5155
800-852-3832
FAX 530-756-7857

Annual directory offering information on over 1,000 growers and wholesalers of organically grown produce and organic products. The new edition includes information on regulations and resources for the industry.
Cost: $34.95
288 Pages
Frequency: Annual
Circulation: 2,500

10874 New Product News
Avtex
N6w23673 Bluemound Rd
Waukesha, WI 53188-1741

262-542-9111
FAX 262-542-8820
E-Mail: info@avtex.com
Home Page: www.avtex.com

Spencer Thomason, President
Martin Friedman, Editor
Diane McBride, Circulation Manager
Chris Kumsher, Chief Financial Officer

Offers food and drug manufacturers up-to-date information on products sold in supermarkets, drug stores, gourmet stores and natural food stores. Includes in-depth analysis of new product trends.
Cost: $359.00
65 Pages
Frequency: Monthly
Mailing list available for rentat $300 per M
Printed in one color on matte stock

10875 Organic Food Mail Order Suppliers
Center for Science in the Public Interest
1875 Connecticut Avenue NW
Suite 300
Washington, DC 20009-5736

202-332-9110
FAX 202-265-4954
Home Page: www.cspinet.org

Michael Jacobson, Executive Director
Jamie Jonker, Director Regulatory Affairs

A directory of organic-food growers and suppliers who make their products available by mail-order.
Founded in 1992

10876 Organic Pages Online
Organic Trade Association

60 Wells Street
PO Box 547
Greenfield, MA 01302

413-774-7511
FAX 413-774-6432
Home Page: www.theorganicpages.com

Christine Bushway, Executive Director/CEO
Linda Lutz, Membership Manager
Laura Batcha, Marketing/Public Relations Manager

Online searchable directory
Founded in 1984

10877 PMMI Packaging Machinery Directory
Packaging Machinery Manufacturers Institute (PMMI)
4350 Fairfax Dr
Suite 600
Arlington, VA 22203-1632

703-243-8555
FAX 703-243-8556
E-Mail: maria@pmmi.org
Home Page: www.pmmi.org

Chuck Yuska, President
Alaina Sacramo, Services Coordinator

Contains information on all 500+ member companies, who are committed to producing quality products and providing world class service to their customers.
Cost: $5.00
Frequency: Non-Members Fee

10878 Packer: Produce Availability and Merchandising Guide
Vance Publishing
10901 W 84th Ter
Suite 200
Lenexa, KS 66214-1631

913-438-5721
800-255-5113
FAX 913-438-0697
E-Mail: info@vancepublishing.com
Home Page: www.vancepublishing.com

Cliff Becker, Vice President, Director
Ben Wood, Editor
Lance Jungmeyer, Managing Editor
Leanne Ball, Manager
Lori Eppel, Chief Financial Officer

Publication of about 6,000 fruit and vegetable suppliers and sales agents.
Cost: $35.00
Frequency: Annual

10879 Parity Corp
11812 N Creek Pkwy N
Suite 204
Bothell, WA 98011-8202

425-487-0997
FAX 425-487-2317
E-Mail: info@paritycorp.com
Home Page: www.paritycorp.com

Arvid Tellevik, Owner

Integrated business information system and services designed specifically for the food industry.
Founded in 1985

10880 Pasta Industry Directory
National Pasta Association
1156 15th St NW
Suite 900
Washington, DC 20005-1717

202-367-1861
FAX 202-367-1865
E-Mail: info@ilovepasta.org
Home Page: www.civilwar.org

Jim Lighthizer, President

Lists by category pasta manufacturers and industry suppliers, including contact names.
Cost: $25.00
Frequency: Annual
Circulation: 1,000

10881 Pickle Packers International Directory

1620 Eye St NW
Suite 925
Washington, DC 20006-4076

202-293-5800
FAX 202-463-8998
Home Page: www.hazmatshippers.org

Glenn Roberts, President
Frequency: Annual

10882 Pioneers of the Hospitality Industry

CHRIE
2810 N Parham Road
Suite 230
Richmond, VA 23294

804-346-4800
FAX 804-346-5009
E-Mail: info@chrie.org
Home Page: www.chrie.org
Social Media: *Facebook, Twitter, LinkedIn*

Susan Fournier, President
Josette Katz, Vice President
Chris Roberts, Secretary
John Drysdale, Treasurer
Kathy McCarty, CEO

Lessons from Leaders, Innovators and Visionaries. A tribute to those dedicated individuals who have shaped the hospitality industry through their colorful lives, their foresight, and their leadership. These profiles offer readers the opportunity to analyze successful leadership and entrepreneurial characteristics, and to evaluate the significance of their contributions.
Cost: $45.00

10883 Pizza Today: Pizza Industry Buyer's Guide

National Association of Pizzeria Operators (NAPO)
908 S 8th Street
Suite 200
Louisville, KY 40203

502-736-9530
800-489-8324
FAX 502-736-9531
Home Page: www.pizzatoday.com

Pete Lachapelle, Publisher
Joe Straughan, Association Executive Director

A directory listing over 3,000 manufacturers and suppliers of products, equipment and services to the pizza industry.
Cost: $25.00
Frequency: Annual
Circulation: 40000
Founded in 1984

10884 Pork Guide to Hero Health Issue

Vance Publishing
10901 W 84th Ter
Suite 200
Lenexa, KS 66214-1631

913-438-5721
FAX 913-438-0697
E-Mail: info@vancepublishing.com
Home Page: www.vancepublishing.com

Cliff Becker, Vice President, Director
Lori Eppel, Chief Financial Officer

This comprehensive directory offers a list of manufacturers of swine health products.
Cost: $25.00
Frequency: Annual
Circulation: 77,000

10885 Poultry Digest: Buyer's Guide Issue

WATT Publishing Company
122 S Wesley Ave
Mt Morris, IL 61054-1451

815-734-7937
FAX 815-734-4201
E-Mail: olentine@wattmm.com
Home Page: www.wattnet.com

Charles Perry, Editor
James Watt, Owner

A list of suppliers to the poultry industry of the US and Canada are listed.
Cost: $6.00
Frequency: Annual
Circulation: 20,000

10886 Poultry International: Who's Who International

WATT Publishing Company
303 N Main Street
Suite 500
Rockford, IL 61101

815-966-5400
FAX 815-966-6416
Home Page: www.wattnet.com

James Watt, Chairman/CEO
Greg Watt, President/COO
Jeff Swanson, Publishing Director

A guide offering information on over 2,500 manufacturers and suppliers of poultry equipment, services and products.
Cost: $15.00
Frequency: Annual
Circulation: 20,000
ISSN: 0032-5767

10887 Poultry Price Book

Urner Barry Publications
PO Box 389
Toms River, NJ 08754-0389

732-240-5330
800-932-0617
FAX 732-341-0891
E-Mail: help@urnerbarry.com
Home Page: www.urnerbarry.com

Paul B Brown Jr, President
Sheila M Deane, Marketing Manager

Seven year price history of selected turkey and chicken items as quoted in Urner Barry's Price— Current.
Cost: $55.00
Frequency: Annual
Circulation: 400

10888 Poultry Processing: Buyer's Guide Issue

WATT Publishing Company
122 S Wesley Ave
Mt Morris, IL 61054-1451

815-734-7937
FAX 815-734-4201
E-Mail: olentine@wattmm.com
Home Page: www.wattnet.com

Virginia Lazar, Editor
James Watt, Owner

Annual reference offering information on over 800 manufacturers and suppliers of equipment, machinery and raw materials for the poultry packing industry.

10889 Prepared Foods

Delta Communications
455 N Cityfront Plaza Drive
Chicago, IL 60611-5503

312-836-2000
FAX 312-222-2026

This database offers information of interest to the processed food industry.
Frequency: Full-text

10890 Proceedings

Flavor & Extract Manufacturers Assn of the US
1620 Eye St NW
Suite 925
Washington, DC 20006-4076

202-293-5800
FAX 202-463-8998
Home Page: www.hazmatshippers.org

Glenn Roberts, President
Kim Earle, Contact

Updates and reports on the proceedings of the association.
Frequency: Annual

10891 Produce Marketing Association Membership Directory & Buyer's Guide

Produce Marketing Association
1500 Casho Mill Road
PO Box 6036
Newark, DE 19711-3547

302-738-7100
FAX 302-731-2409

Kathy Means, VP Membership
Dan Henderson, Marketing
Bryan Silbermann, President

A directory offering information on over 2,000 members involved in retail grocery and food service marketing.
Cost: $70.00
280 Pages
Frequency: Annual

10892 Produce Services Sourcebook

Vance Publishing
10901 W 84th Ter
Suite 200
Lenexa, KS 66214-1631

913-438-5721
800-255-5113
FAX 913-438-0697
E-Mail: info@vancepublishing.com
Home Page: www.vancepublishing.com

Cliff Becker, Vice President, Director
Lori Eppel, Chief Financial Officer

The produce industry's directory of allied services and products. Content is a balance between practical reference information, allied trends and supplier or source listings.
Cost: $20.00

10893 Professional Workers in State Agricultural Experiment Stations

US Department of Agriculture
PO Box 2022
Washington, DC 20250-0001

202-690-7650
FAX 202-512-2250
Home Page: www.access.gpo.gov

This directory offers information on academic and research personnel in all agricultural, forestry, aquaculture and home economics industries.
Cost: $15.00
289 Pages
Frequency: Annual

10894 Purebred Picture: Breeders Directory Issue

American Berkshire Association
PO Box 2346
W Lafayette, IN 47996-2346

765-497-3618
FAX 765-497-2959

Lois Wall, Managing Editor

Annual guide offering information on cattle and hog breeders in the US.
Cost: $12.00
Frequency: Annual
Circulation: 4,000

10895 Quick Frozen Foods Annual Processors Directory & Buyer's Guide
Frozen Food Digest, Saul Beck Publications
271 Madison Ave
Suite 1402a
New York, NY 10016-1014

212-557-8600
FAX 212-986-9868
Saul Beck, Owner
Audrey Beck, General Manager

A buyer's guide listing over 10,000 frozen food processors, associations, equipment manufacturers and suppliers, and public refrigerated warehouses, transportation, freezing & refrigerated equipment, manufacturers, packagers and railroad lines, brokers, etc.
Cost: $140.00
400 Pages
Frequency: Annual
Circulation: 5,000

10896 RIFM/FEMA Fragrance and Flavor Database
Flavor & Extract Manufacturers Association
1620 I Street NW
Suite 925
Washington, DC 20006

202-293-5800
FAX 202-462-8998
Home Page: www.femaflavor.org
Social Media: *YouTube, RSS Feed*

Ed R. Hays, Ph.D., President
George C. Robinson, III, President Elect
Mark Scott, Treasurer
Arthur Schick, VP & Secretary
John Cox, Executive Director

The Database currently contains over 50,000 references and more than 103,000 human health and environmental studies.
Frequency: Annual
Founded in 1909

10897 Refrigerated Transporter: Warehouse Directory Issue
Tunnell Publications
PO Box 66010
Houston, TX 77266

713-523-8124
FAX 713-523-8384
Home Page: http://www.refrigeratedtrans.com

Gary Macklin, Editor

Listing of approximately 265 refrigerated warehouses in the US and Canada.

10898 Restaurant Hospitality: Hospitality 500 Issue
Penton Media
1300 E 9th St
Suite 316
Cleveland, OH 44114-1503

216-696-7000
FAX 216-696-6662
E-Mail: information@penton.com
Home Page: www.penton.com

Jane Cooper, Marketing

500 independent restaurants selected on basis of sales.
Cost: $25.00
Frequency: Annual June
Circulation: 123,000

10899 Restaurant TrendMapper
National Restaurant Association

1200 17th St Nw
Washington, DC 20036-3006

202-331-5900
800-424-5156
FAX 202-331-2429
Home Page: www.restaurant.org
Social Media: *Facebook, Twitter, LinkedIn, YouTube, Flickr*

Sally Smith, Chair
Rosalyn Mallet, Vice Chair
Phil Hickey, Treasurer
Dawn Sweeney, President & CEO

Contains detailed analysis of the economic trends that impact the restaurant industry, as well as forecasts of key industry indicators on the national and state levels.
60000 Members
Founded in 1919

10900 Restaurants and Institutions: Annual Issue
Reed Business Information
1350 E Touhy Avenue
Suite 200E
Des Plaines, IL 60018-3358

847-962-2200
FAX 630-288-8686
Home Page: www.reedbusiness.com

Roland Dietz, CEO
Stuart Whayman, CFO
Cost: $25.00
Frequency: Annual
Circulation: 16,000

10901 Santa Gertrudis Breeders International Membership Directory
PO Box 1257
Kingsville, TX 78364-1257

361-592-9357
FAX 361-592-8572
Home Page: http://www.santagertrudis.com

Ervin Kaatz, Executive Director

Annual guide offering information on over 4,5000 producers of Santa Gertrudis beef and cattle throughout the world.

10902 Santa Gertrudis USA
Santa Gertrudis Breeders International
PO Box 1257
Kingsville, TX 78364-1257

361-592-9357
FAX 361-592-8572
Home Page: http://www.santagertrudis.com

Ervin Kaatz, Executive Director

Monthly publication offering information on over 1,000 producers of Santa Gertrudis beef cattle throughout the United States.
Cost: $30.00
125 Pages
Frequency: Monthly
Circulation: 2,500
Founded in 1998
Printed in on glossy stock

10903 Sauces and Gravies
MarketResearch.com
641 Avenue of the Americas
3rd Floor
New York, NY 10011

212-807-2629
800-298-6699
FAX 212-807-2676

This market profile analyzes US shipments, retail sales, consumer demographics, and food service and food processor purchases for 22 product lines. Also analyzes the sauce and gravy product line, retail sales, brand share, and customer demographics for 16 major mar-

keters.
Cost: $2250.00
250 Pages

10904 Seafood Buyer's Handbook
Diversified Business Communications
PO Box 7438
Portland, ME 04112-7438

207-842-5500
FAX 207-842-5505
Home Page: www.divbusiness.com

Nancy Gelette, VP Operations

This comprehensive directory lists about 1,200 North American fish and shellfish suppliers, distributors and suppliers of related services and equipment to the seafood industry.
Cost: $18.00
250 Pages
Frequency: Annual
Circulation: 15,000

10905 Seafood Price Book
Urner Barry Publications
PO Box 389
Toms River, NJ 08754-0389

732-240-5330
800-932-0617
FAX 732-341-0891
E-Mail: help@urnerbarry.com
Home Page: www.urnerbarry.com

Paul B Brown Jr, President
Sheila M Deane, Marketing Manager

Seven year price history of selected fresh/frozen seafood items as quoted in Urner Barry's Seafood Price— Current.
Cost: $95.00
Frequency: Annual
Circulation: 400

10906 Seafood Shippers' Guide
American Seafood Institute
25 Fairway Circle
Hope Valley, RI 02832

401-491-9017
FAX 401-491-9024
Home Page: www.americanseafood.org

Trucking, freight and cold storage companies that directly affect the seafood packing and shipping industry.
Cost: $29.95
100 Pages
Circulation: 2,000

10907 Seed Technologist Training Manual
Society of Commercial Seed Technologists
101 E State Street
Suite 214
Ithaca, NY 14850

607-256-3313
FAX 607-256-3313
E-Mail: scst@twcny.rr.com
Home Page: www.seedtechnology.net

Anita Hall, Executive Director
Dr Wayne Guerke, Editor

This manual represents the most comprehensive treatment of seed testing technology anywhere.
Cost: $175.00
450 Pages
Frequency: Bi-Annually
Circulation: 500
Founded in 1922

10908 Single Unit Supermarkets Operators Directory
Chain Store Guide

3922 Coconut Palm Dr
Suite 300
Tampa, FL 33619-1389

813-627-6700
800-778-9794
FAX 813-627-7094
E-Mail: info@csgis.com
Home Page: www.csgis.com

Mike Jarvis, Publisher
Shami Choon, Manager

Discover more than 7,100 single-unit supermarkets with annual sales topping $500,000
dollars. This comprehensive desktop reference
makes it easy to reach our compiled list of
21,000 key executives and buyers, plus their
primary wholesalers.
Cost: $335.00
725 Pages
Frequency: Annual

10909 Soya & Oilseed Bluebook

Soyatech Inc
P.O.Box 1307
Southwest Harbor, ME 04679-1307

207-288-4969
800-424-7692
FAX 207-288-5264
E-Mail: subscribe@soyatech.com
Home Page: www.soyatech.com

Provides the world with information on the
processing industry that supports development
and value creation along each step of the supply chain.

10910 Supermarket News Distribution Study of Grocery Store Sales

Fairchild Publications
7 W 34th St
3rd Floor
New York, NY 10001-8100

212-630-3880
FAX 212-630-3868

Directory of services and supplies to the indus-
try.
Cost: $75.00
Frequency: Annual

10911 Supermarket News Retailers & Wholesalers Directory

Fairchild Publications
7 W 34th St
New York, NY 10001-8100

212-630-3880
800-360-1700
FAX 212-630-3868

Over 2,200 US and Canadian retailers, including supermarkets, discount department stores,
membership clubs, drug stores, plus voluntary,
cooperative and nonsponsoring wholesalers.

10912 Supermarket, Grocery & Convenience Store Chains

Lebhar-Friedman
425 Park Ave
New York, NY 10022-3526

212-756-5088
FAX 212-838-9487
E-Mail: info@lf.com
Home Page: www.lf.com

Heather Martin, Manager

Directory of US and Canadian supermarket
chains.
Cost: $335.00

10913 Supermarket, Grocery & Convenience Stores

Chain Store Guide

3922 Coconut Palm Dr
Suite 300
Tampa, FL 33619-1389

813-627-6700
800-778-9794
FAX 813-627-7094
E-Mail: info@csgis.com
Home Page: www.csgis.com

Mike Jarvis, Publisher
Shami Choon, Manager

Contains information on close to 3,400 U.S.
and Canadian supermarket chains, each with at
least $2 million in annual sales - one of the
most profitable segments in this sector of the
economy. The companies in this database operate over 41,000 individual supermarket, super-
store, club store, gourmet supermarkets and
combo-store units. A special convenience store
section profiles 1,700 convenience store chains
operating over 85,000 stores.
Cost: $335.00
Frequency: Annual

10914 Technomic Top 500 Chain Restaurant Report

International Food Service Manufacturers
180 North Stetson Avenue
Suite 4400
Chicago, IL 60601-6766

312-540-4400
FAX 312-540-4401
E-Mail: ifma@ifmaworld.com
Home Page: www.ifmaworld.com
Social Media: *Facebook, LinkedIn, YouTube*

Larry Oberkfell, President & CEO
Jennifer Tarulis, CFO
Michael Hickey, Chairman
Mark Bendix, 1st Vice Chairman
Loren Kimura, Treasurer

Provides a comprehensive ranking, analysis
and overview of the US chain resaurant industry, helping readers develop sales and marketing strategies, identify growth opportunities,
and monitor performance. All data is compiled
for US operations and adjusted to calendar-year
basis, making it an accurate and easy-to-use resource.
Cost: $850.00
Frequency: Annual

10915 Top 100 Fast Casual Chain Restaurant Report

International Food Service Manufacturers
180 North Stetson Avenue
Suite 4400
Chicago, IL 60601-6766

312-540-4400
FAX 312-540-4401
E-Mail: ifma@ifmaworld.com
Home Page: www.ifmaworld.com
Social Media: *Facebook, LinkedIn, YouTube*

Larry Oberkfell, President & CEO
Jennifer Tarulis, CFO
Michael Hickey, Chairman
Mark Bendix, 1st Vice Chairman
Loren Kimura, Treasurer

Provides rankings, analysis and profiles of the
leading Fast Casual chain restaurants and gives
manufacturers a handle on the evolving trends.
Also featuring an in-depth industry overview, a
segment performance review and update on
emerging chains, performance report, key
trends, and individual profiles and sales rankings.
Cost: $850.00
Frequency: Annual

10916 Trade Dimensions

45 Danbury Rd
Wilton, CT 06897-4445

203-563-3000
FAX 203-563-3131
Home Page: www.tradedimensions.com

Hal Clark, Owner

Trade Dimensions has over 30 years of experience and innovation in developing some of the
most sophisticated, reliable and widely used directories and retail site data bases available.

10917 US Agriculture

WEFA Group
800 Baldwin Tower Boulevard
Eddystone, PA 19022-1368

610-490-4000
FAX 610-490-2770
E-Mail: info@wefa.com
Home Page: www.wefa.com

Harry Baurnes

This large database offers information on US
macroeconomic farm crop and related agricultural data.

10918 US Alcohol Beverage Industry Category CD

Beverage Marketing Corporation
2670 Commercial Ave
Mingo Junction, OH 43938-1613

740-598-4133
800-332-6222
FAX 740-598-3977
Home Page: www.beveragemarketing.com

Andrew Standardi III, Director of Operations
Kathy Smurthwaite, Editor

Contains information on approximately 3,030
companies including breweries,
microbreweries, wineries, distilleries, wholesalers and importers.
Cost: $3010.00
Frequency: Annual

10919 US Bagel Industry

Leading Edge Reports/Industry Reports
2171 Jericho Turnpike
Suite 200
Commack, NY 11725-2937

631-462-5454
FAX 631-462-1842
E-Mail: bta@li.net
Home Page: www.businesstrendanalysts.com

Charles J Ritchie, Executive VP
Donna Priani, Marketing Director
Linda Sherman, Production Manager
Vincent Seeno, Research Director

A comprehensive investigation of the dynamics
of the US Bagel Industry. Both historical and
current market data is presented.
Cost: $1995.00
150 Pages
Founded in 2000

10920 US Beer Industry Category CD

Beverage Marketing Corporation
2670 Commercial Ave
Mingo Junction, OH 43938-1613

740-598-4133
800-332-6222
FAX 740-598-3977
Home Page: www.beveragemarketing.com

Andrew Standardi III, Director of Operations
Kathy Smurthwaite, Editor

Contains information on approximately 2,084
companies including breweries,
microbreweries, beer wholesalers and beer importers.
Cost: $2070.00
Frequency: Annual

10921 US Beverage Distribution Landscape Category CD

Beverage Marketing Corporation
2670 Commercial Ave
Mingo Junction, OH 43938-1613

740-598-4133
800-332-6222
FAX 740-598-3977
Home Page: www.beveragemarketing.com

Andrew Standardi III, Director of Operations
Kathy Smurthwaite, Editor

Contains information on approximately 3,340 companies distributing soft drinks, bottled water, beer, wine and spirits.
Cost: $3320.00
Frequency: Annual

10922 US Beverage Manufacturers and Filling Locations Category CD

Beverage Marketing Corporation
2670 Commercial Ave
Mingo Junction, OH 43938-1613

740-598-4133
800-332-6222
FAX 740-598-3977
Home Page: www.beveragemarketing.com

Andrew Standardi III, Director of Operations
Kathy Smurthwaite, Editor

Contains information on approximately 2,402 companies including breweries, microbreweries, wineries, distilleries, soft drink fillers and franchise companies, bottled water fillers, juice, sports beverages and energy drinks, soy, coffee, tea, and milk manufacturers.
Cost: $2390.00
Frequency: Annual

10923 US Bottled Water Industry

Business Trend Analysts/Industry Reports
2171 Jericho Tpke
Suite 200
Commack, NY 11725-2937

631-462-5454
FAX 631-462-1842
E-Mail: bta@li.net
Home Page: www.businesstrendanalysts.com

Charles J Ritchie, Executive VP
Donna Priani, Marketing Director
Linda Sherman, Production Manager
Vincent Seeno, Research Director

BTA continues its pioneering coverage of the bottled water industry with this updated and dramatically expanded edition.
Cost: $1550.00
Founded in 1997

10924 US Bottled Water Operations Category CD

Beverage Marketing Corporation
2670 Commercial Ave
Mingo Junction, OH 43938-1613

740-598-4133
800-332-6222
FAX 740-598-3977
Home Page: www.beveragemarketing.com

Andrew Standardi III, Director of Operations
Kathy Smurthwaite, Editor

Contains information on approximately 3,010 companies including bottled water fillers and distributors.
Cost: $2995.00
Frequency: Annual

10925 US Bread Market

MarketResearch.com

641 Avenue of the Americas
3rd Floor
New York, NY 10011

212-807-2629
800-298-6699
FAX 212-807-2676

This study covers packaged, fresh and frozen bread products, including a growing number of specialty bread products. Major marketing, retailing and demographic trends are all explored in-depth. Special attention is given to the in-store bakery phenomenon.
Cost: $2750.00
197 Pages

10926 US Candy and Gum Market

MarketResearch.com
641 Avenue of the Americas
3rd Floor
New York, NY 10011

212-807-2629
800-298-6699
FAX 212-807-2676

This report dissects the 23.5 billion market for chocolate candy, hard candy, soft candy, mints and gum, covering both the mass-market and gourmet levels. Market size, growth and composition are tabulated, with sales projections through 2004. Competition at the retail level as a major impetus to market growth is covered in full, as are consumer demographics by product type, brand and usage levels.
Cost: $2750.00
351 Pages

10927 US Carbonated Soft Drink Operations Category CD

Beverage Marketing Corporation
2670 Commercial Ave
Mingo Junction, OH 43938-1613

740-598-4133
800-332-6222
FAX 740-598-3977
Home Page: www.beveragemarketing.com

Andrew Standardi III, Director of Operations
Kathy Smurthwaite, Editor

Contains information on approximately 2,713 companies including CSD bottlers, canners, franchise companies and distributors.
Cost: $2700.00
Frequency: Annual

10928 US Cheese Market

Business Trend Analysts/Industry Reports
2171 Jericho Tpke
Suite 200
Commack, NY 11725-2937

631-462-5454
800-866-4648
FAX 631-462-1842
Home Page: www.bta-ler.com

Charles J Ritchie, Executive VP
Donna Priani, Marketing Director
Linda Holm, Production Manager
Jennifer Wichert, Research Director

Survey offering the size and growth of markets for natural, process, cottage and substitute cheeses.
Cost: $1395.00
480 Pages
Founded in 2001

10929 US Confectionary Market

Business Trend Analysts/Industry Reports
2171 Jericho Tpke
Suite 200
Commack, NY 11725-2937

631-462-5454
FAX 631-462-1842

E-Mail: bta@li.net
Home Page: www.businesstrendanalysts.com

Charles J Ritchie, Executive VP
Donna Priani, Marketing Director
Linda Sherman, Production Manager
Vincent Seeno, Research Director

Profiles markets for chocolate and nonchocolate candies, gum, snack nuts, and seeds, as well as providing information on distribution, trends and future opportunities.
Cost: $1250.00
760 Pages
Founded in 1996

10930 US Date Code Directory for Product Labeling

Danis Research
1 Gothic Plaza
Fairfield, NJ 07004-2411

973-575-3509
FAX 973-575-5366

Over 500 companies using date code labeling on their food products; over 500 quality control managers and consumer affairs managers from companies that produce snack foods, baked goods, confectioneries and other food products.
Cost: $295.00

10931 US Ethnic Foods Market

Business Trend Analysts/Industry Reports
2171 Jericho Tpke
Suite 200
Commack, NY 11725-2937

631-462-5454
FAX 631-462-1842
E-Mail: bta@li.net
Home Page: www.businesstrendanalysts.com

Charles J Ritchie, Executive VP
Donna Priani, Marketing Director
Linda Sherman, Production Manager
Vincent Seeno, Research Director

A detailed analysis of the expanding US markets for Italian, Hispanic/Mexican, Oriental, Indian and Kosher foods.
Cost: $995.00
Founded in 1995

10932 US Hot Beverage Market

Business Trend Analysts/Industry Reports
2171 Jericho Tpke
Suite 200
Commack, NY 11725-2937

631-462-5454
FAX 631-462-1842
E-Mail: bta@li.net
Home Page: www.businesstrendanalysts.com

Charles J Ritchie, Executive VP
Donna Priani, Marketing Director
Linda Sherman, Production Manager
Vincent Seeno, Research Director

A survey offering profiles of the coffee, tea and cocoa products market.
Cost: $1995.00
330 Pages
Founded in 1998

10933 US Market for Cereal & Other Breakfast Foods

Business Trend Analysts/Industry Reports
2171 Jericho Tpke
Suite 200
Commack, NY 11725-2937

631-462-5454
800-866-4648
FAX 631-462-1842
Home Page: www.businesstrendanalysts.com

Charles J Ritchie, Executive VP
Donna Praini, General Manager
Linda Sherman, Production Manager
Jennifer Wichert, Research Director

Provides up-to-date information on consumer attitudes and buying patterns, new product development, marketing strategies and current and projected sales trends for all types of hot and cold cereals, baked breakfast foods and frozen breakfast products.
Cost: $1495.00
396 Pages
Founded in 1986

10934 US Market for Fats & Oils

Business Trend Analysts/Industry Reports
2171 Jericho Tpke
Suite 200
Commack, NY 11725-2937

631-462-5454
FAX 631-462-1842
E-Mail: bta@li.net
Home Page: www.businesstrendanalysts.com

Charles J Ritchie, Executive VP
Donna Priani, Marketing Director
Linda Sherman, Production Manager
Vincent Seeno, Research Director

Analyzes the markets for different oils (corn, soybean, peanut, canola, linseed, cottonseed, fish and others), edible and inedible tallow, grease and lard.
Cost: $1295.00
540 Pages
Founded in 1998

10935 US Market for Fruit and Vegetable Based Beverages

MarketResearch.com
641 Avenue of the Americas
3rd Floor
New York, NY 10011

212-807-2629
800-298-6699
FAX 212-807-2676

This new study covers refrigerated juices and juice drinks, aseptic juices, frozen and unfrozen concentrates, shelf-stable juices and juice drinks in bottles and cans. It provides the latest available sales and volume by category and retail outlet, as well as detailed marketer/brand shares. The report unveils the competitive strategies, advertising and promotional campaigns and new product launches of major players; tracks trends in packaging, flavor-blending, health drinks, and other niches.
Cost: $2750.00
258 Pages

10936 US Market for Juices, Aides & Noncarbonated Drinks

Business Trend Analysts/Industry Reports
2171 Jericho Tpke
Suite 200
Commack, NY 11725-2937

631-462-5454
FAX 631-462-1842
E-Mail: bta@li.net
Home Page: www.businesstrendanalysts.com

Charles J Ritchie, Executive VP
Donna Priani, Marketing Director
Linda Sherman, Production Manager
Vincent Seeno, Research Director

A comprehensive market analysis covering all types of fresh and frozen fruit juices, fruit drinks, vegetable juices and canned ades.
Cost: $1195.00
810 Pages
Founded in 1998

10937 US Market for Pizza

Leading Edge Reports/Industry Reports

2171 Jericho Turnpike
Suite 200
Commack, NY 11725-2937

631-462-5454
FAX 631-462-1842
E-Mail: bta@li.net
Home Page: www.businesstrendanalysts.com

Charles J Ritchie, Executive VP
Donna Priani, Marketing Director
Linda Sherman, Production Manager
Vincent Seeno, Research Director

This report examines the size and growth of the US Pizza market through all channels.
Cost: $1995.00
225 Pages
Founded in 1999

10938 US Market for Salted Snacks

MarketResearch.com
641 Avenue of the Americas
3rd Floor
New York, NY 10011

212-807-2629
800-298-6699
FAX 212-807-2676

This new study provides a coherent view of the market as well as its individual segments: potato chips, tortilla chips, corn chips, pretzels, popcorn, snack nuts and extruded snacks. It explains not only what the industry does, but how it works: how shelf life shapes the entire industry; how hundreds of smaller companies manage to thrive in a market dominated by Frito-Lay. This study profiles the giant companies and regional players.
Cost: $2750.00
263 Pages

10939 US Non-Alcoholic Beverage Industry Category CD

Beverage Marketing Corporation
2670 Commercial Ave
Mingo Junction, OH 43938-1613

740-598-4133
800-332-6222
FAX 740-598-3977
Home Page: www.beveragemarketing.com

Andrew Standardi III, Director of Operations
Kathy Smurthwaite, Editor

Contains information on approximately 4,206 companies including CSD and bottled water operations, sports beverages and energy drinks, juice, soy, coffee, tea, and milk manufacturers.
Cost: $4185.00
Frequency: Annual

10940 US Organic Food Market

MarketResearch.com
641 Avenue of the Americas
3rd Floor
New York, NY 10011

212-807-2629
800-298-6699
FAX 212-807-2676

This report covers the booming organic market as it expands into mainstream and gains increased public awareness. The report covers the market size and composition, important trends, and projections for future growth. The information contained in this report will help players in the organic arena make informed decisions to complete successfully in this exciting market.
Cost: $2750.00
275 Pages

10941 US Pasta Market

Business Trend Analysts/Industry Reports

2171 Jericho Tpke
Suite 200
Commack, NY 11725-2937

631-462-5454
FAX 631-462-1842
E-Mail: bta@li.net
Home Page: www.businesstrendanalysts.com

Charles J Ritchie, Executive VP
Donna Priani, Marketing Director
Linda Sherman, Production Manager
Vincent Seeno, Research Director

Quantifies historial, current and projected sales trends in the ever-expanding market for pasta products. Covers all typed of dry, canned, frozen and fresh pasta, as well as shelf-stable noodle dishes and pasta meals.
Cost: $ 1395.00
380 Pages
Founded in 2000

10942 US Poultry and Small Game Market

Business Trend Analysts/Industry Reports
2171 Jericho Tpke
Suite 200
Commack, NY 11725-2937

631-462-5454
FAX 631-462-1842
E-Mail: bta@li.net
Home Page: www.businesstrendanalysts.com

Charles J Ritchie, Executive VP
Donna Priani, Marketing Director
Linda Sherman, Production Manager
Vincent Seeno, Research Director

Profiles market for poultry and small game products and provides information on pricing, foreign trade, and advertising and promotion.
Cost: $1995.00
280 Pages
Founded in 1999

10943 US Processed Fruits & Vegetables Market

Business Trend Analysts/Industry Reports
2171 Jericho Tpke
Suite 200
Commack, NY 11725-2937

631-462-5454
FAX 631-462-1842
E-Mail: bta@li.net
Home Page: www.businesstrendanalysts.com

Charles J Ritchie, Executive VP
Donna Priani, Marketing Director
Linda Sherman, Production Manager
Vincent Seeno, Research Director

A comprehensive marketing, economic and financial analysis of the processed fruits and vegetables industry, covering all types of canned, frozen, dried and dehydrated fruits and vegetables.
Cost: $1195.00
815 Pages
Founded in 1997

10944 US Processed Meat Market

Business Trend Analysts/Industry Reports
2171 Jericho Tpke
Suite 200
Commack, NY 11725-2937

631-462-5454
FAX 631-462-1842
E-Mail: bta@li.net
Home Page: www.businesstrendanalysts.com

Charles J Ritchie, Executive VP
Donna Priani, Marketing Director
Linda Sherman, Production Manager
Vincent Seeno, Research Director

Profiles markets for processed meat products, including sausage, processed pork products,

canned meats, and meat snacks.
Cost: $1295.00
800 Pages
Founded in 2000

10945 US Snack Food Market
Business Trend Analysts/Industry Reports
2171 Jericho Tpke
Suite 200
Commack, NY 11725-2937

631-462-5454
FAX 631-462-1842
Home Page: www.businesstrendanalysts.com

Charles J Ritchie, Executive VP
Donna Priani, Marketing Director
Linda Sherman, Production Manager
Vincent Seeno, Research Director

A product-by-product analysis of the intensely
competitive US snack food industry.
Cost: $1495.00
860 Pages
Founded in 1999

10946 US Soyfoods Market
MarketResearch.com
641 Avenue of the Americas
3rd Floor
New York, NY 10011

212-807-2629
800-298-6699
FAX 212-807-2676

This report covers five product categories:
meat alternatives, dairy alternatives, snacks, cereals, breads, bulk soybeans, meal replace-
ments/protein powders and other soyfoods
including soy sauce and miso. It profiles leading soyfoods producers such as Kellog's, White
Wave and Lightlife Foods. The report projects
sales trends through 2005 and provides insight
into the factors shaping this market. Distributor
trends and consumer attitudes and behaviors
are also covered in detail.
Cost: $2750.00
150 Pages

10947 US Sweeteners Market
Business Trend Analysts/Industry Reports
2171 Jericho Tpke
Suite 200
Commack, NY 11725-2937

631-462-5454
FAX 631-462-1842
E-Mail: bta@li.net
Home Page: www.businesstrendanalysts.com

Charles J Ritchie, Executive VP
Donna Priani, Marketing Director
Linda Sherman, Production Manager
Vincent Seeno, Research Director

In-depth coverage of the continually evolving
sweetener industry, providing up-to-date information on the latest product developments.
Cost: $1995.00
375 Pages
Founded in 1998

10948 US Vitamins & Nutrients Market
Business Trend Analysts/Industry Reports
2171 Jericho Tpke
Suite 200
Commack, NY 11725-2937

631-462-5454
FAX 631-462-1842
E-Mail: bta@li.net
Home Page: www.businesstrendanalysts.com

Charles J Ritchie, Executive VP
Donna Priani, Marketing Director
Linda Sherman, Production Manager
Vincent Seeno, Research Director

Statistical report on the vitamin and health food
industries.
Cost: $1995.00
410 Pages
Founded in 1999

**10949 US Wine & Spirits Industry Category
CD**
Beverage Marketing Corporation
2670 Commercial Ave
Mingo Junction, OH 43938-1613

740-598-4133
800-332-6222
FAX 740-598-3977
Home Page: www.beveragemarketing.com

Andrew Standardi III, Director of Operations
Kathy Smurthwaite, Editor

Contains information on approximately 1,484
companies including wineries, distilleries, wine
& spirit wholesalers, and wine & spirit importers.
Cost: $1475.00
Frequency: Annual

10950 US Wine Market
Business Trend Analysts/Industry Reports
2171 Jericho Tpke
Suite 200
Commack, NY 11725-2937

631-462-5454
FAX 631-462-1842
Home Page: www.businesstrendanalysts.com

Charles J Ritchie, Executive VP
Donna Priani, Marketing Director
Linda Sherman, Production Manager
Jennifer Wichert, Research Director

An analysis of the wine industry, domestic and
imported.
Cost: $1295.00
470 Pages
Founded in 1996

**10951 Uker's International Tea and Coffee
Buyer's Guide & Directory**
Lockwood Trade Journal
26 Broadway
Suite 1050
New York, NY 10004-1777

212-269-7053
FAX 212-827-0945
E-Mail: teacof@aol.com
Home Page: www.lockwoodpublications.com

Robert Lockwood, CEO
Jane McCabe, Editor

A directory covering firms that are involved in
importing and exporting coffee and tea; manufacturers, suppliers and retailers to the industry; and specialty roasters and their suppliers.
Cost: $48.00
Frequency: Annual
Printed in 4 colors on glossy stock

**10952 Urner Barry's Meat & Poultry
Directory**
Urner Barry Publications
PO Box 389
Toms River, NJ 08754-0389

732-240-5330
800-932-0617
FAX 732-341-0891
E-Mail: help@urnerbarry.com
Home Page: www.urnerbarry.com

Paul B Brown Jr, President
Karen Mick, Circulation Director

National business directory of traders in the
meat and poultry industry.
Cost: $95.00
760 Pages
Frequency: Annual

Circulation: 2,000
ISSN: 0738-6745

10953 Vinegar Institute Directory
1100 Johnson Ferry Road
Suite 300
Atlanta, GA 30342

404-252-3663
FAX 404-252-0774
E-Mail: vi@kellencompany.com
Home Page: www.versatilevinegar.org

Pamela A Chumley, President
Jeannie Milewski, Executive Director

Online membership directory for members only

**10954 Vinegar Institute: Basic Reference
Manual**
Vinegar Institute
1100 Johnson Ferry Road
Suite 300
Atlanta, GA 30342

404-252-3663
FAX 404-252-0774
E-Mail: vi@kellencompany.com
Home Page: www.verstailevinegar.org

Looseleaf service guide to vinegar products for
technical personnel such as shop foremen and
production managers.
Cost: $250.00

**10955 Vineyard & Winery Management
Magazine**
Vineyard & Winery Services
PO Box 2358
Windsor, CA 95492

707-836-6820
800-535-5670
FAX 707-836-6825
Home Page: vwm-online.com

Robert Merletti, President
Jennifer Merletti, Sales/Marketing Manager

A leading technical trade publication serving
the North American Wine Industry and designed for today's serious wine business
professional.
Founded in 1975

**10956 Warehouses Licensed Under US
Warehouse Act**
Farm Service Agency-US Dept. of
Agriculture
PO Box 2415
Washington, DC 20013-2415

FAX 202-690-0014

Agricultural warehouses voluntarily licensed
under the US Warehouse Act governing public
storage facilities.
Frequency: Annual

**10957 Western Fruit Grower: Source Book
Issue Agriculture**
Meister Publishing Company
37733 Euclid Ave
Willoughby, OH 44094-5992

440-942-2000
800-572-7740
FAX 440-975-3447
Home Page: www.meisternet.com

Gary Fitzgerald, President

This annual resource offers information on
manufacturers and distributors of suppliers and
supplies for the fruit growing industry.
Cost: $5.00
Frequency: Annual
Circulation: 57,000

10958 Western Growers Export Dirctory
Western Growers Association

PO Box 2130
Newport Beach, CA 92658-8944

949-863-1000
FAX 949-863-9028
Home Page: www.wga.com

Heather Flower, Editor

A directory offering information on shippers of fresh produce and fruit in the states of California and Arizona.
32 Pages
Frequency: Annual

10959 Who is Who: A Directory of Agricultural Engineers Available for Work
American Society of Agricultural Engineers
2950 Niles Rd
St Joseph, MI 49085-8607

269-429-0300
800-371-2723
FAX 269-429-3852
Home Page: www.asabe.org

Mark D Zielke, CEO
Donna Hukk, Publication Director

This directory pertains to the availability of agricultural engineers to work in developing countries. The directory lists over 650 individuals from 60 countries, primarily engineers, available for work in land or water management, farm structures and other aspects of the field.
Cost: $27.50
210 Pages

10960 Who's Who International
WATT Publishing Company
303 N Main Street
Suite 500
Rockford, IL 61101

815-966-5400
FAX 815-966-6416
Home Page: www.wattnet.com

James Watt, Chairman/CEO
Greg Watt, President/COO
Jeff Swanson, Publishing Director
Founded in 1917

10961 Who's Who in Beer Wholesaling Directory
National Beer Wholesalers Association
1101 King Street
Suite 600
Alexandria, VA 22314-8965

703-683-4300
FAX 703-683-8965
E-Mail: info@nbwa.org
Home Page: www.nbwa.org
Social Media: *Facebook, Twitter*

Craig A Purser, President & CEO
Michael Johnson, EVP/Chief Advisory Officer
Rebecca Spicer, VP Public Affairs/Chief
Paul Pisano, SVP Industry Affairs & Gen. Counsel

A listing of more than 3,000 beer distributors and suppliers in the industry.
Cost: $50.00

10962 Who's Who in the Egg & Poultry Industries in the USA & Canada
WATT Publishing Company
303 N Main Street
Suite 500
Rockford, IL 61101

815-966-5400
FAX 815-966-6416
Home Page: www.wattnet.com

James Watt, Chairman/CEO
Greg Watt, President/COO
Jeff Swanson, Publishing Director

Annual directory offering information on producers, processors, and distributors of poultry meat and eggs in the US and Canada.
Cost: $75.00
170 Pages
Frequency: Annual
Circulation: 10,000

10963 Who's Who in the Egg & Poultry Industry
WATT Publishing Company
303 N Main Street
Suite 500
Rockford, IL 61101

815-966-5400
FAX 815-966-6416
Home Page: www.wattnet.com

James Watt, Chairman/CEO
Greg Watt, President/COO
Jeff Swanson, Publishing Director

10964 Who's Who in the Fish Industry
Urner Barry Publications
PO Box 389
Toms River, NJ 08754-0389

732-240-5330
800-932-0617
FAX 732-341-0891
E-Mail: help@urnerbarry.com
Home Page: www.urnerbarry.com

Paul B Brown Jr, President
Sheila M Deane, Marketing Manager

A business directory of Canadian traders in the seafood industry.
Cost: $125.00
Frequency: Annual
Circulation: 2,000

10965 Whole Foods Annual Source Book
Wainer Finest Communications
3000 Hadley Road
2nd Floor
South Plainfield, NJ 07080-1183

908-769-1160
FAX 908-769-1171
E-Mail: info@wfcinc.com
Home Page: www.wfcinc.com

Howard Wainer, Publisher
Alan Richman, Editor
Heather Wainer, Associate Publisher
Cost: $75.00
135 Pages
Frequency: Monthly
Circulation: 16,000
Founded in 1979
Mailing list available for rent: 16000 names at $125 per M

10966 Wholesale Beer Association Executives of America Directory
Wholesale Beer Association Executives of America
2805 E Washington Avenue
Madison, WI 53704-5165

608-255-6464
FAX 608-255-6466

7 Pages
Frequency: Annual

10967 Wholesale Grocers Directory
Chain Store Guide
3922 Coconut Palm Dr
Suite 300
Tampa, FL 33619-1389

813-627-6700
800-972-0292
FAX 813-627-7094

E-Mail: info@csgis.com
Home Page: www.csgis.com

Mike Jarvis, Publisher
Shami Choon, Manager

We have uncovered the facts on more than 1,900 grocery suppliers in the U.S. and Canada in this database. This targeted database allows you to reach food wholesalers, cooperatives and voluntary group wholesalers, non-sponsoring wholesalers, and cash and carry operators who serve grocery, convenience, discount and drug stores. You will also find information regarding company headquarters, divisions, branches, and over 11,000 key executives and buyers.
Cost: $335.00
Frequency: Annual

10968 Wine & Spirits Industry Marketing
Jobson Publishing Corporation
100 Avenue of the Americas
9th Floor
New York, NY 10013-1678

212-274-7000
FAX 212-431-0500

Michael J Tansey, CEO

List of about 300 wine and liquor firms including wineries, producers, distillers and importers.
Cost: $150.00
Frequency: Annual April

10969 Wines and Vines Directory of the Wine Industry in North America Issue
Hiaring Company
1800 Lincoln Avenue
San Rafael, CA 94901-1221

415-453-9700
FAX 415-453-2517
E-Mail: info@winesandvines.com
Home Page: www.winesandvines.com

Dorthy Kubota-Cordery, Editor
Phil Hiaring, Publisher
Debbie Hennessy, Editor
Renee Skiadas, Circulation Director
Chet Klingensmith, Owner

Annual guide offering listings of wineries and wine industry suppliers in the US, Canada and Mexico.
Cost: $85.00
505 Pages
Frequency: Annual
Circulation: 5000

10970 Yogurt Market
MarketResearch.com
641 Avenue of the Americas
3rd Floor
New York, NY 10011

212-807-2629
800-298-6699
FAX 212-807-2676

Brand share and brand consumer profiles are supplemented with profiles of major US manufacturers and new product information in order to provide the reader with competitor intelligence.
Cost: $2250.00
140 Pages

10971 Zagat.Com Restaurant Guides
Zagat Survey
4 Columbus Cir
3rd Floor
New York, NY 10019-1180

212-977-6000
FAX 212-977-9760

E-Mail: customerservice@zagat.com
Home Page: www.zagat.com

Tim Zagat, CEO

Zagat.com was launched in May of 1999 and contains the most trusted and authoritive dining information online for over 20,000 restaurants in dozens of cities worldwide. Based in New York City, the Zagat survey was founded in 1979 by Tim and Nina Zagat.

Industry Web Sites

10972 http://gold.greyhouse.com
G.O.L.D Grey House OnLine Databases

Grey House Publishing's online database platform, GOLD, offers Quick Search, Keyword Search and Expert Search for most business sectors including food, beverage and agriculture markets. The GOLD platform makes finding the information you need quick and easy - whether you're a novice searcher or an experienced database user. All of Grey House's directory products are available for subscription on the GOLD platform.

10973 www.aaccnet.org
American Association of Cereal Chemists

Non profit international organization of nearly 4,000 members who are specialists in the use of cereal grains in foods. AACC has been an innovative leader in gathering and disseminating scientific and technical information to professionals in the grain-based foods indusrty wordwide for over 85 years. We know it's hard to keep up with the latest technology, that's why AACC is here to help you. We're a tool unlike any other in your lab or office. Industry leaders turn to and trust AACC.

10974 www.aaea.org
American Agricultural Economics Association

The professional association for agricultural economists and related fields.

10975 www.aaicc.org
National Alliance of Independent Crop Consultants

Represents individual crop consultants and contract researchers.

10976 www.aaminc.org
American Agriculture Movement

An umbrella organization composed of state organizations representing family farm producers.

10977 www.aamp.com
American Association of Meat Processors

Membership consists of small to medium sized meat, poultry and food businesses including: packers, processors, wholesalers, home food service businesses, retailers, deli and catering operators and suppliers to the industry. AAMP is also affiliated with 34 states, regional and provincial organizations which represent meat and poultry businesses.

10978 www.aanc.net
American Association of Nutritional Consultants

An association combating public ignorance and adverse legislation.

10979 www.aapausa.org
American Alfalfa Processors Association

Information for the processors and suppliers in the alfalfa industry.

10980 www.abfnet.org
American Beekeeping Federation

For honey producers, packers, suppliers and shippers of honey products.

10981 www.aceweb.org
Agricultural Communicators in Education

For writers, editors, broadcasters and communicators who are involved in the dissemination of agricultural, food sciences and natural resource information in land-grant colleges, federal and state agencies, international agencies and other private communications work.

10982 www.acfsa.org
American Correctional Food Service Affiliates

International, professional association created to serve the needs and interests of food service personnel in the correctional environments. The association brings together highly skilled food service workers and their vendors who are interested in the common goal of providing nutritious, cost-efficient meal service for confined populations.

10983 www.acsh.org
American Council on Science and Health

A nonprofit, consumer education organization concerned with issues related to food, nutrition, chemicals, pharmaceuticals, lifestyles, the environment and health.

10984 www.adpi.org
American Dairy Products Institute

An association for manufactured dairy products, including dry milks, whey, lactose, evaporated and condensed milk. ADPI's main purpose is to effectively communicate the many positive attributes and benefits of our members' products. Additionally, we serve our membership by offering the most current industry information available and by collaborating with dairy associations to represent members' interests before state and federal regulatory agencies.

10985 www.adsa.uiuc.edu
American Dairy Science Association
Publications, information, etc.

10986 www.aeb.org
American Egg Board

Facts, recipes, industry and nutrition information.

10987 www.afco.org
Association of American Feed Control Officials

Officials of government agencies at the state and federal levels engaged in the regulation and distribution of products, animal feeds and livestock remedies.

10988 www.affi.com
American Frozen Food Institute
News and events, facts, tips, and recipes, etc.

10989 www.afia.org
Animal Industry Foundation

Works to improve animal production practices in the US, to dispel misconceptions that a diet containing meat, milk and eggs is unhealthy and that animals raised for foods in the US are mistreated.

10990 www.afius.org
Association of Food Industries

The association is a trade association serving the food import trade.

10991 www.ag.ohio-state.edu/~farmshow
North American Farm Show Council

Agriculture trade shows and suppliers of services to these shows. Strives to improve education, communication and evaluation and provide the best possible marketing showcase for exhibitors and related products to the farmer/rancher/producer customer.

10992 www.agnic.org/

Access to experts in various fields of agriculture as well as links to agricultural databases. Find out about conferences, meetings and seminars in your area.

10993 www.agribsuiness.com
National Agri-Marketing Association
Industry information, member directory and links to member sites.

10994 www.agriwashington.org
Apple Processors Association

Organization consisting of processors and suppliers which provides a forum for discussion regarding legislation, regulations and new technology.

10995 www.agriwashington.org/aagiwa.html
American Association of Grain Inspection

Established to provide a liaison between the Federal Grain Inspection Service and designated agencies.

10996 www.agview.com/

All aspects of agriculture: Usenet groups, Web resources, archives, mailing lists, etc.

10997 www.ahpa.org
American Herbal Products Association

For manufacturers, importers and distributors of herbs and herbal products. AHPA seeks self-regulation, establishment of standards and rules of ethical conduct, member enrichment and public outreach.

10998 www.aibonline.org
American Institute of Baking Technical Bulletin

This organization provides research, education, training and consulting for the baking and food industries worldwide.

10999 www.aiccbox.org
International Corrugated Packaging Foundation

Videos, promotional materials, demonstrating support of the corrugated packaging industry worldwide. Place corrugated equipment into universities and technical colleges to provide students with corrugated industry skills.

11000 www.aicr.org
American Institute for Cancer Research

Third largest cancer charity in the US, focusing exclusively on research and education in regard to diet and cancer.

11001 www.aiwf.org
American Institute of Wine & Food

A non-profit educational organization devoted to improving the appreciation, understanding and accessibility of food and drink.

11002 www.ala-national.org
American Logistics Association

A nonprofit trade organization supporting the Military Resale and Morale, Welfare & Recreation industry.

11003 www.alaskaseafood.org
Alaska Seafood Marketing Institute

Organization of private industry and government fishing. Markets only Alaskan seafood. This association also offers educational and promotional materials on fresh and frozen seafood.

11004 www.allied-purchasing.com
Allied Purchasing

A group of ice cream plants, soft drink bottlers, dairies, brewries and water companies collaborating to obtain group purchasing rates on equipment, services, ingredients and supplies.

11005 www.almond-growers.com
California Independent Almond Growers

Association for almond growers, processors, packers and shippers

11006 www.almondsarein.com
Almond Board of California

This association provides production research, mandatory inspection and marketing promotion statistics for the almond/nut industry.

11007 www.americanbakers.org
American Bakers Association

Association comprised of wholesale bakers.

11008 www.americanberkshire.com
American Berkshire Association

Association for cattle and hog breeders in the US.

11009 www.americandairyproducts.com
American Dairy Products Institute

A national trade association representing the processed dairy products industry.

11010 www.americanhoneyproducers.org
American Honey Producers Association

Represents the interests of major USA honey producers and pollinators.

11011 www.americanwineries.org
American Vintners Association

11012 www.amif.org
American Meat Institute Foundation

11013 www.amseed.com
American Seed Trade Association

Producers of seeds for planting purposes.

11014 www.amsey.org
American Soybean Association

To improve US soybean farmer profitability. Publishes a monthly newsletter

11015 www.angus.org
American Angus Association

Industry and member links, information, etc.

11016 www.animalagriculture.org
National Institute for Animal Agriculture

11017 www.aob.org
Association of Brewers

Membership, publications, news, events, etc.

11018 www.aomillers.org
International Association of Operative Millers

An international organization, comprised of flour millers, cereal grain and seed processors and allied trades representatives and companies devoted to the advancement of technology in the flour milling and cereal grain processing industries.

11019 www.apics.org
APICS Association for Operations Management

The primary purpose of this specific industry group is to educate food and beverage manufacturers on effective marketing strategies, market trends and material management.

11020 www.applejuice.org
Processed Apples Institute

Producers of processed apple products; suppliers of equipment, packaging or ingredients to the industry and brokers and concentrate manufacturers.

11021 www.appleprocessors.org
Apple Processors Association

A national association of companies that manufacture quality apple products from whole apples. Members are either apple grower/processor cooperatives, or proprietary firms.

11022 www.appleproducts.org
Processed Apples Institute

Links to related industry sites.

11023 www.apricotproducers.com
Apricot Producers of California

11024 www.ari.org/crm
Commercial Refrigerator Manufacturers Division

Provides information, instruction, education to members in technical and business areas; also specializes in solving common problems and stimulating growth within the industry.

11025 www.asac.org
American Society of Agricultural Consultants

For agricultural consultants acting as an information base for members.

11026 www.asae.org
American Society of Agricultural Engineers

Information on agricultural engineering, biological engineering and food process engineering.

11027 www.asas.org
American Society of Animal Society

For professional researchers, publishes journals and holds seminars in the Animal Science field.

11028 www.asbe.org
American Society of Baking

Research and development of machinery for baking applications.

11029 www.asfsa.org
American School Food Service Association

An association focused on good nutrition for all children.

11030 www.ashrae.org
American Society of Heating, Refrigerating and
Air Conditioning

An international membership organization of engineers who create the worlds we live in.

11031 www.asifood.com
ASI Food Safety Consultants

ASI Food Safety Consultants is a full service provider of food safety audits, seminars and HACCP programs.

11032 www.asmc.org
Association of Sales & Marketing Companies

Members are representatives for producers of food, packaged goods, and other consumer products.

11033 www.astaspice.org
American Spice Trade Association

United States based organization whose worldwide membership is comprised of the leading firms in the spice industry.

11034 www.atsea.org
AT-SEA Processors Association

The At-sea Association represents US flag catcher/processor vessels that participate in the healthy and abundant ground fish fisheries of the Bering Sea.

11035 www.australian-beef.com
Meat & Livestock Australia

Promotes comsumption of Australian beef, lamb, mutton and goat in Canada, US and Mexico. The company is funded by Australian producers. They key focus is to increase access for Australian meat producers to the North American market and to raise awareness of its nutritional value, quality and safety.

11036 www.australian-lamb.com
Meat & Livestock Australia

Promotes comsumption of Australian beef, lamb, mutton and goat in Canada, US and Mexico. The company is funded by Australian producers. They key focus is to increase access for Australian meat producers to the North American market and to raise awareness of its nutritional value, quality and safety.

11037 www.australianmeatsafety.com
Meat & Livestock Australia

Promotes comsumption of Australian beef, lamb, mutton and goat in Canada, US and Mexico. The company is funded by Australian producers. They key focus is to increase access for Australian meat producers to the North American market and to raise awareness of its nutritional value, quality and safety.

11038 www.avocado.org
California Avacado Commission

A resource for the California avocado industry.

11039 www.awmanet.org
American Wholesale Marketers Association

An international trade organization working on behalf of convenience distributors in the United States.

11040 www.awwpa.com
American White Wheat Producers Association

Organization of white wheat producers promoting and introducing new white wheat products.

11041 www.bakeryonline.com
Bakery Online

A database for bakers, food scientists, food engineers, process engineers, plant managers, business managers, executives and other professionals involved in the bakery industry. Features a comprehensive buyer's guide, interactive discussion forums and daily news updates and reports on business, regulatory and technology trends vital to the industry.

11042 www.bbga.org
Bread Bakers Guild of America

Links to member sites.

11043 www.beef.org
National Cattlemen's Beef Association

Related industry information.

11044 www.beerinstitute.org
Beer Institute

National trade association for the malt beverage industry. Represents the diversity of brewers and suppliers.

11045 www.beertown.org
American Homebrewers Association
Devoted to the education of home-brewed beer. Publishes magazine devoted exclusively to education, art and science of homebrewing. Services include: Beer Judge Certification Program, Sanctioned Competitions, World's Largest Homebrew Competition.

11046 www.bema.org
Bakery Equipment Manufacturers Association
An international nonprofit association representing leading bakery and food equipment manufacturers and suppliers whose combined efforts in research and development have led to the continual improvement of the baking and food industries.

11047 www.bestapples.com
Washington Apple Commission
Marketing professionals promote apples through retail marketing, advertising, public relations, health and food communications.

11048 www.beverageonline.com
Beverage Online
A database for beverage chemists, food scientists, food technologists, process engineers, plant managers, business managers, executives and other professionals involved in the beverage processing industry.

11049 www.biodynamics.com
Bio-Dynamic Farming and Gardening Association
Supporting biodynamic growers and processors in North America and acts to safeguard and promote the biodynamic method of agriculture.

11050 www.bisoncentral.com
National Bison Association
The National Bison Association was formed to promote the production, marketing and preservation of bison.

11051 www.bissc.org
Baking Industry Sanitation Standards Committee
Develops and promotes sanitation standards for the design and construction of bakery equipment. Offers self certification and third party certification programs for member companies whose equipment conforms to the BISSC standards.

11052 www.blueberry.org
North American Blueberry Council
History, crop information, products, international markets and berry sites.

11053 www.bottledwater.org
Bottled Water Association

11054 www.brownswissusa.com
Brown Swiss Cattle Breeders Associ of the USA

11055 www.bsdf-assbt.org
Beet Sugar Development Foundation
Association specializing in beet sugar research and the advertisement of seed companies.

11056 www.butterinstitute.org
American Butter Institute
Represents butter manufacturers and conducts research.

11057 www.ca-seafood.org
California Seafood Council

11058 www.caa-aqua.org
California Aquaculture Association

11059 www.cacheeseandbutter.org
California Cheese & Butter Association
Membership directory along with links.

11060 www.calbeef.org
California Beef Council

11061 www.californiadates.org
California Date Commission

11062 www.californiafigs.com
California Fig Advisory Board
History and facts, nutritional information, recipes and contests.

11063 www.calolive.org
California Olive Committee

11064 www.caloriecontrol.org
Calorie Control Council

11065 www.calpear.com
California Pear Association
Consumer information, research reports, marketing and promo information.

11066 www.calstrawberry.com
California Strawberry Commission
Health and nutrition, contests, recipes, news, etc.

11067 www.cancentral.com
Can Manufacturers Institute
Serves can manufacturers and can industry suppliers

11068 www.candyhalloffame.com
National Confectionery Sales Association
Association of salespersons, brokers, sales managers, wholesalers and manufacturers in the confectionery industry.

11069 www.candyusa.org
National Confectioners Association
Association news, candy stats, health information, and candy history.

11070 www.cannedveggies.org
Canned Vegetable Council
An educational and promotional organization of vegetable canners whose goals are to raise the awareness of consumer and food service buyers regarding canned vegetables.

11071 www.canonline.org
Composite Can & Tube Institute
Serving the composite cans and tube industry.

11072 www.cast-science.org
Council for Agricultural Science and Technology
Identifies food, fiber, environmental and other agricultural issues for all stake holders.

11073 www.cawineclub.com
California Wine Club
A wine of the month club that features only California's small boutique wineries. Each month members receive two bottles of award-winning wine.

11074 www.ccpgab.com
California Cling Peach Advisory Board

11075 www.cdfa.ca.gov
North American Agricultural Marketing
For state and provincial officials responsible for agricultural products marketing programs in the US, Canada and ultimately Mexico.

11076 www.cemanet.org
Conveyor Equipment Manufacturers Association

11077 www.cheesesociety.org
American Cheese Society
Promotes cheese industry. Holds cheese tasting and workshops on cheesemaking. Sponsors competition.

11078 www.chicagomidwestmeatasso.com
Chicago-Midwest Meat Association
The CMMA conducts its activities as a not-for-profit trade association for meat companies in the midwest. Its purpose is to support and promote the meat industry

11079 www.chocolateandcocoa.org
American Cocoa Research Institute

11080 www.choosecherries.org
Cherry Marketing Institute
Association representing the cherry industry. Provides promotional material to food service operators, brokers, retailers and manufacturers.

11081 www.chowbaby.com
This web site is a search engine for restaurants. Provides help in finding the perfect eatery close to your home or travel destination. Online reservations, maps, menus and more. Can be searched by International Location, US Location, US Map or Cuisine type.

11082 www.chrie.org
Int'l Council on Hotel, Restaurant Institute Edu.
To enhance professionalism at all levels of the hospitality and tourism industry through education and training.

11083 www.christree.org
National Christmas Tree Association
Provides industry leaders a chance to work directly with their suppliers and distributors.

11084 www.ciachef.edu
Culinary Institute of America

11085 www.clm1.org
Council of Logistics Management

11086 www.coffeeindustry.org
Specialty Coffee Association of America
Association offering business, professional, promotional and educational assistance in the areas of cultivation, processing, and marketing of specialty coffees. The association also hosts the largest event in the world dedicated to coffee, the SCAA Annual Conference and exhibition.

11087 www.colborne.com/apc/home.htm
American Pie Council
Membership, recipes, coupons, etc.

11088 www.corn.org
Corn Refiners Association
Stats, career opportunities, publications and newsbriefs.

11089 www.cosmos.com.mx:80
Index of Food
Manufacturers indexed by industry, company name, products and brands.

11090 www.cottonseed.com
National Cottonseed Products Association
National association of cottonseed products.

11091 www.countryham.org
National Country Ham Association
The NCHA encourages promotion, development, and improvement at the businesses of country ham carvers and encourages the use of country carved meats through cooperative

methods of production, promotion, education and advertisement.

11092 www.cpif.org
California Poultry Industry Federation
Links to other associations.

11093 www.cpma.ca
Canadian Produce Marketing Association
Profile and services, links, technical resources, etc.

11094 www.cranberries.org
Cranberry Institute
Association which gathers and disseminates information about cranberry growing, horticultural and environmental issues to cranberry growers and handlers in the US and Canada.

11095 www.crnusa.org
Council for Responsible Nutrition
Vitamin manufacturers.

11096 www.cropinsurance.org
Crop Insurance Research Bureau
Crop insurance trade organization.

11097 www.croplifeamerica.org
CropLife America
Information on protecting crops and environmentally fragile agriculture.

11098 www.crops.org
Crop Science Society of America
Seeks to advance research, extension and teaching of all basic and applied phases of the crop sciences.

11099 www.csce.com
Coffee, Sugar and Cocoa Exchange
Acts as a financial exchange where futures and options are traded, the CSCE provides hedging and investing, opportunities in the coffee, sugar, cocoa and dairy markets.

11100 www.css.orst.edu/weeds/iwss
International Weed Science Society
For institutions and individuals concerned with the study of weeds and their control.

11101 www.culinary.com
Louisiana Sweet Potato Commission
Links to member sites.

11102 www.dairyinfo.com
Dairy Management
Links to related associations.

11103 www.dairynetwork.com
Dairy Network
Searchable database of food industry related items.

11104 www.delianet.com
Deli Associates
Association for manufacturers or suppliers of confectionary, candy and bakery products.

11105 www.delicouncil.com
Dairy, Deli-Bakery Council of Southern California

11106 www.dhia.org
National Dairy Herd Improvement Association
Sets policies, holds meetings and offers seminars for dairymen.

11107 www.diamondwalnut.com
Diamond Walnut Growers

11108 www.doitwithdairy.com
Dairy Management — American Dairy Association, National Dairy Council, US Dairy Export Council

11109 www.dressings-sauces.org
Association for Dressings and Sauces
This association is comprised of manufacturers of mayonnaise, salad dressings and condiment sauces, as well as industry suppliers.

11110 www.drink-milk.com
American Dairy Association Mideast
We represent dairy farmers and serve as the local affiliate for the American Dairy Association and the National Dairy Council. We work closely with Dairy Management Inc. and the Milk Processors Education Program to extend national dairy promotion programs to the local level.

11111 www.duckling.org
Duckling Council
Consortium of duckling producers located coast-to-coast, whose goal is to increase consumption of duckling nationwide and increase awareness of duckling's nutritionally improved profile.

11112 www.eatchicken.com
National Broiler Council
Recipes, industry information and statistics.

11113 www.eatright.org
American Dietetic Association
Nutrition resources, hot topics, FAQ's.

11114 www.eatturkey.com
National Turkey Federation
Advocate for all segments of the US turkey industry, providing services and conducting activities that increase demand for its members' products. The federation also protects and enhances members' ability to effectively and profitably provide wholesome, high quality, nutritious turkey products.

11115 www.eddal.com
Eastern Dairy Deli Bakery Association
This association encourages growth and education regarding dairy, deli and bakery industries. It promotes the sales of Dairy, Deli and Bakery products through supermarkets and specialty stores and acts as a resource and information center for the industry.

11116 www.eggs.org
Egg Clearing House
Links to related members and associations.

11117 www.ejkrause.com
EJ Krause & Associates
Association for suppliers of hotel and restaurant food and beverages.

11118 www.elettric80.com
Electric 80
Supports automated material handling systems, robotic palletizers and laser-guided vehicles.

11119 www.eppainc.org
Eastern Dairy Perishable Products Association
This association encourages growth and education regarding perishable products. It promotes the sales of perishable products through supermarkets and specialty stores and acts as a resource and information center for the industry.

11120 www.fancyfoodshows.com
Nat'l Association for the Specialty Food Trade

Members are manufacturers, importers, distributors and retailers of specialty gourmet and fancy foods. Has an annual budget of approximately $15 million.

11121 www.fb.com
American Farm Bureau Federation
For state Farm Bureaus in the 50 states and Puerto Rico.

11122 www.fbminet.ca/agnews.htm
Agricultural news releases.

11123 www.fcsi.org
Food Service Consultants Society International
Membership, publications, industry links etc.

11124 www.fda.gov
Food and Drug Administration
The official website of FDA.

11125 www.fdi.org
Food Service Distributors International

11126 www.fdrs.ag.utk.edu/
Food Distribution Research Society
Investigates how food is distributed and traded.

11127 www.feda.com
Food Service Equipment Distributors Association
Dealers and distributors of foodservice equipment and supplies.

11128 www.femaflavor.org
Flavor & Extract Manufacturers Assn of the US
1620 I Street NW
Suite 925
Washington, DC 210006

202-293-5800
FAX 202-463-8998

Ed R. Hayes, President
George C. Robinson III, President Elect
Mark Scott, Treasurer
Arthur Schick, Vice President & Secretary

FEMA is comprised of flavor manufacturers, flavor users, flavor ingredient suppliers, and others with an interest in the U.S. flavor industry. FEMA workds with legislators and regulators to assure that the needs of members and consumers are continuously addressed and is committed to assuring a substantial supply of safe flavoring substances.

11129 www.fewa.org
Farm Equipment Wholesalers Association
For wholesale/distributors of ag equipment and related products.

11130 www.ffane.org
Frozen Food Association of New England
Promotes the frozen food industry.

11131 www.fiae.com
Food Industry Association Executives

11132 www.fightbac.org
Fight Bac
Sound advice for better food safety.

11133 www.fl-citrus-mutual.com
Florida Citrus Mutual
History and mission, member information.

11134 www.foodallergy.org
Food Allergy & Anaphylaxis Network
The only nonprofit organization in the US devoted solely to patient education for food allergies. Mission is to create public awareness about food allergies and anaphylaxis to provide

education, and to advance research on behalf of all those affected by food allergy.

11135 www.foodcontact.com
Food Contact
Searchable directory of food and beverage processors and exporters.

11136 www.foodexplorer.com
Food Explorer
Database of industry related materials.

11137 www.foodfront.com
Internet Foodfront
Searchable database of food industry related items and resources.

11138 www.foodindustry.com
Industry Guides.net
Link directory for related industry.

11139 www.foodingredientsonline.com
Food Ingredients Online
International forum where buyers and sellers connect. Highly targeted and focused site offers original material, daily news updates, a product showcase, projects for bid, employment opportunities, downloadbale software, and a free interactive buyers guide which produces instant leads.

11140 www.foodinstitute.com
American Institute of Food Distribution
Serves as a central information service for food trades. Issues, reports, studies and statistical data and maintains a library. Member companies throughout the US and over 40 foreign countries.

11141 www.foodnet.gr
FoodNet
Searchable database of food industry related items and resources.

11142 www.foodonline.com
Food Online
Searchable database of food industry related items.

11143 www.foodproductdesign.com
Food product design magazine

11144 www.foodprotection.org
International Association for Food Protection
The International Association for Food Protection, founded in 1911, is a nonprofit educational association with a mission to provide food safety professional worldwide with a forum to exchange information on protecting the food supply. The Association is comprised of over 3,000 members from 50 nations. Affiliate chapters are located in the US, Canada, Mexico and South Korea.

11145 www.foodservice.com/doorway.htm
Foodservice.com
Database of information and resources for food industry buyers and sellers.

11146 www.foodserviceworld.com
Food Service World
Food associations, suppliers and events.

11147 www.foodshow.com
Foodshow
Electronic food show with booths for manufacturers.

11148 www.foodweb.com
Foodweb

Links to suppliers of food and equipment, distributors, unions, etc.

11149 www.foodwine.com/digest
Netfood Directory (The BLUE Directory)
List of relevant food and food service internet sites.

11150 www.fourhcouncil.edu
National 4-H Council
Focuses on diverse groups of young people in a variety of urban and suburban locales while continuing to serve youth in rural areas. Helps provide hands-on co-educational programs and activities to young people nationwide.

11151 www.fpaota.org
Fresh Produce Association of the Americas
Trade association for Mexican produce. Formerly known as West Mexico Vegetable Distributors Association.

11152 www.fpfc.org
Fresh Produce and Floral Council
Promotes through communication and education, fresh fruit, vegetable and floral products.

11153 www.fpi.org
Food Service & Packaging Institute
A national association comprised of manufacturers and suppliers of disposables for the food service industry.

11154 www.fpmsa.org (or www.iefp.org)
Food Processing Machinery Association
List of exhibitors from IEFP (links included).

11155 www.fresh-cuts.org
International Fresh-Cut Produce Association
IFPA advances the fresh-cut produce industry by supporting members with technical information, representation, and knowledge to provide convenient safe and wholesome food. Members are processor companies, suppliers and researchers.

11156 www.freshcut.com
Columbia Publishing
Information on carrot production, growers and shippers.

11157 www.frozenfoodcouncil.com
Frozen Food Council of Northern California
Coupons, promotions, contests, member information and events.

11158 www.fsgroup.com
Food Service Group
This organization is comprised of food service brokerage companies meeting the needs and offering a national exchange of ideas and information of food service sales professionals.

11159 www.fspronet.com
Food Service Professionals Network
Database of food industry related items including directories, etc.

11160 www.georgiapecans.org
Georgia Pecan Commission

11161 www.gmabrands.com
Grocery Manufacturers of America
Government affairs, industry regulations, news, etc.

11162 www.gpi.org
Glass Packaging Institute
Serves the glass container suppliers for the beer, juice, RTD tea, liquor, wine and dairy businesses.

11163 www.grains.org
US Feed Grains Council
For grain sorghum, barley and corn producer associations and representatives of the agricultural community. Provides commodity export market development.

11164 www.greyhouse.com
Grey House Publishing
Authoritative reference directories for most business sectors including food, beverage and agriculture markets. Users can search the online databases with varied search criteria allowing for custom searches by product category, geographic area, sales volume, keyword, subject and more. Full Grey House catalog and online ordering also available.

11165 www.hazelnut.com
Hazelnut Growers of Oregon
Recipes, health and ingredient information, etc.

11166 www.hazelnutcouncil.org
Hazelnut Council
Promotion to commercial information exhibiting ingredient users and recipies, formulas and food service

11167 www.healthfinder.gov
Association of Food and Drug Officials
Promotes the enforcement of laws and regulations at all levels of government. Fosters understanding and cooperation between industry and regulators. Develops model laws and regulations and seeks their adoption.

**11168 www.herbnet.com/,
www.herbworld.com**
Herb Growing and Marketing Network
Trade assocation information services for herb related businesses. Hosts national conference for those in the herb industry with seminars covering commercial production, medicinal herbs and general business topics.

11169 www.herbs.org
Herb Research Foundation
Provides scientific-based and traditional information about use and safety of herbs for health. Fee-based hotline, information packs and literature are available to members.

11170 www.herbsociety.org
Herb Society of America
Educates its members and the public on the cultivation of herbs, as well as the history and uses of herbs.

11171 www.hereford.org
American Hereford Association
For people in the Hereford cattle industry.

11172 www.holsteinusa.com
Holstein Association
For people with strong interests in breeding, raising and milking Holstein cattle.

11173 www.iacp.com
International Association of Culinary
A not-for-profit organization whose members represent virtually every profession in the culinary universe: teachers, cooking school owners, caterers, writers, chefs, media cooking personalities, editors, publishers, food stylists, food photographers, restauranteurs, leaders of major food corporations and vintners. Literally a who's who of the food world. Founded in 1978.

11174 www.iacsc.org
International Association of Cold Storage

11175 www.iafenet.org
International Association of Fairs & Expositions

Membership consists of individual agricultural fairs and regional associations of agricultural fairs.

11176 www.iaff.ttu.edu/aals
Association for Arid Land Studies

11177 www.iafis.org
Int'l Association of Food Industry Suppliers

Serves the dairy food and beverage industries, and related sanitary processing industries addressing the marketing and business information needs of the food supply channel.

11178 www.iaicv.org
International Association of Ice Cream Vendors

Members are manufacturers and distributors of ice cream novelties and street vendors.

11179 www.iarw.org
International Association of Refrigerated

Trade association of public refrigerated warehouse storing of all types of perishable products.

11180 www.ibdea.org
International Beverage Dispensing Equipment

Serves independent purveyors of equipment, service and products for the food and beverage industry.

11181 www.iddanet.org
International Dairy-Deli-Bakery Association

Newsletter, training information, publications, member list and FQA's.

11182 www.iddba.org
International Dairy-Deli-Bakery Association

Furthers relationship between manufacturing, production, marketing used in delivery of goods to marketplace. Presents awards and maintains a hall of fame.

11183 www.idfa.org
International Dairy Foods Association

IDFA represents the best interests of the U.S. dairy processing and manufacturing industry, as well as its supplier members and industry's leading suppliers companies.

11184 www.ifas.ufl.edu
Agricultural Communicators of Tomorrow

For college students professionally interested in communications related to agriculture, food, natural resources and allied fields.

11185 www.ific.org
International Food Information Council

Food safety and nutritional information, press releases and publications.

11186 www.ifmaworld.com
International Foodservice Manufacturers

Trade association for food, beverage, equipment and supply manufacturers and ancillary service companies serving the food service industry.

11187 www.ifse.tamu.edu/sma.html
Southwest Meat Association

Newsletter, member information and links.

11188 www.ifsea.org
International Food Service Executives

Provides education and community service to the foodservice industry.

11189 www.ift.org
Institute of Food Technologists

Member information, publications, calender of expos and meetings.

11190 www.iherb.org
International Herb Association

Supports the herb businesses and educates the public.

11191 www.iiar.org
International Institute of Ammonia Refrigeration

Promotes the safe use of ammonia as a refrigerant. Offers educational, promotional and standards development programs and legislative/regulatory support to manufacturers, contractors, consulting engineers, wholesalers and end users.

11192 www.ilovepasta.org
National Pasta Association

List of members, FAQ's, pasta nutrition and recipes.

11193 www.ilovepickles.org
Pickle Packers International

Addresses the concerns of pickle packers, shippers and manufacturers.

11194 www.ilsi.org
International Life Sciences Institute

Scientific institution that supports research on nutrition, food safety and toxicology.

11195 www.independentbaker.org
Independent Bakers Association

Organization of member bakers.

11196 www.insca.org
International Natural Sausage Casing Association

11197 www.iopp.org
Institute of Packaging Professionals

11198 www.ipmwww.ncsu.edu/cernag/
All aspects of agriculture: Usenet groups, Web resources, archives, mailing lists, etc.

11199 www.irrigation.org
Irrigation Association

Irrigation industry information.

11200 www.iseo.org
Institute of Shortening & Edible Oils

11201 www.jps.net/ahaherb
American Herb Association

Membership is comprised of professional herablists and herbal enthusiasts. The goal is to increase knowledge and offer updated scientific information on herbs.

11202 www.juanvaldez.com
National Federation of Coffee Growers of Colombia

This organization is comprised of coffee growers from Colombia whose goal is to promote Colombian coffee in the US.

11203 www.kab.org
Keep America Beautiful

National nonprofit education organization whose corporate members include packagers, retailers, bottlers, and makers of chemical, steel, glass, paper and aluminum products.

11204 www.kiwifruit.org
California Kiwifruit Commission

News, recipes, export information, etc.

11205 www.kla.org
Kansas Livestock Association

11206 www.lambchef.com
American Lamb Council

11207 www.larw.org
Refrigeration Research and Education Foundation

Sponsors graduate-level scientific research on the refrigeration of perishable commodities. Offers annual training institute for public refrigerated warehouse personnel.

11208 www.leafy-greens.org
Leafy Greens Council

Made up of growers and shippers. This association promotes the consumption of leafy greens and vegetables for battling diseases like cancer.

11209 www.llovepecans.org
National Pecan Shellers Association

An association aimed at promoting the pecan shelling and processing industry.

11210 www.mainelobsterpromo.com
Maine Lobster Promotion Council

11211 www.mainpotatoes.com
Maine Potato Board

11212 www.meatami.com
American Meat Institute

A leading trade association for the meat processing industry.

11213 www.meatandpoultryonline.com
Meat and Poultry Online

Searchable database of food industry related items.

11214 www.meatnz.co.nz
Meat New Zealnd

11215 www.meatpoultry.com
Meat and poultry magazine

11216 www.mhia.org
Material Handling Industry

11217 www.micausa.org
Meat Importers Council of America

11218 www.michiganapples.dcom
Michigan Apple Committee

11219 www.militaryfood.org
Research and Development Associates for Military

Founded as a forum for the interchange of technical data on food products, feeding systems, food and feeding equipment and food packaging between industry and professors of Food Science and Technology and the US Armed Forces and Government.

11220 www.mindspring.com/~independentb aker
Independent Bakers Association

Links, issue papers, etc.

11221 www.msgfacts.com
Glutamate Association— US

Members are manufacturers, distributors and processed food users of glutamate, glutamate acid and its salts in the food industry.

11222 www.mtgplace.com
Source of information for food product developers

11223 www.mushroomcouncil.com
Mushroom Council

11224 www.mwfpa.org
Midwest Food Processors Association

This association offers member companies information on legislation and industry matters.

11225 www.naab-css.org
National Association of Animal Breeders

For farmer co-ops and others interested in livestock improvement.

11226 www.nabi-inc.gpg.com
National Association of Beverage Importers

Members hold a Federal Basic Importer's permit.

11227 www.nabronline.org
National Association of Beverage Retailers

Represents over 15,000 off-premise licensees in the 'open' or 'license' states and on-premise proprietors in markets across the nation. Offers members information on legislation and industry matters.

11228 www.nacaa.com
National Association County Agricultural Agents

For agents focusing on educational programs for the youth of the community.

11229 www.naconline.org
National Association of Concessionaires

This association works to professionalize the concession industry by providing information services and training programs for concession managers and employees. Holds conventions, seminars, trade shows, and certification programs for the leisure time food and beverage industry. Produces newsletters and magazines for its international membership.

11230 www.nacufs.org
National Assn of College & University Food Service

Educational programs, conferences, publications, etc.

11231 www.nadefa.org
North American Deer Farmers Association

A nonprofit organization that offers representation of US and Canadian breeders and producers of venison. Velvet and trophy stock.

11232 www.nafem.org
Food Equipment Manufacturers Association

A trade association of foodservice equipment and supplies manufacturers, that provide products for food preparation, cooking, storage and table service.

11233 www.naffs.org
National Association of Fruits, Flavors & Syrups

Industry information, member directory and links to member sites.

11234 www.nama.org
National Agri-Marketing Association

Marketing and communication suppliers, including trade publications, radio and television broadcast sales organizations, premium/incentive manufacturers, printers, marketing research firms, photographers and related professionals.

11235 www.namamillers.org
North American Millers' Association

11236 www.namp.com
North American Meat Processors Association

Represents processors and distributors of meat, poultry, seafood and game to the food service industry.

11237 www.nanca.org
North American Natural Casing Association

The NANCA responds to issues and service needs that are unique to the North American segment of the industry.

11238 www.nas.edu
National Research Council/National Academy

11239 www.nasda-hq.org
National Association of State Departments of Agriculture

11240 www.nationalgrange.org
National Grange

Promotes general welfare and agriculture through local organizations. Presides over the advancement and promotion of the farming and agriculture industry.

11241 www.nationalgrocers.org
National Grocers of America

This association services as the information network to the National Grocers Association. Purposes of this organization: handling government affairs regarding the operation of retail groceries; developing educational programs and literature regarding the industry; and supports women in the retail distribution industry.

11242 www.navigator.tufts.edu
Tufts University Nutrition Navigator

A rating guide for more than 300 nutrition websites.

11243 www.nbva.org
National Bulk Vendors Association

An organization comprised of manufacturers, distributors and operators of bulk vending merchandise and equipment.

11244 www.nbwa.org
National Beer Wholesalers Association

Research and development, quality control and ingredients.

11245 www.nca-cna.org
National Confectioners Association

Manufacturers of confectionary products and services.

11246 www.ncausa.org and www.coffeescience.org
National Coffee Association of USA

This association promotes business relations among members of the trade. Also collects and publishes information on the coffee industry, maintaining a library of 1000 science and medical books and literature about coffee and caffeine.

11247 www.ncga.com
National Corn Growers Association

11248 www.neffa.com
Northeast Fresh Foods Alliance

11249 www.nfdffa.org
National Frozen Dessert and Fast Food Association

This association is made up of small, independent owners and operators of ice cream and fast food establishments.

11250 www.nffa.org
National Frozen Food Association

Training, research, networking services, etc.

11251 www.nfi.org
National Aquaculture Council

For farmers, food processors and food distributors with an interest in aquaculture.

11252 www.nfo.org
National Farmers Union

Promotes educational, cooperative and legislative activities of farm families in 44 states.

11253 www.nfpa-food.org
National Food Processors Association

A leading food industry trade association.

11254 www.nfraweb.org
National Frozen & Refrigerated Foods Association

Nonprofit trade association comprised of 650 member companies representing all segments of the frozen and refrigerated food industry. NFRA has been serving the frozen food industry since 1945 and just recently in 2001 began serving the refrigerated foods industry. The mission of NFRA is to promote the sales and consumption of frozen and refrigerated foods through: educations, training, research, sales planning and menu development and providing a forum for industry dialogue.

11255 www.nhb.org
National Honey Board

This organization offers information and support to members in the honey producing industry.

11256 www.nicra.org
National Ice Cream Retailers Association

A trade organization whose members are in the retail ice cream; frozen custard; gelato; frozen yogurt and water ice business. Members are located all across the United States, Canada and several other countries.

11257 www.nims.com
Network of Ingredient Marketing Specialists

This organization has established a network of ingredient manufacturers' representatives that offers ingredient manufacturers the most cost effective access to US, Canadian and European markets.

11258 www.njpa.com
National Juice Products Association

11259 www.nmaonline.org
National Meat Association

Provides it members unique one-on-one assistance resolving regulatory issues. Mission is to be proactive and responsive in serving members both individually and collectively.

11260 www.nmpf.org
National Milk Producers Federation

11261 www.noble.net
Noble & Associates

Advertising agency for food industry professionals.

11262 www.nopa.org
National Oilseed Processors Association

11263 www.npcspud.com
National Potato Council

Represents US potato growers on federal legislative and regulatory issues.

11264 www.nppc.org
National Pork Producers Council

Nutrition information, educational resources and research results.

11265 www.nsda.org
National Soft Drink Association
Industry, product and recycling information, issues and events.

11266 www.nwcherries.com
Northwest Cherry Growers

11267 www.nwfpa.com
Northwest Food Processors Association
Conventions and exhibits, member listings and links.

11268 www.nwfpa.org
Northwest Food Processors Association
An organization that aims to develop and promote the food processing industry located in Oregon, Idaho, and Washington.

11269 www.nyapplecounty.com
New York Apple/New York Cherry Growers

11270 www.oamp.org
Ohio Association of Meat Processors

11271 www.ocia.org
Organic Crop Improvement Association
For farmers, processors, manufacturers and traders of organic crops.

11272 www.oilseeds.org
American Soybean Association
Consumption statistics, related associations.

11273 www.onions-usa.org
National Onion Association
Recipes, member information and allied industry and export information.

11274 www.opensecrets.org
Cheese Association of America
The Center for Responsive Politics is a nonpartisan, nonprofit research group based in Washington, DC that tracks money in politics, and its effect on campaign finance issues for the news media, academics, activists and the public at large.

11275 www.oregon-berries.com
Oregon Rasberry & Blackberry Commission
Supports the rasberries, blackberries, marionberries and boysenberries industries.

11276 www.oregonhazelnuts.org
Hazelnut Marketing Board
This organization was established to promote and provide for the Oregon hazelnut industry.

11277 www.organic.org
Organic Alliance

11278 www.ostriches.org
American Ostrich Association
Organization that provides leadership for the ostrich industry and its future through the promotion of ostrich products.

11279 www.osu.orst.edu/dept/iifet
International Institute of Fisheries Economics
Promotes discussion, research projects and sponsors educational courses. Publications available.

11280 www.ota.org
Organic Trade Association
For businesses involved in the organic agriculture and products industry. Seeks to promote the industry and establish production and marketing standards.

11281 www.ou.org
Orthodox Union

11282 www.pabeef.org
Pennsylvania Cattlemen's Association

11283 www.packagingeducation.org
Packaging Education Forum
A membership organization through which industry guides the development of, establishes quality standards for, and provides financial assistance to packaging education programs, curricula and students at the university.

11284 www.packagingnetwork.com
Packaging Network
Searchable database of food industry related items.

11285 www.packexpo.com
Packging Machinery Manufacturers Institute
Members are manufacturers of packaging and packaging related coconverting machinery in the US and Canada. PMMI offers meetings, an inquiry service, statistics and surveys and a business to business service on it's website. PMMI also sponsors several Pack Expos (packaging related tradeshows).

11286 www.packinfo-world.com
World Packaging Organization
Information regarding the packaging industry internationally.

11287 www.packinfo-world.org
Contract Packaging and Manufacturing Association
Information on major packaging associations.

11288 www.peanutbutterlovers.com
Peanut Advisory Board
This organization conducts the marketing and promotion of peanut and peanut butter products.

11289 www.peanutsusa.com
American Peanut Council
Association members include growers and manufacturers of peanuts and peanut products.

11290 www.pigglywiggly.com
National Piggly Wiggly Operators Association
An association of independent grocers operating under Piggly Wiggly franchises in 24 states. Includes both small operators of one to five supermarkets as well as multiple store organizations of as many as 90 or more supermarkets.

11291 www.pistachios.org
California Pistachio Commission
Commodity board representing California pistachio growers.

11292 www.pizzatoday.com
National Association of Pizza Operators
The membership of this organization is independent and franchised pizza operators, manufacturers and suppliers of pizza equipment.

11293 www.plma.com
Private Label Manufacturers Association (PLMA)
Trade Association promoting the private label industry.

11294 www.pma.com
Produce Marketing Association
For those who market fresh fruits, vegetables, and floral products worldwide; involved in the production, distribution, retail, and food service sectors of the industry.

11295 www.popcorn.org
Popcorn Institute

A trade association representing the popcorn industry. Institute activites include projects to improve popcorn growing and processing technology, serving as a liasion with several government regulatory agencies and a generic marketing program to promote product awareness and consumption.

11296 www.poultryegg.org
US Poultry & Egg Association

11297 www.ppws.vt.edu/newss/society.htm
Northeastern Weed Science Society

11298 www.processfood.com
Food Processing Machinery & Supplies Association

11299 www.prunes.org
California Prune Board

11300 www.ptnpa.org
Peanut and Tree Nut Processors Association

11301 www.qba.com
Quality Bakers of America Cooperative
Members are independent wholesale bakeries and their suppliers.

11302 www.qchekd.com
Quality Checked Dairies
A cooperative of Dairy foods processors who use the Quality Checked trademark on their products and engage in group purchasing of ingredients and supplies.

11303 www.raisins.org
California Raisin Marketing Food Tech. Program

11304 www.rbanet.com
Retail Bakers Association
Links to other associations.

11305 www.realbutter.com
American Dairy Association
Recipes, media information, celebrity chefs and industry news.

11306 www.redangus1.org
Red Angus Association of America
Association for breeders of Red Angus cattle.

11307 www.redraspberry.com
Washington Red Raspberry Commisson

11308 www.refrigeratedfoods.com
Refrigerated Foods Association
Formerly called the Salad Manufacturers Association, the Refrigerated Foods Association is an international organization comprised of manufacturers and suppliers of prepared, refrigerated, ready-to-eat food products.

11309 www.register.com/food
Food Institute
Member and industry links.

11310 www.renderers.org
National Renderers Association
Members recycle animal by-products only, also provide services to renderers.

11311 www.restaurant.org
National Restaurant Association
Trends, government affairs, training, research, dining guides and links.

11312 www.reta.com
Refrigerating Engineers & Technicians Association

11313 www.retailconfectioners.org
Retail Confectioners International

Provides education, promotion and legislative services. Holds courses and bestows awards.

11314 www.saltinstitute.org
Salt Institute
Industry information and member businesses.

11315 www.sbsonline.org
Society for Biomolecular Screening
Supports research and discovery in pharmaceutical biotechnology and the agrichemical industry that utilize biomolecular screening procedures.

11316 www.scaa.com
Specialty Coffee Association of America
Training programs, newsletter, member websites, etc.

11317 www.scisoc.org/asbc
American Society of Brewing Chemists
Annual scientific meeting for professionals in the brewing industry.

11318 www.seafwa.org
Southeastern Association of Fish and Wildlife
The Southeastern Association of Fish and Wildlife Agencies is an organization whose members are the state agencies with primary responsibility for management and protection of the fish and wildlife resources in 16 states, Puerto Rico and the US Virgin Islands.

11319 www.seedtechnology.net
Society of Commercial Seed Technologists
Professionals involved in the testing and analysis of seeds, including research, production and handling based on botanical and agricultural sciences.

11320 www.sheepusa.org
American Sheep Industry Association
For state associations dedicated to the welfare and profitability of the sheep industry.

11321 www.shellfish.org
National Shellfisheries Association
Organization comprised of scientists, public health workers, shellfish producers and fishery administrators. To promote and advance shellfisheries research and the application of results to the shellfish industry

11322 www.snax.com
Snack Food Association
Facts, stats and trivia about snack food industry.

11323 www.southeastdairy.org
Southeast United Dairy Industry Association
Promotes milk and milk products in the southeastern states.

11324 www.southerncottonginners.org
Southern Cotton Ginners Association
Operates in a five state area as an information center covering safety and governmental regulations.

11325 www.soyfoods.com
US Soy Food Directory
Searchable database of soy food processors, suppliers, and industry information.

11326 www.soyfoods.org
Soyfoods Association of North America
Sponsors April as soy foods month. Conducts annual seminar on soy foods in fall.

11327 www.spcouncil.org
Soy Protein Council

Members of this association include persons, firms and corporations regularly engaged within the US in the processing and sale of vegetable proteins or vegetable protein products derived from agricultural services.

11328 www.specialityfoods.org
Speciality Food Distributors & Manufacturers

11329 www.state.id.us/bean
Idaho Bean Commission
Directory of dealers, recipes, nutritional values and research.

11330 www.steel.org
American Iron and Steel Institute
Develops and implements market development programs for appropriate food and beverage packaging applications.

11331 www.suebeehoney.com
Sioux Honey Association

11332 www.sugar.org
Sugar Association
Represents processors and refiners of beet and cane sugar in nutrition and health matters.

11333 www.sugaralliance.org
American Sugar Alliance
For domestic producers, processors, suppliers and labor organizations in the sugar and sugarcane industry.

11334 www.sunflowernsa.com
National Sunflower Association
For companies associated with sunflower products.

11335 www.sunmaid.com
Sun-Maid Growers of California

11336 www.susta.org
Southern US Trade Association
A non-profit agricultural export trade development association comprised of the Departments of Agriculture of the 15 southern states and the Commonwealth of Puerto Rico.

11337 www.teausa.com
Tea Council of the USA
International companies and governments interested in cultivating and expanding the demand for the sale and consumption of tea in the US.

www.teleport.com/~hazelnut
Hazelnut Marketing Board
This organization was established to promote and provide for the Oregon hazelnut industry.

11339 www.tfi.org
Fertilizer Institute
For brokers, producers, importers, dealers and manufacturers of fertilizer and fertilizer-related equipment.

11340 www.theamericancenter.org
American Center for Wine, Food & the Arts

11341 www.thebcma.org
Biscuit & Cracker Manufacturers Association
An organization that represents and promotes the cookie and cracker manufacturing industry.

11342 www.therestaurantfinder.com
This search engine help to find restaurants by type or location.

11343 www.tianet.org
Transportation Intermediaries Association

Education and policy organization for North American transportation intermediaries representing the interests of all third party transportation service providers. Members include logistics management firms, property brokers, perishable commodities brokers, freight forwarders, intermodal marketers, ocean and air forwarders, and NVOCC's.

11344 www.tortilla-info.com
Tortilla Industry Association
News, trade information, 'where to buy' and recipes.

11345 www.turkeyfed.org
National Turkey Federation
Member site links and industry information.

11346 www.txbeef.com
Texas Beef Council
Recipes, ranching information, tips and links.

11347 www.uark.edu/depts/ifse/ofpa
Ozark Food Processors Association
This association is comprised of regional food processors and national suppliers for the food service industry. Hosts an annual convention in the spring which includes at attendence of over 700 and over 100 exhibitors.

11348 www.uffva.org
United Fresh Fruit & Vegetable Association
Equipment, supplies, cartons, packaging machinery, computers, sorting and sizing equipment, harvesting equipment, film wrap manufacturing and commodity organizations.

11349 www.usapears.com
Pear Bureau Northwest
Promotes fresh pears grown in the Pacific Northwest area.

11350 www.usapple.org
US Apple Association
Members are US and foreign firms, other than retailers, that handle apples.

11351 www.usarice.com
USA Rice Federation

11352 www.usda.gov
US Department of Agriculture
The official website of USDA.

11353 www.usda.gov/fcs/fcs.html
Food & Nutrition Service

11354 www.usguernsey.com
American Guernsey Association
Register and deliver guernsey cattle throughout the US.

11355 www.usmef.org
US Meat Export Federation

11356 www.uspastry.org
US Pastry Alliance

11357 www.uspotatoes.com
National Potato Promotion Board
Also known as the potato board. Organized to operate a national promotion plan to position potatoes as low calorie, nutritious vegetables and to facilitate market expansion into domestic and export sales.

11358 www.vealfarm.com
American Veal Association
For veal producers and processors.

11359 www.vending.org
National Automatic Merchandising Association

Serves merchandising, vending, contract foodservice management and office coffee service industries.

11360 www.versatilevinegar.org
Vinegar Institute
Manufacturers and bottlers of vinegar and suppliers to the industry are the members of this association. Publications available only to members.

11361 www.vrg.org
Vegetarian Resource Group

11362 www.vtcheese.com
Vermont Cheese Council

11363 www.walnut.org
Walnut Marketing Board
History, statistics, supplier listings, etc.

11364 www.warehouselogistics.org
American Warehouse Association

11365 www.watermelon.org
National Watermelon Promotional Board

11366 www.wawgg.org
Washington Association of Wine Grape Growers
Guidance in research and education, and maintaining leadership in local, state and national wine grape issues.

11367 www.wdairycouncil.com
Western Dairyfarmers' Promotion Association
Promotes dairy products for the dairy farmer.

11368 www.westernassn.com
Western Retail Implement and Hardware Association
For manufacturers, suppliers and distributors of equipment, supplies and services relating to the agricultural industry.

11369 www.wflo.com
World Food Logistics Organization
The activities of the WFLO include improving the application of refrigeration technology for the preservation and distribution of food and other commodities, stimulating and supporting research in the science of food refrigeration through grants, training and educating industry personnel, growing its bank of scientific information on the storage and distribution of perishable goods, and developing and supporting national associations.

11370 www.wga.com
Western Growers Association
Links and news, safety and legal information.

11371 www.wheatfoods.org
Wheat Foods Council
Links, nutrition and product information, news and tips.

11372 www.wheatworld.org
National Association of Wheat Growers
Member information, government agencies, research information, etc.

11373 www.whybiotech.com
Council for Biotechnology Information
Our vision and mission is to improve understanding and acceptance of biotechnology by collecting balanced, credible and science based information, then communicating this information through a variety of channels. Plant biotechnology has the potential to provide more and better food for a growing world population while helping steward the environment.

11374 www.wicdirectors.org
National Association of WIC Directors
Members are geographic state, Native American state and local agency directors of the special supplement nutrition program for women, infants and children.

11375 www.wildblueberries.com
Wild Blueberry Association of North America
Sources, recipes, news and product ideas.

11376 www.wineinstitute.org
Wine Institute
Organization that represents the wine and spirit industry to state and federal lawmaking bodies.

11377 www.wislink.org
Wisconsin Milk Marketing Board

11378 www.worldfoodnet.com
Source of information for food product developers

11379 www.wssa.com
Wine and Spirits Shippers Association
Provides members, importers and exporters with efficient and economical ocean transportation and other logistic services.

11380 www.wusata.org
Western US Agricultural Trade Association
This organization offers information and support to increase exports of US agricultural products.

Associations

11381 A Philanthropic Partnership for Black Communities

333 Seventh Avenue
14th Floor
New York, NY 10001

646-230-0306
FAX 646-230-0310
E-Mail: info@abfe.org
Home Page: www.abfe.org
Social Media: *Facebook*

Gary Cunningham, Chair
Samuel Cargile, PH.D., Vice Chair
Kenneth Jones, Treasurer
Towalame Austin, Secretary
Susan TAYLOR BATTEN, President

Encourages blacks in the grantmaking field and helps members improve their job effectiveness.
Founded in 1971

11382 American Society of Association Executives

1575 I St NW
Washington, DC 20005

202-371-0940
888-950-2723
FAX 202-371-8315
E-Mail: service@asaenet.org
Home Page: www.asaecenter.org
Social Media: *Facebook, Twitter, LinkedIn*

Abe Eshkenazi, Chairman
Scott D. Wiley, Chairman-Elect
Matthew R. Shay, Secretary-Treasurer
Francine Alestock, Executive Coordinator
Dana Anaman , CAE, Marketing Manager

ASAE is the premier source of learning, knowledge and future-oriented research for the association and nonprofit profession, and provides resources, education, ideas and advocacy to enhance the power and performance of the association and nonprofit community.
21M Members
Founded in 1920

11383 Arthritis Foundation

1330 W Peachtree St.
Suite 100
Atlanta, GA 30309

404-872-7100
Home Page: www.arthritis.org
Social Media: *Facebook, Twitter, LinkedIn, Instagram*

Ann M. Palmer, President & CEO
Michael V. Ortman, Chair

The Arthritis Foundation is the voice of the arthritis community.

11384 Association for Healthcare Philanthropy

313 Park Avenue
Suite 400
Falls Church, VA 22046

703-532-6243
FAX 703-532-7170
E-Mail: ahp@ahp.org
Home Page: www.ahp.org
Social Media: *Facebook, LinkedIn*

David L. Flood, Chair
Jory Pritchard-Kerr, Vice Chair
Steven W. Churchill, MNA, President & CEO
Randy A. Varju, Secretary/Treasurer
Norman Flores, Finance Director

Represents health care fundraising professionals through education and eventually bestows the credentials upon them.
4100 Members
Founded in 1967

11385 Association of Fund-Raising Professionals

4300 Wilson Blvd.
Suite 300
Arlington, VA 22203

703-684-0410
800-666-3863
FAX 703-684-0540
E-Mail: mbrship@afpnet.org
Home Page: www.afpnet.org
Social Media: *Facebook, Twitter, LinkedIn, YouTube, Pinterest, Instagram*

Patrick J. Feeley, Chair
Ann M. Hale, Chair-Elect
Susan Earl Hosback, Vice Chair,Resource Dev.
Joshua R. Newton, Secretary
Joseph Goepfrich, Treasurer

Supports all involved in the fundraising profession. Publishes monthly newsletter.
26000 Members
Founded in 1965

11386 Association of Fundraising Professionals

4300 Wilson Blvd.
Suite 300
Arlington, VA 22203

703-684-0410
800-666-3863
FAX 703-684-0540
Home Page: www.afpnet.org

Andrew Watt, President & CEO
Terry Rauh, Chief Operating Officer

The Association promotes the professional development of fundraising professionals and advocates for high ethical standards in the industry.
30000 Members
Founded in 1960

11387 Association of Small Foundations/ASF

1720 N St NW
Washington, DC 20036

202-580-6560
888-212-9922
FAX 202-580-6579
E-Mail: info@exponentphilanthropy.org
Home Page: www.exponentphilanthropy.org
Social Media: *Twitter*

Christopher Petermann, Chair
Jean Buckley, Vice Chair
Shirish Dayal, Officer-at-Large
Megan McTiernan, Secretary
Janis A. Reischmann, Treasurer

ASF enhances the power of small foundation giving by providing the donors, trustees, and staff of member foundations with peer learning opportunities, targeted tools and resources, and a collective voice in and beyond the philanthropic community.
3000 Members

11388 BoardSource

750 9th Street, NW
Suite 650
Washington, DC 20001-4793

202-349-2500
877-892-6873
FAX 202-349-2599
E-Mail: mail@boardsource.org
Home Page: www.boardsource.org

John Griswold, Chair
Philip Henderson, Vice Chair
Anne Wallestad, President & CEO
Sharon Rossmark, Treasurer
Kimberly Roberson, Secretary

Formerly the National Center for Nonprofit Boards, is the premier resource for practical information, tools and best practices, training, and leadership development for board members of nonprofit organizations worldwide.
7000 Members
Founded in 1988

11389 Bond Market Foundation

360 Madison Avenue
New York, NY 10017-7111

646-637-9200
FAX 646-637-9120
E-Mail: kedmundson@bondmarkets.com
Home Page:
www.bondmarkets.org/default.shtml

Michael D McCarthy, Chairman
Kathryn L Edmundon, Executive Director
Robert E Foran, Vice Chairman
Hugh Moore, Treasurer
Brian Macwilliams, Assistant Secretary

The Bond Market Foundation is a charitable and educational not for profit (501-c-3) association. The Foundation develops and enhances the public's access to quality saving and investor education in addition to providing credible non-proprietary research capacity and expert discussion on public issues relevant to the bond markets. The Bond Market Foundation is partner to the Securities Industry and Financial Markets Association (SIFMA).

11390 Center for Effective Philanthropy

675 Massachusetts Avenue
7th Floor
Cambridge, MA 02139

617-492-0800
FAX 617-492-0888
E-Mail: addya@effectivephilanthropy.org
Home Page: www.effectivephilanthropy.org
Social Media: *Facebook, Twitter, LinkedIn, Youtube, Flickr*

Phil Buchanan, President
Latia King, Executive Assistant to President
Ellie Beteau, Vice President, Research
Kevin Bolduc, Vice President, Assessment Tools
Grant Oliphant, Chair

To provide management and governance tools to define, assess, and improve overall foundation performance
Mailing list available for rent

11391 Council for Advancement & Support of Education

1307 New York Ave NW
Suite 1000
Washington, DC 20005

202-328-2273
FAX 202-387-4973
E-Mail: memberservicecenter@case.org
Home Page: www.case.org
Social Media: *Facebook, Twitter, LinkedIn, Blog*

Sue Cunningham, President/CEO
Brett Chambers, Executive Director of Volunteers
Donald Falkenstein, VP business and finance
Ron Mattocks, VP marketing, membership
Norma Walker, VP advancement programs

Supports all those involved in campus fund raising, public relations,and alumni administration. Publishes monthly magazine.
Founded in 1974

11392 Council on Foundations

2121 Crystal Drive
Suite 700
Arlington, VA 22202

800-673-9036
E-Mail: MEMBERSHIP@COF.ORG

Home Page: www.cof.org
Social Media: *Facebook, Twitter*

Sherry P. Magill, Chair
JAVIER SOTO, Vice Chair
Vikki Spruill, President & CEO
SHERRY ELISE RISTAU, Secretary
EUGENE W. COCHRANE JR., Treasurer

Supports all those involved in the foundation business. Publishes monthly magazine. We provide leadership expertise, legal services and networking opportunities among other services to our members and to the general public.
2000 Members
Founded in 1949

11393 Foundation Center

32 Old Slip
24th Floor
New York, NY 10005

212-620-4230
800-424-9836
FAX 212-807-3677
E-Mail: feedback@foundationcenter.org
Home Page: www.foundationcenter.org
Social Media: *Facebook, Twitter, YouTube, Flickr, Googleplus, Fo*

Bradford K. Smith, President
Lisa Philip, VP for Strategic Philantropy
Lawrence T. McGill, VP for Research
Jeffery Falkenstein, VP for Data Architecture
R. Nancy Albilal, VP Development

A national association for those interested in fund raising related to government agencies. The leading source on philanthropy worldwide.
Founded in 1956

11394 Giving Institute

225 W. Wacker Drive
Chicago, IL 60606-3396

312-981-6794
800-462-2372
FAX 312-265-2908
E-Mail: info@givinginstitute.org
Home Page: www.givinginstitute.org
Social Media: *Facebook, Twitter*

Jeffrey D. Byrne, Chair
Rachel Hutchison, 1st Vice Chair
Sarah J. Howard, 2nd Vice Chair
Derek Alley, Secretary
Peter J. Fissinger, Treasurer

Formerly the American Association of Fundraising Counsel (AAFRC). Mission is to educate and engage members in the ethical delivery of counsel and related services to non-profits through research, advocacy, and best practices.
Founded in 1935
Mailing list available for rent

11395 Independent Sector

1602 L St NW
Suite 900
Washington, DC 20036

202-467-6100
888-860-8118
FAX 202-467-6101
E-Mail: info@independentsector.org
Home Page: www.independentsector.org
Social Media: *Facebook, Twitter*

Stephen B. Heintz, Chair
Ralph B. Everett, Vice Chair
Diana Aviv, President & CEO
Lorie A. Slutsky, Treasurer
Kelvin H. Taketa, Secretary

The leadership forum for charities, foundations, and corporate giving programs committed to advancing the common good in America and around the world.
700 Members
Founded in 1980

11396 MacArthur Foundation

140 S Dearborn Street
Chicago, IL 60603-5285

312-726-8000
FAX 312-920-6258
E-Mail: 4answers@macfound.org
Home Page: www.macfound.org/site/htm
Social Media: *Facebook, Twitter, YouTube, RSS*

Majorie M. Scardino, Chair
Julia M. Stasch, President
Marc P. Yanchura, Vice President & CFO
Elizabeth Kane, Secretary
Angela Abbott, Communications Assistant

Private, independent grant-making institution dedicated to helping groups and individuals foster lasting improvement in the human condition. Through the support it provides, the Foundation fosters the development of knowledge, nurtures individual creativity, strengthens institutions, helps improve public policy, and provides information to the public, primarily through support for public interest media.
Founded in 1978

11397 Music Performance Trust Fund

1501 Broadway
Suite 600
New York, NY 10036

212-391-3950
FAX 212-221-2604
E-Mail: sramos@musicpf.org
Home Page: www.musicpf.org
Social Media: *Facebook*

Dan Beck, Trustee
Vidrey Blackburn, Contact
Al Elvin, Director of Finance
Samantha Ramos, Contact

Foundation allocates money for the promotion of live music for the general public. The concerts must be free of charge and have no admittance restrictions.
Founded in 1948

11398 National Catholic Development Conference Inc.

734 15th St NW
Suite 700
Washington, DC 20005-1013

202-637-0470
888-879-6232
FAX 202-637-0471
E-Mail: glehmuth@ncdcusa.org
Home Page: www.ncdc.org
Social Media: *Facebook, Twitter, LinkedIn*

Chad McEachern, Chair
Greg Griffin, Vice-Chair
Georgette Lehmuth, President & CEO
Daniel McCormack, Treasurer
Dolly Sokol, Ph.D., Secretary

Members include development officers and key fund raisers of charitable institutions and agencies.
400 Members
Founded in 1968
Mailing list available for rent

11399 National Committee for Responsive Philanthropy

1331 H Street NW
Suite 200
Washington, DC 20005

202-387-9177
FAX 202-332-5084
E-Mail: info@ncrp.org
Home Page: www.ncrp.org
Social Media: *Facebook, Twitter, RSS*

Sherece Y. West-Scantlebury, Chair
Gara LaMarche, Vice Chair
Judy Hatcher, Treasurer

Priscilla Hung, Secretary
Aaron Dorfman, Executive Director

Supports all those involved in the philanthropy field. Publishes quarterly newsletter.
Founded in 1976

11400 National Council of Nonprofits

1001 G St. NW
Suite 700E
Washington, DC 20001

202-962-0322
FAX 202-962-0321
Home Page: www.councilofnonprofits.org

Tim Delaney, President & CEO
Kyle Caldwell, Chair

The Council is a resource for the nation's nonprofits, identifying trends, sharing best practices and promoting solutions.

11401 National School Foundation Association (NSFA)

509 Aurora Ave
Ste 406
Naperville, IL 60540

516-971-2324
866-824-8513
FAX 813-280-4820
E-Mail: bill@billhoffmanandassociates.com
Home Page: www.schoolfoundations.org
Social Media: *Facebook, Twitter*

Bill Hoffman, Board Chair
Nina Menis, Executive Director
David Else, Vice Chair
Shanon Solava, Membership Director
Jennifer Nihart, Accounting & Website Updates

The mission of the National School Foundation Association is to encourage K-12 school and school foundation personnel in the very rewarding and important process of establishing, developing and maintaining school foundations.
Founded in 2001

11402 Northwest Development Officers Association

2150 N 107th Street
Suite 205
Seattle, WA 98133-9009

206-971-3605
FAX 206-367-8777
E-Mail: office@afpadvancementnw.org
Home Page: www.ndoa.org
Social Media: *Facebook, Twitter, LinkedIn*

Anne Marie MacPherson, Co President
Jodie Miner, Co President
Ray Li, President Elect
Kirk Laughlin, Secretary
Linda Hunt, Treasurer

To provide its members and other fundraising professionals with collegial peer support, networking, and comprehensive training opportunities to advance philanthropy and strengthen community. Provides fellowship, targeted training, and a sounding board for development officers, volunteers, board members, students, nonprofit managers and others who are committed to fundraising and philanthropy.
800+ Members
Founded in 1978

11403 Partnership for Philanthropic Planning

233 S McCrea St
Suite 300
Indianapolis, IN 46225

317-269-6274
FAX 317-269-6268
E-Mail: info@pppnet.org
Home Page: www.pppnet.org

Social Media: *Facebook, Twitter, LinkedIn, YouTube, Flickr,Googleplus*

Gregory Sharkey, Chair
Melanie J. Norton, Chair Elect
Michael Kenyon, President & CEO
Alexandra Brovey, Treasurer
Thomas Armstrong, Secretary

Serving people and organizations that work together to make charitable giving most meaningful.
112 Members
Founded in 1988

11404 Society for Non-Profits
P.O.Box 510354
Livonia, MI 48151

734-451-3582
FAX 734-451-5935
E-Mail: submit@feedbackform
Home Page: www.snpo.org
Social Media: *Facebook, Twitter, LinkedIn, Yahoo*

Katie Burnham Laverty, President

Provides busy nonprofit leaders with concise and practical articles whose advice can be easily implemented .
Cost: $69.00
6000 Members
Frequency: Bi-Monthly
Circulation: 7000
ISSN: 8755-7614
Founded in 1983

11405 Society for Nonprofit Organizations
PO Box 510354
Livonia, MI 48151

734-451-3582
FAX 734-451-5935
E-Mail: submit@feedbackform
Home Page: www.snpo.org
Social Media: *Facebook, Twitter, LinkedIn, Yahoo*

Katie Burnham Laverty, President

Dedicated to bringing together those who serve in the nonprofit world in order to build a strong network of professionals throughout the country. Publishes Nonprofit World Magazine and has an on-line certificate in Nonprofit Management in partnership with Michigan State University.
6000 Members
Founded in 1983

11406 The Association of Fund-Raising Distributors & Suppliers
1100 Johnson Ferry Rd
Suite 300
Atlanta, GA 30342

404-252-3663
FAX 404-252-0774
E-Mail: afrds@kellencompany.com
Home Page: www.afrds.org
Social Media: *Facebook*

Kurt Koehler, President
Russ Colombo, Vice President Distributor Affairs
Mark Van Wyk, Vice President Supplier Affairs
Paul Mahler, Treasurer
Lisa Dieltz, Secretary

Association for manufacturers or suppliers of fundraising products, supplies and services. Its members manufacturer, supply or distribute products that are resold by not-for-profit organizations for fundraising purposes.
700+ Members

11407 The Grantsmanship Center
350 South Bixel St., Suite 110
PO Box 17220
Los Angeles, CA 90017

213-482-9860
800-421-9512
FAX 213-482-9863
E-Mail: info@tgci.com
Home Page: www.tgci.com
Social Media: *Facebook, Twitter, YouTube,Pinterest,Googleplus*

Cathleen Kiritz, President & Publisher
Barbara Floersch, Director
Susan Andres, Editor
Mariano Diaz, VP Strategic Innovation
Gail Brauner, Training Program Coordinator

Provides training and publications about obtaining funidng for nonprofit and government agencies. Free e-magazine, Centerd, offers a digest of useful articles for grant proposal writers, as well as expert advice from The Grantsmanship Center's trainers.
Founded in 1972

Newsletters

11408 AFP eWire
Association of Fund-Raising Professionals
4300 Wilson Blvd.
Suite 300
Arlington, VA 22203

703-684-0410
800-666-3863
FAX 703-684-0540
E-Mail: mbrship@afpnet.org
Home Page: www.afpnet.org
Social Media: *Facebook, Twitter, LinkedIn, YouTube*

Andrew Watt, President & CEO
Tom Clark, COO
Rebecca A. Knight, Director
Mike Eason, CFO

Delivers the latest fundraising news and information.
26000 Members
Frequency: Weekly
Founded in 1965

11409 AHP E-Connect
Association for Healthcare Philanthropy
313 Park Avenue
Suite 400
Falls Church, VA 22046

703-532-6243
FAX 703-532-7170
E-Mail: ahp@ahp.org
Home Page: www.ahp.org
Social Media: *Facebook, LinkedIn*

Susan J. Doliner, Chair
William S. Littlejohn, Chair Elect
Merv D. Webb, Secretary/Treasurer

Provides updates on industry news and research, educational and professional opportunities, book reviews and articles related to health care philanthropy.
Cost: $60.00
4100 Members
Frequency: 8x Yearly
Founded in 1967

11410 AID for Education
CD Publications
8204 Fenton St
Silver Spring, MD 20910-4571

301-588-6380
800-666-6380
FAX 301-588-6385

E-Mail: info@cdpublications.com
Home Page: www.cdpublications.com

Michael Gerecht, President
Frank Kalimko, Editor

Private and federal funding opportunities and news for all levels of education including grants for bilingual education, special education, literacy, minorities and more.
Cost: $419.00
18 Pages
Founded in 1991
Mailing list available for rent: 2,000 names at $160 per M

11411 Board Source
Board Source
1828 L St Nw
Suite 900
Washington, DC 20036-5114

202-452-6262
800-883-6262
FAX 202-452-6299
E-Mail: mail@boardsource.org
Home Page: www.boardsource.org

Linda Crompton, CEO
Betsy Rosenblatt, Senior Editor

National newsletter for board members and staff leaders of nonprofit organizations includes strategies for building effective nonprofit boards. Comentaries from nonprofit leaders, case studies, and nonprofit governance news.
Cost: $139.00
Founded in 1988

11412 BoardSource E-Newsletter
BoardSource
750 9th Street, NW
Suite 650
Washington, DC 20001-4590

202-349-2500
877-892-6873
FAX 202-349-2599
E-Mail: mail@boardsource.org
Home Page: www.boardsource.org

Linda C. Crompton, President & CEO
Fred Sherman, CFO
Anne Wallestad, COO
David J. Nygren, Ph.D, Chair
Roxanne Spillett, Vice Chair

Members-only benefit, offering timely news and information on nonprofit governance issues and trends affecting nonprofit boards.
7000 Members
Frequency: Monthly
Founded in 1988

11413 CEO Connection
Association for Healthcare Philanthropy
313 Park Avenue
Suite 400
Falls Church, VA 22046

703-532-6243
FAX 703-532-7170
E-Mail: ahp@ahp.org
Home Page: www.ahp.org
Social Media: *Facebook, LinkedIn*

Susan J. Doliner, Chair
William S. Littlejohn, Chair Elect
Merv D. Webb, Secretary/Treasurer

From AHP President to health care organization CEOs discussing issues affecting health care philanthropy.
4100 Members
Frequency: Quarterly
Founded in 1967

11414 Centered
The Grantsmanship Center

1125 W 6th Street 5th Floor
PO Box 17220
Los Angeles, CA 90017

213-482-9860
800-421-9512
FAX 213-482-9863
E-Mail: centered@tgci.com
Home Page: www.tgci.com

Susan Andres, Editor
Cathleen Kiritz, Publisher

Provides a digest of useful articles for grantseekers and proposal writers, as well as expert advice from The Grantsmanship Center's trainers. Our goal is to deliver practical information that will help you sharpen your grant research, proposal-writing, evaluation, and team-building skills.
Frequency: Monthly
Circulation: 35000

11415 Chronicle of Philanthropy
1255 23rd St Nw
Suite 700
Washington, DC 20037-1146

202-466-1200
800-728-2819
FAX 202-452-1033
E-Mail: press@philanthropy.com
Home Page: www.philanthropy.com

Robin Ross, Publisher
Phil Semas, Editor
Michael Solomon, Manager of External Communications

A newspaper providing news and information for executives of nonprofit, tax-exempt organizations in health, education, religion, the arts, social services and other fields, as well as fund raisers, professional employees of foundation, and corporate grant makers. Features news, lists of grants, fundraising ideas and techniques, statistics, updates on regulations, reports on tax and court rulings, book summaries, calendar of events.
Cost: $72.00
Frequency: Fortnightly
Circulation: 100000
Founded in 1997

11416 Community Health Funding Report
CD Publications
8204 Fenton St
Silver Spring, MD 20910-4571

301-588-6380
800-666-6380
FAX 301-588-6385
E-Mail: info@cdpublications.com
Home Page: www.cdpublications.com

Michael Gerecht, President
Amy Bernstein, Editor
Jessica Cha, Owner

Highlights sources of funding for healthcare ranging from AIDS education to teen pregnancy to minority health care. Plus national and local community health news.
Cost: $339.00
Mailing list available for rent: 2,000 names at $160 per M

11417 Connections
Foundation Center
79 5th Ave
New York, NY 10003-3076

212-620-4230
800-424-9836
FAX 212-807-3677
E-Mail: feedback@foundationcenter.org
Home Page: www.foundationcenter.org
Social Media: *Facebook, Twitter, YouTube, Flickr*

Melissa Berman, President & CEO

The best philanthropy-related content the Web has to offer.
Frequency: Bi-Weekly
Founded in 1956

11418 Contributions
Contributions
28 Park St
Suite A
Medfield, MA 02052-2518

508-359-0019
FAX 508-359-2703
E-Mail: kbrennan@contributionsmagazine.com
Home Page: www.contributionsmagazine.com

Jerry Cianciolo, Editor
Kathleen Brennan, Director of Communications
Robert Riordan, Director of Communications

Offers full coverage of fund raising campaigns.
Cost: $40.00
Circulation: 22,000
Founded in 1987

11419 Corporate Giving Directory
Information Today Inc
143 Old Marlton Pike
Medford, NJ 08055-8750

609-654-6266
FAX 609-654-4309
E-Mail: custserv@infotoday.com
Home Page: www.infotoday.com

Thomas H Hogan, President

Delivers the latest information on program priorities, giving preferences, evaluation criteria, corporate and foundation officers and directors, and all the other data you need to help your nonprofit organization gain a crucial edge as corporate philanthropy budgets tighten.

11420 Corporate Philanthropy Report
LRP Publications
PO Box 24668
West Palm Beach, FL 33416-4668

561-622-6520
FAX 561-622-0757
E-Mail: webmaster@lrp.com
Home Page: www.lrp.com

Kenneth Kahn, President
Eileen Banashek, Editor

A report for both the corporate and nonprofit communities, spotlighting a different field or industry in each issue.
Cost: $235.00
Frequency: Monthly
Founded in 1977

11421 Development and Alumni Relations Report
LRP Publications
747 Dresher Road Suite 500
PO Box 980
Horsham, PA 19044-980

215-784-0912
800-341-7874
FAX 215-784-9639
E-Mail: webmaster@lrp.com
Home Page: www.lrp.com

Anne Checkosky, Editor
Dionne Ellis, Marketing

Gives innovative ideas for improving annual giving, endowment and capital campaigns, planned giving, and alumni relations. Offers suggestions on new ways to spur participation and increase total contributions from alumni, corporate donors and foundations.
Cost: $185.00
Frequency: Monthly
Founded in 1977

11422 Dimensions
National Catholic Development Conference

86 Front St
Hempstead, NY 11550-3667

516-481-6000
888-879-6232
FAX 516-489-9287
E-Mail: glehmuth@ncdcusa.org
Home Page: www.ncdc.org

Rachel Donofrio, Editor
Richard Reale, Director Membership
Georgette Lehmuth, CEO
Patricia Newman, Manager

Offers information on development and fund raising including direct mail, planned giving and major gifts and capitol campaigns.
Cost: $1000.00
16 Pages
Circulation: 550
Founded in 1968
Printed in 2 colors on matte stock

11423 Disability Funding News
CD Publications
8204 Fenton St
Silver Spring, MD 20910-4571

301-588-6380
800-666-6380
FAX 301-588-6385
E-Mail: info@cdpublications.com
Home Page: www.cdpublications.com

Michael Gerecht, President
Martha McPartlin, Editor

Alerts the reader to funding for programs for the disabled, including housing, transportation, rehabilitation, research and special education. Plus advice on successful grantseeking and news updated on national and local developments.
Cost: $419.00
Founded in 1993
Mailing list available for rent: 2,000 names at $160 per M

11424 E-ssentials
National Catholic Development Conference
86 Front St
Hempstead, NY 11550-3667

516-481-6000
888-879-6232
FAX 516-489-9287
E-Mail: glehmuth@ncdcusa.org
Home Page: www.ncdc.org

Mark Melia, Chair
Curtis Yarlott, Vice-Chair
Keith Zekind, Treasurer

Connects NCDC members together by providing news about upcoming NCDC events, workshops, and webinars; membership committee news; member success stories; award notifications; fundraising white papers and quick tips; and CFRE exam information.
400 Members
Frequency: Weekly
Founded in 1968

11425 Funding Alert Newsletter
Society for Nonprofit Organizations
PO Box 510354
Livonia, MI 48151

734-451-3582
FAX 734-451-5935
Home Page: www.snpo.org
Social Media: *Facebook, Twitter, LinkedIn*

Katherine Burnham Leverty,
Co-Founder/President/CEO

The leading e-newsletter for current grant and funding opportunities.
7000 Members
Founded in 1983

11426 Giving USA Update
American Association of Fund-Raising
Counsel
4700 W Lake Avenue
Glenview, IL 60025

847-375-4709
800-462-2372
FAX 866-263-2491
E-Mail: info@aafrc.org
Home Page: www.aafrc.org

Ann Kaplan, Publisher
John J Glier, Chair

Contains analysis, data and comments on chari-
table giving.
Cost: $125.00
Frequency: Quarterly
Founded in 1935

11427 Health Grants Funding Alert
Health Resources Publishing
1913 Atlantic Ave
Suite 200
Manasquan, NJ 08736-1067

732-292-1100
888-843-6242
FAX 732-292-1111
E-Mail: info@healthresourcesonline.com
Home Page: www.healthresourcesonline.com

Robert K Jenkins, Publisher
Barbara Brown, Regional Director
Brett Powell, Regional Director
Alice Burron, Director

Monthly report sharing news of critical federal
and foundation funding opportunities and
trends, read by development directors and
grants officers.
Cost: $495.00
8 Pages
Frequency: Monthly
ISSN: 0193-7928
Founded in 1978

11428 Kaleidoscope
Association of Fund-Raising Professionals
4300 Wilson Blvd.
Suite 300
Arlington, VA 22203

703-684-0410
800-666-3863
FAX 703-684-0540
E-Mail: mbrship@afpnet.org
Home Page: www.afpnet.org
Social Media: *Facebook, Twitter, LinkedIn,
YouTube*

Andrew Watt, President & CEO
Tom Clark, COO
Rebecca A. Knight, Director
Mike Eason, CFO

Supports AFP's strategic goal of connecting
communities around the world by promoting
diversity to donors, boards and fundraisers.
26000 Members
Frequency: Quarterly
Founded in 1965

**11429 National Center for Nonprofit
Boards: Board Member Newsletter**
1828 L Street NW
Washington, DC 20036

202-452-6262
800-883-6262
FAX 202-452-6299
Home Page: www.ncnb.org

Monthly newsletter for board members and
staff leaders of nonprofit organizations includes news updates, case studies, checklists,
interviews and opinion pieces to increase the

effectiveness of nonprofit boards.
Cost: $99.00
Frequency: Monthly
Circulation: 6800
Printed in 2 colors on matte stock

11430 Philanthropy News Digest
Foundation Center
79 5th Ave
New York, NY 10003-3076

212-620-4230
800-424-9836
FAX 212-807-3677
E-Mail: feedback@foundationcenter.org
Home Page: www.foundationcenter.org
Social Media: *Facebook, Twitter, YouTube,
Flickr*

Melissa Berman, President & CEO

Long-running, award-winning news digest of
the Foundation Center.
Frequency: Weekly
Founded in 1956

11431 RFP Bulletin
Foundation Center
79 5th Ave
New York, NY 10003-3076

212-620-4230
800-424-9836
FAX 212-807-3677
E-Mail: feedback@foundationcenter.org
Home Page: www.foundationcenter.org
Social Media: *Facebook, Twitter, YouTube,
Flickr*

Melissa Berman, President & CEO

A roundup of recently announced Requests for
Proposals (RFPs) from private, corporate, and
government funding sources.
Frequency: Weekly
Founded in 1956

11432 Responsive Philanthropy
National Committee for Responsive
Philanthropy
2001 S St Nw
Suite 620
Washington, DC 20009-1165

202-387-9177
FAX 202-332-5084
E-Mail: info@ncrp.org
Home Page: www.ncrp.org

Aaron Dorfman, Executive Director
Naomi Tacuyan, Editor

With news and feature articles about philan-
thropy, fund raising and social justice, covering
issues often unreported in mainstream philan-
thropic publications.
Cost: $25.00
16 Pages
Frequency: Quarterly
Circulation: 5000
Founded in 1976
Mailing list available for rent: 10000 names
Printed in 2 colors on matte stock

11433 Smith Funding Report
SFR
20 O'Neill Circle
Monroe, NY 10950-3210

914-774-4449

Melanie Smith, President

Quarterly guide to private foundation re-
search/project grant opportunities for education
and health institutions.
Cost: $195.00
40 Pages
Frequency: Quarterly
Printed in one color on matte stock

11434 Substance Abuse Funding News
CD Publications

8204 Fenton St
Silver Spring, MD 20910-4571

301-588-6380
800-666-6380
FAX 301-588-6385
E-Mail: info@cdpublications.com
Home Page: www.cdpublications.com

Michael Gerecht, President
Joseph Smith, Editor

Detailed coverage of private and federal funding opportunities nationwide for alcohol and
substance abuse programs. Advice on successful grantmaking strategies and roundup of national news.
Cost: $419.00
Founded in 1992
*Mailing list available for rent: 2,000 names at
$160 per M*

11435 Te Informa
Association of Fund-Raising Professionals
4300 Wilson Blvd.
Suite 300
Arlington, VA 22203

703-684-0410
800-666-3863
FAX 703-684-0540
E-Mail: mbrship@afpnet.org
Home Page: www.afpnet.org
Social Media: *Facebook, Twitter, LinkedIn,
YouTube*

Andrew Watt, President & CEO
Tom Clark, COO
Rebecca A. Knight, Director
Mike Eason, CFO

AFP's Spanish-language e-newsletter covering
issues of fundraising pertinent to Mexico and
other Latin American countries.
26000 Members
Frequency: Quarterly
Founded in 1965

Magazines & Journals

11436 Advancing Philanthropy
Association of Fund-Raising Professionals
4300 Wilson Blvd.
Suite 300
Arlington, VA 22203

703-684-0410
800-666-3863
FAX 703-684-0540
E-Mail: mbrship@afpnet.org
Home Page: www.afpnet.org
Social Media: *Facebook, Twitter, LinkedIn,
YouTube*

Andrew Watt, President & CEO
Tom Clark, COO
Rebecca A. Knight, Director
Mike Eason, CFO

Provides practical information, useful tools and
other resources to help members succeed and
advance.
26000 Members
Frequency: Bi-Monthly
Founded in 1965

11437 Association Management
American Society of Association Executives
1575 I St NW
Washington, DC 20005-1103

202-626-2700
FAX 202-408-9635
E-Mail: publicpolicy@asaenet.org
Home Page: www.asaenet.org

Keith C Skillman, Editor
Karl Ely, Publisher

Association Management strives to provide timely, practical information to help association executives succeed in their dual role as manager and visionary.
Cost: $50.00
106 Pages
Frequency: Monthly
Circulation: 24678
ISSN: 0004-5578
Founded in 1920
Printed in 4 colors on glossy stock

11438 Association for Healthcare Philanthropy

313 Park Avenue
Suite 400
Falls Church, VA 22046-3303

703-532-6243
FAX 703-532-7170
E-Mail: ahp@ahp.org
Home Page: www.ahp.org

Kathy Renzetti, Marketing Manager/Editor
William C McGinly, CEO/President
Yvette Banks, Membership Manager
Alison Shaffer, Administrative Assistant

Written for development professionals, fundraisers, trustees, public relations professionals and executives in health care fundraising. Provides timely information on fundraising, career enhancement, planned giving, donor relations, organizational strategies and the effect of health care reform on philanthropy.
Founded in 1967
Mailing list available for rent: 3000 names at $200 per M

11439 BBB Wise Giving Guide

BBB Wise Giving Alliance
4200 Wilson Boulevard
Suite 800
Arlington, VA 22203-1838

703-276-0100
FAX 703-525-8277
Home Page: www.bbb.org

Margery Heitbrink, Editor

Includes a summary of the latest results of the Alliance's national charity evaluations along with a cover story about giving tips and or charity accountability issues.
Frequency: 3x Yearly
Circulation: 35000

11440 Centered

The Grantsmanship Center
350 South Bixel St., Suite 110
PO Box 17220
Los Angeles, CA 90017

213-482-9860
800-421-9512
FAX 213-482-9863
E-Mail: info@tgci.com
Home Page: www.tgci.com
Social Media: *Facebook, Twitter, MySpace*

Cathleen Kiritz, President
Barbara Floersch, Director
Susan Andres, Editor
Cathleen Kiritz, Publisher

Provides a digest of useful articles for grantseekers and proposal writers, as well as expert advice from the Center's trainers.
Frequency: Monthly
Founded in 1972

11441 Currents

Council for Advancement & Support of Education

1307 New York Ave NW
Suite 1000
Washington, DC 20005-4726

202-393-1301
FAX 202-387-4973
E-Mail: memberservicecenter@case.org
Home Page: www.case.org

John Lippincott, President
Deborah Bangiorno, Editor-in-Chief
Andrea Gabrick, Senior Editor
Toni Lewis-Bennett, Director of Membership
Anne Brown, Executive Director

Offers information on campus fund raising, public relations, and alumni administration.
Cost: $115.00
Circulation: 15,000
Founded in 1994

11442 Essentials

Association of Small Foundations/ASF
1720 N St NW
Washington, DC 20036-2907

202-580-6560
888-212-9922
FAX 202-580-6579
E-Mail: asf@smallfoundations.org
Home Page: www.smallfoundations.org
Social Media: *Twitter*

Henry L. Berman, CEO
Floyd S. Keene, Chair

Provides practical articles on a range of information in one easy read.
3000 Members
Frequency: Quarterly

11443 Foundation News & Commentary

Council on Foundations
2121 Crystal Drive
Suite 700
Arlington, VA 22202

8006739036
Home Page: www.foundationnews.org

Offers news and information for foundations, legislation news and fundraising campaign reviews.
Cost: $24.00
Frequency: Monthly

11444 Fundraising EDGE

Association of Fund-Raising Distributors
1100 Johnson Ferry Rd
Suite 300
Atlanta, GA 30342-1733

404-252-3663
FAX 404-252-0774
E-Mail: afrds@kellencompany.com
Home Page: www.afrds.org
Social Media: *Facebook*

Kurt Koehler, President
Leslie Lawrence, Secretary
Steve Wienkers, Treasurer

Published by the Association of Fund-Raising distributors and suppliers, offers the latest information about product fundraising.
700+ Members

11445 Fundraising: Hands on Tactics for Nonprofit Groups

McGraw-Hill Trade
2 Penn Plz
New York, NY 10121-0101

212-904-4450
877-833-5524
FAX 212-904-2348
E-Mail: Philip_Ruppel@mcgraw-hill.com
Home Page: www.aviationdaily.com

L Peter Edles, Editor
Philip Ruppel, VP & Group Publisher
Jeffrey Krames, Publisher & Editor-in-Chief

William Garvey, Managing Editor
Iain Blackhall, Managing Director

This hands-on operations manual remedies the funding crisis by showing nonprofit professionals and volunteers how to design and run successful fundraising campaigns for their organizations. Combines sound, cost-effective strategies for building better organizational, management, sales, and marketing practices.
Cost: $19.95
288 Pages
ISBN: 0-070189-28-5
Founded in 1992

11446 Giving USA

American Association of Fund-Raising Counsel
4700 W Lake Avenue
Glenview, IL 60025-7406

847-375-4709
800-462-2372
FAX 866-263-2491
E-Mail: info@aafrc.org
Home Page: www.aafrc.org/

Ann Kaplan, Editor

An annual report on charitable giving in the United States, tracking total charitable giving from four categories of sources to seven kinds of organizations.
Cost: $125.00
Frequency: Quarterly
Circulation: 9000
Founded in 1935

11447 Grant Funding for Elderly Health Services

Health Resources Publishing
1913 Atlantic Ave
Suite 200
Manasquan, NJ 08736-1067

732-292-1100
888-843-6242
FAX 732-292-1111
E-Mail: info@healthresourcesonline.com
Home Page: www.healthresourcesonline.com

Robert K Jenkins, Publisher
Lisa Mansfield, Marketing Assistant
Caroline Pense, Editor
Brett Powell, Regional Director
Alice Burron, Director

This report will give insight into which proposals will get funds for which organization. Lists the organizations that will recieve the most funds from grantmakers during this decade and beyond. Also studies different case histories of successful grant proposals.
Cost: $95.00
Frequency: Monthly
ISBN: 1-882364-46-5
Founded in 1978

11448 Grants Magazine

Plenum Publishing Corporation
233 Spring St
New York, NY 10013-1522

212-242-1490
FAX 212-463-0742
E-Mail: info@plenum.com
Home Page: www.plenum.com

Ricot Paillent, Manager

A magazine listing sources for grants, offering legislative news for the fundraising community, and foundation listings.
Founded in 1946

11449 Healthcare Philanthropy

Association for Healthcare Philanthropy

313 Park Avenue
Suite 400
Falls Church, VA 22046

703-532-6243
FAX 703-532-7170
E-Mail: ahp@ahp.org
Home Page: www.ahp.org
Social Media: *Facebook, LinkedIn*

Susan J. Doliner, Chair
William S. Littlejohn, Chair Elect
Merv D. Webb, Secretary/Treasurer

Previously called the AHP Journal. Contains articles on health care fundraising and development, including ideas and methods for creating successful development programs, analyses of the current health care environment and projections of future trends.
Cost: $50.00
4100 Members
Frequency: Bi-Annually
Founded in 1967

11450 International Journal of Educational Advancement

Association of Fundraising Professionals
Henry Stewart Publications
PO Box 10812
Birmingham, AL 35202-0812

205-995-1567
800-633-4931
FAX 205-995-1588
E-Mail: brenda@hspublications.co.uk
Home Page: www.afpnet.org /
www.henrystewart.com

Joyce O'Brien, VP of Communications & Marketing
Brenda Rouse, Publisher

Features new ideas, shares examples of best practices and develops a body of knowledge in educational advancement.
Cost: $250.00
Frequency: 4x/year

11451 Journal of Gift Planning

National Committee on Planned Giving
233 S McCrea St
Suite 400
Indianapolis, IN 46225-1068

317-269-6274
FAX 317-269-6276
Home Page: www.ncpg.org

Tanya Howe Johnson, President

Provides in-depth analysis of issues of daily concern to both nonprofit planners and for-profit donor advisors. Each issue provides an orientation to national issues and trends affecting the profession, such as the release of major research related to planned gift fundraising or the debate over professional certification for gift planners.
Cost: $45.00
Frequency: Quarterly

11452 Nonprofit World

Society for Nonprofit Organizations
PO Box 510354
Livonia, MI 48151

734-451-3582
FAX 734-451-5935
E-Mail: info@snpo.org
Home Page: www.snpo.org
Social Media: *Facebook, Twitter, LinkedIn*

Katherine Burnham Laverty, President
Jason Chmura, Membership Director
Jill Muehrcke, Editor

Contains original articles and departments on all aspects of running an effective nonprofit organization. Accepts advertising. Now includes the Directory of Service and Product Providers and the Resource Center Catalog with dis-

counted resources for nonprofit organizations.
Cost: $79.00
40 Pages
Frequency: Bi-Monthly
Circulation: 4000
ISSN: 8755-7614
Founded in 1983
Printed in 2 colors

11453 Philanthropy Monthly

Non-Profit Report
PO Box 989
New Milford, CT 06776

860-354-7132
860-354-7132
FAX 860-354-7132

Henry Suhrke, Publisher

Editorial range covers concerns of nonprofits; legislative, economic, fund raising, nonprofit accounting, litigation, etc.
Cost: $84.00
Circulation: 6208

11454 Responsive Philanthropy

National Committee for Responsive Philanthropy
1331 H Street NW
Suite 200
Washington, DC 20005

202-387-9177
FAX 202-332-5084
E-Mail: info@ncrp.org
Home Page: www.ncrp.org
Social Media: *Facebook, Twitter*

Diane Feeney, Chair
Dave Beckwith, Vice Chair
Cynthia Guyer, Secretary
Robert Edgar, Treasurer

Looks at ending homelessness, funding direct services, supporting re0enfranchisement efforts and more.
Frequency: Quarterly
Founded in 1976

Trade Shows

11455 AFP International Conference on Fundraising

Association of Fundraising Professionals
1101 King Street
Suite 700
Alexandria, VA 22314-2944

703-684-0410
800-666-3863
FAX 703-684-0540
E-Mail: webmaster@afpnet.org
Home Page: www.afpnet.org

Shannon Watson, Director Meetings & Expositions
Myrlin Young, Conferences Coordinator
Paulette Maehara, President
Michael Nilsen, senior Director public affairs

The largest gathering of fundraisers in the profession. The Conference has become the premier resource for fundraisers to network, learn, and discover new products and services.
Frequency: April
Founded in 1962

11456 ASF Annual National Conference

Association of Small Foundations/ASF
1720 N St NW
Washington, DC 20036-2907

202-580-6560
888-212-9922
FAX 202-580-6579
E-Mail: asf@smallfoundations.org

Home Page: www.smallfoundations.org
Social Media: *Twitter*

Henry L. Berman, CEO
Floyd S. Keene, Chair

Dozens of educational sessions, preconference workshops, networking opportunities, and inspiring site visits and service projects.
3000 Members
Frequency: Biennial

11457 Annual AFRDS Convention & Trade Show

Association of Fund-Raising Distributors
1100 Johnson Ferry Rd
Suite 300
Atlanta, GA 30342-1733

404-252-3663
FAX 404-252-0774
E-Mail: afrds@kellencompany.com
Home Page: www.afrds.org
Social Media: *Facebook*

Kurt Koehler, President
Leslie Lawrence, Secretary
Steve Wienkers, Treasurer

The biggest event in product fundraising.
700+ Members
1000+ Attendees
Frequency: Annual/January

11458 Annual NCDC Conference and Exposition

National Catholic Development Conference
86 Front St
Hempstead, NY 11550-3667

516-481-6000
888-879-6232
FAX 516-489-9287
E-Mail: glehmuth@ncdcusa.org
Home Page: www.ncdc.org

Mark Melia, Chair
Curtis Yarlott, Vice-Chair
Keith Zekind, Treasurer

Network, learn and be inspired by the amazing community gathered in the spirit of the ministry of fundraising.
400 Members
Frequency: Weekly
Founded in 1968

11459 Annual Winter & Spring Conferences

Northwest Development Officers Association
2150 N 107th Street
Suite 205
Seattle, WA 98133

206-367-8704
FAX 206-367-8777
E-Mail: office@ndoa.org
Home Page: www.ndoa.org

Lara Littlefield, President
Louise S. Miller, Executive Director
Jenny Poast, Secretary

Educational meetings focusing on fundraising issues, skills, and best practices. 30 exhibitiors.
400 Attendees
Frequency: Annual Winter & Spring

11460 CEP Bi-Annual Conference

Center for Effective Philanthropy
675 Massachusetts Avenue
7th Floor
Cambridge, MA 02139

617-492-0800
FAX 617-492-0888
E-Mail: addya@effectivephilanthropy.org
Home Page: www.effectivephilanthropy.org

Phil Buchanan, President

To provide management and governance tools to define, assess, and improve overall foundation performance.
Frequency: Bi-Annual

11461 Council on Foundations Annual Conference

Council on Foundations
1828 L Street NW
Washington, DC 20036-5104

202-466-6512
FAX 202-785-3926
E-Mail: jonee@cof.org
Home Page: www.cof.org

Edward Jones, Program Director
Heidi Lyn Capati, Conference Logistics
Michelle Dunston, Registration
Dorothy Ridings, President

Annual conference and exhibits relating to trends and legislation in the field of philanthropy.
Frequency: April

11462 Fall Conference for Community Foundations

Council on Foundations
2121 Crystal Drive
Suite 700
Arlington, VA 22202

800-673-9036
E-Mail: info@cof.org
Home Page: www.cof.org
Social Media: *Facebook, Twitter*

Carol Larson, Chair
Kevin Murphy, Vice Chair
Sherece West, Secretary
Will Ginsberg, Treasurer

Three days of bold steps, original ideas, and new solutions for community foundations.
2000 Members
Frequency: Annual/September

11463 Independent Sector Annual Conference

Independent Sector
1602 L Street NW
Suite 900
Washington, DC 20036

202-467-6100
888-860-8118
FAX 202-467-6101
E-Mail: info@independentsector.org
Home Page: www.independentsector.org
Social Media: *Facebook, Twitter*

Stephen B. Heintz, Chair
Ralph B. Everett, Vice Chair
Kelvin H. Taketa, Treasurer
Lorie A. Slutsky

The conference focuses on the social compact of the charitable community's role.
1000 Attendees
Frequency: Annual/November

11464 National Conference on Planned Giving

National Committee on Planned Giving
233 McCrea Street
Suite 400
Indianapolis, IN 46225-1030

317-269-6274
FAX 317-269-6276
Home Page: www.ncpg.org

Shana McMahon, Meetings Manager
Kathryn J Ramsey, Meetings Director
Tanya Howe Johnson, President

Annual conference and exhibits of fundraising equipment, supplies and services.
Frequency: September-October

11465 Rural Philanthropy Conference

Council on Foundations
2121 Crystal Drive
Suite 700
Arlington, VA 22202

800-673-9036
E-Mail: info@cof.org
Home Page: www.cof.org
Social Media: *Facebook, Twitter*

Carol Larson, Chair
Kevin Murphy, Vice Chair
Sherece West, Secretary
Will Ginsberg, Treasurer

Each session encourages defining rural philanthropy's role, focusing on successful case studies, providing the tools needed to replicate them in the communities.
2000 Members
Frequency: Annual/July

11466 Windows Annual Conference

Council on Foundations
2121 Crystal Drive
Suite 700
Arlington, VA 22202

800-673-9036
E-Mail: info@cof.org
Home Page: www.cof.org
Social Media: *Facebook, Twitter*

Carol Larson, Chair
Kevin Murphy, Vice Chair
Sherece West, Secretary
Will Ginsberg, Treasurer

Features three days of transparency, honesty, and candor in the field of philanthropy.
2000 Members
Frequency: Annual/April

Directories & Databases

11467 Annual Register of Grant Support: A Directory of Funding Services

Information Today
143 Old Marlton Pike
Medford, NJ 08055-8750

609-654-6266
800-300-9868
FAX 609-654-4309
E-Mail: custserv@infotoday.com
Home Page: www.infotoday.com

Beverley McDonough, Editor
Daniel Bazikian, Editor

Contains more that 3,500 grant giving organziations. IS also the definitive resource for researching and uncovering a full range of available grant sources.Also directs you to traditional corporate, private, and public funding programs, it also shows you the way to little known, nontraditional grant sources such as educational associations and unions.
Cost: $240.00
1476 Pages
Frequency: Annual
ISBN: 1-573872-04-0

11468 Charitable Trust Directory

Office of the Secretary of State
Charitable Trust Program
801 Capitol Way South
Olympia, WA 98504-0234

360-753-0863
800-332-GIVE
Home Page: www.secstate.wa.gov/charities

Sam Reed, Chairman/Secretary of State
Linda Vallegos Bremer, Director of General Administration

Directory of charitable trusts regulations in the State of Washington.
Cost: $27.00
290 Pages
Frequency: CD-ROM Available

11469 Corporate Giving Directory

Information Today Inc
143 Old Marlton Pike
Medford, NJ 08055-8750

609-654-6266
FAX 609-654-4309
E-Mail: custserv@infotoday.com
Home Page: www.infotoday.com

Thomas H Hogan, President

Delivers the latest information on program priorities, giving preferences, evaluation criteria, corporate and foundation officers and directors, and all the other data you need to help your nonprofit organization gain a crucial edge as corporate philanthropy budgets tighten.
1610 Pages
Frequency: Biennial
ISBN: 1-573872-93-5

11470 Directory of Research Grants

Greenwood Publishing Group
130 Cremona Drive
PO Box 1911
Santa Barbara, CA 93117

800-368-6868
FAX 866-270-3856
E-Mail: CustomerService@abc-clio.com
Home Page: www.abc-clio.com

Directory containing information for more than 5,100 programs being offered through 1,880 sponsors. Includes contact info for grants and examples of past grants awarded, all of which is divided by subject, program, location, and sponsoring organization.
Cost: $151.95
1208 Pages
ISBN: 9-780897-74-9

11471 Environmental Grantmaking Foundations Directory

Resources for Global Sustainability
PO Box 3665
Cary North, NC 27519-3665

800-724-1857
FAX 919-363-9841
Home Page: www.environmentalgrants.com

Corrine Szymko, President

Over 900 private foundations, community foundations and corporate giving programs that provide funding for environmental interests.
Cost: $115.00
Frequency: Annual
ISBN: 0-976788-00-4

11472 Financial Aid for African Americans

Reference Service Press
5000 Windplay Dr
Suite 4
El Dorado Hills, CA 95762-9319

916-939-9620
FAX 916-939-9626
E-Mail: info@rspfunding.com
Home Page: www.rspfunding.com

Gail Schlachter, Editor
Martin Sklar, Manager

This directory describes nearly 1,450 scholarships, fellowships, loans, grants, awards and internships for African Americans
Cost: $40.00
522 Pages
Frequency: Biennial
ISBN: 1-588410-68-5
Founded in 1997

11473 Financial Aid for Asian Americans
Reference Service Press
5000 Windplay Dr
Suite4
El Dorado Hills, CA 95762-9319

916-939-9620
FAX 916-939-9626
E-Mail: info@rspfunding.com
Home Page: www.rspfunding.com

Gail Schlachter, Editor
Martin Sklar, Manager

Use this source to find funding for Americans of Chinese, Japanese, Korean, Vietnamese, Filipino, or other Asian origins. Nearly 1,000 funding opportunities are described.
Cost: $37.50
346 Pages
Frequency: Biennial
ISBN: 1-588410-69-2
Founded in 1997
Printed in on matte stock

11474 Financial Aid for Hispanic Americans
Reference Service Press
5000 Windplay Dr
Suite 4
El Dorado Hills, CA 95762-9319

916-939-9620
FAX 916-939-9626
E-Mail: info@rspfunding.com
Home Page: www.rspfunding.com

Gail Schlachter, Editor
Martin Sklar, Manager

This directory describes nearly 1,300 funding opportunities open to Americans of Mexican, Puerto Rican, Central American, or other Latin American heritage.
Cost: $30.00
402 Pages
Frequency: Biennial
ISBN: 1-588410-70-6
Founded in 1997
Printed in on matte stock

11475 Financial Aid for Native Americans
Reference Service Press
5000 Windplay Dr
Suite 4
El Dorado Hills, CA 95762-9319

916-939-9620
FAX 916-939-9626
E-Mail: info@rspfunding.com
Home Page: www.rspfunding.com

Gail Schlachter, Editor
Martin Sklar, Manager

In this directory you will find 1,500 funding opportunities set aside just for American Indians, Native Alaskans, and Native Pacific Islanders.
Cost: $40.00
546 Pages
ISBN: 1-588410-71-4
Founded in 1997

11476 Financial Aid for Veterans, Military Personnel and their Dependents
Reference Service Press
5000 Windplay Dr
Suite 4
El Dorado Hills, CA 95762-9319

916-939-9620
FAX 916-939-9626
E-Mail: info@rspfunding.com
Home Page: www.rspfunding.com

Gail Schlachter, Editor
Martin Sklar, Manager

This one-stop directory identifies 1,200 scholarships, fellowships, loans, awards, grants and internships.
Cost: $40.00
418 Pages
Frequency: Biennial
ISBN: 1-588410-97-8
Founded in 1988
Printed in on matte stock

11477 Financial Aid for the Disabled and their Families
Reference Service Press
5000 Windplay Dr
Suite 4
El Dorado Hills, CA 95762-9319

916-939-9620
FAX 916-939-9626
E-Mail: info@rspfunding.com
Home Page: www.rspfunding.com

Gail Schlachter, Editor
Martin Sklar, Manager

A comprehensive directory identifies 1,200 scholarships, fellowships, loans, internships, awards, and grants for these groups.
Cost: $40.00
502 Pages
Frequency: Biennial
ISBN: 0-918276-65-9

11478 Foundation Directory
Foundation Center
79 5th Ave
New York, NY 10003-3076

212-620-4230
800-424-9836
FAX 212-807-3677
E-Mail: feedback@foundationcenter.org
Home Page: www.foundationcenter.org

Bradford K Smith, President
Laura Cascio, Chief Information Officer
Patrick Collins, Chief Information Officer
Nancy Kami, Executive Director

Key facts on the nation's top 10,000 foundations by total giving. And, with over 46,000 descriptions of selected grants, the Directory provides fundraisers with unique insight into foundation giving priorities.
Cost: $215.00
2,533 Pages
ISBN: 1-595420-18-5

11479 Foundation Directory Online Database
Foundation Center
79 5th Ave
New York, NY 10003-3076

212-620-4230
800-424-9836
FAX 212-807-3677
E-Mail: feedback@foundationcenter.org
Home Page: www.foundationcenter.org

Bradford K Smith, President
Laura Cascio, Chief Information Officer
Patrick Collins, Chief Information Officer
Nancy Kami, Executive Director

Search our databases online to get detailed information on up to nearly 80,000 foundations, links to current foundation 990-PF returns, crucial facts on more than half a million grants, including the purpose of grants.
Cost: $ 19.95
Frequency: Monthly

11480 Foundation Directory Supplement
Foundation Center
79 5th Ave
New York, NY 10003-3076

212-620-4230
800-424-9836
FAX 212-807-3677

E-Mail: feedback@foundationcenter.org
Home Page: www.foundationcenter.org

Bradford K Smith, President
Laura Cascio, Chief Information Officer
Patrick Collins, Chief Information Officer
Nancy Kami, Executive Director

Provides revised entries for hundreds of foundations in The Foundation Directory and The Foundation Directory Part 2. Any alterations in giving interests, or updates on staff, financial data, contact information, and more, will be reflected in the Supplement.
Cost: $125.00
1000 Pages
ISBN: 1-931923-89-2

11481 Foundation Grants Index
Foundation Center
79 5th Ave
New York, NY 10003-3076

212-620-4230
800-424-9836
FAX 212-807-3677
E-Mail: feedback@foundationcenter.org
Home Page: www.foundationcenter.org

Bradford K Smith, President
Laura Cascio, Fulfillment Manager
Michael Seltver, President
Patrick Collins, Chief Information Officer
Nancy Kami, Executive Director

Covers the grants of over 1,000 of the largest independent, corporate, and community foundations in the U.S. and features approximately 125,000 grant descriptions in all.
Cost: $175.00
Frequency: CD-ROM
ISBN: 1-595420-09-6

11482 Foundation Grants to Individuals
Foundation Center
79 5th Ave
New York, NY 10003-3076

212-620-4230
800-424-9836
FAX 212-807-3677
E-Mail: feedback@foundationcenter.org
Home Page: www.foundationcenter.org

Bradford K Smith, President
Laura Cascio, Fulfillment Manager
Michael Seltver, President
Patrick Collins, Chief Information Officer
Nancy Kami, Executive Director

Featuring over 6,200 entries packed with current information for individual grantseekers.
Cost: $65.00
1,117 Pages
Frequency: Biennial
ISBN: 1-595420-42-8

11483 Foundation Operations and Management Report
Association of Small Foundations/ASF
1720 N St NW
Washington, DC 20036-2907

202-580-6560
888-212-9922
FAX 202-580-6579
E-Mail: asf@smallfoundations.org
Home Page: www.smallfoundations.org
Social Media: *Twitter*

Henry L. Berman, CEO
Floyd S. Keene, Chair

The tool for small foundation benchmarking. Easy-to-read data and commentary on small foundation administration, boards, grantmaking and investments.
3000 Members
50+ Pages
Frequency: Annual

11484 Foundation Salary & Benefits Report
Association of Small Foundations/ASF
1720 N St NW
Washington, DC 20036-2907

202-580-6560
888-212-9922
FAX 202-580-6579
E-Mail: asf@smallfoundations.org
Home Page: www.smallfoundations.org
Social Media: *Twitter*

Henry L. Berman, CEO
Floyd S. Keene, Chair

Small foundations use this annual report to benchmark base salaries by region, gender, experience, asset size, and more. Data includes information on health insurance premiums, retirement contributions, paid leave, and more.
3000 Members
50+ Pages
Frequency: Annual

11485 Funding for Persons with Visual Impairments
Reference Service Press
5000 Windplay Dr
Suite 4
El Dorado Hills, CA 95762-9319

916-939-9620
FAX 916-939-9626
E-Mail: info@rspfunding.com
Home Page: www.rspfunding.com

Gail Schlachter, Editor
Martin Sklar, Manager

For low-vision readers, we have prepared a large-print listing of the scholarships, fellowships, loans, grants-in-aid, awards, and internships that are set aside just for persons with visual impairments (from high school seniors through professionals and others). Nearly 270 funding opportunities are described in detail here.
Cost: $30.00
274 Pages
Frequency: Annual
ISBN: 1-588411-29-X
Founded in 1997

11486 Grants for Foreign and International Programs
Foundation Center
79 5th Ave
New York, NY 10003-3076

212-620-4230
800-424-9836
FAX 212-807-3677
E-Mail: feedback@foundationcenter.org
Home Page: www.foundationcenter.org

Bradford K Smith, President
Michael Seltver, Chief Information Officer
Patrick Collins, Chief Information Officer
Nancy Kami, Executive Director

A customized list of thousands of recent grants of $10,000 or more that have been awarded to organizations in foreign countries and to domestic recipients for international activities in such areas as: development and relief, peace and security, arms control, human rights, conferences and research, and more.
Cost: $75.00
436 Pages
ISBN: 1-595420-23-1

11487 Guide to Funding for International and Foreign Programs
Foundation Center
79 5th Ave
New York, NY 10003-3076

212-620-4230
800-424-9836
FAX 212-807-3677

E-Mail: feedback@foundationcenter.org
Home Page: www.foundationcenter.org

Bradford K Smith, President
Patrick Collins, Chief Information Officer
Nancy Kami, Executive Director

Includes up-to-date information on over 1,000 foundations and corporate givers that have supported a wide range of projects with an international focus both in the U.S. and in foreign countries.
Cost: $125.00
358 Pages
ISBN: 1-931923-95-7

11488 Guide to US Foundations, Their Trustees, Officers and Donors
Foundation Center
79 5th Ave
New York, NY 10003-3076

212-620-4230
800-424-9836
FAX 212-807-3677
E-Mail: feedback@foundationcenter.org
Home Page: www.foundationcenter.org

Bradford K Smith, President
Patrick Collins, Chief Information Officer
Nancy Kami, Executive Director

The only published source of data on all active grantmaking foundations and the individuals who run them, provides current information on over 68,000 foundations. Featuring a master list of the decision-makers who direct America's foundations, the Guide is a powerful fundraising reference tool.
Cost: $350,00
4,235 Pages
Frequency: Annual
ISBN: 1-595420-35-5

11489 Matching Gift Details
Council for Advancement & Support of Education
1307 New York Ave NW
Suite 1000
Washington, DC 20005-4726

202-393-1301
FAX 202-387-4973
E-Mail: memberservicecenter@case.org
Home Page: www.case.org

Silvia France, Matching Gifts Coordinator

Compiled and maintained by the Matching Gifts Clearinghouse, a comprehensive annual directory of more than 8,600 companies that match employee charitable gifts.
Cost: $100.00
286 Pages
ISBN: 0-899643-83-3

11490 National Directory of Corporate Giving
Foundation Center
79 5th Ave
New York, NY 10003-3076

212-620-4230
800-424-9836
FAX 212-807-3677
E-Mail: feedback@foundationcenter.org
Home Page: www.foundationcenter.org

Bradford K Smith, President
Patrick Collins, Chief Information Officer
Nancy Kami, Executive Director

This comprehensive directory features up-to-date information that helps fundraisers tap into their share of grant money earmarked by companies for nonprofit support. Detailed portraits of close to 2,500 corporate foundations and some 1,400 direct giving programs

feature essential information.
Cost: $195.00
1,165 Pages
Frequency: Annual
ISBN: 1-595420-04-5

11491 New Foundation Guidebook
Association of Small Foundation
4905 Del Ray Avenue
Suite 200
Bethesda, MD 20814

301-073-3337
888-212-9922
FAX 301-907-0980
E-Mail: asf@smallfoundations.org
Home Page: www.smallfoundations.org

Carmen Wong, Director of Communications
Deborah Brody Hamilton, CEO
Hanh Le, Director Member Services
Kathryn Petrillo-Smith, Managing Director

Contains articles and advice from over 40 foundation respresentatives and experts included in the Association of Small Foundations' newsletters and publications.
Cost: $40.00
86 Pages

11492 New Nonprofit Almanac & Desk Reference
Independent Sector
1602 L St NW
Suite 900
Washington, DC 20036-5682

202-467-6100
888-860-8118
FAX 202-467-6101
E-Mail: info@independentsector.org
Home Page: www.independentsector.org

Provides managers, researchers, volunteers, and the press with the essential facts and figures needed to understand the size, scope, and nature of the nonprofit sector and its contributions to American society.
Cost: $42.00
288 Pages
ISBN: 9-780787-95-7

11493 The Complete Guide to Grantmaking Basics: A Field Guide for Funders
Council on Foundations
2121 Crystal Drive
Suite 700
Arlington, VA 22202

800-673-9036
E-Mail: info@cof.org
Home Page: www.cof.org
Social Media: *Facebook, Twitter*

Carol Larson, Chair
Kevin Murphy, Vice Chair
Sherece West, Secretary
Will Ginsberg, Treasurer

A practical guide to honing your grantmaking effectiveness and adapting to the changing nonprofit world.
Cost: $65.00
2000 Members

11494 The Foundation Guidebook
Association of Small Foundations/ASF
1720 N St NW
Washington, DC 20036-2907

202-580-6560
888-212-9922
FAX 202-580-6579
E-Mail: asf@smallfoundations.org
Home Page: www.smallfoundations.org
Social Media: *Twitter*

Henry L. Berman, CEO
Floyd S. Keene, Chair

Gain the baseline knowledge to operate your foundation smoothly and effectively.
Cost: $69.00
3000 Members

Industry Web Sites

11495 http://gold.greyhouse.com
G.O.L.D Grey House OnLine Databases
Grey House Publishing's online database platform, GOLD, offers Quick Search, Keyword Search and Expert Search for most business sectors including foundation and fund raising markets. The GOLD platform makes finding the information you need quick and easy - whether you're a novice searcher or an experienced database user. All of Grey House's directory products are available for subscription on the GOLD platform.

11496 www.aafrc.org
American Association of Fund-Raising Counsel
To promote ethical practice and professional standards in the fund-raising consultant field.

11497 www.ahp.org
Association for Healthcare Philanthropy
Represents health care fundraising professionals through education and eventually bestows the credentials upon them.

11498 www.boardsource.org
BoardSource
Formerly the National Center for Nonprofit Boards, is the premier resource for practical information, tools and best practices, training, and leadership development for board members of nonprofit organizations worldwide.

11499 www.cof.org
Council on Foundations
Supports all those involved in the foundation business. Publishes monthly magazine. We provide leadership expertise, legal services and networking opportunities among other services to our members and to the general public.

11500 www.grantsmart.org
Grantsmart
An online resource database that contains 96,337 private foundations and charitable trusts.

11501 www.greyhouse.com
Grey House Publishing
Authoritative reference directories for most business sectors including foundation and fund raising markets. Users can search the online databases with varied search criteria allowing for custom searches by product category, geographic area, sales volume, keyword, subject and more. Full Grey House catalog and online ordering also available.

11502 www.guidestar.org
GuideStar
A database of more than 1 million nonprofit organizations in the United States. It's the world's most comprehensive source of information about American nonprofit organizations.

11503 www.idealist.org
Action Without Borders
Over 45,000 nonprofit and community organizations in 165 countries, which you can search or browse by name, location or mission.

11504 www.independentsector.org
Independent Sector
The leadership forum for charities, foundations, and corporate giving programs committed to advancing the common good in America and around the world.

11505 www.naspl.org
North American Assn of State & Provincial Lottery
Represents 47 lottery organizations throughout North America. Provides information and benefits of state and provincial lottery organizations.

11506 www.ncdcusa.org
National Catholic Development Conference
Members include development officers and key fund raisers of charitable institutions and agencies.

11507 www.philanthropy.org
A Philanthropic Partnership for Black Communities
Providing information on innovative vehicles for the black communities.

11508 www.snpo.orgorg/snpo
Society for Nonprofit Organizations
Dedicated to bringing together those who serve in the nonprofit world in order to build a strong network of professional throughout the country.

11509 www.tgci.com
The Grantsmanship Center
Launched the world's first training program for grantseekers in 1972 and continues to set the standard in the field.

11510 www.uwex.edu/li
Learning Institute
The Center provides you with a number of resources on the web that could provide you with assistance in a variety of nonprofit management and leadership issues. In the nonprofit web sites section you will find a number of useful annotated resources organized by topic.

Associations

11511 American Chemistry Council
700 Second St, NE
Washington, DC 20002

202-249-7000
FAX 202-249-6100
Home Page:
plastics.americanchemistry.com/pfpg
Social Media: *Facebook, Twitter*

Calvin M. Dooley, President
Raymond J. O Bryan, CFO & Chief
Administrative Officer
Rudy Underwood, Vice President, State Affairs
Bryan Zumwalt, Vice President of Federal
Affairs
Anne Womack Kolton, Vice President of
Communications

Promotes effective use of recycling of polystyrene. Works to provide effective information
about waste disposal and offers technical
assistance.
Founded in 1988

11512 American Trucking Associations
950 North Glebe Road
Suite 210
Arlington, VA 22203-4181

703-838-1700
E-Mail: nafc@trucking.org
Home Page: www.trucking.org

Pat Thomas, Chairman
Bill Graves, President & CEO
Kevin Burch, First Vice Chairman
Karla Hulett, Secretary
G. Tommy Hodges, Treasurer

Largest national trade association for the trucking industry.
1000 Members
Founded in 1933

11513 Association of Independent Corrugated Converters
113 S. West Street
3rd Floor
Alexandria, VA 22314

703-836-2422
877-836-2422
FAX 703-836-2795
E-Mail: info@aiccbox.org
Home Page: www.aiccbox.org
Social Media: *Facebook, Twitter, LinkedIn, YouTube*

Mark Williams, Chairman
Tony Schleich, First Vice Chairman
Joseph M. Palmeri, Vice Chairman
Jeff Pallini, Associate Vice Chairman
John Forrey, Director at Large

Provides a forum for discussion of problems
and offers educational programs and seminars.
1100 Members
Founded in 1974

11514 Composite Can and Tube Institute
50 S Pickett Street
Suite 110
Alexandria, VA 22304-7206

703-823-7234
FAX 703-823-7237
E-Mail: ccti@cctiwdc.org
Home Page: www.cctiwdc.org

Kristine Garland, Executive Vice President
Janine Marczak, Associate Manager, Events
Wayne Vance, Association Counsel

CCTI is an international nonprofit trade association representing the interests of manufacturers of composite paperboard cans, containers,
canisters, tubes, cores, edgeboard and related
or similar composite products and suppliers to
those manufacturers of such items as paper,
machinery, adhesives, labels and other services
and materials.
Founded in 1934

11515 Containerization & Intermodal Institute
960 Holmdel Road
Bldg 2, Suite 201
Holmdel, NJ 07733

732-817-9131
FAX 732-817-9133
E-Mail: connie@containerization.org
Home Page: www.containerization.org
Social Media: *LinkedIn*

Brendan McCahill, Sr., Chairman
Allen Clifford, Vice Chairman
Michael DiVirgilio, President
Steven Blust, Vice President
Sue Coffey, Treasurer

Provides educational opportunities through existing programs and initiatives, including educational outreach, scholarships, and award
programs.
Founded in 1960

11516 Contract Packaging Association
One Parkview Plaza
Suite 800
Oakbrook Terrace, IL 60181

630-544-5053
FAX 630-544-5055
E-Mail: info@contractpackaging.org
Home Page: www.contractpackaging.org
Social Media: *Twitter, LinkedIn*

Vicky Smitley, President
Tim Koers, Vice President
Mark O'Malley, Treasurer
Chris Nutley, Past-President
John Mazelin, Executive Director

A national, not-for-profit trade association that
includes dynamic and growing companies offering contract packaging services.
155 Members
Founded in 1992

11517 Corrugated Packaging Alliance
25 Northwest Point Blvd
Suite 510
Elk Grove Village, IL 60007

847-364-9600
FAX 847-364-9739
E-Mail: inquiries@corrugated.org
Home Page: www.corrugated.org
Social Media: *LinkedIn*

Rachel K Kenyon, Vice President
Dennis Colley, Executive Director

Develops and coordinates industry-wide programs to address corrugated packaging issues.
The Council's mission is to inform consumers,
manufacturers, retailers and government officials of corrugated packaging's performance
and environmental attributes.
Founded in 1994

11518 EPS Industry Alliance (EPS-IA)
1298 Cronson Blvd.
Suite 201
Crofton, MD 21114

800-607-3772
E-Mail: info@epscentral.org
Home Page: www.epspackaging.org
Social Media: *Facebook, Twitter*

EPS-IA is a union of 60 companies dedicated
to the sustainability of the expanded polystyrene (EPS) industry and environmental
protection.
Founded in 2012

11519 Envelope Manufacturers Association
500 Montgomery St.
Suite 550
Alexandria, VA 22314

703-739-2200
FAX 703-739-2209
Home Page: www.envelope.org

Maynard H. Benjamin, President & CEO

Association representing the interests of the en-
velope manufacturing industry.
Founded in 1933

11520 Express Carriers Association
9532 Liberia Avenue
Suite 752
Manassas, VA 20110

703-361-1058
866-322-7447
FAX 703-361-5274
E-Mail: eca@expresscarriers.org
Home Page: www.expresscarriers.org

Paul Steffes, President
Jim Luciani, 1st Vice President
Mike Coyle, 2nd Vice President
Jim King, Treasurer
Jim Bernecker, Secretary

Trade association representing regional carriers. Presents annual marketplace to bring together carriers and shippers

11521 Fibre Box Association
25 Northwest Point Blvd
Suite 510
Elk Grove Village, IL 60007

847-364-9600
FAX 847-364-9639
E-Mail: fba@fibrebox.org
Home Page: www.fibrebox.org
Social Media: *LinkedIn*

John Davis, Chairman
Mike Waite, First Vice Chairman
Bill Hoel, Second Vice Chairman
Dennis Colley, President
Rachel Kenyon, Vice President1

Represents 90 percent of the US corrugated paper board, packaging, manufacturing industry.
141 Members
Founded in 1940

11522 Flexible Intermediate Bulk Container Association
PO Box 241894
Saint Paul, MN 55124-7019

952-412-8867
FAX 661-339-0023
E-Mail: info@fibca.com
Home Page: www.fibca.com
Social Media: *Facebook, Twitter, LinkedIn, Youtube, Googleplus, blogspot*

Lewis Anderson, Executive Director

Works to develop minimum standards of testing and performance for FIBC. Acts as a forum
through seminars and other programs and
serves as an advocate for the industry.
50 Members
Founded in 1983

11523 Flexible Packaging Association
185 Admiral Cochrane Drive
Suite 105
Annapolis, MD 21401

410-694-0800
FAX 410-694-0900
E-Mail: fpa@flexpack.org
Home Page: www.flexpack.org

Marla Donahue, President

One of the leading trade associations for converters of flexible packaging and suppliers to
the industry. Also provides a wealth of infor-

mation to its members through focused services and benefits of membership.

11524 Foodservice & Packaging Institute

7700 Leesburg Pike
Suite 421
Falls Church, VA 22043

703-592-9889
FAX 703-592-9864
E-Mail: fpi@fpi.org
Home Page: www.fpi.org
Social Media: *Facebook, Twitter, LinkedIn*

Lynn Dyer, President
Natha Freiburg, Vice President
Rob Kittredge, Chair
Michael Evans, 1st Vice Chair
Tracy Pearson, 2nd Vice Chair

Manufacturers, suppliers and distributors of one-time use products used for food service, as well as packaging products made from paper, plastic, aluminum and other materials.
37 Members
Founded in 1933

11525 Gemini Shippers Group

137 West 25th Street
3rd Floor
New York, NY 10001

212-947-3424
FAX 212-629-0361
E-Mail: info@geminishippers.com
Home Page: www.geminishippers.com

Sara L. Mayes, CEO and President
Kenneth O'Brien, Chief Operating Officer
Nicole Uchrin, Managing Director
Rich Moore, Sales Director
Arlene L. Blocker, Membership Director

Shippers association with global contracts for all commodities.
200 Members
Founded in 1916

11526 Glass Packaging Institute

1220 North Fillmore Street
Suite 400
Arlington, VA 22201

703-684-6359
FAX 703-546-0588
E-Mail: info@gpi.org
Home Page: www.gpi.org
Social Media: *Facebook, Twitter*

Andres Lopez, Chairman
Lynn M. Bragg, President
John Riordan, Board Member
Sanjay Gandhi, Board Member
John Gallo, Board Member

Develops and evaluates testing procedures and equipment, conducts advertising campaigns for generic products.
Founded in 1945

11527 Healthcare Compliance Packaging Council

2711 Buford Road
#268
Bon Air, VA 23235-2423

804-338-5778
FAX 888-812-4272
Home Page: www.hcpconline.org
Social Media: *Facebook, LinkedIn*

Walt Berghahn, Executive Director

Promotes the many benefits of unit dose blister and strip packaging, especially its ability to be designed in compliance, promoting formats that help people take their medications properly.
Founded in 1990

11528 Institute of International Container Lessors

1120 Connecticut Avenue
Suite 440
Washington, DC 20036-3946

202-223-9800
FAX 202-223-9810
E-Mail: info@iicl.org
Home Page: www.iicl.org

Philip Brewer, Chairman
Steven Blust, President & Secretary
Simon Vernon, 1st Vice President
Keith Lovetro, 2nd Vice President
George Elkas, Treasurer

Represents international container and chassis leasing industry in technical, governmental and legal matters. Publishes leading worldwide manuals on inspection and repair of containers and inspector and maintenance of chassis. Sponsors container and chassis inspection examination once a year in over 40 countries and chassis examination in North America.
Founded in 1971

11529 Institute of Packaging Professionals

One Parkview Plaza
Suite 800
Oakbrook Terrace, IL 60181

630-544-5050
FAX 630-544-5055
E-Mail: info@iopp.org
Home Page: www.iopp.org
Social Media: *Facebook, Twitter, LinkedIn, YouTube*

Jane Chase, Chair
Dan Alexander, Vice Chair
Dana Alexander, Executive VP- Finance & Operations
Robert Meisner, Executive VP- Education
Suzanne Simmons, Executive VP- Membership

Dedicated to creating networking and educational opportunities that help packaging professionals succeed.

11530 International Air Transport Association

800 Place Victoria
PO Box 113
Montreal, CA H4Z 1M1

514-874-0202
FAX 514-874-9632
Home Page: www.iata.org/
Social Media: *Twitter, LinkedIn, YouTube*

Tony Tyler, Director General & CEO

Seeks to improve understanding of the industry among decision makers and increase awareness of the benefits that aviation brings to national and global economies. It fights for the interests of airlines across the globe, challenging unreasonable rules and charges, holding regulators and governments to account, and strivign for sensible regulation.
240+ Members
Founded in 1945

11531 International Molded Fiber Association

355 Lexington Avenue
Floor 15
New York, NY 10017

212-297-2150
FAX 262-241-3766
E-Mail: Alan@IMFA.org
Home Page: www.imfa.org
Social Media: *Facebook, Twitter, LinkedIn*

Cassandra Niesing, Asst. Director
Joseph Grygny, Chairman

Acts as an information center for the molded fiber industry with worldwide membership of users and manufacturers of molded fiber producs. Promotes use of natural and recycled fibers.
Founded in 1997

11532 Keep America Beautiful

1010 Washington Blvd
Stamford, CT 06901

203-659-3000
FAX 203-659-3001
E-Mail: info@kab.org
Home Page: www.kab.org
Social Media: *Facebook, Twitter, Youtube*

Howard Ungerleider, Chairman
Jennifer M. Jehn, President and CEO
Steve Navedo, VP Development
Mike Rogers, Chief Development Officer
Becky Lyons, Chief Operating Officer

National, nonprofit, education organization whose corporate members include packagers, retailers, bottlers, and makers of chemical, steel, glass, paper and aluminum products.
Founded in 1953

11533 Lake Carriers Association

20325 Center Ridge Road
Suite 720
Rocky River, OH 44116

440-333-4444
FAX 440-333-9993
E-Mail: info@lcaships.com
Home Page: www.lcaships.com

James H I Weakley, President
Glen Nekvasil, Vice President
Harold W. Henderson, General Counsel
Katie Gumeny, Administrative Assistant
Katherine A. Gumeny, Secretary/Treasurer

Members are US-Flag Great Lakes vessel operators engaged in transporting iron ore, coal, grain, limestone, cement and petroleum products.
Founded in 1880

11534 National Customs Brokers and Forwarders Association of America, Inc.

1200 18th St NW
Suite 901
Washington, DC 20036

202-466-0222
FAX 202-466-0226
E-Mail: staff@ncbfaa.org
Home Page: www.ncbfaa.org

Darrell Sekin, Jr., Chairman
Geoffrey Powell, President
Amy Magnus, Vice President
Scott E. Larson, Treasurer
William S. App. Jr., Secretary

Learn about new business leads, stay on top of Customs Service and other agency regulations that will impact your operations and provide invaluable professional development resources for your employees.
600+ Members
Founded in 1897

11535 National Institute of Packaging, Handling, and Logistics Engineers

5903 Ridgeway Drive
Grand Prairie, TX 75052

817-466-7490
866-464-7490
E-Mail: admin@niphle.com
Home Page: www.niphle.com
Social Media: *Facebook, Twitter, LinkedIn*

Sean Kernis, President
Anna Boulware, Board Member
Michael Werneke, Board Member
Sher Paul Singh, Board Member
Brian Ramsey, Board Member

An assemblage of professionals whose interest in the complex and diverse practice of distribution and logistics is a common bond.
600 Members
Founded in 1956

11536 Paperboard Packaging Council

1350 Main Street
Suite 1508
Springfield, MA 01103-1670

413-686-9191
FAX 413-747-7777
E-Mail: paperboardpackaging@ppcnet.org
Home Page: www.ppcnet.org
Social Media: *Facebook, Twitter, LinkedIn, Youtube*

Kyle Eldred, Chair
Charles Johnson, Vice Chair
Marc Anderson, Director at large
Michael Ukropina, Director at large
Steven Levkoff, Treasurer

The leading industry association serving suppliers and converters of all forms of paperboard packaging, works to grow, promote, and protect the paperboard packaging industry while providing its members with resources and tools to compete effectively and successfully in the marketplace.
Founded in 1967

11537 Petroleum Packaging Council

ATD Management Inc.
1519 Via Tulipan
San Clemente, CA 92673

949-369-7102
FAX 949-366-1057
E-Mail: PPC@ATDmanagement.com
Home Page: www.ppcouncil.org
Social Media: *LinkedIn*

John Whittenhall, President
Elizabeth Wagg, Vice President
Sam Merenda, Secretary/ Treasurer
Darren Booth, Assistant Treasurer
Carolyn Booms, Director

Provides technical leadership and education to the petroleum packaging industry.
400 Members
Founded in 1950

11538 Pressure Sensitive Tape Council

One Parkview Plaza
Suite 800
Oakbrook Terrace, IL 60181

630-544-5048
FAX 630-544-5055
E-Mail: info@pstc.org
Home Page: www.pstc.org
Social Media: *Twitter, LinkedIn, Flickr*

Michael Merkx, President
Curt Rutsky, Vice President
Charlie McKenna, Treasurer
Brad Boelkins, Directors
Tom Boyle, Directors

Trade association for tape manufacturers and affiliate suppliers, dedicated to helping the industry produce quality pressure sensitive adhesive tape products in the global marketplace. PSTC provides education and training, works with ASTM and global trade organizations to harmonize test methods and monitors legislative and regulatory activities.
Founded in 1953

11539 Recycled Paperboard Technical Association

P.O. Box 5774
Elgin, IL 60121-5774

847-622-2544
FAX 847-622-2546

E-Mail: rpta@rpta.org
Home Page: www.rpta.org

David Briere, President
Mark Sklar, Vice President
Peter Traeger, Treasurer
Amy E. Schaffer, Ex-Officio
Tim Hagenbuch, Chair

An association of US, Canadian and overseas companies interested in cooperative research and development in the industry.
33 Members
Founded in 1953

11540 Retail Packaging Association

105 Eastern Avenue
Suite 104
Annapolis, MD 21403

410-940-6459
FAX 410-263-1659
E-Mail: info@retailpackaging.org
Home Page: www.retailpackaging.org

Tony Van Belkom, President
Jatin Patel, Treasurer
Denise Cabrera, Secretary
Don Smith, Executive Director
Amy Luckado, Membership Director

Serves its members and the entire retail packaging industry. Also organizes the largest trade show and conference of its kind in the US. A self-governed not-for-profit organization comprised of professionals involved in all facets of production and distribution of retail packaging products.
Founded in 1989
Mailing list available for rent

11541 Reusable Industrial Packaging Association

51 Monroe Street
Suite 812
Rockville, MD 20850

301-577-3786
FAX 301-577-6476
E-Mail: prankin@ripaus.com
Home Page: www.reusablepackaging.org
Social Media: *Facebook, Twitter*

Ricky Buckner, Chair
Jerry Butler, Vice Chair
Paul W. Rankin, President
Dan Burek, Treasurer
Tim O'Bryan, Secretary
Founded in 1942

11542 Technical Association of the Pulp & Paper Industry

15 Technology Parkway South
Suite 115
Peachtree Corners, GA 30092

770-446-1400
800-322-8686
FAX 770-446-6947
E-Mail: webmaster@tappi.org
Home Page: www.tappi.org
Social Media: *Facebook, Twitter, LinkedIn*

Chris Luettgen, Chair
Paul R. Durocher, Vice Chair
Larry N. Montague, President & CEO
Peter R. Augustine, Director
Medwick V. Byrd, Director

To engage the people and resources of our association in providing technically sound solutions to the workplace problems and opportunities that challenge our current and future members.
12000 Members
Founded in 1915

11543 The Adhesive and Sealant Council, Inc.

7101 Wisconsin Avenue
Suite 990
Bethesda, MD 20814

301-986-9700
FAX 301-986-9795
E-Mail: info@ascouncil.org
Home Page: www.ascouncil.org
Social Media: *Twitter, LinkedIn*

Traci Jensen, Chair
Matt Croson, President
Charles R. Williams, Jr., Treasurer
Steve Duren, Senior Director, Member Services
Malinda Armstrong, Director, Meetings & Expositions

ASC is a North American trade association dedicated to representing the adhesive and sealant industry. ASC is bound by the collective efforts of its members, and strives to improve the industry operating environment and strengthen its member companies.

11544 Transportation Intermediaries Association

1625 Prince St
Suite 200
Alexandria, VA 22314-2883

703-299-5700
FAX 703-836-0123
E-Mail: info@tianet.org
Home Page: www.tianet.org

Robert Voltmann, President
Jeff Tucker, Chair
Jason Beardall, Vice Chair
Michael Riccio, Treasurer
Barcy Vidt, Secretary

Education and policy organization for North American transportation intermediaries. The only national association representing the interests of all third party transportation service providers. Members include logistics management firms, property brokers, perishable commodities brokers, freight forwarders, intermodal marketers and ocean and air forwarders.
700 Members
Founded in 1977

11545 Transportation Marketing Communications Association (TMCA)

9382 Oak Avenue
Waconia, MN 55387

952-442-5638
FAX 952-442-3941
E-Mail: brian07@tmcatoday.org
Home Page: www.tmcatoday.org

John Ferguson, President
Tom Nightingale, VP
Tracy Robinson, Treasurer
Edward Moritz, Secretary
Brian Everett, Executive Director

The only association serving transportation marketing, sales and communications pros in all modes and market segments of the North American transportation industry.
225 Members
Founded in 1924

Newsletters

11546 ASC e-Catalyst

The Adhesive and Sealant Council, Inc.
7101 Wisconsin Avenue
Suite 990
Bethesda, MD 20814

301-986-9700
FAX 301-986-9795

E-Mail: info@ascouncil.org
Home Page: www.ascouncil.org

Glenn E. Frommer, Chair
C. Russell Thompson, Jr., Treasurer
Matthew E. Croson, President

Delivers the latest ASC news, industry information and end-user trends.
Frequency: Monthly

11547 Air Cargo Report
Phillips Publishing
1201 Seven Locks Road
Potomac, MD 20854-2931

301-541-1400
FAX 301-424-2098
E-Mail: info@accessintel.com
Home Page: www.accessintel.com

Richard Koulbanis, Publisher
Donald Pazour, CEO/President

Reports on emerging trends and business strategies for airline cargo, integrator, freight forwarding and all-cargo carrier operations.
Circulation: 1430

11548 CanTube Bulletin
Composite Can and Tube Institute
50 S Pickett Street
Suite 110
Alexandria, VA 22304-7206

703-823-7234
FAX 703-823-7237
E-Mail: ccti@cctiwdc.org
Home Page: www.cctiwdc.org

Excellent source of information about issues affecting this industry, as well as updates on CCTI activities.
Frequency: Bi-Monthly
Circulation: 800+

11549 Mail Center Management Report
Institute of Management and Administration
3 Bethesda Metro Center
Suite 250
Bethesda, MD 20814-5377

800-372-1033
FAX 800-253-0332
Home Page: www.ioma.com

Shows you how to improve mail center productivity, reduce costs, and get you the recognition you deserve through buying and leasing new equipment, negotiating rates with carriers, and much more. Shows proven techniques to improve relations with the USPS and other service vendors. You'll find tactics for improving your dealing with senior management, purchasing, marketing and logistics.

11550 Packaging Strategies
Packaging Strategies
600 Willowbrook Lane
Suite 610
West Chester, PA 19382

610-436-4220
800-524-7225
FAX 610-436-6277
E-Mail: packinfo@packstrat.com
Home Page: www.packstrat.com
Social Media: *Facebook, Twitter, LinkedIn*

Joe Pryweller, Editor/Conference Director
Janet Martinelli, Conference/Study Support Manager
Randy Green, Publisher
Karen Vaillancourt, Sales Manager
Karen Close, Senior Events Manager

A subscription newsletter focusing on news and analysis of technology and business issues in the packaging industry. Also producer of 4 conferences per year: structural packagingsummit, food packaging technologies summit, global pouch firum, sustainable packaging forum and

multi-client industry studies.
Cost: $497.00
8 Pages
ISSN: 8755-6189
Founded in 1983
Printed in 2 colors on matte stock

11551 Transportation Intermediaries Update
Transportation Intermediaries Association
1625 Prince St
Suite 200
Alexandria, VA 22314-2883

703-299-5700
FAX 703-836-0123
E-Mail: voltmann@tianet.org
Home Page: www.tianet.org

Robert Voltmann, President

Education and policy organization for North American transportation intermediaries. TIA is the only national association representing the interests of all third party transportation service providers. The members of TIA include logistics management firms, property brokers, perishable commodities brokers, freight forwarders, intermodal marketers, ocean and air forwarders, and NVOCC's.
700 Pages
Frequency: Monthly

Magazines & Journals

11552 Advanced Packaging
PennWell Publishing Company
98 Spit Brook Rd
Suite L11
Nashua, NH 03062-5737

603-891-0123
FAX 603-891-9294
E-Mail: lwilliam@pennwell.com
Home Page: www.pennwell.com

Christine Shaw, VP
Gail Flower, Editor

Focuses on materials, assembly, design and reliability issues facing the global packaging community.
Cost: $88.00
Frequency: Monthly
Circulation: 22,000
Founded in 1910

11553 Air Cargo Focus
Cargo Network Services Corporation
703 Waterford Way
Suite 680
Miami, FL 33126-4677

786-413-1000
FAX 786-413-1005
E-Mail: cns@cnsc.us
Home Page: www.cnsc.net

Fernando Garcia, VP
Anthony P Calabrese, President

A forum for professionals involved in the sale , marketing, services and movement of air cargo.
Frequency: Quarterly
Circulation: 8000
Founded in 1986

11554 Air Cargo News
PO Box 98
Portage, MI 49081-98

718-479-0716
FAX 718-740-0761
E-Mail: judy@aircargonews.com
Home Page: www.aircargonews.com

Geoffrey Arend, Publisher

CAB regulations, and other news of interest to those in the air cargo industry.
Cost: $39.95
Frequency: Monthly
Circulation: 100,000
Founded in 1975

11555 American Shipper
Howard Publications
300 W Adams Street Suite 600
PO Box 4728
Jacksonville, FL 32201-4728

904-355-2601
800-874-6422
FAX 904-791-8836
Home Page: www.americanshipper.com

Hayes H Howard, Publisher
Gary G. Burrows, Managing Editor

Provides those involved in domestic and global supply chain management with news and information of a strategic nature, useful in the formation of logistics polices and partnerships.
Cost: $30.00
100 Pages
Frequency: Monthly
Circulation: 13487
ISSN: 1074-8350
Founded in 1951
Printed in 4 colors on glossy stock

11556 Cargo Facts
Air Cargo Managment Group
520 Pike St
Suite 1010
Seattle, WA 98101-4058

206-587-6537
FAX 206-587-6540
E-Mail: news@cargofacts.com
Home Page: www.cargofacts.com

Edwin Laird, Manager
David Harris, Editor
Jackie Edinger, Circulation Manager

Includes fiscal reports, freighter aircraft transactions, short segments, international perspectives, and industry updates.
Cost: $395.00
24 Pages
Frequency: Monthly
Circulation: 7500
ISSN: 0278-0801
Founded in 1980

11557 Contract Packaging
Contract Packaging Association
1833 Centre Point Circle
Suite 123
Naperville, IL 60563-4848

630-544-5053
FAX 630-544-5055
E-Mail: info@contractpackaging.org
Home Page: www.contractpackaging.org

Joe Jaruszewski, President
Chris Nutley, Vice President
Vicky Smitley, Treasurer

Covers conract packaging issues and news, and is an excellent source of CPA news and industry developments, trends, analysis, and information for buyers and sellers of contract packaging.
155 Members
Founded in 1992

11558 Cosmetic Personal Care Packaging
O&B Communications
11444 W Olympic Boulevard
Los Angeles, CA 90064-1303

310-445-4200
FAX 310-445-4299

E-Mail: info@cpcpkg.com
Home Page: www.cpcpkg.com

Patricia Spinner, Publisher
John Bethune, Editorial Director
Jennifer Kwok, Managing Editor

Provides information on new packaging containers, materials, equipment and services that are involved with the cosmetic industry.
Cost: $60.00
Frequency: Monthly
Circulation: 12,500
Founded in 1996

11559 Courier Times
Courier Times
27-16 168th Street
Flushing, NY 11358-1130

718-291-1253
FAX 718-359-1959
Home Page: www.couriertimes.com

Bill Goodman, Editor
C Tsamis, Owner

New products vital to the industry, discusses insurance and technology updates, also offers customer service guidelines.
Cost: $39.00
Frequency: Monthly
Circulation: 1100

11560 Electronic Packaging & Production
Reed Business Information
360 Park Ave S
New York, NY 10010-1737

646-746-6400
FAX 646-756-7583
E-Mail:
corporatecommunications@reedbusiness.com
Home Page: www.reedbusiness.com

John Poulin, CEO
Michael Sweeney, Editorial Director
James Reed, Owner

Edited for engineers and managers who are involved in packaging design, printed circuit board fabrication and assembly, and production testing of electronic circuits, systems, products and equipment.
Founded in 1960

11561 Flexible Packaging
Flexible Packaging Association
971 Corporate Blvd
Suite 403
Linthicum, MD 21090-2253

410-694-0800
FAX 410-694-0900
E-Mail: fpa@flexpack.org
Home Page: www.flexpack.org

Marla Donahue, President

Offering subscribers up-to-the-minute information on industry news and trends, material and substrate developments, innovations in equipment, and the latest in business management. The only magazine in the market that dedicates 100 percent of its editorial content and circulation to flexible packaging converters.
Frequency: Monthly

11562 Food & Beverage Packaging
155 Pfingsten Road
Suite 205
Deerfield, IL 60015

847-405-4000
FAX 847-405-4100
Home Page:
www.foodandbeveragepackaging.com

Randy Green, Publisher

Identifies and analyzes the market trends and packaging solutions that matter to food and beverage processors.
Frequency: Monthly
Circulation: 75140
Founded in 1959

11563 Harbour & Shipping
Progress Publishing Company, Ltd
1489 Marine Drive
Suite 510
West Vancouver, BC V7 T1

604-922-6717
FAX 604-922-1739

Allison Smith, Editor
Murray McLellan, Publisher/Marketing

Serves the deep sea and coastal shipping, and ship building, repair and supply industries of Canada and worldwide. Accepts advertising.
Cost: $60.00
Frequency: Monthly
Circulation: 2200
ISSN: 0017-7637
Printed in 4 colors on glossy stock

11564 International Paper Board Industry
Brunton Publications & NV Public
43 Main Street
Avon By The Sea, NJ 07717-1051

732-502-0500
FAX 732-502-9606
E-Mail: jcurley@NVPublications.com
Home Page: nvpublications.com

Mike Brunton, Publisher
Jim Curley, Editor
Tom Vilardi, President

Information on corrugated paper and converting industry, encompassing news and production worldwide.
Cost: $60.00
Frequency: Monthly
Circulation: 6500

11565 Journal of HazMat Transportation
Packaging Research International
404 Price St
West Chester, PA 19382-3531

610-436-8292
877-429-7447
FAX 610-436-9422
Home Page: www.hazmatship.com

Vincent A Vitollo, Owner

A professionally prepared technical reporting system, focused exlusively on explaining changes to the hazardous materials transportation regulations. Thoroughly covers and provides technical reviews of the US 49CFR, International Civil Aviation Organization Technical Instructions, the International Maritime Dangerous Goods Code, and the European Road and Rail Regulations.
Cost: $209.00
Circulation: 1000
Founded in 1990
Printed in 4 colors on matte stock

11566 MAIL: The Journal of Communication Distribution
1 Elmcoft Road
Stamford, CT 06926-700

203-356-5000
800-672-6937
FAX 203-739-3488
Home Page: www.pb.com

Meg Reiley, President
Ina Steiner, Publisher

Manages change and positions customers for both tactical and long-term success with innovative, cost-effective, end-to-end messaging solutions.

11567 Modern Bulk Transporter
Tunnell Publications
PO Box 66010
Houston, TX 77266

713-523-8124
FAX 713-523-8384
Home Page: www.bulktransporter.com/
Social Media: Facebook, Twitter

Charles Wilson, Editor
Martine Ewing, Advertising Director
Mary Davis, Associate Editor

Serves the truck industry that transports petroleum and petroleum products. Accepts advertising.
Frequency: Monthly
Circulation: 15000

11568 PARCEL
RB Publishing
2901 International Lane
Madison, WI 53704-3102

608-778-8785
800-536-1992
FAX 608-241-8666
Home Page: www.parcelindustry.com
Social Media: LinkedIn

Marll Thiede, CEO
Chad Griepentrog, President
Mike Beacom, Editor

Brings the insights needed to improve parcel operations and keep costs under control. PARCEL gives you access to experts who look at the entire process, from order entry to the shipping dock to customer delivery, to give you information you can use.
Circulation: 30000
Founded in 1988

11569 Packaging Digest Magazine
UBM Canon
1200 Jorie Blvd.
Suite 230
Oak Brook, IL 60523-2260

630-990-2371
FAX 630-990-8894
E-Mail: packagingdigest@ubm.com
Home Page: www.packagingdigest.com

John Kalkowski, Editorial Director
Lisa McTigue Pierce, Editor
Jenni Spinner, Senior Editor

Serves the manufacturing, wholesale and service industries.
Cost: $75.00
Frequency: Monthly
Founded in 1963

11570 Packaging Technology & Engineering
North American Publishing Company
1500 Spring Garden St
12th Floor
Philadelphia, PA 19130-4094

215-238-5300
800-777-8074
FAX 215-238-5342
E-Mail: customerservice@napco.com
Home Page: www.napco.com

Ned S Borowsky, CEO
Richard Soloway, CEO/President
Glen Reynolds, Circulation Manager
Nolle Skodzinski, Editor

Reports on environmental concerns, legislation and regulation, product design, material availability, and economic trends.
Cost: $69.00
Frequency: Monthly
Circulation: 20271
Founded in 1958

11571 Packaging World
Summit Publishing Company

330 N Wabash Ave
Suite 2401
Chicago, IL 60611-7618

312-222-1010
FAX 312-222-1310
E-Mail: reynolds@packworld.com
Home Page: www.packworld.com

Lloyd Ferguson, Owner
Joseph Angel, Vice President
Patrick Reynolds, VP/Editor
Timothy Hammack, Circulation Director
Jim George, Marketing & Design Editor

Serves the manufacturing, wholesaling, and service industries.
Frequency: Monthly
Circulation: 92547
ISSN: 1073-7367
Founded in 1994
Printed in 4 colors on matte stock

11572 Paperboard Packaging
2835 North Sheffield Avenue
Suite 226
Chicago, IL 60657

773-880-2234
FAX 773-880-2244
Home Page: www.packaging-online.com
Social Media: *Facebook, Twitter*

Marisa Palmieri, Editor

Publication edited for management and other key personnel involved in the manufacturing and marketing segments of the paperboard packaging industry.
Cost: $39.00
Frequency: Monthly
ISSN: 0031-1227

11573 Pharmaceutical & Medical Packaging News
Canon Communications
11444 W Olympic Blvd
Suite 900
Los Angeles, CA 90064-1555

310-445-4200
FAX 310-445-4299
E-Mail: sales@devicelink.com
Home Page: www.devicelink.com

Charlie Mc Curdy, President
Daphne Allen, Managing Editor
Bob Michaels, Managing Editor
Nicole Welter, Account Executive

Information and news on events, new technology, industry trends, regulatory matters, and health care trade associations for professionals involved in the pharmaceutical and medical product packaging industry.
Cost: $150.00
Frequency: Monthly
Circulation: 20000
ISSN: 1081-5481
Founded in 1978

11574 Refrigerated Transporter
4200 S. Shepherd Dr.
Suite 200
Houston, TX 77098-2901

713-523-8124
800-880-0368
FAX 713-523-8384
E-Mail: jay.miller@penton.com
Home Page: www.refrigeratedtrans.com

The information source for those involved in the transportation and distribution of refrigerated products ranging from food to pharmaceuticals, from film and cosmetics to chemicals. Provides practical information derived from the experience of businesses in the field as well as up-to-the-minute news on developments and equipment for the industry.
Frequency: Monthly
Circulation: 15023
Founded in 1905

11575 TAPPI Journal
Technical Association of the Pulp & Paper Industry
15 Technology Parkway South
Norcross, GA 30092

770-446-1400
800-322-8686
FAX 770-446-6947
E-Mail: webmaster@tappi.org
Home Page: www.tappi.org

Larry N. Montague, President & CEO

Serves domestic and international pulp, paper, paperboard, packaging and converting industries; manufacturers and suppliers of machinery, equipment, chemicals and other material.
Cost: $350.00
130 Pages
Frequency: Monthly
Circulation: 5300
ISSN: 0734-1415
Founded in 1949
Printed in 4 colors on glossy stock

11576 Trucker's Connection
Megan Cullingford
5960 Crooked Creek Road
Suite 15
Norcross, GA 30092

770-416-0927
FAX 770-416-1734
Home Page: www.truckersconnection.com

Megan Cullingford, General Manager
Dan Barnhill, Editor
Reid Ramsay, Production Manager

Published for the use of long haul, over-the-road truck drivers, owner operators, small trucking company fleet owners, safety and recruiting of personnel for trucking companies in the US and Canada.
Frequency: Monthly
Circulation: 165000
Founded in 1986
Printed in 4 colors on glossy stock

11577 World Wide Shipping (WWS)
World Wide Shipping Guide
16302 Byrnwyck Ln
Odessa, FL 33556-2807

813-920-4788
FAX 813-920-8268
E-Mail: info@wwship.com
Home Page: www.wwship.com

Lee Di Paci, Publisher
Barbara Edwards, Marketing Manager
Bob Susor, Marketing Manager

Dedicated to the interests of North American exporters, importers, distributors, freight forwarders, NVOCC's and customs brokers requiring freight tranportation services and equipment.
Cost: $32.00
32 Pages
Frequency: Fortnightly
Circulation: 9000
ISSN: 1060-7900
Founded in 1919
Printed in 4 colors on glossy stock

Trade Shows

11578 Contract Packaging Association Annual Meeting
Contract Packaging Association

1833 Centre Point Circle
Suite 123
Naperville, IL 60563-4848

630-544-5053
FAX 630-544-5055
E-Mail: info@contractpackaging.org
Home Page: www.contractpackaging.org

Joe Jaruszewski, President
Chris Nutley, Vice President
Vicky Smitley, Treasurer

Includes experts discussing success patterns that work, uncovering winning and learning attitudes and methods that will guide your business toward lasting results.
155 Members
Founded in 1992

11579 International Molded Fiber Packaging Seminar
International Molded Fiber Association
1425 W Mequon Rd
Suite C
Mequon, WI 53092-3262

262-241-0522
FAX 262-241-3766
E-Mail: info@imfa.org
Home Page: www.imfa.org
Social Media: *Facebook, Twitter, LinkedIn*

Cassandra Niesing, Asst. Director
Joseph Grygny, Chairman

Opportunity to network, learn, and grow in the molded fiber industry.
Founded in 1996

11580 LabelExpo
Tarsus Group
9501 W Devon Avenue
Rosemont, IL 60018-4811

847-292-3700
FAX 847-318-1506
Home Page: www.labelresource.com

Steve Krogulski, Manager

The largest event for the lable, web printing, product decoration, converting and packaging industry in the Americas.
13700 Attendees
Frequency: Annual/September

11581 Outlook & Strategies Conference
Paperboard Packaging Council
1350 Main Street
Suite 1508
Springfield, MA 01103-1670

413-686-9191
FAX 413-747-7777
Home Page: www.ppcnet.org

Ben Markens, President
Lou Kornet, Vice President/Chief of Staff

Industry leaders specializing in sustainability, the economy, and education will come together to impart their knowledge, experience, and business predictions.
325 Attendees
Frequency: Annual/March

11582 PROPAK Asia
Reed Exhibition Companies
383 Main Avenue
PO Box 6059
Norwalk, CT 06851

203-840-4800
FAX 203-840-9628

One hundred and seventy four exhibitors for an audience of manufacturers, packaging design and development professionals. International food processing and packaging technology exhibition.
Frequency: Annual

11583 Shipper/Carrier Marketplace
Express Carriers Association
9532 Liberia Ave
Suite 752
Manassas, VA 20110-1719

703-361-1058
866-322-7447
FAX 703-361-5274
Home Page: www.expresscarriers.org

Stuart Hyden, President
Lance Adams, First VP
Fiona Morgan, Executive Director

Brings about 500 representatives from regional and national companies together to explore business relationships through face-to-face interviews
500 Attendees
Frequency: Annual

11584 Transportation Intermediaries Annual Convention & Trade Show
Transportation Intermediaries Association
1625 Prince Street
Suite 200
Alexandria, VA 22314

703-299-5700
FAX 703-836-0123
E-Mail: voltmann@tianet.org
Home Page: www.tianet.org
Social Media: *Facebook, Twitter, LinkedIn*

Robert Voltmann, President/CEO

The only meeting for third-party logistics providers. A once a year opportunity to interact with representatives from throughout North America and abroad. Key decision makers with buying authority attend this meeting.
700 Attendees
Frequency: Annual/March
Founded in 1978

11585 World Packaging Conference
Reed Business Information
2000 Clearwater Drive
Oak Brook, IL 60523

630-740-0825
FAX 630-288-8686
Home Page: www.reedbusiness.com

Jay Singh, Conference Chair
Bruce Harte, Consultant

One thousand three hundred and fourteen booths.
500 Attendees
Frequency: Annual/June

Directories & Databases

11586 ABS International Directory of Offices
American Bureau of Shipping
16855 Northchase Dr
Houston, TX 77060-6006

281-673-2800
FAX 281-877-5801
Home Page: www.abs-group.com

Tony Nassif, CEO

Over 175 operations offices of the bureau worldwide are listed.
122 Pages
Frequency: Semiannual

11587 Air Freight Directory
Air Cargo

1819 Bay Ridge Avenue
Suite 1
Annapolis, MD 21403-2899

410-805-5578
800-747-6505
FAX 410-268-3154

Debbi Mayes

Gives contact details for 35,000 global air cargo companies including 24,000 freight forwarders and 1700 airports. Track and trace shipments, locate airfreight personnel, or just follow the latest air cargo industry news.
Cost: $84.00
Frequency: Bi-Monthly

11588 American Drop-Shippers Directory
World Wide Trade Service
PO Box 283
Medina, WA 98039-0283

206-236-4795

Over 200 firms are listed that are willing to drop ship single item orders at wholesale prices for mail order and other direct marketers.
Cost: $15.00
36 Pages
Frequency: Biennial
Circulation: 5,000

11589 Commercial Carrier Journal: Buyers' Guide Issue
Reed Business Information
1 Chilton Way
Wayne, PA 19089-0002

646-746-6400
FAX 646-746-7433
Home Page: www.reedbusiness.com
Social Media: *Facebook, Twitter, LinkedIn*

Gerald F Standley, Editor
Stuart Whayman, CFO

List of vehicles, components and accessories suppliers for the truck and bus fleet markets.
Cost: $10.00
Frequency: Annual/October
Circulation: 85,000

11590 Commercial Carrier Journal: Top 100 Issue
Reed Business Information
360 Park Avenue
New York, NY 10010

212-450-0067
FAX 646-746-7433
Home Page: www.ccjdigital.com

List of top 100 for-hire motor carriers, ranked by gross revenues; also the next 200 carriers in gross revenue.
Cost: $10.00
Frequency: Annual/August
Circulation: 85,000

11591 Directory of Contract Packagers and their Facilities
Institute of Packaging Professionals
Ste 123
1833 Centre Point Cir
Naperville, IL 60563-4848

630-544-5050
800-432-4085
FAX 630-544-5055
E-Mail: info@iopp.org
Home Page: www.iopp.org

Edwin Landon, Executive Director
Patrick Farrey, General Manager

More than 400 contract packagers in the US and abroad.
Frequency: Biennial

11592 Directory of Corrugated Plants
Fibre Box Association

25 Northwest Point Blvd
Suite 510
Elk Grove Village, IL 60007

847-364-9600
FAX 847-364-9639
E-Mail: fba@fibrebox.org
Home Page: www.fibrebox.org
Social Media: *LinkedIn*

Over 1,600 manufacturing facilities in the North American corrugated and solid fibre industry. Distributed in microsoft excel spreadsheet.
Cost: $200.00

11593 Directory of Freight Forwarders and Custom House Brokers
International Wealth Success
PO Box 186
Merrick, NY 11566-0186

516-766-5850
800-323-0548
FAX 516-766-5919
E-Mail: admin@iwsmoney.com
Home Page: www.iwsmoney.com
Social Media: *Facebook, LinkedIn*

Tyler G Hicks, President

Lists hundreds of these firms throughout the U.S. who help in the export/import business.
Cost: $20.00
106 Pages
Frequency: Annual
ISBN: 1-561503-46-0
Founded in 1980

11594 Directory of Packaging Consultants
Institute of Packaging Professionals
Ste 123
1833 Centre Point Cir
Naperville, IL 60563-4848

630-544-5050
800-432-4085
FAX 630-544-5055
E-Mail: info@iopp.org
Home Page: www.iopp.org
Social Media: *Facebook, Twitter, LinkedIn*

Edwin Landon, Executive Director
Patrick Farrey, General Manager

Packaging consultants in the US.
Cost: $25.00
Frequency: Annual

11595 Directory of US Flexographic Packaging Sources
JPC Directories
PO Box 488
Plainview, NY 11803-0488

516-822-6861

Joel J Shulman, Editor

Offers information on narrow web and wide web printer/converters and suppliers to the printing industry.
125 Pages
Frequency: Annual
Circulation: 50,000

11596 Flexible Packaging Association Membership Directory
Flexible Packaging Association
971 Corporate Boulevard
Suite 403
Linthicum, MD 21090-4769

410-694-0800
FAX 410-694-0900
E-Mail: fpa@flexpack.org

Over 200 member companies that manufacture flexible packaging and supplies used in this industry are profiled.
Frequency: Annual
Circulation: 20,000

11597 Food & Beverage Market Place
Grey House Publishing
4919 Route 22
PO Box 56
Amenia, NY 12501

518-789-8700
800-562-2139
FAX 845-373-6390
E-Mail: books@greyhouse.com
Home Page: www.greyhouse.com
Social Media: *Facebook, Twitter*

Leslie Mackenzie, Publisher
Richard Gottlieb, Editor

This information packed three-volume set is
the most powerful buying and marketing guide
for the US food and beverage industry. Includes thousands of industry and transportation
listings. Contains a significant chapter on food
and beverage transportation.
Cost: $595.00
2000 Pages
Frequency: Annual
ISBN: 1-592373-61-5
Founded in 1981

**11598 Food & Beverage Marketplace:
Online Database**
Grey House Publishing
4919 Route 22
PO Box 56
Amenia, NY 12501

518-789-8700
800-562-2139
FAX 845-373-6390
E-Mail: gold@greyhouse.com
Home Page: http://gold.greyhouse.com
Social Media: *Facebook, Twitter*

Richard Gottlieb, President
Leslie Mackenzie, Publisher

This complete updated Food & Beverage Market Place: Online Database is the go-to source
for the food and beverage industry. Anyone involved in the food and beverage industry needs
this 'industry bible' and the important contacts
to develop critical research data that can make
for successful business growth.
Frequency: Annual
Founded in 1981

**11599 Modern Bulk Transporter: Buyers
Guide**
Tunnell Publications
PO Box 66010
Houston, TX 77266

713-523-8124
FAX 713-523-8384

Charles Wilson, Editor

Directory of suppliers of products or services
for companies operating tank trucks.
Frequency: Annual/October
Circulation: 16,000

11600 NCBFAA Membership Directory
National Customs Brokers & Forwarders
Association
1200 18th St NW
Suite 901
Washington, DC 20036-2572

202-466-0222
FAX 202-466-0226
E-Mail: staff@ncbfaa.org
Home Page: www.ncbfaa.org

About 600 customs brokers, international air
cargo agents, and freight forwarders in the
United States.
Cost: $24.00
Frequency: Annual

**11601 National Highway and Airway
Carriers Directory**
National Highway Carriers Directory
PO Box 6099
Buffalo Grove, IL 60089-6099

847-634-0606
FAX 847-634-1026
Home Page: www.national-highway.com

Pam W Ferreira, President/Editor

Provides information on: LTL motor freight
carriers - with over 250,000 detailed routing
points and terminals for US and Canada, contract carriers (truckload), airline cargo companies, transportation brokers, intermodal
trucking companies, freight forwarders, warehousing companies, Canadian carriers, refrigerated carriers, railroads and ocean carriers.
Cost: $195.00
1400 Pages
Frequency: Biannually
Circulation: 5000
Founded in 1942
Printed in 2 colors on newsprint stock

**11602 National Motor Carrier Directory and
Additional Products**
Transportation Technical Services
500 Lafayette Boulevard
Fredericksburg, VA 22401-6070

540-899-9872
888-665-9887
FAX 540-899-1948
E-Mail: truckinfo@ttstrucks.com
Home Page:
www.ttstrucks.com/www.fleetseek.com

Ronald D Roth, Executive VP

Over 46,000 motor carriers with revenues of
$100,000 or more.
Cost: $495.00
1781 Pages
Frequency: Annual/November
Founded in 1989

11603 Official Container Directory
Advanstar Communications
641 Lexington Ave
8th Floor
New York, NY 10022-4503

212-951-6600
FAX 212-951-6793
E-Mail: info@advanstar.com
Home Page: www.advanstar.com

Joseph Loggia, CEO

Directory of services and supplies to the industry.
200 Pages
Circulation: 5,000

11604 Official Freight Shippers Guide
Official Motor Freight Guides
1700 W Cortland Street
Chicago, IL 60622-1121

773-342-1000
800-621-4650
FAX 773-489-0482

E Koch, Editor
Eric J Robison, Editor

Major air, rail, water and motor carriers pub-
lished in three local editions covering Chicago,
New York and St. Louis.
Cost: $55.00
516 Pages
Frequency: Annual

11605 Official Motor Carrier Directory
Official Motor Freight Guides

1700 W Cortland Street
Chicago, IL 60622-1121

773-342-1000
800-621-4650
FAX 773-489-0482

Edward K Koch, Editor

Approximately 2,100 general and specialized
motor carriers and air cargo carriers; federal
and state agencies concerned with the trucking
industry; tariff publishing bureaus, US and Canadian port authorities; state associations.
Cost: $59.50
Frequency: SemiAnnual
Circulation: 6,000

11606 Official Motor Freight Guide
C&C Publishing Company
1700 W Cortland Street
Chicago, IL 60622-1121

773-536-2050

This directory is published in over 21 regional
editions that list air and water freight transportation, motor carriers and warehouse facilities
for the metropolitan areas of Baltimore,
Boston, Chicago, Cincinnati, Cleveland, Denver, Detroit, Evansville, Ft. Wayne, Indianapolis, Kansas City, Philadelphia, Pittsburgh, Quad
Cities and Toledo.
Cost: $45.00
500 Pages
Frequency: Semiannual

**11607 PMMI Packaging Machinery
Directory**
Packaging Machinery Manufacturers
Institute (PMMI)
4350 Fairfax Dr
Suite 600
Arlington, VA 22203-1632

703-243-8555
FAX 703-243-8556
E-Mail: pmmiwebhelp@pmmi.org
Home Page: www.pmmi.org

Chuck Yuska, President
Sara Kryder, Manager Communications

Contains information on all 500+ member companies, who are committed to producing quality
products and providing world class service to
their customers.

**11608 Packaging Digest: Machinery
Materials Guide Issue**
Delta Communications
Ste 300
20900 Swenson Dr
Waukesha, WI 53186-4050

262-429-9111
FAX 262-546-8820
E-Mail: delta@deltacommunications.com
Home Page: www.deltacommunicatons.com

Barbara McDonough, Editor

List of more than 3,100 manufacturers of machinery and materials for the packaging industry, and about 260 contract packagers.
Frequency: Annual

**11609 Rauch Guide to the US Packaging
Industry**
Impact Marketing Consultants
PO Box 1226
Manchester Center, VT 05255

802-362-2325
802-362-3693
E-Mail: comments@impactmarket.com
Home Page: www.impactmarket.com

Donald R Dykes, Editor
C Verbanic, Editor

Analyzes the US packaging industry, with data
on industry economics, raw materials, major

885

products, and unique profiles of 50% producers.
Cost: $495.00
Frequency: Triennial

11610 Transportation Telephone Tickler
Commonwealth Business Media
50 Millstone Rd
Building 400, Suite 200
East Windsor, NJ 08520-1418

609-371-7700
800-215-6084
FAX 609-371-7879
Home Page: www.cbizmedia.com

Alan Glass, CEO
Edith Chaudoin-Stahlberger, Editor

Provides vital contact information for 24,000 suppliers of 160 types of transportation services in the US, Canada, Caribbean and parts of Latin America.
Cost: $124.95
2425 Pages
Frequency: Annual
Founded in 1949

11611 Who's Who & What's What in Packaging
481 Carlisle Drive
Herndon, VA 20170-4830

703-471-8922

Offers information on members of the Institute of Packaging Professionals, including placement firms, colleges that offer packaging curricula, and related organizations.
Cost: $125.00
240 Pages
Frequency: Annual

Industry Web Sites

11612 http://gold.greyhouse.com
G.O.L.D Grey House OnLine Databases

Grey House Publishing's online database platform, GOLD, offers Quick Search, Keyword Search and Expert Search for most business sectors including freight, packaging and transportation markets. The GOLD platform makes finding the information you need quick and easy - whether you're a novice searcher or an experienced database user. All of Grey House's directory products are available for subscription on the GOLD platform.

11613 plastics.americanchemistry.com
Polystyrene Packaging Council
Links to other associations.

11614 www.adhesives.org
Adhesive and Sealant Council, Inc.
Association for the packaging industry.

11615 www.aiccbox.org
Association of Independent Corrugated Converters

Provides a forum for discussion of problems and offers educational programs and seminars.

11616 www.corrugated.org
Corrugated Packaging Council

Develops and coordinates industry-wide programs to address corrugated packaging issues. The Council's mission is to inform consumers, manufacturers, retailers and government officials of corrugated packaging's performance and environmental attributes.

11617 www.fibca.com
Flexible Intermediate Bulk Container Association

Social Media: *Facebook, Twitter*

11618 www.fibrebox.org
Fibre Box Association

Represents 90 percent of the US corrugated paper board, packaging, manufacturing industry.

11619 www.flexpack.org
Flexible Packaging Association

Trade association of manufacturers, converters and suppliers of paper, metal foil and plastic or cellulose film.

11620 www.fpi.org
Foodservice & Packaging Institute

Sanitation and environmental information, plus programs and services.

11621 www.ftd.com
Florists' Transworld Delivery Association

Has an annual budget of approximately $140 million.

11622 www.geminishippers.com
Gemini Shippers Group

Shippers association with global contracts for all commodities.

11623 www.graysonassociates.com
Grayson Associates

Association for those interested in marketing analysis of the package goods industry.

11624 www.greyhouse.com
Grey House Publishing

Authoritative reference directories for most business sectors including freight, packaging, and transportation markets. Users can search the online databases with varied search criteria allowing for custom searches by product category, geographic area, sales volume, keyword, subject and more. Full Grey House catalog and online ordering also available.

11625 www.homefair.com

Offers comprehensive content and services for people moving to a new home or relocating to another community.

11626 www.iicl.org
Institute of International Container Lessors

Represents international container and chassis leasing industry in technical, governmental and legal matters. Publishes leading worldwide manuals on inspection and repair of containers and inspector and maintenance of chassis. Sponsors container and chassis inspection examination once a year in over 40 countries and chassis examination in North America.

11627 www.lcaships.com
Lake Carriers Association

Members are US- Flag Great Lakes vessel operators engaged in transporting iron ore, coal, grain, limestone, cement and petroleum products.

11628 www.mfsanet.org/
Mailing & Fulfillment Service Association

For over 80 years, this national trade association has been serving the mailing and fulfillment services industry by providing opportunities for learning and professional development of the managers of these companies.

11629 www.niphle.com
National Institute of Packaging, Handling and

Logistics

Originally the DC chapter of the Society of Packaging and Handling engineers, the Institute became independent in an effort to give more emphasis on the governmental responsibilities of its members.

11630 www.nmaonline.org
National Meat Association

Association for meat packers, processors and jobbers through out the USA.

11631 www.packagingnetwork.com
Packaging Network

Searchable database of food industry related items.

11632 www.palletcentral.com
National Wooden Pallet & Container Association

Membership roster, tech talk, publications and industry watch.

11633 www.pmmi.org
Packaging Machinery Manufacturers Institute (PMMI)

For manufacturers of packaging and packaging-related converting equipment.

11634 www.polysort.com
Polysort LLC
Links to related companies.

11635 www.ppcnet.org
Paperboard Packaging Council

Represents industry before legislative and regulatory bodies. Conducts technical seminars on sales, marketing, costs and management methods. Publishes a quarterly newsletter

11636 www.ppcouncil.org
Petroleum Packaging Council
Provides technical leadership and education to the petroleum packaging industry.

11637 www.tianet.org
Transportation Intermediaries Association

Education and policy organization for North American transportation intermediaries. TIA is the only national association representing the interests of all third party transportation service providers. The members of TIA include logistics management firms, property brokers, perishable commodities brokers, freight forwarders, intermodal marketers, ocean and air forwarders, and NVOCC's.

11638 www.unitdose.org
Healthcare Compliance Packaging Council

A not-for-profit trade association that was established in 1990 to promote the many benefits of unit dose blister and ship packaging - especially its ability to be designed in compliance-promoting formats that help people take their medications properly.

11639 www.unitedfresh.org
United Fresh Fruit & Vegetable Association

Equipment, supplies, cartons, packaging machinery, computers, sorting and sizing equipment, harvesting equipment, film wrap manufacturing and commodity organizations.

Associations

11640 American Innerspring Manufacturers Association
1918 N Parkway
Memphis, TN 38112

901-749-9030
800-882-5604
E-Mail: aimy@aiminfo.org
Home Page: www.aiminfo.org

Members make and sell innerspring units and box springs to mattress manufacturers. Also conducts year round public relations program directed at consumers, encouraging purchase of innerspring mattresses.
Founded in 1966

11641 American Society of Furniture Designers
PO Box 5445
4136 Coachmans Court
High Point, NC 27262-5445

336-307-0999
FAX 910-576-1573
E-Mail: info@asfd.com
Home Page: www.asfd.com

Jason Phillips, President
John Conrad, Executive Director
Jena Hall, Editor-in-Chief
Rick Schroeder, Chairman
Tim O'Hare, Vice President

An international non-profit professional organization dedicated to advancing, improving, and supporting the profession of furniture design and its positive impact in the marketplace.
Founded in 1981

11642 Association of Progressive Rental Organizations
1504 Robin Hood Trail
Austin, TX 78703

800-204-2776
FAX 512-794-0097
E-Mail: cferguson@rtohq.org
Home Page: www.rtohq.org
Social Media: *Facebook, Twitter, Youtube, Flickr*

Gary Ferriman, President
Gopal Reddy, 1st Vice President
Mark Connelly, 2nd Vice President
Jonathan Rose, Secretary
Ernie Lewallen, Treasurer

Members include television, appliance and furniture dealers who rent merchandise with an option to purchase.
2000 Members
Founded in 1980
Mailing list available for rent

11643 Authentic Home Furnishings Association
PO Box 520
Spofford, NH 03462

518-832-7939
800-487-8321
FAX 518-824-5719
E-Mail: ufa@unfinishedfurniture.org
Home Page: www.unfinishedfurniture.org

Fred Moriarty, Executive Director
Tim Case, President
Lara Lindner, Secretary
Steve Cavanaugh, Treasurer
Anthony Sabatino, Vice President

Our mission is to promote the common business interests of the unfinished furniture industry, encourage the most efficient and professional organization and administration of firms in the unfinished furniture industry; and

to conduct meetings and educational programs, and to collect and publish information about the unfinished furniture industry.
600 Members
Founded in 1990

11644 Business and Institutional Furniture Manufacturers Association
678 Front Ave NW
Suite 150
Grand Rapids, MI 49504-5368

616-285-3963
FAX 616-285-3765
E-Mail: email@bifma.org
Home Page: www.bifma.org
Social Media: *Twitter, LinkedIn*

Dan Tuohy, President
Sylvain Garneau, Vice President
Franco Bianchi, Treasurer
Tom Reardon, Executive Director
Roxanne DeBoer, Administrator

BIFMA is a not-for-profit trade association of furniture manufacturers and suppliers, addressing issues of common concern.
245+ Members
Founded in 1973

11645 Futon Association International
PO Box 593730
Orlando, FL 32859

800-327-3262

Members are retailers, manufacturers, distributors, associates, sales representatives of their country in the industry.
400 Members
Founded in 1984

11646 Illuminating Engineering Society of North America
120 Wall St
Floor 17
New York, NY 10005-4001

212-248-5000
FAX 212-248-5017
E-Mail: ies@ies.org
Home Page: www.ies.org
Social Media: *Facebook, Twitter, LinkedIn*

Daniel Salinas, President
Paul Mercier, President-Elect
William Hanley, Executive Vice President
Nick Bleeker, Treasurer
Nicole DeGirolamo, Executive Assistant

To advance knowledge and disseminate information for the improvement of the lighted environment to the benefit of society. Publishes a monthly magazine.

11647 International Furniture Rental Association
5008 Pine Creek Drive
#6
Westerville, OH 43081-4848

614-755-3910
800-367-7368

A non-profit trade organization devoted exclusively to furniture rental and leasing.
Founded in 1967

11648 International Furniture Transportation and Logistics Council
PO Box 889
Gardner, MA 01440-0889

978-632-1913
FAX 978-630-2917
E-Mail: jsears@iftlc.org
Home Page: www.iftlc.org

Raynard F Bohman Jr, Managing Director

Members are furniture manufacturers, retailers, carriers, wholesalers and warehouses of allied products.
150 Members

11649 International Home Furnishings Representatives Association
PO Box 670
High Point, NC 27261

336-889-3920
FAX 336-802-1959
E-Mail: ihfra@ihfra.org
Home Page: www.ihfra.org

Matthew Keepers, Chairman
Kathy Parks, Executive Director

Association for the professional development of home furnishings representatives and the improvement of the home furnishings industry as a whole.

11650 International Home Furnishings Center
210 E Commerce Ave
High Point, NC 27260

336-888-3700
336-801-6102
FAX 336-882-1873
Home Page: www.ifsa-info.com

Nonprofit trade association of wholesale distributors, importers and manufacturers of finished goods. Supports furniture retailers by continuous improvement of the industry through advocacy, research and the exchange of ideas. Membership is open to any legitimate furniture wholesaler, importer, manufacturer, agent or any other firm operating within the supply chain of finished goods.
150 Members
Founded in 1928

11651 International Housewares Association
6400 Shafer Ct
Suite 650
Rosemont, IL 60018

847-292-4200
FAX 847-292-4211
E-Mail: pbrandl@housewares.org
Home Page: www.housewares.org
Social Media: *Facebook, Twitter, LinkedIn, YouTube*

Gary Seehoff, Chairman
Gregory C. Cairo, Vice Chairman
Philip J. Brandl, President/CEO
Brett Bradshaw, Treasurer
Dean Kurtis, Vice President, Finance

A full-service trade association dedicated to promoting the sales and marketing of housewares.
Founded in 1938

11652 International Sleep Products Association
501 Wythe Street
Alexandria, VA 22314-1917

703-683-8371
FAX 703-683-4503
E-Mail: info@sleepproducts.org
Home Page: www.sleepproducts.org
Social Media: *Facebook, Twitter, LinkedIn, Googleplus, Pinterest, Youtube*

Ryan Trainer, President

Maintains a strong organization to influence government actions, inform and educate the membership and act on industry issues to enhance the growth, profitability and stature of the sleep products industry. Provides members with information and services to manage their business more effectively and efficiently. Publishes a magazine devoted exclusively to the mattress industry, BEDtimes covers a broad range of issue and news important to the indus-

try.
Cost: $65.00
650 Members
Frequency: Monthly
Circulation: 3,500
Founded in 1915

11653 Juvenile Products Manufacturers Association

15000 Commerce Parkway
Suite C
Mt. Laurel, NJ 08054

856-638-0420
FAX 856-439-0525
E-Mail: jpma@jpma.org
Home Page: www.jpma.org/
Social Media: *Facebook, Twitter, LinkedIn*

Mark Messner, Chairman
Andy Newmark, Vice Chairman
Michael Dwyer-CAE, President
Rob Conley, Treasurer
Kelly Mariotti, Executive Director

The Juvenile Products Manufacturers Association exists to advance the interests, growth and well-being of the juvenile products industry through advocacy,public relations, information sharing and business devrlopment opportunities.
Founded in 1962

11654 National Association of Display Industries

4651 Sheridan Street
Suite 200
Hollywood, FL 33021

954-893-7300
FAX 954-893-7500
E-Mail: nadi@nadi-global.com
Home Page: www.nadi-global.com

Klein Merriman, Executive Director
Tracy Dillon, Director Communications

Sponsors seminars and annual contests. Conducts research programs and maintains placement services.
400 Members
Founded in 1937

11655 National Cotton Batting Institute

4322 Bloombury St
Southaven, MS 38672

901-218-2393
FAX 662-449-0046
E-Mail: info@natbat.com
Home Page: www.natbat.com

Weston Arnall, President
Greg Windsperger, VP
Fred Middleton, Executive Secretary-Treasurer

NCBI respresents U.S. companies that manufacture and sell batting for use in mattresses, futons, home furnishing, and upholstered products. It provides a range of services to assist its members in expanding markets, monitoring and contributing to legislative and regulatory decisions that affect the industry, and conducting consumer education and information programs.
27 Members
Founded in 1954

11656 National Unfinished Furniture Institute

1850 Oak Street
Northfield, IL 60093-3042

847-784-1225
FAX 847-446-3523

Ray Passis, Executive Director

Provides publicity and insurance for industry, offers educational seminars and bestows awards.
1.2M Members
Founded in 1979

11657 National Waterbed Retailers Association

2 Greentree Center
Suit 225
Marlton, NJ 08053-3102

312-236-6662
800-832-3553
FAX 312-236-1140

Promotes industry through educational seminars, sells educational materials on waterbeds, health care and conducts surveys.
500 Members
Founded in 1972

11658 North America Home Furnishings Association

2050 N Stemmons Fwy
Suite 292
Dallas, TX 75207

800-422-3778
FAX 916-784-7697
E-Mail: info@hfia.com
Home Page: www.nahfa.org
Social Media: *Facebook, Twitter, LinkedIn*

Richard Howard, Chairman
Marty Cramer, President
Jeff Child, President-Elect
Sharron Bradley, CEO
Steve Kidder, Vice President

Committed to strengthening the home furnishing industry trhough collective support, services, and leadership.
Founded in 1923

11659 Paint & Decorating Retailers Association

1401 Triad Center Dr
St Peters, MO 63376

636-326-2636
FAX 636-326-1823
E-Mail: info@pdra.org
Home Page: www.pdra.org
Social Media: *Facebook, Twitter, LinkedIn*

Phil Merlo, President
Bahia Taylor, Executive Vice President
Craig Bond, Treasurer
Jeff Baggaley, Past-President
Robert Mueller, Director at Large

Provides members with the tools they need and prosper such as information, sales training, and business operations programs.
1500 Members
Founded in 1947

11660 Quarters Furniture Manufacturers Association

1211 Popes Head Drive
Fairfax, VA 22030

240-215-9700
FAX 276-632-7894
E-Mail: matt.yanson@cma-gsa.com
Home Page: www.qfma.net

Michael Gittinger, President
Chris Arndt, Vice President
Malcolm Wilson, Secretary
Allyn Richert, Treasurer
Tom Chapman, Board Member

Represents companies who produce furniture for military markets. Monitors federal procurement policy as it relates to prison industries.
20 Members
Founded in 1995

11661 Society of Glass & Ceramic Decorated Products

PO Box 2489
Zanesville, OH 43702

740-588-9882
FAX 740-588-0245

E-Mail: info@sgcd.org
Home Page: www.sgcd.org

Chad Yaw, President
Jan Weyrich, Vice President
Mike Gervais, Treasurer
David Stanton, Secretary
Myra Warne, Executive Director

Provides designers, decorators and marketers of glass, ceramic and related products with resources for maximizing profitability, technical applications and regulatory compliance.
525 Members

11662 Summer and Casual Furniture Manufacturers Association

1912 Eastchester Drive
Suite 100
High Point, NC 27265

336-884-5000
FAX 336-884-5303
E-Mail: jlogan@ahfa.us
Home Page: www.ahfa.us
Social Media: *Facebook, LinkedIn*

Ken Burrows, Chairman
George Revington, Immediate Past Chairman
KEVIN O'CONNOR, 1st Vice President
RICHARD MAGNUSSEN, 2nd Vice President
ROGER BLAND, Board Member

Sponsors the International Casual Furniture and Accessories Market in Chicago, the Apollo Awards, recognizing excellence in casual furniture retailing and the Casual Furniture Design Excellence Awards.
500+ Members
Founded in 1959

11663 The American Home Furnishings Alliance

1912 Eastchester Drive
Suite 100
High Point, NC 27265

336-884-5000
FAX 336-884-5303
E-Mail: pbowling@ahfa.us
Home Page: www.ahfa.us
Social Media: *Facebook, LinkedIn*

Ken Burrows, Chairman
George Revington, Immediate Past Chairman
KEVIN O'CONNOR, 1st Vice President
RICHARD MAGNUSSEN, 2nd Vice President
ROGER BLAND, Board Member

The world's largest and most influential trade organization serving the home furnishings industry. AHFA is dedicated to fostering the growth and global well being of its member companies.
450 Members
Founded in 1905

11664 The Association of Woodworking & Furnishings Suppliers

2400 E Katella Ave
Suite 340
Anaheim, CA 92806

323-838-9440
800-946-2937
FAX 323-838-9443
Home Page: www.awfs.org
Social Media: *Facebook, Twitter, LinkedIn*

Wade Gregory, President
Archie Thompson, Vice President
Philip Martin, Secretary/Treasurer
Joan Kemp, IMMEDIATE PAST PRESIDENT
Daniel Hershberger, TRADE SHOW CHAIR

The largest national trade association in the US representing the interests of the broad array of companies that supply the home and commercial furnishings industry. Members include manufacturers and distributors of machinery, hardware, lumber, upholstery materials, bedding components, wood products and other

supplies to furnishings and wood products manufacturers.
Founded in 1979

11665 Upholstered Furniture Action Council
PO Box 2436
High Point, NC 27261

336-885-5065
FAX 336-885-5072
E-Mail: info@ufac.org
Home Page: www.ufac.org

Joseph Ziolkowski, Executive Director

Conducts research and disseminates information about adoption of guidelines for cigarette-resistant furniture. Educates public about safe use of smoking materials.
Founded in 1972

11666 World Floor Covering Association
2211 E Howell Ave
Anaheim, CA 92806

714-978-6440
800-624-6880
FAX 714-978-6066
E-Mail: wfca@wfca.org
Home Page: www.wfca.org
Social Media: *Facebook, Twitter*

Scott Humphrey, CEO
Terry Hearne, Director of Operations
Cammie Weitzel, Director of Finance/Administration
Donna Archambault, Membership Operations Manager

Shapes and defines public policy through agressive, national legislative advocacy on behalf of our members. Provides continuing professional educational programming through educational forums and the Regional Installation and Training Education (RITE) program.
45 Members
Founded in 1973

Newsletters

11667 AWFS Suppliers' Edge
Association of Woodworking & Furnishings Suppliers
500 Citadel Drive
Suite 200
Commerce, CA 90040

323-838-9440
800-946-2937
FAX 323-838-9443
Home Page: www.awfs.org
Social Media: *Facebook, Twitter, LinkedIn*

Joan Kemp, President
Wade Gregory, Vice President
Archie Thompson, Secretary/Treasurer

Industry events, manufacturing news, AWFS Fair news, member news and more.
Frequency: Tri-Annually
Founded in 1979

11668 At The Table
American Home Furnishings Alliance
317 High Avenue
10th Floor
High Point, NC 27260

336-884-5000
FAX 336-884-5303
E-Mail: pbowling@ahfa.us
Home Page: www.ahfa.us
Social Media: *Facebook, LinkedIn*

Andy Counts, CEO

News from legislative and regulatory forums where AHRA is at the table, serving as the voice of the home furnishings industry.
450 Members
Frequency: Quarterly
Founded in 1905

11669 Focus on Benefits
American Furniture Manufacturers Association
PO Box Hp7
High Point, NC 27261

336-884-5000
FAX 336-884-5303
E-Mail: pbowling@ahfa.us
Home Page: www.ahfa.us

Patricia Bowling, VP Communications

Adresses timely benefits subjects along with developing trends.
Frequency: Quarterly

11670 Furniture Executive
American Furniture Manufacturers Association
PO Box Hp7
High Point, NC 27261

336-884-5000
FAX 336-884-5303
E-Mail: pbowling@ahfa.us
Home Page: www.ahfa.us

Patricia Bowling, VP Communications

Includes news on all upcoming programs and events, a message from the AHFA President, news from Washington, updates on the AHFA public relations program, and updates on AHFA member benefits and programs.
Frequency: Monthly

11671 Human Resources Close-Up
American Home Furnishings Alliance
317 High Avenue
10th Floor
High Point, NC 27260

336-884-5000
FAX 336-884-5303
E-Mail: pbowling@ahfa.us
Home Page: www.ahfa.us
Social Media: *Facebook, LinkedIn*

Andy Counts, CEO

Online newsletter, addresses pertinent legal subjects in the employment/labor relations arena, along with relevant court and National Labor Relations Board cases.
450 Members
Frequency: Monthly
Founded in 1905

11672 National Association of Display Industries Newsletter
4651 Sheridan Street
Suite 470
Hollywood, FL 33021

954-893-7300
FAX 954-893-7500
E-Mail: nadi@nadi-global.com
Home Page: www.nadi-global.com

Klein Merriman, Executive Director
Tracy Dillon, Director Communications

Accepts advertising.
Cost: $45.00
16 Pages
Circulation: 8000
Founded in 1956

11673 Square Yard
American Floorcovering Association

2211 E Howell Avenue
Anaheim, CA 92806-6009

714-572-8370
FAX 714-780-0488

Edward Korczak, Publisher

Offers full coverage of interior design in association with floor coverings, carpets and rug manufacturers.
8 Pages
Frequency: Monthly

11674 Suppliers on Demand
American Home Furnishings Alliance
317 High Avenue
10th Floor
High Point, NC 27260

336-884-5000
FAX 336-884-5303
E-Mail: pbowling@ahfa.us
Home Page: www.ahfa.us
Social Media: *Facebook, LinkedIn*

Andy Counts, CEO

Online newsletter designed to help manufacturer members find the product and service suppliers they need, when they need them.
450 Members
Frequency: Quarterly
Founded in 1905

Magazines & Journals

11675 Architectural Lighting
One Thomas Circle, NW
Suite 600
Washington, DC 20005

202-452-0800
FAX 202-785-1974
Social Media: *Twitter*

Ned Cramer, Editor-in-Chief
Elizabeth Donoff, Editor

Covers design specifications and application of electrical lighting and daylighting systems.
Frequency: Monthly
Circulation: 54,000

11676 BEDtimes Magazine
International Sleep Products Association
501 Wythe Street
Alexandria, VA 22314-1917

703-683-8371
FAX 703-683-4503
E-Mail: info@sleepproducts.org
Home Page: www.sleepproducts.org

Julie Palm, Editor
Kerri Bellias, Administrative Assistant
Dana Jackson, Administrative Assistant
Mary Best, Managing Editor

A magazine covering the bedding industry. Target audience as mattress suppliers and manufacturers.
Cost: $50.00
Frequency: Monthly
Circulation: 3000
ISSN: 0893-5556
Founded in 1915
Printed in 4 colors on glossy stock

11677 Designer
HDC Publications
429 Montague Ave
Caro, MI 48723-1921

989-673-4121
800-843-6394
FAX 989-673-2031
E-Mail: info@hdc-caro.org
Home Page: www.hdc-caro.org

Maryann Vandemark, Executive Director

A magazine offering information on interior design.
Frequency: Monthly

11678 Draperies and Window Coverings

840 US Highway One
Suite 330
North Palm Beach, FL 33408

561-627-3393
847-548-3900
FAX 561-694-6578
Home Page: www.dwcdesignet.com

Carolyn Silberman, Publisher
Howard Shingle, Editor
Sarah Christy, Associate Editor

Covers trends and specific industry topics.
Cost: $33.00
160 Pages
Frequency: Monthly
Circulation: 28,000
Founded in 1981

11679 Eastern Floors Magazine

Specialist Publications
22801 Ventura Boulevard
Suite 115
Woodland Hills, CA 91364-1230

818-224-8035
800-835-4398
FAX 818-224-8042
Home Page: www.icsmag.com
Social Media: *Facebook, Twitter*

Howard Olansky, Editor
Phil Johnson, Group Publisher
Evan Kessler, Publisher
Amy Levin, Production Manager

Serving the floor covering and tile industry.
Cost: $140.00
Frequency: Monthly
Founded in 1990

11680 Furniture Today

Reed Business Information
PO Box 2754
High Point, NC 27261-2754

336-605-1000
800-395-2329
FAX 336-605-1143
Home Page: www.reedbusiness.com
Social Media: *Facebook, Twitter*

Kevin Castellani, President
Ray Allegeeza, Editor-in-Chief
Helene Checinski, Circulation Manager
Kim Bashford, Production Manager
Delaney Rudd, Ower

Business and fashion newspaper of the furniture industry, edited for retail furniture executives in furniture stores, department stores, mass merchants, furniture specialty stores and catalog showrooms, as well as manufacturing executives at all levels. Focus is on the business and fashion news that these executives need at key decision times in their merchandising and marketing cycles.
Cost: $159.97
Frequency: Weekly
Circulation: 21212
Founded in 1976
Printed in on glossy stock

11681 Home Accents Today

Reed Business Information
360 Park Ave S
New York, NY 10010-1737

646-746-6400
FAX 646-756-7583
Home Page: www.homeaccentstoday.com
Social Media: *Facebook, Twitter*

John Poulin, CEO
Marion Kelly, Publisher
Gerard Van de Aast, CEO

Becky Boswell Smith, Editor-in-Chief
James Reed, Owner

Enables home furnishing retailers to develop merchandising programs, define new style statements, make buying decisions, and create retail strategies. Editorially covers the broad fashion mix of home accent products.
Cost: $24.94
Frequency: Monthly
Circulation: 21300

11682 Home Furnishing Retailer

National Home Furnishings Association
3910 Tinsley Drive
Suite 101
Highpoint, NC 27265-3610

336-886-6100
800-888-9590
FAX 336-801-6102
E-Mail: info@nhfa.org
Home Page: www.nhfa.org
Social Media: *Facebook, Twitter, LinkedIn, YouTube*

Provides the latest information specifically for industry retailers; current trends and strategies to keep business profitable.
Cost: $70.00
Frequency: Monthly
Circulation: 10000
ISSN: 1073-5585

11683 Home Lighting & Accessories

Doctorow Communications
1011 Clifton Ave
Suite 1
Clifton, NJ 07013-3518

973-779-1600
FAX 973-779-3242
E-Mail: email@homelighting.com
Home Page: www.homelighting.com

Jeffrey Doctorow, President
Jon Doctorow, Circulation Director

Home Lighting & Accessories is a magazine of lamps, lighting fixtures, shades and decorative home accessories. Articles cover marketing and retailing aspects applied to portable lamps, lamps shades, residential lighting fixtures and decorative home accessories - customer relations, sales training, trends, lighting showroom laycut, design and operations. Plus industry and company news, new promotions, appointments, literature, patents
Cost: $15.00
Founded in 1953

11684 ICS Cleaning Specialist

Business News Publishing Company
22801 Ventura Blvd
Suite 115
Woodland Hills, CA 91364-1230

818-224-8035
800-835-4398
FAX 818-224-8042
Home Page: www.bnpmedia.com

Phil Johnson, Publisher
Evan Kessler, Publisher
Jeffrey Stouffer, Editor
Amy Levin, Production Manager

For carpet cleaning, restoration and floor care service providers.
68 Pages
Frequency: Monthly
Circulation: 24250
ISSN: 1522-4708
Founded in 1963
Printed in 4 colors on glossy stock

11685 Journal of Family & Consumer Sciences

American Association of Family & Consumer Sciences

400 N Columbus St
Suite 202
Alexandria, VA 22314-2264

703-706-4600
800-424-8080
FAX 703-706-4663
E-Mail: pr@aafcs.org
Home Page: www.aafcs.org
Social Media: *Facebook, Twitter, LinkedIn, Flickr*

Carolyn Jackson, Executive Director

Contains scholarly peer-reviewed articles, practical information geared toward family and consumer sciences professionals, and news and information about AAFCS.
Frequency: Quarterly

11686 Metropolis

Bellerophon Publications
61 W 23rd St
Floor 4
New York, NY 10010-4246

212-627-9977
FAX 212-627-9988
E-Mail: edit@metropolismag.com
Home Page: www.metropolismag.com

Horace Havemeyer, Publisher
Susan Szenasy, Editor in Chief
Julie Taraska, Editor
Denise Csaky, Marketing Director

The only magazine that covers all facets of design: architecture, interiors, furniture, preservation, urban design, graphics and crafts.
Cost: $27.95
Circulation: 51000
Founded in 1981

11687 NHFA Trade Show

National Home Furnishings Association
3910 Tinsley Drive
Suite 101
Highpoint, NC 27265-3610

336-886-6100
800-888-9590
FAX 336-801-6102
E-Mail: info@nhfa.org
Home Page: www.nhfa.org

Steve DeHaan, Executive VP
Karin Mayfield, Senior Director for Membership
Frequency: Annual

11688 Panel World

Hatton-Brown Publishers
PO Box 2268
Montgomery, AL 36102-2268

334-834-1170
800-669-5613
FAX 334-834-4525
E-Mail: mail@hattonbrown.com
Home Page: www.hattonbrown.com/

D K Knight, Editor-in-chief
Rich Donnell, Editor
David Ramsey, President
Rhonda Thomas, Marketing

A magazine covering the interior design community.
Cost: $40.00
Frequency: Monthly
Circulation: 12000
Printed in 4 colors on matte stock

11689 RTOHQ: The Magazine

Association of Progressive Rental Merchandise
1540 Robinhood Trail
Austin, TX 78703-2624

512-794-0095
800-204-APRO
FAX 512-794-0097

E-Mail: cferguson@rtohq.org
Home Page: www.rtohq.org

Bill Keese, Executive Director
John C Cleek, President
Bill Kelly, Secretary

Emphasis on larger issues facing it players in the rent-to-own industry. Readers are rent-to-own dealers, owners, managers, employees, manufacturers and suppliers to the industry.
Frequency: Bi-Monthly
Circulation: 11000

Trade Shows

11690 AAFCS Annual Conference & Exposition
American Association of Family & Consumer Sciences
400 N Columbus Street
Suite 202
Alexandria, VA 22314

703-706-4600
FAX 703-706-4663
E-Mail: connect@aafcs.org
Home Page: www.aafcs.org
Social Media: *Facebook, Twitter, LinkedIn, Flickr*

Johnny Reynolds, Project Manager
Roxana Ayona, Manager

Informative speakers, cutting-edge workshops, and a panel discussion.
Frequency: Annual/June

11691 APRO Rent-To-Own Convention & Trade Show
Association of Progressive Rental Organizations
1504 Robin Hood Trail
Austin, TX 78703

512-794-0095
800-204-APRO
FAX 512-794-0097
Home Page: www.rtohq.org

Shannon Strunkec, President
John C Cleek, First VP
Jeannie Hutchison, Program Coordinator
Bill Keese, Manager

Seminar, reception and tours, plus 280 exhibits of products and services of interest to rent to own dealers: stereos, televisions, furniture, fabric protection and more.
1400 Attendees
Frequency: Annual

11692 Association of College Unions International Conference
120 W. Seventh St.
Suite 200
Bloomington, IN 47404

812-245-2284
FAX 812-245-6710
Home Page: www.acui.org

Rich Steele, President
Marsha Herman-Betzen, Executive Director
Andrea Langeveld, Marketing

One hundred exhibits of graphic supplies, recreation equipment, computer hardware and software, furnishings, entertainment and speaker bureau information, food service equipment, and more related information and supplies.
1000 Attendees
Frequency: Annual

11693 Canyon County Home & Garden Show
Spectra Productions

837 E State Street
PO Box 333
Eagle, ID 83616

208-939-6426
FAX 208-939-6437
E-Mail: david@spectraproductions.com
Home Page: www.spectraproductions.com

David Beale, Show Manager

Features exhibitors displaying building materials, contractors, decorators, doors and windows, pools and spas, heating and cooling systems and much more.
150 Attendees
Frequency: April

11694 Denver Home Show
Industrial Expositions
PO Box 480084
Denver, CO 80248-0084

303-892-6800
800-457-2434
FAX 303-892-6322
E-Mail: info@iei-expos.com
Home Page: www.bigasalloutdoors.com

Formerly the Spring Home & Patio Show.
23000 Attendees
Frequency: Annual/March

11695 Evergreen Home Show
Westlake Promotions
6020 Seaview Avenue NW
Seattle, WA 98107

206-783-5957
FAX 206-782-6250
Home Page: www.westlakepromo.com

Bill Bradley, VP

See what's new and what you can do for your home. Fresh ideas and practical advice from our remodeling and construction specialists. See demonstrations on how to make dramatic improvements to your home.
7500 Attendees

11696 Fall Home and Garden Expo
Mid-America Expositions, Inc
7015 Spring Street
Omaha, NE 68106

402-346-8003
800-475-7469
FAX 402-346-5412
E-Mail: info@showofficeonline.com
Home Page: www.showofficeonline.com

Robert P Mancuso, CEO
Mike Mancuso, VP/Manager

Displays on everything for the home including kitchens, room additions, bathrooms, interior decorating, fireplaces, outdoor equipment, heating and air conditioning, remodeling contractors, security, siding, appliances, windows, doors, fencing, roofing, fitness equipment, spas and much more.
Frequency: Annual/October

11697 Furniture Expo
Glahe International
PO Box 2460
Germantown, MD 20875-2460

301-515-0012
FAX 301-515-0016

Annual show and exhibits of furniture making.

11698 Glass & Ceramic Decorators Annual Seminar & Exposition
Society of Glass & Ceramic Decorators

47 N 4th Street
PO Box 2489
Zanesville, OH 43702

202-298-8660
FAX 740-588-0245
Home Page: www.sgcd.org

Myra Warne, Exhibit

The SGCD show attracts major suppliers to the decorating industry, including several firms from overseas. With a full seminar program and first step program that attracts attendees on their own merits.
525 Attendees

11699 Great Northeast Home Show
Osborne/Jenks Productions
936 Silas Deane Highway
Wethersfield, CT 06109-4273

860-563-2111
800-955-7469
FAX 860-563-3472

Two hundred and fifty booths.
25M Attendees
Frequency: Annual/February

11700 Home World Home & Garden Show
Show Biz Productions
16520 Harbor Blouevard
Fountain Valley, CA 92708

714-418-2000
FAX 714-418-2009
E-Mail: marlene@sbhomeshow.com
Home Page: www.sbhomeshow.com

Marlene Thorne, VP

Featuring vendors of window, doors, painting, heating, air conditioning, kitchens and baths, flooring, furniture, remodeling services and more.
40000 Attendees
Frequency: Annual/May
Founded in 1991

11701 Home and Outdoor Living Expo
Tower Show Productions
800 Roosevelt Road
Building A, Suite 109
Glen Ellyn, IL 60137

630-469-4611
800-946-4611
FAX 630-469-4811
E-Mail: jaylake20@towershow.com
Home Page: www.towershow.com

J Lake, VP Home Shows

The largest and longest running home improvement show.
15000 Attendees
Frequency: January
Founded in 1977

11702 ICFF International Contemporary Furniture
George Little Management
10 Bank Street
White Plains, NY 10606-1933

914-486-6070
800-272-7469
FAX 914-948-6180
E-Mail: info@icff.com
Home Page: www.icff.com
Social Media: *Facebook, Twitter*

Troy Hansen, Show Manager
Alex Cabat, Show Coordinator
George Little II, President
Tony Orlando, Operations Manager

More than 500 exhibitors will display contemporary furniture, seating, lighting, carpet and flooring, wall coverings, textiles, accessories, kitchen and bath, outdoor furniture, and materials for residential and commercial interiors. The combination of domestic and international

exhibitors provides easy access to the best and hippest home and contract products.
12000 Attendees
Frequency: Annual/December

11703 International Bedding Exposition
International Sleep Products Association
501 Wythe Street
Alexandria, VA 22314-1917

703-683-8371
FAX 703-683-4503
E-Mail: info@sleepproducts.org
Home Page: www.sleepproducts.org

Susan Perry, Executive VP, Business Development
Dana Jackson, Administrative Assistant
Mary Best, Managing Editor

200 booths, net 120,000 square feet with 200 exhibitors participating.
4M Attendees
Frequency: Annual/March

11704 International Home Furnishings Market
International Home Furnishings Market Authority
101 S Main Street
High Point, NC 27262

336-691-1000
FAX 336-889-6999
Home Page: www.highpointmarket.org

Judy Mendenhall, President
Jan Wellmon, Executive Assistant
Shannon Kennedy, Director of Marketing

Large home furnishings trade show with a variety of new opportunities to make your visit easy, cost effective and productive. Ten million square seet of exhibition space with 2,500 manufacturers represented.
75000 Attendees
Frequency: Bi-Annual
Founded in 1921

11705 International Housewares Show
National Housewares Manufacturers Association
6400 Shafer Court
Suite 650
Rosemont, IL 60018

708-292-4200
FAX 847-292-4211
Home Page: www.housewares.org

Mia Rampersad, VP Trade Show & Meetings

See first-hand consumer lifestyle and product trends for all areas of the home, both inside and out, under one roof.
60000 Attendees

11706 International Woodworking Machinery and Furniture Supply Fair: USA
Reed Exhibition Companies
1350 E Touhy Avenue
Des Plaines, IL 60018-3303

847-294-0300
FAX 847-635-1571

Paul Pajor, National Marketing Manager

The largest woodworking machinery and furniture supply manufacturing exposition held in the Western Hemisphere. Exhibitors interface with North American furniture, cabinet, and woodworking manufacturers. One thousand booths.
37M Attendees
Frequency: Biennial/August

11707 Juvenile Products Manufacturers Association Trade Show
PO Box 955
Marlton, NJ 08053-0955

856-231-8500
FAX 856-985-2878

William Macmillan, Show Manager

Home acessories and products for children's rooms.
2.5M Attendees
Frequency: Annual/October

11708 Kitchen & Bath Industry Show
National Kitchen & Bath Association
687 Willow Grove Street
Hackettstown, NJ 07840

908-520-0033
800-843-6522
FAX 908-852-1695
Home Page: www.kbis.com

Lee Hershberg, Sales Manager
Grayson Lutz, Operations Manager

Targeting dealers, designers, distributors, retailers, consumers, home centers and many other high-quality kitchen and bath professionals. Showcasing the latest products and cutting-edge design ideas of the kitchen and bath industry.
40000 Attendees
Frequency: Annual/April

11709 Kitchen/Bath Industry Show & Multi-Housing World Conference
VNU Expositions
1145 Sanctuary Parkway
Suite 355
Alpharetta, GA 30004

770-691-1540
800-933-8735
FAX 770-777-8700

Lee Hershberg, Sales Manager

The latest products and technologies, industry and consumer trends, design and business tools and more to stay ahead of your competitors.
35000 Attendees

11710 LightFair
AMC
120 Wall Street
17th Floor
New York, NY 10005

212-843-8358
FAX 212-248-5017
Home Page: www.iesna.org

Pamela R Weess, Circulation Director
Nini Schwenk, Manager

A major lighting trade show in North America featuring architectural lighting products from all spectrons of the industry. Containing 600 booths and 400 exhibits.
17M Attendees
Frequency: June
Mailing list available for rent: 10M names at $100 per M
Printed in 4 colors on glossy stock

11711 Mid-Atlantic Industrial Woodworking Expo Supply Show
Trade Shows
PO Box 2000
Claremont, NC 28610-2000

828-459-9894
FAX 828-459-1312
E-Mail: tsi@tsishows.com
Home Page: www.tsishows.com

Keith Eidson, Show Manager

Annual show of 300 manufacturers of woodworking and furniture industry equipment, supplies and services.
4500 Attendees
Frequency: Annual/April

11712 National City Home & Garden Show
Expositions
PO Box 550
Edgewater Branch
Cleveland, OH 44107-0550

216-529-1300
FAX 216-529-0311
E-Mail: showinfo@expoinc.com
Home Page: www.expoinc.com

Featuring showcases on how to make your dream home a reality. Create the garden oasis, backyard retreat or a relaxing sanctuary.
35000 Attendees
Frequency: Annual/February

11713 National Hardware Show
Reed Exhibition Companies
383 Main Avenue
Norwalk, CT 06851

203-840-4800
FAX 203-840-4824

The prime time and place for face to face sourcing, trading and learning for the US home improvement and DIY markets.
70000 Attendees

11714 Old House New House Home Show
Kennedy Productions
1208 Lisle Place
Lisle, IL 60532-2262

630-515-1160
FAX 630-515-1165
Home Page: www.kennedyproductions.com

Laura McNamara, Event Producer

Over 300 home improvement exhibitors displaying cutting-edge home enhancements for kitchens, baths, home and garden including landscape, interior remodeling, pools, spas, floors, doors and more.
8000 Attendees
Frequency: Biannual
Founded in 1984

11715 PDRA Paint & Decorating Show
Paint & Decorating Retailers Association
403 Axminister Drive
Fenton, MO 63026

636-326-2636
800-737-0107
FAX 636-326-1823
E-Mail: tina@pdra.org
Home Page: www.pdra.org

Dan Simon, Executive Vice President

Retailers from the paint and decorating products industry to discuss a variety of business topics. Gain insight from retailers who face the same problems that you do everyday.
1000 Attendees
Frequency: Annual/May

11716 Remodeling and Decorating Expo
893 N Jan Mar Ct
Olathe, KS 66061-3693

913-768-8148
FAX 785-780-4777

Tom Reno, VP
Mary Jo Doherty, Executive Director

Four hundred booths of the latest products and services related to remodeling and decorating. Also a presentation of How-To stage presentations on remodeling, decorating and home repair.
40M Attendees
Frequency: Annual/February

11717 Southern Home & Garden Show
Home Builders Association
702 E McBee Avenue
Greensville, SC 29601

864-229-7722
FAX 864-232-3541

Exhibitors include professional landscapers, nurseryment, interior designers and home and garden experts.
40000 Attendees
Frequency: Biannual

11718 Spring Home Show
Osborne/Jenks Productions
936 Silas Deane Highway
Wethersfield, CT 06109

860-563-2111
FAX 860-563-3472

Exhibitors include remodelers, homebuilders, custom cabinets, kitchens & baths, chimneys, wood stoves, sunrooms, awnings & decks, duct & vent maintenance, storage buildings, heating & cooling services, windows, doors & siding, water treatment systems, banks & mortgage companies, home theatre systems, security systems, financial planners, building supplies, insulation, energy management companies and so much more.
Frequency: Annual/March

11719 Surfaces Conference
World Floor Covering Association
2211 E Howell Avenue
Anaheim, CA 92806

714-978-6440
800-624-6880
FAX 714-978-6066
E-Mail: wfca@wfca.org
Home Page: www.wfca.org

Casey Voorhees, Executive Director
Tina Krulich, Administrative Assistant

The event for the floor covering industry with the latest trends to keep your business competitive, proven strategies to increase sales and profitability and all the critical industry information you need to make the right decisions.
40000 Attendees
Frequency: Annual/January

11720 West Week
Pacific Design Center
8687 Melrose Avenue
West Hollywood, CA 90069

310-652-6992
FAX 310-652-9576

Show featuring the top interior designers and decorators.
Frequency: Annual/March

11721 Woodworking and Furniture Expo
Glahe International
PO Box 2460
Germantown, MD 20875-2460

301-515-0012
FAX 301-515-0016

Annual show and exhibits of woodworking and furniture making.

Directories & Databases

11722 AHFA's Industry Resource Guide
American Home Furnishing Alliance

PO Box HP-7
High Point, NC 27261

336-884-5000
FAX 336-884-5303
Home Page: www.ahfa.us

Andy Counts, Executive VP

A who's who in the furniture industry, supplying information on over 500 furniture manufacturers and their suppliers.
80 Pages
Founded in 1966

11723 Casual Living: Casual Outdoor Furniture and Accessory Directory Issue
Reed Business Information
360 Park Ave S
New York, NY 10010-1737

646-746-6400
FAX 646-756-7583
Home Page: www.reedbusiness.com

John Poulin, CEO
Toni Agpar, Editor

List of manufacturers, manufacturers' trepresentatives, and suppliers of outdoor furniture, wicker and rattan furniture, and backyard accessories such as barbecue grills, picnic accessories, outdoor lighting cushions, pads, patio umbrellas, vinyl refinishing, and maintenance, products.
Cost: $10.00
Frequency: Annual
Circulation: 13,000

11724 Complete Directory of Discount & Catalog Merchandisers
Sutton Family Communications & Publishing Company
920 State Route 54 East
Elmitch, KY 42343

270-276-9500
E-Mail: jlsutton@apex.net

Theresa Sutton, Publisher
Lee Sutton, Editor

Print-out from database of wholesalers, manufacturers, distributors, importers and close-out houses. Database is updated daily to guarantee the most current and up-to-date sources available.
Cost: $125.00
100 Pages

11725 Complete Directory of Home Furnishings
Sutton Family Communications & Publishing Company
920 State Route 54 East
Elmitch, KY 42343

270-276-9500
E-Mail: jlsutton@apex.net

Theresa Sutton, Publisher
Lee Sutton, Editor

Print-out from database of wholesalers, manufacturers, distributors, importers and close-out houses. Database is updated daily to guarantee the most current and up-to-date sources available.
Cost: $44.50
100 Pages

11726 Complete Directory of Kitchen Accessories
Sutton Family Communications & Publishing Company

920 State Route 54 East
Elmitch, KY 42343

270-276-9500
E-Mail: jlsutton@apex.net

Theresa Sutton, Editor
Lee Sutton, General Manager

Print-out from database of wholesalers, manufacturers, distributors, importers and close-out houses. Database is updated daily to guarantee the most current and up-to-date sources available.
Cost: $49.50
100+ Pages

11727 Complete Directory of Lamps, Lamp Shades & Lamp Parts
Sutton Family Communications & Publishing Company
955 Sutton Lane
20 State Route 54 East
Elmitch, KY 42343

270-276-9500
E-Mail: jlsutton@apex.net

Theresa Sutton, Editor
Lee Sutton, General Manager

Print-out from database of wholesalers, manufacturers, distributors, importers and close-out houses. Database is updated daily to guarantee the most current and up-to-date sources available.
Cost: $39.50
100+ Pages

11728 Complete Directory of Serving Ware
Sutton Family Communications & Publishing Company
920 State Route 54 East
Elmitch, KY 42343

270-276-9500
E-Mail: jlsutton@apex.net

Theresa Sutton, Editor
Lee Sutton, General Manager

Print-out from database of wholesalers, manufacturers, distributors, importers and close-out houses. Database is updated daily to guarantee the most current and up-to-date sources available.
Cost: $39.50
100+ Pages

11729 Complete Directory of Showroom Fixtures and Equipment
Sutton Family Communications & Publishing Company
920 State Route 54 East
Elmitch, KY 42343

270-276-9500
E-Mail: jlsutton@apex.net

Theresa Sutton, Publisher
Lee Sutton, Editor

Print-out from database of wholesalers, manufacturers, distributors, importers and close-out houses. Database is updated daily to guarantee the most current and up-to-date sources available.
Cost: $39.50
100 Pages

11730 Complete Directory of Small Furniture
Sutton Family Communications & Publishing Company
920 State Route 54 East
Elmitch, KY 42343

270-276-9500
E-Mail: jlsutton@apex.net

Theresa Sutton, Publisher
Lee Sutton, Editor

Print-out from database of wholesalers, manufacturers, distributors, importers and close-out houses. Database is updated daily to guarantee the most current and up-to-date sources available.
Cost: $39.50
100 Pages

11731 Complete Directory of Upholstery Materials Supplies and Equipment
Sutton Family Communications & Publishing Company
920 State Route 54 East
Elmitch, KY 42343

270-276-9500
E-Mail: jlsutton@apex.net

Theresa Sutton, Publisher
Lee Sutton, Editor

Print-out from database of wholesalers, manufacturers, distributors, importers and close-out houses. Database is updated daily to guarantee the most current and up-to-date sources available. Over 600 American wholesale direct supplies in 3-ring binder.
Cost: $67.50
100 Pages

11732 Furniture Retailer Resource Guide
Pace Communications
PO Box 13607
Suite 100
Greensboro, NC 27415-3607

336-378-6065
FAX 336-275-2864
Home Page: www.pacecommunications.com

Bonnie McElveen, CEO

Directory of services and supplies to the industry.
Cost: $20.00
Frequency: Annual;
Circulation: 16,000

11733 Hearth & Home: Furnishings Issue
Village West Publishing
PO Box 1288
Laconia, NH 03247-2008

603-528-4285
800-258-3772
FAX 603-524-0643
E-Mail: avignone@villagewest.com

Richard Wright, Publisher/Editor
Jackie Avignone, Advertising Director
Karen Dipietro, Owner

Trade journal for hearth, barbecue and patio retailing. July issue is Buyer's Guide for the three industries, available separately for $15.
Cost: $6.00
Frequency: Annual
Circulation: 17,000
ISSN: 0273-5695

11734 Home Furnishing Retailers
Chain Store Guide
3922 Coconut Palm Dr
Suite 300
Tampa, FL 33619-1389

813-627-6700
800-972-0292
FAX 813-627-7094
E-Mail: info@csgis.com
Home Page: www.csgis.com

Mike Jarvis, Publisher
Shami Choon, Manager

This database features detailed information on over 2700 companies in the U.S. and Canada, with contact information for over 8600 key executives and buyers.
Cost: $275.00
Frequency: Annual

11735 IFRA Member Directory
International Furniture Rental Association
5008 Pine Creek Drive
#6
Westerville, OH 43081-4848

614-755-3910
800-367-7368
Home Page: www.ifra.org

About 100 member furniture rental companies.

11736 Market Resource Guide
International Home Furnishings Center
PO Box 828
High Point, NC 27261-0828

336-888-3700
FAX 336-882-1873
E-Mail: marketing@ihfc.com
Home Page: www.ihfc.com

Bruce Miller, CEO

Two-volume directory offers over 1,500 manufacturers and distributors in the furniture industry with exhibits at the International Home Furnishings Market.
Cost: $25.00
624 Pages
Frequency: Semiannual
Founded in 1974
Printed in 4 colors on glossy stock

11737 Specialized Furniture Carriers Directory
National Furniture Traffic Conference
PO Box 889
Gardner, MA 01440-0889

978-632-1913
FAX 978-630-2917

Ray Bohman, Editor

Nearly 200 trucking firms specializing in transportation of new furniture, not including household moving firms.
Cost: $39.95

Industry Web Sites

11738 http://gold.greyhouse.com
G.O.L.D Grey House OnLine Databases

Grey House Publishing's online database platform, GOLD, offers Quick Search, Keyword Search and Expert Search for most business sectors including furnishing, fixture and decorating markets. The GOLD platform makes finding the information you need quick and easy - whether you're a novice searcher or an experienced database user. All of Grey House's directory products are available for subscription on the GOLD platform.

11739 www.ahfa.us
American Home Furnishings Alliance

The largest and most influential trade organization serving the home furnishings industry. Dedicated to fostering the growth and global well being of its member companies.

11740 www.ahfa.us/divisions/scfma.asp
Summer & Casual Furniture Manufacturers Assn

Sponsors the International Casual Furniture and Accessories Market in Chicago, the Apollo Awards recognizing excellence in casual furniture retailing and the Casual Furniture Design Excellence Awards.

11741 www.awfs.org
Association of Woodworking & Furnishings Suppliers

Organization for furniture and accessories manufacturers and suppliers that are covered in this comprehensive journal.

11742 www.bifma.org
Business and Institutional Furniture Manufacturers

The voice of the office furniture industry, BIFMA members are manufacturers and suppliers of goods and services to the industry.

11743 www.greyhouse.com
Grey House Publishing

Authoritative reference directories for most business sectors including furnishings, fixtures and decorating marekts. Users can search the online databases with varied search criteria allowing for custom searches by product category, geographic area, sales volume, keyword, subject and more. Full Grey House catalog and online ordering also available.

11744 www.hfia.com/
Home Furnishings International Association

Product categories include residential casegoods, upholstery, gift and decorative accessories, lighting and area floor coverings and beddings.

11745 www.natbat.com
National Cotton Batting Institute

Association representing members of the cotton batting industry.

11746 www.nhfa.org
National Home Furnishings Association

Trade association of furniture retailers which works to improve retailer's business opportunities and management practices.

11747 www.ofdanet.org
Office Furniture Dealers Association

Explores the effect of office environment on productivity and uses contract sales staff to anticipate changes in market.

11748 www.rtohq.org/
Association of Progressive Rental Organizations

Members include television, appliance and furniture dealers who rent merchandise with an option to purchase.

11749 www.unfinishedfurniture.org
Unfinished Furniture Association

Associations

11750 American Herbal Products Association

8630 Fenton St
Suite 918
Silver Spring, MD 20910

301-588-1171
FAX 301-588-1174
E-Mail: ahpa@ahpa.com
Home Page: www.ahpa.org

Graham Rigby, Chair
Steven Dentali, Vice Chair
Michael McGuffin, President
Steven Yeager, Secretary
Mitch Coven, Treasurer

A organization that only focuses on herbs and herbal products.
200 Members
Founded in 1982

11751 American Horticultural Society

7931 E Boulevard Dr
Alexandria, VA 22308

703-768-5700
800-777-7931
FAX 703-768-8700
E-Mail: dhundley@ahs.org
Home Page: www.ahs.org
Social Media: *Facebook, Twitter, Flickr*

Amy Bolton, Chair
Jane Diamantis, 1st Vice Chair
Mary Pat Matheson, 2nd Vice Chair
Nancy Hargroves, Secretary
J. Landon Reeve, Treasurer

Educates and inspires people of all ages to become successful and environmentally responsible gardeners by advancing the art and science of hoticulture. It is an education, nonprofit, 501 organization that recognizes and promotes best practices in American horticulture. AHS is known for its educational programs and the dissemination of horticultural information.
27M Members
Founded in 1922
Mailing list available for rent

11752 American Horticultural Therapy Association

610 Freedom Business Centre
#110
King of Prussia, PA 19406

610-992-0020
800-634-1603
FAX 610-225-2364
Home Page: www.ahta.org
Social Media: *Facebook, Twitter, LinkedIn, Youtube, Pinterest*

MaryAnne McMillan, President
Leigh Anne Starling, Vice President
Todd Schappell, Treasurer
Patricia Cassidy, Secretary

Advancing the practice of hortieulture as therapy to improve human well-being.
Founded in 1973

11753 American Institute of Floral Designers

720 Light Street
Baltimore, MD 21230

410-752-3318
FAX 410-752-8295
E-Mail: aifd@assnhqtrs.com
Home Page: www.aifd.org
Social Media: *Facebook, Twitter, LinkedIn, YouTube*

Joyce Mason-Monheim, President
Anthony Vigliotta, President-Elect
Kim Oldis, Vice President

Frank Feysa, Secretary
Tom Simmons, Treasurer

Nonprofit association to support the floral design industry.
1300 Members
Founded in 1962

11754 American Nursery & Landscape Association

1200 G Street NW
Suite 800
Washington, DC 20005

202-789-2900
FAX 202-789-1893
E-Mail: info@anla.org
Home Page: www.anla.org
Social Media: *Facebook*

Bob Terry, President
Dale Deppe, President Elect
Michael V. Geary, Executive Vice President

The American Nursery and Landscape Association serves firms who grow, sell or use plants. ANLA advocates the industry's interests before government and provides its members with unique business knowledge essential to long-term growth and profitability.
2000 Members
Founded in 1876

11755 American Rose Society

8877 Jefferson Paige Road
PO Box 30000
Shreveport, LA 71130

318-938-5402
800-637-6534
FAX 318-938-5405
E-Mail: ars@ars-hq.org
Home Page: www.rose.org
Social Media: *Facebook, Twitter, Flickr,Pinterest,Youtube*

Steve Jones, President
Jeff Wycoff, VP
Laura Seabaugh, Executive Director
Carol Spiers, Assistant to Executive Director
Peggy Spivey, Administrative Assistant

Striving to provide educational services to encourage the greater use of our national flower in private and public gardens throughout the country.
24000 Members
ISSN: 1078-5833
Founded in 1892

11756 American Society for Horticultural Science

1018 Duke Street
Alexandria, VA 22314

703-836-4606
FAX 703-836-2024
E-Mail: webmaster@ashs.org
Home Page: www.ashs.org
Social Media: *Facebook, Twitter, LinkedIn, Pinterest*

Michael A Arnold, Chair
Curt Rom, President
John Dole, President-Elect
Larry Knerr, Treasurer
Kimberly Moore, Member-At-Large

A cornerstone of research and education in horticulture and an agent for active promotion of horticultural science.
1200 Members
Founded in 1908

11757 American Society of Consulting Arborists

9707 Key West Avenue
Suite 100
Rockville, MD 20850-3222

301-947-0483
FAX 301-990-9771

E-Mail: asca@mgmtsol.com
Home Page: www.asca-consultants.org
Social Media: *Facebook, Twitter, LinkedIn, Pinterest*

Barbara Neal, President
Michael F. Galvin, President Elect
Jan C Scow, Treasurer
Beth W Palys, Executive Director
Chris D. Ahlum,, Director

The industry's premier professional association focusing solely on arboricultural consulting. Consulting Arborists are authoritative experts on trees, consulting property owners, municipalitites, attorneys, insurance professionals and others on tree disease, placement, preservation and dispute resolution in addition to providing consulting and experto testimony in the legal, insurance and environmental arenas.

11758 American Society of Irrigation Consultants

4700 S. Hagadorn
Suite 195D
East Lansing, MI 48823

508-763-8140
866-828-5174
FAX 508-763-8102
E-Mail: info@asic.org
Home Page: www.asic.org

Carol Colein, Executive Director
Ivy Munion, President
Corbin Schneider, Vice President
Stacy Gardner, Secretary
Michael Krones, Treasurer

Provides a forum wherein irrigation design professionals can meet to exchange information and advance skills and techniques in irrigation design, installation and product application.

11759 American Society of Landscape Architects

636 Eye Street, NW
Washington, DC 20001-3736

202-898-2444
800-787-2752
FAX 202-898-1185
E-Mail: info@asla.org
Home Page: www.asla.org
Social Media: *Facebook, Twitter, LinkedIn, Pinterest, Instagram, RSS*

Thomas R Tavella, President
Mark A Focht, President Elect
Mark H Hough, VP, Communications
David L Lycke, VP, Finance
K Richard Zweifel, VP, Education

Residential and commercial real estate developers, federal and state agencies, city planning commissions and individual property owners are all among the thousands of people and organizations in America and Canada that will retain the services of landscape architect this year.
13500 Members
Founded in 1899

11760 Association of Specialty Cut Flower Growers

17 1/2 W. College St.
MPO Box 268
Oberlin, OH 44074

440-774-2887
FAX 440-774-2435
E-Mail: mail@ascfg.org
Home Page: www.ascfg.org
Social Media: *Facebook*

John Dole, Executive Advisor
Frank Arnosky, President
Mike Hutchison, Vice-President
Josie Crowson, Treasurer
Barb Lamborne, Secretary

Trade association that provides cultural and marketing information to specialty cut flower growers.
700 Members
Founded in 1988

11761 Floral Trade Council
101 N Main Street
Ovid, MI 48866

989-341-1322
FAX 517-339-1393

Will Carlson, Executive Director

Association of US fresh cut flower growers.
70 Members
Founded in 1988

11762 Garden Centers of America
2873 Saber Dr.
Clearwater, FL 33759

800-721-0024
E-Mail:
memberservices@gardencentersofamerica.co
Home Page: www.gardencentersofamerica.org

Kris Shepard, President

National association focused on the needs of retail nurseries.

11763 Garden Writers Association of America
7809 FM 179
Shallowater, TX 79363

806-832-1870
FAX 806-832-5244
E-Mail: webtech@gardenwriters.org
Home Page: www.gwaa.org
Social Media: *Facebook, Twitter*

Kirk Brown, President
Becky Health, Vice President
Jo Ellen Meyers Sharp, Treasurer
Maria Zampini, Secretary
Robert LaGasse, Executive Director

A organization with materials of interest to garden writers and news on members of the Association.
1800 Members

11764 Illinois Landscape Contractors Association
Illinois Landscape Contractors Association
2625 Butterfield Road
Suite 204W
Oak Brook, IL 60523

630-472-2851
FAX 630-472-3150
E-Mail: information@ilca.net
Home Page: www.ilca.net

Kevin Vancina, President
Michael Schmechtig, Secretary/Treasurer
Rusty Maulding, Vice President
Charlie Keppel, Immediate Past President
Scott Grams, Executive Director

ILCA's mission is to enhance the professionalism and capabilities of members by providing leadership, education and valued services while promoting environmental awareness within the landscape industry. Sponsor or Mid-Am Horticulture Trade Show.
Founded in 1959

11765 International Society of Arboriculture
1400 W Anthony Drive
PO Box 3129
Champaign, IL 61826

217-355-9411
888-472-8733
FAX 217-355-9516
E-Mail: isa@isa-arbor.com
Home Page: www.isa-arbor.com

Social Media: *Facebook, Twitter, LinkedIn, YouTube, RSS*

Jim Skiera, Executive Director
Karin Phelps, Executive Assistant
Mark Bluhm, Director, Finance & Operations
Keely Roy, Director, Marketing
Sharon Lilly, Director, Educational Goods

A worldwide professional organization dedicated to fostering a greater appreciation for trees and to promoting research, technology, and the professional practice of arboriculture.

11766 Los Angeles Community Garden Council
4470 W Sunset Blvd
#381
Los Angeles, CA 90027

847-864-5781
FAX 847-448-8805
Home Page: www.lagardencouncil.org
Social Media: *Facebook*

Glen Dake, President
Ada Berman, Treasurer
Eileen Zwiers, Secretary
David De La Torre, Contact
Francesca de la Rosa, Contact

Connect people with community garden space in their neighborhoods.

11767 Mailorder Gardening Association
PO Box 429
LaGrange, GA 30241

706-298-0022
FAX 706-883-8215
E-Mail: satkinson@asginfo.net
Home Page:
www.directgardeningassociation.com
Social Media: *Facebook, Twitter, LinkedIn*

Noel Valdes, President
Polly Welch, 1st VP
Ken Oakes, 2nd VP
Matt Bollinger, Secretary
Alisa Meggison, Treasurer

Mail-order suppliers of gardening and nursery stock and supplies.
210 Members
Founded in 1934

11768 National Council of Commercial Plant Breeders
1701 Duke Street
Suite 275
Alexandria, VA 22314

703-299-6633
E-Mail: ajorss@amseed.org
Home Page: www.nccpb.org

Stephen Smith, President
Andrew LaVigne, Executive Vice President
Tom Koch, 1st Vice President
Marcelo Queijo, 2nd Vice President
Ann Jorss, Secretary/Treasurer

A non-profit organization to promote the achievement and interest of American plant breeders both in the United States and abroad.

11769 National Gardening Association
237 Commerce St.
Suite 101
Williston, VT 05495

802-863-5251
FAX 802-864-6889
Home Page: assoc.garden.org

Nichole Rothaupt, Chief Operating Officer
Jennifer Tedeschi, Executive Director

A nonprofit promoting garden-based education.
Founded in 1982

11770 National Pest Management Association
10460 North Street
Fairfax, VA 22030

703-352-6762
800-678-6722
FAX 703-352-3031
Home Page: www.npmapestworld.org
Social Media: *Facebook, Twitter, Flickr*

Gary McKenzie, CFO
Bob Rosenberg, EVP
Jean Baum, Executive Assistant
Gene Harrington, VP, Govt. Affairs
Alexis Wirtz, VP, Conventions & Professional Dev

Represents the interests of its members and the structural pest control industry.
7000 Members
3500 Attendees
Founded in 1933

11771 North American Horticultural Supply Association
100 North 20th Street
Suite 400
Philadelphia, PA 19103-3572

215-320-3877
FAX 215-564-2175
E-Mail: nahsa@fernley.com
Home Page: www.nahsa.org

Neal Farnham, President
Richard Smith, Vice President
Charles Germano, Treasurer

Promotes full service distributors in the greenhouse and nursery hard good supply market.
120 Members
Founded in 1988

11772 Professional Grounds Management Society
720 Light St
Baltimore, MD 21230-3850

410-223-2861
800-609-7467
FAX 410-752-8295
E-Mail: pgms@assnhqtrs.com
Home Page: www.pgms.org
Social Media: *Facebook, Twitter, LinkedIn, YouTube, RSS*

John Burns, President
Marion Bolick, President-Elect
Gerald Landby, Vice President
Jeff McManus, Treasurer/Secretary
John Burns, Past President

Members are professionals involved in the care and maintenance of public and private sites.
1400 Members
Founded in 1911

11773 Professional Landcare Network
950 Herndon Parkway
Suite 450
Herndona, GA 20170

703-736-9666
800-395-2522
FAX 703-736-9668
E-Mail: webmaster@landcarenetwork.org
Home Page: www.landscapeprofessionals.org
Social Media: *Facebook, Twitter, LinkedIn, YouTube*

Scott Jamieson, President
Brett Lemcke, President-Elect
Jason Becker, Directors at Large
Sabeena Hickman, CEO
Scott Lindley, VP Sales

PLANET emerged from the joining of the PLCAA and the ALCA in 2005. It is an educational, professional resource for landcare, exterior maintenance and interiorscape

professionals and the lawn and landscape industry.
1200 Members
Founded in 1979

11774 Society of American Florists
1601 Duke St
Alexandria, VA 22314-3406

703-836-8700
800-336-4743
FAX 703-836-8705
E-Mail: info@safnow.org
Home Page: www.safnow.org
Social Media: *Facebook, Twitter, LinkedIn*

Robert Williams, Chairman
Shirley Lyons, President
Martin Meskers, President-Elect
Dwight Larimer, Treasurer
Peter J Moran, EVP/CEO

Represents all segments of the U.S. floral industry.
12K Members
Founded in 1884

11775 The United States Lawn Mower Racing Association
PO Box 628
Northbrook, IL 60065

Home Page: www.letsmow.com
Social Media: *Facebook, Twitter, Instagram, YouTube*

An association run for racing enthusiasts who love to tinker and compete.
Founded in 1992

11776 Turf Grass Producers International
2 East Main Street
East Dundee, IL 60118

847-649-5555
800-405-8873
FAX 847-649-5678
E-Mail: info@turfgrasssod.org
Home Page: www.turfgrasssod.org
Social Media: *Facebook*

Den Gardner, Editor
Lynn Grooms, Managing Editor
Veronica Iwanski, Membership & Marketing Manager
Jim Novak, Public Relations Manager
Geri Hannah, Accounting & Office Manager

An organization featuring business news and updates on legislation and agronomics concerning the turf industry.
1000 Members
Founded in 1967

Newsletters

11777 Bulletin
Garden Club of America
590 Madison Ave
Suite 19
New York, NY 10022-2544

212-872-1000
FAX 212-872-1002
Home Page: www.akingump.com

Daniel H Golden, Partner

GCA's oldest publication, articles include news from GCA member clubs around the country, with reports from national committees, zones, and GCA conferences and meetings.
Cost: $8.00
Frequency: Bi-Monthly

11778 Front Page News
Professional Landcare Network, Inc

950 Herndon Parkway
Suite 450
Herndon, VA 20170

703-736-9666
800-395-2522
FAX 703-736-9668
Home Page: www.landcarenetwork.org

Dan Foley, Publisher

E-newsletter with timely association and industry news and topics.
16 Pages
Frequency: Monthly

11779 Landscape Architect and Specifier News
George Schmok
14771 Plaza Dr
Suite M
Tustin, CA 92780-8012

714-979-5276
FAX 714-979-3543
E-Mail: webmaster@landscapeonline.com
Home Page: www.landscapeonline.com

George Schmok, Publisher
Jim Lipot, Circulation Manager
Leslie McGuire, Managing Editor

A photographically oriented professional journal featuring topics of concern and state of the art projects designed or influenced by registered landscape architects worldwide.
Frequency: Monthly
Circulation: 29162
Printed in 4 colors on glossy stock

11780 PLANET News Magazine
Professional Landcare Network, Inc
950 Herndon Parkway
Suite 450
Herndon, VA 20170

703-736-9666
800-395-2522
FAX 703-736-9668
E-Mail: info@actionletter.com
Home Page: www.landcarenetwork.org

News and information of the gardening and landscaping industries.
Frequency: Monthly

11781 Quill and Trowel
Garden Writers Association of America
10210 Leatherleaf Ct
Manassas, VA 20111-4245

703-257-1032
FAX 703-257-0213
E-Mail: webmaster@gardenwriters.org
Home Page: www.gwaa.org

Robert C La Gasse, Executive Director
Ann Marie Van Nest, Vice President
Seymour Jordan, Publisher

Material of interest to garden writers and news of members of the Association.
12 Pages
Frequency: Monthly
Circulation: 1800
Founded in 1848

11782 The Cut Flower Quarterly
Association of Specialty Cut Flower Growers
17 1/2 W. College St.
MPO Box 268
Oberlin, OH 44074

440-774-2887
FAX 440-774-2435

E-Mail: ascfg@oberlin.net
Home Page: www.ascfg.org

Newsletter
Cost: $175.00
Frequency: Quarterly
Circulation: 1200
ISSN: 1068-8013

11783 The Dirt
American Society of Landscape Architects
636 Eye Street, NW
Washington, DC 20001-3736

202-898-2444
800-787-2752
FAX 202-898-1185
E-Mail: info@asla.org
Home Page: www.dirt.asla.org

Covers the latest news on the build and natural environments and features stories on landscape architecture.
13500 Members
Frequency: Weekly
Founded in 1899

Magazines & Journals

11784 American Nurseryman
American Nurseryman Publishing Company
223 W Jackson Blvd
Suite 500
Chicago, IL 60606-6911

312-427-7318
800-621-5727
FAX 312-427-7346
E-Mail: editors@amerinursery.com
Home Page: www.amerinursery.com
Social Media: *Facebook, Twitter*

Allen Seidel, President
Sally Benson, Editor

Focuses on topics relevant to professional growers, landscapers and retail garden center operators.
Cost: $48.00
100 Pages
Frequency: Fortnightly
Circulation: 16000
ISSN: 0003-0198
Founded in 1904
Printed in 4 colors on glossy stock

11785 American Rose Magazine
American Rose Society
PO Box 30000
Shreveport, LA 71130

318-221-5026
800-637-6534
FAX 318-938-5405
Home Page: www.ars.org

Mike Kromer, Executive Director
Beth Smiley, Editor
Benny Ellerbe, Executive Director
Marny Fife, Marketing Director

Publication focusing on rose growing, culture and enjoyment. Accepts advertising.
Cost: $37.00
Frequency: Monthly
Circulation: 21000
ISSN: 1078-5833
Founded in 1894

11786 Casual Living
Reed Business Information
PO Box 2754
Suite 200
High Point, NC 27261-2754

336-605-1000
800-652-2948

FAX 336-605-1143
Home Page: www.reedbusiness.com

Kevin Castellani, President
Becky B Smith, Editor-in-Chief
Delaney Rudd, Owner
Stuart Whayman, CFO

Content includes industry lifestyle features, business analysis and product trend information.
Frequency: Monthly
Circulation: 10000
Founded in 1958

11787 Fine Gardening

Taunton Press
63 South Main St
PO Box 5506
Newtown, CT 06470-5506

203-706-6206
800-888-8286
FAX 203-426-3434
E-Mail: fg@taunton.com
Home Page: www.taunton.com

LeeAnne White, Editor
Cathy Austermann, Advertising Manager
Todd Meier, Publisher
John Lagan, National Account Manager

Landscaping and ornamental gardening are the magazine's primary editorial focus. Step-by-step in-depth information for the country. Articles written by gardening experts and enthusiasts.
Cost: $29.95
83 Pages
Circulation: 202163
Founded in 1988

11788 Florists' Review

PO Box 4368
Topeka, KS 66604

785-266-0888
800-367-4708
FAX 785-266-0333
E-Mail: mail@floristsreview.com
Home Page: www.floristsreview.com
Social Media: *Facebook*

Frances Dudley, President / Publisher
David L Coake, Editorial Director
Heather Kline, Circulation Coordinator
Lisa Strydom, Advertising Sales Director
Sue Lafferty, Account Executive

For wholesalers and retailers and designers of fresh and dried flowers.
Cost: $42.00
Frequency: Monthly
Circulation: 28000
Founded in 1897

11789 Flowers&

Richard Salvaggio
11444 W Olympic Boulevard
Los Angeles, CA 90064-1549

310-966-3518
800-321-2665
FAX 310-966-3610
E-Mail: flowersand@teleflora.com
Home Page: www.flowersandmagazine.com

Bruce Wright, Editor
Jill Fox, Circulation Manager
Richard Salvaggio, Publisher

Business information and tips for the retail florist.
Cost: $54.00
Frequency: Monthly
Circulation: 30,000
Founded in 1985
Printed in 4 colors on glossy stock

11790 Garden Center Magazine

GIE Media

801 Cherry St.
Suite 960 Unit 2
Fort Worth, TX 76102

817-882-4110
800-456-0707
FAX 817-882-4121
E-Mail: greenbeam@branchsmith.com
Home Page: www.gardencentermagazine.com
Social Media: *Facebook*

Yale Youngblood, Publisher
Sarah Martinez, Managing Editor

Garden Center magazine has made the business decision to be the voice to serve the total market with the content to serve common needs; the business of buying, merchandising and selling of trees, ornamentals, bedding plants and related garden materials and accessories to homeowner consumers.
Cost: $90.00
Frequency: Monthly
Circulation: 16249

11791 Garden Center Merchandising & Management

Branch-Smith Publishing
120 St. Louis Avenue
PO Box 1868
Fort Worth, TX 76101

817-882-4120
800-433-5612
FAX 817-882-4121
E-Mail: kneal@branchsmith.com
Home Page: www.greenbeam.com

Carol Miller, Editor
Patricia Kuhl, Publisher
Tiffany O'Kelley, Media Manager
Mike Branch, President
Frequency: Monthly

11792 Green Industry PRO

Cygnus Publishing
1233 Janesville Avenue
Fort Atkinson, WI 53538-0803

920-000-1111
800-547-7377
FAX 920-563-1699
E-Mail: Grant.Dunham@cygnuspub.com
Home Page: www.cygnusb2b.com

Rick Monogue, Publisher
Gregg Wartgow, Associate Publisher
Lisa Danes, Associate Editor

A national trade publication providing the critical business information landscape contractors need for success. Readership includes the leaders of companies performing landscape management, installation, lawn care, irrigation and maintenance. Covers how to topics such as surviving and thriving through the pinch-points of growth, maximizing productivity, matching the right tools and equipment to the appliation at ahnd, and taking innovative approaches to the marketplace.
Frequency: Monthly
Circulation: 55000
Founded in 1937

11793 Greenhouse Management

GIE Media
4020 Kinross Lakes Pkwy
Richfield, OH 44286

800-456-0707
Home Page:
www.greenhousemanagementonline.com

Richard Foster, Publisher
Todd Davis, Editorial Director
Kristy O'Hara, Editor
Kelli Rodda, Managing Editor

National magazine for commercial greenhouse growers. Accepts advertising.
Frequency: Monthly

11794 Grounds Maintenance

Penton Media
249 W. 17th Street
New York, NY 10011

212-204-4200
Home Page: www.grounds-mag.com

Keeping readers informed on the latest techniques and products for gounds care. The most popular source of information for grounds maintenance professionals. Readership includes golf course superintendants, corporate/municipal groundskeepers and landscape professionals, providing them with content they trust and creating a deep source of reference and how-to information.
Frequency: Monthly
Circulation: 70000
Founded in 1966

11795 Hearth & Home

Village West Publishing
PO Box 1288
Laconia, NH 03247

603-284-4285
800-258-3772
FAX 603-524-0643

Richard Wright, Editor
Jackie Avignone, Advertising Director

Magazine for retailers, including specialty, hardware, patio and barbecue.
Frequency: Monthly
Circulation: 17,000
Founded in 1980

11796 HortScience

American Society for Horticultural Science
1018 Duke Street
Alexandria, VA 22314-2851

703-836-4606
FAX 703-836-2024
E-Mail: webmaster@ashs.org
Home Page: www.ashs.org
Social Media: *Facebook*

Michael W. Neff, Executive Director
Ruth Gaumond, Managing Editor
Tecola Forbes, Publications Coordinator

Journal of interest to a broad array of horticultural scientists and others interested in horticulture. Goals are to provide information on significant research, education, extension findings and methods, and developments and trends that affect the profession.
Frequency: Monthly
ISSN: 0018-5345
Founded in 1903

11797 HortTechnology

American Society for Horticultural Science
1018 Duke Street
Alexandria, VA 22314-2851

703-836-4606
FAX 703-836-2024
E-Mail: webmaster@ashs.org
Home Page: www.ashs.org
Social Media: *Facebook*

Michael W. Neff, Executive Director
Ruth Gaumond, Managing Editor
Tecola Forbes, Publications Coordinator

Brings reliable, current, peer-reviewed technical information to help solve problems and deal with current challenges in production, education, and extension.
Frequency: Bi-Monthly
Founded in 1903

11798 Horticulture Magazine

F+W Media

10151 Carver Road
Suite 200
Cincinnati, OH 45242

513-531-2690
FAX 513-891-7153
E-Mail: edit@hortmag.com
Home Page: www.hortmag.com
Social Media: *Facebook, Twitter*

Dedicated to celebrating the passion of avid gardeners, who take delight not just in gardens but in garden-making. Our informative, engaging writing and brilliant photography enables gardeners to create spaces that make them proud, beautify their hometowns and provide a gathering place for family and friends.
Frequency: Monthly

11799 Journal of Arboriculture
International Society of Arboriculture
1400 W Anthony Drive
PO Box 3129
Champaign, IL 61826

217-355-9411
888-472-8733
FAX 217-355-9516
E-Mail: isa@isa-arbor.com
Home Page: www.isa-arbor.com

Jim Skiera, Executive Director
Jerri Moorman, Executive Assistant
Refereed journal devoted to the dissemination of knowledge in the science and art of planting and caring for trees in the urban environment. Published by the International Society of Arboriculture, whose mission is to foster a greater appreciation for trees and to promote the research, technology, and practice of professional arboriculture.
Cost: $105.00
Frequency: Bi-Monthly
Circulation: 17000
ISSN: 0278-5226
Founded in 1924

11800 Journal of the American Society for Horticultural Science
American Society for Horticultural Science
113 S West St
Suite 200
Alexandria, VA 22314-2851

703-836-4606
FAX 703-836-2024
E-Mail: journal@ashs.org
Home Page: journal.ashspublications.org/

Neal D. De Vos, Editor in Chief
Michael W. Neff, Publisher
Ruth Gaumond, Managing Editor
Publishes papers on the results of original research on horticultural plants and their products or directly related research areas. Its prime function is to communicate mission-oriented, fundamental research to other researchers. The journal includes detailed reports of original research results on various aspects of horticultural science and directly related subjects.
Frequency: Bi-Monthly
ISSN: 0003-1062
Founded in 1903
Mailing list available for rent: 2500 names at $100 per M

11801 Landscape & Irrigation
Adams Business Media
111 W Jackson Blvd
7th Floor
Chicago, IL 60604-3589

312-846-4600
FAX 312-977-1042
Home Page: www.adamsbusinessmedia.com

John Kmitta, Editor
Steve Brackett, VP/Group Publisher
Joanne Juda, Circulation Manager

Targets decision-makers throughout the landscape industry, from residential contractors to commercial grounds managers, to public works professionals and irrigation and water management professionals. Information includes advice from industry professionals, coverage of specific projects, details on the latest products and innovations, and news from around the world.
Cost: $57.50
Frequency: 9x Yearly
ISSN: 0745-3795

11802 Landscape Illinois
Illinois Landscape Contractors Association
2625 Butterfield Road
Suite 204W
Oak Brook, IL 60523

630-472-2851
FAX 630-472-3150
E-Mail: information@ilca.net
Home Page: www.ilca.net

Scott Grams, Executive Director
An annual publication geared toward homeowners, business owners and consumers
36 Pages
Frequency: Monthly
Circulation: 40,000
Printed in 4 colors on glossy stock

11803 Landscape Management
Advanstar Landscape Group
7500 Old Oak Blvd
Cleveland, OH 44130-3343

440-243-8100
800-225-4569
FAX 440-891-2740
Home Page: www.act-europe.org
Social Media: *Facebook, Twitter*

Tony D Avino, General Manager
Kevin Stoltman, Publisher
Michael Harris, Sales Manager
Stephanie Ricca, Managing Editor
Ron Hall, Editor In Chief
Covers news, market trends, business and operations management, technical information on horticulture and agronomy for 51,000 professional landscape contractors, lawncare operators and inhouse grounds managers.
Cost: $46.00
Frequency: Monthly
Circulation: 60,000
Founded in 1965
Printed in 4 colors on glossy stock

11804 Lawn & Landscape
Gie Publishing
4012 Bridge Avenue
Cleveland, OH 44113

216-961-4130
800-456-0707
FAX 216-961-0364
Home Page: www.gie.net

Ron Lowy, Publisher
Dan Moreland, Executive Vice President

National trade magazine for the landscape professional. Accepts advertising.
120 Pages
Frequency: Monthly
Circulation: 73000
Founded in 1980

11805 Nursery Management
GIE Media
4020 Kinross Lakes Pkwy
Richfield, OH 44286

800-456-0707
Home Page:
www.nurserymanagementonline.com

Todd Davis, Publisher
Kelli Rodda, Editor

Nurserymen, landscapers and garden centers. Accepts advertising.
Cost: $24.00
136 Pages
Frequency: Monthly
Founded in 1910

11806 Nursery Retailer
Brentwood Publications
3023 Eastland Boulevard
Clearwater, FL 33761-4106

727-724-0200
FAX 727-724-0021
Home Page: www.nurseryretailer.com

Jeff Morey, President & Publisher
Cheryl Morey, Vice President & Publisher
News of retail growers.
Cost: $15.00
Frequency: Bi-Monthly
Founded in 1955

11807 Power Equipment Trade
Hatton-Brown Publishers
225 Hanrick Street
PO Box 2268
Montgomery, AL 36102-2268

334-834-1170
800-669-5613
FAX 334-834-4525
E-Mail: rich@hattonbrown.com
Home Page: www.poweret.com

David H Ramsey, Co-Publisher
DK Knight, CEO
Rich Donnell, Editor

Leading publication in the power equipment community. Articles include profiles on successful power equipment retailers (dealers) and manufacturers and accounts pertaining to technology, market trends and timely issues.
Frequency: 10x Yearly
Circulation: 21788
ISSN: 0163-0414
Founded in 1952

11808 Southern Nursery Digest
Betrock Information Systems
7770 Davie Road Ext
Hollywood, FL 33024-2516

954-810-0300
FAX 954-438-2632

Irv Betrock, Editor
Sean Patrick, Manager
This comprehensive magazine covers the gardening and nursery business in the south.
Frequency: Monthly

11809 The American Gardener
Amerian Horticultural Society
7931 E Boulevard Dr
Alexandria, VA 22308-1300

703-768-5700
800-777-7931
FAX 703-768-8700
E-Mail: dhundley@ahs.org
Home Page: www.ahs.org

Tom Underwood, Executive Director
Harry Rissetto, Chair
Mary Pat Matheson, 1st Vice Chair
Leslie Ariail, Secretary
J. Landon Reeve, Treasurer

Features inspiring color photographs and in-depth articles on new and native plants, influetial garden personalities, garden history, and earth friendly gardening techniques and products. Also regular departments on design, children's gardening, conservation issues, and reviews of the latest gardening books, as well as a calendar of gardening events nationwide.
27M Members
Founded in 1922

11810 The Cut Flower Quarterly

Association of Specialty Cut Flower
Growers
17 1/2 W. College St.
MPO Box 268
Oberlin, OH 44074

440-774-2887
FAX 440-774-2435
E-Mail: ascfg@oberlin.net
Home Page: www.ascfg.org

Judy Laushman, Executive Director
Vicki Stamback, President
Leah Cook, Vice-President
Andrea Gagnon, Treasurer
Carolyn Tschetter, Secretary

The only regular publication dedicated to information about the production, postharvest care
and marketing of cut flowers.
700 Members
Frequency: Quarterly
Founded in 1988

11811 The Landscape Contractor

Illinois Landscape Contractors Association
2625 Butterfield Road
Suite 204W
Oak Brook, IL 60523

630-472-2851
FAX 630-472-3150
E-Mail: information@ilca.net
Home Page: www.ilca.net

Scott Grams, Executive Director

Providing readers with news and developments
in the industry with emphasis on regional concerns. Read by ILCA members and nonmembers who own, manage or supervise exterior
and interior design/guild and maintenance
firms, nurseries and garden centers, landscape
architectural firms, as well as the staffs of
parks and recreation districts and landscape industry professionals throughout the Midwest.
Cost: $75.00
Frequency: Monthly
Founded in 1959

11812 Tomato Country

Columbia Publishing
8405 Ahtanum Rd
Yakima, WA 98903-9432

509-248-2452
800-900-2452
FAX 509-248-4056
Home Page: www.tomatomagazine.com

Brent Clement, Editor/Publisher
Mike Stoker, Publisher

Includes information on tomato production and
marketing, grower and shipper feature stories,
tomato research, from herbicide and pesticide
studies to new varieties, market reports, feedback from major tomato meetings and conventions, along with other key issues and points of
interest for USA and Canada tomato growers.
Cost: $12.00

11813 Turf News

Turf Grass Producers International
2 East Main Street
East Dundee, IL 60118

847-649-5555
800-405-8873
FAX 847-649-5678
E-Mail: info@turfgrasssod.org
Home Page: www.turfgrasssod.org

Kirk T Hunter, Executive Director

The only magazine devoted exclusively to
turfgrass sod production. focuses on the business of turfgrass by targeting farm owners and
managers. A valuable tool for suppliers and
manufacturers, featuring industry trends, product news, technical information, marketing, re-

search, government issues, human resources,
seed & planting stock, equipment/machinery,
farm profiles, as well as vital industry and
association news.
Frequency: Bi-Monthly
Circulation: 1600
Founded in 1977

11814 Yard and Garden

Cygnus Publishing
PO Box 803
Fort Atkinson, WI 53538-0803

920-000-1111
800-547-7377
FAX 920-563-1699
E-Mail: noel.brown@cygnuspub.com
Home Page: www.cygnusb2b.com

John French, CEO
Dan Newman, Director of Public Relations
Kathy Scott, Director of Public Relations
Paul Bonaiuto, CFO

A national trade publication providing the critical business information independent outdoor
power equipment servicing dealers need for
success. Readership includes the owners and
managers of full-service outdoor power equipment dealerships serving both commercial and
residential customers. Focuses on retail trends,
management strategies, dealer best practices,
supplier news, and the latest products and
services to hit the lawn and garden
marketplace.
Frequency: 8x Yearl
Circulation: 17504
Founded in 1977

Trade Shows

11815 ASCA's Annual Conference

American Society of Consulting Arborists
9707 Key West Avenue
Suite 100
Rockville, MD 20850-3222

301-947-0483
FAX 301-990-9771
E-Mail: asca@mgmtsol.com
Home Page: www.asca-consultants.org

James R. Clark, Ph.D, President
Gordon Mann, President Elect

Recognized as a high quality, in depth conference with cutting edge speakers. Combining
the best forum for discussion of current and relevant arboricultural issues, as well as consulting practice management issues and key
consulting topics such as the role of the expert
witness, risk assessment and tree appraisal.

11816 ASHS Annual Conference

American Society for Horticultural Science
1018 Duke Street
Alexandria, VA 22314-2851

703-836-4606
FAX 703-836-2024
E-Mail: webmaster@ashs.org
Home Page: www.ashs.org
Social Media: *Facebook*

Fred T. Davies, Chair
Dewayne Ingram, President
Paul Bosland, President-Elect

Attracts US and international horticulturists
who attend to learn about research and new developments in horticulture.
Frequency: Annual/August

11817 American Nursery & Landscape Association Convention

American Nursery & Landscape Association

1200 G Street NW
Suite 800
Washington, DC 20005

202-789-2900
FAX 202-789-1893
Home Page: www.anla.org
Social Media: *Facebook*

Robert S. Lyons, President
Robert Terry, President-Elect

Serves firms who grow, sell or use plants.
ANLA advocates the industry's interests before
government and provides its members with
unique business knowledge essential to
long-term growth and profitability.
Frequency: Annual/July

11818 American Society of Irrigation Consultants Conference

PO Box 426
Byron, CA 94514-0426

925-516-1124
FAX 925-516-1301

Wanda M Sarsfield, Secretary

Addressing major industry issues and learn
from each other and leading experts in irrigation, water management and related fields.
Member participate in the conference to showcase the latest in irrigation solution technology
and services.
Frequency: Annual
Founded in 1970

11819 American Society of Landscape Architects Annual Meeting & Educational Expo

636 Eye Street NW
Washington, DC 20001-3736

202-898-2444
800-787-2752
FAX 202-898-1185
E-Mail: info@asla.org
Home Page: www.asla.org

Nancy Somerville, Executive Vice President
Gerald Beaulieu, CFO/Director Business
Operations

Landscape architect ecucational session and
workshop plus 500 exibits of outdoor lighting,
playground and park equipment, landscape
maintanence equipment, computer hardware
and software and much more.
4700 Attendees

11820 Annual Convention of the International Lilac Society

9500 Sperry Road
Kirtland, OH 44094

440-946-4400
FAX 216-256-1655

Exhibits on lilacs, including innovative cultivation and the use of lilacs in public and private
landscaping.
Frequency: Annual
Founded in 1974

11821 Annual Fort Worth Home & Garden Show

International Exhibitions
1635 W Alabama
Houston, TX 77006

713-295-5366
FAX 713-529-0936

The place to experience what's new in home,
gardening, remodeling, home decor, and much
more. Meet over 400 experts and experience
thousands of products and services.
40000 Attendees

11822 Annual Gulf Coast Home & Garden Expo
Exposition Enterprises of Alabama
PO Box 430
Pinson, AL 35126

205-680-0234
FAX 205-680-0615
Like a well tended garden, the show keeps growing and growing.
12000 Attendees

11823 Central Environmental Nursery Trade Show (CENTS)
Ohio Nursery & Landscape Association
72 Dorchester Square
Westerville, OH 43081-3350

614-991-1195
800-825-5062
FAX 614-899-9489
E-Mail: info@onla.org
Home Page: www.onla.org/cents
Social Media: *Facebook, LinkedIn*

Jay Daley, President
Andy Harding, President-Elect
Kevin Thompson, Executive Director
Tracie Zody, Trade Show/Even Manager
Innovations and ideas in an expanded market.
Frequency: Annual/January

11824 Farwest
2780 SE Harrison Street
Suite 102
Milwaukie, OR 97222-7574

FAX 503-653-1528
Clayton Hannon, Executive Director
775 booths promoting the sale and exchange of nursery/landscape products and services.
13M Attendees
Frequency: August

11825 GIE+EXPO - Green Industry & Equipment Expo
Professional Lawncare Network, Inc
222 Pearl Street
Suite 300
New Albany, IN 47150

812-949-9200
800-558-8767
FAX 812-949-9600
E-Mail: info@gie-expo.com
Home Page: www.gie-expo.com

Anna Demoret, Trade Show Coordinator
Annual show of 400 manufacturers, suppliers and distributors of lawn care equipment, supplies and services, including fertilizers, weed control materials, insurance information and power equipment. Take advantage of the education sessions and presentations and demos, as well as six-hundred and fifty booths.
Frequency: Annual

11826 Green Industry Conference - GIC
Professional Lawncare Network, Inc (PLANET)
950 Herndon Parkway
Suite 450
Herndon, VA 20170

703-736-9666
800-395-2522
FAX 703-736-9668
E-Mail: info@gie-expo.com
Home Page:
www.landcarenetwork.or/cmc/gic.html

Keep current as a green industry professional. Stay tuned in to the new technology, products and services hitting the market every year. Hone your skills with applicable education that you can practice immediately. Green industry firms in all market segments including land-

scape management, lawn care, design, build and installation, irrigation and water management should attend.
Frequency: Annual

11827 Green Industry Great Escape
Professional Landcare Network
950 Herndon Parkway
Suite 450
Herndona, GA 20170

703-736-9666
800-395-2522
FAX 703-736-9668
E-Mail: webmaster@landcarenetwork.org
Home Page: www.landcarenetwork.org
Social Media: *Facebook, Twitter, LinkedIn, YouTube*

Gerald J. Grossi, President
Norman Goldenberg, President-Elect
An annual destination meeting for upper-level management, owners, and key personnel.
1200 Members
Founded in 1979

11828 Green Profit's Retail Experience
Green Profit Magazine
335 N River Street
Batavia, IL 60510

630-208-9080
888-888-0013
FAX 630-208-9350
E-Mail: info@ballpublishing.com
Home Page:
www.ballpublishing.com/conferences

Michelle Mazza, Show Manager
Educational event and tradeshow dedicated exclusively to garden center retailing. Covers topics from store layout and design to merchandising strategies and business management. 20 booths
300 Attendees
Frequency: Annual/September
Founded in 2006

11829 Interior Plantscape Symopsium
Professional Landcare Network
950 Herndon Parkway
Suite 450
Herndon, VA 20170

703-736-9666
800-395-2522
FAX 703-736-9668
E-Mail: webmaster@landcarenetwork.org
Home Page: www.plcaa.org/conference
Social Media: *Facebook, Twitter, LinkedIn, YouTube*

Education will offer practical training for the front line with opportunities to earn CEUs toward Landscape Industry Certified Technician recertification as well as pesticide credits. Attendees will walk away with knowledge on how to run their businesses more effectively and keep customers happy. Technicians will learn cutting-edge techniques to make their jobs easier.
Frequency: Annual/April

11830 International Floriculture Expo
207-842-5508
FAX 207-842-5509
E-Mail: floriexpo@divcom.com
Home Page: www.floriexpo.com

Where buyers and suppliers from each stage of the floriculture production cycle come together to network, teach and learn from one another. With the live products, equipment, technology and education necessary for cultivating and retailing, find the ideas, new products, suppliers, trends and tools to flourish in the US market.

Open to all buyers within the floriculture industry.
Frequency: Annual

11831 International Floriculture Trade Fair (IFTF)
Trade Show Bookings
PO Box 499
Fresh Meadows, NY 11365-0499
George Birne, Show Manager

The industry wide event serving all segments of the floriculture chain, from breeders, propagators, growers to the fresh flower trade.
40M Attendees
Frequency: Annual/November

11832 International Lawn Garden & Power Equipment Expo
Andry Montgomery and Associates
550 S 4th Avenue
#200
Louisville, KY 40202-2504

FAX 502-473-1999
Warren Sellers, Show Manager
The dream trade show for those interested in the concept of more power. The show is filled with outdoor lawn equipment that could do more faster, more quietly, more efficiently, and with the least amount of emissions.
25M Attendees
Frequency: Annual/July

11833 International Symposium on Orchids and Ornamental Plants
Home Page: www.orchidsociety.com
There are 75 booths and 50 exhibits that include bonsai trees, pots, tools and supplies, orchids, live plants and supplies for orchids and more.
Frequency: Annual/January

11834 Lawn & Garden Marketing & Distribution Summit Conference
2105 Laurel Bush Road
Suite 200
Bel Air, MD 21015

443-640-1080
FAX 443-640-1031
Home Page: www.lgmda.org
Steven T King, Executive VP
Marci L Hickey, Director Meetings/Member Services
Amy Chetelat, Financial Manager
Lawn and garden products. 120 booths.
500 Attendees
Frequency: Bi-Annual

11835 Lawn, Flower and Patio Show
Mid-America Expositions, Inc
7015 Spring Street
Omaha, NE 68106-3518

402-346-8003
800-475-7469
FAX 402-346-5412
E-Mail: info@showofficeonline.com
Home Page: www.showofficeonline.com
Robert P Mancuso, CEO
Mike Mancuso, VP/Manager
Annual show and exhibits of equipment, supplies and services for the lawn, flower and patio.
Frequency: Annual/February

11836 Mid Atlantic Nursery Trade Show
PO Box 11739
Baltimore, MD 21206-0339

410-882-5300
Carville Akehurst, Executive VP

Landscaping materials and horticultural tools. 750 booths, nursery stock, garden center and greenhouse supplies. 750 booths.
7.1M Attendees
Frequency: Annual/January

11837 Mid-Atlantic Nursery Trade Show
Mid Atlantic Nurserymen's Trade Shows
PO Box 818
Brooklandville, MD 21022

800-431-0066
FAX 410-296-8288

Widely known as the masterpiece of trade shows.
11M Attendees
Founded in 1970

11838 Midwest Herb and Garden Show
PO Box 3434
Omaha, NE 68103-0434
Jane Booth, Show Manager

With vendors from throughout the midwest and nationally known speakers, this event is geared for everyone from the novice to master gardeners. Exhibitors display a variety of items including fresh herbs, herbs for culinary, medicinal, and decorative use, bulbs, seeds, books on birds, herbs and gardening, plans, herbal cookbooks, gardening magazines, bird feeders, houses and baths, antiques, china, spices, trellises, gourds, orchids, fudge, and much more.
15M Attendees
Frequency: Annual/February

11839 National City Home & Garden Show
Expositions
PO Box 550
Edgewater Branch
Cleveland, OH 44107-0550

216-529-1300
FAX 216-529-0311
E-Mail: showinfo@expoinc.com
Home Page: www.expoinc.com

Featuring showcases on how to make your dream home a reality. Create the garden oasis, backyard retreat or a relaxing sanctuary.
35000 Attendees
Frequency: Annual/February

11840 National Lawn & Garden Trade Show
Great American Exhibitions
112 Main Street
Norwalk, CT 06851

203-498-8735
FAX 203-845-9183

Ronald Gratt, Manager

Sole mission has been to provide an affordable, efficient, alternative to traditional tradeshows which assures buyer/vendor introductions in preset scheduled appointments.
5000 Attendees
Frequency: Annual

11841 National Lawn and Garden Show
Controlled Marketing Conferences
PO Box 1771
Monument, CO 80132

719-488-0226
888-316-0226
FAX 719-488-8168
Home Page: www.nlgshow.com
Social Media: *Facebook, Twitter, LinkedIn*

Bob Mikulas, President

This is the lawn and gardens premier headlines event and features both a pre-set scheduled appointment division and a traditional booth division.
300 Attendees
Frequency: June
Founded in 1995

11842 National Pest Management Association Annual Eastern Conference
10460 North Street
Fairfax, VA 22030

703-352-6762
FAX 703-352-3031
E-Mail: info@pestworld.org
Home Page: www.npmapestworld.org
Social Media: *Facebook, Twitter*

Robert Lederer, Executive VP
7000 Members
3500 Attendees
Frequency: January
Founded in 1933

11843 Novi Expo Backyard, Pool and Spa Show
Show Span
1400 28th Street SW
Grand Rapids, MI 48509

616-530-1919
800-328-6550
FAX 616-530-2122
E-Mail: events@showspan.com
Home Page: www.showspan.com

Melissa Moore
Mike Wilbraham, President
Adam Starr, Manager
Molly Harrison, Administrative Assistant

Held at the Novi Expo Center in Novi, Michigan.

11844 Nursery/Landscape Expo
Texas Nursery & Landscape Association
7730 S IH-35
Austin, TX 78745-6698

512-280-5182
800-880-0343
FAX 512-280-3012
E-Mail: info@txnla.org
Home Page: www.txnla.org

Ed Edmonson, Show Manager
Amy Prenger, President
Nancy Sollohub, Executive Assistant
Darlene Lanham, Communications Manager

Learn about industry trends, experience the breadth and depth of the green industry all under one roof, network, hear about industry best practices from peers and industry experts, and find the best deals from the best dealers in the southwest and beyond.
11M Attendees
Frequency: Annual/August

11845 Old House New House Home Show
Kennedy Productions
1208 Lisle Place
Lisle, IL 60532

630-515-1160
FAX 630-515-1165
E-Mail: info@kennedyproductions.com
Home Page: www.kennedyproductions.com
Social Media: *Facebook*

Laura McNamara, Event Producer

Over 300 home improvement exhibitors displaying cutting-edge home enhancements for kitchens, baths, home and garden including landscape, interior remodeling, pools, spas, floors, doors and more.
8000 Attendees
Frequency: Bi-Annual
Founded in 1984

11846 Perennial Production Conference
335 N River Street
Batavia, IL 60510

630-208-9080
888-888-0013

FAX 630-208-9350
Home Page: ofaconferences.org

Michelle Mazza, Show Manager

Perennial producers of all levels are urged to attend this unique event, which offers an educational and networking experience focused 100 percent on perennials. Learn everything about perennial production and retailing through workshops, seminars, tours, and a trade show.
600 Attendees
Frequency: Annual/September
Founded in 2003

11847 Tropical Plant Industry Exhibition
Florida Nursery Growers Landscape Association
1533 Park Center Drive
Orlando, FL 32835

407-295-7994
800-375-3642
FAX 407-295-1619
E-Mail: info@fngla.org
Home Page: www.fngla.org/tpie/
Social Media: *Facebook, Twitter, LinkedIn*

Linda Adams, Show Manager
Sabrina Haines, Trade Show Coordinator

The trade event showcasing the latest trends in foliage, floral and tropicals. More than an exhibit area, it's 200,000 square feet of living and vibrant plants creating a virtual indoor garden of showstopping displays.
8,000 Attendees
Frequency: Annual/January

Directories & Databases

11848 Complete Directory of Home Gardening Products
Sutton Family Communications & Publishing Company
920 State Route 54 East
Elmitch, KY 42343

270-276-9500
E-Mail: jlsutton@apex.net

Theresa Sutton, Editor
Lee Sutton, General Manager

Print-out from database of wholesalers, manufacturers, distributors, importers and close-out houses. Database is updated daily to guarantee the most current and up-to-date sources available.
Cost: $39.50
100+ Pages

11849 Complete Directory of Horticulture
Sutton Family Communications & Publishing Company
920 State Route 54 East
Elmitch, KY 42343

270-276-9500
E-Mail: jlsutton@apex.net

Theresa Sutton, Editor
Lee Sutton, General Manager

Print-out from database of wholesalers, manufacturers, distributors, importers and close-out houses. Database is updated daily to guarantee the most current and up-to-date sources available.
Cost: $39.50
100+ Pages

11850 DGA Membership Directory
Mailorder Gardening Association

5836 Rockburn Woods Way
Elkridge, MD 21075-7302

410-540-9830
FAX 410-540-9827
Home Page: www.mailordergardening.com

Camille Cimino, Executive Director

Member catalogers who sell gardening and
nursery stock and supplies to consumers.
Cost: $2.00
Frequency: Annual

Industry Web Sites

11851 KidsGardening.org
National Gardening Association
237 Commerce St.
Suite 101
Williston, VT 05495

800-538-7476
FAX 802-864-6889
Home Page: www.kidsgardening.org

Jennifer Tedeschi, Executive Director
Sarah Pounders, Youth Education Specialist

Educational resources and garden grants for
youth.

11852 http://gold.greyhouse.com
G.O.L.D Grey House OnLine Databases

Grey House Publishing's online database platform, GOLD, offers Quick Search, Keyword
Search and Expert Search for most business
sectors including garden and lawncare markets.
The GOLD platform makes finding the information you need quick and easy - whether
you're a novice searcher or an experienced database user. All of Grey House's directory
products are available for subscription on the
GOLD platform.

11853 www.ahs.org
American Horticultural Society

Individuals, institutions and businesses interested in a wide range of horticultural concerns.

11854 www.ahta.org
American Horticultural Therapy Association

Professional therapists, rehabilitation specialists and others using horticulture as a medium
of rehabilitation.

11855 www.aifd.org
American Institute of Floral Designers

Non-profit association to support the floral design industry.

11856 www.anla.org
American Nursery & Landscape Association

The American Nursery and Landscape Association serves firms who grow, sell or use plants.
ANLA advocates the industry's interests before
government and provides its members with
unique business knowledge essential to
long-term growth and profitability.

11857 www.ascfg.org
Association of Specialty Cut Flower
Growers

Trade association that provides cultural and
marketing information to specialty cut flower
growers.

11858 www.asla.org
American Society of Landscape Architects

Landscape architects.

11859 www.emda.net
Farm Equipment Wholesalers Association

International trade association of whole-
sale/distributors of ag equipment and related
products.

11860 www.gardenwriters.org
Garden Writers Association of America

A organization with materials of interest to garden writers and news on members of the Association.

11861 www.greyhouse.com
Grey House Publishing

Authoritative reference directories for most
business sectors including garden and lawncare
markets. Users can search the online databases
with varied search criteria allowing for custom
searches by product category, geographic area,
sales volume, keyword, subject and more. Full
Grey House catalog and online ordering also
available.

11862 www.landcarenetwork.org
Professional Landcare Network

Lawn care companies, manufacturers/suppliers,
ground managers and university personnel
comprise membership of PLCAA. PLCAA is
an educational, professional resource for the
lawn and landscape industry.

11863 www.mailordergardening.com
Mailorder Gardening Association

Mail-order suppliers of gardening and nursery
stock and supplies.

11864 www.nahsa.org
North American Horticultural Supply
Association

Promotes full service distributors in the greenhouse and nursery hard good supply market.

11865 www.pgms.org/
Professional Grounds Management Society

Members are professionals involved in the care
and maintenance of public and private sites.

11866 www.safnow.org
Society of American Florists

Represents all segments of the U.S. floral industry.

11867 www.turfgrasssod.org
Turf Grass Producers International

An organization featuring business news and
updates on legislation and agronomics concerning the turf industry.

11868 www.turfzone.com
Turf Zone

Includes, commerical lawn care, consumer
lawn care, irrigation equipment, fertilizer and
other turf products.

11869 www2.gcamerica.org
Garden Club of America

Bestows awards, maintains a library and more.

Associations

11870 American Craft Council
1224 Marshall St. NW
Suite 200
Minneapolis, MN 55413

612-206-3100
800-836-3470
FAX 612-355-2330
E-Mail: council@craftcouncil.org
Home Page: www.craftcouncil.org
Social Media: *Facebook, Twitter, Flickr, YouTube, RSS*

Chris Amundsen, Executive Director
Alanna Nissen, Office Coordinator
Greg Allen, Director, Finance &
Administration
Claudia Cackler, Director, Development
Pamela Diamond, Director, Marketing &
Communication

The American Craft Council is a national, non-profit educational organization to champion craft.
Founded in 1943

11871 Gift & Home Trade Association
2550 Sandy Plains Road
Suite 225, PO Box 214
Marietta, GA 30066

877-600-4872
E-Mail: info@giftandhome.org
Home Page: www.giftandhome.org
Social Media: *Facebook, Twitter, LinkedIn*

Todd Litzman, Chairman
Bob Ricciardi, President
Joe Harris, Vice President
Fred Schmidt, Treasurer
Allison Barrows, Secretary

The association was designed to help and encourage vendors, sales agencies, industry affiliates and retailers to work together, improving relationships and making business better by providing members with the opportunity to exchange ideas and network with industry leaders.
Founded in 2000

11872 Gift Association of America
115 Rolling Hills Road
Johnstown, PA 15905-5225

814-288-3893

Michael Russo, President

Gift association comprised of retailers and wholesalers in the gift industry.
Founded in 1592

11873 Greeting Card Association
1444 I St. NW
Suite 700
Washington, DC 20005

202-216-9627
FAX 202-216-9646
E-Mail: gca@greetingcard.org
Home Page: www.greetingcard.org

Peter Doherty, Executive Director

Trade association representing American and international publishers - large and small - and production and distribution providers.
Founded in 1941

11874 Museum Store Association
3773 E Cherry Creek North Drive
#755
Denver, CO 80246-3055

303-504-9223
FAX 303-504-9585
E-Mail: info@museumstoreassociation.org
Home Page: www.museumstoreassociation.org

Social Media: *Facebook, Twitter, LinkedIn, Pinterest*

Jama Rice, CEO/Executive Director
Andrea Miller, Manager Of Learning
Kathy Cisar, Communications Manager
Jennifer Anderson, Meetings & Conference
Manager
David Duddy, President

Providing member representatives with the professional opportunities and educational resources they need to operate effectively and ethically.
2500 Members
Founded in 1955

11875 National Gift Organization
332 Hurst Mill N
Bremen, GA 30110

505-798-0375
800-446-2533
Home Page: www.naled.org

Ken Shirley, President

Trade association for the gift and collectibles industry. Offers once yearly expositions, a newsletter, software, low cost credit card processing, telephone service discounts and more to help you run your business profitably.
350 Members

11876 National Specialty Gift Association
PO Box 843
Norman, OK 73070

405-329-7847

Joni Damico, Executive Director

Specialty gift resource center for retailers, wholesale vendors and related professionals.
Cost: $29.95
400 Members
Founded in 1998

**11877 Organization of Associated
Salespeople in the Southwest/OASIS**
15591 W Yucatan Drive
Surprise, AZ 85379

602-952-2050
800-424-9519
FAX 602-952-2244
E-Mail: information@oasis.org
Home Page: www.oasis.org
Social Media: *Facebook*

Kristi Thomas, Media Relations

A gift trade association which represents the manufacturing, sales and distribution side of the giftware industry. OASIS exhibitors offer trend setting general merchandise, world imports, home d,cor, jewelry, Native American art and crafts, western flair and southwestern gifts.
Founded in 1976

Magazines & Journals

11878 American Craft Magazine
American Craft Council
1224 Marshall St. NW
Suite 200
Minneapolis, MN 55413

612-206-3100
800-836-3470
FAX 612-355-2330
E-Mail: council@craftcouncil.org
Home Page: www.craftcouncil.org

Chris Amundsen, Executive Director
Alanna Nissen, Office Coordinator
Greg Allen, Director, Finance &
Administration
Claudia Cackler, Director, Development

Pamela Diamond, Director, Marketing &
Communication

Official magazine of the American Craft Council containing contemporary craft art and happenings of the Council.
Cost: $25.00
Frequency: 6x/Year
Founded in 1943

11879 Gift Basket Review
Festivities Publications
815 Haines Street
Jacksonville, FL 32206-6025

904-634-1902
800-729-6338
FAX 904-633-8764
Home Page: www.festivities-pub.com

Debra Paulk, Publisher
Kathy Horak, Managing Editor

Magazine devoted to issues relating to the gift basket and gift packing industries.
Cost: $29.94
Frequency: Monthly
Circulation: 15000
Founded in 1990

11880 Gifts & Decorative Accessories
Reed Business Information
360 Park Ave S
4th Floor
New York, NY 10010-1737

646-805-0234
FAX 646-756-7583
E-Mail:
corporatecommunications@reedbusiness.com
Home Page: www.giftsanddec.com

Caroline Kennedy, Editor in Chief
Kathy Krassner, Editor at Large
Pamela Brill, Editor at Large

Serves retailers of stationery, greeting cards, collectibles, china, glass, lamps, and accessories.
Cost: $49.95
Frequency: Monthly
Circulation: 23737
ISSN: 0016-9889
Founded in 1946
Printed in 4 colors on glossy stock

11881 Giftware News
Talcott Communications Corporation
20 W Kinzie St
12th Floor
Chicago, IL 60654-5827

312-849-2220
800-229-1967
FAX 312-849-2174
Home Page: www.talcott.com
Social Media: *Twitter*

Daniel Von Rabenau, Executive Director
Claire Weingarden, Associate Editor
John Saxton, Editor in Chief

Edited for gift, stationery and department stores.
Cost: $39.00
Frequency: 18x Yearly
Circulation: 60000
Founded in 1982

11882 Museum Store
Museum Store Association
4100 E Mississippi Ave
Suite 800
Denver, CO 80246-3055

303-504-9223
FAX 303-504-9585
E-Mail: info@museumstoreassociation.org
Home Page: www.museumstoreassociation.org
Social Media: *Facebook, Twitter, LinkedIn*

Beverly J Barsook, Executive Director
Valerie Troyansky, President

Beth Ricker, 1st Vice President
Stacey Stachow, 2nd Vice President

Providing ideas, tips, insights and unique product sources for nonprofit retailers.
2500 Members
Frequency: Quarterly
Founded in 1955

11883 Souvenirs, Gifts & Novelties Magazine

Kane Communications
7000 Terminal Square
Suite 210
Upper Darby, PA 19082-2330

610-734-2420
FAX 610-734-2423
Home Page: www.souvmag.com

Scott Borowsky, President
Mary Anne Peacocti, Director Circulation
Caroline Burns, Managing Editor
Larry White, VP Marketing

Serves the general gift and trend marketplace with a core readership in the tourism and resorts gift and apparel stores.
Cost: $30.00
140 Pages
Frequency: 8x Yearly
Circulation: 43085
Founded in 1962
Printed in 4 colors on glossy stock

Trade Shows

11884 ASD/AMD National Trade Show

ASD/AMD Merchandise Group
2950 31st Street
Suite 100
Santa Monica, CA 90405

310-255-4633
FAX 310-396-8476

The nation's largest, most comprehensive merchandise trade show. Featuring thousands of exhibitors, carrying products in more than 100 catebories, from jewelry and home decor to fashion accessories and general discount merchandise items.
10000 Attendees
Frequency: Annual/March

11885 ASD/AMD's Gift Expo

ASD/AMD Merchandise Group
2950 31st Street
Suite 100
Santa Monica, CA 90405

310-396-6006
800-421-4511
FAX 310-399-2662
Home Page: www.merchandisegroup.com

Julie Ichiba, Show Director

A general merchandise event which attracts over 50,000 buyers to Las Vegas. Tens of thousands of unique products in hundreds of popular consumer product categories are on display at this event.
55000 Attendees
Frequency: Bi-Annual

11886 Accent on Design

George Little Management
10 Bank Street
Suite 1200
White Plains, NY 10606-1954

914-486-6070
800-272-7469
FAX 914-948-2867
Home Page: www.nyigf.com

Elizabeth Murphy, Manager
George Little II, President

370 booths of the latest and most innovative gift lines such as decorative accessories and home furnishings.
50M Attendees
Frequency: Annual/August
Founded in 1999

11887 American Craft Council Show

American Craft Council
1224 Marshall St. NW
Suite 200
Minneapolis, MN 55413

612-206-3100
800-836-3470
FAX 612-355-2330
E-Mail: council@craftcouncil.org
Home Page: www.craftcouncil.org

Chris Amundsen, Executive Director
Alanna Nissen, Office Coordinator
Greg Allen, Director, Finance & Administration
Claudia Cackler, Director, Development
Pamela Diamond, Director, Marketing & Communication

The American Craft Council Show presents outstanding works by America's leading craftspeople for purchase by the public and to the trade
Founded in 1943

11888 Annual Dickens Christmas Show and Festival

Leisure Time Unlimited
2101 N. Oak Street
Myrtle Beach, SC 29577

843-448-9483
800-261-5991
FAX 843-626-1513
E-Mail: dickensshow@sc.rr.com
Home Page: www.dickenschristmasshow.com
Social Media: *Facebook, Twitter*

Linda Cremer, Show Director

Victorian craft and gift show.
28000 Attendees
Frequency: Annual/November
Founded in 1981

11889 Annual Spring New Products Show

Pacific Expositions
1580 Makaola Street
Suite 1200
Honnolulu, HI 96814-3801

808-945-3594
FAX 808-946-6399

Pat Shine, General Sales Manager
Kimalar K Carrol, Show Director/Coordinator

Over 200 New Products Booth Displays featuring for the entire family. All categories of consumer products and service are presented: roofing, siding, jewerly, cosmetics, cars, boats, home improvement products. Over 75 Food & Crafts displays, Sportscards & memorabilia displays.
18000 Attendees
Frequency: Annual/April
Founded in 1974

11890 GHTA Annual Conference

Gift & Home Trade Association
4380 Brockton Drive SE
Suite 1
Grand Rapids, MI 49512

877-600-4872
E-Mail: info@giftandhome.org
Home Page: www.giftandhome.org

Marc Rice, Chairman of the Board
Julie Dix, President
John Keiser, Vice President
Todd Litzman, Treasurer
Denny King, Secretary

GHTA has partnered with the Gift Associates Interchange Network, Inc. (GAIN) to form a new credit reporting interchange. The interchange will give GHTA members access to retailer payment experiences, flash notices, predictive payment scoring, educational resources and more.
Frequency: Annual
Founded in 2000

11891 General Gifts: A Division of the New York International Gift Fair

George Little Management
10 Bank Street
White Plains, NY 10606-1954

914-486-6070
800-272-7469
FAX 914-948-6180
Home Page: www.nyigf.com

George Little II, President

Featuring stationary, collectibles, ceramic giftware, toys, pet items, party lines, trend merchandise, premiums, trim-a-tree, souvenirs and novelties, specialty foods, home office, floral & garden accessories, Judaica, and general items.
Frequency: Biennial

11892 Grand Strand Gift and Resort Merchandise Show

Fairchild Urban Expositions
5500 Interstate N Parkway
Suite 520
Atlanta, GA 30328

770-952-6444
FAX 770-956-9644
Social Media: *Facebook*

Bringing the nation's retailers an unrivaled selection of themed merchandise, resort apparel, gifts and souvenirs.
300 Attendees
Frequency: Annual/December

11893 Gulf Coast Gift Show

Fairchild Urban Expositions
5500 Interstate N Parkway
Suite 520
Atlanta, GA

770-952-6444
FAX 770-956-9644
Home Page: www.urban-expo.com
Social Media: *Facebook*

Offering retailers from the Florida Panhandle and surrounding Gulf Coast areas to New Orleans an opportunigy to buy last minute holiday merchandise and get a jump on their spring/summer resort buying.
4000 Attendees
Frequency: Annual/October

11894 Holiday Market

Gilmore Enterprises
3514 Drawbridge Pkwy
Suite A
Greensboro, NC 27410-8584

336-282-5550
FAX 336-282-0555
E-Mail: contact@gilmoreshows.com
Home Page: www.gilmoreshows.com
Social Media: *Facebook*

Tami Gilmore, Show Manager
Clyde Gilmore, Executive Director
Jan Donovon, Marketing Manager

There are two Holiday Market Shows, one in Greensboro, NC and the others in N. Cahrleston, SC. celebrate the season at Holiday Market. Children visit with santa and you will come away with ideas, recipes, samples, beauty makeovers and treats and holiday gifts.
35000 Attendees
Frequency: Annual/November
Founded in 1989

11895 Immediate Delivery Show: Fall
AMC Trade Shows/DMC Expositions
240 Peachtree Street NW
Suite 2200
Atlanta, GA 30303

404-220-3000
FAX 404-220-3030

Mary Ellen Jackson, Show Manger

A trade show that allows you to move discontinued merchandise, overstocked inventory, samples and one of a kind items.
9000 Attendees
Frequency: Annual/November

11896 Indoor/Outdoor Home Show
True Value
PO Box 17
Bethel Park, PA 15102

412-276-6292
FAX 412-851-6975
E-Mail: EllenDiOrio@aol.com
Home Page: www.pitthomeshow.com

Plenty of exhibits and vendors, and the ultimate displays for the home office, garage, backyard and patio, dream windows, home flooring, and bathroom.
61000 Attendees
Frequency: Annual/January

11897 International Jewelry Fair/General Merchandise Show
Helen Brett Enterprises
5111 Academy Drive
Lisle, IL 60532

630-241-9865
800-541-8171
FAX 630-241-9870
E-Mail: dharrington@helenbrett.com
Home Page: www.gift2jewelry.com

Dave Harrington, Show Manager

Containing 1500 booths during the fall show and 800 booths during the spring show. Tradeshow open to wholesale buyers only (credentials required to attend).
44000 Attendees
Frequency: Bi-Annual

11898 Licensing International Expo
310-857-7544
888-644-2022
Home Page: www.licensingexpo.com

Talia Loggia, Marketing Manager

Annual show of 220 exhibitors of logos, corporate trademarks, characters, designs and other advertising techniques that require licensing.
7000 Attendees
Frequency: Annual/July

11899 Memphis Gift & Jewelry Show-Fall
Helen Brett Enterprises
5111 Academy Drive
Lisle, IL 60532

630-241-9865
800-541-8171
FAX 630-241-9870
E-Mail: dharrington@helenbrett.com
Home Page: www.gift2jewelry.com

Dave Harrington, Show Manager

Containing over 350 booths during the fall show and 350 booths during the spring show. Tradeshow open to wholesale buyers only (credentials required to attend).
9000 Attendees
Frequency: Annual/August

11900 Memphis Gift & Jewelry Show-Spring
Helen Brett Enterprises

5111 Academy Drive
Lisle, IL 60532

630-241-9865
800-541-8171
FAX 630-241-9870
E-Mail: dharrington@helenbrett.com
Home Page: www.gift2jewelry.com

Dave Harrington, Show Manager

Containing over 350 booths during the spring show and 350 booths during the fall show. Tradeshow open to wholesale buyers only (credentials required to attend).
9000 Attendees
Frequency: Annual/February

11901 Mid-South Jewelry & Accessories Fair -Spring
Helen Brett Enterprises
5111 Academy Drive
Lisle, IL 60532

630-241-9865
800-541-8171
FAX 630-241-9870
E-Mail: dharrington@helenbrett.com
Home Page: www.gift2jewelry.com

Dave Harrington, Show Manager

Containing over 300 booths during the spring show and 500 booths during the fall show. Tradeshow open to wholesale buyers only (credentials required to attend).
8500 Attendees
Frequency: Annual/May

11902 Mid-South Jewelry & Accessories Fair-Fall
Helen Brett Enterprises
5111 Academy Drive
Lisle, IL 60532

630-241-9865
800-541-8171
FAX 630-241-9870
E-Mail: dharrington@helenbrett.com
Home Page: www.gift2jewelry.com

Dave Harrington, Show Manager

Containing 500 booths during the fall show and over 300 booths during the spring show. Tradeshow open to wholesale buyers only (credentials required to attend).
16000 Attendees
Frequency: Annual/November

11903 Motivation Show
Hall-Erickson
98 E Naperville Road
Westmont, IL 60559

630-963-9185
800-752-6312
FAX 630-434-1216
E-Mail: moti@heiexpo.com
Home Page: www.motivationshow.com

Nancy A Petitti, Show Director

Connecting engagement, loyalty, and financial results, learn from professional seminars on the latest trends, topics and best practices from some of America's leading organizations.
24000 Attendees
Frequency: Annual/September
Founded in 1929

11904 Museum Source
George Little Management
10 Bank Street
Suite 1200
White Plains, NY 10606-2867

914-486-6070
800-272-7469
FAX 914-948-6180

E-Mail: customer_relations@glmshows.com
Home Page: www.glmshows.com/nyigf

Chelsea A Weinert, Divisional Manager
George Little II, President

Semi-annual show devoted to manufacturers, importers and publishers whose products are appropriate for museum gift shops, bookshores, specialty shops, zoos, aquariums and galleries. Items displayed include calendars, novelties, ethnic and craft items, historical interpretational products, art objects, children's educational items and posters.
Frequency: SemiAnnual

11905 Museum Source: West
George Little Management
10 Bank Street
Suite 1200
White Plains, NY 10606-1954

914-486-6070
800-272-7469
FAX 914-948-6180
E-Mail: customer_relations@glmshows.com
Home Page: www.glmshows.com/sfig

Elizabeth Murphy, Division Manager
George Little II, President

Semi-annual show devoted to manufacturers, importers and publishers whose products are appropriate for museum gift shops, bookshores, specialty shops, zoos, aquariums and galleries. Items displayed include calendars, novelties, ethnic and craft items, historical interpretational products, art objects, children's educational items and posters.
Frequency: SemiAnnual

11906 Museum Store Association Trade Show
Museum Store Association
4100 E Mississippi Avenue
Suite 800
Denver, CO 80246

303-504-9223
FAX 303-504-8585
Home Page: www.museumdistrict.com

Beverly Barsook, Executive Director
Stacey Woldt, Assistant Director Programs

Identify new sales leads, enhance your image and visibility in this niche market, reach your target audience, personally meet your customers, introduce a new product or service, generate sales, and network.
2500 Attendees
Frequency: Annual/April
Founded in 1955

11907 National Halloween Convention
Transworld Exhibits
1850 Oak Street
Northfield, IL 60093

847-784-6905
800-323-5462
FAX 847-446-3523
Home Page:
www.nationalhalloweenconvention.com

This once a year event is where over 10,000 attendees will converge on Chicago from all across the US and over 50 foreign countries to see what over 700 manufacturers and distributors are showcasing as new and exciting for parties, shops and haunted houses. Free educational seminars and workshops.
Frequency: Annual/May

11908 National Stationery Show
Gerorge Little Management
10 Bank Street
Suite 1200
White Plains, NY 10606

741-421-3200
800-272-7469

FAX 914-948-2918
E-Mail:
nationalstationeryshow@gmshows.com
Home Page: www.nationalstationeryshow.com

Lori Robinson, Show Manager

The National Stationery Show is the premiere market for stationery resources in the Unite States. The National Stationery Show presents more than 1,400 exhibitors and product in five distinctive sections; Presents, Celebrate, Take Note, HomeWork, and Indulgences. The show draws 15,000 domestic and international retailers representing department, chain and specialty stores, museum shops, galler and craft retailers, boutiques, stationery, greeting card and gift shops, bookstores, bridal shops
15000 Attendees
Frequency: Annual/May

11909 New Orleans Gift & Jewelry Show-Fall
Helen Brett Enterprises
5111 Academy Drive
Lisle, IL 60532

630-241-9865
800-541-8171
FAX 630-241-9870
E-Mail: dharrington@helenbrett.com
Home Page: www.gift2jewelry.com
Social Media: *Facebook*

Dave Harrington, Show Manager

Containing 850 booths during the fall show and 750 booths during the spring show. Tradeshow open to wholesale buyers only (credentials required to attend).
27000 Attendees
Frequency: Annual/August

11910 New Orleans Gift & Jewelry Show-Spring
Helen Brett Enterprises
5111 Academy Drive
Lisle, IL 60532

630-241-9865
800-541-8171
FAX 630-241-9870
E-Mail: dharrington@helenbrett.com
Home Page: www.gift2jewelry.com

Dave Harrington, Show Manager

Containing 750 booths during the spring show and 850 booths during the fall show. Tradeshow open to wholesale buyers only (credentials required to attend).
20000 Attendees
Frequency: Annual/January

11911 New Yorks Newest: A Division of the New York International Gift Fair
George Little Management
10 Bank Street
White Plains, NY 10606-1954

914-486-6070
800-272-7469
FAX 914-948-6180
Home Page: www.nyigf.com

George Little II, President

Showcasing 250 exhibitors new to the NYIGF spanning all categories and featuring fresh and innovative lines.
Frequency: SemiAnnual

11912 OASIS Gift Show
Organization of Assn Salespeople in the Southwest
1250 E Missouri Avenue
Phoenix, AZ 85014

602-952-2050
800-424-9519
FAX 602-952-2244

E-Mail: information@oasis.org
Home Page: www.oasis.org

Brings success, opportunity, and convenience to buyers and exhibitors. Each show features an expansive product selection on the main floor, the jury-chosen artisans' showcase, and the gifts 2 go cash and carry area. Exhibitors offer trend setting general merchandise, world imports, home decor, jewelry, native american arts and crafts, western flair and southwestern gifts. OASIS is dedicated to providing a wholesale gift marketplace.
6000+ Attendees
Frequency: Annual/January

11913 Offinger's Handcrafted Martketplace
Offinger Management Company
1100-H Brandywine Boulevard
Zanesville, OH 43701-7303

888-878-4438
FAX 740-452-2552
E-Mail: gift@offinger.com
Home Page: www.offingershandcrafted.com

Providing safe, convenient and inexpensive trade shows with rich collections of handmades, limited-production creations, traditional crafts and gifts, home furnishings, furniture and home accents. Meet the country's top producers of folk art, rustic primitives, museum quality replicas, handmade country collectibles, as well as one-of-a-kind, contemporary works of art.
3300 Attendees
Frequency: Triannual

11914 San Francisco International Gift Fair
San Francisco, CA

Home Page: sfigf.com

Top name manufacturers, innovative newcomers, and cutting edge designs.
2500 Attendees

11915 Smoky Mountain Gift Show: Fall
Smoky Mountain Gift Show
PO Box 50
Gatlinburg, TN 37738

865-436-4418
800-441-7889
FAX 865-436-2878
Home Page:
www.smokymountaingiftshow.com

Eva Havlicek, Owner

The most beloved, most popular trade shows for the souvenir, resort and gift industry. Brings the top-name product selection, buyer base, service levels, and spirit of fun and hospitality that defined the show at its prime.
3000 Attendees
Frequency: Annual/November
Founded in 1966

11916 Smoky Mountain Gift Show: Spring
Smoky Mountain Gift Show
PO Box 50
Gatlinburg, TN 37738

865-436-4418
800-441-7889
FAX 865-436-2878
Home Page:
www.smokymountaingiftshow.com

Eva Havlicek, Owner

Geared to the gift and souvenier market. Wholesale trade show open only to buyers in the retail industry. Buyers must present credentials upon registration.
12000 Attendees
Frequency: Annual/March

11917 Southern Christmas Show
Southern Shows

PO Box 36859
Charlotte, NC 28236

704-566-1898
FAX 703-376-6345

Check out the holiday trees, mantels and doors, stroll the Christmas Village, munch on tasty treats and sway with yuletide entertainment.
13200 Attendees

11918 Southern Ideal Home Show: Fall
Southern Shows
PO Box 36859
Charlotte, NC 28236

704-566-1898
800-849-0248
FAX 704-676-6345
E-Mail: dzimmerman@southernshows.com
Home Page: www.southershows.com

David Zimmerman, Show Manager
Brenda Crofts, Assistant Show Manager

Gardens, designer rooms, seminars, exhibitors, and experts on remodeling, decorating, home improvement and landscaping
20000 Attendees
Frequency: Annual/September

11919 Toy Fair
Toy Industry Association
1115 Broadway
Suite 400
New York, NY 10010

212-675-1141
FAX 212-645-3246
E-Mail: toyfairs@toy-tia.org
Home Page: www.toy-tia.org

Thomas Conley, President
Diane Cardinale, Public Information Manager

Products include: games, toys, puzzles, dolls, science and hobby craft kits, books, bicycles and ride-ons, computer and video games and software, playground and sporting equipment, costumes and holiday decorations.
22000 Attendees
Frequency: Annual/February

11920 Variety Merchandise Show
Miller Freeman Publications
One Penn Plaza
PO Box 2549
New York, NY 10116

212-714-1300
FAX 212-714-1313

An emphasis on customer service, community building forums and practical business education seminars.
20000 Attendees

11921 Western States Toy and Hobby Show
Western Toy and Hobby Representative Association
9397 Reserve Drive
Corona, CA 92883

951-771-1598
FAX 909-277-1599
Home Page: www.wthra.com

Phylis St. John, Manager

The biggest assortment of toys, games, hobbies and educational fun.
3000 Attendees
Frequency: March

Directories & Databases

11922 AR100 Award Show Guide
Black Book Marketing Group

10 Aston Place
6th Floor
New York, NY 10003

212-956-1425
FAX 212-539-9801

H Huntington Stehli, President/Publisher

Lists of winners at the AR100 Award Show, which recognizes excellence in the field of annual reports; includes photographers, design firms, illustrators, printers and paper companies; includes listings and ads for winners of past shows.
Cost: $60.00
Frequency: Annual
Circulation: 10,000

11923 Complete Directory of Giftware Items
Sutton Family Communications & Publishing Company
920 State Route 54 East
Elmitch, KY 42343

270-276-9500
E-Mail: jlsutton@apex.net

Theresa Sutton, Publisher
Lee Sutton, Editor

Print-out from database of wholesalers, manufacturers, distributors, importers and close-out houses. Database is updated daily to guarantee the most current and up-to-date sources available. Approximately 1,500 American direct wholesale sources in a three-ring binder.
Cost: $107.50
100 Pages

11924 Complete Directory of Tabletop Items
Sutton Family Communications & Publishing Company
920 State Route 54 East
Elmitch, KY 42343

270-276-9500
E-Mail: jlsutton@apex.net

Theresa Sutton, Editor
Lee Sutton, General Manager

Print-out from database of wholesalers, manufacturers, distributors, importers and close-out houses. Database is updated daily to guarantee the most current and up-to-date sources available.
Cost: $54.50
100+ Pages

11925 Gift Associates Interchange Database
1100 Main Street
Buffalo, NY 14209

716-885-4444
FAX 716-878-2866

J Warren Wright, Secretary

An online credit interchange database.
240 Pages
Founded in 1974

11926 Gift Associates Interchange Network
716-887-9508
800-746-9428
E-Mail: info@gaingroup.com
Home Page: www.gaingroup.com

Donna Mosteller, Director, Member Group Services
Rosanne Battaglia, Member, Development Representative

GAIN is an online credit interchange database designed by and for credit managers in giftware, greeting card, silk floral, and related industries.
200 Members

11927 Giftware Manufacturers Credit Interchange
1100 Main Street
Buffalo, NY 14209-2356

716-885-4444
FAX 716-878-2866
Home Page: www.gaingroup.com

J Warren Wright, Executive Secretary

Manufacturers and importers of giftware and china.
60 Pages

Industry Web Sites

11928 http://gold.greyhouse.com
G.O.L.D Grey House OnLine Databases

Grey House Publishing's online database platform, GOLD, offers Quick Search, Keyword Search and Expert Search for most business sectors including home and corporate gift markets. The GOLD platform makes finding the information you need quick and easy - whether you're a novice searcher or an experienced database user. All of Grey House's directory products are available for subscription on the GOLD platform.

11929 www.greyhouse.com
Grey House Publishing

Authoritative reference directories for most business sectors including home and corporate gift markets. Users can search the online databases with varied search criteria allowing for custom searches by product category, geographic area, sales volume, keyword, subject and more. Full Grey House catalog and online ordering also available.

11930 www.museumstoreassociation.org
Museum Store Association

Providing member representatives with the professional opportunities and educational resources they need to operate effectively and ethically.

11931 www.naled.org
National Gift Organization

Trade association for the gift and collectibles industry. Offers once yearly expositions, a newsletter, software, low cost credit card processing, telephone service discounts and more to help you run your business profitably.
350 Pages

11932 www.oasis.org
Organization of Associated Salespeople Southwest

A gift trade association which represents the manufacturing, sales and distribution side of the giftware industry.

11933 www.shop.com
Altura International

CatalogCity.com is a powerful and flexible e-commerce technology. This site includes recognized brand names such as Blair, Bombay, Chef's Catalog, Fisher-Price, Gump's by Mail, Hammacher Schlemmer, Ross-Simmons, The Sharper Image, and many more.

Associations

11934 ASM International Everything Material

Materials Information Society
9639 Kinsman Rd
Materials Park, OH 44073-0002

440-338-5151
800-336-5152
FAX 440-338-4634
E-Mail: memberservicecenter@asminternational.org
Home Page: www.asminternational.org

Jon D. Tirpak, President-Elect
Dr. William E. Frazier, Vice President-Elect
Craig D. Clauser, Treasurer-Elect
Ellen K. Cerreta, Trustee-Elect
Ryan M. Deacon, Trustee-Elect

The society for materials engineers and scientists, a worldwide network dedicated to advancing industry, technology and applications of metals and materials.
35000 Members
Founded in 1913

11935 American Art Pottery Association

Home Page: aapa.info
Social Media: *Facebook, Pinterest*

Arnie Small, President

Association of dealers and collectors of American Art Pottery.
Founded in 1983

11936 American Ceramic Society

600 N. Cleveland Ave.
Suite 210
Westerville, OH 43082

240-646-7054
866-721-3322
FAX 301-206-9789
E-Mail: customerservice@ceramics.org
Home Page: www.ceramics.org
Social Media: *Facebook, Twitter, LinkedIn, RSS*

Charles Spahr, Executive Director
10000 Members
Founded in 1898

11937 American Cut Glass Association

PO Box 482
Ramona, CA 92065

760-789-2715
FAX 760-789-7112
E-Mail: acgakathy@aol.com
Home Page: www.cutglass.org
Social Media: *Facebook, YouTube*

Kathy Emmerson, Executive Secretary
Judy Northrop, President

A non-profit organization devoted to the study and research of American Brilliant Cut Glass.
1500 Members
Founded in 1978

11938 American Flint Glass Workers Union

1440 S Byrne Road
Toledo, OH 43614-2363

419-385-6687
FAX 419-385-8839
E-Mail: ljs@primenet.com

Timothy Tuttle, President

Organized as the United Flint Glass Workers.
21.7M Members
Founded in 1878

11939 American Scientific Glassblowers Society

PO Box 453
Machias, NY 14101

716-353-8062
FAX 716-353-4259
E-Mail: natl-office@asgs-glass.org
Home Page: www.asgs-glass.org
Social Media: *Facebook*

Skip Huckaby, President
Joe Gregar, President-Elect
Philip Legge, Secretary
Victor Mathews, Treasurer
Jerry Cloninger, Executive Secretary

A not for profit organization that is dedicated to sharing the knowedge,techniques, and skills of scientific glassblowing to its worldwide membership.
650 Members
Founded in 1952

11940 Art Glass Association

5610 Pleasant View Dr.
Nashport, OH 43830

740-450-6547
866-301-2421
FAX 661-264-5277
E-Mail: bbird@artglassassociation.com
Home Page: www.artglassassociation.com

Steve Shupper, Chairman
Jennifer Urbaniak, Vice Chair
Bill Bird, Treasurer
Craig Bradley, Secretary
Vickie Gillespie, Membership

International, nonprofit organization whose purpose is to create awareness, knowledge and involvement for the growth and prosperity of the art glass industry. Programs include an annual conference, group health insurance, marchant listings on our website and more.
Founded in 1986

11941 Ceramic Tile Distributors Association

800 Roosevelt Rd
Building C, Suite 312
Glen Ellyn, IL 60137-5899

630-545-9415
800-938-2832
FAX 630-790-3095
E-Mail: info@ctdahome.org
Home Page: www.ctdahome.org

Tom Kotel, President
Heidi Martin, VP
Robert DeAngelis, Treasurer
Bill Ives, Legal Counsel
Rick Church, Executive Director

An international association of distributors, manufacturers and allied professionals of ceramic tile and related products. Mission is to provide educational and networking opportunities for distributors of ceramic tile and their suppliers to further the consumption of ceramic tile.
500 Members
Founded in 1978

11942 Ceramic Tile Institute of America

12061 Jefferson Blvd.
Culver City, CA 90230-6219

310-574-7800
FAX 310-821-4655
E-Mail: ctioa@earthlink.net
Home Page: www.ctioa.org

Thomas Brady, Board Member
Michael J, Nisenbaum, Board Member
Thomas Domenici, Board Member
Lindell Lummer, Board Member
Bill Klaser, Board Member

Promoting excellence in tile installation and encouraging greater consumption of tile

through education, public relations and liaison with all facets of the construction industry as well as the general public.
Founded in 1992

11943 China Clay Producers Association-CCPA

113 Arkwright Landing
Macon, GA 31210

478-757-1211
FAX 478-757-1949
E-Mail: info@georgiamining.org
Home Page: www.kaolin.com/

Lee Lemke, Executive VP

Organized to advance and encourage the development and production of kaolin-based products, and to work together with the people of Georgia in the communities where the mineral is mined and products manufactured.
Founded in 1978

11944 Glass Art Society

6512 23rd Ave. NW
Suite 329
Seattle, WA 98117

206-382-1305
FAX 206-382-2630
E-Mail: info@glassart.org
Home Page: www.glassart.org
Social Media: *Facebook, Twitter, LinkedIn, Pinterest*

Cassandra Straubing, President
Kim Harty, Vice President
Natali Rodrigues, VP
Roger MacPherson, Treasurer
Kelly Conway, Director

International nonprofit organization encouraging excellence, advancing education, promoting appreciation and development of the glass arts, and supporting the worldwide community of artists who work with glass. Members are artists, students, educators, collectors, gallery and museum personnel, writers and critics.
3100 Members
Founded in 1971

11945 Glass Association of North America

800 SW Jackson St.
Suite 1500
Topeka, KS 66612-1200

785-271-0208
FAX 785-271-0166
E-Mail: gana@glasswebsite.com
Home Page: www.glasswebsite.com

William M Yanek, Executive VP
Ashley M Charest, Account Executive
Urmilla Sowell, Technical Director
Sara Neiswanger, Technical Coordinator
Erin Roberts, Director of Marketing

Offers education on blueprint reading, labor and glass estimating and analysis; manuals on glazing guidelines, sealant compatibility and labor hours and a quarterly newsletter. Serves distributors, installers and fabricators of glass for use in the construction automotive and industrial industries.
250 Members
Founded in 1994

11946 Insulating Glass Certification Council

PO Box 730
Sackets Harbor, NY 13685

315-646-2234
FAX 315-646-2297
E-Mail: erin@amscert.com
Home Page: www.igcc.org

Erin Ackley, Administrative Staff
John G Kent, Administrative Staff
Don Boutelle, President
Bruce Kaskel, Vice President
Brian Burnet, Secretary

IGCC sponsors and directs an independent, true third-party certification program. Periodic accelerated laboratory tests, per American Society for Testing and Materials specifications, and unannounced plant quality audits and inspections assure the quality and performance of sealed insulating glass products.
48 Members
Founded in 1977

11947 National Glass Association

1945 Old Gallows Rd
Suite 750
Vienna, VA 22182

703-442-4890
866-342-5642
FAX 703-442-0630
E-Mail: nga@glass.org
Home Page: www.glass.org
Social Media: *Facebook, Twitter, LinkedIn*

Philip J. James, President & CEO
Nicole Harris, Vice President & Publisher
Denise M Sheehan, VP, Industry Events
James Gandorf, VP, Association Services
Pamela S Paroline, Director, Administration & Finance

The National Glass Association is the largest trade association representing the flat (architectural and automotive) glass industy. Member companies and locations reflect the entire vertical flat glass market. To support this ever changing industry, NGA produces products and services specifically for the industry.
4900 Members
Founded in 1948

11948 National Industrial Sand Association

2011 Pennsylvania Avenue, NW
Suite 301
Washington, DC 20006

202-457-0200
FAX 202-457-0287
E-Mail: info@sand.org
Home Page: www.sand.org

Mark Ellis, President
Darrell K. Smith, Ph.D, Executive Vice President
Chris Greissing, VP Government Affairs
Paige Huggins, Financial Assistant

Trade association representing major manufacturers of industrial sand in North America. Committed to the safe use of industrial sand products and to advancing research and maintaining a dialogue with industry, legislators, regulatory agencies and the scientific community in support of the safety of empoyees and customers.
Founded in 1936

11949 Porcelain Enamel Institute

PO Box 920220
Norcross, GA 30010

770-676-9366
FAX 770-409-7280
E-Mail: penamel@aol.com
Home Page: www.porcelainenamel.com
Social Media: *Twitter, LinkedIn, RSS*

Cullen Hackler, Executive Director
Kevin Coursin, Chairman
Glenn Pfendt, President
Phil Flasher, Treasurer
Cullen Hackler, Executive VP and Secretary

Dedicated to advancing the common interests of porcelain enameling plants and suppliers of porcelain enameling materials and equipment.
85 Members
Founded in 1930

11950 Refractory Ceramic Fiber Coalition

1200 Seventeenth Street, NW
Room 07-54
Washington, DC 20036-3006

202-663-9188
FAX 202-354-4982
E-Mail: info@htiwcoalition.org
Home Page: www.htiwcoalition.org

An association of the leading US producers of refractory ceramic fibers(RCFs). The RCF Coalition develops and promotes proper work practices and standards for the RCF industry, conducts RCF health research and disseminates information on the proper handling and use of refractory ceramic fiber.
Founded in 1992

11951 Safety Glazing Certification Council

100 West Main Street
PO Box 730
Sackets Harbor, NY 13685

315-646-2234
FAX 315-646-2297
E-Mail: staff@amscert.com
Home Page: www.sgcc.org

Bill Nugent, President
Bernie Herron, Vice President
June Willcott, Secretary
Elaine S. Rodman, Treasurer

A nonprofit corporation that provides for the certification of safety glazing materials. Comprised of safety glazing manufacturers and other parties concerned with public safety.
105 Members
Founded in 1971

11952 Society of Glass and Ceramic Decorated Products (SGCDpro)

47 N 4th Street
PO Box 2489
Zanesville, OH 43702

740-588-9882
FAX 740-588-0245
E-Mail: info@sgcd.org
Home Page: www.sgcd.org

Ed Weiner, President

Membership gives decorators and marketers of glass, ceramic and related products the confidence that they are part of a network of professionals who have shared knowledge and resources for nearly 50 years. Helps industry professionals identify new and profitable technology, keeps members abreast of the latest regulatory mandates and works with government and industry to provide reasonable solutions to regulatory compliance.
525 Members

11953 Stained Glass Association of America

9313 East 63rd Street
Raytown, MO 64133

816-737-2090
800-438-9581
FAX 816-737-2801
E-Mail: headquarters@sgaaonline.com
Home Page: www.stainedglass.org
Social Media: *Facebook, Twitter*

Membership consists of the finest architectural stained and decorative art glass artists and studios in the US and around the world. Actively works for the betterment of the craft of stained glass and architectural art glass through various programs that are designed to benefit the members of the SGAA and the clients whom we serve.
Founded in 1903

11954 Technical Ceramics Manufacturers Association

25 N Broadway
Tarrytown, NY 10591-3221

914-332-0040
FAX 914-332-1541
E-Mail: webmaster@tecma.org

A organization of manufacturers of custom and standard technical ceramic products for use in commercial, residential or industrial applications.

11955 The American Ceramic Society

600 N Cleveland Ave.
Suite 210
Westerville, OH 43082

240-646-7054
866-721-3322
FAX 240-396-5637
E-Mail: customerservice@ceramics.org
Home Page: ceramics.org
Social Media: *Facebook, Twitter, LinkedIn, Google+, YouTube*

Charlie Spahr, Executive Director

The National Institute of Ceramic Engineers, the Ceramic Manufacturing Council and the Ceramic Education Council are affiliated groups. All are leading organizations dedicated to the advancement of ceramics.
10000 Members
Founded in 1898

11956 United States Advanced Ceramics Association

1020 19th St NW
Suite 375
Washington, DC 20036-6118

202-467-5459
FAX 202-467-5469
E-Mail: usaca@strategicmi.com
Home Page: www.advancedceramics.org

Todd E Steyer, Chairman
Steve Johnson, Vice Chair
Tom Foltz, Treasurer
Kent W Buesking, Secretary
Glen Mandigo, Executive Director

The premier association that champions the common business interests of the advanced ceramic producer and end user industries.
Founded in 1985

11957 Wedgwood Society of Boston

E-Mail: wedgwoodboston@gmail.com
Home Page: wedgwoodsociety.org

Jeremy Hagger, 1st Vice President
Lorraine C. Horn, Corporate Secretary
Edward C. McCabe, Recording Secretary
Ronald F. Frazier, Treasurer

Organization for those who appreciate the work of the potter Josiah Wedgwood and related decorative arts.
Founded in 1969

11958 Wedgwood Society of New York

7 Palatine Ct.
Syosset, NY 11791-1105

E-Mail: info@wsny.org
Home Page: www.wsny.org

Organization for collectors of Wedgwood. Holds auctions and publishes a widely read newsletter.
Founded in 1957

Newsletters

11959 American Ceramic Society Bulletin

The American Ceramic Society

600 N. Cleveland Ave.
Suite 210
Westerville, OH 43082

866-720-3322
FAX 301-206-9789
E-Mail: customerservice@ceramics.org
Home Page: www.ceramics.org

L David Pye, President
Scott Steen, Executive Director

The undisputed authority on news and new developments in the Ceramics and Glass industries, focuses on five end-use industries: transportation, electronics, defense, energy and construction.
Cost: $75.00
Frequency: 9x Yearly
Circulation: 10,000
ISSN: 0002-7812
Founded in 1898
Printed in 4 colors on glossy stock

11960 The Hobstar
American Cut Glass Association
PO Box 482
Ramona, CA 92065

760-789-2715
FAX 760-789-7112
E-Mail: acgakathy@aol.com
Home Page: www.cutglass.org

ACGA's highly educational journal.
Frequency: 10x Yearly
Founded in 1876
Printed in 2 colors on glossy stock

11961 WDweekly
National Glass Association
1945 Old Gallows Rd
Suite 750
Vienna, VA 22182

703-442-4890
866-342-5642
FAX 703-442-0630
E-Mail: nga@glass.org
Home Page: www.glass.org
Social Media: *Facebook, Twitter, LinkedIn*

Philip J. James, President & CEO
Nicole Harris, Vice President & Publisher
John Swanson, Editor & Associate Publisher

E-newsletter for manufacturers, distributors and dealers. The most thorough, convenient source for the latest industry news and insights on market, design, technology and economic trends.
4900 Members
Frequency: Weekly
Circulation: 30000
Founded in 1948

Magazines & Journals

11962 AGRR Magazine
Key Communications
PO Box 569
Garrisonville, VA 22463

540-577-7174
FAX 540-720-5687
E-Mail: info@agrrmag.com
Home Page: www.agrrmag.com
Social Media: *Facebook, Twitter, LinkedIn*

Debra Levy, Publisher
Megan Headley, President

Source of unbiased, accurate information about auto glass repair and replacement industry.
Cost: $49.95
Frequency: 6x Yearly
Circulation: 10000+
Founded in 1993

11963 Advanced Materials & Processes
ASM International
9639 Kinsman Rd
Materials Park, OH 44073

440-338-5151
800-336-5152
FAX 440-338-4634
Home Page: www.asminternational.org

Joseph M Zion, Publisher
Joanne Miller, Managing Editor
Margaret Hunt, Editor-in-Chief

Covers the latest developments in materials technology.
Frequency: Monthly
Circulation: 32M
Founded in 1977

11964 American Flint Magazine
American Flint Glass Workers Union
1440 S Byrne Road
Toledo, OH 43614-2363

419-385-6687
FAX 419-385-8839

Timothy Tuttle, President

Union news and information for the glass industry.
Frequency: Monthly

11965 Ceramic Bulletin
American Ceramic Society
600 N. Cleveland Avenue
Suite 210
Westerville, OH 43082

240-646-7054
866-721-3322
FAX 240-396-5637
E-Mail: customerservice@ceramics.org
Home Page: www.ceramics.org

L David Pye, President
Scott Steen, Executive Director

Written for ceramic and materials engineers and production management teams involved in industrial ceramics manufacturing. Topics covered include government relations, environmental issues, developing technology, industry statistics, cutting-edge manufacturing processes and technology.
Cost: $75.00
Frequency: Monthly
Circulation: 50000
ISSN: 0027-812
Founded in 1953
Printed in 4 colors on glossy stock

11966 Ceramic Industry
Business News Publishing Company
6075 B Glick Rd
Powell, OH 43065

281-550-5855
FAX 248-244-6439
E-Mail: ci@halldata.com
Home Page: www.ceramicindustry.com

Amy Vallance, Publisher
Susan Sutton, Editor in Chief/Integrated Media
Teresa Mcpherson, Managing Editor
Cory Emery, Art Director
Karen Telan, Production Manager

Serves manufacturers of advanced ceramics, glass, whitewares, refractories and other ceramic businesses. CI's offerings include practical, real-world solutions to manufacturing problems, information on the latest technological advancements, and up-to-date coverage of news, issues and trends.
Frequency: Monthly
Circulation: 10000
Founded in 1926

11967 Ceramics Monthly
American Ceramic Society

735 Ceramic Pl
Suite 100
Westerville, OH 43081-8728

614-895-4213
FAX 614-891-8960
E-Mail: editorial@ceramicsmonthly.org
Home Page: www.ceramicsmonthly.org

Sherman Hall, Editor
Rich Guerrein, Publisher
Jennifer Poellot, Assistant editor
Susan Enderle, Marketing Manager
Erin Pfeifer, Advertising Manager

An internationally distributed magazine covering ceramic arts and crafts. Includes lists of conferences, exhibitions, festivals, fairs, sales and workshops for crafts people.
Cost: $32.00
Frequency: Monthly
Circulation: 35000
ISSN: 0009-0328
Founded in 1953
Printed in on glossy stock

11968 Fired Arts and Crafts
Jones Publishing
N7450 Aanstad Road
PO Box 5000
Iola, WI 54945-5000

715-445-5000
800-331-0038
FAX 715-445-4053
E-Mail: jonespub@jonespublishing.com
Home Page: www.jonespublishing.com

Joe Jones, CEO/President
Mick Harbridge, Editor
Branden Hardy, Marketing

Features on projects and patterns, celebrity clips, new products, show listings, industry news and book reviews.
Cost: $32.95
Frequency: Monthly
Circulation: 15000

11969 Fusion
American Scientific Glassblowers Society
PO Box 778
Madison, NC 27025

336-427-2406
FAX 336-427-2496
E-Mail: natl-office@asgs-glass.org
Home Page: www.asgs-glass.org

Marylin Brown, Editor

Contains technical articles, references and abstracts from other publications, book reviews, new product information, local section reports and announcements, committee reports, and information about health and safety concerns. An excellent source for vendor information with ads of goods and services.
Cost: $40.00
Frequency: Quarterly
Circulation: 850
Founded in 1954

11970 Glass Craftsman
Arts & Media
10 Canal Street
Suite 300
Bristol, PA 19007

215-826-1799
FAX 215-826-1788
E-Mail: webmaster@artglassworld.com
Home Page: www.artglassworld.com

Joe Porcelli, Publisher

Providing the best professionally produced, technical, aesthetic and practical information to its readers and a strong, committed audience of glass enthusiasts and professionals to its family

of advertisers.
Cost: $25.00
Circulation: 12000
ISSN: 1079-199X

11971 Glass Magazine

National Glass Association
1945 Old Gallows Rd
Suite 750
Vienna, VA 22182

703-448-1319
FAX 703-442-0630
Home Page: www.glassmagazine.com

Nicole Harris, VP
Nancy Davis, Editor-in-Chief

Provides subscribers informative coverage of glass industry news, trends and analysis, product introductions, and best business practices, in addition to glass industry statistics and supplier resource guides.
Cost: $34.95
Frequency: 11x Yearly
Circulation: 27098
Founded in 1948

11972 Journal of Materials Engineering and Performance

ASM International
9639 Kinsman Road
Materials Park, OH 44073-0002

440-338-5151
800-336-5152
FAX 440-338-4634
Home Page: www.asminternational.org

Jeffrey A. Hawk, Editor
Rajiv Asthana, Associate Editor
Narandra Dahotre, Associate Editor
Omar S. Es-Said, Associate Editor

Covers all aspects of materials selection, design, processing, characterization and evaluation, including how to improve materials properties through processes and process control of casting, forming, heat treating, surface modification and coating, and fabrication.
Cost: $1965.00
Frequency: Bimonthly
Circulation: 305
Founded in 1992

11973 Journal of Phase Equilibria and Diffusion

ASM International
9639 Kinsman Rd
Materials Park, OH 44072

440-338-5151
800-336-5152
FAX 440-338-4634
Home Page: www.asminternational.org

J.F. Smith, Editor
John Morral, Deputy Editor
H. Okamoto, Supplemental Lit. Review Editor

Covers the significance of diagrams as well as new research techniques, equipment, data evaluation, nomenclature, presentation and other aspects of phase diagram preparation and use. Content includes information on phenomena such as kinetic control of equilibrium, coherency effects, impurity effects, and thermodynamic and crystallographic characteristics.
Frequency: Bimonthly
Circulation: 305

11974 Journal of the American Ceramic Society

American Ceramic Society
735 Ceramic Pl
Suite 100
Westerville, OH 43081

866-721-3322
FAX 301-206-9789

E-Mail: customerservice@ceramics.org
Home Page: www.ceramics.org

David J. Green, Associate Editor
David W. Johnson, Jr., Associate Editor
Lisa Klein, Associate Editor
John Halloran, Associate Editor

Contains records of original research that provide or lead to fundamental principles in the science of ceramics and ceramic-based composites. These papers include reports of the discovery of new phases, phase relationships, processing approaches and microstructures that relate to ceramic materials and processes.
Cost: $1190.00
Frequency: Monthly
ISSN: 0002-7820
Founded in 1905

11975 Pottery Making Illustrated

Ceramic Publications Company
735 Ceramic Pl
Suite 100
Westerville, OH 43081

866-721-3322
FAX 301-206-9789
E-Mail: customerservice@ceramics.org
Home Page: www.ceramics.org

Charlie Spahr, Publisher
Bill Jones, Editor
Mona Thiel, Advertising Manager
Steve Hecker, Marketing Manager
Erin Pfeifer, Editorial Assistant

Provides intermediate to advanced potters with practical techniques, tips and information for the studio in a well-illustrated format. With articles on throwing, handbuilding, sculpture, decorating and firing, PMI covers every aspect of the studio ceramic process. In addition, PMI provides up-to-date information on tools, supplies and materials for the ceramic studio.
Cost: $22.00
Frequency: Bi-Monthly
Circulation: 20000
Founded in 1905

11976 Stained Glass

Stained Glass Association of America
9313 East 63rd Street
Raytown, MO 64133

816-737-2090
800-438-9581
FAX 816-737-2801
E-Mail: headquarters@sgaonline.com
Home Page: www.stainedglass.org
Social Media: *Facebook, Twitter*

Features articles about historical and contemporary installations that will show you what others in the field are doing.
Frequency: Quarterly
Founded in 1903

11977 The Hobstar

American Cut Glass Association
PO Box 482
Ramona, CA 92065

760-789-2715
FAX 760-789-7112
E-Mail: acgakathy@aol.com
Home Page: www.cutglass.org
Social Media: *Facebook, YouTube*

Kathy Emmerson, Executive Secretary
Karen Parker, President

ACGA's highly educational journal.
1500 Members
Frequency: 10x Yearly
Founded in 1978

11978 US Glass, Metal & Glazing

Key Communications

PO Box 569
Garrisonville, VA 22463

540-577-7174
FAX 540-720-5687
E-Mail: scarpenter@glass.com
Home Page: www.usglassmag.com
Social Media: *Facebook, Twitter, LinkedIn*

Penny Stacey, Advertising Coordinator
Ellen Giard Chilcoat, Editor
Debra Levy, President

Serves manufactures/fabricators, contract glaziers, distributors and wholesalers, retailers/dealers of glass/metal and/or glass/metal products and others allied to the field.
Frequency: Monthly
Circulation: 25572
ISSN: 0041-7661
Founded in 1965
Printed in 4 colors on glossy stock

11979 Window & Door

National Glass Association
1945 Old Gallows Rd
Suite 750
Vienna, VA 22182

703-442-4890
866-342-5642
FAX 703-442-0630
E-Mail: nga@glass.org
Home Page: www.glass.org
Social Media: *Facebook, Twitter, LinkedIn*

Philip J. James, President & CEO
Nicole Harris, Vice President & Publisher
John Swanson, Editor & Associate Publisher

Serves the entire fenestration industry, including manufacturers, distributors, and dealers. Offers readers focused news coverage, insightful articles on market and design trends, regular columns on codes, legal issues, and marketing ideas, full coverage of new products, expert articles on operations and technology, and much more.
4900 Members
Frequency: 8x Yearly
Founded in 1948

Trade Shows

11980 ACGA Annual Convention

PO Box 482
Ramona, CA 92065-0482

760-789-2715
FAX 760-789-7112
E-Mail: acgakathy@aol.com
Home Page: www.cutglass.org

Kathy Emmerson, Executive Secretary
Karen Parker, President

Opportunity to learn about cut glass.
Frequency: Annual/July

11981 ASM Heat Treating Society Conference & Exposition

ASM International
9639 Kinsman Road
Materials Park, OH 44073-0002

440-338-5151
800-336-5152
FAX 440-338-4634
E-Mail: pamela.kleinman@asminternational.org
Home Page: www.asminternational.org

Pamela Kleinma, Senior Manager, Events
Kellye Thomas, Exposition Account Manager

The ASM Heat Treating Society and the American Gear Manufacturers Association partner to

create a mix of education, technology, networking and exposition opportunities.
3500 Attendees
Frequency: Bi-Annual
Founded in 1974

11982 AeroMat Conference and Exposition
ASM International
9639 Kinsman Road
Materials Park, OH 44073-0002

440-338-5151
800-336-5152
FAX 440-338-4634
Home Page: www.asminternational.org

Kim Schaefer, Event Manager
Kelly Thomas, Exposition Account Manager

Brings together hundreds of delegates and exhibiting companies to discuss and display the latest advances in materials and processes for aerospace applications. AeroMat is the world's leading aerospace conference devoted entirely to materials and processes used in the fabrication of flight vehicles. Learn the latest technologies in aerospace materials, research and processes.
1500 Attendees
Frequency: Annual/June
Founded in 1984

11983 American Ceramic Society Annual Meeting and Expo
600 N. Cleveland Ave.
Suite 210
Westerville, OH 43082

866-721-3322
FAX 240-396-5637
E-Mail: customerservice@ceramics.org
Home Page: www.ceramics.org

George Wicks, President
Richard Brow, President-Elect
Ted Day, Treasurer
Charlie Spahr, Executive Director

Three-hundred booths of ceramic materials, products manufacturing, testing, processing, research, components and software. Technical conference on ceramic materials research and development with over 1000 papers presented in more than 25 topical areas.
2,500 Attendees
Frequency: Annual/April

11984 American Scientific Glassblowers Exhibition
American Scientific Glassblowers Society
PO Box 453
Machias, NY 14101

716-353-8062
FAX 716-353-4259
E-Mail: natl-office@asgs-glass.org
Home Page: www.asgs-glass.org

Patrick DeFlorio, President
Frank Meints, President-Elect
Steven Moder, Secretary
Victor Mathews, Treasurer
Jerry Cloninger, Executive Secretary

Great opportunity to expand glassblowing knowledge through seminars, demonstrations, technical papers and posters.
650 Members
Frequency: Annual/June
Founded in 1952

11985 BEC Conference
Glass Association of North America

800 SW Jackson St.
Suite 1500
Topeka, KS 66612-1200

785-271-0208
FAX 785-271-0166
Home Page: www.glasswebsite.com

William M Yanek, Executive VP
Ashley M Charest, Account Executive
Urmilla Sowell, Technical Director

Features educational seminars for glazing contractors and executives in contracting companies.
Frequency: Annual/March

11986 DECO
Society of Glass & Ceramic Decorators
4340 E West Highway
Suite 200
Bethesda, MD 20814

301-986-9800
FAX 301-951-3801
Home Page: www.sgcd.org

Focusing on technical and regulatory issues affecting glass and ceramic decorators.

11987 Dealers Show of the American Cut Glass Association
American Cut Glass Association
PO Box 482
Ramona, CA 92065-0482

760-789-2715
FAX 760-789-7112
E-Mail: acgakathy@aol.com
Home Page: www.cutglass.org

Kathy Emmerson, Executive Secretary

Annual show and exhibits of American brilliant period cut glass and related articles.

11988 Electronic Materials and Applications
American Ceramic Society
600 N. Cleveland Ave.
Suite 210
Westerville, OH 43082

240-646-7054
866-721-3322
FAX 301-206-9789
E-Mail: customerservice@ceramics.org
Home Page: www.ceramics.org

Charles Spahr, Executive Director

Focuses on electronic materials for energy generation, conversion and storage applications.
10000 Members
Frequency: Annual/January
Founded in 1898

11989 GANA Annual Conference
Glass Association of North America
800 SW Jackson St.
Suite 1500
Topeka, KS 66612-1200

785-271-0208
FAX 785-271-0166
Home Page: www.glasswebsite.com

William M Yanek, Executive VP
Ashley M Charest, Account Executive
Urmilla Sowell, Technical Director

Seven Divisions of GANA have meetings planned at this event, along with the non-Division Committees including Fire-Rated Glazing, Glazing Industry Code Committee, Marketing, and Protective Glazing.
250 Members
Founded in 1994

11990 Glass & Optical Materials Division Annual Meeting
American Ceramic Society

600 N. Cleveland Ave.
Suite 210
Westerville, OH 43082

240-646-7054
866-721-3322
FAX 301-206-9789
E-Mail: customerservice@ceramics.org
Home Page: www.ceramics.org

Charles Spahr, Executive Director

Involving the physical properties and technological processes important to glasses, amorphous solids and optical materials.
10000 Members
Frequency: Annual/May
Founded in 1898

11991 Glass Art Society Conference
Glass Art Society
6512 23rd Ave. NW
Suite 329
Seattle, WA 98117

206-382-1305
FAX 206-382-2630
E-Mail: info@glassart.org
Home Page: www.glassart.org

Jeremy Lepisto, President
Jutta-Annette Page, Vice-President
Caroline Madden, Secretary
Lance Friedman, Treasurer

Annual conference and exhibits for those who make, collect, exhibit and appreciate objects made with glass.
2000 Attendees
Frequency: Annual/June

11992 Glass Craft Exposition
Las Vegas Management
2408 Chapman Drive
Las Vegas, NV 89104

702-734-0070
800-217-4527
FAX 702-734-0636
Home Page: www.glasscraftexpo.com

Shirley Harvey, Director

Learn new techniques and create new things.
3500 Attendees
Frequency: Annual/March

11993 Glass Expo Midwest
US Glass Magazine
PO Box 569
Garrisonville, VA 22463

540-720-5584
FAX 540-720-5687
E-Mail: expos@glass.com
Home Page: www.glassexpos.com/

Patrick Smith, Marketing Manager

Annual show and exhibits of flat, container, heavy insulated and tempered glass, architectural sealants and hardware, mirror products and windows and doors.
800 Attendees
Frequency: Annual/August

11994 Glass TEXpo
Key Communications, Inc.
PO Box 569
Garrisonville, VA 22463-0569

540-720-5584
FAX 540-720-5687
E-Mail: expos@glass.com
Home Page: www.glassexpos.com

Patrick Smith, Marketing Manager

Annual show and exhibits of flat, container, heavy insulated and tempered glass, architectural sealants and hardware, mirror products and windows and doors. Hosted in Dallas, TX.
700 Attendees
Frequency: Annual/October

11995 International Conference and Expo on Advanced Ceramics and Composites

American Ceramic Society
600 N. Cleveland Ave.
Suite 210
Westerville, OH 43082

240-646-7054
866-721-3322
FAX 301-206-9789
E-Mail: customerservice@ceramics.org
Home Page: www.ceramics.org

George Wicks, President
Richard Brow, President-Elect
Ted Day, Treasurer
Charlie Spahr, Executive Director

Showcases cutting-edge research and product developments in advanced ceramics, armor ceramics, solid oxide fuel cells, ceramic coating, bioceramics and more.
Frequency: Annual/January

11996 International Conference and Exposition on Advanced Ceramics & Composites

American Ceramic Society
600 N. Cleveland Ave.
Suite 210
Westerville, OH 43082

240-646-7054
866-721-3322
FAX 301-206-9789
E-Mail: customerservice@ceramics.org
Home Page: www.ceramics.org

Charles Spahr, Executive Director

Showcases cutting-edge research and product developments in advanced ceramics, armor ceramics, solid oxide fuel cells, ceramic coatings, bioceramics and more.
10000 Members
Frequency: Annual/January
Founded in 1898

11997 International Glass Show

Dame Associates
100 Lincoln Street
Boston, MA 02135

617-783-4777
800-843-3263
FAX 617-783-4787
Home Page: www.dameassoc.com

Annual show of 115 manufacturers and suppliers of windows, doors, sun enclosures, windshields and mirrors, glass, machinery, hardware and insulating units, sealants, adhesives, mastic, security glazing and thermal barriers, aluminum, curtain wall computers and trucks.
2500 Attendees
Frequency: Annual/May

11998 International Symposium for Testing and Failure Analysis

ASM International
9639 Kinsman Road
Materials Park, OH 44073-0002

440-338-5151
800-336-5152
FAX 440-338-4634
E-Mail: pamela.kleinman@asminternational.org
Home Page: www.asminternational.org

Pamela Kleinman, Senior Manager, Events
Kelly Thomas, Exposition Account Manager

Annual event focusing on testing, analysis, characterization and research of materials such as engineered materials, high performance met-als, powdered metals, metal forming, surface modification, welding and joining.
4,000 Attendees
Frequency: Annual/October
Founded in 2005

11999 International Thermal Spray Conference & Exposition

ASM International
9639 Kinsman Road
Materials Park, OH 44073

440-338-5151
800-336-5152
FAX 440-338-4634
E-Mail: natalie.nemec@asminternational.org
Home Page: www.asminternational.org

Natalie Neme, Event Manager
Kelly Thomas, Exposition Account Manager

Global annual event attracting professional interested in thermal spray technology focusing on advances in HVOF, plasma and detonation gun, flame spray and wire arc spray processes, performance of coatings, and future trends. 150 exhibitors.
1000 Attendees
Frequency: Annual/May

12000 International Window Film Conference and Expo

Window Film Magazine
PO Box 569
Garrisonville, VA 22463-0569

540-720-5584
FAX 540-720-5687
E-Mail: expos@glass.com
Home Page: www.glassexpos.com

Patrick Smith, Marketing Manager

Numerous opportunities to network, socialize, and learn from others in the window film industry.
Frequency: Annual/March

12001 MCARE: Materials Challenges in Alternative & Renewable Energy

American Ceramic Society
600 N. Cleveland Ave.
Suite 210
Westerville, OH 43082

240-646-7054
866-721-3322
FAX 301-206-9789
E-Mail: customerservice@ceramics.org
Home Page: www.ceramics.org

Charles Spahr, Executive Director

Facilitates information sharing on the latest developments involving materials for alternative and renewable energy systems. Emphasis will be on materials challenges and innovations in areas of solar energy, wind power, hydro, geothermal, biomass, nuclear, hydrogen, electric grid, materials availability, nanocomposites/manomaterials, and battery and energy storage.
10000 Members
Frequency: Annual/February
Founded in 1898

12002 Porcelain Enamel Institute Technical Forum & Suppliers Mart

4004 Hillsboro Pike
Suite B224
Nashville, TN 37215-2722

615-385-5357
FAX 615-385-5463
E-Mail: penamel@aol.com
Home Page: www.porcelainenamel.com

Cullen Hackler, Executive VP
Patricia Melton, Executive Secretary

Members include suppliers and makers of porcelain enamel products and raw materials. At-tendees of the PEI conference and workshops attend this show. There will be 20 booths.
250 Attendees
Frequency: Annual/May
Founded in 1989

12003 Seattle Gift Show

George Little Management
10 Bank Street
Suite 1200
White Plains, NY 10606

914-486-6070
800-272-7469
FAX 914-948-2918
Home Page: www.washingtongiftshow.com

Louise Seeber, Show Manager
Laura Scott, Exhibit Sales Manager
George Little II, President

See new products and proven bestsellers that cater to the eclectic tastes of the discerning Pacific Northwest consumer.
6000 Attendees
Frequency: Annual/January

Directories & Databases

12004 Ceramic Abstracts

American Ceramic Society
600 N. Cleveland Ave.
Suite 210
Westerville, OH 43081

240-646-7054
866-721-3322
FAX 240-396-5637
E-Mail: customerservice@ceramics.org
Home Page: www.ceramics.org

Charles Spahr, Executive Director

Abstracting/indexing publication covering ceramic materials-related literature. 15,000 entries published annually.
Frequency: Bi-Monthly
Circulation: 2,500

12005 CeramicSOURCE

American Ceramic Society
735 Ceramic Pl
Suite 100
Westerville, OH 43081-8728

614-904-4700
FAX 614-794-5892
Home Page: www.ceramicsource.org

Patricia Janeway, Editor
Marc Bailey, Director Global Marketing

Annual buyer's guide/directory of equipment and materials' suppliers to the industrial ceramic manufacturing market.
Cost: $25.00
Frequency: 1 issue
Circulation: 14,500
ISSN: 0002-7812
Founded in 1985
Printed in 4 colors on glossy stock

12006 Complete Directory of Glassware & Glass Items

Sutton Family Communications & Publishing Company
920 State Route 54 East
Elmitch, KY 42343

270-276-9500
E-Mail: jlsutton@apex.net

Theresa Sutton, Publisher
Lee Sutton, Editor

Print-out from database of wholesalers, manufacturers, distributors, importers and close-out houses. Database is updated daily to guarantee the most current and up-to-date sources avail-

able. Over 800 American firms which sell direct to small retailers, in three-ring binder format.
Cost: $94.50
100 Pages

12007 Complete Guide: US Advanced Ceramic Industry
Business Communications Company
49 Walnut Park
Building 2
Wellesley, MA 02481-1713

866-285-7215
FAX 781-489-7308
E-Mail: sales@bccresearch.com
Home Page: www.bccresearch.com

David Nydam, President
Kevin R. Fitzgerald, Editorial Director
Andrew Hunt, Marketing Director

Approximately 450 companies and institutions involved in the advanced ceramic industry in the US.

12008 Data Book and Buyers' Guide
Ceramic Industry
2540 Billingsley Road
Business News Publishing Company
Columbus, OH 43235-1990

FAX 440-498-9121

List of over 1300 suppliers of equipment and materials for the advanced and traditional ceramics and heavy clay products.
Cost: $25.00
Frequency: Biennially

12009 Glass Factory Directory of North America
Glass News
Box 2267
Hempstead, NY 11551-2267

516-481-2188
Home Page: www.glassfactorydir.com

Liz Scott, Editor

Over 600 glass manufacturers and plants in the US, Canada and Mexico.
Cost: $25.00
Frequency: Annually
Circulation: 1,500

12010 Porcelain Enamel Institute Source List
4004 Hillsboro Pike
Suite B224
Nashville, TN 37215-2722

615-385-5357
FAX 615-385-5463
E-Mail: penamel@aol.com
Home Page: www.porcelainenamel.com

Tom Sanford, Executive VP
Patricia Melton, Executive Secretary
Frequency: Annual/Fall
Founded in 1930

12011 Society of Glass & Ceramic Decorating Products Directory
Society of Glass & Ceramic Decorating Products
PO Box 2489
Zanesville, OH 43702

740-588-9882
FAX 740-588-0245
E-Mail: info@sgcd.org
Home Page: www.sgcd.org

Directory of more than 700 member manufacturers, suppliers, decorators and designers of glass and ceramics; international coverage indexed by product type and decorating technol-

ogy.
Cost: $250.00
172 Pages
Frequency: Annual
Circulation: 800
Founded in 1964

12012 US Glass, Metal & Glazing: Buyers Guide
Key Communications
PO Box 569
Garrisonville, VA 22463-0569

540-577-7174
FAX 540-720-5687
Home Page: www.usglass.com

Debra A Levy, Publisher

About 3,000 suppliers of glass and glazing supplies for the glass, metal and glazing industry.
Cost: $20.00
Frequency: Annual
Circulation: 21,000

Industry Web Sites

12013 Ceramic Arts Daily
Ceramic Publications Company
600 N Cleveland Ave.
Suite 210
Westerville, OH 43082

614-794-5843
FAX 614-794-5842
Home Page: ceramicartsdaily.org

The online community of potters and ceramic artists provides a daily newsletter promoting related products and services as well as tools for learning.

12014 http://gold.greyhouse.com
G.O.L.D Grey House OnLine Databases
Grey House Publishing's online database platform, GOLD, offers Quick Search, Keyword Search and Expert Search for most business sectors including glass and ceramic markets. The GOLD platform makes finding the information you need quick and easy - whether you're a novice searcher or an experienced database user. All of Grey House's directory products are available for subscription on the GOLD platform.

12015 www.acers.org
American Ceramic Society
The National Institute of Ceramic Engineers, the Ceramic Manufacturing Council and the Ceramic Education Council are affiliated classes.

12016 www.advancedceramics.org
United States Advanced Ceramics Association
Promotes the use of advanced ceramic materials in industrial applications.

12017 www.asgs-glass.org
American Scientific Glassblowers Society
Encourages the free exchange of knowledge and the broadening of scientific glassblowing skills to assist scientists, educators and the industry by designing and constructing glass components and scientific apparatus.

12018 www.ceramics.org
American Ceramic Society
The National Institute of Ceramic Engineers, the Ceramic Manufacturing Council and the Ceramic Education Council are affiliated groups.

12019 www.ctdahome.org
Ceramic Tile Distributors Association
Promotes the sales of ceramic tile and similar products.

12020 www.ctioa.org
Ceramic Tile Institute of America
This organization has over 500 member manufacturers of ceramic tile in the western United States.

12021 www.cutglass.org
American Cut Glass Association
A non-profit organization devoted to the study and research of American Brilliant Cut Glass.

12022 www.dameassoc.com
Dame Associates
An organization with a biennial show w/250 manufacturers and suppliers of windows, doors, sun enclosures, windshields, mirrors, glass machinery, hardware, insulating units, sealants, adhesives, mastic, security glazing, thermal barriers, aluminum, curtain wall computers and trucks.

12023 www.glass.org
National Glass Association
An organization with an annual show of 325 manufacturers, suppliers and distributors of glass and glass-related products, supplies, equipment, tools and machinery, automotive glazing, equipment/machinery, curtain wall, store front systems, doors/hardware, windows, mirrors, shower/tub enclosures and tools.

12024 www.glasswebsite.com
Glass Association of North America
Offers educational on blueprint reading, labor, and glass estimating and analysis; manuals on glazing guidelines, sealant compatibility and labor hours; and a quarterly newsletter. Serves distributors, installers, fabricators of glass for use in the construction automotive and industrial industries.

12025 www.glasswebsite.com/gicc
Glazing Industry Code Committee
Protects the glass and glazing interests by monitoring, testifying and developing code proposals at the model building and energy codes.

12026 www.greyhouse.com
Grey House Publishing
Authoritative reference directories for most business sectors including glass and ceramic markets. Users can search the online databases with varied search criteria allowing for custom searches by product category, geographic area, sales volume, keyword, subject and more. Full Grey House catalog and online ordering also available.

12027 www.igcc.org
Insulating Glass Certification Council
Sponsors and directs a program of laboratory testing and unannounced plant inspection to ensure continuing product information.

12028 www.igmaonline.org
Insulating Glass Manufacturers Alliance

12029 www.porcelainenamel.com
Porcelain Enamel Institute
Members include suppliers and makers of porcelain enamel products and raw materials.

12030 www.sgcc.org
Safety Glazing Certification Council
Information center for this nonprofit corporation that provides for the certification of safety glazing materials.

Associations

12031 Academy for State and Local Government

444 N Capitol St NW
Washington, DC 20001-1512

202-434-4850
FAX 202-434-4851

The policy center for the national organizations for the chief elected and appointed officials for state and local governments, functioning as their joint technical assistance, training and research organization. Its mission is to promote cooperation among federal, state and local governments.

12032 American Association of State Highway and Transportation Officials

444 N Capitol St NW
Suite 249
Washington, DC 20001-1539

202-624-5800
FAX 202-624-5806
E-Mail: info@aashto.org
Home Page: www.transportation.org
Social Media: *Facebook, Twitter*

Mike Hancock, President
John Cox, Vice-President
Carlos Braceras, Secretary/ Treasurer
Bud Wright, Executive Director
Selim Amah, Accounts Payable Specialist

Membership is composed of highway and transportation departments in the 50 states, the District of Columbia, and Puerto Rico.
52 Members

12033 American Conference of Governmental Industrial Hygienists (NCGIH)

1330 Kemper Meadow Drive
Cincinnati, OH 45240

513-742-2020
FAX 513-742-3355
E-Mail: mail@acgih.org
Home Page: www.acgih.org
Social Media: *Facebook, Twitter, LinkedIn, Google+*

J Torey Nalbone, Chair
John S. Morawetz, ScM, Treasurer
Jeff Washington, Deputy Executive Director
A Anthony Rizzuto, Executive Director
India Vargas, Administrative Assistant

A professional society of government and university employees engaged in a full program of industrial hygiene.
Founded in 1938

12034 American Correctional Association

206 N Washington St
Alexandria, VA 22314-2528

703-224-0000
800-222-5646
FAX 703-224-0179
E-Mail: jeffw@aca.org
Home Page: www.aca.org
Social Media: *Facebook, Twitter*

Jeff Washington, Deputy Executive Director
James Gondles Jr, Executive Director
Debbi Seeger, Director of the Executive Office
Hok Gao, Director of Finance
Larry Strother, Director of Management

For individuals involved in the correctional field.
20000 Members
Founded in 1870

12035 American Federation of Government Employees

80 F St NW
Washington, DC 20001-1528

202-737-8700
FAX 202-639-6490
E-Mail: comments@afge.org
Home Page: www.afge.com
Social Media: *Facebook, Twitter, Youtube, Flickr, RSS*

J David Cox Sr., President
Eugene Hudson, Secretary/Treasurer
Augusta Thomas, VP for Women's & Fair Practices

The largest federal employee union representing workers nationwide and overseas. Workers in virtually all functions of government at every federal agency depend upon AFGE for legal representation, legislative advocacy, technical expertise and informational services.
600K Members
Founded in 1932

12036 American Federation of State, County & Municipal Employees

1625 L Street NW
Washington, DC 20036-5687

202-429-1000
FAX 202-429-1293
E-Mail: afsa@afsaadmin.org
Home Page: www.afscme.org
Social Media: *Facebook, Twitter, YouTube, RSS*

Lee Saunders, President
Laura Reyes, Secretary/ Treasurer

With members in hundreds of different occupations, AFSCME advocates for fairness in the workplace, excellence in public services and prosperity and opportunity for all working families.

12037 American Foreign Service Association

2101 E St Nw
Washington, DC 20037-2990

202-338-4045
FAX 202-338-6820
E-Mail: member@afsa.org
Home Page: www.afsa.org
Social Media: *Facebook, Twitter, Youtube, RSS*

Hon. Barbara Stephenson, President
Hon. Charles A Ford, Treasurer
William Haugh, Secretary
Steve Morrison, FCS Vice President
Mark Petry, FAS Vice President

Missions are to enhance the effectiveness of the Foreign Service, to protect the professional interests of its members, to ensure the maintenance of high professional standards for both career diplomats and political appointeese, and to promote understanding of the critical role of the Foreign service in promoting America's national security and economic prosperity.
11M Members
Founded in 1924

12038 American Judges Association

300 Newport Ave
Williamsburg, VA 23185-4147

757-259-1841
FAX 757-259-1520
E-Mail: aia@ncsc.dni.us
Home Page: aja.ncsc.dni.us

Judge Brian MacKenzie, President
Judge John E Conery, President-Elect
Justice Russell Otter, Vice President
Judge Catherine Shaffer, Secretary
Jugde Kevin S Burke, Treasurer

The objective and purpose of the Association is: to promote and improve the effective administration of justice; to maintain the status and independance of the judiciary; to provide a forum for the continuing education of its members and the general public; and for the exchange of new ideas among all judges.
2500 Members
Founded in 1959

12039 American League of Lobbyists

300 North Washington Street
Suite 205
Alexandria, VA 22314

703-960-3011
888-712-1357
E-Mail: info@agrp.org
Home Page: grprofessionals.org
Social Media: *Facebook, Twitter, LinkedIn*

Monte Ward, President
James Hickey, 1st Vice President
Paul T Kelly, 2nd Vice President
Wright Andrews, Secretary
Paul Kangas, Treasurer

National association dedicated to serving government relations and public affairs professionals. Provides programs and conferences of interest to lobbyists.
600+ Members
Founded in 1979

12040 American Logistics Association

1101 Vermont Ave NW
Suite 1002
Washington, DC 20005-2710

202-466-7636
FAX 202-296-4419
E-Mail: membership@ala-national.org
Home Page: www.ala-national.org

Patrick B Nixon, President
Russ Moffett, VP, Member Relations
Maurice Branch, VP, Operations
Tracey Durand, Director, Meetings & Expositions
Joseph Campagna, Chair

Organization that represents the private industry to promote food sales to commissaries on military bases.
Cost: $828.00
400 Members
Frequency: Membership Dues Vary
Founded in 1972

12041 American National Standards Institute

1889 L Street NW
11th Floor
Washington, DC 20036-3864

202-293-8020
FAX 202-293-9287
E-Mail: info@ansi.org
Home Page: www.ansi.org
Social Media: *Facebook, Twitter, LinkedIn, Youtube, Google+*

James T Pauley, Chairman
Joe Bhatia, President & CEO
Kemi Allston, Program Administrator

Promotes the knowledge for approved standards for industry, engineering and safety design.
1000 Members
Founded in 1918

12042 American Public Human Services Association

1133 19th Street NW
Suite 400
Washington, DC 20036-3623

202-682-0100
FAX 202-289-6555

Government / Associations

Home Page: www.aphsa.org
Social Media: *Facebook, Twitter, LinkedIn*

Reggie Bicha, President
Uma Ahluwalia, Treasurer
Tracy Wareing, Secretary

APHSA pusues excellence in health and human services by supporting state and local agencies, informing policymakers, and working with partners to drive innovative, integrated and efficient solutions in policy and practice.
Founded in 1930

12043 American Society for Public Administration
1301 Pennsylvania Avenue NW
Suite 700
Washington, DC 20004

202-393-7878
FAX 202-638-4952
E-Mail: info@aspanet.org
Home Page: www.aspanet.org
Social Media: *Facebook, Twitter, LinkedIn*

Maria Aristigueta, President
Susan T. Gooden, President Elect
William P. Shields Jr., Executive Director
Lisa Sidletsky, Chief of Program Operations
Janice Lachance, Vice President

Offers a wide range of services and membership options for individuals in public administration careers. Sponsors 127 local chapters and 16 sections on specific areas of governments, such as the Section of Natural Resources and Environmental Administration and the Section on Human Resource Administration.
15M Members
Founded in 1939

12044 American Society of Access Professionals
1444 I(Eye) St. NW
Suite 700
Washington, DC 20005-6542

202-712-9054
FAX 202-216-9646
E-Mail: asap@bostrom.com
Home Page: www.accesspro.org
Social Media: *Facebook, Twitter*

Amy Bennett, President
Cindy Allard, Vice President
Amy McNulty, Treasurer
Ginger McCall, Secretary
Jonathan Cantor, Director

Members are government employees, lawyers, journalists and others concerned with access to government data under current personal privacy and public informaiton statues.
Founded in 1980

12045 Americans for Democratic Action
1629 K Street NW
Suite 300
Washington, DC 20006-1611

202-785-5980
FAX 202-204-8637
E-Mail: info@adaction.org
Home Page: www.adaction.org
Social Media: *Facebook, Twitter, Flickr, YouTube*

Lynn Woolsey, President
David Card, Treasurer
Mary Von Euler, Secretary
Elijah Cummings, VP
James K. Galbraith, VP
Liberal lobbying group.

12046 Association for Federal Information Resources Management
400 North Washington St.
Suite 300
Alexandria, VA 22314

703-778-4646
FAX 703-683-5480
E-Mail: info@affirm.org
Home Page: www.affirm.org
Social Media: *Facebook, Twitter, LinkedIn, Flickr*

Robert Foster, President
Richard Young, Vice President
Deirdre Murray, VP, Industry
Christopher Hamm, VP
James Maas, VP

A non-profit, volunteer, educational organization whose overall purpose is to improve the management of information, and related systems and resources, within the Federal government. Members include information resource management professionals from the Federal, academic, and industry sectors.
350 Members
Founded in 1979

12047 Association for Postal Commerce
1800 Diagonal Rd.
Suite 320
Alexandria, VA 22314-2862

703-524-0096
FAX 703-997-2414
Home Page: www.postcom.org
Social Media: *Facebook*

National organization representing those who use, or who support, the use of mail as a medium for communication and commerce. Publishes a weekly newsletter covering postal policy and operational issues.
Founded in 1947

12048 Association of Boards of Certification
2805 SW Snyder Blvd.
Suite 535
Ankeny, IA 50023

515-232-3623
FAX 515-965-6827
E-Mail: abc@abccert.org
Home Page: www.abccert.org

Ray Olson, President
Mike Gosselin, President-Elect
Michael Bolt, Vice President
Brian Thorburn, Immediate Past-President
Paul D. Bishop, CAE, Ex-Officio

The Association of Boards of Certification is dedicated to protecting public health and the environment by advancing the quality and integrity of environmental certification programs through innovative technical support services, effective information exchange, professional and cost-effective examination services, and other progressive services for certifying members.
Founded in 1972

12049 Association of Civilian Technicians (ACT)
12620 Lake Ridge Dr
Lake Ridge, VA 22192-2335

703-494-4845
FAX 703-494-0961
E-Mail: actnational@actnat.com
Home Page: www.actnat.com
Social Media: *Facebook*

Terry Garnett, President
Raul Toro, Treasurer

Labor organization of civilian employees of Air Force, Army, National Guard and Reserves.
12M Members

12050 Association of Fish and Wildlife Agencies
1100 First Street, NE
Suite 825
Washington, DC 20002

202-838-3474
FAX 202-350-9869
E-Mail: info@fishwildlife.org
Home Page: www.fishwildlife.org
Social Media: *Facebook, Twitter, Blogger*

Ron Regan, Executive Director
Carol Bambery, Association Counsel
Kathy Boydston, Wildlife & Energy Liasion
John Bloom, Accounting Manager
Arpita Choudhury, Science & Research Liasion

The organization that represents all of North America's fish and wildlife agencies that promotes sound management and conservation, and speaks with a unified voice on important fish and wildlife issues.
Founded in 1902

12051 Association of Food and Drug Officials
2550 Kingston Rd
Suite 311
York, PA 17402-3734

717-757-2888
FAX 717-650-3650
E-Mail: afdo@afdo.org
Home Page: www.afdo.org
Social Media: *Twitter*

Joseph Korby, Executive Director
Krystal Reed, Association Manager
Pat Smith, Support Staff
Randy Young, IT Administrator
Patty Fitzgerald, Admin/Special Projects Assistant

Promotes the enforcement of laws and regulations at all levels of government. Fosters understanding and cooperation between industry and regulators. Develops model laws and regulations and seeks their adoption.
800 Members
Founded in 1986

12052 Association of Former Agents of the US Secret Service
6919 Vista Drive West
Des Moines, IA 50266

515-282-8192
FAX 515-282-9117
Home Page: www.oldstar.org

Founded to bring together former and current employees of the Secret Service for comradeship, friendship and support in time of need. Members include Special Agents, Technical Specialists and other support personnel who carried out the investigative and protective responsibilities of the United States Secret Service.
950 Members
Founded in 1971

12053 Association of Labor Relations Agencies
38 Wolcott Hill Road
Wethersfield, CT 06109

860-263-6860
FAX 860-263-6875
Home Page: www.alra.org

Pat Sims, President
Ginette Brazeau, President-Elect
Sylvie Guilbert, VP, Administration
Scot Beckenbaugh, VP, Finance
Jennifer Abruzzo, Board Member

An association of impartial government agencies in the US and Canada responsible for administering labor-management relations laws or services. Promotes cooperation among these

917

agencies, high professional standards, public interest in labor relations, improved employer-employee relationships, peaceful resolution of employment and labor disputes, and the exchange of information regarding the administration and improvement of agency services.

12054 Center for Neighborhood Enterprise

1625 K. Street NW
Suite 1200
Washington, DC 20006

202-518-6500
FAX 202-588-0314
E-Mail: info@cneonline.org
Home Page: www.cneonline.org
Social Media: *Facebook, Twitter, YouTube, Flickr*

Robert L Woodson Sr, President
Clifford Ehrlich, Chair

Founded to help the residents of low-income neighborhoods address the problems of their communities. Mission is to transform lives, schools, and troubled neighborhoods, from the inside out. Current programs are the Violence-Free Zone youth violence reduction program; Training and Technical Assistance for Community-Based Organizations; and Adult Financial Literacy.
Founded in 1981

12055 Center for the Study of the Presidency and Congress (CSPC)

601 Thirteenth St, NW
Suite 1050N
Washington, DC 20005

202-872-9800
FAX 202-872-9811
E-Mail: email@thepresidency.org
Home Page: www.thepresidency.org
Social Media: *Facebook, Twitter, YouTube*

David M Abshire, Vice Chair
Maxmillian Angerholzer III, President/CEO
Dan Mahaffee, Director, Policy & Board Relations
Jonathan Murphy, Director, External Affairs
Elizabeth Perch, COO & CFO

CSPC strives to: promote leadership in the Presidency and Congress to generate innovative solutions to current national challenges; preserve the historic memory of the Presidency by identifying lessons from successes and failures of such leadership; draw on a wide range of talent to offer ways to better organize an increasingly compartmentalized Federal Government; educate and inspire the next generation of America's leaders to incorporate civility, inclusiveness, and character into their lives.

12056 Citizens Against Government Waste

1301 Pennsylvania Ave
Suite 1075
Washington, DC 20004

202-467-5300
FAX 202-467-4253
E-Mail: membership@cagw.org
Home Page: www.cagw.org
Social Media: *Facebook, Twitter, Youtube*

Thomas A Schatz, President
Ariane E Sweeney, VP, Membership & Development
Leslie K Paige, VP Policy & Communications
Robert J Tedeschi, Treasurer/CFO
William M. Christian, Director of Government Affairs

Public advocacy, non-partisan organization committed to eliminate government waste, fraud, abuse, mismanagement and inefficiency.
1MM+ Members
Founded in 1984
Mailing list available for rent

12057 Citizens for Global Solutions

420 7th St SE
Washington, DC 20003-2707

202-546-3950
FAX 202-546-3749
E-Mail: info@globalsolutions.org
Home Page: www.globalsolutions.org
Social Media: *Facebook, Twitter, YouTube*

Marvin Perry, CEO
Jordan Bankhead, MS, Chairman
Scott Paul,, Vice-Chair
Shirley Lee Davis, Secretary
Evan Freund, Treasurer

Nonprofit, tax deductible memebership organization of 50 chapters and groups throughout the United States. We work to educate policy-makers and the American public on issues of global governance, international law and grassroots activism.
11000 Members
Founded in 1978

12058 Coalition for Government Procurement

1990 M St NW
Suite 450
Washington, DC 20036-3466

202-331-0975
FAX 202-822-9788
E-Mail: info@thecgp.org
Home Page: www.thecgp.org
Social Media: *Facebook, Twitter, LinkedIn, Flickr, RSS*

Roger Waldron, President
Carolyn Alston, EVP & General Counsel
Robert Rendely, CFO
Denise Meliski, Director, Business Development
Matt Cahill, VP, Membership & Marketing

Representing commercial contractors in the Federal market. Advocating for common sense policies that improve the acquisition environment for government, industry and ultimately the American taxpayer. Focusing outreach efforts on the General Services Administration, Department of Veterans Affairs, Office of Management and Budget, Department of Defense, and Capitol Hill.
350 Members
Founded in 1979

12059 Commissioned Officers Association of the United States Public Health Service

8201 Corporate Dr
Suite 200
Landover, MD 20785-2230

301-731-9080
866-366-9593
FAX 301-731-9084
E-Mail: gfarrell@coausphs.org
Home Page: www.coausphs.org
Social Media: *Facebook*

Jim Currie, Executive Director
John McElligott, Deputy Executive Director
Teresa Hayden Foley, Chief Financial Officer
Judith Rensberger, Government Relations Director
Erica Robinson, Administrative Assistant

Protects the interests of the Commissioned Corps officers of the US Public Health Service, who are leaders in the realms of public and global health. Dedicated to improving and protecting the public health of the US by addressing unmet health needs and providing support.
7M Members

12060 Community Leadership Association

1240 S Lumpkin Street
Athens, GA 30602

706-542-0301
FAX 706-542-7007
E-Mail: sheena@claweb.org
Home Page: www.claweb.org

Gene A Honn, Executive Director

Organization dedicated to nurturing leadership in communities throughout the US and internationally. Members include hundreds of diverse community leadership organizations at local, state and national levels, thousands of individual graduates of these organizations and others interested in community leadership development.
2M Members
Founded in 1979

12061 Conference of Minority Public Administrators

PO Box 1552
Norfolk, VA 23510

301-333-5282
FAX 202-638-4952
E-Mail: info@compahr.org
Home Page: www.compahr.org
Social Media: *Facebook*

Stanley Skinner, President
Linda A. Harmon, President-Elect
Pamela Alexxander, Treasurer
Tiffany L. Smith, Recording Secretary
Lynn Cherry-Miller, Corresponding Secretary

COMPA is one of America's leading national organizations committed to excellence in public service and public administration in city, county, state and federal government.
500 Members
Founded in 1977

12062 Contract Services Association of America

1000 Wilson Boulevard
Suite 1800
Arlington, VA 22209-3920

703-243-2020
FAX 703-243-3601

Christopher Jahn, President

Represents the government services contracting industry. Membership ranges from small businesses and corporations servicing federal and state government in numerous capacities. CSA acts to foster the effective implementation of the government's policy of reliance on the private sector for support services.
650 Members
Founded in 1965

12063 Council of Chief State School Officers

One Massachusetts Ave. NW
Suite 700
Washington, DC 20001-1431

202-336-7000
FAX 202-408-8072
E-Mail: communications@ccsso.org
Home Page: www.ccsso.org
Social Media: *Facebook, Twitter, LinkedIn*

Chris Minnich, Executive Director
Bruce Buterbaugh, Chief Financial Officer

Nationwide, nonprofit organization is a voice for elementary and secondary school heads of departments to government and the public.

12064 Council of State Community Development Agencies
1825 K St NW
Suite 515
Washington, DC 20006-1261

202-293-5820
FAX 202-293-2820
E-Mail: info@coscda.org
Home Page: www.coscda.org

Steve Charleston, President
Keith Heaton, VP
Alison George, Secretary
Leslie Leager, Treasurer
Dianne E Taylor, Executive DIrector

The premier national association advocating and enhancing the leadership role of states in community development through innovative policy development and implementation, customer-driven technical assistance, education, and collaborative efforts.
Founded in 1974

12065 Council of State Governments
2760 Research Park Drive
PO Box 11910
Lexington, KY 40578-1910

859-244-8000
800-800-1910
FAX 859-244-8001
Home Page: www.csg.org
Social Media: *Facebook, Twitter, YouTube, RSS*

David Adkins, Executive Director & CEO
Brian Sandoval, President
Luis Fortuno, President-Elect
Sen. Carl Marcellino, Chair
Sen. Beau McCoy, Chair-Elect

Members include every elected and appointed state and territorial official in the US. A nonpartisan organization that brings state leaders together to share capitol ideas, providing them the chance to learn valuable lessons from each other. Also foster innovation in state government and shine a spotlight on examples of how ingenuity and leadership are transforming the way state government serves residents of the states and territories.
Founded in 1933

12066 Council of State Housing Agencies
Hall of States
444 N Capitol St NW
Suite 438
Washington, DC 20001-1505

202-624-7710
FAX 202-624-5899
E-Mail: bthompson@ncsha.org
Home Page: www.ncsha.org
Social Media: *Facebook, Twitter*

Brian A Hudson, President
Thomas R Gleason, Vice President
Grant S Whitaker, Secretary/Treasurer
Barbara J. Thompson, Executive Director
Cary D Knox, Executive Office Admin

A nonprofit, nonpartisan organization created to represent members in Washingtong before Congress, the Administration, and the several federal agencies concerned with housing, including the Department of Housing and Urban Development, the Department of Agriculture, and the Treasury, and with other advocates for affordable housing.

12067 Council on Licensure, Enforcement and Regulation
403 Marquis Ave
Suite 200
Lexington, KY 40502-2104

859-269-1289
FAX 859-231-1943
E-Mail: jhorne@clearhq.org

Home Page: www.clearhq.org
Social Media: *Facebook, Twitter, LinkedIn*

Robin Jenkins, President
Steve Hart, President-Elect
Adam Parfitt, Executive Director
Janet Horne, Office Manager
Rosa Brown, Administrative Associate

Members include occupational and professional licensing boards and agencies and private interests in the 50 states, territories and Canada.
380 Members
Founded in 1980

12068 Digital Government Institute
1934 Old Gallows Road
Suite 350
Vienna, VA 22182

703-752-6243
FAX 703-752-6201
E-Mail: info@digitalgovernment.com
Home Page: www.digitalgovernment.com
Social Media: *Facebook, Twitter, LinkedIn, Flickr*

Specializes in the design and production of leading edge educational programs on emerging trends and technologies for government IT management professionals. A trusted source for education, networking and results.
Founded in 1998

12069 Energy Bar Association
2000 M Street, N.W.,
Suite 715
Washington, DC 20036-3429

202-223-5625
FAX 202-833-5596
E-Mail: admin@eba-net.org
Home Page: www.eba-net.org
Social Media: *Facebook*

Richard Meyer, President
Emma Hand, President-Elect
Robert A. Weishaar, JR, Vice President
Caileen N. Gamache, Secretary
Noha Sidhom, Treasurer

An international, nonprofit association of attorneys and non-attorney professionals active in all areas of energy law. EBA's voluntary membership is comprised of government, corporate and private attorneys, as well as non-attorney professionals from across the globe, and includes law students interested in energy law.
2600 Members
Founded in 1946

12070 Federal Bar Association
1220 North Fillmore St.
Suite 444
Arlington, VA 22201

571-481-9100
FAX 571-481-9090
E-Mail: fba@fedbar.org
Home Page: www.fedbar.org
Social Media: *Facebook, Twitter, LinkedIn*

Karen Silberman, Executive Director
Stacy King, Executive Deputy Director
Heather Gaskins, Director, Development
Monique Dennis, Membership Coordinator
Maria Conticelli, Sections and Divisions Manager

Members are attorneys in the Federal Government or who have interest in federal law.
16000 Members
Founded in 1920

12071 Federal Criminal Investigators Association
5868 Mapledale Plaza
Suite 104
Woodbridge, VA 22193

630-969-8537
800-403-3374

E-Mail: info@fedcia.org
Home Page: www.fedcia.org

Mission of FCIA is to ensure that Federal Law Enforcement Professionals have the tools and the support network to meet the challenges of future criminal investigations while becoming more community oriented.
1500 Members
Founded in 1953

12072 Federal Facilities Council
500 Fifth St. NW
Washington, DC 20001

202-334-3374
FAX 202-334-3370
E-Mail: coskvig@nas.edu
Home Page:
sites.nationalacademies.org/DEPS/FFC/
Social Media: *Facebook, Twitter*

James Rispoli, Chair
Carmelo Melendez, Vice Chair

Operating under the auspices of the BICE, the FFC's mission is to identify and advance technologies, processes, and management practices that improve the performance of federal facilities over their entire life-cycle, from planning to disposal.
130 Members
Founded in 1953

12073 Federal Managers Association
1641 Prince St
Alexandria, VA 22314-2818

703-683-8700
FAX 703-683-8707
E-Mail: info@fedmanagers.org
Home Page: www.fedmanagers.org

Patricia A Niehaus, President
Dora L. Quinlan, VP
Christine C. Parker, Secretary
Katie L Smith, Treasurer
Todd V Wells, Executive Director

Advocates excellence in public service through effective management and professionalism, as well as the active representation of its members' interests and concerns.
15M Members
Founded in 1913

12074 Federal Physicians Association
12427 Hedges Run Drive
Suite 104
Lake Ridge, VA 22192

703-426-8400
877-333-7497
FAX 703-426-8400
E-Mail: info@fedphy.org
Home Page: www.fedphy.com

Brian J Ribiero, MD, President
Indira Jevaji, MD, VP
Michael Nesemann, MD, Treasurer
Michael Borecky, MD, Secretary

Represents and advocates for Physicians employed by the Federal Government.
400 Members
Founded in 1979

12075 Federation of Tax Administrators
444 N Capitol St NW
Suite 348
Washington, DC 20001-1538

202-624-5890
FAX 202-624-7888
Home Page: www.taxadmin.org

Gale Garriott, Executive Director
Michael Reissig, President
Dawn Cash, First Vice President
Julie Magee, Second Vice President
Kevin Sullivan, Secretary

Members are the tax agencies of the 50 state governments, the District of Columbia & New York City.
53 Members

12076 Fund for Constitutional Government

122 Maryland Ave NE
Washington, DC 20002-5610

202-546-3799
FAX 202-543-3156
E-Mail: info@fcgonline.org
Home Page: www.fcgonline.org

Anne B. Zill, President
John Cavanagh, Chairperson
Conrad Martin, Executive Director
Kat Saunders, Secretary
Steven Aftergood, Board Member

Seeks to expose and correct illegal activities, corruption, and lack of accountability in the federal government.
Founded in 1974

12077 Government Finance Officers Association

203 N La Salle St
Suite 2700
Chicago, IL 60601-1210

312-977-9700
FAX 312-977-4806
E-Mail: inquiry@gfoa.org
Home Page: www.gfoa.org

Heather A. Johnston, President
Marc Gonzales, President Elect
Jeffrey Esser, Executive Director, CEO
Robert Bishop, Finance Director
Frank C. Gambosi, Finance Director

The purpose of the Government Finance Officers Association is to enhance and promote the professional management of governments for the public benefit by identifying and developing financial policies and practices and promoting them through education, training and leadership.
17300 Members
Founded in 1906

12078 Hispanic Elected Local Officials

National League of Cities
1301 Pennsylvania Ave NW
Suite 550
Washington, DC 20004-1747

202-626-3169
FAX 202-626-3103
Home Page:
www.nlc.org/build-skills-and-networks/networks/constituency-group
Social Media: *Facebook, Twitter, LinkedIn, Youtube, RSS, Google+*

Oscar Trevino, President
Joel Navarro, 1st Vice President
Lydia N. Martinez, 2nd Vice President
Clarence E Anthony, Executive Director

Serves as a forum for communication and exchange among Hispanic local government officials within the framework of the National League of Cities.
100+ Members
Founded in 1976

12079 Housing Assistance Council

1025 Vermont Ave NW
Suite 606
Washington, DC 20005-3516

202-842-8600
FAX 202-347-3441
E-Mail: hac@ruralhome.org
Home Page: www.ruralhome.org
Social Media: *Facebook, Twitter, LinkedIn*

Moises Loza, Executive Director
Joe Belden, Senior Policy Analyst
Lilla Sutton, Executive Coordinator

Leslie Strauss, Senior Policy Analyst
Stephen Sugg, Government Relations

Expands the pool of decent housing available to the rural poor. Creates and sustains interest and action from all levels of government concerning rural housing for low-income people and helps rural housing organizations become more productive and professional.
30 Members
Founded in 1971

12080 Industry Coalition on Technology Transfer

1400 L St NW
Suite 800
Washington, DC 20005-3502

202-371-5994
FAX 202-371-5950

Coalition of major high technology trade associations concerned with the US Government export controls. Monitors and addresses federal regulations on technology transfer.
4 Members
Founded in 1983

12081 International Association of Correctional Training Personnel

PO Box 81826
Lincoln, NE 68501

312-341-6340
Home Page: www.iactp.org

Pete Norris, President
Tracy Reveal, President Elect
Mary O'Connor, Secretary
Terry Satterfield, Conference Coordinator
Joe Bouchard, Higher Education

Correctional officers and juvenile administrators.
9.5M Members
Founded in 1974

12082 International Association of Fire Chiefs

4025 Fair Ridge Drive
Fairfax, VA 22033-2868

703-273-0911
FAX 703-273-9363
Home Page: www.iafc.org
Social Media: *Facebook, LinkedIn*

Rhoda Mae Kerr, President & Chairman
John D. Sinclair, 1st Vice President
Thomas Jenkins, 2nd Vice President
Richard R. Carrizzo, Treasurer
Dan Eggleston, Director-at-Large

Represents the leadership of firefighters and emergency responders worldwide; members are the world's leading experts in firefighting, emergency medical services, terrorism response, hazardous materials spills, natural disasters, search and rescue, and public safety policy.
12000 Members
Founded in 1873

12083 International Association of Official Human Rights Agencies

444 N Capitol Street NW
Suite 536
Washington, DC 20001

202-624-5410
FAX 202-624-8185
E-Mail: iaohra@sso.org
Home Page: www.iaohra.org

Jean Kelleher Niebauer, President
Alisa Warren, 2nd Vice President
Paula Haley, Secretary
Merrill Smith, Jr., Treasurer
Robin S. Toma, First Vice-President

Private non-profit corporation consisting of human rights agencies in the US and Canada. Pro-

vides opportunities and forums for the exchange of ideas and information among human rights advocates. Also provides training opportunities for members and other concerned groups and organizations.
200 Members
Founded in 1968

12084 International City/County Management Association (ICMA)

777 North Capitol St. NE
Suite 500
Washington, DC 20002-4201

202-289-4262
800-745-8780
FAX 202-962-3500
Home Page: icma.org
Social Media: *Facebook, Twitter, LinkedIn, YouTube, Pinterest, Flickr*

Robert J. O'Neill, Executive Director

A worldwide organization for the advancement of professional local government.
Founded in 1914

12085 International Code Council

500 New Jersey Ave NW
6th Floor
Washington, DC 20001-2005

888-422-7233
FAX 202-783-2348
E-Mail: webmaster@iccsafe.org
Home Page: www.iccsafe.org
Social Media: *Facebook*

Alex Olszowy III, President
Dwayne Garriss, Vice President
Jay Elbettar, Secretary/Treasurer

A nonprofit membership association dedicated to preserving the public health, safety and welfare in the built environment through the promulgation of model codes suitable for adoption by governmental entities and assisting code enforcement officials, design professionals, builders, manufacturers and others involved in the design, construction and regulatory processes.
16M Members
Founded in 1915

12086 International Downtown Association

1025 Thomas Jefferson Street, NW
Sutie 500W
Washington, DC 20007

202-393-6801
FAX 202-393-6869
E-Mail: customerservice@ida-downtown.org
Home Page: www.ida-downtown.org
Social Media: *Facebook, Twitter, LinkedIn*

David Downey, President & CEO
Kevin Moran, Communications & IT Manager
Rebecca Bishophall, Manager, Membership Services
Tracie Clemmer, Development & Exhibits Director
Patricia Stephenson, Director, Finance & Administration

The International Downtown Association has member organizations worldwide in North America, Europe, Asia and Africa. Through a network of committed individuals, a rich body of knowledge and unique capacity to nurture community-building partnerships, IDA is a guiding force in creating healthy and dynamic centers that anchor the well being of towns, cities and regions of the world.
650+ Members
Founded in 1954

12087 International Economic Development Council

734 15th Street NW
Suite 900
Washington, DC 20005

202-223-7800
FAX 202-223-4745
Home Page: www.iedconline.org/
Social Media: *Facebook, Twitter, LinkedIn*

Dyan Lingle Brasington, CEc, Chair
Jeff Finkle, CEcD, President/CEO
Katelyn Palomo, Executive Assistant
Swati Ghosh, Director, Research
Carrie Mulcaire, Director, Federal Grants

Nonprofit membership organization dedicated to helping economic developmers do their job more effectively and raising the profile of the profession. Members create more high-quality jobs, develop more vibrant communities, and generally improve the quality of life in their regions.
1.8M Members
Founded in 1967

12088 Interstate Council on Water Policy

505 North Ivy Street
Arlington, VA 22220-1707

703-243-7383
FAX 301-984-5841
E-Mail: rpmueller1@mchsi.com
Home Page: www.icwp.org
Social Media: *Facebook, Twitter*

Dru Buntin, 2nd Vice-Chairman
Ryan Mueller, Executive Director
Andrew Dehoff, Secretary & Treasurer
Jerry Schulte, 1st Vice Chairman

The ICWP is the national organization of state and regional water resources management agencies. It provides a means for members to exchange information, ideas and experience to work with federal agencies which share water management responsibilities.
70 Members
Founded in 1959

12089 Interstate Oil and Gas Compact Commission

900 NE 23rd Street
Oklahoma City, OK 73105

405-525-3556
800-822-4015
FAX 405-525-3592
E-Mail: communications@iogcc.ok.gov
Home Page: www.iogcc.state.ok.us

Mike Smith, Executive Director
Gerry Baker, Associate Executive Director
Hannah Barton, Member Services Coordinator
Amy Childers, Federal Projects Manager
Carol Booth, CommunicationsÿManager

A multi-state government agency that champions the conservation and efficient recovery of domestic oil and natural gas resources.
700 Members
Founded in 1935

12090 National Academy of Public Administration

1600 K Street, NW
Suite 400
Washington, DC 20006

202-347-3190
FAX 202-223-0823
E-Mail: feedback@napawash.org
Home Page: www.napawash.org
Social Media: *Facebook, Twitter, LinkedIn, Vimeo*

Robert J. Shea, Chair
Nancy R. Kingsbury, Vice Chair
Dan G. Blair, President and CEO

Tom Reidy, Chief Financial Officer
Lisa Trahan, Director of Fellow Relations

Through its trusted and experienced leaders, the Academy improves the quality, performance, and accountability of governments in the nation and the world.
500 Members
Founded in 1967

12091 National Affordable Housing Management Association

400 N Columbus Street
Suite 203
Alexandria, VA 22314

703-683-8630
FAX 703-683-8634
Home Page: www.nahma.org

Kris Cook, Executive Director
Larry Keys, Jr., Director, Government Affairs
Rajni Agarwal, Director, Finance
Brenda Moser, Director, Meetings & Membership
Scott McMillen, Coordinator, Government Affairs

The leading voice for affordable housing, advocating on behalf of multifamily property managers and owners whose mission is to provide quality affordable housing. Membership includes the industry's most distinguished multi-family managers, owners, and industry stakeholders.
3000 Members
Founded in 1990

12092 National Alliance of State and Territorial AIDS Directors

444 N Capitol St NW
Suite 339
Washington, DC 20001

202-434-8090
FAX 202-434-8092
E-Mail: nastad@nastad.org
Home Page: www.nastad.org
Social Media: *Facebook, Twitter, LinkedIn, Blogger, Youtube*

Julie Scofield, Executive Director
Addis Tilahun, Senior Manager Finance & Accounting
Anna Carroll, Manager Global Program
Anne Redmond Sites, Manager Global Program
Brent Parker, Senior Director

NASTAD strengthens state and territory-based leadership, expertise, and advocacy and brings them to bear in reducing the incidence of HIV and viral hepatitis infections and on providing care and support to all who live with HIV/AIDS and viral hepatitis. NASTAD's vision is a world free of HIV/AIDS and viral hepatitis.
59 Members
Founded in 1992

12093 National Assembly of State Arts Agencies

1200 18th Street NW
Suite 1100
Washington, DC 20036

202-347-6352
FAX 202-737-0526
E-Mail: nasaa@nasaa-arts.org
Home Page: www.nasaa-arts.org
Social Media: *Facebook*

Pam Breaux, Chief Executive Officer
Kelly J. Barsdate, Chief Program and Planning Officer
Laura S. Smith, CFRE, Chief Advancement Officer
Sharon Gee, Director of Meetings and Events

Unites, represents and serves the nation's state and jurisdictional arts agencies. Representing state arts agencies by empowering their work

through knowledge, and advance the arts as an essential public benefit.
56 Members
Founded in 1968

12094 National Association for County Community and Economic Development

2025 M St NW
Suite 800
Washington, DC 20036-3309

202-367-1149
FAX 202-367-2149
Home Page: www.nacced.org

John Murphy, Executive Director
Tony Agliata, President
Jim Vazquez, Vice President
Chuck Robbins, Secretary/Treasurer
Bill J. Lake, Director

Purpose is to develop the technical capacity of county government practitioners to professionally administer federally-funded affordable housing, community development, and economic development programs that benefit their low- and moderate-income households.
120+ Members
Founded in 1989

12095 National Association for Search and Rescue

PO Box 232020
Centreville, VA 20120-2020

703-222-6277
877-893-0702
FAX 703-222-6277
E-Mail: meganr@nasar.org
Home Page: www.nasar.org

Monty Bell, President
Christopher Boyer, Executive Director
Ross Robinson, Chief Financial Officer
Ellen Wingerd, Customer Care Manager
Mike Vorachek, Secretary

A not-for-profit membership association dedicated to advancing professional, literary, and scientific knowledge in fields related to search and rescue.
3M Members

12096 National Association of Clean Air Agencies

444 N Capitol Street NW
Suite 307
Washington, DC 20001-1506

202-624-7864
FAX 202-624-7863
E-Mail: 4cleanair@4cleanair.org
Home Page: www.4cleanair.org

Stu A Clark, Co-President
Merlyn Hough, Co-President
Bill Becker, Executive Director
Nancy Kruger, Deputy Director
Dave Klemp, Co-Vice President

Represents state and local air pollution control officers from over 150 major metropolitan areas and 53 states and territories.

12097 National Association of Conservation Districts (NACD)

509 Capitol Court, NE
Washington, DC 20002-4937

202-547-6223
FAX 202-547-6450
Home Page: www.nacdnet.org
Social Media: *Facebook, Twitter, LinkedIn, Vimeo, Google Plus, Flickr*

Earl Garber, President
Lee McDaniel, First Vice President
Brent Van Dyke, Second Vice President
John Larson, Chief Executive Officer

Laura Wood Peterson, Director of Government Affairs

NACD develops national conservation policies, influences lawmakers and builds partnerships with other agencies and organizations. NACD also provides services to its districts to help them share ideas in order to better serve their local communities.
17000 Members
Founded in 1946

12098 National Association of Counties
25 Massachusetts Ave NW
Suite 500
Washington, DC 20001-1450

202-393-6226
888-407-6226
FAX 202-393-2630
E-Mail: nacomeetings@naco.org
Home Page: www.naco.org/
Social Media: *Facebook, Twitter, LinkedIn, YouTube*

Linda Langston, President
Riki Hokama, 1st Vice President
Sallie Clark, 2nd Vice President
Matthew D. Chase, Executive Director
Karen McRunnel, Executive Assistant to the CEO

The National Association of Counties (NACo) is an organization that represents county governments in the United States. NACo advances issues with a unified voice before the federal government, improves the public's understanding of county government, and assists counties in finding and sharing innovative solutions through education and research. NACo's membership totals more than 2,000 counties, representing over 80 percent of the nation's population.
Founded in 1935

12099 National Association of County Engineers
25 Mass. Ave, NW
Suite 580
Washington, DC 20001-1454

202-393-5041
FAX 202-393-2630
E-Mail: nace@naco.org
Home Page: www.countyengineers.org

Brian C Roberts, Executive Director
Rebecca Page, Director of Marketing & Membership
Constantine Connie Radoulovitch, Office Manager
Duane J. Ratermann, President
Brian D. Stacy, President Elect

Members are county engineering professionals or road management authorities.
1900 Members
Founded in 1956

12100 National Association of Development Organizations (NADO)
400 N Capitol St NW
Suite 390
Washington, DC 20001-6505

202-624-7806
FAX 202-624-8813
E-Mail: info@nado.org
Home Page: www.nado.org
Social Media: *Facebook, Twitter, RSS*

Terry Bobrowski, President
Vicki Glass, Director of Meetings and Membership
Susan Howard, Director of Government Relations
Brian Kelsey, Director of Economic Development
Carrie Kissel, Associate Director

The National Association of Development Organizations (NADO) serves as the national voice for regional development organizations. NADO helps its members achieve their goals by providing effective advocacy and lobbying services at the federal level, producing timely information and research, and offering opportunities for professional and organizational growth.

12101 National Association of Government Archives & Records Administrators
444 N. Capitol Street, NW
Suite 237
Washington, DC 20001-6505

202-508-3800
FAX 202-508-3801
E-Mail: nagara@caphill.com
Home Page: www.nagara.org
Social Media: *LinkedIn*

Pari Swift, President
Patty Davis, Vice President
Jannette Goodall, Secretary
Galen R. Wilson, Treasurer
Steve Grandin, Membership Services & Publications

Professional association dedicated to the improvement of federal, state, and local government records and information management and the professional development of government records administrators and archivists. Members include county, municipal, and special district governments, state agencies, the National Archives and Records Administration; individual federal employees; the General Archives of Puerto Rico; and a number of provincial and institutional programs.
Founded in 1974

12102 National Association of Housing and Redevelopment Officials
630 Eye Street, NW
Washington, DC 20001-3736

202-289-3500
877-866-2476
FAX 202-289-8181
E-Mail: nahro@nahro.org
Home Page: www.nahro.org

Saul Ramirez, Executive Director
Donald J Cameron, Senior VP
Joseph E Gray Jr, VP
Elizabeth C Morris, VP Housing
Saul Ramirez, Manager

A professional membership association representing local housing authorities, community development agencies and individual professionals in the housing, community development and redevelopment fields.
700 Members
Founded in 1933

12103 National Association of Local Housing Finance Agencies
2025 M St NW
Suite 800
Washington, DC 20036-2422

202-367-1197
FAX 202-367-2197
E-Mail: info@nalhfa.org
Home Page: www.nalhfa.org

Ron Williams, President
W. D. Morris, Vice President
Vivian Benjamin, Treasurer
Tom Cummings, Secretary

The national association of professionals working to finance affordable housing in the broader community development context at the local level. Nonprofit association working as an advocate before Congress and federal agencies on legislative and regulatory issues affecting affordable housing and provides technical assistance and educational opportunities to its members and the public.
Founded in 1982

12104 National Association of Neighborhoods
1300 Pennsylvania Ave NW
Suite 700
Washington, DC 20004-3024

202-332-7766
FAX 202-588-5881
E-Mail: info@nanworld.org
Home Page: www.nanworld.org

Sam Thompson Jr., Board Member
Debra K. Powell, Board Member

Mission is to improve the quality of life in the nation's most important communities- its neighborhoods. Remains an organization of neighborhood coalitions, block clubs, community councils, and individuals, united by a love of neighborhoods and a strong determination to make them better.
2500+ Members
Founded in 1975

12105 National Association of Postmasters of the United States
8 Herbert St
Alexandria, VA 22305-2600

703-683-9027
FAX 703-683-6820
E-Mail: napusinfo@napus.org
Home Page: www.napus.org

Robert J. Rapoza, President
Michael E. Quinn, Secretary/ Treasurer

Mission is to represent, promote, and protect postmasters. To foster a favorable image of public service and to assure users of the mail the best possible service. To be an advocate with the Congress of the United States. And to work closely with the United States Postal Service in the development of strategies for the enhancement of Postmasters and the Postal Service.
41M Members
Founded in 1898

12106 National Association of Regional Councils
777 North Caoitol Street NE
Suite 305
Washington, DC 20002

202-618-5696
FAX 202-986-1038
E-Mail: lindsey@narc.org
Home Page: www.narc.org
Social Media: *Twitter*

Joanna Turner,, Executive Director
Lindsey Riley, Deputy of Communications
Leslie Wollack,, Deputy Executive Director
Mia Colson,, Grants Manager

State of regional repositories of instructional materials or services.
250 Members
Founded in 1965

12107 National Association of Regulatory Utility Commissioners (NARUC)
1101 Vermont Ave NW
Suite 200
Washington, DC 20005-3553

202-898-2200
FAX 202-898-2213
E-Mail: admin@naruc.org
Home Page: www.naruc.org

Lisa Polak Edgar, President
Travis Kavulla, 1st Vice President
Robert F Powellson, 2nd Vice President
Charles D. Gray, Executive Director
David E. Ziegner, Treasurer

Representing the State Public Service Commissioners who regulate essential utility services, including energy, telecommunications, and water. Members are responsible for assuring reliable utility service at fair, just, and reasonable rates. The Association is an invaluable resource for members and the regulatory community, providing a venue to set and influence public policy, share best practices, and foster innovative solutions to improve regulation.
Founded in 1889

12108 National Association of State Development

12884 Harbor Drive
Woodbridge, VA 22192

703-490-6777
FAX 703-880-0509

Miles Friedman, President/CEO
Sally Pope, Director Finance
Pofen Salem, Project Manager

Established to provide a forum for directors of state economic development agencies to exchange information, compare programs, and establish an organizational base to approach the Federal Government on issues of mutual interest.
250 Members
Founded in 1946

12109 National Association of State Facilities

2760 Research Park Drive
PO Box 11910
Lexington, KY 40578-1910

859-244-8000
800-800-1910
FAX 859-244-8001
E-Mail: membership@csg.org
Home Page: www.csg.org
Social Media: *Facebook, Twitter, YouTube, RSS*

Carl Marcellino, Chair
Gov. Brian Sandoval, President
Sen. Kelvin Atkinson, Vice Chair
Sen. Beau McCoy, Chair-Elect
David Adkins, Executive Director/CEO

Brings state leaders together to share capitol ideas, providing them the chance to learn valuable lessons from each other. Fosters innovation in state government and shining a spotlight on examples of how ingenuity and leaderhsip are transforming the way state government serves residents of the states and territories.
Founded in 1933

12110 National Association of Towns and Townships

1130 Connecticut Ave NW
Suite 300
Washington, DC 20036-3981

202-454-3950
866-830-0008
FAX 202-331-1598
Home Page: www.natat.org

Larry Merrill, President
Matthew DeTemple, Vice President
Jennifer Imo, Federal Director
Bill Hanka, Deputy Federal Director
Mark Limbaugh, Senior Advisor

Seeks flexible and alternative approaches to federal policies to ensure that small communities can meet federal requirements. Advocates for fair share funding, technical assistance, and other affirmative steps to address the inherent disadvantages that small governments face in our present intergovernmental system.
13M Members

12111 National Border Patrol Council

2445 Fifth Ave.
Suite 350
San Diego, CA 92101

520-219-5152
800-620-1613
FAX 520-219-5154
Home Page: www.nbpc1613.org
Social Media: *Facebook*

James Harlan, President
Dan Mais, 1st Vice President
Terence Shigg, 2nd Vice President
Robert Lopez, 3rd Vice President
Victor Cantu, Treasurer

Exlusive representative for non-supervisory Border Patrol Agents and support personnel assigned to the San Diego Sector of the United States Border Parol.
69000 Members
Founded in 1965

12112 National Community Development Association

522 21st St NW
#120
Washington, DC 20006-5012

202-293-7587
FAX 202-887-5546
Home Page: www.ncdaonline.org
Social Media: *LinkedIn*

Cardell Cooper, Executive Director
Vicki Watson, Assistant Director
Karen Parker, Operations Manager

National nonprofit organization at the forefront in securing effective and responsive housing and community development programs for local governments. Provides timely, direct information and technical support to its members on federal housing and community development programs.
550+ Members

12113 National Conference of State Legislatures

National Conference of State Legislatures
7700 E 1st Pl
Denver, CO 80230-7143

303-364-7700
FAX 303-364-7800
E-Mail: ncslnet-admin@ncsl.org.
Home Page: www.ncsl.org
Social Media: *Facebook, Twitter, LinkedIn, Youtube*

Terie Norelli, President
Jean Cantrell, Vice President
Patsy Spaw, Secretary/Treasurer

A bipartisan organization that serves the legislators and staffs of the nation's 50 states, its commonwealths and territories.
Cost: $49.00
15000 Members
Circulation: 18000
ISSN: 0147-0644
Founded in 1975
Printed in 4 colors

12114 National Council of State EMS Training Coordinators

201 Park Washington Court
Falls Church, VA 22046

888-240-4696
FAX 703-241-5603
Home Page: www.nscemstc.org

Members are supervisors or coordinators of state EMS training programs, and limited to three from each state.

12115 National Council of State Housing Agencies

Hall of States

444 N Capitol St NW
Suite 438
Washington, DC 20001-1505

202-624-7710
FAX 202-624-5899
E-Mail: bthompson@ncsha.org
Home Page: www.ncsha.org
Social Media: *Facebook, Twitter*

Thomas R. Gleason, President
Grant S. Whitaker, Vice President
Barbara J. Thompson, Executive Director
Maury L. Edwards, Director of Meetings
Kevin B. Burke, CPA, Director of Finance and Operations

NCSHA represents its members in Washington before Congress, the Administration, and the several federal agencies concerned with housing, including the Department of Housing and Urban Development, the Department of Agriculture, and the Treasury, and with other advocates for affordable housing.
350 Members
Founded in 1974

12116 National District Attorneys Association

99 Canal Center Plaza
Suite 330
Alexandria, VA 22314-1548

703-549-9222
FAX 703-836-3195
Home Page: www.ndaa.org
Social Media: *Facebook*

Kay Chopard Cohen, Executive Director
Rick Hasey, CFO
Richard Hanes, Chief of Staff
Duane Kokesch, Director, Traffic Program
Allie Phillips, Deputy Director

Serves as a nationwide, interdisciplinary resource center for training, research, technical assistance, and publications reflecting the highest standards and cutting-edge practices of the prosecutorial profession.
7000 Members
Founded in 1950

12117 National Emergency Management Association

2760 Research Park Drive
Lexington, KY 40578

859-244-8000
FAX 859-244-8239
E-Mail: nemaadmin@csg.org
Home Page: www.nemaweb.org
Social Media: *Facebook*

Bryan Koon, President
Wendy Smith-Reeve, Vice President
Trina R. Sheets, NEMA Executive Director
Beverly Bell, Senior Policy Analyst
Karen Cobuluis, Meeting & Marketing Coordinator

A nonpartisan, nonprofit association dedicated to enhancing public safety by improving the nation's ability to prepare for, respond to, and recover from all emergencies, disasters, and threats to our nation's security. Provides national leadership and expertise in comprehensive emergency management, serves as a vital emergency management information and assistance resource, and advances continuous improvement in emergency management.
263 Members
Founded in 1970

12118 National Forum for Black Public Administrators

777 N Capitol St NE
Suite 807
Washington, DC 20002-4291

202-408-9300
FAX 202-408-8558

E-Mail: webmaster@nfbpa.org
Home Page: www.nfbpa.org
Social Media: *Facebook, YouTube*

Verdenia C. Baker, President
Bruce T. Moore, 1st Vice President
Regina V. K. Williams, Interim Executive Director
Malick Diagne, Fiscal Director
Yvette Harris, Membership Coordinator

Committed to strengthening the position of Blacks within the field of public administration; increasing the number of Blacks appointed to executive positions in public service organizations; and, to groom and prepare younger, aspiring administrators for senior public management posts in the years ahead.
2.8M Members
Founded in 1983

12119 National Governors' Association
Hall of States
444 N Capitol St
Suite 267
Washington, DC 20001-1512

202-624-5300
FAX 202-624-5313
E-Mail: webmaster@nga.org
Home Page: www.nga.org
Social Media: *Facebook, Twitter*

Governor Mary Fallin, Chair
Governor John Hickenlooper, Vice Chair
Dan Crippen, Executive Director
Barry Anderson, Deputy Director
David Quam, Deputy Director, Policy

Coordinates the formulation of state policies by governors, and works to ensure consideration of these positions in the development of national policies and programs. The governors belong to seven standing committees: agriculture; community and economic development; justice and public protection; energy and environment; human resources; international trade; and foreign relations.
Founded in 1908

12120 National Housing Law Project
703 Market Street
Suite 2000
San Francisco, CA 94103

415-546-7000
FAX 415-546-7007
E-Mail: nhlp@nhlp.org
Home Page: www.nhlp.org

Robert C. Pearman, Jr., Chairperson
John Relman, Vice Chair
Gideon Anders, Senior Staff Attorney
Catherine M. Bishop, Senior Staff Attorney
James R. Grow, Deputy Director

A nonprofit corporation that provides assistance on public and private housing and community development matters to Legal Services attorneys and housing specialists throughout the country. The project's goals are to produce, maintain and conserve low and moderate income housing and protect and expand the rights of lower income persons to decent and affordable housing.
Founded in 1968

12121 National Institute of Governmental Purchasing/NIGP
2411 Dulles Corner Park
Suite 350
Herndon, VA 20170-5223

703-736-8900
800-367-6447
FAX 703-736-9639
E-Mail: grante@co.cape-may.nj.us

Home Page: www.nigp.org
Social Media: *Facebook, Twitter, LinkedIn*

Marcheta E. Gillespie, CPPO, CPPB,; President
Rick Grimm, CPPO, CPPB, Chief Executive Officer
Brent Maas, Executive Director, Business
Catherine Patin, Communications Manager
Carol Hodes, CAE, Executive Director

An international not-for-profit educational and technical organization of public purchasing agencies. NIGP develops, supports and promotes the public procurement profession through premier educational and research programs, professional support, and advocacy initiatives that benefit members and constituents.
2600+ Members
Founded in 1944

12122 National League of Cities
1301 Pennsylvania Ave NW
Suite 550
Washington, DC 20004-1747

202-626-3180
877-827-2385
FAX 202-626-3043
E-Mail: info@nlc.org
Home Page: www.nlc.org
Social Media: *Facebook, Twitter, LinkedIn, RSS, Youtube, Google Plus*

Ralph Becker, President
Melodee Colbert Kean, 1st Vice President
Matt Zone, 2nd Vice President
Clarence Anthony, Executive Director
David DeLorenzo, Chief Digital Officer

Dedicated to helping city leaders build better communities. The NLC advocates for cities and towns, provides programs and services, provides opportunities for involvement and networking, keeps leaders informed, strengthens leadership skills, recognizes municipal achievements, partners with state leagues, and promotes cities and towns.
1700 Members
Founded in 1924

12123 National Public Employer Labor Relations Association
1012 South Coast Highway
Suite M
Oceanside, CA 92054

760-433-1686
877-673-5721
FAX 760-433-1687
E-Mail: mike@npelra.org
Home Page: www.npelra.org
Social Media: *Facebook, Twitter, LinkedIn*

Michael T. Kolb, Executive Director
Yvonne Gillengerten, Operations Manager
Janessa Stephens, Association Specialist
Allison Wittwer, Administrative Assistant
Stephanie Biggs, Administrative Assistant

Provides Professional Development, Networking, and Advocacy Services to Labor Relations & Human Resources professionals, so that public sector employers may deliver the most efficient and effective services to citizens & taxpayers.
2000+ Members
Founded in 1971

12124 National Rural Housing Coalition
1331 G St NW
10th FL
Washington, DC 20002

202-393-5229
FAX 202-393-3034
Home Page: www.nrhcweb.org
Social Media: *Facebook, Twitter*

Karen Speakman, President
Marty Miller, 1st Vice President
Kathleen Tyler, 2nd Vice President

Hope Cupit, Secretary
Lee Beaulac, Treasurer

Works to focus policy makers on the needs of rural areas by direct advocacy and by coordinating a network of rural housing advocates around the nation. National Rural Housing Coalition is supported entirely by donations, contributions and subscriptions.
300 Members
Founded in 1969

12125 National Urban League
120 Wall St.
New York, NY 10005

212-558-5300
FAX 212-344-5332
Home Page: nul.iamempowered.com
Social Media: *Facebook, Twitter, LinkedIn, YouTube*

Marc H. Morial, President & CEO
Paul Wycisk, SVP & Chief Financial Officer
Nicolaine M. Lazare, SVP & General Counsel

Historic civil rights organization focused on improving quality of life in underserved urban communities.
Founded in 1911

12126 National WIC Association
2001 S Street NW
Suite 580
Washington, DC 20009-1165

202-232-5492
FAX 202-387-5281
E-Mail: crichardson@nwica.org
Home Page: www.nwica.org
Social Media: *Facebook, Twitter, Pinterest*

Jacqueline Marlette-Boras, Chair
Douglas Greenaway, President & CEO
Cecilia Richardson, Staff/Nutrition Programs Director
Robert A. Lee, Membership Coordinator
Samantha Lee, Communications, Media and Marketing

NWA is the proactive voice supporting, inspiring and empowering the WIC Community through creativity, teamwork and leadership to serve America's low-income, high-risk women, infants and children.
900 Members
Founded in 1979

12127 North American Gaming Regulators Association
1000 Westgate Drive
Suite 252
St Paul, MN 55114-8612

651-203-7244
FAX 651-290-2266
E-Mail: info@nagra.org
Home Page: www.nagra.org

Lisa M. Christiansen, President
Dave Jeseritz, Vice President
Tracy L. Bigelow, Treasurer
Craig Durbin, Secretary

A nonprofit professional association of gaming regulators throughout North America. The organization brings together agencies that regulate gaming activities and provides them a forum for the mutual exchange of regulatory information and techniques. Collecting and disseminating regulatory and enforcement information, procedures, and experiences from all jurisdictions provides on-going gaming education and training for all members.
120 Members
Founded in 1984

12128 North American Securities Administrators Association, Inc.

750 First Street NE
Suite 1140
Washington, DC 20002-8034

202-737-0900
FAX 202-783-3571
Home Page: www.nasaa.org
Social Media: *Facebook, RSS*

Judith Shaw, President
Russ Iuculano, Executive Director
John H. Lynch, Deputy Executive Director
Joseph Brady, General Counsel
Michael Canning, Director of Policy

NASAA is the international organization representing securities administrators from all 50 states, the District of Columbia, Canada, Mexico and Puerto Rico, and is responsible for investor protection and education. NASAA recommends national policies in the securities industry and provides model legislation for state securities agencies to adopt affecting the regulation of broker/dealers and investment advisers. Consumers can contact NASAA to get phone numbers of state securities regulators.
66 Members
Founded in 1919

12129 Patent and Trademark Office Society

PO Box 2089
Arlington, VA 22202-0089

703-305-8340
Home Page: www.ptos.org

Matthew Troutman, President
Brandon Rosati, Vice President
David Sosnowski, Secretary
Fred Guillermety, Administrator
Tsung-Yin Tsai, Treasurer

Internationally recognized for its activities in the patent and trademark fields. The Society has actively influenced the patent and trademark systems- promoting the systems' growth and well-being.
1800 Members
Founded in 1917
Mailing list available for rent

12130 Procurement Round Table

1464 Nieman Road
Shady Side, MD 20764

301-261-9918
Home Page: www.procurementroundtable.org

Allan V. Burman, Chairman
Bill Gormley, Vice Chair
Kenneth J. Oscar, Treasurer

Chartered by former federal acquisition officials concerned about the economy, efficiency and effectiveness of the federal acquisition system. Its Directors and Officers are private citizens who serve pro bono with the objective of advising and assisting the government in making improvements in federal acquisition.
40 Members
Founded in 1984

12131 Public Employees Roundtable

PO Box 75248
Washington, DC 20013-5248

202-927-4926
FAX 202-927-4920
Home Page: www.theroundtable.org

Committed to helping future public servants reach their goals. Supporting young people planning careers in public service through the scholarship, fellowship and internship programs of its members.

12132 Public Housing Authorities Directors Association

511 Capitol Court NE
Washington, DC 20002-4947

202-546-5445
FAX 202-546-2280
Home Page: www.phada.org

Timothy Kaiser, Executive Director
Ted Van Dyke, Director of Government Affairs
Yaniv Goury, Director of Communications
Jim Armstrong, Policy Analyst
Kathleen Whalen, Policy Analyst

Represents and serves the needs of executive directors of housing authorities of all sizes, in all regions of the nation. In pursuing the Association's goal of improving assisted housing, the corporation works with Congress and federal agencies as well as with all interested groups to improve the nation's housing programs.
1.6M Members
Founded in 1979

12133 Republican Communications Association

Longworth House Office Building
1317 Longworth
PO Box 550
Washington, DC 20515-0001

E-Mail: RCA@mail.house.gov
Home Page: www.rcaweb.org

Neal Patel, President
Tom Wilbur, Vice-President
Shea Snider, Treasurer
Michael Marinaccio, Digital Director
John Cummins, Professional Development Director

Sponsors professional development and networking programs. Conducts seminars, briefings, and tours.
165 Members
Founded in 1970

12134 Society of Government Economists

PO Box 77082
Washington, DC 20013

202-643-1743
E-Mail: sge@sge-econ.org
Home Page: www.sge-econ.org

Robert Lerman, President
Julia Lane, Vice-President
Marvin Ward, Executive Director
Andrew Felton, Website Director
Brian Sloboda, Outreach Director and Event Planner

Supports the professional development of government economists, and those who are interested in public policy economics, by providing them with research, publications, and professional communication opportunities.
500 Members
Founded in 1970

12135 State Government Affairs Council

515 King Street
Suite 325
Alexandria, VA 22314

703-684-0967
FAX 703-684-0968
E-Mail: eloudy@sgac.org
Home Page: www.sgac.org
Social Media: *Facebook, Twitter, LinkedIn*

Gerard Dehrmann, President
Elizabeth A. Loudy, Executive Director
Donna Gehlhaart, Vice President
Crislyn Lumia, Director, Education & Training
Kate Necaise, Manager, Communications

The premier national association for multi-state government affairs professionals, providing op-

portunities for networking and professional development.
260 Members
Founded in 1981

12136 State Higher Education Executive Officers Association

3035 Center Green Drive
Suite 100
Boulder, CO 80301-2205

303-541-1600
FAX 303-541-1639
E-Mail: sheeo@sheeo.org
Home Page: www.sheeo.org
Social Media: *Twitter*

Peter A. Blake, Chair
George Pernsteiner, President
Julie Carnahan, Senior Associate
Glady Kerns, Director of Administration
Eileen I. Klein, Treasurer

A nonprofit, nationwide association of the chief executive officers serving statewide coordinating boards and governing boards of postsecondary education.
56 Members
Founded in 1954

12137 The National Association for State Community Services Programs

111 K Street NE
Suite 300
Washington, DC 20002

202-624-5866
FAX 202-624-8472
E-Mail: nascsp@nascsp.org
Home Page: www.nascsp.org
Social Media: *Facebook, Twitter*

Jenae Bjelland, Executive Director
Joan Harris, Director
Brad Penney, General Counsel
Gretchen Knowlton, Policy Director
Tabitha Beck, Research Director

The premier national association charged with advocating and enhancing the leadership role of states in preventing and reducing poverty.
100 Members
Founded in 1968

12138 Trust for Public Land

101 Montgomery Street
Suite 900
San Francisco, CA 94104

415-495-4014
FAX 415-495-4103
E-Mail: info@tpl.org
Home Page: www.tpl.org
Social Media: *Facebook, Twitter, Youtube*

William Rogers, President & CEO
Brian Beitner, Chief Investment Officer
Sean Connolly, Chief Marketing Officer
Ernest Cook, Senior Vice President
Kathy DeCoster, Vice President

A nonprofit land acquisition and conservation organization, working with community groups, landowners, public land management agencies and rural groups to preserve open space lands and to pioneer methods of community ownership of land. Through its Investment Lands Program, the Trust for Public Land also acquires underutilized properties by gift or bargain sales.
Founded in 1972

12139 U.S. Chamber of Commerce

1615 H St Nw
Washington, DC 20062-2000

202-659-6000
800-638-6582
FAX 202-463-5836
E-Mail: press@uschamber.com

Home Page: www.uschamber.org
Social Media: *Facebook, Twitter*

Thomas J Donohue, President & CEO
David C. Chavern, Executive Vice President
Myron Brilliant, Executive Vice President
Lily Fu Claffee, Senior Vice President
Shannon DiBari, Senior Vice President

The mission of the Chamber of Commerce is to advance human progress through an economic, political and social system based on individual freedom, incentive, initiative, opportunity, and responsibility. The Chamber of Commerce provides a voice of experience and influence in Washington, D.C., and around the globe, fighting for business and free enterprise before Congress, the White House, regulatory agencies, and the courts.

12140 United States Conference of Mayors
1620 Eye Street, NW
Washington, DC 20006-4033

202-293-7330
FAX 202-293-2352
E-Mail: info@usmayors.org
Home Page: www.usmayors.org
Social Media: *Facebook, Twitter*

Mayor Scott Smith, President
Mayor Kevin Johnson, Vice President
Mayor Stephanie Rawlings-Blake, 2nd Vice President
Tom Cochran, CEO and Executive Director

Primary roles are to promote development of policies, strengthen federal-city relationships, ensure federal policy meets urban needs, provide mayors with leadership and management tools, and create a forum in which mayors can share ideas and information.
30000 Members
Founded in 1987

12141 United States Interagency Council on Homelessness
Federal Center SW
409 Third St. SW Suite 310
Washington, DC 20024

202-708-4663
FAX 202-708-1216
E-Mail: usich@usich.gov
Home Page: www.ich.gov
Social Media: *Facebook, Twitter*

Barbara Poppe, Executive Director

Mission is to coordinate the federal response to homelessness and to create a national partnership at every level of government and with the private sector to reduce and end homelessness in the nation while maximizing the effectiveness of the Federal Government in contributing to the end of homelessness.
Founded in 1987

12142 Urban Land Institute
1025 Thomas Jefferson St NW
Suite 500 West
Washington, DC 20007-5230

202-624-7000
FAX 202-624-7140
E-Mail: ulifoundation@uli.org
Home Page: www.uli.org
Social Media: *Facebook, Twitter, LinkedIn, YouTube, Flickr, Google Plus*

Randall Rowe, Chairman
Patrick L. Phillips, Chief Executive Officer
Michael Terseck, CFO
Kathleen B. Carey, Chief Content Officer
Jason Ray, Chief Technology Officer

Founded to provide a land-use information resource for both the professionals and the public. ULI conducts seminars, workshops, semiannual meetings, research programs and publishes books on all aspects of land use and development issues. ULI offers an advisory

service, and gives annual Awards for Excellence.
14M Members
Founded in 1936

12143 Urban and Regional Information Systems Association
701 Lee Street
Suite 680
Des Plaines, IL 60016-4508

847-824-6300
FAX 847-824-6363
E-Mail: info@urisa.org
Home Page: www.urisa.org
Social Media: *Facebook, Twitter, LinkedIn*

Rebecca Somers, President
Wendy Nelson, Executive Director
Keri Brennan, GISP, Education Manager
Patricia Francis, Meeting Coordinator
Verlanda McBride, Registrar & Database Manager

Concerned with the effective use of information systems technology at the state, regional and local levels. Members informed of current developments in the information systems field. Its goal is to stimulate and encourage the advancement of an interdisciplinary professional approach to planning, designing and operating information systems.
3000 Members
Founded in 1963

12144 Western Governor's Association
1600 Broadway
Suite 1700
Denver, CO 80202

303-623-9378
FAX 303-534-7309
Home Page: www.westgov.org
Social Media: *Facebook, Twitter, LinkedIn, Google+, Pinterest*

James Ogbury, Executive Director
Holly Propst, Deputy Executive Director

Association for policy development, information exchange and collective action by the Governors of 19 Western states and 3 US-flag Pacific islands.
Founded in 1984

Newsletters

12145 ADA Today
Americans for Democratic Action
1625 K St NW
Suite 102
Washington, DC 20006-1611

202-785-5980
FAX 202-785-5969
E-Mail: info@adaction.org
Home Page: www.adaction.org

David Card, Editor

The nation's oldest liberal lobbying group. This newsletter describes national and local chapter activities and updates federal legislative action.
Cost: $20.00
Frequency: Quarterly
Circulation: 65000
Mailing list available for rent: 65000 names
Printed in 2 colors on matte stock

12146 ADAction News and Notes
Americans for Democratic Action
1625 K St NW
Suite 210
Washington, DC 20006-1611

202-785-5980
FAX 202-785-5969

E-Mail: info@adaction.org
Home Page: www.adaction.org

Allen Kukovich, Executive Committee Chair
Jim McDermott, CEO
Don Kufler, Circulation Manager

Offers information on legislative issues and lobbying.
Cost: $20.00
Frequency: Weekly
Circulation: 3000
Founded in 1948
Mailing list available for rent: 3000 names
Printed in one color on matte stock

12147 AJA Benchmark
American Judges Association
300 Newport Ave
Williamsburg, VA 23185-4147

757-259-1841
FAX 757-259-1520
Home Page: aja.ncsc.dni.us

Judge Kevin S. Burke, President
Judge Toni Manning Higginbotham, President-Elect
Judge Elliott L. Zide, Vice President
Judge Brian MacKenzie, Secretary
Judge Harold V. Froehlich, Treasurer

Latest news from the American Judges Association.
2500 Members
Frequency: Quarterly
Founded in 1959

12148 ANSI Congressional Standards Update
American National Standards Institute
1819 L St NW
11th Floor
Washington, DC 20036-3864

202-293-8020
FAX 202-293-9287
E-Mail: info@ansi.org
Home Page: www.ansi.org

Arthur E. Cote, Chairman
Joe Bhatia, President & CEO

Designed to provide members of Congress and their staff with timely information on key standards and conformity assessment issues that impact the global competitiveness of US business and the US quality of life.
1000 Members
Frequency: Monthly
Founded in 1918

12149 ASAP Newsletter
American Society of Access Professionals
1444 I St Nw
Suite 700
Washington, DC 20005-6542

202-712-9054
FAX 202-216-9646
E-Mail: asap@bostrom.com
Home Page: www.accesspro.org

Claire Shanley, Executive Director

Provides information about upcoming and recent ASAP events, insights, and information about changes in the laws, and court decisions.
Frequency: Yearly

12150 Advocate
PHADA
511 Capitol Court NE
Washington, DC 20002-4947

202-546-5445
FAX 202-546-2280
Home Page: www.phada.org

Timothy Kaiser, Executive Director

Provides members with insights into HUD and Congressional actions, funding opportunities,

job vacancies, and major developments in the public housing field.
1.6M Members
Frequency: Bi-Weekly
Founded in 1979

12151 American Planning Association
American Planning Association
1030 15th St.
Suite 750 W
Washington, DC 20005

202-872-0611
FAX 202-872-0643
E-Mail: CustomerService@planning.org
Home Page: www.planning.org/
Social Media: *Facebook, Twitter, LinkedIn*

Paul Farmer, CEO
Ann Simms, CFO/EOO

The American Planning Association(APA) brings together thousands of people- practicing planners, citizens, elected officials-committed to making great communities.
Cost: $645.00
40000 Members
Frequency: Monthly
Founded in 1917

12152 Assisted Housing Accounts & Audits Insider
Brownstone Publishers
149 5th Ave
16th Floor
New York, NY 10010-6832

212-473-8200
800-643-8095
FAX 212-473-8786
E-Mail: info@vendomegrp.com
Home Page: www.vendomegrp.com

David B Klein, Editor
John M Striker, Publisher

Explains how to comply with regulatory STET requirements for accounting and auditing for HUD-assisted housing. Includes accounting control policies, audit preparation checklists, model accounting book entries, forms, staff memos and model letters.
Cost: $195.00
Frequency: Monthly
Founded in 1980
Printed in 2 colors on matte stock

12153 Assisted Housing Management Insider
Brownstone Publishers
149 5th Ave
16th Floor
New York, NY 10010-6832

212-473-8200
800-643-8095
FAX 212-473-8786
E-Mail: info@hcmarketplace.com
Home Page: www.hcmarketplace.com

John Striker, Publisher

Explains HUD regulatory requirements for federally-assisted housing, and gives advice on how to stay in compliance. Includes sample copies of model leases, clauses, letters, eviction notices, authorization forms, checklists and signs.
Printed in 2 colors on matte stock

12154 BNA's Eastern Europe Reporter
Bureau of National Affairs
1801 S Bell St
Arlington, VA 22202-4501

703-341-3000
800-372-1033
FAX 800-253-0332

E-Mail: customercare@bna.com
Home Page: www.bnabooks.com

Paul N Wojcik, CEO
William A. Beltz

This is just one of many biweekly notification services covering legislative, regulatory and legal developments affecting business, trade and investment in Eastern Europe and the former Soviet Union.
Cost: $1750.00
Frequency: Bi-annually

12155 CQ Congressional Quarterly
Congressional Quarterly
1414 22nd Street NW
Washington, DC 20037-1003

202-887-8500

Offers information on House and Senate committee hearings scheduled for up to two months from publication date.
Cost: $1299.00

12156 CQ Schedules
Congressional Quarterly
77 K Street NE
Washington, DC 20002-4681

202-650-6500
800-432-2250
E-Mail: customerservice@cqrollcall.com
Home Page: www.cq.com

Susan Benkelman, Executive Editor
Randy Wynn, Deputy Executive Editor
Anne Q Hoy, Managing Editor, Spec. Publications
Caitlin Hendel, Managing Editor, CQ Today
Melanie Starkey, Editor, Daily News

A daily guide to what's happening in Washington.

12157 CQ Today
Congressional Quarterly
77 K Street NE
Washington, DC 20002-4681

202-650-6500
800-432-2250
E-Mail: customerservice@cqrollcall.com
Home Page: www.cq.com

Susan Benkelman, Executive Editor
Randy Wynn, Deputy Executive Editor
Anne Q Hoy, Managing Editor, Spec. Publications
Caitlin Hendel, Managing Editor, CQ Today
Melanie Starkey, Editor, Daily News

CQ Today, available in print and online, delivers unparalleled coverage and analysis from the floor, committee markups, hearings and more. Subscribers receive updates throughout the day as news breaks on Capitol Hill.

12158 Census and You
Census Bureau
4700 Silver Hill Rd
Washington, DC 20233-0001

301-763-3030
FAX 301-457-3670
E-Mail: NPC.Call.Center.Info@census.gov
Home Page: www.census.gov

Thomas E Zebelsky, Plant Manager

Highlights data products and program of the US Census Bureau. Shows which reports, CD-ROMs, tapes, etc. to choose and also highlights releases on the Internet.
Cost: $21.00
12 Pages
Frequency: Monthly
Circulation: 11000
Founded in 1790
Printed in 2 colors on matte stock

12159 Civil Rights: From the State Capitals
Wakeman Walworth
PO Box 7376
Alexandria, VA 22307-7376

703-768-9600
FAX 703-768-9690
Home Page: www.statecapitals.com/civilrights.html

Keyes Walworth, Publisher

Covers ethnic, race and gender discrimination; including hate crime legislation, racial profiling, the current battle over affirmative action plus gay rights, domestic partner issues, rights of the disabled, rights of minors, women in the workforce, Hispanic issues. Includes legislation, judicial and administrative decisions across the country, as well as federal actions that affect the states.
Cost: $245.00
4 Pages
Frequency: Weekly
Founded in 1962
Printed in one color on matte stock

12160 Clearinghouse
NAGARA
1450 Western Avenue
Suite 101
Albany, NY 12203

518-694-8472
FAX 518-463-8656
E-Mail: nagara@caphill.com
Home Page: www.nagara.org

Paul R. Bergeron, President
Daphne DeLeon, Vice President
Caryn Wojcik, Secretary
Nancy Fortna, Treasurer

Illustrated newsletter of NAGARA. Features lively articles, informative announcements, a wide variety of news, and a column by the Archivist of the United States. Provides a forum for archivists to share information and learn from each other. Electronic publication only.
Frequency: Quarterly

12161 Connections
National Public Employer Labor Relations Assoc
1012 South Coast Highway
Suite M
Oceanside, CA 92054

760-433-1686
877-673-5721
FAX 760-433-1687
E-Mail: mike@npelra.org
Home Page: www.npelra.org

The outstanding monthly e-newsletter, your connection to national, regional and local developments. For members only
Frequency: Monthly
Circulation: 2000

12162 Cooperative Housing Bulletin
National Association of Housing Cooperatives
1444 I St Nw
Suite 700
Washington, DC 20005-6542

202-737-0797
FAX 202-216-9646
E-Mail: info@nahc.coop
Home Page: www.coophousing.org

Provides up-to-date information on issues of interest to the cooperative housing community. Accepts advertising.
Frequency: Monthly
Circulation: 2500
Printed in 2 colors on matte stock

12163 Divisions Digest
Federal Bar Association

1220 North Fillmore St.
Suite 444
Arlington, VA 22201

571-481-9100
FAX 571-481-9090
E-Mail: fba@fedbar.org
Home Page: www.fedbar.org
Social Media: *Facebook, Twitter, LinkedIn*

Fern C. Bomchill, President
Robert J. DeSousa, President-Elect
Hon. Gustavo Gelpi, Jr., Treasurer

Serves the Corporate and Association Counsel,
Federal Career Service, Senior Lawyers, and
the Younger Lawyers Divisions of the FBA.
16000 Members
Frequency: Bi-Annually
Founded in 1920

12164 Downtown Idea Exchange

Alexander Communications Group
1916 Park Ave
8th Floor
New York, NY 10037-3733

212-281-6099
800-232-4317
FAX 212-283-7269
E-Mail: info@downtowndevelopment.com
Home Page: www.downtowndevelopment.com

Laurence Alexander, Owner
Nadine Harris, Marketing Manager

News of downtown revitalization for downtown leaders and officials in local and state
government.
Cost: $167.00
8 Pages
Frequency: Monthly
ISSN: 0012-5822

12165 Downtown Promotion Reporter

Alexander Communications Group
1916 Park Ave
8th Floor
New York, NY 10037-3733

212-281-6099
800-232-4317
FAX 212-283-7269
E-Mail: info@downtowndevelopment.com
Home Page: www.downtowndevelopment.com

Romauld Alexander, Owner
Laurence Alexander, CEO
Sarah Benardos, Production Manager
Paul Felt, Editor

Proven promotion ideas and methods to bring
shoppers to downtown stores.
Cost: $189.00
12 Pages
Frequency: Monthly
Circulation: 1000
ISSN: 0363-2830
Founded in 1954

12166 EBA UPDATE

Energy Bar Association
1990 M St NW
Suite 350
Washington, DC 20036-3429

202-223-5625
FAX 202-833-5596
E-Mail: admin@eba-net.org
Home Page: www.eba-net.org
Social Media: *Facebook*

Derek A. Dyson, President
Susan A. Olenchuk, President-Elect
Jason F. Leif, Vice President
Emma F. Hand, Secretary
Hugh E. Hilliard, Treasurer

Providing members with the latest news regarding the energy industry.
2600 Members
Frequency: Quarterly
Founded in 1946

12167 EENR Pursuits

Federal Bar Association
1220 North Fillmore St.
Suite 444
Arlington, VA 22201

571-481-9100
FAX 571-481-9090
E-Mail: fba@fedbar.org
Home Page: www.fedbar.org
Social Media: *Facebook, Twitter, LinkedIn*

Fern C. Bomchill, President
Robert J. DeSousa, President-Elect
Hon. Gustavo Gelpi, Jr., Treasurer

EENR Section newsletter.
16000 Members
Frequency: Bi-Annually
Founded in 1920

12168 Economic Development Now

International Economic Development
Council
734 15th Street NW
Suite 900
Washington, DC 20005

202-223-7800
FAX 202-223-4745
Home Page: www.iedc.org

Jeff Finkle, President & CEO
Dennis G. Coleman, Chair
Jay C. Moon, Vice Chair
Paul Krutko, Secretary/Treasurer

Member publication providing a survey of current economic development news, original reports examining best practices, and updates
concerning federal funding and activity.
1.8M Members
Frequency: Bi-Monthly
Founded in 1967

12169 Economic Development: From the State Capitals

Wakeman Walworth
PO BOX 7376
Alexandria, VA 22307-7376

703-768-9600
FAX 703-768-9690
Home Page: www.statecapitals.com/

Keyes Walworth, Publisher

Covers environmental requirements, land use
regulation, mass transportation, highway construction plans, utility rates, changes in labor
laws, tax policies, enterprise zones, parkland
development, taxes, licensing and fees. Includes vital urban development programs:
growth control legislation, state construction
programs involving airports, stadiums, and
building codes.
Cost: $245.00
8 Pages
Frequency: Weekly
Founded in 1963
Printed in one color on Y stock

12170 Employee Policy for the Public and Private Sector: From the State Capitals

Wakeman Walworth
PO Box 7376
Alexandria, VA 22307-7376

703-768-9600
FAX 703-549-1372
Home Page:
www.statecapitals.com/employeepolicy.html

Keyes Walworth, Publisher

Provides a nationwide perspective on employee
health insurance programs, sexual harassment
policies, unemployment and workers' compensation, retirement policies, family medical
leave, new ergonomic rules, pay equity programs, collective bargaining, dismissal prac-

tices, minimum wages, drug testing, background checks, day care centers, domestic partner rules.
Cost: $245.00
4 Pages
Frequency: Weekly
Printed in one color on matte stock

12171 EuroWatch

WorldTrade Executive
PO Box 761
Concord, MA 01742

978-287-0301
FAX 978-287-0302
E-Mail: info@wtexec.com
Home Page: www.wtexec.com

Alison French, Production Manager

Analyzes the most recent EU judicial and legislative developments. Covers EU trade issues,
labor issues, single market and currency issues,
EU and individual country business law, trademark issues.
Cost: $797.00

12172 Federal Action Affecting the States: From the State Capitals

Wakeman Walworth
PO Box 7376
Alexandria, VA 22307-7376

703-768-9600
FAX 703-768-9690
Home Page:
www.statecapitals.com/fedaction.html

Keyes Walworth, Publisher

Gives a state perspective on Federal court rulings, overseer programs, changes in state jurisdiction, federal funds for state programs,
highway, drug abuse control, disaster, environmental and other programs that involve both
the states and the Feds.
Cost: $245.00
4 Pages
Frequency: Weekly
Founded in 1955
Printed in one color on matte stock

12173 Federal Assistance Monitor

CD Publications
8204 Fenton St
Silver Spring, MD 20910-4571

301-588-6380
800-666-6380
FAX 301-588-6385
Home Page: www.cdpublications.com

Michael Gerecht, President
Dave Kittross, Editor

Comprehensive review of federal funding an-
nouncements, private grants, rule changes and
legislative actions affecting the community
programs.
Cost: $419.00
Frequency: Monthly
Founded in 1961
*Mailing list available for rent: 2,000 names at
$160 per M*

12174 Federal Employees News Digest

1850 Centennial Park Drive
Suite 520
Reston, VA 20191

703-648-9551
800-989-3363
FAX 703-648-0265

Publishes weekly newsletter and self-help
books for federal and postal employees on retirement and pay, as well as other benefit-re-
lated topics. Accepts advertising.
Cost: $49.00
4 Pages
Frequency: 5x Yearly
Founded in 1951

12175 Federal Times

6883 Commercial Dr
Springfield, VA 22159

800-368-5718
E-Mail: armylet@atpco.com
Home Page: www.defensenews.com

Mark Winans, VP
Elaine Howard, President/CEO
Alex Neill, Managing Editor
Jim Tice, Senior Writer
David Smith, Marketing

Timely news and information on the rapid
changes impacting today's federal managers,
managing staff, the latest technology, and financial and career decisions.
Cost: $55.00
Frequency: Weekly
Circulation: 1MM

12176 Friday Flash

Coalition for Government Procurement
1990 M St Nw
Suite 450
Washington, DC 20036-3466

202-331-0975
FAX 202-822-9788
E-Mail: info@thecgp.org
Home Page: www.thecgp.org

A weekly newsletter published by the Coalition
for Government Procurement.
38387 Pages
Frequency: Weekly
Circulation: 1200
Founded in 1979

12177 From the State Capitals

Wakeman Walworth
PO BOX 7376
Alexandria, VA 22307-7376

703-768-9600
FAX 703-768-9690
Home Page: statecapitals.com/

Keyes Walworth, Publisher

Keeps readers informed of national trends in
domestic lawmaking. Issues dealing with taxes,
the environment, economic development, drug
abuse, abortion and education.
Founded in 1955

12178 GovManagement Daily

American Society for Public Administration
1301 Pennsylvania Avenue NW
Suite 700
Washington, DC 20004

202-393-7878
FAX 202-638-4952
E-Mail: info@aspanet.org
Home Page: www.aspanet.org
Social Media: *Facebook, Twitter, LinkedIn*

Erik O. Bergrud, President
Stephen E. Condrey, Vice-President
Kuotsai Tom Liou, President-Elect

Presenting headlines and brief summaries of
news and other information and analysis on
public-sector management at all levels of
government.
15M Members
Frequency: Daily
Founded in 1939

12179 Government Employee Relations Report

Bureau of National Affairs
1801 S Bell St
Arlington, VA 22202-4501

703-341-3000
800-372-1033
FAX 800-253-0332

E-Mail: customercare@bna.com
Home Page: www.bnabooks.com

Paul N Wojcik, CEO

A notification service that covers federal, state
and municipal government employee relations.
Cost: $1479.00
Frequency: Weekly

12180 Government PROcurement

Penton Media
1300 E 9th St
Suite 316
Cleveland, OH 44114-1503

216-696-7000
FAX 216-696-6662
Home Page: www.govpro.com

Jane Cooper, Marketing
Kristin M Atwater, Managing Editor
Kay Ross Baker, Publisher

Specifically for the public sector purchasing
professional.
58 Pages
Circulation: 20000
ISSN: 1078-0769
Founded in 1892
Printed in 4 colors on glossy stock

12181 Government Waste Watch Newspaper

Citizens Against Government Waste
1301 Pennsylvania Ave NW
Suite 1075
Washington, DC 20004-1707

202-467-5300
FAX 202-467-4253
E-Mail: membership@cagw.org
Home Page: www.cagw.org

Thomas A. Schatz, President
Robert J. Tedeschi, Treasurer & CFO

A quarterly newspaper published by Citizens
Against Government Waste.
Cost: $25.00
Frequency: Quarterly
Circulation: 108000
Founded in 1984
Mailing list available for rent

12182 HAC News

Housing Assistance Council
1025 Vermont Ave NW
Suite 606
Washington, DC 20005-3516

202-842-8600
FAX 202-347-3441
E-Mail: hac@ruralhome.org
Home Page: www.ruralhome.org

Moises Loza, Executive Director
Janice Clark, Editor

Newsletter publishing issues of rural and
low-income housing. Free.
ISSN: 1093-8036

12183 HOTLINE

National Journal
The Watergate
600 New Hampshire Ave., NW
Washington, DC 20037

202-739-8400
800-207-8001
FAX 202-833-8069
E-Mail: webmaster@asahq.org
Home Page: www.nationaljournal.com

Julie Abramson, Associate Production Editor
Tim Alberta, Sr Editor, National Journal
Hotline
Ronald Brownstein, Editorial Director

Online daily newsletter offers information on
US national, state and local political campaigns
and issues.
Frequency: Weekly
Founded in 1987

12184 Health Officer News

US Conference of Local Health Officers
1620 I Street NW
Washington, DC 20006-4005

202-887-6120
FAX 202-293-2352

Alan Campbell, Publisher
Stephen Horn, Editor

The official publication of the US conference
of local health officers. Accepts advertising.
Cost: $35.00
12 Pages
Frequency: BiWeekly

12185 Housing Law Bulletin

National Housing Law Project
703 Market Street
Suite 2000
San Francisco, CA 94103

415-546-7000
FAX 415-546-7007
E-Mail: nhlp@nhlp.org
Home Page: www.nhlp.org

Marcia Rosen, Executive Director
James Grow, Deputy Director
Susan Stern, Deputy Director, Administration

Updates in housing law information for use by
legal services organizations.
Cost: $175.00
Frequency: Monthly
Circulation: 400

12186 ICBA NewsWatch Today

Independent Community Bankers of
America
1615 L Street NW
Suite 900
Washington, DC 20036

800-422-8439
FAX 202-659-3604
E-Mail: info@icba.org
Home Page: www.icba.org

Salvatore Marranca, Chairman
Jeffrey L. Gerhart, Chairman-Elect
William A. Loving, Jr., Vice Chairman
Steven R. Gardner, Secretary
Jack Hartings, Treasurer

Free electronic news bulletin highlighting
breaking industry news and information.
Frequency: Daily

12187 In Hot Pursuit

Federal Bar Association
1220 North Fillmore St.
Suite 444
Arlington, VA 22201

571-481-9100
FAX 571-481-9090
E-Mail: fba@fedbar.org
Home Page: www.fedbar.org
Social Media: *Facebook, Twitter, LinkedIn*

Fern C. Bomchill, President
Robert J. DeSousa, President-Elect
Hon. Gustavo Gelpi, Jr., Treasurer

Criminal Law Section newsletter.
16000 Members
Frequency: Bi-Annually
Founded in 1920

12188 Inside Energy

Platts, McGraw Hill Companies
1221 Avenue of the Americas
New York, NY 10020-1001

212-512-2000
FAX 212-512-3840
E-Mail: support@platts.com
Home Page: www.mcgraw-hill.com

Glenn S Goldberg, President
Georgia Safos, Circulation Director

Covers the Department of Energy including energy, science/technology, and environmental management programs as well as energy programs at the Interior Department.
Cost: $1395.00
16 Pages
Frequency: Weekly
Founded in 1884

12189 International Association of Emergency Managers

201 Park Washington Court
Falls Church, VA 22046-4513

703-538-1795
FAX 703-241-5603
E-Mail: info@iaem.com
Home Page: www.iaem.com

Elizabeth B Armstrong, Executive Director
Sharon L Kelly, Member Director
Elizabeth B Armstrong, CEO
Karen Thompson, Editor
Dawn Shiley, Communication Manager

Representatives of city and county government departments responsible for emergency management and disaster preparedness.
Cost: $160.00
20 Pages
Frequency: Monthly
Circulation: 2700
Founded in 1952
Printed in 2 colors on matte stock

12190 Lottery, Parimutuel & Casino Regulation: From the State Capitals

Wakeman Walworth
PO BOX 7376
Alexandria, VA 22307-7376

703-768-9600
FAX 703-768-9690
Home Page:
www.statecapitals.com/lotterypari.html

Keyes Walworth, Publisher

Covers regulation, or attempts to regulate every form of internet gambling to cockfighting. It covers state lottery prize structures, ticket marketing policies, distribution of revenues, new games and equipment; Indian gaming, gambling compacts with tribes and revenue sharing; regulation and taxation of casinos, pari-mutuel wagering operations plus horse racing, dog racing, jai alai, riverboat gambling, bingo and other forms of gaming.
Cost: $345.00
4 Pages
Frequency: Weekly
Founded in 1962
Printed in one color on matte stock

12191 Managing Today's Federal Employees

LRP Publications
PO Box 980
Horsham, PA 19044-0980

215-784-0912
800-341-7874
FAX 215-784-9639
E-Mail: webmaster@lrp.com
Home Page: www.lrp.com

Todd Lutz, CFO
Patrick Byrne, Editor
Chris Donohue, Legal Editor

Keeping supervisors informed of their personnel management responsibilities has always been one of the most difficult tasks facing federal agency personnel officers. This newsletter is a working resource as well as a comprehensive training tool. Gives sensible solutions to common management challenges and covers controversial issues such as sexual harassment, contracting out of federal jobs, alternative dis-

pute resolutions and more.
Cost: $155.00
8 Pages
Frequency: Monthly
Founded in 1977
Printed in 2 colors on matte stock

12192 Mediaite

584 Broadway
Suite 510
New York, NY 10012

E-Mail: info@mediaite.com
Home Page: www.mediaite.com

Dan Abrams, Founder
Jon Nicosia, Senior Editor & Video Director
Nando Di Fino, Senior Editor & TV Reporter
Tommy Christopher, Political Editor & WH Correspondent
Colby Hall, Editor at Large

Mediaite is the site for news, information and smart opinions about print, online and broadcast media, offering original and immediate assessments of the latest news as it breaks.

12193 Motor Vehicle Regulation: From the State Capitals

Wakeman Walworth
PO Box 7376
Alexandria, VA 22307-7376

703-768-9600
FAX 703-768-9690
Home Page:
www.statecapitals.com/motorreg.html

Keyes Walworth, Publisher

Covers all fifty states regarding inspections, tags, fees and taxes, emissions standards, drunken driving laws, motorist licensing, insurance and education . We report on helmet , seat belt, and child restraint seat laws; regulation of all motor vehicles including autos, trucks, motorcycles, school buses, electric vehicles, watercraft. We also cover motor vehicle department administrative changes.
Cost: $245.00
4 Pages
Frequency: Weekly
Founded in 1962
Printed in one color on matte stock

12194 NACCED Alerts

Nat'l Assoc. for County & Economic Development
2025 M St NW
Suite 800
Washington, DC 20036-3309

202-367-1163
FAX 202-367-2149
Home Page: www.nacced.org

John Murphy, Executive Director
Brian Paulson, President
Jack Exler, Vice President
Tony Agliata, Secretary/Treasurer
Bill J. Lake, Director

Analyze federal legislation and regulations, highlight innovative county activities, report on current developments in the field, and provide updates on association activities.
120+ Members
Frequency: Bi-Weekly
Founded in 1989

12195 NADC News

National Association of Development Companies
6764 Old McLean Village Dr
Mc Lean, VA 22101-3906

703-748-2575
FAX 703-748-2582
E-Mail: merril@nadco.org
Home Page: www.nadco.org

Chris Crawford, President

Provides long-term fixed asset financing to small businesses. Publishes newsletter.
Frequency: Monthly
Circulation: 244
Founded in 1981

12196 NAHMA News

National Affordable Housing Management Association
400 N Columbus Street
Suite 203
Alexandria, VA 22314

703-683-8630
FAX 703-683-8634
Home Page: www.nahma.org

Trade association for professional property managers of federally assisted housing. Publishes a newsletter.
Cost: $95.00
Frequency: Bimonthly
Circulation: 3000

12197 NASAA Insight

NA Securities Administrators Association
750 First Street NE
Suite 1140
Washington, DC 20002-8034

202-737-0900
FAX 202-783-3571
Home Page: www.nasaa.org
Social Media: *Facebook*

Jack Herstein, President
Preston DuFauchard, President-Elect
Rick Hancox, Secretary
Fred J. Joseph, Treasurer

Designed to keep readers informed of recent NASAA activities.
Frequency: Quarterly
Founded in 1919

12198 NASCSP Newsletter

Nat'l Assoc. for State Community Service Programs
444 N Capitol St NW
Suite 846
Washington, DC 20001-1556

202-624-5866
FAX 202-624-7745
E-Mail: nascsp@nascsp.org
Home Page: www.nascsp.org
Social Media: *Facebook, Twitter*

Steve Payne, President
William Brand, Vice President
Jennifer Sexson, Treasurer
Ditzah Wooden-Wade, Secretary

Updates the Community Action Network on pertinent legislation, best practices, CSBG and WAP program highlights, and the latest events.
100 Members
Founded in 1968

12199 NASFA News

Natl' Assoc. of State Facilities Administrators
2760 Research Park Drive
PO Box 11910
Lexington, KY 40578-1910

859-311-1877
800-800-1910
FAX 859-244-8001
E-Mail: nasfa@nasfa.net
Home Page: www.nasfa.net/

Marcia Stone, Executive Director

State administrators of facilities and property. A newsletter is published for members.
Cost: $1800.00
Frequency: Quarterly
Circulation: 2000
Founded in 1987

12200 NATAT's Reporter

National Association of Towns and
Townships
444 N Capitol St Nw
Suite 397
Washington, DC 20001-1512

202-624-8195
FAX 202-624-3554
E-Mail: natat@sso.org
Home Page: www.natat.org

Kelly Aylward, Manager
Larry Merrill, Vice President
Matthew DeTemple, Secretary, Treasurer

Covers federal legislation and regulation that
pertain to local governments, with emphasis on
compact or small towns (under 50,000; many
under 1,000); also includes case studies of exemplary, creative local government, programs
and association news from the National Association of Towns & Townships.
Cost: $36.00
24 Pages
Frequency: BiWeekly
Circulation: 15,200
*Mailing list available for rent: 11700 names at
$85 per M*
Printed in 2 colors on newsprint stock

12201 NCDA News

National Community Development
Association
522 21st St NW
Suite 120
Washington, DC 20006-5012

202-293-7587
FAX 202-887-5546
Home Page: www.ncdaonline.org

Shandra Western, Editor

A national nonprofit membership organization
representing local governments that implement
community development programs. The members administer federally supported community
development, housing and human services programs. NCDA provides counsel at the federal
level on new program design and current program implementation and advocates on behalf
of responsive community development.
13 Pages

12202 Nation's Cities Weekly

National League of Cities
1301 Pennsylvania Ave NwW
Suite 550
Washington, DC 20004-1747

202-626-3180
FAX 202-626-3043
E-Mail: info@nlc.org
Home Page: www.nlc.org

Donald J Borut, Executive Director

News for and about cities.
Cost: $96.00
Frequency: Weekly
Circulation: 30000
ISSN: 0164-5935

**12203 National Association of Conservation
Districts**

NACD
509 Capitol Court, NE
Washington, DC 20002-4937

202-547-6223
FAX 202-547-6450
Home Page: www.nacdnet.org

John Larson, CEO

Highlights forestry issues of importance to districts and to showcase district-related forestry
projects and success stories.
17000 Members
Frequency: Monthly
Founded in 1946

**12204 National Association of Regional
Councils**

National Association of Regional Councils
1666 Connecticut Ave NW
Suite 305
Washington, DC 20002

202-986-1032
FAX 202-986-1038
E-Mail: lindsey@narc.org
Home Page: www.narc.org

Fred Abousleman, Executive Director
Lindsey Riley, Deputy of Communications
Frequency: Weekly
Circulation: 2000

12205 Navy Times

Gannett Government Media
6883 Commercial Drive
Springfield, VA 22159-500

703-750-7400
800-368-5718
FAX 703-750-8622
E-Mail: tnaegele@atpco.com
Home Page: www.navytimes.com

Elaine Howard, President
Judy McCoy, Associate Publisher
David Smith, VP Marketing/Business Dev
Dick Howlett, AVP Circulation Operations
Tobias Naegele, Executive Editor

The trusted, independent source for news and
information of the Navy community. Breaking
news, personal finance information, healthcare,
recreational resources, exclusive videos and
photos, Guard and Reserve information, and an
expanded community area connecting service
members, military families and veterans.
Cost: $143.00
Frequency: Weekly

12206 Outlook: From the State Capitals

Wakeman Walworth
PO Box 7376
Alexandria, VA 22307-7376

703-768-9600
FAX 703-549-1372
Home Page:
www.statecapitals.com/theoutlook.html

Keyes Walworth, Publisher

Gives an excellent perspective of trend- setting
topics in state lawmaking: internet taxes,
school choice, economic development, abortion, environmental issues, gambling laws.
Each week is devoted to a different subject. In
addition, a special feature called In the Works
Around The Nation provides current highlights
from other State Capitals newsletters.
Cost: $245.00
4 Pages
Frequency: Weekly
Printed in one color on matte stock

12207 PA TIMES

American Society for Public Administration
1301 Pennsylvania Avenue NW
Suite 700
Washington, DC 20004

202-393-7878
FAX 202-638-4952
E-Mail: info@aspanet.org
Home Page: www.aspanet.org
Social Media: *Facebook, Twitter, LinkedIn*

Erik O. Bergrud, President
Stephen E. Condrey, Vice-President
Kuotsai Tom Liou, President-Elect

ASPA's newspaper covering developments in
the professional field of public administration.
Article topics include successful local state and
federal government programs, PA trends and
new PA methods. Focuses on the issues that
face public managers today. Also highlights
best practices in the field and updates members

on how ASPA plays a role in the support of the
public sector.
15M Members
Frequency: Monthly
Founded in 1939

12208 Politico

Capitol News Company
1100 Wilson Blvd
Suite 610
Arlington, VA 22209

703-647-7999
E-Mail: newsrelease@politico.com
Home Page: www.politico.com

Robert L Allbritton, Publisher
Frederick J Ryan Jr, President & CEO
Kim Kingsley, Chief Operating Officer
John F Harris, Editor-In-Chief
Jim VandeHei, Executive Editor

Provides insider-like access to Washington and
the latest from the world of politics.

**12209 Public Health: From the State
Capitals**

Wakeman Walworth
PO Box 7376
Alexandria, VA 22307-7376

703-768-9600
FAX 703-768-9690
Home Page: www.statecapitals.com

Keyes Walworth, Publisher

Reports on a wide range of health care legislation such as AIDS disclosure and testing, drug
programs, abortion rulings, cancer prevention
including smoking restrictions in public places,
mental health and disability programs, disease
control, regulation of hospitals and nursing
homes, clinics, food inspection policies, organ
donor management and Medicare. It covers
such current issues as mail order through pharmacies on the internet.
Cost: $245.00
4 Pages
Frequency: Weekly
Printed in one color on matte stock

**12210 Public Safety and Justice Policies:
From the State Capitals**

Wakeman Walworth
PO Box 7376
Alexandria, VA 22307-7376

703-768-9600
FAX 703-768-9690
Home Page:
www.statecapitals.com/publicsafety.html

Keyes Walworth, Publisher

Covers gun control on school grounds,
buy-back programs, gunmaker lawsuits, law
enforcement, arrest procedures, drug law enforcement and penalties; financing and administration of substance-abuse counseling, school
violence , police administration, truth in sentencing , prison administration, prisoner drug
testing and AIDS testing, new evidence such as
DNA, inmate work programs, gender bias in
the courtroom, family and juvenile justice, victim compensation laws, inmate living conditions
Cost: $245.00
4 Pages
Frequency: Weekly
Printed in one color on matte stock

12211 Roads and Bridges

Scranton Gillette Communications
3030 W Salt Creek Lane
Suite 201
Arlington Heights, IL 60005-5025

847-391-1000
FAX 847-390-0408

E-Mail: bwilson@sgcmail.com
Home Page: www.roadbridges.com

Bill Wildon, Editorial Director
Allen Zeyher, Managing Editor
Rick Schwer, Publisher

Provides engineers, contractors and government officials with the latest advancements in the road and bridge industry, timely news coverage and important information on products beneficial to the job site of office.
Cost: $40.00
92 Pages
Frequency: Monthly
Circulation: 70000
ISSN: 8750-9229
Founded in 1905

12212 SideBAR

Federal Bar Association
1220 North Fillmore St.
Suite 444
Arlington, VA 22201

571-481-9100
FAX 571-481-9090
E-Mail: fba@fedbar.org
Home Page: www.fedbar.org
Social Media: *Facebook, Twitter, LinkedIn*

Fern C. Bomchill, President
Robert J. DeSousa, President-Elect
Hon. Gustavo Gelpi, Jr., Treasurer

Federal Litigation Section Newsletter
16000 Members
Frequency: Quarterly
Founded in 1920

12213 Standards Action

American National Standards Institute
1819 L St NW
11th Floor
Washington, DC 20036-3864

202-293-8020
FAX 202-293-9287
E-Mail: info@ansi.org
Home Page: www.ansi.org

Arthur E. Cote, Chairman
Joe Bhatia, President & CEO

Published to assure a complete consensus of ANSI members and the general public by facilitating review of proposed standards. Also included is information on draft American National Standards, governmental and other foreign standards and conformity assessment activities.
1000 Members
Frequency: Weekly
Founded in 1918

12214 Tax Administrators News

Federation of Tax Administrators
444 N Capitol St NW
Suite 348
Washington, DC 20001-1538

202-624-5890
FAX 202-624-7888
Home Page: www.taxadmin.org

Harley Duncan, Executive Director
Rian Turruss, Editor

Covers state and federal legislation, US Supreme Court and state court cases, and developments relating to state tax administration.
Cost: $40.00
12 Pages
Frequency: Monthly
Circulation: 2000
Founded in 1930
Printed in one color on matte stock

12215 Taxes-Property: From State Capitals

Wakeman Walworth

PO Box 7376
Alexandria, VA 22307-7376

703-689-9600
FAX 703-768-9690
Home Page:
www.statecapitals.com/taxprop.html

Keyes Walworth, Publisher

Covers new property tax legislation, initiatives, referenda, property assessment programs, tax exemptions, tax incentives, and tax collection methods. This newsletter emphasizes the use of property taxes for school financing including state aid formulas, alternative school financing methods, budget issues related to teacher pay and class sizes.
Cost: $345.00
4 Pages
Frequency: Weekly
Printed in one color on matte stock

12216 The Certifier

Association of Boards of Certification
2805 SW Snyder Blvd.
Suite 535
Ankeny, IA 50023

515-232-3623
FAX 515-965-6827
E-Mail: abc@abccert.org
Home Page: www.abccert.org

Paul Bishop, Executive Director
Bob Hoyt, Vice President
Cheryl Bergener, President
Kathy Cook, VP

The newsletter for environmental certification authorities, filled with news and updates on the latest in certification and focuses on state and provincial certification programs, certification issues, and association events.
Frequency: Monthly
Founded in 1972

12217 The Government Standard

American Federation of Government Employees
80 F St NW
Washington, DC 20001-1528

202-737-8700
FAX 202-639-6490
E-Mail: comments@afge.org
Home Page: www.afge.com

John Gage, President
J. David Cox, Secretary/Treasurer
Augusta Thomas, VP for Women's & Fair Practices

AFGE's official membership publication keeping members up to date on what their local government is up to.
Frequency: Quarterly
Founded in 1932

12218 The Resolver

Federal Bar Association
1220 North Fillmore St.
Suite 444
Arlington, VA 22201

571-481-9100
FAX 571-481-9090
E-Mail: fba@fedbar.org
Home Page: www.fedbar.org
Social Media: *Facebook, Twitter, LinkedIn*

Fern C. Bomchill, President
Robert J. DeSousa, President-Elect
Hon. Gustavo Gelpi, Jr., Treasurer

Turning conflict into resolution, Alternative Dispute Resolution Section newsletter.
16000 Members
Frequency: Bi-Annually
Founded in 1920

12219 The Resource

National Association of Conservation Districts
509 Capitol Ct. NE
Washington, DC 20002-4937

202-547-6223
FAX 202-547-6450
Home Page: www.nacdnet.org

Krysta Harden, CEO
Bob Cordova, Second Vice President

NACD's print publication provides in depth coverage of the association's recent activities and features columns by the NACD CEO and President, in addition to guest and partnership columns.
Cost: $35.00
12 Pages
Frequency: Monthly
Circulation: 25000
Founded in 1937

12220 This Week in Washington

American Public Human Services Association
1133 19th Street NW
Suite 400
Washington, DC 20036-3623

202-682-0100
FAX 202-289-6555
Home Page: www.aphsa.org

Tracy Wareing, Executive Director

Gives readers concise updates on initiatives of the administration, legislative action in human service programs, the latest information on federal regulations, and state agency personnel changes- everything the human service administrator needs to know from the nation's capital.
Frequency: Weekly
Founded in 1930

12221 URISA Newsletter

Association for GIS Professionals
701 Lee St.
Suite 680
Des Plaines, IL 60016-4508

847-824-6300
FAX 847-824-6363
E-Mail: info@urisa.org
Home Page: www.urisa.org

Susan Johnson, President
Wendy Nelson, Executive Director

Effective use of information systems technology at the state, regional and local levels Newsletter is published.
Frequency: Monthly
Founded in 1963

12222 US Mayor

US Conference of Mayors
1620 I St Nw
Suite 40
Washington, DC 20006-4034

202-464-0790
FAX 202-293-2352
E-Mail: info@usmayors.org
Home Page: www.usmayors.org

Don Plusquellic, President
Tom Cochan, Editor
Guy Smith, Managing Editor
Michael Guido, Chair Advisory Board
J Thomas Cochran, CEO

Federal government and congressional activities.
Cost: $35.00
16 Pages
Circulation: 6000
Founded in 1933

12223 USNC News and Notes

American National Standards Institute

1819 L St NW
11th Floor
Washington, DC 20036-3864

202-293-8020
FAX 202-293-9287
E-Mail: info@ansi.org
Home Page: www.ansi.org

Arthur E. Cote, Chairman
Joe Bhatia, President & CEO

For the electrotechnology community summarizing activities, events, and items of interest for the US National Committee of the International Electrotechnical Commission, keeping US stakeholders informed about the latest standards and conformity assessment updates in the domestic, regional and global arenas.
1000 Members
Frequency: Quarterly
Founded in 1918

12224 United Nations Jobs Newsletter
Thomas F Burola & Associates
6477 Telephone Road
Suite 7R
Ventura, CA 93003-4459

805- 64- 725
FAX 805-654-1708

Thomas F Burola, Publisher

Focus of this newsletter is employment conditions within the United Nations System and vacancy notices.
Cost: $145.00
Circulation: 3,500
Founded in 1994
Printed in 2 colors on matte stock

12225 United States Confernce of Mayors News
United States Conference of Mayors
1620 Eye Street, NW
Washington, DC 20006-4005

202-293-7330
FAX 202-293-2352
E-Mail: info@usmayors.org
Home Page: www.usmayors.org/uscm/

J Thomas Cochran, President
William Fay, CEO

City government officials. Newsletter is available for members.
Circulation: 30000
Founded in 1932

12226 Washington Report
Federal Managers Association
1641 Prince St
Alexandria, VA 22314-2818

703-683-8700
FAX 703-683-8707
E-Mail: info@fedmanagers.org
Home Page: www.fedmanagers.org

Todd Wells, Manager
Darryl A Perkinson, President

News bulletin detailing the latest developments on Capitol Hill and in the nation's capital.
15M Members
Frequency: Quarterly
Founded in 1913

12227 Washington Spectator
Public Concern Foundation
PO Box 20065
New York, NY 10011

212-741-2365
E-Mail:
subscriptions@washingtonspectator.com
Home Page: www.washingtonspectator.com/

Kevin Walter, Publisher
Ben A Franklin, Editor
Lisa Vandepaer, Associate Editor

Marvin Shanken, Owner
Ruth Shikes, Co-Founder

News, comment and analysis on current national and international affairs; politics, economics, environment and social issues.
Cost: $15.00
4 Pages
Circulation: 60,000
Founded in 1974
Mailing list available for rent: 60000 names at $75 per M
Printed in one color on matte stock

12228 Washington Trade Daily
Trade Reports International Group
PO Box 1802
Wheaton, MD 20915-1802

301-946-0817
FAX 301-946-2631
E-Mail: trigtrig@aol.com
Home Page: www.washingtontradedaily.com/
Social Media: *Twitter*

Jim Berger, CEO
D Kanth, Editor

The only faxed daily newsletters of its kind that covers the goings-on in the nation's Capital related to imports, exports and foreign investment. It reports daily to readers on the Executive Branch - including the US Trade Representative's office and the Commerce Department - as well as Congress. Readers can gain insight every morning on what are likely to be new laws and regulations governing international business tomorrow.
Cost: $650.00
16 Pages
Frequency: Daily
Founded in 1991
Printed in one color

12229 What's New?
American National Standards Institute
1819 L St NW
11th Floor
Washington, DC 20036-3864

202-293-8020
FAX 202-293-9287
E-Mail: info@ansi.org
Home Page: www.ansi.org

Arthur E. Cote, Chairman
Joe Bhatia, President & CEO

Electronic newsletter distributed to members and constituents free of charge. Includes synopses and links to the most recent news, events and publications available from ANSI Online.
1000 Members
Frequency: Weekly
Founded in 1918

12230 Worldwide Government Report
Worldwide Government Directories
7979 Old Georgetown Road
Suite 900
Bethesda, MD 20814-2429

301-258-2677
800-332-3535
FAX 301-718-8494

Jonathan Hixon, Publisher

Each issue provides detailed reports of elections, government and military turnover. Events covered include ousted heads of state, reshuffled governments, changes in ruling majorities, analyses of recent elections, outlooks for upcoming elections, and senior military appointments.
Cost: $247.00
Frequency: Monthly

12231 eNotes
National Association of Conservation
Districts

509 Capitol Ct. NE
Washington, DC 20002-4937

202-547-6223
FAX 202-547-6450
Home Page: www.nacdnet.org

Krysta Harden, CEO
Bob Cordova, Second Vice President

NACD's weekly news briefs.
Cost: $35.00
12 Pages
Frequency: Monthly
Circulation: 25000
Founded in 1937

Magazines & Journals

12232 AASHTO Daily Transportation Update
Amer. Assoc. of State Highway & Trans. Officials
444 N Capitol St NW
Suite 249
Washington, DC 20001-1539

202-624-5800
FAX 202-624-5806
E-Mail: info@aashto.org
Home Page: www.transportation.org
Social Media: *Facebook, Twitter*

Kirk T. Steudle, President
Michael P. Lewis, Vice-President
Carlos Braceras, Secretary/ Treasurer
John Horsley, Executive Director

To help members and other transportation professionals stay informed about critical industry happenings and events.
52 Members
Frequency: Daily

12233 AASHTO Journal
Amer. Assoc. of State Highway & Trans. Officials
444 N Capitol St NW
Suite 249
Washington, DC 20001-1539

202-624-5800
FAX 202-624-5806
E-Mail: info@aashto.org
Home Page: www.transportation.org
Social Media: *Facebook, Twitter*

Kirk T. Steudle, President
Michael P. Lewis, Vice-President
Carlos Braceras, Secretary/ Treasurer
John Horsley, Executive Director

Electronic journal to help members and other transportation professionals stay informed about critical industry happenings and events.
52 Members

12234 ANSI's Annual Report
American National Standards Institute
1819 L St NW
11th Floor
Washington, DC 20036-3864

202-293-8020
FAX 202-293-9287
E-Mail: info@ansi.org
Home Page: www.ansi.org

Arthur E. Cote, Chairman
Joe Bhatia, President & CEO

Designed to inform members of the standards community of the Institute's accomplishments and financial activities of the past year, while also laying out goals for the future as presented by the chairman and president.
1000 Members
Frequency: Annually
Founded in 1918

12235 APWA Reporter
American Public Works Association
1275 K Street NW
Suite 750
Washington, DC 20005

202-408-9541
800-848-2792
FAX 202-408-9542
E-Mail: ddancy@apwa.net
Home Page: www.apwa.net

Peter King, Executive Director
David Dancy, Director Of Marketing
Connie Hartline, Publisher

Prime communication link uniting the community of public works professionals that make up APWA.
Cost: $100.00
Frequency: Monthly
Circulation: 25000
ISSN: 0092-4873
Founded in 1937
Mailing list available for rent

12236 American Public Human Services Association Public Human Services Directory
American Public Human Services Association
1133 19th St NW
Suite 400
Washington, DC 20036-3623

202-682-0100
FAX 202-204-0071
E-Mail: memberservice@aphsa.org
Home Page: www.aphsa.org

Tracy L. Wareing, Executive Director

A must-have for all human service professionals. Backed by APHSA, the Directory has consistently help steer people to the right contacts. Program contacts for such programs as Temporary Assistance for Needy Families, Child Welfare, Medicaid, Nutrition Assistance, Long-Term Care, Mental Health, Workforce Investment Act, and the Social Services Block Grant are available at a glance.
Cost: $115.00
Founded in 1930

12237 Armed Forces Journal
6883 Commercial Dr
Springfield, VA 22159

800-368-5718
E-Mail: armylet@atpco.com
Home Page: www.defensenews.com

Mark Winans, VP
Elaine Howard, President/CEO
Alex Neill, Managing Editor
Jim Tice, Senior Writer
David Smith, Marketing

The leading joint service monthly magazine for officers and leaders in the US military community. AFJ has been providing essential review and analysis on key defense issues for more than 140 years. Offers in-depth coverage of military technology, procurement, logistics, strategy, doctrine and tactics. Also covers special operations, US Coast Guard and US National Guard developments.
Cost: $55.00
Frequency: Monthly
Circulation: 1MM

12238 Army Magazine
2425 Wison Boulevard
Arlington, VA 22201-3326

703-841-4300
800-336-4570
FAX 703-525-9039

E-Mail: membersupport@ausa.org
Home Page: www.ausa.org

Gen. Gordon Sullivan, President
Mary Blake French, Editor
Millie Hurlbut, Director of Marketing
Founded in 1950

12239 Army Times
Army Times Publishing Company
6883 Commercial Dr
Springfield, VA 22151-4202

703-750-9000
800-368-5718
FAX 703-750-8622
E-Mail: jmccoy@atpco.com
Home Page: www.armytimes.com

Elaine Howard, CEO
Judy McCoy, Associate Publisher
Tobias Naegele, Executive Editor
David Smith, Marketing Manager

Magazine soldiers and their families rely on as trusted, independent sources for news and information on the most important issues affecting their careers and personal lives. A single source for breaking news; personal finance information; healthcare; recreational resources; exclusive videos and photos; Guard and Reserve information; and an expanded community area connecting service members, military families and veterans.
Cost: $52.00
Frequency: Weekly

12240 C4ISR Journal
Defense News
6883 Commercial Dr
Springfield, VA 22159

800-368-5718
E-Mail: armylet@atpco.com
Home Page: www.defensenews.com

Mark Winans, VP
Elaine Howard, President/CEO
Alex Neill, Managing Editor
Jim Tice, Senior Writer
David Smith, Marketing

Dedicated to the rapidly advancing, high-tech realm of military intelligence, surveillance and reconnaissance. It was the first major periodical to specifically serve this key area of military growth and development, and has a strong following in the world's network-centric warfare community.
Cost: $55.00
Frequency: Monthly
Circulation: 1MM

12241 CQ Weekly
Congressional Quarterly
77 K Street NE
Washington, DC 20002-4681

202-650-6500
800-432-2250
E-Mail: customerservice@cqrollcall.com
Home Page: www.cq.com

Susan Benkelman, Executive Editor
Randy Wynn, Deputy Executive Editor
Anne Q Hoy, Managing Editor, Spec. Publications
Caitlin Hendel, Managing Editor, CQ Today
Melanie Starkey, Editor, Daily News

This award-winning publication provides a clear perspective on how legislation is shaped, who is shaping it and how the process could affect your interests.

12242 Capitol Ideas
National Association of State Facilities

2760 Research Park Drive
PO Box 11910
Lexington, KY 40578-1910

859-244-8000
800-800-1910
FAX 859-244-8001
Home Page: www.csg.org
Social Media: *Facebook, Twitter, YouTube*

Gov. Brian Schweitzer, President
Gov. Luis Fortuno, President-Elect
Bob Godfrey, Chair
Jay Emler, Chair-Elect
Gary Stevens, Vice Chair

Includes member-driven content, including a targeted focus for each issue, news from each region and association news, focusing on what is going on in the states that might be of interest to other states.

12243 Code Official
International Code Council
4051 Flossmoor Rd
Country Club Hl, IL 60478-5771

708-799-2300
800-214-4321
202-783-2348
FAX 708-799-4981
Home Page: www.bocai.org

Paul K Myers, CEO
Margaret M Leddin, Managing Editor

Serves a wide-ranging readership of professionals who are interested in the development, maintenance and enforcement of progressive and reponsive building regulations.
Cost: $30.00
Frequency: Monthly
Circulation: 16000
Founded in 1994
Printed in on glossy stock

12244 Congressional Digest
Congressional Digest Corporation
4416 East-West Highway
Suite 400
Bethesda, DC 20814-3389

301-634-3113
800-638-8380
FAX 301-634-3189
Home Page: www.congestionaldigest.com

Griff Thomas, President
Page Robinson, Publisher
Kathy Thorne, Circulation Manager
Sarah Orrick, Editor

The only publication about Congress that concentrates each month on a single legislative issue in a unique Pro and Con format. It is an indispensable education tool for students of national and world affairs.
Cost: $62.00
36 Pages
ISSN: 0010-5899
Founded in 1921
Printed in 2 colors on glossy stock

12245 Contract Management
National Contract Management Association
8260 Greensboro Drive
Suite 200
McLean, VA 22102-3728

571-382-0082
800-344-8096
FAX 703-448-0939
E-Mail: cm@ncmahq.org
Home Page: www.ncmahg.org

Neal J Couture, Executive Director
Kathryn Mullan, Assistant Editor

It covers the myriad aspects of government and commercial contract management. News and features provide information on such topics as procurement policy, on-the-job techniques, regulations, case law, ethics, contract administra-

tion, electronic commerce, international and small business matters, education and career development.
Cost: $178.00
80 Pages
Frequency: Monthly
Circulation: 22000
Founded in 1959
Printed in 4 colors on glossy stock

12246 Cooperative Housing Bulletin

National Association of Housing Cooperatives
1444 I Street, NW
Suite 700
Washington, DC 20005-6542

202-737-0797
FAX 202-216-9646
E-Mail: info@nahc.coop
Home Page: www.coophousing.org

Member benefit conatining articles for co-op board members and professionals, up-to-date news on legislative issues that NAHC is monitoring, and practical information on issues facing housing cooperatives.
Frequency: Quarterly
Printed in 2 colors on matte stock

12247 Correctional Health Today

American Correctional Association
206 N Washington St
Suite 200
Alexandria, VA 22314-2528

703-224-0000
800-222-5646
FAX 703-224-0179
E-Mail: jeffw@aca.org
Home Page: www.aca.org

Jeff Washington, Deputy Executive Director
James Gondles Jr, Executive Director

An interdisciplinary, peer-reviewed, academic publication devoted to examining all areas of health care within corrections. Available in print and electronically.
20000 Members
Frequency: Monthly
Founded in 1870

12248 Corrections Compendium

American Correctional Association
206 N Washington St
Suite 200
Alexandria, VA 22314-2528

703-224-0000
800-222-5646
FAX 703-224-0179
E-Mail: jeffw@aca.org
Home Page: www.aca.org

Jeff Washington, Deputy Executive Director
James Gondles Jr, Executive Director

The peer-reviewed, research-based journal of the American Correctional Association. Presents research findings and trends and examines events in corrections and criminal justice.
20000 Members
Frequency: Quarterly
Founded in 1870

12249 Corrections Today

American Correctional Association
206 N Washington St
Suite 200
Alexandria, VA 22314-2528

703-224-0000
FAX 703-224-0179
E-Mail: execoffice@aca.org
Home Page: www.aca.org
Social Media: *Facebook, Twitter*

James Gondles, Executive Director

The professional membership publication of the ACA. Its international readership includes

individuals involved in every sector of the corrections and criminal justice fields.
Frequency: 6x Yearly

12250 Court Review

American Judges Association
300 Newport Ave
Williamsburg, VA 23185-4147

757-259-1841
FAX 757-259-1520
Home Page: aja.ncsc.dni.us

Judge Kevin S. Burke, President
Judge Toni Manning Higginbotham, President-Elect
Judge Elliott L. Zide, Vice President
Judge Brian MacKenzie, Secretary
Judge Harold V. Froehlich, Treasurer

Court technology, managing your staff, controlling your docket-a bench's eye view of information you won't find anywhere else.
2500 Members
Frequency: Quarterly
Founded in 1959

12251 Defense News

6883 Commercial Dr
Springfield, VA 22151-4202

703-750-9000
800-424-9335
FAX 703-658-8412
E-Mail: armylet@atpco.com
Home Page: www.defensenews.com

Mark Winans, VP
Elaine Howard, President/CEO
Alex Neill, Managing Editor
Jim Tice, Senior Writer
David Smith, Marketing

Provides the global defense community with the latest news and analysis on defense programs, policy, business and technology. With bureaus and reporters around the world, Defense News sets the standard for accuracy, credibility and timeliness in defense reporting. Circulates to top leaders and decisionmakers in North America and in Europe, Asia and the Middle East.
Cost: $55.00
Frequency: Weekly
Circulation: 1MM

12252 Democratic Communique

Union for Democratic Communications
777 Glades Rd
Boca Raton, FL 33431

Home Page:
www.democraticcommunications.net

Janet Wasko, Publisher

News of Democratic and grassroots communications projects, issues and publications.
Cost: $20.00
12 Pages
Frequency: BiWeekly

12253 Economic Development Journal

International Economic Development Council
734 15th Street NW
Suite 900
Washington, DC 20005

202-223-7800
FAX 202-223-4745
Home Page: www.iedc.org

Jeff Finkle, President & CEO
Dennis G. Coleman, Chair
Jay C. Moon, Vice Chair
Paul Krutko, Secretary/ Treasurer

Premier publication of IEDC's diverse and dynamic discipline, featuring in-depth accounts of

important programs, projects, and trends from the US and around the world.
1.8M Members
Frequency: Quarterly
Founded in 1967

12254 Energy Law Journal

Energy Bar Association
1990 M St NW
Suite 350
Washington, DC 20036-3429

202-223-5625
FAX 202-833-5596
E-Mail: admin@eba-net.org
Home Page: www.eba-net.org
Social Media: *Facebook*

Derek A. Dyson, President
Susan A. Olenchuk, President-Elect
Jason F. Leif, Vice President
Emma F. Hand, Secretary
Hugh E. Hilliard, Treasurer

Providing members with the latest news regarding the energy industry.
2600 Members
Frequency: Bi-Annually
Founded in 1946

12255 Federal Criminal Investigator

P.O. Box 23400
Washington, DC 20026

800-403-3374
630-969-8537
FAX 800-528-3492
E-Mail: fcianat@aol.com
Home Page: www.fedcia.org

Richard Zehme, President
William Paulin, Vice President
Rich Ahern, National Treasurer/Secretary

This comprehensive publication covers legislation and federal information for the police official and officer.
Frequency: Quarterly
Founded in 1956

12256 Federal Manager

Federal Managers Association
1641 Prince St
Alexandria, VA 22314-2818

703-683-8700
FAX 703-683-8707
E-Mail: info@fedmanagers.org
Home Page: www.fedmanagers.org

Todd Wells, Manager
Darryl A Perkinson, President

Magazine focusing on current management issues.
15M Members
Frequency: Quarterly
Founded in 1913

12257 Foreign Service Journal

American Foreign Service Association
2101 E St NW
Washington, DC 20037-2990

202-338-4045
800-704-2572
FAX 202-338-6820
E-Mail: member@afsa.org
Home Page: www.afsa.org

Susan R. Johnson, President
Andrew Winter, Treasurer

Each issue covers foreign affairs from an insider's perspective, providing thoughtful articles on international issues, the practice of diplomacy and the US Foreign Service.
Cost: $40.00
68 Pages
Frequency: Monthly
Circulation: 12500
ISSN: 0146-3543

Founded in 1924
Printed in on glossy stock

12258 Government Executive

National Journal
600 New Hampshire Ave NW
Suite 4
Washington, DC 20037-2403

202-739-8400
FAX 202-833-8069
E-Mail: webmaster@govexec.com
Home Page: www.govexec.com
Social Media: *Facebook, Twitter*

John Fox Sullivan, President
Shane Harris, Editor

Serving senior executives and managers in the federal government's departments and agencies. Subscribers are high-ranking civilian and military officials who are responsible for defending the nation and carrying out the many laws that define the government's role in our economy and society. Covers the business of the federal government and its huge departments and agencies.
Cost: $48.00
72 Pages
Frequency: Monthly
Circulation: 75,000
Founded in 1970

12259 Government Product News

Penton Media
1300 E 9th St
Suite 316
Cleveland, OH 44114-1503

216-696-7000
FAX 216-696-6662
Home Page: www.penton.com

Jane Cooper, Marketing
Kristin M Atwater, Managing Editor
Vaughn Rockhold, Group Publisher
Kay Ross-Baker, Publisher
Sarah Arnold, Marketing Director

Serves officials in the executive, legislative, administrative, engineering, purchasing, financial and other operational departments, within government agencies.
40 Pages
Frequency: Monthly
Circulation: 85000
ISSN: 0017-2642
Founded in 1962
Printed in 4 colors on glossy stock

12260 Government Recreation & Fitness

Executive Business Media
825 Old Country Road
PO Box 1500
Westbury, NY 11590

516-334-3030
FAX 516-334-3059
E-Mail: mail@ebmpubs.com
Home Page: www.ebmpubs.com

Murry Greenwald, Publisher
Paul Ragnoz, Managing Editor

Government Recreation and Fitness reaches recreation and fitness professionals in every department and agency of the federal government, goes directly to the people who purchase your products, with deep market penetration, and covers both appropriated and nonappropriated fund budgets.
Cost: $35.00
42 Pages
Frequency: 10x Yearly
Circulation: 8521
ISSN: 1086-7899
Founded in 1996
Printed in 4 colors on glossy stock

12261 Government Technology

GT Publications

150 Almaden Blvd
Suite 600
San Jose, CA 95113-2016

408-275-9000
FAX 408-275-0582
Home Page: www.grantthornton.com
Social Media: *Facebook*

Jeffrey S Pera, Managing Partner
Sherese Graves, Advertising Director
Dennis McKenna, Publisher
Micki Gerardi, Manager

Covering information technology's role in state and local governments. Through in-depth coverage of IT case studies, emerging technologies, and the implications of digital technology on the policies and management of public sector organizations, Government Technology chronicles the dynamics of governing in the information age. Readers include managers, elected officials, CIOs and technology staff at all levels of government.
56 Pages
Frequency: Monthly

12262 ICBA Independent Banker

Independent Community Bankers of America
1615 L Street NW
Suite 900
Washington, DC 20036

800-422-8439
FAX 202-659-3604
E-Mail: info@icba.org
Home Page: www.independantbanker.org

Salvatore Marranca, Chairman
Jeffrey L. Gerhart, Chairman-Elect
William A. Loving, Jr., Vice Chairman
Steven R. Gardner, Secretary
Jack Hartings, Treasurer

Covers the news topics and trends that are important to the nation's community bank senior executives. Keeping members informed about and connected with their national association and its activities; and providing them with timely, relevant information on developments to growth their business franchise within the rapidly evolving financial services industry.
Frequency: Monthly

12263 International Debates

Congressional Digest Corporation
4416 E West Hwy
Suite 400
Bethesda, MD 20814-4568

301-634-3113
800-637-9915
FAX 301-634-3189
E-Mail: info@congressionaldigest.com
Home Page: www.pro-and-con.org/

Griff Thomas, President
Page Robinson, Publisher

Independent journal featuring controversies before the United Nations and other international forums. Each issue covers an important and timely international issue and includes in-depth background information, key documents, and diverse global perspectives.
Frequency: 9x Yearly
Founded in 1921

12264 Journal of Food Protection

International Association for Food Protection
6200 Aurora Ave
Suite 200W
Urbandale, IA 50322-2864

515-276-3344
800-369-6337
FAX 515-276-8655
E-Mail: info@foodprotection.org

Home Page: www.foodprotection.org
Social Media: *Facebook, Twitter, LinkedIn*

Lisa Hovey, Managing Editor
Didi Loynachan, Administrative Editor

Internationally recognized as the leading publication in the field of food microbiology, each issue contains scientific research and authoritative review articles reporting on a variety of topics in food science pertaining to food safety and quality.
Cost: $335.00
Frequency: Monthly
Circulation: 11000+
ISBN: 0-362028-X -
Founded in 1911
Mailing list available for rent: 3000+ names at $150 per M
Printed in 4 colors on glossy stock

12265 Journal of Housing Economics

630 Eye St NW
Washington, DC 20001-3736

202-289-3500
877-866-2476
FAX 202-289-8181
Home Page: www.journals.elsevier.com

Saul Ramirez, Executive Director
Donald J Cameron, CEO

Provides a focal point for the publication of economic research related to housing and encourages papers that bring to bear careful analytical technique on important housing-related questions. The journal covers the broad spectrum of topics and approaches that constitute housing economics, including analysis of important public policy issues.
Cost: $33.00
Founded in 1933

12266 Journal of Medical Regulation

Federation of State Medical Boards
400 Fuller Wiser Rd
Suite 300
Euless, TX 76039-3856

817-868-4043
FAX 817-868-4099
E-Mail: dcarlson@fsmb.org
Home Page: www.fsmb.org

Rhonda Olsobrook, Manager

Peer-reviewed scholarly publication that helps raise awareness of important trends and challenging issues in the regulatory community.
Frequency: Monthly

12267 Journal of Occupational and Environmental Hygiene (JOEH)

ACGIH
1330 Kemper Meadow Drive
Cincinnati, OH 45240

513-742-2020
FAX 513-742-3355
E-Mail: mail@acgih.org
Home Page: www.acgih.org

Lisa M. Brosseau, Chair
Bill R. McArthur, Vice Chair
Robert F. Herrick, Vice Chair-Elect
Heather D. Borman, Secretary/ Treasurer
A. Anthony Rizzuto, Executive Director

Focuses on publishing information that practicing professionals can apply in their day-to-day activities.
Founded in 1938

12268 Journal of the Association of Food and Drug Officials

2550 Kingston Road
Suite 311
York, PA 17402

717-757-2888
FAX 717-755-8089

E-Mail: afdo@afdo.org
Home Page: www.afdo.org

News and the latest legislation for the Food and Drug Association.
Cost: $80.00
Frequency: Quarterly
Founded in 1896

12269 Legislative Update
1250 Eye St NW
Suite 902
Washington, DC 20005-3947

202-393-5225
FAX 202-393-3034
Home Page: www.nrhcweb.org

Robert A Rapoza, Publisher/Executive Director

Published by the National Rural Housing Coalition.
Cost: $250.00
Frequency: 25x Yearly
Circulation: 300
Founded in 1969

12270 McGraw-Hill's Federal Technology Report
McGraw Hill
1200 G St Nw
Suite 900
Washington, DC 20005-3821

202-383-2377
800-223-6180
FAX 202-383-2438
Home Page: www.aviationnow.com

Jennifer Michels, Manager
Georgia Safos, Circulation Director

Brings readers inside those areas of the federal government where federal technology policy and legislation is made; also identifies commercial opportunities at federal labs.
Cost: $1015.00
16 Pages
Frequency: Weekly

12271 NCOA Journal
Todays NCOA
10635 N 35th
San Antonio, TX 78233-6627

210-653-6161
800-662-2620
FAX 210-637-3337
E-Mail: membsvc@ncoausa.org
Home Page: www.uag-inc.com

Gene Overstreet, President/CEO
Cathy John, Advertising Manager

The official magazine for the Non Commissioned Officers Association.
Frequency: Quarterly
Circulation: 60000
Founded in 1960

12272 NIST Tech Beat
National Institute of Standards & Technology
Public & Business Affairs
100 Bureau Drive, Stop 1070
Gaithersburg, MD 20899-1070

800-877-8339
FAX 301-926-1630
E-Mail: media@nist.gov
Home Page: www.nist.gov
Social Media: *Facebook, Twitter, YouTube, Flickr*

Michael Baum, Segments Editor
Ben Stein, Segments Editor
Michael E Newman, Segments Editor
Evelyn Brown, Segments Editor
Laura Ost, Segments Editor

A biweekly lay-language newsletter of recent research results and other news from the National Institute of Standards and Technology.

NIST is the nation's physical sciences and engineering measurement laboratory. Archives available online.
Frequency: Biweekly

12273 Nation's Cities Weekly
National League of Cities
1301 Pennsylvania Ave NW
6th Floor, Suite 550
Washington, DC 20004-1747

202-626-3180
FAX 202-626-3043
E-Mail: memberservices@nlc.org
Home Page: www.nlc.org

Donald J Borut, Executive Director
Cyndy Hogan, Managing Editor

Delivers top stories about advocacy activities, successful and innovative city programs, new research and networking opportunities for local elected officials and city employees.
Cost: $96.00
12 Pages
Frequency: Weekly
Circulation: 27000
Founded in 1978

12274 National Journal
National Journal
600 New Hampshire Ave NW
Suite 4
Washington, DC 20037-2403

202-739-8400
800-207-8001
FAX 202-833-8069
Home Page: nationaljournal.com
Social Media: *Facebook, Twitter*

John Fox Sullivan, President

Delivers highly engaged consumers with all of the information and insights that they need to know to conduct business successfully in Washington. Trusted professional resource for Members of Congress and their senior staffs, the Executive branch, federal agency executives, government affairs professionals, corporate and association leaders, and the political news media.
Cost: $1799.00
Founded in 1969

12275 Navy News and Undersea Technology
Pasha Publications
1616 N Fort Myer Drive
Suite 1000
Arlington, VA 22209-3107

703-528-1244
800-424-2908
FAX 703-528-1253

Harry Baisden, Group Publisher
Thomas Jandl, Editor
Tod Sedgwick, Publisher

This report on the Navy, as well as the Marine Corps and naval developments overseas. Frequently cited by experts in the field as the source for breaking developments in submarine and anti-submarine warfare technology, this newsletter sets the standard for Navy reporting.
Cost: $545.00
Frequency: Weekly

12276 Off the Shelf
Coalition for Government Procurement
1990 M St NW
Suite 450
Washington, DC 20036-3466

202-331-0975
FAX 202-822-9788
E-Mail: info@thecgp.org
Home Page: www.thecgp.org

Larry Allen, Executive VP

Providing vital updates on rules, regulations, and GSA Schedule developments that may impact your business.
Frequency: Monthly
Founded in 1979

12277 Parameters
US Army War College
122 Forbes Ave
Suite C34
Carlisle, PA 17013-5220

717-245-3131
FAX 717-245-3323
Home Page: www.carlisle.army.mil

Robert J Ivany, Manager

Refereed journal of ideas and issues. Provides a forum for mature thought on the art and science of land warfare, joint and combined matters, national and international security affairs, military strategy, military leadership and management, military history, ethics, and other topics of significant and current interest to the US Army and the Department of Defense.
Cost: $26.00
Frequency: Quarterly
Circulation: 1300

12278 Policy & Practice
American Public Human Services Association
1133 19th Street NW
Suite 400
Washington, DC 20036-3623

202-682-0100
FAX 202-289-6555
Home Page: www.aphsa.org

Tracy Wareing, Executive Director

Presents a lively and comprehensive look at key human service issues. Its aim is to highlight the experiences of those who administer public assistance programs and services; to examine cutting-edge public human service research and demonstration projects; and to provide readers with a variety of resources to guide them in their challenging roles in the human service arena.
Frequency: Bi-Monthly
Founded in 1930

12279 Presidential Studies Quarterly
Center for the Study of the Presidency & Congress
1020 19th St NW
Suite 250
Washington, DC 20036-6120

202-872-9800
FAX 202-872-9811
E-Mail: email@thepresidency.org
Home Page: www.thepresidency.org
Social Media: *Facebook, Twitter, YouTube*

George C Edwards III, Editor

Available in print and online, PSQ is widely viewed by scholars and professionals as an indispensable resource for understanding the Presidency. The only scholarly journal that focuses on the most powerful political figure in the world - the President of the United States. Offers articles, features, review essays, and book reviews covering Presidential decision making, the operations of the White House, and much more.
Frequency: Quarterly
Circulation: 6000
ISSN: 0360-4918

12280 Prosecutor
National District Attorneys Association

44 Canal Center Plaza
Suite 110
Alexandria, VA 22314-1548

703-549-9222
FAX 703-836-3195
Home Page: www.ndaa.org

Jean Hemphill, Publications Director/Editor

Fascinating articles, names in the news, upcoming conferences, capital perspective, profiles, course announcements, message from the President, message from the Executive Director, and much more.
Frequency: Quarterly
Circulation: 7000

12281 Public Administration Review (PAR)

American Society for Public Administration
1301 Pennsylvania Avenue NW
Suite 700
Washington, DC 20004

202-393-7878
FAX 202-638-4952
E-Mail: info@aspanet.org
Home Page: www.aspanet.org
Social Media: *Facebook, Twitter, LinkedIn*

Erik O. Bergrud, President
Stephen E. Condrey, Vice-President
Kuotsai Tom Liou, President-Elect

The preeminent journal in the field of public administration research and theory.
15M Members
Frequency: Bi-Monthly
Founded in 1939

12282 Public Integrity

American Society for Public Administration
1301 Pennsylvania Avenue NW
Suite 700
Washington, DC 20004

202-393-7878
FAX 202-638-4952
E-Mail: info@aspanet.org
Home Page: www.aspanet.org
Social Media: *Facebook, Twitter, LinkedIn*

Erik O. Bergrud, President
Stephen E. Condrey, Vice-President
Kuotsai Tom Liou, President-Elect

Furthering the understanding of ethics in government by publishing articles of interest to practitioners and scholars.
15M Members
Frequency: Monthly
Founded in 1939

12283 Public Risk

Public Risk Management Association
500 Montgomery St
Suite 750
Alexandria, VA 22314-1565

703-647-6244
FAX 703-739-0200
E-Mail: info@primacentral.org
Home Page: www.primacentral.org
Social Media: *Facebook, LinkedIn*

Jim Hirt, Executive Director
Jon Ruzan, Manager
Kerry Langley, Manager

Provides risk managers in the public sector with timely, focused information in an easy-to-read format. Features articles from risk management practitioners as well as industry experts.
Frequency: 10x Yearly
Circulation: 8000+
Founded in 1978

12284 Pull Together

1306 Dahlgren Avenue SE
Washington Navy Yard, DC 20374-5055

202-678-4333
FAX 202-889-3565
E-Mail: nhfwny@navyhistory.org
Home Page: www.navyhistory.org

Captain Charles Creekman, Executive Director
Robert F Dunn, President
Cost: $25.00
Founded in 1926

12285 Rural Housing Reporter

1250 Eye St NW
Suite 902
Washington, DC 20005-3947

202-393-5225
FAX 202-393-3034
Home Page: www.nrhcweb.org

Robert A Rapoza, Publisher/Executive Director

Published by the National Rural Housing Coalition.
Cost: $250.00
Frequency: Monthly
Founded in 1969

12286 Rural Voices

Housing Assistance Council
1025 Vermont Ave NW
Suite 606
Washington, DC 20005-3516

202-842-8600
FAX 202-347-3441
E-Mail: hac@ruralhome.org
Home Page: www.ruralhome.org
Social Media: *Twitter, LinkedIn*

Moises Loza, Executive Director

Written in non-technical language for a general audience.
Frequency: Quarterly
Founded in 1971

12287 Society of Cost Estimating and Analysis Journal

Society of Cost Estimating and Analysis
527 Maple Ave E
Suite 301
Vienna, VA 22180-4753

703-938-5090
FAX 703-938-5091
E-Mail: scea@sceaonline.org
Home Page: www.sceaonline.net

Elmer Cleg, Executive Director
Joseph Dean, National VP

Subscribers are professionals engaged primarily in the field of government contract estimating and pricing.
Cost: $40.00
Frequency: Annual+
Circulation: 4500
ISSN: 0882-3871
Founded in 1984

12288 State Legislatures

National Conference of State Legislatures
7700 E 1st Pl
Denver, CO 80230-7143

303-364-7700
FAX 303-364-7800
E-Mail: pubs-info@ncsl.org
Home Page: www.ncsl.org
Social Media: *Twitter, LinkedIn*

William Pound, Executive Director
Edward Smith, Managing Editor
LeAnn Hoff, Director, Revenue & Sales

The national magazine of state government and policy.
Cost: $49.00
15000 Members
Circulation: 18000
ISSN: 0147-0644
Founded in 1975
Printed in 4 colors

12289 Supreme Court Debates

Congressional Digest Corporation
4416 E West Hwy
Suite 400
Bethesda, MD 20814-4568

301-634-3113
800-637-9915
FAX 301-634-3189
E-Mail: info@congressionaldigest.com
Home Page: www.pro-and-con.org/

Griff Thomas, President
Page Robinson, Publisher

Independent journal featuring controversies before the US Supreme Court. Each issue covers a current prominent case, along with in-depth historical and legal background and excerpts from lawyers' arguments before the Court. Each issue also lists cases expected to be considered by the High Court during the current term.
Frequency: 9x Yearly
Founded in 1921

12290 The Federal Lawyer

Federal Bar Association
1220 North Fillmore St.
Suite 444
Arlington, VA 22201

571-481-9100
FAX 571-481-9090
E-Mail: fba@fedbar.org
Home Page: www.fedbar.org
Social Media: *Facebook, Twitter, LinkedIn*

Fern C. Bomchill, President
Robert J. DeSousa, President-Elect
Hon. Gustavo Gelpi, Jr., Treasurer

The only magazine written and edited for lawyers who practice in federal courts or have an interest in federal law as well as judges who sit on the federal bench. Editorial content covers immigration, Indian, antitrust, labor and employment, bankruptcy, criminal, intellectual property, environmental, and other types of law that fall within federal jurisdiction.
Cost: $35.00
16000 Members
Frequency: Monthly
Founded in 1920

12291 The Forum

National Forum for Black Public Administrators
777 N Capitol St NE
Suite 807
Washington, DC 20002-4291

202-408-9300
FAX 202-408-8558
E-Mail: webmaster@nfbpa.org
Home Page: www.nfbpa.org
Social Media: *Facebook, YouTube*

Aretha R. Ferrell-Benavides, President
Verdenia C. Baker, 1st Vice President
Bruce T. Moore, 2nd Vice President
Jelynne LeBlanc Burley, Secretary/Treasurer
John E. Saunders, III, Executive Director

Has been used as a means of polishing and honing the skills of capable and experienced administrators by providing practical advice on professional development and insight on social and economic concerns impacting the Black community. Strives to present timely, factual, and comprehensive information on subjects of critical importance to its readers who share a

common commitment to excellence in public service.
2.8M Members
Frequency: Quarterly
Founded in 1983

12292 Training & Simulation Journal
6883 Commercial Dr
Springfield, VA 22159

800-368-5718
E-Mail: armylet@atpco.com
Home Page: www.defensenews.com

Mark Winans, VP
Elaine Howard, President/CEO
Alex Neill, Managing Editor
Jim Tice, Senior Writer
David Smith, Marketing

About trends in the global military training and simulation market, and a forum for market leaders to obtain and exchange information on emerging issues, new technologies, and new products.
Cost: $55.00
Frequency: Bi-Monthly
Circulation: 1MM

12293 Translog
200 Stovall Street
Hoffman Building Room 11N57
Alexandria, VA 22332-5000

703-428-3207
FAX 703-428-3312

An authorized online publication for members of the Department of Defense, published under supervision of the SDDC Director of Command Affairs to provide timely, relevant information concerning SDDC people, missions, policies, operations, technical developments, trends, and ideas of and about SDDC and the US Army.

12294 Urban Land
Urban Land Institute
1025 Thomas Jefferson St NW
Suite 500 West
Washington, DC 20007-5230

202-624-7000
FAX 202-624-7140
E-Mail: ulifoundation@uli.org
Home Page: www.uli.org
Social Media: *Facebook, Twitter, LinkedIn, YouTube*

Patrick Phillips, CEO
Richard Rosan, President
Michael Terseck, CFO

Focuses on the information needs of land use and development professionals worldwide, providing them with timely, objective, practical, and accessible articles on a wide variety of subjects related to their professional interests.
14M Members
Frequency: Monthly
Founded in 1936

12295 Washington Law & Politics
100 W Harrison St
Suite 340
Seattle, WA 98119-4196

206-282-9527
FAX 206-282-9601
Home Page: www.superlawyers.com

Keith Goben, Publisher
Beth Taylor, Editor
Paul Englund, Circulation Manager
Tina Justison, Production Manager

A magazine for those who care about, or have a stake in, the public policy debate that is the basis of our editorial. Readers consist of those in positions of power in media, government, politics, law and business. Attracts a curious blend

of readers ranging from corporate CEOs to political junkies.
48 Pages
Frequency: 6x Yearly
Circulation: 18000
Founded in 1977
Printed in 4 colors on glossy stock

12296 Washington Remote Sensing Letter
Dr. Murray Felsher
1057B National Press Building
Washington, DC 20045-2001

202-393-3640

Dr. Murray Felsher, Publisher
Murray Felsher, Editor
Dr. Murray Felsher, Publisher
Dr. Murray Felsher, Marketing
Dr. Murray Felsher, Circulation Manager

The recognized leader in reporting and analysis of US and international news dealing with all phases and applications of satellite remote sensing of the earth and global analyses research, including imagery, photography, surveillance and monitoring the Earth from space.
Cost: $1100.00
4 Pages
ISSN: 0739-6538
Founded in 1980
Printed in 2 colors on matte stock

12297 Western City Magazine
League of California Cities
1400 K St
4th Floor
Sacramento, CA 95814-3971

916-658-8200
800-262-1801
FAX 916-658-8289
E-Mail: info@westerncity.com
Home Page: www.cacities.org
Social Media: *Facebook*

Pam Blodgett, Ad Manager
Eva Spiegel, Managing Editor
Chris McKenzie, Executive Director

The magazine of the League of California Cities.
Cost: $39.00
Frequency: Monthly
Circulation: 10500
Founded in 1924
Printed in 4 colors on glossy stock

Trade Shows

12298 ACAP National Training Conference
American Society of Access Professionals
1444 I(Eye) St. NW
Suite 700
Washington, DC 20005-6542

202-712-9054
FAX 202-216-9646
E-Mail: asap@bostrom.com
Home Page: www.accesspro.org

Anne Weismann, President
Will Kammer, Vice President
Karen Finnegan, Treasurer
Carmen L. Mallon, Secretary

Created to bring educational opportunities beyond the Washington, D.C. area. Combines training topics with the thought-provoking and practical issues associated with FOIA and Privacy Act processing and requesting.
Frequency: Annual/March
Founded in 1980

12299 ASPA Annual Conference
American Society for Public Administration

1301 Pennsylvania Avenue NW
Suite 840
Washington, DC 20004

202-393-7878
FAX 202-638-4952
E-Mail: info@aspanet.org
Home Page: www.aspanet.org

Antoinette Samuel, Executive Director
Lyric Jonze, Administration Assistant

Offers cuttin-edge educational programming at this year's conference. There are over 150 educational options to choose from - Panel Sessions, Best Practice Workshops, and Roundtable Discussions.
550 Attendees
Frequency: Annual/May

12300 AURP International Conference
Association of University Research Parks
6262 N. Swan Road
Suite 100
Tucson, AZ 85718-8936

520-529-2521
FAX 520-529-2499
E-Mail: info@aurp.net
Home Page: www.aurp.net
Social Media: *Facebook, Twitter*

Eileen Walker, CEO
Victoria Palmer, Events Manager
Chelsea Simpson, Membership & Marketing Manager

Bringing together the world's leaders in high-tech economic development, this conference features professional development for university research park professionals.
Frequency: Annual/September

12301 America's Town Meeting
National Association of Towns and Townships
1130 Connecticut Ave NW
Suite 300
Washington, DC 20036-3981

202-454-3954
866-830-0008
FAX 202-331-1598
Home Page: www.natat.org

NATaT's national conference is the largest national conference for grassroots government leaders. Educational workshops and legislative workshops help officials be more effective representatives for the citizens they serve. The conference provides a time for attendees to lobby members of Congress on issues important to their towns.
13M Members
Frequency: Annual

12302 American Association of Port Authorities Annual Convention
1010 Duke Street
Alexandria, VA 22314-3589

703-684-5700
FAX 703-684-6321
E-Mail: info@aapa-ports.org
Home Page: www.aapa-ports.org

Kurt Nagle, President/CEO

AAPA's largest membership meeting of the year. It includes technical and policy committee meetings, business sessions and social networking opportunities for port professionals and others in the marine transportation industry.
700 Attendees
Frequency: Annual/September
Founded in 1912

12303 American Industrial Hygiene Conference and Exposition
ACGIH

1330 Kemper Meadow Drive
Cincinnati, OH 45240

513-742-2020
FAX 513-742-3355
E-Mail: mail@acgih.org
Home Page: www.acgih.org

Lisa M. Brosseau, Chair
Bill R. McArthur, Vice Chair
Robert F. Herrick, Vice Chair-Elect
Heather D. Borman, Secretary/ Treasurer
A. Anthony Rizzuto, Executive Director

One of the world's premier conferences for occupational and environmental safety and health
professionals. Committees and individual members contribute their expertise in professional
development courses, technical sessions, and
poster sessions.
8000 Attendees
Founded in 1938

12304 American Political Science Association Annual Meeting

1527 New Hampshire Avenue NW
Washington, DC 20036-1206

202-483-2512
FAX 202-483-2657
E-Mail: apsa@apsanet.org
Home Page: www.apsanet.org

G. Bingham Powell, Jr., President
Jane Mansbridge, President-Elect
Jonathan Benjamin-Alvarado, Treasurer
Lisa L. Martin, Secretary
Michael A. Brintnall, Executive Director

Workshop, luncheon and 150 plus exhibits of
publications and software relating to political
science.
6500 Attendees
Frequency: Annual
Founded in 1903

12305 CLEAR Annual Educational Conference

Council on Legislative Enforcement &
Regulation
403 Marquis Ave
Suite 200
Lexington, KY 40502-2104

859-269-1289
FAX 859-231-1943
E-Mail: jhorne@clearhq.org
Home Page: www.clearhq.org
Social Media: *Facebook*

Bruce Matthews, President
Michelle Pedersen, President-Elect

Conference content focuses on compliance and
discipline, credentialing and licensing, examination issues, and legislative and policy issues/
reulatory administration.
380 Members
400+ Attendees
Frequency: Annual/September
Founded in 1980

12306 CSG National Conference & North American Summit

Council of State Governments
2760 Research Park Drive
PO Box 11910
Lexington, KY 40578-1910

859-244-8000
800-800-1910
FAX 859-244-8001
Home Page: www.csg.org
Social Media: *Facebook, Twitter*

Key officials that shape and make today's economic decisions.
1000+ Attendees
Frequency: Annual/October

12307 Congress of Cities & Exposition

National League of Cities
1301 Pennsylvania Avenue NW
Suite 550
Washington, DC 20004

202-626-3100
800-564-4220
FAX 202-626-3043
Home Page: www.nlc.org

Ted Ellis, President
Marie Lopez Rogers, 1st Vice President
Chris Coleman, 2nd Vice President
Don Borut, Executive Director

Provides educational content on the most pressing challenges facing city leaders. Conference
attendees hear from prominent speakers and issue experts, participate in leadership training
sessions, attend issue-specific workshops, visit
best practices keynote speakers, issue workshops, mobile workshops, and leadership
training sessions.
4200 Attendees
Frequency: Annual/December
Founded in 1924

12308 EANGUS National Conference

Exhibit Promotions Plus
11620 Vixens Path
Ellicott City, MD 21042

301-596-3028
FAX 410-997-0764
Home Page: www.eangus.org

Kevin Horowitz, Exhibit Mgmt.

General conference and exhibition for the En-
listed Association of the National Guard of the
United States. All attendees are either National
Guard members, retirees or their families.
2000+ Attendees
Frequency: Annual/August
Founded in 1971

12309 Energy - Exhibit Promotions Plus

US Dept. of Energy/US Dept. of
Defense/GSA
11620 Vixens Path
Ellicott City, MD 21042

301-596-3028
FAX 410-997-0764
Home Page: www.energy2003.ee.doe.gov

Harve Horowitz, President
Kevin Horowitz, Senior Association Manager

Energy is an exclusive Federal Grant sponsored
annual educational forum and exhibition.
1000+ Attendees
Frequency: Annual/August

12310 FOSE

Contingency Planning & Management
Conference
3141 Fairview Park Drive
Suite 777
Falls Church, VA 22042

703-876-5100
800-638-8510
Home Page: www.fose.com
Social Media: *Facebook, Twitter, LinkedIn*

Sylvia Griffiths, Customer Supervisor

Vendors in different marketplaces & pavilions,
providing the opportunity to source effective &
actionable IT solutions, in-depth conferences,
workshops, camps, keynote & theater education designed to help achieve sucess with government IT mandates & initiatives. Association
meetings, CIO Summits and peer networking
opportunities, bringing the government IT
community together.
80M Attendees
Frequency: April

12311 Government Finance Officers Association Annual Conference

203 N LaSalle Street
Suite 2700
Chicago, IL 60601-1210

312-977-9700
FAX 312-977-4806
E-Mail: inquiry@gfoa.org
Home Page: www.gfoa.org

Jeffrey Esser, Executive Director/CEO
Barbara Mollo, Director Operations &
Marketing
Anne Spray Kinney, Director Research &
Consulting
John Jurkash, CFO/Financial Administration
Barrie Tabin Berger, Federal Liaison
Coordinator

The Government Finance Officers Association's Annual Conference provides training and
networking opportunities for public sector finance professionals from across the United
States and Canada. 250 booths with 200
exhibitors.
4000 Attendees
Frequency: June

12312 HFA Institute

National Council of State Housing Agencies
444 N Capitol St NW
Suite 438
Washington, DC 20001-1505

202-624-7710
FAX 202-624-5899
E-Mail: bthompson@ncsha.org
Home Page: www.ncsha.org
Social Media: *Facebook, Twitter*

Gerald M. Hunter, President
Brian A. Hudson, Vice President
Thomas R. Gleason, Secretary/ Treasurer
Barbara J. Thompson, Executive Director

Premier training event providing an unprecedented chance to network with peers and receive top-notch education and invaluable
advice from key federal officials, leading trainers and consultants, noted industry professionals, and experienced HFA practitioners.
350 Members
Frequency: Annual/December
Founded in 1974

12313 Housing Credit Conference & Marketplace

National Council of State Housing Agencies
444 N Capitol St NW
Suite 438
Washington, DC 20001-1505

202-624-7710
FAX 202-624-5899
E-Mail: bthompson@ncsha.org
Home Page: www.ncsha.org
Social Media: *Facebook, Twitter*

Gerald M. Hunter, President
Brian A. Hudson, Vice President
Thomas R. Gleason, Secretary/ Treasurer
Barbara J. Thompson, Executive Director

The industry event of the year. Only NCSHA
brings leaders and top development and compliance staff from the state Housing Credit allocating agencies together with government
officials, developmers, lenders syndicators, investors, attorneys, accountants, property managers, compliance experts, owners, and
nonprofits.
350 Members
Frequency: Annual/June
Founded in 1974

12314 IAEM Annual Conference

International Association of Emergency
Managers

201 Park Washington Court
Falls Church, VA 22046

703-538-1795
FAX 703-241-5603
E-Mail: info@iaem.com
Home Page: www.iaem.com

Provides a forum for current trends and topics, information about the latest tools and technology in emergency management and homeland security, and advances IAEM-USA committee work. Sessions encourage stakeholders at all levels of government, the private sector, public health and related professions to exchange ideas on collaborating to protect lives and property from disaster.
1000 Attendees
Frequency: Annual/November

12315 ICMA Annual Conference
International City/County Management Association
777 N Capitol Street NE
Suite 500
Washington, DC 20002

202-624-4600
800-745-8780
FAX 202-962-3500
E-Mail: amahoney@icma.org
Home Page: www.icma.org

Robert J. O'Neill, Executive Director
David Ellis, Conference Committee Co-Chair
Maria A. Hurtado, Conference Committee Co-Chair

The largest annual event in the world for local government managers and staff.
3814 Attendees
Frequency: Annual/September
Founded in 1914

12316 ICMA Regional Summit
International City/County Management Association
777 N Capitol Street NE
Suite 500
Washington, DC 20002-4239

202-289-4262
800-745-8780
FAX 202-962-3500
E-Mail: customerservices@icma.org
Home Page: www.icma.org
Social Media: *Facebook, Twitter, LinkedIn, YouTube, Flickr*

Barry Sacks, Show Manager
Robert J. O'Neill, Executive Director

A networking and professional development opportunity for members and state officers in the four regions.
3.5M Attendees
Frequency: Annual/September

12317 Legislative Conference
National Council of State Housing Agencies
444 N Capitol St NW
Suite 438
Washington, DC 20001-1505

202-624-7710
FAX 202-624-5899
E-Mail: bthompson@ncsha.org
Home Page: www.ncsha.org
Social Media: *Facebook, Twitter*

Gerald M. Hunter, President
Brian A. Hudson, Vice President
Thomas R. Gleason, Secretary/ Treasurer
Barbara J. Thompson, Executive Director

Join HFA leaders and their board members and stakeholders in Washington to learn about NCSHA's legislative priorities and strategize the best way to communicate our message to Congress with one unified voice. Hear from

key Congressional staff and industry leaders about the issues of the day.
350 Members
Frequency: Annual/March
Founded in 1974

12318 MMA Annual Meeting and Trade Show
Massachusetts Municipal Association
One Winthrop Square
Boston, MA 02110

617-426-7272
FAX 617-695-1314
Home Page: www.mma.org

The largest regular gathering of Massachusetts local government officials. Features educational workshops, nationally recognized speakers, awards programs, a large trade show, and an opportunity to network with municipal officials from across the state.
1000 Attendees
Frequency: Annual/January

12319 Marine West Military Expo
Nielsen Business Media, USA
1145 Sanctuary Parkway
Suite 355
Alpharetta

703-488-2762

Ron Bates, Event Organizer

This event is fully dedicated to the defense industry. The event will showcase the latest products and equipments used for marine and related industry at one place. The visitors will be the military professionals, equipment buyers, decision makers and the other people related to the field of defense.
Frequency: Annual/February

12320 NACE Annual Conference
National Association County Engineers
25 Mass. Avenue NW
Suite 580
Washington, DC 20001

202-393-5041
FAX 202-393-2630
E-Mail: nace@naco.org
Home Page: www.countyengineers.org

Mark A. Craft, President
Richie Beyer, President-Elect
Mark K. Servi, Secretary/ Treasurer

Attendees will have many opportunities to meet road and bridge professionals and their counterparts from other counties around the country, to exchange ideas and have some fun. The exhibit show offers a friendly environment for delegates to learn about the latest products and services.
450 Attendees
Frequency: Annual/April

12321 NACo Annual Conference and Exposition
National Association of Counties
25 Massachusetts Avenue, NW
Suite 500
Washington, DC 20001

202-393-6226
888-407-6226
FAX 202-393-2630
E-Mail: nacomeetings@naco.org
Home Page: admin.naco.org

Larry E. Naake, Executive Director

Provides an opportunity for all county leaders and staff to learn, network and guide the direction of the association. Provides county officials with a great opportunity to vote on NACo's policies related to federal legislation and regulation; elect officers; network with colleagues; learn about innovative county programs; find out about issues impacting counties

across the country; and view products and services from participating companies and exhibitors.
Frequency: Annual/July

12322 NACo's Annual Conference and Exposition
National Association of Counties
440 1st Street NW
Washington, DC 20001-2028

202-393-6226
FAX 202-393-2630
E-Mail: webmaster@naco.org
Home Page: www.naco.org

Amanda Clark, Conference & Meetings Associate
Kim Struble, Conference & Meetings Director
Larry Naake, CEO

The place for elected and appointed county officials to network, attend educational sessions and meet with companies that sell products to counties. It includes a variety of activities designed to meet the needs of all delegates. In addition to strong educational sessions, the conference includes affiliate, steering and subcommittee meetings, state association meetings and social events.
4000 Attendees
Frequency: Annual

12323 NAHRO National Conference
Nat'l Assn of Housing & Redevelopment Officials
630 Eye Street NW
Washington, DC 20001-3736

202-289-3500
877-866-2476
FAX 202-289-8181
E-Mail: nahro@nahro.org
Home Page: www.nahro.org

A wide array of products and services needed by the housing and community development field.
3M Attendees
Frequency: Annual/October

12324 NARC Conference and Exhibition
National Association of Regional Councils
1666 Connecticut Ave NW
Suite 305
Washington, DC 20002

202-986-1032
FAX 202-986-1038
E-Mail: lindsey@narc.org
Home Page: www.narc.org

Fred Abousleman, Executive Director
Lindsey Riley, Deputy of Communications
500+ Attendees
Frequency: Annual/June

12325 NASTAD Annual Conference
Nat'l Alliance of State/Territorial AIDS Directors
444 N Capitol St NW
Suite 339
Washington, DC 20001

202-434-8090
FAX 202-434-8092
E-Mail: nastad@nastad.org
Home Page: www.nastad.org

Julie Scofield, Executive Director

Apprenticeship directors from around the nation come together to problem solve, share innovative ideas to the Registered Apprenticeship model as well as to bring the association up to date on each state's activities.
Frequency: Annual/May

12326 NCBM Annual Convention
National Conference of Black Mayors

191 Peachtree Street, NE
Suite 849
Atlanta, GA 30303

404-765-6444
FAX 404-765-6430
E-Mail: info@ncbm.org
Home Page: www.ncbm.org

Vanessa R. Williams, Executive Director
Robert L. Bowser, President
Jamie Mayo, Treasurer
Johnny L. DuPree, Ph.D, Secretary
John White, Sergeant-at-Arms

Serving as a catalyst for bringing together mayors and municipal leaders, including several international delegations, state and federal officials, as well as leaders in the public and private sectors for the purpose of networking and obtaining information on the latest policies and strategies for enhancing municipal government.
542 Members
Founded in 1974

12327 NCSHA Housing Credit Conference & Marketplace

444 N Capitol Street NW
Suite 438
Washington, DC 20001-1512

202-624-7710
FAX 202-624-5899
Home Page: www.ncsha.org

Louise Moors, Membership Coordinator
William Pound, Executive Director

Brings leaders and top development and compliance staff from the state Housing Credit allocating agencies together with government officials, developers, lenders, syndicators, investors, attorneys, accountants, property managers, compliance experts, owners, and nonprofits. Heavy hitters of the industry and their partners will deliver the latest news on how to make the housing Credit work in these unprecedented times.
700 Attendees
Frequency: Annual/June

12328 NCSL Fall Forum

National Conference of State Legislatures
7700 East First Place
Denver, CO 80230

303-364-7700
FAX 303-364-7800
Home Page: www.ncsl.org

Peg Coniglio, Manager
Deana Blackwood, Circulation Director

Focuses on how best to advance the States' Agenda and tackle the difficult policy issues of our time, including budget gaps, health care coverage, education affordability, transportation funding, energy costs and many others.
6700 Attendees
Frequency: Annual/November

12329 NCSL Legislative Summit

National Conference of State Legislatures
444 North Capitol Street NW
Suite 515
Washington, DC 20001

202-624-5400
FAX 202-737-1069
E-Mail: deana.blackwood@ncsl.org
Home Page: www.ncsl.org

William T Pound, Executive Director
Leticia Van de Putte, President
Steven Rauschenberger, VP
Max Arinder, Staff Chair

Four days of 150 policy sessions on the most pressing issues facing state legislatures. Some of the topics include budget conditions, educa-

tion reform, health care implementation and renewable energy.
13M+ Members
4800+ Attendees
Frequency: Annual/August
Founded in 1975

12330 NCWM Annual Meeting

National Conference on Weights and Measures
1135 M Street
Suite 110
Lincoln, NE 68508

402-434-4880
FAX 402-434-4878
E-Mail: info@ncwm.net
Home Page: www.ncwm.net

Don Onwiler, Executive Director

Technical presentations are a way to stay on the cutting edge of new developments in the weights and measures community. Complete the business of the conference through open hearings and voting on national standards.

12331 NEMA Mid-Year Conference

National Emergency Management Association
PO Box 11910
Lexington, KY 40578

859-244-8000
FAX 859-244-8239
E-Mail: nemaadmin@csg.org
Home Page: www.nemaweb.org

Jim Mullen, President
John Madden, Vice President
Charley English, Treasurer
Tom Sands, Secretary
Brenda Bergeron, Legal Counsel

Gives the opportunity to discuss important issues in the field of emergency management and homeland security. Also hear from respected leaders working on many of these issues. Opportunities to meet and network with peers are invaluable in these times of rapid change and economic challenges.
Frequency: Annual/March

12332 NFBPA FORUM

National Forum for Black Public Administrators
777 N Capitol Street NE
Suite 807
Washington, DC 20002-4239

202-289-5851
800-745-8780
FAX 202-962-3500
E-Mail: webmaster@nfbpa.org
Home Page: www.nfbpa.org

Aretha R. Ferrell-Benavides, President
Verdenia C. Baker, 1st Vice President
Bruce T. Moore, 2nd Vice President
Jelynn LeBlanc Burley, Secretary/ Treasurer

Waves of change, oceans of opportunity repositioning our communities for the future. Plenary sessions and luncheons, public policy forum, workshops, banquet and brunch, corporate exhibit, vendor showcase, artist's gallery and more.
1.4M Attendees
Frequency: Annual/April

12333 NPELRA Annual Training Conference

National Public Employer Labor Relations Assoc.
1620 I Street NW
4th Floor
Washington, DC 20006-4005

202-591-1190
FAX 202-293-2352

Home Page: www.npelra.org
Social Media: *Facebook, Twitter, LinkedIn*

Sam Penrod, President
Michael S. Bates, Executive Vice President
Christa Ballowe, Vice President
Walt Pellegrini, Vice President
Joel Kuhl, Secretary/ Treasurer

Attend the best training available for public sector Labor Relations & Human Resources professionals with over 30 program sessions; in addition the conference provides credit hours for CLE and HRCI recertification. Interact with colleagues representing public sector labor relations professionals from across the country.
350 Attendees
Frequency: Annual

12334 NPELRA Training Conference

National Public Employer Labor Relations Assoc
1012 South Coast Highway
Suite M
Oceanside, CA 92054

760-433-1686
877-673-5721
FAX 760-433-1687
E-Mail: mike@npelra.org
Home Page: www.npelra.org
Social Media: *Facebook, Twitter, LinkedIn*

Michael T Kolb, Executive Director
Janessa Stephens, Association Specialist
Yvonne Gillengerten, Operation Manager
Stephanie Biggs, Administrative Assistant
Allison Wittwer, Administrative Assistant

Attend the best training available for public sector Labor Relations and Human Resources professionals with over 30 program sessions; in addition the conference provides credit hours for CLE and HRCI recertification. Interact wth colleagues representing public sector labor relations professionals from across the country.
Frequency: Annual

12335 NSCL Legislative Summit

National Conference of State Legislatures
7700 E 1st Pl
Denver, CO 80230-7143

303-364-7700
FAX 303-364-7800
E-Mail: pubs-info@ncsl.org
Home Page: www.ncsl.org
Social Media: *Twitter, LinkedIn*

William Pound, Executive Director
Edward Smith, Managing Editor
LeAnn Hoff, Director, Revenue & Sales

A bipartisan organization that serves the legislators and staffs of the nation's 50 states, its commonwealths and territories.
15000 Members
5500 Attendees
Founded in 1975

12336 National Association Regional Councils

1666 Conneticut Ave NW
Suite 305
Washington, DC 20002

202-986-1032
FAX 202-986-1038
Home Page: www.narc.org

Shawn Sample, Show Manager

80 booths.
1.2M Attendees
Frequency: June
Founded in 1965

12337 National Council of State Housing Agencies Conference
444 N Capitol St NW
Suite 438
Washington, DC 20001-1505

202-624-7710
FAX 202-624-5899
E-Mail: bthompson@ncsha.org
Home Page: www.ncsha.org
Social Media: *Facebook, Twitter*

Gerald M. Hunter, President
Brian A. Hudson, Vice President
Thomas R. Gleason, Secretary/ Treasurer
Barbara J. Thompson, Executive Director

The premier gathering of state HFAs and NCSHA affiliate members. It is the main networking event of the year for HFAs and the partners who work with them to increase housing opportunities through the financing, developemnt, and preservation of affordable housing.
350 Members
Frequency: Annual/October
Founded in 1974

12338 National Electricity Forum
NARUC
1101 Vermont Ave NW
Suite 200
Washington, DC 20005-3553

202-898-2200
FAX 202-898-2213
E-Mail: admin@naruc.org
Home Page: www.naruc.org

David A. Wright, Chairman & President
Philip B. Jones, 1st Vice President
Colette D. Honorable, 2nd Vice President
David E. Ziegner, Treasurer
Charles D. Gray, Executive Director

Addressing cutting-edge issues and discuss how collaboration can successfully modernize the nation's electricity infrastructure. The forum will feature national thought leaders from all sectors of the electric power industry, academia, policymakers, equipment manufacturers, consumers, and other affected parties.
Frequency: Annual/February
Founded in 1889

12339 National League of Postmasters Annual National Convention
National League of Postmasters
5904 Richmond Highway
Suite 500
Alexandria, VA 22303-1864

703-329-4550
FAX 703-329-0466
E-Mail: exhibit@epponline.com
Home Page: www.epponline.com

Mark W. Strong, President

Extensive training and educational opportunities.
1400 Attendees
Frequency: Annual/August
Founded in 1903

12340 National Postal Forum
3998 Fair Ridge Drive
Suite 300
Fairfax, VA 22033

703-218-5015
FAX 703-218-5020
E-Mail: info@npf.org
Home Page: www.npf.org
Social Media: *Facebook, Twitter, LinkedIn, Flickr*

Mary Guthrie, Director, Marketing & Exhibits
Laurie Woodhams, Exhibits Assistant

The premier educational event and tradeshow available to mail professionals today. Attend the National Postal Forum to get a complete education in the Business of Mail.
Frequency: Annual/April

12341 Norfolk NATO Festival
440 Bank Street
Norfolk, VA 23510

757-282-2800
FAX 757-282-2787
Home Page: www.azaleafestival.org

Kelly Harlan, General Manager

A salute to the NATO's Allied Command Atlantic forces in order to create new friendships, provide a basis for cultural exchange, recognize the military's role in maintaining peace in the world and pursue new lines of trade between Norfolk and the world.
5M Attendees
Frequency: Canada
Founded in 1953

12342 PHADA Annual Convention and Exhibition
Public Housing Authorities Directors Association
511 Capitol Court NE
Washington, DC 20002-4937

202-546-5445
FAX 202-546-2280
Home Page: www.phada.org

Timothy G. Kaiser, Executive Director
Stephanie White, Director of Meetings

Provides the latest information and tools housing authorities need to run their agencies in these changing times. Also, many exciting housing suppliers and vendors will be on-hand to showcase their services. There are many sessions to provide attendees with important information emanating from Congress and HUD headquarters.
800 Attendees
Frequency: Annual/May

12343 Transforming Local Government Conference
Mid-America Regional Council
6604 Harney Road, Suite L
PO Box 16645
Tampa, FL 33687-6645

813-622-8484
FAX 813-664-0051
Home Page: www.tlgconference.org
Social Media: *Facebook, Twitter, Flickr, YouTube*

Mary Laird, Executive Assistant
David Warm, Executive Director

Through innovative case study sessions, conference attendees will take an in-depth look at the ingenuity and creativity of successful government programs. TLG attracts participation from local governments that are deliberately seeking new and innovative ways to connect people, information and ideas that support their efforts to be the best communities in which to live, work, and prosper.
800 Attendees
Frequency: Annual
Printed in one color on matte stock

12344 UDT: Undersea Defense Technology Conference and Exhibition
Reed Exhibition Companies
255 Washington Street
Newton, MA 02458-1637

617-584-4900
FAX 617-630-2222
Social Media: *Facebook, Twitter, LinkedIn*

Elizabeth Hitchcock, International Sales

The world's leading exhibition and conference for undersea defence and security. Gain access to the latest technologies, connect with existing suppliers and create new business relationships. Gives the invaluable opportunity to network across the global maritime community. Suppliers exhibiting; UUVs and components, acoustic technologies, maritime surveillance solutions, harbour and port security products, mine detection systems, and submarine hardware and electronics.
Frequency: Annual/May

12345 UNA-USA Annual Meeting
United Nations Association of the USA
1800 Massachusetts Avenue NW
Suite 400
Washington, DC 20036

202-887-9040
FAX 202-887-9021
E-Mail: inquiries@un.org
Home Page: www.unausa.org

Patrick Madden, Executive Director

Brings together UNA-USA's constituencies for a variety of skills trainings, issue briefings, networking opportunities and capacity-building.
400 Attendees
Frequency: Annual/November

12346 Western Legislative Conference
1107 9th Street
Suite 730
Sacramento, CA 95814

916-553-4423
FAX 916-446-5760
E-Mail: csgw@csg.org
Home Page: www.csgwest.org

Rosie Berger, Chair
Kelvin Atkinson, Chair-Elect
Craig Johnson, Vice Chair

Brings together legislators from western states to learn from each other and collaborate on issues of regional concern such as water, public lands, energy and transportation. Also offers training and professional development opportunities for all legislators.
500 Attendees
Frequency: Annual/July
Founded in 1933

Directories & Databases

12347 Almanac of American Politics
National Journal
1730 M St NW
Suite 800
Washington, DC 20036-4551

202-828-0300
FAX 202-457-5160

Marcia Coyle, Manager

The definitive guide to understanding the forces that shape American politics. Has been established as a Washington institution in its own right and an indespensable resource for anyone involved or interested in the American political scene.
Cost: $59.95
1500 Pages
Frequency: Biennial

12348 Almanac of the Federal Judiciary
Prentice Hall Law & Business
270 Sylvan Avenue
Englewood Cliffs, NJ 07632-2521

201-569-0006

Providing balanced, responsible judicial profiles of every federal judge and all the key bankruptcy judges and magistrate judges- profiles that include reliable inside information based on interviews with lawyers who have ar-

gued cases before the federal judiciary.
Cost: $1715.00
2130 Pages
Frequency: Annual
ISBN: 9-780735-56-8

12349 American Bench
Forster-Long
3280 Ramos Cir
Sacramento, CA 95827-2513

916-362-3276
800-328-5091
FAX 916-362-5643
Home Page: www.forster-long.com

Jay Long, Vice President, Marketing

Over 19,000 judges who sit in local, state and federal courts are profiled. The definitive biographical reference to the American judiciary.
Cost: $595.00
Frequency: Daily
Founded in 1977

12350 BRB Publications
BRB Publications
PO Box 27869
Tempe, AZ 85285-7869

480-829-7475
800-929-3811
FAX 800-929-4981
E-Mail: mike@brbpublications.com
Home Page: www.BRBpublications.com

Mike Sankey, President

Comprehensive listing of government agencies that have placed public records online, both free and fee based.
Founded in 1988

12351 Billcast Archive
George Mason University, Public Choice Center
4400 University Dr
Fairfax, VA 22030-4444

703-993-1120

Clayton Austin, Manager

This database contains information on public bills introduced in the US House of Representatives and Senate during the preceding session of Congress.

12352 Book of the States
Council of State Governments
2760 Research Park Drive
PO Box 11910
Lexington, KY 40578-1910

859-244-8000
800-800-1910
FAX 859-244-8001
E-Mail: research@csg.org
Home Page: www.csg.org

Jodi Rell, President
Carol Juett, Director of Development
Roger Werholtz, Secretary

A reference tool of choice and includes comparative information on everything from highway miles to state government employment and everything in between.
Cost: $99.00
Frequency: Annually
Founded in 1935

12353 CSG State Directories
Council of State Governments
2760 Research Park Drive
PO Box 11910
Lexington, KY 40578-1910

859-244-8000
800-800-1910
FAX 859-244-8001

E-Mail: research@csg.org
Home Page: www.csg.org

Jodi Rell, President
Carol Juett, Director of Development
Roger Werholtz, Secretary

Includes the names and contact information for key state government officials.
Frequency: Annually

12354 Canadian Almanac & Directory
Grey House Publishing Canada
555 Richmond Street West
Suite 301
Toronto, ON M5V 3B1

416-644-6479
866-433-4739
FAX 416-644-1904
E-Mail: info@greyhouse.ca
Home Page: www.greyhouse.ca
Social Media: *Facebook, Twitter, LinkedIn*

Richard Gottlieb, President
Leslie Mackenzie, Publisher

A combination of textual material, charts, colour photographs and directory listings, the Canadian Almanac & Directory provides the most comprehensive picture of Canada, from physical attributes to economic and business summaries to leisure and recreation.
Cost: $360.00
1936 Pages
Frequency: Annual
ISBN: 1-592377-69-5

12355 Canadian Parliamentary Guide
Grey House Publishing Canada
555 Richmond Street West
Suite 301
Toronto, ON M5V 3B1

416-644-6479
866-433-4739
FAX 416-644-1904
E-Mail: info@greyhouse.ca
Home Page: www.greyhouse.ca
Social Media: *Facebook, Twitter, LinkedIn*

Richard Gottlieb, President
Leslie Mackenzie, Publisher

Canadian Parliamentary Guide provides the most complete and comprehensive information on elected and appointed members in federal and provincial government.
Cost: $229.00
1152 Pages
Frequency: Annual
ISBN: 1-592377-65-7

12356 Capital Source
National Journal
600 New Hampshire Ave NW
Suite 4
Washington, DC 20037-2403

202-739-8400
FAX 202-833-8069
E-Mail: capitalsource@nationaljournal.com

John Fox Sullivan, President

Directory brimming with key information on the most important players and institutions Inside-the-Beltway, The Capital Source is the place for essential and current contact information all year round. A must-have resource for anyone in the business of politics, policy, government relations or the media.
Cost: $29.95
160 Pages
Frequency: Monthly

12357 Carroll's County Directory
Carroll Publishing

4701 Sangamore Rd
Suite S-155
Bethesda, MD 20816-2532

301-263-9800
800-336-4240
FAX 301-263-9805
E-Mail: customersvc@carrollpub.com
Home Page: www.carrollpub.com
Social Media: *Twitter, LinkedIn*

Bill Wade, President/COO
Kathleen Undegraff, VP Marketing
Cost: $350.00
Founded in 1973

12358 Carroll's Federal Directory
Carroll Publishing
4701 Sangamore Rd
Suite 155S
Bethesda, MD 20816-2532

301-263-9800
800-336-4240
FAX 301-263-9805
E-Mail: info@carrollpub.com
Home Page: www.carrollpub.com

Tom Carroll, President

Offers complete coverage of the headquarter offices of the Executive, Legislative, and Judicial branches of government. Includes over 38,000 positions offering direct contact information for all Executive departments, independent agencies, Congressional Agencies and US Federal Courts.
Cost: $500.00
450 Pages
Frequency: Annual

12359 Carroll's Federal Regional Directory
Carroll Publishing
4701 Sangamore Rd
Suite 155S
Bethesda, MD 20816-2532

301-263-9800
800-336-4240
FAX 301-263-9805
E-Mail: info@carrollpub.com
Home Page: www.carrollpub.com

Tom Carroll, President

The one regional resource that has it all. Covering regional and field offices of Federal government departments, home-state offices for members of Congress, federal district courts and more. Reach over 32,000 government people located outside of Washington.
Cost: $170.00
370 Pages
Frequency: Bi-Annually

12360 Carroll's Municipal Directory
Carroll Publishing
4701 Sangamore Rd
Suite 155S
Bethesda, MD 20816-2532

301-263-9800
800-336-4240
FAX 301-263-9805
E-Mail: info@carrollpub.com
Home Page: www.carrollpub.com

Tom Carroll, President

The most comprehensive municipal directory available anywhere. It includes more than 60,000 appointed officials, career officials and local authorities across the US. Covering more cities than any other source, this has nearly 8,000 cities, towns and villages.
Cost: $170.00
550 Pages
Frequency: Bi-Annually

12361 Carroll's State Directory
Carroll Publishing

4701 Sangamore Rd
Suite 155S
Bethesda, MD 20816-2532

301-263-9800
800-336-4240
FAX 301-263-9805
Home Page: www.carrollpub.com
Social Media: *Twitter, LinkedIn*

Bill Wade, President/COO
Kathleen Updegraff, VP Marketing

Provides complete contact information for over 68,000 key officials in all 50 states, plus the District of Columbia, Puerto Rico and the American Territories.
Cost: $210.00
530 Pages
Frequency: TriAnnual

12362 Congress at Your Fingertips: Congressional Directory
Capitol Advantage
1255 22nd St NW
Washington, DC 20037-1217

703-899-9636
800-659-8708
FAX 703-289-4678
E-Mail: sales@capitoladvantage.com
Home Page: www.capitoladvantage.com

Dr. John Hansan, Production Manager

Comprehensive directory lists members of the US Senate and House of Representatives, complete with color photos and a fold-out map of Capitol Hill.
Cost: $13.95
Frequency: Annual

12363 Congressional Staff Directory
Leadership Directories, Inc.
1167 K Street NW
Suite 801
Washington, DC 20006

202-628-7757
FAX 202-628-3430
E-Mail: infoleadershipdirectories.com
Home Page: www.leadershipdirectories.com

Gretchen Teichgraeber, CEO
William Cressey, Chairman

Locate key decision-makers and support staff that work behind the scenes on important legislative issues. Pinpoint key contacts on committees who work day-to-day on legislation that's most important.
Cost: $69.00
1200 Pages
Frequency: SemiAnnual

12364 Daily Defense News Capsules
United Communications Group
11300 Rockville Pike
Suite 1100
Rockville, MD 20852-3030

301-816-8950
FAX 301-816-8945

Greg Beaudoin, Editor

This database offers the complete text of Periscope - Daily Defense News Capsules, that provide abstracts of international press coverage of military and defense news.

12365 Defense Industry Charts
Carroll Publishing
4701 Sangamore Rd
Suite 155S
Bethesda, MD 20816-2532

301-263-9800
800-336-4240
FAX 301-263-9805
E-Mail: info@carrollpub.com
Home Page: www.carrollpub.com

Tom Carroll, President

19000 key personnel in top US defense contractors, including major aerospace, electronic, military hardware, information technology and systems integration companies. Serves as a road map to the critical players in this important industry.
Cost: $2050.00
Frequency: Quarterly

12366 Defense Programs
Carroll Publishing
4701 Sangamore Rd
Suite 155S
Bethesda, MD 20816-2532

301-263-9800
800-336-4240
FAX 301-263-9805
E-Mail: info@carrollpub.com
Home Page: www.carrollpub.com

Tom Carroll, President

Detailed description of more than 2,000 military research, development, test and evaluation programs and projects.
Cost: $1060.00
Frequency: Quarterly

12367 Defense and Foreign Affairs Handbook
International Strategic Studies Association
PO Box 19289
Alexandria, VA 22320-0289

703-548-1070
FAX 703-684-7476
E-Mail: dfa@strategicstudies.org
Home Page: www.strategicstudies.org

Gregory Copley, Editor

Important global reference encyclopedia for most world leaders .Comprehensive chapters on 238 countries and territories worldwide, with each chapter giving full cabinet and leadership listings, history, recent developments, demographics, economic statistics, political and constitutional data, news media,defense overview, defense structure.
Cost: $297.00
2500 Pages
Frequency: Monthly
Circulation: 4,000
ISBN: 1-892998-06-8
Founded in 1976

12368 Directory of Congressional Voting Scores and Interest Group Ratings
1414 22nd Street NW
Washington, DC 20037-1003

202-887-8500
800-432-2250
FAX 800-380-3810
Home Page: www.cqpress.com

Complete compilation of CQ voting studies and interest group rating data for every legislator who has served in Congress since 1947. This resource is perfect for quick or in-depth research and provides the easiest, most accurate way to gauge the political orientation of members of Congress over time. This is the best source for understanding the political preferences of US senators and representatives, and what it means about their choices on future votes.
Cost: $450.00
1700 Pages
Frequency: Triennial

12369 Encyclopedia of Governmental Advisory Organizations
Gale/Cengage Learning
PO Box 6904
Florence, KY 41022-6904

800-354-9706
FAX 800-487-8488

E-Mail: gale.galeord@cengage.com
Home Page: www.gale.com

Patrick C Sommers, President

Contains entries which describe the activities and personnel of groups and committees that function to advise the President of the United States and various departments and bureaus of the federal government, as well as detailed information about historically significant committees.
Frequency: Annual

12370 Federal Benefits for Veterans, Dependents and Survivors
US Department of Veterans Affairs
810 Vermont Ave NW
Washington, DC 20420-0002

202-273-5400
FAX 202-273-4880

John R Gingirch, CEO

Health care benefits, disability benefits, pensions, home loan, insurance, and much more.
Cost: $3.25
Frequency: Annual

12371 Federal Buyers Guide
Gold Crest
650 Ward Dr # A
Santa Barbara, CA 93111-2395

805-683-9000
800-922-3233
FAX 805-683-7661
Home Page: www.goldcrestinc.com

Roger Edgar, CEO
Gunnar Sundstrom, OPS Manager

Companies that serve or wish to serve as vendors to the federal government. Reading specialty lights, giftware, manufacturer, distributor, Mighty Bright brand.
170 Pages
Frequency: Quarterly
ISSN: 1043-7568
Founded in 1979

12372 Federal Directory of Contract Administration Services Components
Contract Mgmt. Command/Defense
Logistics Agency
Caremon Station
Alexandria, VA 22304

703-781-9807

Lists the names and telephone numbers of those DCMA and other agency offices that offer contract administration services within designated geographic areas and at specified contractor plants.
110 Pages
Frequency: Annually

12373 Federal Government Certification Programs
US National Institute of Standards & Technology
Administration Building
Room 629
Gaithersburg, MD 20899-0001

301-975-2281
FAX 301-963-2871

A directory available certification programs.
Cost: $18.95
229 Pages

12374 Federal Staff Direcotry
1414 22nd Street NW
Washington, DC 20037-1003

202-887-8500
800-432-2250

FAX 800-380-3810
Home Page: www.cqpress.com

Penny Perry, Editor

Pinpoint senior officials and top aides working directly with the President and Vice President using the most well-researched information available. Find all the information needed to locate high-ranking policy-makers, their deputies, bureau chiefs, and division heads. Connect with top-level officials at agencies ranging from the American Red Cross to the Environmental Protection Agency.
Cost: $450.00
1700 Pages
Frequency: Monthly

12375 Federal Technology Source

Government Executive- National Journal Group
600 New Hampshire Ave NW
Suite 4
Washington, DC 20037-2403

202-739-8500
800-356-4838
FAX 202-739-8511
E-Mail: webmaster@govexec.com
Home Page: www.govexec.com

Matt Dunie, President
Sue Fourney, Managing Editor

A directory of most important people and organizations in the federal technology community.
Cost: $9.95
168 Pages
Frequency: Annual
Circulation: 73,500
ISSN: 0017-2626
Printed in 4 colors on glossy stock

12376 Foreign Consular Offices in the United States

Bureau of Public Affairs/US Department of State
2201 C Street NW
Washington, DC 20520-0001

202-647-6141

A complete and official listing of the foreign consular offices in the US, and recognized consular officers. Compiled by the US Department of State, with the full cooperation of the foreign missions in Washington, it is offered as a convenience to organizations and persons who must deal with consular government agencies, state tax officials, international trade organizations, chamber of commerce, and judicial authorities.
Cost: $4.00
290 Pages
Frequency: Annual

12377 Getting Started in Federal Contracting: A Guide Through the Federal Maze

Panoptic Enterprises
PO Box 11220
Burke, VA 22009-1220

703-451-5953
800-594-4766
FAX 703-451-5953
Home Page: www.fedgovcontracts.com

Vivina Mcvay, President
Barry L McVay, Editor

Information is given on over 65 government procurement offices, Department of Labor offices, General Services Administration business services and Small Business Administration regional and branch offices.
Cost: $39.95
395 Pages
ISBN: 0-912481-24-2
Founded in 1984

12378 Government Assistance Almanac: Guide to all Federal Financial Programs

Omnigraphics
615 Griswold
Detroit, MI 48226

313-961-1340
800-234-1340
FAX 313-961-1383
E-Mail: editorial@omnigraphics.com
Home Page: www.omnigraphics.com

Robert Dumouchel, Editor

Provides updated information on all 1,613 federal domestic assistance programs available. These programs represent $1.675 trillion worth of federal assistance earmarked for distribution to consumers, children, parents, veterans, senior citizens, students, businesses, civic groups, state and local agencies, and others.
Cost: $240.00
1,000 Pages
Frequency: Annual
ISBN: 0-780807-00-6

12379 Government Phone Book USA

Omnigraphics
615 Griswold Street
Detroit, MI 48226

313-961-1340
800-234-1340
FAX 313-961-1383
E-Mail: editorial@omnigraphics.com
Home Page: www.omnigraphics.com

David Bianco, Marketing Director

Key federal, state and local government offices in the US are profiled. More than 270,000 listings with complete contact data.
Cost: $275.00
2,700 Pages
Frequency: Annual
ISBN: 0-780806-93-X
Founded in 1992

12380 Government Research Directory

Gale/Cengage Learning
PO Box 09187
Detroit, MI 48209-0187

248-699-4253
800-877-4253
FAX 248-699-8049
E-Mail: gale.galeord@cengage.com
Home Page: www.gale.com

Patrick C Sommers, President

In this vital resource you'll find research facilities and programs of the US and Canadian federal governments. Listings include e-mail addresses, information on patents available for licensing and expanded coverage of key personal contact.
ISBN: 1-414420-23-4

12381 Governments Canada

Grey House Publishing Canada
555 Richmond Street West
Suite 301
Toronto, ON M5V 3B1

416-644-6479
866-433-4739
FAX 416-644-1904
E-Mail: info@greyhouse.ca
Home Page: www.greyhouse.ca
Social Media: Facebook, Twitter, LinkedIn

Richard Gottlieb, President
Leslie Mackenzie, Publisher

Governments Canada is the most complete and comprehensive tool for locating people and programs in Canada. It provides regularly updated listings on federal, provincial and territorial government departments, offices and agencies across Canada. Branch and regional

offices are also included, along with all associated agencies, boards, commissions and crown corporations. Listings include contact names, full address, telephone and fax numbers, as well as e-mail addresses.
Cost: $299.00
600 Pages
Frequency: 2x/Year
ISBN: 1-592379-85-9

12382 Grey House Safety & Security Directory

Grey House Publishing
4919 Route 22
PO Box 56
Amenia, NY 12501

518-789-8700
800-562-2139
FAX 845-373-6390
E-Mail: books@greyhouse.com
Home Page: www.greyhouse.com
Social Media: Facebook, Twitter

Leslie Mackenzie, Publisher
Richard Gottlieb, Editor

Comprehensive guide to the safety and security industry, including articles, checklists, OSHA regulations and product listings. Focuses on creating and maintaining a safe and secure enviroment, and dealing specifically with hazardous materials, noise and vibration, workplace preparation and maintenance, electrical and lighting safety, fire and rescue and more.
Cost: $165.00
1600 Pages
ISBN: 1-592373-75-5
Founded in 1981

12383 Guide to Management Improvement Projects in Local Government

ICMA Publications
777 N Capitol St NE
Suite 600
Washington, DC 20002-4240

202-216-9408
800-745-8780
FAX 202-962-3500
Home Page: www.icma.org

Joan Mc Callen, President

Projects conducted by municipal governments that have resulted in improvements in efficiency or cost reductions are listed.
Cost: $65.00
50 Pages
Frequency: Quarterly

12384 Hudson's Washington News Media Contacts Directory

Grey House Publishing
4919 Route 22
PO Box 56
Amenia, NY 12501

518-789-8700
800-562-2139
FAX 845-373-6390
E-Mail: books@greyhouse.com
Home Page: www.greyhouse.com
Social Media: Facebook, Twitter

Leslie Mackenzie, Publisher
Richard Gottlieb, President

A comprehensive guide to the entire Washington, D.C. press corps, broken down into categories.
Cost: $289.00
350 Pages
ISBN: 1-592378-53-6
Printed in one color on matte stock

12385 Hudson's Washington News Media Contacts - Online Database

Grey House Publishing

4919 Route 22
PO Box 56
Amenia, NY 12501

518-789-8700
800-562-2139
FAX 845-373-6390
E-Mail: gold@greyhouse.com
Home Page: http://gold.greyhouse.com
Social Media: *Facebook, Twitter*

Leslie Mackenzie, Publisher
Richard Gottlieb, President

With 100% verification of data, Hudson's is the most accurate, most up-to-date source for media contacts in our nation's capital. With the largest concentration of news media in the world, having access to Washington's news media will get your message heard by these key media outlets.

12386 IAEM Directory
International Association of Emergency Managers
111 Park Pl
Falls Church, VA 22046-4513

703-538-1795
FAX 703-241-5603
E-Mail: info@iaem.com
Home Page: www.iaem.com

Shan Coffin, Editor
Sharon L Kelly, Circulation Director
Cost: $100.00
Circulation: 8,000

12387 Immediate Need Resource Directory
Gold Crest
650 Ward Dr
Suite A
Santa Barbara, CA 93111-2395

805-683-9000
800-922-3233
FAX 805-683-7661
Home Page: www.goldcrestinc.com

Roger Edgar, CEO
Gunnar Sundstrom, OPS Manager

A directory catering to the immediate needs of Federal government purchasing agents. Reading and speciality lights, giftware, manufacturer, distributor, Mighty Bright brand.
Cost: $20.00
50 Pages
Frequency: Monthly
Founded in 1990

12388 Judicial Yellow Book
Leadership Directories
104 5th Ave
New York, NY 10011-6901

212-627-4140
FAX 212-645-0931
E-Mail: judicial@leadershipdirectories.com
Home Page: www.leadershipdirectories.com

David Hurvitz, CEO
James M Petrie, Associate Publisher

Contact information for over 3,250 federal and state judges in federal and state appellate courts, including staff and law clerks, and the law schools they attended.
Cost: $245.00
1,100 Pages
Frequency: SemiAnnual
ISSN: 1082-3298
Founded in 1995
Mailing list available for rent: 13,000 names at $125 per M

12389 Kaleidoscope: Current World Data
ABC-CLIO

PO Box 1911
Santa Barbara, CA 93102-1911

805-968-1911
FAX 805-685-9685
E-Mail: CustomerService@abc-clio.com
Home Page: www.abc-clio.com

Ron Boehm, CEO

This comprehensive database takes a look at all aspects of the American culture. Listings of information include statistics and factual information on the population, culture, economy, military forces, government, and political systems of countries around the world, the US States and Canadian provinces.
Frequency: Full-text

12390 Leadership Directories
104 5th Ave
New York, NY 10011-6901

212-627-4140
FAX 212-645-0931
E-Mail: info@leadershipdirectories.com
Home Page: www.leadershipdirectories.com

David Hurvitz, CEO
Barry Graubart, Executive VP/CMO

The mission of Leadership Directories is to compile, produce and offer subscribers, in all media and in easily usable form, the most current and accurate directories of leaders in the major categories of American activity, including government, business, the professions, and the nonprofits.
Founded in 1969

12391 Leadership Library in Print
Leadership Directories
104 5th Ave
New York, NY 10011-6901

212-627-4140
FAX 212-645-0931
E-Mail: info@leadershipdirectories.com
Home Page: www.leadershipdirectories.com

David Hurvitz, CEO

Complete set of all 14 leadership directories. Provides subscribers with complete contact information for the 400,000 individuals who constitute the institutional leadership of the US.
Cost: $2300.00
Frequency: Semiannually
Founded in 1996

12392 Leadership Library on Internet and CD-ROM
Leadership Directories
104 5th Ave
New York, NY 10011-6901

212-627-4140
FAX 212-645-0931
E-Mail: info@leadershipdirectories.com
Home Page: www.leadershipdirectories.com

David Hurvitz, CEO

Makes all 14 leadership directories available over the Internet and on CD-ROM in one integrated directory. They provide subscribers with complete contact information, in one database. Subscription includes Internet access and four CD-ROM editions quarterly.
Cost: $3065.00
Frequency: Updated Daily
ISSN: 1075-3869
Founded in 1999
Mailing list available for rent
Printed in A colors on B stock

12393 Local Court & County Record Retrievers
BRB Publications

PO Box 27869
Tempe, AZ 85285

480-677-7200
800-929-3811
FAX 480-829-8505
Home Page: www.brbpub.com

Mark Sankey, President

Who's who of the public record retrieval industry. Over 2,700 companies profiled and indexed, can search alphabetically and by location.
Cost: $39.95
632 Pages
Frequency: Annual
ISBN: 1-879792-76-1
Founded in 1994

12394 Member Data Disk
CQ Staff Directories
815 Slaters Lane
Alexandria, VA 22314-1219

800-252-1722
FAX 703-739-0234

Bruce B Brownson, Editor

Covers all members of the US Congress and their key staff members in Washington, DC and principal district offices.
Cost: $395.00
Frequency: Quarterly

12395 Military Biographical Profiles
CTB/McGraw Hill
20 Ryan Ranch Rd
Monterey, CA 93940-5770

831-393-0700
800-538-9547
FAX 831-393-6528
E-Mail: CTBTechnicalSupport@CTB.com
Home Page: www.ctb.com

Ellen Haley, President
Sandor Nagy, Chief Operating Officer

Offers valuable information on US military officers and Department of Defense officials.
Frequency: Full-text

12396 Municipal Year Book
ICMA Publications
777 N Capitol St NE
Suite 600
Washington, DC 20002-4240

202-216-9408
800-745-8780
FAX 202-962-3500
E-Mail: cpmmail@icma.org
Home Page: www.icma.org

Joan Mc Callen, President
Gary Huff, Founder

Directory of services and supplies to the industry.
Cost: $79.95
416 Pages
Frequency: Annual

12397 Municipal Yellow Book
Leadership Directories
104 5th Ave
New York, NY 10011-6901

212-627-4140
FAX 212-645-0931
E-Mail: municipal@leadershipdirectories.com
Home Page: www.leadershipdirectories.com

David Hurvitz, CEO
James M Petrie, Associate Publisher

Contact information for over 33,000 elected and administrative officials of US cities, counties, and local authorities.
Cost: $245.00
1,200 Pages
Frequency: SemiAnnual
ISSN: 1054-4062

Founded in 1991
Mailing list available for rent: 30,000 names at
$125 per M

12398 National Directory of Corporate Public Affairs

Columbia Books
PO Box 251
Annapolis Junction, MD 20701-0251

888-265-0600
FAX 240-646-7020
E-Mail: info@columbiabooks.com
Home Page: www.columbiabooks.com

J Valerie Steele, Senior Editor

Tracks the public/government affairs programs of about 1,900 major US corporations and lists the 14,00 people who run them, Also lists: Washington area offices, corporate PACs, federal and state lobbyists, outside contract lobbyists. Indexed by subject and geographic area. Includes membership directory of the Public Affairs Council.
Cost: $109.00
Frequency: Annual January

12399 National Directory of Women Elected Officials

National Women's Political Caucus
1630 Connecticut Avenue NW
Suite 201
Washington, DC 20009

202-785-1100
FAX 202-785-3605
E-Mail: info@nwpc.org
Home Page: www.nwpc.org

Directory of services and supplies to the industry.
230 Pages
Frequency: Biennial

12400 National and Federal Employment Report

Federal Reports
1010 Vermont Ave NW
Suite 408
Washington, DC 20005-4945

202-393-1552
FAX 202-393-1553
Home Page: www.attorneyjobs.com

Richard L Hermann, Owner

Over 600 current attorney and law-related job opportunities with the US government are listed.
Cost: $111.20
Frequency: Monthly

12401 New York State Directory

Grey House Publishing
4919 Route 22
PO Box 56
Amenia, NY 12501

518-789-8700
800-562-2139
FAX 845-373-6390
E-Mail: books@greyhouse.com
Home Page: www.greyhouse.com
Social Media: *Facebook, Twitter*

Leslie Mackenzie, Publisher
Richard Gottlieb, Editor

A comprehensive and easy-to-use guide to accessing public officials and private sector organizations and individuals who influence public policy in the state of New York. Includes important information on all New York state legislators and congressional representatives, including biographies and key committee as-

signments.
Cost: $145.00
800 Pages
ISBN: 1-592373-58-5
Founded in 1981

12402 New York State Directory - Online Database

Grey House Publishing
4919 Route 22
PO Box 56
Amenia, NY 12501

518-789-8700
800-562-2139
FAX 845-373-6390
E-Mail: gold@greyhouse.com
Home Page: http://gold.greyhouse.com
Social Media: *Facebook, Twitter*

Leslie Mackenzie, Publisher
Richard Gottlieb, Editor

A comprehensive and easy-to-use guide to accessing public officials and private sector organizations and individuals who influence public policy in the state of New York. Includes important information on all New York state legislators and congressional representatives, including biographies and key committee assignments. With a subscription to the online database, you'll have immediate access to this wealth of contact information.
Founded in 1981

12403 Organization Charts

Carroll Publishing
4701 Sangamore Rd
Suite 155S
Bethesda, MD 20816-2532

301-263-9800
800-336-4240
FAX 301-263-9805
Home Page: www.carrollpub.com

Tom Carroll, President

Provide a unique graphic visualization of the personnel relationships in Federal, Defense and Defense Industry organizations. Traditionally used to display report relationships between individuals, these charts are the #1 authoritative source for getting an up-to-date picture of the hierarchy within government, defense and defense contractors, including major aerospace, military hardware and IT companies.
Cost: $1160.00
185 Pages
Frequency: 8x Yearly

12404 Politics in America

Congressional Digest
4416 East West Highway
Suite 400
Bethesda, MD 20814-4568

301-634-3113
800-637-9915
FAX 301-634-3189
Home Page: www.pro-and-con.org

Offers information on United States senators and representatives.
Cost: $89.95
1700 Pages
Frequency: Biennial

12405 Profiles of Worldwide Government Leaders

Worldwide Government Directories
7979 Old Georgetown Road
Suite 900
Bethesda, MD 20814-2429

301-258-2677
800-332-3535
FAX 301-718-8494

Jonathan Hixon, Publisher

Spanning 195 countries, includes comprehensive biographical snapshots of as many as 30 or more ministers from each country. The material is obtained from primary and secondary sources including embassies, government ministries, offices of the United States government and proprietary global network of correspondents.
Cost: $297.00
850+ Pages
Frequency: Annual

12406 Public Human Services Directory

American Public Human Services Association
1133 19th Street NW
Suite 400
Washington, DC 20036-3623

202-682-0100
FAX 202-289-6555
Home Page: www.aphsa.org

Tracy Wareing, Executive Director

State-by-state guide to people, programs and a must-have for all human service professionals.
Frequency: Annual
Founded in 1930

12407 Public Record Research System

BRB Publications
PO Box 27869
Tempe, AZ 85285

480-677-7200
800-929-3811
FAX 480-829-8505
E-Mail: brb@brbpub.com
Home Page: www.publicrecordsources.com

Mark Sankey, President

Comprehensive public records locator, over 26,000 government agencies and institutions profiled.
Cost: $119.00

12408 Public Records Online

BRB Publications
PO Box 27869
Tempe, AZ 85285-7869

480-677-7200
800-929-3811
FAX 800-929-4981
Home Page: www.brbpub.com

Mark Sankey, President

Comprehensive listing of government agencies that have placed public records online, both free and fee based.
Cost: $20.95
520 Pages
ISBN: 1-889150-21-5
Founded in 2000

12409 Public Risk Management Association Membership Directory

500 Montgomery Street
Suite 750
Alexandria, VA 22314

703-528-7701
FAX 703-739-0200
E-Mail: info@primacentral.org
Home Page: www.primacentral.org

Jim Hirt, Executive Director
Jon Ruzan, Manager
Kerry Langley, Manager

Lists all members alphabetically; by state/country; by category; government; private; associate. Yellow pages give vender and service provider 50-wind thumbnail descriptions. Advertising sold.
Circulation: 2,000

12410 The Guide to County Court Records

BRB Publications

PO Box 27869
Tempe, AZ 85285-7869

480-829-7475
800-929-3811
FAX 800-929-4981
E-Mail: mike@brbpublications.com
Home Page: www.BRBpublications.com

Mike Sankey, President
Founded in 1988

12411 The MVR Access and Decoder Digest
BRB Publications
PO Box 27869
Tempe, AZ 85285-7869

480-829-7475
800-929-3811
FAX 800-929-4981
E-Mail: mike@brbpublications.com
Home Page: www.BRBpublications.com

Mike Sankey, President
Founded in 1988

12412 The Manual to Online Public Records
BRB Publications
PO Box 27869
Tempe, AZ 85285-7869

480-829-7475
800-929-3811
FAX 800-929-4981
E-Mail: mike@brbpublications.com
Home Page: www.BRBpublications.com

Mike Sankey, President
Founded in 1988

12413 US Congress Handbook
8120 Woodmont Ave.
Suite 110
Bethesda, MD 20814

E-Mail: info@uscongresshandbook.com
Home Page: www.uscongresshandbook.com
Social Media: *Facebook, Twitter*

Washington's most trusted source for information on Congressional offices and their staff. The most comprehensive Congressional directory available.
Frequency: Annually
Founded in 1974

12414 United States Government Manual
Office of the Federal Register
National Archives Administration
Washington, DC 20408-0001

202-564-2480
FAX 202-501-0599

The official handbook of the United States government; includes descriptions and lists of principal personnel of agencies and government bodies.
Cost: $30.00
935 Pages
Frequency: Annual

12415 Washington Information Directory
Congressional Quarterly
1414 22nd Street NW
Washington, DC 20037-1003

202-887-8500
FAX 202-822-6583

Paul McClure, Editor
Will Gardner, Associate Editor

5,000 governmental agencies, congressional committees and non-governmental associations considered competent sources of specialized information.
Cost: $105.00
Frequency: Annual June

12416 Washington: Comprehensive Directory of the Key Institutions and Leaders
Columbia Books
1212 New York Avenue NW
Suite 330
Washington, DC 20005-3969

202-641-1662
888-265-0600
FAX 202-898-0775
E-Mail: info@columbiabooks.com
Home Page: www.columbiabooks.com

Buck Downs, Senior Editor

Over 5,000 federal and district government offices, businesses, associations, publications, radio and television stations, labor organizations, religious and cultural institutions, health care facilities and community organizations in the District of Columbia area.
Cost: $75.00
Frequency: Annual May

12417 Worldwide Directory of Defense Attorneys
Worldwide Government Directories
7979 Old Georgetown Road
Suite 900
Bethesda, MD 20814-2429

301-258-2677
800-332-3535
FAX 301-718-8494

Jonathan Hixon, Publisher

One-of-a-kind resource covering military and civilian defense and national security agencies from the ministry of defense down to service branches in 195 countries worldwide.
Cost: $647.00
1,100 Pages
Frequency: Annual

12418 Worldwide Government Directory
Worldwide Government Directories
7979 Old Georgetown Road
Suite 900
Bethesda, MD 20814-2429

301-258-2677
800-332-3535
FAX 301-718-8494

Jonathan Hixon, Publisher

Offers valuable information on every senior government official in the executive, legislative, and judicial branches as well as the diplomatic and defense communities of 195 countries worldwide. Plus senior officials in over 100 international organizations. Each entry includes name, address, title, telephone, telex, facsimile number, and more. Also included are current state agencies and corporations, official forms of address, international dialing codes and central bank information.
Cost: $347.00
1,400 Pages
Frequency: Annual

12419 Worldwide Government Directory with International Organizations
1414 22nd Street NW
Washington, DC 20037-1003

202-887-8500
800-432-2250
FAX 800-380-3810
Home Page: www.cqpress.com

Linda Dziobek, Editor

Coverage includes over 1800 pages of executive, legislative and political branches; heads of state, ministers, deputies, secretaries and spokespersons as well as state agencies, diplomats and senior level defense officials. Also covers the leadership of more than 100 interna-

tional organizations.
Cost: $450.00
1700 Pages
Frequency: Annually

Industry Web Sites

12420 http://gold.greyhouse.com
G.O.L.D Grey House OnLine Databases

Grey House Publishing's online database platform, GOLD, offers Quick Search, Keyword Search and Expert Search for most business sectors including govenment markets. The GOLD platform makes finding the information you need quick and easy - whether you're a novice searcher or an experienced database user. All of Grey House's directory products are available for subscription on the GOLD platform.

12421 www.aashto.org
American Association of State Highway and Transportation

Membership is composed of highway and transportation departments in the 50 states, the District of Columbia, and Puerto Rico.

12422 www.abccert.org
Association of Boards of Certification

The Association of Boards of Certification is dedicated to protecting public health and the environment by advancing the quality and integrity of environmental certification programs through innovative technical support services, effective information exchange, professional and cost-effective examination services, and other progressive services for certifying members.

12423 www.access.digex.net/fedbar
Federal Bar Association
Members are attorneys in the Federal Government or who have interest in federal law.

12424 www.accesspro.org
American Society of Access Professionals
Members are government employees, lawyers, journalists and others concerned with access to government data under current personal privacy and public informaiton statues.

12425 www.acsp.uic.edu/iaco
International Association of Correctional Officers
Correctional officers and juvenile administrators.

12426 www.actnat.com
Association of Civilian Technicians
Union of civilian employees of the Army and National Guard and Air Reserve.

12427 www.admin.org
American Federation of School Administrators
Established in 1971 as the school administrators and supervisors organizing committee. Information of interest to those in public education.

12428 www.affirm.org
Associ for Federal Information Resources Mngt
Seeks to improve the management of information systems and resources of the Federal Government.

12429 www.afge.org
American Federation of Government Employees
The largest federal employee union representing 700,000 workers nationwide and overseas.

12430 www.afscase.org
American Federation of State, County and Municipal Employees

Sponsors their own Political Action Committee.

12431 www.aglf.org/
Association for Governmental Leasing and Finance
Provides an exchange of information among tax-exempt issuers, investment banking firms and party lease brokers.

12432 www.aja.ncsc.dni.cs
American Judges Association
An independent organization of judges in all jurisdictions in Canada, Mexico and the United States.

12433 www.alexandriagroup.com
National Association of Government Communicators
A merger of Federal Editors association, the Government Information Organization, and the Armed Forces Writers League.

12434 www.alldc.org
American League of Lobbyists
National association dedicated to serving government relations and public affairs professionals. Provides programs and conferences of interest to lobbyists.

12435 www.ansi.org
American National Standards Institute
Promotes the knowledge for approved standards for industry, engineering and safety design.

12436 www.aphf.org
American Federation of Police & Concerned Citizens
Operates the American police Academy as its educational arm. Maintains the American Police Hall of Fame & Museum in Miami, Florida.

12437 www.aspanet.org
American Society for Public Administration
Offers a wide range of services and membership options for individuals in public administration careers. Sponsors 127 local chapters and 16 sections on specific areas of governments, such as the Section of Natural Resources and Environmental Administration and the Section on Human Resource Administration.

12438 www.aspehhs.gov
Interagency Council on the Homeless
Seeks to evaluate and monitor federal activities for the homeless, collect information, study problems related to homelessness and disseminate information. Provides technical and professional assistance to the State and local governments and other public and private organizations to maximize resources and develop innovative programs to help the homeless.

12439 www.brbpub.com
BRB Publications
Over 700 reviewers are indexed and profiled by county of expertise. Includes the membership of The Public Record Retriever Network, links to hundreds of sites with free public records and you may order research books online.

12440 www.cagw.com
Citizens Against Government Waste
Public advocacy, non-partisan organization committed to eliminate government waste, fraud, abuse, mismanagement and inefficiency.

12441 www.clearhq.org
Council on Licensure, Enforcement and Regulation
Members include occupational and professional licensing boards and agencies and private interests in the 50 states, territories and Canada.

12442 www.communityleadership.org
Community Leadership Association
Founded by 40 community leadership organizations.

12443 www.coscda.org
Council for State Community Development Agencies
Employees of state community affairs agencies.

12444 www.csa-dc.org
Contract Services Association of America
Represents the government services contracting industry in Washington, DC. Members range from small businesses to large corporations servicing federal and state government in numerous capacities. CSA acts to foster effective implementation of the government's policy of reliance on the private sector for support services.

12445 www.cued.org
National Council for Urban Economic Development
National membership organization serving public and private participants in economic development across the United States and in international settings. CUED provides information to its members who build local economies through the tools used for job creation, attraction and retention. Members include public economic development directors, chamber of commerce staff, utility executives and academicians, plus the many other professionals who help design and implement development programs.

12446 www.eba-net.org
Energy Bar Association
Lawyers engaged in promoting proper administration of federal laws relating to the production, development and economic regulation of energy.

12447 www.epic.org
Fund for Constitutional Government
Seeks to expose and correct illegal activities, corruption, and lack of accountability in the federal government.

12448 www.fbi.gov
Federal Investigators Association
Formerly the United States Treasury Agents.

12449 www.fedphy.org
Federal Physicians Association
The purpose of the Federal Physicians Association is to improve the practice of medicine within the federal government; and to improve the working conditions and benefits of Federal Civil Service Physicians.

12450 www.foodprotection.org
International Association for Food Protection
The International Association for Food Protection founded in 1911, is a nonprofit educational association with a mission to provide food safety professional worldwide with a forum to exchange information on protecting the food

supply. The Association is comprised of a cross-section of over 3,000 members from 50 nations. Affiliate chapters are located in the United States, Canada and South Korea.

12451 www.ginniemae.gov/about/contract.htm
Government National Mortgage Association - Ginnie Mae

Supports government housing objectives by establishing secondary markets for residential mortgages. Through its mortgage-backed securities programs, Ginnie Mae creates a vehicle for channeling funds from the securities markets into the mortgage market and helps to increase the supply of credit available for housing.

12452 www.govexec.com
National Journal
The website of Government Executive Magazine.

12453 www.greyhouse.com
Grey House Publishing
Authoritative reference directories for most business sectors including government markets. Users can search the online databases with varied search criteria allowing for custom searches by product category, geographic area, sales volume, keyword, subject and more. Full Grey House catalog and online ordering also available.

12454 www.healthfinder.gov
Association of Food and Drug Officials
Promotes the enforcement of laws and regulations at all levels of government. Fosters understanding and cooperation between industry and regulators. Develops model laws and regulations and seeks their adoption.

12455 www.ida-downtown.org
International Downtown Association
Represents organizations and individuals involved in downtown development. Members include city center redevelopment organizations and local officials, businesses, property owners, financiers, planners, university and foundation representatives, and legal and accounting professionals. Offers conferences, technical assistance, consulting services and extensive information services.

12456 www.ihs.com
International Code Council
Nonprofit membership association with more than 16,000 members who span the building community, from code enforcement officials to materials manufacturers. Dedicated to preserving the public health, safety and welfare in the built environment through the effective use and enforcement of model codes.

12457 www.imsasafety.org
International Municipal Signal Association
International resource for information, education and certification for public safety.

12458 www.iogcc.state.ok.us
Interstate Oil and Gas Compact Commission
Represents the governors of 37 states that produce virtually all the domestic oil and natural gas in the United States.

12459 www.leadershipdirectories.com
Leadership Directories
Offers free online directory of Presidential Transition Team, free online roster of newly elected congressman and subscription information.

12460 www.liberty.uc.wlu.edu
Journalism Resources

Lists of newspapers, film resources, jobs and internships and political advocacy groups.

12461 www.nacced.org
National Association for County Community and Economic Development

Members are directors and staff members of county, community and economic development agencies.

12462 www.naco.org
Nat'l Assn of County Information Technology Admin

12463 www.nagra.org
North American Gaming Regulators Association

Members are government entities involved in local, state, federal and provincial regulation of gambling activities.

12464 www.nahma.org
National Affordable Housing Management Association

Trade association representing companies and individuals involved in the management of affordable multifamily housing.

12465 www.nahro.org
Ntl Assoc of Housing & Redevelopment Officials

A professional membership association representing local housing authorities, community development agencies, and individual professionals in the housing, community development, and redevelopment fields.

12466 www.nalhfa.org
National Assn. of Local Housing Finance Agencies

County and city agencies which finance affordable housing using tax-exempt annual tools such as the low income housing tax credit and private activity bonds.

12467 www.napawash.org
National Academy of Public Administration

An independent, non-profit organization chartered by Congress to improve governance at all levels- local, regional, state, national and international.

12468 www.napus.org
National Association of Postmasters of the US

Sponsors and supports the Political Education for Postmasters Political Action Committee.

12469 www.narc.org
National Association of Regional Councils

State of regional repositories of instructional materials or services.

12470 www.nasaa-arts.org
National Assembly of State Arts Agencies

NASAA's mission is to advance and promote a meaningful role for the arts in the lives of individuals, families and communities throughout the United States. We empower state art agencies through strategic assistance that fosters leadership, enhances planning and decision making, and increases resources. TTD 202-347-5948.

12471 www.nasaa.org
North American Securities Administrators Assoc

NASAA is the international organization representing 66 securities administrators from all 50 states, the District of Columbia, Canada, Mexico and Puerto Rico, and is responsible for investor protection and education. NASAA recommends national policies in the securities industry and provides model legislation for state securities agencies to adopt affecting the regulation of broker/dealers and investment advisers. Consumers can contact NASAA to get phone numbers of state securities regulators.

12472 www.nasar.org
National Association for Search and Rescue

Members belong to various emergency medical, fire or survival rescue services.

12473 www.nasda.com
National Association of State Development Agencies

Established to provide a forum for directors of state economic development agencies to exchange information, compare programs, and establish an organizational base to approach the Federal Government on issues of mutual interest.

12474 www.nast.net
Ntl Assoc of State Facilities Administrators

State administrators of facilities and property.

12475 www.nastad.org
Nat'l Alliance of State/Territorial AIDS Directors

NASTAD strengthens state and territory-based leadership, expertise, and advocacy and brings them to bear in reducing the incidence of HIV and viral hepatitis infections and on providing care and support to all who live with HIV/AIDS and viral hepatitis. NASTAD's vision is a world free of HIV/AIDS and viral hepatitis.

12476 www.natat.org
National Association of Towns and Townships

A nonprofit membership organization offering technical assistance, educational services and public policy support to local officials from more than 13,000 town and township governments across the country. The purpose is to strengthen the effectiveness of town and township governments and promote their interests in the public and private sectors.

12477 www.nbpc.net
National Border Patrol Council

A labor union representing employees of the US border patrol.

12478 www.ncne.com
National Center for Neighborhood Enterprise

A research demonstration and development organization providing support and technical assistance to grassroots organizations who are working toward revitalization of urban communities. The Center accomplishes this goal by promoting, and explaining alternative approaches to community development; identifies successful transferable program principles, strategies and techniques; and encouraging policy recommendations to assist neighborhood revitalization.

12479 www.ncsha.org
National Council of State Housing Agencies

Represents the views of state housing finance agencies in 48 states. A high priority for the Council is promoting the views of state housing agencies on the issue of delivery of housing financing for low and moderate income people. Other priorities include increasing the stock of affordable rental units and generating innova-

tive approaches to providing public housing acceptable to residents and communities.

12480 www.ncsl.org
National Conference of State Legislatures

A bipartisan organization dedicated to serving the lawmakers and staffs of the nations 50 states, its commonwealths and territories.

12481 www.ndaa-apri.org
Prosecutor

To be the voice of America's prosecutors and to support their efforts to protect the rights and safety of the people.

12482 www.ndaa.org
National District Attorneys Association

Voice of America's prosecutors and to support their efforts to protect the rights and safety of the people.

12483 www.nedaonline.org
National Community Development Association

A national nonprofit membership organization representing local governments that implement community development programs. The members administer federally supported community development, housing and human services programs. NCDA provides counsel at the federal level on new program design and current program implementation and advocates on behalf of responsive community development.

12484 www.nemaweb.org
National Emergency Management Association

Members include federal agencies, local emergency management representatives and interested individuals, associations and corporations.

12485 www.nfbpa.org
National Forum for Black Public Administrators

An association for public administrators.

12486 www.nhlp.org
National Housing Law Project

A nonprofit corporation that provides assistance on public and private housing and community development matters to Legal Services attorneys and housing specialists throughout the country. The project's goals are to produce, maintain and conserve low and moderate income housing and protect and expand the rights of lower income persons to decent and affordable housing.

12487 www.nlc.org
National League of Cities

Advocates on behalf of cities and regularly monitors all three branches of the federal government. Promotes the National Municipal Policy developed and adopted by member cities at the annual Congress of Cities.

12488 www.npelra.org
National Labor Relations Board of Professionals

Represents members in contract negotiations and grievance laws.

12489 www.nrhcweb.org
National Rural Housing Coalition

A national membership organization that advocates improved housing for low-income rural families and works to increase public awareness of rural housing problems. The Coalition works with a network of state coalitions and nonprofit organizations to promote federal housing policy that benefits both rural housing and community development programs.

12490 www.patriot.net/users/permail
Public Employees Roundtable

Demonstrates the value of government employees. Develop an 'espirit de corps' among public service employees and encourages public service careers.

12491 www.phada.org
Public Housing Authorities Directors Association

Represents and serves the needs of executive directors of housing authorities of all sizes, in all regions of the nation. In pursuing the Association's goal of improving assisted housing, the corporation works with Congress and federal agencies as well as with all interested groups to improve the nation's housing programs.

12492 www.postcom.org
Association for Postal Commerce

National Organization representing those who use, or support the use, of mail as a medium for communication and commerce. Postcom publishes a weekly newsletter covering postal policy and operational issues.

12493 www.ptos.org
Patent and Trademark Office Society

Members are examiners in the US Patent & Trademark Office, registered patent attorneys and agents, agencies, judges and other patent professionals.

12494 www.publicrecordsources.com
BRB Publications

The BRB Public Record Vendor search tool indexes and categorizes: Over 450 search firms, gateways, proprietary database managers and online public record vendors, over 250 pre employment and tenant screening companies, has links to free public sites, and locates industry trade associations.

12495 www.ruralhome.org
Housing Assistance Council

Expands the pool of decent housing available to the rural poor. Creates and sustains interest and action from all levels of government concerning rural housing for low-income people and helps rural housing organizatins become more productive and professional.

12496 www.sgac.org
State Government Affairs Council

Seeks to improve the state legislative process through interaction with major state governmental conferences. Conducts educational programs on public policies to further understanding between private sector businesses and state legislations.

12497 www.sge-econ.org
Society of Government Economists

Membership benefits economists employed in the public sector or who are interested in the economic aspects of government policies.

12498 www.sheeo.org
State Higher Education Executive Officers

Members are the full-time chief executive officers serving statewide coordinating or governing boards of postsecondary education.

12499 www.sso.org
Intl Assoc of Official Human Rights Agencies

Members are state and local government human rights and human relations agencies.

12500 www.sso.org/iafwa
Intl Assoc of Fish and Wildlife Agencies

Established as the National Association of Game Commissioners.

12501 www.statenews.org
Council of State Governments

Research and service agency for state governments and state officials.

12502 www.theiacp.org
International Association of Chiefs of Police

Has an annual budget of approximately $7 million.

12503 www.urisa.org
Urban & Regional Information Systems Association

Concerned with the effective use of information systems technology at the state, regional and local levels. Members informed of current developments in the information systems field. Its goal is to stimulate and encourage the advancement of an interdisciplinary professional approach to planning, designing and operating information systems.

12504 www.usmayors.org/uscm/
United States Conference of Mayors

An organization of city government officials.

12505 www.water.dnr.state.sc.us/water/icwp
Interstate Council on Water Policy

Members are state and regional agencies concerned with conservation and environmental issues.

12506 www.wicdirectors.org
National Association of WIC Directors

Members are geographic state, Native American state and local agency directors of the Special Supplement nutrition program for woman,infants and children.

Associations

12507 ACM SIGGRAPH
Association for Computing Machinery

Home Page: www.siggraph.org
Social Media: *Facebook, Twitter, LinkedIn,
YouTube, Google Plus, RSS*

Jeff Jortner, President
Paul Debevec, VP
Tony Baylis, Treasurer

The Association for Computing Machinery's
Special Interest Group on Computer Graphics
and Interactive Techniques promotes the generation and dissemination of information on computer graphics and interactive techniques.
Fostering a membership community whose
core values help them to catalyze the innovation and application of computer graphics and
interactive techniques.
8300+ Members
Founded in 1974

12508 American Institute of Graphic Arts
164 Fifth Avenue
New York, NY 10010-5989

212-807-1990
FAX 212-807-1799
Home Page: www.aiga.org
Social Media: *Facebook, Twitter, LinkedIn*

Richard Grefe, Executive Director
Katie Baker, Director of chapter development
Jennifer Bender, Director of Communications
Elaine Bowen, Director of strategic
partnerships
Kathleen Bundy, Program director

To further excellence in design as a broadly defined discipline, strategic tool for business and
cultural force. A professional association committed to stimulating thinking about design
through the exchange of ideas and information,
the encouragement of critical analysis and research and the advancement of education and
ethical practice.
18575 Members
Founded in 1922

**12509 Association of Graphic
Communications**
330 7th Ave
9th Floor
New York, NY 10001-5010

212-279-2100
FAX 212-279-5381
Home Page: www.agcomm.org

Serves as a provider of graphic arts education
and training, a network for industry information and idea exchange, an advocate for legislative and regulatory/environmental issues, and a
vehicle for industry promotion.
560 Members
Founded in 1865

12510 Design Management Institute
38 Chauncy St.
Suite 800
Boston, MA 02111

617-338-6380
Home Page: www.dmi.org
Social Media: *Facebook, Twitter, LinkedIn,
YouTube, Flickr*

International nonprofit seeking to improve organizations through design management.
Founded in 1975

12511 Graphic Artists Guild
32 Broadway
Suite 1114
New York, NY 10004-1612

212-791-3400
FAX 212-791-0333
E-Mail: admin@graphicartistsguild.org
Home Page: www.graphicartistsguild.org
Social Media: *Facebook, Twitter, LinkedIn,
Google Plus*

Haydn Adams, President
Chuck Schultz, Vice President
Lauren Rabinowitz, Treasurer
Lara Kisielewska, Secretary
Patricia McKiernan, Executive Director

Promotes and protects the economic interests
of member artists and is committed to improving conditions for all ceators of graphic arts
and raising standards for the enitre industry.
1400 Members
Founded in 1967

12512 Graphic Arts Association
1210 Northbrook Dr
Suite 200
Trevose, PA 19053-8406

215-396-2300
FAX 215-396-9890
E-Mail: gaa@gaaonline.org
Home Page: www.graphicartsassociation.org
Social Media: *Facebook, Twitter*

Melissa Jones, President
Bill Scotese, Director of Credit and Collections
Stephen Stankavage, Environmental, Health
Rita Donlan, Bookkeeper/Office Manager
Patti Rose, Administrative Assistant

Mission is to be the leading resource for the
printing and graphic communications industry
in advocacy, education, and information to enhance the strength and profitability of its
members.
400 Members
Founded in 1886

12513 Guild of Natural Science Illustrators
Guild of Natural Science Illustrators
P.O. Box 42410
Ben Franklin Station
Washington, DC 20015

301-309-1514
FAX 301-309-1514
E-Mail: gnsihome@his.com
Home Page: www.gnsi.org

Amelia Janes, President
Britt Griswold, Vice President
Gail Guth, Membership Secretary
Ikumi Kayama, Secretary
Marjorie Leggitt, Treasurer

A nonprofit organization of persons employed
or genuinely interested in the field of natural
science illustration. It maintains and encourages high standards of competence and professional ethics by increasing communication
among its members. Provides opportunities for
professional and scholarly development, and
seeks to promote better understanding of the
profession among the general public and potential clients requiring the services of natural
science illustrators.
1.1M Members
Founded in 1968

**12514 International Digital Enterprise
Alliance**
1600 Duke Street
Suite 420
Alexandria, VA 22314-2805

703-837-1070
FAX 703-837-1072
E-Mail: dsteinhardt@idealliance.org

Home Page: www.idealliance.org
Social Media: *Facebook, Twitter, LinkedIn*

Laura C Reid, Board Chair
David J Steinhardt, President & CEO
Joe Duncan, Board Vice Chair
Debbie Cooper, Treasurer
Penny Sullivan, Secretary

A global community of content and media creators, and their service providers, material suppliers, and technology partners. Association
identifies best practices for efficient end-to-end
digital media workflows, from content creation
through distribution. Providing members the
forum for the exchange of information that results in the creation of the industry's most
valued standards.
300+ Members
Founded in 1966

**12515 National Association for Printing
Leadership (NAPL)**
One Meadowlands Plaza
Suite 1511
East Rutherford, NJ 07073

201-634-9600
800-642-6275
FAX 201-634-0324
E-Mail: webmaster@napl.org
Home Page: www.napl.org
Social Media: *Facebook, Twitter, LinkedIn,
YouTube, Google Plus, Pinteres*

Nigel Worme, Chairman
Niels Winther, Vice Chairman
Joseph P. Truncale, Ph.D., CAE,, President &
CEO
Mike Philie, Senior Vice President
Mark R. Hahn, Senior Vice President

A not-for-profit national trade association serving companies in the $100 billion+ graphic
communications industry. NAPL offers a comprehensive slate of business and building solutions that provides company leaders with the
strategies, insights, and guidance they can use
to make informed business decisions, minimize
risk, anticipate change, and profitably grow
their business.
2000 Members
Founded in 1933

**12516 Pacific Printing & Imaging
Association**
6825 SW Sandburg Street
Portland, OR 97223

877-762-7742
FAX 503-221-5691
E-Mail: info@ppiassociation.org
Home Page: www.ppiassociation.org
Social Media: *Facebook, Twitter, LinkedIn,
YouTube*

Jules Van Sant, Executive Director

Dedicated to promoting members and their industries while providing a variety of benefits
and money saving programs to Visual &
Graphic Communications Companies and individuals in six states. Purpose is to deliver what
it takes to help members become more successful and profitable in their businesses.
200 Members
Founded in 1948

12517 Printing Industries of America
200 Deer Run Rd
Sewickley, PA 15143-2600

412-741-6860
800-910-4283
FAX 412-741-2311
E-Mail: info@printing.org
Home Page: www.printing.org

Social Media: *Facebook, Twitter, LinkedIn, Pinterest*

Michael F. Makin, President & CEO
Mary Garnett, Executive Vice President
Nicholas Stratigos, CFO
Ronnie Davis Senior, Vice President & Chief Economist
Lisbeth Lyons, Vice President, Government Affairs

A graphic arts trade association representing our members in this industry. Printing Industries of America, along with its affiliates, delivers products and services that enhance the growth, efficiency and profitability of its members and the industry through advocacy, education, research and technical information
10000 Members
Founded in 1887

12518 Society for Environmental Graphic Design
1900 L Street NW
Suite 710
Washington, DC 20036

202-638-5555
FAX 202-478-2286
E-Mail: segd@segd.org
Home Page: www.segd.org
Social Media: *Facebook, Twitter, LinkedIn, RSS*

Clive Roux, CEO
Ann Makowski, COO

Members work in the planning, design, fabrication, and implementation of communications in the built environment. SEGD is the global community of people working at the intersection of communication design and the built environment.
1600+ Members
Founded in 1974

12519 Society of Publication Designers
27 Union Square West
Suite 207
New York, NY 10003

212-223-3332
FAX 212-223-5880
E-Mail: mail@spd.org
Home Page: www.spd.org
Social Media: *Twitter, RSS*

Tim Leong, President
David Curcurito, Vice President
Allyson Torrisi, Vice President
Leah Bailey, Secretary
Courtney Murphy, Treasurer

The only organization specifically addressing the visual concerns of print and online editorial professionals. Activities promote the role of members as journalists and partners in the editorial process, as well as fostering new generations of publication designers through educational outreach and scholarship opportunities.
550 Members
Founded in 1965

12520 Technical Association of the Graphic Arts
200 Deer Run Road
Sewickley, PA 15143

412-259-1706
800-910-4283
FAX 412-741-2311
Home Page: www.printing.org/taga
Social Media: *Facebook, Twitter, LinkedIn, Pinterest, Google Plus*

Michael F. Makin, President & CEO
Mary Garnett, Executive Vice President
Nicholas Stratigos, CFO
Ronnie Davis Senior, Vice President & Chief Economist

Lisbeth Lyons, Vice President, Government Affairs

Provides a worldwide forum for sharing and disseminating theoretical, functional and practical information on current and emerging technologies for Graphic Arts print production and related processes
900+ Members
Founded in 1948

Newsletters

12521 Graphic News
Printing Industry of Minnesota
2829 University Avenue SE
Suite 750
Minneapplis, MN 55414-3222

612-379-3360
800-448-756
FAX 618-379-6030
E-Mail: davidr@pimn.org
Home Page: www.pimn.org

David Radziej, President
Arlene Roth, Director Public Relations
John Connelly, Director of Membership
Carla Steuck, Director of Education Services
Patricia Barnum, CFO

For the printing and graphic arts industries.
16 Pages
Frequency: Bi-Monthly
Circulation: 12000
Founded in 1955

12522 Graphics Update
Printing Association of Florida
6095 NW 167 Street
Suite D-7
Miami, FL 33015

305-558-4855
800-331-0461
FAX 305-823-8965
E-Mail: printpaf@ix.netcom.com
Home Page: www.pafgraf.org
Social Media: *Facebook, Twitter, LinkedIn, Flickr, YouTube*

Gene Strul, Editor
Michael H Streibig, Staff Executive
Ron Davis, Chief Economist

A monthly newsletter to the members of the Printing Association of Florida. Full color publication with attractive advertising purchases and a focused buying circulation.
Cost: $200.00
Frequency: Monthly

12523 Guild News
Graphic Artists Guild
32 Broadway
Suite 1114
New York, NY 10004-1612

212-791-3400
FAX 212-791-0333
Home Page: www.graphicartistsguild.org

Patricia McKiernan, Executive Director
Haydn Adams, President
Chuck Schultz, Vice President
Lauren Rabinowitz, Treasurer
Lara Kisielewska, Secretary

Designed to keep individuals abreast of what's going on with the Guild, the industry, and in the area.
Frequency: Bimonthly

12524 Holography News
Reconnaissance International Consulting

PO Box 40976
Denver, CO 80204

303-628-5568
FAX 303-628-5594
Home Page: www.reconnaissance-intl.com

Ian Lancaster, Director
Jon Senft, VP
Lewis Kontnik, Publisher

Leading global source of business intelligence on holography and authentication for document security, personal identification and brand protection. Unique knowledge and experience of these highly-specialized and rapidly-changing industries, this newsletter is offering invaluable insight into and authoritative information on markets, strategic management and technical issues through reports, newsletters, conferences, executive briefings and consultancy.
Cost: $774.00
Frequency: Monthly
Founded in 1987

12525 Messages
Society of Environmental Graphic Designers
1000 Vermont Ave Nw
Suite 400
Washington, DC 20005-4903

202-638-0891
FAX 202-638-0891
E-Mail: segd@segd.org
Home Page: www.segd.org
Social Media: *Facebook, Twitter, LinkedIn*

Be the first to hear about new SEGD initiatives, events, and educational resources. Also learn about new contracts, new products, personnel changes, and other news from SEGD member companies. Messages is also the conduit for special SEGD publications and resources such as the ADA White Papers, the SEGD Green Paper, and other valuable educational materials.
Frequency: Monthly

Magazines & Journals

12526 Animation Magazine
Animation Magazine
30941 Agoura Rd
suite 102
Westlake Villag, CA 91361-4637

818-991-2884
FAX 818-991-3773
E-Mail: info@animationmagazine.net
Home Page: www.animationmagazine.net

Jean Thoren, President

Covers the animation industry trends, technology, new products, historical perspectives coverage of current animated programming and features, and general news.
Cost: $65.07
Frequency: Monthly
Founded in 1985
Printed in 4 colors on glossy stock

12527 Before & After: How to Design Cool Stuff
Pagelab
323 Lincoln Street
Roseville, CA 95678-2229

956-78 -229
800-266-5783
FAX 916-784-3995
E-Mail: contact@bamagazine.com
Home Page: www.bamagazine.com
Social Media: *Facebook, Twitter, YouTube*

John McWade, Publisher
Gaye McWade, Editor

Practical approach to graphic design. Dedicated to making graphic design understandable, use-

ful and even fun for everyone.
Cost: $36.00
Circulation: 26000
Founded in 1990

12528 Bulletin Magazine
International Digital Enterprise Alliance
1421 Prince St
Suite 230
Alexandria, VA 22314-2805

703-837-1070
FAX 703-837-1072
Home Page: www.idealliance.org
Social Media: *Facebook, Twitter, LinkedIn*

David Steinhardt, President & CEO
Lisa Bos, Chair
Chip Harding, Vice Chair
Paul Clancy, Treasurer
Jim Mikol, Secretary

The voice of IDEAlliance+IPA, keeping members abreast of business challenges and opportunities, assuring workflows are state-of-the-art, speeding information across the end-to-end digital media supply chain, from content creation through delivery. Since its founding, the Bulletin has played a significant role in the dissemination of information for the graphic communications industry.
300+ Members
Frequency: Bi-Monthly
Founded in 1966

12529 Cadalyst
Longitude Media

Home Page: www.cadalyst.com
Social Media: *Facebook, Twitter*

Nancy Spurling Johnson, Editor-in-Chief
Cyrena Respini-Irwin, Senior Editor

The most complete source of essential information about computer-aided design and related software and hardware technologies for the fields of AEC, manufacturing, and GIS. Delivers timely, objective, and practical product reviews and updates, tips, tutorials, insight, and advice to help CAD managers and users make informed decisions about technology, get productive, and get the job done.
Cost: $39.95
100 Pages
Frequency: Monthly
Circulation: 90000
ISSN: 0360-3520
Founded in 1987
Printed in 4 colors

12530 Communication Arts
Coyne & Blanchard
110 Constitution Dr
Menlo Park, CA 94025-1107

650-326-6040
FAX 650-326-1648
E-Mail: editorial@commarts.com
Home Page: www.commarts.com

Patrick Coyne, Publisher
Ernie Schenck, Creative Director
Mike Krigel, Marketing Executive

Features profile individuals, studios and agencies with examples of their work. Includes reviews of software, books and products, as well as discussing the latest in digital and broadcast design.
Cost: $53.00
Frequency: 8 issues per ye
Circulation: 71927
ISSN: 0010-3519
Founded in 1959
Printed in 4 colors

12531 Computer Graphics World
COP Communications, Inc.

620 W. Elk Ave
Glendale, CA 91204

603-432-7568
E-Mail: karen@cgw.com
Home Page: www.cgw.com

Karen Moltenbrey, Chief Editor
William R. Rittwage, Publisher, President & CEO
Kelly Ryan, Marketing Coordinator
Michael Viggiano, Art Director

Covers specific applications of computer graphics, written by users and vendors of equipment and services to the industry. The magazine of 3D computer graphics for engineering and animation professionals.
Cost: $55.00
Frequency: Monthly
Circulation: 40597
Founded in 1977
Printed in 4 colors on glossy stock

12532 Critique
Neumeier Design Team
120 Hawthorne Avenue
#102
Palo Alto, CA 94301-1000

650-326-4396
FAX 650-323-3298
Home Page: www.critiquemag.com

Marty Neumeier, Editor

Features include methods and products to increase the creativity and technological advance of graphic artwork.
Cost: $60.00
Frequency: Quarterly
Circulation: 10000

12533 Desktop Publishers Journal
Desktop Publishing Institute
462 Boston Street
Topsfield, MA 01983-1200

FAX 978-887-9245

Thomas Tetreault, Publisher
Barry Harrigan, Editor

Desktop publishing topics and issues and association information.
Frequency: Weekly
Circulation: 60000

12534 Digital Imaging
Cygnus Publishing
3 Huntington Quadrangle
Suite 301N
Melville, NY 11747

631-845-2700
800-308-6397
FAX 631-845-2798
Home Page: www.cygnuspub.com

Laureen Delaney, Associate Publisher
Kathy Schneider, Group Publisher
Andrew Darlow, Editorial Director
Liz Vickers, Advertising Sales Manager
Paul Bonaiuto, CFO

For the imaging professional. Dedicated to bridging the digital imaging gap between graphics and photography while providing in-depth solutions.
Circulation: 30,000
Founded in 1966

12535 Dynamic Graphics
Dynamic Graphics
6000 N Forest Park Drive
Peoria, IL 61614-3592

309-888-8851
888-698-8542

FAX 800-488-3492
Home Page: www.dynamicgraphics.com

Alan Meckler, President, JupiterMedia
David Moffly, President/CEO
Marcy Slane, Managing Editor

Encourages users to take their electronic tools to the next level of productivity and creativity. Emphasizes practical and real-world solutions.
Cost: $36.00
72 Pages
Frequency: 6
Circulation: 66143
ISSN: 1094-2548
Founded in 1964
Printed in on glossy stock

12536 GATFWORLD Magazine
Graphic Arts Technical Foundation Association
200 Deer Run Road
Sewickley, PA 15143-2324

412-741-6860
800-910-4283
FAX 412-741-2311
E-Mail: gain@piagatf.org
Home Page: www.gain.net

George Ryan, Executive VP/COO
Michael Makin, President/CEO
Deanna Gentile, Editor

A bi-monthly magazine for GATF members and subscribers that reports on research and technical trends in the graphic arts (printing) industry, environmental and safety news, developments in graphic communications education and news of emerging products, programs and services.
Cost: $75.00
Circulation: 18000
Founded in 1924

12537 Gasp Report
GASP Engineering
234 Benjamin W Avenue
Swarthmore, PA 19081-1421

610-543-5194
800-256-4282
FAX 610-328-1358
Home Page: www.gaspnet.com

Steve Hannaford, Publisher

Covers new technology, financing, marketing and other business concerns of the printing, graphics and publishing industries. In-depth articles highlight strategies for industry professionals.
Cost: $195.00
Frequency: Monthly
Circulation: 400

12538 Graphic Arts Monthly
360 Park Avenue S
New York, NY 10010

212-636-6834
800-217-7874
FAX 646-746-7422
Home Page: www.worldleadersinprint.com

Phil Saran, Publisher
Roger Ynostroza, Editorial Director

The magazine of the printing industry including commercial, in-plant and related operations, such as color separations, composition, binding and pre-press service bureaus.
Frequency: Monthly
Circulation: 75,000

12539 Graphic Design: USA
Kaye Publishing Corporation
641 Lexington Ave
Suite 1202
New York, NY 10022-4503

212-259-0400
FAX 212-489-4736

E-Mail: gkaye@gdusa.com
Home Page: www.gdusa.com

M Kaye, Owner
Maria Mohamed, Circualtion Manager
Gordon D. Kaye, Publisher

A publication for the graphic designer, offering information and news of the industry.
Cost: $60.00
120 Pages
Frequency: Monthly
ISSN: 0274-7499
Founded in 1965

12540 Graphic Impressions
Pioneer Communications
218 6th Ave
Fleming Building, Suite 610
Des Moines, IA 50309-4009

515-246-0402
FAX 515-282-0125
Home Page:
www.pioneercommunicationsinc.com

Rick Thomas, President

Provides providing industry news and information including in-depth coverage of PIM, and PIAMS association news and events. Features cover technology, legal, environmental, niche printing, education, new products, marketing, distribution, finance and insurance.
Cost: $20.00
32 Pages
Frequency: 10 per year
Circulation: 7,000
Founded in 1995
Printed in 4 colors on glossy stock

12541 Graphics Pro
Graphic Products Association
4709 N El Capitan Avenue
Suite 103
Fresno, CA 93722

559-276-8494
800-276-8428
FAX 559-276-8496
E-Mail: info@graphicspro.org
Home Page: www.graphicspro.org

Michael R Neer, Publisher
Steven V Neer, Associate Publisher
Damara Torres, Owner

A bi-monthly journal published by the Graphic Products Association.
Cost: $55.00
Circulation: 7500
Founded in 1994
Printed in on glossy stock

12542 Graphis
Graphis Press
307 5th Ave
10th Floor
New York, NY 10016-6517

212-532-9387
866-648-2915
FAX 212-213-3229
E-Mail: info@graphis.com
Home Page: www.graphis.com

Martin Pederson, Owner
Walter Herdeg, Editor

Graphis is an international journal of design and visual communication, covering graphic arts, design, photography, architecture and related topics. The targeted readership includes professionals in these disciplines as well as all creative visual communicators.
Cost: $90.00
Circulation: 22000
Founded in 1944

12543 HOW Magazine
F&W Publications

4700 E Galbraith Rd
Cincinnati, OH 45236-2726

513-531-2690
FAX 513-531-1843
E-Mail: editorial@howdesign.com
Home Page: www.fwpublications.com

David Nussbaum, CEO
Bryn Mooth, Editor
William R. Reed, President
Jim Ogle, Chief Financial Officer
Kate Rados, Marketing Director

Business and creative resource for graphic designers. Latest business, technological and creative information.
Cost: $49.00
194 Pages
Circulation: 39946
ISSN: 0886-0483
Founded in 1900
Printed in 4 colors on glossy stock

12544 ID Magazine
38 East 29th Street
Floor 3
New York, NY 10016

212-447-1400
800-258-929
FAX 212-447-5231
E-Mail: gary.lynch@id-mag.com
Home Page: www.id-mag.com

Kelly N Kofron, Executive Editor
Dave Richmond, Executive Editor

Leading critical magazine covering the art, business and culture of design.
Frequency: 8 per year

12545 PC Graphics & Video
Advanstar Communications
Ste 300
17770 Cartwright Rd
Irvine, CA 92614-5815

714-513-8400
FAX 714-513-8481
E-Mail: info@advanstar.com
Home Page: www.advanstar.com

Michael Forcillo, Publisher
Gene Smarte, Chief Executive Officer

Covers graphics and video for personal computers.
Cost: $5.00
Circulation: 10,699

12546 Print Magazine
RC Publications
38 E 29th Street
3rd Floor
New York, NY 10016

212-447-1400
FAX 212-447-5231
E-Mail: info@printmag.com
Home Page: www.printmag.com

Joyce Rutter Kay, Editor in Chief
Joel Toner, Publisher
Stephany Skirvin, Art Director
Steven Kent, CEO
William Reed, President

News and information for the graphic design industry.
Cost: $53.00
160 Pages
Circulation: 45000
ISSN: 0032-8510
Founded in 1940
Printed in 4 colors on glossy stock

12547 Printer's Northwest Trader
Eagle Newspapers

650 N 1st Street
PO Box 96
Woodburn, OR 97071-450

503-981-3441
FAX 503-981-1253
Home Page: www.eaglenewspapers.com

Rod Stollery, Publisher
Sandy Hubbard, Founder
Elmo Smith, Founder

Reviews new equipment and techniques and highlights industry leaders of note. Serves the northwestern portion of the United States.
Cost: $10.00
Frequency: Monthly
Circulation: 16000
Founded in 1933

12548 Publication Design Annual #39
Society of Publication Designers
17 East 47th Street
6th Floor
New York, NY 10017

212-223-3332
FAX 212-223-5880
E-Mail: mail@spd.org
Home Page: wwww.spd.org

Bruce Ramsay, President
Amid Capeci, Treasurer
Gail Bichler, Treasurer
Nancy Stamatopoulos, Secretary

A compendium of the best designed magazine/trade and consumer newspapers. Annual reports of the year as judged by a panel. Also includes web and interactive design sites and annual reports.
Cost: $195.00
Frequency: Monthly
Circulation: 15000
ISBN: 1-564966-21-6
Founded in 1969
Printed in 4 colors on matte stock

12549 Publish How-to Magazine
MacWorld Communications
501 2nd St
Suite 310
San Francisco, CA 94107-1496

415-243-0505
FAX 415-442-0766

Mike Kisseberth, CEO
Susan Gubemat, Editor

The definitive source on how to use personal computers to integrate text and graphics into printed communication.
Cost: $4.00
Circulation: 98,819

12550 Sign & Digital Graphics
National Business Media
PO Box 1416
Broomfield, CO 80038-1416

303-469-0424
800-669-0424
FAX 303-465-3424
Home Page: www.sdgmag.com

Mary Tohill, Publisher
Ken Mergentime, Executive Editor
Matt Dixon, Managing Editor
James Kochevar, Associate Publisher
Sara Siauw, Production Coordinator

The most widely read industry trade publication covering the business of visual communications and offering a broad range of in-depth reporting for sign industry and wide-format digital graphics professionals. This distinguished and unique magazine provides comprehensive professional coverage on all aspects of commercial signage, commercial graphics production, electric LED-based signage and letter

systems, architectural signage, electronic digital displays, vehicle wraps, and much more.
Frequency: Monthly

12551 Southern Graphics
PTN Publishing Company
445 Broadhollow Road
Suite 21
Melville, NY 11747-3601

FAX 631-845-7109

Rob Schweiger, Publisher
KJ Moran, Editor
Edited for those in the graphic arts industry throughout the southeastern US and the Caribbean.
Cost: $5.00
Circulation: 21,000

12552 TAGA Journal of Graphic Technology
Technical Association of the Graphic Arts
200 Deer Run Road
Sewickley, PA 15143

412-259-1706
FAX 412-741-2311
Home Page: www.taga.org

Mark Bohan, Managing Director
A peer-reviewed journal designed to meet the needs of the global professional graphic applications industries and to bring together the multi-disciplinary community in further development of printing as a manufacturing process. Embraces the fundamental science and technology, application and technology transfer and the generic problems and experience associated with the management and implementation of graphic applications.
900+ Members
Frequency: Bi-Annually
Founded in 1948

12553 Trade Show Times
Fichera Communications
441 S State Road
Suite 14
Margate, FL 33063

954-971-4360
800-327-8999
FAX 954-971-4362
Home Page: www.tradeshowtimes.com

Orazio Fichera, Publisher
Rick Kelly, Contact
Hand distributed to attendees at major graphic arts trade shows. Accepts advertising.
32 Pages
Frequency: Monthly
Founded in 1974

12554 Visual Communications Journal
Graphic Arts Technical Foundation
Association
200 Deer Run Road
Sewickley, PA 15143-2324

412-741-6860
800-910-4283
FAX 412-741-2311
E-Mail: gain@piagatf.org
Home Page: www.gain.net

George Ryan, Executive VP/COO
Michael Makin, President/CEO
Peter Oresick, VP Publishing
Educational guide and news for scholars and students studying the graphic arts industry.

12555 segdDESIGN
Society for Environmental Graphic Design
1000 Vermont Ave NW
Suite 400
Washington, DC 20005-4921

202-638-5555
FAX 202-638-0891

E-Mail: pat@segd.org
Home Page: www.segd.org

Ann Makowski, Manager
The magazine of choice for creative professionals working at the intersection of communication design and the built environment. A rich source of information on the key people, research, technologies, materials, and resources that influence communications in the built environment. International Journal of Environmental Graphic Design
Frequency: Quarterly

Trade Shows

12556 3D Design & Animation Conference & Expo
Miller Freeman Publications
525 Market Street
Suite 500
San Francisco, CA 94110

415-955-5533
FAX 415-278-5341
Home Page: www.mfi.com

For animators and digital content creators, exibits include equipment supplies and services for the 3D design and animation industry. Conferences, reception and publications. Space rental available.
Frequency: Annual

12557 Annual Automated Imaging Associates Business Conference
Appliance Manufacturer
5900 Harper Road
Suite 105
Solon, OH 44139-1935

440-349-3060
FAX 440-498-9121
E-Mail: jburnstein@robotics.org
Home Page: www.machinevisiononline.org

Jeff Burnstein, Executive Director
The industry's leading conference and networking event. This conference gathers over 150 top industry executives to do business with their peers and hear presentations on issues affecting the global economy in general and the machine vision industry specifically.
Frequency: Annual, February

12558 Grafix
Conference Management Corporation
200 Connecticut Avenue
Norwalk, CT 06854-1940

800-342-3238
FAX 203-831-8446

Annual show of 200 exhibitors of computer hardware and software for graphic design and computer publishing, paper supplies, typesetting equipment and services, stock photography, clip art service and related equipment, supplies and services.
4000 Attendees

12559 Graph Expo
Graphic Arts Show Company
1189 Preston White Drive
Reston, VA 20191-5435

703-264-7200
FAX 703-620-9187
Home Page: www.graphexpo.com

Where top executives come to learn, network and make informed intelligent purchasing decisions. Leading manufacturers and suppliers will be exhibiting at the show and many of them will be showcasing newly released products, technologies and services. The year's

largest and most exciting display of live running equipment in the Americas.
40000 Attendees
Frequency: Annual/September

12560 Graph Expo West
Graphic Arts Show Company
1899 Preston White Drive
Reston, VA 20191

703-264-7200
FAX 703-620-9187
E-Mail: info@gasc.org
Home Page: www.gasc.org

Lilly Kinney, Conference Manager
Chris Theil, Administrative Assistant
Erin Omwake, Administrative Assistant
Deborah Vieder, Director of Communications
Two hundred booths for the graphics industry.
13M Attendees
Frequency: November
Founded in 1982

12561 Graphics Trade Show Expo Southwest
910 W Mockingbird Lane
Dallas, TX 75247-5182
Jim Weinstein, Show Manager
Six hundred and fifty booths.
13M Attendees
Frequency: June

12562 Graphics of the Americas
Printing Association of Florida
6275 Hazeltine National Drive
Orlando, FL 32822

407-240-8009
FAX 407-240-8333
Home Page: www.pafgraf.org

Holly Price, Booth Sales & Marketing
Michelle Torres, Attendee Info.
Largest annual international graphic commincations education and exhibit showplace. Over 450 exhibitors in 500,000 square feet.
22000 Attendees
Frequency: February

12563 Gutenberg & Digital Outlook
Graphic Arts Show Company
1189 Preston White Drive
Reston, VA 22091

703-264-7200
FAX 703-620-9187
E-Mail: info@gasc.org
Home Page: www.gasc.org

Chris Thiel, VP
Kelly Kilga, Administrative Assistant
Erin Omwake, Administrative Assistant
Deborah Vieder, Director of Communications
Largest graphic design, digital prepress, printing, publishing, and converting trade show in the Westen United States. Over 100 exhibitors with the widest selection of vendors.
8000 Attendees
Frequency: Annual, June

12564 IMPA Annual Conference
In-Plant Printing and Mailing Association
125 S. Jefferson
Suite B-4
Kearney, MO 64060

816-903-4762
FAX 816-902-4766
E-Mail: ipmaininfo@ipma.org
Home Page: www.ipma.org

John Sarantakos, Administrator
Larry Wright, Treasurer
Annual educational conference and vending show.

12565 Printing Expo Conference Mid America
Graphics Arts Show Company
1899 Preston White Drive
Reston, VA 20191

703-264-7200
FAX 703-620-9187
E-Mail: info@gasc.org
Home Page: www.gasc.org

Paul Kaplan, Show Manager
Erin Omwake, Administrative Assistant
Deborah Vieder, Director of Communications

Exhibits by manufacturers and dealers of the latest graphics equipment and services.
3000 Attendees
Frequency: June
Founded in 1982

12566 Sunbelt Computer and Graphics
Printing Industry Association of Georgia
5020 Highlands Parkway
Smyrna, GA 30082

770-433-3050
800-288-1894
FAX 770-433-3062
Home Page: www.sunbeltshow.org

Dianne McPherson, Trade Show Director
Denise Holland, VP Communications

Two hundred and fifty exhibitors of current printing technology.
18M Attendees

Directories & Databases

12567 365: AIGA Year In Design
American Institute of Graphic Arts
164 Fifth Avenue
New York, NY 10010-5989

212-807-1990
Home Page: www.aiga.org
Social Media: *Facebook, Twitter, LinkedIn*

Doug Powell, President
Zia Khan, Secretary/ Treasurer
Richard Grefe, Executive Director

About 500 works of graphic designers that have been cited for outstanding design by the American Institute of Graphic Arts.
Cost: $45.00
Frequency: Annual

12568 Graphic Artist's Guide to Marketing and Self-Promotion
North Light Books
1557 Dana Avenue
Cincinnati, OH 45207-1005

FAX 513-531-4082

A list of publishers of resources about marketing for the graphic artist.
Cost: $19.95

12569 Graphic Arts Blue Book
AF Lewis & Company
360 Lexington Ave
Suite 21
New York, NY 10017-6529

212-682-8448
FAX 212-682-2442
Home Page: www.d-net.com/graphartsbb

Andrew Lewis, Owner
Timothy Lewis, Editor

Offers information on printing plants, bookbinders, imagesetters, platemakers, paper merchants, paper manufacturers, printing machinery manufacturers and dealers and oth-

ers serving the graphic arts industry.
Cost: $85.00
Frequency: 8 Annual Editions
Circulation: 51500

12570 Graphic Arts Monthly Sourcebook
Reed Business Information
2000 Clearwater Dr
Oak Brook, IL 60523-8809

630-574-0825
FAX 630-288-8781
Home Page: www.reedbusiness.com

Jeff Greisch, President
Bill Esler, Editor-in_Chief
Roger Ynostroza, Editorial Director

About 1,400 manufacturers and distributors of graphic arts equipment, supplies and services, as well as over 700 graphic arts dealers.
Cost: $50.00
Frequency: Annual March
Circulation: 85,000

12571 Graphic Communications Association Bar Code Reporter
International Digital Enterprise Alliance
1421 Prince St
Suite 230
Alexandria, VA 22314-2805

703-837-1060
FAX 703-548-2867
Home Page: www.idealliance.org

David Steinhardt, CEO

The authoritative quarterly journal of bar codes, electronic data interchange, and related electronic commerce technologies in the publishing, printing, and paper industries.
Cost: $95.00
Frequency: Quarterly
Circulation: 150

12572 Publication Design Annual
Society of Publication Designers
27 Union Square West
Suite 207
New York, NY 10003

212-223-3332
FAX 212-223-5880
E-Mail: mail@spd.org
Home Page: www.spd.org
Social Media: *Twitter*

Josh Klenert, President
Andrea Dunham, Vice President
Jennifer Pastore, Vice President
Nancy Stamatopoulos, Secretary
Gail Bichler, Treasurer

Celebrates the journalists, editorial directors, photographers, and other talented individuals who brought the year with all its triumphs and disasters to light. Featuring work published in a wide range of mediums and created by journalistic, design, and publishing talent from around the world.
Cost: $14.49
ISBN: 1-592531-81-4
Founded in 1965

12573 RSVP: Directory of Illustration and Design
RSVP
PO Box 050314
Brooklyn, NY 11205

718-857-9267
E-Mail: info@rsvpdirectory.com
Home Page: www.rsvpdirectory.com

Kathleen Creighton, Co-Publisher/Co-Editor
Richard Lebenson, Co-Publisher/Co-Editor

Fully illustrated resource book for the graphic arts/media industry. Showcases work of illustrators and designers, nationwide.
Circulation: 18,000

Industry Web Sites

12574 Creative Business
38 Indian Rd.
Suite 200
Marshfield, MA 02050

617-451-0041
E-Mail: mail@creativebusiness.com
Home Page: www.creativebusiness.com
Social Media: *Facebook, LinkedIn, YouTube*

Cameron S. Foote, Editor

Business resources - forms, articles, books - for creative services organizations and freelancers.

12575 http://gold.greyhouse.com
G.O.L.D Grey House OnLine Databases

Grey House Publishing's online database platform, GOLD, offers Quick Search, Keyword Search and Expert Search for most business sectors including graphic design markets. The GOLD platform makes finding the information you need quick and easy - whether you're a novice searcher or an experienced database user. All of Grey House's directory products are available for subscription on the GOLD platform.

12576 www.agcomm.org
Association of Graphic Communications

Promtes the interest of graphic communication professionals.

12577 www.aiga.org
American Institute of Graphic Arts

The purpose of the AIGA is to further excellence in a communication design as a broadly defined discipline, as a strategic tool for business and as a cultural force. The AIGA is the place design professionals turn first to exchange ideas and information, participate in critical analysis and research and advance education and ethical practice.

12578 www.gaa1900.com
Graphic Arts Association

Promotes the interests of graphic art professionals. Members consist of suppliers and distributors of graphic arts equipment.

12579 www.gatf.org
Graphic Arts Technical Foundation Association

To serve the graphic comunications community as the leading source for the technical information and services through research and education.

12580 www.graphicartistsguild.org
Graphic Artists Guild

Promotes and protects the economic interests of member artists and is committed to improving conditions for all ceators of graphic arts and raising standards for the enitre industry.

12581 www.greyhouse.com
Grey House Publishing

Authoritative reference directories for most business sectors including graphic design markets. Users can search the online databases with varied search criteria allowing for custom searches by product category, geographic area, sales volume, keyword, subject and more. Full Grey House catalog and online ordering also available.

12582 www.idealliance.org
International Digital Enterprise Alliance

Provides the opportunity for those who create, produce, manage, and deliver content to interface with those who develop the software tools to facilitate these functions.

12583 www.myfonts.com

MyFonts.com

Allows a user to find fonts with simple keywords. The user can test a font. The site also offers a MyFonts forum, where users can ask the experts

12584 www.nagasa.org

North American Graphic Arts Suppliers Association

The association for the channel that distributes printing and imaging technologies.

12585 www.napl.org

National Association for Printing Leadership

NAPL publishes industry specific books and periodicals for the graphic arts community. Topics cover management in the areas of sales, marketing, human resources, finance and operations technology.

12586 www.ppi-assoc.org

Pacific Printing & Imaging Association

To provide programs, offer services, and promote an environment, which assists members to see and adapt to the future, while continuing to improve and profit in the present.

12587 www.recouncil.org

Research and Engineering Council of the National

Association for Printing Leadership

A technical trade association established to identify graphic arts industry problems, coordinate graphic arts technical activities and develop industry associated technical/education programs, conference and seminars.

12588 www.siggraph.org

Special Interest Group on Computer Graphics

A forum for the promotion and distribution of current computer graphics research and technology.

12589 www.taga.org

Technical Association of the Graphic Arts

Organized to advance the science and technology of graphic arts. Disseminates graphic arts research internationally via annual technical conference and proceedings.

Associations

12590 American Hardware Manufacturers Association
801 N Plaza Drive
Schaumburg, IL 60173-4977

847-605-1025
FAX 847-605-1030
E-Mail: info@ahma.org
Home Page: www.ahma.org
Social Media: *Twitter, LinkedIn*

A leading industry trade association providing a wide range of programs and services for member firms as well as the entire industry, including industry conferences, events and workshops; legislative representation in Washington; domestic and international marketing support; technology initiatives; cost-saving programs; targeted publications; networking opportunities; and many other industry-directed services.
Founded in 1901

12591 Associated Locksmiths of America
3500 Easy St
Dallas, TX 75247

214-819-9733
800-532-2562
FAX 214-819-9736
E-Mail: webmaster@aloa.org
Home Page: www.aloa.org
Social Media: *Facebook*

International professional organization of highly qualified security professionals engaged in consulting,sales,installation and maintenance of locks,keys,safes,premises security,access controls,alarms, and other secutriy relates endeavors.
10000 Members

12592 Builders Hardware Manufacturers Association
355 Lexington Avenue
15th Floor
New York, NY 10017

212-297-2122
FAX 212-370-9047
Home Page: www.buildershardware.com
Social Media: *LinkedIn*

Scott James, President
Dan Picard, 1st Vice President
Patricia Yulkowksi, 2nd Vice President
John Cringole, 3rd Vice President

The trade association for North American manufacturers of commercial builders hardware. Nationally recognized for its leadership role in ensuring the quality and performance of builders hardware. Any organization that manufactures and sells builders hardware in the United States is eligible for Association membership.
Founded in 1925

12593 Builders' Hardware Manufacturers
355 Lexington Avenue
15th Floor
New York, NY 10017

212-297-2122
FAX 212-370-9047
Home Page: www.buildershardware.com
Social Media: *LinkedIn*

Sandy Johnson, President
Scott James, 1st Vice President
Dan Picard, 2nd Vice President
Ed Pruitt, 3rd Vice President
Founded in 1925

12594 Door and Hardware Institute
14150 Newbrook Drive
Chantilly, VA 20151-2232

703-222-2010
FAX 703-222-2410
E-Mail: info@dhi.org
Home Page: www.dhi.org
Social Media: *Facebook, Twitter, LinkedIn*

Jerry Heppes, Sr, CAE, Chief Executive Officer
Stephen R Hildebrand, FDHI, Executive Vice President
Sharon Newport, Director of Operations
Kathleen Fite, CPA, Director of Finance
Julie Walter, Director of Events

Represents the architectural openings industry. Membership consists of individuals and consultants involved in the architectural openings industry, representing distributors, manufacturers and sales representatives/agency firms, as well as architects, specifiers and contractors who rely on such professionals. Advancing the safety and security of the built environment.
5000 Members
Founded in 1975

12595 Hand Tools Institute
25 North Broadway
Tarrytown, NY 10591-3221

914-332-0040
FAX 914-332-1541
E-Mail: info@hti.org
Home Page: www.hti.org

Trade association of North American manufacturers of non-powered hand tools and tool boxes. The objectives of the Institute are to promote and further the interests of its members relative to manufacturing, safety, standardization, international trade and government relations.
Founded in 1935

12596 International Door Association
PO Box 246
West Milton, OH 45383-0246

937-698-8042
800-355-4432
FAX 937-698-6153
E-Mail: info@longmgt.com
Home Page: www.doors.org
Social Media: *Facebook, Twitter, LinkedIn, YouTube*

Chris Long, Managing Director
Roe Long-Wagner, Meetings/Exposition Manager
Dawn Jennings, Accounting Manager
Jane Treiber, Membership Manager
Shawn Hicks, Marketing Manager

Supports all those in the door and door operator industry, especially garage doors, installation hardware, roller shades and garage door openers. Publishes bimonthly magazine.
Founded in 1996

12597 Midwest Hardware Association
2301 Country Club Dr.
Suite A
Stevens Point, WI 54481

E-Mail: johnh@midwesthardware.com
Home Page: www.midwesthardware.com

John Haka, Managing Director

Nonprofit supporting independent hardware, lumber and building supply retailers.
Founded in 1896

12598 National Lumber & Building Material Dealers Association (NLBMDA)
2025 M Street, NW
Suite 800
Washington, DC 20036-3309

202-367-1169
FAX 202-367-2169
E-Mail: info@dealer.org
Home Page: www.dealer.org
Social Media: *Facebook, Twitter, LinkedIn*

JD Saunders, Chair
Jonathan M Paine, President
Ben Gann, Director of Legislative Affairs
Frank Moore, Regulatory Counsel

Promoting the industry and educating legislators and public policy personnel, assising legislative, regulatory, standard-setting and other government or private bodies in the development of laws, regulations and policies affecting lumber and building material dealers, its customers and suppliers.
6M Members
Founded in 1917

12599 North American Retail Hardware Association
6325 Digital Way
#300
Indianapolis, IN 46278-1679

317-275-9400
800-772-4424
FAX 317-275-9403
E-Mail: nrha40@nrha.org
Home Page: www.nrha.org
Social Media: *Facebook, Twitter, YouTube*

Serving the needs of independent hardware retailers in the United States and Canada. Purpose is to help independent home improvement retailers become better and more profitable merchants. Providing members with a wide array of educational and training programs, financial management resources and human resource tools that are all available online with unlimited access.
Founded in 1805

12600 Pacific Northwest Association
PO Box 17819
Salem, OR 97305

503-375-9024
800-933-7437
FAX 888-686-6271
Home Page: www.pnwassoc.com

Ronald F. Moore, President
Newell Weatherly, Vice President

Serving as a bureau of information for its members, offering health and other insurance coverage. Membership is available to any person, firm or corporation regularly engaged in the retail hardware, home center, lumber, farm equipment, outdoor power and industrial equipment industry.
Founded in 1899

Newsletters

12601 American Hardware Manufacturers Association Newsletter
American Hardware Manufacturers Association
801 N Plaza Dr
Schaumburg, IL 60173-4977

847-605-1025
FAX 847-605-1030
E-Mail: info@ahma.org
Home Page: www.ahma.org

Timothy Farrell, CEO

Industry association news.
36 Pages
Frequency: Monthly
Founded in 1900

12602 MLA LINE
Mid-America Lumbermens Association
638 W 39th St
Kansas City, MO 64111

816-561-5323
800-747-6529
FAX 816-561-1249
E-Mail: mail@themla.com
Home Page: www.themla.com

Olivia Holcombe, Executive Vice President

Lumber Industry News Express is the e-news-letter of the MLA.
Frequency: Monthly

Magazines & Journals

12603 Asian Sources Hardwares
Asian Sources
PO Box 2118
Santa Fe Springs, CA 90670

562-945-4612
FAX 562-906-2420
Home Page: www.globalsources.com

Dianna Corriero, US Circulation Manager

The leading publication providing the latest product and market information on home cen-ter/DIY, lighting, security and safety, auto parts and accessories, and machinery and industrial supplies from around the world for volume buyers worldwide.
Frequency: Monthly
Founded in 1976

12604 Brushware
Centaur Company
5515 Dundee Rd
Huddleston, VA 24104

540-297-1517
FAX 540-297-1519

Carl Wurzer, Owner
Tom Goldberg, Editor

Accepts advertising.
Cost: $35.00
88 Pages
Circulation: 1200

12605 Hardware Retailing
National Retail Hardware Association
6325 Digital Way
#300
Indianapolis, IN 46278-1787

317-290-0338
800-772-4424
FAX 317-328-4354
Home Page: www.nrha.org

The hardware and home improvement indus-try's leading trade publication. Covers hard hit-ting issues many retailers in the industry face. Content includes practical profitability advice and up-and-coming new products from the in-dustry's leading manufacturers.
Cost: $50.00
Frequency: Monthly
Circulation: 36000
Founded in 1901

12606 Hearth & Home
Village West Publishing

PO Box 2008
Laconia, NH 03247

800-258-3772
FAX 603-524-0643

Richard Wright, Editor

Magazine for retailers, including specialty, hardware, patio and barbecue.

12607 Home Channel News
Lebhar-Friedman
425 Park Ave
6th Floor
New York, NY 10022-3526

212-756-5088
FAX 212-838-9487
E-Mail: info@lf.com
Home Page: www.lf.com

Heather Martin, Manager
Terry Evans, Editor
J.Roger Friedman, CEO

Merchandising, marketing, management, and product trends that are important to owners, managers, and buyers.
Cost: $120.00
Frequency: 50 issues per y
Circulation: 50,000
Founded in 1925

12608 International Door & Operator Industry
International Door Association
PO Box 246
West Milton, OH 45383-0246

800-355-4432
FAX 937-698-6153
Home Page: www.doors.org

Art Komorowksi, Publications Manager
Shawn Hicks, Marketing Manager

The first magazine published specifically for the door and access systems industry. Inform-ing the industry about new products, new ser-vices, and the latest industry news. In addition, the publication features articles directed to help both door and access systems dealers and those who provide them products and services.
Circulation: 14000
Founded in 1996

12609 Keynotes
Associated Locksmiths of America
3003 Live Oak Street
Dallas, TX 75204-6189

214-827-1701
800-532-2562
FAX 214-827-1810
Home Page: www.aloa.org

Betty Handerson, Editor
Charles Gibson, CEO

Technical magazine for locksmiths.
Frequency: Monthly
Circulation: 8000
Founded in 1956

12610 Modern Paint & Coatings
2 Grand Central Tower
140 East 45th Street 40th Floor
New York, NY 10017

212-884-9528
FAX 212-884-9514
E-Mail: jmennella@chemweek.com
Home Page: www.chemweek.com

Joe Mennella, Global Sales Director
Lyn Tattum, Vice President/ Publisher

Keep up with the latest trends in the paint/dec-orating industry. Read about hot topics, suc-cessful business practices, industry performance & compliance. Covers topics re-lating to everything from sales and marketing to business and finance to wholesale and retail

trade.
Cost: $59.00
Frequency: Monthly

12611 Outdoor Power Equipment
Adams Business Media
111 W Jackson Blvd
7th Floor
Chicago, IL 60604-3589

312-846-4600
FAX 312-846-4634
Home Page: www.adamsbusinessmedia.com

Joanne Juda, Circulation Manager
Steve Brackett, VP/Group Publisher
Steve Noe, Editor

Serves retailers and distributors who sell and service outdoor power equipment products, in-cluding retailers, lawn and garden supply re-tailers, farm supply retailers, hardware store retailers, home centers, and building supply retailers.

12612 Power Equipment Trade
Hatton-Brown Publishers
PO Box 2268
Montgomery, AL 36102-2268

334-834-1170
FAX 334-834-4525
E-Mail: petnet@powerequipmenttrade.com
Home Page: www.powerequipmenttrade.com

David Knight, Co-Owner/Editor-in-Chief
Dan Shell, Managing Editor
Rich Donnell, Editor
Dianne Sullivan, General Manager
Dave Ramsey, Co-Owner Advertising Sales Manager

Service-oriented and technical articles, product evaluations, industry news, dealer surveys and business management information.
Cost: $55.00
Circulation: 21441
ISSN: 0163-0414
Founded in 1952
Printed in on glossy stock

Trade Shows

12613 Ace Hardware Fall Convention and Exhibit
Ace Hardware Corporation
2200 Kensington Court
Oak Brook, IL 60521

630-990-6600
FAX 708-990-0278

Over 950 exhibitors with hardware related products for Ace Hardware dealers. Seminar and dinner are part of the event.
17000 Attendees
Frequency: Annual/October

12614 Ace Hardware Spring Convention and Exhibit
Ace Hardware Corporation
2200 Kensington Court
Oak Brook, IL 60521

630-990-6600
FAX 708-990-0278

David Myer, Senior VP

Over 900 exhibitors with hardware related products for Ace Hardware dealers.
8000 Attendees
Frequency: Annual

12615 Door & Hardware Exposition & Convention
Door & Hardware Institute

14170 Newbrook Drive
Suite 200
Chantilly, VA 20151

703-222-2010
FAX 703-222-2410
E-Mail: info@dhi.org
Home Page: www.dhi.org

Stephen R Hildebrand, Director Business
Development
Garld Heppes Sr, Executive Assistant
Cathy Jones, Executive Assistant

Over 150 exhibitors bringing the latest in industry trends, education and developments to
safely secure the built environment.
4200 Attendees
Frequency: Annual

12616 Equipment Leasing Association Annual Meeting

1825 K Street NW
Suite 900
Washington, DC 20006

202-238-3400
FAX 202-238-3401
E-Mail: rscoggins@elfaonline.org
Home Page: www.elfaonline.org

Sally Maloney, Meeting Manager
Michael Fleming, President

25 booths.
1,200 Attendees
Frequency: October

12617 Florida Building Products and Design Show

Florida Lumber & Building Material Dealers
1303 Limit Avenue
Mount Dora, FL 32757

352-383-0366
FAX 352-383-8756
Home Page: www.fbma.org

Bill Tucker, President
Kair Hebrank, VP Government Relations
Betty Askew, Director of Operations

A place for members of the Building Supply Industry to gather. It provides an affordable opportunity to learn about new and innovative
equipment and products.
3000 Attendees
Frequency: Annual
Founded in 1920

12618 Gemstate Industrial and Construction Show

Trade Shows West
360 S Fort Ln
Suite 2C
Layton, UT 84041-5708

801-485-0176
800-794-3706
FAX 801-485-0241
E-Mail: jeffwfredericks@hotmail.com
Home Page: www.facetofacemarketing.net

Exhibit focusing on the needs of the industrial,
construction, and plant maintenance industries.
6049 Attendees
Frequency: Annual/November

12619 Hardware Wholesalers: Merchandise Mart

Hardware Wholesalers
Nelson Road
Box 868
Ft.Wayne, IN 46801

260-748-5300
FAX 260-496-1245

11500 Attendees

12620 International Hardware Week

American Hardware Manufacturers
Association
801 N Plaza Drive
Schaumburg, IL 60173-4977

847-605-1025
FAX 847-605-1030
E-Mail: info@ahma.org
Home Page: www.ahma.org

William Farrell, Vice Chairman Of The Board
Timothy Farrell, President/CEO

3,000 exhibitors.
62.5M Attendees
Frequency: August
Founded in 2001

12621 Iowa Lumber Convention

Northwestern Lumber Association
5905 Golden Valley Road
Suite 110
Minneapolis, MN 55422-4535

763-544-6822
888-544-6822
FAX 763-595-4060
Home Page: www.nlassn.org

Jodie Fleck, Director of Conventions

Hosts educational seminars and trade show.
Frequency: Annual/March

12622 Lumber and Hardware Show Mid-America

PO Box 1828
Columbus, OH 43216

614-460-6000
FAX 614-833-6983

Joe Bailey, Show Manager

300 booths for retail lumber yard stores.
7M Attendees
Frequency: February

12623 National Building Products Exposition & Conference

American Hardware Manufacturers
Association
801 N Plaza Drive
Schaumburg, IL 60173-4977

847-605-1025
FAX 847-605-1030
E-Mail: info@ahma.org
Home Page: www.ahma.org

William Farrell, Vice Chairman Of The Board
Timothy Farrell, President/CEO
70000 Attendees

12624 National Hardware Show

Association Expositions & Services
383 Main Avenue
Norwalk, CT 06851

203-840-5622
888-425-9377
FAX 203-840-4824
E-Mail: inquiry@hardware.reedexpo.com
Home Page: www.nationalhardwareshow.com

Timothy Farrell, Executive VP
Martin O'Rourke, Membership Manager

Held in conjunction with International Hardware Week, this is the industry's leading hard-
ware/home improvement event, with products
from over 2,000 manufacturers from around the
world. Includes hardware and allied lines,
plumbing, paint and home decorating, lawn and
garden, building products and housewares.
Also international pavilions.
70000 Attendees
Frequency: August
Founded in 1945

12625 National Hardware Show/National Building Products Exposition & Conference

Reed Exhibition Companies
383 Main Avenue
Norwalk, CT 06851

203-840-4800
FAX 203-840-4801
E-Mail: inquiry@reedexpo.com
Home Page: www.reedexpo.com

12626 Service Specialists Association Annual Convention

Service Specialists Association
4015 Marks Road
Suite 2B
Medina, OH 44256-8316

330-725-7160
800-763-5717
FAX 330-722-5638
E-Mail: trucksvc@aol.com
Home Page: www.truckservice.org

Cara R Giebner, Manager

Containing 70 booths and 70 exhibits.
400 Attendees

12627 Servistar Corporation Lumber & Home Center: Fall

Servistar Corporation
PO Box 1510
Butler, PA 16001

773-695-5000
FAX 773-695-5172

1500 Attendees

12628 Servistar Corporation Lumber & Home Center : Spring

Servistar Corporation
8600 W Bryn Mawr Avenue
Chicago, IL 60631-3505

773-695-5000
FAX 773-695-5172

1500 Attendees

12629 Servistar Market

Truserv Corporation
8600 W Bryn Mawr Avenue
Chicago, IL 60631-3505

773-695-5000
FAX 773-695-5172

Johnathan Mills, Show Manager

Hardware manufacturers, suppliers and distributors.
5M Attendees
Frequency: September

Directories & Databases

12630 Complete Directory of Hardware Items

Sutton Family Communications &
Publishing Company
920 State Route 54 East
Elmitch, KY 42343

270-276-9500
E-Mail: jlsutton@apex.net

Theresa Sutton, Editor
Lee Sutton, General Manager

Print-out from database of wholesale distributors, importers, manufacturers, close-out houses,
and liquidators. Database is updated daily to
guarantee the most current and up-to-date

sources available.
Cost: $109.00
100+ Pages

12631 Complete Directory of Household Items
Sutton Family Communications &
Publishing Company
920 State Route 54 East
Elmitch, KY 42343

270-276-9500
E-Mail: jlsutton@apex.net

Theresa Sutton, Editor
Lee Sutton, General Manager

Print-out from database of wholesalers, manufacturers, distributors, importers and close-out houses. Database is updated daily to guarantee the most current and up-to-date sources available.
Cost: $109.00
100+ Pages

12632 Directory and Buyer's Guide of the Door and Hardware Institute
Door and Hardware Institute
14150 Newbrook Dr
Suite 200
Chantilly, VA 20151-2232

703-222-2010
FAX 703-222-2410
E-Mail: info@dhi.org
Home Page: www.dhi.org

Gerald S Heppes Sr, Executive Director
Cathy Jones, Executive Assistant

More than 700 firms which supply doors, hinges, locks, cabinets and closet hardware, door motors, smoke clothing and detection devices.
Frequency: Annual

12633 Door and Hardware Institute: Membership Directory
Door and Hardware Institute
14150 Newbrook Dr
Suite 200
Chantilly, VA 20151-2232

703-222-2010
FAX 703-222-2410
E-Mail: info@dhi.org
Home Page: www.dhi.org

Gerald S Heppes Sr, Executive Director
Cathy Jones, Executive Assistant

Includes names and addresses of more than 5,000 members, including 700 manufacturing firms. Excellent resource for networking and staying in touch with your colleagues. Advertising is available.
Frequency: Annually
Founded in 1999

12634 Home Center Operators & Hardware Chains
Chain Store Guide
3922 Coconut Palm Dr
Suite 300
Tampa, FL 33619-1389

813-627-6700
800-927-9292
FAX 813-627-7094
E-Mail: info@csgis.com
Home Page: www.csgis.com

Mike Jarvis, Publisher
Arthur Rosenberg, Editor
Shami Choon, Manager

The facts on more than 4,600 company headquarters and subsidiaries operating almost 23,500 units in the vast Home Improvement Building Material Industry. Also included are 19 major buying/marketing groups and coops that contribute approximately $30 billion and

serve 103,243 accounts.
Cost: $30.00
Frequency: Annual, Paperback

12635 MLA Buyer's Guide & Dealer Directory
Mid-America Lumbermens Association
638 W 39th St
Kansas City, MO 64111

816-561-5323
800-747-6529
FAX 816-561-1249
E-Mail: mail@themla.com
Home Page: www.themla.com

Olivia Holcombe, Executive Vice President

Industry Web Sites

12636 http://gold.greyhouse.com
G.O.L.D Grey House OnLine Databases
Grey House Publishing's online database platform, GOLD, offers Quick Search, Keyword Search and Expert Search for most business sectors including hardware markets. The GOLD platform makes finding the information you need quick and easy - whether you're a novice searcher or an experienced database user. All of Grey House's directory products are available for subscription on the GOLD platform.

12637 www.ahma.org
American Hardware Manufacturers Association
Over 280 manufacturer representatives in the hardware industry.

12638 www.aloa.org
Associated Locksmiths of America
Strives to educate and provide information to industry. Maintains referral service and offers insurance and bonding programs. Holds technical training.

12639 www.americanladderinstitute.org
American Ladder Institute
Members include manufacturers of wood, metal and fiberglass ladders. Represents US companies engaged in the research, development, manufacture and safety ladders.

12640 www.greyhouse.com
Grey House Publishing
Authoritative reference directories for most business sectors including hardware markets. Users can search the online databases with varied search criteria allowing for custom searches by product category, geographic area, sales volume, keyword, subject and more. Full Grey House catalog and online ordering also available.

12641 www.hti.org
Hand Tools Institute
Provides safety education and concerned with product standards.

12642 www.nrha.org
National Retail Hardware Association
An organization which features news and information for hardware retailers.

Associations

12643 ALS Association
1275 K Street NW
Suite 250
Washington, DC 20005

202-407-8580
FAX 202-289-6801
Home Page: www.alsa.org
Social Media: *Facebook, Twitter, LinkedIn, YouTube*

Barbara Newhouse, President, CEO
Gregory L. Mitchell, Chief Financial Officer
Carrie Martin Munk, Chief Comm. & Marketing Officer
Lucie Bruijn, PhD, Chief Scientist
Steve Gibson, Chief Public Policy Officer

National nonprofit organization fighting Lou Gehrig's Disease—leads the way in research, care services, public education, and public policy.
Founded in 1869

12644 ARMA International
11880 College Blvd
Suite 450
Overland Park, KS 66210

913-341-3808
800-422-2762
FAX 913-341-3742
E-Mail: headquarters@armaintl.org
Home Page: www.arma.org
Social Media: *Twitter*

Komal Gulich, CRM, Chairman
Julie J. Colgan, CRM, President
Brenda Prowse, CRM, Treasurer
Nicholas De Laurentis, Chair

ARMA is a not-for-profit professional association and the authority on managing records and information. Members include records managers, archivists, corporate librarians, imaging specialists, legal professionals, IT managers, consultants, and educators, all of whom work in a wide variety of industries, including government, legal, healthcare, financial services, and petroleum.
11M Members
Founded in 1955

12645 ASET - The Neurodiagnostic Society
402 East Bannister Road
Suite A
Kansas City, MO 64131-3019

816-931-1120
FAX 816-931-1145
E-Mail: info@aset.org
Home Page: www.aset.org
Social Media: *Facebook, Twitter*

Arlen Reimritz, Executive Director
Cheryl Plummer, President
Susan Agostini,, President-Elect
Cherie Young, Secretary-Treasurer
Brian Markley, Past President

ASET is the largest national professional association for individuals involved in the study and recording of electrical activity in the brain and nervous system. ASET's mission is to provide leadership, advocacy and professional excellence for members, creating greater awareness of the profession and establishing standards and best practices to ensure quality patient care.
4200 Members
Founded in 1959

12646 Academy of Dental Materials
21 Grouse Terrace
Lake Oswego, OR 97035

503-636-0861
FAX 503-675-2738
Home Page: www.academydentalmaterials.org

Objectives of the Academy are; to provide a forum for the exchange of information on all aspects of dental materials, to enhance communication between industry, researchers and practicing dentists, to encourage dental materials research and its applications and to promote dental materials through its activities.
Founded in 1941

12647 Academy of General Dentistry
560 W. Lake Street
Sixth Floor
Chicago, IL 60611-6600

888-243-3368
FAX 312-440-0559
E-Mail: abgd@agd.org
Home Page: www.agd.org

Linda J Edgar, DDS, MEd, MAGD, President
W. Mark Donald, DMD, MAGD, Vice-President
Manuel A Cordero, DDS, MAGD, Secretary
Maria A Smith, DMD, MAGD, Treasurer
W. Carter Brown, DMD, FAGD, President-Elect

Mission is to serve the needs and represent the interest of general dentists, to promote the oral health of the public, and to foster continued proficiency of general dentists through quality continuing dental education in order to better serve the public.
37M Members
Founded in 1952

12648 Academy of Nutrition and Dietetics
120 South Riverside Plaza
Suite 2000
Chicago, IL 60606

312-899-0040
800-877-1600
E-Mail: info@eatright.org
Home Page: www.eatright.org
Social Media: *Facebook, Twitter, Google Plus, Youtube*

Striving to improve the nation's health and advance the profession of dietetics through research, education, and advocacy.
70M Members
Founded in 1917

12649 Academy of Osseointegration
85 W Algonquin Rd
Suite 550
Arlington Hts, IL 60005-4460

847-439-1919
800-656-7736
FAX 847-439-1569
E-Mail: academy@osseo.org
Home Page: www.osseo.org

Russell D. Nishimura DDS, President
Michael R. Norton,, Vice President
Kevin P. Smith, MA, MBA, Executive Director
Jean Lynch, Director of Exhibits
Gina Seegers, Director of Meeting Services

Established to provide a focus for the rapidly advancing biotechnology involving the natural bond between bone and certain alloplastic reconstructive materials.
5200 Members
Founded in 1987

12650 Acoustic Neuroma Association
600 Peachtree Pkwy
Suite 108
Cumming, GA 30041-6899

770-205-8211
877-200-8211
FAX 770-205-0239
FAX 877-202-0239
E-Mail: info@anausa.org
Home Page: www.anausa.org
Social Media: *Facebook, Twitter, YouTube*

Alan Goldberg, President
Karla Jacobus, Vice President
John Gigliello, Treasurer
David Puzzoÿ, Secretary
Jeffrey D. Barr, Immediate Past President

A patient organization that provides education and support to thosediagnosed with an acoustic neuroma.
Founded in 1981

12651 Adult Congenital Heart Association
6757 Greene Street,
Suite 335
Philadelphia, PA 19119-3508

215-849-1260
888-921-ACHA
FAX 215-849-1261
E-Mail: info@achaheart.org
Home Page: www.achaheart.org
Social Media: *Facebook, Twitter*

John C. Fernie, Chair
Cindy Huie, Vice Chair
Kevin Gordon, Treasurer
Denise Garvy, Secretary
Curt J. Daniels, MD, Medical Advisory Board Chair

Information, resources, and support for adults with congenital heart disease.
Founded in 1998

12652 Advanced Medical Technology Association
701 Pennsylvania Ave, NW
Suite 800
Washington, DC 20004-2654

202-783-8700
FAX 202-783-8750
E-Mail: info@advamed.org
Home Page: www.advamed.org
Social Media: *Facebook, Twitter, LinkedIn, Youtube*

David C. Dvorak, Chairman of the Board
Stephen J. Ubl, President &ÿChief Executive Officer
David H. Nexon, Senior Executive Vice President
JC Scott, Senior Executive Vice President
Kenneth Mendez, Senior Executive VP

Advocates for a legal, regulatory and economic environment that advances global health care by assuring worldwide patient access to the benefits of medical technology. Promoting policies that foster the highest ethical standards, rapid product approvals, appropriate reimbursement, and access to international markets.
1100 Members
Founded in 1980

12653 Aerospace Medical Association
320 S Henry St
Alexandria, VA 22314-3579

703-739-2240
FAX 703-739-9652
E-Mail: rrayman@asma.org
Home Page: www.asma.org

Jeffrey C. Sventek, MS, CAsP, Executive Director
Gisselle Vargas, Operations Manager
Gloria Carter, Director, Member Services

Sheryl Kildall, Subscriptions Manager
Frederick Bonato, PhD, Editor-in-Chief

Organized exclusively for charitable, educational, and scientific purposes. It is the largest, most-representative professional membership organization in the fields of aviation, space, and environmental medicine.
3200 Members
Founded in 1929
Mailing list available for rent

12654 Alexander Graham Bell Association for the Deaf and Hard of Hearing
3417 Volta Place, NW
Washington, DC 20007

202-337-5220
FAX 202-337-8314
E-Mail: info@agbell.org
Home Page:
www.listeningandspokenlanguage.org
Social Media: *Facebook, Twitter, YouTube, Pinterest*

Emilio Alonso-Mendoza, Chief Executive Officer
Lisa Chutjian, Chief Development Officer
Susan Boswell, Director of Communications
Robin Bailey, Programs Specialist
Judy Harrison, Director of Programs

A resource, support network and advocate for listening, learning, talking, and living independently with hearing loss.
Founded in 2005

12655 Alzheimer's Association
225 N. Michigan Ave.
Floor 17
Chicago, IL 60601-7633

312-335-8700
FAX 866-699-1246
E-Mail: advocate@alz.org
Home Page: www.alz.org/
Social Media: *Facebook, Twitter, YouTube*

Michelle Helton, Vice President, Financial Operation
Christine Foh, Vice President, Legal
Beth Kallmyer, Vice President, Constituent Service
Maria Carrillo, Chief Science Officer
Richard Hovland, Chief Operations Officer

Information on Alzheimer's disease and dementia symptoms, diagnosis, stages, treatment, care and support resources.

12656 Ambulatory Surgery Center Association
1012 Cameron Street
Alexandria, VA 22314-2427

703-836-8808
FAX 703-549-0976
E-Mail: asc@ascassociation.org
Home Page: www.ascassociation.org
Social Media: *Facebook, Twitter, LinkedIn*

Nap Gary, President
Michael A. Guarino, Vice President
David S. George, MD, Secretary

Membership and advocacy organization that provides member benefits and services, combats legislative, regulatory and other challenges at the federal and state level, assists state ASC association, enhances ASC representation at the state and federal level, and has established a political action committee.

12657 America's Health Insurance Plans (AHIP)
601 Pennsylvania Avenue
NW South Building, Suite 500ÿ
Washington, DC 20004

202-778-3200
FAX 202-331-7487

E-Mail: ahip@ahip.org
Home Page: www.ahip.org/

The national trade association representing the health insurance industry. Members provide health and supplemental benefits to more than 200 million Americans through employer-sponsored coverage, the individual insurance market, and public programs such as Medicare and Medicaid. Advocates for public policies that expand access to affordable health care coverage to all Americans through a competitive marketplace that fosters choice, quality and innovation.

12658 American Academy for Cerebral Palsy and Developmental Medicine
555 East Wells
Suite 1100
Milwaukee, WI 53202-3800

414-918-3014
FAX 414-276-2146
E-Mail: info@aacpdm.org
Home Page: www.aacpdm.org
Social Media: *Facebook, Twitter*

Richard Stevenson, MD, President
Darcy Fehlings, MD MSc FRCPC, First Vice President
Eileen Fowler, PhD PT, Second Vice President
Johanna Darrah, PhD PT, Secretary
Joshua Hyman, MD, Treasurer

Mission is to provide multidisciplinary scientific education for health professionals and promote excellence in research and services for the benefit of people with cerebral palsy and childhood-onset disabilities. A global leader in the multidisciplinary scientific education of health professionals and researchers.
1100 Members
Founded in 1947

12659 American Academy of Allergy, Asthma and Immunology
555 E Wells St
Suite 1100
Milwaukee, WI 53202-3823

414-272-6071
E-Mail: info@aaaai.org
Home Page: www.aaaai.org
Social Media: *Facebook*

The largest professional medical specialty organization in the United States, representing allergists, asthma specialists, clinical immunologists, allied health professionals, and others with a special interest in the research and treatment of allergic disease.
6M Members
Founded in 1943

12660 American Academy of Child and Adolescent Psychiatry
3615 Wisconsin Ave NW
Washington, DC 20016-3007

202-966-7300
FAX 202-966-2891
E-Mail: cme@aacap.org
Home Page: www.aacap.org
Social Media: *Facebook, Twitter*

Martin J. Drell, President
Paramjit T. Joshi, President-Elect
David R. DeMaso, Secretary
Steven P. Cuffe, Treasurer

Membership based organization, composed of child and adolescent psychiatrists and other interested physicians. Members actively research, evaluate, diagnose, and treat psychiatric disorders and pride themselves on giving direction to and responding quickly to new developments in addressing the health care needs of children and their families.
7500 Members
Founded in 1953

12661 American Academy of Dermatology
930 E. Woodfield Road
Schaumburg, IL 60173

847-240-1280
866-503-7546
FAX 847-240-1859
E-Mail: jbarnes@aad.org
Home Page: www.aad.org
Social Media: *Facebook, Twitter, Pinterest, Youtube*

Dirk M Elston, MD, President
Lisa A Garner, MD, Vice President
Suzanne M Olbricht, MD, Secretary-Treasurer
Brett M Coldiron, MD, President-Elect
Elise A Olsen, MD, Vice President-Elect

The largest, most influential and most representative dermatology group in the United States. Represents virtually all practicing dermatologists in the US, as well as a growing number of international dermatologists.
13700 Members
Founded in 1938

12662 American Academy of Family Physicians
11400 Tomahawk Creek Pkwy.
Leawood, KS 66211-2680

913-906-6205
FAX 913-906-6086
E-Mail: contactcenter@aafp.org
Home Page: www.aafp.org
Social Media: *Facebook, Twitter*

Douglas E. Henley, EVP & CEO
Todd C. Dicus, Dep. EVP & COO

The national association of family doctors.
Founded in 1947

12663 American Academy of Fixed Prosthodontics
6661 Merwin Road
Columbus, OH 43235

614-761-1927
FAX 614-292-0941
E-Mail: aafpsec@gmail.com
Home Page: www.fixedprosthodontics.org
Social Media: *Twitter*

Steven Morgagno, D.M.D., President
David Burns, Vice President
Stephen F Rosenstiel, Secretary
Richard D Jordan, Treasurer
Gerry Santulli, President-Elect

Mission is to foster excellence in the field of prosthodontics, implants and esthetic dentistry through mutual study, participation, and cooperation.
Founded in 1950

12664 American Academy of Forensic Sciences
410 North 21st Street
Colorado Springs, CO 80904-2712

719-636-1100
FAX 719-636-1993
E-Mail: awarren@aafs.org
Home Page: www.aafs.org
Social Media: *Facebook, RSS, YouTube*

Victor W. Weedn, MD, JD, President
Norm Sauer, PhD, Vice President
Susan M. Ballou, MS, Secretary
Betty Layne DesPortes, JD, Treasurer
John E. Gerns, MFS, President-Elect

Committed to the promotion of education and the elevation of accuracy, precision, and specificity in the forensic sciences. Membership consists of physicians, attorneys, dentists, toxicologists, physical anthropologists, document examiners, digital evidence experts, and others.
5M Members
Founded in 1948

12665 American Academy of Home Care Physicians
PO Box 1037
Edgewood, MD 21040-0337

410-676-7966
FAX 410-676-7980
E-Mail: aahcp@comcast.net
Home Page: www.aahcp.org/
Social Media: *Facebook, Twitter, LinkedIn, YouTube*

Bruce Leff, President
Thomas Cornwell, President-Elect
Kathy A. Kemle, Secretary
Brent T. Feorene, Treasurer

Mission is to promote the art, science, and practice of medicine in the home. Members include home care physicians, physicians who make house calls, care for homebound patients, act as home health agency medical directors, or who refer patients to home care agencies.
Founded in 1988

12666 American Academy of Implant Dentistry
211 East Chicago Avenue
Suite 750
Chicago, IL 60611

312-335-1550
877-335-2243
FAX 312-335-9090
E-Mail: info@aaid.com
Home Page: www.aaid.com
Social Media: *Facebook, Twitter, LinkedIn, YouTube, Google Plus*

John Da Silva, President
Shankar Iyer, DDS, Vice President
David G. Hochberg, DDS, Treasurer
Natalie Wong, DDS, Secretary
Richard Mercurio, DDS, President-Elect

AAID offers a rigorous implant dentistry credentialing program which requires at least 300 hours of post-docroal or continuing education instruction in implant dentistry, passing a comprehensive exam, and presenting successful cases of different types of implants to a group of examiners. It is one of the most comprehensive credentialing programs in dentistry.
4000 Members
Founded in 1951

12667 American Academy of Medical Administrators
330 N Wabash Avenue
Suite 2000
Chicago, IL 60611

312-321-6815
FAX 312-673-6705
E-Mail: info@aameda.org
Home Page: aama.socious.com

John Garrity, MHA, CFAAMA, Chairman
Jennifer Smith, Vice Chair
Thomas Draper, Treasurer
David Schmahl, Executive Director
Bruce Hammond, CRA, CFAAMA, Appointed Director

To advance excellence in healthcare leadership through individual relationships, multi-disciplinary interaction, practical business tools and active engagement.
Founded in 1957

12668 American Academy of Neurology
201 Chicago Avenue
Minneapolis, MN 55415

612-928-6000
800-879-1960
FAX 612-454-2746
E-Mail: memberservices@aan.com
Home Page: www.aan.com

Social Media: *Facebook, Twitter, LinkedIn, YouTube, Pinterest, Google+*

Bruce Sigsbee, President
Timothy A. Pedley, President Elect
Lisa M. DeAngelis, Vice President
Terrence L. Cascino, Treasurer
Lisa M. Shulman, Secretary

An international professional association of neurologists and neuroscience professionals dedicated to promoting the highest quality patient-centered neurologic care. The AAN is strongly committed to its mission and focuses its efforts on ensuring the reality of the principles and standards set forth in AAN mission statement.
18000 Members
Founded in 1948

12669 American Academy of Ophthalmology
655 Beach Street
San Francisco, CA 94109

415-561-8500
FAX 415-561-8533
E-Mail: customer_service@aao.org
Home Page: www.aao.org
Social Media: *Facebook, Twitter, LinkedIn, YouTube, RSS, Google+*

Richard L. Abbott, Chair

Mission is to advance the lifelong learning and professional interests of opthalmologists to ensure that the public can obtain the best possible eye care.
80000 Members
Founded in 1979

12670 American Academy of Optometry
2909 Fairgreen Street
Orlando, FL 32803

321-710-3937
800-969-4226
FAX 407-893-9890
E-Mail: aaoptom@aaoptom.org
Home Page: www.aaopt.org
Social Media: *Facebook, Twitter, LinkedIn, Youtube*

Brett G. Bence, OD, FAAO, President
Lois Schoenbrun, CAE, FAAO, Executive Director
Barbara Caffery, OD, PhD, FAAO, Secretary-Treasurer
Joseph P. Shovlin, OD, FAAO, President-Elect
Richard Jones, CPA, Senior Director, Finance

A philanthropic organization that develops and provides financial support for optometric research and education in vision and eye health.
5000 Members
Founded in 1922

12671 American Academy of Oral and Maxillofacial Surgeons
9700 West Bryn Mawr Avenue
Rosemont, IL 60018-5701

847-678-6200
800-822-6637
FAX 847-678-6286
Home Page: www.aaoms.org
Social Media: *Facebook, Twitter, YouTube, Vimeo*

Louis K. Rafetto, DMD, President
Robert C Rinaldi, PhD, CAE, Secretary / Executive Director
J. David Johnson, Jr., DMD, Treasurer
Douglas W.ÿ Fain, DDS, MD, FACS, President-Elect
Brett L. Ferguson, DDS, Vice President

The professional organization representing oral and maxillofacial surgeons in the US, supporting its members' ability to practice their specialty through education, research, and advocacy. Members comply with rigorous con-

tinuing education requirements and submit to periodic office examinations, ensuring the public that all office procedures and personnel meet stringent national standards.
9000+ Members
Founded in 1946

12672 American Academy of Orofacial Pain
174 S. New York Ave
PO Box 478
Oceanville, NJ 08231

609-504-1311
FAX 609-573-5064
E-Mail: steve@benderdds.com
Home Page: www.aaop.org
Social Media: *Facebook, Twitter*

Steven D. Bender, President
Gary Dÿ Klasser, President-Elect
Maureen Lang, Council Chair
Barry Rozenberg, Treasurer
Kenneth Sÿ Cleveland, Executive Director

Dedicated to alleviating pain and suffering through the promotion of excellence in education, research and patient care in the field of orofacial pain and associated disorders.
Founded in 1975

12673 American Academy of Orthopaedic Surgeons
9400 West Higgins Rd.
Rosemont, IL 60018

847-823-7186
FAX 847-823-8125
Home Page: www.aaos.org
Social Media: *Facebook, Twitter*

David Teuscher, President
Karen L. Hackett, Chief Executive Officer

Provider of medical education to orthopaedic surgeons.
Founded in 1933

12674 American Academy of Osteopathy
3500 DePauw Boulevard
Suite 1100
Indianapolis, IN 46268-1136

317-879-1881
800-875-6360
FAX 317-879-0563
E-Mail: info@academyofosteopathy.org
Home Page: www.academyofosteopathy.org/
Social Media: *Facebook, Twitter, LinkedIn, YouTube*

Doris B. Newman, DO, FAAO, President
Laura E. Griffin, DO, FAAO, President-Elect
Judith A. O'Connell, DO, FAAO, Treasurer, Secretary
Kenneth J. Lossing, DO, Immediate Past President
Michael E. Fitzgerald, Executive Director

Mission is to teach, advocate, and research the science, art and philosophy of osteopathic medicine, emphasizing the integration of osteopathic principles, practices and manipulative treatment in patient care.
Founded in 1937

12675 American Academy of Otolaryngology-Head and Neck Surgery
1650 Diagonal Road
Alexandria, VA 22314-2857

703-836-4444
E-Mail: membership@entnet.org
Home Page: www.entnet.org
Social Media: *Facebook, Twitter, LinkedIn, YouTube*

Richard Waguespack, MD, President
J Gavin Setzen, MD, Secretary/Treasurer
David R. Nielsen, MD, Executive Vice President and CEO

Paul T Fass, MD, Director - Private Practice
Bradley F Marple, MD, Director - Academic

The world's largest organization representing specialists who treat the ear, nose, throat, and related structures of the head and neck. Represents otolaryngologist- head and neck surgeons who diagnose and treat disorders of those areas.
12M Members
Founded in 1896

12676 American Academy of Pain Medicine
8735 W. Higgins Rd.
Suite 300
Chicago, IL 60631-2738

847-375-4731
FAX 847-375-6477
E-Mail: info@painmed.org
Home Page: www.painmed.org
Social Media: *LinkedIn*

Perry Fine, President
Martin Grabois, President-Elect
Lynn Webster, Treasurer
Zahid H. Bajwa, Secretary

Has evolved as the primary organization for physicians practicing the specialty of Pain Medicine in the US. Purpose is to optimize the health of patients in pain and eliminate the major public health problem of pain by advancing the practice and the specialty of pain medicine.
Founded in 1983

12677 American Academy of Pediatric Dentistry
211 East Chicago Avenue
Suite 1600
Chicago, IL 60611-2637

312-337-2169
FAX 312-337-6329
E-Mail: info@aapd.org
Home Page: www.aapd.org
Social Media: *Facebook, Twitter*

Robert L. Delarosa, D.D.S., President
Robert L Delarosa, D.D.S., Vice President
Jade Miller, D.D.S., Secretary-Treasurer
Edward J. Moody, President-Elect

Mission is to advocate policies, guidelines, and programs that promote optimal oral health and oral health care for infants and children through adolescence, including those with special health care needs. Serves and represents its membership in the areas of professional development and governmental and legislative activities. It is a liaison to other health care groups and the public.
8M Members
Founded in 1948

12678 American Academy of Periodontology
737 N. Michigan Avenue
Suite 800
Chicago, IL 60611-6660

312-787-5518
FAX 312-787-3670
E-Mail: staff@abperio.org
Home Page: www.perio.org
Social Media: *Facebook, Twitter, YouTube, Google Plus*

Joan Otomo-Corgel, President
Terrence J.ÿ Griffin, Vice President
Steven R.ÿ Daniel, Secretary/ Treasurer
Wayne A.ÿ Aldredge, President-Elect
Stuart J.ÿ Froum, Immediate Past President

Purpose is to advance the periodontal and general health of the public and promote excellence in the practice of periodontics. Membership includes periodontists and general dentists from all 50 states as well as around the world.
8,400 Members
Founded in 1914

12679 American Academy of Physical Medicine and Rehabilitation (AAPMR)
9700 West Bryn Mawr Avenue
Suite 200
Rosemont, IL 60018-5701

847-737-6000
877-227-6799
FAX 847-754-4368
E-Mail: info@aapmr.org
Home Page: www.aapmr.org
Social Media: *Facebook, Twitter*

Kurt M Hoppe, MD, President
Thomas E Stautzenbach, CAE, Executive Director
Gregory M Worsowicz, MD, MBA, Vice President
Darryl L Kaelin, MD, Secretary
David G. Welch, MD, Treasurer

Exclusively serving the needs of today's physical medicine and rehabilitation physician.
9000+ Members
Founded in 1938

12680 American Academy of Physician Assistants
2318 Mill Road
Suite 1300
Alexandria, VA 22314

703-836-2272
FAX 703-684-1924
E-Mail: aapa@aapa.org
Home Page: www.aapa.org
Social Media: *Facebook, Twitter, LinkedIn, Youtube, Huddle*

Jeffrey A. Katz, PA-C, DFAAPA, President and Chair
John G. McGinnity, President Elect
L Gail Curtis, Vice President/Speaker of the House
Tillie Fowler, SVP, Advocacy
Jennifer L Dorn, Chief Executive Officer

Advocates and educates on behalf of the profession and the patients PAs serve. AAPA works to ensure the professional growth, personal excellence and recognition of physician assistants. It also works to enhance their ability to improve the quality, accessibility and cost-effectiveness of patient-centered health care.
81M Members
Founded in 1968

12681 American Academy of Professional Coders
2233 S Presidents Dr.
Salt Lake City, UT 84120

801-236-2200
800-626-2633
FAX 801-236-2258
E-Mail: info@aapc.com
Home Page: www.aapc.com
Social Media: *Facebook, Twitter, LinkedIn*

Jaci Johnson Kipreos, President
Ann M. Bina, CPC, COC, CPC-I, Secretary
Michael D. Miscoe, President-elect
Angela Clements, Member Relations Officer

Founded to provide education and professional certification to physician-based medical coders and to elevate the standards of medical coding by providing student training, certification, ongoing education, networking, and job opportunities.
111M Members
Founded in 1988

12682 American Alliance for Health, Physical Education, Recreation and Dance
1900 Association Drive
Reston, VA 20191-1598

703-476-3400
800-213-7193
FAX 703-476-9527
Home Page: www.shapeamerica.org
Social Media: *Facebook, Twitter, Instagram*

Steven Jefferies, President
E. Paul Roetert, Chief Executive Officer
Dolly D Lambdin, President-Elect

Mission is to promote and support leadership, research, education, and best practices in the professions that support creative, healthy, and active lifestyles. AAHPERD envisions a society in which all individuals enjoy an optimal quality of life through appreciation of and participation in an active and creative, health-promoting lifestyle.
25M Members
Founded in 1885

12683 American Art Therapy Association
4875 Eisenhower Avenue
Suite 240
Alexandria, VA 22304

703-548-5860
888-290-0878
FAX 703-783-8468
E-Mail: info@arttherapy.org
Home Page: www.arttherapy.org
Social Media: *Facebook, Twitter, LinkedIn, RSS*

Donna Betts, PhD, ATR-BC, President
Christianne Strang, PHD, ATR-BC, President Elect
Stephanie Wise, Treasurer
Cynthia Woodruff, Executive Director
Michelle Dean, Secretary

A U.S. national professional association of over 5,000 practicing art therapy professionals, including students, educators, and related practitioners in the field art therapy.

12684 American Association for Cancer Research
615 Chestnut St.
17th Fl.
Philadelphia, PA 19106-4404

215-440-9300
866-423-3965
FAX 215-440-9313
E-Mail: aacr@aacr.org
Home Page: www.aacr.org
Social Media: *Facebook, Twitter, LinkedIn, YouTube*

Margaret Foti, Chief Executive Officer
Jos, Baselga, President

The AACR is the oldest and largest cancer research organization in the world.
Founded in 1907

12685 American Association for Clinical Chemistry
900 Seventh Street, NW
Suite 400
Washington, DC 20001

202-857-0717
800-892-1400
FAX 202-887-5093
E-Mail: custserv@aacc.org
Home Page: www.aacc.org
Social Media: *Facebook, Twitter, LinkedIn, YouTube, Google+*

David D.ÿ Koch, PhD, DABCC, FACB, President
Patricia M. Jones, PhD, President-Elect
David G. Grenache, Secretary

Michael J. Bennett, Treasurer
Stevenÿ Wong, PhD, DABCC, FACB, Past President

An international scientific/ medical society of clinical laboratory professionals, physicians, research scientists and other individuals involved with clinical chemistry and related disciplines. Vision is to provide leadership in advancing the practice and profession of clinical laboratory science and its application to health care.
10M Members
Founded in 1948

12686 American Association for Continuity of Care

342 N. Main Street
West Hartford, CT 06117-2500

860-586-7525
E-Mail: info@continuityofcare.org
Home Page: www.continuityofcare.org
Social Media: *Facebook, LinkedIn, RSS*

A national nonprofit multidisciplinary professional organization dedicated to providing leadership and supporting excellence in practice among those involved in continuity of care within the health care system through education and patient focused advocacy.
Founded in 1982

12687 American Association for Geriatric Psychiatry

6728 Old McLean Village Drive
McLean, VA 22101

703-556-9222
FAX 703-556-8729
E-Mail: main@aagponline.org
Home Page: www.aagponline.org
Social Media: *Facebook, Twitter, LinkedIn*

Gary W. Small, MD, President
Dan Sewell, MD, President Elect
Susan K. Schultz, MD, Past President
Amita Patel, Secretary/Treasurer
Christopher N. Wood, Executive Director

National association that has products, activities, and publications which focus exclusively on the challenges of geriatric psychiatry.
Founded in 1978

12688 American Association for Hand Surgery

500 Cummings Center
Suite 4550
Beverly, MA 1915

978-927-8330
FAX 978-524-8890
Home Page: www.handsurgery.org
Social Media: *LinkedIn*

Michael W Neumeister, M.D., President
William Cÿ Pederson, M.D., Vice President
John D. Lubahn, M.D., Treasurer
Robert Spinner, M.D., Secretary
Peter M. Murray, M.D., President Elect

Resource for hand surgeons and patients.

12689 American Association for Laboratory Animal Science

9190 Crestwyn Hills Drive
Memphis, TN 38125-8538

901-754-8620
FAX 901-753-0046
E-Mail: info@aalas.org
Home Page: www.aalas.org
Social Media: *Facebook, Twitter, LinkedIn, YouTube*

Scott Mischler, Past President

An association of professionals that advances responsible laboratory animal care and use to benefit people and animals. Dedicated to the humane care and treatment of laboratory animals and the quality research that leads to scientific gains that benefit people and animals.
11M+ Members
Founded in 1950

12690 American Association for Marriage and Family Therapy

112 South Alfred Street
Alexandria, VA 22314-3061

703-838-9808
FAX 703-838-9805
E-Mail: central@aamft.org
Home Page: www.aamft.org
Social Media: *Facebook, Twitter, LinkedIn, Youtube*

Marvareneÿ Oliver, EdD, President
Christopher Habben, PhD, President-Elect
Michaelÿ Chafin, MEd, Past President
Thomas Smith, PhD, Secretary
Mike Fitzpatrick, MSW, Treasurer

The professional association for the field of marriage and family therapy. Representing the professional interests of marriage and family therapists throughout the US, Canada, and abroad. The Association facilitates research, theory development and education.
25M Members
Founded in 1942

12691 American Association for Pediatric Ophthalmology and Strabismus

655 Beach Street
San Francisco, CA 94109-1336

415-561-8505
FAX 415-561-8531
E-Mail: aapos@aao.org
Home Page: www.aapos.org
Social Media: *Facebook, Twitter, Google+*

M. Edwardÿ Wilson, MD, President
Robert E.ÿ Wiggins, Jr, MD, Vice President
Derek T.ÿ Sprunger, MD, Vice President Elect
Sherwin J.ÿ Isenberg, MD, Past President
Christie L. Morse MD, Executive Vice President

An academic association of pediatric ophthalmologists and strabismus surgeons.

12692 American Association for Respiratory Care

9425 N MacArthur Blvd
Suite 100
Irving, TX 75063-4706

972-243-2272
FAX 972-484-2720
E-Mail: info@aarc.org
Home Page: www.aarc.org

Tom Kallstrom, Executive Director/CEO
Doug Laher, Associate Executive Director
Sherry Milligan, Associate Executive Director
Tim Myers, Associate Executive Director
Steve Nelson, Associate Executive Director

Leading the respiratory care profession in science, education and research. Its members are committed to providing exemplary respiratory care and improving lung health worldwide.
38M Members
Founded in 1947

12693 American Association for Thoracic Surgery

500 Cummings Center
Suite 4550
Beverly, MA 01915

978-927-8330
FAX 978-524-0498
E-Mail: aats@prri.com
Home Page: www.aats.org
Social Media: *Facebook, Youtube*

Joseph S. Coselli, President
Thoralf M. Sundt, III, President-Elect

Marc R. Moon, Secretary
Shaf Keshavjee, Treasurer
Duke E. Cameron, Vice President

The promotion and fostering of education and research in the field of cardiothoracic surgery, membership consists of the world's foremost cardiothoracic surgeons representing 35 countries. Surgeons must have a proven record of distinction within the cardiothoracic surgical field and have made meritorious contributions to the extant knowledge base about cardiothoracic disease and its surgical treatment to be considered for membership.
1231 Members
Founded in 1917

12694 American Association for the Advancement of Science

1200 New York Ave NW
Washington, DC

202-326-6400
Home Page: www.aaas.org
Social Media: *Facebook, Twitter, Google+, YouTube*

Gerald Fink, Chair
Geraldine Richmond, President
Barbara A.ÿ Schaal, President-Elect
David Evans Shaw, Treasurer
Rush D. Holt, Chief Executive Officer

A nonprofit organization that has research news, issue papers, educational programs, etc.
Founded in 1848

12695 American Association for the Study of Liver Disease

1001 North Fairfax Street
Suite 400
Alexandria, VA 22314

703-299-9766
FAX 703-299-9622
E-Mail: aasld@aasld.org
Home Page: www.aasld.org
Social Media: *Facebook, Twitter, LinkedIn, Instagram, YouTube*

Gyongyi Szabo, MD, PhD, FAASLD, President
Keith D. Lindor, MD, FAASLD, President Elect
Adrian M. Di Bisceglie, Past President
W. Ray Kim, Treasurer
Gary L. Davis, MD, FAASLD, Secretary

Organization of scientists and health care professionals committed to preventing and curing liver disease.
Founded in 1950

12696 American Association of Bioanalysts

906 Olive Street
Suite 1200
Saint Louis, MO 63101-1448

314-241-1445
FAX 314-241-1449
E-Mail: aab@aab.org
Home Page: www.aab.org

Mark S Birenbaum PhD, Administrator

Professional Association representing clinical laboratory directors, owners, managers and supervisors, medical technologistsm medical laboratory technicians,and physical office laboratory technicians. AAB provides a broad range of services, including representation before federal and state legislative and regulatory agencies, educational programs, and publications.
Founded in 1956

12697 American Association of Blood Banks

8101 Glenbrook Road
Bethesda, MD 20814-2749

301-907-6977
FAX 301-907-6895
E-Mail: aabb@aabb.org

Home Page: www.aabb.org
Social Media: *Facebook, Twitter, LinkedIn, YouTube*

Lynne Uhl, MD, President
Graham Sher, MD, PhD, Past Presidentÿ
Zbigniew M. Szczepiorkowski, Vice President
Donald Berglund, MHA, FACHE, Treasurer
Lynne Uhl, MDÿ, President-Elect

Advances the practice and standards of transfusion medicine and cellular therapies to optimize patient and donor care and safety. AABB vision is to be the pre-eminent knowledge-based organization focused on improving health through advancing the science and practice of transfusion medicine and cellular therapies.
Founded in 1947

12698 American Association of Cardiovascular & Pulmonary Rehabilitation

330 N. WabashÿAvenue
Suite 2000
Chicago, IL 60611

312-321-5146
FAX 312-673-6924
E-Mail: aacvpr@aacvpr.org
Home Page: www.aacvpr.org
Social Media: *Facebook*

Adam T. deJong, President
Thomas A. Draper, MBA, FAACVPR, President Elect
Todd Brown, MD, MSPH, Secretary
Zack Klint, MS, CES, Treasurer
Megan Cohen, Executive Director

Mission is to reduce morbidity, mortality, and disability from cardiovascular and pulmonary diseases through education, prevention, rehabilitation, research, and disease management.
Founded in 1985

12699 American Association of Clinical Endocrinologists

245 Riverside Avenue
Suite 200
Jacksonville, FL 32202-4933

904-353-7878
FAX 904-353-8185
E-Mail: info@aace.com
Home Page: www.aace.com
Social Media: *Facebook, Twitter, LinkedIn*

George Grunberger, President
Donald C Jones, Chief Executive Officer
Dan Kelsey, MS,MBA,CAE, Deputy CEO
Michael Avallone, CPA, Chief Financial Officer
Pauline M. Camacho, MD, FACE, President-Elect

Professional medical organization devoted to the enhancement of the practice of clinical endocrinology. Maintains high standards in a society of qualified medical, pediatric, reproductive and surgical endocrinologists to futher the practice through advocacy and education.
6200 Members
Founded in 1991

12700 American Association of Colleges of Nursing

One Dupont Circle, NW
Suite 530
Washington, DC 20036

202-463-6930
FAX 202-785-8320
E-Mail: info@aacn.nche.edu
Home Page: www.aacn.nche.edu
Social Media: *Facebook, Twitter, LinkedIn*

Eileen Breslin, PhD, RN, FAAN, President
Juliann Sebastian, President-Elect
Teri Murray, PhD, RN, FAAN, Treasurer

Judy Beal, DNSc, RN, FAAN, Secretary
Jennifer Ahearn, COO

Education, research, federal advocacy, data collection, publications, and special programs for nursing education.
765 Members
Founded in 1969

12701 American Association of Critical-Care Nurses

101 Columbia
Aliso Viejo, CA 92656-4109

949-362-2000
800-899-2226
FAX 949-362-2020
E-Mail: info@aacn.org
Home Page: www.aacn.org
Social Media: *Facebook, Twitter, RSS*

Karen McQuillan, President
Clareen Wiencek, President-Elect
Deborah Klein, Secretary
Paula S. McCauley, Treasurer
Teri Lynn Kiss, Immediate Past President

The largest specialty nursing organization in the world, representing the interests of nurses who are charged with the responsibility of caring for acutely and critically ill patients. The Association is dedicated to providing members with the knowledge and resources necessary to provide optimal care to critically ill patients.
Founded in 1969

12702 American Association of Diabetes Educators

200 W Madison Street
Suite 800
Chicago, IL 60606

800-338-3633
E-Mail: info@diabeteseducator.org
Home Page: www.diabeteseducator.org
Social Media: *Facebook, Twitter, LinkedIn, Google+, Pinterest*

Tami Ross, RD, LD, CDEÿ, President
Charles Macfarlane, FACHE, CAE, Chief Executive Officer
Laura Downes, CAEÿ, Chief Operating Officerÿ
Ruth Lipman, PhDÿ, Chief Science and Practice Officerÿ
Ken Widelka, CAE, CPAÿ, Chief Financial Officerÿ

A multidisciplinary association of healthcare professionals dedicated to integrating self-management as a key outcome in the care of people with diabetes and related chronic conditions.
10M Members
Founded in 1973

12703 American Association of Healthcare Administrative Management

11240 Waples Mill Road
Suite 200
Fairfax, VA 22030-6078

703-281-4043
FAX 703-359-7562
E-Mail: info@aaham.org
Home Page: www.aaham.org
Social Media: *Facebook, Twitter, LinkedIn, YouTube, Google+, Pinterest*

Victoria Di Tomaso, CRCE-I, President
Christine Stottlemyer, CRCE-I, Chair of the Board
John Currier, CRCE-I, National First Vice President
Lori Sickelbaugh, National Second Vice President
Amy Mitchell, CRCE-I, National Treasurer

The premier professional organization in healthcare administrative management. Actively represents the interests of healthcare administrative management professionals through

a comprehensive program of legislative and regulatory monitoring and its participation in industry goups such as ANSI, DISA, and NUBC. AAHAM is a major force in shaping the future of health care administrative management.
Founded in 1968

12704 American Association of Hip and Knee Surgeons

9400 W. Higgins Rd.
Suite 230
Rosemont, IL 60018-4976

847-698-1200
FAX 847-698-0704
Home Page: www.aahks.org
Social Media: *Facebook, Twitter, LinkedIn*

Jay R. Lieberman, MD, President
William A. Jiranek, MD, First Vice President
David A. Halsey, MD, Second Vice President
Mark I. Froimson, MD, Third Vice President
C. Lowryÿ Barnes, MD, Treasurer

Specialty society for orthopedic surgeons who specialize in hip andknee replacements.
Founded in 1991

12705 American Association of Immunologists

9650 Rockville Pike
Bethesda, MD 20814

301-634-7178
FAX 301-634-7887
E-Mail: infoaai@aai.org
Home Page: www.aai.org
Social Media: *Facebook*

Marc K Jenkins, Ph.D., President
Linda A Sherman, Ph.D., Vice President
Mitchell Kronenberg, Ph.D., Secretary-Treasurer
M. Michele Hogan, Ph.D., Executive Director
David G. Jackson, CPA, MBA, Director of Finance

An association of professionally trained scientists from all over the world dedicated to advancing the knowledge of immunology and its related disciplines, fostering the interchange of ideas and information among investigators, and addressing the potential integration of immunologic principles into clinical practice.
Founded in 1913

12706 American Association of Integrated Healthcare Delivery Systems

4435 Waterfront Drive
Suite 101
Glen Allen, VA 23060

804-747-5823
FAX 804-747-5316
Home Page: www.aaihds.org
Social Media: *Facebook, Twitter, LinkedIn, Google+*

A nonprofit organization dedicated to the educational advancement of provider-based managed care professionals involved in integrated healthcare delivery. Mission is to provide managed healthcare professionals in IPAs, PHOs, health systems, hospitals and other integrated delivery systems with the tools, education, skills and resources to be successful in the marketplace.
1000 Members
Founded in 1993

12707 American Association of Managed Care Nurses

4435 Waterfront Drive
Suite 101
Glen Allen, VA 23060-3393

804-747-9698
FAX 804-747-5316
E-Mail: keads@aamcn.org

Home Page: www.aamcn.org
Social Media: *Facebook, Twitter, LinkedIn, Google+*

Jacquelyn Smith, President
Gloria J. Hayman, RN, CMCN, Board of Director
LaNita Knoke RN, BS, CMCN, Board of Director
Veronica Sheffield, CMCN, Board of Director
Joyce Thiem, RN, BSN, CCM, Board of Director

Nonprofit organization representing Registered Nurses, Nurse Practitioners and Licensed Practical Nurses. AAMCN seeks to offer those nurses the opportunity to become more successful, both in their workplace and their community, through interactive membership services, quality educational resources and unparalleled networking with other managed care nurses throughout the industry.
Founded in 1994

12708 American Association of Medical Assistants

20 N Wacker Dr
Suite 1575
Chicago, IL 60606-2963

312-899-1500
800-228-2262
FAX 312-899-1259
Home Page: www.aama-ntl.org
Social Media: *Facebook, YouTube, WordPress*

Ann Naegele, President
Chris Hollander, Vice President
Charlene Couch, Secretary/ Treasurer

Mission is to provide the medical assistant professional with education, certification, credential acknowledgment, networking opportunities, scope-of-practice protection, and advocacy for quality patient-centered health care.
Founded in 1955

12709 American Association of Naturopathic Physicians

818 18th Street, NW
Suite 250
Washington, DC 20006

202-237-8150
866-538-2267
FAX 202-237-8152
E-Mail: member.services@naturopathic.org
Home Page: www.naturopathic.org
Social Media: *Facebook, Twitter, LinkedIn, Google+*

Kasra Pournadeali, ND, President
Jaclyn Chasse, ND, President-Elect
Michelle Simon, ND, PhD, AANP Treasurer
Michael Cronin, ND, Board of Director
Laura Farr, Board of Director

Vision is to transform the healthcare system from a disease management system to a comprehensive health program incorporating the principles of naturopathic medicine.
1800 Members
Founded in 1985

12710 American Association of Neurological Surgeons

5550 Meadowbrook Drive
Rolling Meadows, IL 60008-3852

847-378-0500
888-566-2267
FAX 847-378-0600
E-Mail: info@aans.org
Home Page: www.aans.org
Social Media: *Facebook, Twitter, LinkedIn, Youtube, iTunesU*

H. Hunt Batjer, President
Deborah L. Benzil, Vice President
Frederick A. Boop,ÿMD, FAANS, FACS,

President-Elect
Alex B. Valadka, Treasurer
Christopher I. Shaffrey,ÿMD, FAANS, Secretary

The organization that speaks for all of neurosurgery. The AANS is dedicated to advancing the specialty of neurological surgery in order to promote the highest quality of patient care.
6500+ Members
Founded in 1931

12711 American Association of Neuromuscular and Electrodiagnostic Medicine

2621 Superior Drive NW
Rochester, MN 55901

507-288-0100
FAX 507-288-1225
E-Mail: aanem@aanem.org
Home Page: www.aanem.org
Social Media: *Facebook, Twitter, LinkedIn, YouTube*

Vincent J. Tranchitella, MD, President
Vern C. Juel, MD, President Elect
Francis O. Walker, MD, Past President
Shirlyn A. Adkins, JDÿ, Executive Director
Anthony E.ÿ Chiodo, MD, Secretary-Treasurer

A nonprofit membership association dedicated to the advancement of neuromuscular, musculoskeletal medicine.
Founded in 1953

12712 American Association of Neuromuscular and Electrodiagnostic Medicine

2621 Superior Drive NW
Rochester, MN 55901-8350

507-288-0100
FAX 507-288-1225
E-Mail: aanem@aanem.org
Home Page: www.aanem.org
Social Media: *Facebook, Twitter, LinkedIn, Youtube*

Vincent J. Tranchitella, MD, President
Vern C. Juel, MD, President Elect
Francis O. Walker, MD, Past President
Shirlyn A. Adkins, JDÿ, Executive Director
Anthony E.ÿ Chiodo, MD, Secretary-Treasurer

Dedicated to the advancement of neuromuscular, musculoskeletal, and electrodiagnostic medicine. Physician members- primarily neurologists and physiatrists- now are joined by allied health professionals and PhD Researchers working to improve the quality of medical care provided to patients with muscle and nerve disorders.
5200 Members
Founded in 1953

12713 American Association of Neuroscience Nurses

8735 W. Higgins Road
Suite 300
Chicago, IL 60631

847-375-4733
888-557-2266
FAX 847-375-6430
FAX 732-460-7313ÿ
E-Mail: info@aann.org
Home Page: www.aann.org

Jan Hinkle, RN PhD CNRN, President
Cindy M.ÿ Sullivan, President Elect
Sandra J. Brettler, MSN RN CNRN, Secretary/Treasurer
Megan Keiser, RN DNP CNRN, Immediate Past President
Joan Kram, MBA RN FACHE, Executive Director

The leading authority in neuroscience nursing, inspires passion in nurses and creates the future for the specialty. AANN is committed to the

advancement of neuroscience nursing as a specialty through the development and support of nurses to promote excellence in patient care.
3000 Members
Founded in 1968

12714 American Association of Nurse Anesthetists

222 South Prospect Avenue
Park Ridge, IL 60068-4001

847-692-7050
855-526-2262
FAX 847-692-6968
E-Mail: info@aana.com
Home Page: www.aana.com
Social Media: *Facebook, Twitter, LinkedIn, Youtube*

Juan F. Quintana, President
Bruce A.ÿ Weiner, MS, CRNA, Vice President
Kathryn L.ÿ Jansky, CRNA, ARNP, Treasurer
Cheryl L.ÿ Nimmo, CRNA, DNP, President-Elect
Robertÿ Gauvin, CRNA, MS, Director, Region 1

The AANA promulgates education and practice standards and guidelines, and affords consultation to both private and governmental entities regarding nurse anesthetists and their practice.
Founded in 1931

12715 American Association of Occupational Health Nurses

7794 Grow Drive
Pensacola, FL 32514

850-474-6963
800-241-8014
FAX 850-484-8762
E-Mail: AAOHN@aaohn.org
Home Page: www.aaohn.org/
Social Media: *Facebook, Twitter, LinkedIn*

Jeannie Tomlinson, MSN, RN, President
Ronda Weiss, MS, MPH, MBA, Secretary
Mary Gene Ryan, President-Elect
Phyllis Berryman, Director
David Allcott, Director

Dedicated to advancing and maximizing the health, safety and prductivity of domestic and global workforces by providing education, research, public policy and practice resources for occupational and environmental health nurses. Mission is to advance the profession of occupational and environmental health nursing.

12716 American Association of Orthodontists

401 North Lindbergh Boulevard
St. Louis, MO 63141-7816

314-993-1700
800-424-2841
FAX 314-997-1745
E-Mail: info@aaortho.org
Home Page: www.aaoinfo.org/
Social Media: *Facebook, Twitter, LinkedIn*

Jill Nowak, Director Of Finance & Admin
Linda Gladden, Director Of Comm. & Marketing
Sarah Dvorak, Meetings Coordinator
Sherry Nappier, Member Coordinator
Mike Nappier, Shipping And Receiving Coordinator

Official organization for board qualified and board certified orthodontists.
Founded in 1900

12717 American Association of Physician Specialists Inc.

5550 West Executive Drive
Suite 400
Tampa, FL 33609

813-433-2277
FAX 813-830-6599

E-Mail: wcarbone@aapsus.org
Home Page: www.aapsus.com

Martin E. Thornton, D.O., FAAEP, President
Surinder K. Kad, M.D., FAAIM,
Secretary/Treasurer
Craig S. Smith, M.D., President-Elect
Mark DeSantis, D.O., Membership Officer
Kenneth A. Wallace, III, M.D., Vice President

AAPS was founded to fill a professional need among physicians practicing in medical specialities. Distinct from other medical societies, the AAPS accepts qualified physicians into membership who have either an allopathic (MD) or osteopathic (DO) degree.
Founded in 1950

12718 American Association of Poison Control Centers

515 King St.
Suite 510
Alexandria, VA 22314

703-894-1858
800-222-1222
E-Mail: info@aapcc.org
Home Page: www.aapcc.org
Social Media: *Facebook, Twitter, RSS, WordPress*

Jay L. Schauben, PharmD, President
William Banner, MD, PhD, President Elect
Marsha Ford, MD, FACMT, Past President
Stuart Heard, PharmD, FCSHP, Treasurer
Julie Weber, RPh, CSPIÿ, Secretary

National voluntary health organization that supports poison centersto prevent poisonings, provide education, conduct scientific research and treat individuals exposed to poisoning.

12719 American Association of Public Health Physicians

1605 Pebble Beach Blvd.
Green Cove Springs, FL 32043-8077

888-447-7281
FAX 202-333-5016
E-Mail: membership@aaphp.org
Home Page: www.aaphp.org

Ryung Suh, President

The AAPHP speaks on behalf of all public health physicians on major issues affecting public health.
Founded in 1954

12720 American Association of Retired Persons

601 E Street NW
Washington, DC 20049-0003

202-434-3525
888-687-2277
FAX 202-434-7599
E-Mail: member@aarp.org
Home Page: www.aarp.org
Social Media: *Facebook, Twitter, YouTube*

Jo Ann Jenkins, CEO
Lawrence Flanagan, President, AARP Services
Scott Frisch, Chief Operating Officer
Nancy Smith, Corporate Secretary
Martha M. Boudreau, Chief Comm. & Marketing Officer

A nonprofit, nonpartisan membership organization for people age 50 and over. AARP is dedicated to enhancing quality of life for all.
21 Members
Founded in 1958

12721 American Association of Sexuality Educators, Counselors & Therapists

1444 I Street NW
Suite 700
Washington, DC 20005

202-449-1099
FAX 202-216-9646

E-Mail: info@aasect.org
Home Page: www.aasect.org

Konnie McCaffree, President
Debby Herbenick, President Elect
Douglas Braun-Harvey, LMFT, Treasurer
Chris F. Fariello, PhD, MA, Secretary
Michael Chan, Executive Director

A not-for-profit, interdisciplinary professional organization that is devoted to the promotion of sexual health by the development and advancement of the fields of sexual therapy, counseling and education.
Founded in 1967

12722 American Association of Suicidology

5221 Wisconsin Avenue, NW
Washington, DC 20015

202-237-2280
800-273-TALK
FAX 202-237-2282
Home Page: www.suicidology.org
Social Media: *Facebook, Twitter, YouTube*

David Miller, PhD, President
Julie Cerel, PhDÿ, President Elect
Amy Boland, CPAÿ, Treasurer
Marnin J. Heisel, Secretary
Michelle Cornette, PhDÿ, Executive Director

A membership organization for those involved in suicide prevention and intervention, or touched by suicide.

12723 American Association on Intellectual and Developmental Disabilities

501 3rd Street, NW
Suite 200
Washington, DC 20001

202-387-1968
FAX 202-387-2193
Home Page: www.aaidd.org/
Social Media: *Facebook, Twitter, LinkedIn, YouTube*

Susan B. Palmer, PhD, President
William Gaventa, MDiv, President Elect
Susan Havercamp, PhD, VP
Patti N. Martin, MEd, Secretary-Treasurer
Amy S. Hewitt, PhD, Immediate Past President

An American nonprofit professional organization concerned with intellectual disability and related developmental disabilities.
Founded in 1876

12724 American Autoimmune Related Diseases Association

22100 Gratiot Ave.
Eastpointe, MI 48021

586-776-3900
FAX 586-776-3903
Home Page: www.aarda.org
Social Media: *Facebook, Twitter, YouTube, RSS*

Betty Diamond, M.D., Chairperson
Noel R. Rose, M.D., Ph.D., Chairman Emeritus
Edward K. Christian, Advisor
Stephanie P. Halesÿ, Advisor
Virginia T. Ladd, President and Executive Director

Includes patient information about autoimmunity and autoimmune related diseases.

12725 American Behcet's Disease Association

PO Box 80576
Rochester, MN 48308

631-656-0537
800-723-4238
FAX 480-247-5377

E-Mail: info@behcets.com
Home Page: www.behcets.com

Deb Kleber, President
Mary Burke, VP
Belinda Rivasÿ, Treasurer
Marcia Wiseÿ, Executive Secretary
Mirta Avila Santos, MD, Executive Dir. & Comm Coordinator

Provides information and support for patients with Behcet's Diseaseand for their family members and caretakers.

12726 American Brain Tumor Association

8550 W. Bryn Mawr Ave.
Suite 550
Chicago, IL 60631

773-577-8750
800-886-2282
FAX 773-577-8738
E-Mail: info@abta.org
Home Page: www.abta.org
Social Media: *Facebook, Twitter, YouTube*

Jeff Fougerousse, Chair
Brian Olson, Vice Chair
Carla Varner, Treasurer
James Reilly, Secretary
Elizabeth M. Wilson, MNA, President and CEO

National nonprofit organization dedicated to providing support services and programs to brain tumor patients and their families, as well as the funding of brain tumor research.
Founded in 1973

12727 American Burn Association

311 S. Wacker Drive
Suite 4150
Chicago, IL 60606

312-642-9260
FAX 312-642-9130
Home Page: www.ameriburn.org
Social Media: *Facebook, Twitter*

Edward E. Tredget, MD, MSc, President
Michael D. Peck, MD, ScD, FACS, President Elect
Linwood R. Haith, MD, FACS, First Vice President
Ernest J. Grant, RN, BSN, MSNÿ, Second Vice President
William L. Hickerson, MD, FACS, Treasurer

Involved in research in the methods of treating burn injuries and fostering prevention efforts.
3500+ Members

12728 American Chronic Pain Association

PO Box 850
Rocklin, CA 95677

800-533-3231
FAX 916-632-3208
E-Mail: ACPA@theacpa.org
Home Page: theacpa.org
Social Media: *Facebook, Twitter, YouTube, Pinterest*

Penney Cowan, Founderÿ& CEO
Mary Jane Bentÿ, Board of Director
Chris Duncan, Board of Director
Daniel Galia, Board of Director
Steve Feinberg, MD, Board of Director

Information is provided concerning services, conditions, and pain management issues.
Founded in 1980

12729 American College Health Association

1362 Mellon Road
Suite 180
Hanover, MD 21076

410-859-1500
FAX 410-859-1510
E-Mail: contact@acha.org

Home Page: www.acha.org
Social Media: *Facebook, Twitter, YouTube*

Jake Baggott, MLS, 1SG, President
Jamie Davidson, PhD, President Elect
Stephanieÿ Hanenberg, RN, MSN, Vice President
Beverly Kloeppel, MD, MBA, Treasurer
Sarah Van Orman, MD, MMM, FA, Immediate Past President

The American College Health Association (ACHA) is the principal advocate and leadership organization for college and university health. The association provides advocacy, education, communications, products, and services, as well as promoting research and culturally competent practices to enhance its members' ability to advance the health of all students and the campus community.
2600 Members
Founded in 1920

12730 American College of Allergy, Asthma and Immunology

85 West Algonquin Road
Suite 550
Arlington Heights, IL 60005-4460

847-427-1200
FAX 847-427-1294
E-Mail: mail@acaai.org
Home Page: www.acaai.org
Social Media: *Facebook, Twitter, LinkedIn, YouTube, Pinterest*

Michael B Foggs, MD, President
Bryan L Martin, MD*, Vice President
Bradley E Chipps, MD, FACAAI*, Treasurer
James L Sublett, MD, FACAAI*, President-Elect
Bob Q Lanier, MD, Executive Medical Director

Information and news service for patients, parents of patients, members, the news media, and purchasers of health care programs.
5200 Members
Founded in 1942

12731 American College of Cardiology

Heart House
2400 N Street NW
Washington, DC 20037-1153

202-375-6000
800-253-4636
FAX 202-375-7000
E-Mail: resource@acc.org
Home Page: www.acc.org
Social Media: *Facebook, Twitter, LinkedIn, YouTube*

Robert A.ÿ Shor, MD, FACC, Chair
Matthewÿ Phillips, MD, FACC, Chair-Elect
Michael Mansour, MD, FACC, Immediate Past Chairÿ
Kim Allan Williams, President
Richard A.ÿ Chazal, MD, FACC, President-Elect

The mission is to advocate for quality cardiovascular care-through education, research promotion, development and application of standards and guidelines-and to influence health care policy.
39M Members
Founded in 1949

12732 American College of Cardiovascular Administrators (ACCA)

American Academy of Medical Administrators
701 Lee Street
Suite 600
Des Plaines, IL 60016-4516

847-759-8601
FAX 312-673-6705
E-Mail: info@aameda.org
Home Page:

www.aameda.org/Colleges/ACCA/cardiology.html

Renee L. Mazeroll, President
Kathy A. Miller, President-Elect

Mission is to advance ACCA members and the field of cardiovascular management and promote excellence and integrity in cardiovascular leadership.

12733 American College of Emergency Physicians

1125 Executive Circle
Irving, TX 75038-2522

972-550-0911
800-798-1822
FAX 972-580-2816
E-Mail: membership@acep.org
Home Page: www.acep.org
Social Media: *Facebook*

Rebecca B. Parker, MD, FACEP, Chair
Michael J. Gerardi, President
Paul D. Kivela, MD, FACEP, VP
Jay A. Kaplan, MD, FACEP, President-Elect
John J. Rogers, MD, FACEP, Secretary-Treasurer

Promoting the highest quality emergency care, ACEP is the leading advocate for emergency physicians and their patients.
28M Members
Founded in 1968

12734 American College of Healthcare Executives

One North Franklin Street
Suite 1700
Chicago, IL 60606-3529

312-424-2800
FAX 312-424-0023
E-Mail: contact@ache.org
Home Page: www.ache.org
Social Media: *Facebook, Twitter, LinkedIn, Youtube*

Richard D.ÿ Cordova, FACHE, Chairman
Edward H. Lamb, FACHE, Chairman-Elect
Deborah J.ÿ Bowen, FACHE, President and CEO
Christine M. Candio, RN, FACHE, Immediate Past Chairman
James W. Connolly, FACHE, Governor

An international professional society of healthcare executives who lead hospitals, healthcare systems and other healthcare organizations.
40M Members
Founded in 1933

12735 American College of Healthcare Information Administrators (ACHIA)

701 Lee Street
Suite 600
Des Plaines, IL 60016-4516

847-759-8601
FAX 847-759-8602
E-Mail: info@aameda.org
Home Page:
www.aameda.org/Colleges/ACHIA/healthcareinformation.html

Charles D. Chapdelaine, President

Develops innovative concepts in the field of healthcare information and promotes the advancement of its members in knowledge, professional standing, and personal achievements through continuing education and research in healthcare information administration. ACHIA focuses on providing education, support and opportunity for information technology leaders in the healthcare industry.
300 Members
Founded in 1991

12736 American College of Medical Practice

104 Inverness Terrace East
Englewood, CO 80112-5306

303-799-1111
877-275-6462
E-Mail: support@mgma.org
Home Page: www.mgma.com
Social Media: *Facebook, Twitter, LinkedIn, Google+*

Stephen A. Dickens, JD, FACMPE, F, Board Chair
Debra J. Wiggs, FACMPE, Vice Chair
Susan L. Turney, MD, MS, FACP,, President and CEO
Ronald W. Holder, Jr., MHA, FACM, Finance/Audit Chair

Delivering networking, professional education and resources and political advocacy for medical practice management.
3000 Members
Founded in 1926

12737 American College of Medical Quality

5272 River Road
Suite 630
Bethesda, MD 20816

301-718-6516
FAX 301-656-0989
Home Page: www.acmq.org
Social Media: *Facebook, Twitter, LinkedIn*

Prathibha Varkey, President
Mark Lyles, MD, MBA, FACMQ, President Elect
Donald E. Casey, Jr MD, MPH, Vice President
John Vigorita, Secretary
Henry C. L. Johnson, Jr., MD, MPH, Treasurer

The mission of the American College of Medical Quality is to provide leadership and education in healthcare quality management.
Founded in 1973

12738 American College of Oncology Administrators

701 Lee Street
Suite 600
Des Plaines, IL 60016-4516

847-759-8601
FAX 847-759-8602
E-Mail: info@aameda.org
Home Page:
www.aameda.org/Colleges/ACOA/oncology.html

Margaret A. O'Grady, President
Bonnie J. Miller, President-Elect

Focuses on providing support and opportunity for oncology administrators and managers in all types of healthcare institutions.
300 Members
Founded in 1991

12739 American College of Oral and Maxillofacial Surgeons

2025 M Street NW
Suite 800
Washington, DC 20036

202-367-1182
800-522-6676
FAX 202-367-2182
E-Mail: admin@acoms.org
Home Page: www.acoms.org
Social Media: *Facebook, Twitter, LinkedIn, RSS*

Bernard Dreiman, President
Leonard Spector, President-Elect
Charles Hasse, Vice President
Cyntia Battel, Treasurer
Steven C. Kemp, CAE, Executive Director

The diplomates have joined together in the College for the purpose of enhancing the level of patient care. This enhancement of surgical care

through the furthering of research and education in OMS surgery is achieved by the College's sponsoring of educational programs, research activities, and fellowships as a service to not only the members of the College, but to the profession at large.
2M+ Members
Founded in 1975

12740 American College of Osteopathic Family Physicians

330 E. Algonquin Road
Suite 1
Arlington Heights, IL 60005-4665

800-323-0794
FAX 847-228-9755
E-Mail: membership@acofp.org
Home Page: www.acofp.org
Social Media: *Facebook, Twitter, LinkedIn, Youtube*

Kevin D. de Regnier, DO, FACOFP, President
Peter L Schmelzer, CAE, Executive Director
Rodney M. Wiseman, DO, FACOFPÿ, Vice President
Duane G. Koehler, DO, FACOFP, Secretary/Treasurer
Annie DeVries, Sr. Administrative Assistant

Works to promote excellence in osteopathic family medicine through quality education, visionary leadership and responsible advocacy.
20M Members
Founded in 1950

12741 American College of Osteopathic Surgeons

123 North Henry Street
Alexandria, VA 22314-2903

703-684-0416
800-888-1312
FAX 703-684-3280
E-Mail: info@facos.org
Home Page: www.facos.org
Social Media: *Facebook, Twitter, LinkedIn, YouTube*

Linda Ayers, MHCM, CAE, CEO
Don Kaveny, Director of Postdoctoral Trainingÿ
Sonjya Johnson, Director of Membership Recruitment
Brandon Roberts, Director of Finance
Allison Hamrick, Manager, Marketing & Communication

Committed to assuring excellence in osteopathic surgical care through education, advocacy, leadership, development and the fostering of professional and personal relationship.
2147 Members
Founded in 1927

12742 American College of Physician Executives

400 North Ashley Drive
Suite 400
Tampa, FL 33602

813-287-2000
800-562-8088
FAX 813-287-8993
E-Mail: acpe@acpe.org
Home Page: www.acpe.org
Social Media: *Facebook, Twitter, LinkedIn, YouTube*

Peter B. Angood, CEO

The nation's largest health care organization for physician executives who want to boost their leadership skills while adding weight to their CVs. The primary focus of the College is to provide superior leadership and management skills to physicians and encouraging them to

assume more active roles in the leadership and management of their organizations.
10M Members
Founded in 1975

12743 American College of Physicians

190 North Independence Mall West
Philadelphia, PA 19106-1572

215-351-2400
800-523-1546
FAX 215-351-2759
E-Mail: archives@acponline.org
Home Page: www.acponline.org
Social Media: *Facebook, Twitter, LinkedIn, RSS*

Tanveer P.ÿ Mir, MD, MACP, Chair, Board of Regents
Wayne J. Riley, President
Steven E. Weinberger, EVP/CEO
Robert A Gluckman, MD, FACP, Treasurer
David A. Fleming, MD, MA, FACP, Immediate Past President

Mission is to enhance the quality and effectiveness of health care by fostering excellence and professionalism in the practice of medicine.
Founded in 1915

12744 American College of Rheumatology

2200 Lake Boulevard NE
Atlanta, GA 30319

404-633-3777
FAX 404-633-1870
E-Mail: acr@rheumatology.org
Home Page: www.rheumatology.org/
Social Media: *Facebook, Twitter, LinkedIn, YouTube*

E. William St.Clair, MD, President
Joan Von Feldt, MD, MSEd, President Elect
Mark Andrejeski, Executive Director
Steve Echard, CAE, IOM,, Foundation Executive Director
David I. Daikh, MD, PhD, Foundation Secretary

Mission is advancing rheumatology. The organization is for physicians, health professionals, and scientists that meets the mission through programs of education, research, advocacy and practice support.
Founded in 1934

12745 American College of Sports Medicine

401 West Michigan Street
Indianapolis, IN 46202-3233

317-637-9200
FAX 317-634-7817
Home Page: www.acsm.org
Social Media: *Facebook, Twitter, YouTube, Pinterest, Instagram*

Lawrence E. Armstrong, President
NiCole Keith, Ph.D., FACSM, First Vice President
Walter Thompson, Ph.D., FACSM, First Vice President
Craig Harms, Ph.D., FACSM, Second Vice Presidentÿ
Kathryn Schmitz, Ph.D., FACSM, Second Vice Presidentÿ

From academicians to students and from personal trainers to physicians, the association of sports medicine, exercise science, and health and fitness professionals is dedicated to helping people worldwide live longer, healthier lives.
50,00 Members
Founded in 1954

12746 American College of Surgeons

633 N Saint Clair Street
Chicago, IL 60611-3211

312-202-5000
800-621-4111

FAX 312-202-5001
E-Mail: postmaster@facs.org
Home Page: www.facs.org
Social Media: *Facebook, Twitter, LinkedIn, Youtube*

Fabrizio Michelassi, MD, FACS, Chair, Board of Governors
Diana Farmer, MD, FACS, Vice-Chair, Board of Governors
Steven Stain, MD, FACS, Secretary, Board of Governors
David B. Hoyt, MD, FACS, Executive Director
Felix Niespodziewanski, Convention and Meetings Director

Dedicated to improving the care of the surgical patient and to safeguarding standards of care in an optimal and ethical practice environment.
Founded in 1913

12747 American Congress of Obstetricians and Gynecologists

409 12th Street SW
PO Box 70620
Washington, DC 20024-2188

202-638-5577
800-673-8444
E-Mail: sales@acog.org
Home Page: www.acog.org
Social Media: *Facebook, Twitter, Youtube, RSS*

Mark S. DeFrancesco, MD, MBA, President
Dr. Hal C Lawrence IIIÿ, EVP, CEO
Richard C Bailey, CPA, MBA, CFO, VP - Finance
Thomas M. Gellhaus, MD, President Elect
Dr Sandra Ann Carson, MD, Vice President, Education

Serving as a strong advocate for quality health care for women, maintaining the highest standards of clinical practice and continuing education for its members, promoting patient education and stimulating patient understanding of and involvement in medical care, and increasing awareness among its members and the public of the changing issues facing women's health care.
45M Members
Founded in 1951

12748 American Congress of Rehabilitation Medicine

11654 Plaza America Drive
Suite 535
Reston, VA 20190-4700

703-435-5335
FAX 866-692-1619
E-Mail: info@ACRM.org
Home Page: www.acrm.org
Social Media: *Facebook, Twitter, LinkedIn, Google+*

Sue Ann Sisto, PT, MA, PhD, President
Jon W Lindberg, MBA, CAE, Chief Executive Officer
Douglas Katz, MD, FACRM, FAAN, Vice President
Wayne A. Gordon, PhD ABPP-CN, Treasurer
Cindy Harrison-Felix, Secretary

An organization of rehabilitation professionals dedicated to serving people with disabling conditions by supporting research that; promotes health, independence, productivity, and quality of life, and meets the needs of rehabilitatio clinicians and people with disabilities.
Founded in 1923

12749 American Council of Academic Plastic Surgeons

500 Cummings Center
Suite 4550
Beverly, MA 01915

978-927-8330
FAX 978-524-0498
Home Page: www.acaplasticsurgeons.org/

W. John Kitzmiller, M.D., President
C. Scottÿ Hultman, M.D., President-Elect
Michael L. Bentz, M.D., VP Finance and Communication
Donald R.ÿ Mackay, MD, FACS, VP Academic Administration
Anthony Aÿ Smith, M.D., Vice President of Education

Goal is to provide leadership and support for educational programs for plastic surgery residents.

12750 American Counseling Association (ACA)

6101 Stevenson Ave
Suite 600
Alexandria, VA 22304-3302

703-823-9800
800-347-6647
FAX 703-823-0252
E-Mail: membership@counseling.org
Home Page: www.counseling.org
Social Media: *Facebook, Twitter, LinkedIn*

Thelma Duffey, Ph.D., President
Catherine Roland, President-Elect
Elias Zambrano, Treasurer
Richard Yep, CEO
Robert L. Smith, Past President

Dedicated to the growth and development of the counseling profession and those who are served.
45M Members
Founded in 1952

12751 American Dance Therapy Association

10632 Little Patuxent Parkway
Suite 108
Columbia, MD 21044

410-997-4040
FAX 410-997-4048
Home Page: www.adta.org
Social Media: *Facebook, LinkedIn, YouTube, Pinterest*

Jody Wager, MS, BC-DMT, President
Margaret Migliorati, R-DMT, VP
Meghan Dempsey, MS, BC-DMT, Treasurer
Gail Wood,ÿMA, BC-DMT, NCC, Secretary
Susan D. Imus, Board of Director

Establishes and maintains standards of professional education in the field of dance/movement therapy.
Founded in 1966

12752 American Dental Association

211 East Chicago Avenue
Chicago, IL 60611-2678

312-440-2500
FAX 312-440-2800
E-Mail: affiliates@ada.org
Home Page: www.ada.org
Social Media: *Facebook, Twitter, LinkedIn, YouTube*

Dr. Maxine Feinberg, President
Dr. Carol Gomez Summerhays, President Elect
Dr. Kathleen T. T. O'Loughlin, Executive Director

The oldest and largest national dental society in the world. Becoming the leading source of oral health related information for dentists and their patients. The professional association of dentists that fosters the success of a diverse mem-

bership and advances the oral health of the public.
156M Members
Founded in 1859

12753 American Dental Education Association

655 K Street, NW
Suite 800
Washington, DC 20001ÿ

202-289-7201
FAX 202-289-7204
E-Mail: membership@adea.org
Home Page: www.adea.org
Social Media: *Facebook, Twitter, YouTube*

Huw F. Thomas, Chair of the Board
Cecile A. Feldman, Chair-elect of the Board
Lily T Garcia, Immediate Past Chair of the Boardÿ
David M. Shafer, D.M.D.ÿ, Board Director for Hospitals
Richard W. Valachovic, President and CEO

The voice of dental education. Members include all US and Canadian dental schools and many allied and postdoctoral dental education programs, corporations, faculty, and students. Mission is to lead individuals and institutions of the dental education community to address contemporary issures influencing education, research, and the delivery of oral health care for the health of the public.
21,00 Members
Founded in 1983

12754 American Dental Hygenists Association

444 North Michigan Avenue
Suite 3400
Chicago, IL 60611-3980

312-440-8900
FAX 312-440-8929
E-Mail: member.services@adha.net
Home Page: www.adha.org
Social Media: *Facebook, Twitter, LinkedIn, YouTube, Instagram*

Jill Rethman, RDH, BA, President
Betty Kabel, RDH, BS, President Elect
Tammy Filipiak, RDH, MS, VP
Donnellaÿ Miller, RDH, BS, MPS, Treasurer
Kelli Swanson Jaecks, Immediate Past President

Mission is to advance the art and science of dental hygiene, and to promote the highest standards of education and practice in the profession.
Founded in 1993

12755 American Dental Society of Anesthesiology

211 E Chicago Ave
Suite 780
Chicago, IL 60611-6983

312-664-8270
877-255-3742
FAX 312-224-8624
E-Mail: adsahome@mac.com
Home Page: www.adsahome.org
Social Media: *Facebook, Twitter, Vimeo, Instagram*

Kenneth L. Reed, DMD, President
Edward C. Adlesic, DMD, Board of Director
Michael Rollert, DDSÿ, President-Elect
Morton B. Rosenberg, DMD, Treasurer
Daniel S. Sarasin, DDS, VP

Mission is to provide a forum for education, research, and recognition of achievement in order to promote safe and effective patient care for all dentists who have an interest in anesthesiol-

ogy, sedation and the control of anxiety and pain.
5000 Members
Founded in 1953

12756 American Diabetes Association

1701 North Beauregard Street
Alexandria, VA 22311-1742

703-549-1500
800-342-2383
FAX 703-739-0290
E-Mail: meetings@diabetes.org
Home Page: www.diabetes.org
Social Media: *Facebook, Twitter, Vimeo, Instagram*

Janel Wright, MD, Chair
Robin J. Richardson, Chair Elect
David G. Marrero, PhD, President, Health Care & Education
Samuel Dagogo-Jack, MD, President, Medicine & Science
Richard Farber, MBA, Secretary/Treasurer

Leading the fight against the deadly consequences of diabetes and fight for those affected. Funding research to prevent, cure and manage diabetes. Delivering services to hundreds of communitites. Providing objective and credible information. Giving a voice to those denied their rights because of diabetes.
Founded in 1940

12757 American Gastroenterological Association

4930 Del Ray Avenue
Bethesda, MD 20814

301-654-2055
FAX 301-654-5920
E-Mail: member@gastro.org
Home Page: www.gastro.org
Social Media: *Facebook, Twitter, LinkedIn, YouTube*

Michael Camilleri, MD, AGAF, President
Sheila E. Crowe, MD, AGAF, Vice President
Francis M. Giardiello, MD, AGAF, Secretary/Treasurer
Timothy C.ÿ Wang, MD, AGAF, President-Elect
Martin Brotman, MD, AGAF, Foundation Chair

Advancing the science and practice of gastroenterology.
16000 Members
Founded in 1897

12758 American Head and Neck Society

11300 W Olympic Boulevard
Suite 600
Los Angeles, CA 90064

310-437-0559
FAX 310-437-0585
E-Mail: admin@ahns.info
Home Page: www.headandneckcancer.org
Social Media: *Facebook, Twitter, YouTube*

Dennis Kraus, MD, President
Jonathan Irish, MD, Vice President
Brian B Burkey, MD MEd, Secretary
Ehab Hanna, MD, Treasurer
Jeffery Myers, MD, President-Elect

The single largest organization in North American for the advancement of research and education in head and neck oncology.
Founded in 1998

12759 American Headache Society

19 Mantua Road
Mount Royal, NJ 08061

856-423-0043
FAX 856-423-0082
E-Mail: achehq@talley.com
Home Page:

www.americanheadachesociety.org
Social Media: *Facebook, Twitter*

Paul Winner, DO, Chair

Professional society of health care providers dedicated to the study and treatment of headache and face pain. Members collaborate in producing educational programs and materials, coordinating the support groups, and undertaking public awareness initiatives all aimed at improving care for headache sufferers.
1500 Members
Founded in 1990

12760 American Health Care Association

1201 L Street, N.W.
Washington, DC 20005-4046

202-842-4444
FAX 202-842-3860
E-Mail: webmaster@ahca.org
Home Page: www.ahcancal.org
Social Media: *Facebook, Twitter, YouTube, Flickr, Blogspot*

Represents the long term care community to the nation at large- to government, business leaders, and the general public. Serves as a force for change, providing information, education, and administrative tools that enhance quality at every level.
12M Members
Founded in 1949

12761 American Health Information Management Association

233 N. Michigan Avenue
21st Floor
Chicago, IL 60601-5809

312-233-1100
800-335-5535
FAX 312-233-1090
Home Page: www.ahima.org
Social Media: *Facebook, Twitter, LinkedIn, RSS, YouTube*

Cassi Birnbaum, President/Chair
Melissa M. Martin, President/Chair-elect
Laura Pait, RHIA, CDIP, CCS, Speaker of The HoD
Lynne Thomas Gordon, CEO
Susan W.ÿ Carey, RHIT, PMP, Treasurer

Professional organization for the field of effective management of health data and medical record needed to deliver quality healthcare to the public management.
71,00 Members
Founded in 1928

12762 American Health Information Management Association

233 N. Michigan Avenue
21st Floor
Chicago, IL 60601-5809

312-233-1100
800-335-5535
FAX 312-233-1090
E-Mail: info@ahima.org
Home Page: www.ahima.org
Social Media: *Facebook, Twitter, LinkedIn, RSS, YouTube*

Cassi Birnbaum, President/ Chair
Melissa M. Martin, President/ Chair-Elect
Laura Pait, RHIA, CDIP, CCS, Speaker of The HoD
Lynne Thomas Gordon, CEO
Susan W.ÿ Carey, RHIT, PMP, Treasurer

Mission is to be the professional community that improves healthcare by advocating best practices and standards for health information management and the trusted source for education, reasearch, and professional credentialing.
46M Members
Founded in 1928

12763 American Health Quality Association

7918 Jones Branch Drive
Suite 300
McLean, VA 22102

202-331-5790
FAX 202-331-9334
E-Mail: info@ahqa.org
Home Page: www.ahqa.org

Dawn FitzGerald, MS, MBA, President
Jane Brock, MD, MSPH, President Elect
Kathleen D.ÿ Merrill, Immediate Past President
Rick Potter, Treasurer
Colleenÿ Delaney Eubanks, CAE, Executive Director

Represents Quality Improvement Organizations and professionals working to improve the quality of health care in communities across America. QIOs share information about best practices with physicians, hospitals, nursing homes, home health agencies, and others. Working together with health care providers, QIOs identify opportunities and provide assistance for improvement.

12764 American Heart Association

7272 Greenville Ave
Dallas, TX 75231-4596

214-373-6300
800-242-8721
FAX 214-570-5930
E-Mail: Review.personal.info@heart.org
Home Page: www.americanheart.org
Social Media: *Facebook, Twitter, YouTube, Google Plus*

Bernie Dennis, Chairman
Mariell Jessup, President
Nancy Brown, CEO
Sunder Joshi, Chief Administrative Officer
Suzie Upton, Chief Development Officer

A nonprofit organization funding research and providing information on the diagnosis, treatment, and prevention of heart diseases and stroke. Mission is to build healthier lives, free of cardiovascular diseases and stroke.
Founded in 1924

12765 American Horticultural Therapy Association (AHTA)

610 Freedom Business Center
Suite 110
King of Prussia, PA 19406

610-992-0020
FAX 610-225-2364
E-Mail: martha@ahta.org
Home Page: www.ahta.org
Social Media: *Facebook, Twitter, LinkedIn, Pinterest, Youtube, RSS*

MaryAnne McMillan, HTR, President
Leigh Anne Starling, MS, CRC, Vice President
Todd Schappell, OTR/L, Treasurer
Patricia Cassidy, HTR, Secretary
Gabriela Harvey, HTR, Immediate Past President

A champion of barrier-free, therapeutic gardens that enable everyone to work, learn, and relax in the garden. Horticultural therapists are skilled at creating garden spaces that accommodate people with a wide range of abilities.
Founded in 1973

12766 American Hospital Association

155 N. Wacker Dr.
Chicago, IL 60606

312-422-3000
800-424-4301
FAX 312-422-4500
E-Mail: ddavidson@aha.org
Home Page: www.aha.org
Social Media: *Facebook, Twitter, YouTube*

Benjamin K Chu, M.D., Chairman
Richard J Pollack, President and CEO

John Evans, CFO, SVP
Alicia Mitchell, SVP, Communications
Richard Umbdenstock, Past President, CEO

Represents and serves all types of hospitals, health care networks, and their patients and communities. Provides education for health care leaders and is a source of information on health care issues and trends.
43,00 Members
Founded in 1898

12767 American Industrial Hygiene Association

3141 Fairview Park Drive
Suite 777
Falls Church, VA 22042

703-849-8888
FAX 703-207-3561
E-Mail: infonet@aiha.org
Home Page: www.aiha.org
Social Media: *Facebook, Twitter, LinkedIn, RSS, YouTube*

Daniel H. Anna, PhD, CIH, CS?P, President
Deborah Imel Nelson, PhD, CIH, Vice President
Cynthia A. Ostrowski, CIH, Treasurer
Kathleen S. Murphy, CIH, Secretary
Steven E. Lacey, PhD, CIH, CSP, President-Elect

Organization of professionals in the science of occupational and environmental health and safety. Devoted to achieving and maintaining the highest professional standards for members. Promoting certification of industrial hygienists.
10,00 Members
Founded in 1939

12768 American Institute of Ultrasound in Medicine

14750 Sweitzer Lane
Suite 100
Laurel, MD 20707-5906

301-498-4100
800-638-5352
FAX 301-498-4450
E-Mail: cvalente@aium.org
Home Page: www.aium.org
Social Media: *Facebook, Twitter, LinkedIn, YouTube, Instagram*

Beryl R. Benacerraf, MD, President
Joseph R Wax, MD, First Vice President
Charlotte G. Henningsen, Second Vice President
Michael Blaivas, MD, Third Vice President
Brian D. Coley, MD, President-Electÿ

A multidisciplinary association dedicated to advancing the safe and effective use of ultrasound in medicine through professional and public education, research, development of guidelines, and accreditation.
85M Members
Founded in 1952

12769 American Institute of Ultrasound in Medici ne

14750 Sweitzer Lane
Suite 100
Laurel, MD 20707-5906

301-498-4100
800-638-5352
FAX 301-498-4450
E-Mail: cvalente@aium.org
Home Page: www.aium.org
Social Media: *Facebook, Twitter, LinkedIn, YouTube, Instagram*

Beryl R. Benacerraf, MD, President
Joseph R Wax, MD, First Vice President
Charlotte G. Henningsen, Second Vice President
Michael Blaivas, MD, Third Vice President
Brian D. Coley, MD, President-Electÿ

A multidisciplinary association dedicated to advancing the safe and effective use of ultrasound in medicine through professional and public education, research, development of guidelines, and accreditation.
9.8M Members
Founded in 1952

12770 American Lung Association

1301 Pennsylvania Ave. NW
Suite 800
Washington, DC 20004

202-785-3355
FAX 202-452-1805
E-Mail: info@lungusa.org
Home Page: www.lung.org
Social Media: *Facebook, Twitter, YouTube, Google Plus, RSS*

Albert A. Rizzo, Chair
Ross P. Lanzafame, Esq., Chair-Elect
Christine L. Bryant, Secretary/ Treasurer

Dedicated to the prevention, cure, and control of lung diseases such as asthma, emphysema, tuberculosis, and lung cancer. The Association offers community service, public health education, advocacy, and research.
Founded in 1904

12771 American Massage Therapy Association

500 Davis Street
Suite 900
Evanston, IL 60201

847-864-0123
877-905-0577
FAX 847-864-5196
E-Mail: info@amtamassage.org
Home Page: www.amtamassage.org/
Social Media: *Facebook, Twitter, LinkedIn, RSS, YouTube*

Jeff Smoot, President
Nathan J. Nordstrom, President Elect
Nancy M. Porambo, Immediate Past President
Glyn Desmond, Board of Director
Maureen P.ÿ Hoock, Board of Director

Nonprofit, professional association serving massage therapists, massage students and massage schools.

12772 American Medical Association

330 N. Wabash Avenue
Chicago, IL 60611-5885

800-621-8335
E-Mail: robin_rusell@ama-assn.org
Home Page: www.ama-assn.org
Social Media: *Facebook, Twitter, LinkedIn, Google+*

James L. Madara, MD, CEO, EVP
Bernard L. Hengesbaugh, Chief Operating Officer
Denise M Hagerty, SVP, CFO
Robert W Davis, SVP, HR & Corporate Services
Kenneth J. Sharigian, SVP, Chief Strategy Officer

Mission is to promote the art and science of medicine and the betterment of public health. The American Medical Association helps doctors help patients by uniting physicians nationwide to work on the most important professional and public health issues.
Founded in 1847

12773 American Medical Directors Association

11000 Broken Land Parkway
Suite 400
Columbia, MD 21044

410-740-9743
800-876-2632
FAX 410-740-4572

E-Mail: info@amda.com
Home Page: www.amda.com
Social Media: *Facebook, Twitter, LinkedIn*

Naushira Pandya, MD, FACP, CMD, President
Heidi K. White, Vice President
Daniel Haimowitz, Secretary
Arif Nazir, MD, FACP, CMD, Treasurer
Susan M. Levy, MD, CMD, AGSF, President-Elect

Professional association of medical directors, attending physicians, and others practicing in the long term care continuum, is dedicated to excellence in patient care and provides education, advocacy, information, and professional development to promote the delivery of quality long term care medicine.
Founded in 1978

12774 American Medical Group Association

One Prince Street
Alexandria, VA 22314-3318

703-838-0033
FAX 703-548-1890
E-Mail: dfisher@amga.org
Home Page: www.amga.org
Social Media: *Facebook, Twitter, LinkedIn, YouTube, Flickr*

Don L. Wreden, M.D., Chair
Donald W Fisher, Ph.D., CAE, President and CEO
Donn E. Sorensen, Chair Elect
Barbara A. Walters, D.O., M.B.A., Treasurer
Clyde L. Morris, C.P.A., CFO

Represents medical groups and organized systems of care, including some of the nation's largest, most prestigious integrated healthcare delivery systems. Mission is to improve health care for patients by supporting multispecialty medical groups and other organized systems of care.
113M Members
Founded in 1950

12775 American Medical Informatics Association

4720 Montgomery Lane
Suite 500
Bethesda, MD 20814

301-657-1291
FAX 301-657-1296
E-Mail: mail@amia.org
Home Page: www.amia.org
Social Media: *Facebook, Twitter, LinkedIn, YouTube*

Blackford Middleton, Chair
Thomas H. Payne, MD, FACMI, Chair Elect
Douglas B. Fridsma, President, CEO
Karen Greenwood, Executive Vice President, COO
Steven Labkoff, Treasurer

Aims to lead the way in transforming health care through trusted science, education, and the practice of informatics. Connecting a broad community of professionals and students interested in informatics, AMIA is the bridge for knowledge and collaboration across a continuum, from basic and applied research to the consumer and public health arenas.
3200 Members
Founded in 1990

12776 American Medical Student Association

45610 Woodland Road
Suite 300
Sterling, VA 20166

703-620-6600
800-767-2266
FAX 703-620-6445
E-Mail: members@amsa.org

Home Page: www.amsa.org
Social Media: *Facebook, Twitter, Inex, Youtube*

Deborah Vozzella Hall, MD, National President
Kelly Thibert, President Elect
Joshua Weinstock, VP for Internal Affairs
Rinku Skaria, VP for Membership
Perry Tsai, VP for Program Development

The oldest and largest independent association of physicians-in-training in the United States. Committed to improving the lives of medical students.
40M Members
Founded in 1950

12777 American Medical Technologists

10700 West Higgins Road
Suite 150
Rosemont, IL 60018-3722

847-823-5169
800-275-1268
FAX 847-823-0458
E-Mail: mail@americanmedtech.org
Home Page: www.americanmedtech.org
Social Media: *Facebook, Twitter, LinkedIn, Youtube*

Everett Bloodworth, President
Jeffrey Lavender, Vice President
Heather Herring, Secretary
Jeannette Hobson, Treasurer
Edna Anderson, Executive Councillor

Mission is to manage, promote, expand upon and continuously improve their certification programs for allied health professionals who work in a variety of disciplines and settings, to administer certification examinations in accordance with the highest standards of accreditation, and to provide continuing education, information, advocacy services and other benefits to members.
Founded in 1939

12778 American Medical Women's Association

12100 Sunset Hills Road
Suite 130
Reston, VA 20190

703-234-4069
866-564-2483
FAX 703-435-4390
E-Mail: associatedirector@amwa-doc.org
Home Page: www.amwa-doc.org
Social Media: *Facebook, Twitter, LinkedIn, Flickr*

Theresa Rohr-Kirchgraber, MD, President
Eliza Lo Chin, MD, MPH, Executive Director
Shahnaz Fatteh, MD, Treasurer
Laura McCann, MD, Secretary
Kimberly Templeton, MD, President-Elect

An organization of women physicians, medical students and other persons dedicated to serving as the unique voice for women's health and the advancement of women in medicine.
Founded in 1915

12779 American Music Therapy Association (AMTA)

8455 Colesville Road
Suite 1000
Silver Spring, MD 20910-3392

301-589-3300
FAX 301-589-5175
E-Mail: info@musictherapy.org
Home Page: www.musictherapy.org
Social Media: *Facebook, Twitter, YouTube*

Andrea Farbman, Executive Director
Mary Ellen Wylei, AMTA President

AMTA's purpose is the progressive development of the therapeutic use of music in rehabilitation, special education, and community settings. AMTA is committed to the advancement of education, training, professional stan-

dards, credentials, and research in support of the music therapy profession.
3800 Members
Founded in 1998

12780 American Nephrology Nurses Association

East Holly Avenue
Box 56
Pitman, NJ 08071-0056

856-256-2320
FAX 856-589-7463
E-Mail: anna@annanurse.org
Home Page: www.annanurse.org
Social Media: *Facebook, Twitter, RSS*

Cindy A. Richards, BSN RN CNN, President
Sheila J.ÿ Doss-McQuitty, President-Elect
Sharon M.ÿ Longton, Immediate Past President
Susan Cary, MN APRN NP CNN, Treasurer
Lynda K. Ball, MSN RN CNN, Secretary

Mission is to promote excellence by advancing nephrology nursing practice and positively influence outcomes for individuals with kidney disease.
Founded in 1969

12781 American Nurses Association

8515 Georgia Avenue
Suite 400
Silver Spring, MD 20910-3492

800-274-4ANA
FAX 301-628-5001
E-Mail: anf@ana.org
Home Page: www.nursingworld.org
Social Media: *Facebook, Twitter, LinkedIn, YouTube*

Pamela F. Cipriano, PhD, RN, President
Cindy R. Balkstra, MS, RN, Vice President
Gingy Harshey-Meade, MSN, Treasurer
Patricia Travis, PhD, RN, CCRP, Secretary
Andrea C. Gregg, PhD, RN, Director at Large

Advances the nursing profession by fostering high standards of nursing practice, promoting the rights of nurses in the workplace, projecting a positive and realistic view of nursing, and by lobbying the Congress and regulatory agencies on health care issues affecting nurses and the public.

12782 American Occupational Therapy Association

4720 Montgomery Lane
Ste 200
Bethesda, MD 20814-3449

301-652-6611
800-729-2682
FAX 301-652-7711
Home Page: www.aota.org
Social Media: *Facebook, Twitter, LinkedIn, RSS*

Florence Clark, President
Ginny Stoffel, Vice President
Paul A. Fontana, Secretary
Saburi Imara, Treasurer

Representing the interests and concerns of occupational therapy practitioners and students of occupational therapy and to improve the quality of occupational therapy services.
42M Members
Founded in 1917

12783 American Optometric Association

243 N Lindbergh Blvd
Flr. 1
St Louis, MO 63141-7881

314-991-4100
800-365-2219
FAX 314-991-4101
Home Page: www.aoa.org

Social Media: *Facebook, Twitter, LinkedIn, RSS, Youtube*

Mitchell T. Munson, O.D, President
Steven A. Loomis, O.D., Vice President
Andrea P. Thau, O.D., Secretary/ Treasurer

National organization of optometrists, evaluates ophthalmic products and sponsors continuing education programs.
36M Members
Founded in 1898

12784 American Optometric Student Association

243 N Lindbergh Blvd
Suite 311
St Louis, MO 63141-7881

314-983-4231
E-Mail: rfoster@theaosa.org
Home Page: www.theaosa.org/

Robert Foster, Executive Director
Alan Wegener, Vice President
Vicky Wong, Secretary
Elizabeth Turnage, Treasurer

Committed to promoting the optometric profession, enhancing the education and welfare of optometry students, as well as enhancing the vision and ocular health of the public.
6M Members

12785 American Orthopaedic Foot & Ankle Society

9400 West Higgins Road
Suite 220
Rosemont, IL 60018-4263

847-698-4654
800-235-4855
FAX 847-823-8125
Home Page: www.aofas.org
Social Media: *Facebook, Twitter, LinkedIn*

Mark E. Easley, MD, President
Jeffrey E.ÿ Johnson, MD, President-Elect
ThomasÿH. Lee, MD, Vice President
J. Chris Coetzee, MD, Treasurer
Bruce J. Sangeorzan, MD, Immediate Past President

Mission is to promote quality, ethical and cost effective patient care through education, research and training of orthopaedic surgeons and other health care providers, create public awareness for the prevention and treatment of foot and ankle disorders, provide leadership, and serve as a resource for government, industry and the national and international health care community.
35000 Members
Founded in 1969

12786 American Orthopaedic Foot and Ankle Society

9400 West Higgins Road
Suite 220
Rosemont, IL 60018-4975

847-698-4654
800-235-4855
FAX 847-692-3315
E-Mail: aofasinfo@aofas.org
Home Page: www.aofas.org/
Social Media: *Facebook, Twitter, LinkedIn*

Mark E. Easley, MD, President
Jeffrey E.ÿ Johnson, MD, President-Elect
ThomasÿH. Lee, MD, Vice President
J. Chris Coetzee, MD, Treasurer
Bruce J. Sangeorzan, MD, Immediate Past President

Specialty society for orthopedic surgeons with training and interest in the prevention and treatment of foot and ankle conditions.
Founded in 1969

12787 American Orthopaedic Society for Sports Medicine

9400 W. Higgins Road
Suite 300
Rosemont, IL 60018ÿ

847-292-4900
877-321-3500
FAX 847-292-4905
Home Page: www.sportsmed.org
Social Media: *Facebook, Twitter*

Irvin E. Bomberger, Executive Director
Camille Petrick, Managing Director
Heather Hodge, Education Director
Kevin M. Boyer, MPHÿÿ, Director of Research
Lisa Weisenberger, Director of Communications

Promotes sports medicine education, research, communication, and fellowship and includes national and international orthopaedic sports medicine leaders.

12788 American Orthopsychiatric Association

C/o Clemson University, IFNL
225 S. Pleasantburg Dr.
Suite B-11
Greenville, SC 29607

864-250-4622
FAX 864-250-4633
E-Mail: orthocontact@aoatoday.com
Home Page: www.aoatoday.org

Andres J. Pumariega, President
Donald Wertlieb, President-Elect
Jan L. Culbertson, Secretary
William Reay, Treasurer
Robin Kimbrough-Melton, Executive Officer

Provides a common ground for collaborative study, research, and knowledge exchange among individuals from a variety of disciplines engaged in preventive, treatment, and advocacy approaches to mental health.
Founded in 1923

12789 American Orthotic & Prosthetic Association

330 John Carlyle Street
Suite 200
Alexandria, VA 22314

571-431-0876
FAX 571-431-0899
E-Mail: info@aopanet.org
Home Page: www.aopanet.org
Social Media: *Facebook, Twitter, LinkedIn, Youtube*

Charles H. Dankmeyer, Jr., CPO, President
Michael Oros, CPO, FAAOP, Vice President
James Campbell, CO, Ph.D., President Elect
Jeff Collins, CPA, Treasurer
Anita Liberman-Lampear, MA, Immediate Past President

A national trade association committed to providing high quality, unprecedented business services and products to O&P professionals.
Founded in 1917

12790 American Osteopathic Association

142 E Ontario St
Chicago, IL 60611-2864

312-202-8000
800-621-1773
FAX 312-202-8200
E-Mail: info@osteotech.org
Home Page: www.osteopathic.org
Social Media: *Facebook, Twitter, LinkedIn, Youtube, Pinterest*

John W. Becher, DO, President
Adrienne White-Faines, MPA, CEO
Geraldine O'Shea, DO, Second Vice President
Frank M. Tursi, DO, Third Vice President
Boyd R. Buser, DO, President-Electÿ

Promotes public health, encourages scientific research, and is the accrediting agency for all osteopathic medical schools and health care facilities.
52M Members
Founded in 1897

12791 American Osteopathic College of Dermatology

2902 North Baltimore Street
P.O. Box 7525
Kirksville, MI 63501

660-665-2184
800-449-2623
FAX 660-627-2623
Home Page: www.aocd.org/
Social Media: *Facebook, Twitter, Tumblr*

Marsha Wise, Executive Director
John Grogan, Resident Coordinator
Shelley Wood, Grants Coordinator

Specialty college that promotes the practice of osteopathic dermatology.
Founded in 1958

12792 American Pain Society

8735 W. Higgins Road
Suite 300
Chicago, IL 60631

847-375-4715
FAX 847-375-6479
FAX 732-460-7318
E-Mail: info@americanpainsociety.org
Home Page: www.americanpainsociety.org/
Social Media: *Facebook, Twitter, LinkedIn, Youtube*

Roger Fillingim, PhD, President
Catherine H Underwood, MBA CAE, Executive Director
David A. Williams, PhD, Treasurer
Kathleen Sluka, PT PhD, Secretary
Gregory W Terman, MD PhD, President-Elect

The American Pain Society is a multidisciplinary community that brings together a diverse group of scientists, clinicians and other professionals to increase the knowledge of pain and transform public policy and clinical practice to reduce pain-related suffering.
Founded in 1977

12793 American Pediatric Society/Society for Pediatric Research

3400 Research Forest Drive
Suite B7
The Woodlands, TX 77381

281-419-0052
FAX 281-419-0082
E-Mail: info@aps-spr.org
Home Page: www.aps-spr.org
Social Media: *Facebook, Twitter, Instagram*

Eileen G. Fenton, Executive Director
Belinda Thomas, PAS Education Program Director
Stephanie Dean, Managing Editor, Pediatric Research
Antonio Moreno, Information Technology Director
Belinda Thomas, Information Services Manager

Coordinates meetings, research and further education of health professionals. Features policies, publications and details of research programs.
Founded in 1888

12794 American Pediatric Surgical Association

One Parkview Plaza
Suite 800
Oakbrook Terrace, IL 60181

847-686-2237
FAX 847-686-2253
E-Mail: eapsa@eapsa.org
Home Page: www.eapsa.org/
Social Media: *Twitter*

Mary Fallat, Presidentÿ
Diana Farmer, President-Elect
Michael D. Klein, Immediate Past Presidentÿ
Daniel Von Allmen, Treasurer
John H.T. Waldhausen, Secretary

Pediatric surgical care of patients and their families.

12795 American Pharmacists Association (APhA)

2215 Constitution Avenue NW
Suite 400
Washington, DC 20037-2985

202-628-4410
800-237-2742
FAX 202-783-2351
Home Page: www.pharmacist.com
Social Media: *Facebook, Twitter, LinkedIn, RSS, Youtube*

Stacie Maass, SVP, Pharmacy Practice
Thomas E. Menighan, BSPharm, MBA, Chief Executive Officer
Jule Miller, SVP, Human Resources
Joseph J. Janela, Chief Financial Officer
Elizabeth K. Keyes, Chief Operating Officer

The American Pharmacists Association (APhA) is an organization whose members are recognized in society as essential in all patient care settings for optimal medication use that improves health, wellness, and quality of life. Through information, education, and advocacy, APhA empowers its members to improve medication use and advance patient care.
60000 Members
Founded in 1852

12796 American Physical Therapy Association

1111 North Fairfax Street
Alexandria, VA 22314-1488

703-683-6748
800-999-2782
FAX 703-684-7343
E-Mail: memberservices@apta.org
Home Page: www.apta.org
Social Media: *Facebook, Twitter, LinkedIn, Youtube*

Sharon L.ÿ Dunn, PT, PhD, OCS, President
Lisa K. Saladin, Vice President
J. Michael Bowers, CEO
Rob Batarla, MBA, CPA, CAE, EVP, Financial and Business Affairs
Elmer Platz, PT, Treasurer

The principal membership organization representing and promoting the profession of physical therapy, is to furhter the profession's role in the prevention, diagnosis, and treatment of movement dysfunctions and the enhancement of the physical health and functional abilities of members of the public.
74000 Members

12797 American Physiological Society

9650 Rockville Pike
Bethesda, MD 20814-3991

301-634-7164
FAX 301-634-7241
E-Mail: webmaster@the-aps.org
Home Page: www.the-aps.org

Social Media: *Facebook, Twitter, LinkedIn, YouTube*

Patricia Molina, M.D., Ph.D.ÿ, President
David M.ÿ PollockÿPh.D, Past President
Jane Reckelhoff, Ph.D., President Elect
Martin Frank, PhD, Executive Director
Robert Price, Director of Finance

A nonprofit devoted to fostering education scientific research and dissemination of information in the physiological sciences. A member of the Federation of American Societies for Experimental Biology (FASEB) a coalition of 18 independent societies that plays an active role in lobbying for the interests of biomedical scientists.
10,50 Members
Founded in 1887

12798 American Podiatric Medical Association

9312 Old Georgetown Road
Bethesda, MD 20814-1621

301-581-9200
FAX 301-530-2752
E-Mail: mskulick@apma.org
Home Page: www.apma.org
Social Media: *Facebook, Twitter, LinkedIn, YouTube*

Matthew G. Garoufalis, DPM, President
Phillip E. Ward, DPM, Vice President
R. Daniel Davis, DPM, Treasurer
Glenn B. Gastwirth, DPM, Secretary

An association of podiatrists providing services and information on foot problems and foot health.
11000 Members
Founded in 1912

12799 American Porphyria Foundation

4900 Woodway
Suite 780
Houston, TX 77056-1837

713-266-9617
866-APF-3635
FAX 713-840-9552
E-Mail: porphyrus@porphyriafoundation.com
Home Page: www.porphyriafoundation.com

James V. Young, Chairman, Board of Trustee
Desiree H. Lyon, Executive Director
Dr. William McCutchen, Board Member
Warren Hudson, Board Member
Andrew Turell, Board Member

Dedicated to improving the health and well-being of individuals andfamilies affected by Porphyria. Also advocates for public, private, and government agencies interested in funding research and educational programs.
Founded in 1982

12800 American Psychiatric Association

1000 Wilson Boulevard
Suite 1825
Arlington, VA 22209-3901

703-907-7300
888-357-7924
FAX 703-907-1085
E-Mail: apa@psych.org
Home Page: www.psych.org
Social Media: *Facebook, Twitter, LinkedIn*

Saul M. Levin, M.D., M.P.A., CEO, Medical Director

Association for manufacturers, suppliers, distributors, publishers, state/federal agencies and psychiatric facilities.
Founded in 1844

12801 American Psychological Association

750 First St. NE
Washington, DC 20002-4242

202-336-5500
800-374-2721

FAX 202-336-5518
Home Page: www.apa.org
Social Media: *Facebook, Twitter, LinkedIn, YouTube, Google+, RSS*

Barry S. Anton, PhD, President
Norman B. Anderson, PhD, Chief Executive Officer, EVP
Susan McDaniel, PhD$\ddot{y}$, President Elect
Nadine J. Kaslow, PhDÿ, Past President
Bonnie Markham, PhD, PsyDÿ, Treasurer

The largest scientific and professional organization representing psychology in the United States and the largest association of psychologists in the world, dedicated to advancing psychology as a science and as a means of promoting health, education, and human welfare.
12250 Members
Founded in 1892

12802 American Public Health Association

800 I Street, NW
Washington, DC 20001

202-777-2742
FAX 202-777-2534
Home Page: www.apha.org
Social Media: *Facebook, Twitter*

Pamela Aaltonen, PhD, RN, Chair
Jose Ramon Fernandez-Pena, Vice Chair
Joyce R. Gaufin, BS, Immediate Past President
Shiriki Kumanyika, PhD, MPH, President
Richard J. Cohen, PhD, FACHE, Treasurer

Professional association dedicated to improving the public's healththrough education.
24 Members

12803 American Public Human Services Association

1133 19th Street, NW
Suite 400
Washington, DC 20036-3623

202-682-0100
FAX 202-289-6555
Home Page: www.aphsa.org
Social Media: *Facebook, Twitter, LinkedIn*

Reggie Bicha, President
Tracy Wareing, Executive Director
Nicole Lobban, Human Resources Director
Raymond Washington III, Director of Finance
Anita Light, Senior Deputy Executive Director

Pursues excellence in health and human services by supporting state and local agencies, informing policymakers, and working wtih our partners to drive innovative, integrated and efficient solutions in policy and practice.
Founded in 1930

12804 American Rhinologic Society

PO Box 495
Warwick, NY 10990

845-988-1631
FAX 845-986-1527
Home Page: www.american-rhinologic.org/

Roy Casiano, MD, President
Joseph Jacobs, MD, Executive Vice President
Peter Hwang, MD, President-elect
John DelGaudio, MD, 1st Vice President
Richard Orlandi, MD, 2nd Vice President

Physician organization whose focus is upon the medical and surgicaltreatment of patients with diseases of the nose and paranasal sinuses.

12805 American School Health Association

7918 Jones Branch Drive
Suite 300
McLean, VA 22102

703-506-7675
FAX 703-503-3266
E-Mail: info@ashaweb.org
Home Page: www.ashaweb.org

Social Media: *Facebook, Twitter, LinkedIn, YouTube*

Linda Morse, RN, MA, CHES, President
Ty Oehrtman, VP
Sharon Murray, MHSE, FASHA, Treasurer
Sharon Miller, Secretary
Sandy Klarenbeek, Chair of Advocacy

Concerned with all health factors that are necessary for students to be ready to learn, including optimum nutrition, physical fitness, emotional well-being, and a safe and clean environment.
2000 Members
Founded in 1927

12806 American Sleep Apnea Association

1717 Pennsylvania Avenue, NW
Suite 1025
Washington, DC 20006

888-293-3650
FAX 888-293-3650
Home Page: www.sleepapnea.org/
Social Media: *Facebook, Twitter, Google+, YouTube, Vimeo*

Will Headapohl, Chair
Adam Amdurÿ, COO
Addison Closson, Treasurer
Nancy Rothstein, Secretary
Tracy R. Nasca, Executive Director

A nonprofit organization that promotes education, awareness and research into sleep apnea.
Founded in 1990

12807 American Society for Aesthetic Plastic Surgery

36 W 44th Street
New York, NY 10036

212-921-0500
FAX 212-921-0011
E-Mail: media@surgery.org
Home Page: www.surgery.org
Social Media: *Facebook, Twitter, LinkedIn*

Jack Fisher, MD, President
James C. Grotting, MD, Vice President
Daniel C. Mills, II, MD, Treasurer
Clyde H. Ishii, MD, Secretary

Organization of plastic surgeons certified by the American Board of Plastic Surgery who specialize in cosmetic surgery of the face and body.

12808 American Society for Cell Biology

8120 Woodmont Avenue
Suite 750
Bethesda, MD 20814-2762

301-347-9300
FAX 301-347-9310
E-Mail: ascbinfo@ascb.org
Home Page: www.ascb.org
Social Media: *Facebook, Twitter, LinkedIn, Vimeo*

Shirley M. Tilghman, President
Stefano Bertuzzi, PhD, Executive Director
Thea Clarke, Director of Comm. & Education
John Fleischman, Senior Science Writer
Christina Szalinski, Science Writer/Program Coordinator

A nonprofit membership organization of biologists studying the cell, the fundamental unit of life. Membership is open to all research scientists, students, educators, and technicians who have education or research experience in cell biology or an allied field.
10M Members
Founded in 1960

12809 American Society for Dermatologic Surgery

5550 Meadowbrook Drive
Suite 120
Rolling Meadows, IL 60008

847-956-0900
FAX 847-956-0999
E-Mail: info@asds.net
Home Page: www.asds.net
Social Media: *Facebook, Twitter, LinkedIn, YouTube*

Naomi Lawrence, MDÿ, President
Lisa M. Donofrio, MD, Vice President
Katherine J. Duerdoth, CAE, Executive Director
Thomas Rohrer, MD, President Elect
Mathew M. Avram, MD, JD, Treasurer

To promote optimal quality care for patients as well as support and develop investigative knowledge in the field of dermatologic surgery.
5,800 Members
Founded in 1973

12810 American Society for Histocompatability and Immunogenetics

1120 Route 73
Suite 200
Mt. Laurel, NJ 08054

856-638-0428
FAX 856-439-0525
E-Mail: kmiranda@ahint.com
Home Page: www.ashi-hla.org
Social Media: *Facebook, Twitter, LinkedIn*

Kathy Miranda, Executive Director
Deb Dupnik, Assistant Executive Director
Melissa Weeks, Accreditation Manager
Caitlin O'Brien, Meeting Manager
Cecilia Blair, Director of Operations

Dedicated to advancing the practice and science of inherited aspects of immunity, and its impact on the quality of human life.
Founded in 1972

12811 American Society for Laser Medicine and Surgery, Inc.

2100 Stewart Avenue
Suite 240
Wausau, WI 54401-1709

715-845-9283
877-258-6028
FAX 715-848-2493
E-Mail: information@aslms.org
Home Page: www.aslms.org
Social Media: *Facebook, Twitter, LinkedIn, Google+, YouTube, Pinterest*

Dianne Dalsky, Executive Director
Corri Marschall, Conference Specialist
Paula Deffner, Accounting Specialist
Diane Dodds, Member and Customer Service
Andrea Alstad, Marketing & Communications Mgr.

Promotes excellence in patient care by advancing biomedical application of lasers and other related technologies worldwide.
Founded in 1980

12812 American Society for Microbiology

1752 N Street, N.W.
Washington, DC 20036-2904

202-737-3600
FAX 202-942-9341
E-Mail: service@asmusa.org
Home Page: www.asm.org
Social Media: *Facebook, Twitter, LinkedIn, Instagram, Youtube*

Jeffery Miller, President
Joseph M. Campos, Secretary,

The world's largest scientific society of individuals interested in the microbiological sciences.
39,00 Members

12813 American Society for Nutrition

9650 Rockville Pike
Bethesda, MD 20814

301-634-7050
FAX 301-634-7894
Home Page: www.nutrition.org
Social Media: *Facebook, LinkedIn, Youtube, RSS*

Patrick J. Stover, PhD, President
Marian Neuhouser, PhD, RD, Vice-President
Simin Nikbin Meydani, Past President
Barbara Lyle, PhD, Treasurer
Susan Percival, PhD, Secretary

A non-profit organization dedicated to bringing together the world's top researchers, clinical nutritionists and industry to advance our knowledge and application of nutrition for the sake of humans and animals.
Founded in 1928

12814 American Society for Pharmacology and Experimental Therapeutics

9650 Rockville Pike
Bethesda, MD 20814-3995

301-634-7060
FAX 301-634-7061
E-Mail: info@aspet.org
Home Page: www.aspet.org
Social Media: *Facebook, Twitter, LinkedIn, Flickr*

Judith A. Siuciak, Ph.D., Executive Director
Matthew Hilliker, Chief Financial Officer
Suzie Thompson, Director of Marketing
Richard Dodenhoff, Director of Journals
Cecilia Fox, Meetings and Admin. Coordinator

Members research efforts help develop new medicines and therapeutic agents to fight existing and emerging diseases.
5,000 Members
Founded in 1909

12815 American Society for Surgery of the Hand

822 W. Washington Boulevard
Suite 600
Chicago, IL 60607

312-880-1900
FAX 847-384-1435
E-Mail: info@assh.org
Home Page: www.assh.org
Social Media: *Facebook, Twitter, LinkedIn*

Mark C. Anderson, FASAE, CAE, EVP, CEO
Pamela Schroeder, CAE, Deputy EVP
Angie Legaspi, CMP, VP, Professional Development
Bill Chandler, Director of Finance
Tara Spiess, Director of Publishing, Marketingÿ

The oldest medical specialty society in the United States devoted entirely to continuing medical education related to hand surgery.
3,500 Members
Founded in 1946

12816 American Society for Therapeutic Radiology And Oncology

8280 Willow Oaks Corporate Drive
Suite 500
Fairfax, VA 22031

703-502-1550
800-962-7876
FAX 703-502-7852
E-Mail: meetings@astro.org
Home Page: www.astro.org

Social Media: *Facebook, Twitter, LinkedIn, YouTube*

Bruce D. Minsky,ÿ MD, FASTRO, Chairman
David C. Beyer,ÿ MD, FASTRO, President
Jeff M. Michalski, Secretary/Treasurer
Brian Kavanagh, President-elect
Bruce G. Haffty,ÿ MD, FASTRO, Immediate Past Chair

Provides members with the continuing medical education, health policy analysis, patient information resources and advocacy that they need to succeed in today's ever-changing health care delivery system.
10M Members
Founded in 1958

12817 American Society of Addiction Medicine

4601 North Park Ave.
Upper Arcade, Suite 101
Chevy Chase, MD 20815-4520

301-656-3920
FAX 301-656-3815
E-Mail: email@asam.org
Home Page: www.asam.org
Social Media: *Facebook, Twitter, LinkedIn*

Penny S. Mills, Executive Vice President
Carolyn C. Lanham, Chief Operating Officer

ASAM represents professionals in the addiction field. It promotes research and prevention, education for physicians and the public and improving access to, and quality of, treatment.
3600+ Members
Founded in 1954

12818 American Society of Anesthesiologists

1061 American Lane
Schaumburg, IL 60173-4973

847-825-5586
FAX 847-825-1692
E-Mail: info@asahq.org
Home Page: www.asahq.org
Social Media: *Facebook, Twitter, LinkedIn, YouTube*

J.P. Abenstein, President
Daniel J.ÿ Cole, MD, President Elect
Jane C. K. Fitch, M.D., Immediate Past President
Jeffrey Plagenhoef, M.D.ÿ, First Vice President
James D.ÿ Grant, MD, Treasurer

An educational, research and scientific association of physicians organized to raise and maintain the standards of the medical practice of anesthesiology and improve the care of the patient.
39M Members
Founded in 1905
Mailing list available for rent

12819 American Society of Angiology

708 Glen Cove Ave
Glen Head, NY 11545

516-671-1975
FAX 516-759-5524
E-Mail: anngailius@amsocang.org
Home Page: www.amsocang.org/

David K Jackson, MD, President
Ann Gailius, Director, Membership

Striving to incorporate a variety of disciplines to encourage education and interaction in our common fields of endeavor.

12820 American Society of Bariatric Physicians

2821 S Parker Rd
Suite 625
Aurora, CO 80014-2735

303-770-2526
877-266-6834
FAX 303-779-4834

E-Mail: info@asbp.org
Home Page: www.asbp.org
Social Media: *Facebook, Twitter, LinkedIn, Youtube, RSS*

David Bryman, D.O., F.A.S.B., Chairman
Eric C. Westman, M.D., M.H.S., President
Wendy Scinta, M.D., M.S., Vice President
Laurie Traetow, CAE, CPA, Executive Director
Heidi Gordon, Director of Marketing

ASBP is a nonprofit international professional medical association headquartered in Aurora, Colorado. The ASBP was awarded a seat in the House of Delegates of American Medical Association. The American Society of Bariatric Physicians has members worldwide.
Founded in 1950

12821 American Society of Cataract & Refractive Surgery

4000 Legato Rd
Suite 700
Fairfax, VA 22033-4055

703-591-2220
800-451-1339
FAX 703-591-0614
E-Mail: ascrs@ascrs.org
Home Page: www.ascrs.org
Social Media: *Facebook, Twitter, YouTube, Flickr*

Robert J. Cionni, MD, President
Kerry D. Solomon, MD, Vice President/President Elect
Richard A. Lewis, MD, Immediate Past President
Bonnie An Henderson, MD, Treasurer
Thomas W. Samuelson, MD, Secretary

The mission of the American Society of Cataract and Refractive Surgery is to advance the art and science of ophthalmic surgery and the knowledge and skills of ophthalmic surgeons. It does so by providing clinical and practice management education and by working with patients, government, and the medical community to promote the delivery of quality eye care.
9,000 Members
Founded in 1974

12822 American Society of Clinical Oncology

2318 Mill Road
Suite 800
Alexandria, VA 22314

571-483-1300
FAX 703-299-1044
E-Mail: abstracts@asco.org
Home Page: www.asco.org
Social Media: *Facebook, Twitter, LinkedIn, Youtube*

Julie M. Vose, MD, MBA, FASCO, President
Craig R. Nichols, MD, Treasurer
Daniel F. Hayes, MD, FASCO, President-Elect
Peter Paul Yu, Past-President
Richard L. Schilsky, Chief Medical Officer

Goal is to improve cancer care and prevention. Members include physicians and health-care professionals in all levels of the practice of oncology.
30M Members
Founded in 1964
Mailing list available for rent

12823 American Society of Clinical Pathologists

33 West Monroe Street
Suite 1600
Chicago, IL 60603

312-541-4999
FAX 312-541-4998
E-Mail: info@ascp.org
Home Page: www.ascp.org

Social Media: *Facebook, Twitter, LinkedIn, Youtube*

William G. Finn, MD, FASCP, President
William E. Schreiber, MD, FASCP, Vice President
Melissa Perry Upton, MD, FASCP, Secretary
Gregory N. Sossaman, MD, FASCP, Treasurer
David N.B. Lewin, MD, FASCP, President Elect

Mission is to provide excellence in education, certification and advocacy on behalf of patients, pathologists and laboratory professionals across the globe.
100M+ Members

12824 American Society of Colon and Rectal Surgeons

85 West Algonquin Road
Suite 550
Arlington Heights, IL 60005

847-290-9184
800-791-0001
FAX 847-290-9203
E-Mail: ascrs@fascrs.org
Home Page: www.fascrs.org
Social Media: *Facebook, Twitter, LinkedIn*

Charles Littlejohn, MD, President
Patricia L. Roberts, MD, President-Elect
Terry C. Hicks, MD, Past President
Guy R. Orangio, MD, Vice President
Neil H. Hyman, MD, Treasurer

The premier society for colon and rectal surgeons and other surgeons dedicated to advancing and promoting the science and practice of the treatment of patients with diseases and disorders affecting the colon, rectum and anus.
3,300 Members
Founded in 1899

12825 American Society of Cytopathology

100 West 10th Street
Suite 605
Wilmington, DE 19801-6604

302-543-6583
FAX 302-543-6597
E-Mail: asc@cytopathology.org
Home Page: www.cytopathology.org
Social Media: *Facebook, Twitter, LinkedIn, YouTube*

Michael R. Henry, MD, President
Eva M. Wojcik, MD, MIAC, President Elect
Edmund S. Cibas, MD, Vice President
Daniel F. I. Kurtycz, MD, Treasurer
Elizabeth Jenkins, Executive Director

A professional organization dedicated to the science and study of cells. Membership includes physicians, cytotechnologists and scientists who practice the cytologic method of diagnostic pathology. Committed to education, research, and advocacy on behalf of its membership, with the ultimate goal of improving the standards and quality of patient care.
3,000 Members
Founded in 1951

12826 American Society of ExtraCorporeal Technology

2209 Dickens Road
Richmond, VA 23230-2005

804-565-6363
FAX 804-282-0090
E-Mail: stewart@amsect.org
Home Page: www.amsect.org
Social Media: *Facebook, Twitter, LinkedIn, YouTube*

Jeffrey B. Riley MHPE CCT CCP, President
Kenny Shann CCP, President-Elect
Robert C. Groom MS CCP, Treasurer
Susan J. Englert RN CCP CPBMT, Secretary
Stewart Hinckley, Executive Director

Enhancing the quality of extracorporeal (involving heart and lung machines) technology rendered to the public by engaging in the programmatic activities that will further the knowledge, skills, abilities and general proficiency of practitioners.
2000 Members
Founded in 1964

12827 American Society of Forensic Odontology

4414 82nd Street
Suite 212
Lubbock, TX 79424

Home Page: www.asfo.org
Social Media: *Facebook, Twitter*

Dr. Roger Metcalf, President
Dr. Bruce Schrader, Executive Director
Dr.ÿJacquelineÿ Reid, Secretary
Dr. Eric Wilson, Treasurer
Dr.ÿDavid Senn, President Elect

ASFO is one of the largest organizations representing all of those interested in forensic dentistry worldwide. Mission and goal to encourage and stimulate investigation and research in forensic odontology and related disciplines.
Founded in 1970

12828 American Society of Health-System Pharmacists

7272 Wisconsin Avenue
Bethesda, MD 20814-4861

301-657-3000
866-279-0681
FAX 301-664-8877
E-Mail: custserv@ashp.org
Home Page: connect.ashp.org
Social Media: *Facebook, Twitter, LinkedIn, YouTube, RSS*

John A. Armitstead, President
Philip J. Schneider, Treasurer
Lisa M. Gersema, President-Elect
Paul W. Abramowitz, CEO
Christene M. Jolowsky, Immediate Past President

ASHP is a national professional association that represents pharmacists who practice in hospitals, health maintenance organizations, long-term care facilities, home care, and other compnents of health care systems.
30K Members
Founded in 1936

12829 American Society of Hematology

2021 L Street NW
Suite 900
Washington, DC 20036-3508

202-776-0544
FAX 202-776-0545
E-Mail: ash@hematology.org
Home Page: www.hematology.org
Social Media: *Facebook, Twitter, LinkedIn, Youtube*

David A. Williams, MD, President
Charles S. Abrams, MD, President-Elect
Kenneth C. Anderson, MD, Vice President
Stephanie J. Lee, MD, MPH, Secretary
Susan B. Shurin, MD, Treasurer

Mission is to further the understanding, diagnosis, treatment, and prevention of disorders affecting the blood, bone marrow, and the immunologic, hemostatic and vascular systems, by promoting research, clinical care, education, training, and advocacy in hematology.
15,00 Members
Founded in 1958

12830 American Society of Human Genetics, Inc.

9650 Rockville Pike
Bethesda, MD 20814-3998

301-634-7300
866-HUM-GENE
FAX 301-634-7079
E-Mail: society@ashg.org
Home Page: www.ashg.org
Social Media: *Facebook, Twitter, LinkedIn, YouTube, RSS*

Neil J. Risch, PhD, President
Cynthia C. Morton, PhD, Past President
Harry C. Dietz, MD, President-Elect
Geoffrey M. Duyk, MD PhDÿ, Treasurer
Brendan Lee, MD PhD, Secretary

The primary professional membership organization for human genetics worldwide. Members include researchers, academicians, clinicians, laboratory practice professionals, genetic counselors, nurses and others involved in or with special interest in human genetics.
8000 Members
Founded in 1948

12831 American Society of Nephrology

1510 H Street, NW
Suite 800
Washington, DC 20005

202-640-4660
FAX 202-637-9793
E-Mail: email@asn-online.org
Home Page: www.asn-online.org
Social Media: *Facebook, Twitter, LinkedIn, YouTube, Google+, Flickr, RSS*

Jonathan Himmelfarb, MD, FASN, President
Sharon M. Moe, MD, FASN, Past President
Raymond C. Harris, MD, FASN, President-Elect
John R. Sedor, MD, FASN, Secretary-Treasurer
Tod Ibrahim, Executive Director

Leads the fight against kidney disease by educating health professionals, sharing new knowledge, advancing research, and advocating the highest quality care for patients.

12832 American Society of Neuroradiology

800 Enterprise Dr.
Suite 205
Oak Brook, IL 60523

630-574-0220
FAX 630-574-0661
E-Mail: ltannehill@asnr.org
Home Page: www.asnr.org
Social Media: *RSS*

Laurie A. Loevner, MD, President
Howard A. Rowley, MD, President-Elect
Joshua A. Hirsch, MD, Treasurer
Tina Y. Poussaint, MD, Secretary
James B. Gantenberg, FACHE, Executive Director

Active members must devote approximately one half or more of their professional practice to nueroradiology. Publishes a monthly journal and holds an annual meeting.
3000 Members
Founded in 1962

12833 American Society of Ophthalmic Administrators

4000 Legato Road
Suite 700
Fairfax, VA 22033

703-788-5777
800-451-1339
FAX 703-547-8827
E-Mail: asoa@asoa.org

Home Page: www.asoa.org
Social Media: *Facebook, Twitter*

John S. Bell, MBA, COE, CMPE, President
William T. Koch, COE, COA, CPC, Vice
President
Daniel Chambers, MBA, COE, President-Elect
Sondra Soffman, COE, CPC, Immediate Past
President
Laureen Rowland, CAE, Executive Director

The premier organization for the business side
of the ophalmic practice.
Founded in 1986

12834 American Society of Plastic Surgeons

444 E Algonquin Road
Arlington Heights, IL 60005

847-228-9900
888-475-2784
FAX 847-228-9131
E-Mail: webmaster@plasticsurgery.org
Home Page: www.plasticsurgery.org
Social Media: *Facebook, Twitter, YouTube,
Google+, Instagram, P*

Scot Bradley Glasberg, MD, President
Michael D. Costelloe, JD, Executive Vice
President
Keith M. Hume, Staff Vice President
Carol L. Lazier, Staff Vice President
Mark Espinosa, Staff Vice President

Promotes the specialty of plastic surgery and
supports the highest quality patient care, professionalism and ethical standards through our
role as patient and physician advocates.
Founded in 1931

12835 American Speech-Language-Hearing Association

2200 Research Boulevard
Rockville, MD 20850-3289

301-897-5700
800-638-8255
FAX 301-296-8580
E-Mail: actioncenter@asha.org
Home Page: www.asha.org
Social Media: *Facebook, Twitter, LinkedIn,
YouTube, Instagram, Pinterest*

Patricia A. Prelock, PhD, CCC-SLP, President
Donna Fisher Smiley, PhD, CCC-A, Vice
President for Audiology
Howard Goldstein, PhD, CCC-SL, Vice
President for Science
Carolyn W. Higdon, EdD, CCC-SLP, Vice
President for Finance
Barbara J. Moore, EDD, CCC-SLP, Vice
President for Planning

Represents the interests of medical specialists
in speech, language, and hearing science and
advocates for people with communication-related disorders.
Founded in 1925

12836 American Stroke Association (ASA)

7272 Greenville Ave
Dallas, TX 75231-5129

214-706-1556
888-478-7653
FAX 214-570-5930
Home Page: www.strokeassociation.org
Social Media: *Facebook, Twitter, YouTube,
RSS*

Lee Schwamm, Chairman

The American Stroke Association (ASA) is the
division of the American Heart Association
that's solely focused on reducing disability and
death from stroke through research, education,
fundraising and advocacy. The ASA offers a
wide array of programs, products and services,
from patient education materials to scientific
statements.

12837 American Tinnitus Association

522 SW Fifth Avenue
Suite 825
Portland, OR 97204-2143

503-248-9985
800-634-8978
FAX 503-248-0024
E-Mail: tinnitus@ata.org
Home Page: www.ata.org/
Social Media: *Facebook, Twitter, YouTube*

Melanie F. West, Chair
Scott C. Mitchell, J.D., C.P.A., Vice Chair
Gary P. Reul, Ed.D., Treasurer
David M. Sykes, Secretary
Paul F. Morris, CFRE, Development Director

The American Tinnitus Association (ATA) exists to cure tinnitus through the development of
resources that advance tinnitus research. ATA
board and staff work with researchers, tinnitus
sufferers, donors, legislators and other concerned individuals to support vital tinnitus
research.
Founded in 1971

12838 American Urological Association

1000 Corporate Boulevard
Linthicum, MD 21090-2260

410-689-3700
866-746-4282
FAX 410-689-3800
E-Mail: aua@AUAnet.org
Home Page: www.auanet.org
Social Media: *Facebook, Twitter, LinkedIn,
YouTube*

William F. Gee, MD, FACS, President
Richard K. Babayan, MD, President-Elect
William W. Bohnert, MD, FACS, Immediate
Past President
Manoj Monga, MD, FACS, Secretary
Steven M. Schlossberg, MD, MBA, Treasurer

The premier professional association for the
advancement or urologic patient care, and
works to ensure that its members are current on
the latest research and practices in urology.

12839 Arthroscopy Association of North America

9400 W. Higgins Road
Suite 200
Rosemont, IL 60018

847-292-2262
FAX 847-292-2268
E-Mail: info@aana.org
Home Page: www.aana.org

Jeffrey S. Abrams, MDÿÿ, President
John C. Richmond, MD, First Vice-President
Robert E. Hunter, MDÿÿÿÿÿÿ, Second
Vice-President ÿ
Louis F. McIntyre, MD, Treasurerÿÿÿÿ
Larry D. Field, MD, Secretary

Goal is to promote, encourage, support and foster through continuing medical education functions, the development and dissemination of
knowledge in the discipline of arthroscopic
surgery.

12840 Association for Gerontology in Higher Education

1220 L Street NW
Suite 901
Washington, DC 20005-4018

202-289-9806
FAX 202-289-9824
E-Mail: aghe@aghe.org
Home Page: www.aghe.org
Social Media: *Facebook, Twitter, LinkedIn,
YouTube, Google+*

Donna L. Wagner, President
Christine A. Fruhauf, Treasurer
Lydia Manning, Secretary

Nina M. Silverstein, President-Elect
M Angela Baker, Director

A membership organization devoted primarily
to gerontological education, the Association for
Gerontology in Higher Education (AGHE)
strives to develop and sponsor education and
training initiatives and to involve students, educators, researchers, and officials from across
the country in providing resources for older
adults and for those who serve them.
Founded in 1974

12841 Association for Healthcare Documentation Integrity

4230 Kiernan Avenue
Suite 120
Modesto, CA 95356

209-527-9620
800-982-2182
FAX 209-527-9633
E-Mail: ahdi@ahdionline.org
Home Page: www.ahdionline.org
Social Media: *Facebook, Twitter, LinkedIn,
Pinterest*

Jay Vance, President
Sheila Guston, CHDS, AHDI-F,
President-Elect
Sheryl Williams, CHDS, AHDI-F, Treasurer
Diane Warth, CHDS, RHIT, CPC, Secretary
Susan Dooley, Immediate Past President

AHDI works tirelessly to give thousands of
medical transcriptionists a voice before legislative and regulatory agencies and to ensure MTs
are recognized for their contributions to patient
safety and risk management.
7000 Members
Founded in 1978

12842 Association for Medical Imaging Management

490B Boston Post Rd
Suite 200
Sudbury, MA 01776-3367

978-443-7591
800-334-2472
FAX 978-443-8046
E-Mail: memberservices@ahraonline.org
Home Page: www.ahraonline.org
Social Media: *Facebook, Twitter, LinkedIn,
YouTube*

Ernie Cerdena, CRA, FAHRA, President
Chris Tomlinson, CRA, FAHRA, Finance
Director
Edward J Cronin, Jr., Chief Executive Officer
Kerri Hart-Morris, Associate Editor
Jason Newmark, CRA, FAHRA, President
Elect

Professional association of radiology administrators from the US, Canada and several other
countries. AHRA is a resource and catalyst for
the development of professional leaders in imaging sciences and other health care
disciplines.
5,000 Members
Founded in 1973

12843 Association for Professionals in Infection Control and Epidemiology, Inc.

1275 K St NW
Suite 1000
Washington, DC 20005-4006

202-789-1890
FAX 202-789-1895
E-Mail: info@apic.org
Home Page: www.apic.org
Social Media: *Facebook, Twitter, LinkedIn,
Youtube*

Mary Lou Manning, President
Marc Oliver Wright, MT, MS, Treasurer
Connie Steed, RN, MSN, CICÿ, Secretary

Susan A. Dolan, RN, MS, CICÿ, President-Elect
Katrina Crist, MBA, CEO

Mission is to improve health and patient safety by reducing risks of infection. APIC advances its mission through education, research, collaboration, practice guidance, public policy, and credentialing.
15,00 Members
Founded in 1972

12844 Association for the Advancement of Medical Instrumentation

4301 N. Fairfax Drive
Suite 301
Arlington, VA 22203-1633

703-525-4890
FAX 703-276-0793
E-Mail: customerservice@aami.org
Home Page: www.aami.org
Social Media: *Facebook, Twitter, LinkedIn, Youtube*

Michael Scholla, PhD, Chair
Mary Logan, JD, CAE, President
Eamonn V. Hoxey, PhD BPharm, Treasurer/Secretary
C. Phillip Cogdill, Chair Elect
Ray Laxton, Immediate Past Chair

Mission is to increase the understanding and beneficial use of medical instrumentation through effective standards, educational programs, and publications.
Founded in 1967

12845 Association of Air Medical Services

909 N. Washington Street
Suite 410
Alexandria, VA 22314-3143

703-836-8732
FAX 703-836-8920
E-Mail: information@aams.org
Home Page: www.aams.org/
Social Media: *RSS*

Martin F. Arkus, CMTE, Chair
Dave Evans, EMT-P, CMTE, Vice Chair
Rick Sherlock, President, CEO (ex-officio)
Christopher Hall, BS, FP-C, CMTE, Treasurer
Douglas A.ÿ Garretson, Secretary

Voluntary, nonprofit organization, encourages and supports its members in maintaining a standard of performance reflecting safe operations and efficient, high quality patient care. Built on the idea that representation from a variety of medical transport services and businesses can be brought together to share information, collectively resolve problems and provide leadership in the medical transport community.
Founded in 1980

12846 Association of American Physicians and Surgeons

1601 N Tucson Boulevard
Suite 9
Tucson, AZ 85716-3450

800-635-1196
FAX 520-325-4230
E-Mail: aaps@aapsonline.org
Home Page: www.aapsonline.org
Social Media: *Facebook, Twitter*

Tom Kendall, Sr., M.D., President, Executive Director
David Stumph

AAPS is a nonpartisan professional association of physicians in all types of practices and specialties across the country.
Founded in 1943

12847 Association of Applied Psychophysiology and Biofeedback

10200 West 44th Avenue
Suite 304
Wheat Ridge, CO 80033-2837

303-422-8436
800-477-8892
FAX 303-422-8894
E-Mail: info@aapb.org
Home Page: www.aapb.org
Social Media: *Facebook, Twitter*

Richard Harvey, PhD, President
Thomas Collura, PhD, President-Elect
Stuart C. Donaldson, PhD, Past-President
Fred B. Shaffer, PhD, Treasurer
David Stumph, CAE, AAPB, Executive Director

Goals of the association are to promote a new understanding of biofeedback and advance the methods used in this practice. Mission is to advance the development, dissemination and utilization of knowledge about applied psychophysiology and biofeedback to improve health and the quality of life through research, education and practice.
Founded in 1969

12848 Association of Family Medicine Administration

11400 Tomahawk Creek Parkway
Leawood, KS 66211-2672

800-274-2237
FAX 913-906-6084
E-Mail: cestes@aafp.org
Home Page: www.afmaonline.org/

Star Andrews, C-TAGME, President
Eileen Morroni, C-TAGME, President-Elect
Debbie Blackburn, C-TAGME, Immediate Past President
Gina Silvey, C-TAGME, Co-Treasurer
Bobbi Kruse, AA, Edu. Comm.ÿ-ÿRAD Workshop, Chair

Promotes professionalism in family practice administration. Serves as a network for sharing information and fellowship among members. Provides technical assistance to members, functions as a liaison to related professional organizations.

12849 Association of Family Medicine Residency Directors

11400 Tomahawk Creek Parkway
Suite 670
Leawood, KS 66211-2672

913-906-6000
800-274-2237
FAX 913-906-6105
E-Mail: afmrd@aafp.org
Home Page: www.afmrd.org/i4a/pages/index.cfm?pageid=1

Michael Mazzone, MD, President
Todd D. Shaffer, MD, MBA,ÿ, Immediate Past President
Lisa Maxwell, MD, President Elect
Karen Mitchell, MD, Treasurer
Katy Kirk, MD, MPH, Resident Representative

Inspires and empowers family medicine residency program directors to achieve excellence in family medicine residency training.
410 Members
Founded in 1990

12850 Association of Healthcare Internal Auditors

10200 W 44th Avenue
Suite 304
Wheat Ridge, CO 80033

303-327-7546
888-275-2442
FAX 720-881-6101

E-Mail: info@ahia.org
Home Page: www.ahia.org
Social Media: *LinkedIn, Youtube*

Cavell Alexander, Chair
David Richstone, Vice Chair
Bryon Neaman, CPA, CIA, Secretary/Treasurer
Heidi Crosby, CPA, CIA, CHFP, Immediate Past Chair
David Stumph, Executive Director

Promotes cost containment and increased productivity in health care institutions through internal auditing. Serves as a forum for the exchange of experience, ideas, and information among members, provides continuing professional education courses and informs members of developments in health care internal auditing. Offers employment clearinghouse services.
1000 Members
Founded in 1981

12851 Association of Otolaryngology Administrators

2400 Ardmore Boulevard
Suite 302
Pittsburgh, PA 15221

412-243-5156
FAX 412-243-5160
E-Mail: AOA@oto-online.org
Home Page: www.oto-online.org
Social Media: *Facebook, LinkedIn*

Jo Ann LoForti, President
Jeff Dudley, President-Elect
James Benson, Secretary-Treasurer
Robin L. Wagner, Executive Director

Seeks to promote the concept of professional management in otolaryngology, provide a forum for interaction and exchange of information between otolaryngological managers and present educational programs. Maintains data exchange service for members researching specific topics.
1000 Members
Founded in 1983

12852 Association of Pediatric Hematology/Oncology Nurses

8735 W. Higgins Rd
Ste 300
Chicago, IL 60631

847-375-4724
FAX 847-375-6478
E-Mail: info@aphon.org
Home Page: www.aphon.org

Jami Gattuso, MSN RN CPON, President
Dave Bergeson, PhD CAE, Executive Director
Nicole Wallace, Senior Operations Manager
Jennifer Schap, Education Manager
Stephanie Sayen, Marketing Manager

Members are dedicated to promoting optimal nursing care for children, adolescents, and young adults with cancer and blood disorders, and their families. APHON provides the leadership and expertise to pediatric hematology/oncology nurses by defining and promoting the highest standards of practice and care to the pediatric, adolescent, and young adult communities.
3,000 Members
Founded in 1973

12853 Association of Perioperative Registered Nurses

2170 South Parker Rd
Suite 400
Denver, CO 80231-5711

303-755-6300
800-755-2676
FAX 800-847-0045
E-Mail: custserv@aorn.org
Home Page: www.aorn.org

Social Media: *Facebook, Twitter, LinkedIn, Slideshare, Pinterest, Youtube*

Renae Battie, MN, RN, CNOR, President
Martha Stratton, President-Elect
Nathalie Walker, MBA, RN, CNOR, Secretary
Stephanie S.ÿ Davis, MSHA, RN, CNOR, Treasurer
Callie Craig, VP

A nonprofit membership association that represents the interests of perioperative nurses by providing nursing education, standards, and clinical practice resources.
41,00 Members
Founded in 1954

12854 Case Management Society of America

6301 Ranch Drive
Little Rock, AR 72223

501-225-2229
FAX 501-221-9068
E-Mail: cmsa@cmsa.org
Home Page: www.cmsa.org
Social Media: *Facebook, Twitter, LinkedIn*

Kathy Fraser, President
Rebecca Perez, RN, BSN, CCM, Secretary
Catherine Campbell, RN, MSN, MBA, Treasurer
Cheri A Lattimer, RN, BSN, Executive Director
Mary McLaughlin-Davis, President-Elect

The leading membership association providing professional collaboration across the health care continuum to advocate for patients' wellbeing and improved health outcomes.
Founded in 1990

12855 Catholic Health Association

4455 Woodson Road
St Louis, MO 63134-3797

314-427-2500
FAX 314-427-0029
E-Mail: khewitt@chausa.org
Home Page: www.chausa.org
Social Media: *Facebook, Twitter, LinkedIn, YouTube*

Carol Keehan, DC, President
Adele Gianino, Director, Meetings & Travel
Ana Hilton, Government Relations Coordinator
Betsy Taylor, Associate Editor, Catholic Health
Betty Crosby, Executive Assistant

Led by dedicated women and men, both religious and lay, who combine advanced technology and innovative treatment with caring tradidtion. As provider, employer, and advocate, Catholic health care is committed to improving the health status of communities and creating quality and compassionate health care that works for everyone, especially the vulnerable.
2000+ Members
ISSN: 0882-1577
Founded in 1915

12856 Christopher & Dana Reeve Paralysis Resource Center

636 Morris Turnpike
Suite 3A
Short Hills, NJ 07078-2608

973-467-8270
800-225-0292
FAX 973-912-9433
E-Mail: info@crpf.org
Home Page: www.christopherreeve.org
Social Media: *Facebook, Twitter, LinkedIn, YouTube, Google+, Pinterest, F*

John M. Hughes, Chairman
John E. McConnell, Vice Chairman
Peter T. Wilderotter, President and CEO
Susan Howley, Executive Vice President, Research
Maggie Goldberg, Vice President, Policy and Programs

The Christopher & Dana Reeve Paralysis Resource Center (PRC) promotes the health and well-being of people living with paralysis and their families by providing comprehensive information resources and referral services.
Founded in 2001
Mailing list available for rent

12857 Clinical Laboratory Management Association

330 N. Wabash Avenue
Suite 2000
Chicago, IL 60611

312-321-5111
FAX 610-995-9568
E-Mail: info@clma.org
Home Page: www.clma.org
Social Media: *Facebook, Twitter, LinkedIn, YouTube*

Patty Eschliman, President
Jane Mÿ Hermansen, President Elect
Rodney W Forsman, Treasurer
Paul L. Epner, Past-President
Deborah Wells, Board Member
Founded in 1976

12858 Consumer Healthcare Products Association

1625 Eye Street, NW
Suite 600
Washington, DC 20006-2105

202-429-9260
FAX 202-223-6835
E-Mail: eassey@chpa-info.org
Home Page: www.chpa.org
Social Media: *Twitter, YouTube, Pinterest*

Scott Melville, President and CEO
Brian Green, Vice President, Finance, CFO
John F Gay, Vice President, Government Affairs
Barbara A Kochanowski, Ph.D, Vice President, Regulatory Affairs
Theodore L Peterson, Vice President, Corporate Dev

Promotes industry growth through consumer understanding, appreciation, and acceptance of responsible self-care in America's health care system by developing and sustaining a climate that provides consumers with convenient access to safe and effective nonprescription medicines and other self-care products marketed without undue restrictions.
Founded in 1881

12859 Cremation Association of North America

499 Northgate Parkway
Wheeling, IL 60090-2646

312-245-1077
FAX 312-321-4098
E-Mail: info@cremationassociation.org
Home Page: www.cremationassociation.org
Social Media: *Facebook, Twitter, LinkedIn, Youtube*

Sheri Stahl, President
Michael Sheedy, First Vice President
Mitch Rose, Second Vice Presidentÿ
Timothy R. Borden, President-Elect (Treasurer)
Robert M Boetticher, Jr.ÿ, Past Presidentÿ

An International organization of over 1300 members, composed of cemeterians, cremationists, funeral directors, industry suppliers and consultants. CANA'members believe that cremation is preparation for memorialization.

12860 Dental Group Management Association

North Point Dental Group

2525 E Arizona Biltmore Circle
Suite 127
Phoenix, AZ 85016

602-381-8980
FAX 602-381-1093
Home Page: www.dgma.org

Vincent Cardillo, President
Jill Nesbtt, Vice President

The DGMA is a national organization which recognizes the importance of professional management in group dental practices. The purpose of the Association is to advance dental group management and practice administration.
200 Members
Founded in 1951

12861 Digital Phenom

700 Princess Street
Suite 2M
Alexandria, VA 22314

202-393-0000
800-432-3247
FAX 202-737-8406
E-Mail: staff@digitalphenom.com
Home Page: www.digitalphenom.com

Atilla Kocsis, President
Ismaila Togola, Sr. Developer - Content Management
James Patterson, Project Management
Siaka Togola, Junior Dev. -ÿContent Management

A non-profit educational foundation with a membership of companies engaged in the manufacture, preparation, compounding or processing of aspirin and aspirin products. AFA serves as a central source of information on the health benefits of aspirin and aspirin products, when used as directed.
Founded in 1995

12862 Emergency Nurses Association

915 Lee Street
Des Plaines, IL 60016-6569

847-460-4100
800-900-9659
FAX 847-698-9406
E-Mail: membership@ena.org
Home Page: www.ena.org
Social Media: *Facebook, Twitter, Google Plus*

JoAnn Lazarus, MSN, RN, CEN, President
Susan M. Hohenhaus, LPD,ÿRN, CE, Executive Director
Matthew F Powers, MS, BSN, RN, M, Secretary/Treasurer
Deena Brecher, ÿMSN, RN, APRN, President-Elect
Founded in 1968

12863 Federation of American Health Systems

750 9th Street, NW
Suite 600
Washington, DC 20001-4524

202-624-1500
FAX 202-737-6462
E-Mail: info@fah.org
Home Page: www.fah.org
Social Media: *Facebook, Twitter, LinkedIn, RSS*

Chip Kahn, President and CEO
Keith Pitts, Vice Chairman
Matthew D. Klein, Treasurer
William F. Carpenter III, Secretary
Michael D. Bromberg, Vice Chair of the Board
Founded in 1966

12864 Gerontological Society of America
1220 L Street NW
Suite 901
Washington, DC 20005

202-842-1275
FAX 202-842-1150
E-Mail: geron@geron.org
Home Page: www.geron.org
Social Media: *Facebook, Twitter, LinkedIn, YouTube, Google+*

Rita Effros, President
Nancy Morrow, President Elect
Rosemary Blieszner, Past President
Suzanne Kunkel, Treasurer
Tamara Baker, Secretary
800+ Members
Founded in 1945

12865 Health Industry Distributors Association
310 Montgomery Street
Alexandria, VA 22314-1516

703-549-4432
FAX 703-549-6495
E-Mail: rowan@hida.org
Home Page: www.hida.org

Matthew Rowan, President and CEO
Jennifer Gilbertson, Director, Marketing
Ian Fardy, Executive Vice President
Elizabeth Hilla, Sr. Vice President, Education
Linda Rouse O'Neill, Vice President, Government Affairs

The trade association representing medical products distributors. Provides leadership in the healthcare distribution industry.
Founded in 1902

12866 Health Industry Manufacturers Association
1200 G Street NW
Washington, DC 20005-3814

FAX 202-783-8750

Established as the Wholesale Surgical Trade Association. Represents manufacturers of health care technology, including medical devices, diagnostic products, and health care information systems.

12867 Healthcare Compliance Packaging Council
2711 Buford Road
#268
Bon Air, VA 23235-2423

804-338-5778
FAX 888-812-4272
E-Mail: pgmayberry@aol.com
Home Page: www.hcpconline.org
Social Media: *Facebook, LinkedIn*

Peter G Mayberry, Executive Director
Kathleen Hemming, Staff Consultant

Nonprofit trade association promoting the benefits of unit dose blister and strip packaging — especially its ability to be designed in compliance prompting formats that help people take their medications properly.
Founded in 1990

12868 Healthcare Convention & Exhibitors Association
1100 Johnson Ferry Rd.
Suite 300
Atlanta, GA 30342-1733

678-298-1183
FAX 404-836-5595
E-Mail: hcea@kellencompany.com
Home Page: www.hcea.org
Social Media: *Facebook, Twitter, LinkedIn*

Christine Farmer, President
Kyle Wood, Vice President

Sue Huff, Secretary/Treasurer
Don Schmid, MBA, CME/H, President-Elect
Diane Benson, CTSM, Immediate Past President

Trade association of organizations involved in health care exhibiting or providing services to health care conventions, exhibitions and/or meetings.
600 Members
Founded in 1930

12869 Healthcare Distribution Management Association
901 North Glebe Road
Suite 1000
Arlington, VA 22203-1853

703-787-0000
FAX 703-812-5282
Home Page: www.healthcaredistribution.org
Social Media: *Twitter, LinkedIn*

Ted Scherr, Chairman and President/CEO
Jon Giacomin, Vice Chairman & CEO
Peri L Fri, Senior Vice President
Patrick M Kelly, Senior Vice President, Government
Karen J Ribler, Executive Vice President

An organization representing all major constituents of healthcare product distribution management.
Founded in 1876

12870 Healthcare Financial Management Association
3 Westbrook Corporate Center
Suite 600
Westchester, IL 60154-5723

708-531-9600
800-252-4362
FAX 708-531-0032
E-Mail: jfifer@hfma.org
Home Page: www.hfma.org
Social Media: *Facebook, Twitter, LinkedIn, YouTube*

Joseph J Fifer, FHFMA, CPA, CEO & President
Edwin P Czopek, FHFMA, CPA, Executive Vice President & CFO
Susan Brenkus, Vice President, Human Resources
Richard L Gundling, FHFMA, CMA, Vice President, Healthcare
Todd Nelson, Vice President, Education

Brings perspective and clarity to the industry's complex issues for the purpose of preparing our members to succeed. Through our programs, publications and partnerships we enhance the capabilities that strengthen not only individual careers, but also the organizations from which our members come.
34000 Members
Founded in 1946

12871 Healthcare Marketing & Communications Council
1525 Valley Center Parkway
Bethlehem, PA 18017

610-868-8299
FAX 610-868-8387
E-Mail: info@hmc-council.org
Home Page: www.hmc-council.org

Janis Cohen, President/CEO
Gary J Gyss, Founder

Enhancing the professional development of its members by providing continuing education and career development opportunities. The council also works toward a better understanding of the role of marketing, education, and communications in health care.

12872 Home Medical Equipment and Services Association of New England
515 Kempton St
New Bedford, MA 02740-3852

508-993-0700
FAX 508-993-0797
E-Mail: info@homesne.org
Home Page: www.homesne.org

Karyn Estrella, Executive Director
Brian Simonds, President
Jim Greatorex, VP
Rebecca Godley, Secretary
Paula Finamore, Treasurer

Works together supporting the common goals and interests of the home medical equipment, respiratory, and rehab/assistive techology and home infusion therapy industry.
15 Members
Founded in 1988

12873 Infectious Diseases Society of America
1300 Wilson Blvd.
Suite 300
Arlington, VA 22209

703-299-0200
FAX 703-299-0204
Home Page: www.idsociety.org
Social Media: *Facebook, Twitter, Flickr*

Johan S. Bakken, President

The IDSA represents health care professionals specializing in infectious diseases.

12874 Infusion Nurses Society
315 Norwood Park South
Norwood, MA 02062-4694

781-440-9408
800-694-0298
FAX 781-440-9409
E-Mail: ins@ins1.org
Home Page: www.ins1.org
Social Media: *Facebook, Twitter, LinkedIn, Youtube*

Cheryl Dumont, PhD, RN, CRNI, President
Mary Alexander, MA, RN, Chief Executive Officer
Christopher Hunt, Executive Vice President
Lisa Bruce, BSN, RN, CRNI, Secretary/Treasurer
Richelle Hamblin, MSN, RN, CRNI, President-Elect

The INS is committed to bringing innovative new resources and opportunities to a wide range of healthcare professionals who are involved with the specialty practice of infusion therapy.
6000 Members
Founded in 1973

12875 International Anesthesia Research Society
44 Montgomery Street
Suite 1605
San Francisco, CA 94104-4703

415-296-6900
FAX 415-296-6901
E-Mail: info@iars.org
Home Page: www.iars.org

Alex Evers, MD, Chair
Thomas A Cooper, Executive Director
Davy C H Cheng, MD, Treasurer
Makoto Ozaki, MD, PhD, Secretary
Laura J Kuhar, Education Director
Founded in 1922

12876 International Association For Healthcare Security & Safety
PO Box 5038
Glendale Heights, IL 60139

630-529-3913
888-353-0990

FAX 630-529-4139
E-Mail: info@iahss.org
Home Page: www.iahss.org
Social Media: *Facebook, Twitter, LinkedIn*

David LaRose, CHPA, CPP, President
Dana Frentz,ÿCHPA,
Vice-President/Treasurerÿ
Ben Scaglione, CHPA, CPP,
Vice-President/Secretaryÿ
Jeff A. Young, CHPA, CPP, President-Electÿ
Colleen Kucera, Executive Director

The International Association for Healthcare
Security and Safety, (IAHSS) is an organization dedicated to professionals involved in
managing and directing security and safety programs in healthcare institutions. Its members
have joined together to develop educational
and credentialing programs and create a body
of knowledge that meets the needs of today's
fast paced and ever changing environment.
2000 Members
Founded in 1968

12877 International Association for Worksite Health Promotion

401 West Michigan Street
Indianapolis, IN 46202

317-637-9200
E-Mail: iawhp@acsm.org
Home Page: www.acsm-iawhp.org/
Social Media: *Facebook, LinkedIn*

George Pfeiffer, MSE, President
Stephen Cherniak, MS, MBA,
Secretary/Treasurer
Charlie Estey, MS, President Elect
Wolf Kirsten, MSÿ, Past President
Kristine Holbrook, MEd, Board of Director

Mission is to advance the global community of
worksite health promotion practitioners
through high-quality information, services, educational activities, personal and professional
development and networking opportunities.

12878 International Association of Healthcare Central Service Material Management

213 W Institute Place
Suite 307
Chicago, IL 60610-3195

312-440-0078
800-962-8274
FAX 312-440-9474
E-Mail: mailbox@iahcsmm.com
Home Page: www.iahcsmm.com

Sharon Greene-Golden, CRCST,, President
Susan Adams, Executive Director
Marilyn T Conde, CRCST, MAOM, FC,
Secretary/Treasurer
Nick Baker, Certification Manager
Elizabeth Berrios, Member Services
Coordinatorÿ

Membership consists of persons serving in a
technical, supervisory or management capacity
in hospital central service departments responsible for the sterilization management and
distribution of supplies.
9000 Members
Founded in 1958
Mailing list available for rent: 13000 names

12879 International Bone and Mineral Society

330 N Wabash
Suite 1900
Chicago, IL 60611

312-321-5113
FAX 312-673-6934
E-Mail: info@ibmsonline.org

Home Page: www.ibmsonline.org
Social Media: *Twitter*

John Eisman, President
Theresa Guise, Immediate Past President
Anna Teti, Vice Presidentÿ
Richard Eastell, Treasurer Secretary
David Schmahl, Executive Director
3600 Members
Founded in 1960

12880 International Oxygen Manufacturers Association

1025 Thomas Jefferson Street, NW
Suite 500 East
Washington, DC 20007

202-521-9300
FAX 202-833-3636
E-Mail: ioma@iomaweb.org
Home Page: www.iomaweb.org

The International Oxygen Manufacturers Association is the truly worldwide trade association
of companies in the industrial and medical gas
business
190 Members
Founded in 1943

12881 International Sleep Products Association

501 Wythe Street
Alexandria, VA 22314-1917

703-683-8371
FAX 703-683-4503
E-Mail: info@sleepproducts.org
Home Page: www.sleepproducts.org
Social Media: *Facebook, Twitter, LinkedIn,
Youtube, Flickr, Google Plus,*

Debi Sutton, VP, Marketing & Member
Services

Maintains a strong organization to influence
government actions, inform and educate the
membership and act on industry issues to enhance the growth, profitability and stature of
the sleep products industry. Provides members
with information and services to manage their
business more effectively and efficiently. Publishes a magazine devoted exclusively to the
mattress industry, BEDtimes covers a broad
range of issue and news important to the industry.
Cost: $65.00
650 Members
Frequency: Monthly
Circulation: 3,500
Founded in 1915

12882 International Society for Quality-of-Life Studies

2056 Pamplin
Virginia Tech
Blacksburg, VA 24061-0236

540-231-5110
FAX 540-231-3076
E-Mail: sirgy@vt.edu
Home Page: www.isqols.org
Social Media: *RSS*

Rhonda Phillips, President
Mariano Rojas, President Elect
Denis Huschka, Executive Director/Treasurer
Peter Krause, VP-Programs
Don Rahtz, VP-Publications

Was founded to stimulate interdisciplinary research in quality-of-life studies and closer cooperation among scholars. Members are
academic and government social/behavioral
science researchers drawn from such fields as
marketing, management, applied psychology,
applies sociology, political science, economics,
public administration, educational administration family/child development lei-

sure/recreation studies and technology
development.
Founded in 1995

12883 Interstate Postgraduate Medical Association

PO Box 5474
Madison, WI 53705

608-231-9045
866-446-3424
FAX 877-292-4489
E-Mail: cmehelp@ipmameded.org
Home Page: www.ipmameded.org
Social Media: *Facebook*

Carolyn C. Lopez, MD, Board Chair
Robert A.ÿ Lee, MD, Vice Chair
William E.ÿ Kobler, MD, Board Treasurer
Don Klitgaard, MD, Board of Trustee
Rodney A. Erickson, MD, Board of Trustee

Dedicated to sponsoring clinically relevant education for primary care clinicians.
Founded in 1916

12884 Leading Age

2519 Connecticut Avenue NW
Washington, DC 20008-1520

202-783-2242
FAX 202-783-2255
E-Mail: info@leadingage.org
Home Page: www.leadingage.org
Social Media: *Facebook, Twitter, LinkedIn,
Google+, RSS*

William L. Minnix, Jr., President & CEO
Katrinka Smith Sloan, COO & Sr. Vice
President
Robyn I. Stone, Senior Vice President of
Research
Cheryl Phillips, Senior Vice President
Majd Alwan, Senior Vice President of
Technology

Focused on advocacy, leadership development,
and applied research and promotion of effective
services, home health, hospice, community services, senior housing, assisted living resi-
dences, continuing care communities, nursing
homes, as well as technology solutions, to seniors, children, and others with special needs.
6M Members
Founded in 1961

12885 Leukemia & Lymphoma Society

1311 Mamaroneck Ave.
Suite 310
White Plains, NY 10605

914-949-5213
FAX 914-949-6691
Home Page: www.lls.org
Social Media: *Facebook, Twitter, LinkedIn,
Instagram, Pinterest, YouTube*

Louis J. DeGennaro, President & CEO
Rosemarie Loffredo, CAO & CFO
Mark Roithmayr, Chief Development Officer

Volunteer organization dedicated to funding
blood cancer research and ensuring access to
treatment.
Founded in 1949

12886 Medical Group Management Association

104 Inverness Terrace East
Englewood, CO 80112-5306

303-799-1111
877-275-6462
FAX 303-643-9599
E-Mail: support@mgma.org
Home Page: www.mgma.com
Social Media: *Facebook, Twitter, LinkedIn,
Google+*

William Jessee, CEO
Nicholas H Kupferle, Board Chair
Jyl D Bradley, Chair

Warren C White Jr, Chair
Nicholas H Kupferle III, Chair

The mission of the MGMA is to continually improve the performance of medical group practice professionals and the organizations they represent.
19000 Members
Founded in 1926

12887 Medical Library Association

65 East Wacker Place
Suite 1900
Chicago, IL 60601-7246

312-419-9094
FAX 312-419-8950
E-Mail: info@mlahq.org
Home Page: www.mlanet.org
Social Media: *Facebook, Twitter, LinkedIn, Youtube*

Michelle Kraft, AHIP, President
Kevin Baliozian, Executive Director
Teresa L.ÿ Knott, AHIP, President-Elect
Linda Walton, AHIP, Immediate Past President
Chris Shaffer, AHIP, Treasurer

A nonprofit, educational organization that is a leading advocate for health sciences information professionals worldwide. Through it's programs and services, we provide lifelong educational opportunities, supports a knowledgebase of health information research and works with a global network of partners to promote the importance of quality information for improved health to the health care community and the public.
4500 Members
Founded in 1898
Mailing list available for rent

12888 Medical Marketing Association

10293 N Meridian Street
Suite 175
Indianapolis, IN 46290

317-816-1640
FAX 317-816-1633
Home Page:
www.medicalmarketingassociation.org/
Social Media: *Facebook, Twitter, Google+, RSS*

Michael L Boner, President
Steve Hamburger, Treasurer
Stewart Marsden, Secretary

Builds diagnostic industry leadership by providing market education, professional development and a forum for fellowship and the exchange of ideas.

12889 National Association Medical Staff Services

2025 M Street NW
Suite 800
Washington, DC 20036-2422

202-367-1196
FAX 202-367-2196
E-Mail: info@namss.org
Home Page: www.namss.org
Social Media: *Facebook, LinkedIn, YouTube, Flickr, RSS*

Sharon Kimbrough, CPCS, CPMSM, President
Lynn Boyd, Executive Director
Tiffany Boykin, Operations Manager
Andrew Miller, Member Services Coordinator
Chris Murphy Peck, Education & Learning Services

NAMSS' vision is to advance a healthcare environment that maximizes the patient experience through the delivery of quality services.
4000 Members
Founded in 1978

12890 National Association for Healthcare Recruitment

18000 W. 105th St.
Suite 103
Olathe, KS 66061-7543

913-895-4627
FAX 913-895-4652
E-Mail: nahcr@goAMP.com
Home Page: www.nahcr.com
Social Media: *Facebook, Twitter, LinkedIn, Blogger, youtube*

Jude Hill, President
Sheilaÿ O'Neal, Executive Director
Christie Ross, CAE, Education Director
Candice Miller, Administrative Assistant
Debbie Jennings, Meeting Planner

Individuals employed directly by hospitals and other health care organizations which are involved in the practice of professional health care recruitment. Promotes sound principles of professionals health care recruitment. Provides financial assistance to aid members in planning and implementing regional educational programs. Offers technical assistance and consultation services. Compiles statistics.
800 Members
Founded in 1975

12891 National Association for Home Care and Hospice

228 Seventh Street, SE
Washington, DC 20003-4306

202-547-7424
FAX 202-547-3540
E-Mail: ads@nahc.org
Home Page: www.nahc.org
Social Media: *Facebook, Twitter, Pinterest*

Denise Schrader, Chairman
Lucy Andrews, Vice Chair
Val J. Halamandaris, President
Walter W. Borginis, Treasurer
Karen Marshall Thompson, Secretary

12892 National Association for Medical Direction of Repiratory Care (NAMDRC)

8618 Westwood Center Drive
Suite 210
Vienna, VA 22182-2222

703-752-4359
FAX 703-752-4360
E-Mail: ExecOffice@namdrc.org
Home Page: www.namdrc.org

Timothy A. Morris, MD, President
Phillip Porte, Executive Director
Vickie Parshall, Director Member Services
Charles W. Atwood, MD, President-Elect
Karen Lui, RN, Associate Executive Director

The National Association for Medical Direction of Respiratory Care, our mission is to improve access to quality care for patients with respiratory disease by removing regulatory and legislative barriers to appropriate treatment. It advises on coding issues and federal reimbursement policies; provides economic and regulatory updates; and offers unique educational opportunities.
700 Members
Founded in 1977

12893 National Association of County & City Health Officials

1100 17th Street NW
Seventh Floor
Washington, DC 20036-4619

202-783-5550
FAX 202-783-1583
E-Mail: info@naccho.org

Home Page: www.naccho.org
Social Media: *Facebook, Twitter*

Paul Yeghiayan, President, NACCHO Foundation
Mark Jorritsma, COO
John Mericsko, Chief Financial Officer
LaMar Hasbrouck, Executive Director
William Barnes, Chief Program Officer

Administrators of freestanding and hospital-based long-term care facilities owned and operated by county governments or city-county consolidations; elected local officials. Promotes interests of county long-term care facilities; offers guidance in relevant legislative and regulatory areas. Provides technical assistance; conducts training workshops. Compiles statistics on public policy changes, such as changes in the Medicaid program, which affect long-term care facilities.
250 Members
Founded in 1977

12894 National Association of School Nurses

1100 Wayne Avenue
Suite 925
Silver Spring, MD 20910

240-821-1130
866-627-6767
FAX 301-585-1791
E-Mail: nasn@nasn.org
Home Page: www.nasn.org

Beth Mattey, MSN, RN, NCSN, President
Susan Zacharski, Vice President
Donna J. Mazyck, RN, MS, NCSN, Executive Director
Catherine Davis, BSN, RN, NCSN, Secretary/Treasurer
Nina Fekaris, President Elect
15500 Members
Founded in 1968

12895 National Athletic Trainers Association

1620 Valwood Parkway
Suite 115
Carrollton, TX 75006

214-637-6282
860-437-5700
FAX 214-637-2206
E-Mail: webmaster@nata.org
Home Page: www.nata.org

Scott Sailor, EdD, ATC, President
MaryBeth Horodyski, Vice President
Kathy Dieringer, Secretary/Treasurer
Dave Saddler, Executive Director
Rachael Oats, Associate Executive Director
35,00 Members
Founded in 1950

12896 National Cancer Institute

9609 Medical Center Drive
Bethesda, MD 20892-9760

800-422-6237
E-Mail: cancergovstaff@mail.nih.gov
Home Page: www.cancer.gov
Social Media: *Facebook, Twitter, LinkedIn, Google+, YouTube, Instagram, R*

Douglas R. Lowy, M.D., Acting Director
Lynn Austin, PhD, Deputy Director for Management
Jeffrey S. Abrams, MD, Acting Director, Clinical Research
Stephen J. Chanock, MD, Director
Peter Greenwald, MD, Associate Director, Prevention

Conducts and supports research, training, health information dissemination and other programs with respect to the cause, diagnosis, prevention and treatment of cancer, rehabilitation from cancer and the continuing care of cancer patients.

12897 National Council for Behavioral Health

1701 K Street NW
Suite 400
Washington, DC 20005

202-684-7457
FAX 202-386-9391
E-Mail:
communications@thenationalcouncil.org
Home Page: www.TheNationalCouncil.org
Social Media: *Facebook, Twitter, LinkedIn,*
YouTube, Pinterest, Google+

Susan Blue, Chair
Donald Miskowiec, Vice Chair
Jeff Richardson, Second Vice Chair
Linda Rosenberg, President & CEO
Jeannie Campbell, Executive Vice President
and COO

Advocates for public policies in mental and behavioral health that ensure that people who are
ill can access comprehensive healthcare
services.
2,500 Members

12898 National Council on the Aging

251 18th Street South
Suite 500
Arlington, VA 22202

571-527-3900
FAX 202-479-0735
E-Mail: info@ncoa.org
Home Page: www.ncoa.org
Social Media: *Facebook, Twitter, LinkedIn,*
Youtube, RSS

Carol Zernial, Chair
James Firman, EdD, President and CEO
Richard Browdie, Immediate Past-Chair
Donna Whitt, SVP, CFO
Wendy Zecker, SVP, Public/Private Programs
Founded in 1950

**12899 National Environmental Health
Association**

720 S Colorado Blvd
Suite 1000-N
Denver, CO 80246-1926

303-756-9090
866-956-2258
FAX 303-691-9490
E-Mail: staff@neha.org
Home Page: www.neha.org
Social Media: *Facebook, Twitter, LinkedIn*

Bob Custard REHS, CP-FS, President
David Riggs, President Elect
Adam London MPA, RS, First VP
Vince Radke, 2nd VP
David T. Dyjack Dr.PH, CIH, Executive
Director

NEHA offers a variety of programs that are all
in keeping with the association's mission which
is as relevant today as it was when the organization was founded. The mission of NEHA is
to advance the environmental health and protection professional for the purpose of providing a healthful environment for all.
5000 Members
Founded in 1937

**12900 National Managed Health Care
Congress**

71 2nd Avenue
3rd Floor
Waltham, MA 02154

888-882-2500
FAX 941-365-0157
Home Page: www.nmhcc.org

12901 National Medical Association

8403 Colesville Road
Suite 820
Silver Spring, MD 20910

202-347-1895
800-257-8290
FAX 202-347-0722
E-Mail: cme@nmanet.org
Home Page: www.nmanet.org
Social Media: *Facebook, Twitter, LinkedIn,*
YouTube

Garfield Clunie, M.D, Chair of the Board
Edith P. Mitchell, M.D., President
Lawrence Sanders, Immediate Past President
Richard Allen Williams, M.D., President-Elect
Traci C. Burgess, M.D., M.P.H., Secretary

The mission of the NMA is to advance the art
and science of medicine for people of African
descent through education, advocacy, and
health policy to promote health and wellness,
eliminate health disparities, and sustain
physician viability.
Founded in 1895

**12902 National Renal Administrators
Association**

100 North 20th Street
Suite 400
Philadelphia, PA 19103-1462

215-320-4655
FAX 215-564-2175
E-Mail: nraa@nraa.org
Home Page: www.nraa.org/index.php
Social Media: *Facebook, Twitter, LinkedIn*

Helen Currier, President
Karen Kelley, MHA, BSN, CNN,
President-Elect
Anthony Messana, Secretary
Rob Bomstad, ÿRN, BSBA, MS, Treasurer
Deb Cote, Past-President

Administrative personnel involved with dialysis programs for patients suffering from kidney
failure. Provides a vehicle for the development
of educational and informational services for
members. Maintains contact with health care
facilities and government agencies. Operates
placement serve; compiles statistics; conducts
political action committee.
475 Members
Founded in 1977

12903 National Rural Health Association

4501 College Blvd
#225
Leawood, KS 66211-1921

816-756-3140
FAX 816-756-3144
E-Mail: mail@NRHArural.org
Home Page: www.ruralhealthweb.org
Social Media: *Facebook, Twitter, LinkedIn*

Jodi Schmidt, President
Lisa Kilaweeÿ, President-Elect
Dave Pearson, Treasurer
Tommy Barnhart, Secretary
Raymond G. hristensen, MD, Past-President

A national membership organization, whose
mission is to improve the health care of rural
Americans and to provide leadership on rural
issues through advocacy, communications, education and research.
20,00 Members

**12904 National Society Of Certified
Healthcare Business Consultants**

12100 Sunset Hills Road
Suite 130
Reston, VA 20190-3233

703-234-4099
FAX 703-435-4390
E-Mail: info@nschbc.org
Home Page: www.nschbc.org

Social Media: *Facebook, Twitter, LinkedIn,*
Pinterst, Youtube

H. Christoperÿ Zaenger, CHBC, President
Michael J. Dejno, CHBC, CPA, President-Elect
Robert C. Scroggins, Secretary/Treasurer
Reed Tinsley, Immediate Past-President
Carol Wynne, Executive Director

Maintains code of ethics, rules of professional
conducts, and certification program; administers exams and conduct certification course.
Membership by successful completion of certification examination only.
350 Members
Founded in 1975

12905 National Society for Histotechnology

8850 Stanford Boulevard
Suite 2900
Columbia, MD 21045

443-535-4060
FAX 443-535-4055
E-Mail: histo@nsh.org
Home Page: www.nsh.org
Social Media: *Facebook, Twitter, LinkedIn*

Elizabeth Sheppard, President
Sharon Kneebone, Executive Director
Jerry Santiago, Vice President
Diane Sterchi, Secretary
Monty Hyten, Treasurer

A non-profit organization, committed to the
advacement of histotechnology, its practitioners
and quality standards of practice through leadership, education and advocacy.
Founded in 1974

**12906 National Strength and Conditioning
Association**

1885 Bob Johnson Drive
Colorado Spring, CO 80906-4000

719-632-6722
800-815-6826
FAX 719-632-6367
E-Mail: nsca@nsca.com
Home Page: www.nsca.com/Home/

G. Gregory Haff, President
Colin Wilborn, PhD, ATC, VP
Joel T. Cramer, PhD, CSCS, Treasurer
Lee Madden, Sr. Director of Admin. Services
Wayde Rivinius, Sr. Director of Technology

Develops and presents the most advanced information regarding strength training and conditioning practices, injury prevention, and
research findings.
30000 Members
Founded in 1978

12907 Northwest Urological Society

914 164th St. SE
Suite 145
Mill Creek, WA 98012

866-800-3118
FAX 800-808-4749
E-Mail: support@nwurologicalsociety.org
Home Page: www.nwurologicalsociety.org/

William Ellis, MD, President
John Corman, MD, VP
Stan Myers, MD, VP
John Corman, MD, Secretary-Treasurer
Michael Conlin, MD, Immediate Past President

12908 OMA: Optical Industry Association

6055A Arlington Boulevard
Falls Church, VA 22044-2721

703-237-8433
FAX 703-237-0643

Members are makers and importers of spectacle
frames, and related products.
57 Members
Founded in 1916

12909 Optical Society of America
2010 Massachusetts Ave, NW
Washington, DC 20036-1023

202-223-8130
FAX 202-223-1096
E-Mail: info@osa.org
Home Page: www.osa.org
Social Media: *Facebook, Twitter, LinkedIn, YouTube, Blog*

Philip Russell, President
Elizabeth A. Rogan, Chief Executive Officer
Sean Bagshaw, COO, Chief Information Officer
Melissa Russell, Chief Industry Relations Officer
Tracy Schario, Chief External Relations Officer

OSA was organized to increase and diffuse the knowledge of optics, pure and applied; to promote the common interests of investigators of optical problems, of designers and of users of optical apparatus of all kinds; and to encourage cooperation among them.
Founded in 1916

12910 Orthopedic Surgical Manufacturers Association
BioMet
7302 Texas Heights Ave
Kalamazoo, MI 49009

269-303-3831
FAX 574-372-1790
E-Mail: secretary@osma.net
Home Page: www.osma.net/

Sharon Starowicz, President
Lynnette Jackson, Vice President
Lori Burns, Secretary
Ed Chin, Treasurer
Susan Krasny, Past President

Members are manufacturers of orthopedic surgical items. Sponsors research, information and ethics programs.
25 Members
Founded in 1954

12911 Pacific Dermatological Association
575 Market Street
Suite 2125
San Francisco, CA 94105

415-927-5729
888-388-8815
FAX 415-764-4915
E-Mail: pda@hp-assoc.org
Home Page: www.pacificderm.org

Janellen Smith, MD, President
Tina Suneja, MD, President Elect
Keith Duffy, MD, Vice President
Hege Grande Sarpa, MD, Secretary-Treasurer
Catherine Ramsay, MD, Immediate Past President

Provides opportunities for exchange of information and advancement of knowledge of dermatology among physicians within the membership area. Exclusively for education, scientific and charitable purposes.
Founded in 1948

12912 Pacific Northwest Radiological Society
2001 6th Ave
Ste 2700
Seattle, WA 98121

206-956-3650
800-552-0612
FAX 206-441-5863
E-Mail: lmk@wsma.org
Home Page: www.pnwrs.org

Tess Chapman, MD, President
Greg Kicska, MD, First Vice President
Debra Alderman, Association Director

12913 Professional Association of Health Care Office Management
1576 Bella Cruz Drive
Suite 360
Lady Lake, FL 32159

847-375-4717
800-451-9311
FAX 407-386-7006
E-Mail: info@pahcom.com
Home Page: www.pahcom.com
Social Media: *Facebook, Twitter, LinkedIn, Youtube*

Richard Blanchette, MS, Founder
Daniel Labelle, CISSP CEH, Chief Technology Officer
Karen Blanchette, MBA, Association Director
Darlene Born, CMM, HITCM-PP, Business Development
Aaron Miller, Web Developer

A national organization dedicated to promoting professionalism in physician office practice by providing professional development opportunities, continuing education in health care office management principles and practice, and certification for health care office managers.
Founded in 1988

12914 Radiological Society of North America
820 Jorie Blvd
Oak Brook, IL 60523-2251

630-571-2670
800-381-6660
FAX 630-571-7837
Home Page: www.rsna.org
Social Media: *Facebook, Twitter, LinkedIn, Flickr, Youtube*

Richard L. Ehman, MD, Chairman
Ronald L. Arenson, MD, President
Richard L.ÿ Baron, MD, President-Elect/Secretary-Treasurer
William P. Dillon, MD, First Vice-President
William G. Bradley Jr, MD, PhD, Second Vice-President

The mission is to promote and develop the highest standards of radiology and related sciences through education and research. The society seeks to provide radiologists and allied health scientists with educational programs and materials of the highest quality and to constantly improve the content and value of these educational activities.
54,00 Members

12915 Radiology Business Management Association
10300 Eaton Place
Suite 460
Fairfax, VA 22030

703-621-3355
888-224-7262
FAX 703-621-3356
E-Mail: info@rbma.org
Home Page: www.rbma.org
Social Media: *Facebook, Twitter, LinkedIn*

Suzanne Taylor, BS, FRMBA, President
Keith E. Chew, MHA, CMPEÿÿ, Immediate Past President
Jim Hamilton, President Elect
Thomas C. Dickerson, Treasurer, MidWestern Director
Michael R.ÿ Mabry, Executive Director

The only radiology-specific business organization in existence today. Dedicated to providing managers with information, resources, educatio

and networking to run a successful radiology business.
2200 Members
Founded in 1968

12916 Sisters Network: National Headquarters
2922 Rosedale Street
Houston, TX 77004

713-781-0255
866-781-1808
FAX 713-780-8998
E-Mail: infonet@sistersnetworkinc.org
Home Page: www.sistersnetworkinc.org
Social Media: *Facebook, Twitter, Youtube*

Karen Eubanks Jackson, Founder & CEO
Bettie Eubanks, Vice Chair
Dr John Green, Treasurer
Erie E. Calloway, Executive Director
Monica Jones, Administrative Assistant

Committed to increasing local and national attention to the devastating impact that breast cancer has in the African American community.
3000 Members
Founded in 1994

12917 Society for Healthcare Strategy and Market Development
155 North Wacker Drive
Chicago, IL 60606-3421

312-422-3888
FAX 312-278-0883
E-Mail: shsmd@aha.org
Home Page: www.shsmd.org/
Social Media: *Facebook, Twitter, LinkedIn*

Christine Gallery, President
Lawrence Margolis, President Elect
Mark Parrington, Immediate Past Presidentÿ
Diane Weber, RN, Executive Director
Lisa Hinkle, Education Manager

The society of choice for thousands of healthcare marketing, public relations, strategic planning, communications and business development professionals.
4,000 Members
Founded in 1996

12918 Society for Imaging Informatics In Medicine
19440 Golf Vista Plaza
Suite 330
Leesburg, VA 20176-8264

703-723-0432
FAX 703-723-0415
E-Mail: info@siim.org
Home Page: www.siim.org
Social Media: *Facebook, Twitter, LinkedIn, Google+, YouTube, Instagram*

David E. Brown, CIIP, Chair
William W Boonn, MD, Secretary
Rasu B. Shrestha, MD, MBA, Treasurer
Paul G. Nagy, PhD, FSIIM, CIIP, Chair-Elect
Anna Marie Mason, MS,CAE, Executive Director

Devoted to advance informatics and information technology in medical imaging through education and research. Provides an open environment for imaging information professionals to access expert and cutting edge resources in a collegial and practical atmosphere.
2200 Members
Founded in 1980

12919 Society of Critical Care Medicine
500 Midway Drive
Mount Prospect, IL 60056-5811

847-827-6869
FAX 847-827-6886
E-Mail: info@sccm.org

Home Page: www.sccm.org
Social Media: *Facebook, Twitter, Google+*

Carol Thompson, President
David Julian Martin, CAE, CEO, EVP
Brian Schramm, CAE, Director Business
Affairs
James Flanigan, CAE, Director, Marketing
Pamela S. Dallstream, CMP, CMM, Director of
Education

Professional organization devoted exclusively
to the advancement of multidisciplinary,
multiprofessional intensive care through excellence in patient care, education, research, and
advocacy.
11000 Members
Founded in 1972

**12920 Society of Medical-Dental
Management**
125 Strafford Avenue
Suite 300
Wayne, PA 19087-3318

800-826-2264
FAX 610-687-7702
E-Mail: patricia01@aol.com
Home Page: www.smdmc.org

Joseph Cobo, President
Richard G Bock, Regional
Director/Coordinator
Rex Stanley, Secretary/Treasurer

Professional medical and/or dental management consultants associated for educational and
information sharing purposes. Objectives are
to: advance the profession; share management
techniques; improve individual skills; provide
clients with competent and capable business
management. Provides information on insurance and income tax. Conducts surveys;
compiles statistics.
60+ Members
Founded in 1968

**12921 Society of NeuroInterventional
Surgery**
3975 Fair Ridge Drive
Suite 200 North
Fairfax, VA 22033

703-691-2272
FAX 703-537-0650
E-Mail: info@snisonline.org
Home Page: www.snisonline.org
Social Media: *Facebook, Twitter*

Donald F. Frei, MD, President
Blaise W. Baxter, MD, Vice President
Charles J. Prestigiacomo, MD, President Elect
Richard P. Klucznik, MD, Treasurer
Adam S. Arthur, MD, Secretary

Formerly the American Society of
Interventional and Therapeutic Neuroradiology,
mission is to promote excellence in patient
care, provide education, support research, influence health care policy, and foster the
growth of the specialty.
3000 Members
Founded in 1992

**12922 Society of Nuclear Medicine &
Molecular Imaging**
1850 Samuel Morse Dr
Reston, VA 20190-5316

703-708-9000
FAX 703-708-9015
E-Mail: volunteer@snmmi.org
Home Page: www.snm.org
Social Media: *Facebook, Twitter, LinkedIn,
Youtube*

Hossein Jadvar, MD,PhD,MPH,MBA,
President
Sally W. Schwarz, MS, RPh, BCNP,
President-Elect
Bennett S. Greenspan, Vice President-Elect

Michael L. Middleton, MD, FACNMÿ,
Secretary/Treasurer
Peter Herscovitch, Immediate Past President

International scientific and professional organization that promotes the science, technology
and practical applications of nuclear medicine.
18,00 Members
Founded in 1954

12923 Southern Medical Association
35 W. Lakeshore Drive
Suite 201
Birmingham, AL 35209-7254

205-945-8903
800-423-4992
FAX 205-945-1840
E-Mail: CustomerService@sma.org
Home Page: www.sma.org
Social Media: *Facebook, Twitter, Youtube*

Mark S. Williams, President
Benjamin M. Carmichael, President-Elect
Ajoy Kumar, President-Electÿ
Stuart J. Goodman, Immediate Past President
William L. Hartsfield FLMI, Executive
Director

Physician's choice for education and support to
enhance practice and performance and career
development.
88 Members
Founded in 1906

**12924 TLPA Annual Convention & Trade
Show**
Taxicab, Limousine & Paratransit
Association
3200 Tower Oaks Boulevard
Suite 220
Rockville, MD 20852

301-984-5700
FAX 301-984-5703
E-Mail: info@tlpa.com
Home Page: www.tlpa.org

James Campolongo, PA, President
Alfred LaGasse, MD, Chief Executive Officer
Carl Ward, KY, Treasurer
Robert McBride, CO, Vice President
Harold Morgan, MD, Secretary

Shares information vital to owners or taxicab,
limousine, airport shuttle, paratransit and
nonemergency medical transportation fleets.
100 supplier exhibits of the newest products
available to the industry.
1000 Attendees
Frequency: Annual
Founded in 1917

**12925 The American Association of Tissue
Banks**
8200 Greensboro Drive
Suite 320
McLean, VA ÿ22102

703-827-9582
FAX 703-356-2198
Home Page: www.aatb.org
Social Media: *Facebook, Twitter, LinkedIn*

Daniel Schultz, MD, Chairman
Frank Wilton, President & Chief Executive
Officer
Louis Barnes III, Chairman-Elect
Kevin Cmunt, Immediate Past Chairman
Diana Buck, Secretary/Treasurer

Transplant trade organization dedicated to ensuring that human tissues intended for transplantation are safe and free of infectious
disease and available in quantities sufficient to
meet national needs.
Founded in 1976

12926 The American Board of Surgery
1617 John F. Kennedy Blvd.
Suite 860
Philadelphia, PA 19103

215-568-4000
FAX 215-563-5718
Home Page: www.absurgery.org
Social Media: *Facebook, Twitter*

Stephen R. T. Evans, Chair
Frank R. Lewis Jr., Executive Director

Independent, nonprofit organization promoting
excellence in surgical practice.
Founded in 1937

**12927 The American Chiropractic
Association**
1701 Clarendon Boulevard
Suite 200
Arlington, VA 22209

703-276-8800
FAX 703-243-2593
E-Mail: memberinfo@acatoday.org
Home Page: www.acatoday.org
Social Media: *Facebook, Twitter, LinkedIn,
RSS, YouTube, Instagram*

John Falardeau, SVP, Public Policy and
Advocacy
Janet Ridgely, Deputy Executive Vice President
Kim Hodes, Senior Director, Finance
Felicity Clancy, SVP, Communications
Dean Millard, Vice President, Information
Systems

Professional organization representing chiro-
practors.

12928 The American Geriatrics Society
40 Fulton St.
New York, NY 10038

212-308-1414
FAX 212-832-8646
E-Mail: info.amger@americangeriatrics.org
Home Page: www.americangeriatrics.org
Social Media: *Facebook, Twitter, LinkedIn,
Instagram, Pinterest*

Nancy E. Lundebjerg, Chief Executive Officer
Steven Counsell, President

AGS is a nonprofit dedicated to improving the
lives of the elderly.
6000 Members

Newsletters

12929 AAB Bulletin
American Association of Bioanalysts
906 Olive Street
Suite 1200
Saint Louis, MO 63101-1448

314-241-1445
FAX 314-241-1449
E-Mail: aab@aab.org
Home Page: www.aab.org

Mark S Biernbaum PhD, Administrator

Newsletter that provides the latest information
on meetings, conferences, legislative and
regulatoryy issues and developments.
Frequency: Quarterly
Founded in 1956

12930 AABB News
American Association of Blood Banks
8101 Glenbrook Rd
Suite 2
Bethesda, MD 20814-2747

301-907-6977
FAX 301-907-6895

E-Mail: aabb@aabb.org
Home Page: www.aabb.org

Karen Lipton, CEO
Frequency: Monthly

12931 AAMI News
Assoc for the Advancement of Medical
Instrumentat
4301 N. Fairfax Drive
Suite 301
Arlington, VA 22203-1633

703-525-4890
FAX 703-276-0793
E-Mail: publications@aami.org
Home Page: www.aami.org

Sean Loughlin, Publications Director
Robert King, Editor

Keeps individuals up-to-date with timely and
relevant infustry news, breaking information
about new standards activities and AAMI benefits, and guidance from experts in the field.
Cost: $160.00
Frequency: Monthly
Circulation: 6000

12932 AAMI News Extra!
Assoc for the Advancement of Medical
Instrumentat
4301 N. Fairfax Drive
Suite 301
Arlington, VA 22203-1633

703-525-4890
FAX 703-276-0793
E-Mail: publications@aami.org
Home Page: www.aami.org

Sean Loughlin, Publications Director

Online newsletter that includes the top stories
of the month; an up-to-date listing of career opportunities in the field; and updates on AAMI's
standards, benefits, and services.
Frequency: Monthly

12933 ACOG Clinical Review
American College of
Obstetricians/Gynecologists
409 12th Street SW
PO Box 96920
Washington, DC 20090-6920

202-638-5577
FAX 202-484-5107
E-Mail: resources@acog.org
Home Page: www.acog.org

Kathleen Harrison, Advertising
Frequency: 6 X

12934 ACOS News
American College of Osteopathic Surgeons
123 N Henry Street
Alexandria, VA 22314-2903

703-684-0416
FAX 703-684-3280
E-Mail: info@facos.org
Home Page: www.facos.org

Guy Beaumont, Executive Director
Judith T Mangum, Director Finance
Frequency: Monthly

12935 ACOS Review
American College of Osteopathic Surgeons
330 E Algonquin Rd
Suite 1
Arlington Hts, IL 60005-4665

847-228-6090
800-323-0794
FAX 847-228-9755
Home Page: www.acofp.org

Peter Schmelzer, Executive Director
Frequency: Monthly

12936 AMGA's Advocacy ENewS
American Medical Group Association
One Prince Street
Alexandria, VA 22314-3318

703-838-0033
FAX 703-548-1890
Home Page: www.amga.org

Don Fisher, CEO
Ryan O'Connor, VP, Membership/Marketing
Timely analysis on the latest issues that affect
medical groups on the federal legislative and
regulatory front.
375 Members

12937 AOA News
American Optometric Association
243 N Lindbergh Blvd
Suite 1
St Louis, MO 63141-7881

314-991-4100
FAX 314-991-4101
E-Mail: info@iacconline.org
Home Page: www.aoa.org

Barry Barresi, Executive Director
Tom Cappucci, First Vice President
Michael Jones, CEO

Official newspaper of the American Optometric
Association
Cost: $93.50
Circulation: 30000
ISSN: 0094-9620
Founded in 1896
*Mailing list available for rent: 22,500 names at
$70 per M*
Printed in 4 colors on glossy stock

12938 Adult Day Services Letter
Health Resources Publishing
1913 Atlantic Ave
Suite 200
Manasquan, NJ 08736-1067

732-292-1100
FAX 732-292-1111
E-Mail: info@healthresourcesonline.com
Home Page: www.healthresourcesonline.com

Robert K Jenkins, Publisher
Brett Powell, Regional Director
Alice Burron, Director

A monthly newsletter that contains management information, reports on trends and new
developments and information about other
adult day care programs across the country.
Cost: $147.00
38574 Pages
Frequency: Monthly
ISSN: 0885-4572
Founded in 1985

12939 BNA's Health Law Reporter
Bureau of National Affairs
1801 S Bell St
Arlington, VA 22202-4501

703-341-3000
800-372-1033
FAX 800-253-0332
E-Mail: customercare@bna.com
Home Page: www.bnabooks.com

Paul N Wojcik, CEO

Of many newsletters from BNA, this contains
information on health care policy, bankruptcy,
antitrust, insurance and state developments,
employment issues as well as a congressional
and a regulatory calendar.
Cost: $1782.00
Frequency: Weekly

12940 Biomedical Market Newsletter
Biomedical Market

3237 Idaho Pl
Costa Mesa, CA 92626-2207

714-434-9500
800-875-8181
FAX 714-434-9755
E-Mail: info@biomedical-market-news.com
Home Page:
www.biomedical-market-news.com

David G Anast, President
Steve Baker, Director of Marketing/Sales
Richard Guiss, Senior Editor
George Anast, CFO

New business development, FDA, regulatory,
financial, and marketing NL on medical equip-
ment, device, diagnostic test and instrument in-
dustries worldwide.
Cost: $199.00
Frequency: Monthly
ISSN: 1064-4180
Founded in 1991
Printed in 4 colors on matte stock

12941 Bulletin on Long-Term Care Law
Health Resources Publishing
1913 Atlantic Ave
Suite 200
Manasquan, NJ 08736-1067

732-292-1100
FAX 732-292-1111
E-Mail: info@healthresourcesonline.com
Home Page: www.healthresourcesonline.com

Robert K Jenkins, Publisher
Lisa Mansfield, Regional Director
Brett Powell, Regional Director
Alice Burron, Director

A newsletter that covers compliance problems,
Medicaid and Medicare overhauls, charges of
abuse, fraud, negligence, needless litigation
and other concerns of those involved in
long-term health care.
Cost: $227.00
Frequency: Monthly
ISSN: 1093-6939
Founded in 1978

12942 Communique
213 W Institute Place
Suite 307
Chicago, IL 60610-3195

312-440-0078
800-962-8274
FAX 312-440-9474
E-Mail: mailbox@iahcsmm.com
Home Page: www.iahcsmm.com

Betty Hanna, Executive Director
Marilyn Corida, Secretary/Treasurer
Lisa Huber, President

Bi-monthly publication separates supervi-
sors/directors from technicians.
Cost: $40.00
Frequency: 6/Annual
Circulation: 15M
ISBN: 1-605309-30-9
Mailing list available for rent: 13000 names

**12943 Diagnostic Testing & Technology
Report**
Institute of Management and Administration
1 Washington Park
Suite 1300
Newark, NJ 07102

212-244-0360
FAX 973-622-0595
Home Page: www.ioma.com

Contains up-to-the minute information and
unique perspectives on where diagnostic testing is headed, covering every innovation, new
product, manufacturer, market and end-user applications.
Cost: $549.00
Frequency: Monthly

12944 Directions: Looking Ahead in Healthcare

Health Resources Publishing
1913 Atlantic Ave
Suite 200
Manasquan, NJ 08736-1067

732-292-1100
888-843-6242
FAX 732-292-1111
E-Mail: info@healthresourcesonline.com
Home Page: www.healthresourcesonline.com

Robert K Jenkins, Publisher
Lisa Mansfield, Marketing Assistant
Carolin Pense, Publisher
Brett Powell, Regional Director
Alice Burron, Director

Provides management news on such topics as alerts, trends, forecasts, profitable innovations, facts and statistics.
Cost: $127.00
Frequency: Monthly
ISSN: 1093-6920
Founded in 1978

12945 Dispatch & Division Newsletters

Taxicab, Limousine & Paratransit Association
3200 Tower Oaks Blvd
Suite 220
Rockville, MD 20852

301-984-5700
FAX 301-984-5703
E-Mail: info@tlpa.org
Home Page: www.tlpa.org

Alfred LaGasse, CEO
Victor Dizengoff, President

Dispatch features articles on industry business issues, provides advice on running a transportation company, and comes with division specific bi-monthly newsletters.
Frequency: Bimonthly
Circulation: 6000

12946 Elderly Health Services Letter

Health Resources Publishing
1913 Atlantic Ave
Suite 200
Manasquan, NJ 08736-1067

732-292-1100
888-843-6242
FAX 732-292-1111
E-Mail: info@themcic.com
Home Page: www.healthresourcesonline.com

Robert K Jenkins, Publisher
Lisa Mansfield, Regional Director
Brett Powell, Regional Director
Alice Burron, Director

A newsletter on projections and trends for health services provided for the elderly. Subjects include inpatient care, long-term care, outpatient, home care, primary care, ambulatory care, day care, health promotion, disease prevention, support groups, health education and residental care.
Cost: $227.00
Frequency: Monthly
ISSN: 0891-9275

12947 Emergency Department Law

Business Publishers
8737 Colesville Road
Suite 1100
Silver Spring, MD 20910-3928

301-876-6300
800-274-6737
FAX 301-589-8493
E-Mail: custserv@bpinews.com
Home Page: www.bpinews.com

Leonard A Eiserer, Publisher
James Lawlor, Editor

Devoted entirely to legal issues pertinent to emergency medicine, and covers monthly the latest case law, legal trends, risk management, tort reform and explains how they could impact your emergency care facility.
Cost: $357.00
Frequency: Monthly

12948 Employee Assistance Program Management Letter

Health Resources Publishing
1913 Atlantic Ave
Suite 200
Manasquan, NJ 08736-1067

732-292-1100
888-843-6242
FAX 732-292-1111
E-Mail: info@themcic.com
Home Page: www.healthresourcesonline.com

Robert K Jenkins, Publisher
Lisa Mansfield, Regional Director
Brett Powell, Regional Director
Alice Burron, Director

A briefing published monthly on the range of influences surrounding your employee assistance program.
Cost: $237.00
Frequency: Monthly
ISSN: 0896-0941
Founded in 1978

12949 Executive Report on Integrated Care & Capitation

Managed Care Information Center
1913 Atlantic Ave
Suite 200
Manasquan, NJ 08736-1067

732-292-1100
888-843-6242
FAX 732-292-1111
E-Mail: info@themcic.com
Home Page: www.themcic.com

Robert K Jenkins, Publisher
Joseph Schmidt, Editor

A newsletter published twice a month to keep readers informed of the competitive market. Gives facts on strategic issues, mergers and acquisitions, market facts, economics, network alliances and plan affiliations.
Cost: $447.00
Frequency: Monthly
ISSN: 1085-3103

12950 Executive Report on Managed Care

Managed Care Information Center
1913 Atlantic Ave
Suite 200
Manasquan, NJ 08736-1067

732-292-1100
888-843-6242
FAX 732-292-1111
E-Mail: info@themcic.com
Home Page: www.themcic.com

Robert K Jenkins, Publisher

A monthly report that gives news of how major employers are implementing their managed care programs. The report also aids companies in preparing to evaluate and monitor different managed care proposals to determine cost effectiveness, quality and liability to the employer.
Cost: $437.00
ISSN: 0898-9753

12951 Executive Report on Physician Organizations

Managed Care Information Center

1913 Atlantic Ave
Suite 200
Manasquan, NJ 08736-1067

732-292-1100
888-843-6242
FAX 732-292-1111
E-Mail: info@themcic.com
Home Page: www.themcic.com

Robert K Jenkins, Publisher

The newsletter covers mergers, acquisitions, practice management agreements and strategic planes implemented in the physician marketplace. Also provides information about the ways that managed care and goverment regulations affect the physician marketplace.
Cost: $257.00
8-10 Pages
Frequency: 12 per year
ISSN: 1097-7309
Founded in 1998

12952 Eye-Mail Monthly

American Academy of Optometry
6110 Executive Blvd
Suite 506
Rockville, MD 20852-3929

301-984-1441
FAX 301-984-4737
E-Mail: aaoptom@aaoptom.org
Home Page: www.aaopt.org

Lois Schoenbrun, Executive Director
Frequency: Monthly

12953 G-2 Compliance Report

Institute of Management and Administration
1 Washington Park
Suite 1300
Newark, NJ 07102

212-244-0360
FAX 973-622-0595
Home Page: www.ioma.com

Designed to guide hospital, lab, and pathology professionals in developing, implementing and revising compliance programs to meet federal standards.
Cost: $469.00

12954 HCEA Edge

Healthcare Convention & Exhibitors Association
5775 Peachtree Dnwdy Rd
Building G, Suite 500
Atlanta, GA 30342-1556

404-252-3663
FAX 404-252-0774
E-Mail: hcea@kellencompany.com
Home Page: www.hcea.org

Eric Allen, Executive Vice President
Nancy Hoppe, President

News and events of the trade association of over 600 organizations involved in healthcare exhibiting or providing services to healthcare conventions, exhibitions and/or meetings.
Frequency: Monthly, Members Only

12955 HFMA's The Business of Caring

Healthcare Financial Management Association
Two Westbrook Corporate Center
Suite 700
Westchester, IL 60154-5700

708-319-9600
800-252-4362
FAX 708-531-0032
Home Page: www.hfma.org/boc

Robert Fromberg, Editor-in-Chief
Maggie Van Dyke, Product Manager & Editor
Chris Burke, Advertising Manager
Kurt Belisle, Sponsorhip Manager

Helps nurse managers navigate the business side of health care to become successful hospital leaders. Topics discussed include: budgeting, workforce management, cost containment, and IT implementation. Available Free Online.
Frequency: Quarterly

12956 HMFA Healthcare Cost Containment Newsletter
Healthcare Finance Management Association
3 Westbrook Corporate Center
Suite 600
Westchester, IL 60154

708-531-9600
FAX 708-531-0032
Home Page:
www.hfma.org/publications/healthcarecost

Issues illustrate how to implement strategic cost management that will reduce labor and supply expenses, enhance operational efficiency, satisfy your patients, and improve your competitive position.
Cost: $125.00
Frequency: Quarterly
Mailing list available for rent

12957 HMFA Revenue Cycle Stragetist Newsletter
Healthcare Finance Management Association
3 Westbrook Corporate Center
Suite 600
Westchester, IL 60154

708-531-9600
FAX 708-531-0032
Home Page: www.hfma.org/publications/

Improve your organization's bottom line while maintaining regulatory compliance.
Cost: $165.00
Frequency: Quarterly
Mailing list available for rent

12958 Health Care Reimbursement Monitor
Health Resources Publishing
1913 Atlantic Ave
Suite 200
Manasquan, NJ 08736-1067

732-292-1100
888-843-6242
FAX 732-292-1111
E-Mail: info@themcic.com
Home Page: www.healthresourcesonline.com

Robert K Jenkins, Publisher
Lisa Mansfield, Regional Director
Brett Powell, Regional Director
Alice Burron, Director

A monthly newsletter that covers the latest details of actions taken or proposals in Washington concerning changes to the BBA; updates on Medicaid and Medicare budget and reimbursement issues; reimbursement news for hospital operations executives as well as top financial management. Reimbursement briefings cover hospitals, home health care, long-term care, hospice, ambulatory care and physician payment.
Cost: $257.00
Frequency: Monthly

12959 Health Product Marketing
PRS Group
6320 Fly Rd
Suite 102
East Syracuse, NY 13057-9792

315-431-0511
FAX 315-431-0200
E-Mail: custserv@prsgroup.com
Home Page: www.prsgroup.com

Mary Lou Walsh, President
Ben McTernan, Managing Editor

Patti Davis, Circulation Manager
Patty Redhead, Production Manager
Provides current information, analysis and ideas for strategic planning in the health industry.
ISSN: 1520-3271
Founded in 1979

12960 Healthcare Market Reporter
Managed Care Information Center
1913 Atlantic Ave
Suite 200
Manasquan, NJ 08736-1067

732-292-1100
888-843-6242
FAX 732-292-1111
E-Mail: info@themcic.com
Home Page: www.themcic.com

Robert K Jenkins, Publisher

Twice-a-month newsletter to help you abreast of the fiercely competitive market. Get the facts and details you'll need on strategies issues, market facts, mergers and acquisitions, economics, network alliances and plan affiliations.
Cost: $457.00
10 Pages
ISSN: 1073-6816

12961 Healthcare Marketers Executive Briefing
Health Resources Publishing
1913 Atlantic Ave
Suite 200
Manasquan, NJ 08736-1067

732-292-1100
FAX 732-292-1111
E-Mail: info@healthresourcesonline.com
Home Page: www.healthresourcesonline.com

Robert K Jenkins, Publisher
Lisa Mansfield, Regional Director
Brett Powell, Regional Director
Alice Burron, Director

Helps managers stay informed of the latest innovations and changes in the health care field. Gives contact information for other community relations, publication practioners, administrators and marketing and advertising professonals.
Cost: $237.00
Frequency: Monthly
ISSN: 0894-9980

12962 Healthcare PR & Marketing News
Phillips Business Information
1201 Seven Locks Road
Potomac, MD 20854-2931

301-354-1400
888-707-5814
FAX 301-309-3847
Home Page: www.prandmarketing.com

Matthew Schwartz, Editor
Diane Schwartz, Publisher
Amy Urban, Marketing Manager

Issues faced by health care executives in PR firms and hospitals. Regular features include industry surveys, case studies and executive profiles.
Cost: $397.00
Founded in 1944

12963 Healthcare e-Business Manager
Managed Care Information Center
1913 Atlantic Ave
Suite 200
Manasquan, NJ 08736-1067

732-292-1100
888-843-5242
FAX 732-292-1111
E-Mail: info@themcic.com
Home Page: www.themcic.com

Robert K Jenkins, Publisher

Monthly executive briefing on the latest developments in the proliferation of electronic commerce among healthcare and managed care organization. Focuses on the internet marketplace, reports on trends in the industry and predictions of where the market seems to be heading.
Cost: $477.00
10 Pages
ISSN: 1526-6052

12964 Hospice Letter
Health Resources Publishing
1913 Atlantic Ave
Suite 200
Manasquan, NJ 08736-1067

732-292-1100
888-843-6242
FAX 732-292-1111
E-Mail: info@themcic.com
Home Page: www.healthresourcesonline.com

Robert K Jenkins, Publisher
Lisa Mansfield, Regional Director
Brett Powell, Regional Director
Alice Burron, Director

Monthly newsletter reporting the latest development in the rapidly hospice concept of caring for the terminally ill. Ready by administrators and directors who follow Medicare reimbursement and hospice accreditation. How hospices are raising money and staging community events; new legislation and regulations and the latest on nursing care, volunteers and counseling programs. Delivery options: via mail or e-mail (indicate PDF or HTML format)
Cost: $227.00
10 Pages
Frequency: Monthly
ISSN: 0913-6816
Founded in 1978

12965 Integrated Healthcare News
American Association of Integrated Healthcare
4435 Waterfront Drive
Suite 101
Glen Allen, VA 23060

804-747-5823
FAX 804-747-5316
E-Mail: bwilliams@aainds.org
Home Page: www.aaihds.org

Jerry Williams, Editorial
Mark Abernathy, Managing Director
Dalal Haldeman, PhD, MBA, Director, Marketing Operations

12966 Journal of the American Association of Forensic Dentists
1000 N Avenue
Waukegan, IL 60085

847-244-0292
E-Mail: info@andent.net
Home Page: www.andent.net

Quarterly journal that brings forensic dental knowledge not only to dentists and their staff, but also to anthropologists, attorneys and law enforcement personnel.
3000 Pages
Founded in 1978

12967 Legislative Alert
Taxicab, Limousine & Paratransit Association
3200 Tower Oaks Blvd
Suite 220
Rockville, MD 20852

301-984-5700
FAX 301-984-5703

E-Mail: info@tlpa.org
Home Page: www.tlpa.org

Alfred LaGasse, CEO
William Rouse, President
Harold Morgan, Executive Vice President
Michelle A. Hariston, CMP, Manager of Meetings
Leah New, Manager of Communications

TLPA's members-only bulletin of early alerts to critical changes in the industry, announcing threats and opportunities on issues that are before Congress and federal agencies. Organizes operators to take action, and provides knowledge and awareness.
Circulation: 6000
Founded in 1917
Mailing list available for rent

12968 Medical Group Management Update
Medical Group Management Association
104 Inverness Ter E
Englewood, CO 80112-5313

303-799-1111
FAX 303-643-9599
E-Mail: infocenter@mgma.com
Home Page: www.mgma.com

William Jessee, CEO
Eileen Barker, senior Vice President
Anders Gilberg, senior Vice President
Natalie Jamieson, Administrative Assistant

Monthly association newspaper offering up-to-the-minute articles on current legislation, practical management, health care trends, association activities and other timely subjects.
Frequency: Monthly

12969 National Intelligence Report
Institute of Management and Administration
1 Washington Park
Suite 1300
Newark, NJ 07102-3130

212-244-0360
FAX 973-622-0595
E-Mail: customercare@bna.com
Home Page: www.ioma.com

Provides concise, independent coverage and analysis of fast-breaking lab, pathology, blood banking, imaging and diagnostic radiology news from the Nation's Capital.
Cost: $489.00
Frequency: Biweekly

12970 Nephrology News and Issues
Nephrology News and Issues
17797 N Perimeter Dr
Suite 109
Scottsdale, AZ 85255-5455

480-443-4635
FAX 480-443-4528
E-Mail: info@nephnews.com
Home Page: www.nephronline.com

Melissa Laudenschlager, Publisher
Mark Neumann, Editor
Marcia Coutts, Circulation Manager
Cost: $55.00
Frequency: Monthly
Circulation: 22000
Founded in 1986

12971 News Now
American Physical Therapy Association
1111 N Fairfax St
Alexandria, VA 22314-1488

703-684-2782
FAX 703-706-8536
E-Mail: memberservices@apta.org
Home Page: www.apta.org
Social Media: Facebook, Twitter, LinkedIn

Maryann DiGiacomo, Editor
John D. Barnes, Chief Executive Officer
Janet Bezner, VP, Education, Governance

Rob Batarla, VP, Finance & Business Development
Felicity Clancy, VP, Communications & Marketing

Reports timely legislative, health care, and Association news to APTA members and subscribers.
80000 Members
Frequency: Weekly
Mailing list available for rent

12972 Nurses' Notes
American Association of Managed Care Nurses
4435 Waterfront Dr
Suite 101
Glen Allen, VA 23060-3393

804-747-9698
FAX 804-747-5316
E-Mail: keads@aamcn.org
Home Page: www.aamcn.org

Bill Williams, President

A quarterly newsletter published by the American Association of Managed Care Nurses. Available to members only.
Circulation: 2000

12973 Nursing News Update
American Association of Managed Care Nurses
4435 Waterfront Dr
Suite 101
Glen Allen, VA 23060-3393

804-747-9698
FAX 804-747-5316
E-Mail: keads@aamcn.org
Home Page: www.aamcn.org

Bill Williams, President
Laura Givens, Executive Admin

A weekly electronic newsletter published by the American Association of Managed Care Nurses. Available to members only.
Circulation: 2000

12974 Physician's News Digest
Physician's New Digest
230 Windsor Ave
Suite 216
Narberth, PA 19072-2217

610-668-1040
800-220-6109
FAX 610-668-9177
E-Mail: info@physiciansnews.com
Home Page: www.physiciansnews.com

Jeffery Barg, CEO/President
Christopher Gaudagnino, Business Manager
Ben Birenbaum, Business Manager
Cost: $35.00
Frequency: Monthly
Circulation: 40000
ISSN: 1079-6312
Founded in 1987
Printed in 4 colors on newsprint stock

12975 Public Health
State Capitals Newsletters
PO Box 7376
Alexandria, VA 22307-7376

703-768-9600
FAX 703-768-9690
Home Page: statecapitals.com
Cost: $245.00

Frequency: Weekly

12976 Sisters Network/National Newsletter
Sisters Network

2922 Rosedale St
Suite 4206
Houston, TX 77004-6188

713-781-0255
866-781-1808
FAX 713-780-8998
E-Mail: infonet@sistersnetworkinc.org
Home Page: www.sistersnetworkinc.org

Erie Calloway, Executive Director
Karen E. Jackson, CEO
Caleen Burtonalleen, Public Relations Manager
Cherlyn K Latham, Project Director
Kelly P. Hodges, National Program Director

Publication of the group committed to awareness of the impact that breast cancer has on the African American community, with the latest information, medical research and news about events taking place within the Sisters National Network of affiliate chapters.
Frequency: Monthly
Founded in 1994

12977 Today's School Psychologist
LRP Publications
747 Dresher Road
PO Box 980
Horsham, PA 19044-2247

215-784-0912
800-341-7874
FAX 215-784-9639
E-Mail: webmaster@lrp.com
Home Page: www.lrp.com

Caroline Miller, Editor

In-depth guide to a school psychologists job, offering proactive strategies and tips for handling day-to-day tasks and responsibilities, encouraging change and improving professional standing and performance.
Cost: $135.00
Frequency: Monthly

12978 US Medicine Newsletter
US Medicine
39 York Street
Suite 400
Lambertville, NJ 08530

609-397-5522
FAX 609-397-4237
E-Mail: usmedicine@usmedicine.com
Home Page: www.usmedicine.com

James F Breuning, Publisher
Brenda L. Mooney, Editorial Director
Stephen Spotswood, Correspondent
Beth Scholz, Account Manager
Anita Crandall, Production Manager

US Medicine is an organization that supports physicians and healthcare workers with medical and legal information. Publishes a newspaper. Founded in 1964.
9 Members
Founded in 1964

12979 Walking Tomorrow
Christopher Reeve Paralysis Foundation
500 Morris Ave
Springfield, NJ 07081-1027

973-467-5915
800-225-0292
FAX 973-912-9433
Home Page: www.christopherreeve.org/

Julie Kwon, Director of Marketing
Kathy Lewis, Controller
Ed Jobst, Controller

Newsletter of the Christopher Reeve Paralysis Foundation.
Frequency: Monthly
Founded in 1982

12980 Wellness Program Management Advisor
Health Resources Publishing

1913 Atlantic Ave
Suite 200
Manasquan, NJ 08736-1067

732-292-1100
888-843-6242
FAX 732-292-1111
E-Mail: info@themcic.com
Home Page: www.healthresourcesonline.com

Robert K Jenkins, Publisher
Lisa Mansfield, Regional Director
Brett Powell, Regional Director
Alice Burron, Director

A newsletter that is designed to help professionals manage their organization's health promotion and wellness programs. Gives information about how other wellness programs are doing in such areas as strategies adopted, expenses and return on investments. Also included are in depth profiles of wellness programs around the country that list the problems that they encountered and the steps that they took to alter them.
Cost: $247.00
Frequency: Monthly
ISSN: 1085-7125

Magazines & Journals

12981 24 X 7
HealthTech Publishing Company
6100 Center Drive
Suite 1000
Los Angeles, CA 90045

310-642-4400
FAX 310-641-4444
E-Mail: tantikadjian@medpubs.com
Home Page: www.24x7mag.com

Tony Ramos, Publisher
Kelly Stephens, Editor
Jennifer Bezahler, Circulation Manager

News and business magazine for the healthcare service support and technology management industry.
Frequency: Monthly
Circulation: 15000
ISSN: 1091-1626
Founded in 1996
Printed in 4 colors on glossy stock

12982 AAMA Executive
American Academy of Medical Administrators
701 Lee St
Suite 600
Des Plaines, IL 60016-4516

847-759-8601
800-621-6902
FAX 847-759-8602
E-Mail: info@aameda.org
Home Page: www.aameda.org

Renee Schleichar, CEO
Nancy L Anderson, Director of Education
Guy Snyder, Director of Education
Rhonda Guptill, Chief Financial Officer
Cost: $90.00
Frequency: Quarterly
Founded in 1957

12983 AAPS Newsmagazine
American Association of Pharmaceutical Scientists
2107 Wilson Blvd
Suite 700
Arlington, VA 22201-3042

703-243-2800
FAX 703-243-9054

E-Mail: aaps@aaps.org
Home Page: www.aaps.org

John Lisack, Executive Director
Joy Metcalf, Managing Editor
Janelle Kihlstrom, Editorial Assistant
Ken Corch, Executive Assistant

Exclusive to AAPS members. Features expanded coverage of the industry, complete with expert information on marketplace trends, regulatory matters, and career opportunities.
Mailing list available for rent

12984 AAPS PharmSciTech Journal
American Association of Pharmaceutical Scientists
2107 Wilson Blvd
Suite 700
Arlington, VA 22201-3042

703-243-2800
FAX 703-243-9054
E-Mail: aaps@aaps.org
Home Page: www.aaps.org

John Lisack, Executive Director
Joy Metcalf, Managing Editor
James Greif, Communications Specialist
Ken Corch, Executive Assistant

An online-only journal published and owned by the American Association of Pharmaceutical Scientists. The journal's mission is to disseminate scientific and technical information on drug product design, development, evaluation and processing to the global pharmaceutical research community, taking full advantage of web-based publishing by presenting innovative text with 3-D graphics, interactive figures and databases, video and audio files.
ISSN: 1530-9932
Mailing list available for rent

12985 AARP The Magazine
American Association of Retired Persons
601 E St NW
Washington, DC 20049-0003

202-434-2277
888-687-2277
202-434-3525
FAX 202-434-7599
E-Mail: member@aarp.org
Home Page: www.aarp.org

Hop Backus, Executive Vice President
Steve Cone, Executive Vice President
Joann Jenkins, Foundation President
A. Barry Rand, Chief Executive Officer
Cindy Lewin, General Counsel

AARP is a nonprofit, nonpartisan organization with a membership that helps people age 50 and over have independence, choice and control in ways that are beneficial and affordable to them and society as a whole, ways that help people 50 and over improve their lives. Founded through support from staffed offices in all 50 states.
Frequency: Monthly
Founded in 1958
Mailing list available for rent

12986 ACSM's Health & Fitness Journal
Lippincott Williams & Wilkins
351 W Camden St
Baltimore, MD 21201-2436

410-949-8000
800-222-3790
FAX 410-528-4414
Home Page: www.lww.com

J Arnold Anthony, Operations
Michael Hargrett, Publisher
Edward Howley, Editor-in-Chief

The Journal strives to help health and fitness practitioners improve their knowledge and experience through reports and recommendations from experts, CEC offerings, opportunities to

question the experts, listings of job openings and more.
Cost: $40.00
Frequency: Fortnightly
Circulation: 11144
ISSN: 1091-5397
Founded in 1997
Printed in 4 colors on matte stock

12987 ADA Courier
American Dietetic Association
120 South Riverside Plaza
Suite 2000
Chicago, IL 60606-6995

312-990-0040
800-877-1600
FAX 312-899-4757
E-Mail: affiliate@eatright.org
Home Page: www.eatright.org

Susan H Laramee, President
Ronald S Moen, CEO
Patricia M. Babjak, Executive VP
Jennifer Herendeen, Editorial Director
Jason Switt, Editor

Readers look to the Courier for current association activities, membership news, updates on continuing education opportunities, ADA policies and coverage of the Associations' lobbying efforts in Washington.
Cost: $315.00
10 Pages
Frequency: Monthly
Circulation: 80000
ISSN: 1050-7434
Founded in 1917
Printed in 4 colors on glossy stock

12988 ADA News
American Dental Association
211 E Chicago Ave
Chicago, IL 60611-2678

312-440-2897
FAX 312-440-3538
Home Page: www.ada.org

Judy Jakush, Editor
Jill Philbein, Circulation Manager
James Bramson, CEO
Cost: $64.00
Founded in 1859

12989 AHA News
AHA
1 N Franklin St
Suite 700
Chicago, IL 60606-4425

312-895-2500
800-242-2626
FAX 312-895-2501
E-Mail: storeservice@aha.org
Home Page: www.aha.org

Anthony Burke, CEO
Cliff Lehman, Director Membership Services

Provides extensive coverage of regulatory, judicial and legislative developments while also providing news and information from the AHA.
Cost: $45.00
Frequency: Weekly
Circulation: 40000
Founded in 1917

12990 AMA Alliance Today
AMA
515 N State St
Chicago, IL 60654-9104

312-464-4470
FAX 312-464-5020
E-Mail: amaa@ama-assn.org
Home Page: www.ama-assn.org

Jo Posselt, Executive Director
Megan Pellegrini, General Counsel

Jon Ekdahl, General Counsel
Bernard Hengesbaugh, Chief Operating Officer
Jacqueline Drake, Secretary
Circulation: 30,000
Founded in 1922

12991 AdvaMed SmartBrief
Advanced Medical Technology Association
1200 G St NW
Suite 400
Washington, DC 20005-3832

202-408-9788
FAX 202-408-9793
E-Mail: info@advamed.org
Home Page: www.avamed.org

Andrea Levre, President

12992 Advance for Health Information Executives
Advance Newsmagazines/Merion Publications
2900 Horizon Dr
King of Prussia, PA 19406-2651

610-265-8249
800-355-5627
FAX 610-962-0639
Home Page: www.advanceforhie.com

Frank Irving, Editor
Maryann Kurkowski, Circulation Manager

Coverage of emerging e-health and computer-based patient record technologies.
Frequency: Monthly
Founded in 1997

12993 Aesthetic Plastic Surgery
6277 Sea Harbor Drive
Orlando Florida
Orlando, Fl 32887-7703

407-345-4000
800-364-2147
FAX 407-363-9661
E-Mail: elspcs@elsevier.com
Home Page: www.surgery.org/

Elizabeth Sadati, Executive Editor
Paul Bernstein, Scientific Forum Editor
Stanley A Klatsky, Managing Director
Cost: $196.00
Frequency: Monthly
Founded in 1996

12994 Air Medical Journal
Mosby
11830 Westline Industrial Drive
Saint Louis, MO 63146-3318

314-453-4307
800-325-4307
FAX 314-872-9164
E-Mail: elspcs@elsevier.com
Home Page: www.mosby.com/airmedj

David Dries, Editor
Liz Bennett-Bailey, Publisher
Eric Ferguson, Issue Manager
Cost: $85.00
Frequency: bi-monthly
Founded in 1986

12995 American Family Physician
American Academy of Family Physicians
11400 Tomahawk Creek Pkwy.
Leawood, KS 66211-2672

913-906-6205
FAX 913-906-6086
E-Mail: afpjournal@aafp.org
Home Page: www.aafp.org/journals/afp.html
Social Media: *Facebook, Twitter, YouTube*

Jay Siwek, Editor

Peer-reviewed clinical journal of the American Academy of Family Physicians.
Cost: $240.00
Frequency: Monthly
ISSN: 0002-838X
Founded in 1947

12996 American Health Line
600 New Hampshire Avenue NW
Washington, DC 20037

202-295-5381
800-717-3245
FAX 202-266-5700
E-Mail: ahl@advisory.com
Home Page: www.americanhealthline.com

Joshua Perin, Editor-in-Chief
Josh Kotzman, Editors
Frequency: Weekly
Founded in 1992

12997 American Imago: Studies In Psychoanalysis and Culture
Johns Hopkins University Press
2715 N Charles St
Baltimore, MD 21218-4319

410-516-6900
800-548-1784
FAX 410-516-6998
E-Mail: webmaster@jhupress.jhu.edu
Home Page: www.press.jhu.edu/journals

William Brody, President
Kathleen Keane, Director
William M. Breichner, Publisher
Founded in 1878

12998 American Journal of Clinical Medicine
American Association of Physician Specialists, Inc
5550 West Executive Drive
Suite 400
Tampa, FL 33609

813-433-2277
FAX 813-830-6599
E-Mail: wcarbone@aapsus.org
Home Page: www.aapsus.com

Nadine Simone, Executive Administrative Assistant
Debi Colmorgen, Communications Coordinator
William Carbone, Chief Executive Officer
Anthony Durante, Director of Finance & Operations
Sandy Martin, Finance & Operations Coordinator

The official peer-reviewed journal of the AAPS, an organization dedicated to promoting the highest intellectual, moral, and ethical standards of its members.
1000 Attendees

12999 American Journal of Cosmetic Surgery
737 N Michigan Ave
Suite 2100
Chicago, IL 60611-5641

312-981-6760
FAX 312-981-6787
E-Mail: info@cosmeticsurgery.org
Home Page: www.cosmeticsurgery.org

Jeffrey Knezovich, Executive VP
Charlie Baase, Marketing Manager

13000 American Journal of Health Education (AJHE)
1900 Association Dr
Reston, VA 20191-1502

703-476-3400
800-213-7193
FAX 703-476-9527
E-Mail: info@aahperd.org

Home Page: www.aahperd.org
Social Media: *Facebook, Twitter, YouTube*

Monica Mize, President
Judith C Young, VP
Paula Kun, Marketing

Covers today's health education and health promotion issues head on with timely, substantive, and thought provoking articles for professionals working in medical care facilities, professional preparation, colleges and universities, community and public health agencies, schools, and businesses.
25000 Members
Founded in 1885

13001 American Journal of Human Genetics
American Society of Human Genetics
9650 Rockville Pike
Bethesda, MD 20814-3998

301-634-7300
866-HUM-GENE
FAX 301-634-7079
E-Mail: society@ashg.org
Home Page: www.ashg.org
Social Media: *Facebook, Twitter, LinkedIn*

Joann Boughman, PhD, Executive VP
Chuck Windle, Director of Finance/Administration
Karen Goodman, Executive Assistant
Pauline Minhinnett, Dir. of Meetings/Exhibit Management
Mary Shih, Membership Manager

ASHG is the primary professional membership organization for human genetics specialists worldwide.
8000 Members
Frequency: Monthly
Circulation: 7,199
ISSN: 0002-9297
Founded in 1948
Mailing list available for rent

13002 American Journal of Hypertension
148 Madison Ave
Fifth Floor
New York, NY 10016-6700

212-532-0537
FAX 212-696-0711
E-Mail: journal@ash-us.org
Home Page: www.ash-us.org

John H Laragh, Editor In Chief
Ellen Twyne, President
Cost: $246.00
Frequency: Monthly
Founded in 1985

13003 American Journal of Managed Care
American Medical Publishing
241 Forsgate Drive
Jamesburg, NJ 08831

732-656-1006
FAX 732-656-0818
E-Mail: info@ajmc.com
Home Page: www.ajmc.com

Jim King, Publisher
Lyn Beamesderfer, Editor

The American Journal of Managed Care is an independent, peer-reviewed forum for the publication of clinical research and opinion related to quality, value, and policy in health care delivery. The Journal delivers original research on patient outcomes, clinical effectiveness, cost effectiveness, quality management, and health policy to managed care decision makers.
Frequency: Monthly
Circulation: 53000
ISSN: 1088-0224
Founded in 1995

13004 American Journal of Neuroradiology
2210 Midwest Rd
Suite 207
Oak Brook, IL 60523-8205

630-574-1487
800-783-4903
FAX 630-786-6251
Home Page: www.ajnr.org

Karen Halm, Managing Editor
Victor M Haughton MD, VP

Relays news and schedules of events for members.
Cost: $235.00
Circulation: 7000
Founded in 1937

13005 American Journal of Roetgenology
American Roentgen Ray Society
1891 Preston White Dr
Reston, VA 20191-4326

703-729-3353
800-438-2777
FAX 703-729-4839
E-Mail: info@arrs.org
Home Page: www.arrs.org

Susan Brown, Executive Director
Connie Wolfe, Publications Assistant
Fran Schuweiler, Managing Editor
Charles Kahn, Vice President
Melissa Rosado, Secretary

A monthly journal published by the American
Roentgen Ray Society.
Cost: $275.00
Frequency: Monthly
Circulation: 25,000
Founded in 1900
*Mailing list available for rent: 10000 names at
$160 per M*

13006 American Medical News
American Medical Association
515 N State St
9th Floor
Chicago, IL 60654-9104

312-464-4429
800-621-8335
FAX 312-464-4445
E-Mail: ben_mindell@ama-assn.org
Home Page: www.ama-assn.org

Ben Mindell, Vice President
John Nelson, CEO/President
Kathryn Trombatore, Manager
Jon Ekdahl, General Counsel
Bernard Hengesbaugh, Chief Operating Officer

Intended to serve as an impartial forum for information affecting physicians and their practices. The views expressed in AMNews are not necessarily endorsed by the American Medical Association.
Cost: $95.00
Frequency: Weekly
Circulation: 230,000
Founded in 1847

13007 American Nurse Today
American Nurses Association
600 Maryland Avenue SW
Washington, DC 20024-2571

202-651-7000
FAX 202-651-7003
Home Page: www.NursingWorld.org

Pamela Cipriano PhD RN FAAN,
Editor-in-Chief

Serves registered nurses in North America.
Frequency: 6 per year
Printed in 4 colors on glossy stock

13008 Anesthesiology News
545 W 45th St
8th Floor
New York, NY 10036-3409

212-957-5300
FAX 212-957-7230
E-Mail: marsap@mcmahonmed.com
Home Page: www.anesthesiologynews.com

Adam Marcus, Managing Editor
Raymond E. McMahon, CEO/Publisher
Marsha Radebaugh, Circulation Coordinator
Cost: $65.00
Frequency: Monthly
Circulation: 39720
Founded in 1975

**13009 Annals of Allergy, Asthma &
Immunology**
85 W Algonquin Road
Suite 550
Arlington Heights, IL 60005-4460

847-427-1200
FAX 847-427-1294
E-Mail: mail@acaai.org
Home Page: www.acaai.org
Social Media: *Facebook, Twitter, LinkedIn,
YouTube*

Dana Wallace, MD, President
Stanley Fineman, MD, MBA, President-Elect

Information and news service for patients, parents of patients, members, the news media, and purchasers of health care programs.
5200 Members
Frequency: Monthly
Circulation: 5100
ISSN: 1081-1206
Founded in 1942

13010 Annals of Emergency Medicine
Elsevier Publishing
1125 Executive Circle
P.O. Box 619911
Irving, TX 75038-2522

972-550-0911
800-798-1822
FAX 972-580-2816
E-Mail: customerservice@acep.org
Home Page: www.acep.org

Nancy B Medina, CAE, Editorial Director
Tracy Napper, Managing Editor
Michael L Callaham, MD, Editor-in-Chief
Dean Wilkerson, Executive Director
Marco Coppola, Council Speaker

An international, peer-reviewed journal dedicated to improving the quality of care by publishing the highest quality science for emergency medicine and related medical specialties.
Frequency: Monthly
Circulation: 30000
ISSN: 0196-0644
Mailing list available for rent

13011 Annals of Opthalmology
Am. Society of Cont. Medicine, Surgery &
Opth.
North Cisero Avenue
Suite 208
Chicago, IL 60712

847-677-9093
800-621-4002
FAX 847-677-9094
E-Mail: iaos@aol.com
Home Page: www.medlit.ru/medeng/vof5.htm

Mikhail Krasnov, Editor-in-Chief
Randall Bellows MD, CEO/President

Exclusive articles written and peer-reviewed by doctors.
Frequency: bi-monthly
Founded in 1884

13012 Annals of Periodontology
737 N Michigan Ave
Suite 800
Chicago, IL 60611-2690

312-787-5518
FAX 312-787-3670
E-Mail: member.services@perio.org
Home Page: www.perio.org

Alice Deforest, Executive Director
Julie Daw, Managing Editor
Vincent J. Iacono, President
Sarah Schneider, Administrative Assistant
Cost: $365.00
Frequency: Monthly

13013 Annals of Plastic Surgery
530 Walnut St
Philadelphia, PA 19106-3603

215-521-8300
FAX 215-521-8411
Home Page: www.lww.com

Melissa Ricks, Manager
Cost: $375.00
Frequency: Monthly

13014 Applied Clinical Trials
Advanstar Communications
6200 Canoga Avenue
2nd Floor
Woodland Hills, CA 91367

818-593-5000
FAX 818-593-5020
Home Page:
www.appliedclinicaltrialsonline.com
Social Media: *Facebook, Twitter, LinkedIn*

Joseph Loggia, President
Chris DeMoulin, VP
Susannah George, Marketing Director

Practical information for clinical research professionals in industry and academia who develop, execute and manage clinical trials worldwide. Regular topics include regulatory affairs, protocol development, data management and harmonization updates.
Frequency: Monthly
Circulation: 16255
ISSN: 1064-8542
Founded in 1987
Mailing list available for rent

**13015 Archives of Physical Medicine and
Rehabilitation**
American Congress of Rehabilitation
Medicine
11654 Plaza America Drive
Suite 535
Reston, VA 20190

703-435-5335
FAX 866-692-1619
E-Mail: acrm@acrm.org
Home Page: www.acrm.org

Jon W. Lindberg, Executive Director
Dinara Suleymanova, Director of Operations
Judy Reuter, Publications & Web Development
Cindy Robinson, Marketing Coordinator
Margo Holen, Chief Meetings Officer

Available with membership to American Congress of Rehabilitation Medicine.
Frequency: Monthly
Circulation: 900
Founded in 1923

13016 Arthritis Hotline
2824 Swift Avenue
Dallas, TX 75204

972-286-6664
FAX 214-363-2817

13017 Aviation, Space and Environmental Medicine
Aerospace Medical Association
320 S Henry St
Alexandria, VA 22314-3579

703-739-2240
FAX 703-739-9652
E-Mail: asemjournal@att.net
Home Page: www.asma.org

Gisselle Vargas, Manager
Jeffrey C. Sventek, Executive Director
Gisselle Vargas, Operations Manager
Gloria Carter, Director, Member Services
Sheryl Kildall, Subscriptions Manager

Provides contact with physicians, life scientists, bioengineers and medical specialists working in both basic medical research and in its clinical applications.
Frequency: Monthly
Mailing list available for rent

13018 BNA's Health Care Policy Report
3 Bethesda Metro Center
Suite 250
Bethesda, MD 20814

202-452-4107
800-372-1033
FAX 202-452-4084
E-Mail: edcontactslitigation@bna.com
Home Page: www.bna.com

Greg McCaffey, President, Bloomburg BNA
Frequency: Weekly
Founded in 1929

13019 Behavioral Health Management
MEDQUEST Communications
3800 Lakeside Ave E
Suite 201
Cleveland, OH 44114-3857

216-391-9100
FAX 216-391-9200
Home Page: www.behavioral.net

Mark Goodman, Manager
Monica E Oss, Editor-in-Chief

Largest publication reporting on the cutting edge trends and management practices in the behavioral health field.
Cost: $94.00
52 Pages
Circulation: 21615
ISSN: 1075-6701
Printed in 4 colors on glossy stock

13020 Behavioral Neuroscience
750 1st St NE
Washington, DC 20002-4242

202-336-5500
800-374-2721
FAX 202-336-5549
E-Mail: journals@apa.org
Home Page:
www.apa.org/pubs/journals/bne/index.aspx

Rebecca Burwell, Editor
Cost: $235.00
Circulation: 200,000
Founded in 1988

13021 Biomedical Instrumentation & Technology
Assoc for the Advancement of Medical Instrumentat
4301 N. Fairfax Drive
Suite 301
Arlington, VA 22203-1633

703-525-4890
FAX 703-276-0793
E-Mail: publications@aami.org
Home Page: www.aami.org

Sean Loughlin, Managing Editor

Filled with practical guidance and regular features on troubleshooting, certification, career trends, management issues, sterilization, quality assurance, and more.
Cost: $182.00
Frequency: Bimonthly
Circulation: 6000
Mailing list available for rent

13022 Biomedical Safety & Standards
Aspen Publishers
280 Orchard Ridge Drive
Suite 200
Gaithersburg, MD 20878-1978

301-417-7591

Jack Bruggeman, Publisher

13023 Birth-Issues in Perinatal Care
350 Main Street
6th Floor
Malden, MA 02148-5023

781-388-8200
800-759-6102
FAX 781-388-8210
E-Mail: books@blackwellpublishingasia.com
Home Page: www.blackwellpublishing.com

Diony Young, Editor
Gordon Tibbitts III, President
Robert Campbell, Publisher
Ginny Foley, Manager
Cost: $36.00
Frequency: Quarterly
Circulation: 1709
Founded in 1897

13024 Body Positive
19 Fulton Street
Suite 308 B
New York, NY 10038-2100

212-566-7333
800-566-6599
FAX 212-566-4539
Home Page: www.bodypos.org/

Raymond A Smith, Editor
Eric Rodriguez, Executive Director
Cost: $40.00
Frequency: Quarterly
Circulation: 10000
Founded in 1987

13025 Bulletin
1650 Diagonal Road
Alexandria, VA 22314-3357

703-836-4444
FAX 703-683-5100
E-Mail: membership@entnet.org
Home Page: www.entnet.org
Social Media: *Facebook, Twitter*

Marty Stewart, Sr Manager, Media/Public Relations
James L. Netterville, President
J. Gavin Setzen, Secretary/Treasurer
David R. Nielsen, Executive Vice President and CEO
Paul T. Fass, Director - Private Practice

Features articles written by member otolaryngologists and Academy staff, as well as regular segments on political advocacy, the grassroots member network, practice management, and the latest specialty news and information.
Frequency: Monthly
Circulation: 12,000
ISSN: 0731-8359
Mailing list available for rent

13026 Business and Health
Medical Economics Publishing
131 West First Street
Duluth, Mi 55802-2065

218-723-9200
888-346-0085

FAX 218-723-9437
E-Mail: info@advanstar.com
Home Page: www.advanstar.com

Tracey Walker, Senior Editor
Julie Miller, Managing Editor
Daniel Corcoran, Publisher
Joseph Loggia, Chief Executive Officer
Thomas Ehardt, Chief Administrator

Provides the business and industry fields with information on manufacturing, wholesale, retail and financial, insurance companies, law/accounting firms, hospitals, HMO/PPOs, labor unions, consulting firms, and Medicare/Medicade.
Cost: $64.00
Frequency: Monthly
Circulation: 39736
Founded in 1987
Printed in 4 colors on glossy stock

13027 CA: A Cancer Journal for Clinicians
1599 Clifton Road NE
Atlanta, GA 30329-4251

404-929-6902
FAX 404-325-9341
E-Mail: journals@cancer.org
Home Page: caonline.amcancersoc.org

Harmon J Eyre, Editor
Vickie Thaw, Publisher
John R. Seffrin, CEO
Circulation: 90,000
Founded in 1913

13028 CVS InStep with Healthy Living
Drug Store News Consumer Health Publications
425 Park Ave
New York, NY 10022-3526

212-756-5220
845-426-7612
FAX 212-756-5250
E-Mail: jtanzola@lf.com
Home Page: www.drugstorenews.com

Lebhar Friedman, Publisher
John Tanzola, National Sales Manager

Helps educate and inform over 25 millions 45+ shoppers that visit CVS every month. Topics include health, nutrition, fitness, lifestyle, travel, coupons and CVS programs and events.
Frequency: Quarterly
Circulation: 950000
Founded in 2002

13029 Case Manager
Mosby
10801 Executive Center Drive
Suite 509
Little Rock, AR 72211

501-223-5165
FAX 501-220-0519
Home Page: www.mosby.com

Catherine Mullahy, Editor
Tom Strickland, Editor-in-Chief
Cheri Lattimer, Executive Director

Exclusively for the case management profession.
Cost: $52.00
80 Pages
Frequency: Bi-Monthly
Circulation: 20M
Founded in 1990
Printed in 4 colors on glossy stock

13030 Circulation Research
PO Box 1620
Suite 230
Hagerstown, MD 21741

301-223-2300
800-638-3030
FAX 301-223-2400

E-Mail: educsales@lww.com
Home Page: www.lww.com

Eduardo Marb n, Editor
Cost: $377.00
Founded in 1792

13031 CleanRooms Magazine

PennWell Publishing Company
98 Spit Brook Rd
Nashua, NH 03062-5737

603-891-0123
FAX 603-891-9294
E-Mail: georgem@pennwell.com
Home Page: www.pennwell.com

Christine Shaw, VP
John Haystead, Editor
James Enos, Publisher
Adam Japko, President
Heidi Barnes, Circulation Manager

Serves the contamination control and ultrapure materials and process industries. Written for readers in the microelectronics, pharmaceutical, biotech, health care, food processing and other user industries. Provides technology and business news and new product listings.
Circulation: 34019
Founded in 1910

13032 Clinical Chemistry

American Association for Clinical Chemistry
1850 K St NW
Suite 625
Washington, DC 20006-2215

202-857-0717
800-892-1400
FAX 202-887-5093
E-Mail: custserv@aacc.org
Home Page: www.aacc.org

Richard Flaherty, VP
8,000 Members
Mailing list available for rent

13033 Clinical Lab Products

MWC Allied Healthcare Group
6100 Center Drive
Suite 1000
Los Angeles, CA 90045

310-642-4400
FAX 310-641-4444
E-Mail: tantikadjian@ascendmedia.com
Home Page: www.clpmag.com

Scott Anderson, Publisher
Carol Andrews, Editor
Sharon Marsee, Production Manager
Tony Ramos, President
Jennifer Bezahler, Circulation Director

CLP is the leading monthly product news magazine on key decision makers in the clinical diagnostic laboratory. New product annoucements and editorial features assist lab professionals in providing cost effective timely and accurate patient diagnostic information.
Cost: $125.00
Frequency: Monthly
Circulation: 45000
Founded in 1976
Printed in 4 colors on glossy stock

13034 Clinical Pulmonary Medicine

530 Walnut St
Philadelphia, PA 19106-3603

215-521-8300
800-638-6423
FAX 215-521-8411
Home Page: www.lww.com

Barry Morrill, Publisher
Michael S Niederman MD, Editor-in-Chief
Jay Lippincott, President

Provides a forum for the discussion of important new knowledge in the field of pulmonary medicine that is of interest and relevance to the practitioner.

13035 Computers and Biomedical Research

525 B Street
Suite 1900
San Diego, CA 92101-4401

619-231-6616
800-321-5068
FAX 619-699-6422
Home Page: www.elsevier.com

Gilbert Laporte, Editor
Bill Godfrey, Chief Information Officer
David Clark, Senior Vice President
Frequency: Monthly
Founded in 1974

13036 Computers, Informatics, Nursing

Lippincott Williams & Wilkins
10 A Beech Street
Suite 2
Portland, ME 04101

207-553-7750
FAX 207-553-7751
E-Mail: CustomerService@NursingCenter.com
Home Page: www.nursingcenter.com

Leslie H. Nicoll, Editor
Lippin Cott, Publisher/President

Computer and informatics applications and product selection in nursing and education for nurse managers, patient care executives, nurses in direct patient care, nurse educators and researchers.
Cost: $63.00
Circulation: 4112
Founded in 1985

13037 Consultant Pharmacist

American Society of Consultant Pharmacists
1321 Duke St
Alexandria, VA 22314-3563

703-739-1300
800-355-2727
FAX 703-739-1321
E-Mail: info@ascp.com
Home Page: www.ascp.com

John Feather, Executive Director
Patti Thompson, Production Manager
Marlene Bloom, Editor
Debbie Furman, Circulation

Official peer reviewed journal of the American Society of Consultant Pharmacists. Editorial deals with geriatric pharmacotherapy.
Cost: $210.00
76 Pages
Frequency: Monthly
Circulation: 11000
Printed in 4 colors on glossy stock

13038 Contemporary Urology

Medical Economics Publishing
5 Paragon Dr
Montvale, NJ 07645-1791

973-944-7777
888-581-8052
FAX 973-944-7778
Home Page: www.contemporaryurology.com

Curtis Allen, President
Culley C Carson MD, Editor-in-Chief
Matthew J Holland, Publisher
Don Berman, Director Business Development

Comtemporary Urology serves medical and osteopathic physicians specializing in urology.
Cost: $120.00
Frequency: Monthly
Circulation: 4276
ISSN: 1042-2250
Founded in 1992
Printed in 4 colors on glossy stock

13039 Contingency Planning & Management

Witter Publishing Corporation
20 Commerce Street
Flemington, NJ 08822

908-788-0343
FAX 908-788-3782
Home Page: www.witterpublishing.com

Bob Joudanin, Publisher
Paul Kirvan, Editor-in-Chief
Mike Viscel, Production Manager
Andrew Witter, President

Serves the fields of financial/banking, manufacturing industrial, transportation, utilities, telecommunications, health care, government, insurance and other allied fields.
Cost: $195.00
Frequency: Monthly
Founded in 1987

13040 Continuing Care

Stevens Publishing Corporation
5151 Belt Line Rd
10th Floor
Dallas, TX 75254-7507

972-687-6700
FAX 972-687-6767
Home Page: www.stevenspublishing.com

Craig S Stevens, President/CEO
Mike Valenti, Executive Vice President
Angela Neville, Editor

To provide case management and discharge planning professions with practical and professional information to ensure quality patient services at a cost-effective price.
Cost: $119.00
Founded in 1925

13041 Coping with Allergies and Asthma

Media America
PO Box 682268
Franklin, TN 37068-2268

615-790-2400
FAX 615-794-0179
E-Mail: info@copingmag.com
Home Page: www.copingmag.com

Michael D Holt, Publisher
Julie McKenna, Editor
Michael D Holt, CEO

Information, tips and news for sufferers of allergies or asthma.
Cost: $13.95
36 Pages
Circulation: 30,000
Founded in 1998

13042 Coping with Cancer

Media America
PO Box 682268
Franklin, TN 37068-2268

615-790-2400
FAX 615-794-0179
E-Mail: info@copingmag.com
Home Page: www.copingmag.com

Michael D Holt, Publisher
Julie McKenna, Editor

A magazine for people whose lives have been touched by cancer. Provides knowledge, hope and inspiration to its readers including cancer patients (survivors) and their families, caregivers, healthcare teams and support group leaders.
Cost: $19.00
Circulation: 572,000
Founded in 1987

13043 Cosmetic Surgery Times

Advantstar Communications

7500 Old Oak Blvd
Cleveland, OH 44130-3343

440-243-8100
888-527-7008
FAX 440-891-2740
E-Mail: info@advanstar.com
Home Page: www.advanstar.com

Claudia Shayne-Ferguson, Group Publisher
Maureen Hrehocik, Editor-in-Chief
Michelle Tackla, Senior Editor
Ray Lender, General Manager
Carol Bessick, Manager

Provides cosmetic surgeons with the most current clinical news available. Covers latest surgical techniques, medicolegal issues, updates on new technologies, and suggestions for practice management.
Cost: $95.00
Frequency: 10x/yr
Circulation: 10,003
ISSN: 1094-6810
Founded in 1987

13044 Cost Reengineering Report

National Health Information
PO Box 15429
Atlanta, GA 30333-0429

404-607-9500
800-597-6300
FAX 404-607-0095
Home Page: www.nhionline.com

David Schwartz, President

Contains strategies for reengineering clinical and operational functions, and cutting costs while maintaining or improving quality.
Cost: $299.00
Frequency: Monthly

13045 Counseling Today

5999 Stevenson Ave
Alexandria, VA 22304-3302

703-823-9800
800-347-6647
FAX 703-823-0252
E-Mail: membership@counseling.org
Home Page: www.counseling.org
Social Media: *Facebook, Twitter*

Marvin D. Kuehn, Executive Director
Tom Evenson, President

The mission of the American Counseling Association (ACA) is to enhance the quality of life in society by promoting the development of professional counselors, advancing the counseling profession, and using the profession and practice of counseling to promote respect for human dignity and diversity. ACA is a not-for-profit, professional and educational organization.
Frequency: Monthly
Circulation: 50000
Founded in 1952
Mailing list available for rent: 60M names

13046 Critical Strategies: Psychotherapy in Managed Care

Bill Cohen
10 Alice Street
Binghamton, NY 13904-1580

607-722-5857
800-342-9678
FAX 607-722-6362
E-Mail: getinfo@haworthpressinc.com
Home Page: www.haworthpressinc.com

Frank DePiano, Editor
Sandra J Sickels, Marketing VP
William Cohen, Owner

Resource for innovative and effective approaches to clinical practice in relation to managed care.
Cost: $35.00
Frequency: 2 per year

13047 Data Strategies & Benchmarks

National Health Information
PO Box 15429
Atlanta, GA 30333-429

404-607-9500
800-597-6300
FAX 404-607-0095
E-Mail: nhi@nhionline.net
Home Page: www.nhionline.net

David Schwartz, Publisher
Steve Larose, Editor
David Schwartz, CEO
Edgardo Rivera, Director

Provides insightful guidance and how-to advice to help them meet all the key challenges faced under managed care.
Cost: $339.00
Frequency: Monthly
Founded in 1994

13048 Dental Economics

PennWell Publishing Company
1421 S Sheridan Rd
Tulsa, OK 74112-6619

918-831-9421
800-331-4463
FAX 918-831-9476
E-Mail: joeb@pennwell.com
Home Page: www.pennwell.com

Robert Biolchini, President
Lyle Hoyt, Publisher
Cost: $105.76
Frequency: Monthly
Founded in 1910

13049 Dental Lab Products

MEDEC Dental Communications
2 Northfield Plaza
Suite 300
Northfield, IL 60093-1219

847-441-3700
800-225-4569
FAX 847-441-3702
Home Page: www.dentalproducts.net

Bob Kehoe, Editorial Director
Gail Weisman, Editor
Fran Martin, Managing Editor
Richard Fischer, Publisher
Tom Delaney, National Sales Manager

Serves the dental profession and the dental industry, list rentals, classifieds and other services to complete your marketing plan.$35 subscription per year
35 Pages
Circulation: 19,000
ISSN: 0146-9738
Founded in 1967
Printed in 4 colors on glossy stock

13050 Dental Materials

Academy of Dental Materials
21 Grouse Terrace
PO Box 980566
Lake Oswego, OR 97035

503-636-0861
FAX 503-675-2738
E-Mail: admabstr@vcu.edu
Home Page: www.academydentalmaterials.org

David C Watts PhD FADM, Editor-in-Chief
Dr. Lorenzo Breschi, President
J. Robert Kelly, Vice President
Paulo F. Cesar, Secretary
Tom Hilton, Treasurer

13051 Dental Practice

MEDEC Dental Communications

2 Northfield Plaza
Suite 300
Northfield, IL 60093-1219

847-441-3700
800-225-4569
FAX 440-826-2865
Home Page: www.dentalproducts.net

Richard Fischer, Publisher
Bob Kehoe, Editorial Director
Steven Diogo, Editor
Daniel McCann, Senior Editor
Tom Delaney, National Sales Manager

Serves the dental industry. Subscription
75 Pages
Circulation: 120,000
ISSN: 1078-1250
Printed in 4 colors on glossy stock

13052 Dental Products Report

MEDEC Dental Communications
2 Northfield Plaza
Suite 300
Northfield, IL 60093-1219

847-441-3700
FAX 847-441-3702
Home Page: www.dentalproducts.net

Dolph Sharp, Publisher
Gail Weisman, Editor
Matthew LaFleur, Illustrator

Serves the dental profession and the dental industry. $120 subscription per year
141 Pages
Frequency: 12 per year
ISSN: 0011-8737
Founded in 1967
Printed in 4 colors on glossy stock

13053 Dental Products Report Europe

MEDEC Dental Communications
Two Northfield Plaza
Suite 300
Northfield, IL 60093-1219

847-441-3700
FAX 847-441-3702
Home Page: www.dentalproducts.net

Richard Fisher, Publisher
Pam Johnson, Editor
Keith Easty, Circulation Director
Dennis Spaeth, Editor
Bob Kehoe, Editorial Director

Designed to inform dentists in Europe and selected Middle Eastern and North African countries and dental distributors and depot personnel worldwide of new developments and ongoing trends in the dental market.
Cost: $40.00
Circulation: 50000
Founded in 1987

13054 Dentistry Today

100 Passaic Ave
Fairfield, NJ 07004-3508

973-882-4700
FAX 973-783-7112
E-Mail: admin@dentistrytoday.com
Home Page: www.dentistrytoday.com/

Paul Radcliffe, Owner
Phillip Bonner, Editor
Susan Oettinger, Treasurer, Manager
Jan Nigro, Production Manager
Janice Yawdoszyn, Director

The nation's leading clinical news magazine for dentists
Cost: $65.00
122 Pages
Frequency: Monthly
Circulation: 150,000
ISSN: 8750-2186
Founded in 1981
Printed in 4 colors on glossy stock

13055 Devices and Diagnostics Letter
300 N Washington Street
Suite 200
Falls Church, VA 22046-3431

703-538-7600
888-838-5578
FAX 703-538-7676
E-Mail: customerservice@fdanews.com
Home Page: www.fdanews.com

Robert Barton, Editorial Director
Matt Salt, Publisher
Maritza Lizama, Marketing Director
Cynthia Carter, President
Cost: $987.00
Frequency: Weekly
Circulation: 3300
Mailing list available for rent

13056 Diabetes Care
1701 N Beauregard St
Alexandria, VA 22311-1742

703-549-1500
800-342-2383
FAX 703-739-0290
E-Mail: askada@diabetes.org
Home Page: www.diabetes.org

Donna Lucas, Human Resources
Joseph Scheffer, Editor
Peter Banks, Publisher
Joe Herget, Marketing Manager
Cost: $314.00
Frequency: Monthly
Circulation: 13637
Founded in 1940

13057 Diabetes Digest Family
Drug Store News Consumer Health
Publications
425 Park Ave
New York, NY 10022-3526

212-756-5220
FAX 212-756-5250
Home Page: www.drugstorenews.com

Lebhar Friedman, Publisher
Contains health news of importance to those
with diabetes.
Frequency: Annual
Circulation: 6.8mm

13058 Diabetes Educator
American Association of Diabetes Educators
100 W Monroe Street
Suite 400
Chicago, IL 60603

312-424-2426
800-338-3633
FAX 312-424-2427
E-Mail: aade@aadenet.org
Home Page: www.diabeteseducator.org

James Sain, Editor
Chris Laxton, CEO
Michael Warner, Marketing Director
Tami Ross, Vice President
Published by the American Association of Dia-
betes Educators.
Founded in 1973
Mailing list available for rent: 10000 names at
$160 per M

13059 Diabetes Interview
6 School St
Suite 160
Fairfax, CA 94930-1655

415-258-2828
800-234-1218
FAX 415-258-2822
E-Mail: webmaster@diabeteshealth.com
Home Page: www.diabeteshealth.com

Nadia Al-Samarrie, Publisher
Scott King, Editorial

Daniel Trecroci, Managing Editor
Dick Young, Production
Susan Art, Director
Cost: $12.00
Frequency: Monthly
Circulation: 120,000
Founded in 1989

13060 Diagnostic Imaging
Miller Freeman Publications
600 Harrison Street
San Francisco, CA 94107

415-947-6478
FAX 415-947-6099
Home Page: www.diagnosticimaging.com

John C. Hayes, Editor
Gary Marshall, President
Suzanne Johnston, Publisher
Kathy Mischak, Associate Publisher
The news magazine of imaging innovation and
economics.
Cost: $113.00
90 Pages
Frequency: Monthly
Circulation: 31240
ISSN: 0194-2514
Founded in 1984
Printed in 4 colors on glossy stock

13061 Diagnostic Imaging America Latina
Miller Freeman Publications
600 Harrison Street
San Francisco, CA 94107

415-947-6478
FAX 415-947-6099
Home Page: www.diagnosticimaging.com

Suzanne Johnston, Editor/Publisher
John Hayes, Editorial
Buckley Dement, Circulation
Heidi Torpey, Marketing
Cost: $113.00
Frequency: Monthly
Founded in 1996

13062 Diagnostic Imaging Asia Pacific
Miller Freeman Publications
600 Harrison Street
San Francisco, CA 94107

415-947-6491
FAX 415-947-6099
Home Page: www.diagnosticimaging.com

Philip Ward, Editor
David E Lese, Publisher
A newsmagazine aimed at radiologists and allied medical professionals involved in the practice of diagnostic imaging, and provides timely
articles on new diagnostic and technical developments in the field mixed with extensive coverage of important political, commercial and
economic trends in the specialty.
Cost: $120.00
42 Pages
Frequency: Quarterly
Circulation: 10,000
Printed in 4 colors on glossy stock

13063 Diagnostic Imaging Europe
Miller Freeman Publications
600 Harrison Street
San Francisco, CA 94107

415-947-6478
FAX 415-947-6099
Home Page: www.diagnosticimaging.com

Philip Ward, Editor
Suzanne Johnston, Publisher
Jose Joaquin, Circulation
Kim Spinoso, National Sales Manager
A newsmagazine aimed at radiologists and al-
lied medical professionals involved in the prac-
tice of diagnostic imaging. Provides a balanced
mix of timely articles on new diagnostic and

technical developments in the field mixed with
extensive coverage of important political, com-
mercial and economic trends in the specialty.
Cost: $125.00
58 Pages
Circulation: 10062
Founded in 1996
Printed in 4 colors on glossy stock

13064 Dialysis and Transplantation
Creative Age Publications
7628 Densmore Ave
Van Nuys, CA 91406-2042

818-782-7560
800-442-5667
FAX 818-782-7450
Home Page: www.creativeage.com

Deborah Carver, Publisher/CEO
Joseph G Herman, Executive Editor
Carlos Benskin, Circulation Manager
Gail Edwards, Accounting Manager
Diane Jones, Advertising Director
Serves the renal care community. Subscription:
$17.50.
Cost: $35.00
Frequency: Monthly
Founded in 1975
Printed in 4 colors on glossy stock

13065 Director
National Funeral Director Association
13625 Bishops Dr
Brookfield, WI 53005-6607

262-789-1880
800-228-6332
FAX 262-789-6977
E-Mail: nfda@nfda.org
Home Page: www.nfda.org

Coverage concentrates on funeral service edu-
cation and licensure, community service and
public relations as well as public health con-
cerns and legal, ethical and moral issues.
Cost: $45.00
84 Pages
Frequency: Monthly
Circulation: 13906
ISSN: 0199-3186
Founded in 1882
Printed in 4 colors on glossy stock

13066 Diseases of the Colon & Rectum
American Society of Colon & Rectal
Surgeons
85 W Algonquin Road
Suite 550
Arlington Heights, IL 60005

847-290-9184
800-791-0001
FAX 847-290-9203
E-Mail: ascrs@fascrs.org
Home Page: www.fascrs.org
Social Media: *Facebook*

Pat Oldenburg, Managing Editor
Rick Slawny, Executive Director
Stella Zedalis, Associate Executive Director
Julie Weldon, Assistant Director
John Nocera, Chief Financial Officer
2800 Members
Mailing list available for rent

13067 Drug Store News
Lebhar-Friedman
425 Park Ave
New York, NY 10022-3526

212-756-5088
800-216-7117
FAX 212-838-9487
E-Mail: info@lf.com
Home Page: www.lf.com

Heather Martin, Manager
Tony Lisanti, Editor/Associate Publisher
Terry Nicosia, Senior Production Manager

K Dement, Circulation Manager
Wayne Bennett, Advertising Manager

Publication consists of merchandising trends and pharmacy developments. Provides extensive coverage of every major segment of chain drug retailing and combination stores.
Frequency: Monthly
Circulation: 44372
Founded in 1925

13068 Emergency Medicine

7 Century Dr
Siute 302
Parsippany, NJ 07054-4609

973-206-3434
FAX 973-206-9378
Home Page: www.quadranthealth.com

Susan Alburtus, Manager
Michael Pepper, Publisher
Martin Dicarlantonio, Editor
Donna Sickles, Circulation Manager
Kathleen Corbett, Advertising Coordinator
Cost: $90.00
Frequency: Monthly
Circulation: 158000
Founded in 1967

13069 Emerging Trends

Trends Analysis Group
1 N Franklin
29th Floor
Chicago, IL 60606-3421

312-422-3990
FAX 312-422-4569

Marcia Foley, Editor

Published as a community hospital trends which focuses on financial performance, personnel, utilization and facilities.
Cost: $135.00
Frequency: Quarterly
Circulation: 1,700

13070 EndoNurse

Virgo Publishing LLC
3300 N Central Ave
Suite 300
Phoenix, AZ 85012-2532

480-990-1101
FAX 480-990-0819
E-Mail: jsiefert@vpico.com
Home Page: www.vpico.com

Jenny Bolton, President
John Siefert, CEO
Jennifer Janos, Controller
Kelly Ridley, Executive VP, CFO, Copado

EndoNurse provides the practical information and updated protocol for those practicing in hospitals and freestanding facilities.
Mailing list available for rent: 13000+ names at $var per M

13071 Endocrine

505 NW 185th Avenue
Beaverton, OR 97006-3448

503-690-5350
FAX 503-690-5245
E-Mail: journals@ohsu.edu
Home Page: www.bioscience.org

P Michael Conn, Editor-in-Chief
Peter O Kohler, President
Cost: $365.00
Founded in 1867

13072 Endocrine Practice

American Association of Clinical
Endocrinologists

245 Riverside Avenue
Suite 200
Jacksonville, FL 32202

904-353-7878
FAX 904-353-8185
E-Mail: info@aace.com
Home Page: www.aace.com

Donald Jones, CEO
Donna Beasley, CPA, Finance Manager
Michael Avallone, CPA, Chief Financial Officer
Lynn Blanco, Executive Assistant
Lucille Killgore, Director of College Activities

To enhance the health care of patients with endocrine diseases through continuing education of practicing endocrinologists
Cost: $350.00
Frequency: Bi-Monthly
Circulation: 5000
Mailing list available for rent

13073 Endocrine Reviews

The Endocrine Society
8401 Connecticut Ave
Suite 900
Chevy Chase, MD 20815-5817

301-941-0200
888-363-6274
FAX 301-941-0259
E-Mail: societyservices@endo-society.org
Home Page: www.endo-society.org

Scott Hunt, Executive Director
Anthony R. Means, Secretary
John Marshall, Secretary
Cost: $252.00
Circulation: 5907
Founded in 1916

13074 European Medical Device Manufacturer

Canon Communications
11444 W Olympic Blvd
Los Angeles, CA 90064-1555

310-445-4200
FAX 310-445-4299
Home Page: www.cancom.com

Charlie Mc Curdy, President
Cost: $150.00
Circulation: 15,048
Founded in 1978

13075 Exercise and Sport Sicence Reviews

Lippincott Williams & Wilkins
530 Walnut St
Philadelphia, PA 19106-3604

215-521-8300
FAX 215-521-8902
E-Mail: support@ovid.com
Home Page: www.lww.com

Gordon Macomber, CEO
Lori A Tish, Editorial Assistant
Michael A. Hargrett, Associate Publisher

This Journal provides premier reviews of the most contemporary scientific, medical and research-based topics emerging in the field of sports medicine and exercise science, targeted to students, professors, clinicians, scientists and professionals for practical and research applications.
192 Pages
Frequency: Quarterly
ISSN: 0091-6331
Founded in 1998
Printed in 4 colors on matte stock

13076 Extended Care Product News

HMP Communications

83 General Warren Blvd
Suite 100
Malvern, PA 19355-1252

610-560-0500
800-237-7285
FAX 610-560-0502
E-Mail: pnorris@hmpcommunications.com
Home Page: www.hmpcommunications.com

Christine Franey, VP
Elizabeth Klumpp, Executive Editor
Peter Treaill, CEO/President
Bonnie Shannon, Manager
Michelle Koch, Circulation Manager

Serves purchasing professionals in acute, long term, and home care, offering product information, reimbursement updates, legislative news, industry trends, and a health care business focus.
24 Pages
Circulation: 100000
ISSN: 0895-2906
Founded in 1989
Printed in 4 colors on glossy stock

13077 Family Medicine

11400 Tomahawk Creek Parkway
Leawood, KS 66211

913-906-6000
800-274-2237
FAX 913-906-6096
E-Mail: fmjournal@stfm.org
Home Page: www.stfm.org

Traci Nolte, Publisher
John Saultz, President/Editor
Stacy Brungardt, Executive Director
Circulation: 6000
Founded in 1967

13078 Family Therapy Magazine

American Assoc for Marriage and Family
Therapy
112 S Alfred Street
Alexandria, VA 22314-3061

703-838-9808
FAX 703-838-9805
E-Mail: central@aamft.org
Home Page: www.aamft.org
Social Media: *Facebook, Twitter, LinkedIn*

Linda S. Metcalf, PhD, President
Michael L. Chafin, President-Elect
Michael Bowers, Executive Director
Robin Stillwell, MA, Secretary
Silvia M. Kaminsky, MsED,, Treasurer

AAMFT Association has been involved with the problems, needs and changing patterns of couples and family relationships. The assocation leads the way to increasing understanding, research and education in the field of marriage and family therapy, and ensuring that the public's needs are met by trained practitioners. The AAMFT provides individuals with the tools and resources they need to succeed as marriage and family therapists.
25000 Members
Frequency: Bi-Monthly
Circulation: 25,000
Founded in 1942

13079 First Messenger

American Association of Clinical
Endocrinologists
245 Riverside Avenue
Suite 200
Jacksonville, FL 32202

904-353-7878
FAX 904-353-8185
E-Mail: info@aace.com
Home Page: www.aace.com

Donald Jones, CEO
Donna Beasley, CPA, Finance Manager
Michael Avallone, CPA, Chief Financial

Officer
Lynn Blanco, Executive Assistant
Lucille Killgore, Director of College Activities

Serves as a fast track communications tool for AACE members. AACE members utilize The First Messenger to remain in touch with the latest news that may impact their practices, including legislative and socioeconomic issues, cutting edge educational programs, practice management issues and new coding changes.
Frequency: Bi-Monthly
Circulation: 5000
Mailing list available for rent

13080 General Dentistry

211 E Chicago Ave
Suite 900
Chicago, IL 60611-2637

312-440-4300
888-243-3368
FAX 312-440-0559
E-Mail: executiveoffice@agd.org
Home Page: www.agd.org

John Maher, Manager
Mark Heiss, AGD Member
Jay Donohue, Executive Director
Circulation: 37,000
Founded in 1951

13081 General Surgery News

545 W 45th St
8th Floor
New York, NY 10036-3409

212-957-5300
FAX 212-957-7230
E-Mail: cdahnke@mcmahonmed.com
Home Page: www.mcmahonmed.com

Raymond E Mc Mahon, CEO
Van Velle, Director
James Prudden, Director
Megan Roloff, Managing Editor
Cost: $60.00
Frequency: Monthly
Circulation: 37,268
Founded in 1974

13082 Grant Funding for Elderly Health Services

Health Resources Publishing
1913 Atlantic Ave
Suite F4
Manasquan, NJ 08736-1067

732-292-1100
888-843-6242
FAX 732-292-1111
E-Mail: info@healthresourcesonline.com
Home Page: www.healthresourcesonline.com

Robert K Jenkins, Publisher
Lisa Mansfield, Marketing Assistant
Robert Jenkins, Editor
Brett Powell, Regional Director
Alice Burron, Director

This report will give insight into which proposals will get funds for which organization. Lists the organizations that will recieve the most funds from grantmakers during this decade and beyond. Also studies different case histories of successful grant proposals.
Cost: $147.00
Frequency: Monthly
ISBN: 1-882364-46-5
Founded in 1969

13083 Group Practice Data Management

SourceMedia

550 W Van Buren
Suite 1100
Chicago, IL 60607-6680

312-913-1334
FAX 312-913-1959
Home Page: www.sourcemedia.com

Howard Anderson, Publisher/Editor
Melissa Sefic, Director of Sales

Analyses of trends, insights on technology and practice advice from automation pioneers for executive and physician administrators of medical groups in charge of making decisions about information technology investments. Profiles on practices, new software development updates, and ideas on plans for implementing information technology.
Frequency: Semiannual
Circulation: 15M

13084 Harvard Mental Health Letter

Harvard Health Publcations
10 Shattuck Street
Boston, MA 02115

617-432-1485
877-649-9457
FAX 617-432-1506
E-Mail: mental_health@hms.harvard.edu
Home Page: www.health.harvard.edu/mental

Michael Craig Miller, Editor in Chief
Edward Coburn, Publishing Director
Cost: $59.00
Frequency: Monthly
Circulation: 50000
Founded in 1985

13085 Harvard Public Health Review

Harvard School of Public Health
665 Huntington Ave
Boston, MA 02115-6018

617-495-1000
FAX 617-384-8989
E-Mail: fphelps@hsph.harvard.edu
Home Page: www.hsph.harvard.edu/review

Martha Cassin, Manager
Barry R. Bloom, Dean of the School
Martha Cassin, Manager

Flagship magazine of the Harvard School of Public Health.
60 Pages
Frequency: Bi-annually
Circulation: 10000
Founded in 1922
Printed in 4 colors on glossy stock

13086 Health Data Management

SourceMedia
550 W Van Buren
Suite 1100
Chicago, IL 60607-6680

312-913-1334
FAX 312-913-1959
Home Page: www.healthdatamanagement.com/

Howard J Anderson, Publisher
Bill Siwicki, Editorial Director
Greg Gillespie, Managing Editor
Bill Briggs, Senior Editor
Jim Siebert, Sales/Marketing Manager

Reporting on important information technology issues in health care with emphasis on computerization trends that improve health care efficiency.
Frequency: Monthly
Circulation: 41116
Founded in 1994

13087 Health Facilities Management

American Hospital Publishing

1 N Franklin St
29th Floor
Chicago, IL 60606-3530

312-893-6800
800-821-2039
FAX 312-422-4500
E-Mail: hfcustsvc@healthforum.com
Home Page: www.hfmmagazine.com

Mary Grayson, Publisher
Mike Hrickiewicz, Managing Editor
Gary A. Mecklenburg, Chairman
Neil J. Jesuele, Director

Reflects their highly specialized needs such as changes in codes and standards, industry news, new products and technical developments of suppliers.
Cost: $30.00
Frequency: Monthly
Circulation: 28160
Founded in 1998

13088 Health Management Technology

Nelson Publishing
2500 Tamiami Trl N
Nokomis, FL 34275-3476

941-966-9521
FAX 941-966-2590
E-Mail: rblair@healthmgttech.com
Home Page: www.healthmgttech.com
Social Media: *Facebook, Twitter*

A Verner Nelson, Owner
Robin Blair, Editor

Serves the health care industry including hospitals/multi-hospital systems, managed care organizations and others allied to the field.
Cost: $60.00
66 Pages
Frequency: Monthly
Circulation: 45751
ISSN: 0745-1075
Founded in 1965
Printed in 4 colors on glossy stock

13089 Health Progress

Catholic Health Association
4455 Woodson Rd
St Louis, MO 63134-3797

314-427-2500
FAX 314-427-0029
E-Mail: rmueller@chausa.org
Home Page: www.chausa.org

Rhonda Mueller, Senior Vice President of Operations
Monica Heaton, Editor
Martha Slover, Circulation Manager

Focuses on management concepts, ethical issues, legislative trends, and theological issues.
Cost: $50.00
Frequency: Monthly
Circulation: 12000
Founded in 1914

13090 Healthcare Executive

American College of Healthcare Executives
1 N Franklin St
Chicago, IL 60606-3529

312-424-2800
FAX 312-424-0023
E-Mail: contact@ache.org
Home Page: www.ache.org

Thomas C Dolan, CEO
Deborah A Labb, Editor-in-Chief
Michael C Waters, Chairman
Deborah Sprindzunas, Executive Director

Serves members of the American College of Health care executives, whose primary business/industries include hospitals, managed care organizations, long-term care facilities and oth-

ers allied to the field.
Cost: $65.00
Frequency: Bi-Monthly
ISSN: 0883-5381
Printed in 4 colors on glossy stock

13091 Healthcare Financial Management

2 Westbrook Corporate Ctr
Westchester, IL 60154-5723

708-531-9614
FAX 708-531-0032
Home Page: www.hfma.org

Richard L Clarke, President

13092 Healthcare Foodservice Magazine

International Publishing Company of America
664 La Villa Dr
Miami Springs, FL 33166-6030

305-887-1700
800-525-2015
FAX 305-885-1923
Home Page: www.healthcare-services.com

Alexander Morton, Owner
Melora Grattan, Assistant Editor

Devoted to foodservice topics for foodservice directors, foodservice managers, dieticians, foodservice supervisors, chefs, purchasing managers, purchasing agents, administrators and others.
Cost: $25.00
24 Pages
Frequency: Quarterly
Printed in 4 colors on glossy stock

13093 Healthcare Informatics

McGraw Hill
4530 W 77th St
Suite 350
Edina, MN 55435-5018

952-832-7887
FAX 952-832-7908

Jim Dougherty, Publisher

13094 Healthcare Purchasing News

Nelson Publishing
7650 S Tamiami Trail N
Suite 10
Sarasota, FL 34275

941-927-9345
FAX 941-927-9588
Home Page: www.hpnonline.com

Rick Dana Barlow, Senior Editor
Jeannie Akridge, New Products Editor
Kristine Russell, Publisher
Julie Williamson, Features Editor
Susan Cantrell, Infection Control Editor

Serves the field of hospital materials management, purchasing, central services and administration.
Cost: $63.00
27 Pages
Frequency: Monthly
Circulation: 33000
ISSN: 0279-4799
Founded in 1965
Printed in 4 colors on glossy stock

13095 Healthplan

American Association of Health Plans
601 Pennsylvania Ave NW
Suite 500
Washington, DC 20004-2601

202-778-3200
FAX 202-955-4394
E-Mail: ahip@ahip.org
Home Page: www.ahip.org

Kevin New, Editor

A magazine of trends, insights and best practices.
Cost: $60.00
Circulation: 19000
Founded in 2004

13096 Home Health Products

Stevens Publishing Corporation
5151 Belt Line Rd
Dallas, TX 75254-7507

972-687-6700
FAX 972-687-6767
Home Page: www.stevenspublishing.com

Craig S Stevens, President
Mike Valenti, Executive Vice President
Randy Dye, Publisher
Sandra Bienkowski, Editor
Cost: $119.00
Circulation: 20000
Founded in 1925

13097 Home Medical Equipment News

United Publications
106 Lafayette Street
PO Box 998
Yarmouth, ME 04096

207-846-0600
FAX 207-846-0657
E-Mail: hmenews@hmenews.com
Home Page: www.hmenews.com

Rick Rector, Publisher
Brook Taliaferro, Editorial Director
Brenda Boothby, Circulation Director
James G. Taliaferro, President
Jim Sullivan, Editor

Serves home medical equipment providers.
Cost: $84.00
Frequency: Monthly
Circulation: 17100
Founded in 1995

13098 HomeCare

Penton Media Inc
249 W 17th St
New York, NY 10011-5390

212-204-4200
FAX 212-206-3622
E-Mail: gwalker@homecaremag.com
Home Page: www.penton.com

Sharon Rowlands, CEO
Gail Walker, Editor
David Kieselstein, Chief Executive Officer
Kurt Nelson, Vice President, Human Resources
Andrew Schmolka, Senior Vice President

For business leaders in home medical equipment
Frequency: Monthly
Founded in 1989
Mailing list available for rent

13099 Hospital Law Manual

Publishers
111 Eighth Avenue
7th Floor
New York, NY 10011-1978

212-771-0600
800-234-1660
FAX 212-771-0885
E-Mail: customer.service@aspenpubl.com
Home Page: www.aspenpub.com

Robert Becker, CEO
Stacey Caywood, Publisher
Richard H Kravitz, VP

Hospital law.
Cost: $1325.00
Frequency: Quarterly
Founded in 1965

13100 Hospital Outlook

801 Pennsylvania Ave NW
Suite 245
Washington, DC 20004-2697

202-624-1500
202-624-1500
FAX 202-737-6462
E-Mail: info@fah.org
Home Page: www.fah.org

Charles Kahn, President
LaQuanda Washington, Editor Asst.
Richard P Coorsh, Publisher
Letitia Faison-Mahoney, Controller
Founded in 1966

13101 Hypertension

1516 Jefferson Highway
BH 514
New Orleans, LA 70121

504-842-3700
FAX 504-842-3258

13102 Immediate Care Business

Virgo Publishing LLC
3300 N Central Ave
Suite 300
Phoenix, AZ 85012-2532

480-990-1101
FAX 480-990-0819
E-Mail: jsiefert@vpico.com
Home Page: www.vpico.com

Jenny Bolton, President
John Siefert, CEO
Jennifer Janos, Controller
Kelly Ridley, Executive VP, CFO, Copado

Immediate Care Business provides practical business solutions to professionals who own, operate or are planning to open an urgent care/immediate care facility.
Mailing list available for rent

13103 Infection Control Today

Virgo Publishing LLC
3300 N Central Ave
Suite 300
Phoenix, AZ 85012-2532

480-990-1101
FAX 480-990-0819
E-Mail: jsiefert@vpico.com
Home Page: www.vpico.com

Jenny Bolton, President
John Siefert, CEO
Jennifer Janos, Controller
Kelly Ridley, Executive VP, CFO, Copado

Infection Control Today provides science based articles for the general ward, operating room, sterile processing and environmental services departments of healthcare facilities as well as for the public health community.
Mailing list available for rent: 30000+ names at $var per M

13104 Information Management Magazine

ARMA International
11880 College Blvd
Suite 450
Overland Park, KS 66210

913-341-3808
800-422-2762
FAX 913-341-3742
E-Mail: hq@arma.org
Home Page: www.arma.org

Marilyn Bier, Executive Director
Jody Becker, Associate Editor
Kerrianne Aulet, Education Program Administrator
Michael Avery, Chief Operating Officer
Paula Banes, Sales Project Manager

The leading source of information on topics and issues central to the management of records and information worldwide. Each issue features insightful articles written by experts in the management of records and information.
Cost: $115.00
10,00 Members
Frequency: Bi-monthly
Circulation: 11000
ISSN: 1535-2897
Founded in 1955
Mailing list available for rent: 9000 names
Printed in 4 colors on glossy stock

13105 International Journal of Trauma Nursing

Mosby/Professional Opportunities
11830 Westline Industrial Drive
St Louis, MO 63146-3318

314-453-4338
800-237-9851
FAX 314-872-9164
E-Mail: c.kilzer@elsevier.com
Home Page: www.mosby.com/trauma

Judith Stoner Halpern, Editor
Sarah Papke Kalamazoo, EDITORIAL ASSISTANT
Carol Kilzer, Advertising Sales Service

Reaches today's trauma nurses, coordinators,and managers who direct the nursing aspects of patient care. The journal's multidisciplinary and collaborative approach to the unique needs of the trauma patient represents the vision and clinical expertise of each nursing specialty. These professionals influence the purchase of supplies and equipment for use in emergency and trauma departments.
Cost: $42.00
Frequency: Quarterly
Circulation: 1298
Founded in 1995

13106 Internet Healthcare Strategies

Dean Anderson
PO Box 50507
Santa Barbara, CA 93150

805-564-2177
FAX 805-564-2146
Home Page: www.corhealth.com

13107 JAAPA

Medical Economics Publishing
131 W 1st Street
Duluth, MN 55802-2065

877-922-2022
FAX 218-723-9437
E-Mail: aapa@aapa.org
Home Page: www.jaapa.com

Leslie A Kole, Editor-in-Chief
Tanya Gregory, Editor
Dominic Barone, Publisher
Miguel Van Brakle, Circulation manager
Lee Maniscalco, CEO

Official journal of the American Academy of Physician Assistants.
92 Pages
Frequency: Monthly
Circulation: 52500
ISSN: 0893-7400

13108 Journal Of Oncology Management

Alliance Communications Group
810 E 10th St
Lawrence, KS 66044-3018

785-843-1235
800-627-0932
FAX 785-843-1274
Home Page: www.acgpublishing.com

Gerald Lillian, CEO
Jorgene Hallett, Chief Financial Officer

Rob Chestnut, Chief Financial Officer
Barbara Buzzi, Manager

Bi-monthly, peer-reviewed journal. Includes original research, case studies and other features pertinent to improving performance of oncology administrators.
Cost: $87.00
32 Pages
Circulation: 10000
ISSN: 1061-9364
Founded in 1935
Printed in 4 colors on glossy stock

13109 Journal Watch

860 Winter Street
Waltham, MA 02154

781-893-3800
800-843-6356
FAX 781-893-3914
E-Mail: jwatch@mms.org
Home Page: www.jwatch.org

Allan S Brett, Editor In Chief
Alberta L Fitzpatrick, Publisher
Founded in 1987

13110 Journal of Allergy and Clinical Immunology

American Academy of Allergy, Asthma and Immunology
555 E Wells St
Suite 1100
Milwaukee, WI 53202-3800

414-272-6071
E-Mail: info@aaaai.org
Home Page: www.aaaai.org

Thomas B. Casale, MD, Executive VP
Kay A. Whalen, Executive Director
Roberta Silvensky, Associate Executive Director
Amy Flanders, Director of Grants & Development
Rachel McCormick, Executive Assistant

The official scientific journal of the American Academy of Allergy, Asthma and Immunology and the premiere journal in the field. Each issue features the very latest and best research in the allergy/immunology specialty.
6000+ Members
Frequency: Monthly
Founded in 1943

13111 Journal of American Dietetic Association

American Dietetic Association
120 South Riverside Plaza
Suite 2000
Chicago, IL 60606-6995

312-990-0040
800-877-1600
FAX 312-899-4757
E-Mail: elspcs@elsevier.com
Home Page: www.adajournal.org

Linda Van Horn, Editor-in-Chief
Jason T Switt, Editors:

The Journal of American Dietetic Association serves the dietetic field.
Cost: $220.00
Frequency: Monthly
Circulation: 65000
ISSN: 0002-8223
Founded in 1925
Printed in 4 colors on glossy stock

13112 Journal of Cardiovascular Management

Alliance Communications Group
810 E 10th St
Lawrence, KS 66044-3018

785-843-1235
800-627-0932
FAX 785-843-1274

E-Mail: info@aameda.org
Home Page: www.acgpublishing.com

Gerald Lillian, CEO
Jorgene Hallett, Publishing Manager
Renee S Schleicher, CEO/President
Rob Chestnut, Chief Financial Officer

Bi-monthly, peer-reviewed journal of articles pertinent to cardiovascular administration.
Cost: $87.00
32 Pages
Circulation: 12,500
ISSN: 1053-5330
Founded in 1957
Mailing list available for rent: 400 names at $350 per M
Printed in 4 colors on glossy stock

13113 Journal of Clinical Epidemiology

Elsevier Publishing
PO Box 28430
St Louis, MO 63146-0930

314-872-8370
800-545-2522
FAX 314-432-1380
Home Page: www.elsevier.com

Erik Engstrom, CEO
Bill Godfrey, Chief Information Officer
David Clark, Senior Vice President

13114 Journal of Clinical Investigation

11830 Westline Industrial Drive
St Louis, MO 63146

314-453-7010
800-460-3110
FAX 314-453-7095
Home Page: www.elsevier.com

A Knottnerus, Editor
P Tugwell, Editor
Laurence Zipson, Group Advertisement Manag
Karlyn Messinger, Communications Manager
Cost: $274.00
Frequency: Monthly
Founded in 1955

13115 Journal of Craniofacial Surgery

Lippencott Williams & Wilkins
16522 Hunters Green Pkwy
Hagerstown, MD 21740-2116

301-223-2300
800-638-3030
FAX 301-223-2398
E-Mail: service@lww.com
Home Page: www.nursingdrugguide.com

Mutaz B Habal MD, Editor
Jay Lippioctt, CEO

An international journal dedicated to the art and science essential to the practice of craniofacial surgery. Online version available.
Cost: $586.00
ISSN: 1049-2275
Founded in 1998

13116 Journal of Digital Imaging

Society for Imaging Informatics in Medicine
19440 Golf Vista Plaza
Suite 330
Leesburg, VA 20176-8264

703-723-0432
FAX 703-723-0415
E-Mail: info@siimweb.org
Home Page: www.siimweb.org

Janice Honeyman-Buck PhD, Editor-in-Chief

Goal is to enhance the exchange of knowledge encompassed by the general topic of Imaging Informatics in Medicine such as research and practice in clinical, engineering, information technologies and techniques in all medical imaging environments. JDI topics are of interest to researchers, developers, educators, physicians, and imaging informatics professionals.
Frequency: Bi-Monthly

13117 Journal of Emergency Nursing

Mosby/Professional Opportunities
PO Box 1510
Clearwater, FL 33757-1510

727-443-3047
800-237-9851
FAX 727-445-9380
Home Page: www.mosby.com/trauma

Presents original, peer-reviewed clinical articles as well as the annual ENA Scientific Assembly program.
Circulation: 27240

13118 Journal of ExtraCorporeal Technology

American Society of ExtraCorporeal Technology
2209 Dickens Road
Richmond, VA 23230-2005

804-565-6363
FAX 804-282-0090
E-Mail: judyr@amsect.org
Home Page: www.amsect.org

Stewart Hinckley, Executive Director
Donna Pendarvis, Associate Manager
Michael Troike, Government Relations Chairman
Kimberly Robertson, CPA, Controller
Greg Leasure, Membership Services
Cost: $225.00
2,000 Members
Frequency: Quarterly
Circulation: 2000
ISSN: 0022-1058
Founded in 1964

13119 Journal of Forensic Psychology Practice

Bill Cohen
10 Alice Street
Binghamton, NY 13904-1580

607-225-5857
607-722-5857
FAX 607-771-0012
E-Mail: getinfo@haworthpress.com
Home Page: www.haworthpressinc.com

Bill Cohen, President/Publisher
Jim Hom, Editor

Provides the forensic psychology practicioner and professional with timely information and regional research that examines the impact of new knowledge in the field as it relates to their practice.
Cost: $60.00
Frequency: Quarterly
Circulation: 700
Founded in 1978

13120 Journal of Hand Surgery

American Society for Surgery of the Hand
822 W. Washington Boulevard
Suite 600
Chicago, IL 60607

312-880-1900
FAX 847-384-1435
E-Mail: info@assh.org
Home Page: www.assh.org

Roy A Meals, Editor-in-Chief

Publishes original, peer-reviewed articles related to the diagnosis, treatment, and pathophysiology of diseases and conditions of the upper extremity; these include both clinical and basic science studies, along with case reports.
Frequency: Monthly
Mailing list available for rent

13121 Journal of Healthcare Quality

National Association for Healthcare Quality

4700 W Lake Ave
Glenview, IL 60025-1468

847-375-4732
800-966-9392
FAX 888-576-4349
E-Mail: info@nahq.org
Home Page: www.nahq.org

Sheila Lee, Manager
John D Hartley, President

Professional forum that advances quality in a diverse and changing health care environment. Health care professionals worldwide depend upon the Journal for its creative solutions and scientific konwledge in the pursuit of quality.
Cost: $115.00
54 Pages
ISSN: 1062-2551
Founded in 1976
Printed in 4 colors on glossy stock

13122 Journal of Magnetic Resonance

525 B Street
Suite 1900
San Diego, CA 92101-4401

619-231-6616
800-321-5068
FAX 619-699-6280
Home Page: www.elsevier.com/

S.J. Opella, Editor
JJH Ackerman, Associate Editor
L Frydman, Associate Editor
W.S. Brey, Founding Editor
Founded in 1880

13123 Journal of Managed Care Medicine

American Assoc of Integrated Healthcare Delivery
4435 Waterfront Drive
Suite 101
Glen Allen, VA 23060

804-747-5823
FAX 804-747-5316
E-Mail: phulcher@aaihds.org
Home Page: www.aaihds.org

Bill Edwards, Managing Editor
Jeremy Williams, Communications Director
Mark Abernathy, Managing Director
David Tyler, Manager
Steven M. Abramson, Senior Manager

13124 Journal of Marriage & Family Therapy

American Assoc for Marriage and Family Therapy
112 S Alfred Street
Alexandria, VA 22314-3061

703-838-9808
FAX 703-838-9805
E-Mail: central@aamft.org
Home Page: www.aamft.org
Social Media: *Facebook, Twitter, LinkedIn*

Linda S. Metcalf, PhD, President
Michael Chafin, President-Elect
Michael Bowers, Executive Director
Robin K. Stillwell, MA, Secretary
Silvia M. Kaminsky, MSEd, Treasurer

The AAMFT has been involved with the problems, needs and changing patterns of couples and family relationships. The association leads the way to increasing understanding, research and education in the field of marriage and family therapy, ensuring that the public's needs are met by trained practitioners.
25000 Members
Frequency: Quarterly
Circulation: 25,000
Founded in 1942

13125 Journal of Midwifery & Women's Health

American College of Nurse-Midwives
8403 Colesville Road,Suite 1550
Silver Spring, MD 20910

240-485-1815
FAX 240-485-1817
E-Mail: jmwh@acnm.org
Home Page: www.jmwh.org/

tekoa king, Editor
Tekoa King, President, Chief Executive Officer
Kalpana Raina, Managing Partner
Cost: $130.00
Circulation: 8000

13126 Journal of Music Therapy

8455 Colesville Rd
Suite 1000
Silver Spring, MD 20910-3392

301-589-3300
FAX 301-589-5175
E-Mail: info@musictherapy.org
Home Page: www.musictherapy.org
Social Media: *Facebook, Twitter*

Andrea Farbman, Executive Director
Mary Ellen Wylei, AMTA President

Founded in 1998, AMTA's purpose is the progressive development of the therapeutic use of music in rehabilitation, special education, and community settings. AMTA is committed to the advancement of education, training, professional standards, credentials, and research in support of the music therapy profession.
3800 Members
Frequency: 4 Issues Per Year
Founded in 1998

13127 Journal of Neurotherapy

Taylor & Francis Group LLC
325 Chestnut Street
Suite 800
Philadelphia, PA 19106

215-625-8900
800-354-1420
FAX 215-625-2940
E-Mail: haworthorders@taylorandfrancis.com
Home Page: www.haworthpressinc.com

Timothy Tinius PhD, Editor
David Kaiser PhD, Editor

Provides an integrated multidisciplinary perspective on clinically relevant research, treatment and public policy for neurotherapy. The journal reviews important findings in clinical neurotherapy and electroencephalography for use in assessing baselines and outcomes of various procedures.
Frequency: Monthly

13128 Journal of Nuclear Medicine

Society of Nuclear Medicine
1850 Samuel Morse Dr
Reston, VA 20190-5316

703-708-9000
FAX 703-708-9015
E-Mail: volunteer@snm.org
Home Page: www.snm.org

Virginia Pappas, Executive Director
Vincent Pistilli, Chief Financial Officer
Matt Dickens, Director, Information Services
Judy Brazel, Director, Meeting Services
Joanna Spahr, Director, Marketing

13129 Journal of Occupational and Environmental Hygiene

American Industrial Hygiene Association
2700 Prosperity Ave
Suite 250
Fairfax, VA 22031-4321

703-849-8267
FAX 703-207-3561

E-Mail: infonet@aiha.org
Home Page: www.aiha.org

Peter J Oneil, Executive Director
Michael T Brandt, President

A joint publication of AIHA and ACGIH that is published to enhance the knowledge and practice of occupational and environmental hygiene and safety.

13130 Journal of Oral Implantology
American Academy of Implant Dentistry
211 E Chicago Avenue
Suie 750
Chicago, IL 60611

312-335-1550
877-335-2243
FAX 312-335-9090
Home Page: www.aaid.org
Social Media: *Facebook, Twitter, LinkedIn*

James Rutkowski, Editor-in-Chief
Sheldon Winkler, Senior Editor

Dedicated to providing valuable information to general dentists, oral surgeons, prosthodontists, periodontists, scientists, clinicians, laboratory owners and technicians, manufacturers, and educators
Cost: $140.00
Frequency: Bimonthly
Circulation: 4200
ISSN: 0160-6972

13131 Journal of Prosthetics and Orthotics
351 W Camden St
Baltimore, MD 21201-7912

410-528-4000
800-638-6423
FAX 410-528-4452
E-Mail: webmaster@lww.com
Home Page: www.lww.com

Jeffrey A Nemeth, Editor
Cost: $91.00
Frequency: Quarterly
Founded in 1792

13132 Journal of School Nursing (JOSN)
Sage Publications
2455 Teller Rd
Newbury Park, CA 91320-2234

805-499-9774
800-818-7243
FAX 805-499-0871
E-Mail: info@sagepub.com
Home Page: www.sagepub.com

Blaise R Simqu, CEO
Janice Denehy, Executive Editor

A forum for advancing the specialty of school nursing, promoting professional growth of school nurses, and improving the health of children in school. Published bi-monthly, this is the official journal of the National Association of School Nurses.
Cost: $164.00
Frequency: bi-Monthly
Mailing list available for rent

13133 Journal of Social Behavior & Personality
Drawer 37
Corte Madera, CA 94976

415-209-9838
FAX 415-209-6719
Home Page: www.rickcrandall.com

Rick Crandall, CEO/President
Rick Crandall, Editor
Cost: $70.00
Frequency: Quarterly
Founded in 1985

13134 Journal of Thoracic and Cardiovascular Surgery
American Association for Thoracic Surgery
500 Cummings Center
Suite 4550
Beverly, MA 01915

978-927-8330
FAX 978-524-8890
E-Mail: aats@prri.com
Home Page: www.aats.org
Social Media: *Facebook*

G Alexander Patterson, President
Elizabeth Dooley Crane, Executive Director
Cost: $354.00
Frequency: Monthly
Circulation: 6000
Founded in 1917
Mailing list available for rent

13135 Journal of Trauma & Dissociation
Taylor & Francis Group LLC
325 Chestnut Street
Suite 800
Philadelphia, PA 19106

215-625-8900
800-354-1420
FAX 215-625-2940
E-Mail: haworthorders@taylorandfrancis.com
Home Page: www.haworthpressinc.com

Jennifer J Freyd PhD, Editor

Dedicated to publishing peer reviewed scientific literature on psychological trauma, dissociation, and traumatic memory in children and adults. The journal addresses issues ranging from controlled management of traumatic memories and successful interventions to the ethical and philosophical issues entailed by trauma.
Frequency: Quarterly

13136 Journal of Ultrasound in Medicine
American Institute of Ultrasound in Medicine
14750 Sweitzer Ln
Suite 100
Laurel, MD 20707-5906

301-498-4392
800-638-5352
FAX 301-498-4450
E-Mail: admin@aium.org
Home Page: www.aium.org

Dr Beryl R Benacenraf, Editor-in-Chief
Bruce Totaro, Director of Publications
Thomas R. Nelson, Deputy Editor

Dedicated to the rapid, accurate publication of original articles dealing with all aspects of diagnostic ultrasound, particularly its direct application to patient care, but also relevant basic science, advances in instrumentation and biologic effects. Research papers, case reports, review articles, technical notes and letters to the editor are published.
Cost: $265.00
Frequency: Monthly
Circulation: 8200
ISSN: 0278-4297
Founded in 1952
Mailing list available for rent
Printed in 4 colors on glossy stock

13137 Journal of the American Academy of Child and Adult Psychiatry
American Academy of Child and Adult Psychiatry
3615 Wisconsin Ave NW
Washington, DC 20016-3007

202-966-7300
FAX 202-966-2891
E-Mail: communications@aacap.org

Home Page: www.aacap.org
Social Media: *Facebook, Twitter*

Eva Brown, Manager
Martin J. Drell, President
Virginia Anthony, Executive Director
Founded in 1953
Mailing list available for rent

13138 Journal of the American Academy of Child & Adolescent Psychiatry
Lippincott Williams & Wilkins
351 W Camden St
Baltimore, MD 21201-2436

410-949-8000
FAX 410-528-4414
Home Page: www.lww.com
Social Media: *Facebook, Twitter*

J Arnold Anthony, Operations
AndrSs Martin, MD/MPH, Editor-Elect
Rebecca Jensen, Managing Editor

The official journal of the American Academy of Child & adolescent Psychiatry, the journal is recognized as the major journal exclusivley on todays psychiatric research and treatment of the child and adolescent.
Frequency: Monthly
ISSN: 0890-8567

13139 Journal of the American College of Surgeons
633 N St. Clair Street
Chicago, IL 60611

312-202-5136
800-440-5227
FAX 312-202-5027

13140 Journal of the American Dental Association
American Dental Association
211 E Chicago Ave
Chicago, IL 60611-2678

312-440-2897
FAX 312-440-2800
Home Page: www.ada.org

Lawrence H Meskin, Editor
Daniel M Castagna, Editorial Board

Serves the dental profession and dental industry.
Cost: $95.00
Frequency: Monthly
Circulation: 135361
ISSN: 0002-8177
Founded in 1859
Printed in 4 colors on glossy stock

13141 Journal of the American Health Information Management Association
American Health Information Management Association
633 N St. Clair Street
Chicago, IL 60611-3211

312-202-5000
800-621-4111
FAX 312-202-5001
E-Mail: postmaster@facs.org
Home Page: www.facs.org/

Barry M. Manuel, Editor-in-chief
Paul F. Nora, Editor

Provides information in the field of health information and medical record management in all health care settings. Subscription: non-members $72,
Cost: $25.00
Frequency: Monthly
Founded in 1913
Printed in 4 colors on glossy stock

13142 Journal of the Medical Library Association

Medical Library Association
65 E Wacker Drive
Suite 1900
Chicago, IL 60601-7246

312-419-9094
FAX 312-419-8950
E-Mail: info@mlahq.org
Home Page: www.mlanet.org

Elizabeth Lund, Director Publication
Carla J Funk, Executive Officer
Susan Talmage, Editorial Assistant
Scott Plutchak, Editor
Cost: $163.00
Frequency: Quarterly
Circulation: 5000
Founded in 1898
Mailing list available for rent

13143 Journal of the National Medical Association

4930 Del Ray Avenue
Bethesda, MD 20814

301-654-2055
FAX 301-654-5920
E-Mail: member@gastro.org
Home Page: www.gastro.org

Robert Greenberg, Executive Vp
Michael Stolar, Senior Vp

13144 MS Connection

Lippincott Williams & Wilkins
351 W Camden St
Baltimore, MD 21201-2436

410-949-8000
800-787-8981
FAX 410-528-4414
Home Page: www.lww.com

J Arnold Anthony, Operations
Michael Levin-Epstein, Managing Editor
Michele Swain, Marketing Manager

13145 Managed Healthcare

Advanstar Communications
7500 Old Oak Blvd
Cleveland, OH 44130-3343

440-243-8100
FAX 440-891-2740
E-Mail: info@advanstar.com

Daniel J. Corcoran, Publisher
Michael T. McCue, Editor-In-Chief
Craig Roth, Group Publisher
Tracey L. Walker, Senior Editor
Julie Miller, Managing Editor

Valuable resource for managers charged with
controlling health care costs and quality.
Cost: $64.00
Frequency: Monthly
Circulation: 40000
ISSN: 1060-1392
Founded in 1987

13146 McKnight's Long-Term Care News

McKnight Medical Communications
1 Northfield Plz
Suite 300
Northfield, IL 60093-1216

847-784-8706
800-558-1703
FAX 847-784-9346
E-Mail: ltcn-webmaster@mltcn.com
Home Page: www.mcknightsonline.com

William Pecover, CEO
Lee Maniscalco, Executive VP
Jim Berklan, Editor
Jeff Hartford, Circulation Director

Serves the field of long term care including
nursing homes, senior housing centers, assisted
living facilities, hospitals with LTC units, continuing care retirement communities, nursing
home chains and other allied organizations in
the field.
35 Pages
Frequency: Weekly
Circulation: 46000
ISSN: 1048-3314
Printed in 4 colors on glossy stock

13147 Medical Economics

Advanstar Communications
5 Paragon Dr
Montvale, NJ 07645-1791

973-944-7777
FAX 973-944-7778

Curtis Allen, President
Marianne Dekker Mattera, Editor-in-Chief
Mike Graziani, Publisher
Sean Keating, Managing Editor
Laura Wagner, VP Operations

Medical Economics guides physicians in the
business of practicing by giving advice about
malpractice, third-party reimbursement, managed care, tax strategies, legal information and
counseling, fraud, abuse and anti-trust strategies. It helps them manage their practice more
efficiently so they can be more effective in delivering patient care.
Cost: $109.00
Frequency: Monthly
Circulation: 154897
Founded in 1987

13148 Medical Reference Services Quarterly

Taylor & Francis Group LLC
325 Chestnut Street
Suite 800
Philadelphia, PA 19106

215-625-8900
215-625-8900
FAX 215-625-2940
E-Mail: haworthorders@taylorandfrancis.com
Home Page: www.haworthpress.com

M Sandra Wood, Editor

Covers topics of current interest and practical
value in the areas of reference in medicine and
related specialties, the biomedical sciences,
nursing and allied health.
Cost: $60.00
Frequency: Quarterly
ISSN: 0276-3869
Founded in 1978

13149 Medical Research Funding Bulletin

PO Box 7507
New York, NY 10150-7507

212-371-3398
FAX 801-761-4200

John Connolly, CEO
Carroll Gordon, Circulation Manager
Cost: $75.00
Frequency: Fortnightly
Circulation: 4500
Founded in 1972

13150 Modern Healthcare

Crain Communications
360 N Michigan Ave
Chicago, IL 60601-3800

312-649-5200
FAX 312-649-7937
E-Mail: info@crain.com
Home Page: www.crain.com

Keith Crain, CEO

Examines and reports on the issues that have a
direct impact on the business decisions
healthcare professionals make every day.
Frequency: Weekly
Circulation: 70180

13151 Molecular Endocrinology

Molecular Society Journals
8401 Connecticut Avenue
Suite 900
Chevy Chase, MD 20815-4410

301-941-0200
888-363-6274
FAX 301-941-0259
E-Mail: societyservices@endo-society.org
Home Page: www.endo-society.org

John A Cidlowski, Editor-in-chief
Scott Hunt, Executive Director
Maggie Haworth, Managing Editor
Jessica Peterson, Marketing Manager
John Marshall, Secretary
Cost: $376.00
Frequency: Weekly
Circulation: 11000
Founded in 1916

13152 NASN Newsletter

National Association of School Nurses
163 US Route 1
PO Box 1300
Scarborough, ME 04074-9060

207-883-2117
877-627-6476
FAX 207-883-2683
E-Mail: nasn@nasn.org
Home Page: www.nasn.org

Devin Dinkel, Editor
Wanda Miller, Executive Director
Donna Mazyck, President
Gloria Durgin, Administrator/Sponsorship
Kenny Lull, Communications Manager
Cost: $2.00
Founded in 1968

13153 New England Journal of Medicine

Massachusetts Medical Society
10 Shattuck St
Boston, MA 02115-6094

617-734-9800
FAX 617-739-9864
E-Mail: comments@nejm.org
Home Page: www.nejm.org

Debra Weinstein, Chair
Jeffrey M Drazen, Editor-in-Chief
Gregory Curfman, Executive Editor

General medicine journal that publishes new
medical research findings, review articles, and
editorial opinion on a wide variety of topics of
importance to biomedical science and clinical
practice. Published with an emphasis on internal medicine and specialty areas including al-
lergy/immunology, cardiology, endocrinology,
gastroenterology, hematology, kidney disease,
oncology, pulmonary disease, rheumatology,
HIV, and infectous diseases.
Cost: $149.00
Frequency: Weekly

13154 Nursing

Ambler Office of Lippincott Williams and
Wilkins
323 Norristown Rd
Suite 200
Ambler, PA 19002-2758

215-646-8700
800-346-7844
FAX 215-654-1328
Home Page: www.lww.com

Mary Gill, Human Resources
Cheryl Mee, Publisher & Editor
Keith Sollweiler, Marketing
Cost: $34.00
Frequency: Monthly
Circulation: 300000
Founded in 1971

13155 Nursing News
48 W Street
Concord, NH 03301-3595

603-225-3783
FAX 603-228-6672
Home Page: www.nhnurses.org

Bob Desc, CEO
Susan Fetzer, President
Cost: $26.00
Frequency: Quarterly
Circulation: 18000
Founded in 1906

13156 Nursing Outlook
1111 Middle Drive
Indiana, IN 46202

317-274-1486
FAX 317-278-1842
E-Mail: mbroome@iupui.edu
Home Page: www.nursiniupui.edu

Marion Broome, Editor
Adam Herberg, President, Circulation Manager

13157 Nutrition Business Journal
4452 Park Boulevard
Suite 306
San Diego, CA 92116

619-295-7685
FAX 619-295-5743
E-Mail: info@nutritionbusiness.com
Home Page: www.nutritionbusiness.com

David Nussbaum, CEO
Preston Vice, CFO
Cost: $995.00
Frequency: Monthly
Founded in 1892

13158 O&P Almanac
American Orthotic & Prosthetic Association
330 John Carlyle Street
Suite 200
Alexandria, VA 22314

571-431-0876
FAX 571-431-0899
E-Mail: info@aopanet.org
Home Page: www.aopanet.org
Social Media: *Facebook, Twitter, LinkedIn*

Tom DiBello, President
Anita Liberman, VP
Thomas F Fise, Executive Director
Don DeBolt, Chief Operating Officer
Devon Bernard, Manager of Reimbursement
Cost: $59.00
84 Pages
Frequency: Monthly
Circulation: 13000
ISSN: 1061-4621
Founded in 1951
Mailing list available for rent
Printed in 4 colors on glossy stock

13159 Occupational Health & Safety
Stevens Publishing Corporation
5151 Belt Line Rd
10th Floor
Dallas, TX 75254-7507

972-687-6700
FAX 972-687-6767
E-Mail: jlaws@stevenspublishing.com
Home Page: www.stevenspublishing.com

Craig S Stevens, President
Jerry Laws, Executive Vice President
Mike Valenti, Executive Vice President
Craig Stevens, CEO
Margaret Perry, Circulation Director

Practical advice on workplace safety and compliance with laws and regulations. Feature articles and product information.
Frequency: Monthly
Circulation: 84000
Founded in 1925

13160 Oncology Times
333 7th Ave
19th Floor
New York, NY 10001-5015

646-674-6544
800-933-6525
FAX 646-674-6500
E-Mail: ot@lww.com
Home Page: www.lww.com

Serena Stockwell, Manager
Ken Senerth, Publisher
Frank Cox, Advertising Manager
Larry Klein, Director
Cost: $189.00
Circulation: 45000
Founded in 1972

13161 Optometry: Journal of the American Optometric Association
American Optometric Association
243 N Lindbergh Blvd
St Louis, MO 63141-7881

314-991-4100
FAX 314-991-4101
E-Mail: journalsonlinesupport-usa@elsevier.com
Home Page: www.optometryjaoa.com

Paul B. Freeman, OD, Editor-in-Chief

Most widely circulated scholarly optometry journal, provides a forum for research that advances the art and science of the practice of primary care optometry.
Cost: $95.00
68 Pages
Frequency: Monthly
Circulation: 34000
ISSN: 1529-1839
Founded in 1898
Printed in 4 colors on glossy stock

13162 Ostomy Wound Management
HMP Communications
83 General Warren Blvd
Suite 100
Malvern, PA 19355-1252

610-560-0500
800-237-7285
FAX 610-560-0502
E-Mail: subscriptions@hmpcommunications.com
Home Page: www.hmpcommunications.com
Social Media: *Facebook, Twitter, LinkedIn*

Jeff Hennessy, CEO
Barbara Zeiger, Editor
Jeremy Bowden, Publisher
Bonnie Shannon, Circulation Manager

Information on the disciplines of ostomy care, wound care, incontinence care, and related skin and nutritional issues.
Cost: $39.95
Frequency: Monthly
Circulation: 230000
ISSN: 0889-5099
Founded in 1980
Printed in 4 colors on glossy stock

13163 PT in Motion
American Physical Therapy Association
1111 N Fairfax St
Alexandria, VA 22314-1488

703-684-2782
FAX 703-706-8536
E-Mail: memberservices@apta.org

Home Page: www.apta.org
Social Media: *Facebook, Twitter, LinkedIn*

Don Tepper, Editor
John D. Barnes, Chief Executive Officer
Janet Bezner, VP, Education, Governance
Rob Batarla, VP, Finance & Business Development
Felicity Clancy, VP, Communications & Marketing

Formerly PT Magazine, published to meet the needs and interests of APTA members and to promote physical therapy as a vital professional career, PT provides legislative, health care, human interest, and Association news and serves as a forum for discussion of professional issues and ideas in physical therapy practice.
80000 Members
Mailing list available for rent

13164 Patient Care
Medical Economics Publishing
5 Paragon Dr
Montvale, NJ 07645-1791

973-944-7777
FAX 973-944-7778
Home Page: www.patientcareonline.com

Curtis Allen, President
Stuart Williams, Publisher
Christine Shappell, Circulation Manager
Don Berman, Director Business Development

Patient care serves selected medical and osteopathic physicians.
Cost: $51.50
Frequency: Monthly
Founded in 1967
Printed in 4 colors

13165 Physicians & Computers
Moorhead Publications
810 S Waukegan Road
#200
Lake Forest, IL 60045-2672

847-615-8333
FAX 847-615-8345
Home Page: www.physicians-computers.com

Tom Moorhead, Publisher

Provides physicians with information on computer advances helpful in the private practice of medicine. Practice management, current medical and non-medical software, computer diagnostics, etc.
Cost: $40.00
Frequency: Monthly
Circulation: 90M

13166 Pneumogram
1961 Main Street
#246
Sacramento, CA 95076

916-441-2222
888-730-2772
FAX 916-442-4182
E-Mail: arosenberg@csrc.org
Home Page: www.csrc.org/

Janyth Bolden, President
Abbie Rosenberg, Secretary
Sherry Blansfield, Secretary
Frequency: Quarterly
Founded in 1968

13167 Psychoanalytic Psychology
211 E 70th Street
Suite 17 H
New York, NY 10021

212-633-9162
FAX 212-628-8453

Lori Sloan, Executive Director

13168 Psychology of Addictive Behaviors
University of South Florida

BEH 339
Department of Psychology
Tampa, FL 33620

813-974-4826
800-374-2721
FAX 202-336-5568
Home Page: www.apa.org
Social Media: *Facebook, Twitter*

Stephen A. Maisto, Editor
Norman B. Anderson, Chief Executive Officer
L. Michael Honaker, Chief Operating Officer
Cynthia D. Belar, Executive Director
Tony Habash, Chief Information Officer
Mailing list available for rent

13169 Public Health Nursing

350 Main Street
6th Floor
Malden, MA 02148

781-388-8200
FAX 781-388-8210
E-Mail:
mspencer@bos.blackwellpublishing.com
Home Page: www.blackwellpublishing.com/

Sarah E Abrams, Editor
Judith C Hays, Editor
Otis Dean, Publisher
Alice Meadows, Senior Manager, Circulation
Paige Larkin, Sr. Marketing Manager
Cost: $149.00
Founded in 1922

13170 Quality Matters

385 Highland Colony Parkway
Suite 120
Ridgeland, MS 39157

601-957-1575
800-844-0500
FAX 601-956-1713

13171 RDH

PennWell Publishing Company
1421 S Sheridan Rd
Tulsa, OK 74112-6619

918-831-9421
FAX 918-831-9476
Home Page: www.pennwell.com

Robert Biolchini, President
Mark Hartley, Editor

National magazine for dental hygiene professionals.
Cost: $48.00
60 Pages
Frequency: Monthly
Founded in 1910

13172 RN Magazine

Medical Economics Publishing
5 Paragon Dr
Montvale, NJ 07645-1791

973-944-7777
888-581-8052
FAX 973-944-7778
Home Page: www.rnweb.com

Curtis Allen, President
Wendy Raupers, Associate Publisher
Joy Puzzo, Marketing/Circulation Manager
Don Berman, Director Business Development

Published to serve professional nurses in hospitals, physician's offices, extended care facilities, schools of nursing, occupational and community health agencies and other professional nurses.
Cost: $35.00
Frequency: Monthly
Circulation: 2500
ISSN: 0033-7021
Founded in 1937

13173 Radiology

820 Jorie Boulevard
Oak Brook, IL 60523-2251

630-571-2670
800-381-6660
FAX 630-571-7837
E-Mail: reginfo@rsna.org
Home Page: www.rsna.org

Anthony V. Proto, Editor
Michael Ulezlo, Senior Marketing Manager
Cost: $250.00
Frequency: Monthly
Circulation: 35000
Founded in 1915

13174 Radiology Management

American Healthcare Radiology
Administrators
490B Boston Post Rd
Suite 200
Sudbury, MA 01776-3367

978-443-7591
800-334-2472
FAX 978-443-8046
E-Mail: info@ahraonline.org
Home Page: www.ahraonline.org
Social Media: *Facebook, Twitter, LinkedIn*

Edward Cronin, Jr., CEO
Sarah Murray, Executive Assistant
Emily Ryan, Membership Coordinator
Debra Murphy, Publications Director

A peer reviewed journal with an editorial review board of AHRA members.
Cost: $65.00
64 Pages
Circulation: 4,000
ISSN: 0198-7097
Founded in 1978
Printed in 4 colors on glossy stock

13175 Remington Report

Remington Report
30100 Town Center Drive
Suite 421
Laguna Niguel, CA 92677

800-247-4781
800-247-4781
FAX 949-715-1797
E-Mail: remrptedit@aol.com
Home Page: www.remingtonreport.com

Lisa Remington, Publisher
Cost: $44.50
Founded in 1993

13176 Renal Business Today

Virgo Publishing LLC
3300 N Central Ave
Suite 300
Phoenix, AZ 85012-2532

480-990-1101
FAX 480-990-0819
E-Mail: jsiefert@vpico.com
Home Page: www.vpico.com

Jenny Bolton, President
John Siefert, CEO
Jennifer Janos, Controller
Kelly Ridley, Executive VP, CFO, Copado

Renal Business Today delivers editorials for practice management professionals. Editorials include the latest business and technology trends in renal care, expert advice, strategic business solutions written by industry leaders and human interest articles.
Mailing list available for rent

13177 Research Quarterly for Exercise and Sport

AAHPERD

1900 Association Dr
Reston, VA 20191-1598

703-476-3400
800-213-7193
FAX 703-476-9527
Home Page: www.aahperd.org

E. Paul Roetert, CEO
Judith C Young, VP
Paula Kun, Marketing

RQES is a professional journal providing members with numerous articles and research on subjects that focus on the art and science of human movement studies.
Cost: $295.00
128 Pages
Frequency: Quarterly
Circulation: 6000
ISSN: 0270-1367
Mailing list available for rent
Printed in one color on glossy stock

13178 Respiratory Care

9425 N Macarthur Blvd
Suite 100
Irving, TX 75063-4725

972-243-2272
FAX 972-484-2720
E-Mail: info@aarc.org
Home Page: www.aarc.org

Sam Giordano, CEO

Journal for the professional respiratory care therapist. Member publication of the American Association for Respiratory Care.
Cost: $89.95
Frequency: Monthly
Founded in 1947

13179 Review of Optometry

11 Campus Boulevard
Newton Square, PA 19073

610-492-1000
FAX 610-492-1039
E-Mail: reviewofoptometry@jobson.com
Home Page: www.revoptom.com

Amy Hellem, Editor-in-Chief
Jeffrey S Eisenberg, Director
Paul Karpecki, Director
Frequency: Monthly

13180 Risk Management Handbook

NACHA: The Electronic Payments
Association
13450 Sunrise Valley Drive
Suite 100
Herndon, VA 20171

703-561-1100
FAX 703-787-0996
E-Mail: info@nacha.org
Home Page: www.nacha.org

Janet O Estep, CEO
Marcie Haitema, Chairperson

A comprehensive guide to ACH Risk Issues and Control Procedures. Explains the types of ACH payments risk, assesses the operational implications, and provides best practices for developing an effective risk management program.
Cost: $65.00
Frequency: Monthly
Founded in 1991

13181 Rite Aid Be Healthy & Beatiful

Drug Store News Consumer Health
Publications
425 Park Ave
New York, NY 10022-3526

212-756-5220
FAX 212-756-5250

E-Mail: jtanzola@lf.com
Home Page: www.drugstorenews.com

Lebhar Friedman, Publisher

Provides health and beauty tips to millions of women who visit Rite Aid stores.
Frequency: Quarterly
Circulation: 950,000
Founded in 2002

13182 Scrip Magazine
270 Madison Ave
New York, NY 10016-0601

212-262-8230
FAX 212-262-8234
E-Mail: pharmabooks@pharmabooks.com
Home Page: www.pjbpubs.com

Ken May, Executive Director
Alice Dunmore, Circulation Manager
Jenefer Trevena, Marketing Manager
Phillip Every, Worldwide Advertising Sales

An in-depth view of the issues and challenges facing all sectors of the pharmaceutical industry worldwide. Analytical features are written by pharmaceutical experts and opinion leaders as well as specialist journalists.
Cost: $ 1190.00

13183 Sports Medicine Digest
351 W Camden St
Baltimore, MD 21201-7912

410-528-4000
800-787-8981
FAX 410-528-4452
Home Page: www.lww.com

Daniel Schwartz, Publisher
Michael Levin-Epstein, Managing Editor
Cost: $125.00
12 Pages
Frequency: Monthly
ISSN: 0731-9770
Founded in 1978
Printed in one color on matte stock

13184 SurgiStrategies
Virgo Publishing LLC
3300 N Central Ave
Suite 300
Phoenix, AZ 85012-2532

480-990-1101
FAX 480-990-0819
E-Mail: jsiefert@vpico.com
Home Page: www.vpico.com

Jenny Bolton, President
John Siefert, CEO
Jennifer Janos, Controller
Kelly Ridley, Executive VP, CFO, Copado

SurgiStrategies identifies and analyzes the high level trends impacting physician and corporation owned outpatient healthcare facilities with relevant, timely, ahead of the curve content.
Mailing list available for rent: 22000+ names at $var per M

13185 Surgical Products
Reed Business Information
100 Enterprise Drive
Suite 600
Rockaway, NJ 07866-912

973-920-7000
FAX 630-288-8686
E-Mail: rritsma@reedbusiness.com
Home Page: www.surgprodmag.com/

Noreen Costelloe, Group VP/Publisher
Richard Ritsma, Editor-in-Chief
James Reed, Owner
Sabrina Crow, Managing Director
Steve Koppelman, Circulation Manager

Surgical products provides surgeons, OR supervisors and OR materials managers working in hospitals and surgi-centers with new product technology and equipment.
Frequency: Monthly
Circulation: 71000
Founded in 1946

13186 The Neurodiagnostic Journal
American Society of Electroneurodiagnostic Tech
402 East Bannister Road
Suite A
Kansas City, MO 64131-3019

816-931-1120
FAX 816-931-1145
E-Mail: info@aset.org
Home Page: www.aset.org

Arlen Reimritz, Executive Director
Lucy Sullivan, Managing Editor

Peer-reviewed journal that contains research articles, case studies, technical articles and book reviews.
Cost: $110.00
Frequency: Quarterly
Circulation: 5000
ISSN: 1086-508X

13187 Transplantation
351 W Camden St
Baltimore, MD 21201-7912

410-528-4000
800-222-3790
FAX 410-528-4452
Home Page: www.lww.com

Sherry Reed, Manager
Mark A Hardy, Editor
Jim Mulligan, Publisher
Taron Buttler, National Sales Manager
Jeff Hargrove, Manager
Cost: $657.00
Circulation: 2556

13188 Transportation Leader
Taxicab, Limousine & Paratransit Association
3200 Tower Oaks Blvd
Suite 220
Rockville, MD 20852

301-984-5700
FAX 301-984-5703
E-Mail: info@tlpa.org
Home Page: www.tlpa.org

Alfred LaGasse, CEO
William Rouse, President
Harold Morgan, Executive Vice President
Michelle A. Hariston, CMP, Manager of Meetings
Leah New, Manager of Communications

Leading resource for news and information on issues, trends, and people in the private, for-hire passenger transportation industry. Provides readers with an array of features, articles, and columns that include information on managing a transportation company, industry trends, driver's tips, an industry calendar of events, coverage of TLPA events, and advertisements from the industry's leading suppliers.
Cost: $4.00
48 Pages
Frequency: Quarterly
Circulation: 6000
Founded in 1917
Mailing list available for rent: 6,000 names at $100 per M
Printed in 4 colors on glossy stock

13189 Urologic Nursing
Society of Urologic Nurses and Associates
East Holly Avenue
PO Box 56
Pitman, NJ 08071

856-256-2300
FAX 856-589-7463

E-Mail: uronsg@ajj.com
Home Page: www.suna.org

Nancy Mueller, President
Robert McIlvaine, Circulation Manager
Mike Cunningham, Marketing
Jane Hokanson Hawks, Editor
Anthony Jannetti, Executive Director
Cost: $40.00
Circulation: 4500
Founded in 1981
Printed in 4 colors on glossy stock

13190 Virology
125 Park Avenue
23rd Floor
New York, NY 10017

212-309-5498
800-821-5068
FAX 212-309-5480
E-Mail: d.weerd@elsevier.com
Home Page: www.reed-elsevier.com/

A Pinczuk, Editor-in-Chief
Karlyn Messinger, Communications Manager
Cost: $139.00
Frequency: Monthly
Circulation: 280
Founded in 1993

13191 Volunteer
119 W 24th Street
9th Floor
New York, NY 10011-1913

212-870-4940
FAX 212-367-1236

Esperanza Jorge-Garcia, Executive Director

13192 Walgreens Diabetes & You
Drug Store News Consumer Health Publications
425 Park Ave
New York, NY 10022-3526

212-756-5220
FAX 212-756-5250
E-Mail: jtanzola@lf.com
Home Page: www.drugstorenews.com

Lebhar Friedman, Publisher
Edward H King, Director

Contains health news of importance to those with diabetes.

13193 World Disease Weekly
2900 Paces Ferry Road
Bldg D 2nd Floor
Atlanta, GA 30339

770-507-7777
800-726-4550
FAX 770-435-6800
E-Mail: subscribe@newsrx.com
Cost: $2329.00

Frequency: Weekly
Founded in 1984

Trade Shows

13194 AAAAI Annual Conference and Exhibition
American Academy Allergy, Asthma, and Immunology
555 E Wells Street
Suite 100
Milwaukee, WI 53202-3823

414-272-6071
800-822-2762
FAX 414-272-6070
E-Mail: info@aaaai.org
Home Page: www.aaaai.org

Katie Ferguson, Sr. Meetings Manager

Exhibits, pharmaceuticals, medical supplies and books.
7000 Attendees
Frequency: Annual
Founded in 1943

13195 AAAAI Annual Meeting

American Academy of Allergy, Asthma and Immunology (AAAAI)
555 E. Wells Street, Suite 1100
Milwaukee, WI 53202-3823

414-272-6071
E-Mail: info@aaaai.org
Home Page: www.aaaai.org

Thomas B. Casale, MD, Executive Vice President
Kay A. Whalen, Executive Director
Roberta Slivensky, Associate Executive Director
Amy Flanders, Director of Grants & Development
Rachel McCormick, Executive Assistant

Annual gathering of immunology and allergy experts. Those attending the annual meeting include academicians, allied health professionals and clinicians.
6000+ Members
Founded in 1943

13196 AAB Annual Meeting and Educational Conference

American Association of Bioanalysts
906 Olive Street
Suite 1200
Saint Louis, MO 63101-1448

314-241-1445
FAX 314-241-1449
E-Mail: aab@aab.org
Home Page: www.aab.org

Mark S Biernbaum PhD, Administrator

Educational programs, abstract presentations, poster presentations and exhibits.
Founded in 1956

13197 AACAP Annual Meeting

American Academy of Child & Adolescent Psychiatry
3615 Wisconsin Avenue NW
Washington, DC 20016-3007

202-966-7300
FAX 202-966-2891
E-Mail: communications@aacap.org
Home Page: www.aacap.org
Social Media: *Facebook, Twitter*

Thomas F Anders, MD, President
Virginia Anthony, Executive Director
Martin J. Drell, President
Founded in 1953
Mailing list available for rent

13198 AAHP Institute & Display Forum

American Association of Health Plans
1129 20th Street NW
Washington, DC 20036

202-778-3200
FAX 202-778-8506

13199 AAID Annual Meeting

American Academy of Implant Dentistry
211 E Chicago Avenue
Suite 750
Chicago, IL 60611

312-335-1550
877-335-2243
FAX 312-335-9090
E-Mail: info@aaid.com

Home Page: www.aaid.com
Social Media: *Facebook, Twitter, LinkedIn*

Sharon Bennett, Executive Director
Max Moses, Director Communications

The 2012 meeting will be in Washington, DC.
1500 Attendees
Frequency: October 3-6, 2012

13200 AAMFT Conference

American Assoc for Marriage and Family Therapy
112 S Alfred Street
Alexandria, VA 22314-3061

703-838-9808
FAX 703-838-9805
E-Mail: central@aamft.org
Home Page: www.aamft.org
Social Media: *Facebook, Twitter, LinkedIn*

Linda S. Metcalf, PhD, President
Michael L. Chafin, President-Elect
Michael Bowers, Executive Director
Robin K. Stillwell, MA, Secretary
Silvia M. Kaminsky, MSEd, Treasurer

AAMFT represents the professional interests of more than 25,000 marriage and family therapists throughout the United States, Canada and abroad.
25000 Members
1500 Attendees
Frequency: Annual
Founded in 1942

13201 AAMI Conference & Expo

Assoc for the Advancement of Medical Instrumenta
4301 N. Fairfax Drive
Suite 301
Arlington, VA 22203-1633

703-525-4890
FAX 703-276-0793
E-Mail: customerservice@aami.org
Home Page: www.aami.org

Michael Miller, President
Ed Leonardo, Meetings/Expositions Director

Offers educational, networking, and personal-development opportunities that wil lenable you to expand your expertise, increasr your productivity, develop lasting relationships with peers, and ultimately advance your career.
Frequency: Annual

13202 AANEM Annual Meeting

American Assoc of Neuromuscular & Electro Medicine
2621 Superior Drive NW
Rochester, MN 55902-3018

507-288-0100
FAX 507-288-1225
E-Mail: aanem@aanem.org
Home Page: www.aanem.org

Shirlyn A Adkins, Executive Director
Patrick D Aldrich, Finance Director
Emily Spaulding, Executive Assistant
Loretta Bronson, Senior Director of Operations
Catherine French, Director of Health Policy

Forty exhibits of electromyographic and electrodiagnosis equipment and accessories. Seminar, workshop and breakfast.
1000 Attendees
Mailing list available for rent

13203 AAO-HNSF Annual Meeting & OTO Expo

American Academy of Otolaryngology
1650 Diagonal Road
Alexandria, VA 22314-3357

703-836-4444
FAX 703-683-5100

E-Mail: membership@entnet.org
Home Page: www.entnet.org

Jessica Mikulski, Sr Manager, Media/Public Relations
Matt Daigle, Media & Public Relations Manager
James L. Netterville, President
J. Gavin Setzen, Secretary/Treasurer
David R. Nielsen, Executive Vice President and CEO

The largest gathering of otolaryngologists, together with the world's largest collection of products and services for the specialty
Frequency: Septemer
Mailing list available for rent

13204 AAOMS Scientific Meeting

American Assn. of Oral & Maxillofacial Surgeons
9700 W Bryn Mawr Avenue
Rosemont, IL 60018-5701

847-678-6200
800-822-6637
FAX 847-678-6286
E-Mail: inquiries@aaoms.org
Home Page: www.aaoms.org

Edwin Slade, Treasurer
Ira Cheifetz, Vice President

Educational session, reception, tours. Over 275 exhibits relating to the profession.
4000 Attendees
Frequency: Annual
Founded in 1918

13205 AAOS Annual Meeting

American Academy of Orthopaedic Surgeons
9400 West Higgins Rd.
Rosemont, IL 60018

847-823-7186
FAX 847-823-8125
Home Page: www.aaos.org

David Teuscher, President
Karen L. Hackett, Chief Executive Officer

Three hundred and fifty-five exhibits of surgical equipment, supplies and services used by the orthopedic professional.
28000 Attendees
Frequency: Annual
Founded in 1933

13206 AAPS Annual Scientific Meeting

American Association of Physician Specialists, Inc
5550 West Executive Drive
Suite 400
Tampa, FL 33609-1035

813-433-2277
FAX 813-830-6599
E-Mail: wcarbone@aapsus.org
Home Page: www.aapsus.com

Esther Berg, Director of CME/Meetings/Membership
Keely Clarke, Membership/CME Coordinator
William Carbone, Chief Executive Officer

The American Association of Physician Specialists, Inc.(AAPS) annual meeting is used to educate medical professionals on relevant medical topics that include continuing medical education(CME) credits. The association also holdsbusiness meetings at this time.
1000 Attendees

13207 AARC International Respiratory Congress

American Association for Respiratory Care
9425 N MacArthur Boulevard
Suite 100
Irving, TX 75063-4706

972-243-2272
FAX 972-484-2720

E-Mail: info@aarc.org
Home Page: www.aarc.org

Sam P Giordano, Executive Director/Executive VP
Beth Binkley, Communication Coordinator
Steve Bowden, Web developer
Kathy Blackmon, Convention and Meetings Manager
Asha Desai, Customer Service Manager

Largest respiratory care meeting in the world. Offers the latest information in all aspects of respiratory care. The congress offers you an opportunity to earn all the continuing education hours required for your state license annually.
7000 Attendees
Frequency: December
Founded in 1947
Mailing list available for rent

13208 ACA Annual Conference & Expo

Journal of Counseling and Development
5999 Stevenson Ave
Alexandria, VA 22304-3302

703-823-9800
FAX 703-823-0252
E-Mail: membership@counseling.org
Home Page: www.counseling.org
Social Media: *Facebook, Twitter*

Marvin D. Kuehn, Executive Director
Tom Evenson, President

The mission of the American Counseling Association (ACA) is to enhance the quality of life in society by promoting the development of professional counselors, advancing the counseling profession, and using the profession and practice of counseling to promote respect for human dignity and diversity. ACA is a not-for-profit, professional and educational organization. The annual expo features over 100 exhibitors.
4000 Attendees
Frequency: Annual
Founded in 1952
Mailing list available for rent

13209 ACOFP Convention & Scientific Seminar

American College of Osteopathic Family Physicians
330 E Algonquin Road
Arlington Heights, IL 60005

847-228-6090
FAX 800-323-0794

2500 Attendees

13210 AHRA Annual Meeting and Exposition

Association for Medical Imaging Management
490B Boston Post Road
Suite 200
Sudbury, MA 01776

978-443-7591
800-334-2472
FAX 978-443-8046
E-Mail: info@ahraonline.org
Home Page: www.ahraonline.org
Social Media: *Facebook, Twitter, LinkedIn*

Edward Cronin, Jr., CEO
Sarah Murray, Executive Assistant
Emily Ryan, Membership Coordinator
Debra Murphy, Publications Director

Educational event for Radiology Administration. Topics that are covered include human resources, finance, operations and communication.
3000 Attendees
Frequency: Annual

13211 AMGA's Annual Conference

American Medical Group Association
One Prince Street
Alexandria, VA 22314-3318

703-838-0033
FAX 703-548-1890
Home Page: www.amga.org
Social Media: *Facebook, Twitter, LinkedIn*

Donald W Fisher PhD, CAE, President/CEO
Ryan O'Connor, VP Membership/Marketing
April Noland, Assistant to the President/CEO
Clyde L. Morris, C.P.A., CFO
Nanette Lewis, Administrative Asst/Office Manager

Brings together physician and nonphysician executives from the nation's leading health care organizations, medical groups and physician owned and operated IPAs. It offers both an interactive exhibit area and a relaxed environment for meeting one-on-one with management from the nation's leading health care organizations. National conference dedicated to leadership development in multispecialty medical groups.
375 Members
1100+ Attendees
Frequency: March, Arizona
Founded in 1949
Mailing list available for rent: 600 names

13212 AORN Congress

Association of PeriOperative Registered Nurses
2170 S Parker Road
Suite 300
Denver, CO 80231-5711

303-755-6300
800-755-2676
FAX 303-755-4511
E-Mail: sales@aorn.org
Home Page: www.aorn.org

Garth Jordan, VP Marketing/Business
Lori Ropa, Manager

Surgical tradeshow featuring medical devices and supplies for the operating room and facilities recruiting for open OR nursing positions.
7000 Attendees
Frequency: Annual
Founded in 1954

13213 AORN World Conference of Perioperative Nurses

Association of PeriOperative Registered Nurses
2170 S Parker Road
Suite 300
Denver, CO 80231-5711

303-755-6300
FAX 303-755-5411
E-Mail: sales@aorn.org
Home Page: www.aorn.org

Christine Lindmark, Exhibits Director
Lori Ropa, Manager

Seminar and 82 equipment & supplies displays used in operating room suites, and pre-surgical areas.
2500 Attendees
Frequency: Biennial
Founded in 1978

13214 APTA Annual Conference & Exposition

American Physical Therapy Association
1111 N Fairfax Street
Alexandria, VA 22314

703-684-2782
FAX 703-706-3396
E-Mail: memberservices@apta.org
Home Page: www.apta.org

R Scott Ward, President
John Barnes, CEO

The national event for physical therapy.
Frequency: June

13215 ARMA International Conference & Expo

ARMA International
11880 College Blvd
Suite 450
Overland Park, KS 66210

913-341-3808
800-422-2762
FAX 913-341-3742
E-Mail: hq@arma.org
Home Page: www.arma.org/conference
Social Media: *Facebook, Twitter, LinkedIn*

Carol Jorgenson, Meetings/Education Coordinator
Wanda Wilson, Senior Manager, Conferences
Elizabeth Zlitni, Exposition Manager

Conference, seminar, workshop, banquet, award ceremony and 175 exhibits of micrographics, optical disk, automated document storage and retrieval systems and more technology of interest to information professionals.
3500 Attendees
Frequency: Annual
Founded in 1956
Mailing list available for rent

13216 ARVO

FASEB/OSMC
9650 Rockville Pike
Bethesda, MD 20814

301-634-7100
FAX 301-634-7014
E-Mail: info@faseb.org
Home Page: www.faseb.org/meetings

Jacquelyn Roberts, Marketing Manager
David Craven, Executive Director

13217 ASC Association Annual Conference

Ambulatory Surgery Center Association
1012 Cameron Street
Alexandria, VA 22314-2427

703-836-8808
FAX 703-549-0976
E-Mail: asc@ascassociation.org
Home Page: www.ascassociation.org
Social Media: *Facebook, Twitter, LinkedIn*

Kathy Bryant, President
Sarah Silberstein, Executive Director
71000 Attendees
Frequency: April
Founded in 1970

13218 ASCRS Annual Meeting

American Society of Colon & Rectal Surgeons
85 W Algonquin Road
Suite 550
Arlington Heights, IL 60005

847-290-9184
800-791-0001
FAX 847-290-9203
E-Mail: ascrs@fascrs.org
Home Page: www.fascrs.org
Social Media: *Facebook*

James W J Felshman MD, President
John H Pemberton MD, VP
Alan G Thorson MD, Treasurer
Rick Slawny, Executive Director
Stella Zedalis, Associate Executive Director
2800 Members
Mailing list available for rent

13219 ASCRS Symposium & ASOA Congress

American Society of Cataract & Refractive Surgery

American Society of Opthalmic Administrators
4000 Legato Road, # 850
Fairfax, VA 22033-4003

703-912-2220
800-451-1339
FAX 703-591-0614
E-Mail: ascrs@ascrs.org
Home Page: www.ascrs.org

Jane Krause, Show Manager

Seminar and 700 exhibits of opthalmic related
intruments of interest to opthalmologists, administrators, nurses and technicians.
7000 Attendees
Frequency: June
Founded in 1986

**13220 ASHCSP Annual Conference:
American Society for Heathcare
Central Servi**
American Hospital Association
One N Franklin
Chicago, IL 60601

312-422-2000
FAX 312-422-4572

Conference and exhibition of health care administration supplies and services.

**13221 ASHHRA'S Annual Conference &
Exposition**
American Society of Healthcare & Human
Resources
155 North Wacker
Suite 400
Chicago, IL 60606

312-422-3720
FAX 312-422-4577
E-Mail: ricky@corcexpo.com
Home Page: www.ashhra.org
Social Media: *Facebook, Twitter, LinkedIn*

Ricky Iovino, Exhibit Manager

ASHHRA's Annual Conference & Exposition
is the opportunity to connect face-to-face with
the top human resource executives and decision-makers in the healthcare field. The attendees come from hospital, hospital system,
ambulatory care, long-term care and hospice
organizations. Attendee job titles include:
Chief Human Reosurce Officer; Vice Presi-
dent/Director of Human Resources; Direc-
tor/Manager of Recruitment, Compensation,
Benefits, Organizational Development or
Employee Relations
500 Attendees
Frequency: September, Disneyland
Mailing list available for rent

13222 ASHP Midyear Clinical Meeting
American Society of Health-System
Pharmacists
7272 Wisconsin Avenue
Bethesda, MD 20814-4836

301-657-3000
866-279-0681
FAX 301-657-1641
E-Mail: ipa@ashp.org
Home Page: www.ashp.org
Social Media: *Facebook, Twitter, LinkedIn*

Kathryn R. Schultz, President
Paul W. Abramowitz, Chief Executive Officer
Philip J. Schneider, Treasurer
Gerald Meyer, Vice-Chairman

Containing 1,160 booths and 320 exhibits.
Mailing list available for rent

13223 ASNP Convention & Exhibition
American Association of Naturopathic
Physicians

4435 Wisconsin Avenue NW
Suite 403
Washington, DC 20016

202-237-8150
866-538-2267
FAX 202-237-8152
E-Mail: member.services@naturopathic.org
Home Page: www.naturopathic.org

Karen Howard, Executive Director
Michael Cronin, ND, President
Joe Pizzorno, ND, Treasurer
Shelly Nichols, Executive Administrator
Stephanie Geller, Membership Associate
900 Attendees
Frequency: Annual/August
Mailing list available for rent

13224 ASPET Annual Meeting
ASPET
9650 Rockville Pike
Bethesda, MD 20814

301-347-7060
FAX 301-634-7061
E-Mail: info@aspet.org
Home Page: www.aspet.org

Jean Lash, Exhibit Manager
Christine Carrico, Secretary, Treasurer
Paul Czoty, Secretary, Treasurer

The American Society for Pharmacology & Experimental Therapeutics annual meeting consisting of four-hundred exhibits of
pharmacology and toxicology equipment,
supplies and services.
13000 Attendees
Frequency: April

**13225 ASPRS/PSEF/ASMS Annual
Scientific Meeting**
American Society of Plastic Surgeons
444 E Algonquin Road
Arlington Heights, IL 60005

847-228-9900
888-475-2784
FAX 847-228-9131
E-Mail: webmaster@plasticsurgery.org
Home Page: www.plasticsurgery.org

Bonnie Burkoth, Exhibit Manager

Close to four hundred exhibits of plastic surgery products, patient education and software
to assist plastic surgeons, nurses and paramedical staff.
4000 Attendees
Frequency: October
Mailing list available for rentat $750 per M

13226 ASSH Annual Meeting
American Society for Surgery of the Hand
822 W. Washington Boulevard
Suite 600
Chicago, IL 60607

312-880-1900
FAX 847-384-1435
E-Mail: info@assh.org
Home Page: www.assh.org

Mark Anderson, CEO
Daniel Nagle, President
W P Andrew Lee, Secretary/VP
3500 Members
Frequency: September
Mailing list available for rent

**13227 Academy of General Dentistry
Annual Meeting**
Academy of General Dentistry
211 E Chicago Avenue
Suite 900
Chicago, IL 60611

312-440-4300
888-243-3368
FAX 312-440-0559

E-Mail: executiveoffice@agd.org
Home Page: www.agd.org

Heather Nash CMP, Director Meetings
Jay Donohue, Executive Director

Educational session and over 225 dental manufacturers and supplier exhibits. Attended by
dentists and the general public.
5000 Attendees
Frequency: Annual
Founded in 1954

**13228 Academy of Osseointegration
Convention**
Smith, Bucklin and Associates
401 N Michigan Avenue
Chicago, IL 60611-4267

312-644-6610
FAX 312-245-1082
E-Mail: info@smithbucklin.com
Home Page: www.smithbucklin.com

Henry S. Givray, President & CEO
C. Albert Koob, Executive Vice President
Carolyn Dolezal, Executive Vice President
Michael L. Payne, Executive Vice President
Cele Fogarty, Vice President - Event Services

Osseointegration medical exhibition.
Founded in 1949

13229 Adult Day Services Exposition
VNU Expositions
Dulles International Airport
PO Box 17413
Washington, DC 20041

703-318-0300
800-765-7616
FAX 703-318-8833
Home Page: www.vnuexpo.com

Luellen Hoffman, Show Director

Adult/geriatric health care professionals gather
to see exhibits of equipment, supplies, services
and consulting for those who represent senior
centers, adult day centers, nursing homes, hospitals and other health care markets.
300 Attendees
Frequency: Annual

13230 Air Medical Transport Conference
Association of Air Medical Services
526 King Street
Sutie 415
Alexandria, VA 22314-3143

703-836-8732
FAX 703-836-8920
E-Mail: information@aams.org
Home Page: www.aams.org

Johanna VanArsdall, Education/Meetings
Manager
Blair Marie Kelly, Commuications/Marketing
Director
Andy Papovie, Member Serives Coordinator
John Fiegel, Director

Annual exhibit of air medical transport equipment, supplies and services.
1500 Attendees
Frequency: November

13231 AmSECT International Conference
American Society of ExtraCorporeal
Technology
2209 Dickens Road
Richmond, VA 23230-2005

804-565-6363
FAX 804-282-0090
E-Mail: judyr@amsect.org
Home Page: www.amsect.org

Stewart Hinckley, Executive Director
Donna Pendarvis, Associate Manager
Michael Troike, Government Relations
Chairman

Kimberly Robertson, CPA, Controller
Greg Leasure, Membership Services
2000 Members
600 Attendees
Frequency: Annual
Founded in 1964
Mailing list available for rent

13232 American Academy for Cerebral Palsy and Developmental Medicine Meeting

Amer. Academy for Cerebral Palsy/Dev.
Medicine
555 E Wells St
Suite 1100
Milwaukee, WI 53202-3800

414-918-3014
FAX 414-276-2146
E-Mail: info@aacpdm.org
Home Page: www.aacpdm.org

Maureen O'Donnell, President
Scott Hoffinger, Treasurer
Richard Stevenson, First Vice President
Darcy Fehlings, Second Vice President
Annette Majnemer, Secretary

Provides dissemination of current and emerging information in the basic sciences, prevention, diagnosis, treatment and technical advances as applied to persons with cerebral palsy and developmental disabilities.
800 Attendees
Frequency: Yearly
Founded in 1940

13233 American Academy of Dermatology Annual Meeting

American Academy of Dermatology
930 N Meacham Road
PO Box 4014
Shaumburg, IL 60168-4014

708-330-1090
FAX 708-330-1090

Seven hundred exhibits from 300 technical companies relating to skin care, professional and scientific organizations.
Frequency: Annual
Founded in 1940

13234 American Academy of Environmental Medicine Conference

American Academy of Environmental
Medicine
7701 E Kellog
Suite 625
Wichita, KS 67207-1705

316-684-5500
FAX 316-684-5709
E-Mail: centraloffice@aaem.com
Home Page: www.aaem.com

D E Rodgers, Executive Director

Environmental medicine equipment, supplies and services of interest to physicans.
175 Attendees
Frequency: October
Mailing list available for rent

13235 American Academy of Family Physicians Scientific Assembly

American Academy of Family Physicians
11400 Tomahawk Creek Parkway
Leawood, KS 66211-2680

913-906-6000
800-274-2237
FAX 913-906-6082
E-Mail: sbiggs@aafp.org
Home Page: www.aafp.org

Sondra Biggs CMP, Meetings/Convention
Director
20000 Attendees
Frequency: Annual

13236 American Academy of Fixed Prosthodontics Scientific Session

American Academy of Fixed Prosthodontics
6661 Merwin Road
Columbus, OH 43235

614-761-1927
800-860-5633
FAX 614-292-0941
E-Mail: aafpsec@gmail.com
Home Page: www.fixedprosthodontics.org
Social Media: *Facebook, Twitter*

Stephen F. Rosenstiel, Secretary
Richard D. Jordan, Treasurer
Carl F. Driscoll, President
Jack Lipkin, VP

Thirty-two exhibits of prosthodontics equipment, supplies and services. Luncheon and meeting.
800 Attendees
Frequency: Annual Feb.
Founded in 1951

13237 American Academy of Forensic Sciences Annual Meeting

American Academy of Forensic Sciences
410 N 21st St
Colorado Springs, CO 80904-2712

719-636-1100
FAX 719-636-1993
E-Mail: awarren@aafs.org
Home Page: www.aafs.org

Anne Warren, Executive Director
Nancy Jackson, Director Development

Professionals in the forensic science field attend meeting and see 120 exhibits of scientific instruments.
2300 Attendees
Frequency: Annual

13238 American Academy of Implant Dentistry Annual Meeting

American Academy of Implant Dentistry
211 E Chicago Avenue
Chicago, IL 60611

312-335-1550
877-335-2243
FAX 312-335-9090
Home Page: www.aaid.org
Social Media: *Facebook, Twitter, LinkedIn*

Sharon Bennett, Executive Director
Joyce Sigmon, Director Administrative
Activities
Max Moses, Director Communications
1500 Attendees
Frequency: Annual

13239 American Academy of Neurology: Annual Meeting

American Academy of Neurology
1080 Montreal Avenue
Suite 335
Saint Paul, MN 55116-2325

651-951-1940
800-879-1960
FAX 651-695-2791
E-Mail: aan@aan.com
Home Page: www.aanos.org

Judy Larson

One hundred and seventy-four publishers, pharmaceutical companies, and related suppliers have exibits, along with the seminar, workshop, banquet and reception.
6500 Attendees
Frequency: Annual, August

13240 American Academy of Ophthalmology Annual Meeting

American Academy of Ophthalmology

655 Beach Street
P.O. Box 7424
San Francisco, CA 94109

415-618-8500
FAX 415-561-8533
E-Mail: meetings@aao.org
Home Page: www.aao.org

Karen Cristello, Promotions Coordinator
Dunbar Hoskins, Executive VP
25000 Attendees
Frequency: November
Founded in 1896
Mailing list available for rent

13241 American Academy of Optometry Annual Meeting

American Academy of Optometry
2909 Fairgreen Street
Suite 506
Orlando, FL 32803

301-984-1441
FAX 407-893-9890
E-Mail: aaoptom@aaoptom.org
Home Page: www.aaopt.org

Bernard J. Dolan, President
Lois Schoenbrun, Executive Director
Jenny Brown, Program Manager, Membership
Randy Consola, Office Manager
Dana Edwards, MLIS, Database Administrator

Two hundred exhibits focusing on the latest patient treatment and research. Workshop and banquet.
4000 Attendees
Frequency: Annual

13242 American Academy of Oral and Maxillofacial Radiology Annual Session

American Academy of Oral & Maxillofacial
Radiology
PO Box 55722
Jackson, MS 39296

601-984-6060
FAX 601-984-6086
Home Page: www.aaomr.org

Dr M Kevin O'Carroll, Executive Secretary
Charles Hildebolt, Treasurer
Steven Singer, Director

Over 20 exhibits relating to dental radiology, equipment, software and accessories.
120 Attendees
Frequency: November
Founded in 1949

13243 American Academy of Orofacial Pain Annual Scientific Meeting

American Academy of Orofacial Pain
19 Mantua Road
Mount Royal, NJ 00861

856-233-3629
FAX 856-423-3420

Donna Blackmore, Manager Meetings
Bob Talley, President

Ten exhibits relating to orofacial pain and temporomandibular disorders. Medical and dental doctors attend meeting, luncheon, tours and a reception.
350 Attendees
Frequency: Annual

13244 American Academy of Otolaryngology Mid-Winter Meeting

American Academy of
Otolaryngology-Head & Neck

19 Mantua Road
Mt. Royal, NJ 08061

856-423-0041
E-Mail: headquarters@aro.org
Home Page: www.aro.org

Darla Dobson, Executive Director

Over 300 exhibits of otolaryngology, diseases
of the ear, nose and throat, head and neck surgery equipment, supplies and services plus
seminar.
9000+ Attendees
Frequency: February
Founded in 1896

13245 American Academy of Pain Medicine Annual Conference and Review Course

American Academy of Pain Medicine
4700 Lake Avenue
Glenview, IL 60025

847-375-4731
FAX 847-375-4777
E-Mail: info@painmed.org
Home Page: www.painmed.org

Samuel Hassenbusch, President
Frederick Burgess, Treasurer

Meeting and exhibits relating to pain medicine,
particularly related socioeconomic and governmental issues.
Frequency: Annual

13246 American Academy of Pediatric Dentistry Annual Meeting

American Academy of Pet Owners
830 Taylor Street
Suite 1700
Ft. Worth, TX 76102

312-337-2169
800-992-8044
FAX 312-337-6329
E-Mail: info@aapd.org
Home Page: www.aapo.org
Social Media: *Facebook, Twitter*

Keith Morley, President
William Berlocher, Vice President
John Rutkauskas, Executive Director

Seventy-five to 100 displays of dental products
and publications.
2500 Attendees
Frequency: May
Founded in 1948

13247 American Academy of Pediatrics Annual Meeting

American Academy of Pediatrics
141 NW Point Boulevard
Elk Grove Village, IL 60009

847-434-4000
FAX 847-434-8000
E-Mail: kidsdocs@aap.org
Home Page: www.aap.org

E Stephen Edwards MD FAAP, President
Joe M Sanders Jr, MD FAAP, Executive
Director
Joann Barbour, Manager

Three hundred and fifty exhibits relating to
prescription and over the counter drugs, infant
formulas medical equipment and publications.
Reception, tours and meeting.
10000 Attendees
Frequency: Annual

13248 American Academy of Periodontology Annual Meeting & Exhibition

American Academy of Periodontology

737 N Michigan Avenue
Suite 800
Chicago, IL 60611

312-787-5518
FAX 312-573-3225
E-Mail: member.services@perio.org
Home Page: www.perio.org

Melody Anderson, Meetings Manager
Alice Deforest, Administrative Assistant
Sarah Schneider, Administrative Assistant

Two hundred and seventy-five exhibits of products and services relating to periodontics, including dental instruments, literature, X-ray
equipment, furniture, software and more.
5800 Attendees
Frequency: Annual
Founded in 1914

13249 American Academy of Physical Medicine and Rehabilitation Annual Assembly

330 N Wabash Avenue
Suite 2500
Chicago, IL 60611-7617

312-464-9700
FAX 312-464-0227
Home Page: www.aapmr.org/assembly.htm

Steve M Gnatz MD/MHA, President
Thomas E Stautzenbach CAE, Executive
Director
Joanne Constantine, Assembly Press
Releases/Media
Elsa Lightfoot, Assembly Registration
Coordinator
Linda Griffin, Assembly Technical Information

One hundred twenty-five exhibitors representing pharmceutical companies, diagnostics, rehabilitation equipment manufacturers and
more.
2500 Attendees
Frequency: Annual/November
Founded in 1938

13250 American Academy of Professional Coders National Conferences

2480 South 3850 West
Suite B
Salt Lake City, UT 84120

801-236-2200
800-626-2633
FAX 801-236-2258
E-Mail: info@aapc.com
Home Page: www.aapc.com

Reed Pew, CEO
Sandra Nestman, Conference Coordinator
Amy Pistorius, Conference Coordinator
Kira Golding, Conference Coordinator
Raemarie Jimenez, Conference Coordinator

Provides the opportunity to meet the National
Advisory Board, members, staff and management. Mingle with local chapters from all over
the country. Get education on the most popular
and needed subject matter taught by industry
experts.
Frequency: January and June
Founded in 1988
Mailing list available for rent

13251 American Alliance for Health, Physical Education, Recreation & Dance Expo

AAHPERD
1900 Association Drive
Reston, VA 20191

703-476-3400
800-213-7193

FAX 703-476-9527
Home Page: www.aahperd.org

E. Paul Roetert, CEO
Judith C Young, VP
Paula Kun, Marketing

National convention and exposition that features many exhibits focusing on products, services and equipment within the fields of health,
physical education, recreation and dance.
5000 Attendees
Frequency: Annual
Mailing list available for rent

13252 American Ambulance Association Annual Conference & Trade Show

Executive Management Services
1255 23rd Street NWrd
Suite 200
Washington, DC 20037

202-213-3999
800-523-4447
FAX 202-452-0005
Home Page: www.the-aaa.org

David Saunders, Executive Director
Maria Bianchi, Executive Vice President
6100 Attendees
Frequency: Annual, October

13253 American Association for Continuity of Care Annual Conference

American Association for Continuity of
Care
638 Prospect Avenue
Hartford, CT 06105-4250

860-867-7525
FAX 203-586-7550

Seminar, reception and 35 exhibits of suppliers
of health care delivery resources, products and
services.
Frequency: Annual
Founded in 1982

13254 American Association for Laboratory Animal Science National Meeting

American Association for Laboratory
Animal Science
9190 Crestwyn Hills Drive
Memphis, TN 38125

901-754-8620
FAX 901-753-0046
E-Mail: info@aalas.org
Home Page: www.aalas.org

Ann Turner, Executive Director

Two-hundred and seventy exhibits of
pharmaceuticals and laboratory animal supplies.
4,500 Attendees
Frequency: October

13255 American Association for Medical Transcription Annual Meeting

PO Box 576187
Modesto, CA 95357-6187

209-551-0883
800-982-2182
FAX 209-551-9317
E-Mail: aamt@sns.com
Home Page: www.aamt.org

Daryl Ochs, Director Marketing
Terri White, Operations Manager

Exhibitors are medical transcription businesses,
hardware, software, publishers and services.
750 Attendees
Frequency: Annual
Founded in 1978

13256 American Association for Thoracic Surgery Annual Meeting

American Association for Thoracic Surgery

500 Cummings Center
Suite 4550
Beverly, MA 01915

978-927-8330
FAX 978-524-8890
E-Mail: aats@prri.com
Home Page: www.aats.org
Social Media: *Facebook*

G Alexander Patterson, President
Elizabeth Dooley Crane, Executive Director
4700 Attendees
Frequency: Annual
Founded in 1917
Mailing list available for rent

13257 American Association for the Study of Headache Meeting
19 Mantua Road
Mount Royal, NJ 08061

856-423-0043
FAX 856-423-0082
E-Mail: ahshq@talley.com
Home Page:
www.americanheadachesociety.org

Paul Winner, President
David Dodick, Treasurer

Twenty-five exhibits of research equipment supplies, and services related to headache study.
650 Attendees
Frequency: Annual
Founded in 1958

13258 American Association of Nurse Anesthetists Midyear Assembly
222 S Prospect Avenue
Park Ridge, IL 60068-4001

847-927-7055
FAX 847-692-6968
E-Mail: info@aana.org
Home Page: www.aana.com

Wanda Wilson, President
Daniel Vigness, Vice President

Exhibits relating to nurse anesthetists.
350 Attendees

13259 American Association of Blood Banks Annual Meeting
American Association of Blood Banks
8101 Glenbrook Road
Bethesda, MD 20814-2749

301-907-6977
FAX 301-907-6895
E-Mail: aabb@aabb.org
Home Page: www.aabb.org

Daniel Connor, President
Jacquelyn Fredrick, VP

Four hundred and eighty-nine exhibits relating to blood banking and transfusion medicine, gloves, donor coaches, chairs and equipment. Seminar, workshop and banquet.
7500 Attendees
Frequency: November
Founded in 1947
Mailing list available for rent

13260 American Association of Cardiovascular & Pulmonary Rehabilitation Conf.
American Assoc of Cardiovascular & Pulmonary Rehab
7611 Elmwood Avenue
Suite 201
Middleton, WI 53562

608-316-6989
FAX 608-831-5122
E-Mail: aacvpr@tmahq.org
Home Page: www.aacvpr.org

Sheil Kirshbaum, Director Meetings

Seminar and workshop, plus 70 exhibits of cardiovascular and pulmonary rehabilitation equipment, supplies and services.
1800 Attendees
Frequency: Annual
Founded in 1985

13261 American Association of Diabetes Educators Annual Meeting & Educational Prog.
American Association of Diabetes Educators
100 W Monroe
Chicago, IL 60603

312-424-2426
800-338-3633
FAX 312-424-2427
Home Page: www.diabeteseducator.org

Christopher Laxton, Executive Director
Tami Ross, Vice President

Six hundred exhibits of dietary food and beverages, testing and screening tools, educational programs and publications. Banquet and reception available.
Mailing list available for rent: 10000 names at $160 per M

13262 American Association of Homes and Services for the Aging Convention
American Association of Homes and Services/Aging
901 E Street NW
Suite 500
Washington, DC 20004-2037

202-661-5700
FAX 202-783-2255
E-Mail: mraynor@aahsa.org
Home Page: www.aahsa.org

Daniel Smith, VP
Mary-Louise Raynor, Secretary
Bonnie Gauthier, Secretary
Douglas Struyk, Treasurer

One thousand eight hundred exhibitors of equipment, supplies and services for housing and long term care facilities for the aged, conference and tours.
4000 Attendees
Frequency: Annual
Founded in 1980

13263 American Association of Immunologists Annual Meeting
American Association of Immunologists
9650 Rockville Pike
Bethesda, MD 20814

301-634-7178
FAX 301-634-7887
E-Mail: infoaai@aai.org
Home Page: www.aai.org
Social Media: *Facebook*

M Michele Hogan PhD, Executive Director
Gail A. Bishop, President

Exhibits related to immunological research, equipment and supplies.
7,600 Members
10000 Attendees
Frequency: May
Founded in 1913

13264 American Association of Managed Care Nurses Annual Conference
American Association of Managed Care Nurses
4435 Waterfront Drive
Suite 101
Glen Allen, VA 23060

804-747-9698
FAX 804-747-5316

E-Mail: keads@aamcn.org
Home Page: www.aamcn.org

Sloane Reed, VP Sales
Laura Givens, Executive Admin

The AAMCN Annual Conference is designed to provide registered nurses, licensed practical nurses, advanced practice, executive nurses and other healthcare professionals with current information they can use to influence their marketplace.

13265 American Association of Medical Assistants National Convention
American Association of Medical Assistants
20 N Wacker Drive
Suite 1575
Chicago, IL 60606-2963

312-899-1500
800-228-2262
FAX 312-899-1259
E-Mail: info@aama-ntl.org
Home Page: www.aama-ntl.org

David Balasa, Executive Director
Kathy Langley, Director Of Board Services

Main exhibits, data processing equipment, pharmaceuticals, publications, insurance services, text books, coding system reference guides, health care services and more.
500 Attendees
Frequency: Annual

13266 American Association of Naturopathic Physicians Convention
American Association of Naturopathic Physicians
4435 Wisconsin Avenue NW
Suite 403
Washington, DC 20016

202-237-8150
FAX 202-237-8152
Home Page: www.naturopathic.org

Karen Howard, Executive Director
Michael Cronin, ND, President
Joe Pizzorno, ND, Treasurer
Shelly Nichols, Executive Administrator
Stephanie Geller, Membership Associate

One hundred and twenty exhibits of Naturopathic medicine, supplies and services plus conference and banquet.
750 Attendees
Frequency: Annual
Founded in 1986
Mailing list available for rent

13267 American Association of Neurological Surgeons Annual Meeting
American Association of Neurologists
5550 Meadowbrook Drive
Rolling Meadows, IL 60008

847-378-0500
888-566-2267
FAX 847-378-0600
E-Mail: info@aans.org
Home Page: www.aans.org

John Robertson, President
Troy Tippett, Vice President
Griffith R. Harsh, Chairperson

Two hundred manufacturers and suppliers have 500 booths of equipment, publications and supplies.
2400 Attendees
Frequency: Annual
Mailing list available for rent

13268 American Association of Neuroscience Nurses Convention

224 N Des Plaines
#601
Chicago, IL 60661

312-258-1200
800-477-2266
FAX 312-993-0362
E-Mail: info@aann.org
Home Page: www.aann.org

Thomas O'Dowd, Manager Meetings

Sixty exhibits of nuerological and neurosurgical supplies, services and industry related recruiters.
900 Attendees
Frequency: Annual
Founded in 1968

13269 American Association of Nurse Anesthetists Annual Meeting

222 S Prospect Avenue
Park Ridge, IL 60068-4001

847-985-5400
FAX 847-692-6968
E-Mail: meetings@aana.com
Home Page: www.aana.com

Cindy Wood, Director Programs

325 exhibits of equipment, supplies, publications and recruiters. Seminar and workshop, as well as a banquet.
3500 Attendees

13270 American Association of Nurse Anesthetists Assembly of School Faculty

222 S Prospect Avenue
Park Ridge, IL 60068-4001

847-927-7055
FAX 847-692-6968
E-Mail: info@aana.com
Home Page: www.aana.com

Wanda Wilson, President
Daniel Vigness, Vice President

Nurse anesthetist related exhibits
250 Attendees
Frequency: Annual

13271 American Association of Office Nurses Annual Meeting & Convention

52 Park Avenue
Suite B4
Park Ridge, NJ 07656

201-391-2600
800-457-7504
FAX 201-573-8543
Home Page: www.aanon.org

Michelle Aronowitz, Managing Director
Sherry Levy, Associate Managing Director

American Association of Office Nurses annual meeting and convention at the Eden Roc Hotel in Miami Beach, Florida.
150 Attendees
Frequency: Sept
Founded in 1988

13272 American Association of Orthodontists Trade Show and Scientific Session

401 N Lindbergh Boulevard
Saint Louis, MO 63141-7816

314-993-1700
FAX 314-997-1745
E-Mail: info@aaortho.org
Home Page: www.aaortho.org

Chris Varanas, Manager

Five hundred and fifty exhibits of orthodontic equipment, publications, supplies and services.
9000 Attendees
Frequency: Annual

13273 American Association of Suicidology Conference

4201 Connecticut Avenue NW
Suite 408
Washington, DC 20008

202-237-2280
FAX 202-237-2282
Home Page: www.suicidology.org

Alan Berman PhD, Executive Director

Exhibits relating to the advancement of studies to prevent suicide and life threatening behavior.
Frequency: Annual
Founded in 1969

13274 American Association of Tissue Banks Meeting

1320 Old Chain Bridge Road
Suite 450
Mc Lean, VA 22101

703-827-9582
FAX 703-356-2198
E-Mail: aatb@aatb.org
Home Page: www.aatb.org

Robert Rigney, CEO
Scott Brubaker, Chief Policy Officer

Exhibits for the revival, preservation, storage, and distribution of tissues for transplantation.

13275 American Association on Mental Retardation Annual Meeting

444 N Capitol Street
Suite 846
Washington, DC 20001-1512

202-387-1968
800-424-3688
FAX 202-387-2193
E-Mail: dcroser@aamr.org
Home Page: www.aamr.org

Doreen Croser, Executive Director
Paul Aitken, Director Of Finance Administration
2000 Attendees
Founded in 1876

13276 American Chiropractic Association Annual Convention and Exhibition

1701 Clarendon Boulevard
Arlington, VA 22209

703-276-8800
800-986-4636
FAX 703-243-2593
Home Page: http://www.acatoday.org

Kevin Corcoran, VP

Fifty displays of chiropractic tables and products, mattress companies, nutritional supplements, computer software, services and supplies.
500 Attendees
Frequency: Annual
Founded in 1963

13277 American Cleft Palate Craniofacial Association Annual Meeting

104 S Estes Drive
Suite 204
Chapel Hill, NC 27514

919-933-9044
FAX 919-933-9604
E-Mail: meetings@acpa-cpf.org
Home Page: www.acpa-cpf.org

Kathy Bogie, Manager Meetings
Nancy Smythe, Administrative Assistant
Hillary Jones, Administrative Assistant

Scientific meeting.
600 Attendees
Frequency: March
Founded in 1943

13278 American Clinical Neurophysiology Society Convention

1 Regency Drive
PO Box 30
Bloomfield, CT 06002

860-447-9408
FAX 860-286-0787
E-Mail: info@acns.org
Home Page: www.acns.org

Mark Ross, President
Alan Legatt, First Vice President

Over 40 exhibits of electroencephalographic and neurophysiology equipment, seminar, workshop and conference.
400 Attendees
Frequency: Annual
Founded in 1946

13279 American College Health Association Annual Meeting

American College Health Association
1362 Mellon Road
Suite 180
Hanover, MD 21076

410-859-1500
FAX 410-859-1510
E-Mail: contact@acha.org
Home Page: www.acha.org/annualmeeting13/index
Social Media: *Facebook, Twitter*

Jenny Haubenreiser, President
Pat Ketcham, President-Elect
Doyle Randall, Executive Director

The largest conference for college professionals. This year we honor the spirit of service and compassion that college health professionals have shown in their dedication to serving college students and their campus communities.
1800 Attendees
Frequency: Annual
Founded in 1922

13280 American College of Allergy, Asthma and Immunology Annual Meeting

85 W Algonquin Road
Suite 550
Arlington Heights, IL 60005-4460

847-427-1200
FAX 847-427-1294
E-Mail: mail@acaai.org
Home Page: www.acaai.org

Richard G Gowes MD, President
Sami L Bahna MD, President-Elect

2006 Annual Meeting will be held November 9-15 in Philadelpia, Pennsylvania
Frequency: November
Founded in 1942
Mailing list available for rent: 4500 names at $100 per M

13281 American College of Angiology Conference

295 Northern Boulevard
Suite 104
Great Neck, NY 11021-4701

516-466-4055
FAX 516-466-4099
Home Page: www.collegeofangiology.org

Joan Shaffer, Executive Director

CME Seminars and 50 exhibits from commercial and scientific suppliers.
300 Attendees
Frequency: October
Founded in 1954

13282 American College of Cardiology Annual Scientific Session
American College of Cardiology
2400 N Street, NW
Washington, DC 20037-1699

202-375-6000
800-253-4636
FAX 202-375-7000
E-Mail: resource@acc.org
Home Page: www.acc.org

Christine McEntee, CEO
Julie Miller, Assistant Professor of Medicine

Seminar, workshop, dinner and 385 exhibits of products, supplies and services related to cardiovascular medicine.
30000 Attendees
Founded in 1949

13283 American College of Cardiovascular Administrator Leadership Conference
American Academy of Medical Administrators
701 Lee Street
Suite 600
Des Plaines, IL 60016

847-759-8601
FAX 847-759-8602
E-Mail: info@aameda.org
Home Page: www.ammeda.org

Holly Estal Ed M, Director Education
Gen Hedland, Manager of Exhibits
S. Patrick Alford, Chairman
Linda R. Larin, Treasurer
Tina R. Brinton, Vice Chairman

Featuring keynote and concurrent sessions on human relations, finance and business developments, CV program development technology plus exhibitors that include the latest technological and innovative systems and products in cardiovascular health care. There are 30-40 booths.
300 Attendees
Frequency: March
Mailing list available for rent: 3,000 names at $150 per M

13284 American College of Emergency Physicians Scientific Assembly
American College of Emergency Physicians
PO Box 619911
Dallas, TX 75261-9911

972-550-0911
800-798-1822
FAX 972-580-2816
E-Mail: publicaffairs@acep.org
Home Page: www.acep.org

Dana Bellantone, Manager Meetings

Five hundred and twenty-five exhibits of products and services related to emergency medicine.
4400 Attendees
Frequency: Annual
Founded in 1972

13285 American College of Medical Quality Annual Meeting
4334 Montgomerey Avenue
2nd Floor
Bethesda, MD 20814-4402

301-913-9149
800-924-2149
FAX 301-656-0989
E-Mail: acmq@aol.com
Home Page: www.acmq.org

Louis H. Diamond MB, ChB, President
Alan Krumholz, MD, Vice President

Seminar, reception and exhibits of computer hardware and software, publications, phamaceuticals and supplies. Medical professionals and others involved in quality assurance and utilization review and risk management attend.
150 Attendees
Founded in 1973
Mailing list available for rent

13286 American College of Nurse Practitioners
J Spargo & Associates
11208 Waples Mill Road
Suite 112
Fairfax, VA 22030

703-631-6200
800-564-4220
FAX 703-654-6931
E-Mail: acnp@jspargo.com
Home Page: www.afcea.org
Social Media: *Facebook, Twitter, LinkedIn*
June LaMountain, Exhibit Sales Account Manager
Kent Schneider, President and CEO
Pat Miorin, Chief Financial Officer
Al Grasso, Chairman

The premier educational offering for nurse practitioners. It offers the opportunity to earn a full scope of continuing education contact hours at sessions led by top clinical experts in many areas.
1200 Attendees
Frequency: October
Mailing list available for rent

13287 American College of Obstetricians and Gynecologists Clinical Meeting/Expo
American College of Obstetricians
409 12th Street SW
Washington, DC 20024

202-857-3288
FAX 202-484-3933
Home Page: http://www.acog.org

Professionally related exhibits.

13288 American College of Oral and Maxillofacial Surgeons Annual Conference
2025 M Street Nw
Washington, DC 20036

202-367-1182
800-522-6676
FAX 202-367-2182
E-Mail: admin@acoms.org
Home Page: www.acoms.org
Social Media: *Facebook, Twitter, LinkedIn*

Dr Steven Guttenberg, President
Dr Leonard Spector, Secretary/Treasurer
Sunny Patel, Staff Accountant
Tina Hochberg, Sr. Director of Event Services
Steven C. Kemp, Executive Director

Fifty exhibits for oral and maxillofacial surgery.
250 Attendees
Frequency: Annual

13289 American College of Physicians Annual Convention
American College of Physicians
Independence Mall W
6th Street & Race
Philadelphia, PA 19106

215-351-2400
Home Page: http://www.acponline.org

John Tooker, CEO

Five hundred exhibits of medical supplies and services, as well as a seminar.
8000 Attendees

13290 American College of Rheumatology Scientific Meeting
Slack

4930 Del Ray Avenue
Bethesda, MD 20814

301-654-2055
FAX 301-654-5920
E-Mail: member@gastro.org
Home Page: www.gastro.org

Robert Greenberg, Executive Vp
Michael Stolar, Senior Vp

Two hundred and ten exhibits of diagnostic testing kits, pharmaceuticals, equipment and supplies, of interest to professionals in Rheumatology.
4500 Attendees
Frequency: Annual
Founded in 1934

13291 American College of Surgeons Annual Clinical Congress
American College of Surgeons
633 N Saint Clair Street
Chicago, IL 60611

312-202-5000
FAX 312-440-7143
E-Mail: postmaster@facs.org
Home Page: www.facs.org

Felix P Niespodziewanski, Conventions Manager
Thomas Russell, Chairman
Andrew Warshaw, Treasurer
Courtney Townsend, Secretary

One thousand one hundred exhibits of medical and patient care products, equipment and supplies. Conference, seminar and workshop, as well as luncheon and tours.
10000 Attendees
Frequency: Annual
Founded in 1914

13292 American Congress of Rehabilitation Medicine Annual Meeting
6801 Lake Plaza Drive
Suite B- 205
Indianapolis, IN 46220

317-915-2250
FAX 317-915-2245
E-Mail: crobinson@acrm.org
Home Page: www.acrm.org

Richard D Morgan, Executive Director

Seminar, workshop and conference with 20 exhibits of rehabilitation supplies and equipment.
250 Attendees
Frequency: September/October
Founded in 1923
Mailing list available for rent: 750 names at $275 per M

13293 American Dental Association Annual Session & Technical Exhibition
211 E Chicago Avenue
Suite 200
Chicago, IL 60611-2678

312-440-2500
FAX 312-440-2707
E-Mail: donovanj@ada.org
Home Page: www.ada.org

James P Donovan, Exhibit Manager
Patricia A Johnson, Manager Program Development
Vicki Guinta, Director
James Bramson, CEO

The annual session scientific program consists of over 180 programs, including science of dentistry, practice of dentistry, dental technology and general insterest programs as well as participation workshops. The leading suppliers will showcase their products and services. Dental professionals can compare products, see demonstrations, and make decisions about applying the latest technology. Attendees visiting

the Technical Exhibition can also look for the ADA Seal which has long been recognizd
30000 Attendees
Frequency: October

13294 American Dental Education Association Annual Session and Exposition
1400 K Street NW
Suite 1100
Washington, DC 20005

202-289-7201
FAX 202-289-7204
Home Page: www.adea.org

Rhonda Buford, Meetings Manager
Renee Latimer, Meeting Manager
Simone Smith, Meetings Manager
Novella Abrams, Senior Administrative Associate
Cassandra Allen, Program Associate

One hundred commercial and educational exhibits of supplies, video equipment, publications and more.
3000 Attendees
Frequency: Annual
Founded in 1983

13295 American Dental Hygienists Association Conference
444 N Michigan Avenue
Suite 3400
Chicago, IL 60611

312-440-8900
FAX 312-440-8929
E-Mail: mail@adha.org
Home Page: www.adha.org

Ann Battrell, Executive Director
Kathy Madryk, Marketing Manager
Katie Powell, Director, Members Service
Ann Lynch, Director, Governmental Affairs
Isaac Carpenter, Director, Finance and MIS

Educational session and 120 exhibits of dental products.
1500 Attendees
Frequency: Annual
Founded in 1993
Mailing list available for rent

13296 American Dental Society of Anesthesiology Scientific Meeting
211 E Chicago Avenue
Suite 948
Chicago, IL 60611

312-664-8270
800-722-7788
FAX 312-642-9713

R Knight Charlton, Executive Director

Meeting and over 15 exhibits of anesthetics and monitoring equipment.
200 Attendees
Frequency: Annual
Founded in 1954

13297 American Diabetes Association Annual Meeting and Scientific Sessions
1701 N Beauregard Street
PO Box 25757
Alexandria, VA 22311

703-549-1500
800-676-4065
FAX 703-683-1351
E-Mail: meetings@diabetes.org
Home Page: www.afassano.com/ada

Anna Fassano, Director Exhibits
Lynn Nicholas, CEO

Three hundred and fifty exhibits of medical and dietary products and services, seminar and workshop.
Frequency: June
Founded in 1940

13298 American Health Care Association Annual Convention and Exhibition
1201 L Street NW
Washington, DC 20005

202-842-4444
FAX 202-842-3860
E-Mail: webmaster@ahca.org
Home Page: www.ahcancal.org
Social Media: *Facebook, Twitter, LinkedIn*

Dave Kyllo, VP

Three hundred and fifty exhibits of supplies and information for the long term health care industry, banquet, luncheon and tours.
5000 Attendees
Frequency: Annual
Mailing list available for rent

13299 American Health Information Management Association National Convention
American Health Information Management Association
233 N Michigan Avenue
21st Floor
Chicago, IL 60601-5809

312-233-1100
FAX 312-233-1090
E-Mail: info@ahima.org
Home Page: www.ahima.org
Social Media: *Facebook, Twitter, LinkedIn*

Erin Toth, Exhibition Manager
Linda Kloss, Executive Director
Patty Thierry Sheridan, President
Lynne Thomas Gordon, Chief Executive Officer
Beth Kost-Woodrow, Treasurer

Five hundred exhibits of interest to health information management professionals, reception.
3500 Attendees
Frequency: Annual
Founded in 1928
Mailing list available for rent

13300 American Health Quality Association Annual Session
1140 Connecticut Avenue NW
Washington, DC 20036

202-331-5790
E-Mail: info@ahqa.org
Home Page: www.ahqa.org

David Thomas MD, President
David Adler, Public Affairs Associate

Quality Improvement Organizations (QIOs) and professionals working to improve the quality of health care in communities across America gather for educational sessions and networking.
Frequency: March

13301 American Heart Association Scientific Sessions
American Heart Association
7272 Greenville Avenue
Dallas, TX 75231

214-736-6300
FAX 214-373-3406
Home Page: www.amhrt.org

M Cass Wheeler, CEO

Conference, seminar and tours, plus 325 exhibits relating to exercise, equipment, pharmceuticals and services related to cardiovascular health care.
29000 Attendees

13302 American Hospital Association Convention
155 N. Wacker Dr.
Chicago, IL 60606

312-422-3000
800-424-4301
FAX 312-422-4500
E-Mail: ddavidson@aha.org
Home Page: www.aha.org
Social Media: *Twitter, YouTube*

Richard Umbdenstock, President & CEO
Richard Pollack, VP, Advocacy
Neil Jesuelo, SVP Business Development

Exhibits of equipment, supplies and services for the medical and hopsital industry.

13303 American Industrial Hygiene Conference & Exposition (AIHce)
American Industrial Hygiene Association
2700 Prosperity Avenue
Suite 250
Fairfax, VA 22031

703-849-8888
FAX 703-207-3561
E-Mail: infonet@aiha.org
Home Page: www.aiha.org

Carol Tobin, Education/Meetings Director
Caroline Lacey, Expositions Manager

Attracts OEHS professionals that are industrial hygienists, EHS specialists, safety professionals, risk management professionals and other who are esponsible for safety, health and the environment at their organization.
7000 Attendees
Frequency: Annual/May

13304 American Lung Association/American Thoracic Society Int Conference
1740 Broadway
New York, NY 10019-4374

212-315-8700
FAX 212-265-5642

John Kirkwood, CEO

Two hundred and fifty exhibits of pharmaceuticals, equipment and books.
8500 Attendees
Frequency: Annual
Founded in 1904

13305 American Medical Directors Association Annual Symposium
American Medical Directors Association
11000 Broken Land Parkway, Suite 400
Suite 760
Columbia, MD 21044

410-740-9743
800-876-2632
FAX 410-740-4572
E-Mail: info@amda.com
Home Page: www.amda.com

Megan Brey, Director Meetings
Lorraine Tarnove, Manager

Exhibits relating to geriatrics, pharmaceuticals and medical administration of long term care facilities. Long term health care physicians and professionals attend educational sessions, receptions and special events. Spouse/guest program offered.
1400 Attendees
Frequency: April
Founded in 1978

13306 American Medical Informatics Association Fall Symposium
American Medical Informatics Association

4915 Saint Elmo
Suite 401
Bethesda, MD 20814

301-657-1291
FAX 301-657-1296

Megan Brey, Meeting Coordinator
Karen Greenwood, Manager

One hundred ten commercial and scientific medical informatics software and hardware, supplies and service dealers. Attended by medical professionals and the general public.
2500 Attendees
Frequency: Annual
Founded in 1977

13307 American Medical Student Association Convention

American Medical Student Association
1902 Association Drive
Reston, VA 20191

703-620-6600
800-767-2266
FAX 703-620-5873
E-Mail: amsa@amsa.org
Home Page: www.amsa.org

One hundred exhibits relating to medical supplies and equipment, residency programs, physician recruitment and professional associations.
1500 Attendees

13308 American Medical Technologists Convention

American Medical Technologists
10700 West Higgins Road
Rosemont, IL 60018

847-823-5169
800-275-1268
FAX 847-823-0458
E-Mail: dianepowell.amt@juno.com
Home Page: www.amtc.com

Diane Powell, Show Manager

Forty eight exhibits of clinical laboratory books, supplies and equipment, seminar, workshop, banquet and tours.
600 Attendees
Frequency: Annual
Founded in 1991

13309 American Medical Women's Association Annual Meeting

12100 Sunset Hills Road, Suite 130
4th Floor
Reston, VA 20190

703-234-4069
866-564-2483
FAX 215-564-2175
E-Mail: info@amwa-doc.org
Home Page: www.amwa-doc.org

Gayatri Devi, President
Beatrice S Desper MD, President-Elect
Ana Maria Lopez, Secretary
Mary Fitzsimmons MD, Treasurer

Seminar, banquet, tours and 60 exhibits of medical equipment, supplies and services.
1000 Attendees
Frequency: Annual
Founded in 1915
Mailing list available for rent

13310 American Nephrology Nurses Association Symposium

Society of Urologic Nurses and Associates
E Holly Avenue
Box 56
Pittman, NJ 08071

856-256-2350
FAX 856-589-7463

Mike Cunningham, Manager

One hundred fifteen companies have exhibits of equipment, supplies, pharmaceuticals and services for nephrology.
2000 Attendees
Frequency: Annual
Founded in 1970

13311 American Nurses Association Convention

600 Maryland Avenue SW
Suite 100
Washington, DC 20024-2571

202-651-7000
FAX 301-628-5001
E-Mail: exhibits@ana.org
Home Page: www.nursingworld.org

Exhibits of nursing professional equipment, supplies and services.
Frequency: Annual

13312 American Occupational Health Conference & Exhibits

Slack
4930 Del Ray Avenue
Bethesda, MD 20814

301-654-2055
FAX 301-654-5920
E-Mail: member@gastro.org
Home Page: www.gastro.org
Social Media: *Facebook, Twitter, LinkedIn*

Robert Greenberg, Executive Vp
Michael Stolar, Senior Vp
Derek Randolph, Director of Building Services
Arceli Bacsinila, Senior Director of Finance
Hillina Fetehawoke, Staff Accountant

Four hundred exhibits of pharmaceuticals, equipment, software and supplies for health professionals, offices and labs.
4500 Attendees
Mailing list available for rent

13313 American Occupational Therapy Association Annual Conference

American Occupation Therapy Association
4720 Montgomery Lane
PO Box 31220
Bethesda, MD 20824-1220

301-652-2682
FAX 301-652-7711
Home Page: www.aota.org

M Carolyn Baum, President
Lizette Rosales, Manager
7000 Attendees
Frequency: May
Founded in 1919

13314 American Optometric Student Association Annual Meeting

243 N Lindbergh Boulevard
Saint Louis, MO 63141

314-993-8575
FAX 314-993-8919
E-Mail: info@iacconline.org
Home Page: www.iaccnorthamerica.org
Social Media: *Facebook, Twitter, LinkedIn*

James Mahon, Director Marketing
Tom Cappucci, First Vice President

Optometry equipment, supplies and services.
Frequency: Annual

13315 American Organization of Nurse Executives Meeting and Exposition

American Hospital Association
1 N Franklin
Suite 27
Chicago, IL 60606

312-222-2000
312-422-4519

E-Mail: aone@aha.org
Home Page: www.aha.org

Pamela Thompson, CEO
Cliff Lehman, Director Membership Services

One hundred fifty exhibits of patient care equipment and supplies, computer hardware and software, communications systems and information for the professional in health care.
Frequency: Annual

13316 American Orthopsychiatric Association Annual Meeting

330 7th Avenue
18th Floor
New York, NY 10001

212-564-5930
FAX 212-564-6180

Rachel L MacAulay, Program Associate

Meeting and exhibits by social service agencies, publications, computer software companies and more.
1928 Members
700 Attendees
Frequency: Annual
Founded in 1923

13317 American Orthotic & Prosthetic Association on National Assembly

American Orthotic & Prosthetic Association
330 John Carlyle Street
Suite 200
Alexandria, VA 22314

571-431-0876
FAX 571-431-0899
E-Mail: info@aopanet.org
Home Page: www.aopanet.org

Thomas V. Di Bello, President
Bart Herman, VP
Thomas F Fise, Executive Director
Michael Chapman, Coord Membership Operations/Meeting

AOPA's goal is to advocate for policies that improve patient care.
1928 Members
2200 Attendees
Frequency: Annual
Founded in 1917

13318 American Osteopathic Association Meeting & Exhibits

American Osteopathic Hospital Association
142 E Ontario Street
Chicago, IL 60611

312-587-3709
FAX 312-202-8212

John Crosby, Executive Director

Over 25 exhibits of products and services relating to the osteopathic health care industry, including building and finacing, marketing and operations.
500 Attendees
Founded in 1983

13319 American Pain Society Scientific Meeting

4700 W Lake Avenue
Glenview, IL 60025

847-375-4715
FAX 877-734-8758
E-Mail: info@ampainsoc.org
Home Page: www.ampainsoc.org

Judith A Paice, President
Catherine Underwood, Executive Director
Marilyn Rutkowski, Marketing Manager
Kathryn Checea, Director of Sales
Deborah Pinkston, Managing Editor

Designed for a diverse group of pain clinicians, scientists and other professionals, the Annual Scientific Meeting features a prominent faculty

presenting basic, translational, and clinical research advancements. Seminar, banquet, luncheon, breakfast and 150 exhibits of pharmceutical and medical instruments, medical equipment, products, supplies, services, and alternative delivery systems.
Frequency: Annual
Founded in 1977

13320 American Physical Therapy Association Annual Conference
American Physical Therapy Association
1111 N Fairfax Street
Alexandria, VA 22314

703-684-2782
800-999-2782
FAX 703-706-8575
E-Mail: webmaster@apta.org
Home Page: www.apta.org

Kelly Glascoe, Director/Exposition
Frank Mallon, CEO

450 exhibits of physical therapy equipment, supplies and services.
4000 Attendees
Frequency: Annual

13321 American Physical Therapy Association: Private Practice Session
1111 N Fairfax Street
Alexandria, VA 22314

703-684-2782
800-999-2782
FAX 703-706-8575
Home Page: http://www.apta.org

Frank Mallon, CEO

Seminar, workshop, dinner and 120 exhibits of physical therapy and rehabilitation equipment, supplies and services.
1200 Attendees
Frequency: Annual
Founded in 1983

13322 American Podiatric Medical Association Annual Meeting
9312 Old Georgetown Road
Bethesda, MD 20814

301-581-9200
FAX 301-530-2752
Social Media: *Facebook, Twitter, LinkedIn*

Anne Martinez CMP, Meetings Administrator

One-hundred and fifty exhibits of medical and laser equipment, supplies and podiatric services.
1,500 Attendees
Frequency: August

13323 American Psychiatric Association Annual Meeting
1400 K Street NW
Washington, DC 20005

202-682-6100
FAX 202-682-6132
E-Mail: gank@psych.org
Home Page: www.psych.org

Ken Robinson, Manager Meetings

Conference, seminar, workshop and 850 exhibits of computer online service and software, media products, criminal justice, dianostic tools and much more.
18000 Attendees
Frequency: Annual
Founded in 1844

13324 American Psychological Association Annual Convention
American Psychological Association

750 1st Street NE
Washington, DC 20002-4242

202-336-5500
800-374-2721
FAX 202-336-5568
Home Page: www.apa.org

James H Bray PhD, President
Norman Anderson PhD, Executive VP/CEO
Paul L Craig PhD, Treasurer
12000 Attendees
Frequency: Annual, August

13325 American Public Health Association Annual Exhibition
American Public Health Association
800 I Street NW
Washington, DC 20001

202-777-2742
FAX 202-777-2534
E-Mail: lynn.schoen@apha.org
Home Page: www.apha.org

Lynn Schoen, Exhibition Manager
Georges Benjamin, Executive Director

Five-hundred seventy exhibits of medical interest, pharmaceuticals, publishers, educational, governmental, software, helth promotion products and more. Scientific Sessions available.
13000 Attendees
Frequency: November

13326 American Roentgen Ray Society Meeting
American Roentgen Ray Society
44211 Slatestone Court
Leesburg, VA 20176

703-729-3353
800-438-2777
FAX 703-729-4839
E-Mail: info@arrs.org
Home Page: www.arrs.org

Maureen Robertson, Show Manager
Noel Montesa, Vice President
Charles Kahn, Vice President
Melissa Rosado, Secretary

Forty-one and a half hours of Category ICME credits available; Categorical course on Body CT; 30 commercial exhibits; 300 scientific exhibits; scientific paper presentations.
2,500 Attendees
Frequency: April-May

13327 American School Health's Annual School Health Conference
American School Health Association
4340 East West Highway
Suite 403
Bethesda, MD 20814

301-652-8072
800-445-2742
FAX 301-652-8077
E-Mail: info@ashaweb.org
Home Page: www.ashaweb.org
Social Media: *Facebook, Twitter, LinkedIn*

Mary Bamer Ramsier, Meeting Planner
Thomas Reed, Manager
Stephen Conley, Executive Director
Julie Greenfield, Marketing and Conferences Director
Lori Lawrence, Membership/Database Manager

Join school health professionals who will come together to learn, share perspectives and resources, and network during the more than 120 educational sessions and workshops. General Sessions, multiple break-outs, and exhibits.
800 Attendees
Frequency: Annual
Founded in 1927
Mailing list available for rent: 650 names

13328 American Society for Aesthetic Plastic Surgery Conference
American Society for Aesthetic Plastic Surgery
36 W 44th Street
Suite 630
New York, NY 10036

212-921-0500
FAX 212-921-0011
E-Mail: media@surgery.org
Home Page: www.surgery.org

Educational sessions and displays of the latest prdoucts and developments.
2500 Attendees
Frequency: May

13329 American Society for Artificial Internal Organs Meeting and Exhibits
PO Box C
Boca Raton, FL 33429-8589

561-391-8589
FAX 561-368-9153
Home Page: www.asaio.org

Workshop, and over 30 exhibits of interest to physicians, nurses, engineers, perfusionists and technicians.
1000 Attendees
Frequency: Annual
Founded in 1954

13330 American Society for Bone and Mineral Research Congress
1200 19th Street NW
Suite 300
Washington, DC 20036

202-289-5900
FAX 202-857-1880
Home Page: www.asbmr.org

Joan Goldberg, Executive Director

Exhibits for the research of bone and mineral diseases.
Frequency: Annual
Founded in 1977

13331 American Society for Cell Biology Annual Meeting
9650 Rockville Pike
Bethesda, MD 20814

301-530-7153
FAX 301-530-7139
E-Mail: enewman@ascb.org
Home Page: www.ascb.org/ascb

Edward Newman, Director Marketing
Joan Goldberg, Manager
Jean Schwarzbauer, Secretary

Conference and 425 exhibits of interest to biomedical researchers, scientists, and related trade professionals.
8000 Attendees
Frequency: Annual
Founded in 1961

13332 American Society for Dermatologic Surgery Annual Meeting
American Society for Dermatologic Surgery
5550 Meadowbrook Drive
Suite 120
Rolling Meadows, IL 60008

847-956-0900
FAX 847-956-0999
E-Mail: info@asds.net
Home Page: www.asds-net.org

Alastair Carruthers, President
Kimberly Butterwick, Board of Directors

Educational session, banquet and tours plus 80 exhibits of surgical instruments, dressings, clo-

sure materials and dermatologic pharmceuticals.
800 Attendees
Founded in 1973

13333 American Society for Health Care Human Resources Administration Meeting
American Hospital Association
1 N Franklin
Chicago, IL 60606

312-222-2000
FAX 312-422-4519
Home Page: www.aha.org

Human resources administration in health care exhibition.

13334 American Society for Healthcare Management Convention
Corcoran Expositions
100 W Monroe Street
Suite 1001
Chicago, IL 60603

312-541-0567
FAX 312-541-0573

13335 American Society for Histocompatability and Immunogenetics
PO Box 15804
Lexana, KS 66285-5804

913-541-0009
FAX 913-541-0156

Michael P Flanigan CAE, Executive Director
Fifty exhibits from medical suppliers relating to tissue typing.
1000 Attendees
Frequency: Annual
Founded in 1974

13336 American Society for Laser Medicine and Surgery Conference
2100 Stewart Avenue
Suite 240
Wausau, WI 54401-1709

715-845-9283
FAX 715-848-2493
E-Mail: information@aslms.org
Home Page: www.aslms.org

Richard O Gregory MD, Board Secretary
Dianne Dalsky, Executive Director
Seventy five exhibits of laser medicine and supplies of interest to physicians, physicists, nurses, veterinarians, dentists, podiatrists and technicians.
Frequency: Annual
Founded in 1980

13337 American Society for Microbiology: General Meeting
1325 Massachusetts Anvenue NW
Washington, DC 20005

202-942-9252
FAX 202-942-9340

Professionally related exhibits.

13338 American Society for Nutrition Annual Meeting
9650 Rockville Pike
Bethesda, MD 20814-3998

301-634-7050
FAX 301-634-7892
Home Page: www.nutrition.org

Teresa A. Davis, President
John E Courtney PhD, Executive Officer
Gordon L. Jensen, VP

Cheryl Rock, Treasurer
Catherine Field, Secretary
Exhibits relating to clinical nutrition of interest to physicians and scientists.
Frequency: Annual
Mailing list available for rent

13339 American Society for Surgery of the Hand Annual Meeting
American Society for Surgery of the Hand
6300 N River Road
Suite 600
Rosemont, IL 60018

847-384-8300
FAX 847-384-1435
E-Mail: info@assh.org
Home Page: www.assh.org

Carissa Wehrman, Meetings/Exhibits Coordinator
Mark Anderson, Executive Director
Meeting plus exhibits of microsurgical instruments, finger splinting devices, surgical telescopes, trauma products, external fixation systems and more.
2,000 Attendees
Frequency: September

13340 American Society for Therapeutic Radiology and Oncology Annual Meeting
American Society for Therapeutic Radiology & Onc.
12500 Fairlakes Circle
Suite 375
Fairfax, VA 22033

703-502-1550
800-962-7876
FAX 703-502-7852
E-Mail: meetings@astro.org
Home Page: www.astro.org

Laura Mulay, ASTRO Meetings Manager
Eight-hundred exhibits of products, supplies and services for the treatment of cancer.
10000 Attendees
Frequency: October

13341 American Society of Aesthetic Plastic Surgery Meeting
11081 Winners Circle
Suite 200
Los Alamitos, CA 90720-2813

562-799-2356
FAX 310-427-2234

Robert Stanton, Manager
Meeting and 100 exhibits of plastic surgery medical instruments and equipment.
Frequency: Annual

13342 American Society of Anesthesiologists Annual Meeting
American Society of Anesthesiologists
520 N Northwest Highway
Park Ridge, IL 60068-2573

847-825-5586
FAX 847-825-1692
E-Mail: mail@asahq.org
Home Page: www.asahq.org

Ronald Bruns, Executive Director
18000 Attendees
Frequency: Annual, October

13343 American Society of Clinical Oncology Annual Convention
J Spargo & Associates
11208 Waples Mill Road
Suite 112
Fairfax, VA 22030

703-631-6200
800-564-4220

FAX 703-299-1044
E-Mail: info@jspargo.com
Home Page: www.jspargo.com

John Spargo, President
Three hundred exhibits of medical equipment, supplies and services used in the practice of clinical oncology.
20000 Attendees
Frequency: Annual
Founded in 1964

13344 American Society of Clinical Pathologists and College of American Pathologist
American Society of Clinical Pathologists
2100 W Harrison Street
Chicago, IL 60612

312-738-1336
FAX 312-738-1619

John Ball, Executive VP
4500 Attendees

13345 American Society of Cytopathology Annual Scientific Meeting
100 West 10th Street
Suite 605
Wilmington, DE 19801

302-543-6583
FAX 302-543-6597
E-Mail: asc@cytopathology.org
Home Page: www.cytopathology.org
Social Media: *Facebook, Twitter, LinkedIn*

Christy Myers, Meetings Manager
Elizabeth Jenkins, Manager
Andrew Renshaw, President
Premier event in the field of cytopathology. The objectives of the Annual Meeting are to update cytologists on the current practice of cytopathology, foster research in early diagnosis and effective treatment of human disease and provide a forum for advocacy on behalf of cytologists and their patients.
850 Attendees
Frequency: November
Founded in 1951

13346 American Society of Directors of Volunteer Services Leadership Training Conf
1 N Franklin
Chicago, IL 60606

312-223-3937
FAX 312-442-4575

Audrey Harris, Executive Director
Workshop, banquet, luncheon and 55 exhibits of health care administration equipment, supplies and services.
700 Attendees
Frequency: Annual
Founded in 1964

13347 American Society of Electroneurodiagnostic Technologists Convention
American Society of Electroneurodiagnostic Tech
402 E Bannister Rd
Suite A
Kansas City, MO 64131-3019

816-931-1120
FAX 816-931-1145
E-Mail: info@aset.org
Home Page: www.aset.org
Social Media: *Facebook, Twitter*

Arlen Reimnitz, Executive Director
Sarah Ecker, Marketing/Communications Manager
The premier education and exposition opportunity for the Neurodiagnostic technologists in

the country. A must attend event for all neurodiagnostic professionals whether you are a technologist, laboratory manager, physician or representing a supplier. The 2012 convention will be in St. Paul, MN.
500 Attendees
Frequency: Annual

13348 American Society of Extra-Corporeal Tech. International Conference

503 Carlisle Drive
Suite 125
Herndon, VA 20170-4838

703-435-8556
FAX 703-435-0056
E-Mail: webmaster@amsect.org
Home Page: www.amsect.org

Judy Luther, Deputy Executive Director

Seminar, workshop, conference and 75 exhibits relating to the practice of extra-corporeal technology (involving heart and lung machines).
Frequency: Annual

13349 American Society of Hand Therapists Convention

Smith, Bucklin and Associates
401 N Michigan Avenue
Chicago, IL 60611-4267

312-644-6610
FAX 312-245-1082
E-Mail: info@smithbucklin.com
Home Page: www.smithbucklin.com

Henry S. Givray, President & CEO
C. Albert Koob, Executive Vice President
Carolyn Dolezal, Executive Vice President
Michael L. Payne, Executive Vice President
Cele Fogarty, Vice President - Event Services

Workshop and 40 - 60 exhibits of books, and hand therapy equipment.
800 Attendees
Frequency: Annual
Founded in 1949

13350 American Society of Health Care Marketing & Public Relations

1 N Franklin Street
31st Floor
Chicago, IL 60606-3421

773-327-1064
FAX 312-422-4579

Lauren Barnett, Executive Director

Sixty booths of communications, printing, computer equipment, public relations and fund raising consultants in the health care profession.
600 Attendees
Frequency: September

13351 American Society of Hematology Annual Meeting & Exposition

1200 19th Street NW
Suite 300
Washington, DC 24226

202-857-1118
FAX 202-847-1164

Gail Sparks

Four hundred fifty exhibits of equipment and supplies of interest to hematologists and related professionals.
15000 Attendees
Founded in 1958

13352 American Society of Human Genetics Annual Meeting

American Society of Human Genetics
9650 Rockville Pike
Bethesda, MD 20814-3998

301-634-7300
FAX 301-634-7079

E-Mail: society@ashg.org
Home Page: www.ashg.org
Social Media: *Facebook, Twitter, LinkedIn*

Joann Boughman, PhD, Executive VP
Chuck Windle, Director of Finance/Administration
Karen Goodman, Executive Assistant
Pauline Minhinnett, Dir. of Meetings/Exhibit Management
Mary Shih, Membership Manager

A meeting of researchers, clinicians, trainees and others who share the most recent research findings in human genetics. Includes invited speaker sessions and about 3000 contributed abstracts; 266 to platform and the remainder to poster presentations.
8000 Members
6,000 Attendees
Founded in 1948

13353 American Society of Nephrology

American Society of Nephrology
1200 19th Street NW
Suite 300
Washington, DC 20036

202-857-1190
FAX 202-429-5112
13000 Attendees

13354 American Society of PeriAnesthesia Nurses

American Gastroenterological Association
4930 Del Ray Avenue
Bethesda, MD 20814

301-654-2055
FAX 301-654-5920
E-Mail: member@gastro.org
Home Page: www.gastro.org

13355 American Society of Post Anesthesia Nurses Meeting

Slack
4930 Del Ray Avenue
Bethesda, MD 20814

301-654-2055
FAX 301-654-5920
E-Mail: member@gastro.org
Home Page: www.gastro.org

Robert Greenberg, Executive Vp
Michael Stolar, Senior Vp

One hundred seventy exhibits of pharmaceuticals and recovery room supplies.
1700 Attendees
Frequency: Annual
Founded in 1981

13356 American Society of Psychoprophylaxis in Obstetrics/Lamaze Conference

Smith, Bucklin and Associates
1200 19th Street NW
Suite 300
Washington, DC 20036-2412

202-861-6416
FAX 202-429-5112

Leigh McMillan, Senior Convention Director

One hundred exhibitors of educational materials for Lamaze method of prepared childbirth, obstetric equipment and supplies, infant products, breast pumps and more.
500 Attendees
Frequency: Annual
Founded in 1960

13357 American Society of Transplant Physicians Scientific Meeting

Slack

4930 Del Ray Avenue
Bethesda, MD 20814

301-654-2055
FAX 301-654-5920
E-Mail: member@gastro.org
Home Page: www.gastro.org

Robert Greenberg, Executive Vp
Michael Stolar, Senior Vp

Fifty exhibits of medical supplies and services of interest to physicans and others actively involved with transplantaion.
800 Attendees
Frequency: Annual
Founded in 1981

13358 American Society of Transplant Surgeons Annual Meeting

Wright Organization
716 Lee Street
Des Plaines, IL 60016-4515

847-245-5700
FAX 708-824-0394

Sixty exhibitors of medical equipment, supplies and services relating to renal and cardiac transplants.
750 Attendees
Founded in 1974

13359 American Society of Tropical Medicine and Hygiene Annual Scientific Meeting

60 Revere Drive
Suite 500
Northbrook, IL 60062

847-480-9592
FAX 847-480-9282
E-Mail: info@astmh.org
Home Page: www.astmh.org

Madhuri Carson, Conference Administrator
Judy DeAcetis, Director
Karen Goraleski, Executive Director

Reception and over 20 exhibits related to tropical medicine and hygiene, including the areas of arboviology, entomology, medicine, nursing and parasitology.
1500 Attendees
Frequency: November
Founded in 1951

13360 American Speech-Language-Hearing Association Annual Convention

American Speech- Language Hearing Association
10801 Rockville Pike
Rockville, MD 20852

301-897-5700
800-498-2071
FAX 301-296-8580
E-Mail: productsales@asha.org
Home Page: www.asha.org

Mary Harding, Exhibition Manager
Arlene Pietranton, Associate Director
Amy Hasselkus, Associate Director

Four hundred exhibits of medical, educational and testing equipment, plus publications.
12000 Attendees

13361 American Urological Association Convention

1000 Corporate Boulevard
Linthicum, MD 21090

410-689-3700
FAX 410-689-3800
E-Mail: convention@auanet.org
Home Page: www.auanet.org/

Jane Conway, Advertising & Exhibit Sales
Sarah Hardy, Exhibitor Customer Service
Andrew Niles, Exhibit Operations
Michael T Sheppard, Executive Director

Paul F Schellhammer, Board of Directors President

At the American Urological Association (AUA)'s Annual Meeting there are more than 10,000 urologists and health care professionals in attendance and over 300 exhibitors showcasing their urological products or services- there is no better place to learn about the latest advances in urology.
10000 Attendees
Frequency: Annual

13362 Annual Clinical Assembly of Osteopathic Specialists
American College of Osteopathic Surgeons
123 N Henry Street
Alexandria, VA 22314

703-684-0416
FAX 703-684-3280
E-Mail: info@facos.org
Home Page: www.facos.org
Social Media: *Facebook, Twitter, LinkedIn*

Guy Beaumont, Executive Director
Judith T Mangum, Director Finance
Jennifer B. Colwell, Director of Continuing Education
Sonjya Johnson, Director of Membership Recruitment
Brandon Roberts, Director of Finance
700 Members
Frequency: Annual
Mailing list available for rent

13363 Annual Conference on Healthcare Marketing
Alliance for Healthcare Strategy & Marketing
11 S LaSalle Street
Suite 2300
Chicago, IL 60603

312-704-9700
FAX 312-704-9709
Home Page: www.alliancehlth.org/hlthmktg

Workshop and social events plus 50 exhibits of marketing communications, health care information lines, strategic planning and more.
600 Attendees
Frequency: Annual
Founded in 1984

13364 Annual Contact Lens and Primary Care Seminar, MOA
Michigan Optometric Association
530 W Ionia Street
Suite A
Lansing, MI 48933-1062

517-482-0616
FAX 517-482-1611
E-Mail: mioptoassn@aol.com
Home Page: www.themoa.org

William D Dansby CAE, Executive VP
Mark Margolies, Treasurer

Continuing education program and trade show for optometrists and optometric technicians/assistants.
1100 Attendees
Frequency: October, Annually
Founded in 1968

13365 Annual Convention of American Institute of Ultrasound in Medicine
American Institute of Ultrasound in Medicine
14750 Sweitzer Lane
Suite 100
Laurel, MD 20707

301-498-4392
800-638-5352
FAX 301-498-4450

E-Mail: conv_edu@aium.org
Home Page: www.aium.org

Jenny Clark, Director of Development
Brenda Kinney, Meeting Coordinator
Lisa Shendan, Sales Manager
Frequency: June

13366 Annual Convention of the American College of Osteopathic Obstetricians
American College Of Osteopathic Obstetricians
900 Auburn Road
Pontiac, MI 48342

248-332-6360
800-875-6360
FAX 248-332-4607
Home Page: www.acoog.com

Jaki Britton, Administrator

Workshop, reception and banquet as well as exhibits relating to women's health, medical equipment and supplies.
350 Attendees
Frequency: Annual
Founded in 1934

13367 Annual Critical Care Update
National Professional Education Institute
2525 Ossen Fort Road
PO Box 118
Glencoe, MO 63068-1107

636-735-5570
800-575-5575
FAX 561-743-9596
E-Mail: JJMcDaid@aol.com
Home Page: www.npeinursing.com

Judie McDaid, Exhibitor Relations Manager
Leslie Brock, Registration Manager
The Annual Critical Care Update and Nurse Managers Conference/EXPO provides a fully integrated program dedicated to the continuing education of critical care nurses, nurse managers and other healthcare professionals. Exhibitors showcase their latest healthcare products, pharmaceuticals, services, research and facilities. Knowledge gained in the informative, entertaining EXPO Hall, will influence these nurses' purchasing decisions throughout the year.
1500 Attendees
Frequency: Annual, April
Founded in 1973

13368 Annual Disease Management Congress: Innnovative Strategies
National Managed Health Care Congress
71 2nd Avenue
3rd Floor
Waltham, MA 02154

888-882-2500
FAX 941-365-0157
Home Page: www.nmhcc.org

Frances Pratt, Director/Marketing

One hundred exhibits of targeted disease management and services.
1700 Attendees
Frequency: Annual
Founded in 1996

13369 Annual Educational Conference and Exhibits
Society for Healthcare Strategy & Market Dev.
One N Franklin
Chicago, IL 60606

312-422-3840
FAX 312-422-4579
E-Mail: stratsoc@aha.org
Home Page: www.stratsociety.org

Frequency: September

13370 Annual Meeting & Clinical Lab Exposition
American Association for Clinical Chemistry
1850 K St NW
Suite 625
Washington, DC 20006-2215

202-857-0717
800-892-1400
FAX 202-887-5093
E-Mail: custserv@aacc.org
Home Page: www.aacc.org

Jean Rhame, Director Professional Affairs

Six hundred exhibitors of clincal laboratory equipment, supplies and services for lab automation, information, robotics and OEM products. Seminar, worhshop and conference.
20000 Attendees
Frequency: Annual
Mailing list available for rent: 11000 names at $150 per M

13371 Annual Meeting & Homecare Expo
National Association for Home Care and Hospice
228 7th Street SE
Washington, DC 20003

202-547-7424
FAX 202-547-3540
E-Mail: webmaster@nahc.org
Home Page: www.nahc.org

Gathering of Home Care and Hospice professionals.
4000 Attendees
Frequency: October

13372 Annual Meeting & OTO Expo
American Academy of Otolaryngology-Head & Neck
1650 Diagonal Road
Alexandria, VA 22314-3357

703-836-4444
FAX 703-683-5100
E-Mail: membership@entnet.org
Home Page: www.entnet.org

Marty Stewart, Sr Manager, Media/Public Relations
James L. Netterville, President
J. Gavin Setzen, Secretary/Treasurer
David R. Nielsen, Executive Vice President and CEO
Paul T. Fass, Director - Private Practice
Frequency: September
Mailing list available for rent

13373 Annual Meeting of the American Association on Mental Retardation
American Association on Mental Retardation
444 N Capitol Street NW
Suite 846
Washington, DC 20001-1512

202-387-1968
800-424-3688
FAX 202-387-2193
E-Mail: dcroser@aamr.org
Home Page: www.aamr.org

Doreen Croser, Executive Director
Paul Aitken, Director Of Finance Administration
2000 Attendees
Frequency: Annual, May

13374 Annual Meeting of the Microscopy Society of America
Bostrom Corporation

230 E Ohio
Suite 400
Chicago, IL 60611-3265

312-644-1527
800-538-3672
FAX 312-644-8557
E-Mail:
BusinessOffices@MSA.Microscopy.com
Home Page: www.msa.microscopy.com

Judy Janes, Manager

Microscopes and related supplies of interest to medical, biological, metalurgical, and polymer research scientists, technicians and physicists interested in instrument design and improvement.
Frequency: Annual, August

13375 Annual National Managed Health Care Congress

71 2nd Avenue
3rd Floor
Waltham, MA 02154

888-882-2500
FAX 941-365-0157
E-Mail: register@mnhcc.com
Home Page: www.nmhcc.org

Seminar, workshop, conference, and 600 exhibits of services and products dedicated to improving the quality of health care.
10000 Attendees
Frequency: Annual
Founded in 1989

13376 Annual PPO Forum

American Assn of Preferred Provider Organizations
222 South First Street
Suite 303
Louisville, KY 40202

502-403-1122
FAX 502-403-1129
E-Mail: mcox@aappo.org
Home Page: www.aappo.org

Melissa Cox, Event Coordinator
Michael Taddeo, Chairperson
Keith Vangeison, Vice-Chairman
Kenneth Hamm, Treasurer
William Ross, Secretary
Frequency: San Diego
Founded in 1983

13377 Annual Scientific & Clinical Congress

American Association of Clinical Endocrinologists
245 Riverside Avenue
Suite 200
Jacksonville, FL 32202

904-353-7878
FAX 904-353-8185
E-Mail: info@aace.com
Home Page: www.aace.com

Donald Jones, CEO
Jeffrey Garber, President

Clinical endocrinologists and endocrine surgeons gather for meeting and exhibits of equipment, supplies and services.
2000 Attendees
Frequency: April

13378 Annual Scientific Meeting

Aerospace Medical Association
320 S Henry Street
Alexandria, VA 22314-3579

703-739-2240
FAX 703-739-9652
E-Mail: rrayman@asma.org
Home Page: www.asma.org

Sheryl Kildall, Subscriptions Manager
Warren Silberman DO, VP
Jeffrey C. Sventek, Executive Director

Gisselle Vargas, Operations Manager
Gloria Carter, Director, Member Services

Provides a multi-faceted forum for all aerospace medical disciplines and concurrently provides continuing education credits for those attending the meeting.
3000 Attendees
Frequency: Annual/May
Mailing list available for rent

13379 Annual Scientific Meeting of the Gerontological Society of America

Gerontological Society of America
1030 15th Street NW
Suite 250
Washington, DC 20005

202-842-1275
FAX 202-842-1150
Home Page: www.geron.org

Carol Schutz, Executive Director

13380 Applied Ergonomics Conference

Institute of Industrial Engineers
3597 Parkway Lane
Suite 200
Norcross, GA 30097

770-449-0461
800-494-0460
FAX 770-263-8532
E-Mail: webmaster@iienet.org
Home Page: www.iienet.org/annual

Carol LeBlanc, Conference Manager

An exclusive event for ergonomists, engineers, and safety professionals. The conference focuses on how companies have successfully implemented programs that provide excellent return on their ergonomics investment.
800 Attendees
Frequency: March
Founded in 1998

13381 Arthroscopy Association of North America Annual Meeting

6300 N River Road
#104
Rosemont, IL 60018

847-292-2262
FAX 847-292-2268
E-Mail: holly@aana.org
Home Page: www.aana.org

Holly Albert, Meetings Manager
Edward Goss, Executive Director

Seminar, reception and 100 exhibits of video and arthroscopy equipment, braces, books and more.
1000 Attendees

13382 Assisted Living Expo

VNU Expositions
Dulles International Airport
PO Box 17413
Washington, DC 20041

703-318-0300
800-765-7616
FAX 703-318-8833
Home Page: www.vnuexpo.com

Displays of assisted living information and equipment.

13383 Association for Applied Psychophysiology & Biofeedback Annual Meeting

Association for Applied Psychophysiology
10200 W 44th Avenue
Suite 304
Wheat Ridge, CO 80033

303-228-8436
800-477-8892
FAX 303-422-8894

E-Mail: info@aapb.org
Home Page: www.aapb.org

Tina Watkins, Meetings Manager
Francine Butler, Treasurer
Fred Schaffer, Treasurer

Exhibits of biofeedback equipment, supplies, and training programs, medical supplies and software, as well as annual meeting.
500 Attendees
Frequency: March
Founded in 1969

13384 Association for Healthcare Philanthropy Annual Int'l Educational Conference

Association for Healthcare Philanthropy
313 Park Avenue
Suite 400
Falls Church, VA 22046

703-532-6243
FAX 703-532-7170
E-Mail: ahp@ahp.org
Home Page: www.ahp.org

Conference and 120 exhibits with information about equipment and services for the fundraising and helatcare development community, including computer software, recognition gifts, direct mail companies, executive recruiters, special events and more.
900 Attendees
Frequency: September

13385 Association for Professionals in Infection Control & Epidemiology

Association for Professionals in Infection Control
1275 K Street NW
Suite 1000
Washington, DC 20005-4006

202-789-1890
800-650-9570
FAX 202-789-1899
E-Mail: apicinfo@apic.org
Home Page: www.apic.org

Christine J Nutty, President
Carolyn E Jackson, Secretary
Katrina Crist, CEO
Jacqueline Manson, Accounting
Sara Haywood, Education

Workshop, banquet, reception and 150 exhibits of infection control products, pharmaceuticals, disinfectants, soaps, dataprocessing software, housekeeping equipment and supplies.
2700 Attendees
Frequency: Annual
Founded in 1974

13386 Association for Worksite Health Promotion Annual International Conference

60 Revere Drive
Suite 500
Northbrook, IL 60062-1577

847-480-9574
FAX 847-480-9282
Home Page: www.awhp.org

Liz Freyn, Conference Manager

One hundred twenty two booths of information and supplies to promote and develop quality programs of health and fitness in business and industry. Seminar, workshop, conference, tours and luncheon.
950 Attendees
Founded in 1974

13387 Association of Behavioral Healthcare Management Convention

60 Revere Drive
Suite 500
Northbrook, IL 60062

847-480-9626
FAX 847-480-9282

Exhibits related to the administration of services for the emotionally disturbed, mentally ill, mentally retarded, developmentally disabled, and those with substance abuse problems.
Frequency: Annual

13388 Association of Healthcare Internal Auditors Conference

PO Box 449
Onstead, MI 49265-0449

517-467-7729
FAX 517-467-6104
E-Mail: ahia@ahia.org
Home Page: www.ahia.org

Thomas Monahan, Executive Director
Michelle Cunningham, Account Executive
Robert Michalski, Secretary, Treasurer

Exhibits concerning cost containment and increased productivity in health care institutions through internal auditing.
1000 Attendees
Founded in 1981

13389 Association of Pediatric Oncology Nurses Annual Conference

Association of Pediatric Nurses
4700 W Lake Avenue
Glenview, IL 60025-1485

847-375-4724
FAX 847-375-4777
E-Mail: info@apon.org
Home Page: www.apon.org

Pamela Asfahani, Product Manager
Elizabeth Sherman, senior marketing Manager

Exhibits on caring for children who have cancer.

13390 Association of Rehabilitation Nurses Annual Educational Conference

4700 W Lake Avenue
Glenview, IL 60025-1485

847-375-4710
800-229-7530
FAX 847-375-4777

Conference, educational session, workshop and 225 exhibits of rehabilitational aids and supplies, medical equipment, hospitals and rehbilitation facilities and publications of interest to rehabilitation nurses.
2300 Attendees
Founded in 1974

13391 Benefits Health Care New York Show

Flagg Management
353 Lexington Avenue
New York, NY 10016

212-286-0333
FAX 212-286-0086
E-Mail: flaggmgmnt@msn.com
Home Page: www.flaggmgmt.com

Russell Flagg, President

Sponsored by Employee Benefit News, the conference will focus on the recent health care reform, as well as coping with the economic downturn. Human resources, personnel, administration and training marketplace. HRMS, systems and services 250 exhibits. $295.
Frequency: Annual
Mailing list available for rent

13392 Building Bridges VII

American Association of Health Plans

1129 20th Street NW
Washington, DC 20036

202-778-3200
FAX 202-778-8506

13393 CHPA Annual Executive Conference

Consumer Health Care Products Association
900 19th St NW
Suite 700
Washington, DC 20006-2105

202-429-9260
FAX 202-223-6835
E-Mail: eassey@chpa-info.org
Home Page: www.chpa-info.org

Paul L. Sturman, Chair

Join top healthcare executives from across the nation and participate in high-level education sessions focused on the industry's rapidly shifting environment.

13394 Center for School Mental Health Assistance National Convention

Exhibit Promotions Plus
11620 Vixens Path
Ellicott City, MD 21042

301-596-3028
FAX 410-997-0764

Harve C Horowitz, President

Supports school health, mental health professionals by offering ongoing consutation to address administrative, clinical and systems issues relevant to school health services.
Frequency: October

13395 Clinical Laboratory Expo

AACC; c/o Scherago International
11 Penn Plaza
Suite 1003
New York, NY 10001

212-643-1750
FAX 212-643-1758
E-Mail: tonym@scherago.com
Home Page: www.scherago.com/AACC

Tony Maiorino, Vice President
20000 Attendees
Frequency: July-August

13396 Clinical Laboratory Management Association Annual Conference & Exhibition

Clinical Laboratory Management Association
989 Old Eagle School Road
Suite 815
Wayne, PA 19087

610-995-9580
FAX 610-995-9568
E-Mail: info@clma.org
Home Page: www.clma.org

Dana Procsal, VP
Ruth Nelson, Director of Operations

CLMA-ASCP have combined forces to offer the largest, most comprehensive laboratory conference and exhibition ever, specifically designed for laboratory professionals at all levels.
4800 Attendees
Frequency: June

13397 Clinical and Scientific Congress of the Int'l Anesthesia Research Society

International Anesthesia Research Society
2 Summit Park Drive
Suite 140
Cleveland, OH 44131

216-642-1124
FAX 216-642-1127

E-Mail: info@iars.org
Home Page: www.iars.org

Donald S Prough, Chair
Hugo Van Aken, Chairman
1200 Attendees
Frequency: March

13398 Congress on Invitro Biology

Society for Invitro Biology
9315 Lango Drive W
Suite 255
Lango, MD 20774

301-324-5054
800-741-7476
FAX 301-324-5057
E-Mail: sivb@sivb.org
Home Page: www.sivb.org

Marietta Ellis, Managing Director
Richard Heller, Treasurer

Focus on issues pertinent to the Vertebrate, Invertebrate, and Cellular Toxicology Sections and will give participants a unique learning experience on animal cell culture and biotechnology.
1,000 Attendees
Frequency: June

13399 Consumer Directed Health Care Conference

Po Box 448, East Cary Street
Suite 102
Richmond, VA 23219

804-266-7422
FAX 804-225-7458
Home Page: www.cdhcc.com or www.consumerhealthworld.com

Carlotta Farmer, Director of Programming
Frequency: December, Washington

13400 Digestive Disease Week Meeting & Exhibition

American Gastroenterological Association
4930 Del Ray Avenue
Bethesda, MD 20814

301-654-2055
FAX 301-652-3890
E-Mail: member@gastro.org
Home Page: www.gastro.org

14000 Attendees
Frequency: March

13401 Distribution Management Conference & Expo

Healthcare Distribution Management Association
900 N Glebe Road
Suite 1000
Arlington, VA 22203

703-787-0000
FAX 703-935-3200
Home Page: www.healthcaredistribution.org

Lori Burke, Director Meetings/Conferences
Denise Woodson, Managing Director
Laurel Todd, Managing Director

Provides the latest information on the most important topics affecting healthcare distribution.
Frequency: June

13402 Drug Discovery Technology

Hynes Convention Center
900 Boylston Street
Boston, MA 02115

617-954-2000
800-845-8800
FAX 617-954-2125
E-Mail: info@mccahome.com
Home Page: www.mccahome.com

2000 Attendees
Frequency: August

13403 Emergency Nurses Association Scientific Assembly & Exhibits
Emergency Nurses Association
915 Lee Street
Des Plaines, IL 60016-6569

847-460-4100
800-900-9659
FAX 847-460-4001
E-Mail: webmaster@ena.org
Home Page: www.ena.org

David Westman, CEO
Anita Dorr, Co-Founder
Kathy Szumanski, Director
3500 Attendees
Frequency: Annual, September

13404 Endocrine Society Annual Meeting
Scherago International
11 Penn Plaza
Suite 1003
New York, NY 10001

212-643-1750
FAX 212-643-1758

6500 Attendees

13405 Experimental Biology
FASEB/OSMC
9650 Rockville Pike
Bethesda, MD 20814

301-634-7100
FAX 301-634-7014
E-Mail: info@faseb.org
Home Page: www.faseb.org/meetings

Pauline Minhinnett, Meeting Manager
Jean Lash, Marketing Manager
Jacquelyn Roberts, Marketing Manager
David Craven, Executive Director
12M Attendees
Frequency: April

13406 FASEB Conference Federation for American Societies for Experimental Biology
FASEB/OSMC
9650 Rockville Pike
Bethesda, MD 20814

301-634-7100
FAX 301-634-7014
E-Mail: info@faseb.org
Home Page: www.faseb.org/meetings

Jean Lash, Exhibit Manager
Marcella Jackson, Marketing Manager
Jacquelyn Roberts, Marketing Manager
David Craven, Executive Director
900 Attendees
Frequency: March

13407 Fall Symposium
American College of Emergency Physicians
PO Box 619911
Dallas, TX 75261

972-550-0911
FAX 972-580-2816

325 Attendees

13408 Federation of Hospitals Public Policy Conference & Business Exposition
Federation of American Health Systems
801 Pennsylvania Avenue NW
Suite 245
Washington, DC 20004-2604

202-624-1500
FAX 202-737-6462
E-Mail: info@fah.org
Home Page: www.fah.org

Bonnie Moneypenny, Senior VP Administrative Services
Letitia Faison-Mahoney, Controller

The conference brings together hospital executives and leading policymakers each Spring for important discussions. It also affords an important opportunity for suppliers to meet face-to-face with hospital managers and buyers.
Frequency: Annual, March
Founded in 1966

13409 Fire-Rescue International
International Association of Fire Chiefs
4025 Fair Ridge Drive
Fairfax, VA 22033

703-273-0911
FAX 703-273-9363
Home Page: www.iafc.org/conference.shtml

William Walton, CFO

Conference and exposition of the fire service industry.
16000 Attendees
Frequency: August

13410 Food & Nutrition Conference & Expo
American Dietetic Association
120 South Riverside Plaza
Suite 2000
Chicago, IL 60606

312-899-0040
800-877-1600
FAX 312-899-0008
E-Mail: gandruch@eatright.org
Home Page: www.eatright.org
Social Media: *Facebook, Twitter*

Greg Andruch, Exhibits Manager
Allison MacMunn, Public Relations Manager
Donna Wickstrom, Manager
Karen Didriksen, Purchasing Manager

More than 8,000 professionals come to the Food & Nutrition Conference & Expo for the latest technological and nutritional advancements. This is the premier selling opportunity in the fields of nutrition and food service management. The event continues to expand-attracting a wider audience of professionals, including hotel and restaurant managers, sports, health and nutrition professionals and executive chefs.
8000 Attendees
Frequency: September, Pennsylvania
Circulation: 65000

13411 HCEA Annual Meeting
Healthcare Convention & Exhibitors Association
1100 Johnson Ferry Rd NE
Suite 300
Atlanta, GA 30342-1733

404-252-3663
FAX 404-252-0774
E-Mail: hcea@kellencompany.com
Home Page: www.hcea.org

Eric Allen, Executive Vice President
Jackie Beaulieu, Associate Director
Michelle Hall, Staff Associate
Carol Wilson, Meetings Director
Frank Skinner, Executive Director

Cost varies; approximately 50 booths; 800 attendees.
200 Attendees
Frequency: Annual
Founded in 1930
Mailing list available for rent: 1400 names

13412 HCEA Marketing Summit
Healthcare Convention & Exhibitors Association
1100 Johnson Ferry Rd NE
Suite 300
Atlanta, GA 30342-1733

404-252-3663
FAX 404-252-0774

E-Mail: hcea@kellencompany.com
Home Page: www.hcea.org

Eric Allen, Executive Vice President
Jackie Beaulieu, Associate Director
Michelle Hall, Staff Associate
Carol Wilson, Meetings Director
Frank Skinner, Executive Director

Cost varies; no exhibits; 200-250 attendees.
200 Attendees
Frequency: Annual
Founded in 1930
Mailing list available for rent: 1400 names

13413 HDMA Annual Meeting
Healthcare Distribution Management Association
900 N Glebe Road
Suite 1000
Arlington, VA 22203

703-787-0000
FAX 703-935-3200
Home Page: www.healthcaredistribution.org

Lori Burke, Director Meetings/Conferences
Denise Woodson, Managing Director
Laurel Todd, Managing Director

Provides a unique opportunity for senior-level retailer and supplier member executives to interact and discuss strategic issues.
Frequency: October

13414 HIDA Conference & Expo
Health Industry Distributors Association
310 Montgomery Street
Alexandria, VA 22314-1516

703-549-4432
FAX 703-549-4695
E-Mail: rowan@hida.org
Home Page: www.hida.org

Matt Rowan, CEO

Includes education sessions, training rotation, and the best-attended trade show in the industry.
8000 Attendees
Frequency: October

13415 HMFA's ANI: The Healthcare Finance Conference
Healthcare Finance Management Association
3 Westbrook Corporate Center
Suite 600
Westchester, IL 60154

708-531-9600
FAX 708-531-0032
Home Page: www.hfma.org/events/ani

Access to education programs, speaker sessions and hundreds of vendors, as well as networking and best practices sharing opportunities.
Mailing list available for rent

13416 HMFA's Virtual Healthcare Finance Conference & Career Fair
Healthcare Finance Management Association
3 Westbrook Corporate Center
Suite 600
Westchester, IL 60154

708-531-9600
800-252-4362
FAX 708-531-0032
E-Mail: virtualhcfc@hfma.org
Home Page: www.hfma.org
Social Media: *Facebook, Twitter, LinkedIn*

Access live education programs and on-demand sessions from your office. Keynote speakers and presenters, and a virtual exhibit hall and career fair.
39000 Members
Founded in 1991
Mailing list available for rent

13417 Healthcare Information and Management Systems Society
HIMSS/Healthcare Information and Management
230 E Ohio
Suite 500
Chicago, IL 60611

312-664-4467
FAX 312-664-6143

13418 IAHCSMM Annual Conference
213 W Institute Place
Suite 307
Chicago, IL 60610-3195

312-440-0078
800-962-8274
FAX 312-440-9474
E-Mail: mailbox@iahcsmm.com
Home Page: www.iahcsmm.com

Betty Hanna, Executive Director
Marilyn T. Conde, Secretary/Treasurer
Bruce T. Bird, President
David Jagrosse, Executive Board Member
David Narance, Executive Board Member
International Association of Healthcare
Central Service Material Management - 125
EXHIBITORSlication separates supervisors/directors from technicians.
600+ Attendees
Frequency: Annual

13419 IAHSS Annual General Meeting
International Association for Healthcare
Security
PO Box 5038
Glendale Heights, IL 60139

888-353-0990
888-353-0990
FAX 630-529-4139
E-Mail: info@iahss.org
Home Page: www.iahss.org

Bryan Warren, President
Evelyn Meserve, Executive Director
Jim Stankevich, President-Elect
Lisa Pryse, VP/Treasurer
Bryan Warren, VP/Secretary

Non-profit organization of healthcare security and safety executives from around the world. The association works to improve and professionalize security and safety in healthcare facilities through the exchange of information and experiences among members.
1700 Members
Founded in 1968

13420 INTERPHEX - The World's Forum for the Pharmaceutical Industry
Reed Exhibition Companies
383 Main Avenue
Norwalk, CT 06851

203-840-4800
FAX 203-840-4804

Chet Burchett, President
11000 Attendees

13421 Infusion Nurses Society
Infusion Nurses Society
315 Norwood Park South
Norwood, MA 02062

781-440-9408
800-694-0298
FAX 781-440-9409
E-Mail: ins@ins1.org
Home Page: www.ins1.org
Social Media: *Facebook, Twitter, LinkedIn*

Britt Meyer, President
Mary Alexander, CEO
Chris Hunt, Executive VP

Michaelle Frost, Accounting Manager
Chelsea McCue, Accounting Coordinator
7000 Members
1000 Attendees
Frequency: Annual
Founded in 1973
Mailing list available for rentat $200 per M

13422 Infusion Nurses Society Annual Meeting
Infusion Nurses Society
315 Norwood Park South
Norwood, MA 02062

781-440-9408
800-694-0298
FAX 781-440-9409
E-Mail: ins@ins1.org
Home Page: www.ins1.org
Social Media: *Facebook, Twitter, LinkedIn*

Cora Vizcarra, President
Mary Alexander, CEO
Chris Hunt, Executive VP
Michaelle Frost, Accounting Manager
Chelsea McCue, Accounting Coordinator
Mailing list available for rentat $200 per M

13423 International Conference on Head and Neck Cancer
American Head and Neck Society
1805 Ardmore Boulevard
Pittsburgh, PA 15221

412-243-5156
FAX 412-243-5160
E-Mail: rwagnercme@aol.com
Home Page: www.headandneckcancer.org

Robin Wagner, Show Manager

Sixty exhibits of equipment and supplies, conference, luncheon and reception.
2,500 Attendees
Frequency: August

13424 International Congress on Ambulatory Surgery Conference
Hynes Convention Center
900 Boylston Street
Boston, MA 02115

617-954-2000
FAX 617-954-2125
E-Mail: info@mccahome.com
Home Page: www.mccahome.com

1500 Attendees
Frequency: May

13425 International Society for Magnetic Resonance in Medicine
International Society for Magnetic
Resonance
2118 Milvia Street
Suite 201
Berkeley, CA 94704

510-841-1899
FAX 510-841-2340
E-Mail: info@ismrm.org
Home Page: www.ismrm.org

Frequency: May

13426 International Vision Exposition & Conference
Association Expositions & Services
383 Main Avenue
Norwalk, CT 06851

203-840-4820
800-811-7151
FAX 203-840-4824
Home Page: visionexpo.com

Eileen Baird
Ed Gallo, Sales Manager
Tracy Flacherty, Marketing Director

As the most comprehensive vision care show and conference in the US, International Vision Expo is where today's eye care professionals meet, learn and conduct business. International vision expo draws optical professionals from all career path including: Ophthalmologist, Optometrist, Opticians, Lab Personnel, Practice managers, Ophthalmic Medical Personnel, Retailers, Manufacturing Executives, Import Export buyers, Ophthalmic Assistants, Optical Interns and more.
15000 Attendees
Frequency: March/September

13427 Managed Care Institute & Display Forum
American Association of Health Plans
601 Pennsylvania Avenue, NW
South Building, Suite 500
Washington, DC 20004

202-778-3200
FAX 202-331-7487
E-Mail: ahip@ahip.org
Home Page: www.aahp.org
Social Media: *Twitter*

Michael Abbott, President
William Cameron, Chairman

Two hundred exhibits by suppliers to the managed health care industry, conference and reception.
2000 Attendees
Frequency: Annual
Founded in 1986

13428 Managed Care Law Conference
American Association of Health Plans
1129 20th Street NW
Washington, DC 20036

202-778-3200
FAX 202-778-8506

13429 Medical Design & Manufacturing Conference & Exhibition West
Canon Communications
11444 W Olympic Boulevard
Los Angeles, CA 90064

310-445-4200
FAX 310-996-9499
Home Page: www.cancom.com

Diane O'Conner, Trade Show Director
Dan Cutrone, Show Marketing Manager

Devoted to the design, development, and manufacture of medical products. Visitors can preview the latest advances in medical-grade materials, assembly components, machinery, electronics, systems, software, services and more. Held at the Anaheim Convention Center in Anaheim, California.
8,500 Attendees
Frequency: January

13430 Medical Design and Manufacturing Minneapolis Conference
Canon Communications
11444 W Olympic Boulevard
Los Angeles, CA 90064

310-445-4200
FAX 310-996-9499
Home Page: www.mdm-minneapolis.com

Diane O'Connor, Trade Show Director
Dan Cutrone, Show Marketing Manager

Four hundred thirty three exhibitors in 52,500 square feet of the Minneapolis Convention Center. Medical supplies and information promotional opportunities in show directory, web site advertising, conference program, sponsorships and product previews.
3374 Attendees
Frequency: October
Founded in 1994

13431 Medical Equipment Design & Technology Exhibition & Conference
Canon Communications
11444 W Olympic Boulevard
Los Angeles, CA 90064-1549

310-445-4200
FAX 310-445-4299
Home Page: www.medtecshow.com

Diane O'Conner, Trade Show Director
Dan Cutrone, Show Marketing Manager

Devoted to the design, development and manufacture of medical products. Visitors can preview the latest advances in medical-grade materials, assembly components, electronics, machinery, software, systems, services and more. Held at the RAI International Exhibition and Congress Center in Amsterdam, Netherlands.
2231 Attendees
Frequency: October

13432 Medical Group Management Association
Medical Group Management Association
104 Inverness Terrace E
Englewood, CO 80112-5306

303-991-1111
800-275-6462
FAX 877-329-6462
E-Mail: infocenter@mgma.com
Home Page: www.mgma.com

William Jessee, President, Chief Executive Officer
Anders Gilberg, senior Vice President
Natalie Jamieson, Administrative Assistant
3800 Attendees
Frequency: Annual, October

13433 Medical Meetings
Penton Media Inc
249 W. 17th St., third floor
New York, NY 10011

847-763-9504
866-505-7173
E-Mail: shatch@meetingsnet.com
Home Page: www.meetingsnet.com

Susan Hatch, Editor
Betsy Bair, Director, Content and Media
Melissa Fromento, Group Publisher
Regina McGee, Religious Conference Manager
Susan Hatch, Executive Editor

International guide for health care and meeting planners.
Cost: $57.00
106 Pages
Circulation: 12000
Founded in 1989
Printed in 4 colors on glossy stock

13434 Medicare and Medicaid Conference
American Association of Health Plans
1129 20th Street NW
Washington, DC 20036

202-778-3200
FAX 202-778-8506

13435 Medtrade West
VNU Expositions
Dallas International Airport
PO Box 17413
Washington, DC 20041

703-318-0300
FAX 703-318-8833

13436 Medtrade/Comtrade
VNU Communications

1130 Hightower Trail
Atlanta, GA 30350

770-569-1540
FAX 703-318-8833

13437 NCPA Rx Exposition
NCPA
100 Daingerfield Road
Alexandria, VA 22314

703-683-8200
800-544-7447
FAX 703-683-3619
E-Mail: info@ncpanet.com
Home Page: www.ncpanet.org

Donnie Calhoun, President
B. Douglas Hoey, Chief Executive Officer
2000 Attendees
Frequency: Annual, October
Mailing list available for rent

13438 National Athletic Trainers Association
National Athletic Trainers
2952 Stemmons Freeway
#200
Dallas, TX 75247

214-637-6282
FAX 214-637-2206
E-Mail: webmaster@nata.org
Home Page: www.nata.org

Charles Kimmel, President
Charles Rozanski, VP
Mailing list available for rent

13439 National Convention: Opticians Association of America
Opticians Association of America
10341 Democracy Lane
Fairfax, VA 22030

703-916-8856
FAX 703-691-8929

13440 National Council on the Aging Annual Conference
National Council on the Aging
1901 L Street Nw
4th Fl
Washington, DC 20036

202-479-1200
FAX 202-479-0735
E-Mail: info@ncoa.org
Home Page: www.ncoa.org
Social Media: *Facebook, Twitter*

James Firman, President/CEO
Richard Browdie, Chair
Andrew Greene, Treasurer
Jay Greenberg, Senior Vice President
Donna Whitt, Senior Vice President
Mailing list available for rent

13441 National Managed Healthcare Congress
Po Box 3685
Boston, MA 02441-3685

888-670-8200
FAX 941-365-2507
Home Page: www.nmhcc.com

Frequency: March Atlanta

13442 National Medical Association Annual Convention & Scientific Assembly
National Medical Association
8403 Colesville Road
Suite 920
Silver Spring, MD 20910

703-631-6200
800-564-4220
FAX 703-654-6931

E-Mail: nma@jspargo.com
Home Page: www.nmanet.org
Social Media: *Facebook, Twitter*

June LaMountain, Exhibit Sales Account Manager
Rahn K. Bailey, President
C. Freeman, Treasurer
Darryl R. Matthews, Executive Director

Promotes the collective interests of physicians and patients of African descent. NMA carries out this mission by serving the collective voice of physicians of African descent and a leading force for purity in medicine, elimination of health disparities and optimal health.
3000 Attendees
Frequency: August
Founded in 1895

13443 National Safety Council Congress Expo
National Safety Council
1121 Spring Lake Drive
Itasca, IL 60143

630-775-2213
800-621-7619
FAX 630-285-0798
E-Mail: customerservice@nsc.org
Home Page: www.congress.nsc.org

Nancy Gavin, Expo Manager
Bill Steinbach, Exhibit Sales
Janet Froetscher, CEO

Annual event for safety, health and the environment.
16000 Attendees
Frequency: September

13444 National Society for Histotechnology Symposium/Convention
National Society for Histotechnology
8850 Stanford Blvd
Suite 2900
Columbia, MD 21045

443-535-4060
FAX 443-535-4055
E-Mail: histo@nsh.org
Home Page: www.nsh.org

Aubrey M J Wanner, Meeting Manager
Carrie Diamond, Executive Director
Kerry Crabb, President
Kristin Ramseur, Administrative Assistant
Beth Wise, Administrative Assistant

National gathering for all chapters, advancing professional growth through educational sessions and the exchange of ideas.
1500 Attendees
Frequency: October
Founded in 1964

13445 Neocon South
Designfest/NeoCon South
200 World Trade Center Chicago
Chicago, IL 60654

312-527-7999
FAX 312-527-7782
Home Page: http://www.neocon.com

Chris Kennedy, President

13446 Neocon West
Designfest/Neocon South
200 World Trade Center
Chicago, IL 60654

312-527-7999
FAX 312-527-7782
Home Page: http://www.neocon.com

Chris Kennedy, President

13447 Neocon's World Trade Fair
Design/Neocon South

200 World Trade Center
Chicago, IL 60654

312-527-7999
FAX 312-527-7782

Chris Kennedy, President

13448 New England Grows

Hynes Convention Center
900 Boylston
Boston, MA 07115

617-954-2000
FAX 617-954-2125
E-Mail: info@mccahome.com
Home Page: www.mccahome.com

1500 Attendees
Frequency: February

13449 Northwest Urological Society

Northwest Urological Society
914 164th Street Se
Suite B-12 #145
Mill Creek, WA 98012

866-800-3118
FAX 800-808-4749
Home Page: www.nwus.org

S Larry Goldenberg, President
Martin Gleave, VP
180 Attendees

13450 Nurse Managers Update

National Professional Education Institute
2525 Ossen Fort Road
PO Box 118
Glencoe, MO 63068-1107

636-735-5570
800-575-5575
FAX 561-743-9596
E-Mail: JJMcDaid@aol.com
Home Page: www.npeinursing.com

Judie McDaid, Exhibitor Relations Manager
Leslie Brock, Registration Manager

The Nurse Managers Update and Critical Care
Conference/EXPO provides a fully integrated
program dedicated to the continuing education
of critical care nurses, nurse managers and
other healthcare professionals. Exhibitors
showcase their latest healthcare products,
pharmaceuticals, services, research and facilities. Knowledge gained in the informative, entertaining EXPO Hall, will influence these
nurses' purchasing decisions throughout the
year.
1500 Attendees
Frequency: Annual, April
Founded in 1989

13451 Obesity and Associated Conditions Symposium

American Society of Bariatric
Physicians/ASBP
5453 E Evans Place
Denver, CO 80222

303-794-4833
FAX 303-779-4834
E-Mail: info@asbp.org
Home Page: www.asbp.org

Cathy Suski, Communications
Stacy Schmidt, Director

Learn about the latest research in obesity treatment and how to use it in your practice.
500 Attendees
Frequency: Annual

13452 Optometry's Meeting

American Optometric Association
243 N Lindbergh Boulevard
Saint Louis, MO 63141

314-993-8575
FAX 314-993-8919

E-Mail: info@iacconline.org
Home Page: www.iaccnorthamerica.org

Tom Bolman, Executive VP
Jerry White, Director of Education

Main exhibits: optometric equipment, supplies
and services.
8000 Attendees
Frequency: June

13453 Osteopathic Physicians & Surgeons Annual Convention

Osteopathic Physicians & Surgeons of
California
455 Capitol Mall
Suite 230
Sacramento, CA 95814

916-561-0724

Kathleen Creason, Executive Director

13454 Pacific Dermatological Association

Pacific Dermatological Association
575 Market Street
Suite 2125
San Francisco, CA 94105

415-927-5729
888-388-8815
FAX 415-764-4915
E-Mail: pda@hp-assoc.com
Home Page: www.pacificderm.org

Edgar F. Fincher, President
Catherine Ramsay, VP
Anita Gilliam, Secretary/Treasurer
Kent Lindeman, Executive Director
Ben Hsu, Executive Committee

Exclusively for education, scientific and charitable purposes. Provides opportunities for exchange of information and advancement of
knowledge of dermatology among physicians
within the membership area.
Frequency: August
Founded in 1948
Mailing list available for rent

13455 Pacific Northwest Radiological Society

Pacific Northwest Radiological Society
2033 6th Avenue
Suite 1100
Seattle, WA 98121

206-441-9762
800-552-0612
FAX 206-441-5863
E-Mail: lmk@wsma.org
Home Page: www.pnwrs.org

Gautham Reddy, President
Eric Stern, VP
Pauline Proulx, Association Executive
Jason Clement, Secretary/Treasurer

13456 Pediatric Academic Societies Annual Meeting

American Pediatric Society & Society for
Pediatric
3400 Research Forest Drive
Suite B7
The Woodlands, TX 77381

281-419-0052
FAX 281-419-0082
E-Mail: info@aps-spr.org
Home Page: www.aps-spr.org

Debbie Anagnostelis, Executive Director
Kathy Cannon, Associate Executive Director
Belinda Thomas, Information Services Director
Kate Culliton, Accounting Manager
Rachael Vogler, Executive Assistant
4500 Attendees
Frequency: May

13457 Pediatric Perfusion

American Society of ExtraCorporeal
Technology
2209 Dickens Road
Richmond, VA 23230-2005

804-565-6310
FAX 804-282-0090
E-Mail: judyr@amsect.org
Home Page: www.amsect.org

Stewart Hinckley, Executive Director
Donna Pandarvis, Manager
Michael Troike, Government Relations
Chairman
Kimberly Robertson, CPA, Controller
Greg Leasure, Membership Services
2000 Members
100 Attendees
Frequency: Bi-Annual
Founded in 1964
Mailing list available for rent

13458 Perfusion Safety & Best Practices in Perfusion

American Society of ExtraCorporeal
Technology
2209 Dickens Road
Richmond, VA 23230-2005

804-532-2323
FAX 804-282-0090
E-Mail: judyr@amsect.org
Home Page: www.amsect.org

Stewart Hinckley, Executive Director
Donna Pandarvis, Manager
Michael Troike, Government Relations
Chairman
Kimberly Robertson, CPA, Controller
Greg Leasure, Membership Services
2000 Members
150 Attendees
Frequency: Annual/October
Founded in 1964
Mailing list available for rent

13459 Policy Conference

American Association of Health Plans
1129 20th Street NW
Washington, DC 20036

202-778-3200
FAX 202-778-8506

13460 Postgraduate Assembly in Anesthesiology

New York State Society of
Anesthesiologists
85 5th Avenue
8th Floor
New York, NY 10003

212-867-7140
FAX 212-867-7153
Home Page: www.nyssa-pga.org

Kurt G Becker, Executive Director
David Wlody, Director

Annual conference for anesthesia professionals,
held each December in New York City.
7000 Attendees
Frequency: December

13461 Primary Care Update

Interstate Postgraduate Medical Association
PO Box 5474
Madison, WI 53705

608-231-9045
866-446-3424
FAX 877-292-4489
E-Mail: cmehelp@ipmameded.org
Home Page: www.ipmameded.org

Designed to enhance your practice and improve
the patient's health.
Frequency: November

13462 Radiological Society of North America's Scientific Assembly
Radiological Society of North America
2021 Spring Road
Suite 600
Oak Brook, IL 60521

630-571-5424
62000 Attendees

13463 SCCM Educational & Scientific Symposium
Society of Critical Care Medicine
8101 E Kaiser Blouevard
Anaheim, CA 92808

714-282-6000
2500 Attendees

13464 SIIM Annual Meeting & Conference
Society for Imaging Informatics in Medicine
19440 Golf Vista Plaza
Suite 330
Leesburg, VA 20176-8264

703-723-0432
FAX 703-723-0415
E-Mail: info@siimweb.org
Home Page: www.siimweb.org
Social Media: *Facebook, Twitter, LinkedIn*

Andrea Saris, Meetings Director

Provides a vibrant community and collegial forum for learning and networking with peers and thought leaders in the imaging informatics field. This is where physicians, health care IT decision-makers, PACS administrators, and vendors from around the world come together to explore the emerging field of informatics.
2000 Members
1800 Attendees
Frequency: June
Founded in 1980

13465 Society for Disability Studies Annual Meeting
Exhibit Promotions Plus
11630 Vixens Path
Ellicott City, MD 21042

301-596-3028
FAX 410-997-0764
Home Page: www.epponline.com

Harve C Horowitz, President
Frequency: June

13466 Society for Neuroscience
Herlitz Company
1890 Palmer Avenue
Suite 202 A
Larchmont, NY 10538

914-833-1979
FAX 914-833-0920

Bruce Herlitz, President

13467 Society of Nuclear Medicine Annual Meeting
Society of Nuclear Medicine
1850 Samuel Morse Drive
Reston, VA 20190

703-708-9000
FAX 703-708-9015
E-Mail: volunteer@snm.org
Home Page: www.snm.org

Rebecca Maxey, Director
Vincent Pistilli, Chief Financial Officer
Matt Dickens, Director, Information Services
Judy Brazel, Director, Meeting Services
Joanna Spahr, Director, Marketing
7000 Attendees

13468 Society of Thoracic Surgeons Annual Meeting
Society of Thoracic Surgeons

633 N Saint Clair Street
Suite 2320
Chicago, IL 60611

312-202-5800
FAX 312-202-5801
E-Mail: sts@sts.org
Home Page: www.sts.org
Social Media: *Facebook, Twitter*

Robert A Wynbrandt, Executive Director
Cheryl D. Wilson, Administrative Manager & Executive
Natalie Boden, Director of Marketing
Phillip A. Bongiorno, Director of Government Relations
Courtney Donovan, Director of Meetings
4200 Attendees
Mailing list available for rent

13469 Society of Toxicology Annual Meeting
Society of Toxicology
1821 Michael Faraday Drive
Suite 300
Reston, VA 20190

703-438-3115
FAX 703-438-3113
E-Mail: sothq@toxicology.org
Home Page: www.toxicology.org

Shawn Lamb, Executive Director
Clarissa Russell Wilson, Contact

Professional and scholarly organization meeting of scientists from academic institutions, government and industry representing the great variety of scientists who practice toxicology in the US and abroad.
5000 Attendees
Frequency: March

13470 Southeastern Surgical Congress Annual Assembly
South Med. Associates
PO Box 330
Pelham, AL 35124

205-991-3552
FAX 205-991-6771

13471 Southern Association for Primary Care
Southern Medical Association
35 Lake Shore Drive
Birmingham, AL 35209

205-945-1840
800-423-4992
FAX 205-945-1830
E-Mail: ewaldron@sma.org
Home Page: www.sma.org
Social Media: *Facebook, Twitter, LinkedIn*

Michael C. Gosney, President
Ed Waldron, Administration
G. Richard Holt, Editor-in-Chief

13472 Southern Medical Association Meeting
Southern Medical Association
PO Box 190088
Birmingham, AL 35219

205-451-1840
800-423-4992
FAX 205-945-1830

Ed Waldron, CEO
2500 Attendees

13473 Symposium of the Protein Society
FASEB
9650 Rockville Pike
Bethesda, MD 20814

301-634-7100
FAX 301-530-7001

E-Mail: info@faseb.org
Home Page: www.faseb.org

David Craven, Executive Director
Jacquelyn Roberts, Marketing Manager
Richard Dunn, Director

13474 Symposium on New Advances in Blood Management
American Society of ExtraCorporeal Technology
2209 Dickens Road
Richmond, VA 23230-2005

804-532-2323
FAX 804-282-0090
E-Mail: judyr@amsect.org
Home Page: www.amsect.org

Stewart Hinckley, Executive Director
Donna Pandarvis, Manager
Michael Troike, Government Relations Chairman
Kimberly Robertson, CPA, Controller
Greg Leasure, Membership Services
2000 Members
150 Attendees
Frequency: Annual/August
Founded in 1964
Mailing list available for rent

13475 Synergist
American Industrial Hygiene Association
2700 Prosperity Ave
Suite 250
Fairfax, VA 22031-4321

703-849-8267
FAX 703-207-3561
E-Mail: infonet@aiha.org
Home Page: www.aiha.org

Peter J Oneil, Executive Director
Michael T Brandt, President
Frequency: Monthly

13476 TLPA Annual Convention & Trade Show
Taxicab, Limousine & Paratransit Association
3200 Tower Oaks Boulevard
Suite 220
Rockville, MD 20852

301-984-5700
FAX 301-984-5703
E-Mail: info@tlpa.com
Home Page: www.tlpa.org

Alfred LaGasse, CEO
William Rouse, President
Harold Morgan, Executive Vice President
Michelle A. Hariston, CMP, Manager of Meetings
Leah New, Manager of Communications

Shares information vital to owners or taxicab, limousine, airport shuttle, paratransit and nonemergency medical transportation fleets. 100 suppliers and exhibitors of the newest products available to the industry.
1000 Attendees
Frequency: Annual
Founded in 1917
Mailing list available for rent

13477 Today's Surgicenter Conference
Virgo Publishing LLC
3300 N Central Avenue
Suite 300
Phoenix, AZ 85012

480-675-8177
FAX 602-567-6841
E-Mail: mikes@vpico.com
Home Page: www.xchangemag.com
Social Media: *Facebook, Twitter, LinkedIn*

Mike Saxby, Group Publisher
Craig Galbraith, Senior Online Managing Editor

Buffy Naylor, Managing Editor
Khali Henderson, Contributing Editor
Melissa Budwig, Online Advertising

Offers owners and operators of ambulatory surgery centers high-caliber instructive seminars by leading industry veterans, exhibits, and networking opportunities. Decision makers attend to learn more about construction and design, technology, equipment, legal and regulatory issues, marketing and finance and development. Approximately 50 booths.
200+ Attendees
Frequency: September
Founded in 2004
Mailing list available for rent: 15000+ names

13478 United States and Canadian Academy of Pathology

Herlitz Company
1890 Palmer Avenue
Suite 202A
Larchmont, NY 10538

914-833-1979
FAX 914-833-0929
E-Mail: kris@herlitz.com
Home Page: www.herlitz.com

Kris Herlitz, Show Manager
3000 Attendees
Frequency: March

13479 Vision New England

Hynes Convention Center
900 Boylston Street
Boston, MA 07115

617-954-2000
FAX 617-954-2125
E-Mail: info@mccahome.com
Home Page: www.mccahome.com

24000 Attendees
Frequency: January

13480 World Congress on Pediatric & Intensive Care

Hynes Convention Center
900 Boylston Street
Boston, MA 02115

617-954-2000
800-845-8800
FAX 617-954-2125
E-Mail: info@mccahome.com
Home Page: www.mccahome.com

2500 Attendees
Frequency: June

13481 Yankee Dental Congress

Hynes Convention Center
900 Boylston Street
Boston, MA 07115

617-954-2000
FAX 617-954-2125
E-Mail: info@mccahome.com
Home Page: www.mccahome.com

2400 Attendees
Frequency: January

Directories & Databases

13482 ARMA International's Buyers Guide

ARMA International
11880 College Blvd
Suite 450
Overland Park, KS 66210

913-341-3808
800-422-2762
FAX 913-341-3742

E-Mail: hq@arma.org
Home Page: www.arma.org/conference

Marilyn Bier, Executive Director
Jody Becker, Associate Editor
Kerrianne Aulet, Education Program Administrator
Michael Avery, Chief Operating Officer
Paula Banes, Sales Project Manager

75-100 companies listed. Free.
10,00 Members
Founded in 1955
Mailing list available for rent

13483 American Academy of Forensic Sciences Membership Directory

410 N 21st St
Colorado Spring, CO 80904-2712

719-636-1100
FAX 719-636-1993
E-Mail: awarren@aafs.org
Home Page: www.aafs.org

Anne Warren, Executive Director
Nancy Jackson, Director Development
Offers valuable information on over 5,000 persons qualified in forensic sciences including law, anthropology and psychiatry.
Cost: $50.00
250 Pages
Frequency: Annual

13484 Antimicrobial Therapy in Otolaryngology Head and Neck Surgery

American Academy of Otolaryngology
1650 Diagonal Road
Alexandria, VA 22314-3357

703-836-4444
FAX 703-683-5100
E-Mail: membership@entnet.org
Home Page: www.entnet.org

Richard Carson, Senior Manager, Board of Govenors
Paul T. Fass, Director - Private Practice
J. Gavin Setzen, Secretary/Treasurer
David R. Nielsen, Executive Vice President and CEO
James L. Netterville, President
Frequency: Yearly
Mailing list available for rent

13485 Catalog of Professional Testing Resources

Psychological Assessment Resources
PO Box 998
Odessa, FL 33556

800-331-8378
FAX 800-727-9329
Home Page: www.parinc.com

13486 Comparative Guide to American Hospitals

Grey House Publishing
4919 Route 22
PO Box 56
Amenia, NY 12501

518-789-8700
800-562-2139
FAX 845-373-6390
E-Mail: books@greyhouse.com
Home Page: www.greyhouse.com
Social Media: *Facebook, Twitter*

Leslie Mackenzie, Publisher
Richard Gottlieb, Editor

This new edition compares all of the nation's hospitals by 24 measures of quality in the treatment of heart attack, heart failure, pneumonia, and, new to this edition, surgical procedures and pregnancy care. Plus, this edition is now available in regional volumes, to make locating

information about hospitals in your area quicker and easier than ever before.
Cost: $350.00
2000 Pages
ISBN: 1-532371-82-5
Founded in 1981

13487 Complete Directory for Pediatric Disorders

Grey House Publishing
4919 Route 22
PO Box 56
Amenia, NY 12501

518-789-8700
800-562-2139
FAX 845-373-6390
E-Mail: books@greyhouse.com
Home Page: www.greyhouse.com
Social Media: *Facebook, Twitter*

Leslie Mackenzie, Publisher
Richard Gottlieb, Editor

Provides parents and caregivers with information about pediatric conditions, disorders, diseases and disabilities. Contains understandable descriptions of major bodily systems, descriptions of more than 200 disorders and a resource section.
Cost: $165.00
1200 Pages
ISBN: 1-592371-50-7
Founded in 1981

13488 Complete Directory for People with Disabilities

Grey House Publishing
4919 Route 22
PO Box 56
Amenia, NY 12501

518-789-8700
800-562-2139
FAX 845-373-6390
E-Mail: books@greyhouse.com
Home Page: www.greyhouse.com
Social Media: *Facebook, Twitter*

Leslie Mackenzie, Publisher
Richard Gottlieb, Editor

Comprehensive resource for people with disabilities, detailing independent living centers, rehabilitation facilities, state and federal agencies, associations and support groups. This one-stop resource also provides immediate access to the latest products and services for people with disabilities, such as periodicals and books, assistive devices, employment and education programs and travel groups.
Cost: $165.00
1200 Pages
ISBN: 1-592373-67-4
Founded in 1981

13489 Complete Directory for People with Chronic Illness

Grey House Publishing
4919 Route 22
PO Box 56
Amenia, NY 12501

518-789-8700
800-562-2139
FAX 845-373-6390
E-Mail: books@greyhouse.com
Home Page: www.greyhouse.com
Social Media: *Facebook, Twitter*

Leslie Mackenzie, Publisher
Richard Gottlieb, Editor

This directory provides a comprehensive overview of the support services and information resources available for people diagnosed with a chronic illness. It details the wide range of organizations, educational materials, books, newsletters, web sites, periodicals and data-

bases that address 88 specific chronic illness.
Cost: $165.00
1200 Pages
ISBN: 1-952371-83-3
Founded in 1981

13490 Complete Learning Disabilities Directory
Grey House Publishing
4919 Route 22
PO Box 56
Amenia, NY 12501

518-789-8700
800-562-2139
FAX 845-373-6390
E-Mail: books@greyhouse.com
Home Page: www.greyhouse.com
Social Media: *Facebook, Twitter*

Leslie Mackenzie, Publisher
Richard Gottlieb, Editor

The most comprehensive database of programs, services, curriculum materials, professional meetings and resources, camps, newsletters and support groups for teachers, students and families concerned with learning disabilities. Includes information about associations and organizations, schools, colleges and testing materials, government agencies, legal resources and more.
Cost: $145.00
800 Pages
ISBN: 1-592373-68-2
Founded in 1981

13491 Complete Learning Disabilities Directory - Online Database
Grey House Publishing
4919 Route 22
PO Box 56
Amenia, NY 12501-0056

518-789-8700
800-562-2139
FAX 518-789-0556
E-Mail: gold@greyhouse.com
Home Page: www.gold.greyhouse.com
Social Media: *Facebook, Twitter*

Leslie Mackenzie, Publisher
Richard Gottlieb, President

The most comprehensive database of important learning disability resources, details associations and organizations, national and state programs, schools, colleges and learning centers, publishers, publications and periodicals, classroom resources, testing materials, exchange programs, and more. Locating learning disability resources has never been easier - it's only a click away.
Founded in 1981

13492 Complete Mental Health Directory
Grey House Publishing
4919 Route 22
PO Box 56
Amenia, NY 12501

518-789-8700
800-562-2139
FAX 845-373-6390
E-Mail: books@greyhouse.com
Home Page: www.greyhouse.com
Social Media: *Facebook, Twitter*

Leslie Mackenzie, Publisher
Richard Gottlieb, Editor

Comprehensive information covering the field of behavioral health, with critical information for both the layman and mental health professional. Provides the layman with understandable descriptions of 25 mental health disorders, as well as detailed information on associations, media, support groups and mental health facilities. Offers the professional critical and comprehensive information on managed care organizations, information systems, govern-

ment agencies and provider organizations.
Cost: $165.00
800 Pages
ISBN: 1-592372-85-6
Founded in 1981

13493 Complete Mental Health Directory - Online Database
Grey House Publishing
4919 Route 22
PO Box 56
Amenia, NY 12501-0056

518-789-8700
800-562-2139
FAX 518-789-0556
E-Mail: gold@greyhouse.com
Home Page: www.gold.greyhouse.com
Social Media: *Facebook, Twitter*

Leslie Mackenzie, Publisher
Richard Gottlieb, President

This award-winning directory, now available in a quick-to-search, easy-to-use, online database provides the most comprehensive compilation of mental health resources available anywhere, with data for both layman and mental health professionals.
Founded in 1981

13494 Detwiler's Directory of Health and Medical Resources
Information Today
143 Old Marlton Pike
Medford, NJ 08055-8750

609-654-6266
800-300-9868
FAX 609-654-4309
E-Mail: custserv@infotoday.com
Home Page: www.infotoday.com

Thomas H Hogan, President
Roger R Bilboul, Chairman Of The Board
Joe Menendez, Marketing Manager
John Brokenshire, Chief Financial Officer
Michael V. Zarrello, Advertising Director

A comprehensive guide to over 2,000 health and medical corporations,associations, state and federal agencies, helathcare market research firms, foundations, institutes, and more.
Cost: $195.00
ISBN: 1-573871-55-9

13495 Directory for Pediatric Disorders - Online Database
Grey House Publishing
4919 Route 22
PO Box 56
Amenia, NY 12501-0056

518-789-8700
800-562-2139
FAX 518-789-0556
E-Mail: gold@greyhouse.com
Home Page: www.gold.greyhouse.com
Social Media: *Facebook, Twitter*

Leslie Mackenzie, Publisher
Richard Gottlieb, President

The Complete Directory for Pediatric Disorders - Online Database is an important reference tool that provides parents and caregivers with information about common pediatric and adolescent conditions, disorders, diseases, and disabilities. This comprehensive, informative database is designed to meet the growing consumer demands for current, understandable medical information on pediatric disorders.
Founded in 1981

13496 Directory for People with Chronic Illness - Online Database
Grey House Publishing

4919 Route 22
PO Box 56
Amenia, NY 12501-0056

518-789-8700
800-562-2139
FAX 518-789-0556
E-Mail: gold@greyhouse.com
Home Page: www.gold.greyhouse.com
Social Media: *Facebook, Twitter*

Leslie Mackenzie, Publisher
Richard Gottlieb, President

This important database is structured around the 80 most prevalent chronic illnesses and provides a comprehensive overview of the support services and information resources available for people diagnosed with a chronic illness. With a subscription to the Complete Directory for People with Chronic Illness - Online Database, your organization will have immediate access to a wealth of resources available for people diagnosed with a chronic illness, their families and support systems.
Founded in 1981

13497 Directory for People with Disabilities - Online Database
Grey House Publishing
4919 Route 22
PO Box 56
Amenia, NY 12501-0056

518-789-8700
800-562-2139
FAX 518-789-0556
E-Mail: gold@greyhouse.com
Home Page: www.gold.greyhouse.com
Social Media: *Facebook, Twitter*

Leslie Mackenzie, Publisher
Richard Gottlieb, President

Comprehensive resource for people with disabilities, detailing independent living centers, rehabilitation facilities, state and federal agencies, associations and support groups. This one-stop resource also provides immediate access to the latest products and services for people with disabilities, such as periodicals and books, assistive devices, and more. With a subscription to the online databse, your organization will have immediate access to a wealth of resources available.
Founded in 1981

13498 Directory of Health Care Group Purchasing Organizations
Grey House Publishing
4919 Route 22
PO Box 56
Amenia, NY 12501

518-789-8700
800-562-2139
FAX 845-373-6390
E-Mail: books@greyhouse.com
Home Page: www.greyhouse.com
Social Media: *Facebook, Twitter*

Leslie Mackenzie, Publisher
Richard Gottlieb, Editor

This comprehensive directory profiles over 800 Purchasing Organizations that negotiate more than 65% of all health care products purchased by hospitals and related facilities, and the institutions they represent.
Cost: $465.00
800 Pages
ISBN: 1-592372-87-2
Founded in 1981

13499 Directory of Health Care Group Purchasing Organizations - Online Database
Grey House Publishing

4919 Route 22
PO Box 56
Amenia, NY 12501-0056

518-789-8700
800-562-2139
FAX 518-789-0556
E-Mail: gold@greyhouse.com
Home Page: www.gold.greyhouse.com
Social Media: *Facebook, Twitter*

Leslie Mackenzie, Publisher
Richard Gottlieb, President

This interactive online database offers immediate access to detailed information about over 800 GPOs, over 3,000 key contacts and 16,000 member hospitals and institutions they represent. These 800+ organizations represent billions of dollars in purchasing power for the medical and device supplies industry. This data is so critical for market research, sales plans and market development.
Founded in 1981

13500 Directory of Hospital Personnel

Grey House Publishing
4919 Route 22
PO Box 56
Amenia, NY 12501

518-789-8700
800-562-2139
FAX 845-373-6390
E-Mail: books@greyhouse.com
Home Page: www.greyhouse.com
Social Media: *Facebook, Twitter*

Leslie Mackenzie, Publisher
Richard Gottlieb, Editor

A Who's Who of the hospital universe, The Directory of Hospital Personnel puts you in touch with over 100,000 key decision makers. This comprehensive directory contains listings of over 6,000 hospitals within the US, arranged alphabetically by city within state.
Cost: $325.00
2300 Pages
ISBN: 1-592372-86-4
Founded in 1981

13501 Directory of Hospital Personnel - Online Database

Grey House Publishing
4919 Route 22
PO Box 56
Amenia, NY 12501-0056

518-789-8700
800-562-2139
FAX 518-789-0556
E-Mail: gold@greyhouse.com
Home Page: www.gold.greyhouse.com
Social Media: *Facebook, Twitter*

Richard Gottlieb, President
Leslie Mackenzie, Publisher

The DHP Online Database is the best resource you can have at your fingertips when researching or marketing a product or service to the hospital market. A 'Who's Who' of the hospital universe, this database puts you in touch with over 140,000 key decision-makers at 5,800 hospitals nationwide.
Founded in 1981

13502 Employee Assistance Program Management Yearbook

Health Resources Publishing
1913 Atlantic Ave
Suite 200
Manasquan, NJ 08736-1067

732-292-1100
888-843-6242
FAX 732-292-1111

E-Mail: info@themcic.com
Home Page: www.healthresourcesonline.com

Robert K Jenkins, Publisher
Lisa Mansfield, Regional Director
Brett Powell, Regional Director
Alice Burron, Director

Explore major areas of involvement for EAPS. Investigate tools for effectively managing your EAP. Learn how screening tools for mental illness can help EAPS manage care. Learn how to help families deal with workplace changes. Learn how to identify potentially violent situations in the workplace and much more.
Cost: $149.00
ISBN: 1-882364-25-2

13503 HCEA Directory of Healthcare Meetings and Conventions

Healthcare Convention & Exhibitors Association
1100 Johnson Ferry Rd NE
Suite 300
Atlanta, GA 30342-1556

404-252-3663
FAX 404-252-0774
E-Mail: hcea@kellencompany.com
Home Page: www.hcea.org

Susan Huff, President
Carol Wilson, Meetings Director
Michelle Hall, Staff Associate
Jackie Beaulieu, Associate Director
Frank Skinner, Executive Director

Information on 6,000 health care meetings, available to members only.
500 Pages
Founded in 1930
Mailing list available for rent: 1400 names

13504 HMO/PPO Directory

Grey House Publishing
4919 Route 22
PO Box 56
Amenia, NY 12501

518-789-8700
800-562-2139
FAX 845-373-6390
E-Mail: books@greyhouse.com
Home Page: www.greyhouse.com
Social Media: *Facebook, Twitter*

Leslie Mackenzie, Publisher
Richard Gottlieb, Editor

The HMO/PPO Directory is a comprehensive source that provides detailed information about Health Maintenance Organizations and Preferred Provider Organizations nationwide. Within the HMO/PPO Profiles, over 1,300 HMOs, PPOs and affiliated companies are listed, arranged alphabetically by state.
Cost: $325.00
600 Pages
ISBN: 1-592373-69-0
Founded in 1981

13505 HMO/PPO Directory - Online Database

Grey House Publishing
4919 Route 22
PO Box 56
Amenia, NY 12501-0056

518-789-8700
800-562-2139
FAX 518-789-0556
E-Mail: gold@greyhouse.com
Home Page: www.gold.greyhouse.com
Social Media: *Facebook, Twitter*

Leslie Mackenzie, Publisher
Richard Gottlieb, President

The HMO/PPO Directory - Online Database is your in-depth searchable guide to health plans nationwide - their contact information, key executives, plan information and more. The on-

line database is a necessary tool when researching or marketing a product or service to this important industry.
Founded in 1981

13506 Health Funds Grants Resources Yearbook

Health Resources Publishing
1913 Atlantic Ave
Suite 200
Manasquan, NJ 08736-1067

732-292-1100
888-843-6242
FAX 732-292-1111
E-Mail: info@themcic.com
Home Page: www.healthresourcesonline.com

Robert K Jenkins, Publisher
Judy Granholm, Regional Director
Brett Powell, Regional Director
Alice Burron, Director

A resource book that gives dollar amounts, descriptions of previous grant recipients and programs that attract funding and details of future funding trends.
Cost: $165.00
ISBN: 1-882364-30-9

13507 Managed Care Yearbook

Health Resources Publishing
1913 Atlantic Ave
Suite 200
Manasquan, NJ 08736-1067

732-292-1100
888-843-6242
FAX 732-292-1111
E-Mail: info@themcic.com
Home Page: www.healthresourcesonline.com

Robert K Jenkins, Publisher
Judy Granholm, Regional Director
Brett Powell, Regional Director
Alice Burron, Director

Resource book that includes critical facts, statistics cost, analysis, comparisions, enrollment and trends studies on managed care. Topics also include member retention, international markets and disease management.
Cost: $29.00
608 Pages
ISBN: 1-882364-26-0

13508 Medical Abbreviations: 24,000

Niel M Davis Associates
2049 Stout Dr
B-3
Warminster, PA 18974-3861

215-442-7430
FAX 888-333-4915
E-Mail: med@neilmdavis.com
Home Page: www.neilmdavis.com

Neil M Davis, Owner

This current edition paperback pocket book contains 16,000 medical related abbreviations and 24,000 of their possible meanings. It is current, comprehensive, and formatted so that it is easy to use. It also contains a cross-referenced listing of 3,300 generic and trade drug names.
Cost: $24.95
Frequency: Monthly
ISBN: 0-931431-09-3
Founded in 1981

13509 Medical Device Register

Grey House Publishing
4919 Route 22
PO Box 56
Amenia, NY 12501

518-789-8700
800-562-2139
FAX 845-373-6390
E-Mail: books@greyhouse.com

Home Page: www.greyhouse.com
Social Media: *Facebook, Twitter*

Leslie Mackenzie, Publisher
Richard Gottlieb, Editor

The only one-stop resource of every medical supplier licensed to sell products in the US. This edition offers fast access to over 13,000 companies - and more than 65,000 products. This comprehensive resource saves you hours of time and trouble when searching for the equipment and supplies you want and the manufacturers who provide them.
Cost: $350.00
3000 Pages
ISBN: 1-592373-73-9
Founded in 1981

13510 National Directory of Integrated Healthcare Delivery Systems

Health Resources Publishing
1913 Atlantic Ave
Suite 200
Manasquan, NJ 08736-1067

732-292-1100
888-843-6242
FAX 732-292-1111
E-Mail: info@themcic.com
Home Page: www.healthresourcesonline.com

Robert K Jenkins, Publisher
Lisa Mansfield, Regional Director
Brett Powell, Regional Director
Alice Burron, Director

Gives facts and stastics on more than 850 health care delivery systems and affiliations. Includes profiles of IHDSs by state and by alphabetical order. Also includes a directory of health care associations, a ranking of systems by revenues and an analysis of IHDSs growth projections.
Cost: $995.00
ISBN: 1-882364-31-7

13511 National Directory of Managed Care Organzatons

Health Resources Publishing
1913 Atlantic Ave
Suite 200
Manasquan, NJ 08736-1067

732-292-1100
888-843-6242
FAX 732-292-1111
E-Mail: info@themcic.com
Home Page: www.healthresourcesonline.com

Robert K Jenkins, Publisher
Lisa Mansfield, Regional Director
Brett Powell, Regional Director
Alice Burron, Director

Published by Health Resources Publishing. Available in print ($325), database ($1695) or CD-Rom ($695).
Cost: $325.00
ISSN: 0898-9753

13512 National Directory of Physician Organizations Database On Cd-Rom

Health Resources Publishing
1913 Atlantic Ave
Suite 200
Manasquan, NJ 08736-1067

732-292-1100
888-843-6242
FAX 732-292-1111
E-Mail: info@themcic.com
Home Page: www.healthresourcesonline.com

Robert K Jenkins, Publisher
Judy Granholm, Regional Director
Brett Powell, Regional Director
Alice Burron, Director

Detailed profiles on over 1,800 physician organizations. Listings include physician hospitals organizations (PHOs), independent practice as-

sociations, management services organizations and physician practice management companies. Key elements of the data profile include: executive officers; year founded; profits status, statue of incorporation; numbers of associates physician; market area; market analysis; affiliated/participating hospital; management service organizations used.
Cost: $995.00
ISBN: 1-882364-18-X

13513 Older Americans Information Directory

Grey House Publishing
4919 Route 22
PO Box 56
Amenia, NY 12501

518-789-8700
800-562-2139
FAX 845-373-6390
E-Mail: books@greyhouse.com
Home Page: www.greyhouse.com
Social Media: *Facebook, Twitter*

Leslie Mackenzie, Publisher
Richard Gottlieb, Editor

Important resources for older americans, including national, regional, state and local organizations, government agencies, research centers, legal resources, discount travel information, continuing education programs, disability aids and assistive devices, health, print media and electronic media.
Cost: $165.00
1200 Pages
ISBN: 1-592373-57-7
Founded in 1981

13514 Older Americans Information Directory - Online Database

Grey House Publishing
4919 Route 22
PO Box 56
Amenia, NY 12501-0056

518-789-8700
800-562-2139
FAX 518-789-0556
E-Mail: gold@greyhouse.com
Home Page: www.gold.greyhouse.com
Social Media: *Facebook, Twitter*

Leslie Mackenzie, Publisher
Richard Gottlieb, President

The Older Americans Information Directory is an easy to use source that offers up-to-date information on the prevalent social, health and financial issues facing older Americans in the 21st century, as well as recreational and educational opportunities to enrich their lives. With a subscription to the online database, you'll have immediate access to over 8,000 resources including national, regional, state and local organziations, government agencies, health facilities and more.
Founded in 1981

13515 Wellness Program Management Yearbook

Health Resources Publishing
1913 Atlantic Ave
Suite 200
Manasquan, NJ 08736-1067

732-292-1100
888-843-6242
FAX 732-292-1111
E-Mail: info@themcic.com
Home Page: www.healthresourcesonline.com

Robert K Jenkins, Publisher
Lisa Mansfield, Regional Director
Brett Powell, Regional Director
Alice Burron, Director

This yearbook highlights such issues as obtaining senior management support, encouraging

employment participation in programs, finding, funding and developing different programs. Also helps in planning initiatives by providing details of the components that will be important to include about the programs that will help you to meet your goals.
Cost: $155.00
ISBN: 1-882364-39-2

Industry Web Sites

13516 http://gold.greyhouse.com

G.O.L.D Grey House OnLine Databases

Grey House Publishing's online database platform, GOLD, offers Quick Search, Keyword Search and Expert Search for most business sectors including healthcare markets. The GOLD platform makes finding the information you need quick and easy - whether you're a novice searcher or an experienced database user. All of Grey House's directory products are available for subscription on the GOLD platform.

13517 www.aaaai.org

American Academy of Allergy, Asthma And Immunology

The largest professional medical specialty organization in the United States, representing allergists, asthma specialists, clinical immunologists, allied health professionals, and others with the special interest in the research and treatment of allergic disease.

13518 www.aaham.org

American Association of Healthcare Administrative Management

Business offices, credit and collection managers, and admitting officers for hospitals, clincis and other health care organizaitons. To educate members, exchange information and techniques, and keep members abreast of new regulations relating to their field. Seeks proper recognition for the financial aspect of hospital and clinic managememnt.

13519 www.aahperd.org

American Alliance for Hlth, Phys. Edu. Rec. Dance
Recreation & Dance

13520 www.aaid.org

American Academy of Implant Dentistry

Offers a rigorous implant dentistry credentialing program which requires at least 300 hours of post-docroal or continuing education instruction in implant dentistry, passing a comprehensive exam, and presenting successful cases of different types of implants to a group of examiners. It is one of the most comprehensive credentialing programs in dentistry.

13521 www.aaihds.org

American Association of Integrated Healthcare Delivery Systems

Physicians, hospital executives and board members, health plan executives, and other key entities and professionals employed by all forms of IDDSs including PHOS, IPA POSOS, and MSOS. Seeks to provide advocacy for issues related to integrated health care through research, education, and communication. Conducts educational and research programs; maintains speakers' bureau and information clearinghouse.

13522 www.aameda.org
American Academy of Medical Administrators

Individuals involved in medical administration at the executive- or midele-management levels. Promotes educational courses for the training of persons in medical administration. Conducts research. Offers placement service.

13523 www.aamft.org
American Assoc for Marriage and Family Therapy

AAMFT represents the professional interests of more than 25,000 marriage and family therapists in the United States, Canada and abroad.

13524 www.aami.org
Assoc for the Advancement of Medical Instrumentati

The Association for the Advancement of Medical Instrumentation (AAMI), founded in 1967, is a unique alliance of over 6,000 members united by the coommon goal of increasing the understanding and use of medical instrumentation. AAMI is the primary source of consensus and timely information on medical instrumentation and technology for the industry, professionals, and the government for national and intemational standrards.

13525 www.aaos.org
American Academy for Cerebral Palsy and Developmental Medicine

13526 www.aap.org
American Academy of Pediatrics

13527 www.academydentalmaterials.org
Academy of Dental Materials

Formerly known as American Academy for Plastics Research in Dentistry.

13528 www.ache.org
American College of Healthcare Executives

International professional society of more than 30,000 healthcare executives. Credentialing and educational programs, Congress on Healthcare Management. ACHE's publishing division, Health Administration Press, is one of the largest publishers of books.

13529 www.acpe.org
American College of Physician Executives

Physicians whose primary professional responsibility is the management of health care organizations. Provides for continuing education and certification of the physician executive and the profession. Offers specialized career planning, counseling, recruitment and placement services, and research and information data on physican managers.

13530 www.acrm.org
American Congress of Rehabilitation Medicine

13531 www.acsm.org
American College of Sports Medicine

The ACSM promotes and integrates scientific research, education, and practical applications of sports medicine and exercise science to maintain and enhance physical performance, fitness, health, and quality of life.

13532 www.afprd.org
Association of Family Practice Residency Directors

Provides representation for residency directors at a national level and provides a political voice

for them to approprite arenas. Promotes cooperation and communication between residency programs and different branches of the family practice specialty. Dedicated to improving of education of family physicians. Provides a network for mutual assistance among FP, residency directors.

13533 www.aha.org
American Hospital Association

13534 www.ahia.org
Association of Healthcare Internal Auditors

Promotes cost containment and increased productivity in health care institutions through internal auditing. Serves as a forum for the exchange of experience, ideas, and information among members; provides continuing professional education courses and informs members of developments in health care internal auditing. Offers employment clearinghouse services.

13535 www.ahqa.org
American Health Quality Association

Central news area for the group that represents quality inprovement organizations and professionals working to improve the quality of health care in communities across America.

13536 www.ahraonline.org
Association for Medical Imaging Management

For radiology administrators from the US, Canada, and several other countries.

13537 www.ama-assn.org
American Medical Association

A partnership of physicians and their professional associations dedicated to promoting the art and science of medicine and the betterment of the public health. To serve physicians and their patients by establishing and promoting ethical, educational, and clinical standards for the medical profession and by advocating for the highest principle of all - the integrity of the physician/patient relationship.

13538 www.amga.org
American Medical Group Association

13539 www.apta.org
American Physical Therapy Association

The principal membership organization representing and promoting the profession of physical therapy, is to furhter the profession's role in the prevention, diagnosis, and treatment of movement dysfunctions and the enhancement of the physical health and functional abilities of members of the public.

13540 www.arrs.org
American Roentgen Ray Society

102 years strong radiological association for all subspecialties.

13541 www.ascrs.org
American Society of Ophthalmic Administrators

A division of the American Society of Cataract and Retractive Surgery. Persons involved with the administration of an ophthalmic office or clinic. Facilitates the exchange of idease and information in order to improve management practices and working conditions. Offers placement services.

13542 www.asma.org
Aerospace Medical Association

Our mission is to apply and advance scientific knowledge to promote and enhance the health, safety and performance of those involved in aerospace and related activities.

13543 www.asnr.org
American Society of Neuroradiology

13544 www.asrm.org
American Society for Reproductive Medicine

Organization devoted to advancing knowledge and expertise in reproductive medicine and biology. Members of this voluntary nonprofit organization must demonstrate the high ethical principals of the medical profession, evince an interest in reproductive medicine and biotechnology, and adhere to the objectives of the Society.

13545 www.assh.org
American Society for Surgery of the Hand

The oldest medical specialty society in the United States devoted entirely to continuing medical education related to hand surgery.

13546 www.awhp.org
Association for Worksite Health Promotion

Exists to advance the profession of worksite health promotion and the career development of its practitioners and to improve the performance of the programs they administer. Represents a variety of disciplines and worksites, for decision-makers in the areas of health promotion/disease prevention and health-care cost management.

13547 www.cdc.gov
Centers for Disease Control and Prevention

The official website of CDC, the government's public health agency.

13548 www.chpa-info.org
Consumer Healthcare Products Association

Members are producers of nonprescription medicines and dietary supplements for self-care. Has an annual budget of approximately $10 million.

13549 www.claims.org
Alliance of Claims Assistance Professionals

Professionals dedicated to the effective management of health insurance claims. Our members are claims assistance professionals who work for patients.

13550 www.cleftline.org
American Cleft Palate Craniofacial Association

Organization of plastic surgeons, dentists, orthodontists, speech pathologists, geneticists, social workers and others.

13551 www.cmsa.org
Case Management Society of America

Exclusively for the case management profession.

13552 www.crnusa.com
Council for Responsible Nutrition

Government relations, scientific and regulatory affairs, publications.

13553 www.docinfo.org

A national data bank of disciplinary histories on US licensed physicians from the Federation of State Medical Boards; charges $9.95 per report

13554 www.entnet.org
American Academy of Otolarygngology-Head & Neck

13555 www.fascrw.org
American Society of Colon & Rectal Surgeons

13556 www.foodallergy.org
Food Allergy & Anaphylaxis Network
Facts, common questions, resources and news.

13557 www.gretmar.com/webdoctor/
General medical information.

13558 www.greyhouse.com
Grey House Publishing
Authoritative reference directories for most
business sectors including healthcare markets.
Users can search the online databases with varied
search criteria allowing for custom searches
by product category, geographic area, sales volume,
keyword, subject and more. Full Grey
House catalog and online ordering also
available.

13559 www.hcea.org
Healthcare Convention & Exhibitors
Association
Trade association of over 650 organizations involved
in health care exhibiting or providing
services to health care conventions, exhibitions
and/or meetings.

13560 www.healthfinder.gov
A comprehensive guide to resources for health
information from the federal government and
related agencies

13561 www.hfma.org
Healthcare Financial Management
Association
Brings perspective and clarity to the industry's
complex issues for the purpose of preparing
our members to succeed. Through our programs,
publications and partnerships, we enhance
the capabilities that strengthen not only
individuals careers, but also the organizations
from which our members come.

13562 www.hida.org
Health Industry Distributors Association
The trade association representing medical
products distributors. Provides leadership in
the healthcare distribution industry.

13563 www.iahss.org
International Association for Healthcare
Security
Non-profit professional organization of
healthcare security and safety executives from
around the world.

13564 www.ichbc.org
Institute of Healthcare Business Consultants
Maintains code of ethics, rules of professional
conducts, and certification program, administers
examination and conducts certification
course. Membership by successful completion
of certification examination only.

13565 www.jamesbeard.org
James Beard Foundation
Not-for-profit organization dedicated to preserving
the country's culinary heritage and fostering
the appreciation and development of
gastronomy by recognizing and promoting excellence
in all aspects of the culinary arts.

13566 www.managedcaremarketplace.com
Managed Care Information Center
An online yellow pages for companies providing
services to MCOs, hospitals and physicians
groups. There are more than three dozen targeted
categories, offering information on vendors
from claims processing to transportation
services to health care compliance.

13567 www.medicaid.apwa.org
National Association of Medicaid Directors
Promotes effective Medicaid policy and program
administration; works with the federal
government on issues through technical advisory
groups. Conducts forums on policy and
technical issues.

13568 www.mgma.com
American College of Medical Practice
Executives
Professional credentialing organization. Works
to encourage medical group practice administrators
to improve and maintain their proficiency
and to provide appropriate recognition;
to establish a program with uniform standards
of admission, advancement, certification and
fellowship in order to achieve the highest possible
standards in the profession of medical
group practice administration; to participate in
the development of educational and research
programs.

13569 www.mwsearch.com/
Medical world search.

13570 www.mywebmd.com
The largest commercial health site, offers easy
- to read information on health and wellness issues
and latest medical news

13571 www.naher.com
National Association for Healthcare
Recruitment
Individuals employed directly by hospitals and
other health care organizations which are involved
in the practice of professional health
care recruitment. Promotes sound principles of
professionals health care recruitment. Provides
financial assistance to aid members in planning
and implementing regional educational programs.
Offers technical assistance and
consultation services. Compiles statistics.

13572 www.namdrc.org
National Association of Medical Directors
for
Respiratory Care

Works to provide educational opportunities to
fit the needs of medical directors of respiratory
care and represents the interests of members to
regulatory agencies to ensure that the needs of
respiratory patients are not overlooked. Offers
educational programs; maintains speakers'
bureau.

13573 www.namss.org
National Association Medical Staff Service
Individuals involved in the management and
administration of health care provider services.
Seeks to enhance the knowledge and experience
of medical staff services professionals and
promote the certification of those involved in
the profession.

13574 www.nerf.org
National Eye Research Center
Improving your vision through eyecare, education
and research.

**13575 www.nlm.nih.gov/databases/medline.h
tml**
Vast bibliographic database maintained by the
US National Library of Medicine. Medline contains
citations and abstracts from several thousand
biomedical journals, covering medicine,
nursing, dentistry, vetinary medicine and other
fields.

13576 www.nraa.org/renal/
National Renal Administrators Association

Administrative personnel involved with dialysis
programs for patients suffering from kidney
failure. Provides a vehicle for the development
of educational and informational services for
members. Maintains contact with health care
facilities and government agencies. Operates
placement serve; compiles statistics; conducts
political action committee.

13577 www.oncolink.com
Founded by specialist at the University of
Pennsylvania, provides information on wide
range of childhood and adult cancers

13578 www.pahcom.com
Professional Association of Health Care
Office
Management

Office managers of small group and solo medical
practices. Operates certification program
for health care office managers.

13579 www.paralysis.org
Christopher Reeve Paralysis Foundation
Our mission is to raise money to help fing spinal
cord injury research.

13580 www.quackwatch.com
A nonprofit corporation whose purpose is to
combat health - related frauds, myths, fads, and
fallacies and investigate phony medical news

13581 www.rbma.org
Radiology Business Management
Association
Business managers for private radiology
groups; corporate members include: vendors of
equipment, services, or supplies. Purposes are
to improve business administration of radiologists'
practices to better serve patients and the
medical profession; and to provide opportunities
for professional development and recognition.
Offers extensive educational and
networking opportunities and informal placement
service. Maintains information services
emphasizing those aspects unique to the
business.

13582 www.siim.org
Society for Imaging Informatics in Medicine
Devoted to advance informatics and information
technology in medical imaging through education
and research. Provides an open
environment for imaging information professionals
to access expert and cutting edge resources
in a collegial and practical atmosphere.

13583 www.sleepproducts.org
International Sleep Products Association
Maintains a strong organization to influence
government actions, inform and educate the
membership and act on industry issues to enhance
the growth,profitability and stature of the
sleep products industry. Provides members
with information and services to manage their
business more effectively and efficiently. Publishes
a magazine devoted exclusively to the
mattress industry, BEDtimes covers a broad
range of issue and news important to the
industry.

13584 www.smamc.org
Society of Medical-Dental Management
Consultants
Professionals medical and/or dental management
consultants associated for educational and
information sharing purposes. Objectives are
to: advance the profession; share management
techniques; improve individual skills; provide
clients with competent and capable business
management. Provides information on insur-

ance and income tax. Conducts surveys; compiles statistics.

13585 www.themcic.com

Healthcare IS/IT Yearbook

The Health care IS/IT Market Yearbook is a unique and valuable sales and marketing reference tool for IT companies selling into the health and managed care industries. Great for sales and marketing research; developing reports or preparing presentations. Now, it's easy to identify what hospitals are contracting for, get information on hundreds of millions of dollars in healthcare. IT contract deals, discover what other companies are doing.

13586 www.toxicology.org

Society Of Toxicology

Members are scientists concerned with the effects of chemicals on man and the environment. Promotes the aquisition and utilization of knowledge in toxicology, aids in the protection of public health and facilitates disiplines. The society has a strong commitment to education in toxicology and to the recruitment of students and new members into the profession.

13587 www.uams.edu/afpa/

Association of Family Practice Administrators

Promotes professionalism in family practice administration. Serves as a network for sharing of information and fellowship among network for sharing of information and fellowship among members. Provides technical assistance to members; functions as a liaison to related professional organizations.

Associations

13588 ASHRAE
1791 Tullie Circle, N.E.
Atlanta, GA 30329-2398

404-636-8400
800-527-4723
FAX 404-321-5478
E-Mail: ashrae@ashrae.org
Home Page: www.ashrae.org
Social Media: *Facebook, Twitter*

T. David Underwood, P.Eng., President
Timothy G. Wentz, P.E.ÿ, President-Elect
Walid Chakroun, Ph.D., P.E., VP
Patricia T. Graef, P.E., VP
James K. Vallort, VP

An international organization that fulfills its mission of advancing heating, ventilation, air conditioning and refrigeration to serve humanity and promote a sustainable world through research, standards writing, publishing and continuing education.
55000 Members
Founded in 1894
Mailing list available for rent

13589 Air Conditioning Contractors of America
2800 S Shirlington Rd
Suite 300
Arlington, VA 22206-3607

703-575-4477
888-290-2220
E-Mail: info@acca.org
Home Page: www.acca.org
Social Media: *Facebook, Twitter, LinkedIn, YouTube*

Paul T. Stalknecht, President/CEO
Don Langston, Secretary/Treasurer
Kevin W. Holland, SVP, Business Operations
Glenn Hourahan, SVP, Research & Technology
Charlie McCrudden, SVP, Government Relations

Represents HVAC contractors and holds annual meetings and exhibits for heating, air conditioning and refrigeration equipment, supplies and services.

13590 Air Diffusion Council
1901 North Roselle Road
Suite 800
Schaumburg, IL 60195

847-706-6750
FAX 847-706-6751
E-Mail: info@flexibleduct.org
Home Page: www.flexibleduct.org

Jack Lagershausen, President

The purpose of the Air Diffusion Council is to promote and further the interests of the manufacturers of air distribution equipment, more specifically, flexible air ducts and related products, and the interests of the general public in the areas of safety, quality, efficiency and energy conservation. Also, to develop programs approved and supported by the membership that legally promote and further these interests.
40 Members
Founded in 1961

13591 Air Movement and Control Association International, Inc.
30 West University Dr.
Arlington Heights, IL 60004

847-394-0150
Home Page: www.amca.org
Social Media: *Facebook, Twitter, LinkedIn*

Dr. Geoff Sheard, Chairman
Patrick Cockrum, President
Mark Stevens, Executive Director

AMCA represents manufacturers of air movement devices from 34 countries.
330 Members
Founded in 1917

13592 Air-Conditioning, Heating, Refrigeration
2111 Wilson Boulevard
Suite 500
Arlington, VA 22201

703-524-8800
FAX 703-562-1942
E-Mail: ahri@ahrinet.org
Home Page: www.ahrinet.org
Social Media: *Facebook, Twitter, RSS*

Stephen Yurek, President and CEO
Amanda M Donahue, Executive Assistant
Stephanie Murphy, CFO
Cade Clark, Vice President, Government Affairs
Henry Hwong, Senior Vice President
300+ Members
Founded in 1953

13593 Air-Conditioning, Heating, and Refrigeration Institute (AHRI)
2111 Wilson Blvd.
Suite 500
Arlington, VA 22201

703-524-8800
Home Page: www.ahrinet.org
Social Media: *Facebook, Twitter, YouTube*

Stephen Yurek, President & CEO
Stephanie Murphy, Chief Financial Officer

Institute members manufacture 90 percent of the residential and commercial HVAC equipment in North America.

13594 American Boiler Manufacturers Association
8221 Old Courthouse Road
Suite 380ÿ
Vienna, VA 22015

703-356-7172
FAX 703-356-4543
E-Mail: info@abma.com
Home Page: www.abma.com
Social Media: *Facebook, Twitter, LinkedIn*

Robert Stemen, Chairman of the Board
Robert Forslund, Vice Chairman
Scott Lynch, President/Chief Executive Officer
Thomas Giaier, Secretary/ Treasurer
Kevin Hoey, Immediate Past Chair

Manufacturers' trade association representing companies involved in utility, industrial and commercial steam generation. Includes associate memberships for companies who sell to or work with these companies and those who own boilers. Holds technical and production conferences and publishes technical guideline publications.
Founded in 1888

13595 American Supply Association
1200 North Arlington Heights Road
Suite 150
Itasca, IL 60143

630-467-0000
FAX 630-467-0001
E-Mail: info@asa.net
Home Page: www.asa.net
Social Media: *Facebook, Twitter, LinkedIn*

John Strong, Chairman
Rick Fantham, President
Tim Milford, President Elect
Steve Cook, Treasurer
Brian Tuohey, VP

The national association of full-service plumbing, heating, cooling, and piping products for wholesalers, manufacturers, and distributors.
4000 Members
Founded in 1969

13596 Association of Professional Energy
3916 W Oak Street
Suite D
Burbank, CA 91505

818-972-2159
FAX 818-972-2863
E-Mail: buschre@earthlink.net
Home Page: www.apem.org

John Sykes, Communications
Mark Martinez, Chair/Chapter Development
Bernell Loveridge, Chair/Treasurer
Lynne Eichner Kelley, Chair/Membership

Members include individuals responsible for energy production, consumption or management decisions.
1.5M Members
Founded in 1982

13597 Cooling Technology Institute
PO Box 681807
Houston, TX 77268

281-583-4087
FAX 281-537-1721
E-Mail: vmanser@cti.org
Home Page: www.cti.org

Jack Bland, President
Frank Michell, Vice-President
Steven Chaloupka, Treasurer
Thomas Toth, Secretary
Helene Troncin, Director

Seeks to improve technology, design and performance of water conservation apparatus. Provides inspection services and conducts research.
400 Members
Founded in 1950

13598 Heating, Air Conditioning & Refrigeration Distributors International
3455 Mill Run Drive
Suite 820
Columbus, OH 43026

614-345-4328
888-253-2128
FAX 614-345-9161
E-Mail: hardimail@hardinet.org
Home Page: www.hardinet.org
Social Media: *Facebook, Twitter, LinkedIn, Flickr, Youtube, Instagram*

William Bergamini, President
Tom Roberts, Vice President
Troy Meachum, Secretary / Treasurer
Michael Meier, President-Elect
Royce Henderson, Immediate Past President

Nonprofit organization dedicated to advancing the science of wholesale distribution in the HVACR industry.
1200 Members
Founded in 1947

13599 International Microwave Power Institute
PO Box 1140
Mechanicsville, VA 23111-5007

804-559-6667
FAX 804-559-4087
E-Mail: info@impi.org
Home Page: www.impi.org
Social Media: *Facebook, Twitter, LinkedIn*

Bob Schifmann, President
Ben Wilson, VP
Dorin Boldor, Secretary

Amy Lawson, Treasurer
Molly Poisant, Executive Director

To be the global organization that provides a forum for the exchange of information on all aspects of microwave and RF heating technologies.
Founded in 1966

13600 Masonry Heater Association of North America

2180 S Flying Q Lane
Tuscon, AZ 85731

520-883-0191
FAX 480-371-1139
E-Mail: execdir@mha-net.org
Home Page: www.mha-net.org

Richard Smith, Executive Director
Tim Seaton, VP
Rod Zander, Treasurer
Beverly Marois, Administrator

Promotes use of masonry heaters, increases public awareness and encourages reasonable governmental regulation.
115 Members
Founded in 1989

13601 Mechanical Contractors Association of America

1385 Piccard Drive
Rockville, MD 20850-4329

301-869-5800
FAX 301-990-9690
Home Page: www.mcaa.org

John Gentille, Executive VP

Represents heating, piping and air conditioning professionals.
1.4M Members

13602 Mobile Air Conditioning Society Worldwide

225 South Broad Street
PO Box 88
Lansdale, PA 19446

215-631-7020
FAX 215-631-7017
E-Mail: info@macsw.org
Home Page: www.macsw.org
Social Media: *Facebook, Twitter, LinkedIn, Youtube, WordPress, Google+, T*

Elvis L. Hoffpauir, President, Chief Operating Officer
Marion J. Posen, VP Marketing & Member Relations
Pam Smith, Events Manager
Maria Whitworthÿ, Director of Operations
Laina Casey, Manager of Graphics and Design

Non-profit organization provides technical training, information and communication for the professionals in the automotive air-conditioning industry.
1700 Members
Founded in 1981

13603 National Air Duct Cleaners Association

1120 Route 73
Suite 200
Mt Laurel, NJ 08054

856-380-6810
855-GON-ADCA
FAX 856-439-0525
E-Mail: info@nadca.com
Home Page: www.nadca.com
Social Media: *Facebook, Twitter, LinkedIn, Youtube*

Michael Vinick,ÿASCS, President
Jodi Araujo, CEM, Executive Director
Mike Dwyer, CAE, Chief Relationship Officer
Richard Lantz,ÿASCS, 1st Vice President
Rick MacDonald, ASCS, 2nd Vice President

The trade association of the HVAC/Heating-Ventilation-Air Conditioning industry.
1000 Members
Founded in 1989

13604 National Association of Plumbing, Heating and Cooling Contractors Association

180 S Washington Street
Suite 100
Falls Church, VA 22046

703-237-8100
800-533-7694
FAX 703-237-7442
E-Mail: naphcc@naphcc.org
Home Page: www.phccweb.org
Social Media: *Facebook, Twitter, LinkedIn*

Dawn Dalton, Administrative Coordinator
Katie Gilbert, Membership Coordinator
Merry Beth Hall, Director, Apprentice and Journeyman
Don Hawkins, Accounts Receivable Clerk
Patrice L Jackson, Coordinator, QSC Member Services

National organization designed for suppliers of equipment, supplies and services for the plumbing, heating and cooling industries.
3700 Members
Founded in 1883

13605 National Association of Power Engineers

One Springfield Street
Chicopee, MA 01013-2672

413-592-6273
FAX 413-592-1998
E-Mail: nape@powerengineers.com
Home Page: www.powerengineers.com
Social Media: *Facebook, Twitter, LinkedIn*

Michael Morin, National President
Shawn Fitzpatrick, National Vice President
William Love, National Treasurer/Secretary

Members include power plant operators and maintenance personnel who supply the industry with process power and related building and plant services.

13606 National Environmental Balancing Bureau

8575 Grovemont Circle
Gaithersburg, MD 20877-4121

301-977-3698
866-497-4447
FAX 301-977-9589
E-Mail: glenn@nebb.org
Home Page: www.nebb.org

Jean Paul Le Blanc, President
Donald E. Hill, Vice President
Jim Kelleher, President Elect
Jim Whorton, Treasurer
James Huber, Past President

NEBB is an international certification association for firms that deliver high performance building systems. Members perform testing, adjusting and balancing (TAB) of heating, ventilating and air-conditioning systems, commission and retro-commission building systems commissioning, execute sound and vibration testing, and test and certify lab fume hoods and electronic and bio clean rooms. NEBB holds the highest standards in certification.
Founded in 1971

13607 Wholesalers Association of the Northeast

1200 N. Arlington Heights Rd.
Suite 150
Itasca, IL 60143

630-467-0000
FAX 508-923-1044

E-Mail: wane5@asa.net
Home Page: www.wane5.org

Chris Murin, Executive Director

Presently comprised of the leading wholesale distributors of pluming, heating, cooling and industrial pipe supplies, located throughout the northeast states.
Founded in 1932

Newsletters

13608 HVACR News

Trade News International
4444 Riverside Drive
Suite 202
Burbank, CA 91505

818-848-6397
FAX 818-848-1306
Home Page: www.hvacrnews.com

Gary McCarty, Editor-in -Chief
Mark Deitch, Publisher
Jordan Tolila, Associate Publisher
Barb Kerr, Executive Assistant

A monthly national trade newspaper serving contractors, technicians, mechanical engineers, manufactures, manufacturer representatives, wholesalers, distributors, trade associations, government representatives, schools, students and other in the heating, ventilating, air conditioning, refrigerating, hydronics, sheet metals, solar, and allied trades.
Frequency: Monthly
Circulation: 50000
Founded in 1981
Printed in 4 colors on n stock

13609 Heating/Combustion and Equipment News

Business Communications Company
1 Penn Plz
Suite 42
New York, NY 10119-4200

212-273-7100
800-685-4488
FAX 212-244-3721
Home Page: www.firstalbany.com

Equipment, materials and supplies for the heating and air conditioning industry.
Cost: $12.00
Frequency: Monthly

13610 Impact Compressor/Turbines News And Patents

Impact Publishers
PO Box 3113
Ketchum, ID 83340-3113

208-726-2332
FAX 208-726-2115

Mary Jo Helmeke, Publisher

Regular features include new product announcements, patent information and up-to-date industry news and information on current books, brochures, software, seminars and meetings.
Cost: $60.00
30 Pages
Frequency: Annual

13611 Impact Pump News and Patents

Impact Publishers
PO Box 3113
Ketchum, ID 83340-3113

208-720-4876
FAX 208-726-2115

Mary Jo Helmeke, Publisher

Regular features include new product announcements, patent information and

up-to-date industry news and information on current books, brochures software, seminars and meetings.
Cost: $100.00
25 Pages

13612 Indoor Air Quality Update
Cutter Information Corporation
37 Broadway
Suite 1
Arlington, MA 02474-5500

718-648-8700
FAX 718-648-8707
Home Page: www.cutter.com
Social Media: *Facebook, Twitter*

Karen Coburn, President and CEO
Paul Bergeron, CFO and COO
Israel Gat, Director, Agile Practice
Anne Mullaney, VP, Prodct Development
Cuitlahuac Osorio, Director, Cutter Latin America

Practical control of indoor air problems.
Cost: $287.00
Frequency: Monthly

13613 MACS Action!
Mobile Air Conditioning Society Worldwide
225 S Broad Street
PO Box 88
Lansdale, PA 19446

215-631-7020
FAX 215-631-7017
E-Mail: info@macsw.org
Home Page: www.macsw.org

Elvis Hoffpauir, President/COO
Marion Posen, VP Marketing/Sales

Industry informational newsletter of Mobile Air Conditioning Society Worldwide.
Cost: $5.00
Frequency: 8x Yearly
Circulation: 13000
ISSN: 1949-3436

13614 MACS Service Reports
Mobile Air Conditioning Society Worldwide
PO Box 100
East Greenville, PA 18041

215-679-2220
FAX 215-541-4635
E-Mail: elvis@macsw.org
Home Page: www.macsw.org

Elvis Hoffpauir, Editor
Paul DeGuiseppi, Manager of Training
Amy Anderson, Production Designer
Pam Smith, Manager
Maria Whitworth, Director of Operations

Technical newsletter for mobile air conditioning industry.
Frequency: Monthly
Circulation: 1600
Founded in 1981

13615 Residential Heat Recovery Ventilators Directory
Cutter Information Corporation
37 Broadway
Suite 1
Arlington, MA 02474-5500

781-648-1950
FAX 781-648-1950
Home Page: www.cutter.com

Verna Allee, Senior Consultant

A comprehensive comparative guide and product directory to heat exchangers and ventilators.
Cost: $75.00

13616 Superinsulated House Design and Construction Workbook
Cutter Information Corporation

37 Broadway
Suite 1
Arlington, MA 02474-5500

781-648-1950
FAX 781-648-1950
Home Page: www.cutter.com

Verna Allee, Senior Consultant

Detailed, graphic information to design and build superior houses.
Cost: $85.00

Magazines & Journals

13617 AHRI Trends Magazine
Air Conditioning & Refrigeration Institute
2111 Wilson Boulevard
Suite 500
Arlington, VA 22201

703-524-8800
FAX 703-528-3816
E-Mail: ahri@ahri.net
Home Page: www.ahrinet.org

A resource for HVAC contractors and technicians.
Frequency: Monthly

13618 ASHRAE Journal
1791 Tullie Circle NE
Atlanta, GA 30329

404-636-8400
800-527-4723
FAX 404-321-5478
E-Mail: ashrae@ashrae.org
Home Page: www.ashrae.org
Social Media: *Facebook*

Ronald Jarnagin, President
Thomas Watson, President-Elect
William Bahnfleth, Tresurer
Constantinos A Balaras, VP
Ross D Montgomery, VP

Explores topical technical issues, such as: indoor air quality, energy management, thermal storage, alternative refrigerants, fire and life safety and more.
Printed in 4 colors on matte stock

13619 Air Conditioning Today
PO Box 311776
New Braunfels, TX 78131

830-627-0605
877-669-4228
FAX 830-627-0614
E-Mail: info@ac-today.com
Home Page: ac-today.com

Joe Eaton, Editor

Updates readers on the latest products, materials and technologies available.
Frequency: Monthly
Circulation: 19000
Founded in 1986

13620 Air Conditioning, Heating & Refrigeration News
Business News Publishing Company
1050 IL Route 83
Suite 200
Bensenville, IL 60106-1096

630-377-5909
Home Page: www.bnpmedia.com

Katie Rotella, Manager

Timely information to contractors, wholesalers, distributors, manufacturers, owner/operators and consulting engineers. Features technical, marketing, design, engineering, installation, management, governmental and labor aspects of the heating and cooling industry. Regular columns highlight new products and literature,

legal rulings, manufacturer announcements, industry events and the latest HVAC/r patents.
Cost: $49.00
Frequency: Weekly
Circulation: 32854
Founded in 1926
Mailing list available for rent: 35M names
Printed in 4 colors on glossy stock

13621 American Supply Association News
222 Merchandise Mart Plaza
Suite 1400
Chicago, IL 60654-1203

312-464-0090
FAX 312-464-0091
E-Mail: info@asa.net
Home Page: www.asa.net

Joel Becker, President
Bob Christian, Vice President
Kevin Neupert, Marketing
Joel Becker, Editor

Articles on plumbing, heating, cooling, and piping products.
50 Pages
Frequency: Monthly
Circulation: 2500
Founded in 1969
Mailing list available for rent: 4,000 names
Printed in 4 colors on matte stock

13622 Automotive Cooling Journal
National Automotive Radiator Service Association
3000 Villiage Run Rd
Suite 103, #221
Wexford, PA 15090-6315

412-847-5747
800-551-3232
FAX 724-934-1036
E-Mail: info@narsa.org
Home Page: www.narsa.org

Jim Holowka, National President
Chuck Braswell, National Chairman-Past President
Rick Fuller, National 1st VP
Maarten Taal, National 2nd VP
Angelo Miozza, National Treasurer

Auto cooling system service data. Free to members.
Cost: $30.00
60 Pages
Frequency: Monthly
Circulation: 10,000
Founded in 1954

13623 Boiler Systems Engineering Magazine
HPAC Engineering
1300 E 9th Street
Cleveland, OH 44144

216-696-7000
FAX 216-696-3432
E-Mail: hpac@penton.com
Home Page: www.hpac.com
Social Media: *Facebook, Twitter*

Mike Well, Editorial Director
Scott Arnold, Executive Editor
Ron Rajecki, Senior Editor

The official publication of the American Boiler Manufacturers Association, assists consulting engineers, in-house engineers, and building managers with the design, installation, operations, maintenance and commissioning of steam and hot water systems for institutional, commercial and industrial buildings.

13624 Contracting Business
Penton Media
249 W 17th St
New York, NY 10011

212-204-4200
FAX 216-696-6662

E-Mail: information@penton.com
Home Page: www.penton.com

Jane Cooper, Marketing
Michael S Weil, Editor-in-Chief
Gwen Hostnik, Marketing Manager

Directed to the residential, commercial and industrial mechanical systems contracting marketplace. HVAC mechanical systems and Design/Build/Maintain contractors, wholesalers and commercial/industrial in-house service organizations.
Cost: $75.00
120 Pages
Frequency: Monthly
Circulation: 49,001
Founded in 1944
Printed in 4 colors on glossy stock

13625 Contractor Magazine
Penton Media
1300 E 9th St
Cleveland, OH 44114-1503

216-696-7000
FAX 216-696-6662
E-Mail: information@penton.com
Home Page: www.contractormag.com
Social Media: *Facebook, Twitter*

Jane Cooper, Marketing
Bob Mader, Managing Editor
David B. Nussbaum, CEO

For contractors who sell, install, service air conditioning, heating, piping, plumbing, air handling, heat transfer and fluid controls equipment. Accepts advertising.
70 Pages
Frequency: Monthly
Circulation: 50000
Founded in 1892

13626 District Energy
International District Enery Association
(IDEA)
24 Lyman Streetad
Suite 230
Westborough, MA 01581

508-366-9339
FAX 508-366-0019
E-Mail: idea@districtenergy.org
Home Page: www.districtenergy.org

Peter Myers, Editor
Rob Thornton, President

Journal of district heating and cooling industry, congeneration, physical plants and energy efficiency. Accepts advertising.
Cost: $40.00
Frequency: Quarterly

13627 Energy Engineering
Association of Energy Engineers
4025 Pleasantdale Rd
Suite 420
Atlanta, GA 30340-4264

770-447-5083
FAX 770-446-3969
E-Mail: info@aeecenter.org
Home Page: www.aeecenter.org
Social Media: *Facebook, Twitter, LinkedIn, YouTube*

Jennifer Venola, Controller
Ruth Whitlock, Executive Admin
Albert Thumann, Executive Director
Kate Feltgen, Executive Director's Assistant

Engineering solutions to cost efficiency problems and mechanical contractors who design, specify, install, maintain, and purchase non-residential heating, ventilating, air conditioning and refrigeration equipment and components.
Cost: $40.00
Circulation: 8000

13628 Engineered Systems
Business News Publishing Company
1050 IL Route 83
Suite 200
Bensenville, IL 60106-1096

630-377-5909
Home Page: www.esmagazine.com

Katie Rotella, Manager
Peter E Moran, Publisher

Research conducted by us shows that end users, consulting engineers, and contractors work together closely on the specification and selection of engineered HVAC/r systems and components. We give this receptive audience solid editorial information about real-world solutions to the everyday situations faced in the industry.
72 Pages
Frequency: Monthly
Circulation: 57515
Founded in 1985
Mailing list available for rent: 57.5M names
Printed in 4 colors on glossy stock

13629 Fuel Oil News
Hunter Publishing Limited
3100 S King Dr
7th Floor
Chicago, IL 60616-3483

312-567-9981
FAX 312-846-4632
Home Page: www.fueloilnews.com

Luke Hunter, Partner
Joanne Juda, Circulation Director
Kate Kenny, Publisher
Chris Traczek, Editor-in-Chief
Patricia McCartney, Associate Editor

For home heating oil retailers.
Cost: $28.00
70 Pages
Frequency: Monthly
Circulation: 15200
Founded in 1935
Printed in 4 colors on glossy stock

13630 HVAC Insider
Retailing Newspapers
PO Box 81489
Conveyors, GA 30013

770-787-0115
FAX 770-787-1213
E-Mail: insider@mindsprin.com
Home Page:
www.mindspring.com/~insider/insider

Jerry M Lawson, Publisher
Robert Scott, Chief Information Officer

Up to date information on technical tips, product reviews, commercial and industrial industry new, a job bulletin, new businesses and promotions, and a calendar of events. Retailing Newspapers issues a monthly publication for the Appliance and Electronics trade. Insiders Newspapers issues a quarterly national and 14 monthly regionals for the HVAC trade and a monthly regional publication for the plumbing trade.
Frequency: Monthly
Circulation: 118740
Founded in 1969
Printed in 4 colors on newsprint stock

13631 HVAC/R Distribution Today
HARDI
3455 Mill Run Dr
Suite 820
Columbus, OH 43026-7578

614-345-4328
888-253-2128
FAX 614-345-9161

E-Mail: HARDImail@Hardinet.org
Home Page: www.hardinet.org

Talbot H Gee, Executive VP & COO
Donald L Frendberg, Chairman
Susan Little, Director of Marketing
Mary Gustafson, Director of Operations
Alan Beaulieu, Chief Economist

Official publication of Heating, Air Conditioning and Refrigeration International. Uniting world class distribution.
Frequency: Quarterly
Founded in 1960

13632 HVACR & Plumbing Distribution
Penton Media
1300 E 9th St
Cleveland, OH 44114-1503

216-696-7000
FAX 216-696-6662
E-Mail: information@penton.com
Home Page: www.penton.com

Jane Cooper, Marketing
Perry Clark, Publisher

Exclusively for plumbing and heating equipment distributors.
Circulation: 10,000
Founded in 1890

13633 Hearth & Home
Village West Publishing
PO Box 1288
Laconia, NH 03246

603-528-4285
800-258-3772
FAX 603-524-0643
E-Mail: info@hearthnhome.com
Home Page: villagewest.com

Richard Wright, Editor
Susan Salls, Publisher

Magazine for retailers, including specialty, hardware, patio and barbecue.
Cost: $36.00
Frequency: Monthly
Circulation: 18000

13634 Industrial Heating
Business News Publishing Company
1910 Cochran Road
Manor Oak One, Suite 450
Pittsburgh, PA 15220

412-531-3370
FAX 412-531-3375
E-Mail: europesales@industrialheating.com
Home Page: www.industrialheating.com
Social Media: *Facebook, Twitter*

Ed Kubel, Editor
Beth McClelland, Production Manager
Doug Glenn, Publisher
Kathy Pisano, Advertising Director
Patrick Connolly, Sales Representative

We have been applying the latest advances in thermal technology to practical use since 1931. With over 22,000 BPA audited circulation comprised of mostly thermal processing engineers, technical articles cover heat treatments, brazing, sintering, melting, process control, instrumentation, refractories, burners, heating elements, and other thermal processes typically in excess of 1000 degrees.
Cost: $55.00
70 Pages
Circulation: 22100
ISSN: 0019-8374
Founded in 1931
Printed in 4 colors on glossy stock

13635 PM Engineer
Business News Publishing Company

1050 IL Route 83
Suite 200
Bensenville, IL 60106-1096

630-377-5909
Home Page: www.pmengineer.com
Social Media: *Facebook, Twitter*

Bob Miodonski, Group Publisher & Editor
Mike Miazga, Senior Editor
Julius Ballanco, Editorial Director
Suzette Rubio, Online Editor
John Siegenthaler, Hydronics Editor

Provides technical sheets, manufacturer product brochures, news features and analysis of useful industry information on the engineering and design of plumbing, piping, hydronics, cooling/heating, and fire protection/sprinkler systems. Free to trade engineers.
Cost: $64.00
80 Pages
Frequency: Monthly
Circulation: 25000
Founded in 1926
Printed in 4 colors on glossy stock

13636 RSES Journal
Refrigeration Service Engineers Society
1666 Rand Rd
Des Plaines, IL 60016-3552

847-297-6464
800-297-5660
FAX 847-297-5038
E-Mail: general@rses.org
Home Page: www.rses.org
Social Media: *Facebook, Twitter, LinkedIn*

John Iwanski, Publishing Director
Lori A Kasallis, Editor

Providing quality technical content in digital and printed forms that can be applied on the job site.
Frequency: Monthly
Circulation: 15231

13637 Reeves Journal
23421 S Pointe Drive
Suite 280
Laguna Hills, CA 92654

949-830-0881
FAX 949-859-7845
Home Page: www.reevesjournal.com

Ellyn Fishman, Publisher
John Fultz, Editor
Tagg Henderson, CEO

An invaluable tool for Western plumbing contractors and industry professionals for more than 80 years.
Frequency: Monthly
Circulation: 13545
Founded in 1926

13638 Refrigerated Transporter
Primedia
4200 S Shepherd Drive
Suite 200
Houston, TX 77098

713-233-3826
FAX 713-523-8384
Home Page: www.refrigeratedtrans.com/

Gary Macklin, Editor-in-Chief
Tom Rogers, Chief Executive Officer
John Wilkins, executive Vice-President
Frequency: Monthly
Circulation: 15,023

13639 Refrigeration
John W Yopp Publications
73 Sen Island Parkway Suite 21
PO Box 1147
Beaufort, SC 29901-1147

843-521-0239
800-849-9667

FAX 843-521-1398
E-Mail: cgraffo@jwyopp.com
Home Page: www.refrigeration-magazine.com

John W Yopp, Chairman
Joe Cronley, Publisher
Mary Yopp Cronley, Associate Publsiher
Cheryl Graffo, Editor

About the plants and processes used in ice manufacture, marketing and merchandising information, news of associations, meetings and new products available.
Cost: $20.00
Frequency: Monthly
Circulation: 3200
Founded in 1919
Printed in 4 colors on glossy stock

13640 Snips
Business News Publishing Company
2401 W. Big Beaver Road
Suite 700
Troy, MI 48084

248-362-3700
FAX 248-362-0317
E-Mail: snips@halldata.com
Home Page: www.snipsmag.com

Katie Rotella, Manager
Sally Fraser, Advertising Sales
Karen Koppins, Advertising Productions
Ann Kalb, Customer Service
Michael McConnel, Editorial Director

Magazine directed to the heating, air conditioning, sheet metal and ventilation industry. Accepts advertising.
Cost: $18.00
120 Pages
Frequency: Monthly
Circulation: 22000
Founded in 1926
Printed in 4 colors on glossy stock

13641 Tab Journal
Associated Air Balance Council
1518 K Street NW
Washington, DC 20005-1203

202-737-0202
FAX 202-638-4833
Home Page: www.aabchq.com/

Kenneth M Sufka, Publisher
Mike Young, President

Case studies, industry updates, as well as other news of importance to engineers.
Cost: $24.00
Frequency: Quarterly
Circulation: 12000
Founded in 1965

13642 Todays A/C and Refrigeration News
Todays Trade Publications
PO Box 521247
130 W Pine Ave
Longwood, FL 32750-1247

407-332-4959
866-320-2773
FAX 407-332-5319
Home Page: www.todays-ac.com

Thomas Fatchell, Editor

Covers industry legislation, building codes, licensing requirements and continuing educations. New product reviews and personnel changes are also included.
Frequency: Monthly
Circulation: 20000
Founded in 1988

Trade Shows

13643 ABMA Annual Meeting
American Boiler Manufacturers Association
8221 Old Courthouse Road
Suite 207
Vienna, VA 22182-3839

703-356-7172
FAX 703-356-4543
Home Page: www.abma.com

W Randall Rawson, President/CEO
Diana McClung, Executive Assistant
Cheryl Jamall, Director of Meetings
Geoffrey Halley, Director of Technical Affairs
Hugh K Webster, Association General Counsel

The association's premier membership networking events. In casual and relaxed settings, members have the opportunity to not only learn about developments and trends, both inside and outside their industry, that are likely to influence their business, members are also afforded the opportunity, through committee and product/market group meetings to focus on issues and concerns of specific relevance to their product and market segments.
Frequency: Bi-Annual
Founded in 1888

13644 ABMA Manufacturers Conference
American Boiler Manufacturers Association
8221 Old Courthouse Road
Suite 207
Vienna, VA 22182-3839

703-356-7172
FAX 703-356-4543
Home Page: www.abma.com

W Randall Rawson, President/CEO
Diana McClung, Executive Assistant
Cheryl Jamall, Director of Meetings
Geoffrey Halley, Director of Technical Affairs
Hugh K Webster, Association General Counsel

Designed to bring together manufacturing plant, office and others concerned with the design, fabrication, sales and distribution of ABMA'products and services to network, discuss trends and developments, and problem solve with others in the industry and with outside experts.
Frequency: Annual/October
Founded in 1888

13645 AMCA Annual Meeting
Air Movement and Control Assoc. Intl., Inc.
30 West University Dr.
Arlington Heights, IL 60004

847-394-0150
Home Page: www.amca.org
Social Media: *Facebook, Twitter, LinkedIn*

Dr. Geoff Sheard, Chairman
Patrick Cockrum, President
Mark Stevens, Executive Director

13646 ASA Convention and ISH North America Trade Show
American Supply Association
222 Merchandise Mart Plaza
Suite 1400
Chicago, IL 60654

312-640-0090
FAX 312-464-0091
E-Mail: info@asa.net
Home Page: www.asa.net or www.ish-na.com

Ruth Mitchell, Manager/Convention Director
Bob Jarvie, Show Manager

Annual conference for wholesalers, distributors and manufacturers of plumbing and heating pipes, valves and fittings.
1800 Attendees
Frequency: Annual/September

13647 Air Conditioning Contractors of America Annual Conference
Air Conditioning Contractors of America
1712 New Hampshire Avenue NW
Washington, DC 20009-2502

202-518-3236
FAX 202-332-5293
Home Page: www.acca.org

Christopher Holelzel, Director Marketing
Rosemary Graeme, Executive Assistant

Annual meeting and exhibits of heating, air conditioning and refrigeration equipment, supplies and services. Over 140 exhibitors, plus seminar, workshop and banquet.
1000 Attendees

13648 Air Conditioning Heating & Refrigeration Expo Mexico - AHR
Industrial Shows of America
164 Lake Front Drive
Hunt Valley, MD 21030-2215

410-771-1445
800-638-6396
FAX 410-771-1158
Home Page: www.isoa.com

Bryan Mayes, President
Phillip McKay, Managing Director

300 exhibitors with air conditioning, heating and refrigerating equipment, supplies and information. Attended by professionals.
5000 Attendees
Frequency: Annual

13649 Annual Campus Energy Conference
International District Energy Association
24 Lyman Street
Suite 230
Westborough, MA 01581

508-366-9339
FAX 508-366-0019
E-Mail: idea@districtenergy.org
Home Page: www.districtenergy.org

Robert Thornton, President
Vincent Bedeli, Chair
Leonard Phillips, Director of Business Development

IDEA fosters the success of its members as leaders in providing reliable, economical, and environmentally sound district energy services.
600 Attendees
Frequency: Annual/June
Founded in 1909

13650 Hearth Products Association
1555 Wilson Boulevard
Suite 300
Arlington, VA 22209-2405

703-522-0086
FAX 703-812-8875
Social Media: *Facebook, Twitter*

Joan Letch Worth, Show Manager

900 booths of products related to the residential alternative fuel heating industry.
8M Attendees
Frequency: Annual/March

13651 Heating, Air Conditioning & Refrigeration Distributors International
3455 Mill Run Drive
Suite 820
Columbus, OH 43026

614-345-4328
888-253-2128
FAX 614-345-9161
Home Page: www.hardinet.org

Talbot H Gee, Executive VP & COO
Donald L Frendberg, Chairman
Susan Little, Director of Marketing
Mary Gustafson, Director of Operations
Alan Beaulieu, Chief Economist

Annual show of 200 exhibitors of heating and air conditioning equipment, supplies and services.
1200 Attendees
Founded in 2003

13652 International Air Conditioning, Heating, & Refrigerating Expo
ASHRAE
1791 Tullie Circle NW
Atlanta, GA 30329

404-636-8400
800-527-4723
FAX 404-321-5478
E-Mail: ashrae@ashrae.org
Home Page: www.ashrae.org

William A Harrison, President
Jeff H Littleton, Executive VP

The largest HVAC&R event in America featuring over 1,600 exhibiting companies. Held every year in conjunction with the ASHRAE Winter Meeting.
30000 Attendees
Frequency: Annual/January
Founded in 1894

13653 International District Energy Association (IDEA) Show
1200 19th Street NW
Suite 300
Washington, DC 20036-2428

202-429-5131
FAX 202-429-5113
Home Page: www.energy.rochester.edu/idea

John L Fiegel, Editor
Tammie Jackson, Advertising Manager

Show of the district heating and cooling industry, cogeneration, physical plants, energy efficiency. 40 booths.
450 Attendees
Frequency: Annual/June

13654 International Institute of Ammonia Refrigeration Annual Conference
1001 N Fairfax St
suite 503
Alexandria, VA 22314

703-312-4200
FAX 202-857-1104
E-Mail: iiar_request@iiar.org

Adolfo Blasquez, Chair
Robert Port Jr, Vice Chair
Joe Mandato, Chair Elect
Marcos Braz, Treasurer
Bruce Badger, President

Show of the district heating and cooling industry, cogeneration, physical plants, energy efficiency. 40 booths.
750 Attendees
Frequency: Annual/March

13655 International Thermal Spray Conference & Exposition
ASM International

9639 Kinsman Road
Materials Park, OH 44073-0002

440-338-5151
800-336-5152
FAX 440-338-4634
E-Mail: natalie.nemec@asminternational.org
Home Page: www.asminternational.org

Carole Chesla, Administrator, Awards
Thom Passek, Associate Managing Director
Leslie Taylor, Executive Office Manager
Stanley Theobald, Managing Director

Global annual event attracting professional interested in thermal spray technology focusing on advances in HVOF, plasma and detonation gun, flame spray and wire arc spray processes, performance of coatings, and future trends. 150 exhibitors.
1000 Attendees
Frequency: Annual/May

13656 MACS Convention & Trade Show
Mobile Air Conditioning Society Worldwide
225 S Broad Street
PO Box 88
Lansdale, PA 19446

215-631-7020
FAX 215-631-7017
E-Mail: info@macsw.org
Home Page: www.macsw.org

Pam Smith, Events Manager
2000 Attendees
Frequency: Annual

13657 Midwest Contractors Expo
Kansas Assn of Plumbing, Heating & Cooling Contr
320 Laura Street
Wichita, KS 67211-1517

316-262-8860
FAX 316-262-2782

Ray Katzenmeier, Owner

Annual show and exhibits of plumbing, heating and cooling equipment, supplies and services.

13658 National Plumbing, Heating, Cooling and Piping Products Exposition
Nat'l Assn of Plumbing-Heating-Cooling Contractors
180 S Washington Street
PO Box 6808
Falls Church, VA 22046

703-237-8100
800-533-7694
FAX 703-237-7442
Home Page: www.phccweb.org
Social Media: *Facebook, LinkedIn*

Elicia Magruder, VP of Member Services
Cynthia A Sheridan, Foundation Chief Operating Officer
Charlotte R Perham, Senior Director of Communications

Annual show of 500 manufacturers and suppliers of equipment, supplies and services for the plumbing, heating and cooling industries.
15M Attendees
Frequency: Annual/October

13659 North American Thermal Analysis Society
Complete Conference
1540 River Park Drive
Suite 111
Sacramento, CA 95815-4608

916-922-7032
FAX 916-922-7379

Marilyn Hauck, President

30 booths.
300 Attendees
Frequency: Annual/September

13660 Oil Heat Business and Industry Expo
20 Summer Street
#9137
Watertown, MA 02472-3468

FAX 781-924-1022

Bernard A Smith, Executive VP
Nancy Spinney, Expo Manager

This show provides a marketplace for prime purchasers of heating oil; oil heating, and air conditioning, as well as accessory equipment; fuel oil distribution equipment, trucks, transports, service and salesmen's vehicles; computers, office equipment; insurance programs and more.
8.5M Attendees
Frequency: Annual/June

13661 RSES Annual Conference and HVAC Technology Expo
Refrigeration Service Engineers Society
1666 Rand Road
Des Plaines, IL 60016-3552

847-297-6464
800-297-5660
E-Mail: general@rses.org
Home Page: www.rses.org
Social Media: *Facebook, Twitter, LinkedIn*

Mark Lowry, Executive Vice President
Josh Flaim, Operations Manager
Jean Birch, Conference & Seminar Manager
80 booths consisting primarily of products and services.

13662 Sheet Metal Air Conditioning Contractors National Association Show
4201 Lafayette Center Drive
Chantilly, VA 20151-1209

703-032-2980
Home Page: http://www.smacna.org

Mary Lou Taylor, Convention Director
John Sroka, Executive VP

250 booths.
2.3M Attendees
Frequency: Annual/October

13663 Southwestern Ice Association Show
823 Congress Avenue
1300
Austin, TX 78701

512-479-0425
FAX 512-495-9031

Andrea Barnard, Executive Director

30 booths.
200 Attendees
Frequency: Annual/February
Founded in 1891

Directories & Databases

13664 Air Conditioning, Heating & Refrigeration News Directory Issue
The Air-Conditioning, Heating & Refrigeration New
2401 W. Big Beaver Road
Suite 700
Troy, MI 48084

248-362-3700
Home Page: www.achrnews.com

John Conrad, Publisher
Mike Murphy, Editor-in-Chief
Kyle Gargaro, Managing Editor
Greg Mazurkiewicz, Web Editor
Barbary Checket-Hanks, Service & Maintenance Editor

This issue offers a list of over 2,000 manufacturers, 5,000 wholesalers and factory outlets. Over 10,000 HVAC/R products, exporters and related trade organizations are also covered.
Cost: $35.00
618 Pages
Frequency: Annual
Circulation: 38,000
Printed in 4 colors on glossy stock

13665 Annual Member Directory
Air Conditioning & Heating Contractors of America
1712 New Hampshire Avenue NW
Washington, DC 20009-2502

202-483-9370
FAX 202-234-4721

Rae Dorsey, Production Manager

A publication for the members of the Air Conditioning and Heating Contractors of America.
Circulation: 5,000

13666 Directory of Certified Applied Air-Conditioning Products
Air-Conditioning & Refrigeration Institute
4301 Fairfax Drive
Suite 425
Arlington, VA 22203-1634

703-248-8800

A list of 50 manufacturers of air conditioning and heating products.
Cost: $8.50
Frequency: Bi-Annual

13667 Directory of Certified Unitary Air-Conditioners & Heat Pumps
Air-Conditioning & Refrigeration Institute
4301 Fairfax Drive
Suite 425
Arlington, VA 22203-1634

703-248-8800

Air and coil heating and cooling units and air-to-air heat pumps manufacturers are profiled.
Cost: $13.00
Frequency: Bi-Annual

13668 HPAC Engineering Information
Penton Media
1300 E 9th St
Cleveland, OH 44114-1501

216-696-7000
FAX 216-696-1752
E-Mail: information@penton.com
Home Page: www.penton.com

Jane Cooper, Marketing
Cost: $30.00
300 Pages
Frequency: Annual
Circulation: 56,000
ISSN: 1527-4055
Printed in 4 colors on glossy stock

13669 Industrial Heating Buyers Guide and Reference Handbook
Business News Publishing
1050 IL Route 83
Suite 200
Bensenville, IL 60106-1096

630-377-5909
Home Page: www.industrialheating.com
Social Media: *Facebook, Twitter, LinkedIn*

Katie Rotella, Manager

Companies are profiled that have over 1,200 heating products, and heat treating, and other services in the worldwide industrial heating market.
Cost: $25.00
250 Pages
Circulation: 20,000

13670 LP/Gas: Industry Buying Guide Issue
Advanstar Communications
131 W 1st St
Duluth, MN 55802-2065

218-740-7200
800-346-0085
FAX 218-723-9122
E-Mail: info@advanstar.com
Home Page: www.advanstar.com

Kent Akervik, Manager

List of about 1,000 liquid propane gas equipment manufacturers and suppliers; list of about 700 distributors of gas appliances and equipment.
Cost: $50.00
Frequency: Annual
Circulation: 16,000
Printed in 4 colors on glossy stock

13671 PM Directory & Reference Issue
Business News Publishing
1050 IL Route 83
Suite 200
Bensenville, IL 60106-1096

630-377-5909
Home Page: www.bnpmedia.com

Katie Rotella, Manager

Manufacturers, wholesalers, exporters, associations, products, consultants and manufacturers' representatives in the industries of plumbing, piping and hydronic heating.
Cost: $30.00
Frequency: Annual/December
Circulation: 42,000

13672 Refrigeration: Ice Industry's Buyer's Guide Issue
John W Yopp Publications
PO Box 1147
Beaufort, SC 29901-1147

843-521-0239
800-849-9677
FAX 800-849-8418

Joe Cronley

Directory of services and supplies to the industry.
Cost: $3.00
Frequency: Annual
Circulation: 3,000

Industry Web Sites

13673 http://gold.greyhouse.com
G.O.L.D Grey House OnLine Databases
Grey House Publishing's online database platform, GOLD, offers Quick Search, Keyword Search and Expert Search for most business sectors including heating and air conditioning markets. The GOLD platform makes finding the information you need quick and easy - whether you're a novice searcher or an experienced database user. All of Grey House's directory products are available for subscription on the GOLD platform.

13674 www.abma.com
American Boiler Manufacturers Association
Manufacturers trade association representing companies involved in utility, industrial and commercial steam generation. Includes associate memberships for companies who sell to or work with these companies and those who own boilers. Holds technical and production conferences, and publishes technical guideline publications.

13675 www.achrnews.com
BNP Media

News, tips and a calendar of events for the heating & cooling industry.

13676 www.aga.com

American Gas Association

Events, publications, information, etc.

13677 www.ari.org

Air Conditioning & Refrigeration Institute

Trade association representing manufacturers of more than 90% of North American produced air-conditioning and commercial refrigeration equipment.

13678 www.asa.net

American Supply Association

The National association of full-service plumbing, heating, cooling, and piping products for wholesalers, manufacturers, and distributors.

13679 www.ashrae.org

American Society of Heating, Refrigeration, AC

Research, activities, education and publications.

13680 www.construction.com

McGraw-Hill Construction (MHC), part of The McGraw-Hill Companies, connects people and projects across the design and construction industry, serving owners, architects, engineers, general contractors, subcontractors, building product manufacturers, suppliers, dealers, distributors and adjacent markets.

13681 www.districtenergy.org

International District Energy Association

Journal of district heating and cooling industry, congeneration, physical plants and energy efficiency. Accepts advertising.

13682 www.gamanet.org

Gas Appliance Manufacturers Association

Represents manufacturers of residential, commercial and industrial gas and oil fired appliances, associated controls and accessories, as well as equipment used in the production, transmission and distribution of fuel gases.

13683 www.greyhouse.com

Grey House Publishing

Authoritative reference directories for most business sectors including heating and air conditioning markets. Users can search the online databases with varied search criteria allowing for custom searches by product category, geographic area, sales volume, keyword, subject and more. Full Grey House catalog and online ordering also available.

13684 www.impi.org

International Microwave Power Institute

IMPI's members include scientists, researchers, lab technicians, product developers, marketing managers and a variety of other professionals in the microwave industry. The Institute serves the information needs of all specialists working with dielectric (microwave and RF) heating sytems, and was expanded in 1977 to meet the information needs relating to consumer microwave ovens and related products.

13685 www.macsw.org

Mobile Air Conditioning Society Worldwide

Information on technical training for professionals in the automotive air-conditioning industry.

13686 www.mha-net.org

Masonry Heater Association of North America

Promotes use of masonry heaters, increases public awareness and encourages reasonable governmental regulation.

13687 www.sweets.construction.com

McGraw Hill Construction

In depth product information that lets you find, compare, select, specify and make purchase decisions in the industrial product marketplace.

Associations

13688 American Camping Association
5000 State Road 67 North
Martinsville, IN 46151-7902

765-342-8456
800-428-2267
FAX 765-342-2065
E-Mail: shallway@aca-camps.org
Home Page: www.acacamps.org
Social Media: *Facebook, Twitter, LinkedIn, YouTube, Pinterest, Google+*

Tisha Bolger, Chair
Rue Mapp, Vice Chair
Craig Whiting, Treasurer
Tom Holland, CEO
Steve Baskin, Board Member
6600+ Members
Founded in 1910
Mailing list available for rent

13689 American Craft Council
1224 Marshall Street NE.
Suite 200
Minneapolis, MN 55413

612-206-3100
800-836-3470
FAX 612-355-2330
E-Mail: council@craftcouncil.org
Home Page: www.craftcouncil.org
Social Media: *Facebook, Twitter, LinkedIn, YouTube, Pinterest, Google+, I*

Stuart Kestenbaum, Board Chair
Gariel Ofiesh, Board Vice Chair
Libba Evans, Board Secretary
Kevin Buchi, Board Treasurer
Barbara Berlin, Board of Trustee Member

National nonprofit, educational organization dedicated to promotion, understanding and appreciation of contemporary American craft. Sponsors annual wholesale and retail shows, a magazine, a library and seminars.
Founded in 1943
Mailing list available for rent

13690 American Home Sewing and Craft Association
PO Box 369
Monroeville, PA 15146

412-372-5950
FAX 212-714-1655
E-Mail: info@sewing.org
Home Page: www.sewing.org

13691 American Philatelic Society
100 Match Factory Place
Bellefonte, PA 16823-1367

814-933-3803
FAX 814-933-6128
E-Mail: webmaster@stamps.org
Home Page: www.stamps.org
Social Media: *Facebook, Twitter, LinkedIn, YouTube, Pinterest*

Stephen Reinhardÿ, President
Scott English, Executive Director
Alex Haimann, Board of Vice Presidents
Yamil Kouri, Board of Vice Presidents
Mick Zais, Board of Vice Presidents

National organization for postage stamp collectors, monthly magazine, the American Philatelist; lending library; insurance for philatelic materials; sales division, seminars and annual conventions open to the public.
32,00 Members
Founded in 1886

13692 American Quilt Study Group
American Quilt Study Group

1610 L Street
Lincoln, NE 68508-2509

402-477-1181
FAX 402-477-1181
E-Mail: aqsg2@americanquiltstudygroup.org
Home Page: www.americanquiltstudygroup.org
Lisa Erlandson, President
Lenna DeMarco, Vice President
Kathy Moore, Vice President
Judy J. Brott Buss, Ph.D., Executive Director
Anne E. Schuff, Member Services Coordinator

Establishes, sustains, and promotes the highest standards for quilt-related studies. We stimulate, nurture, and affirm engagement in quilt studies and provide opportunities for its dissemination.
1000 Members
Founded in 1980
Mailing list available for rent

13693 American Specialty Toy Retailing Association
432 N. Clark St.ÿ
Suite 305
Chicago, IL 60654

312-222-0984
800-591-0490
FAX 312-222-0986
E-Mail: info@astratoy.org
Home Page: www.astratoy.org
Social Media: *Facebook, Twitter*

Dean May, Chair
Michael Levins, Past Chair
Ann Kienzle, Chair Electÿ
Tim Holliday, Treasurer
Erik Quam, Secretary

Providing a unified voice for the specialty toy industry, and opportunities to exchange information and ideas with counterparts. Membership benefits include workshops and seminars, vendor representative roundtables, membership directory and annual convention.
1000 Members
Founded in 1992

13694 American Stamp Dealers Association
PO Box 858
Suite 205
Morris Plains, NJ 07950

973-267-1644
800-369-8207
FAX 800-369-8207
E-Mail: asda@americanstampdealer.com
Home Page: www.asdaonline.com

Mark Reasoner, President
Stanley Piller, Vice President
Richard A. Friedberg, Secretary
James F. Bardo, Treasurer
Robert Prager, Director
800 Members
Founded in 1914

13695 Archery Trade Association
PO Box 70
101 N German St
New Ulm, MN 56073-0070

507-233-8130
866-266-2776
FAX 507-233-8140
E-Mail: jaymcaninch@archerytrade.org
Home Page: www.archerytrade.org
Social Media: *Facebook, Twitter*

Jay McAninch, President/CEO
Kurt Weber, Director of Marketing
Patrick Durkin, Contributing Editor and Writer
Mitch King, Director of Government Relations
John Nelson, Director of Finance and Operations

Provides core funding and direction for two new foundations critical to the future of archery and bowhunting: Arrow Sport and the

Bowhunting Preservation Alliance. In addition the ATA continues to direct the industry's annual archery and bowhunting trade show.
Founded in 1953
Mailing list available for rent

13696 Association of Traditional Hooking Artists
600 1/2 Maple Street
Endicott, NY 13760

E-Mail: jcahill29@aol.com
Home Page: www.rughookersnetwork.com
Social Media: *Facebook*

Joan Cahill, Membership Chairperson
Karen Balon, Guild Secretary
Mary Henck, President

Provides educational material about rug hooking, free patterns, supplies information, chapter/rug camp meetings and teacher information that is not available through any other source. Membership includes all 50 states, England, Japan and Australia.
Founded in 1996

13697 Embroidery Trade Association
PO Box 793967
Dallas, TX 75379-3967

972-247-0415
888-628-2545
FAX 972-755-2561
E-Mail: info@embroiderytrade.org
Home Page: www.embroiderytrade.org

John Swinburn, Executive Director
Dolores Cheek, Director of Membership
Keith Amen, VP

An organization with the objective to continually strengthen the commercial embroidery business.
1200 Members
Founded in 1990

13698 Game Manufacturers Association
240 N. Fifth St.
Suite 340
Columbus, OH 43215

614-255-4500
FAX 614-255-4499
E-Mail: president@gama.org
Home Page: www.gama.org
Social Media: *Facebook*

Justinÿ Ziran, President
Jamie Chambers, Vice President
Aaron Witten, Treasurer
Brian Dalrymple, Secretary
John Ward, Executive Director

A non-profit trade association dedicated to the advancement of the hobby game business.
Founded in 1977
Mailing list available for rent

13699 Hobby Industry Association
319 E 54th Street
Elmwood Park, NJ 07407-2712

201-835-1200
FAX 201-797-0657
E-Mail: info@craftandhobby.org
Home Page: www.craftandhobby.org
Social Media: *Facebook, Twitter, LinkedIn, Pinterest, Youtube*

David Murray, Chair
Mark Hill, Interim President, CEO
Chuck McGonigle, Vice Chair
Natalie Cohn, Vice President, Finance & Admin.
Maureen Walsh, Vice President, Marketing

Trade association in the craft and hobby market. The group produces an international trade

show open to qualified professionals and is the industry's only market research show.
4000 Members
Founded in 1940
Mailing list available for rent

13700 Hobby Manufacturers Association
1410 East Erie Avenue
Philadelphia, PA 07405-0315

267-341-1604
FAX 215-744-4699
E-Mail: heather.stoltzfus@hmahobby.org
Home Page: www.hmahobby.org

Richard Janyszek, President
Bill Jeric, Vice President
Fred Hill, Treasurer
Abby Robey, Secretary
Mike MacDowell, Board of Director

The mission of the Hobby Manufacturers Association is to stimulate the growth of the model hobby industry.
292 Members
Founded in 2005

13701 International Council of Toy Industries
ICTI Secretariat, c/o Toy Industry Association
1115 Broadway, Suite 400
New York, NY 10010

212-675-1141
E-Mail: info@toy-icti.org
Home Page: www.toy-icti.org

May Liang, President

Association of toy brands from 20 countries acting on issues of importance to the toy industry.
Founded in 1975

13702 Major League Gaming
Home Page: www.majorleaguegaming.com
Social Media: *Facebook, Twitter, YouTube*

Sundance DiGiovanni, Co-Founder & CEO
Greg Chisholm, Chief Financial Officer

A professional eSports organization. MLG.tv, its free video streaming eSports showcase, attracts 27 million users per month.
Founded in 2002

13703 Museum Store Association
3773 E. Cherry Creek North Drive
Suite 755
Denver, CO 80209-3804

303-504-9223
FAX 303-504-9585
E-Mail: info@museumstoreassociation.org
Home Page: www.museumdistrict.com
Social Media: *Facebook, Twitter, LinkedIn, Pinterest*

David Duddy, President
Jama Rice, MBA, CAE, Executive Director/ CEO
Stuart Hata, 1st Vice President
Julie Steiner, 2nd Vice President
Alice McAuliffe, Treasurer

Providing member representatives with the professional opportunities and educational resources they need to operate effectively and ethically.
2500 Members
Founded in 1955

13704 National School Supply Equipment Association
8380 Colesville Rd
Suite 250
Silver Spring, MD 20910-6225

301-495-0240
800-395-5550
FAX 301-495-3330
E-Mail: memberservices@nssea.org

Home Page: www.nssea.org
Social Media: *Facebook, Twitter, LinkedIn, Youtube*

Jim McGarry, President/CEO
Bill Duffy, Vice President - Operations
Adrienne Dayton, Vice President - Marketing
Joe Tucker, CEM, CMP, Director of Meetings & Experiences
Michael Nercesian, Exhibits Manager

Trade Association for the educational products industry.
1400+ Members
Founded in 1916

13705 Toy Industry Association
1115 Broadway
Suite 400
New York, NY 10010-3466

212-675-1141
FAX 212-633-1429
E-Mail: info@toyassociation.org
Home Page: www.toyassociation.org/
Social Media: *Facebook, Twitter, LinkedIn, Youtube*

John Gessert, Chairman
David Hargreaves, Vice Chairman
Steve Pasierb, President and CEO
Bob Wann, Secretary-Treasurer
Shirley Price, Member of the Executive Committeeÿ

National organization with toy, game and holiday decoration manufacturers and their representatives, as well as toy designers, testing laboratories, licensors, sales representatives and trade magazines.
400+ Members
Founded in 1916

13706 Western Toy & Hobby Representatives Association
PO Box 2250
Pomona, CA 91786

909-899-3753
FAX 909-697-2014
E-Mail: toyshow@wthra.com
Home Page: www.wthra.com

Phylis St John, Show Director

A nonprofit association organization. Produces and promotes the Western States Toy & Hobby Show.
Founded in 1961

Newsletters

13707 American Stamp Dealers Association Newsletter
American Stamp Dealers Association
3 School St
Suite 205
Glen Cove, NY 11542-2548

516-759-7000
FAX 800-369-8207
Home Page: www.asdaonline.com

Joseph Savarese, Executive VP
Elizabeth Pope, Secretary
Kim Kellermann, Secretary
Thomas Jacks, Treasurer

Association news.
Frequency: Monthly
Circulation: 810
Founded in 1914
Printed in on matte stock

13708 Bill Nelson Newsletter
Nelson Newsletter Publishing Corporation

PO Box 90890
Tucson, AZ 85752-0890

520-297-8240
800-368-8434
FAX 520-629-0387
Home Page: www.billnelsonnewsletter.com/

James Lee, President

Features news on the pin collecting hobby.
Cost: $20.00
8 Pages
Frequency: Monthly
Printed in one color on matte stock

13709 Guild of Natural Science Illustration
Guild of Natural Science Illustrators
PO Box 652
Ben Franklin Station
Washington, DC 20044-652

301-309-1514
FAX 301-309-1514
E-Mail: gnsihome@his.com
Home Page: www.gnsi.org

Gretchen Kai Halpert, President
Erica Beade, Vice President

Non-profit organization for those interested in the field of natural science illustrations. Newsletter is published 10 times a year.
Cost: $75.00
Frequency: 10x Yearly
Circulation: 1000
Founded in 1968

13710 This Time
Homeworkers Organized for More Employment
PO Box 10
Orland, ME 04472

207-469-7961
FAX 207-469-1023
E-Mail: info@homecoop.net
Home Page: www.homecoop.net/

Lucy Toulin, President
J Ralph, Editor
F Eldridge, Volunteer Coordinator

Home community newsletter, part of the world Emmaus movement, offering information on craft store items and antiques. Member of rural coalition , Washington D.C..
Cost: $5.00
16 Pages
Frequency: Quarterly
Circulation: 300
Founded in 1970

Magazines & Journals

13711 ABCs of Retailing
Hobby Industry Association
319 E 54th St
Suite 348
Elmwood Park, NJ 07407-2712

201-794-1133
FAX 201-797-0657
E-Mail: afliss@rfcp.com
Home Page: www.craftandhobby.org

Steve Berger, CEO

Guide to opening and maintaining a craft/hobby retail store.
20 Pages
Founded in 1940

13712 American Craft Magazine
72 Spring St
New York, NY 10012-4090

212-274-0630
FAX 212-274-0650

E-Mail: council@craftcouncil.org
Home Page: www.craftcouncil.org

Andrew Wagner, Manager
John Gourlay, Publisher
Lois Moran, Editor-in-Chief

Celebrates the excellence of contemporary craft, focusing on masterful achievements in the craft media — clay, fiber, metal, glass, wood and other materials — with the goal to create intellectual and visual interest for the reader on today's craft.
Cost: $40.00
Founded in 1943

13713 American Philatelist

American Philatelic Society
100 Match Factory Pl
Bellefonte, PA 16823-1367

814-237-3803
FAX 814-933-6128
E-Mail: kpmartin@stamps.org
Home Page: www.stamps.org

Ken Martin, Executive Director

One hundred page monthly magazine for stamp collectors.
Cost: $80.00
34000 Members
100 Pages
Frequency: Monthly
Circulation: 37500
ISSN: 0003-0473
Founded in 1886

13714 Antiques and Collecting Hobbies

Lightner Publishing Corporation
1006 S Michigan Ave
Chicago, IL 60605-2216

312-939-4767
FAX 312-939-0053

Antiques and collectible news articles.
Cost: $32.00
88 Pages
Frequency: Monthly
Circulation: 18,000
Founded in 1931

13715 Bank Note Reporter

F+W Media
38 E. 29th Street
New York, NY 10016

212-447-1400
FAX 212-447-5231
E-Mail: contact_us@fwmedia.com
Home Page: www.fwpublications.com
Social Media: *Facebook, Twitter, LinkedIn*

Bill Bright, General Manager
Dave Harper, Editor
Buddy Redling, Manager
Chad Phelps, Chief Digital Officer
Stacie Berger, Communications Director

Recognized as the finest publication for paper money collectors available. Contains news on market values, 'Bank Note Clinic' (a collector Q&A), an up-to-date foreign exchange chart, 'Fun Notes' (interesting, odd & unusual notes), a price guide, a world currency section, historical features on paper money worldwide (emphasizing US issues), & hundreds of display & classified ads offering to buy, sell, & trade bank notes of all kinds. Contributors include some of the top experts in the field.
Cost: $21.98
84 Pages
Frequency: Monthly
Circulation: 8072
Founded in 1952
Mailing list available for rent

13716 Blade

F+W Media

38 E. 29th Street
New York, NY 10016

212-447-1400
FAX 212-447-5231
E-Mail: contact_us@fwmedia.com
Home Page: www.fwpublications.com
Social Media: *Facebook, Twitter, LinkedIn*

David Nussbaum, CEO/Chairman
Steve Shackleford, Editor
Jim Ogle, Chief Financial Officer
Chad Phelps, Chief Digital Officer
Stacie Berger, Communications Director

Provides knifemakers, collectors, and knife enthusiasts with information concerning new knife-making techniques and processes, field tests, and the latest news and features on knives and their makers. Also includes a Q&A section, letters to the editor, features about individual knifemakers, an extensive listing of upcoming knife shows, and a reader feature entitled, 'The Knife I Carry.'
Cost: $25.98
140 Pages
Frequency: Monthly
Circulation: 38068
ISSN: 1064-5853
Founded in 1973
Mailing list available for rent

13717 Cast On Magazine

The Knitting Guild Association (TKGA)
1100-H Brandywine Blvd.
Zanesville, OH 43701-7303

740-452-4541
E-Mail: tkga@tkga.com
Home Page: www.tkga.com
Social Media: *Facebook, Twitter, LinkedIn*

Penny Sitler, Executive Director

Educational journal for knitters.
10000 Members
Frequency: Quarterly
Circulation: 11,000
Mailing list available for rent

13718 Coin Prices

F+W Media
38 E. 29th Street
New York, NY 10016

212-447-1400
FAX 212-447-5231
E-Mail: contact_us@fwmedia.com
Home Page: www.fwpublications.com
Social Media: *Facebook, Twitter, LinkedIn*

Bill Bright, General Manager
Bob Van Ryzin, Editor
Jim Ogle, Chief Financial Officer
Chad Phelps, Chief Digital Officer
Stacie Berger, Communications Director

Coin Prices is a complete guide to retail values for collectible US coins. A market update section (value guide) by market editor Joel Edler beings each issue. Rotating special sections provide values for Canadian and Mexican coins, Colonial coins, territorial coins, errors and varieties and selected issues of US paper money. Regular departments include a guide to grading US coins.
Cost: $18.98
96 Pages
Circulation: 56611
Founded in 1952
Mailing list available for rent

13719 Coins

F+W Media
38 E. 29th Street
New York, NY 10016

212-447-1400
FAX 212-447-5231
E-Mail: contact_us@fwmedia.com

Home Page: www.fwpublications.com
Social Media: *Facebook, Twitter, LinkedIn*

Bill Bright, General Manager
Bob Van Ryzin, Editor
Jim Ogle, Chief Financial Officer
Chad Phelps, Chief Digital Officer
Stacie Berger, Communications Director

Covers market trends, buying tips, and historical perspectives on all aspects of numismatics. The news section, 'Bits and Pieces,' wraps up the latest happenings in numismatics. Regular columns and departments include 'Basics& Beyond,' 'Budget Buyer,' 'Coin Clinic' (Q&A), the editor's column, coin finds, a calendar of upcoming shows nationwide, 'Coin Values Guide' and 'Market Watch.'
Cost: $20.98
120 Pages
Frequency: Monthly
Circulation: 52660
Founded in 1955
Mailing list available for rent

13720 Comics & Games Retailer

F+W Media
38 E. 29th Street
New York, NY 10016

212-447-1400
FAX 212-447-5231
E-Mail: contact_us@fwmedia.com
Home Page: www.fwpublications.com
Social Media: *Facebook, Twitter, LinkedIn*

Mark Williams, Publisher
John Miller, Editor
Norma Jean Fochs, Ad Manager

Provides information to retailers about marketing, industry news, and practical how-to tips on selling comics and games at the retail level. Regular columns include 'Suggested for Mature Retailers,' 'Small Store Strategy,' 'Trade Show Calendar,' 'Retailer News,' and 'Distributor News.' Special issue focus on the comic book industry, trade shows, trading cards, gaming, display racks, and other retail store supplies. 'Market Beat' gives a national overview of the comics market.
Cost: $29.95
72 Pages
Frequency: Monthly
Circulation: 5,201
Founded in 1971
Mailing list available for rent

13721 Comics Buyer's Guide

F+W Media
38 E. 29th Street
New York, NY 10016

212-447-1400
FAX 212-447-5231
E-Mail: contact_us@fwmedia.com
Home Page: www.fwpublications.com
Social Media: *Facebook, Twitter, LinkedIn*

David Nussbaum, CEO/Chairman
Maggie Thompson, Editor
Jim Ogle, Chief Financial Officer
Chad Phelps, Chief Digital Officer
Stacie Berger, Communications Director

The longest-running magazine about comic books. Each 200+ page monthly issue features new comic reviews, nostalgic retroviews, interviews and the largest monthly price guide. Aslo included is the latest convention news, opinion pieces from celebrity columnists and expanded coverage of anime, manga and other comics-related auctions.
Cost: $38.95
244 Pages
Frequency: Monthly
Circulation: 30,000
ISSN: 1064-5853
Founded in 1952
Mailing list available for rent

13722 Craftrends

Primedia Enthusiast Group Publishing
741 Corporate Circle
Suite A
Golden, CO 80401

303-278-1010
800-881-6634
FAX 303-277-0370
Home Page: www.craftrends.com

Bill Gardner, Editorial Director
Beth Hess, Managing Editor
Dave O'Neil, VP Group Publishing
Kelly P. Conlin, President/CEO

Includes new products, coverage of industry trade shows, merchandising and promotion ideas. Also has timely information to operate a craft business and stay on top of a rapidly changing retail environment.
Cost: $26.00
Frequency: Monthly
Circulation: 22000
Founded in 1989

13723 Crafts Magazine

Primedia Enthusiast Group Publishing
PO Box 420494
Palm Coast, FL 32142-9524

800-727-2387
FAX 386-447-2321
E-Mail: papercrafts@palmcoastd.com
Home Page: www.craftsmag.com

Valerie Pingree, Editor-in-Chief
Mike Irish, Associate Publisher
Kelly P Conlin, CEO/President

Monthly craft consumer magazine reaching the crafting enthusiast.
Cost: $15.97
112 Pages
Circulation: 300272
ISSN: 0148-9127
Founded in 1989
Printed in 4 colors on glossy stock

13724 Crafts Report

Crafts Reports Publishing
100 Rogers Road
Wilmington, DE 19801

302-656-2209
800-777-7098
FAX 302-656-4894
E-Mail: theeditor@craftsreport.com
Home Page: www.craftsreport.com

Lammot Copeland Jr, Publisher
Heather Skelly, Editor
Stewart Abowitz, Marketing Director
Deborah Copeland, Co-Publisher

Monthly business magazine for the crafts professional, providing information on marketing, growing your craft business, time management, studio safety, retail relationships, artist/retailer profiles, show listings and more.
Cost: $29.00
Frequency: Monthly
Circulation: 30000
ISSN: 0160-7650
Founded in 1975
Printed in 4 colors on glossy stock

13725 Creative Knitting

House of White Birches
306 E Parr Rd
Berne, IN 46711-1100

260-589-8741
800-829-5865
FAX 260-589-8093
E-Mail: customer_service@drgbooks.com
Home Page: www.whitebirches.com

David J McKee, CEO
John Boggs, Advertising Sales Director
Carl Musselman, Editor

David J McKee, Publishing Director
Greg Deily, Marketing Director

Serves the knitting industry.
Cost: $13.00
64 Pages
Frequency: Monthly
Founded in 1947

13726 Doll Artisan

Jones Publishing
N7 450 Aanstad Road
PO Box 5000
Iola, WI 54945-5000

715-445-5000
FAX 715-445-4053
E-Mail: joejones@jonespublishing.com
Home Page: www.dollmakingartisian.com

Edited to entertain, fascinate and educate the doll maker in reproduction of antique porcelain dolls. Encourages and promotes efforts to make porcelain doll making easier, safer and more accessible to a growing number of enthusiasts.
Cost: $5.95
Frequency: Bi-Monthly

13727 Doll World

Jones Publishing
N7 450 Aanstad Road
PO Box 5000
Iola, WI 54945-5000

715-445-5000
800-331-0038
FAX 715-445-4053
E-Mail: jonespub@jonespublishing.com
Home Page: www.jonespublishing.com

Joe Jones, President
Nayda Rondon, Editor
Trina Laube, Assistant Editor
Virginia Adams, Marketing
Brandan Hardie, Circulation Manager
Cost: $32.95
Frequency: Monthly

13728 Dollmaking

Jones Publishing
N7 450 Aanstad Road
PO Box 5000
Iola, WI 54945-5000

715-445-5000
FAX 715-445-4053
E-Mail: jonespub@jonespublishing.com
Home Page: www.Dollmaking/Artisan.com

Resource for makers of porcelain and sculpted modern dolls, is edited for the serious costume and doll maker.
Cost: $4.95
Frequency: Bi-Monthly

13729 Essentials Magazine

National School Supply Equipment
8300 Colesville Rd
Suite 250
Silver Spring, MD 20910-6225

301-495-0240
800-395-5550
FAX 301-495-3330
E-Mail: customerservice@nssea.org
Home Page: www.nssea.org
Social Media: *Facebook, Twitter, LinkedIn*

Jim McGarry, President/CEO
Rashad Cheeks, Meetings Coordinator
Tamara Davis, Bookkeeper/Office Manager
Karen Prince, Director of Membership
Bill Duffy, Vice President - Operations

13730 Family Tree

B&W Publications

1507 Dana Avenue
Cincinnati, OH 45207-1056

513-943-9464
FAX 513-531-1843

Ideas and advice for discovering, preserving and celebrating family history.

13731 Family Tree Magazine

F+W Media
38 E. 29th Street
New York, NY 10016

212-447-1400
FAX 212-447-5231
E-Mail: contact_us@fwmedia.com
Home Page: www.fwpublications.com
Social Media: *Facebook, Twitter, LinkedIn*

David Nussbaum, CEO/Chairman
Allison Stacy, Editor
Kelly Klener, Marketing
Chad Phelps, Chief Digital Officer
Stacie Berger, Communications Director

America's most popular family history magazine. It covers all areas of potential interest to family history enthusiasts, reaching beyond strict genealogy research to include ethnic heritage, family reunions, memoirs, oral history, scrapbooking, historical travel and other ways that families connect with their pasts. Each issue features the latest tools, how-to tips and expert advice to guide readers through the journey of discovering, preserving and celebrating their roots.
Cost: $27.00
84 Pages
Circulation: 80050
Founded in 1952
Mailing list available for rent

13732 Fine Woodworking

Taunton Press
63 S Main Street
PO Box 5506
Newtown, CT 06470-5506

203-270-6206
800-926-8776
FAX 203-426-3434
E-Mail: fw@taunton.com
Home Page: www.taunton.com

David Grey, Publisher
Linda Abbett, Advertising Manager
Anatole Burkin, Editor
John Lagan, National Account Manager

Published since 1975, written by woodworkers for woodworkers regularly shows the finest work in wood being done today.
Cost: $34.95
120 Pages
Circulation: 295000
Founded in 1975
Mailing list available for rent: 185M names
Printed in 4 colors on glossy stock

13733 Gun Digest

F+W Media
38 E. 29th Street
New York, NY 10016

212-447-1400
FAX 212-447-5231
E-Mail: contact_us@fwmedia.com
Home Page: www.fwpublications.com
Social Media: *Facebook, Twitter, LinkedIn*

David Nussbaum, CEO/Chairman
Steve Hudziak, Marketing
Jim Ogle, Chief Financial Officer
Chad Phelps, Chief Digital Officer
Stacie Berger, Communications Director

An all-advertising, nationwide marketplace for buyers and sellers of new, used and antique firearms. Display advertising from the nation's top dealers, manufacturers, distributors, and suppliers is found in each bi-weekly issue,

along with thousands of classified word ads, organized alphabetically, from collectors all over the world. The nation's leading indexed firearms paper. Hundreds of gun show listings and knife show listings are included to help readers schedule their show attendance.
Cost: $37.98
136 Pages
Circulation: 81120
Founded in 1952
Mailing list available for rent

13734 HIA Craft/Hobby Consumer Study

Hobby Industry Association
319 E 54th St
Elmwood Park, NJ 07407-2712

201-794-1133
FAX 201-797-0657
E-Mail: info@craftandhobby.org
Home Page: www.craftandhobby.org

Steve Berger, CEO

An extensive study of consumer behavior and buying habits relevant to the hobby/craft/creative industry. Executive summary is available on-line.
Cost: $400.00
Circulation: 5000
Founded in 2004

13735 Hobby Merchandiser

Hobby Publications
207 Commercial Court
PO Box 102
Morganville, NJ 07751-102

732-536-5160
800-969-7176
FAX 732-536-5761
E-Mail: info@hobbymerchandiser.com
Home Page: www.hobbymerchandiser.com/

Robert Gherman, Publisher
Jeff Troy, Editor
Patrick Sarver, Associate Publisher

Trade magazine for the model hobby industry, available to professionals only.
Cost: $20.00
96 Pages
Frequency: Monthly
Circulation: 7000
ISSN: 0744-1738
Founded in 1947
Mailing list available for rent: 8,300 names at $241 per M
Printed in 4 colors on glossy stock

13736 Hobby Rocketry

California Rocketry Publishing
PO Box 1242
Claremont, CA 91711-1242

760-389-2233
FAX 661-824-0868
E-Mail: info@v-serv.com
Home Page: www.v-serv.com/crp

Jerry Irvine, Publisher

Covers consumer rocket products which are available in hobby, toy and retail outlets. Product reviews, manufacturers notes, consumer feedback and more. Back issues available.
Cost: $16.00
16 Pages
Frequency: Quarterly
Circulation: 8M
Founded in 1992
Printed in on newsprint stock

13737 Horizons

Hobby Industry Association

319 E 54th St
Elmwood Park, NJ 07407-2712

201-794-1133
FAX 201-797-0657
Home Page: www.craftandhobby.org

Steve Berger, CEO

Available only to members of the Hobby Association of America. This magazine offers information and updates on what is happening in the industry.
6 Pages
Frequency: Quarterly

13738 Master Embroidery Manual

Embroidery Trade Association
P.O. Box 794534
Suite 414
Dallas, TX 75379-4534

972-247-0415
888-628-2545
FAX 972-755-2561
E-Mail: info@embroiderytrade.org
Home Page: www.embroiderytrade.org
Social Media: *Twitter, LinkedIn*

John Swinburn, Executive Director
Dolores Cheek, Director Of Membership
Keith Amen, VP

Developed and published by ETA, this manual is an embroiderer's encyclopedia, especially for those new to the embroidery industry. Chapters include hooping & framing, backings & toppings, common goods and fabrics, and much more.
1200 Members
Founded in 1990

13739 Model Retailer

Kalmbach Publishing Company
21027 Crossroads Circle
PO Box 1612
Waukesha, WI 53187

262-796-8776
800-533-6644
FAX 262-796-8776
E-Mail: hmiller@modelretailer.com
Home Page: www.modelretailer.com

Kevin Keefe, Publisher
Hal Miller, Editor
Rick Albers, Advertising Sales Manager
Jim Meinhardt, Circulation Manager

The business of hobbies, from financial and shop management issues to industry news and trends, as well as the latest in product releases. Provides hobby shop entreprenuers with the information, ideas and examples they need in order to be successful retailers.
Frequency: Monthly
Circulation: 6350
Founded in 1934

13740 Needlework Retailer

Yarn Tree Designs
117 Alexander Avenue
PO Box 2438
Ames, IA 50010-2438

515-232-3121
800-247-3952
FAX 515-232-0789
E-Mail: info@needleworkretailer.com
Home Page: www.needleworkretailer.com

Larry Johnson, VP
Megan Chriswisser, Editor

Highlights a variety of new products and designs in needlework. Includes information on upcoming needlework trade shows and association news.
Cost: $12.00
Circulation: 11000

13741 Numismatic News

F+W Media

38 E. 29th Street
New York, NY 10016

212-447-1400
FAX 212-447-5231
E-Mail: contact_us@fwmedia.com
Home Page: www.fwpublications.com
Social Media: *Facebook, Twitter, LinkedIn*

Bill Bright, General Manager
Dave Harper, Editor
Jim Ogle, Chief Financial Officer
Chad Phelps, Chief Digital Officer
Stacie Berger, Communications Director

Provides timely reports on market happenings and news concerning collectible coins. 'Coin Clinic' is a very popular weekly Q&A column that gives readers a chance to learn all about numismatics. The 'Coin Market' section provides comprehensive pricing monthly. Each issue also includes columns with practical how-to advice and historical features by some of the top experts in the field including 'Making the Grade' and 'Facts about Fakes.' Sponsors the annual Mid-America Coin Convention.
Cost: $35.99
72 Pages
Frequency: Weekly
Circulation: 34392
Founded in 1952
Mailing list available for rent

13742 Play Meter

Skybird Publishing Company
PO Box 337
Metairie, LA 70004-0337

504-488-7003
888-473-2376
FAX 504-488-7083
E-Mail: news@playmeter.com
Home Page: www.playmeter.com
Social Media: *Facebook, Twitter, LinkedIn*

Bonnie Theard, Editor
Carol P. Lally, Publisher
Carol Ann Lally, President
Bonnie Theard, Managing Editor
Courtney McDuff, Assistant Editor

Trade publication that provides members with information on the coin-operated entertainment industry, including upcoming trade shows, new products, ongoing trends and more.
Cost: $60.00
Frequency: Monthly
Circulation: 60000
Founded in 1974

13743 Playthings

Reed Business Information
360 Park Ave S
4th Floor
New York, NY 10010-1737

646-746-6400
800-309-3332
FAX 646-756-7583
E-Mail: mlaporte@reedbusiness.com
Home Page: www.reedbusiness.com
Social Media: *Twitter, LinkedIn*

John Poulin, CEO
Larry Oliver, VP/Group Publisher
Micki LaPorte, Circulation Director
James Reed, Owner
Andrew Rak, Senior Vice President

Emphasizes a merchandising approach for improving sales and promotional techniques. Features include new product listings, market reports, licensing updates and general industry trends.
Cost: $33.95
80 Pages
Frequency: Monthly
Founded in 1903
Printed in 4 colors on glossy stock

13744 SCRYE
F+W Media
38 E. 29th Street
New York, NY 10016

212-447-1400
FAX 212-447-5231
E-Mail: contact_us@fwmedia.com
Home Page: www.fwpublications.com
Social Media: *Facebook, Twitter, LinkedIn*

Mark Williams, Publisher
Joyce Greenholdt, Editor
Jim Ogle, Chief Financial Officer
Chad Phelps, Chief Digital Officer
Stacie Berger, Communications Director

The most respected price guide in the industry for collectible card games and collectible miniatures. SCRYE also provides collectors and players the latest news, checklists, player strategies, deck building tips and tricks for collectible card games. The latest collectible card games are reviewed in each issue in addition to related role-playing and board games.
Cost: $29.98
160 Pages
Frequency: Monthly
Circulation: 47000
Founded in 1994
Mailing list available for rent

13745 Snapshot Memories
PRIMEDIA Consumer Magazine & Internet Group
2 News Plaza
PO Box 1790
Peoria, IL 61656-1790

309-682-6626
FAX 309-679-5057

Mike Irish, Associate Publisher
Miram Olson, Editor-in-Chief
Scrapbook page idea magazine.
Cost: $16.98
92 Pages
Frequency: Quarterly
Circulation: 90,000
Founded in 1998
Printed in 4 colors on glossy stock

13746 Sports Collectors Digest
F+W Media
38 E. 29th Street
New York, NY 10016

212-447-1400
FAX 212-447-5231
E-Mail: contact_us@fwmedia.com
Home Page: www.fwpublications.com
Social Media: *Facebook, Twitter, LinkedIn*

Dean Listle, Publisher
TS O'Connell, Editor
Jim Ogle, Chief Financial Officer
Chad Phelps, Chief Digital Officer
Stacie Berger, Communications Director

The Bible of Hobby covers every aspect of modern sports collecting, including cards, memorabilia, equipment, lithographs, figurines, and autographed material. Online collecting, graded cards, memorabilia and auction news are covered each week in specially designed sections that complement columns from some of the most respected experts in the hobby and up-to-date card pricing checklisting data from expert analysts, along with display advertisements from all the major dealers in the country.
Cost: $49.95
96 Pages
Frequency: Weekly
Circulation: 23356
Founded in 1973
Mailing list available for rent

13747 Stamp Collector
F+W Media

38 E. 29th Street
New York, NY 10016

212-447-1400
FAX 212-447-5231
E-Mail: contact_us@fwmedia.com
Home Page: www.fwpublications.com
Social Media: *Facebook, Twitter, LinkedIn*

Wayne Youngblood, Publisher
Jill Ruesch, Ad Manager
Jim Ogle, Chief Financial Officer
Chad Phelps, Chief Digital Officer
Stacie Berger, Communications Director

Covers a wide variety of US & foreign stamp news. Sepcial inserts cover topicals, errors, postal history, and many others. Regular columns and features include 'Decoding the Catalog,' 'Q&A,' 'Meet the Designer,' 'Postal History,' 'New Stamps of the World,' 'Stamp Values Today,' an auction guide and the most extensive stamp show calendar in the hobby. The first issue each month cotains Stamp Wholesaler - stamp dealer info that is used as a 'philatelic phone book' by the entire industry.
Cost: $32.98
60 Pages
Circulation: 13251
Founded in 1931
Mailing list available for rent

13748 Stitches
Advertising Specialty Institute
4800 E Street Rd
Langhorne, PA 19053-6698

215-953-4000
800-546-1350
FAX 215-953-3045
E-Mail: info@asicentral.com
Home Page: www.asicentral.com
Social Media: *Facebook*

Timothy M Andrews, CEO

The voice and vision of the embroidery industry and the single most referenced magazine in the business.
Frequency: 13x/Year
Circulation: 40000

13749 Tole World
EGW.com
4075 Papazian Way
Suite 208
Fremont, CA 94538-4372

510-668-0268
FAX 510-668-0280
Home Page: www.toleworld.com

Chris Slaughter, VP
Rickie Wilson, Advertisement Manager

Serving crafters in the decorative painting field; each issue features 10 to 12 projects complete with full color photographs, step-by-step instructions and line art patterns. Project designs come from the nation's leading decorative artists, many of whom are also teachers in the field.
Cost: $35.94
84 Pages
Frequency: Quarterly
Circulation: 85956
Founded in 1977

13750 Toy Book
Adventure Publishing Group
1107 Broadway
Suite 1204
New York, NY 10010

212-575-4510
FAX 212-575-4521
Home Page: www.adventurepub.com

Owen Shorts, Owner
Nelson Lombardi, Editor
A Schwartz, Marketing
Anthony Guardiola, Production Manager

Keeps readers abreast of new products and marketing information related to the industry.
Cost: $48.00
Frequency: Monthly
Circulation: 18000
Founded in 1980

13751 Toy Shop
F+W Media
38 E. 29th Street
New York, NY 10016

212-447-1400
FAX 212-447-5231
E-Mail: contact_us@fwmedia.com
Home Page: www.fwpublications.com
Social Media: *Facebook, Twitter, LinkedIn*

Mark Williams, Publisher
Tom Bartsch, Editor
David Nussbaum, CEO/Chairman
Chad Phelps, Chief Digital Officer
Stacie Berger, Communications Director

A complete marketplace for buyers and sellers of toys, action figures, Barbie, Hot Wheels, character toys, and more. Offers thousands of easy-to-read, categorized classified ads, display ads, and a complete editorial package covering baby-boomer collectibles, vintage collectibles, TV toys, action figures, and many helpful Q&A columns. Also contains up-to-date market trends as well as thorough auction updates and reports from toy shows nationwide.
Cost: $33.98
76 Pages
Circulation: 11577
Founded in 1988
Mailing list available for rent

13752 Trapper & Predator
F+W Media
38 E. 29th Street
New York, NY 10016

212-447-1400
FAX 212-447-5231
E-Mail: contact_us@fwmedia.com
Home Page: www.fwpublications.com
Social Media: *Facebook, Twitter, LinkedIn*

Hugh McAloon, Publisher
Paul Wait, Editor
Jim Ogle, Chief Financial Officer
Chad Phelps, Chief Digital Officer
Stacie Berger, Communications Director

Contains news, in-depth features, and how-to tips on trapping, the art of predator calling, and animal damage control. Contributors include the top names in the business. Regular columns and departments include 'The Fure Shed,' 'Let's Swap Ideas,' 'Q&A,' and news from state trapping associations nationwide.
Cost: $18.95
80 Pages
Circulation: 38260
Founded in 1975
Mailing list available for rent

13753 Tuff Stuff
F+W Media
38 E. 29th Street
New York, NY 10016

212-447-1400
FAX 212-447-5231
E-Mail: contact_us@fwmedia.com
Home Page: www.fwpublications.com
Social Media: *Facebook, Twitter, LinkedIn*

Dean Listle, Publisher
Rocky Landsverk, Editor
Jim Ogle, Chief Financial Officer
Chad Phelps, Chief Digital Officer
Stacie Berger, Communications Director

A guide to the sports card and collectibles hobby. Coverage of sports cards includes the latest prices on baseball, football, basketball, hockey, racing, and more. Each issue lists pric-

ing information on Hall of Fame baseball and football memorabilia, autographed items, and commentary on the sports card industry. Columns and opinion pieces include a Q&A section, directories to professional teams, geographical and product directories, and hobby dealer listings for the US and Canada.
Cost: $29.95
Frequency: Monthly
Circulation: 175,682
Founded in 1983
Mailing list available for rent

13754 Turkey & Turkey Hunting
F+W Media
38 E. 29th Street
New York, NY 10016

212-447-1400
FAX 212-447-5231
E-Mail: contact_us@fwmedia.com
Home Page: www.fwpublications.com
Social Media: *Facebook, Twitter, LinkedIn*

David Nussbaum, CEO/Chairman
James Schlender, Editor
Jim Ogle, Chief Financial Officer
Chad Phelps, Chief Digital Officer
Stacie Berger, Communications Director

Edited for serious, technical, year-round, gun and bow turkey hunters. Features emphasize success and enjoyment of the sport. Articles focus on hunting, scouting, turkey behavior and biology, hunting ethics, new equipment, methodologies, turkey management, and current research. Columns include 'Tree Call,' 'Mail Pouch,' 'Turkey Biology,' a Q&A column, 'Hunter's Library,' 'Turkey Gear,' and 'Last Call.'
Cost: $15.95
72 Pages
Circulation: 68962
Founded in 1975
Mailing list available for rent

13755 Weekend Woodcrafts
EGW.com
1041 Shary Circle
Concord, CA 94518-2407

925-671-9852
FAX 925-671-0692
E-Mail: info@egw.com
Home Page: www.weekendwoodcrafts.com

Chris Slaughter, Circulation Director
Rickie Wilson, Advertising

Wide selection of easy-to-finish wood projects ranging from craft fair novelties and decorative home-accents to useful housewares and wooden toys.
Cost: $35.94
68 Pages
Frequency: Monthly
Founded in 1980

13756 Wood Strokes
EGW.com
1041 Shary Circle
Concord, CA 94518-2407

925-671-9852
FAX 925-671-0692
E-Mail: info@egw.com
Home Page: www.egw.com

Chris Slaughter, Circulation Manager

Wide selection of easy-to-finish decorative wood painting projects ranging from craft fair novelties and decorative home accents to useful housewares and wooden toys.
Cost: $5.99
76 Pages
Circulation: 110437

13757 World Coin News
F+W Media

38 E. 29th Street
New York, NY 10016

212-447-1400
FAX 212-447-5231
E-Mail: contact_us@fwmedia.com
Home Page: www.fwpublications.com
Social Media: *Facebook, Twitter, LinkedIn*

Bill Bright, General Manager
Dave Harper, Editor
Jim Ogle, Chief Financial Officer
Chad Phelps, Chief Digital Officer
Stacie Berger, Communications Director

Recognized as the leading authority on world coins. It regularly reports on new issues, auctions and other coin news from around the world. Features by some of the top experts in the field provide in-depth historical information on coins and the countries that issue them. Regular features include World Coin Clinic (Q&A), World Coin Roundup (newly issued coins), Rule Britannia, Nautical Numismatics, Mexican Potpourri, and Coin Critters. Each issue provides a calendar of shows.
Cost: $30.99
84 Pages
Frequency: Monthly
Circulation: 8729
Founded in 1952
Mailing list available for rent

Trade Shows

13758 ACC Craft Show
American Craft Council
21 S Eltings Corner Road
Highland, NY 12528

845-883-6100
800-836-3670
FAX 845-883-6130
E-Mail: shows@craftcouncil.org
Home Page: www.craftcouncil.org

Craft fair.
Frequency: Annual

13759 APS Stampshow
American Philatelic Society
100 Match Factory Place
Ballefonte, PA 16823

814-373-3803
FAX 814-933-6128
E-Mail: stampshow@stamps.org
Home Page: www.stamps.org

Kenneth P Martin, Executive Director
Dana Guyer, Shows/Exhibits

Annual show for postage stamp collectors. Includes 150 dealers buying and selling material, more than 100 seminars, and 10,000 pages of stamps in collection.
6,000 Attendees
Frequency: Annual

13760 AQSG Conference and Annual Meeting
American Quilt Study Group
1610 L St
Lincoln, NE 68508-2509

402-477-1181
FAX 402-477-1183
E-Mail: aqsg2@americanquiltstudygroup.org
Home Page: www.americanquiltstudygroup.org
Social Media: *Twitter, LinkedIn*

Lisa Erlandsonn, President
Lenna DeMarco, VP
Flavin Glover, VP
Judy J. Brott Buss, Ph.D., Executive Director
Anne E. Schuff, Member Services Coordinator

For members. Research presentations and quilt and textile study
200 Attendees
Frequency: Annual
Mailing list available for rent

13761 ASD/AMD Group
Flectcher
2950 31st Street
Suite 100
Santa Monica, CA 90405

310-255-4633
FAX 310-396-8476

15000 Attendees

13762 AmeriStamp Expo
American Philatelic Society
100 Match Factory Place
Bellafonte, PA 16823

814-373-3803
FAX 814-933-6128
E-Mail: stampshow@stamps.org
Home Page: www.stamps.org

Ken Martin, Director Shows/Exhibitions

Annual event for postage stamp collectors, featuring 75 dealers, 50 meetings and services, auction, 5,000 pages of exhibits and beginner actions.
2,500 Attendees
Frequency: Annual
Founded in 1998

13763 American Camping Association Conference & Exhibits
5000 State Road 67 N
Martinsville, IN 46151-7902

765-342-8456
800-428-2267
FAX 765-342-2065
E-Mail: bwilliems@aca-camps.org
Home Page: http://www.acacamps.org

Peg Smith, CEO
Bill Willems, Director Business

One hundred fifty booths of arts and crafts, computer software, sporting goods, waterfront equipment and more plus a seminar and workshop.
1,200 Attendees
Frequency: Annual
Founded in 1943

13764 American Craft Council Fairs
ACC
21 S Elting Corners Road
Highland, NY 12528-2805

845-883-6100
800-836-3470
FAX 612-355-2330
E-Mail: shows@craftcouncil.org
Home Page: www.craftcouncil.org

Nine fairs nationwide each year. Each show incorporates crafts from the ceramics, wood, metal, mixed media, fiber, glass, jewelry, accessories and related industries. Most fairs include retail portion (public sales); some fairs also have wholesale (trade) component.

13765 American International Toy Fair
Toy Industry Association
1115 Broadway
Suite 400
New York, NY 10010

212-675-1141
FAX 212-675-3246
Home Page: www.toy-tia.org

Laura Green, VP Trade Shows/Meetings
Diane Cardinale, Public Information Manager

1,800-2,000 booths for producers of all types of toys and games, party and holiday items, models, hobby products, as well as collectibles,

dolls, plush and miniatures. Attendees are retail buyers and trade professionals. Seminar and program.
20000 Attendees
Frequency: Annual
Founded in 1903

13766 American Needlepoint Guild Show
3410 Valley Creek Circle
Middleton, WI 53562-1990

608-831-3328
FAX 608-831-0651
E-Mail: seminars@needlepoint.org
Home Page: www.needlepoint.org

Estelle Kelley, Seminars Director

Two hundred exhibits of needlework pieces, banquet and luncheon.
830 Attendees
Frequency: Annual
Founded in 1972

13767 American Numismatic Association Trade Show
8181 N Cascade Avenue
Colorado Springs, CO 80903

719-632-2646
E-Mail: webmaster@money.org
Home Page: www.money.org

Brenda Bishop, Show Manager
Nancy Green, Manager

Four hundred twenty five booths of coins, medals and paper money.
15M Attendees
Frequency: August

13768 American Quilt Study Group
American Quilt Study Group
1610 L St
Lincoln, NE 68508-2509

402-477-1181
FAX 402-477-1181
E-Mail: aqsg2@americanquiltstudygroup.org
Home Page: www.americanquiltstudygroup.org
Social Media: *Twitter, LinkedIn*

Lisa Erlandsonn, President
Lenna DeMarco, Vice President
Kathy Moore, VP
Judy J. Brott Buss, Ph.D., Executive Director
Anne E. Schuff, Member Services Coordinator

Annual Seminar, Annual Journal member organization
Frequency: October, Kansas
Founded in 1980
Mailing list available for rent

13769 American Stamp Dealers Association Stamp Shows
3 School Street
Suite 201
Glen Cove, NY 11542-2548

516-759-7000
FAX 800-369-8207

Joseph Savarese, Show Manager/Executive VP

Two hundred booths.
12.5M Attendees

13770 Americover
American First Day Cover Society
PO Box 1335
Maplewood, NJ 07040

973-762-2012
FAX 973-762-7916
E-Mail: webmaster@afdcs.org
Home Page: www.afdcs.org

Steve Ripley, Show Manager

US and international first day postal covers, USPS first day ceremonies at most shows, 50

stamp dealers, cover dealers, cachetmalchers philatelic suppliers.
1500 Attendees
Frequency: Annual

13771 Annual Spring-Easter Arts & Crafts Show & Sale
Finger Lakes Craftsmen Shows
1 Freshour Road
Shortsville, NY 14548

585-289-9439
FAX 585-289-9440

Ronald L Johnson, President

Annual show of 150 exhibitirs of arts and crafts manufacturers. Exhibits include hand-crafted arts and crafts, including photos and prints.
9000 Attendees
Frequency: March
Founded in 1999

13772 Antique Arms Show
P.O. Box 2917
Cathedral City, CA 92234

760- 20- 448
FAX 760-202-4793
Home Page: www.antiquearmsshow.com

Wallace Beinfield

Public show with 850 booths of antiques and collectibles.
4M Attendees
Frequency: January

13773 Association of Crafts and Creative Industries Show: ACCI Show
Offinger Management Company
1100-H Brandywine Boulevard
PO Box 3388
Zanesville, OH 43702

740-452-4541
888-360-2224
FAX 740-452-2552
E-Mail: accishow@offinger.com
Home Page: www.accicrafts.org
Social Media: *Facebook, Twitter, LinkedIn*

Marrijane Jones, Executive Director
Erica McKenzie, ACCI Communications Manager

The ACCI Show is sponsored by the Association of Crafts and Creative Industries. Over 1,300 booths are represented, featuring general crafts, softcrafts, art materials and framing, scrapbooking materials and floral, home and garden items.
8000+ Attendees
Frequency: Annual

13774 Christmas Gift & Hobby Show
HSI Show Productions
PO Box 502797
Indianapolis, IN 46250

317-576-9933
800-215-1700
FAX 317-576-9955
E-Mail: info@hsishows.com
Home Page: www.hsishows.com

Donell Hebererwalton, Sales Director
Todd Jameson, Show Manager
45000 Attendees

13775 Christmas Gift and Hobby Show
HSI Show Productions
PO Box 502797
Indianapolis, IN 46250-7797

317-576-9933
800-215-1700
FAX 317-576-9955

E-Mail: info@hsishows.com
Home Page: www.hsishows.com

Donell Hebererwalton, Sales Director
Todd Jameson, Show Manager

Annual show of 360 exhibitors of arts, crafts and giftware.
70M Attendees

13776 Coin and Stamp Exposition: San Francisco
Bick International
PO Box 854
Van Nuys, CA 91408

818-997-6496
FAX 818-988-4337
E-Mail: iibick@sbcglobal.net
Home Page: www.bick.net

Israel I Bick, Managing Director
5000 Attendees
Frequency: June/September, Annually

13777 Doll, Teddy Bear & Toy Show & Sale
Jones Publishing
9572 Forest Hills Lodge & Route 173
Rockford, IL 54945-5000

715-445-5000

JoAnn Reynolds, Contact

Great assortment of toys featuring teddy bears of all kinds.

13778 Eastern States Doll, Toy, and Teddy Bear Show and Sale
Maven Company
PO Box 937
Plandome, NY 11030

914-248-4646
FAX 914-248-0800
Home Page: www.mavencompany.com

N Chittenden, VP

Wide variety of dolls, toys and teddy bears. Largest show of its kind in the northeast.
5000 Attendees
Frequency: November/April
Founded in 1982

13779 Ed Expo
National School Supply & Equipment Association
8380 Colesville Road
Suite 250
Silver Spring, MD 20910

301-495-0240
800-395-5550
FAX 301-495-3330
E-Mail: nssea@nssea.org
Home Page: www.nssea.org

Bill Duffy, VP Operations
Adrienne Dayton, VP Marketing

The world's premier back-to-school purchasing event, specifically geared toward helping the educational products/parent-teacher retailer, cataloger and full-line distributor find the best teaching tools and resources for the classrooms of today, tomorrow and the future.
3000 Attendees
Frequency: Annual/April

13780 Evolution Championship Series
Home Page: evo.shoryuken.com
Social Media: *Facebook, Twitter*

Annual open eSports tournament focused on fighting games.
Frequency: Annual
Founded in 1996

13781 HIA: Hobby Industries of America Trade Show
Hobby Industries of America

319 E 54th Street
PO Box 348
Elmwood Park, NJ 07407

201-794-1133
FAX 201-798-0657
E-Mail: sberger@craftandhobby.org
Home Page: www.hobby.org

Steve Berger, Executive Director
International trade show open to qualified professionals and is the industry's only market research show.
10000 Attendees

13782 Halloween Costume and Party Show
TransWorld Exhibits
1850 Oak Street
Northfield, IL 60093

847-784-6905
800-323-5462
FAX 847-446-3523
Home Page: www.transworldexhibits.com

Don Olstinske, Manager
Stephanie Geitner, Operations Director

13783 International Coin + Stamp Collection Society
Bick International
PO Box 854
Van Nuys, CA 91408

818-997-6496
FAX 818-988-4337
E-Mail: iibick@sbcglobal.net
Home Page: www.bick.net

Israel I Bick, Managing Director
5000 Attendees
Frequency: Annual/December/May, NV

13784 International Gift and Collectible Expo
F+W Media
38 E. 29th Streett
New York, NY 10016

212-447-1400
FAX 212-447-5231
E-Mail: contact_us@fwmedia.com
Home Page: www.fwpublications.com
Social Media: *Twitter, LinkedIn*

Claude Chmiel, Show Producer
John Swinburn, Executive Director
17000 Attendees
Frequency: June

13785 International JPMA Show
Juvenile Products Manufacturers Association
15000 Commerce Parkway
Suite C
Mt Laurel, NJ 08054

856-439-0500
FAX 856-439-0525
Home Page: www.jpma.org

Linda Still, Director of Trade Show
Items of interest to retailers of children's apparel and toys.
3000 Attendees
Frequency: Annual

13786 International Miniature Collectibles Trade Show
10 Estes Street
Ipswich, MA 1938

978-356-6500
800-653-2726
FAX 978-356-6565
Home Page: www.connection.ebscohost.com
Social Media: *Facebook, Twitter, LinkedIn*

Frequency: August

13787 Just Kidstuff & The Museum Source
George Little Management
10 Bank Street
Suite 1200
White Plains, NY 10606

914-486-6070
800-272-7469
FAX 914-948-2918

George Little II, President
45000 Attendees

13788 Knitting Guild Association Conference
The Knitting Guild Association (TKGA)
1100-H Brandwine Blvd.
Zanesville, OH 43701-7303

740-452-4541
FAX 740-452-2552
E-Mail: tkga@tkga.com
Home Page: www.tkga.com
Social Media: *Facebook, Twitter, LinkedIn*

Penny Sitler, Executive Director

The TKGA conference is held twice each year and offers items such as fiber, stitching tools, patterns, books, finishing accessories and more.
10000 Members
Mailing list available for rent

13789 National Dollhouse & Miniatures Trade Show & Convention
Miniatures Association of America
10 Estes Street
Ipswich, MA 1938

978-356-6500
800-653-2726
FAX 978-356-6565
Home Page: www.connection.ebscohost.com
Social Media: *Facebook, Twitter, LinkedIn*

1400 Attendees

13790 National Merchandise Show
Miller Freeman Publications
One Penn Plaza
PO Box 2549
New York, NY 10119

212-714-1300
FAX 212-714-1313

16000 Attendees

13791 National NeedleArts Association Trade Show
National Needlework Association
PO Box 3388
Zanesville, OH 43702-3388

740-452-4541
800-889-8662
FAX 740-452-2552
E-Mail: tnna.info@offinger.com
Home Page: www.tnna.org

Joel Woodcock, VP
Frequency: January

13792 National Sewing Show: Home Sewing Association
American Home Sewing and Craft Association
1350 Broadway
Suite 1601
New York, NY 10018

212-714-1633
FAX 212-714-1655
E-Mail: info@sewing.org
Home Page: www.sewing.org

Pat Kobishyn, Show Manager

Two hundred exhibits of fabric, notions, patterns, sewing and trimmings. Attended by professionals from major chain stores, independent retailers, wholesalers and manufacturers.
3000 Attendees
Frequency: Annual

13793 SHOPA
SHOPA
3131 Elbee Road
Dayton, OH 45439-1900

937-297-2250
800-854-7467
FAX 937-297-2254
Home Page: www.shopa.org

Steven Jacober, President
Doris Condron, Director of Communications
7500 Attendees
Frequency: November

13794 School Equipment Show
National School Supply & Equipment Association
8380 Colesville Rd
Suite 250
Silver Spring, MD 20910-6225

301-495-0240
800-395-5550
FAX 301-495-3330
E-Mail: customerservice@nssea.org
Home Page: www.nssea.org
Social Media: *Facebook, Twitter, LinkedIn*

Jim McGarry, President/CEO
Rashad Cheeks, Meetings Coordinator
Tamara Davis, Bookkeeper/Office Manager
Karen Prince, Director of Membership
Bill Duffy, Vice President - Operations

Source new products, engage in industry discussion, hear perspectives on current issues, and network with existing and potential new suppliers, distributors and purchasing influencers.
Frequency: Annual/November

13795 Souvenirs Gifts & Novelties Trade Association
Kane Communications
7000 Terminal Square
Suite 210
Upper Darby, PA 19082-2330

610-734-2420
FAX 610-734-2423
Home Page: www.souvmag.com

Al Barry, Show Manager
Larry White, VP Marketing

Trade show serving amusements, museums, zoos, entertainment, bowling, and retailers. Seminars and networking party.
5000 Attendees
Frequency: July

13796 Variety Merchandise Show
Miller Freeman Publications
One Penn Plaza
PO Box 2549
New York, NY 10119

212-714-1300
FAX 212-714-1313

20000 Attendees

13797 Western States Toy and Hobby Show
Western Toy and Hobby Representative Association
9397 Reserve Drive
Corona, CA 92883

951-771-1598
FAX 909-277-1599
Home Page: www.wthra.com

Phylis St. John, Contact

If it's for kids, it's here. Show is for trade members only, not open to the public.
3000 Attendees
Frequency: March

13798 iHobby Expo
Hobby Manufacturers Association
PO Box 315
Butter, NJ 07405-0315

973-283-9088
FAX 973-838-7124
E-Mail: pat.koziol@hmahobby.org
Home Page: www.hmahobby.org
Social Media: *Twitter, LinkedIn*

Patricia S. Koziol, Executive Director
Jodi Araujo, Expositions and Events Manager
Models, trains, rc, cars, boats, planes and more
Frequency: October

Directories & Databases

13799 American International Toy Fair Official Directory of Showrooms & Exhibits
Toy Industry Association
1115 Broadway
Suite 400
New York, NY 10010-3466

212-675-1142
FAX 212-633-1429
E-Mail: info@toy-tia.org
Home Page: www.toy-tia.org

Thomas Conley, President
Diane Cardinale, Public Information Manager
Over 1,500 toy, game and hobby decoration manufacturers and their representatives are profiled.
Cost: $50.00
400 Pages
Frequency: Annual
Circulation: 12,000

13800 Complete Directory of Collectibles
Sutton Family Communications &
Publishing Company
920 State Route 54 East
Elmitch, KY 42343

270-276-9500
E-Mail: jlsutton@apex.net

Theresa Sutton, Publisher
Lee Sutton, Editor
Print-out from database of wholesalers, manufacturers, distributors, importers and close-out houses. Database is updated daily to guarantee the most current and up-to-date sources available.
Cost: $67.50
100 Pages

13801 Complete Directory of Crafts and Hobbies
Sutton Family Communications &
Publishing Company
920 State Route 54 East
Elmitch, KY 42343

270-276-9500
E-Mail: jlsutton@apex.net

Theresa Sutton, Editor
Lee Sutton, General Manager
Print-out from database of wholesalers, manufacturers, distributors, importers and close-out houses. Database is updated daily to guarantee the most current and up-to-date sources available.
Cost: $54.50
100+ Pages

13802 Complete Directory of Figurines
Sutton Family Communications &
Publishing Company
920 State Route 54 East
Elmitch, KY 42343

270-276-9500
E-Mail: jlsutton@apex.net
Theresa Sutton, Publisher
Lee Sutton, Editor
Print-out from database of wholesalers, manufacturers, distributors, importers and close-out houses. Database is updated daily to guarantee the most current and up-to-date sources available.
Cost: $44.50
100 Pages

13803 Complete Directory of Games
Sutton Family Communications &
Publishing Company
920 State Route 54 East
Elmitch, KY 42343

270-276-9500
E-Mail: jlsutton@apex.net

Theresa Sutton, Publisher
Lee Sutton, Editor
Print-out from database of wholesalers, manufacturers, distributors, importers and close-out houses. Database is updated daily to guarantee the most current and up-to-date sources available.
Cost: $39.50
100 Pages

13804 Complete Directory of Novelties
Sutton Family Communications &
Publishing Company
920 State Route 54 East
Elmitch, KY 42343

270-276-9500
E-Mail: jlsutton@apex.net

Theresa Sutton, Publisher
Lee Sutton, Editor
Print-out from database of wholesalers, manufacturers, distributors, importers and close-out houses. Database is updated daily to guarantee the most current and up-to-date sources available.
Cost: $79.50
100 Pages

13805 Complete Directory of Pewter Items
Sutton Family Communications &
Publishing Company
920 State Route 54 East
Elmitch, KY 42343

270-276-9500
E-Mail: jlsutton@apex.net

Theresa Sutton, Publisher
Lee Sutton, Editor
Print-out from database of wholesalers, manufacturers, distributors, importers and close-out houses. Database is updated daily to guarantee the most current and up-to-date sources available.
Cost: $39.50
100 Pages

13806 Complete Directory of Plush and Stuffed Toys and Dolls
Sutton Family Communications &
Publishing Company
920 State Route 54 East
Elmitch, KY 42343

270-276-9500
E-Mail: jlsutton@apex.net

Theresa Sutton, Editor
Lee Sutton, General Manager

Print-out from database of wholesalers, manufacturers, distributors, importers and close-out houses. Database is updated daily to guarantee the most current and up-to-date sources available.
Cost: $39.50
100+ Pages

13807 Complete Directory of Posters, Buttons and Novelties
Sutton Family Communications &
Publishing Company
920 State Route 54 East
Elmitch, KY 42343

270-276-9500
E-Mail: jlsutton@apex.net

Theresa Sutton, Editor
Lee Sutton, General Manager
Print-out from database of wholesalers, manufacturers, distributors, importers and close-out houses. Database is updated daily to guarantee the most current and up-to-date sources available.
Cost: $39.50
100+ Pages

13808 Complete Directory of Toys and Games
Sutton Family Communications &
Publishing Company
920 State Route 54 East
Elmitch, KY 42343

270-276-9500
E-Mail: jlsutton@apex.net

Theresa Sutton, Editor
Lee Sutton, General Manager
Print-out from database of wholesalers, manufacturers, distributors, importers and close-out houses. Database is updated daily to guarantee the most current and up-to-date sources available.
Cost: $44.50
100+ Pages

13809 Directory of Manufacturer Representatives Service Suppliers
Hobby Industry Association
319 E 54th St
Elmwood Park, NJ 07407-2712

201-794-1133
FAX 201-797-0657
E-Mail: sberger@craftandhobby.org
Home Page: www.craftandhobby.org

Steve Berger, CEO

Two hundred manufacturers representatives and 105 trade show booth demonstrators working in the hobby equipment industry.
Cost: $25.00
Frequency: Biennial

13810 Game Manufacturers Association Membership Directory
Game Manufacturers Association
240 N. Fifth St.
Suite 340
Columbus, OH 43215

614-255-4500
FAX 614-255-4499
Home Page: www.gama.org
Social Media: *Twitter, LinkedIn*

Justin Ziran, President
Jamie Chambers, Vice President
Aaron Witten, Treasurer
Brian Dalrymple, Secretary

Approximately 350 member manufacturers and distributors of adventure games.
Frequency: Annual
Founded in 1977
Mailing list available for rent

13811 Games and Entertainment on CD-ROM

Mecklermedia Corporation
20 Ketchum Street
Westport, CT 06880-5908

203-341-2806
FAX 203-454-5840

Over 1,300 multimedia encyclopedias, children's educational software and interactive 'board games'.
Cost: $29.95

13812 Hobby Industries of America Trade Show Program and Buyers Guide

Hobby Industry Association
319 E 54th St
Elmwood Park, NJ 07407-2712

201-794-1133
FAX 201-797-0657
E-Mail: hia@ihobby.org
Home Page: www.craftandhobby.org

Steve Berger, CEO

Over 1000 manufacturers are listed that exhibit at the HIA trade show.
Cost: $25.00
170 Pages
Frequency: Annual
Founded in 1940

13813 Hobby Merchandiser Annual Trade Directory

Hobby Publications
207 Commercial Ct
Morganville, NJ 07751-1099

732-536-5160
FAX 732-536-5761
Home Page: www.hobbypub.com

David Gherman, President
Jeff Troy, Editor
Ellen Gherman, Circulation Director
Tracey Decesure, Production Manager

Offers valuable information on manufacturers, wholesalers, industry suppliers and publishers of books and periodicals in the hobby trade industry.
Cost: $35.00
140 Pages
Frequency: Annual
Circulation: 7,000
Founded in 1945
Mailing list available for rent: 8M names
Printed in 4 colors on glossy stock

13814 Hobby RoundTable

GE Information Services
401 N Washington Street
Rockville, MD 20850-1707

301-388-8284

Cathy Ge, Owner

This database offers a forum enabling participants to share information on hobby-related topics, the hobby industry and hobby-related software.
Frequency: Bulletin Board

13815 Radio Control Hobby Membership Directory

Radio Control Hobby Trade Association
31632 N Ellis Avenue
Unit 111
Volo, IL 60073

847-740-1111
FAX 847-740-1111
Home Page: www.rchta.org

Members and manufacturers of radio control products.
Founded in 1983

Industry Web Sites

13816 http://gold.greyhouse.com
G.O.L.D Grey House OnLine Databases

Grey House Publishing's online database platform, GOLD, offers Quick Search, Keyword Search and Expert Search for most business sectors including hobby and game markets. The GOLD platform makes finding the information you need quick and easy - whether you're a novice searcher or an experienced database user. All of Grey House's directory products are available for subscription on the GOLD platform.

13817 www.amo-archery.org
Archery Manufacturers & Merchants Organization

Members are producers and sellers to the archery consumer.

13818 www.asdaonline.com
American Stamp Dealers Association

Holds annual International Philatelic Exhibition Interpex. Sponsors the annual International Dealers course. Postage stamp mega event twice a year (spring and fall).

13819 www.craftdesigners.org
Society of Craft Designers

The Society of Craft Designers (SCD), founded in 1975, is a professional organization for those who believe that quality craft design is the basis of a strong and viable craft industry. It is the only membership organization exclusively serving those who design for the consumer craft industry.

13820 www.greyhouse.com
Grey House Publishing

Authoritative reference directories for most business sectors including hobby and game markets. Users can search the online databases with varied search criteria allowing for custom searches by product category, geographic area, sales volume, keyword, subject and more. Full Grey House catalog and online ordering also available.

13821 www.hobby.org
Hobby Industry Association

The world's largest trade association in the craft and hobby market. The group produces an International Trade Show open to qualified professionals and is the industrys only market research show.

13822 www.hubcityhobby.com
5182 Old Highway 11
Suite 3
Hattiesburg, MS 39402

601-264-1040
Home Page: www.hubcityhobby.com
Social Media: *Facebook, Twitter*

Links to clubs, events, races and shows of interest to hobbyists.

13823 www.mria.org
Model Railroad Industry Association

Works to publicize the hobby and to keep members informed on the industry. Assists clubs and retailers in their shows.

13824 www.nssea.org
Naitonal School Supplu Equipment

Trade Association for the educational products industry.

13825 www.rchta.org
Radio Control Hobby Trade Association

For manufacturers and distributors of model hobby kits and hobby equipment, supplies and services and products associated with retail hobby stores.

13826 www.stamps.org
American Philatelic Society

National organization for stamp collectors; lending library; insurance for philatelic materials; sales division, seminars and annual conventions open to the public.

13827 www.tkga.com
The Knitting Guild Association (TKGA)

Membership organization for knitters with focus on knitting education and enhancing knitter's skills

13828 www.tnna.org
National Needlework Association

For maufacturers, suppliers and distributers of needlework and related equipment, supplies and services.

13829 www.toyassociation.org
Toy Industry Association

National organization for U.S. producers and importers of toys, games and children's entertainment products. Represents more than 500 member companies including designers, safety consultants, testing laboratories, licensors, communication professionals and inventors.

13830 www.wccwis.gr.jp/home.html
World Craft Council

A national organization for Handicraft

Associations

13831 African American Association of Innkeepers International

877-422-5777
E-Mail: africanamericaninns@yahoo.com
Home Page: www.africanamericaninns.com

Association dedicated to increasing awareness of African American-owned inns.

13832 American Hotel & Lodging Association

1250 I Street, N.W.
Suite 1100
Washington, DC 20005-3931

202-289-3100
FAX 202-289-3199
E-Mail: membership@ahla.com
Home Page: www.ahla.com
Social Media: *Facebook, Twitter, LinkedIn*

Jim Abrahamson, CHA, CEO, Chair of the Board
Mark Carrier, CHA, Vice-Chair
Katherine Lugar, President/CEO
Geoff Ballotti, Secretary/ Treasurer
Kimberly Miles, CMP, Senior Vice President, Operations

Supports all those involved in managing or franchising properties worldwide. Publishes annual directory.
10000 Members
Founded in 1910

13833 American Hotel & Lodging Educational Institute

800 N. Magnolia Avenue
Suite 300
Orlando, FL 32803

407-999-8100
800-344-4381
FAX 407-236-7848
E-Mail: info@ahlei.org
Home Page: www.ahlei.org/
Social Media: *Facebook, Twitter, LinkedIn, Google Plus, Youtube, Instagra*

Minaz Abji, Board Chairman
S. Kirk Kinsell, Vice Chairman
Paul Kirwin, Secretary/Treasurerÿ
Joori Jeon, Chief Executive Officer
Brenda Moons, CMHS, Senior Vice President, Sales

Fosters education, research programming, and information regarding operating techniques in the lodging industry.
11000 Members
Founded in 1953

13834 Asian American Hotel Owners Association

1100 Abernathy Rd.
Suite 1100
Atlanta, GA 30328

404-816-5759
FAX 404-816-6260
Home Page: www.aahoa.com
Social Media: *Facebook, Twitter, LinkedIn, YouTube, Instagram, Google+*

Chip Rogers, President & CEO
Jay R. (Jimmy) Patel, Chairman

Members own 40 percent of all hotels in the United States and employ 600,000 people.
14000 Members
Founded in 1989

13835 Asian/American Hotel Owners Association

Asian American Hotel Owners Association

1100 Abernathy Road
Suite 1100
Atlanta, GA 30328-6707

404-816-5759
FAX 404-816-6260
E-Mail: info@aahoa.com
Home Page: www.aahoa.com
Social Media: *Facebook, Twitter, LinkedIn, YouTube, Instagram*

Jay R. Patel, CHO, Chairman
Bharat Patel, CHO, Vice Chairman
Chip Rogers, President & CEO
Bhavesh B. Patel, CHO, Treasurer
Hitesh Patel, CHA, CHO, Secretary

Supports Asian/American hotel and motel owners and operators.
8,700 Members
Founded in 1989

13836 Associated Luxury Hotels International

1667 K Street, NW
Suite 610
Washington, DC 20006

202-887-7020
FAX 202-887-0085
E-Mail: midatlantic@alhi.com
Home Page: www.alhi.com
Social Media: *Facebook, Twitter, YouTube*

Jim Schultenover, President
David Gabri, Chief Executive Officer
Chris Riccardi, Division VP
Mike Coutu, Executive VP & CFO
Ashly Balding, Division VP - East

Provided a National Sales Network to associations and corporations in America for the distinguished hotels and resorts now in 26 states, Canada, Mexico, and the Caribbean.
Founded in 1986

13837 Bed and Breakfast League

PO Box 9490
Washington, DC 20016-9490

202-363-7767
FAX 202-363-8396
E-Mail:
bedandbreakfast/washingtondc@erols.com

Millie Groobey, Director

A reservation service for bed and breakfasts in Washington, DC, that welcome selected travelers into their homes.
Founded in 1976

13838 Educational Institute of the American Hotel & Lodging Association

2113 N High St
Lansing, MI 48906-4221

517-372-8800
800-752-4567
FAX 517-372-5141
E-Mail: info@ei-ahla.org
Home Page: www.ei-ahla.org
Social Media: *Facebook, Twitter*

George Glazer, VP
Anthony Farris, Chairman
Thomas J. Corcoran Jr., Vice Chair
Brenda Moons, Senior Vice President of Sales
K.V. Simon, Regional Vice President

A nonprofit educational foundation of the American Hotel & Lodging Association and the world's largest provider of hospitality education training resources, videos, books, workbooks, seminars, management courses, complete training systems and professional certification programs.
120 Members
Founded in 1953

13839 Green Hotels Association

PO Box 420212
Houston, TX 77242-0212

713-789-8889
FAX 713-789-9786
E-Mail: green@greenhotels.com
Home Page: www.greenhotels.com
Social Media: *Facebook, Twitter*

Patricia Griffin, President

Association of hoteliers for environmentally-friendly properties.
Founded in 1993

13840 Hospitality Financial & Technology Professionals

11709 Boulder Lane
Suite 110
Austin, TX 78726-1832

512-249-5333
800-646-4387
FAX 512-249-1533
E-Mail: membership@hftp.org
Home Page: www.hftp.org
Social Media: *Facebook, Twitter, LinkedIn*

Daniel N. Conti, Jr., CHAE, CAM, President
Arlene Ramirez, Vice President
Lyle Worthington, CHTP, Treasurer
Jerry M. Trieber, Immediate Past President
Connie Hong, Executive Services Administrator

Professional society for those in the financial segment of the hospitality industry.
4,700 Members
Founded in 1952
Mailing list available for rent

13841 Hotel Employees and Restaurant Employees

275 7th Avenue
16th Floor
New York, NY 10001-6708

212-265-7000
E-Mail: ccarrera@unitehere.org
Home Page: www.unitehere.org
Social Media: *Facebook, Twitter, Google Plus*

D. Taylor, General President
Jo Marie Agriesti, General VP
Sherriÿ Chiesa, Secretary-Treasurerÿ
Maria Elena Durazo, General VP for Immigration
Peter Ward, Recording Secretary

Hosts a diverse membership, comprised largely of immigrants and including high percentages of African-American, Latino, and Asia-American workers. The majority of members are women.
850m Members
Founded in 1891

13842 International Council on Hotel, Restaurant and Institutional Education

2810 North Parham Road
Suite 230
Richmond, VA 23294

804-346-4800
FAX 804-346-5009
E-Mail: webmaster@chrie.org
Home Page: www.chrie.org
Social Media: *Facebook, Twitter, LinkedIn*

Maureen Brookes, President
Martin O'Neillÿ, Immediate Past President
Margaret Steiskal, ViceÿPresident
Wanda Costen, Secretary
Stephanie Hein, Treasurer

A nonprofit professional association which provides programs and services to continually improve the quality of global education, research,

service, and business operations in the hospitality and tourism industry.
Founded in 1946

13843 International Executive Housekeepers Association

1001 Eastwind Drive
Suite 301
Westerville, OH 43081-3361

614-895-7166
800-200-6342
FAX 614-895-1248
E-Mail: excel@ieha.org
Home Page: www.ieha.org
Social Media: *Facebook, Twitter, LinkedIn*

Michael Patterson, President
Wayne Bledy, Director at Large
Wanda Joyce, Secretary/Treasurer
Lorrie Tripp, President-Elect
Sarah Larsen Miller, Convention Manager

An organization for persons working in the housekeeping area of the lodging industry.
3,500 Members
Founded in 1930

13844 International Facility Management Association

800 Gessner Rd
Suite 900
Houston, TX 77024-4257

713-623-4362
FAX 713-623-6124
E-Mail: ifma@ifma.org
Home Page: www.ifma.org
Social Media: *Facebook, Twitter, LinkedIn, Flickr, Youtube, RSS*

Michael D. Feldman, FMP, CM, Chair
Tony Keane, CAE, President and CEO
Maureen Ehrenberg, FRICS, CRE, First Vice Chair
William M. O'Neill, CFM, Second Vice Chair
John Perry, Chief Operating Officer

Certifies facility managers, conducts research, provides educational programs, recognizes facility management degree and certificate programs and produces World Workplace, the world's largest facility management conference and exposition.
24,00 Members
Founded in 1980
Mailing list available for rent

13845 NEWH: The Hospitality Industry Network

PO Box 322
Shawano, WI 54166

800-593-6394
FAX 800-693-6394
Home Page: newh.org
Social Media: *Facebook, Twitter, LinkedIn*

Shelia Lohmiller, Executive Director
Jena Seibel, Deputy Director

The Network of Executive Women in Hospitality promotes the professional development of women in hospitality and related industries.
Founded in 1984

13846 National Bed & Breakfast Association

1011 W Fifth Street
Suite 300
Austin, TX 78703

512-322-2710
FAX 512-320-0883
E-Mail: Sales@BedandBreakfast.com
Home Page: www.bedandbreakfast.com
Social Media: *Facebook, Twitter, Pinterest, Google Plus*

John Banczac, Vice President
Denis Kashkin, Sr. Directory of Technology
Eric Goldreyer, Founder & President

An organization of services and supplies to the industry offering a list of the best in bed and breakfast accommodations in the USA, Canada and the Caribbean.
Founded in 1981
Mailing list available for rent

13847 Preferred Hotels and Resorts Worldwide

311 S Wacker Dr
Suite 1900
Chicago, IL 60606-6676

312-913-0400
866-990-9491
FAX 312-913-5124
E-Mail: info@preferredhotels.com
Home Page: www.preferredhotels.com
Social Media: *Facebook, Twitter, Pinterest, Instagram*

John Ubberoth, CEO
Nora Gainer, Director Marketing

Independently owned luxury hotels and resorts. Each provides the highest standards of quality and extraordinary service.
120 Members
Founded in 1968

13848 Professional Association of Innkeepers International

295 Seven Farms Drive
Suite 236-C
Charleston, SC 29492

856-310-1102
800-468-7244
FAX 856-895-0432
E-Mail: questions@paii.org
Home Page: www.paii.org
Social Media: *Facebook, Twitter, Pinterest, Google+*

Jay Karen, CEO
Isabel Abreu, Membership Sales Manager
Brook Patterson, Director of Vendor Services
Ingrid Thorson, Marketing & Communications Manager
Kris Ullmer, Executive Director

Serving bed and breakfast/country inn owners, aspiring innkeepers, inn sitters, vendors with educational and consultative services. International conference.
3000 Members
Founded in 1988

13849 Select Registry

295 Seven Farms Drive
Suite C-279
Charleston, SC 29492

269-789-0393
800-344-5244
FAX 269-789-0970
E-Mail: maincontact@selectregistry.com
Home Page: www.selectregistry.com/
Social Media: *Facebook, Twitter*

Emily Cisewski, Content Manager
Carol Riggs, Director of Membership Services
Renee Flowers, Director of Marketing
Susan Galvin, Director of Membership Development
Susan Butler, Operations Manager

Represents the finest country inns, B&Bs, and unique small hotels from California to Nova-Scotia. The very best the travel industry has to offer.
400 Members
Founded in 1968
Mailing list available for rent

13850 Small Luxury Hotels

370 Lexington Avenue
Suite 1506
New York, NY 10017

212-953-2064
800-608-0273
E-Mail: reservation@slh.com
Home Page: www.slh.com
Social Media: *Facebook, Twitter, LinkedIn, Pinterest, Instagram, Google+*

Members are independent owners and managers of deluxe hotels with fewer than 200 rooms.
233 Members
Founded in 1991

13851 Small Luxury Hotels of the World

370 Lexington Avenue
Suite 1506
New York, NY 10017

212-953-2064
800-608-0273
FAX 212-953-0576
E-Mail: reservation@slh.com
Home Page: www.slh.com
Social Media: *Facebook, Twitter, LinkedIn, Pinterest, Instagram, Google+,*

Lanny Grossman, Marketing
Johnathan Slater, Chairman
Ed Donaldson, Manager

Collection of independently owned exclusive hotels in more than 50 countries. Selected for style and comfort, properties include spas, country houses, golf resorts, island retreats, city sanctuaries, game and wilderness lodges. Publishes directory.
300 Members
Founded in 1991

13852 Textile Rental Services Association

1800 Diagonal Road
Suite 200
Alexandria, VA 22314-2842

703-519-0029
877-770-9274
FAX 703-519-0026
E-Mail: trsa@trsa.org
Home Page: www.trsa.org
Social Media: *Facebook, Twitter, LinkedIn, RSS, YouTube*

Roger Cocivera, President
George F. Ferencza, VP

Develops new programs and services to help textile rental operators meet today's challenges.
1400 Members
Founded in 1913

Newsletters

13853 AHA Hotline Newsletter

American Hospitality Association
603 S Pulaski
PO Box 3866
Little Rock, AR 72201

501-376-2323
800-472-5022
FAX 501-376-6517
Home Page: www.arhospitality.org
Social Media: *Facebook, Twitter, LinkedIn*

Montine McNulty, Executive Director
Rita Walker, Executive Assistant
Amanda Glover, Education Coordinator
Holly Heer, Director of Membership
Kristen Smith, Director of Finance

For members, focuses on trends in the hospitality industry, upcoming events, training and education opportunities and more.
Frequency: Monthly

13854 AHF Developments
American Hotel & Lodging Association
1201 New York Ave Nw
Suite 600
Washington, DC 20005-3931

202-289-3100
FAX 202-289-3199
E-Mail: webmaster@ahla.com
Home Page: www.ahla.com

Joseph Mc Inerney, President
Pam Inman, Executive Vice President & COO
Joori Jeon, Executive Vice President & CFO
Marlene M. Colucci, Executive Vice President
Lisa Costello, Vice President, Gov Affairs

AHF Developments is published three times a year with circulation to donors, scholarship recipients and members of the American Hotel and Motel association.
Frequency: Quarterly
Founded in 1910

13855 Cameron's Foodservice Marketing Reporter
Cameron's Publications
5423 Sheridan Drive
PO Box 676
Williamsville, NY 14231

519-586-8785
FAX 519-586-8816
E-Mail: mail@cameronpub.com
Home Page: www.cameronpub.com

Bob McClelland, CEO
Nina Cameron, Editor

Successful promotion and advertising case histories for the restaurant and hotel industry.

13856 Epicurean Revue
PO Box 35128
Sarasota, FL 34242-5128

FAX 941-349-4370

Jean-Noel Prade, Publisher
Georgia Brown, Editor
JN Prade, Circulation Manager

The publication for the jetsetters exclusive recommendations on top class hotels and restaurants. Total analysis of the various issues of the Michelin Guide and results of the wine auctions.
Cost: $79.00
8 Pages
Frequency: Monthly
Circulation: 5,000
Printed in one color on matte stock

13857 Hospitality Law
LRP Publications
PO Box 24668
West Palm Beach, FL 33416-4668

561-622-6520
800-341-7874
FAX 561-622-0757
E-Mail: webmaster@lrp.com
Home Page: www.lrp.com

Kenneth Kahn, President
Dave Light, Editor

Details and analyzes significant cases in the hospitality industry so you can learn from the mistakes that landed other properties in court. You receive summaries of the latest court cases - without legalese - involving hotels, inns, resorts and restaurants.
Cost: $229.00
12 Pages
Frequency: Monthly
Circulation: 1400

13858 Hotel Technology Newsletter
Chervenak, Keane and Company

307 E 44th Street
New York, NY 10017

212-986-8230
FAX 212-983-5275
Home Page:
www.e-hospitality.com.storefronts/ckchoteltech.html

J Christmas, Publisher
L Chervenak, Editor

Covers hotel information processing, telecommunications, security, fire safety, energy and audio-visual systems.
Cost: $180.00
Frequency: Annual

13859 Hotel and Casino Law Letter
William F Harrah College of Hotel Administration
4505 Maryland Parkway
Box 456013
Las Vegas, NV 89154-6013

702-895-3161
FAX 702-895-4109
E-Mail: hoaadvise@ccmail.nevada.edu
Home Page: hotel.unlv.edu/

Annette Kannenberg, Business Manager
Stuart H Mann, Dean
Alice Baker, Administrative Assistant
Pat Merl, Management Assistant
Sherri Theriault, Director

Legislative news for executive level management of hotels and motels.

13860 Hyatt Overseas
Hyatt International Corporation
71 S Wacker Dr
Chicago, IL 60606-4637

312-701-7063
FAX 312-750-8578

Thomas Pritzker, CEO

A summary of news, packages and events happening at Hyatt Hotels.
2 Pages

13861 Inn Side Issues
Hotel and Motel Brokers of America
10220 N Executive Boulevard
Suite 610
Kansas City, MO 64153

816-891-8776
FAX 816-891-7071

Robert Kralicek, Editor

News of hotel owners and investors with articles about hospitality real estate.

Magazines & Journals

13862 Bottomline
Hospitality Financial & Technology Professionals
11709 Boulder Lane
Suite 110
Austin, TX 78726-1832

512-249-5333
800-646-4387
FAX 512-249-1533
E-Mail: Sales@hftp.org
Home Page: www.hftp.org

Jen Gonzales, Communications Manager
Theresa Pulley, Advertising Director

Official publication of the international association for individuals employed as controllers and financial officers in the hospitality industry. Articles include topics such as technology, personnel management, financial analysis, eth-ics and financial controls.
Cost: $200.00
Circulation: 4300
Founded in 1952
Printed in on glossy stock

13863 Cameron's Worldwide Hospitality Marketing Reporter
53256 Sheridan Drive
Williamsville, NY 14221-3503

416-636-5666
FAX 416-636-5026

13864 Cheers
257 Park Avenue S
3rd Floor, Suite 303
New York, NY 10010

212-967-1551
FAX 646-654-2099

John Eastman, Owner

Every issue is designed to help on-premise operators enhance the profitability of their beverage operations.

13865 Club Management Magazine
Finan Publishing Company
107 W Pacific
Saint Louis, MO 63119-3776

314-961-6644
FAX 314-961-4809
Home Page: www.club-mgmt.com

Thomas J Finan, IV, Managing Editor
Dee Kaplan, Publisher
Dianne Dierkes, Circulation Manager

The resource for successful club operations.
Cost: $26.95
150 Pages
Founded in 1921
Mailing list available for rent: 21,000 names
Printed in 4 colors on glossy stock

13866 Consortium of Hospitality Research Information Services
Quanta Press
1313 5th St SE
Suite 223A
Minneapolis, MN 55414-4513

612-379-3618

Nancy J Hall, Owner

Consists of academic and industry groups which together have produced a comprehensive index of hospitality literature in CD-ROM format. Over 47,000 bibliographic records with abstracts from over 50 journals serving the hospitality industry.

13867 Cornell Hotel & Restaurant Administration Quarterly
Elsevier Science Publishing Company
415 Horsham Road
Horsham, PA 19044

212-633-3730
888-437-4636
FAX 212-633-3680
E-Mail: nicole@leonardmedia.com
Home Page: www.hotelschool.cornell.edu/

Glenn Withiam, Executive Editor
Dr. Michael Sturman, Editor
Thomas Cullen, Associate Professor

A journal devoted to the development and exchange of management ideas for the hospitality industry.
Cost: $113.00
Frequency: Quarterly
Circulation: 4500
Founded in 1960

13868 Developments Magazine
American Resort Development Association
1201 15th St NW
Suite 400
Washington, DC 20005-2842

202-371-6700
FAX 202-289-8544
E-Mail: customerservice@arda.org
Home Page: www.ardafoundation.org

Howard Nusbaum, President/CEO
Lou Ann Burney, Vice President of Marketing
Robert Craycraft, Vice President of Industry
Relation
Rob Dunn, Vice President of Finance
Jason C. Gamel, Vice President of State
Governments

13869 Executive Housekeeping Today (EHT)
International Executive Housekeepers
Association
1001 Eastwind Dr
Suite 301
Westerville, OH 43081-3361

614-895-7166
800-200-6342
FAX 614-895-1248
E-Mail: excel@ieha.org
Home Page: www.ieha.org
Social Media: *Facebook, Twitter, LinkedIn*

Beth Risinger, CEO
Laura DiGiulio, Advertising/Sales/Ed

Magazine for management personnel in the institutional housekeeping industry. Highlighting
products, services, association news and industry trends.
Cost: $40.00
3500 Members
30 Pages
Frequency: Monthly
Circulation: 4130
ISSN: 0738-6583
Founded in 1930

**13870 Foodservice Equipment & Supplies
Specialist**
Reed Business Information
2000 Clearwater Dr
Oak Brook, IL 60523-8809

630-574-0825
FAX 630-288-8781
E-Mail: 411_webmaster@reedbusiness.com
Home Page: www.reedbusiness.com

Jeff Greisch, President
Maureen Slocum, Publisher
Paulette Cortopassi, Managing Editor
Victoria Jones, Production Manager
Andrew Rak, Senior Vice President

Magazine for professionals who specify, sell
and distribute foodservice equipment, supplies
and furnishings.
Frequency: Monthly
Circulation: 22719
Founded in 1948
Printed in 4 colors on glossy stock

13871 Hospitality News
PO Box 11960
Prescott, AZ 86304-1960

206-686-7378
800-685-1932
FAX 206-463-0090
Home Page: www.hospnews.com

Linda Sanders, Publisher
Miles Small, Editor-in-Chief

Serves restaurants, lodges, health care facili-
ties, schools, clubs, casino's, caterers, and culi-
nary and beverage marketplaces.
Circulation: 105000
ISSN: 1084-2551
Founded in 1988

13872 Hospitality Product News
Advantstar Communications
2501 Colorado Avenue
Suite 280
Santa Monica, CA 90404

310-857-7500
888-527-7008
FAX 310-857-7510
E-Mail: info@advanstar.com
Home Page: www.advanstar.com/

Doug Ferguson, Group Publisher
Helen Gardner, General Manager
Georgiann Decenzo, Director of Corporate mar
Joseph Loggia, CEO
Thomas Ehardt, Chief Administrator

Contains ADA compliance, maintenance and
cleaning, fitness, leisure and entertainment,
food and beverage, foodservice equipment and
supplies, furnishings and fixtures, guest amenities, tabletop, technology, uniforms, and bedding and linens.
Cost: $35.00
Circulation: 30019
Founded in 1987

13873 Hospitality Technology
Edgell Communications
4 Middlebury Boulevard
Randolph, NJ 07869

973-252-0100
FAX 973-252-9020
Home Page: www.htmagazine.com

Lenore O'Meara, Associate Publisher
Reid Paul, Editor
Gerald Ryerson, President
Jan Miciak, Production Manager
Leah Segarra, Account Executive

Aimed at owners/operators, franchise and chain
executives, and managers in operations, finance, sales/marketing and information systems. Emphasis on applications, new products,
industry news and trade show highlights.
Circulation: 16000
Founded in 1984
Printed in 4 colors on glossy stock

13874 Hotel & Motel Management
Advantstar Communications
757 3rd Avenue
New York, NY 10017-2013

212-951-6600
FAX 212-951-6793
E-Mail: info@advanstar.com
Home Page: www.advanstar.com

Scott E Pierce, President
Mike Malley, Publisher
Jeff Higley, Editor-in-Chief
Mary M. Malloy, National Sales Manager

Publication reaching more than 57,000 man-
agement personnel in hotels, motels, motor
inns and other related businesses.
Circulation: 53058
ISSN: 0018-6082
Founded in 1875

13875 Hotels
Reed Business Information
2000 Clearwater Dr
Oak Brook, IL 60523-8809

605-3 8-09
FAX 630-288-8781
E-Mail: hotels_webmaster@reedbusiness.com
Home Page: www.reedbusiness.com

Jeff Greisch, President
Andrew Rak, Senior Vice President
Jeff Weinstein, Editor

The magazine for the worldwide hotel industry
Cost: $125.90
Frequency: Monthly
Circulation: 62000

ISSN: 1047-2975
Printed in 4 colors on glossy stock

13876 Infoline
Hospitality Financial & Technology
Professionals
11709 Boulder Lane
Suite 110
Austin, TX 78726-1832

512-249-5333
800-646-4387
FAX 512-249-1533
E-Mail: eliza.selig@hftp.org
Home Page: www.hftp.org

Eliza Selig, Editor
Lance Peterson, Director Marketing
Frank Wolfe, Executive ViP

Chapter and officer activities.
Frequency: Monthly
Circulation: 4000
Founded in 1952

**13877 Journal of Quality Assurance in
Hospitality & Tourism**
Bill Cohen
10 Alice Street
Binghamton, NY 13904-1580

607-722-5857
800-342-9678
FAX 607-722-6362
E-Mail: getinfo@haworthpressinc.com
Home Page: www.haworthpressinc.com

Timothy R Hinkin, Editor
Pyo Sungsoo, Editor
William Cohen, Owner

Serves as a medium to share and disseminate
information coming from new research findings and superior practices in tourisim and
hospiality; covers planning, development, management and marketing.
Cost: $50.00
Frequency: Quarterly
Founded in 1978

**13878 Journal of Teaching in Travel &
Tourism**
Bill Cohen
10 Alice Street
Binghamton, NY 13904-1580

607-722-5857
800-342-9678
FAX 607-722-6362
E-Mail: getinfo@haworthpress.com
Home Page: www.haworthpressinc.com

Timothy R Hinkin, Editor
Pyo Sungsoo, Editor
Cathy HC Hsu, Editor
William Cohen, Owner

Serves as an international interdisiplinary forum and reference source for travel and
tourisim education at professional schools and
universities.
Founded in 1978

13879 Lodging Hospitality
Penton Media
1300 E 9th St
Cleveland, OH 44114-1503

216-696-7000
FAX 216-696-6662
E-Mail: ewatkins@penton.com
Home Page: www.penton.com

Jane Cooper, Marketing
Edward Watkins, Editor
David Kieselstein, CEO
Preston L. Vice, Chief Financial Officer
Andrew Schmolka, Senior Vice President

Serving the US hotel, motel and resort industry.
Published 16 times per year, LH provides owners and operators with the latest trends and in-

formation on the development, operations and marketing of lodging properties
Frequency: Monthly
Circulation: 50,976
ISSN: 0148-0766
Founded in 1892
Mailing list available for rent
Printed in 4 colors on glossy stock

13880 Market Watch
M Shanken Communications
387 Park Ave S
Floor 8
New York, NY 10016-8872

212-684-4224
FAX 212-684-5424
Home Page: www.cigaraficionado.com

Marvin Shanken, Publisher
Felicia Bedoya, President
Up-to-date information for individuals and businesses working in the beverage and alcohol industry.
Cost: $75.42
200 Pages
Circulation: 65000
Founded in 1981
Printed in 4 colors

13881 Nation's Restaurant News
Lebhar-Friedman Publications
425 Park Ave
New York, NY 10022-3526

212-756-5220
FAX 212-756-5250
E-Mail: info@lf.com

Lebhar Friedman, Publisher
Michael Cardillo, VP Sales
Ellen Koteff, Editor
Serves commercial and onsite food service and lodging establishments including restaurants, schools, universities, hospitals, nursing homes and other health and welfare facilities, hotels and motels with food service, government installations, clubs and other related firms.
Cost: $44.95
Circulation: 85,999
Founded in 1925
Mailing list available for rent: 100,000 names at $100 per M
Printed in 4 colors on matte stock

13882 National Culinary Review
American Culinary Federation
180 Center Place Way
St Augustine, FL 32095-8859

904-824-4468
800-624-9458
FAX 904-825-4758
E-Mail: acf@acfchefs.net
Home Page: www.acfchefs.org

Heidi Cramb, Executive Director
Kay Orde, Editor
Edward Leonard, Presient
Michael Feierstein, Administrative Assistant
Bryan Hunt, Graphic Designer
Accepts advertising.
Cost: $50.00
Frequency: Monthly
Circulation: 20000
Founded in 1929

13883 Restaurant Hospitality
Penton Media
1300 E 9th St
Cleveland, OH 44114-1503

216-696-7000
FAX 216-696-6662
E-Mail: information@penton.com
Home Page: www.penton.com

Jane Cooper, Marketing
Jennifer Daugherty, Communications Manager

David Kieselstein, Chief Executive Officer
Kurt Nelson, Vice President, Human Resources
Andrew Schmolka, Senior Vice President
A national trade publication that covers the full-service restaurant industry. If offers cover story features, an extensive food section with recipes, a multi-page news section and a variety of one page profiles on rising stars, equipment, food safety, beverages, design and more.
130 Pages
Frequency: Monthly
Circulation: 117721
ISSN: 0147-9989
Founded in 1892
Mailing list available for rent
Printed in 4 colors on glossy stock

13884 Restaurants & Institutions
Reed Business Information
2000 Clearwater Dr
Oak Brook, IL 60523-8809

605-3 8-09
FAX 630-288-8781
E-Mail: privacymanager@reedbusiness.com
Home Page: www.reedbusiness.com

Patricia B Dailey, Editor-in-Chief
Scott Hume, Managing Editor
Jim Casella, CEO
Brion Palmer, Publisher
Andrew Rak, Senior Vice President
Commercial and noncommercial foodservice establishments including restaurant, hotels, motels, fast-food chains, coffee shops, food stores with foodservice
Cost: $477.00
Frequency: Monthly
Circulation: 154,110
Founded in 1937
Printed in 4 colors on glossy stock

13885 Ski Area Management
Beardsley Publishing Corporation
PO Box 644
Woodbury, CT 06798-644

203-263-0888
FAX 203-266-0452
Home Page: www.saminfo.com

Jennifer Rowan, Publisher
Rick Kahl, Editor
Donna Jacobs, Production Manager
Content includes technologies of skilifts, snowmaking and slope grooming, at year-round resort operations. Other features include product and supplier directories, resort architecture and design, new products, marketing, real estate and rental.
Cost: $42.00
Frequency: Monthly
Circulation: 3100
Printed in 4 colors on glossy stock

13886 Textile Rental Magazine
Textile Rental Services Association
1800 Diagonal Rd
Suite 200
Alexandria, VA 22314-2842

703-519-0029
877-770-9274
FAX 703-519-0026
E-Mail: trsa@trsa.org
Home Page: www.trsa.org
Social Media: *Facebook, Twitter, LinkedIn*

Roger Cocivera, President/CEO
Jack Morgan, Editor
Packed with valuable tips and ideas.
Frequency: Monthly
Founded in 1912

Trade Shows

13887 American Hotel & Motel Association Annual Conference/Leadership Forum
1201 New York Avenue NW
Suite 600
Washington, DC 20005-3931

202-289-3100
FAX 202-289-3158
E-Mail: webmaster@ahla.com
Home Page: www.ahlef.org

Gerald Petitt, Chairman
Joseph A. McInerney, President/Ceo
Pam Inman, Executive Vice President & COO
Joori Jeon, Executive Vice President & CFO
Marlene M. Colucci, Executive Vice President
189 exhibits of hotel supplies, equipment and information, conference and workshop.
1500 Attendees
Frequency: Annual
Founded in 1910

13888 American Hotel & Motel Association Annual Convention
1201 New York Avenue NW
Suite 600
Washington, DC 20005-3931

202-289-3100
FAX 202-289-3199
E-Mail: webmaster@ahla.com
Home Page: www.ahlef.org

Gerald Petitt, Chairman
Joseph A. McInerney, President/Coo
Pam Inman, Executive Vice President & COO
Joori Jeon, Executive Vice President & CFO
Marlene M. Colucci, Executive Vice President
125 booths consisting of telecommunication systems, supplies and equipment for the hotel and motel industry.
1.5M Attendees
Frequency: April

13889 American Resort Development Association Convention
1201 15th Street NW
Suite 400
Washington, DC 20005-2842

202-371-6700
FAX 202-289-8544
E-Mail: customerservice@arda.org
Home Page: www.arda.org

Howard C Nusbaum, President/CEO
Lou Ann Burney, Vice President of Marketing
Robert Craycraft, Vice President of Industry Relation
Rob Dunn, Vice President of Finance
Jason C. Gamel, Vice President of State Government
One hundred fifty booths.
3600 Attendees
Frequency: April

13890 Annual Council on Hotel, Restaurant and Institutional Education Conference
Int'l Council on Hotel & Restaurant Education
2810 North Parham Roaf
Suite 230
Richmond, VA 23294

804-346-4800
FAX 804-346-5009

E-Mail: publications@chrie.org
Home Page: www.chrie.org

Kathy McCarty, Executive VP/CEO
Bill Shoemaker, Treasurer
Joseph Bradley, Treasurer

Terrific opportunity to gain knowledge, exchange ideas, and enjoy the camaraderie and fellowship of colleagues in the hospitality industry
6MM Attendees
Frequency: July

13891 Annual Hotel, Motel and Restaurant Supply Show of the Southeast
Leisure Time Unlimited
708 Main Street
PO Box 332
Myrtle Beach, SC 29577

843-448-9483
800-261-5991
FAX 843-626-1513
E-Mail: hmrss@sc.rr.com
Home Page: www.hmrsss.com

Brooke P Baker, Show Director

Trade show for the hospitality industry.
23000 Attendees
Frequency: January
Founded in 1975

13892 Fall Conference for Hospitality Supply Management
Institute for Supply Management
Po Box 22160
Tempe, AZ 85285-2160

480-752-6276
800-888-6276
FAX 480-752-7890
Home Page: www.ism.ws
Social Media: *Facebook, Twitter, LinkedIn*

Sidney Johnson, Chairman
Thomas W. Derry, Chief Executive Officer
Debbie Webber, Senior VP/Corporate Treasurer
Holly LaCroix Johnson, Senior VP/Corporate Secretary
Nora Neibergall, CPM, Senior VP
Frequency: Oct, Dallas, TX
Mailing list available for rent

13893 Great Southwest Lodging & Restaurant Show
Arizona Hotel and Lodging Association
1240 East Missouri Avenue
Phoenix, AZ 85014

602-604-0729
800-788-2462
FAX 520-604-0769
E-Mail: info@azhla.com
Home Page: www.azhla.com

Britt Kimball, Show Manager

Seminars, workshops and 450+ exhibits of food service and lodging equipment, marketing, decorations, berverage services (alcoholic and non), cleaning services and pest control, furnishings, lighting, insurance, transportation and more.
5000 Attendees
Frequency: Annual
Founded in 1970

13894 IEHA's Association Convention/in Conjunction with ISSA Interclean
International Executive Housekeepers Association
1001 Eastwind Drive
Suite 301
Westerville, OH 43081-3361

614-895-7166
800-200-6342
FAX 614-895-1248
E-Mail: excel@ieha.org

Home Page: www.ieha.org
Social Media: *Facebook, Twitter, LinkedIn*

Beth Risinger, CEO

Educational seminars and exhibits by firms engaged in manufacturing, marketing and distribution of cleaning and maintenance suppliers. Containing 750 exhibits.
3500 Members
15M Attendees
Frequency: Oct 23-26 Orlando Florida

13895 Innkeeping
PAII
Box 97010
Santa Barbara, CA 93190

805-965-4525

JoAnn Bell, Publisher

Offers a forum for innkeepers, hotel and motel managers, owners and operators.
500 Attendees
Frequency: March/April

13896 International Hotel/Motel & Restaurant Show
George Little Management
10 Bank Street
Suite 1200
White Plains, NY 10606-1954

914-486-6070
800-272-7469
FAX 914-948-6180
E-Mail: ihmrs@glmshows.com
Home Page: www.ihmrs.com

Christian Falkemberg, Show Manager
George Little II, President

Products and services for lodging and food service properties organized in 12 categories: Technology; Uniforms, Linens and Bedding; Tabletop; Guest amenities and services; Food and Beverage; Cleaning and Maintenance; Food Service Equipment and Supplies; Franchise, Finance and Management; Furnishings and Fixturtes; Fitness, Leisure and Entertainment; The Environment; Advertising and Promotion
45000 Attendees
Frequency: Early November

13897 Marine Hotel Catering Duty Free Conference
PO Box 1659
Sausalito, CA 94966

415-332-1903
FAX 415-332-9457
E-Mail: mha@mhaweb.org
Home Page: www.mhaweb.org

Caroline Prichard, Administrator

100 booths.
700 Attendees
Frequency: April

13898 National Restaurant Association: Restaurant, Hotel-Motel Show
Convention Office
150 North Michigan Avenue
Suite 2000
Chicago, IL 60601

312-853-2525
Home Page: www.restaurant.org

Mary Pat Heftman, Sr VP Conventions
Jamie Schaefer, Treasurer
Phil Hickey, Treasurer

1,800 booths.
Frequency: Annual, May

13899 Pacific Hospitality Expo Convention Center
1801 Kalakaua Avenue
Honolulu, HI 96815-2558

808-973-9790

Joanie Gribbin, Director

220 booths.
2.5M Attendees
Frequency: June

13900 Rocky Mountain Hospitality Convention and Expo
899 Logan Street
Suite 300
Denver, CO 80203-3155

303-792-9621

Bruce Whiticker, Convention Director

413 booths.
7M Attendees
Frequency: June

Directories & Databases

13901 All Suite Hotel Guide
Ten Speed Press
PO Box 7123
Berkeley, CA 94707-0123

510-559-1600
800-841-2665
FAX 510-559-1629
Home Page: www.tenspeedpress.com

Phil Wood, President

Over 1,600 hotels are offered which have suites available consisting of two or more rooms for rent.
Cost: $14.95
336 Pages
Frequency: Annual
ISBN: 1-580080-91-

13902 America's Wonderful Little Hotels & Inns
St. Martin's Press
175 5th Ave
4th Floor
New York, NY 10010-7703

212-674-5151
FAX 212-674-3179

John Sargent, CEO

A directory listing hotels and inns that are located throughout the United States and Canada in various volumes. Prices vary per region, per volume.
ISBN: 0-312081-30-8
Founded in 1952

13903 Bed & Breakfast Home Directory: Homes Away from Home, West Coast
Knighttime Publications
890 Calabasas Road
Watsonville, CA 95076-0418
Diane Knight, Author
Suzy Blackaby, Author
Kevin McElvain, Author

Over 250 bed and breakfast homes are listed that are located in the areas of California, Oregon, Washington and British Columbia, Canada.
Cost: $12.95
203 Pages
Frequency: Biennial
ISBN: 0-942902-03-3

13904 Bed and Breakfast Guest Houses and Inns of America
PO Box 38066
Germantown, TN 38183-0066

901-946-1902
FAX 901-758-0816
Directory of services and supplies to the industry.
Cost: $45.00
350 Pages
Frequency: Annual
ISSN: 1056-8069

13905 Cabin Guide to Wilderness Lodging
Hammond Publishing
1500 E Tropicana Ave
Suite 110
Las Vegas, NV 89119-6515

702-878-2008
Home Page: www.prosofrealty.com

Jim Smith, Manager
Information is given on over 500 cabins in national and state forests, preserves and other wildlife areas.
Cost: $14.95
250 Pages
Frequency: Annual

13906 Complete Guide to Bed & Breakfasts, Inns and Guesthouses in US & Canada
Lanier Publishing International
963 Transport Way
Petaluma, CA 94954-8011

707-763-0271
FAX 707-763-5762
E-Mail: lanier@travelguides.com
Home Page: www.travelguides.com

Pamela Lanier, Owner
Directory of services and supplies to the industry.
Cost: $16.95
536 Pages
Frequency: Annual

13907 Country Inns and Back Roads, North America
HarperCollins
10 E 53rd St
Cellar 1 Floor
New York, NY 10022-5299

212-207-7000
FAX 212-207-6964
E-Mail: feedback2@harpercollins.com
Home Page: www.harpercollins.com

Brian Murray, CEO
Over 200 country inns in the United States and Canada are listed.
Cost: $13.00
450 Pages
Frequency: Annual

13908 Directory of Hotel & Lodging Companies
American Hotel & Lodging Association
1201 New York Ave NW
Suite 600
Washington, DC 20005-3931

202-289-3100
FAX 202-289-3199
E-Mail: webmaster@ahla.com
Home Page: www.ahla.com

Joseph McInerney, President
Joori Jeon, Executive Vice President & CFO
Pam Inman, Executive Vice President & COO
Marlene M. Colucci, Executive Vice President
Lisa Costello, Vice President, Government Affairs

Lists over 1,000 companies that own, manage or franchise properties worldwide. Also lists, in 7 sections: companies by type, company/brand web site, company listings, geographical, company rankings, hotel brokers, and vendors.
Cost: $100.00
Frequency: Annual
Founded in 1931

13909 Hotel Development Guide
Hospitality Media
17950 Preston Rd
Suite 710
Dallas, TX 75252-5637

972-934-2040
FAX 972-934-2070
E-Mail: Info@hospitalitymgt.com
Home Page: www.hospitalitymgt.com

Leo Spriggs, CEO
John Connor, Director of Operations
Bill Sullivan, Chief Financial Officer
Offers a list of suppliers of equipment, fixtures and services needed for new motels.
Cost: $100.00

13910 Hotel and Travel Index
Reed Travel Group
904 Haddonfield Rd
Subscription Department
Cherry Hill, NJ 08002-2745

856-665-4455
800-442-0900
FAX 856-488-4867
Over 45,000 hotels worldwide are profiled in this travel directory.
Cost: $125.00
2000 Pages
Frequency: Quarterly
Circulation: 60,000

13911 Inspected, Rated and Approved Bed and Breakfast Country Inns
American Bed & Breakfast Association
10800 Midlothian Tpke
Suite 254
Richmond, VA 23235-4700

Home Page: www.abba.com

Beth Burgreen Stuhlman, Editor
Information on over 500 overnight accommodations in North American bed and breakfast locations are listed.
Cost: $17.95
350 Pages
ISBN: 0-934473-27-7
Founded in 1996

13912 National Directory of Budget Motels
Pilot Books
127 Sterling Avenue
#2102
Greenport, NY 11944-1439

631-477-0978
800-79-ILOT
FAX 631-477-0978
Guide to the best in economy-priced chain motel accommodations in the United States and Canada.
Cost: $12.95
346 Pages
Frequency: Annual

13913 National Trust Guide to Historic Bed & Breakfasts, Inns & Small Hotels
Preservation Press
1785 Massachusetts Ave NW
Washington, DC 20036-2117

202-588-6083
FAX 202-588-6172

James Schwartz, Manager

Directory of services and supplies to the industry.
Cost: $13.95
416 Pages
Frequency: Biennial

13914 Official Bed and Breakfast Guide
National Bed & Breakfast Association
148 E Rocks Road
Norwalk, CT 06851

203-847-6196
FAX 203-847-0469
Home Page: www.nbba.com

Phyllis Featherston, President
A who's who directory of services and supplies to the industry offering a list of the best in bed and breakfast accommodations in USA, Canada and the Carribbean.
Cost: $17.95
560 Pages

13915 Official Hotel Guide
Reed Hotel Directories Network
500 Plaza Drive
Secaucus, NJ 07094-3619

201-902-1960
FAX 201-319-1628

Wilma Goldenberg, Editor
3 volumes of 25,000 hotels, motels and resorts worldwide.
Cost: $385.00
Frequency: Annual
Circulation: 20,000

13916 Pelican's Select Guide to American Bed and Breakfast
Pelican Publishing Company
1000 Burmaster St
Gretna, LA 70053-2246

504-368-1175
FAX 504-368-1195
E-Mail: sales@pelicanpub.com
Home Page: www.pelicanpub.com

Milburn Calhoun, Publisher
Joseph Billingsley, Sales Manager
Independent guest houses, inns and bed and breakfast accommodations are profiled.
Cost: $14.95
216 Pages
ISBN: 1-589800-61-8
Printed in 2 colors on matte stock

13917 Preferred Hotels Directory
Preferred Hotels & Resorts Worldwide
311 S Wacker Dr
Suite 1900
Chicago, IL 60606-6676

312-913-0400
800-323-7500
FAX 312-913-5124
Home Page: www.preferredhotels.com

John Ubberoth, CEO
Casey Ueberroth, Managing Director
80 Pages
Frequency: Annual
Circulation: 25,000

13918 Recommended Country Inns
Globe Pequot Press
246 Goose Lane
PO Box 480
Guilford, CT 06437

203-458-4500
888-249-7586
FAX 800-820-2329
Home Page: www.globepequot.com

Elizabeth Squier
Elenor Berman
This series of directories offers information on country inns located in certain parts of the

United States.
Cost: $18.95
416 Pages
Frequency: Biennial
ISBN: 0-762728-48-5

13919 Where to Stay USA
Prentice Hall Law & Business
1 Lake St
Upper Saddle Rv, NJ 07458-1828

201-236-7000
FAX 201-236-3381
Information is given on over 1,200 places to
stay and eat from $4 to $35 a night.
Cost: $16.00
350 Pages
Frequency: Biennial

Industry Web Sites

13920 http://gold.greyhouse.com
G.O.L.D Grey House OnLine Databases
Grey House Publishing's online database platform, GOLD, offers Quick Search, Keyword
Search and Expert Search for most business
sectors including hotel, motel and hospitality
markets. The GOLD platform makes finding
the information you need quick and easy -
whether you're a novice searcher or an experienced database user. All of Grey House's directory products are available for subscription on
the GOLD platform.

13921 www.abba.com
American Bed & Breakfast Association
National organization with information on over
500 overnight accomodations in North American bed and breakfast locations.

13922 www.ahma.com
American Hotel & Lodging Foundation
Trade association covering news, issues and ac-
tivities of related industry groups.

13923 www.biztravel.com
Biztravel.com
Internet travel service offering discounts on
flights, hotels, car rentals, packages and
cruises.

13924 www.chrie.org
Int'l Council on Hotel & Restaurant
Education
To enhance professionalism at all levels of the
hospitality and tourism industry through educa-
tion and training.

13925 www.ei-ahla.org
American Hotel&Lodging Educational
Foundation
A non-profit educational foundation of the
American Hotel & Lodging Association and
the world's largest provider of hospitality education training resources, videos, books, workbooks, seminars, management courses,
complete training systems and professional
certification programs.

13926 www.expedia.com
Expedia.com
Internet travel service offers access to airlines,
hotels, car rentals, vacation packages, cruises
and corporate travel.

13927 www.goworldnet.com/cgi-bin
Worldnet USA
A database of states with hotels, theaters and
museums.

13928 www.greyhouse.com
Grey House Publishing
Authoritative reference directories for most
business sectors including hotel, motel and
hospitality markets. Users can search the online
databases with varied search criteria allowing
for custom searches by product category, geographic area, sales volume, keyword, subject
and more. Full Grey House catalog and online
ordering also available.

13929 www.hanyc.org
Hotel Association of New York City
One of the oldest professional trade associa-
tions in the nation.

13930 www.hotels.com
Hotels.com
Provides discount accommodations worldwide.

13931 www.hotwire.com
Hotwire.com
Internet travel service offering discounts on
flights, hotels, car rentals, packages and
cruises.

13932 www.ieha.org
International Executive Housekeepers
Association
An organization for persons working in the
housekeeping area of the lodging industry.

13933 www.innbook.com
Bed and Breakfast Inns & Small Luxury
Hotels
Includes the finest inns, B&Bs, and getaway retreats in Canada and the Us, carefully chosen
and inspected to maintain the highest standards.

13934 www.masslodging.com
Massachusetts Lodging Association
A trade association representing and promoting
the lodging industryin Massachusetts.

13935 www.nmhotels.com
New Mexico Lodging Association
New Mexico's trade association representing
the lodging industry.

13936 www.orbitz.com
Orbitz.com
Internet travel service offering discounts on
flights, hotels, car rentals, packages and
cruises.

13937 www.paii.org
Professional Association of Innkeepers
International

Serving bed and breakfast/country inn owners,
aspiring innkeepers, inn sitters, vendors with
educational and consultative services. International conference.

13938 www.preferredhotels.com
The Luxury Hotels of Preferred Hotels &
Resorts
Worldwide

An exclusive group of independent luxury hotels in the United States.

13939 www.travel.lycos.com
Lycos.com
Internet travel service offering discounts on
flights, hotels, car rentals, packages and
cruises.

13940 www.travel.yahoo.com
Yahoo.com

Internet travel service providing access to
flights, hotels, car rentals, vacation packages
and cruises.

13941 www.travelocity.com
Sabre Holdings
Travel service offering consumers access to
hundreds of airlines and thousands of hotels, as
well as cruises, last-minute and vacation packages and best-in-class car rental companies.

13942 www.travelweb.com
Travelweb.com
Internet provider of hotel accommodations.

Associations

13943 ASM International
9639 Kinsman Road
Materials Park, OH 44073-0002

440-338-5151
800-336-5152
FAX 440-338-4634
E-Mail: memberservices@asminternational.org
Home Page: www.asminternational.org
Social Media: *Facebook, Twitter, LinkedIn*

Stanley Theobald, Senior Director, Business
Tom Passek, Managing Director
Nichol Campana, Director of Development
Skip Wolfe, Membership Product Manager
Norina Columbaro, Senior Manager, Education

The society for materials engineers and scientists, a worldwide network dedicated to advancing industry, technology and applications of metals and materials.
35000 Members
Founded in 1913

13944 American Coatings Association
1500 Rhode Island Ave., NW
Washington, DC 20005

202-462-6272
FAX 202-462-8549
E-Mail: members@paint.org
Home Page: www.coatingstech.org
Social Media: *Facebook, Twitter, LinkedIn, Reddit, Digg, MySpace, Stumble*

J. Andrew Doyle, President & CEO
Thomas J. Graves, Vice President, General Counsel
Allen Irish, Counsel / Director
Alison Keane, Vice President, Government Affairs
Robin Eastman Caldwell, Senior Gov. Affairs Specialist

Provides technical education and professional development to its members and to the global industry through its multinational Constituent Societies and collectively as a Federation
Founded in 1922

13945 American Composites Manufacturers Association
3033 Wilson Blvd.
Suite 420
Arlington, VA 22201-4749

703-525-0511
FAX 703-525-0743
E-Mail: info@acmanet.org
Home Page: www.acmanet.org
Social Media: *Facebook, Twitter, LinkedIn, RSS*

Jeff Craney, Chairman
Leon Garoufalis, Vice Chairman
Tom Dobbins, CAE, President
John Schweitzer, Vice President, Government Affairs
Heather Rhoderick, CMP, CAE, SVP, Events & Information

A trade association serving the composites industry.
1100 Members
Founded in 1979

13946 American Electroplaters and Surface Finishers Society (AESF)
1155 15th Street NW
Suite 500
Washington, DC 20005

202-457-8401
FAX 202-530-0659
E-Mail: info@aesf.org
Home Page: www.aesf.org

Social Media: *Facebook, Twitter, LinkedIn, Google+, RSS*

John Flatley, Executive Director
Courtney Mariette, Bookstore/Education
Holly Wills, Membership
Carrie Hoffman, Deputy Executive Director
Cheryl Clark, Director of Events

AESF is an international society that advances the science of surface finishing to benefit industry and society through education, information and social involvement, as well as those who provide services, supplies and support to the industry.
5000 Members
Founded in 1909

13947 American Society of Industrial Security
1625 Prince Street
Alexandria, VA 22314-2882

703-519-6200
FAX 703-519-6299
E-Mail: asis@asisonline.org
Home Page: www.asisonline.org
Social Media: *Facebook, Twitter, LinkedIn, YouTube*

Richard E. Widup, Jr., CPP, Chairman
Dave N. Tyson, CPP, President
Michael J. Stack, ASIS Chief Executive Officer
Thomas J. Langer, CPP, Treasurer
Richard E. Chase, CPP, PCI, PSP, Secretary

The largest international organization for professionals who are responsible for security, including managers and directors of security.
38000 Members
Founded in 1955
Mailing list available for rent

13948 Asphalt Recycling and Reclaiming Associates
15 Harold Court
Suite 250
Bayshore, NY 11706

631-231-8400
FAX 631-434-1116
E-Mail: sales@arra.com
Home Page: www.arra.com

Mike Krissoff, Executive Director

Promotes the interest of owners and manufacturers of recycling equipment, engineers, suppliers and businesses involved in the asphalt recycling industry. Newsletter published quarterly.
200 Members
Founded in 1957
Mailing list available for rent

13949 Associated Equipment Distributors
600 22nd Street
Suite 220
Oak Brook, IL 60523-8807

630-574-0650
800-388-0650
FAX 630-574-0132
E-Mail: info@aednet.org
Home Page: www.aednet.org
Social Media: *Facebook, Twitter, YouTube, Google+*

Don Shilling, Chairman
Whit Perryman, Vice Chairman
Brian P. McGuire, President, CEO
Bob Henderson, Executive VP & COO
Jason Blake, Senior VP & CFO

Membership organization of independent distributors, manufacturers and other organizations involved in the distribution of construction equipment and related products

and services in North America and throughout the world.
1200 Members
Founded in 1919
Mailing list available for rent

13950 Association for Manufacturing Excellence
3701 Algonquin Rd.
Suite 225
Rolling Meadows, IL 60008-3150

224-232-5980
FAX 224-232-5981
E-Mail: info@ame.org
Home Page: www.ame.org
Social Media: *Facebook, Twitter, LinkedIn, YouTube*

Jerry Wright, Chairman
Greg Williams, Vice Chairman

Organization promoting personal and enterprise improvement in the manufacturing industry.
4000 Members
Founded in 1985

13951 Association of Equipment Manufacturers
6737 West Washington Street
Suite 2400
Milwaukee, WI 53214-5647

414-272-0943
866-236-0943
FAX 414-272-1170
E-Mail: aem@aem.org
Home Page: www.aem.org
Social Media: *Twitter*

John Patterson, Chair
Leif J. Magnusson, Vice Chair
Goran Lindgren, Treasurer
Dennis J Slater, Secretary
Judy Gaus, Vice President, Human Resources

The trade and business development resource for companies that manufacture equipment, products and services used worldwide in the construction, agricultural, mining, forestry, and utility fields.
Founded in 2002
Mailing list available for rent

13952 Association of Machinery and Equipment Appraisers
315 South Patrick Street
Alexandria, VA 22314-3532

703-836-7900
800-537-8629
FAX 703-836-9303
E-Mail: amea@amea.org
Home Page: www.amea.org
Social Media: *LinkedIn, YouTube*

Jack Mendenhall, CEA, President
Randy Koster, CEA, 1st Vice President
Don Bentley, 2nd Vice President
Dave Troutman, Treasurer
James Zvonar, CEA, Immediate Past President

Certifies and accredits the most qualified capital equipment appraisers in the appraisal industry through promotion of standards of professional practice, ethical conduct, and marketing based experience.
300 Members
Founded in 1983
Mailing list available for rent

13953 Association of Technology Management and Applied Engineering

1390 Eisenhower Place
Suite 220
Ann Arbor, MI 48108

734-677-0720
FAX 734-677-0046
E-Mail: atmae@atmae.org
Home Page: www.atmae.org
Social Media: *Facebook, Twitter, LinkedIn*

Rick Coscarelli, Executive Director
Dave Monforton, Associate Director
Mary Lee, Association Manager
Keith Bretzius, Publications Coordinator

Provides support to all those involved in the industrial technology industry. Hosts trade shows and publishes various materials.
Mailing list available for rent

13954 Athletic Equipment Managers Association

207 E. Bodman
Bement, IL 13068-9643

217-678-1004
FAX 217-678-1005
E-Mail: aema@frontiernet.nen
Home Page: www.equipmentmanagers.org

Dan Siermine E.M., C., President
Mike Royster, Executive Director
Matthew Althoff E.M.,C., Associate Executive Director
Meli Resendiz E.M.,C, Vice Presidentÿ
Clifton Perry, Vice President

The purpose of the AEMA is to promote, advance, and improve the Equipment Managers Profession in all of its many phases
700 Members
Founded in 1974

13955 Casting Industry Suppliers Association

14175 West Indian School Road
Suite B4-504
Goodyear, AZ 85395

623-547-0920
FAX 623-536-1486
E-Mail: lsfish@asbury.comg
Home Page: www.cisa.org
Social Media: *RSS*

Lew Fish, President
Roger A Hayes, Executive Director
Lew Fish, 2nd Vice President
Mike Bartol, 1st Vice President

Fosters better trade practices. Serves as industry representative before the government and public. Encourages member research into new processes and methods of foundry operation. Association of suppliers to the worldwide metal casting industry.
70 Members
Founded in 1919
Mailing list available for rent

13956 Composite Can and Tube Institute

50 South Pickett Street
Suite 110
Alexandria, VA 22304-7206

703-823-7234
FAX 703-823-7237
E-Mail: ccti@cctiwdc.org
Home Page: www.cctiwdc.org

Kristine Garland, Executive Vice President
Wayne Vance, Association Councel
Janine Marczak, Associate Manager, Events

CCTI is an international nonprofit trade association representing the interests of manufacturers of composite paperboard cans, containers, canisters, tubes, cores, edgeboard and related or similar composite products and suppliers to those manufacturers of such items as paper, machinery, adhesives, labels and other services and materials.
Founded in 1933

13957 Conveyor Equipment Manufacturers Association

5672 Strand Ct.
Suite 2
Naples, FL 34110

239-514-3441
FAX 239-514-3470
E-Mail: phil@cemanet.org
Home Page: www.cemanet.org
Social Media: *Facebook, Twitter, LinkedIn*

Jerry Heathman, President
Garry Abraham, VP
Robert Reinfried, Executive VP
E.A. (Ned) Thompson, Treasurer
Paul Ross, Secretary

Involved in writing industry standards, the CEMA seeks to promote among its members and the industry standardization of design manufacture and application on a voluntary basis and in such manner as will not impede development of conveying machinery and component parts or lessen competition. CEMA sponsors an annual Engineering Conference that allows Member Company Engineers to meet and develop or improve CEMA Consensus Industry Standards and National Standards that affect the conveyor industry.
96 Members
Founded in 1933

13958 Equipment Leasing and Finance Association

1825 K Street NW
Suite 900
Washington, DC 20006

202-238-3400
FAX 202-238-3401
E-Mail: jbenson@elfaonline.org
Home Page: www.elfaonline.org
Social Media: *Facebook, Twitter, LinkedIn, RSS, YouTube*

William G. Sutton, CAE, President and CEO
Amy Vogt, Vice President of Communications
Paul Stilp, Vice President of Finance
Lesley Sterling, Vice President-Business
Andy Fishburn, VP, Federal Government Relations

Represents companies involved in the dynamic equipment leasing and finance industry to the business community, government and media.
700+ Members
Founded in 1961
Mailing list available for rent

13959 Fluid Controls Institute

1300 Sumner Avenue
Cleveland, OH 44115-2851

216-241-7333
FAX 216-241-0105
E-Mail: fci@fluidcontrolsinstitute.org
Home Page: www.fluidcontrolsinstitute.org

Manufacturers of equipment for fluid (liquid or gas) control and conditioning. This institute is organized into product specific sections which address issues that are relevant to particular products and or/or technologies.
Founded in 1921

13960 Fluid Sealing Association

994 Old Eagle School Rd
Suite 1019
Wayne, PA 19087-1802

610-971-4850
FAX 610-971-4859
E-Mail: info@fluidsealing.com
Home Page: www.fluidsealing.com

Robert Ecker, Executive Director
Hope Silverman, Administrative Director

Influence and support the development of related standards and to provide education in the fluid sealing area.
57 Members
Founded in 1933
Mailing list available for rent

13961 Hoist Manufacturers Institute

8720 Red Oak Boulevard
Suite 201
Charlotte, NC 28217-3996

704-676-1190
FAX 704-676-1199
E-Mail: cmiller@mhi.org
Home Page: www.mhi.org
Social Media: *Facebook, Twitter, LinkedIn*

E Larry Strayhorn, Last Retiring Executive Chairman
Dave Young, Executive Vice Chairman
John Paxton, President
Gregg E. Goodner, VP
Carol Miller, VP, Marketing

An affiliate of Material Handling Industry, also a trade association of maufacturers of overhead handling hoists. The products of member companies include hand chain hoists, ratchet lever hoists, trolleys, air chain and air rope hoists, and electric chain and electric wire rope hoists.
800 Members
Founded in 1945
Mailing list available for rent

13962 Independent Lubricant Manufacturers Association

400 N. Columbus Street
Suite 201
Alexandria, VA 22314-2264

703-684-5574
FAX 703-836-8503
E-Mail: tmack@ilma.org
Home Page: www.ilma.org
Social Media: *Facebook, Twitter*

Barbara A. Bellanti, President
Frank H. Hamilton III, VP
Beth Ann Jones, Treasurer
Lon Fanning, Immediate Past President
Dave Croghan, Secretary

Independent blenders and compounders of lubricants.
320 Members
Founded in 2004
Mailing list available for rent: 2000 names at $750 per M

13963 Industrial & Municipal Cleaning Association

906 Olive Street
Suite 1200
Saint Louis, MO 63101-1448

314-241-1445
FAX 314-241-1449
E-Mail: wjta-imca@wjta.org
Home Page: www.wjta.org

Bill Gaff, Chairman
George Savanick, Ph.D., President
Bill McClisterÿ, VP
Larry Loper, Treasurer
Kathy Krupp, Secretary

International association of professionals involved in high/ultra-high waterjet technology and industrial cleaning. Members are contractors, end users, job shops, manufacturers, researchers, and academicians.
Founded in 1983

13964 Industrial Diamond Association of America

PO Box 29460
Columbus, OH 43229

614-797-2265
FAX 614-797-2264
E-Mail: tkane-ida@insight.rr.com
Home Page: www.superabrasives.org

Mike Mustin, President
Terry M Kane, Executive Director
Troy Heuermann, Vice President
Keith Reckling, Secretary/Treasurer

Trade association for those in the superabrasives industry. Products and services provided and used in most manufacturing and constuction industries such as: stone processing, glass, construction, woodworking, electronics, medical, etc.
Founded in 1946

13965 Industrial Heating Equipment Association

5040 Old Taylor Mill Rd., PMB 13
Taylor Mill, KY 41015

859-356-1575
FAX 859-356-0908
E-Mail: ihea@ihea.org
Home Page: www.ihea.org
Social Media: *Facebook*

Anne Goyer, Executive Vice President
Amanda Goyer, Marketing
Mark Gentry, Membership Director
Kelly LeCount, Conference Manager
Leslie Muck, Webmaster and Database Management

A voluntary national trade association representing the major segments of the industrial heat processing equipment industry. Provides services to member companies that will enhance member company capabilities to serve end users in the industrial heat processing industry and improve the member company's business performance as well.
Founded in 1929
Mailing list available for rent

13966 Industrial Supply Association

100 North 20th Street
Suite 400
Philadelphia, PA 19103

215-320-3862
866-460-2360
FAX 215-564-2175
FAX 877-460-2365
E-Mail: info@isapartners.org
Home Page: www.isapartners.org
Social Media: *Facebook, Twitter, LinkedIn, RSS, YouTube*

Craig Vogely, Chairman
John Wiborg, Vice Chairman
Derek Yurgaitis, Treasurer
William Henricks, Secretary
Tommy Thompson, Immediate Past Chairman

ISA goal is to help members increase sales, reduce expenses and improve profitability.
600 Members
Founded in 1988

13967 Institute for Supply Management

2055 E. Centennial Circle
Tempe, AZ 85284-1802

480-752-6276
800-888-6276
FAX 480-752-7890
E-Mail:
custsvc@instituteforsupplymanagement.org
Home Page: www.ism.ws

Social Media: *Facebook, Twitter, LinkedIn, Youtube, Google Plus*

Thomas Derry, CEO
Nora Neibergall, CPSM CPO
Cindy Urbaytis, Managing Director
Mary Lue Peck, Managing Director

The mission of ISM is to enhance the value and performance of procurement and supply chain management practitioners and their organizations worldwide.
45000 Members
Founded in 1915
Mailing list available for rent

13968 Institute of Industrial Engineers

3577 Parkway Lane
Suite 200
Norcross, GA 30092

770-449-0460
800-494-0460
FAX 770-441-3295
E-Mail: cs@iienet.org
Home Page: www.iienet.org
Social Media: *Facebook, Twitter, LinkedIn, Google+, YouTube*

Don Greene, P.E., C.A.E., Chief Executive Officery
Donna Calvert, Chief Operating Officer
Hope Teaque, Dir. - Multimedia Advertising Sales
Nancy LaJoice, Director of Membership
Monica Elliott, Director of Communications

Supports all industrial engineers with training, education, publications, conferences, etc.
15000 Members
Founded in 1948
Mailing list available for rent

13969 International Staple, Nail and Tool

8735 W. Higgins Road
Suite 300
Chicago, IL 60631ÿ

847-375-6454
FAX 847-375-6455
E-Mail: info@isanta.org
Home Page: www.isanta.org

John Kurtz, Executive VP
David Rapp, Codes/Technical Services

An international organization of premier power fastening companies involved in the design, and manufacturing, and sales of power fastening tools and the fasteners they drive.
22 Members
Founded in 1966

13970 Machinery Dealers National Association

315 S. Patrick Street
Alexandria, VA 22314-3532

703-836-9300
800-872-7807
FAX 703-836-9303
E-Mail: office@mdna.org
Home Page: www.mdna.org
Social Media: *Facebook, Twitter, LinkedIn, Youtube*

Kim Khoury, CEA, President
Joe Lundvick, CEA, First Vice President
John Greene, CEA, Second Vice President
Terry Yoder, Treasurer
Mark Robinson, Executive Vice President

An international, non-profit trade association dedicated to the promotion of the used machinery industry.
400+ Members
Founded in 1941

13971 NIBA - The Belting Association

6737 W Washington St
Suite 1300
Milwaukee, WI 53214-5648

414-389-8606
800-488-4845
FAX 414-276-7704
E-Mail: staff@niba.org
Home Page: www.niba.org
Social Media: *Facebook, Twitter, LinkedIn*

John Shelton, President
Tom Pientok, First Vice President
Vernon Smith, Second Vice President
Bill Hornsby, Second Vice President
Jennifer Rzepka, Executive Director

A voluntary association of individuals and organizations who have joined together to further the interests of all fabricators, distriubtors and manufacturers of belting and related products. Promtes common business interests of all distriubtors/fabricators and manufacturers of conveyor and flat power transmission belting and material that enhances/changes belt.
Founded in 1927
Mailing list available for rent

13972 National Corrugated Steel Pipe Association

14070 Proton Road
Suite 100 LB9
Dallas, TX 75244

972-850-1907
FAX 972-490-4219
E-Mail: info@ncspa.org
Home Page: www.ncspa.org
Social Media: *Twitter, LinkedIn, Youtube, RSS*

Mike Mihelick, President
Dan Kadrmas, First Vice President
Roger Loding, Treasurer
Wallace Johnson, Immediate Past President
Pat Loney, Secretary

Seeks to promote sound public policy relating to the use of corrugated steel drainage structures in private and public construction.
60 Members
Founded in 1956

13973 National Spray Equipment Manufacturers

PO Box 2147
Skokie, IL 60076

440-366-6808
FAX 847-763-9538
E-Mail: ipp@halldata.com
Home Page: www.ippmagazine.com

Bruce Bryan, Advertising Director
Ted Klaiber, Sales Manager

Serves as a technical forum for safety and environmental matters pertaining to the spray finishing industry.
16 Members
Founded in 1922

13974 New England Equipment Dealers Association

PO Box 895
Concord, NH 03302-0895

603-225-5510
FAX 603-225-5510

George M Becker, Managing Director

The New England Equipment Association serve equipment manufacturing companies who provide products and services to the food and beverage industry.

13975 North American Equipment Dealers Association
1195 Smizer Mill Road
Fenton, MO 63026-3480

636-349-5000
FAX 636-349-5443
E-Mail: naeda@naeda.com
Home Page: www.naeda.com
Social Media: *Facebook, Twitter, LinkedIn*

Blaine Bingham, Chairman
Brian Carpenter, First Vice Chairman & Treasurer
Mark Foster, Second Vice Chairman & Secretary
Tom Nobbe, Immediate Past Chairman
Richard Lawhun, President and CEO

NAEDA and its affiliates provides a variety of educational, financial, legislative and legal services to equipment dealers in the United States and Canada.
5000 Members
Founded in 1900

13976 North American Sawing Association
1300 Sumner Avenue
Cleveland, OH 44115-2851

216-241-7333
FAX 216-241-0105
E-Mail: nasa@sawing association.com
Home Page: www.sawingassociation.com

Charles M Stockinger, Secretary/Treasurer

The purpose of this association is to improve the band sawing and power tool accessoried industries.
8 Members
Founded in 1959

13977 Society of Tribologists & Lubrication Engineers
840 Busse Hwy
Park Ridge, IL 60068-2302

847-825-5536
FAX 847-825-1456
E-Mail: information@stle.org
Home Page: www.stle.org
Social Media: *Facebook, Twitter, LinkedIn, Youtube*

Dr. Martin N. Webster, President
Dr. Aliÿ Erdemir, Vice President
Mr. Michaelÿ Anderson, Secretary
Greg Croce, Treasurer
Dr. Maureen E. Hunter, Past President

Purpose is to advance the science of tribology and the practice of lubrication engineering in order to foster innovation, improve the performance of equipment and products, conserve resources and protect the environment.
4000 Members
Founded in 1944
Mailing list available for rent

13978 The National Council for Advanced Manufacturing (NACFAM)
2025 M St. NW
Suite 800
Washington, DC 20036

202-367-1178
Home Page: www.nacfam.org

Robert (Rusty) Patterson, Chairman & CEO
Fred Wentzel, Executive Vice President
The non-partisan Council advocates for federal policies that will spur innovation in U.S. manufacturing and make it more competitive globally.

13979 ToolBase Services
NAHB Research Center

400 Prince George's Boulevard
Upper Marlboro, MD 20774

301-494-4000
800-898-2842
E-Mail: toolbase@nahbrc.org
Home Page: www.toolbase.org

The housing industry's resource for technical information on building products, materials, new technologies, business management, and housing systems.
Mailing list available for rent

13980 Unified Abrasive Manufacturers' Association
30200 Detroit Road
Cleveland, OH 44145-1967

440-899-0010
FAX 440-892-1404
E-Mail: contact@uama.org
Home Page: www.uama.org

Jeff Wherry, Executive Director

The purpose is to undertake those activities that can be pursued more effectively by an association than individual companies in order to enable the industry to freely create and market safe, productive abrasive products throughout the world.
30 Members
Founded in 1999

13981 WaterJet Technology Association Industrial & Municipal Cleaning Association
906 Olive Street
Suite 1200
Saint Louis, MO 63101-1448

314-241-1445
FAX 314-241-1449
E-Mail: wjta-imca@wjta.org
Home Page: www.wjta.org

Bill Gaff, Chairman
George Savanick, Ph.D., President
Bill McClisterÿ, VP
Larry Loper, Treasurer
Kathy Krupp, Secretary

A professional association of high pressure waterjet and industrial vacuum equipment users, manufacturers, distributors, researchers, regulators and consultants.
Founded in 1983

13982 Web Sling & Tiedown Association
9 Newport Drive
Suite 200
Forest Hill, MD 21050

443-640-1070
FAX 443-640-1031
E-Mail: wstda@stringfellowgroup.net
Home Page: www.wstda.com
Social Media: *LinkedIn*

Jeff Iden, President
Greg Pilgrim, Vice-President
Jim Bailey, Secretary/Treasurer
Kathleen A.ÿ DeMarco, CAE, Executive Director
Amy Chetelat, CAE, Director of Finance

Manufacturers of web slings which are used as hoists in various industrial lifting operations.
79 Members
Founded in 1973

Newsletters

13983 Asphalt Recycling and Reclaiming Association
Asphalt Recycling and Reclaiming Association

3 Church Cir
PMB Box 250
Annapolis, MD 21401-1933

410-267-0023
FAX 410-267-7546
Home Page: www.arra.com

Mike Krissoff, Executive Director

Promotes the interest of owners and manufacturers of recycling equipment, engineers suppliers and businesses involved in the asphalt recycling industry.
Frequency: Quarterly
Circulation: 1200
Founded in 1976
Mailing list available for rent

13984 Can Tube Bulletin
Composite Can & Tube Institute
50 S Pickett Street
Suite 110
Alexandria, VA 22304-7206

703-823-7234
FAX 703-823-7237
E-Mail: ccti@cctiwdc.org
Home Page: www.cctiwdc.org

Kristine Garland, Executive VP
Wayne Vance, Association Counsel
Janine Marczak, Associate Manager, Events
Frequency: Bi-monthly
Circulation: 800+

13985 Fastener Industry News
Business Information Services
5028 Dumont Place
Woodland Hills, CA 91364-2407

818-248-5023
800-929-5586
FAX 818-249-1169
E-Mail: info@biscomputer.com
Home Page: www.biscomputer.com

Richard Callahan, Publisher
John Wolz, Editor
Miro Macho, CEO/President

Publication written for executives and administrators in the fastener industry. Focuses on providing readers with business and financial news from within the industry. Includes personnel notices, management ideas and related materials.
Cost: $200.00
8 Pages
Frequency: Monthly
Founded in 1971
Mailing list available for rent
Printed in 2 colors on matte stock

13986 Instrumentation and Automation News
Chilton Company
201 King of Prussia Rd
Radnor, PA 19087-5147

610-964-4762
800-274-2207
FAX 610-964-1888

Matt DeJulio, Publisher
The control technology/instrumentation market's only product news tabloid.

13987 Journal of the National Spray Equipment Manufacturers Association
550 Randall Road
Elyria, OH 44035-2974

440-366-6808
FAX 440-892-2018

Don R Scarbrough, Executive Secretary

Includes editorial on safety and environmental matters pertaining to the spray finishing industry. Regular monthly features.
16 Pages
Founded in 1922

13988 Manufacturing Automation

Vital Information Publications
754 Caravel Lane
Foster City, CA 94404-1712

650-345-7018
Home Page: www.sensauto.com

Peter Adrian, Owner
Gary Kuba, Marketing Director

Provides market research data and vital information about key products, applications, and technologies for a wide range of industrial automation segments, such as CAD/CAM, supply chain management, e-Commerce solutions, enterprise resource planning, automation software, manufacturing technology, industrial controls, and manufacturing systems.

13989 Sensor Business Digest

Vital Information Publications
754 Caravel Lane
Foster City, CA 94404-1712

650-345-7018
Home Page: www.sensauto.com

Peter Adrian, Owner
Gary Kuba, Marketing Director

A widely recognized as a major source of information about the sensors industry-provides unique information about vital sensor markets, products, and applications, sensor technology, as well as in-depth company profiles
Frequency: Monthly

13990 Sensor Technology

John Wiley & Sons
111 River St
Hoboken, NJ 07030-5774

201-748-6000
800-825-7550
FAX 201-748-6088
E-Mail: info@wiley.com
Home Page: www.wiley.com

William J Pesce, CEO

Written for companies and enterprises involved in a broad range of industrial disciplines. Publication follows advances in sensor technologies and their applications, along with opportunities for their use in the industrial marketplace.
Cost: $565.00
10 Pages
Frequency: Daily
Founded in 1807
Mailing list available for rent: 25000 names at $180 per M
Printed in 2 colors on newsprint stock

13991 Waterjet Technology Association-Industrial and Municipal Cleaning Association

906 Olive Street
Suite 1200
Saint Louis, MO 63101-1448

314-241-1445
FAX 314-241-1449
E-Mail: wjta-imca@wjta.org
Home Page: www.wjta.org

George A Savanick PhD, President, Jet News Editor
Kenneth C Carroll, Association Manager

A professional association of high pressure waterjet and industrial cleaning equipment users, manufacturers, distributors, researchers, regulators, consultants and academicians.
Founded in 1983

Magazines & Journals

13992 Advanced Materials & Processes

ASM International
9639 Kinsman Rd
Materials Park, OH 44073-0002

440-338-5151
800-336-5152
FAX 440-338-4634
E-Mail: memberservices@asminternational.org
Home Page: www.asminternational.org

Joseph M Zion, Publisher
Joanne Miller, Managing Editor
Margaret Hunt, Editor-in-Chief
Gernant E. Maurer, President
Thomas S. Passek, Managing Director

AM&P, the monthly technical magazine from ASM International, is designed to keep readers aware of leading-edge developments and trends in engineering materials - metals and alloys, engineering polymers, advanced ceramics, and composites - and the methods used to select, process, fabricate, test, and characterize them.
Frequency: Monthly
Circulation: 32M
Founded in 1977

13993 American Industry

Publications for Industry
21 Russell Woods Road
Great Neck, NY 11021-4644

516-487-0990
FAX 516-487-0809
Home Page: www.publicationsforindustry.com

Jack S Panes, Publisher

Created for those executives responsible for overall plant operations and maintenance. Editorial focus is on new products and related services.
Cost: $25.00
Circulation: 300000
Founded in 1946
Printed in 4 colors on newsprint stock

13994 American Tool, Die & Stamping News

Eagle Publications
42400 Grand River Ave
Suite 103
Novi, MI 48375-2572

248-347-3487
800-783-3491
FAX 248-347-3492
E-Mail: info@ameritooldie.com
Home Page: www.ameritooldie.com

Applications, techniques, equipment and accessories of metal stamping, moldmaking, electric discharge machining; and new product information relating to the tool and die industry. Accepts advertising.
70 Pages
Frequency: Monthly
Circulation: 30000
ISSN: 0192-5709
Founded in 1971
Printed in 5 colors on glossy stock

13995 Asian Industrial Report

Keller International Publishing Corporation
150 Great Neck Rd
Great Neck, NY 11021-3309

516-829-9722
FAX 516-829-9306

Gerald E Keller, President
Bryan DeLuca, Editorial Director
Terry Beirne, Publisher
Bob Herlihy, Sales manager

English language tabloid presenting new products, equipment and services.
36 Pages
Circulation: 37107
ISSN: 1076-8351
Founded in 1882
Printed in 4 colors on glossy stock

13996 Business & Industry

Business Magazines
1720 28th Street
Suite B
West Des Moines, IA 50266-1400

515-225-2545
FAX 515-225-2318
Home Page: www.busindmag.com

James V Snyder, Publisher
RJ Balch, Editor

Industrial news publication
Cost: $24.00
56 Pages
Frequency: Monthly
Circulation: 14M
ISSN: 0021-0463
Founded in 1946
Printed in 4 colors on glossy stock

13997 Cleaner

COLE Publishing
1720 Maple Lake Dam Road
PO Box 220
Three Lakes, WI 54562-0220

715-546-3346
800-257-7222
FAX 715-546-3786
E-Mail: info@cleaner.com
Home Page: www.cleaner.com
Social Media: *Facebook, Twitter*

Jeff Bruss, President
Winnie May, Advertising Sales/Subscriptions
Ted Rulseh, Editor
Bob Kendall, Co-founder

The latest tools and equipment promoting safety and efficiency, employment and enviromental concerns, as well as industry profiles.
Cost: $15.50
Frequency: Monthly
Circulation: 22780
Founded in 1979

13998 Composites Manufacturers Magazine

American Composites Manufacturers Association
1010 N Glebe Rd
Suite 450
Arlington, VA 22201-5761

703-525-0511
FAX 703-525-0743
E-Mail: info@acmanet.org
Home Page: www.acmanet.org

Tom Dobbins, Chief Staff Executive
Patti Washburn, Deputy Chief Staff Executive
Frequency: Monthly

13999 Crane & Hoist Canada

Capamara Communications
815 1st Ave
#301
Seattle, WA 98104

250-474-3982
800-936-2266
FAX 250-478-3979
E-Mail: jeremy@capamara.com
Home Page: www.naqua.com

Peter Chetteburgh, Editor-in-Chief
Jeremy Thain, Sales Manager
James Lewis, Production Department

Only magazine focused exclusively on Canada's crane and hoist sectors. Provides essential news and information that Canadian crane and

hoist professionals need in order to operate successfully and profitably. Articles on company profiles, practical crane & rigging information, new product news, industry trends, policy & regulations, safety/training/certification, and risk management.
Cost: $27.95
Frequency: Bi-monthly
Circulation: 3,500
Founded in 1985

14000 Filtration News

Eagle Publishers
42400 Grand River Ave
Suite 103
Novi, MI 48375-2572

248-347-3487
FAX 248-347-3492
E-Mail: info@filtnews.com

Arthur Brown, Editor
Antoinette DeWaal, Associate Publisher/VP
Ken Norberg, Editor-in-Chief

New products and events on the special aspects of filtraion ranging from new equipment applications to new trends in the filtraion industry.
Cost: $65.00
Frequency: Bi-Monthly
Founded in 1981

14001 Finer Points Magazine

Industrial Diamond Association of America
PO Box 29460
Columbus, OH 43229

614-797-2265
FAX 614-797-2264
E-Mail: tkane-ida@insight.rr.com
Home Page: www.superabrasives.org

Terry Kane, Publisher/Editor
Joe Tabling, President

Information for people who are involved in superabrasives or superabrasive products in some way.
Cost: $35.00
Frequency: Quarterly
Circulation: 7,500
Founded in 1946

14002 Flow Control

Grand View Media Group
200 Croft Street
Suite 1
Birmingham, AL 35242

888-431-2877
FAX 205-408-3799
E-Mail: flowcontrol@grandviewmedia.com
Home Page: www.flowcontrolnetwork.com
Social Media: *Facebook, Twitter, LinkedIn*

John P Harris, Publisher
Matt Migliore, Editor
Matt Migliore, Executive Director of Content
Amy W. Richardson, Managing Editor
Mary Beth Timmerman, Marketing Manager

Technology information and new products for fluid handling engineers

14003 Hauler

Hauler Magazine
166 S Main Street
PO Box 508
New Hope, PA 18938

800-220-6029
800-220-6029
FAX 215-862-3455
E-Mail: mag@thehauler.com
Home Page: www.thehauler.com

Thomas N Smith, Publisher/Editor
Barbara Gibney, Circulation Manager
Leslie T Smith, Marketing Director

Dedicated to the refuse and solid waste industry. It is the acknowledged leader in the new and used refuse truck and equipment market-

place, and now lists hundreds of new and used trash trucks, trailers, containers, services, plus parts and accessories from the best suppliers in the industry.
Cost: $12.00
Frequency: Monthly
Circulation: 18630
Founded in 1978

14004 High Performance Composites

Ray Publishing
P.O.Box 992
Morrison, CO 80465-0992

303-467-1776
FAX 303-467-1777
E-Mail: info@raypubs.com
Home Page: www.compositeworld.com

Approach is technical, offering cutting-edge design, engineering, prototyiping, and manufacturing solutions for aerospace and other traditional and emerging structural applications for advanced composites.

14005 I&CS-Instrumentation & Control Systems

PennWell Publishing Company
1421 S Sheridan Rd
Tulsa, OK 74112-6619

918-831-9421
800-331-4463
FAX 918-831-9476
E-Mail: headquarters@pennwell.com
Home Page: www.pennwell.com

Robert Biolchini, President

Regular issue features include new systems analyses, new products listings, application ideas, and tutorial technology features.
Cost: $65.00
Frequency: Monthly
Circulation: 92,618
Founded in 1910

14006 ICS Cleaning Specialist

BNP Media
22801 Ventura Boulevard
#115
Woodland Hills, CA 91364

818-224-8035
800-835-4398
FAX 818-224-8042
E-Mail: kesslere@bnpmedia.com
Home Page: www.icsmag.com
Social Media: *Facebook, Twitter, LinkedIn*

Phil Johnson, Group Publisher
Evan Kessler, Publisher
Jeffrey Stouffer, Editor

Dedicated to providing cleaning and restoration/remediation professionals with the most current and relevant information available to the industry.
Frequency: Annual+
Circulation: 25000
Mailing list available for rent

14007 Industrial Distribution

199 East Badger Road
Suite 201
Madison, WI 53713

781-734-8000
FAX 781-734-8070
Home Page: www.manufacturing.net/ind
Social Media: *Facebook, Twitter*

Eric Wixom, Publisher
Jeff Reinke, Editorial Director
Joel Hans, Managing Editor
Mary Ann Gajewski, Production Manager

Provides current, comprehensive, issues-oriented editorial unique to the distribution industry including news, product updates, profitable product selection, management techniques, features on distribution-manufacturer relation-

ships, legal issues and sales improvement.
Cost: $89.90
Frequency: Monthly
Circulation: 38000+
Mailing list available for rent

14008 Industrial Equipment News

Thomas Publishing Company
5 Penn Plaza
Manhattan, NY 10001

212-695-0500
800-733-1127
FAX 212-290-7206
E-Mail: dmaskin@tpmgnet.com
Home Page: www.ienonline.com

Mark Maskin, Editorial Director
Deborah Maskin, Managing Editor
Ciro Buttacavoli, Publisher
Marie Urbanowicz, Marketing Director

Serves the industrial field including manufacturing, mining, utilities, construction, transportation,governmental establishments, and educational services.
Frequency: Monthly
Circulation: 205,000+
ISSN: 0019-8258
Founded in 1898

14009 Industrial Laser Solutions

PennWell Publishing Company
1421 S Sheridan Rd
Tulsa, OK 74112-6619

918-831-9421
FAX 918-831-9476
E-Mail: belforte@penwell.com
Home Page: www.pennwell.com

Robert Biolchini, President
Laureen Belleville, Associate Publisher/Senior Editor

Devoted exclusively to global coverage of industrial laser applications, technology, and the people and companies who participate in this, the largest commerical portion of the global laser market.
45 Pages
Frequency: Monthly
Circulation: 10000
ISSN: 1523-4266
Founded in 1910

14010 Industrial Literature Review

Thomas Publishing Company
5 Penn Plz
12th Floor
New York, NY 10001-1860

212-695-0500
FAX 212-290-7362
E-Mail: businesslists@thomaspublishing.com
Home Page: www.thomaspublishing.com

Carl Holst-Knudsen, CEO

Created to provide the dissemination of manufacturer catalogs and literature and mailed to buyers and specifies at plants with more than twenty employees.
Founded in 1976

14011 Industrial Maintenance & Plant Operation

Advantage Business Media
199 E Badger Road
Suite 201
Madison, WI 53713

973-920-7787
FAX 973-607-5599
Home Page: www.impomag.com

Tom Lynch, Group Publisher
Eric Wixom, Associate Publisher
Anna Wells, Editor
Jeff Reinke, Editorial Director

provides timely, relevant coverage of manufacturing news, technology breakthrough, and

in-plant advancements for plant managers and engineers looking to increase productivity, operate more efficiently and improve competitiveness.
Frequency: Monthly
Founded in 1940

14012 Industrial Management
Institute of Industrial Engineers
3577 Parkway Lane
Suite 200
Norcross, GA 30092

770-449-0460
800-494-0460
FAX 770-441-3295
E-Mail: cs@iienet.org
Home Page: www.iienet.org

Elaine Fuerst, Marketing Director
Don Greene, Chief Executive Officer
Donna Calvert, Chief Operating Officer
Heather Bradley, Director of Membership
Monica Elliott, Director of Communications

Directed to the full range of management issues including adapting and evaluating new technologies, improving productivity and quality, and motivating employees.
Cost: $35.00
Frequency: Monthly
Circulation: 8500
Founded in 1948
Mailing list available for rent

14013 Industrial Market Place
Wineberg Publications
7842 Lincoln Avenue
Skokie, IL 60077

847-676-1900
800-323-1818
FAX 847-676-0063
E-Mail: info@industrialmktpl.com
Home Page: www.industrialmktpl.com

Joel Wineberg, President
Jakie Bitensky, Editor

Has advertisements on machinery, industrial and plant equipment, services and industrial auctions in each issue.
Cost: $175.00
Frequency: Bi-Weekly
Circulation: 14,000
Founded in 1951
Mailing list available for rent: 120 names at $70 per M
Printed in 4 colors on glossy stock

14014 Industrial Purchasing Agent
Publications for Industry
21 Russell Woods Road
Great Neck, NY 11021-4644

516-487-0990
FAX 516-487-0809
Home Page: www.PublicationsforIndustry.com

Jack Panes, Publisher
Pearl Shaine, Editor

New products publication for industrial purchasing agent executives in largest plants in the United States. Contains new releases on products, brochures, materials handling, etc.
Cost: $25.00
Frequency: Monthly
Circulation: 27000
Founded in 1958
Printed in 4 colors on newsprint stock

14015 International Journal of Purchasing & Materials Management
National Association of Purchasing Management

2055 E Centennial Circle
PO Box 22160
Tempe, AZ 85285-2160

480-752-2277
FAX 480-491-7885
Home Page: www.capsresearch.com
Social Media: *Twitter*

Phillip L Carter, CEO/President
Richard A. Boyle, Director of Corporate
Kristina Cahill, Research Specialist
Phillip L. Carter, Executive Director
Kim Dixon-Williams, Executive Programs Manager

Publishes articles dealing with concepts from business, economics, operations management, information systems, the behavioral sciences, and other disciplines which contribute to the advancement of knowledge in the various areas of purchasing, materials management, and related fields.
Cost: $59.00
Frequency: Quarterly
Circulation: 2800
Founded in 1986

14016 Journal of Coatings Technology
Federation of Societies for Coatings Technology
1500 Rhode Island Ave., NW
Suite 415
Washington, DC 20005

202-462-6272
FAX 202-462-8549
E-Mail: fsct@coatingstech.com
Home Page: www.coatingstech.org

J. Andrew Doyle, President & CEO
Thomas J. Graves, VP, General Counsel
Allen Irish, Counsel / Director, Industry Affair
Alison Keane, Vice President, Government Affairs
Robin Eastman Caldwell, Senior Government Affairs

Includes practical articles, Q&A features, and roundtable discussions with coatings professionals related to industry segments, manufacturing processes, business operations, environmental concerns, and other pertinent topics.
Frequency: 11x/Year

14017 Journal of Materials Engineering and Performance
ASM International
9639 Kinsman Road
Materials Park, OH 44073-0002

440-338-5151
800-336-5152
FAX 440-338-4634
E-Mail: memberservice@asminternational.org
Home Page: www.asminternational.org

Gernant E. Maurer, President
Thomas S. Passek, Managing Director

Peer-reviewed journal that publishes contributions on all aspects of materials selection, design, characterization, processing and performance testing. The journal for solving day-to-day engineering challenges - especially those involving components for larger systems.
Cost: $1965.00
Frequency: Bimonthly
Circulation: 305
Founded in 1992

14018 Journal of Phase Equilibria
ASM International
9639 Kinsman Rd
Materials Park, OH 44073-0002

440-338-5151
800-336-5152
FAX 440-338-4634

E-Mail: memberservices@asminternational.org
Home Page: www.asminternational.org

Gernant E. Maurer, President
Thomas S. Passek, Managing Director

Peer-reviewed journal that contains basic and applied research results, evaluated phase diagrams, a survey of current literature, and comments or other material pertinent to the previous three areas. The aim is to provide a broad spectrum of information concerning phase equilibria for the materials community.
Cost: $1965.00
Frequency: Bimonthly
Circulation: 305

14019 Journal of Protective Coatings & Linings
Technology Publishing Company
2100 Wharton St
Suite 310
Pittsburgh, PA 15203-1951

412-431-8300
800-837-8303
FAX 412-431-5428
E-Mail: webmaster@paintsquare.com
Home Page: www.paintsquare.com
Social Media: *Facebook, Twitter*

Harold Hower, Owner
Karen Kapsanis, Editor
Milissa Bogats, Production Director
Pam Simmons, Director of Marketing
Julie Birch, Marketing Manager

Focuses on good practice in the use of protective coatings for steel and concrete surfaces. Features articles on such topics as coatings selection for specific service environments, surface preparation, coating application, quality control, cost-effectiveness in maintenance programs, safety issues, and environmental regulations.
Cost: $80.00
Frequency: Monthly
Circulation: 15000
Mailing list available for rent

14020 Journal of Thermal Spray Technology
ASM International
9639 Kinsman Rd
Novelty, OH 44073-0002

440-338-5151
800-336-5152
FAX 440-338-4634
E-Mail: Cust-Srv@asminternational.org
Home Page: www.asminternational.org

Gernant E. Maurer, President
Thomas S. Passek, Managing Director

Peer-reviewed journal which publishes contributions on all aspects, fundamental and practical, of thermal spray science, including processes, feedstock manufacture, testing and characterization. As the primary vehicle for thermal spray information transfer, its mission is to synergize the rapidly advancing thermal spray industry and related industries by presenting research and development efforts leading to advancements in implementable engineering applications of the technology.
Cost: $1577.00
Frequency: Bimonthly
Circulation: 680
Founded in 1952

14021 Lift Equipment
Group III Communications

204 W Kansas Street
Suite 103
Independence, MO 64050

816-254-8735
FAX 816-254-2128

Terry Ford, President
Michael Scheibach, Publisher
Tracy L Bennett, Editor/Associate Publisher

The buyer's source for equipment, technology
and trends. Free to qualified subscribers.
Cost: $24.00
80 Pages
Frequency: 10 per year
Circulation: 18,000
ISSN: 1056-0149
Printed in 4 colors on glossy stock

14022 Lubes-N-Greases

LNG Publishing Company
6105 Arlington Blvd
Suite G
Falls Church, VA 22044-2708

703-536-0800
FAX 703-536-0803
E-Mail: info@LNGpublishing.com
Home Page: www.lngpublishing.com

Gloria Stienberg, Owner
Tim Sullivan, Managing Editor
Sheryl Unangst, Circulation Manager
Michele Persaud, Senior Editor
Richard Beercheck, Senior Editor

Features and informed opinions covering automotive and industrial lubricants, metalworking
fluids, greases, base stocks, additives, packaging, biodegradable and synthetic products,
companies, people, issues and trends affecting
the industry.
Frequency: Monthly
Circulation: 16000
ISSN: 1080-9449
Founded in 1995
Printed in 4 colors

14023 Lubricating Engineering

Society of Tribologists & Lubrication
Engineers
840 Busse Hwy
Park Ridge, IL 60068-2376

847-825-5536
FAX 847-825-1456
E-Mail: information@stle.org
Home Page: www.stle.org

Ed Salek, Executive Director
Karl Phipps, Associate Managing Editor
Tracy Nicholas, National Sales Manager

Technical papers and news articles with up to
date developments in the lubrication industry.
Frequency: Monthly
Circulation: 6000

14024 MRO Today

Pfingsten Publishing
730 Madison Avenue
Fort Atkinson, WI 53538-606

920-563-5225
800-932-7732
FAX 920-563-4269
Home Page: www.mrotoday.com

Todd Rank, VP
Tom Hammel, Associate Publisher/Editorial
Dir
John Mansavage, Circulation and Research
Jill Sheppard, Marketing Manager

Provides best practices for industrial
maintenance, production, MRO purchasing,
quality and safety personnel. MRO Today helps
these pros do their jobs cheaper, better, faster
and smarter.
Circulation: 120,000
ISSN: 1091-0638

Founded in 1996
Printed in on glossy stock

14025 Maintenance Technology

Applied Technology Publications
1300 S Grove Ave
Suite 105
Barrington, IL 60010-5246

847-382-8100
FAX 847-304-8603
Home Page: www.mt-online.com

Arthur Rice, President/CEO
Bill Kiesel, Vice President/Publisher
Jane Alexander, Editor-In-Chief
Rick Carter, Executive Editor
Randy Buttstadt, Director of Creative Services

Maintenance Technology magazine serves the
business and technical information needs of
managers and engineers responsible for assuring availability of plant equipment and systems. It provides readers with articles on
advanced technologies, strategies, tools, and
services for the life-cycle management of
capital assets.
Frequency: Monthly
Circulation: 50,827
*Mailing list available for rent: 35,263 names at
$$15 per M*

14026 Measurements & Control

100 Wallace Avenue
Suite 100
Sarasota, FL 34237

941-954-8405
800-883-8894
FAX 941-366-5743

14027 Modern Paint & Coatings

Cygnus Publishing
445 Broad Hollow Road
Melville, NY 11747-3601

631-845-2700
FAX 631-845-2723
Home Page: www.cygnuspub.com

Esther D'Amico, Editor
Paul Bonaiuto, CFO
Kathy Scott, Director of Public Relations

The latest technology and news including
chemical innovations, new production equip-
ment,new trends and coverage of regulatory af-
fairs.
Cost: $45.00
Frequency: Monthly
Circulation: 14,000

14028 NAEDA Equipment Dealer

North American Equipment Dealers
Association
1195 Smizer Mill Rd
Fenton, MO 63026-3480

636-349-5000
FAX 636-349-5443
E-Mail: naeda@naeda.com
Home Page: www.naeda.com
Social Media: *Twitter, LinkedIn*

Paul Kindinger, President/CEO
Michael Williams, VP, Government
Relations/Treasurer
Terry Leath, Executive Assistant
Roger Gjellstad, First Vice Chair
Lester Killebrew, Chairman

A monthly management and merchandising
magazine features articles about successful
dealers, new products, new technology, indus-
try news, insurance loss control solutions, and
top management tips.
Cost: $45.00
5000 Members
32 Pages
Frequency: Monthly

ISSN: 1074-5017
Founded in 1959
Printed in 4 colors on glossy stock

14029 New Equipment Digest

Penton Media
1300 E 9th St
Cleveland, OH 44114-1503

216-696-7000
FAX 216-696-6662
E-Mail: information@penton.com
Home Page: www.penton.com

Jane Cooper, Marketing
Diane Madzelonka, Production Manager
David Kieselstein, Chief Executive Officer
Kurt Nelson, Vice President, Human Resources
Andrew Schmolka, Senior Vice President

Serves the general industrial field which in-
cludes manufacturing, processing, engineering
services, construction, transportation, mining,
public utilities, wholesale distributors, educa-
tional services, libraries, and governmental
establishments.
Frequency: Monthly
Circulation: 206154
Founded in 1936
Mailing list available for rent

14030 OEM Off-Highway

1233 Janesville Avenue
PO Box 803
Fort Atkinson, WI 53538-803

920-563-6388
800-547-7377
FAX 920-328-9029
E-Mail: Leslie.Shalabi@cygnuspub.com
Home Page: www.oemoff-highway.com

Richard Reiff, Executive VP
Leslie Shalabi, Publisher/Editor
Paul Mackler, President/CEO
Barb Hesse, Circulation Manager

Offers information on off-road machinery and
farm equipment.
Founded in 1965

14031 Purchasing Magazine's Buying Strategy Forecast

Reed Business Information
275 Washington St
Newton, MA 02458-1611

617-964-3030
FAX 617-558-4327
E-Mail: kbecker@reedbusiness.com

Kathy Doyle, Publisher
Paul Teague, Chief Editor
Kathy Becker, Publisher's Assistant

Provides insight and forecasts of numerous in-
dustrial and commercial raw materials
products.
Circulation: 95,095
Founded in 1960

14032 Rental Product News

Cygnus Business Media
3 Huntington Quadrangle
Suite 301N
Melville, NY 11747

631-845-2700
800-308-6397
FAX 631-845-2741
E-Mail: info@cygnus.com
Home Page: www.cygnusb2b.com

Dave Davel, VP Publishing
Kris Flitcroft, Group Publisher
Carrier Grall, Publisher
Paul Bonaiuto, Chief Financial Officer
John French, Chief Executive Officer

Provides professional rental operators with the
latest insights on equipment asset management
so they can make their businesses more produc-
tive and competitive. Also provides insight on

how leaders in the equipment rental field are getting the best return from their assets through better equipment selection, application, maintenance and safety techniques.
Circulation: 20000
Founded in 1966

14033 Robotics World
Douglas Publications
2807 N Parham Road
Suite 200
Richmond, VA 23294

804-762-9600
800-791-8699
570-567-1982
FAX 570-320-2079
E-Mail:
briefingsweborders@publishersserviceasso
Home Page: www.douglaspublications.com

Jack Browne, Editor
Andrew Dwyer, Publisher
Covers key developments in the field of flexible automation and intelligent machines for an audience of management level automation professionals.
Frequency: Monthly
Circulation: 87000
Founded in 1985

14034 Twin Plant News
5400 Suncrest
Suite D-5
El Paso, TX 79912

915-532-1567
FAX 915-544-7556
E-Mail: tpn@twinplantnews.com
Home Page: www.twinplantnews.com

Michele Lee, President
Rosa Ma Nibbe, Executive Publisher
Mike Patten, Managing Editor
Focuses on the operations of major companies in the United States and the maquiladoras in Mexico. Includes articles about changes affecting the automotive, electronics, plastics and metal industries, as well as information about customs regulations on both sides of the border and other relevant topics.
Frequency: Monthly
Founded in 1985

14035 World Industrial Reporter
Keller International Publishing Corporation
150 Great Neck Rd
Great Neck, NY 11021-3309

516-829-9722
FAX 516-829-9306
Home Page: www.supplychainbrain.com

Bryan DeLuca, Editor
Terry Beirne, Publisher
Jerry Keller, President
Mary Chavez, Director of Sales
New equipment, machinery and techniques for the industry.
34 Pages
Circulation: 37,107
Founded in 1882

Trade Shows

14036 AMSE Internation Manufacturing Science & Engineering Conference
American Society of Mechanical Engineers
Three Park Avenue
New York, NY 10016-5990

973-882-1170
800-843-2763
E-Mail: infocentral@asme.org
Home Page: www.asme.org

David Walsh, Editor
Chitra Sethi, Managing Editor
John Kosowatz, Senior Editor
The MSEC highlights cutting edge manufacturing research in technical paper, poster and panel sessions.
3200 Attendees
Frequency: Annual/Fall
Founded in 1880
Mailing list available for rentat $125 per M

14037 ASIS Annual Conference and Exhibits
American Society of Industrial Security
1625 Prince Street
Alexandria, VA 22314-2818

703-519-6200
703-519-6299
FAX 703-519-6299
E-Mail: asis@asisonline.org
Home Page: www.asisonline.org

Eduard J. Emde, President
Michael J Stack, CEO
The most comprehensive educational and networking event in the security industry that offers high-quality and insightful educational sessions on every aspect of security; exhibits featuring the latest security technology and innovations and providing a forum for 900 companies to demonstrate the cutting-edge security products and services that are shaping the security industry.
38000 Members
14M Attendees
Frequency: September
Founded in 1955
Mailing list available for rent

14038 ASM Heat Treating Society Conference & Exposition
Materials Information Society
9639 Kinsman Road
Materials Park, OH 44073-0002

440-385-5151
800-336-5152
FAX 440-338-4634
E-Mail:
pamela.kleinman@asminternational.org
Home Page: www.asminternational.org

Pamela Kleinma, Senior Manager, Events
Kellye Thomas, Exposition Account Manager
Gernant E. Maurer, President
Thomas S. Passek, Managing Director
Conference and exhibits of heat treating equipment and supplies plus information of interest to metallurgists, manufacturing, research and design technical professionals. 300 exhibitors.
3500 Attendees
Frequency: September, Bi-Annual
Founded in 1974

14039 ASM Materials Science & Technology (MS&T)
Materials Information Society
9639 Kinsman Road
Materials Park, OH 44073-0002

440-338-5151
800-336-5152
FAX 440-338-4634
E-Mail:
pamela.kleinman@asminternational.org
Home Page: www.asminternational.org

Pamela Kleinman, Senior Manager, Events
Kelly Thomas, Exposition Account Manager
Gernant E. Maurer, President
Thomas S. Passek, Managing Director
Annual event focusing on testing, analysis, characterization and research of materials such as engineered materials, high performance met-

als, powdered metals, metal forming, surface modification, welding and joining. 350 exhibitors.
4,000 Attendees
Frequency: Annual/October
Founded in 2005

14040 ASME Annual Meeting
American Society of Mechanical Engineers
Three Park Avenue
New York, NY 10016

973-882-1170
800-843-2763
FAX 212-591-7856
E-Mail: infocentral@asme.org
Home Page: www.asme.org

Melissa Torres, Meetings Manager
Mary Jakubowski, Meetings Manager
David Walsh, Editor
Chitra Sethi, Managing Editor
John Kosowatz, Senior Editor
Frequency: Annual/June
Founded in 1880
Mailing list available for rent

14041 ASME Gas Turbine Users Symposium (GTUS)
American Society of Mechanical Engineers/IGTI
6525 The Corners Pkwy
Ste. 115
Norcross, GA 30092

404-847-0072
FAX 404-847-0151
E-Mail: igti@asme.org
Home Page: www.asme.org/igti

Stephanie Searsr, Coordinator, IGTI Conferences
Judy Osborn, Manager, IGTI Conferences & Expos
Michael Ireland, Managing Director
Charity Golden, Operations Director
Shirley Barton, Manager, Professional Development
A show focused on the role gas turbines will play in meeting the nation's future energy demands, provides the information related to gas turbine operations, maintenance, advances, and design.
2000 Attendees
Frequency: Annual
Mailing list available for rent

14042 AeroMat Conference and Exposition
ASM International
9639 Kinsman Road
Materials Park, OH 44073-0002

440-385-5151
800-336-5152
FAX 440-338-4634
E-Mail: kim.schaefer@asminternational.org
Home Page: www.asminternational.org

Kim Schaefer, Event Manager
Kelly Thomas, Exposition Account Manager
Gernant E. Maurer, President
Thomas S. Passek, Managing Director
Conference for Aerospace Materials Engineers, Structural Engineers and Designers. The annual event focuses on affordable structures and low-cost manufacturing, titanium alloy technology, advanced intermetallics and refractory metal alloys, materials and processes for space applications, aging systems, high strength steel, NDT evaluation, light alloy technology, welding and joining, and engineering technology. 150 exhibitors.
1500 Attendees
Frequency: Annual/June
Founded in 1984

14043 Association of Machinery and Equipment Appraisers Annual Conference

315 S Patrick Street
Alexandria, VA 22314-3501

703-836-7900
800-537-8629
FAX 703-836-9303
E-Mail: amea@amea.org
Home Page: www.amea.org

Lorna Lindsey, Manager
Charles J. Winternitz, President
Pamela Reid, Director, Member Services

Exhibits of interest to machinery and equipment appraisers.
300 Members
Founded in 1983
Mailing list available for rent

14044 CCTI Annual Meeting

Composite Can & Tube Institute
50 S Pickett Street
Suite 110
Alexandria, VA 22304-7206

703-823-7234
FAX 703-823-7237
E-Mail: ccti@cctiwdc.org
Home Page: www.cctiwdc.org

Kristine Garland, Executive VP
Wayne Vance, Association Counsel
Janine Marczak, Associate Manager, Events
Frequency: May

14045 Capital Industrial Show

Industrial Shows of America
1794 The Alameda
San Jose, CA 95126-1729

408-947-0233
FAX 408-286-8836

Annual show and exhibits of industrial equipment, supplies and services.
4000 Attendees

14046 Dynamic Positioning Conference

Marine Technology Society
1100 H St., Nw
Suite LL-100
Washington, DC 20005

202-717-8705
FAX 202-347-4302
E-Mail: membership@mtsociety.org
Home Page: www.mtsociety.org
Social Media: *Facebook, Twitter, LinkedIn*

Jerry Boatman, President
Drew Michel, President-Elect
Jerry Wilson, VP of Industry and Technology
Jill Zande, VP of Education and Research
Justin Manley, VP of Gov. & Public Affairs

Recognized as the leading symposium covering developments and technology associated with Dynamic Positioning. Industry leaders discuss DP-related vessel design, and operations, and DP manufacturers and service companies exhibit their products and services to a highly targeted and focused audience.
2M Members
Founded in 1963

14047 FABFORM

Industrial Shows of America
164 Lake Front Drive
Hunt Valley, MD 21030-2215

410-771-1445
800-638-6396
FAX 410-771-1158

This is the most effective way to reach forming, fabricating and welding equipment buyers in the Northern California area.
3000 Attendees
Frequency: April

14048 Federation of Societies for Coatings Technology

Federation of Societies for Coatings Technology
492 Norristown Road
Blue Bell, PA 19422-2350

610-940-0777
FAX 610-940-0292
Home Page: www.coatingstech.com

Robert Ziegler, Publisher
Patricia D Ziegler, Semior Editor
Ray Dickie, Editor

Provides a major service to the coatings industry, serves as a link between users and supplies of raw materials, production equipment, coatings, adhesives, inks, sealants, testing equipment, containers and laboratory apparatus.International Coating Expo November, Georgia World Congress Center in Atlanta, Georgia.

14049 Great Lakes Industrial Show

North American Expositions Company
33 Rutherford Avenue
Boston, MA 02129

617-242-6092
800-225-1577
FAX 617-242-1817
E-Mail: dnovack@naexpo.com
Home Page: www.naexpo.com

Denise Novack, Contact

With over 300 companies exhibiting, showcases the latest technology, products, services and solutions for your manufacturing needs.
14319 Attendees
Frequency: November
Founded in 1972

14050 ISMA/IDA Spring & Fall Conventions

Industrial Distribution Association
100 N 20th Street
Suite 400
Philadelphia, PA 19103

215-320-3862
866-460-2360
FAX 215-963-9785
E-Mail: info@isapartners.org
Home Page: www.isapartners.org
Social Media: *Facebook, Twitter, LinkedIn*

John Duffy, Director
Ed Gerber, President
Michael Carr, Vice President
Tommy Thompson, Treasurer

Semi-annual conventions for distributors and manufacturers of industrial (MROP) supplies.

14051 Industrial Marketing Expo

Lobos Services
16016 Perkins Road
Baton Rouge, LA 70810

225-751-5626

Debbie Balough, Show Manager

250 booths.
6M Attendees
Frequency: April

14052 Industrial Products Expo and Conference

Key Productions
94 Murphy Road
Hartford, CT 06114-2121

860-247-8363
880-753-9776
FAX 860-947-6900
E-Mail: webadmin@keypro.com
Home Page: www.keypro.com

Maura Lewis, Show Manager

This show features exhibits and/or services used in manufacturing, management and warehousing.
6M Attendees
Frequency: September

14053 Industrial Show Pacific Coast

Industrial Shows of America
164 Lake Front Drive
Hunt Valley, MD 21030-2215

410-771-1445
800-638-6396
FAX 410-771-1158

James K Donahue, President

Four hundred booths.
11M Attendees
Frequency: November

14054 International Fastener and Precision Formed Parts Manufacturing Expo

Pemco
383 Main Avenue
Norwalk, CT 06851-1543

203-840-7700
800-323-5155
FAX 630-260-0395

Biennial show and exhibits of cold headers and header tooling, tools and dies, forming machines, parts feeding and handling equipment and test equipment for the industrial fastener and precision formed parts manufacturing industry.

14055 International Off-Highway and Power Plant Meeting and Exposition

Society of Automotive Engineers
400 Commonwealth Drive
Warrendale, PA 15096-0001

724-776-4841
FAX 724-776-4026
Home Page: www.sae.org

Diane Rogne, Show Manager
Sam Barill, Treasurer
Andrew Brown, Treasurer

Annual show of 270 suppliers of parts, components, materials and systems utilized in farm and industrial machinery and off-road and recreational vehicles.
5000 Attendees
Circulation: 84,000

14056 International Symposium for Testing & Failure Analysis

ASM International
9639 Kinsman Road
Materials Park, OH 44073-0002

440-338-5151
800-336-5152
FAX 440-338-4634
E-Mail: kim.schaefer@asminternational.org
Home Page: www.asminternational.org

Kim Schaefer, Event Manager
Kelly Thomas, Exposition Account Manager
Gernant E. Maurer, President
Thomas S. Passek, Managing Director

Annual event focusing on microelectronic and elcetronic device failure analysis, techniques, EOS/ESD testing and descretes aimed at failure analysis engineers and managers, technisians and new failure analysis engineers. 200 exhibitors.
1100 Attendees
Frequency: Annual/November

14057 Mid South Industrial, Material Handling and Distribution Expo

Industrial Shows of America

164 Lake Front Drive
Hunt Valley, MD 21030-2215

410-771-1445
800-638-6396
FAX 410-771-1158

James K Donahue, President
300 booths of industrial and business related products and services.
8M Attendees
Frequency: June

14058 National Association of Industrial Technology Convention

National Association of Industrial Technology
3300 Washtenaw Avenue
Suite 220
Ann Arbor, MI 48104-4294

734-677-0720
FAX 734-677-2407
E-Mail: nait@nait.org
Home Page: www.nait.org

Dr. Alvin Thadisill, Show Manager
Dave Monporan, Exhibit Manager
Rick Coscarelli, Executive Director

Annual convention of National Association of Industrial Technology, professional association of two and four year Industrial Technology program, faculty, standards and professionals in industry. Exhibitors desired in textbooks, training manuals, software and video; testing and training equipment, computer hardware and software, ISP's and distance learning hosts; CAD/CAM; Rapid Protyping; PC's. There are 25 booths. Next show is in Pittsburgh, Pennsylvania.
500 Attendees
Frequency: November

14059 Pacific Coast Industrial and Machine Tool Show

ISOA
1794 The Alameda
San Jose, CA 95126-1729

408-947-0233
800-286-2882
FAX 408-286-8836

Annual show of 260 exhibitors of industrial equipment, machine tools, business services, hand tools and related equipment, supplies and services.
12M Attendees
Frequency: November, Santa Clara

14060 Rocky Mountain Industrial and Machine Tool Show

Trade Shows West
360 S Fort Ln
Suite 2C
Layton, UT 84041-5708

801-485-0176
FAX 801-485-0241
Home Page: www.facetofacemarketing.net

A three day exhibit focusing on the needs of the industrial, manufacturing and plant maintenance industries.
8463 Attendees
Frequency: Annual/May

14061 Salt Lake Machine Tool & Manufacturing Exposition

Trade Shows West
2880 S Main Street
Suite 110
Salt Lake City, UT 84115

801-485-0176
FAX 801-485-0241
E-Mail: jeffwfredericks@hotmail.com
Home Page: www.facetofacemarketing.net

14062 Tidewater Industrial & Manufacturing Technology Show

Industrial Shows of America
164 Lake Front Drive
Hunt Valley, MD 21030-2215

410-771-1445
800-638-6396
FAX 410-771-1158
Home Page: www.isoa.com

Annual show of 250 suppliers and distributors of industrial and marine equipment, machine and hand tools, business services and related equipment, supplies and services.
Frequency: September, VA Beach

14063 Tri-State Industrial & Machine Tools Show

Industrial Shows of America
164 Lake Front Drive
Hunt Valley, MD 21030-2215

410-771-1445
800-638-6396
FAX 410-771-1158

This show will bring together exhibitors and customers to preview products and discuss new technologies for the metalworking and manufacturing industries. The show will feature machine tools, metalworking equipment, services for manufacturing industrial products and supplies. Thousands of qualified decision-makers involved in management, engineering, purchasing and manufacturing will attend.
Frequency: April

14064 USA/Mexico Industrial Expo

Industrial Shows of America
164 Lake Front Drive
Hunt Valley, MD 21030-2215

410-771-1445
800-638-6396
FAX 410-771-1158

This event draws attendees from avariety of manufacturing and assembly companies. Product categories include material handling, safety equipment, compressors, maintenance equipment, industrial water products, hydraulic/pneumatics, tools and many more. On average, attendees spend over $100,000 per year obn these products.
9000 Attendees
Frequency: June

Directories & Databases

14065 Capital Cities Regional Industrial Buying Guide

Thomas Publishing Company
5 Penn Plaza
New York, NY 10001-1810

212-950-0500

A who's who directory of supplies to the industry.
Cost: $65.00
1200 Pages
Frequency: Annual

14066 Directory of the Association of Machinery and Equipment Appraisers

Association of Machinery and Equipment Appraisers
315 S Patrick St
Alexandria, VA 22314-3532

703-836-7900
800-537-8629
FAX 703-836-9303

E-Mail: amea@amea.org
Home Page: www.amea.org

Pamela Reid, Director, Member Services
Lorna Lindsey, Manager
Charles J. Winternitz, President
Nearly 300 member certified machinery appraisers.
300 Members
Frequency: Annual January
Founded in 1983
Mailing list available for rent

14067 IGWB Buyer's Guide

BNP Media
PO Box 1080
Skokie, IL 60076-9785

847-763-9534
FAX 847-763-9538
E-Mail: igwb@halldata.com
Home Page: www.igwb.com

James Rutherford, Editor
Lynn Davidson, Marketing
Nikki Smith, Director

A comprehensive resource listing over 1000 gaming products and services suppliers.
Frequency: Annual

14068 Industrial Machinery Digest

Cygnus Interactive
262 Yeager Parkway
Suite C
Pelham am, AL 35124

866-833-5346
FAX 866-826-5918
E-Mail: william.strickland@cygnusb2b.com
Home Page: www.indmacdig.com
Social Media: *Facebook, Twitter, LinkedIn*

William Strickland, Publisher
Adrienne Gallender, Associate Publisher
Lisa Hanschu, Sales Consultant
Amy Boelk, Art Director / Print Product
Susan Hopkins, Accounting

A leader among industrial trade publications distributed to machine shops, job shops, fabricating shops, gear manufacturers, industrial warehouses & distribution centers, large industrial facilities & manufacturing plants, material handling, retro & rebuilding machine maintenance, pipe & tube manufacturers and manchinery dealers and wholesalers.

14069 SBC Industrial Purchasing Guide

100 E Big Beaver Rd
Suite 700E
Troy, MI 48083-1248

248-524-4800
800-331-1385
FAX 248-524-4849
Home Page: www.smartpages.com

Susan Wright, Industrial Operations Manager
Nicole Howard-Combs, Director

Providers of industrial products and services; seperate regional editions cover Illinois, Wisconsin, Indiana, Michigan, and Ohio.

14070 Sweets Directory

Grey House Publishing/McGraw Hill Construction
1221 Avenue of the Americas
New York, NY 10020-1095

212-512-2000
800-442-2258
FAX 212-512-3840
E-Mail: webmaster@mcgraw-hill.com
Home Page: www.mcgraw-hill.com
Social Media: *Facebook, Twitter*

Harold W McGraw III, CEO

The leading desktop reference and preliminary research guide, featuring more than 10,000 building product manufacturers and their prod-

ucts.
Cost: $145.00
950 Pages
Frequency: Annual
ISBN: 1-592378-50-1
Founded in 1906

14071 ThomasNet

Thomas Publishing Company, LLC
User Services Department
5 Penn Plaza
New York, NY 10001

212-695-0500
800-699-9822
FAX 212-290-7362
E-Mail: contact@thomaspublishing.com
Home Page: www.thomasnet.com
Social Media: *Facebook, Twitter, LinkedIn*

Carl Holst-Knudsen, President
Robert Anderson, VP, Planning
Mitchell Peipert, VP, Finance
Ivy Molofsky, VP, Human Resources

A way to reach qualified businesses that list
their company information on ThomasNet.com.
Detailed profiles promote their products, services, capabilities and brands carried. The
ThomasNet.com web site is the most up-to-date
compilation of 650,000 North American manufacturers, distributors, and service companies
in 67,000 industrial categories.
Founded in 1898
Mailing list available for rent

14072 World Industrial Reporter: Directory of Distributors Issue

Keller International Publishing Corporation
150 Great Neck Rd
Great Neck, NY 11021-3309

516-829-9722
FAX 516-829-9306
Home Page: www.supplychainbrain.com

Jerry Keller, President
Mary Chavez, Director of Sales

A list of over 3,000 international advertisers
and their distributors with product line related
to the industrial supplies and equipment industry.
Cost: $45.00
Frequency: Annual

14073 World Industrial Reporter: International Buyer's Guide Issue

Keller International Publishing Corporation
150 Great Neck Rd
Great Neck, NY 11021-3309

516-829-9722
FAX 516-829-9306
Home Page: www.supplychainbrain.com

Jerry Keller, President
Mary Chavez, Director of Sales

Over 275 international advertisers are listed
that offer industrial supplies and equipment for
export.
Cost: $5.00
Frequency: Annual
Circulation: 40,000

Industry Web Sites

14074 http://gold.greyhouse.com

G.O.L.D Grey House OnLine Databases

Grey House Publishing's online database platform, GOLD, offers Quick Search, Keyword
Search and Expert Search for most business
sectors including industrial equipment markets.
The GOLD platform makes finding the information you need quick and easy - whether
you're a novice searcher or an experienced da-

tabase user. All of Grey House's directory
products are available for subscription on the
GOLD platform.

14075 www.amea.org

Association of Machinery and Equipment
Appraisers

The premier international association of appraisers who specialize in appraising machinery and equipment.

14076 www.arra.org

Asphalt Recycling and Reclaiming
Association

Promotes the interest of owners and manufacturers of recycling equipment, engineers suppliers and businesses involved in the asphalt
recycling industry.

14077 www.atmae.org

Assoc of Tech, Management, and Applied
Engineering

Faculty, students and industry professionals
dedicated to solving complex technological
problems and developing the competitive technologist and applied engineering workforce.

14078 www.greyhouse.com

Grey House Publishing

Authoritative reference directories for most
business sectors including industrial equipment
markets. Users can search the online databases
with varied search criteria allowing for custom
searches by product category, geographic area,
sales volume, keyword, subject and more. Full
Grey House catalog and online ordering also
available.

14079 www.ida-assoc.org

Industrial Supply Association

To help members increase sales, reduce expenses and improve profiyability

14080 www.mdna.org

Machinery Dealers National Association

Represents dealers of used industrial equipment.

14081 www.mt-online.com

Applied Technology Publications

MT-online.com is the premier source of capacity assurance and best practice solutions for
manufacturing, process and service operations
worldwide. Online home of Maintenance Technology magazie, the dynamic MT-online.com
portal serves the critical technical, business and
professional-development needs of engineers,
managers and technicians from across all industrial, institutional and commercial sectors.

14082 www.polysort.com

Polysort.com

A portal for the plastics and rubber industry,
providing news, information about plastics and
rubber industry trade shows, company links, as
well as plastics and rubber classified
advertising

14083 www.sweets.construction.com

McGraw Hill Construction

In depth product information that lets you find,
compare, select, specify and make purchase decisions in the industrial product marketplace.

14084 www.thomasregister.com Thomas Register

Thomas Register

Comprehensive online resource for defining
companies and products manufactured in North
America. Use it for placing orders, downloading computer-aided design drawings, and
viewing thousands of online company catalogs
and websites.

Associations

14085 Alliance of Claims Assistance Professionals

9600 Escarpment
Suite 745-65
Austin, TX 78749

512-394-0008
888-394-5163
E-Mail: capinfo@claims.org
Home Page: www.claims.org
Social Media: *Twitter*

Rebecca Stephenson, Co-President
Katalin Goencz, Co-President

Professionals dedicated to the effective management of health insurance claims. Our members are claims assistance professionals who work for patients.
50 Members
Founded in 1991

14086 America's Health Insurance Plans

601 Pennsylvania Ave., NW
South Building, Suite 500
Washington, DC 20004-2601

202-778-3200
FAX 202-331-7487
E-Mail: ahip@ahip.org
Home Page: www.ahip.org
Social Media: *Twitter*

Karen M Ignagni, President/CEO

Mission is to be an effective advocate for a workable legislative and regulatory environment at the federal and state levels in which our members can advance their vision of a health care system that meets the needs of consumers, employers and public purchasers.
1300 Members
Founded in 2003
Mailing list available for rent

14087 American Academy of Actuaries

1850 M Street NW
Suite 300
Washington, DC 20036

202-223-8196
FAX 202-872-1948
E-Mail: webmaster@actuary.org
Home Page: www.actuary.org
Social Media: *Facebook, Twitter, LinkedIn, Youtube*

Mary D. Miller, President
Tom Wildsmith, President-Elect
Tom Terry, Immediate Past President
Art Panighetti, Treasurer
John Moore, Secretary

AAA is a public policy organization for actuaries within the US. The Academy acts as the public information organization for the profession. Assisting public policy process through the presentation of clear actuarial analysis, the Academy regularly prepares testimony for Congress, provides information to federal elected officials, regulators and congressional staff, comments on proposed federal regulations, and works closely with state officials on issues related to insurance.
18,00 Members
Founded in 1965
Mailing list available for rent

14088 American Agents Alliance

1231 I Street
Suite 201
Sacramento, CA 95814

916-283-9473
866-497-9222
FAX 916-283-9479
E-Mail: info@agentsalliance.com

Home Page: www.agentsalliance.com
Social Media: *Facebook, Twitter, LinkedIn, Google Plus*

Ken May, President
Brady Harrigan, Vice President
Charlie Garrison, Chief Financial Officer
Debra Jackson, Immediate Past President
Toni Damberger, Secretary

Founded on the philosophy that independent producers speaking with one united voice can accomplish mch more than separate individuals. A member-driven organization dedicated to protect and serve independent insurance producers and consumers.
Founded in 1962

14089 American Association for Long Term Care Insurance

3835 E. Thousand Oaks Blvd.
Suite 336
Westlake Village, CA 91362

818-597-3227
FAX 818-597-3206
E-Mail: info@aaltci.org
Home Page: www.aaltci.org

Jesse Slome, Media Inquiries
Joseph Howard, Board of Advisor
Don Hansen, Board of Advisor
Tom Hebrank, Board of Advisor
Larry Thomas, Board of Advisor

National trade organization for the long term care insurance industry in the United States.
Founded in 1998

14090 American Association of Crop Insurers

1 Massachusetts Ave NW
Suite 800
Washington, DC 20001-1401

202-789-4100
FAX 202-408-7763
E-Mail: aaci@mwmlaw.com
Home Page: www.cropinsurers.com

Mike McLeod, Executive Director
David Graves, Manager/Secretary

A organization that represents companies involved with the Federal crop insurance program.
25 Members
Founded in 1980

14091 American Association of Dental Consultants

10032 Wind Hill Drive
Greenville, IN 47124

812-923-2600
800-896-0707
FAX 812-923-2900
Home Page: www.aadc.org

Dr.ÿMichael D. Weisenfeld, President
Dr. Marc K. Zweig, President-Elect
Dr. Lawrence M Hoffman, Secretary-Treasurer
Dr. Kay D. Eckroth, PastÿPresident
Judith K. Salisbury, Executive Director

Members are dentists, insurance consultants, benefits programs administrators and other dental professionals.
350 Members
Founded in 1979

14092 American Association of Insurance Management Consultants

Eaglemark Consulting Group
PO Box 20
Lemoyne, PA 17043

717-763-7717
FAX 717-763-7989

E-Mail: lesley.Perkins@aaimco.com
Home Page: www.aaimco.com

Lee M Hoffman, President
Mary LaPorte, Membership Director
Lesley Perkins, Executive Director
Kevin Hromas, Membership Inquiries
Van Hedges, General Inquiries

THe premier association of consultants to the insurance industry: insurance companies, agents, brokers, and their consumers. Also dedicated to helping the insurance industry operate more efficiently and more profitably, thus enabling improved service to the buying public.
35 Members
Founded in 1979

14093 American Association of Insurance Services

701 Warrenville Roady
Lisle, IL 60532

630-681-8347
800-564-AAIS
FAX 630-681-8356
Home Page: www.aaisonline.com
Social Media: *Facebook, LinkedIn*

Edmund J. Kelly, President, CEO
Joan Zerkovich, SVP, Operations
Robin Westcott, VP, Govt. Affairs
John Kadous, CPCU, CPM, VP, Personal Lines
Bill Bickerton, VP, Data Analytics

A member-owned, nonprofit national insurance advisory organization that provides specialized services to property/casualty insurers.

14094 American Association of Managing General Agents

610 Freedom Business Center
Suite 110
King of Prussia, PA 19406-2832

610-992-0022
FAX 610-992-0021
E-Mail: bernie@aamga.org
Home Page: www.aamga.org
Social Media: *Facebook, Twitter, LinkedIn*

Roger Ware, Jr., ARM, President
Ed Dickerson, III, CIC, Senior Vice President
Corinne Jones, CPCU, Senior Vice President
Edward Levy, CIW, President Elect
Mark Maucere, CIW, Vice President

A trade association of the premier wholesale property and casualty agents and companies in the insurance industry, committed to fostering the business partnerships, networking, professionalism, trusted expertise and exchange of knowledge among its members.
Founded in 1926
Mailing list available for rent

14095 American Association of Retired Persons (AARP)

American Association of Retired Persons
601 E Street NW
Suite A1-200
Washington, DC 20049-0003

202-434-2277
888-687-2277
202-434-3525
FAX 202-434-7599
E-Mail: member@aarp.org
Home Page: www.aarp.org
Social Media: *Facebook, Twitter, RSS*

Gail E. Aldrich, Board Chair
Josh Collett, VP, International Affairs
Jeffrey Gullo, Policy Analyst
Holly Schulz, Editorial Manager
Bradley Schurman, Senior Advisor

AARP is a nonprofit membership organization of persons 50 and older dedicated to addressing their needs and interests. Services include: informing members and the public on issues important to this age group; advocating on

legislative, consumer and legal issues; promoting community service, and offering a wide range of special products and services to members. There are 39+ million members within the United States.
Founded in 1958
Mailing list available for rent

14096 American Association of State Compensation Insurance Funds
P.O. Box 20073
Towson, MD 21284

877-494-3237
FAX 800-925-9420
E-Mail: dgarfield@wcf.com
Home Page: www.aascif.org/
Social Media: *Facebook*

Ray Pickup, President and CEO
Tom Phelan, Past President
Kristin Walls, Vice President
Gerard Adams, Vice President
Dennis Lloyd, Treasurer/Secretary

An association of workers' compensation insurance companies from 27 different states, plus 11 workers' compensation boards in Canada.

14097 American Cargo War Risk Reinsurance
30 Broad Street
7th floor
New York, NY 10004

212-405-2835
FAX 212-344-1664
E-Mail: amich@amich.org
Home Page: www.amich.org

TD Montgomery, Chairman
RJ Decker, Vice Chairman
TA Haig Dick, Secretary/Director
Warren C Dietz, Treasurer

Reinsurance pool of member companies.
Founded in 1939

14098 American Council of Life Insurance
101 Constitution Avenue, NW
Suite 700
Washington, DC 20001-2133

202-624-2000
FAX 202-624-2115
E-Mail: contact@acli.com
Home Page: www.acli.com
Social Media: *Facebook, Twitter, YouTube, RSS*

Dirk Kempthorne, President & Chief Executive Officer
Brian Waidmann, Chief of Staff
Gary E. Hughes, EVP, General Counsel
J. Bruce Ferguson, SVP, State Relations
Don Walker, SVP, Administration & CFO

Works to advance the interests of the life insurance industry and to provide effective government relations. Conducts investment and social research programs.
631 Members
Founded in 1976
Mailing list available for rent

14099 American Fraternal Alliance
1301 West 22nd Street
Suite 700
Oak Brook, IL 60523-6022

630-522-6322
FAX 630-522-6326
E-Mail: info@fraternalalliance.org
Home Page: www.fraternalalliance.org
Social Media: *Facebook, Twitter*

Harald Borrmann, Chair
Patrick Dees, Vice Chair
Joseph J. Annotti, President, CEO
Allison Koppel, Executive Vice President
Melanie Hinds, Director, Advocacy

The trade association of America's fraternal benefit societies.
69 Members
Founded in 1886

14100 American Institute of Marine Underwriters
14 Wall Street
Suite 820
New York, NY 10005-2145

212-233-0550
FAX 212-227-5102
E-Mail: aimu@aimu.org
Home Page: www.aimu.org

Frank Costa, Chairman of the Boardÿ
Drew Feldman, Vice Chairman
John A Miklus, President
Michael McKenna, Director of Finances
Eileen Monreale, Education/Training Specialist

Provides information of interest to marine underwriters and promotes their interests.

14101 American Insurance Association
2101 L Street, NW
Suite 400
Washington, DC 20037-1542

202-828-7100
FAX 202-293-1219
E-Mail: info@aiadc.org
Home Page: www.aiadc.org
Social Media: *Facebook, Twitter, Youtube*

Leigh Ann Pusey, President & CEO
J. Stephen Zielezienski, Senior Vice President
Joseph Digiovanni, Senior VP, State Affairs
Peter R Foley, Vice President, Claims Admin.
Eric M Goldberg, Vice President, State Govt Affairs

The leading property and casualty insurance trade organization. Member companies offer all types of property and casualty insurance, as well as personal and commercial auto insurance, commercial property and liability coverage for small businesses, worker's compensation, homeowners' insurance, medical malpractice coverage, and product liability insurance.
Founded in 1886

14102 American Insurance Marketing & Sales Society
PO Box 35718
Richmond, VA 23235

804-674-6466
877-674-2742
FAX 703-579-8896
E-Mail: info@aimssociety.org
Home Page:
www.aimssociety.org/cpiaseminars.html
Social Media: *Facebook, Twitter, LinkedIn, RSS*

Craig Most, CPIA, CIC, President
Jim Mansfield, CPIA, Vice President
June Taylor, Immediate Past President
Carlos Vargas, CPIA, Secretary
Bob Klinger, CPIA LUTCF, Treasurer

A sales training organization that is managed by agents for agents; makes an active effort to ensure that its sales training material is current and takes into consideration today's agency sales approaches.
Founded in 1968

14103 American Nuclear Insurers
95 Glastonbury Boulevard
Suite 300
Glastonbury, CT 06033-4453

860-682-1301
FAX 860-659-0002
E-Mail: info@nuclearInsurance.com

Home Page: www.amnucins.com
Social Media: *Facebook, Twitter*

George Turner, President/CEO
John Quatrocchi, Senior VP

A joint underwriting association, and and organization created by some of the largest stock insurance companies in the United States. The purpose is to pool the financial assets pledged by these member companies to provide significant amount of property and liability insurance we make available to nuclear power plants and related facilities throughout the world.
60 Members
Founded in 1957

14104 American Risk and Insurance Association ARIA
716 Providence Road
Malvern, PA 19355-3402

610-640-1997
FAX 610-725-1007
E-Mail: aria@TheInstitutes.org
Home Page: www.aria.org

Andreas Richter, President
Richard Phillips, Vice President
Paul Thistle, President-Elect
Patricia Born, Immediate Past President
Anthony Biacchi, Executive Director

ARIA is the premier academic organization devoted to the study and promotion of knowledge about risk management and insurance.
500 Members
Founded in 1932

14105 American Society for Healthcare Risk Management
155 N. Wacker Drive
Suite 400
Chicago, IL 60606-4425

312-422-3980
FAX 312-422-4580
E-Mail: ashrm@aha.org
Home Page: www.ashrm.org
Social Media: *Facebook, Twitter, LinkedIn, YouTube*

Ellen Grady Venditti, President
Ann Gaffey, President Elect
Jacque Mitchell, Past-President
Kimberly Hoarle, MBA, CAE, Executive Director
Virginia Petrancosta, CAE, Director, Marketing & Comm.

National organization for the health care industry risk management equipment, supplies and services.
4400+ Members
Founded in 1980
Mailing list available for rent

14106 American Society of Appraisers
11107 Sunset Hills Rd
Suite 310
Reston, VA 20190

703-478-2228
800-272-8258
FAX 703-742-8471
E-Mail: asainfo@appraisers.org
Home Page: www.appraisers.org
Social Media: *Facebook, Twitter, LinkedIn, YouTube*

Jim Hirt, CEO
Bonny Price, Chief Operations Officer
Joseph Noselli, MBA, CPA, Chief Financial Officer
Todd Paradis, Dir., Marketing & Comm.
Susan Fischer, Governance Operations Manager

Organization provides education and accreditation for appraisers, plus an appraiser locator service.

14107 American Society of Pension Professionals and Actuaries

4245 N. Fairfax Drive
Suite 750
Arlington, VA 22203

703-516-9300
FAX 703-516-9308
E-Mail: customercare@asppa.org
Home Page: www.asppa.org
Social Media: *Facebook, LinkedIn, RSS, YouTube*

Kyla M. Keck, CPC, QPA, QKA, President
Joseph A. Nichols, MSPA, President-Elect
Richard A. Hochman, APM, VP
David M. Lipkin, MSPA, Immediate Past President
Brian H. Graff, Esq., APMÿ, Executive Director

(ASPPA) ia a national organization for career retirement plan professionals. The membership consists of the many disciplines supporting retirement income management and benefits policy. Its members are part of the diversified, technical, and highly regulated benefits industry. ASPPA represents those who have made a career of retirement plan and pension policy work.
7,000 Members
Founded in 1966

14108 American Society of Safety Engineers

520 N. Northwest Hwy
Park Ridge, IL 60068

847-699-2929
FAX 847-768-3434
E-Mail: customerservice@asse.org
Home Page: www.asse.org
Social Media: *Facebook, Twitter, LinkedIn, Instagram, Blog*

Michael Belcher, CSP, President
Thomas F. Cecich, CSP, CIHÿ, President Elect
James D. Smith, CSP, M.S., Senior Vice President
Stephanie A. Helgerman, CSP, Vice President, Financeÿ
Fred J. Fortman, Jr., LL.M., Secretary & Executive Director

The oldest and largest professional safety organization. Its members manage, supervise and consult on safety, health, and environmental issues in industry, insurance, government and education.
30000 Members
Founded in 1911

14109 Appraisers Association of America

212 West 35th Street
11th Floor South
New York, NY 10001

212-889-5404
FAX 212-889-5503
E-Mail: aaa@appraisersassoc.org
Home Page: www.appraisersassoc.org
Social Media: *Facebook, Twitter, LinkedIn*

Deborah G. Spaniermann, AAA, President
Cynthia D. Herbert, AAA, First Vice President
Edward Yee, AAA, Second Vice President
Sharon Chrust, AAA, Recording Secretary
Erica Hartman, AAA, Treasurer

The oldest non-profit professional association of personal property appraisers. The mission and primary purpose of the association is to develop and promote standards of excellence in the profession of appraising through education and the application of the highest form of professionals practice, which results in enhancing the visibility and standing of appraisers within

the private and professional communities in which they serve.
900 Members
Founded in 1949
Mailing list available for rent

14110 Arbitration Forums

3820 Northdale Boulevard
Suite 200A
Tampa, FL 33624

813-915-2263
866-977-3434
FAX 813-915-4153
E-Mail: status@arbfile.org
Home Page: www.arbfile.org

Russ Smith, President & CEO
Jay Arcila, CFO/Secretary Treasurer
John Shedd, Director of Information Technology
Geoff Engert, Director of Mktg, Corp Compliance
Ken Butler, Director, Human Resource

Arbitration Forums is a not-for-profit provider of intercompany insurance dispute resolution services. More than 2,000 insurers and self-insurers participate in AF's programs. AF resolves over 250,000 disputes with a claim value approaching one billion dollars.
Founded in 1943

14111 Associated Risk Managers International

Two Pierce Place
20th Floor
Itasca, IL 60143-3141

630-285-4324
FAX 630-285-3590
E-Mail: Scott.Spangler@armiweb.com
Home Page: www.armiweb.com
Social Media: *Facebook, LinkedIn*

Priscilla Hottle, Chairman
Greg Easley, Vice Chairman
Brenda Case, Immediate Past President
Richard Simmons, Treasurer
Mary Pursell, Secretary

Develops specialized insurance/risk management services for trade associations, professional groups and other industry organizations. Conducts seminars and sponsors competitions.
505 Members
Founded in 1969

14112 Association of Advanced Life Underwriters

11921 Freedom Drive
Suite 1100
Reston, VA 20190

703-641-9400
888-275-0092
FAX 703-641-9885
E-Mail: stertzer@aalu.org
Home Page: www.aalu.org

Mark B. Murphy, President
Richard A. DeVita, Vice President & Treasurer
David J Stertzer, Chief Executive officer
David F. Byers Jr., Secretary
Chris Foster, President - Elect

Offers services in complex fields of estate analysis, business, insurance, pension planning, employee benefit plans.
1.4M Members
Founded in 1957

14113 Association of Average Adjusters of the United States and Canada

126 Midwood Avenue
Farmingdale, NJ 11735

973-597-0824
E-Mail: averageadjusters@aol.com
Home Page: www.averageadjustersusca.org/

Phil Gran, Chair
Richard P Carney, Executive Chairman
Eileen M Fellin

Marine insurance and general average adjusters, ship and cargo surveyors and admiralty lawyers. Has no paid staff. Membership principally in New York area.
700+ Members
Founded in 2011

14114 Association of Finance and Insurance Professionals

4104 Felps Drive
Suite H
Colleyville, TX 76034

817-428-2434
FAX 817-428-2534
E-Mail: info@afip.com
Home Page: www.afip.com
Social Media: *Facebook, Twitter, LinkedIn*

David N Robertson, Executive Director
Tarrah Lett, Sr VP
Heather M Barnett, Communications Director

A nonprofit educational foundation that serves the needs of in-dealership finance and insurance personnel for the automobile, RV, commercial truck and equipment, motorcycle, and motorized sports industries while assisting the lenders, vendors, and independent general agents who support the F&I function.
Cost: $95.00
3500 Members
Frequency: $2,500 for Company's
Founded in 1989
Mailing list available for rent

14115 Association of Financial Guaranty Insurers

139 Lancaster Street
Albany, NY 12210-1903

518-449-4698
FAX 212-391-6920
E-Mail: tcasey@mackinco.com
Home Page: www.afgi.org

Bruce E.ÿ Stern, AFGI Chairman
Teresa M.ÿ Casey, Executive Director
Margaret Towers, Contact Person

A trade association of the insurers and reinsurers of municipal bonds and asset-backed securities.
10 Members
Founded in 1986

14116 Association of Home Office Underwriters

1155 15th Street, Nw
Suite 500
Washington, DC 20005

202-962-0167
FAX 202-530-0659
E-Mail: memberservices@ahou.org
Home Page: www.ahou.org
Social Media: *Facebook, Twitter, LinkedIn*

Cheryl Johns, FALU, CLU, FLMI, President
Traci Davis, AALU, ACS, FLMI, Executive Vice President
Jean Pfundtner, RN, BSN, VP, Publications & Secretary
Tim Ranfranz, Vice President, Treasurer
Bob Cicchi, Vice President, Program Development

Founded when the Home Office Life Underwriters Association and Institute of Homes Of-

fice Underwriters joined forces to provide one unified underwriting voice. The mission is to advance the knowledge of sound underwriting of life and disability insurance risks, toward which end it holds meetings, publishes papers and discussions, and promotes educational programs.
Cost: $100.00
1,400 Members
Frequency: Membership Fee
Founded in 2002
Mailing list available for rent

14117 Association of Insurance Compliance Professionals

12100 Sunset Hills Road
Suite 130
Reston, VA 20190

703-437-4377
FAX 703-435-4390
E-Mail: aicp@aicp.net
Home Page: www.aicp.net

Sue Eckler-Kerns, President
Roger Osgood, AINS, BA, MBA, Vice President
Karen L. Pollitt, AIRC, CCP, Secretary
Jim Morgan, Treasurer
Elaine Douglas, Past President

Formerly the Society of State Filers. AICP represents individuals involved or interested in statutes, state filing methods, and/or regulatory requirements. Associate members are consultants, attorneys, association managers, education/service organizations and other interested individuals.
Cost: $175.00
1200 Members
Frequency: Membership Fee
Founded in 1985

14118 Association of Life Insurance Counsel

14350 Mundy Drive
Ste. 800 #258
Noblesville, IN 46060

317-774-7500
FAX 317-614-7147
E-Mail: pcarey@alic.cc
Home Page: www.alic.cc/

Teresa J. Rasmussen, President
Raymond J.ÿ Manista, President-Elect
William J. Forgione, Past President
Carl Wilkerson, Treasurer/Secretary
Paula L. Carey, Executive Director

Association for life insurance counsel.
Founded in 1913

14119 Association of Professional Insurance Women

990 Cedar Bridge Avenue
suite B7 PMB210
Brick, NJ 08723-4157

973-941-6024
FAX 732-920-1260
E-Mail: scb@thebeaumontgroup.com
Home Page: www.apiw.org
Social Media: *LinkedIn*

Cheryl Vollweiler, President
Susan Zdroik, CPCU, ARe, First Vice President
Bina Dagar, Senior Vice President
Lucy Mendieta, Treasurer
Kathryn Turck-Rose, Corporate Secretary

Provides women in the insurance insudtry with opportunities for professional development and assistance in advancing their careers. Our membership consists of professional insurance women, highly regarded, decision makers with primary insurers, reinsurers, insurance brokers, risk management, professional services firms and other industry related organizations.
135 Members
Founded in 1976

14120 Association of Professional Insurance Agen ts

400 North Washington Street
Alexandria, VA 22314

703-836-9340
FAX 703-836-1279
E-Mail: web@pianet.org
Home Page: www.pianet.com
Social Media: *Facebook, Twitter, LinkedIn, RSS*

Richard A. Clements, President
Robert W Hansen, President-Elect
Gareth W Blackwell, Jr., Vice President/Treasurer
John G. Lee, Past President
Mike Becker, Executive Vice President & CEO

Represents professional independent insurance agents in all 50 states, Puerto Rico and the District of Columbia. Our members are local Main Street Agents who serve their communities throughout America
Founded in 1931
Mailing list available for rent

14121 Automobile Insurance Plans Service Office

302 Central Ave
Johnston, RI 02919-4995

401-275-1000
FAX 401-528-1350
Home Page: www.aipso.com

David Kohlhammer, President

AIPSO's mission is to provide high quality services for the insurance residual market at the lowest possible cost.

14122 Aviation Insurance Association

7200 W. 75th Street
Overland Park, KS 66204

913-627-9632
FAX 913-381-2515
E-Mail: mandie@aiaweb.org
Home Page: www.aiaweb.org
Social Media: *Facebook, Blog*

David Sales, President
Paul Herbers, Vice President
James Gardner, Secretary
Christopher R. Zanette, Treasurer
Amanda Bannwarth, Executive Director

A not-for-profit association dedicated to expanding the knowledge of and promoting the general welfare of the aviation insurance industry through numerous educational programs and events.
900 Members
Founded in 1976

14123 Blue Cross and Blue Shield Association

225 North Michigan Avenue
Chicago, IL 60601-6026

312-540-0460
FAX 312-297-6609
E-Mail: bcbswebmaster@bcbsa.com
Home Page: www.bcbs.com
Social Media: *Facebook, Twitter, RSS, YouTube*

Scott P Serota, Presidentÿ & Chief Executive Officer
William A. Breskin, VP, Govt. Programs
Bhaskar Bulusu, VP, Enterprise Information
Kathy Didawick, VP, Congressional Relations
John T. Ericksen, VP, Federal Relations

Formerly Blue Cross Association and National Association of Blue Shield Plans. Members must be medical and/or hospital plans and operate according to established standards. Offers information, consulting, representation and operation services to members. Member plans

represent over 68.1 million health care consumers.
55 Members
Founded in 1946
Mailing list available for rent

14124 Captive Insurance Companies Association

4248 Park Glen Road
Minneapolis, MN 55416

952-928-4655
FAX 952-929-1318
E-Mail: info@cicaworld.com
Home Page: www.cicaworld.com
Social Media: *Facebook, Twitter, LinkedIn*

Scott Beckman, Board Chair
Michael Bemi, Board Vice Chair
Joel Chansky, Secretary/Treasurer
Dennis P. Harwick, President
Amy Sellheim, CICA Staff

An organization dedicated to networking, educating, and promoting the captive insurance industry. Its mission is to be the first and best source of unbiased information, knowledge, and leadership for captive insurance decision makers.
Founded in 1972

14125 Casualty Actuarial Society

4350 N. Fairfax Drive
Suite 250
Arlington, VA 22203-1620

703-276-3100
FAX 703-276-3108
E-Mail: office@casact.org
Home Page: www.casact.org
Social Media: *Facebook, Twitter, LinkedIn, RSS, YouTube, Flickr*

Robert S. Miccolis, President
Stephen P. Lowe, President Elect
G. Chris Nyce, Vice President- Administration
Steven D. Armstrong, Vice President- Admissions
Jeff Courchene, Vice President- Internation

The purpose is to advance the body of knowledge of actuarial science applied to property, casualty and similar risk exposures, to establish and maintain standards of qualification for membership, to promote and maintain highstandards of conduct and competence for the members, and to increase the awareness of actuarial science.
6,300 Members
Founded in 1914
Mailing list available for rent

14126 Certified Claims Professional Accreditation Council

PO Box 550922
Jacksonville, FL 32255-0922

301-292-1988
FAX 301-292-1787
E-Mail: animag@lattmag.com
Home Page: www.ccpac.com

Dave Nordt, CCP, President
Judy R. Johnson, CCP, Vice President - Certifications
Deborah Baker, CCP, Vice President - Membership
Brenda Baker, CCP, Secretary
Jean Zimmerman, CCP, Treasurer

A nonprofit organization that seeks to raise the professional standards of individuals who specialize in the administration and negotiation of freight claims. Specifically it seeks to give recognition to those who have acquired the necessary degree of experience, education, and expertise in domestic and international freight claims to warrant acknowledgment of their professional stature.
Founded in 1981

14127 Chartered Property Casualty Underwriters
720 Providence Road
Suite 100
Malvern, PA 19355-3446

610-251-2733
800-932-2728
FAX 610-725-5969
E-Mail: MemberResources@theinstitutes.org
Home Page: www.cpcusociety.org
Social Media: *Facebook, Twitter, LinkedIn*

Jane M. Wahl, President and Chairman
Kevin H Brown, Esq., CPCU, CAE, SVP, Executive Director
Brian P. Savko, CPCU, CLU, ChFC, President Elect
Stanley W. Plappert, Secretary/Treasurer
Cynthia A. Baroway, CPCU, M.Ed., Immediate Past President, Chairman

A community of credentialed property and casualty insurance professionals who promote excellence through ethical behavior and continuing education. Mission is to meet the career development needs of a diverse membership pf professionals who have earned the CPCU designation, so that they may serve others in a competent and ethical manner
22,00 Members
Founded in 1944

14128 Coalition Against Insurance Fraud
1012 14th St. NW
Suite 200
Washington, DC 20005

202-393-7330
E-Mail: info@insurancefraud.org
Home Page: www.insurancefraud.org
Social Media: *Facebook, Twitter*

Frank Sztuk, Co-Chair
Don Rounds, Co-Chair

The Coalition fights insurance fraud on behalf of consumers, insurance companies and government.
Founded in 1993

14129 Conference of Consulting Actuaries
3880 Salem Lake Drive
Suite H
Long Grove, IL 60047-5292

847-719-6500
FAX 847-719-6506
E-Mail: conference@ccactuaries.org
Home Page: www.ccactuaries.org
Social Media: *Twitter, LinkedIn*

Philip A. Merdinger, President
Donald E. Fuerst, President-Elect
Donald J. Segal, President-Elect
Edward M. Pudlowski, Treasurer
John H. Lowell, Secretary

The Conference advances the quality of consulting practice, supports the needs of consulting actuaries, and represents their interests.
1200+ Members
Founded in 1950

14130 Consumer Credit Industry Association
6300 Powers Ferry Road
Suite 600-286
Atlanta, GA 30339

678-858-4001
E-Mail: webmaster@cciaonline.com
Home Page: www.cciaonline.com

Dick Williams, Chair
Jim Pangburn, President
Rebecca Smart, VP
Tom Keepers, EVP
Stephanie Neal, Director of Member Services

Preserves, promotes and enhances the availability, utility and integrity of insurance and related products and services delivered in connection with financial transactions.
140+ Members
Founded in 1951

14131 Council on Employee Benefits
1501 M Street, N.W
Suite 620
Washington, DC 20005

202-861-6025
FAX 202-861-6027
E-Mail: info@ceb.org
Home Page: www.ceb.org
Social Media: *LinkedIn*

Donna A Sexton, President
Shane Canfield, Executive Director
Karen M Welch, Vice President
John R. Collins, Treasurer
Julie R Sheehy, Secretary

Composed of major corporations having a common interest in the management of employee benefits. Stimulates the development and improves the adminstration of sound, progressive employee benefit plan among its members. Also provides an excellent medium for the exchange of ideas, thought and information on the design, operation and financing of such plans.
Founded in 1946

14132 Crop Insurance and Reinsurance Bureau
440 First St NW
Suite 500
Washington, DC 20001

202-544-0067
FAX 202-330-5255
E-Mail: mtorrey@cropinsurance.org
Home Page: www.cropinsurance.org

Sheri Bane, Chairwoman
Ron Rutledge, Vice Chairman
Zane Vaughn, Treasurer
Greg Mills, Immediate Past Chairman
Mike Torrey, Executive Vice President

National trade association made up of insurance providers and related organization who provide a variety of insurance products for our Nation's Farmers.
Founded in 1964

14133 Eastern Claims Conference
PO Box 863902
Ridgewood, NY 11386

732-922-7037
FAX 212-615-7345
E-Mail: easternclaimsconference@gmail.com
Home Page: www.easternclaimsconference.com

Jennifery Cobb, Conference Chair
Christine Prutting, Program
Melissa J Thomas, Marketing
Ann Healy, Ad Journal/Publications
Arlene Walsh, Ad Journal/Publications

Provides education and training to examiners, managers, and officers who review medical and disability claims. Holds seminars for life, health and disability clinics.
Founded in 1977

14134 Employee Benefit Research Institute
1100 13th St NW
Suite 878
Washington, DC 20005-4051

202-659-0670
FAX 202-775-6312
E-Mail: info@ebri.org
Home Page: www.ebri.org

Dallas L Salisburyÿ, President
Stephen Blakely, Communications Director
Martha Bobbino, Director, Library Resourcesÿ

Marcene Pugh, Director of Finance and Admin.
Jack VanDerhei, Director of Researchÿ

Mission is to contribute to, to encourage, and to enhance the development of sound employee benefit programs and sound public policy through objective research and education.
Founded in 1978
Mailing list available for rent

14135 Federal Insurance Administration
500 C Street SW
Washington, DC 20472-2110

202-646-3535
FAX 202-646-4320

Bud Schaurte, Administrator

Administers the federal flood insurance and crime insurance programs.

14136 Federation of Defense & Corporate Counsel
11812 North 56th Street
Tampa, FL 33617-1528

813-983-0022
FAX 813-988-5837
E-Mail: mstreeper@thefederation.org
Home Page: www.thefederation.org
Social Media: *Facebook, Twitter, LinkedIn*

Victoria H. Roberts, Board Chair
Steven E. Farrar, President
J. Scott Kreamer, Secretary-Treasurer
H. Mills Gallivan, President-Elect
Walter Dukes, Senior Director

The Federation is an organization of recognized leaders in the legal community dedicated to representation of insurers and corporations.
1400+ Members
Founded in 1936

14137 Financial & Insurance Conference Planners
330 N. Wabash Avenue
Suite 2000
Chicago, IL 60611

312-245-1023
FAX 312-321-5150
E-Mail: info@icpanet.com
Home Page: www.ficpnet.com
Social Media: *Facebook, Twitter, LinkedIn, YouTube, Flickr*

Shelia R. Cleary, Chair
Caryn Taylor Lucia, Chair Elect and Treasurer
Marla Hannigan, CMP, Chair Elect and Treasurer
Sherri Lindenberg, CLU, Chair Elect and Treasurer
Kathy Roche, Chair Elect and Treasurer

An association of insurance and financial services industry meeting planners who exchange proven meeting management techniques and explore trends and new ideas that may enhance the value of conferences.
Founded in 1957

14138 Financial Planning Association
7535 E. Hampden Ave.
Suite 600
Denver, CO 80231

303-759-4900
800-322-4237
FAX 303-759-0749
E-Mail: info@onefpa.org
Home Page: www.fpanet.org
Social Media: *Facebook, Twitter, LinkedIn*

Mary Tuttle, CEO
Maureen Peck, Executive Communications Manager
Lauren Schadle, Assoc Exec Dir, COO
Curt Niepoth, Assoc Exec Dir, CFO
Ian MacKenzie, Managing Dir Bus Dev, CMO

Members include accountants, financial planners, lawyers, bankers, stockbrokers, insurance professionals and others who provide financial advice and services to individuals.
15M Members
Founded in 2000
Mailing list available for rent

14139 Fraternal Field Managers' Association

Concordia Mutual Life
3020 Woodcreek Drive
Downers Grove, IL 60515

630-971-8000
FAX 630-971-9332
Home Page: www.ffma.info

William J. Murray, President
Jay Schenk, VP

FFMA is dedicated to the promotion of higher ethical standards and the professional development of the fraternal field force, fostering harmony, unity of purpose and the exchange of ideas among the member societies.
70 Members
Founded in 1935

14140 GAMA International

2901 Telestar Ct
Suite 140
Falls Church, VA 22042-1205

703-770-8184
800-345-2687
FAX 571-499-4302
E-Mail: membership@gamaweb.com
Home Page: www.gamaweb.com
Social Media: *Facebook, Twitter, LinkedIn*

Bonnie Godsman, Chief Executive Officer
Debra Grommons, Chief of Staff / EVP
John Behn, Executive Vice President
Steven Mandurano, Sr. Director, Media & Marketing
Kathryn Kellam, CEO, GAMA Foundation

The only association dedicated to promoting the professional development needs of managers in the insurance and financial services industry. Also the only volunteer organization that focuses on the agency building tasks and skills of successful career agenices and firms.
Cost: $300.00
5500 Members
Frequency: Membership Fee
Mailing list available for rent

14141 General Agents and Managers Conference of NALU

2901 Telestar Ct
Suite 140
Falls Church, VA 22042-1205

703-770-8184
800-345-2687
FAX 571-499-4302
E-Mail: membership@gamaweb.com
Home Page: www.gamaweb.com
Social Media: *Facebook, Twitter, LinkedIn*

Bonnie Godsman, Chief Executive Officer
Debra Grommons, Chief of Staff / EVP
John Behn, Executive Vice President
Steven Mandurano, Sr. Director, Media & Marketing
Kathryn Kellam, CEO, GAMA Foundation

Seeks to improve quality of management and life insurance selling through educational programs, code of ethical practices, and research programs.
7.2M Members
Founded in 1951
Mailing list available for rent

14142 Great American Insurance Group Tower

301 E Fourth Street
Cincinnati, OH 45202

513-369-5000
800-545-4269
FAX 212-885-1535
E-Mail: service@fcia.com
Home Page:
www.greatamericaninsurancegroup.com
Social Media: *Facebook, LinkedIn, YouTube*

Lindley M Franklin, CEO

To provide credit insurance covering teh risk of non-payment on foreign and,in certain cases, domestic receivables.
Founded in 1961

14143 Group Underwriters Association of America

P.O. Box 735
Northbrook, IL 60065-0735

205-427-2638
FAX 205-981-2901
E-Mail: info@guaa.com
Home Page: www.guaa.com/

Libby Corcillo, President
Shawn R. Dutremble, Vice President
Steve Ginsburg, Treasurer
Patty Marshall, Secretary
Jennifer Kyle, Past President

Comprised of industry professionals that promote the study, analysis, and discussion of all matters relating to the underwriting of group products.

14144 Health Insurance Association of America

601 Pennsylvania Avenue, NW South Building
Suite 500
Washington, DC 20004

202-778-3200
FAX 202-331-7487
E-Mail: ahip@ahip.org
Home Page: www.ahip.org

A national political advocacy and trade association with about 1,300 member companies that sell health insurance coverage to Americans.

14145 Highway Loss Data Institute

1005 N. Glebe Road
Suite 800
Arlington, VA 22201-5759

703-247-1500
FAX 703-247-1588
E-Mail: rrader@iihs.org
Home Page: www.iihs.org
Social Media: *Twitter, YouTube, RSS*

Adrian Lund, President
Russ Rader, Senior Vice President
Shelley M.ÿ Shelton, CAP, Senior Legal & Admin. Associate
Brenda O'Donnell, Vice President, Insurer Relations
Andrew Hauff, Communications Specialist

Provides the public with insurance industry data concerning human and economic loss resulting from crashes.
12 Members
Founded in 1959
Mailing list available for rent

14146 Home Office Life Underwriters Association

Minnesota Mutual Life

400 Robert Street N
Suite A
Saint Paul, MN 55101-2098

651-665-3500
FAX 651-665-4488

Lynn Patterson, President
Jane Hall, Executive Vice President

Offers educational programs through the Academy Life Underwriting designed for professional home office underwriters.
560 Members
Founded in 1930

14147 I-Car

5125 Trillium Blvd
Hoffman Estates, IL 60192-3600

847-590-1198
800-422-7872
FAX 800-590-1215
E-Mail: tom.mcgee@i-car.com
Home Page: www.i-car.com
Social Media: *LinkedIn, Google+, YouTube*

William Brower, Chair
John S. Van Alstyne, CEO & President
Rollie Benjaminÿ, Vice Chair
Dustin Wombleÿ, Secretaryÿ
Bob Keith, Treasurer

Formed by the collision industry, an international not-for-profit training organization. Develops and delivers technical training programs to professionals in all areas of the collision industry. Also provides a communication forum for anyone interested in proper collision repair.
100 Members
Founded in 1979

14148 IMCA Annual Meeting

Insurance Marketing Communications Association
4248 Park Glen Road
Minneapolis, MN 55416

206-219-9811
FAX 866-210-2481
E-Mail: tseibert@imcanet.com
Home Page: www.imcanet.com
Social Media: *Facebook, Twitter, LinkedIn*

Rob Martin, President
Gloria Grove, Executive Director
Mark Friedlander, Executive Vice President
Anna Hargis, Treasurer

To promote education and development of its members.
Cost: $795.00
Frequency: Registration Fee
Mailing list available for rent

14149 Independent Automotive Damage Appraisers Association

PO Box 12291
Columbus, GA 31917-2291

800-369-IADA
FAX 888-423-2669
E-Mail: admin@iada.org
Home Page: www.iada.org

Mark Nathan, President
Bill Ambrosino, First Vice President
John Williams, Executive Vice President
Michael M. Sellman, Secretary/Treasurer
Mike Wilson, Regional Vice President

A nationwide network of appraiser specialists with the knowledge and experience to assess vehicle damage and to make unbiased repair decisions based on the manufacturer's specifications, accepted industry procedures, and safety concerns.
731 Members
Founded in 1947

14150 Independent Insurance Agents & Brokers of America

127 S Peyton Street
Alexandria, VA 22314-2803

703-683-4422
800-221-7917
FAX 703-683-7556
E-Mail: info@iiaa.org
Home Page: www.independentagent.com/
Social Media: *Facebook, Twitter, LinkedIn, Vimeo*

Robert A Rusbuldt, CEO
Ronald Tubertini, Chairman

A national alliance of business owners and their employees who offer all types of insurance and financial services products. IIABA agents and brokers not only advise clients about insurance, they recommend loss-prevention ideas that can cut costs.
300M+ Members
Founded in 1896
Mailing list available for rent

14151 Information, Incorporated

2025 M Street NW
Washington, DC 20036

301-215-4688
800-497-5636
FAX 301-215-4600
E-Mail: acarr@mail.infoinc.com
Home Page: www.infoinc.com

Alain Carr, Manager

Organization offers evaluations of companies on their claims-paying ability. Association news services.
Founded in 1979
Mailing list available for rent

14152 Inland Marine Underwriters Association

14 Wall Street
8th Floor
New York, NY 10005

212-233-0550
FAX 212-227-5102
E-Mail: lcolson@imua.org
Home Page: www.imua.org
Social Media: *Facebook, Twitter, LinkedIn*

Michelle Hoehn, Chair
Kevin O'Brien, President & CEO
William Rosa, Deputy Chair
Lloyd J. Stoik, Vice Chair
Lillian L. Colson, Vice President & Secretary

Serves as the collective voice of the U.S. inland marine insurance industry. Also provides its members with education, research and communications services that support the inland marine underwriting discipline.
Cost: $1750.00
400+ Members
Frequency: Membership Fee
Founded in 1930
Mailing list available for rent

14153 Institute of Home Office Underwriters

General American Life Insurance Company
1155 15th Street, Nw
Suite 500
Washington, DC 20005

202-962-0167
FAX 202-530-0659
E-Mail: memberservices@ahou.org
Home Page: www.ahou.org
Social Media: *Facebook, Twitter, LinkedIn*

Cheryl Johns, FALU, CLU, FLMI, President
Traci Davis, AALU, ACS, FLMI, Executive Vice President
Jean Pfundtner, RN, BSN, VP, Publications & Secretary

Tim Ranfranz, Vice President, Treasurer
Bob Cicchi, Vice President, Program Development

Goals are to increase underwriting knowledge of members through educational programs. Prepares program and examinations leading to Fellowship in Academy of Life Underwriting.
1,400 Members
Founded in 1937
Mailing list available for rent

14154 Insurance Accounting Systems Association

3511 Shannon Rd, Suite 160
PO Box 51340
Durham, NC 27707-6330

919-489-0991
FAX 919-489-1994
E-Mail: info@iasa.org
Home Page: www.iasa.org
Social Media: *Facebook, Twitter, LinkedIn, YouTube*

Forrest Mills, Jr., Board Chair
Tim Morgan, President
Joseph Pomilia, Executive Director
Margaret McKeon, VP-Conference
Kim Morris, Director-Exhibits

Membership includes insurance companies of all types, as well as companies that serve the insurance industry, regulators and also organizations more broadly representative of the financial services industry, including banks and investment brokerage firms.
1.7M Members
Founded in 1928
Mailing list available for rent

14155 Insurance Accounting and Systems Association

3511 Shannon Road, Suite 160
PO Box 51340
Durham, NC 27707

919-489-0991
FAX 919-489-1994
E-Mail: info@iasa.org
Home Page: www.iasa.org/
Social Media: *Facebook, Twitter, LinkedIn, YouTube*

Forrest Mills, Jr., Chairman of the Board
Tim Morgan, President
Rod Travers, President-Elect
Tom Ewbank, CFO
Joe Pomilia, Executive Director

A nonprofit education association that strives to enhance the knowledge of insurance professionals and participants from similar organizations closely allied with the insurance industry.

14156 Insurance Committee for Arson Control

3601 Vincennes Road
Indianapolis, IN 46268

317-575-5601
FAX 317-879-8408
E-Mail: info@arsoncontrol.org
Home Page: www.arsoncontrol.org
Social Media: *Facebook, Twitter, LinkedIn, Google+*

Jerry Mulhearn, Chairman
Scott Sanderson, Vice Chairman
Rick Hammond, Executive Director
Don Hancock, Technical Director
Larry Baile, Event Director

Serves as a national resource, education and communications organization. ICAC works to increase public awareness of the arson problem, what can be done and how the industry is responding on both the national and local levels.
Founded in 1978
Mailing list available for rent

14157 Insurance Consumer Affairs Exchange

PO Box 746
Lake Zurich, IL 60047

847-991-8454
E-Mail: nbrebner@icae.com
Home Page: www.icae.com

Kendra Franklin, President
Kristi Colbert, Secretary
Erica Hiemstra, Treasurer
Joan Holson, VP
Nancy Brebner, Executive Director

A not-for-profit organization that promotes professionalism and shapes the standards of behavior in relationships between insurance organizations, regulators and customers through proactive dialogue, research, communication and education.
110 Members
Founded in 1976

14158 Insurance Cost Containment Service

330 S Wells
Chicago, IL 60606-4701

312-427-2520
FAX 312-368-8336

Robert Kissane, President

Assists insurance companies with property claims adjustment and arson and fraud claims investigation.

14159 Insurance Information Institute

110 William Street
New York, NY 10038-3908

212-346-5500
800-942-4242
FAX 212-732-1916
E-Mail: members@iii.org
Home Page: www.iii.org
Social Media: *Facebook, Twitter, LinkedIn, Google+, YouTube, Flickr*

Andrea C. Basora, Executive Vice President
Jeanne M Salvatore, SVP, Public Affairs
Michael Barry, VP, Media Relations
Loretta Worters, Vice President, Communications
James P. Ballot, Director, Digital Communications

A factfinding communication and media organization for all lines of insurance except life and health insurance. Affiliated with Western Insurance Information Services offering consumer information services to 10 western states. Also offers a national insurance consumer helpline.
250 Members
Founded in 1959

14160 Insurance Loss Control Association

PO Box 346
Morton, IL 61550

309-696-2551
FAX 317-879-8408
E-Mail: president@insurancelosscontrol.org
Home Page: www.insurancelosscontrol.org

Ron Huber, CSP, ALCM, President
Robert J. Cruse, CSP, ARM, ALCM, First Vice President
Daniel Finn, ALCM, CFPS, AIM, Second Vice President
Mark Bates, CSP, Secretary
Stig T Ruxlow, CSP, Financial Secretary

Supports loss control professionals. Publishes quarterly newsletter.
Founded in 1931

14161 Insurance Marketing Communications Association

4248 Park Glen Road
Minneapolis, MN 55416

206-219-9811
FAX 866-210-2481
E-Mail: tseibert@imcanet.com
Home Page: www.imcanet.com
Social Media: *Facebook, Twitter, LinkedIn, Youtube*

Rob Martin, President
Gloria Grove, Executive Director
Mark Friedlander, Executive Vice President
Anna Hargis, Treasurer

An international organization of insurance communications professionals who specialize in marketing, marketing communications, advertising, sales promotion, and public relations.
Cost: $500.00
180 Members
Frequency: Annual Membership Fee
Founded in 1923
Mailing list available for rent

14162 Insurance Premium Finance Association

2890 Niagara Falls Boulevard
PO Box 726
Amherst, NY 14226

716-695-8757
FAX 716-695-8758

Eric Bouskill, Contact

Firms licensed by New York State to finance property and casualty insurance premiums.
16 Members
Founded in 1961

14163 Insurance Research Council

718 Providence Road
Malvern, PA 19355-0725

610-644-2212
FAX 610-640-5388
E-Mail: irc@theinstitutes.org
Home Page: www.ircweb.org
Social Media: *Facebook, Twitter, LinkedIn, Pinterest, Google+*

Victoria McCarthy, Chairperson
Elizabeth A. Sprinkel, SVP
David Corum, Vice President
Victoria Kilgore, Director of Research
Patrick Schmid, PhD, Director of Research

Non profit division of the American Institute for Chartered Property Casualty Underwriters and the Insurance Institute of America. Addresses subjects relating to all lines of property-casualty insurance, including coverages of automobiles, homes, businesses, municipalities, and professionals.
Founded in 1977

14164 Insurance Value Added Network Services

1455 E Putnam Avenue
Old Greenwich, CT 06870-1307

203-698-1900
800-548-2675
FAX 203-698-7299
E-Mail: ivans.info@ivans.com
Home Page: www.ivans.com
Social Media: *Twitter, LinkedIn*

Clare DeNicola, President/CEO
Jeffery K Dobish, Sr VP/CFO
Linda Welsh, CAO

Industry-sponsored organization offering value added data communications network linking agencies, companies and healthcare providers to the insurance industry.
Founded in 1983

14165 Insured Retirement Institute

1100 Vermont Avenue, NW
10th Floor
Washington, DC 20005

202-469-3000
FAX 202-469-3030
Home Page: www.irionline.org
Social Media: *Twitter, LinkedIn, YouTube, RSS*

Nick Lane, Chairman
William Benjaminÿ, Vice Chairman
Catherine J Weatherford, President, CEO
Lee Covington, SVP, General Counsel
Danielle Holland, SVP, Communications, Marketing

An association for the retirement income industry.

14166 Intermediaries and Reinsurance Underwriters Association

3626 East Tremont Avenue
Suite 203
Throggs Neck, NY 10465

718-ÿ89- 022
FAX 908-203-0213
E-Mail: mcs@irua.com
Home Page: www.irua.com

Mike Sowa, President
Amy Barra, Executive Director

A not-for-profit corporation, organized for the purposes of reinsurance education and research and the dissemination of information relevant to the reinsurance industry.
60 Members
Founded in 1967

14167 International Association for Insurance Law: United States Chapter

Chase Communications
PO Box 3028
Malvern, PA 19355-0728

FAX 914-966-3264

Stephen C Acunto, VP

Members are attorneys, professors, regulators and others who are interested in international or comparative aspects of insurance law.
700 Members
Founded in 1963

14168 International Association of Accident Reconstruction Specialists

1036 Gretchen Lane
Grand Ledge, MI 48837-1873

517-622-3135
E-Mail: brandtb@benchmarktrafficservices.com
Home Page: www.iaars.org

Fred Rice, President
Eino Butch Thompson, Vice President

Composed of members and associates from 38 states, as well as abroad. Membership comprised of law enforcement officers and civilian personnel.
152 Members
Founded in 1980

14169 International Association of Arson Investigators

2111 Baldwin Avenue
Suite 203
Crofton, MD 21114

410-451-3473
800-468-4224
FAX 410-451-9049
E-Mail: iaai@firearson.com
Home Page: www.firearson.com

Social Media: *Facebook, Twitter, LinkedIn, Youtube*

Daniel Heenan, President
George Codding, First Vice President
Scott Bennett, Second Vice President
Peter Mansi, IAAI-CFI, MIAAI, Immediate Past President
Deborah Keeler, Executive Director

Dedicated to improving the professional development of fire and explosion investigators by being the global resource for fire investigation, technology and research.
7500 Members
Founded in 1949

14170 International Association of Defense Counsel

303 West Madison
Suite 925
Chicago, IL 60606-3300

312-368-1494
FAX 312-368-1854
E-Mail: info@iadclaw.org
Home Page: www.iadclaw.org
Social Media: *Facebook, Twitter, LinkedIn*

Joseph E. O'Neil, President
John T. Lay, Jr., President Elect
Tripp Haston, Immediate Past President
Albert C. Hilber, Vice President of Insurance
Alfred R. Paliani, Vice President of Corporate

Formerly the International Association of Insurance Counsel. Members are defense attorneys and insurance and corporate counsels, by invitation only.
Cost: $650.00
2400 Members
Frequency: Membership Fee
Founded in 1920

14171 International Association of Industrial Accident Boards and Commissions

5610 Medical Circle
Suite 24
Madison, WI 53719

608-663-6355
FAX 608-663-1546
E-Mail: webmaster@iaiabc.org
Home Page: www.iaiabc.org
Social Media: *Facebook, Twitter, LinkedIn*

R.D. Maynard, President
Dave Threedy, President Elect
Dwightÿ Lovan, Immediate Past President
Matt Carey, Secretary/Treasurer
Jennifer Wolf Horejsh, Executive Director

A not for profit trade association representing government agencies charged with the administration of workers' compensation systems throughout most of the United States and Canada, and other nations and territories.
300+ Members
Founded in 1914

14172 International Association of Insurance Receivers

610 Freedom Business Center
Suite 110
King of Prussia, PA 19406

610-992-0017
FAX 610-992-0021
E-Mail: nancy@iair.org
Home Page: www.iair.org

Bart Boles, President
Alan Gamse, Esq., First Vice President
Bruce Gilbert, Second Vice President
Donna Wilson, CIR-ML, Treasurer
James Kennedy, Esq., Corporate Secretary

Founded to provide an association to individuals involved with insurance receiverships in order to receive education, promote information

exchange, and enhance the standards followed those who work in this position.
Founded in 1991

14173 International Association of Insurance Pro fessionals Corporate Centre

3525 Piedmont Road
Building Five, Suite 300
Atlanta, GA 30305ÿ

404-789-3153
800-766-6249
FAX 404-240-0998
E-Mail: joinnaiw@naiw.org
Home Page:
www.internationalinsuranceprofessionals.org
Social Media: *Facebook, Twitter, LinkedIn*

Rebecca Clusserathÿÿ, Education
Beth Chitnis, CAE, Managementÿ
John C McColloch, Membership
Michael North, Accounting
Betsey Blimlineÿÿ, Marketing

Serves its members by providing professional education, an environment in which to build business alliances and the opportunity to make connections with people of differing career paths and levels of experience within the insurance industry.
2000 Members
Founded in 1940
Mailing list available for rent

14174 International Association of Special Investigation Units (IASIU)

N83 W13410 Leon Road
Menomonee Falls, WI 53051

414-375-2992
FAX 414-359-1671
E-Mail: info@iasiu.org
Home Page: www.iasiu.org
Social Media: *Facebook, LinkedIn*

Wade Wickre, CIFI, FCLA, President
J. Michael Skiba, Vice President
Ellen Withers, Secretary
John D. Kloc, FCLS, Treasurer
Bill Elliott, Executive Director

An association of more than 870 insurance company SIU professionals representing 130 of the largest property and casualty companies in the country.
4000 Members
Founded in 1984

14175 International Claim Association

1155 15th Street NW
Suite 500
Washington, DC 20005

202-452-0143
FAX 202-530-0659
E-Mail: cmurphy@claim.org
Home Page: www.claim.org
Social Media: *Facebook*

Emily E. Sudermann, Chairperson
David W. Grannan, CFE, President
Erin M. Worthington, President Elect
Rebecca L. Huerta, Secretary
Lester L. Bohnert, ALHC, FLMI, Treasurer

Provides a forum for information exchange and a program of education tailored to the needs of its member life and health insurance companies, reinsurers, managed care companies, TPAs, and Blue Cross and Blue Shield organizations worldwide
Founded in 1909
Mailing list available for rent

14176 International Claim Association Newsletter

International Claim Association

1155 15th Street NW
Suite 500
Washington, DC 20005

202-452-0143
FAX 202-530-0659
E-Mail: cmurphy@claim.org
Home Page: www.claim.org
Social Media: *Facebook*

Emily E. Sudermann, Chairperson
David W. Grannan, CFE, President
Erin M. Worthington, President Elect
Rebecca L. Huerta, Secretary
Lester L. Bohnert, ALHC, FLMI, Treasurer
Frequency: Quarterly
Founded in 1909
Mailing list available for rent

14177 International Cooperative and Mutual Insurance Federation

8400 Westpark Drive
Second Floor
McLean, VA 22102-5116

703-245-8077
FAX 703-610-0211
Home Page: www.aacmis.org

Edward L Potter, CAE, Executive Director

Formerly the North American Association of the International Cooperative Insurance Federation.

14178 International Foundation of Employee Benefit Plans

18700 W. Bluemound Rd
P.O. Box 69
Brookfield, WI 53045

262-786-6700
888-334-3327
FAX 262-786-8780
E-Mail: pr@ifebp.org
Home Page: www.ifebp.org
Social Media: *Facebook, Twitter, LinkedIn, Youtube*

Thomas T. Holsman, President and Chair of the Board
Michael Wilson, Chief Executive Officer
Thomas W. Stiedeÿ, Treasurer
Regina C Reardon, President-Elect
Kenneth R Boyd, Immediate Past President

The largest educational association serving the employees and compensation industry.
Cost: $295.00
35000 Members
Frequency: $575/Organization Fee
Founded in 1954

14179 International Insurance Society

101 Astor Place
Suite 202
New York, NY 10003

212-277-5171
FAX 212-277-5172
E-Mail: ej@iisonline.org
Home Page: www.iisonline.org
Social Media: *Facebook, Twitter, LinkedIn*

Greig Woodring, Chairman
Michael Morrissey, President & Chief Executive Officer
Takeo Inokuchi, Vice Chairman
Chang Jae Shin, Vice Chairman
Yassir Albaharna, Board Member

Provides a world forum for leading insurance executives, academicians and others interested in insurance to share interests and ideas on timely global issues.
1000 Members
Founded in 1965

14180 International Risk Management Institute

12222 Merit Drive
Suite 1600
Dallas, TX 75251-3297

972-996-0800
800-827-5991
FAX 972-371-5128
Home Page: www.zeroriskhr.com
Social Media: *Facebook, Twitter, LinkedIn, Google+*

Jack P Gibson, Chairman
Mike Poskey, President
Dr. Robert Kinsel Smith, Senior Adviser/Consultant
Heath Hilliard, National Sales Manager
Michelle Lima, Operations Manager

Provides important risk and insurance information to business, legal, risk management, and insurance professionals
Founded in 1978

14181 International Society of Appraisers

225 West Wacker Drive
Suite 650
Chicago, IL 60606ÿ

312-981-6778
FAX 312-265-2908
E-Mail: isa@isa-appraisers.org
Home Page: www.isa-appraisers.org/
Social Media: *Facebook, Twitter, LinkedIn, RSS*

Christine Guernsey, ISA CAPP, President
Perri Guthrie, ISA CAPP, Vice President
Steven R. Roach, JD, ISA CAPP, Treasurer
Karen S. Rabe, ISA CAPP, Secretary
Hughene D. Acheson, ISA AM, Director

A nonprofit, professional personal property appraisal association representing appraisers in the United States and Canada.
Founded in 1979

14182 International Tax and Investment Center

1800 K St NW
Suite 718
Washington, DC 20006-2202

202-530-9799
FAX 202-530-7987
E-Mail: Washington@iticnet.org
Home Page: www.iticnet.org
Social Media: *Facebook, Twitter, RSS*

Daniel A. Witt, President
Blake Marshall, Vice President
Irene Savitsky, Vice President
Brian Mandel, Program Manager
Diana McKelvey, Communications Manager

A trade association that advances the use of structured settlements as a means of using periodic payments to resolve personal injury claims, workers compensation, and other types of claims.
600+ Members
Founded in 1993

14183 Intersure Ltd

3 Hotel St
Warrenton, VA 20186-3221

540-349-0969
FAX 540-349-0971
E-Mail: info@intersurepartners.com
Home Page: www.intersurepartners.com
Social Media: *Vimeo*

Millie Curtis, Executive Officer

Formerly the Association of International Insurance Agents. Founded to promote the principles of a free exchange of ideas and mutual

cooperation based on the highest standards of intergrity, confidentiality and trust.
45 Members
Founded in 1965

14184 LIMRA International
300 Day Hill Road
Windsor, CT 6095

860-688-3358
800-235-4672
FAX 860-298-9555
E-Mail: customer.service@limra.com
Home Page: www.limra.com
Social Media: *Facebook, Twitter, LinkedIn, Google+, RSS, YouTube*

Tim Stonehocker, Chair
Deanna Strable, Vice Chair
Robert A. Kerzner, CLU, ChFC, President
Alison Salka, Ph.D., SVP, Director - Research
Sean F. O'Donnell, Vice President, Member Relations
800 Members
Founded in 1916
Mailing list available for rent

14185 LOMA: Life Office Management Association
6190 Powers Ferry Road
Suite 600
Atlanta, GA 30339

770-951-1770
800-275-5662
FAX 770-984-0441
E-Mail: askloma@loma.org
Home Page: www.loma.org
Social Media: *Facebook, Twitter, LinkedIn, YouTube*

Robert A Kerzner, CLU, ChFC, President and CEO
Jeffrey Hasty, FLMI, ACS, SVP, Corporate Secretary
Michele LaBouff, SVP, Human Resources
Kathy Milligan, FLMI, ACS, Senior Vice President, Education
Ian J Watts, SVP, Managing Director

Insurance worldwide association of insurance companies specializing in research and education.
1200+ Members
Founded in 1924
Mailing list available for rent

14186 Life Insurance Marketing & Research Association (LIMRA)
300 Day Hill Rd.
Windsor, CT 06095

860-688-3358
FAX 860-285-7792
E-Mail: customer.service@limra.com
Home Page: www.limra.com
Social Media: *Facebook, Twitter, LinkedIn, Google+, YouTube*

Catherine Theroux, Director, Public Relations

We offer our clients insight in the form of cooperative research and value added marketing and distribution expertise. Insight that helps you identify trends, evaluate options and implement solutions. All of which leads to one clear outcome; the growth of your company.
800 Members
Founded in 1916
Mailing list available for rent

14187 Life Insurance Settlement Association
225 South Eola Drive
Orlando, FL 32801

407-894-3797
Home Page: www.lisa.org/

Social Media: *Facebook, Twitter, LinkedIn, Google+, RSS, YouTube*

Cynthia Poveda, Chairman
Michael Freedman, Vice Chairman
Phil Loy, Treasurer
James W. Maxson, Secretary
Alan Buerger, Board Member

Promotes the development, integrity, and reputation of the life settlement industry and promotes a competitive market for the people it serves.
85+ Members
Founded in 1994

14188 Life Insurers Council
2300 Windy Ridge Parkway
Suite 600
Atlanta, GA 30339

770-984-3724
800-275-5662
FAX 770-984-3780
E-Mail: askloma@loma.org
Home Page: www.loma.org/lic/

Robert A Kerzner, CLU, ChFC, President and CEO
Jeffrey Hasty, FLMI, ACS, Senior Vice President, Assessment
Michele LaBouff, Senior Vice President
Kathy Milligan, FLMI, ACS, A, Senior Vice President, Education
Ian J Watts, Senior Vice President

In 1997, the LIC merged with (LOMA) Life Office Management Association which added extensive benefits for all LIC members. Serving the basic insurance needs of the general public, including the underserved market, through various distribution methods.
62 Members
Founded in 1910
Mailing list available for rent

14189 Lightning Protection Institute
25475 Magnolia Drive
PO Box 99
Maryville, MO 64468

804-314-8955
800-488-6864
FAX 660-582-0430
E-Mail: lpi@lightning.org
Home Page: www.lightning.org
Social Media: *Facebook, Twitter*

Harold VanSickle III, Executive Director
Kim Loehr, Communications Director

A not-for-profit organization whose members are dedicated to insuring that today's lightning protection systems are the best possible quality in design, materials and installation, so that precious live and property can be protected from the damaging and costly effects of one of nature's most exciting phenomenons, lightning.
100 Members
Founded in 1955

14190 Loss Executives Association
Industrial Risk Insurers
P.O. Box 37
Tenafly, NJ 07670

201-569-3346
E-Mail: info@lossexecutives.com
Home Page: www.lossexecutives.com

Edward J. Ryan, President
Jean L. Broderick, Vice President
Paul Aviles, Treasurer
Raymond Mattia, Secretary
Harris E. Berenson, Esq., Board Member

A professional association of property loss executives providing education to the industry.

14191 Mass Marketing Insurance Institute
3007 Tilden Street, NW
Suite 7M-103
Washington, DC 20008

816-221-7575
FAX 816-772-7765
E-Mail: gregc@robstan.com
Home Page: www.mi2.org
Social Media: *Facebook, Twitter, LinkedIn, Google Plus, Youtube, Pinteres*

Mark Smith, Director
Laurie Weber, Associate Director
Jim Barrett, First VP
Mary Walsh, VP Membership
Jennifer Branfort, Associate Director

The oldest not-for-profit membership organization that promotes the voluntary benefits industry by providing a forum for education, business development and fellowship.
300 Members
Frequency: Annual Meeting (Spring)
Founded in 1970

14192 Massachusetts Association of Insurance Agents
91 Cedar Street
Milford, MA 01757

508-634-2900
800-972-9312
FAX 508-634-2929
E-Mail: info@massagent.com
Home Page: www.massagent.com
Social Media: *Facebook, LinkedIn, Google+*

Raymond Sirois, AAI, Chairman
G. L. Gaudette, III, CPCU, Chairman Elect
Glen E. Davis, CIC, CRM, LIA, Vice Chairman
Ely Kaplansky, Secretary-Treasurer
Raymond D.ÿ Gallant, National Director

Trade show for everyday use in the insurance agency office.
1800 Members
Frequency: November
Mailing list available for rent

14193 Million Dollar Round Table
325 West Touhy Ave
Park Ridge, IL 60068-4265

847-692-6378
FAX 847-518-8921
E-Mail: info@mdrt.org
Home Page: www.mdrt.org
Social Media: *Facebook, Twitter, LinkedIn, Pinterest*

Brian Heckert, CLU, ChFC, President
Caroline Banks, FPFS, Immediate Past President
Mark Hanna, CLU, ChFC, First Vice President
James Douglas Pittman, Second VP
Ross Vanderwolf, CFP, Secretary

Provides its members with resources to improve their technical knowledge, sales and client service while maintaining a culture of high ethical standards. Mission is to be a valued, member-driven international network of leading insurance and investment financial services professionals/advisors who serve their clients by exemplary performance and the highest standards of ethics, knowledge, service and productivity.
35000 Members
Founded in 1927
Mailing list available for rent

14194 Mortgage Bankers Association of America
1919 M Street NW
5th Floor
Washington, DC 20036

202-557-2700
800-793-6222
Home Page: www.mortgagebankers.org

Social Media: *Facebook, Twitter, LinkedIn, YouTube*

Thomas Dennardÿ, Chairman
Kurt Pfotenhauerÿ, Vice Chairman
David H. Stevens, President, Chief Executive Officer
Bill Killmer, SVP, Legislative & Pol. Affairs
Marcia Davies, Chief Operating Officer

United States national association representing all facets of the real estate finance industry.
2200 Members

14195 Mortgage Insurance Companies of America

1425 K St Nw
Suite 210
Washington, DC 20005-3590

202-682-2683
FAX 202-842-9252
E-Mail: info@privatemi.com
Home Page: www.privatemi.com

Suzanne Hutchinson, Executive VP

Representing the private mortgage insurance industry.
4 Members
Founded in 1973

14196 National African American Insurance Association

1718 M Street, NW
Box #1110
Washington, DC 20036

866-56 -AAIA
FAX 513-563-9743
E-Mail: info@naaia.org
Home Page: www.naaia.org
Social Media: *Facebook, Twitter, LinkedIn*

Leslie L. Skinner-Leslieÿ, Chairman
Jerald L. Tillman,ÿLUTCF, Founder
Quincy Branch, Vice Chair
Cherie Coffey, Treasurer
Henry Pippins, Secretary

Helps create a network among minorities who are employed by insurance companies or self-employed in the insurance industry.
Founded in 1997

14197 National Alliance for Insurance Education & Research

3630 North Hills Drive
PO Box 27027
Austin, TX 78755-2027

512-457-7932
800-633-2165
FAX 512-349-6194
E-Mail: alliance@scic.com
Home Page: www.scic.com/
Social Media: *Facebook, Twitter, LinkedIn, Google Plus, RSS*

William T Hold, Ph.D, CIC, CPCU, President and CEO
Skyla Badger, Assistant Vice President, Marketing
Theresa Bucek, CISR, Assistant Vice President
Paula Cook, CISR, SVP, Program Administration
Bettie Duff, SVP, Customer Care

National education providers offering programs for all insurance and risk management professionals in property, liability and life insurance, with a continuing education requirement upon designation.
75000 Members
Founded in 1969

14198 National Association of Professional Agents

8430 Enterprise Circle
Suite 200
Lakewood Ranch, FL 34202

800-593-7657
FAX 800-411-4771
Home Page: www.napa-benefits.org/
Social Media: *Facebook, Twitter, LinkedIn*

Offers insurance agents direct access to insurance benefits and professional services.
Founded in 1989

14199 National Association of Bar-Related Title Insurers

1430 Lee Street
Des Plaines, IL 60018

847-298-8300
FAX 847-298-8388
E-Mail: joanne@elliottlaw.com
Home Page: www.nabrti.com

Joanne P Elliott, Executive Vice President
Kathleen Waters, Secretary/Treasurer

Members are bar-related title insurance companies registered with the US Patent Office.
10 Members
Founded in 1965

14200 National Association of Casualty and Surety Agents

316 Pennsylvania Avenue SE
Suite 400
Washington, DC 20003-1172

202-543-7500
FAX 202-293-1219

Lawrence Zippin, Executive Director

A trade organization of insurance agentswho represent and sell for stock insurers. Its purpose is to foster the growth of its members through cooperation with the insurers its members represent.

14201 National Association of Catastrophe Adjusters

PO Box 499
Alvord, TX 76225

817-498-3466
FAX 817-498-0480
E-Mail: naca@nacatadj.org
Home Page: www.nacatadj.org
Social Media: *Facebook, Twitter, LinkedIn*

Woody Britton, Chairman
Shari Brittonÿ, President
Chris Hatcherÿ, VP
Jon Joyce, Secretary/Treasurerÿ
John Postava, Past President

Provides a professional organization focused on excellence in catastrophe insurance adjusting for members through education, shared resources, and technology.
347 Members
Founded in 1976

14202 National Association of Dental Plans

12700 Park Central Drive
Ste. 400
Dallas, TX 75251

972-458-6998
FAX 972-458-2258
E-Mail: info@nadp.org
Home Page: www.nadp.org
Social Media: *Facebook, Twitter, LinkedIn, Youtube*

Chris Swanker, FSA, MAAA, Chair
Theresa McConeghey, Vice Chair
Dr Gene Sherman, Secretary
Kirk Andrews, Treasurer
Evelyn F. Ireland, CAEÿÿ, Executive Director

Non profit trade association representing the entire dental benefits industry; dental HMOs, dental PPOs, discount dental plans and dental indemnity products. Members include major commercial carriers, regional and single state companies, as well as companies organized as Delta and Blue Cross Blue Shield plans.
80 Members
Founded in 1989

14203 National Association of Disability Evaluating Professionals

13801 Village Mill Drive
Midlothian, VA 23113

804-378-7275
Home Page: www.nadep.com

Virgil Robert May III, Executive Director

Members are lawyers, medical doctors and other professionals involved in the evaluation and rehabilitation of persons with disabilities resulting from work or personal injuries.
Cost: $150.00
1000 Members
Frequency: Membership Fee
Founded in 1984

14204 National Association of Fire Investigators , International

857 Tallevast Road
Sarasota, FL 34243

941-359-2800
877-506-6234
FAX 941-351-5849
E-Mail: info@nafi.org
Home Page: www.nafi.org
Social Media: *Facebook, Twitter, LinkedIn*

Heather Kennedy, Director Membership Services
Christine Kennedy, Director Training Program

Primary purpose of this association is to increase the knowledge and improve the skills of persons engaged in the investigation and analysis of fires, explosions, or in the litigation that ensues from such investigations. The Association also originated and implemented the National Certification Board.
6000 Members
Founded in 1961

14205 National Association of Fraternal Insurance Counselors

211 Canal Road
Waterloo, WI 53594

920-458-1996
866-478-3880
FAX 920-457-4661
E-Mail: office@nafic.org
Home Page: www.nafic.org
Social Media: *Facebook*

Robert Cooper, FICF, President
James Dietrich, FIC, AFA, Vice President
Joy Collins, FICF, Secretary/Treasurer
Randall Kolarik, FIC, LUTCF, Immediate Past President
Anna Maenner, Executive Director

Promotes and educates the sales force in fraternal life insurance. Bestows quality service award and production awards annually.
3.1M Members
Founded in 1950

14206 National Association of Health Underwriters

1212 New York Avenue NW
Suite 1100
Washington, DC 20005

202-552-5060
FAX 202-747-6820
E-Mail: info@nahu.org
Home Page: www.nahu.org

Social Media: *Facebook, Twitter, LinkedIn, Youtube, RSS, B2B*

Janet Trautwein, Executive Vice President & CEO
Jennifer B Murphy, CFO, COO
Illana Maze, Senior Vice President of Technology
Brooke Willson, Vice President of Leadership
Melanie Gibson, VP, Member & Corporate Relations

The mission is to improve its members' ability to meet the health, financial and retirement security needs of all Americans through education, advocacy and professional development.
18000 Members
Founded in 1930
Mailing list available for rent: 18000 names at $350 per M

14207 National Association of Independent Insurance Adjusters (NAIIA)

1880 Radcliff Ct.
Suite 117-C&B
Tracy, CA 95376

209-832-6962
FAX 209-832-6964
E-Mail: admin@naiia.com
Home Page: www.naiia.com

Matt Ouellette, President
Peter Crosa, President Elect
Susan Daniels, Secretary/Treasurer
James Hunt, Immediate Past President
Brenda Reisinger, Executive Director

Members are companies and individuals adjusting claims for insurance companies on a fee basis.
300 Members
Founded in 1937

14208 National Association of Independent Insura nce Adjusters (NAIIA)

1880 Radcliff Ct.
Suite 117-C & B
Tracy, CA 95376

209-832-6962
FAX 209-832-6964
E-Mail: admin@naiia.com
Home Page: www.naiia.com

Matt Ouellette, President
Peter Crosa, President Elect
Susan Daniels, Secretary/Treasurer
James Hunt, Immediate Past President
Brenda Reisinger, Executive Director

Membership consists of property-liability companies Supports the National Association of Independent Insurers Political Action Committee.

14209 National Association of Independent Life Brokerage Agencies

11325 Random Hills Road
Suite 110
Fairfax, VA 22030

703-383-3081
FAX 703-383-6942
E-Mail: jnormandy@nailba.org
Home Page: www.nailba.org
Social Media: *Facebook, Twitter, LinkedIn, RSS*

David Long, Chairman
Jack Chiasson, CAE, Chief Executive Officer
George C. Van Dusen IV, Chair Elect
James Sorebo, Secretary/Treasurerÿ
Susan D. Haning, CEM, CMP, Director, Business Development

Influencing the independent life and health brokerage community.
300+ Members
Founded in 1981

14210 National Association of Insurance Commissioners

1100 Walnut Street
Suite 1500
Kansas City, MO 64106-2197

816-842-3600
FAX 816-783-8175
E-Mail: news@naic.org
Home Page: www.naic.org
Social Media: *Facebook, Twitter, LinkedIn, YouTube, RSS*

Monica J. Lindeen, NAIC President, Commissioner
Sharon P. Clark, NAIC Vice President Commissioner
John M. Huff, NAIC President Elect Director
Sen. Ben Nelson, NAIC Chief Executive Officer
Ted Nickel, NAIC Secretary-Treasurer

Assists state insurance regulators, individually and collectively, in serving the public interest and achieving the following fundamental insurance regulatorygoals in a responsive, efficient and cost effective manner, consistent with the wishes of its members.
Founded in 1871
Mailing list available for rent

14211 National Association of Insurance and Financial Advisors

2901 Telestar Court
PO Box 12012
Falls Church, VA 22042-1205

877-866-2432
877-866-2432
FAX 703-770-8201
E-Mail: membersupport@naifa.org
Home Page: www.naifa.org
Social Media: *Facebook, Twitter, LinkedIn, Youtube*

Jules O. Gaudreau, President
Kevin M. Mayeux, CAE, Chief Executive Officer
Paul R. Dougherty, President Elect
Matthew S. Tassey, Treasurer
Keith M. Gillies, Secretary

Mission is to advocate for a positive legislative and regulatory environment, enhance business and professional skills, and promote the ethical conduct of our members.
Founded in 1890

14212 National Association of Mortgage Brokers

2701 W. 15th Street
Suite 536
Plano, TX 75075

972-758-1151
FAX 530-484-2906
E-Mail: membership@namb.org
Home Page: www.namb.org
Social Media: *Facebook, Twitter, LinkedIn, Youtube, RSS*

John Councilman, CMC, CRMSÿ, President
Fred Kreger, CMC, Vice President
Rocke Andrews, CMC, CRMS, President Elect
Andy W. Harris, CRMS, Treasurer
Rick Bettencourt, CRMS, Secretary

The only national trade association representing the mortgage broker industry. Promotes the industry through programs and services such as education, professional certification and government affairs representation.
25000 Members
Founded in 1973
Mailing list available for rent

14213 National Association of Mutual Insurance Companies

3601 Vincennes Road
Indianapolis, IN 46268-0700

317-875-5250
FAX 317-879-8408
Home Page: www.namic.org
Social Media: *Facebook, Twitter, LinkedIn, YouTube, RSS*

Charles M Chamness, President/CEO
Neil Alldredge, SVP, State & Policy Affairs
Gregg Dykstra, COO, General Counsel
Michael Ulmer, VP, Business Developmentÿ
Pam Keeney, Vice President - Underwriting

A full service nationaltrade association with more than 1,400 member companies that underwrite 43 percent of the property/casualty insurance premium in the United States.
1400 Members
Founded in 1985
Mailing list available for rent

14214 National Association of Professional Surplus Lines Offices, Ltd.

4131 N. Mulberry Drive
Suite 200
Kansas City, MO 64116

816-741-3910
FAX 816-741-5409
E-Mail: info@napslo.org
Home Page: www.napslo.org
Social Media: *Facebook, Twitter, LinkedIn*

Gilbert C. Hine, Jr., CPCU, CFP, President
David E. Leonard, CPCU, Are, Vice President
Hank Haldeman, Immediate Past President
Jacqueline M.ÿ Schaendorf, CPCU, Treasurer
James C. Drinkwater, Secretary

A national trade association representing the surplus lines industry and the wholesale insurance marketing system. Acting as a source of information, spends a great deal of time identifying and explaining to regulatory, other segments of the insurance industry, the media and the public the vital role surplus lines in the insurance industry.
Founded in 1975
Mailing list available for rent

14215 National Association of Professional Insur ance Agents

400 North Washington Street
Alexandria, VA 22314

703-836-9340
FAX 703-836-1279
E-Mail: web@pianet.org
Home Page: www.pia.org/
Social Media: *Facebook, Twitter, LinkedIn, RSS*

Mike Becker, Executive Vice President & CEO
Ted Besesparis, SVP, Comm./Public Relations
Patricia A. Borowski, CPIW, SVP, Government/Industry Affairs
Alexi Papandon, CAE, SVP, Products & Services
Jon Gentile, Director of Federal Affairs

Voluntary, membership based, trade association representing professional independent insurance agents throughout the United States.
Founded in 1931

14216 National Association of Public Insurance Adjusters

21165 Whitfield Place
Suite 105
Potomac Falls, VA 20165

703-433-9217
FAX 703-433-0369

E-Mail: info@napia.com
Home Page: www.napia.com

Scott deLuise, SPPAÿ, President
Diane Swerling, SPPA, First Vice President
Jeff Gould, CPA, Second Vice President
Damon Faunce, Third VP
Greg Raab, Fourth VP

Experts on property loss adjustment who are retained by policy holders to assist in preparing, filing and adjusting insurance claims. NAPIA members have joined together for the purpose of professional education, certification, and promotion of a code of professional conduct.
Founded in 1951
Mailing list available for rent

14217 National Association of State Comprehensive Health Insurance

580-512-1488
Home Page: www.naschip.org/

Tanya Case, Chair
Vic Kensler, Chair-Elect/Vice President
Cecil Bykerk, Treasurerÿ
Vernita McMurtrey, Secretary
Michele Eberle, Board Member

Provides educational opportunities and information for state high risk health insurance pools that have been, or are yet to be, established by state governments to serve the medically "uninsurable" population.

14218 National Association of Surety Bond Producers

1140 19th Street
Suite 800
Washington, DC 20036-5104

202-686-3700
FAX 202-686-3656
E-Mail: info@nasbp.org
Home Page: www.nasbp.org
Social Media: *Facebook, Twitter, LinkedIn*

Susan Hecker, President
Lynne Cook, First Vice President
Howard Cowan, Second VP
Robert Shaw, Third VP
Mark McCallum, CEO

International organization of professional surety bond producers and brokers.
500+ Members
Founded in 1942

14219 National Cargo Bureau

17 Battery Place
Suite 1232
New York, NY 10004-1110

212-785-8300
FAX 212-785-8333
E-Mail: ncbnyc@natcargo.org
Home Page: www.natcargo.org

Ian J. Lennard, President
Kristian Wiede, Corporate Secretary
Philip Anderson, Chief, Technical Department
Capt. Thomasÿ Sheridan, Deputy Chief Surveyor
Capt. Peter Ho, Deputy Chief Surveyor

The Bureau was created to render assistance to the United States Coast Guard in discharging its responsibilities under the 1948 International Convention for Safety of Life at Sea and for other purposes closely related thereto.
Founded in 1952

14220 National Conference of Insurance Legislators

385 Jordan Road
Troy, NY 12180

518-687-0178
FAX 518-687-0401
E-Mail: info@ncoil.org

Home Page: www.ncoil.org
Social Media: *Facebook, Twitter*

Sen. Neil Breslin, President
Sen. Travis Holdman, IN, Vice President
Rep. Steve Riggs, Secretary
Sen. Jason Rapert, Treasurer

NCOIL is an organization of state legislators whose main area of public policy concern is insurance legislation and regulation. Many legislators active in NCOIL either chair or are members of the committees reponsible for insurance legislation in their respective state houses across the country.
Founded in 1969

14221 National Conference of Insurance Legislato rs (NCOIL)

1100 13th Street NW
Suite 1000
Washington, DC 20005

202-955-3500
FAX 202-955-3599
E-Mail: customersupport@ncqa.org
Home Page: www.ncqa.org
Social Media: *Facebook, Twitter, LinkedIn, YouTube, Google+, Pinterest*

David Chin, MD, Chair
Margaret E. O'Kane, President
Michael S. Barr, MD, MBA, FACP, EVP, Quality Measurement
Tom Fluegel, Chief Operating Officer
Patricia Barrett, VP, Product Design and Support

Independent, non profit organization dedicated to improving healthcare quality.
Founded in 1990
Mailing list available for rent

14222 National Council of Self-Insurers

P.O. Box 98248
Des Moines, WA 98198

206-409-6995
FAX 206-212-9488
E-Mail: dave.kaplan@natcouncil.com
Home Page: www.natcouncil.com

Dave Kaplan, Executive Director
Robin R Obetz, VP

The Council believes that the workers' compensation system, properly administered by the states, is a vital part of the economic and social fabric of the United States. The Council aime to preserve it and protect it as the most effective means of resolving claims for industrial injuries and occupational diseases between employers and employees.
3500 Members
Founded in 1946

14223 National Council on Compensation Insurance

901 Pennisula Corporate Circle
Boca Raton, FL 33487-1362

561-893-1000
FAX 561-893-1191
E-Mail: robert_pierson@ncci.com
Home Page: www.ncci.com

Cheryl Budd, Chief Communications Officerÿ
Robert Pierson, Affiliate Services Executive
Jennie Dennison, Account Manager
Gregory Quinn, Media Relations Directorÿ
Judy Joffe, Community Relations Directorÿ

Manages the nation's largest database of workers' compensation insurance information. They analyze industry trends, prepares workers compensation insurance rate recommendations, determines the cost of propsed legislation, and provides a variety of services and tools to maintain a healthy workers compensation system.
Founded in 1922

14224 National Independent Statistical Service

3601 Vincennes Road
PO Box 68950
Indianapolis, IN 46268-0950

317-876-6200
FAX 317-876-6210
E-Mail: questions@niss-stat.org
Home Page: www.niss-stat.org

Theresa Szwast, President

A unique resource for the property/casualty insurance industry. Collect and report timely, quality insurance data, and perform other related functions, at a reasonable cost.
Founded in 1966

14225 National Insurance Association

1133 Desert Shale Avenue
Las Vegas, NV 89120

702-269-2445
FAX 702-269-2446

Josephine King, Executive Director

Organization of about 14 insurance companies owned or controlled by African Americans.
14 Members
Founded in 1921

14226 National Insurance Crime Bureau

1111 E Touhy Ave
Suite 400
Des Plaines, IL 60018-5804

847-544-7000
800-447-6282
FAX 847-544-7100
E-Mail: rjones@nicb.org
Home Page: www.nicb.org
Social Media: *Facebook, Twitter, LinkedIn, Youtube*

Joseph H Wehrle, Jr, President
James K Schweitzer, SVP, COO
Daniel G Abbott, SVP, Chief Information Officer
Robert Jachnicki, SVP, CFO
Andrew J Sosnowski, SVP, General Counsel

Not for profit organization that receives support from property/casualty insurance companies. Partners with insurers and law enforcement agencies to facilitate the identification, detection and prosecution of insurance criminals. Formed from the merging of the National Automobile Theft Bureau and the Insurance Crime Prevention Institute.
1000 Members
Founded in 1992

14227 National Organization of Life and Health Insurance Guaranty Associations

13873 Park Center Road
Suite 329
Herndon, VA 20171

703-481-5206
FAX 703-481-5209
E-Mail: info@nolhga.com
Home Page: www.nolhga.com/

Deborah J.ÿ Long, Esq., Chair
Lee Douglassÿ, Vice Chair
Deborah Bello, Treasurer
Margaret M . Parker, Secretary
Melody R. J.ÿ Jensen, Esq., Immediate Past Chair

A voluntary, U.S. association made up of the life and health insurance guaranty associations of all 50 states and the District of Columbia.
Founded in 1983

14228 National Risk Retention Association
16133 Ventura Blvd.
Suite 1055
Encino, CA 91436

818-995-3274
800-928-5809
FAX 818-995-6496
FAX 800-421-5981
E-Mail: joe@riskretention.org
Home Page: www.nrra-usa.org

Dan Labrie, Chair
Michael J. Schroeder, Chair Elect/Vice Chair
Sanford Elsass, Immediate Past Chair
Jon Harkavy, Secretary
Nancy Gray, Treasurer

Promotes Risk Retention Act-authorized group
insurance programs as a practical, economical,
efficient and financially sound option for distributing the liability risks of member insuerds.
Founded in 1987

14229 National Underwriter Company
5081 Olympic Blvd
Erlanger, KY 41018-3164

859-692-2100
800-543-0874
FAX 859-692-2295
E-Mail: webmistress@nuco.com
Home Page: www.nationalunderwriter.com

Charlie Smith, CEO

Organization with listings which include companies, brokers and agents in each area handling all lines of insurance.

14230 National Viatical Association
1030 15th Street NW
Washington, DC 20005

202-347-7361
800-741-9465
FAX 202-393-0336

Charles C Reely, Executive Director

NVA is dedicated to financially assisting and
effectively promotingthe needs of people coping with terminal illnesses in a compassionate,
professional and ethical manner. The National
Viatical Association is further dedicated to educating and informing the public on the viatical
settlement processs.
60 Members
Founded in 1993

**14231 New England Professional Insurance
Agents Association**
1 Ash Street
Hopkinton, MA 01748-1822

508-497-2590

Stella Di Camilo, Manager

Supports all those in professional agents in the
insurance industry in the New England region.
Hosts annual trade show.

14232 Nonprofit Risk Management Center
204 South King Street
Leesburg, VA 20175

202-785-3891
FAX 703-443-1990
E-Mail: info@nonprofitrisk.org
Home Page: www.nonprofitrisk.org
Social Media: *Twitter*

Peter Andrew, President
Lisa Prinz, Treasurer
Carolyn Hayes-Gulston, Secretary
Melanie Lockwood Herman, Executive
Director
Kay Nakamura, Director of Client Solutions

Provides assistance and resources for commu-
nity serving organizations.
Founded in 1990
Mailing list available for rent

**14233 North American Pet Health Insurance
Association**
200 - 692 Osborne Street
Winnipeg, MB R3L 2B9

877-962-7442
E-Mail: info@naphia.org
Home Page: www.naphia.org
Social Media: *Facebook, Twitter, LinkedIn,
YouTube*

Dennis Rushovich, President and Past
Treasurer
Laura Bennett, Past President
Steve Popovich, Treasurer
Tim Graff, Secretary
Randy Valpy, Board Member

Represents experienced and reputable pet
health insurance companiesand pet health professionals.

**14234 Physician Insurers Association of
America**
2275 Research Blvd
Suite 250
Rockville, MD 20850-6213

301-947-9000
FAX 301-947-9090
E-Mail: membership@piaa.us
Home Page: www.piaa.us
Social Media: *Twitter*

Gloria H. Everett, Chair
Paul C. McNabb, II, MD, Vice Chair
Richard E. Anderson, MD, Secretary
Brian Atchinson, President & CEO
Eric Anderson, VP of Marketing &
Communications

An organization of healthcare liability insurance entities which share the common values of
its founders to advocate on behalf of physicians, dentists, and other healthcare providers
in the areas of legislation, education, risk
management and research.
1000 Members
Founded in 1977

**14235 Professional Insurance
Communicators of America**
3601 Vincennes Road
Po Box 60700
Indianapolis, IN 46268-0700

317-875-5250
FAX 317-879-8408
Home Page: www.pica.pro/
Social Media: *Twitter, LinkedIn*

Janet EH Wright, Secretary/Treasurer

Members are editors of insurance company
newsletters.
90 Members
Founded in 1955

**14236 Professional Insurance Marketing
Association**
35 E. Wacker Dr.
Suite 850
Chicago, IL 60601-2106

817-569-7462
FAX 312-644-8557
E-Mail: mona@pima-assn.org
Home Page: www.pima-assn.org
Social Media: *Twitter, LinkedIn*

Michael Mercer, President
Mark Kelsey, President-Elect
Daniel O'Brien, CLU, Imm. Past President
William Suneson, Treasurer
Mona Buckley, CEO (ex-officio)

The leading national membership association
of third-party administrators, insurance carriers
and allied business partners involved in the direct marketing of insurance products. Also provides educational conferences, legislative
updates, networking opportunities, publications

and manuals to all those whose primary
business is insurance marketing.
117 Members
Founded in 1974

**14237 Professional Liability Underwriting
Society**
5353 Wayzata Blvd
Suite 600
Minneapolis, MN 55416-1335

952-746-2580
800-845-0778
FAX 952-746-2599
E-Mail: info@plusweb.org
Home Page: www.plusweb.org
Social Media: *Twitter, LinkedIn, RSS*

James Skarzynski, President
Heather Fox, President-Elect
Peter Herron, Imm. Past President
Debbie Schaffel, RPLU, Secretary-Treasurer
Robbie Thompson, Executive Director

Enhances the professionalism of its members
through education and other activities and to
responsibly address issues related to professional liability.
7000 Members
Founded in 1986

**14238 Property Casualty Insurers
Association of America**
8700 West Bryn Mawr Avenue
Suite 1200S
Chicago, IL 60631-3512

847-297-7800
FAX 847-297-5064
E-Mail: pcinet@pciaa.net
Home Page: www.pciaa.net
Social Media: *Facebook, Twitter, YouTube*

David A. Sampson, President
Paul C. Blume, Senior Vice President
Nathaniel Wienecke, Senior Vice President
Randi Cigelnik, Senior Vice President
Joanne M. Orfanos, Senior Vice President

Established by the Merger of the Alliance of
American Insurers and the National Association Association of Independent Insurers. Provides a responsible and effective voice on
public policy questions affecting insurance
products and services, fosters a competitive insurance marketplace for the benefit of insurers
and consumers, and provides members with the
highest quality products, information and
services at a reasonable cost.
1000 Members
Founded in 2004

14239 Property Insurance Loss Register
700 New Brunswick Avenue
Rahway, NJ 07065-3819

732-388-0332
FAX 732-388-0537

Lawrence Zippin, President

A voluntary nonprofit organization administered by the American Insurance Services
Group; maintains a computerized registry of
property loss claims which can be used by its
subscribers to fight insurance fraud, and provides data for nonactuarial/statistical research.

**14240 Property Loss Research Bureau
(PLRB/LIRB)**
3025 Highland Parkway
Suite 800
Downers Grove, IL 60515-1291

630-724-2200
888-711-7572
FAX 630-724-2260

Home Page: www.plrb.org
Social Media: *Facebook, Twitter, Instagram*

Tom Mallin, President
Paul C Despensa, VP/General Counsel

PLRB/LIRB provides legal research, consulting and educational services in auto liability and CGL lines, in addition to promoting education and new, beneficial developments within the property and casualty insurance industry. Members are stock and mutual insurance companies.
252 Members
Founded in 1990
Mailing list available for rent

14241 Public Agency Risk Managers Association

PO Box 6810
San Jose, CA 95150

888-907-2762
FAX 888-412-5913
E-Mail: Info@parma.com
Home Page: www.parma.com
Social Media: *Facebook, Twitter, LinkedIn, Vimeo, Instagram*

Jim Thyden, President
Kim Hunt, Vice President
Susan Eldridge, Secretary Treasurer
Coni Hernandez, Alliance of Schools
Jeff J Rush, Senior Claims Administrator

A forum promoting, developing and advancing education and leadership in public agency risk management. PARMA is dedicated to facilitating the exchange of ideas and innovative solutions toward risk management in government.
600+ Members
Founded in 1974

14242 Registered Mail Insurance Association

100 William Street
New York, NY 10038-4512

212-612-4000
800-969-7462
FAX 212-425-2539

Cheryl Martinez, Assistant VP

Insurance companies providing insurance for shipments of currency, securities and other valuables. LSTD Instrument Bonds are provided to facilitate the reproduction of lost documents.
3 Members
Founded in 1921

14243 Reinsurance Association of America

1445 New York Ave
7th Floor
Washington, DC 20005

202-638-3690
FAX 202-638-0936
E-Mail: infobox@reinsurance.org
Home Page: www.reinsurance.org
Social Media: *Facebook, Twitter, LinkedIn*

Franklin W Nutter, President
Dennis C Burke, Vice President, State Relations
Marsha A Cohen, SVP, Director of Education
Tracey W Laws, SVP, General Counsel
Karalee C Morell, VP, Assistant General Counsel

Non profit association committed to an activist agenda that represents the interests of reinsurance professionals across the United States.
Founded in 1968

14244 Risk and Insurance Management Society

5 Bryant Park
13th Floor
New York, NY 10018-0713

212-286-9292
FAX 212-986-9716
Home Page: www.rims.org
Social Media: *Facebook, Twitter, LinkedIn*

Mary Roth, Executive Director
Deborah Flam, Human Resources Manager
Lynn Chambers, CFO
Stephanie Orange, Chief Marketing Officer
Valerie Cammiso, Membership/Chapter Services

Dedicated to advancing the practice of risk management, a professinal discipline that protects physical, financial and human resources.
3900 Members
Founded in 1950
Mailing list available for rent

14245 SNL Financial

212 7th Street NE
One SNL Plaza
Charlottesvle, VA 22902

434-977-1600
FAX 434-977-4466
E-Mail: customerservice@snl.com
Home Page: www.snl.com
Social Media: *Facebook, Twitter, LinkedIn, YouTube, Google+*

Michael Chinn, President
Reid Nagle, CEO
Bjorn Turnquist, Director Product Management

This organization offers the most up-to-date information available in the insurance industry featuring the latest news releases, filings and important events. Provides current data on top-performing stocks, insider trades, ownership filings, company news and events and legislative issues.
Founded in 1987
Mailing list available for rent

14246 Securities Industry and Financial Markets Association (SIFMA)

1101 New York Avenue, NW
8th Floor
Washington, DC 20005-4279

202-962-7300
FAX 202-962-7305
Home Page: www.sifma.org
Social Media: *Facebook, Twitter, LinkedIn*

William A.ÿ Johnstone, Chair
John F.ÿ W. Rogers, Chair Elect
Timothy C. Scheve, Vice Chair
Kenneth E. Bentsen, Jr., President, CEO
Gerard McGraw, Treasurer

SIFMA's mission is to champion policies and practices that benefit investors and issuers, expand and perfect global capital markets, and foster the development of new products and services. SIFMA provides an enhanced member network of access and forward-looking services, as well as premiere educational resources for the professionals within the industry and the investors whom they serve.
Mailing list available for rent

14247 Self Insurance Institute of America

PO Box 1237
Simpsonville, SC 29681

800-851-7789
FAX 864-962-2483
E-Mail: administration@siia.org
Home Page: www.siia.org
Social Media: *Facebook, Twitter*

Donald K. Drelich, Chairman of the Board
Steven J. Link, Chairman Elect

Ronald K. Dewsnup, Treasurer/Corporate Secretary
Mike Ferguson, President, CEO
Erica Massey, EVP

Dedicated to protecting and promoting the self insurance and alternative risk transfer industry.
1500 Members
Founded in 1981

14248 Shipowners Claims Bureau

1 Battery Park Plaza
31st Floor
New York, NY 10004-1487

212-847-4500
FAX 212-847-4599
E-Mail: info@american-club.com
Home Page: www.american-club.com

J. Arnold Witte, Chairman
Markos K. Marinakis, Deputy Chairman
Arpad A. Kadi, Senior Vice President - Treasurer
Donald R. Moore, Senior Vice President

Members are claim managers and adjusters for shipping lines and protection and indemnity clubs.
31 Members
Founded in 1917
Mailing list available for rent

14249 Society of Actuaries

475 North Martingale Rd.
Suite 600
Schaumburg, IL 60173-2252

847-706-3500
888-697-3900
FAX 847-706-3599
E-Mail: customerservice@soa.org
Home Page: www.soa.org
Social Media: *Twitter, LinkedIn, YouTube*

Craig W. Reynoldsÿÿ, President
Jeremy J. Brown, President-Elect
Joan C. Barrett, Vice-President
Susan E. Pantely, Vice-President
Susan R. Sames, Vice-President

An educational, research and professional organization dedicated to serving the public and Society members. The vision is for actuaries to be recognized as the leading professionals in the modeling and management of finanacial risk and contingent events.
17000 Members
Founded in 1949

14250 Society of Certified Insurance Counselors

3630 North Hills Drive
Austin, TX 78731-3028

512-457-7932
800-633-2165
FAX 512-349-6194
E-Mail: alliance@scic.com
Home Page: www.scic.com
Social Media: *Facebook, Twitter, LinkedIn, Google+, RSS*

William Hold, Ph.D, CIC, CPCU, President/CEO
Skyla Badger, Assistant Vice President, Marketing
Theresa Bucek, CISR, Assistant Vice President
Paula Cook, CISR, SVP, Program Administration
Bettie Duff, SVP, Customer Care

National education program in property, liability and life insurance, with a continuing education requirement upon designation.

14251 Society of Financial Examiners
12100 Sunset Hills Rd
Suite 130
Reston, VA 20190-3221

703-234-4140
800-787-7633
FAX 888-436-8686
E-Mail: sofe@sofe.org
Home Page: www.sofe.org
Social Media: *Facebook, LinkedIn*

Annette Knief, CFE, President
Richard Nelson, CFE, VP
Susan Bernard, CFE, AES, VP
James Kattman, CFE, Treasurer
Mark Murphy, CFE, Secretary

The one organization where financial examiners of inusrance companies, banks, savings and loans, credit unions come together for training and to share exchange information on a formal and informal level.
1600 Members
Founded in 1973

14252 Society of Financial Service Professionals
3803 West Chester Pike
Suite 225
Newtown Square, PA 19073-3230

610-526-2500
FAX 610-359-8115
E-Mail: info@financialpro.org
Home Page: www.financialpro.org
Social Media: *Facebook, Twitter, LinkedIn, Flickr, RSS*

Michael P. Dow, President
James M. Christian, CLU, ChFC, Immediate Past President
Anthony R. Bartlett, ChFC, CASL, President Elect
Joseph E. Frack, CPA, CGMA, CEO
James S. Aussem, JD, AEP, Secretary

Members are dedicated to the highest standards of competence and service in insurance and financial services.
11,00 Members
Founded in 1928
Mailing list available for rent

14253 Society of Insurance Research
631 Eastpoint Drive
Shelbyville, IN 46176-2291

317-398-3684
FAX 317-642-0535
E-Mail: sir.mail@comcast.net
Home Page: www.sirnet.org

Sharon Markovsky, President
Tom Forristell, CPA, Vice President - Controller
Karen Imbrogno, Vice President - Annual Conference
Michael Warner, VP Marketing
Carol Smith, Vice President - Membership

Provides a forum for the free exchange of ideas in all areas of insurance research. The Society includes representation from many different organizations such as insurance and non-insurance companies, government agencies, institutions of higher education, and trade associations.
350 Members
Founded in 1970
Mailing list available for rent

14254 Society of Insurance Trainers and Educators
1821 University Ave W
Ste S256
St. Paul, MN 55104

651-999-5354
FAX 651-917-1835
E-Mail: ed@insurancetrainers.org

Home Page: www.insurancetrainers.org
Social Media: *Facebook, Twitter, LinkedIn, Instagram*

Deborah Davenport, CIC, ITP, President
Brad Gutcher, Immediate Past President
Elise Quadrozzi, CPCU, AIC,, VP Annual Conference
Treg Camper, VP Membership Services
Heather Hubbard, MSHRM, Vice President - Marketing

Professional organization of trainers and educators in insurance.
600 Members
Founded in 1953

14255 Society of Professional Benefit Administrators
2 Wisconsin Circle
Suite 670
Chevy Chase, MD 20815

301-718-7722
FAX 301-718-9440
E-Mail: info@spbatpa.org
Home Page: www.spbatpa.org
Social Media: *Twitter*

Anne C Lennan, President

National Association of Third Party Administrators (TPAs) of employee benefit health and pension plans. SPBA represents TPAs who offer comprehensive services.
300 Members
Founded in 1975

14256 Society of Risk Management Consultants
621 North Sherman Avenue
Madison, WI 53704

800-765-SRMC
FAX 212-572-6499
E-Mail: webmaster@srmcsociety.org
Home Page: www.srmcsociety.org

Susan Kaufman, Public Relations
Mark R. Forsythe, CPCU, President
Robert Harder, ARM, Secretary
Michael Norek, Treasurer
Joy M. Gander, CPCU, ARM, President Elect

The mission is to advance these professions to benefit the consultants themselves, their clients and the public through research, education, the exchange of information, anf the promotion of professional and ethical guidlines.
150 Members
Founded in 1984

14257 Sun States Professional Insurance Agents Association
13416 N 32nd Street
Suite 106
Phoenix, AZ 85032-6000

602-482-3333

Maryls M Graser, Executive VP

Supports all those professional insurance agents who serve the southern region of the country. Hosts annual trade show.

14258 Teachers Insurance and Annuity Association
730 Third Avenue
New York, NY 10017

800-842-2252
FAX 800-842-2252
Home Page: www.tiaa-cref.org
Social Media: *Facebook, Twitter, LinkedIn, YouTube, Google+*

Roger Ferguson, President, CEO
Gina Wilson, EVP, CFO
Connie Weaver, EVP, Chief Marketing Officer
Ron Pressman, EVP, Chief Operating Officer
Annabelle Bexiga, EVP, Chief Information Officer

Financial services organization that is a retirement provider for people who work in the academic, research, medical and cultural fields.

14259 The American Council of Life Insurers
101 Constitution Avenue, NW
Suite 700
Washington, DC 20001-2133

202-624-2000
FAX 202-624-2115
E-Mail: contact@acli.com
Home Page: www.acli.com
Social Media: *Facebook, Twitter, RSS, YouTube*

Dirk Kempthorne, President, CEO
Brian Waidmann, Chief of Staff
Gary E. Hughes, EVP, General Counsel
J. Bruce Ferguson, SVP, State Relations
Don Walker, SVP, Administration & CFO

A Washinton, D.C.-based lobbying and trade group for the life insurance industry.
300 Members
Founded in 1976

14260 The American Society of Law, Medicine & Ethics
765 Commonwealth Avenue
Suite 1634
Boston, MA 02215-1401

617-262-4990
FAX 617-437-7596
E-Mail: info@aslme.org
Home Page: www.aslme.org
Social Media: *Facebook, Twitter, LinkedIn*

Ted Hutchinson, Executive Director
Margo Smith, Membership Department
Katie Kenney Johnson, Conference Director
Courtney McClellan, Assistant Editor
Arthur R. Derse, MD, JD, FACEP, Board of Director

Provides high-quality scholarship, debate, and critical thought to the community of professionals at the nexus of law, medicine, and ethics.
Founded in 1972
Mailing list available for rent

14261 The Blue Cross and Blue Shield Association
225 North Michigan Avenue
Chicago, IL 60601

E-Mail: bcbswebmaster@bcbsa.com
Home Page: www.bcbs.com/
Social Media: *Facebook, Twitter, YouTube, RSS*

Scott P. Serota, President, CEO
William A.ÿ Breskin, VP, Government Programs
Doug Porter, SVP, Operations, CIO
Maureen E. Sullivan, SVP, Strategic Services
Robert Kolodgy, SVP, Financial Services, CFO

Trade association for the independent, locally operated Blue Cross and Blue Shield plans in the USA.

14262 The Council of Insurance Agents & Brokers
701 Pennsylvania Avenue NW
Suite 750
Washington, DC 20004-2661

202-783-4400
FAX 202-783-4410
E-Mail: ciab@ciab.com
Home Page: www.ciab.com
Social Media: *Facebook, Twitter, LinkedIn*

Bill D. Henry, Chairman
Ken A Crerar, President/CEO
Robert Cohen, Vice Chairman

David L. Eslick, Treasurer
Martin P.ÿ Hughes, Secretary

Formerly the National Association of Casualty and Surety agents. The council represents the nation's largest commercial property and casualty insurance agencies and brokerage firms. Council members annually place some 80% of the commercial property/casualty insurance premiums in the United States. Council members who operate both nationally and internationally, specialize in a wide range of insurance products and risk management services for business, industry, government and the public.
300 Members
Founded in 1913

14263 The Griffith Insurance Education Foundation

720 Providence Rd
Suite 100
Malvern, PA 19355

855-288-7743
FAX 610-725-5967
E-Mail: info@griffithfoundation.org
Home Page: www.griffithfoundation.org
Social Media: *Facebook, Twitter*

Susan Krieger, Chair
James Jones, MBA, CPCU, ARM, Vice Chair
Dana Rudmose, CPA, Treasurer
Janice M. Abraham, Immediate Past Chairman
Kevin Brown, Esq., CAE, Executive Director

Nonprofit, nonadvocacy, educational organization that provides riskmanagement and insurance education for students and public policymakers.
Founded in 1960

14264 The Institutes

720 Providence Road
Suite 100
Malvern, PA 19355-3433

610-644-2101
800-644-2101
610-640-2100ÿ
FAX 610-640-9576
E-Mail: cserv@cpcuiia.org
Home Page: www.theinstitutes.org
Social Media: *Facebook, Twitter, LinkedIn*

Peter L. Miller, CPCU, President
Anita Z. Bourke, CPCU, AINS, EVP
Kevin H. Brown, Esq., CPCU, CAE, SVP, General Counsel, Exe. Dir.
Jeffrey Scheidt, SVP
Elizabeth A. Sprinkel, CPCU, SVP

An independent, nonprofit organization offering educational programs and professional certification to people in all segments of the property and liability insurance business. More than 150,000 insurance practitioners around the world are involved in Institute programs.
Mailing list available for rent

14265 The National Association for Fixed Annuities

1155 F Street NW
Suite 1050
Washington, DC 20004

414-332-9306
FAX 415-946-3532
E-Mail: bailey@nafa.com
Home Page: www.nafa.com
Social Media: *Facebook, Twitter, LinkedIn*

S. Christopher Johnson, NAFA Chair
Nathan Zuidema, NAFA Vice Chair
Dominicÿ Cursio, NAFA Treasurer
Brian D. Mann, Secretaryÿ
Chip Anderson, Executive Director

Trade association dedicated to promoting fixed annuities.

14266 The National Association of Independent Insurance Adjusters

1880 Radcliff Ct.
Tracy, CA 95376

209-832-6962
FAX 209-832-6964
E-Mail: admin@naiia.com
Home Page: www.naiia.com

Matt Ouellette, President
Peter Crosa, President Elect
Susan Daniels, Secretary/Treasurer
James Hunt, Immediate Past President
Brenda Reisinger, Executive Director

Trade group of property and casualty claims companies.

14267 The National Association of Mutual Insurance Companies

122 C Street N.W.ÿ
Suite 540
Washington, DC 20001

202-628-1558
FAX 202-628-1601
Home Page: www.namic.org
Social Media: *Facebook, Twitter, LinkedIn, RSS, YouTube*

Paul G. Stueven, PFMMÿ, Chairman
Paul A. Ehlert, J.D.ÿ, Vice Chairman
Stuart Henderson, J.D., CPCU, Immediate Past Chairman
Charles Chamnessÿ, President, CEO
Steve Linkousÿ, Chairman Elect

National trade association of mutual property and casualty insurance companies.

14268 The Society of Chartered Property and Casualty Underwriters (CPCU)

720 Providence Road
Malvern, PA 19355

800-932-2728
FAX 610-725-5969
E-Mail: MemberResources@theinstitutes.org
Home Page: www.cpcusociety.org/
Social Media: *Facebook, Twitter, LinkedIn*

Jane M. Wahl, CPCU, CSSBB, President, Chair
Brian P. Savko, CPCU, CLU, ChFC, President-Elect
Stanley W. Plappert, JD, CPCU, Treasurer, Secretary
Cynthia A. Baroway, CPCU, M.Ed., Immediate Past President, Chairman
Kevin H. Brown, Esq., CPCU, CAE, SVP, Executive Director

A community of credentialed property and casualty insurance professionals.
22,00 Members

14269 Think Believe Act

220 West 42nd Street
10th Floor
New York, NY 10036

646-445-7000
FAX 646-445-7001
E-Mail: losangeles@tbaglobal.com
Home Page: www.tbaglobal.com
Social Media: *Facebook, Twitter, LinkedIn, Instagram*

Robert Geddes, CEO

TBA is a privately-held company that is now one of the world's leading producers and marketers of brand events and experiences for Fortune 1000 companies

14270 Transportation & Logistics Council

120 Main Street
Huntington, NY 11743

631-549-8988
FAX 631-549-8962

E-Mail: tlc@transportlaw.com
Home Page: www.tlcouncil.org

Reed Tepper, Chairman
Nadia Martin, CCP, President
Curtis Hart, VP
Phillip Lamb, Secretary/Treasurer
George CarlÿPezold, Executive Director

Formerly the Transportation Consumer Protection Council, a not for profit trade association dedicated to the education of shippers, carriers and others involved in the transportation of goods, the prevention of transit loss and damage, the promulgation of reasonable practices, laws and regulations, and the equitable resolution of disputes invloving frieght claims, freight charges and related maters.
250 Members
Founded in 1974

14271 US Travel Insurance Association

2080 Western Avenue
Guilderland, NY 12084

800-224-6164
E-Mail: president@ustia.org
Home Page: www.ustia.org

Bruce Kirby, President
Mark Carney, Vice President
Linda Finkle, Treasurer
Mike Kelly, Past President
Henry Carpenter, Secretary

National association of insurance carriers, third-party administrators, insurance agencies and related businesses involved in the development, administration and marketing of travel insurance and travel assistance products.
Founded in 2004

14272 Underwriters Laboratories

333 Pfingsten Road
Northbrook, IL 60062-2096

847-272-8800
877-854-3577
FAX 847-272-8129
E-Mail: CustomerExperienceCenter@ul.com
Home Page: www.ul.com
Social Media: *Facebook, Twitter, LinkedIn, YouTube, Google+, Pinterest*

Keith E Williams, President/CEO
Michael Saltzman, SVP & CFO
Christian Anschuetz, Senior VP and CIO
Adrian Groom, Senior Vice President
Terry Brady, SVP & Chief Legal Officer

An independent, not for profit product safety testing and certification organization. They have also tested products for public safety for more than a century.
Founded in 1894
Mailing list available for rent

14273 Women In Insurance and Financial Services

136 Everett Road
Albany, NY 12205

518-694-5506
866-264-9437
FAX 518-935-9232
E-Mail: office@wifsnational.org
Home Page: www.w-wifs.org
Social Media: *Facebook, Twitter, LinkedIn*

Susan L. Combs, PPACA, President
Susan Glass, LUTC, President-Elect
Evelyn Gellar, LUTCF, Secretary
Lisa Pilgrim, Deputy Treasurer
Angelia Z. Shay, Immediate Past President

Vision is to provide a strong network of women helping each other develop the success that lies within each of us.
1.5M Members
Founded in 1987

14274 Women in Insurance and Financial Services
136 Everett Road
Albany, NY 12205

518-694-5506
866-264-9437
FAX 518-935-9232
E-Mail: office@wifsnational.org
Home Page: www.wifsnational.org
Social Media: *Facebook, Twitter, LinkedIn*

Susan L. Combs, PPACA, President
Susan Glass, LUTC, President-Elect
Evelyn Gellar, LUTCF, Secretary
Lisa Pilgrim, Deputy Treasurer
Angelia Z. Shay, Immediate Past President

National organization devoted to the success of women in the insurance and financial services fields.

14275 Workers Compensation Reinsurance Bureau
2 Hudson Place
Hoboken, NJ 07030-5515

201-798-6312
FAX 201-792-4441

Alfred O Weller, President

An association of insurance companies which pool their workers compensation excess losses as an alternative to purchasing reinsurance.
Founded in 1912

14276 Workers Compensation Research Institute
955 Massachusetts Ave.
Cambridge, MA 02139

617-661-9274
FAX 617-661-9284
E-Mail: wcri@wcrinet.org
Home Page: www.wcrinet.org

Vincent Armentano, Chair
Richard A. Victor, President & CEO

WCRI conducts research into public policy issues surrounding workers' compensation systems.

Newsletters

14277 ARIA Newsletter
American Risk and Insurance Association
716 Providence Road
Malvern 19355-3402

610-640-1997
FAX 610-725-1007
E-Mail: diana.lee@pciaa.net
Home Page: www.aria.org

Frequency: 2x/Year

14278 AWCP Newsletter
Association of Workers' Compensation Professionals
PO Box 760
Rancho Cordova, CA 95741-0760

916-290-8017
FAX 916-914-1706
E-Mail: info@awcp.org
Home Page: www.awcp.org

Debra Real, President
Connie Conley, Executive Director

An educational newsletter with information about our constantly changing industry, how to contact our sponsors as well as announcing our upcoming events.
Frequency: Monthly

14279 Actuarial Studies in Non-Life Insurance
Astin Bulletin
B641 Locust Walk
Philadelphia, PA 19104-6218

215-898-2741

Jean Lemaire, Chairman
Promotes actuarial research and study and publishes the ASTIN Bulletin.
2.2M Pages
Founded in 1957

14280 Advanced Underwriting Services
Dearborn Financial Publishing
155 N Wacker Drive
Floor 1
Chicago, IL 60606-6819

312-836-4400
FAX 312-836-1146

Georgia Mann, Publisher
Information on the law.
Cost: $395.00
Frequency: Monthly

14281 Best's Agents Guide to Life Insurance Companies
AM Best Company
Ambest Rd
Oldwick, NJ 08858

908-439-2200
800-544-2378
FAX 908-439-3296
E-Mail: webmaster@ambest.com
Home Page: www.ambest.com

Arthur Snyder, CEO
Offers information on over 1,400 life and health insurance companies nationwide.
Cost: $150.00
Frequency: Monthly
Founded in 1899

14282 Compensation & Benefits for Law Offices
Institute of Management and Administration
1 Washington Park
Suite 1300
Newark, NY 07102-3130

212-244-0360
FAX 973-622-0595
E-Mail: customercare@bna.com
Home Page: www.ioma.com

An indespensible reference for law firm recruitment, training, compensation, benefits, and HR managers who want and need to keep pace with what it takes to successfully, recruit, retain, train, reward, recognize, and compensatetop legal talent.
Cost: $449.00

14283 Crittenden Insurance Markets Newsletter
Crittenden Publishing
45 Leveroni Court
Suite 204
Novato, CA 94949-5721

415-475-1522
800-421-3483
FAX 619-923-3518
E-Mail: ins@crittendenonline.com
Home Page: www.crittendenonline.com
Social Media: *Twitter*

Offers readers a behind-the-scenes look at everything going on in the commercial insurance market. Provides all the coverage necessary for agents to be successful in the board field of commercial insurance
Frequency: Weekly
Founded in 1972

14284 Disability Eval and Rehab Review
National Association of Disability Evaluating
13801 Village Mill Drive
Midlothian, VA 23113

804-378-7275
Home Page: www.nadep.com

This periodical is peer reviewed and addresses issues which are impacting the field of medicine and rehabilitation and which specifically address impairment rating, disability determination, functional capacity evaluation, vocational evaluation and current trends in reimbursement and how the Americans with Disabilities Act of 1990 has changed the practice of medicine and rehabilitation.
Frequency: Quarterly

14285 HELP Newsletter
Insurance Loss Control Association
PO Box 346
Morton, IL 61550

309-696-2551
FAX 317-879-8408
E-Mail: ccarson@namic.org
Home Page: www.insurancelosscontrol.org

Brock Bell, President
Daniel Finn, VP
Stig Ruxlow, Financial Secretary

Association news and activities.
Frequency: Quarterly
Circulation: 325
Founded in 1931
Printed in 2 colors on matte stock

14286 Highlights
American Association of Retired Persons
601 E St Nw
Washington, DC 20049-0003

202-434-2277
FAX 202-434-7599
E-Mail: PCMNationalOffice@aarp.org
Home Page: www.aarp.org

A Barry Rand, CEO
Ethel Andrus, Founder

Offers information and updates on the association, tax information and legal statistics.
4 Pages
Frequency: BiWeekly

14287 IOMA's Report on Hourly Compensation
Institute of Management and Administration
1 Washington Park
Suite 1300
Newark, NJ 07102-3130

212-244-0360
FAX 973-622-0595
E-Mail: customercare@bna.com
Home Page: www.ioma.com

RHC is a sister publication for IOMA's Report on Salary Surveys and takes compensation and salary dates from major surveys produced by firms like Watson Wyatt Data Services, the Big Six Accounting firms and local HR groups to show benefits and compensation managers the going rate for hourly workers in a variety of positions.

14288 Insurance Daily
SNL Financial
One SNL Plaza
PO Box 2124
Charlottesville, VA 22902

434-977-1600
FAX 434-293-0407
E-Mail: salesdept@snl.com

Home Page: www.snl.com
Social Media: *Facebook, Twitter, LinkedIn*

Akash Sinha, Editor
Tom Mason, Editor

The most comprehensive news source on the insurance sector. The news desk researches filings and investor presentations, conducts exclusive interviews with industry executives and analysts for the stories that impact the insurance market
Cost: $995.00
Frequency: Daily
Mailing list available for rent

14289 Insurance Finance & Investment
Institutional Investor
488 Madison Ave
New York, NY 10022-5701

212-303-3100
800-715-9195
FAX 212-224-3491
E-Mail: iieditor@institutionalinvestor.com
Home Page: www.institutionalinvestor.com

Erik Kolk, Publisher
Chris Brown, CEO/President
Stuard Wise, Senior Editor
Nick Ferris, Marketing Director

Provides reviews of investment performance, financing strategies, overviews of ratings, and highlights of new issues.
Cost: $1495.00
Frequency: Monthly
Founded in 1905

14290 Insurance Forum
Insurance Forum
PO Box 245
Ellettsville, IN 47429

812-876-6502
FAX 812-876-6572
Home Page: www.theinsuranceforum.com

Joseph M Belth, Editor
Ann I Belth, Business Manager
Jeffrey E Belth, Circulation Manager

Provides objective information and incisive analysis of important insurance topics.
Cost: $120.00
Frequency: Monthly
Founded in 1974

14291 Insurance Performance Graph
SNL Financial
PO Box 2124
Charlottesvle, VA 22902-2124

434-977-1600
FAX 434-977-4466
E-Mail: isales@snl.com
Home Page: www.snl.com

Mike Deane, Editor
Matt Mueller, Chief Operating Officer
Nick Cafferillo, Chief Operating Officer
Adam Hall, Managing Director

For publicly traded insurance companies and law, accounting and consulting firms. Compares the investment performance of an insurance company to a specific SNL index or to a selected peer group and the appropriate broad multi-industry index. Covers a 5-year period or the period beginning with the IPO date.
Cost: $399.00
Frequency: Monthly
Founded in 1987

14292 Insurance Regulation
Wakeman Walworth Inc

PO Box 7376
Alexandria, VA 22307-7376

703-768-9600
FAX 703-768-9690
Home Page: statecapitals.com

Keyes Walworth, Publisher

The best way to track day-to-day changes and innovations at the state level ☐ covers health insurance including HMOs, CHIP programs and the battle to increase health insurance benefits. It also covers life, automobile, homeowner, unemployment insurance, workers compensation and malpractice. It reports on tort reform, licensing, self-insurance, plus new approaches such as lifestyle considerations.
Cost: $245.00
Frequency: Weekly

14293 Insurance Weekly: Life & Health
SNL Financial
One SNL Plaza
PO Box 2124
Charlottesville, VA 22902-2124

434-977-1600
FAX 434-977-4466
E-Mail: subscriptions@snlnet.com
Home Page: www.snl.com
Social Media: *Facebook, Twitter, LinkedIn*

Akash Sinha, Editor
Tom Mason, Editor

Super-focused coverage of the dynamic life and health, managed care and insurance agency sectors
Cost: $396.00
Frequency: Weekly
ISSN: 1098-8149
Mailing list available for rent

14294 Insurance Weekly: Property & Casualty
SNL Financial
One SNL Plaza
PO Box 2124
Charlottesville, VA 22902-2124

434-977-1600
FAX 434-977-4466
E-Mail: subscriptions@snlnet.com
Home Page: www.snl.com
Social Media: *Facebook, Twitter, LinkedIn*

Akash Sinha, Editor
Tom Mason, Editor

Complete, current coverage of the property and casualty, title, financial and mortgage guaranty and insurance agency sectors
Cost: $396.00
Frequency: Weekly
ISSN: 1098-8130
Mailing list available for rent

14295 Journal for Insurance Compliance Professionals Newsletter
Association of Insurance Compliance Professionals
12100 Sunset Hills Road
Suite 130
Reston, VA 20190

703-234-4074
FAX 703-435-4390
E-Mail: aicp@aicp.net
Home Page: www.aicp.net

Doug Simino, President
Darrell Turner, Editor
Elaine Douglas, Vice President
Dawn Murphy, Secretary
Doug Geraci, Treasurer

Includes topical information for members, covering regulatory and industry issues, along with

the latest techniques in filings nad news from each Association Region and Chapter
Frequency: Quarterly
Founded in 1998

14296 LIC Newsletter
Life Insurers Council
2300 Windy Ridge Pkwy SE
Suite 600
Atlanta, GA 30339-5665

770-951-1770
800-275-5662
FAX 770-984-0441
E-Mail: askloma@loma.org
Home Page: www.loma.org

Jeff Shaw, Executive Director
Rose Hoyt, Administrative Assistant

Includes news and analysis about issues of concern to executives and those involved in operations, plus information on upcoming events and company activities
Frequency: Monthly
Mailing list available for rent

14297 Mealey's Catastrophic Loss
LexisNexis Mealey's
555 W 5th Avenue
Los Angeles, CA 90013

213-627-1130
800-253-4182
E-Mail: mealeyinfo@lexisnexis.com
Home Page: www.lexisnexis.com/mealeys
Social Media: *Facebook, Twitter, LinkedIn, RSS, Youtube*

Tom Hagy, CEO
Maureen McGuire, Editorial Director
Gina Cappello, Editor
Mike Wash, Chief Executive Officer, Legal
Lisa Agona, Chief Marketing Officer

This report focuses on business interruption insurance claims in the aftermath of the Hurricane Katrina, September 11th, and other catastrophic loss tragedies. Additionally, the report will go beyond these claims and will offer important business interruption insurance coverage news related to computer viruses, computer failures, and natural disasters.
Cost: $1075.00
100 Pages
Frequency: Monthly
Founded in 2001
Mailing list available for rent

14298 Mealey's Emerging Insurance Disputes
LexisNexis Mealey's
555 W 5th Avenue
Los Angeles, CA 90013

213-627-1130
800-253-4182
E-Mail: mealeyinfo@lexisnexis.com
Home Page: www.lexisnexis.com/mealeys
Social Media: *Facebook, Twitter, LinkedIn, RSS, Youtube*

Tom Hagy, CEO
Maureen McGuire, Editorial Director
Gina Cappello, Editor
Mike Wash, Chief Executive Officer, Legal
Lisa Agona, Chief Marketing Officer

The report tracks new areas of coverage liability, novel policy applications, and conflicting policy language interpretations as they arise in insurance litigation. Some areas of coverage featured are: sexual harassment and discrimination, assault and battery, professional liability, patent and trademark infringement, construction defects, directors and officers claims, emotional distress, intentional acts, technology, and insurance business practices.
Cost: $ 1229.00
100 Pages
Frequency: Semi-Monthly

Founded in 1996
Mailing list available for rent

14299 Mealey's Litigation Report: Asbestos

LexisNexis Mealey's
555 W 5th Avenue
Los Angeles, CA 90013

213-627-1130
800-253-4182
E-Mail: mealeyinfo@lexisnexis.com
Home Page: www.lexisnexis.com/mealeys
Social Media: *Facebook, Twitter, LinkedIn, RSS, Youtube*

Tom Hagy, CEO
Maureen McGuire, Editorial Director
Bryan Redding, Editor
Mike Wash, Chief Executive Officer, Legal
Lisa Agona, Chief Marketing Officer

The report offers unsurpassed coverage of litigation arising from asbestos-related injury and death. Key issues include: massive class action settlements involving present and future claimants, state and federal verdicts, litigation experts, medical monitoring claims, suits against the tobacco industry, discovery battles, discovery rule decisions, insurance coverage rulings, and asbestos property decisions.
Cost: $1789.00
100 Pages
Frequency: Semi-Monthly
Founded in 1984
Mailing list available for rent

14300 Mealey's Litigation Report: California Insurance

LexisNexis Mealey's
555 W 5th Avenue
Los Angeles, CA 90013

213-627-1130
800-253-4182
E-Mail: mealeyinfo@lexisnexis.com
Home Page: www.lexisnexis.com/mealeys
Social Media: *Facebook, Twitter, LinkedIn, RSS, Youtube*

Tom Hagy, CEO
Maureen McGuire, Editorial Director
Jennifer Hans, Editor
Mike Wash, Chief Executive Officer, Legal
Lisa Agona, Chief Marketing Officer

The Report focuses on ever-changing California and federal Ninth Circuit insurance coverage disputes and developments. Topics include California developments in bad faith litigation, earthquake damage coverage, disability insurance, products liability coverage, environmental insurance coverage, mold coverage, asbestos coverage, aviation litigation coverage, entertainment law and more.
Cost: $949.00
100 Pages
Frequency: Monthly
Founded in 2001
Mailing list available for rent

14301 Mealey's Litigation Report: Disability Insurance

LexisNexis Mealey's
555 W 5th Avenue
Los Angeles, CA 90013

213-627-1130
800-253-4182
E-Mail: mealeyinfo@lexisnexis.com
Home Page: www.lexisnexis.com/mealeys
Social Media: *Facebook, Twitter, LinkedIn, RSS, Youtube*

Tom Hagy, CEO
Maureen McGuire, Editorial Director
Karen Miehle, Editor
Mike Wash, Chief Executive Officer, Legal
Lisa Agona, Chief Marketing Officer

This report tracks the burgeoning number of disputes involving complex disability coverage claims. Topics covered include: claims for chronic fatigue, chronic pain, stress, psychiatric disabilities, chemical dependency and risk of relapse, plus key issues like total disability, own occupation, bad faith, ERSA, class actions and much more.
Cost: $849.00
100 Pages
Frequency: Monthly
Founded in 2000
Mailing list available for rent

14302 Mealey's Litigation Report: Insurance

LexisNexis Mealey's
555 W 5th Avenue
Los Angeles, CA 90013

213-627-1130
800-253-4182
E-Mail: mealeyinfo@lexisnexis.com
Home Page: www.lexisnexis.com/mealeys
Social Media: *Facebook, Twitter, LinkedIn, RSS, Youtube*

Tom Hagy, CEO
Maureen McGuire, Editorial Director
Vivi Gorman, Editor
Shawn Rice, Co-Editor
Mike Wash, Chief Executive Officer, Legal

The report tracks declaratory judgment actions regarding coverage for litigation arising from long-tail claims, including environmental contamination and latent damage and injury allegedly caused by asbestos, tox chemicals and fumes, lead, breast implants, medical devices, construction defects, and more. Key issues: allocation, occurrence, policy exclusion, choice of law, discovery, duty to defend, notice, trigger of coverage and known loss.
Cost: $2115.00
100 Pages
Frequency: Weekly
Founded in 1984
Mailing list available for rent

14303 NACA NEWS

National Association of Catastrophe Adjusters
PO Box 821864
North Richland Hills, TX 76182

817-498-3466
FAX 817-498-0480
E-Mail: naca@nacatadj.org
Home Page: www.nacatadj.org

Lori Ringo, Executive Administrator
Robert Uhler, Vice President
John Postava, Secretary/Treasurer
Wanda Hogan, President

Contains information of interest and benefit to the members of NACA and the president of the association provides his insights for the quarter.
Frequency: Quarterly
Circulation: 2500
Founded in 1976

14304 NAPIA Newsletter

National Association of Public Insurance Adjusters
21165 Whitfield Place
Suite 105
Potomac Falls, VA 20165

703-433-9217
FAX 703-433-0369
E-Mail: info@napia.com
Home Page: www.napia.com

David W Barrack, Executive Director
Ronald R. Reitz, President
Frequency: Quarterly
Circulation: 600
Mailing list available for rent

14305 NCOILetter

National Conference of Insurance Legislators
385 Jordan Road
Troy, NY 12180

518-687-0178
FAX 518-687-0401
E-Mail: info@ncoil.org
Home Page: www.ncoil.org

Susan F. Nolan, Executive Director
Candace Thorson, Deputy Executive Director
Simone Smith, Director, Operations/Administration
Mike Humphreys, Director,State-Federal Relations
Jordan Estey, Dir, Legislative Affairs/Education

NCOIL is an organization of state legislators whose main area of public policy concern is insurance legislation and regulation. Many legislators active in NCOIL either chair or are members of the committees responsible for insurance legislation in their respective state houses across the country.
Frequency: Monthly
Circulation: 2500
Founded in 1969

14306 NFPA Journal Update

National Fire Protection Association
1 Batterymarch Park
Quincy, MA 02169-7471

617-770-3000
800-344-3555
FAX 617-770-0700
E-Mail: publicaffairs@nfpa.org
Home Page: www.nfpa.org

James M. Shannon, President/CEO
Peg O'Brien, Administrator - Public Affairs
Sharon Gamache, Executive Director
Bruce Mullen, CFO
Paul Crossman, VP, Marketing

Member newsletter that contains the latest articles, features, and special online exclusives from NFPA Journal , as well as quick access to the information and resources on NFPA's codes and standards-making process, research, training, safety information, and more.
75000 Members
Frequency: Monthly
Founded in 1896

14307 PIA Connection

Association of Professional Insurance Agents
400 N Washington Street
Alexandria, VA 22314-2312

703-836-9340
FAX 703-836-1279
E-Mail: web@pianet.org
Home Page: www.pianet.com
Social Media: *Facebook, Twitter, LinkedIn*

Andrew C. Harris, President
John G. Lee, President-elect
Richard A. Clements, Vice President, Treasurer
Robert W. Hansen, Secretary/Assistant Treasurer

Contains current insurance industry news that is particularly relevant to independent insurance agents
Cost: $24.00
Frequency: 10x/Year
Mailing list available for rent

14308 Report on Property/Casualty Rates & Ratings

Institute of Management and Administration

1 Washington Park
Suite 1300
Newark, NJ 07102-3130

212-244-0360
FAX 973-622-0595
E-Mail: customercare@bna.com
Home Page: www.ioma.com

Helps agents and brokers get competitive premium rates for their clients.
Cost: $389.00
16 Pages
Frequency: Monthly
Founded in 1755

14309 Risk Management Essentials
Nonprofit Risk Management Center
15 N King Street
Suite 203
Leesburg, VA 20176

202-785-3891
FAX 703-443-1990
E-Mail: info@nonprofitrisk.org
Home Page: www.nonprofitrisk.org

Melanie Herman, Executive Director
Erin Gloeckner, Project Manager
Sue Weir Jones, Office Manager
Jennifer Walther, Director of Client Solutions

Each issue covers a selection of issues, showcases the Center's training and workshops, and/or highlights new publications offering risk management advice from a nonprofit perspective
16 Pages
Frequency: 3 times a year
Mailing list available for rent

14310 Riskwatch
Public Risk Management Association
700 S. Washington St.
Suite 218
Alexandria, VA 22314-1565

703-528-7701
FAX 703-739-0200
E-Mail: info@primacentral.org
Home Page: www.primacentral.org
Social Media: *Facebook, Twitter, LinkedIn*

Marshall Davies, Executive Director
Jennifer Ackerman, Deputy Executive Director
Bles Dones, Manager, Member Services
Jennifer W. Morris, Manager, Meetings and Conferences
Paulette Washington, Office Administrator

E-news service that delivers handpicked, high-quality news articles relating to the public risk management industry. Provides PRIMA members with valuable association-related news. Keeps you on top of the latest news and trends in the public sector risk management field.
Frequency: Weekly
Mailing list available for rent

14311 SFFA Newsletter
Surety & Fidelity Association of America
1101 Connecticut Avenue NW
Suite 800
Washington, DC 20036

202-463-0600
FAX 202-463-0606
E-Mail: information@surety.org
Home Page: www.surety.org
Social Media: *Facebook, Twitter*

Lynn Schubert, President
Mailing list available for rent

14312 Surety Association of America
Surety Association of America

1101 Connecticut Ave Nw
Suite 800
Washington, DC 20036-4347

202-463-0600
FAX 202-463-0606
E-Mail: information@surety.org
Home Page: www.surety.org

Lynn Schubert, President

14313 UPDATE
Insurance Marketing Communications Association
PO Box 473054
Charlotte, NC 28247

704-755-5551
FAX 704-543-6345
E-Mail: tseibert@imcanet.com
Home Page: www.imcanet.com

September J Seibert, Executive Director

Contains reviews and previews of meetings, articles on communications issues and techniques, and news of IMCA members.
Frequency: For Members Only

Magazines & Journals

14314 AHIP Solutions Directory Resource Directory of Health Plans
America's Health Insurance Plans
601 Pennsylvania Ave NW
South Building, Suite 500
Washington, DC 20004-2601

202-778-3200
877-291-2247
FAX 202-331-7487
E-Mail: ahip@ahip.org
Home Page: www.ahip.org
Social Media: *Twitter*

Karen M Ignagni, President/CEO
Susan Pisano, VP Communications

More than 3,400 key executives listed, types of products offered such as HMO, PPO, POS, etc., company contact information, national enrollment by type of products, and national and state level enrollment data by company. There is also a CD-ROM availablie for $1,495.00
Cost: $492.00
Mailing list available for rent

14315 ASPPA Journal
American Society of Pension Professionals & Act
4245 Fairfax Dr
Suite 750
Arlington, VA 22203-1648

703-516-0512
FAX 703-516-9308
E-Mail: asppa@asppa.org
Home Page: www.asppa.org

Thomas Finnegan, President

A technical publication providing critical insight into legislative and regulatory developments. Also features technical analysis of benefit plan matters as well as information regarding ASPPA's programs.
Frequency: Quarterly
Circulation: 7500

14316 Actuarial Digest
Actuarial Digest Publishing Company
PO Box 1127
Ponte Vedra, FL 32004-1127

904-273-1245
Home Page: www.theactuarialdigest.com

Gene Hubbard, Editor

Covers fields such as life, group, health, reinsurance, pension/employee benefits, government regulations and educational institutions.
Founded in 1982

14317 Actuarial Studies in Non-Life Insurance
Peeters
1600 Arch St
Philadelphia, PA 19103-2032

215-567-0097
FAX 215-567-0107
E-Mail: webmaster@actuaries.org
Home Page: www.actuaries.org

Lucy Peters, Owner
Andrew Cairns, Editor
David G Hartman, Chairman
Carla Melvin, Executive Assistant
Katy Martin, Project Manager

Promotes actuarial research and study and publishes the ASTIN Bulletin.
Cost: $65.00
500 Pages
Frequency: Quarterly
Circulation: 3000
Founded in 1957

14318 Advisor Today
Natl Assoc of Insurance and Financial Advisors
2901 Telestar Court
Falls Church, VA 22042

703-770-8100
877-866-2432
E-Mail: membersupport@naifa.org
Home Page: www.advisortoday.com
Social Media: *Facebook, Twitter, LinkedIn*

Ayo Mseka, Editor-In-Chief
Julie Britt, Senior Editor
Preeti Vasishtha, Editor
Tara Heuser, Publication and Circulation

Provides practical information, sales idas resources and business strategies to hel pinsurance and financial advisors succeed.
Founded in 1906
Mailing list available for rent

14319 American Journal of Law & Medicine
American Society of Law, Medicine and Ethics
765 Commonwealth Ave
Suite 1634
Boston, MA 02215-1401

617-262-4990
FAX 617-437-7596
E-Mail: info@aslme.org
Home Page: www.aslme.org
Social Media: *Facebook, Twitter, LinkedIn*

Ted Hutchinson, Executive Director
Courtney McClellan, Assistant Editor
Katie Kenney Johnson, Conference Director
Margo Buege, Membership Department
Courtney McClellan, Assistant Editor

A law review fulfilling the need to improve communication between leagal and medical professionals. Contains professional articles and case notes on themes in health law and policy, and on the legal, ethical, and economic aspects of medical practice, research, and education-and health law court decisions and book reviews.
Cost: $150.00
Frequency: Quarterly
Mailing list available for rent

14320 Annuity Shopper
Annuity Shopper

28 Harrison Ave.
D209
Englishtown, NJ 07726

732-521-5110
877-206-8141
FAX 732-521-5113
Home Page: www.annuityshopper.com

Hersh Stern, Owner
Laura Stern, Editor

Helps consumers purchase the safest and most reliable lifetime income annuities for their retirement.
Frequency: Semi-annually
ISSN: 1071-4510
Founded in 1986
Mailing list available for rent

14321 Beacon
American Association of Dental Consultants
10032 Wind Hill Dr
Greenville, IN 47124-9673

812-923-2600
800-896-0707
FAX 812-923-2900
Home Page: www.aadc.org

Judith Salisburty, Executive Director
Dr Larry Hoffman, Secretary/Treasurer

Informs members about the latest issues affecting dentistry and dental benefits.
Frequency: Twice/Year
Circulation: 350

14322 Benefits Magazine
International Foundation of Employee Benefit Plans
18700 W Bluemound Road
Brookfield, WI 53045

262-786-6700
888-334-3327
FAX 262-786-8670
E-Mail: pr@ifebp.org
Home Page: www.ifebp.org
Social Media: *Facebook, Twitter, LinkedIn*

Michael Wilson, CEO
Terry Davidson, VP, Business Development
Beth Harwood, VP, Educ Program/Content Management

Covers issues such as healthcare, retirement and related trends. Authors are experienced professionals in the field.
Cost: $175.00
35000 Members
Frequency: Monthly
Circulation: 28336
ISSN: 2157-6157
Founded in 1954

14323 Benefits Quarterly
Int'l Society of Certified Employee Benfit Special
18700 W Bluemound Road
PO Box 209
Brookfield, WI 53008-0209

262-786-8771
FAX 262-786-8650
E-Mail: iscebs@iscebs.org
Home Page: www.iscebs.org
Social Media: *Facebook, Twitter, LinkedIn*

Daniel W Graham, CEBS, Executive Director
Sandra L. Becker, Director
Jennifer Mathe, Manager Member Services
Kathy Frank, Administrative Assistant
Julie Dickow, Department Assistant

Offers comprehensive coverage of the latest trends and innovations in benefits and compensation. Features articles on health care, retirement and total compensation, each issue includes a section focused on a topic of special

interest.
Cost: $125.00
Frequency: Quarterly
Circulation: 15000
Founded in 1981
Mailing list available for rent

14324 Best's Review
AM Best Company
Ambest Rd
Oldwick, NJ 08858

908-439-2200
800-424-2378
FAX 908-439-3296
E-Mail: editor_br@bestreview.com
Home Page: www.ambest.com

Arthur Snyder, Chairman & President
Paul Tinnirello, CIO
Larry Mayewski, Chief Rating Officer

Best's Review, the insurance industry's premier news magazine, contains insightful, award-winning coverage of the worldwide insurance industry, giving you the information you need to make informed decisions about your business and career.
Cost: $60.00
Frequency: Monthly
ISSN: 1527-5914
Founded in 1900

14325 BestWeek
AM Best Company
Ambest Rd
Oldwick, NJ 08858

908-439-2200
FAX 908-439-3296
E-Mail: bestweek@ambest.com
Home Page: www.ambest.com

Arthur Snyder, Chairman and President
Paul Tinnirello, CIO
Larry Mayewski, Chief Rating Officer

BestWeek, the cornerstone of a Best's Insurance News & Analysis subscription, now provides even more ratings information and A.M. Best-generated analytical content in three region-focused editions.
Frequency: Weekly
ISSN: 1945-4139
Founded in 1953

14326 Broker World
Insurance Publications
9404 Reeds Road
PO Box 11310
Overland Park, KS 66207-1010

913-383-9191
800-762-3387
FAX 913-383-1247
E-Mail: info@brokerworldmag.com
Home Page: www.brokerworldmag.com

Rita S Reeves, Sales Manager
Sharon A Chace, Editor
Stephen P Howard, Publisher
Betsy Masters, Production Manager
Patty L Godfrey, Director of Circulation

The first and only national insurance magazine founded, focused and edited to specifically address the unique informational needs of independent like and health producers.
Frequency: Monthly
Circulation: 28600
Founded in 1980

14327 Business Insurance
Crain Communications
711 3rd Ave
New York, NY 10017-4014

212-210-0785
FAX 212-210-0200

E-Mail: info@crain.com
Home Page: www.businessinsurance.com

Norm Feldman, Manager
Charmain Benton, Assistant Managing Editor
Paul Bomberger, Managing Editor
Roberto Ceniceros, Senior Editor
Matt Dunning, Associate Editor

Reports on risk management, risk financing, employee benefits management and workers compensation. Our audience also includes insurance brokers, agents, consultants, insurers, reinsurers, and others concerned with corporate insurance, risk management, alternative risk financing, employee benefits, workers compensation and reinsurance.
Frequency: Weekly
Circulation: 44639
Mailing list available for rent at $89y per M

14328 CICA International Conference
Captive Insurance Companies Association
4248 Park Glen Road
Minneapolis, MN 55416

952-928-4655
FAX 952-929-1318
E-Mail: info@cicaworld.com
Home Page: www.cicaworld.com

Dennis Harwick, President

2012 International Conference is located in Scottsdale, AZ during March 11-13.
500 Attendees
Frequency: Annual

14329 CPCU Journal
Chartered Property Casualty Underwriters
720 Providence Rd
Malvern, PA 19355-3446

610-251-2733
FAX 610-251-2761
Home Page: www.cpcusociety.org

Steve McElhiney, President
Cynthia Barouex, Vice President

14330 CPCU e-Journal
Chartered Property Casualty Underwriter Society
720 Providence Road
Suite 100
Malvern, PA 19355

610-512-2728
800-932-2728
FAX 610-725-5969
E-Mail: membercenter@cpcusociety.org
Home Page: www.cpcusociety.org
Social Media: *Facebook, Twitter, LinkedIn*

James R Marks, CEO
David C Marlett, Editor
Mark A. Robinson, President and Treasurer

Provides information on practical and timely issues of interest to financial services and property and casualty insurance professionals.
Frequency: Monthly

14331 Contingencies
American Academy of Actuaries
1850 M Street NW
Suite 300
Washington, DC 20036

202-223-8196
FAX 202-872-1948
E-Mail: webmaster@actuary.org
Home Page: www.actuary.org

Linda Mallon, Editor
Cindy Johns, Marketing/Publications Production

Magazine of the actuarial profession, available in print and digital editions; its circulation includes legislators, regulators, CEOs, and all

Academy members
Cost: $24.00
Frequency: Bi-Monthly
ISSN: 1048-9851
Founded in 1965
Printed in 4 colors on glossy stock

14332 Contingency Planning & Management

Witter Publishing Corporation
20 Commerce Street
Flemington, NJ 08822

908-788-0343
FAX 908-788-3782
Home Page: www.witterpublishing.com

Bob Joudanin, Publisher
Paul Kirvan, Editor-in-Chief
Mike Viscel, Production Manager
Courtney Witter, Circulation Manager
Andrew Witter, President

Serves the fields of financial/banking, manufacturing industrial, transportation, utilities, telecommunications, health care, government, insurance and other allied fields.
Cost: $275.00
Frequency: Monthly
Circulation: 62000
Founded in 1987

14333 Crittenden Excess & Surplus Insider

Crittenden Publishing
250 Bel Marin Keys Boulevard
PO Box 1150, #A
Novato, CA 94948-1150

415-382-2400
FAX 415-382-2476
E-Mail: ins@crittendenonline.com
Home Page: www.crittendenonline.com

Robert Fink, Publisher

Focuses on new products, trade literature, industry news, and personnel changes.
Cost: $411.00
Frequency: Weekly
Circulation: 20,000

14334 EXAMINER Magazine

Society of Financial Examiners
174 Grace Blvd
Altamonte Spgs, FL 32714-3210

407-682-4930
800-787-7633
FAX 407-682-3175
Home Page: www.sofe.org
Social Media: Facebook, LinkedIn

L. Brackett, Executive Director
Stephen J Szypula, Financial Administrator
Judy Estus, Administrator
Ryan Havick, President
Eric Dercher, Treasurer

A quarterly magazine offering association news and information.
Cost: $65.00
Frequency: Quarterly
Circulation: 2500
Founded in 1973
Printed in 2 colors on glossy stock

14335 GAMA International Journal

GAMA International
2901 Telestar Ct
Suite 140
Falls Church, VA 22042-1261

703-770-8184
800-345-2687
FAX 703-770-8182
E-Mail: rwolpert@gama.naifa.org
Home Page: www.gamaweb.com
Social Media: Facebook, Twitter, LinkedIn

Mary Barnes, Director of Communications / Editor
Jeff Hughes, CEO

Miriam Hankins, Marketing Director
Stephanie Beattie, Membership and Awards Coordinator
Jen D'Alessio, Program Manager

Devoted to the professional development of leaders in the insurance and financial services industry.
Cost: $300.00
56 Pages
Circulation: 5000
ISSN: 1095-7367
Founded in 1951
Mailing list available for rent
Printed in 4 colors on glossy stock

14336 Health Insurance Underwriters

National Association of Health Underwriters
1212 New York Avenue NW
Suite 1100
Washington, DC 20005

202-552-5060
FAX 202-747-6820
E-Mail: editor@nahu.org
Home Page: www.nahu.org
Social Media: Facebook, Twitter, LinkedIn

Martin Carr, Publisher/Editor

Covers technology, legislation and product news-everything that affects how health insurance professionals do business
Cost: $40.00
Frequency: Monthly
Circulation: 30,000
ISSN: 0017-9019
Founded in 1930
Mailing list available for rent: 19000 names at $350 per M
Printed in 4 colors on glossy stock

14337 IAIABC Journal

Int'l Assoc of Industrial Accident Boards/Commis.
5610 Medical Circle
Suite 24
Madison, WI 53719

608-663-6355
FAX 608-663-1546
E-Mail: hlore@iaiabc.org
Home Page: www.iaiabc.org

Robert Aurbach, Editor
Jennifer Wolf Horejsh, Executive Director
Faith Howe, Manager
Christina Klein, Events and Office Administrator
Heather Lore, Manager of Membership and Marketing

Advances the understanding and management of workers' compensation system administration through the availability of data, research, policy analysis, and thoughtful opinion.
Frequency: 2x/Year
Mailing list available for rent

14338 Independent Agent Magazine

Independent Insurance Agents & Brokers of America
127 S Peyton St
Alexandria, VA 22314-2803

703-683-4422
800-221-7917
FAX 703-683-7556
E-Mail: info@iiaba.net
Home Page: www.iiaba.net
Social Media: Facebook, Twitter

Robert A Rusbuldt, CEO
Ronald Tubertini, Chairman

Regular issue features include agency management and automation, insurance products and markets, legislative issues, and analysis of industry trends.
Cost: $24.00
Frequency: Monthly
Circulation: 57,814
Mailing list available for rent

14339 Inquiry

Excellus Health Plan
1807 Glenview Rd
Suite 100
Glenview, IL 60025-2944

847-724-9280
FAX 847-729-2199
E-Mail: inquiry@hartleydata.com
Home Page: www.inquiryjournal.org

Howard J Berman, Publisher
Kevin P Kane, Editor-In-Chief
Alan Monheit, Editor
Ronny G. Frishman, Managing Editor

Seeks to contribute to the continued improvement of the nation's health care system by providing a thoughtful forum for the communication and discussion of relevant public policy issues, innovative concepts, and original research and demonstrations in the areas of health care organization, provision and financing
Cost: $1.00
Frequency: Quarterly
ISSN: 0046-9580

14340 Insurance & Financial Meetings Managment

Coastal Communications Corporation
2700 N Military Trail
Suite 120
Boca Raton, FL 33431

561-989-0600
FAX 561-989-9509
E-Mail: ccceditor@att.net
Home Page: www.themeetingmagazines.com

Harvey Grotsky, Publisher/Editor-In-Chief
Susan Wyckoff Fell, Managing Editor
Susan Gregg, Managing Editor

The executive source for planning meetings and incentives for the financial and insurance sectors. With regular features and special focus on site selection, destinations, industry-related studies and activities, motivational and incentive programs, program and event planning.
Frequency: Monthly
Circulation: 40,000
Founded in 1983

14341 Insurance & Technology

TechWeb
240 West 35th Street
New York, NY 10011

212-600-3000
FAX 212-600-3060
Home Page: www.insurancetech.com

Katherine Burger, Editorial Director
Anthony O'Donnell, Executive Editor
Nathan Golia, Associate Editor
Cara Latham, Online Managing Editor

Information on how technology can help life, health, property and casualty and multi-line insurance companies perform more productively, profitably, and competitively.
Frequency: Monthly
ISSN: 1054-0733
Mailing list available for rent

14342 Insurance Advocate

PO Box 14367
Cincinatti, OH 45250-0367

908-859-0893
E-Mail: cluke@nuco.com
Home Page: www.nationaunderwriter.com

Chris Luke, Publisher
Phil Gusman, Editor

Eric V Gilkey, Assistant Editor
Steve Acunto, Associate Publisher

Covers the people and issues affecting the insurance industry in New York, New Jersey, Connecticut and beyond. Also the source for new markets and coverages, financial trends, legislative isssues, M&A, insurance law and industry developments.
Cost: $59.00
Frequency: Weekly
Circulation: 7200
Founded in 1889
Printed in 4 colors on glossy stock

14343 Insurance Conference Planner
Penton Media Inc
249 W. 17th St., third floor
New York, NY 10011

847-763-9504
866-505-7173
E-Mail: shatch@meetingsnet.com
Home Page: www.meetingsnet.com

Susan Hatch, Editor
Betsy Bair, Director, Content and Media
Melissa Fromento, Group Publisher
Regina McGee, Religious Conference Manager
Susan Hatch, Executive Editor

Meeting and incentive strategies for the financial services industry.
Cost: $57.00
148 Pages
Circulation: 9000
Founded in 1989
Printed in 4 colors on glossy stock

14344 Insurance Insight
Professional Independent Insurance Agents of IL
4360 Wabash Ave
Springfield, IL 62711-7009

217-793-6660
800-628-6436
FAX 217-793-6744
E-Mail: info@IIAofIllinois.org
Home Page: www.iiaofillinois.org

Sandy Cuffle, Manager
Dennis Garrett, VP Marketing/Membership
Mark Kuchar, CPA, CFO
Mike Tate, CAE, Chief Operating Officer
Peter Gulatto, Marketing Representative

Features articles that are relevant to the Illinois insurance industry, and includes topics such as industry news, technology, markets and coverages, financial planning, sales and marketing, state and federal issues, agency management, The Middleton Letter, and education.
Cost: $65.00
68 Pages
Frequency: Monthly
Circulation: 2500
Founded in 1993
Mailing list available for rent

14345 Insurance Journal West
3570 Camino Del Rio N
Suite 200
San Diego, CA 92108-1747

619-584-1100
800-897-9965
FAX 619-584-5889
E-Mail: info@insurancejournal.com
Home Page: www.insurancejournal.com
Social Media: *Facebook, Twitter, LinkedIn*

Mark Wells, Publisher
Mitch Dunford, Chief Operating Officer
Katie Robley, Circulation Manager
Suzie Song, Marketing Manager
Andrea Ortega-Wells, Editor-In-Chief

Insurance Journal is written for the independent agent and broker. Insurance Journal West covers California and the western states, while Insurance Journal Texas/South Central covers

Texas, Arkansas, Oklahoma & Louisiana. We cover legal issues, people, markets, regulations and legistation, the very things that affect our readers.
Cost: $58.00
Circulation: 40000
Founded in 1923
Printed in 4 colors on matte stock

14346 Insurance Networking News
SourceMedia
550 W. Van Buren St.
Suite 1110
Chicago, IL 60607

847-933-5183
FAX 312-566-0656
Home Page: www.insurancenetworking.com
Social Media: *Facebook, Twitter*

Carrie Burns, Editor-In-Chief

A trusted source for information on how technology is being implemented to support insurers' strategic business objectives, providing insightful analysis of-and case studies on-how technology is being innovatively utilized to automate critical processes.
Frequency: Monthly
Founded in 1997
Mailing list available for rent

14347 Journal of Healthcare Risk Management
American Society for Healthcare Risk Management
1 N Franklin St
Chicago, IL 60606-4425

312-422-3840
FAX 312-422-4573
Home Page: www.aha.org

Deborah Sprindzunas, Executive Director
Cliff Lehman, Director Membership Services
Cost: $80.00
Circulation: 4500
Mailing list available for rent: 4400 names

14348 Journal of Law, Medicine & Ethics
American Society of Law, Medicine and Ethics
765 Commonwealth Ave
Suite 1634
Boston, MA 02215-1401

617-262-4990
FAX 617-437-7596
E-Mail: info@aslme.org
Home Page: www.aslme.org
Social Media: *Facebook, Twitter, LinkedIn*

Ted Hutchinson, Executive Director
Ted Hutchinson, Publications Director
Katie Kenney Johnson, Conference Director
Margo Buege, Membership Department
Courtney McClellan, Assistant Editor

Provides articles on such timely topics as health care quality and access, managed care, pain relief, genetics, child/maternal health, reproductive health, informed consent, assisted dying, ethics committees, HIV/AIDS, and public health. Issues review significant policy developments, health law court decisions, and books.
Cost: $140.00
Frequency: Quarterly
Circulation: 4,500+
Mailing list available for rent

14349 Journal of Reinsurance
Intermediaries and Reinsurance Underwriters Assoc
971 Rte 202 North
Branchburg, NJ 08876

908-203-0211
FAX 908-203-0213

E-Mail: info@irua.com
Home Page: www.irua.com

Paul Walther, Editor

To encourage an exchange of ideas and to disseminiate educational information for the benefit and betterment of the Intermediaries & Reinsurance Underwriters Association membership and the reinsurance community.
Cost: $195.00
Frequency: Quarterly

14350 Journal of Risk and Insurance
Wiley-Blackwell Publishing
111 River Street
Hoboken, NJ 07030-5774

201-748-6000
FAX 201-748-6088
E-Mail: info@wiley.com
Home Page: www.wiley.com

Georges Dionne, Editor

The flagship journal for the American Risk and Insurance Association. The JRI is the most well recognized academic risk management and insurance journal in the world and is currently indexed by the American Economic Association's Economic Literature Index, the Finance Literature Index, RePEc, the Social Sciences Citation Index, ABI/Inform, Business and Company ASAP, Lexis-Nexis, Dow Jones Interactive, and others.
Frequency: Quarterly
ISSN: 0022-4367

14351 LIMRA's MarketFacts Quarterly
LIMRA
300 Day Hill Rd.
Windsor, CT 06095

860-688-3358
FAX 860-285-7792
E-Mail: bragaglia@limra.com
Home Page: www.limra.com

Wendy Weston, Contact

Features in-depth, timeless articles devoted to the critical issues of the day, including such topics as distribution, technology, marketing strategies, retirement, globalization, demographics, financial integration and products and services.
Cost: $500.00
Frequency: Quarterly
Circulation: 7500

14352 Leader's Edge Magazine
Council of Insurance Agents & Brokers
701 Pennsylvania Ave NW
Suite 750
Washington, DC 20004-2661

202-783-4400
FAX 202-783-4410
E-Mail: webmaster@ciab.com
Home Page: www.ciab.com

Ken A Crerar, President
Pat Wade, Director of Communications
Brianne Mallaghan, Director of Communications
Scott Sinder, General Counsel

Comprised of vital information and news for the industry of insurance agents and brokers.
Cost: $100.00
Frequency: Bi-Monthly

14353 Liability & Insurance Week
JR Publishing
PO Box 6654
McLean, VA 22106-6654

703-532-2235
FAX 703-532-2236
E-Mail: jvreistrup@erols.com

John Reistrup, Publisher

Reports on political, legislative and regulatory actions affecting the insurance and legal industries.

14354 Life & Health Advisor
JonHope Communications
71 Emerson Road
PO Box 613
Walpole, MA 02081

508-668-8025
888-578-8025
FAX 508-668-8056
E-Mail: pkelley@lifehealth.com
Home Page: www.lifehealth.com
Social Media: *Facebook, Twitter, LinkedIn*

Sally O'Connell, Publisher/Ad Sales Manager
Peter Kelley, Editor

Access, exposure & market visibility for financial services, investment and retirement income planningo.
Frequency: Monthly
Founded in 1995
Mailing list available for rent

14355 Life Insurance Selling
Summit Buiness Media
5081 Olympic Blvd.
Suite 550
Erlanger, KY 41018

859-692-2100
FAX 859-692-2000
E-Mail: lis@pfpublish.com
Home Page: www.lifeinsuranceselling.com
Social Media: *Facebook, Twitter, LinkedIn, RSS*

Dave O'Neil, Group Publisher
John K Moore, Publisher
Brian Anderson, Editor
Tashawna Rodwell, Publisher
Bill Coffin, Group Editorial Director

The leading sales publication for life, health and financial planning professionals.

14356 Life and Health Insurance Sales Magazines
Rough Notes Company
11690 Technology Drive
Carmel, IN 46032-5600

317-582-1600
800-321-1909
FAX 317-816-1000
E-Mail: rnc@roughnotes.com
Home Page: www.roughnotes.com

Walter Gdowski, Owner
Nancy Doucette, Senior Editor
Elisabeth Boone, CPCU, Associate Editor
Dennis Pillsbury, Associate Editor

For life and health agents, general agents, managers and brokers with prospects to culivate and clients to serve. Accepts advertising.
48 Pages
Frequency: Monthly
Founded in 1878
Mailing list available for rent

14357 Long-Term Care Insurance Sales Strategies
Sales Creators
3835 E Thousand Oaks Boulevard
Suite 336
Westlake Village, CA 91362

818-597-3205
888-599-5997
FAX 818-597-3206
E-Mail: jslome@ltcsales.com
Home Page: www.ltcsales.com

Jesse Sloame, Publisher/President
Mindy Hartman, Ad Director

Content covers successful sales approaches, new and unexplored marekts, industry trends,

and upcoming training seminars.
Cost: $24.00
Frequency: Quarterly
Circulation: 7500
Founded in 1998

14358 Momentum
Metropolitan Life Insurance Company
1 Madison Ave
New York, NY 10010-3603

212-867-2165
FAX 212-685-8042
Home Page: www.metlife.com

Robert H Benmosche, CEO

Magazine covering the Metropolitan Life Insurance Company.
Frequency: Monthly
Founded in 1970

14359 NRRA News
National Risk Retention Association
4248 Park Glen Road
Minneapolis, MN 55416-4758

952-284-4643
800-999-4505
FAX 952-929-1318
Home Page: www.captive.com

Judith Harrington, Editor
Cost: $195.00
Frequency: Quarterly
Circulation: 250,000

14360 National Underwriter Life & Health Financial Services Edition
33-41 Newark Street
2nd Floor
Hoboken, NJ 07030

201-526-1230
FAX 201-526-1260
E-Mail: spiontek@nuco.com
Home Page: cms.nationalunderwriter.com

Stephen Piontek, Editor-In-Chief
Jim Connolly, Senior Editor

Uniquely positioned to provider producers, brokers, marketers and company executives with timely, insightful information. Each week, identifies, analyzes and comments on the latest trends and developments for their significance to the market-giving our readers the information they need to make critical business decisions.
Frequency: Weekly

14361 National Underwriter: Life & Health Insurance Edition
National Underwriter Company
5081 Olympic Blvd
Erlanger, KY 41018-3164

859-692-2100
800-543-0874
FAX 859-692-2295
Home Page: www.nationalunderwriter.com

Charlie Smith, CEO

Offers features on agent activities, stocks and marketing, brokers and financial planners, trade meetings, business trends and outside developments in the industry.
Cost: $75.00
Frequency: Weekly
Circulation: 48,5070

14362 National Underwriter: Property & Casualty Risk & Benefits Management
National Underwriter Company
5081 Olympic Blvd
Erlanger, KY 41018-3164

859-692-2100
800-543-0874

FAX 859-692-2295
Home Page: www.nationalunderwriter.com

Charlie Smith, CEO

Covers industry trends, risk management, state and federal legislation, and judicial affairs.
Cost: $149.00
Frequency: Weekly
Circulation: 485070
Founded in 1897

14363 POA Bulletin/Merritt Risk Management News and Review
POA Publishing
1625 Prince Street
Alexandria, VA 22314-2818

703-519-6200
877-663-4890
FAX 703-519-6299
E-Mail: asis@asisonline.org
Home Page: www.asisonline.org

Michael E. Knoke, Managing Editor
Sherry Harowitz, Editor-In-Chief
Denny White, Director/Publishing

Editorial content is designed to keep security managers and risk managers abreast of legal, legislative and insurance issues, and contains features that identify security and risk management trends and present analysis of insurance coverage and needs.
Cost: $690.00
Frequency: Quarterly
Circulation: 3400
Founded in 1955

14364 Proceedings
Conference of Consulting Actuaries
3880 Salem Lake Drive
Suite H
Long Grove, IL 60047-5292

847-719-6500
FAX 847-719-6506
E-Mail: conference@ccactuaries.org
Home Page: www.ccactuaries.org

Rita K DeGraaf, Executive Director
Keith G Stewart, Director of Operations
Patricia D Johnson, Project Manager
Matthew D Noncek, Member Services Manager

The professional journal of the Conference of Consulting Actuaries. Promotes the interchange of information among actauries and the various actuarial organizations, and to keep its publics informed of the viewpoints and activities of the professional consulting actuary.
Cost: $95.00
500 Pages
Circulation: 1,200
Founded in 1950

14365 Professional Agent
Association of Professional Insurance Agents
400 N Washington Street
Alexandria, VA 22314-2312

703-836-9340
FAX 703-836-1279
E-Mail: piainfo@pianet.org
Home Page: www.pianet.com

Magazine for the insurance professional.
Cost: $24.00
65 Pages
Frequency: Monthly
Circulation: 35000
Founded in 1931

14366 Property/Casualty Insurance
National Association of Mutual Insurance Companies

3601 Vincennes Road
PO Box 68700
Indianapolis, IN 46268

317-875-5250
FAX 317-879-8408
E-Mail: webmaster@namic.org
Home Page: www.namic.org

Bart Anderson, Publisher
Laura Biddle-Bruckman, Managing Editor
Matt Keating, Editor
Kristen Eichhorn, Program Director

Highlights insurance industry news, personnel
announcements, industry events, and new prod-
ucts in the field.
Cost: $20.00
Frequency: Monthly
Circulation: 2500
Founded in 1895

14367 Public Risk

Public Risk Management Association
700 S. Washington St.
Suite 218
Alexandria, VA 22314-1565

703-528-7701
FAX 703-739-0200
E-Mail: info@primacentral.org
Home Page: www.primacentral.org
Social Media: *Facebook, Twitter, LinkedIn*

Marshall Davies, Executive Director
Jon Ruzan, Editor
Jennifer Ackerman, Deputy Executive Director
Bles Dones, Manager, Member Services
Paulette Washington, Office Administrator

Magazine exclusively targeting risk manage-
ment practitioners in the public sector: state
and local governments.
Cost: $130.00
Frequency: 1 Year 10 Issue
Circulation: 8250
ISSN: 0891-7183
Founded in 1978
Mailing list available for rent

14368 Resource Magazine

Life Office Management Association
2300 Windy Ridge Pkwy SE
Suite 600
Atlanta, GA 30339-5665

770-951-1770
800-275-5662
FAX 770-984-0441
E-Mail: resource@loma.org
Home Page: www.loma.org

Thomas P Donaldson, President/CEO
Jerry Woo, Director
Robert Lai, Managing Director

Covers every topic of interest to management
of insurance and financial services companies.
Frequency: Monthly

14369 Risk & Insurance

LRP Publications
PO Box 980
Horsham, PA 19044-0980

215-784-0912
800-341-7874
FAX 215-784-9639
E-Mail: custserv@lrp.com
Home Page: www.lrp.com

Todd Lutz, CFO
Jack Roberts, Editor-in-Chief
Cyril Tuohy, Managing Editor

Provides business executives and insurance
professionals with the insight, information and
strategies they need to mitigate challenging
business risks. Published monthly and
semi-monthly in April when publish two special editions focusing on the Risk and Insur-

ance Management Society's annual RIMS
conference.
Frequency: Monthly
Circulation: 51541
Founded in 1977

14370 Risk Management

Risk Management Society Publishing
1065 Avenue of the Americas
13th Floor
New York, NY 10018-5637

212-286-9292
FAX 212-986-9716
E-Mail: tdonovan@rims.org
Home Page: www.rims.org
Social Media: *Facebook, Twitter, LinkedIn*

Ted Donovan, Publisher
Bill Coffin, Editor-In-Chief
Morgan O'Rouke, Managing Editor
Jared Wade, Editor
Callie Nelson, Circulation Manager

The premier source of analysis, insight and
news for corporate risk managers. RM strives
to explore existing and emerging techniques
and concepts that address the needs of those
who are tasked with protecting the physical, financial, human and intellectual assets of their
companies.
Cost: $64.00
Frequency: Monthly
Circulation: 17000
Founded in 1950
Mailing list available for rent

**14371 Risk Management and Insurance
Review**

Wiley Publications
111 River Street
Hoboken, NJ 07030-5774

201-748-6000
FAX 201-748-6088
E-Mail: info@wiley.com
Home Page: www.wiley.com

Mary A Weiss, Editor

Publishes respected, accessible, and high-quality applied research, and well-reasoned opinion
and discussion in the field of risk and insurance. The Review's Feature Articles section includes original research involving applications
and applied techniques. The Perspectives section contains articles providing new insights on
the research literature, business practice, and
public policy.
Frequency: Bi-Annual
ISSN: 1098-1616

14372 Risk Report

International Risk Management Institute
12222 Merit Dr
Suite 1450
Dallas, TX 75251-3297

972-996-0800
800-827-5991
FAX 972-371-5128
Home Page: www.zeroriskhr.com
Social Media: *Facebook, Twitter, LinkedIn*

Mike Poskey, Vice President
Jack P Gibson, President
Paul D Murray, VP Marketing/Sales
Robert Kinsel Smith, Senior
Adviser/Consultant
Mike Wojcik, Information Technology Director

Helps risk and insurance professionals in both
of these areas with analysis and interpretation
of the latest innovations in insurance
Cost: $219.00
Frequency: Monthly
Founded in 1987

14373 Rough Notes

Rough Notes Company

PO Box 1990
Carmel, IN 46082-1990

317-582-1600
800-428-4384
FAX 317-816-1000
E-Mail: rnc@roughnotes.com
Home Page: www.roughnotes.com

Monthly sales and management magazine for
property and casualty insurance agents.
Cost: $357.00
120 Pages
Frequency: Monthly
Founded in 1878
Printed in 4 colors on glossy stock

14374 Round the Table Magazine

Million Dollar Round Table
325 W Touhy Ave
Park Ridge, IL 60068-4265

847-692-6378
FAX 847-518-8921
E-Mail: editor@mdrt.org
Home Page: www.mdrt.org

Guy E Baker, President
Kathryn F Keuneke, Associate Editor
John Prast, Executive VP
Scott Brennan, Secretary

Productivity ideas, reaching your clients, professional knowledge, motivational stories, all
this to share with clients and to help you make
the sale.
Cost: $14.00
Frequency: Bi-Monthly

14375 Standard

Standard Publishing Corporation
155 Federal St
13th Floor
Boston, MA 02110-1752

617-457-0600
FAX 617-457-0608
E-Mail: e.ayers@spcpub.com
Home Page: www.standardpub.com

John Cross, President/Publisher

Content focuses on all aspects involving legislative and regulatory developments at the state
and federal levels, court decisions, trade association positions and more. Coverage includes
news, feature articles and opinion pieces, with
an emphasis on property/casualty insurance.
Cost: $80.00
Frequency: Weekly
Circulation: 5000
Founded in 1870

**14376 The Brief (Tort & Insurance Practice
Section)**

American Bar Association
321 N Clark St
Chicago, IL 60654-7598

312-988-5000
800-285-2221
FAX 312-988-6281
E-Mail: askaba@abanet.org
Home Page: www.abanet.org
Social Media: *Facebook, Twitter*

Jane Harper-Alport, Staff Editor
John Warren May, Editor
Janet Jackson, Director
Bill Pritchard, Assistant to the Director

The Brief explores all aspects of tort and insur-
ance law, including the many facets of trial
practice essential to the profession.
Cost: $50.00
400,0 Members
60 Pages
Frequency: Quarterly
Circulation: 30000
ISSN: 0273-0995
Founded in 1878
Printed in 4 colors

14377 Today's Insurance Woman
National Association of Insurance Women
1847 E 15th Street
PO Box 4410
Tulsa, OK 74159-0410

918-744-5195
FAX 918-743-1968

Melissa Carlson, Editor

Focus is on business careers, legislation, leadership, management and social issues facing women in the industry.
Cost: $15.00
Frequency: Bi-Monthly
Circulation: 12,887

14378 Underwriters' Report
National Underwriters Company
5081 Olympic Boulevard
Erlanger, KY 41018

859-922-2100
800-543-0874
FAX 800-874-1916
Home Page: www.nationalunderwriter.com

Charlie Smith, CEO

Offering complete information on fire, casualty and life insurance every week.
Cost: $45.00
40 Pages
Frequency: Weekly
Circulation: 5000

14379 Weight Loss Solutions
Field Media Publishing
200 S Main Street
Alpharetta, GA 30004

770-475-9770
FAX 678-990-5565
Home Page: www.bcsolutionsmag.com

Doug Field, CEO/Publisher
Steve Milano, Editor

A business magazine that addresses real-world issues by delivering best-practice solutions and information to those involved in benefits and compensation decisions. Free to members.
Frequency: Monthly

14380 Worker's Compensation Monitor
LRP Publications
PO Box 24668
West Palm Beach, FL 33416-4668

561-622-6520
FAX 561-622-0757
E-Mail: webmaster@lrp.com
Home Page: www.lrp.com

Kenneth Kahn, President
Leslie Lake, Managing Editor
Josh Clifton, Editor

Information on worker's compensation laws.
Cost: $210.00
Frequency: Monthly
Founded in 1977

Trade Shows

14381 AADC Annual Spring Workshop
American Association of Dental Consultants
10032 Wind Hill Drive
Greenville, IN 47124

812-923-2600
800-896-0707
FAX 812-923-2900
Home Page: www.aadc.org

Dr George Koumaras, President
Dr Larry Hoffman, Secretary/Treasurer
Judith K. Salisbury, Executive Director

These meetings provide a forum to discuss topical subjects involving the Dental Benefit Industry and Clinical Dentistry as a whole. AADC presenters and lectures are recognized as leaders in the Dental Industry. 10 exhibitors.
300 Attendees
Frequency: Annual/May
Founded in 1979

14382 AHIP Annual Meeting
America's Health Insurance Plans
601 Pennsylvania Avenue NW
South Building, Suite 500
Washington, DC 20004

202-778-3200
877-291-2247
FAX 202-331-7487
E-Mail: ahip@ahip.org
Home Page: www.ahip.org

Karen M Ignagni, President/CEO
Susan Pisano, VP Communications

This meeting continues to be the nation's leading health care conference where all segments of the health insurance industry convene to share perspectives on, and analysis of, the most recent developments in health care.
300 Attendees

14383 AHOU Annual Conference
Association of Home Office Underwriters
22300 Windy Ridge Parkway
Suite 600
Atlanta, GA 30339-8443

770-984-3715
FAX 770-984-6418
E-Mail: ahou@loma.org
Home Page: www.ahou.org

Jennifer Richards, Convention VP
Lee Janecek, Convention Assistant VP

Providing career development, underwriting solutions, the latest medical issues and valuable insight to keep you prepared.
Frequency: Annual/October
Founded in 2001

14384 AIA Annual Conference
Aviation Insurance Association
400 Admiral Blvd
Suite 200
Kansas City, MO 64106-1508

816-221-8488
FAX 816-472-7765
E-Mail: mandie@robstan.com
Home Page: www.aiaweb.org
Social Media: *Facebook*

Paul Leonard, President
Todd McCredie, Vice President
Patrick Bailey, Secretary
Mary D'Alauro, Treasurer
Mandie Bannwarth, Executive Director

Provides a forum for the biggest names and best minds in the aviaiton insurance industry. Offers top-notch speakers, continuing education classes, time with vendors and opportunities to network and develop relationships that last a lifetime.
900 Members
Frequency: April/May
Founded in 1976

14385 AICP Annual Conference
Association of Insurance Compliance Professionals
12100 Sunset Hills Road
Suite 130
Reston, VA 20190

703-234-4074
FAX 703-435-4390

E-Mail: aicp@aicp.net
Home Page: www.aicp.net

Richard A Guggolz, Executive Director
Elaine Bailey, Conference Chair

Learning opportunities for a broad range of compliance professionals, sessions for beginners and seasoned professionals and networking opportunities with colleagues, peers and state regulators.
680 Attendees
Frequency: Annual/Sept-Oct

14386 ASPPA Annual Conference
American Society of Pension Professionals & Act
4245 N Fairfax Drive
Suite 750
Arlington, VA 22203

703-160-0512
FAX 703-516-9308
E-Mail: asppa@asppa.org
Home Page: www.asppa.org

Tom Finnegan, President

Attendees of this conference share quality time with representatives from every aspect of the retirement plan industry. Offers 20 hours of ASPPA continuing education credits and provides Joint Board for the Enrollemnt of Actuaries credit hours for enrolled actuaries.
1600 Attendees

14387 ASSE Annual Conference & Exposition
American Society of Safety Engineers
1800 E Oakton Street
Des Plaines, IL 60018

847-699-2929
FAX 847-768-3434
E-Mail: customerservice@asse.org
Home Page: www.asse.org
Social Media: *Facebook, Twitter, LinkedIn, Blogger, Pinterest, Tumblr*

Fred Fortman, Executive Director
Jim Drzewiecki, Finance/Controller Director
Diane Hurns, Manager Public Relations Department
Richard A. Pollock, President
Stephanie A. Helgerman, Vice President, Finance

Featuring more than 200 sessions, an exposition with 300 exhibitors, special pre- and post-conference seminars, conference proceedings on CD, numerous networking events and more! Learn the latest strategies to expand your knowledge base and network with other safety, health and environmental professionals
3500 Attendees
Frequency: Annual/June
Mailing list available for rent

14388 Advanced Life Underwriting Association
1922 F Street NW
Washington, DC 20006-4302

202-331-6099
FAX 202-331-2164

Karen G Keating, Director

22 booths.
1.1M Attendees
Frequency: February

14389 Alliance of Insurance Agents and Brokers Convention & Expo
1029 J. Street
Suite 120
Sacramento, CA 95814

916-283-9473
866-497-9222
FAX 916-283-9479
E-Mail: info@agentsalliance.com

Home Page: www.agentsalliance.com
Social Media: *Facebook, Twitter*

Joe Jimenez, President
David Nelson, Executive Direcetor
Mike D'Arelli, Executive Vice President
Yolanda Olquin, Sales/Marketing Manager

The largest insurance industry trade show in the western U.S. Offers the perfect blend of business networking opportunities, education seminars, and fun and laughs with old and new friends.
Frequency: Annual
Founded in 1962

14390 American Association of Managing General Agents Annual Meeting

American Association of Managing General Agents
9140 Ward Parkway
Kansas City, MO 64114-3306

816-444-3500
FAX 816-444-0330

Jeanne Corlew-Knox, Director Meetings

Annual meeting and exhibits for managing general agents of insurance companies.
1000 Attendees
Frequency: Annual

14391 American Fraternal Alliance Annual Meeting

American Fraternal Alliance
1301 W 22nd St
Suite 700
Oak Brook, IL 60523-6022

630-522-6322
FAX 630-522-6326
E-Mail: info@fraternalalliance.org
Home Page: www.fraternalalliance.org
Social Media: *Facebook, Twitter*

Joseph Annotti, President & CEO
Linda McLaughlin, Admin Services Manager
Melanie Hinds, Director, Advocacy
Allison Koppel, Executive Vice President
Andrea Litewski, Executive Administrator

Keeps members abreast of industry trends, to promote the spirit of fraternalism and to resolve mutual concerns.
Frequency: September

14392 American Society for Healthcare Risk Management Convention

American Society for Healthcare Risk Management
American Hospital Association
1 N Franklin
Chicago, IL 60606

312-422-3840
FAX 312-422-4580
Home Page: www.aha.org

Deborah Sprindzunas, Executive Director
Cliff Lehman, Director Membership Services

Annual convention and exhibits of health care industry risk management equipment, supplies and services.
Frequency: Annual

14393 American Society of CLU and CHFC Annual Conference

American Society of CLU and CHFC
270 S Bryn Mawr Avenue
Suite 2
Bryn Mawr, PA 19010-2195

215-726-3160
FAX 610-527-1400

Annual conference and exhibits for insurance agents and financial services professionals who hold Chartered Life Underwriter or Chartered Financial Consultant designations.
Frequency: October, San Diego

14394 Annual Conference for Public Agencies

Public Risk Management Association
1815 Fort Myer Drive
Suite 1020
Arlington, VA 22209-1805

703-527-5546
FAX 703-528-7966
E-Mail: info@primacentral.org
Home Page: www.primacentral.org

James F Coyle, Executive Director
Tony D'Alba, Manager
Kerry Langley, Manager

Largest conference in North America for state and local government risk managers who purchase insurance, safety and training products, computer software, TPA and consultant services. 150 booths.
2000 Attendees
Frequency: June
Founded in 1979
Mailing list available for rent: 2000 names

14395 Annual National Association of Insurance Women International

1847 E 15th
PO Box 4410
Tulsa, OK 74159

918-744-5195
800-766-6249
FAX 918-743-1968
E-Mail: naiw@ionet.net
Home Page: www.naiw.org

Mark Adams, Executive Vice-President

Equipment, information and supplies for women in the insurance industry.
900 Attendees
Frequency: Annual

14396 Appraisers Association of America National Conference

386 Park Avenue S
Suite 2000
New York, NY 10016-8804

212-889-5404
FAX 212-889-5503
Home Page: www.appraisersassoc.org

Aleya Lehmann, Executive Director

A unique opportunity to connect with fellow appraisers as well as with allied professionals in insurance companies, law firms, government agencies, auction houses, galleries, museums, and libraries to debate and discuss the latest issues impacting the appraisal profession. We'll offer panels, specialist sessions, roundtable discussions, networking, and behind-the-scenes tours.

14397 Association for Advanced Life Underwriting

2901 Telester Court
Falls Church, VA 22042

703-641-9400
888-275-0092

Karen Keating, Communications Director
David Stertzer, Executive VP

Twenty two booths.
1M Attendees
Frequency: March

14398 CEB Spring Conference

Council on Employee Benefits
1311 King Street
Alexandria, VA 22314

703-549-6025
FAX 703-549-6027

E-Mail: scanfiled@ceb.org
Home Page: www.ceb.org

Shane Canfield, Executive Director
Robert B. Arthur, President
John R. Collins, Treasurer
Donna A. Sexton, Vice President
Charles A. Jordan, Secretary

For members only and affords a great opportunity to exchange ideas in an interactive workshop format.
Frequency: April

14399 CIRB Annual Meeting

Crop Insurance Research Bureau
201 Massachusetts Avenue, NE
Suite C5
Washington, DC 20002

202-544-0067
FAX 202-330-5255
E-Mail: mtorrey@cropinsurance.org
Home Page: www.cropinsurance.org

Mike Torrey, Executive VP/Federal Affairs Rep
Naomi Watson, Operations Manager
W. Kurt Henke, Legal Counsel

The annual meeting brings together crop industry leaders to learn from expert speakers and newtwork with others in their industry.
Frequency: Annual/January-February

14400 CPCU Annual Meeting & Seminar

Chartered Property Casualty Underwriter Society
720 Providence Road
PO Box 3009
Malvern, PA 19355-0709

610-251-2728
800-932-2728
FAX 610-251-2780
E-Mail: lrizzo@cpcusociety.org
Home Page: www.cpcusociety.org

Liliana Rizzo, CMP, Meeting Services Director

Join your fellow society members, new designees and industry leaders for the best in education, networking and leadership the property and casualty insurance industry has to offer.
2600 Attendees
Frequency: Annual/October
Founded in 1944

14401 CPCU Conferment Ceremony

American Institute for CPCU
720 Providence Road
PO Box 3016
Malvern, PA 19355

610-251-2733
800-644-2101
FAX 610-640-9576
E-Mail: cserv@cpcuiia.org
Home Page: www.aicpcu.org

Karen Burger CPCU CPIW, Public Relations
Roch Parayre, Senior Partner

Annual graduation ceremony for people who have earned the Chartered Property Casualty Underwriter - CPCU - designation.
Frequency: October

14402 Captive Insurance Companies Association Conference

Captive Insurance Companies Association
4248 Park Glen Road
Minneapolis, MN 55416

952-928-4655
FAX 952-928-1318
Home Page: www.captiveassociation.com

Annual conference and exhibits of captive insurance equipment, supplies and services.

14403 Chartered Property Casualty Underwriters Society Fall Seminar
Chartered Property Casualty Underwriter Society
720 Providence Road
Malvern, PA 19355-3402

610-512-2728
Home Page: http://www.cpcusociety.org

Joseph Wisniewski, VP Finance
Jim Marks, Executive Director

Offers a forum for the exchange of ideas between insurance representatives.
3M Attendees
Frequency: October

14404 Employee Benefits Annual Conference
International Foundation of Employee Benefit Plans
18700 W Bluemound Road
Brookfield, WI 53045

262-786-6700
888-334-3327
FAX 262-786-8780
E-Mail: pr@ifebp.org
Home Page: www.ifebp.org
Social Media: *Facebook, Twitter, LinkedIn*

Michael Wilson, CEO
Terry Davidson, VP, Business Development
Beth Harwood, VP, Educ Program/Content Management

This conference is designed to meet the specific needs of multiemployer and public sector plan trustees and administrators, attorneys, accountants, actuaries, investment managers and others who provide services or who are involved in the overall management and administration of benefit trust funds. The 2011 conference will be in New Orleans, LA.
35000 Members
4500 Attendees
Frequency: Annual/Nov 4-7

14405 FICP Conference
Financial & Insurance Conference Planners
330 N. Wabash Avenue
Suite 2000
Chicago, IL 60611

312-245-1023
FAX 312-321-5150
E-Mail: jschultze@ficpnet.com
Home Page: www.ficpnet.com

James Schultze, CMP, Conference Manager
Laura Vanderbur, Conference Associate
Steve Bova, CAE, Executive Director
Mark Swets, Membership Manager
Ellie Hurley, Events Senior Manager

Exhibits, education and networking activities.
Frequency: Annual/November

14406 Financial Service Forum
Society of Financial Service Professionals
19 Campus Blvd
Suite 100
Newtown Square, PA 19073-3230

610-526-2500
800-392-6900
FAX 610-526-2538
E-Mail: info@financialpro.org
Home Page: www.financialpro.org
Social Media: *Facebook, Twitter, LinkedIn*

Joseph E Frack, CEO
Donna Conrad, CFO
Anthony Smith, VP Marketing/Corporate Services
Jill Von Czoernig, Managing Director
Sherry Chester, Director, Professional Development

Composed of motivational speakers, break-out educational session with continuing education

for insurance, CFP, PACE, CLE, CPE, ICB, and EA. Exhibithall includes demo theaters.
3000+ Attendees
Frequency: October

14407 General Agents and Managers Life Agency Management Program
1922 F Street NW
Washington, DC 20006-4302

202-331-6099
FAX 202-785-5612

Jo Anne Kohler, Show Manager
80 booths including publishers, computer software and hardware manufacturers and office management services.
2.7M Attendees
Frequency: March

14408 Health Law Professors Conference
American Society of Law, Medicine and Ethics
765 Commonwealth Avenue
16th Floor
Boston, MA 02215

617-262-4990
FAX 617-437-7596
E-Mail: conferences@aslme.org
Home Page: www.aslme.org
Social Media: *Facebook, Twitter, LinkedIn*

Ted Hutchinson, Executive Director
Katie Kenney Johnson, Conference Director
Margo Buege, Membership Department
Courtney McClellan, Assistant Editor
Frequency: June
Mailing list available for rent

14409 I-Car International Annual Meeting
3701 W Algonquin Road
Suite 400
Rolling Meadows, IL 60008

925-961-0393
800-422-7872
FAX 800-590-1215
E-Mail: webmaster@i-car.com
Home Page: www.i-car.com

Pat Perren, Meetings Manager
Matt Forpanek, Customer Care Manager

A important event that brings together collision industry leaders from across the United States, Canada and New Zealand to address current trends and issues in the industry. Attendees will have the opportunity to learn about new products and technologies and share ideas with other industry leaders.
Frequency: Annual/July

14410 IAAI Annual Conference and General Meeting
International Association of Arson Investigators
12770 Boenker Road
Bridgeton, MO 63044

314-739-4224
FAX 314-739-4219
E-Mail: orders@firearson.com
Home Page: www.firearson.com

Marsha Sipes, Conference/Meeting Services
Dolores Nelson, Executive Director
Dave Allen, Executive Director

Provides the means to stay abreast of the latest techniques and theories in the investigation of the crime of arson.
Frequency: Annual/April

14411 IADC Annual Meeting
International Association of Defense Counsel

303 West Madison
Suite 925
Chicago, IL 60606

312-368-1494
FAX 312-368-1854
E-Mail: info@iadclaw.org
Home Page: www.iadclaw.org
Social Media: *Facebook, Twitter, LinkedIn*

Mary Beth Kurzak, Executive Director
Mathew Hornberger, Director Membership/Administration
Liz Anderson, Administrative Assistant
Carmela Balice, Senior Manager, Member Services
Ashley Fitzgerald, Communications Coordinator

Offering interests CLE and excellent networking opportunities in family friendly environment.
Frequency: Annual/July

14412 IAIABC Annual Convention
Int'l Assoc of Industrail Accident Boards/Commissi
5610 Medical Circle
Suite 24
Madison, WI 53719

608-663-6355
FAX 608-663-1546
E-Mail: hlore@iaiabc.org
Home Page: www.iaiabc.org

Jennifer Wolf Horejsh, Executive Director
Faith Howe, EDI Manager
Christina Klein, Events/Education Coordinator
Christina Klein, Events and Office Administrator
Heather Lore, Manager of Membership and Marketing

Brings together regulators and administrators of workers' compensation agencies and private sector professionals to discuss the industry's most common and pressing problems.
Frequency: August
Mailing list available for rent

14413 IAIR Roundtable and Meetings
International Association of Insurance Receivers
174 Grace Boulevard
Altamonte Springs, FL 32714

407-682-4513
FAX 407-682-3175
E-Mail: info@iair.org
Home Page: www.iair.org

Daniel A Orth III, Meetings VP
Mary Cannon Veed, Vice President
Douglas Hartz, Vice President

Quarterly meetings that provides an opportunity to share information about important industry issues and topics in insurance and reinsurance as they relate specifically to insurance receiverships.
Frequency: June, Sept, December

14414 IASA Annual Conference
Insurance, Accounting & Systems Association
3511 Shannon Road
Suite 160
Durham, NC 27707

919-489-0991
FAX 919-489-1994
E-Mail: info@iasa.org
Home Page: www.iasa.org

Thom Hoffman, Exhibit Manager
R Iovino, Account Manager

Providing the most comprehensive education program and business show targeted for finan-

cial and technology professionals in the industry.
1800 Attendees
Frequency: June

14415 ICAE's Annual Exchange
Insurance Consumer Affairs Exchange
PO Box 746
Lake Zurich, IL 60047

847-997-8454
E-Mail: nbrebner@icae.com
Home Page: www.icae.com

Mike Hammond, President
Kendra Franklin, VP
Nancy Brebner, Executive Director
Chad Batterson, Executive Committee
Gail Cleary, Secretary

A not-for-profit organization that promotes professionalism and shapes the standards of behavior in relationships between insurance organizations, regulators and customers through proactive dialogue, research, communication and education.
110 Members
Frequency: Annual/October
Founded in 1976

14416 IRU Spring Conference
Intermediaries and Reinsurance Underwriters Assoc
971 Rte 202 North
Branchburg, NJ 08876

908-203-0211
FAX 908-203-0213
E-Mail: info@irua.com
Home Page: www.irua.com

Amy Barra, Executive Director
Frequency: Annual, March

14417 Insurance and Financial Communications Association Annual Conference
1037 N 3rd Ave
Tucson, AZ 85705

602-350-0717
E-Mail: info@ifcaonline.com
Home Page: www.ifcaonline.com
Social Media: *Facebook, Twitter, LinkedIn, YouTube*

Susan o'Neill, President
Ralph Chaump, VP
Kim Schultz, Secretary
Kim Schultz, Secretary

An international organization dedicated to the ongoing professional development of its members in life insurance and related financial services communications.
700 Members
Founded in 1933

14418 International Claim Association Conference
International Claim Association
1155 15th Street NW
Suite 500
Washington, DC 20005

202-452-0143
FAX 202-530-0659
E-Mail: cmurphy@claim.org
Home Page: www.claim.org

Marlon Nettleton, President
Christopher Murphy, Executive Director
Lisa Phillips, Secretary
400 Attendees
Frequency: Annual
Founded in 1909
Mailing list available for rent

14419 LAMP Annual Meeting
GAMA International

2901 Telestar Court
Suite 140
Falls Church, VA 22042-1205

703-770-8184
FAX 703-770-8182
E-Mail: gamamail@gamaweb.com
Home Page: www.gamaweb.com

Nicole Travers, Meetings/Products Administrator
Delaine Everett, Meetings/Convention Director

The event for field leaders in the insurance and financial services industry. Featuring top-notch main platform speaker presentations, more than 30 leading practices concurrent sessions, resource center with more than 50 exhibitors that will be offering valuable products and services and networking opportunities with your peers.
Frequency: Annual/March
ISSN: 1095-7367
Printed in 4 colors on glossy stock

14420 LIC Annual Meeting
Life Insurers Council
2300 Windy Ridge Parkway
Suite 600
Atlanta, GA 30339-8443

770-984-3724
800-275-5662
FAX 770-984-3780
E-Mail: askloma@loma.org
Home Page: www.loma.org/IndexPage-LIC.asp

Michael H Siris, Executive Director
Rose Hoyt, Administrative Assistant

Designed to educate members about critical issues for competing in today's regulatory, legislative and business climates.
Frequency: Annual/May
Mailing list available for rent

14421 MDRT Annual Meeting
Million Dollar Round Table
325 W Touhy Avenue
Park Ridge, IL 60068-4265

847-926-6378
FAX 847-518-8921
E-Mail: meetings@mdrt.org
Home Page: www.mdrt.org

Ray Kopcinski, Meeting Services Director
Jody Egel, Meeting Coordinator
Kathryn H Pagura, Meeting Coordinator
John Prast, Executive Vice President
Scott Brennan, Secretary

Known throughout the industry as the premier meeting for financial professionals. Motivational stories, educational sessions, experienced colleagues, networking opportunities come together at these annual meetings.
Frequency: Annual/June

14422 NACA Convention
National Association of Catastrophe Adjusters
PO Box 821864
North Richland Hills, TX 76182-1864

817-498-3466
FAX 817-498-0480
E-Mail: nacatadj@aol.com
Home Page: www.nacatadj.org

Lori Ringo, Executive Administrator

Annual convention and business meeting offering continuing education credits for some states; also a vendor show. Convention is held in Las Vegas, NV.
200 Attendees
Frequency: January
Founded in 1976

14423 NADP Annual Conference
National Association of Dental Plans

8111 LBJ Freeway
Suite 935
Dallas, TX 75251-1347

972-458-6998
FAX 972-458-2258
E-Mail: info@nadp.org
Home Page: www.nadp.org

Evelyn F Ireland, CAE, Executive Director
Tim Brown, Executive Assistant
Jeremy May, Executive Assistant

Get the greater industry insight, re-energized creativity and influential contacts.
Frequency: Annual/September

14424 NAIFA Convention and Career Conference
Ntl Association of Insurance & Financial Advisors
2901 Telestar Court
PO Box 12012
Falls Church, VA 22042-1205

703-770-8100
877-866-2432
FAX 703-770-8201
E-Mail: membersupport@naifa.org
Home Page: www.naifa.org

Robert O. Smith, President
Matthew S. Tassey, Treasurer
Juli McNeely, Secretary
Susan B. Waters, CEO
Susan B Waters, Deputy Chief Executive Officer

Features educational workshops from more than a dozen prominent speakers and the NAIFA Expo, one of the largest exhibits of financial services and products in the nation.
2000 Attendees
Frequency: Annual/September
Founded in 1890

14425 NAIIA Annual Conference
National Association of Independent Insurance Adj.
825 W State Street
Suite 117-C&B
Geneva, IL 60134

630-397-5012
FAX 630-397-5013
E-Mail: assist@naiia.com
Home Page: www.naiia.com

David F Mehren, Executive Director
Brenda Reisenger, President
Mark Nixon, Secretary, Treasurer

Attendance is open to claims handling professionals.
Frequency: Annual

14426 NAPIA Annual Meeting
National Association of Public Insurance Adjusters
21165 Whitfield Place
Suite 105
Potomac Falls, VA 20165

703-433-9217
FAX 703-433-0369
E-Mail: info@napia.com
Home Page: www.napia.com

David W Barrack, Executive Director
Ronald R. Reitz, President

Education sessions, networking and social events and exhibits by industry suppliers.
Frequency: Annual/June
Mailing list available for rent

14427 National Association of Independent Life Brokerage Agencies Conference
National Assn of Independent Life Brokerage Agents

8201 Greensboro Drive
Suite 300
Mc Lean, VA 22102-3814

703-610-9011
FAX 703-524-2303

Annual conference and exhibits of equipment, supplies and services for licensed independent life insurance brokerage agencies that represent at least 3 insurance companies, but are not controlled or owned by an underwriting company.
Frequency: November, San Diego

14428 National Association of Life Underwriters Conference
1922 F Street NW
Washington, DC 20006-4394

202-331-6099
FAX 202-331-2179

William V Regan III, Executive VP
Teresa Bonnema, Advertising Account

Sales professionals in life and health insurance and other financial services. 110 booths.
3.5M Attendees
Frequency: September

14429 National Association of Mutual Insurance Companies Annual Convention & Expo
National Association of Mutual Insurance Companies
3601 Vincennes Road
#68700
Indianapolis, IN 46268-1154

317-875-5250
FAX 317-879-8408
E-Mail: bnastally@namic.org
Home Page: www.namic.org

Charles Chamness, President
Barbara Nastally, Program Director
Kristen Eichhorn, Program Director
Gregg Dykstra, COO

Convention and exhibit show for property/casualty insurance executives. Four day event.
1700 Attendees
Frequency: Fall
Founded in 1895

14430 New England Professional Insurance Agents Association Conference
1 Ash Street
Hopkinton, MA 01748-1822

508-497-2590

Stella Di Camilo, Show Manager

100 booths of insurance-related products.
1.5M Attendees
Frequency: November

14431 PIA Annual Convention and Trade Fair
Professional Insurance Agents Association of
VA & DC
8751 Park Central Dr., Suite 140
Richmond, VA 23227

804-264-2582
FAX 804-266-1075
E-Mail: pia@piavadc.com
Home Page: www.piavadc.com
Social Media: *Facebook, Twitter*

Dennis Yooom, Executive VP
Lori Lohr, Education Manager
Carol Throokmorton, Accounting Manager
Founded in 1936

14432 PLRB/LIRB Claims Conference & Insurance Expo
PLRB/LIRB-Property Loss Research Bureau

3025 Highland Parkway
Suite 800
Downers Grove, IL 60515-1291

630-242-2250
888-711-7572
FAX 630-724-2260
E-Mail: pdispensa@lirb.org
Home Page: www.lirb.org

Tom Mallin, President
Paul C Despensa, VP/General Counsel

Concept sessions that feature a thorough presentation of a topic by expert panelists. A forum of experts/panels that will discuss controversial topics in response to questions and comments from participants on a range of subjects outlined in the agenda for that forum. Participants form a small discussion group to reach consensus on hypothetical problems. Each table debates and defends its conclusions with other groups.
Frequency: April
Mailing list available for rent

14433 PRIMA Annual Conference Trade Show
700 S. Washington St.
Suite 218
Alexandria, VA 22314

703-528-7701
FAX 703-739-0200
E-Mail: info@primacentral.org
Home Page: www.primacentral.org
Social Media: *Facebook, Twitter, LinkedIn*

Marshall Davies, Executive Director
Jon Ruzan, Editor
Jennifer Ackerman, Deputy Executive Director
Bles Dones, Manager, Member Services
Paulette Washington, Office Administrator

Containing 150 exhibits concerning insuring the public.
2,200 Attendees
Frequency: June
Founded in 1976
Mailing list available for rent

14434 Physician Insurers Association of America Annual Conference
Physician Insurers Association of America
2275 Research Boulevard
Rockville, MD 20850-3268

301-947-9000
FAX 301-947-9090

Annual exhibits related to physician liability insurance.

14435 Professional Insurance Agents National Annual Conference & Exhibition
National Association of Prof. Insurance Agents
400 N Washington Street
Alexandria, VA 22314-2312

703-836-9340
FAX 703-836-1279
Home Page: http://www.pianet.com

Ted Besesparis, VP

Annual conference and exhibits of equipment, supplies and services for independent property and casualty agents.

14436 Public Agency Risk Managers Association Convention
Public Agency Risk Managers Association
PO Box 6810
San Jose, CA 95150-6810

Annual convention and exhibits of risk management equipment, supplies and services.

14437 Risk Insurance Management Society
1065 Avenue of Americas
13th Floor
New York, NY 10018

212-286-9292
E-Mail: chapterservices@RIMS.org
Home Page: www.rims.org

Brian Stevenson, Show Manager
Mary Roth, Manager
Fran Jordan, Manager

500 booths of premier insurance companies and associated service companies.
5M Attendees

14438 Securities Industry and Financial Markets Association (SIFMA) Annual Meeting
1101 New York Avenue Nw
8th Floor
Washington, DC 20005

202-962-7300
FAX 202-962-7305
Home Page: www.sifma.org
Social Media: *Facebook, Twitter, LinkedIn*

T Timothy Ryan Jr, President/CEO
Randy Snook, Senior Managing Director/EVP
Cheryl Crispen, Executive VP, Communications
Ira D. Hammerman, Senior Managing Director
David Krasner, Chief Financial Officer

The Securities Industry and Financial Markets Association/SIFMA Annual Meeting and Conference program addresses a variety of topics that may include competitiveness of the U.S. capital markets, global exchange consolidation, regulatory and legal initiatives, and trends in the fixed-income and capital markets.
Mailing list available for rent

14439 Society of Insurance Trainers and Educators Conference
2120 Market Street
Suite 108
San Francisco, CA 94114

415-621-2830
FAX 415-621-0889
E-Mail: ed@insurancetrainers.org
Home Page: www.insurancetrainers.org

Lois A Markovich, Executive Director

Forty booths. A major conference for those involved with training and education in the insurance industry.
200 Attendees
Frequency: June-July
Founded in 1953

14440 Sun States Professional Insurance Agents Association
13416 N 32nd Street
Suite 106
Phoenix, AZ 85032-6000

602-482-3333
Social Media: *Facebook, Twitter, LinkedIn*

Maryls M Graser, Executive VP

50 booths.
300 Attendees
Frequency: May

14441 VCIA Annual Meeeting
Vermont Captive Insurance Association
180 Battery Street
Suite 200
Burlington, VT 05401-5212

802-658-8242
FAX 802-658-9365
E-Mail: vcia@vcia.com
Home Page: www.vcia.com

Richard Smith, President
Diane Leach, Education/Program Planning

Director
Janice Valgoi, Membership/Development
Director
Elizabeth Halpern, Communications Director
Peggy Companion, Director of Finance
Frequency: August
Founded in 1985

**14442 WCRI Annual Issues & Research
Conference**
Workers Compensation Research Institute
955 Massachusetts Ave.
Cambridge, MA 02139

617-661-9274
FAX 617-661-9284
E-Mail: wcri@wcrinet.org
Home Page: www.wcrinet.org/conference.html

Vincent Armentano, Chair
Richard A. Victor, President & CEO

**14443 Women Life Underwriters
Confederation**
1126 S 70th Street
Suite S-106
Milwaukee, WI 53214-3151

800-776-3008
FAX 414-475-2585

Ann Wells, Managing Director

For women insurance agents, their managers
and their companies. 20 booths.
100 Attendees
Frequency: September

Directories & Databases

14444 ADP Parts Exchange New
ADP Claims Services Group
2010 Crow Canyon Place
San Ramon, CA 94583

925-866-1100
Home Page: www.adpclaims.com

Provides an electronic link from your ADP estimating system to comprehensive database of
new replacement parts. Data on over three and
a half million parts facilitates the writing of
complete, cost-effective damage reports.

14445 Adjusters Reference Guide
Bar List Publishing Company
425 Huehl Road
Building 6B
Northbrook, IL 60062-2323

847-498-6133
800-726-1007
FAX 847-498-6695
E-Mail: info@barlist.com
Home Page: www.barlist.com

Bruce Rodgers, President
Leslie Rodgers, Production Manager

A professional service for anyone who handles
insurance claims. It contains a complete set of
ISO Policy and Forms and is divided into two
major categories; Personal Lines and Commercial Lines.
Frequency: Annual

**14446 Best's Directory of Recommended
Insurance Attorneys and Adjusters**
AM Best Company
Ambest Rd
Oldwick, NJ 08858

908-439-2200
FAX 908-439-3296
E-Mail: webmaster@ambest.com
Home Page: www.ambest.com

Arthur Snyder, CEO

Includes over 5,300 insurance defense law
firms and over 1,200 insurance adjusters companies recommended by the insurance industry.
Includes a section on expert services providers,
insurance company groups or fleets, legal and
claims services, officials and a digest of insurance laws.
Cost: $1205.00
5100 Pages
Frequency: Annual
Circulation: 19,000
Founded in 1928

14447 Best's Insurance News & Analysis
AM Best Company
Ambest Rd
Oldwick, NJ 08858

908-439-2200
800-424-2378
FAX 908-439-3296
E-Mail: editor_br@bestreview.com
Home Page: www.ambest.com

Arthur Snyder, Chairman & President
Paul Tinnirello, CIO
Larry Mayewski, Chief Rating Officer

Best's Insurance News & Analysis makes it
easy to take advantage of A.M. Best's extensive insurance news and industry research. A
Best's Insurance News & Analysis subscription
grants you access to a full range of news products as well as unique statistical studies and
special reports - all of which are accessible
from one convenient online location. Allows
access to receive BestDay, BestWeek, Best's
Review, and Best's Special Reports.

14448 Best's Insurance Reports
AM Best Company
Ambest Rd
Oldwick, NJ 08858

908-439-2200
FAX 908-439-3296
E-Mail: webmaster@ambest.com
Home Page: www.ambest.com

Arthur Snyder, CEO

Published in two editions - life-health insur-
ance and property-casualty insurance, United
States and Canada.
Cost: $570.00
Frequency: Annual

**14449 Best's Insurance Reports:
International Edition**
AM Best Company
Ambest Rd
Oldwick, NJ 08858

908-439-2200
FAX 908-439-3296
E-Mail: webmaster@ambest.com
Home Page: www.ambest.com

Arthur Snyder, CEO

Offers information on over 800 insurance companies in Canada, Europe, Asia, Africa, Australia, and South America that offer life/health
and property/casulaty insurance policies.
Cost: $495.00
1200 Pages
Frequency: Annual

14450 Best's Key Rating Guide
AM Best Company
Ambest Rd
Oldwick, NJ 08858

908-439-2200
FAX 908-439-3296
E-Mail: webmaster@ambest.com
Home Page: www.ambest.com

Arthur Snyder, CEO
Larry Mayewski, Editor

Financial and operating characteristics on over
2,600 major property/casualty insurance com-

panies, over 1,750 major life and health
insurance companies.
Cost: $95.00
Frequency: Annual August

14451 Best's Market Guide
AM Best Company
Ambest Rd
Oldwick, NJ 08858

908-439-2200
FAX 908-439-3296
E-Mail: webmaster@ambest.com
Home Page: www.ambest.com

Arthur Snyder, CEO

In each volume, separate volumes for corporate
stocks, corporate bonds, and municipal bonds,
a list of insurance company investment officers
are offered.
Cost: $1425.00
Frequency: 3-Volume Set

**14452 Business Insurance Directory of
Reinsurance Intermediaries**
Crain Communications
360 N Michigan Ave
Chicago, IL 60601-3800

312-649-5200
800-678-9595
FAX 312-649-7937
Home Page: www.crain.com

Keith Crain, CEO
Sandra L Budde, Editor

Lists nearly 100 reinsurance intermediaries in
the United States and Bermuda.
Cost: $4.00
Frequency: Annual
Circulation: 53,000

**14453 Captive Insurance Company
Directory**
Tillinghast/Towers Perrin Company
263 Tresser Boulevard
Stamford, CT 06901-3236

203-631-1900
FAX 203-326-5498

Corinne Ramming, Editor

Lists over 3,000 captive insurance companies
and their parent or sponsor companies; management companies and insurance subsidiary
investment advisors.
Cost: $210.00
270 Pages
Frequency: Annual

**14454 Certified Claims Professional
Accreditation Council**
PO Box 441110
Fort Washington, MD 20749-1110

301-292-1988
FAX 301-292-1787
Home Page: www.lattmag.com

Dale L Anderson, Editor

Offers a variety of information on members of
the CCPAC and certified claims professionals.
76 Pages
Circulation: 350

14455 Claim Service Guide
Bar List Publishing Company
425 Huehl Road
Building 6B
Northbrook, IL 60062-2323

847-498-6133
800-726-1007
FAX 847-498-6695
E-Mail: info@barlist.com
Home Page: www.barlist.com

Bruce Rodgers, President
Edna MacMillan, Editor

National Directory of Independent Insurance Adjusters, Appraisers, Expert Consultants and Property Specialists. Distributed to every home and branch office insurance company claims manager.
Cost: $80.00
Frequency: Annual
Circulation: 13,000

14456 Corporate Yellow Book
Leadership Directories
104 5th Ave
New York, NY 10011-6901

212-627-4140
FAX 212-645-0931
E-Mail: corporate@leadershipdirectories.com
Home Page: www.leadershipdirectories.com
Social Media: *Facebook, Twitter*

David Hurvitz, CEO

Contact information for over 48,000 executives at over 1,000 companies and more than 9,000 board members and their outside affiliations.
Cost: $360.00
1,400 Pages
Frequency: Quarterly
ISSN: 1058-2098
Founded in 1969

14457 Custom Publishing & News Services
Information
7707 Old Georgetown Rd
Suite 700
Bethesda, MD 20814

301-215-4688
FAX 301-215-4600
E-Mail: acarr@mail.infoinc.com
Home Page: www.infoinc.com
Alain Carr, Owner
Offers evaluations of companies on their claims-paying ability.

14458 Directory of Corporate Buyers
Crain Communications Inc
360 N Michigan Ave
Chicago, IL 60601-3800

312-649-5200
FAX 312-649-7937
Home Page: www.crain.com

Keith Crain, CEO

Provides complete contact information for more that 3,200 top level corporate executives from Fortune 500 companies involved in risk management and employee benefits.
Frequency: Annual

14459 Directory of Employee Assistance Program Providers
Crain Communications Inc
360 N Michigan Ave
Chicago, IL 60601-3800

312-649-5200
FAX 312-649-7937
Home Page: www.crain.com

Keith Crain, CEO

Lists organizations that provide a variety of EAP services to employers on a direct, stand alone basis.
Frequency: Annual
Circulation: 50,000

14460 Directory of Property Loss Control Consultants
Crain Communications
360 N Michigan Ave
Chicago, IL 60601-3800

312-649-5200
FAX 312-649-7937
Home Page: www.crain.com

Keith Crain, CEO

Lists companies that provide loss control services on a direct, unbundled basis. Consultants that provide loss control assistance only in conjunction with other services such as brokering insurance are not listed.
Frequency: Annual
Circulation: 53,000

14461 Directory of Specialty Markets Issue
Insurance Journal
9191 Towne Centre Drive
Suite 550
San Diego, CA 92122-1231

619-584-1100
FAX 619-584-1200

Mark Wells, Editor

Lists about 200 insurance companies and surplus lines brokers offering specialty lines to insurance agents and brokers in California, Arizona, Alaska, Oregon, Hawaii and Washington.
Cost: $10.00
Frequency: SemiAnnual
Circulation: 10,400

14462 HMO/PPO Directory
Grey House Publishing
4919 Route 22
PO Box 56
Amenia, NY 12501

518-789-8700
800-562-2139
FAX 845-373-6390
E-Mail: books@greyhouse.com
Home Page: www.greyhouse.com
Social Media: *Facebook, Twitter*

Leslie Mackenzie, Publisher
Richard Gottlieb, Editor
The HMO/PPO Directory is a comprehensive source that provides detailed information about Health Maintenance Organizations and Preferred Provider Organizations nationwide. Within the HMO/PPO Profiles, over 1,300 HMOs, PPOs and affiliated companies are listed, arranged alphabetically by state.
Cost: $325.00
600 Pages
ISBN: 1-592373-69-0
Founded in 1981

14463 HMO/PPO Directory - Online Database
Grey House Publishing
4919 Route 22
PO Box 56
Amenia, NY 12501-0056

518-789-8700
800-562-2139
FAX 518-789-0556
E-Mail: gold@greyhouse.com
Home Page: www.gold.greyhouse.com
Social Media: *Facebook, Twitter*

Leslie Mackenzie, Publisher
Richard Gottlieb, President
The HMO/PPO Directory - Online Database is your in-depth searchable guide to health plans nationwide - their contact information, key executives, plan information and more. The online database is a necessary tool when researching or marketing a product or service to this important industry.
Founded in 1981

14464 III Data Base Search
Insurance Information Institute

110 William St
New York, NY 10038-3908

212-346-5500
FAX 212-732-1916
Home Page: www.iii.org

Gary Johnson, Manager
Cary Schneider, Executive Vice President
Provides citations and abstracts of insurance-related literature appearing in magazines, newspapers and trade publications and books.

14465 III Insurance Daily
Insurance Information Institute
110 William St
New York, NY 10038-3908

212-346-5500
FAX 212-732-1916
Home Page: www.iii.org

Gary Johnson, Manager
Cary Schneider, Executive Vice President
This insurance database provides summaries of news and articles relating to the property and casualty insurance industry.
Frequency: Full-text

14466 IRU Members +
Intermediaries and Reinsurance
Underwriters Assoc
971 Rte 202 North
Branchburg, NJ 08876

908-203-0211
FAX 908-203-0213
E-Mail: info@irua.com
Home Page: www.irua.com

Jim Brost, President
List of all member companies and contacts; conference and attendee list provided to attendees only.
Founded in 1967

14467 Independent Insurance
Independent Insurance Agents of America
127 S Peyton St
Alexandria, VA 22314-2803

703-683-4422
800-221-7917
FAX 703-683-7556
E-Mail: info@iiaba.net
Home Page: www.independentagent.com
Social Media: *Facebook, Twitter*

Robert A Rusbuldt, CEO
Alex Soto, President
This web site contains information for consumers on property and casualty insurance including homeowner, renter, landlord, and automobile insurance.
Frequency: Full-text
Founded in 1896
Mailing list available for rent

14468 Insurance Almanac
Underwriter Printing & Publishing Company
244 North Main St.
P.O. Box 622
New City, NY 10956

845-634-2720
FAX 845-634-2989
E-Mail: jgcrothers@criterionpub.com
Home Page: www.criterioninsurancedirectory.com

Over 3,000 insurance companies that write fire, casualty, accident, health and life insurance policies.
650 Pages
Frequency: Annual
Circulation: 10,000

14469 Insurance Bar Directory
Bar List Publishing Company

425 Huehl Road
Building 6B
Northbrook, IL 60062-2323

847-498-6133
800-726-1007
FAX 847-498-6695
E-Mail: info@barlist.com
Home Page: www.barlist.com

Bruce Rodgers, President
Edna MacMillin, Editor
Leslie Rodgers, Production Manager

National Directory of Insurance Defense Attorneys that is distributed to all insurance company home office and branch office company executives and claims personnel.
Cost: $80.00
Frequency: Annual
Circulation: 40,000

14470 Insurance Companies' Directory List of Mortgage Directors
Communication Network International
3918 Avenue T
Brooklyn, NY 11234-5028

718-396-6245

Listing of 210 mortgage offices of major insurance companies that make real estate mortgages and related investments.
Cost: $75.00
Founded in 1993

14471 Kelly Casualty Insurance Claims Directory
Francis B Kelley & Associates
123 Veteran Avenue
Los Angeles, CA 90024-1900

800-328-4144
FAX 310-472-1290
Home Page: www.fbka.com

Francis B Kelley, Editor

Lists only casualty insurance claims payment offices. Workers' Compensation and Auto Insurance can pay health care providers for their services. Directory covers Casualty Insurance Companies, Independent Claims Companies, Insurance Commissioners with their Web sites.
Cost: $150.00
280 Pages
Frequency: Annual

14472 LEXIS Insurance Law Library
Mead Data Central
9443 Springboro Pike
Dayton, OH 45401

888-223-6337
FAX 518-487-3584
Home Page: www.lexis-nexis.com

Andrew Prozes, CEO
Rebecca Schmitt, Chief Financial Officer

This full database contains the complete text of the insurance statutes for 50 states, the District of Columbia and Puerto Rico.
Frequency: Full-text

14473 LOMA's Information Center Database
Life Office Management Association
2300 Windy Ridge Pkwy SE
Suite 600
Atlanta, GA 30339-5665

770-951-1770
800-275-5662
FAX 770-984-0441
E-Mail: infoctr@loma.org
Home Page: www.loma.org

Thomas P Donaldson, President/CEO
Jerry Woo, Director
Robert Lai, Managing Director

A team of experienced researchers provide current data utilizing our comprehensive database. More than 10,000 documents are maintained and updated. A comprehensive list of Industry Research Links can also be found in this area.
Frequency: Available to Members

14474 Life Insurance Selling: Sources Issue
Commerce Publishing Company
330 N 4th Street
Suite 200
Saint Louis, MO 63102-2041

314-421-5445
FAX 314-421-1070

Larry Albright, Editor

Lists life insurance companies, publishers of software used in the insurance field and financial planning corporations.
Cost: $7.00
Frequency: 45000

14475 Life Office Management Association Directory
5770 Powers Ferry Road NW
Atlanta, GA 30327-4350

770-953-6872
FAX 770-984-0441

Philippa Griffith, Editor

Offers information on life insurance and financial service companies.
190 Pages
Frequency: Annual

14476 Morningstar
Morningstar
225 W Washington Street
Chicago, IL 60602

312-384-4000
FAX 312-696-6001
E-Mail: productinfo@morningstar.com
Home Page: www.morningstar.com

Joe Mansueto, Chairman & CEO
Chris Boruff, President, Software Division
Peng Chen, President, Global Investment Div.
Bevin Desmond, President, International Operations
Scott Cooley, Chief Financial Officer

Morningstar provides data on approximately 330,000 investment offerings, including stocks, mutual funds, and similar vehicles, along with real-time global market data on more than 5 million equities, indexes, futures, options, commodities, and precious metals, in addition to foreign exchange and Treasury markets. Morningstar also offers investment management services and has more than $167 billion in assets under advisement and management.

14477 NAIC Database
National Association of Insurance Commissioners
1100 Walnut Street
Suite 1500
Kansas City, MO 64106-2197

816-842-3600
FAX 816-783-8175
Home Page: www.naic.org

Sandy Praeger, President
Andrew Beal, CEO
Kevin M. McCarty, President
James J. Donelon, President-Elect
Monica J. Lindeen, Secretary-Treasurer
Mailing list available for rent

14478 National Association of Catastrophe Adjusters Membership Directory
National Association of Catastrophe Adjusters

PO Box 821864
North Richland Hills, TX 76182-1864

817-498-3466
FAX 817-498-0480
E-Mail: nacatadj@aol.com
Home Page: www.nacatadj.org

Lori Ringo, Executive Administrator
Frequency: Annual
Circulation: 2000
Founded in 1976

14479 National Insurance Law Service/Insource Insurance
NILS Publishing Company
PO Box 2507
Chatsworth, CA 91313-2507

818-998-8830
800-423-5910
FAX 818-718-8482
Home Page: www.nils.com

Jon Fish, Circulation Director
Karen G Beaudoin, VP Marketing
Jonathon K Fish, Production Manager

This insurance database contains the complete text of insurance codes, related laws, regulations, bulletins and selected attorney general opinions for all 50 states and the federal government. Available on CD-ROm and in looseleaf print. The CD-ROM service 'Insource Insurance' is accessible for licensed users on the NILS Publishing Website.
Cost: $520.00
Frequency: Monthly Updates
Circulation: 5,000

14480 National Underwriter Kirschner's Insurance Directories (Red Book)
National Underwriter Company
5081 Olympic Blvd
Erlanger, KY 41018-3164

859-692-2100
FAX 859-692-2295
Home Page: www.nationalunderwriter.com

Charlie Smith, CEO
Charlie Smith, Chief Executive Officer

This series of 24 directories are published by state or region. Listings include companies, brokers and agents and services for each state handling property and casualty.
Cost: $19.95
150+ Pages
Frequency: Semi-Annual/Annual
Printed in on matte stock

14481 Profiles: Health Insurance Edition
National Underwriter Company
5081 Olympic Blvd
Erlanger, KY 41018-3164

859-692-2100
800-543-0874
FAX 859-692-2295
Home Page: www.nationalunderwriter.com

Charlie Smith, CEO

Your reliable resource for up-to-date news and information in the life & health insurance/financial services industry.
Cost: $39.95
300 Pages
Frequency: Annual

14482 Profiles: Property and Casualty Insurance Edition
National Underwriter Company
505 Gest Street
Cincinnati, OH 45203-1716

513-723-0012

Edward A Lyon, Editor

Offers information on more than 1,500 property and liability insurance companies.
Cost: $39.95
852 Pages
Frequency: Annual

14483 Register of North American Insurance Companies

American Preeminent Registry
PO Box 622
Old Bridge, NJ 08857-0622

732-225-5533

Brian Axelrod, Publisher

Directory of services and supplies to the industry.
Cost: $125.00
450 Pages
Frequency: Annual

14484 Risk Retention Group Directory and Guide

Insurance Communications
PO Box 50147
Pasadena, CA 91115-0147

626-796-4972
FAX 626-796-4972
Home Page: http://www.rrr.com

Karen Cutts, Editor

Offers information on over 80 risk retention groups formed under the 1986 Risk Retention Act or the 1981 Product Liability Risk Retention Act through 1990.
Cost: $165.00
144 Pages
Frequency: Annual

14485 Shortcut 2: Insurance Markets Tracking Systems

National Underwriter Company
505 Gest Street
Cincinnati, OH 45203-1716

513-723-0012

Directory of services and supplies to the industry.
Cost: $300.00

14486 Society of Professional Benefit Administrators

Society of Professional Benefit
Administrators
2 Wisconsin Circle
Suite 670
Chevy Chase, MD 20815

301-718-7722
FAX 301-718-9440
E-Mail: info@spbatpa.org
Home Page: www.spbatpa.org

Anne Lennan, President

For members only. Discusses and analyzes government compliance requirements of administration and plan design and industry and market trends
300 Members
350 Attendees
Frequency: 2x/Year
Founded in 1975

14487 Statistics of Fraternal Benefit Societies

1240 Iroquois Avenue
Suite 300
Naperville, IL 60563-8476

630-355-6633
FAX 630-355-0042
Home Page: www.nfcanet.org

Anthony Snyder, Communications Director

NFCA membership is currently made up of 82 fraternal benefit societies in the United States and Canada. Each of these societies pay annual membership dues to belong to the organization and it is their executives, employees and grass-roots members who serve on the NFCA Board of Directors and various NFCA committees and sections.
Cost: $11.00

14488 TPA Directory

Society of Professional Benefit
Administrators
2 Wisconsin Circle
Suite 670
Chevy Chase, MD 20815

301-718-7722
FAX 301-718-9440
E-Mail: info@spbatpa.org
Home Page: www.spbatpa.org

Frederick D Hunt Jr, President
Anne C Lennan, President-Elect

Detailed description of contact information and types of plans and services and size of each firm in an easy-to-cross-reference and compare format.
Cost: $495.00
Mailing list available for rent

14489 WESTLAW Insurance Library

West Publishing Company
610 Opperman Drive
Eagan, MN 55123-1340

651-687-7327
Home Page: www.westgroup.com

This database offers information on US state laws relating to the insurance industry.
Frequency: Full-text

14490 Weiss Ratings Consumer Box Set

Grey House Publishing
4919 Route 22
PO Box 56
Amenia, NY 12501

518-789-8700
800-562-2139
FAX 845-373-6390
E-Mail: books@greyhouse.com
Home Page: www.greyhouse.com
Social Media: *Facebook, Twitter*

Leslie Mackenzie, Publisher
Richard Gottlieb, Editor

Each guide in the Weiss Ratings Consumer Box Set is packed with accurate, unbiased information, including helpful, step-by-step Worksheets & Planners. The set consists of Consumer Guides to Variable Annuities, Elder Care Choices, Medicare Supplement Insurance, Medicare Prescription Drug Coverage, Homeowners Insurance, Automobile Insurance, Long-Term Care Insurance, and Term Life Insurance.
Cost: $249.00
600 Pages
Frequency: Quarterly
Founded in 1981

14491 Weiss Ratings Guide to Health Insurers

Grey House Publishing
4919 Route 22
PO Box 56
Amenia, NY 12501

518-789-8700
800-562-2139
FAX 845-373-6390
E-Mail: books@greyhouse.com
Home Page: www.greyhouse.com
Social Media: *Facebook, Twitter*

Leslie Mackenzie, Publisher
Richard Gottlieb, Editor

Weiss Ratings Guide to Health Insurers is the first and only source to cover the financial stability of the nation's health care system, rating the financial safety of more than 6,000 health maintenance organizations (HMOs) and all of the Blue Cross Blue Shield plans - updated quarterly to ensure the most accurate, up-to-date informations.
Cost: $249.00
600 Pages
Frequency: Quarterly
Founded in 1981

14492 Weiss Ratings Guide to Life & Annuity Insurers

Grey House Publishing
4919 Route 22
PO Box 56
Amenia, NY 12501

518-789-8700
800-562-2139
FAX 845-373-6390
E-Mail: books@greyhouse.com
Home Page: www.greyhouse.com
Social Media: *Facebook, Twitter*

Leslie Mackenzie, Publisher
Richard Gottlieb, Edtior

Each easy-to-use edition provides independent, unbiased ratings on the financial strength of 1,000 life and annuity insurers, including companies providing life insurance, annuities, guaranteed investment contracts (GICs) and other pension products.
Cost: $249.00
600 Pages
Frequency: Quarterly
Founded in 1981

14493 Weiss Ratings Guide to Property & Casualty Insurers

Grey House Publishing
4919 Route 22
PO Box 56
Amenia, NY 12501

518-789-8700
800-562-2139
FAX 845-373-6390
E-Mail: books@greyhouse.com
Home Page: www.greyhouse.com
Social Media: *Facebook, Twitter*

Leslie Mackenzie, Publisher
Richard Gottlieb, Editor

Updated quarterly, this publication is the only resource that provides independent, unbiased ratings and analyses on the 2,400 insurers offering auto & homeowners, business, worker's compensation, product liability, medical malpractice and other professional liability insurance in the United States.
Cost: $249.00
600 Pages
Frequency: Quarterly
Founded in 1981

14494 Yearbook of the Insurance Industry

American Association of Managing General Agents
150 S Warner Rd
Suite 156
King of Prussia, PA 19406-2832

610-225-1999
FAX 610-225-1996
Home Page: www.aamga.org

Bernie Heinz, Executive Director

250 managing general agents of insurance companies and more than 500 branch offices; coverage includes Canada.
Frequency: Annual Spring

Industry Web Sites

14495 http://gold.greyhouse.com

G.O.L.D Grey House OnLine Databases

Grey House Publishing's online database platform, GOLD, offers Quick Search, Keyword Search and Expert Search for most business sectors including insurance markets. The GOLD platform makes finding the information you need quick and easy - whether you're a novice searcher or an experienced database user. All of Grey House's directory products are available for subscription on the GOLD platform.

14496 www.aaimco.com

American Association of Insurance Management Consultants

Supports the insurance management industry.

14497 www.aaimedicine.org

American Academy of Insurance Medicine

This organization offers information and legislative updates for people in the medical insurance field.

14498 www.actuary.org

American Academy of Actuaries

The AAA is a public policy organization for actuaries within the US The Academy acts as the public information organization for the profession. Assisting public policy process through the presentation of clear actuarial analysis, the Academy regularly prepares testimony for Congress, provides information to federal elected officials, regulators and congressional staff, comments on proposed federal regulations, and works closely with state officials on issues related to insurance.

14499 www.aha.org

American Society for Healthcare Risk Management

National organization for the health care industry risk management equipment, supplies and services.

14500 www.aicpcu.org

Insurance Institute of America

Sponsors programs for property and casualty insurance firms, conducts exams and award certificates. Maintains a library.

14501 www.aicpeu.org

American Institute for CPCU

An independent, nonprofit educational organization that confers the Chartered Property Casualty Underwriter professional designation on those individuals who meet its education and ethics requirements.

14502 www.allianceai.org

Alliance of American Insurers

Trade association of property and casualty insurers providing educational, legislative and safety services to its members.

14503 www.apiw.org

Association of Professional Insurance Women

Promotes cooperation and understanding among members. Maintains high professional standards and provides a network of professional contacts. Encourages women in industry.

14504 www.arbifile.org

Arbitration Forums

Arbitration Forums is a not-for-profit provider of intercompany insurance dispute resolution services. More than 2,000 insurers and self-insurers participate in AF's programs. AF resolves over 250,000 disputes with a claim value approaching 1 billion dollars.

14505 www.arminet.com

Associated Risk Managers International

Develops specialized insurance/risk management services for trade associations, professional groups and other industry organizations. Conducts seminars and sponsors competitions.

14506 www.asppa.org

American Society of Pension Professionals & Act

(ASPPA) ia a national organization for career retirement paln professionals. The membership consists of the many disciplines supporting retirement income management and benefits policy. Its members are part of the diversified, technical, and highly regulated benefits industry. ASPPA represents those who have made a career of retirement plan and pension policy work.

14507 www.awpc.org

Association of Workers' Compensation Professionals

A nonprofit organization for those engaged in the field of workers' compensation, providing members with training and certification.

14508 www.ccactuaries.org

Conference of Consulting Actuaries

Full-time consulting actuaries.

14509 www.easternclaimsconference.com

Eastern Claims Conference

Provides education and training to examiners, managers, and officers who review medical and disability claims. Holds seminars for life, health and disability clinics.

14510 www.financialpro.org

Society of Financial Service Professionals

Members are dedicated to the highest standards of competence and service in insurance and financial services.

14511 www.financialratingsseries.com

Grey House Publishing

Financial Ratings Series Online combines the strength of Weiss Ratings and TheStreet Ratings to offer the library community with a single source for financial strength ratings and financial planning tools covering Banks, Insurers, Mutual Funds and Stocks. This powerful database will provide the accurate, independent information consumers need to make informed decisions about their financial planning.

14512 www.fraternalalliance.org

American Fraternal Alliance

The trade association of America's fraternal benefit societies.

14513 www.greyhouse.com

Grey House Publishing

Authoritative reference directories for most business sectors including insurance markets. Users can search the online databases with varied search criteria allowing for custom searches by product category, geographic area, sales volume, keyword, subject and more. Full Grey House catalog and online ordering also available.

14514 www.highwaysafety.org

Insurance Institute for Highway Safety

Traffic and motor vehicle safety organization supported by auto insurers.

14515 www.hwsafety.org

Highway Loss Data Institute

Provides the public with insurance industry data concerning human and economic loss resulting from crashes.

14516 www.iasa.org

Insurance Accounting Systems Association

Facilitates the exchange of ideas among insurance industry professionals and their industry-related associates.

14517 www.icae.com

Insurance Consumer Affairs Exchange

Promotes professionalism and shapes the standards of behavior in relationships between insurance organizations, regulators and customers through proactive dialogue, research, communication and education.

14518 www.insuranceallnations.com

Allnations Insurance

Provides financial and technical assistance to new and developing cooperative insurance facilities. Promotes and develops all types of cooperative insurance organizations.

14519 www.irua.org

Intermediaries & Reinsurance Underwriters Assoc

A not-for-profit corporation, organized for the purposes of reinsurance education and research and the dissemination of information relevant to the reinsurance industry.

14520 www.ivans.com

Insurance Value Added Network Services

Industry-sponsored organization offering value added data communications network linking agencies, companies and providers of data to the insurance industry.

14521 www.nacatadj.org

National Association of Catastrophe Adjusters

Association of Catstrophe Insurance Adjusters and independent adjustment companies.

14522 www.nafi.org

National Association of Fire Investigators

Primary purpose of this association is to increase the knowledge and improve the skills of persons engaged in the investigation and analysis of fires, explosions, or in the litigation that ensues from such investigations. The Association also originated and implemented the National Certification Board.

14523 www.nafi921.org

National Association of Fire Investigators

Primary purpose is to increase the knowledge and improve the skills of persons engaged in the investigation and analysis of fires, explosions, or in the litigation that ensues from such investigations.

14524 www.nahu.org

National Association of Health Underwriters

Sponsors advanced health insurance underwriting and research seminars. Testifies before federal and state committees on pending health insurance legislation. Presents numerous awards.

14525 www.naiw.org

National Association of Insurance Women

Professional membership association for employees in all facets of the insurance industry. The association exists to promote continuing education and networking for the professional advancement of its members, and offers education programs, meetings, publications, services and leadership opportunities for its members' benefits.

14526 www.ncci.com
National Council on Compensation Insurance
Develops and administers rating plans and systems for workers compensation insurance.

14527 www.ncoil.org
National Conference of Insurance Legislators
NCOIL is an organization of state legislators whose main area of public policy concern is insurance legislation and regulation. Many legislators active in NCOIL either chair or are members of the committees responsible for insurance legislation in their respective state houses across the country.

14528 www.nonprofitrisk.org
Nonprofit Risk Management Center
Publishes materials and delivers workshops and conferences on risk management, liability and insurance issues of special concern to nonprofit organizations.

14529 www.ontherisk.org/houla/
Home Office Life Underwriters Association
Offers educational programs through the Academy Life Underwriting designed for professional home office underwriters.

14530 www.plrb.org
Property Loss Research Bureau
Provides access to legal and technical databases, legal research on property and inland marine coverage issues countrywide, claims education, and daily catastrophe information for a membership of 570 property/casualty insurance companies.

14531 www.sirnet.org
Society of Insurance Research
Members are individuals actively engaged in some form of insurance research.

14532 www.snl.com
SNL Securities
News articles on banks and thrifts, insurance and other financial services. Also features vital company information.

14533 www.snlnet.com
SNL Securities
This organization offers the most up-to-date information available in the insurance industry featuring the latest news releases, filings and important events. Provides current data on top-performing stocks, insider trades, ownership filings, company news and events and legislative issues.

14534 www.soa.org
Society of Actuaries
Nonprofit professional society of 17,000 members involved in the modeling and management of financial risk and contingent events. The mission of the SOA is to advance actuarial knowledge and to enhance the ability of actuaries to provide expert advice and relevant solutions for financial, business and societal problems involving uncertain future events.

14535 www.spbatpa.org
Society of Professional Benefit Administrators
National Association of Third Party Administrators (TPAs) of employee benefit health and pension plans. SPBA represents TPAs who offer comprehensive services.

14536 www.thefederation.org
Federation of Insurance and Corporate Counsel
For members of the bar who are actively engaged in the legal aspects of the insurance business, executives of insurance companies and associations and corporate counsel engaged in the defense of claims.

14537 www.thepiaa.org
Physician Insurers Association
Represents domestic and international medical malpractice insurance companies which are practioner-owned or controlled.

14538 www.transportlaw.com
Transportation Consumer Protection Council
Dedicated to the reduction of transit losses and the improvement of freight claim and freight charge payment procedures in domestic and international commerce.

14539 www.users.erols.com/spba
Society of Professional Benefit Administrators
Third-party contract administration (TPA) administers employee benefit plans for client employers and unions. It is estimated that 66 percent of US workers with employee benefits are in plans administered by TPA.

Associations

14540 American Floorcovering Alliance
210 West Cuyler Street
Dalton, GA 30720

706-278-4101
800-288-4101
FAX 706-278-5323
E-Mail: afa@americanfloor.org
Home Page: www.americanfloor.org
Social Media: *Facebook, RSS*

Wanda J. Ellis, Executive Director

Promotes the industry's products and services to the world, and educates the members and others through seminars, press releases, and trade shows.
Founded in 1979

14541 American Lighting Association
2050 N Stemmons Freeway
Ste 10046
Dallas, TX 75207

214-698-9898
800-605-4448
Home Page: www.americanlightingassoc.com
Social Media: *Facebook, YouTube*

Ray S. Angelo, Chair
Eric Jacobson, CAE, President/CEO
W. Lawrence Lauck, Vice President, Communications
Michael Weems, Vice President, Government Affairs
Beth Bentley, CMP, LA, Director of Confrences

A trade association uniting lighting; component manufacturers, showrooms/distributors, manufacturer representatives; industry related companies dedicated to providing quality residential illumination in the U.S., Canada and the Caribbean.
700 Members
Founded in 1945

14542 American Society of Interior Designers
608 Massachusetts Avenue NE
Washington, DC 20002-6006

202-546-3480
FAX 202-546-3240
E-Mail: membership@asid.org, asid@asid.org
Home Page: www.asid.org
Social Media: *Facebook, Twitter, LinkedIn, Stagram*

Thom Banks, COO
Randy Fiser, EVP/ CEO
Kevin Mulavaney, Marketing/Communications
Don Davis, Government/Public Affairs
Rick Peluso, CFO

The American Society of Interior Designers (ASID) is a community of people-designers, industry representatives, educators and students committed to interior design. Through education, knowledge sharing, advocacy, community building and outreach, the Society strives to advance the interior design profession and, in the process, to demonstrate and celebrate the power of design to positively change people's lives.
34500 Members
Founded in 1975

14543 Association of University Interior Design
1652 Cross Center Drive
Norman, OK 73019-5050

FAX 405-325-4164
Home Page: www.auid.org

Debra Barresse, President
Sara Powell, First VP

Debi Miller, Second VP
Susan Carlyle, Secretary
Lisa Kring, Treasurer

Provides a network for individuals who work within institutions of higher education and to promote activities designed to benefit its members through education, research, and communication.
Founded in 1979

14544 Association of the Wall and Ceiling Industry
513 West Broad Street
Suite 210
Falls Church, VA 22046

703-538-1600
FAX 703-534-8307
E-Mail: info@awci.org
Home Page: www.awci.org
Social Media: *Facebook, Twitter, LinkedIn, YouTube*

Scott Casabona, President
John Hinson, VP
Mike Taylor, Treasurer
Ed Sellers, Secretary
Steven A. Etkin, Executive Vice President/CEO

Represents acoustic systems, ceiling systems, drywall systems, exterior insulation and finishing systms, fireproofing, flooring systems, insulation, and stucco contractors, suppliers and manufacturers and those in allied trades.
2400 Members
Founded in 1918
Mailing list available for rent

14545 Carpet Cushion Council
5103 Brandywine Drive
Eagleville, PA 19043

484-687-5170
FAX 610-885-5131
Home Page: www.carpetcushion.org

Chris Bradley, President
Gary Lanser, Vice President
Bob Ambrose, Secretary
Mark Vitale, Treasurer
G. William Haines, Executive Director

Encourages distribution and use of seperate carpet cushions. Works with regulatory agencies at the national, state and local levels.
33 Members
Founded in 1976

14546 Carpet and Rug Institute
100 South Hamilton Street
P.O. Box 2048
Dalton, GA 30720

706-278-3176
FAX 706-278-8835
Home Page: www.carpet-rug.org
Social Media: *Facebook, Twitter, LinkedIn, YouTube, Google+*

Jim Jolly, CEO
Georgina Sikorski, Executive Director
Werner Braun, President

CRI is a nonprofit trade association representing the manufacturers of more than 95 percent of all carpet made in the United States, as well as service providers and their suppliers. To help increase consumers' satisfaction with carpet and to show them how carpet creates a better environment, they coordinate with other segments of the industry, such as installers, distributors, and retailers.
115 Members
Founded in 1969

14547 Certified Interior Decorators International, Inc.
649 SE Central Pkwy.
Stuart, FL 34994

772-287-1855
800-624-0093
FAX 772-287-0398
Home Page: www.cidinternational.org
Social Media: *Facebook, Twitter, LinkedIn*

Ron Renner, President

Worldwide certifying body and professional association for interior decorators.

14548 Council for Interior Design Accreditation
206 Grandville Avenue
Suite 350
Grand Rapids, MI 49503-4014

616-458-0400
FAX 616-458-0460
E-Mail: info@accredit-id.org
Home Page: www.accredit-id.org
Social Media: *Facebook*

Pamela K. Evans, Ph.D., FIDEC, Chair
Jan Johnson, FIIDA, Industry Rep.
Secretary-Treasurer
Holly Mattson, Executive Director
Laura Hozeska, Office Manager
Stacy I. Peck, Director of Public Relations

Leads the interior design profession to excellence by setting standards and accrediting academic programs.
135 Members
Founded in 1970

14549 Custom Electronic Design & Installation Association
7150 Winton Drive
Suite 300
Indianapolis, IN 46268

317-328-4336
800-669-5329
FAX 317-735-4012
E-Mail: info@cedia.org
Home Page: www.cedia.net
Social Media: *Facebook, Twitter, RSS*

Larry Pexton, Chairman
Dennis Erskine, Chairman Elect
David Humphries, Treasurer
Richard Millson, Secretary
Vin Bruno, CEO

The Custom Electronic Design & Installation Association (CEDIA) is an international trade association of companies that specialize in planning and installing electronic systems for the home. CEDIA provides educational conferences, industry professional training, and certification focused on the installation and integration of residential electronic systems that consumers use to enhance their lifestyles.
3,500 Members
Mailing list available for rent

14550 Designer Society of America
866-721-7857
E-Mail: support@dsasociety.org
Home Page: www.dsasociety.org

The Society offers networking and showcasing opportunities for practicing designers.

14551 Foundation for Design Integrity

1950 N Main Street
Suite 139
Salinas, CA 93906

650-326-1867
FAX 408-449-7040
Home Page: www.ffdi.org

Justin Binnix, President
Eleanor McKay, Chairman
Susan E. Farley, Esquire

Promotes original design and to fight the un-
ethical and illegal practice of manufacturing
knockoffs. Honors those who conceive, design,
engineer and develop innovative new products
for the Interior and Architectural Design
Community and their clients.
150+ Members
Founded in 1994

14552 Home Fashion Partners, LLC

524 Canterbury Rd
Bay Village, OH 44140-2410

727-443-2702
Home Page: www.homefashionpartners.com

Pam Costantini, Business Manager
John James, Manager

This organization has a list of wallcovering
manufacturers and distributors aimed at the interior design community.
Founded in 1977

14553 Home Fashion Products Association

355 Lexington Ave.
Suite 1500
New York, NY 10017

212-297-2122
Home Page: www.homefashionproducts.com

Association for the promotion of manufacturers
of bedding, window, floor and wall coverings,
kitchen textiles and allied home fashion
products.
Founded in 1996

14554 Illuminating Engineering Society

120 Wall St
17th Floor
New York, NY 10005-4001

212-248-5000
FAX 212-248-5017
E-Mail: ies@ies.org
Home Page: www.iesna.org

Daniel Salinas, President
Clayton Gordon, Marketing Manager
William Hanley, Executive Vice President
Calyton Gordon, Marketing Manager
Nick Bleeker, Treasurer

To advance knowledge and disseminate information for the improvement of the lighted environment to the benefit of society. Publishes a
monthly magazine.
8500 Members
Founded in 1906

**14555 Institute of Inspection Cleaning and
Restoration Certification**

4317 NE Thurston Way
Ste 200
Vancouver, WA 98662

360-693-5675
800-835-4624
FAX 360-693-4858
E-Mail: info@iicrc.org
Home Page: www.iicrc.org
Social Media: *Facebook, Twitter, LinkedIn,
Google+*

Patrick Winters, President & CEO
Hank Unck, 1st Vice President
Pete Duncanson, 2nd Vice President
Norm Maia, Treasurer
Kevin Pearson, Secretary

Sets standards of skill and ethics in fabric restoration industry. Works with regulatory bodies
to develop proficiency standards and issues
certification.
1.6M Members
Founded in 1972

14556 Interior Design Educators Council

One Parkview Plaza
Suite 800
Oakbrook Terrace, IL 60181

630-544-5057
FAX 317-280-8527
E-Mail: info@idec.org
Home Page: www.idec.org
Social Media: *Facebook, Twitter, LinkedIn,
YouTube, Google+, Yahoo, Flick*

Cynthia Mohr, President
Katherine Ankerson, Past President
Migette Kaup, President Electy
Cindy Martimo, Secretary/Treasurer
Jill Pable, IDEC Director

Dedicated to the advancement of education and
research in interior design. IDEC fosters exchange of information, improvement of educational standards, and development of the body
of knowledge relative to the quality of life and
human performance in the interior
environment.
Founded in 1963

14557 Interior Design Society

164 S. Main St.
Suite 404
High Point, NC 27260

336-884-4437
FAX 336-885-3291
E-Mail: info@interiordesignsociety.org
Home Page: www.interiordesignsociety.org
Social Media: *Facebook, Twitter, LinkedIn,
YouTube, Blogspot, Instagram,*

Bruce Knott, President
Anna Mavrakis, Past President
Jan Cregier, Vice President
Kimberly Joi McDonald, Treasurer/Secretary
Snoa Garrigan, Executive Director

The largest design organization exclusively
dedicated to serving the residential interior design industry. Promote retail interior design,
emphasizing education and skills improvement.
2500 Members
Founded in 1973

14558 International Feng Shui Guild

705-B SE Melody Ln.
Suite 106
Lees Summit, MO 64063

816-246-1898
E-Mail: office@ifsguild.org
Home Page: ifsguild.org

Mia Staysko, Chair
Bridget Saraka, Chief Executive Officer

Professional organization for Feng Shui consultants of all perspectives.

**14559 International Furnishings and Design
Association**

610 Freedom Business Center
Suite 110
King of Prussia, PA 19406

610-992-0011
FAX 610-992-0021
E-Mail: info@ifda.com
Home Page: www.ifda.com
Social Media: *Facebook, Twitter, LinkedIn*

Diane Nicolson, FIFDA, President
Linda Kulla, FIFDA, Treasurer
Jennifer Jones, MPA, Executive Director
Diane Fairburn, Immediate Past President
Athena Charis, Immediate Past Treasurer

The only all-industry association whose members provide services and products to the furnishings and design industry. IFDA is the
driving force, through its programs and services, to enhance the professionalism and
strature of the industry worlwide.
1400 Members
Founded in 1947

**14560 National Association of Decorative
Fabric Distributors**

One Windsor Cove
Suite 305
Columbia, SC 29223

800-445-8629
FAX 803-765-0860
E-Mail: info@nadfd.com
Home Page: www.nadfd.com

Ted Sargetakis, President
Debbye Lustig, Vice President, Membership
Chair
Frank Governal, 1st Vice Presiden
Dee Duncan, Director
Kathy Gowdy, Secreatry-Treasurer

Comprised of the leading fabric distributors
who reach the reupholsterers, made to order
drapery and home decorator markets, and more
than fifty of their major suppliers, fabric mills,
fabric finishers, manufacturers of upholstery
and drapery supplies.
75 Members
Founded in 1968

**14561 National Council for Interior Design
Qualification, Inc.**

1602 L Street, NW
Suite 200
Washington, DC 20036-5681

202-721-0220
FAX 202-721-0221
E-Mail: inquiries@ncidqexam.org
Home Page: www.ncidq.org
Social Media: *Facebook, Twitter, LinkedIn,
Pinterest*

Laurie McRae, President
David Hanson, President Elect
Victoria Horobin, Past President
Carol Williams-Nickelson, Executive Director
Lola Liao, Director of Finance & Admin.

Serves to identify to the public those interior
designers who have met the minimum standards for professional practice by passing the
NCIDQ examination in addition to protecting
the public by identifying those individuals who
are competent to practice interior design.
10000 Members
Founded in 1974

**14562 National Guild of Professional
Paperhangers, Inc.**

136 S Keowee Street
Dayton, OH 45402

937-222-6477
800-254-6477
FAX 937-222-5794
E-Mail: ngpp@ngpp.org
Home Page: www.ngpp.org
Social Media: *Facebook, Twitter, LinkedIn*

Kimberly Fantaci, Executive Director
Bob Banker, Secretary
Cyndi Green, President
Carl Bergaman, Treasurer
Vincent LaRusso, Vice President

Promotes products, upgrades skills of paperhangers and encourages good business ethics.
Holds workshops and seminars.
650 Members
Founded in 1974

14563 National Home Furnishings Association

3910 Tinsley Drive
Suite 101
High Point, NC 27265-3610

336-886-6100
800-422-3778
FAX 916-784-7697
E-Mail: info@nhfa.org
Home Page: www.nhfa.org
Social Media: *Facebook, Twitter, LinkedIn, YouTube*

Rick Howard, Chairman
Marty Cramer, President
Jeff Child, President Elect
Steve Kidder, Vice President
Jim Fee, Secretary/Treasurer

The nation's largest organization devoted specifically to the needs and interests of home furnishings retailers. Also to provide members with the information, education, products and services they need to remain successful.
2800 Members
Founded in 2013

14564 North American Association of Floor Covering Distributors

330 N. Wabash Ave.
Suite 2000
Chicago, IL 60611-4267

312-321-6836
800-383-3091
FAX 312-673-6962
E-Mail: info@nafcd.org
Home Page: www.nafcd.org
Social Media: *LinkedIn, YouTube*

Rosana Chaidez, President
Heidi Cronin Mandell, Vice President
Geoff Work, Treasurer
Torrey Jaeckle, President Elect
Craig Folven, Immediate Past President

Organized to foster trade and commerce for those having a business, financial, or professional interest as wholesale distributors or manufacturers of floor coverings and allied products.
557 Members
Founded in 1971

14565 Paint and Decorating Retailers Association

1401 Triad Center Drive
St Peters, MO 63376

636-326-2636
800-737-0107
FAX 636-229-4750
E-Mail: info@pdra.org
Home Page: www.pdra.org
Social Media: *Facebook, Twitter, LinkedIn*

Phil Merlo, President
Bahia Taylor, VP
Craig Bond, Treasurer
Jeff Baggaley, Past President
Dan Simon, Executive Vice President/Publisher

PDRA serves the independent dealer through education, membership benefits and trade shows. The Board of Director's initiative to bring top-quality, efficient education to all independent dealers has resulted in development of a new online seminar. The PDRA Coatings Specialist course eliminates the time and expense of traveling to a seminar site. This new course can be taken right in the store, during slow times or at the dealer's convenience.
1500 Members
Founded in 1947

14566 Painting and Decorating Contractors of America

2316 Millpark Drive
Maryland Heights, MO 63043

314-514-7322
800-332-7322
FAX 314-890-2068
E-Mail: bhoran@pdca.org
Home Page: www.pdca.org
Social Media: *Facebook, Twitter, LinkedIn, YouTube*

Dave Ryker, BOD Chair
Tony Severinoÿ, BOD Vice Chair
Mark Adams, BOD Treasurer
Richard Bright, National Sales Director
Chris Shank, Education Manager

PDCA exists to lead the industry by providing quality products, programs, services, and opportunities essential to the success of our members.
5M Members
Founded in 1884
Mailing list available for rent

14567 Professional Picture Framers Association

2282 Springport Road
Suite F
Jackson, MI 49202

517-788-8100
800-762-9287
FAX 517-788-8371
E-Mail: info@ppfa.com
Home Page: www.ppfa.com
Social Media: *Facebook, Twitter, LinkedIn*

John Pruitt, President
Elaine Truman, Administrative
Jeff Frazine, Trade Exhibit Sales
Nick Shaver, Membership
Sheila Pursglove, FMO

An international trade association for the art and framing industry. Supporting a membership of custom picture framers, art galleries, manufacturers, and distibutors.
3000+ Members
Founded in 1971

14568 Society of Glass & Ceramic Decorated Products

PO Box 2489
Zanesville, OH 43702

740-588-9882
FAX 740-588-0245
E-Mail: sgcd@sgcd.org
Home Page: www.sgcd.org

Mark Kelly, President
Walter Lumley, VP
Nancy Klinefelter, Secretary/Treasurer

Provides decorating professionals with a competitive edge in business by providing opporotunities for networking to learn about new decorating technologies and techniques.
525 Members

14569 Window Coverings Association of America

P.O. Box 731
Wake Forest, NC 27588

919-263-9850
888-298-9222
FAX 919-426-2047
E-Mail: solutions@wcaa.org
Home Page: www.wcaa.org
Social Media: *Facebook, LinkedIn, YouTube, Google+*

Michele Williams, President
Julie A. Wood, VP
Sandra VanSickle, Treasurer
Ronica VanGelder, Secretary
Linda Principe, Past President

The only national non-profit trade association dedicated to the retail window covering industry and to the dealers, decorators, and workrooms that are our members.
1200 Members
Founded in 1987

Newsletters

14570 Architectural Lighting

1515 Broadway
34th Floor
New York, NY 10036-8901

212-360-0660
847-763-9050
FAX 646-654-4484
E-Mail: archl@halldata.com
Home Page: www.archlighting.com

Gary Gyss, Group Publisher
Emilie Worth Sommerhoff, Editor-in-Chief
Elizabeth Donoff, Managing Editor
Carolyn Cunningham, Brand Manager
Cliff Smith, Sales Manager

Showcases the application of lighting in architectural and interior design applications.
Circulation: 25,000
Founded in 1964

14571 Installer

National Guild of Professional Paperhangers
136 S Keowee Street
Dayton, OH 45402

937-222-6477
800-254-6477
FAX 937-222-5794
E-Mail: ngpp@ngpp.org
Home Page: www.ngpp.org

Elsie Kaptetna CP, President
Phil Curtis CP, First VP
Vincent Larusso CP, Second VP

Promotes products, upgrades skills of paperhangers and encourages good business ethics.
Frequency: Bimonthly
Circulation: 900

14572 Mirror News

Market Power
103 2nd Street N
Hopkins, MN 55343-9276

E-Mail: feedback@mirror.co.uk
Home Page: www.mirror.co.uk

Wil Tiller, Publisher
Paul Hodd, Head of Digital

Offers interior design news and developments for professionals in the industry.
Cost: $16.00
24 Pages
Frequency: Monthly

14573 National Guild of Professional Paperhangers

136 S Keowee Street
Dayton, OH 45402

937-222-6477
800-254-6477
FAX 937-222-5794
E-Mail: ngpp@ngpp.org
Home Page: www.ngpp.org

Kim Fantaci, Executive VP
Joseph Parker, President

Accepts advertising.
16 Pages
Founded in 1974

14574 NewsFash

American Society of Interior Designers

608 Massachusetts Avenue NE
Washington, DC 20002-6006

202-546-3480
FAX 202-546-3240
E-Mail: asid@asid.org
Home Page:
www.asid.org/designer/ASID+Member+Benefi
ts.htm

Julie Warren, Editor
Jennifer Lipner, Associate Editor
Rick McCosh, Director of Chapter Services
Thom Banks, COO
Rick Peluso, CFO

Bi-weekly newsletter published by the American Society of Interior Designers (ASID) that provides need-to-know design and Society news delivered biweekly. Through education, knowledge sharing, advocacy, community building and outreach, the Society strives to advance the interior design profession and, in the process, to demonstrate and celebrate the power of design to positively chang
Frequency: Bi-Weekly
Founded 1975
Mailing list available for rent

Magazines & Journals

14575 ASID ICON

American Society of Interior Designers
608 Massachusetts Avenue NE
Washington, DC 20002-6006

202-546-3480
FAX 202-546-3240
E-Mail: asid@asid.org
Home Page:
www.asid.org/designer/ASID+Member+Benefi
ts.htm

Julie Warren, Editor
Jennifer Lipner, Associate Editor
Rick McCosh, Director of Chapter Services
Thom Banks, COO
Rick Peluso, CFO

ASID ICON, the magazine of the American Society of Interior Designers/ASID, provides readers with success strategies bi-monthly. ASID is a community of people-designers, industry representatives, educators and students committed to interior design. Through education, knowledge sharing, advocacy, community building and outreach, the Society strives to advance the interior design profession and, in the process, to demonstrate and celebrate the power of design to positively change people's lives.
Frequency: Monthly
Circulation: 40,000
Founded in 1975
Mailing list available for rent

14576 Better Homes and Gardens

Meredith Corporation
1716 Locust St
Des Moines, IA 50309-3023

515-284-3000
800-678-8091
FAX 515-284-3371
E-Mail: shareholderhelp@meredith.com
Home Page: www.meredith.com

Stephen M Lacy, CEO
Daniel M. Lagani, V.P./Publisher
Karol DeWulf Nickell, Editor in Chief

Ideas and how-to information on both new and remodeled kitchen and bath.
Cost: $11.00
Frequency: Monthly
Circulation: 7.6 mill
Founded in 1902

14577 Country Home Product Guide

Meredith Corporation
1716 Locust St
Des Moines, IA 50309-3023

515-284-2015
FAX 515-284-3684
E-Mail: shareholderhelp@meredith.com
Home Page: www.meredith.com

David Kahn, Publisher

Offers information on residential projects focusing on innovative design work for homes with a country motif.
Frequency: Monthly

14578 Decor

Pfingsten Publishing
330 N 5th Street
Saint Louis, MO 63102-2036

314-421-5445
800-867-9285
FAX 314-421-1070
Home Page: www.decormagazine.com

Gary S Goldman, Publisher
Alice C Gibson, Editor

In the business of furnishing helpful information, education, and marketing services that will assist art and framing retailers, distributors, and wholesalers in the manufacture and sale of their products and services, and in the successful management of their business. Every article of Decor must give art and framing retailers helpful information that they can use to make their business stronger.
Cost: $20.00
Frequency: 13 per year
Circulation: 27,000

14579 Design Solutions Magazine

Architectural Woodwork Institute
46179 Westlake Drive
Suite 120
Potomac Falls, VA 20165-5874

571-323-3636
FAX 571-323-3630
E-Mail: awiweb@vt.edu
Home Page: www.awinet.org

David Ritchey, Editor
Judith Durham, Executive VP
Matthew Lundahl, President
Randy Jensen, Vice President
Bruce Spitz, Treasurer

Covers new commercial construction, as well as renovation. Updates on doors, paneling, laminatem plywood, architectural hardware and finishes.
Cost: $25.00
Frequency: Quarterly
Circulation: 25000
Mailing list available for rent

14580 Designers West

Designers World Corporation
8914 Santa Monica Boulevard
Los Angeles, CA 90069-4902

213-748-8291
FAX 213-748-0039

Carol Soucek King, Editor
Rafael Nadal, President

For interior designers, architects and other design professionals involved in residential, office and hospitality projects. Accepts advertising.
Cost: $30.00
120 Pages
Frequency: Monthly
Founded in 1953

14581 Designing with Tile and Stone

Tile & Stone

20 Beekman Pl
20th Floor
New York, NY 10022-8043

212-929-0500
FAX 212-376-7723
E-Mail: ashleepub@aol.com
Home Page: www.ashlee.com

Michelle Tillou, Owner

Articles on design, selection, installation and maintenance.
Frequency: Quarterly
Circulation: 12000

14582 Donna Dewberry's One-Day Decorating

F+W Media
38 E. 29th Street
New York, NY 10016

212-447-1400
FAX 212-447-5231
E-Mail: contact_us@fwmedia.com
Home Page: www.fwpublications.com
Social Media: *Facebook, Twitter, LinkedIn*

Colleen Cannon, Publisher
David Nussbaum, CEO
Jim Ogle, Chief Financial Officer
Chad Phelps, Chief Digital Officer
Stacie Berger, Communications Director

A how-to magazine for decorative painters, crafters, and do-it-yourself home decorators. Its goal is to inspire anyone interested in embellishing their home, and it features easy-to-complete, step-by-step project ideas using decorative painting, stamping, faux finishing, stenciling, and other crafting techniques.
Cost: $27.00
76 Pages
Frequency: Monthly
Circulation: 100000
Founded in 1945
Mailing list available for rent

14583 Eye on Design

American Society of Interior Designers
608 Massachusetts Avenue NE
Washington, DC 20002-6006

202-546-3480
FAX 202-546-3240
E-Mail: asid@asid.org
Home Page:
www.asid.org/designer/ASID+Member+Benefi
ts.htm

Julie Warren, Editor
Jennifer Lipner, Associate Editor
Rick McCosh, Director of Chapter Services
Thom Banks, COO
Rick Peluso, CFO

Eye on Design, provided by the American Society of Interior Designers\ASID, focuses on industry news and developments and is delivered electronically on a weekly basis. Through education, knowledge sharing, advocacy, community building and outreach, the Society strives to advance the interior design profession and, in the process, to demonstrate and celebrate the power of design to positively change people's lives.
Founded in 1975
Mailing list available for rent

14584 Facilities Design & Management

1515 Broadway
34th Floor
New York, NY 10036-8901

212-840-0595
800-950-1314
FAX 212-302-6273

Anne Fallucchi, Editor-in-Chief

Covers all aspects of the planning, design and management of facilities for corporate offices

and related facilities, health care, government, hospitality and education.
Frequency: Monthly

14585 Floor Care Professional

Vacuum Dealers Trade Association
2724 2nd Ave
Des Moines, IA 50313-4933

515-282-9101
800-367-5651
FAX 515-282-4483
E-Mail: mail@vdta.com
Home Page: www.vdta.com

Charles Dunham, Owner
Beth Vitiritto, Managing Editor
Rob Heater, Managing Editor
Sherry Graham, Administrative Assistant
Judy Patterson, Vice President

Offers news and information for the distributers and dealers of vacuum and sewing machines.
Cost: $100.00
Frequency: Monthly
Circulation: 18000
Founded in 1981
Printed in 4 colors on glossy stock

14586 Flora-Line

Berry Hill Press
7336 Berry Hill Drive
Palos Verdes Estates, CA 90275-4404

310-377-7040

Dody Lyness, Editor

Targeted to the home-based business person engaged in dried floral design. Its format keeps readers abreast of the floral trends in herbal growing and the most modern techniques for drying and designing with flowering herbs. Accepts advertising.
Cost: $16.95
20 Pages
Frequency: Quarterly
Circulation: 1,000
Founded in 1981

14587 Furniture Style

400 Knightsbridge Parkway
Lincolnshire, IL 60069-3613

847-634-4339
800-621-2845
FAX 847-634-4379
E-Mail: info@vancepublishing.com
Home Page: www.vancepublishing.com

Michael R Reckling, Publisher
Judy Riggs, Director
Steve Chair, Marketing Manager
Douglas A. Riemer, Circulation Manager
William C Vance, Chairman
Cost: $49.95
Frequency: Monthly
Circulation: 25000
Founded in 1937

14588 HOW Design Ideas at Work

F&W Publications
4700 E Galbraith Rd
Cincinnati, OH 45236-2726

513-531-2690
800-333-1115
FAX 513-531-1843
E-Mail: editorial@howdesign.com
Home Page: www.fwpublications.com

David Nussbaum, CEO
Bryn Mooth, Chief Financial Officer
Jim Ogle, Chief Financial Officer
Kate Rados, Marketing Director
Stacie Berger, Communications Director

HOW reaches visual communicators, including art directors, graphic designers, type designers, typographers, illustrators, advertising and sales promotion managers, and other design-minded

executives; also manufacturers and suppliers of graphic arts products and services.
Cost: $29.96
194 Pages
Frequency: Monthly
Circulation: 39946
ISSN: 0886-0483
Founded in 1990
Printed in 4 colors on glossy stock

14589 Home Furnishings Executive

305 W High Ave
Suite 400
High Point, NC 27260-4950

336-885-6981
800-888-9590
FAX 336-885-4424

14590 Home Lighting & Accessories

Doctorow Communications
1011 Clifton Ave
Clifton, NJ 07013-3518

973-779-1600
FAX 973-779-3242
E-Mail: email@homelighting.com
Home Page: www.homelighting.com

Jeffrey Doctorow, President
Cost: $15.00
Frequency: Monthly
Founded in 1953

14591 Homeworld Business

45 Research Way
Suite 106
East Setauket, NY 11733

631-246-9300
FAX 631-246-9496
Home Page: www.homeworldbusiness.com

Ian Gittlitz, Publisher/Editor-in-Chief
Peter Giannetti, Editor
Bill McLoughlin, Executive Editor
Peter Chamberlin, Circulation Manager
Hope Rosenzweig, Classified Advertising
Cost: $185.00

14592 House Beautiful

959 8th Ave
New York, NY 10019-3737

212-649-2098
FAX 212-765-3528
Home Page: www.hearstcorp.com

Kate Kelly Smith, Publisher
Victor F Ganzi, CEO
Bruce Paisner, VP
Michael A Hurley, Marketing Director
Cost: $19.97
Frequency: Monthly
Circulation: 854627
Founded in 1887

14593 Interior Design

Reed Business Information
360 Park Avenue South
17th floor
New York, NY 10010

212-772-8300
FAX 630-288-8686
E-Mail: custserv@espcomp.com
Home Page: www.interiordesignmag.com
Social Media: *Facebook, Twitter, LinkedIn, RSS*

Lawrence S Reed
Woody Goldfien, Owner
Jim Casella, CEO

Offers information on quality residential and contract design work. Recent issues include corporate offices, remodeling/restoration, kitchen and bath design, health care and hospi-

tality.
Cost: $64.95
250 Pages
Frequency: Monthly
Circulation: 59,000
Founded in 1932
Printed in 4 colors on glossy stock

14594 Interiors and Sources

840 US Highway 1
Suite 330
North Pal Beach, FL 33408

561-627-3393
FAX 561-694-6578
Home Page: www.isdesignet.com

Robert Nieminen, Editor
Guy De Silva, Publisher
Charlotte Vann, Circulation Manager
Adam Moore, Managing Editor

Offers national commercial and residential design work articles. Emphasizes design solutions and focuses on challenges encountered by designers.
Cost: $27.00
Frequency: Monthly
Circulation: 28,000
Founded in 1990

14595 Kitchen & Bath Design News

Cygnus Publishing
PO Box 803
Fort Atkinson, WI 53538-0803

920-000-1111
FAX 920-563-1699
E-Mail: ESefrin@kbdn.net
Home Page: www.cygnusb2b.com

John French, CEO
Eliot Sefrin, Director of Public Relations
Kathy Scott, Director of Public Relations
Paul Bonaiuto, CFO

Offers articles for kitchen and bath dealers, interior designers and architects.
Frequency: Monthly
Circulation: 50000
Founded in 1966

14596 Laminating Design & Technology

Cygnus Publishing
PO Box 803
Fort Atkinson, WI 53538-0803

920-000-1111
FAX 920-563-1699
Home Page: www.cygnusb2b.com

John French, CEO
Rich Reiff, Director of Public Relations
Kathy Scott, Director of Public Relations
Paul Bonaiuto, CFO

Global design and color trends, as well as surfacing solutions for furniture architecture and interior design. Focuses on surface design, performance and application.
Cost: $30.00
44 Pages
Frequency: Monthly
Circulation: 40006
Founded in 1937

14597 Lighting Dimensions

Primedia
PO Box 12901
Shawnee Mission, KS 66282-2901

913-341-1300
FAX 913-514-6895
E-Mail: djohnson@primediabusiness.com

Eric Jacobson, Senior VP
David Barbour, Editorial Director
Cost: $34.97
Frequency: Monthly

14598 Metropolis

Bellerophon Publications

61 W 23rd St
23rd Street
New York, NY 10010-4246

212-627-9977
800-344-3046
FAX 212-627-9988
E-Mail: info@metropolismag.com
Home Page: www.metropolismag.com

Horace Havemeyer, Publisher
Susan S Szenasy, Editor-in-Chief
Denise Csaky, Marketing Director
Tamara Costa, Advertising Manager
Peter Sangiorgio, Circulation Controller

The only magazine that covers all facets of design: architecture, interiors, furniture, preservation, urban design, graphics and crafts.
Cost: $32.95
Circulation: 54000
Founded in 1980

14599 Michaels Create!
F+W Media
38 E. 29th Streett
New York, NY 10016

212-447-1400
FAX 212-447-5231
E-Mail: contact_us@fwmedia.com
Home Page: www.fwpublications.com

Debbie Knauer, Publisher
Jane Beard, Editor

Features contemporary designs reflecting the latest trends with clear instructions. The home decorating, fashion, and gift ideas will inspire experienced crafters as well as seasonal crafters to explore new possibilities. Step-by-step instructions, tips, and techniques will engage crafters of all ages - including kids - with the creative skills of crafting to be enjoyed as a year-round activity.
Cost: $21.97
116 Pages
Frequency: Monthly
Circulation: 24991
Founded in 1952

14600 Midwest Retailer
8528 Columbus Ave S
Bloomington, MN 55420-2460

952-854-7610
FAX 952-854-6460

Joan Thomasberg, Owner
Cost: $10.00
38588 Pages
Circulation: 5000
Founded in 1972
Printed in 2 colors on newsprint stock

14601 NHFA Trade Show
National Home Furnishings Association
3910 Tinsley Drive
Suite 101
Highpoint, NC 27265-3610

336-886-6100
800-888-9590
FAX 336-801-6102
E-Mail: info@nhfa.org
Home Page: www.nhfa.org

Steve DeHaan, Executive VP
Karin Mayfield, Senior Director for Membership
Frequency: Annual

14602 National Floor Trends
Business News Publishing Company
22801 Ventura Blvd
Suite 113
Woodland Hills, CA 91364-1230

818-224-8035
FAX 818-224-8042

E-Mail: privacy@BNPMedia.com
Home Page: www.bnpmedia.com

Phil Johnson, Publisher
Rick Arvidson, Director
For interior designers.
Frequency: Monthly
Founded in 1952

14603 Paint & Decorating Retailer Magazine
Paint and Decorating Retailers Association
1401 Triad Center Dr
St. Peters, MO 63376-7353

636-326-2636
800-737-0107
FAX 636-229-4750
E-Mail: info@pdra.org
Home Page: www.pdra.org

Dan Simon, Executive VP/Publisher
Tina Sullivan, Dir Membership/Education/Tradeshows
Diane Capuano, Managing Editor
Renee Nolte, Director, Finance/Human Resources
Tony Sarantakis, Account Executive

Monthly trade magazine dedicated to the informational needs of paint and decorating store owners, managers and employees.
1500 Members
Frequency: Annual May
Circulation: 26,000+
Founded in 1947

14604 Panel World
Hatton-Brown Publishers
225 Hanrick Street
PO Box 2268
Montgomery, AL 36102

334-834-1170
FAX 334-834-4525
E-Mail: rich@hattonbrown.com
Home Page: www.hattonbrown.com

Rich Donnell, Editor
David Knight, Co-Owner
Rhonda Thomas, Circulation Director
Dianne Sullivan, Chief Operating Officer
Phil Grissett, Operations Manager
Cost: $30.00
Frequency: Monthly
Circulation: 12754
ISSN: 1048-826X
Founded in 1948
Printed in on glossy stock

14605 Perspective
13-500 Merchandise Mart
Chicago, IL 60654-1104

312-467-1950
888-799-4432
FAX 312-467-0779
E-Mail: ahq@iida.org
Home Page: www.iida.org

John Lijewski, President
Cheryl Durst, Executive Vice President
Jocelyn Pysarchuk, Managing Director, Communications
Suzanne Murphy, Director, Membership & Chapter
Robert Friedman, Editor
International magazine of IIDA.
Cost: $30.00
Frequency: Monthly
Circulation: 10000
Founded in 1994
Mailing list available for rent: 10000 names
Printed in on matte stock

14606 Picture Framing Magazine
Hobby Publications

225 Gordon's Corner Road
PO Box 420
Manalapan, NJ 07726

732-446-4900
800-969-7176
FAX 732-446-5488
E-Mail: gcoughlin@hobbypub.com
Home Page:
www.pictureframingmagazine.com

Bruce Gherman, Executive Publisher
Anne Vazquez, Editor
Deborah Salmon, Circulation Director
Alan Pegler, Production Manager of Advertising

News and trends in the picture framing trade, marketing strategies, and economic developments.
Cost: $20.00
Frequency: Monthly
Circulation: 23000
ISSN: 1052-9977
Founded in 1995

14607 Progressive Architecture
Progressive Scale
382 S Beach Avenue
Old Greenwich, CT 06870-2223

203-792-2854
FAX 203-748-2456

Valerie Kanter Sisca, Managing Editor

This magazine has been covering the fields of architecture and interiors for more than 60 years and publishes projects that illustrate both current trends and innovative design solutions.
Cost: $48.00
Frequency: Monthly
Circulation: 65,000

14608 Upholstery Journal
Industrial Fabrics Association International
1801 County Road B W
Roseville, MN 55113-4061

651-222-2508
800-225-4324
FAX 651-631-9334
E-Mail: generalinfo@ifai.com
Home Page: www.ifai.com

Stephen Warner, CEO
JoAnne Farris, Marketing Director

Serves as the industry resource for after-market furniture, marine and automotive upholstery. Provides education for both the craft and business of upholstery.
Frequency: Bimonthly
Circulation: 5,000

14609 Wall Paper
Waldman Publishers
570 Fashion Ave
New York, NY 10018-1603

212-730-9590
FAX 212-391-6610

Edited for wallcovering retailers and the wallcovering industry. Accepts advertising.
Cost: $25.00
40 Pages
Frequency: Monthly
Circulation: 18,000
Founded in 1980

14610 Wallcoverings, Windows and Interior Fashion
Cygnus Publishing
445 Broad Hollow Road
Melville, NY 11747-3669

631-845-2700
FAX 631-845-2723
Home Page: www.cygnuspub.com

Paul Bonaiuto, CFO
Kathy Scott, Director of Public Relations

14611 Walls & Ceilings
Business News Publishing Company
2401 W. Big Beaver Rd
Suite 700
Troy, MI 48084

248-362-3700
Home Page: www.bnpmedia.com
Social Media: *Facebook, Twitter, LinkedIn*

Katie Rotella, Manager

Information regarding management, building methods, technology, government regulations, consumer trends, and product information for the contractor involved in exterior finishes, waterproofing, insulation, metal framing, drywall, fireproofing, partitions, stucco and plaster.
Cost: $49.00
140 Pages
Frequency: Monthly
Circulation: 32800
Founded in 1939
Printed in 4 colors

Trade Shows

14612 Accent on Design
George Little Management
10 Bank Street
Suite 1200
White Plains, NY 10606-1954

914-486-6070
800-272-7469
FAX 914-948-2867
Home Page: www.nyigf.com

George Little II, President
Elizabeth Murphy, Show Manager

370 booths of the latest and most innovative gift lines such as decorative accessories and home furnishings.
50M Attendees
Frequency: August
Founded in 1984

14613 Aidex: Asian International Interior Design Exposition
Reed Exhibition Companies
383 Main Avenue
PO Box 6059
Norwalk, CT 06851

203-840-4800
FAX 203-840-9628

Audio visual systems, bathroom equipment, supplies and services, plus interior decorations. More than 22 exhibitors, for trade professionals.
Frequency: Annual

14614 American Society of Interior Designers National Conference
American Society of Interior Designers
608 Massachusetts Avenue NE
Washington, DC 20002-6006

202-546-3480
FAX 202-546-3240
E-Mail: asid@asid.org
Home Page: www.asid.org

Randy Fiser, Executive Vice President/CEO
Thom Banks, COO
Rick Peluso, CFO
Deanna Waldron, Government/Public Affairs
Willie Pugh, Information Technology

Workshop and annual conference with 100 manufacturers and suppliers. Exhibits include interior design merchandise, wall coverings, laminates, lighting fixtures, plumbing fixtures, carpets, furniture, office systems and fabrics.
3000 Attendees
Frequency: Annual

Founded in 1975
Mailing list available for rent

14615 Dickens Christmas Show & Festival
Leisure Time Unlimited
708 Main Street
Myrtle Beach, SC 29577

843-448-9483
FAX 843-362-6153
E-Mail: dickensshow@sc.rr.com
Home Page: www.dickenschristmasshow.com

Offers a unique blend of craft and gift exhibits presented in a 19th century setting
25000 Attendees
Frequency: Annual November

14616 Evergreen Home Show
Westlake Promotions
8740 Golden Gardens Dr. NW
Seattle, WA 98117

206-783-5957
FAX 206-708-7406
Home Page: www.westlakepromo.com
Social Media: *Facebook, Twitter*

Bill Bradley, VP
Sam Scott, Marketing Director, Operations
Michael R. Scott, President

See what's new and what you can do for your home. Fresh ideas and practical advice from our remodeling and construction specialists. See demonstrations on how to make dramatic improvements to your home.
7500 Attendees

14617 Fall Decor
Paint & Decorating Retailers Association
403 Axminister Drive
Fenton, MO 63026

636-326-2636
FAX 314-991-5039
E-Mail: info@pdra.org
Home Page: www.pdra.org

Tina Sullivan, Show Coordinator
Kathy Witmeyer, Director of Trade Shows

Annual show of 350 manufacturers, suppliers and distributors of decorating and office products and related equipment, supplies and services.
4000 Attendees
Frequency: October

14618 Galeria
Decor Magazine
330 N 4th Street
Saint Louis, MO 63102

314-421-5445
FAX 314-421-1070

12000 Attendees

14619 Holiday Fair
Textile Hall Corporation
25 Woodslake Road
Greenville, SC 29607

864-331-2277
FAX 864-293-0619
Home Page:
http://www.holidayfairgreenville.com

25000 Attendees

14620 Home Furnishings Summer Market
1355 Market Street
San Francisco, CA 94103-1324

415-934-1380

Donald Preiser, Show Manager
600 booths.
30M Attendees

14621 Home World Home & Garden Show
Show Biz Productions

16600 Harbor Blouevard
Suite F
Fountain Valley, CA 92708

714-418-2000
877-418-2001
FAX 714-418-2009
E-Mail: marlene@sbhomeshow.com

Rachel Perry, President
Marlene Thorne, VP

Featuring vendors of window, doors, painting, heating, air conditioning, kitchens and baths, flooring, furniture, remodeling services and more.
30000 Attendees
Founded in 1991

14622 Home and Garden Show
Reed Exhibition Companies
255 Washington Street
Newton, MA 02458-1637

617-584-4900
FAX 617-630-2222

Elizabeth Hitchcock, International Sales

Home products and services.
75M Attendees
Frequency: March

14623 IDS National Conference
Interior Design Society
164 S Main Street
Suite 404
High Point, NC 27260

336-884-4437
888-884-4469
FAX 336-885-3291
E-Mail: info@interiordesignsociety.org
Home Page: www.interiordesignsociety.org
Social Media: *Facebook, Twitter, Youtube, Blogger*

Domnick Minella, President
Snoa Garrigan, Executive Director
Dennis Novosel, Treasurer
Anna Mavrakis, VP

IDS is the largest design organization exclusively dedicated to serving the residential interior design industry. Promotes retail interior design, emphasizing education and skills improvement.
3000 Members
Founded in 1973

14624 IFAI Annual Expo
Industrial Fabrics Association International
1801 County Road BW
Roseville, MN 55113-4061

651-222-2508
800-225-4324
FAX 651-631-9334
E-Mail: generalinfo@ifai.com
Home Page: www.ifai.com
Social Media: *Facebook, Twitter, LinkedIn, Youtube*

Beth Wistrcill, Conference Manager
Mary J. Hennessy, President and CEO
Pam Egan-Blahna, Director of Human Resources
Todd V. Lindemann, Vice President
Susan R. Niemi, Publisher

Trade event in the American for the technical textiles and specialty fabrics industry.
Frequency: Annual/September

14625 International Home Furnishings Market
International Home Furnishings Market Authority
POBox 5243
High Point, NC 27262

336-888-3794
800-874-6492

FAX 336-889-6999
Home Page: www.highpointmarket.org

Judy Mendenhall, President
G Bruce Miller, CEO
Tammy Covington, Director Operations
Jan Wellmon, Executive Assistant
Shannon Kennedy, Director of Marketing

Large home furnishings trade show with a variety of new opportunities to make your visit easy, cost effective and productive. Ten million square feet of exhibition space with 2,500 manufacturers represented.
80000 Attendees
Frequency: April & October
Founded in 1921

14626 International Silk Flower Accessories Exhibition

Dallas Market Center
2000 N Stemmons Freeway
Dallas, TX 75207

214-655-6100
800-325-6587
FAX 214-655-6238

8000 Attendees

14627 LightFair

AMC
120 Wall Street
17th Floor
New York, NY 10005

212-843-8358
FAX 212-248-5017
Home Page: www.iesna.org

Pamela R Weess, Circulation Director
Nini Schwenk, Manager

A major lighting trade show in North America featuring architectural lighting products from all spectrons of the industry. Containing 600 booths and 400 exhibits.
17M Attendees
Frequency: June
Mailing list available for rent: 10M names at $100 per M
Printed in 4 colors on glossy stock

14628 Museum Store Association

4100 E Mississippi Avenue
Suite 800
Denver, CO 80246-3055

303-504-9223
FAX 303-504-9585
E-Mail: expo@msaweb.org
Home Page: www.museumdistrict.com

Beverly Barsook, Executive Director
Stacey Woldt, Assistant Director Programs
Eric Curtis, Conference & Expo Manager
2500 Attendees
Frequency: April, Annually
Founded in 1955

14629 NGPP National Convention & Trade Show

National Guild of Professional Paperhangers
136 S Keowee Street
Dayton, OH 45402

937-222-6477
800-254-6477
FAX 937-222-5794
E-Mail: ngpp@ngpp.org
Home Page: www.ngpp.org

Elsie Kaptetna CP, President
Phil Curtis CP, First VP
Vincent Larusso CP, Second VP

Promotes products, upgrades skills of paperhangers and encourages good business ethics. Workshops and product launches with over 130 vendors.
Frequency: Annual

14630 National Decorating Product Show

Paint & Decorating Retailers Association
403 Axminister Drive
Fenton, MO 63026-2941

636-326-2636
FAX 314-991-5039

James B Savens III, Executive Director

430 booths for home supplies, equipment and services.
10M Attendees
Frequency: November

14631 National Decorating Products Association: Western Show

1050 N Lindbergh Boulevard
Saint Louis, MO 63132-2912

314-432-6001
FAX 314-991-5039

Ruth Williams, Convention Manager

230 booths of decorating products such as paint, furniture and more.
2.5M Attendees
Frequency: March

14632 National Decorating Products Southern Show

Paint & Decorating Retailers Association
403 Axminister Drive
Fenton, MO 63026-2941

636-326-2636
FAX 314-991-5039

Ruth Williams, Convention Manager

850 display booths of floor coverings, paint, furniture and various interior decorating products.
4M Attendees
Frequency: February

14633 Needlework Markets

Needlework Markets
PO Box 533
Pine Mountain, GA 31822

706-663-0140
FAX 706-663-0202
Home Page: www.stitching.com

Emily Castleberry, Owner
Frequency: February

14634 Old House New House Home Show

Kennedy Productions
1208 Lisle Place
Lisle, IL 60532-2262

630-515-1160
FAX 630-515-1165
E-Mail: info@kennedyproductions.com
Home Page: www.kennedyproductions.com

Laura McNamara, Event Producer
Joanne Kennedy, President

Over 300 home improvement exhibitors displaying cutting-edge home enhancements for kitchens, baths, home and garden including landscape, interior remodeling, pools, spas, floors, doors and more.
8000 Attendees
Frequency: Feb/Sept
Founded in 1977

14635 PDCA Painting & Decorating Expo

Paint and Decorating Retailers Association
1401 Triad Center Dr
St. Peters, MO 63376-7353

636-326-2636
800-737-0107
FAX 636-229-4750
E-Mail: info@pdra.org
Home Page: www.pdra.org

Dan Simon, Executive VP/Publisher
Tina Sullivan, Dir

Membership/Education/Tradeshows
Diane Capuano, Managing Editor
Renee Nolte, Director, Finance/Human Resources
Tony Sarantakis, Account Executive

Over thiry education sessions, multiple special networking events and the latest in products and services to support the trade.
2000 Members
Frequency: May
Founded in 1947

14636 Paint Industries Show

492 Norristown Road
Blue Bell, PA 19422-2355

610-940-0777
FAX 215-840-0292

Robert F Ziegler, Show Manager

Exhibits of raw materials, production equipment, instrumentation and testing apparatus for the coatings, inks and adhesives manufacturing industries. 920 booths.
3.5M Attendees
Frequency: October

14637 Painting and Decorating Contractors of America National Convention

3913 Old Lee Highway
Suite 301
Fairfax, VA 22030-2433

703-359-0826
FAX 703-359-2976

Mary S DePersig, Director Meetings

200 booths of painting, wallcoverings, coatings and sundries.
1.2M Attendees
Frequency: March

14638 Surtex

George Little Management
10 Bank Street
Suite 1200
White Plains, NY 10606-1954

914-486-6070
800-272-7469
FAX 914-948-6180
E-Mail: SURTEX@glmshows.com
Home Page: www.SURTEX.com

Gina DeLuca, Show Coordinator
Rita Malek, Show Manager
George Little II, President

Annual show of 350 exhibitors featuring prints and patterns for all applications-decorative fabrics, linens, and domestics, apparel and contract textiles, wall and floor coverings, greeting cards, giftwrap and other paper products, tabletop, ceramics and packaging. Available for sale and/or license.
5000 Attendees
Frequency: May

14639 TEXBO

Reed Exhibition Companies
255 Washington Street
Newton, MA 02458-1637

617-584-4900
FAX 617-630-2222

Elizabeth Hitchcock, International Sales

International trade fair for the interior design industry.
7M Attendees
Frequency: January

14640 Tabletop Market

George Little Management
577 Airport Boulevard
Burlingame, CA 94010-2020

650-548-1200
800-272-SHOW
FAX 650-344-5270

E-Mail: customer_relations@glmshows.com
Home Page: www.glmshows.com/table

Susan Corwin, VP

Annual show of 90 exhibitors featuring table-ware, table linens, better housewares and decorative accessories.
1500 Attendees
Frequency: October

14641 West Coast Art and Frame

Art Trends/Picture Framing/Digital Fine Arts
PO Box 594
Lynbrook, NY 11563

516-596-3937
FAX 516-596-3941

3500 Attendees

Directories & Databases

14642 Carpet & Rug Industry Buyers Guide Issue

Rodman Publishing
17 S Franklin Tpke
Ramsey, NJ 07446-2522

201-252-2552

More than 300 suppliers of machinery, equipment and colors and dyes used in the making of carpets and rugs.
Cost: $7.00
Frequency: Annual
Circulation: 5,500

14643 Carpet Cleaners Institute of the Northwest Membership Roster

Carpet Cleaners Institute of the Northwest
PMB #40 2421 South Union Avenue
Suite L-1
Tacoma, WA 98405

253-759-5762
877-692-2469
FAX 253-761-9134
E-Mail: info@ccinw.org
Home Page: www.ccinw.org

Lyle Neville, President
Matt O'Haleck, Treasurer
Jim Thomas, Secretary
Mike Elias, Director of Education

Over 330 member companies involved in the carpet cleaning industry in Washington, Oregon, and Montana, USA and Alberta and British Columbia, Canada.
Frequency: Annual

14644 Decor-Sources Issue

Commerce Publishing Company
330 N 4th Street
Suite 200
Saint Louis, MO 63102-2041

314-421-5445

Over 1,200 wholesale suppliers of pictures, frames, interior accessories and mirrors to art galleries and home accessories retailers are profiled.
Cost: $5.00
Frequency: Annual
Circulation: 35,000

14645 Decorating Registry

Paint and Decorating Retailers Association
1401 Triad Center Dr
St. Peters, MO 63376-7353

636-326-2636
800-737-0107
FAX 636-229-4750

E-Mail: info@pdra.org
Home Page: www.pdra.org

Dan Simon, Executive VP/Publisher
Tina Sullivan, Dir Membership/Education/Tradeshows
Diane Capuano, Managing Editor
Renee Nolte, Director, Finance/Human Resources
Tony Sarantakis, Account Executive

A searchable industry database listing paint and decorating companies, products, trademarks, distributors and manufacturer reps.
Cost: $15.00
1500 Members
200 Pages
Frequency: Annual, Magazine
Founded in 1947
Printed in on glossy stock

14646 Decorating Retailer's Decorating Registry

National Decorating Products Association
1050 N Lindbergh Boulevard
Saint Louis, MO 63132-2912

314-432-6001
800-737-0107
FAX 314-991-5039

Ernest Stewart, Executive VP
Cindy Nusbaum, Directories Editor

Trademark and brand name directory covering paint, wallcovering, window covering, floor covering and related sundries.
Cost: $9.00
Frequency: Annual
Circulation: 30,000
Mailing list available for rent: 30,000+ names
Printed in 4 colors on glossy stock

14647 Decorating Retailer: Directory of the Wallcoverings Industry Issue

National Decorating Products Association
1050 N Lindbergh Boulevard
Saint Louis, MO 63132-2912

314-432-6001
800-737-0107
FAX 314-991-5039

Ernest Stewart, Publisher
Cindy Nusbaum, Editor

Over 1,000 manufacturers and distributors of wallcoverings and related products are listed.
Cost: $25.00
Frequency: Annual
Circulation: 5,000
Printed in 4 colors

14648 DesignSource: Official Specifying and Buying Directory

PO Box 5059
Hoboken, NJ 07030-1501

201-963-9000

More than 10,000 companies that manufacture or supply products or services for interior designers.
Cost: $25.00
Frequency: Annual
Circulation: 40,000

14649 Directory of African American Design Firms

San Francisco Redevelopment Agency
770 Golden Gate Avenue
San Francisco, CA 94102

415-749-2400
FAX 415-749-2526

Over 100 architectural, engineering, planning and landscape design firms.
Frequency: Annual December

14650 Draperies & Window Coverings: Directory and Buyer's Guide Issue

LC Clark Publishing Company
840 US Highway 1
Suite 330
North Palm Beac, FL 33408-3878

561-627-3393
FAX 561-694-6578

John Clark, Owner
Sarah Christy, Associate Editor
Katie Sosnowchik, Senior Editor

Over 2,000 manufacturers and distributors of window coverings and other products used in the window coverings and interior fashions industry.
Cost: $15.00
Frequency: Annual

14651 ENR Directory of Design Firms

McGraw Hill
PO Box 182604
Columbus, OH 43272

877-833-5524
FAX 614-759-3749
E-Mail: customer.service@mcgraw-hill.com
Home Page: www.mcgraw-hill.com
Social Media: *Facebook, Twitter, LinkedIn, Blog, Youtube, Social*

Paul Hermannsfeldt, Editor
Harold McGraw III, Chairman, President
Jack F. Callahan, Executive Vice President
John Berisford, Executive Vice President
Mary Jo Vittor, Executive Vice President

Profiles of 88 architects, architectural engineers, consultants and other design firms; limited to advertisers.
Cost: $95.00
Frequency: Biennial
Mailing list available for rent

14652 ENR: Top 500 Design Firms Issue

McGraw Hill
1221 Avenue of the Americas
Suite C3A
New York, NY 10020-1095

212-512-2000
FAX 212-512-3840
E-Mail: webmaster@mcgraw-hill.com
Home Page: www.mcgraw-hill.com

Harold W McGraw III, CEO

List of 500 leading architectural, engineering and specialty design firms selected on basis of annual billings.
Cost: $35.00
Frequency: Annual April
Circulation: 71,000

14653 Flooring: Buying and Resource Guide Issue

Leo Douglas
9609 Gayton Road
Suite 100
Richmond, VA 23233-4904

Lists various manufacturers, workrooms, manufacturers' representatives and distributors of floor, and other interior surfacing products and equipment.
Cost: $38.50
Frequency: Annual
Circulation: 24,000

14654 Home Lighting & Accessories Suppliers Directory

Doctorow Communications
1011 Clifton Ave
Clifton, NJ 07013-3518

973-779-1600
FAX 973-779-3242

E-Mail: info@homelighting.com
Home Page: www.homelighting.com

Jeffrey Doctorow, President
Linda Longo, Editor-in-Chief
Susan Grisham, Managing Editor
Dina Tamburro, Associate Publisher

A list of over 1,000 suppliers of lighting fixtures and other products for use in the retail lighting industry are provided.
Cost: $6.00
Frequency: Semi-Annual
Circulation: 9,690

14655 Interior Decorators Handbook

EW Williams Publications
370 Lexington Ave
Suite 1409
New York, NY 10017-6583

212-661-1516
FAX 212-661-1713
Home Page: www.williamspublications.com

Philippa Hochschild, Publisher
Phillip Russo, Publishing Director
Lynne Lancaster, Advertising Sales Director

Designers resource guide with over 600 product/service categories. 3,000 suppliers are listed with their headquarters, showrooms. Addresses, phone numbers, fax numbers and e-mail.
Cost: $36.00
230 Pages
Frequency: Bi-annual
Circulation: 25,000
Founded in 1922
Printed in 4 colors on glossy stock

14656 LDB Interior Textiles Annual Buyers' Guide

EW Williams Publications
370 Lexington Ave
Room 1409
New York, NY 10017-6583

212-661-1516
FAX 212-661-1713
Home Page: www.williamspublications.com

Philippa Hochschild, Publisher

Over 2,000 manufacturers and importers of home accessories and interior design products are listed.
Cost: $40.00
Frequency: Monthly
Circulation: 14000
Founded in 1927

14657 Market Resource Guide

International Home Furnishings Center
PO Box 828
High Point, NC 27261-0828

336-888-3700
FAX 336-882-1873
E-Mail: marketing@ihfc.com
Home Page: www.ihfc.com

Bruce Miller, CEO

Two-volume directory offers over 1,500 manufacturers and distributors in the furniture industry with exhibits at the International Home Furnishings Market.
Cost: $25.00
624 Pages
Frequency: Semiannual
Founded in 1974
Printed in 4 colors on glossy stock

14658 Painting and Wallcovering Contractor

Painting and Decorating Contractors of America

2316 Millpark Drive
Suite 220
Maryland Heights, MO 63043

314-514-7322
800-332-7322
FAX 314-514-9417
E-Mail: bhoran@pdca.org
Home Page: www.pdca.org
Social Media: *Facebook*

Beth Horan, VP Operations
David Ayala, Chairman
David Ryker, Vice Chairman
Darylene Dennon, Treasurer

Offers a list of over 3,300 member contractors engaged in painting, decorating and special coatings applications.
Frequency: Annual
Circulation: 3,500
Mailing list available for rent

14659 Rauch Guide to the US Paint Industry

Grey House Publishing
4919 Route 22
PO Box 56
Amenia, NY 12501

518-789-8700
800-562-2139
FAX 845-373-6390
E-Mail: books@greyhouse.com
Home Page: www.greyhouse.com
Social Media: *Facebook, Twitter*

Leslie Mackenzie, Publisher
Richard Gottlieb, Editor

Provides industry structure and current market information about this $16.6 billion industry. The report is divided into five major chapters with 100+ tables and 20 figures in its 500 pages. Unique to the Guide is a profile over 800 industry manufacturers, with sales estimates, products, mergers and acquisitions, divestitures and other information for the 400 largest companies.
Cost: $595.00
500 Pages
ISBN: 1-592371-27-2
Founded in 1981

14660 Specifiers' Guide and Directory of Contract Wallcoverings

Wall Publications
570 Fashion Ave
New York, NY 10018-1603

212-730-9590

Anne Gober, Owner

A who's who directory of services and supplies to the industry.
Cost: $15.95
Frequency: Annual
Circulation: 15,000

14661 Tile & Decorative Surfaces

18 E 41st Street
New York, NY 10017-6222

212-376-7722
FAX 212-376-7723
E-Mail: publisher@ashlee.com
Home Page: www.ashlee.com/tile

Jordan M Wright, President/Publisher

The Tile industry including ceramic, natural stone, terrazzo, agglomerated, cement glasstiles and others allied to the field. Architects, designers, importers, retail floor covering dealers, distributors, installers and contractors. Also, firms involved with renovation and restoration of tile. Accepts advertising.
Cost: $25.00
Frequency: Monthly
Circulation: 24,000
ISSN: 0192-9550
Founded in 1950

14662 Wallcovering Pattern Guide and Source Directory

Home Fashion Information Network
557 S Duncan Avenue
Clearwater, FL 33756-6255

A list of wallcovering manufacturers and distributors are offered in this comprehensive directory aimed at the interior design community.
Cost: $78.00
Frequency: Semiannual
Circulation: 10,000

14663 Western Floors: Buyers Guide & Directory

Specialist Publications
17835 Ventura Boulevard
Suite 312
Encino, CA 91316-3634

818-709-1437

A list of firms which manufacture, import or distribute floor coverings.
Cost: $15.00
Frequency: Annual
Circulation: 17,000

14664 Who's Who in Floor Covering Distribution

National Association of Floor Covering Distributor
122 S. Michigan Avenue
Suite 1040
Chicago, IL 60603

312-461-9600
FAX 312-461-0777
E-Mail: info@nafed.org
Home Page: www.nafed.org

Jack Lidenschmidt, President
Danny Harris, Executive Director/CEO
Norbert Makowka, Vice President, Technical
Tamara Matthews, Communications Coordinator
Socorro Garcia, Office Manager

Offers information on over 400 member distributors and suppliers of floor coverings.
40 Pages
Frequency: Annual
Mailing list available for rent

Industry Web Sites

14665 http://gold.greyhouse.com

G.O.L.D Grey House OnLine Databases

Grey House Publishing's online database platform, GOLD, offers Quick Search, Keyword Search and Expert Search for most business sectors including interior design, decorating and lighting markets. The GOLD platform makes finding the information you need quick and easy - whether you're a novice searcher or an experienced database user. All of Grey House's directory products are available for subscription on the GOLD platform.

14666 www.carpet-rug.com

Carpet and Rug Institute

National association of carpet and rug manufacturers. Source for product information.

14667 www.fider.org

Foundation for Interior Design Education Research

Promotes excellence in interior design education through research and the accreditation of academic programs.

14668 www.greyhouse.com

Grey House Publishing

Authoritative reference directories for most business sectors including interior design, decorating and lighting markets. Users can search the online databases with varied search criteria allowing for custom searches by product category, geographic area, sales volume, keyword, subject and more. Full Grey House catalog and online ordering also available.

14669 www.homeshows.net
Home Show Management

Organizes three annual south Flordia home design and remodeling shows in Coconut Grove, Ft. Lauderdale and Miami Beach convention centers. Open to the trade and public.

14670 www.i-d-d.com
Interior Design Directory

Sources and links for the interior designer.

14671 www.iesna.org
Illuminating Engineering Society of North America

To advance knowledge and disseminate information for the improvement of the lighted environment to the benefit of society. Publishes a monthly magazine.

14672 www.iida.org
International Interior Design Association

Members are professionals from various facets of the interior design trade.

14673 www.interiordesignsociety.org
Interior Design Society

The largest design organization exclusively dedicated to serving the residential interior design industry. Promotes retail interior design, emphasizing education and skills improvement.

14674 www.nadfd.com
National Assn of Decorative Fabric Distributors

Promotes the textile and home furnishings manufacturers and distributors.

14675 www.nafcd.org
National Assn of Floor Covering Distributors

This organization offers information on over 500 member distributors and suppliers of floor coverings. Publications available to members.

14676 www.ncidq.org
National Council for Interior Design Qualification

Serves to identify to the public those interior designers who have met the minimum standards for professional practice by passing the NCIDQ examination.

14677 www.ngpp.org
National Guild of Professional Paperhangers

Promotes products, upgrades skills of paperhangers and encourages good business ethics. Holds workshops and seminars.

14678 www.nhfa.org
National Home Furnishings Association

A federation of local home furnishings representatives association.

14679 www.oikos.com
Oikos

Devoted to serving professionals whose work promotes sustainable design and construction. Oikos is a Greek word meaning house. Oikos serves as the root for two English words: ecology and economy. That may seem contradictory at first, but it makes perfect sense. Ecology is the science of interactions in natural communities. It examines the web of life where plants, animals, rocks and gases all affect one another.

Healthy communities, healthy ecosystems exist ina dynamic equilibrium.

14680 www.pdra.org
Paint and Decorating Retailers Association

This organization lists 1,500 manufacturers, manufacturers' representatives, distributors, and suppliers of decorating merchandise.

14681 www.resources.com
Resources

Organized into easy point and click directories under a highly interactive database.

Associations

14682 Academy of International Business

The Eli Broad College of Businesss, Eppley Cent
645 N. Shaw Ln Rm 7
East Lansing, MI 48824

517-432-1452
FAX 517-432-1009
E-Mail: webmaster@aib.msu.edu
Home Page: aib.msu.edu
Social Media: *Facebook, Twitter, LinkedIn*

Rosalie Tung, President
Masaaki Kotabe, President-Elect
Nakiye Boyacigiller, Past President
Charles Dhanaraj, Vice President Program
Jeremy VP, Administration, VP, Administration

Leading association of scholars and specialists in the field of international business. Members include academics, consultants, researchers, and NGO representatives. AIB has chapters worldwide to facilitate networking and information exchange at a local level.
3,089 Members
Founded in 1959
Mailing list available for rent: 3000 names at $250 per M

14683 American Association of Exporters and Importers

1717 K Street, NW
Suite 1120
Washington, DC 20006

202-857-8009
FAX 202-857-7843
E-Mail: hg@aaei.org
Home Page: www.aaei.org
Social Media: *Facebook, Twitter, LinkedIn, Google+*

Phyliss Wigginton, Chair
Karen Kelly, Vice Chair
Lori Goldberg, Vice Chair
Theresa Walker, Secretary/Treasurer
Marianne Rowden, President, CEO

Supports those involved in trade development with other countries and conducting business in the United States, as well as developments affecting trade originating from Treasury, Customs, US Courts, Commerce Department, International Trade Commission, Federal Maritime Commission and other regulatory agencies. Hosts annual trade show.
Founded in 1921

14684 American Foreign Service Association

2101 E Street NW
Washington, DC 20037

202-338-4045
FAX 202-338-6820
Home Page: www.afsa.org
Social Media: *Facebook, Twitter, YouTube, Flickr*

Barbara Stephenson, President
Sharon Wayne, Vice President
Angie Bryan, State Vice President
Hon. Charles A. Ford, Treasurer
Ian Houston, Executive Director

Organization dedicated specifically to preserving and enhancing theintegrity of the U.S. Foreign Service.
31000 Members
Founded in 1924

14685 American League for Exports and Security Assistance

122 C St NW
Suite 740
Washington, DC 20001-2109

202-393-3903
FAX 202-737-4727

David Lewis, President

Encourages and supports the sale of American defense products abroad in agreement with foreign policy, security and economic goals of the nation.
38 Members
Founded in 1976

14686 Assist International

90 John Street
Room 505
New York, NY 10038

212-244-2074
FAX 831-439-9602
E-Mail: info@assist-intl.com
Home Page: www.assist-intl.com

International trade promotion and consulting firm: mailing lists, seminars, conferences, international business expo.

14687 Association Of American Chambers of Commerce in Latin America

1615 H. Street, NW
Washington, DC 20062-2000

202-463-5485
E-Mail: info@aaccla.org
Home Page: www.aaccla.org

Nicholas Galt, Chair
Thomas H. Kenna, Vice Chair
Aldo Defilippi, VP for Executive Management
Neil Herrington, Executive Vice President
Reuben Smith-Vaughan, Executive Director

Promotes trade and investment between the United States and the countries of the region through free trade, free markets, and free enterprise.
20000 Members

14688 CalChamber Council for International Trade

1215 K Street
Suite 1400
Sacramento, CA 95814

916-444-6670
800-649-4921
FAX 916-325-1272
Home Page: www.calchamber.com
Social Media: *Facebook, Twitter, LinkedIn*

Allan Zaremberg, President/CEO
Ann Amioka, VP, Communications
Drew Savage, VP, Corporate Relations
Karen Olson, VP, Marketing
Denise Davis, Vice President, Media Relationsÿ

Formed by the merging of California Council for International Trade and California Chamber of Commerce International Trade Committee. The foundation is dedicated to preserving and strengthening the California business climate and private enterprise through accurate, impartial research and education on public policy issues of interest to the California business and public policy communities.
15000 Members
Founded in 1890
Mailing list available for rent

14689 Customs and International Trade Bar Association

Home Page: www.citba.org

Joseph W. Dorn, President
Lawrence M. Friedman, Vice President

Melvin S. Schwechter, Chair, Export Committee
Kathleen W. Cannon, Secretary
William Sjoberg, Treasurer

Members represent importers, exporters, and domestic producers in matters involving U.S. customs laws, antidumping and countervailing duty laws, safeguards, export licensing, and other federal laws and regulations that affect imported or exported merchandise or international commerce.
Founded in 1917

14690 FSC/DISC Tax Association

Council for International Tax Education
PO Box 1012
White Plains, NY 10602

914-328-5656
800-207-4432
FAX 914-328-5757
E-Mail: info@citeusa.org
Home Page: www.citeusa.org

Robert Ross, Owner

The only organization operating on a national level devoted to educational interests of companies that have set up a foreign sales corporation.
300 Members
Founded in 1984
Mailing list available for rent

14691 Foreign Trade Association

437 S. Cataract Avenue
Suite #4B
San Dimas, CA 91773

888-223-6459
FAX 310-220-4474
E-Mail: info@foreigntradeassociation.com
Home Page: www.foreigntradeassociation.com
Social Media: *Facebook, Twitter, LinkedIn*

Keith Sanchez, Chairman
Tom Gould, President
Adonna Martin, 1st VP
Cameron Roberts, 2nd VP
Glenn Patton, Treasurer

Business association of European and International commerce that promotes the values of free trade.

14692 Forum for International Trade Training

116 Lisgar Street
Suite 100
Ottawa, ON K2P 0C2

613-230-3553
800-561-3488
FAX 613-230-6808
E-Mail: info@fitt.ca
Home Page: www.fitt.ca
Social Media: *Facebook, Twitter, LinkedIn, Google+*

Bill Walsh, Chair
Leslie Meingast, Vice Chair
Paloma Healey, Board Member
Scott Forbes, Board Member
Carl Burlock, Treasurer

Nonprofit organization that develops international business programs, sets competency standards, designs the certification and accreditation programs for the Certified International Trade Professional (CITP) designation, and generally ensures continuing professional development in the practice of international trade.
Founded in 1992

14693 Futures Industry Association

2001 Pennsylvania Avenue NW
Suite 600
Washington, DC 20006-1823

202-466-5460
FAX 202-296-3184

E-Mail: info@fia.org
Home Page: www.futuresindustry.org/
Social Media: *Facebook, Twitter, LinkedIn, Flickr*

Gerald Corcoran, Chair
Walter L. Lukken, President & CEO
Mary Ann Burns, EVP & COO
M. Clarkÿ Hutchison, Treasurer
Emily Portney, Secretary

Trade association in the United States composed of futures commission merchants.
Founded in 1955

14694 Gemini Shippers Group National Fashion Accessories Assoc

137 West 25th Street
3rd Floor
New York, NY 10001

212-947-3424
FAX 212-629-0361
E-Mail: info@geminishippers.com
Home Page: www.geminishippers.com
Social Media: *Facebook, Twitter, LinkedIn, Google+*

Sara L.ÿ Mayes, President
Kenneth O'Brien, Chief Operating Officer
Nicole Uchrin, Managing Director
Rich Moore, SalesÿDirector
Arlene L. Blocker, Membership Director

Offers membership to importers and exporters of various products.
200 Members
Founded in 1916

14695 Hong Kong Association of New York

115 East 54th Street
New York, NY 10022-4563

646-770-1676
E-Mail: contact@hkany.org
Home Page: www.hkany.org
Social Media: *Facebook, LinkedIn, Instagram*

Mary Wadsworth Darby, Chairman
Sylvia S. Ng, Vice Chairman
Amy Shang, Vice Chairman
Sebastien J.ÿ Granier, Treasurer
Raymond H. Wong, Secretary

Nonprofit organization that promotes global cooperation, communication exchange and synergy among the Hong Kong business associations worldwide.
1100 Members
Founded in 1987

14696 Hong Kong Trade Development Council

38/F, Office Tower
Convention Plaza, 1 Harbour Road
Wanchai, HK 10017-2951

852-183- 668
800-820-5188
FAX 852-282-0249
E-Mail: hktdc@hktdc.org
Home Page: www.hktdc.com
Social Media: *Facebook, Twitter, LinkedIn, Google+, YouTube, RSS, Weibo*

Margaret Fong, Executive Director
Benjamin Chau, Deputy Executive Director
Raymond Yip, Deputy Executive Director
Lawrence Yipp, Asst. Executive Director
Sophia Chong, Asst. Executive Director

Promotes trade between the United States and Hong Kong.
Founded in 1966
Mailing list available for rent

14697 International Chamber of Commerce (ICC)

33-43 Ave. du President Wilson
Paris, Fr 75116

33- 0 -1 49
FAX 3- 0- 1 4
E-Mail: icc@iccwbo.org
Home Page: www.iccwbo.org
Social Media: *Facebook, Twitter, LinkedIn, Google+, YouTube*

Harold McGraw III, Chairman
Sunil Bharti Mittalÿ, Vice Chairman
Frederico Fleury Curadoÿ, Vice Chairman
Dennis M. Nally, Vice Chairman
Gerard Worms, Honorary Chairman
Founded in 1919
Mailing list available for rent

14698 International Reciprocal Trade Association

524 Middle Street
Portsmouth, VA 23704

FAX 757-257-4014
E-Mail: ariggs@comcast.net, ron@irta.com
Home Page: www.irta.com
Social Media: *Facebook, LinkedIn, Google+, YouTube*

Annette Riggs, President
Scott Whitmer, Vice President
Ron Whitney, Executive Director
Chong Kee Tan, Secretary
Mary Ellen Rosinski, Treasurer

A nonprofit organization committed to promoting just and equitable standards of practice and operation within the Modern Trade and Barter and otherAlternative Capital Systems Industry.
Founded in 1979

14699 International Trade Administration

U.S. Department of Commerce
1401 Constitution Ave NW
Washington, DC 20230

800-USA-TRAD
Home Page: trade.gov
Social Media: *Facebook, Twitter, LinkedIn, Blog*

Tim Rosado, CFO & CAO
Arthur Paiva, Chief Information Officer
Stefan M. Selig, Under Secretary
Kenneth E. Hyatt, Deputy Under Secretary
Arun Venkataraman, Policy Director

An agency in the United States Department of Commerce that promotesUnited States exports of nonagricultural U.S. services and goods.

14700 International Trade and Finance Association

PO Box 2145
Kingsville, TX 78363

E-Mail: itfaconf@ymail.com
Home Page: www.itfaconf.org

Khosrow Fatemi, President
Janina Witkowska, VP of Membership
Alfred Eckes, EVP
Scheherazade Rehman, President Elect
Pompeo Della Posta, Board Member

A multidisciplinary association for academics and professionals interested in studying international trade and finance and in promoting a general awareness of these fields and related global economic issues.
Founded in 1988

14701 International Trademark Association

655 Third Avenue
10th Floor
New York, NY 10017

212-642-1700
FAX 212-768-7796
E-Mail: memberservices@inta.org

Home Page: www.inta.org/
Social Media: *Facebook, Twitter, LinkedIn*

J. Scott Evans, President
Joseph Ferrettiÿ, Vice President
Ronald Van Tuijlÿ, President Elect
Tish Berard, VP
Etienne Sanz de Acedo, CEO

A global association of trademark owners and professionals dedicated to supporting trademarks and related intellectual property in order to protectconsumers and to promote fair and effective commerce.
6400 Members
Founded in 1878

14702 International Warehouse Logistics Association

2800 S. River Road
Suite 260
Des Plaines, IL 60018

847-813-4699
FAX 847-813-0115
E-Mail: mail@iwla.com
Home Page: www.iwla.com
Social Media: *Facebook, Twitter, LinkedIn, YouTube*

Steve DeHaan, President/CEO
Jay Strother, Vice President
John Levi, Executive Director
Jennifer Rezny, Membership Director
Ben Fairbank, Senior Coordinator, Strategic Data

The unified voice of the global logistics outsourcing industry, representing third party warehousing, transportation and logistics service providers. Our member companies provide the most timely and cost-effective global logistics solutions for their customers and are committed to protecting the free flow of products across international borders.
500 Members
Founded in 1891
Mailing list available for rent

14703 Italian Trade Agency

33 East 67th Street
New York, NY 10065-5949

212-980-1500
FAX 212-758-1050
E-Mail: newyork@ice.it
Home Page: www.italtrade.com

Maurizio Forte, Trade Commissioner & Executive Dir.
Gemma Di Gangi, Executive Secretary
Gioia Gatti, Food and Wine section
Marc Littell, Graphic Design
Alessandro Greco, Fashion and Start Up

Trade promotion section of the Italian Consulate.

14704 Latin American Studies Association

University of Pittsburgh
416 Bellefield Hall
University of Pittsburgh
Pittsburgh, PA 15260

412-648-7929
FAX 412-624-7145
E-Mail: lasa@pitt.edu
Home Page: lasa.international.pitt.edu/
Social Media: *Facebook, Twitter, LinkedIn*

Gilbertÿ Joseph, President
Joanne Rappaport, Vice President-President Elect
Timothy J. Power, Treasurer
Debra Castillo, Past President
Milagros Pereyra-Rojas, Executive Director

To foster intellectual discussion, research, and teaching on Latin America, the Caribbean, and its people throughout the Americas, promote the interests of its diverse membership, and en-

courage civic engagement through network building and public debate.
5000+ Members
Mailing list available for rent

14705 MIQ Logistics, LLC
11501 Outlook Street
Suite 500
Overland Park, KS 66211

913-696-7100
877-246-4909
FAX 913-696-7501
E-Mail: contact_us@miq.com
Home Page: www.meridianiq.com
Social Media: *Facebook, Twitter, LinkedIn, Google+, RSS Feed*

John E. Carr, President/CEO
Dan Bentzinger, Senior VP Transportation Services
Brenda Stasiulis, Chief Financial Officer
Reid Schultz, General Counsel & CAO
Clint Dvorak, Managing Director

Plans and coordinates the movement of goods throughout the world.

14706 NEXCO, Inc.
Grand Central Station
PO Box 3949
New York, NY 10163

877-291-4901
FAX 646-349-9628
E-Mail: director@nexco.org
Home Page: www.nexco.org
Social Media: *Facebook, Twitter, LinkedIn, YouTube*

Barney Lehrer, President
David Reiff, Secretary
Susan T.ÿ Gilligan, B.O.D.
Henry Lapidos, Director
Neil Lenok, B.O.D.

Members are import and export trading and import and export management companies, international trade service vendors and other international trade companies.
300 Members
Founded in 1963

14707 National Association of College Stores
500 E. Lorain Street
Oberlin, OH 44074

800-622-7498
FAX 440-775-4769
Home Page: nacs.org

Brian Cartier, CEO
Tony Ellis, VP, Industry Advancement
Jenny Febbo, VP, Strategic Communications
Rich Hershman, VP, Government Relations
Cindy Thompson, Director, Assocation Relations

14708 National Council on International Trade Development
1901 Pennsylvania Ave. NW
Suite 804
Washington, DC 20006

202-872-9280
FAX 202-293-0495
E-Mail: cu@ncitd.org
Home Page: www.ncitd.org

Mary Fromyer, Executive Director
David Joy, Senior Counsel
Cathleen Ryan, Asst. Dir. Of Enforcement
kevin J. Wolf, Asst. Secretary of Commerce
Gerard Horner, Head of Economic Analysis Program

Non-profit membership organization dedicated to providing direct expertise on a wide range of international trade topics. Our mission is to identify impediments to all aspects of interna-

tional commerce and to provide solutions to faciliting the global process.
Founded in 1967

14709 National Foreign Trade Council
1625 K Street, NW
Suite 200
Washington, DC 20006

202-887-0278
FAX 202-452-8160
E-Mail: nftcinformation@nftc.org
Home Page: www.nftc.org
Social Media: *Facebook, Twitter*

William A. Reinsch, President & CEO
J. Daniel O'Flaherty, Vice President
Marshall Lane, Sr Director of Operations
Andrew Watrous, Program Manager
Catherine Schultz, VP, Tax Policy

Business organization advocating a rules-based world economy.
300 Members
Founded in 1914

14710 PromaxBDA
5700 Wilshire Blvd
Suite 275
Los Angeles, CA 90036

310-788-7600
FAX 310-788-7616
E-Mail: steve.kazanjian@promaxbda.org
Home Page: www.promaxbda.org
Social Media: *Facebook, Twitter, LinkedIn, RSS*

Steve Kazanjian, President/CEO
Randy Smith, SVP & CFO
Stacy La Cotera, General Manager and Vice President
Lucian Cojescu, CIO
Stephen Earley, VP, Strategic Partnerships

International association of promotion and marketing, professionals in electronic media. Promotes the effectiveness of promotion and marketing within the industry and the academic community.
2400 Members
Founded in 1952

14711 Russian Trade Development Association
Palms & Company
6421 Lake Washington Boulevard North East
Penthouse Suite 408
Kirkland, WA 98033-6876

425-828-6774
FAX 425-821-9101
E-Mail: Palms@PeterPalms.com
Home Page: www.peterpalms.com

Variety of industrial trade shows by SIC code occuring in the Russian Federation throughout the year. Export services from USA to purchasing agent services in Russia for buyers worldwide.
25000 Members
Founded in 1934

14712 Small Business Exporters Association
800-345-6728
E-Mail: info@sbea.org
Home Page: www.sbea.org

Jody Milanese, Government Affairs
Patrick Post, Membership
Molly Day, Media/ Press Inquires

Association for small and mid-sized exporters and serves as the international trade arm of the National Small Business Association (NSBA), the nation's first small-business advocacy organization with more than 65,000 members across the country.
65000 Members

14713 The Association of Women in International Trade
4070 52nd Street NW
Washington, DC 20016

202-293-2948
E-Mail: info@wiit.org
Home Page: www.wiit.org
Social Media: *Twitter, LinkedIn*

Stefanie Holland, President
Rowan M. Dougherty, VP of Programming
Jennifer Shore, VP of Communications
Dana Watts, VP of Professional Development
Peggy A. Clarke, Secretary

Provides educational and networking opportunities to professional women involved in international trade and business.
Founded in 1987

14714 The Federation of International Trade Associations
172 Fifth Avenue
#118
Brooklyn, NY 11217

888-491-8833
E-Mail: info@fita.org
Home Page: www.fita.org

Kimberly Park, President & CEO

Provides resources, benefits and services to the international trade community.
45000 Members
Founded in 1984

14715 The Women in International Trade Charitable Trust
Home Page: www.wiittrust.org

Nicole Bivens Collinson, Chair
Amy Breeman-Rhodes, Treasurer
Emily Ruger-Beline, Advisory Committee
Amanda DeBusk, Advisory Committee
Cami Mazard, Advisory Committee

Funds charitable, scientific, and educational activities in international trade.
Founded in 2001

14716 US China Business Council
1818 N Street, NW
Suite 200
Washington, DC 20036

202-429-0340
FAX 202-775-2476
E-Mail: info@uschina.org
Home Page: www.uschina.org
Social Media: *Facebook, Twitter, LinkedIn, Google+*

Mark Fields, Chair
Robert A. Iger, Vice Chair
Paul D. Conway, Vice Chair
Indra K. Nooyi, Vice Chair
John Frisbie, President

Membership association for US companies doing business with the People's Republic of China. Provides representation, practical assistance, and up-to-date information to members.
240 Members
Founded in 1973
Mailing list available for rent

14717 US Council for International Business
1212 Avenue of the Americas
New York, NY 10036

212-354-4480
FAX 212-575-0327
E-Mail: info@uscib.org
Home Page: www.uscib.org
Social Media: *Facebook, Twitter, LinkedIn, RSS, Flickr, YouTube*

Harold McGraw III, Chair
Dennis Nally, Vice Chair
Thomas M. T. Niles, Vice Chair

Donald Monks, Treasurer
Peter M. Robinson, President, CEO

Addresses a broad range of policy issues with the objective of promoting an open system of world trade, finance and investment in which business can flourish and contribute to economic growth, human welfare and protection of the environment.
300 Members
Founded in 1945

14718 US International Trade Association
1401 Constitution Ave Nw
U.S. Department of Commerce
Washington, DC 20230

202-482-2867
800-USA-TRAD
FAX 202-482-2867
Home Page: www.trade.gov
Social Media: *Facebook, Twitter, LinkedIn, Blog, YouTube*

Tim Rosado, CFO & CAO
Arthur Paiva, Chief Information Officer
Stefan M. Selig, Under Secretary
Kenneth E. Hyatt, Deputy Under Secretary
Arun Venkataraman, Policy Director

Association for those interested in export opportunities for United States businesses.

14719 US Russia Business Council
1110 Vermont Avenue, NW
Suite 350
Washington, DC 20005

202-739-9180
FAX 202-659-5920
E-Mail: info@usrbc.org
Home Page: www.usrbc.org
Social Media: *LinkedIn*

Klaus Kleinfield, Chairman of the Board
Daniel A. Russell, President, CEO
Randi Levinas, EVP, Chief Operating Officer
Jeff Barnett, Senior Director of Policy
Marc Luet, Board Member

A Washington-based trade association that provides significant business developme, dispute resolution, government relations, and market intelligence services to its American and Russian member companies.

14720 United States Council for International Business
1212 Avenue of the Americas
New York, NY 10036

212-354-4480
FAX 212-575-0327
E-Mail: info@uscib.org
Home Page: www.uscib.org
Social Media: *RSS, Flickr, YouTube*

Harold McGraw III, Chair
Dennis Nally, Vice Chair
Thomas M. T. Niles, Vice Chair
Donald Monks, Treasurer
Peter M. Robinson, President, CEO

Promotes open markets, competitiveness and innovation, sustainable development and corporate responsibility, supported by international engagement and regulatory coherence.
300 Members
Founded in 1945

14721 WESTCONN International Trade Association
Home Page: www.westconn.org
Social Media: *Facebook, Twitter, LinkedIn*

George Woods, President
Edward Carey, Vice President
Sam Fischel, Treasurer
Mark Bishop, Co-Secretary
Susan Leavitt, Co-Secretary

Promotes industrial and academic awareness of the importance of international trade to our national economy.
Founded in 1972

14722 Women's International Shipping & Trading Association
Home Page: www.wista.net
Social Media: *Facebook, Twitter*

Karin Orsel, President
Rachel Lawton, Treasurer
Despina Panayiotou Theodosiou, Secretary
Katerina Stathopoulou, Board Member
Sanjam Gupta, Board Member

An international organization for women in management positions involved in the maritime transportation business and related trades worldwide.
2,100 Members
Founded in 1997

Newsletters

14723 AAMA News
Asian American Manufacturers Association
3300 Zanker Road
Maildrop Sj2f8
San Jose, CA 95134

408-955-4505
FAX 408-955-4516
E-Mail: aama@aamasv.com

Robert M Lee, Executive Director
Cost: $30.00
Frequency: Monthly
Circulation: 1000

14724 AIB Newsletter
Academy of International Business
Michigan State University
7 Eppley Center
East Lansing, MI 48824-1121

517-432-1452
FAX 517-432-1009
E-Mail: aib@aib.msu.edu
Home Page: aib.msu.edu

G Tomas M Hult, Executive Director
Tunga Kiyak, Managing Director
Irem Kiyak, Treasurer

Provides feature reports and news articles. Information on upcoming events such as conference announcements, calls for papers, and publishing opportunities are also featured.
Frequency: Quarterly
ISSN: 1520-6262

14725 Asahi Shimbun Satellite Edition
Japan Access
757 3rd Avenue
Front 3
New York, NY 10017-2013

212-869-7018
FAX 212-317-3025

Mo Matsuchita, Publisher
Cost: $3.00
Circulation: 12,000

14726 Asian Economic News
Kyodo News International
50 Rockefeller Plz
Room 803
New York, NY 10020-1605

212-603-6600
FAX 212-397-3721
E-Mail: kni@kyodonews.com
Home Page: www.kyodonews.com

Economic business news of Asian countries and regions.

14727 Buisness IP Services in Brazil
Probe Research
3 Wing Drive
Suite 240
Cedar Knolls, NJ 07927-1000

973-285-1500
FAX 973-285-1519
Home Page: www.proberesearch.com

Provides an overview of the business IP services market in Brazil; one of the most active IP markets in South America. Breakdown of Brazil companies. IT investment in B2B and networking applications. We discuss cable and ADSL broadband services and the e-government project. Profile of over 15 service providers.

14728 Business Russia
Economist Intelligence Unit
111 W 57th Street
New York, NY 10019-2211

212-586-1115
800-938-4685
FAX 212-586-1181
Home Page: www.eiu.com

Hyunkyu Lee, Owner

Monthly newsletter providing financial and market information as well as current business statistics, economic forecasts and political risk analysis for Russia.
Cost: $865.00
12 Pages
Frequency: Monthly
ISSN: 1357-0293

14729 Business Africa
Economist Intelligence Unit
111 W 57th Street
New York, NY 10019-2211

212-861-1115
800-938-4685
FAX 212-586-1181
Home Page: www.eiu.com

Daniel Franklin, Editorial Director
Richard Epstein, Director
Ingersoll Rand, Managing Director
Jane Morley, Senior Editor

Fortnightly newsletter identifying key business issues across Africa; forecasting future developments and trends and analysing their implications on Africa's business environment.
Cost: $1095.00
12 Pages
ISSN: 0968-4468
Founded in 1946

14730 Business Asia
Economist Intelligence Unit
111 W 57th Street
New York, NY 10019-2211

212-861-1115
800-938-4685
FAX 212-586-1181
Home Page: www.eiu.com

Daniel Franklin, Editorial Director
David Butter, Editor
Euan Rellie, Executive Director

Fortnightly newsletter focusing on operating issues and analyzing current political, business and economic developments across Asia.
Cost: $1055.00
12 Pages
Frequency: Fortnightly
ISSN: 0572-7545
Founded in 1946

14731 Business China
Economist Intelligence Unit

111 W 57th Street
New York, NY 10019-2211

212-586-1115
800-938-4685
FAX 212-586-1181
Home Page: www.eiu.com

Daniel Franklin, Editorial Director
Richard Epstein, Advertising Manager

Fortnightly newsletter alerting business executives to the political economic and legal changes that will affect corporate interests. Provides corporate case studies. Analysis financial issues in, and affecting, China. Offers practical, detailed advice.
Cost: $895.00
12 Pages
Frequency: 50 issues per y
ISSN: 1016-9766
Founded in 1946

14732 Business Eastern Europe
Economist Intelligence Unit
111 W 57th Street
New York, NY 10019-2211

212-861-1115
800-938-4685
FAX 212-586-1181
Home Page: www.eiu.com

Daniel Franklin, Editorial Director
Richard Epstein, Advertising Manager

Fortnightly newsletter providing information for business planning on the latest political and economic developments in Eastern Europe on a country-by-country basis.
Cost: $1395.00
12 Pages
Frequency: Weekly
ISSN: 1351-8763
Founded in 1946

14733 Business Europe
Economist Intelligence Unit
111 W 57th Street
New York, NY 10019-2211

212-861-1115
800-938-4685
FAX 212-586-1181
Home Page: www.eiu.com/

Lou Hencken, CEO/President
Paul Lewis, Editor
Nina Andrikian, Marketing

Fortnightly newsletter providing hard facts about changes in the EU's business environment; identifying opportunities for growth and analysing the impact of current issues on business in Europe.
Cost: $1435.00
12 Pages
Frequency: 44 issues per y
ISSN: 1351-8755
Founded in 1946

14734 Business India Intelligence
Economist Intelligence Unit
111 W 57th Street
New York, NY 10019-2211

212-586-1115
800-938-4685
FAX 212-586-1181
Home Page: www.eiu.com

Helen Alexander, CEO
Lou Kelly, Marketing Manager
Louis Ceil, VP

Monthly newsletter tracking the issues and trends in India's business environment; providing information on infrastructure and industries, tariffs, taxes and economic policy and consumer markets.
Cost: $660.00
16 Pages
Frequency: Monthly

ISSN: 1352-8335
Founded in 1946

14735 Business Latin America
Economist Intelligence Unit
111 W 57th Street
New York, NY 10019-2211

212-861-1115
800-938-4685
FAX 212-586-1181
Home Page: www.eiu.com

Daniel Franklin, Editorial Director
Richard Epstein, Director, Business Development

Weekly newsletter covering vital issues affecting business in Latin America, identifying the opportunities, and forecasting the risks to help executives make competetive corporate decisions.
Cost: $1370.00
12 Pages
Founded in 1946

14736 Caribbean Update
52 Maple Avenue
Maplewood, NJ 07040-2626

973-762-1565
FAX 973-762-9585
E-Mail: mexcarib@cs.com
Home Page: www.caribbeanupdate.org

Kal Wagenheim, Editor/Publisher

Monthly newsletter focusing on trade and investment opportunities in the Caribbean and Central America.
Cost: $267.00
24 Pages
Frequency: Monthly
Founded in 1985
Mailing list available for rent: 2500 names
Printed in one color on newsprint stock

14737 Country Finance
Economist Intelligence Unit
111 W 57th Street
New York, NY 10019-2211

212-861-1115
800-938-4685
FAX 212-586-1181
Home Page: www.eiu.com

Daniel Franklin, Editorial Director
Richard Epstein, Director, Business Development

Covering 47 countries, this service is a comprehensive overview of global financial issues and conditions. Provides case studies and resources to help companies find and manage finances in countries around the globe. A weekly alert service highlights changes as they happen.
Cost: $445.00
Frequency: 41 issues per y
Founded in 1946

14738 Country Forecasts
Economist Intelligence Unit
111 W 57th Street
New York, NY 10019-2211

212-861-1115
800-938-4685
FAX 212-586-1181
Home Page: www.eiu.com

Daniel Franklin, Editorial Director

Five-year forecasts of political, economic and business trends in 60 countries. Each quarterly updated forecast focuses on the key factors affecting a country's political and economic outlook and its business environment over the next five years.
Cost: $845.00
36 Pages
Frequency: Quarterly

14739 Country Monitor
Economist Intelligence Unit
111 W 57th Street
New York, NY 10019-2211

212-861-1115
800-938-4685
FAX 212-586-1181
Home Page: www.eiu.com

Daniel Franklin, Editorial Director
Richard Epstein, Director, Business Development

Weekly newsletter analysing the latest global economic and political events; providing risk assessment in emerging markets and facts on global trends and markets.
Cost: $895.00
12 Pages
Frequency: Weekly
Founded in 1946

14740 Country Reports
Economist Intelligence Unit
111 W 57th Street
New York, NY 10019-2211

212-861-1115
800-938-4685
FAX 212-586-0248
Home Page: www.eiu.com

Daniel Franklin, Editorial Director
Emily Morris, Senior Editor

Quarterly updates on the situation in over 180 countries. Each report includes and analysis of a country's current political and economic climate as well as 12-18 month economic projection.
Cost: $425.00
Founded in 1946

14741 Country Risk Service
Economist Intelligence Unit
111 W 57th Street
New York, NY 10019-2211

212-861-1115
800-938-4685
FAX 212-586-1181
Home Page: www.eiu.com

Daniel Franklin, Editorial Director

Information to assist financial risk management in emerging countries. Country Risk Service is an exclusive two-year forecasting service, assessing the solvency of 100 indebted countries. Each report includes projections of GDP, the budget deficit, trade and current account balances, financing requirements and debt-service ratio.
Cost: $760.00
60 Pages
Frequency: Quarterly
Founded in 1946

14742 East Asian Business Intelligence
International Executive Reports
717 D St Nw
Suite 300
Washington, DC 20004-2815

202-737-6366
FAX 202-628-6618
E-Mail: execrep@aol.com

William Hearn, Publisher

Twice-a-month newsletter containing business leads and market studies on Far East business.
Cost: $345.00
8 Pages
Frequency: 22 per year
Circulation: 300
ISSN: 0888-058X
Founded in 1986
Printed in on matte stock

14743 East/West Executive Guide
WorldTrade Executive

PO Box 761
Concord, MA 01742

978-287-0301
FAX 978-287-0302
E-Mail: info@wtexec.com
Home Page: www.wtexec.com

Alison French, Production Manager

Provides detailed information on how to do business in Russia, the CIS, and East/Central Europe. Focuses on key mechanical issues such as accounting and tax matters, local sourcing, the due diligence process, labor, finance, permits, environmental issues etc.
Cost: $656.00
Frequency: Monthly

14744 European Community
US Council for International Business
1212 Ave of the Americas
Suite 1800
New York, NY 10036-1689

212-354-4480
FAX 212-575-0327
Home Page: www.uscib.org

Peter Robinson, President

Newssheet on developments in the European community affecting business on council activities.
Circulation: 2,800

14745 Export Update
Trade Communications
733 15th Street NW
Suite 1100
Washington, DC 20005-2112

202-737-1060
FAX 202-783-5966

Stephen Pfeiderer, Publisher

Includes significant buying trends, specific sales leads, in-depth country market profiles, latest figures on trade activity, schedules for trade affairs and missions and insight on the affects of international news.

14746 Hong Kong Trade Development Council Newsletter
Hong Kong Development Council
219 E 46th St
Suite 1
New York, NY 10017-2951

212-838-8688
FAX 212-838-8941
E-Mail: new.york.office@tdc.org.hk
Home Page: www.tdctrade.com

Louis Ho, Executive Director

Promotes trade between United States and Hong Kong.
Frequency: Weekly
Founded in 1966

14747 Hong Kong Trader
Hong Kong Trade Development Council
219 E 46th St
Suite 1
New York, NY 10017-2951

212-838-8688
FAX 212-838-8941
E-Mail: new.york.office@tdc.org.hk
Home Page: www.tdctrade.com

Louis Ho, Executive Director
8 Pages
Frequency: Monthly
Printed in on glossy stock

14748 Indonesia Letter
Asia Letter Group

12508 Whitley Street
Whittier, CA 90601-2729

FAX 852-526-2950

14749 International Finance & Treasury
WorldTrade Executive
PO Box 761
Concord, MA 01742

978-287-0301
FAX 978-287-0302
E-Mail: info@wtexec.com
Home Page: www.wtexec.com

Alison French, CEO

Focus on techniques used by leading firms to manage worldwide financial resources. Topics covered include: tax, accounting and regulatory changes, currency and interest rate risk, cash management techniques, risk management strategies, regional treasury alerts.
Cost: $1245.00
Frequency: Weekly

14750 International Observer
PO Box 5997
Washington, DC 20016-1597

202-244-7050
FAX 202-244-5410

J Wagner, Publisher

Informs on world developments in political, diplomatic, government, security, and economic origins.
Cost: $240.00
10 Pages
Frequency: Monthly
Printed in one color

14751 International Securitization & Structured Finance
WorldTrade Executive
PO Box 761
Concord, MA 01742

978-287-0301
FAX 978-287-0302
E-Mail: info@wtexec.com
Home Page: www.wtexec.com

Jill McKenna, Production Manager
George Veoger, Editor
Pierre Brown, Publisher
Alleesa Aughas, Marketing Manager

A twice monthly report devoted exclusively to asset-backed securities in international markets. Covers all aspects of international asset-backed securitization, including innovative product trends, issuer considerations, regulatory matters, and tax and accounting considerations. Examines what is working in emerging markets and spotlights unique US transactions.
Cost: $1296.00
Frequency: Bi-monthly
Founded in 1996

14752 International Trade Alert
American Association of Importers and Exporters
1200 G Street NW
Suite 800
Washington, DC 20005

212-944-2230
FAX 202-661-2185
Home Page: www.aaei.org

Mathew Mermigousis, Production Manager
Stuart Iserber, Director of Events
Michelle Measel, Director of Events

Reports on current trade developments and advance notices of changes in rules for conducting business in the United States, as well as developments affecting trade originating from Treasury, Customs, US Courts, Commerce Department, International Trade Commission,

Federal Maritime Commission and other regulatory agencies.
10 Pages
Frequency: Monthly
Circulation: 2,200

14753 International Trade Reporter Current Reports
Bureau of National Affairs
1801 S Bell St
Arlington, VA 22202-4501

703-341-3000
800-372-1033
FAX 800-253-0332
E-Mail: customercare@bna.com
Home Page: www.bnabooks.com
Social Media: *Facebook, Twitter, LinkedIn*

Paul N Wojcik, Chairman
Gregory C. McCaffery, President and CEO
John Camp, Vice President
Lisa A. Fitzpatrick, Vice President
Audrey Hipkins, Vice President

A comprehensive source that reports and analyzes legislative and regulatory developments as well as private sector activities affecting international trade (both export and import).
Cost: $1744.00
Frequency: Weekly
Founded in 1929

14754 International Trade Reporter Decisions
Bureau of National Affairs
1801 S Bell St
Arlington, VA 22202-4501

703-341-3000
800-372-1033
FAX 800-253-0332
E-Mail: customercare@bna.com
Home Page: www.bnabooks.com
Social Media: *Facebook, Twitter, LinkedIn*

Paul N Wojcik, Chairman
Gregory C. McCaffery, President and CEO
John Camp, Vice President
Lisa A. Fitzpatrick, Vice President
Audrey Hipkins, Vice President

Only available source of digested, classified and indexed judicial and administrative decisions dealing with legal issues arising from US trade law (mostly import cases).
Cost: $2265.00
ISSN: 0748-0709

14755 International Trade Reporter Import Reference Manual
Bureau of National Affairs
1801 S Bell St
Arlington, VA 22202-4501

703-341-3000
800-372-1033
FAX 800-253-0332
E-Mail: customercare@bna.com
Home Page: www.bnabooks.com
Social Media: *Facebook, Twitter, LinkedIn*

Paul N Wojcik, Chairman
Gregory C. McCaffery, President and CEO
John Camp, Vice President
Lisa A. Fitzpatrick, Vice President
Audrey Hipkins, Vice President

A complete guide to the entire import process with analysis and full text of statutes, regulations, and executive orders on subjects such as customhouse brokers, dumping, countervailing duties, escape clauses, and presidential retaliation.
Cost: $1781.00

14756 Investing, Licensing & Trading
Economist Intelligence Unit

111 W 57th Street
New York, NY 10019-2211

212-586-1115
800-938-4685
FAX 212-586-1181
Home Page: www.eiu.com

Updated twice a year, ILT outlines business requirements for operating successfully in the world's major markets. This reference service, shows how the laws work in practice, with case studies of how leading multinationals obtain government approvals, set up local companies, calculate corporate and personal taxes and overcome restrictions and other legal hurdles in 60 countries and the European Union.
Cost: $345.00

14757 Managing Imports and Exports

Institute of Management and Administration
1 Washington Park
Suite 1300
Newark, NJ 07102-3130

212-244-0360
FAX 973-622-0595
E-Mail: customercare@bna.com
Home Page: www.ioma.com

The source of information on customs policies and procedures, BIS rules and regulations, and how to best enhance the compliance programs.
Cost: $437.00

14758 Market Europe

PRS Group
6320 Fly Rd
Suite 102
East Syracuse, NY 13057-9792

315-431-0511
FAX 315-431-0200
E-Mail: custserv@prsgroup.com
Home Page: www.prsgroup.com

Mary Lou Walsh, President
Doris Walsh, Chairman

Demographic and lifestyle information about consumers in Europe to help businesses do a better job marketing to those consumers.
Cost: $397.00
Frequency: Monthly
Circulation: 325
Founded in 1985
Printed in one color on matte stock

14759 Mexican Forecast

WorldTrade Executive
2250 Main St
Suite 100
Concord, MA 01742-3838

978-287-0301
FAX 978-287-0302
E-Mail: info@wtexec.com
Home Page: www.wtexecutive.com

Gary Brown, President
Jay Stanley, Sales Manager

Provides up-to-date information and forecasts on Mexican business. Includes coverage of foreign trade, currency, major industry sectors, market trends and investment climates.
Cost: $535.00

14760 Middle East Business Intelligence

International Executive Reports
717 D St Nw
Suite 300
Washington, DC 20004-2815

202-737-6366
FAX 202-628-6618
E-Mail: execrep@aol.com

William Hearn, Publisher

Twice-a-month newsletter containing business leads and market studies on Middle East busi-

ness.
Cost: $345.00
8 Pages
Circulation: 400
ISSN: 0731-5305
Printed in one color on matte stock

14761 Middle East Trade Letter

PO Box 472986
Charlotte, NC 28247-2986

704-536-9847
FAX 704-543-6161

Leslie B Cohen, Publisher
Business in the Middle East.
Cost: $139.00
4 Pages
Frequency: Quarterly
Circulation: 500
Printed in one color on newsprint stock

14762 Nielsen's International Investment Letter

Nielsen & Nielsen
1901 South Bay Rd Ne
Olympia, WA 98506-3532

360-352-7485
FAX 360-352-7485
Home Page: www.nelsonfurnitureworks.com

Paul Nelson, President

Tracks domestic and international stock markets and economics, precious metals and other commodities, USA and foreign bonds, interest rates, foreign currencies and real estate; offers clients specific buy and sell recommendations on domestic and international investments for both traders and investors.
Cost: $360.00
10 Pages
Frequency: Monthly
Printed in on matte stock

14763 North American Free Trade & Investment

WorldTrade Executive
PO Box 761
Concord, MA 01742

978-287-0301
FAX 978-287-0302
E-Mail: info@wtexec.com
Home Page: www.wtexec.com

Alison French, Production Manager
Gary Brown, CEO/President
Gary Brown, Editor
Dana Pierce, Marketing Manager
Dana Pierce, Circulation Manager

Covers NAFTA trade and investment developments. Key topics include rules of origin, tariff phaseouts, intellectual property protection, compliance and planning options, and business opportunities.
Cost: $734.00
Frequency: Annual+
Circulation: 100
Founded in 1992

14764 Practical Latin American Tax Strategies

WorldTrade Executive
PO Box 761
Concord, MA 01742

978-287-0301
FAX 978-287-0302
E-Mail: info@wtexec.com
Home Page: www.wtexec.com

Alison French, Production Manager

A monthly report on how leading companies are reacting to changes and developments in Latin American tax practice. Includes commentary from senior practitioners at major law and accounting firms and case studies from major

corporations.
Cost: $645.00
Frequency: Monthly

14765 Practical US/International Tax Strategies

WorldTrade Executive
PO Box 761
Concord, MA 01742-761

978-287-0301
FAX 978-287-0302
E-Mail: info@wtexec.com
Home Page: www.wtexec.com

Dana Pierce, Production Manager
Gary Brown, CEO/Publisher
David Cooper, Editor
John Nartel, Marketing Manager
Jay Stanley, Sales Manager

Analyzes how leading companies are reacting to changes in US-international tax practice. Leading experts provide practical guidance covering every area of international transactions.
Cost: $614.00
Frequency: Fortnightly
Circulation: 200
Founded in 1992

14766 Russian Far East Update

Russian Far East Update
PO Box 22126
Seattle, WA 98122-0126

206-447-2668
FAX 206-628-0979
Home Page: www.russianfareast.com

Trade and economic information plus news analysis of Russia's far east.
Cost: $20.00
Circulation: 1,300

14767 Vietnam Business Info Track

Vietnam Access
PO Box 1210
Port Hueneme, CA 93044-1210

FAX 805-985-0839

Kahn Le, Editor

Comprehensive coverage of Vietnam market. Focuses on trade, investment and sector reports. Gives you an immediate advantage in evaluating the potential of doing business in Vietnam and operating in a timely and cost effective matter.

14768 Vietnam Market Watch

Vietnam Market Resources
375 Lexington Avenue
New York, NY 10017

212-499-2000
FAX 203-256-9790
E-Mail: mail@inc.com
Home Page: www.inc.com/

Khoung Ho, Publisher
Aaron Goldstein, Chief Operating Officer
Caroline Basquez, Owner

For companies and professionals doing business in Vietnam.
Cost: $295.00
Frequency: Monthly
Circulation: 500
Founded in 2004

14769 Weekly International Market Alert

International Business Communications
114 E 32nd Street
#602
New York, NY 10016

212-686-1460

Johnathan Block, Publisher
International trade news.
Frequency: Monthly

14770 World Trade
Taipan Press
4199 Campus Drive
Suite 230
Irvine, CA 92612-4684

949-410-0980
FAX 949-725-0306

Will Swaim, Publisher

Articles aim to help companies expand international opportunities. Accepts advertising.
Cost: $24.00
96 Pages
Frequency: Monthly

Magazines & Journals

14771 AIB Insights
Academy of International Business
Michigan State University
7 Eppley Center
East Lansing, MI 48824-1121

517-432-1452
FAX 517-432-1009
E-Mail: aib@aib.msu.edu
Home Page: aib.msu.edu

Ilan Alon, Editor

Provides an outlet for short, interesting, topical, current, and thought provoking articles. Articles can discuss theoretical, empirical, practical or pedagogical issues affecting the international business community.
Frequency: Quarterly
ISSN: 1938-9590

14772 Aaonline
Africa-America Institute
420 Lexington Ave
Suite 1706
New York, NY 10170-0007

212-949-5666
FAX 212-682-6174
E-Mail: aainy@aaionline.org
Home Page: www.aaionline.org

Amber Jones, Executive Assistant
Mora McLean, Vice President
Joy Phumaphi, Vice President
Frequency: Quarterly
Circulation: 3000
Founded in 1953

14773 American Business in China
Caravel
23545 Crenshaw Blvd
Suite 101E
Torrance, CA 90505-5201

310-325-0100
FAX 310-325-2583
E-Mail: info@china4us.com
Home Page: www.china4us.com

Directory of US firms operating in China and Hong Kong; Hong Kong: a special administrative region; exporting to China - best US exporting prospects; China's major cities for foreign investments; marketing, advertising and exhibiting in China.
Cost: $99.00
288 Pages
Circulation: 10,000
ISBN: 0-964432-29-3
Founded in 1993
Mailing list available for rent: 2,000 names at $95 per M

14774 Asian Finance
Asian Finance Publications
14 Davis Drive
Armonk, NY 10504-3005

Focuses on international banking and finance.
Circulation: 13147

14775 Asian Industrial Report
Keller International Publishing Corporation
150 Great Neck Rd
Great Neck, NY 11021-3309

516-829-9722
FAX 516-829-9306
E-Mail: mcamca@rad.net.id

Robert Herihly, Publisher
Brian Deluca, Editor
Jerry Keller, President

New machinery and equipment.
Cost: $85.00
36 Pages
Frequency: Monthly
Circulation: 20000
Founded in 1882
Printed in 4 colors on matte stock

14776 Business America: the Magazine of International Trade
US Department of Commerce
200 Constitution Ave NW
Washington, DC 20210-0001

202-693-5000
FAX 202-219-8822
Home Page: www.dol.gov
Social Media: *Facebook, Twitter, LinkedIn, Pinterest, Blogger, Tumblr*

Hilda L Solis, CEO

Designed to help American exporters penetrate overseas markets by providing them with timely information on opportunities for trade and methods of doing business in foreign countries.
Cost: $2.00
Circulation: 13,000
Mailing list available for rent

14777 Cross Border
Economist Intelligence Unit
111 W 57th Street
New York, NY 10019-2211

212-586-1115
FAX 212-586-1181

Debrah Langley, Publisher

Focuses on multinational management issues faced by managers of international businesses.
Circulation: 55,000

14778 East Asian Executive Report
International Executive Reports
717 D St NW
Suite 300
Washington, DC 20004-2815

202-737-6366
FAX 202-628-6618
E-Mail: execrep@aol.com

William Hearn, Publisher

Monthly magazine covering the legal and practical requirements of doing business in Far Eastern countries.
Cost: $455.00
28 Pages
Frequency: Monthly
Circulation: 600
ISSN: 0272-1589
Founded in 1979
Printed in on matte stock

14779 Economist
PO Box 58524
Boulder, CO 80322-8524

303-945-1917
800-456-6086
FAX 303-604-7455

E-Mail: ukpressoffice@economist.com
Home Page: www.economist.com

Helen Alexander, CEO
Kate Cooke, Group Communications Manager
David Hanger, Publisher
James Wilson, Founder

The Economist is a news and business publication written for top business decision-makers and opinion leaders who need a wide range of information and views on world events. It explores the close links between domestic and international issues, business, finance, current affairs, science and technology.
160 Pages
Frequency: Weekly
Circulation: 1009759
ISSN: 0013-0613
Founded in 1843
Printed in 4 colors on glossy stock

14780 Export
Adams/Hunter Publishing
2101 S Arlington Heights Road
Suite 150
Arlington Heights, IL 60005-4142

FAX 847-427-2006

David Thayer, Publisher

Covers all aspects of international trade for distributors of consumer durables in 183 countries.

14781 Foreign Affairs
Foreign Affairs
58 E 68th St
New York, NY 10065-5953

212-434-9522
800-829-5539
FAX 212-861-2759
E-Mail: order@wshein.com
Home Page: www.foreignaffairs.org

David Kellogg, Publisher
Gideon Rose, Editor
Michael Pasuit, Marketing Coordinator
Eugnia Chang, Circulation Director

Reviews on events, news, people, and foreign relations.
Cost: $44.00
Founded in 1921

14782 Global Trade
North American Publishing Company
1500 Spring Garden St
Suite 1200
Philadelphia, PA 19130-4094

215-238-5300
FAX 215-238-5342
Home Page: www.napco.com

Ned S Borowsky, President and CEO
Bennett Zucker, Publisher

Assists international cargo decision makers in planning, financing and documenting goods and commodities in international trade. Accepts advertising.
Cost: $45.00
Frequency: Monthly
Founded in 1958

14783 IGT Magazine
World Trade Winds
610 Old Campbell Rd
Suite 108
Richardson, TX 75080-3379

972-994-9816
877-861-1188
FAX 972-699-1189
Home Page: www.asiatrademart.com

Offers information for exporters to find international buyers.
ISSN: 0259-9880
Founded in 1975

14784 Journal of International Business Studies
Academy of International Business
Michigan State University
7 Eppley Center
East Lansing, MI 48824-1121

517-432-1452
FAX 517-432-1009
E-Mail: managing-editor@jibs.net
Home Page: www.aib.msu.edu

Lorraine Eden, Editor

The leading peer-reviewed, scholarly journal that publishes research across the entire range of topics encompassing the domain of international business studies.
Frequency: 9x/Year
ISSN: 0047-2506

14785 LASA Forum
Latin American Studies Association
946 William Pitt Union
University of Pittsburgh
Pittsburgh, PA 15260

412-648-7929
FAX 412-624-7145
E-Mail: lasa@pitt.edu
Home Page: lasa.international.pitt.edu/

Hane Horowitz, Exhibit Management Head
Arturo Arias, Associate Editor
Sonia E Alvarez, President/Editor
Charles R Hale, VP
Milagros Pereyra-Rojas, Managing Editor

Published by the Latin American Studies Association.
Cost: $30.00
Frequency: Quarterly
Founded in 1969
Mailing list available for rent

14786 Latin Trade Magazine
Freedom Latin America
1001 Brickell Bay Drive
Suite 2700
Miami, FL 33131

305-749-0880
FAX 786-513-2407
E-Mail: info@latintrade.com
Home Page: www.latintrade.com
Social Media: *Facebook, Twitter, LinkedIn, RSS*

Rosemary Winters, Chief Executive Officer
Maria Lourdes Gallo, Executive Director & Publisher
Santiago Gutierrez, Executive Editor
Elida Bustos, Managing Editor
Manny Melo, Art & Production Director

Comprehensive news coverage and analysis of business issues in Latin America and the Caribbean. Available in English or Spanish.
Cost: $64.00
Frequency: Monthly
Circulation: 92,319
Founded in 1993

14787 Middle East Executive Reports
International Executive Reports
717 D St NW
Suite 300
Washington, DC 20004-2815

202-737-6366
FAX 202-628-6618
E-Mail: execrep@aol.com

William Hearn, Publisher

Monthly magazine covering the legal and practical requirements of doing business in the Middle East.
Cost: $455.00
28 Pages
Frequency: Monthly
Circulation: 1,000

ISSN: 0271-0498
Founded in 1978
Printed in 2 colors on matte stock

14788 Showcase USA
Bobit Publishing Company
23210 Crenshaw Blvd
Torrance, CA 90505-3181

310-539-1969
FAX 310-539-4329
Home Page: www.bobit.com

John Bebout, Owner

International marketing vehicle for American manufacturing.
Cost: $12.00
165 Pages
Founded in 1979

14789 Trade and Culture Magazine
Key Communications
PO Box 569
Garrisonville, VA 22463-0569

540-657-7174
800-544-5684
FAX 540-720-5687
Home Page: www.key-com.com

Debra Levy, Owner
Kim White, Managing Editor
Penny Stacey, Advertising Coordinator

Published to help executives make their companies competitive worldwide, featuring 22 trade zone presentations in each issue covering every country. Trade and Culture blends cultural insight with practical how-to business information.
Cost: $39.95
96 Pages
Frequency: Quarterly
Circulation: 45000
Founded in 1993

14790 US Council for International Business
1212 Avenue of the Americas
Suite 1805
New York, NY 10036-1689

212-354-4480
FAX 212-575-0327
E-Mail: info@uscib.org
Home Page: www.uscib.org

Peter Robinson, President
Davis Hodge, Marketing & Advertising

Monthly newsletter that supports those involved in the developments in the European community affecting business on council activities.
Frequency: Monthly
Founded in 1945

14791 US-China Business Council
US China Business Council
1818 N St NW
Suite 200
Washington, DC 20036-2470

202-429-0340
FAX 202-775-2476
E-Mail: info@uschina.org
Home Page: www.uschina.org

John Frisbie, President
Erin Ennis, VP
Ryan Ong, Director/Business Advisory Services

Covers all aspects of doing business with China and Hong Kong.
Cost: $100.00
240+ Members
Circulation: 6000
ISSN: 0163-7169
Founded in 1973
Printed in on glossy stock

14792 Vietnam Business Journal
VIAM Communications Group
535 W 114th Street
New York, NY 10027

212-854-2271
FAX 212-854-9099

Kenneth Felderbaum, Publisher

Research and experience based articles and graphics produces by journalists.

14793 World Trade
Freedom Magazine
2401 W. Big Beaver Rd
Suite 700
Troy, MI 48084

248-362-3700
Home Page: www.bnpmedia.com
Social Media: *Facebook, Twitter, LinkedIn*

Steve Beyer, Director

Articles are aimed at helping companies to expand their international opportunities.
Frequency: Monthly
Circulation: 70590
Founded in 1987

Trade Shows

14794 AIB Annual Meeting
Academy of International Business
645 N. Shaw Ln
Rm 7
East Lansing, MI 48824-1121

517-432-1452
FAX 517-432-1009
E-Mail: aib@aib.msu.edu
Home Page: www.aib.msu.edu

G Tomas M Hult, Executive Director
Tunga Kiyak, Managing Director
Irem Kiyak, Treasurer
Robert Grosse, President
Elizabeth Rose, Vice President Administration

Features a combination of plenaries, panels, and papers.
Frequency: June-July

14795 American-Turkish Council Annual Meeting
Ideea
6233 Nelway Drive
McLean, VA 22101

703-760-0762
FAX 703-760-0764
E-Mail: qwhiteree@ideea.com
Home Page: www.ideea.com

Quentin C Whiteeree, President

High level military and government officials and businessmen from Turkey and the United States. Seminar and over 25 exhibits of trade, defense, banking, investments and tourism.
1000 Attendees
Frequency: Annual
Founded in 1983

14796 Annual Convention and Trade Show
American Association of Exporters and Importers
1050 17th Street NW
Suite 810
Washington, DC 20036

202-857-8009
FAX 202-857-7843
E-Mail: hq@aaei.org
Home Page: www.aaei.org
Social Media: *Facebook, Twitter*

Kathy Corrigan, Director Meetings/Events
Marianne Rowden, President and CEO

Terri A Lankford, Director Membership & Marketing
David A Potts, Manager Office Administration
Megan Montgomery, Director of Government Affairs

Reports on current trade developments and advance notices of changes in rules for conducting business in the United States, as well as developments affecting trade originating from Treasury, Customs, US Courts, Commerce Department, International Trade Commission, Federal Maritime Commission and other regulatory agencies. 50 exhibitors with 50 booths.
550 Attendees
Frequency: May
Founded in 1921

14797 International Business Expo

Assist International
90 John Street
Room 505
New York, NY 10038

212-442-2074
FAX 212-725-3312
Home Page: www.assist-intl.com

Peter Robinson, Director

This expo has 170 exhibitors with 170 booths.
1800 Attendees
Frequency: April
Founded in 1999

14798 Showcase USA Trade Show

Bobit Publishing Company
3520 Challenger Street
Torrance, CA 90503

310-533-2400
FAX 310-533-2500
E-Mail: webmaster@bobit.com
Home Page: www.bobit.com

Mike Spivak, Editor
Ty Bobit, CEO

International marketing vehicle for American manufacturing.
165 Attendees
Founded in 1979

14799 USRBC Annual Meeting

US Russia Business Council
1701 Pennsylvania Avenue NW
Suite 520
Washington, DC 20006

202-739-9180
FAX 202-659-5920
E-Mail: lawson@usrbc.org
Home Page: www.usrbc.org

Eugene K Lawson, President

Highlights the opportunities and risks that are emerging in the Russian market as it enters a new stage of development.

Directories & Databases

14800 A Basic Guide to Exporting

World Trade Press
1450 Grant Avenue
Suite 204
Novato, CA 94945

415-549-9934
800-833-8586
FAX 415-898-1080
Home Page: www.worldtradepress.com

Alexandra Woznick

Includes significant new information on export regulations, customs benefit, and tax incentives. There are also hundreds of new sources

of assistance available with updated addresses and telephone numbers.
188 Pages
ISBN: 1-885073-83-6
Founded in 1999

14801 American Business in China

Caravel
23545 Crenshaw Blvd
Sutie 101E
Torrance, CA 90505-5201

310-325-0100
FAX 310-325-2583
E-Mail: info@china4us.com
Home Page: www.china4us.com

Davisson Chang, Owner
Sheryl Chang, Production Manager
Betty Yao, Marketing Manager

Directory of US firms operating in China and Hong Kong; Hong Kong as a special administrative region; exporting to China - best US exporting prospects; China's major cities for foreign investments; marketing, advertising and exhibiting in China. Also contains 1,000+ US contacts and 1,800+ China & Hong Kong contacts
Cost: $99.00
288 Pages
Frequency: Annual
ISBN: 0-964432-29-3
Founded in 1995
Mailing list available for rent: 2,000 names at $95 per M

14802 Arthur Andersen North American Business Sourcebook

Triumph Books
601 S La Salle St
Suite 500
Chicago, IL 60605-1725

312-939-3330
FAX 312-663-3557
Home Page: www.triumphbooks.com

Mitch Rogatz, President/Publisher
Tom Bast, Editorial Director
Blythe Hurley, Managing Editor
Kelley Thornton, Associate Editor

Government and trade agencies and trade-related databases in the United States, Canada and Mexico are profiled.
Cost: $150.00
Founded in 1994

14803 AtoZ World Business

World Trade Press
800 Lindberg Lane
Suite 190
Petaluma, CA 94952

707-778-1124
800-833-8586
FAX 707-778-1329
E-Mail: egh@worldtradepress.com
Home Page: www.worldtradepress.com

Edward Hinkelman, Publisher

The world's most comprehensive country-by-country resource for success in international business and trade. Consists of 100 Country Business Guides and 76 World Trade Resources. Offers entrepreneurs, business professionals and researchers access to vetted international business and trade intelligence, compiled into a single, reliable source.
Founded in 1993

14804 Brazil Tax, Law, & Business Briefing

WorldTrade Executive
2250 Main St
Suite 100
Concord, MA 01742-3838

978-287-0301
FAX 978-287-0302

E-Mail: info@wtexec.com
Home Page: www.wtexecutive.com

Gary Brown, Owner
Jay Stanley, Sales Manager

Coverage includes economic analysis and risk assessment, new transfer pricing rules, foreign direct investment, labor regulation, environment, privatization, accessing the Mercosur market, litigation, arbitration, and debt collection in Brazil, antitrust concerns for foreign acquisition, securitizing infrastructure projects, foreign investor access to the telecommunications market, and choices in creating Brazilian subsidiaries.
Cost: $297.00
340 Pages
ISBN: 1-893323-57-9

14805 CSI Market Statistics

Commodity Systems
200 W Palmetto Park Rd
Suite 200
Boca Raton, FL 33432-3788

561-392-1556
800-274-4727
FAX 561-392-7761
E-Mail: info@csidata.com
Home Page: www.csidata.com

Bob Pelletier, President

Offers information on daily, weekly and monthly time series of price and trading data for commodity markets worldwide, cash, futures options, index options, US stocks and mutual funds and government instruments.

14806 Chinese Business in America

Caravel
23545 Crenshaw Blvd
Suite 101E
Torrance, CA 90505-5201

310-325-0100
FAX 310-325-2583
E-Mail: info@china4us.com
Home Page: www.china4us.com

Davisson Chang, Owner
Sheryl Chang, CEO

Directory of ethnic Chinese importers and exporters in the US; marketing, sourcing and establishing a business in the US; US business laws and immigration regulations; money saving tips and business bargains.
Cost: $88.00
288 Pages
Frequency: Annual
Circulation: 5,000
ISBN: 0-964432-26-9
Founded in 1997

14807 DACA Directory

Distributors & Consolidators of America
2240 Bernays Drive
York, PA 17404

888-519-9195
FAX 717-764-6531
E-Mail: daca@comcast.net
Home Page: www.dacacarriers.com

Mike Wichert, Chairman
Mike Oliver, President
Steve Hubbard, VP
Andy Delaney, Secretary
Rich Eberhart, Treasurer

Firms and individuals active in the shipping, warehousing, receiving, distribution or consolidation of freight shipments.

14808 DRI Europe

DRI/McGraw-Hill
24 Hartwell Ave
Lexington, MA 02421-3103

781-860-6060
FAX 781-860-6002

E-Mail: support@construction.com
Home Page: www.construction.com

Walt Arvin, President

Subjects covered in this database include macroeconomic, microeconomic, and financial indicators for the European countries.

14809 DRI Middle East and African Forecast

DRI/McGraw-Hill
24 Hartwell Ave
Lexington, MA 02421-3103

781-860-6060
FAX 781-860-6002
E-Mail: support@construction.com
Home Page: www.construction.com

Walt Arvin, President

This large database offers more than 500 annual historical and forecast time series for 10 Middle Eastern and African economies.

14810 DRI/TBS World Sea Trade Forecast

DRI/McGraw-Hill
24 Hartwell Ave
Lexington, MA 02421-3103

781-860-6060
FAX 781-860-6002
E-Mail: support@construction.com
Home Page: www.construction.com

Walt Arvin, President

This comprehensive database covers cargo movements over major water trade routes worldwide.

14811 DRI/TBS World Trade Forecast

DRI/McGraw-Hill
24 Hartwell Ave
Lexington, MA 02421-3103

781-860-6060
FAX 781-860-6002
E-Mail: support@construction.com
Home Page: www.construction.com

Walt Arvin, President

Offers over 82,000 annual historical and forecast time series on import and export volumes, and prices in current US dollars.

14812 Dictionary of International Trade

World Trade Press
1450 Grant Avenue
Suite 190
Petaluma, CA 94952

707-778-1124
800-833-8586
FAX 707-778-1329
E-Mail: egh@worldtradepress.com
Home Page: www.worldtradepress.com

Edward G Hinkelman

The most respected and largest-selling dictionary of trade in the world. It is in use in more than 100 countries by importers, exporters, bankers, shippers, logistics professionals, attorneys, economists, and government officials.
Cost: $55.00
688 Pages
ISBN: 1-885073-72-0
Founded in 2004

14813 Directory of US Exporters

Journal of Commerce
33 Washington Street
Floor 13
Newark, NJ 07102

973-848-7000
E-Mail: amiddlebrook@cbizmedia.com
Home Page: www.cbizmedia.com

Amy Middlebrook, Group Publisher

Provides logistics professionals with active confirmed leads for over 60,000 US companies

involved in world trade.
Cost: $450.00
Frequency: Annual

14814 Directory of US Importers

Journal of Commerce
33 Washington Street
13 Floor
Newark, NJ 07102

973-848-7000
E-Mail: amiddlebrook@cbizmedia.com
Home Page: www.cbizmedia.com

Amy Middlebrook, Group Publisher

Provides logistics professionals with active confirmed leads for over 60,000 US companies involved in world trade.
Cost: $450.00

14815 Export Yellow Pages

US West Marketing Resources Group
1101 30th Street NW
Suite 200
Washington, DC 20007-3769

202-934-4584
800-228-2582
FAX 202-944-4680

David Lee, President

Approximately 16,000 US suppliers distributed worldwide through US commerce department channels.

14816 Foreign Exchange Forecast Data Base

Global Insight
800 Baldwin Tower
Eddystone, PA 19022

610-490-4000
FAX 610-490-2770
E-Mail: info@wefa.com
Home Page: www.wefa.com

Ben G Hackett, International Trade/Transportation

This large database covers over 130 monthly and 60 quarterly time series of historical and forecast data for foreign exchange rates.

14817 Foreign Representatives in the US Yellow Book

Leadership Directories
104 5th Ave
New York, NY 10011-6901

212-627-4140
FAX 212-645-0931
E-Mail: info@leadershipdirectories.com
Home Page: www.leadershipdirectories.com
Social Media: *Facebook, Twitter*

David Hurvitz, CEO
James M Petrie, Associate Publisher

Contact information for foreign representatives of over 187 nations at embassies, consulates, and intergovernmental organizations in the US, US executives of over 1,100 foreign corporations, over 275 foreign financial institutions with offices in the US, and over 300 international media outlets with bureaus in the US.
Cost: $245.00
850+ Pages
Frequency: SemiAnnual
ISSN: 1089-5833
Founded in 1969
Mailing list available for rent: 12,000 names at $125 per M

14818 GIN International Database

Global Information Network
146 W 29th St
Suite 7E
New York, NY 10001-5303

212-244-3123
Home Page: www.globalinfo.org

Lisa Vives, Owner

This large database offers all sorts of information on developing countries, ranging from economics and finance to health and social trends.
Frequency: Full-text

14819 GLOBAL Vantage

Standard & Poor's Corporation
55 Water St
New York, NY 10041-0003

212-438-1000
800-525-8640
FAX 212-438-0299

Deven Sharma, President

This database provides corporate financial data covering more than 2,500 US companies and over 1,500 companies in 23 other countries.

14820 Global Report

Citicorp
800 3rd Ave
New York, NY 10022-7669

212-688-1308
Home Page: www.citibank.com

One of the most comprehensive databases in the world offering information on foreign exchange, country reports, money markets, bonds, companies, industries and news.
Frequency: Full-text

14821 Importers Manual USA

World Trade Press
800 Lindberg Lane
Suite 190
Petaluma, CA 94952

707-778-1124
800-833-8586
FAX 707-777-1329
E-Mail: egh@worldtradepress.com
Home Page: www.worldtradepress.com

Edward Hinkelman, Publisher
James Nolan, Editor
Karla Shippey, Editor

Lists of trade fairs, embassies, chambers of commerce, banks, and other sources of information on various aspects of international trade.
Cost: $145.00
960 Pages
Frequency: 2-3 per year
Circulation: 3,000
ISBN: 1-885073-93-3
Founded in 1993

14822 International Directory of Importers

1741 Kekamek NW
Poulsbo, WA 98730

360-779-1511
800-818-0140
FAX 360-697-4696
Home Page: www.export-leads.com

Esther Camacho, Circulation

Publishes reference guides for worldwide importers, wholesalers, agents, and distributors.
Cost: $250.00
5000 Pages
Frequency: Annual
Founded in 1978

14823 Japan Economic Daily

Kyodo News International
747 3rd Ave
Suite 1803
New York, NY 10017-2803

212-935-4440
FAX 212-508-5441

E-Mail: kni@kyodonews.com
Home Page: www.kyodonews.com

This full coverage database contains news on Japanese business, industry, economics and finance developments.
Frequency: Full-text

14824 LEXIS International Trade Library
Mead Data Central
9443 Springboro Pike
Dayton, OH 45401

888-223-6337
FAX 518-487-3584
Home Page: www.lexis-nexis.com

Andrew Prozes, CEO
Rebecca Schmitt, Chief Financial Officer

This database contains information on international trade regulation decisions handed down from the Supreme Court and other legislative bodies.
Frequency: Full-text

14825 Local Chambers of Commerce Which Maintain Foreign Trade Services
US Chamber of Commerce-International Division
1615 H St NW
Washington, DC 20062-0002

202-659-6000
FAX 202-463-5836
Home Page: www.uschamber.org

Thomas J Donohue, CEO
Jean Hunt, Administrative Assistant
Cost: $15.00

14826 Mexico Tax, Law,& Business Briefing
WorldTrade Executive
2250 Main St
Suite 100
Concord, MA 01742-3838

978-287-0301
FAX 978-287-0302
E-Mail: info@wtexec.com
Home Page: www.wtexecutive.com

Gary Brown, Owner
Jay Stanley, Sales Manager

A single volume special report that provides guidance on tax and legal issues investors should consider when evaluating a possible company aquisition, starting a business or entering into a joint venture or strategic alliance in Mexico. Also featuring important guidance prepared by major accounting and law firms.
Cost: $297.00
291 Pages
ISBN: 1-893323-67-6

14827 North American Export Pages
US West Marketing Resources Group
1101 30th Street NW
Suite 200
Washington, DC 20007-3769

202-934-4584
800-288-2582
FAX 202-944-4680

David Lee, President

Approximately 50,000 suppliers from the United States, Canada, and Mexico wishing to export products worldwide.
Cost: $39.95

14828 Official Export Guide
North American Publishing Company
1500 Spring Garden St
Suite 1200
Philadelphia, PA 19130-4094

215-238-5300
FAX 215-238-5342
Home Page: www.napco.com

Ned S Borowsky, President and CEO

Offers information on customs officials, port authorities, embassies and consulates, chambers of commerce and other organizations involved in international trade.
Cost: $399.00
1800 Pages
Frequency: Annual
Founded in 1958

14829 Political Handbook of the World
McGraw Hill
PO Box 182604
Columbus, OH 43272

614-866-5769
FAX 614-759-3759
E-Mail: webmaster@mcgraw-hill.com
Home Page: www.mcgraw-hill.com

Arthur S Banks, Editor
Thomas C Muller, Editor

Annual reference book containing separate sections on every country in the world and more than 100 intergovernment organizations. Each edition completely updates political developments over the past year while retaining the extensive background information necessary for researchers to place current events in a comprehensive historical perspective.
1400 Pages
Founded in 1979

14830 Practical Guide: Doing Business in Ukraine
WorldTrade Executive
PO Box 761
Concord, MA 01742-0761

978-287-0301
FAX 978-287-0302
E-Mail: info@wtexec.com
Home Page: www.wtexec.com

Alison French, Production Manager

Topics covered include: common business structures, registration procedures, real property transactions, tax and foreign investment legislation, currency reforms and regulations, privatization programs, intellectual property.
Cost: $145.00

14831 Protecting Intellectual Property in Latin America
WorldTrade Executive
PO Box 761
Concord, MA 01742-0761

978-287-0301
FAX 978-287-0302
E-Mail: info@wtexec.com
Home Page: www.wtexec.com

Alison French, Production Manager

A complete guide to the protection of intellectual property in Latin America, including in-depth coverage of copyright law, patents and trademarks, software, pharmaceuticals, etc. Also deals with issues of enforcement and prosecution.
Cost: $235.00

14832 Russian Far East: A Business Reference Guide
Russian Far East Advisory Group
PO Box 22126
Seattle, WA 98122-0126

206-447-2668
FAX 206-628-0979
Home Page: www.russianfareast.com

Elisa Miller, Editor
Alexander Karp, Editor

Sourcebook for business people, travelers, and researchers focusing on trends and economic developments in the Russian Far East. Includes reviews of each of the ten administrative re-

gions and 27 maps
Cost: $79.00
270 Pages
ISBN: 0-964128-63-2

14833 Selling Successfully in Mexico
WorldTrade Executive
PO Box 761
Concord, MA 01742-0761

978-287-0301
FAX 978-287-0302
E-Mail: info@wtexec.com
Home Page: www.wtexec.com

Alison French, Production Manager

A detailed guide to market research, advertising, direct marketing, and trade show exhibition in Mexico, written by marketing professionals and supplemented by extensive data and key contracts.
Cost: $129.00

14834 Showcase USA: American Export-Buyers Guide and Membership
Bobit Publishing Company
3623 Artesia Boulevard
Redondo Beach, CA 90278

FAX 310-376-9043

List of member companies and organizations of Sell Overseas America.

14835 Trade Opportunity
US International Trade Association
1401 Constitution Ave NW
Washington, DC 20230-0001

202-482-2867
800-872-8723
FAX 202-482-2867
Home Page: www.ita.doc.gov

David L Aaron, Manager
Renee Macklin, Chief Information Officer

Leads to export opportunities for United States businesses.

14836 Trade Shows Worldwide
Gale/Cengage Learning
PO Box 09187
Detroit, MI 48209-0187

248-699-4253
800-877-4253
FAX 248-699-8049
E-Mail: gale.galeord@cengage.com
Home Page: www.gale.com
Social Media: *Facebook, Twitter, Google+, Youtube*

Patrick C Sommers, President

Each edition of this resource includes listings for more than 10,000 trade shows; approximately 6,000 trade show sponsoring organizations and more than 5,900 facilities, services and information sources on trade shows and exhibitions held in the United States and around the globe.
Frequency: Annual
ISBN: 1-414435-24-X

14837 US Custom House Guide
U.S. Custom House Guide

609-371-7825
888-215-6084
FAX 609-371-7885
E-Mail: mmcarthy@ubmglobaltrade.com
Home Page: www.uscustomhouseguide.com

Monica McCarthy, Associate Editor
Amy Middlebrook, Vice President, Directories
Dennis Ferrere, Advertising Sales Rep

List of ports having customs facilities, customs officials, port authorities, chambers of commerce, embassies and consulates, foreign trade zones and other organizations; related trade

services.
Cost: $399.00
Frequency: Annual January

14838 World Trade Almanac
World Trade Press
1450 Grant Avenue
Suite 204
Novato, CA 94945

415-454-9934
415-898-1124
Home Page: www.worldtradepress.com

Gayle Madison
Peter Jones

Industry Web Sites

14839 http://gold.greyhouse.com
G.O.L.D Grey House OnLine Databases

Grey House Publishing's online database platform, GOLD, offers Quick Search, Keyword Search and Expert Search for most business sectors including international trade markets. The GOLD platform makes finding the information you need quick and easy - whether you're a novice searcher or an experienced database user. All of Grey House's directory products are available for subscription on the GOLD platform.

14840 www.aib.msu.edu/
Academy of International Business

Members are executives and teachers in the international business field.

14841 www.fancyfoodshows.com
National Association for the Specialty Food Trade

Members are manufacturers, importers, distributors and retailers of specialty gourmet and fancy foods. Has an annual budget of approximately $15 million. Publications available to members.

14842 www.geminishippers.com
Gemini Shippers Group

Shippers association with global contracts for all commodities.

14843 www.greyhouse.com
Grey House Publishing

Authoritative reference directories for most business sectors including international trade markets. Users can search the online databases with varied search criteria allowing for custom searches by product category, geographic area, sales volume, keyword, subject and more. Full Grey House catalog and online ordering also available.

14844 www.iwla.com
International Warehouse Logistics Association

14845 www.ncitd.org
National Council on Int'l Trade Development

For exporters and importers and other professionals serving the international commerce industry.

14846 www.tdctrade.com
Hong Kong Trade Development Council

Promotes trade between United States and Hong Kong.

14847 www.uschina.org
US China Business Council

Membership association for US companies doing business with the People's Republic of China. Provides representation, practical assistance, and up-to-date information to members.

14848 www.vita.com
VMEbus International Trade Association (VITA)

Association for manufacturers of microcomputer boards, hardware, software, military products, controllers, bus interfaces and other accessories compatible with VMEbus architecture.

International Trade Resources

14849 Albania to the United Nations
320 E 79th Street
New York, NY 10075

212-249-2059
FAX 212-535-2917
E-Mail: mission.newyork@mfa.gov.al
Home Page: www.albania-un.org
Social Media: *Facebook, Twitter, LinkedIn, RSS Feed, Google+*

Geronimo Albano, Owner
Petrik Jorgji, Minister Counselor
Olisa Cifligu, Second Secretary
Ermal Frasheri, Adviser, legal Issues
Admira Jorgji, Counselor

14850 Antigua and Barbuda Department of Tourism and Trade
25 S.E. 2nd Avenue
Suite 300
Miami, FL 33131

305-381-6762
FAX 305-381-7908
E-Mail: cganuear@bellsouth.net
Home Page: www.antigua-barbuda.org

Byron Spencer, Manager

14851 Austrian Trade Commission
120 West 45th Street
9th Floor
New York, NY 10036

212-421-5250
FAX 212-421-5251
E-Mail: newyork@advantageaustria.org
Home Page: www.advantageaustria.org/us
Social Media: *Facebook, Twitter, RSS Feed*

Peter Athanasiadis, Manager
Sabine Miller, Project Manager
Walter HAfle, Director

14852 Azerbaijan - Permanent Mission to the United Nations
866 United Nations Plaza, Ste 560
48 str. & 1 Avenue
New York, NY 10017

212-371-2559
FAX 212-371-2784
E-Mail: azerbaijan@un.int,
az.protocol@yahoo.com
Home Page: www.un.int/azerbaijan/

Eldar Kouliev, Manager

14853 Bahamas Consulate General
231 E 46th Street
New York, NY 10017

212-421-6420
FAX 212-688-5926
E-Mail: consulate@bahamasny.com
Home Page: www.un.it/bahamas

Hon Eldred E Bethel, Contact
Forrester J. Carroll, JP, Consul General
Sandra N. McLaughlin, Vice Consul

Clemmy Eneas-varence, Sr. Information Clerk
Carolyn Young-Miller, Administrative Asst.

14854 Bulgarian General Consulate
121 E 62nd Street
New York, NY 10021

212-935-4646
FAX 212-319-5955
E-Mail: consulate.newyork@mfa.bg
Home Page: www.consulbulgaria-ny.org

14855 Business Council for the United Nations
801 2nd Avenue
Ste 900
New York, NY 10017

212-697-3315
FAX 212-682-9185
E-Mail: unahq@unausa.org
Home Page: www.unfoundation.org
Social Media: *Facebook, Twitter, YouTube, RSS Feed*

Allison B MacEachron, Executive Director
Kathy Calvin, President & CEO
Richard S. Parnell, COO
Walter Cortes, CFO
Aaron Sherinian, VP, Communications

14856 Chile Trade Commission
866 United Nations Plaza
Suite 603
New York, NY 10017

212-207-3266
FAX 212-207-3649

Alejandro Cerda, Trade Commissioner

14857 Consulate General of Bahrain
866 2nd Avenue
14th Floor
New York, NY 10017

212-223-6200
FAX 212-319-0687
Home Page:
www.un.int/bahrain/consulate.html

Jassim Buallay, Manager

14858 Consulate General of Belgium in New York
1065 Avenue of Americas
22nd Floor
New York, NY 10018

212-586-5110
212-586-7472
FAX 212-582-9657
E-Mail: NewYork@diplobel.fed.be
Home Page: www.diplomatie.be/newyork/

Piet Morisse, Manager
Marc Calcoen, Consul General
Leon Cortens, Deputy Consul General

14859 Consulate General of Brazil
220 E. 42nd St.
26th Floor
New York, NY 10017

917-777-7777
FAX 212-827-0225
E-Mail: cg.novayork@itamaraty.gov.br
Home Page:
http://novayork.utamaraty.gov.br/en-us/

Julio Cesar Gomes Dos Sant, Manager

14860 Consulate General of Costa Rica
14 Penn Plaza, #1202
225 West 34th Street
New York, NY 10122

212-509-3066
212-509-3066
FAX 212-509-3068

FAX 212-509-3068
Home Page: www.costariica-embassy.org

Otto Barcas, Manager

14861 Consulate General of Germany
871 United Nations Plaza
New York, NY 10017

212-610-9700
FAX 212-940-0402

Bernhard Von Der Planit, Manager

14862 Consulate General of Haiti
815 2nd Ave.
6th Floor
New York, NY 10017

212-697-9767
FAX 212-681-6991
E-Mail: contact@haitianconsulate-nyc.org,
cg.new
Home Page: www.haitianconsulate-nyc.org

Marie Therese, Manager
Charles A. Forbin, Consul General

14863 Consulate General of Honduras
255 West 36th Street
First Level
New York, NY 10018

212-714-9451
FAX 212-714-9453
Home Page: www.hondurasemb.org
Social Media: *Facebook, Twitter*

14864 Consulate General of India
3 E 64th Street
New York, NY 10065

212-774-0600
FAX 212-861-3788
Home Page: www.indiacgny.org

Ambassador Prabhu Dayal, Consul General
Mr. P.K. Bajaj, Consul (Head of Chancery)
Shambhu Amitabh, Vice Consul (Passport &
Consular)
Ajay Purswani, Consul (Visa)
Dhirendra Singh, Counsel

14865 Consulate General of Indonesia
5 E 68th Street
New York, NY 10021

212-879-0600

**14866 Consulate General of Israel in New
York**
800 Second Avenue
New York, NY 10017

212-499-5000
E-Mail: info@newyork.mfa.gov.il
Home Page: www.israelfm.org
Social Media: *Facebook, Twitter, YouTube,
flickr*

Ido Aharoni, Consul General
Founded in 1948

14867 Consulate General of Kenya
866 UN Plaza
Suite 4016
New York, NY 10017

212-421-4741
FAX 212-486-1985
Home Page:
www.kenya.embassy-online.net/kenya-consulat
e-general-new-york.php

Rolando Visconti, Manager

**14868 Consulate General of Lebanon in New
York**
9 E 76th Street
New York, NY 10021

212-744-7905
FAX 212-794-1510
E-Mail: lebconsny@aol.com
Home Page: www.lebconsny.org

Hassan Saad, Manager

14869 Consulate General of Lithuania
420 5th Avenue
3rd Floor
New York, NY 10018

212-354-7840
FAX 212-354-7911
E-Mail: kons.niujorkas@urm.lt
Home Page: ny.mfa.lt

Rimantas Morkvenas, Manager
Valdemaras Sarapinas, Consul General

14870 Consulate General of Malta
249 E 35th Street
New York, NY 10016

212-725-2345
FAX 212-779-7097

14871 Consulate General of Morocco
10 East 40th Street
New York, NY 10016

212-758-2625
FAX 646-395-8077
E-Mail: info@moroccanconsulate.com
Home Page: www.moroccanconsulate.com

Ramon Xilotl, Manager
Mohammed Benabdeljalil, Consul general
Sidi Mohammed El Bakkari, Deputy Consul

14872 Consulate General of Nigeria
828 2nd Avenue
New York, NY 10017

212-808-0301
FAX 212-687-1476
E-Mail: cgnny@nigeriahouse.com
Home Page: www.nigeriahouse.com

14873 Consulate General of Paraguay
801 2nd . Ave.
Suite 600
New York, NY 10017

212-682-9441
212-682-9442
FAX 212-682-9443
E-Mail: info@consulparny.com
Home Page:
www.consulparny.com/ingles/html/visas.html

Juan Baiardi, Manager

14874 Consulate General of Peru
241 East 49th St.
New York, NY 10017

646-735-3828
FAX 646-735-3866
E-Mail: consulado@conperny.org
Home Page: www.consuladoperu.com

Fortunato Ricar Quesada Seminario, Consul
General

14875 Consulate General of Qatar
2555 M St NW
Washington, DC 20037-1305

202-274-1600
FAX 202-237-9880
E-Mail: info@qatarembassy.net
Home Page: www.qatarembassy.net

Mohammad Al-Madadi, Consul

14876 Consulate General of Saudi Arabia
866 United Nations Plaza
Suite 480
New York, NY 10017

212-752-2740

Abdulrahman Gdaia, Execellency

14877 Consulate General of Slovenia
120 East 56th Street
Suite 320
New York, NY 10022

212-370-3006
FAX 212-421-1532
E-Mail: nky@gov.si

Reimo Pettai, Manager

14878 Consulate General of South Africa
333 E 38th Street
9th Floor
New York, NY 10016

212-213-4880
FAX 212-213-0102
E-Mail: consulate.ny@foreign.gov.za
Home Page: www.southafrica-newyork.net

Fikile Magubane, Consul-General
Thami Sono, Consul
Leon Naidoo, Consul
George Monyemangene, Consul General

14879 Consulate General of St. Lucia
2005 Massachusetts Ave., NW
Washington, DC 20036-1030

202-558-2216
800-345-6541
202-364-6795
FAX 202-318-0771
E-Mail: info@visahq.com
Home Page: saint-lucia.visahq.com

Julian Hunte, Manager

14880 Consulate General of Switzerland
633 3rd Avenue
30th Floor
New York, NY 10017-6706

212-599-5700
FAX 212-599-4266
Home Page: www.eda.admin.ch

Raymond Loretan, Excellency

**14881 Consulate General of Trinidad &
Tobago**
125 Maidan Lane
4th Floor
New York, NY 10038

212-682-7272
FAX 212-232-0368
E-Mail: consulate@ttcgny.com
Home Page: www.ttcgnewyork.com
Social Media: *Facebook, Twitter, YouTube,
RSS Feed*

Hon Harold Robertson, Contact
Rudrawatee Nan Ramgoolam, Consul General

14882 Consulate General of Ukraine
240 E 49th Street
New York, NY 10017

212-371-5690
FAX 212-371-5547
E-Mail: gc_usn@mfa.gov.ua
Home Page: ny.mfa.gov.ua

Serhii Pohoreltsev, Consul General

14883 Consulate General of Uruguay
420 Madison Street
6th Floor
New York, NY 10017

212-753-8581
212-753-8192

FAX 212-753-1603
E-Mail:
consulado@consuladouruguaynewyork.com
Home Page:
www.consuladouruguaynewyork.com

Basil Bryan, Manager
Carlos Orlando, Consul General

14884 Consulate General of Venezuela
7 E 51st Street
New York, NY 10022

212-826-1660
FAX 212-644-7471
E-Mail: ven.newyork@gmail.com
Home Page: newyork.embavenez-us.org

Carol Delgado Arria, Consul General

14885 Consulate General of the Dominican Republic
1715 22nd Street, NW
Washington, DC 20008

202-332-6280
202-332-7670
FAX 202-265-8057
E-Mail: embassy@us.serex.gov.do,
consular@us.ser
Home Page: www.domrep.org
Social Media: *Facebook, Blogspot*

Jose Luis Dominguez, Minister Counselor
Felipe Herrera, Cunselor
Morela Baez, Commercial Affairs
Alejandra Hernandez, Minister Counselor
Ligia Reid Bonetti, Minister Counselor

14886 Consulate General of the Netherlands
666 Third Avenue
19th floor
New York, NY 10017

877-388-2443
FAX 212-333-3603
E-Mail: nyc@minbuza.nl
Home Page: ny.the-netherlands.org
Social Media: *Facebook, Twitter, YouTube, RSS Feed*

Wanda Fleck, Manager

14887 Consulate General of the Principality of Monaco
565 5th Avenue
23rd Floor
New York, NY 10017

212-286-0500
FAX 212-286-1574
E-Mail: info@monaco-consulate.com
Home Page: www.monaco-consulate.com
Social Media: *Facebook, Twitter*

Maguy Maccario-Doyle, Consul General,
Minister Cousellor

14888 Consulate General of the Republic of Belarus
708 3rd Avenue
20th Floor
New York, NY 10017

212-682-5392
FAX 212-682-5491
E-Mail: gcny@belembassy.org
Home Page: www.belarusconsul.org
Social Media: *RSS Feed*

Sergei Kolos, Manager

14889 Consulate General of the Russian Federation
2343 Massachusettes Ave, NW
Washington, DC 20008-2803

202-588-5899
FAX 202-588-8937
Home Page: www.croatiaemb.org

14890 Consulate of Guyana
370 7th Avenue
New York, NY 10017

212-947-5110
FAX 212-573-6225
Home Page: www.guyana.org
Social Media: *Facebook, Twitter, Gmail, StumbleUpon,Pinterest,G*

Samuel Insanally, Ambassador, Permanent Rep
Edwin Carrington, Secretary
Mohammed A. O. Ishmael, Managing Director
Amral Khan, Administrator & Editor

14891 Consulate of the Republic of Uzbekistan in New York City
801 Second Ave
20th Floor
New York, NY 10017

212-754-7403
FAX 212-838-9812
E-Mail: info@uzbekconsulny.org
Home Page: www.uzbekconsulny.org

14892 Croatia Consulate, United States
369 Lexington Avenue
11th Floor
New York, NY 10017

212-599-3066
FAX 212-599-3106
E-Mail: croatian.consulate@gte.net
Home Page:
www.croatia.visahq.com/embassy/United-State s/

Abdul Seraj, Manager

14893 Ecuadorian Consulate
2535 15th Street NW
Washington, DC 20009

202-234-7200
866-ECU-DOR
FAX 202-667-3482
E-Mail: consuladodc@ecuador.org
Home Page: www.ecuador.us

Pablo Yanez, Consul General

14894 Egyptian Consulate Economic & Commercial Office
3521 International Ct. NW
Washingotn, DC 20008

202-895-5400
FAX 202-244-5131
E-Mail: embassy@egyptembassy.net
Home Page: www.egyptembassy.net
Social Media: *Facebook*

Ayden Nour, Executive Director
Mohamed M. Tawfik, Ambassador

14895 Embassy of Australia
1601 Massachusetts Avenue NW
Washington, DC 20036

202-797-3000
FAX 202-797-3168
Home Page: www.usa.embassy.gov.au
Social Media: *Facebook, Twitter*

Kim Beazley, Ambassador

14896 Embassy of Benin
2124 Kalorama Road NW
Washington, DC 20008

202-232-6656
FAX 202-232-2611
E-Mail: info@beninembassy.us
Home Page: www.beninembassy.us

Boni T. Yayi, President
Cyrille S. Oguin, Ambassador

14897 Embassy of Bosnia and Herzegovina
2109 E Street NW
Washington, DC 20037

202-337-1500
FAX 202-337-1502
E-Mail: info@bhembassy.org,
consularaffairs@bhem
Home Page: www.bhembassy.org
Social Media: *Facebook, Twitter, Google +, Pinterest*

Yayi Kujundzic, Ambassador Extraordinary
Jadranka Negodic, Ambassador
Edic Sehic, Minister-Counselor Head
Haris Bazdarecic, Counselor
Adnan Hadrovic, Minister-Counselor

14898 Embassy of Cambodia
4530 16th Street NW
Washington, DC 20011

202-726-7742
202-726-7824
FAX 202-726-8381
E-Mail: camemb.usa@mfa.gov.kh
Home Page: www.embassyofcambodia.org
Social Media: *Facebook*

Hem Heng, Ambassador
Mouth Keo Thida, Commercial Counselor
Koeut navuth, Defense Attache
Neang Chanthou, Finance Attache
Theam Vuth, Second Secretary

14899 Embassy of Estonia
2131 Massachusetts Avenue NW
Washington, DC 20008

202-588-0101
FAX 202-588-0108
E-Mail: embassy.washington@mfa.ee
Home Page: www.estemb.org
Social Media: *Facebook, Twitter, Flickr*

Marina Kaljurand, Ambassador

14900 Embassy of Ethiopia
3506 International Drive NW
Washington, DC 20008

202-364-1200
FAX 202-587-0195
E-Mail: ethiopia@ethiopianembassy.org
Home Page: www.ethiopianenmbassy.org/

Girma Birru, Ambassador
Tsegab Kebebew, Minister Counselor
Kidist Yakob, Counselor (Politcal Affairs)
Wahide Belay, Minister Counselor
Yohannes Getahun, Minster Counselor

14901 Embassy of Finland
3301 Massachusetts Avenue NW
Washington, DC 20008

202-298-5800
FAX 202-298-6030
E-Mail: sanomat.was@formin.fi
Home Page: www.finland.org
Social Media: *Facebook, Twitter*

Ritva Koukku-Ronde, Ambassador

14902 Embassy of Georgia
2209 Massachusettes Avenue, NW
Washington, DC 20008

202-387-2390
FAX 202-387-0864
E-Mail: embgeo.usa@mfa.gov.ge
Home Page: www.embassy.mfa.gov.ge

Temur Yakobashvili, Ambassador
David Rakviashvili, Envoy
Mikheil Darchiashvili, Minister
Thea Kentchadze, Sr. Counselor
Mariam Lebanidze, Counselor

14903 Embassy of Grenada
1701 New Hampshire Ave, NW
Washington, DC 20009-2501

202-265-2561
FAX 292-265-2468
E-Mail: gdaembassydc@gmail.com
Home Page: www.grenadaembassyusa.org
Social Media: *Facebook, Twitter, Google+*

E. Angus Friday, Ambassador
Patricia D.M. Clarke, Counsellor
Dianne C. Perrotte, Adminstrative Asst
Lucia Amedee, Receptionist/ Clerical Asst.

14904 Embassy of Jamaica (JAMPRO)
1520 New Hampshire Ave, NW
Washington, DC 20036

202-452-0660
FAX 202-452-0036
E-Mail: firstsec@jamaicaembassy.org
Home Page: www.embassyofjamaica.org

Audrey P. Marks, Ambassador

14905 Embassy of Jordan
3504 International Drive NW
Washington, DC 20008

202-966-2664
FAX 202-966-3110
E-Mail:
HKJEmbassyDC@jordanembassyus.org
Home Page: www.jordanembassyus.org
Social Media: *Facebook, Twitter, YouTube,
RSS Feed, Pinterest,*

Alia Hatoung Bouran, Ambassador
Amjad Hatem Al-Mbideen, Consul
Fawaz Bilbesi, Deputy Chief of Mission
Aishabint Al hussein, Military Attache
Qais Biltaji, Fist Secretary

14906 Embassy of Mali
2130 R Street NW
Washington, DC 20008

202-332-2249
FAX 202-332-6603
E-Mail: info@maliembassy.us
Home Page: www.maliembassy.us

Al Maamoun Baba Lamine Kehta, Ambassador
Muhamed Ouzouna Maiga, 1st Counselor
Ahmadou Barazi Maiga, 2nd Counselor
Colonel Bourama Sangare, Defence Attache
Mahama Dicko, Financial Attache

14907 Embassy of Mongolia
2833 M Street NW
Washington, DC 20007

202-333-7117
FAX 202-298-9227
E-Mail: dc@mongolianembassy.us
Home Page: www.mongolianembassy.us

Khasbazaryn Bekhbat, Ambassador

14908 Embassy of Panama
2862 McGill Terrace NW
Washington, DC 20008

202-483-1407
202-483-1407
FAX 202-483-8413
E-Mail: info@embassyofpanama.org
Home Page: www.embassyofpanama.org
Social Media: *Facebook*

Mario E. Jaramillo, Ambassador

14909 Embassy of Tanzania
1232 22nd St, NW
Washington, DC 20037

202-884-1080
202-939-6125, 202-
FAX 202-797-7408
E-Mail: ubalozi@tanzaniaembassy-us.org

Home Page: www.tanzaniaembassy-us.org
Social Media: *Facebook, Twitter*

Liberata Mulamula, Ambassador
Lily Munanka, Minister/ Head of Chancery
Paul Mwafongo, Minister, Economic Affairs
B.G. Emmanuel Maganga, Defense Attache
Edward Masanja, Finacial Attache

14910 Embassy of Tunisia
1515 Massachusetts Avenue NW
Washington, DC 20005

202-862-1850
FAX 202-862-1858
E-Mail: info@tunconusa.org
Home Page: www.tunconsusa.org/

Gordon Gray, Ambassador

14911 Embassy of Uganda
5911 16th Street NW
Washington, DC 20011

202-726-7100
FAX 202-726-1727
E-Mail: info@ugandaembassyus.org
Home Page: www.ugandaemb.org

Oliver Wonekha, Ambassador
Alfred Nnam, Deputy Chief of Commission
Dickson Ogwang, Minister Counselor
Patrick Muganda Guma, Counselor
Sam Bhoi Omara, 1st Secretary

14912 Embassy of Vietnam
1233 20th Street NW
Suite 400
Washington, DC 20036

202-861-0737
FAX 202-861-0917
E-Mail: info@vietnamembassy.us,
vnconsular@vietn
Home Page: www.vietnamembassy-usa.org

Nguyen Quoc Cuong, Ambassador

14913 Embassy of Zimbabwe
1608 New Hampshire Avenue NW
Washington, DC 20009

202-332-7100
FAX 202-483-9326
E-Mail: info33@zimbabwe-embassy.us
Home Page: www.zimbabwe-embassy.us

Dr. Machivenyik Mapuranga, Ambassador
Richard T. Chibuwe, Minister Counselor &
Deputy Chief
Whatmore Goora, Counselor (Political)
R. Matsika, Counselor
Lt. Col. George Chinoingira, Defence Attache

**14914 Embassy of the Lao People's
Democratic Republic**
2222 S Street NW
Washington, DC 20008

202-332-6416
202-667-0076
FAX 202-332-4923
E-Mail: embasslao@gmail.com
Home Page: www.laoembassy.com

H.E. Seng Soukhathivong, Ambassador
Thongmoon Phongphailath, 1st Secretary
Somxai Kittanouvong, 2nd Secretary
(Consular)
Kerlor Yangko, 3rd Secretary (Economy And
Culture)
Sounthone Duangxaty, Attache (Economic &
Culture)

**14915 Embassy of the People's Republic of
China**
3505 International Place NW
Washington, DC 20008

202-495-2266
FAX 202-495-2138

E-Mail: chinaembpress_us@mfa.gov.cn
Home Page: www.china-embassy.org

Cui Tiankai, Ambassador
Lu Kang, Minister

14916 Embassy of the Republic of Angola
2100-2108 16th Street, NW
Washington, DC 20009

202-785-1156
FAX 202-822-9049
E-Mail: angola@angola.org
Home Page: www.angola.org

Alberto do Carmo Bento Ribeiro, Ambassador
Sofia Pegado da Silva, Minster Counselor
Manuel Fransisco Lourenco, 1st Secretary
Ismael Filipe, 2nd secretary- Political Affairs
Gil Cardoso, Financial Attache

**14917 Embassy of the Republic of Botswana
and GlobeScope, Inc.**
1531-1533 New Hampshire Avenue NW
Washington, DC 20036

202-244-4990
E-Mail: smautle@botswanaembassy.org
Home Page: www.botswanaembassy.org

H.E. Dr.Tebelel Mazile Seretse, Ambassador
Ms. Sophie Heide Mautle, Deputy Head of
Mission
Innocent Matengu, Counselor (Politcal Affairs)
Dineo Mpuchane, 1st Secretary
(Administration)
Mighty Mohurutshe, Administrative Attache
Founded in 1965

14918 Embassy of the Republic of Fiji
2000 M Street,NW
Suite 710
Washington, DC 20036

202-466-8320
FAX 202-466-8325
E-Mail: info@fijiembassydc.com
Home Page: www.fijiembassydc.com

Winston Thompson, Ambassador
Akuila Vuira, 1st Secretary
Teresita R. Sauler-Cooke, Executive Asst.
Lathanzuala Phillips, Chauffer

14919 Embassy of the Republic of Latvia
2306 Massachusettes Ave, NW
Washington, DC 20008

202-328-2840
FAX 202-328-2860
E-Mail: embassy.usa@mfa.gov.lv
Home Page: www.latvia-us.org

Andrejs Pildegovics, Ambassador

14920 Embassy of the Republic of Yemen
2319 Wyoming Ave, NW
Washington, DC 20008

202-965-4760
FAX 202-337-2017
E-Mail: ambassador@yemenembassy.org
Home Page: www.yemenembassy.org

Abdulwahab Abdulla Al-Hajjri, Ambassador
Nadia Fhashem, Asst to the Ambassador

**14921 Embassy of the Republic of the
Marshall Islands**
2433 Massachusetts Avenue NW
Washington, DC 20008

202-234-5414
FAX 202-232-3236
E-Mail: info@rmiembassyus.org
Home Page: www.rmiembassyus.org

Charles R. Paul, Ambassador
Dixie Lomae, 1st Secretary
Donna Dizon, Office Manager

14922 Export-Import Bank of the United States

800-565-3946
Home Page: www.exim.gov
Social Media: *Twitter, LinkedIn, YouTube*

Fred P. Hochberg, Chairman & President
An agency of the Executive Branch of the U.S. Government, EXIM is the official export credit agency of the United States.

14923 Export.gov

Home Page: www.export.gov
Export.gov is managed by the U.S. Department of Commerce's International Trade Administration. It connects businesses with U.S. Government resources that will assist them in their international sales efforts.

14924 Fair Trading Commission

Good Hope, Green Hill
St. Michael, Ba BB12003

246-424-0260
FAX 246-424-0300
E-Mail: info@ftc.gov.bb
Home Page: www.ftc.gov.bb

Peggy Griffith, CEO
Sir Neville Nicholls, Chairman
Andrew Downes, Deputy chairman
Monique Taitt, Commissioner
Kendrid Sargeant, Commissioner

14925 French Trade Commission

200 N Colombus Dr.
Chicago, IL 60601

312-565-8000
FAX 312-856-1032
Home Page: www.firmafrance.com
Social Media: *Facebook, Twitter, LinkedIn, RSS Feed, Google +*

14926 Gambia Mission to the United Nations

800 2nd Avenue
Suite 400 F
New York, NY 10017

212-949-6640
FAX 212-856-9820
E-Mail: gambia@un.int
Home Page:
www.un.int/wcm/content/site/gambia

Tamsir Jallow, Ambassador

14927 General Consulate of Luxembourg

17 Beekman Place
New York, NY 10022

212-888-6664
FAX 212-888-6116
E-Mail: newyork.cg@mae.etat.lu
Home Page: www.newyork-cg.mae.lu/

Jean-Claude Knebelar, Consul General
Saba Amroun-Forbes, Consular Officer

14928 Gibraltar Information Bureau

1156 15th Street NW
Suite 1100
Washington, DC 20005

202-452-1108
FAX 202-452-1109

Perry Stieglitz, Executive Director

14929 Greek Trade Commission

150 E 58th Street
17th Floor
New York, NY 10155

212-751-2404
FAX 212-593-2278

Yannis Papadimitriou, Manager

14930 Hungarian Trade Commission

425 Bloor Street, East
Suite 501
Toronto-Ontario M4W 3R4

416-923-3596
FAX 416-923-2097
E-Mail: itdtoronto@hungariantrade.org

Gyula Cseko, Trade Commissioner

14931 Icelandic Consulate General

800 3rd Avenue
36th Floor
New York, NY 10022

646-282-9360
FAX 646-282-9369
E-Mail: icecon.ny@mfa.is
Home Page: www.iceland.is/us/nyc

Hlynur Gudjonsson, Consul & Trade Commissioner

14932 International Chamber of Commerce (ICC)

1212 Avenue of the Americas
New York, NY 10036-1689

212-703-5065
FAX 212-575-0327
Home Page: www.iccwbo.org
Social Media: *Facebook, Twitter, LinkedIn, Google+, YouTube*

Sunil Bharti Mittal, Vice-Chairman
Harold McGraw III, Chairman
Gerard Worms, Honorary Chairman
Jean-Guy Carrier, Secretary General
Founded in 1919
Mailing list available for rent

14933 Irish Trade Board

345 Park Avenue
17th Floor
New York, NY 10154

212-180-0800

Jean McCluskey, Marketing Executive

14934 Japanese External Trade Organization

1221 Avenue of the Americas
McGraw Hill Building, 42nd Floor
New York, NY 10020

212-997-0400
FAX 212-997-0464
E-Mail: jetrony@jetro.go.jp
Home Page: www.jetro.org
Social Media: *Facebook, Twitter*

Hiroyuki Ishige, Chairman
Masaki Fujihara, Dir., Business Development
Daiki Nakajima, ICT/ Environment

14935 Kazakhstan Mission to the United Nations

305 East 47th Street
3rd Floor
New York, NY 10017

212-230-1900
FAX 212-230-1172
E-Mail: kazakhstan@un.int
Home Page: www.kazakhstanun.org

Byrganym Aitimova, Ambassador
Akan Rakhmetulin, Deputy Permanent Rep
Israil Tilegen, Minister Counsellor
Ruslan Bultrikov, Counsellor
Col. Alexander Kabentayev, Counsellor Military Adviser

14936 Korea Trade Promotion Center (KOTRA)

460 Park Avenue
14th Floor
New York, NY 10022

212-826-0900
FAX 212-888-4930
E-Mail: kotrany@hotmail.com
Home Page: www.kotrana.org

Sungpil Um, Presiden/North America
Il Hoon Ko, Deputy Director

14937 Kyrgyzstan Mission to the United Nations

866 United Nations Plaza
Room 477
New York, NY 10017

212-486-4214
FAX 212-486-5259
Home Page:
www.un.int/wcm/content/site/kyrgyzstan

Talaibek Kydyrov, Ambassador
Nuran Niyazaliev, Counsellor/DPR
Nurbek Kasymov, 1st secretary
Asel Davydova, Chief Administrative Specialist
Salamat Supataev, Administrative Officer

14938 Malaysia Mission to the United Nations

313 E 43rd Street
3rd Floor
New York, NY 10017

212-986-6310
FAX 212-490-8576
E-Mail: malnyun@kln.gov.my
Home Page: www.kln.gov.my
Social Media: *RSS Feed*

Hussein Haniff, Ambassador

14939 Mexico Trade Commission

757 3rd Ave
Suite 2400
New York, NY 10017-2042

212-826-2978
FAX 212-826-2979
Home Page: www.mexconnect.com
Social Media: *Facebook, Twitter*

14940 Moldova Mission to the United Nations

35 East 29th Street
New York, NY 10016

212-447-1867
FAX 212-447-4067
E-Mail: unmoldova@aol.com
Home Page:
www.un.int/wcm/content/site/moldova

Vlad Lupan, Ambassador
Larisa Miculet, Counsellor, Deputy Permanent Rep
Carolina Podoroghin, 3rd Secretary
Tatiana Dudnicenco, CFO,Head of Chancery
Litvac Sergiu, Administrator

14941 New Zealand Trade Development Board

222 East 41st Street
New York, NY 10017-6739

212-497-0200

14942 Norwegian Trade Council

2720 34th Street NW
Washington, DC 20008

202-333-6000
FAX 202-469-3990
E-Mail: emb.washington@mfa.no
Home Page: www.norway.org

Social Media: *Facebook, Twitter, Flickr, Instagram*

Kare A. Aas, Ambassador
Berit Enge, Minister Counselor
Beate Anderson Varrecchia, Officer for Administrative
Harald W. Storen, Counselor
Olav Heian-Engdal, 1st Secretary

14943 Pakistan Trade Commission

12 E 65th Street
4th Floor
New York, NY 10021

212-879-5800

Abbas Zaidi, Manager

14944 Permanent Mission of Armenia to the United Nations

119 E 36th Street
New York, NY 10016

212-686-9079
FAX 212-686-3934
Home Page: www.un.mfa.am/
Social Media: *RSS*

Andrezej Towpik, Manager
Garen Nazarian, Permanent Representative to the UN
Tigran Samvelian, Counsell, Deputy Permanent Rep
Nikolay Sahakov, 1st Secretary
Sahak Sargsyan, 2nd Secretary

14945 Permanent Mission of Bangladesh to the United Nations

820 East 2nd Avenue, Diplomat Centre
4th Floor
New York, NY 10017

212-867-3434
FAX 212-972-4038
E-Mail: bangladesh@un.int
Home Page:
www.un.int/wcm/content/site/bangladesh

Sheikh Hasina, Prime Minister

14946 Permanent Mission of Belize to the United Nations

675 Third Avenue
Suite 1911
New York, NY 10017

212-986-1240
FAX 212-593-0932
E-Mail: belize@un.int
Home Page: www.belizemission.com
Social Media: *Facebook, Twitter*

Mohamed Latheef, Manager
Paulette Erlington, Counselor
Han Dean Barrow, Prime Minister
Lois M. Young, Ambassador
Janine felson, Deputy Permanent Representative

14947 Permanent Mission of Ghana to the United Nations

19 E 47th Street
New York, NY 10017

212-832-1300
FAX 212-751-6743
E-Mail: ghanaperm@aol.com
Home Page: www.un.int/ghana

Ken Kanda, Ambassador
William A. Awinador-Kanyirige, Minister
Henry Tachie-Menson, Minister-Counsellor
N.A. Abayena, Counsellor
A. Ayebi Arthur, 1st Secretary

14948 Permanent Mission of Myanmar (Formerly Burma)

10 E 77th Street
New York, NY 10075

212-744-1271
FAX 212-744-1290
E-Mail: myanmarmission@verizon.net, myanmarconsu
Home Page: www.myanmarmissionny.org

Janis Priedkalns, Manager
U Han Thu, Deputy Permanent Representative
U Aung Kyaw Zan, Minister Counsellor
U kyaw Tin, Permanent representative
U Ko Ko Shein, Minister Counselor

14949 Permanent Mission of Saint Vincent & the Grenadines

800 2nd Avenue
Suite 400-G
New York, NY 10017

212-599-0950
FAX 212-599-1020
Home Page: www.suv-un.org
Social Media: *Facebook, Twitter, YouTube*

Camillo M. Gonsalves, Ambassador
Nedra Miguel, Minister Counsellor
Mozart Carr, Attache
Maglyn Carrington, Secretary/ Accountant
N. Pepper Alexander, Security Officer/ Aide de Camp

14950 Permanent Mission of Slovakia to the United Nations

801 2nd Ave.
New York, NY 10017

212-286-8880
E-Mail: un.newyork@mzv.sk
Home Page: www.mzv.sk/unnewyork

Founded in 1993

14951 Permanent Mission of Tajikistan to the United Nations

216 East 49th St.
4th Floor
New York, NY 10017

212-207-3315
FAX 212-207-3855
E-Mail: tajikistan@un.int, tajikistanun@verizon.
Home Page: www.un.int/

Khamrokhon Zaripov, President
Sirodjidin Aslov, Ambassador

14952 Permanent Mission of the Czech Republic to the United Nations

1109-1111 Madison Avenue
New York, NY 10028

646-981-4000
FAX 646-981-4099
E-Mail: un.newyork@embassy.mzv.cz
Home Page: www.mzv.cz/un.newyork
Social Media: *RSS*

Edita Hrda, Ambassador
David Cervenka, Minister Counsellor
Peter Urbanek, Counsellor
Ladislav Steinhubel, 1st Secretary
Petra Benesova, 3rd Secretary

14953 Permanent Mission of the Kingdom of Bhutan to the United Nations

343 East 43rd Street
New York, NY 10017

212-682-2268
FAX 212-661-0551
E-Mail: bhutan@un.int
Home Page:
www.un.int/wcm/content/site/bhutan

Lhatu Wangchuk, Ambassador

14954 Permanent Mission of the Republic of Sudan to the United Nations

305 East 47th Street
3 Dag Hammarskjold Plaza, 4th Floor
New York, NY 10017

212-573-6033
FAX 212-573-6160
E-Mail: sudan@sudanmission.org
Home Page:
www.un.int/wcm/content/site/sudan

Jenine Selson, Manager

14955 Permanent Mission of the Solomon Islands to the United Nations

800 2nd Avenue
Suite 400
New York, NY 10017-4709

212-599-6192
FAX 212-661-8925
E-Mail: simun@foreignaffairs-solomons.org
Home Page:
www.un.int/wcm/content/site/solomonislands/cache/offonce/pid/4707

B Jagne, Manager

14956 Philippines Commercial Office

556 5th Avenue
New York, NY 10036

212-764-1330

14957 Poland Trade Commission

675 3rd Avenue
19th Floor
New York, NY 10017

212-351-1713

Phyllis Poland, Owner

14958 Portuguese Trade Commission

590 5th Avenue
3rd Floor
New York, NY 10036

212-354-4627
FAX 212-575-4737

Soto Moura, Manager

14959 Romanian Consulate General

11766 Wilshire Blvd
Suite 560
Los Angeles, CA 90025

310-444-0043
FAX 310-445-0043
E-Mail: losangeles@mae.ro, losangeles.cons@mae.r
Home Page: http://www.romanian.com
Social Media: *RSS*

Corina Suteu, Manager
Eugen Chivu, Consul General

14960 Singapore Trade Commission

55 E 59th Street
Suite 21-B
New York, NY 10022

212-421-2200

Kc Yeoh, Executive Director

14961 Swedish Trade Council

150 N Michigan Avenue
Chicago, IL 60601

312-781-6222

Stefam Bergstrom, Manager

14962 Syrian Arab Republic Embassy

2215 Wyoming Avenue NW
Washington, DC 20008

202-232-6316
FAX 202-265-4585

E-Mail: consular@syrembassy.net,
info@syrembassy
Home Page: www.syrianembassy.us/

14963 Taiwan Trade Center
1 Penn Plaza
Suite 2025
New York, NY 10119

212-904-1677
FAX 212-904-1678
E-Mail: newyork@taitra.org.tw
Home Page:
http://newyork.taiwantrade.com.tw/,

Kevin K. H. Wei, Director

14964 Thailand Trade Center-Consulate General of Thailand
401 N Michigan Avenue
Suite 544
Chicago, IL 60611

312-467-0044
FAX 312-467-1690
E-Mail: ttcc@wwa.com

14965 Trade Commission of Denmark
3565 Piedimont Rd
NE #1-400
Atlanta, GA 30305

404-588-1588
FAX 404-835-0799
E-Mail: atlhkt@um.dk
Home Page: /www.dtcatlanta.um.dk

Henrik Bronner, Manager

14966 Trade Commission of Spain
500 N Michigan Avenue
Suite 1500
Chicago, IL 60611

312-644-1154

14967 Turkish Trade Commission
821 United Nations Plaza
4th Floor
New York, NY 10017

212-687-1530

14968 Turkmenistan Mission to the United Nations
866 United Nations Plaza
Suite 424
New York, NY 10017

212-486-8908
FAX 212-486-2521

Aksoltan Ataeva, Manager

14969 UK Trade & Investment
1 Victoria St.
London, UK SW1H OET

212-745-0495
E-Mail: uktiusa@ukti.gsi.gov.uk
Home Page: www.ukti.gov.uk
Social Media: *Twitter, LinkedIn, Youtube, Flickr, Open to Expor*

Nick Baird, CEO
Sandra Rogers, Managing Dir., Marketing
Jon Harding, COO
Charu Gorasia, Dir., Finance & IT
Michael W. Boyd, MD, Strategic Investments

14970 United Nations Mission to El Salvador
46 Park Avenue
New York, NY 10016

212-679-1616
FAX 212-725-3467

E-Mail: elsalvador@un.int
Home Page:
www.un.int/wcm/content/site/elsalvador

Antonio Montiero, Manager
Mauricio Fiunes, President

Associations

14971 American Gem Society Laboratories

8917 W Sahara Ave
Las Vegas, NV 89117-5826

702-233-6120
FAX 702-233-6125
E-Mail: support@agslab.com
Home Page: www.agslab.com
Social Media: *Facebook, Twitter, RSS, Youtube, Tumblr, Blogger,*

Frank Delahan, CEO
Donna Jolly, Marketing Executive

Seeks to build consumer confidence in the retail jeweler by promoting ethical business standards and professional excellence.
4.4M Members
Founded in 1996

14972 American Gem Trade Association

3030 LBJ Freeway
Ste 840
Dallas, TX 75342-643

214-742-4367
800-972-1162
FAX 214-742-7334
E-Mail: info@agta.org
Home Page: www.agta.org
Social Media: *Facebook, Twitter, YouTube*

Ruben Bindra, Board President
Jeffrey Bilgore, Board VP
Gerry Manning, Board VP
Douglas K. Hucker, CEO
Joan Allen, Chief Financial Officer

Trade association for the colored gemstone industry in North America. Operates a gemological testing laboratory in New York.
750+ Members
Founded in 1981
Mailing list available for rent

14973 American Jewelry Design Council

P.O. Box 1149
Hermitage, PA 16148

724-979-4992
800-376-3609
E-Mail: info@ajdc.org
Home Page: www.ajdc.org
Social Media: *Facebook, RSS*

Barbara Heinrich, President
Alishan Halebian, VP
Jane Bohan, Secretary
Mark Schneider, Treasurer
Pascal Lacroix, Board Member

The American Jewelry Design Council is a non-profit educational corporation that recognizes and promotes the understanding of original jewelry designs as art.
Founded in 1988

14974 American Watch Association

1201 Pennsylvania Avenue NW
PO Box 464
Washington, DC 20044

434-963-7773
FAX 434-963-7776
E-Mail: egcollado@earthlink.net
Home Page:
www.americanwatchassociation.com

David Periman, Chairman
Timothy Michno, First Vice President
Mark Goldberg, Second Vice President
Michael Kaplan, Treasurer
Steven Kaiser, Secretary

Trade association for communication among professionals and legislative advocacy.
45 Members
Founded in 1933

14975 American Watchmakers-Clockmakers Institute

701 Enterprise Drive
Harrison, OH 45030-1696

513-367-9800
866-367-2924
FAX 513-367-1414
E-Mail: awci@awci.com
Home Page: www.awci.com
Social Media: *Facebook, RSS, Instagram*

Fred White, President
Drew Zimmerman, VP
Manuel Yazijian, Treasurer
Chris Carey, Secretary
Paul Wadsworth, Immediate Past President

Examines and certifies master watchmakers and clockmakers. Maintains a placement service. Conducts home study courses.
2500 Members
Founded in 1892
Mailing list available for rent

14976 Appraisers Association of America

212 West 35th Street
11th Floor South
New York, NY 10001

212-889-5404
FAX 212-889-5503
E-Mail: aaa@appraiserassoc.org
Home Page: www.appraisersassoc.org
Social Media: *Facebook, Twitter, LinkedIn*

Deborah G. Spanierman, AAA, President
Cynthia D. Herbert, AAA, First Vice President
Edward Yee, AAA, Second Vice President
Erica Hartman, AAA, Treasurer
Sharon Chrust, AAA, Recording Secretary

The oldest non-profit professional association of personal property appraisers. The mission and primary purpose of the association is to develop and promote standards of excellence in the profession of appraising through education and the application of the highest form of professional practice, which results on enhancing the visibility and standing of appraisers within the private and professional communities in which they serve.
900 Members
Founded in 1949

14977 Brotherhood of Traveling Jewelers

Leys, Christie & Company
342 Madison Avenue
Suite #1530
New York, NY 10013

212-869-9162

Represents traveling jewelers.
300 Members

14978 Cultured Pearl Information Center

331 E 53rd Street
New York, NY 10022-4923

212-688-5580
FAX 212-688-5857
Home Page: www.pearlinfo.com

Devin MacNow, Executive Director

Conference information and buying guide for pearls.

14979 Diamond Council of America

3212 West End Ave
Suite 400
Nashville, TN 37203

615-385-5301
877-283-5669
FAX 615-385-4955
Home Page: www.diamondcouncil.org
Social Media: *Facebook*

Peter Engel, Chairman
Terry Chandler, President/CEO

Provides courses in diamontology and gemology to retail jewelers and their employees who are DCA members. Sixty-six retailers representing 1,800 locations.
70 Members
Founded in 1944

14980 Diamond Dealers Club

580 Fifth Avenue
Floor 10
New York, NY 10036

212-790-3600
FAX 212-869-5164
E-Mail: mhochbaum@nyddc.com
Home Page: www.nyddc.com
Social Media: *Facebook, Twitter, LinkedIn*

Reuven Kaufman, President
Israel Ashkenazy, VP
Abraham Einhorn, Treasurer
Elliot Krischer, Secretary
William Lerner, General Counsel

Seeks to foster the interest of the diamond industry, promote equitable trade principles and eliminate abuses and unfair trading practices.
Founded in 1931

14981 Diamond Manufacturers and Importers Association of America

580 Fifth Avenue
Suite 2000
New York, NY 10036

212-944-2066
800-223-2244
FAX 212-202-7525
E-Mail: info@dmia.net
Home Page: www.dmia.net

Ronald VanderLinden, President
Stuart Samuels, Secretary
Parag Shah, Treasurer
Eli Haas, VP
Steve Eisen, Director, Board Member

Represents and promotes manufacturers and importers of diamonds and rare gems.
150 Members
Founded in 1931

14982 Diamond Peacock Club Kebadjian Brothers

Kebadjian Brothers
333 Washington Street
Suite 638
Boston, MA 02108-5111

617-523-5565
FAX 617-523-7193
E-Mail: info@kebadjian.com
Home Page: www.kebadjian.com

Claude Kebadjian, Founder And Designer
Seta Kebadjian, Designing
Michael Kebadjian, Jewelry Design
Founded in 1957

14983 Diamond Promotion Service

466 Lexington Avenue
New York, NY 10017-9998

800-370-6789
FAX 877-276-1224
E-Mail: newyorkdps@jwt.com
Home Page: www.diamondpromotions.com
Social Media: *Facebook, Twitter*

Resource for the tools and strategies to sell more diamonds. Buy marketing materials, train your staff, find the suppliers of advertised jewelry and more.

14984 Estate Jewelry Association of America
209 Post Street
Suite 718
San Francisco, CA 94108-5209

415-834-0718
800-584-5522
FAX 212-840-1644
E-Mail: jaa@aol.com

14985 Fashion Jewelry Association of America
3 Davol Sq
Unit 135
Providence, RI 02903-4710

401-273-1515

Nick Macris, President
150 Members
Founded in 1985

14986 Gem & Lapidary Dealers Association
120 Derwood Circle
Rockville, MD 20850

301-294-1640
FAX 301-294-0034
E-Mail: info@glda.com
Home Page: www.glda.com
Social Media: *Facebook, Twitter, Google+, Pinterest*

Arnold Duke, President
Brandy Swanson, Customer Service
Jennifer Guillot, Exhibit Sales/Services
Monique Anderson, PR/ Marketing & New Media
Don Wyatt, PR/ Marketing & New Media
G.L.D.A. is a firmly established, successful wholesale gem & jewelry show promotion company. For the past 30 years, our Tucson show has enjoyed a booming success growth rate. Our show has included 400 exhibit booths which is the maximum that this facility would accomodate.

14987 Gold Prospectors Association of America
43445 Business Park Drive
Suite #113
Temecula, CA 92590

951-699-4749
800-551-9707
FAX 951-699-4062
E-Mail: info@goldprospectors.org
Home Page: www.goldprospectors.org
Social Media: *Facebook, Twitter, LinkedIn, YouTube*

Thomas Massie, CEO

GPAA is the largest recreational gold prospecting club. Owner of The Outdoor Channel, a cable TV channel featuring real outdoors for real people.
35M Members
Founded in 1985
Mailing list available for rent

14988 Independent Jewelers Organization
136 Old Post Road
Southport, CT 06890-1302

203-846-4215
800-624-9252
FAX 203-254-7429
E-Mail: ijo@ijo.com
Home Page: www.ijo.com
Social Media: *Facebook, Twitter, LinkedIn*

Penny Palmer, Member Services Director

Jewelry buying group and service organization for retail jewelers.
850 Members
Founded in 1972

14989 Indian Arts & Crafts Association
4010 Carlisle NE
Suite C
Albuquerque, NM 87107

505-265-9149
FAX 505-265-8251
E-Mail: info@iaca.com
Home Page: www.iaca.com
Social Media: *Facebook, Twitter*

Jacque Foutz, President
Joseph P. Zeller, President
Kathi Ouellet, Treasurer
Georgia Fischel, Secretary
Beth Hale, Membership Director

Nonprofit trade association whose mission is to promote, protect and preserve Indian arts.
700 Members
Founded in 1974
Mailing list available for rent

14990 Industrial Diamond Association of America
PO Box 29460
Columbus, OH 43229

614-797-2265
FAX 614-797-2264
E-Mail: tkane-ida@insight.rr.com
Home Page: www.superabrasives.org

Terry M. Kane, Executive Director
Mike Mustin, President
Keith Reckling, Secretary/Treasurer
Troy Heuermann, Vice President
Edward E. Galen, Executive Director

Association of industrial diamond, cvd diamond and polycrystalling supplies, toolmakers. Products and services provided and used in most manufacturing and constuction industries such as: stone processing, glass construction, electronics, medical, woodworking, etc.
190 Members
Founded in 1946

14991 International Colored Gemstone Association
30 West 47th Street
Suite 201
New York, NY 10036

212-352-8814
FAX 212-352-9054
E-Mail: claudiu@gemstone.org
Home Page: www.gemstone.org
Social Media: *RSS Feed*

Benjamin Hackmanÿ, President
Damien Cody, VP
Santpal Sinchawla, Vice-President
Marcelo Ribeiro Fernandes, Treasurer
Ehud Harel, Secretary

Nonprofit association representing the international gemstone industry. Works to increase the understanding, appreciation and sales of colored gemstones worldwide.
Founded in 1984

14992 International Fine Jewelers Guild
257 Adams Lane
Hewlett, NY 11557

516-295-2516
FAX 516-374-5060
E-Mail: Info@InternationalFineJewelersGuild.com
Home Page: www.internationalfinejewelersguild.com

Bertram Kalisher, Chairman
Olivia Cornell, President
Berge Abajian, Jewelry Industry Advisory Board
Kari Allen, Jewelry Industry Advisory Board
Zoltan David, Jewelry Industry Advisory Board

14993 International Precious Metals Institute
5101 North 12th Avenue
Suite C
Pensacola, FL 32504

850-476-1156
FAX 850-476-1548
E-Mail: mail@ipmi.org
Home Page: www.ipmi.org
Social Media: *Facebook, LinkedIn, YouTube*

Robert Bullen Smith, Chairman
Jon Potts, Vice Chairman
Sascha Biehl, Treasurer
Bodo Albrecht, Secretary
Chris Jones, Immediate Past Chairman

International association of producers, refiners, fabricators, scientists, users, financial institutions, merchants, private and public sector groups and the general precious metals community created to provide a forum for the exchange of information and technology.
Founded in 1976

14994 International Society of Appraisers
225 West Wacker Drive
Suite 650
Chicago, IL 60606

312-981-6778
FAX 312-265-2908
E-Mail: isa@isa-appraisers.org
Home Page: www.isa-appraisers.org
Social Media: *Facebook, Twitter, LinkedIn*

Christine Guernsey, ISA CAPP, President
Perri Guthrie, ISA CAPP, Vice President
Steven R. Roach, JD, ISA CAPP, Treasurer
Karen S. Rabe, ISA CAPP, Secretary
Hughene D. Acheson, ISA AM, Director

Nonprofit professional association of personal property appraisers. ISA provides education and organizational support to its members, to serve the public by producing highly qualified and ethical appraisers who are recognized authorities in personal property appraising.
1400+ Members
Founded in 1979
Mailing list available for rent

14995 Jewelers Board of Trade
95 Jefferson Boulevard
Warwick, RI 02888

401-467-0055
FAX 401-467-6070
E-Mail: jbtinfo@jewelersboard.com
Home Page: www.jewelersboard.com
Social Media: *Twitter*

Dione Kenyen, President

Trade Association: credit and collection for the jewelry industry.
3300 Members
Founded in 1884

14996 Jewelers Vigilance Committee
801 2nd Avenue
Suite 303
New York, NY 10017

212-997-2002
FAX 212-997-9148
E-Mail: clg@jvclegal.org
Home Page: www.jvclegal.org
Social Media: *Facebook, LinkedIn*

Berylÿ Raff, Chairman
Steven P. Kaiser, 1st Vice President
Scott Berg, 2nd Vice President
Mark Goldberg, Treasurer
Cecilia L. Gardner, President, CEO, General Counsel

The sole legal compliance association in the jewelry industry. Educates the trade to under-

stand complex rules governing the manufacture, sale and marketing of fine jewelry.
1300 Members
Founded in 1917

14997 Jewelers of America
120 Broadway
Suite 2820
New York, NY 10271

646-658-0246
800-223-0673
FAX 646-658-0256
E-Mail: info@jewelers.org
Home Page: www.jewelers.org
Social Media: *Facebook, Twitter, LinkedIn*

Ryan Berg, Chairman
David J. Bonaparte, President and CEO
John Henne, Chair Elect
Mark Light, Vice Chair
Coleman Clark, Treasurer

Center of knowledge for the jeweler and an advocate for professionalism and high social, ethical and environmental standards in the jewelry trade. Our mission is to assist all members in improving their business skills and profitability. JA will provide acess to meaningful educational programs and services, leadership in public and industry affairs, and encourage members with common interests to act in the industry's best interest.
Founded in 1906
Mailing list available for rent

14998 Jewelry Industry Distributors Association
701 Enterprise Drive
Harrison, OH 45030

513-367-2357
FAX 513-367-1414
E-Mail: info@jida.info
Home Page: www.jida.info

Bill Nagle, President
Harvey Cobrin, First VP
Rick Foster, Secretary/Treasurer

Sets standards of service and facilitates the exchange of information of all types among members in order to improve business, maximize opportunities, and minimize risks.
150 Members
Founded in 1946

14999 Jewelry Information Center
120 Broadway
Suite 2820
New York, NY 10271

646-658-0246
800-223-0673
FAX 646-658-0256
E-Mail: info@jewelers.org
Home Page: www.jic.org
Social Media: *Facebook, Twitter, RSS*

Matthews Runzi, President and CEO
Robert Headley, Vice President & COO
Carlon Alexandr, Administrative Assistant
Carey Miller, Membership Manager

Identifies deceptive trade practices and misleading advertising. Provides advice on marketing and assists in prosecution of violations. The media side of the Jewelers Vigilance Committee.
1000 Members
Founded in 1946
Mailing list available for rent

15000 Jewelry Manufacturers Guild
PO Box 46099
Los Angeles, CA 90046

909-769-1820
800-359-0340
FAX 909-769-1920

Paula Glick Hill, Operations Manager

Promotes and improves conditions in the fine jewelry manufacturing industry.
400 Members

15001 Leading Jewelers Guild
PO Box 64609
Los Angeles, CA 90064

310-820-3386
FAX 310-820-3530
E-Mail: jimmywest828 @ gmail.com
Home Page: www.love-story.com
Social Media: *Facebook, Twitter, Google+, Pinterest*

James West, President
Mailing list available for rent

15002 Manufacturing Jewelers & Suppliers of America
8 Hayward St.
Attleboro, MA 2703

508-316-2132
800-444-6572
FAX 508-316-1429
E-Mail: info@mjsa.org
Home Page: www.mjsa.org
Social Media: *Facebook, Twitter, LinkedIn, Pinterest*

Ann Arnold, Chair
Darrell Warren, Vice Chair
Steven A. Cipolla, Vice Chair
David W. Cochran, President, CEO
James K. McCarty, Chief Operating Officer & CFO

National trade association for the manufacturing jewelers and silversmiths. Sponsors trade shows, expositions and social events.
1.8M Members
Founded in 1903

15003 Manufacturing Jewelers and Silversmiths
8 Hayward St.
Attleboro, MA 2703

508-316-2132
800-444-6572
FAX 508-316-1429
E-Mail: info@mjsa.org
Home Page: www.mjsa.org
Social Media: *Facebook, Twitter, LinkedIn*

Ann Arnold, Chair
Darrell Warren, Vice Chair
Steven A. Cipolla, Vice Chair
David W. Cochran, President, CEO
James K. McCarty, Chief Operating Officer & CFO

The trade association for all segments of the American jewelry manufacturing and supply industry.
Founded in 1903

15004 National Association of Jewelry Appraisers
PO Box 18
Rego Park, NY 11374-0018

718-896-1536
FAX 718-997-9057
E-Mail: office@NAJAAppraisers.com
Home Page: www.najaappraisers.com
Social Media: *Facebook*

Gail Brett Levine, Executive Director

Purpose is to maintain professional standards and education in the field of jewelry appraising and provide members benefits at lower cost than can be attained individually.
720 Members
Founded in 1981

15005 Platinum Guild International USA
620 Newport Center Dr
Suite 800
Newport Beach, CA 92660-6420

212-404-1600
800-207-PLAT
FAX 949-760-8780
E-Mail: info@pgiusa.com
Home Page: www.preciousplatinum.com
Social Media: *Facebook, Twitter, Google+, Pinterest*

Laurie A Hudson, President

Organization promoting platinum jewelry. Maintains a website where the press and the public can find helpful information.
Founded in 1975

15006 Plumb Club
157 Engle Street
Englewood, NJ 07631

201-816-8881
FAX 201-816-8882
E-Mail: susan@plumbclub.com
Home Page: www.plumbclub.com

Jonathan Goodman Cohen, President
Michael Lerche, VP
Michael Langhammer, Treasurer
Roger Forman, Secretary
Jeffrey Cohen, Director

Exclusive social organization within the jewelry industry holding black tie events for members and their clients and exhibitor shows.

15007 Schneider National
3101 S Packerland Drive
Po Box 2545
Green Bay, WI 54306-2545

920-592-2000
800-558-6767
Home Page: www.schneider.com
Social Media: *RSS*

Don Schneider, Chairman
Christopher Lofgren PhD, President & CEO

A leading provider of transportation and logistics services with a comprehensive reach across North America and a growing presence in Europe and Asia.
Founded in 1935

15008 Silver Institute
1400 I Street, NW
Suite #550
Washington, DC 20005

202-835-0185
FAX 202-835-0155
E-Mail: info@silverinstitute.org
Home Page: www.silverinstitute.org

Fernando Alanis, President
Michael DiRienzo, Executive Director and Secretary
Mitchell Krebs, Vice President
Thomas Angelos, Treasurer
Mark Spurbeck, Assistant Treasurer

International association of miners, refiners, fabricators and wholesalers of silver and silver products.
Founded in 1971

15009 Silver Users Association
3930 Walnut Street
Suite 210
Fairfax, VA 22030

703-930-7790
800-245-6999
FAX 703-359-7562
E-Mail: pmiller@mwcapitol.com
Home Page: www.silverusersassociation.org

Bill LeRoy, President
Mike Huber, VP
Jack Gannon, Immediate Past President

Bill Hamelin, Treasurer
John King, Secretary

Represents manufacturers and distributors of products in which silver is an essential element, such as photographic materials, medical and dental supplies, batteries and electronic and electrical equipment, silverware, mirrors, commemorative art and jewelry.
27 Members
Founded in 1947

15010 Society of American Silversmiths
P.O.Box 786
West Warwick, RI 02893

401-461-6840
FAX 401-828-0162
E-Mail: sas@silversmithing.com
Home Page: www.silversmithing.com

Jeffrey Herman, Founder/Executive Director

Organization devoted to the preservation and promotion of the silversmithing art and craft.
240 Members
Founded in 1989
Mailing list available for rent

15011 Society of North American Goldsmiths
PO Box 1355
Eugene, OR 97440

541-345-5689
FAX 541-345-1123
E-Mail: info@snagmetalsmith.org
Home Page: www.snagmetalsmith.org
Social Media: *Facebook, Twitter, LinkedIn, Pinterest, Flickr, RSS, YouTub*

Renee Zettle-Sterling, President
Anne Havel, Treasurer
Gwynne Rukenbrod, Executive Dir.
Tara Jecklin, Operations Manager
John Garbett, Advertising & Production Director

Promotes a favorable and enriching environment in which contemporary metalsmiths practice their art. One aspect of this process is educating the public about the quality and rich diversity within the field of metalsmithing. Exhibitions, public forums, lectures, and published documents are our primary methods of reaching out to the public. SNAG sponsors workshops, seminars, audio-visual services and an annual conference.
Founded in 1968

15012 The Fashion Jewelry & Accessories Trade Association (FJATA)
25 Sea Grass Way
North Kingstown, RI 02852

401-667-0520
FAX 401-267-9096
E-Mail: bcleaveland@fjata.org
Home Page: www.fjata.org
Social Media: *Twitter*

Brent Cleaveland, Executive Director

The voice of jewelry and accessories manufacturers, suppliers and retailers to regulatory agencies.
225 Members

15013 Women's Jewelry Association
80 Washington Street
Suite 205
Poughkeepsie, NY 12601

845-473-7323
FAX 646-355-0219
E-Mail: info@womensjewelryassociation.com
Home Page:
www.womensjewelryassociation.com

Andrea Hansen, President
Brandee Dallow, President Elect
Tryna Kochanek, Immediate Past President

Kristie Nicolosi, Treasurer
Bernadette Mack, Executive Director

To empower women to achieve their highest goals in the international jewelry, watch and related businesses.
Founded in 1983

15014 World Gold Council
685 Third Avenue
27th Floor
New York, NY 10017

212-317-3800
FAX 212-688-0410
E-Mail: info@gold.org
Home Page: www.gold.org
Social Media: *Facebook, Twitter, LinkedIn, YouTube Flickr, RSS Feed, Goog*

Aram Shishmanian, CEO
Brenda Bates, Managing Director, Corporate Comm.
Natalie Dempster, Managing Director, Central Banks
Roland Wang, Managing Director, China
William Rhind, Managing Director, Investment

Organization formed and funded by the world's leading gold mining companies with the aim of stimulating and maximizing the demand for, and holding of gold by consumers, investors, industry and the official sector.
23 Members
Founded in 1987

Newsletters

15015 Benchmark
Manufacturing Jewelers & Suppliers of America
57 John L Dietsch Sq
Attleboro Falls, MA 02763-1027

401-274-3840
800-444-6572
FAX 401-274-0265
E-Mail: info@mjsa.org
Home Page: www.mjsa.org

James McCarthy, COO
Bruce Coltin, Operations Manager
Kristin Kopaz, Operations Manager
Corrie Berry, Sales Manager

Offers details of association activities and industry events for members.
4 Pages
Frequency: Bi-Monthly

15016 Costume Jewelry Review
Retail Reporting Bureau
302 5th Ave
11th Floor
New York, NY 10001-3604

212-279-7000

Offers news and information on the costume jewelry industry, suppliers and manufacturers.
Cost: $108.00
Frequency: Monthly

15017 Diamond Insight
Tryon Mercantile
790 Madison Avenue
New York, NY 10021-6124

212-288-9011
FAX 212-772-1286
Home Page: www.newsletteraccess.com

Guido Giovannini-Torelli, Editor

Penetrates the multifaceted world of diamonds, giving intelligence on the world's important stones, future price indicators, key individuals behind the trends, jewelry auctions and

DeBeers/CSO Activities.
Cost: $325.00
12 Pages
Frequency: Monthly
Circulation: 250
Printed in one color on glossy stock

15018 Diamond Registry Bulletin
Diamond Registry
580 5th Avenue
New York, NY 10036-4701

212-575-0444
800-223-7955
FAX 212-575-0722
E-Mail: info@diamondregistry.com
Home Page: www.diamondregistry.com

Joseph Schlussel, President

Monthly newsletter offering the latest trends, prices and forecasts concerning diamonds, diamond jewelry and diamond mining.
Cost: $97.00
Frequency: Monthly
ISSN: 0199-9753
Founded in 1961

15019 Jewelers' Security Alliance Newsletter
Jewelers' Security Alliance
6 E 45th St
Suite 1305
New York, NY 10017-2469

212-687-0328
800-537-0067
FAX 212-808-9168
E-Mail: jsa2@jewelerssecurity.org
Home Page: www.jewelerssecurity.org

John J Kennedy, President
Robert W. Frank, Vice President
Helen M. Buck, Manager of Membership Services

Principal activity is providing education and information to jewelers so they can guard against loss through crimes, including burglary, robbery and theft.
Cost: $375.00
Frequency: Annual+
Founded in 1883

15020 Jewelers' Security Bulletin
Jewelers' Security Alliance
6 E 45th St
Suite 1305
New York, NY 10017-2469

212-687-0328
800-537-0067
FAX 212-808-9168
E-Mail: jsa2@jewelerssecurity.org
Home Page: www.jewelerssecurity.org

John J Kennedy, President
Robert W. Frank, Vice President
Helen M. Buck, Manager of Membership Services

Principal activity is providing education and information to jewelers so they can guard against loss through crimes, including burglary, robbery and theft.
19500 Members
Founded in 1883
Mailing list available for rent

15021 Jewelry Newsletter International
Newsletters International
7710 T Cherry Park Drive
#421
Houston, TX 77095

888-972-4662
Home Page: www.j-i.com

Len Fox, Editor

Informs manufacturers, wholesalers, suppliers, and retailers of jewelry how to stimulate sales,

increase profits, and cut costs.
Cost: $250.00
4-8 Pages
Frequency: Monthly
Founded in 1975
Printed in on matte stock

15022 Precious Metals News
International Precious Metals Institute
5101 N 12th Avenue
Suite C
Pensacola, FL 32504

850-476-1156
FAX 850-476-1548
E-Mail: mail@ipmi.org
Home Page: www.ipmi.org

Robert Ianniello, President
Frequency: Quarterly
Circulation: 1000

15023 Spectra
American Gem Society
8917 W Sahara Ave
Las Vegas, NV 89117-5826

702-233-6120
FAX 702-233-6125
E-Mail: support@agslab.com
Home Page: www.agslab.com

Frank Delahan, CEO

Society news covering all aspects of the jewelry world.
12 Pages
Frequency: Quarterly
Founded in 1934

Magazines & Journals

15024 AJM Magazine: The Authority on Jewelry Manufacturing
Manufacturing Jewelers & Suppliers of America
57 John L Dietsch Sq
Attleboro Falls, MA 02763-1027

401-274-3840
800-444-6572
FAX 401-274-0265
E-Mail: info@mjsa.org
Home Page: www.mjsa.org

James McCarthy, COO
Corrie Silvia Berry, Director of Sales & Business
David W. Cochran, President & CEO
Kristin Kopaz, Operations Manager
Dawn Britland, Assistant Controller

This is the only magazine dedicated solely to jewelry manufacturers. It delivers the three T's of jewelry manufacturing: trends, technology and techniques.
Cost: $47.00
Frequency: Monthly
Founded in 1903
Printed in 4 colors on glossy stock

15025 Accent Magazine
Larkin Group
485 Fashion Ave
Suite 1400
New York, NY 10018-6804

212-594-1439
FAX 212-594-8556

AJ Larkin, Publisher

Provides trend analysis and market forecasts for buyers and designers, for accessories, clothing, and footwear. Also covers convention and tradeshow news, and new product launches.
Cost: $24.00
Frequency: Monthly
Circulation: 13,000

15026 Adornment: Newsletter of Jewelry and Related Arts
1333A N Avenue
New Rochelle, NY 10804

914-636-3784
E-Mail: ekarlin@usa.net

Elyse Karlin, Publisher/Editor/CEO
Cost: $60.00
Frequency: Quarterly
Circulation: 800
Founded in 1999

15027 Chronos
Golden Bell Press
2403 Champa St
Denver, CO 80205-2621

303-296-1600
FAX 303-295-2159
E-Mail: print@goldenbellpress.com
Home Page: www.goldenbellpress.com

Editorial material looks at timepieces of the past, present and future, bringing you the latest, the best and the most intriguing creation from the leading international watch and clock makers. The history of timepiece manufacturers and their significant milestones are also reported as well as armchair tours of the world's most prestigious horological museums.
Cost: $2250.00
Frequency: Quarterly
Circulation: 20000
Founded in 1933

15028 Colored Stone
PRIMEDIA
60 Chestnut Avenue
Suite 201
Devon, PA 19333-1312

610-964-6300
610-232-5700
FAX 610-293-1717
Home Page: www.colored-stone.com

Joseph Breck, Publisher
Morgan Beard, Editor-in-Chief

Contains news and information on the gem and gemstone jewelry industry.
Cost: $29.95
64 Pages
Circulation: 10000
Founded in 1986

15029 Couture International Jeweler
Miller Freeman Publications
770 Broadway
5th Floor
New York, NY 10003-9595

212-780-0400
FAX 847-763-9037
E-Mail: ijmag@halldata.com
Home Page: www.couturejeweler.com

Debra De Roo Ballard, Publisher
Lynda Roguso, Operations Director
Karen Stewart, Operations Director

Publication features information on hot trends in fine jewelry and fashion.
Cost: $60.00
Circulation: 20000
Founded in 1964

15030 GZ (European Jeweler)
JCK International Publishing Group
360 Park Ave S
New York, NY 10010-1710

646-746-6400
FAX 646-746-7131
Home Page: www.jckgroup.com

Ted Smith, CEO
Donna Borrelli, Associate Publisher
Hedda Schupak, Editor-in-Chief
Tracey Peden, Marketing Manager

Nancy Walsh, Senior Vice President
Cost: $49.95
Frequency: Monthly
Founded in 1874

15031 High-Volume Jeweler
Reed Business Information
201 King of Prussia Road
Radnor, PA 19087-5114

610-889-9577
FAX 630-288-8686
Home Page: www.reedbusiness.com

Shawn Mery, Publisher
Lisa Reed, CFO
Stuart Whayman, CFO

Provides original market research and in-depth analysis of current news and industry trends affecting this segment of the jewelry and watch market. Features operational strategies and new technological developments that can make and save money for retailers and vendors.
Cost: $60.00
Frequency: Bi-Monthly
Circulation: 5,000

15032 Horological Times
American Watchmakers-Clockmakers Institute
701 Enterprise Drive
Harrison, OH 45030-1696

513-367-9800
866-367-2924
FAX 513-367-1414
Home Page: www.awci.com
Social Media: *Facebook, RSS*

James Lubic, Executive Director
Tom Pack, Operations Director
Jennifer Bilodeau, Assistant Editor
Elizabeth Janszen, Membership Coordinator

Contains articles dealing with the techniques of servicing and repairing watches and clockes; the uses of shop tool and equipment; the functional characteristics of mechanical, electronic, and antique timepieces.
Frequency: Monthly
Founded in 1892
Mailing list available for rent

15033 International Wristwatch Magazine USA
International Publishing Corporation
979 Summer Street
PO Box 110204
Stamford, CT 06905

203-259-8100
FAX 203-295-0847
E-Mail: wristwatch@snet.net
Home Page: www.intlwristwatch.com

Gary George, Editor-in-Chief
Patricia Russo, General Manager

Editorial content provides a consumer-oriented focus on new, vintage, and collectable watches.
Cost: $7.95
150 Pages
Frequency: Bi-Monthly
Circulation: 30,000
ISBN: 0-744706-22-2
Founded in 1989
Printed in 4 colors on glossy stock

15034 JCK Magazine
JCK International Publishing Group
1018 W Ninth Avenue
King of Prussia, PA 19406-1

610-205-1100
800-305-7759
FAX 610-205-1139
E-Mail: JCK@pub-serv.com
Home Page: www.jckgroup.com

Nancy Walsh, Senior VP
Fran Pennella, Marketing Director

Mark Smelzer, Publisher
Hedda Schupak, Editor-in-chief
Jay Jackson, Chief Operating Officer

Serves retailers, manufacturers, and vendors of fine jewelry and selected upscale gift categories, providing valuable market and design trend information and how-to information about gemology, financial management, employee relations, marketing, advertising, and visual merchandising, e-commerce, and other topics.
Cost: $49.95
Frequency: Monthly
Founded in 1869

15035 JQ Limited Edition
JQ Publishing
585 5th Street W
Sonoma, CA 95476-6831

707-938-1082
FAX 707-935-6585
Home Page: www.retailmerchandising.net

Audrey Bromstad, Publisher
Cynthia Unninayar, Editor
Deborah Rittenberg, Marketing Manager

Issues contain articles presented with illustrations on precious colored gems and diamonds, creative jewelry designs, designers, and luxury watches.
Frequency: Monthly
Circulation: 300000
Founded in 1985

15036 Jewelers' Circular: Keystone
Reed Business Information
360 Park Ave S
New York, NY 10010-1737

646-746-6400
FAX 646-756-7583
E-Mail: hschupak@reedbusiness.com
Home Page: www.reedbusiness.com
Social Media: *Twitter, LinkedIn*

John Poulin, CEO
Hedda Schupak, Editor
Victoria Jones, Production Manager
James Reed, Owner
Andrew Rak, Senior Vice President

Discusses news of interest mainly to the jewelry shop owner and manager. Covers such topics as; product notices, manufacturer news and tips on operating a successful business.
Cost: $49.95
Frequency: Monthly
Circulation: 25000
Founded in 1874
Printed in on glossy stock

15037 Jewelry Appraiser
National Association of Jewelry Appraisers
P. O. Box 18
Rego Park, NY 11374-0018

718-896-1536
FAX 718-997-9057
E-Mail: naja.appraisers@netzero.net
Home Page: www.najaappraisers.com
Social Media: *Facebook, LinkedIn*

Gail Brett Levine, Executive Director

An important source for all jewelry appraisers.
Frequency: Quarterly
Founded in 1981

15038 Lapidary Journal
300 Chesterfield Parkway
Suite 100
Malvern, PA 19355-937

610-232-5700
800-676-4336

FAX 610-232-5754
Home Page: www.lapidaryjournal.com

Merle White, Editor
Karen Nuckols, Sales Director
Joe Breck, Publisher

This publication focuses fundamentally on the all aspects of the jewelry industry.
Cost: $29.95
Frequency: Monthly
Circulation: 45000
Founded in 1947

15039 Link
National Cuff Link Society
PO Box 5970
Vernon Hills, IL 60061-5970

847-816-0035
FAX 847-816-0035
Home Page: www.cufflink.com

Gena Klompus, President
Founded in 1990

15040 Lustre
Cygnus Publishing
19 W 44th St
Suite 1405
New York, NY 10036-6101

212-921-1091
FAX 212-921-5539
E-Mail: lorraine.depasque@cygnuspub.com
Home Page: www.cygnusb2b.com

Tim Murphy, Publisher
Roy Kim, Sales Director
Lorraine DePasque, Editor In Chief
Barb Hesse, Circulation Manager
Paul Mackler, President/CEO
Circulation: 4000
Founded in 1966

15041 Modern Jeweler
3 Huntington Quadrangle
Suite 301N
Melville, NY 11747-3602

631-845-2700
800-255-5113
FAX 631-845-7109
E-Mail: tim.murphy@cygnuspub.com
Home Page: www.modernjeweler.com

Matthew Kramer, Managing Editor
Timothy Murphy, Publisher
Cheryl Kremkow, Editor in Chief
Barb Hesse, Circulation Manager
Jeff Prine, Executive Editor

A trade publication serving retail jewelers, wholesalers and manufacturers of jewelry, watches and related items. Accepts advertising.
Cost: $66.00
90 Pages
Frequency: Monthly
Circulation: 30000

15042 Monroe Originals
Karen Monroe
14014 Moorpark Street
Apartment 122
Sherman Oaks, CA 91423-3492

FAX 818-783-5009

Handmade wholesale jewelry designs magazine.
Cost: $2.00
50 Pages
Frequency: Monthly

15043 Ornament
PO Box 2349
San Marcos, CA 92079-9806

760-599-0222
800-888-8950
FAX 760-599-0228
E-Mail: ornament@sbcglobal.net

Home Page:
beadwrangler.com/mag-ornament.htm

Robert Liu, Co-Editor
Carolin Denish, Co-Editor

Offers information on contemporary, ethnic, ancient jewelry and costumes.
Cost: $26.00
Frequency: Quarterly
Circulation: 38,000
Founded in 1976

15044 Professional Jeweler
Bond Communications
1500 Walnut Street
Suite 1200
Philadelphia, PA 19102-3523

215-670-0727
888-557-0727
FAX 215-545-9629
E-Mail: askus@professionaljeweler.com
Home Page: www.professionaljeweler.com

Lee Lawrence, Publisher/President
Peggy Jo Donahue, Editor-in-Chief
Peter James, Manager
Carole Masciantonio, Marketing Coordinator
Lisa Pastore, Advertising Manager

Editorial content provides these professionals with the information they need to meet business objectives and ensure success. Regular departments offer the latest news, trends, technical and practical information on all aspects of the jewelry industry.
Cost: $49.95
105 Pages
Frequency: Monthly
Circulation: 24000
ISSN: 1097-5314
Founded in 1998
Printed in 4 colors on glossy stock

15045 Southern Jewelry News
Mullen Publications
9629 Old Nations Ford Rd
Charlotte, NC 28273-5719

704-527-5111
800-738-5111
FAX 704-527-5114
Home Page: www.mullenpublications.com

Chip Smith, Publisher
Bill Newnam, Production Manager
Robert Cutshaw, Production Manager
Elesa Dillon, Sales Manager

Dedicated to the southern jewelry industry and contains industry news, local and regional events, personnel announcements, and pricing information.
Frequency: Monthly
Circulation: 13,431
Founded in 1945

15046 Watch and Clock Review
Golden Bell Press
2403 Champa St
Denver, CO 80205-2621

303-296-1600
FAX 303-295-2159
E-Mail: print@goldenbellpress.com
Home Page: www.goldenbellpress.com

Offers news and information on fashion accessories and jewelry.
Cost: $19.50
48 Pages
ISSN: 1082-2453
Founded in 1935

Trade Shows

15047 ASD/AMD Las Vegas Variety Merchandise Show
ASD/AMD Merchandise Group
Las Vegas Convention Center
3150 Paradise Road
Las Vegas, NV 89109

702-892-0711
FAX 702-892-2933
Home Page: www.lvcva.com

Features tens of thousands of unique products in hundreds of popular categories.
10000 Attendees
Frequency: March

15048 Accent on Design
George Little Management
10 Bank Street
Suite 1200
White Plains, NY 10606-1954

914-486-6070
800-272-7469
FAX 914-948-2867
Home Page: www.nyigf.com

Elizabeth Murphy, Show Manager
George Little II, President

Three hundred and seventy booths of the latest and most innovative gift lines such as decorative accessories and home furnishings.
50M Attendees
Frequency: August
Founded in 1984

15049 American Gem Society Conclave
8881 W Sahara Avenue
Las Vegas, NV 89117

702-255-6500
FAX 702-255-7420
Home Page: www.ags.org

Glory Wade, Show Manager

One hundred and sixty booths. Conference and exhibitors.
1M Attendees
Frequency: April

15050 American Gem Trade Association Expo
3030 LBJ Freeway
Suite 840
Dallas, TX 75234

214-742-4367
800-972-1162
FAX 214-742-7334
E-Mail: info@agta.org
Home Page: www.agta.org

Elizabeth Ross, Marketing Manager
Rick Krementz, President

Two booths featuring exhibits of loose colored gemstones and diamonds.
10.3M Attendees
Frequency: February

15051 Annual Spring New Products Show
Pacific Expositions
1600 Kapiolani Boulevard
Suite 1660
Honnolulu, HI 96814

808-945-3594
FAX 808-946-6399

48000 Attendees
Frequency: Annual

15052 Bead and Button Show
Kalmbach Publishing Company

21027 Crossroads Circle
PO Box 1612
Waukesha, WI 53187-1612

262-796-8776
800-553-6644
262-796-8776
FAX 262-796-1615
Home Page: www.beadandbuttonshow.com
Social Media: *Facebook, Pinterest*

3500 Attendees

15053 Best Bead Show
Crystal Myths
PO Box 3243
Albuquerque, NM 87190

505-883-9295
FAX 505-889-9553

15054 Business to Business Gem Trade Show
Gem & Lapidary Wholesalers
Holiday Inn Palo Verde/Holidome
Tucson, AZ

601-879-8832
FAX 601-879-3282
E-Mail: info@glwshows.com
Home Page: www.glwshows.com

Frequency: February

15055 Catalog in Motion
Bell Group
Tucson E Hilton
Tucson, AZ

505-839-3249
FAX 505-839-3248
Home Page: www.riogrande.com

Frequency: February

15056 Fashion Accessories Expo
Business Journals
50 Day Street
Norwalk, CT 06854

203-853-6015
FAX 203-852-8175
Home Page: www.busjour.com

Britton Jones, President
Lizette Chin, Show Director Market
14000 Attendees

15057 Fashion Accessories Expo Accessories to Go
Business Journals
50 Day Street
Norwalk, CT 06854

203-853-6015
FAX 203-852-8175
Home Page: www.busjour.com

Britton Jones, President
Lorrie Frost, Accessories Publisher
14000 Attendees

15058 GJX Gem and Jewelry Show
198 S Granada Avenue
Tucson, AZ

520-824-4200
FAX 520-882-4203
Home Page: www.gjxusa.com

Allan Norville, President
Frequency: February

15059 GLDA Gem and Jewelry Show
Gem & Lapidary Dealers Association
PO Box 2391
Tucson, AZ 85702

520-792-9431
FAX 520-882-2836

E-Mail: info@glda.com
Home Page: www.glda.com

Paul Page, Director Marketing

Qualified buyers receive free admission. Buyers are jewelry retailers, manufacturers, wholesalers, gem dealers.
16000 Attendees
Frequency: February

15060 Gem & Jewelry Show
International Gem & Jewelry Show
120 Derwood Circle
Rockville, MD 20850-1264

301-294-1640
FAX 301-294-0034

Herb Duke, Owner

Annual show and exhibits of jewelry and gemstones and related equipment, supplies and services.
Frequency: October, Denver

15061 Gem, Jewelry & Mineral Show
Trade Shows International
PO Box 8862
Tucson, AZ 85738

520-791-2210
FAX 520-825-9115

15062 IJO Trade Show & Seminars
Independent Jewelers Organization
25 Seir Hill Rd
Norwalk, CT 06850-1322

203-846-4215
800-624-9252
FAX 203-846-8571
E-Mail: ijo@ijo.com
Home Page: www.ijo.com

Penny Palmer, Member Services Director
For members only
3500 Attendees
Frequency: Semi-Annual

15063 IPMI Conference
International Precious Metals Institute
5101 N 12th Avenue
Suite C
Pensacola, FL 32504

850-476-1156
FAX 850-476-1548
E-Mail: mail@ipmi.org
Home Page: www.ipmi.org

Robert Ianniello, President
Frequency: Annual

15064 International Gem & Jewelry Show
120 Derwood Circle
Rockville, MD 20850

301-294-1640
FAX 301-294-0034
Home Page: www.intergem.net

Herb Duke, Owner

Jewelry, gemstones and related equipment, supplies and services.

15065 International Gift Show: The Jewelry & Accessories Expo
Business Journals
50 Day Street
Norwalk, CT 06854

203-853-6015
FAX 203-852-8175

14000 Attendees

15066 International Jewelry Fair/General Merchandise Show-Spring
Helen Brett Enterprises

5111 Academy Drive
Lisle, IL 60532-2171

630-241-9865
800-541-8171
FAX 630-241-9870
E-Mail: dharrington@helenbrett.com
Home Page: www.gift2jewelry.com
Social Media: *Facebook*

Dave Harrington, Show Manager

Containing 800 booths during the spring show and 1500 booths during the fall show. Tradeshow open to wholesale buyers only (credentials required to attend).
24000 Attendees
Frequency: May
Founded in 1946
Mailing list available for rent

15067 International Watch and Jewelry Show

Burley and Olg Bullock
5901-Z Westheimer Road
Houston, TX 77057

713-783-8188
800-554-4992
FAX 281-589-8987
E-Mail: info@iwjg.com
Home Page: www.iwjg.com

JJ Gilbreath
Christina LeDoux
Frequency: June-Nov./January-March

15068 JA International Jewelry Show

Jewelers of America
52 Vanderbuilt Avenue
19th Floor
New York, NY 10017

646-580-0255
FAX 212-768-8087
E-Mail: info@jewelers.org
Home Page: www.jewelers.org

Matthew Runci, President
Donald Jackson, Controller
Timothy Haake, Founder
Lauren Thompson, Communications Manager
Showcase of fine jewelry open to the trade only.
11000 Attendees
Frequency: Febuary/July

15069 JCK Orlando International Jewelry Show

Reed Exhibition Companies
383 Manin Avenue
Norwalk, CT 06850

203-404-4800
FAX 203-840-5830
Home Page: www.jckgroup.com

Jay Jackson, Chief Operating Officer
Matthew Stuller, Founder
John Bachman, Secretary
Conference and exhibition.
2000 Attendees
Frequency: February

15070 Jewelers International Showcase (JIS)

6421 Congress Avenue
Suite 105
Boca Raton, FL 33487-2858

561-998-0205
FAX 561-998-0209
E-Mail: jisshow@aol.com
Home Page: www.jisshow.com

Michael G Breslow CEM, President
Jordan Tuchband, Sales Director
Vito J. Miceli, Sales Manager
Cindy Corrente, Financial Coordinator
Michele Carter, Show Director

Worldwide manufacturers and wholesalers of jewelry exhibit to trade buyers from Florida, Caribbean, Central and South America, plus other USA states. Exhibits of 1000 suppliers of fine jewelry, fashion jewelry and related products and services. The leading and largest independent Jewelery Trade-Only Show in the Western Hemisphere.
12000 Attendees
Frequency: October, January, April
Founded in 1979

15071 Merchandise Mart Gift/Jewelry/Resort Show

Denver Merchandise Mart
451 E 58th Avenue #470
Suite 4270
Denver, CO 80216

303-292-6278
800-289-6278
FAX 303-298-8473
E-Mail: bridget@denvermart.com
Home Page: www.denvermart.com

Bridget Oakes, Gift Show Exhibit Manager

A wholesale market for retail store buyers for resorts, theme parksand national parks, specialty gift stores and interior designers. Semi - Annual Show.
7000 Attendees
Frequency: February/August

15072 Mid-South Jewelry & Accessories Fair -Spring

Helen Brett Enterprises
5111 Academy Drive
Lisle, IL 60532-2171

630-241-9865
800-541-8171
FAX 630-241-9870
E-Mail: dharrington@helenbrett.com
Home Page: www.gift2jewelry.com
Social Media: *Facebook*

Dave Harrington, Show Manager

Containing over 300 booths during the spring show and 500 booths during the fall show. Tradeshow open to wholesale buyers only (credentials required to attend).
8500 Attendees
Frequency: May
Founded in 1946
Mailing list available for rent

15073 Mid-South Jewelry & Accessories Fair-Fall

Helen Brett Enterprises
5111 Academy Drive
Lisle, IL 60532-2171

630-241-9865
800-541-8171
FAX 630-241-9870
E-Mail: dharrington@helenbrett.com
Home Page: www.gift2jewelry.com
Social Media: *Facebook*

Dave Harrington, Show Manager

Containing 500 booths during the fall show and over 300 booths during the spring show. Tradeshow open to wholesale buyers only (credentials required to attend).
16000 Attendees
Frequency: November
Founded in 1946
Mailing list available for rent

15074 Midwest Jewelry Expo

Wisconsin Jewelry Assocation

1 East Main Street
Suite 305
Madison, WI 53703

608-257-3541
FAX 608-257-8755
Home Page: www.midwestjewelryexpo.com

Mary Kaja, Executive Director

The next jewelry trade show exposition is scheduled for March 24th to March 25th in 2007.
3000 Attendees
Frequency: March

15075 National Accessory Maintenance Exposition

240 Peachtree Street NW
Suite 2200
Atlanta, GA 30303-1327

404-203-3000
FAX 404-607-8682

Jeff Portman, CEO
Charles Sydney, Manager

Offers a forum for the exchange of ideas between manufacturers and suppliers of fashion accessories.
10M Attendees
Frequency: January

15076 Pacific Jewelry Show

California Jewelers Association
911 Wilshire Boulevard
Suite 1740
Los Angeles, CA 90017-3446

213-235-5722
FAX 213-623-5742

Richard Trujillo, Owner
Alberta E Hultman, Manager
Annual show of 250 exhibitors of jewelry and related items.
3000 Attendees
Frequency: August
Founded in 1999

15077 Stylemax

Merchandise Mart Properties Inc
222 Merchandise Mart Plaza
Suite 470
Chicago, IL 60654

312-527-4141
800-677-6278
E-Mail: sglick@mmart.com
Home Page: www.mmart.com
Social Media: *Facebook*

Susan Glick, VP

A women's apparel and accessory trade show with over 4,000 exhibitors.
5000 Attendees
Founded in 1920
Mailing list available for rent

15078 The Whole Bead Show

PO Box 1100
Nevada City, CA 95959

530-652-2725
800-292-2577
FAX 530-265-2776
E-Mail: info@wholebead.com
Home Page: www.wholebead.com
Social Media: *Facebook*

Ava Motherwell, Owner

An international bread trade show that occurs thirteen times per year. Contemporary pieces made from glass, stone, metal, pearl, amber and porcelain. Offering antique beads, handmade, findings, buttons, charms and beaded jewelry. Access merchants, bead makers and importers

who are direct suppliers of many professional and novice jewelry makers.
N/A Attendees
Frequency: Jan/Feb/Mar/Apr
Founded in 1993
Mailing list available for rent

15079 Trade Show for Jewelry Making

Manufacturing Jewelers & Suppliers of America
57 John L Dietsch Sq
Attleboro Falls, MA 02763-1027

401-274-3840
800-444-6572
FAX 401-274-0265
E-Mail: info@mjsa.org
Home Page: www.mjsa.org

James McCarthy, COO
Corrie Silvia Berry, Director of Sales & Business
David W. Cochran, President & CEO
Kristin Kopaz, Operations Manager
Dawn Britland, Assistant Controller

New regional trade show designed to service jewelry makers and manufacturers of all sizes throughout New England and surrounding areas. Providing a full range of products that industry professionals need to make their jewelry and operate their business.
1000 Attendees
Frequency: September
Founded in 1903

15080 Transworld's Jewelry, Fashion & Accessories Show

Transworld Exhibits
1850 Oak Street
Northfield, IL 60093

847-446-8434
800-323-5462
FAX 847-446-3523
Home Page: www.tweshows.com/jfa

Don Olstinske, Show Manager
Yianna Manokas, Creative Director
Donna Connolly, Customer Service Rep
Ron Carlson, Logistics Manager

Hundreds of the country's finest exhibitors. Thousands of the best buyers nationwide. The perfect venue for the latest jewelry collections, the most current fashion ideas and new accessories.
25000 Attendees
Frequency: July/October/December

15081 Tucson Gem and Mineral Show (tm)

Tucson Gem and Mineral Society
PO Box 42588
Tucson, AZ 85733

520-322-5773
FAX 520-322-6031
E-Mail: tgms@tgms.org
Home Page: www.tgms.org

Sponsored by the Tucson Gem and Mineral Society. Retail show open to the public at the Tucson Convention Center every February for four days. Over 200 dealers, over 100 exhibitors, children's activities.
25000 Attendees
Frequency: February
Founded in 1946

Directories & Databases

15082 AJM Technology Sourcebook

Manufacturing Jewelers & Suppliers of America

57 John L Dietsch Sq
Attleboro Falls, MA 02763-1027

401-274-3840
800-444-6572
FAX 401-274-0265
E-Mail: info@mjsa.org
Home Page: www.mjsa.org

James McCarthy, COO
Corrie Silvia Berry, Director of Sales & Business
David W. Cochran, President & CEO
Kristin Kopaz, Operations Manager
Dawn Britland, Assistant Controller

This publication provides listings and specs on machinery, equipment, raw materials, and software specifically geared to jewelry manufacturing.
Cost: $4.50
Frequency: Annual
Circulation: 5,000
Founded in 1903
Printed in 4 colors on glossy stock

15083 Accent Source Book

Larkin Group
100 Wells Avenue
Newton, MA 02459-3210

617-326-6525
800-869-7469
FAX 617-964-2752

Lauren Parker, Editor
Michael Corkin, Owner

Information on over 1,500 manufacturers of jewelry, watches and accessories is available in this comprehensive directory aimed at the gemology and related industries.
Cost: $25.00
200 Pages
Frequency: Annual
Circulation: 15,000
ISSN: 0192-7507

15084 Accessories Resource Directory

Business Journals
50 Day Street
Norwalk, CT 06854-3100

203-853-6015
FAX 203-852-8175
Home Page: www.busjour.com

Britton Jones, President

Over 1,500 manufacturers, importers and sales representatives that produce accessories are profiled.
Frequency: Annual
Circulation: 10,000

15085 Complete Directory of Cubic Zirconia Jewelry

Sutton Family Communications & Publishing Company
920 State Route 54 East
Elmitch, KY 42343

270-276-9500
E-Mail: jlsutton@apex.net

Theresa Sutton, Editor
Lee Sutton, General Manager

Print-out from database of wholesalers, manufacturers, distributors, importers and close-out houses. Database is updated daily to guarantee the most current and up-to-date sources available.
Cost: $39.50
100+ Pages

15086 Complete Directory of Earrings & Necklaces

Sutton Family Communications & Publishing Company

920 State Route 54 East
Elmitch, KY 42343

270-276-9500
E-Mail: jlsutton@apex.net

Theresa Sutton, Editor
Lee Sutton, General Manager

Print-out from database of wholesalers, manufacturers, distributors, importers and close-out houses. Database is updated daily to guarantee the most current and up-to-date sources available.
Cost: $37.00
100+ Pages

15087 Complete Directory of Jewelry Close-Outs

Sutton Family Communications & Publishing Company
920 State Route 54 East
Elmitch, KY 42343

270-276-9500
E-Mail: jlsutton@apex.net

Theresa Sutton, Editor
Lee Sutton, General Manager

Print-out from database of wholesalers, manufacturers, distributors, importers and close-out houses. Database is updated daily to guarantee the most current and up-to-date sources available.
Cost: $34.50
100+ Pages

15088 Complete Directory of Jewelry: General

Sutton Family Communications & Publishing Company
920 State Route 54 East
Elmitch, KY 42343

270-276-9500
E-Mail: jlsutton@apex.net

Theresa Sutton, Editor
Lee Sutton, General Manager

Print-out from database of wholesalers, manufacturers, distributors, importers and close-out houses. Database is updated daily to guarantee the most current and up-to-date sources available.
Cost: $54.50
100+ Pages

15089 Complete Directory of Low-Price Jewelry & Souvenirs

Sutton Family Communications & Publishing Company
920 State Route 54 East
Elmitch, KY 42343

270-276-9500
E-Mail: jlsutton@apex.net

Theresa Sutton, Editor
Lee Sutton, General Manager

Print-out from database of wholesalers, manufacturers, distributors, importers and close-out houses. Database is updated daily to guarantee the most current and up-to-date sources available.
Cost: $39.50
100+ Pages

15090 Complete Directory of Watches and Watch Bands

Sutton Family Communications & Publishing Company
920 State Route 54 East
Elmitch, KY 42343

270-276-9500
E-Mail: jlsutton@apex.net

Theresa Sutton, Editor
Lee Sutton, General Manager

Print-out from database of wholesalers, manufacturers, distributors, importers and close-out houses. Database is updated daily to guarantee the most current and up-to-date sources available.
Cost: $39.50
100+ Pages

15091 Diamond Report
Rapaport Diamond Corporation
15 W 47th Street
Suite 600
New York, NY 10036-3305

212-540-0575
FAX 212-840-0243
E-Mail: rap@diamonds.net
Home Page: www.diamond.net

Amber Michelle, Editor
Eillene Furrel, Advertising Manager

This large directory database offers background information and current prices for more than 100,000 stores.
Cost: $185.00
Frequency: Annual

15092 International Society of Appraisers
International Society of Appraisers
Ste 400
230 E Ohio St
Chicago, IL 60611-3646

206-241-0359
FAX 312-265-2908
E-Mail: isa@isa-appraisers.org
Home Page: www.isa-appraisers.org

Nan B Shelton, President
Connie Davenport, Vice President
Charles Pharr, Treasurer
Philip Hawkins, Secretary

Be Certain of its Value - A Consumer's Guide To Hiring a Competent Personal Property Appraiser is available complimentary to the public. Alphabetical list of appraisers with specialty areas plus indexes: area of expertise, zip code, state and city, company, and related services.
Cost: $15.00
305 Pages
Frequency: Annual
Circulation: 1500
Founded in 1979
Printed in 2 colors

15093 Jewelers Board of Trade: Confidential Reference Book
Jewelers Board of Trade
95 Jefferson Blvd
Warwick, RI 02888-1046

401-467-0055
FAX 401-467-1199
E-Mail: jbtinfo@jewelersboard.com
Home Page: www.jewelersboard.com

Dione Kenyen, President

Importers, distributors and retailers, close to 45,000, are profiled that are directly related to the jewelry industry.
Frequency: Semiannual
Circulation: 3,400

15094 Jewelers' Circular/Keystone: Brand Name and Trademark Guide
Chilton Company
1 Chilton Way
Wayne, PA 19089-0002

610-964-4243
800-866-0206
FAX 610-964-4481

L Roberts, Editor

Over 5,000 manufacturers of jewelry store products.
Cost: $49.95

15095 Jewelers' Circular/Keystone: Jewelers' Directory Issue
Chilton Company
PO Box 2045
Radnor, PA 19089

610-964-4000
FAX 610-964-4512

Kathleen Ellis, Editor

About 10,000 manufacturers, importers and wholesale jewelers providing merchandise and supplies to the jewelry retailing industry and related trade organizations.
Cost: $32.00
Frequency: Monthyly
Circulation: 30,000

15096 Lapidary Journal: Annual Buyers' Directory Issue
Lapidary Journal
60 Chestnut Avenue
Suite 201
Devon, PA 19333-1312

610-325-5700
800-676-GEMS
FAX 610-293-1717

Michele Erazo, Marketing Executive

List of 4,000 suppliers and retailers of gem-cutting and jewelry making and mineral collecting equipment, beads, fossils, minerals and gems, gem and mineral clubs, bead societies, museums, schools and shops.
Cost: $6.50
Frequency: Annual May
Circulation: 67,000

15097 MJSA Buyers' Guide
Manufacturing Jewelers & Suppliers of America
57 John L Dietsch Sq
Attleboro Falls, MA 02763-1027

401-274-3840
800-444-6572
FAX 401-274-0265
E-Mail: info@mjsa.org
Home Page: www.mjsa.org

James McCarthy, Coo
Bruce Coltin, Operations Manager
Kristin Kopaz, Operations Manager
Corrie Berry, Sales Manager

Contains finished jewelry as well as equipment, supplies, and components necessary for jewelry manufacturing.
Cost: $45.00
Frequency: BiAnnual
Circulation: 5,000

15098 National Jeweler: Industry Yellow Pages
Miller Freeman Publications
28 East 28th Street
12th Floor
New York, NY 10016

212-378-0400
FAX 212-378-0470
E-Mail: sedorusa@optonline.net
Home Page: www.governmentvideo.com
Social Media: *RSS*

Gary Rhodes, International Sales Manager

Approximately 5,000 companies providing products and services in the jewelry and watch industries.
Cost: $10.00
Frequency: Annual December
Circulation: 36,000

Industry Web Sites

15099 Gemological Institute of America
The Robert Mouawad Campus
5345 Armada Dr.
Carlsbad, CA 92008

760-603-4000
800-421-7250
FAX 760-603-4080
Home Page: www.gia.edu
Social Media: *Facebook, Twitter, LinkedIn, Google+, YouTube*

John A. Green, Chair
Susan M. Jacques, President & CEO

The jewellery industry's source for knowledge, standards and education since 1931.
Founded in 1931

15100 http://gold.greyhouse.com
G.O.L.D Grey House OnLine Databases

Grey House Publishing's online database platform, GOLD, offers Quick Search, Keyword Search and Expert Search for most business sectors including jewelry and watch markets. The GOLD platform makes finding the information you need quick and easy - whether you're a novice searcher or an experienced database user. All of Grey House's directory products are available for subscription on the GOLD platform.

15101 www.agta.org
American Gem Trade Association

A trade association for the colored gemstone industry in North Africa. Operates gemological testing in New York.

15102 www.awi-net.org
American Watchmakers Institute

Examines and certifies master watchmakers and clockmakers. Maintains a placement service. Conducts home study courses.

15103 www.cufflink.com
National Cuff Link Society

For cuff link wearers and collectors.

15104 www.glda.com
Gem & Lapidary Dealers Association

15105 www.goldinstitue.org
Gold Institute

15106 www.greyhouse.com
Grey House Publishing

Authoritative reference directories for most business sectors including jewelry and watch markets. Users can search the online databases with varied search criteria allowing for custom searches by product category, geographic area, sales volume, keyword, subject and more. Full Grey House catalog and online ordering also available.

15107 www.iaca.com
Indian Arts & Crafts Association

Not for profit trade association. Our mission is to promote, protect and preserve Indian arts.

15108 www.independentjewlers.com
Independent Jewelers

Works to aid independent jewelers in competing in local markets through advertising, promotion, and buyers assistance.

15109 www.ipmi.org
International Precious Metals Institute

International association of producers, refiners, fabricators, scientists, users, financial institutions, merchants, private and public sector groups and the general precious metals community created to provide a forum for the exchange of information and technology.

15110 www.isa-appraisers.org
International Society of Appraisers

A not-for-profit professional association of personal property appraisers. ISA provides education and organizational support to its members, to serve the public by producing highley qualified and ethical appraisers who are recognized authorities in personal property appraising.

15111 www.jewelers.org
Jewelers of America

15112 www.jewelersboard.com
Trade association providing credit reporting, collections and marketing services to the US and overseas jewelry industries. Our members are wholesalers, manufacturers and service providers to the jewelry industry.

15113 www.jewelerssecurity.org
Jewelers' Security Alliance

Principal activity is providing education and information to jewelers so they can guard against loss through crimes, including burglary, robbery and theft.

15114 www.jewelryinfo.org
Jewelery Information Center

Identifies deceptive trade practices and misleading advertising. Provides advice on marketing and assists in prosecution of violations. The media side of the Jewelers Vigilance Committee.

15115 www.jvclegal.org
Jewelers Vigilance Committee

Identifies deceptive trade practices and misleading advertising. Provides advice on marketing and assists in prosecution of violations.

15116 www.love-story.com
Leading Jewelers Guild

15117 www.silverinstitute.org
Silver Institute

15118 www.silversmithing.com
Society of American Silversmiths

15119 www.silverusersassociation.org
Silver Users Association

Represents manufacturers and distributors of products in which silver is an essential element, such as photographic materials, medical and dental supplies, batteries and electronic and electrical equipment, silverware, mirrors, commemorative art and jewelry.

15120 www.superabrasives.org
Industrial Diamond Association of America

15121 www.womensjewelry.org
Women's Jewelry Association

For jewelry industry professionals.

15122 National Academy of Television Journalists

PO Box 289
Salisbury, MD 21803

410-251-2511
FAX 410-543-0658
E-Mail: wolske@shore.intercom.net
Home Page: www.angelfire.com/md/NATJ/

Dr Catherine North, Executive Director
Dr Cathy Roche, Director

Works with newly graduated journalist school students to assist them as they enter in the world of television news. Honors those in the industtry for excellence in their field of endeaver.
Founded in 1985

Associations

15123 Accrediting Council on Education in Journalism and Mass Communications

1435 Jayhawk Blvd
Lawrence, KS 66045-7575

785-864-3973
FAX 785-864-5225
Home Page: www2.ku.edu/~acejmc/

Christopher Callahan, Chair
Marie Hardin, Vice Chair
David Boardman, President
Doug Anderson, Vice President
Cindy Reinardy, Assistant to the Executive Dir.

ACEJMC members are journalism and media departments, education associations and professional organizations.
113 Members
Founded in 1945

15124 American Agricultural Editors' Association

120 Main Street W
PO Box 156
New Prague, MN 56071

952-758-6502
FAX 952-758-5813
E-Mail: aaea@gandgcomm.com
Home Page: www.ageditors.com
Social Media: *Facebook, Twitter, LinkedIn*

Elaine Shein, President
Kurt Lawton, Immediate Past President
Mike Wilson, President Elect
Den Gardner, Executive Director
Doug Rich, Board Member

National professional development member association for agricultural communicators.
Founded in 1921

15125 American Association of Sunday & Feature Editors

1921 Gallows Road
Suite 600
Vienna, VA 22182-3900

703-902-1639
FAX 703-620-4557
E-Mail: contact@aasfe.org
Home Page: www.aasfe.org

Chris Beringer, President
Gina Seay, VP
Denise Joyce, VP
Kim Marcum, Secretary-Treasurer

An organization of editors from the United States and Canada dedicated to the quality of features in newspapers and the craft of feature writing.

15126 American Copy Editors Society

155 E. Algonquin Road
Arlington Heights, IL 60005-4617

E-Mail: info@copydesk.org
Home Page: www.copydesk.org
Social Media: *Facebook, Twitter, LinkedIn, RSS*

Teresa Schmedding, President
David Sullivan, Vice President
Sara Ziegler, Treasurer
Brady Jones, Secretary
Christine Steele, Director of Membership

A professional nonprofit association for copy editors at U.S. newspapers, magazines, websites, and corporations.
Founded in 1997

15127 American Copy Editors Society (ACES)

7 Avenida Vista Grande
Suite B7 #467
Santa Fe, NM 87508

E-Mail: info@copydesk.org
Home Page: www.copydesk.org
Social Media: *Facebook, Twitter, LinkedIn, RSS*

Teresa Schmedding, President
Lisa McLendon, Vice President Conferences
Sara Ziegler, Treasurer
Rudy Bahr, Executive Director
David F. Sullivan, Secretary

ACES is a professional organization working toward the advancement of editors. Their aim is to provide opportunities through training, discussion and advocacy that promote the editing profession.
Founded in 1997

15128 American Medical Writers' Association

30 W Gude Dr
Suite 525
Rockville, MD 20850-4347

240-238-0940
FAX 301-294-9006
E-Mail: amwa@amwa.org
Home Page: www.amwa.org
Social Media: *Facebook, Twitter, LinkedIn*

Susan Krug, CAE, Executive Director
Ann Silveira, Membership Manager & Database Coor
Shari Rager, CAE, Deputy Director
Julia Shedlin, Membership Program Assistant
Josie Zeman, Education Program Assistant

Concerned with the advancement and improvement of medical communications.
5000+ Members
Founded in 1940
Mailing list available for rent

15129 American Newspaper Representatives

2075 W Big Beaver Rd
Suite 310
Troy, MI 48084-3439

248-643-9910
800-550-7557
FAX 248-643-9914
E-Mail: accountsales@gotoanr.com
Home Page: gotoanr.com

Hilary Howe, President
Robert Sontag, Executive VP/COO
John Jepsen, Controller
Melanie Cox, Regional Sales Manager

Supports those newspaper representatives and distributors in the United States. Hosts annual trade show.
Founded in 1943

15130 American Press Institute

4401 Wilson Boulevard
Suite 900
Arlington, VA 22203

571-366-1200
E-Mail: hello@pressinstitute.org
Home Page: www.americanpressinstitute.org/
Social Media: *Facebook, Twitter, YouTube, RSS*

Robert J. Weil, Chair
Michael G. Abernathy, Vice Chair
Tom Rosenstiel, Executive Director
Jeff Sonderman, Deputy Director
Jane Elizabeth, Senior Research Project Manager

Conducts research, training, convenes thought leaders and creates tools to help chart a path ahead for journalism in the 21st century.
Founded in 1946

15131 American Press Institute (API)

4401 Wilson Blvd.
Ste 900
Arlington, VA 22203

571-366-1200
FAX 571-366-1195
E-Mail: hello@pressinstitute.org
Home Page: www.americanpressinstitute.org
Social Media: *Facebook, Twitter, RSS, YouTube*

Robert J. Weil, Chair
Michael G. Abernathy, Vice Chair
Tom Rosenstiel, Executive Director
Jeff Sonderman, Deputy Director
Jane Elizabeth, Senior Research Project Manager

API is the trusted source for career leadership development for the newsmedia industry in North America and around the world. They help companies innovate and leaders realize their full potential.
Founded in 1946

15132 American Society of Business Press Editors

214 North Hale Street
Wheaton, IL 60187

630-510-4588
FAX 630-510-4501
E-Mail: info@asbpe.org
Home Page: www.asbpe.org
Social Media: *Facebook, Twitter, LinkedIn, RSS*

Jessica Zemler, President
Dominick Yanchunas, Vice President
Janet Svazas, Executive Director
Steve Ross, Treasurer
Robin Sherman, Associate Dir. & Newsletter Editor

ASBPE is the professional association for full-time and freelance editors and writers employed in the business, trade, and specialty press. It is widely known for its annual Awards of Excellence competition, which recognizes the best editorial, design, and online achievement.
Founded in 1964
Mailing list available for rent

15133 American Society of Business Publication Editors

214 North Hale St.
Wheaton, IL 60187

630-510-4588
FAX 630-510-4501
E-Mail: info@asbpe.org
Home Page: www.asbpe.org

Social Media: *Facebook, Twitter, LinkedIn, YouTube*

Jessica Zemler, President
Dominick Yanchunas, Vice President
Janet Svazas, Executive Director
Steve Ross, Treasurer

Professional association for full-time and freelance editors and writers employed in the business, trade, and specialty press.
Founded in 1964

15134 American Society of Journalists and Authors

355 Lexington Avenue
15th Floor
New York, NY 10017-6603

212-997-0947
FAX 212-937-2315
E-Mail: webeditor@asja.org
Home Page: www.asja.org
Social Media: *Facebook, Twitter, LinkedIn, Google+, Instagram*

Randy Dotinga, President
Sherry Beck Paprocki, Vice President
Alexandra Cantor Owens, Executive Director
Meredith Taylor, General Manager
Neil O'Hara, Treasurer

For freelance nonfiction writers whose bylines appear in periodicals and in books.
1000+ Members
Founded in 1948

15135 American Society of Magazine Editors

757 Third Avenue
11th Floor
New York, NY 10017

212-872-3700
E-Mail: mpa@magazine.org
Home Page: www.magazine.org/
Social Media: *Facebook, Twitter, LinkedIn, YouTube, Google+*

Mary G. Berner, President, CEO
Nancy Telliho, Interim CEO
Sid Holt, Chief Executive
Eric John, SVP, Digital Strategy & Initiatives
Rita Cohen, SVP/ Legislative & Reg Policy

An industry trade group for editors of magazines published in the United States.
Founded in 1919

15136 American Society of Media Photographers (ASMP)

150 North 2nd Street
Philadelphia, PA 19106

215-451-2767
FAX 215-451-0880
E-Mail: info@asmp.org
Home Page: asmp.org
Social Media: *Facebook, Twitter, LinkedIn*

Tom Kennedy, Executive Director
Victor Perlman, General Counsel
Elena Goertz, General Manager
Chris Chandler, Bookkeeper
Ellen Khlystova, IT Specialist

ASMP is the premier trade association for the world's most respectd photograhers. ASMP is the leader in promoting photographers' rights, providing education in better business practices, producing business publications for photographers, and helping to connect purchasers with professional photographers.
7000 Members
Founded in 1944

15137 American Society of News Editors (ASNE)

209 Reynolds Journalism Institute
Mission School of Journalism
Columbia, MO 65211

573-884-2405
FAX 573-884-3824
E-Mail: asne@asne.org
Home Page: www.asne.org
Social Media: *Facebook, Twitter, Storify*

Pam Fine, President
Mizell Stewart III, Vice President
Teri Hayt, Executive Director
Arnie Robbins, Senior Adviser
Cindy L. Roe, Finance Director

ASNE is a membership organization for editors, producers or directors in charge of journalistic organizations or departments, deans or faculty at university journalism schools, and leaders and faculty of media-related foundations and training organizations.
Founded in 1922

15138 Asian American Journalists Association (AAJA)

5 Third Street
Suite 1108
San Francisco, CA 94103

415-346-2051
FAX 415-346-6343
E-Mail: national@aaja.org
Home Page: www.aaja.org
Social Media: *Facebook, Twitter, LinkedIn*

Paul Cheung, President
Kathy Chow, Executive Director
Glenn E. K. Sugihara, Accounting Consultant
Karen A. Sugihara, Accounting Consultantÿ
Derric Jones, Event Manager Consultant

AAJA provides support among Asian American and Pacific Islander journalists. It provides encouragement, information, advice and scholarship assistance to Asian American and Pacific Islander students who aspire to professional journalism careers.
Founded in 1981

15139 Associated Press

1825 K Street NW
Suite 800
Washington, DC 20006-1202

212-621-1500
FAX 202-736-1107
E-Mail: info@ap.org
Home Page: www.ap.org
Social Media: *Facebook, Twitter, LinkedIn, Google+, Youtube*

Mary Junck, Chairman
Gary Pruitt, President and CEO
Jessica Bruce, SVP, Director of Human Resources
Ken Dale, Senior Vice President and CFO
Ellen Hale, SVP, Director of Corporate Comm.

Seeks to advance journalism through radio and television, and cooperates with the AP to promote accurate and impartial news.
5.9m Members
Founded in 1846

15140 Associated Press Media Editors

450 West 33rd Street
New York, NY 10001

212-621-7007
E-Mail: sjacobsen@ap.org
Home Page: www.apme.com/
Social Media: *Facebook, Blog*

Alan D. Miller, President
Laura Sellers-Earl, Vice President
Bill Church, Secretary
Dennis Anderson, Treasurer
Jim Simon, Journalism Studies Chair

Members are managing editors or executives of Associated Press News Executives.
Founded in 1930

15141 Associated Press Media Editors (APME)

450 West 33rd Street
New York, NY 10001

212-621-7007
E-Mail: sjacobsen@ap.org
Home Page: www.apme.com
Social Media: *Facebook, Twitter, Blog*

Alan D. Miller, President
Laura Sellers-Earl, Vice President
Bill Church, Secretary
Dennis Anderson, Treasurer
Jim Simon, Journalism Studies Chair

APME is an association of U.S. and Canadian editors, broadcasters and educators whose entitites are members of The Associated Press.
Founded in 1930

15142 Associated Press Sports Editors

9000 N. Broadway
Oklahoma City, OK 73114

405-475-3164
FAX 405-475-3315
E-Mail: msherman@oklahoman.com
Home Page: apsportseditors.org
Social Media: *Facebook, Twitter, RSS*

Mike Sherman, Chairman
Mary Byrne Byrne, President
Tommy Deas, First Vice President
John Bednarowski, Third VP
Jack Berninger, Executive Director

A national organization that strives to improve professional standards of sports departments.

15143 Association for Education in Journalism and Mass Communication

234 Outlet Pointe Boulevard
Suite A
Columbia, SC 29210-5667

803-798-0271
FAX 803-772-3509
E-Mail: aejmchq@aol.com
Home Page: www.aejmc.org/
Social Media: *Facebook, Twitter, LinkedIn, Friendfeed, YouTube, RSS*

Lori Bergen, President
Jennifer McGill, Executive Director
Kathy Bailey, Association Business Manager
Felicia G. Brown, Desktop Publisher
Lillian Coleman, Newsletter Editor/Project Manager

AEJMC promotes the highest possible standards for education in journalism and mass communication, encouraging the widest possible range of communication research and the implementation of a multi-cultural society in the classroom and curriculum, defending and maintaining the freedom of expression in day-to-day living.
Founded in 1912

15144 Association for Women in Communications

3337 Duke Street
Alexandria, VA 22314

703-370-7436
FAX 703-342-4311
Home Page: www.womcom.org
Social Media: *Facebook, Twitter, LinkedIn, Google+, YouTube*

Mitzie Zerr, Chair
Missy Kruse, Vice Chair
Pat Meads, Treasurer
Hannah Schmuckler, AWC Membership & Comm. Coordinator
Pamela Valenzuela, AWC Executive Director

Supports all those professional women in the fields of journalism online media, public relations, advertising, marketing, educational communications, graphic and web design, photography and film. Hosts bi-annual conference.
Founded in 1909

15145 Association for Women in Sports Media

7742 Spalding Dr.
#377
Norcross, GA 30092

E-Mail: info@awsmonline.org
Home Page: www.awsmonline.org
Social Media: *Facebook, Twitter, LinkedIn, Instagram*

Lydia Craver, Chair of the Board
Jennifer Overman, President
Rachel Whittaker, VP, Administration
Jill Ann Bouffard, VP, Convention
Allison Creekmore, VP, Digital

Nonprofit organization founded as a support network and advocacy group for women who work in sports writing, editing, broadcast and production, andpublic and media relations.

15146 Association of Alternative Newsmedia

116 Cass Street
Traverse City, MI 49684ÿ

703-470-2996
FAX 866-619-9755
E-Mail: web@aan.org
Home Page: www.altweeklies.com/
Social Media: *Facebook, Twitter, RSS, Google+*

Blair Barna, President
Chuck Strouse, Vice President
Ellen Meany, Treasurer
Tiffany Shackelford, Executive Director
Jason Zaragoza, Deputy Director

Trade association of alternative weekly newspapers in North America.
Founded in 1978

15147 Association of American Editorial Cartoonists

PO Box 460673
Fort Lauderdale, FL 33346

717-703-3003
FAX 717-703-3008
Home Page: www.editorialcartoonists.com
Social Media: *Twitter*

Jack Ohman, President
Jen Sorensen Sorensen, Vice President
R.C. Harvey, Secretary-Treasurer

15148 Association of Food Journalists

Home Page: www.afjonline.com
Social Media: *Facebook*

Debbie Moose, President
Bob Batz, Jr., Vice President
Jennifer Palcher-Silliman, Executive Director
Nancy Stohs, Secretary
Patricia West-Barker, Treasurer
Founded in 1974

15149 Association of Health Care Journalists

Missouri School of Journalism
10 Neff Hall
Columbia, MO 65211

573-884-5606
FAX 573-884-5609
E-Mail: info@healthjournalism.org
Home Page: www.healthjournalism.org
Social Media: *Facebook, Twitter*

Karl Stark, President
Ivan Oransky, M.D., Vice President
Len Bruzzeseÿ, Executive Director

Jeff Porter, Special Projects Director
Pia Christensen, Managing Editor/Online Services
1,400 Members
Founded in 1997

15150 Association of Magazine Media

757 Third Avenue
11th Floor
New York, NY 10017

212-872-3700
FAX 212-906-0128
E-Mail: mpa@magazine.org
Home Page: www.magazine.org
Social Media: *Facebook, Twitter, LinkedIn, Youtube, Pinterst*

Mr. Stephen M. Lacy, Chairman
Ms. Nancy Telliho, Interim President and CEO
Sid Holt, Chief Executive
Nina Fortuna, Director, ASME
Julie Ryu, Marketing and Events Coordinator

ASME is the principal organization for magazine journalists in the United States. ASME works to defend the First Amendment, protect editorial independence and support the development of journalism.
700 Members
Founded in 1919

15151 Association of Opinion Journalists

2301 Vanderbilt Place
VU Station B 351669
Nashville, TN 37233-1699

E-Mail: opinionjournalists@gmail.com
Home Page: www.opinionjournalists.org/
Social Media: *Facebook, Twitter*

David D. Haynes, President
Jennifer Hemmingsen, Secretary
Dan Morain, Treasurer
Founded in 1947

15152 Baptist Communicators Association

1519 Menlo Drive
Kennesaw, GA 30152

770-425-3728
E-Mail: office@baptistcommunicators.org, webmast
Home Page: www.baptistcommunicators.org
Social Media: *Facebook, RSS*

Brian Hobbs, Program Chair
Eric Yarbrough, Awards Chairman
Ian Richardson, President
Neisha Fuson Roberts, Membership Vice President
Brooke Zimny, Communications Vice President

PR and journalism profesionals.
300 Members
Founded in 1953

15153 Center for Investigative Reporting

1400 65th St.
Suite 200
Emeryville, CA 94608

510-809-3160
FAX 510-849-6141
E-Mail: jalvarado@cironline.org
Home Page: www.revealnews.org
Social Media: *Facebook, Twitter, Tumblr, RSS*

Phil Bronstein, Executive Chair
Joaquin Alvarado, CEO
Laurel Leichter, Human Resources Consultant
Robert J. Rosenthal, Executive Director
Christa Scharfenberg, Head of Studio
Founded in 1977

15154 Center for Media Literacy

22837 Pacific Coast Highway
#472
Malibu, CA 90265

310-804-3985
E-Mail: cml@medialit.com

Home Page: www.medialit.org
Social Media: *YouTube*

Elizabeth Thoman CHM, Founder
Tessa Jolls, President, CEO
Beth Thornton, Communications
Founded in 1977

15155 Collegiate Press Association

330 21st Avenue S
Minneapolis, MN 55455-0480

612-625-3500
FAX 612-626-0720

Tom Rolnicki, Manager

Supports all those involved in the development and betterment of collegiate press. Hosts annual trade show.

15156 Committee of Concerned Journalists

Administrative Offices
Suite 300
Columbia, MO 65211

573-884-9121
FAX 573-884-3824
E-Mail: rji@rjionline.org
Home Page: www.rjionline.org
Social Media: *Facebook, Twitter, LinkedIn, Google+, YouTube*

Randy Picht, Executive Director
Roger Gafke, Director of Program Development
Edward McCain, Digital Curator of Journalism
Brian Steffens, Director, Communications
Esther Thorson, Director, Research
Founded in 2004

15157 Committee to Protect Journalists

330 7th Avenue
11th Floor
New York, NY 10001

212-465-1004
FAX 212-465-9568
E-Mail: info@cpj.org
Home Page: www.cpj.org/
Social Media: *Facebook, Twitter, YouTube, Tumblr, RSS*

Joel Simon, Executive Director
Robert Mahoney, Deputy Director
John Weis, Development & Outreach Director
Sue Marcoux, Director, Finance & Admin.
Kavita Menon, Senior Program Officer
Founded in 1981

15158 Dart Center for Journalism & Trauma

Columbia University
Graduate School of Journalism, 2950
New York, NY 10027

212-854-8056
E-Mail: bruce.shapiro@dartcenter.org
Home Page: www.dartcenter.org
Social Media: *Facebook, Twitter*

Bruce Shapiro, Executive Director
Kate Black, Associate Director
Kelly Boyce, Administrative Coordinator
Ariel Ritchin, Website Editor

15159 Education Writers Association

3516 Connecticut Avenue NW
Washington, DC 20008

202-452-9830
FAX 202-452-9837
Home Page: www.ewa.org
Social Media: *Facebook, Twitter, LinkedIn, Google+*

Scott Elliott, President
Greg Toppo, Vice President (Journalists)
Christine Tebben, Vice President (Community Members)
Caroline W. Hendrie, Executive Director
George Dieter, Chief Operating Officer

The Education Writers Association is the national professional organization of education reporters and intent of improving education reporting to the public.

15160 First Amendment Center

555 Pennsylvania Ave. N.W.
Washington, DC 20001

202-292-6288
FAX 202-292-6295
E-Mail: kcatone@newseum.org
Home Page: www.firstamendmentcenter.org
Social Media: *Facebook, Twitter, RSS*

Ken Paulson, President and CEO
Gene Policinski, SVP and Executive Director
John Seigenthaler, Founder
Karen Catone, Director
Ashlie Hampton, Event Coordinator

15161 Football Writers Association of America

18652 Vista del Sol
Dallas, TX 75287

972-713-6198
E-Mail: webmaster@sportswriters.net
Home Page: www.sportswriters.net
Social Media: *Twitter*

Kirk Bohls, President
Steve Richardson, Executive Director
Lee Barfknecht, 1st VP
Mark Anderson, Second VP
1,000 Members
Founded in 1941

15162 Garden Writers Association of America

7809 FM 179
Shallowater, TX 79363

806-832-1870
FAX 806-832-5244
E-Mail: webtech@gardenwriters.org
Home Page: www.gardenwriters.org/
Social Media: *Facebook, Twitter, LinkedIn, Pinterest, Google+*

Kirk Brown, President
Becky Heath, Vice President
Jo Ellen Meyers Sharp, Treasurer
Robert LaGasse, Executive Director
Debra Prinzing, Past President

15163 Gay and Lesbian Press Association

PO Box 8185
Universal City, CA 91618-8185

FAX 818-902-9576

Supports those gay and lesbian professionals in the field of journalism. Publishes quarterly newsletter.

15164 Hollywood Foreign Press Association

646 N Robertson Blvd
West Hollywood, CA 90069

310-657-1731
FAX 310-939-9034
E-Mail: info@hfpa.org
Home Page: www.hfpa.org
Social Media: *Facebook, Twitter, Youtube, RSS*

Lorenzo Soria, President
Meher Tatna, VP
Serge Rakhlin, Executive Secretary
Jorge Camara, Treasurer
Meher Tatna, Treasurer

Foreign correspondents covering Hollywood and the entertainment industry.
Mailing list available for rent

15165 Inland Press Association

701 Lee Street
Suite 925
Des Plaines, IL 60016

847-795-0380
FAX 847-795-0385
E-Mail: inland@inlandpress.org
Home Page: www.inlandpress.org/
Social Media: *Facebook, Twitter, LinkedIn*

Tom Slaughter, Executive Director
Patty Slusher, Director, Membership & Programming
Tim Mather, Financial Studies Manager
Mark Fitzgerald, Publications Editor
Maria Choronzuk, Graphic Designer
Founded in 1885

15166 Inter American Press Association

Jules Dubois Building
1801 Sw 3rd Ave
Miami, FL 33129

305-634-2465
FAX 305-635-2272
E-Mail: info@sipiapa.org
Home Page: www.sipiapa.org
Social Media: *Facebook, Twitter, Blogger, Youtube*

Ricardo Trotti, Executive Director
Martha Estrada, Assistant Executive Director
Melba Jimenez, Assistant Press Freedom Committee
Carlos Fernandez, Financial counselor
Ana Maria Perez, Accounting

Supports all those involved in the media and journalism industry. Hosts annual trade show.
Founded in 1926

15167 International Center for Journalists

2000 M St. NW
Suite 250
Washington, DC 20036

202-737-3700
FAX 202-737-0530
Home Page: www.icfj.org
Social Media: *Facebook, Twitter, LinkedIn, YouTube, Instagram, Google+*

Michael Golden, Chairman
James F. Hoge, Jr., Vice Chair
Pamela Howard, Vice Chair
Matthew Winkler, Vice Chair
Joyce Barnathan, President

15168 International Communications Association

1500 21st St Nw
Washington, DC 20036

202-955-1444
FAX 202-955-1448
E-Mail: icahdq@icahdq.org
Home Page: www.icahdq.org
Social Media: *Facebook, Twitter, LinkedIn, Google+, Tumblr, Reddit*

Michael L. Haley, Executive Director
Francois Heinderyckx, President
John Paul Gutierrez, Communication Director
Jennifer Le, Executive Assistant
Michael J. West, Publications Manager

Supports all students and professionals in the international communications industry. Publishes bi-monthly newsletter.
3400 Members
Founded in 1950
Mailing list available for rent

15169 International Food, Wine and Travel Writers Association

39252 Winchester Rd.
Ste 107 #418
Murrieta, CA 92563

877-439-8929
951-970-8326
FAX 909-396-0014
E-Mail: admin@ifwtwa.org
Home Page: www.ifwtwa.org
Social Media: *Facebook, Twitter, LinkedIn, RSS, Youtube, Instagram*

Linda Kissam, President, Officer, Chair Marketing
Allen Cox, VP, Officer, Chair Excellence Award
Elizabeth Willoughby, Secretary
Michelle M. Winner, Director
Andrew M. Harris, Director, Culinary Advisor

Staff and/or freelance writers in the food, wine and travel field. Also includes other media professionals and industry associate members in 28 countries worldwide.
300 Members
Founded in 1956

15170 International Food, Wine and Travel Writer

39252 Winchester Rd
Ste 107 #418
Murrieta, CA 92563

877-439-8929
951-970-8326
FAX 877-439-8929
E-Mail: admin@ifwtwa.org
Home Page: www.ifwtwa.org/
Social Media: *Facebook, Twitter, LinkedIn, YouTube, RSS, Instagram*

Linda Kissam, President, Officer, Chair Marketing
Allen Cox, VP, Officer, Chair Excellence Award
Elizabeth Willoughby, Secretary
Michelle M. Winner, Director
Andrew M. Harris, Director, Culinary Advisor

15171 International News Media Association

PO Box 740186
Dallas, TX 75374

214-373-9111
972-991-3151
FAX 214-373-9112
E-Mail: inma@inma.org
Home Page: www.inma.org
Social Media: *Facebook, Twitter, LinkedIn, RSS*

Ross McPherson, Executive Chairman
Mark Challinor, President
Yasmin Namini, Senior VP, Chief Consumer Officer
Earl J. Wilkinson, Executive Director/CEO
Brie Logsdon, Social Media Editor

Individuals in marketing, circulation, research and public relations of newspapers.
1100 Members
Founded in 1930
Mailing list available for rent

15172 Investigative Reporters and Editors

141 Neff Annex
Missouri School of Journalism
Columbia, MO 65211

573-882-2042
FAX 573-882-5431
E-Mail: info@ire.org
Home Page: www.ire.org

Sarah Cohen, Board President
Matt Goldberg, Vice President
Andrew Donohue, Treasurer
Mark Horvit, Executive Director
Jaimi Dowdell, Senior Training Directory

For individuals involved in investigative journalism.
Founded in 1975

15173 Journalism Center on Children and Families

Knight Hall, Room 1100
College Park, MD 20742

301-405-8808
E-Mail: info@journalismcenter.org
Home Page: www.journalismcenter.org
Social Media: *Facebook, Twitter, LinkedIn*

Julie Drizin, Director
Aysha Khan, Editorial Intern
Zoe King, Editorial Intern
Fatimah Waseem, Editorial Intern
Founded in 1993

15174 Magazine Publishers of America

757 Third Avenue
11th Floor
New York, NY 10017

212-872-3700
E-Mail: mpa@magazine.org
Home Page: www.magazine.org
Social Media: *Facebook, Twitter, LinkedIn, YouTube, Google+*

Mr. Stephen M. Lacy, Chairman
Ms. Nancy Telliho, Interim President and CEO
Sid Holt, Chief Executive
Eric John, SVP
Rita Cohen, SVP / Legislative & Reg Policy
Founded in 1919

15175 Media Financial Management Association

550 W. Frontage Road
Ste. 3600
Northfield, IL 60093

847-716-7000
FAX 847-716-7004
E-Mail: info@mediafinance.org
Home Page: www.infe.org

Ralph Bender, Chairman
Mary M. Collins, President & CEO
Jamie L. Grande, Director of Operations
Arcelia Pimentel, Director of Sales
Caitlin Hahne, Membership Coordinator

Focuses on newspaper financial management, with members representing most North American newpaper companies, as well as many off-shore. INFE's activities include publishing, conferences, workshops, industry surveys and studies, and offers members networking opportunities.
1200 Members
Founded in 1961

15176 National Association of Black Journalists

1100 Knight Hall
Suite 3100
College Park, MD 20742

301-405-0248
FAX 301-314-1714
E-Mail: drmatthews@nabj.org
Home Page: www.nabj.org
Social Media: *Facebook, Twitter*

Sarah Glover, President
Dorothy Tucker, Vice President/Broadcast
Marlon A. Walker, Vice President/Print
Ben,t Wilson, Vice President/Digital
Sherlon Christie, Secretary

An organization of journalists, students and media-related professionals that provides quality programs and services and advocates on behalf of black journalists worldwide.
Founded in 1975

15177 National Association of Broadcast Employees & Technicians

501 3rd St Nw
Washington, DC 20001

202-434-1254
FAX 202-434-1426
E-Mail: guild@cwa-union.org
Home Page: www.nabetcwa.org
Social Media: *Facebook, Youtube, RSS, Flickr*

Charles G. Braico, Sector President
Lou Marinaro, Sector Vice President
William Murray, Staff Representative
Eric Seggi, Staff Representative
Jodi Fabrizio-Clontz, Assistant to the President

Organization covering the newspaper industry, its employment practices, press freedom and labor movement.
Founded in 1934

15178 National Association of Hispanic Journalists

1050 Connecticut Avenue NW
10th Floor
Washington, DC 20036

202-662-7145
FAX 202-662-7144
E-Mail: nahj@nahj.org
Home Page: www.nahj.org
Social Media: *Facebook, Twitter, LinkedIn, YouTube*

Mekahlo Medina, President
Rebecca Aguilar, VP, Online
Barbara Rodriguez, VP Print
Francisco Cortes, Financial Officer
Sid Garcia, Secretary

NAHJ is dedicated to the recognition and professional advancement of Hispanics in the news industry. NAHJ created a national voice and unified vision for all Hispanic journalists.
2300 Members
Founded in 1984

15179 National Association of Hispanic Journalis ts

1050 Connecticut Avenue NW
10th Floor
Washington, DC 20036

202-662-7145
E-Mail: NAHJ@nahj.org
Home Page: www. nahj.org/
Social Media: *Facebook, Twitter, LinkedIn, YouTube*

Mekahlo Medina, President
Rebecca Aguilar, VP, Online
Barbara Rodriguez, VP, Print
Francisco Cortes, Financial Officer
Sid Garcia, Secretary
Founded in 1984

15180 National Association of Science Writers

P.O. Box 7905
Berkeley, CA 94707

510-647-9500
Home Page: www.nasw.org
Social Media: *Facebook, Twitter, LinkedIn, Google+*

Robin Marantz Henig, President
Laura Helmuth, Vice President
Jill Adams, Treasurer
Deborah Franklin, Secretary
Tinsley Davis, Executive Director
Founded in 1934

15181 National Book Critics Circle

160 Varick Street
11th Floor
New York, NY 10013

E-Mail: info@bookcritics.org
Home Page: www.bookcritics.org
Social Media: *Twitter*

Tom Beer, President
Jane Ciabattari, VP, Online
Rigoberto Gonzalez, VP/Awards
Michael Miller, VP/Treasurer
Karen Long, VP/Secretary
Founded in 1974

15182 National Federation of Press Women

200 Little Falls Street
Ste.405
Falls Church, VA 22046

703-237-9804
800-780-2715
FAX 703-237-9808
E-Mail: presswomen@aol.com
Home Page: www.nfpw.org
Social Media: *Facebook, Twitter, LinkedIn, RSS, Flickr, Youtube*

Teri Ehresman, President
Marsha Hoffman, 1st VP
Marianne Wolf, 2nd VP (Membership Adviser)
Gay Porter DeNileon, Secretary
Ellen Crawford, Treasurer (Financial Advisor)

Members are writers, editors and other communication professionals for newspapers, magazines, wire services, agencies and freelance.
2000 Members
Founded in 1937
Mailing list available for rent: 1700 names at $40 per M

15183 National Journalism Center

11480 Commerce Park Dr.
Suite 600
Reston, VA 20191

800-872-1776
FAX 703-318-9122
Home Page:
www.yaf.org/NationalJournalismCenter.aspx

Journalism training with a conservative edge.
Founded in 1977

15184 National Lesbian & Gay Journalists Association

2120 L St, NWÿ
Suite 850
Washington, DC 20037ÿ

202-588-9888
E-Mail: info@nlgja.org
Home Page: www.nlgja.org/
Social Media: *Facebook, Twitter, LinkedIn*

Jen Christensen, President
Sarah Blazucki, Vice President of Print & Online
Ken Miguel, Vice President of Broadcast
Sharif Durhams, Treasurer
Rick Stuckey, Secretary
Founded in 1990

15185 National Lesbian and Gay Journalists Association (NLGJA)

2120 L Street NW
Suite 850
Washington, DC 20037

202-588-9888
E-Mail: info@nlgja.org
Home Page: www.nlgja.org
Social Media: *Facebook, Twitter*

Jen Christensen, President
Sarah Blazucki, Vice President of Print & Online
Ken Miguel, Vice President of Broadcast

Sharif Durhams, Treasurer
Rick Stuckey, Secretary

NLGJA is an organization of journalists, media professionals, educators and students working within the news industry to foster fair and accurate coverage of LGBT issues. NLGJA opposes all forms of workplace bias and provides professional development to its members.
220 Members
Founded in 1990
Mailing list available for rent

15186 National Newspaper Association

PO Box 7540
Columbia, MO 65205-7540

573-777-4980
800-829-4662
FAX 703-237-9808
Home Page: www.nnaweb.org
Social Media: *Facebook, Twitter, RSS Feeds*

Chip Hutcheson, President
Matthew (Matt) Paxton, Vice President
Tonda Rush, CEO
Carol Pierce, Managing Director
Lynn Edinger, Associate Director

To protect, promote and enhance America's community newspapers.
2000 Members
Founded in 1885

15187 National Press Club

529 14th St NW
13th Floor
Washington, DC 20045

202-662-7500
FAX 202-662-7512
Home Page: press.org/
Social Media: *Facebook, Twitter, Google+, RSS*

angela Greiling Keane, President
Myron Belkind, Vice President
Joel Whitaker, Secretary
John Hughes, Treasurer
Marc Wojno, Membership Secretary

A private organization composed of professional journalists who are directly related to the media. Persons must qualify to be admitted.
4.6M Members
Founded in 1921

15188 National Press Foundation

1211 Connecticut Ave NW
Suite 310
Washington, DC 20036

202-663-7280
FAX 202-662-1232
E-Mail: maha@nationalpress.org
Home Page: www.nationalpress.org
Social Media: *Facebook, Twitter, Flickr, Youtube, Google+, Scri*

Sandy Johnson, President/COO
Amun Nadeem, Program Manager
Linda Topping Streitfeld, Director of Training and Content
Jenny Ash-Maher, Director of Operations
Reyna Abigale Levine, Digital Media Manager

Supports all those involved with national press and the media. Publishes bi-weekly newsletter.
Founded in 1976

15189 National Scholastic Press Association

2221 University Ave SE
Suite 121
Minneapolis, MN 55414

612-625-8335
FAX 612-605-0072
E-Mail: info@studentpress.org
Home Page: www.studentpress.org
Social Media: *Facebook, Twitter, Flickr, RSS*

Diana mitsu Klos, Executive Director
Paul Schwarzkopf, Dir. Of Communications &

Technology
Lindasy Grome, Dir. Of Community Engagement
Albert R. Tims, President
Christopher J. Ison, Treasurer

Supports all those involved in yearbook printing and photographic services, college journalism departments and video yearbook production services. Hosts annual trade show.
Founded in 1921
Mailing list available for rent

15190 Native American Journalists Association (NAJA)

OU Gaylord College
395 W. Lindsey St.
Norman, OK 73019-4201

405-325-1649
FAX 405-325-6945
Home Page: www.naja.com/
Social Media: *Facebook, Twitter, RSS*

Jason Begay, President
Bryan Pollard, Vice President
Tristan Ahtone, Treasurer
Shannon Shaw-Duty, Secretary

NAJA serves and empowers Native journalists through programs and actions designed to enrich journalism and promote Native cultures. NAJA educates and unifies its membership through journalism programs that promote diversity and defends challenges to free press.
Founded in 1983

15191 New England Newspaper and Press Association

370 Common Street, Barletta Hall
3rd Floor, Suite 319
Dedham, MA 02026

781-320-8050
FAX 781-320-8055
E-Mail: info@nepa.org
Home Page: www.nenpa.org
Social Media: *Facebook, Twitter*

Peter Haggerty, President
Mark S. Murphy, VP
Linda Conway, Executive Director
Megan Sherman, PR and Events Manager
Robin LaPolla, Business Manager

This organization offers a publication about the newspaper industry specifically focusing on New England newspapers and the issues that affect them, which goes to every newspaper in New England.
460 Members
Founded in 1950

15192 New Jersey Press Association

810 Bear Tavern Rd
Suite 307
West Trenton, NJ 08628-1022

609-406-0600
FAX 609-406-0300
E-Mail: foundation@njpa.org
Home Page: www.njpa.org

Stanley M. Ellis, Chairman
Thomas M. Donovan, President
Brett Ainsworth, 1st Vice President
Michael Lawson, 2nd Vice President
George H. White, Executive Director/Secretary

Supports all those involved in the development and betterment of collegiate press. Hosts annual trade show.
49 Members
Founded in 1857

15193 Newspaper Association Managers

New England Press Association

32 Dunham Rd.
Beverly, MA 01929

978-338-2555
FAX 978-744-0333
E-Mail: mlpiper52@comcast.net
Home Page: www.nammanagers.com

Lisa Hills, President
Layne Bruce, VP
Tom Newton, Director
Michelle Rea, Director
George H. White, Secretary

Executives of state, regional, national and international newspaper associations.
65 Members
Founded in 1923

15194 Newspaper Association of America

4401 Wilson Blvd
Suite 900
Arlington, VA 22203

571-366-1000
FAX 571-366-1195
E-Mail: joan.mills@naa.org
Home Page: www.naa.org
Social Media: *Facebook, Twitter, LinkedIn, RSS, Youtube, Google+*

Donna Barrett, Chairman
Stephen P. Hills, Vice Chairman
Tony W. Hunter, Secretary
Michael J. Klingensmith, Treasurer
Robert M. Nutting, Chairan

Newspaper Association of America maintains close, cooperative relations with other newspaper and journalism organizations.
2000 Members
Founded in 1992

15195 Overseas Press Club of America

40 W 45th St
New York, NY 10036

212-626-9220
FAX 212-626-9210
E-Mail: sonya@opcofamerica.org
Home Page: www.opcofamerica.org
Social Media: *Facebook, Twitter, LinkedIn, Yahoo, Stumbleupon, Google, Di*

Marcus Mabry, President
Calvin Sims, First Vice-President
Abigail Pesta, Second Vice-President
Pancho Bernasconi, Third Vice-President
Tim Ferguson, Treasurer

OPC is a private non-profit membership organization of journalists engaged in international news.
600 Members
Founded in 1939

15196 Pulic Radio News Directors Incorporated

PO Box 838
Sturgis, SD 57785

605-490-3033
FAX 605-490-3085
E-Mail: info@prndi.org
Home Page: www.prndi.org
Social Media: *Facebook, Twitter, RSS*

George Bodarky, President
Rachel Osier Lindley, Treasurer
Teresa Collier, Large Station Rep
Catherine Welch, Medium Station Rep
Christine Paige Diers, Business Manager

A non-profit professional association that exists to improve local news and information programming by serving public radio journalists.
Founded in 1985

15197 Society for Features Journalism

Home Page: www.featuresjournalism.org
Social Media: *Facebook, Twitter, RSS*

Lisa Glowinski, President
Kathy Lu, First Vice-President
Jim Haag, Second Vice-President
Margaret Myers, Secretary-Treasurer
Andrew Nynka, Executive Director
Founded in 1947

15198 Society for News Design

424 E. Central Blvd.
Suite 406
Orlando, FL 32801

407-420-7748
FAX 407-420-7697
E-Mail: snd@snd.org
Home Page: www.snd.org
Social Media: *Facebook, Twitter, LinkedIn,
RSS, Pinterest*

Lee Steele, President
Sara Quinn, Vice President
Douglas Okasaki, Secretary/Treasurer
Stephen Komives, Executive Director
Jonathon Berlin, Immediate Past President

An international professional organization that
encourage high standards of journalism
through design. An international forum and resource for all those interested in news design,
SND works to recognize excellence and
strengthen visual journalism as a profession.
1500 Members
Founded in 1979
Mailing list available for rent

**15199 Society of American Business Editors
and Writers**

ASU, Walter Cronkite School of Journalism &
Mas
555 North Central Ave, Suite 302
Phoenix, AZ 85004-1248

602-496-7862
FAX 602-496-7041
E-Mail: sabew@sabew.org
Home Page: www.sabew.org
Social Media: *Facebook, Twitter, RSS*

Joanna Ossinger, President
Cory Schouten, VP
Kathleen Graham, Executive Director
Spring Eselgroth, Web/ Membership Director
Liisa Straub, Fiscal Manager

Members are financial and economic news
writers and editors for print and broadcast outlets.
3200 Members
Founded in 1964

15200 Society of American Travel Writers

One Parkview Plaza
Suite 800
Oakbrook Terrace, IL 60181

414-359-1625
FAX 414-359-1671
E-Mail: info@satw.org
Home Page: www.satw.org
Social Media: *Facebook, Twitter, LinkedIn*

Paul Lasley, President
Barbara Orr, Vice President, Membership
Marla Schrager, Executive Director
John Kingzette, Membership Coordinator
Cindy Lemek, Executive Director

Photographers and 35 associate member representatives of airlines, hotels, resorts, tourist
agencies and public relations firms.
Founded in 1955

15201 Society of Environmental Journalists

PO Box 2492
Jenkintown, PA 19046

215-884-8174
FAX 215-884-8175
E-Mail: sej@sej.org
Home Page: www.sej.org
Social Media: *Facebook, Twitter, RSS*

Jeff Burnside, President
Beth Parke, Executive Director
Jennifer Bogo, First Vice Pres. & Programs
Chair
Kate Sheppard, SVP/Membership Chair
Gloria Gonzalez, Treasurer & Finance Chair

To advance public understanding of environmental issues by improving the quality, accuracy, and visibility of environmental reporting.
Founded in 1990
Mailing list available for rent

15202 Society of Professional Journalists

3909 N Meridian Street
Indianapolis, IN 46208

317-927-8000
FAX 317-920-4789
E-Mail: webmaster@spj.org
Home Page: www.spj.org
Social Media: *Facebook, Twitter, LinkedIn,
RSS, Pinterest, Flickr, Storif*

Paul Fletcher, President
Rebecca Baker, Secretary/Treasurer
Joe Skeel, Executive Director
Chris Vachon, Associate Executive Director
Linda Hall, Director of Membership

Broad-based journalism organization, dedicated
to encouraging the free practice of journalism
and stimulating high standards of ethical
behavior.
7500 Members
Founded in 1909
Mailing list available for rent

**15203 The American Society of Journalists
and Authors**

355 Lexington Avenue
15th Floor
New York, NY 10017-6603

212-997-0947
Home Page: www.asja.org/
Social Media: *Facebook, Twitter, LinkedIn,
Instagram, Google+*

Randy Dotinga, President
Sherry Beck Paprocki, Vice President
Neil O'Hara, Treasurer
Alexandra Cantor Owens, Executive Director
Meredith Taylor, General Manager
Founded in 1948

**15204 The Fund for Investigative
Journalism**

529 14th Street NW
13th Floor
Washington, DC 20045

202-662-7564
E-Mail: fundfij@gmail.com
Home Page: www.fij.org
Social Media: *Facebook, Twitter, RSS*

Ricardo Sandoval Palos, President
Marcia Bullard, Vice President
Peter Eisler, Treasurer
Founded in 1969

15205 The Gridiron Club

Prestigious organization of Washington, D.C.
journalists. Membership is by invitation only.
The Club is best known for its annual dinner
featuring skits and speeches by politicians of
both parties.
Founded in 1885

**15206 The Poynter Institute for Media
Studies**

801 Third St. S
St. Petersburg, FL 33701

727-821-9494
Home Page: www.poynter.org
Social Media: *Facebook, Twitter*

Tim Franklin, President

Non-profit journalism school begun by Nelson
Poynter, owner of the St. Petersburg Times
(now the Tampa Bay Times).
Founded in 1975

**15207 The Society of Environmental
Journalists**

PO Box 2492
Jenkintown, PA 19046

215-884-8174
FAX 215-884-8175
E-Mail: sej@sej.org
Home Page: www.sej.org
Social Media: *Facebook, Twitter, RSS*

Jeff Burnside, President
Beth Parke, Executive Director
Jennifer Bogo, First Vice Pres. & Programs
Chair
Kate Sheppard, SVP/Membership Chair
Gloria Gonzalez, Treasurer & Finance Chair

Mission is to strengthen the quality, reach and
viability of journalism across all media to advance public understanding of environmental
issues.
Founded in 1990
Mailing list available for rent

15208 UNITY Journalists for Diversity, Inc.

PO Box 511783
Milwaukee, WI 53203

414-335-1478
E-Mail: info@unityjournalists.org
Home Page: unityjournalists.org
Social Media: *Facebook, Twitter, LinkedIn,
Google+, Tumblr*

Alliance of Asian American Journalists Association, National Lesbian and Gay Journalists
Association and the Native American Journalists Association. Advocates fair and accurate
coverage of diversity issues.
Founded in 1994

Newsletters

**15209 AEJMC News Association for
Education in Journa**

234 Outlet Pointe Boulevard
Columbia, SC 29210-5667

803-798-0271
FAX 803-772-3509
E-Mail: meirick@ou.edu
Home Page: www.aejmc.org

Jenniffer Mcgrill, CEO
Kyshra Brown, Executive Director
Jennifer McGill, Executive Director

Supports all those scholars and educators of
journalism and mass communications.
Frequency: Monthly
Circulation: 3425
Founded in 1912

15210 AGENDA

National Federation of Press Women
PO Box 34798
Alexandria, VA 22334-0798

800-780-2715
FAX 703-812-4555
E-Mail: jane@janeleecomm.com
Home Page: www.nfpw.org

Social Media: *Facebook, Twitter, LinkedIn, RSS, Flickr, Youtube*

Lori Potter, President

A quarterly newletter published by the National Federation of Press Women.
Cost: $51.50
4 Pages
Frequency: Quarterly
Circulation: 2000
Founded in 1937
Mailing list available for rent: 1700 names at $40 per M

15211 ASBPE News
American Society of Business Publication Editors
214 North Hale Street
Wheaton, IL 60187

630-510-4588
FAX 630-510-4501
E-Mail: info@asbpe.org
Home Page: www.asbpe.org
Social Media: *Facebook, Twitter, LinkedIn, RSS*

Amy Florence Fischbach, President
Erin Erickson, Vice President
Tina Grady Barbaccia, Secretary/Treasurer
Janet Svazas, Executive Director
Robin Sherman, Associate Dir. & Newsletter Editor

ASBPE is the professional association for full-time and freelance editors and writers employed in the business, trade, and specialty press. It is widely known for its annual Awards of Excellence competition, which recognizes the best editorial, design, and online achievement.
Founded in 1964
Mailing list available for rent

15212 ASJA Newsletter
American Society of Journalists and Authors
1501 Broadway
Suite 403
New York, NY 10036-5505

212-997-0947
FAX 212-937-2315
E-Mail: staff@asja.org
Home Page: www.asja.org
Social Media: *Facebook, Twitter, LinkedIn, Goggle+*

Alexandra Cantor Owens, Executive Director
Minda Zetlin, President
Barbara DeMarco- Barrett, Newsletter Editor
Dave Mosso, Art Director

Confidential news for journalists and authors, available only to members of the Society.
Frequency: Monthly
Founded in 1948
Mailing list available for rent

15213 ASMP Bulletin
American Society of Media Photographers
150 North 2nd Street
Philadelphia, PA 19106

215-451-2767
E-Mail: info@asmp.org
Home Page: www.asmp.org
Social Media: *Facebook, Twitter, LinkedIn, Pinterest, Blogger, Tumblr*

Peter Dyson, Director of Communications
Victor Perlman, General Counsel
Eugene Mopsik, Executive Director
Elena Goertz, General Manager
Khaisha Allford, Member Services Coordinator

ASMP is the premier trade association for the world's most respectd photograhers. The ASMP Bulletin is a newsletter benefit for members.
Founded in 1944
Mailing list available for rent

15214 Associated Press Media Editors (APME) Newsletter
450 West 33rd Street
New York, NY 10001

212-621-7007
E-Mail: sjacobsen@ap.org
Home Page: www.apme.com
Social Media: *Facebook, Twitter*

Brad Dennison, President
Debra Adams Simmons, Vice President
Alan D. Miller, Journalism Studies Chair
Jan Touney, Treasurer
Mark Mittelstadt, Executive Director

APME is an association of U.S. and Canadian editors, broadcasters and educators whose entitites are members of The Associated Press.
Founded in 1933

15215 Bulldog Reporter
James Sinkinson/InfoCom Group
124 Linden Street
Suite L
Oakland, CA 94607

510-596-9300
800-959-1059
Home Page: www.bulldogreporter.com
Social Media: *Facebook, Twitter, RSS, Pinterest, Google+*

James Sinkson, President
Jacques Guatreaux, Vice President

Journalist contact updates and intelligence on how to successfully place stories with the most influential business media and journalists in the US.
Cost: $449.00
Frequency: 24 issues per y
Founded in 1980
Mailing list available for rent

15216 Clio Among the Media
Association for Education in Journalism
234 Outlet Pointe Blvd
Suite A
Columbia, SC 29210-5667

803-798-0271
FAX 803-772-3509
E-Mail: aejmc@aejmc.org
Home Page: www.asjmc.org

Georgia NeSmith, Assistant Editor
Jennifer McGill, Executive Director

This newsletter is aimed directly at scholars and educators of Journalism and Mass Communications.
Cost: $107.50
24 Pages
Frequency: Quarterly
Circulation: 450
Founded in 1966

15217 Communicator
American Institute of Parliamentarians
550m Ritchie Highway #271
Severna Park, MD 21146

888-664-0428
FAX 410-544-4640
E-Mail: aip@aipparl.org
Home Page: www.aipparl.org

Rob James, Vice President
Alison Wallis, President
Mary Remson, Treasurer
Jim Jones, CPP-T, Accrediting Director
Jeanette Williams, CP-T, Education Director

Quarterly newsletter listing AIP's board of directors, committees, parliamentary activities, chapter news and activities.
Founded in 1958

15218 GP Reporter
Star Reporter Publishing Company

PO Box 60193
Staten Island, NY 10306-0193

718-981-5700
FAX 718-981-5713

RA Lindberg, Publisher

Covers journalism for educational purposes.
Cost: $9.00
20 Pages

15219 Guild Reporter
Newspaper Guild: CWA
501 3rd St Nw
6th Floor
Washington, DC 20001-2760

202-434-1254
FAX 202-434-1426
E-Mail: guild@cwa-union.org
Home Page: www.nabetcwa.org
Social Media: *Facebook, Youtube, RSS, Flickr*

John Clark, President
Carol D Rothman, Secretary/Treasurer
Andy Zipser, Guild Reporter
Charles G. Braico, Sector Vice President

Covers the newspaper industry, its employment practices, press freedom and labor movement.
Cost: $20.00
6 Pages
Frequency: Monthly
Founded in 1933

15220 ICA Newsletter
International Communications Association
1500 21st St Nw
Washington, DC 20036-1000

202-955-1444
FAX 202-530-9851
E-Mail: icahdq@icahdq.org
Home Page: www.icahdq.org
Social Media: *Facebook, Twitter, LinkedIn, Google+*

Michael L. Haley, Executive Director
Sam Luna, Member Services Director
John Paul Gutierrez, Communication Director
Jennifer Le, Executive Assistant
Michael J. West, Publications Manager

Trade association publication for scholars in the field of communication.
Cost: $20.00
Frequency: 10 times a year
Founded in 1950
Mailing list available for rent
Printed in on matte stock

15221 Journalist and Financial Reporting
TJFR Publishing Company
82 Wall Street
Suite 1105
New York, NY 10005-3600

212-422-2456
FAX 212-663-3260

Dean Rotbart, Publisher

Financial and business news.
Cost: $549.00
12 Pages
Frequency: BiWeekly

15222 Media Reporter
Gay and Lesbian Press Association
PO Box 8185
Universal City, CA 91618-8185

FAX 818-902-9576

RJ Curry, Publisher

Accepts advertising.
Cost: $40.00
16 Pages
Frequency: Quarterly

15223 N2 Newspaper Next:
American Press Institute

4401 Wilson Boulevard
Suite 900
Arlington, VA 22203

703-620-3611
FAX 703-620-5814
E-Mail: info@americanpressinstitute.org
Home Page: www.americanpressinstitute.org
Social Media: *Facebook, Twitter, LinkedIn*

Thomas A. Silvestri, Chairman
Peter Bhatia, Editor
Caroline H. Little, President and CEO
Margaret G. Vassilikos, Finance & Operations
Mary Peskin, Training Programs

N2 Newspaper Next: is the forward-thinking project undertaken by API - to identify and test new business models for newspaper companies. It has grown to include not just research, but two reports of the project's findings as well as cuountless seminars, worksops, tailored programs offerings and special events.
Founded in 1946
Mailing list available for rent

15224 National Press Foundation Update
National Press Foundation
1211 Connecticut Ave Nw
Suite 310
Washington, DC 20036-2709

202-663-7280
FAX 202-662-1232
E-Mail: maha@nationalpress.org
Home Page: www.nationalpress.org
Social Media: *Facebook, Twitter, RSS, Youtube, Google+, Scribd,*

Bob Meyers, President/COO
Gerald Seib, Vice Chairman
Linda Topping Streitfeld, Director of Programs
Maha Masud, Programs Manager
Kerry Buker, Director of Operations

News.
4 Pages
Frequency: BiWeekly
Founded in 1993

15225 New England Press Association Bulletin
New England Press Association
360 Huntington Avenue
428CP
Boston, MA 02115-5005

617-254-4880
FAX 617-373-5615
Home Page: www.nepa.org

Brenda Need, Publisher
Linda Conway, Marketing Director
Thomas Guenette, Circulation Manager
Brenda Need, Editor

A monthly publication about the newspaper industry specifically focusing on New England newspapers and the issues that affect them.
Cost: $15.00
Frequency: Monthly
Circulation: 1500
Founded in 1950
Printed in 4 colors on newsprint stock

15226 OCP Bulletin
Overseas Press Club of America
40 W 45th St
New York, NY 10036-4202

212-626-9220
FAX 212-626-9210
Home Page: www.opcofamerica.org

Sonya Fry, Executive Director
David Andelman, President
Jacqueline Albert-Simon, Treasurer

Foreign correspondence news and features.
Frequency: Monthly

15227 Publisher's Auxiliary
National Newspaper Association

PO Box 7540
Columbia, MO 65205-7540

800-829-4662
E-Mail: lynnedinger@nws.org
Home Page: www.nnaweb.org
Social Media: *Facebook, Twitter*

Lynn Edinger, Associate Director
Merle Baranczyk, President
Robert M. Williams Jr., Vice President
John Edgecombe Jr., Treasurer

The only national publication serving America's community newspapers. First published in 1865, Publishers' Auxiliary is also the oldest newspaper serving the newspaper industry.
2000 Members
Founded in 1885

Magazines & Journals

15228 Alternative Press Review
CAL Press
PO Box 6245
Arlington, VA 22206

E-Mail: alternativepressreview@comcast.net
Home Page: www.altpr.org

Jason McQuinn, Editor

Covers alternative press including humor, opinion and art.
Cost: $16.00
Frequency: Quarterly
Circulation: 7000

15229 American Editor
American Society of Newspaper Editors
11690B Sunrise Valley Drive
Reston, VA 20191-1409

703-453-1122
FAX 703-453-1133
Home Page: www.asne.org

Arnie Robbins, Executive Director
Kathy Bates, Development Director
Cindy L. Roe, Finance Director
Diana Mitsu Klos, Senior Project Director
Megan Schumacher, Sr. Information Specialist

A magazine published by the American Society of Newspaper Editors.
30 Pages
Frequency: Daily
Founded in 1922

15230 American Journalism Review
University of Maryland
1117 Journalism Building
College Park, MD 20742-1

301-405-8803
800-827-0771
FAX 301-405-8323
E-Mail: editor@ajr.org
Home Page: www.ajr.org

Tom Kunkel, President
Rem Rieder, Editor
Reese Cleghorn, Publisher
Kathy Darragh, Circulation Manager
Kevin Klose, Senior Vice President

Monthly magazine for media professionals.
Cost: $24.00
Circulation: 25000
Founded in 1972

15231 American Prospect
5 Broad Street
Boston, MA 02109

617-570-8030
FAX 617-570-8028

E-Mail: editors@prospect.org
Home Page: www.prospect.org

Robin Hutson, Publisher
Tim Lysler, Associate Publisher
Robert Kuttner, President

Progressive liberal publication
Cost: $19.95
Frequency: Monthly
Circulation: 55000
Founded in 1990
Printed in 4 colors on matte stock

15232 Brilliant Ideas for Publishers
Creative Brilliance Associates
Mathey Road
PO Box 32
Clam Lake, WI 94517

715-749-2186
800-975-5474
FAX 715-749-2180

Naomi Shapiro, Editor

Edited and published for the newspaper industry.

15233 Catholic Journalist
3555 Veterans Memorial Highway
Unit O
Ronkonkoma, NY 11779

631-471-4730
FAX 631-471-4804
E-Mail: cathjourn@catholicpress.org
Home Page: www.catholicpress.org

Penny Wiegert, President
Tim Walker, Executive Director
Cost: $12.00
Frequency: Quarterly

15234 Columbia Journalism Review
Columbia University
2960 Broadway
New York, NY 10027-6900

212-854-1754
888-425-7782
FAX 212-749-0397
E-Mail: subscriptions@cjr.org
Home Page: www.columbia.edu

Robert Kasdin, Executive VP
Evan Cornog, Publisher
Michael Hoyt, Executive Editor

Evaluates all of the media as well as establishes standards for the profession.
Cost: $19.95
72 Pages

15235 ESD Technology
Kelvin Publishing
22700 Wood Street
Saint Clair Shores, MI 48080-1762

586-777-0440
FAX 586-774-3892

John Kelvin, Editor
Kevin Campbell, VP Marketing

Technical articles highlighting new applications and research.
Founded in 1936

15236 Ideas
International Newspaper Marketing Association
10300 N Central Expressway
Suite 467
Dallas, TX 75231

214-373-9111
FAX 214-373-9112
E-Mail: inma@inma.org
Home Page: www.inma.org

Social Media: *Facebook, Twitter, LinkedIn, RSS*

Earl Wilkinson, Executive Director
Marise Trevino, Editor
Earl Wilkinson, CEO/President
Dawn McMullan, Editor
Ravi Dhariwal, President

Marketing and promotion ideas for newspaper executives.
32 Pages
Frequency: Monthly
Circulation: 1200
Founded in 1930
Mailing list available for rent

15237 International Communications Association

1500 21st St NW
Washington, DC 20036-1000

202-955-1444
FAX 202-955-1448
E-Mail: icahdq@icahdq.org
Home Page: www.icahdq.org
Social Media: *Facebook, Twitter, LinkedIn, Google+*

Michael L. Haley, Executive Director
Sam Luna, Member Services Director
John Paul Gutierrez, Communication Director
Jennifer Le, Executive Assistant
Michael J. West, Publications Manager

Bi-monthly newsletter that supports all students and professionals in the international communications industry.
Mailing list available for rent
Printed in on matte stock

15238 Journalism & Mass Communication Quarterly (JMC)

234 Outlet Pointe Road
Columbia, SC 29210-5667

803-798-0271
FAX 803-772-3509
E-Mail: aejmchq@aol.com
Home Page: www.aejmc.org/
Social Media: *Facebook, Twitter, LinkedIn, FriendFeed, Flickr, Youtube, R*

Lillian Coleman, JMC Production Manager (AEJMC)
Dan Riffe, Editor (JMCQ Contact)
Jennifer McGill, Executive Director
Pamela Price, Membership/Subscription Coordinator
Kysh Anthony, Website Content Manager

Published by the Association for Education in Journalism and Mass Communication, the JMC Quarterly focuses on research in journalism and mass communication. Each issue features reports of original investigation, presenting the latest developments in theory and methodology of communication, international communication, journalism history, and social and legal problems. Also contains book reviews. Refereed. Four times per year. (est. 1924)
Cost: $80.00
Circulation: 4800
Mailing list available for rent

15239 Latinos in the US: A Resource Guide for Journalists

National Association of Hispanic Journalists
529 14th St Nw # 1240
Washington, DC 20045-2520

202-789-1157
FAX 202-347-3444
E-Mail: rnutting@marketwatch.com
Home Page: www.marketwatch.com

Rex Nutting, Manager
Joseph Torres, Communications Director
Rex Nutting, Manager

Purposes are to increase educational and career opportunities in journalism for Hispanic Amer-

icans.
Cost: $8.50
Mailing list available for rentat $500 per M

15240 Magazine Media Factbook (ASME)

American Society of Magazine Editors
810 Seventh Avenue
24th Floor
New York, NY 10019

212-872-3700
FAX 212-906-0128
E-Mail: info@magazine.org
Home Page: www.magazine.org
Social Media: *Facebook, Twitter, LinkedIn, Youtube, Pinterst*

Mary Berner, President & CEO
Nina Fortuna, Program Coordinator
Larry Hackett, President
Peggy Northrop, Vice President
Lucy Danziger, Secretary

A comprehensive guide of magazine media facts for advertisers, advertising agencies, media planners and consumer magazine marketers.
700 Members
Founded in 1963

15241 Newspaper Financial Executive Journal

Interactive & Newsmedia Financial Executives
550 W. Frontage Road
Ste. 3600
Northfield, IL 60093

847-716-7000
FAX 703-421-4068
Home Page: www.infe.org

Mary M. Collins, President & CEO
Jamie L. Smith, Director of Operations
Arcelia Pimentel, MFM Membership Manager & Sales
Debi Borden, Administrative Manager
Cindy Laser, Sales Account Executive

Trade publication for financial management of newspapers. More than 800 members.
Frequency: Weekly
Circulation: 1000
Founded in 1947
Mailing list available for rent

15242 Newspapers & Technology

Conley Magazines
1623 Blake Street
Suite 250
Denver, CO 80202

303-575-9595
FAX 303-575-9555
E-Mail: letters@newsandtech.com
Home Page: www.newsandtech.com/

Mary Van Meter, Publisher
Chuck Moozakis, Editor-in-Chief
Tara McMeekin, Editor
Hays Goodman, Associate Editor/Webmaster
Jessica Shade, Creative Services Assistant

Newspapers & Technology is a monthly trade publication for newspaper publishers and department managers involved in applying and integrating technology. Written by industry experts, News & Tech provides regular coverage of the following departments: prepress, press, postpress and new media.
Circulation: 16,874
Mailing list available for rent

15243 Overseas Press Club of America Magazine

Overseas Press Club of America
40 W 45th St
New York, NY 10036-4202

212-626-9220
FAX 212-626-9210

Home Page: www.opcofamerica.org
Social Media: *Facebook, Twitter, LinkedIn*

Sonya Fry, Executive Director
David Andelman, President
Jacqueline Albert-Simon, Treasurer
600 Members
Frequency: Annual
Circulation: 600
Founded in 1939

15244 Parliamentary Journal

American Institute of Parliamentarians
550m Ritchie Highway #271
Severna Park, MD 21146

888-664-0428
FAX 410-544-4640
E-Mail: aip@aipparl.org
Home Page: www.aipparl.org

Rob James, Vice President
Alison Wallis, President
Mary Remson, Treasurer
Jim Jones, CPP-T, Accrediting Director
Jeanette Williams, CP-T, Education Director

Wide range of subjects for AIP members
Founded in 1958

15245 Ways With Words

American Society of News Editors
11690B Sunrise Valley Drive
Reston, VA 20191-1409

703-453-1122
E-Mail: asne@asne.org
Home Page: www.asne.org
Social Media: *Facebook, Twitter, Storify*

Cindy L. Roe, Finance Director
Arnie Robbins, Executive Director
Diana Mitsu Klos, Senior Project Director
Megan Schumacher, Sr. Information Specialist
Kevin Goldberg, Legal Counsel

Ways With Words is the result of unusual, perhaps unique, collaboration among a diverse group of people who care about newspapers and reading. It may well be a model for joint research and development by journalism scholars and practitioners into the future of newspaper journalism.
Cost: $1.00
Founded in 1922

Trade Shows

15246 AWC National Conference

Association for Women in Communications
3337 Duke Street
Alexandria, VA 22314

703-370-7436
FAX 703-342-4311
E-Mail: info@womcom.org
Home Page: www.womcom.org
Social Media: *Facebook, Twitter, LinkedIn, Youtube*

Patricia Valenzuela, National Administrator
Judy Arent-Morency, Board Chair
Pamela Valenzuela, Executive Director
Liz Booth, Membership Coordinator
Beth Veney, Communications and Programs Manager

Annual conference and exhibits of journalism, public relations, advertising, marketing, educational communications and film.
Mailing list available for rent

15247 American Society of Journalists and Authors Conference
1501 Broadway
Suite 403
New York, NY 10036-5501

212-997-0947
FAX 212-937-2315
E-Mail: director@ajsa.org
Home Page: www.asja.org
Social Media: *Facebook, Twitter, LinkedIn, Goggle+*

Alexandra Cantor Owens, Executive Director
Minda Zetlin, President
Barbara DeMarco- Barrett, Newsletter Editor
Dave Mosso, Art Director
Bruce Miller, Web Master

A forum for the exchange of ideas between journalists.
700 Attendees
Frequency: May
Mailing list available for rent

15248 American Society of News Editors (ASNE) Convention
11690B Sunrise Valley Drive
2660 Woodley Road, NW
Reston, VA 20191-1409

703-453-1122
800-656-4622
E-Mail: registrar@naa.org
Home Page: www.asne.org
Social Media: *Facebook, Twitter*

Cindy L. Roe, Finance Director
Arnie Robbins, Executive Director
Diana Mitsu Klos, Senior Project Director
Megan Schumacher, Sr. Information Specialist
Kevin Goldberg, Legal Counsel

ASNE's annual convention is the largest annual gathering of newsroom leaders from daily newspapers and other news organizations. Editors and leaders in the field of journalism education will gather to refresh their spirits and create a roadmap to transform their newsrooms and shape the future of professional journalism.
Frequency: April
Founded in 1922

15249 Annual Multimedia Convention & Career Expo (NAHJ)
National Association of Hispanic Journalists
Disney's Coronado Spings Resort
1000 W Buena Vista Drive
Lake Buena Vista, FL 32830

866-257-5990
Home Page: www.nahjconvention.org
Social Media: *Facebook, Twitter, LinkedIn, YouTube*

Michele Salcedo, President
Manuel De La Rosa, Vice President/Broadcast
Russell Contreras, VP Print/Financial Officer

NAHJ is dedicated to the recognition and professional advancement of Hispanics in the news industry. NAHJ created a national voice and unified vision for all Hispanic journalists.
2300 Members
Frequency: August
Founded in 1984

15250 Associated Press Media Editors (APME) Conference
The John Seigenthaler Center, Vanderbilt Univ.
1207 18th Avenue S.
Nashville, TN 37212

615-727-1600
E-Mail: sjacobsen@ap.org
Home Page: www.apme.com
Social Media: *Facebook, Twitter*

Brad Dennison, President
Debra Adams Simmons, Vice President
Alan D. Miller, Journalism Studies Chair

Jan Touney, Treasurer
Mark Mittelstadt, Executive Director

APME is an association of U.S. and Canadian editors, broadcasters and educators whose entitites are members of The Associated Press.
Frequency: September
Founded in 1933

15251 Association for Education in Journalism and Mass Communication Annual Show
234 Outlet Pointe Boulevard
Suite A
Columbia, SC 29210-5667

803-798-0271
FAX 803-772-3509
Home Page: www.aejmc.org/

Fred Williams, Communications & Convention Manager
Richard Burke, Business Manager/Convention Manager
Jennifer McGill, Executive Director

Annual show of publishers and educational groups. Exhibits include publications, information retrieval services and special programs.
2000 Attendees
Frequency: August
Founded in 1912

15252 Collegiate Press Association Trade Show
330 21st Avenue S
Minneapolis, MN 55455-0480

612-625-3500
FAX 612-626-0720

Tom Rolnicki, Show Manager

20 booths including learning sessions and press conferences.
1.2M Attendees
Frequency: November

15253 Edward R. Murrow Forum on Issues in Journalism
Tufts University
95 Talbot Ave.
Medford, MA 02155

617-627-2155
FAX 617-627-3449
E-Mail: fms@tufts.edu
Home Page: ase.tufts.edu/cms/murrow.html

Annual interdisciplinary panel reflecting on contemporary issues in journalism.
Frequency: Annual
Founded in 2006

15254 International American Press Association Trade Show
2911 NW 39th Street
Miami, FL 33142-5148

305-634-2465

Julio Munoz, Executive Director

12 booths.
500 Attendees
Frequency: September
Mailing list available for rent

15255 International Newspaper Marketing Association Central
World-Herald Square
Omaha, NE 68102

402-734-7632
FAX 402-444-1370

Terry Ausenbaugh

20 booths.
100 Attendees
Frequency: October

15256 Magazine Media Factbook (ASME)
American Society of Magazine Editors

810 Seventh Avenue
24th Floor
New York, NY 10019

212-872-3700
FAX 212-906-0128
E-Mail: info@magazine.org
Home Page: www.magazine.org
Social Media: *Facebook, Twitter, LinkedIn, Pinterest, Youtube*

Sid Holt, Chief Executive
Nina Fortuna, Program Coordinator
Larry Hackett, President
Peggy Northrop, Vice President
Lucy Danziger, Secretary

A comprehensive guide of magazine media facts for advertisers, advertising agencies, media planners and consumer magazine marketers.
700 Members
Founded in 1963

15257 National Conference of the American Copy Editors Society
Sheraton New Orleans Hotel
500 Canal Street
Nw Orleans, LA 70130

504-525-2500
866-716-8106
FAX 504-595-5552
Home Page: www.sheratonneworleans.com
Social Media: *Facebook, Twitter, LinkedIn*

Teresa Schmedding, President
Lisa McLendon, Vice President Conferences
Sara Hendricks, Vice President Membership
Rudy Bahr, Executive Director
Gerri Berendzen, Content Editor

ACES is a professional organization working toward the advancement of editors. Their aim is to provide opportunities through training, discussion and advocacy that promote the editing profession.
Frequency: April
Founded in 1997

15258 National Convention & Annual LGBT Media Summit
National Lesbian and Gay Journalists Association
2120 L Street NW
Suite 850
Washington, DC 20037

202-588-9888
E-Mail: info@nlgja.org
Home Page: www.nlgja.org
Social Media: *Facebook, Twitter*

Bach Polakowski, National Office Administrator
Matthew Rose, Membership Coordinator
Michael Tune, Executive Director
David Steinberg, President
Jen Christensen, Vice President/Broadcast

NLGJA is an organization of journalists, media professionals, educators and students working within the news industry to foster fair and accurate coverage of LGBT issues. NLGJA opposes all forms of workplace bias and provides professional development to its members.
220 Members
Founded in 1990
Mailing list available for rent

15259 National Editorial Conference
American Society of Business Publication Editors
The Gleacher Center
450 N. Cityfront Plaza Drive
Chicago, IL 60611

312-464-8787
FAX 312-464-8683
E-Mail: info@gleachercenter.com

Home Page: www.gleachercenter.com
Social Media: *Facebook, Twitter, LinkedIn*

Amy Florence Fischbach, President
Erin Erickson, Vice President
Tina Grady Barbaccia, Secretary/Treasurer
Janet Svazas, Executive Director
Robin Sherman, Associate Dir. & Newsletter Editor

The National Editorial Conference focuses on the skills and ideas you need to weather the down economy and thrive in the new B2B publishing landscape.
Frequency: August

15260 National Magazine Awards

American Society of Magazine Editors
810 Seventh Avenue
24th Floor
New York, NY 10019

212-872-3700
FAX 212-906-0128
E-Mail: info@magazine.org
Home Page: www.magazine.org
Social Media: *Facebook, Twitter, LinkedIn, Pinterest, Youtube*

Sid Holt, Chief Executive
Nina Fortuna, Program Coordinator
Larry Hackett, President
Peggy Northrop, Vice President
Lucy Danziger, Secretary

The National Magazine Awards honor magazines, published in print and on digital platforms, that consistently demonstrate superior execution of editirial objectives, innovative techniques, noteworthy journalistic enterprise and imaginative art direction.
Founded in 1966

15261 National Scholastic Press Association Conference

National Scholastic Press Association
330 21st Avenue S
Suite 620
Minneapolis, MN 55455-0479

612-625-8335
FAX 612-626-0720

Tom Rolnicki, Executive Director

Annual conference and exhibits of information on yearbook printing and photographic services, college journalism departments and video yearbook production services.
1800 Attendees

15262 Newspaper Association of America/ Circulation Managers International

1921 Gallows Road
Suite 600
Vienna, VA 22182-3995

703-902-1600
FAX 703-902-1600

James Abbott, VP
Newspaper management forum.
1M Attendees

15263 SABEW Annual Conference

Society of American Business Editors & Writers
ASU, Walter Cronkite School of Journalism
555 North Central Ave, Suite 302
Phoenix, AZ 85004-1248

602-496-7862
FAX 602-496-7041
E-Mail: sabew@sabew.org
Home Page: www.sabew.org
Social Media: *Facebook, Twitter, LinkedIn, RSS*

Warren Watson, Executive Director
Lacey Clements, Marketing Director
Mark Scarp, Membership Director

Spring Eselgroth, Web/ Membership Coordinator
Defines and inspires excellence in business journalism.
Frequency: April

15264 West Coast Practicum

American Institute of Parliamentarians
550m Ritchie Highway #271
Severna Park, MD 21146

888-664-0428
FAX 410-544-4640
E-Mail: aip@aipparl.org
Home Page: www.aipparl.org

Rob James, Vice President
Alison Wallis, President
Mary Remson, Treasurer
Jim Jones, CPP-T, Accrediting Director
Jeanette Williams, CP-T, Education Director

Topics being covered are convention committees, boards and problems related to boards, reference committees and the parliamentarian's role in consulting with boards.
Founded in 1958

Directories & Databases

15265 1,000 Worldwide Newspapers

Albertsen's
PO Box 339
Nevada City, CA 95959-0339

Over 500 English-language newspapers overseas and in the United States are listed.
Cost: $10.00
54 Pages
Frequency: Annual

15266 American Society of Journalists and Authors Directory

ASJA
1501 Broadway
Suite 403
New York, NY 10036-5505

212-997-0947
FAX 212-937-2315
Home Page: www.asja.org
Social Media: *Facebook, Twitter, LinkedIn, Goggle+*

Alexandra Cantor Owens, Executive Director
Minda Zetlin, President
Barbara DeMarco- Barrett, Newsletter Editor
Dave Mosso, Art Director

Lists over 800 member freelance nonfiction writers.
Cost: $75.00
90 Pages
Mailing list available for rent

15267 American Society of News Editors (ASNE) Database

11690B Sunrise Valley Drive
Reston, VA 20191-1409

703-453-1122
E-Mail: asne@asne.org
Home Page: www.asne.org
Social Media: *Facebook, Twitter, Storify*

Cindy L. Roe, Finance Director
Arnie Robbins, Executive Director
Diana Mitsu Klos, Senior Project Director
Megan Schumacher, Sr. Information Specialist
Kevin Goldberg, Legal Counsel

Free access to ASNE's extensive online archive of reports and journalism studies, the gold standard in newsroom-related research.
Founded in 1922

15268 Asian American Journalists Accountants Directory

1182 Market St
Suite 320
San Francisco, CA 94102-4919

415-346-2051
FAX 415-346-6343
Home Page: www.aaja.org

Ellen Endo, Executive Director
Luke Stangel, Co-Founder
Christine Choy, Director
Marcus Brauchli, Executive Editor

Student development, job referrals, fellowship and internship reports.
700 Pages
Founded in 1981

15269 Bacon's Newspaper & Magazine Directories

Cision U.S., Inc.
322 South Michigan Avenue
Suite 900
Chicago, IL 60604

312-263-0070
866-639-5087
E-Mail: info.us@cision.com
Home Page: us.cision.com

Joe Bernardo, President & CEO
Heidi Sullivan, VP & Publisher
Valerie Lopez, Research Director
Jessica White, Research Director
Rachel Farrell, Research Manager

Two volume set listing all daily and community newspapers, magazines and newsletters, news service and syndicates, syndicated columnists, complete editorial staff listings of each publication provided, covers U.S., Canada, Mexico, and Carribean.
Cost: $350.00
4,700 Pages
Frequency: Annual
ISSN: 1088-9639
Founded in 1951
Printed in one color on matte stock

15270 Bacon's Radio/TV/Cable Directory

Cision U.S., Inc.
332 South Michigan Avenue
Suite 900
Chicago, IL 60604

312-263-0070
866-639-5087
E-Mail: info.us@cision.com
Home Page: www.us.cision.com

Joe Bernardo, President & CEO
Heidi Sullivan, VP & Publisher
Valerie Lopez, Research Director
Jessica White, Research Director
Rachel Farrell, Research Manager

Includes comprehensive coverage for contact and programming information for more than 3,500 televsion networks, cable networks, television syndicators, television stations, and cable systems in the United States and Canada.
Cost: $350.00
Frequency: Annual
ISSN: 1088-9639
Printed in one color on matte stock

15271 Burrelle's Media Directory

BurrellesLuce
75 E Northfield Rd
Livingston, NJ 07039-4532

973-992-6600
800-631-1160
FAX 973-992-7675
Home Page: www.burrellesluce.com

Social Media: *Facebook, Twitter, LinkedIn, RSS*

Robert C Waggoner, CEO
Johna Burke, Senior Vice President, Marketing
Approximately 60,000 media listings in North America. Listings cover newspapers, magazines (trades and consumer), broadcast, and internet outlets.
Cost: $795.00
Frequency: Annual

15272 Directory of Selected News Sources Issue
American Journalism Review
8701 Adelphi Road
Suite 310
Adelphi, MD 20783-1716

800-827-0771
FAX 301-405-8323

Rem Reider, Editor
List of about 400 companies, organizations and associations that provide information to newspapers and freelance reporters.
Cost: $2.95
Frequency: Annual
Circulation: 28,295

15273 FYI Directory of News Sources and Information
JSC Group
PO Box 868
Severna Park, MD 21146-0868

410-647-1013
FAX 410-647-9557
Home Page: www.fyinews.com

Julia Stocks Corneal, Editor
About 400 associations, corporations, individuals and sources for background story gathering for journalists.
Cost: $19.95
Frequency: Annual
Circulation: 20,000

15274 Find A Photographer Database
American Society of Media Photographers
150 North 2nd Street
Philadelphia, PA 19106

215-451-2767
E-Mail: info@asmp.org
Home Page: www.asmp.org
Social Media: *Facebook, Twitter, LinkedIn, Pinterest, Blogger, Tumblr*

Peter Dyson, Director of Communications
Victor Perlman, General Counsel
Eugene Mopsik, Executive Director
Elena Goertz, General Manager
Khaisha Allford, Member Services Coordinator
Find a Photographer is a search engine to help ASMP members connect with the most respected photographers in the industry.
Founded in 1944
Mailing list available for rent

15275 Journalism Forum
CompuServe Information Service
5000 Arlington Centre Blvd
Columbus, OH 43220-5439

614-326-1002
800-848-8199

This database provides information on all aspects of professional journalism.
Frequency: Full-text

15276 National Directory of Community Newspapers
American Newspaper Representatives

1000 Shelard Parkway
Suite 360
Minneapolis, MN 55426-4933

612-545-1116
800-752-6237
FAX 612-545-1116

Hilary Howe, President
A directory of community and weekly newspapers in the United States offering rates, circulation, etc.
Cost: $85.00
550 Pages
Frequency: Annual
Circulation: 2,000

15277 News Media Yellow Book
Leadership Directories
104 5th Ave
New York, NY 10011-6901

212-627-4140
FAX 212-645-0931
E-Mail: newsmedia@leadershipdirectories.com
Home Page: www.leadershipdirectories.com
Social Media: *Facebook, Twitter*

David Hurvitz, CEO
James M Petrie, Associate Publisher
Contact information for over 39,000 journalists at over 2,500 new services, networks, newspapers, television, radio stations, as well as independent journalists and syndicated columnists.
Cost: $325.00
1,200 Pages
Frequency: Quarterly
ISSN: 1071-8931
Founded in 1969
Mailing list available for rent: 32,000 names at $125 per M

15278 Newswire ASAP
Information Access Company
362 Lakeside Drive
Foster City, CA 94404-1171

650-378-5200
800-227-8431

Provides citations and the complete text of more than 1 million news releases and wire stories from the international news wire agencies. Subjects covered include banking, commodities, companies, currency and economics.
Frequency: Full-text
Founded in 1983

15279 Overseas Press Club of America Directory
Overseas Press Club of America
40 W 45th St
New York, NY 10036

212-626-9220
FAX 212-626-9210
E-Mail: sonya@opcofamerica.org
Home Page: www.opcofamerica.org
Social Media: *Facebook, Twitter, LinkedIn*

Sonya Fry, Executive Director
David Andelman, President
Jacqueline Albert-Simon, Treasurer
OPC is a private non-profit membership organization of journalists engaged in international news.
600 Members
Founded in 1939

Industry Web Sites

15280 http://gold.greyhouse.com
G.O.L.D Grey House OnLine Databases
Grey House Publishing's online database platform, GOLD, offers Quick Search, Keyword Search and Expert Search for most business

sectors including communication, broadcast and journalism markets. The GOLD platform makes finding the information you need quick and easy - whether you're a novice searcher or an experienced database user. All of Grey House's directory products are available for subscription on the GOLD platform.

15281 www.aarwba.org
American Auto Racing Writers and Broadcasters Association

Members are professional journalists who regularly cover auto racing and other related sports events.

15282 www.ajr.newslink.org
American Journalism Review
Provides links to sources, journalism organizations, search tools and media newsletters.

15283 www.apme.com
Associated Press Managing Editors
Members are executives of Associated Press News Executives.

15284 www.asja.org
American Society of Journalists and Authors
For freelance nonfiction writers whose bylines appear in periodicals and in books.

15285 www.asne.org
American Society of Newspaper Editors
Directing editors who determine editorial and news policy on daily newspapers and news gathering operations of daily newspapers.

15286 www.cjr.org/resources
Columbia Journalism Review
Contains resource guides and other journalism-related lists.

15287 www.drudgereport.com
Links to international news sources and columnists.

15288 www.greyhouse.com
Grey House Publishing
Authoritative reference directories for most business sectors including communication, broadcast and journalism markets. Users can search the online databases with varied search criteria allowing for custom searches by product category, geographic area, sales volume, keyword, subject and more. Full Grey House catalog and online ordering also available.

15289 www.house.gov
Association of House Democratic Press Assistants
Promotes education and professional standards of members through speakers, series, seminars and papers. Offers placement services.

15290 www.infesecure.org
International Newspaper Financial Executives
Controllers, chief accountants, auditors, business managers, treasurers, secretaries and related newspaper executives, educators and public accountants.

15291 www.inma.org
International Newspaper Marketing Association
Individuals in marketing, circulation, research and public relations of newspapers.

15292 www.ire.org
Investigative Reporters and Editors

For individuals involved in investigative journalism.

15293 www.jour.missouri.edu/home.nsf/

Resources at the University of Missouri's School of Journalism and beyond.

15294 www.jrn.columbia.edu/ressources

Columbia University School of Journalism

Access to Columbia University's Journalism School, the library's bibliographies and reference works, job listings and other associations.

15295 www.kausfiles.com

Site for journalists and media specialists.

15296 www.liberty.uc.wlu.edu

Journalism Resources

Lists of newspapers, film resources, jobs and internships and political advocacy groups.

15297 www.naa.org

Newspaper Association of America

Focuses on the major issues that affect today's newspaper industry public policy and legal matters, advertising revenue growth and audience development across the medium's broad portfolio of products and digital platforms.

15298 www.nepa.org

New England Press Association

This organizatiom offers a publication about the newspaper industry specifically focusing on New England newspapers and the issues that affect them, which goes to every newspaper in New England.

15299 www.nna.org

National Newspaper Association

Representatives of community newspapers. Founded 1885.

15300 www.nnaweb.org

National Newspaper Association

To protect, promote and enhance America's community newspapers.

15301 www.opcfamerica.org

Overseas Press Club of America

A media/journalist organization.

15302 www.poynter.org

Poynter Institute is dedicated to teaching and inspiring journalists and media leaders. Promotes excellence and integrity in the practice of craft and in the practical leadership of successful businesses.

15303 www.press.org

National Press Club

A private organization composed of professional journalists who are directly related to the media. Persons must qualify to be admitted.

15304 www.ukans.edu/~acejmc/

Accrediting Council on Education in Journalism
and Mass Communications

ACEJMC members are journalism and media departments, education associations and professional organizations.

Associations

15305 Academy of Criminal Justice Science

PO Box 960
Suite A
Greenbelt, MD 20768-0960

301-446-6300
800-757-2257
FAX 301-446-2819
E-Mail: info@acjs.org
Home Page: www.acjs.org

Brandon Applegate, President
Lorenzo M. Boyd, First Vice-President
Nicole Leeper Piquero, Second Vice President
Mary K. Stohr, Executive Director
Cathy L. Barth, Association Manager

An international association established to foster professional and scholarly activities in the field of criminal justice.
2800 Members
Founded in 1963

15306 Air Force Security Forces Association

818 Willow Creek Cir
San Marcos, TX 78666

512-396-5444
888-250-9876
FAX 512-396-7328
Home Page: afsfaonline.com

Scott Castillo, President
Jim Saulnier, Vice President
John Probst, Executive Director
Jerry Bullock, Executive Director Emeritus
Lucille Bullock, Executive Treasurer-Secretary

The mission is to bring together all those currently serving in the US Air Force as Security Forces members, past Air Police and Security Police members, as well as future Security forces members.
Founded in 1947

15307 Airborne Law Enforcement Association

50 Carroll Creek Way
Suite 260
Frederick, MD 21701

301-631-2406
FAX 301-631-2466
E-Mail: webmaster@alea.org
Home Page: www.alea.org
Social Media: *Facebook, Twitter, LinkedIn*

Steve Roussell, Chair:Executive Committee
Daniel B. Schwarzbach, Executive Director/CEO
Benay Osborne, CEM, CMP, Operations Manager
Don Ruby, Training Program Manager
Bryan Smith, Safety Program Manager

Supports and encourages the use of aircraft in public safety and provides networking systems, educational seminars and product expositions.
3500 Members
Founded in 1968

15308 American Academy of Forensic Sciences

410 N 21st St
Colorado Spring, CO 80904

719-636-1100
FAX 719-636-1993
E-Mail: awarren@aafs.org
Home Page: www.aafs.org
Social Media: *Facebook, YouTube, RSS*

Victor W. Weedn, President
Norm Sauer, PhD, Vice President
Zeno J. Geradts, PhD, Vice President
Anne Warren, Executive Director
Nancy Jackson, Director of Dev. & Accreditation

The need to identify forensic scientists unequivocally qualified to provide essential professional services for the Nation's judicial and executive branches of government has long been recognized. In response to this professional mandate, The American Board of Forensic Odontology was organized under the auspices of the National Institute of Justice.
Founded in 1948
Mailing list available for rent

15309 American Association of Motor Vehicle Administrators

4401 Wilson Boulevard
Suite 700
Arlington, VA 22203

703-522-4200
FAX 703-522-1553
E-Mail: info@aamva.org
Home Page: www.aamva.org
Social Media: *Facebook, Twitter, YouTube, Flickr*

Neil D Schuster, President & CEO
Sandy Bloomfield, Executive Asst.
Philip Quinlan, VP, Business Solutions
Marc Saitta, Vice President & CFO
Kathy King, Director, Program Business Services

A nonprofit association that supports both state and provincial official members throughout North America who oversee the administration and enforcement of motor vehicle laws. Services include development and research in motor vehicle administration, law enforcement and highway safety as well as being an information clearinghouse.
Founded in 1933
Mailing list available for rent

15310 American Association of Police Polygraphists

3223 Lake Ave
Unit 15c-168
Wilmette, IL 60091-1069

847-635-3980
888-743-5479
FAX 937-488-1046
E-Mail: NOM@policepolygraph.org
Home Page: www.policepolygraph.org
Social Media: *Facebook*

Karen Clark, Chairperson
James Wardwell, President
Tracey Hilton, Vice President
Robert C. Heard, Secretary
Gordon W. Moore, Treasurer

Promote and maintain the highest standards of ethics, integrity, honor and conduct in the polygraph profession; provide an opportunity and forum for the exchange of information regarding polygraph experiences, studies and research; cooperate with other national, regional and state polygraph associations and other professional organizations in matters of mutual interest and benefit to the profession.
900 Members
Founded in 1977

15311 American Association of Police Officers

1109 W 6th St
Suite 205
Austin, TX 78703

800-961-9773
FAX 800-227-1042
E-Mail: policeusa@gmail.com
Home Page: www.policeusa.com
Social Media: *Facebook*

Phil LeConte, Executive Officer
David Dierks, Financial Officer
Suzanne D'Ambrose, Law Enforement Instructor

Dennis Haley, Veteran Homicide Investigator
Curt Schwake, General Counsel & Advisor

Dedicated to bringing the wisdom of America's law enforcement veterans to the next generation of police officers and citizens. AAPO has provided a national stage for veteran law enforcement officers to share their wisdom and experience. Guided by an advisory council of law enforcement veterans and distinguished citizens, AAPO is committed to tapping into this often overlooked resource - veteran law enforcers both active duty and retired - and putting this unique knowledge to a useful purpose.

15312 American Association of State Troopersÿ

1949 Raymond Diehl Road
Tallahassee, FL 32308

800-765-5456
850-765-5456
FAX 850-385-8697
E-Mail: joan@statetroopers.org
Home Page: www.statetroopers.orgÿ
Social Media: *Facebook*

Keith Barbier, President
Jeffrey Lane, First Vice President
Lee Burch, Second Vice President
Noel Houze Jr., Secretary
Kenneth Musick, Treasurer
Founded in 1989

15313 American Correctional Association

206 N Washington St
Alexandria, VA 22314

703-224-0000
800-222-5646
FAX 703-224-0179
E-Mail: jeffw@aca.org
Home Page: www.aca.org
Social Media: *Facebook, Twitter, LinkedIn, YouTube*

Mary L Livers, President
Michael Wade, Vice President
Gary C Mohr, Treasurer
James A Gondles, Jr., Secretary

For individuals involved in the correctional field.
20000 Members
Founded in 1870
Mailing list available for rent

15314 American Criminal Justice Association

PO Box 601047
Sacramento, CA 95860-1047

916-484-6553
FAX 916-488-2227
E-Mail: acjalae@aol.com
Home Page: www.acjalae.org

Preston Koelling, President
Steve Atchley, VP
Jeanne Church-Elson, Region 1 President
Karen Campbell, Executive Secretary
David Redford, Region 2 President

Objectives are to improve criminal justice through educational activities, foster professionalism in law enforcement personnel and agencies, promote professional, academic and public awareness of criminal justice issues and promote high standards of ethical conduct, professional training and higher education within the criminal justice field.
7200 Members
Founded in 1937

15315 American Jail Association

1135 Professional Ct
Hagerstown, MD 21740-5853

301-790-3930
FAX 301-790-2941
E-Mail: rickn@aja.org

Home Page: www.aja.org
Social Media: *Facebook, Twitter, LinkedIn, YouTube, Instagram*

Robert J. Kasabian, Executive Director
Steve Custer, Director of Communications
Patty Vermillion, Program Manager
Lauren Pirri, Marketing and Sales Coordinator
Nico Gentile, Dir. Of Business Development

Dedicated to supporting those who work in and operate our nations's jails. AJA is the only national association that focuses exclusively on issues specific to the operations of local correctional facilities.
5000 Members
Founded in 1981

15316 American Police Hall of Fame and Museum

6350 Horizon Drive
Titusville, FL 32780

321-264-0911
FAX 321-264-0033
E-Mail: policeinfo@aphf.org
Home Page: www.aphf.org
Social Media: *Facebook*

Donna Shepherd, CEO
Barry Shepherd, Executive Director
Debra Chitwood, CFO
Jamie Maynard, Dir. Of Communications
Brent Shepherd, Director of Operations

Offers benefits and various types of awards to members, magazine, line of duty benefits, film and training library as well as support services, scholarships and financial assistance for police family survivors.
Founded in 1960

15317 American Police Hall of Fame and Museum

6350 Horizon Drive
Titusville, FL 32780

321-264-0911
FAX 321-264-0033
E-Mail: policeinfo@aphf.org
Home Page: www.aphf.org
Social Media: *Facebook*

Donna Shepherd, CEO
Barry Shepherd, Executive Director
Debra Chitwood, Chief Financial Officer
Brent Shepherd, Director of Operations
Jamie Maynard, Director of Communications

The nation's first national police museum dedicated to law enforcement officers who have died in the line of duty.
104M Members
Founded in 1960

15318 American Polygraph Association

PO Box 8037
Chattanooga, TN 37414-0037

423-892-3992
800-APA-8037
FAX 423-894-5435
E-Mail: manager@polygraph.org
Home Page: www.polygraph.org
Social Media: *Facebook, Twitter, LinkedIn, Pinterest, Google+, Myspace*

Ray Nelson, Chairman
Walt Goodson, President
Lisa Jacocks, Office Manager and Secretary
Mark Handler, Editor & Web Administer
Darry Starks, VP, Govt

Representing experienced polygraph examiners in private business, law enforcement and government. Professional APA polygraph examiners administer hundreds of thousands of polygraph exams each year worldwide. The APA establishes standards of ethical practices, techniques, instrumentation and research, as

well as provides advanced training and continuing education programs.
3200 Members
Founded in 1966
Mailing list available for rentat $125 per M

15319 American Probation and Parole Association

2760 Research Park Drive
Lexington, KY 40511-8482

859-244-8203
FAX 859-244-8001
E-Mail: appa@csg.org
Home Page: www.appa-net.org
Social Media: *Facebook, Twitter, LinkedIn*

Dee Bell, Executive Director
Diane Kincaid, Deputy Director/Info. Specialist
Tracy Mullins, Deputy Director
Adam Matz, Research Associate
John Higgins, Graphic Designer

An international association composed of members from the United States, Canada and other countries actively involved with probation, parole and community based corrections, inboth adult and juvenile sectors
2200 Members
Founded in 1975

15320 American Psychiatric Association

1000 Wilson Blvd
Suite 1825
Arlington, VA 22209-3901

703-907-7300
888-35 -7792
FAX 703-907-1085
E-Mail: apa@psych.org
Home Page: www.psychiatry.org
Social Media: *Facebook, Twitter, LinkedIn*

Ren,e Binder, M.D., President
Saul Levin, M.D., M.P.A., CEO and Medical Director
Altha J. Stewart, M.D., Secretary
Frank W. Brown, M.D., Treasurer

U.S. and international member physicians work together to ensure humane care and effective treatment for all persons with mental disorder, including mental retardation and substance-related disorders. It is the voice and conscience of modern psychiatry. Its vision is a society that has available, accessible quality psychiatric diagnosis and treatment.
3500 Members
Founded in 1966

15321 American Society of Crime Laboratory Directors

139A Technology Drive
Garner, NC 27529

919-773-2044
FAX 919-861-9930
E-Mail: asclddirector@gmail.com
Home Page: www.ascld.org
Social Media: *Twitter, LinkedIn, RSS*

Jody Wolf, President
Jean Stover, Executive Director
Kris Deters, Training & Education Chair
Andrea Swiech, Treasurer
Cecilia Doyle, Secretary
Founded in 1974

15322 American Society of Criminology

1314 Kinnear Rd
Suite 212
Columbus, OH 43212-1156

614-292-9207
FAX 614-292-6767
E-Mail: asc@asc41.com

Home Page: www.asc41.com
Social Media: *Twitter, LinkedIn*

Bonnie Fisher, Treasurer
Joanne Belknap, President-Elect
Christopher Uggen, Executive Secretary
Robert Agnew, President
Becky Block, VP

Objectives are to encourage the exchange, in a multidisciplinary setting, of those engaged in research, teaching, and practice so as to foster criminological scholarship, and to serve as a forum for the dissemination of criminological knowledge.
Founded in 1941

15323 American Speaker Association

32 East Riverhead Drive
Houstan, TX 77042-2501

713-914-9444
800-636-2722
E-Mail: info@americanspeakers.com
Home Page: www.americanspeakers.com
Social Media: *Facebook, LinkedIn*

Don Akers, Customer Service/Sales
Richard Alderman, Director of Consumer Law

Assists in proceedings involving legislation and arbitration.
37 Members
Founded in 1979
Mailing list available for rent

15324 American Traffic Safety Services Association

15 Riverside Parkway
Suite 100
Fredericksburg, VA 22406-1022

540-368-1701
800-272-8772
FAX 540-368-1717
E-Mail: foundation@atssa.com
Home Page: www.atssa.com
Social Media: *Facebook, Twitter, LinkedIn, Pinterest, Google+, YouTube*

Sue Reiss, President
Kathleen Holst, Vice President
Chad England, Traffic Director
john Tobin, Director, Manufacturers & Suppliers
Juan Arvizu, At-Large Director

Promotes uniform use of lights, signs, pavement markings and barricades. Distributes technical information and sponsors training courses for worksite traffic supervisors.
1600 Members
Founded in 1969

15325 Americans for Effective Law Enforcement

P.O. Box 75401
Chicago, IL 60675-5401

847-685-0700
FAX 847-685-9700
E-Mail: info@aele.org
Home Page: www.aele.org
Social Media: *RSS*

Daniel B. Hales, President
Wayne W. Schmidt, Esq., Executive Director
Bernard J. Farber, Editor/ Research Counsel
Helen Finkel, Staff Vice President
Missy Taki, Supervisor/Manager

Incorporated as a not for profit educational organization for the purpose of establishing an organized voice for the law-abiding citizens regarding this country's crime problem, and to lend support to professional law enforcement.
Founded in 1966

15326 Association of Firearm and Tool Mark Examiners
525 Carter Hill Rd.
Montgomery, AL 36106

334-242-2938
FAX 334-240-3284
E-Mail: kathy.richert@adfs.alabama.gov
Home Page: www.afte.org

Brandon Giroux, President
Travis Spinder, 1st Vice President
Justine Kreso, Secretary
Alison Quereau, Membership Secretary
Melissa Oberg, Treasurer

15327 Association of Paroling Authorities Inernational
Sam Houston State University
Huntsville, TX 77341-2296

877-318-2724
FAX 936-294-1671
E-Mail: keith@apaintl.org
Home Page: www.apaintl.org

Cyndi Mausser, President
Tena Pate, Vice President
Keith Hardison, Chief Administrative Officer
David Blumberg, Treasurer
Dan Fetsco, Secretary
511 Members
Founded in 1970

15328 Association of Public-Safety Communication s Officials International (APCO)
351 N Williamson Boulevard
Daytona Beach, FL 32114-1112

386-322-2500
888-272-6911
FAX 386-322-2501
E-Mail: apco@apcointl.org
Home Page: www.apcointl.org/
Social Media: *Facebook, Twitter, LinkedIn*

Brent Lee, President
Cheryl J. Greathouse, RPL, 1st Vice President
Martha K. Carter, ENP, 2nd Vice President
Doreen Geary, Accounting
Sarah Hill, Awards

International, nonprofit organization fostering the development and progress of the art of public safety communications by means of research, planning, training and education. Promotes cooperation between towns, cities, counties, states and federal, public safety agencies in the area of communications.
15000 Members
Founded in 1935

15329 Border Patrol Supervisors' Association
3755 Avocado
Blvd #404
La Mesa, CA 91941

Home Page: www.bpsups.org

Richard Haynes, President
Richard Marzec, Vice President
Linwood Knowles, Secretary
Logan Snider, Treasurer
Mike Diaz, Sergeant at Arms
500 Members
Founded in 1990

15330 Central Station Alarm Association
8150 Leesburg Pike
Suite 700
Vienna, VA 22182

703-242-4670
FAX 703-242-4675
E-Mail: techadmin@csaaintl.org
Home Page: www.csaaintl.org

Social Media: *Facebook, Twitter, LinkedIn, RSS*

Pamela Petrow, President
Joe Nuccio, First Vice President
Graham Westphal, Secretary
Ivan Spector, Treasurer
Peter Lowitt, Secretary

Represents companies offering security (alarm) monitoring systems through a central station. It also represents companies that provide services and products to the industry.
300+ Members
Founded in 1950
Mailing list available for rent

15331 Commission on Accreditation for Law Enforcement Agencies, Inc.
13575 Heathcote Boulevard
Suite 320
Gainesville, VA 20155

703-352-4225
800-368-3757
FAX 703-890-3126
E-Mail: calea@calea.org
Home Page: www.calea.org
Social Media: *RSS, Pinterest, Google+, Myspa*

W. Craig Hartley, Jr., Executive Director
Travis Parrish, Dir, Client Services and Relations
Antonio T. Beatty, Administrative Services Manager
Margaret Giglio, Program Specialist
Wendi Jones, Contract Specialist

Established as an independent accrediting authority by the four major law enforcement membership associations: International Association of Chiefs of Police; National Organization of Black Law Enforcement Executives; National Sheriffs' Association; and Police Executive Research Forum.
21 Members
Founded in 1979

15332 Concerns of Police Survivors
846 Old South 5
PO Box 3199
Camdenton, MO 65020

573-346-4911
FAX 573-346-1414
E-Mail: cops@nationalcops.org
Home Page: www.nationalcops.org
Social Media: *Facebook, Twitter, Youtube*

Brenda Donner, President
Dianne Bernhard, Executive Director
Sarah Slone, Director of Public Relations
Shelley Jones, Director of Operations
Lynn Kuse, Financial Manager

Resources are offered in the rebuilding of the lives of surviving families of law enforcement officers killed in the line of duty or determined by federal criteria. Futhermore, COPS provides training to law enforcement agencies on survivor victimizationa issues and educates the public of the need to support the law enforcement profession and its survivors.

15333 Congressional Fire Services Institute
900 2nd St NE
Suite 303
Washington, DC 20002-3557

202-371-1277
FAX 202-682-3473
E-Mail: update@cfsi.org
Home Page: www.cfsi.org
Social Media: *Facebook*

William Jenaway, President
Jim Estepp, Vice President
Bill Webb, Executive Director
Sean Carroll, Director of Government Affairs
Brian Goldfeder, Special Events Manager

Designed to educate members of Congress about the needs and challenges of our nation's fire and emergency services so that the federal government provides the types of training and funding needed by our first responders.
Founded in 1989

15334 Cops Who Careÿ
PO Box 20688
Wickenburg, AZ 85358

860-500-8926
Home Page: www.copswhocare.org

Founded in 1982

15335 Criminal Justice Center
Sam Houston State University
PO Box 2296
Huntsville, TX 77341

936-294-1635
FAX 281-294-1653
E-Mail: icc_www@shsu.edu

Vincent Webb, Director/Dean
Kristi Kreier, Business Office Director

Established to provide an educational program for students seeking careers in law enforcement, cours and corrections and for the development of a continuing education program for professionals working in the field.

15336 D.A.R.E. America
PO Box 512090
Los Angeles, CA 90051-0090

310-215-0575
800-223-DARE
FAX 310-215-0180
E-Mail: webmaster@dare.com
Home Page: www.dare.com

Louis Miller, Chair
David M. Horn, Vice Chair
Francisco X Pegueros, President and CEO
Thomas Hazelton, President of Development
Anita Bryan, Deputy Director of Education

A police officer led series of classroom lessons that teaches children from kindergarten through 12th grad how to resist peer pressure and live productive drug and violence free lives.
Mailing list available for rent

15337 Dogs Against Drugs/Dogs Against Crime National Law Enforcement K9 Assn.
3320 Main St.
Suite G
Anderson, IN 46013

765-642-9447
888-323-3227
FAX 765-642-4899
E-Mail: office@daddac.com
Home Page: daddac.tripod.com
Social Media: *Facebook*

Darron Sparks, President/National Director

Dedicated to the betterment of law enforcement K9 operations and to educating the youth on the dangers of drug abuse. DAD/DAC provides grants to officers for purchasing highly trained special purpose dogs and related training equipment and supplies and to provide training for the officer and/or dog. Working/training seminars are offered for K9 officers on numerous topics related to police service dogs.

15338 Evidence Photographers International Council
229 Peachtree St. NE
Ste #2200
Atlanta, GA 30303

570-253-5450
866-868-3742
FAX 404-614-6404
E-Mail: EPICheadquarters@verizon.net

Home Page: www.evidencephotographers.com
Social Media: *Facebook*

Robert F Jennings, Executive Director

Nonprofit scientific/educational organization with a primary purpose of advancement of forensic photography/videography in civil evidence and law enforcement.
Founded in 1968

15339 FBI National Academy Associates

422 Garrisonville Road
Suite 103
Stafford, VA 22554

540-628-0834
FAX 703-632-1993
E-Mail: info@fbinna.org
Home Page: www.fbinaa.org

Barry Thomas, Association President
Steve Tidwell, Executive Director
Korri Roper, CFO/COO
Denise MacLane, Financial Accountant
Ashley Sutton, Communications Manager

A non-profit international organization of senior law enforcement professionals dedicated to providing the communities and profession with the highest degree of law enforcement expertise, training, education and information.
17000 Members
Founded in 1935

15340 Federal Criminal Investigators Association

5868 Mapledale Plaza
Suite 104
Woodbridge, VA 22193

800-403-3374
E-Mail: info@fedcia.org
Home Page: www.fedcia.org
Founded in 1991

15341 Federal Law Enforcement Officers Association

7945 MacArthur Blvd
Suite 201
Cabin John, MD 20818

202-870-5503
866-553-5362
E-Mail: fleoa@fleoa.org
Home Page: www.fleoa.org
Social Media: *Facebook, Twitter, Reddit, Pinterest*

Jon Adler, National President
Nate Catura, Executive Vice President
Chris Schoppmeyer, Vice President - Agency Affairs
Frank Terreri, Vice President- Legislative Affairs
John Ramsey, Vice President - Membership Benefit
Founded in 1977

15342 Fire Equipment Manufacturers' Association

1300 Sumner Avenue
Cleveland, OH 44115

216-241-7333
FAX 216-241-0105
E-Mail: fema@femalifesafety.org
Home Page: www.femalifesafety.org
Social Media: *YouTube, Wikipedia, Slideshare*

The premier trade association representing leading brands, and spanning dozens of product categories, related to fire protection.
24 Members
Founded in 1925

15343 Fire Suppression Systems Association

3601 East Joppa Road
Baltimore, MD 21234

410-931-8100
FAX 410-931-8111
E-Mail: fssa@clemonsmgmt.com
Home Page: www.fssa.net
Social Media: *Facebook, Twitter, LinkedIn, Reddit, Pinterest, Blooger*

Tim Carman, President
Ray Aldridge, Vice President
Helen Lowery, Secretary/Treasurer
Tim Carman, Secretary/Treasurer
Eric Burkland, VP

An organization of manufacturers, suppliers, and design-installers, dedicated to providing a higher level of fire protection. Members are specialists in protecting high value special hazardareas from fire.
Founded in 1982

15344 Fire and Emergency Manufacturers and Services Association

PO Box 147
Lynnfield, MA 01940-0147

781-334-2771
FAX 781-334-2771
E-Mail: info@femsa.org
Home Page: www.femsa.org
Social Media: *Twitter, LinkedIn*

Dan Reese, President
William Lawson, VP

The leading trade association for the fire and emergency services industry whose members provide products and services to millions of fire and EMS professionals throughout the world. Works to strengthen its membership, planning for future development and directing programs that build industry opportunities.
150 Members
Founded in 1966

15345 Flight Safety Foundation

801 N. Fairfax Street
Suite 400
Alexandria, VA 22314-1774

703-739-6700
FAX 703-739-6708
Home Page: www.flightsafety.org
Social Media: *Facebook, Twitter, LinkedIn*

Ken Hylander, Chairman
Jon Beatty, President and CEO
David Barger, Treasurer
Kenneth P. Quinn, General Counsel & Secretary
David McMillan, Chairman

Independent, nonprofit, international organization engaged in research, auditing, education, advocacy and publishing to improve aviation safety.
Founded in 1947

15346 Fraternal Order of Police

701 Marriott Dr
Nashville, TN 37214-5043

615-399-0900
FAX 615-399-0400
E-Mail: webmaster@grandlodgefop.org
Home Page: www.fop.net

Chuck Canterbury, National President
Ed Brannigan, National VP
Les Neri, National Second Vice President
Tom Penoza, National Treasurer
Patrick Yoes, National Secretary

This is the world's largest organization of sworn law enforcement officers, with more than 324,000 members in more than 2,100 lodges. It is the voice of those who dedicate their lives to protecting and serving our communities, and is committed to improving the working conditions of law enforcement officers and the safety of those served through education, legislation, information, community involvement,and employeee representation.
324M Members
Founded in 1915
Mailing list available for rent

15347 Hispanic National Law Enforcement Association

PO Box 766
Cheltenham, MD 20623

240-244-9189
E-Mail: President@hnlea.zzn.com
Home Page: www.hnlea.com

Mike Rodriguez, President
Luis Rodriguez, Executive Director
Miguel I. Core, Vice President
Jose Perez, Treasurer
Adriane Clayton, Secretary

Non-profit organization of professionals involved in the administration of justice and dedicated to the advancement of Hispanic(Latino) and minority interests within the law enforcement profession.
Founded in 1988

15348 Institute of Investigative Technology

AccuQuest
6950 Phillips Hwy, #46
Jacksonville, FL 32216-6087

904-296-0212
FAX 904-296-7385
Home Page:
www.aqonline.com/iitframeset.html

John Ramming, Director

Provides training for law enforcement and corporate clients. Programs can be designed from one-day to multiple week training courses.

15349 Institute of Police Technology and Management

University of North Florida
12000 Alumni Dr
Jacksonville, FL 32224-2678

904-620-4786
FAX 904-620-2453
E-Mail: info@iptm.org
Home Page: www.iptm.org
Social Media: *Facebook*

Teresa R. Dioquino, Management Section Coordinator
Cameron Pucci, Diector
Tony Becker, Administration
Kenin Al Roop, Marketing
Harry Walters, Traffic Enforcement

Mission of the Institute is to provide the law enforcement community with the highest quality of training at competitive prices. By providing this service, IPTM continues to support law enforcement's efforts in building and maintaining safer communitites.
Founded in 1980

15350 Insurance Institute for Highway Safety

1005 N Glebe Rd
Suite 800
Arlington, VA 22201

703-247-1500
FAX 703-247-1588
E-Mail: rrader@iihs.org
Home Page: www.iihs.org
Social Media: *Twitter, RSS, YouTube*

Adrian Loud, President
Russ Rader, Senior Vice President
Shelley Shelton, Executive Assistant, Legal Affairs
Brenda O'Donnell, Vice President, Insurer Relations
Chamelle Matthew, Communications Associate

Independent, nonprofit, scientific and educational organization dedicated to reducing the losses (deaths, injuries, and property damage) from crashes on the nation's highways.
Founded in 1959
Mailing list available for rent

15351 International Association for Identification

2131 Hollywood Blvd.,
Suite 403
Hollywood, FL 33020

954-589-0628
FAX 954-589-0657
Home Page: www.theiai.org
Social Media: *Facebook*

Bridget Lewis, President
Harold Ruslander, 1st Vice President
Ray Jorz, 2nd Vice President
Lisa Hudson, 3rd Vice President
Glen Calhoun, Chief Operations Officer
Founded in 1915

15352 International Association for Property Evidence, Inc.

903 N San Fernando Boulevard
Suite 4
Burbank, CA 91504-4327

818-846-2926
800-449-4273
FAX 818-846-4543
E-Mail: Mail@IAPE.org
Home Page: www.iape.org
Social Media: *Facebook*

Joseph T. Latta, Executive Director/Lead Instructor
William Kiley, Board Member, Instructor
Steve Campbell, Secretary, Instructor
Suzanne Cox, Tresurer
Robin Lynn Trench, Founder

Established to further the education, training and professional growth of Law Enforcement Property and Evidence Personnel.
Founded in 1993

15353 International Association of Arson Investigators

2111 Baldwin Avenue
Suite 203
Crofton, MD 21114

410-451-3473
800-468-4224
FAX 410-451-9049
E-Mail: Dan.Heenan@firearson.com
Home Page: www.firearson.com
Social Media: *Facebook, Twitter, LinkedIn, YouTube*

Daniel Heenan, President
George Codding, 1st Vice President
Scott Bennett, 2nd Vice President
Deborah Keeler, Executive Director
Debra Miller, Accounting & Finanace Manager

Dedicated to improving the professional development of fire and explosion investigators by being the global resource for fire investigation, technology and research.
7500 Members
Founded in 1949

15354 International Association of Auto Theft Investigators

PO Box 223
Clinton, NY 13323-0223

315-853-1913
FAX 315-883-1310
E-Mail: jvabounader@iaati.org
Home Page: www.iaati.org

Todd M. Blair, President
Robert C. Hasbrouck, Treasurer
John V Abounader, Executive Director

Heidi M. Jordan, 1st VP
Todd M. Blair, 3rd VP

Provides members who are auto theft investigators with resources to develop and maintain professional standards within the industry.
3604 Members
Founded in 1952

15355 International Association of Bloodstain Pattern Analysts

Home Page: www.iabpa.org

Pat Laturnus, President
Donald Schuessler, VP
Norman Reeves, Secretary/ Treasurer
Jeff Scozzafava, Sergeant at Arms
Stuart H James, Historian

15356 International Association of Bomb Technicians and Investigators

1120 International parkway
Fredricksburg, VA 22406

540-752-4533
FAX 540-752-2796
E-Mail: admin@iabti.org
Home Page: www.iabti.org
Social Media: *Facebook, Twitter, LinkedIn*

Ralph Way, Executive Director

An independent professional association formed for countering the criminal use of explosives. This is sought through the exchange of training, expertise and information among personnel employed in the fields of law enforcement, fire and emergency services, the military, forensic science and other related fields.
4000 Members
Founded in 1973

15357 International Association of Campus Law Enforcement Administrators

342 N Main Street
West Hartford, CT 06117-2507

860-586-7517
FAX 860-586-7550
E-Mail: info@iaclea.org
Home Page: www.iaclea.org
Social Media: *Facebook*

William F. Taylor, President
Christopher Blake, CAE, Executive Director
Kendra Pheasant, CAE, Associate Director
Susan Koczka, Corporate Relations
Eva Storrs, Membership Services

Advances public safety for educational institutions by providing educational resources, advocacy and professional development.
Founded in 1958
Mailing list available for rent

15358 International Association of Directors of Law Enforcement Standards/Training

1330 N. Manship Pl.
Meridian, ID 83642

208-288-5491
FAX 517-857-3826
E-Mail: mikebecar@iadlest.org,
pjudge@att.net
Home Page: www.iadlest.org

David Harvey, President
Brian Grisham, First Vice-President
Dan Zivkovich, Second Vice-President
Michael N. Becar, Executive Director
Mark Damitio, Secretary

An international organization of training managers and executives dedicated to the improvement of public safety personnel. The Association serves as the national forum of Peace Officer Standards and Training (POST) agencies, boards and commissions as well as

statewide training academies throughout the United States.
Mailing list available for rent

15359 International Association of Law Enforcement Firearms Instructors

25 Country Club Road
Suite 707
Gilford, NH 03249

603-524-8787
FAX 603-524-8856
E-Mail: info@ialefi.com
Home Page: www.ialefi.com

R Steven Johnson, President
Robert D Bossey, Executive Director/Treasurer
Michial Dunlap, Secretary
John T. Meyer, 1st VP
Emanuel Kapelson, 2nd VP

An independent, non-profit association whose mission is to update and modernize the instruction and teaching techniques used to train the majority of law enforcement officers.
Founded in 1981

15360 International Association of Undercover Officers

142 Banks Drive
Brunswick, GA 31523

800-876-5943
FAX 800-876-5912
E-Mail: charlie@undercover.org
Home Page: www.undercover.org

Brian Sallee, President
Brian Sallee, President
Steve Cook, First Vice-President
David Redemann, Second Vice-President
Frank Swirko, Treasurer

Established for the purpose of promoting safety and professionalism among undercover officers. The association continues to foster mutual cooperation, discussion and interests among its members. It provides vast international network of intelligence gathering means for today's undercover officer and sponsors high quality training programs for undercover officers.

15361 International Association of Women

1352 NE 47th Avenue
Portland, OR 97213

301-464-1402
FAX 301-464-1402
E-Mail: carolpaterick@gmail.com
Home Page: www.iawp.org
Social Media: *Twitter*

Margaret Shorter, President
Deborah Friedl, First Vice President
Andrea Humphrys, Executive Director
Michelle Lish, Foundation Treasurer
Julia Jaeger, Recording Secretary
Founded in 1915

15362 International Association of Women Police

1352 NE 47th Avenue
Portland, OR 97213

301-464-1402
FAX 301-464-1402
E-Mail: carolpaterick@gmail.com
Home Page: www.iawp.org
Social Media: *Twitter*

Margaret Shorter, President
Deborah Friedl, First Vice President
Andrea Humphrys, Executive Director
Michele Lish, Foundation Treasurer
Julia Jaeger, Recording Secretary

To strengthen, unite, and raise the profile of women in criminal justice internationally.
24000 Members
Founded in 1915

15363 International Board of Certification for Safety Managers

173 Tucker Road
Suite 202
Helena, AL 35080

205-664-8412
FAX 205-663-9541
E-Mail: info@ibfcsm.org
Home Page: www.ibfcsm.org
Social Media: *Facebook*

James Tweedy, Executive Director

A professional credentialing organization that promotes the application of managerial techniques to eliminate or control unsafe and unhealthy conditions, behavior and other factors detrimental to people and property. Offers credentials in safety, product safety, healthcare safety, patient safety, and healthcare emergency management.
2500 Members
Founded in 1976

15364 International Crime Scene Investigator's Association

15774 S. LaGrange Road
Orland Park, IL 60462

708-460-8082
Home Page: www.icsia.org

Hayden B Baldwin, Executive Director
Christopher Anderson, Caribbean Director
Paul Echols, Board of Directors
Chad Pitfield, Board of Directors
Steven W Hulsey, Board of Directors

15365 International Critical Incident Stress Foundation

3290 Pine Orchard Ln
Suite 106
Ellicott City, MD 21042

410-750-9600
FAX 410-750-9601
E-Mail: info@icisf.org
Home Page: www.icisf.org
Social Media: *Facebook, Twitter*

Dave Evans, CPA, Chairman
Lisa Joubert, Finance Director
Richard Barton, CEO
C. Kenneth Bohn, Director of Operations
Jeannie Gow, General Information Requests

A foundation dedicated to the prevention and mitigation of disabling stress through the provision of; Education, training and support services for all Emergency Services professions, continuing education and training in Emergency Mental Health Services for Psychologists, Psychiatrists, Social Workers and Licensed Professional Counselors and Consultation in the establishment of Crisis and Disaster Response Programs for varied organizations and communities worldwide.

15366 International Footprint Association

PO Box 1652
Walnut, CA 91788

323-981-1488
877-432-3668
FAX 323-265-4657
E-Mail: footprint@footprinter.org
Home Page: www.footprinter.org

Robert H. Hubbell, Grand President
Doug Partlow, First Grand Vice President
Michael Leary, Second Grand Vice President
Maura Mattson, Grand Secretary/Treasurer
Michael Leary, Assistant Grand
Secretary/Treasurer

A non-profit association that promotes and encourages fellowship, respect, cooperation, and helpfulness between all arms of law enforcement and all others who are sympathetic with

and understanding toward law enforcement and all of its agencies.
4000 Members
Founded in 1929

15367 International Law Enforcement Educators & Trainers Association

4742 79 Street
Kenosha, WI 53142

262-767-1406
FAX 262-767-1813
E-Mail: info@ILEETA.org
Home Page: www.ileeta.org
Social Media: *Facebook*

Harvey Hedden, Executive Director
Brian Wills, Deputy Executive Dir.
Alexis Artwohl, Advisory Board Member
Massad Ayoob, Advisory Board Member
Steve Ashley, Advisory Board Member

An organization by, for and about instructors and training for the criminal justice professions. Committed to the reduction of law enforcement risk through the enhancement of training for criminal justice practitioners.
Founded in 2003

15368 International Narcotic Enforcement Officers Association

112 State Street
Suite 1200
Albany, NY 12207-2079

518-463-6232
E-Mail: ineoa@iopener.net
Home Page: www.ineoa.org

John J Bellizer Jr, Executive Director
Michael Harris, President

Basic purpose is to promote and foster mutual interest in the problems of narcotic control; provide a medium for the exchange of ideas, conduct seminars, conferences and study groups and issue publications.

15369 International Police Associationÿÿ

PO Box 516
Greystone Station
Yonkers, NY 10703-0516

855-241-9998
Home Page: www.ipa-usa.org
Social Media: *Facebook, Twitter*

Kevin Gordon, President
Calvin Chow, 1st VP
Cory Freadling, 2nd VP
Joe Johnson, 3rd VP
Viola Powrie, Treasurer
Founded in 1950

15370 International Union of Police Associations

1549 Ringling Blvd.
Suite 600
Sarasota, FL 35236

800-247-4872
FAX 941-487-2570
E-Mail: iupa@iupa.org
Home Page: iupa.org
Social Media: *Facebook, Twitter, LinkedIn, YouTube*

Samuel A. Cabral, President

The voice of the law enforcement community within the organized labor movement.
Founded in 1954

15371 Law Enforcement & Emergency Services Video Association

84 Briar Creek Road
Whitesboro, TX 76273

469-285-9435
FAX 469-533-3659
E-Mail: commngr@leva.org

Home Page: www.leva.org
Social Media: *Facebook, Twitter, LinkedIn*

Alan Salmon, Chairman of the Board
Tracy Peloquin, Vice Chairman
Juan Ruano, President
Scott Olar, Executive Vice President
Scott Sullivan, Forensic Training, Program Manager

Committed to improving the quality of video training and promoting the use of state-of-the-art, effective equipment in the law enforcement and emergency services community.
Mailing list available for rent

15372 Law Enforcement Alliance of America

12427 Hedges Run Drive
Suite 113
Lake Ridge, VA 22192-1715

202-706-9218
FAX 703-556-6485
E-Mail: membership@leaa.org
Home Page: www.leaa.org

Jim Fotis, Executive Director
Kevin Watson, Communications Director

Nation's largest nonprofit, non-partisan coalition of law enforcement professionals. Crime victims, and concerned citizens united for justice; with a major focus on public education, LEAA is dedicated to providing hard facts and real world insights into the world of law enforcement and the battle against violent crime. Fighting at every level of government for legislation that reduces violent crime while preserving the rights of honest citizens, particularly the right of self-defense.
Founded in 1992

15373 Law Enforcement Bloodhound Association

PO Box 190442
Anchorage, AL 99519-0442

907-602-3542
E-Mail: leba@gci.net
Home Page: www.leba98.com

Gerry Nichols, President

LEBA is a professional nonprofit organization dedicated to the promotion of bloodhounds in law enforcement. Also provides beginning, continuing and advanced education to law enforcement professionals and thier bloodhound partners.
Founded in 1998
Mailing list available for rent

15374 Law Enforcement Executive Development Association, Inc.

5 Great Valley Pkwy.
Suite 125
Malvern, PA 19355

484-321-7821
877-772-7712
FAX 610-644-3193
E-Mail: info@fbileeda.org
Home Page: www.fbileeda.org
Social Media: *Facebook, Twitter, LinkedIn*

Chief David Boggs, President
Paul Shastany, First Vice President
Thomas Alber, Second Vice President
Chief John Horsman, Third Vice President
Charles Robb, Executive Director

Purpose of the association is to advance the Science and Art of Police Management and Administration; to develop and disseminate improved administrative and technical practices; promote the exchange of information and training for executives of law enforcement.

15375 Law Enforcement Legal Defense Fundÿ

1428 Duke Street
Alexandria, VA 703-807-18

E-Mail: info@leldf.org
Home Page: www.policedefense.orgÿ
Social Media: *Facebook, Twitter, LinkedIn, YouTube*

Alfred S Regnery, Chairman
John J Burke, Vice Chairman
Ron Hosko, President
Edwin Meese, Director
Daniel J DeSimone, Secretary-Treasurer
Founded in 1995

15376 Law Enforcement Standards Office

100 Bureau Drive
MS 8102
Gaithersburg, MD 20899-8102

301-975-6478
FAX 301-948-0978
E-Mail: inquiries@nist.gov
Home Page: www.nist.gov/oles/

Patrick D. Gallagher, Director
Michael D. Herman, Executive Officer
Kevin Kimball, Chief of Staff
Henry N. Wixon, Chief Counsel
Mary Saunders, Associate Director

OLES's mission is to serve as the principal agent for standards development for the criminal justice and public safety communities. Helping criminal justice and public safety agencies acquire, on a cost-effective basis, the high quality resources they need to do their jobs.
Founded in 1901

15377 Major Cities Chiefs Police Association

E-Mail: stephens@majorcitieschiefs.com
Home Page: www.majorcitieschiefs.com

J. Thomas Manger, President
Garry McCarthy, 1st Vice President
George Turner, 2nd Vice President
J. Thomas Manger, Chief of Police
Darrel Stephens, Executive Director
Founded in 1949

15378 Metropolitan Alliance of Police

215 Remington Blvd.
Suite C
Bolingbrook, IL 60440

630-759-4925
FAX 630-759-1902
E-Mail: mapunion@msn.com
Home Page: www.mapunion.org

Joseph Andalina, President
Keith George, Vice President
Richard Tracy, Secretary
Joseph R. Mazzone, Chief Counsel
Richard J. Reimer, Co-Counsel

15379 Narcotic Enforcement Officers Association

29 N Plains Hwy
Suite 10
Wallingford, CT 06492

203-269-8940
FAX 203-284-9103
Home Page: www.neoa.org

Michael R Rinaldi, President
Gabriel Lupo, VP
Richard Stook, Treasurer
Duane Tompkins, Secretary

A non-profit educational organization of more than a thousand law enforcement personnel and others in the criminal justicce system, includin state and local police, D.E.A., F.B.I. and customs.

15380 National Asian Peace Officers' Association

1776 I Street, NW,
Suite 900
Washington, DC 20006

646-632-5384
FAX 202-756-1301
E-Mail: james.ng@napaoonline.com
Home Page: www.napoaonline.org

James Ng, President
Taerance Oh, 1st Vice President
Thomas Masters, 3rd Vice President
Rolland Ogawa, Secretary
Siamone Bangphraxay, Treasurer

15381 National Association School Resource Officers

2020 Valleydale Road
Suite 207A
Hoover, AL 35244

205-739-6060
888-316-2776
FAX 205-536-9255
E-Mail: kevin.campana@nasro.org
Home Page: www.nasro.org
Social Media: *Facebook, Twitter, RSS, Youtube*

Joe Carter, President
Don Bridges, 1st Vice President
Bill West, 2nd Vice President
Jon Carrier, Secretary
Jennifer Thornton, Marketing Manager

A not-for-profit organization for school based law enforcement officers, school administrators, and school security/safety professionals working as partners to protect students, school faculty and staff and the schools they attend.

15382 National Association of Attorneys General

2030 M Street NW
8th Floor
Washington, DC 20036

202-326-6000
FAX 202-331-1427
E-Mail: feedback@naag.org
Home Page: www.naag.org
Social Media: *Facebook, Twitter*

Jim McPherson, Executive Director
Theresia Heller, Chief Financial Officer
Janet Fernandes, Accounting Manager
Al Lama, Chief of Staff
Marjorie Tharp, Director of Communications

Founded to help Attorneys General fulfill the responsibilities of their office and to assist in the delivery of high quality legal services to the states and territorial jurisdictions.
Founded in 1907
Mailing list available for rent

15383 National Association of Chiefs of Police

6350 Horizon Drive
Titusville, FL 32780-8002

321-264-0911
FAX 321-264-0033
E-Mail: policeinfo@aphf.org
Home Page: www.aphf.org

Jamie Maynard, Director of Communications
Barry Shepherd, Executive Director
Debra Chitwood, Chief Financial Officer
Brent Shepherd, Director of Operations

The mission is to encourage through the leadership of persons who hold a command law enforcement or security position within the United States and her territories and possessions, educational activities and services to upgrade law enforcement and security on a professional level.
Founded in 1967
Mailing list available for rent

15384 National Association of Drug Court Professionals

1029 N. Royal St
Suite 201
Alexandria, VA 22314

703-575-9400
FAX 703-706-0577
Home Page: www.nadcp.org
Social Media: *Facebook, Twitter, YouTube, Instagram*

West Huddleston, CEO
Meghan Wheeler, Project Director

Seeks to reduce substance abuse, crime and recidivism by promoting and advocating for the establishment and funding of Drug Courts and providing for collection and dissemination of information, technical assistance, and mutual support to association members.
Founded in 1997
Mailing list available for rent

15385 National Association of Field Training Officers

7942 W. Bell Rd.
Suite C5 #463
Glendale, AZ 85308

812-483-6588
E-Mail: info@nafto.org
Home Page: www.nafto.org
Social Media: *Facebook, Twitter, RSS*

Lt. Bob Smith, President
Officer Jeff Crippen, First VP
Sgt. Daniel Greene, Second VP
Sgt. Jeff Chapman, Executive Director

An educational and professional association concerned with apprenticeship and advance ongoing training for law enforcement, communications, and corrections personnel. Educators, administrators and other criminal justice practitioners are also encouraged to participate.

15386 National Association of Fleet Administrators

125 Village Boulevard
Suite 200,Princeton Forrestal Villa
Princeton, NJ 08540

609-720-0882
FAX 609-452-8004
E-Mail: info@nafa.org
Home Page: www.nafa.org
Social Media: *Facebook, Twitter, LinkedIn, Youtube, RSS*

Charles A Gibbens, President
Gayle Pratt, Senior VP

Serving the needs of those managing fleets of automobiles, light duty trucks and/or vans for US and Canadian organizations. Offers statistical research, publications, including NAFA's Fleet Executive monthly magazine, regional meetings, government representation, conferences, trade shows and seminars.
2600+ Members
Mailing list available for rent

15387 National Association of Police Organizations

317 S Patrick St
Alexandria, VA 22314-3501

703-549-0775
FAX 703-684-0515
E-Mail: info@napo.org
Home Page: www.napo.org
Social Media: *Facebook, Twitter*

Mick McHale, President
John Flynn, Vice President
William J. Johnson, Executive Director
Craig Lally, Executive Secretary
Sean Smoot, Treasurer

A coalition of police unions and associations from across the United States that serves to advance the interests of America's law enforcement officers through legislative and legal advocacy, political action and education.

241k Members
Founded in 1978
Mailing list available for rent

15388 National Black Police Association

3100 Main Street
#256
Dallas, TX 75226

855-879-6272
FAX 202-986-0410
E-Mail: nationaloffice@blackpolice.org
Home Page: www.blackpolice.org

Malik Aziz, Chairperson
Rochelle Bilal, Vice Chairperson
Carlos Bratcher, Sergeant at Arms
Sherri V. Lockett, Secretary
Donna Ross, Fiscal Officer

Law enforcement association to improve the relationship between Police Departments as institutions and the minority.

35000 Members
Founded in 1972

15389 National Burglar & Fire Alarm Association

2300 Valley View Lane
Suite 230
Irving, TX 75062-1733

214-260-5970
888-447-1689
FAX 214-260-5979
E-Mail: MerlinG@alarm.org
Home Page: www.alarm.org
Social Media: *Facebook, Twitter, Youtube*

Merlin Guilbeau, Executive Director
Georgia Calaway, Communications/PR Director

Representing, promoting and enhancing the growth and professional development of the electronic life safety, security, and integrated systems industry. In cooperation with a federation of state associations, NBFAA provides government advocacy and delivers timely information, professional development tools, products and services that members use to grow and prosper their businesses.

Founded in 1948

15390 National Constables Association (NCA)

16 Stonybrook Drive
Levittown, PA 19055-2217

215-943-3110
800-292-1775
FAX 215-943-0979
E-Mail: lefcourtapr@juno.com
Home Page:
www.angelfire.com/la/nationalconstable

Hal Lefcourt APR, Executive Director
John Sindt, President
Leo Bullock, Secretary

Helping to preserve and clearly define the significant role of the constable in the delivery of justice system in the United States; to train, educate and upgrade the quality of performance of the constable; to serve as a clearing house for all positive actions to give a continued rebirth to the dignity, respect, status and duties and responsibilities of the position of constable as the heritage of the law enforcement community.

Founded in 1973

15391 National Correctional Industries Association

800 North Charles Street
Suite 550B
Baltimore, MD 21201

410-230-3972
FAX 410-230-3981
E-Mail: memberservices@nationalcia.org
Home Page: www.nationalcia.org
Social Media: *Facebook*

Gina Honeycutt, Executive Director
Wil Heslop, Director of Operations
Karl Wiley, Accounting Manager
Rebekah Zinno, Sales and Marketing Manager
Farrah Marriott, Systems Coordinator

An affiliate body of the American Correctional Association, the Jail Industries Association and The Workman Fund. The mission is to promote excellence and credibility in correctional industries through professional development and innovative business solutions.

Founded in 1941
Mailing list available for rent

15392 National Crime Prevention Council

1201 Connecticut Avenue, NW
Suite 200
Washington, DC 20036

202-466-6272
FAX 202-296-1356
E-Mail: webmaster@ncpc.org
Home Page: www.ncpc.org

David A. Dean, Chairman
Robert F. Diegelman, Vice Chairman
Ann M. Harnkins, President/CEO
John P. Box, Treasurer
Jean Adnopoz, Secretary

Aids people in keeping themselves, their families, and their communities safe from crime. NCPC produces tools that communities can use to learn crime prevention strategies, engage community members, and coordinate with local agencies.

136 Members
Founded in 1982
Mailing list available for rent

15393 National Crime and Punishment Learning Center

300 S 25th Ave
Hattiesburg, MS 39401-7301

228-447-0285
FAX 228-896-8696
E-Mail: ncplc@crimeandpunishment.net
Home Page: www.crimeandpunishment.net

William H Sanford, President/Founder

Provide free information on the most common crimes and their punishments in each state. The center is unique in its dedicated endeavor to accomplish this task by providing information to bridge the gap between the legal justice system and the American people.

15394 National Criminal Justice Association

720 7th St Nw
3rd Floor
Washington, DC 20001-3902

202-628-8550
FAX 202-448-1723
E-Mail: info@ncja.org
Home Page: www.ncja.org
Social Media: *Facebook, Twitter, LinkedIn, RSS*

Jeanne Smith, President
Karhlton Moore, Vice President
Cabell Cropper, Executive Director
David Fredenburgh, Director of Program Services
Bethany Broida, Director of Communications

A national voice in shaping and implementing criminal justice policy since its founding. As the representative of state, tribal and local criminal and juvenile justice practitioners, the NCJA works to promote a balanced approach to communities' complex public safety and criminal and juvenile justice system problems.

Founded in 1971

15395 National Criminal Justice Reference Service

PO Box 6000
Rockville, MD 20849-6000

301-519-5500
800-851-3420
202-836-6998
FAX 301-240-5830
Home Page: www.ncjrs.gov
Social Media: *Facebook, Twitter, LinkedIn, RSS, Youtube, Google+, Vimeo,*

Dolores Kozloski, Executive Director

A federally funded resource offering justice and substance abuse information to support research, policy, and program development worldwide.

Founded in 1972
Mailing list available for rent

15396 National District Attorneys Association

99 Canal Center Plz
Suite 330
Alexandria, VA 22314-1548

703-549-9222
FAX 703-836-3195
E-Mail: berryb@co.yamhill.or.us
Home Page: www.ndaa.org
Social Media: *Facebook, Twitter*

William Fitzpatrick, President
Kay Chopard Cohen, Executive Director
Rick Hanes, Chief of Staff

Development resource for prosecutors at all levels of government. APRI has become a vital resource and national clearinghouse for information on the prosecutorial function. The Institute is committed to providing interdisciplinary responses to the complex problems of criminal justice. It is also committed to supporting the highest professional standards among officials entrusted with the crucial responsibility for public safety.

Founded in 1950

15397 National Drug Court Institute

1029 N. Royal St
Suite 201
Alexandria, VA 22314

703-575-9400
FAX 703-575-9402
E-Mail: webmaster@nadcp.org
Home Page: www.ndci.org
Social Media: *Facebook, Twitter, RSS, Youtube*

Lars Levy, President
Milly Merrigan, President-Elect

Promote education, research and scholarship for drug court and other court-based intervention programs.

15398 National Drug Enforcement Officers Association

Drug Enforcement Administration
Office of Training/TRDS
FBI Academy, PO Box 1475
Quantico, VA 22134-1475

202-298-9653
E-Mail: paul.stevens@state.mn.us
Home Page: www.ndeoa.org

Paul Stevens, President
Steve Peterson, First VP

NDEOA's purpose and objective is to promote the cooperation, education and exchange of information among all Law Enforcement Agencies involved in the enforcement of controlled substance laws.
Founded in 1970

15399 National Emergency Number Association
1700 Diagonal Road
Suite 500
Alexandria, VA 22314

202-466-4911
FAX 202-618-6370
E-Mail: rhixson@nena.org
Home Page: www.nena.org
Social Media: *Facebook, Twitter, YouTube*

Christy Williams, President
Renee Hardwick, ENP, 1st Vice President
Rob McMullen, ENP, 2nd Vice President
Brian Fontes, Chief Executive Officer
Trey Forgety, Director of Government Affairs

15400 National Fire Protection Association
1 Batterymarch Park
Quincy, MA 02169-7471

617-770-3000
800-344-3555
FAX 617-770-0700
E-Mail: custserv@nfpa.org
Home Page: www.nfpa.org
Social Media: *Facebook, Twitter, LinkedIn, Youtube, RSS, Google+, Flickr*

Ernest J. Grant, RN, MSN, PhD, Chair
Randolph W. Tucker, First Vice Chair
Jim Pauley, President and CEO
Amy R. Acton, Secretary
Thomas A. Lawson, Treasurer

Mission is to reduce the worldwide burden of fire and other hazards on the quality of life by providing and advocating scientifically based concensus codes and standards, research, training, and education. Also serves as the world's leading advocate of fire prevention and is an authoritive source on public safety.
70000 Members
Founded in 1896

15401 National Gang Crime Research Center
Research Center
PO Box 990
Peotone, IL 60468-0090

708-258-9111
FAX 708-258-9546
E-Mail: gangcrime@aol.com
Home Page: www.ngcrc.com

George W Knox, Director

Research on gangs and gang members, disseminate information through publications and reports, and provide training and consulting services.
Founded in 1990

15402 National Institute of Justice
US Department Of Justice
810 7th Street NW
Washington, DC 20531

202-664-4000
800-851-3420
FAX 202-307-6394
E-Mail: askncjrs@ncjrs.org
Home Page: www.ojp.usdoj.gov
Social Media: *Facebook, Twitter, RSS, YouTube*

Leigh Benda, Chief Financial Officer
Karol Virginia Mason, Assistant Attorney General
Phillip Merkle, Director
Mary Lou Leary, Principal Deputy Assistant Attorney

James H. Burch, II, Deputy Assistant Attorney General

Research, development and evaluation agency of the US department of Justice. Supports all those in the justice industry with education and training, publications and trade shows.
Mailing list available for rent

15403 National Insurance Crime Bureau
1111 E Touhy Ave
Suite 400
Des Plaines, IL 60018-5804

847-544-7002
800-447-6282
FAX 708-544-7100
E-Mail: rjones@nicb.org
Home Page: www.nicb.org
Social Media: *Facebook, Twitter, LinkedIn, Youtube*

Joseph H. Wehrle, President/CEO
James K. Schweitzer, Senior Vice President
Daniel G. Abbott, Senior Vice President
Robert Jachnicki, Senior Vice President
Andrew J. Sosnowski, Senior Vice President

A not for profit organization that recieves support from approximately 1,000 property/casualty insurance companies. NICB partners with insurers and law enforcement agencies to facilitate the identification, detection and prosecution of insurance criminals.
1000 Members
Founded in 1992

15404 National Latino Peace Officers Association
PO Box 23116
23116
Santa Ana, CA 92711

E-Mail: nlpoamgr@gmail.com
Home Page: www.nlpoa.com
Social Media: *Facebook*

Andrew P Peralta, National President
Alfredo Dean, Vice President
Maria B. Thomas, Secretary
Cindy Rodriguez, Treasurer
Vicente Calderon, Founder
Founded in 1972

15405 National Native American Law Enforcement Association
PO Box 171
Washington, DC 20040

202-207-3065
FAX 866-506-7631
E-Mail: info@nnalea.org
Home Page: www.nnalea.org

Joseph Wicks, President
Mark Murtha, Vice President
Gary Edwards, CEO
Dave Nichols, CFO
Daryll Davis, Senior Director

NNALEA is a nonprofit organization that promotes and fosters mutual cooperation between American Indian Law Enforcement Officers/Agents/Personnel, their agencies, tribes, private industry and public.
Founded in 1993

15406 National Organization for Victim Assistance
510 King St
Suite 424
Alexandria, VA 22314-3132

703-535-6682
800-879-6682
FAX 703-535-5500
E-Mail: nova@trynova.org

Home Page: www.trynova.org
Social Media: *Facebook, Twitter, RSS*

Will Marling, Executive Director
Claire Ponder Selib, Director of Education
James Gierke, Director of Victim Services
Deborah Baroch, Director of Finance and Operations
Barbara Kendall, Director of Training

A private, non-profit organization of victim and witness assistance programs and practitioners, criminal justice agencies and professionals, mental health professionals, researchers, former victims and survivors, and others committed to the recognition and implementation of victim rights and services.

15407 National Organization of Black Law Enforcement Executives
4609 Pinecrest Office Park Dr
Alexandria, VA 22312-1442

703-658-1529
FAX 703-658-9479
E-Mail: jakers@noblenatl.org
Home Page: www.noblenatl.org
Social Media: *Facebook, Twitter, LinkedIn, Tumblr, Stumbleupon, Pinterest*

Gregory Thomas, National President
Perry Tarrant, National First Vice President
Clarence Cox, National Second Vice President
Hubert Bell, Treasurer
Thomas Nelson, National Recording Secretary

Ensure equity in the administration of justice in the provision of public service to all communities, and to serve as the conscience of law enforcement by being committed to justice by action.
Founded in 1976

15408 National Police Athletic/Activities League , Inc.
1662 N. US Highway 1
Suite C
Jupiter, FL 33469

561-745-5535
FAX 561-745-3147
E-Mail: mdillhyon@nationalpal.org
Home Page: www.nationalpal.org
Social Media: *Facebook, Twitter*

Christopher Hill, President
Barbara Bonilla, 1st Vice President
Ronald Allen, 2nd Vice President
Donna Miller, 3rd Vice President
Frank Williams, Secretary

Exists to prevent juvenile crime and violence by providing civic, athletic, recreational, and educational opportunities and resources to PAL Chapters.
Founded in 1940

15409 National Police Bloodhound Association

E-Mail: president@npba.com
Home Page: www.npba.com
Social Media: *Facebook*

Doug Lowry, President
Roger G. Titus, Vice President
Kevin Osuch, Secretary
Coby Webb, Treasurer
Roger G. Titus, Training
Founded in 1966

15410 National Police Institute
Central Missouri State University
200 Ming Street
Warrensburg, MO

660-543-4090
FAX 660-543-4709
E-Mail: wiggins@cmsu.edu
Home Page: www.cmsu.edu/x4869.xml

Dr Mike Wiggins, Director

An internationally recognized police training center. Provides advanced police training in a number of areas as well as housing the Regional Police Academy.

15411 National Public Safety Information Bureau

PO Box 365
Stevens Point, WI 54481

715-345-2772
800-647-7579
FAX 715-345-7288
E-Mail: info@safetysource.com
Home Page: www.safetyresource.com

Steve Cywinski, President/Publisher
Ronald Tippel, VP Information Services
Laura Gross, VP Data Procurement
Celia Piesik, Data Procurement Specialist
Christina Scott, Data Procurement Specialist

Working hand in hand with law enforcement, fire and emergency departments to develop the most accurate database in the public safety industry with over 70,000 contacts. The result is; the most current and comprehensive reference tools available.
Founded in 1964

15412 National Public Safety Telecommunications Council

8191 Southpark Lane
Unit 205
Littleton, CO 80120-4641

407-836-9668
866-907-4755
FAX 303-649-1844
E-Mail: support@npstc.org
Home Page: www.npstc.org
Social Media: *Facebook, Twitter, LinkedIn, YouTube, Blogger*

Don Root, Committee Vice Chair
Stu Overby, Committee Vice Chair
Marilyn Ward, Ecexutive Director
Charles Bryson, Outreach News Editor
Mark Grubb, Participant Development Coordinator

NPSTC is a federation of associations representing public safety telecommunications. They follow up on the recommendations of the Public Safety Wireless Advisory Committee.
Founded in 1997
Mailing list available for rent

15413 National Reserve Law Officers Association

PO Box 6505
San Antonio, TX 78209

210-805-8917
FAX 210-653-9655
E-Mail: nrloa01@earthlink.net
Home Page: www.nrlo.net

Capt. Chuck Mantkus, Director of Training

Provides members with training information and services plus the best, most extensive, and lowest cost in-line-of-duty accidental insurance coverage available.

15414 National Safety Council

1121 Spring Lake Dr
Itasca, IL 60143-3201

630-285-1121
800-621-7615
FAX 630-285-1434
E-Mail: info@nsc.org,
customerservice@nsc.org
Home Page: www.nsc.org
Social Media: *RSS*

John P. Surma, Chairman
Deborah Hersman, President & CEO
Patrick Phelan, Chief Financial Officer
Shay Gallagher, Vice President, General Manager

Michael Pollock, VP, Relationship Management

Provides information sharing opportunities, continuing education and professional fellowship to people with environmental health and safety responsibilities in higher education.
936 Members
Founded in 1912
Mailing list available for rent

15415 National Sheriffs' Association

1450 Duke St
Alexandria, VA 22314-3490

703-836-7827
800-424-7827
FAX 703-683-5349
E-Mail: jthompson@sheriffs.org
Home Page: www.sheriffs.org
Social Media: *Facebook, Twitter, LinkedIn, Google+*

Aaron D. Kennard, Executive Director
John Thompson, Chief of Staff and Deputy Executive
Fred G. Wilson, Director of Operations
Ed Hutchison, Director of Traffic Safety & Triad
Greg J. MacDonald, Director of Homeland Security

Devoted to helping sheriffs and other law enforcers to execute their duties most effectively and professionally.
21M Members
Founded in 1940
Mailing list available for rent: 3M names

15416 National Tactical Officers Association

PO Box 797
Doylestown, PA 18901

215-230-7552
800-279-9127
FAX 215-230-7552
E-Mail: membership@ntoa.org
Home Page: www.ntoa.org
Social Media: *Facebook, Twitter*

Deputy Chief Bo Chabali, Board Chairman
Mark Lomax, Executive Director
Rob Cartner, Director of Training
Corey Luby, Marketing Director
Marsha Martello, Membership Coordinator

Enhance the performance and professional status of law enforcement personnel by providing a credible and proven training resource, as well as a forum for the development of tactics and information exchange. The Association's ultimate goal is to improve public safety and domestic security through training, education, and tactical excellence.
32000 Members
Founded in 1983

15417 National Technical Investigators Association (NATIS)

1069 West Broad Street
Box 757
Falls Church, VA 22046

703-237-9338
800-966-2842
770-485-1820
FAX 703-832-2600
E-Mail: admin@natia.org
Home Page: www.natia.org

Michael Woods, President

The purpose of NATIA is to further knowledge, develop skills and promote fellowship between those law enforcement and intelligence professionals who support their agencies' and departments' technical surveillance, tactical operations, and forensic activities.

15418 National United Law Enforcement Officers

256 E McLemore Avenue
Memphis, TN 38106-2833

901-774-1118
FAX 901-774-1139
E-Mail: clydevenson@bellsouth.org

Clyde Venson, Executive Director
Samantha Macklin, Secretary

Protects the needs and interests of persons in the law enforcement industry.
5000 Members
Founded in 1969

15419 National White Collar Crime Center

10900 Nuckols Rd
Suite 325
Glen Allen, VA 23060-9288

804-967-6200
Home Page: www.nw3c.org
Social Media: *Facebook, Twitter, Youtube*

Don Brackman, Director
Ken Brooks, Deputy Director

Through a combination of training and critical support services, law enforcement agencies are given the skills and resources they need to tackle emerging economic and cyber crime problems.
Mailing list available for rent

15420 Naval Criminal Investigative Services

27130 Telegraph Road
Suite 2000
Quantico, VA 22134

202-433-8800
FAX 724-794-3293
Home Page: www.ncis.navy.mil

Andrew L. Traver, Director
John Beattie, Senior Intelligence Officer
Mark D. Ridley, Deputy Director
Rod Baldwin, Executive Assistant Director
Charlton Howard, Chief Intelligence Officer

Primary law enforcement and counterintelligence arm of the United States Department of the Navy. It works closely with other local, state, federal and foreign agencies to counter and investigate the most serious crimes.

15421 Organized Crime Task Force

The Capitol
Albany, NY 12224-0341

518-474-7330
FAX 914-422-8795
Home Page: www.ag.ny.gov

John Amodeo, Assistant Attorney General
Colleen Glavin, Public Integrity Officer

A forum that brings government, law enforcement and a range of agencies together to set priorities for tackling organized crime.
Founded in 1970

15422 Park Law Enforcement Association

E-Mail: nielsen4397@com.cast.net
Home Page: www.myparkranger.org

Tom Wakolbinger, President
William Westerfield, Vice President
Dale Steele, Secretary
Capt. Carl Nielsen, Executive Director
Steve Newsom, Treasurer
Founded in 1979

15423 Police & Firemen's Insurance Association

101 E 116th St
Carmel, IN 46032-5629

317-581-1913
800-221-7342

FAX 317-571-5946
Home Page: www.pfia.net

Mark Kemp, President
Jeanie Williams, Operations VP

Mission of the association is to create and operate a Supreme Lodge and Subordinate Branches for the purpose of inculcating principles of friendship and brotherhood among police officers and fire fighters. Providing financial assistance to its members through disability certificates and pay final expenses for members with legal reserve life insurance policies.

15424 Police Executive Research Forum
1120 Connecticut Ave NW
Suite 930
Washington, DC 20036-3951

202-466-7820
FAX 202-466-7826
Home Page: www.policeforum.org

Chief J. Scott Thomson, President
Chief Tom Manger, VP
Chief Robert White, Secretary
Chief Roberto Villase¤or, Treasurer
Shannon Branly, Deputy Chief of Staff

A national membership organization of progressive police executives from the largest city, county and state law enforcement agencies. Dedicated to improving policing and advancing professionalism through research and involvement in public policy debate.
100 Members
Founded in 1976
Mailing list available for rent

15425 Police Foundation
1201 Connecticut Ave NW
Suite 200
Washington, DC 20036-2636

202-833-1460
FAX 202-659-9149
E-Mail: info@policefoundation.org
Home Page: www.policefoundation.org
Social Media: *Facebook, Twitter, RSS, Google+, YouTube*

Weldon J. Rougeau, Chairman
Chief Jim Bueermann, President
Karen L. Amendola, PhD, Chief Behavioral Scientist
Tari Lewis, CPA, Chief Financial Officer
Blake Norton, VP/COO

A national, nonpartisan, nonprofit organization dedicated to supporting innovation and improvement in policing through its research and evaluation, technical assistance, training, technology, professional services, and communication programs.
Founded in 1970
Mailing list available for rent

15426 Public Safety Diving Association
904-743-3025
E-Mail: psdahq@bellsouth.net
Home Page:
www.publicsafetydivingassociation.comÿ

David Scoggins, President
Mark Reese, Director
Founded in 1972

15427 Public Services Health and Safety Association
4950 Yonge Street
Suite 902
Toronto, ON M2N 6K1

416-250-2131
877-250-7444
FAX 416-250-7484

E-Mail: elearning@pshsa.ca
Home Page: www.pshsa.ca

Michael Papadakis, Chair
Thomas Hayes, Vice Chair
Ron Kelusky, CEO
Joanne Clark, Director, Marketing and Comm.
Susan Sun, Director, Finance & Administration
Founded in 2009

15428 Reserve Police Officers Association
89 Rockland Ave
Yonkers, NY 10705

800-326-9416
800-326-9416
FAX 212-555-1234
Home Page: www.reservepolice.org

Brooke Webster, President

Dedicated to the support of law enforcement with an emphasis on the role of the reserve and auxiliary law enforcement officer.
Founded in 1996

15429 Texas Department of Public Safety Officer's Association
5821 Airport Boulevard
Austin, TX 78752

512-451-0571
800-933-7762
FAX 512-451-0709
E-Mail: info@dpsoa.com
Home Page: www.dpsoa.com
Social Media: *Facebook, Twitter, RSS, Google+, Tumblr*

Sgt. Gary Chandler, President
Lt. Jimmy Jackson, VP
John M. Pike, Executive Director
Trooper Clay Taylor, Secretary/Treasurer
Patti Benson, Membership Services

Offers and executes programs that benefit Texas Troppers and the communitites around them. Also publishes DPSOA a quarterly magazine.
2650 Members
Founded in 1974

15430 The Association of Certified Fraud Specialists
4600 Northgate Blvd.
Suite 105
Sacramento, CA 95834

916-419-6319
FAX 916-419-6318
E-Mail: headquarters@acfsnet.org
Home Page: www.acfsnet.org
Social Media: *Facebook, LinkedIn*

Bill Cramer, President
Mark Menz, National Vice President
Charles Raborn, Executive Director
Jeremy Krater, Information Technology Specialist
Brittany Cyrus, Graphic Designer
Founded in 1993

15431 The Commission on Accreditation forÿLaw Enforcement Agencies
13575 Heathcote Boulevard
Suite 320
Gainesville, VI 20155

703-352-4225
FAX 703-890-3126
E-Mail: jgregory@calea.org
Home Page: www.calea.org
Social Media: *Facebook, Twitter, LinkedIn, Reddit, Google+, Tumblr*

J. Grayson Robinson, President
Craig Webre, Vice-President
W. Craig Hartley, Jr., Executive Director
Richard Myers, Secretary
Gary Margolis, Treasurer

15432 The Federal Law Enforcement Associationÿ
7945 MacArthur Blvd
Suite 201
Cabin John, MD 20818

202-870-5503
866-553-5362
E-Mail: fleoa@fleoa.org
Home Page: www.fleoa.org
Social Media: *Facebook, Twitter, Reddit, Google+, Tumblr*

Jon Adler, National President
Nate Catura, Executive Vice President
Chris Schoppmeyer, Vice President - Agency Affairs
Frank Terreri, Vice President- Legislative Affairs
Enid Febus, National Secretary
Founded in 1977

15433 The International Association of Chiefs of Police
44 Canal Center Plaza
Suite 200
Alexandria, VA 22314

703-836-6767
E-Mail: beckmann@theiacp.org
Home Page: www.theiacp.org
Social Media: *Facebook, Twitter, LinkedIn, YouTube*

Richard Beary, President
Vincent Talucci, Executive Director/CEO
Gwen Boniface, Deputy Executive Director
John Firman, Director of Strategic Partnerships
Jacqueline Gooding, Director of Human Resources
Founded in 1893

15434 The United Deputy Sheriffs' Association
319 S. Hydraulic St.,
Suite B
Wichita, KS 67211

316-263-2583
E-Mail: info@usdeputy.org
Home Page: www.usdeputy.org
Social Media: *Facebook*

Mike Willis, Executive Director
David Hinners, Deputy Director

15435 Theÿ AssociationÿofÿPublic-Safety Communications Officials
351 N. Williamson Blvd
Daytona Beach, FL 32114-1112

386-322-2500
FAX 386-322-2501
E-Mail: apco@apcointl.org
Home Page: www.apcointl.org
Social Media: *Facebook, Twitter*

Brent Lee, President
Cheryl J. Greathouse, RPL, First Vice President
Martha K. Carter, ENP, Second Vice President
Gigi Smith, Immediate Past President
Derek Poarch, Executive Director
Founded in 1982

15436 Transportation Research Board National Research Council
500 Fifth Stret NW
Washington, DC 20001

202-334-2934
FAX 202-334-2003
Home Page: www.trb.org
Social Media: *Facebook, Twitter, LinkedIn, RSS, Blogger, Pinterest, Tumbl*

Neil Pedersen, Executive Director
Rosa Allen, Administrative Coordinator
Stephen J. Andrle, Deputy Director
Javy Awan, Director, Publications
Terri M. Baker, Senior Program Assistant

A division of the National Research Council, which serves as an independent advisor to the federal government and others on scientific and technical questions of national importance.

15437 Transportation Technology Center

55500 DOT Rd.
Pueblo, CO 81001-0130

719-584-0750
FAX 719-584-0711
E-Mail: ttci_marketing@ttci.aar.com
Home Page: www.aar.com
Social Media: *Facebook, Twitter, Youtube*

Roy Allen, Manager
Michele Johnson, Administrative Assistant
Mark Nordling, Assistant Director Business
Ron Lang, Manager Business Development
Michele Johnson, Executive Assistant

A wholly owned subsidiary of the Association of American Railroads. TTCI is a world-class transportation research and testing organization, providing emerging technology solutions for the railway industry throughout North America and the world.

15438 U.S. First Responders Association

420 Kimbrel Avenue
Panama City, FL 32404

E-Mail: Corporate@usfra.org
Home Page: www.usfra.org
Social Media: *Facebook, Twitter, LinkedIn, RSS*

15439 United States Conference of Mayors

1620 Eye St NW
Washington, DC 20006

202-293-7330
FAX 202-293-2352
E-Mail: info@usmayors.org
Home Page: www.usmayors.org
Social Media: *Facebook, Twitter*

Mayor Stephanie Rawlings-Blake, President
Mick Cornett, VP
Mitchell J. Landrieu, Second Vice President
Tom Cochran, CEO and Executive Director

An organization of city government officials whose primary roles are to promote the development of effective national urban/suburban policy; strengthen federal-city relationships; ensure that federal policy meets urban needs; provide mayors with leadership and management tools; and create a forum in which mayors can share ideas and information.
Founded in 1932

15440 United States Deputy Sheriff's Association

319 S. Hydraulic St.
Suite B
Wichita, KS 67211

316-263-2583
877-800-8854
FAX 281-578-0669
E-Mail: info@usdeputy.org
Home Page: www.usdeputy.org

Mike Willis, Executive Director/Training
David Hinners, Deputy Director/National Trainer

Provides needed equipment, free of charge, to the mostly rural, underfunded county law enforcement agencies. All members are given an Emergency Disaster Relief of $2,000, if killed in the line of duty.
Founded in 1995

15441 United States Deputy Sheriffs' Association

319 S. Hydraulic St.,
Suite B
Wichita, KS 67211

316-263-2583
E-Mail: info@usdeputy.org
Home Page: www.usdeputy.org
Social Media: *Facebook*

Mike Willis, Executive Director
David Hinners, Deputy Director

Survival training for men and women in law enforcement.

15442 United States Police Canine Association

PO Box 80
Springboro, OH 45066

937-751-6469
800-531-1614
E-Mail: uspcadir@aol.com
Home Page: www.uspcak9.com
Social Media: *Facebook*

Russ Hess, Executive Director
Kevin Johnson, President
Melinda Roupp, Secretary
James Matarese, Treasurer

Nonprofit organization striving for the establishment of minimum standards for Police K-9 dogs through proper methods of training. Police K-9 dogs, properly trained and handled, give Law Enforcement officers one of the finest non-lethal aids in the prevention and detection of crime.
Founded in 1971

Newsletters

15443 CGAA Signals

Central Station Alarm Association
8150 Leesburg Pike
Suite 700
Vienna, VA 22182-2721

703-242-4670
FAX 703-242-4675
E-Mail: communications@csaaul.org
Home Page: www.csaaul.org
Social Media: *Facebook, Twitter, LinkedIn*

Stephen P Doyle, Executive VP/CEO
Celia Besore, VP Marketing & Programs
Robert R. Bean, President
Jay Hauhn, First Vice President
Peter Lowitt, Secretary
300+ Members
Frequency: Quarterly
Circulation: 1200
Founded in 1950
Mailing list available for rent

15444 Correctional Education Bulletin

LRP Publications
747 Dresher Road Suite 500
PO Box 980
Horsham, PA 19044

215-784-0912
800-341-7874
FAX 215-784-9639
E-Mail: webmaster@lrp.com
Home Page: www.lrp.com

Kim Yablonski, Editor

Combines and analyzes corrections education issues and management topics. You'll learn how educators are coping with shrinking budgets and the growing number of youths being sentenced as adults. Expert analysis of current legal issues and the latest regulatory updates

given.
Cost: $125.00
Frequency: Monthly
Founded in 1977

15445 Corrections Professional

LRP Publications
PO Box 980
Horsham, PA 19044

215-840-0912
800-341-7874
FAX 215-784-9639
E-Mail: webmaster@lrp.com
Home Page: www.lrp.com

Debi Pelletier, Editor
Kenneth Kahn, President

Tracks innovative strategies, proven techniques and legal developments impacting correction facilities across the country. Gives profiles of other professionals and their institutions, giving an opportunity to learn from their experiences and avoid costly mistakes. Contains Q-A section that addresses difficult situations.
Cost: $210.00
Frequency: 104 issues per
Founded in 1977

15446 Criminal Justice Newsletter

Pace Publications
443 Park Ave S
New York, NY 10016-7322

212-685-5450
FAX 212-679-4701

Sid Goldstein, Publisher
Craig Fischer, Editor
Peter Kiers, Executive Director

Independent publication providing system-wide perspective of law enforcement.
Cost: $219.00
Frequency: BiWeekly

15447 Emergency Preparedness News

Business Publishers
2222 Sedwick Dr
Suite 101
Durham, NC 27713

800-223-8720
FAX 800-508-2592
E-Mail: custserv@bpinews.com
Home Page: www.bpinews.com

Dedicated solely to disaster management: from securing pre-disaster mitigation and counter terrorism funds, to staying prepared for hurricanes, terrorist threats, fires, floods and other natural disasters.
Cost: $327.00

15448 FEMSA News

Fire and Emergency Manufacturers and Services Asso
PO Box 147
Lynnfield, MA 01940-0147

781-334-2771
FAX 781-334-2771
E-Mail: info@femsa.org
Home Page: www.femsa.org
Social Media: *Twitter, LinkedIn*

Dan Reese, President
William Lawson, VP

Member newsletter
Frequency: 3x/Year
Circulation: 600

15449 FLEOA Newsletter

Federal Law Enforcement Officers Association
PO Box 326
Lewisberry, PA 17339-2900

717-938-2300
FAX 717-932-2262

E-Mail: fleoa@fleoa.org
Home Page: www.fleoa.org
Social Media: *Facebook, Twitter*

Jon Adler, National President
Nate Catura, National Executive VP

Federal newsletter offering information, legislative updates and news for law enforcement officers nationwide.
12 Pages
Circulation: 2400
Founded in 1976

15450 Journal of the American Association of Forensic Dentists
1000 N Avenue
Waukegan, IL 60085

847-223-5077
E-Mail: info@andent.net
Home Page: www.andent.net
Social Media: *RSS*

Quarterly journal that brings forensic dental knowledge not only to dentists and their staff, but also to anthropologists, attorneys and law enforcement personnel.
Cost: $8.00
Frequency: Quarterly
Founded in 1978

15451 Keepers' Voice
International Association of Correctional Officers
PO Box 53
Chicago, IL 60690

312-996-5401
FAX 312-413-0458

Jim Clark, Publisher
Jess Maghan, Editor

Of special interest to correctional officers because it focuses on current developments in the field, including practical, day-to-day training topics, current legislation, resources, conference notices and job openings.

15452 Law Enforcement Legal Publications
421 Ridgewood Avenue
Suite 100
Glen Ellyn, IL 60137-4900

630-858-6092
FAX 630-858-6392
E-Mail: lelp@xnet.com
Home Page: www.lelp.com

James Manak, Publisher/President

Publication for law enforcement, legal professional civil liability, personnel law, labor law, criminal law and law libraries.
ISSN: 1070-9967
Founded in 1970
Printed in 3 colors on newsprint stock

15453 Law Enforcement Legal Review
Law Enforcement Legal Publications
421 Ridgewood Avenue
Suite 100
Glen Ellyn, IL 60137-4900

630-858-6392
FAX 630-858-6392
E-Mail: lelp@xnet.com
Home Page: www.lelp.com/

James Manak, Publisher
Glen Manak, VP Marketing

Case reporter for law enforcement, legal profession and law libraries, covering criminal law, civil liability and personnel law.
Cost: $98.00
16 Pages
Frequency: Bi-monthly
Circulation: 500
ISSN: 1070-9967
Founded in 1975

15454 Legal Employment Weekly Law Bulletin Publishing Company
415 N State Street
Chicago, IL 60610-4674

312-644-7800
FAX 312-644-1215
E-Mail: editor@lbpc.com
Home Page: www.lawbulletin.com

Bernard Judge, Publisher
Stephen Brown, Managing Editor
Lanning Macfarland, Chairman

Legal employment opportunities.
Frequency: Weekly
Founded in 1854
Printed in 2 colors on newsprint stock

15455 National Constables Association Newsletter
National Constables Association
PO Box 1172
Haverhill, MA 01831-1572

978-373-5234
800-272-1775
FAX 978-373-1191
E-Mail: mike@constables.com
Home Page: www.constables.com

Hal Lefcourt, Executive Director
John Sindt, President

A newsletter published for the members of National Constables Association.
4 Pages
Frequency: Quarterly
Printed in one color on glossy stock

15456 Police Executive Research Forum
1120 Connecticut Avenue NW
Suite 930
Washington, DC 20036

202-466-7820
FAX 202-466-7826
Home Page: www.policeforum.org

Chuck Wexler, Executive Director
Chief John Timoney, VP
Daniel Woods, Research Associate
Jessica Toliver, Deputy Director
Raquel Rodriguez, Accounting Manager

Members are chief executives of city, county and state police agencies. Membership dues are general $300.00, subscribing $125.00.
Cost: $35.00
Frequency: Monthly
Circulation: 1000
Founded in 1977
Mailing list available for rent

15457 Signal
American Traffic Safety Services Association
15 Riverside Parkway
Suite 100
Fredericksburg, VA 22406-1022

540-368-1701
800-272-8772
FAX 540-368-1717
Home Page: www.atssa.com

James Baron, Communications Director
Douglas Danko, Chairman

Covers legislative updates, industry news and meeting information, as well as other items of interest to the roadway safety industry as is a full-color publication.
Frequency: Quarterly
Mailing list available for rent

15458 Women Police
International Association of Women Police

PO Box 690418
Tulsa, OK 74169

918-234-6445
E-Mail: jvanland@aol.com
Home Page: www.iawp.org/

Mona Moore, Publisher
Kim Covert, Treasurer

Accepts advertising.
Cost: $25.00
50 Pages
Frequency: Quarterly

Magazines & Journals

15459 Air Beat Magazine
Airborne Law Enforcement Association
50 Carroll Creek Way
Suite 260
Frederick, MD 21701-4786

301-631-2406
FAX 301-631-2466
Home Page: www.alea.org

Steven Ingley, Executive Director
Kevin R. Caffery, VP
Nicole Gentile, Operations Manager
Keith Johnson, Safety Program Director
Carrie Cosens, Membership Manager

Dedicated to Airborne Law Enforcement. The subscription also includes the annual Buyer's Guide and special Convention issue with membership.
Cost: $40.00
3500 Members
Frequency: Bi-Monthly
Circulation: 6500
Founded in 1968

15460 Campus Safety Journal
Bricepac
12228 Venice Boulevard
PO Box 66515
Los Angeles, CA 90066

310-390-5277
FAX 310-390-4777
E-Mail: tnelson@campusjournal.com
Home Page: www.campusjournal.com

John Van Horn, Publisher
Tom Nelson, Managing Editor
Wendy Rackley, Production Manager

Provides a vehicle for communicating campus safety and security issues to all interested parties at the middle, secondary, college and university levels.
40 Pages
Frequency: Monthly
Circulation: 20100
Founded in 1992
Printed in 4 colors on glossy stock

15461 Contingency Planning & Recovery Journal
Management Advisory Services & Publications
PO Box 81151
Wellesley Hills, MA 02481-0001

781-235-2895
FAX 781-235-5446
E-Mail: info@masp.com
Home Page: www.masp.com/

An independent, subscription supported to all issues of contingency planning, disaster recovery and business continuity. Includes tutorial extensive literature review on the fields of business continuity.
Cost: $75.00
Frequency: Quarterly
Founded in 1972
Printed in on glossy stock

15462 Corrections Today

4380 Forbes Boulevard
Lanham, MD 20706

301-918-1800
800-222-5646
FAX 301-918-1900
E-Mail: customerservice@corrections.com
Home Page: www.corrections.com/aca

Susan Clayton, Editor
Gwendolyn C Chunn, President
Harry Wilhelm, Marketing Manager
Alice Heiserman, Publications and Research Manager

Published by the American Correctional Association.
Cost: $25.00
200 Pages
Circulation: 20000
Founded in 1870
Mailing list available for rent

15463 Credit Card Crime, Law Enforcement Kit

9770 S Military Trail
Suite 380
Boynton Beach, FL 33436-4011

561-737-8700
FAX 561-737-5800
E-Mail: sales@fraudandtheftinfo.com
Home Page: www.fraudandtheftinfo.com

Larry Schwartz, Editor

Ways to catch and punish the thieves, including corporate support of police, reverse sting operations, paying informants. Case histories, specific recommendations.
Cost: $59.95
ISBN: 0-914801-05-8
Founded in 1982

15464 Crime & Delinquency

Sage Publications
2455 Teller Rd
Newbury Park, CA 91320-2234

805-499-9774
800-818-7243
FAX 805-499-0871
E-Mail: info@sagepub.com
Home Page: www.sagepub.com

Blaise R Simqu, CEO
Janice Denehy, Executive Editor

Offers information to probation and parole executives as well as criminologists and lawyers.
Cost: $105.00
Frequency: Quarterly
Circulation: 3250
Founded in 1965
Mailing list available for rent

15465 Law Enforcement Legal Review

Law Enforcement Legal Publications
421 Ridgewood Avenue
Suite 100
Glen Ellyn, IL 60137-4900

630-858-6392
FAX 630-858-6392
E-Mail: lelp@xnet.com
Home Page: home.xnet.com/~lelp

James Manak, President
Glen P Manak, VP Marketing

Civil liability, criminal law and personnel law case reporter for law enforcement, legal professional and law libraries.
Cost: $98.00
Circulation: 1000
ISSN: 1070-9967
Founded in 1970
Printed in on n stock

15466 Law Enforcement Product News

100 Garfield Street
2nd Floor
Denver, CO 80206

303-322-6400
800-291-3911
FAX 303-322-0627
Home Page: www.law-enforcement.com

Michael George, Publisher
Jeannine Heinecke, Editor
Paul Mackler, CEO
Chuck Cummings, Sales Manager
Circulation: 57000
Founded in 1966

15467 Law Enforcement Technology

Cygnus Publishing
PO Box 803
Fort Atkinson, WI 53538-0803

920-000-1111
FAX 920-563-1699
E-Mail: Patrick.Bernardo@cygnuspub.com
Home Page: www.cygnusb2b.com

John French, CEO
Scott Cravens, Circulation Director
Gordon Gavin, VP
Ronnie Garrett, Editor
Kathy Scott, Director of Public Relations

Covers the innovative products and technology available to the law enforcement manager. Accepts advertising.
64 Pages
Frequency: Monthly
Circulation: 30,000
Founded in 1966

15468 Law and Order

Hendon
130 Waukegan Rd
Deerfield, IL 60015-4912

847-444-3300
800-843-9764
FAX 847-444-3333
E-Mail: info@hendonpub.com
Home Page: hendonpub.com

Henry Kingwill, Owner
Bruce Cameron, Editor
Pete Kingwill, National Director
Yesenia Salcedo, Managing Editor
Tim Davis, Graphic Designer

Tailored to the law enforcement officer, the magazine updates professionals on trends, covers new methods and incorporates articles with special focuses.
Cost: $24.00
100 Pages
Frequency: Monthly
Circulation: 32304
Founded in 1953

15469 Materials Evaluation

American Society for Nondestructive Testing
PO box 28518
1711 Arlingate Lane
Columbus, OH 43228-518

614-274-6003
800-222-2768
FAX 614-274-6899
Home Page: www.asnt.org

Paul McIntire, Publication Manager
Betsy Blazar, Marketing Manager
Wayne Holliday, Executive Director
Shelby Reeves, Owner

Research, reviews and information of nondestructive testing materials. Provides members and subscribers the latest news and technical information concerning this industry.
Frequency: Monthly
Circulation: 10200
Founded in 1941

15470 National Fire Protection Association Newsletter

1 Batterymarch Park
Quincy, MA 02169-7471

617-770-3000
800-344-3555
FAX 617-770-0700
E-Mail: custserv@nfpa.org
Home Page: www.nfpa.org

James M. Shannon, President/CEO
Peg O'Brien, Administrator - Public Affairs
Lorraine VP - Communications, Executive Director
Bruce Mullen, CFO
Paul Crossman, VP, Marketing

Written for various fire safety professionals and covers major topics in fire protection and suppression. The Journal carries investigation reports written by NFPA specialists, special NFPA statistical studies on large-loss fires, multiple deaths, fire fighter deaths and injuries, and others annually. Articles on fire protection advances, public education and information of interest to NFPA members.
Cost: $135.00
70000 Members
Circulation: 85000
Founded in 1896

15471 Peace Officer

Dale Corporation
22150 W 9 Mile Road
Southfield, MI 48034

248-204-2244
FAX 248-204-2240
Home Page: www.salesdoctors.com

Dale Jabolonski, President

Covers areas of interest to law enforcement personnel.
Cost: $12.00
40 Pages
Founded in 1958

15472 Perspectives Journal

American Probation and Parole Association
PO Box 11910
Lexington, KY 40578-1910

859-244-8203
FAX 859-244-8001
E-Mail: appa@csg.org
Home Page: www.appa-net.org
Social Media: *Facebook, Twitter, LinkedIn*

Carl Wicklund, Executive Director
Barbara Broderick, President
Diane Kincaid, Deputy Director
Carrie Abner, Research Associate
John Higgins, Graphic Designer

Mailing list includes mailing addresses only, no email
Frequency: Quarterly
Circulation: 2200
Mailing list available for rent: 2200 names

15473 Police

Bobit Publishing Company
3520 Challenger St
Torrance, CA 90503-1640

310-533-2400
FAX 310-533-2500
E-Mail: webmaster@bobit.com
Home Page: www.bobit.com

Edward J Bobit, CEO

The law officer's magazine. Accepts advertising.
Cost: $35.00
104 Pages
Frequency: Monthly
Circulation: 50000
Founded in 1961

15474 Police Chief
International Association of Chiefs of Police
515 N Washington St
Alexandria, VA 22314-2340

703-836-6767
800-843-4227
FAX 703-836-4543
E-Mail: information@theiacp.org
Home Page: www.theiacp.org
Social Media: *Facebook, Twitter, RSS, Youtube*

Dan Rosenblatt, Executive Director
Mark L. Whitman, Chair Commissioner

A monthly magazine published by the International Association of Chiefs of Police.
Cost: $25.00
80 Pages
Frequency: Monthly
Circulation: 21300
Founded in 1893
Mailing list available for rent

15475 Police Times
American Federation of Police & Concerned Citizens
6350 Horizon Drive
Titusville, FL 32780

321-264-0911
FAX 321-573-9819
E-Mail: policeinfo@aphf.org
Home Page: www.aphf.org
Social Media: *Facebook*

Barry Shepard, Executive Director
Deputy Dennis Wise, National President
Debra Chitwood, CEO
Brent Shephard, Director of Operations

Quarterly publication focusing on law enforcement, security and police survivors.
Circulation: 31,000
Founded in 1978

15476 Public Safety Communications/APCO Bulletin
Assn of Public Safety Communication Officials
351 N Williamson Boulevard
Daytona Beach, FL 32114-1112

386-322-2500
888-272-6911
FAX 386-322-2501
E-Mail: apco@apcointl.org
Home Page:
www.apcointl.org/services/publications/

Toni Edwards, Editor
George S Rice Jr, President
Susan Stowell, Member Services Director
Garry Mendez, Marketing/Communications Director
Robert Gurss Esq., Legal/Government Affairs Director

The world's oldest and largest professional organization dedicated to the enhancement of public safety communications and to serving its more than 15,000 members, the people who use public safety communications systems and services.
Cost: $12.00
Frequency: Monthly
Circulation: 13000
ISSN: 1526-1646
Founded in 1935

15477 Public Safety Product News
Cygnus Publishing
PO Box 803
Fort Atkinson, WI 53538-0803

920-000-1111
800-547-7377
FAX 920-563-1699

E-Mail: Patrick.Bernardo@cygnusB2B.com
Home Page: www.cygnusb2b.com

John French, CEO
Sharon Haberkorn, Development Manager
Ronnie Garrett, Editor-in-Chief
Kathy Scott, Director of Public Relations
Paul Bonaiuto, CFO
Frequency: Monthly

15478 Sheriff
National Sheriff's Association
1450 Duke St
Alexandria, VA 22314-3490

703-836-7827
800-424-7827
FAX 703-836-6541
E-Mail: nsamail@sheriffs.org
Home Page: www.sheriffs.org

Suzanne Kitts, Editor
Aaron Kennard, President
Thomas N Faust, Executive Director

Published for the law enforcement official.
Cost: $25.00
Circulation: 20,000
Founded in 1948

15479 Tactical Edge
National Tactical Officers Association
PO Box 797
Doylestown, PA 18901

215-230-7616
800-279-9127
FAX 215-230-7552
E-Mail: membership@ntoa.org
Home Page: www.ntoa.org
Social Media: *Facebook, Twitter, LinkedIn, Google+, Blogger, Bloggy, Pint*

Phil Hansen, Board Chairman
Jim Torkar, Treasurer
Bob Chabali, Secretary
Mark Lomax, Executive Director
Rob Cartner, Director of Training
Cost: $40.00
Frequency: Quarterly
Circulation: 12000
Mailing list available for rent

15480 Today's Policeman
Towerhigh Productions
PO Box 875108
Los Angeles, CA 90087-208

Donald Mack, President

General philosophy of the police services.
Cost: $9.00
40 Pages
Founded in 1961

Trade Shows

15481 ACFSA International Conference
American Correctional Food Service Affiliates
210 N Glenoaks Blvd
Suite C
Burbank, CA 91502

818-843-6608
FAX 818-843-7423
E-Mail: jonnichols@acfsa.org
Home Page: www.acfsa.org

Jon Nichols, Executive Director
150 Attendees
Frequency: Annual/August
Founded in 1969

15482 APCO Annual Conference & Expo
351 N Williamson Boulevard
Daytona Beach, FL 32114-1112

386-322-2500
888-272-6911
FAX 386-322-2501
E-Mail: apco@apcointl.org
Home Page: www.apcointl.org/

Barbara Myers, Director Conference Services
Casey Epton Roush, Conference/Meeting Services Manager
Brigid Blaschak, Tradeshow Manager
Patricia Giannini, Senior Meeting Coordinator
Garry Mendez, Marketing/Communications Director

APCO's Annual Conference and Exposition brings together more than 300 vendors to provide hands-on demonstrations of new technologies you might use in your agency or call centers. The Conference also offers sessions on personal and professional development and a variety of technical skills. Banquet, breakfast and exhibitors of radio, computer, and supporting equipment companies.
6000 Attendees
Frequency: Annual
Founded in 1935

15483 Academy of Criminal Justice Sciences Annual Meeting
Academy of Criminal Justice Sciences
7339 Hanover Parkway
Suite A
Greenbelt, MD 20770

301-446-6300
800-757-2257
FAX 301-446-2819
E-Mail: info@acjs.org
Home Page: www.acjs.org

Mittie Southerland, Executive Director
Cathy Barth, Association Manager
Craig Hemmens, President
James Frank, 1st Vice President
David F. Owens, Treasurer

Criminal justice educators, researchers, practicioners, students and the general public visit 45 exhibits and seminars.
2000 Attendees
Frequency: Annual
Founded in 1963

15484 Airborne Law Enforcement Annual Conference & Expo
Airborne Law Enforcement Association
50 Carroll Creek Way
Suite 260
Frederick, MD 21701-4786

301-631-2406
FAX 301-631-2466
Home Page: www.alea.org

Steven Ingley, Executive Director
Kevin R. Caffery, VP
Nicole Gentile, Operations Manager
Keith Johnson, Safety Program Director
Carrie Cosens, Membership Manager

Containing 157 booths.
1100 Attendees
Frequency: July
Founded in 1968

15485 American Academy of Forensic Sciences Annual Meeting
American Academy of Forensic Sciences
410 N 21st St
Colorado Springs, CO 80904-2712

719-636-1100
FAX 719-636-1993

E-Mail: awarren@aafs.org
Home Page: www.aafs.org

Nancy Jackson, Director Development
Anne Warren, Executive Director
Sondra Bynoe-Doolittle, Assistant Meetings Manager
Addie Arellano, Meetings/Exposition Assistant
Anne Warren, Executive Director

Professionals in the forensic science field attend meeting and see 120 exhibits of scientific instruments.
2300 Attendees
Frequency: Annual,February
Mailing list available for rent

15486 American Correctional Association Congress
206 N Washington St
Suite 200
Alexandria, VA 22314

703-224-0000
800-222-5646
FAX 703-224-0179
E-Mail: pres@aca.org
Home Page: www.aca.org

Daron Hall, President
James Gondles Jr, Executive Director
Jeff Washington, Deputy Executive Director

Five hundred booths featuring association whose membership is concerned with correctional services.
3900 Attendees
Mailing list available for rent

15487 American Correctional Association Winter Conference
206 N Washington St
Suite 200
Alexandria, VA 22314

703-224-0000
800-222-5646
FAX 703-224-0179
E-Mail: pres@aca.org
Home Page: www.aca.org

James Gondles Jr, Executive Director
Daron Hall, President
Jeff Washington, Deputy Executive Director

Three hundred and fifty booths.
3M Attendees
Frequency: January
Founded in 1935
Mailing list available for rent

15488 American Criminal Justice Association National Conference
American Criminal Justice Association
PO Box 601047
Sacramento, CA 95860-1047

916-484-6553
FAX 916-488-2227
E-Mail: acjalae@aol.com
Home Page: www.acjalae.org

Joe Davenport, President
Karen Campbell, Executive Secretary
Abby Schofield, Region 1 President
Preston Koelling, Vice-President

Business meetings, awards, competitions, job fairs, physical agility competitions, safety meetings and crime scene competitions.
7200 Members
Founded in 1937

15489 American Jail Association Training Conference & Jail Expo
1135 Professional Court
Hagerstown, MD 21740

301-790-3930
FAX 301-790-2941
E-Mail: dorothyd@aja.org

Home Page: www.aja.org
Social Media: *Facebook*

Dorothy Drass, Marketing Director
Holly Nicarry, Assistant Marketing Director
Robert J. Kasabian, Executive Director
Patty Vermillion, Training Coordinator
Leslie Brozna, Marketing and Sales Coordinator

Brings together more than 2,200 participants from around the world and over 275 companies who provide products and services to jails.
2200 Attendees
Frequency: May
Founded in 1981

15490 American Society of Criminology Show
1314 Kinnear Road
Columbus, OH 43212

614-292-9207
FAX 614-292-6767
E-Mail: webmaster@asc41.com
Home Page: www.asc41.com

Bonnie Fisher, Treasurer

Twenty-five tables.
1.5M Attendees
Frequency: October

15491 Convention & Traffic Expo
American Traffic Safety Services Association
15 Riverside Parkway
Suite 100
Fredericksburg, VA 22406-1022

540-368-1701
800-272-8772
FAX 540-368-1717
Home Page: www.atssa.com

Douglas Danko, Chairman

The premier meeting place for roadway professionals around the world. The program and exhibits are dedicated to issues and products related to all aspects of temporary traffic control and roadway safety.
Frequency: Annual/February
Mailing list available for rent

15492 FBINAA Conference
FBI National Academy Associates
422 Garrisonville Road
Suite 103
Stafford, VA 22554

540-628-0834
FAX 703-632-1993
E-Mail: info@fbinaa.org
Home Page: www.fbinaa.org

Timothy D Overton, National President
Steve Tidwell, Executive Director
Rhonda Stites, Administrative Assistant
Becky Storm, Business Manager
Nell Cochran, Financial Manager
Frequency: July
Mailing list available for rent

15493 FEMSA Annual Meeting
Fire and Emergency Manufacturers and Services Asso
PO Box 147
Lynnfield, MA 01940-0147

781-334-2771
FAX 781-334-2771
E-Mail: info@femsa.org
Home Page: www.femsa.org
Social Media: *Twitter, LinkedIn*

Dan Reese, President
William Lawson, VP

Works to strengthen its membership, planning for future development, and directing programs that build industry opportunities
100+ Attendees
Frequency: Fall

15494 GovSec: The Govenment Security Conference & Expo
1105 Media
9201 Oakdale Avenue
Suite 101
Chatsworth, CA 91311

818-734-5200
FAX 818-734-1522
E-Mail: info@1105media.com
Home Page: www.1105media.com

Jules Gagne, Exhibits & Sponsorships
Deborah Lovell, Conference Program
Brad Wills, Press & Media
Neal Vitale, President & Chief Executive Officer
Richard Vitale, Senior Vice President & CFO

GovSec is the premier government security conference & expo that has joined forces with the Contingency Planning & Management Network (Centric Security) and U.S. Law Enforcement Conferences, to strengthen its focus on critical infrastructure protection, cybercrime and cyberterrorism, counterterrorism and homeland security. Washington Convention Center, Washington, DC.
Frequency: Annual/April
Founded in 2001

15495 Int'l Assn of Campus Law Enforcement Administrators Annual Conference
International Assn of Campus Law Enforcement Admin
342 North Main Street
West Hartford, CT 06117-2507

860-586-7522
FAX 860-586-7550
E-Mail: info@iaclea.org
Home Page: www.iaclea.org

Pamela Hayes, Exhibitor Contact
Peter Berry, Executive Director

Offers members an opportunity to attend informative programs to learn more about current issues and developments in campus public safety, network with peers, visit exhibitor booths, and enjoy special events.
Frequency: Annual

15496 International Association of Chiefs of Police Annual Conference
International Association of Chiefs of Police
515 N Washington Street
Alexandria, VA 22314-2357

703-836-6767
800-843-4227
FAX 703-836-4543
E-Mail: information@theiacp.org
Home Page: www.theiacp.org
Social Media: *Facebook, Twitter, RSS, Youtube*

Lia Muwwakkil, Exhibits & Conferences
Colleen Phalen, Exhibits & Sponsorships
Dan Rosenblatt, Executive Director

Enables professionals to examine the state of the police industry through highly rated seminars, forums, and technical workshops. Only open to IACP members and their guests.
Frequency: Annual,September
Mailing list available for rent

15497 National Education & Training Conference
National Black Police Association

3100 Main Street
#256
Dallas, TX 75226

855-879-6272
FAX 202-986-0410
Home Page: www.blackpolice.org

Ronald Hampton, Executive Director
Malik Aziz, Chairperson
Walter L Holloway, Vice Chairperson
Sherri Lockett, Secretary
Donna Ross, Fiscal Officer
400 Attendees
Frequency: Annual

15498 National Forensic League
125 Watson Street
PO Box 38
Ripon, WI 54971

920-748-6206
FAX 920-748-9478
E-Mail: nflcustomerservice@nflonline.org
Home Page: www.nflonline.org

Diane Rasmussen, Associate Secretary
J Scott, Executive Director
Ten booths.
2.8M Attendees
Frequency: June

15499 National Sheriff's Association
1450 Duke Street
Alexandria, VA 22314-3490

703-836-7827
800-424-7827
E-Mail: kbright@sheriffs.org
Home Page: www.sheriffs.org

Kimberly Bright, Director, Marketing & Exhibits
Thomas Faust, Executive Director
More than 500 exhibits.
3M Attendees
Frequency: June

15500 Tactical Operations Conference
National Tactical Officers Association
PO Box 797
Doylestown, PA 18901

215-230-7616
800-279-9127
FAX 215-230-7552
E-Mail: membership@ntoa.org
Home Page: www.ntoa.org
Social Media: *Facebook, Twitter, LinkedIn, Google+, Blogger, Bloggy, Pint*

Mark Lomax, Executive Director
Laura Gerhart, Conference Coordinator
Rob Cartner, Director of Training
Mary Heins, Editor
Michelle Griffin, Assistant Editor
1000 Attendees
Frequency: September
Mailing list available for rent

Directories & Databases

15501 American Academy of Forensic Sciences Membership Directory
410 N 21st St
Colorado Spring, CO 80904-2712

719-636-1100
FAX 719-636-1993
E-Mail: awarren@aafs.org
Home Page: www.aafs.org

Anne Warren, Executive Director
Offers valuable information on over 5,000 persons qualified in forensic sciences including

law, anthropology and psychiatry.
Cost: $50.00
250 Pages
Frequency: Annual

15502 Directory of Law Enforcement and Criminal
Law Enforcement Standards Office
US National Institute of Standards
100 Bureau Drive M/S 8102
Gaithersburg, MD 20899-8102

301-975-2757
FAX 301-948-0978
Marilyn Leach, Editor
Ruth Joel, Editor
More than 200 local, national and international organizations involved in the fields of law enforcement, corrections, forensic science and criminal justice in the US.

15503 Fire Chief: Equipment and Apparatus Directory Issue
Primedia
1300 E 9th St
Cleveland, OH 44114-1503

216-696-7000
FAX 216-696-6662
Home Page: www.penton.com

Eric Jacobson, Senior VP
Jane Cooper, Marketing
David Kieselstein, Chief Executive Officer
Kurt Nelson, Vice President, Human Resources
Andrew Schmolka, Senior Vice President
List of approximately 1,000 suppliers of fire protection equipment, including ladder trucks, protective clothing, alarms, alternators and others.
Cost: $10.00
Frequency: Monthly
Circulation: 52901
Mailing list available for rent

15504 Grey House Homeland Security Directory
Grey House Publishing
4919 Route 22
PO Box 56
Amenia, NY 12501

518-789-8700
800-562-2139
FAX 845-373-6390
E-Mail: books@greyhouse.com
Home Page: www.greyhouse.com
Social Media: *Facebook, Twitter*

Leslie Mackenzie, Publisher
Richard Gottlieb, Editor
Features the latest contact information for government and private organizations involved with Homeland Security along with the latest product information. The directory provides detailed profiles of nearly 1,500 Federal & State Organizations & Agencies and over 3,000 Officials and Key Executives involved with Homeland Security.
Cost: $195.00
800 Pages
ISBN: 1-592370-75-6
Founded in 1981

15505 Grey House Homeland Security Directory - Online Database
Grey House Publishing
4919 Route 22
PO Box 56
Amenia, NY 12501-0056

518-789-8700
800-562-2139
FAX 518-789-0556
E-Mail: gold@greyhouse.com

Home Page: www.gold.greyhouse.com
Social Media: *Facebook, Twitter*

Leslie Mackenzie, Publisher
Richard Gottlieb, President
This comprehensive database presents a wide range of information that is scattered and hard to find elsewhere, providing subscribers with access to the most comprehensive, up-to-date and detailed information on the nation's homeland security contacts and services. This online database contains over 1,100 profiles of Federal and State agencies and companies along with the names of 11,000 key contacts.
Founded in 1981

15506 Grey House Safety & Security Directory
Grey House Publishing
4919 Route 22
PO Box 56
Amenia, NY 12501

518-789-8700
800-562-2139
FAX 845-373-6390
E-Mail: books@greyhouse.com
Home Page: www.greyhouse.com
Social Media: *Facebook, Twitter*

Leslie Mackenzie, Publisher
Richard Gottlieb, Editor
Comprehensive resource guide to the safety and security industry, including articles, checklists, OSHA regulations and product listings. Focuses on creating and maintaing a safe and secure enviroment, and dealing specifically with hazardous materials, noise and vibration, workplace preparation and maintenance, electrical and lighting safety, fire and rescue and more.
Cost: $165.00
1600 Pages
ISBN: 1-592373-75-5
Founded in 1981

15507 Law Enforcement Technology Directory
Hendon
130 Waukegan Rd
Deerfield, IL 60015-4912

847-444-3300
800-843-9764
FAX 847-444-3333
E-Mail: info@hendonpub.com
Home Page: www.lawandordermag.com

Henry Kingwill, Owner
Directory of manufacturers and suppliers of one type of law enforcement equipment such as computers, weapons, training, surveillance, forensics and radio and communications equipment.
Cost: $60.00
Frequency: Annual December

15508 Law and Order Magazine: Police Management Buyer's Guide Issue
Hendon
130 Waukegan Rd
2nd Floor
Deerfield, IL 60015-4912

847-444-3300
800-843-9764
FAX 847-444-3333
E-Mail: esanow@hendonpub.com
Home Page: www.hendonpub.com

Henry Kingwill, Owner
Jennifer Gavigan, Managing Editor
Yesenia Salcedo, Managing Editor
Tim Davis, Graphic Designer
Marilou Go, Office Manager
Monthly publication for police managers, covering all aspects of law enforcement including a list of manufacturers, dealers and distributors

of products and services for police departments.
Cost: $15.00
Frequency: Annual February

15509 National Directory of Law Enforcement Administrators Correctional Inst
National Public Safety Information Bureau
PO Box 365
Stevens Point, WI 54481

715-345-2772
800-647-7579
FAX 715-345-7288
E-Mail: info@safetysource.com
Home Page: www.safetysource.com

Steve Cywinski, Publisher
John Diser, Account Manager
Christina Scott, Business Development Manager

Listing of police departments, sheriffs, criminal prosecutors, state law enforcement, criminal investigation agencies, federal law enforcement and homeland security.
Cost: $129.00
924 Pages
Frequency: Annual, paperback
Circulation: 9,000
ISBN: 1-880245-22-1
ISSN: 1066-5595
Founded in 1964

15510 National Employment Listing Service Bulletin
Criminal Justice Center
Sam Houston State University
1803 Avenue I
Huntsville, TX 77341

936-295-6371

Kay Billingsley, Editor

Job openings in police departments, sheriff's departments, courts and other law enforcement and security agencies.

15511 Police: Buyer's Guide Issue
Bobit Publishing Company
23210 Crenshaw Blvd
Torrance, CA 90505-3181

310-539-1969
FAX 310-539-4329
E-Mail: police@bobit.com

John Bebout, Owner

List of suppliers of police products and services.
Cost: $10.00
Frequency: Annual August

15512 Transportation Security Directory & Handbook
Grey House Publishing
4919 Route 22
PO Box 56
Amenia, NY 12501

518-789-8700
800-562-2139
FAX 845-373-6390
E-Mail: books@greyhouse.com
Home Page: www.greyhouse.com
Social Media: *Facebook, Twitter*

Leslie Mackenzie, Publisher
Richard Gottlieb, Editor

Provides information on everything from Regulatory Authorities to Security Enforcement, this top-flight directory brings together the relevant information necessary for creating and maintaining a security plan for a wide range of

transportation facilities.
Cost: $195.00
800 Pages
ISBN: 1-592370-75-6
Founded in 1981

15513 Who's Who in Jail Management Jail Directory
American Jail Association
1135 Professional Ct
Hagerstown, MD 21740-5853

301-790-3930
FAX 301-790-2941
Home Page: www.aja.org

Gwyn Smith-Ingley, Executive Director
Kelton Chapman, Manager
Sheryl Ebersole, Business Manager
Connie Lacy, Director

Offers the most current information available on local jails in the US. Also offers an up-to-date listing of all the jails in the US that is available for rent electronically and a valuable resource for sheriffs, jail administrators and vendors.
Cost: $85.00

Industry Web Sites

15514 http://gold.greyhouse.com
G.O.L.D Grey House OnLine Databases
Grey House Publishing's online database platform, GOLD, offers Quick Search, Keyword Search and Expert Search for most business sectors including law enforcement and public safety markets. The GOLD platform makes finding the information you need quick and easy - whether you're a novice searcher or an experienced database user. All of Grey House's directory products are available for subscription on the GOLD platform.

15515 www.aamva.org
American Assn. of Motor Vehicle Administrators
Nonprofit organization represents state and provincial officials in the US and Canada who administer and enforce motor vehicle laws. Strives to develop model programs in motor vehicle administration, police traffic services and highway safety.

15516 www.aca.org
American Correctional Association
This organization offers information on the correctional field.

15517 www.alea.org
Airborne Law Enforcement Association
Members are law enforcement officers who use both fixed and rotary wing air craft, in law enforcement, and equipment suppliers.

15518 www.apco911.org
Association of Public-Safety Communications
Officials International

The world's oldest and largest professional organization dedicated to the enhancement of public safety communications and to serving its more than 15,000 members, the people who use public safety communications systems and services.

15519 www.aphf.org
American Police Hall of Fame
Offers benefits, and various types of awards to members, magazine, line of duty death benefits, film and training library as well as support ser-

vices, scholarships and financial assistance for police family survivors.

15520 www.atssa.org
American Traffic Safety Services Association
Promotes uniform use of lights, signs, pavement markings and barricades. Distributes technical information and sponsors training courses for worksite traffic supervisors.

15521 www.blr.com
Business & Legal Reports
Provides essential tools for safety and environmental compliance and training needs

15522 www.corrections.com/
Corrections Professionals
Information about events, careers, news, legal happenings and newsletters.

15523 www.dpsoa.com
Texas Department of Public Safety Officer's Association

15524 www.fema.gov
Federal Emergency Management Agency.

15525 www.femsa.org
Fire and Emergency Manufacturers and Services Asso
The leading trade association for the fire and emergency services industry whose members provides products and services to millions of fire and EMS professionals throughout the world.

15526 www.footprinter.org
International Footprint Association

15527 www.fssa.net
Fire Suppression Systems Association
Designers, suppliers and installers of special hazard fire suppression equipment, gases and detectors.

15528 www.greyhouse.com
Grey House Publishing
Authoritative reference directories for most business sectors including law enforcement and public safety markets. Users can search the online databases with varied search criteria allowing for custom searches by product category, geographic area, sales volume, keyword, subject and more. Full Grey House catalog and online ordering also available.

15529 www.highwaysafety.org
Insurance Institute for Highway Safety
Traffic and motor vehicle safety organization supported by auto insurers.

15530 www.home.xnet.com/~lelp
Law Enforcement Legal Publications
Publication for law enforcement, legal professional and law libraries.

15531 www.iaati.org
International Association of Auto Theft Investigators

Provides members who are auto theft investigators with resources to develop and maintain professional standards within the industry.

15532 www.iawp.org
International Association of Women Police
To strengthen, unite and raise the profile of women in criminal justice internationally.

15533 www.ncpc.org
National Crime Prevention Council

15534 www.neoa.org
Narcotic Enforcement Officers Association

A non-profit educational organization of more than a thousand law enforcement personnel and others in the criminal justicce system, includin state and local police, D.E.A., F.B.I. and customs.

15535 www.nist.gov/oles/
Law Enforcement Standards Office

15536 www.ntoa.org
National Tactical Officers Association

Enhance the performance and professional status of law enforcement personnel by providing a credible and proven training resource as well as a forum for the development of tactics and information exchange.

15537 www.policeforum.org
Police Executive Research Forum

For chief executives of city, county and state police agencies.

15538 www.polygraph.org
American Polygraph Association

A merger of Academy of Scientific Interrogation, American Academy of Polygraph Examiners and National Board of Polygraph examiners.

15539 www.psa.com
Production Services Associates,Inc.

Dealers and dealer banks who underwrite and trade federal, state and local government securities and mortgage-backed securities.

15540 www.sheriffs.org
National Sherriff's Association

Devoted to helping sheriffs and other law enforcers to execute their duties most effectively and professionally.

15541 www.theiacp.org
International Association of Chiefs of Police

Organization that focuses on topics of interest to professional law enforcers.

15542 www.toxicology.org
Society of Toxicology

Members are scientists concerned with the effects of chemicals on man and the environment. Promotes the aquisition and utilization of knowledge in toxicology, aids in the protection of public health and facilitates disiplines. The society has a strong commitment to education in toxicology and to the recruitment of students and new members into the profession.

Associations

15543 American Leather Chemists Association
1314 50th Street
Suite 103
Lubbock, TX 79412

806-744-1798
FAX 806-744-1785
E-Mail: alca@leatherchemists.org
Home Page: www.leatherchemists.org

Steve Lange, President
Sarah Drayna, Vice President
Robert F. White, JALCA Editor
Carol Adcock, Executive Secretary

Group of leather chemists who are interested in the development of methods that could be utilized to standardize both the supply and application of the tanning agents utilized by the industry.
500 Members
Founded in 1903
Mailing list available for rent

15544 American Saddle Makers Association
12155 Donovan Lane
Black Forest, CO 80908

729-494-2848
E-Mail: info@saddlemakers.org
Home Page: www.saddlemakers.org

Cheryl Rifkin, President
Bob Brenner, Executive Director
Steve Bowen, Director of Membership

Representing manufacturers of Western and English saddles in the US.

15545 International Federation Leather Guild
2264 Logan Drive
New Palestine, IN 46163

317-691-0321
E-Mail: eddjanlucas@sbcglobal.net
Home Page: www.ifolg.org

David Smith, Executive Director
Alex Madson, Assistant Director
Carol Higgins, Secretary
Monica Nibbes, Treasurer
Roger Bligan, Web Master

Supports all leather craftsmen via education, training, publications and trade shows.

15546 Leather Apparel Association
19 W 21st Street
Suite 403
New York, NY 10010

212-727-1210
FAX 212-727-1218
E-Mail: info@leatherassociation.com
Home Page: www.leatherassociation.com

Morris Goldfarb, President
Richard Harrow, Executive Director

Represents the nation's leading leather retailers, manufacturers, cleaners and other businesses in promoting leather apparel in the US.
Founded in 1990

15547 Leather Industries of America
3050 K St NW
Suite 400
Washington, DC 20007-5100

202-342-8497
FAX 202-342-8583
E-Mail: info@leatherusa.com
Home Page: www.leatherusa.com

John Wittenborn, President
John M. Pike, Executive Director

A trade association representing the leather industry: tanners; chemical suppliers; hide, skin and leather suppliers; and product manufacturers. Provides environmental, technical, educational, statistical, and marketing services.
Founded in 1917

15548 Leathercraft Guild
9108 Garvey Ave
Rosemead, CA 91770

Home Page: www.theleathercraftguild.com
Social Media: *Facebook, Twitter, Myspace*

Preserves and promotes the art of leather carving and stamping. Seeks to improve skills of members, raise standards of crafts and promote the product.
200 Members
Founded in 1949

15549 National Shoe Retailers Association
7386 N. La Cholla Blvd.
Suite G
Tucson, AZ 85741

520-209-1710
800-673-8446
FAX 410-381-1167
E-Mail: info@nsra.org
Home Page: www.nsra.org
Social Media: *Facebook, Twitter, LinkedIn, Pinterest, Google Plus*

Rick Ravel, Board Chairman
Lenny Comeras, Vice Chairman
Jeff Greenberg, Vice Chairman
Chuck Schuyler, President
Tanja Towne, Membership Director

Membership association for independent shoe ratailers. Provides business services such as credit-card processing and shipping at special low members only prices. Also provides educational and training programs, consulting and other services.
63 Members
Founded in 1912

15550 Pedorthic Footwear Association
1610 East Forsyth Street
Suite D
Americus, GA 31709

229-389-3440
703-995-4456
FAX 888-563-0945
E-Mail: info@pedorthics.org
Home Page: www.pedorthics.org
Social Media: *Facebook, Twitter, LinkedIn, Google+, Blogger, Bloggy, Pint*

Rob Sobel, C. Ped., President
Dean Mason, Vice President
Matt Almeida, Secretary
Christopher J. Costantini, C. Ped., Treasurer
Rebecca Fazzari, Meeting and Convention Manager

Membership organization for individuals and companies involved in the design, manufacture, modification and fit of therapeutic footwear. Provides educational programs, publications, legislative monitoring, marketing materials, professional liason and business operations services.
Cost: $55.00
2000 Members
Founded in 1958

15551 Proleptic, Inc.
PO Box 17817
Asheville, NC 28816

828-505-8474
FAX 828-505-8476
E-Mail: shoptalk@proleptic.net
Home Page: www.proleptic.net
Social Media: *Facebook*

Daniel S Preston, PhD, Director

A Comprehensive Source for Sewing Machines, Leather working Equipment, Supplies, Tools, Horse Healthcare and Finished Products Repair Shops Retailers, Crafters, Collectors.
320 Members
Founded in 1984

15552 Sponge and Chamois Institute
10024 Office Center Ave
Suite 203
Saint Louis, MO 63128

314-842-2230
FAX 314-842-3999
E-Mail: scwaters@swbell.net
Home Page: www.chamoisinstitute.org

Members are suppliers and dealers of natural sponges and chamois leather.

15553 Travel Goods Association
301 North Harrison Street
#412
Princeton, NJ 08540-3512

609-720-1200
FAX 877-842-1938
E-Mail: info@travel-goods.org
Home Page: www.travel-goods.org
Social Media: *Facebook, Twitter, LinkedIn, YouTube*

Michele Marini Pittenger, President/CEO
Rob Holmes, Vice President/ CFO
Kim Wong, Creative Director
Kate Ryan, Media Relations
Nate Herman, Director, Government Relations

Trade association that represents manufacturers of luggage, business and computer cases,handbags and accessories. Formerly the Luggage and Leather Goods Association.
450 Members
Founded in 1938
Mailing list available for rent

15554 Western-English Trade Association
451 East 58th Avenue
Suite 4323
Denver, CO 80216-8468

303-295-2001
FAX 303-295-6108
E-Mail: weta@netway.net
Home Page: www.wetaonline.org

Glenda Chipps, Executive Director

Members are manufacturers and retailers of western and english style riding equipment and clothes.
158 Members
Founded in 1963

Newsletters

15555 Leather Conservation News
Minnesota Historical Society
345 Kellogg Blvd W
St Paul, MN 55102-1906

651-259-3000
FAX 651-296-1004
E-Mail: webmaster@mnhs.org
Home Page: www.mnhs.org

Nina Archabal, Executive Director
Jackie Swanson, Secretary
Sue Leas, Executive Assistant

Research and advancements in the specialty of leather conservation and preservation; articles on materials science research and treatments; news of conferences and workshops.
Cost: $15.00
24 Pages
Frequency: 2 per year
Circulation: 250

ISSN: 0898-0128
Printed in on matte stock

15556 Leather Facts
US Hide, Skin & Leather Association
1700 N Moore Street
Suite 1600
Arlington, VA 22209

703-841-2400
FAX 703-527-0938
E-Mail: jreddington@meatami.com
Home Page: www.meatami.com

John Reddington, President
Association news covering the leather and hide industry.

15557 Leather International

Home Page: www.leathermag.com

Carl Friedmann, Editor
In-depth coverage of every aspect of the international leather industry.

Magazines & Journals

15558 Journal of the American Leather Chemists Association (JALCA)
American Leather Chemists Association
1314 50th Street
Suite 103
Lubbock, TX 79412

806-744-1798
FAX 806-744-1785
E-Mail: alca@leatherchemists.org
Home Page: www.leatherchemists.org

Carol Adcock, Executive Secretary
Robert F. White, Editor
Steven Gilberg, President
Steve Lange, Vice President
Cost: $175.00
Frequency: Monthly
Circulation: 500
Founded in 1903
Mailing list available for rent

15559 Leather Crafters & Saddlers Journal
222 Blackburn St
Rhinelander, WI 54501

715-362-5393
888-289-6409
FAX 715-362-5391
E-Mail: journal@newnorth.net
Home Page: www.leathercraftersjournal.com
Social Media: *Facebook*

Dot Reis, Editor
Publication for leather workers. Sponsors several trade shows throughout the year which attract vendors of leather, tools, equipment and supplies.
Cost: $32.00
Frequency: Bi-Monthly
Circulation: 6000
ISSN: 1082-4480

15560 Travel Goods Showcase
Travel Goods Association
301 North Harrison St.
Suite 412
Princeton, NJ 08540-3512

877-842-1938
FAX 877-842-1938
Home Page:
travel-goods.org/travel-goods-showcase
Social Media: *Facebook, Twitter, LinkedIn, YouTube*

Michele Marini Pittenger, Editor-in-chief
Founded in 1975

Trade Shows

15561 ALCA Annual Meeting
American Leather Chemists Association
1314 50th Street
Suite 103
Lubbock, TX 79412

806-744-1798
FAX 806-744-1785
E-Mail: alca@leatherchemists.org
Home Page: www.leatherchemists.org

Carol Adcock, Executive Secretary
Robert F. White, Editor
Steven Gilberg, President
Steve Lange, Vice President
100 Attendees
Mailing list available for rent

15562 International Federation Leather Guild Trade Show
748 NW Wood Street
Burleson, TX 76028-2619

817-478-2335

Ernie Wayman, Executive Director
Open exhibition of leather craftsmen.
400 Attendees

15563 Leather Allied Trade Show
2214 S Brentwood Boulevard
Saint Louis, MO 63144-1804

314-961-2829

Virginia Breen, Secretary
Exhibition of leathers and components.
2.1M Attendees
Frequency: February

15564 PFA Annual Symposium & Exhibition
Pedorthic Footwear Association
1610 E Forsyth St.
Suite D
Americus, GA 31709

229-389-3440
FAX 888-563-0945
E-Mail: pedorthicsusa@gmail.com
Home Page: www.pedorthics.org
Social Media: *Facebook, Twitter, LinkedIn*

Robert Sobel, President
One hundred fifty booths plus educational sessions regarding the design, manufacture or modification and fit of shoes and foot orthoses to alleviate foot problems caused by disease, congenital condition, overuse or injury.
1000 Attendees
Frequency: November

15565 The International Travel Goods Show
Travel Goods Association
301 North Harrison St.
Suite 412
Princeton, NJ 08540-3512

877-842-1938
FAX 877-842-1938
Home Page: www.thetravelgoodsshow.org

Michele Marini Pittenger, President/CEO
Cathy Hays, VP/Trade Show

Directories & Databases

15566 Complete Directory of Leather Goods & Luggage
Sutton Family Communications & Publishing Company

920 State Route 54 East
Elmitch, KY 42343

270-276-9500
E-Mail: jlsutton@apex.net

Theresa Sutton, Publisher
Lee Sutton, Editor

Print-out from database of wholesalers, manufacturers, distributors, importers and close-out houses. Database is updated daily to guarantee the most current and up-to-date sources available.
Cost: $39.50
100 Pages

15567 LIA Member Directory & Buyer's Guide
Leather Industries of America
3050 K St. NW
Suite 400
Washington, DC 20007

202-342-8497
FAX 202-342-8583
E-Mail: info@leatherusa.com
Home Page: www.leatherusa.com

John Wittenborn, President
30 Pages
Frequency: Annual/March
Founded in 1917

15568 Leather Manufacturer Directory
Shoe Trades Publishing Company
323 Cornelia
Suite 274
Plattsburg, NY 12901

514-457-8787
800-973-7463
FAX 514-457-5832
Home Page: www.shoetrades.com

George McLeish, Group Publisher
Inta Huns, Managing Editor

Classified directory of major leather finishers, tanneries and hide processors in the United States and Canada, and their suppliers.
Cost: $61.00
413 Pages
Frequency: Annual
Circulation: 1,200

15569 U.S. Leather Industry Statistics
Leather Industries of America
3050 K St. NW
Suite 400
Washington, DC 20007

202-342-8497
FAX 202-342-8583
E-Mail: info@leatherusa.com
Home Page: www.leatherusa.com

John Wittenborn, President
Statistical record of the U.S. leather industry for over 85 years.
Cost: $18.00
10 Pages
Frequency: Annual
Founded in 1917

Industry Web Sites

15570 http://gold.greyhouse.com
G.O.L.D Grey House OnLine Databases
Grey House Publishing's online database platform, GOLD, offers Quick Search, Keyword Search and Expert Search for most business sectors including leather markets. The GOLD platform makes finding the information you need quick and easy - whether you're a novice searcher or an experienced database user. All of

Grey House's directory products are available for subscription on the GOLD platform.

15571 www.greyhouse.com
Grey House Publishing

Authoritative reference directories for most business sectors including leather markets. Users can search the online databases with varied search criteria allowing for custom searches by product category, geographic area, sales volume, keyword, subject and more. Full Grey House catalog and online ordering also available.

15572 www.hidenet.com
Hidenet

Furnishes detailed information on the daily hide market worldwide.

15573 www.leatherusa.com
Leather Industries of America

Works to promote the leather industry through collection of statistics, chemical and technical research and public relations.

15574 www.meatami.org
US Hide, Skin & Leather Association

15575 www.ssia.info
Shoe Service Institute of America

Shop to shop chat room, links and listings of manufacturers and wholesalers plus shoe care tips.

15576 www.travel-goods.org
Travel Goods Association

Manufacturers of luggage and other leather goods.

Associations

15577 ABA Young Lawyers Division
American Bar Association
321 N Clark St
Chicago, IL 60654-7598

312-988-5000
800-285-2221
FAX 312-988-5280
E-Mail: yld@staff.abanet.org
Home Page: www.abanet.org/yld/home.html
Social Media: *Facebook, Twitter, LinkedIn, Youtube*

James R. Silkenat, President
Robert M. Carlson, Chair, House of Delegates
Jack L. Rives, Executive Director
Hon. Cara Lee T Neville, Secretary
Lucian T. Pera, Treasurer

The Division is committed to assuring it is best able to represent the newest members of the profession, ensuring that it reflects the society it serves, and providing young lawyers wth the tools and opportunities for professional and personal success.
150M Members
Founded in 1878

15578 AILA's Immigration Lawyer Search
E-Mail: ils@aila.org
Home Page: www.ailalawyer.com

12,00 Members

15579 Academy of Family Mediators
PO Box 51090
Eugene, OR 97405

541-345-1629
E-Mail: admin@mediate.com
Home Page: www.mediate.com
Social Media: *Facebook, Twitter, LinkedIn, Google+*

Jim Melamed, CEO
Carol Knapp, CTO
Josh Remis, COO
John Blair, Business Advisor & Board Member
Byron Knapp, Systems Administrator

Produce conflict management specialists who can advance conflict resolution and engagement, as well as a functional approach to conflict within our communities and society.
2M Members
Founded in 1981
Mailing list available for rent

15580 Adjutants General Association of the United States
One Massachusetts Ave, N.W.
Washington, DC 20001

504-278-8357
FAX 302-326-7196
E-Mail: agausinfo@gmail.com
Home Page: www.agaus.org

MG Glenn H. Curtis, President
MG Robert E. Livingston, Jr., VP Army
H. Michael Edwards, VP Air
MG Kenneth Reiner, Treasurer
MG Timothy A. Reisch, Secretary

Composed of the commander of the National Guard in each state.
55 Members

15581 Alliance for Justice
11 Dupont Cir NW
2nd Floor
Washington, DC 20036-1206

202-822-6070
FAX 202-822-6068
E-Mail: alliance@afj.org
Home Page: www.afj.org

Social Media: *Facebook, Twitter, Youtube, Google Plus*

Ken Grossinger, Chair
Nan Aron, President
Paulette Meyer, Vice-Chair
Elizabeth Posner, Director of Foundation Relations
Kyle Barry, Director of Justice Programs

Nonprofit association of public interest advocacy organization. Offers workshops, advocacy projects, legal guides, techinical assistance and public education. Publishes a directory of public interest law centers.
Founded in 1979
Mailing list available for rent

15582 American Academy of Psychiatry and the Law
One Regency Drive
PO Box 30
Bloomfield, CT 06002-2310

860-242-5450
800-331-1389
FAX 860-286-0787
E-Mail: office@aapl.org
Home Page: www.aapl.org

Graham D. Glancy, MB, President
Christopher Thompson, MD, Vice President
Barry W. Wall, MD, Vice President
Susan Hatters Friedman, MD, Secretary
Douglass Mossman, MD, Treasurer

Members are psychiatrists who have a professional interest in psychiatry and the law.
1500 Members
Founded in 1969

15583 American Alliance of Paralegals
4023 Kennett Pike
Suite 146
Wilmington, DE 19807-2018

E-Mail: info@aapipara.org
Home Page: www.aapipara.org
Social Media: *Facebook, Twitter, LinkedIn*

Carolyn M. Saenz, AACP, President
Sandra M. Herdler, Vice President
Patricia S. Carr, AACP, Treasurer
Keelie J. Fike, Secretary
Leslie L. Adams, AACP, Director of Education
Founded in 2003

15584 American Arbitration Association
1633 Broadway
Floor 10
New York, NY 10019-6707

212-716-5800
FAX 877-304-8457
E-Mail: websitemail@adr.org
Home Page: www.adr.org

William K Slate II, CEO
Debi Miller-Moore, VP

Available to resolve a wide range of disputes through mediation, arbitration, elections and other out-of-court settlement procedures.
Founded in 1996

15585 American Association for Justice
777 6th Street, NW
Suite 200
Washington, DC 20001

202-965-3500
800-424-2725
E-Mail: membership@justice.org
Home Page: www.justice.org
Social Media: *Facebook, Twitter, LinkedIn*

Burton LeBlanc, President
Larry Tawwater, Vice President
Charles Jeffress, Chief Operating Officer

Kathi Berge, Chief Financial Officer
Anjali Jesseramsing, Executive Vice President
56000 Members
Founded in 1972
Mailing list available for rent

15586 American Association for Paralegal
19 Mantua Road
Suite 241
Mt. Royal, NJ 08061

856-423-2829
FAX 856-423-3420
E-Mail: info@aafpe.org
Home Page: www.aafpe.org
Social Media: *Facebook, Twitter, LinkedIn*

Patricia Lyons, President
Leslie Vincent, Executive Director
Wendy Stevens, Exhibits & Meetings Manager
Kathy Suckiel, Administrative Assistant
Marcy Delesandri, Secretary

National organization serving paralegal education and institutions which offer paralegal education programs.
Founded in 1981

15587 American Association for Paralegal Educati on
19 Mantua Road
Mt. Royal, NJ 8061

856-423-2829
FAX 856-423-3420
E-Mail: info@aafpe.org
Home Page: www.aafpe.org
Social Media: *Facebook, Twitter, LinkedIn*

Patricia Lyons, President
Leslie Vincent, Executive Director
Wendy Stevens, Exhibits & Meetings Manager
Kathy Suckiel, Administrative Assistant
Marcy Delesandri, Secretary
Founded in 1981

15588 American Association of Attorney-Certified Public Accountants
PO Box 706
Ste. 639
Warrendale, PA 15095

703-352-8064
888-288-9272
FAX 703-352-8073
E-Mail: info@attorney-cpa.com
Home Page: www.attorney-cpa.com
Social Media: *Facebook, Twitter, LinkedIn*

John W. Pramberg, President
David M. Berger, President Elect/Vice President
Eric J. Rollinger, Treasurer
Jo Ann M. Koontz, Secretary
William B. Le Vay, Assistant Treasurer/Secretary

Seeks to safeguard the professional and legal rights of CPA attorneys.
1400 Members
Founded in 1964

15589 American Association of Law Libraries
105 W Adams Street
Suite 3300
Chicago, IL 60603-6225

312-939-4764
FAX 312-431-1097
E-Mail: aallhq@aall.org
Home Page: www.aallnet.org
Social Media: *Facebook, Twitter, LinkedIn, RSS*

Kate Hagan, Executive Director
Emily Feltren, Director of Government Relations
Paula Davidson, Director of Finance and Admin

Cara Schillinger, Director
Ashley St. John, Director
Marketing/Communications

Promotes and enhances the value of law libraries to the legal and public communities, fosters the profession of law librarianship and provides leadership in the field of legal information.
5000+ Members
Founded in 1906

15590 American Bail Coalition
3857 Lewiston Place
Fairfax, VA 22030

877-385-9009
FAX 703-385-1809
Home Page: www.americanbailcoalition.com
Social Media: *Facebook, Twitter, LinkedIn, Youtube*

William B Carmichael, President
Thomas Ritchey, Treasurer

Dedicated to the long term growth and continuation of the surety bail bond industry.
Founded in 1992

15591 American Bar Association
321 N Clark St
Chicago, IL 60654-7598

312-988-5000
800-285-2221
FAX 312-988-5280
E-Mail: askaba@abanet.org
Home Page: www.abanet.org
Social Media: *Facebook, Twitter, LinkedIn*

Patricia Lee Refo, Chairman
Paulette Brown, President
Jack L. Rives, Executive Director
G. Nicholas Casey, Jr., Treasurer
Mary T. Torres, Secretary

The American Bar Association is the largest coluntary professional association in the world, with over 400,000 members. The ABA provides law school accreditation, continuing legal education, information about the law, programs to assist lawyerd and judges in their work, and initiatives to improve the legal system for the public.
400M Members
Founded in 1878
Mailing list available for rent

15592 American Bar Foundation
750 N Lake Shore Dr
Chicago, IL 60611-4403

312-988-6500
FAX 312-988-6579
E-Mail: khannaford@abfn.org
Home Page: www.americanbarfoundation.org

David A. Collins, President
Ellen J. Flannery, Vice President
David S. Houghton, Secretary
George S. Frazza, Treasurer
Katharine Hannaford, Senior Writer & Grants Officer

Memberships are elected and limited to one third of one percent of the lawyers in the United States.
Founded in 1955
Mailing list available for rent

15593 American Civil Liberties Union
125 Broad St
18th Floor
New York, NY 10004-2427

212-549-2500
FAX 212-549-2646
E-Mail: membership@aclu.org
Home Page: www.aclu.org
Social Media: *Facebook, Twitter, RSS, Youtube*

Susan N. Herman, President
Anthony D Romero, Executive Director

Steven Shapiro, Legal Director
Mark Wier, Chief Development Officer
Dorothy M. Ehrlich, Deputy Executive Director

Protection of civil liberties and constitutional rights through litigation, public education and legislative lobbying.
Founded in 1920
Mailing list available for rent

15594 American College of Legal Medicine
1100 E Woodfield Rd
Suite 520
Schaumburg, IL 60173

847-969-0283
FAX 847-517-7229
E-Mail: info@aclm.org
Home Page: www.aclm.org

Vicky A. Trompler, Chairman, Counsel
Victoria L. Green, President
Wendy J. Weiser, Executive Director
Sue O'Sullivan, Associate Director
Christopher White, Secretary

Organization related to the field of health law, legal medicine or medical jurisprudence.
1400 Members
Founded in 1960

15595 American Health Lawyers Association
1620 Eye Street, NW
6th Floor
Washington, DC 20006-4010

202-833-1100
FAX 202-833-1105
Home Page: www.healthlawyers.org
Social Media: *Facebook, Twitter, LinkedIn*

Lois Dehls Cornell, President
Hon. Wiliam C. Koch, Jr., Executive Vice President
BG Malinda E. Dunn, Executive Director
David W. Akridge, CAE, Deputy Executive Director
Rita Denniston Zimmerman, Communications Coordinator

Health Lawyers offers numerous services for their members and most are freely available to nonmembers as well.
Mailing list available for rent

15596 American Immigration Lawyers Association
1331 G St NW
Suite 300
Washington, DC 20005-3142

202-507-7600
FAX 202-783-7853
E-Mail: info@aila.org
Home Page: www.aila.org
Social Media: *Facebook, Twitter, LinkedIn, Youtube*

Victor D. Nieblas Pradis, President
Annaluisa Padilla, First Vice President
Anastasia Tonello, Second Vice President
Marketa Lindt, Treasurer
Jennifer Minear, Secretary

Attorneys practicing in the field of immigration and naturalization law.
11200 Members
Founded in 1946
Mailing list available for rent

15597 American Inns of Court
225 Reinekers Lane
Suite 770
Alexandria, VA 22314

703-684-3590
FAX 703-684-3607
E-Mail: info@innsofcourt.org
Home Page: home.innsofcourt.org

Social Media: *Facebook, Twitter, LinkedIn, Pinterest, Tumblr, Blogger, St*

Hon. Carl E. Stewart, President
Carl E. Stewart, Vice President
Malinda E. Dunn, Executive Director
Cindy Dennis, Awards & Scholarships Coordinator
Andrew Young, Director of Knowledge Resources

AIC is designed to improve skills, professionalism and ethics of the bench and bar. The American Inns of Court is an amalgam of judges, lawyers, and in some cases, law professors and law students.
Mailing list available for rent

15598 American Institute of Parliamentarians
618 Church Street
Suite 220
Nashville, TN 37219

888-664-0428
FAX 615-248-9253
E-Mail: aip@aipparl.org
Home Page: www.aipparl.org

Kay Allison Crews, CP, PRP, President
Daniel Ivey-Soto, CP-T, PRP, Vice President
Barbara J. Rosi, PRP, Treasurer
Lucy Hicks Anderson, Secretary
Jeanette Williams, CP-T, Education Director

Promotes the use of effective, democratic and parliamentary practices by teaching of parliamentary procedures; training and certification of parliamentarians; promoting the use of parliamentarians; and maintaining a representative, democratic organization.
1.4M Members
Founded in 1958

15599 American Intellectual Property Law Association
241 18th Street, South
Suite 700
Arlington, VA 22202

703-415-0780
FAX 703-415-0786
E-Mail: aipla@aipla.org
Home Page: www.aipla.org
Social Media: *Facebook, Twitter, LinkedIn, Pinterest, Tumblr, Blogger, St*

Sharon A. Israel, President
Lisa Jorgenson, Executive Director
Meghan Donohoe, Chief Operating Officer
Cathleen Clime, Director of Meetings & Events
Meghan Donohoe, Chief Operating Officer

Lawyers whose specialty is trademark, patent or copyright laws.
Founded in 1897
Mailing list available for rent

15600 American Judicature Society
Center Building2014 Broadway
Suite 100
Nashville, TN 37203

615-873-4675
800-626-4089
FAX 615-873-4671
E-Mail: sandersen@ajs.org
Home Page: www.ajs.org
Social Media: *Facebook, Twitter, Youtube*

Martha Hill Jamison, President
Rebecca Lee Wiggs, Vice President
Jon Comstock, Vice President
James Alfini, Interim Executive Director
Cynthia Gray, Director, Center Judicial Ethics

Lawyers, judges and educators interested in the effective administration of justice.
5000 Members
Founded in 1913

15601 American Law & Economics Association
PO Box 208245
New Haven, CT 06520-8245

203-432-7801
FAX 203-432-7225
E-Mail: ALEA@yale.edu
Home Page: www.amlecon.org

Kathryn Spier, President
Ian Ayres, Vice President
Keith N. Hylton, Secretary-Treasurer

Dedicated to the advancement of economic understanding of law and related areas of public policy and regulation.
Founded in 1991

15602 American Law Institute
4025 Chestnut St
Suite 5
Philadelphia, PA 19104-3099

215-243-1600
800-253-6397
FAX 215-243-1636
E-Mail: ali@ali.org
Home Page: www.ali.org
Social Media: *Facebook, Twitter, LinkedIn, Vimeo*

Roberta Cooper Ramo, President
Douglas Laycock, 1st Vice President
Lee H. Rosenthal, 2nd Vice President
Julie Scribner, Chief Financial Officer
Stephanie A. Middleton, Deputy Director

A private, nonprofit organization that seeks to promote the clarification and simplification of the law through legal research and reform activities.
Founded in 1923
Mailing list available for rent

15603 American Law Institute Continuing Legal Education Group (ALI CLE)
4025 Chestnut St
Suite 5
Philadelphia, PA 19104

215-243-1600
800-253-6397
FAX 215-243-1664
E-Mail: ali@ali.org
Home Page: www.ali-cle.org

Julie Scribner, CFO and Director
Nancy Mulloy-Bonn, Chief CLE Content Officer
Nancy Cline, Customer Service/MCLE Director
Diane Schnitzer, Director of Human Resources
Frank Paul Tomasello, Director

Provides continuing legal education courses, books, and periodicals for practicing attorneys and others in the legal profession. This organization is a collaborative effort of the ALI and the ABA.
Founded in 2012

15604 American Lawyers Auxiliary
321 North Clark Street
Chicago, IL 60610-4714

312-988-6387
FAX 312-988-5494
E-Mail: moisantj@staff.abanet.org
Home Page:
www.americanlawyersauxiliary.org
Social Media: *Facebook, RSS*

Sue Patterson, President
Anne Santorelli, First Vice President
Marilyn McDowell, Second Vice President
Connie Meigs, Secretary
Sharon Chappelear, Treasurer

Acts as a clearinghouse for state and local groups throughout the country and suggests ed-

ucational programs pertaining to the law. Encourages members to volunteer their services.
75M Members
Founded in 1958

15605 American Lawyers Newspapers Group
1730 M Street NW
Washington, DC 20036-4513

202-457-0686

Supports all those involved in the reporting of legal issues. Publishes a weekly newsletter.
Founded in 1977

15606 American Prepaid Legal Services Institute
321 N Clark Street
Chicago, IL 60654

312-988-5751
FAX 312-932-6436
E-Mail: info@aplsi.org
Home Page: glsaonline.org
Social Media: *Facebook, Twitter, LinkedIn*

Nicolle Schippers, President
Stephen Ginsberg, Treasurer
Jean Clauson, Secretary

Professional trade organization representing the legal services plan industry. The members include lawyers, sponsor representatives, administrators and marketers of legal service plans. These people have invested their time, money and organizational resources to build legal service plans into the premier mechanism for supplying affordable legal services.
Founded in 1975

15607 American Society for Legal History
185 West Broadway
PO Box R
New York, NY 10013

574-631-6984
FAX 574-631-3595
E-Mail: walter.f.pratt.1@nd.edu
Home Page: www.aslh.net

Michael Grossberg, President
Sally Hadden, Secretary
Craig Evan Klafter, Treasurer
Rebecca J. Scott, President-Elect

Exhibits relating to legal history and its uses in formulating legal policy, decisions and actions; unearthing historical items; and preserving legal and legislative records.
1200 Members
Founded in 1956
Mailing list available for rent

15608 American Society of Comparative Law
University of Baltimore
1420 N. Charles Street
Baltimore, MD 21201

410-837-4689
FAX 410-837-4560
E-Mail: lschnitzer@ubalt.edu
Home Page: www.comparativelaw.org

David J. Gerber, President
Vivian Curran, Vice President
Franklin Gervurtz, Secretary
Mortimer Sellers, Treasurer
Helge Dedek, Editor

An organization of institutional and individual members devoted to study, research, and write on foreign and comparative law as well as private international law.
60 Members
Founded in 1951
Mailing list available for rent

15609 American Society of International Law
2223 Massachusetts Ave Nw
Washington, DC 20008-2864

202-939-6000
FAX 202-797-7133
E-Mail: services@asil.org
Home Page: www.asil.org
Social Media: *Facebook, Twitter, LinkedIn, Youtube*

Lori Fisler Damrosch, President
Gabrielle Kirk McDonald, Honorary President
Mark Agrast, Executive Director
Matthew Gomez, Membership Manager
Michael Farley, Director of Development

Supports all those involved with overseas litigation. Publishes monthly newsletter.
4000 Members
Founded in 1906
Mailing list available for rent

15610 American Society of Notaries
PO Box 5707
Tallahassee, FL 32314-5707

850-671-5164
FAX 850-671-5165
Home Page: www.asnnotary.org

Kathleen Butler, Executive Director
Carly Hayes, Member Services Director

Helps to organize, improve and uphold high standards for notaries public.
21M Members
Founded in 1965

15611 American Society of Trial Consultants
10534 York Road
Suite 102
Hunt Valley, MD 21030

410-560-7949
FAX 410-560-2563
E-Mail: ASTCOffice@astcweb.org
Home Page: www.astcweb.org

Richard Jenson, President
Ronald Matlon, Ph.D., Executive Director
Bill Grimes, Treasurer & Board Member
Carol Bauss, J.D., Secretary & Board Member

Members come from diverse professional fields: communication, psychology, theatre, marketing, linguistics, political science and law.
500+ Members
Founded in 1982
Mailing list available for rent

15612 American Society of Trial Consultants Foundation
10951 West Pico Blvd.
Suite 203
Los Angeles, CA 90064

424-832-3641
E-Mail: info@astcfoundation.org
Home Page: www.astcfoundation.org

Daniel Wolfe, J.D., Ph.D., Board of Director
Karen Ohnemus Lisko, Ph.D., Board of Director
Mark Modlin, M.S., N.C.C., Board of Director
Ken Broda-Bahm, Ph.D., Board of Director
Ted Donner, Esq., Board of Director
Founded in 2004

15613 Association of American Law Schools
1614 20th Street, Northwest
Washington, DC 20009-1001

202-296-8851
FAX 202-296-8869
E-Mail: aals@aals.org
Home Page: www.aals.org

Social Media: *Facebook, Twitter, LinkedIn, YouTube, RSS*

Brian Harrison, Staff Accountant
Judith Areen, Executive Director/CEO
Pablo Molina, Chief Information Officer
Melinda Price, Communications Coordinator
Tim Bloomquist, Facilities Manager

An association of law schools that serves as the law teachers' learned society.
Founded in 1900
Mailing list available for rent

15614 Association of Corporate Counsel
1025 Connecticut Ave NW
Suite 200
Washington, DC 20036-5425

202-293-4103
FAX 202-293-4701
E-Mail: acc.chair@acc.com
Home Page: www.acc.com
Social Media: *Facebook, Twitter, LinkedIn, RSS*

Sabine Chalmers, Chair
Iohann Le Frapper, Vice-Chair
William Mordan, Treasurer
Mary Kennard, Secretary
Jan Alonzo, Director

Lawyers who practice law in a corporation or other private sector entity and do not hold themselves out to the public to practice law.
15000 Members
Founded in 1982
Mailing list available for rent

15615 Association of Family and Conciliation
6525 Grand Teton Plaza
Madison, WI 53719

608-664-3750
FAX 608-664-3751
E-Mail: afcc@afccnet.org
Home Page: www.afccnet.org
Social Media: *Facebook, Twitter, LinkedIn, RSS*

Hon. Peter Boshier, President
Annette T. Burns, JD, Vice President
Peter Salem, MA, Executive Director
Leslye Hunter, MA, LMFT, Associate Director
Carly Wieman, BA, Program Director

AFCC is an interdisciplinary, international association of professionals dedicated to improving the lives of children and families through the resolution of family conflict.
3700 Members
Founded in 1963

15616 Association of Insolvency and Restructuring Advisors
221 Stewart Ave
Suite 207
Medford, OR 97501-3647

541-858-1665
FAX 541-858-9187
E-Mail: aira@aira.org
Home Page: www.aira.org
Social Media: *Facebook, Twitter, LinkedIn*

Matthew Schwartz, CIRA, Chairman
Thomas Morrow, CIRA, President
David Payne, CIRA, CDBV, Vice President - Conferences
Joel Waite, Vice President - Development
Grant Newton, Executive Director

Disseminates judicial and financial information relating to insolvency proceedings as well as offering methods to increase skills needed in these cases. Also administers the (CIRA) Certified Insolvency and Reorganization Account Program.
1250 Members
Founded in 1984

15617 Association of Legal Administrators
8700 W. Bryn Mawr Ave.
Suite 110S
Chicago, IL 60631-3512

847-267-1252
FAX 847-267-1329
E-Mail: publications@alanet.org
Home Page: www.alanet.org
Social Media: *Facebook, Twitter, LinkedIn*

Paul Farnsworth, President
Oliver Yandle, JD, CAEÿ, Executive Director
Renee Tibbettsÿ, Director of Administration
Gwen Biasi, CAEÿ, Director of Marketing
Michelle Goldberg, Sr. Director Marketing

Professional support for management of private law firms and other legal organizations worldwide.
10000 Members
Founded in 1971

15618 Association of Professional Responsibility Lawyers (APRL)
20 South Clark Street
Suite 1050
Chicago, IL 60603

312-782-4396
FAX 312-782-4725
E-Mail: admin@aprl.net
Home Page: aprl.net

Arthur J Lachman, President
Charles Lundberg, President-Elect
Lynda C Shely, Secretary
Donald Campbell, Treasurer

An organization of lawyers who concentrate on professional responsibilities issues.
300 Members
Founded in 1990

15619 Association of Prosecuting Attorneys
1615 L St. NW
Suite 1100
Washington, DC 20036

202-861-2480
FAX 202-223-4688
E-Mail: info@apainc.org
Home Page: www.apainc.org
Social Media: *Facebook, Twitter*

David LaBahn, President & CEO
Steven Jansen, VP & COO

Advocacy body and global forum focused on proactive and innovative prosecutorial practices.

15620 Biz Law Association
PO Box 247
Springdale, UT 84767-0247

FAX 435-635-9817

Suppports all those involved in business law, especially business owners and managers. Publishes newsletter.

15621 Business & Legal Reports
100 Winners Circle
Suite 300
Brentwood, TN 37027

860-510-0100
800-727-5257
FAX 860-510-7225
E-Mail: service@blr.com
Home Page: www.blr.com
Social Media: *Facebook, Twitter, LinkedIn*

Robert L Brady, JD, Founder
Dan Oswald, Chief Executive Officer
Elizabeth Petersen, Vice President of Healthcare
Lawton Miller, Chief Financial Officer
Brad Forrister, VP, Training and Legal

Provides essential tools for safety and environmental compliance and training needs.
32 Members
Mailing list available for rent

15622 Center for Professional Responsibility
American Bar Association
321 North Clark Street
Chicago, IL 60654

312-988-5000
800-285-2221
FAX 312-988-5491
E-Mail: cpr@staff.abanet.org
Home Page: www.americanbar.org
Social Media: *Facebook, Twitter, LinkedIn*

James R. Silkenat, President
Jack L. Rives, Executive Director
Robert M. Carlson, Chair, House of Delegates
Lucian T. Pera, Treasurer
Cara Lee T. Neville, Secretary

Since 1978, the Center has provided national leadership and vision in developing and interpreting standards and scholarly resources in legal ethics, professional regulation, professionalism and client protection mechanisms.
Founded in 1878
Mailing list available for rent

15623 Center on Children and the Law
American Bar Association Young Lawyers Division
1050 Connecticut Ave. N.W.
Suite 400
Washington, DC 20036

202-662-1000
800-285-2221
FAX 202-662-1755
E-Mail: ctrchildlaw@abanet.org
Home Page: www.americanbar.org
Social Media: *Facebook, Twitter, LinkedIn*

James R. Silkenat, President
Jack L. Rives, Executive Director
Robert M. Carlson, Chair, House of Delegates
Lucian T. Pera, Treasurer
Cara Lee T. Neville, Secretary

This is a program of the Young Lawyers Division that aims to improve children's lives through advances in law, justice, knowledge, practice and public policy. Areas of expertise include child abuse and neglect, child welfare and protective services system enhancement, foster care, family preservation, termination of parental rights, parental substance abuse, adolescent health, and domestic violence.
15 Members
Founded in 1878

15624 Commercial Law League of America
1000 N. Rand Rd.
Suite 214
Wauconda, IL 60084

312-240-1400
800-978-2552
FAX 847-526-3993
E-Mail: info@clla.org
Home Page: www.clla.org
Social Media: *Facebook, Twitter, LinkedIn, YouTube*

Robert S. Bernstein, President
Jeff Henderson, Executive Vice President
Casey Henderson, Executive Assistant
Kate Friedman, Marketing Manager
Ann Scheible, Membership Services

Supports those involved in bankruptcy, collections, debt and insolvency legislation. Publishes quarterly magazine and weekly e-newsletter.
1500 Members
Founded in 1895
Mailing list available for rent

15625 Commission on Mental & Physical Disability Law

American Bar Association
1050 Connecticut Ave. N.W.
Suite 400
Washington, DC 20036

202-662-1000
800-285-2221
FAX 202-442-3439
E-Mail: cdr@americanbar.org
Home Page: www.americanbar.org
Social Media: *Facebook, Twitter, LinkedIn*

Mark D. Agrast, Esq., Chair
Amy L. Allbright, Director
M. Tovah Miller, Program Specialist
Michael J. Stratton, Administrative
Coordinator
Brandon M. Moore-Rhodes, Technology
Associate

The Commission's mission is 'to promote the
ABA's commitment to justice and the rule of
law for persons with mental, physical, and sensory disabilities and to promote their full and
equal participation in the legal profession.' The
Commission consists of 15 members appointed
by the ABA President-elect on an annual basis.
It meets bi-annually at its headquarters in
Washington, D.C., to map out future plans and
to direct the current activities.
15 Members
Founded in 1973
Mailing list available for rent

15626 Copyright Society of The USA

1 East 53rd Street
8th Floor
New York, NY 10022

Home Page: www.csusa.orgÿ
Social Media: *Facebook, Twitter, LinkedIn*

Eric J. Schwartz, President
Nancy E. Wolff, Vice President
Michael Donaldson, Treasurer
Judith Finell, Secretary
Kaitland Kubat, Director of Operations
Founded in 1953

15627 Council of State Governments

2760 Research Park Drive
PO Box 11910
Lexington, KY 40578-1910

859-244-8000
800-800-1910
FAX 859-244-8001
E-Mail: press@csg.org
Home Page: www.csg.org
Social Media: *Facebook, Twitter, LinkedIn,*
YouTube, RSS

Sen. Carl Marcellino, Chair
Brian Sandoval, President
David Adkins, Executive Director/CEO
Carl Marcellino, Vice Chair
Mark Norris, Chair-Elect
Founded in 1933
Mailing list available for rent

15628 Council on Legal Education Opportunity

1101 Mercantile Lane
Suite 294
Largo, MD 20774

240-582-8600
866-886-4343
FAX 240-582-8605
E-Mail: cleo@cleoinc.org
Home Page: www.cleoscholars.org
Social Media: *Facebook, Twitter*

Cassandra Sneed Ogden, Executive Director
Bernetta J Hayes, Admissions Administrator
Leigh R. Allen II, Mentoring & Development
Director

Lynda Cevallos, Pre-Law Coordinator
Julie D Long, Project Research Assistant

Provides law school preparation assistance for
minority and disadvantaged students. Program
is six-week summer institute paid for by the
program. Scholarship of approximately
$16,000 for the three years of law study is
granted to selected and certified students, after
completion of the summer program.

15629 Council on Licensure, Enforcement and Regulation

403 Marquis Ave
Suite 200
Lexington, KY 40502-2104

859-269-1289
FAX 859-231-1943
E-Mail: rbrown@clearhq.org
Home Page: www.clearhq.org
Social Media: *Facebook, Twitter, LinkedIn*

Robin Jenkins, President
Adam Parfitt, Executive Director
Rosa Brown, Administrative Associate
Lisa Eads, Marketing & Communications
Jodie Markey, Senior Program Coordinator

Supports all those involved in occupational and
professional testing and credentialing. Publishes bi-annual magazine.
Mailing list available for rent

15630 DRI-The Voice Of The Defense Bar

55 W. Monroe Street
Suite 2000
Chicago, IL 60603

312-951-1101
FAX 312-795-0749
E-Mail: dri@dri.org
Home Page: www.dri.org
Social Media: *Facebook, Twitter, LinkedIn,*
Youtube

Laura E. Proctor, President
John F. Kuppens, First Vice President
Toyja E. Kelley, Second Vice President
Kathleen M. Guilfoyle, Secretary-Treasurer
John Parker Sweeney, President-Elect

Service organization to improve the administration of justice and defense lawyers' skills.
Founded in 1960

15631 Education Law Association

2121 Euclid Avenue
LL 212
Cleveland, OH 44115-2214

216-523-7377
FAX 216-687-5284
E-Mail: ela@educationlaw.org
Home Page: www.educationlaw.org
Social Media: *Facebook, Twitter, LinkedIn*

Patrick D. Pauken, J.D., Ph.D., President
Lynn Rossi Scott, J.D, Vice President
Cate K. Smith, J.D., M.P.A, Executive Director
Pat Petrusky, Member Services Coordinator
Pamela Hardy, Publications Specialist

Brings together educational and legal scholars
and practitioners to inform and advance educational policy and practice through knowledge
of the law. Together, our professional community anticipates trends in educational law and
supports scholarly research through the highest
value print and electronic publications, conferences, seminars and professional forums.
1400 Members
Founded in 1954

15632 Environmental Law Alliance Worldwide

1412 Pearl St.
Eugene, OR 97401

541-687-8454
FAX 541-687-0535

E-Mail: elawus@elaw.org
Home Page: www.elaw.org

Bern Johnson, Executive Director

Attorneys, scientists and others advocating for
a healthy planet.

15633 Equal Justice Works

1730 M Street NW
Suite 1010
Washington, DC 20036-4511

202-466-3686
FAX 202-429-9766
E-Mail: mail@equaljusticeworks.org
Home Page: www.equaljusticeworks.org
Social Media: *Facebook, Twitter, LinkedIn,*
Youtube, Flickr

Kim Koopersmith, Chair
David Stern, Executive Director
Jeanne Van Vlandren, Chief Operating Officer
Tammy Sun, Senior Manager, Fellowships
Anne Bloom, Director of Public Programs

Founded by law students dedicated to sur-
mounting barriers to equal justice that affect
millions of low income individuals and families. Equal Justice organizes, trains and supports public service minded law students, and
in creating summer and postgraduate public
interest jobs.
Founded in 1986
Mailing list available for rent

15634 Federal Bar Association

1220 North Fillmore St.
Suite 444
Arlington, VA 22201ÿ

571-481-9100
FAX 571-481-9090
E-Mail: fba@fedbar.org
Home Page: www.fedbar.org
Social Media: *Facebook, Twitter, LinkedIn*

Matthew B. Moreland, President
Mark K. Vincent, President Elect
Michael J. Newmanÿ, Treasurer
Karen Silberman, Executive Director
Heather Gaskins, Director of Development
Founded in 1920

15635 Federal Circuit Bar Association

1620 Eye St NW
Suite 801
Washington, DC 20006-4035

202-466-3923
FAX 202-833-1061
E-Mail: ehaugFCBA@FLHlaw.com
Home Page: www.fedcirbar.org

Edgar H. Haug, Esquire, President
James E. Brookshire, Executive Director
Marcia Foster, Office Operations
Jeremy Atkinson, IT/Administration
Darren Davis, Membership Coordinator

FCBA is a national organization of attorneys
who practice before the United States Court of
Appeals for the Federal Circuit.
Mailing list available for rent

15636 Federal Communications Bar Association

1020 19th St NW
Suite 325
Washington, DC 20036-6101

202-293-4000
FAX 202-293-4317
E-Mail: fcba@fcba.org
Home Page: www.fcba.org

Christopher J. Wright, President
Julie M. Kearney, Secretary
Natalie G. Roisman, Assistant Secretary
Erin L. Dozier, Treasurer
Lee G. Petro, Assistant Treasurer

A nonprofit organization of attorneys and other professionals involved in the development, interpretation, implementation and practice of communications law and policy.
3000 Members
Founded in 1936
Mailing list available for rent

15637 Federal Mediation & Conciliation Service

2100 K St NW
Washington, DC 20427

202-606-8100
FAX 202-606-4251
E-Mail: jpinto@fmcs.gov
Home Page: www.fmcs.gov

John Pinto, Manager of Field Operations

15638 Federation of Defense & Corporate Counsel

11812 N 56th St
Tampa, FL 33617-1528

813-983-0022
FAX 813-988-5837
E-Mail: mstreeper@thefederation.org
Home Page: www.thefederation.org
Social Media: *Facebook, Twitter, LinkedIn*

Victoria H. Roberts, Board Chair
Smith Moore Leatherwood, President
Martha J. Streeper, FDCC Executive Director
Michael W. Streeper, FDCC Financial Director
Susan J. Coone, Executive Administration

The objective and purposes of this Federation are to establish and maintain an organization consisting of members of the bar who are actively engaged in the legal aspects of the insurance business, executives of insurance companies an associations and corporate counsel engaged in the defense of claims; to assist in establishing standards for providing competent, efficient and economical legal services; to encourage and provide for legal education of the members of this Federation.
Founded in 1960

15639 First Amendment Lawyers Association

123 W. Madison St.
Suite 3100
Chicago, IL 60602

312-236-0606
FAX 312-236-9264
E-Mail: wgiampietro@wpglawyers.com
Home Page: www.firstamendmentlawyers.org

Wayne Gianpetro, General Counsel

Lawyers concentrating on defending clients under the first amendment of the Constitution.
180 Members
Founded in 1972

15640 Hispanic National Bar Association

1020 19th Street NW
Suite 505
Washington, DC 20036

202-223-4777
FAX 202-223-2324
E-Mail: info@hnba.com
Home Page: www.hnba.com
Social Media: *Facebook, Twitter, RSS*

Robert Maldonado, President
Alba Cruz-Hacker, HNBA COO & Executive Director
Anjanette Cabrera, VP of Membership
Jaime Areizaga-Soto, VP of Regions & Affiliates
Raquel Matas, VP of External Affairs

Supports all Latino attorneys and legal professionals with publications and educational conferences.
25000 Members
Founded in 1972
Mailing list available for rent

15641 Institute of Management & Administration

3 Bethesda Metro Center
Suite 250
Bethesda, MD 20814-5377

703-341-3500
800-372-1033
FAX 800-253-0332
E-Mail: customercare@bna.com
Home Page: www.ioma.com
Social Media: *Facebook, Twitter, LinkedIn, YouTube*

Gregory C. McCaffery, CEO & President
Sue Martin, Chief Operating Officer
Jean Lockhart, Chief of Staff
Michael Newborn, VP/Chief Security Officer
Rich Thompson, Chief Technology Officer

An independent source of exclusive business management information for experienced senior and middle management professionals.

15642 Inter-American Bar Association

1889 F Street, NW
3rd. Floor, Suite 355
Washington, DC 20006

202-466-5944
FAX 202-466-5946
E-Mail: iaba@iaba.org
Home Page: www.iaba.org
Social Media: *Facebook, Twitter, LinkedIn, YouTube*

Alejandro Lapad£, President
Alejandro Solano, Vice President
Tina di Battista, Secretary

The main purposes of this association are to establish and maintain relations among organizations of lawyers, national and local, in the Americas; to provide a forum for the exchange of views; to advance the science of jurisprudence particularly in the study of comparative law; to promote uniformity of the law; to disseminate knowledge of the laws; to promote the Rule of Law and the administration of justice; to preserve and defend human rights and liberties.
3M Members
Founded in 1940

15643 International Association of Defense Counsel

303 West Madison
Suite 925
Chicago, IL 60606-3401

312-368-1494
FAX 312-368-1854
E-Mail: info@iadclaw.org
Home Page: www.iadclaw.org
Social Media: *Facebook, Twitter, LinkedIn*

Joseph E. O'Neil, President
Mary Beth Kurzak, Executive Director
Amy O'Maley, Esq., Director, Professional Development
Carmela Balice, Senior Manager, Member Services
Ashley Fitzgerald, Manager, Communications

Offers continuing legal education and conducts research projects.
Cost: $650.00
2.5M Members
Founded in 1920

15644 International Bar Association

1667 K Street, NW
Suite 1230
Washington, DC 20006

202-827-3250
FAX 202-733-5657
E-Mail: iba@int-bar.org
Home Page: www.ibanet.org
Social Media: *Facebook, Twitter, LinkedIn, YouTube*

David W Rivkin, President
Martin Solc, Vice President
Horacio Bernardes-Neto, Secretary-General
Mark Ellis, Executive Director
Ele Dexter, Executive Assistant
Founded in 1947

15645 International BarÿAssociation

1667 K Street, NW
Suite 1230
Washington, DC 20006

202-827-3250
FAX 202-733-5657
Home Page: www.ibanet.org
Social Media: *Facebook, Twitter, LinkedIn, YouTube*

David W Rivkin, President
Martin Solc, Vice President
Horacio Bernardes-Neto, Secretary-General
Mark Ellis, Executive Director
Ele Dexter, Executive Assistant
Founded in 1947

15646 International Paralegal Management Association

980 N. Michigan Ave
Suite 1400
Chicago, IL 60611

312-214-4991
FAX 888-662-9155
Home Page: www.theipma.org
Social Media: *Facebook, Twitter, LinkedIn*

Victoria L.ÿ Snook, President
Gary L. Melhuish, Vice President - Membership
Lynda S. McNie, Secretary-Treasurer
Jennifer Karns, Vice President - Trends & Positions
Larry C. Smith, CAE, Executive Director
Founded in 1984

15647 International Probate Research Association

c/o Josh Butler & Company
PO Box 27
Cuyahoga Falls, OH 44222-0027

330-506-6400
E-Mail: inforequest@joshbutler.com
Home Page: www.lostheir.com/ipa.htm

Josh Butler, President

IPRA members are probate research companies.
Founded in 1989

15648 International Society of Barristers

210 Science Drive
802 Legal Research Building
Durham, NC 27708-0360

919-613-7085
FAX 734-764-8309
E-Mail: reedj@umich.edu
Home Page: isob.com

John W Reed, Administrative Secretary

Members are trial lawyers interested in encouraging advocacy under the adversary system and preserving trial by jury.
750 Members
Founded in 1965

15649 Investigative Professionals, Inc.
PO Box 35
Hardyville, KY 42746

928-451-1598
FAX 877-657-6691
Home Page:
www.investigativeprofessionals.com
Social Media: *Facebook, Twitter, Google+, Blogger*

Larry Troxel

NALI was formed with its primary focus to conduct investigations related to litigation. Membership in NALI is open to all professional legal investigators who are actively engaged in negligence investigations for the plaintiff and/or criminal defense, and who are employed by investigative firms, law firms or public defender agencies.
Founded in 1996
Mailing list available for rent

15650 Japanese American Society for Legal Studies
University of WA Law School-1100 NE Cam.
Seattle, WA 98105

206-233-9292
FAX 206-685-4469
John Haley, Editor
Association for those interested in Japanese law and legal issues.

15651 Law and Society Association
383 South University Street
Suite 205
Salt Lake City, UT 84112

801-581-3219
FAX 888-292-5515
E-Mail: lsa@lawandsociety.org
Home Page: www.lawandsociety.org
Social Media: *Facebook, Twitter, LinkedIn*

Valerie Hans, President
Susan Olson, Executive Director
Kris Monty, Administrative and Events Manager
Megan Crowley, Communication Specialist
Susan Olson, Executive Director
Founded in 1964

15652 Legal Education and Admissions to the Bar Association
321 N Clark Street
21st Floor
Chicago, IL 60611-4403

312-988-5000
800-285-2221
FAX 312-988-5681
Home Page: www.abanet.org/legaled/resources
Social Media: *Facebook, Twitter*

Barry Currier, Managing Director
William E. Adams, Deputy Managing Director
Camille deJorna, Associate Consultant
Carl A. Brambrink, Director of Operations
Beverly Holmes, Program Associate

Association for state bar admission administrators in the United States and its territories.
10000 Members
Founded in 1878
Mailing list available for rent

15653 Legal Marketing Association
330 North Wabash Ave.
Suite 2000
Chicago, IL 60611

312-321-6898
FAX 312-673-6894
E-Mail: membersupport@legalmarketing.org
Home Page: www.legalmarketing.org

Social Media: *Facebook, Twitter, LinkedIn, YouTube*

Timothy B. Corcoran, President
Susan Lane, Director of Operations
Lisa Rottler, Membership Services Coordinator
Adrianne Stokes, Membership Services Associate
Betsi Roach, Executive Directory
Founded in 1985

15654 Maritime Law Association of the United States
400 Poydras Street
27th Floor Texaco Center
New Orleans, LA 70130-324

504-680-8433
FAX 904-421-8437
Home Page: www.mlaus.org

Robert B. Parrish, President
Robert G. Clyne, First VP
Harold K. Watson, Second VP
William Robert Connor III, Treasurer
David J. Farrell, Secretary

To advance reforms in the Maritime Law of the United States, to facilitate justice in its administration to promote uniformity in its enactment and interpretation, to furnish a forum for the discussion and consideration of problems affecting the Maritime Law and its administration to participate as a constituent member of the Comite Maritime International and as an affiliated organization of the American Bar Association.
Founded in 1899
Mailing list available for rent

15655 Mid-America Association of Law Libraries
E-Mail: jeri_hopkins@ca8.uscourts.gov
Home Page: www.aallnet.org/chapter/maall/

Cynthia Bassett, President
Jennifer Prilliman, Vice President/ President Elect
Erika Cohn, Secretary
Jenny Watson, Treasurer

Association for suppliers of law library equipment, supplies and services.
Founded in 1973

15656 NALS/The Association For Legal Professionals
8159 East 41st Street
#210
Tulsa, OK 74145

918-582-5188
FAX 918-582-5907
E-Mail: info@nals.org
Home Page: www.nals.org
Social Media: *Facebook, Twitter, LinkedIn, RSS, Youtube, Google+, Flickr*

Carl H. Morrison, PP-SC, AACP, President
Tammy Hailey, CAE, Executive Director
April Collins, Meetings & Communications Manager
Saundra Bates, Membership Services Manager
Melissa Wells, Certification/Education

Supports all those involved with the technology of the legal profession and the education and training of the legal administrative staff. Publishes quarterly magazine. NALS is dedicated to enhancing the competencies and contributions of members in the legal field.
Founded in 1929
Mailing list available for rent

15657 National Academy of Elder Law Attorneys
1577 Spring Hill Road
Suite 220
Vienna, VA 22182-2223

703-942-5711
FAX 703-563-9504
E-Mail: naela@naela.org
Home Page: www.naela.org

Shirley Berger Whitenack, President
Hyman G. Darling, CELA, CAP, Vice President
Peter G. Wacht, CAE, Executive Director
Ann Watkins, Operations Manager
Courtney White, Marketing Coordinator

Non-profit association for attorneys specializing in Elder Law and Special Needs Law.
4200 Members
Founded in 1987

15658 National American Indian Court Clerks Association
National Association of Tribal Court Personnel
920 Spring Creek Circle
Green Bay, WI 54311

E-Mail: RMJ143@compuserve.com
Robert Miller, President

Devoted to upgrading the integrity capabilities and management of tribal courts through training, testing and certification of court clerks and court administrators.
257 Members

15659 National American Indian Court Judges
1942 Broadway
Suite 215
Boulder, CO 80303

303-449-4112
FAX 303-449-4038
E-Mail: info@naicja.org
Home Page: www.naicja.org
Social Media: *Facebook, Youtube*

Hon. Jill E. Tompkins, President
Richard Blake, First VP
Kevin Briscoe, Second VP
Winona Tanner, Treasurer
Catherine Bryan, Associate Director

National voluntary association of tribal court judges. Primarily devoted to the support of the American Indian and Alaska Native justice systems through education, information sharing and advocacy.
256 Members
Founded in 1969
Mailing list available for rent

15660 National Association for Community Mediation
PO Box 3376
STE 252
Cumming, GA 30028

602-633-4213
FAX 202-545-8873
E-Mail: jordway@nafcm.org
Home Page: www.nafcm.org
Social Media: *Facebook, Twitter, LinkedIn, Youtube, Blogger, Google+*

Joanne Galindo, Senior Director
Victoria Tobin, Executive Director
D.G. Mawn, Associate Executive Director
LaDessa Croucher, Secretary
Laura Jeffords, Treasurer

Supports the maintenance and growth of community-based mediation program and processes: presents a compelling voice in appropriate policy-making, legislative, professional, and other arenas; and encourages the

development and sharing of resources for these efforts.
779 Members
Founded in 1994
Mailing list available for rent

15661 National Association for Court Management
300 Newport Avenue
Williamsburg, VA 23185-4147

757-259-1841
800-616-6165
FAX 757-259-1520
E-Mail: nacm@ncsc.org
Home Page: www.nacmnet.org
Social Media: *Facebook, Twitter, LinkedIn*

David W. Slayton, President
Stephanie Hess, Vice President
Scott C. Griffith, Secretary/Treasurer

Members are clerks of court, court administration and others serving in a court management capacity.
1700 Members
Founded in 1985
Mailing list available for rent

15662 National Association for Legal Career Professionals
1220 19th Street NW
Suite 401
Washington, DC 20036-2405

202-835-1001
FAX 202-835-1112
E-Mail: info@nalp.org
Home Page: www.nalp.org
Social Media: *Facebook, Twitter, LinkedIn, YouTube*

Jean A. Durling, President
Beth Moeller, Vice-President for Member Services
Christina Fox, Vice-President for Finance
James G. Leipold, Executive Director
Frederick E. Thrasher, Deputy Director

Deals with issues such as career planning, recruiting and ethics.
Founded in 1971

15663 National Association of Attorneys General
2030 M Street Nw
8th Floor
Washington, DC 20036

202-326-6000
FAX 202-331-1427
E-Mail: feedback@naag.org
Home Page: www.naag.org
Social Media: *Facebook, Twitter*

Jim McPherson, NAAG Executive Director
Chris Toth, NAAG Deputy Executive Director
Al Lama, NAAG Chief of Staff
Jeffrey Hunter, NAAG Executive Assistant
Marjorie Tharp, NAAG Communications Director

Fosters interstate cooperation on legal and law enforcement issues, conducts policy research and analysis, provides advocacy.
56 Members
Founded in 1907
Mailing list available for rent: 56 names

15664 National Association of Black Criminal
1801 Fayetteville Street 106
Whiting Criminal Justice Building
Durham, NC 27707

919-683-1801
866-846-2225
FAX 919-683-1903
E-Mail: office@nabcj.org

Home Page: www.nabcj.org
Social Media: *Facebook, Twitter, RSS*

Carlyle I. Holder, President
Terri Mcgee, Vice President
Vernise Robinson, Secretary
Charles Lockett, Treasurer
Andre Turner, Assistant Treasurer
Founded in 1974

15665 National Association of Blacks in Criminal Justice
1801 Fayetteville St.
106 Whiting Criminal Justice Bldg.
Durham, NC 27707

919-683-1801
866-846-2225
FAX 919-683-1903
E-Mail: office@nabcj.org
Home Page: www.nabcj.org
Social Media: *Facebook, Twitter, RSS*

Carlyle Holder, President
Terrie McGee, Vice President
Vernise Robinson, Secretary
Charles Lockett, Treasurer

Supports all black persons who are involved in the criminal justice system. Hosts annual trade show.
Founded in 1974

15666 National Association of College and University Attorneys
One Dupont Circle
Suite 620
Washington, DC 20036-1134

202-833-8390
FAX 202-296-8379
E-Mail: nacua@nacua.org
Home Page: www.nacua.org

Kathleen Curry, CEO
Jeanna L. Grimes, Manager of Membership and Marketing
John R. Bishop, Director of Information Services
Meredith L. McMillan, Meetings and Events Planner
Paul L. Parsons, Deputy CEO

Educates attorneys and administrative executives about campus legal issues.
Mailing list available for rent

15667 National Association of Consumer Advocates
1215 17th Street NW
5th Floor
Washington, DC 20036

202-452-1989
FAX 202-452-0099
E-Mail: info@consumeradvocates.org
Home Page: www.consumeradvocates.org
Social Media: *Facebook, Twitter*

Stuart Rossman, Co-Chair
Kirsten Keefe, Co-Chair
Daniel Blinn, Treasurer
Leslie Bailey, Secretary
Ira Rheingold, Executive Director

15668 National Association of Counsel for Children
13123 E. 16th Avenue
B390
Aurora, CO 80045

303-864-5320
E-Mail: Advocate@NACCchildlaw.org
Home Page: www.nacchildlaw.org
Social Media: *Facebook, LinkedIn, Blog*

Gerard Glynn, MS, JD / LLM, President
H.D. Kirkpatrick, Vice President
Kendall Marlowe, Executive Director

Daniel Trujillo, Certification Director
Sara Whalen, Membership Director
Founded in 1977

15669 National Association of County Civil Attorneys
1100 17th St NW
Second Floor
Washington, DC 20036-4619

202-783-5550
FAX 202-783-1583
E-Mail: info@naccho.org
Home Page: www.naccho.org
Social Media: *Facebook, Twitter, LinkedIn, RSS, Blogger, Pinterest, Tumbl*

Paul Yeghiayan, President
Mark Jorritsma, Chief Operating Officer
John Mericsko, Chief Financial Officer
LaMar Hasbrouck, Executive Director
Laura Hanen, Chief, Government & Public Affairs

An affiliate of the National Association of Counties.
240 Members
Founded in 1994
Mailing list available for rent

15670 National Association of Criminal Defense Lawyers
1660 L St NW
12th Floor
Washington, DC 20036-5632

202-872-8600
FAX 202-872-8690
E-Mail: assist@nacdl.org
Home Page: www.nacdl.org
Social Media: *Facebook, Twitter, LinkedIn, YouTube*

E. G. Morris, President
Rick Jones, First Vice President
Drew Findling, Second Vice President
Chris Wellborn, Treasurer
Norman L. Reimer, Executive Director

America's preeminent voluntary nar association supporting the Criminal Defense profession.
10000 Members
Founded in 1958

15671 National Association of Legal Assistants
7666 E. 61st Street
Suite 315
Tulsa, OK 74133

918-587-6828
FAX 918-582-6772
E-Mail: nalanet@nala.org
Home Page: www.nala.orgÿ

Kelly A. LaGrave, ACP, President
Cassandra Oliver, ACP, First Vice President
Jill Francisco, ACP, Second Vice President
Debra L. Overstreet, ACP, Treasurer
Marge Dover, CAE, Executive Director

15672 National Association of Legal Investigator s
235 N. Pine Street
Lansing, MI 48933

517-702-9835
866-520-NALI
FAX 517-372-1501
E-Mail: info@nalionline.org
Home Page: www.nalionline.org
Social Media: *Facebook, LinkedIn*

David W. Luther, CLI, National Director
Don C. Johnson, CLI, CII, Assistant National Director
Neeta McClintock, National Secretary
Julian Vail, LLC, Association Management
John Hoda, CLI, Regional Director, Northeast Region
Founded in 1967

15673 National Association of Legal Vendors
Juris
5106 Maryland Way
Brentwood, TN 37027-7501

615-377-3740

Mel Goldenburg, Chairman

Trade association of organizations who sell products to the legal community.
100 Members

15674 National Association of Parliamentarians (NAP)
213 South Main Street
Independence, MO 64050-3808

816-833-3892
888-627-2929
FAX 816-833-3893
E-Mail: hq@nap2.org
Home Page: www.parliamentarians.org
Social Media: *Facebook, Twitter, RSS*

Mary Randolph, President
James Jones, VP
Cyndy Launchbaugh, Executive Director
Courtney Emery, Membership Marketing & Comm.
Stefanie Luttrell, Administrative Coordinator

An association for those interested in parliamentary law and procedure, NAP's primary objectives are teaching, promoting, and disseminating the philosophy and principles underlying the rules of deliberative assemblies.
3500 Members
Founded in 1930

15675 National Association of Women Lawyers
321 North Clark Street
Chicago, IL 60654

312-988-6186
FAX 312-932-6450
E-Mail: nawl@nawl.org
Home Page: www.nawl.org

Marsha L. Anastasia, President
Angela Beranek Brandt, Vice President
Jennifer A. Waters, Executive Director
Caitlin Kepple, Marketing and Development Director
Karen M. Richardson, Program Director

Promotes the advancement and welfare of women in the legal profession. NAWL is a professional association of attorneys, judges and law students serving the educational, legal and practical interests of the organized bar and women generally. Founded in 1899, long before most local and national bar associations admitted women.
800 Members
Founded in 1899

15676 National Bar Association
1225 11th St Nw
Washington, DC 20001-4217

202-842-3900
FAX 202-289-6170
E-Mail: headquarters@nationalbar.org
Home Page: www.nationalbar.org
Social Media: *Facebook, Twitter, LinkedIn, YouTube*

Benjamin Crump, President
Keith Andrew Perry, Executive Director
Chris Tinker, CFO
Heidi Franklin, Director
Nanjiba Hlemi, Director of Membership and Programs

Represents the interests of minority attorneys, offers education and research programs.
18000 Members
Founded in 1925
Mailing list available for rent

15677 National Center for State Courts
300 Newport Ave
Williamsburg, VA 23185-4147

757-259-1819
800-616-6164
FAX 757-220-0449
E-Mail: mmcqueen@ncsc.org
Home Page: www.ncsc.org
Social Media: *Facebook, Twitter, LinkedIn, Google+, Flickr, Vimeo, Pinter*

David Gilbertson, Chair
Patricia W. Griffin, Vice-Chair
Mary McQueen, President
Thomas Clarke, VP, Research and Technology
Daniel Hall, Vice President of Court Consulting

Provides a forum for the state courts.
Founded in 1971
Mailing list available for rent

15678 National College of District Attorneys
99 Canal Center Plaza
Suite 330
Alexandria, VA 22314

703-549-9222
FAX 703-836-3195
Home Page: www.ndaa.org
Social Media: *Facebook, Yahoo*

William Fitzpatrick, President
Rick Hasey, Chief Financial Officer
Rick Hanes, Chief of Staff
Kay Chopard Cohen, Executive Director
Ann Ratnayake, Staff Attorney

Provides continuing legal education and training for prosecuting attorneys and their investigators and office administrators through programs specifically tailored to meet their needs. Programs include resident courses held each summer at the University of Houston Law Center, short courses conducted in locations throughout the country, and courses presented cooperatively with state associations and local offices.
Founded in 1950
Mailing list available for rent

15679 National Conference of Bar Examiners
302 South Bedford Street
Madison, WI 53703-3622

608-280-8550
FAX 608-280-8552
E-Mail: contact@ncbex.org
Home Page: www.ncbex.org

Erica Moeser, President

A non-profit organization offering tests and services to state boards of bar examiners.
Founded in 1931

15680 National Conference of Bar Foundations
ABA Division For Bar Services
321 North Clark Street
Suite 2000
Chicago, IL 60654

312-988-5344
FAX 312-988-5492
E-Mail: info@ncbf.org
Home Page: www.ncbf.org

Leonard Pataki, President
Leslie Barineau, Secretary
Alison Belfrage, Treasurer
Lorrie Albert, Secretary

Serves bar foundations in the United States and Canada; conducts biannual conferences; maintains information clearinghouses.
Founded in 1977
Mailing list available for rent

15681 National Conference of Bar Presidents
321 North Clark Street
Suite 2000
Chicago, IL 60654-7598

312-988-5344
FAX 312-988-5492
E-Mail: bware@staff.abanet.org
Home Page: www.ncbp.org
Social Media: *Facebook, Twitter*

Lanneau W. Lambert Jr., President
Christine H. Hickey, Treasurer
Jennifer L. Parent, Secretary

Provides a forum for the exchange of ideas and seeks to stimulate work in bar associations.
1M Members
Founded in 1950

15682 National Conference of Commissioners on US Law
211 E Ontario St
Suite 1300
Chicago, IL 60611-3242

312-283-5200
FAX 312-915-0187
E-Mail: nccusl@nccusl.org
Home Page: www.nccusl.org

John A. Sebert, Executive Director
J. Elizabeth Cotton-Murphy, Chief Administrative Officer
Robert Stein, Secretary
Carl Lisman, Treasurer
Elizabeth Cotton, Manager

Designed to foster interstate cooperation in legal issues.
Founded in 1892
Mailing list available for rent

15683 National Conference of Women's Bar Associations
PO Box 82366
Portland, OR 97282

503-775-4396
E-Mail: info@ncwba.org
Home Page: www.ncwba.org
Social Media: *Facebook, Twitter, LinkedIn*

Katherine L. Brown, President
Barbara L. Harris Chiang, Vice President - Membership
Robin Bresky, VP, Fundraising & Strategic Part.
Monica Parham, Vice-President-Finance
Celia J. Collins, Secretary

To promote and assist the growth of local and statewide women's bar associations and ideas among women's bar associations and women's bar sections of local and statewide bar associations; to serve as a vehicle for the exchange and dissemination of information and ideas among women's bar associations and women's bar sections of local and statewide bar associations.

15684 National Conference of Womens' Bar Associations
PO Box 82366
Portland, OR 97282

503-775-4396
FAX 503-657-3932
E-Mail: info@ncwba.org
Home Page: www.ncwba.org
Social Media: *Facebook, Twitter, LinkedIn*

Katherine L. Brown, President
Barbara L. Harris Chiang, Vice President - Membership
Robin Bresky, VP, Fundraising & Strategic Part.
Monica Parham, Vice-President-Finance
Celia J. Collins, Secretary

Supports women who are involved in the legal community and provides a forum for the ex-

change of ideas, thus stimulating work in bar associations.
30000 Members
Founded in 1981
Mailing list available for rent

15685 National Court Reporters Association

12030 Sunrise Valley Drive
Suite 400
Reston, VA 20191

703-556-6272
800-272-6272
FAX 703-391-0629
E-Mail: msic@ncra.org
Home Page: www.ncraonline.org
Social Media: *Facebook, Twitter, LinkedIn, Youtube, RSS*

Stephen A. Zinone, RPR, President
Christine J. Willette, Vice President
Doreen Sutton, RPR, Secretary-Treasurer
Stephen A. Zinone, RPR, Secretary/Treasurer
Toni O'Neill, FAPR, RPR, Director
18000 Members
Founded in 1899

15686 National District Attorneys Association

99 Canal Center Plaza
Suite 330
Alexandria, VA 22314-1548

703-549-9222
FAX 703-836-3195
Home Page: www.ndaa.org
Social Media: *Facebook, Yahoo*

William Fitzpatrick, President
Rick Hasey, Chief Financial Officer
Mary McQueen, President
Thomas Clarke, VP, Research and Technology
Daniel Hall, Vice President of Court Consulting

Supports district attorneys nationwide with education, publications, and regular conferences.
7000 Members
Founded in 1950

15687 National Federation of Paralegal Associations, Inc.

23607 Highway 99
Suite 2-C
Edmonds, WA 98026

425-967-0045
FAX 425-771-9588
E-Mail: info@paralegals.org
Home Page: www.paralegals.org
Social Media: *Facebook, LinkedIn*

Lisa Vessels, RP, CP, FRP, President
Allen F. Mihecoby, CLAS, RP, VP/Director of Profession Dev
Lynne-Marie Reveliotis, VP/Director of Positions and Issues
Yvonne DeAntoneo, VP/Director of Membership
Nita Serrano, RP, VP/Director of Paralegal Cert.

Nonprofit, professional organization comprising state and local paralegal associations throughout the United States and Canada. NFPA affirms the paralegal profession as an independent, self-directed profession which supports increased quality, efficiency and accessibility in the delivery of legal services. NFPA promotes the growth, development and recognition of the profession as a integral partner in the delivery of legal services.
15000 Members
Founded in 1974

15688 National Forensic Center

17 Temple Terrace
Lawrenceville, NJ 08648

609-883-0550
800-526-5177
E-Mail: jon@midi.com
Home Page: expertindex.com

Association for those interested in the application of scientific knowledge in litigation.

15689 National Institute for Trial Advocacy

1685 38th Street
Suite 200
Boulder, CO 80301-2735

800-225-6482
FAX 720-890-7069
E-Mail: support@nita.org
Home Page: www.nita.org

Karen Lockwood, Executive Director
Michelle Rogness, Director of Programs
Katie Grosso, Program Specialist, Public Programs
Jennifer Schneider, Director of Publications
Daniel McHugh, Director of Sales & Marketing
60 Members
Founded in 1971

15690 National Law Foundation

P. O. Box 218
Montchanin, DE 19710

302-656-4757
FAX 302-764-8697
Home Page: www.nlfcle.com

15691 National Lawyers Association

PO Box 327
Suite 400
Lee's Summit, MO 64063

844-917-1787
E-Mail: info@nla.org
Home Page: www.nla.org
Social Media: *Facebook, Twitter, LinkedIn, Pinterest, Google+*

Joshua McCaig, President
Paul Brodersen, Vice President
Lenny A. Best, CEO
Jeremiah Morgan, Board Member
Cynthia Dunbar, Board Member
Founded in 1993

15692 National Lawyers Guild

132 Nassau St
Room 922
New York, NY 10038-2486

212-679-5100
FAX 212-679-2811
E-Mail: nlgno@nlg.org
Home Page: www.nlg.org
Social Media: *Facebook, Twitter*

Azadeh Shahshahani, President
Heidi Boghosian, Executive Director
Natasha Bannan, Executive Vice President
Bina Ahmad, National Vice President
Camilo Romero, National Vice President

Dedicated to seeking economic justice, social equality and the right to political dissent.
5000 Members
Founded in 1937
Mailing list available for rent

15693 National Legal Aid and Defender Associatio n

1901 Pennsylvania Avenue NW
Suite 500
Washington, DC 20006

202-452-0620
FAX 202-872-1031

E-Mail: info@nlada.org
Home Page: www.nlada100years.org

John Mauldin, Chairperson
Rosita Stanley, Vice-Chairperson
Alex Gulotta, Vice-Chairperson
Jo-Ann Wallace, President & CEO
Helen Katz, Chief Development Officer

Private, nonprofit association that dedicates all its resources to ensuring the availability of high quality legal assistance for the poor.
3500 Members
Founded in 1911
Mailing list available for rent

15694 National Notary Association

9350 De Soto Avenue
Chatsworth, CA 91311-4926

818-739-4000
800-876-6827
FAX 818-700-1942
E-Mail: hotline@nationalnotary.org
Home Page: www.nationalnotary.org
Social Media: *Facebook, Twitter, LinkedIn, Google+*

Milton G Valera, Chairman
Thomas A. Heymann, President And CEO
Deborah M Thaw, Executive VP
Rob Clarke, Chief Financial Officer
Dave Stephenson, Vice President, CIO/CTO

Supports all those involved in identity fraud and electronic notarization. Publishes newlsetter.
200M Members
Founded in 1957

15695 National Organizations of Bar Counsel

275 N. York Street
Ste 401
Elmhurst, IL 60126

630-617-5153
E-Mail: BloomL@dcobc.org
Home Page: www.nobc.org
Social Media: *Facebook, Twitter*

Paul J. Burgoyne, President
Kathleen M. Uston, Treasurer
Melinda Bentley, Secretary

NOBC is a non-proft of legal professionals whose members enforce ethics rules that regulate the professional conduct of lawyers who practice in the U.S., Canada and Australia. Via the website, locate your local member office for information.
Founded in 1965

15696 National Paralegal Association

23607 Highway 99
Suite 2-C
Edmonds, WA 98026

425-967-0045
FAX 425-771-9588
E-Mail: info@paralegals.org
Home Page: www.paralegals.org
Social Media: *Facebook, LinkedIn*

Lisa Vessels, RP, CP, FRP, President
Allen F. Mihecoby, CLAS, RP, VP/Director of Profession Dev.
Lynne Marie Reveliotis, VP & Director of Positions
Yvonne DeAntoneo, VP, Director of Membership
Nita Serrano, RP, VP, Dir. of Paralegal Certification
Founded in 1974

15697 Native American Rights Fund

1506 Broadway St
Boulder, CO 80302-6296

303-447-8760
FAX 303-443-7776
E-Mail: webmaster@narf.org

Home Page: www.narf.org
Social Media: *Facebook*

Moses K. N. Haia III, Chairman
Mark Macarro, Board Vice-Chairman
John E. Echohawk, Executive Director
Michael Kennedy, Chief Financial Officer
Eric Anderson, Legal Administrative Assistant

National legal defense fund. Provides legal services and technical assistance to Indian tribes, organizations and individuals in the areas of preservation of tribal existence, protection of tribal natural resources, promotion of human rights, accountability of governments and development of Indian law.
35000 Members
Founded in 1971
Mailing list available for rent

15698 People Against Racist Terror

PO Box 70447
Oakland, CA 94612

510-893-4648
FAX 818-848-2680
E-Mail: info@prisonactivist.org
Home Page:
www.prisonactivist.org/resources/anti-racist-action-lapart-people

Michael Novick, Publisher

Association for those interested in anti-racist activism, research and education covering neo-nazi and other racist violence, efforts at conflict resolution and social justic reforms.

15699 Practising Law Institute

1177 Avenue of the Americas
2nd Floor
New York, NY 10036

212-824-5700
800-260-4754
FAX 212-581-4670
E-Mail: cfbook@loc.gov
Home Page: www.pli.edu
Social Media: *Facebook, Twitter, LinkedIn, YouTtube, Pinterest*

John Y Cole, Director
Anne Boni, Program Specialist

Nonprofit continuing legal education organization chartered by the Regents of the University of the State of New York. Dedicated to providing the legal community and allied professionals with the most up-to-date, revelant information and techniques which are critical to the development of a professional, competitive edge.
Founded in 1977
Mailing list available for rent

15700 RAND Institute for Civil Justice

1776 Main Street
Santa Monica, CA 90407-3208

310-393-0411
FAX 310-393-4898
E-Mail: webmaster@monroecc.edu
Home Page: www.rand.org/icj
Social Media: *Facebook, Twitter, LinkedIn, Instagram, YouTube*

John L. Bartolotta, Chair
Grace S. Tillinghast, Vice Chair
Anne M. Kress, Ph.D., President
Andrea C. Wade, Ph.D., Provost/VP, Academic Services
Lloyd A. Holmes, Ph.D., Vice President, Student Services

Nonprofit research organization within the RAND Corporation dedicated to interdisciplinary, empirical research to facilitate change in the civil justice system.
1.1M Members
Founded in 1961

15701 Rocky Mountain Mineral Law Foundation

9191 Sheridan Blvd
Suite 203
Westminster, CO 80031-3011

303-321-8100
FAX 303-321-7657
E-Mail: igor@dramaguild.com
Home Page: www.rmmlf.org
Social Media: *Facebook, Twitter, Flickr, Tumblr, Youtube*

Stephen Schwartz, President
Ralph Sevush, Executive Director, Business
Gary Garrisonÿ, Executive Director
Joey Stocks, Director of Publications
Deborah Murad, Director of Business Affairs
6M+ Members
Founded in 1920
Mailing list available for rent

15702 The Center for HIV Law & Policy

65 Broadway
Suite 832
New York, NY 10006

212-430-6733
FAX 212-430-6734
Home Page: www.hivlawandpolicy.org
Social Media: *Facebook, Twitter, LinkedIn, Instagram*

Catherine Hanssens, Executive Director
Allison Nichol, Co-Director

Center works to reduce impact of HIV on vulnerable communities.

15703 The International Association for Conflict Management

E-Mail: office@the-efa.org
Home Page: www.iacm-conflict.orgÿ
Social Media: *Facebook, Twitter, LinkedIn*

Karen Williams, Secretary
Robin Martin, Chapter Development
Jennifer Maybin, Education
Sheila Buff, Job List
Cassie Tuttle, Membership
Founded in 1970

15704 The Sports Lawyers Association

12100 Sunset Hills Road
Suite 130
Reston, VA 20190

703-437-4377
FAX 703-435-4390
E-Mail: ewa@ewa.org
Home Page: www.sportslaw.org

Scott Elliott, President
Caroline W. Hendrie, Executive Director
George Dieter, Chief Operating Officer
Tracee Eason, Administrative Coordinator
Kenneth Terrell, Project Director
800 Members
Founded in 1947

15705 Trial Lawyers Marketing

1 Boston Place
Suite 1260
Boston, MA 02108-4471

617-720-5356
FAX 617-742-5417

James Sokolve, President

Provides education and marketing information to personal injury attorneys.
300 Members
Founded in 1986

Newsletters

15706 ABA Child Law Practice

ABA Center on Children and the Law
740 15th Street, NW
Washington, DC 20005

202-662-1000
800-285-2221
FAX 202-662-1755
E-Mail: teaguec@staff.abanet.org
Home Page: www.abanet.org
Social Media: *Facebook, Twitter*

Laurel Bellows, President
Jack L. Rives, Executive Director
Robert M. Carlson, Chairman
Lucian T. Pera, Treasurer
Cara Lee T. Neville, Secretary

An online periodical for lawyers who advocate for children and youth, judges handling child protection-related cases, and other professionals who want to keep abreast of cutting edge legal issues affecting children. Includes litigation strategies, analyses of new laws, policies and research, and how they apply to practice, expert interviews, advice from judges, and more.
Cost: $50.00
Frequency: Online
Founded in 1878
Mailing list available for rent

15707 ABA Washington Letter

American Bar Association Government Affairs Office
321 N Clark St
Chicago, IL 60654-7598

312-988-5000
800-285-2221
FAX 202-662-1762
E-Mail: mcmillionr@staff.abanet.org
Home Page:
www.abanet.org/poladv/home.html
Social Media: *Facebook, Twitter*

Thomas M. Susman, Director, GAO
Denise A. Cardman, Deputy Director
Jared D. Hess, Legislative Coordinator
Laurel Bellows, President
Jack L. Rives, Executive Director

A monthly publication produced by the GAO to report and analyze congressional and executive branch action on legislation issues of interest to the ABA and the legal profession, highlighting ABA involvment in the federal legislative process.
Cost: $30.00
Frequency: Monthly
Founded in 1957
Mailing list available for rent

15708 ACC Docket

American Corporate Counsel Association
1025 Connecticut Ave Nw
Suite 200
Washington, DC 20036-5425

202-293- 410
FAX 202-293-4701
E-Mail: acc.chair@acc.com
Home Page: www.acc.com

Tiffani Alexander, Managing Editor
Ken Lawrence, Director Publishing
Fred Krebs, President/CEO
Moustafa W. Abdel-Kader, Marketing Manager
David Barre, Director Communications
Frequency: Monthly
Mailing list available for rent

15709 ALA News

Association of Legal Administrators

75 Tri-State International
Suite 222
Lincolnshire, IL 60069-4435

847-267-1252
FAX 847-267-1329
E-Mail: publications@alanet.org
Home Page: www.alanet.org

Larry Smith, Executive Director
Debbie Thomas, Director, Accounting &
Finance
Renee Mahovsky, Director,
Administration/Operations
Bob Abramson, Director, Marketing &
Communication
Jan Waugh, Director, Member Services

Member magazine focusing on association
news and career improvements for administra-
tors in the association.
Cost: $36.00
40 Pages
Circulation: 9000
Founded in 1971
Mailing list available for rent
Printed in 4 colors on glossy stock

15710 ATLA Advocate
Association of Trial Lawyers of America
1050 31st Street NW
Washington, DC 20007

202-965-3500
800-424-2725
Home Page: www.atla.org

Kathleen Flynn Peterson, President
Linda Lipsen, Chief Executive Officer
Charles Jeffress, Chief Operating Officer
Kathi Berge, Chief Financial Officer
Anjali Jesseramsing, Executive Vice President

Keeps association members abreast of associa-
tion news. Not available by subscription. No
advertising or announcements.
Cost: $5.00
Frequency: Monthly
Mailing list available for rent
Printed in 2 colors

**15711 Administrative & Regulatory Law
News**
American Bar
Association-Administrative/Regulatory
740 15th St NW
11th Floor
Washington, DC 20005-1022

202-662-1000
800-285-2221
FAX 202-662-1592
E-Mail: knightk@staff.abanet.org
Home Page: www.abanet.org
Social Media: *Facebook, Twitter*

Laurel Bellows, President
Jack L. Rives, Executive Director
Robert M. Carlson, Chairman
Lucian T. Pera, Treasurer
Cara Lee T. Neville, Secretary

Newsletter for Section members providing information about recent developments affecting
clients and practices with features such as Supreme Court News, News From the Circuits,
and more.
16 Pages
Frequency: Quarterly
Circulation: 6000
Founded in 1878
Mailing list available for rent

15712 Admiralty Law Newsletter
American Bar Association - TIPS
Admiralty/Maritime
321 N Clark St
Chicago, IL 60654-7598

312-988-5000
800-285-2221

FAX 312-988-5280
E-Mail: askaba@abanet.org
Home Page: www.abanet.org
Social Media: *Facebook, Twitter*

Laurel Bellows, President
Jack L. Rives, Executive Director
Robert M. Carlson, Chairman
Lucian T. Pera, Treasurer
Cara Lee T. Neville, Secretary

Focuses on summaries of recent case law development, CLE programs in maritime law
area, and information and articles on programs
and projects.
Frequency: Quarterly
Founded in 1878
Mailing list available for rent

15713 Allen's Trademark Digest
Congressional Digest Corporation
152413 29th Street NW
Washington, DC 20007-2756

202-333-7332
800-637-9915
FAX 202-625-6670
E-Mail: ededitor@aol.com
Home Page: www.trademarkdigest.com

Griff Thomas, President
Page Robinson, Publisher
Brooke Beyer, Editor

Monthly digest of citable and uncitable
tradmark decisions issues by the US Patent and
Trademark Office.
Cost: $695.00
Frequency: 12 per year
ISSN: 8990-191X
Founded in 1989

**15714 American Association of Visually
Impaired Attorneys**
American Blind Lawyers Association
c/o American Council of the Blind
2220 Wilson Blvd, Suite 650
Arlingtonn, VA 22201

202-467-5081
800-424-8666
FAX 703-465-5085
E-Mail: info@acb.org
Home Page: www.acb.org

Melanie Brunson, Executive Director
12000 Members
Frequency: Audio
Circulation: 150
Founded in 1961

**15715 American Corporate Counsel
Association Newsletter**
Americna Corporate Counsel Association
1025 Connecticut Ave NW
Suite 200
Washington, DC 20036-5425

202-293-8439
FAX 202-331-7454
Home Page: http://www.acc.com

Deneen Stambone, Editor

Association news.
16 Pages
Frequency: Bi-Monthly
Circulation: 9,700
Printed in 2 colors on matte stock

**15716 American Foreign Law Association
Newsletter**
Forman Law School
140 W 62nd Street
New York, NY 10023

212-636-6844
FAX 212-636-6899

James Maxelner, Publisher

Reports on programs sponsored by the Association of American Foreign Law.
Cost: $20.00
4 Pages
Frequency: Monthly

**15717 American Lawyers Newspapers
Group**
American Lawyers Newspapers
1730 M St Nw
Suite 802
Washington, DC 20036-4550

202-296-1995
FAX 202-457-0718

Ted Goldman, Manager

Supports all those involved in the reporting of
legal issues.
Founded in 1977

15718 American Notary
American Society of Notaries
PO Box 5707
Tallahassee, FL 32314

850-671-5164
800-522-3392
FAX 850-671-5165
Home Page: www.notaries.org

Lisa K Fisher, Publisher
Joanna Lilly, Executive Director
Kathleen Butler, Executive Director

Legislation news.
Cost: $21.00
20 Pages
Frequency: Quarterly
Circulation: 21000
Printed in 4 colors on glossy stock

**15719 American Society of International
Law Newsletter**
American Society of International Law
2223 Massachusetts Ave Nw
Washington, DC 20008-2864

202-939-6000
FAX 202-797-7133
Home Page: http://www.asil.org

Charlotte Ku, Executive Director

Association news and updates on overseas litigation.
6 Pages
Frequency: Monthly

**15720 Antitrust and Trade Regulation
Report**
Bureau of National Affairs
1801 S Bell St
Arlington, VA 22202-4501

703-341-3000
800-372-1033
FAX 800-253-0332
E-Mail: customercare@bna.com
Home Page: www.bnabooks.com
Social Media: *Facebook, Twitter, LinkedIn*

Paul N Wojcik, Chairman
Gregory C. McCaffery, President and CEO
John Camp, Vice President and Chief
Technology
Lisa A. Fitzpatrick, Vice President
Audrey Hipkins, Vice President

Weekly comprehensive coverage of significant
competition and deceptive trade practice law
developments on the federal, state and international levels.
Cost: $1894.00
Frequency: Weekly

15721 Attorneys Marketing Report
James Publishing

3505 Cadillac Avenue
Suite H
Costa Mesa, CA 92626

714-755-5450
800-440-4780
FAX 714-751-2709
E-Mail:
customer-service@jamespublishing.com
Home Page: www.jamespublishing.com

Jim Pawell, Founder/President
Linda Standke, Editor

The latest practice development tips and news
for law firms from Yellow Pages advertising to
referral management.
Founded in 1981
Mailing list available for rent

15722 BNA's Bankruptcy Law Reporter
Bureau of National Affairs
1801 S Bell St
Arlington, VA 22202-4501

703-341-3000
800-372-1033
FAX 800-253-0332
E-Mail: customercare@bna.com
Home Page: www.bnabooks.com
Social Media: *Facebook, Twitter, LinkedIn*

Paul N Wojcik, Chairman
Gregory C. McCaffery, President and CEO
John Camp, Vice President and Chief
Technology
Lisa A. Fitzpatrick, Vice President
Audrey Hipkins, Vice President

Weekly notification service covering various
areas of bankruptcy law.
Cost: $1331.00
Frequency: Weekly

15723 BNA's Corporate Counsel Weekly Corporate Practice Series
Bureau of National Affairs
1801 S Bell St
Arlington, VA 22202-4501

703-341-3000
800-372-1033
FAX 800-253-0332
E-Mail: customercare@bna.com
Home Page: www.bnabooks.com
Social Media: *Facebook, Twitter, LinkedIn*

Paul N Wojcik, Chairman
Gregory C. McCaffery, President and CEO
John Camp, Vice President and Chief
Technology
Lisa A. Fitzpatrick, Vice President
Audrey Hipkins, Vice President

A weekly roundup of the latest developments in
law that affect business, including coverage of
the courts, federal regulatory agencies, the executive branch, states and professional associations.
Cost: $722.00
8 Pages
Frequency: Weekly
Printed in one color on matte stock

15724 BNA's Medicare Report
Bureau of National Affairs
1801 S Bell St
Arlington, VA 22202-4501

703-341-3000
800-372-1033
FAX 800-253-0332
E-Mail: customercare@bna.com
Home Page: www.bnabooks.com
Social Media: *Facebook, Twitter, LinkedIn*

Paul N Wojcik, Chairman
Gregory C. McCaffery, President and CEO
John Camp, Vice President and Chief
Technology
Lisa A. Fitzpatrick, Vice President
Audrey Hipkins, Vice President

Biweekly notification service covering legislative, regulatory and legal developments affecting or pertaining to the Medicare program; also
provides information about relevant developments in the Medicaid program that could have
implications for Medicare.
Cost: $1108.00
Frequency: Weekly

15725 Bankruptcy Court Decisions
LRP Publications
PO Box 980
Horsham, PA 19044-0980

215-784-0912
800-341-7874
FAX 215-784-9639
E-Mail: webmaster@lrp.com
Home Page: www.lrp.com

Todd Lutz, CFO
Kenneth Khan, CEO

Full-text loose leaf bankruptcy reporting ser-
vice with an expanded and informative news-
letter.
Cost: $900.00
Founded in 1977
Mailing list available for rent
Printed in one color on matte stock

15726 Bankruptcy Law Letter
Thomson West Publishing
610 Opperman Dr
Eagan, MN 55123-1340

651-687-7000
800-344-5008
FAX 651-687-5581
Home Page: www.west.thomson.com
Social Media: *Facebook, Twitter, LinkedIn,
Blogger, Pinterest, Tumblr, St*

Charles B Cater, Executive VP
Laurie Zenner, VP

Highly specialized coverage of case develop-
ments in the bankruptcy field. No outside sub-
missions accepted.
Cost: $621.00
Frequency: Monthly
Circulation: 3000

15727 Biotechnology Law Report
Mary Ann Liebert
2 Madison Ave
Larchmont, NY 10538-1947

914-834-4348
800-6 5-3 23
FAX 914-834-3688
E-Mail: info@liebertpub.com
Home Page: www.liebertpub.com/

Mary Ann Liebert, President
Gerry J Elman, Editor
Harry Matisco, Marketing

Legislative news for the world of biotechnol-
ogy and science.
Cost: $1858.00
96 Pages
ISSN: 0730-031X
Founded in 1980

15728 Business Crime: Criminal Liability of the Business Community
Matthew Bender and Company
11 Penn Plz
Suite 5101
New York, NY 10001-2006

212-000-1111
FAX 212-244-3188

Eric Blood, Data Processing

The most complete guide to the many criminal
questions that can arise in modern business
practice.

15729 Business Information Alert
Alert Publications

401 W Fullerton Parkway
Suite 1403E
Chicago, IL 60614-2801

773-525-7594
866-492-5266
FAX 773-525-7015
E-Mail: info@alertpub.com
Home Page: www.alertpub.com/

Donna T Heroy, Publisher/Editor
Nina Wendt, Director Marketing

Newsletter for business and law librarians to
help them make purchasing decisions for their
companies. Includes product reviews and columns on industry news. Discounted price of
$99 for non-profit organizations.
Cost: $167.00
12 Pages
ISSN: 1042-0746
Founded in 1981

15730 CLE Guidebook
Law Bulletin Publishing Company
415 N State St
Suite 1
Chicago, IL 60654-8116

312-644-7800
FAX 312-644-4255
Home Page: www.lawbulletin.com

Lanning Macfarland Jr, President
Bernard M Judge, Publisher
Michael Loquercio, Sales Manager

Lists hundreds of CLE courses by date, subject
and provider.
Cost: $219.00
34 Pages
Printed in 4 colors on matte stock

15731 Chapter 11 Update
Federal Managers Association
1641 Prince St
Alexandria, VA 22314-2818

703-683-8700
FAX 703-683-8707
E-Mail: info@fedmanagers.org
Home Page: www.fedmanagers.org

Todd Wells, Executive Director
George J. Smith, National VP
Patricia J. Niehaus, National President
Richard J. Oppedisano, National Secretary
Katie L. Smith, National Treasurer

Management issues and concerns.
Frequency: Monthly
Mailing list available for rent

15732 Civil RICO Report
LRP Publications
PO Box 24668
West Palm Beach, FL 33416-4668

561-622-6520
800-341-7874
FAX 561-622-0757
E-Mail: webmaster@lrp.com
Home Page: www.lrp.com

Kenneth Kahn, President
Robert K Latzko, Editor

Weekly report and analysis of litigation under
the civil provisions of the Racketeer Influenced
and Corrupt Organizations Act as well as legislative developments and state little RICO laws.
Cost: $812.00
Printed in 2 colors on matte stock

15733 Client Counseling Update
American Bar Association
321 N Clark St
Chicago, IL 60654-7598

312-988-5000
800-285-2221
FAX 312-988-5280
E-Mail: askaba@abanet.org

Home Page: www.abanet.org
Social Media: *Facebook, Twitter*

Laurel Bellows, President
Jack L. Rives, Executive Director
Robert M. Carlson, Chairman
Richard J. Oppe Pera, Treasurer
Cara Lee T. Neville, Secretary

e-Newsletter contains summaries of publications and news articles concerning client counseling.
Founded in 1878
Mailing list available for rent

15734 Collective Bargaining Negotiations and Contracts
Bureau of National Affairs
1801 S Bell St
Arlington, VA 22202-4501

703-341-3000
800-372-1033
FAX 800-253-0332
E-Mail: customercare@bna.com
Home Page: www.bnabooks.com
Social Media: *Facebook, Twitter, LinkedIn*

Paul N Wojcik, Chairman
Gregory C. McCaffery, President and CEO
John Camp, Vice President and Chief Technology
Lisa A. Fitzpatrick, Vice President
Audrey Hipkins, Vice President

A biweekly notificaiton and reference service containing information designed to help unions and management prepare, negotiate and administer contracts.
Cost: $1541.00
Frequency: Monthly
Founded in 1929

15735 Commercial Law Bulletin
Commercial Law League of America
205 N. Michigan
Suite 2212
Chicago, IL 60601-5961

312-240-1400
800-978-2552
FAX 312-240-1408
E-Mail: info@clla.org
Home Page: www.clla.org

Oliver Yandle, VP
Charles R Johnson III, Treasurer

Provides news and information on bankruptcy, collections, debt and insolvency information, as well as reports from Washington DC and updates on resolutions.
Cost: $65.00
Circulation: 5000
Founded in 1895

15736 Commercial Laws of the World
Foreign Tax Law
PO Box 2189
Ormond Beach, FL 32175-2189

386-341-7405
Home Page: www.foreignlaw.com

Contains company laws, commercial codes, and related law for over 100 countries.
Cost: $100.00

15737 Communications Lawyer
American Bar Association Forum - Communication Law
321 N Clark St
Chicago, IL 60654-7598

312-988-5000
800-285-2221
FAX 312-988-5280
E-Mail: askaba@abanet.org

Home Page: www.abanet.org
Social Media: *Facebook, Twitter*

Laurel Bellows, President
Jack L. Rives, Executive Director
Robert M. Carlson, Chairman
Lucian T. Pera, Treasurer
Cara Lee T. Neville, Secretary

Newsletter reviews significant activities and developments in communications law and reports on Forum activities.
Cost: $45.00
30 Pages
Frequency: Quarterly
ISSN: 0737-7622
Founded in 1878
Mailing list available for rent

15738 Computer & Internet LAWCAST
Vox Juris
PO Box 389
Pennington, NJ 08534

609-737-6543
800-LAW-CAST
FAX 609-737-3860
E-Mail: INFO@lawcast.com
Home Page: www.lawcast.com

Jason Meyer, Publisher

Groundbreaking law arising from life and commerce in the digital age,...in licensing, torts, intellectual property securities, contracts, privacy, joint ventures, antitrust, content regulation and more. If your clients use email or the internet, have their own websites, produce hardware or software or provide on-line service, listen up here. 60 minute audio and outline twice monthly
Cost: $25.00

15739 Computer Industry Litigation Reporter
Andrews Publications
175 Strafford Avenue
Building 4 Suite 140
Wayne, PA 19087

610-225-0510
800-345-1101
FAX 610-225-0501
Home Page: www.andrewspub.com

Donna Higgins, Editor
Mary Ellen Fox, Publisher
Jodine Mayberry, Executive Editor

Covers litigation involving copyright, patent, trade secrets, employment, securities, trademark, contracts and other issues related to the computer industry.
Cost: $1226.00
Founded in 1983

15740 Construction Claims Monthly
Business Publishers
2222 Sedwick Dr
Suite 101
Durham, NC 27713

800-223-8720
FAX 800-508-2592
E-Mail: custserv@bpinews.com
Home Page: www.bpinews.com

Contains summaries of important decisions from the federal and state courts, boards of contract appeals, and the Office of Comptroller General on such topics as change orders, design problems, inspection, delay, home office overhead, claims administration, termination, waivers, differing site conditions, subcontractors and insurance.
Cost: $244.00
8 Pages
Frequency: Monthly
Founded in 1962

15741 Construction Litigation Reporter
McGraw Hill
1221 Avenue of the Americas
New York, NY 10020-1095

212-512-2000
800-352-3566
FAX 212-512-3840
E-Mail: webmaster@mcgraw-hill.com
Home Page: www.mcgraw-hill.com

Harold W McGraw III, CEO

Summaries of judicial and agency decisions.
Cost: $300.00
24 Pages
Frequency: Monthly

15742 Consumer Financial Services Law Report
LRP Publications
PO Box 980
Horsham, PA 19044-0980

215-784-0912
800-341-7874
FAX 215-784-9639
E-Mail: webmaster@lrp.com
Home Page: www.lrp.com

Todd Lutz, CFO
Kenneth Kahn, President

Keeps you up-to-date with the latest changes and developments in the area of consumer financial services litigation. Provides timely coverage of legal developments involving fair lending, debt collection, state UDAP laws and fraud, automobile lending and leasing, damage theories and class actions, and more.
Cost: $220.00
Founded in 1977

15743 Consumer Product Litigation Reporter
Andrews Publications
175 Strafford Avenue
Building 4, Suite 140
Wayne, PA 19087-3331

610-225-0510
800-345-1101
FAX 610-225-0501
Home Page: www.andrewspub.com

Robert Maroldo, Publisher
Eileen Gonyeau, Editor

Covers areas such as strict liability, assumption of risk, insurance coverage, adequacy of warning merchantability, punitive damages, component liability, forseeability and more.
Cost: $46.00

15744 Controlling Law Firm Costs
Institute of Management and Administration
1 Washington Park
Suite 1300
Newark, NJ 07102-3130

212-244-0360
FAX 973-622-0595
E-Mail: customercare@bna.com
Home Page: www.ioma.com

Laurel Bellows, President

Shows law office administrators how to reduce overhead, improve the firm's profitability and efficiency, get more value for the firm's budget dollar, and improve their own professional standing. Includes strategies to control the costs of support staff, insurance, leases, taxes, computers and more.
Cost: $300.00
Frequency: Annual+

15745 Corporate Counsel LAWCAST
Vox Juris

PO Box 389
Pennington, NJ 08534

609-737-6543
800-LAW-CAST
FAX 609-737-3860
E-Mail: INFO@lawcast.com
Home Page: www.lawcast.com

Jason Meyer, Publisher

Everything for the in-house counsel in one lively and substantive program. In-house ethics and privileges, the law of the workplace, intellectual property, corporate governance, contracts, regulations, and more...close-ups on how top counsel meet the demands of the in-house practice. 75 minute audio and online, 15 times per year
Cost: $25.00

15746 Corporate Legal Times

Corporate Legal Times
656 West Randolph Street
Suite 500 East
Chicago, IL 60611

312-654-3500
FAX 312-654-3525
Home Page: www.cltmag.com

Nat Slavin, Publisher
Larry Lannon, CEO

Written for general counsel and other in house corporate attourneys to provide information relevant to strategic planning and day-to-day operation of legal departments including in-house counsel's relationships with outside law firms.
Cost: $10.00
Frequency: Monthly
Circulation: 40000
Founded in 1991

15747 Corporate Practice Series

Bureau of National Affairs
1801 S Bell St
Arlington, VA 22202-4501

703-341-3000
800-372-1033
FAX 800-253-0332
E-Mail: customercare@bna.com
Home Page: www.bnabooks.com
Social Media: *Facebook, Twitter, LinkedIn*

Paul N Wojcik, Chairman
Gregory C. McCaffery, President and CEO
John Camp, Vice President and Chief Technology
Lisa A. Fitzpatrick, Vice President
Audrey Hipkins, Vice President

A corporate law reference service organized into a series of portfolios written by legal experts, with a weekly newsletter. Each portfolio covers a different legal subject with detailed analyses, working papers and a bibliography.
Cost: $2426.00
ISSN: 0162-5691

15748 Criminal Law Reporter

Bureau of National Affairs
1801 S Bell St
Arlington, VA 22202-4501

703-341-3000
800-372-1033
FAX 800-253-0332
E-Mail: customercare@bna.com
Home Page: www.bnabooks.com
Social Media: *Facebook, Twitter, LinkedIn*

Paul N Wojcik, Chairman
Gregory C. McCaffery, President and CEO
John Camp, Vice President and Chief Technology
Lisa A. Fitzpatrick, Vice President
Audrey Hipkins, VP

A weekly notification service providing coverage of court decisions, federal legislative activ-

ities and administrative developments in the field of criminal law. Fulltext of the cases highlighted in each issue are available free on CrL's web site. Subscribers can also recieve free email notification of Supreme Court decisions.
Cost: $1108.00
Frequency: Weekly
Founded in 1929

15749 DataLaw Report

Clark Boardman Company
155 Pflingsten Road
Deerfield, IL 60015

847-374-0400
FAX 847-948-7099

Amelia Boss, Editor

Analyzes the changing global legal environment for electronic information.

15750 Death Care Business Advisor

LRP Publications
747 Dresher Road
PO Box 980
Horsham, PA 19044-980

215-784-0912
800-341-7874
FAX 215-784-9639
E-Mail: webmaster@lrp.com
Home Page: www.lrp.com

Jay Kravetz, Editor
Dionne Ellis, Managing Editor

The only twice a month newsletter that offers you in-depth business coverage of memorialization and remembrance issues. You'll recieve news and tips on the latest trends and developments in funeral service, cemetery management and cremation and learn innovative strategies to capture the expanding preneed market and more.
Cost: $215.00
Founded in 1977

15751 Digest of Environmental Law

Strafford Publications
PO Box 13729
Atlanta, GA 30324-0729

404-881-1141
800-926-7926
FAX 404-881-0074
E-Mail: customerservice@straffordpub.com
Home Page: www.straffordpub.com

Richard Ossoff, Presdient
Jennifer Vaughan, Managing Editor

Monthly digest of nationally significant litigation related to the full range of environmental issues, includes annual index.
Cost: $547.00
Frequency: Monthly
ISSN: 1073-9521
Founded in 1984

15752 Disability Compliance for Higher Education

LRP Publications
747 Dresher Road
PO Box 980
Horsham, PA 19044-980

215-784-0912
800-341-7874
FAX 561-622-2423
E-Mail: webmaster@lrp.com
Home Page: www.lrp.com

Marsha Jaquays, Editor
Nancy Grover, Managing Editor

Helps colleges determine if they are complying with the Americans with Disabilities Act (ADA) and section 504 of the Rehabilitation Act. Readers find out how to fulfill legal obligations under the law and save their college

from costly litigation.
Cost: $198.00
Frequency: Monthly
Founded in 1977

15753 ELA Notes

Education Law Association
300 College Park Ave
Dayton, OH 45469-0001

937-229-3589
FAX 937-229-3845
E-Mail: ela@educationlaw.org
Home Page: www.educationlaw.org

Mandy Schrenk, Executive Director
Jody Thornburg, Publications Editor
Cate K Smith, Executive Director
Judy Pleiman, Member Services Coordinator
Jody Thornburg, Publications Manager

ELA is a nonprofit, nonadvocacy, member-based organization found in 1954 to provide an unbiased forum for the dissemination of information about current issues in education law. Membership is open to all individuals and organizations with a special interest in education law. ELA's mission is to bring together educational and legal scholars and practioners to inform and advance educational policy and practice through knowledge of the law.
Cost: $125.00
Frequency: Quarterly
Circulation: 1300
ISSN: 0047-8997
Founded in 1954
Printed in 2 colors on matte stock

15754 Employee Benefits Cases

Bureau of National Affairs
1801 S Bell St
Arlington, VA 22202-4501

703-341-3000
800-372-1033
FAX 800-253-0332
E-Mail: customercare@bna.com
Home Page: www.bnabooks.com
Social Media: *Facebook, Twitter, LinkedIn*

Paul N Wojcik, Chairman
Gregory C. McCaffery, President and CEO
John Camp, Vice President and Chief Technology
Lisa A. Fitzpatrick, Vice President
Audrey Hipkins, VP

A weekly decisional service that reports the full text of federal and state court opinions and selected decisions of arbitrators and the NLRB on employee benefits issues.
Cost: $1582.00
54 Pages
Frequency: Weekly
Circulation: 6000+
ISSN: 0273-236X
Founded in 1929
Printed in on matte stock

15755 Employment Law Report Strategist

Data Research
PO Box 490
Rosemount, MN 55068-0490

952-452-8694
800-365-4900
FAX 952-452-8694

Covers the latest court cases and late-breaking legislation along with the most recent law review articles affecting employment.
Cost: $120.00
Frequency: Monthly
ISSN: 1058-1308

15756 Entertainment Law and Finance

345 Park Avenue S
New York, NY 10010-1707

212-779-6611
800-888-8300
FAX 212-696-1848

Stan Soocher, Editor
Stuart M Wise, Production Manager
Kerry Kyle, Circulation Director

Laws and news in the entertainment field.
Cost: $195.00
8 Pages
Frequency: Monthly
ISSN: 0883-2455
Printed in 2 colors

15757 Entertainment and Sports Lawyer

American Bar Association
Forum-Entertainment/Sport
321 N Clark St
Chicago, IL 60654-7598

312-988-5000
800-285-2221
FAX 312-988-5280
E-Mail: askaba@abanet.org
Home Page: www.abanet.org
Social Media: *Facebook, Twitter*

Laurel Bellows, President
Vered Yakovee, Editor
Jack L. Rives, Executive Director
Robert M. Carlson, Chairman
Lucian T. Pera, Treasurer

Newsletter on recent developments in the
sports and entertainment industries, public pol-
icy and scholarly viewpoints.
Cost: $60.00
40 Pages
Frequency: Quarterly
ISSN: 0732-1880
Founded in 1878
Mailing list available for rent

15758 Estate Planner's Alert

Thomson Reuters
2395 Midway Rd
Suite 4
Carrollton, TX 75006

646-822-2000
800-231-1860
FAX 646-822-2800
E-Mail: trta.lei-support@thomsonreuters.com
Home Page: www.ria.thomsonreuters.com

Laurel Bellows, President
Thomas H Glocer, CEO & Director
Robert D Daleo, Chief Financial Officer
Kelli Crane, Senior Vice President & CIO

Offers complete coverage of estate planning
and law.
Cost: $195.00
Frequency: Monthly
Founded in 1935

**15759 Exercise Standards and Malpractice
Reporter**

PRC Publishing
3976 Fulton Dr Nw
Canton, OH 44718-3043

330-492-6063
800-336-0083
FAX 330-492-6176
Home Page: www.prcpublishingcorp.com

Molly Romig, VP
Dr. Doyice Cotton, Publisher
Mary Cotton, Publisher

Designed to cover topics of interest and con-
cern to the exercise professionals.
Cost: $39.95
16 Pages
Circulation: 750
ISSN: 0891-0278

Founded in 1997
Printed in 2 colors on matte stock

15760 FCBA Newsletter

Federal Communications Bar Association
1020 19th St Nw
Suite 325
Washington, DC 20036-6113

202-293-4000
FAX 202-293-4317
E-Mail: fcba@fcba.org
Home Page: www.fcba.org

Stanley Zenor, Executive Director
Kerry Loughney, Director of Membership
Services
Diane J Cornell, Treasurer
Wendy Jo Parish, Administrative Assistant
Beth Phillips, Bookkeeper

A non-profit organization of attorneys and
other professionals involved in the development, interpretation, implementation and practice of communications law and policy.
Frequency: Monthly
Founded in 1936
Mailing list available for rent

15761 Family Law Reporter

Bureau of National Affairs
1801 S Bell St
Arlington, VA 22202-4501

703-341-3000
800-372-1033
FAX 800-253-0332
E-Mail: customercare@bna.com
Home Page: www.bnabooks.com
Social Media: *Facebook, Twitter, LinkedIn*

Paul N Wojcik, Chairman
Gregory C. McCaffery, President and CEO
John Camp, Vice President and Chief
Technology
Lisa A. Fitzpatrick, Vice President
Audrey Hipkins, VP

A weekly notification and reference service
dealing with all significant state and federal de-
velopments in the field of family law.
Cost: $974.00
Frequency: Weekly
Founded in 1929

15762 Federal Contract Disputes

Business Publishers
2222 Sedwick Dr
Suite 101
Durham, NC 27713

800-223-8720
FAX 800-508-2592
E-Mail: custserv@bpinews.com
Home Page: www.bpinews.com

A monthly newsletter designed to help you
avoid disputes, and successfully resolve those
you can't avoid. Each issue brings you concise
synopses of a dozen major decisions, from the
courts, the Comptroller General, and the boards
of contract appeals.
Cost: $285.00
Frequency: Monthly

15763 Federal Contracts Report

Bureau of National Affairs
1801 S Bell St
Arlington, VA 22202-4501

703-341-3000
800-372-1033
FAX 800-253-0332
E-Mail: customercare@bna.com
Home Page: www.bnabooks.com
Social Media: *Facebook, Twitter, LinkedIn*

Paul N Wojcik, Chairman
Gregory C. McCaffery, President and CEO
John Camp, Vice President and Chief
Technology

Lisa A. Fitzpatrick, Vice President
Audrey Hipkins, VP

A weekly reporting service providing compre-
hensive coverage of the latest significant devel-
opments affecting federal contracts and grants.
Cost: $1887.00
Frequency: Weekly
Founded in 1929

15764 Federal Discovery News

LRP Publications
747 Dresher Road
PO Box 980
Horsham, PA 19044-980

215-784-0912
800-341-7874
FAX 215-784-9639
E-Mail: webmaster@lrp.com
Home Page: www.lrp.com

John Massaro, Editor
Dionne Ellis, Managing Editor

Each issue covers the whole realm of pretrial
case management and discovery, especially the
impact of the new civil procedure rules on discovery in federal cases. Provides a timely review of how district developments pertain to
your practice.
Cost: $275.00
Frequency: Monthly
Founded in 1977

15765 Federal EEO Advisor

LRP Publications
747 Dresher Road
PO Box 980
Horsham, PA 19044-980

215-784-0912
800-341-7874
FAX 215-784-9639
E-Mail: webmaster@lrp.com
Home Page: www.lrp.com

Allison Uehling, Editor
Clarrisa Spasyk, Staff Writer

One-of-a-kind publication provides readers
with essential tips, strategies and news about
the constanly changing EEO profession. Each
issue includes insightful coverage on topics
such as: details on major developments and
trends in federal EEO; tips on how to accomplish specific objectives within the EEO program; synopses of decisions by the EEOC and
related courts, etc.
Cost: $220.00
Frequency: Monthly
Founded in 1977

15766 Federal Human Resources Week

LRP Publications
747 Dresher Road Suite 500
PO Box 980
Horsham, PA 19044

215-840-0912
800-341-7874
FAX 215-784-9639
E-Mail: custserve@lrp.com
Home Page: www.feds.com

Daniel J Gephart, Editorial Director
Julie Davidson, Managing Editor
Kathleen Filipczyk, Staff Writer

Federal Human Resources Week helps you stay
on top of changes affecting you and your workplace. This revolutionary resource enables you
to experience each major development as it occurs.
Cost: $365.00
12 Pages
Frequency: Weekly
Founded in 1977
Printed in 2 colors on matte stock

15767 Financial Management Newsletter

Association of Legal Administrators

75 Tri-State International
Suite 222
Lincolnshire, IL 60069-4435

847-267-1252
FAX 847-267-1329
E-Mail: publications@alanet.org
Home Page: www.alanet.org

Larry Smith, Executive Director
Debbie Thomas, Director, Accounting &
Finance
Renee Mahovsky, Director,
Administration/Operations
Bob Abramson, Director, Marketing &
Communication
Jan Waugh, Director, Member Services
8 Pages
Frequency: Monthly
Founded in 1971

15768 Forum
Federal Bar Association
1220 North Fillmore St.
Ste. 444
Arlington, VA 22201

571-481-9100
FAX 571-481-9090
E-Mail: fba@fedbar.org
Home Page: www.fedbar.org
Social Media: *Facebook, Twitter, LinkedIn*

Karen Silberman, Executive Director
Lori Beth Gorman, Executive Assistant
Stacy King, Deputy Executive Director
April Davis, Staff Accountant
Patty Richardson, Receptionist

A forum for the exchange of ideas, news, up-
dates, and cases for lawyers.
Cost: $35.00
8 Pages
Frequency: Monthly
Founded in 1920
Mailing list available for rent

15769 General Aviation Accident Report
Andrews Communications
175 Stafford Street Building 4
Suite 140
Wayne, PA 19087

610-225-0510
800-345-1101
FAX 610-225-0501
E-Mail: nick.sullivan@thomson.com
Home Page: www.andrewsonline.com/

Thomson West, Publisher
Nick Sullivan, Editor

General aviation laws.
Cost: $99.00
20 Pages
Founded in 1872

15770 HRFocus
Institute of Management and Administration
1 Wasington Park
Suite 1300
Newark, NJ 07102-3130

212-244-0360
FAX 973-622-0595
E-Mail: customercare@bna.com
Home Page: www.ioma.com

Provides HR managers with timely information
on a variety of topics, including talent management, HR legal and compliance issues, performance reviews, and workplace policies and
standards.
Cost: $429.00
16 Pages
Frequency: Monthly
Printed in 4 colors

**15771 Hastings Communications &
Entertainment Law Journal**
Hastings College of Law

200 McAllister St
2nd Floor, Room 213
San Francisco, CA 94102-4978

415-565-4600
FAX 415-565-4854
Home Page: www.uchastings.edu

Nell Jessup Newton, Manager
Karen Gibbs, Editor

Specializing in a host of legal issues generally
grouped under the rubric of communications
and entertainment law. Focuses on, but is not
limited to, telecommunications, broadcasting,
cable and other non-broadcast video, and the
print media.
Cost: $7.00
Frequency: Monthly
Circulation: 1300
Founded in 1878

15772 Health Law Week
Strafford Publications
PO Box 13729
Atlanta, GA 30324-0729

404-881-1141
800-926-7926
FAX 404-881-0074
E-Mail: customerservice@straffordpub.com
Home Page: www.straffordpub.com

Richard Ossoff, President

Case digest of judicial decision affecting all as-
pects of health care operations. Topics covered
include AIPS abortion antitrust, drugs, ERISA,
expert testimony, informed consent, amd much
more.
Cost: $1397.00
Frequency: Weekly
ISSN: 1063-4061
Founded in 1984
Mailing list available for rent: 25M names

15773 Hospital Litigation Reporter
Strafford Publications
PO Box 13729
Atlanta, GA 30324-0729

404-881-1141
800-926-7926
FAX 404-881-0074
E-Mail: customerservice@straffordpub.com
Home Page: www.straffordpub.com

Richard Ossoff, President
Jennifer Vaughan, Editor

Monthly digest of judicial decisions that con-
cern or affect the hospital environment. Cases
are screened and selected to provide concise,
comprehensive coverage of issues important to
hospital attorneys and administrators.
Cost: $397.00
18 Pages
Frequency: Monthly
ISSN: 1048-5201
Founded in 1984
Mailing list available for rent: 11M names
Printed in one color

15774 Human Resources Report
Bureau of National Affairs
1801 S Bell St
Arlington, VA 22202-4501

703-341-3000
800-372-1033
FAX 800-253-0332
E-Mail: customercare@bna.com
Home Page: www.bnabooks.com
Social Media: *Facebook, Twitter, LinkedIn*

Paul N Wojcik, Chairman
Gregory C. McCaffery, President and CEO
John Camp, Vice President and Chief
Technology
Lisa A. Fitzpatrick, Vice President
Audrey Hipkins, VP

Covers current developments in every area of
human resources; includes in-depth analysis of
important events, developments or trends af-
fecting human resource professionals.
Cost: $1140.00
28 Pages
Frequency: Weekly
ISSN: 1095-6239
Founded in 1929
Printed in one color on matte stock

15775 I-CBC Newsletter
Institute of Certified Business Counselors
18831 Willamette Dr
West Linn, OR 97068-1711

503-751-1856
877-422-2674
FAX 503-292-8237
E-Mail: inquiry@i-cbc.org
Home Page: www.i-cbc.org

Roger Murphy, Director, Newsletter

For counselors, brokers and attorneys qualified
to act as advisors for persons with business
problems. Regular editorial features.
Frequency: 6/Year
Mailing list available for rent

**15776 IOMA's Report on Controlling Law
Firm Costs**
Institute of Management and Administration
1 Washington Park
Suite 1300
Newark, NJ 07102-3130

212-244-0360
FAX 973-622-0595
E-Mail: customercare@bna.com
Home Page: www.ioma.com

Information to control costs of law firms management.
Cost: $175.00
12 Pages
Frequency: Monthly

15777 IRR News Report
ABA Section - Individual Rights &
Responsibilities
740 15th Stree, NW
10th Floor
Washington, DC 20005

202-662-1000
800-285-2221
FAX 202-662-1031
E-Mail: askaba@abanet.org
Home Page: www.abanet.org
Social Media: *Facebook, Twitter*

Laurel Bellows, President
Jack L. Rives, Executive Director
Robert M. Carlson, Chairman
Lucian T. Pera, Treasurer
Cara Lee T. Neville, Secretary

A quarterly newsletter including updates on
Section events, news about members, a review
of recent legislative events and decision by the
Supreme Court.
Circulation: 6000
Founded in 1878
Mailing list available for rent

15778 Individual Employment Rights
Bureau of National Affairs
1801 S Bell St
Arlington, VA 22202-4501

703-341-3000
800-372-1033
FAX 800-253-0332
E-Mail: customercare@bna.com
Home Page: www.bnabooks.com
Social Media: *Facebook, Twitter, LinkedIn*

Paul N Wojcik, Chairman
Gregory C. McCaffery, President and CEO
John Camp, Vice President and Chief

Technology
Lisa A. Fitzpatrick, Vice President
Audrey Hipkins, VP

Case reference and notification on individual
employment rights issues including employment at will, privacy, polygraph testing, and
other employee rights issues outside the traditional labor-management relations context.
Cost: $1227.00
Frequency: Monthly
ISSN: 0148-7981
Founded in 1929

15779 Intellectual Property LAWCAST
Vox Juris
PO Box 389
Pennington, NJ 08534-389

609-737-6543
FAX 609-737-3860
E-Mail: INFO@lawcast.com
Home Page: www.lawcast.com

Jason Meyer, Publisher

US legal news in patents, trademarks, copyrights, trade secrets, unfair trade, etc. including
comprehensive coverage of PTO policies and a
regular Listening Post on legal issues in the
digital age. The buzz for thousands of IP lawyers, nationwide. 60 minute audio and online,
twice monthly.
Cost: $488.00

15780 Intellectual Property Law Review
Clark Boardman Company
375 Hudson St
Room 201
New York, NY 10014-3658

585-546-5530
800-323-1336

David Doughty, Publisher

Compilation of the best law review articles.
Frequency: Monthly
Founded in 1916

**15781 Intellectual Property Litigation
Reporter**
Andrews Publications
175 Strafford Avenue
Building 4 Suite 140
Wayne, PA 19087-3331

610-225-0510
800-345-1101
FAX 610-225-0501
Home Page: www.andrewspub.com

Robert Maroldo, Publisher
Jodine Mayberry, Editor

Covers litigation and regulation of intellectual
property issues including patents, copyrights,
and tradeworks.
Cost: $83.00

15782 Intellectual Property Today
Omega Communications
29 E Maryland Street
Indianapolis, IN 46204-7258

317-264-4010
FAX 317-264-4020
E-Mail: planet@iptoday.com
Home Page: www.omegac.com

Douglas Dean, Editor
Steve Barnes, Vice President
Laura Moore, Vice President

Emphasizes developments in leading edge tech-
nology, including multimedia, genetic engi-
neering and computer software, and how they
effect disciplines of law.
Cost: $96.00
Frequency: Monthly
Circulation: 20000
Founded in 1971

**15783 Inter-American Bar Association
Newsletter**
Inter-American Bar Association
1211 Connecticut Ave Nw
Suite 202
Washington, DC 20036-2712

202-466-5944
FAX 202-466-5946
E-Mail: iaba@iaba.org
Home Page: www.iaba.org
Social Media: *Facebook*

Marianne Cordier, Secretary General
Rafael Veloz, President
Cost: $60.00
Frequency: Quarterly

15784 International Law News
American Bar Association Internat'l Law &
Practice
321 N Clark St
Chicago, IL 60654-7598

312-988-5000
800-285-2221
FAX 312-988-5280
E-Mail: askaba@abanet.org
Home Page: www.abanet.org
Social Media: *Facebook, Twitter*

Angela Gwizdala, Managing Editor
Laurel Bellows, President
Jack L. Rives, Executive Director
Robert M. Carlson, Chairman
Lucian T. Pera, Treasurer

Provides information concerning current, im-
portant developments pertaining to interna-
tional law and practice, Section news, and other
information of professional interest.
28 Pages
Frequency: Quarterly
Circulation: 15000
ISSN: 0047-0813
Founded in 1878
Mailing list available for rent

15785 Internet Lawyer
GoAhead Productions
123 7th Avenue
#137
Brooklyn, NY 11215-1301

718-399-6136
FAX 718-499-6039
Home Page: www.internetlawyer.com

Tatia L Gordon-Troy, Editor-in-Chief
Christopher Eddings, Publisher

Gives legal advice and examines how to use the
Net for research, marketing and communications purposes. Includes book reviews as well
as information on current law office technology.
Cost: $149.00
Frequency: Monthly

15786 Judicial Division Record
American Bar Association Judicial Division
321 N Clark St
Chicago, IL 60654-7598

312-988-5000
800-285-2221
FAX 312-988-6281
E-Mail: askaba@abanet.org
Home Page: www.abanet.org
Social Media: *Facebook, Twitter*

Laurel Bellows, President
Jack L. Rives, Executive Director
Robert M. Carlson, Chairman
Lucian T. Pera, Treasurer
Cara Lee T. Neville, Secretary

The Record is the only newsletter published by
the Division, providing news about Division
activites, products, publications and programs.
It contains sections for each Division Confer-

ence, and an insert.
Cost: $25.00
Frequency: Free Online
Founded in 1878
Mailing list available for rent

**15787 Labor Arbitration and Dispute
Settlements**
Bureau of National Affairs
1801 S Bell St
Arlington, VA 22202-4501

703-341-3000
800-372-1033
FAX 800-253-0332
E-Mail: customercare@bna.com
Home Page: www.bnabooks.com
Social Media: *Facebook, Twitter, LinkedIn*

Paul N Wojcik, Chairman
Gregory C. McCaffery, President and CEO
John Camp, Vice President and Chief
Technology
Lisa A. Fitzpatrick, Vice President
Audrey Hipkins, VP

Contains the full-text of arbitration cases, and
digests of court decisions involving arbitration.
Cost: $1686.00
Frequency: Weekly
ISSN: 1043-5662
Founded in 1929

15788 Labor Arbitration in Government
LRP Publications
PO Box 980
Horsham, PA 19044-0980

215-784-0912
800-341-7874
FAX 215-784-9639
E-Mail: webmaster@lrp.com
Home Page: www.lrp.com

Todd Lutz, CFO
Dionne Ellis, Marketing

Selected awards involving city, state, and fed-
eral employers (other than those employed by
schools) are covered by this reporting service.
Some of the issues arbitrated include: absentee-
ism, smoking policies, layoffs, and substance
abuse.
Cost: $120.00
Frequency: Monthly
Founded in 1977
Printed in 2 colors on glossy stock

15789 Labor Lawyer
American Bar Association - Labor &
Employment Law
321 N Clark St
Chicago, IL 60654-7598

312-988-5000
800-285-2221
FAX 312-988-5814
E-Mail: laborempllaw@abanet.org
Home Page: www.abanet.org
Social Media: *Facebook, Twitter*

Laurel Bellows, President
Jack L. Rives, Executive Director
Robert M. Carlson, Chairman
Lucian T. Pera, Treasurer
Cara Lee T. Neville, Secretary

Substantive articles on developments in labor
and employment law.
Frequency: Quarterly
Circulation: 2300
Founded in 1878
Mailing list available for rent

15790 Labor Relations Reporter
Bureau of National Affairs
1801 S Bell St
Arlington, VA 22202-4501

703-341-3000
800-372-1033

FAX 800-253-0332
E-Mail: customercare@bna.com
Home Page: www.bnabooks.com
Social Media: *Facebook, Twitter, LinkedIn*

Paul N Wojcik, Chairman
Gregory C. McCaffery, President and CEO
John Camp, Vice President and Chief
Technology
Lisa A. Fitzpatrick, Vice President
Audrey Hipkins, VP

A multi-part notification and reference service covering labor-management relations, wages and hours, labor arbitration, fair employment practices, individual employment rights and more.
Cost: $6175.00
Frequency: Weekly
ISSN: 0148-7981
Founded in 1929

15791 Labor Relations Week
Bureau of National Affairs
1801 S Bell St
Arlington, VA 22202-4501

703-341-3000
800-372-1033
FAX 800-253-0332
E-Mail: customercare@bna.com
Home Page: www.bnabooks.com
Social Media: *Facebook, Twitter, LinkedIn*

Paul N Wojcik, Chairman
Gregory C. McCaffery, President and CEO
John Camp, Vice President and Chief
Technology
Lisa A. Fitzpatrick, Vice President
Audrey Hipkins, VP

A weekly reporting service that provides a comprehensive overview of developments influencing labor relations in the private sector.
Cost: $1472.00
Frequency: Weekly
ISSN: 0891-4141
Founded in 1929

15792 Labor and Employment Law
American Bar Association - Labor &
Employment Law
321 N Clark St
Chicago, IL 60654-7598

312-988-5000
800-285-2221
FAX 312-988-6281
E-Mail: askaba@abanet.org
Home Page: www.abanet.org
Social Media: *Facebook, Twitter*

Laurel Bellows, President
Jack L. Rives, Executive Director
Robert M. Carlson, Chairman
Lucian T. Pera, Treasurer
Cara Lee T. Neville, Secretary

Offers news items of interest to members and information on the latest developments in the labor field.
Cost: $5.00
16 Pages
Frequency: Quarterly
Circulation: 22000
ISSN: 0193-5739
Founded in 1878
Mailing list available for rent

15793 Labor and Employment Law News
American Bar Association - Labor &
Employment Law
321 N Clark St
Chicago, IL 60654-7598

312-988-5000
800-285-2221
FAX 312-988-5280
E-Mail: service@abanet.org

Home Page: www.abanet.org
Social Media: *Facebook, Twitter*

Laurel Bellows, President
Jack L. Rives, Executive Director
Robert M. Carlson, Chairman
Lucian T. Pera, Treasurer
Cara Lee T. Neville, Secretary

Legal issues and trends of interest to lawyers who represent employees, unions, and management.
Cost: $5.00
16 Pages
Frequency: Monthly
Circulation: 22000
ISSN: 0193-5739
Founded in 1878
Mailing list available for rent
Printed in 4 colors

15794 Labor-Management Relations
Bureau of National Affairs
1801 S Bell St
Arlington, VA 22202-4501

703-341-3000
800-372-1033
FAX 800-253-0332
E-Mail: customercare@bna.com
Home Page: www.bnabooks.com
Social Media: *Facebook, Twitter, LinkedIn*

Paul N Wojcik, Chairman
Gregory C. McCaffery, President and CEO
John Camp, Vice President and Chief
Technology
Lisa A. Fitzpatrick, Vice President
Audrey Hipkins, VP

Contains a table of cases, digest-summaries of all published NLRB decisions and full-text of opinions of the US Supreme Court, US Courts of Appeals and other courts, in one bound volume, issued several times a year.
Cost: $ 1776.00
Frequency: Monthly
ISSN: 1043-5506
Founded in 1929

15795 Labor-Management Relations Analysis/News and Background Information
Bureau of National Affairs
1801 S Bell St
Arlington, VA 22202-4501

703-341-3000
800-372-1033
FAX 800-253-0332
E-Mail: customercare@bna.com
Home Page: www.bnabooks.com
Social Media: *Facebook, Twitter, LinkedIn*

Paul N Wojcik, Chairman
Gregory C. McCaffery, President and CEO
John Camp, Vice President and Chief
Technology
Lisa A. Fitzpatrick, Vice President
Audrey Hipkins, VP

This weekly section of the Labor Relations Reporter summarizes developments and rulings in the field of labor law, covers major non-decisional developments and recent significant arbitration awards, and provides in-depth analysis and evaluation of the week's labor news.
Cost: $507.00
Frequency: Weekly
Founded in 1929

15796 Land Use Law Report
Business Publishers
8737 Colesville Road
10th Floor
Silver Spring, MD 20910-3928

301-876-6300
800-274-6737
FAX 301-589-8493

E-Mail: custserv@bpinews.com
Home Page: www.bpinews.com/

Leonard Eiserer, Publisher
James Esq, Editor

Zoning and land use decisions at all levels of government; impact on business community and environment.
Cost: $397.00
Founded in 1963

15797 Latin America Law and Business Report
WorldTrade Executive
2250 Main St
Suite 100
Concord, MA 01742-3838

978-287-0301
FAX 978-287-0302
E-Mail: info@wtexec.com
Home Page: www.wtexecutive.com

Gary Brown, President
Jay Stanley, Sales Manager

Provides practical, current information on how to do business in Latin America. Covers areas such as capital markets, accounting matters, labor issues, privatization, project finance techniques, joint venture regulation, local sourcing, export/import, taxation, intellectual property, environment.
Cost: $893.00
Frequency: Monthly

15798 Law Bulletin
Andrews Publications
175 Strafford Avenue
Building 4, Suite 140
Wayne, PA 19087-3331

610-225-0510
800-345-1101
FAX 610-225-0501
Home Page: www.andrewspub.com

Donna Higgins, Editor
Rose MacDonald, Production Manager

Newsletter covering the legal issues raided by the Millenium. Bug along with insightful commentary from attorneys and other experts.
Cost: $25.00
Frequency: Monthly
Founded in 1872

15799 Law Firm Profit Report
James Publishing
3505 Cadillac Avenue
Suite H
Costa Mesa, CA 92626

714-755-5450
800-440-4780
FAX 714-751-2709
E-Mail:
customer-service@jamespublishing.com
Home Page: www.jamespublishing.com

Jim Pawell, Founder/President
Lorraine Thinnes, Editor

How to manage a small to medium-sized law firm profitably, with tips on cost-cutting, managing automation, personnel and more.
Founded in 1981
Mailing list available for rent

15800 Law Office Management & Administration Report
Institute of Management and Administration
1 Washington Park
Suite 1300
Newark, NJ 07102-3130

212-244-0360
FAX 973-622-0595

E-Mail: customercare@bna.com
Home Page: www.ioma.com

Covers the daily management concerns relevant for law firm administrators, office managers, and others.
Cost: $489.00
Frequency: Monthly
Founded in 1983

15801 Law Practice Today
American Bar Association
321 N Clark St
Chicago, IL 60654-7598

312-988-5000
800-285-2221
FAX 312-988-5280
E-Mail: askaba@abanet.org
Home Page: www.abanet.org
Social Media: *Facebook, Twitter*

Laurel Bellows, President
Jack L. Rives, Executive Director
Robert M. Carlson, Chairman
Lucian T. Pera, Treasurer
Cara Lee T. Neville, Secretary

An e-newsletter focusing on how lawyers can improve their personal productivity in the hands-on practice of law.
Frequency: Monthly
Founded in 1878
Mailing list available for rent

15802 Law and Society Association Newsletter
Denver College of Law
1900 Olive Street
Denver, CO 80220-1857

303-871-6306
E-Mail: Exec_Office@lawandsociety.org
Home Page: www.lawandsociety.org

Joyce Sterling, Publisher

Legal updates and information on the Society.
Frequency: Monthly

15803 LawPractice.news
American Bar Association - Law Practice Management
321 N Clark St
Chicago, IL 60654-7598

312-988-5000
800-285-2221
FAX 312-988-5280
E-Mail: askaba@abanet.org
Home Page: www.abanet.org/lpm/home.shtml
Social Media: *Facebook, Twitter, Youtube*

Laurel Bellows, President
Jack L. Rives, Executive Director
Robert M. Carlson, Chairman
Lucian T. Pera, Treasurer
Cara Lee T. Neville, Secretary

A monthly e-newsletter for Law Practice Management Section members, keeping them abreast of Section events, publications, promotions and member news.
Frequency: Monthly
Founded in 1974
Mailing list available for rent

15804 Lawyer's PC
West Group
1428 Dewey Ave
Rochester, NY 14613-1128

585-254-9585
800-327-2665
FAX 585-258-3707
E-Mail: west.support@thomson.com
Home Page: www.west.thomson.com

Computer and electronics information aimed at the legal profession.
Cost: $299.00
16 Pages
Circulation: 4000

Founded in 1872
Printed in one color

15805 Lawyering Tools and Techniques
American Bar Association
321 N Clark St
Chicago, IL 60654-7598

312-988-5000
800-285-2221
FAX 312-988-5280
E-Mail: askaba@abanet.org
Home Page: www.abanet.org
Social Media: *Facebook, Twitter*

Laurel Bellows, President
Jack L. Rives, Executive Director
Robert M. Carlson, Chairman
Lucian T. Pera, Treasurer
Cara Lee T. Neville, Secretary

Focuses on specific tools lawyers can use to improve the productivity of their work including electronic communications, laptops, desk publishing and resources.
Cost: $50.00
Frequency: Quarterly
Founded in 1878
Mailing list available for rent

15806 Lawyers Tax Alert
Research Institute of America
90 5th Avenue
2nd Floor
New York, NY 10011-7696

212-367-6300

Peter Grean, Manager

Tax laws and news.
Frequency: Monthly

15807 Lawyers' Letter
American Bar Association
321 N Clark St
Chicago, IL 60654-7598

312-988-5000
800-285-2221
FAX 312-988-5280
E-Mail: askaba@abanet.org
Home Page: www.abanet.org
Social Media: *Facebook, Twitter*

Laurel Bellows, President
Jack L. Rives, Executive Director
Robert M. Carlson, Chairman
Lucian T. Pera, Treasurer
Cara Lee T. Neville, Secretary

Newsletter informing lawyers of new developments in court improvement and reports on Conference activities.
Founded in 1878
Mailing list available for rent

15808 Legal Advisory
WPI Communications
55 Morris Ave
Suite 300
Springfield, NJ 07081-1422

973-467-8700
800-323-4995
FAX 973-467-0368
E-Mail: info@wpicomm.com
Home Page: www.wpicomm.com

Steve Klinghoffer, President
Marilyn Lang, Chairman

Offers updates, news and the latest legislation for lawyers.
Frequency: Monthly
Founded in 1952

15809 Legal Assistant Today Magazine
James Publishing

3505 Cadillac Avenue
Suite H
Costa Mesa, CA 92626

714-755-5450
800-440-4780
FAX 714-751-2709
E-Mail:
customer-service@jamespublishing.com
Home Page: www.jamespublishing.com

Jim Pawell, Founder/President
Rod Hughes, Managing Editor

Written exclusively for paralegals and legal assistants. Each issue includes coverage if industry news and trends, how-to articles as well as colorful and informative pieces on unique areas and persons in the profession and sound advice for becoming more efficient in the workplace., buy wisely and use their investments to maximize productivity and profitability.
Cost: $47.98
56 Pages
Circulation: 13000
ISSN: 1055-128X
Founded in 1981

15810 Legal Review
Native American Rights Fund
1506 Broadway St
Boulder, CO 80302-6296

303-447-8760
FAX 303-443-7776
E-Mail: webmaster@narf.org
Home Page: www.narf.org
Social Media: *Facebook*

John E Echohawk, Executive Director
Carly Hare, Director Development
Rose Cuny, Office Manager
Katrina Mora, Office Services Assistant
Mireille Martinez, Development Projects Manager

A bi-annual case update published by the Native American Rights Fund.
Frequency: Bi-annually
Circulation: 30000
ISSN: 0739-862x
Mailing list available for rent
Printed in 4 colors on matte stock

15811 Litigation LAWCAST
Vox Juris
PO Box 389
Pennington, NJ 08534

609-737-6543
800-529-2278
FAX 609-737-3860
E-Mail: info@lawcast.com
Home Page: www.lawcast.com

Jason Meyer, Editor & Publisher
Linda Delp, General Manager

Analysis of legal departments and advanced strategic ideas for the most demanding litigators - whatever the subject of your litigation. Stay up to date on substance and tactics in evidence, discovery, advocacy, damages, client management and selection, settlement, ADR, and ethics, plus coverage of groudbreaking decisions affecting personal injury, commercial, and employment law. 60 min./monthly
Cost: $399.00
Frequency: Monthly
Founded in 1994

15812 Litigation News
American Bar Association Section of Litigation
321 N Clark St
Chicago, IL 60654-7598

312-988-5000
800-285-2221
FAX 312-988-5280
E-Mail: askaba@abanet.org

Home Page: www.abanet.org
Social Media: *Facebook, Twitter*

Laurel Bellows, President
Jack L. Rives, Executive Director
Robert M. Carlson, Chairman
Lucian T. Pera, Treasurer
Cara Lee T. Neville, Secretary

Present articles on the latest developments in law, litigation trends, and topics of interest to litigators.
Frequency: Quarterly
Circulation: 60000
Founded in 1878
Mailing list available for rent

15813 Marketing for Lawyers
Leader Publications
345 Park Avenue S
New York, NY 10010-1707

212-799-9200
FAX 212-696-1848

Sam Adler, Editor
Kerry Kyle, Circulation Director

Helps lawyers expand their practice through marketing.
Cost: $17.50

15814 Mealey's Asbestos Bankruptcy Report
LexisNexis Mealey's
555 W 5th Avenue
Los Angeles, CA 90013

213-627-1130
800-253-4182
E-Mail: mealeyinfo@lexisnexis.com
Home Page: www.lexisnexis.com/mealeys
Social Media: *Facebook, Twitter, LinkedIn, RSS, Youtube*

Tom Hagy, CEO
Maureen McGuire, Editorial Director
Lisa Schaeffer, Editor
Mike Wash, Chief Executive Officer, Legal
Lisa Agona, Chief Marketing Officer

The report provides in-depth news and analysis of asbestos bankruptcy law and the progress of bankrupt asbestos companies through the ever-evolving Chapter 11 process. Topics include: insurance issues, impacts on settlements, how asbestos bankruptcies are affecting the landscape of the litigation and which companies may be forced to file for Chapter 11 protection in the future.
Cost: $475.00
100 Pages
Frequency: Quarterly
Founded in 2000
Mailing list available for rent

15815 Mealey's California Section 17200 Report
LexisNexis Mealey's
555 5th Avenue
Los Angeles, CA 90013

213-627-1130
800-253-4182
E-Mail: mealeyinfo@lexisnexis.com
Home Page: www.lexisnexis.com/mealeys
Social Media: *Facebook, Twitter, LinkedIn, RSS, Youtube*

Tom Hagy, CEO
Maureen McGuire, Editorial Director
Bryan Redding, Editor
Mike Wash, Chief Executive Officer, Legal
Lisa Agona, Chief Marketing Officer

Monitors litigation and provides legislative updates on California's Unfair Competition Law. This monthly report will offer readers hard-to-find filings and briefs, new complaints, breaking news, concise case summaries, and trial updates. All major cases involving Section 17200 of the state's Business and Professions Code will be reported, including those dealings

with insurance, employment, consumer law, the Internet, telecommunications, securities, fraud, product liability and many more.
Cost: $959.00
100 Pages
Frequency: Monthly
Founded in 2002
Mailing list available for rent

15816 Mealey's Catastrophic Loss
LexisNexis Mealey's
555 W 5th Avenue
Los Angeles, CA 90013

213-627-1130
800-253-4182
E-Mail: mealeyinfo@lexisnexis.com
Home Page: www.lexisnexis.com/mealeys
Social Media: *Facebook, Twitter, LinkedIn, RSS, Youtube*

Tom Hagy, CEO
Maureen McGuire, Editorial Director
Gina Cappello, Editor
Mike Wash, Chief Executive Officer, Legal
Lisa Agona, Chief Marketing Officer

This report focuses on business interruption insurance claims in the aftermath of the Hurricane Katrina, September 11th, and other catastrophic loss tragedies. Additionally, the report will go beyond these claims and will offer important business interruption insurance coverage news related to computer viruses, computer failures, and natural disasters.
Cost: $1075.00
100 Pages
Frequency: Monthly
Founded in 2001
Mailing list available for rent

15817 Mealey's Daubert Report
LexisNexis Mealey's
555 W 5th Avenue
Los Angeles, CA 90013

213-627-1130
800-253-4182
E-Mail: mealeyinfo@lexisnexis.com
Home Page: www.lexisnexis.com/mealeys
Social Media: *Facebook, Twitter, LinkedIn, RSS, Youtube*

Tom Hagy, CEO
Maureen McGuire, Editorial Director
Kristin Casler, Editor
Mike Wash, Chief Executive Officer, Legal
Lisa Agona, Chief Marketing Officer

This newsletter covers the interpretation, adoption and/or rejection of the Supreme Court's landmark expert admissibility ruling, Daubert v. Merrell Dow Pharmaceutical Inc. As the nation's jurisdictions grapple with so called junk science testimony, this monthly newsletter offers subscribers the latest key rulings in this contentious components of civil and criminal litigation.
Cost: $735.00
100 Pages
Frequency: Monthly
Founded in 1997
Mailing list available for rent

15818 Mealey's Emerging Drugs & Devices
LexisNexis Mealey's
555 W 5th Avenue
Los Angeles, CA 90013

213-627-1130
800-253-4182
E-Mail: mealeyinfo@lexisnexis.com
Home Page: www.lexisnexis.com/mealeys
Social Media: *Facebook, Twitter, LinkedIn, RSS, Youtube*

Tom Hagy, CEO
Maureen McGuire, Editorial Director
Tom Moylan, Editor

Mike Wash, Chief Executive Officer, Legal
Lisa Agona, Chief Marketing Officer

The report covers cases involving a variety of prescription drug vaccines, implants and devices. Duract, Parlodel, Accutane, fen-phen, Rezulin, Propulsid, dietary supplements and blood products are among the topics tracked. Medical devices covered include heart catheters, breast implants, heart valves, intraocular lenses, jaw implants, joint replacements, latex gloves, pacemakers, pedicle screws, penile implants, and surgical lasers.
Cost: $1249.00
100 Pages
Frequency: Semi-Monthly
Founded in 1996
Mailing list available for rent

15819 Mealey's Emerging Insurance Disputes
LexisNexis Mealey's
555 W 5th Avenue
Los Angeles, CA 90013

213-627-1130
800-253-4182
FAX 610-768-0880
E-Mail: mealeyinfo@lexisnexis.com
Home Page: www.lexisnexis.com/mealeys
Social Media: *Facebook, Twitter, LinkedIn, RSS, Youtube*

Tom Hagy, CEO
Maureen McGuire, Editorial Director
Gina Cappello, Editor
Mike Wash, Chief Executive Officer, Legal
Lisa Agona, Chief Marketing Officer

The report tracks new areas of coverage liability, novel policy applications, and conflicting policy language interpretations as they arise in insurance litigation. Some areas of coverage featured are: sexual harassment and discrimination, assault and battery, professional liability, patent and trademark infringement, construction defects, directors and officers claims, emotional distress, intentional acts, technology, and insurance business practices.
Cost: $ 1229.00
100 Pages
Frequency: Semi-Monthly
Founded in 1996
Mailing list available for rent

15820 Mealey's Emerging Securities Litigation
LexisNexis Mealey's
555 W 5th Avenue
Los Angeles, CA 90013

213-627-1130
800-253-4182
FAX 610-768-0880
E-Mail: mealeyinfo@lexisnexis.com
Home Page: www.lexisnexis.com/mealeys
Social Media: *Facebook, Twitter, LinkedIn, RSS, Youtube*

Tom Hagy, CEO
Maureen McGuire, Editorial Director
Mike Lello, Editor
Mike Wash, Chief Executive Officer, Legal
Lisa Agona, Chief Marketing Officer

The report covers fiduciary duties to shareholders, 401k and pension implications, class actions, damage calculations, causation questions, Daubert issues, debt bondholder implications, bankruptcy issues and accountant liability in the securities law context.
Cost: $875.00
100 Pages
Frequency: Monthly
Founded in 2002
Mailing list available for rent

15821 Mealey's Emerging Toxic Torts
LexisNexis Mealey's

555 W 5th Avenue
Los Angeles, CA 90013

213-627-1130
800-253-4182
FAX 610-768-0880
E-Mail: mealeyinfo@lexisnexis.com
Home Page: www.lexisnexis.com/mealeys
Social Media: *Facebook, Twitter, LinkedIn, RSS, Youtube*

Tom Hagy, CEO
Maureen McGuire, Editorial Director
Bill Lowe, Editor
Mike Wash, Chief Executive Officer, Legal
Lisa Agona, Chief Marketing Officer

The report focuses on the hottest areas of toxic tort litigation including: chemical sensitivity; indoor air quality; groundwater, soil and air contamination; radiation; workplace exposure; pesticides; solvents; latex gloves; EMF's; MTBE; endocrine disruptors, and more. The report provides in-depth coverage of medical monitoring; fear of cancer/disease; stigma damages; expert admissibility; federal preemption; class actions; punitive damages and market share theory.
Cost: $1539.00
100 Pages
Frequency: Semi-Monthly
Founded in 1992
Mailing list available for rent

15822 Mealey's International Arbitration Quarterly Law Review

LexisNexis Mealey's
555 W 5th Avenue
Los Angeles, CA 90013

213-627-1130
800-253-4182
FAX 610-768-0880
E-Mail: mealeyinfo@lexisnexis.com
Home Page: www.lexisnexis.com/mealeys
Social Media: *Facebook, Twitter, LinkedIn, RSS, Youtube*

Tom Hagy, CEO
Maureen McGuire, Editorial Director
Edie Scott, Editor
Mike Wash, Chief Executive Officer, Legal
Lisa Agona, Chief Marketing Officer

The report provides thought-provoking commentary articles authored by aribitrators, scholars and attorneys with first-hand knowledge of the complex field of commercial dispute resolution. Each issue contains analytical discussions and practical insights on current case law, new treaties and statues, arbitration principles, dispute resolution techniques, and more from our prestigious international authors.
Cost: $475.00
100 Pages
Frequency: Quarterly
Founded in 2000
Mailing list available for rent

15823 Mealey's International Arbritation Report

LexisNexis Mealey's
555 W 5th Avenue
Los Angeles, CA 90013

213-627-1130
800-253-4182
FAX 610-768-0880
E-Mail: mealeyinfo@lexisnexis.com
Home Page: www.lexisnexis.com/mealeys
Social Media: *Facebook, Twitter, LinkedIn, RSS, Youtube*

Tom Hagy, CEO
Maureen McGuire, Editorial Director
Edie Scott, Editor
Mike Wash, Chief Executive Officer, Legal
Lisa Agona, Chief Marketing Officer

The report examines arbitration and related litigation in courts world-wide. Covers enforce-

ment, jurisdictional disputes, forum selection, use of experts by arbitral parties, enforcement, judicial supervision, the Iran-US Claims Tribunal, the United Nations Compensation Commission, and events of interest at arbitration institutions around the globe.
Cost: $2049.00
100 Pages
Frequency: Monthly
Founded in 1986
Mailing list available for rent

15824 Mealey's International Asbestos Liability Report

LexisNexis Mealey's
555 W 5th Avenue
Los Angeles, CA 90013

213-627-1130
800-253-4182
FAX 610-768-0880
E-Mail: mealeyinfo@lexisnexis.com
Home Page: www.lexisnexis.com/mealeys
Social Media: *Facebook, Twitter, LinkedIn, RSS, Youtube*

Tom Hagy, CEO
Maureen McGuire, Editorial Director
Lisa Schaeffer, Editor
Mike Wash, Chief Executive Officer, Legal
Lisa Agona, Chief Marketing Officer

The report covers the latest litigation, regulatory, and medical news related to worldwide asbestos exposure - including the emerging issue of subsidiary liability and the question of US jurisdiction - with in-depth case summaries and news of medical findings, full-text court documents, and exclusive expert commentary articles.
Cost: $959.00
100 Pages
Frequency: Monthly
Founded in 2003
Mailing list available for rent

15825 Mealey's Litigation Report: Insurance Fraud

LexisNexis Mealey's
555 W 5th Avenue
Los Angeles, CA 90013

213-627-1130
800-253-4182
FAX 610-768-0880
E-Mail: mealeyinfo@lexisnexis.com
Home Page: www.lexisnexis.com/mealeys
Social Media: *Facebook, Twitter, LinkedIn, RSS, Youtube*

Tom Hagy, CEO
Maureen McGuire, Editorial Director
Teresa Kent Zink, Editor
Mike Wash, Chief Executive Officer, Legal
Lisa Agona, Chief Marketing Officer

The report reviews civil and criminal cases arising from efforts by policyholders and third parties to defraud insurance carriers. Topics include false and fraudulent claims, arson, reverse bad faith, restitution, RICO, incontestability clauses, material misrepresentation, rescission, qui tam actions and fraud rings. Readers receive reports on schemes involving property & casualty, health care, automobile, life, homeowners, and workers' compensation fraud.
Cost: $839.00
100 Pages
Frequency: Monthly
Founded in 1994
Mailing list available for rent

15826 Mealey's Litigation Report: Asbestos

LexisNexis Mealey's

555 W 5th Avenue
Los Angeles, CA 90013

213-627-1130
800-253-4182
FAX 610-768-0880
E-Mail: mealeyinfo@lexisnexis.com
Home Page: www.lexisnexis.com/mealeys
Social Media: *Facebook, Twitter, LinkedIn, RSS, Youtube*

Tom Hagy, CEO
Maureen McGuire, Editorial Director
Bryan Redding, Editor
Mike Wash, Chief Executive Officer, Legal
Lisa Agona, Chief Marketing Officer

The report offers unsurpassed coverage of litigation arising from asbestos-related injury and death. Key issues include: massive class action settlements involving present and future claimants, state and federal verdicts, litigation experts, medical monitoring claims, suits against the tobacco industry, discovery battles, discovery rule decisions, insurance coverage rulings, and asbestos property decisions.
Cost: $1789.00
100 Pages
Frequency: Semi-Monthly
Founded in 1984
Mailing list available for rent

15827 Mealey's Litigation Report: Baycol

LexisNexis Mealey's
555 W 5th Avenue
Los Angeles, CA 90013

213-627-1130
800-253-4182
FAX 610-768-0880
E-Mail: mealeyinfo@lexisnexis.com
Home Page: www.lexisnexis.com/mealeys
Social Media: *Facebook, Twitter, LinkedIn, RSS, Youtube*

Tom Hagy, CEO
Maureen McGuire, Editorial Director
Dylan McGuire, Editor
Mike Wash, Chief Executive Officer, Legal
Lisa Agona, Chief Marketing Officer

This report tracks the litigation surrounding Baycol and other statin-based anti-cholesterol drug cases. Since the voluntary withdrawl of Bayer's Baycol and Lipobay brand cerivastatin anti-cholesterol drugs, numerous complaints have been filed. The report will cover hard-to-find filings, new complaints, class actions, MDL developments, trial updates and more.
Cost: $950.00
100 Pages
Frequency: Monthly
Founded in 2002
Mailing list available for rent

15828 Mealey's Litigation Report: California Insurance

LexisNexis Mealey's
1016 W Ninth Avenue
1st Floor
King of Prussia, PA 19406-1221

215-564-1788
800-448-1515
FAX 610-768-0880
E-Mail: mealeyinfo@lexisnexis.com
Home Page: www.lexisnexis.com/mealeys
Social Media: *Facebook, Twitter, LinkedIn, Itunes, Youtube*

Kumsal Bayazit, Global Senior Vice President
Haywood Talcove, Chief Executive Officer, Government
Ian McDougall, Executive Vice President
Mike Walsh, CEO
Alex Watson, Executive Vice President

The Report focuses on ever-changing California and federal Ninth Circuit insurance coverage disputes and developments. Topics include

California developments in bad faith litigation, earthquake damage coverage, disability insurance, products liability coverage, environmental insurance coverage, mold coverage, asbestos coverage, aviation litigation coverage, entertainment law and more.
Cost: $949.00
100 Pages
Frequency: Monthly
Founded in 2001

15829 Mealey's Litigation Report: Class Actions
LexisNexis Mealey's
1016 W Ninth Avenue
1st Floor
King of Prussia, PA 19406-1221

215-564-1788
800-448-1515
FAX 610-768-0880
E-Mail: mealeyinfo@lexisnexis.com
Home Page: www.lexisnexis.com/mealeys
Social Media: *Facebook, Twitter, LinkedIn, Itunes, Youtube*

Kumsal Bayazit, Global Senior Vice President
Haywood Talcove, Chief Executive Officer, Government
Ian McDougall, Executive Vice President
Mike Walsh, CEO
Alex Watson, Executive Vice President
This report will provide in-depth coverage of class action litigation involving mass torts and beyond - including consumer law, employment law, securities litigation and e-commerce disputes. Get the latest on: hard-to-find filings, notice plans, fairness hearings, class certification rulings, settlements, trial news and verdicts, attorney fee news, appeals, breaking news stories, new complaints, Supreme Court battles, and much more.
Cost: $1195.00
100 Pages
Frequency: Semi-Monthly
Founded in 1997

15830 Mealey's Litigation Report: Construction Defects
LexisNexis Mealey's
1016 W Ninth Avenue
1st Floor
King of Prussia, PA 19406-1221

215-564-1788
800-448-1515
FAX 610-768-0880
E-Mail: mealeyinfo@lexisnexis.com
Home Page: www.lexisnexis.com/mealeys
Social Media: *Facebook, Twitter, LinkedIn, Itunes, Youtube*

Kumsal Bayazit, Global Senior Vice President
Haywood Talcove, Chief Executive Officer, Government
Ian McDougall, Executive Vice President
Mike Walsh, CEO
Alex Watson, Executive Vice President
The Report tracks the growing area of construction defect litigation, including cases involving water intrusion, building settlement, concrete corrosion, mold and other defects. Topics covered include: recovery of damages, warranty issues, contractor liability, sub-contractor liability, developer liability, architect liability and related insurance cover actions.
Cost: $979.00
100 Pages
Frequency: Monthly
Founded in 2000

15831 Mealey's Litigation Report: Copyright
LexisNexis Mealey's

1016 W Ninth Avenue
1st Floor
King of Prussia, PA 19406-1221

215-564-1788
800-448-1515
FAX 610-768-0880
E-Mail: mealeyinfo@lexisnexis.com
Home Page: www.lexisnexis.com/mealeys
Social Media: *Facebook, Twitter, LinkedIn, Itunes, Youtube*

Kumsal Bayazit, Global Senior Vice President
Haywood Talcove, Chief Executive Officer, Government
Ian McDougall, Executive Vice President
Mike Walsh, CEO
Alex Watson, Executive Vice President
The report offers timely and practical analysis on the hot issues in the field. Also features in-depth reporting of copyright law, including court decisions, new suits, settlements, and trials, plus full-text court documents.
Cost: $849.00
100 Pages
Frequency: Monthly
Founded in 2002

15832 Mealey's Litigation Report: Cyber Tech & E -Commerce
LexisNexis Mealey's
1016 W Ninth Avenue
1st Floor
King of Prussia, PA 19406-1221

215-564-1788
800-448-1515
FAX 610-768-0880
E-Mail: mealeyinfo@lexisnexis.com
Home Page: www.lexisnexis.com/mealeys
Social Media: *Facebook, Twitter, LinkedIn, Itunes, Youtube*

Kumsal Bayazit, Global Senior Vice President
Haywood Talcove, Chief Executive Officer, Government
Ian McDougall, Executive Vice President
Mike Walsh, CEO
Alex Watson, Executive Vice President
The Report covers disputes arising from e-commerce. The report tracks emerging legal issues, including: Internet security, data destruction and/or alteration, defamation on the Web, software errors, hardware failure, electronic theft, e-mail trespass, online privacy, government action, shareholder lawsuits, Internet jurisdiction issues, file sharing (copyright) disputes and much more.
Cost: $999.00
100 Pages
Frequency: Monthly
Founded in 1999

15833 Mealey's Litigation Report: Disability Insurance
LexisNexis Mealey's
1016 W Ninth Avenue
1st Floor
King of Prussia, PA 19406-1221

215-564-1788
800-448-1515
FAX 610-768-0880
E-Mail: mealeyinfo@lexisnexis.com
Home Page: www.lexisnexis.com/mealeys
Social Media: *Facebook, Twitter, LinkedIn, Itunes, Youtube*

Kumsal Bayazit, Global Senior Vice President
Haywood Talcove, Chief Executive Officer, Government
Ian McDougall, Executive Vice President
Mike Walsh, CEO
Alex Watson, Executive Vice President
This report tracks the burgeoning number of disputes involving complex disability coverage claims. Topics covered include: claims for chronic fatigue, chronic pain, stress, psychiatric

disabilities, chemical dependency and risk of relapse, plus key issues like total disability, own occupation, bad faith, ERSA, class actions and much more.
Cost: $849.00
100 Pages
Frequency: Monthly
Founded in 2000

15834 Mealey's Litigation Report: Discovery
LexisNexis Mealey's
1016 W Ninth Avenue
1st Floor
King of Prussia, PA 19406-1221

215-564-1788
800-448-1515
FAX 610-768-0880
E-Mail: mealeyinfo@lexisnexis.com
Home Page: www.lexisnexis.com/mealeys
Social Media: *Facebook, Twitter, LinkedIn, Itunes, Youtube*

Kumsal Bayazit, Global Senior Vice President
Haywood Talcove, Chief Executive Officer, Government
Ian McDougall, Executive Vice President
Mike Walsh, CEO
Alex Watson, Executive Vice President
This report covers all of the discovery litigation essentials, including how different districts and judges interpret federal discovery rules, procedural changes, the work product, attorney-client and common interest privileges, and discovery abuse.
Cost: $785.00
100 Pages
Frequency: Monthly
Founded in 2003

15835 Mealey's Litigation Report: ERISA
LexisNexis Mealey's
1016 W Ninth Avenue
1st Floor
King of Prussia, PA 19406-1221

215-564-1788
800-448-1515
FAX 610-768-0880
E-Mail: mealeyinfo@lexisnexis.com
Home Page: www.lexisnexis.com/mealeys
Social Media: *Facebook, Twitter, LinkedIn, Itunes, Youtube*

Kumsal Bayazit, Global Senior Vice President
Haywood Talcove, Chief Executive Officer, Government
Ian McDougall, Executive Vice President
Mike Walsh, CEO
Alex Watson, Executive Vice President
The report focuses on the hottest areas of ERISA litigation, including preemption, health plan actions, exhaustion of administrative remedies, contingent worker litigation, class actions 401k plans, attorney's fees, breach of fiduciary duty, what courts consider to be equitable relief, downsizing and benefit cutbacks, blackout periods and bad faith claims against disability insurers.
Cost: $875.00
100 Pages
Frequency: Monthly
Founded in 2002

15836 Mealey's Litigation Report: Ephedra/PPA
LexisNexis Mealey's
1016 W Ninth Avenue
1st Floor
King of Prussia, PA 19406-1221

215-564-1788
800-448-1515
FAX 610-768-0880
E-Mail: mealeyinfo@lexisnexis.com
Home Page: www.lexisnexis.com/mealeys

Social Media: *Facebook, Twitter, LinkedIn, Itunes, Youtube*

Kumsal Bayazit, Global Senior Vice President
Haywood Talcove, Chief Executive Officer, Government
Ian McDougall, Executive Vice President
Mike Walsh, CEO
Alex Watson, Executive Vice President

The report tracks every facet of the growing area of litigation resulting from injuries and deaths associated with over-the-counter decongestant and appetite suppressant, phenylpropanolamine (PPA), and the chemically similar weight-loss herb, ephedra. The report offers true litigation reporting of new complaints, answers, discovery motions, appeals, trials, verdicts, settlements, plus covers the latest regulatory news.
Cost: $995.00
100 Pages
Frequency: Monthly
Founded in 2001

15837 Mealey's Litigation Report: Fen-Phen/Redux

LexisNexis Mealey's
1016 W Ninth Avenue
1st Floor
King of Prussia, PA 19406-1221

215-564-1788
800-448-1515
FAX 610-768-0880
E-Mail: mealeyinfo@lexisnexis.com
Home Page: www.lexisnexis.com/mealeys
Social Media: *Facebook, Twitter, LinkedIn, Itunes, Youtube*

Kumsal Bayazit, Global Senior Vice President
Haywood Talcove, Chief Executive Officer, Government
Ian McDougall, Executive Vice President
Mike Walsh, CEO
Alex Watson, Executive Vice President

The report provides detailed coverage of the litigation surrounding fen-phen, Redux and other diet drugs. The report covers new filings, class actions, MDL proceedings, trials, settlements, rulings, medical studies, FDA activity and more.
Cost: $995.00
100 Pages
Frequency: Monthly
Founded in 1997

15838 Mealey's Litigation Report: Insurance

LexisNexis Mealey's
1016 W Ninth Avenue
1st Floor
King of Prussia, PA 19406-1221

215-564-1788
800-448-1515
FAX 610-768-0880
E-Mail: mealeyinfo@lexisnexis.com
Home Page: www.lexisnexis.com/mealeys
Social Media: *Facebook, Twitter, LinkedIn, Itunes, Youtube*

Kumsal Bayazit, Global Senior Vice President
Haywood Talcove, Chief Executive Officer, Government
Ian McDougall, Executive Vice President
Mike Walsh, CEO
Alex Watson, Executive Vice President

The report tracks declaratory judgment actions regarding coverage for litigation arising from long-tail claims, including environmental contamination and latent damage and injury allegedly caused by asbestos, tox chemicals and fumes, lead, breast implants, medical devices, construction defects, and more. Key issues: allocation, occurrence, policy exclusion, choice of law, discovery, duty to defend, notice, trig-

ger of coverage and known loss.
Cost: $2115.00
100 Pages
Frequency: Weekly
Founded in 1984

15839 Mealey's Litigation Report: Insurance Bad Faith

LexisNexis Mealey's
1016 W Ninth Avenue
1st Floor
King of Prussia, PA 19406-1221

215-564-1788
800-448-1515
FAX 610-768-0880
E-Mail: mealeyinfo@lexisnexis.com
Home Page: www.lexisnexis.com/mealeys
Social Media: *Facebook, LinkedIn, Itunes, Youtube*

Kumsal Bayazit, Global Senior Vice President
Haywood Talcove, Chief Executive Officer, Government
Ian McDougall, Executive Vice President
Mike Walsh, CEO
Alex Watson, Executive Vice President

The report details insurance coverage disputes arising from alleged breaches of the implied covenant of good faith and fair dealing. The topics covered involve third-party and first-party actions, statutory suits, punitive damage claims, coverage denials and delays, the definition of bad faith, relevant legislation, verdicts, and discovery disputes.
Cost: $1325.00
100 Pages
Frequency: Semi-Monthly
Founded in 1987

15840 Medical Liability Advisory Service

Business Publishers
8737 Colesville Road
10th Floor
Silver Spring, MD 20910-3928

301-876-6300
800-274-6737
FAX 301-589-8493
E-Mail: custserv@bpinews.com
Home Page: www.bpinews.com

Eric Easton, Publisher
Bonita Becker, Editor

Gives you practical information on just what triggers a lawsuit. Information you can pass on to your staff to claim-proof your procedures.
Founded in 1963

15841 Medical Malpractice Reports

Matthew Bender and Company
11 Penn Plz
Suite 5101
New York, NY 10001-2006

212-000-1111
FAX 212-244-3188

Eric Blood, Data Processing

All the facts, background information and expert analysis you need to keep on top of new legislation, new theories of liability, the impact of new medical technology and more.

15842 Mental and Physical Disability Law Reporter: On-Line

American Bar Association
740 15th Street NW
Washington, DC 20005-1019

202-662-1000
FAX 202-442-3439
Social Media: *Facebook, Twitter, LinkedIn*

Stephen N. Zack, President
Katherine H. O'Neil, Commission Chair
John W. Parry, Commission Director
Jack L. Rives, Executive Director
Alice Richmond, Treasurer

A new online searchable database allows subscribers to research disability law cases and legislation by case name, federal or state legislation, subject area, jurisdiction, and year (beginning 2003). There are 22 subject areas that cover three main areas: civil mental disability law; criminal mental disability law; and disability discrimination law. The database, which is updated every two months, contains over 12,000 summaries of key cases and legislation.
Cost: $299.00
15 Members
Frequency: 6 X/Year
ISSN: 0883-7902
Founded in 1973

15843 Mergers & Acquisitions Litigation Reporter

Thomson Reuters
610 Opperman Dr
St Paul, MN 55123-1340

651-687-7000
800-344-5008
FAX 651-687-5581
Home Page: www.store.westlaw.com/default.aspx

Charles B Cater, Executive VP
Laurie Zenner, VP

Provides summaries and fulltext documents in key litigation concerning mergers and acquisitions. Offers general buyout and acquisition coverage as well as cases related to leveraged buyouts.
Cost: $1234.20
Frequency: Monthly
Mailing list available for rent

15844 Money Laundering Alert

Alert Global Media
80 SW 8th Street
Suite 2300
Miami, FL 33130-3031

305-530-0500
800-232-3652
FAX 305-530-9434
E-Mail: customerservice@moneylaundering.com
Home Page: www.moneylaundering.com

Charles Intriago, President

Covers legal issues, including new laws, regulations and cases related to money laundering and the bank secrecy act in the US and worldwide. Provides practical guidance and analysis and serves as a training tool. Also full text on the internet.
Cost: $945.00
15 Pages
Frequency: Monthly
ISSN: 1046-3070
Founded in 1989

15845 Municipal Litigation Reporter

Strafford Publications
PO Box 13729
Atlanta, GA 30324-0729

404-881-1141
800-926-7926
FAX 404-881-0074
E-Mail: customerservice@straffordpub.com
Home Page: www.straffordpub.com

Richard Ossoff, President
Jennifer Vaughan, Managing Editor

Monthly digest of key court decisions on litigation involving local governments. Cases are screened and selected to provide concise, comprehensive coverage of issues important to municipal attorneys and others involved with the local government.
Cost: $497.00
16 Pages
ISSN: 0278-1301
Founded in 1984

Mailing list available for rent: 7.4M names
Printed in one color

15846 NAELA News
National Academy of Elder Law Attorneys
1577 Spring Hill Road
Suite 220
Vienna, VA 22182-2223

703-942-5711
FAX 703-563-9504
E-Mail: naela@naela.org
Home Page: www.naela.org

Peter G Wacht, CAE, Executive Director
Nancy Sween, Director Publications
Kirsten Brown Simpson, Director, Membership
& Marketing
Ann Watkins, Operations Manager
Roger Naoroji, Meetings & Education
Coordinator

Communicates the activities, goals, and mis-
sion of its publisher, the National Academy of
Elder Law Attorneys and seeks out and pub-
lishes information and diverse views related to
Elder Law and Special Needs.
Frequency: 6x Year

15847 NCWBA Newsletter
National Conference of Women's Bar
Associations
PO Box 82366
Portland, OR 97282

E-Mail: info@ncwba.org
Home Page: www.ncwba.org

Jeanne Cezanne Collins, President
Pamela Berman, President-Elect
Diane Rynerson, Executive Director

To promote and assist the growth of local and
statewide women's bar associations and ideas
among women's bar associations and women's
bar sections of local and statewide bar associations; to serve as a vehicle for the exchange
and dissemination of information and ideas
among women's bar associations and women's
bar sections of local and statewide bar
associations.
Frequency: Monthly

15848 National Bankruptcy Reporter
Andrews Communications
175 Stafford, Building 4
Suite 140
Wayne, PA 19087

610-225-0510
800-345-1101
FAX 610-225-0501
Home Page: www.andrewspub.com

Robert Maroldo, Publisher

Commercial bankruptcy news.
Frequency: Monthly

15849 National Bar Bulletin
National Bar Association
1225 11th St Nw
Washington, DC 20001-4217

202-842-3900
FAX 202-289-6170
Home Page: www.nationalbar.org

John Crump, Executive Director
Kim M Keenan, Manager
Teka Miller, Manager

Association news and activities, legislative up-
dates and information for lawyers.
Cost: $20.00
8 Pages
Frequency: Monthly
Founded in 1925

15850 National Financing Law Digest
Strafford Publications

PO Box 13729
Atlanta, GA 30324-0729

404-881-1141
800-926-7926
FAX 404-881-0074
E-Mail: customerservice@straffordpub.com
Home Page: www.straffordpub.com

Richard Ossoff, President
Jennifer Vaughan, Managing Editor

Monthly digest of nationally significant litiga-
tion concerning secured and unsecured financ-
ing transactions, including bonds, bankruptcy
collection, and lender liability.
Cost: $597.00
Frequency: Monthly
ISSN: 1073-953X
Founded in 1984

15851 National Notary
National Notary Association
9350 DeSoto Avenue
PO Box 2402
Chatsworth, CA 91311-2402

818-394-4000
800-876-6827
FAX 800-833-1211
E-Mail: publications@nationalnotary.org
Home Page: www.nationalnotary.org

Deborah Thaw, Executive VP
Armando Aguirre, Editor
Milton G. Valera, Chairman
Thomas A. Heymann, President /CEO
Deborah M. Thaw, Executive Vice President

Contents range from indentity fraud and elec-
tronic notarization, to legislation and practicing
tips. Also includes human interest stories in-
volving notaries.
Circulation: 250,000
ISSN: 0894-7872
Founded in 1957
Printed in 4 colors on glossy stock

15852 National On-Campus Report
Magna Publications
2718 Dryden Drive
Madison, WI 53704-3086

608-246-3590
800-433-0499
FAX 608-246-3597
E-Mail: support@magnapubs.com
Home Page: www.magnapubs.com

William Haight, President
Jody Glynn Patrick, VP
Therese Kattner, Editor
David Burns, Publisher
Debra Art, Director

The campus legal monthly.
Cost: $169.00
8 Pages
Founded in 1972
Printed in 2 colors on matte stock

15853 National Paralegal Reporter
National Federation of Paralegal
Associations
2815 Eastlake Ave E
Suite 160
Seattle, WA 98102-3278

206-285-1851
FAX 206-284-3481
E-Mail: info@akpreparedness.com
Home Page: www.akproductions.com

Founded in 1981

15854 National Property Law Digests
Strafford Publications
PO Box 13729
Atlanta, GA 30324-0729

404-881-1141
800-926-7926

FAX 404-881-0074
E-Mail: customerservice@straffordpub.com
Home Page: www.straffordpub.com

Richard Ossoff, Presdient

Case digests of national significant court deci-
sions affecting the acquisition, development,
management, transfer and financing of real
property.
Cost: $697.00
Frequency: Monthly
ISSN: 0363-8340
Founded in 1984
Mailing list available for rent: 25M names

15855 National Report on Substance Abuse
National Retail Federation
325 7th St Nw
Suite 1000
Washington, DC 20004-2808

202-783-7971
800-673-4692
FAX 202-737-2849
Home Page: www.nrf.com

Tracy Mullin, President
Terry Peters, Editor
Matthew Shay, President and CEO
Vicki Cantrell, Senior Vice President,
Communities
Mallory Duncan, Senior Vice President

Biweekly review of federal and state laws, regulations and court cases involving alcohol and
drug abuse, with an emphasis on workplace
drug testing. Also covers treatment and prevention, EAPs, ADA, local laws and policies.
Cost: $377.00
Circulation: 36000
Founded in 1981
Printed in 2 colors on matte stock

15856 National Report on Work & Family
Business Publishers
2222 Sedwick Dr
Suite 101
Durham, NC 27713

800-223-8720
FAX 800-508-2592
E-Mail: custserv@bpinews.com
Home Page: www.bpinews.com

Independent, authoritative resource covering
the latest federal and state legislative, legal and
regulatory developments concerning work/fam-
ily issues. Includes case studies of organizations that have implemented family-friendly
policies.
Cost: $497.00
Frequency: 25 per year

15857 National Security Law Report
American Bar Association-Law & National
Security
740 15th St Nw
Suite 8
Washington, DC 20005-1022

202-662-1000
FAX 202-662-1032
E-Mail: orders@abanet.org
Home Page: www.americanbar.org/aba.html
Social Media: *Facebook, Twitter*

Laurel G. Bellows, President

The Report includes reports of committee conferences, pertinent law and national security
updates, recent cases, book reviews, pending
legislation, and other writing relevant to the
field.
Frequency: Monthly
Circulation: 4000
Founded in 1991

**15858 Nolo News: Legal Self-Help
Newspaper**
Nolo Press

950 Parker St
Berkeley, CA 94710-2576

510-704-2248
FAX 510-859-0027
E-Mail: LibraryCS@nolo.com
Home Page: www.nolo.com

Maggie Wang, Manager
Mary Randolph, Editor

Self-help legal newspaper.
Cost: $39.99
Frequency: Weekly
Circulation: 120000
Founded in 1971

15859 On the Line: Union Labor Reports Guide

Bureau of National Affairs
1801 S Bell St
Arlington, VA 22202-4501

703-341-3000
800-372-1033
FAX 800-253-0332
E-Mail: customercare@bna.com
Home Page: www.bnabooks.com
Social Media: *Facebook, Twitter, LinkedIn*

Paul N Wojcik, CEO

Reports on shopfloor issues affecting union
stewards. Includes summaries of arbitration
awards and court cases. $4.00 per year each
subscription.
Cost: $4.00
ISSN: 1526-2863
Founded in 1929

15860 Parascope

American Bar Association
321 N Clark St
Chicago, IL 60654-7598

312-988-5000
800-285-2221
FAX 312-988-6281
E-Mail: askaba@abanet.org
Home Page: www.americanbar.org/aba.html
Social Media: *Facebook, Twitter*

Tommy H Wells Jr, President
Laurel G. Bellows, President

Newsletter for nation's appellate staff attorneys. Contains book reviews and articles on
matters concerning appellate courts.
Cost: $19.00
Frequency: Quarterly

15861 Partner's Report for Law Firm Owners

Institute of Management and Administration
3 Bethesda Metro Center
Suite 250
Bethesda, MD 20814-5377

703-341-3500
800-372-1033
FAX 800-253-0332
Home Page: www.ioma.com

Keeps partners up to date on salary guidelines
and benefits, aw well as provide the reader with
tips on increasing profit margins and exercising
leadership skills.
Frequency: Monthly
Founded in 1984

15862 Patent/Trade/Copyright Newsletter

American Bar Association
321 N Clark St
Chicago, IL 60654-7598

312-988-5000
800-285-2221
FAX 312-988-6281
E-Mail: askaba@abenet.com

Home Page: www.americanbar.org/aba.html
Social Media: *Facebook, Twitter*

Tommy H Wells Jr, President
Laurel G. Bellows, President

Activities of the Section, recent developments
in intellectual property law and calendar of
events.
Frequency: Quarterly
Founded in 1878

15863 People and Programs

American Bar Association
321 N Clark St
Chicago, IL 60654-7598

312-988-5000
800-285-2221
FAX 312-988-6281
E-Mail: askaba@abanet.org
Home Page: www.americanbar.org/aba.html
Social Media: *Facebook, Twitter*

Tommy H Wells Jr, President
Laurel G. Bellows, President

A newsletter for donors and volunteers for the
ABA fund for Justice and Education, which
supports over 150 public service and law-related education programs.
Founded in 1878

15864 People-to-People Newsletter

Association of Legal Administrators
75 Tri-State International
Suite 222
Lincolnshire, IL 60069-4435

847-267-1252
FAX 847-267-1329
E-Mail: publications@alanet.org
Home Page: www.alanet.org

Larry Smith, Executive Director
Debbie Thomas, Director, Accounting &
Finance
Renee Mahovsky, Director,
Administration/Operations
Bob Abramson, Director, Marketing &
Communication
Jan Waugh, Director, Member Services

Offers the newest information and legislative
updates for legal administrators.
Frequency: Monthly
Founded in 1971

15865 Personal Injury Verdict Reviews

LRP Publications
PO Box 980
Horsham, PA 19044-0980

215-784-0912
800-341-7874
FAX 215-784-9639
E-Mail: webmaster@lrp.com
Home Page: www.lrp.com

Todd Lutz, CFO
David Light, Managing Editor
Brooke Doran, Research Associate

Each twice-monthly issue contains a statisti-
cally based feature article backed by nationwide personal injury case summaries. Each
case summary includes description of the incident, names and locations of counsel and expert witnesses, verdict or settlement amount,
amount of medical expense and wage loss and
date and docket number.
Cost: $375.00
Founded in 1977

15866 Personal Legal Alert

Alexander Hamilton Institute
70 Hilltop Rd
Suite 2200
Ramsey, NJ 07446-2816

201-825-3377
800-879-2441
FAX 201-825-8696

E-Mail: editorial@ahipubs.com
Home Page: www.ahipubs.com

Schuyler T Jenks, President

Deals with legal aspects of personnel.
Cost: $97.00
4 Pages
Frequency: Fortnightly
Circulation: 4000
Founded in 1989
*Mailing list available for rent: 7,000 names at
$125 per M*
Printed in 2 colors on matte stock

15867 Personnel Manager's Legal Letter

Institute of Management and Administration
3 Bethesda Metro Center
Suite 250
Bethesda, MD 20814-5377

703-341-3500
800-372-1033
FAX 800-253-0332
Home Page: www.ioma.com

PMLL regularly covers title VII, the Americans
with Disabilities Act, ERISA, the Family and
Medical Leave Act, and human resources legal
issues around hiring, teminations, compensation and much more.

15868 Practical Law Books Reviews

Library Managemental Services
5914 Highland Hills Drive
Austin, TX 78731-4057

512-320-0320

Judith Helburn, Publisher

Reference book separated by field specification.

15869 Premises Liability Report

Strafford Publications
PO Box 13729
Atlanta, GA 30324-0729

404-881-1141
800-926-7926
FAX 404-881-0074
E-Mail: customerservice@straffordpub.com
Home Page: www.straffordpub.com

Richard Ossoff, President
Jennifer Vaughan, Managing Editor

Digest of legal developments offering liability
of property owners and managers. Warning sys-
tem for potential lawsuits for injuries resulting
from conditions on or near premises.
Cost: $287.00
Frequency: Monthly
ISSN: 1055-730X
Founded in 1984

15870 Preservation Law Reporter

National Trust for Historic Preservation
1785 Massachusetts Ave Nw
Washington, DC 20036-2189

202-588-6000
800-944-6847
FAX 202-588-6038
E-Mail: members@nthp.org
Home Page: www.nationaltrust.org

Richard Moe, CEO
Andrew Carroll, Production Manager
Bob Barron, Publisher
Doug Loescher, Director

The definitive source on preservation law. It
provides informative and reliable reports on re-
cent court decisions, tax rulings, new publica-
tions and new legislation.
Cost: $95.00
Frequency: Monthly
Circulation: 400
Founded in 1949

15871 Preview of US Supreme Court Cases
American Bar Association
321 N Clark St
Chicago, IL 60654-7598

312-988-5000
800-285-2221
FAX 312-988-6281
E-Mail: askaba@abanet.org
Home Page: www.americanbar.org/aba.html
Social Media: *Facebook, Twitter*

Tommy H Wells Jr, President
Laurel G. Bellows, President
Previews cases coming before the US Supreme
Court.
Cost: $130.00
Frequency: Annual

15872 Private Security Case Law Reporter
Strattford Publishers
590 Dutch Valley Road NE
Atlanta, GA 30324-729

404-881-1141
800-926-7926
FAX 404-881-0074
E-Mail: customerservice@straffordpub.com
Home Page: www.straffordpub.com

Richard Ossoff, Publisher
Albert J Pucciarelli, VP

Monthly digest decisions on litigation involving private security operations; includes insights and trend analysis by nations leading
security expert.
Cost: $347.00
Frequency: Monthly
Founded in 1984

15873 Probate and Property
American Bar Association
321 N Clark St
Chicago, IL 60654-7598

312-988-5000
800-285-2221
FAX 312-988-6281
E-Mail: askaba@abanet.org
Home Page: www.americanbar.org/aba.html
Social Media: *Facebook, Twitter*

Tommy H Wells Jr, President
Laurel G. Bellows, President
Aimed at lawyers who devote a large part of
their practice to real estate law and laws deal-
ing with wills, trusts and estates.
Cost: $60.00
Founded in 1978

15874 Public Contract Newsletter
American Bar Association
321 N Clark St
Chicago, IL 60654-7598

312-988-5000
800-285-2221
FAX 312-988-6281
E-Mail: askaba@abanet.org
Home Page: www.americanbar.org/aba.html
Social Media: *Facebook, Twitter*

Tommy H Wells Jr, President
Laurel G. Bellows, President
Contains informative articles on a wide range
of timely topics including current developments in federal and grant law, recent developments in state and local public contract law,
upcoming educational programs and legislative
developments.
Cost: $60.00
Frequency: Quarterly

15875 Purchasing Law Report
Institute of Management and Administration

3 Bethesda Metro Center
Suite 250
Bethesda, MD 20814-5377

703-341-3500
800-372-1033
FAX 800-253-0332
Home Page: www.ioma.com

Purchasing Law Report is the most practical,
least expensive and quickest way to understand
and apply new purchasing laws and regulations
in your day-to-day operations without wasting
time sorting through hundreds of legal
documents.

15876 Report on Disability Programs
Business Publishers
8737 Colesville Road
Suite 1100
Silver Spring, MD 20910-3928

301-876-6300
800-274-6737
FAX 301-589-8493
E-Mail: custserv@bpinews.com
Home Page: www.bpinews.com

Leonard A Eiserer, Publisher

Follows legislation, regulations, legal actions
and funding in areas import to all persons with
disabilities including health care, employment,
civil rights, housing, and transportation.
Cost: $227.00
8 Pages
Frequency: Monthly
Founded in 1963
Printed in on matte stock

15877 School Law Reporter
Education Law Association
300 College Park Ave
Dayton, OH 45469-0001

937-229-3589
FAX 937-229-3845
E-Mail: ela@educationlaw.org
Home Page: www.educationlaw.org
Social Media: *Facebook, Twitter, LinkedIn*

W Brad Colwell, President
Mandy Schrank, Executive Director
Cate K. Smith, Executive Director
Judy Pleiman, Member Services Coordinator
Jody Thornburg, Publications Manager

Member association for those with an iunterest
in school law issues, such as attorneys, law
professors, education professors, school administrators, and teachers.
Frequency: Monthly
ISSN: 1059-4094
Founded in 1954

15878 Search and Seizure Law Report
Clark Boardman Company
375 Hudson St
Room 201
New York, NY 10014-3658

585-546-5530
800-323-1336

Robert Bouchard, Publisher
Elizabeth Brooks, Editor

Provides detailed, current coverage of the law,
procedure, trends, and developments evolving
in search and seizure law.
Cost: $175.00
8 Pages
Frequency: Monthly
Circulation: 2,000
Printed in 2 colors on matte stock

15879 Section of Taxation Newsletter
American Bar Association

321 N Clark St
Chicago, IL 60654-7598

312-988-5000
800-285-2221
FAX 312-988-6281
E-Mail: askaba@abanet.org
Home Page: www.americanbar.org/aba.html
Social Media: *Facebook, Twitter*

Tommy H Wells Jr, President
Laurel G. Bellows, President

Update on current tax developments, committee projects, meeting information and order
forms.
Cost: $15.00
Frequency: Quarterly

15880 Security Law
Strafford Publications
PO Box 13729
Atlanta, GA 30324-0729

404-881-1141
800-926-7926
FAX 404-881-0074
E-Mail: customerservice@straffordpub.com
Home Page: www.straffordpub.com

Richard Ossoff, President

Monthly updates on security law without all the
legal jargon.
Cost: $297.00
Frequency: Monthly
ISSN: 0889-0625
Founded in 1984
Mailing list available for rent: 31.6M names
Printed in one color

**15881 Sexual Harassment Litigation
Reporter**
Andrews Publications
175 Strafford Avenue
Building 4 Suite 140
Wayne, PA 19087-3317

610-225-0510
800-345-1101
FAX 610-225-0501
Home Page: www.andrewspub.com

Robert Maroldo, Publisher
Linda Coady, Editor
Cost: $49.00
Frequency: Monthly

**15882 Small Firm Profit Report: Attorney
Edition**
Professional Newsletters
Atlanta, GA 30366-1143

770-819-4151

Robert Palmer, Publisher

Practice management and marketing help for
small law firms and solo practitioners.

15883 Software Law Bulletin
Andrews Publications
1735 Market Street
Suite 1600
Wayne, PA 19087

610-225-0510
800-345-1101
FAX 610-225-0501
Home Page: www.andrewspub.com

Donna Higgins, Editor

As pantenting becomes the predominant
method of protecting software, and as cases involving technological copy protection measures wind through the court system, Andrews'
Software Law Bulletin provides coverage of
decisions and opinions in the key cases. Detailed articles put individual developments into

the big picture of the changing law landscape.
Cost: $588.00
Frequency: Monthly
Founded in 1972

15884 Special Court News
American Bar Association
321 N Clark St
Chicago, IL 60654-7598

312-988-5000
800-285-2221
FAX 312-988-6281
E-Mail: askaba@abanet.org
Home Page: www.abanet.org

Tommy H Wells Jr, President

Newsletter apprises members of the current activities and plans of the Conference. Also provides active, continual contact with members and solicits more active participation.
Cost: $11.00
Frequency: Quarterly

15885 Special Education Law Monthly
LRP Publications
747 Dresher Road Suite 500
PO Box 980
Horsham, PA 19044-980

215-784-0912
800-341-7874
FAX 215-784-9639
E-Mail: webmaster@lrp.com
Home Page: www.lrp.com

Jessyca Harrington, Editor
Dionne Ellis, Managing Editor

Covers court decisions and administrative rulings affecting the education of students with disabilities. Each issue begins with a brief overview of the case summaries covered allowing you to quickly focus on the decisions and hearings that affect you most.
Cost: $140.00
Frequency: Monthly
Founded in 1977

15886 Sports & Entertainment Litigation Reporter
Andrews Publications
175 Strafford Avenue
Building 4 Suite 140
Wayne, PA 19087-3317

610-225-0510
800-345-1101
FAX 610-225-0501
Home Page: www.andrewspub.com

Robert Maroldo, Publisher
Robert Sullivan, Editor

Covers the latest news in the fast-changing world of entertainment litigation.
Cost: $775.00
Frequency: Monthly
Founded in 1960

15887 Sports Medicine Standards and Malpractice Reporter
PRC Publishing
3976 Fulton Dr Nw
Canton, OH 44718-3043

330-492-6063
800-336-0083
FAX 330-492-6176
Home Page: www.prcpublishingcorp.com

Molly Romig, VP

Designed to keep sports medicine professionals informed about current trends in their challenging professions. Accepts advertising.
Cost: $29.95
16 Pages
Frequency: Quarterly
Circulation: 500
ISSN: 0141-696X

Founded in 1984
Printed in 2 colors on matte stock

15888 Sports, Parks and Recreation Law Reporter
PRC Publishing
3976 Fulton Dr Nw
Canton, OH 44718-3043

330-492-6063
800-336-0083
FAX 330-492-6176
Home Page: www.prcpublishingcorp.com

Molly Romig, VP

For those professionals in the sports, parks and recreational law. Accepts advertising.
Cost: $39.95
16 Pages
Frequency: Quarterly
Circulation: 500
ISSN: 0893-8210
Founded in 1997
Printed in 2 colors on matte stock

15889 State Legislative Report
American Bar Association
1800 M Street NW
#450S
Washington, DC 20036-5802

202-662-1000
FAX 202-331-2220

Patrick Sheehan, Publisher
Diane Gibson, Editor

A summary of key legislative developments of interest to attorneys.
Cost: $50.00
4 Pages
Circulation: 800

15890 State and Local Law News
American Bar Association
321 N Clark St
Chicago, IL 60654-7598

312-988-5000
800-285-2221
FAX 312-988-6281
E-Mail: askaba@abanet.org
Home Page: www.americanbar.org/aba.html
Social Media: *Facebook, Twitter*

Tommy H Wells Jr, President
Laurel G. Bellows, President
Richard W. Bright, Staff Editor

Informs members regarding Section activities and important issues of law.
Cost: $40.00
Frequency: Quarterly
Circulation: 6000
Founded in 1878

15891 Summary and Reports
American Bar Association
321 N Clark St
Chicago, IL 60654-7598

312-988-5000
800-285-2221
FAX 312-988-6281
E-Mail: askaba@abanet.org
Home Page: www.americanbar.org/aba.html
Social Media: *Facebook, Twitter*

Tommy H Wells Jr, President
Laurel G. Bellows, President

Contains recommendations and informational reports to the ABA House of Delegates.

15892 Summary of Labor Arbitration Awards
LRP Publications
PO Box 980
Horsham, PA 19044-0980

215-784-0912
800-341-7874

FAX 215-784-9639
E-Mail: webmaster@lrp.com
Home Page: www.lrp.com

Todd Lutz, CFO
Ken Kahn, CEO
Dana Eynon, Marketing Director
Claude Werder, VP
Marcy Witt, Marketing Director

Since 1959, the summary has been providing digests of private-sector labor arbitration decisions, covering the latest topics in collective bargaining with non-governmental employers.
Cost: $120.00
16 Pages
Frequency: Monthly
Founded in 1977
Printed in 2 colors on glossy stock

15893 Syllabus
American Bar Association
321 N Clark St
Chicago, IL 60654-7598

312-988-5000
800-285-2221
FAX 312-988-6281
E-Mail: askaba@abanet.org
Home Page: www.americanbar.org/aba.html
Social Media: *Facebook, Twitter*

Tommy H Wells Jr, President
Laurel G. Bellows, President

Newspaper describing and commenting on developments in legal education.
Cost: $15.00
Frequency: Quarterly
Founded in 1978

15894 Tax Laws of the World
Foreign Tax Law
PO Box 2189
Ormond Beach, FL 32175-2189

386-253-5785
FAX 386-257-3003
Home Page: www.foreignlaw.com

Income, corporate and related tax laws for over 100 countries. Many full text translations.
Cost: $100.00

15895 Testifying Expert
LRP Publications
747 Dresher Road
PO Box 980
Horsham, PA 19044-2247

215-784-0912
800-341-7874
FAX 215-784-9639
E-Mail: webmaster@lrp.com
Home Page: www.lrp.com

Patrick Byrne, Editor
Gary Bagin, Circulation Manager

A newsletter designed to help experts develop a reputation or improve their present standing as an expert. Each monthly issue contains relevant decisions affecting the expert, book reviews and seminar listings.
Cost: $140.00
Frequency: Monthly
Founded in 1977

15896 The ALI Reporter
American Law Institute-American Bar Association
Continuing Professional Education
4025 Chestnut Street, Suite 5
Philadelphia, PA 19104

215-243-1600
FAX 215-243-1664
E-Mail: ali@ali.org
Home Page: www.ali-aba.org
Social Media: *Facebook, Twitter, LinkedIn*

Julene Franki, Executive Director
Lawrence F. Meehan, Deputy Executive

Director
Judith Cole, Executive Assistant
Bennett Boskey, Treasurer

This newsletter reports on the activities of the ALI and is primarily for its members.
Frequency: Quarterly
Founded in 1947

15897 The Air and Space Lawyer

American Bar Association Forum on Air & Space Law
321 N Clark St
Chicago, IL 60654-7598

312-988-5000
800-285-2221
FAX 312-988-6281
E-Mail: askaba@abanet.org
Home Page: www.americanbar.org/aba.html
Social Media: *Facebook, Twitter*

Kenneth P. Quinn, Editor-in-Chief
John Palmer, Staff Editor
Laurel G. Bellows, President

Newsletter of significant developments in the field of air and space law as well as reports of Forum Committee activities.
Cost: $40.00
24 Pages
Frequency: Quarterly
Circulation: 2000
ISSN: 0747-7449
Printed in 4 colors

15898 The Construction Lawyer

American Bar Association
321 N Clark St
Chicago, IL 60654-7598

312-988-5000
800-285-2221
FAX 312-988-5280
E-Mail: askaba@abanet.org
Home Page: www.americanbar.org/aba.html
Social Media: *Facebook, Twitter*

Thomas J. Campbell, Staff Editor
John W. Ralls, Editor-in-Chief
Laurel G. Bellows, President

Newsletter containing articles on recent developments in the construction industry as well as announcements pertaining to the Forum Committee or to other organizations in the field.
Cost: $50.00
48 Pages
Frequency: Quarterly

15899 The Health Lawyer

American Bar Association Section on Health Law
321 N Clark St
Chicago, IL 60654-7598

312-988-5000
800-285-2221
FAX 312-988-5280
E-Mail: askabanet@abanet.org
Home Page: www.americanbar.org/aba.html
Social Media: *Facebook, Twitter*

Laurel G. Bellows, President

Provides informative articles that focus on a wide range of areas in the health law field and offers incisice analysis of key issues.
Cost: $60.00
Frequency: Bi-monthly

15900 The National Notary

Po Box 2402
Chatsworth, CA 91313-2402

818-739-4000
800-876-6827
FAX 818-700-1942
E-Mail: hotline@nationalnotary.org

Home Page: www.nationalnotary.org
Social Media: *Facebook, Twitter, LinkedIn*

Milton G Valera, President
Deborah M Thaw, Executive VP
Marc Reiser, CEO
Jane Eagle, Executive VP & CFO
Ron Johnson, VP Systems & Operations

The National Notary addresses pertinent cutting-edge notarial issues in depth, and also features helpful how-to articles on every phase of operating as a professional Notary Public in the venue of American law and commerce.
200M Members
Frequency: Bi-Monthly
Circulation: 200,000
Founded in 1957

15901 The Procurement Lawyer

American Bar Association - Public Contract Law
321 N Clark St
Chicago, IL 60654-7598

312-988-5000
800-285-2221
FAX 312-988-5280
E-Mail: pubcontract@abanet.org
Home Page: www.americanbar.org/aba.html
Social Media: *Facebook, Twitter*

John A. Burkholder, Editor-in-Chief
Laurel G. Bellows, President

Newsletter providing news on federal, state and local government procurement professionals.
Frequency: Quarterly

15902 The SciTech Lawyer

American Bar Association Science & Technology Law
321 N Clark St
Chicago, IL 60654-7598

312-988-5533
800-285-2221
E-Mail: sciencetech@abanet.org
Home Page: www.americanbar.org/aba.html
Social Media: *Facebook, Twitter*

Shawn T Kaminski, Section Director
Julie Fleming, Co-Editor-in-Chief
Eleanor Kellett, Co-Editor-in-Chief
Laurel G. Bellows, President

Quarterly practice specific magazine featuring cutting edge news.

15903 Tobacco Products Litigation Reporter

TPLR
PO Box 1162
Back Bay Annex
Boston, MA 02117-1162

617-373-2026
FAX 617-373-3672
Home Page: www.tplr.com

Lissy Friedman, Publisher
Richard Daynard, Editor

Tobacco industry news.
Cost: $995.00
Founded in 1975

15904 Transnational Bulletin

Lewis, D'Amato, Brisbois & Bisgaard
221 N Figueroa St
Suite 1200
Los Angeles, CA 90012-2663

213-250-1800
FAX 213-250-7900

Legal information for the international business community written by lawyers of the firm.

15905 Trial Judges News

American Bar Association

321 N Clark St
Chicago, IL 60654-7598

312-988-5000
800-285-2221
FAX 312-988-6281
E-Mail: askaba@abanet.org
Home Page: www.americanbar.org/aba.html
Social Media: *Facebook, Twitter*

Tommy H Wells Jr, President
Laurel G. Bellows, President

This newsletter informs membership of the National Conference of State Trial Judges of the activities and programs of that conference.
Frequency: Quarterly
Founded in 1978

15906 Turning the Tide

People Against Racist Terror
PO Box 1990
Burbank, CA 91507-1990

FAX 818-848-2680

Michael Novick, Publisher

Bimonthly newsletter of anti-racist activism, research and education covering neo-nazi and other racist violence, efforts at conflict resolution and social justic reforms.
Cost: $10.00
24 Pages
Frequency: BiWeekly
Circulation: 7,500
Printed in 2 colors on newsprint stock

15907 Urban Lawyer

American Bar Association
321 N Clark St
Chicago, IL 60654-7598

312-988-5000
800-285-2221
FAX 312-988-6281
E-Mail: askaba@abanet.org
Home Page: www.americanbar.org/aba.html
Social Media: *Facebook, Twitter*

Tommy H Wells Jr, President
Laurel G. Bellows, President

Articles on various areas of urban, state and local government law.
Cost: $49.95
Frequency: Quarterly
Circulation: 6000
Founded in 1879

15908 Utility Section Newsletter

American Bar Association
321 N Clark St
Chicago, IL 60654-7598

312-988-5000
800-285-2221
FAX 312-988-6281
E-Mail: askaba@aba.org
Home Page: www.americanbar.org/aba.html
Social Media: *Facebook, Twitter*

Tommy H Wells Jr, President
Laurel G. Bellows, President

Articles pertaining to the field of public utility law.
Frequency: Quarterly
Founded in 1878

15909 Washington Employment Law Letter

M Lee Smith Publishers
PO Box 5094
Brentwood, TN 37219-2407

615-737-7517
800-274-6774
FAX 615-256-6601
Home Page: www.mleesmith.com

M Lee Smith, Publisher
Michael Reynvaan, Editor

Reviews of employment laws.
Cost: $157.55
8 Pages
Frequency: Monthly
Circulation: 54,000
Founded in 1975
Mailing list available for rent
Printed in 2 colors on matte stock

15910 Washington Summary

American Bar Association
740 15th St Nw
Suite 8
Washington, DC 20005-1022

202-662-1000
FAX 202-662-1032
E-Mail: cmpdi@abanet.org
Home Page: www.americanbar.org/aba.html
Social Media: *Facebook, Twitter*

Stephanie A Marella, Editor
Laurel G. Bellows, President

Tracks legislation and federal regulations of interest to lawyers by abstracting the Congressional Record and Federal Register.
Cost: $55.00
Frequency: Daily
Founded in 1878

15911 White-Collar Crime Reporter

Andrews Publications
175 Strafford Avenue
Building 4, Suite 140
Wayne, PA 19087-3317

610-225-0510
800-345-1101
FAX 610-225-0501
Home Page: www.andrewspub.com

Robert Maroldo, Publisher
Edith McFail, Editor

Major articles guest written by practitioners in the area of white collar crame and covering such topics as sentencing guidelines, corporate liability, banking and securities fraud and government contract fraud.
Cost: $66.00
Frequency: Monthly
Founded in 1872

15912 Word Progress

American Bar Association
321 N Clark St
Chicago, IL 60654-7598

312-988-5000
800-285-2221
FAX 312-988-6281
E-Mail: askaba@abanet.org
Home Page: www.americanbar.org/aba.html
Social Media: *Facebook, Twitter*

Tommy H Wells Jr, President
Laurel G. Bellows, President

Newsletter of the Word Processing User Group, includes updates on more effective word processing in the law office.
Cost: $50.00
Frequency: Quarterly

15913 World Jurist

World Jurist Assn of the World Peace Through Law
1000 Connecticut Avenue NW
Suite 202
Washington, DC 20036

202-466-5428
FAX 202-452-8540
E-Mail: wja@worldjurist.org
Home Page: http://www.worldjurist.net

Sona Pancholy, Editor
M Henneberry, Executive VP

Research for international development as a basis for future world peace.
Cost: $80.00
Frequency: Fortnightly
Circulation: 6000
Founded in 1963
Printed in on glossy stock

15914 Your School and the Law

LRP Publications
747 Dresher Road Suite 500
PO Box 980
Horsham, PA 19044-2247

215-840-0912
800-341-7874
FAX 215-784-9639
E-Mail: webmaster@lrp.com
Home Page: www.lrp.com

Stephen Bekiiacqwa, Editor

A monthly newsletter providing practical information on current judicial decisions affecting schools.
Cost: $190.00
Founded in 1977
Mailing list available for rent
Printed in one color on matte stock

Magazines & Journals

15915 AALL Spectrum

American Association of Law Libraries
105 W Adams Street
Suite 3300
Chicago, IL 60603

312-939-4764
FAX 312-431-1097
E-Mail: support@aall.org
Home Page: www.aallnet.org
Social Media: *Facebook, Twitter*

Mark Estes, Editorial Director
Hillary Baker, Marketing and Communications
Kate Hagan, Executive Director
Kim Rundle,, Executive Assistant
Emily Feltren,, Director of Government Relations

Publishes substantive, well-written articles on topics of real interest to law librarians, as well as news about the American Association of Law Libraries, including its chapters, committees and Special Interest Sections
Cost: $ 75.00

15916 ABA Journal

American Bar Association
321 N Clark St
6th Floor
Chicago, IL 60654-7598

312-988-5000
800-285-2221
FAX 312-988-6281
E-Mail: abajournal@abanet.org
Home Page: www.abanet.org

Tommy H Wells Jr, President
Robert Brouwer, Associate Publisher
Elizabeth Sullivan, Marketing Manager

Its editorial materials include news of interest to members of the legal profession. Editorial highlights include reviews of general interest and legal books, a US Supreme Court Digest section, a section listing significant rulings of other courts and news from government agencies.
Cost: $75.00
Frequency: Monthly
Circulation: 389420
Founded in 1878

15917 APA Magazine

American Polygraph Association

PO Box 8037
Chattanooga, TN 37414-0037

423-892-3992
800-272-8037
FAX 423-894-5435
E-Mail: office@polygraph.org
Home Page: www.polygraph.org

Robbie S Bennett, National Office Manager
Gordon L. Vaughan, General Counsel
Donald Krapohl, Editor
Robbie S. Bennett, National Office Manager
Barry Cushman, President
Cost: $125.00
Frequency: Bi-Monthly
Founded in 1966

15918 Administrative Law Review

American University Washington College of Law
4801 Massachusetts Ave Nw
Suite 622
Washington, DC 20016-8180

202-274-4433
FAX 202-274-4130
E-Mail: alr-editor-in-chief@wcl.american.edu
Home Page:
www.wcl.american.edu/journal/alr/
Social Media: *Facebook, LinkedIn*

Stacey L.Z. Edwards, Editor-In-Chief
Keeley McCarty, Executive Editor
Brittany Ericksen, Managing Editor
Sharon Wolfe, Journal Coordinator

Scholarly legal journal on developments in the field of administrative law and regulatory practice.
Cost: $40.00
Frequency: Quarterly
Founded in 1949

15919 Advance Sheet

150 Lincoln Street
Boston, MA 02111

617-695-3660
FAX 617-695-3656

15920 AmLaw Tech

American Lawyer Media
345 Park Avenue S
New York, NY 10010

212-799-9434
800-888-8300
FAX 212-972-6258
E-Mail: customersvc@amlaw.com
Home Page: www.americanlawyermedia.com

William L Pollak, President
Aric Press, Editorial Director
Kevin Vermeulen, Senior Vice President of Legal
Frequency: Annual+
Circulation: 16,500
Founded in 1997

15921 American Bankruptcy Law Journal

American Bankruptcy Institute
235 Secret Cove
Lexington, SC 29072

803-576-6225
FAX 703-739-1060
E-Mail: Support@abiworld.org
Home Page: www.abiworld.org

Christine Molick, Executive Director
Marilyn Shea-Stonum, Editor-in-Chief
J Rich Leonard, Associate Editor

Offers information on bankruptcy, legislation and financial information.
Cost: $65.00
Frequency: Quarterly
Founded in 1982

15922 American Lawyer
American Lawyer Corporation
Lbby L5
120 Broadway
New York, NY 10271-0096

917-562-2000
800-603-6571
FAX 212-696-1845
E-Mail: lawcatalog@amlaw.com
Home Page: www.americanlawyermedia.com

Barbara Eskin, Circulation Director

Issues affecting lawyers and the legal profession, with an emphasis on the business aspect of law firms.
Cost: $349.00
102 Pages
Frequency: Monthly

15923 American Lawyers Quarterly
American Lawyers Company
853 Westpoint Pkwy
Suite 710
Cleveland, OH 44145-1546

440-871-8700
800-843-4000
FAX 440-871-9997
E-Mail: alq@alqlist.com
Home Page: www.alqlist.com

Thomas W Hamilton, Executive VP
Frequency: Quarterly
Founded in 1899

15924 American University Business Law Review
American University Washington College of Law
4801 Massachusetts Ave Nw
Suite 615-A
Washington, DC 20016-8180

202-274-4433
FAX 202-274-4130
Home Page: www.wcl.american.edu/blr/

Averell Sutton, Editor-In-Chief
Cameron Chong, Executive Editor
Sara Hill, Managing Editor
Sharon Wolfe, Journal Coordinator

Scholarly legal journal publishing articles providing cutting-edge legal analysis for the business law community, scholarly articles, case law analysis, and coverage of developing trends in a variety of areas to include financial regulation, international trade, antitrust, communications, healthcare and energy.
Cost: $40.00
Frequency: Quarterly
Founded in 2011

15925 American University International Law Review
American University Washington College of Law
4801 Massachusetts Ave Nw
Suite 610
Washington, DC 20016-8180

202-274-4433
FAX 202-274-4130
Home Page: www.auilr.org
Social Media: *LinkedIn*

Lauren R Dudley, Editor-In-Chief
Daniel F Martini, Executive Editor
Michelle Mora Rueda, Managing Editor
Sharon Wolfe, Journal Coordinator

Scholarly legal journal publishing articles, critical essays, comments, and casenotes on a wide variety of international law topics, including public and private international law, the law of international organizations, international trade law, international arbitration, and international human rights. AUILR also publishes pieces on topics of foreign and comparative law that are

of particular interest to the international legal community.
Cost: $40.00
Frequency: Quarterly
Founded in 1986

15926 American University Journal of Gender, Social Policy & the Law
American University Washington College of Law
4801 Massachusetts Ave Nw
Suite 632
Washington, DC 20016-8180

202-274-4433
FAX 202-274-4130
Home Page:
www.wcl.american.edu/journal/genderlaw/
Social Media: *Facebook*

Rafael Roberti, Editor-In-Chief
J. Peter Bodri, Executive Editor
Claire Griggs, Managing Editor
Sharon Wolfe, Journal Coordinator

Scholarly legal journal that publishes articles addressing social and political equality under the law.
Cost: $40.00
Frequency: Quarterly
Founded in 1992

15927 American University Law Review
American University Washington College of Law
4801 Massachusetts Ave Nw
Suite 616
Washington, DC 20016-8180

202-274-4433
FAX 202-274-4130
E-Mail: alr-editor-in-chief@wcl.american.edu
Home Page:
www.wcl.american.edu/journal/alr/
Social Media: *Facebook, Twitter, LinkedIn*

Brian R Westley, Editor-In-Chief
Mary M Gardner, Executive Editor
Christopher J Walsh, Managing Editor
Sharon Wolfe, Journal Coordinator

Scholarly legal journal, which publishes articles from professors, judges, practicing lawyers, and renowned legal thinkers. It is the only jounal in the nation to publish an annual issue dedicated to decisions of the Court of Appeals for the Federal Circuit regarding patent law, international trade, government contracts, and trademark law.
Cost: $40.00
Frequency: Quarterly
Founded in 1952

15928 Animal Law Report
American Bar Association
321 N Clark St
Chicago, IL 60654-7598

312-988-5000
800-285-2221
FAX 312-988-6281
E-Mail: askaba@abanet.org
Home Page: www.americanbar.org/aba.html
Social Media: *Facebook, Twitter*

Tommy H Wells Jr, President
Laurel G. Bellows, President

Summarizes recent legislation, case decisions and literature.
Cost: $10.00
Frequency: SemiAnnual

15929 AntiShyster
AntiShyster
PO Box 540786
Dallas, TX 75354-786

FAX 972-386-8604

Alfred Adask, Editor

Critical examination of the American legal system.
Circulation: 10000

15930 Antitrust Law Journal
American Bar Association
321 N Clark St
Chicago, IL 60654-7598

312-988-5000
800-285-2221
FAX 312-988-6281
E-Mail: askaba@abanet.org
Home Page: www.americanbar.org/aba.html
Social Media: *Facebook, Twitter*

Tommy H Wells Jr, President
Laurel G. Bellows, President
MaryAnn Dadisman, Staff Editor

Covers proceedings of Section meetings, Section reports and positions on legislation, as well as content of National Institutes on antitrust law.
Cost: $120.00
Circulation: 10,000
Founded in 1878

15931 Arbitration Journal
American Arbitration Association
1633 Broadway
Suite 2c1
New York, NY 10019-6707

212-716-5800
800-778-7879
FAX 212-716-5905
Home Page: www.adr.org

William K Slate II, CEO
Christine Newhall, Senior Vice President
Harry Kaminsky, Vice President
Cost: $30.00
Frequency: Quarterly
Founded in 1926

15932 Association of Legal Administrators
Association of Legal Administrators
75 Tri-State International
Suite 222
Lincolnshire, IL 60069-4435

847-267-1252
FAX 847-267-1329
E-Mail: publications@alanet.org
Home Page: www.alanet.org

Larry Smith, Executive Director
Debbie Thomas, Director, Accounting & Finance
Renee Mahovsky, Director, Administration/Operations
Bob Abramson, Director, Marketing & Communication
Jan Waugh, Director, Member Services

Professional support for management of private law firms and other legal organizations worldwide.
Cost: $10.00
9500 Members
Founded in 1971
Printed in 4 colors on glossy stock

15933 Attorney/CPA
3921 Old Lee Highway
Suite71A
Fairfax, VA 22030-3926

703-352-8064
FAX 703-352-8073
E-Mail: cmulligan@attorney-cpa.com
Home Page: www.attorney-cpa.com

Bernard Eizen, Publisher
Clark Mulligan, Executive Director

Promotes high ethical standards of dual licensed professionals.
Cost: $44.37
Founded in 1964

15934 BNA's Patent, Trademark and Copyright Journal
Bureau of National Affairs
1801 S Bell St
Arlington, VA 22202-4501

703-341-3000
800-372-1033
FAX 800-253-0332
E-Mail: cuatomercare@bna.com
Home Page: www.bnabooks.com
Social Media: *Facebook, Twitter, LinkedIn*

Paul N Wojcik, CEO

Provides an in-depth review of significant current developments in the intellectual property field. Covers congressional activity, court decisions, relevant conferences, professional associations, international developments, plus actions of the Patent and Trademark Office and the Copyright Office.
Cost: $1968.00
Frequency: Weekly

15935 Barrister
American Bar Association
321 N Clark St
Chicago, IL 60654-7598

312-988-5000
800-285-2221
FAX 312-988-6281
E-Mail: askaba@aba.net
Home Page: www.americanbar.org/aba.html
Social Media: *Facebook, Twitter*

Tommy H Wells Jr, President
Laurel G. Bellows, President

Magazine containing general articles about the profession, the law and society in general.
Cost: $19.95
Frequency: 5 per year

15936 Broadcasting and the Law
One SE 3rd Avenue
#1450
Miami, FL 33131-1714

305-530-1322
FAX 305-539-0013
E-Mail: broadlaw@aol.com

Matthew L Leibowitz

Addresses legal issues within the broadcasting industry.
Frequency: Monthly
Circulation: 400

15937 Business Law Today
American Bar Association Section on Business Law
321 N Clark St
Chicago, IL 60654

312-988-5000
800-285-2221
FAX 312-988-5280
E-Mail: askaba@abanet.org
Home Page: www.americanbar.org/aba.html
Social Media: *Facebook, Twitter*

John Palmer, Staff Editor
Arthur F. Ferguson, Editor
Laurel G. Bellows, President

The Business Law Section's magazine edited for busy professionals: no footnotes and lots of the latest in business law.
64 Pages
Frequency: Bimonthly
Circulation: 55000
ISSN: 1059-9436
Printed in 4 colors

15938 Business Lawyer
American Bar Association

321 N Clark St
Chicago, IL 60654-7598

312-988-5000
800-285-2221
FAX 312-988-6281
E-Mail: askaba@abanet.org
Home Page: www.americanbar.org/aba.html

Tommy H Wells Jr, President

Journal of business and financial law, with articles on current legal topics and substantive section programs.
Cost: $20.00
Frequency: Quarterly
Circulation: 60000
Founded in 1915

15939 Business Lawyer's Computer News
American Bar Association
321 N Clark St
Chicago, IL 60654-7598

312-988-5000
800-285-2221
FAX 312-988-6281
E-Mail: askaba@abanet.org
Home Page: www.americanbar.org/aba.html

Tommy H Wells Jr, President

Information on new developments in technology for the business lawyer and news on how business lawyers are applying technology in their practices.
Cost: $50.00
Frequency: Quarterly

15940 Champion Magazine
National Association of Criminal Defense Lawyers
1660 L St Nw
Suite 1200
Washington, DC 20036-5632

202-872-8600
FAX 202-872-8690
E-Mail: assist@nacdl.org
Home Page: www.nacdl.org

Quintin Chatman, Editor

Offers timely, informative articles written for and by criminal defense lawyers, featuring the latest developments in search and seizure laws, DUI/DWI, grandy jury proceedings, habeas, the exclusionary rule, death penalty, RICO, federal sentencing guidelines, forfeiture, white-collar crime, and more
Cost: $70.00
Frequency: 10x/Year
Circulation: 13000

15941 Chinese Law and Government
ME Sharpe
80 Business Park Dr
Suite 202
Armonk, NY 10504-1715

914-273-1800
800-541-6563
FAX 914-273-2106
E-Mail: info@mesharpe.com
Home Page: www.mesharpe.com

Myron E Sharpe, President
James Tong, Executive Editor
George Lobell, Executive Editor

Translations of significant works and policy documents, primarily from the Peoples Republic of China.
Cost: $144.00
Frequency: 1 Year 6 Issues

15942 Clearinghouse Reference Guide
American Bar Association

1800 M Street NW
Washington, DC 20036-5802

202-662-1000
FAX 202-331-2220

Patrick Sheehan, Editor
Diane Gibson, Publications Coordinator

A summary of key state legislative developments of interest to attorneys.
Frequency: Annual
Circulation: 800

15943 Columbia Law School Magazine
Columbia Law School
435 West 116 Street
Box A-2
New York, NY 10027

212-854-2640
FAX 212-854-7801
E-Mail: webmaster@law.columbia.edu
Home Page: http://web.law.columbia.edu
Social Media: *Facebook, Twitter, LinkedIn*

Matthew Malady, Editor
Joy Wang, Managing Editor

Features contributions that promotes ongoing discussion of social change and related issues.
Frequency: Biennial
Founded in 1754

15944 Commercial Law Journal
Commercial Law League of America
205 N. Michigan
Suite 2212
Chicago, IL 60601

312-240-1400
800-978-2552
FAX 312-240-1408
E-Mail: info@clla.org
Home Page: www.clla.org
Social Media: *Facebook, Twitter, LinkedIn*

Oliver Yandle, VP
Charles R Johnson III, Treasurer

Law review journal covering such issues as credit, debt, insolvency, banking and the Uniform Commercial Code.
Frequency: Quarterly
Circulation: 6000
Founded in 1895

15945 Communications and the Law
Fred B Rotham Company
10368 W Cenntenial Road
Littleton, CO 80127-4205

800-828-7971
FAX 716-883-8100

Theodore Kupfeman, Publisher

Features articles and book reviews on communications law, new technologies and law.
Cost: $25.00
Circulation: 585

15946 Complete Lawyer
American Bar Association
321 N Clark St
Chicago, IL 60654-7598

312-988-5000
800-285-2221
FAX 312-988-6281
E-Mail: askaba@abanet.org
Home Page: www.americanbar.org/aba.html

Tommy H Wells Jr, President

Magazine provides practical articles directed to general practitioners, on substantive areas of law, news of council and committee activities.
Cost: $23.00
Frequency: Quarterly
Circulation: 16743

15947 Computer Industry Litigation Reporter
Andrews Publications
175 Strafford Avenue
Building 4, Suite 140
Wayne, PA 19087-3331

610-225-0510
800-345-1101
FAX 610-225-0501
Home Page: www.andrewspub.com

Robert Maroldo, Publisher

Legal issues as they relate to hardware, software electronic databaes and the computer industry in general.
Cost: $875.00

15948 Computer Law Strategist
Leader Publications
345 Park Avenue S
New York, NY 10010-1707

212-799-9200
FAX 212-696-1848

Stuart Wise, Publisher

For lawyers operating in the area of computer law and intellectual property.
Frequency: Monthly

15949 Corporate Control Alert
The Deal, LLC.
14 Wall Street
New York, NY 10005

212-313-9200
888-667-3325
FAX 212-481-8128
E-Mail: customerservice@thedeal.com
Home Page: www.thedeal.com
Social Media: *Twitter*

Mickey Hernandez, Advertising Sales
Elena Freed, Marketing
Frequency: Monthly
Founded in 1999

15950 Corporate Counsel
American Lawyer Media
345 Park Avenue S
New York, NY 10010

212-779-9434
800-234-4256
FAX 212-696-1845
Home Page: www.americanlawyermedia.com

15951 Court Review
American Judges Association
300 Newport Ave
Williamsburg, VA 23185-4147

757-259-1841
FAX 757-259-1520
E-Mail: aja@ncsc.dni.us
Home Page: aja.ncsc.dni.us

James McKay, President

Highlights court decicions and precedents through articles written by US jurists and legal scholars.
Cost: $35.00
Frequency: Quarterly
Circulation: 2000
ISSN: 0011-0647
Founded in 1959

15952 Criminal Justice
American Bar Association
321 N Clark St
Chicago, IL 60654-7598

312-988-5000
800-285-2221
FAX 312-988-6281

E-Mail: askaba@abanet.org
Home Page: www.americanbar.org/aba.html

Tommy H Wells Jr, President

Magazine providing practical treatment of aspects of the criminal law and reporting on legislative, policy-making and educational activities of the ABA Criminal Justice Section.
Cost: $38.00
Frequency: Quarterly
Circulation: 9000
Founded in 1915

15953 Cyber Esq.
Daily Journal Corporation
PO Box 54026
Los Angeles, CA 90054-0026

213-229-5300
FAX 213-229-5481
Home Page: www.dailyjournal.com

Gerald L Salzman, CEO

Cyber Esq. is a guide for lawyers who use technology and whose practices are affected by the impact on the latest hardware and software and analysis of cutting-edge legal issues.
52 Pages
Frequency: Quarterly
Printed in 4 colors on n stock

15954 Daily Journal
Daily Journal Corporation
PO Box 54026
Los Angeles, CA 90054-0026

213-229-5300
FAX 213-229-5481
Home Page: www.dailyjournal.com

Gerald L Salzman, CEO
Ray Chagolla, Circulation Manager

The Daily Journal Corporation provides lawyers with concise, comprehensive and intelligent coverage of legal news throughout the city, state, and nation. Through our family of publications we are able to serve the nation's largest legal markets.
Cost: $628.00
28 Pages
Frequency: Daily
Circulation: 11000
ISSN: 1059-2636
Founded in 1888
Printed in on n stock

15955 Decisions & Developments
PO Box 98
Bolton, MA 01740-0098

781-890-5678
FAX 781-890-1150

15956 Dispute Resolution
American Bar Association Sec. Dispute Resolution
321 N Clark St
Chicago, IL 60654-7598

312-988-5000
800-285-2221
FAX 312-988-5280
E-Mail: askaba@abanet.org
Home Page: www.americanbar.org/aba.html

Thomas J. Campbell, Staff Editor
Chip Stewart, Editor

A clearinghouse of information on programs related to the study of existing methods for prompt and effective resolution of disputes.
Cost: $45.00
32 Pages
Frequency: Quarterly
Founded in 1978

15957 Dispute Resolution Journal
206 Hulston Hall
University of Missouri
Columbia, MO 65211

573-823-3645
FAX 212-716-5906
E-Mail: umclawcdr@missouri.edu
Home Page: www.law.missouri.edu

Jonathan R Bunch, Editor-in-Chief
Cassandra A Rogers, Managing Editor
Leonard Riskin, Manager
Cost: $21.00
Founded in 1984

15958 Docket
150 Lincoln Street
Boston, MA 02111

617-695-3660
FAX 617-695-3656

15959 Duke Law Journal
Duke University School of Law
210 Science Drive
Box 90362
Durham, NC 27708

919-613-7006
FAX 919-681-8460
E-Mail: dlj@law.duke.edu
Home Page: www.law.duke.edu
Social Media: *Facebook, Twitter, LinkedIn, Youtube*

Sarah Boyce, Editor-in-Chief
Julia Wood, Managing Editor
Jennifer Brady, Executive Editor
Philip Alito, Research Editor

The journal's purpose is to publish legal writing of superior quality, to publish a collection of outstanding scholarship from established legal writers, up and coming authors, and student editors.
Frequency: 8x/year
Founded in 1951

15960 EEOC Compliance Manual
Bureau of National Affairs
1801 S Bell St
Arlington, VA 22202-4501

703-341-3000
800-372-1033
FAX 800-253-0332
E-Mail: customercare@bna.com
Home Page: www.bnabooks.com
Social Media: *Facebook, Twitter, LinkedIn*

Paul N Wojcik, CEO

A two-binder monthly service containing the complete text of the EEOC Compliance Manual, as issued by the EEOC, with monthly notification to related developments.
Cost: $410.00

15961 Education Law Association
Education Law Association
300 College Park Ave
Dayton, OH 45469-0001

937-229-3589
FAX 216-687-5284
E-Mail: ela@educationlaw.org
Home Page: www.educationlaw.org
Social Media: *Facebook, Twitter, LinkedIn*

Mandy Schrenk, Executive Director
Cate K. Smith, Executive Director
Judy Pleiman, Member Services Coordinator
Jody Thornburg, Publications Manager

Brings together educational and legal scholars and practitioners to inform and advance educational policy and practice through knowledge of the law. Together, our professional community anticipates trends in educational law and supports scholarly research through the highest

value print and electronic publications, conferences, seminars and professional forums.
Cost: $125.00
1400 Pages
Frequency: Monthly
Circulation: 1200
Founded in 1954

15962 Energy Law Journal
Federal Energy Bar Association
1990 M St Nw
Suite 350
Washington, DC 20036-3429

202-223-5625
FAX 202-833-5596
E-Mail: admin@eba-net.org
Home Page: www.eba-net.org

Lorna Wilson, Administrator
Clinton A. Vince, Secretary, Treasurer
Michelle Grant, Secretary, Treasurer
Peter Trombley, Vice President

Lawyers and consultants engaged in energy and public utility law.
Cost: $35.00
Frequency: Monthly
Circulation: 2600
ISSN: 0270-9163
Founded in 1946
Printed in 2 colors on matte stock

15963 Environmental Forum
Environmental Law Institute
2000 L St Nw
Suite 620
Washington, DC 20036-4919

202-939-3800
800-433-5120
FAX 202-939-3868
E-Mail: law@eli.org
Home Page: www.eli.org

John Cruden, President
Stephen R. Dujack, Editor
Linda Ellis, Manager Customer Service
Carolyn Fischer, Editorial Associate

Uses diverse points of view to stimulate the exchange of ideas and foster solutions for pressing environmental issues.
Cost: $115.00
60 Pages
Circulation: 2100
Founded in 1985
Printed in 4 colors on matte stock

15964 Environmental Law Journal
State Bar of Texas
1515 S Capitol of Texas Highway
Suite 415
Austin, TX 78746-6544

512-322-5800
FAX 512-478-7750

Jimmy Alan Hall, Editor-in-Chief
Charles Jordan, Chairman

Provides members with current legal activities, recent developments and information pertaining to environmental and natural resource law, as well as section activities and other events pertaining to this area of the law.
Cost: $ 10.00
68 Pages
Frequency: Monthly
Founded in 1969

15965 Experience
American Bar Association
321 N Clark St
Chicago, IL 60654-7598

312-988-5000
800-285-2221
FAX 312-988-6281

E-Mail: askaba@abanet.org
Home Page: www.americanbar.org/aba.html

Tommy H Wells Jr, President

News magazine for one of the fastest-growing sections in the ABA. Articles cover elderlaw, Council relationships, aspects of retirement including housing and health, and other topics of interest to lawyers pre- and post retirement.
Cost: $45.00
Frequency: Quarterly
Founded in 1878

15966 Expert and the Law
National Forensic Center
17 Temple Terrace
Lawrenceville, NJ 08648-3254

800-562-5177
E-Mail: info@nfstc.org
Home Page: www.nfstc.org/

Betty Lipscher, Publisher
David Epstein, Chief Operations Officer
Mike Berry, Program Manager

Appilcation of scientific, medical and technical knowledge to litigation.

15967 Fair Employment Practices/Labor Relations Reporter
Bureau of National Affairs
1801 S Bell St
Arlington, VA 22202-4501

703-341-3000
800-372-1033
FAX 800-253-0332
E-Mail: customercare@bna.com
Home Page: www.bnabooks.com
Social Media: *Facebook, Twitter, LinkedIn*

Paul N Wojcik, CEO

A guide to the regulation of fair employment practices, including federal laws, orders and regulations; policy guides and ground rules; and state and local fair employment practice laws.
Cost: $1576.00
Frequency: Weekly
Founded in 1929

15968 Family Advocate
American Bar Association
321 N Clark St
Chicago, IL 60654-7598

312-988-5000
800-285-2221
FAX 312-988-6281
E-Mail: askaba@abanet.com
Home Page: www.americanbar.org/aba.html
Social Media: *Facebook, Twitter*

Tommy H Wells Jr, President
Laurel G. Bellows, President
Amelia Stone, Marketer
Adrienne Cook, Development Editor

A practical journal in magazine format, containing information on divorce, mental health, juveniles, custody, support and problems of the aging as well as current trends, recent court decisions and new legislation.
Cost: $39.50
Frequency: Quarterly
Circulation: 11000
Founded in 1984

15969 Family Law Quarterly
American Bar Association
321 N Clark St
Chicago, IL 60654-7598

312-988-5000
800-285-2221
FAX 312-988-6281
E-Mail: askaba@abanet.org

Home Page: www.americanbar.org/aba.html
Social Media: *Facebook, Twitter*

Tommy H Wells Jr, President
Laurel G. Bellows, President

A scholarly journal, including regular coverage of judicial decisions, legislation, taxation, summaries of state and local bar association projects and book reviews.
Cost: $79.95
Frequency: Quarterly
Circulation: 11000
Founded in 1998

15970 Federal Communications Law Journal
University of California-Los Angeles
Box 951476
Los Angeles, CA 90095-1476

310-825-7768
FAX 310-206-6489
E-Mail: webmaster@law.ucla.edu
Home Page: www.law.ucla.edu

John Alden, Editor in Chief
David Matheson, Advertising Director

Articles on legal issues relating to the communications industry.
Cost: $10.00
Circulation: 2500

15971 Federal Lawyer
Federal Bar Association
1220 North Fillmore St.
Ste. 444
Arlington, VA 22201

571-481-9100
FAX 571-481-9090
E-Mail: fba@fedbar.org
Home Page: www.fedbar.org
Social Media: *Facebook, Twitter, LinkedIn*

Jack D. Lockridge, Executive Director
Lori Beth Gorman, Executive Assistant
Lisa Sidletsky, Director Membership
Robert J. DeSousa, President
Hon. Gustavo Gelpi, Jr., President-Elect

Chronicles the news of the association and its members as well as providing practical coverage of issues affecting federal attorneys.
Cost: $35.00
Circulation: 15200
Founded in 1931

15972 Fidelity and Surety News
American Bar Association
321 N Clark St
Chicago, IL 60654-7598

312-988-5000
800-285-2221
FAX 312-988-6281
E-Mail: askaba@abanet.org
Home Page: www.americanbar.org/aba.html
Social Media: *Facebook, Twitter*

Tommy H Wells Jr, President
Laurel G. Bellows, President

Summarizes selected recent cases on fidelity and surety law for professionals and lawyers.
Cost: $165.00
Frequency: Quarterly
Circulation: 1000
Founded in 1878

15973 Firestation Lawyer
Quinlan Publishing Company
23 Drydock Avenue
Boston, MA 02215-2336

617-542-0048
FAX 617-345-9646
Home Page: www.quinlan.com

E Michael Quinlan, Publisher
Hoss Homaier, President, Chief Executive Officer

Case summaries of recent lawsuits involving fire departments. Discusses residency requirements of firefighters, worker's compensation, pensions, discrimination, and fire department rules and regulations.
Frequency: Monthly
Founded in 1950

15974 Franchise Law Journal
American Bar Association
321 N Clark St
Chicago, IL 60654-7598

312-988-5000
800-285-2221
FAX 312-988-6281
E-Mail: askaba@abanet.com
Home Page: www.americanbar.org/aba.html
Social Media: *Facebook, Twitter*

Tommy H Wells Jr, President
Laurel G. Bellows, President
Robert A Stein, Executive Director

Journal in newsletter format primarily on current legal trends in franchising; also reports on activities of the Forum.
Cost: $50.00
Frequency: Quarterly

15975 Health Law Litigation Reporter
Andrews Publications
175 Strafford Avenue
Building 4, Suite 140
Wayne, PA 19087-3331

610-225-0510
800-345-1101
FAX 610-225-0501
Home Page: www.andrewspub.com/

John E Backe, Publisher

Focus on cases involving ERSA, experimental insurance coverage, patient dumping, Medicare and Medicaid, medical devices, and federal and state legislation.
Frequency: Monthly
Circulation: 4100

15976 Hospital Law Manual
Publishers
200 Orchard Ridge Drive
Gaithersburg, MD 20878-1978

301-417-7500
800-234-1660
FAX 301-698-7931
E-Mail: customer.service@aspenpubl.com
Home Page: www.aspenpub.com

Patricia Younger, Director

Hospital law.
Cost: $1325.00
Frequency: Quarterly
Founded in 1959

15977 Human Rights
American Bar Association
321 N Clark St
Chicago, IL 60654-7598

312-988-5000
800-285-2221
FAX 312-988-6281
E-Mail: askaba@abanet.org
Home Page: www.americanbar.org/aba.html
Social Media: *Facebook, Twitter*

Tommy H Wells Jr, President
Laurel G. Bellows, President

Magazine containing news articles, features and commentary with relevance to human rights and individual rights and responsibilities.
Cost: $17.00
Frequency: Quarterly
Circulation: 6000
Founded in 1878

15978 IP Worldwide
American Lawyer Media
345 Park Avenue S
New York, NY 10010

212-779-9434
FAX 212-592-4900
Home Page: www.americanlawyermedia.com

Steve Pressman, Editor
William L Pollak, CEO/President
Kevin Vermeulen, Publisher
Frequency: Quarterly
Circulation: 8000
Founded in 1997

15979 Institute of Management & Administration Newsletter
Institute of Management and Administration
3 Bethesda Metro Center
Suite 250
Bethesda, MD 20814-5377

703-341-3500
800-372-1033
FAX 800-253-0332
Home Page: www.ioma.com

Monthly newsletter that supports law office administrators by offering training on how to reduce overhead, improve the firm's profitability and efficiency, get more value for the firm's budget dollar, and improve their own professional standing.
Frequency: Monthly

15980 International Commercial Litigation
Euromoney Publications
173 W 81st Street
New York, NY 10024-7227

212-874-4265
FAX 212-501-8926

International litigation and dispute resolution news and developments in commercial law.

15981 International Lawyer
American Bar Association
321 N Clark St
Chicago, IL 60654-7598

312-988-5000
800-285-2221
FAX 312-988-6281
E-Mail: askaba@abanet.org
Home Page: www.americanbar.org/aba.html
Social Media: *Facebook, Twitter*

Tommy H Wells Jr, President
Laurel G. Bellows, President

Practical issues facing lawyers engaged in an international practice.
Cost: $7.00
Circulation: 11000

15982 Journal of Court Reporting
National Court Reporters
8224 Old Courthouse Rd
Vienna, VA 22182-3808

703-556-6272
800-272-6272
FAX 703-556-6291
Home Page: www.ncraonline.org
Social Media: *Facebook, Twitter*

Melanie Humphrey-Sonntag, President
Mark Golden, Executive Director & CEO
Tami Smith, VP
Bruce Matthews, Secretary/Treasurer

Covers information and views on matters related to the court recording and captioning professions.
20000 Members
Circulation: 34000
Founded in 1905

15983 Journal of Internet Law
Apen Publishers

111 Eighth Avenue
7th Floor
New York, NY 10011

212-771-0600
800-638-8437
FAX 212-771-0885
Home Page: www.aspenpublishers.com

Mark F Radcliffe, Editor-in-Chief
Stacey Caywood, VP/Publisher
Mark Radcliffe, Editor
Gerry Centrowitz, VP Marketing And Communication
Robert Becker, CEO

Discusses strategies utilized by top intellectual property, computer law and information technology industry experts.
Cost: $380.00
Frequency: Monthly

15984 Journal of Paralegal Education and Practice
American Association for Paralegal Education
407 Wekiva Springs Road
Suite 241
Longwood, FL 32779

407-834-6688
FAX 407-834-4747
E-Mail: info@aafpe.org
Home Page: www.americanbar.org/aba.html

Ronald Goldfarb, President

A journal offering news and information, pertaining to paralegal education.
Frequency: Annual

15985 Judges' Journal
American Bar Association
321 N Clark St
Chicago, IL 60654-7598

312-988-5000
800-285-2221
FAX 312-988-6281
E-Mail: askaba@abanet.org
Home Page: www.americanbar.org/aba.html
Social Media: *Facebook, Twitter*

Tommy H Wells Jr, President
Laurel G. Bellows, President

Created to help judges and lawyers improve the administration of justice.
Cost: $23.00
Frequency: Quarterly
Founded in 1878

15986 Judicature
American Judicature Society
The Opperman Center at Drake University
2700 University Avenue
Des Moines, LA 50311

515-271-2281
800-626-4089
FAX 515-279-3090
E-Mail: sandersen@ajs.org
Home Page: www.ajs.org

Seth S. Andersen, Executive Director
Krista Maeder, Assistant to the Executive Director
Laury Lieurance, Accountant/Membership Coordinator
Danielle Mitchell, Program Manager
David Richert, Editor

A forum for fact and opinion relating to all aspects of the administration of justice and its improvement.
Cost: $60.00
Frequency: Bi-Monthly
ISSN: 0022-5800

15987 Jurimetrics: Journal of Law, Science and Technology
American Bar Association

321 N Clark St
Chicago, IL 60654-7598

312-988-5000
800-285-2221
FAX 312-988-6281
E-Mail: askaba@abanet.org
Home Page: www.americanbar.org/aba.html
Social Media: *Facebook, Twitter*

Tommy H Wells Jr, President
Laurel G. Bellows, President

Covers a wide range of topics on legal issues in science and technology.
Cost: $29.00
Frequency: Quarterly

15988 Juvenile and Child Welfare Law Reporter

American Bar Association
321 N Clark St
Chicago, IL 60654-7598

312-988-5000
800-285-2221
FAX 312-988-6281
E-Mail: askaba@abanet.org
Home Page: www.americanbar.org/aba.html
Social Media: *Facebook, Twitter*

Tommy H Wells Jr, President
Laurel G. Bellows, President

Contains abstracts of case law on juvenile delinquency, abuse and neglect, adoption, termination of parental rights and other topics on child welfare.
Cost: $145.00
Frequency: Monthly

15989 Law

National Association of Legal Professionals
314 E 3rd Street
Suite 210
Tulsa, OK 74120-2409

918-582-5188
FAX 918-582-5907
E-Mail: moore@nals.org
Home Page: www.nals.org

Jay Moore, Editor
Tammy Hailey, Publisher
Jay Moore, Communications Manager
Tammy Hailey, Executive Director
Cindy Rosser, Executive Assistant

Published content focuses on new products, technology and items of interest to the administrative staff within the legal profession.
Cost: $40.00
Frequency: Quarterly
Circulation: 7000
Founded in 1929

15990 Law Office Computing Magazine Services Section

James Publishing
PO Box 25202
Santa Ana, CA 92799-5202

714-755-5450
800-440-4780
FAX 714-751-2709
E-Mail: customer-service@jamespublishing.com
Home Page: www.jamespublishing.com

Jim Pawell, Founder/President
Tina Dhamija, Assistant Editor
Adrianne Choi, Production Manager

Focuses on law office automation. Issues contain independent reviews of legal software with side-by-side comparisons of the top programs, plus how-to articles and expert columns. Targeted editorial attracts legal technology buyers and helps them plan effectively for their purchases, buy wisely and use their investments to maximize productivity and profitability.
Cost: $49.00
96 Pages
Founded in 1981

15991 Law Practice Management

American Bar Association
321 N Clark St
Chicago, IL 60654-7598

312-988-5000
800-285-2221
FAX 312-988-6281
E-Mail: askaba@abanet.org
Home Page: www.americanbar.org/aba.html
Social Media: *Facebook, Twitter*

Tommy H Wells Jr, President
Laurel G. Bellows, President
Jody Thornburg, Publications Editor

The pre-eminent magazine on all phases of law office management. Includes feature articles, book reviews, reports on technical innovations and announcements of forthcoming events.
Cost: $40.00
Founded in 1878

15992 Law Reporter

The American Association for Justice
777 6th Street, NW
Washington, DC 20001

202-965-3500
800-424-2725
E-Mail: membership@justice.org
Home Page: www.justice.org/

Peter C Quinn, Editor-in-Chief
Linda Lipsen, Chief Executive Officer
Charles Jeffress, Chief Operating Officer
Kathi Berge, Chief Financial Officer
Anjali Jesseramsing, Executive Vice President

Covers civil law, including automobile ,civil rights, insurance, commercial, employment and family law, medical negligence, premises liability and products liability, and workplace safety.
Cost: $135.00
40 Pages
Circulation: 53000
ISSN: 1052-4649
Founded in 1947
Printed in 2 colors

15993 Law Technology News

American Lawyer Media
345 Park Avenue S
New York, NY 10010

212-779-9434
FAX 212-592-4900
E-Mail: subscribe@lawtechnews.com
Home Page: www.americanlawyermedia.com

Kevin Vermuellen, Publisher
Monica Bay, Editor
William L Pollak, President/CEO

Covers the use of technology in the law profession.
Cost: $99.00
Frequency: Monthly
Circulation: 40000
Founded in 1997

15994 Law and Social Inquiry: Journal of the American Bar Foundation

American Bar Association
321 N Clark St
Chicago, IL 60654-7598

312-988-5000
800-285-2221
FAX 312-988-6281
E-Mail: askaba@abanet.org
Home Page: www.americanbar.org/aba.html
Social Media: *Facebook, Twitter*

Tommy H Wells Jr, President
Laurel G. Bellows, President

An academic and legal journal containing a wide range of research reports relating to the law, the profession and legal institutions.
Frequency: Weekly
Circulation: 4,00,000
Founded in 1878

15995 Law in Japan

Japanese American Society for Legal Studies
University of WA Law School-1100 NE Cam.
Seattle, WA 98105

206-233-9292
FAX 206-685-4469

John Haley, Editor

Academic journal with translation, original articles, comments and case notes on Japanese law and legal issues.
Cost: $13.00
Circulation: 1,400

15996 Lawyers Weekly USA

Lawyers Weekly Publications
10 Milk Street
Suite 1000
Boston, MA 02111-1203

617-451-7300
366-294-8963
FAX 617-451-1466
E-Mail: comments@lawyersweekly.com
Home Page: www.lawyersweeklyusa.com
Social Media: *Facebook, Twitter, LinkedIn*

Scott Murdock, Circulation Manager
Susan Bocamazo, Editor
Reni Germer, Managing Editor

Features profiles, practice tips, technology, marketing, management and other topics related to law practice.
Cost: $249.00
Frequency: Monthly
Circulation: 2500
Founded in 1972

15997 Lawyers' Professional Liability Update

American Bar Association
321 N Clark St
Chicago, IL 60654-7598

312-988-5000
800-285-2221
FAX 312-988-6281
E-Mail: askaba@abanet.org
Home Page: www.americanbar.org/aba.html
Social Media: *Facebook, Twitter*

Tommy H Wells Jr, President
Laurel G. Bellows, President

Current reports and articles on legal malpractice insurance marketplace and other aspects of legal malpractice.
Cost: $45.00
Circulation: 23,000

15998 Leadership and Management Directions

American Bar Association
321 N Clark St
Chicago, IL 60654-7598

312-988-5000
800-285-2221
FAX 312-988-6281
E-Mail: askaba@abanet.org
Home Page: www.americanbar.org/aba.html
Social Media: *Facebook, Twitter*

Tommy H Wells Jr, President
Laurel G. Bellows, President

Focuses on trends, principles, and practices in law office management including financial matters, marketing, human resources, facilities

and technology.
Cost: $50.00
Frequency: Quarterly

15999 Legal Management: Journal of the Association of Legal Administrators
Association of Legal Administrators
75 Tri-State International
Suite 222
Lincolnshire, IL 60069-4435

847-267-1252
FAX 847-267-1329
E-Mail: publications@alanet.org
Home Page: www.alanet.org

Larry Smith, Executive Director
Debbie Thomas, Director, Accounting & Finance
Renee Mahovsky, Director, Administration/Operations
Bob Abramson, Director, Marketing & Communication
Jan Waugh, Director, Member Services

Covers personnel management, finance, strategic planning, the legal industry, business software, technology. leadership, interpersonal communication, time and stress management, and disaster planning.
Circulation: 25000
Founded in 1971

16000 Legal Tech
Leader Publications
345 Park Avenue S
New York, NY 10010-1707

212-799-9200
800-888-8300
FAX 212-696-1848

Stuart Wise, Publisher
Frequency: Monthly

16001 Legal Times
American Lawyers Newspapers Group
1730 M St Nw
Suite 802
Washington, DC 20036-4550

202-296-1995
FAX 202-457-0718
Home Page: www.legaltimes.com

Peter Scheer, Editor
Ann Pelham, Publisher
Eva Rodriguev, Editor-in-Chief
Gwen Jones, Circulation Manager
Rose Mahoney, Sales Manager

Covers law, lobbying and politics.
Cost: $349.00
36 Pages
Frequency: Weekly
Circulation: 6200
Founded in 1977

16002 Lender Liability Litigation Reporter
Andrews Communications
175 Stafford Building 4
Suite 140
Wayne, PA 19087

610-225-0510
800-328-4880
FAX 610-225-0501

Robert Maroldo, Publisher
Journal of record, of litigation proceedings involving lender liability issues.
Cost: $650.00
Frequency: Monthly

16003 License
1 Park Avenue
2nd Floor
New York, NY 10016

212-951-6600
888-527-7008

FAX 212-951-6714
E-Mail: info@advanstar.com
Home Page: www.licensemag.com

Joyceann Cooney, Editor-in-Chief
Lorri Freifeld, Managing Editor
Steven Ekstract, Publisher
Sharon Weisman, Sales Manager

Patents, trademarks and copyrights
Frequency: Monthly
Circulation: 25000
Founded in 1987

16004 Litigation
American Bar Association
321 N Clark St
Chicago, IL 60654-7598

312-988-5000
800-285-2221
FAX 312-988-6281
E-Mail: askaba@abanet.org
Home Page: www.americanbar.org/aba.html
Social Media: *Facebook, Twitter*

Tommy H Wells Jr, President
Laurel G. Bellows, President

A journal for trial lawyers and judges, each issue of which focuses on a particular topic involving trial practice.
Cost: $39.50
Frequency: Quarterly

16005 M and A Lawyer
Glasser LegalWorks
150 Clove Road
Little Falls, NJ 07424-2138

973-890-0008
FAX 973-890-0042
Home Page: www.legalwks.com

Steven E Bochner, Editor
Stephen W Seemer, President

News affecting all types of mergers and acquisitions transactions, including securities law, state law, international, taxation, accounting and practice areas like intellectual property, employee benefits/compensation, antitrust and environmental.
Cost: $317.00
Circulation: 500
Founded in 1995

16006 Mental & Physical Disability Law
American Bar Association
740 15th St Nw
Suite 8
Washington, DC 20005-1022

202-662-1000
FAX 202-662-1032
E-Mail: cmpdi@abanet.org
Home Page: www.americanbar.org/aba.html
Social Media: *Facebook, Twitter*

William Neukom, President
Laurel G. Bellows, President
John Parry, Executive Director

A bi-monthly journal published by the Commission on Mental and Physical Disability Law, containing timely summaries of reported legal developments in 22 disability subject areas - over 1600 summaries annually.
Founded in 1878

16007 Mental & Physical Disability Law Reporter
American Bar Association
740 15th Street NW
Washington, DC 20005-1019

202-662-1570
FAX 202-442-3439
E-Mail: cmpdl@abanet.org

Home Page: www.abanet.org/disability
Social Media: *Facebook, Twitter, LinkedIn*

Stephen N. Zack, President
Katherine H. O'Neil, Commission Chair
John W. Parry, Commission Director
Jack L. Rives, Executive Director
Alice Richmond, Treasurer

Published since 1976, the Reporter is the only periodical that comprehensively covers civil and criminal mental disability law and disability discrimination law. Organized by 22 subject areas, the Reporter allows you to target your research and save time. A perfect complement to your online legal research databases.
Cost: $325.00
15 Members
Frequency: 6 X/Year
Circulation: 300+
ISSN: 0883-7902
Founded in 1973

16008 Mental Health Law Reporter
Business Publishers
2222 Sedwick Drive
Durham, NC 27713

800-223-8720
FAX 800-508-2592
E-Mail: custserv@bpinews.com
Home Page: www.bpinews.com

Sarah Terry, Managing Editor

Court decisions affecting mental health professionals.
Cost: $277.00
Frequency: Monthly
Founded in 1963

16009 Midwest Alternative Dispute Resolution Guide
Law Bulletin Publishing Company
415 N State St
Suite 1
Chicago, IL 60654-8116

312-644-7800
FAX 312-644-4255
Home Page: www.lawbulletin.com

Lanning Macfarland Jr, President

Profiles of midwest attorneys.
Cost: $219.00
156 Pages
Frequency: Monthly
Founded in 1854

16010 Midwest Legal Staffing Guide
Law Bulletin Publishing Company
415 N State St
Suite 1
Chicago, IL 60654-8116

312-644-7800
FAX 312-644-4255
E-Mail: editor@lbpc.com
Home Page: www.lawbulletin.com

Lanning Macfarland Jr, President
Bernard Judge, Editor
Stephen E Brown, Publisher

Monthly magazine about law, people and opportunity.
Frequency: Daily
Founded in 1854
Printed in 4 colors

16011 Midwest Legal Technology Guide
Law Bulletin Publishing Company
415 N State St
Suite 1
Chicago, IL 60654-8116

312-644-7800
FAX 312-644-4255
Home Page: www.lawbulletin.com

Lanning Macfarland Jr, President

Supplement to the Chicago Daily Law Bulletin and Chicago Lawyer. Eliminates the confusion arising from the many new technological service and product providers.
60 Pages

16012 NAELA Journal
National Academy of Elder Law Attorneys
1577 Spring Hill Road
Suite 220
Vienna, VA 22182-2223

703-942-5711
FAX 703-563-9504
E-Mail: naela@naela.org
Home Page: www.naela.org

Peter G Wacht, CAE, Executive Director
Nancy Sween, Director, Comm. & Publications
Kirsten Brown Simpson, Director, Membership & Marketing
Ann Watkins, Operations Manager
Roger Naoroji, Meetings & Education Coordinator

Peer-reviewed, scholarly publication of substantive articles on Elder and Special Needs Law topics.
Frequency: 2x Year

16013 National Bar Association Magazine
National Bar Association
1225 11th St Nw
Washington, DC 20001-4217

202-842-3900
FAX 202-289-6170
E-Mail: headquarters@nationalbar.org
Home Page: www.nationalbar.org
Social Media: *Facebook, Twitter, LinkedIn*

John Crump, Executive Director

Founded in 1925, the National Bar Association (NBA) is the nation's oldest and largest association of African American lawyers and judges.
Cost: $32.00
Circulation: 25,000
Founded in 1925

16014 National Jurist
PO Box 939039
Sandy, CA 92193

858-503-7786
FAX 858-503-7588
E-Mail: jurist@clark.net
Home Page: www.nationaljurist.com

Jack Crittenden, Editor-in-Chief
Keith Carter, Managing Editor
Rebecca Luczycki, Editor
Mike Wright, National Accounts Manager

Information, advice, news and entertainment for law and pre-law students to help them succeed in law school.
Cost: $30.00
Circulation: 100000
Founded in 1996

16015 National Notary
National Notary Association
9350 Desoto Avenue
Post Office Box 2402
Chatsworth, CA 91313-2402

818-739-4000
800-876-6827
FAX 800-833-1211
E-Mail: webmaster@nationalnotary.org
Home Page: www.nationalnotary.org

Deborah M. Thaw, Executive Vice President
Milton Valera, President
Mark Valera, Managing Director
Thomas Hayden, Director of Marketing

Focuses on the importance of notaries as public servants and updates readers on related news.
Founded in 1957

16016 National Paralegal Reporter
National Federation of Paralegal Association
PO Box 2018
Edmonds, WA 98020

425-967-0045
FAX 425-771-9588
E-Mail: info@paralegals.org
Home Page: www.paralegals.org

Features in-depth articles on timely topics such as paralegal roles and choosing vendors; how-toarticles providing readers with practical information that can be directly applied to their careers; and provides legal updated providing information that affects the paralegal profession such as case law, legislation, and technology education.
Cost: $30.00
Frequency: Bi-Monthly
Circulation: 10,000

16017 Natural Resources and Environment
American Bar Association
740 15th St Nw
Suite 8
Washington, DC 20005-1022

202-662-1000
800-285-2221
FAX 202-662-1032
E-Mail: service@abanet.org
Home Page: www.abanet.org

Practical magazine on the latest developments in the field of natural resources law.
Cost: $60.00
Frequency: Quarterly
Circulation: 12000

16018 Negotiation Journal
Plenum Publishing Corporation
513 Pound Hall
Cambridge, MA 02138

617-495-1684
FAX 617-495-7818
Home Page: www.pon.harvard.edu

Michael Wheeler, Editor
Nancy Waters, Managing Editor

Investigates theoretical and practical developments in the conflict resolution field.
Cost: $79.00
Frequency: Quarterly
Founded in 1998

16019 Older Americans Report
Business Publishers
8737 Colesville Road
Suite 1100
Silver Spring, MD 20910-3928

301-876-6300
800-274-6737
FAX 301-589-8493
E-Mail: custserv@bpinews.com
Home Page: www.bpinews.com

Leonard A Eiserer, Publisher
Beth Early, Operations Director
Mark Sherman, Editor

Covers every issue and program that affects your decision-making: Older Americans Act, long term care, Social Security & SSI, nutrition, nursing home regulation, housing, retirement/pension issues, all block grants for the aged, and more.
Cost: $427.00
Frequency: Weekly
Founded in 1963

16020 Payroll Administration Guide
Bureau of National Affairs

1801 S Bell St
Arlington, VA 22202-4501

703-341-3000
800-372-1033
FAX 800-253-0332
E-Mail: customercare@bna.com
Home Page: www.bnabooks.com
Social Media: *Facebook, Twitter, LinkedIn*

Paul N Wojcik, CEO

A notification and reference service for payroll professionals. Covers federal and state employment tax, wage-hour and wage-payment laws.
Cost: $896.00
Frequency: Bi-Weekly
Founded in 1929

16021 Polygraph
American Polygraph Association
PO Box 8037
Chattanooga, TN 37414-0037

423-892-3992
800-272-8037
FAX 423-894-5435
E-Mail: office@polygraph.org
Home Page: www.polygraph.org

Robbie S Bennett, National Office Manager
Gordon L. Vaughan, General Counsel
Donald Krapohl, Editor
Robbie S. Bennett, National Office Manager
Barry Cushman, President

Features articles about the psychophysiological detection of deception, and related areas.
Cost: $125.00
Frequency: Quarterly
Founded in 1966

16022 Preview of United States Supreme Court Cases
American Bar Association
321 N Clark St
Chicago, IL 60654-7598

312-988-5000
800-285-2221
FAX 312-988-6281
E-Mail: askaba@abanet.org
Home Page: www.americanbar.org/aba.html
Social Media: *Facebook, Twitter*

Tommy H Wells Jr, President
Laurel G. Bellows, President

Advance analysis by legal experts of the issues, facts and significance of each case being argued before the Supreme Court, plus special summer issue with all court decisions.
Cost: $340.00
Frequency: 10-12 issues

16023 Probate Lawyer
3415 S Sepulveda Boulevard
Suite 460
Los Angeles, CA 90034-6014

310-478-4454

Offers legislative news for probate courts.
Frequency: Annual

16024 Professional Lawyer
American Bar Association
321 N Clark St
Chicago, IL 60654-7598

312-988-5000
800-285-2221
FAX 312-988-6281
E-Mail: askaba@abanet.org
Home Page: www.americanbar.org/aba.html
Social Media: *Facebook, Twitter*

Tommy H Wells Jr, President
Laurel G. Bellows, President

A magazine providing a forum for exchange of views and ideas on professionalism issues for bar leaders, lawyers, law school education and

others interested in professionalism.
Cost: $40.00
Founded in 1878

16025 Prosecutor

National District Attorneys Association
44 Canal Center Plz
Suite 110
Alexandria, VA 22314-1548

703-549-4253
FAX 703-836-3195
E-Mail: trafficemail@ndaa.org
Home Page: www.ndaa.org

Thomas Charron, Executive Director
Paul F Walsh Jr, Manager
Bill Gibbs, Manager

Covers a variety of criminal justice topics including child abuse, telemarketing fraud, violence against women, vehicular crime, DNA, juvenile justice and community prosecution.
48 Pages
Circulation: 7000
ISSN: 0027-6383
Founded in 1977
Mailing list available for rent: 6,500 names
Printed in 4 colors on glossy stock

16026 Public Contract Law Journal

American Bar Association
321 N Clark St
Chicago, IL 60654-7598

312-988-5000
800-285-2221
FAX 312-988-6281
E-Mail: askaba@abanet.org
Home Page: www.americanbar.org/aba.html
Social Media: *Facebook, Twitter*

Tommy H Wells Jr, President
Laurel G. Bellows, President

Contains articles on all phases of federal, state and local procurement and grant law by leading authoritiies.
Cost: $60.00
Frequency: Annual+

16027 Real Property, Property and Trust Journal

American Bar Association
740 15th St Nw
Suite 8
Washington, DC 20005-1022

202-662-1000
FAX 202-662-1032
E-Mail: collinsj@staff.abanet.org
Home Page: www.americanbar.org/aba.html
Social Media: *Facebook, Twitter*

William Neukom, President
Laurel G. Bellows, President
Jennifer Collins, Advertising Sales Coordinator

Scholarly articles in the fields of estate planning, trust law and real property law.
Cost: $60.00
Frequency: Quarterly

16028 Review of Banking and Financial Services

Standard & Poor's Corporation
55 Water St
New York, NY 10041-0003

212-438-1000
FAX 212-438-0299
E-Mail: clientsupport@standardandpoors.com
Home Page: www.standardandpoors.com

Deven Sharma, President
Hendrik Kranenburg, Executive VP

Focuses on laws and regulations affecting the banking and related industries.
Founded in 1941

16029 Review of Securities & Commodities Regulation

Standard & Poor's Corporation
55 Water St
44th Floor
New York, NY 10041-0003

212-438-1000
FAX 212-438-0299

Deven Sharma, President

Information on the laws and regulations affecting the securities and future industries.
Cost: $8.55
Frequency: 22 per year
Printed in on newsprint stock

16030 Right of Way

International Right of Way
19750 S Vermont Ave
Suite 220
Torrance, CA 90502-1144

310-538-0233
FAX 310-538-1471
E-Mail: info@irwaonline.org
Home Page: www.irwa.net

Mark Rieck, Executive VP
Barbara Billitzer, Publisher
Cost: $425.00
Founded in 1985

16031 Specialization Update

American Bar Association
321 N Clark St
Chicago, IL 60654-7598

312-988-5000
800-285-2221
FAX 312-988-6281
E-Mail: askaba@abanet.org
Home Page: www.abanet.org

Tommy H Wells Jr, President

A compilation of current news briefs and articles of interest on lawyer specialization and related topics.
Circulation: 4,00,000
Founded in 1878

16032 Student Lawyer

American Bar Association
321 N Clark St
Chicago, IL 60654-7598

312-988-5000
800-285-2221
FAX 312-988-6281
E-Mail: askaba@abanet.org
Home Page: www.americanbar.org/aba.html
Social Media: *Facebook, Twitter*

Tommy H Wells Jr, President
Laurel G. Bellows, President

Magazine for law students featuring articles on legal, political, social issues, law school and the profession.
Cost: $20.00
Frequency: Monthly
ISSN: 0039-274X
Founded in 1972
Printed in 4 colors on glossy stock

16033 Tax Lawyer

American Bar Association
321 N Clark St
Chicago, IL 60654-7598

312-988-5000
800-285-2221
FAX 312-988-6281
E-Mail: askaba@abanet.org
Home Page: www.americanbar.org/aba.html
Social Media: *Facebook, Twitter*

Tommy H Wells Jr, President
Laurel G. Bellows, President

Journal of scholarly articles written by highly respected attorneys in the field and a thought-provoking student notes and comments section.
Cost: $53.00
Frequency: Quarterly

16034 Technology and Practice Guide

ABA Publishing
321 N Clark St
Chicago, IL 60654-7598

312-988-5000
800-285-2221
FAX 312-988-6281
E-Mail: askaba@abanet.org
Home Page: www.americanbar.org/aba.html
Social Media: *Facebook, Twitter*

Tommy H Wells Jr, President
Laurel G. Bellows, President

Helps law professionals of general practice in making decisions about legal information management and technology.
Cost: $18.00
Frequency: SemiAnnual
Circulation: 13,477

16035 The Bar Examiner Magazine

National Conference of Bar Examiners
302 South Bedford Street
Madison, WI 53703

608-280-8550
FAX 608-280-8552
E-Mail: contact@ncbex.org
Home Page: www.ncbex.org

Erica Moeser, President

Published by the NCBE as a servuce to courts, academia, bar admissions administrators, members of bar examining boards and character committees, and others with special interest in the bar admissions process. Views and opinions in the articles are not to be taken as official expressions of the NCBE's policy unless so stated.
Frequency: 4/Year
Founded in 1931

16036 The Rules of the Game

Alliance for Justice
11 Dupont Cir Nw
Suite 200
Washington, DC 20036-1206

202-822-6070
FAX 202-822-6068
E-Mail: alliance@afj.org
Home Page: www.afj.org

Nan Aron, President
Mailing list available for rent

16037 Tort and Insurance Law Journal

American Bar Association
740 15th St Nw
Suite 8
Washington, DC 20005-1022

202-662-1000
FAX 202-662-1032
E-Mail: cmpdi@abanet.org
Home Page: www.americanbar.org/aba.html
Social Media: *Facebook, Twitter*

William Neukom, President
Laurel G. Bellows, President
Rick Paszkiet, Development Editor
Jennifer Collins, Advertising Sales Coordinator

Scholarly journal on current or emerging issues of national scope in the fields of tort and insurance law.
Cost: $23.00
Frequency: Quarterly

16038 Trial

The American Association for Justice

777 6th Street, NW
Washington, DC 20001

202-965-3500
800-424-2725
E-Mail: membership@justice.org
Home Page: www.justice.org/

Kathleen Flynn Peterson, President
Linda Lipsen, Chief Executive Officer
Charles Jeffress, Chief Operating Officer
Kathi Berge, Chief Financial Officer
Anjali Jesseramsing, Executive Vice President

In depth articles by experts on socio-legal issues. Evaluates legal practices, points of law, civil law and recent developments in law.
Cost: $79.00
Frequency: Monthly
Circulation: 60000
Founded in 1946

16039 Utilities Law Review
John Wiley & Sons
111 River St
Hoboken, NJ 07030-5790

201-748-6000
800-825-7550
FAX 201-748-6088
E-Mail: info@wiley.com
Home Page: www.wiley.com

William J Pesce, CEO

Edited by a team of specialist UK and European lawyers, it is the leading journal in this fast-changing field. Providing detailed coverage of electricity, gas, telecommunications, transport, water and broadcasting.
Founded in 1807

16040 Verdicts & Settlement
Daily Journal Corporation
PO Box 54026
Los Angeles, CA 90054-0026

213-229-5300
FAX 213-229-5481
Home Page: www.dailyjournal.com

Gerald L Salzman, CEO
Malisha Anderson, Editor
Ray Chagolla, Marketing Head
Ama Sanchev, Circulation Manager
Frequency: Weekly
Circulation: 11000
Founded in 1888

16041 Women Lawyers Journal
National Association of Women Lawyers
American Bar Center 15.2
321 N Clark Street
Chicago, IL 60610-4403

312-988-6186
FAX 312-988-5491
E-Mail: nawl@nawl.org
Home Page:
www.abanet.org/nawl/journal/wlj.html

Janice Sperow, Editor
Peggy Golden, Managing Editor
Stephanie Scharf, President

Published since 1911 as a forum for the exchange of ideas and information of interest to women lawyers. Unsolicited articles and press releases about non members will not be published.
Cost: $45.00
Circulation: 1200
ISSN: 0043-7468
Founded in 1899

16042 Young Lawyers Division Newsletter
Young Lawyers

104 Marietta St Nw
Suite 100
Atlanta, GA 30303-2743

404-527-8700
800-334-6865
FAX 404-527-8717
E-Mail: webmaster@gabar.org
Home Page: www.gabar.org

Cliff Brashier, Executive Director
Bryan Scott, Director
Natalie Kelly, Director
Frequency: Quarterly
Circulation: 21000
Founded in 1978

Trade Shows

16043 ABA Annual Meeting
American Bar Association
740 15th Street NW
9th Floor
Washington, DC 20005

202-662-1570
FAX 202-442-3439
E-Mail: cmpdl@abanet.org
Home Page: www.americanbar.org/aba.html
Social Media: Facebook, Twitter

Carolyn B Lamm, President
Alex J Hurder, Commission Chair
Laurel G. Bellows, President

The meeting includes a CLE event on incompetency and Miranda rights, and also a reception for lawyers with disabilities.

16044 AFCC Annual Conference
Association of Family and Conciliation Courts
6525 Grand Teton Plaza
Madison, WI 53719

608-664-3750
FAX 608-664-3751
E-Mail: afcc@afccnet.org
Home Page: www.afccnet.org

Peter Salem, Executive Director

Over 20 exhibits relating to family judicial issues, including child custody and marriage, family, and divorce counseling. Attended by judges, couselors, attorneys, court personnel, mediators, teachers and researchers.
Frequency: June

16045 AIRA Annual Bankruptcy & Restructuring Conference
Association of Insolvency & Restructuring Advisors
221 Stewart Avenue
Suite 207
Medford, OR 97501

541-858-1665
FAX 541-858-9187
E-Mail: aira@airacira.org
Home Page: www.airacira.org

Grant Newton, Executive Director

Exhibits for professionals involved in insolvency and restructuring.
Frequency: Annual/June
Founded in 1984

16046 ALA Annual Educational Conference and Exposition
Association of Legal Administrators
75 Tri-State International
Suite 222
Lincolnshire, IL 60069-4435

847-267-1252
FAX 847-267-1329

E-Mail: publications@alanet.org
Home Page: www.alanet.org

Larry Smith, Exhibits Manager
Debbie Thomas, Director, Accounting & Finance
Renee Mahovsky, Director, Administration/Operations
Bob Abramson, Director, Marketing & Communication
Jan Waugh, Director, Member Services

Seminar, luncheon, tours and 200 exhibitors of information about computer hardware and software, facilities management, publications, printers, suppliers, litigation support, travel consultants and more.
2000 Attendees
Frequency: May

16047 APA Annual Meeting
American Polygraph Association
PO Box 8037
Chattanooga, TN 37414-0037

423-892-3992
800-272-8037
FAX 423-894-5435
E-Mail: office@polygraph.org
Home Page: www.polygraph.org

Robbie S Bennett, National Office Manager
Gordon L. Vaughan, General Counsel
Donald Krapohl, Editor
Robbie S. Bennett, National Office Manager
Barry Cushman, President
600 Attendees
Founded in 1966

16048 Academy of Criminal Justice Sciences
Northern Kentucky University
402 Nunn Hall
Highland Heights, KY 41099

859-572-5100
800-757-ACJS
FAX 859-572-6665

Patricia Delancey, Executive Director

Exhibits of publications pertaining to criminal justice and related areas. 45 booths.
1.8M Attendees
Frequency: March

16049 Academy of Legal Studies in Business Annual Meeting
School of Business-Forsyth
Western Carolina University
Cullowhee, NC 28723
Daniel Hebron, Executive Secretary

15 booths.
300 Attendees
Frequency: August

16050 Adjutants General Association of the United States Annual Meeting
1 Massachusetts Avenue NW
Washington, DC 20001-1401

302-326-7008
FAX 302-326-7196
Home Page: www.agaus.org

Government legislation.
300 Attendees
Frequency: Spring

16051 American Association for Paralegal Education Convention
American Association for Paralegal Education
2965 Flowers Road S
Suite 105
Atlanta, GA 30341-5520

770-909-9000
FAX 913-381-9308

David Scharf, Executive Director

Annual convention of 20 exhibitors of computer hardware and software, paralegal publications and educational materials and related supplies.
200 Attendees
Founded in 1984

16052 American Association of Attorney-Certified Public Accountants Convention
American Association of Attorney-CPAs
3921 Old Lee Highway
Suite 71a
Fairfax, VA 22030

703-352-8064
888-288-9272
FAX 703-352-8073
E-Mail: info@attorney-cpa.com
Home Page: www.attorney-cpa.com

Kenneth D Goodman, President
Susan Pollock, Membership Coordinator

Exhibits for persons licensed both as attorneys and CPAs.
Frequency: Annual

16053 American Association of Law Libraries Meeting & Conference
American Association of Law Libraries
105 W Adams Street
Suite 3300
Chicago, IL 60603

312-939-4764
FAX 312-431-1097
E-Mail: support@aall.org
Home Page: www.aallnet.org
Social Media: *Facebook, Twitter*

Paul Graller, Exhibits Manager
Susan Fox, Executive Director
Kate Hagan, Executive Director
Kim Rundle,, Executive Assistant
Emily Feltren,, Director of Government Relations

Annual show of 200 booths and 175 exhibitors of library equipment, supplies and services, including computer hardware and software/publishers of legal materials/information.
2000 Attendees
Frequency: July

16054 American Bar Association Annual Meeting/ ABA Expo
American Bar Association
321 N Clark Street
Chicago, IL 60610

312-988-5000
800-285-2221
E-Mail: askaba@abanet.org
Home Page: www.americanbar.org/aba.html
Social Media: *Facebook, Twitter*

William Neukom, President
Laurel G. Bellows, President

Annual meeting and 200 exhibits of legal technology, law books, computers, data processing equipment and other products and services related to the legal profession.
15000 Attendees
Frequency: August
Founded in 1887

16055 American Corporate Counsel Association Conference
1025 Connecticut Avenue NW
Suite 200
Washington, DC 20036-5425

202-318-8327
FAX 202-331-7454
Home Page: http://www.acc.com

Frederick J Krebs, Executive Director

Corporate law.
600 Attendees
Frequency: November

16056 American Immigration Lawyers Association Trade Show
American Immigration Lawyers Association
1331 G Street NW
Suite 300
Washington, DC 20005-3142

202-507-7600
FAX 202-783-7853
E-Mail: executive@aila.org
Home Page: www.aila.org

Charles H Kuck, President
Bernard P Wolfadorf, President-Elect
David W Leopold, First VP
Gregory Chen, Director of Advocacy
Susan D. Quarles, Deputy Executive Director
628 booths.
600 Attendees
Frequency: June

16057 American Society for Legal History Annual Meeting
American Society for Legal History
Notre Dame Law School
PO Box R
Notre Dame, IN 46556-0780

574-631-6627
FAX 574-631-3595
E-Mail: WEBMASTER@ASLH.NET
Home Page: www.aslh.net

Walter F Pratt Jr, Secretary/Treasurer

Annual meeting of scholarly presses. Exhibits relating to legal history and its uses in formulating legal policy, decisions and actions; unearthing historical items; and preserving legal and legislative records.
1200 Attendees
Frequency: Annual
Founded in 1956

16058 American Society of International Law Conference
2223 Massachusetts Avenue NW
Washington, DC 20008-2847

202-939-6005
FAX 202-797-7133
Home Page: http://www.asil.org

Rosemarie Rauzino-Heller, Show Manager
Charlotte Ku, Executive Director
30 tables.
1M Attendees

16059 Annual Conference on Legal Medicine
American College of Legal Medicine
611 E Wells Street
Milwaukee, WI 53202-3816

414-276-1881
800-433-9137
FAX 414-276-3349
E-Mail: info@aclm.org
Home Page: www.aclm.org

Laura Morrone, Meeting/Project Manager

Annual conference and exhibits related to the field of legal medicine or health care related issues.
225 Attendees
Mailing list available for rent: 1400 names at $150 per M

16060 Annual Education Conference & Resource Center Exhibition
National Association for Law Placement

1666 Connecticut Avenue NW
Suite 1110
Washington, DC 20009

202-835-1001
FAX 202-835-1112
E-Mail: info@nalp.org
Home Page: www.nalp.org

Fred Thrasher, Deputy Director
Mark Weber, Senior Vice President
Pamela Malone, Senior Vice President

Annual conference and exhibits relating to recruitment and placement of lawyers.
800 Attendees
Frequency: Annual

16061 Association of American Law Schools Annual Meeting
Association of American Law Schools
1201 Connecticut Avenue NW
Suite 800
Washington, DC 20036-2605

202-296-8851
FAX 202-296-8869
E-Mail: aals@aals.org
Home Page: www.aals.org

Mary E Cullen, Director Meetings
Carl Monk, Executive Director

Annual meeting of 51 book publishers, suppliers and distributors, computer software suppliers.
4100 Attendees
Founded in 1896

16062 Association of Trial Lawyers Annual Summer Meeting
The American Association for Justice
777 6th Street, NW
Washington, DC 20001

202-965-3500
800-424-2725
E-Mail: membership@justice.org
Home Page: www.justice.org/

Kathleen Flynn Peterson, President
Linda Lipsen, Chief Executive Officer
Charles Jeffress, Chief Operating Officer
Kathi Berge, Chief Financial Officer
Anjali Jesseramsing, Executive Vice President
45 booths.
3M Attendees
Frequency: July/August

16063 Association of Trial Lawyers Mid Winter Meeting
The American Association for Justice
777 6th Street, NW
Washington, DC 20001

202-965-3500
800-424-2725
E-Mail: membership@justice.org
Home Page: www.justice.org/

Kathleen Flynn Peterson, President
Linda Lipsen, Chief Executive Officer
Charles Jeffress, Chief Operating Officer
Kathi Berge, Chief Financial Officer
Anjali Jesseramsing, Executive Vice President
55 booths.
1.5M Attendees
Frequency: January/Febuary

16064 Association of Trial Lawyers of America Convention/Exposition
The American Association for Justice
777 6th Street, NW
Washington, DC 20001

202-965-3500
800-424-2725

E-Mail: membership@justice.org
Home Page: www.justice.org/

Kathleen Flynn Peterson, President
Linda Lipsen, Chief Executive Officer
Charles Jeffress, Chief Operating Officer
Kathi Berge, Chief Financial Officer
Anjali Jesseramsing, Executive Vice President

Semi-annual convention and exhibits of 130 manufacturers, suppliers and distributors of legal products/service, including computer animation videos, computer software/hardware, demonstrative evidence products, expert witness services and marketing firms, as well as high end consumer gifts.
3000 Attendees
Frequency: July
Founded in 1946

16065 DRI- Annual Conference
DRI-The Voice of the Defense Bar
55 W. Monroe Street
Suite 2000
Chicago, IL 60603

312-951-1101
FAX 312-795-0749
E-Mail: dri@dri.org
Home Page: www.dri.org
Social Media: *Facebook, Twitter, LinkedIn*

Mary Massaron Ross, President
J. Michael Weston, President-Elect
John Parker Sweeney, First Vice President
Laura E. Proctor, Second Vice President
John E. Cuttino, Secretary/Treasurer

DRI is an international organization of attorneys defending the interests of business and individuals in civil litigation. DRI provides numerous educational and informational resources to DRI members and offers many opportunities for liaison among defense trial lawyers.

16066 Education Law Association Annual Conference
Education Law Association
300 College Park Avenue
Dayton, OH 45469

937-229-3589
FAX 216-687-5284
E-Mail: ela@educationlaw.org
Home Page: www.educationlaw.org
Social Media: *Facebook, Twitter, LinkedIn*

Mandy Schrank, Executive Director
Cate K. Smith, Executive Director
Judy Pleiman, Member Services Coordinator
Jody Thornburg, Publications Manager

Annual conference with over 100 presenters giving presentations on current education law issues. Ten to twelve exhibitors of education law resources.
350 Attendees
Frequency: November

16067 Federal Bar Association Convention
Federal Bar Association
1220 North Fillmore St.
Ste. 444
Arlington, VA 22201

571-481-9100
FAX 571-481-9090
E-Mail: fba@fedbar.org
Home Page: www.fedbar.org
Social Media: *Facebook, Twitter, LinkedIn*

Jack D. Lockridge, Executive Director
Lori Beth Gorman, Executive Assistant
Robert J. DeSousa, President
Hon. Gustavo Gelpi, Jr., President-Elect

Annual convention and exhibits of legal publications, computer software and insurance information.
300 Attendees

16068 Federal Taxation Institute
11 W 42nd Street
New York, NY 10036-8002

212-921-2300

Lorrie Ann England, Show Manager

11 booths.
1M Attendees
Frequency: November

16069 Institute of Federal Taxation
USC Law Center
University Park
Suite 124
Los Angeles, CA 90089-0001

FAX 213-740-9442

Karen Sprague, Director

10 booths.
1M Attendees
Frequency: January

16070 Law and Society Association Annual Meeting
University of Massachusetts
Hampshire House
Amherst, MA 01003

413-545-0111
FAX 413-545-1640
E-Mail: Exec_Office@lawandsociety.org
Home Page: www.lawandsociety.org

Ronald Pipkin, Executive Officer
Lissa Ganter, Administrative Coord

The annual meeting brings together 800-1000 scholars from the US and around the world to present research in the field of socio-legal studies. This includes the place of law in relation to other social institutions, legal decision making, legal systems, and operations, and a variety of research methods and modes of analysis. 50 booths including publishers exhibit, mainly academic, in the fiels of legal studies, and social science.
Frequency: May

16071 Legal Administrators Association
Association of Legal Administrators
75 Tri-State International
Suite 222
Lincolnshire, IL 60069-4435

847-267-1252
FAX 847-267-1329
E-Mail: publications@alanet.org
Home Page: www.alanet.org

Larry Smith, Executive Director
Debbie Thomas, Director, Accounting & Finance
Renee Mahovsky, Director, Administration/Operations
Bob Abramson, Director, Marketing & Communication
Jan Waugh, Director, Member Services

350 booths of products and services related to the legal industry.
2M Attendees
Frequency: April
Founded in 1971

16072 Mid-America Association of Law Libraries Convention
Mid-America Association of Law Libraries
105 W Adams Street
Suite 3300
Chicago, IL 60603

312-939-4764
FAX 312-431-1097

Home Page: www.aallnet.org/chapter/maall/
Social Media: *Facebook, Twitter*

Annual show and exhibits of law library equipment, supplies and services.
Frequency: October, Omaha
Founded in 1973
Mailing list available for rent

16073 NFPA Convention
National Federation of Paralegal Associations
23607 Highway 99
Suite 2-C
Edmonds, WA 98026

425-967-0045
FAX 425-771-9588
E-Mail: info@paralegals.org
Home Page: www.paralegals.org
Social Media: *Facebook, LinkedIn*

Dana Murphy-Love, Managing Director
Celeste Allen, Assistant Director
Rodney Dunham, Assistant Director

The premier annual event for legal professionals to gather for education seminars, dynamic speakers, knowledge sharing, networking, and of course product-shopping.
350 Attendees
Frequency: Annual

16074 National Association of Black Criminal Justice
1900 N Loop W
Suite 255
Houston, TX 77018-8116

713-681-3700
FAX 713-956-8664

Keith Branch Esq, Chairman
Howard Thompson, Owner

60 booths.
700 Attendees
Frequency: July

16075 National Association of Parliamentarians (NAP) Conference
National Association of Parliamentarians
213 South Main Street
Independence, MO 64050-3850

816-833-3892
888-627-2929
FAX 816-833-3893
E-Mail: hq@nap2.org
Home Page: www.parliamentarians.org

Ronald R Stinson, President
Naurice S Henderson, VP
Sandra K Olson, Secretary

The NAP sponsors a conference and exhibit relating to parliamentary law and procedure on a biennial basis. In addition, the Association also holds a national event once each year, providing the opportunities for members, prospective members, and guests to learn more about effective meetings, how to help others learn the fundamentals of parliamentary procedure, and how to be an effective parliamentarian.

16076 National Bar Association Annual Convention
National Bar Association
1225 11th Street NW
Washington, DC 20001-4217

202-842-3900
FAX 202-289-6170
Home Page: www.nationalbar.org
Social Media: *Facebook, Twitter, LinkedIn*

Maurice Foster, Director Special Projects
Reese Marshall, Coordinator Special Projects
John Crump, Executive Director

Annual convention and exhibits of computers and legal software, office products, accounting services, financial planners, temporary employ-

ment agencies, legal publications, travel agencies, luggage and leather goods, fine arts and jewelry. Containing 50 booths.
2500 Attendees
Frequency: July-August
Founded in 1925

16077 National Court Reporters Association Annual Convention & Expo
National Court Reporters Association
8224 Old Courthouse Road
Vienna, VA 22182-3808

703-556-6272
800-272-6272
FAX 703-556-6291
E-Mail: msic@ncra.org
Home Page: www.ncra.org
Social Media: *Facebook, Twitter, LinkedIn, Youtube*

James M. Cudahy, Executive Director & CEO
18000 Members
1200 Attendees
Founded in 1899

16078 National Federation Paralegal Associations
PO Box 33108
Kansas City, MO 64114

816-421-5989
FAX 816-941-2725
E-Mail: info@paralegals.org
Home Page: www.paralegals.org

Tena Nichols, Assistant Managing Director
Thirty-five booths.
300 Attendees
Frequency: April

16079 National Forensic Center Trade Show
National Forensic Center
17 Temple Ter
Lawrenceville, NJ 08648-3254

609-883-0550
800-526-5177
FAX 609-883-7622
E-Mail: ForenExpts@att.net
Home Page: expertindex.com

Betty Lipschner, Director

Coverage of the application of scientific, medical and technical knowledge to litigation.
200 Attendees
Printed in one color on matte stock

16080 National Judges Association
P.O. Box 325
Glendale, OR 97442

FAX 541-832-2674
E-Mail: njaoffice@yahoo.com
Home Page: www.nationaljudgesassociation.org

Whitney Sullivan, Executive Director
Charlene Hewitt, Secretary
Ralph Zeller, Vice President
10 booths.
150 Attendees
Frequency: May

16081 National Notary Association Annual National Conference
Po Box 2402
Chatsworth, CA 91313-2402

818-739-4000
800-876-6827
FAX 818-700-1942
E-Mail: hotline@nationalnotary.org
Home Page: www.nationalnotary.org
Social Media: *Facebook, Twitter, LinkedIn*

Milton G Valera, President
Deborah M Thaw, Executive VP
Marc Reiser, CEO

Jane Eagle, Executive VP & CFO
Ron Johnson, VP Systems & Operations
200M Members
500+ Attendees
Frequency: Bi-Monthly
Circulation: 200,000
Founded in 1957

Directories & Databases

16082 ABA Journal Directory of Legal Software and Hardware
American Bar Association
321 N Clark St
Chicago, IL 60654-7598

312-988-5000
800-285-2221
FAX 312-988-6281
E-Mail: askaba@abanet.org
Home Page: www.americanbar.org/aba.html
Social Media: *Facebook, Twitter*

Tommy H Wells Jr, President
Laurel G. Bellows, President

Directory of supplies to the industry.
Cost: $7.00
Frequency: Annual
Circulation: 400,000

16083 Agricultural Law Update
American Agricultural Law Association
University of Arkansas Law Programs Building
Fayetteville, AR 72701

479-575-4671
FAX 479-575-5830
Home Page: www.aglan-assn.org

Susan Williams, Admininstrative Assistant
Linda McGormic, Editor

Monthly update of legal issues concerning the agricultural industry(members only)
Frequency: Biennial
Circulation: 1,500

16084 American Association of Attorney-Certified Public Accountants Directory
3291 Old Lee Highway
Suite 71a
Fairfax, VA 22030

703-352-8064
888-288-9272
FAX 703-352-8073
E-Mail: info@attorney-cpa.com
Home Page: www.attorney-cpa.com

Kenneth D Goodman, President
Susan Pollock, Membership Coordinator

Offers names, addresses and biographical data on 1,400 individuals licensed as both attorneys and CPAs.
Cost: $175.00
100 Pages
Frequency: Annual

16085 American Bar Association Legal Education Database
American Bar Association
321 N Clark St
Chicago, IL 60654-7598

312-988-5000
800-285-2221
FAX 312-988-6281
E-Mail: askaba@abanet.org
Home Page: www.americanbar.org/aba.html
Social Media: *Facebook, Twitter*

Tommy H Wells Jr, President
Laurel G. Bellows, President

Contains the complete text of the Third Tenative Draft of Law School Library Accreditation Standards.
Frequency: Full-text

16086 American College of Legal Medicine Membership Directory
611 E Wells Street
Milwaukee, WI 53202-3816

414-276-1881
800-433-9137
FAX 414-276-3349
E-Mail: info@aclm.org
Home Page: www.aclm.org

Janet L Haynes, Director

Lists members alphabetically, specialty or area(s) of expertise, and geographic location.
Cost: $75.00
1400 Pages
Circulation: 1,425
Founded in 1960

16087 American Law Reports Library
Lawyers Co-operative Publishing Company
50 Broad Street E
Rochester, NY 14694-0001

585-719-9760

A database, updated periodically, that contains the complete text of analyses of state and federal case law.
Frequency: Full-text

16088 BNA Criminal Practice Manual
Pike & Fischer
8505 Fenton St
Suite 1400
Silver Spring, MD 20910-4499

301-562-1530
800-255-8131
FAX 301-562-1521
E-Mail: pike@pf.com
Home Page: www.pf.com

Meg Hargreaves, President
David Heyman, Director Marketing
Karen James-Cody, Director of Communications
Kirk Swanson, Managing Editor

16089 BNA's Directory of State and Federal Courts, Judges and Clerks
BNA Books
1231 25th Street NW
Washington, DC 20037-1164

732-346-0089
800-960-1220
FAX 732-346-1624
E-Mail: books@bna.com
Home Page: www.bnabooks.com

Margaret Hullinger, Executive Editor
Lois Smith, Marketing Manager
Janie Meidhof, Media Specialist

Complete contact information including e-mail addresses on the nation's judges and clerks, as well as comprehensive details on the structure of federal, state, and territorial courts. Includes 2,201 state courts, 214 federal courts, 14,432 judges, and 5,303 clerks, list of nominations for federal judgeships, federal appellate court jurisdiction map and list, state court structure charts, reports of judicial decisions, directory of electronic public-access services, and personal name index.
714 Pages
Frequency: Annual
Circulation: 1,300
ISBN: 1-570184-11-9
ISSN: 1078-5582
Founded in 1986

16090 Best Lawyers in America
Woodward/White

129 1st Ave Sw
Aiken, SC 29801-4862

803-648-0300
FAX 803-641-4794
E-Mail: info@bestlawyers.com
Home Page: www.bestlawyers.com

Steven Naifeh, President

Over 11,000 attorneys who are selected as the best in their specialities by a survey of over 150,000 lawyers are profiled.
Cost: $110.00
1000 Pages
Frequency: Biennial

16091 Business Litigation Database
Trans Union Credit Information Company
20 Constance Ct
Hauppauge, NY 11788-4200

631-582-2690
FAX 516-582-2767

Over 8 million court records on companies from New York and New Jersey are included in this database.
Frequency: Directory

16092 CEMC/ENR Directory of Law Firms
Construction Education Management Corporation
8133 Leesburg Pike
Suite 700
Vienna, VA 22182-2706

703-734-2399
FAX 703-734-2908

Over 70 construction-oriented law firms located nationwide and overseas are listed.
Cost: $75.00
Frequency: Annual

16093 Common Market Law Review
Kluwer Law and Taxation Publishers
101 Philip Drive
Assinippi Park
Norwell, MA 02061

781-871-6600
866-269-9527
FAX 781-681-9045

Serves as a medium for the dissemination of legal thinking on community law matters, meeting the need of both the academic and the practitioner.

16094 Comprehensive Guide to Bar Admission Requirements
Legal Education and Admissions to the Bar
321 N Clark Street
21st Floor
Chicago, IL 60610

312-988-6738
FAX 312-988-5681
Home Page: www.americanbar.org/aba.html
Social Media: *Facebook, Twitter*

Laurel G. Bellows, President

Offers a list of state bar admission administrators in the United States and its territories.
Cost: $5.00
Frequency: Annual

16095 Corporate Counsel's Law Library
LexisNexis Matthew Bender
1275 Broadway
Menands, NY 12204-2694

518-487-3385
888-223-1940
FAX 518-487-3083
E-Mail: info.in@lexisnexis.com
Home Page: www.lexisnexis.com

George Bearese, VP
Rebecca Schmitt, Chief Financial Officer

This database contains court decisions covering statutory and common law concepts related to the formation, maintenance and dissolution of corporations.
Cost: $2484.00

16096 Criminal Justice Information Exchange Directory
US National Criminal Justice Reference Service
P.O. Box 60769
Harrisburg, PA 17106-0769

717-232-7554
FAX 717-232-2162
Home Page: www.pacounties.org

Carroll Penyak, Director
Lori Dabbondanza, Executive Secretary
Lucas Martsolf, Manager

Over 100 criminal justice-related organizations are listed.
95 Pages
Frequency: Annual

16097 Criminal Justice Periodical Index
University Microfilms International
125 Chapman Hall
1219 University of Oregon
Eugine, OR 97403-1219

541-346-5129
FAX 541-346-2804

Mary Ann Gilbert, Editor

Offers information on more than 180,000 citations to articles in 145 magazines, journals, newsletters and law reporting periodicals on the administration of justice and law enforcement.
Cost: $315.00
Frequency: TriAnnual

16098 Current Index to Legal Periodicals
Marian Gould Gallagher Law Library-Univ. of Wash.
William H Gates Hall
Box 353025
Seattle, WA 98195-3025

206-543-4089
FAX 206-685-2165
Home Page:
lib.law.washington.edu/clip/cilp.html

Susan M Sorensen, Editor
Muriel Quick, Information Specialist

List of publishers of titles indexed in the database.
Cost: $192.00
Frequency: 52 issues
Founded in 1948
Printed in on matte stock

16099 Deskbook Encyclopedia of Employment Law
Data Research
PO Box 490
Rosemount, MN 55068-0490

952-452-8694
800-365-4900
FAX 952-452-8694

An up-to-date compilation of summarized federal and state appellate court decisions which affect employment. The full legal citation is supplied for each case. A brief introductory note on the American judicial system is provided along with updated appendices of recent US Supreme Court cases and recently published law review articles. Also included are portions of the US Constitution which are most frequently cited in employment cases.
Cost: $85.75
500 Pages
Frequency: Annual
ISBN: 0-939675-55-2
Founded in 1996

16100 Deskbook Encyclopedia of Public Employment Law
Data Research
PO Box 490
Rosemount, MN 55068-0490

952-452-8694
800-365-4900
FAX 952-452-8694

An up-to-datre compilation of summarized federal and state appellate court decisions which affect public employment. The full legal citation is cupplied for each case. A brief introductory note on the American judicial system is provided along with updated appendices of recent US Supreme Court cases and recently published law review articles.
Cost: $987.54
531 Pages
Frequency: Annual
ISBN: 0-939675-56-0
Founded in 1996

16101 Directory of Bar Associations
American Bar Association
321 N Clark St
Chicago, IL 60654-7598

312-988-5000
800-285-2221
FAX 312-988-6281
E-Mail: askaba@abanet.org
Home Page: www.americanbar.org/aba.html
Social Media: *Facebook, Twitter*

Tommy H Wells Jr, President
Laurel G. Bellows, President

Offers information on more than 57 state bar associations, local bar associations and other local associations represented in the American Bar Association House of Delegates.
Cost: $95.00
40 Pages
Frequency: Annual

16102 Directory of Certified Business Counselors
Institute of Certified Business Counselors
18831 Willamette Dr
West Linn, OR 97068-1711

503-751-1856
877-422-2674
FAX 503-292-8237
Home Page: www.i-cbc.org

David Finsterwald, President

120 member counselors, brokers and attorneys qualified to act as advisors for persons with business problems.

16103 Directory of Courthouses, Abstract and Title Companies of the USA
Harbors International
7020 S Yale Avenue
Suite 206
Tulsa, OK 74136-5744

918-496-3232
FAX 918-496-8905

A who's who directory of counties, parishes and boroughs with a section on abstract and title companies.
Cost: $95.00
368 Pages
ISSN: 0896-7830

16104 Directory of Law-Related CD-ROMs
Infosource Publishing
140 Norma Road
Teaneck, NJ 07666-4234

201-836-7072

Arlene Eis, Editor

A who's who directory of supplies to the industry.
Cost: $64.00
200 Pages
Frequency: Annual

16105 Directory of Lawyer Disciplinary Agencies & Lawyers' Funds/Client Protection

Center for Professional Responsibility
321 North Clark Street
Chicago, IL 60610

312-988-5000
FAX 312-988-6281
Home Page: www.americanbar.org/aba.html
Social Media: *Facebook, Twitter*

Laurel G. Bellows, President
35 Pages
Frequency: Annual

16106 Directory of Lawyer Referral Services

American Bar Association
321 N Clark St
Chicago, IL 60654-7598

312-988-5000
800-285-2221
FAX 312-988-6281
E-Mail: askaba@abanet.org
Home Page: www.americanbar.org/aba.html
Social Media: *Facebook, Twitter*

Tommy H Wells Jr, President
Laurel G. Bellows, President

Names of services, sponsoring organizations, phones and names of the directors are listed for over 330 services.
Cost: $10.00
40 Pages
Frequency: Annual

16107 Directory of Legal Aid & Defender Offices in the United States & Territories

National Legal Aid and Defender Association
1140 Connecticut Ave NW
Suite 900
Washington, DC 20036-4019

202-452-0620
FAX 202-872-1031
E-Mail: info@nlada.org
Home Page: www.nlada100years.org

Jo Ann Wallace, President & CEO
Julie Clark, Secretary
Alex Gulotta, Treasurer
Cost: $70.00

16108 Directory of Opportunities in International Law

John Bassett Moore Society of International Law
School of Law: University of VA
Charlottesville, VA 22901

Offers hundreds of possible employers in international law.
Cost: $10.00
204 Pages

16109 Directory of Private Bar Involvement Programs

American Bar Association
321 N Clark St
Chicago, IL 60654-7598

312-988-5000
800-285-2221
FAX 312-988-6281
E-Mail: askaba@abanet.org
Home Page: www.americanbar.org/aba.html
Social Media: *Facebook, Twitter*

Tommy H Wells Jr, President
Laurel G. Bellows, President

A list of over 900 programs that provide free or low-cost legal services.
Cost: $7.50
210 Pages
Frequency: Annual

16110 Directory of Public Interest Law Centers

Alliance for Justice
11 Dupont Cir NW
2nd Floor
Washington, DC 20036-1206

202-822-6070
FAX 202-822-6068
E-Mail: alliance@afj.org
Home Page: www.afj.org

Nan Aron, President

Nonprofit association of public interest advocacy organization. Offers workshops, advocacy projects, legal guides, techinical assistance and public education. Lists addresses, branch offices and directors of 200 public interest law centers around the country. Indexed by state and subject area.
Cost: $10.00
48 Pages
Founded in 1996
Mailing list available for rent

16111 Directory of State Court Clerks & County Courthouses

WANT Publishing Company
420 Lexington Ave
Room 300
New York, NY 10170-0002

212-687-3774
FAX 212-687-3779
E-Mail: rwant@msn.com
Home Page: www.wantpublishing.com

Robert S Want, President

Allows easy access to vital information including court decisions, real estate records, UCC and tax liens, and other important documents maintained by State appellate and trial courts and county courthouses nationwide.
Cost: $75.00
380 Pages
Frequency: Annual
ISBN: 0-970122-91-8

16112 FCBA Directory

Federal Communications Bar Association
1020 19th St NW
Suite 325
Washington, DC 20036-6113

202-293-4000
FAX 202-293-4317
E-Mail: fcba@fcba.org
Home Page: www.fcba.org

Stanley Zenor, Executive Director
Kerry Loughney, Director Of Membership Services
Wendy Jo Parish, Administrative Assistant

A nonprofit organization of attorneys and other professionals involved in the development, interpretation, implementation and practice of communications law and policy.
Founded in 1936

16113 Federal Careers for Attorneys

Federal Reports
1010 Vermont Ave NW
Suite 408
Washington, DC 20005-4945

202-393-1552
Home Page: www.attorneyjobs.com

Richard L Hermann, Owner

United States government general counsel and other legal offices throughout the federal sys-

tem.
Cost: $23.95
150 Pages

16114 Federal Law-Related Careers Directory

Federal Reports
1010 Vermont Ave NW
Suite 408
Washington, DC 20005-4945

202-393-1552
800-296-9611
FAX 202-393-1553
Home Page: www.attorneyjobs.com

Richard L Hermann, Owner
Richard L Hermann, Editor

Listings of over 1,000 federal government recruiting offices.
Cost: $16.95

16115 General Bar Law Directory

General Bar
25000 Center Ridge Rd
Suite 3
Cleveland, OH 44145-4108

440-835-2000
800-533-2500
FAX 440-835-3636
E-Mail: service@generalbar.com
Home Page: www.generalbar.com

Charles Sonnhalter, Owner
700 Pages
Circulation: 10000
Founded in 1941

16116 Insider's Guide to Law Firms

Mobius Press
PO Box 3339
Boulder, CO 80307

303-188-8205
800-529-5627
FAX 303-499-5389

Directory of services and supplies to the industry.
Cost: $28.95
740 Pages
Frequency: Annual

16117 Judicial Yellow Book

Leadership Directories
104 5th Ave
New York, NY 10011-6901

212-627-4140
FAX 212-645-0931
E-Mail: judicial@leadershipdirectories.com
Home Page: www.leadershipdirectories.com

David Hurvitz, CEO
James M Petrie, Associate Publisher

Contact information for over 3,250 federal and state judges in federal and state appellate courts, including staff and law clerks, and the law schools they attended.
Cost: $245.00
1,100 Pages
Frequency: SemiAnnual
ISSN: 1082-3298
Founded in 1995
Mailing list available for rent: 13,000 names at $125 per M

16118 Latin American Labor Law Handbook

WorldTrade Executive
PO Box 761
Concord, MA 01742-0761

978-287-0301
FAX 978-287-0302
E-Mail: info@wtexec.com
Home Page: www.wtexec.com

Alison French, Production Manager

Designed to give firms doing business in Latin America some basic knowledge of labor and employment law in the region. Covers countries where US and foreign investment is particularly high: Argentina, Brazil, Venezuela, Colombia, Costa Rica and Chili - providing an overview of the complex network of laws, regulations, and customs affecting social security, wages, employment security, and labor organizing.
Cost: $185.00

16119 Law Books and Serials in Print
R R Bowker LLC
630 Central Ave
New Providence, NJ 07974-1506

908-286-0288
888-269-5372
FAX 908-464-3553
E-Mail: info@bowker.com
Home Page: www.bowker.com

R R Bowker
L Yuster-Freeman, Editor

Focusing on core legal and related titles, Law Books & Serials in Print includes descriptive annotations that provide expert guidance on selecting the right sources for every research need.
ISBN: 0-835249-42-3
Mailing list available for rent

16120 Law Books in Print
Glanville Publishers
75 Main St
Dobbs Ferry, NY 10522-1673

914-693-1320

Publishers of law books in English are listed.
Cost: $750.00
Frequency: Base Edition

16121 Law Firms Yellow Book
Leadership Directories
104 5th Ave
New York, NY 10011-6901

212-627-4140
FAX 212-645-0931
E-Mail: lawfirms@leadershipdirectories.com
Home Page: www.leadershipdirectories.com

David Hurvitz, CEO
James M Petrie, Associate Publisher

Contact information for over 24,000 attorneys and administrators who make the business decisions and manage the practice areas in over 800 of the nation's leading law firms.
Cost: $245.00
1,100 Pages
Frequency: SemiAnnual
ISSN: 1054-4054
Founded in 1991
Mailing list available for rent: 19,000 names at $125 per M

16122 Law Office Computing Directory
James Publishing
Po Box 25202
Suite E
Santa Ana, CA 92799-5202

714-755-5450
FAX 714-751-2709
Home Page: www.jamespublishing.com

Jim Pawell, Owner

Approximately 25 computer products and services designed for use by the legal profession.
Cost: $49.95
Frequency: Bi-Monthly
Circulation: 9,000

16123 Law Office Economics & Management: Directory of Law Office Software
Clark Boardman Callaghan

155 Pfingsten Road
Deerfield, IL 60015

847-374-0400
800-323-1336
FAX 847-948-9340

Paul S Hoffman, Editor

List of about 100 suppliers of data processing equipment and software.
Cost: $15.00
Frequency: Annual June

16124 Law and Legal Information Directory
Gale/Cengage Learning
27500 Drake Road
Farmington Hills, MI 48331-3535

248-699-4253
800-877-4253
FAX 877-363-4253
E-Mail: gale.galeord@cengage.com
Home Page: www.gale.cengage.com
Social Media: *Facebook, Twitter, Youtube*

Patrick C Sommers, President
Jacqueline O'Brien, Editor

Provides descriptions and contact information for more than 21,000 institutions, services and facilities in the law and legal information industry.
Frequency: Annual
ISBN: 1-414421-26-5

16125 Lawyers Referral Directory
PO Box 40335
Cleveland, OH 44140-0335

440-899-8660
800-LAW-LIST
FAX 440-899-1005
E-Mail: Support@LawListIL.com
Home Page: www.lawlistil.com

Ted M McManamon, Editor
Richard T Ostovitz, Production Manager

Bonded reference guide to lawyers specializing in commercial law, creditors' rights and collection litigation. Free to users registering referrals sent.
700 Pages
Frequency: Annual

16126 Lawyers' List
Commercial Publishing Company
PO Box 2430
Easton, MD 21601-2430

410-820-4494
800-824-9911
FAX 410-820-4474

DA Schwartz, President

A listing of law offices engaged in general, corporation and trial practice or patent, trademark and copyright practice.
1700 Pages
Frequency: Annual

16127 Legal Information Alert
Alert Publications
401 W Fullerton Parkway
Apartment 1403E
Chicago, IL 60614-2805

773-525-7594

Donna Tuke-Heroy, President

Publishers of books, databases, CD-ROM products and loose-leaf services for the legal profession are listed.
Cost: $149.00

16128 Legal Looseleafs in Print
Infosource Publishing

140 Norma Road
Teaneck, NJ 07666-4234

201-836-7072
E-Mail: aeis@carroll.com
Home Page: www.infosourcespub.com

Over 230 publishers offering 3,600 looseleaf legal information services.
Cost: $106.00
400 Pages
Frequency: Annual March
Founded in 1981

16129 Legal Newsletters in Print
Infosource Publishing
140 Norma Road
Teaneck, NJ 07666-4234

201-836-7072

Arlene Eis, Editor

Directory of services and supplies to the industry.
Cost: $90.00
400 Pages
Frequency: Annual

16130 Legal Researcher's Desk Reference
Infosource Publishing
140 Norma Road
Teaneck, NJ 07666-4234

201-836-7072

Arlene Eis, Editor

Information is provided on federal and state government officials and departments are listed, as well as publishers and law book dealers and much more.
Cost: $58.00
416 Pages
Frequency: Biennial

16131 Legal Resource Directory
McFarland & Company Publishers
PO Box 611
Jefferson, NC 28640-0611

336-246-4460
FAX 336-246-5018
E-Mail: info@mcfarlandpub.com
Home Page: www.mcfarlandpub.com
Social Media: *Facebook, Twitter, LinkedIn*

Information is given on national, state and local organizations providing free or inexpensive legal advice to low-income families.
Cost: $30.95
148 Pages
Mailing list available for rent

16132 Legal Resources Index
Information Access Company
362 Lakeside Drive
Foster City, CA 94404-1171

650-378-5200
800-227-8431

This database contains more than 500,000 citations, with selected abstracts, to articles published in more than 800 key law journals, bar association publications and legal newspapers.

16133 Martindale-Hubbell Law Directory
Martindale-Hubbell/Reed Reference Publishing
121 Chanlon Rd
New Providence, NJ 07974-1544

908-464-6800
800-526-4902
FAX 908-771-8704
E-Mail: info@martindale.com
Home Page: www.martindale.com

Ralph Colistri, President

Directory of services and supplies to the industry.
Cost: $690.00
50000 Pages
Frequency: 26 Volumes

16134 NALP Directory of Legal Employers

National Association for Law Placement
1025 Connecticut Ave NW
Suite 1110
Washington, DC 20036-5413

202-835-1001
FAX 202-835-1112
E-Mail: info@nalp.org
Home Page: www.nalp.org

M Liepold, Executive Director
Fred Thrasher, Senior Vice President
Pamela Malone, Senior Vice President

Information on more than 1,700 employers nationwide and is an invaluable tool for job searchers, career counselors, and legal recruiters alike. Published both on-line and in print, this directory includes indexes by location and by practice area keyword.
Cost: $75.00
Frequency: Annual
Founded in 1971
Mailing list available for rent: CBC names

16135 NLADA Directory of Legal Aid and Defender Offices in the US & Territories

National Legal Aid and Defender Association
1140 Connecticut Ave NW
Suite 900
Washington, DC 20036-4019

202-452-0620
FAX 202-872-1031
E-Mail: info@nlada.org
Home Page: www.nlada100years.org

Jo Ann Wallace, President & CEO
Julie Clark, Secretary
Alex Gulotta, Treasurer

About 3,600 civil legal aid and indigent defense organizations in the US.
Cost: $70.00
Frequency: Biennial

16136 NSA Directory

National Sheriff's Association
1450 Duke St
Alexandria, VA 22314-3490

703-836-7827

Suzanne B Litts, Editor
David Strigel, Advertising Manager

Sheriffs of the US address phone and fax.
Cost: $50.00
94 Pages
Frequency: Annual

16137 National Directory of Corrections Construction

National Institute of Justice
PO Box 6000
Rockville, MD 20849-6000

301-251-5500

Offers valuable information on over 150 correctional institutions constructed since 1985.
Cost: $32.00
354 Pages

16138 National Directory of Courts of Law

Information Resources

1110 N Glebe Road
Suite 550
Arlington, VA 22201-5762

703-525-4750

Directory of services and supplies to the industry.
Cost: $95.00
888 Pages
Frequency: Biennial

16139 National Employment Listing Service Bulletin

Criminal Justice Center
Sam Houston State University
Huntsville, TX 77341

936-295-6371
FAX 281-294-1653

Kay Billingsley, Editor

Job openings in police departments, sheriff's departments, courts and other law enforcement and security agencies.

16140 National Hispanic American Attorney Directory

Hispanic National Bar Association
100 Seaview Drive
Secaucus, NJ 07094-1800

201-348-4900
FAX 201-348-6609

Carlos G Ortiz

National directory listing Hispanic American Attorneys.
Cost: $65.00
Circulation: 4,000

16141 National Law Journal: Directory of Current Law & Law-Related Books

New York Law Publishing Company
345 Park Avenue S
8th Floor
New York, NY 10010-1700

212-799-9434
FAX 212-696-1875
Home Page: www.ljextra.com

Ben Gerson, Editor
Bill Pollak, General Counsel
Michael Holston, General Counsel
David Hechler, Executive Editor
Paula Martersteck, Managing Editor

Lists over 70 publishers of law and law-related books.
Cost: $124.00
Frequency: Annual January

16142 National List

PO Box 2486
Bismark, ND 58502-2486

701-237-7202
800-227-1675
FAX 701-223-5634
E-Mail: info@nationallist.com
Home Page: www.nationallist.com

Randy Nicola, VP
Gerry Cowgill, President
Kacey Rask, Account Executive
Leslie Herr, Director of Operations

A list of lawyers and law firms handling collections and general practice in the United States, Canada, and most foreign countries.
550 Pages
Frequency: Annual

16143 National Trial and Deposition Directory

321 W Franklin Street
Boise, ID 83702

208-344-3191
FAX 208-345-8800
Cost: $39.95

490 Pages
Circulation: 2,000

16144 National and Federal Legal Employment Report

Federal Reports
1010 Vermont Ave NW
Suite 408
Washington, DC 20005-4945

202-393-1552
800-296-9611
FAX 202-393-1553
Home Page: www.attorneyjobs.com

Richard L Hermann, Owner
Richard L Hermann, Editor

Listings of approximately 600 current attorney and law-related job opportunities with the US government and other public and private employers in Washington DC, nationwide and abroad.
Cost: $35.80
Frequency: Monthly

16145 Nelson's Law Office Directory

Nelson Company
53 West Jackson Blvd.
Chicago, IL 60604

877-464-6656
Home Page: www.nelson.com

Richard Nelson, Owner
Michael Andrews, Chief Financial Officer

A directory of the top rated law firms in the United States. Rated on legal ability, integrity and diligence by the leading lawyers in each state.
Cost: $23.00
210 Pages
Frequency: Annual
Founded in 1968

16146 Now Hiring: Government Jobs for Lawyers

American Bar Association
321 N Clark St
Chicago, IL 60654-7598

312-988-5000
800-285-2221
FAX 312-988-6281
E-Mail: askaba@abanet.org
Home Page: www.americanbar.org/aba.html
Social Media: *Facebook, Twitter*

Tommy H Wells Jr, President
Laurel G Bellows, President

Federal, quasi- and independent government agency jobs for lawyers.
Cost: $17.95
170 Pages

16147 Parole and Probation Compact Administrator Association Mailing List

Council of State Governments
2760 Research Park Drive
PO Box 11910
Lexington, KY 40578-1910

859-244-8000
800-800-1910
FAX 859-244-8001
Home Page: www.csg.org

Jodi Rell, President

16148 Preview of United States Supreme Court Cases

American Bar Association
321 N Clark St
Chicago, IL 60654-7598

312-988-5000
800-285-2221
FAX 312-988-6281
E-Mail: askaba@abanet.org
Home Page: www.americanbar.org/aba.html
Social Media: *Facebook, Twitter*

Tommy H Wells Jr, President
Laurel G. Bellows, President

This database contains full-text reviews of cases orally argued before the US Supreme Court.
Frequency: Full-text

16149 Representative Offices in the Russian Federation

WorldTrade Executive
PO Box 761
Concord, MA 01742-0761

978-287-0301
FAX 978-287-0302
E-Mail: info@wtexec.com
Home Page: www.wtexec.com

Alison French, Production Manager

Combines detailed information on the legal structure within which representative offices must operate, including tax and other requirements, with a user-friendly guide to the accreditation and registration process.
Cost: $135.00

16150 Russell Law List

Commercial Publishing Company
PO Box 2430
Easton, MD 21601-2430

410-820-4494
800-824-9911
FAX 410-820-4474

DA Schwartz, President

A listing of law offices in general practice worldwide.
147 Pages
Frequency: Annual

16151 Russia Business & Legal Briefing

WorldTrade Executive
PO Box 761
Concord, MA 01742-0761

978-287-0301
FAX 978-287-0302
E-Mail: info@wtexec.com
Home Page: www.wtexec.com

Alison French, Production Manager

Topics include: economic analysis; hard currency regulations; investment legislation in St. Petersburg; enforcing foreign judgements in Russia; new laws on limited liability companies and bankruptcy; new commercial arbitration court in St. Petersburg; changes in tax legislation; managing the Russian tax burden.
Cost: $265.00

16152 Sourcebook of Local Court and County Records Retrievers

BRP Publications
200 E Eager Street
Baltimore, MD 21202-3704

202-312-6060
800-822-6338
FAX - - 047

Offers information on firms that specialize in finding court and county records, including civil, criminal, probate and bankruptcy files.
Cost: $45.00
432 Pages

16153 Summer Legal Employment Guide

Federal Reports
1010 Vermont Ave NW
Suite 408
Washington, DC 20005-4945

202-393-1552
Home Page: www.attorneyjobs.com

Richard L Hermann, Owner

Directory of services and supplies to the industry.
Cost: $170.00
36 Pages
Frequency: Annual

16154 US Supreme Court Employment Cases

Data Research
PO Box 490
Rosemount, MN 55068-0490

952-452-8694
800-365-4900
FAX 952-452-8694

A compilation of summarized US Supreme Court decisions which affect employment. The full legal citation is supplied for each case.
Cost: $64.70
288 Pages
Frequency: Annual
ISBN: 0-939675-51-0
Founded in 1995

16155 United States Probation and Pretrial Services Officers Directory

Probation Div./Admin. Office of US Courts
1 Columbus Circle NE
Suite 4-300
Washington, DC 20544-0001

FAX 202-273-1603

Federal probation offices and pretrial services offices.
Frequency: Annual

16156 WESTLAW International Law Library

West Publishing Company
610 Opperman Drive
Eagan, MN 55123-1340

651-687-7327
Home Page: www.westgroup.com

Database containing the complete information of international and US federal court decisions.
Frequency: Full-text

16157 WESTLAW Legal Services Library

West Publishing Company
610 Opperman Drive
Eagan, MN 55123-1340

651-687-7327
Home Page: www.westgroup.com

This database offers the complete text of US federal and state court decisions, statutes and regulations.

16158 WESTLAW Litigation Library

West Publishing Company
610 Opperman Drive
Eagan, MN 55123-1340

651-687-7327
Home Page: www.westgroup.com

Offers information on law reviews, bar association journals and law-related texts.
Frequency: Full-text

16159 Want's Federal-State Court Directory

WANT Publishing Company

420 Lexington Ave
Room 300
New York, NY 10170-0002

212-687-3774
FAX 212-687-3779
E-Mail: rwant@msn.com
Home Page: www.wantpublishing.com

Robert S Want, President

The nation's number one court reference source, offering comprehensive information on the nation's federal, state and county courts.
Cost: $35.00
235 Pages
Frequency: Softcover

Industry Web Sites

16160 http://gold.greyhouse.com

G.O.L.D Grey House OnLine Databases
Grey House Publishing's online database platform, GOLD, offers Quick Search, Keyword Search and Expert Search for most business sectors including legal markets. The GOLD platform makes finding the information you need quick and easy - whether you're a novice searcher or an experienced database user. All of Grey House's directory products are available for subscription on the GOLD platform.

16161 www.aallnet.org

American Association of Law Libraries
Membership consists of national law library professionals.

16162 www.abanet.org

American Bar Association

The largest organization serving lawyers and all professionals involved in the law enforcement and legal industries. Conducts research and educational activities, encourages professional improvement and provides public service.

16163 www.aclm.org

American College of Legal Medicine
Organization related to the field of health law, legal medicine or medical jurisprudence.

16164 www.aclu.org

American Civil Liberties Union
Protection of civil liberties and constitutional rights through litigation, public education and legislative lobbying.

16165 www.afccnet.org

Association of Family and Conciliation
AFCC is an interdisciplinary, international association of professionals dedicated to improving the lives of children and families through the resolution of family conflict.

16166 www.afj.org

Alliance for Justice
Nonprofit association of public interest advocacy organization. Offers workshops, advocacy projects, legal guides, techinical assistance and public education. Publishes a directory of public interest law centers.

16167 www.aipparl.org

American Institute of Parliamentarians
A not-for-profit educational organization for the advancement of the parliamentary procedure.

16168 www.ajs.org

American Judicature Society
Lawyers, judges and educators interested in the effective administration of justice.

16169 www.ali-aba.org
American Law Institute - American Bar Association

Provides continuing legal education courses, books, and periodicals for practicing attorneys and others in the legal profession.

16170 www.ascm.vicsc.dni.us
National Association for Court Management

Members are clerks of court, court administration and others serving in a court management capacity.

16171 www.atlanet.org
Association of Trial Lawyers of America

16172 www.attorney-cpa.com
American Association of Attorney-CPAs

Seeks to safeguard the professional and legal rights of CPA attorneys

16173 www.blr.com
Business & Legal Reports

Provides essential tools for safety and environmental compliance and training needs

16174 www.educationlaw.org
Education Law Association

Association for manufacturers or suppliers of law education equipment, supplies and services.

16175 www.fala.org
First Amendment Lawyers Association

Lawyers concentrating on defending clients under the first amendment of the Constitution.

16176 www.fcba.org
Federal Communications Bar Association

A non-profit organization of attorneys and other professionals involved in the development, interpretation, implementation and practice of communications law and policy.

16177 www.findlaw.com
Online Legal Resources. Legal, Professionals, Students, Business, Legal News, etc.

16178 www.greyhouse.com
Grey House Publishing

Authoritative reference directories for most business sectors including legal markets. Users can search the online databases with varied search criteria allowing for custom searches by product category, geographic area, sales volume, keyword, subject and more. Full Grey House catalog and online ordering also available.

16179 www.honet.msu.edu/~law
American Society for Legal History

Exhibits relating to legal history and its uses in formulating legal policy, decisions and actions; unearthing historical items; and preserving legal and legislative records.

16180 www.lexis-nexis.com
Mead Data Central

Contains the Lexis-Nexis Source Locator, a powerful new tool for retrieving targeted information about the more 31,000 Lexi-Nexis sources.

16181 www.nacdl.org
National Association of Criminal Defense Lawyers

Supports all criminal defense lawyers with education, publications and trade shows.

16182 www.naela.org
National Academy of Elder Law Attorneys

Members are private attorneys, law professors and Title III interest in the provision of legal service to the elderly.

16183 www.narf.org
Native American Rights Fund

Provides legal services to Indian tribes, organizations and individuals in the areas of preservation of tribal existence, protection of tribal natural resources, promotion of human rights , accoutability of governments, development of Indian law.

16184 www.ncraonline.org
National Court Reporters Association

16185 www.ncwba.org
National Conference of Women's Bar Associations

To promote and assist the growth of local and statewide women's bar associations and ideas among women's bar associations and women's bar sections of local and statewide bar associations; to serve as a vehicle for the exchange and dissemination of information and ideas among women's bar associations and women's bar sections of local and statewide bar associations.

16186 www.paralegals.org
National Federation of Paralegal Association

For state and local paralegal associations throughout the United States and Canada.

16187 www.parliamentarians.org
National Association of Parliamentarians

An association for those interested in parliamentary law and procedure, NAP's primary objectives are teaching, promoting, and disseminating the philosophy and principles underlying the rules of deliberative assemblies.

16188 www.rand.org/icj
Institute for Civil Justice

Nonprofit research organization within the RAND Corporation dedicated to interdisciplinary empirical research to facilitate change in the civil justice system.

16189 www.rmmlf.org
Rocky Mountain Mineral Law Foundation

16190 www.romingerlegal.com
Is a Search Engine dedicated to Legal Links, Legal Research Page, Case Law and Professional Directories for Law, etc.

16191 www.searchcrawl.com/legal/justice.html
Searchcrawl
List of legal resources.

16192 www.usfca.edu/law/globaljustice
Web site for the Center for Law and Global Justice. Focus on legal education, judicial training, free and fair elections, and the protection of human rights. The Center is an integral part of the University of San Francisco School of Law.

16193 www.westlaw.com
Westlaw is the premier legal and business research tool on the Internet.

16194 www.worldjurist.org
World Jurist Association of the World Peace Through Law

Association for those interested in future world peace.

Associations

16195 Africana Librarians Council
African Studies Association
54 Joyce Kilmer Avenue
Piscataway, NJ 08854-8045

732-932-8173
FAX 732-445-1366
E-Mail: kramer@tiac.net
Home Page: www.africanstudies.org/

Eileen Kramer, President

Members consist of librarians, archivists or documentalists working with materials from and about Africa or scholars interested in the preseravtionof or access to Africana.
500 Members
Founded in 1983

16196 American Association of Law Libraries
105 W Adams Street
Suite 3300
Chicago, IL 60603

312-939-4764
FAX 312-431-1097
E-Mail: admin@ifwtwa.org
Home Page: www.aallnet.org
Social Media: *Facebook, Twitter, LinkedIn, Youtube, RSS, Instagram*

Linda Kissam, President
Allen Cox, Vice President
Elizabeth Willoughby, Treasurer
Susan J Montgomery, Treasurer, Board Member
Marc d'Entremont, Director

Promotes and enhances the value of law libraries to the legal and public communities, fosters the profession of law librarianship and provides leadership in the field of legal information.
300 Members
Founded in 1956

16197 American Association of School Librarians
American Library Association
50 E Huron Street
Chicago, IL 60611

312-944-6780
800-545-2433
FAX 312-280-5276
E-Mail: ala@ala.org
Home Page: www.ala.org/aasl/
Social Media: *Facebook, Twitter, LinkedIn, Flickr, Pinterest, Google+, In*

Sylvia Knight Norton, Executive Director
Jennifer Habley, Manager, Web Communications
Stephanie Book, Manager, Communications
Allison Cline, Deputy Executive Director
Meg Featheringham, Manager/Editor

Works to ensure that all members of the school library media field collaborate to provide leadership in the total education program, participate as active partners in the teaching and learning process, connect learners with ideas and information and prepare students for life long learning, informed decision making, a love of reading and the use of information technologies.
60000 Members

16198 American Indian Library Association
American Library Association
50 E Huron Street
Chicago, IL 60611

312-944-6780
800-545-2433
FAX 312-664-7459

E-Mail: ala@ala.org
Home Page: www.ala.org

Sari Feldman, President
Keith Michael Fiels, Executive Director
Sara Harris, Manager

Association for Native Americans and Native Alaskans libraries and librarians.
10000 Members
Founded in 1949

16199 American Library Association
American Library Association
50 E Huron St
Chicago, IL 60611-2788

312-944-6780
800-545-2433
E-Mail: ala@ala.org
Home Page: www.ala.org

Sari Feldman, President
Keith Michael Fiels, Executive Director

To provide leadership for the development, promotion, and improvement of library and information services and the profession of librarianship in order to enhance learning and ensure access to information for all.
65000 Members
Founded in 1876

16200 American Society for Information Science
ASIS&T
8555 16th Street
Suite 850
Silver Spring, MD 20910

301-495-0900
FAX 301-495-0810
E-Mail: mwa@mysterywriters.org
Home Page: www.asis.org
Social Media: *Facebook, Twitter, Instagram*

Sara Paretsky, President
Donna Andrews, Executive Vice President
Elaine Viets, Secretary
Tona Perona, Treasurer
3000 Members
Founded in 1945

16201 American Society of Indexing
American Society for Indexing
1628 E. Southern Avenue
Suite 9-223
Tempe, AZ 85282

480-245-6750
FAX 303-422-8894
E-Mail: nahj@nahj.org
Home Page: www.asindexing.org
Social Media: *Facebook, Twitter, YouTube, RSS*

Mekahlo Medina, President
Ivette Davila-Richards, Vice President/Broadcast
Rebecca Aguilar, Vice President, Online
Barbara Rodriguez, Vice President, Print
Francisco Cortes, Financial Officer

A national association with international membership and interests. A nonprofit charitable organization for indexers, librarians, abstractors, editors, publishers, database producers, and organizations concerned with indexing, seeking cooperation and membership of all persons, groups or institutions interested in indexing. Founded in 1968 to promote excellence in indexing and increase awareness of the value of well-written indexes.
2300 Members
Founded in 1984

16202 American Theological Library Association
The American Theological Library Association

300 S Wacker Dr
Suite 2100
Chicago, IL 60606-6701

312-454-5100
888-665-2852
FAX 312-454-5505
E-Mail: presswomen@aol.com
Home Page: www.atla.com
Social Media: *Facebook, Twitter, LinkedIn, Youtube, RSS, Flickr*

Teri Ehresman, President
Marsha Hoffman, 1st Vice President
Marianne Wolf-Astrauskas, 2nd Vice President
Ellen Crawford, Treasurer (Financial Adviser)
Gay Porter DeNileon, Secretary

Provides indexing services in these formats: online database, CD-ROM versions, magnetic tape for OPAC tapeload and print publications. ATLA Religion indexes in print include Religious Index One: Periodicals, Religion Index Two: Multi-Author Works, Index to Book Reviews, Research in Ministry an Index to D. Min. Project Reports and Theses.
2000 Members
Founded in 1937

16203 Americans For Libraries Council
Americans For Libraries Council
347 Congress Street
Boston, MA 02210

855-533-9335
800-542-1918
FAX 646-336-6318
E-Mail: natlwritersassn@hotmail.com
Home Page: www.lff.org

Sandy Whelchel, Executive Director

Americans for Libraries Council (ALC) is a national non-profit organization that advocates for libraries at the national level and develops and promotes programs aimed at realizing the potential of libraries in the 21st century.
2000 Members
Founded in 1937

16204 Art Libraries Society of North America
Art Libraries Society of North America
7044 South 13th Street
Box 11
Oak Creek, WI 53154

403-247-3001
800-817-0621
FAX 414-768-8001
E-Mail: info@owaa.org
Home Page: www.arlisna.org
Social Media: *Facebook, Twitter, LinkedIn, RSS Feeds*

Lisa Ballard, President
Brett Prettyman, 1st Vice President
Phil Bloom, 2nd Vice President
Tom Sadler, Executive Director
Jessica Seitz, Membership & Conference Services

Membership organization for art libraries in the US and Canada.
2.4M Members
Founded in 1927

16205 Asian/Pacific American Librarians
Asian/Pacific American Librarians
PO Box 677593
Orlando, FL 32867

415-422-5379
Home Page: www.apalaweb.org

Alan Di Benedetto, President
Stan Cohen, Vice President / Online Director
Liz Kassler, Treasurer
Chris McDonough, Membership Director
George Kamper, Communications Director

Librarians and information specialists of Asian Pacific descent and those interested in APA librarianship.
Founded in 1984

16206 Association for Library & Information Science Education
Association for Library & Information
2150 N 107th St
Suite 205
Seattle, WA 98133

206-209-5267
FAX 206-367-8777
E-Mail: sabew@sabew.org
Home Page: www.alise.org
Social Media: *Facebook, Twitter, LinkedIn, RSS*

Joanna Ossinger, President
Cory Schouten, VP
Kathleen Graham, Executive Director
Crystal Beasley, Membership
Renee McGivern, Director of conference sponsorship

Provides a forum for library educators to share ideas, discuss issues and seek solutions to common problems.
3200 Members
Founded in 1964

16207 Association for Library Collections & Technical Services
American Library Association
50 E Huron Street
Chicago, IL 60611

312-944-6780
800-545-2433
FAX 312-280-5033
E-Mail: ala@ala.org
Home Page: www.ala.org/alcts

Norm Medeiros, President
Keri Cascio, Executive Director
Keri A Cascio, Director at Large
Norm Medeiros, Director at Large
Timothy T Strawn, Director at Large

Division of the American Library Association.
5M Members
Founded in 1957

16208 Association for Library Service to Children
American Library Association
50 E Huron Street
Chicago, IL 60611

312-944-6780
800-545-2433
FAX 312-944-7671
E-Mail: ala@ala.org
Home Page: www.ala.org/alsc/

Andrew Medlar, President
Betsy Orsburn, Vice-President/President-Elect
Jenna Nemec-Loise, ALSC Division Councilor
Diane Foote, Fiscal Officer
Kristen Sutherland, Program Officer

A network of more than 4,000 children's and youth librarians, children's literature experts, publishers, education and library school faculty members, and other adults committed to improving and ensuring the future of the nation through exemplary library service to children, their families, and others who work with children.
3500 Members

16209 Association for Population/Family Planning
Family Health International Library
PO Box 13950
Research Triangle Park, NC 27709

919-447-7040
FAX 215-898-2124
E-Mail: info@satw.org

Home Page: www.aplici.org
Social Media: *Facebook, Twitter, LinkedIn*

Paul Lasley, President
Barbara Orr, Vice President, Membership
Marla Schrager, Executive Director
John Kingzette, Membership Coordinator
Peggy Bendel, Secretary

Global network of communication, information and resource professionals dedicated to providing assistance and support to members and to other population and reproductive health colleagues, especially in developing nations.
Founded in 1955

16210 Association for Recorded Sound Collections
Association for Recorded Sound Collections
1299 University of Oregon
Eugene, OR 97403-1299

440-564-9340
E-Mail: scwg-jm@cfi.rr.com
Home Page: www.arsc-audio.org
Social Media: *Facebook, Twitter, LinkedIn, Google+*

Scott Tilley, President
Kit Adams, VP
JP Osterman, Secretary
Peggy Insula, Treasurer
Bill Allen, Communications & Publicity

Persons in broadcasting and recording industries, librarians, sound archivists, curators, private collectors and reviewers.
Cost: $40.00
Frequency: 2 Per Year
Circulation: 1000
Founded in 1982
Mailing list available for rent

16211 Association of Christian Libraries
PO Box 4
Cedarville, OH 45314

937-766-2255
FAX 937-766-5499
Home Page: www.acl.org
Social Media: *Facebook, Twitter, Youtube,RSS*

Howard A. Rodman, President
David A. Goodman, Vice President
Aaron Mendelsohn, Secretary-Treasurer

Membership is composed of over 500 evangelical Christian librarians representing primarily evangelical institutions of higher education.
9500 Members
Founded in 1912

16212 Association of College and Research Libraries
American Library Association
50 E Huron Street
Chicago, IL 60611

312-944-6780
800-545-2433
FAX 312-280-2520
E-Mail: acrl@ala.org
Home Page: www.ala.org/acrl/

Ann Campion Riley, President
Irene M. H. Herold, ACRL Vice-President
Margot Sutton Conahan, Manager of Professional Development
David Connolly, Classified Advertising Coordinator
Kathryn Deiss, Content Strategist
13M Members
ISSN: 0099-0086
Founded in 1940

16213 Association of Independent Information Professionals (AAIP)
Association of Independent Information

8550 United Plaza Boulevard
Suite 1001
Baton Rouge, LA 70809

225-408-4400
FAX 225-922-4611
E-Mail: info@writersresearchgroup.com
Home Page: www.aiip.org

Lori Packwood, Director

Provides a forum for information professionals to meet and exchange views.
Founded in 2000

16214 Association of Jewish Libraries
Association of Jewish Libraries
PO Box 1118
Teaneck, NJ 07666

201-371-3255
E-Mail: info@ablusa.org
Home Page: www.jewishlibraries.org
Social Media: *Facebook, Twitter, RSS*

Warren Scheidt, President
John D Bodnovich, Executive Director
Susan Day Duffy, Director of Trade Relations
Jessica Anders, Manager, Comm. & Public Relations
Warren Scheidt, Vice President

Promotes the advancement of the interests of Jewish libraries and publications of Jewish biographical interest.
15000 Members
Founded in 1933

16215 Association of Mental Health Librarians
Cedarcrest Regional Hospital, Medical Libary
One Beach Street
Suite 100
San Francisco, CA 94133

415-955-2157
FAX 845-398-5551
E-Mail: society@asev.org
Home Page: www.mhlib.org
Social Media: *Facebook, Twitter, LinkedIn, Picasa*

Mark Greenspan, President
Dan Howard, Executive Director
Nichola Hall, First Vice President
James Harbertson, Second Vice President
Tom Collins, Secretary/Treasurer

Provides a forum for the introduction of new audiovisual and printed materials in the field of mental health.
2400+ Members
Founded in 1950

16216 Association of Moving Archivists
1313 North Vine Street
Hollywood, CA 90028

323-463-1500
FAX 323-463-1506
E-Mail: asbc@scisoc.org
Home Page: www.amianet.org
Social Media: *Facebook, Twitter, LinkedIn, Pinterest*

Jeffery L Cornell, President
Christina Schoenberger, Vice President
Amy Hope, Executive Officer
Barbara Mock, Vice President of Finance
Kelly A Tretter, Secretary

A non-profit professional association established to advance the field of moving image archiving by fostering cooperation among individuals and organization concerned with the acquistion, description, preservation, exhibition and use of moving image materials.
750 Members
Founded in 1934

16217 Association of Research Libraries
Association of Research Libraries

21 Dupont Circle NW
Suite 800
Washington, DC 20036

202-296-2296
FAX 202-872-0884
E-Mail: info@beerinstitute.org
Home Page: www.arl.org
Social Media: *Facebook, Twitter, YouTtube*

Joe McClain, President
Mary Jane Saunders, VP & General Counsel

Nonprofit organization striving to shape and influence forces affecting the future of research libraries in the process of scholarly communication.
100 Members
Founded in 1986

16218 Beta Phi Mu
University of South Florida
3141 Chestnut Street
Philadelphia, PA 19104

215-895-2000
FAX 215-895-2494
E-Mail: info@brewersassociation.org
Home Page: www.beta-phi-mu.org/
Social Media: *Facebook, Twitter, Youtube*

Charlie Papazian, President
Bob Pease, Chief Operating Officer
Paul Gatza, Director
Erin Glass, Membership Coordinator
Katie Marisic, Federal Affairs Manager

Beta Phi Mu is an organization that recognizes and encourages scholastic achievement among library and information studies students.
1900 Members
Founded in 1978

16219 Black Caucus of ALA
Gladys Smiley Bell
PO Box 5837
Lib. Med. Serv., Rm 161, Kent State
Chicago, IL 60680

330-672-3045
FAX 330-672-3964
Home Page: www.bcala.org
Social Media: *Facebook, Twitter*

Peter H Cressy, President

Association that supports black librarians. Holds annual meeting in conjunction with the American Library Association conference.
32 Members
Founded in 1973

16220 Catholic Library Association
Catholic Library Association
8550 United Plaza Blvd
Ste 1001
Baton Rouge, LA 70809

225-408-4417
855-739-1776
FAX 312-739-1778
Home Page: www.cathla.org
Social Media: *Facebook, Twitter, YouTube, flickr, RSS*

Anthony Perrone, International President
William T. McDonough, Executive Vice President, UFCW
Patrick J. O'Neill, International Secretary-Treasurer
Stuart Appelbaum, Executive Vice President
Paul Meinema, Executive Vice President

International membership organization, providing its members professional development through educational and networking experiences, publications, scholarships and other services.
14M Members
Founded in 1979

16221 Center for Children's Books
Center for Children's Books

501 E Daniel Street
Champaign, IL 61820

217-244-9331
FAX 217-333-5603
E-Mail: dee@hwbta.org
Home Page: ccb.lis.illinois.edu
Social Media: *Facebook, Twitter, Youtube*

Mark Alston, President
Steven Haynes, VP
Ray Ault, Secretary
Allison Babock, Treasurer
Dee Roberson, Executive Director

A crossroads for critical inquiry, professional training and educational outreach related to literature for youth from birth through adolescence. In partnership with The Bulletin of the Center for Children's Books, it aims to inspire and inform adults who connect young people with resources in person, in print, and online.
Founded in 1976

16222 Center for Childrens Books
Center for Children's Books
501 E Daniel Street
Champaign, IL 61820

217-244-9331
FAX 217-333-5603
E-Mail: newyork@ice.it
Home Page: ccb.lis.illinois.edu

Michelle Jones, Editor
Robert Luongo, Executive Director

16223 Chief Officers of State Library Agencies
Chief Officers of State Library Agencies
201 E Main Street
Suite 1405
Lexington, KY 40507

859-514-9151
FAX 859-514-9166
E-Mail: iwfi@aol.com
Home Page: www.cosla.org

Lucio Caputo, President
Vincent Giampaoco, VP

Association for directors of state libraries.
Founded in 1983

16224 Chinese-American Librarians Association
UCI Libraries
PO Box 19557
Irvine, CA 92623-9557

949-824-6836
FAX 949-857-1988
Home Page: www.cala-web.org
Social Media: *Facebook, Twitter, Youtube*

Stephen Larson, Chairman
James M. Sgueo, President & CEO
Jerome J. Janicki, Sr. VP of Operations, COO
Patricia Kelly, Sr. VP of Administration, CFO
Steven L. Schmidt, SVP, Public Policy/Communications
175 Members
Founded in 1938

16225 Church and Synagogue Library Association
10157 SW Barbur Boulevard
Suite 102C
Portland, OR 97219

503-244-6919
800-542-2752
FAX 503-977-3734
E-Mail: info@nbwa.org
Home Page: www.cslainfo.org
Social Media: *Facebook, Twitter, Youtube, Flickr*

Craig A. Purser, NBWA President & CEO
Kimberly McKinnish, CPA, Chief Financial Officer

Rebecca Spicer, SVP Comm. and Public Affairs
Paul Pisano, SVP Industry Affairs & Gen. Counsel
Patti Rouzie, VP, Membership and Meetings

Provides educational guidance in the establishment and maintenance of congregational libraries
Founded in 1938

16226 Coalition for Networked Information
21 Dupont Circle
Suite 800
Washington, DC 20036-1109

202-296-5098
FAX 202-872-0884
Home Page: www.cni.org

Robert P Koch, President / Chief Executive Officer
Nancy Light, Vice President, Communications
Steve Gross, Vice President, State Relations
Allison Jordan, VP, Environmental Affairs
Steve Hayes, VP, Finance and Administration

The Coalition for Networked Information is an organization dedicated to supporting the transformative promise of networked information technology for the advancement of scholarly communication and the enrichment of intellectual productivity.
80 Members
Founded in 1934

16227 Council on Library and Information Resources
Council on Library and Information Resources
1707 L Street NW, Suite 650
Washington, DC 20036-2124

202-939-4750
FAX 202-600-9628
E-Mail: info@wssa.com
Home Page: www.clir.org
Social Media: *Facebook, Twitter, LinkedIn, RSS*

V. James Andretta, Jr., Chairman of the Board
Louis Healey, President
Howard Jacobs, Vice President
Heather Randolph, Director of Operations
Alison Leavitt, Managing Director

The mission of the Council on Library and Information Resources is to expand access to information, however recorded and preserved, as a public good.
460 Members
Founded in 1976

16228 Council on Library/Media Technicians
PO Box 256
Oxon Hill, MD 20748

202-231-3836
FAX 202-231-3838
E-Mail: Info@wswa.org
Home Page: http://colt.ucr.edu/
Social Media: *Facebook, Twitter, YouTube, RSS, Google+*

Brien Fox, Chairman
Doug Epstein, Vice Chairman
Craig Wolf, President and CEO
Jim Rowland, VP, Government Affairs
Dawson Hobbs, Vice President, State Affairs

Supports library and media techicians by offering publications, training, networking and annual conference in conjunction with the American Library Association conference.
450 Members
Founded in 1943

16229 Ethnic Employees of the Library of Congress
6100 Eastview Street
Bethesda, MD 20817-6004
George E Perry, President

Promotes and strengthens brotherhood among ethnic employees and ethnic members of society.
Founded in 1973

16230 Federal Library and Information Network
Library of Congress
101 Independence Ave SE
Washington, DC 20540-4935

202-707-4800
FAX 202-707-4818
E-Mail: help@apawood.org
Home Page: www.loc.gov/flicc
Social Media: *Facebook, Twitter*

Tom Temple, Chairman
Don Grimm, Vice Chairman
Edward Elias, President
Marilyn Thompson, Director of Marketing and Comm.
Tom Kositzky, Director, Field Services Rep.

Representatives of departments and agencies of the federal government.
160 Members
Founded in 1933
Mailing list available for rent

16231 Federal and Armed Forces Libraries Roundtable
American Library Association
50 E Huron Street
Chicago, IL 60611

312-944-6780
800-545-2433
E-Mail: ala@ala.org
Home Page: www.ala.org

Amanda J. Wilson, President
Stephen V. Pomes, Vice President
Theresa Taylor, Armed Forces Director
Bianna E. Ine-Ryan, Armed Forces Director
Anne Harrison, Federal Director

Association for libraries and information services.

16232 Friends of Libraries (FOLUSA)
Association of Library Trustees, Advocates, Friend
50 E Huron Street
Chicago, IL 60611

312-944-6780
800-545-2433
FAX 215-545-3821
E-Mail: jkalonick@ala.org
Home Page: www.ala.org

Ed McBride, President
Sally Gardner Reed, Executive Director
Beth Nawalinski, Deputy Executive Director
Jillian Kalonick, Marketing/PR Specialist
Bette M Kozlowski, Treasurer

Encourages the development of excellent library service to all residents of the US. Aids in forming local and state, friends branches in academic and special libraries.
1.8M Members
Founded in 1979

16233 Herbert Hoover Presidential Library Association
302 Park Side Drive
PO Box 696
West Branch, IA 52358

319-643-5327
800-828-0475
FAX 319-643-2391
E-Mail: afa@fiberboard.org

Home Page: www.hooverassociation.org
Social Media: *Twitter*

Rina P. McGuire, President
Jim Pieczynski, VP
Louis E. Wagner, Executive Director
William C. Ives, Legal Counsel
Blair Ruzicka, Secretary/Treasurer
7 Members
Founded in 1990

16234 Insurance Library Association of Boston
Insurance Library
156 State St
Boston, MA 02109-2584

617-227-2087
FAX 617-723-8524
E-Mail: info@afandpa.org
Home Page: www.insurancelibrary.org
Social Media: *Facebook, Twitter, LinkedIn, Youtube*

Mark R. Gardner, Chairman
Mark W. Kowlzan, President and CEO
Linda Massman, Second Vice Chairman
Samuel Kerns, VP, Administration and CFO
Chuck Fuqua, Executive Director, Strategic Comm.

Founded in 1887, the Insurance Library Association of Boston is a resource for and provider of literature, information services, and quality professional education for the insurance industry and related interests. The Association offers a wide variety of research services and materials. The collection includes contemporary and historical versions of books, pamphlets, articles and reference materials in all areas of the insurance industry.
550 Members
Founded in 1993
Mailing list available for rent

16235 Interagency Council on Information
American Nurses Association Library
8515 Georgia Avenue
Suite 400
Silver Spring, MD 20910-3492

301-628-5143
FAX 301-628-5008
E-Mail: info@forestfoundation.org
Home Page: www.icirn.org
Social Media: *Facebook, Twitter*

Kenneth Stewart, Chairman
Connie Best, Vice-Chair
Nathan Truitt, Vice President of Development
Scott Smiley, Vice President, Finance
Kathy McGlauflin, SVP, Project Learning Tree

To esablish an effective use of information resources available to the nursing community, and to advance the profession through the promotion and use of its literature.
120 Members

16236 International Association of Aquatic & Mar ine Science Libraries
The International Association of Aquatic and Marin
2030 S Marine Science Drive
Newport, OR 97365

772-460-9977
E-Mail: info@americanforests.org
Home Page: www.iamslic.org
Social Media: *Facebook, Twitter, YouTube*

Ann Nichols, Chair
Scott Steen, President & CEO
Matthew Boyer, Vice President, Individual Giving
Peter Hutchins, VP/COO
Greg Meyer, VP, Corporate Partnerships

Encourages members to exchange scientific and technical information and explore issues of

mutual concern. Conducts workshops about on line databases.
Founded in 1990

16237 International Association of School Librarianship
65 E. Wacker Place
Suite 1900
Chicago, IL 60601-7246

814-474-1115
FAX 312-419-8950
Home Page: www.iasl-online.org/

Michael Snow, Executive Director
An Di H Nguyen, Manager of International Programs
Stefani Brown, International Program Coordinator

IASL provides an international forum for those people interested in promoting effective school library media programs as viable instruments in the educational process.

16238 Library Binding Institute
4440 PGA Blvd.
Ste. 600
Palm Beach Gardens, FL 33410

561-745-6821
FAX 561-472-8401
E-Mail: info@aitc-glulam.org
Home Page: www.lbibinders.org

Don DeVisser P.E., Executive VP
Skeet Rominger, Director Quality Services
Mike Schoen, Controller
Robert A Horlacher, Senior District Manager, Eastern
John Zachariou, Senior District Manager, Western

Members are firms binding books for libraries and their suppliers.
Founded in 1952

16239 Library Leadership and Management Association
American Library Association
50 E Huron Street
Chicago, IL 60611

312-944-6780
800-545-2433
FAX 312-280-5033
E-Mail: lama@ala.org
Home Page: www.ala.org/llama/

Jeff Steely, President
Kerry Ward, Executive Director
Fred Reuland, Program Officer
Jim Rettig, Treasurer

Works to improve and develop all aspects and levels of administration in all types of libraries.
5M Members
Founded in 1957

16240 Library and Information Technology Association
American Library Association
50 E Huron Street
Chicago, IL 60611

312-944-6780
800-545-2433
E-Mail: lita@ala.org
Home Page: www.ala.org/lita/

Thomas P. Dowling, President
Jenny Levine, Executive Director
Mark A. Beatty, Staff Liaison
Melissa Prentice, Program Planning and Marketing
Valerie A Edmonds, Program Coordinator

16241 Major Orchestra Librarians' Association
MOLA

1530 Locust Street
PMB 154
Philadelphia, PA 19102

E-Mail: alsc@alsc.org
Home Page: www.mola-inc.org

Thomas D Searles, President, Chief Lumber Inspectory

International organization whose objectives include: to improve communication among orchestra librarians; present a unified voice in publisher relations; and assist librarians in providing better service to their orchestras.
Founded in 1924

16242 Medical Library Association
65 E Wacker Place
Suite 1900
Chicago, IL 60601-7246

312-419-9094
FAX 312-419-8950
E-Mail: info@sportsbuilders.org
Home Page: www.mlanet.org /
www.marketing.mlanet.org
Social Media: *Facebook, LinkedIn, Blog*

Dan Wright, CFB, Chairman
Pete Smith, CTB, Tennis Division President
Troy Rudolph, Track Division President
Joe Covington, Jr, Indoor Division President
Jim Catella, CFB, CTB, Fields Division President

A nonprofit, educational organization that is a leading advocate for health sciences information professionals worldwide. Through it's programs and services, we provide lifelong educational opportunities, supports a knowledgebase of health information research and works with a global network of partners to promote the importance of quality information for improved health to the health care community and the public.
50 Members
Founded in 1965

16243 Mid-America Association of Law Libraries
MidAmerican Energy Holdings Company
Po Box 657
Des Moines, IA 50306-0657

515-242-4300
800-358-6265
FAX 515-242-4261
E-Mail: jackson@purdue.edu
Home Page: www.midamerican.com

Brian Brookshire, Executive Director
Laura Brookshire, Comm. and Membership Manager
Beverly Heidbreder, Accountant

Association for suppliers of law library equipment, supplies and services.
8 Members
Founded in 1912

16244 Middle East Librarians' Association
Middle East Librarians Association
Main Library
Santa Barbara, CA 93106

805-637-7749
E-Mail: mlmoody@stoel.com
Home Page: www.mela.us
Social Media: *Facebook, Twitter, LinkedIn, RSS*

Kris J. Ormseth, Office Managing Partner

Interested in aspects of librarianship that support the study or dissemination of information about the Middle East. Publishes a bulletin (semi-annually) that is distributed to members and subscriber institutions in North America, Europe, the Middle East, Asia and Africa.
5 Members
Founded in 1907

16245 Mountain Plains Library Association
14293 W. Center Drive

Lakewood, CO 80228

303-985-7795
FAX 605-677-5488
E-Mail: email@awpa.com
Home Page: www.mpla.us

Colin McCown, Executive Vice President

Purpose is to promote the development of librarians and libraries by providing significant educational and networking opportunities. The association meets annually in joint conferences with member stats on a rotational basis, and its governed by an elected board of representatives from each member state and a number of selections and roundtables representing interests and types of libraries. In addition to its board and officers, MPLA activities are carried out by a number of committees.
900 Members
Founded in 1904

16246 Music Library Association
1600 Aspen Commons
Suite 100
Middleton, WI 53562

608-836-5825
FAX 608-831-8200
E-Mail: tom@appalachianwood.org
Home Page: www.musiclibraryassoc.org

Tom Inman, President
Dinah Farrington, Administrative Assistant

Promotes growth and establishment in the use of music libraries, musical instruments and musical literature.
154 Members
Founded in 1926

16247 National Association of Media & Technology Centers
PO Box 9844
Cedar Rapids, IA 52409-9844

319-654-0608
FAX 319-654-0609
E-Mail: info@awinet.org
Home Page: www.namtc.org
Social Media: *Facebook, Twitter, LinkedIn, YouTube, Flickr*

Philip Duvic, Executive Vice President
Greg Heuer, Chief Learning Officer
Cassey Gibson, Chief Member Services Officer
Beth Holcomb, Meeting and Event Planner
Katie Allen, Project Manager

The National Association of Media & Technology Centers is an organization committed to promoting leadership among its membership through networking, advocacy, and support activities that will enhance the equitable access to media, technology, and information services to educational committees. Current membership is over 20 million students.
4000 Members
Founded in 1954

16248 National Church Library Association
National Church Library Association
275 3rd St S
Suite 101A
Stillwater, MN 55082-5094

651-430-0770
E-Mail: Mail@WorldMillworkAlliance.com
Home Page: www.churchlibraries.org
Social Media: *Twitter, LinkedIn*

Joe Bayer, President
Dave Ondrasek, First Vice President
Timothy Lyons, Second Vice President
Rosalie Leone, Chief Executive Officer
Brian Welsh, Membership & Marketing Director

Non-profit support organization that endeavours to further the gospel through church libraries. New resources and support programs are always under development to serve the ever changing needs of the church librarian. Membership is open to individuals, churches or libraries of any denomination or size.
1200 Members
Founded in 1935

16249 National Information Standards Organization
3600 Clipper Mill Road
Suite 302
Baltimore, MD 21211

301-654-2512
FAX 410-685-5278
E-Mail: awfsofc@aol.com
Home Page: www.niso.org
Social Media: *Facebook, Twitter, LinkedIn*

Wade Gregory, President
Archie Thompson, VP
Angelo Gangone, Executive Vice President
Amy Bartz, Fair Sales Director
Nancy Fister, Education & Conference Director

A non-profit association accredited by the American National Standards Institute, identifies, develops, maintains, and publishes technical standards to manage information in our changing and ever-more digital environment.
425 Members
Founded in 1979

16250 National Library Service for the Blind
Library of Congress
1291 Taylor Street, NW
Washington, DC 20542

202-707-5100
800-424-8567
FAX 202-707-0712
E-Mail: info@capital-lumber.com
Home Page: www.loc.gov/nls
Social Media: *Facebook, Twitter, LinkedIn, Pinterest*

Dan Merrill, Division Manager
Bill Bieker, Sales Manager
ISSN: 0363-3805
Founded in 1948
Mailing list available for rent

16251 National Media Market
National Media Market
PO Box 87410
Tucson, AZ 85754-7410

520-743-7735
FAX 800-952-0442
E-Mail: info@capital-lumber.com
Home Page: www.nmm.net
Social Media: *Facebook, Twitter, LinkedIn, Pinterest*

Matt Yates, Branch Manager
Darren Henderson, Operations Manager
Bill Butner, Sales Manager
Cindy DeLand, Office Manager
Phillip Floyd, Account Manager

Presents an exceptional opportunity for media professionals who purchase for public libraries, universities, media/technology centers and educational broadcasting to screen the newst and best quality motion medis from fifty-five prominent producers and distributors.
Founded in 1999

16252 New England Library Association
New England Library Association
55 North Main Street, Unit 49
Belchertown, MA 01007

413-813-5254
FAX 978-282-1304
E-Mail: info@cedarbureau.com

Home Page: www.nelib.org
Social Media: *Facebook, Twitter*

Kent Gibson, Chairman
Ed Watkins, Vice-chairman
Terry Kost, Secretary-Treasurer
Lynne Christensen, MBA, CAE, Director of
Operations
Barbara Enns, Accountant

Promotes excellence in library services to the
people of New England and advances the leadership role of it's members. Holds an annual
conference.
350 Members
Founded in 1915

16253 Public Library Association
Public Library Association
50 E Huron Street
Chicago, IL 60611-5295

312-280-5752
800-545-2433
FAX 312-280-5029
E-Mail: pla@ala.org
Home Page: www.ala.org/pla
Social Media: *Facebook*

Vailey Oehlke, President
Barb Macikas, Executive Director
Julianna Kloeppel, Program Director
Melissa Faubel Johnson, CMP, Meeting &
Special Events Planner
Mary Hirsh, Project Manager

Exists to provide a diverse program of communications and programming for its members
and others interested in the advancment of public libaries.
Founded in 1944

**16254 Reference and User Services
Association**
American Library Association
50 E Huron St
Chicago, IL 60611-2729

312-280-4395
800-545-2433
FAX 312-944-8085
E-Mail: rusa@ala.org
Home Page: www.ala.org/RUSA

Susan Hornung, Executive Director
Andrea Hill, Manager, Web Services
Leighann Wood, Membership Assistant
Marianne Braverman, Marketing & Programs
Manager

Reference and User Services Association is responsible for stimulating and supporting excellence in the delivery of general library services
and materials to adults, and the provision of
reference and information services, collection
development, and resource sharing for all ages,
in every type of library.
5000 Members
Founded in 1876

16255 Society of American Archivists
17 North State Street
Suite 1425
Chicago, IL 60602

312-606-0722
866-722-7858
FAX 312-606-0728
E-Mail: admin@decorativesurfaces.org
Home Page: www2.archivists.org/

Jackson Morrill, President
Donald Bisson, VP, Gov. and Industry Affairs
Jeannie Ervin, VP, Membership and
Administration
Gary Heroux, Vice President, Product
Acceptance
Allyson O'Sullivan, Director of Marketing

Association for those interested in archival theory and practice in North America.
232 Members
Founded in 1960

16256 Southeastern Library Association
P.O. Box 950
Rex, GA 30273

678-466-4334
FAX 678-466-4349
E-Mail: FhvaAwmaWc@CompuServe.com
Home Page: www.selaonline.org/

James Mathers, President
Larry R Frye, Executive Director

For over 60 years, the Association has been a
unifying force strong enough to influence legislation and to attract foundation and federal
funds for regional library projects. The accomplishments of the Association include 2 regional library surveys; the adoption of school
library standards; the establishment of state library agencies and the position of state school
library supervisor; the founding of library
schools; the sponsoring of a variety of
informative workshops.
15 Members
Founded in 1933

16257 Special Libraries Association
331 S Patrick St
Alexandria, VA 22314-3501

703-647-4900
FAX 703-647-4901
E-Mail: license@landmobile.com
Home Page: www.sla.org
Social Media: *Facebook, Twitter*

Kevin Mc Carthy, President

International association of information professionals who work in special libraries serving
business, research, government and institutions
that produce specialized information.
600 Members
Founded in 1947

**16258 State University of New York
Librarians Association**
Office of Library & Information Services
SUNY Plaza
Albany, NY 12246

518-443-5577
FAX 518-443-5358
E-Mail: info@forestlandowners.com
Home Page: www.sunyla.org
Social Media: *Facebook, Twitter*

Joe Hopkins, President
Scott P. Jones, Chief Executive Officer
Susan Johnson Klco, Director of
Administration
Kent Sole, Director of Development
Katelin Baker, Marketing Coordinator

Statewide professional librarian organization.
10500 Members
Founded in 1941

**16259 Substance Abuse Librarians and
Information**
Substance Abuse Librarians & Information
Specialis
PO Box 9513
Berkeley, CA 94709-0513

510-865-6225
FAX 510-865-2467
E-Mail: info@forestprod.org
Home Page: www.salis.org
Social Media: *Facebook, Twitter, LinkedIn*

Maureen Puettman, President
David DeVallance, Vice President
Stefan A. Bergmann, Executive Vice President

Provides professional development and exchange of information and concerns about ac-

cess to and dissemination of information on
substance abuse.
Founded in 1947

16260 Theatre Library Association
40 Lincoln Center Plaza
New York, NY 10023

E-Mail: friendsofthetrees@yahoo.com
Home Page: www.tla-online.org

Michael Pilarski, Founder and Director

Supports librarians and archivists affiliated
with theatre, dance, performance studies,
popluar entertainment, motion picture and
broadcasting collections. Promotes professional
best practices in acquistion, organization, access and preservation of performing arts resources in libraries, archives, museums, private
collections, and the digital environment.
Founded in 1978

**16261 U.S. National Commission on
Libraries and Information Science
(NCLIS)**
1800 M Street NW
Suite 350 North Tower
Washington, DC 20036-5841

FAX 202-606-9203
E-Mail: info@timberpa.com
Home Page: www.nclis.gov/
Social Media: *Facebook, Twitter*

Mark Huempfner, President
Guy Longhini, Vice President
Matt Jensen, Vice President
Henry Schienebeck, Executive Director
Aaron Nieman, Event Coordinator

The U.S. National Commission on Libraries
and Information Science is a permanent, independent agency of the federal government
charged with advising the executive and legislative branches and other public and private organizations on national library and information
policies and plans.

16262 Urban Libraries Council
1333 H Street, NW
Suite 1000 West
Washington, DC 20005

202-750-8650
FAX 312-676-0950
E-Mail: jackhillman@woodtank.com
Home Page: www.urbanlibraries.org

Jack Hillman, Company Contact

Works to strengthen public libraries as an essential part of urban life. Serves as a forum for
research widely recognized and used by public
and prrivate sector leaders.
Founded in 1854

Newsletters

16263 AASL Presidential Hotline
American Library Association
50 E Huron St
Chicago, IL 60611-2788

312-280-2518
800-545-2433
E-Mail: kfiels@ala.org
Home Page: www.ala.org

Keith Michael Fiels, Executive Director

School library media association news.
Frequency: Monthly
Founded in 1951

**16264 Church & Synagogue Libraries
Journal**
Church and Synagogue Library Association

10157 SW Barbur Boulevard #102C
Portland, OR 97219

503-244-6919
800-542-2752
FAX 503-977-3734
E-Mail: csla@worldaccessnet.com
Home Page: www.cslainfo.org
Social Media: *Facebook, Twitter*

Judith Jazen, Administrator/Director
Cheryl Cutchin, President
Maria Isabel Garala, Second VP/Membership Chair
Alice Campbell, Treasurer

The Church & Synagouge Library Assn. provides educational guidance in the establishment and maintenance of congreational libraries.
Cost: $35.00
Frequency: Bi-Monthly
ISSN: 0009-6342
Founded in 1967

16265 Church & Synagogue Libraries Newsletter
Church and Synagogue Library Association
10157 SW Barbur Boulevard #102C
Portland, OR 97219

503-244-6919
800-542-2752
FAX 503-977-3734
E-Mail: csla@worldaccessnet.com
Home Page: www.cslainfo.org
Social Media: *Facebook, Twitter*

Judith Jazen, Religious Leader
Evelyn Pockrass, President
Cheryl Cutchin, First Vice President
David Reed, Second Vice President
Dick Burgduff, Treasurer

16266 Corporate Library Update
Reed Business Information
30 Technology Parkway South
Suite 100
Norcross, GA 30092

646-746-6400
800-424-3996
FAX 646-756-7583
E-Mail: webmaster@reedbusiness.com
Home Page: www.reedbusiness.com

John Poulin, CEO
Lynn Blumenstein, Senior Editor
Susan DiMattia, Editor
Cost: $69.95
Frequency: Fortnightly
Circulation: 2500

16267 Libraries Alive
National Church Library Association
275 3rd St S
Suite 101A
Stillwater, MN 55082-5094

651-430-0770
E-Mail: info@churchlibraries.org
Home Page: www.churchlibraries.org
Social Media: *Facebook*

Sue Benish, Executive Director
Chuck Mann, President Board of Directors

Features informative articles, reviews of books and other media, a sharing of ideas, Internet resources, chapter news, news of authors and upcoming regional and national workshops.
Frequency: Quarterly

16268 Library Hotline
Library Journal/School Library Journal
360 Park Ave S
New York, NY 10010-1710

646-746-6819
800-446-6551

FAX 646-746-6734
Home Page: www.libraryjournal.com

Ron Shank, Publisher
Justin Torres, Production Manager
Lynn Blumenstein, Senior Editor
Carol Batt, COO
Patty Braden, Director
Cost: $115.00
Frequency: Weekly
Founded in 1876

16269 MLA News
Medical Library Association
65 E Wacker Place
Suite 1900
Chicago, IL 60601-7298

312-419-9094
FAX 312-419-8950
E-Mail: info@mlahq.org
Home Page: www.mlanet.org

Lynanne Fielen, Director Publications
Carla Funk, Editor
Lynanne Fielen, Circulation Manager
Elizabeth Rodriguez, Graphic Designer

Covers MLA programs and services as well as the medical librarian profession in general.
Cost: $58.00
Frequency: Monthly
Founded in 1898
Mailing list available for rent

16270 Marcato
MOLA/Editor
1530 Locust Street
PMB 154
Philadelphia, PA 19102

202-416-8131
FAX 202-416-8132
E-Mail: sfriedman@kennedy-center.org
Home Page: www.mola-inc.org

Shelley Friedman, Editor
Gordon Rowley, Treasurer
Elena Lence Talley, President

Newsletter of Major Orchestra Librarians' Association.
Cost: $20.00
Frequency: Quarterly

16271 Marketing Treasures
Chris Olson & Associates
857 Twin Harbor Drive
Arnold, MD 21012-1027

410-647-6708
FAX 410-647-0415
Home Page: www.chrisolson.com

Christine Olson, Publisher

Provinding creative ideas, helpful hints and insights on how libraries can promote thier services
6 Pages
Frequency: Monthly
Circulation: 1000
Founded in 1987
Printed in 2 colors on matte stock

16272 Report on Literacy Programs
Business Publishers
8737 Colesville Road
Suite 1100
Silver Spring, MD 20910-3928

301-876-6300
800-274-6737
FAX 301-589-8493
E-Mail: custserv@bpinews.com
Home Page: www.bpinews.com

Dave Speights, Editor
Leonard A Eiserer, Publisher
Beth Early, Operations Director

Covers all aspects of literacy including legislation, funding, training programs, important

conferences, job skills and much more.
Cost: $317.00
Founded in 1963

16273 Research Library Issues
Association of Research Librarics
21 Dupont Circle NW
Suite 800
Washington, DC 20036

202-296-2296
FAX 202-872-0884
E-Mail: arlhq@arl.org
Home Page: www.arl.org
Social Media: *Facebook, Twitter, LinkedIn, Flickr, YouTube*

Charles B Lowry, Executive Director
Prudence S. Adler, Associate Executive Director
Sue Baughman, Deputy Executive Director
Julia Blixrud, Assistant Executive Director
Mary Jane Brooks, Assistant Executive Director

Member representatives
Frequency: Bi-Monthly
ISSN: 1947-4911

16274 State University of New York Librarians Association
Office of Library & Information Services
SUNY Plaza
Albany, NY 12246

518-443-5577
FAX 518-443-5358
E-Mail: drewwe@morrisville.edu
Home Page: www.sunyla.org
Social Media: *Facebook, Twitter*

Wilfred Drew, President
John Schumacher, Electronic Resources Coordinator

Provides news, notes and information from SUNY campus libraries.
Frequency: 2-3/Year

16275 Technicalities
Westport Publishing
802 Broadway Street
Kansas City, MO 64105

816-842-0641

Brian Alley, Editor

A professional journal presenting discussion, opinions, and reviews on library-management topics. Typical issues include articles ranging from computer applications, on-line public access catalogs, library budgets, collection building, book reviews, automation, software, library marketplace trends, and the Library of Congress. Articles are indexed in Library Literature and LISA: Library Information Science Abstracts and are available on microfilm from UMI.
Cost: $ 47.00
16 Pages
Frequency: Monthly
Circulation: 700
Mailing list available for rent
Printed in one color on matte stock

16276 Urban Libraries Council Exchange Letter
1603 Orrington Avenue
Suite 1080
Evanston, IL 60201

847-866-9999
FAX 847-866-9989
E-Mail: info@urbanlibraries.org
Home Page: www.urbanlibraries.org/

Eleanor Rodger, President/CEO
Linda Crismond, Editor

Newsletter for public libraries in cities with over 100,000 people. Free to members, also

available without membership.
Cost: $50.00
150 Pages
Circulation: 6000
Founded in 1971

Magazines & Journals

16277 AALL Spectrum
American Association of Law Libraries
105 W Adams Street
Suite 3300
Chicago, IL 60603

312-939-4764
FAX 312-431-1097
E-Mail: support@aall.org
Home Page: www.aallnet.org
Social Media: *Facebook, Twitter*

Mark Estes, Editorial Director
Hillary Baker, Marketing and Communications
Kate Hagan, Executive Director
Kim Rundle,, Executive Assistant
Emily Feltren,, Director of Government Relations

Publishes substantive, well-written articles on topics of real interest to law librarians, as well as news about the American Association of Law Libraries, including its chapters, committees and Special Interest Sections
Cost: $ 75.00

16278 Advanced Technology/Libraries
GK Hall & Company
1239 Broadway
Suite 1601
New York, NY 10001-4327

212-685-0602
FAX 212-654-4751
E-Mail: sales@gkimport.com
Home Page: www.gkimport.com

Dina Groudan, President
Audrey Ismal, Owner

Concise, practical information on the advances in development, implementation and use of library automation. Articles cover new products, new services, legislation and grant information.
Cost: $95.00
Frequency: Monthly

16279 American Archivist
Society of American Archivists
527 S Wells Street
5th Floor
Chicago, IL 60607-3922

312-922-0140
FAX 312-347-1452
Home Page: www.archivists.org

Susan Fox, Executive Director
Philip B Eppard, Editor
Teresa Brinati, Director of Publications

Offers information and essays on archival theory and practice in North America.
Cost: $85.00
Circulation: 4800+
Founded in 1936

16280 American Libraries
American Library Association
50 E Huron St
Chicago, IL 60611-2788

312-280-2518
800-545-2433
E-Mail: customerservice@ala.org
Home Page: www.ala.org

Claire Knowles, Manager
Carla D Hayden, President

Library development news.
Cost: $60.00
Frequency: Monthly
Founded in 1876

16281 Book Report: Magazine for Secondary School Librarians
Linworth Publishing
480 East Wilson Bridge Road
Suite L
Worthington, OH 43085

614-436-7107
800-786-5017
FAX 614-436-9490
E-Mail: linworth@linworthpublishing.com
Home Page: www.linworth.com

Marlene Woo-Lun, Publisher
Amy Robinson, Marketing Manager

In-depth articles, helpful hints, and reviews on books, software, videos, and CD-Roms for secondary school librarians.
Cost: $49.00
105 Pages
Circulation: 15000
Founded in 1981
Printed in 4 colors on glossy stock

16282 Booklist
American Library Association
50 E Huron St
Chicago, IL 60611-2788

312-280-2518
800-545-2433
E-Mail: customerservice@ala.org
Home Page: www.ala.org

Claire Knowles, Manager

To provide a guide to current library materials in many formats appropriate for use in public libraries and school library media centers.
Cost: $89.95
Circulation: 25000
Founded in 1876

16283 Bulletin of Bibliography
Greenwood Publishing Group
88 Post Road W
P O Box 5007
Westport, CT 06881-5007

203-226-3571
800-225-5800
FAX 203-226-6009
E-Mail: customer-service@greenwood.com
Home Page: www.greenwood.com

Bernard McTigue, Editor-in-Chief
Gerry Katz, Executive Editor
Naomi Caldwell Wood, Author

Offers bibliographies in humanities and social sciences.
Cost: $125.00
100 Pages
Frequency: Quarterly
Circulation: 1000
ISSN: 0190-745X
Printed in 2 colors on matte stock

16284 Bulletin of the Center for Children's Books
501 E Daniel Street
MC-493
Champaign, IL 61820

217-244-0324
FAX 217-244-3302
Home Page: alexia.lis.uiuc.edu

Deborah Stevenson, Editor
Marlow Welshon, Dean

Reviews of children's books for librarians, teachers, booksellers and parents.
Cost: $50.00
34 Pages
Frequency: Monthly

Circulation: 6500
Founded in 1893

16285 CD-ROM Librarian
Mecklermedia Corporation
11 Ferry Lane W
Westport, CT 06880-5808

FAX 203-454-5840

Alan Meckler, Editor

A periodical intended for the library professional.
Cost: $80.00
Frequency: Monthly
Founded in 1986

16286 Catholic Library World
Catholic Library Association
205 W Monroe St, Ste 314
Pittsfield, MA 01201-5178

413-443-2252
FAX 413-442-2252
E-Mail: cla@cathla.org
Home Page: www.cathla.org
Social Media: *Facebook*

Nancy K Schmidtmann, President
Malachy R McCarthy, VP
Jean R Bostley SSJ, Executive Director

Articles and news of interest to the library profession. Extensive section of book and media reviews
Frequency: Quarterly
ISSN: 0008-820X

16287 Choice
Association of College and Research Libraries
575 Main Street
Suite 300
Middletown, CT 06457

800-545-2433
E-Mail: acrl@ala.org
Home Page: www.ala.org/acrl/choice

Lori Goetsch, President
Irving Rockwood, Publisher
Francine Graf, Editorial Director
Lisa Gross, Information/Production Manager
Rita Balasco, Choice Reviews

Publishes reviews of books, internet sites, and microcomputer software suitable for college and university libraries.
Cost: $280.00
Frequency: Monthly
Circulation: 5000
Founded in 1938

16288 Congregational Libraries Today
Church and Synagogue Library Association
2920 SW Dolphin Court
Suite 3A
Portland, OR 97219-4055

503-244-6919
800-542-2752
FAX 503-977-3734
Home Page: www.cslainfo.org

Jeri Zulli, Publications Editor

Contains news about CSLA and its chapters, feature stories about congregational libraries and librarians, promotion ideas, information on using computers and the internet in the library, and reviews of books, videos, CDs, and audiotapes for adults and children.
Frequency: Quarterly
Circulation: 2500

16289 Information Retrieval & Library Automation
Lomond Publications

PO Box 88
Mount Airy, MD 21771-0088

202-362-1361
FAX 202-362-6156

Thomas Hattery, Publisher

New technology, products and equipment that improve information systems and library services, for science, social, social science, law, medicine, academic institutions and the public.
Cost: $75.00
Frequency: Monthly

16290 Journal of the Medical Library Association
Medical Library Association
65 E Wacker Drive
Suite 1900
Chicago, IL 60601-7298

312-419-9094
800-462-6420
FAX 312-419-8950
E-Mail: info@mlahq.org
Home Page: www.mlanet.org

Lynanne Feilen, Director Publication
Carla J Funk, Executive Director
Susan C Talmage, Editorial Assistant
Bleu caldwell, Production Assistant
Barbara Redmond, Advertising Coordinator
Cost: $163.00
Frequency: Quarterly
Mailing list available for rent

16291 Knowledge Quest
American Library Association
50 E Huron St
Chicago, IL 60611-2788

312-280-2518
800-545-2433
E-Mail: kfiels@ala.org
Home Page: www.ala.org

Keith Michael Fiels, Executive Director
Andria Parker, Marketing
Vickie William, Circulation Manager

Articles on teaching, learning process, ideas and information to prepare students for life long learning.
Cost: $40.00
Circulation: 5000
ISSN: 1094-9046
Founded in 1879
Printed in 4 colors on matte stock

16292 Library Bookseller
PO Box 9544
Berkeley, CA 94709-544
Scott Saifer, Publisher
Gail Russin, Editor

A journal focusing on suppliers to libraries.
Cost: $100.00
36 Pages

16293 Library Journal
Media Source
160 Varick Street
11th Floor
New York, NY 10013

646-380-0700
FAX 646-380-0756
E-Mail: ljinfo@mediasourceinc.com
Home Page: www.libraryjournal.com

Ron Shank, Publisher
Francine Fialkoff, Editor-in-Chief
Brian Kenney, Editorial Director
Bette-Lee Fox, Managing Editor
Rebecca Miller, Executive Editor

Provides groundbreaking features and analytical news reports covering technology, management, policy and other professional concerns to public, academic and institutional libraries. Evaluates 8000 reviews annually of books, ebooks, audiobooks, videos/DVDs, databases,

systems and websites.
Cost: $141.00
Circulation: 17936
Founded in 1876
Printed in 4 colors on glossy stock

16294 Library Resources & Technical Services
American Library Association
50 E Huron St
Chicago, IL 60611-2788

312-280-2518
800-545-2433
E-Mail: kfiels@ala.org
Home Page: www.ala.org

Keith Michael Fiels, Executive Director
Steven L Hofman, Circulation Manager
Andrea Parker Parker, Marketing Head

Offers articles to technical service librarians on acquisitions, cataloging and classification.
Cost: $30.00
Frequency: Bi-annually
Circulation: 60000
Founded in 1951

16295 Library Software Review
Sage Publications
Vanderbilt University
419 21st Avenue S
Nashville, TN 37240-0001

615-343-6094
FAX 615-343-8834
E-Mail: info@sagepub.com
Home Page: www.sagepub.com

Marshall Breeding, Editor

Provides the library professional with information necessary to make intelligent software evaluation, procurement, integration and installation decisions. Issues review software and software books and periodicals.
Cost: $52.00
Frequency: Quarterly
Circulation: 1M

16296 Library Talk: Magazine for Elementary School Librarians
Linworth Publishing
480 E Wilson Bridge Road
Suite L
Worthington, OH 43085-2372

614-436-7107
800-786-5017
FAX 614-436-9490
E-Mail: linworth@linworthpublishing.com
Home Page: www.linworth.com

Marlene Woo-Lun, Publisher
Amy Robinson, Marketing Manager
Carol Simpson, Consulting Editor

In-depth articles, helpful hints, and reviews on books, software, and CD-ROMS for elementary school library media and technology specialist.
Cost: $49.00
68 Pages
Circulation: 10000
Founded in 1988
Printed in 4 colors on glossy stock

16297 Library Trends
University of Illinois Press
1325 S Oak St
Champaign, IL 61820-6975

217-333-0950
866-244-0626
FAX 217-244-8082
E-Mail: journals@uillinois.edu
Home Page: www.press.uillinois.edu

Willis Regier, Director
Ann Lowry, Journals Manager
Cheryl Jestis, Manager
Pat Hoefling, Marketing and Sales Director

A journal which offers a medium for current thought and information in the library field.
Cost: $75.00
Frequency: Quarterly
Circulation: 2600
ISBN: 0-252725-23-9
Founded in 1918

16298 Medical Reference Services Quarterly
Taylor & Francis
325 Chestnut Street
Suite 800
Philadelphia, PA 19106

800-354-1420
FAX 215-625-2940
Home Page: www.tandf.co.uk

M Sandra Wood, Editor

An essential working tool for medical and health sciences librarians. Covers topics of current interest and practical value in the areas of reference in medicine and related specialities, the biomedical sciences, nursing and allied health.
Cost: $110.00
Frequency: Quarterly
ISSN: 0276-3869
Founded in 1975

16299 Reference and User Services Quarterly (RUSQ)
American Library Association
50 E Huron St
Chicago, IL 60611-2788

312-280-2518
800-545-2433
FAX 312-664-7459
E-Mail: customerservice@ala.org
Home Page: www.ala.org

Keith Michael Fiels, Executive Director
Andrea Parker, Marketing Specialist
Steven L Hofmann, Manager, Communications
Connie Van Fleet, Editor in Chief

News of interest to reference and adult services librarians.
Cost: $60.00
Frequency: Quarterly
Circulation: 6,246
Founded in 1951

16300 School Library Journal
Media Source
160 Varick Street
11th Floor
New York, NY 10013

646-380-0700
FAX 646-380-0756
E-Mail: sljinfo@mediasourceinc.com
Home Page: www.schoollibraryjournal.com

Ron Shank, Publisher
Francine Fialkoff, Editor-in-Chief
Brian Kenney, Editorial Director
Bette-Lee Fox, Managing Editor
Rebecca Miller, Executive Editor

Provides groundbreaking features and analytical news reports covering technology, management, policy and other concerns to school libraries. Evaluates 8000 reviews annually of books, ebooks, audiobooks, videos/DVDs, databases, systems and websites.
Frequency: Monthly
Circulation: 100000
Founded in 1954
Printed in 4 colors on glossy stock

16301 School Library Media Research
American Library Association
50 E Huron St
Chicago, IL 60611-2788

312-280-2518
800-545-2433

E-Mail: kfiels@ala.org
Home Page: www.ala.org

Keith Michael Fiels, Executive Director
Available online only. Current developments in
the media and library field. Evaluates the most
currently available print and nonprint materials
for library media centers.

16302 Science and Technology Libraries
Taylor & Francis
325 Chestnut Street
Suite 800
Philadelphia, PA 19106

800-354-1420
FAX 215-625-2940
Home Page: www.tandf.co.uk

Tony Stankus, Editor-in-Chief
A peer-reviewed, scholarly journal covering all
aspects of the profession as librarians serving
science, engineering, clinical investigation, and
agriculture.
Cost: $110.00
Frequency: Quarterly
ISSN: 0194-262X
Founded in 1978

16303 Today's Librarian
Virgo Publishing LLC
3300 N Central Ave
Suite 300
Phoenix, AZ 85012-2532

480-990-1101
FAX 480-990-0819
E-Mail: mikes@vpico.com
Home Page: www.vpico.com

Jenny Bolton, President
John Siefert, CEO
Kelly Ridley, Executive VP, CFO
Heather Wood, VP, Human Resources
Jon Benninger, VP, Health & Nutrition
Network
Of interest to librarians and media profession-
als.

16304 Video Librarian
Video Librarian
3435 NE Nine Boulder Drive
Poulsbo, WA 98370

360-626-1259
FAX 360-626-1260
E-Mail: vidlib@videolibrarian.com
Home Page: www.videolibrarian.com

Randy Pitman, Publisher
Anne Williams, Graphic Designer
Carol Kaufman, Graphic Designer

Offers video reviews and news for public,
school, academic and special libraries.
Cost: $64.00
56 Pages
Circulation: 2000
ISSN: 0887-6851
Founded in 1986
Printed in 4 colors on glossy stock

Trade Shows

16305 ACL Conference
Association of Christian Librarians
PO Box 4
Cedarville, OH 45314

937-766-2255
FAX 937-766-5499
E-Mail: info@acl.org
Home Page: www.acl.org
Social Media: *Facebook, Twitter, Delicious*

Jo Ann Rhodes, President
Alice Ruleman, VP

Janelle Mazelin, Executive Director
Sheila O. Carlblom, Treasurer
Carrie Beth Lowe, Secretary
The purpose of the conference is to provide
professional information, promote Christian
philosophy and ethic of librarianship, provide
an opportunity for exchange of ideas and promote service to the academic community
worldwide
550 Members
Founded in 1954

**16306 ALA National Conference on Asian
Pacific American Librarians**
American Library Association
50 E Huron Street
Chicago, IL 60611

800-545-2433
E-Mail: customerservice@ala.org
Home Page: www.ala.org

**16307 American Association of School
Librarians National Conference &
Exhibition**
50 E Huron Street
Chicago, IL 60611-5295

312-280-4386
800-545-2433
FAX 312-664-7459
E-Mail: customerservice@ala.org
Home Page: www.ala.org/aasl

Judy King, Director Program Development
Lissa Salvatierra, Meeting Planner
Biennial continuing education conference and
300-500 exhibits of equipment, supplies and
services for school library media centers, including print and nonprint materials and other
equipment.
3500 Attendees
Frequency: October
Founded in 1876

**16308 American Indian Library Association
Conference**
American Indian Library Assn Univ. of
Pittsburgh
207 Hillman Library
Pittsburgh, PA 15260

412-621-4470
FAX 412-648-1245
Home Page: http://www.ailanet.org

Lisa A Mitten
Annual conference and exhibits relating to the
development, maintenance and cultural information services on reservations and in communities of Native Americans and Native
Alaskans.
Founded in 1979

**16309 American Library Association
Annual Conference**
American Library Association
50 E Huron Street
Chicago, IL 60611

800-545-2433
E-Mail: customerservice@ala.org
Home Page: www.ala.org

Loriene Roy, President
Keith Michael Fiels, Executive Director
Annual meeting and exhibits of books, periodicals, reference works, audio visual equipment,
films, data processing services, computer hardware and software, library equipment and
supplies.

**16310 American Library Association
Midwinter Meeting**
American Library Association

50 E Huron Street
Chicago, IL 60611

800-545-2433
E-Mail: customerservice@ala.org
Home Page: www.ala.org

Loriene Roy, President
Keith Michael Fiels, Executive Director
Annual meeting and 418 exhibits of books, periodicals, reference works, audio visual equipment, films, data processing services, computer
hardware and software, library equipment and
supplies.

**16311 Art Libraries Society of North
America Annual Conference**
Art Libraries Society of North America
4101 Lake Boone Trail
Suite 201
Raleigh, NC 27607-7506

919-518-1919
800-892-7547
FAX 919-787-4916
E-Mail: arlisna@mercury.interpath.com

Annual conference and show of publishers,
book dealers, library suppliers and visual resources suppliers.
500 Attendees
Founded in 1977

**16312 Association for Library &
Information Science Education
Annual Conference**
11250 Roger Bacon Drive
Suite 8
Reston, VA 20190-5202

703-360-0500
FAX 703-435-4390
Home Page: www.alise.org/index.shtml

John Budd, President
Deborah York, Executive Director
Frequency: January

**16313 Association for Population/Family
Planning Libraries & Information
Centers**
Assn for Population Family Planning
Libraries
Surgical Contraception-79 Madison
New York, NY 10016

212-780-2687
FAX 212-779-9439

William Record
Annual conference and exhibits for effective
documentation, information systems and services in the field of population/family
planning.

**16314 Association of College and Research
Libraries**
American Library Association
50 E Huron Street
Chicago, IL 60611-5295

312-280-2511
800-545-2433
FAX 312-280-2520
E-Mail: customerservice@ala.org
Home Page: www.ala.org/acrl

Mary Ellen Davis, Executive Director
Two hundred exhibitors with computers and
web products, audiovisual products, furniture
and library equipment.
3000 Attendees
Frequency: Biennial
ISSN: 0099-0086
Founded in 1978
Mailing list available for rent

16315 CSLA Conference
Church and Synagogue Library Association

2920 SW Dolphin Court
Suite 3A
Portland, OR 97219-4055

503-244-6919
800-542-2752
FAX 503-977-3734
Home Page: www.cslainfo.org

Judith Janzen, Administrator
150 Attendees
Frequency: Annual/July

16316 Culture Keepers: Making Global Connections
Black Caucus of the American Library Association
Newark Public Library
5 Washington Street
Newark, NJ 07101

973-961-2540
FAX 973-522-4827

Dr. Alex Boyd

Biennial show and exhibits of books, journals and library products.

16317 Federal and Armed Forces Libraries Roundtable Conference
American Library Association
50 E Huron St
Chicago, IL 60611-2729

312-944-6780
800-545-2433
FAX 312-944-8085
E-Mail: ala@ala.org
Home Page: www.ala.org/faflrt/front

Emily Sheketoff, Executive Director

Annual conference and exhibits of equipment, supplies and services for libraries and information services.

16318 International Association of Aquatic & Marine Science Libraries Conference
Harbor Branch Oceanographic Institution
5600 US 1 N
Fort Pierce, FL 34946

800-333-4264
FAX 772-465-2446

Annual conference and exhibits of equipment, supplies and services for marine-related libraries and information centers.
Frequency: October, Charleston

16319 Mid-Atlantic Regional Library Federation
South Maryland Regional Library
37 606 New Market Road
Charlotte Hall, MD 20622

301-884-0436

Katharine Hurrey, President

Offers exhibits by vendors who provide services and products useful to libraries and information brokers.
1M Attendees
Frequency: March

16320 Mountain Plains Library Association Annual Conference
Mountain Plains Library Association
University of SD-I D Weeks Library
Vermillion, SD 57069

FAX 605-677-5488

Annual conference and exhibits of publications and library equipment, supplies and services.
600 Attendees

16321 New England Library Association Annual Conference
New England Library Association

14 Main Street
Gloucester, MA 03031

978-820-0787
FAX 978-282-1304
Home Page: www.nelib.org

Mary Ann Rupert, Technology Manager
Barry Blaisdell, Manager

Annual show of publishers, distributors and suppliers of books, media, supplies, furniture, equipment, hardware, software and services used by libraries. Containing 160 booths and 130 exhibits.
1,000 Attendees
Frequency: October

16322 Public Library Association National Conference
Public Library Association
50 E Huron Street
Chicago, IL 60611-5295

312-280-5752
800-545-2433
FAX 312-280-5029
E-Mail: pla@ala.org

Barb Macikas, Show Manager

Biennial show of 200 exhibitors of books and other equipment, supplies and services for libraries.
3500 Attendees
Frequency: March

16323 Southeastern Library Association
Combined Book Exhibit
P.O. Box 950
Rex, GA 30273

678-466-4334
FAX 678-466-4349
Home Page: http://selaonline.org/

This biennial conference, offers attendees from over 12 states. The convention offers exhibits, meetings and an open reception in the exhibit hall. The three biggest states, Georgia, North Carolina and South Carolina spend twice as much of expenditures on CD-ROM and 8% more on books than the national average, which makes this the perfect exhibition for sellers.
2.1M+ Attendees
Frequency: Fall

16324 Special Libraries Association
331 South Patrick St
Alexandria, VA 22314-3501

703-647-4900
FAX 703-647-4901
E-Mail: janice@sla.org
Home Page:
http://www.sla.org/content/SLA/contactus/index.cfm

James Mears, Conference Manager
Janice Lschance, CEO

An international professional association of people working in special libraries serving institutions and organizations that use or produce specialized information.
6M Attendees
Frequency: June

Directories & Databases

16325 Address List, Regional and Subregional Libraries for the Handicapped
Library of Congress

101 Independence Avenue SE
Washington, DC 20540

202-707-4800
888-657-7323
FAX 202-707-0712
E-Mail: nls@loc.gov
Home Page: www.loc.gov/nls
Social Media: *Facebook, Twitter, LinkedIn*

Kurt Cykle, Director
25 Pages
Frequency: Semi-Annual
ISSN: 0363-3805
Mailing list available for rent

16326 American Library Association Handbook
American Library Association
50 E Huron St
Chicago, IL 60611-2788

312-280-2518
800-545-2433
E-Mail: customerservice@ala.org
Home Page: www.ala.org

Claire Knowles, Manager

Offers 56 regional groups comprised of libraries, trustees, librarians and others interested in the responsibilities of libraries in the educational and cultural needs of society.

16327 American Library Directory
Information Today
143 Old Marlton Pike
Medford, NJ 08055-8750

609-654-6266
800-300-9868
FAX 609-654-4309
E-Mail: custserv@infotoday.com
Home Page: www.infotoday.com

Thomas H Hogan, President
Roger R Bilboul, Chariman Of The Board

Detailed profiles for more than 35,000 public, academic, special, and government libraries and library related organizations in the US and Canada. These include addresses, phone and fax numbers, e-mail addresses, network participation, expenditures, holdings and special collections, key personnel, special services and more than 40 categories of library information in all. A two volume set.
Cost: $299.00
4000 Pages
ISBN: 1-573872-04-0
Mailing list available for rent

16328 Association of Jewish Libraries Membership List
Ramaz Upper School Library
60 E 78th St
New York, NY 10075-1838

212-517-2103

Ira Miller, Principal
Cost: $100.00
100 Pages
Frequency: Annual

16329 BookQuest
ABACIS
135 Village Queen Drive
Owings Mills, MD 21117-4470

FAX 410-581-0398

This database offers descriptions of book dealers' offerings and books being sought by libraries, dealers and collectors.
Frequency: Full-text

16330 Chief Officers of State Library Agencies Directory
Chief Officers of State Library Agencies

201 E Main St
Suite 1405
Lexington, KY 40507-2004

859-514-9151
FAX 859-514-9166
Home Page: www.cosla.org

Tracy Tucker, Executive Director

Directors, staff and consultants of state librar-
ies.
Cost: $25.00
Frequency: Annual April

**16331 Computers in Libraries: Buyer's
Guide & Consultants Directory Issue**
Mecklermedia Corporation
11 Ferry Lane W
Westport, CT 06880-5808

This comprehensive directory offers a list of
suppliers of computer products and services for
use in libraries.
Cost: $30.00
Frequency: Annual

16332 DataLinx
Faxon Company
1001 W Pines Road
Oregon, IL 61061-9507

815-732-9001
800-732-9001
FAX 815-732-2132
Home Page: www.faxon.com

This online system was established to provide
technical support to libraries for serials acquisition and control.

**16333 Directory of Special Libraries and
Information Centers**
Gale Research
27500 Drake Road
Farmington Hills, MI 48331-3535

248-699-4253
800-877-4253
FAX 877-363-4253
E-Mail: gale.galeord@cengage.com
Home Page: www.gale.cengage.com
Social Media: *Facebook, Twitter, Youtube*

Patrick C Sommers, President

Provides detailed contact and descriptive information on subject-specific resource collections
maintained by various government agencies,
businesses, publishers, educational and nonprofit organizations, and associations around
the world.
3600 Pages
Frequency: Annual
ISBN: 1-414433-49-2

**16334 Directory of US Government:
Depository Libraries**
Joint Committee on Printing, US Congress
1309 Longworth
Washington, DC 20515

202-225-8281
FAX 202-225-9957

Directory of federal depository libraries, regional and select throughout the United States.
Includes list of GPO bookstores.
91pp Pages
Frequency: Annual

16335 EBSCONET
EBSCO Publishing
Po Box 682
Ipswich, MA 01938-0682

978-356-1372
800-653-2726
FAX 978-356-6565
Home Page: http://www.ebsco.com

Timothy S Collins, President

This database provides technical support to libraries, information centers and purchasing departments for serials acquisitions and control.

**16336 Employment Sources in the Library
and Information Professions**
National Center for Information Media &
Technology
University of Hertfordshire, College Lane
Chicago, IL 60611

773-846-7300
E-Mail: customerservice@ala.org
Home Page: www.ala.org

Directory of services to the industry.
140 Pages
Frequency: Annual

16337 Gale Directory of Databases
Gale/Cengage Learning
27500 Drake Road
Farmington Hills, MI 48331-3535

248-699-4253
800-877-4253
FAX 877-363-4253
E-Mail: gale.galeord@cengage.com
Home Page: www.gale.cengage.com
Social Media: *Facebook, Twitter, Youtube*

Patrick C Sommers, President
Bob Romanick, Editor

Profiles thousands of databases available
worldwide in a variety of formats. Entries include producer name and contact information,
description, cost and more.
ISBN: 1-414420-79-X

16338 Interlibrary Loan Policies Directory
Neal-Schuman Publishers
100 William St
New York, NY 10038-5017

212-925-8650
800-584-2414
FAX 212-219-8916
E-Mail: info@neal-schuman.com
Home Page: www.neal-schuman.com

Patricia Schuman, Owner

A brand new edition of the standard source of
current information about the policies of over
1,425 academic, public and other libraries that
offer books through interlibrary loans in the
United States, Canada and Puerto Rico. Updated to include all the members of the Association of Research Libraries, Internet addresses,
Ariel addresses and libraries that loan periodicals, government documents, microfilms, software, newspapers, media and foreign countries.
Cost: $119.95
800 Pages

16339 Librarian's Yellow Pages
Garance
7823 Stratford Road
Bethesda, MD 20814

240-354-1281
Home Page: www.librarianyellowpages.com

A database offering information on products
and services intended for use by libraries and
information centers in the United States.

16340 Library Fax/Ariel Directory
CBR Consulting Services
PO Box 22421
Kansas City, MO 64113-0421

Over 10,500 libraries with telefacsimile services in the United States and Canada and
worldwide.
Cost: $49.50
475 Pages
Frequency: Annual

**16341 Library Literature & Information
Science**
HW Wilson Company
950 Dr Martin L King Jr Blvd
Bronx, NY 10452-4297

718-588-8405
FAX 718-590-1617
Home Page: www.hwwilson.com

Harold Regan, CEO
Kathleen McEvoy, Director of Public Relations

Comprehensive listings are offered in this database on more than 25,000 citations to articles
and reviews of books, periodicals and audiovisual materials in the library and information
science areas.

**16342 Library Periodicals: An Annual
Guide for Subscribers, Authors and
Publicists**
Periodical Guides Publishing
1633 Pearl Street
Alameda, CA 94501-3065

510-865-7439

Over 150 journals and newsletters in the
United States and Canada of national or inter-
national scope devoted to library science.
Cost: $18.00
55 Pages
Frequency: Annual

**16343 One Hundred and One Software
Packages to Use in Your Library**
American Library Association
50 E Huron St
Chicago, IL 60611-2788

312-280-2518
800-545-2433
E-Mail: customerservice@ala.org
Home Page: www.ala.org

Claire Knowles, Manager

Directory of services and supplies to the industry.

**16344 Subject Directory of Special Libraries
& Information Centers**
Gale/Cengage Learning
27500 Drake Road
Farmington Hills, MI 48331-3535

248-699-4253
800-877-4253
FAX 877-363-4253
E-Mail: gale.galeord@cengage.com
Home Page: www.gale.cengage.com
Social Media: *Facebook, Twitter, Youtube*

Patrick C Sommers, President

Presents entries culled from the Directory of
Special Libraries and Information Centers in
three volumes arranged by subject matter. This
rearrangement is especially important for all
users who frame their searches in a subject context. In addition to expanded international coverage, users will also find fax numbers, E-mail
addresses, Web and Internet addresses and increased reporting of online services
Frequency: Annual/Set
ISBN: 1-414434-59-6

**16345 Univ. of Missouri School of
Journalism: Freedom of Information
Center**
University of Missouri
133 Neff Annex
Columbia, MO 65210-0012

573-882-7539
FAX 573-884-6204
Home Page: www.missouri.edu/~foiwww

Charles N Davis, Executive Director
Kathleen M Edwards, Center Manager

Reference and research library serving the public and media regarding access to government information. The center has a collection of over a million articles and documents concerning access to information at state, federal and local levels and offers a wide variety of online documents through its webpage.

16346 Who's Who in Special Libraries
Special Libraries Association
1700 18th St Nw
Washington, DC 20009-2508

202-234-4700
FAX 202-265-9317

Directory of services and supplies to the industry.
Cost: $50.00
364 Pages
Frequency: Annual

Industry Web Sites

16347 http://gold.greyhouse.com
G.O.L.D Grey House OnLine Databases
Grey House Publishing's online database platform, GOLD, offers Quick Search, Keyword Search and Expert Search for most business sectors including library markets. The GOLD platform makes finding the information you need quick and easy - whether you're a novice searcher or an experienced database user. All of Grey House's directory products are available for subscription on the GOLD platform.

16348 www.aallnet.org
American Association of Law Libraries

16349 www.acl.org
Association of Christian Librarians
Membership is composed of over 500 evangelical Christian librarians representing primarily evangelical institutions of higher education.

16350 www.aiip.org
Association Independent Information Professionals

16351 www.akla.org
Alaska Library Association

16352 www.ala.org
American Library Association
Association for librarians, libraries, trustees, students and academics, encompassing all aspects of librarianship.

16353 www.ala.org./alcts
Assn for Library Collections & Technical Services
A division of the American Library Association.

16354 www.ala.org/aasl
American Association of School Librarians
Works to ensure that all members of the school library media field collaborate to: provide leadership in the total eduction program; participate as active partners in the teaching/learning process; connect learners with ideas and information; and prepare students for life-long learning. The American Association of School Librarians is a division of the American Library Association.

16355 www.ala.org/acrl
Association of College and Research Libraries
A division of the American Library Association. Represents academic and research librarians.

16356 www.ala.org/alsc
Association for Library Service to Children
A division of the American Library Association. For persons interested in the improvement and extension of library services to children.

16357 www.ala.org/lama
Library Administrative Management Association
Works to improve and develop all aspects and levels of administration in all types of libraries. The Library Administrative Management Association is a division of the Young Adult Library Services Association, which is part of the American Library Association.

16358 www.ala.org/yalsa
The Young Adult Library Services Association
Responsible for the evaluation and selection of books and nonbook materials and the interpretation and use of materials for teenagers and young adults. The Young Adult Library Services Association is a division of the American Library Association.

16359 www.alise.org/index.shtml
Association for Library & Information Science
Education

16360 www.allanet.org
Alabama Library Association

16361 www.amianet.org
Association of Moving Image Archivists

16362 www.arl.org
Association of Research Libraries
Non profit organization striving to shape and influence forces affecting the future of research libraries in the process of scholarly communication.

16363 www.arlib.org
Arkansas Library Association
Includes constitution and bylaws, conference information, publication, membership, and links to the Arkansas State Library.

16364 www.arlisna.org
Art Libraries Society of North America
Membership organization for art libraries in the US and Canada.

16365 www.arma.org
Assoc. for Information Management Professionals

16366 www.arsc-audio.org
Association for Recorded Sound Collections
Persons in broadcasting and recording industries, librarians, sound archivists, curators, private collectors and reviewers.

16367 www.asindexing.org
American Society of Indexers
A national association with international membership and interests. A nonprofit charitable organization for indexers, librarians, abstractors, editors, publishers, database producers, and organizations concerned with indexing, seeking cooperation and membership of all persons, groups or institutions interested in indexing. Founded in 1968 to promote excellence in indexing and increase awareness of the value of well-written indexes.

16368 www.atla.com/home.html
American Theological Library Association
Provides indexing services in these formats: online database, CD-ROM versions, magnetic

tape for OPAC tapeload and print publications. ATLA Religion indexes in print include Religious Index One: Periodicals, Religion Index Two: Multi-Author Works, Index to Book Reviews, Research in Ministry: an Index to D. Min. Project Reports and Theses. ETHICS Index, a new ATLA interdisciplinary index on CD-ROM, contains indexing from polygraphs, articles, journals and newspapers.

16369 www.azla.org
Arizona Library Association

16370 www.bcala.org
Black Caucus of the American Library Association
Meets annually in conjunction with the American Library Association in August.

16371 www.beta-phi-mu-org
Beta Phi Mu

16372 www.cal-webs.org/aboutus.html
Colorado Association Of Libraries

16373 www.cala-web.org
Chinese-American Librarians Association

16374 www.cla-net.org
California Library Association

16375 www.clir.org
Council on Library & Information Resources

16376 www.cni.org
Coalition for Networked Information

16377 www.csla.org
Church and Synagogue Library Association
Provides educational guidance in the establishment and maintenance of congregational libraries

16378 www.ctlibraryassociation.org
Connecticut Library Association
Professional organization of librarians, library staff, friends, and trustees working together: to improve library service to Connecticut, to advance the interests of librarians, library staff, and librarianship, and to increase public awareness of libraries and library services.

16379 www.dla.lib.de.us
Delaware Library Association

16380 www.flalib.org
Florida Library Association

16381 www.floridamedia.org
Florida Library Association

16382 www.folgers.edu
Independent Research Libraries Association
Seeks to provide consultation to members concerning mutual problems.

16383 www.folusa.com
Friends of Libraries (FOLUSA)
Encourages the development of excellent library service to all residents of the US Aids in forming local and state friends branches in academic and special libraries.

16384 www.glma-inc.org/
Georgia Media Library Association

16385 www.greyhouse.com
Grey House Publishing
Authoritative reference directories for most business sectors including library markets. Users can search the online databases with varied search criteria allowing for custom searches by product category, geographic area, sales vol-

ume, keyword, subject and more. Full Grey House catalog and online ordering also available.

16386 www.hlaweb.org
Hawaii Library Association

16387 www.hooverassociation.org
Herbert Hoover Presidential Library Association

Foster the collection, interpretation and preservation of historical resources relating to the life, ideas, values, and times of Herbert Hoover, thirty-first President of the United States; we will promote public education about and appreciation for Herbert Hoover, support the Hoover Presidential Library-Museum and the National Historic Site at West Branch, Iowa, effectively garner and prudently manage Association resources, and serve Association members.

16388 www.idaholibaries.org
Idaho Library Association

16389 www.idaholibraries.org
Idaho Library Association

16390 www.ifla.org
International Federation of Library Associations

16391 www.ila.org
Illinois Library Association

16392 www.ilfonline.org
Indiana Library Federation

16393 www.iowalibraryassociation.org
Iowa Library Association

16394 www.kylibasn.org
Kentucky Library Association

16395 www.lff.org
Americans for Libraries Council

16396 www.library.ucr.edu/COLT
Council on Library/Media Technicians

Meets annually in conjunction with the American Library Association in August.

16397 www.lita.org
Library and Information Technology Association

Concerned with information dissemination in the areas of library information technology and automation. The Library and Information Technology Association is a division of the American Library Association.

16398 www.llaonline.org
Louisiana Library Association

16399 www.mainelibraries.org
Maine Library Association

16400 www.masslib.org
Massachusetts Library Association

16401 www.mdlib.org
Maryland Library Association

16402 www.misslib.org
Mississippi Library Association

16403 www.mla.lib.mi.us
Michigan Library Association

16404 www.mlanet.org
Medical Library Association

MLA is dedicated to the dissemination of quality health sciences information for use in education, research, and patient care.

16405 www.mnlibraryassociation.org
Minnesota Library Association

16406 www.molib.org
Missouri Library Association

16407 www.mtlib.org
Montana Library Association

The mission of the Montana Library Association is to develop, promote, and improve library and information services and the profession of librarianship in order to enhance learning and ensure accesss to information to all.

16408 www.musiclibraryassoc.org
Music Library Association

Promotes growth and establishment in the use of music libraries, musical instruments and musical literature.

16409 www.namtc.org
National Association of Media & Technology Centers

16410 www.nativeculture.com/lisamitten/aila.html
American Indian Library Association

Association for Native Americans and Native Alaskans libraries and librarians.

16411 www.nclaonline.org
North Carolina Library Association

16412 www.nclis.gov
U.S. National Commission On Libraries & Information Science

16413 www.ndsl.lib.state.nd.usndla
North Dakota Library Association

16414 www.nelib.org
New England Library Association

16415 www.nevadalibraries.org
Nevada Library Association

16416 www.niso.org
National Information Standards Organization

16417 www.njla.org
New Jersey Library Association

16418 www.nmla.org
New Mexico Library Association

16419 www.nmm.net
National Media Market

16420 www.nol.org/home/nla
Nebraska Library Association

16421 www.nursingworld.org/icirn/indate.htm
Library American Journal of Nursing Compliance

Comprised of representatives from agencies and organizations concerned with library needs of nurses.

16422 www.nyla.org
New York Library Association

16423 www.oelma.org
Ohio Educational Library Media Association

16424 www.oema.net
Oregon Educational Media Association

16425 www.oklibs.org
Oklahoma Library Association

16426 www.olaweb.org
Oregon Library Association

16427 www.olc.org
Ohio Library Council

16428 www.palibraries.org
Pennsylvania Library Association

16429 www.pla.org
Public Library Association

Plans programs on current public library issues and concerns, develops publications for public librarians and disseminates statistics on public libraries. The Public Library Association is a division of the American Library Association.

16430 www.pnla.org
Pacific Northwest Library Association

16431 www.rig.org
Research Libraries Group

16432 www.rusa.org
Reference & User Services Association

16433 www.salis.org
Substance Abuse Librarians & Info. Specialists

Provides professional development and exchange of information and concerns about access to and dissemination of information on substance abuse.

16434 www.scla.org
South Carolina Library Association

16435 www.seflin.org/seflin/aboutsef.cfm
Southeast Florida Library Information Network

16436 www.skyways.lib.ks.us/kla
Kansas Library Association

16437 www.sla.org
Special Libraries Association

International association of information professionals who work in special libraries serving business, research, government and institutions that produce specialized information.

16438 www.state.nh.us/nhla
New Hampshire Library Association

16439 www.taet.org
Texas Association for Educational Technology

16440 www.tla.library.unt.edu/default.asp
Theatre Library Association

16441 www.tnla.org/
Tennessee Library Association

16442 www.txla.org
Texas Library Association

16443 www.ublib.buffalo.edu/libraries/units/cts
University of North Florida, Carpenter Library

For catalogers of audiovisual materials and electronic resources. Provides information exchange, continuing education, and works toward a common understanding of practices and standards.

16444 www.uic.edu/depts/lib/projects/resources
Asian/Pacific American Librarians Association

Librarians and information specialists of Asian Pacific descent working in the United States.

16445 www.ula.org
Utah Library Association

16446 www.urbanlibraries.org
Urban Libraries Council
Works to strengthen public libraries as an essential part of urban life. Serves as a forum for research widely recognized and used by public and private sector leaders.

16447 www.uri.edu/library/rila/rila.html
Rhode Island Library Association

16448 www.usd.edu/mpla
Mountain Plains Library Association

16449 www.usd.edu/sdla
South Dakota Library Association

16450 www.vermontlibraries.org
Vermont Library Association

16451 www.vla.org
Virginia Library Association

16452 www.wla.lib.wi.us
Wisconsin Library Association

16453 www.wla.org
Washington Library Association

16454 www.worldaccessnet.com/nesla
Church and Synagogue Library Association
Religious groups interested in promoting church or synagogue libraries comprise the membership. This association also offers a bi-monthly newsletter to all its members.

16455 www.worldaccessnet.com/netsa
Church and Synagogue Library Association
Religious groups interested in promoting church or synagogue libraries comprise the membership. This association also offers a bi-monthly newsletter to all its members.

16456 www.wvla.org
West Virginia Library Association

16457 www.wyla.org
Wyoming Library Association

Associations

16458 American Agricultural Editors' Association

American Agricultural Editors' Association
120 Main Street W
PO Box 156
New Prague, MN 56071

952-758-6502
FAX 952-758-5813
E-Mail: ljovanovich@hardwood.org
Home Page: www.ageditors.com
Social Media: *Facebook, Twitter, Youtube, Pinterest*

Susan M Regan, Executive VP

National professional development member association for agricultural communicators.
55 Members

16459 American Independent Writers

1001 Connecticut Ave Nw
Suite 701
Washington, DC 20036-5547

202-775-5150
FAX 202-775-5810
E-Mail: hpva@hpva.org
Home Page: www.amerindywriters.org/

Kip Howlett, HPVA President
Eva Mentel, Office Manager
Ketti Tyree, Membership and Conventions Manager
Matthew Windt, Marketing Manager

An association that seeks to create an open and inclusive community of authors, journalists and other writers.
73 Members
Founded in 1921

16460 American Medical Writers' Association

American Medical Writers' Association
30 W Gude Dr
Suite 525
Rockville, MD 20850-4347

240-238-0940
FAX 301-294-9006
E-Mail: paraman@vt.edu
Home Page: www.amwa.org

Philip Araman, President

Concerned with the advancement and improvement of medical communications.

16461 American Society of Journalists and Authors

American Society of Journalists and Authors
355 Lexington Avenue
15th Floor
New York, NY 10017-6603

212-997-0947
FAX 212-937-2315
Home Page: www.asja.org
Social Media: *Facebook, Twitter*

Jack Goldman, President & CEO
David E. Woodbury, Jr., Director - Finance & Operations
Debbie Scerbo, Office Manager
Ryan Carroll, Director - Government Affairs
John Crouch, Director - Public Affairs

Association for journalists and authors.
2600 Members
Founded in 1980

16462 American Translators Association

American Translators Association

225 Reinekers Lane
Suite 590
Alexandria, VA 22314

703-683-6100
FAX 703-683-6122
E-Mail: info@intforest.org
Home Page: www.atanet.org

Tom Troxel, Executive Director
Ben Wudtke, Forest Programs Manager

ATA membership is open to anyone with an interest in translation and interpreting as a profession or as a scholarly pursuit.
Founded in 1986

16463 Association of American Collegiate Literary Societies

Philomathean Society
College Hall
Box G
Philadelphia, PA 19104
Andrew Smith, Governor

Works with literary societies in the United States to promote the creation of new societies, existing societies and reviving old societies.
400 Members
Founded in 1978

16464 Association of Authors' Representatives, Inc.

302A W 12th St.
#112
New York, NY 10014

E-Mail: administrator@aaronline.org
Home Page: aaronline.org

Gail Hochman, President

Professional organization whose members represent book authors and playwrights.
400+ Members

16465 Association of Professional Writing

Professional Writers Association
P.O. Box 7474
Daytona Beach, FL 32116

386-265-4279
E-Mail: info@iwpawood.org
Home Page: www.prowriters.org
Social Media: *Facebook, Twitter, LinkedIn*

Craig Forester, President
Bronson Newburger, Vice President
JoAnn Gillebaard Keller, Treasurer
Cindy L Squires, Esq., Executive Director
Joseph L. O'Donnell, Manager

Organization founded to establish standards for writing consultants. Other goals are to draw new members into the writing consulting field. Also offers a referral system for companies looking for writing consultants.
220 Members
Founded in 1956

16466 Association of Writers & Writing Programs

George Mason University
4400 University Dr., MSN 1E3
Fairfax, VA 22030

703-993-4301
FAX 703-993-4302
Home Page: www.awpwriter.org
Social Media: *Facebook, Twitter, Pinterest*

David W. Fenza, Executive Director

Support, resources and advocacy for writers and creative writing programs, conferences and centers.
Founded in 1967

16467 Before Columbus Foundation

The Raymond House

655 13th Street
Suite 302
Oakland, CA 94612

510-268-9775
E-Mail: infor@lma.org
Home Page: www.beforecolumbusfoundation.com
Social Media: *Facebook, Twitter*

Honorable Carro Breaux, President
Ronnie C Harris, Executive Director
Kerry Landry, Chief Financial Officer
Cliff Palmer, LaMATS Executive Director
Nikki Samrow, Events Coordinator

Participants are individuals interested in promoting contemporary American multicultural literature.
Founded in 1926

16468 Center for the Book

Library of Congress
101 Independence Avenue SE
Washington, DC 20540

202-707-5000
FAX 202-707-0269
Home Page: www.loc.gov/loc/cfbook

Steven Smith, President/Director
Elliott Smith, VP
Richard J Arde, Secretary/Treasurer

This organization strives to stimulate consumer interest in books and reading.
Founded in 1876
Mailing list available for rent

16469 Children's Literature Association (ChLA)

1301 W 22nd St.
Suite 202
Oak Brook, IL 60523

630-571-4520
FAX 708-876-5598
E-Mail: info@childlitassn.org
Home Page: www.childlitassn.org
Social Media: *Facebook, Twitter*

Annette Wannamaker, President

ChLA is a nonprofit dedicated to promoting the study of children's literature.

16470 Council of Biology Editors

1000 East Henrietta Road
Rochester, NY 14623

585-292-2000
E-Mail: info@msrlumber.org
Home Page: www.monroecc.edu

Dan Uskoski, President
Stacy Tiefenbach, Secretary/Treasurer
Sean Shields, Business Manager

Represents those members in life sciences who write for journals, medical science publications, and textbooks.
Founded in 1987

16471 Council on National Literatures

Council on National Literatures
68-02 Metropolitan Avenue
Middle Village, NY 11379

718-821-3916
E-Mail: mfma@maplefloor.org
Home Page: www.cnliteratures.com
Social Media: *Facebook, Twitter, Pinterest*

Daniel F. Heney, Executive Director
Heather Currier, Marketing Communications Director
Daniel J. Krupa, Technical Director
Madhuri Carson, Conference Manager
Amber Montgomery, Order Processing Specialist

Provides a forum for scholars concerned with comparative study of literature.
175 Members
Founded in 1897

16472 Dramatists Guild of America
1501 Broadway
Suite 701
New York, NY 10036-5505

212-398-9366
FAX 212-944-0420
E-Mail: info@nari.org
Home Page: www.dramatistsguild.com/
Social Media: *Facebook, Twitter, Pinterest, Houzz, YouTube*

Kevin Anundson, MCR, CKBR, Chairman
Judy Mozen, CR, GCP, President
Tom Miller, Treasurer
Elsie Iturralde, CAE, Chief Operations Officer
Fred Ulreich, Chief Executive Officer

Protects the rights of its international membership of playwrights, composers and lyricists. Supports fair royalty, maintenance of subsidiary rights, artistic control and ownership of copyright.
Founded in 1983

16473 Editorial Freelancers Association
Editorial Freelancers Association
71 W 23rd St
4th Fl
New York, NY 10010-4102

212-929-5400
866-929-5425
FAX 212-929-5439
E-Mail: info@nofma.org
Home Page: www.the-efa.org
Social Media: *Facebook, Twitter, LinkedIn*

Michael Martin, President & CEO
Bree Urech-Boyle, CFO
Anita Howard, COO
Adam Williams, Marketing Manager
Laura Boyle, Marketing Production Coordinator

National nonprofit, professional organization of self-employed workers in the publishing and communications industries.
27 Members
Founded in 1908

16474 Education Writers Association
Education Writers Association
3516 Connecticut Avenue NW
Suite 201
Washington, DC 20008

202-452-9830
FAX 202-452-9837
E-Mail: info@nfba.org
Home Page: www.ewa.org
Social Media: *Facebook, RSS*

Ken Gieseke, Chair
Todd Carlson, Secretary-Treasurer
Mike Dunipace, Director
Dan Nyberg, Director
Terry Burrow, Director

The Education Writers Association is the national professional organization of education reporters and intent of improving education reporting to the public.
Founded in 1969

16475 Freelance Editorial Association
PO Box 380835
Cambridge, MA 02238-0835

617-643-8626
E-Mail: membership@nhla.com
Home Page: www.freelancepubs.com
Social Media: *Facebook, Twitter, LinkedIn, RSS*

Pem Jenkins, President
Brent Stief, 1st Vice President

Mark Barford, Chief Executive Officer
Kristina Bran, Digital Media Manager
Trisha Clariana, Office Manager

Offers editorial services that include editing, writing, proofreading, graphic design, desktop publishing, and project managemant.
1600 Members
Founded in 1898
Mailing list available for rent

16476 International Food, Wine and Travel Writers Association
39252 Winchester Rd
Ste 107 #418
Murrieta, CA 92563

877-439-8929
909-860-6914
951-970-8326
FAX 877-439-8929
E-Mail: info@dealer.org
Home Page: www.ifwtwa.org
Social Media: *Facebook, Twitter, LinkedIn*

JD Saunders, Chair
Jonathan M. Paine, President/CEO
Laura DeMaria, Membership Services Manager
Ben Gann, VP, Legislative & Political Affairs
Frank Moore, Regulatory Counsel

Staff and/or freelance writers in the food, wine and travel field. Also includes other media professionals and industry associate members in 28 countries worldwide.
6000 Members
Founded in 1916

16477 Mystery Writers of America
1140 Broadway
Suite 1507
New York, NY 10001

212-888-8171
FAX 212-888-8107
E-Mail: info@nwfa.org
Home Page: www.mysterywriters.org
Social Media: *Facebook, Twitter, LinkedIn*

Michael Martin, President & CEO
Anita Howard, COO
Bree Urech-Boyle, CFO
Debbie Edgar, Human Resources Manager
Laura Boyle, Marketing Production Coordinator

Professional writers of crime and mystery stories and novels. Unpublished writers are affiliate members. MWA annually gives the Edgar Awards for excellence in the mystery genre.
3000 Members
Founded in 1985

16478 National Association of Hispanic Journalists
1050 Connecticut Avenue NW
Washington, DC 20036

202-662-7145
FAX 202-662-7144
E-Mail: membersupport@wdma.com
Home Page: www.nahj.org
Social Media: *Facebook, Twitter, LinkedIn, RSS Feeds*

Al Babiuk, Chairman
Michael O'Brien, CAE, President & CEO
John McFee, Vice President, Certification
Jeff Lowinski, Vice President, Technical Services
Jeffrey Inks, VP, Code & Regulatory Affairs

NAHJ is dedicated to the recognition and professional advancement of Hispanics in the news industry. NAHJ created a national voice and unified vision for all Hispanic journalists.
140 Members
Founded in 1926

16479 National Federation of Press Women
National Federation of Press Women

200 Little Falls Street
Suite 405
Falls Church, VA 22046

703-237-9804
800-780-2715
FAX 703-237-9808
E-Mail: pjsherry@nepapallet.com
Home Page: www.nfpw.org
Social Media: *Facebook, Twitter, LinkedIn, YouTube*

Brent J. McClendon, CAE, President/CEO
Isabel Sullivan, VP, Operations and Events
Brad Gething, PhD, Technical and PDS Manager
John A. McLeod III, Director
Annette Ferri, Comm. & Education Director

Members are writers, editors and other communication professionals for newspapers, magazines, wire services, agencies and freelance.
700+ Members
Founded in 1947
Mailing list available for rent: 1700 names at $40 per M

16480 National Writers Association
10940 S Parker Rd
Suite 508
Parker, CO 80134-7440

303-841-0246
FAX 303-841-2607
E-Mail: sales@kiln-direct.com
Home Page: www.nationalwriters.com

William Smith, Executive Director

Exists to enhance the future of writers by fostering continuing education through award winning scholarships and providing no or low cost workshops and seminars. A non-profit organization, we provide education and an ethical resource for writers at all levels of experience.
650 Members
Founded in 1951

16481 Newspaper Features Council
22 Byfield Lane
Greenwich, CT 06830

203-661-3386
FAX 203-661-7337

A forum for editors, writers, columnists, cartoonists and syndicates to exchange views and improve the content of newspapers.
130 Members
Founded in 1955

16482 Outdoor Writers Association of America
615 Oak St
Suite 201
Missoula, MT 59801-1896

406-728-7434
800-692-2477
FAX 406-728-7445
E-Mail: info@nawla.org
Home Page: www.owaa.org
Social Media: *Facebook, Twitter, LinkedIn*

Scott Elston, Chairman
Jim McGinnis, First Vice Chairman
Bill Adams, Second Vice Chairman
Marc Saracco, Executive Director
Ben Barclay, Manager

Nonprofit, international organization representing over 2,000 professional outdoor communicators who report on diverse interests in the outdoors.
600+ Members
Founded in 1893

16483 Self-Employed Writers and Artists Network
PO Box 175
Towaco, NJ 07082

E-Mail: nela@northernlogger.com
Home Page: www.njcreatives.org

Joseph E. Phaneuf, Executive Director
Eric A Johnson, Executive Editor
Mona Lincoln, Coordinator of Training and Safety
Debbie Haehl, Advertising Manager
Nancy E. Petrie, Circulation Manager

For more then 2 decades, companies and agencies alike have relied on the NJ Creatives Network organization as a cost-efficient, reliable source for freelance talent-from writers and artists to designers and photographers, plus film and video producers, and more.
2000 Members
Founded in 1952

16484 Society of American Business Editors and Writers
ASU, Walter Cronkite School of Journalism
555 North Central Ave, Suite 416
Phoenix, AZ 85004-1248

602-496-7862
FAX 602-496-7041
Home Page: www.sabew.org

Tom Partin, President

Members are financial and economic news writers and editors for print and broadcast outlets.
70 Members
Founded in 1987

16485 Society of American Travel Writers
One Parkview Plaza
Suite 800
Oakbrook Terrace, IL 60181

414-359-1625
FAX 414-359-1671
E-Mail: info@nlassn.org
Home Page: www.satw.org
Social Media: *Facebook*

William Wood, Chairman of the Board
Cody Nuernberg, President
Abbie Diekmann, Membership & Financial Assistant
Jodie Fleck, Director of Conventions & Tours
Melanie Hultman, Communications Coordinator

Photographers and 35 associate member representatives of airlines, hotels, resorts, tourist agencies and public relations firms.
1.5M Members
Founded in 1890

16486 Space Coast Writers Guild
PO Box 262
Melbourne, FL 32902

E-Mail: osbguide@tecotested.com
Home Page: www.scwg.org

Nonprofit, tax-exempt organization of writers of all genres.
Cost: $35.00
Frequency: Annual
Founded in 1978

16487 Writers Alliance
12 Skylark Lane
Stony Brook, NY 11790-3121

516-751-7080

Writers' organization.

16488 Writers Guild of America: West
Writers Guild of America

7000 W 3rd St
Los Angeles, CA 90048-4329

323-951-4000
800-548-4532
FAX 323-782-4800
E-Mail: rikki@pacificloggingcongress.com
Home Page: www.wga.org
Social Media: *Facebook, Twitter*

Rikki Wellman, Executive Director
Craig Olson, President
Ron Simon, Treasurer

An independent labor union representing writers in motion pictures, television and radio in the west.
550 Members
Founded in 1909

16489 Writers Research Group LLC
Po Box 891568
Oklahoma City, OK 73189-1568

405-682-2589
FAX 405-685-3390
E-Mail: info@lumber-exporters.org
Home Page: www.writersresearchgroup.com
Social Media: *Facebook, Twitter, LinkedIn, Google+*

David Stallcop, President
Chip Setzer, Vice-President
Mark Rodakowski, Secretary
Chris Knowles, Treasurer

Writers Research Group is a professional writing and research firm. Our knowledgeable employees gather, examine, edit, and compile data to your company's specifications. Our services include research, writing, directory listing updates and new entries, indexing, copyediting, proofreading, data entry, document markup and permissions negotiations.
Founded in 1923

Newsletters

16490 AGENDA
National Federation of Press Women
PO Box 34798
Alexandria, VA 22334-0798

800-780-2715
FAX 703-237-9808
E-Mail: jane@janeleecomm.com
Home Page: www.nfpw.org
Social Media: *Facebook, Twitter, LinkedIn, Youtube*

A quarterly newletter published by the National Federation of Press Women.
Cost: $51.50
4 Pages
Frequency: Quarterly
Circulation: 2000
Founded in 1937
Mailing list available for rent: 1700 names at $40 per M

16491 ASJA Newsletter
American Society of Journalists and Authors
1501 Broadway
Suite 302
New York, NY 10036-5505

212-997-0947
FAX 212-937-2315
E-Mail: staff@asja.org
Home Page: www.asja.org
Social Media: *Facebook, Twitter, LinkedIn*

Alexandra Owens, Executive Director
Lisa Collier Coloradool, President
Barbara Barrett, Newsletter Editor

Confidential news for journalists and authors, available only to members of the Society.
Frequency: Monthly
Founded in 1948

16492 American Writer
American Independent Writers
1001 Connecticut Ave Nw
Suite 701
Washington, DC 20036-5547

202-775-5150
FAX 202-775-5810
E-Mail: info@aiwriters.org
Home Page: www.amerindywriters.org/

Donald Graul, Executive Director

News and information for freelance writers.
Cost: $160.00
8 Pages
Frequency: Monthly
Founded in 1975

16493 Copy Editor
McMurry
1010 E Missouri Ave
Phoenix, AZ 85014-2602

602-395-5850
888-626-8779
FAX 602-395-5853
Home Page: www.mcmurry.com

Chris McMurry, CEO
Barbara Wallraff, Editor

Helps editors stay up-to-date with the changing language. Articles discuss new words, changes in usage and reference books. Each issue contains interviews with copy editors.
Cost: $69.00
8 Pages
Circulation: 2000
Founded in 1990
Printed in one color

16494 EFA Newsletter
Editorial Freelancers Association
71 W 23rd St
Suite 1910
New York, NY 10010-4181

212-929-5400
866-929-5400
FAX 212-929-5439
E-Mail: office@the-efa.org
Home Page: www.the-efa.org

Judi Greenstein, Office Manager
J P Partland, Co-Executive
Mary Ratcliffe, Editor
Martha Schuenman, Executive Director
Pat Molholt, Secretary

Book reviews, news, features and reports on matters of interest to writers, indexers and editors.
Cost: $20.00
Frequency: 6 issues/year
Founded in 1970

16495 Editorial Eye
Editorial Experts
66 Canal Center Plz
Suite 200
Alexandria, VA 22314-5507

703-683-0683
800-683-8380
FAX 703-683-4915
E-Mail: info@eeicommunications.com
Home Page: www.eeicom.com

Jim De Graffenreid, President
Candee Wilson, Director
Robin Cormier, VP Publications
Linda B Jorgensen, Editor
Keith C. Ivey, Technical Editor

Professional standards and practices for editors, writers and publication managers.
Cost: $139.00
12 Pages
Frequency: Monthly
Circulation: 3,000
Founded in 1972

16496 Freelance Writer's Report
CNW Publishing
PO Box A
North Stratford, NH 03590

603-922-8338
800-351-9278
FAX 603-922-8339
E-Mail: info@writers-editors.com
Home Page: www.writers-editors.com

Dana K Cassell, Executive Director

News and marketing information for freelance writers.
Cost: $39.00
Frequency: Monthly
Circulation: 1200

16497 IDEAS Unlimited for Editors
Omniprint
9700 Philadelphia Ct
Lanham, MD 20706-4405

301-731-7000
800-774-6809
FAX 301-731-7001
E-Mail: info@omniprint.net
Home Page: www.omniprint.net

Ken Kaufman, President
Stephen Brownan, VP

Editorial ideas and graphics for editors of in-house, corporate newsletters. Provides 16 pages of fresh, ready-to-use items and ideas editors can use to fill out their publications.
Cost: $5.00
16 Pages
Frequency: Monthly
Circulation: 6310
Founded in 1973
Printed in one color on matte stock

16498 KEYSTROKES
Writers Alliance
12 Skylark Lane
Stony Brook, NY 11790-3121

516-751-7080

Kiel Stuart, Publisher
Howard Austerlitz, Editor
Charles Spataro, Circulation Manager

A writers newsletter containing marketing, how-to and computer information.
Cost: $10.00
16 Pages
Frequency: TriAnnual
Circulation: 250
Mailing list available for rent: 250 names
Printed in one color on matte stock

16499 Linington Lineup
1223 Glen Ter
Glassboro, NJ 08028-1315

856-589-1571

Rinehart S Potts, Editor

Editing, publishing, police procedural.
Cost: $12.00
16 Pages
Frequency: Bi-Monthly
Circulation: 400
Founded in 1984
Printed in one color on matte stock

16500 NWA Newsletter
National Writers Association

10940 S Parker Rd
Suite 508
Parker, CO 80134-7440

303-841-0246
FAX 303-841-2607
E-Mail: natlwritersassn@hotmail.com
Home Page: www.nationalwriters.com

Sandy Whelchel, Executive Director

A monthly e-mail newsletter that includes information on upcoming contests and conferences, announcements and job opportunities
2000 Members
Frequency: Monthly
Founded in 1938

16501 Speechwriter's Newsletter
Ragan Communications
316 N Michigan Ave
Suite 400
Chicago, IL 60601-3773

312-960-4100
800-493-4867
FAX 312-960-4106
E-Mail: cservice@ragan.com
Home Page: www.ragan.com

Jim Ylisela, Publisher
David Murray, Editor
Rebecca Anderson, Managing Editor

Offers speechwriting tips, examples and criticism.
Cost: $307.00
4 Pages
Frequency: Monthly
Founded in 1980

16502 Story Bag: National Storytelling Newsletter
5361 Javier St
San Diego, CA 92117-3215

858-569-9399
FAX 858-569-0205
E-Mail: storybag@juno.com

Professional storytellers, whether freelance or working for a school or library, will find this newsletter stuffed full of tips on techniques, suggestions for handling the business, reviews of storytelling books and tapes, listings of events nationwide, bibliographies of suggested materials, and discussion of issues such as censorship. Note: Above phone is used on e-mail, if busy try again.
Cost: $15.00
8 Pages
Frequency: Bi-Monthly
Circulation: 300
Printed in one color on matte stock

16503 Strategic Employee Publications
Lawrence Ragan Communications
316 N Michigan Ave
Suite 400
Chicago, IL 60601-3773

312-960-4100
800-878-5331
FAX 312-960-4106
E-Mail: cservice@ragan.com
Home Page: www.ragan.com

Jim Ylisela, Publisher
David Murray, Editor
Diane Tillman, Marketing Manager

Designed to help organizational editors produce their company publications.
Cost: $139.00
8 Pages
Frequency: Monthly
Circulation: 2500
Founded in 1970
Printed in 2 colors on matte stock

16504 Writers Connection
Writers Connection

1826 Crossover Roade
PMB 108
Fayetteville, AR 72703

Home Page: www.thewritersconnection.com

Provides how-to information for writers, plus listings of markets, contests and events. Accepts advertising.
Cost: $45.00
16 Pages
Frequency: Monthly

Magazines & Journals

16505 ATA Chronicle
American Translators Association
225 Reinekers Lane
Suite 590
Alexandria, VA 22314

703-683-6100
FAX 703-683-6122
E-Mail: ata@atanet.org
Home Page: www.atanet.org
Social Media: Facebook, Twitter

Nicholas Hartmann, President
Walter Bacak, Executive Director
Kirk Lawson, Accounting Manager
Jamie Padula, Chapter & Division Relations
Teresa Kelly, Meetings Manager

Contains feature articles, announcements, reviews, and association news.
Cost: $65.00
Frequency: Monthly
Circulation: 11,100

16506 Latinos in the US: A Resource Guide for Journalists
National Association of Hispanic Journalists
529 14th St Nw # 1240
Washington, DC 20045-2520

202-789-1157
FAX 202-347-3444
E-Mail: rnutting@marketwatch.com
Home Page: www.marketwatch.com

Rex Nutting, Manager
Joseph Torres, Communications Director
Rex Nutting, Manager

Purposes are to increase educational and career opportunities in journalism for Hispanic Americans.
Cost: $8.50
Mailing list available for rentat $500 per M

16507 Modernism/Modernity
2715 N Charles Street
Baltimore, MD 21218-4319

410-516-6900
800-548-1784
FAX 410-516-6968
E-Mail: claity@drew.edu
Home Page: www.press.ghu.edu/journals

Jeffrey T Schnapp, Editor
Becky Brasington Clark, Marketing Director
Tom Lovett, Circulation Manager
Ken Sabol, Production Manager

Focuses systematically on the methodological, archival, and theoretical exigencies particular to modernist studies. It encourages and interdisciplinary approach linking music, architecture, the visual arts, literature, and social and intellectual history.
Cost: $40.00
Frequency: Quarterly
Founded in 1994

Trade Shows

16508 ATA Annual Conference
American Translators Association
225 Reinekers Lane
Suite 590
Alexandria, VA 22314

703-683-6100
FAX 703-683-6122
E-Mail: ata@atanet.org
Home Page: www.atanet.org
Social Media: *Facebook, Twitter*

Nicholas Hartmann, President
Walter Bacak, Executive Director
Kirk Lawson, Accounting Manager
Jamie Padula, Chapter & Division Relations
eresa Kelly, Meetings Manager
2000 Attendees

16509 AWP Conference & Bookfair
Association of Writers & Writing Programs
George Mason University
4400 University Dr., MSN 1E3
Fairfax, VA 22030

703-993-4301
FAX 703-993-4302
E-Mail: registration@awpwriter.org
Home Page:
www.awpwriter.org/awp_conference/overview
Social Media: *Facebook, Twitter, Pinterest*

The largest literary conference in North America.
12K+ Attendees
Frequency: Annual

16510 Agricultural Publications Summit
American Agricultural Editors' Association
120 Main Street W
PO Box 156
New Prague, MN 56071

952-758-6502
FAX 952-758-5813
E-Mail:
aaea@gardnerandgardnercommunications.com
Home Page: www.ageditors.com

Den Gardner, Executive Director
Holly Martin, President
Kenna Rathai, Associate Executive Director
Frequency: July

16511 American Society of Journalists and Authors Conference
American Society of Journalists and Authors
1501 Broadway
Suite 302
New York, NY 10036-5501

212-997-0947
FAX 212-937-2315
E-Mail: director@ajsa.org
Home Page: www.asja.org
Social Media: *Facebook, Twitter, LinkedIn*

Alexandra Owens, Executive Director
Salley Shannon, President
Barbara DeMarco- Barrett, Newsletter Editor
Stephen Morril, Web Editor
Bruce Miler, Web Master

A forum for the exchange of ideas between journalists.
700 Attendees
Frequency: May

16512 Annual Multimedia Convention & Career Expo (NAHJ)
National Association of Hispanic Journalists

Disney's Coronado Spings Resort
1000 W Buena Vista Drive
Lake Buena Vista, FL 32830

866-257-5990
Home Page: www.nahjconvention.org
Social Media: *Facebook, Twitter, LinkedIn, YouTube*

Michele Salcedo, President
Manuel De La Rosa, Vice President/Broadcast
Russell Contreras, VP Print/Financial Officer
NAHJ is dedicated to the recognition and professional advancement of Hispanics in the news industry. NAHJ created a national voice and unified vision for all Hispanic journalists.
2300 Members
Frequency: August
Founded in 1984

16513 ChLA Conference
1301 W 22nd St.
Suite 202
Oak Brook, IL 60523

630-571-4520
FAX 708-876-5598
Home Page:
www.childlitassn.org/annual-conference
Roberta Seelinger Trites, Chair, Conf. Planning Committee
Jackie Stallcup, Committee Member
Annette Wannamaker, Committee Member
Eric Tribunella, Committee Member
Jennifer Miskec, Committee Member

Academic conference focused on the scholarly study of children's and adolescent literature.
Frequency: Annual/June
Founded in 1973

16514 SABEW Annual Conference
Society of American Business Editors & Writers
ASU, Walter Cronkite School of Journalism
555 North Central Ave, Suite 416
Phoenix, AZ 85004-1248

602-496-7862
FAX 602-496-7041
E-Mail: sabew@sabew.org
Home Page: www.sabew.org
Social Media: *Facebook, Twitter, LinkedIn*

Carrie Paden, Executive Director
Rex Seline, VP
Jon Lansner, Secretary/Treasurer
Brant Houston, Executive Director
Frequency: April

Directories & Databases

16515 AWP Official Guide to Writing Programs
Association of Writers & Writing Programs
Mail Stop 1E3
Fairfax, VA 22030

703-993-4301
FAX 703-993-4302
E-Mail: awp@awpwriter.org

Supriya Bhatngar, Director of Publications

About 300 colleges and universities offering workshops and degree programs in creative writing; approximately 100 writers' conferences, colonies and centers; coverage includes Canada and the United Kingdom.
Cost: $24.95
400 Pages
Frequency: Biennial

16516 American Directory of Writer's Guidelines
Dustbooks

PO Box 100
Paradise, CA 95967-0100

530-877-6110
800-477-6110
FAX 530-877-0222
E-Mail: directories@dustbooks.com
Home Page: www.dustbooks.com

Brigitte M Phillips, Editor
Susan D Klassen, Editor
Doris Hall, Editor

These guidelines help writers target their submissions to the exact needs of the individual publisher. A compilation of information for freelancers from more than 1,500 magazine editors and book publishers.
Cost: $29.95
752 Pages
ISBN: 1-884956-40-8

16517 American Library Directory
Information Today
143 Old Marlton Pike
Medford, NJ 08055-8750

609-654-6266
800-300-9868
FAX 609-654-4309
E-Mail: custserv@infotoday.com
Home Page: www.infotoday.com

Thomas H Hogan, President
Roger R Bilboul, Chariman Of The Board

Detailed profiles for more than 35,000 public, academic, special, and government libraries and library related organizations in the US and Canada. These include addresses, phone and fax numbers, e-mail addresses, network participation, expenditures, holdings and special collections, key personnel, special services and more than 40 categories of library information in all. A two volume set.
Cost: $299.00
4000 Pages
ISBN: 1-573872-04-0
Mailing list available for rent

16518 American Society of Journalists and Authors Directory
American Society of Journalists and Authors
1501 Broadway
Suite 302
New York, NY 10036-5505

212-997-0947
FAX 212-937-2315
Home Page: www.asja.org
Social Media: *Facebook, Twitter, LinkedIn*

Alexandra Owens, Executive Director

Lists over 800 member freelance nonfiction writers.
Cost: $75.00
90 Pages

16519 Applied Science & Technology Index
HW Wilson Company
950 Dr Martin L King Jr Blvd
Bronx, NY 10452-4297

718-588-8405
800-367-6770
FAX 718-590-1617
Home Page: www.hwwilson.com

Harold Regan, CEO
Kathleen McEvoy, Director of Public Relations

Fast, convenient access to the cover-to-cover content of leading trade and industrial publications, journals issued by professional and technical societies, specialized subject periodicals, as well as buyers' guides, directories, and conference proceedings.
Frequency: Monthly on WlisonDisc

16520 Association of Professional Writing Consultants Membership Directory
Northwestern University
2315 Sheridan Rd
Evanston, IL 60201-2920

847-491-5500

Henry Bienen, President
Cost: $75.00
Frequency: Annual

16521 Authors and Artists for Young Adults
Gale/Cengage Learning
27500 Drake Road
Farmington Hills, MI 48331-3535

248-699-4253
800-877-4253
FAX 877-363-4253
E-Mail: gale.galeord@cengage.com
Home Page: www.gale.cengage.com
Social Media: *Facebook, Twitter, Youtube*

Patrick C Sommers, President

A a source where teens can discover fascinating and entertaining facts about the writers, artists, film directors, graphic novelists and other creative personalities that most interest them.
ISBN: 0-787677-96-5

16522 Children's Writer's and Illustrator's Market
Writer's Market
1507 Dana Avenue
Cincinnati, OH 45207-1005

513-396-6160
800-289-0963
FAX 513-531-4082

Offers valuable information about book and magazine publishers that publish works by authors and illustrators for young audiences.
Cost: $22.99
256 Pages
Frequency: Annual

16523 Complete Guide to Self-Publishing
Writer's Market
1507 Dana Avenue
Cincinnati, OH 45207-1005

513-396-6160
800-289-0963
FAX 513-531-4082

Offers, in appendixes, a list of contacts and companies that help see to publication of a book at the author's expense.
Cost: $18.95

16524 Contemporary Authors
Gale/Cengage Learning
27500 Drake Road
Farmington Hills, MI 48331-3535

248-699-4253
800-877-4253
FAX 877-363-4253
E-Mail: gale.galeord@cengage.com
Home Page: www.gale.cengage.com
Social Media: *Facebook, Twitter, Youtube*

Patrick C Sommers, President

Find biographical information on more than 130,000 modern novelists, poets, playwrights, nonfiction writers, journalists and scriptwriters. Sketches typically include personal information, contact information, career history, writings, biographical and critical sources, authors' comments and informative essays about their lives and work.
ISBN: 0-810319-11-X

16525 Directory of Literary Magazines
Council of Literary Magazines and Presses

154 Christopher St
Suite 3C
New York, NY 10014-2840

212-741-9110
FAX 212-741-9112
E-Mail: info@clmp.org
Home Page: www.clmp.org

Contains names, addresses and phone numbers of nearly 600 magazines in the US and abroad that publish poetry, fiction, essays, literary reviews and more.
Cost: $17.00
Frequency: Annual

16526 Directory of Poetry Publishers
Dustbooks
PO Box 100
Paradise, CA 95967-0100

530-877-6110
800-477-6110
FAX 530-877-0222
E-Mail: directories@dustbooks.com
Home Page: www.dustbooks.com

Len Fulton, Editor

Over 2,100 magazines, small and commercial presses and university presses that accept poetry for publication.
Cost: $25.95
300 Pages
Frequency: Annual
Circulation: 2,000
ISBN: 0-916685-47-0

16527 Directory of Small Magazines Press Magazine Editors & Publishers
Dustbooks
PO Box 100
Paradise, CA 95967-0100

530-877-6110
800-477-6110
FAX 530-877-0222
E-Mail: directories@dustbooks.com
Home Page: www.dustbooks.com

Len Fulton, Editor

This directory contains more than 7,500 listings of editors and publishers in alphabetical order, along with their associated publishing companies, their addresses, phones, e-mail addresses and Web pages. Includes self publishers.
Cost: $25.95
460 Pages
Frequency: Annual
Circulation: 1,000
ISBN: 0-913218-28-6
Founded in 1967
Mailing list available for rent

16528 Editor & Publisher International Year Book
Editor & Publisher Company
17782 Cowan
Suite C
Irvine, CA 92614

929-660-6150
888-732-7323
FAX 949-660-6172
E-Mail: circulation@editorandpublisher.com
Home Page: www.editorandpublisher.com

Duncan McIntosh, President/Publisher
Jeff Fleming, Editor-In-Chief
Kristina Ackermann, Managing Editor
Ralph Bayless, Sales Manager

It's the encyclopedia of the newspaper industry with listings for all dailies worldwide and all community and special interest U.S. and Canadian weeklies. Tabbed sections make it easy to find information from U.S. & Canadian dailies to foreign newspapers. Tables profile newspaper ad trends, circulation size by population

groups, rankings by circulation size and more.
Cost: $125.00
600 Pages
Frequency: Annual
Founded in 1884

16529 Editor & Publisher: Directory of Syndicated Services Issue
Editor & Publisher Company
11 W 19th Street
10th Floor
New York, NY 10011-4209

212-929-1259

Michael Parker, President

A directory of several hundred syndicates serving newspapers in the United States and abroad with news, features and comic strips.
Cost: $7.00
Frequency: Annual

16530 Editorial Freelancers Association: Membership Directory
Editorial Freelancers Association
71 W 23rd St
4th Fl
New York, NY 10010-4181

212-929-5400
866-929-5425
FAX 212-929-5439
E-Mail: office@the-efa.org
Home Page: www.the-efa.org
Social Media: *Facebook, Twitter, LinkedIn*

Jp Partland, Co-Executive
Judi Greenstein, Office Manager

1,100 member editorial freelancers.
Cost: $25.00
Frequency: Annual Spring

16531 Guide to Literary Agents
Writer's Market
1507 Dana Avenue
Cincinnati, OH 45207-1005

513-396-6160
800-289-0963
FAX 513-531-4082
Home Page: www.writersmarket.com

Agents and representatives for professional writers.
Cost: $18.95
240 Pages
Frequency: Annual

16532 Guide to Writers Conferences & Workshops
Shaw Guides
PO Box 231295
New York, NY 10023

212-799-6464
FAX 212-724-9287
E-Mail: info@shawguides.com
Home Page: www.shawguides.com

Conferences, workshops, and seminars for amateur and professional writers.
Cost: $19.95
272 Pages

16533 Key Guide to Electronic Resources: Language and Literature
Information Today
143 Old Marlton Pike
Medford, NJ 08055-8750

609-654-6266
800-300-9868
FAX 609-654-4309
E-Mail: custserv@infotoday.com
Home Page: www.infotoday.com

Thomas H Hogan, President
Roger R Bilboul, Chairman Of The Board

Part of the ongoing topic related series of reference guides is an evaluative directory of electronic reference sources in the fields of language and literature.
Cost: $39.50
120 Pages
ISBN: 1-573870-20-x
Mailing list available for rent

16534 Literary Agents of North America
Author Aid/Research Associates International
340 E 52nd St
New York, NY 10022-6728

212-758-4213

Arthur Orrmont, Editor

More than 1,00 US and Canadian literary agencies.
Cost: $33.00

16535 Literary Forum
CompuServe Information Service
5000 Arlington Centre Blvd
Columbus, OH 43220-5439

614-326-1002
800-848-8199

This database covers literature, including books and poetry, writing, stage and screen, journalism and comic books.
Frequency: Bulletin Board

16536 Market Guide for Young Writers: Where and How to Sell What You Write
Writer's Market
1507 Dana Avenue
Cincinnati, OH 45207-1005

513-396-6160
800-289-0963
FAX 513-531-4082
Home Page: www.writersmarket.com

A list of over 150 magazines and writers contests are profiles that all accept work from young writers for publishing purposes.
Cost: $16.95

16537 Mystery Writer's Market Place and Sourcebook
Writer's Market
1507 Dana Avenue
Cincinnati, OH 45207-1005

513-396-6160
800-289-0963
FAX 513-531-4082
Home Page: www.writersmarket.com

Offers various profiles of about 50 publishers of mystery and crime books.
Cost: $17.95

16538 Novel & Short Story Writer's Market
Writer's Market
1507 Dana Avenue
Cincinnati, OH 45207-1005

513-396-6160
800-289-0963
FAX 513-531-4082
Home Page: www.writersmarket.com

More than 2,000 literary magazines, publishers, agents and writer's organizations are profiled.
Cost: $19.95
Frequency: Annual

16539 Poet's Market
Writer's Market
1507 Dana Avenue
Cincinnati, OH 45207-1005

513-396-6160
800-289-0963

FAX 513-531-4082
Home Page: www.writersmarket.com

Over 1,500 publishers, periodicals and other markets that accept poetry for publication are profiled.
Cost: $22.99
528 Pages
ISSN: 0883-5470

16540 Professional Freelance Writers Directory
National Writers Club
314 Peoria
Suite 290
Aurora, CO 80014

303-841-0246

Over 200 professional members selected from the total membership on the basis of significant articles books or movies published.
Cost: $12.50
75 Pages
Frequency: Annual

16541 Science Fiction and Fantasy Writers of America Membership Directory
PO Box 877
Chestertown, MD 21620

E-Mail: exedir@sfwa.org
Home Page: www.sfwa.org

Mary Kowal, Vice-President
Robert Howe, Secretary
Amy Casil, Treasurer
Directory of services and supplies to the industry.
Cost: $60.00
40 Pages
Frequency: Annual

16542 Self-Employed Writers and Artists Network Directory
Po Box 175
Towacos, NJ 07653-0440

Home Page: www.swan-net.com
Social Media: *Facebook, Twitter*

Phil Cantor, President
Wayne Rousck, VP Marketing

Over 140 freelance writers and graphic designers, as well as illustrators, photographers and more in northern New Jersey and Metropolitan New York City are profiled.
20 Pages
Frequency: Annual

16543 Self-Publishing Manual: How to Write, Print and Sell Your Own Book
Para Publishing
PO Box 8206
Santa Barbara, CA 93118-8206

805-968-7277
800-727-2782
FAX 805-968-1379
E-Mail: info@parapublishing.com
Home Page: www.parapublishing.com

Dan Poynter, Publisher

A list of wholesalers, reviewers and exporters, etc, are profiled.
Cost: $19.95
900 Pages
Frequency: Biennial
ISBN: 1-568600-73-9
Founded in 1979
Printed in one color on matte stock

16544 Space Coast Writers Guild: Organization, Activities and Membership
PO Box 262
Melbourne, FL 32902

E-Mail: scwg-jm@cfi.rr.com
Home Page: www.scwg.org
Social Media: *Facebook, Twitter, LinkedIn*

Judy Mammay, President
Bill Allen, VP
Donna Chesher, President
Andy Vazquez, Vice-President
Carol Didier, Secretary

A who's who directory of professional writing services and training to the media industry.
25 Pages
Frequency: Annual

16545 Who's Who in Writers, Editors and Poets: US and Canada
December Press
Apt 406
2800 N Roadrunner Pkwy
Las Cruces, NM 88011-0859

847-940-4122

Curt Johnson, President

Directory of writers and editors.
Cost: $99.00
700 Pages
Frequency: Biennial

16546 Writer's Digest: Writers Conference Issue
F&W Publications
1507 Dana Avenue
Cincinnati, OH 45207-1005

513-531-2222
FAX 513-531-1843

Directory of services and supplies to the industry.
Cost: $2.95
Frequency: Annual
Circulation: 225,000

16547 Writer's Guide to Book Editors, Publishers and Literary Agents
Prima Publishing
3000 Lava Ridge Ct
Roseville, CA 95661-2802

916-787-7000
800-632-8676
FAX 916-787-7004
E-Mail: sales@primapub.com
Home Page: www.primagames.com

Julie Asbury, Publisher

Offers information on more than 200 publishing houses and their editors.
Cost: $19.95
370 Pages
Frequency: Annual

16548 Writer's Handbook
Kalmbach Publishing Company
21027 Crossroads Circle
PO Box 1612
Waukesha, WI 53186-1612

262-796-8776
800-533-6644
FAX 262-796-1615
Home Page: www.writermag.com

A list of more than 3,000 markets for the sale of manuscripts, ads and awards.
Cost: $29.95
Frequency: Annual

16549 Writer's Market: Where and How to Sell What You Write
Writer's Market

1507 Dana Avenue
Cincinnati, OH 45207-1056

513-396-6160
FAX 513-531-4082

Directory of services and supplies to the industry.
Cost: $29.95
1000 Pages
Frequency: Annual
ISSN: 0084-2729

16550 Writer's Northwest Handbook
Media Weavers, Blue Heron Publishing
4140 S.E. 37
#10
Portland, OR 97202

Home Page: www.mediaweavers.net

Over 3,000 markets for writers, including newspapers, magazines and book publishers in Northwestern United States and British Columbia, Canada.
Cost: $18.95
232 Pages
Frequency: Biennial

16551 Writers Conferences
Poets & Writers
150 Broadway
New York, NY 10038-4381

212-566-2424
FAX 212-587-9673
E-Mail: mpettus@pettuswilliams.com
Home Page: www.pettuswilliams.com

Marvin K Pettus
Cost: $7.50
50 Pages
Frequency: Annual

16552 Writers Directory
St. James Press/Gale
27500 Drake Road
Farmington Hills, MI 48331-3535

248-699-4253
800-877-4253
FAX 877-363-4253
E-Mail: gale.galeord@cengage.com
Home Page: www.gale.cengage.com
Social Media: *Facebook, Twitter, Youtube*

Patrick C Sommers, President

This comprehensive resource features uptodate bibliographical, biographical and contact information for approximately 20,000 living authors worldwide who have at least one English publication.
ISBN: 1-558626-20-4

16553 Writers Guild Directory
Writers Guild of America, West
8455 Beverly Blvd
Los Angeles, CA 90048-3445

323-651-2600
FAX 323-782-4802

Bob Waters, Owner

Directory of services and supplies to the industry.
Cost: $17.50
450 Pages
Frequency: Annual

Industry Web Sites

16554 http://gold.greyhouse.com
G.O.L.D Grey House OnLine Databases
Grey House Publishing's online database platform, GOLD, offers Quick Search, Keyword Search and Expert Search for most business sectors including literary markets. The GOLD platform makes finding the information you need quick and easy - whether you're a novice searcher or an experienced database user. All of Grey House's directory products are available for subscription on the GOLD platform.

16555 www.asja.org
American Society of Journalists and Authors
Association for journalists and authors.

16556 www.dramaguild.com
Dramatists Guild
Protects the rights of its international membership of playwrights, composers and lyricists. Supports fair royalty, maintenance of subsidiary rights, artistic control and ownership of copyright.

16557 www.freelancepubs.com
Freelance Editorial Association
Self-employed contractors, or consultants with expertise in editorial functions such as copyediting, researching, indexing and proofreading, writing, illustrating, editing, project managing, desktop publishing, and translating.

16558 www.greyhouse.com
Grey House Publishing
Authoritative reference directories for most business sectors including literary markets. Users can search the online databases with varied search criteria allowing for custom searches by product category, geographic area, sales volume, keyword, subject and more. Full Grey House catalog and online ordering also available.

16559 www.ifwtwa.org
International Food, Wine and Travel Writers Association

Staff and/or freelance writers in the food, wine and travel field. Also includes other media professionals and industry associate members in 28 countries worldwide.

16560 www.loc.gov/loc/cfbook/
Library of Congress
This organization strives to stimulate the consumer interest in books and reading.

16561 www.mysterywriters.org
Mystery Writers of America
Professional writers of crime and mystery stories and novels. Unpublished writers are affiliate members. MWA annually gives the Edagar Awards for excellence in the mystery geare.

16562 www.nationalwriters.com
Membership organization for writers.

16563 www.nfc.council.com
Newspaper Features Council
A forum for editors, writers, columnists, cartoonists and syndicates to exchange views and improve the content of newspapers.

16564 www.nfpw.org
National Federation of Press Women
Members are writers, editors and other communication professionals for newspapers, magazines, wire services, agencies and freelance.

16565 www.owaa.org
Outdoor Writers Association of America
A nonprofit, international organization representing over 2,000 professional outdoor communicators who report on diverse interests in the outdoors.

16566 www.the-efa.org
Editorial Freelancers Association

National nonprofit, professional organization of self-employed workers in the publishing and communications industries.

16567 www.wga.org
Writers Guild of America, West
An independent labor union representing writers in motion pictures, television and radio in the west.

16568 www.writersresearchgroup.com
Writers Research Group

Associations

16569 American Beverage Licensees

5101 River Rd
Suite 108
Bethesda, MD 20816-1560

301-656-1494
FAX 301-656-7539
E-Mail: info@plib.org
Home Page: www.ablusa.org/
Social Media: *Facebook, LinkedIn*

John Blodgett, Chairman
Ken Thorlakson, Vice Chairman
Jeff Fantozzi, President
Ben Haynes, Manager
Hannah Petersen, Corporate Secretary

Represents over 15,000 off-premise licensees in the open or license states and on-premise proprietors in markets across the nation. Offers members information on legislation and industry matters.
65 Members
Founded in 1903

16570 American Craft Spirits Association

PO Box 701414
Louisville, KY 40270

502-299-0238
Home Page: www.americancraftspirits.org
Social Media: *Facebook, Twitter*

Tom Mooney, President
Margie A. S. Lehrman, Interim Executive Director

Trade association of U.S. craft spirits industry.

16571 American Society for Enology and Viticulture

1784 Picasso Avenue
Suite D
Davis, CA 95618-0551

530-753-3142
FAX 530-753-3318
E-Mail: pfpa@paforestproducts.org
Home Page: www.asev.org

Alan Metzler, Chairman
Terry Stockdale, Vice-Chairman
Paul Lyskava, Executive Director
Michelle McManus, Business Manager
Bob Long, Membership Representative

A tax exempt professional society dedicated to the interests of enologists, viticulturists, and others in the fields of wine and grape research and production throughout the world.
Founded in 1980

16572 American Society of Brewing Chemists

3340 Pilot Knob Rd
St Paul, MN 55121-2055

651-454-7250
800-328-7560
FAX 651-454-0766
E-Mail: ties@rta.org
Home Page: www.asbcnet.org

Jim Gauntt, Executive Director
Debbie Corallo, Association Administrator
Barbara Stacey, Committee and Website Coordinator
2500 Members
Founded in 1919

16573 Association of Winery Supplies

21 Tamal Vista Boulevard
Suite 196
Corte Madera, CA 94925-1146

415-924-2640
Social Media: *1983*

Warner Executive Director

United States supplier of services and materials used in the winery industry.
John Members
Founded in 34

16574 Beer Institute

122 C St NW
Suite 350
Washington, DC 20001-2150

202-737-2337
800-379-2739
FAX 202-737-7004
E-Mail: info@calredwood.org
Home Page: www.beerinstitute.org
Social Media: *Youtube*

Christopher Grover, President

The national trade association for the brewing industry. Representing both big and small brewers as well as importers and industry suppliers.
Founded in 1916

16575 Brewers Association

Brewers Association
1327 Spruce Street
Boulder, CO 80302

303-447-0816
888-822-6273
FAX 303-447-2825
E-Mail: membership@safnet.org
Home Page: www.brewersassociation.org
Social Media: *Facebook, Twitter, LinkedIn*

A non-profit educational and trade organization for small and craft brewers. Its mission is to make quality brewing and beer knowledge accessible to all.
Founded in 1900

16576 Distilled Spirits Council of the United States

1250 Eye St NW
Suite 400
Washington, DC 20005-3998

202-628-3544
FAX 202-682-8844
E-Mail: vicki@swst.org
Home Page: www.discus.org
Social Media: *Facebook*

Eric Hansen, President
Bob Smith, Vice-President
Vicki L. Herian, Executive Director
H. Michael Barnes, Editor of Wood and Fiber Science
Barb Hogan, Editorial Assistant

National trade association representing producers and marketers of liquor sold in the US.
450 Members
Founded in 1958

16577 Distillery, Wine and Allied Workers' International Union

66 Grand Avenue
Englewood, NJ 07631-3506

201-894-8444
FAX 201-569-9216
Home Page: www.ufcw.org/

Bryan Smalley, President
Alexis Sivcovich, Member Services Coordinator
Beverly Knight, Accounting Manager
Will Telligman, Government Affairs Manager

Addresses the concerns of wine makers and fellow industry workers.
350 Members
Founded in 1962

16578 Foundation for Advancing Alcohol Responsibility

2345 Crystal Dr.
Suite 710
Arlington, VA 22202

Home Page: responsibility.org
Social Media: *Facebook, Twitter, YouTube, Pinterest, Instagram*

Ralph S. Blackman, President & CEO

Promoting responsible drinking.

16579 Home Wine and Beer Trade Association

PO Box 1373
Valrico, FL 33595

813-685-4261
FAX 813-681-5625
Home Page: www.fermentersinternational.org/
Social Media: *Facebook, Youtube*

Manufacturers, wholesalers, retailers, authors and editors having a commercial interest in the beer and wine trade.
19 Members
Founded in 1905

16580 Italian Trade Commission

33 East 67th Street
New York, NY 10065

212-980-1500
FAX 212-758-1050
E-Mail: mail@sfpa.org
Home Page: www.italtrade.com/countries/americas/usa/newyork.htm
Social Media: *Twitter, Youtube*

Tami Kessler, Executive Director
Richard Wallace, Vice President, Communications
Vernon Barabino, Chief Financial Administrator
Rachel Elton, Admin. Assistant/Program Coor.
Eric Gee, CF, RF, Director

Developments in the Italian wine industry and market, as well as reviews of imported wines from Italy.
265 Members
Founded in 1915

16581 Italian Wine and Food Institute

Italian Wine and Food Institute
60 East 42nd Street, Suite 2214
Suite 2214
New York, NY 10165

212-867-4111
FAX 212-867-4114
E-Mail: spib@spib.org
Home Page: www.italianwineandfoodinstitute.com

T. Furman Brodie, Chairman
Bert H. Jones, Vice Chairman
Steve Singleton, President
Shelly James, Operations & Finance Assistant
Eileen Ehrsam, Accounts Receivable Admin.

Members are producers, distributors and marketers of Italian wines and foods.
Founded in 1940

16582 National Alcohol Beverage Control Association

4401 Ford Avenue
Suite 700
Alexandria, VA 22302-1433

703-578-4200
FAX 703-820-3551
E-Mail: info@forestinfo.org
Home Page: www.nabca.org

Robert M Owens, Chairman
Lee F Freeman, President & CEO

Members include control jurisdictions, supplier members and industry trade associations.
Founded in 1989

16583 National Beer Wholesalers Association

1101 King Street
Suite 600
Alexandria, VA 22314-2944

703-683-4300
800-300-6417
FAX 703-683-8965
E-Mail: tpm@tpmrs.com
Home Page: www.nbwa.org

Russ Vaagen, Chairman
Tom Shaffer, Vice Chairman
Adam Molenda, President
Chris Chathams, Safety Resource Director
Jolene Skjothaug, Office Manager

NBWA represents the interests of America's 2,850 independent, licensed beer distributors which service every congressional district and media market in the country.
250 Members
Founded in 1916

16584 National Wine Distribution Association

2701 E Street
Sacramento, CA 95816-3221

916-979-3051
FAX 916-448-9115

GM Pucilowski, Executive Director

Dedicated to promoting the interests and education of smaller wine wholesalers, importers, wineries, and others who are involved in the wine distribution business.
285 Members
Founded in 1978

16585 Wine Institute

425 Market St
Suite 1000
San Francisco, CA 94105-2487

415-512-0151
FAX 415-356-7569
E-Mail: tcia@tcia.org
Home Page: www.wineinstitute.org
Social Media: *Facebook, Twitter, LinkedIn, Youtube*

Jack W. Guffey, Jr., Chair
Mark Garvin, President
Bob Rouse, Chief Program Officer
Sarah Winslow, Director of Development
Amy Tetreault, Marketing Director

Organization that represents the wine and spirit industry to state and federal lawmaking bodies.
2000 Members
Founded in 1938

16586 Wine and Spirits Shippers Association

11800 Sunrise Valley Dr
Reston, VA 20191-5302

703-860-2300
800-368-3167
FAX 703-860-2422
E-Mail: info@tpinst.org
Home Page: www.wssa.com

Michael A Cassidy, Executive Director

Provides members, importers and exporters with efficient and economical ocean transportation and other logistic services.
300 Members
Founded in 1961
Mailing list available for rent

16587 Wine and Spirits Wholesalers of America

805 15th Street NW
Suite 430
Washington, DC 20005

202-371-9792
FAX 202-789-2405
E-Mail: info@wclib.org
Home Page: www.wswa.org

John Konecny, President
Rod Lucas, Vice President
Don DeVisser, Exec. Vice Pres.
Kyle Freres, Sec./Treasurer

This association is comprised of wholesale distributors of domestic and imported wine and distilled spirits.
189 Members
Circulation: 1,000
Founded in 1941

Newsletters

16588 ASBC Newsletter

American Society of Brewing Chemists
3340 Pilot Knob Rd
Eagan, MN 55121-2055

651-454-7250
800-328-7560
FAX 651-454-0766
E-Mail: asbc@scisoc.org
Home Page: www.asbcnet.org

Steven C Nelson, VP
Jordana Anker, Director of Publications
Karen Cummings, Director Publications
Joan A Raumschuh, Editor
Jody Grider, Director of Operations
Cost: $20.00
Frequency: Quarterly
Founded in 1934

16589 Alcoholic Beverage Control: From the State Capitals

Wakeman Walworth
PO BOX 7376
Alexandria, VA 22307-7376

703-768-9600
FAX 703-768-9690
Home Page:
www.statecapitals.com/alcoholbev.html

Keyes Walworth, Publisher

Covers binge drinking laws, internet sales, advertising, taxes, bottle bills, Sunday sales laws, license regulation, drunk driving laws, under-age drinking, mini-bottles and other state laws affecting beer, liquor and wine distribution.
Cost: $245.00
4 Pages
Frequency: Weekly
Printed in one color on matte stock

16590 Beer Marketer's Insights Newsletter

Beer Marketer's Insights
49 E Maple Ave
Suffern, NY 10901-5507

845-624-2337
FAX 845-624-2340
Home Page: www.beerinsights.com

Benj Steinman, President

Reports on the competitive battle among brewers for a share of the beer market. Analyzes recent legislation and factors that affect the industry.
Cost: $595.00
Frequency: 23/Year
Founded in 1975

16591 Beer Statistics News

Beer Marketer's Insights
49 E Maple Ave
Suffern, NY 10901-5507

845-624-2337
FAX 845-624-2340
E-Mail: bmiexpress@aol.com
Home Page: www.beerinsights.com

Benj Steinman, President
Eric Shephard, Executive Editor
Andy Leinicke, Circulation Manager

Supplies data for major brewers' shipments in 39 reporting states.
Cost: $450.00
Frequency: Monthly
Founded in 1975

16592 Brewers Bulletin

PO Box 677
Thiensville, WI 53092

262-242-6105
FAX 262-242-5133
E-Mail: bulletindigest@milwpc.com

Tom Volke, President/CEO

Brewing industry newspaper.
Cost: $53.00
Frequency: Monthly
Circulation: 500
Founded in 1907

16593 Champagne Wines Information Bureau

KCSA
800 2nd Avenue Frnt 5
New York, NY 10017-4709

212-682-6300
800-642-4267
FAX 212-697-0910
E-Mail: info@champagnes.com
Home Page: www.champagnes.com

Jean-Louis Carbonnier, Editor

Representative of Comite Interprofessionnel duVinde Champagne, Epernay, France.
4 Pages
Frequency: TriAnnual
Circulation: 10,000
Printed in one color on matte stock

16594 Impact International

M Shanken Communications
387 Park Ave S
Suite 8
New York, NY 10016-8872

212-684-4224
800-848-7113
FAX 212-684-5424
Home Page: www.cigaraficionado.com

Marvin Shanken, Publisher
Samantha Shanken, President

Reports on the global alcoholic beverage market.
Cost: $595.00
Frequency: Annual+
Founded in 1972

16595 Kane's Beverage Week

Whitaker Newsletters
313 S Avenue
#340
Fanwood, NJ 07023-1364

908-889-6339
800-359-6049
FAX 415-027-0608

Whitaker Publisher, Anne
Bittner Editor, Fred
Rossi Editor

News on marketing, economic and regulatory factors affecting the alcohol beverage industry.
Cost: $131.00
Joel Members
6 Pages
Frequency: Monthly
ISSN: 0882-2573

16596 Notiziario
Italian Wine and Food Institute
60 East 42nd Street, Suite 2214
Suite 1341
New York, NY 10165

212-867-4111
FAX 212-867-4114
E-Mail: iwfi@aol.com
Home Page:
www.italianwineandfoodinstitute.com

Lucio Caputo, President
Vincent Giampaoco, VP

Provides detailed information on the Italian gastronomy and wines. It distributes information materials and give press interviews for the American radio and television. It carries out an intense public relations program, participates in the most important local promotional initiatives and events and maintains contact with the American and Italian authorities in this sector.
Cost: $250.00
Founded in 1984

16597 On Tap: Newsletter
WBR Publishing
PO Box 71
Clemson, SC 29633

864-654-2300
FAX 864-654-5067

Steve Johnson, Publisher
North America breweries and microbreweries.
Cost: $.95
20 Pages
Frequency: Bi-Monthly
Circulation: 1000
Printed in one color on matte stock

16598 Spirited Living: Dave Steadman's Restaurant Scene
5301 Towne Woods Rd
Coram, NY 11727-2808

631-736-0436
FAX 631-736-0436

Dave Steadman, Editor
Newsletter published Bi-Weekly except January, July, and August.
Cost: $75.00

16599 US Beer Market
Business Trend Analysts/Industry Reports
2171 Jericho Tpke
Suite 200
Commack, NY 11725-2937

631-462-5454
800-866-4648
FAX 631-462-1842
Home Page: www.bta-ler.com

Charles J Ritchie, Executive VP
Donna Priani, Marketing Director

Profiles markets for premium, superpremium, popular and light beers.
Cost: $1495.00

16600 Uncorked
California Wine Club
2175 Goodyear Avenue
Suite 102
Ventura, CA 93006-3699

805-650-4330
800-777-4443
FAX 800-700-1599

E-Mail: info@cawineclub.com
Home Page: www.cawineclub.com

Bruce Boring, Proprietors
Judy Reynolds, Proprietors

Uncorked is an 8 page newsletter that describes the featured winery. It provides an upclose and personal look at a small 'boutique' California Winery.
Frequency: Monthly
Circulation: 10000
Founded in 1990

16601 Vinotizie Italian Wine Newsletter
Italian Trade Commission
33 E 67th St
New York, NY 10065-5949

212-848-0300
FAX 212-758-1050
E-Mail: newyork@newyork.ice.it
Home Page: www.italtrade.com

Aniello Musella, President
Giovanni Mafodda, Operations Manager

This newsletter discusses developments in the Italian wine industry and market, as well as reviews of imported wines from Italy.
Frequency: Monthly
Founded in 1998

16602 Wine Investor Buyers Guide
PGE Publications
1224 N Fairfax Avenue
Apartment 5
Los Angeles, CA 90046-5234
Paul Gillette, Publisher
JD Kronman, Editor

Reviews new releases of wines, recommends the best buys, predicts when wines will be at their peak and surveys markets for pricing trends. Accepts advertising.
Cost: $75.00
10 Pages
Frequency: Monthly

16603 World Beer Review
WBR Publishing
PO Box 71
Clemson, SC 29633-0071

864-654-2300

Steve Johnson, Publisher
Complete coverage of the beer and beermaking industry.

Magazines & Journals

16604 All About Beer
Chautauqua Inc
501 Washington St
Suite H
Durham, NC 27701-2169

919-530-8150
800-977-2337
FAX 919-530-8160
E-Mail: editor@allaboutbeer.com
Home Page: www.allaboutbeer.com

Julie Bradford, Publisher
Natalie Abernethy, Circulation Manager
Quality beers, breweries and restaurants.
Cost: $19.99
64 Pages
Founded in 1981

16605 Atlantic Control States Beverage Journal
Club & Tavern

3 12th Street
Wheeling, WV 26003-3276

304-232-7620
FAX 304-233-1236

Arnold Lazarus, Editor
A magazine for the alcoholic beverage industry. Serving bars, restaurants, clubs and industry personnel with West Virginia, Virginia, and North Carolina state editions. Includes states' liquor price lists.

16606 Bar Business Magazine
Simmons-Boardman Publishing Corporation
345 Hudson St
Suite 1201
New York, NY 10014-7123

212-620-7200
FAX 212-633-1165
E-Mail: cytuarte@sbpub.com
Home Page: www.simmonsboardman.com

Arthur J McGinnis Jr, President

The premier How-To publication covering the best business practices and products for owners and managers of nightclubs, bars and lounges across the US.
Frequency: Monthly
Circulation: 8541

16607 Bartender Magazine
Foley Publishing Corporation
PO Box 157
Spring Lake, NJ 07762

732-449-4499
FAX 732-974-8289
E-Mail: barmag@aol.com
Home Page: www.bartender.com
Social Media: *Facebook, Twitter*

Raymond Foley, Publisher
Jaclyn Wilson Foley, Editor

Serves all full service drinking establishments. Including individual restaurants, hotels, motels, bars, taverns, lounges, and all other full service on premise licenses. Subscription price is $40 for Canada, and $55 for all other foriegn countries.
Cost: $30.00
72 Pages
Frequency: Monthly
Circulation: 149044
Founded in 1979
Printed in 4 colors on glossy stock

16608 Beer Perspectives
National Beer Wholesalers Association
1101 King St
Suite 600
Alexandria, VA 22314-2965

703-683-4300
FAX 703-683-8965
E-Mail: info@nbwa.org
Home Page: www.nbwa.org
Social Media: *Facebook, Twitter*

Craig A Purser, President & CEO
Michael Johnson, EVP Fed Aff/Chief Advisory Office
Rebecca Spicer, VP Public Affairs/Chief
Paul Pisano, SVP Industry Affairs & Gen. Counsel

Trade association for beer wholesalers. Provides government and public affairs outreach as well as education and training for its wholesaler members.
Founded in 1938

16609 Beverage Dynamics
The Beverage Information Group

17 High Street
2nd Floor
Norwalk, CT 06851

203-855-8499
E-Mail: lzimmerman@m2media360.com
Home Page: www.bevinfogroup.com

Liza Zimmerman, Editor-in-Chief
Jeremy Nedelka, Managing Editor

Devoted to the needs of the off-premise beverage alcohol retailer. Covers wine, beer and spirits categories as well as beset practices for retail decision makers.
Cost: $35.00
Frequency: Bi-Monthly
Founded in 1934

16610 Beverage Journal
Michigan Licensed Beverage Association
920 N Fairview Ave
Lansing, MI 48912-3238

517-374-9611
800-292-2896
FAX 517-374-1165
E-Mail: info@mlba.org
Home Page: www.mlba.org

Lou Adado, CEO
Cathy Pavick, Executive Director
Peter Broderick, Director of Communication

Offers information on the alcoholic beverage industry/retail sales
Cost: $52.00
Frequency: Monthly
ISSN: 1050-4427
Founded in 1939
Printed in on glossy stock

16611 Beverage Network
Beverage Media Group
116 John St
Suite 2305
New York, NY 10038-3419

212-571-3232
800-723-8372
FAX 212-571-4443
E-Mail: info@bevmedia.com
Home Page: www.bevmedia.com

Jason Glasser, CEO
S Paley, Circulation Manager
Cost: $99.00
Frequency: Monthly
Circulation: 6000
Founded in 1940

16612 Beverage Retailer Magazine
Oxford Publishing
Ste 1
1903b University Ave
Oxford, MS 38655-4150

662-236-5510
800-247-3881
FAX 662-236-5541
Home Page: www.beverage-retailer.com

Brenda Owen, Editor
Ed Meek, Publisher
Stacy Clark, Production Manager
Jennifer Parsons, Marketing Director
Ruth Ann Wolfe, Circulation Director

A magazine covering the off premise market for retailers in the wine, beer and spirits business.
Cost: $30.00
Circulation: 25000
Founded in 1985
Printed in 4 colors on glossy stock

16613 Cheers
The Beverage Information Group

17 High St
Suite 2
Norwalk, CT 06851

203-855-8499
FAX 203-855-9446
E-Mail: cforman@m2media360.com
Home Page: www.bevinfogroup.com

Charlie Forman, SVP/Group Publisher
Liza Zimmerman, Editor-In-Chief
Jeremy Nedelka, Managing Editor

Business magazine for on-premise hospitality professionals. Coverage includes trends and innovations in operations, merchandising, service and training, as well as new developments in beverage product segments.
Cost: $35.00
Frequency: Monthly
Founded in 1998

16614 Modern Brewery Age
Business Journals
50 Day Street
PO Box 5550
Norwalk, CT 06856-5550

203-853-6015
FAX 203-853-8175
E-Mail: FayS@busjour.com
Home Page: www.breweryage.com

Mac Brighton, Chairman/COO
Britton Jones, President/CEO
Peter V K Reid, Editor/Publisher
Arthur Heilman, Circulation Director
Diane Apicelli, Advertising Director

A magazine for the wholesale and brewing industry.
Cost: $95.00
Founded in 1933

16615 Modern Brewery Age: Tabloid Edition
Business Journals
50 Day Street
PO Box #5550
Norwalk, CT 06856-5550

203-853-6015
FAX 203-853-8175
Home Page: www.breweryage.com

Peter VK Reid, Editor
Peter VK Reid, Publisher
Britton Jones, President/CEO
Diane Apicelli, Advertising Director
Mac Brighton, Chairman & COO

Brewery industry tabloid.
Cost: $95.00
Frequency: Weekly
Founded in 1933

16616 Nightclub & Bar Magazine
Oxford Publishing
Ste 1
1903b University Ave
Oxford, MS 38655-4150

662-236-5510
800-247-3881
FAX 662-281-0104
Home Page: www.nightclub.com

Ed Meek, Production Manager
Mitchell Diggs, Managing Editor
Laura McCreary, Advertising Director
Jennifer Cummins, Production Manager
Adam Alson, Founder

A monthly publication covering the nightclub and bar hospitality industry.
Frequency: Monthly
Circulation: 30,000
Printed in 4 colors on glossy stock

16617 Southern Beverage Journal
Beverage Media Group

14337 Sw 119th Ave
Miami, FL 33186-6006

305-233-7230
FAX 305-252-2580
Home Page: www.bevnetwork.com

Sharon Mijares, President
Sharon Mijares, Circulation Manager

A magazine for the alcoholic beverage industry.
Cost: $35.00
Frequency: Monthly
Circulation: 29000
Founded in 1944

16618 StateWays
The Beverage Information Group
17 High Street
2nd Floor
Norwalk, CT 06851

203-855-8499
E-Mail: lzimmerman@m2media360.com
Home Page: www.bevinfogroup.com

Liza Zimmerman, Editor-In-Chief
Jeremy Nedelka, Managing Editor

Written for commissioners, board members, headquarters personnel, and retail store managers responsible for buying beverage alcohol in the eighteen control states. Covered editorial includes product knowledge, market trends, store operations, merchandising, warehousing, computerization, administration, training, and other topics.
Cost: $20.00
Frequency: Bi-Monthly
Circulation: 8500

16619 US Beer Market: Impact Databank Review and Forecast
M Shanken Communications
387 Park Ave S
Suite 8
New York, NY 10016-8872

212-684-4224
FAX 212-684-5424
Home Page: www.cigaraficionado.com

Marvin Shanken, Publisher
Samantha Shanken, Marketing Manager
Cost: $9.10

16620 US Liquor Industry
Business Trend Analysts/Industry Reports
2171 Jericho Tpke
Suite 200
Commack, NY 11725-2937

631-462-5454
FAX 631-462-1842
E-Mail: bta@li.net
Home Page: www.businesstrendanalysts.com

Charles J Ritchie, Executive VP
Donna Priani, Marketing Director
Linda Sherman, Production Manager
Jennifer Wichert, Research Director

A survey summarizing the past, current and future markets and trends in the liquor industry.
Cost: $1195.00
600 Pages
Founded in 1999

16621 US Wine Market
Business Trend Analysts/Industry Reports
2171 Jericho Tpke
Suite 200
Commack, NY 11725-2937

631-462-5454
800- 86- 464
FAX 631-462-1842
Home Page: www.businesstrendanalysts.com

Charles J Ritchie, Executive VP
Donna Priani, Marketing Director

An analysis of the wine industry, domestic and imported.
Cost: $1995.00
470 Pages
Circulation: 2004
Founded in 1978

16622 Vineyard and Winery Management Magazine
Vineyard & Winery Management
421 E Street
Santa Rosa, CA 95404

707-577-7700
FAX 707-577-7705
Home Page: www.vwm-online.com

Robert Merletti, CEO/Publisher
Dennis Black, General Manager
Tina Caputo, Editor-in-Chief

A leading independent award winning wine trade magazine serving all of North America.
Cost: $37.00
100 Pages
Frequency: Bi-Monthly
Circulation: 6900
ISSN: 1047-4951
Founded in 1975
Printed in 4 colors on glossy stock

16623 Wine Advocate
Robert M Parker Jr
PO Box 311
Monkton, MD 21111

410-329-6477
FAX 410-357-4504
E-Mail: wineadvocate@erobertparker.com
Home Page: www.erobertparker.com

Robert M Parker Jr, Publisher/ Editor
Jacques Robinson, President

An independent magazine covering reviews of wine.
Cost: $60.00
64 Pages
Circulation: 40000
Founded in 1978

16624 Wine and Spirits
Winestate Publications
1748 Market Street
San Francisco, CA 94102-4997

415-255-7736
FAX 415-255-9659
E-Mail:
mlkinney@wineandspiritsmagazine.com
Home Page:
www.wineandspiritsmagazine.com/

Joshua Greene, Editor/Publisher
Michael Kinney, Associate Publisher
Ray Isle, Managing Editor
W. Charles Squires, Circulation Director
Gilian Handelman, Marketing Manager

A consumer magazine for wine enthusiasts.
Cost: $26.00
70 Pages
Circulation: 75000
Founded in 1987
Printed in 4 colors on glossy stock

Trade Shows

16625 ASBC Annual Meeting
American Society of Brewing Chemists
3340 Pilot Knob Road
Saint Paul, MN 55121-2055

651-454-7250
800-328-7560
FAX 651-454-0766

E-Mail: bford@scisoc.org
Home Page: www.meeting.asbcnet.org

Betty Ford, Meetings Director
Sue Casey, Meetings Coordinator
Steven Nelson, VP
300 Attendees
Frequency: June/Non-Members Fee

16626 American Beverage Licensees Annual Convention & Trade Show
American Beverage Licensees
5101 River Road
Suite 108
Bethesda, MD 20816-1560

301-656-1494
FAX 301-656-7539
Home Page: www.nabronline.org

Harry Wiles, Executive Director
Susan Day Pirieda, Office Manager

Annual show of 75 manufacturers, suppliers and distributors of alcoholic beverages.
700 Attendees
Frequency: March

16627 American Society for Enology and Viticulture Annual Meeting
PO Box 1855
Davis, CA 95617-1855

530-753-3142
FAX 530-753-3318
E-Mail: society@asev.org
Home Page: www.asev.org

Bill Mead, Event/Tradeshow Coordinator

With technical sessions, research forums, symposia and a supplier showcase.
Frequency: June
Founded in 1950

16628 American Wine Society
3006 Latta Road
Rochester, NY 14612-3298

585-225-7613
FAX 585-225-7613
E-Mail: angel910@aol.com
Home Page: americanwinesociety.com

Angel E Nardone, Executive Director
12 booths.
600 Attendees
Frequency: November
Founded in 1967

16629 Beer, Wine & Spirits Industry Trade Show
Indiana Association of Beverage
200 S Meridian Street
Suite 350
Indianapolis, IN 46225-3418

317-847-7580
FAX 317-673-4210

Teresa Koch

Annual show of 125 exhibitors of alcohol beverage distillers brewers that are recognized primary sources in the state of Indiana as supplies for retailers.
2500 Attendees

16630 Craft Brewers Conference and Brew Expo America
Brewers Association
736 Pearl Street
Boulder, CO 80302

303-447-0816
888-822-6273
FAX 303-447-2825
E-Mail: info@brewersassociation.org

Home Page: www.brewersassociation.org
Social Media: *Facebook, Twitter, Youtube*

Charlie Papazian, President
Bob Pease, VP
Cindy Jones, Sales/Marketing Director
1,200 Attendees
Frequency: April

16631 Great American Beer Festival
Brewers Association
736 Pearl Street
Boulder, CO 80302

303-447-0816
888-822-6273
FAX 303-447-2825
E-Mail: info@brewersassociation.org
Home Page: www.brewersassociation.org
Social Media: *Facebook, Twitter, Youtube*

Charlie Papazian, President
Bob Pease, VP
Cindy Jones, Sales/Marketing Director
Frequency: September

16632 NABR Tasting & Display Event Annual Convention
American Beverage Licensees
5101 River Road
Suite 108
Bethesda, MD 20816-1560

301-656-1494
FAX 301-656-7539
Home Page: www.nabronline.org

Harry Wiles, Executive Director
Shawn Ross, Office Manager

Offers exhibits on spirits, beer and wine industry supplies, equipment, bar accessories and computers. The NABR Annual Convention is a gathering of alcohol beverage retailers and proprietors for networking and educational opportunities. An exclusive trade display and tasting event is held to promote brands and services of use to retailers and proprietors. There are 25-75 booths.
500+ Attendees
Frequency: March

16633 NBWA Annual Convention
National Beer Wholesalers Association
1101 King Street
Suite 600
Alexandria, VA 22314-8965

703-683-4300
FAX 703-683-8965
E-Mail: info@nbwa.org
Home Page: www.nbwa.org
Social Media: *Facebook, Twitter*

Craig A Purser, President & CEO
Michael Johnson, EVP Fed Aff/Chief Advisory Office
Rebecca Spicer, VP Public Affairs/Chief
Paul Pisano, SVP Industry Affairs & Gen. Counsel

Designed to provide valuable education programs and important networking opportunities for the beer industry. Featuring speakers and seminars on a number of topics of imprtance to beer distributors .
2500 Attendees
Frequency: Fall

16634 National Beer Wholesalers Association Convention and Trade Show
Corcoran Expositions

33 N Dearborn Street
Suite 505
Chicago, IL 60602-3103

312-541-0567
800-541-0359
FAX 312-541-0573

Al Natker, Operations Manager

Biennial show of 166 manufacturers, suppliers
and distributors of brewery software and hardware, trucking, beer cleaning equipment and related equipment, supplies and services.
3000 Attendees

16635 Wineries Unlimited
Vineyard & Winery Services
3883 Airway Drive
Suite 250
Santa Rosea, CA 95403

707-577-7700
800-535-5670
FAX 707-577-7705
Home Page: www.wineriesunlimited.com

The largest, most powerful trade show and conference for the eastern wine industry.
2000 Attendees
Frequency: March

Directories & Databases

16636 Beverage Marketing Directory
Beverage Marketing Corporation
2670 Commercial Ave
Mingo Junction, OH 43938-1613

740-598-4133
800-332-6222
FAX 740-598-3977
Home Page: www.beveragemarketing.com

Andrew Standardi III, Director of Operations
Kathy Smurthwaite, Editor

Publication is available in Print Copy
(Price-$1,465), PDF Format (Price-$1,465),
CD-ROM Format (For pricing, call number
listed for details or visit website), and Online.
1196 Pages

16637 Brewers Resource Directory
Brewers Association
736 Pearl Street
Boulder, CO 80302

303-447-0816
888-822-6273
FAX 303-447-2825
E-Mail: info@brewersassociation.org
Home Page: www.brewersassociation.org
Social Media: *Facebook, Twitter, Youtube*

Charlie Papazian, President
Bob Pease, VP
Cindy Jones, Sales/Marketing Director

Various categories of listees are included that
have a direct relation to the beer and liquor industry.
Mailing list available for rent

16638 Contacts
National Alcohol Beverage Control
Association
4401 Ford Avenue, Suite 700
Alexandria, VA 22302-1507

703-578-4200
FAX 703-820-3551
Home Page: www.nabca.org
Social Media: *Facebook, Twitter*

James M Sgueo, Executive Director
Dixie Jamieson, Executive Assistant

Members include control jurisdictions, supplier
members and industry trade associations.

16639 Directory & Products Guide
Vineyard & Winery Services
PO Box 2358
Windsor, CA 95492

707-836-6820
800-535-5670
FAX 707-836-6825
Home Page: vwm-online.com

Jennifer Merietti, Sales/Marketing Manager
Dennis Black, General Manager
Suzanne Webb, Marketing Director

A must have reference book that belongs on the
desk of every wine professional. Whether it's
tracking down a particular vendor, shopping for
the best deal on oak barrels or searching for
out-of-state winery contacts, the DPG is a powerhouse of information. Over 2,300 supplier
listings and 2,700 winery/vineyard listings, it is
a reliable resource that saves time and money.
Cost: $95.00
450+ Pages
Frequency: Annually

16640 Food & Beverage Market Place
Grey House Publishing
4919 Route 22
PO Box 56
Amenia, NY 12501

518-789-8700
800-562-2139
FAX 845-373-6390
E-Mail: books@greyhouse.com
Home Page: www.greyhouse.com
Social Media: *Facebook, Twitter*

Leslie Mackenzie, Publisher
Richard Gottlieb, Editor

This information-packed 3-volume set is the
most powerful buying and marketing guide for
the US food and beverage industry. Includes
thousands of industry freight and transportation
listings.
Cost: $595.00
2000 Pages
Frequency: Annual
ISBN: 1-592373-61-5
Founded in 1981

16641 Food & Beverage Marketplace:
Online Database
Grey House Publishing
4919 Route 22
PO Box 56
Amenia, NY 12501

518-789-8700
800-562-2139
FAX 518-789-0556
E-Mail: gold@greyhouse.com
Home Page: http://gold.greyhouse.com
Social Media: *Facebook, Twitter*

Richard Gottlieb, President
Leslie Mackenzie, Publisher

This complete updated Food & Beverage Market Place: Online Database is the go-to source
for the food and beverage industry. Anyone involved in the food and beverage industry needs
this 'industry bible' and the important contacts
to develop critical research data that can make
for successful business growth.
Frequency: Annual
Founded in 1981

16642 Impact International Directory:
Leading Spirits, Wine and Beer
Companies
M Shanken Communications

387 Park Ave S
8th Floor
New York, NY 10016-8872

212-684-4224
FAX 212-684-5424
Home Page: www.cigaraficionado.com

Marvin Shanken, Publisher

A directory offering information on the major
players of the alcoholic beverage industry.
Cost: $295.00

16643 Impact Yearbook: Directory of the US
Wine, Spirits & Beer Industry
M Shanken Communications
387 Park Ave S
8th Floor
New York, NY 10016-8872

212-684-4224
FAX 212-684-5424
Home Page: www.cigaraficionado.com

Marvin Shanken, Publisher

A directory offering information on the top 40
American distributors and profiles of compa-
nies.
Cost: $170.00
Frequency: Annual

16644 US Alcohol Beverage Industry
Category CD
Beverage Marketing Corporation
2670 Commercial Ave
Mingo Junction, OH 43938-1613

740-598-4133
800-332-6222
FAX 740-598-3977
Home Page: www.beveragemarketing.com

Andrew Standardi III, Director of Operations
Kathy Smurthwaite, Editor

Contains information on approximately 3,030
companies including breweries,
microbreweries, wineries, distilleries, wholesalers and importers.
Cost: $3010.00
Frequency: Annual

16645 US Beverage Manufacturers and
Filling Locations Category CD
Beverage Marketing Corporation
850 Third Avenue, 18th Floor
New York, NY 10022

212-688-7640
800-332-6222
FAX 212-826-1255
Home Page: www.beveragemarketing.com

Andrew Standardi III, Director of Operations
Kathy Smurthwaite, Editor

Contains information on approximately 2,402
companies including breweries,
microbreweries, wineries, distilleries, soft
drink fillers and franchise companies, bottled
water fillers, juice, sports beverages and energy
drinks, soy, coffee, tea, and milk manufacturers.
Cost: $2390.00
Frequency: Annual
Mailing list available for rent

16646 US Wine & Spirits Industry Category
CD
Beverage Marketing Corporation
2670 Commercial Ave
Mingo Junction, OH 43938-1613

740-598-4133
800-332-6222
FAX 740-598-3977
Home Page: www.beveragemarketing.com

Andrew Standardi III, Director of Operations
Kathy Smurthwaite, Editor

Contains information on approximately 1,484 companies including wineries, distilleries, wine & spirit wholesalers, and wine & spirit importers.
Cost: $1475.00
Frequency: Annual

16647 Vineyard & Winery Management Magazine
Vineyard & Winery Services
421 E Street
Santa Rosa, CA 95404

707-577-7700
800-535-5670
FAX 707-577-7705
Home Page: vwm-online.com

Jennifer Merletti, Sales/Marketing Manager
Robert Merletti, Chairman/Owner
George Christie, President/CEO

A leading technical trade publication serving the North American Wine Industry and designed for today's serious wine business professional.
Founded in 1975
Mailing list available for rent

16648 Who's Who in Beer Wholesaling Directory
National Beer Wholesalers Association
1101 King Street
Suite 600
Alexandria, VA 22314-8965

703-683-4300
FAX 703-683-8965
E-Mail: info@nbwa.org
Home Page: www.nbwa.org
Social Media: *Facebook, Twitter*

Craig A Purser, President & CEO
Michael Johnson, EVP Fed Aff/Chief Advisory Office
Rebecca Spicer, VP Public Affairs/Chief
Paul Pisano, SVP Industry Affairs & Gen. Counsel

A listing of more than 3,000 beer distributors and suppliers in the industry.
Cost: $50.00

16649 Wholesale Beer Association Executives of America Directory
Wholesale Beer Association Executives of America
2805 E Washington Avenue
Madison, WI 53704-5165

608-255-6464
FAX 608-255-6466

7 Pages
Frequency: Annual

16650 Wine & Spirits Industry Marketing
Jobson Publishing Corporation
100 Avenue of the Americas
9th Floor
New York, NY 10013-1678

212-274-7000
FAX 212-431-0500

Michael J Tansey, CEO

List of about 300 wine and liquor firms including wineries, producers, distillers and importers.
Cost: $150.00
Frequency: Annual April

16651 Wine on Line
Wine on Line International

400 E 59th St
Apartment 9F
New York, NY 10022-2342

212-755-4363
FAX 212-755-7365

A database containing information including reviews about wines, production methods, serving advice, and more. Available on the Internet and worldwide web.
Frequency: Daily

16652 Wines and Vines Directory of the Wine Industry in North America Issue
Hiaring Company
1800 Lincoln Avenue
San Rafael, CA 94901-1221

415-453-9700
FAX 415-453-2517
E-Mail: info@winesandvines.com
Home Page: www.winesandvines.com

Dorthy Kubota-Cordery, Editor
Phil Hiaring, Publisher
Debbie Hennessy, Editor
Renee Skiadas, Circulation Director
Chet Klingensmith, Owner

Annual guide offering listings of wineries and wine industry suppliers in the US, Canada and Mexico.
Cost: $85.00
505 Pages
Frequency: Annual
Circulation: 5000

Industry Web Sites

16653 http://gold.greyhouse.com
G.O.L.D Grey House OnLine Databases

Grey House Publishing's online database platform, GOLD, offers Quick Search, Keyword Search and Expert Search for most business sectors including alcoholic beverage markets. The GOLD platform makes finding the information you need quick and easy - whether you're a novice searcher or an experienced database user. All of Grey House's directory products are available for subscription on the GOLD platform.

16654 www.beerinstitute.org
Beer Institute

Protects the market environment from unfair burdens imposed by government bodies. Represents members interest before Congress.

16655 www.beertown.org
American Homebrewers Association

Devoted to the education of home brewed beer. Publishes the only magazine devoted exclusively to education, art and science of homebrewing. Services include: Beer Judge Certification Program, Sanctioned Competitions, World's Largest Homebrew Competition.

16656 www.cawineclub.com
California Wine Club

A wine of the month club that features only California's small boutique wineries. Each month members receive two bottles of award-winning wine.

16657 www.greyhouse.com
Grey House Publishing

Authoritative reference directories for most business sectors including alcoholic beverage markets. Users can search the online databases with varied search criteria allowing for custom searches by product category, geographic area, sales volume, keyword, subject and more. Full

Grey House catalog and online ordering also available

16658 www.nbwa.org
National Beer Wholesalers Association

Research and development, quality control and ingredients.

16659 www.scisoc.org/asbc
American Society of Brewing Chemists

Annual scientific meeting for professionals in the brewing industry.

16660 www.wineinstitute.org
Wine Institute

Organization that represents the wine and spirit industry to state and federal lawmaking bodies.

16661 www.wssa.com
Wine and Spirits Shippers Association

Provides members, importers and exporters with efficient and economical ocean transportation and other logistic services.

Associations

16662 APA - The Engineered Wood Association
7011 S 19th Street
Tacoma, WA 98466-5333

253-565-6600
FAX 253-565-7265
E-Mail: casey@wbma.org
Home Page: www.apawood.org
Social Media: *Facebook, Twitter, LinkedIn*

Casey Voorhees, Executive Director
Stephanie Masters, Office Manager
Tom Rider, Manager Member Services

A nonprofit trade association that represents US and Canadian manufacturers of structural engineered wood products, including plywood, oriented strand board (OSB), glued-laminated timber (glulam), wood i-joists and structural composite lumber.
600 Members
Mailing list available for rent

16663 American Fiberboard Association
2118 Plum Grove Rd.
#283
Rolling Meadows, IL 60008

847-934-8394
E-Mail: richard@westernforestry.org
Home Page: www.fiberboard.org

Richard Zabel, Executive Director

The national trade organization of manufacturers of cellulose fiberboard products used for residential and commercial construction.
125 Members
Founded in 1909

16664 American Forest & Paper Association
AF&PA
1101 K Street, NW
Suite 700
Washington, DC 20005

202-463-2700
800-878-8878
FAX 202-463-2785
E-Mail: wrcla@wrcla.org
Home Page: www.afandpa.org
Social Media: *Facebook, Twitter, Youtube, Pinterest*

Peter Lang, General Manager
Edward Burke, Eastern Field Representative

Represents member companies and related trade associations which grow, harvest and process wood and wood fiber, manufacture pulp, paper and paperboard products from both virgin and recovered fiber and produce solid wood products.
Founded in 1954

16665 American Forest Foundation
2000 M Street, NW
Suite 550
Washington, DC 20036

202-765-3660
FAX 202-827-7924
E-Mail: info@wwpa.org
Home Page: www.forestfoundation.org

Michael O'Halloran, President
Tom Hanneman, VP/Director
Robert Bernhardt Jr, Director Information Services
Kevin CK Cheung, Director Technical Services
Kevin Binam, Director Economic Services

Committed to creating a future where North American forests are sustained by the public that understand and values the social, economic, and environmental benefits they pro-

vide to our communities, our nation, and the world.
135 Members
Founded in 1964
Mailing list available for rent

16666 American Forest Resource Council
5100 SW Macadam
Suite 350
Portland, OR 97239

503-222-9505
FAX 503-222-3255
E-Mail: info@amforest.org
Home Page: www.amforest.org
Social Media: *Facebook, Twitter*

Tom Partin, President

Manufacturers and forest products companies working for responsible forestry.

16667 American Forests
1220 L Street NW
Suite 750
Washington, DC 20005

202-737-1944
E-Mail: membersupport@wdma.com
Home Page: www.americanforests.org
Social Media: *Facebook, Twitter, LinkedIn, RSS*

Michael O'Brien, CAE, President & CEO
Jeff Lowinski, Vice President, Technical Services
Jeffrey Inks, Vice President, Code & Regulatory
John McFee, VP, Certification Programs
Jonathan Paine, VP, Membership & Operations

Restoring watersheds to help provide clean drinking water and replanting forests destroyed by human action and by natural disasters.
Founded in 1927
Mailing list available for rent

16668 American Hardwood Export Council
American Hardwood Export Council
1825 Michael Faraday Dr
Reston, VA 20190

703-435-2900
FAX 703-435-2537
E-Mail: wcma@wcma.com
Home Page: www.ahec.org

Paul Dow, President
Sid Anderson, III, Vice President
Keith Malmstadt, Treasurer

AHEC provides the global hardwood industry with promotional assistance, technical information and sources of supply for American hardwoods from its international offices.
Founded in 1929

16669 American Institute of Timber Construction
American Institute of Timber Construction
7012 S Revere Parkway
Suite 140
Centennial, CO 80112

503-639-0651
FAX 503-684-8928
E-Mail: info@wmma.org
Home Page: www.aitc-glulam.org
Social Media: *Facebook, Twitter, LinkedIn*

Jamison J. Scott, President
Chris Hacker, Vice President
Fred Stringfellow, Executive Director
Diane Schafer, Director of Meetings
Amy Chetelat, Director of Finance

The national trade association of the structural glued laminated (glulam) timber industry.
Founded in 1899

16670 American Lumber Standard Committee
American Lumber Standard Committee
PO Box 210
Germantown, MD 20875-0210

301-972-1700
FAX 301-540-8004
E-Mail: info@wmmpa.com
Home Page: www.alsc.org
Social Media: *Facebook*

Kellie Schroeder, CMP, CAE, CEO / Exec. VP
Clark Malak, Legal Counsel
Sadie Dickinson, Member Services
Scott Biesecker, Finance
Ric Morrison, Technical Advisor

Comprised of manufacturers, distributors, users, and consumers of lumber, serves as the standing committee for the American Softwood Lumber Standard

16671 American Sports Builders Association
American Sports Builders Association
9 Newport Drive
Suite 200
Forest Hill, MD 21050

410-730-9595
888-501-2722
FAX 410-730-8833
E-Mail: info@wmia.org
Home Page: www.sportsbuilders.org
Social Media: *Facebook, Twitter*

Scott Mueller, President
Dave Rakauskas, Vice President
Jim Besonen, Secretary/Treasurer
Liza Wentworth, Program Administrator
Dave Rakauskas, Secretary/Treasurer

Wood flooring manufacturers and distributors.
Founded in 1977

16672 American Walnut Manufacturers Association
American Walnut Manufacturers Association
505 East State Street
Jefferson City, MO 65101

573-635-7877
FAX 573-636-2591
E-Mail: memberservices@asminternational.org
Home Page: www.walnutassociation.org
Social Media: *Facebook, Twitter, LinkedIn*

Dr. Sunniva R. Collins, FASM, President
Jon D. Tirpak, P.E., FASM, Vice President
Craig D. Clauser, P.E., Treasurer
Terry F. Mosier, Managing Director
Virginia Shirk, Foundation Executive Assistant

A national trade group representing manufacturers of walnut lumber, veneer, gunstock and dimensions.
35000 Members
Founded in 1913

16673 American Wood Chip Export Association
Stoel Rives
101 South Capitol Boulevard
Suite 1900
Boise, ID 83702

208-389-9000
FAX 208-389-9040
Home Page: www.stoel.com
Social Media: *Facebook, Wordpress*

Chris Felix, President
Holly Hampton, Vice President
John Schultz, Executive Vice President
Ashley Davis, Administrative Assistant
Tina Schwart, Business & Finance Manager

Researches and compiles data on the wood chip export association.
Founded in 1981

16674 American Wood Council

222 Catoctin Circle SE
Suite 201
Leesburg, VA 20175

202-463-2766
FAX 202-463-2791
Home Page: www.awc.org
Social Media: *Twitter, LinkedIn, YouTube*

Robert Glowinski, President & CEO

The wood products division of the American
Forest & Paper Association promotes the use
and manufacture of structural wood products.

16675 American Wood Protection Association

100 Chase Park S
Suite 116
Birmingham, AL 35244-1851

205-733-4077
FAX 205-733-4075
E-Mail: webmaster@agma.org
Home Page: www.awpa.com
Social Media: *Facebook, Twitter*

Dean Burrows, Chairman
Joe T Franklin Jr, President
Amir Aboutaleb, Vice President, Technical
Division
Jan Alfieri, Director, Education
Mary Ellen Doran, Web Communications
Manager

A non-profit organization which is responsible
for promulgating voluntary wood preservation
standards.
400 Members
Founded in 1916

16676 Appalachian Hardwood Manufacturers

Appalachian Hardwood Manufacturers
PO Box 427
Suite 202
High Point, NC 27272

336-885-8315
FAX 336-886-8865
E-Mail: info@amba.org
Home Page: www.appalachianwood.org/

Todd Finley, President
Troy Nix, Executive Director
Kym Conis, Managing Director

Promotes the use of Appalachian hardwoods.
Provides education and research programs.
400 Members
Founded in 1973

16677 Architectural Woodwork Institute

Architectural Woodwork Institute
46179 Westlake Drive
Suite 120
Potomac Falls, VA 20165-5874

571-323-3636
FAX 571-323-3630
E-Mail: CustomerCare@asme.org
Home Page: www.awinet.org
Social Media: *Facebook, Twitter, LinkedIn*

Julio Guerrero, President
David Soukup, Managing Director, Governance
James W. Coaker, Secretary/Treasurer
John Delli Venneri, Assistant Secretary
William Garofalo, Assistant Treasurer

Members consist of architectural woodworkers,
suppliers, design professionals and students
from around the world
12000 Members
Founded in 1880

16678 Association of Equipment Manufacturers

Association of Equipment Manufacturers

6737 W Washington St
Suite 2400
Milwaukee, WI 53214-5647

414-272-0943
FAX 414-272-1170
E-Mail: aem@aem.org
Home Page: www.aem.org
Social Media: *Twitter*

John Patterson, Chairman
Leif J. Magnusson, Vice Chair
Renee Peters, Chief Financial Officer
Megan Tanel, VP, Exhibitions & Events
Luke, Anne Forristall, VP, Political & Public
Affairs

Representing manufacturers of architectural,
construction, forestry, materials handling and
liabilty equipment.

16679 Association of Millwork Distributors

10047 Robert Trent Jones Pkwy
New Port Richey, FL 34655-4649

727-372-3665
800-786-7274
FAX 727-372-2879
E-Mail: info@atmanet.org
Home Page: www.amdweb.com

Will Motchar, Chairman
Clay D Tyeryar, President/Assistant Treasurer
Harry W. Buzzerd, Jr., ATMA Management
Counsel
Susan A. Denston, ATMA SVP/Secretary
Carlos F. J. Moore, Consultant

Provides leadership, certification, education,
promotion, networking and advocacy to, and
for, the millwork distribution industry.
Founded in 1933

16680 Association of Woodworking & Furnishings Suppliers

Association of Woodworking & Furnishings
2400 E Katella Ave
Suite 340
Anaheim, CA 92806

323-838-9440
800-946-2937
FAX 323-838-9443
E-Mail: info@aednet.org
Home Page: www.awfs.org
Social Media: *Facebook, Twitter, Google+,
YouTube*

Don Shilling, Chair
Whit Perryman, Vice Chair
Brian P. McGuire, President & CEO
Bob Henderson, Executive Vice President /
COO
Jason Blake, SVP/ CFO

Trade association for suppliers to the
woodworking and furnishings industry. Services include three trade shows: Woodworking;
Machinery and Supply Fair; Home and Commercial Furnishings.
500 Members

16681 Capital Lumber Company: Boise

Capital Lumber Company
5110 North 40th Street
Ste 242
Phoenix, AZ 85018

602-381-0709
FAX 602-955-6191
E-Mail: info@AFE.org
Home Page: www.capital-lumber.com
Social Media: *Facebook, Twitter, LinkedIn*

Dennis M. Hydrick, CPMM, President &
Chairman
Wayne P. Saya, CPE, CPMM, Executive
Director
Fred King, Vice Chair of Finance
Virginia N Gibson, Vice Chair of Membership
Wayne P. Saya Sr., CPE, Executive Director

Serves Idaho with a 10,000 square foot warehouse on a five acre site.
Founded in 1915

16682 Capital Lumber Company: Tacoma

Capital Lumber Company
230 East F. Street
Ste 242
Tacoma, WA 98421

602-381-0709
877-479-5077
FAX 602-955-6191
Home Page: www.capital-lumber.com
Social Media: *Twitter, LinkedIn*

Serves Western Washington, Alaska and Western Oregon through a seven acre asphalt covered yard and a 100,000 square foot fully
enclosed warehouse.
Founded in 1991

16683 Cedar Shake and Shingle Bureau

Cedar Shake & Shingle Bureau
PO Box 1178
Sumas, WA 98295-1178

604-820-7700
FAX 604-820-0266
E-Mail: amt@amtonline.org
Home Page: www.cedarbureau.org
Social Media: *Facebook, Twitter, LinkedIn,
Youtube*

Douglas K Woods, President
Amber L Thomas, Vice President - Advocacy
JefferyÿH Traver, Vice President - Business
PeterÿR. Eelman, Vice President - Exhibitions
Rebecca Stahl, Chief Financial Officer

Nonprofit trade association representing manufacturer's, distributors, approved installers and
service suppliers of Certilabel™ cedar shakes
and shingles.
400 Members
Founded in 1925

16684 Composite Panel Association

19465 Deerfield Avenue
Suite 306
Leesburg, VA 20176

703-724-1128
FAX 703-724-1588
E-Mail: acmhelp@acm.org
Home Page: www.compositepanel.org
Social Media: *Facebook, Twitter, LinkedIn,
Google+, YouTube*

Alexander L Wolf, President
Vicki Hanson, Vice President
Erik R Altman, Secretary/Treasurer
Vicki Hanson, Vice President
Erik AR. Altman, Secretary/ Treasurer

Represents Northern American Particle Board
and Manufacturers' sister association, Composite Wood Council. Represents manufacturers
and suppliers of Composite Wood Council.
Founded in 1947

16685 Fine Hardwood Veneer Association

American Walnut Manufacturers
Association
260 S 1st Street
Suite 2
Zionsville, IN 46077

317-873-8780
FAX 317-873-8788
E-Mail: amea@amea.org
Home Page:
www.h-i-solutions.com/wood/detail.htm
Social Media: *LinkedIn, YouTube*

Jack Mendenhall, CEA, President
Randy Koster, CEA, 1st Vice President
Don Bentley, Second VP
Dave Troutman, Treasurer

Represents the decorative veneer industry.
Members are face veneer manufacturers, deal-

ers, veneer custom cutters, rotary face and crossband manufacturers, hardwood industry suppliers, veneer salesman and veneer face plants.
284 Members
Founded in 1983

16686 Forest Industries Telecommunications

1565 Oak St
Eugene, OR 97401-4008

541-485-8441
FAX 541-485-7556
E-Mail: avemexecsec@avem.org
Home Page: www.landmobile.com

David Dedman, Chairman
Ken Harrison, Vice Chairman
Dawn M. Shiley, Executive Director
Clay Tyeryar, MAM, CAE, Assistant Treasurer
Kim Fay, Data Analyst

Organized to assist the forest industry in radio matters before the FCC.
49 Members
Founded in 1969

16687 Forest Landowners Association

900 Circle 75 Pkwy SE
Suite 205
Atlanta, GA 30339-3075

404-325-2954
800-325-2954
FAX 404-325-2955
E-Mail: inquiries@clinicalrobotics.com
Home Page: www.forestlandowners.com

Gyu-Seog Choi, President
Mark Dylewski, Vice President
Rajan Sudan, Vice President
Chung Ngai Tang, Secretary
Joseph Colella, Treasurer

Proactive, progressive, grassroots organization of timberland owners - large and small - who operate more than 47 million acres of timberland in 17 southern and eastern states.
Mailing list available for rent

16688 Forest Products Society

15 Technology Parkway South
Ste. 115
Peachtree Corners, GA 30092

855-475-0291
FAX 608-231-2152
E-Mail: cagi@cagi.org
Home Page: www.forestprod.org

John Addington, Manager

An international non-profit technical association founded to provide an information network for all segments of the forest products industry.
Founded in 1915

16689 Forest Products Trucking Council

1025 Vermont Avenue NW
Suite 1020
Washington, DC 20005-3516

202-149-9250

Douglas Domenech, Secretary

An affiliate of the American Pulpwood Association.
50 Members

16690 Friends of the Trees

PO Box 165
Hot Springs, MT 59845

406-741-5809
E-Mail: info@csda.org
Home Page: www.friendsofthetrees.net
Social Media: *Facebook, LinkedIn, YouTube, Instagram*

Kevin Baron, President
Jack Sondergard, Vice President

Pat O'Brien, Executive Director
Mike Orzechowski, Secretary/ Treasurer
500 Members
Founded in 1971
Mailing list available for rent

16691 Great Lakes Timber Professionals Association

3243 Golf Course Road
PO Box 1278
Rhinelander, WI 54501-1278

715-282-5828
FAX 715-282-4941
E-Mail: aimcal@aimcal.org
Home Page: www.timberpa.com
Social Media: *Facebook, Twitter, LinkedIn, YouTube, Instagram*

Craig Sheppard, Executive Director
Tracey Ingram, Operations Manager
Melissa Crandall, Administrative Assistant
Ashley Wood, Event Planner
Colin Rupp, Web Designer

A nonprofit organization that is committed to leading the Forest Products industry in sustainable forest management through advocacy, professionalism, service to members, education and training.
Founded in 1984

16692 Hall-Woolford Tank Company, Inc.

5500 N. Water Street
PO Box 2755
Philadelphia, PA 19120

215-329-9022
FAX 215-329-1177
E-Mail: kim@cemanet.org
Home Page: www.woodtank.com
Social Media: *Facebook, Twitter, LinkedIn*

Jerry Heathman, President
Garry Abraham, Vice President
Paul Ross, Secretary
Robert Reinfried, Executive Vice President of CEMA
E.A. Thompson, Treasurer

To promote the use and to guide the proper construction methods for wooden tanks as per NWTI S-82.
96 Members
Founded in 1933

16693 Hardwood Manufacturers Association

Hardwood Manufacturers Association
665 Rodi Road
Suite 305
Pittsburgh, PA 15235

412-244-0440
FAX 412-244-9090
E-Mail: info@farmequip.org
Home Page: www.hardwoodinfo.com
Social Media: *Twitter*

Vernon Schmidt, Executive Vice President
Elaina Jackson, Membership Services
Tricia Kidd, Accounting and Meeting Services
Kristi Ruggles, Publications and Communications
Hannah Hamontree, Communications Director

Over 100 companies with over 150 locations in the US.
340 Members

16694 Hardwood Plywood and Veneer Association

1825 Michael Faraday Dr
Reston, VA 20190-5350

703-435-2900
FAX 703-435-2537
E-Mail: fema@femalifesafety.org
Home Page: www.hpva.org
Social Media: *LinkedIn, Youtube*

Provides public relations, advertising, marketing, and technical services to manufacturers

and distributors of hardwood plywood, veneers and engineered hardwood flooring and suppliers who sell to these industries.
24 Members
Founded in 1925

16695 Hardwood Utilization Consortium

USDA Forest Service
Southern Research Station
Blacksburg, VA 24061-0503

540-231-5341
FAX 540-231-8868
E-Mail: info@fluidpowersafety.com
Home Page: www.consortium.forprod.vt.edu

Rory S. McLaren, Founder & Director

The role is to improve hardwood resource viability through better utilization, technology, markets, cooperative extension and education in the eastern United States.

16696 Hearth, Patio & Barbecue Association

1901 N Moore St
Suite 600
Arlington, VA 22209-1708

703-522-0086
FAX 703-522-0548
E-Mail: Askus@ifps.org
Home Page: www.hpba.org

Marti Wendel, CFPE, CFPS, CF, President & Chairperson
Donna Pollander, ACA, Executive Director
Jeff Morrow, Business Development Manager
Adele Kayser, Website/Communications Manager
Sue Dyson, Client Data Manager
2600 Members
Founded in 1960

16697 Intermountain Forest Association

2218 Jackson Blvd
#10
Rapid City, SD 57702

605-341-0875
FAX 605-341-8651
E-Mail: info@fpsa.org
Home Page: www.intforest.org
Social Media: *Facebook, Twitter, LinkedIn, Google+*

Gil Williams, Chairman
David Seckman, President & CEO
Robyn Roche, CFO
Andy Drennan, Senior VP, International Market
Adam Finney, VP of Membership and Communications

Seeks to provide a unified voice for the industry. Promotes a sustained timber yield. Monitors federal legislation.
350+ Members
Founded in 2005

16698 International Wood Products Association

4214 King St
Alexandria, VA 22302-1555

703-820-6696
FAX 703-820-8550
E-Mail: hei@heatexchange.org
Home Page: www.iwpawood.org

John H Addington, Secretary-Treasurer
Craig H Addington, Account Executive

International trade association for the North American imported wood products industry, representing companies and trade organizations engaged in the import of hardwoods and softwoods from sustainably managed forests in more than 30 nations across the globe.
19 Members
Founded in 1933

16699 Laminating Materials Association
Louisiana Municipal Association
700 North 10th street
Baton Rouge, LA 70802

225-344-5001
800-234-8274
FAX 225-344-3057
E-Mail: info@isapartners.org
Home Page: www.lma.org

John Duffy, Director
Ed Gerber, Director

Nonprofit trade group representing all decorative overlays and edgebanding in North America. These products are applied to a composite wood substrate and used in the production of furniture, store fixtures, kitchen cabinets and more.
650 Members
Founded in 1988

16700 Lumbermen's Credit Association
20 N Wacker Dr
Suite 1800
Chicago, IL 60606-2905

312-553-0943
FAX 312-553-2149
E-Mail: staff@iadd.org
Home Page: www.lumbermenscredit.com
Social Media: *Facebook, Twitter, LinkedIn*

Jeremy T. Guest, President
Mauro Tomelleri, VP, International Activities
Ian Young, Vice President, Media & Content
Jennifer Thoroe, Vice President, Membership
Eric B. Anderson, Vice President, Sales & Marketing

Assist credit managers and salesmen by providing listings and credit ratings of companies which deal in lumber and wood products. Also publishes a directory.

16701 MSR Lumber Producers Council
MSR Lumber Producers Council
6300 Enterprise Lane
Madison, WI 53719

888-848-5339
FAX 888-212-5110
E-Mail: websteward@iamaw.org
Home Page: www.msrlumber.org
Social Media: *Facebook, Twitter, RSS, Ucubed*

R Thomas Buffenbarger, CEO
Robert Martinez, Jr., General VP
Robert Roach, Jr., General Secretary-Treasurer
Diane Babineaux, Executive Assistant

Represents the interest of Machine Stress Rated Lumber Producers in the manufacturing, marketing, promotion, utilization and technical aspects of machine stress rated lumber.
Founded in 1888

16702 Maple Flooring Manufacturers Association
Maple Flooring Manufacturers Association
One Parkview Plaza
Suite 800
Oakbrook Terrace, IL 60181

847-480-9138
888-480-9138
FAX 847-686-2251
Home Page: www.maplefloor.org

International non-profit trade organization representing manufacturers of northern hard maple solid strip flooring along with flooring contractors, distributors and providers of installation-related products and services. Maintains technical standards for product quality, grading, shipping and packaging, and quality central.
Founded in 1954

16703 National Association of the Remodeling Industry
P.O. Box 4250
Des Plaines, IL 60016

847-298-9200
800-611-6274
FAX 847-298-9225
E-Mail: office@mdna.org
Home Page: www.nari.org
Social Media: *Facebook, Twitter, LinkedIn, Youtube*

Kim Shuster, AEA, President
Joe Lundvick, CEA, Vice President
John Greene, CEA, Second Vice President
Terry Yoder, Treasurer
Jennifer Gray, Director

Purpose is to establish and maintain a firm commitment to developing and sustaining programs that expand and unite the remodeling industry; to ensure the industry's growth and security; to encourage ethical conduct, sound business practices and professionalism in the remodeling industry; and to present NARI as the recognized authority in the remodeling industry.
383 Members
Founded in 1941

16704 National Food Flooring Association
111 Chesterfield Industrial Boulevard
Suite B
Chesterfield, MO 63005

636-519-9663
800-422-4556
636-519-9663
FAX 636-519-9664
Home Page: www.nofma.org
Social Media: *Facebook, Twitter, LinkedIn, Youtube, RSS*

Carlos M. Cardoso, Chairman
John M. Stropki, Vice Chairman
Stephen V. Gold, President
Cameron L. Mackey, Vice President, Sales and Marketing
Daniel J. Meckstroth, Vice President and Chief Economist

It's warmer with wood. Genuine hardwoods, plus one-of-a-kind beauty. You never get tired of solid hardware floors - provides the perfect setting.
500+ Members
Founded in 1933

16705 National Frame Builders Association
8735 W Higgins Road
Suite 300
Chicago, IL 60631

785-843-2444
800-557-6957
FAX 847-375-6495
E-Mail: jnofsinger@mhia.org
Home Page: www.nfba.org
Social Media: *Facebook, Twitter, LinkedIn, Youtube, Blooger, RSS*

Dave Young, Executive Chairman
John Paxton, President
Gregg E. Goodner, Vice President
Cathy Moose, Executive Assistant
Victoria Wheeler, Director Member Services

Building contractors, suppliers, design and code professionals and academic personnel specializing in the post frame construction industry.
22 Members
Founded in 1945

16706 National Hardwood Lumber Association
National Hardwood Lumber Association

PO Box 34518
Memphis, TN 38184

901-377-1818
800-933-0318
E-Mail: bob@mpta.org
Home Page: www.nhla.com
Social Media: *Youtube*

Robert Reinfried, Executive VP

Founded to establish a uniform system of grading rules for the measurement and inspection of hardwood lumber
23 Members
Founded in 1933

16707 National Lumber and Building Material Dealers Association
2025 M St NW
Suite 800
Washington, DC 20036-3309

202-367-1169
800-634-8645
FAX 202-367-2169
E-Mail: nfpa@nfpa.com
Home Page: www.dealer.org
Social Media: *Facebook, Twitter, LinkedIn, Google+*

Jeff Stuart, Chairman of the Board
Eric Lanke, Chief Executive Officer
Denise Rockhill, OEM Marketing Manager
Pete Alles, Director of Membership & Comm.
Sue Chase, Director of Finance & HR

To advance the national agenda for America's building material suppliers.
Founded in 1955

16708 National Wood Flooring Association
111 Chesterfield Industrial
Suite B
Chesterfield, MO 63005-1219

636-519-9663
800-422-4556
FAX 636-519-9664
E-Mail: info@ntma.org
Home Page: www.nwfa.org
Social Media: *Twitter, LinkedIn*

Rob Akers, CEO
Rich Basalla, Membership Officer
Tiffany Bryson, Sales/Sponsorship Manager
John Capka, Chief Financial Officer

A not-for-profit trade association serving the wood flooring industry
2800 Members
Founded in 1943

16709 National Wood Window and Door Association
330 N. Wabash Avenue
Suite 2000
Chicago, IL 60611-4267

312-321-6802
FAX 847-299-1286
E-Mail: naeda@naeda.com
Home Page: www.wdma.com
Social Media: *Facebook, Twitter, LinkedIn*

Blaine Bingham, Chairman
Richard Lawhun, President/CEO
Joseph Dykes, VP Industry Relations
Michael Williams, VP Operations
Doug Kreienkamp, Coordinator Operations

Members are makers of standard building products such as doors, windows and frames.
5000 Members
Founded in 1900

16710 National Wooden Pallet & Container Association

1421 Prince Street
Suite 340
Alexandria, VA 22314-2805

703-519-6104
FAX 703-519-4720
E-Mail: info@opeesa.com
Home Page: www.palletcentral.com
Social Media: *Twitter, LinkedIn*

Jeff Plotka, President and Director
Nancy Cueroni, Executive Director
David Dollard, Director
Robert Smith, Director
Mark DeShetler, Director

An advocacy organization communicating regularly with key lawmakers and regulators, collaborating with a broad network of business groups and wood product organizations.

16711 New England Kiln Drying Association

SUNY
200A Progress Drive Ext,
Burgaw, NC 28425

910-259-9794
FAX 910-259-1625
E-Mail: pmmiwebhelp@pmmi.org
Home Page: www.kiln-direct.com
Social Media: *Facebook, Twitter, LinkedIn, Youtube*

Charles D. Yuska, President and CEO
Tom Egan, Vice President, Industry Services
Maria Ferrante, VP, Education & Workforce Dev.
Patti Fee, Vice President Meetings And Events
Jim Pittas, Senior Vice President

Disseminates information on the dying of wood to the wood-using industry.
Founded in 1933

16712 North American Wholesale Lumber Association

330 N. Wabash
Suite 2000
Chicago, IL 60611

312-321-5133
800-527-8258
FAX 312-673-6838
E-Mail: info@patmi.org
Home Page: www.nawla.org

Supports the wholesale lumber industry. Publishes monthly NAWLA Bulletin that includes industry and association news, and produces the NAWLA Traders Market, an annual trade show bringing together over 1500 manufacturers and wholesale lumber traders at the premier event in the forest products industry. NAWLA also produces a variety of educational programs designed to enhance professionalism in the lumber industry.
7 Members
Founded in 1951

16713 Northeastern Loggers Association

3311 State Route 28
PO Box 69
Old Forge, NY 13420-0069

315-369-3078
800-318-7561
FAX 315-369-3736
E-Mail: pti@powertoolinstitute.com
Home Page: www.northernlogger.com

Susan Young, Manager

Works to improve the industry in the Northeast and educate the public about policies and products of the industry.
Founded in 1968

16714 Northern Woods Logging Association

PO Box 270
Jackman, ME 04945-0270

Provides members with a workers compensation protection program. Conducts on-site inspections and offers a first aid course and safety training program.
213 Members
Founded in 1974

16715 Northwest Forestry Association

1500 SW 1st Ave
Suite 700
Portland, OR 97201-5837

503-222-9505
FAX 503-222-3255
E-Mail: ptrahq@ptra.org
Home Page: www.nwtrees.org

Doug Landgraf, President
Bill Taylor, First Vice President
Curt Benson, CPMR, Second Vice President
Susan Crolla, Executive Director
Walt Brooks, Treasurer

Promotes forestry throughout the region to assure a permanent industry and stable economy. Works to keep informed on current changes affecting forest products.
Founded in 1972

16716 Northwestern Lumber Association

Northwestern Lumber Association
5905 Golden Valley Road
Suite 110
Minneapolis, MN 55422-4535

763-544-6822
888-544-6822
FAX 763-595-4060
E-Mail: info@pmpa.org
Home Page: www.nlassn.org
Social Media: *Facebook, Twitter, LinkedIn, YouTube, Flickr, RSS*

Tom Bernstein, Jr., President
Harry S Eighmy, First Vice President
Douglas R. Coster, Second Vice President
Bernard Nagle, Executive Director
Miles K. Free, Director, Industry Research & Tech.

Retail lumber dealer in Iowa, Minnesota, North Dakota, and South Dakota.
Mailing list available for rent

16717 OSBGuide

Structural Board Association
25 Valleywood Drive
Unit 27
Markham, L3R 5L9, ON

905-475-1100
FAX 905-475-1101
E-Mail: ria@robotics.org
Home Page: osbguide.tecotested.com
Social Media: *Facebook, Twitter, LinkedIn, YouTube, Google+*

Jeff Burnstein, Executive Director

Members are manufacturers of structural panels.
Founded in 1974

16718 Pacific Logging Congress

Pacific Logging Congress
PO Box 1281
Maple Valley, WA 98038

425-413-2808
FAX 425-413-1359
E-Mail: rbrothers@wade-partners.com
Home Page: www.pacificloggingcongress.com

Matt Thompson, President
Sean Ryan, Vice-President
Bill Wade, Executive Director
Toni Nastali, Treasurer
Randy Brothers, Manager

Logging firms.
140 Members
Founded in 1981

16719 Pacific Lumber Exporters Association

720 NE Flanders
Suite 207
Portland, OR 97232

503-701-6510
FAX 503-467-5273
E-Mail: advertising@sme.org
Home Page: www.lumber-exporters.org
Social Media: *Facebook, Twitter, LinkedIn, Youtube, RSS*

Wayne F. Frost, CMfgE, President/Interim CEO
Jeffrey M. Krause, Chief Executive Officer
Dean L. Bartles, PhD, FSME, Secretary/Treasurer
Debbie Holton, Managing Director
Jeannine Kunz, Managing Director

Provide forum to discuss trade issues and problems; promote member companies through governmental and other trade association channels.
7000 Members
Founded in 1932

16720 Pacific Lumber Inspection Bureau

Pacific Lumber Inspection Bureau
909 S. 336th St.
Ste 203
Federal Way, WA 98003

253-835-3344
FAX 253-835-3371
E-Mail: srs@wjweiser.com
Home Page: www.plib.org
Social Media: *Facebook*

Accredited for grading and grade stamping of softwood lumber. Issues certificates on domestic and export lumber shipments.

16721 Pennsylvania Forest Products Association

301 Chestnut Street
Suite 102
Harrisburg, PA 17101

717-901-0420
800-232-4562
FAX 717-901-0360
E-Mail: pmmiwebhelp@pmmi.org
Home Page: www.paforestproducts.org
Social Media: *Facebook, Twitter*

Charles D. Yuska, President and CEO
Tom Egan, Vice President, Industry Services
Maria Ferrante, VP, Education & Workforce Dev.
Patti Fee, Vice President Meetings And Events
Jim Pittas, Senior Vice President

Created to provide members with a unified voice on state legislative and regulatory issues.
650 Members
Founded in 1933

16722 Railway Tie Association

Railway Tie Association
115 Commerce Dr
Suite C
Fayetteville, GA 30214-7335

770-460-5553
FAX 770-460-5573
E-Mail: info@fpda.org
Home Page: www.rta.org

Tim Gillig, President & Chairman
Patricia A. Lilly, Executive Director
Beth Hiltabidle, Marketing Specialist
Joseph M. Thompson, General Manager
Donald Smith, Accounting Manager

Members include crosstie producers, sawmill owners, chemical manufacturers, wood preser-

vation companies, railroad maintenance engineers, purchasing officials and others.
180 Members
Founded in 1974

16723 Redwood Inspection Service

818 Grayson Road
Suite 201
Pleasant Hill, CA 94523

925-935-1499
888-225-7339
FAX 925-935-1496
E-Mail: contact@uama.org
Home Page: www.calredwood.org

Authorized by Department of Commerce to develop and supervise redwood lumber grading.
Founded in 1999

16724 Society of American Foresters

5400 Grosvenor Lane
Bethesda, MD 20814-2198

301-897-8720
866-897-8720
FAX 301-897-3690
E-Mail: wsandler@vma.org
Home Page: www.safnet.org

Greg Rogowski, Chairman
Bob Kemple, Vice Chairman
William S. Sandler, President
Marc Pasternak, VP/ VRC Executive Director
Malena Malone-Blevins, Meetings Manager

Provides access to information and networking opportunities to prepare members for the challenges and the changes that face natural resource professionals.
100 Members
Founded in 1938

16725 Society of Wood Science & Technology

PO Box 6155
Monona, WI 53716-6155

608-577-1342
FAX 608-467-8979
E-Mail: information@vi-institute.org
Home Page: www.swst.org
Social Media: *Facebook, Twitter, LinkedIn*

Dave Corelli, President
Tom Spettel, Executive Vice President
Robin Ginner, Executive Director
Ellie Murphy, Finance Associate
Ronald L. Eshleman, Ph.D., Technical Director

Promotes policies and procedures which assure the wise use of wood and wood-based products; assures high standards for professional performance of wood scientists and technologists; fosters educational programs at all levels of wood science and technology and further the quality of such programs; represents the profession in public policy development.
3000 Members
Founded in 1972

16726 Southeastern Lumber Manufacturers Association, Inc.

Southeastern Lumber Manufacturers
200 Greencastle Road
Tyrone, GA 30290

770-631-6701
FAX 770-631-6720
E-Mail: info@pli.edu
Home Page: www.slma.org
Social Media: *Facebook, Twitter, LinkedIn, RSS, Google+*

Victor J Rubino, President
Sandra R. Geller, Executive Vice President
William C. Cubberley, Vice President of Publishing
Anita C. Shapiro, Vice President of Programs
Donald F. Berbary, Chief Sales & Marketing Officer

Represents membership in local, regional, and national problems that affect southeastern lumber industry. Conducts marketing and promotional activity.
Founded in 1933

16727 Southern Cypress Manufacturers Association

Southern Cypress Manufacturers Association
400 Penn Center Boulevard
Suite 530
Pittsburgh, PA 15235

877-607-7262
E-Mail: zakaras@rand.org
Home Page: www.cypressinfo.org
Social Media: *Facebook, Twitter*

Michael D Rich, President/CEO
Richard Fallon, SVP and Chief Financial Officer
Andrew R Hoehn, SVP, Research and Analysis
Allison Elder, Vice President, Human Resources
Naveena Ponnusamy, Executive Director, Development

Administrative support provided by the Hardwood Manufacturers Association.
Founded in 1948
Mailing list available for rent

16728 Southern Forest Products Association

6660 Riverside Dr.
Suite 212
Metairie, LA 70003

504-443-4464
FAX 504-443-6612
E-Mail: info@rmmlf.org
Home Page: www.sfpa.org
Social Media: *Facebook, Twitter, LinkedIn*

David Phillips, Executive Director
Mark Holland, Associate Director
Catherine J. Boggs, President
Robert B. Keiter, Vice President
Gregory R. Danielson, Secretary

The Association and its members are committed to quality, and believe that Southern Pine forest products provide a smart, environmentally friendly way to meet our world's needs for a wide range of building and industrial products.
2000 Members
Founded in 1955

16729 Southern Pine Inspection Bureau

Southern Pine Inspection Bureau
Po Box 10915
Pensacola, FL 32524-0915

850-434-2611
FAX 850-434-1290
Home Page: www.spib.org

Anne Lytle, President

Develops grading standards for Southern pine lumber and provides an inspection service and grade marking systems.
Founded in 1984
Mailing list available for rent

16730 Temperate Forest Foundation

528 Hennepin Avenue
Suite 703
Minneapolis, MN 55403

612-333-0430
FAX 612-333-0432
E-Mail: sla@sportslaw.org
Home Page: www.forestinfo.org
Social Media: *Facebook, Twitter, LinkedIn*

Matthew J. Mitten, President
Richard A. Guggolz, Executive Director
Ash Narayan, Treasurer
Vered Yakovee, Secretary

William M. Drohan, CAE, Deputy Executive Director

A tax-exempt, non-profit, public charity. Provides leadership by articulating the current realities, and a positive inspiring vision of the future. Helps people move toward the positive vision of living sustainably.

16731 Timber Products Manufacturers Association (TPM)

951 E 3rd Avenue
Spokane, WA 99202-2287

509-535-4646
FAX 509-534-6106
E-Mail: secretariat@africanstudies.org
Home Page: www.timberassociation.com
Social Media: *Facebook, Twitter, LinkedIn, Flickr*

Toyin Samatar, President
Dorothy Hodgson, Vice President
Suzanne Moyer Baazet, Executive Director
Kathryn Salucka, Program Manager
Kathryn Salucka, Executive Assistant

Association of companies in the Timber and Wood products industry of the pacific northwest. TPM provides human resource and safety consulting, Training and employee benefits.
Founded in 1957

16732 Tree Care Industry Association

Tree Care Industry Association
136 Harvey Road
Suite 101
Londonderry, NH 03053

603-314-5380
800-733-2622
FAX 603-314-5386
E-Mail: aallhq@aall.org
Home Page: www.tcia.org/
Social Media: *Facebook, Twitter, LinkedIn, Flickr*

Kate Hagan, Executive Director
Kim Rundle, Executive Assistant
Emily Feltren, Director Government Relations
Julia O'Donnell, Director Membership Marketing
Ashley St. John, Director Marketing/Communications

Supports all those involved with trees and tree care by offering education and training, community events, and publications.
5000+ Members
Founded in 1906
Mailing list available for rent

16733 Truss Plate Institute

218 North Lee Street
Suite 312
Alexandria, VA 22314-2800

703-683-1010
FAX 866-501-4012
E-Mail: asis@asis.org
Home Page: www.tpinst.org
Social Media: *Facebook, Twitter, LinkedIn*

Dr. Sandra G. Hirsh, President
Richard Hill, Executive Director
Jan Hatzakos, Director of Finance & Admin
Vanessa Foss, Director of Meetings and Membership
Sandra Holder, Receptionist, Office Assistant

The Truss Plate Institute's mission is '...to maintain the truss industry on a sound engineering basis..'. To accomplish its mission, TPI establishes methods of design and construction for trusses in accordance with the American National Standards Institute's accredited consensus procedures for coordination and development of American National Standards in addition to providing a Quality Assurance In-

spection program and by contributing its expertise in other technical areas.
4000 Members
Founded in 1937

16734 West Coast Lumber Inspection Bureau

PO Box 23145
Portland, OR 97281-3145

503-639-0651
FAX 503-684-8928
E-Mail: info@asindexing.org
Home Page: www.wclib.org

Fred Leise, President
Diana Witt, Vice President and President-Elect
Gwen Henson, Executive Director
Janet Perlman, Treasurer
Judi Gibbs, Secretary

Supervises manufacturing practices, grade stamping, and inspecting.
1M Members
Founded in 1957

16735 Western Building Material Association

Western Building Material Association
909 Lakeridge Dr. SW
PO Box 1699
Olympia, WA 98502

360-943-3054
888-551-9262
FAX 360-943-1219
E-Mail: sales@atla.com
Home Page: www.wbma.org
Social Media: *Facebook*

Kelly Campbell, President
Timothy D. Lincoln, Vice President
Brenda Bailey-Hainer, Executive Director
Gillian Harrison Cain, Director of Member Programs
Jim Butler, Director of Information Systems

Regional trade association derving building material dealers throughout the states of Alaska, Idaho, Montana, Oregon and Washington and a federated association of the National Lumber and Building Material Dealers Association.
800 Members
Founded in 1991

16736 Western Forestry and Conservation Association

4033 SW Canyon Rd
Portland, OR 97221

503-226-4562
888-722-9416
FAX 503-226-2515
E-Mail: info@lff.org
Home Page: www.westernforestry.org

Diantha Dow Schull, President
Bruce Astrein, Executive Director
Nina Sonenberg, VP Communications
Sabrina Waldron, Program Manager
William Zeisel, Operations Director

Offers high-quality continuing education workshops and seminars for professional foresters throughout Oregon, Washington, Idaho, Montana, Northern California and British Columbia.
Mailing list available for rent

16737 Western Red Cedar Lumber Association

Western Red Cedar Lumber Association
1501-700 West Pender Street
Pender Place 1, Business Building
Vancouver, BC V6C 1G8

604-891-1262
800-266-1910
FAX 604-687-4930
E-Mail: g.rodriguez@arlisna.org

Home Page: ww.realcedar.com
Social Media: *Facebook, Twitter, LinkedIn*

Kristen Regina, President
Heather Gendron, Vice-President/President Elect
Jamie Lausch Vander Broek, Secretary
Mark Pompelia, Treasurer
Carol Graney, Editorial Director

Mission is to produce quality Western Red Cedar lumber products and support them with technical education and promotion.
Founded in 1972

16738 Western Wood Products Association

1500 SW First Ave.
Suite 870
Portland, OR 97201

503-224-3930
FAX 503-224-3935
E-Mail: webmaster@apalaweb.org
Home Page: www2.wwpa.org
Social Media: *Facebook, Twitter, LinkedIn, Flickr*

Buenaventura Ven Basco, Executive Director

Represents lumber manufacturers in 12 Western states and Alaska. Provides lumber quality control, technical support, and business information to supporting mills.
310 Members
Founded in 1980

16739 Window & Door Manufacturers Association

Window & Door Manufacturers Association
330 N. Wabash Avenue
Suite 2000
Chicago, IL 60611-4267

312-321-6802
800-223-2301
FAX 847-299-1286
E-Mail: office@alise.org
Home Page: www.wdma.com
Social Media: *Facebook, Twitter, LinkedIn*

John Budd, President
Connie Van Fleet, VP/President-Elect
Deborah York, Executive Director
Jeremy Uthank, Information Management

A trade association representing approximately 145 U.S. and Canadian manufacturers and suppliers of windows and doors for the domestic and export markiets.
Founded in 1915

16740 Wood Component Manufacturers Association

Wood Component Manufacturers Association
PO Box 662 Lindstrom
Ste 350
Minneapolis, MN 55045

651-332-6332
FAX 651-400-3502
E-Mail: info@aplici.org
Home Page: www.woodcomponents.org
Social Media: *Twitter*

Allison Burns, President
Debbie Dickson, Vice President
Liz Nugent, Recording Secretary
Joann Donatiello, Acting Treasurer

Represents manufacturers of wood component products for furniture, cabinetry, building products, and decorative wood products.
Founded in 1968

16741 Wood Machinery Manufacturers of America

9 Newport Dr.
Suite 200
Forest Hill, MD 21050

443-640-1052
FAX 443-640-1031
E-Mail: info@wmma.org
Home Page: www.wmma.org
Social Media: *Facebook, Twitter, LinkedIn*

Jamison Scott, President
Chris Hacker, Vice President
Fred Stringfellow, Executive Director

WMMA has worked to increase the productivity and profitability of U.S. machinery and tooling manufacturers and the businesses that support them.
Founded in 1899

16742 Wood Machinery Maufacturers of America

Wood Machinery Maufacturers of America
9 Newport Drive
Suite 200
Forest Hill, MD 21050

443-640-1052
FAX 443-640-1031
E-Mail: execdir@arsc-audio.org
Home Page: www.wmma.org
Social Media: *Facebook, LinkedIn, YouTube*

Sam Brylawski, President
David Seubert, VP
Louise Spear, Second VP/Program Chair
Esther Gillie, Secretary/Editor
1000 Members
Founded in 1966

16743 Wood Moulding and Millwork Producers Association

MMPA
507 1st St
Woodland, CA 95695-4025

530-661-9591
800-550-7889
FAX 530-661-9586
E-Mail: info@acl.org
Home Page: www.wmmpa.com
Social Media: *Facebook, Twitter*

Frank Quinn, President
Janelle Mazelin, Executive Director
Rodney Birch, Vice President
Sheila O Carlblom, Treasurer
Denise Nelson, Secretary

Promote quality products produced by its members, to develop sources of supply, to promote optimum use of raw materials to standardize products, and to increase the domestic and foreign usage of moulding and millwork products.
574 Members
Founded in 1956

16744 Wood Products Manufacturers Association

PO Box 761
Westminster, MA 01473-0761

978-874-5445
FAX 978-874-9946
E-Mail: woodprod@wpma.org
Home Page: www.wpma.org
Social Media: *Facebook, LinkedIn*

Philip Bibeau, Executive Director

Information and services to support businesses in the industry.
Founded in 1929

16745 Woodworking Machinery Industry Association
225 Reinekers Lane
Suite 410
Alexandria, VA 22314

860-350-9642
FAX 860-354-0677
E-Mail: info@aiip.org
Home Page: www.wmia.org
Social Media: *Facebook, Twitter, LinkedIn, YouTube, Instagram*

June Boyle, President
Shelly Azar, Secretary
Marilyn Harmacek, Treasurer
Michelle Rawl, Director - Membership
Jennifer Burke, Director - Marketing - Content

Providing the North American wood products industry with technologically advanced woodworking systems available in the global market. A wide range of special programs provide industry awards, safety publications, scholarships and a host of other methods to support industry initiatives and address industry issues.
700 Members
Founded in 1987

Newsletters

16746 AFRC News
American Forest Resource Council
5100 SW Macadam
Suite 350
Portland, OR 97239

503-222-9505
FAX 503-222-3255
E-Mail: info@amforest.org
Home Page: www.amforest.org

Tom Partin, President
Newsletter of the American Forest Resource Council.
Frequency: Monthly

16747 American Wood Protection Association Newsletter
American Wood Protection Association
100 Chase Park South
Suite 116
Birmingham, AL 35244-1851

205-733-4077
FAX 205-733-4075
E-Mail: info@awpa.com
Home Page: www.awpa.com

John Hall, Publisher

Reports on governmental issues and environmental news.
Cost: $7.50
12 Pages
Frequency: Monthly
Founded in 1921

16748 Association of Millwork Distributors Newsletter
Association Of Millwork Distributors
10047 Robert Trent Jones Pkwy
Trinity, FL 34655-4649

727-372-3665
800-786-7274
FAX 727-372-2879
E-Mail: marketing@amdweb.com
Home Page: www.amdweb.com/

Rosalie Leone, CEO
Kim Cotterman, Director of Membership
Updates for wholesale millwork distribution companies.
Frequency: Monthly
Circulation: 1500

Founded in 1964
Printed in 2 colors on glossy stock

16749 Building Products CONNECTION
Northwestern Lumber Association
5905 Golden Valley Road
Suite 110
Minneapolis, MN 55422-4535

763-544-6822
888-544-6822
FAX 763-595-4060
E-Mail: info@nlassn.org
Home Page: www.nlassn.org

Beth Stoll, Editor
Jodie Fleck, Director of Conventions & Tours
Cody Nuernberg, Manager of Membership

Dedicated to providing information on issues important to the success of the lumber and building material industry in the upper Midwest.
Cost: $300.00
Frequency: Bi-Monthly
Circulation: 2200
Mailing list available for rent

16750 Classified Exchange
Miller Publishing Corporation
PO Box 34908
Memphis, TN 38184-0908

901-372-8280
800-844-1280
FAX 901-373-6180
E-Mail: editor@millerwoodtradepub.com
Home Page: www.millerpublishing.com

Paul J Miller, President
Sue Putnam, Editor

Pages and pages of bargains, several pages on raw material and service sources for everything from lumber to curved plywood, from dry kilns to sawmill equipment and boilers. Special liquidations and auctions offering everything from soup to nuts.
Cost: $65.00
Frequency: Monthly

16751 Connected
Association of Millwork Distributors
10047 Robert Trent Jones Pkwy
Trinity, FL 34655-4649

727-372-3665
800-786-7274
FAX 727-372-2879
E-Mail: marketing@amdweb.com
Home Page: www.amdweb.com

Rosalie Leone, CEO

Keeps you abreast of the latest breaking news within the millwork industry regarding economics & finance; the current housing industry; legislative updates; codes, standards and the AMD Certification Program information, Education special offers as well as comprehensive Millwork News.
Frequency: Weekly

16752 Forestbytes
American Forests
734 15th Street NW
Suite 800
Washington, DC 20005

202-737-1944
Home Page: www.americanforests.org
Social Media: *Facebook, Twitter*

Lynda Webster, Chair
Scott Steen, CEO

Features environmental stories and breakthroughs that impact our forests and trees and news and updates on American Forests projects and programs.
Frequency: Monthly
Founded in 1990

16753 Forestry Source
Society of American Foresters
5400 Grosvenor Ln
Bethesda, MD 20814-2198

301-897-8720
FAX 301-897-3690
E-Mail: safweb@safnet.org
Home Page: www.safnet.org
Social Media: *Facebook, Twitter, LinkedIn*

Michael T Goergen Jr, Executive VP/CEO
Joe Smith, Editor

Offers the latest information on national forestry trends, the latest developments in forestry at the federal, state, and local levels, the newest advances in forestry-related research and technology, and up-to-date information about SAF programs and activities.
Cost: $33.00
Frequency: Monthly
Founded in 1900
Printed in 4 colors

16754 Import/Export Wood Purchasing News
Miller Publishing Corporation
PO Box 34908
Memphis, TN 38184-0908

901-372-8280
800-844-1280
FAX 901-373-6180
E-Mail: editor@millerwoodtradepub.com
Home Page: www.millerpublishing.com

Paul J Miller, President
Sue Putnam, Editor

Read features about overseas buyers, U.S. factories buying imported forest products and North American exporters. Also carries forest products business trends on the domestic and international markets.
Cost: $75.00
Frequency: Bi-Monthly

16755 MSR Council Matters
MSR Lumber Producers Council
6300 Enterprise Lane
Madison, WI 53719

888-848-5339
FAX 888-212-5110
E-Mail: info@msrlumber.org
Home Page: www.msrlumber.org

Steve Hardy, President

Provides updates on issues affecting members and customers
Frequency: Monthly
Founded in 1987

16756 National Frame Builders Association Newsletter
National Frame Builders Association
4700 W. Lake Avenue
Glenview, IL 60025

785-843-2444
800-557-6957
FAX 847-375-6495
E-Mail: info@nfba.org
Home Page: www.nfba.org

John Fullerton, VP
Tom Knight, President

Published by the National Frame Builders Association.

16757 National Wooden Pallet & Container Association: Newsletter
National Wooden Pallet & Container Association

1421 Prince Street
Suite 340
Alexandria, VA 22314-3501

703-519-6104
FAX 703-519-4720
E-Mail: palletcomm@aol.com
Home Page: www.nwpca.com

Bruce N Scholnick, President
Pamela Wilson, Publisher
Kathy Conroy, Marketing Director
Sam McAdow, Interim President
Susan Cheney, Membership Coordinator

Newsletter published by The National Wooden
Pallet and Container Association.
Cost: $2995.00

16758 SFPA E-Newsletter

Southern Forest Products Association
2900 Indiana Ave
Kenner, LA 70065-4605

504-443-4464
FAX 504-443-6612
E-Mail: mail@sfpa.org
Home Page: www.sfpa.org

Digges Morgan, President
Richard Wallace, VP Communications
Tami Kessler, Corporate Secretary
Stephen P. Conwell, President
Tami Kessler, Corporate Secretary & Director

The Association and its members are committed to quality, and believe that Southern Pine
forest products provide a smart, environmentally friendly way to meet our world's needs for
a wide range of building and industrial
products.
265 Members
Frequency: Weekly/Online

16759 Softwood Forest Products Buyer

Miller Publishing Corporation
PO Box 34908
Memphis, TN 38184-0908

901-372-8280
800-844-1280
FAX 901-373-6180
E-Mail: editor@millerwoodtradepub.com
Home Page: www.millerpublishing.com

Paul J Miller, President
Sue Putnam, Editor

Provides you with interesting feature articles
on purchasing, inventory control, marketing,
production, utilization and distribution of Softwood forest products such as lumber, plywood,
moulding, etc.
Cost: $65.00
Frequency: Bi-Monthly

16760 TPM Bulletin

Timber Products Manufacturers Association
951 E 3rd Avenue
Spokane, WA 99202-2287

509-535-4646
FAX 509-534-6106
E-Mail: tpm@tpmrs.com
Home Page: www.tpmrs.com

Dick Molenda, Interim President
Shelley Jeffers, Publications Coordinator

Provides insightful overviews of key employ-
ment issues that can impact every business.
Frequency: Monthly
Circulation: 250

16761 TPM Newsletter

Timber Products Manufacturers (TPM)
Association
951 E 3rd Avenue
Spokane, WA 99202-2287

509-535-4646
FAX 509-534-6106

E-Mail: tpm@tpmrs.com
Home Page: www.tpmrs.com

Dick MoLenda, Interim President
Jeff Bosma, Chairman

Official newsletter of Timber Products Manu-
facturers (TPM) Association.
Cost: $195.00
250 Members
Frequency: Monthly
Circulation: 700
Founded in 1916

16762 Timberline

Bear Creek Lumber
Po Box 669
Winthrop, WA 98862

800-597-7191
FAX 509-997-2040
E-Mail:
customerservice@bearcreeklumber.com
Home Page: www.bearcreeklumber.com
Social Media: *Twitter, LinkedIn*

Features articles about the timber industry, the
construction industry, how-to information, and
it also lets folks know what's new at Bear
Creek Lumber.
Cost: $15.00
6000 Pages

16763 TreeWorker

Tree Care Industry Association
136 Harvey Road
Suite 101
Londonderry, NH 03053

603-314-5380
800-733-2622
FAX 603-314-5386
E-Mail: tcia@tcia.org
Home Page: www.tcia.org
Social Media: *Facebook, Twitter, LinkedIn,
Youtube*

Mark Garvin, Interim CEO/President
Peter Gerstenberger, Sr Adv
Safety/Standards/Compliance
Frequency: Monthly
Founded in 1938

16764 Two-By-Four

Mountain States Lumber & Building
Material Dealers
9034 E Easter Pl
#103
Centennial, CO 80112-2104

303-793-0859
800-365-0919
FAX 303-290-9137
E-Mail: contact@mslbmda.org
Home Page: www.mslbmda.org

Geri Adams, Executive Director

16765 Wood Design Focus

Forest Products Society
2801 Marshall Court
Madison, WI 53705-2295

608-231-1361
FAX 608-231-2152
E-Mail: info@forestprod.org
Home Page: www.forestprod.org
Social Media: *Facebook, Twitter*

Paul Merrick, President
Patrice Tardif, President-Elect
Timothy M. Young, Vice President
Stefan Bergmann, Executive Vice President

Online publication providing a communications link between design professionals, educators, reserachers, building code officials, and
manufacturers of engineered wood products
through the publication of technical articles related to contemporary engineered wood con-

struction.
Cost: $125.00
Frequency: Quarterly
Founded in 1947

16766 Wood Machining News

Wood Machining Institute
PO Box 476
Berkeley, CA 94701

510-448-8363
FAX 925-945-0947
E-Mail: szymani@woodmachining.com
Home Page: www.woodmachining.com

Ryszard Szymani, Editor
Ryszard Szymani, Director

Information on the latest technological ad-
vances in the field of wood machining, includ-
ing sawing, planning and sanding operations as
well as the production of veneers and chips.
Cost: $72.00
Frequency: Fortnightly
Circulation: 600
Founded in 1984

Magazines & Journals

16767 AMD Millwork Magazine

Association of Millwork Distributors
10047 Robert Trent Jones Pkwy
Trinity, FL 34655-4649

727-372-3665
800-786-7274
FAX 727-372-2879
E-Mail: marketing@amdweb.com
Home Page: www.amdweb.com

Rosalie Leone, CEO

Digital news journal distributed to AMD members and industry professionals with an interest
in the millwork industry. An inside look at the
heartbeat of AMD and offers industry insights
found nowhere else.
Frequency: Monthly

16768 American Forests

American Forests
734 15th Street NW
Suite 800
Washington, DC 20005

202-737-1944
FAX 202-955-4588
Home Page: www.americanforests.org
Social Media: *Facebook, Twitter*

Deborah Gangloff, Executive Director
Lydia Scalettar, Art Director

Updates on forest management and environ-
mental policy, as well as news on the programs
and policies of the American Forests organiza-
tion.
Cost: $25.00
Frequency: Quarterly
Circulation: 25000
Founded in 1875

16769 American Forests Magazine

American Forests
734 15th Street NW
Suite 800
Washington, DC 20005

202-737-1944
Home Page: www.americanforests.org
Social Media: *Facebook, Twitter*

Lynda Webster, Chair
Scott Steen, CEO

Topics covered include urban forestry methods
and visiting champion trees, fighting invasive

species and learning about the many incredible creatures that make their homes in forests.
Frequency: Bi-Annually
Founded in 1990

16770 Crossties
Railway Tie Association
115 Commerce Dr
Suite C
Fayetteville, GA 30214-7335

770-460-5553
FAX 770-460-5573
E-Mail: ties@rta.org
Home Page: www.rta.org

Talty O'Connor, President/CEO

Highlights new products, industry news, and personnel changes.
Cost: $35.00
Circulation: 3000
Founded in 1983

16771 Crow's Weekly Market Report
CC Crow Publications
3635 N Farragut St
Portland, OR 97217-5954

503-241-7382
FAX 503-646-9971
E-Mail: info@chadcrowe.com
Home Page: www.chadcrowe.com
Social Media: *Facebook, Twitter, LinkedIn*

Chad Crowe, President
Sam Sherrill, Editor

Tracks the wood and lumber industry, providing customers with accurate and timely pricing and analysis.
Cost: $285.00
Frequency: Weekly
Circulation: 2000
Founded in 1921
Mailing list available for rent

16772 Custom Woodworking Business
Vance Publishing
400 Knightsbridge Parkway
Lincolnshire, IL 60069

847-342-2600
800-343-2016
FAX 847-634-4374
E-Mail: industrialinfo@vancepublishing.com
Home Page: www.iswonline.com
Social Media: *Facebook, Twitter, Youtube*

William C Vance, CEO
Helen Kuhl, Editor
Harry Urban, VP Publishing
Bill Esler, Associate Publisher/Editor-in-Chief
Rich Christianson, Associate Publisher/Editor-at-Large
Founded in 1937

16773 Design Solutions Magazine
Architectural Woodwork Institute
46179 Westlake Drive
Suite 120
Potomac Falls, VA 20165

571-323-3636
FAX 571-323-3630
E-Mail: info@awinet.org
Home Page: www.awinet.org

Judy Durham, Executive VP
Philip Duvic, Marketing Director
Kirsten Ingham, President

Featuring beautiful woodwork projects manufactured by members of the Architectural Woodwork Institute (AWI). Many other related publications, including woodworking quality standards used by woodwork manufacturers and design professionals.
Cost: $25.00
Frequency: Quarterly
Circulation: 27000

16774 Evergreen Magazine
Evergreen Foundations
PO Box 1290
Bigfork, MT 59911

406-837-0966
FAX 406-258-0815
E-Mail: editor@evergreenmagazine.com
Home Page: www.evergreenmagazine.com
Social Media: *Facebook*

James D Petersen, Publisher

Focuses on issues and events impacting forestry, forest communities, and the forest product industry. Includes profiles of industry leaders and advocates.
Frequency: Bi-Monthly
Circulation: 100000

16775 Fine Woodworking
Taunton Press
63 South Main Street
PO Box 5506
Newtown, CT 06470-2355

203-426-8171
800-477-8727
FAX 203-426-3434
E-Mail: fwads@taunton.com
Home Page: www.taunton.com

James Chiavelli, Publisher
Richard West, Advertising Manager

Published since 1975, written by woodworkers for woodworkers regularly shows the finest work in wood being done today.
Cost: $34.95
120 Pages
Frequency: 7 Issues (1yr)
Circulation: 250000
Founded in 1980
Printed in 4 colors on glossy stock

16776 Forest Industries
Miller Freeman Publications
600 Harrison Street
6th Fl
San Francisco, CA 94107

415-947-6000
FAX 415-947-6055
Home Page: www.mfi.com

Directed to foresters, loggers and manufacturers.
Cost: $55.00
90 Pages
Frequency: Monthly

16777 Forest Landowner Magazine
Forest Landowners Association
900 Circle 75 Pkwy Se
Suite 205
Atlanta, GA 30339-3075

404-325-2954
800-325-2954
FAX 404-325-2955
E-Mail: info@forestlandowners.com
Home Page: www.forestlandowners.com

Scott P Jones, Executive VP
Joy Moore, Circulation Director

Provides members with applied, practical and current forestry information written by the most experienced and successful forestry professionals.
Cost: $50.00
Circulation: 9000
Founded in 1941

16778 Forest Products Journal
Forest Products Society
2801 Marshall Ct
Madison, WI 53705-2295

608-231-1361
FAX 608-231-2152
E-Mail: info@forestprod.org

Home Page: www.forestprod.org
Social Media: *Facebook, Twitter, LinkedIn*

Carol Lewis, VP

Covers the latest research and technology from every branch of the forest products industry.
Cost: $155.00
Founded in 1945

16779 Forests and People
Louisiana Forestry Association
PO Drawer 5067
Alexandria, LA 71307

318-443-2558
FAX 318-443-1713
E-Mail: jtompkins@laforestry.com
Home Page: www.laforestry.com
Social Media: *Facebook, Twitter*

Janet Tompkins, Editor
Mike Merritt, President
Buck Vandersteen, Executive Director
Karla Johnson, Admin. Assistant/Annual Meeting
Debbie Dodd, Membership/Tree Farm Magazine
Cost: $250.00
36 Pages
Frequency: Quarterly
Circulation: 5800
ISSN: 0015-7589
Founded in 1947
Printed in 4 colors on glossy stock

16780 Frame Building News
National Frame Builders Association
4700 W. Lake Avenue
Glenview, IL 60025

785-843-2444
800-557-6957
FAX 847-375-6495
E-Mail: info@nfba.org
Home Page: www.nfba.org
Social Media: *Facebook*

John Fullerton, VP
Tom Knight, President

The official publication of National Frame Builders Association.

16781 Great Lakes TPA Magazine
Great Lakes Timber Professionals Association
3243 Golf Course Road
PO Box 1278
Rhinelander, WI 54501-1278

715-282-5828
FAX 715-282-4941
E-Mail: info@timberpa.com
Home Page: www.timberpa.com

Henry Schienebeck, Executive Director & Editor

The magazine provides education and information on the practice and promotion of sustainable forestry and seeks to instill a sense of pride and professionalism among manufacturers, operators, transporters, landowners, and foresters.
Cost: $24.00
Frequency: Monthly
Circulation: 2500

16782 Hardwood Floors
National Wood Flooring Association
111 Chesterfield Industrial
Chesterfield, MO 63005-1219

636-519-9663
800-422-4556
FAX 636-519-9664
E-Mail: info@nwfa.org
Home Page: www.nwfa.org

Ed Korczak, Executive Director

An essential educational tool, with articles on everything from sanding and finishing techniques to industry trends and tips on running a profitable business.
Frequency: 6x/Year
Circulation: 25000

16783 International Journal of Forest Engineering

Forest Products Society
2801 Marshall Court
Madison, WI 53705-2295

608-231-1361
FAX 608-231-2152
E-Mail: info@forestprod.org
Home Page: www.forestprod.org
Social Media: *Facebook, Twitter*

Paul Merrick, President
Patrice Tardif, President-Elect
Timothy M. Young, Vice President
Stefan Bergmann, Executive Vice President

Committed to serving the international forest engineering community as the voice of new ideas and developments in forest engineering. Reporting on existing practices and innovations in forest engineering by scientists and professionals from around the world which promote environmentally sound forestry practices and contribute to sustainable forest management.
Frequency: Semiannually
Founded in 1947

16784 International Wood: The Guide to Applications, Sources & Trends

International Wood Products Association
4214 King St
Alexandria, VA 22302-1555

703-820-6696
FAX 703-820-8550
E-Mail: info@iwpawood.org
Home Page: www.iwpawood.org

Brent McClendon, Executive VP/CAE
Annette Ferri, Member Services
Brigid Shea, Government Affairs
Annette Ferri, Director, Finance & Administration
Ashley A. Amidon, Manager, Government

Formerly Imported Wood, International Wood continues to lead with innovative new designs and new product applications.
Frequency: Annual
Circulation: 25000

16785 Journal of Forestry

Society of American Foresters
5400 Grosvenor Ln
Bethesda, MD 20814-2198

301-897-8720
FAX 301-897-3690
Home Page: www.safnet.org

Michael T Goergen Jr, Executive VP/CEO
Matthew Walls, Publications Dir/Managing Editor

To advance the profession of forestry by keeping professionals informed about significant developments and ideas in the many facets of forestry: economics, education and communication, entomology and pathology, fire, forest ecology, geospatial technologies, history, international forestry, measurments, policy, recreation, silviculture, social sciences, soils anf hydrology, urban and community forestry, utilization and engineering, and wildlife management.
Cost: $85.00
Frequency: 8 Times
ISSN: 0022-1201
Founded in 1902
Printed in 4 colors on glossy stock

16786 Loggers' World

Loggers World Publications

4206 Jackson Hwy
Chehalis, WA 98532-8425

360-262-3376
800-462-8283
FAX 360-262-3337
E-Mail: logworld@aol.com
Home Page: www.loggersworld.com

Mike Crouse, Publisher
Kevin Core, Advertising Manager
Finley Hays, Editor
Darin Burt, Writer
Accepts advertising.
Cost: $12.00
56 Pages
Frequency: Monthly
Circulation: 16,000
Founded in 1966

16787 Logging & Sawmilling Journal

Logging & Sawmilling Journal
Po Box 86670
Vancouver, BC V7L-4L2

604-990-9970
FAX 604-990-9971
E-Mail: stanhope@forestnet.com
Home Page: www.forestnet.com
Social Media: *Facebook*

Rob Stanhope, Publisher
Lil Fawcus, Production Manager
Mailing list available for rent

16788 Logging Management

Baum International Media
203-2323 Boundary Road
Vancouver, Ca V5M 4

604-298-3005
FAX 604-298-3966
E-Mail: editor.lm@bauminternational.com
Home Page: www.bauminternational.com

Kevin Cook, Associate Publisher
Gunner Martin, Editor
Carol Lee, Circulation Manager

Logging equipment information for the United States and Canada.
Circulation: 23000

16789 Lumber Cooperator

Northeastern Retail Lumber Association
585 N Greenbush Rd
Rensselaer, NY 12144-9615

518-286-1010
800-292-6752
FAX 518-286-1755
E-Mail: rferris@nrla.org
Home Page: www.nrla.org

Rita Ferris, President

Includes the latest industry, legislative and regulatory news, as well as issues and trends that most influence the lumber and building materials business. Readers gain insight into the newest methods, management techniques, new product ideas, family owned business concerns and key industry issues.
Cost: $40.00
100 Pages
Circulation: 5000
Founded in 1894

16790 Lumberman's Equipment Digest

Lumbermen Online
PO Box 1146
Columbia, TN 38401

931-381-1638
800-477-7606
FAX 931-388-3564
E-Mail: publisher@lumbermenonline.com
Home Page: www.lumbermenonline.com

Brady Carr, Publisher
Tammy Coffman, Advertising Manager
Shana Hibdon, Internet Technical Support

Gina High, Graphics Department
Cost: $38.00
Frequency: Monthly
Circulation: 35,000

16791 Millwork Magazine

Association of Millwork Distributors
10047 Robert Trent Jones Pkwy
New Port Richey, FL 34655-4649

727-372-3665
800-786-7274
FAX 727-372-2879
Home Page: www.amdweb.com
Social Media: *Twitter, LinkedIn*

Rosalie Leone, CEO/ Secretary
Dan Barber, President
John Crowder, 1st VP
Mark Hefley, Associate VP
George Kessel, Treasurer

Articles of interest to AMD members.
1200 Members
Frequency: Monthly
Founded in 1935

16792 Modern Woodworking

Modern Woodworking
90 West Afton Ave. #117
Yardley, PA 19067

267-519-1705
800-633-5953
FAX 205-391-2081
E-Mail: Admin@tccmedia.com
Home Page: www.modernwoodworking.com

Brooke Wisdom, Executive Editor
W.W. Chip Wisdom, VP/Group Publisher
Mailing list available for rent

16793 National Hardwood Magazine

Miller Publishing Company
PO Box 34908
Memphis, TN 38184-0908

901-372-8280
800-844-1280
FAX 901-373-6180
E-Mail: editor@millerwoodtradepub.com
Home Page: www.millerpublishing.com

Paul J Miller, President
Wayne Miller, VP
Sue Putnam, Editor

A monthly journal serving the hardwood industry including sawmillls, distillation, lumber yards, wholesalers and buyers and woodworkers.
Cost: $45.00
85 Pages
Frequency: Monthly
Circulation: 5000
Founded in 1927
Printed in 4 colors on glossy stock

16794 Northern Journal of Applied Forestry

Society of American Foresters
5400 Grosvenor Ln
Bethesda, MD 20814-2198

301-897-8720
866-897-8720
FAX 301-897-3690
E-Mail: safweb@podi.com
Home Page: www.safnet.org
Social Media: *Facebook, Twitter, LinkedIn*

Matthew Walls, Publications Dir/Managing Editor
Kim C Steiner, Editor

Each regional journal of applies forestry focuses on research, practice, and techniques targeted to foresters and allied professionals in specific regions of the United States and Canada. This journal covers northeastern, midwestern, and boreal forests in the United States and

Canada.
Cost: $75.00
Frequency: 4 Times
ISSN: 0742-6348

16795 Pallet Enterprise
Industrial Reporting
10244 Timber Ridge Dr
Ashland, VA 23005-8135

804-550-0323
800-805-0263
FAX 804-550-2181
E-Mail: ed@ireporting.com
Home Page: www.palletenterprise.com

Edward C Brindley Jr, Publisher
Chris Edwards, Production Manager
Chaille Brindley, Assistant Publisher
Scott Brindley, Marketing Director
Laura Seal, Circulation Manager

Written for those who manufacture, repair, sell
or use wooden pallets and containers. Regular
features include a market column, new prod-
ucts section and industry events.
Cost: $60.00
104 Pages
Frequency: Monthly
Circulation: 15000
Founded in 1981
Printed in 4 colors on glossy stock

16796 PalletCentral
National Wooden Pallet & Container
Association
1421 Prince Street
Suite 340
Alexandria, VA 22314-2805

703-519-6104
FAX 703-519-4720
E-Mail: pjsherry@nepapallet.com
Home Page: www.nwpca.com

John T. Swenby, Chair
James Ruder, Chair-Elect
James Schwab, Secretary/ Treasurer
Bruce N. Scholnick, President

The technical journal for the solid wood packaging industry published by the NWPCA. First
with essential news and innovations affecting
wood packaging companies, going beyond reporting to provide useful analysis and strategies for coping with industry changes.
700+ Members
Frequency: Montly
Circulation: 6000
Founded in 1947

16797 Panel World
Hatton-Brown Publishers
225 Hanrick Street(36104)
PO Box 2268
Montgomery, AL 36102-3317

334-834-1170
800-669-5613
FAX 334-834-4525
E-Mail: mail@hattonbrown.com
Home Page: www.hattonbrown.com

Rich Donnell, Editor
Rhonda Thomas, Circulation Manager
Dan Shell, Managing Editor
Jennifer McCary, Associate Editor
Tonya Cooner, Associate Editor

For people who deal with production, sales,
marketing, distribution, fabrication and utiliza-
tion of veneer, plywood and other panel prod-
ucts.
Cost: $40.00
Circulation: 12850
Founded in 1948
Printed in 4 colors on matte stock

16798 Popular Woodworking
F And W Publications

10151 Carver Road, Suite # 200
Blue Ash, OH 45242

513-531-2690
FAX 513-531-1843
E-Mail: publicity@fwmedia.com
Home Page: www.fwpublications.com

David Nussbaum, CEO
Don Schroder, Ad Manager

Everything woodworkers need to develop their
skills; in-depth tool reviews and tests, shop
tips, finishing secrets, projects and more.
Cost: $28.00
104 Pages
Frequency: Monthly
Circulation: 240151
Founded in 1981

16799 Rural Builder
F And W Publications
10151 Carver Road, Suite # 200
Blue Ash, OH 45242

513-531-2690
FAX 715-445-4087
E-Mail: publicity@fwmedia.com
Home Page: www.fwpublications.com

Steve Shanesy, Publisher
Don Schroder, Advertising Manager

16800 Southern Loggin' Times
Hatton-Brown Publishers
PO Box 2268
Montgomery, AL 36102-2268

334-834-1170
800-669-5613
FAX 334-834-4525
E-Mail: mail@hattonbrown.com
Home Page: www.hattonbrown.com

David H Ramsey, President
Rich Donnell, Editor

Monitors the south's forest products industry.
Cost: $65.00
Frequency: Monthly
Circulation: 13,408
ISSN: 0744-2106
Founded in 1948
Printed in 4 colors on glossy stock

16801 Southern Lumberman
Hatton-Brown Publishers
PO Box 2268
Montgomery, AL 36102-2268

334-834-1170
800-669-5613
FAX 334-834-4525
E-Mail: mail@hattonbrown.com
Home Page: www.hattonbrown.com

David H Ramsey, President
Rich Donnell, Editor

Industry news for sawmill operators and di-
mension manufacturers.
Cost: $21.00
60 Pages
Frequency: Monthly
Circulation: 13500

**16802 Southern Pine Inspection Bureau
Magazine**
Southern Pine Inspection Bureau
PO Box 10915
Pensacola, FL 32524-0915

850-434-2611
FAX 850-433-5594
E-Mail: spib@spib.org
Home Page: www.spib.org

James Loy, President
Tom Jones, Executive Director
Founded in 1940
Mailing list available for rent

16803 Timber Harvesting
Hatton-Brown Publishers
225 Hanrick Street (36104)
PO Box 2268
Montgomery, AL 36102-3317

334-834-1170
800-669-5613
FAX 334-834-4525
E-Mail: mail@hattonbrown.com
Home Page: www.hattonbrown.com

Dave Ramsey, Co-Publisher
D K Knight, Co-Publisher
Rich Donnell, Editor

News and methods reported that are of particu-
lar interest to loggers.
Cost: $40.00
Frequency: Monthly
Circulation: 20130
ISSN: 0160-6433
Founded in 1953
Printed in 4 colors on matte stock

16804 Timber Processing
Hatton-Brown Publishers
225 Hanrick Street
PO Box 2268
Montgomery, AL 36102

334-834-1170
800-669-5613
FAX 334-834-4525
E-Mail: rich@hattonbrown.com
Home Page: www.hattonbrown.com

David H Ramsey, Co-Publisher
Rich Donnell, Editor-in-Chief
Dan Shell, Managing Editor

Timber Processing serves sawmill/chipmill op-
erations; consultants in mill and processing op-
erations; machinery manufacturers, dealers and
distributors, others allied to the field.
Cost: $40.00
44 Pages
Circulation: 20780
ISSN: 0885-906X
Founded in 1948
Printed in 4 colors on glossy stock

16805 Timber West Journal
Logging & Sawmilling Journal
Po Box 86670
Vancouver, BC V7L-4L2

604-990-9970
866-221-1017
FAX 604-990-9971
E-Mail: timberwest@forestnet.com
Home Page: www.forestnet.com/timberwest
Social Media: *Facebook*

Sheila Ringdahl, Publisher
Diane Mettler, Managing Editor

Packed with valuable and useful stories on successful mechanized harvesting and wood processing techniques and equipment, special
editorial features, plus timely information on
legislation, industry news, annual events, and
people and products pertinent to America's
largest forestry market.
Cost: $20.00
48 Pages
Circulation: 10500
ISSN: 0192-0642
Founded in 1975
Mailing list available for rent
Printed in 4 colors

16806 Timberline
Industrial Reporting
10244 Timber Ridge Dr
Ashland, VA 23005-8135

804-550-0323
FAX 804-550-2181

E-Mail: editor@ireporting.com
Home Page: www.palletenterprise.com

Edward C Brindley Jr, Publisher
Tim Cox, Editor
Laura Seal, Circulation

Highlights sawmill, logging, and pallet interests including environmental issues, new machinery and technologies that impact the industry.
52 Pages
Frequency: Monthly
Circulation: 30000
Founded in 1994
Mailing list available for rent: 28,000 names at $250 per M
Printed in 4 colors on newsprint stock

16807 Tree Care Industry

Tree Care Industry Association
136 Harvey Road
Suite 101
Londonderry, NH 03053

603-314-5380
800-733-2622
FAX 603-314-5386
E-Mail: tcia@tcia.org
Home Page: www.tcia.org
Social Media: *Facebook, Twitter, LinkedIn, Youtube*

Mark Garvin, Interim CEO/President
Peter Gerstenberger, Sr Adv Safety/Compliance/Standards

Informative articles on tree care issues, leading advertisers, and industry almanac, and cutting edge product news combine to make TCI Magazine a must-read for tree workers, tree care company owners, and anyone who wants a fresh, insightful look at the industry
Founded in 1938

16808 Tree Farmer Magazine, the Guide to Sustaining America's Family Forests

American Forest Foundation
1111 19th St NW
Suite 780
Washington, DC 20036

202-463-2462
FAX 202-463-2461
E-Mail: info@forestfoundation.org
Home Page: www.forestfoundation.org
Social Media: *Facebook, Twitter, YouTube*

Tom Martin, President & CEO
Brigitte Johnson APR, Director Communications, Editor

The official magazine of ATFS, this periodical provides practical, how-to and hands-on information and techniques, and services to help private fore landowners to become better stewards, save money and time, and add to the enjoyment of their land.

16809 Wood Digest

Cygnus Publishing
1233 Janesville Avenue
Fort Atkinson, WI 53538-0803

920-000-1111
800-547-7377
FAX 920-563-1699
E-Mail: info@cygnus.com
Home Page: www.cygnus.com

John French, CEO
John Anfderhaar, Associate Publisher
Paul Bowers, President
Jay Schneider, Publisher

Trade magazine, Accepts advertising.
64 Pages
Frequency: Monthly
Circulation: 51000
Founded in 1965

16810 Wood Finisher

7616 Banning Way
Inver Grove Heights, MN 55077-5819
Mitchell Kohansek, Editor

Wood finishing information.
Cost: $10.00
20 Pages
Frequency: Monthly
Founded in 1981

16811 Wood and Fiber Science

Society of Wood Science & Technology
PO Box 6155
Monona, WI 53716-6155

608-577-1342
FAX 608-467-8979
E-Mail: vicki@swst.org
Home Page: www.swst.org
Social Media: *Facebook*

Victoria Herian, Executive Director
James Funck, President Elect

Publishes papers with both professional and technical content. Original papers of professional concer, or based on research dealing with the science, processing, and manufacture of wood and composite products of wood or wood fiber origin are considered for publication. All papers are peer-reviewed and must be unpublished research not offered for publication elsewhere.
Cost: $250.00
Frequency: Quarterly
Circulation: 950
ISSN: 0735-6161
Founded in 1958

16812 Wood and Wood Products

Vance Publishing
400 Knightsbridge Pkwy
Lincolnshire, IL 60069

847-634-2600
FAX 847-634-4379
E-Mail: info@vancepublishing.com
Home Page: www.vancepublishing.com

William C Vance, Chairman
Peggy Walker, Wood & Wood Products

Leading woodworking industry publication for solid wood and panel technology.
140 Pages
Frequency: Monthly
Circulation: 48000
ISSN: 0043-7662
Founded in 1937

16813 World Wood Review

Widman Publishing
601 West Broadway
Suite 400
Vancouver, BC V5Z 4C2

604-675-6923
FAX 604-675-6924
E-Mail: tlhaugen@widman.com
Home Page: www.widman.com

Janice Widman, Chair
Jason Roth, Director / Editor
Tamara Haugen, Director / Editor
Dick Brown, Associate Editor
Brian Haugen, Associate Editor

The premier newsletter serving the global wood products industry, with news of trends and developments in the solid wood and panel manufacturing sector.
Cost: $55.00
50 Pages
Frequency: Monthly

Trade Shows

16814 AMD Annual Convention & Tradeshow

Association of Millwork Distributors
10047 Robert Trent Jones Pkwy
Trinity, FL 34655-4649

727-372-3665
800-786-7274
FAX 727-372-2879
E-Mail: marketing@amdweb.com
Home Page: www.amdweb.com

Rosalie Leone, CEO

16815 ATIC Annual Meeting

7012 S Revere Parkway
Suite 140
Centennial, CO 80112

303-379-2955
E-Mail: info@aitc-glulam.org
Home Page: www.aitc-glulam.org
Social Media: *Facebook*

R Michael Caldwell PE, Executive VP
Frequency: Annual
Founded in 1952

16816 American Forestry Association

PO Box 2000
Washington, DC 20013-2000

202-955-4500

Billl Tikkala, Show Manager
Deborah Gangloff, Executive Director

30 booths of tree planting and care equipment.
1M Attendees
Frequency: November

16817 Appalachian Hardwood Expo

Mercer County Technical Education Center
105 Old Bluefield Road
Princeton, WV 24740-8901

304-425-4583

Linda Cox
100 tables.
2M Attendees
Frequency: June

16818 Architectural Woodwork Institute Annual Convention

46179 Westlake Drive
Suite 120
Potomac Falls, VA 20165

571-323-3636
FAX 571-323-3630
E-Mail: info@awinet.org
Home Page: www.awinet.org

Kimberly Haynes, Director Meetings & Conventions

Seminar, workshop and woodwork products such as casework, fixtures and panelings, equipment and supplies.

16819 Forest Expo

Prince George Regional Forest Exhibition Society
850 River Road
Prince George, BC V2L-5S8

250-563-8833
FAX 250-563-3697
E-Mail: info@forestexpo.bc.ca
Home Page: www.forestexpo.bc.ca

Trudy Swaan, General Manager

Provides a showcase to display the latest in new technology, equipment, supplies and services, as well as educate the forest sector and the general public about the importance of our forests.

16820 Forest Products Machinery & Equipment Expo

Southern Forest Products Association
2900 Indiana Avenue
Kenner, LA 70065

504-443-4464
FAX 504-443-6612
E-Mail: mail@sfpa.org
Home Page: www.sfpa.org

Digges Morgan, President
Richard Wallace, VP Communications
Tami Kessler, Corporate Secretary
Stephen P. Conwell, President
Tami Kessler, Corporate Secretary & Director

200+ exhibitors
3000 Attendees
Frequency: June, Biennial

16821 Frame Building Expo

National Frame Builders Association
4700 W. Lake Avenue
Glenview, IL 60025

785-843-2444
800-557-6957
FAX 847-375-6495
E-Mail: info@nfba.org
Home Page: www.nfba.org
Social Media: Facebook

John Fullerton, VP
Tom Knight, President

Containing 200 booths.
2000+ Attendees
Frequency: February

16822 Greenbuild International Conference and Expo

Engineered Wood Association
7011 S 19th Street
Tacoma, WA 98466-5333

253-565-6600
FAX 253-565-7265
E-Mail: tanya.rosendahl@apawood.org
Home Page: www.apawood.org
Social Media: Facebook, Twitter

Tanya Rosendahl, Tradeshow Coordinator

16823 HPVA Spring Conference

Hardwood Plywood & Veneer
1825 Michael Faraday Dr
Reston, VA 20190-5350

703-435-2900
FAX 703-435-2537
E-Mail: hpva@hpva.org
Home Page: www.hpva.org

Clifford Howlett, President
Kip Howlett, HPVA President
Eva Mentel, Office Manager
Frequency: May

16824 HPVA Winter Conference

Hardwood Plywood & Veneer
1825 Michael Faraday Dr
Reston, VA 20190-5350

703-435-2900
FAX 703-435-2537
E-Mail: hpva@hpva.org
Home Page: www.hpva.org

Clifford Howlett, President
Kip Howlett, HPVA President
Eva Mentel, Office Manager
Frequency: November

16825 Hardwood Manufacturers Association

400 Penn Center Boulevard
Suite 530
Pittsburgh, PA 15235-5605

412-244-0440
FAX 412-244-9090

Susan Regan, Executive VP

Offers 20 booths of sawmill and logging machinery and services.
300 Attendees
Frequency: March

16826 IWPA Annual Convention

International Wood Products Association
4214 King St
Alexandria, VA 22302-1555

703-820-6696
FAX 703-820-8550
E-Mail: info@iwpawood.org
Home Page: www.iwpawood.org

Brent McClendon, Executive VP/CAE
Annette Ferri, Member Services
Brigid Shea, Government Affairs
Annette Ferri, Director, Finance & Administration
Ashley A. Amidon, Manager, Government

The largest gathering solely dedicated to the North American imported wood products industry.
Frequency: April

16827 International Woodworking Machinery and Furniture Supply Fair: USA

Reed Exhibition Companies
1350 E Touhy Avenue
Des Plaines, IL 60018-3303

847-294-0300
FAX 847-635-1571

Paul Pajor, National Marketing Manager

The largest woodworking machinery and furniture supply manufacturing exposition held in the Western Hemisphere. Exhibitors interface with North American furniture, cabinet, and woodworking manufacturers. One thousand booths.
37M Attendees
Frequency: August/Biennial

16828 Lake States Logging Congress & Equipment Expo

Great Lakes Timber Professionals Association
3243 Golf Course Road
PO Box 1278
Rhinelander, WI 54501-1278

715-282-5828
FAX 715-282-4941
E-Mail: info@timberpa.com
Home Page: www.timberpa.com

Henry Schienebeck, Executive Director & Editor

Held in either Michigan or Wisconsin, the Logging Congress is a 3-day expo that takes place during the Fall season throughout the Lake States region of the United States.
3500 Attendees
Founded in 1945

16829 Live Woods Show

Pacific Logging Congress
PO Box 1281
Maple Valley, WA 98038

425-413-2808
FAX 425-413-1359

E-Mail: rikki@pacificloggingcongress.com
Home Page: www.pacificloggingcongress.com

Rikki Wellman, Executive Director
Craig Olson, President
Ron Simon, Treasurer
3000+ Attendees
Frequency: September

16830 Logging Congress Pacific

2300 SW 6th Avenue
Suite 200
Portland, OR 97201-4915

FAX 503-612-0344

Al Wilson, Executive Director
50 booths.
800 Attendees
Frequency: September

16831 Lumbermen's Merchandising Conferences

137 W Wayne Avenue
Wayne, PA 19087-4018

610-293-7000
FAX 215-293-7098

Jack Reznor, Show Manager
Anthony Decarlo, President
325 booths.
1.6M Attendees
Frequency: March

16832 MFMA Annual Conference

Maple Flooring Manufacturers Association
111 Deer Lake Road
Suite 100
Deerfield, IL 60015

847-480-9138
888-480-9138
FAX 847-480-9282
E-Mail: mcarson@maplefloor.org
Home Page: www.maplefloor.org

Madhuri Carson, Conference Manager
Containing 50 booths.
300 Attendees
Frequency: Annual/March

16833 NHLA Annual Convention & Exhibit Showcase North American Hardwood Lumber Indu

National Hardwood Lumber Association
6830 Raleigh Lagrange Road
Memphis, TN 38184

901-377-1818
E-Mail: www.natlhardwood.org
Home Page: www.nhla.com

Lisa Browne, Convention Director

The premier networking opportunity for the Hardwood Industry. Provides attendees time for direct, personal contact with industry leaders and exhibitors, giving them from the opportunity to ask meaningful questions, view and compare products and services and strengthen business relationships.
Frequency: Annual

16834 NWFA Wood Flooring Convention and Expo

National Wood Flooring Association
111 Chesterfield Industrial Boulevard
Chesterfield, MO 63005

636-519-9663
800-422-4556
FAX 636-519-9664
E-Mail: convention@nwfa.org
Home Page: www.nwfa.org

Michael Martin, CEO

The Wood Flooring Expo has become the international gathering place for wood flooring professionals: Manufacturers, Distributors, Dealer/Contractors, Inspectors, Installers, Im-

port/Exporters, Architects & Designers of wood flooring.
2000 Attendees
Frequency: April

16835 Northeastern Forest Products Equipment Expo
Northeastern Loggers Association
3311 State Route 28 PO Box 69
Old Forge, NY 13420-0069

315-369-3078
FAX 315-369-3736
E-Mail: nela@northernlogger.com
Home Page: http://nefpexpo.net

Joseph Phaneuf, Show Manager

Annual expo on forest products equipment, suppliers, and services. Always listed as one of the top 100 shows in the U.S. with 200+ exhibitors and indoor/outdoor demonstrations.
6000 Attendees
Frequency: Annual/May

16836 Northeastern Retail Lumber Association
Northeastern Retail Lumber Association
585 N Greenbush Road
Rensselaer, NY 12144

518-286-1010
800-292-6752
FAX 518-286-1755
E-Mail: rferris@nrla.org
Home Page: www.nrla.org

Deborah Talar, Executive Assistant
Rita Ferris, President

500 booths or more of builiding materials and education relating to the lumber and building industry.
8M Attendees
Frequency: January

16837 Northwestern Building Products Expo
Northwestern Lumber Association
5905 Golden Valley Road
Suite 110
Minneapolis, MN 55422-4535

763-544-6822
888-544-6822
FAX 763-595-4060
E-Mail: info@nlassn.org
Home Page: www.nlassn.org

Sally Means, Director of Conventions
Jodie Fleck, Director of Conventions & Tours
Cody Nuernberg, Manager of Membership

Building material retailers and their contractors attend this trade show and conference for continuing education and cammeraderie
1200 Attendees
Frequency: Annual
Mailing list available for rent

16838 Redwood Region Logging Conference California
Redwood Region Logging Conference
5601 South Broadway Street
Eureka, CA 95503

707-443-4091
FAX 707-443-0926
E-Mail: rrlc@sonic.net
Home Page: www.rrlc.net/

Charles Benbow, Show Manager

100 booths of timber and forestry related products and services.
3M Attendees
Frequency: March

16839 Retail Lumbermen's Association Northeast
339 E Avenue
Rochester, NY 14604-2627
John Brill, Show Manager

681 booths of lumber and related services.
10M Attendees
Frequency: January

16840 Sawmill Logging Equipment Expo East Coast
220 E Williamsburg Road
PO Box 160
Sandston, VA 23150-0160

804-737-5625
FAX 804-737-9437
E-Mail: info@exporichmond.com
Home Page: www.exporichmond.com

Mike Washko, Expo Manager

Logging and forestry production and distribution.
12M Attendees
Frequency: May

16841 Southeastern Lumber Manufacturers Association
Southeastern Lumber Manufacturers
200 Greencastle Road
Tyrone, GA 30290

770-631-6701
FAX 770-631-6720
Home Page: www.slma.org/

Steve Roundtree, President
Bryan Smalley, President
Will Telligman, Government Affairs Manager
Beverly Knight, Accounting Manager

50 booths.
350 Attendees
Frequency: July

16842 Southern Forest Products Mid-Year Meeting
Southern Forest Products Association
2900 Indiana Avenue
Kenner, LA 70065

504-443-4464
FAX 504-443-6612
E-Mail: mail@sfpa.org
Home Page: www.sfpa.org

Digges Morgan, President
Richard Wallace, VP Communications
Tami Kessler, Corporate Secretary
Stephen P. Conwell, President
Tami Kessler, Corporate Secretary & Director

200+ exhibitors
3000 Attendees
Frequency: Annual

16843 Southern Forestry Conference
Forest Landowners Association
900 Circle 75 Pkwy Se
Suite 205
Atlanta, GA 30339-3075

404-325-2954
800-325-2954
FAX 404-325-2955
E-Mail: info@forestlandowners.com
Home Page: www.forestlandowners.com

Lisa Newsome, Manager
Stacie Lewis, Managing Editor
Frequency: May
Founded in 1941

16844 TCI Expo
Tree Care Industry Association
136 Harvey Road
Suite 101
Londonderry, NH 03053

603-314-5380
800-733-2622
FAX 603-314-5386
E-Mail: tcia@tcia.org
Home Page: www.tcia.org

Social Media: *Facebook, Twitter, LinkedIn, Youtube*

Mark Garvin, Interim CEO/President
Peter Gerstenberger, Sr Adv Safety/Compliance/Standards
3500 Attendees
Frequency: Annual
Founded in 1938

16845 World of Wood Annual Convention
International Wood Products Association
4214 King Street W
Alexandria, VA 22302-1507

703-820-6696
FAX 703-820-8550
E-Mail: info@iwpawood.org
Home Page: www.iwpawood.org

Brent J McClendon, Executive VP/CAE
Annette Ferri, Member Services
Brigid Shea, Government Affairs
Annette Ferri, Director, Finance & Administration
Ashley A. Amidon, Manager, Government

A gethering for imported wood products industry importers, distributers, manufacturers, offshore suppliers and service providers.
220 Attendees
Frequency: Annual/Spring

Directories & Databases

16846 Cedar Shake and Shingle Bureau Membership Directory/Buyer's Guide
Cedar Shake & Shingle Bureau
PO Box 1178
Sumas, WA 98295-1178

604-820-7700
FAX 604-820-0266
E-Mail: info@cedarbureau.com
Home Page: www.cedarbureau.org

Lynne Christensen, Director of Operations
Barb Enns, Accountant
Dave Mooney, Cedar Quality Auditor
Sharron Beauregard, Accounting Assistant
Suzie Quigley, Customer Service Representative

About 102 member manufacturing mills in the Pacific Northwest and British Columbia, Canada; approximately 163 affiliated roofing applicators, builders, architects, remodelers and suppliers of related products and services.
Cost: $17.00
Frequency: SemiAnnual
Circulation: 450

16847 Dimension & Wood Components Buyer's Guide
Miller Publishing Corporation
Po Box 34908
Memphis, TN 38184-0908

901-372-8280
800-844-1280
FAX 901-373-6180
E-Mail: editor@millerwoodtradepub.com
Home Page: www.millerpublishing.com

Paul J Miller, President
Sue Putnam, Editor

Instant access to manufacturers of furniture parts, mouldings, cabinet doors, stair parts, flooring, turnings, paneling, door parts, window parts, edge glued panels, etc. Gives the information on who to contact, firm name and address, phone number, fax number, number of employees, products manufactured, species of wood used, machining capabilities and marketing areas served.
Cost: $350.00

16848 Forest Products Export Directory
Miller Publishing Corporation
Po Box 34908
Memphis, TN 38184-0908

901-372-8280
800-844-1280
FAX 901-373-6180
E-Mail: editor@millerwoodtradepub.com
Home Page: www.millerpublishing.com

Paul J Miller, President
Sue Putnam, Editor

The only directory published listing all the major exporters of North American forest products. Edited to help the oversease buyer find reliable suppliers for the wide variety of Softwood and Hardwood forest products available in North America.
Cost: $175.00

16849 Forest Products Research Society Membership Directory
2801 Marshall Ct
Madison, WI 53705-2295

608-231-1361
FAX 608-231-2152
E-Mail: info@forestprod.org
Home Page: www.forestprod.org

Carol Lewis, VP
Stefan A. Bergmann, Executive Vice President
Joe Gravunder, Publications Manager
Cost: $125.00
1900 Pages
Frequency: 10 Per Year
Circulation: 3500
Founded in 1947

16850 Gebbie Press: All-In-One Media Directory
Gebbie Press
Po Box 1000
New Paltz, NY 12561

845-255-7560
FAX 888-345-2790
Home Page: www.gebbieinc.com
Social Media: *Facebook, Twitter, LinkedIn*

Mark Gebbie, Associate Editor
Founded in 1955

16851 Green Book's Hardwood Marketing Directory
Miller Publishing Corporation
Po Box 34908
Memphis, TN 38184-0908

901-372-8280
800-844-1280
FAX 901-373-6180
E-Mail: editor@millerwoodtradepub.com
Home Page: www.millerpublishing.com

Paul J Miller, President
Sue Putnam, Editor

A sales booster that lists over 7,900 woodworking plants' Hardwood lumber and other Hardwood forest products purchasing needs. Gives up-to-date, documented facts on species, grades, thicknesses and quantities purchased by each plant annually in the U.S. and Canada.
Cost: $1200.00

16852 Green Book's Softwood Marketing Directory
Miller Publishing Corporation
Po Box 34908
Memphis, TN 38184-0908

901-372-8280
800-844-1280
FAX 901-373-6180

E-Mail: editor@millerwoodtradepub.com
Home Page: www.millerpublishing.com

Paul J Miller, President
Sue Putnam, Editor

Instant access to over 5,000 woodworking and industrial plants' Softwood lumber purchasing needs with complete, up-to-date, documented facts on species, grades, thicknesses, and quantities of Softwood lumber and other Softwood forest products bought regularly.
Cost: $900.00

16853 Hardwood Manufacturers Association: Membership Directory
Hardwood Manufacturers Association
665 Rodi Road
Suite 305
Pittsburgh, PA 15235

412-244-0440
800-373-9663
FAX 412-244-9090
Home Page: www.hardwoodinfo.com

Susan Regan, Executive VP

Over 100 companies with over 160 locations in the US.
Frequency: Annual December

16854 Hardwood Purchasing Handbook
Miller Publishing Corporation
Po Box 34908
Memphis, TN 38184-0908

901-372-8280
800-844-1280
FAX 907-373-6180
E-Mail: editor@millerwoodtradepub.com
Home Page: www.millerpublishing.com

Paul J Miller, President
Sue Putnam, Editor

An easy-to-use digest size directory that has all the major Hardwood suppliers in the U.S.A. and Canada of Hardwood lumber, plywood, veneers, etc. Up-to-date sections describe Hardwood sawmills, wholesalers, distribution yards, etc. Complete mailing addresses, phone numbers, fax numbers, email addresses, names of sales agents, main Hardwood species handled, specialty items listed and information on production facilities and shipping methods are given.
Cost: $175.00

16855 Imported Wood Purchasing Guide
Miller Publishing Corporation
Po Box 34908
Memphis, TN 38184-0908

901-372-8280
800-844-1280
FAX 901-373-6180
E-Mail: editor@millerwoodtradepub.com
Home Page: www.millerpublishing.com

Paul J Miller, President
Sue Putnam, Editor

A wide variety of imported suppliers of lumber, mouldings, veneers, wall paneling, furniture components, flooring, plywood, hardboard, doorskins, millwork, etc.
Cost: $175.00

16856 Imported Wood: Guide To Applications, Sources and Trends
International Wood Products Association
4214 King St
Alexandria, VA 22302-1555

703-820-6696
FAX 703-820-8550
E-Mail: info@iwpawood.org

Home Page: www.iwpawood.org
Social Media: *Facebook, Twitter, LinkedIn*

Brent McClendon, Executive VP/CAE
Annette Ferri, Member Services
Brigid Shea, Government Affairs

An annual magazine featuring imported woods in applications, sustainable Forest Management issues and listing of IWPA members.
84 Pages
Frequency: Annual
Circulation: 15,000

16857 International Green Front Report
Friends of the Trees
PO Box 1064
Tonasket, WA 98855-1064

FAX 509-485-2705
E-Mail: michael@friendsofthetrees.net

Michael Pilarski, Editor

Organizations and periodicals concerned with sustainable forestry and agriculture and related fields.
Cost: $7.00
Frequency: Irregular

16858 Lumbermen's Red Book
Lumbermens Credit Association
20 N Wacker Drive
Suite 1800
Chicago, IL 60606-2905

312-553-0943
FAX 312-533-1842
Home Page: www.lumbermanscredit.com

PD McLaughlin, Editor

Approximately 39,000 manufacturers and distributors of lumber and wood products in the US and Canada.
Cost: $1780.00
Frequency: SemiAnnual

16859 North American Forest Products Export Directory
International Wood Trade Publications
1235 Sycamore View Road
Memphis, TN 38134-7646

901-752-1246
FAX 901-373-6180

Producers, exporters, agents, etc. of lumber, plywood, etc. in the US and Canada.
Cost: $150.00
Frequency: Annual August
Circulation: 10,000

16860 Northeastern Retail Lumber Association Buyer's Guide
Northeastern Retail Lumber Association
585 N Greenbush Rd
Rensselaer, NY 12144-9615

518-286-1010
800-292-6752
FAX 518-286-1755
E-Mail: rferris@nrla.org
Home Page: www.nrla.org

Rita Ferris, President

Offers information on over 2,000 retail dealers in lumber and forest products located in the Northeastern states of the US.
Cost: $125.00
225 Pages
Frequency: Annual
ISSN: 0024-7294

16861 Random Lengths Big Book: Buyers' & Sellers' Directory of the Forest
Random Lengths Publications
PO Box 867
Eugene, OR 97440-0867

541-869-9925
888-686-9925

FAX 800-874-7979
E-Mail: rlmail@rlpi.com
Home Page: www.randomlengths.com

Dave Evans, Editor
Terri Richards, Editor

About 7,500 companies, consultants and associations involved in the softwood forest product industry in the US and Canada, including sawmills, treating plants, manufacturers of panels and specialty products, wholesalers and secondary manufacturers.
Cost: $188.00
Frequency: Annual February
Circulation: 2,200

16862 Rauch Guide to the US and Canadian Pulp & Paper Industry
Grey House Publishing
4919 Route 22
PO Box 56
Amenia, NY 12501

518-789-8700
800-562-2139
FAX 845-373-6390
E-Mail: books@greyhouse.com
Home Page: www.greyhouse.com
Social Media: *Facebook, Twitter*

Leslie Mackenzie, Publisher
Richard Gottlieb, Editor

Provides current market information and trends; industry economics and government regulations; company share data for each of the leading product categories; technology and raw material information; industry sources of further data; and unique profiles of 500+ pulp and paper manufacturers, a section which includes all known companies with pulp and paper sales at or over $15 million annually.
Cost: $595.00
400 Pages
ISBN: 1-592371-31-0
Founded in 1981

16863 Timber Harvesting: Logger's Resource Guide
Hatton-Brown Publishers
Po Box 2268
Montgomery, AL 36102-2268

334-834-1170
800-669-5613
FAX 334-834-4525
E-Mail: mail@hattonbrown.com
Home Page: www.hattonbrown.com

David H Ramsey, President
Rich Donnell, Editor
Cost: $20.00
88 Pages
Frequency: Annually, January
Circulation: 20,179
ISSN: 0160-6433
Printed in on glossy stock

16864 Where to Buy Hardwood Plywood, Veneer & Engineered Hardwood Flooring
Hardwood Plywood and Veneer Association
1825 Michael Faraday Drive
Reston, VA 20190-5350

703-435-2900
FAX 703-435-2537
E-Mail: hpva@hpva.org
Home Page: www.hpva.org

Kip Howlett, President
Eva Mentel, Office Manager
Ketti Tyree, Membership & Conventions Manager

The definitive annual guide to the species and products sold by HPVA members.
120 Pages
Frequency: Annual
Founded in 1921

16865 Wood & Wood Products: Laminating Users Guide Issue
Louisiana Municipal Association
700 North 10th street
Baton Rouge, LA 70802

225-344-5001
800-234-8274
FAX 225-344-3057
E-Mail: infor@lma.org
Home Page: www.lma.org

George Carter, Editor

List of approximately 100 manufacturers and importers of decorative overlays, wood substrates, adhesives, laminating equipment and laminated products.
Frequency: Annual June

16866 Wood Components Buyer's Guide
Wood Component Manufacturers Association
741 Butlers Gate NE
Suite 100
Marietta, GA 30068-4207

770-565-6660
FAX 770-565-6663
E-Mail: wcma@woodcomponents.org
Home Page: www.woodcomponents.org

Steven V Lawser, Executive Director

Over 150 member manufacturers of wood components.
Cost: $5.00
Frequency: Annual Summer

16867 Wood Technology: Buyers' Guide Issue
Miller Freeman Publications
600 Harrison Street
Suite 400
San Francisco, CA 94107-1391

800-227-4675
FAX 415-905-2630
Home Page: www.woodtechmag.com

David A Pease, Editorial Director

Companies supplying machinery, tools and other equipment to manufacturers of wood products worldwide.
Frequency: Annual

16868 Wood and Wood Products: Red Book Issue
Vance Publishing
400 Knightsbridge Parkway
Lincolnshire, IL 60069

847-634-2600
FAX 847-634-4379
Home Page: www.vancepublishing.com

William C Vance, Chairman
Peggy Walker, President

Annual directory that is the editorial and advertising leader for the woodworking industry. Listings and specifications of more than 3,000 industry suppliers.
Cost: $40.00
Frequency: Annual
Circulation: 50,000

Industry Web Sites

16869 http://gold.greyhouse.com
G.O.L.D Grey House OnLine Databases
Grey House Publishing's online database platform, GOLD, offers Quick Search, Keyword Search and Expert Search for most business sectors including lumber and wood markets. The GOLD platform makes finding the information you need quick and easy - whether you're a novice searcher or an experienced database user. All of Grey House's directory products are available for subscription on the GOLD platform.

16870 www.afandpa.org
American Forest and Paper Association
Represents member companies and related trade associations which grow, harvest and process wood and wood fiber, manufacture pulp, paper and paperboard products from both virgin and recovered fiber and produce solid wood products.

16871 www.afma4u.org
American Furniture Manufacturers Association
Provides a uniform voice in the furniture industry.

16872 www.aitc-glulam.org
American Institute of Timber Construction
The national trade association of the structural glued laminated (glulam) timber industry.

16873 www.alsc.org
American Lumber Standard Committee

16874 www.amdweb.com
Association of Millwork Distributors
Provides leadership, certification, education, promotion, networking and advocacy to, and for, the millwork distribution industry.

16875 www.apawood.org
Engineered Wood Association
A nonprofit trade association that represents US and Canadian manufacturers of structural engineered wood products, including plywood, oriented strand board (OSB), glued-laminated timber (glulam), wood i-joists and structural composite lumber.

16876 www.bearcreeklumber.com
Bear Creek Lumber
Publishes a newsletter called the Timberline.

16877 www.big-creek.com
Big Creek
Produces a newspaper

16878 www.calredwood.org
California Redwood Association
Authorized by Department of Commerce to develop and supervise redwood lumber grading.

16879 www.capital-lumber.com
Capital Lumber Company
Dedicated to being the leading distributor of materials in the Western United States.

16880 www.construction.com
McGraw-Hill Construction
McGraw-Hill Construction (MHC), part of The McGraw-Hill Companies, connects people and projects across the design and construction industry, serving owners, architects, engineers, general contractors, subcontractors, building product manufacturers, suppliers, dealers, distributors and adjacent markets.

16881 www.fiberboard.org
American Fiberboard Association
The national trade organization of manufacturers of cellulosic fiberboard products used for residential and commercial construction.

16882 www.forestinfo.org
Temperate Forest Foundation
Source for information which is understandable, unbiased, fast, accurate, and available in a wide variety of formats.

16883 www.forestnet.com
Logging & Sawmilling Journal
A journal that provides information on logginf and sawmilling.

16884 www.forestprod.org
Forest Products Society
Focus is on the development and research of information for the wood industry.

16885 www.fpl.fs.fed.us/swst
Society of Wood Science & Technology
Promotes policies and procedures which assure the wise use of wood and wood-based products; assures high standards for professional performance of wood scientists and technologists; foster educational programs at all levels of wood science and technolgoy and further the quality of such programs; represents the profession in public policy development.

16886 www.gebbieinc.com
Gebbie Press
A directory with all information that is needed for the lumber industry.

16887 www.greyhouse.com
Grey House Publishing
Authoritative reference directories for most business sectors including lumber and wood markets. Users can search the online databases with varied search criteria allowing for custom searches by product category, geographic area, sales volume, keyword, subject and more. Full Grey House catalog and online ordering also available.

16888 www.hardboard.org
American Hardboard Association
Represents major United States producers of hardwood.

16889 www.hlma.org
Pennsylvania Forest Products Association
Represents the state's entire forest products industry, including foresters, loggers, sawmills, and value-added processors.

16890 www.iwpawood.org
International Wood Products Association
International trade association representing companies handling imported wood products of all types.

16891 www.lma.org
Laminating Materials Association
Nonprofit trade group representing manufacturers and importers of decorative overlays, wood substrates, adhesives, laminating equipment and laminated products.

16892 www.loggertraining.com
A reference site for loggers in their pursuit of training programs where they work and live. Maintained by Northeastern Loggers' Association.

16893 www.lumber.org
North American Wholesale Lumber Association
NAWLA Bulletin is published monthly and includes industry and association news. The Association also produces the NAWLA Traders Market, an annual trade show bringing together over 2000 manufacturer and wholesale lumber traders at the premier event in the forest products industry. NAWLA also produces a variety of educational programs designed to enhance professionalism in the lumber industry.

16894 www.maplefloor.org
Maple Flooring Manufacturers Association

For manufacturers of northern hard maple solid strip flooring along with flooring contractors, distributors and providers of instalation-related products and services. Maintains technical standards for product quality, grading, shipping and packaging, and quality central.

16895 www.millerpublishing.com
Miller Publishing Corporation
Publishes many newspapers, magazines, and directories.

16896 www.mslbmda.org
Mountain States Lumber & Building Materials Dealer

16897 www.nari.org
National Association of the Remodeling Industry
Establishes and maintains a firm commitment to developing and sustaining programs that expand and unite the remodeling industry.

16898 www.nlassn.org
Northwestern Lumber Association
Retail lumber dealers in Iowa, Minnesota, North Dakota, and South Dakota.

16899 www.nofma.org
National Oak Flooring Manufacturers Association
Formulates and administers industry standards on hardwood floorings, inspection service, and semiannual Hardwood Flooring installation school.

16900 www.nsdja.com
National Sash and Door Jobbers Association
For wholesale millwork distribution companies.

16901 www.nwfa.org
National Wood Flooring Association
A not-for-profit trade association serving the wood flooring industry

16902 www.nwpca.com
National Wooden Pallet & Container Association
Represents wood and pallet container organizations.

16903 www.osbguide.com
Structural Board Association
Members are manufacturers of structural panels.

16904 www.pacificloggingcongress.org
Pacific Logging Congress
Fulfills the need to provide sound technical education about the forest industry.

16905 www.pbmdf.org
Composite Panel Association
For particle board manufacturers and suppliers.

16906 www.postframe.org
National Frame Builders Association
Building contractors, suppliers, design and code professionals and academic personnel specializing in the post frame construction industry.

16907 www.sfpa.org
Southern Forest Products Association
For lumber manufacturers across the mid-Atlantic and southern states as far west as Texas.

16908 www.spib.org
Southern Pine Inspection Bureau
Develops grading standards for Southern pine lumber and provides an inspection service and grade marking systems.

16909 www.sweets.construction.com
McGraw Hill Construction
In depth product information that lets you find, compare, select, specify and make purchase decisions in the industrial product marketplace.

16910 www.swst.org
Society of Wood Science & Technology
Promotes policies and procedures which assure the wise use of wood and wood-based products; assures high standards for professional performance of wood scientists and technologists; foster educational programs at all levels of wood science and technology and further the quality of such programs; represents the profession in public policy development.

16911 www.toc.org
TOC Management Services
Serves membership in the fields of labor, industrial, and employee relations. Provides counsel in wage and contract negotiations. Provides training and safety programs.

16912 www.tpmrs.com
Timber Products Manufacturers Association
Association of companies in the Timber and Wood products industry of the pacific northwest. TPM provides human resource and safety consulting, Training and employee benefits.

16913 www.wdma.org
Window & Door Manufacturers Association
Trade association representing approximately 145 U.S. and Canadian manufacturers and suppliers of windows and doors for the domestic and export market.

16914 www.westernforestry.org
Western Forestry and Conservation Association
Offers high-quality continuing education workshops and seminars for professional foresters throughout Oregon, Washington, Idaho, Montana, Northern California and British Columbia.

16915 www.woodcomponents.org
Wood Component Manufacturers Association
Represents manufacturers of wood component products for urniture, cabinetry, building products, and decorative wood products.

16916 www.woodfloors.org
National Wood Flooring Association
For distributors, manufacturers, retailers, and contractors.

16917 www.woodtank.com
National Wood Tank Institute
To promote the use and to guide the proper construction methods for wooden tanks as per NWTI S-82.

16918 www.wrcla.org
Western Red Cedar Lumber Association
Association of 26 quality producers of Western Red Cedar lumber products in Washington, Oregon, Canada.

16919 www.wwpa.org
Western Wood Products Association
Represents lumber manufacturers in 12 Western states and Alaska. Provides lumber quality control, technical support, and business information to supporting mills.

16920 www2.dcn.org/orgs/wmmpa.wm
Wood Moulding And Millwork Producers Association
Goal is to promote quality products produced by its members, to develop sources of supply,

to promote optimum use of raw materials to standardize products, and to increase the domestic and foreign usage of moulding and millwork products.

Associations

16921 ASM International
ASM International
9639 Kinsman Rd
Materials Park, OH 44073-0002

440-338-5151
800-336-5152
FAX 440-338-4634
E-Mail: info@jewishlibraries.org
Home Page: www.asminternational.org
Social Media: *Facebook, Twitter, LinkedIn, RSS*

Yossi Galron, Membership

The society for materials engineers and scientists, a worldwide network dedicated to advancing industry, technology and applications of metals and materials.
900 Members
Founded in 1966

16922 American Amusement Machine Association
450 E. Higgins Road
Suite 201
Elk Grove Village, IL 60007

847-290-9088
E-Mail: jtally@alliant.edu
Home Page: www.coin-op.org

Mary L Conlon
140 Members
Founded in 1964

16923 American Gear Manufacturers Association
American Gear Manufacturers Association
1001 N. Fairfax Street
Suite 500
Alexandria, VA 22314-1587

703-684-0211
FAX 703-684-0242
E-Mail: amia@amianet.org
Home Page: www.agma.org
Social Media: *Facebook, Twitter, Youtube*

Caroline Frick, President and Director of the Board
Tyler Leshney, Secretary and Director of the Board
Colleen Simpson, Treasurer and Director of the Board
Laura Rooney, Managing Director
Beverly Graham, Membership Manager

Manufacturers of gears and geared speed changers. Involved in writing industry standards.
750 Members
Founded in 1991

16924 American Mold Builders Association
American Mold Builders Association
7321 Shadeland Station Way
#285
Indianapolis, IN 46256

317-436-3102
FAX 317-913-2445
E-Mail: webmgr@arl.org
Home Page: www.amba.org
Social Media: *Facebook, Twitter, LinkedIn, Flickr, YouTube, Google Plus*

Larry Alford, President
Mary Case, Vice President/ President-Elect
Elliott Shore, Executive Director
Prudence S Adler, Associate Executive Director
Sue Baughman, Deputy Executive Director

Promotes the development, welfare and expansion of businesses engaged in the manufacture of molds and related tooling.
Cost: $50.00
124 Members
Frequency: Annual
Founded in 1932

16925 American Society of Mechanical Engineers
Two Park Avenue
New York, NY 10016-5990

973-882-1170
800-843-2763
FAX 202-429-9417
E-Mail: betaphimu@drexel.edu
Home Page: www.asme.org
Social Media: *Facebook, Twitter, LinkedIn, YouTube, Instagram*

Amanda Ros, President
Eileen G Abels, PhD, Vice-President, President-Elect
Alison M. Lewis, PhD, Executive Director
Kathleen Inman, Treasurer
Erin Gabriele, Program Director

To promote and enhance the technical competency and professional well-being of the members, and through quality programs and activities in mechanical engineering, better enable its practitioners to contribute to the well being of human kind.
Founded in 1948

16926 American Textile Machinery Association
American Textile Machinery Association
201 Park Washington Ct
Falls Church, VA 22046-4527

703-538-1789
FAX 703-241-5603
E-Mail: gladysb@lms.kent.edu
Home Page: www.atmanet.org

Kelvin A Watson, President
Diane Covington, Secretary
Annie M Ford, Treasurer
Diane Covington, Secretary

ATMA's purpose is to advance the common interests of its members, improve business conditions within the US textile machinery industry from a global perspective and market the industry and members' machinery, parts and services.
Founded in 1969

16927 Associated Equipment Distributors
600 22nd Street
Suite 220
Oak Brook, IL 60523

630-574-0650
FAX 630-574-0132
E-Mail: cla@cathla.org
Home Page: www.aednet.org
Social Media: *Facebook*

Mary Kelleher, President
N. Curtis LeMay, Vice President/Treasurer
Melanie Talley, Senior Association Coordinator
Bland O'Connor, Executive Director, CLA Office
1000 Members
Founded in 1921

16928 Association for Facilities Engineering
8200 Greensboro Drive
Suite 400
McLean, VA 22102

571-395-8777
FAX 571-766-2142
E-Mail: ccb@illinois.edu
Home Page: www.afe.org
Social Media: *Facebook*

Dr. Deborah Stevenson, Director of the Center for Children
Michelle Biwer, Graduate Assistant
Lauren Gray, Graduate Assistant
Thaddeus Andracki, CCB Outreach & Communications

16929 Association for Machine Translation in the Americas
E-Mail: ccb@illinois.edu
Home Page: www.amtaweb.org
Social Media: *Facebook*

Dr. Deborah Stevenson, Director of the Center for Children
Michelle Biwer, Graduate Assistant
Lauren Gray, Graduate Assistant
Thaddeus Andracki, CCB Outreach & Communications

16930 Association for Manufacturing Technology
American Machine Tool Distributors
7901 Westpark Drive
McLean, VA 22102-4206

703-893-2900
800-524-0475
FAX 703-893-1151
E-Mail: sbrandenburg@amrms.com
Home Page: www.amtonline.org
Social Media: *Twitter*

Kendall Wiggin, President
Sandra Treadway, Vice President/President Elect
Kurt Kiefer, Secretary
Stacey Aldrich, Treasurer
Timothy Cherubini, Executive Director

Since 1925, the American Machine Tool Distributors' Association has been a major voice within the machine tool industry. The AMTDA represents independent distributors and worldwide builders of machine tools and related products used in the metalworking industry. The Association's mission is to provide marketers of manufacturing technology the essential services necessary to develop and perpetuate distribution businesses that make vital contributions to North American manufacturing.
53 Members
Founded in 1973

16931 Association of Computing Machinery
2 Penn Plaza
Suite 701
New York, NY 10121-0701

212-626-0500
800-342-6626
FAX 212-944-1318
E-Mail: sctseng@uci.edu
Home Page: www.acm.org
Social Media: *Facebook, Youtube*

Sally C Tseng, Executive Director
Founded in 1973

16932 Association of Equipment Manufacturers
6737 West Washington Street
Suite 2400
Milwaukee, WI 53214-5647

414-272-0943
FAX 414-272-1170
E-Mail: aem@aem.org
Home Page: www.aem.org
Social Media: *Twitter*

John Patterson, Chair
Leif J. Magnusson, Vice Chair
Renee Peters, Chief Financial Officer
Megan Tanel, VP, Exhibitions & Events
Luke, Anne Forristall, VP, Political & Public Affairs
850 Members

16933 Association of Machinery and Equipment Appraisers

Association of Machinery and Equipment
315 South Patrick Street
Alexandria, VA 22314-3532

703-836-7900
800-537-8629
FAX 703-836-9303
E-Mail: csla@worldaccessnet.com
Home Page: www.amea.org
Social Media: *Facebook*

Marcia Trauernicht, President
Maria Isabel Garcia, Second Vice President/Membership
Evelyn Pockrass, Treasurer
Dottie Lewis, Archives Coordinator
Judith Janzen, Administrator

Members are appraisers of the metalworking industry.
1500 Members
Founded in 1967
Mailing list available for rent

16934 Association of Vacuum Equipment Manufacturers International

201 Park Washington Court
Falls Church, VA 22046-4527

703-538-3542
FAX 703-241-5603
E-Mail: info@cni.org
Home Page: www.avem.org
Social Media: *Facebook, Twitter, LinkedIn, Youtube, Vimeo*

Clifford A Lynch, Executive Director
Joan K. Lippincott, Asociate Executive Director
Sharon Adams, Administrative Assistant
Maurice-Angelo Cruz, Systems Coordinator
Jacqueline J Eudell, Office Manager

The only non-profit U.S. association dedicated fully to companies that manufacture vacuum equipment and supplies that serve and advance vacuum science and technology. AVEM promotes member interests and provides services to enhance the membership value and understanding of the global market.
202 Members
Founded in 1990

16935 Clinical Robotic Surgery Association

Two Prudential Plaza
180 North Stetson, Suite 3500
Chicago, IL 60601

312-268-5754
E-Mail: gromero@clir.org
Home Page: www.clinicalrobotics.com
Social Media: *Facebook, Twitter, LinkedIn, Youtube*

Charles Henry, President
Alice Anderson, Senior Program Officer
Nicole K. Ferraiolo, Program Officer
Sharon Ivy Weiss, Chief Operations Officer
Lizzi Albert, Administrative Coordinator
Founded in 1997

16936 Compressed Air and Gas Institutue

Compressed Air and Gas Institutue
1300 Sumner Ave
Cleveland, OH 44115-2851

216-241-7333
FAX 216-241-0105
E-Mail: jmhite0@dia.mil
Home Page: www.cagi.org

Jackie Hite, President
Margaret Barron, Executive Direrctor
Chris Eganÿ, Vice-President/President Elect
Robin Martindill, Secretary
Stan Cieplinski, Treasurer

An organization representing manufacturers of compressed air system equipment, including air compressors, blowers, pneumatic tools and air and gasdryingand filtration equipment.
Founded in 1967

16937 Concrete Sawing and Drilling Association

Polycrystalline Products Association
100 2nd Ave S
Suite 402N
St. Petersburg, FL 33701

727-577-5004
FAX 727-577-5012
Home Page: www.csda.org
Social Media: *Facebook, Twitter, LinkedIn, Flickr, YouTube, Pinterest*

Roberta Shaffer, Executive Diretor
Robin Hatziyannis, Editor-in-Chief/Education
Joseph S Banks, Business Manager
Ruby J Thomas, Head, Member Services

An industrial trade association of tool fabricators, machine tool builders, material suppliers, educators and users of polycrystalline products.
40 Members
Founded in 1965

16938 Contractors Pump Bureau

Contractors Pump Bureau
6737 W Washington Street
Suite 2400
Milwaukee, WI 53214-5650

414-272-0943
866-AEM-0442
FAX 414-272-1170
E-Mail: aem@aem.org
Home Page: www.aem.org/Groups/Groups/Group.asp?G=22
Social Media: *Twitter*

Jeff Davis, Chair
Juan Quiros, Senior Vice Chair
Andy Falco, Vice Chair
Nathan Burton, Technical & Safety Services Manager

A product group of the Association of Equipment Manufacturers, the CPB promotes matters of mutual interest to contractor pump users, manufacturers and parts and component suppliers. Membership is open to any AEM member in good standing actively engaged in the manufacture and distribution of portable contractor pumps within the USA, or supplying components to those manufacturers.
20 Members
Founded in 1938

16939 Converting Equipment Manufacturers Association

201 Springs Street
Fort Mill, SC 29715

803-948-9470
FAX 803-948-9471
E-Mail: info@hooverassociation.org
Home Page: www.cema-converting.org
Social Media: *Facebook, Twitter, LinkedIn, YouTube*

Charles Becker, President
Robert Downer, Vice President
Ryan Johnson, Financial Development
Brad Reiners, Communications Manager
Jerry Fleagle, IOM, CAE, Executive Director
Founded in 1939

16940 Conveyor Equipment Manufacturers Association (CEMA)

5672 Strand CT
Suite 2
Naples, FL 34110

239-514-3441
FAX 239-514-3470
E-Mail: shart@insurancelibrary.org
Home Page: www.cemanet.org

Glenn Cryan, Executive Director
Meagan Stefanow, Reference Librarian
Sarah Hart, Reference Librarian

Involved in writing industry standards, the CEMA seeks to promote among its members and the industry standardization of design manufacture and application on a voluntary basis and in such manner as will not impede development of conveying machinery and component parts or lessen competition. CEMA sponsors an annual Engineering Conference that allows Member Company Engineers to meet and develop or improve CEMA Consensus Industry Standards and National Standards that affect the conveyor industry.
760+ Members
Founded in 1887

16941 Farm Equipment Manufacturers Association

Farm Equipment Manufacturers Association
1000 Executive Parkway Dr
Suite 100
St Louis, MO 63141-6369

314-878-2304
FAX 314-732-1480
E-Mail: richard.barry@ana.org
Home Page: www.farmequip.org

Gertrude B. Hutchinson, President
June Levy, President
Warren Hawkes, VP
Wanda Hiestand, Treasurer
Jane Root, Secretary

An information gathering and distributing organization for farm equipment manufacturers and suppliers.
26 Members
Founded in 1960

16942 Fire Equipment Manufacturers' Association

Fire Equipment Manufacturers' Association
1300 Sumner Avenue
Cleveland, OH 44115-2851

216-241-7333
FAX 216-241-0105
E-Mail: janet.webster@oregonstate.edu
Home Page: www.femalifesafety.org

Kristen Anderson, President
Brian Voss, Secretary
Kristen LaBonte, Treasurer
Guillermina Cosulich, President-Elect
Kristen Anderson, President-Elect

The premier trade association representing leading brands, and spanning dozens of product categories, related to fire protection.
200 Members
Founded in 1975

16943 Fluid Power Safety Institute

2170 South 3140 West
West Valley City, UT 84119

801-908-5456
FAX 801-908-5734
E-Mail: iasl@mlahq.org
Home Page: www.fluidpowersafety.com
Social Media: *Twitter*

Dr. Diljit Singh, President
Mihaela Banek Zorica, VP, Association Operations
Kay Hones, VP, Association Relations
Elizabeth Greef, VP, Advocacy & Promotion
Katy Manck, Treasurer

16944 Fluid Power Society

Fluid Power Society

1930 E Marlton Pike
Suite A2
Cherry Hill, NJ 08034-0054

856-489-8983
800-308-6005
FAX 856-424-9248
E-Mail: info@lbibinders.org
Home Page: www.ifps.org

Duncan Campbell, President
Jack Tolbert, Vice President
Debra S. Nolan, CAE, Executive Director
Alan McIntire, Treasurer
Jack McLoraine, Director

International organization for fluid power and motion control professionals.

16945 Food Processing Suppliers Association
Food Processing Suppliers Association
1451 Dolley Madison Blvd
Suite 101
Mc Lean, VA 22101-3850

703-761-2600
FAX 703-761-4334
E-Mail: admin@mola-inc.org
Home Page: www.fpsa.org

Patrick McGinn, President
Mark Millidge, Vice President
Alison Mrowka, Secretary
Shannon Highland, Treasurer

Trade association for food and beverage processing suppliers.
630 Members
Founded in 1983

16946 Heat Exchange Institute
Heat Exchange Institute
1300 Sumner Avenue
Cleveland, OH 44115-2851

216-241-7333
FAX 216-241-0105
E-Mail: info@mlahq.org
Home Page: www.heatexchange.org
Social Media: *Facebook, LinkedIn, Youtube*

Michelle Kraft, AHIP, President
Kevin Baliozian, Executive Director
Chris Shaffer, AHIP, Treasurer
Chris Shaffer, Director and Treasurer
Julia Esparza, Director

A non-profit trade association committed to the technical advancement, promotion and understanding of a broad range of utility and industrial-scale heat exchange and vacuum apparatus.
4500 Members
Founded in 1898

16947 Industrial Distribution Association
Industrial Distribution Association
100 N 20th Street
4th Floor
Philadelphia, PA 19103

215-320-3862
866-460-2360
FAX 215-564-2175
E-Mail: sharon.kern@lawiowa.com
Home Page: www.ida-assoc.org
Social Media: *Facebook, Twitter, YouTube*

William J. Fehrman, President and CEO
Patrick J. Goodman, Executive Vice President
Maureen E. Sammon, Senior Vice President
Douglas L. Anderson, Executive Vice President

Promotes the industry and the use of converting equipment. Conducts research and compiles statistics for wholesalers of industrial equipment.
Founded in 1971

16948 International Association of Diecutting and Diemaking
651 W Terra Cotta Ave
Suite 132
Crystal Lake, IL 60014

815-455-7519
800-828-4233
FAX 815-455-7510
E-Mail: webmaster@mela.us
Home Page: www.iadd.org
Social Media: *Facebook, Twitter, LinkedIn*

Roberta L. Dougherty, President
Jaleh Fazelian, Vice President/ Program Chair
William Kopycki, Secretary/ Treasurer
Marlis J. Saleh, Editor

A not-for-profit international trade association serving diecutters, diemakers, and industry suppliers worldwide. Provides conferences, educational and training programs, networking opportunities, a monthly magazine, technical articles, regional chapter meetings, publications and training manuals, recommended specifications, videos and surveys.
150 Members
Founded in 1972

16949 International Association of Machinists and Aerospace
International Association of Machinists
9000 Machinists Pl
Upper Marlboro, MD 20772-2675

301-967-4500
FAX 301-967-4588
E-Mail: execsecretary@mpla.us
Home Page: www.goiam.org
Social Media: *Facebook, Twitter, LinkedIn, Flickr, YouTube, Google+*

Eric Stroshane, President
Mickey Coalwell, Vice-President/President Elect
Melanie Argo, Recording Secretary
Judy Zelenski, Executive Secretary
Roy Degler, Systems Administrator

Has an annual budget of approximately $101.3 million.
1600+ Members
Founded in 1948

16950 International Association of Professional Mechanical Engineers
55 Public Square
Suite 612
Cleveland, OH 44113

216-453-0500
E-Mail: mla@areditions.com
Home Page: iapme.org
Social Media: *Facebook*

Michael Colby, President
Pamela Bristah, Recording Secretary
Paul Cary, Administrative Officer
Linda W. Blair, Assistant Administrative Officer
Founded in 1951

16951 Machinery Dealers National Association
Machinery Dealers National Association
315 S Patrick St
Alexandria, VA 22314-3532

703-836-9300
800-872-7807
FAX 703-836-9303
E-Mail: bettyge@mchsi.com
Home Page: www.mdna.org
Social Media: *Facebook, Twitter*

Sally Lindgren, President
Betty G. Ehlinge, Executive Director
Barbara Siemaszko, Secretary
Geoff Craven, Treasurer

Represents dealers of used industrial equipment.
Founded in 1984

16952 Manufacturers Alliance for Productivity and Innovation
1600 Wilson Blvd
Suite 1100
Arlington, VA 22209-2594

703-841-9000
FAX 703-841-9514
E-Mail: info@churchlibraries.org
Home Page: www.mapi.net
Social Media: *Facebook*

A policy research organization whose members are companies drawn from the producers and users of capital goods and allied products. Includes leading companies in heavy industry, automotive, electronics, precision instruments, telecommunications, computers, office systems. aerospace, oil/gas, chemicals and similar high technology industries.
Founded in 1958

16953 Material Handling Institute
Crane Manufacturers Association of America
8720 Red Oak Boulevard
Suite 201
Charlotte, NC 28217-3996

704-676-1190
FAX 704-676-1199
E-Mail: nisohq@niso.org
Home Page: www.mhia.org/psc

Mike Teets, Chair
Todd Carpenter, Executive Director / Secretary
Nettie Lagace, Associate Director for Programs
DeVonne Parks, Manager
Keith Webster, Treasurer

Supports crane equipment manufacturers.
70 Members
Founded in 1939

16954 Mechanical Power Transmission Association
Mechanical Power Transmission Association
5672 Strand Ct.
Suite 2
Naples, FL 34110

239-514-3441
FAX 239-514-3470
E-Mail: nls@loc.gov
Home Page: www.mpta.org
Social Media: *Facebook, Twitter, LinkedIn*

Frank Cylke, Manager
Martinez Majors, IT Specialist
Alice G Freeman, Program Management Assistant
Michael M Moodie, Research/Development Officer

Formerly Multiple V-Belt and Mechanical Power Transmission Association.

16955 National Fluid Power Association
National Fluid Power Association
6737 W. Washington Street
Suite 2350
Milwaukee, WI 53214

414-778-3344
FAX 414-778-3361
E-Mail: director@nmm.net
Home Page: www.nfpa.com
Social Media: *Facebook, Twitter, LinkedIn, Flickr, Pinterest*

Ursula Schwarz, Executive Director
Julie Drake, Chair

Members are companies which have designed, manufactured and nationally marketed a fluid

power component for at least two years in the US.
55 Members
Founded in 1978

16956 National Tooling & Machining Association

National Tooling & Machining Association
1357 Rockside Road
Cleveland, OH 44134

301-248-6200
800-248-6862
FAX 216-264-2840
E-Mail: rscheier@gmail.com
Home Page: www.ntma.org
Social Media: *Facebook, Twitter, Flickr, RSS, Instagram*

Deb Hoadley, President
Stephen Spohn, Vice President
David Bryan, Technology Contractor
Mary Ann Rupert, Conference Management Contractor
Robert Scheier, Library Association Administrator

Members are makers of jigs, molds, tools, gages, dies and fixtures for companies doing precision machining. Supports the NTMA - Committee for A Strong Economy.
Founded in 1963

16957 North American Equipment Dealers Association

1195 Smizer Mill Rd
Fenton, MO 63026-3480

636-349-5000
FAX 636-349-5443
E-Mail: info@archivists.org
Home Page: www.naeda.com
Social Media: *Facebook, Twitter, LinkedIn*

Nancy Beaumont, Executive Director
Teresa Brinati, Director of Publishing
Solveig De Sutter, Director of Education
Tom Jurczak, Director of Finance
Matthew Black, Web and Information Systems

NAEDA and its affiliates provides a variety of educational, financial, legislative and legal services to equipment dealers in the United States and Canada.
3400 Members
Founded in 1936

16958 Outdoor Power Equipment and Engine Service Association

Outdoor Power Equipment and Engine
37 Pratt Street
Essex, CT 06426-1159

860-767-1770
FAX 860-767-7932
E-Mail: lfallon@solinet.net
Home Page: www.opeesa.com

Gordon Baker, President
Beverly James, Treasurer
Lorene Flanders, Secretary
Diane N Baird, Treasurer

Members are distributors of outdoor power equipment to retailers with a minimum of $1 million gross sales. Associate membership is available for suppliers and finance companies associated with the industry.

16959 Packaging Machinery Manufacturers Institute

Packaging Machinery Manufacturers
11911 Freedom Drive
Suite 600
Reston, VA 20190

571-612-3200
FAX 703-243-8556
E-Mail: sla@sla.org
Home Page: www.pmmi.org

Social Media: *Facebook, Twitter, LinkedIn, Youtube, Pinterest*

Doug Newcomb, Deputy Chief Executive Officer
Quan O. Logan, Chief Technology Officer
Natasha Kenner, Director
Linda Broussard, Chief Financial Officer
Paula Diaz, Director, Membership

Trade association for manufacturers of packaging and packaging-related converting equipment. PMMI offers meetings, an inquiry service, statistics and surveys, and a business to business survey on its website. PMMI also offers several Pack Expos (packaging related tradeshows).
13M Members

16960 Powder Actuated Tool Manufacturers' Institute

Powder Actuated Tool Manufacturers
136 South Main Street
Suite 2e
Saint Charles, MO 63301

636-578-5510
FAX 314-884-4414
E-Mail: drewwe@morrisville.edu
Home Page: patmi.org
Social Media: *Facebook, Twitter*

Rebecca Hyams, President
Bill Jones, 1st Vice-President/President Elect
Laura Evans, 2nd Vice-President/Conference Chair
Carrie Fishner, Secretary
Greg Bobish, Treasurer

Represents manufacturers of construction tools used to fasten to and into steel and concrete.
348 Members
Founded in 1968

16961 Power Conversion Products Council International

4 Hollis Street
PO Box 378
Sherborn, MA 01770

508-979-5935
FAX 508-651-3920

Elizabeth Bevington-Chambers, Executive Director

Members are manufacturers and suppliers to the wall plug-in transformer/transformer charger/converter industry. Sponsor two meetings each year covering business and engineering topics.
50 Members
Founded in 1974

16962 Power Tool Institute

1300 Sumner Ave
Cleveland, OH 44115-2851

216-241-7333
FAX 216-241-0105
E-Mail: salis@salis.org
Home Page: www.powertoolinstitute.com

Jane Shelling, Chair
Andrea Mitchell, Executive Director and Editor
Sheila Lacroix, Secretary
Karen Palmer, Treasurer

The preeminent organization for building global understanding of power tools and for maintaining high standards of safety and quality control in the industry.
160 Members
Founded in 1988

16963 Power-Motion Technology Representative Association

Power-Motion Technology Representative

5353 Wayzata Blvd.
Suite 350
Minneapolis, MN 55416

949-859-2885
888-817-7872
FAX 952-252-8096
E-Mail: info@tla-online.org
Home Page: www.ptra.org
Social Media: *Facebook, RSS*

Nancy Friedland, President
Angela Weaver, VP
Laurie Murphy, Executive Secretary
Colleen Riley, Treasurer

To promote the science of power transmission/motion control engineering, to promote educational programs and activities and to promote representatives placed in the industry.
300 Members
Founded in 1937

16964 Precision Machined Products Association

Precision Machined Products Association
6880 West Snowville Road
Suite 200
Brecksville, OH 44141

440-526-0300
FAX 440-526-5803
Home Page: www.pmpa.org

Trudi Bellardo Hahn, Executive Director
C. Beth Fitzsimmons, Chairperson

Produces several educational opporunities for members, emphasizing quality assurance and emerging technologies. Sponsors the PMPA Political Action Committee.
Founded in 1970

16965 Robotic Industries Association

Robotic Industries Association
900 Victors Way
Suite 140
Ann Arbor, MI 48108

734-994-6088
FAX 734-994-3338
E-Mail: info@urbanlibraries.org
Home Page: www.roboticsonline.com
Social Media: *Facebook, Twitter*

Matt Poland, Chairman
Michael Sherrod, Vice Chair/Chair Elect
Gary Wasdin, Secretary/Treasurer
Lourdes Aceves, Project Manager, Edge
Mary Colleen Bragiel, Project Manager

Only trade group in North America specifically to serve the rototics industry.
150+ Members
Founded in 1971

16966 Service Dealers Association

PO Box 73796
Houston, TX 77273-3063

281-443-3063
FAX 817-921-3741

Melinda Delgado, Executive Director

Represents dealers and distributors of power equipment.
690 Members
Founded in 1986

16967 Service Specialists Association

PO Box 936
Elgin, IL 60121

847-760-0067
800-763-5717
FAX 330-722-5638
E-Mail: aaea@gandgcomm.com
Home Page: www.truckservice.org
Social Media: *Facebook, Twitter, LinkedIn*

Den Gardner, Executive Director
Kenna Rathai, Associate Director
Kenna Rathai, Associate Executive Director

Members are persons, firms or corporations who have operated a full line heavy duty repair service shop for at least one year with sufficient inventory to service market area, having rebuilding department capable of making all necessary repairs.
Founded in 1921

16968 Society of Manufacturing Engineers
Society of Manufacturing Engineers
1 SME Drive
PO Box 930
Dearborn, MI 48128

313-425-3000
800-733-4763
FAX 313-425-3400
E-Mail: info@washwriter.org
Home Page: www.sme.org

Donald Graul, Executive Director

Serves its members and others in the international manufacturing community by identifying, evaluating and explaining the adoption and integration of emerging information technologies to create business value.
1800 Members
Founded in 1975

16969 Society of Robotic Surgery
Two Woodfield Lake
1100 E Woodfield Road, Suite 350
Schaumburg, IL 60173

847-517-7225
E-Mail: amwa@amwa.org
Home Page: www.srobotics.org
Social Media: *Facebook, Twitter, LinkedIn*

Samantha Nelson, Program Assistant
Rachel Spassiani, Membership Associate & Publications
Melanie Canahuate, Education & Conference Assistant
Becky Phillips, Conference Program Manager
Lauren Ero, Education and Certificate Program
3.4M Members
Founded in 1940

16970 The Association for Packaging and Processing Technologies
11911 Fredom Drive
Suite 600
Reston, VA 20190

571-612-3200
FAX 703-243-8556
E-Mail: webeditor@asja.org
Home Page: www.pmmi.org
Social Media: *Facebook, Twitter, LinkedIn, Google+*

Randy Dotinga, President
Sherry Beck Paprocki, Vice President
Alexandra Cantor Owens, Executive Director, ASJA
Neil O'Hara, Treasurer
Bruce Miller, Webmaster/IT Manager
1000+ Members
Founded in 1948

16971 The FPDA Motion & Control Network
105 Eastern Avenue
Suite 104
Annapolis, MD 21403

410-940-6347
E-Mail: ata@atanet.org
Home Page: www.fpda.org
Social Media: *Facebook, Twitter*

Caitilin Walsh, President
Walter W. Bacak, Executive Director
Boris M. Silversteyn, Secretary
Ted R. Wozniak, Treasurer
Teresa Kelly, Meetings Manager
11100 Members
Founded in 1959

16972 Tooling Component Manufacturers Association
36505 Florida Avenue
Hemet, CA 92545-3534

FAX 909-766-7443

Ray Fuhrer, Executive Secretary
Members are united primarily for the purpose of coordinating and standardizing sizes.
8 Members
Founded in 1958

16973 Unified Abrasives Manufacturers' Association
30200 Detroit Road
Cleveland, OH 44145-1967

440-899-0010
FAX 440-892-1404
E-Mail: pwa@prowriters.org
Home Page: www.uama.org
Social Media: *Twitter*

Lee C Johns, President
400+ Members
Founded in 1983

16974 Valve Manufacturers Association of America (VMA)
Valve Manufacturers Association of America
1050 17th St NW
Suite 280
Washington, DC 20036-5521

202-331-8105
FAX 202-296-0378
E-Mail: beforecolumbusfoundation@gmail.com
Home Page: www.vma.org

Gundars Strads, Executive Director
VMA represents the interests of nearly 100 U.S. and Canadian valve, actuator, and control Manufacturers who account for approximately 80% of the total industrial valve shipments out of U.S. and Canadian facilities. The American valve industry supplies approximately 35% of worldwide valve demand. VMA member companies employ 20,000 men and women directly in supporting jobs. VMA is the only organization exclusively serving U.S. and Canadian manufacturers of industrial valves, controls and actuator
Founded in 1976

16975 Vibration Institute
Vibration Institute
2625 Butterfield Road
Suite 128N
Oak Brook, IL 60523-3415

630-654-2254
FAX 630-654-2271
E-Mail: anneandhenrypaolucci@yahoo.com
Home Page: www.vi-institute.org

Anne Paolucci, President
A not-for-profit organization dedicated to the exchange of practical vibration information on machines and structures.
Founded in 1976

16976 Wood Machinery Manufacturers of America
9 Newport Dr.
Suite 200
Forest Hill, MD 21050

443-640-1052
FAX 443-640-1031
E-Mail: info@wmma.org
Home Page: www.wmma.org
Social Media: *Facebook, Twitter, LinkedIn*

Jamison Scott, President
Chris Hacker, Vice President
Fred Stringfellow, Executive Director

WMMA has worked to increase the productivity and profitability of U.S. machinery and tooling manufacturers and the businesses that support them.
Founded in 1899

16977 Wood Machinery Maufacturers of America
Wood Machinery Maufacturers of America
9 Newport Drive
Suite 200
Forest Hill, MD 21050

443-640-1052
FAX 443-640-1031
E-Mail: info@wmma.org
Home Page: www.wmma.org
Social Media: *Facebook, Twitter, LinkedIn*

Jamison J. Scott, President
Chris Hacker, Vice President
Fred Stringfellow, Executive Director
Diane Schafer, Director of Meetings
Amy Chetelat, Director of Finance
Founded in 1899

16978 Woodworking Machinery Industry Association
225 Reinekers Lane
Suite 410
Alexandria, VA 22314

860-350-WMIA
FAX 860-354-0677
E-Mail: info@wmia.org
Home Page: www.wmia.org
Social Media: *Facebook, Twitter*

Scott Mueller, President
Dave Rakauskas, Vice President
Jim Besonen, Secretary/Treasurer
Larry Hoffer, Executive Vice President
Liza Wentworth, Program Administrator
Founded in 1977

Newsletters

16979 Association of Machinery and Equipment Appraisers - Newsletter
Association of Machinery and Equipment Appraisers
315 S Patrick St
Alexandria, VA 22314-3532

703-836-7900
800-537-8629
FAX 703-836-9303
E-Mail: amea@amea.org
Home Page: www.amea.org

Pamela Reid, Executive Director

Information about appraisers of the machinery equipment.
8 Pages
Circulation: 6800
Founded in 1983
Mailing list available for rent: 282 names at $100 per M
Printed in 2 colors on matte stock

16980 CEMA Bulletin
Conveyor Equipment Manufacturers Association
5672 Strand Ct., Suite 2
Naples, FL 34110

239-514-3441
FAX 239-514-3470
E-Mail: cema@cemanet.org
Home Page: www.cemanet.org

Robert Reinfried, Executive Director
Association and conveyor industry news.
6 Pages
Circulation: 96
Founded in 1933

16981 Caster and Wheel Handbook

Youngs
55 E Cherry Ln
Souderton, PA 18964-1550

215-723-4400
800-523-5454
FAX 800-544-3239
E-Mail: custrep@youngscatalog.com
Home Page: www.youngscatalog.com

Paul O Young Jr, President

Technical news and information.
Frequency: Monthly
Founded in 1945

16982 Computer Aided Design Report

CAD/CAM Publishing
711 Van Nuys Street
San Diego, CA 92109-1053

858-488-0533
FAX 858-488-0361
E-Mail: info@cadcampub.com
Home Page: www.cadcampub.com/

Randall Newton, Editor

Uses of computers by engineers in the manufacturing trades.
Cost: $344.00
Frequency: Monthly
ISSN: 0276-749X
Founded in 1977

16983 Computer Integrated Manufacture and Engineering

Lionheart Publishing
2555 Cumberland Pkwy Se
Suite 299
Atlanta, GA 30339-3921

770-432-2551
FAX 770-432-6969

Explores cutting edge developments in manufacturing systems operation management.
Circulation: 24,000

16984 High-Tech Materials Alert

John Wiley & Sons
111 River St
Hoboken, NJ 07030-5790

201-748-6000
800-825-7550
FAX 201-748-6088
E-Mail: info@wiley.com
Home Page: www.wiley.com

William J Pesce, CEO

Details significant developments in high-performance materials ranging from alloys and metallic whiskers to ceramic and graphite fibers, their fabrication and industrial applications.
Cost: $1152.00
Frequency: Monthly
Founded in 1807

16985 Industrial Health & Hazards Update

InfoTeam
PO Box 15640
Plantation, FL 33318-5640

954-473-9560
FAX 954-473-0544

Merton Allen, Editor

Covers occupational safety, health, hazards, and disease, mitigatioin and control of hazardous situations; waste recycling and treaqtment; environmental pollution and control; product safety and liability; fires and explosions; plant and computer security,; air pollution; surface and ground water; wastewater; soil gases; combustion and incineration; earth warming; ozone layer depletion; electromagnetic radiation; toxic materials; and many other related topics.
Frequency: Monthlyth

16986 Innovators Digest

InfoTeam
PO Box 15640
Plantation, FL 33318-5640

954-473-9560
FAX 954-473-0544

Merton Allen, Editor

A multidisciplinary publication covering developments in science, engineering, products, markets, business development, manufacturing and other technological developments having industrial or commercial significance.
Frequency: Bi-Weekly

16987 Intelligent Manufacturing

Lionheart Publishing
506 Roswell St Se
Suite 220
Marietta, GA 30060-4101

770-422-3139
FAX 770-432-6969
E-Mail: lpi@lionhrtpub.com
Home Page: www.lionhrtpub.com

John Llewellyn, Publisher
David Blanchard, Advertising Sales Manager
Marvin Diamond, Advertising Sales Manager

Provides expert solutions to manufacturing professionals covering production problems, developments in manufacturing systems.
Cost: $20.00
Frequency: Weekly
Circulation: 1598
Founded in 1987

16988 Machinery Outlook

Manfredi & Associates
20934 W Lakeview Pkwy
Mundelein, IL 60060-9502

847-949-9080
FAX 847-949-9910
E-Mail: info@manfredi.com
Home Page: www.machineryoutlook.com

Frank Manfredi, President

A newsletter about and for the construction and mining machinery industry.
Cost: $550.00
14 Pages
Frequency: Monthly
Founded in 1984
Printed in one color on matte stock

16989 Machining Technology

Society of Manufacturing Engineers
1 SME Drive
PO Box 930
Dearborn, MI 48121

313-425-3000
800-733-4763
FAX 313-425-3400
E-Mail: advertising@sme.org
Home Page: www.sme.org

Mark Tomlinson, Executive Director/General Manager
Greg Sheremet, Publisher
Bob Harris, Director Finance

Covers all aspects of machining in manufacturing, milling, grinding, honing, etc.
Cost: $60.00
8 Pages
Frequency: Quarterly
Circulation: 3770
Founded in 1932
Printed in 2 colors on matte stock

16990 Manufacturing Technology

National Technical Information Service
5285 Port Royal Rd
Springfield, VA 22161-0001

703-605-6000
FAX 703-605-6900

E-Mail: info@ntis.gov
Home Page: www.ntis.gov

Linda Davis, VP
Patrik Ekstrom, Business Development Manager
Reuel Avila, Managing Director

Covers CAD/CAM, robotics, robots, productivity, manufacturing, planning, processing and control, plant design and computer software.

16991 NTMA Record

Tooling
9300 Livingston Road
Fort Washington, MD 20744-4905

301-248-5071
800-248-6862
FAX 301-248-7104
E-Mail: tom@ntma.org
Home Page: www.ntma.org

Rob Akers, Operations Director/ Publisher
Richard Wills, CEO
Thomas Garcia, Manager, Marketing

Covers activities of 4,000 member companies of tool, die and precision machining industries.
Cost: $39.00
16 Pages
Frequency: Monthly
Circulation: 2000
Founded in 1943

16992 Wood Machining News

Wood Machining Institute
PO Box 476
Berkeley, CA 94701

510-448-8363
FAX 925-945-0947
E-Mail: szymani@woodmachining.com
Home Page: www.woodmachining.com

Ryszard Szymani, Director

Information on the latest technological advances in the field of wood machining, including sawing, planning and sanding operations as well as the production of veneers and chips and equipment associated with these operations. WMN also reports on new machinery, processes and software, cutting tools and machinery and worker safety.
Cost: $72.00
38448 Pages
Circulation: 600
ISSN: 0743-5232
Founded in 1984

Magazines & Journals

16993 American Society of Mechanical Engineers

American Society of Mechanical Engineers
3 Park Ave
Suite 21
New York, NY 10016-5990

212-591-7000
800-843-2763
FAX 202-429-9417
E-Mail: infocentral@asme.org
Home Page: www.asme.org

Thomas Loughlin, Executive Director
John G Falcioni, Editor-in-Chief
Frequency: Monthly
Founded in 1880

16994 American Tool, Die & Stamping News

Eagle Publications
42400 Grand River Ave
Suite 103
Novi, MI 48375-2572

248-347-3487
800-783-3491

FAX 248-347-3492
E-Mail: info@ameritooldie.com
Home Page: www.ameritooldie.com

Arthur Brown, President
Joan Oakley, CEO

Applications, techniques, equipment and accessories of metal stamping, moldmaking, electric discharge machining; and new product information relating to the tool and die industry. Accepts advertising.
70 Pages
Circulation: 36000
ISSN: 0192-5709
Founded in 1971
Printed in 4 colors on glossy stock

16995 Compressed Air Magazine

Ingersoll Rand Company
200 Chestnut Ridge Road
Woodcliff, NJ 07677

201-573-0123
FAX 201-573-3172
Home Page: www.irco.com

Michele Zayle, Circulation Director
Thomas McAloon, Editor

A magazine of applied technology and industrial management for middle and upper level managers in diversified industries.
Cost: $15.00
44 Pages
Frequency: 8 per year
Circulation: 125,000
Printed in 4 colors on matte stock

16996 Contact

Furnas Electric Company
1000 McKee Street
Batavia, IL 60510-1682

630-879-6000
FAX 630-879-0867

Steve Wilcox, Editor

Application of electric motor controls to electrically operated machinery and equipment.
Circulation: 4,000

16997 Cutting Edge

Int'l Assoc of Diecutting and Diemaking
651 W Terra Cotta Ave
Suite 132
Crystal Lake, IL 60014

815-455-7519
800-828-4233
FAX 815-455-7510
E-Mail: cccrouse@iadd.org
Home Page: www.iadd.org

Cindy Crouse, CEO
Jill May, Chapter Relations Coordinator

A technical journal and trade magazine written and edited specifically for diecutters, diemakers and industry suppliers who are faced with the need to stay ahead of technologies in an industry that is changing at breakneck speed.
Frequency: Monthly

16998 Diesel Progress: North American Edition

Diesel & Gas Turbine Publications
20855 Watertown Rd
Suite 220
Waukesha, WI 53186-1873

262-754-4100
FAX 262-754-4175
E-Mail: mmcneely@dieselpub.com
Home Page: www.dieselspec.com

Michael Osenga, President
S Bollwahn, Circulation Manager

Geared towards readers interested in state-of-the-art systems technology. Features include new product listings, systems design,

research and product testing as well as systems maintenance and rebuilding.
Frequency: Monthly
Circulation: 26011

16999 EE-Evaluation Engineering

Nelson Publishing Inc
2500 Tamiami Trl N
Nokomis, FL 34275-3476

941-966-9521
FAX 941-966-2590
Home Page: www.healthmgttech.com
Social Media: *Facebook*

A Verner Nelson, President

Leading source of information for the electronics testing and evaluation market.
Founded in 1962

17000 Elevator World

Elevator World
PO Box 6507
Mobile, AL 36660-0507

251-479-4514
800-730-5093
FAX 251-479-7043
E-Mail: editorial@elevator-world.com
Home Page: www.elevator-world.com

T Bruce Mackinnon, CEO
Robert S Caporale, Senior VP/Editor
Patricia Cartee, VP/Commercial Operations

International journal for those involved in short-range vertical transportation, including manufacturers, contractors, maintainers, consultants and inspectors.
Cost: $75.00
170 Pages
Frequency: Monthly
Circulation: 7,000
Founded in 1953
Printed in 4 colors on glossy stock

17001 Equip-Mart

Story Communications
116 N Camp Street
Seguin, TX 78155

830-303-3328
800-864-1155
FAX 830-372-3011
Home Page: www.equip-mart.com

Tammy Reilly, Publisher

Largest industrial equipment magazine in North America. Received by manufacturig executives who purchase or sell industrial equipment, tools, supplies and accessories.
Frequency: Monthly
Circulation: 108,000

17002 Gear Technology

Randall Publishing Company
PO Box 1426
Elk Grove Village, IL 60009

847-437-6604
FAX 847-437-6618
Home Page: www.geartechnology.com

Michael Goldstein, Publisher
William R Stott, Managing Editor
Dan Pels, Business Development Mana
Carol Tratar, Circulation Coordinator
Richard Goldstein, Vice President

Gear Technology offers technical articles from the top names in the industry; feature articles dealing with management and technology; top-notch tradeshow coverage; industry and products news.
Circulation: 13025
Founded in 1934
Printed in 4 colors on glossy stock

17003 High Performance Composites

Ray Publishing

P.O.Box 992
Morrison, CO 80465-0992

303-467-1776
FAX 303-467-1777
E-Mail: info@raypubs.com
Home Page: www.compositeworld.com

Approach is technical, offering cutting-edge design, engineering, prototyiping, and manufacturing solutions for aerospace and other traditional and emerging structural applications for advanced composites.

17004 Home Medical Equipment News

United Publications
106 Lafayette Street
PO Box 998
Yarmouth, ME 04096

207-846-0600
FAX 207-846-0657
Home Page: www.hmenews.com

James G Taliaferro, CEO/President
Brenda Boothby, Circulation Director
Joline V Gilman, Production Director
Jim Sullivan, Editor
Rick Rector, Publisher

Serves home medical equipment providers.
Frequency: Monthly
Circulation: 17100
Founded in 1995

17005 Home Shop Machinist

Village Press
2779 Aero Park Drive
PO Box 968
Traverse City, MI 49685-968

231-946-3712
800-327-7377
FAX 231-946-3289
E-Mail: info@villagepress.com
Home Page: www.villagepress.com

Robert Goff, Publisher
Neil Knopf, Editor
Joe D. Rice, Editor in Chief
Angela Sagi, Advertising Director

Articles on precision machining and metal working and how-to projects geared towards the amateur machinist and small commercial machine shops.
Cost: $25.00
Circulation: 28000

17006 IEEE Transactions on Industry Applications

IEEE Operations Center
PO Box 1331
Piscataway, NJ 08855-1331

732-981-0060
FAX 732-981-1721
E-Mail: society-info@ieee.org
Home Page: www.ieee.org

John Vig, CEO
Johnathan Dahl, Director of Sales and Marketing

The development and applications of electrical systems, apparatus, devices and controls to the processes and equipment of industry and commerce.
Cost: $515.00
Circulation: 5100
Founded in 1980

17007 InTech

ISA Services
67 Alexander Drive
PO Box 12277
Research Triangle Park, NC 27709

919-549-8411
FAX 919-990-9434

E-Mail: info@isa.org
Home Page: www.isa.org

Greg Hale, Editor
Richard Simpson, Publisher

Covers the most recent developments in the instrumentation, measurement and control market.
Frequency: Monthly
Circulation: 75000
Founded in 1945

17008 Industrial Machine Trader
Heartland Industrial Group
1003 Central Avenue
PO Box 1415
Fort Dodge, IA 50501

515-955-1600
800-203-9960
FAX 515-955-3753
E-Mail: ads@industrialgroup.com
Home Page: www.imtgetsresults.com/

Tony Smith, Publisher
Gele Mckinney, President
Angi Hesterman, Circulation Manager

Industrial machinery equipment, suppliers and manufacturers.
Cost: $67.85
8 Pages
Frequency: Weekly
Circulation: 234000
Founded in 1970

17009 Industrial Market Place
Wineberg Publications
7842 Lincoln Avenue
Skokie, IL 60077

847-676-1900
800-323-1818
FAX 847-676-0063
E-Mail: info@industrialmktpl.com
Home Page: www.industrialmktpl.com

Joel Wineberg, President
Jackie Bitensky, Editor

Has advertisements on machinery, industrial and plant equipment, services and industrial acution in each issue.
Cost: $175.00
Frequency: Every 2 weeks
Circulation: 14,000
Founded in 1951
Mailing list available for rent: 120 names at $70 per M
Printed in 4 colors on glossy stock.

17010 Journal of Engineering for Industry
American Society of Mechanical Engineers
3 Park Ave
Suite 21
New York, NY 10016-5990

212-591-7000
800-843-2763
FAX 212-591-7674
E-Mail: Infocentral@asme.org
Home Page: www.asme.org

Richard E Feigel, President
David Soukup, Managing Director

Covers interfaces of mechanical engineering.
Cost: $40.00
Founded in 1880

17011 Journal of Materials Engineering and Performance
ASM International
9639 Kinsman Road
Materials Park, OH 44073-0002

440-338-5151
800-336-5152
FAX 440-338-4634
E-Mail: memberservice@asminternational.org

Home Page: www.asminternational.org
Social Media: *Facebook, Twitter, LinkedIn*

Jeane Deatherage, Administrator, Foundation Programs
Virginia Shirk, Foundation Executive Assistant

Peer-reviewed journal that publishes contributions on all aspects of materials selection, design, characterization, processing and performance testing. The journal for solving day-to-day engineering challenges - especially those involving components for larger systems.
Cost: $1965.00
Frequency: Bimonthly
Circulation: 305
Founded in 1992

17012 Journal of Thermal Spray Technology
ASM International
9639 Kinsman Rd
Novelty, OH 44072-9603

440-338-5151
FAX 440-338-4634
E-Mail: Cust-Srv@asminternational.org
Home Page: www.asminternational.org
Social Media: *Facebook, Twitter, LinkedIn*

Jeane Deatherage, Administrator, Foundation Programs
Virginia Shirk, Foundation Executive Assistant

Peer-reviewed journal which publishes contributions on all aspects, fundamental and practical, of thermal spray science, including processes, feedstock manufacture, testing and characterization. As the primary vehicle for thermal spray information transfer, its mission is to synergize the rapidly advancing thermal spray industry and related industries by presenting research and development efforts leading to advancements in implementable engineering applications of the technology.
Cost: $1577.00
Frequency: Bimonthly
Circulation: 680
Founded in 1952

17013 Locator Services
Locator Online
315 S Patrick St
Suite 3
Alexandria, VA 22314-3532

703-836-9700
800-537-1446
FAX 703-836-7665
E-Mail: sales@locatoronline.com
Home Page: www.locatoronline.com

Terry Pitman, Publisher

Used metalworking equipment.
Cost: $38.00
Frequency: Monthly
Circulation: 225000
Founded in 1969

17014 Machine Shop Guide
Worldwide Communications
401 Worthington Avenue
Harrison, NJ 07029-2039

973-977-7555
FAX 253-872-7603
Home Page: www.machineshopguide.com

Robert L Hatschek, Executive Editor
Frederick Mason, Editor

Information on manufacturing technology, new applications for manufacturing technology and new products. Focus is metal cutting machines and tooling.
Frequency: 10 per year
Circulation: 102,893
Founded in 1996
Printed in 4 colors on glossy stock

17015 Machinery Trader
Sandhills Publishing

PO Box 82545
Lincoln, NE 68501-2545

402-479-2181
800-247-4898
FAX 402-479-2195
E-Mail: feedback@sandhills.com
Home Page: www.sandhills.com

Tom Peed, CEO
Marva Wasser, Editor-in-Chief

Covering heavy equipment.
Cost: $59.00
160 Pages
Frequency: Weekly
Circulation: 20000
Founded in 1978

17016 Managing Automation
Thomas Publishing Company
5 Penn Plz
Suite 10
New York, NY 10001-1860

212-695-0500
FAX 212-290-7362
E-Mail: businesslists@thomaspublishing.com
Home Page: www.thomaspublishing.com

Carl Holst-Knudsen, CEO
Robert Malone, Editor
Heather L Mikisch, Publisher
Kim Vennard, Marketing Manager

Serves the needs of those managers and engineers responsible for the planning and implementation of factory automation at both the plant and enterprise levels.
Frequency: Monthly
Circulation: 100246
Founded in 1898

17017 Manufacturing Engineering
Society of Manufacturing Engineers
1 SME Drive
#930
Dearborn, MI 48121

313-425-3000
800-733-4763
FAX 313-425-3400
E-Mail: advertising@sme.org
Home Page: www.sme.org

Mark Tomlinson, Executive Director
Greg Sheremet, Publisher
Gene Nelson, President

Serves metalworking industry machining, forming, inspection, assembly and processing operations.
Frequency: Monthly
Circulation: 111966
Founded in 1932

17018 Modern Machine Shop
Gardner Publications
6915 Valley Ln
Cincinnati, OH 45244-3153

513-527-8800
800-950-8020
FAX 513-527-8801
E-Mail: mmsmkt@gardnerweb.com
Home Page: www.gardnerweb.com

Rick Kline Sr, CEO
Mark D Albert, Manager
John Campos, Manager
Brian Wertheimer, Account Manager
Eddie Kania, Sales Manager

Reaches metalworking plants of all sizes - from small job shops to giant aerospace and automotive plants. It is edited for those involved in metalworking operations, particularly those performed on machine tools.
Cost: $4.00
Frequency: Monthly
Circulation: 107000
Founded in 1928

Mailing list available for rent: 106M names
Printed in 4 colors on glossy stock

17019 Motion Control
ISA Services
PO Box 12277
Durham, NC 27709-2277

919-549-8411
FAX 919-990-9434
E-Mail: info@isa.org
Home Page: www.isa.org

Sam Batman, Editor
Richard Simpson, Publisher
Robert Renner, Executive Director

Information for those who design and maintain
motion control systems.
Cost: $54.00
56 Pages
Circulation: 41000
ISSN: 1058-4644
Founded in 1945
Printed in 4 colors on glossy stock

17020 Motion System Distributor
Penton Media
1166 Avenue of the Americas/10th Fl
New York, NY 10036

212-204-4200
FAX 216-696-6662
E-Mail: information@#penton.com
Home Page: www.penton.com

Jane Cooper, Marketing
Chris Meyer, Director, Corporate
Communications

Provides selling and technical information to
individuals and distributors specializing in
power transmission, motion control and fluid
products.

17021 NAEDA Buyer's Guide
North American Equipment Dealers
Association
1195 Smizer Mill Road
Fenton, MO 63026-3480

636-349-5000
FAX 636-349-5443
E-Mail: naeda@naeda.com
Home Page: www.naeda.com
Social Media: *Twitter, LinkedIn*

Annual directory of contact names, trade and
product names of more than two thousand of
the equipment industry's manufacturers and
suppliers.
Cost: $35.00
5000 Members
Frequency: Annually
Founded in 1900

17022 OEM Worldwide
Cygnus Publishing
PO Box 803
Fort Atkinson, WI 53538-0803

920-000-1111
FAX 920-563-1699
E-Mail: tjheinlein@cableinet.co.uk
Home Page: www.cygnusb2b.com

John French, CEO
Leslie Shalabi, Publisher
James S Rank, VP
Sue Cullen, Advertising Manager
Brett Apold, Corporate Production Director

Designed to be a resource of operational and
general productivity information for original
equipment manufacturers in Europe, competing
in the global marketplace.
Cost: $6.00
Frequency: Monthly
Circulation: 16800
Founded in 1984

17023 Outdoor Power Equipment
1900 Arch Street
Philadelphia, PA 19103-1404

215-564-3484
FAX 215-564-2175

Julie S Burns, Executive Director

Members are distributors of outdoor power
equipment to retailers with a minimum of $1
million gross sales. Associate members are
suppliers and finance companies.
150 Pages
Founded in 1980

17024 Plant Engineering
Reed Business Information
30 Technology Parkway South
Suite 100
Norcross, GA 30092

646-746-6400
800-424-3996
FAX 646-756-7583
E-Mail: webmaster@reedbusiness.com
Home Page: www.reedbusiness.com

John Poulin, CEO
Richard L Dunn, Editor
Gerard Van de Aast, Director
Carel de Bos, Chief Information Officer

The magazine for plant engineering professionals responsible for the maintenance, repair and
operations of plant facilities, equipment and
systems.
Cost: $3.00
Circulation: 116700

17025 Processing Magazine
Grand View Media Group
200 Croft Street
Suite 1
Birmingham, AL 35242

888-431-2877
FAX 205-408-3797
E-Mail: webmaster@grandviewmedia.com
Home Page: www.gvmg.com/

Leading source for up-to-date product and
equipment solutions.

17026 Production Machining
Gardner Publications
6915 Valley Ln
Cincinnati, OH 45244-3153

513-527-8800
800-950-8020
FAX 513-527-8801
E-Mail: jjordan@gardnerweb.com
Home Page: www.gardnerweb.com

Rick Kline Sr, CEO
Leo Rakowski, Senior Editor
John Jordan, Assistant Editor
Lori Beckman, Managing Editor
John Campos, Manager
Frequency: Monthly
Circulation: 200000
Founded in 1928

17027 Pumps & Systems
Randall Publishing Company
1900 28th Ave S
Suite 110
Homewood, AL 35209-2627

205-212-9402
FAX 205-212-9452
Home Page: www.pump-zone.com

Walter Evans, President
George Lake, Associate Publisher
Scott Kidwell, Advertising Sales:
Tom Cory, Circulation
Robert Windle, CEO
Frequency: Monthly
Founded in 2002

17028 Sensors Magazine
Advanstar Communications
7500 Old Oak Blvd
Cleveland, OH 44130-3343

440-243-8100
FAX 440-891-2740
E-Mail: info@advanstar.com
Home Page: www.act-europe.org

Barbara G Goode, Editor-in-Chief
Donna Pellerin George, Associate Editor
Joseph Loggia, CEO
Georgiann Decenzo, Director of Corporate
marketing
Francis Heid, Vice President of Publishing

Primary source among design and production
engineers of information on sensor technologies and products, and topic integral to sensor-based systems and applications. Provides
practical and in-depth yet accessible information on sensor operation, design, application,
and implementation within systems. Covers the
effective use of state-of-the-art resources and
tools that enable readers to get the maximum
benefit from their use of sensors.
Frequency: Monthly
Circulation: 75000
Founded in 1984

17029 Valve Magazine
Valve Manufacturers Association of
America
1050 17th Street NW
Suite 280
Washington, DC 20036-5521

202-331-8105
FAX 202-296-0378
E-Mail: wsandler@vma.org
Home Page: www.vma.org

Bill Sandler, President
Marc Pasternak, VP

Promotion of significance and application of
US and Canadian manufactured industrial
valves and actuators.
Frequency: Quarterly
Circulation: 26000

17030 Vibrations Magazine
Vibration Institute
6262 Kingery Hwy
Suite 212
Willowbrook, IL 60527-2276

630-654-2254
FAX 630-654-2271
E-Mail: information@vi-institute.org
Home Page: www.vi-institute.org

Ronald Eshleman, Executive Director

Provides current information about activities of
the Vibration Institute and news about vibration
technology. Each issue contains practical, technical articles and case histories.
Frequency: Quarterly
Founded in 1975

17031 World Industrial Reporter
Keller International Publishing Corporation
150 Great Neck Rd
Suite 400
Great Neck, NY 11021-3309

516-829-9722
FAX 516-829-9306
Home Page: www.supplychainbrain.com

Bryan DeLuca, Editor
Terry Beirne, Publisher
Jerry Keller, President
Mary Chavez, Director of Sales

New equipment, machinery and techniques for
the industry.
34 Pages
Frequency: Monthly

Circulation: 37107
Founded in 1882

Trade Shows

17032 ASME Annual Meeting
American Society of Mechanical Engineers
Three Park Avenue
New York, NY 10016

973-882-1170
800-843-2763
FAX 212-591-7856
E-Mail: CustomerCare@asme.org
Home Page: www.asme.org

Melissa Torres, Meetings Manager
Mary Jakubowski, Meetings Manager
Frequency: Annual/June

17033 ASME Gas Turbine Users Symposium (GTUS)
American Society of Mechanical
Engineers/IGTI
Three Park Avenue
New York, NY 10016-5990

973-882-1170
800-843-2763
FAX 404-847-0151
E-Mail: CustomerCare@asme.org
Home Page: www.asme.org/igti

Stephanie Searsr, Coordinator, IGTI
Conferences
Judy Osborn, Manager, IGTI Conferences &
Expos

A show focused on the role gas turbines will
play in meeting the nation's future energy demands, provides the information related to gas
turbine operations, maintenance, advances, and
design.
2000 Attendees
Frequency: Annual

17034 Association of Machinery and Equipment Appraisers Annual Conference
315 S Patrick Street
Alexandria, VA 22314-3501

703-836-7900
800-537-8629
FAX 703-836-9303
E-Mail: amea@amea.org
Home Page: www.amea.org

Lorna Lindsey, Manager
Mary Flynn, Executive Director

Exhibits of interest to machinery and equip-
ment appraisers.
Founded in 1982
Mailing list available for rent

17035 FloorTek Expo
American Floorcovering Alliance
210 West Cuyler St
Dalton, GA 30720-8209

706-278-4101
800-288-4101
FAX 706-278-5323
E-Mail: afa@americanfloor.org
Home Page: www.floor-tek.com

Wanda J Ellis, Executive Director

The only internationla flooring manufacturing
tradeshow dedicated to the production and materials of the industry.
3000+ Attendees
Frequency: Bi-Annual

17036 Gear Expo
American Gear Manufacturers Association

500 Montgomery Street
Suite 350
Alexandria, VA 22314-1581

703-684-0211
FAX 703-684-0242
Home Page: www.gearexpo.com

Kurt Medert, VP
Biennial trade show held in October of the
odd-numbered years. It is the only trade show
devoted exclusively to the Gear Manufacturing
process.
4.5M Attendees
Frequency: October
Founded in 1987

17037 IADD/FSEA Odyssey
Int'l Assoc of Diecutting and Diemaking
651 W Terra Cotta Ave
Suite 132
Crystal Lake, IL 60014

815-455-7519
800-828-4233
FAX 815-455-7510
E-Mail: cccrouse@iadd.org
Home Page: www.iadd.org

Cindy Crouse, CEO
Jill May, Chapter Relations Coordinator
The premiere education and technology expo
uniquely focused on diemaking, converting,
foil stamping, embossing and bindery.
Frequency: Annual/May

17038 International Integrated Manufacturing
Reed Exhibition Companies
255 Washington Street
Newton, MA 02458-1637

617-584-4900
FAX 617-630-2222

Elizabeth Hitchcock, International Sales

Expo and conference dedicated to the products
and technology needed by engineering operations and management to automate and integrate manufacturing.
Frequency: March

17039 International Manufacturing Technology Show
7901 Westpark Drive
Mc Lean, VA 22102-4206

703-893-2900
FAX 703-893-1151
Home Page: www.amtonline.org

John Byrd, President
Peter Eelman, VP Exhibitions

Manufacturing equipment trade show.
85M Attendees
Frequency: Biennial
Founded in 1927

17040 International Woodworking Machinery and Furniture Supply Fair: USA
Reed Exhibition Companies
1350 E Touhy Avenue
Des Plaines, IL 60018-3303

847-294-0300
FAX 847-635-1571

Paul Pajor, National Marketing Manager

The largest woodworking machinery and furniture supply manufacturing exposition held in
the Western Hemisphere. Exhibitors interface
with North American furniture, cabinet, and
woodworking manufacturers. One thousand
booths.
37M Attendees
Frequency: August/Biennial

17041 Job Shop Show: Midwest
Edward Publishing LLC
16 Waterbury Road
Prospect, CT 06712-1215

203-758-6658
FAX 203-758-4476
Home Page: www.jobshoptechnology.com

Jennifer Bryda, Production Manager
Christoper Davis, Manager
Gerald Schmidt, President

A source for forming, fabricating, shaping, and
assemblies. The show is designed to attract the
highest caliber engineers and buyers from
product manufacturers. There will be 170 exhibitors and booths.
1500 Attendees

17042 National Technical Training Symposium
Vibration Institute
6262 S Kingery Highway
Suite 212
Willowbrook, IL 60527

630-654-2254
FAX 630-654-2271
E-Mail: information@vi-institute.org
Home Page: www.vi-institute.org

Ronald L Eshlemann, Director

Formerly the annual meeting, provides specific
training in practical vibration technology.
Frequency: Annual

17043 Powder and Bulk Solids Conference and Exhibition
Reed Exhibition Companies
255 Washington Street
Newton, MA 02458-1637

617-584-4900
FAX 617-630-2222

Elizabeth Hitchcock, International Sales

Equipment and technology for processing and
handling of powder and bulk solids.
8.4M Attendees
Frequency: May

17044 South-Tec Machine Tool and Manufacturing Show
Society of Manufacturing Engineers
1 SME Drive
#930
Dearborn, MI 48128

313-425-3000
800-733-4763
FAX 313-425-3400
E-Mail: advertising@sme.org
Home Page: www.sme.org

Mark Tomlinson, Executive Director
Greg Sheremet, Publisher

A professional society dedicated to advancing
scientific knowledge in the field of manufacturing and to applying its resources for researching, writing, publishing and disseminating
information.
70M Attendees
Frequency: March
Founded in 1932

Directories & Databases

17045 American Machine Tool Distributors Association Directory
1445 Research Bowl
Suite 450
Rockville, MD 20852-1421

301-738-1200
Home Page: www.metalworld.com

Greg Safko, Editor
Ralph Nappi, President

Directory of services and supplies to the industry.
Cost: $60.00
150 Pages
Frequency: Annual
Founded in 1925

17046 American Machinist Buyers' Guide
Penton Media
1166 Avenue of the Americas/10th Fl
New York, NY 10036

212-204-4200
FAX 216-696-6662
E-Mail: information@penton.com
Home Page: www.penton.com

Jane Cooper, Marketing
Pat Smith, Managing Editor
Chris Meyer, Director, Corporate Communications

Guide to over manufacturers of products and services used by metalworking industries.
Cost: $6.00
Frequency: Annual
Circulation: 80,000
Printed in 4 colors on glossy stock

17047 American Mold Builders Association
PO Box 404
Medinah, IL 60157-0404

630-980-7667
FAX 630-980-9714
E-Mail: info@amba.org
Home Page: www.amba.org

Jeanette Bradley, Editor
Kym Conis, Managing Director

Directory of services and supplies to the industry.
Cost: $25.00
50 Pages
Frequency: Annual

17048 American Textile Machinery Association Official Directory
201 Park Washington Ct
Falls Church, VA 22046-4527

703-538-1789
FAX 703-241-5603
E-Mail: info@atmanet.org
Home Page: www.atmanet.org

Harry W Buzzerd, Owner
Clay D Tyeryar, President/Assistant Treasurer
Susan Denston, Executive VP/Secretary
Judith O Buzzerd, Meetings Manager

The Directory of the American Textile Machinery Association/ATMA offers information on over 100 member textile machinery and accessory manufacturers. ATMA is a professional trade association devoted to the advancement of manufacturers of textile machinery, parts, and accessories in the textile industry.
100 Pages

17049 Directory of Machine Tools and Manufacturing
Association for Manufacturing Technology

7901 Westpark Drive
Mc Lean, VA 22102-4206

703-893-2900
FAX 703-893-1151

Machine tools and related products built by members of the Association for Manufacturing Technology.
Frequency: Annual

17050 Equip-Mart
116 N Camp Street
Seguin, TX 78155

830-303-3328
800-864-1155
FAX 830-372-3011
Home Page: www.equip-mart.com

Directory of available used metalworking equipment.
Frequency: Weekly

17051 ISA Directory
Instrumentation, Systems, and Automation Society
PO Box 12277
Durham, NC 27709-2277

919-549-8411
FAX 919-990-9434
E-Mail: info@isa.org
Home Page: www.isa.org

Premier guide to instrumentation, systems and automation
Printed in 4 colors

17052 Industrial Machine Trader
Heartland Industrial Group
1003 Central Avenue
PO Box 1415
Fort Dodge, IA 50501

515-955-1600
800-247-2000
FAX 515-955-3753
E-Mail: igproduction@industrialgroup.com
Home Page: www.industrialgroup.com
Social Media: *Facebook, Twitter, LinkedIn*

Virginia Rodriguez, Publisher

Printed directory of available used metalworking equipment.
150+ Members
Frequency: Weekly
Founded in 1966

17053 Locator Services
315 S Patrick St
Alexandria, VA 22314-3532

703-836-9700
800-537-1446
FAX 703-836-7665
E-Mail: sales@locatoronline.com
Home Page: www.locatoronline.com

Terry Pitman, Publisher

Printed directory of available used metalworking equipment.
Frequency: Monthly
Circulation: 225,000

17054 Machine Design Product Locator
Penton Media
1166 Avenue of the Americas/10th Fl
New York, NY 10036

212-204-4200
FAX 216-696-6662
E-Mail: information@penton.com
Home Page: www.penton.com

Jane Cooper, Marketing
Chris Meyer, Director, Corporate Communications

Directory of services and supplies to the industry.
Cost: $35.00
325 Pages
Frequency: Annual
Circulation: 180,000
Printed in 4 colors on glossy stock

17055 Metalworking Machinery Mailer
Tade Publishing Group
29501 Greenfield Road
Suite 120
Southfield, MI 48076

248-552-8583
800-966-8233
FAX 248-552-0466
Home Page: www.tadesite.com

Tom Lynch, Editor

Printed directory of available used metalworking equipment.
Frequency: Monthly

17056 Motion Control Technical Reference and Buyers Guide
ISA Services
PO Box 12277
Durham, NC 27709-2277

919-549-8411
FAX 919-990-9434
E-Mail: info@isa.org
Home Page: www.isa.org

The most comprehensive reference source for motion control market
Founded in 2000
Printed in 4 colors

17057 Multimedia Monograph Series
SIGDA Multimedia

E-Mail: pedram@seng.usc.edu
Home Page: atrak.usc.edu/~sigda-mm/

Massoud Pedram, Program Director

Set of electronic media publications focusing on key talks/presentations given at various ACM sponsored conferences over the last few years.

17058 Orion Blue Book: Tools
Orion Research Corporation
14555 N Scottsdale Rd
Suite 330
Scottsdale, AZ 85254-3487

480-951-1114
800-844-0759
FAX 480-951-1117
Home Page: www.bluebook.com

Roger Rohrs, Owner

List of manufacturers of tools.
Frequency: Annual

17059 Surplus Record Machinery & Equipment Directory
Thomas Scanlan
20 N Wacker Dr
Chicago, IL 60606-3004

312-372-9077
FAX 312-372-6537
E-Mail: surplus@surplusrecord.com
Home Page: www.surplusrecord.com

Thomas Scanlan, Publisher

Listing over 55,000 items of used/surplus machine tools, machinery, electrical apparatus, and capital equipment by more than 1200 suppliers worldwide.
Cost: $33.00
736 Pages
Frequency: Monthly Magazine
Circulation: 150000
ISSN: 0039-615X
Founded in 1924

17060 ThomasNet

Thomas Publishing Company, LLC
User Services Department
5 Penn Plaza
New York, NY 10001

212-695-0500
800-699-9822
FAX 212-290-7362
E-Mail: contact@thomaspublishing.com
Home Page: www.thomasnet.com
Social Media: *Facebook, Twitter, LinkedIn*

Carl Holst-Knudsen, President
Robert Anderson, VP, Planning
Mitchell Peipert, VP, Finance
Ivy Molofsky, VP, Human Resources

A way to reach qualified businesses that list their company information on ThomasNet.com. Detailed profiles promote their products, services, capabilities and brands carried. The ThomasNet.com web site is the most up-to-date compilation of 650,000 North American manufacturers, distributors, and service companies in 67,000 industrial categories.
Founded in 1898

17061 Used Machinery Buyer's Guide

Machinery Dealers National Association
315 S Patrick St
Alexandria, VA 22314-3532

703-836-9300
800-872-7807
FAX 703-836-9303
E-Mail: office@mdna.org
Home Page: www.mdna.org

Mark Robinson, Executive VP
Richard Levy CEA, President

Over 400 dealers in used capital equipment.
Frequency: Annual, September

Industry Web Sites

17062 http://gold.greyhouse.com

G.O.L.D Grey House OnLine Databases

Grey House Publishing's online database platform, GOLD, offers Quick Search, Keyword Search and Expert Search for most business sectors including machinery markets. The GOLD platform makes finding the information you need quick and easy - whether you're a novice searcher or an experienced database user. All of Grey House's directory products are available for subscription on the GOLD platform.

17063 www.amea.org

Association of Machinery and Equipment Appraisers

Members are appraisers of the metalworking industry.

17064 www.americanfloor.org

American Floorcovering Alliance

Promotes the industry's products and services to the world, and educates the members and others through seminars, press releases, and trade shows.

17065 www.avem.org

Association of Vacuum Equipment Manufacturers
International

The only non-profit U.S. association dedicated fully to companies that manufacture vacuum equipment and supplies.

17066 www.cemanet.org

Conveyor Equipment Manufacturers Association

Continues to be considered the resource for conveyor safety dimensional and application standards.

17067 www.fpmsa.org (or www.iefp.org)

Food Processing Machinery & Supplies Association

List of exhibitors from IEFP (links included).

17068 www.greyhouse.com

Grey House Publishing

Authoritative reference directories for most business sectors including machinery markets. Users can search the online databases with varied search criteria allowing for custom searches by product category, geographic area, sales volume, keyword, subject and more. Full Grey House catalog and online ordering also available.

17069 www.iadd.org

Int'l Association of Diecutting and Diemaking

A not-for-profit international trade association serving diecutters, diemakers, and industry suppliers worldwide. IADD provides conferences, educational and training programs, networking opportunities, a monthly magazine, technical articles, regional chapter meetings, publications and training manuals, recommended specifications, videos and surveys.

17070 www.mapi.net

Manufacturers Alliance/MAPI

A policy research organization whose members are companies drawn from the producers and users of capital goods and allied products. Includes leading companies in heavy industry, automotive, electronics, precision instruments, telecommunications, computers, office systems. aerospace, oil/gas, chemicals and similar high technology industries.

17071 www.mdna.org

Machinery Dealers National Association

Represents dealers of used industrial equipment.

17072 www.naeda.com

North American Equipment Dealers Association

Promotes the general welfare of retail agricultural, outdoor power, construction and large property equipment dealers in the United States and Canada.

17073 www.ntma.org

National Tooling and Machining Association

For makers of jigs, molds, tools, gages, dies and fixtures for companies doing precision machining.

17074 www.packexpo.com

Packaging Machinery Manufacturers Institute (PMMI)

For manufacturers of packaging and packaging-related converting equipment.

17075 www.pmpa.org

Precision Machined Products Association

Member companies are producers of high precision component products. Provides educational opportunities for members, emphasizing quality assurance and emerging technologies.

17076 www.polysort.com

Polysort

Includes materials, machinery and equipment, processors and industry services.

17077 www.taol\fema.com

Fire Equipment Manufacturers' Association

Members are companies making devices that control or extinguish fires in residential or commercial buildings.

17078 www.vma.org

Valve Manufacturers Association of America

Associations

17079 AAHC American Association of Healthcare

1205 Johnson Ferry Road
Suite 136-420
Marietta, GA 30068

404-661-1710
888-350-2242
FAX 770-874-4401
E-Mail: info@aahcmail.org
Home Page: www.aahc.net

Linda Campbell, Executive Director

To serve as the preeminent credentialing, professional and practice development organization for the healthcare consulting profession; to advance the knowledge, quality and standards of practice for consulting to management in the healthcare industry; and to enhance the understanding and image of the healthcare consulting profession and member firms among its various publics.
Founded in 1949

17080 AMR Management Services

201 East Main Street
Suite 1405
Lexington, KY 40507

859-514-9150
FAX 859-514-9207
E-Mail: info@amrms.com
Home Page: www.amrms.com
Social Media: *Facebook, LinkedIn*

Rebecca Klemm, President

Seeks to enhance members skills in organizational opportunities and in planning strategies to influence external events on international objectives.
400 Members
Founded in 1982

17081 Academy of Human Resource Development

1000 Westgate Drive
Suite 252
St. Paul, MN 55114

651-290-7466
FAX 651-290-2266
E-Mail: office@ahrd.org
Home Page: www.ahrd.orgÿ
Social Media: *Facebook, Twitter, LinkedIn, RSS*

Ron Jacobs, President
Kathie Pugaczewski, CAE, CMP, Executive Director
Jeanne Demartino, Member Service Specialist
Jazzy McCroskey, Communications Specialist
Carissa Wolf, Meeting Planner
Founded in 1993

17082 Adizes Network International

1212 Mark Ave
Carpinteria, CA 93013

805-565-2901
FAX 805-565-0741
E-Mail: info@adizes.com
Home Page: www.adizes.com
Social Media: *Facebook, Twitter, LinkedIn, Google+*

James C Morgan, Chairman and CEO
Dr Ichak Adizes, Professional Director
James Zukin, Senior Managing Director

Promotes Adizes management consulting as a profession. Facilitates discussion of ideas and conducts lectures and seminars.
115 Members
Founded in 1973

17083 American Academy of Medical Administrators

American Academy of Medical Administrators
330 N Wabash Avenue
Suite 2000
Chicago, IL 60611

312-321-6815
FAX 312-673-6705
E-Mail: info@aameda.org
Home Page: aama.socious.com

John Garrity, Chairman
Kevin Baliozian, Executive Director
Eric Conde, MSA, CFAAMA, Chairman Elect
John Garrity, CFAAMA, Treasurer
Robert McKenney, PhD,FAAMA, Vice Chair

Department heads and administrators in areas of hospital and health administration.
Founded in 1957

17084 American Association of Commerce Executives

American Chambers of Congress Executives
1330 Braddock Place
Suite 300
Alexandria, VA 22314

703-998-0072
FAX 888-577-9883
E-Mail: webmaster@acce.org
Home Page: www.acce.org
Social Media: *Facebook, Twitter, LinkedIn, RSS*

Joe Roman, Chairman of the Board
Mick Fleming, President
Tamara Philbin, COO and Membership Management
Chris Mead, SVP, Member & Sponsor Relations
Jacqui Cook, Chief Financial Officer

National association uniquely serving individuals involved in the management of chambers of all sizes. Chamber executives and professionals hold positions requiring leadership, vision and strong management skills. Devoted to helping chamber executives and their staffs' play a significant leadership role ing their communities.
1300 Members
Founded in 1914

17085 American Business Women's Association

9820 Metcalf Ave
Suite 110
Overland Park, KS 66212

800-228-0007
FAX 913-660-0101
E-Mail: webmail@abwa.org
Home Page: www.abwa.orgÿ
Social Media: *Facebook, Twitter, YouTube*

Nancy Griffin, National President
Meg Bell, National ViceÿPresident
Lisa Montross, National Secretary - Treasurer
Gina Berry, Vice President, District I
Frances Nicholson, Vice President, District II

17086 American Management Association

American Management Association
1601 Broadway
New York, NY 10019-7420

212-586-8100
800-262-9699
FAX 212-903-8168
Home Page: www.amanet.org
Social Media: *Facebook, Twitter, LinkedIn, YouTube*

Edward T Reilly, CEO

Membership-based management development organization. AMA provides valuable and practical action-oriented learning programs to people at all levels, in all industries, from companies and agencies of all sizes. More than 500,000 AMA customers and members a year learn new skills and behaviors, gain more confidence, advance their careers through a wide range of seminars, conferences and executive forums, as well as publications, research, print and online self-study courses.
20000 Members
Founded in 1923

17087 American Productivity and Quality Center

American Productivity and Quality Center
123 N Post Oak Ln
Third Floor
Houston, TX 77024-7797

713-681-4020
800-776-9676
FAX 713-681-8578
E-Mail: cflett@apqc.org
Home Page: www.apqc.org
Social Media: *Facebook, Twitter, LinkedIn, Youtube, RSS*

C. Jackson Grayson, Founder and Executive Chairman
Lisa Higgins, President
Carla O'Dell, Chief Executive Officer
Cindy Hubert, Executive Director
Mike Shea, Chief Financial Officer

Seeks to improve productivity and the quality of work life in the United States. Works with businesses, unions, academics and government agencies to improve productivity and quality.
300 Members
Founded in 1977

17088 American Small Businesses Association

American Small Businesses Association
206 E College
Grapevine, TX 76034-2663

817-488-8770
800-801-2722
FAX 817-251-8578

Bill Hill Sr, President
Wanda Johnson, Bookkeeper

Represents the interests of small businesses.
10M Members
Founded in 1975

17089 American Society for Quality

American Society for Quality
600 N Plankinton Avenue
PO Box 3005
Milwaukee, WI 53201-3005

414-272-8575
800-248-1946
FAX 414-272-1734
E-Mail: help@asq.org
Home Page: www.asq.org
Social Media: *Facebook, Twitter, LinkedIn, Youtube*

Cecilia L. Kimberlin, Chairman
Bill Troy, Chief Executive Officer
Eric Hayler, Treasurer
Laurel Nelson-Rowe, Managing Director
Michelle Mason, Managing Director

ASQ's mission is to facilitate continuous improvement and increase customer satisfaction. Promotes quality principles, concepts and technologies. Provides information, contacts and opportunities to make things better in the workplace, in communities and in people's lives.
100M Members
Founded in 1946

17090 American Society for the Advancement of Project Management

American Society for the Advancement of

6547 North Academy
#404
Colorado Springs, CO 80918

719-488-3850
FAX 719-487-0637
E-Mail: info@asapm.org
Home Page: www.asapm.org

Joel Carboni, President
Tim Jaques, Vice President
Bill Duncan, Director of Certification
Thomas Baumann, Director of Education
John Colville, Director of Member Services

Standards and guidelines to define the work of project management personnel. Requirements to standardize the norms are collection, process and then institutionalization of the applied competence with acceptable protocols in managing the work for optimization of output. This includes the knowledge, experience and attitude of the manpower involved in the handling the assigned project.

17091 American Society of Association Executives

American Society of Association Executives
1575 I St NW
Washington, DC 20005-1103

202-371-0940
888-950-2723
FAX 202-371-8315
E-Mail: ASAEservice@asaecenter.org
Home Page: www.asaecenter.org/

Abe Eshkenazi, Chair
Dana Anaman , CAE, Marketing Manager
Eyitemi Amorighoye, Director, Web Projects
Jenna Allen, Development Operations Manager
Francine Alestock, Executive Coordinator
24.5M Members
Founded in 1920

17092 Association For Strategic Planning

Association for Strategic Planning
191 Clarksville Road
Princeton, NJ 08550

877-816-2080
FAX 609-799-7032
Home Page: www.strategyplus.org
Social Media: *Facebook, Twitter, LinkedIn, Youtube, Picasa*

Neelima Firth, President
Lee Crumbaugh, Vice President
Tom Carter, Treasurer
Kimme Carlos, Executive Director

Dedicated to advancing thought and practice in strategy development and deployment for business, non-profit and government organizations. Provides opportunities to explore cutting-edge strategic planning principles and practices that enhance organizational success and advance members' and organizations' knowledge, capability, capacity for innovations and professionalism.
Founded in 1999

17093 Association for Services Management International (AFSM)

Association for Services Management
17065 Camino San Bernardo
Suite 200
San Diego, CA 92127

858-674-5491
800-333-9786
FAX 239-275-0794
E-Mail: jschoenewald@afsmi.org
Home Page: www.tsia.com
Social Media: *Facebook, Twitter, YouTube, Google+, Blog*

J.B. Wood, President and CEO
Ren, Grossrieder, SVP, Membership Development
Tom Rich, Vice President, IT

Trisha Bright, Vice President, Marketing
Thomas Lah, Executive Director

A global organization dedicated to furthering the knowledge, understanding, and career development of executives, managers and professionals in the high-technology service industry.
5000 Members
Founded in 1975

17094 Association for Systems Management

Association for Systems Management
24587 Bagley Road
Cleveland, OH 44138

216-671-1919
FAX 440-234-2930

Paula Winrod, Public Communication

Offers seminars and conferences in all phases of business systems and management.
5M Members
Founded in 1947

17095 Association of Executive and Administrative Professionals

900 South Washington Street
Suite G-13
Falls Church, VA 22046-4009

703-237-8616
FAX 703-533-1153
E-Mail: headquarters@theaeap.com
Home Page: www.theaeap.com
Social Media: *LinkedIn*

Ruth Ludeman, Director

Has helped thousands of administrative and secretarial professionals grow in their chosen careers, and supported their efforts at becoming the best that they can be. Strives to provide its members with a pathway for setting and achieving accomplishments of all types and at all levels. Publishes a newsletter 11 times per year.
3000 Members
Founded in 1975

17096 Association of Higher Education Facilities Officers (APPA)

1643 Prince St
Alexandria, VA 22314-2818

703-684-1446
FAX 703-549-2772
E-Mail: webmaster@appa.org
Home Page: www.appa.org
Social Media: *Facebook, Twitter, LinkedIn, Youtube*

Peter Strazdas, President
E. Landerÿ Medlin, Executive Vice President
John F Bernhardsÿ, Associate Vice President
Norm Young, VP, Information and Research
Paul Wuebold, VP, Professional Affairs

APPA is an association dedicated to leadership in educational facilities management and the ongoing evolution of its professionals into influential leaders in education.
5500 Members
Founded in 1914

17097 Association of Investment Management Sales Executives

Association of Investment Management
12100 Sunset Hills Road
Suite 130
Reston, VA 20190

703-234-4098
FAX 703-435-4390
E-Mail: lyarborough@drohanmgmt.com
Home Page: www.aimse.org/

P. MacKenzie Hurd, CFA, President
Christopher D. Rae, Vice President
Kathy Hoskins, Executive Director
Katie Earley, Deputy Executive Director
Glenn Beales, Director of Finance

The AIMSE mission is to provide an educational forum for those employed in the investment management sales and marketing services profession worldwide. AIMSE fosters high ethical and professional standards among members regarding representation of investment products and services, with an educational emphasis on improving skills, enabling members to adapt to the changing needs of the marketplace.
1400 Members
Founded in 1977

17098 Association of Management

Association of Management
920 Battlefield Boulevard
Suite 100
Chesapeake, VA 23322

757-482-2273
FAX 757-482-0325
E-Mail: aomgt@aom-iaom.org
Home Page: www.aom-iaom.org

Dr. Karin Klenke, Chairperson, Co-Founder and CEO
Dr. Willem Arthur Hamel, Co-Founder/President
T J Mills, VP Comptroller

Formerly the Association of Human Resources Management and Organizational Behavior (HRMOB).
3.5M Members
Founded in 1979

17099 Association of Management Consulting Firms

Association of Management Consulting Firms
370 Lexington Avenue
Suite 2209
New York, NY 10017

212-262-3055
FAX 212-262-3054
E-Mail: info@amcf.org
Home Page: www.amcf.org
Social Media: *Facebook, Twitter, LinkedIn, YouTube, RSS*

Steve Goodrich, Chairman of the Board
Sally Caputo, President & Chief Operating Officer
Ayaka Sparks, Marketing & Events Coord.
Dina Bystryak, Marketing & Events Coordinator
MaryAnn Dogo, Admin Support & Project Coordinator

Seeks to unite management consulting firms in order to develop and improve professional standards and practice in the field. Offers information and referral services on management consultants.
65 Members
Founded in 1929

17100 Automotive Trade Association Executives

Automotive Trade Association Executives
8400 Westpark Dr
Mc Lean, VA 22102-5116

703-821-7072
FAX 703-556-8581
E-Mail: sjewett@nada.org
Home Page: www.asna-atae.com

Stacey Castle, ATAE Chairman
Joe Rohatynski, Senior Editor

Promotes interests of executives of state and local auto dealers associations.
106 Members
Founded in 2003

17101 Awards and Recognition Association

Awards and Recognition Association

8735 W. Higgins Road
Suite 300
Chicago, IL 60631

847-375-4800
800-344-2148
FAX 847-375-6480
E-Mail: info@ara.org
Home Page: www.ara.org
Social Media: *Facebook, Twitter, Instagram*

Mike May, President
Louise Ristau, CAE, Executive Director
Brian Fitzgerald, Senior Sales Manager
Tom Calvin, Sales Manager
Chris Schroll, Sales Manager

Membership organization of 4,000 companies
dedicated to increasing the professionalism of
recognition specialists and advancing the
awards and engraving industry.
Founded in 1993

17102 Best Employers Association

Best Employers Association
17701 Mitchell North
Irvine, CA 92614-6028

866-706-2225
800-237-8543
FAX 949-553-0883
E-Mail: info@bestlife.com
Home Page: www.beassoc.org/
Social Media: *Facebook, Twitter, LinkedIn*

Steve Course, President
Jennifer Bolton, Sales Account Manager
Ramon Duran, Sales Account Manager
Cristina Rios, Sales Account Manager
Dorothy Sehramm, Salews Account Manager

Providing group medical, dental, long-term disability, vision and life insurance to employers.
Founded in 1970

17103 Business Management Daily

National Institute of Business Management
PO Box 9070
McLean, VA 22102-0070

703-058-8000
800-543-2055
FAX 703-905-8040
E-Mail:
Customer@BusinessManagementDaily.com
Home Page:
www.businessmanagementdaily.com
Social Media: *Facebook, Twitter, LinkedIn,
Google+*

Steve Sturm, President

Career guidance for managers and executives.
Founded in 1937

17104 Center for Breakthrough Thinking

Center for Breakthrough Thinking
PO Box 18012
Los Angeles, CA 90018

213-740-6415
FAX 213-740-1120
E-Mail: info@breakthroughthinking.com
Home Page: www.breakthroughthinking.com
Social Media: *Twitter*

Dr Gerald Nadler, President
George Hathaway, Executive Vice President
Dr. William Chandon, Vice President
Mr. Steven S. Benson, Vice President -
Development

Organized to promote and institutionalize the
teaching and application of Breakthrough
Thinking in universities, corporations and governments for solving problems, leveraging opportunities, and achieving change.
15 Members
Founded in 1988

17105 Center for Creative Leadership

Center for Creative Leadership

One Leadership Place
PO Box 26300
Greensboro, NC 27410-6300

336-545-2810
FAX 336-282-3284
E-Mail: info@ccl.org
Home Page: www.ccl.org/Leadership/
Social Media: *Facebook, Twitter, LinkedIn,
Youtube, Google Plus, Pinteres*

Odd Ingar Skaug, Chairman
John Alexander, President

An international, nonprofit educational institution devoted to behavioral science research, executive development and leadership education.
Founded in 1970
Mailing list available for rent

17106 Center for Management Effectiveness

Center for Management Effectiveness
P. O. Box 1202
Pacific Palisades, CA 90272

310-459-6052
FAX 310-459-9307
E-Mail: info@cmeinc.org
Home Page: www.cmeinc.org
Social Media: *Facebook, Twitter, LinkedIn,
RSS*

Jerry Feist, President
Ron Smith, General Manager
Rob Wood, Publications Director
Sam Erdman, Manager Information Systems
Christie Randolph, Management Consultants

Conducts management training programs and
publishes self-scoring inventories, trainer
guides and workbooks on stress management,
resolution of conflict, risk taking, decision
making and building managerial skills.
Founded in 1981

17107 Center for Management Systems

Center for Management Systems
PO Box 159
Akron, IA 51001-0159

FAX 712-568-3427

Provides specialized education to improve
management skills.
70M Members
Founded in 1978

17108 Center for Third World Organizing

Center For Third World Organizing
900 Alice Street
Suite 300
Oakland, CA 94607

510-433-0908
FAX 510-433-0908
Home Page: www.ctwo.org

Faron Mclurkin, Executive Director
Karey Leung, Research Director
Karissa Lewis, Senior Field Organizerÿ
Avery Bizzell, Organiser

A national organization of books, periodicals
and audiovisuals on transnational corporations
and labor issues.
Founded in 1980

17109 Christian Management Association

Christian Management Association
1825 Hamilton Drive
San Jose, CA 95125

408-703-6568
FAX 408-703-6568
E-Mail: info@cmanational.org
Home Page:
www.christianmanagementassociation.org
Social Media: *Facebook, Twitter, RSS*

Frank Lofaro, CEO
Dick Bahruth, Senior Consultant
Sandy Huston, Member Services Manager

Joe Voorhies, Director Business Development
Charles S Blake, Director Finance

Designed to assist those involved in the management of Christian organizations.
3500+ Members
Founded in 1976

17110 Club Managers Association of America

1733 King St
Alexandria, VA 22314-2720

703-739-9500
FAX 703-739-0124
E-Mail: cmaa@cmaa.org
Home Page: www.cmaa.org
Social Media: *Facebook, Twitter, LinkedIn,
Flickr*

Tony D'Errico, CCM, CCE, President
Jill Philmon, CCM, CCE, Vice President
Jeff Morgan, FASAE, CAE, Chief Executive
Officerÿ
Seth Gregg, Chief Operating Officerÿ
Margaret Meleney, Chief Financial Officer

Advances the professional of club management
by fulfilling the educational and related needs
of its members.
7000 Members
Founded in 1927

17111 Construction Financial Management Association

100 Village Blvd.
Suite 200
Princeton, NJ 8540

609-452-8000
888-421-9996
FAX 609-452-0474
E-Mail: info@cfma.org
Home Page: www.cfma.orgÿ
Social Media: *Facebook, Twitter, LinkedIn,
YouTube*

Stuart Binstock, President, CEO
Erica O'Grady, CAE, Vice President,
Operations
Robert Rubin, CPA, VP, Finance & Admin.
Brian Summers, CAE, VP, Content Mgmt &
Edu.
Ariel Sanchirico, Director, Online Learning
Founded in 1981

17112 Data Processing Sciences Corporation

Data Processing Sciences Corporation
11370 Reed Hartman Hwy
Cincinnati, OH 45241

513-489-4200
FAX 513-791-2371
E-Mail: info@dpsciences.com
Home Page: www.dpsciences.com
Social Media: *Facebook, Twitter, LinkedIn,
Youtube, Google+*

Kurt Loock, President
Scott Nesbitt, CEO
Stephen Vandegriff, EVP
Tim Shelton, CFO

DPS delivers solutions that simplify and manage technology for our clients so they can aggressively pursue their strategic business goals.

17113 Decision Sciences Institute

Decision Sciences Institute
C.T. Bauer College of Business
334 Melcher Hall, Suite 325
Houston, TX 77204-6021

713-743-4815
FAX 713-743-8984
E-Mail: info@decisionsciences.org
Home Page: www.decisionsciences.org
Social Media: *Facebook, Twitter, LinkedIn*

Morgan Swink, Publisher
Janelle Heineke, VP - Finance (Treasurer)
Gyula Vastag, VP - Global Activities

Kaushik Sengupta, VP - Marketing
Hope Baker, VP - Member Services

Scientific quantitative, behavioral and computational approaches to decision making.

17114 Distribution Business Management Association

2938 Columbia Ave
Suite 1102
Lancaster, PA 17603

717-295-0033
FAX 717-299-2154
E-Mail: athorn@dbm-assoc.com
Home Page: www.dcenter.com

17115 Diversified Business Communications

Diversified Business Communications
121 Free Street
Portland, ME 04101

207-842-5500
FAX 207-842-5503
E-Mail: custserv@divcom.com
Home Page: www.divbusiness.com

Theodore Wirth, President & Chief Executive Officer
Paul Clancy, Executive Vice President
Janice Rogers, Vice President, Human Resources
Vicki Hennin, Vice President, Strategic Marketing
Oakley R. Dyer, VP/Business Development

Has over 30 years of experience as trade magazine publishers and exhibition organizers. Provides exposition management services for associations and organizations seeking to expand domestically and overseas, as well as direct mail, internet, telemarketing campaigns and market research.
Founded in 1949

17116 Employer Associations of America

262-696-3473
E-Mail: Vicki.Vought@mranet.org
Home Page: www.eaahub.org

Mary Lynn Fayoumi, Chair
Vicki Vought, Executive Director
Clayton Kamida, Secretary - Treasurer
Cassie Schauer, Web Tech Specialist
Pam Estergard, Financial Services

17117 Employers Group

Employers Group
1150 S Olive St
Suite 2300
Los Angeles, CA 90015-2211

213-748-0421
800-748-8484
FAX 213-742-0301
E-Mail: serviceone@employersgroup.com
Home Page: www.employersgroup.com
Social Media: *Facebook, Twitter, LinkedIn*

Mark Wilbur, CEO

Aims to provide human resources management, management counseling and educational programs. Offers unemployment insurance services, and workers compensation programs.
3.9M Members

17118 Employers of America

Employers of America
310 Meadow Lane
Mason City, IA 50401

641-424-3187
800-728-3187
FAX 641-424-3187
E-Mail: employer@employerhelp.org
Home Page: www.employersgroup.com

Jim Collison, President

Provides information and guidance to employers, managers, and supervisors to empower employees and make great things happen.
1600 Members
Founded in 1976

17119 Financial Management Association International

University of South Florida/College of Business
4202 E Fowler Ave
BSN 3416
Tampa, FL 33620-5500

813-974-2084
FAX 813-974-3318
E-Mail: fma@coba.usf.edu
Home Page: www.fma.org

Kose John, President
William G Christie, VP-Program
Ronald Masulis, VP-Global Services
Javier Estradaÿ, VP-Practitioner Services
Jay R Ritter, President Elect

The mission of the FMA is to broaden the common interests between academicians and practitioners, provide opportunities for professional interaction between and among academicians, practitioners and students, promote the development and understanding of basic and applied research and of sound financial practices, and to enhance the quality of education in finance.
3000 Members
Founded in 1970

17120 Floodplain Management Association

P.O. Box 712080
Santee, CA 92072

760-936-3676
E-Mail: admin@floodplain.org
Home Page: www.floodplain.orgÿ
Social Media: *Facebook, Twitter, LinkedIn, Google+*

Thomas Plummer, Chair
Mark Seits, Vice Chair
Andrew Treleaseÿ, Treasurer
George Booth, Secretary
John Moynier, Director

17121 Fulfillment Management Association

Fulfillment Management Association
225 West 34th Street
Suite 946
New York, NY 10122

818-487-2090
FAX 818-487-4501
E-Mail: info@the-mcma.org
Home Page: the-mcma.org
Social Media: *Facebook, Twitter, LinkedIn*

Rochelle Boorstein, President
Suzanne Nicholas, Vice President
Raymond Dryden, Treasurer
Melissa Borduin, Executive Secretary
Jodi Sentementes, Recording Secretary

Educates, updates and maintains high standards of service in operations management and customer service. Sponsors four seminars per year. Members are direct mail fullfillment, marketing and circulation executives.
425 Members
Founded in 1945

17122 Independent Professional Representatives Organization (IPRO)

Independent Professional Representatives
34157 West 9 Mile Road
Farmington Hills, MI 48335

248-474-0522
800-420-4268
FAX 248-514-4418
E-Mail: ray@avreps.org

Home Page: www.avreps.org
Social Media: *Facebook, LinkedIn*

Dave Humphries, President
Frank Culotta, Vice President
Mark Adams, Secretary
Mike Pecar, Treasurer

The mission of IPRO is to provide new avenues of networking; provide new and emerging resources for sound business management; enhance valuable dialogue and commmunication with business partners; and to continue to develop resources and benefits for individual members beyond the resources of individual firms.

17123 Industrial Asset Management Council

Industrial Asset Management Council
6625 The Corners Parkway
Suite 200
Peachtree Corners, GA 30092

770-325-3461
FAX 770-263-8825
E-Mail: info@iamc.org
Home Page: www.iamc.org
Social Media: *Facebook, Twitter, LinkedIn, Pinterest, Tumblr, Blogger, St*

Samantha L. Turner, Chair
Mr. Russell A. Burton, Vice Chair
J. Tate Godfrey, Executive Director
Rya Hazelwood, Director of Marketing & Conference
Joel Parker, Director of Research & Education

World's leading associates of industrial asset management and corporate real estate executives, their supplies and service providers and economic developers.
135 Members
Founded in 1963

17124 Information Resources Management Association

Information Resources Management Association
701 E Chocolate Ave
Suite 200
Hershey, PA 17033-1240

717-533-8845
FAX 717-533-8661
E-Mail: member@irma-international.org
Home Page: www.irma-international.org

Jan Travers, Executive Director
Sherif Kamel, Communications Director
Lech Janczewski PhD, IRMA World Representative Director
Gerald Grant, IRMA Doctoral Symposium Director
Paul Chalekian, IRMA United States Representative

An international professional organization dedicated to advancing the concepts and practices of information resources management in modern organizations. The primary objective of IRMA is to assist organizations and professionals in enhancing the overall knowledge and understanding of effective information resources management in the early 21st century and beyond.

17125 Institute for Supply Management Association

2055 E Centennial Circle
PO Box 22160
Tempe, AZ 85284-1802

480-752-6276
800-888-6276
FAX 480-752-7890
E-Mail: custsvc@instituteforsupplymanagement.org
Home Page: www.ism.ws

Social Media: *Facebook, Twitter, LinkedIn, Youtube, google Plus*

Thomas K. Linton, Chair
Bill Michels, CPSM, C.P.M., Senior Vice President
Nora Neibergall, CPSM, C.P., Senior Vice President
Thomas W. Derry, Chief Executive Officer, ISM
Janis Kellerman, Senior Vice President/Corporate

The mission of ISM is lead supply management.
43000 Members
Founded in 1915

17126 Institute of Business Appraisers
Institute of Business Appraisers
5217 South State Street
Suite 400
Salt Lake City, UT 84107

954-482-1812
800-299-4130
FAX 866-353-5406
E-Mail: hqiba@go-iba.org
Home Page: www.go-iba.org

Mark Walker, Board of Governor's Chair

The oldest professional society devoted solely to the appraisal of closely-held businesses.
3,000 Members
Founded in 1978

17127 Institute of Certified Business Counselors
Institute of Certified Business Counselors
222 N. LaSalle Street
Suiteÿ300
Chicago, IL 60601

312-856-9590
877-844-2535
FAX 503-292-8237
E-Mail: info@amaaonline.org
Home Page: www.amaaonline.com
Social Media: *Facebook, Twitter, LinkedIn, Google+*

Michael Nail, Founder & Managing Director
Diane Niederman, Vice President of Alliances
MaryÿLou Nall, Operations Manager
Nancy Reyes, Member Services Administrator
Nilla Cooper, Director of Accounting

Premier association of skilled, experienced practitioners focused on the needs of businesses in ownership transition.
120 Members
Founded in 1998

17128 Institute of Management & Administration
Institute of Management & Administration
3 Bethesda Metro Center
Suite 250
Bethesda, MD 20814-5377

703-341-3500
800-372-1033
FAX 800-253-0332
E-Mail: customercare@bna.com
Home Page: www.bna.com
Social Media: *Facebook, Twitter, LinkedIn, YouTube*

Gregory C. McCaffery, CEO & President
Sue Martin, Chief Operating Officer
Paul Albergo, Bureau Chief
Joe Breda, EVP, Product
Daniel M. Fine, EVP, Strategy

An independent source of exclusive business management information for experienced senior and middle management professionals.

17129 Institute of Management Accountant
Institute of Management Accountant

10 Paragon Dr
Suite 1
Montvale, NJ 07645-1760

201-573-9000
800-638-4427
FAX 201-474-1600
E-Mail: ima@imanet.org
Home Page: www.imanet.org
Social Media: *Facebook, Twitter, LinkedIn, Youtube*

Benjamin R.ÿ Mulling, Chair
Marc P. Palker, CMA, Chair - Elect
Jeffrey C. Thomson CMA, CAE, President

A subunit of the Institute of Management Accountants, with a network of 3,000 controllers incorporating newsletters and seminars.
70000 Members
Founded in 1919

17130 Institute of Management Consultants - USA
Institute of Management Consultants - USA
2025 M St NW
Suite 800
Washington, DC 20036-2422

202-367-1261
800-221-2557
FAX 202-367-2134
E-Mail: norm@ecksteinconsult.com
Home Page: www.imcusa.org
Social Media: *Facebook, Twitter, LinkedIn, RSS*

Loraine Huchler CMC, P.E, Chair and CEO
Cynthia E. Currence CMC, Director
Lee Czarapata CMC, Director
Don Matheson, Treasurer
Manola Robinson CMC, Director

IMC is the leading association representing management consultants in the United States, organized to establish consulting as a self-regulating profession, meriting public confidence and respect. Toward the achievement of this goal IMC awards the international appelation CMC for certified management consultants.

17131 Institute of Management and Administration
Institute of Management and Administration
3 Bethesda Metro Center
Suite 250
Bethesda, MD 20814-5377

703-341-3500
800-372-1033
FAX 800-253-0332
E-Mail: customercare@bna.com
Home Page: www.bna.com
Social Media: *Facebook, Twitter, LinkedIn, YouTube*

Gregory C. McCaffery, CEO & President
Sue Martin, Chief Operating Officer
Paul Albergo, Bureau Chief
Joe Breda, EVP, Product
Daniel M. Fine, EVP, Strategy

An independent source of exclusive business management information for experienced senior and middle management professionals.

17132 Int'l. Association of Healthcare Central Services Material Management
Int'l. Association of Healthcare
55 West Wacker Drive
Suite 501
Chicago, IL 60601

312-440-0078
800-962-8274
FAX 312-440-9474
E-Mail: mailbox@iahcsmm.com

Home Page: www.iahcsmm.org
Social Media: *Facebook, Twitter, LinkedIn*

David Jagrosse, CRCST, President
Susan Adams, Executive Director
Nick Baker, Certification Manager
Josephine Colacci, Advocacy
Elizabeth Berrios, Office Manager

Membership consists of persons serving in a technical, supervisory or management capacity in hospital central service departments responsible for the sterilization management and distribution of supplies.
9000 Members
Founded in 1958

17133 International Association for Worksite Health Promotion
Association for Worksite Health Promotion
401 W. Michigan St.
Indianapolis, IN 46202

317-637-9200
FAX 847-480-9282
E-Mail: iawhp@acsm.org
Home Page: ww.acsm-iawhp.org
Social Media: *Facebook, LinkedIn*

George Pfeiffer, MSE, President
Charlie Estey, President-Elect
Stephen Cherniak, MS, MBA, Secretary/Treasurer
Wolf Kirsten, MSÿ, Past President

Exists to advance the profession of worksite health promotion and the career development of its practitioners and to improve the performance of the programs they administer. Represents a variety of disciplines and worksites, for decision makers in the areas of health promotion/disease prevention and health care cost management.
3000 Members

17134 International Association of Administrative Professionals
10502 N. Ambassador Dr.
Suite 100
Kansas City, MO ÿ64153

816-891-6600
FAX 816-891-9118
Home Page: www.iaap-hq.orgÿ
Social Media: *Facebook, Twitter, LinkedIn, Pinterest, RSS, YouTube*

Wendy Melby, CAP-OM, Chair
Kristiÿ Rotvold, CAP-OM, Chair-Elect
Jay Donohue,CAE, CMP, President & CEO
Melissa Mahoney, CAE, Senior Director, Operations
Melissa Sutphin, Executive Admin
Founded in 1942

17135 International Council for Small Business
2201 G Street NW
Funger Hall Suite 315
Washington, DC 20052

202-944-0704
FAX 202-994-4930
E-Mail: info@icsb.org
Home Page: www.icsb.org
Social Media: *Facebook, Twitter, LinkedIn, Google+, RSS*

Ki-Chan Kim, President
Dato' Hafsah Hashim, SVP Development
Geralyn McClure Franklin, SVP Finance & Control
HE. Mohammad M. Al-Zuhair, Ph.D., Vice-President
Dr. Jeffrey R. Alves, Vice-President

Promotes the growth and development of small businesses by bringing together researchers,

practitioners and policy makers from around the world.
2000+ Members
Founded in 1956

17136 International Council of Management Consulting Institutes
International Council of Management
3860 BB NIJKERK Gld
P.O. Box 1058
Netherland

31 -0 3- 247
FAX 31 -0 3- 246
E-Mail: info@icmci.org
Home Page: www.icmci.org

Camera Gaylen, Executive Director
Michael Shays, Manager
John Roethle, Advisory Council

The global association of management consultants. The members of ICMCI are national institutes from around the world that certify professional management consultants. The ICMCI maintains an international code of professional conduct, an international uniform body of knowledge, and strict standards for certification and reciprocity between nations. It promotes professional development and networking between consultants and the highest standards of performance for clients.
39 Members
Founded in 1987

17137 International Facility Management Association
International Facility Management
800 Gessner Rd.
Ste. 900
Houston, TX 77024-4257

713-623-4362
FAX 713-623-6124
E-Mail: ifma@ifma.org
Home Page: www.ifma.org
Social Media: *Facebook, Twitter, LinkedIn, Youtube, Flickr, RSS*

Michael D. Feldman, FMP, CM, Chair
Tony Keane, CAE, President and CEO
Maureen Ehrenberg, FRICS, First Vice President
William M. O'Neill, CFM, Second Vice President
Cheryl White, Director, Corporate Programs

Certifies facility, managers, conducts research, provides educational programs, recognizes facility management degree and certificate programs and produces World Workplace, the world's largest facility management conference and exposition.
Founded in 1980

17138 International Leadership Association
1110 Bonifant Street
Suite 510
Silver Spring, MD 20910-3358

202-470-4818
FAX 202-470-2724
E-Mail: ila@ila-net.org
Home Page: www.ila-net.org
Social Media: *Facebook, Twitter, LinkedIn, Google+, YouTube, Flickr*

Cynthia Cherrey, President & CEO
Shelly Wilsey, Chief Operating Officer
Bridget Chisholm, Director of Conferences
Anita Marsh, Membership Manager
Jean Portianko, I.T. and Office Manager
Founded in 1999

17139 International Personal Management and Association for Human Resources
Int'l Public Management Assoc for Human Resources

1617 Duke St
Alexandria, VA 22314-3406

703-549-7100
FAX 703-684-0948
E-Mail: ipma@ipma-hr.org
Home Page: www.ipma-hr.org
Social Media: *Facebook, Twitter, LinkedIn*

Neil Reichenberg, Executive Director
Sima Hassassian, Deputy Executive Director
Jenny Chang, Director of Communications
Jacob Jackovich, Assessment Services Coordinator
Andrey Pankov, Assessment Research Manager

Human resource professionals, representing the interests of over 6,000 individual and 1,300 agency members, at the federal, state and local levels of government. Promotes excellence in human resource management through the ongoing development of professional and ethical standards, and through its publishing and educational training programs.
6M Members
Founded in 1906

17140 International Public Management Association
1617 Duke Street
Alexandria, VA 22314

703-549-7100
FAX 703-684-0948
E-Mail: nreichenberg@ipma-hr.org
Home Page: www.ipma-hr.orgÿ
Social Media: *Facebook, Twitter, LinkedIn*

Neil Reichenberg, Executive Director
Sima Hassassian, Deputy Executive Director
Gabrielle Voorhees, Controller
Jenny Chang, Director of Communications
Linda Sun, Director of China Programs
Founded in 1906

17141 Life Office Management Association
Life Office Management Association
6190 Powers Ferry Road
Suite 600
Atlanta, GA 30339-5665

770-951-1770
800-968-1738
FAX 770-984-0441
E-Mail: askloma@loma.org
Home Page: www.loma.org
Social Media: *Facebook, Twitter, LinkedIn, Youtube*

Robert A Kerzner, CLU, ChFC, President and CEO
Jeffrey Hasty, FLMI, ACS, SVP/Corporate Secretary
Michele LaBouff, SVP, Human Resources
Kathy Milligan, FLMI, ACS, A, SVP, Education and Training
Ian J Watts, SVP/Managing Director, Intl. Ops

Insurance worldwide association of insurance companies specializing in research and education.
1250 Members
Founded in 1924

17142 Marketing Management Association
Home Page: www.mmaglobal.orgÿ
Social Media: *Facebook, Twitter, LinkedIn, Google+, YouTube*

Brain Vander Schee, President
Roscoe Hightower, Immediate Past President
Pam Kennett-Hensel, President Elect
Susan Geringer, VP, Marketing
Alex Miliovic
Founded in 1977

17143 Medical Group Management Association
Medical Group Management Association

104 Inverness Terrace East
Englewood, CO 80112-5306

303-799-1111
877-275-6462
FAX 303-643-9599
E-Mail: support@mgma.org
Home Page: www.mgma.com
Social Media: *Facebook, Twitter, LinkedIn, Youtube*

Ronald S German, MBA, FACMPE, Chair of the Board
Kevin Spencer, Chief Operating Officer
Stephen A. Dickens, JD, FACMPE, F, Secretary/Treasurer

The oldest and largest professional membership association dedicated to medical practice management. Serves their members by offering timely and relevant networking and educational opportunities that keep the members up-to-date on the practice management field.
18M Members
Founded in 1926

17144 National Association Executive Club
1300 L Street NW
Suite 1050
Washington, DC 20005-4107

202-043-3001
FAX 202-783-4410

Steven Fier, Secretary
Angela West, Manager

Provides networking services and facilities.
500 Members
Founded in 1953

17145 National Association for the Self-Employed
P.O. Box 241
Annapolis Junction, MD 20701-0241

800-649-6273
800-649-6273
E-Mail: advocacy@NASE.org.
Home Page: www.nase.org
Social Media: *Facebook, Twitter, LinkedIn, Youtube*

Keith R. Hall, President/CEO
John K. Hearrell, VP, Membership & Affiliate Programs
Thom Childers, Software Developer/Database Admin
Rosie Farris, Accounts Payable
Cameron T. Brown, Systems Administrator

Goal is to promote small business growth through education and discounts earned through NASE negotiating power.
225M Members
Founded in 1981
Mailing list available for rent

17146 National Association of Corporate Directors
2001 Pennsylvania Ave, NW
Suite 500
Washington, DC 20006

202-775-0509
FAX 202-775-4857
E-Mail: Join@NACDonline.org
Home Page: www.nacdonline.org
Social Media: *Facebook, Twitter, LinkedIn, Youtube, RSS*

Kenneth Daly, President/CEO
Katherine Davis, COO
Peter Gleason, Managing Director, CFO
Henry Stoever, Chief Marketing Officer
Judy Warner, Editor in Chief

A national non-profit membership organization dedicated exclusively to serving the corporate

governance needs of corporate boards and individual board members.
15500 Members
Founded in 1977

17147 National Association of Service Managers

PO Box 250796
Milwaukee, WI 53225

414-466-6060
FAX 414-466-0840
Home Page: www.nasm.com
Social Media: *Facebook*

Ken Cook, Treasurer

Service manager association for professional development
100 Members
Founded in 1955

17148 National Business Owners Association

480 Broadway
PO Box 3373
Saratoga Springs, NY 12866

202-839-9000
866-639-1669
FAX 866-224-0609
Home Page: www.nboaofny.org

Ed Bolen, President
A non-profit organization representing small business owners' interests and offers several money-saving services, valuable benefits and assistance.
4.5M Members
Founded in 1986

17149 National Businesswomens Leadership Association

P.O. Box 419107
Kansas City, MI 64141-6107

913-432-7755
800-258-7246
FAX 913-432-0824
E-Mail: cstserv@natsem.com
Home Page:
www.nationalseminarstraining.com/AboutNBLA.cfm
Social Media: *Facebook, Twitter, LinkedIn, Google+*

Linda Truitt, President

Offers seminars and workshops on business related issues.
Founded in 1986

17150 National Career Development Association

305 N. Beech Circle
Broken Arrow, OK 74012

918-663-7060
866-367-6232
FAX 918-663-7058
E-Mail: webeditor@ncda.org
Home Page: www.ncda.org
Social Media: *Facebook, Twitter, LinkedIn, Pinterest*

Cynthia Marco Scanlon, President
Mark Danaher, Past President
David M. Relie, President Elect
Deneen Pennington, Executive Director
Mary Ann Powell, CDF & Conference Director
Founded in 1913

17151 National Committee for Quality Assurance

1100 13th Street NW
Suite 1000
Washington, DC 20005

202-955-3500
FAX 202-955-3599
E-Mail: customersupport@ncqa.org
Home Page: www.ncqa.org

Social Media: *Facebook, Twitter, LinkedIn, Youtube, Google+, Pinterest*

David Chin, MD, Chair
Margaret E. O'Kane, President
Tom Fluegel, Chief Operating Officer
Scott Hartranft, Chief Financial Officer
Rick Moore, Chief Information Officer

Independent, non profit organization dedicated to improving healthcare quality.
Founded in 1990
Mailing list available for rent

17152 National Conference of Personal Managers

964 2nd Avenue
New York, NY 10022-6304

212-421-2670
866-91N-COPM
FAX 212-838-5105
E-Mail: ncopmse@cox.net
Home Page: www.ncopm.com/

Clinton Ford Billups Jr, National President
Jack Rollins, National First Vice President
Stanley Evans, National Second Vice President
Peggy Becker, National Secretary
Daniel Abrahamson, Eastern Executive Director

A personal manager is engaged in the occupation of advising and counseling talent and personalities in the enternainment industry. personal managers have the expertis to find and develop new talent and create opportunities for those artists which they represent.

17153 National Contract Management Association

21740 Beaumeade Circle
Suite 125
Ashburn, VA 20147

571-382-0082
800-344-8096
FAX 703-448-0939
E-Mail: memberservices@ncmahq.org
Home Page: www.ncmahq.org
Social Media: *Facebook, Twitter, LinkedIn, Youtube,Instagram*

Russell J. Blaine, CPCM, Fellow, President
Michael Fischetti, J.D., CPCM,, Executive Director
John G. Horan, J.D., General Counsel
Penny L. White, J.D., Fellow, Director and Chair
Kim Rupert, CPCM, CFCM, Fe, Director and Chair, Finance

Formed in 1959 to foster the professional growth and educational advancement of its members.
19000 Members
Founded in 1959

17154 National Employee Services and Recreation Association

Employee Services Management Association
568 Spring Road
Suite D
Elmhurst, IL 60126-3896

630-559-0020
E-Mail: esmahq@esmassn.org
Home Page: www.esmassn.org

Pud Belek, President

Manufacturers and distributors offering products and services for employee discount programs and employee store merchandise to members.

17155 National Management Association

2210 Arbor Blvd
Moraine, OH 45439-1580

937-294-0421
FAX 937-294-2374
E-Mail: nma@nma1.org
Home Page: www.nma1.org
Social Media: *Facebook, Twitter, LinkedIn, YouTube*

William T Mahaffey, Chairman
Wendell M Pichon, Vice Chairman
Steve Bailey, CM, President
Sue Kappeler, CM, Vice President
Robin Furlong, Manager

Seeks to develop and recognize management as a profession and to promote the free enterprise system.
22000 Members
Founded in 1925

17156 National Property Management Association

3525 Piedmont Road
Building 5, Suite 300
Atlanta, GA 30305

404-477-5811
FAX 404-240-0998
E-Mail: hq@npma.org
Home Page: www.npma.orgÿ
Social Media: *Facebook, LinkedIn, YouTube*

Marcia Whitson CPPM CF, National Presidentÿ
Cinda Brockman CPPM CF, Executive Vice Presidentÿ
Cheri Cross CPPM CF, Immediate Past Presidentÿ
Ivonne Bachar CPPM CF, VP, Administration
Rosanne Green CPPM CF, VP, Certification
Founded in 1970

17157 National Small Business United

1156 15th St NW
Suite 1100
Washington, DC 20005-1755

202-293-8830
800-345-6728
FAX 202-872-8543
E-Mail: info@nsba.biz
Home Page: www.nsba.biz/
Social Media: *Facebook, Twitter, LinkedIn, Google+, Stumbleupon*

Tim Reynolds, Chair
C. Cookie Driscoll, First Vice Chair
Todd McCracken, President and CEO
Cynthia Kay, Vice Chair for Advocacy
Marc Amato, Vice Chair for Membership

Merged with Small Business United in 1986 and sponsors and supports the NSBU Political Action Committee.

17158 National Training Systems Association

2111 Wilson Boulevard
Suite 400
Arlington, VA 22201-3061

703-247-9471
FAX 703-243-1659
E-Mail: jrobb@ndia.org
Home Page: www.trainingsystems.org
Social Media: *Facebook, Twitter, LinkedIn*

De Voorhees, GD IT, Chairman
Pete Swan, VT MAK, Vice Chairman
James Robb, President
Debbie Dyson, Director/Exhibits
Patrick Rowe, Director of Membership Services

Represents companies in the simulation and training and training support industry. Provides forums, market surveys, and business develop-

ment information and other services to members.
944 Members
Founded in 1988

17159 Newspaper Association Managers
New England Press Association
PO Box 458
Essex, MA 01929

978-338-2555
FAX 978-744-0333
E-Mail: mlpiper52@comcast.net
Home Page: www.nammanagers.com

Lisa Hills, President
Layne Bruce, Vice President
George White, Secretary
Tom Newton, Director
Robin Rhodes, Director

Executives of state, regional, national and international newspaper associations.
65 Members
Founded in 1923

17160 North America Human ResourceÿManagement Association

E-Mail: casandra.merkel@shrm.org
Home Page: www.nahrma.org
Social Media: *Facebook, Twitter, LinkedIn*

Henry Jackson, President
Lic. Jorge Jauregui, HRMP, Immediate Past Presidentÿ
Cheryl Newcombeÿÿÿÿ, Secretary/Treasurer
Founded in 1997

17161 Operations Management Society
5400 Bosque Boulevard
Waco, TX 76710-4414

254-752-6315
FAX 254-776-3767
Home Page: www.poms.orgÿ

Sushil Gupta, Ph.D, Executive Director
Dr. Metin €akanyildirim, Associate Executive Director

Members are senior management and deans of business schools in the field of operations management.
Founded in 1989

17162 Organization Development Institute
11234 Walnut Ridge Road
Chesterland, OH 44026-1240

440-729-7419
FAX 440-729-9319
E-Mail: donwcole@aol.com
Home Page: www.odinstitute.org
Social Media: *Facebook, Twitter, LinkedIn*

Dr. Donald W Cole RODC, President
Jim Gustafson, Editor Journal

Promotes the understanding of organization development and offers three categories of membership: professional consultant, regular and student. Offers the International Registry of O.D. Professionals and O.D. Handbook which lists names, addresses and e-mail addresses, publishes a monthly newsletter plus a quarterly journal of 100-150 pages. There are two conferences held every year, one in the USA and one International.
500 Members
Founded in 1991

17163 Product Development and Management Association
330 N. Wabash Avenue
Suite 2000
Chicago, IL 60611

312-321-5145
800-232-5241
FAX 312-673-6885
E-Mail: pdma@pdma.org

Home Page: www.pdma.org
Social Media: *Facebook, Twitter, LinkedIn*

Charlie Noble, Chair
Charlie Noble, VP Academic Affairs
Peter Bradford, NPDP, VP of Certification
Peter Flentov, VP Chapters
Brad White, VP Conferences & Events

Provides essential information to help foster new product development, giving an overview of the total product innovation process and presenting the latest advancements in product innovation. Also assists managers in innovating and producing products more effectively and efficiently.
3200 Members
Founded in 1976

17164 Production and Operations Management Society

Home Page: www.poms.orgÿ

Sushil Gupta, Ph.D, Executive Director
Dr. Metin €akanyildirim, Associate Executive Director
Founded in 1989

17165 Professional Convention Management Association
35 East Wacker Drive
Suite 500
Chicago, IL 60601

312-423-7262
877-827-7262
FAX 312-423-7222
E-Mail: communications@pcma.org
Home Page: www.pcma.org
Social Media: *Facebook, Twitter, LinkedIn, YouTube,Google+*

Ray Kopcinski, CMP, Chairman of Board
Deborah Sexton, President and CEO
Jason Paganessi, Vice President, Business Innovation
Sherrif Karamat, CAE, BAS, MBA, Chief Operating Officer
Michelle Russell, Editor in Chief

PCMA delivers superior and innovative education, to promote the value of professional convention management.
6100 Members
Founded in 1957

17166 Professional Managers Association
PO Box 77235
Washington, DC 20013

202-803-9597
FAX 202-803-9044
E-Mail: info@promanager.org
Home Page: www.promanager.org

Michael Leszcz, National President
Jeff Eppler, National Vice President
Jackie Jones, National Secretary
Tom Burger, Executive Director
Carlos Zepeda, National Treasurer

National membership association representing the interests of professional managers, management officials and non-bargaining unit employees in the federal government. Promote leadership and management excellence within the federal services.
10000 Members
Founded in 1981

17167 Project Management Institute (PMI)
14 Campus Blvd
Newtown Square, PA 19073-3299

610-356-4600
855-746-4849
FAX 610-482-9971
E-Mail: customercare@pmi.org
Home Page: www.pmi.org

Social Media: *Facebook, Twitter, LinkedIn, YouTube,Google+*

Mark Langley, President & CEO
Michael Deprisco, Vice President
John J Doyle, MBA, Vice President, Finance
Craig Killough, Vice President, Organization Market
Dorothy McKelvy, MA, SPHR, Vice President, Human Resources

Fosters recognition of the need for project management professionalism. Offers professional certification and bestows awards.
105M Members
Founded in 1969
Mailing list available for rent

17168 Public Risk Management Association
700 S. Washington St.
Suite 218
Alexandria, VA 22314

703-528-7701
FAX 703-739-0200
E-Mail: info@primacentral.org
Home Page: www.primacentral.org
Social Media: *Facebook, Twitter, LinkedIn*

Dean Coughenour, ARM, President
Regan Rychetsky, ABCP, Past President
Terri Evans, President-Elect
Marshall Davies, PhD, Executive Director
Jennifer Ackerman, CAEÿ, Deputy Executive Director

17169 Small Business Assistance Center
90 Daniel Drive
Avondale, PA 19311

610-444-1720
FAX 610-444-1724
E-Mail: inquire@sbacnetwork.org
Home Page: www.sbacnetwork.org

Provides information and assistance to small businesses. To train and consult entrepreneurs through information services, seminars and professional consultations.
Founded in 1988

17170 Society for Advancement of Management
6300 Ocean Drive - OCNR 383
Unit - 5808
Corpus Christi, TX 78412-5807

361-825-3045
888-827-6077
FAX 361-825-5609
E-Mail: moustafa@cob.tamucc.edu
Home Page: www.samnational.org
Social Media: *Facebook, LinkedIn*

Moustafa H Abdelsamad, President/CEO
R. Clifton Poole, Secretary
Kent Byus, Treasurer

SAM members come from a variety of disciplines - productions, finance, marketing, accounting and more who all share a common bond of interest in becoming stronger managers. SAM abounds with opportunities for professional development.
3000 Members
Founded in 1912

17171 Society for Human Resource Management
SHRM/Society for Human Resource Management
1800 Duke St
Alexandria, VA 22314-3496

703-535-6000
800-283-7476
703-548-3440
FAX 703-535-6490
E-Mail: shrmeducation@shrm.org.
Home Page: www.shrm.org

Social Media: *Facebook, Twitter, LinkedIn, YouTube, RSS, Google+*

Bette J. Francis, SPHR, Chair
Henry G. Jackson, CPA, President and CEO
J. Robert Carr, J.D., SPHR, SVP, Membership, Marketing
Deb Cohen, Ph.D., SPHR, SVP, Knowledge Development
Brian K. Dickson, SVP, Professional Development

World's largest association devoted to human resource management. Serves the needs of the human resource management professional by providing the most essential and comprehensive set of resources available.
18500 Members
Founded in 1948
Mailing list available for rent

17172 Stage Managers' Association
PO Box 275
Times Square Station
New York, NY 10108-0275

Home Page: www.stagemanagers.org
Social Media: *Facebook, Twitter, LinkedIn*

Elynmarie Kazle, Chair
Mandy L. Berry, 1st Vice Chair
Hope Rose Kelly, 2nd Vice Chair
Eileen Arnold, Treasurer
Melissa A.ÿ Nathan, Secretary
Founded in 1981

17173 Strategic Management Association
19102 South Blackhawk Parkway
Unit 25
Mokena, IL 60448-4066

815-806-4908
E-Mail: slfmcb@telus.net
Home Page: www.strategicleadershipforum.org

Chris Glatz, Executive Director/Administration

The international society for strategic management and planning. Presents awards, conducts seminars and foundation research.
6.5M Members
Founded in 1985

17174 Strategic Management Society
Rice Building, 815 W Van Buren Street
Suite 215
Chicago, IL 60607

312-492-6224
FAX 312-492-6223
E-Mail: sms@strategicmanagement.net
Home Page: www.strategicmanagement.net
Social Media: *Facebook, Twitter, LinkedIn, YouTube*

Robert Hoskisson, President
Marjorie Lyles, President Elect
Jay Barney, Past President
Steven Floyd, Treasurer
Nikolaus Pelka, Executive Director
Founded in 1981

17175 Support Services Alliance
Po Box 130
Schoharie, NY 12157-0130

518-295-7966
800-322-3920
FAX 518-295-8556
E-Mail: membershipservices@ssamembers.com
Home Page: www.ssainfo.com

Steven Cole, President

Multi-state membership organization that provides cost-savings services and legislative representation for small businesses and the self-employed. Also offers services to the memberships of more than 100 affiliated state, regional and national associations.
50 Members
Founded in 1977

17176 The Association of State Floodplain Managers
575 D'Onofrio Drive
Suite 200
Madison, WI 53719

608-828-3000
FAX 608-828-6319
Home Page: www.floods.orgÿ
Social Media: *Facebook, Twitter, LinkedIn*

Bill Nechamen, Chair
Ceil Strauss, Vice Chair
Karen McHugh, Treasurer
Leslie Durham, Secretary
Chad Berginnis, Executive Director
Founded in 1977

17177 The Employers Association
3020 W. Arrowood Road
Charlotte, NC 28273

704-522-8011
FAX 704-522-8105
E-Mail: info@employersassoc.com
Home Page: www.employersassoc.com
Social Media: *Facebook, Twitter, LinkedIn, RSS*

Paul DeVine, Chairman
Paul DeVine, Vice Chairman
Kenny Colbert, President, CEO
Tom L. Barnhardt, Past Chairman
Cathy Graham, SPHR, Director, Benefit Services

17178 The Sales Management Association

E-Mail: support@salesmanagement.org
Home Page: www.salesmanagement.org
Social Media: *Facebook, Twitter, LinkedIn, RSS*

Robert J. Kelly, Chairman
Laura Hall, Managing Director

17179 Theÿ American Societyÿofÿ Administrativeÿ Professionals
121 Free Street
Portland, ME 4101

888-960-ASAP
FAX 207-842-5603
E-Mail: membership@asaporg.com
Home Page: www.asaporg.com
Social Media: *Facebook, Twitter, LinkedIn, Pinterest*

Founded in 2005

17180 Theÿ Associationÿfor Financial Professionals
4520 East West Highway
Suite 750
Bethesda, MD 20814ÿ

301-907-2862
FAX 301-907-2864
Home Page: www.afponline.org
Social Media: *Twitter, LinkedIn, YouTube, RSS*

Anthony Scaglione, CTP, Chairman
Roberta Eiseman, CTP, Vice Chairman
Jeff Johnson, CTP, CPA, Vice Chairman
Ann Anthony, CTP, Board of Director
Terry Crawford, CTP, Board of Director

17181 Turnaround Management Association Headquarters
150 S Wacker Drive
Suite 900
Chicago, IL 60606

312-578-6900
FAX 312-578-8336
E-Mail: info@turnaround.org

Home Page: www.turnaround.org
Social Media: *Facebook, Twitter, LinkedIn*

Ronald R Sussman, Chairperson
Thomas M Kim, President
Gregory J. Fine, CAE, Chief Executive Officer
Jim Gavin, Chief Financial Officer
Jennifer Bethke, Chief Learning & Certification

The only international nonprofit association dedicated to corporate renewal and turnaround management. TMA's 9,000 members in 46 regional chapters comprise a professional community of turnaround practitioners, attorneys, accountants, investors, lenders, venture capitalists, appraiser, liquidators, executive recruiters and consultants. Three international conferences each year offer networking and educational sessions on the latest trends and best practices in the restructuring field.
9000 Members
Founded in 1988

17182 U.S. Workplace Wellness Alliance
1615 H Street NW
Washington, DC 20062-2000

Home Page: www.uswwa.org

17183 WACRA: World Association for Case Method Research & Application
23 Mackintosh Avenue
Needham, MA 02492-1218

781-444-8982
FAX 781-444-1548
E-Mail: hans.klein@wacra.org
Home Page: www.wacra.org

Dr Hans E Klein, President/Executive Director
Denise M. Smith, Executive Assistant
Dr. Amelia J. Klein, Director Education
Dr. Lars Bengtsson, Director Public Relations
Dr. Charles H. Patti, Director of Publications

Advancing the use of the case method and other interactive methodologies in teaching, training and planning.
2000 Members
Founded in 1984

17184 Wiley
John Wiley & Sons
111 River Street
Hoboken, NJ 07030-5774

201-748-6000
800-825-7550
FAX 201-748-6088
E-Mail: info@wiley.com
Home Page: www.wiley.com

Matthew S. Kissiner, Chairman of the Board
Mark Allin, President and CEO
Vincent Marzano, Vice President & Treasurer
Ellis E. Cousens, Executive Vice President
John Kritzmacher, Executive Vice President

Provides information to help executives manage their companies effectively.

17185 Women in Management
Women in Management
PO Box 6690
Elgin, IL 60121-6690

877-946-6285
FAX 847-683-3751
E-Mail: nationalwim@aol.com
Home Page: www.wimonline.org

Dana Vierck, President
Ann Louis, Secretary
Tracey Carlstedt, Treasurer
Jane Gregory, Membership
Chris Awe, Administrator

Aims to promote self-growth in management. Sponsors speakers and discussion groups.
1.7M Members
Founded in 1976

17186 Young Presidents Organization
600 East Las Colinas Boulevard
Suite 1000
Irving, TX 75039ÿ

972-587-1500
800-773-7976
FAX 972-587-1611
E-Mail: askypo@ypo.org
Home Page: www.ypo.orgÿ
Social Media: *Facebook, Twitter, LinkedIn, YouTube, Google+, Instagram*

Scott Mordell, Chief Executive Officer
Sean Magennis, Chief Operating Officer
Cynthia Abbott, Chief Marketing Officer
Terry Wilson, Chief Financial Officer
Dwight Moore, Chief Information Officer
Founded in 1950

17187 Young Presidents' Organization
Young Presidents' Organization
600 East Las Colinas Boulevard
Suite 1000
Irving, TX 75039

972-587-1500
800-773-7976
FAX 972-587-1611
E-Mail: askypo@ypo.org
Home Page: www.ypo.org
Social Media: *Facebook, Twitter, LinkedIn, Youtube, Google+, Instagram*

Fulton Collins, Chairman
Scott Mordell, Chief Executive Officer

Members are corporate presidents under the age of fifty whose companies employ at least fifty employees.
8000 Members
Founded in 1950

Newsletters

17188 American Academy of Medical Administration Executive Newsletter
701 Lee St
Suite 600
Des Plaines, IL 60016-4516

847-759-8601
FAX 847-759-8602
E-Mail: renee@aameda.org
Home Page: www.aameda.org

Renee Schleichar, CEO
Guy Snyder, Director of Education
Rhonda Guptill, Chief Financial Officer

Offers information and news to upper level administration of hospitals and medical institutions.
14 Pages
Frequency: BiWeekly

17189 Best Practices Report
Management Roundtable
92 Crescent St
Waltham, MA 02453-4315

781-891-8080
800-338-2223
FAX 781-398-1889
Home Page: www.pharmcentric.com

A monthly newsletter on the best practices in product development. How to develop and deliver great products at the lowest cost in the shortest time.

17190 Better Supervision
Economics Press

12 Daniel Road
Fairfield, NJ 07004-2565

973-227-1224
FAX 973-227-9742

Robert Guder, Publisher
Techniques for managing people successfully.
Cost: $1.00
Circulation: 43,000

17191 Better Work Supervisor
Clement Communications
Concord Industrial Park
Concordville, PA 19331

610-459-4200
FAX 610-459-0936

Offers important information, articles and news to upper level management.
Cost: $48.50

17192 Blue Ribbon Service
Economics Press
12 Daniel Road
Fairfield, NJ 07004-2565

973-227-1224
FAX 973-227-9742

Robert Guder, Publisher
Shows employees the importance of giving good customer service and methods of providing that service.
Circulation: 27,760

17193 Bridging the Gap
Section for Women in Public Administration
1301 Pennsylvania Avenue NW
Suite 700
Washington, DC 20004

202-393-7878
FAX 202-638-4952
E-Mail: info@aspanet.org
Home Page: www.aspanet.org
Social Media: *Facebook, Twitter, LinkedIn*

Circulation: 400
Founded in 1939
Mailing list available for rent: 400 names

17194 Bulletin to Management
Bureau of National Affairs
1801 S Bell St
Arlington, VA 22202-4501

703-341-3000
800-372-1033
FAX 800-253-0332
E-Mail: customercare@bna.com
Home Page: www.bnabooks.com
Social Media: *Facebook, Twitter, LinkedIn*

Paul N Wojcik, CEO

Features summaries of current developments in human resource/personnel management and labor relations. Discusses real life job situations and provides policy guides on how companies have successfully handled employee related problems. Recurring features include statistics.
Cost: $317.00
Frequency: Weekly
Founded in 1929

17195 Business Journal
Business Journals of North Carolina
120 W Morehead St
Suite 420
Charlotte, NC 28202-1874

704-973-1200
800-948-5323
FAX 704-973-1201

E-Mail: charlotte@bizjournals.com
Home Page: www.citybiznetwork.com

George Conley, President
Robert Morris, Editor
David Harris, Managing Editor
72 Pages
Frequency: Weekly
ISSN: 0887-5588
Printed in 4 colors on newsprint stock

17196 Business Courier
101 W 7th St
Cincinnati, OH 45202-2306

513-621-6665
800-767-3263
FAX 513-621-2462
E-Mail: borben@bizjournals.com
Home Page: www.bizjournals.com/cincinnati/

Douglas Bolton, Publisher
Rob Daumeyer, Editor
Cost: $83.00
Frequency: Weekly
Circulation: 11000
Founded in 1947

17197 Case Strategies
Cutter Information Corporation
37 Broadway
Suite 1
Arlington, MA 02474-5500

781-648-1950
800-888-8939
FAX 781-648-1950
E-Mail: service@cutter.com
Home Page: www.cutter.com/

Paul Harman, Editor
Kim Leonard, Customer Service Director
Karen Coburn, CEO/President
Hillel Glazer, Senior Consultant
Ron Blitstein, Director

Objective, timely information to help you successfully integrate CASE into your organization.
Cost: $387.00
16 Pages
Frequency: Monthly
Founded in 1986

17198 Cash Flow Enhancement Report
Institute of Management and Administration
3 Bethesda Metro Center
Suite 250
Bethesda, MD 20814-5377

703-341-3500
800-372-1033
FAX 800-253-0332
Home Page: www.ioma.com

Focuses on business strategies for increasing liquidity.
Cost: $245.00
16 Pages
Frequency: Monthly

17199 Center for Creative Leadership Newsletter
Center for Creative Leadership
Attn: Client Services
PO Box 26300
Greensboro, NC 27438-6300

336-887-7210
FAX 336-282-3284
E-Mail: info@ccl.org
Home Page: www.ccl.org

Walter Ulmer Jr, Publisher
John Alexander, President, Chief Executive Officer

A newsletter featuring issues and observations on the behavioral science research and development field.
Frequency: Monthly
Circulation: 35000
Founded in 1970

17200 Chief Executive Officers Newsletter

Center for Entreprenuel Management
47 West Street
Suite 5C
New York, NY 10014-4606

212-633-0060
FAX 212-633-0063
E-Mail: mail@ceoclubs.org
Home Page: www.ceoclubs.org

Joseph Mancuso, President
Christopher Jones, Office Manager

Unique management insights and sources for presidents of growing businesses.
Cost: $71.00
Frequency: Monthly
Circulation: 40000
Founded in 1978

17201 Communications Insights

Comquest
112 Schubert Drive
Downingtown, PA 19335-3382

610-269-2100
FAX 610-269-2275

Mark Schubert, Publisher

Tips and techniques for sucessful communication.

17202 Communique

213 W Institute Place
Suite 307
Chicago, IL 60610-3195

312-440-0078
800-962-8274
FAX 312-440-9474
E-Mail: mailbox@iahcsmm.com
Home Page: www.iahcsmm.com

Betty Hanna, Executive Director
Marilyn Corida, Secretary/Treasurer
Lisa Huber, President
Bruce T. Bird, President

Bi-monthly publication separates supervisors/directors from technicians.
Cost: $40.00
Frequency: 6/Annual
Circulation: 15M
ISBN: 1-605309-30-9

17203 Contractor's Business Management Report

Institute of Management and Administration
3 Bethesda Metro Center
Suite 250
Bethesda, MD 20814-5377

703-341-3500
800-372-1033
FAX 800-253-0332
Home Page: www.ioma.com

Delivers practical, relevant, and insightful business management guidance to contractors, subcontractors and their consultants.
Cost: $424.00

17204 Corporate EFT Report

Phillips Publishing
95 Old Shoals Road
Arden, NC 28704

301-340-2100
866-599-9491
E-Mail: feedback@healthydirections.com

Home Page: www.healthydirections.com
Social Media: *Facebook, Twitter*

Newsletter on business, EFT operations for corporate cash managers.

17205 Corporate Examiner

Interfaith Center on Corporate Response
475 Riverside Dr
Suite 1842
New York, NY 10115-0034

212-870-2295
FAX 212-870-2023
E-Mail: info@interfaithcommunity.org
Home Page: www.interfaithcommunity.org

Laura Morrison, Program Coordinator
Diane Bratcher, Editor

Analyzes corporate social responsibility issues and trends, reports corporate action news, reviews publications and media and presents the ideas and opinions of leaders of the corporate social responsibility movement.
Cost: $ 35.00
8 Pages
Circulation: 1500
Founded in 1981
Printed in one color on matte stock

17206 Cost Controller

Siefer Consultants
PO Box 1384
Storm Lake, IA 50588-1384

712-732-7340
FAX 712-732-7906

Dan Siefer, Publisher

Cost cutting techniques and ideas for business and industry.
Cost: $149.00
8 Pages
Frequency: Monthly

17207 Customer Communicator

Alexander Communications Group
1916 Park Ave
Suite 501
New York, NY 10037-3733

212-281-6099
800-232-4317
FAX 212-283-7269
E-Mail: info@customerservicegroup.com
Home Page: www.customerservicegroup.com

Romauld Alexander, President
Adam Reif, Marketing Manager

Provides customer service representatives with the skills, techniques and motivation they need to be more productive.
Cost: $200.00
Frequency: Monthly
ISSN: 0145-8450
Founded in 1990

17208 Customer Service Manager's Letter

Bureau of Business Practice
76 Ninth Avenue
7th Floor
New York, NY 10011

212-771-0600
FAX 212-771-0885
Home Page: www.aspenpublishers.com
Social Media: *Facebook, Twitter, LinkedIn*

Mark Dorman, CEO
Gustavo Dobles, VP Operations

Specially designed to show managers how to reduce their costs, their customer base, and maximize their employee capability.
Cost: $179.00
8 Pages
Frequency: 2 per year
Circulation: 5200

17209 Daily Report for Executives

Bureau of National Affairs
1801 S Bell St
Arlington, VA 22202-4501

703-341-3000
800-372-1033
FAX 800-253-0332
E-Mail: customercare@bna.com
Home Page: www.bnabooks.com
Social Media: *Facebook, Twitter, LinkedIn*

Paul N Wojcik, CEO

A daily notification service covering legislative, regulatory, legal, tax and economic developments which affect both national and international businesses.
Cost: $9399.00
Frequency: Daily
ISSN: 0148-8155
Founded in 1929

17210 Deal

The Deal, LLC.
14 Wall Street
New York, NY 10005

212-313-9200
888-667-3325
E-Mail: customerservice@thedeal.com
Home Page: www.thedeal.com
Social Media: *Twitter*

Mickey Hernandez, Advertising Sales
Elena Freed, Marketing

Dedicated solely to reporting and analyzing all the aspects of the booming, high stakes world of the deeal economy. Areas of coverage include mergers and acquisitions, IPO's, private equity, venture capital and bankruptcies. Published in newsletter and on website.
Cost: $249.00
26 Pages
Founded in 1999

17211 Delphi Insight Series

Delphi Group
Ten Post Office Square
Suite 580
Boston, MA 02109-4603

617-247-1511
800-335-7440
FAX 617-247-4957
Home Page: www.delphigroup.com

Thomas Koulopoulos, President
Hadley Reynolds, Director Research
Mary Ann Kozlowski, Director Public Relations

Timely and insightful analysis and review of the markets, developments, and business cases for knowledge management, corporate portals and e-business solutions. Incorporates original Delphi research findings. Written for all management titles. Includes weekly email news update on relevant issues and access to DelphiWeb, an extensive online resource of product and market information.
Cost: $20000.00
Frequency: Daily

17212 Directorship

Directorship Search Group
8 Sound Shore Drive
Suite 250
Greenwich, CT 06830-7276

203-618-7000
FAX 203-618-7007
Home Page: www.directorship.com

Russell Reynolds Jr, CEO/President
Barrett Stephens, VP
J.P. Donlon, Editor-in-Chief

Articles and news of interest to CEOs and directors of public companies, on every aspect of

corporate governance.
Cost: $395.00
12 Pages
ISSN: 0193-4279
Founded in 1975
Printed in 4 colors on glossy stock

17213 EAP Link

International Education Services and
Publishing
1537 Franklin Street
#201-203
San Francisco, CA 94109-4571

415-239-4171
800-551-3005

Kendall Van Blarcom, Publisher

International news for human resource professionals.
Cost: $197.00
8 Pages
Frequency: Monthly

17214 Employee Assistance Program Management Letter

Health Resources Publishing
1913 Atlantic Ave
Suite 200
Manasquan, NJ 08736-1067

732-292-1100
888-843-6242
FAX 732-292-1111
E-Mail: info@healthresourcesonline.com
Home Page: www.healthresourcesonline.com

Robert K Jenkins, Publisher
Lisa Mansfield, Regional Director
Brett Powell, Regional Director
Alice Burron, Director

A monthly briefing on guidelines to help companies make decisions on managing their EAP programs. Contains information on what EAP's across the country are doing; help on policy issues dealing with and monitoring costs; framing coverages and limitations; and case histories.
Cost: $227.00
Frequency: Monthly
ISSN: 0896-0941
Founded in 1978

17215 Enrollment Management Report

LRP Publications
747 Dresher Road Suite 500
PO Box 980
Horsham, PA 19044-980

215-840-0912
800-341-7874
FAX 215-784-9639
E-Mail: webmaster@lrp.com
Home Page: www.lrp.com

Jay Margolis, Editor

Provides solutions and strategies for recruitment, admissions, retention and financial aid for higher-education institutions. Shows readers how to face the challenge of working across departmental lines to improve retention rates and how to respond to the upcoming surge in non-traditional students who apply.
Cost: $198.00
Frequency: Monthly
Founded in 1977

17216 Executive Administrator

Seifer Consultants
P.O.Box 1384
Storm Lake, IA 50588-1384

712-732-7340
FAX 712-732-7906

John Siefer, Publisher

Management, job opportunities and news.
Cost: $70.00
Frequency: Monthly

17217 Executive Advantage

Briefings Publishing Group
1101 King St
Suite 110
Alexandria, VA 22314-2944

703-548-3800
800-888-2084
FAX 703-684-2136
Home Page: www.briefings.com

Tina Ragland, Editorial Assistant
Lois Willingham, Marketing Manager
Deirdre Hackett, Executive Editor
William Dugan, Group Publisher
Michelle Cox, Publisher

A publication designed to help you learn the key interpersonal secrets to business success through proper etiquette and protocol.
Cost: $147.00
8 Pages
Frequency: Monthly
Founded in 1981
Mailing list available for rent: 6000 names at $125 per M
Printed in 2 colors on matte stock

17218 Executive Edge

28 W 23rd Street
10th Floor
New York, NY 10010

212-367-4100
FAX 212-367-4137

Rich Karlgaard, Publisher
David Hallerman, Editor

Covers quality customer service and marketing techniques.

17219 Executive Issues

Wharton School
255 S 38th St
Philadelphia, PA 19104-3706

215-386-8300
FAX 215-573-6138
E-Mail: editor@wharton.upenn.edu
Home Page: www.wharton.upenn.edu

Jason Fisher, President

Discusses current business issues, business continuing information.
Circulation: 40000

17220 Executive Recruiter News

Kennedy Information
1 Phoenix Mill Lane
Floor 3
Peterborough, NH 03458

603-924-1006
800-531-0007
E-Mail: customerservice@kennedyinfo.com
Home Page: www.kennedyinfo.com

Joseph McCool, Editor
William Allen, Managing Director

The authoritative voice of the recruiting industry, covering news, analysis, practice, advice, proprietary data and opinion.
Cost: $229.00
8 Pages
Frequency: Monthly
ISSN: 0271-0781
Founded in 1980
Printed in 2 colors on matte stock

17221 Executive Report on Managed Care

Health Resources Publishing
1913 Atlantic Ave
Suite 200
Manasquan, NJ 08736-1067

732-292-1100
888-843-6242
FAX 732-292-1111

E-Mail: info@themcic.com
Home Page: www.healthresourcesonline.com

Robert K Jenkins, Publisher
Lisa Mansfield, Regional Director
Brett Powell, Regional Director
Alice Burron, Director

Bi-monthly report giving news of how major employers are implementing managed care programs. Helps companies prepare to evaluate and monitor various managed care proposals in terms of their cost effectiveness, quality and liability to the employer.
Cost: $497.00
Frequency: Weekly
ISSN: 0898-9753
Founded in 1978

17222 Executive Report on Physician Organizations

Health Resources Publishing
1913 Atlantic Ave
Suite 200
Manasquan, NJ 08736-1067

732-292-1100
800-516-4343
FAX 732-292-1111
E-Mail: info@themcic.com
Home Page: www.healthresourcesonline.com

Robert K Jenkins, Publisher
Lisa Mansfield, Marketing Assistant
Caroline Pense, Editor
Brett Powell, Regional Director
Alice Burron, Director

A bi-monthly newsletter published by Health Resources Publishing.
Cost: $197.00
Frequency: Monthly
Circulation: 5000
ISSN: 0898-9753
Founded in 1978

17223 Executive Solutions

Dartnell Corporation
4660 N Ravenswood Avenue
Chicago, IL 60640-4510

773-907-9500
800-727-1227
FAX 561-622-2423
E-Mail: customerservice@dartnellcorp.com
Home Page: www.dartnellcorp.com

Clark Fertridge, Publisher
John Aspley, Founder

Modern management techniques for executive training.

17224 Executive Wealth Advisory

National Institute of Business Management
Po Box 906
Williamsport, PA 17703-9933

703-058-8000
800-433-0622
FAX 570-567-0166
E-Mail: customer@nibm.net
Home Page: www.nibm.net

10 Pages
Frequency: Monthly
ISSN: 1049-4855

17225 Federal Personnel Guide

LRP Publications
360 Hiatt Drive
Palm Beach Gardens, FL 33418

561-622-6520
800-341-7874
FAX 561-622-0757
E-Mail: webmaster@lrp.com
Home Page: www.lrp.com

Kenneth Kahn, President

Annual almanac for US civilian federal personnel and training officers and individual federal

and postal employees. An up-to-the-minute summary of rules and regulations affecting federal employees, including employment, pay and benefits.
Cost: $12.95
Circulation: 55000
ISBN: 1-881097-12-9
ISSN: 0163-7665
Founded in 1978

17226 Financial Management Association International (FMA)
University of South Florida
4202 E Fowler Ave
Tampa, FL 33620-9951

813-974-2011
FAX 813-974-5530
E-Mail: fma@coba.usf.edu OR info@fma.org
Home Page: www.usf.edu

Judy L Genshaft, President
William Christie, Financial Management Editor
Keith M Howe, Journal of Applied Finance Editor
James Schallheim, FMA Survey Synthesis Series Editor
John Finnerty, Editor FMA Online

Financial books, textbooks, databases, newspapers, research services, software and related products and services.
Frequency: Quarterly
Founded in 1970
Mailing list available for rent

17227 Global Environmental Change Report
Cutter Information Corporation
111 Eighth Avenue 7th Floor
New York, NY 10011-5552

212-771-0600
FAX 212-771-0885
E-Mail: jrohaly@aspenpublishers.com
Home Page: www.aspenpublishers.com

Wolters Kluwer, CEO
Richard Richard, Executive VP

An exclusive international service reporting on policy trends, industry actions and global environmental change.
Cost: $565.00
8 Pages
Frequency: Monthly

17228 HIPAA Bulletin for Management
Health Resources Publishing
1913 Atlantic Ave
Suite 200
Manasquan, NJ 08736-1067

732-292-1100
888-843-6242
FAX 732-292-1111
E-Mail: info@healthresourcesonline.com
Home Page: www.healthresourcesonline.com

Robert K Jenkins, Publisher
Lisa Mansfield, Regional Director
Brett Powell, Regional Director
Alice Burron, Director

A monthly newsletter published by Health Resources Publishing.
Cost: $147.00
Frequency: Monthly
ISSN: 0898-9753
Founded in 1978

17229 HMFA Healthcare Cost Containment Newsletter
Healthcare Finance Management Association
3 Westbrook Corporate Center
Suite 600
Westchester, IL 60154

708-531-9600
FAX 708-531-0032

Home Page:
www.hfma.org/publications/healthcarecost

Issues illustrate how to implement strategic cost management that will reduce labor and supply expenses, enhance operational efficiency, satisfy your patients, and improve your competitive position.
Cost: $125.00
Frequency: Quarterly

17230 HMFA Revenue Cycle Stragetist Newsletter
Healthcare Finance Management Association
3 Westbrook Corporate Center
Suite 600
Westchester, IL 60154

708-531-9600
FAX 708-531-0032
Home Page: www.hfma.org/publications/

Improve your organization's bottom line while maintaining regulatory compliance.
Cost: $165.00
Frequency: Quarterly

17231 HR Briefings
Bureau of Business Practice
111 8th Avenue
New York, NY 10011

212-771-0733
800-243-1660
FAX 800-901-9075
Home Page: www.aspenpublishers.com/

Alicia Pierce, President

Designed to help HR professionals become more effective on the job. It offers hands-on advice from other personnel managers who have experienced the kinds of problems facing readers.
Cost: $259.00
8 Pages
Frequency: Monthly
Founded in 1925

17232 HR News
Int'l Public Management Assoc for Human Resources
1617 Duke St
Alexandria, VA 22314-3406

703-549-7100
FAX 703-684-0948
E-Mail: ipma@pma-hr.org
Home Page: www.ipma-hr.org

Neil Reichenberg, Executive Director
Sima Hassassian, COO
Tina Chiappetta, Sr Director Gov't Affairs/Comm
Frequency: Monthly
Circulation: 8000

17233 HR Weekly
SHRM/Society for Human Resource Management
1800 Duke St
Alexandria, VA 22314-3494

703-535-6000
866-898-4724
FAX 703-535-6474
E-Mail: shrmeducation@shrm.org.
Home Page: www.shrm.org
Social Media: Facebook, Twitter, LinkedIn, Youtube

Susan R Meisinger, CEO

Weekly e-newsletter highlighting critical HR/Human Resourace issues.

17234 HR on Campus
LRP Publications

747 Dresher Road
PO Box 980
Horsham, PA 19044-980

215-784-0912
800-341-7874
FAX 215-784-9639
E-Mail: webmaster@lrp.com
Home Page: www.lrp.com

Jay Margolis, Editor/publisher

Gives you the tools you need to solve your institution's human resource challenges. Provides pratical tips for handling real-life, day-to-day problems, along with the latest news and significant developments in higher education.
Cost: $165.00
Frequency: Monthly
Founded in 1977

17235 HRmadeEasy
Employers of America
310 Meadow Lane
Mason City, IA 50401

641-424-3187
800-728-3187
FAX 641-424-3187
E-Mail: employer@employerhelp.org
Home Page: www.employerhelp.org

Jim Collison, President

A weekly e-newsletter published by Employers of America.
Cost: $149.00
Frequency: Weekly
Circulation: 600
Founded in 1976

17236 Hiring the Best
Briefings Publishing Group
1101 King St
Suite 110
Alexandria, VA 22314-2944

703-548-3800
800-888-2084
FAX 703-684-2136
Home Page: www.briefings.com

Deirdre Hackett, Editor
William G Dugan, Publisher
Tina Ragland, Editorial Assistant
Lois Willingham, Marketing Manager

A publication designed to help executives recruit, screen, and retain the best employees.
Cost: $697.00
8 Pages
Frequency: Monthly
Circulation: 1300
Founded in 1981
Mailing list available for rent: 6000 names at $125 per M
Printed in 2 colors on matte stock

17237 Human Resource Department Management Report
Institute of Management and Administration
3 Bethesda Metro Center
Suite 250
Bethesda, MD 20814-5377

703-341-3500
800-372-1033
FAX 800-253-0332
Home Page: www.ioma.com

Shows HR department heads how to boost staff motivation and productivity, improve department automation, and cut costs while improving service.
Cost: $299.00
Frequency: Monthly

17238 Human Resources Management Reporter
Thomson Reuters

2395 Midway Rd
Carrollton, TX 75006

646-822-2000
800-431-9025
FAX 888-216-1929
E-Mail: trta.lei-support@thomsonreuters.com
Home Page: www.ria.thomsonreuters.com

Elaine Yadlon, Plant Manager
Thomas H Glocer, CEO & Director
Robert D Daleo, Chief Financial Officer
Kelli Crane, Senior Vice President & CIO

For personnel practitioners.
Founded in 1935

17239 IOMA's Pay for Performance Report

Institute of Management and Administration
3 Bethesda Metro Center
Suite 250
Bethesda, MD 20814-5377

703-341-3500
800-372-1033
FAX 800-253-0332
Home Page: www.ioma.com

Helps human resource and compensation executives improve their company's productivity through the use of variable pay and bonus programs for all types of employees.

17240 IOMA's Report on Managing Flexible Benefit Plans

Institute of Management and Administration
3 Bethesda Metro Center
Suite 250
Bethesda, MD 20814-5377

703-341-3500
800-372-1033
FAX 800-253-0332
Home Page: www.ioma.com

Information to manage a firm's flex plan.
Cost: $245.00
16 Pages
Frequency: Monthly

17241 IT Services Business Report

Staffing Industry Analysts
881 Fremont Ave
Suite A3
Los Altos, CA 94024-5637

650-948-9303
800-950-9496
FAX 650-232-2360
Home Page: www.sireport.com

Ron Mester, President/CEO
Peter Yessne, Chairman/Publisher

Business news and industry trends analysis for professionals.
Cost: $297.00
Frequency: Monthly
Founded in 1989

17242 Information Advisor

Information Advisory Services
143 Old Marlton Pike
Medford, NJ 08055-8750

609-654-6266
FAX 609-654-4309
E-Mail: dpanara@infotoday.com
Home Page: www.informationadvisor.com

Robert Berkman, Editor

Compares and evaluates business information services - print, online and CD-ROM. Covers international data, information quality, and new noteworthy products.
Frequency: Monthly
Circulation: 700

17243 International Council for Small Business

2201 G Street NW
Suite 315
Washington, DC 20052

202-944-0704
FAX 202-994-4930
E-Mail: icsb@gwu.edu
Home Page: www.icsb.org

David Smallbone, President
Don B. Bradley, III, President-Elect
Rita Grant, VP/Finance/Control
Ayman El Tarabishy, Executive Director
Michael Bataglia, Operations Manager

Promotes the growth and development of small businesses by bringing together researchers, educators, practitioners, and policy makers from around the world.
2000+ Members
Founded in 1956
Printed in 2 colors on glossy stock

17244 International Management Council

608 S 114th Street
Omaha, NE 68154-3153

402-330-6310
800-688-9622
FAX 402-330-7424
E-Mail: imcoffice@msn.com
Home Page: www.imc-ymca.org/join.html

Jodeen Sterba, National Administrator

Information on developing leadership and management skills through a network of shared experiences and education.
Printed in 2 colors on matte stock

17245 International Quality

Underwriters Laboratories
2600 N.W. Lake Rd.
Camas, WA 98607-8542

847-412-0136
877-854-3577
FAX 360-817-6278
E-Mail: cec.us@us.ul.com
Home Page: www.ul.com

Keith E Williams, CEO
John Drengenberg, Manager Consumer Affairs

Free standards and other quality management topics.
Frequency: Monthly
Circulation: 18000
Founded in 1894

17246 Inventory Reduction Report

Institute of Management and Administration
3 Bethesda Metro Center
Suite 250
Bethesda, MD 20814-5377

703-341-3500
800-372-1033
FAX 800-253-0332
Home Page: www.ioma.com

Focuses on reducing inventory costs, JIT methods and improving profitability.
Cost: $245.00
16 Pages
Frequency: Monthly

17247 Issues and Observations

Center for Creative Leadership & Jossay-Bass
350 Sansome Street
San Francisco, CA 94104-1304

415-334-4700
888-378-2537
FAX 800-605-2665

E-Mail: info@ccl.org
Home Page: www.ccl.org

John Alexander, President
Patricia Ohlott, President, Chief Executive Officer

Contains articles about leadership and management.
Cost: $99.00
Frequency: Quarterly
Circulation: 3000
ISSN: 1093-6092
Founded in 1970

17248 Job Safety and Health

Bureau of National Affairs
1801 S Bell St
Arlington, VA 22202-4501

703-341-3000
800-372-1033
FAX 800-253-0332
E-Mail: customercare@bna.net
Home Page: www.bnabooks.com
Social Media: *Facebook, Twitter, LinkedIn*

Paul N Wojcik, CEO

A biweekly review of workplace health and safety regulations, policies, practices and trends.
Cost: $898.00
ISSN: 0149-7510
Founded in 1929

17249 Jots and Jolts

Economics Press
12 Daniel Road
Fairfield, NJ 07004-2565

973-227-1224
FAX 973-227-9742

John Beckley, Publisher

Monthly planner for supervisors; includes information management theory.
Cost: $1.00
Circulation: 32000

17250 Kennedy's Career Strategist

Career Strategies
1150 Wilmette Avenue
Wilmette, IL 60091-2603

847-251-1661
800-728-1709
FAX 847-251-5191
E-Mail: mmkcareer@aol.com
Home Page:
www.moatskennedy.com/newsletter.html

Marilyn Moat Kennedy, Editor
Linda Mitchell, Production Manager
Cost: $65.00
Frequency: Monthly
ISSN: 0891-2572
Founded in 1986

17251 Laboratory Industry Report

Institute of Management and Administration
3 Bethesda Metro Center
Suite 250
Bethesda, MD 20814-5377

703-341-3500
800-372-1033
FAX 800-253-0332
Home Page: www.ioma.com

An insider's view of the lab industry's most important business and financial trends.
Cost: $449.00

17252 Law Office Management & Administration Report

Institute of Management and Administration

3 Bethesda Metro Center
Suite 250
Bethesda, MD 20814-5377

703-341-3500
800-372-1033
FAX 800-253-0332
Home Page: www.ioma.com

Covers the daily management concerns relevant for law firm administrators, office managers, and others.
Cost: $489.00
Frequency: Monthly
Founded in 1983

17253 Leadership Strategies
Briefings Publishing Group
1101 King St
Suite 110
Alexandria, VA 22314-2944

703-548-3800
800-888-2084
FAX 703-684-2136
Home Page: www.briefings.com

Deirdre Hackett, Editor
Jacqueline Stonis, Production Manager
William G. Duggan, Group Publisher
Lois Willingham, Marketing Manager

A publication designed to sharpen your management and leadership abilities, improve your productivity, and accelerate your professional success.
Cost: $199.00
8 Pages
Frequency: Monthly
Circulation: 8500
Founded in 1981
Mailing list available for rent: 7000 names at $125 per M
Printed in 2 colors on matte stock

17254 Management Policies and Personnel Law
Business Research Publications
1533 H Street NW
Suite 200W
Washington, DC 20005-1005

202-364-6473
800-822-6338
FAX 202-466-3509

Susan Sonnesyn-Brooks, Editor

Leading newsletter designed to give managers an inside view into the best run companies.
Frequency: BiWeekly

17255 Manager's Legal Bulletin
Alexander Hamilton Institute
70 Hilltop Rd
Suite 220
Ramsey, NJ 07446-2816

201-825-3377
800-879-2441
FAX 201-825-8696
E-Mail: custsvc@ahipubs.com
Home Page: www.ahipubs.com

Schuyler T Jenks, President

Shows managers how to handle problems in the workplace without provoking lawsuits for illegal discrimination in hiring, firing, promotions, sexual harassment or discipline decisions.
Cost: $66.00
4 Pages
Frequency: Fortnightly
Circulation: 20000
Founded in 1909
Mailing list available for rent: 8M names at $125 per M
Printed in 2 colors on matte stock

17256 Managing Benefits Plans
Institute of Management and Administration

3 Bethesda Metro Center
Suite 250
Bethesda, MD 20814-5377

703-341-3500
800-372-1033
FAX 800-253-0332
Home Page: www.ioma.com

The result of combining two newsletters into one, stronger report. Managers who oversee the enrollment, communications, and administration of employee benefits are the best subscribers to MBP.
Cost: $399.00
Founded in 1982

17257 Managing Customer Service
Institute of Management and Administration
3 Bethesda Metro Center
Suite 250
Bethesda, MD 20814-5377

703-341-3500
800-372-1033
FAX 800-253-0332
Home Page: www.ioma.com

Boost the productivity, efficiency and visibility of your department, and keep it on the cutting edge.

17258 Managing Logistics
Institute of Management and Administration
3 Bethesda Metro Center
Suite 250
Bethesda, MD 20814-5377

703-341-3500
800-372-1033
FAX 800-253-0332
Home Page: www.ioma.com

Covers new technologies and strategies, how to negotiate with outsourced service providers.

17259 Managing Training & Development
Institute of Management and Administration
3 Bethesda Metro Center
Suite 250
Bethesda, MD 20814-5377

703-341-3500
800-372-1033
FAX 800-253-0332
Home Page: www.ioma.com

Covers all aspects of measuring, learning, development, getting employees trained for their jobs, and justifying the cost of training to upper management.

17260 Medical Group Management Update
Medical Group Management Association
104 Inverness Ter E
Englewood, CO 80112-5313

303-799-1111
FAX 303-643-9599
E-Mail: infocenter@mgma.com
Home Page: www.mgma.com

William Jessee, CEO
Eileen Barker, senior Vice President
Anders Gilberg, senior Vice President
Natalie Jamieson, Administrative Assistant

Monthly association newspaper offering up-to-the-minute articles on current legislation, practical management, health care trends, association activities and other timely subjects.
Frequency: Monthly

17261 Object-Oriented Strategies
Cutter Information Corporation
37 Broadway
Suite 1
Arlington, MA 02474-5500

781-648-1950
800-888-8939
FAX 781-648-1950

E-Mail: service@cutter.com
Home Page: www.cutter.com

Paul Harman, Editor
Kim Leonard, Customer Service Director
Karen Coburn, CEO
Hillel Glazer, Senior Consultant
Ron Blitstein, Director

Designed for managers and developers of object-oriented systems.
Cost: $495.00
16 Pages
Frequency: Monthly
Founded in 1986

17262 Orlando Business Journal
Business Journals
Ste 700
255 S Orange Ave
Orlando, FL 32801-5007

407-649-8470
888-649-6254
FAX 407-420-1625
E-Mail: orlando@bizjournals.com
Home Page: www.bizjournals.com/orlando

Ann Sonntag, Publisher
Ken Cogburn, Editor
Cindy Barth, Managing Editor
Sue Ross, Ad Director
Alan Byrd, Director of Marketing/Circulation
Cost: $79.00
64 Pages
Frequency: Weekly
ISSN: 8750-8686
Founded in 1995
Printed in 4 colors on newsprint stock

17263 PMI Today
Project Management Institute
14 Campus Blvd
Newtown Square, PA 19073-3299

610-356-4600
FAX 610-356-4647
Home Page: www.pmi.org

Gregory Balestrero, CEO
Mark Langley, Managing Director
Louis Mercken, Chairman
Van Goldfisher, Editor
Jane Farley, Secretary

A monthly newsletter published by the Project Management Institute.
6 Pages
Frequency: Monthly
Circulation: 150000
Founded in 1969
Mailing list available for rent

17264 PSMJ Principal Strategies
PSMJ Resources
10 Midland Avenue
Newton, MA 02458-1000

617-965-0055
800-537-7765
FAX 617-965-5152
E-Mail: info@psmj.com
Home Page: www.psmj.com

Frank Stasiowski, Production Manager

Offers management tactics and techniques for the design industry.
Cost: $195.00
8 Pages
Frequency: Monthly
Founded in 1974
Mailing list available for rent at $125 per M
Printed in 2 colors on matte stock

17265 PSMJ Project Delivery
PSMJ Resources
10 Midland Avenue
Newton, MA 02458-1000

617-965-0055
800-537-7765

FAX 617-965-5152
E-Mail: info@psmj.com
Home Page: www.psmj.com

Frank Stasiowski, Production Manager

Offers project management tactics and techniques to the design industry.
Cost: $196.00
8 Pages
Frequency: Monthly
Mailing list available for rental $125 per M
Printed in 2 colors on matte stock

17266 Payroll Manager's Letter

Bureau of Business Practice
111 8th Avenue
7th Floor
New York, NY 10011

212-771-0600
800-638-8437
E-Mail: rfecustomer@aspenpubl.com
Home Page: www.aspenpublishers.com

Marc Jennings, VP
Gerry Centrowitz, VP, Marketing and Commu

Contains concise, plain-English explanations of the latest federal payroll developments which helps companies comply with rapidly changing employment tax and minimum wage/overtime laws.
Cost: $235.00
8 Pages
Circulation: 7000
Founded in 1920
Printed in one color on glossy stock

17267 Personal Report for the Administrative Professional

National Institute of Business Management
1750 Old Meadow Rd
Suite 302
Mc Lean, VA 22102-4304

703-905-8000
800-543-2049
FAX 703-905-8042
E-Mail: customer@nibm.net
Home Page: www.nibm.net

Steve Sturm, President
Phil Ash, Marketing Director
Cost: $54.00
10 Pages
Frequency: Monthly
ISSN: 1049-4855
Founded in 1937

17268 Preventing Business Fraud

Institute of Management and Administration
3 Bethesda Metro Center
Suite 250
Bethesda, MD 20814-5377

703-341-3500
800-372-1033
FAX 800-253-0332
Home Page: www.ioma.com

Stop corporate fraud before it happens. Get guidance on how to avoid supplier collusion and kickbacks, false invoicing, health insurance and workers' compensation fraud, payroll, petty cash and T and E overstatements, theft of equipment and materials and more.

17269 Professional Advisor

Int'l Society of Speakers, Authors & Consultants
PO Box 6432
Kingwood, TX 77325-6432

281-441-3558
FAX 281-441-3538

Bernard Zick, Publisher

Includes information of the consulting industry.
Cost: $120.00
10 Pages
Frequency: Monthly

17270 Profit Line

Ernst and Young
9920 Pacific Heights Blvd
Suite 200
San Diego, CA 92121

858-452-6800
800-200-7763
FAX 858-452-6998
E-Mail: media@profitline.com
Home Page: www.profitline.com

Gary Martino, Chief Financial Officer
Business information newsletter for entrepreneurs.

17271 Quality Assurance Bulletin

Bureau of Business Practice
76 Ninth Avenue
7th Floor
New York, NY 10011

212-771-0600
FAX 212-771-0885
Home Page: www.aspenpublishers.com
Social Media: *Facebook, Twitter, LinkedIn*

Mark Dorman, CEO
Gustavo Dobles, VP Operations

Helps quality professionals improve the company's question-answer function.
Cost: $118.80
8 Pages
Frequency: 2 per year

17272 Real Estate & Leasing Report

Business Journals
120 W Morehead St
Suite 420
Charlotte, NC 28202-1874

704-973-1200
FAX 704-973-1201
Home Page: www.citybiznetwork.com

George Conley, President
Joanne Skoog, Editor
Cost: $70.00
70 Pages
Frequency: Weekly
ISSN: 0887-5588
Printed in 4 colors on newsprint stock

17273 Report on Salary Surveys

Institute of Management and Administration
3 Bethesda Metro Center
Suite 250
Bethesda, MD 20814-5377

703-341-3500
800-372-1033
FAX 800-253-0332
Home Page: www.ioma.com

Analyzes data from major salary surveys released during the year by the biggest compensation survey companies, WorldatWork, SHRM, state HR societies, and the Big Four accounting firms, to give readers an overview of those expensive, hard-to-manage services.
Cost: $429.00
Founded in 1993

17274 Rodenhauser Report

Consulting Information Services
191 Washington Street
Keene, NH 03431

603-355-1560
Home Page: www.consultinginfo.com

Tom Rodenhauser, President

Rodenhauser Report is a monthly electronic briefing that forecasts consulting trends for se-

nior management advisors and business executives.
Frequency: Monthly
Founded in 1998

17275 Servicing Management

LDJ Corporation
70 Edwin Avenue
PO Box 2180
Waterbury, CT 06708-2180

203-755-0158
800-325-6745
FAX 203-755-3480
Home Page: www.sm-online.com/

Paul Zackin, Publisher
Michael Bates, Editor
June Han, Circulation Manager
Jeanette Laliberte, Subscriptions

Delivers news and how-to advice to executives and personnel in the servicing of mortgage loans nationwide.
Cost: $48.00
Frequency: Monthly
Circulation: 18000
Founded in 1969

17276 Small-Biz Growth

Support Services Alliance
PO Box 130
Schoharie, NY 12157-0130

518-295-7966
800-322-3920
FAX 518-295-8556
E-Mail: info@ssamembers.com
Home Page: www.smallbizgrowth.com

Steven Cole, President

Keeps SSA members and their employees up-to-date on developments affecting small-business communities.
Cost: $25.00
Frequency: Monthly
Circulation: 17,000
Founded in 1977

17277 Small-Business Strategies

Page Group
PO Box 116
Dundee, IL 60118-0116

847-695-7887

Phillip Grisolia, Publisher

Contains practical ideas for use in successfully starting and profitably managing small businesses. Accepts advertising.
Cost: $95.00
4 Pages
Frequency: BiWeekly

17278 Sound Thinking

Jay Mitchell Associates
PO Box 1285
Fairfield, IA 52556-0022

641-472-4087
FAX 641-472-2071

Jay Mitchell, Publisher

Notes and comments on the radio industry and related fields, specializing in an outside-in view.
Cost: $65.00
2 Pages
Frequency: Monthly

17279 Source

Rachel PR Services
1650 S Pacific Coast Highway
Suite 200C
Redondo Beach, CA 90277-5625
Janis Brett-Elspas, Editor
Jamie Steiner, Advertising/Sales

Annual reference guide for job hunters in advertising, public relations, marketing and jour-

nalism offering more than 2,000 resources for finding jobs at all levels in all 50 states. Listings includes job banks, job hotlines, executive recruiters, books/directories, trade publications, industry associations and more.
Cost: $39.00
40 Pages
Frequency: Annual
Circulation: 30,000
Printed in on matte stock

17280 Southeastern Association Executive
Special Edition Publishing
999 Douglas Ave
Suite 3317
Altamonte Spgs, FL 32714-2063

407-862-7737
FAX 407-862-8102
E-Mail: specedpub@earthlink.net
Home Page: www.specedpub.com

A Sciuto, Publisher
Nichole Wunduke, Editor
Betty Harper, Director of Sales & Marke

Monthly news magazine serving associations meetings and hospitality executives in the southeast .
25 Pages
Frequency: Monthly
Circulation: 5200
Founded in 1973
Printed in 4 colors on glossy stock

17281 Staffing Industry Report
Staffing Industry Analysts
881 Fremont Ave
Suite A3
Los Altos, CA 94024-5637

650-948-9303
800-950-9496
FAX 650-232-2360
E-Mail: memberservices@staffingindustry.com
Home Page: www.staffingindustry.com

Ron Mester, Managing Director
Tim Murphy, Editor
Joyce Routson, Managing Editor
Greg Palmer, CEO
Jason Ezratty, Managing Partner

A twice monthly newsletter for temporary help, staff leasing and employment service companies. Industry information, company news, training and automation resource reviews, financial coverage, labor demand and supply analysis, key interviews. Association news, public company stock tables. SI Report sponsors an annual Staffing Industry Executive Forum in April. Emphasis is on business news. Includes advertising supplement.
Cost: $385.00
Circulation: 3000
Founded in 1989
Mailing list available for rent: 3500 names
Printed in 2 colors on matte stock

17282 Success in Recruiting and Retaining
National Institute of Business Management
1750 Old Meadow Rd
Suite 302
Mc Lean, VA 22102-4304

703-905-8000
800-543-2049
FAX 703-905-8042
E-Mail: customer@nibm.net

Steve Sturm, President
10 Pages
Frequency: Monthly
ISSN: 1049-4855

17283 Successful Self-Management
Stahlka Associates

60 Westchester Road
Williamsville, NY 14221-5021

716-347-7070
FAX 716-626-4188
E-Mail: wendystahlka@verizon.net
Home Page: www.stahlkamarketing.com

Clayton A Stahlka, Production Manager
Wendy Stahlka, President

Mastering changes in yourself and your environment to be the best you can be with what you have.
Cost: $24.00
5 Pages
Frequency: Quarterly
Circulation: 1800
Founded in 1975
Printed in one color on matte stock

17284 Supplier Selection and Management Report
Institute of Management and Administration
3 Bethesda Metro Center
Suite 250
Bethesda, MD 20814-5377

703-341-3500
800-372-1033
FAX 800-253-0332
Home Page: www.ioma.com

Focuses on supplier selection, partnering and management issues.
Cost: $289.00
16 Pages
Frequency: Monthly
Circulation: 180,000
Founded in 1980

17285 Travel Manager's Executive Briefing
Health Resources Publishing
1913 Atlantic Ave
Suite 200
Manasquan, NJ 08736-1067

732-292-1100
888-843-6242
FAX 732-292-1111
E-Mail: info@themcic.com
Home Page: www.healthresourcesonline.com

Robert K Jenkins, Publisher
Judith Granholm, Regional Director
Brett Powell, Regional Director
Alice Burron, Director

A digest published twice a month that covers developments in the field of travel and expense cost control. Topics include discounts in air fare, car rentals, hotel bills, travel alternatives, phone savings, planning for meetings trends in government legislation affecting business travel costs, and case histories of companies that have successfully cut costs. Ideal for travel managers of corporations, small businesses and nonprofit organizations.
Cost: $447.00
ISSN: 0272-569X
Founded in 1978

17286 WACRA News
World Assoc for Case Method Research & Application
23 Mackintosh Avenue
Needham, MA 02492-1218

781-444-8982
800-523-6468
FAX 781-444-1548
E-Mail: wacra@rcn.com
Home Page: www.wacra.org

Dr Hans E Klein, President/Executive Director
Dr Charles H Patti, Publications Director

17287 WACRA Newsletter
World Assoc for Case Method Research & Application

23 Mackintosh Avenue
Needham, MA 02492-1218

781-444-8982
800-523-6468
FAX 781-444-1548
E-Mail: hans.klein@wacra.org
Home Page: www.wacra.org

Dr Hans E Klein, President/Executive Director
Dr Charles H Patti, Publications Director
Frequency: Biannual

17288 Wage-Hour Compliance Report
Institute of Management and Administration
3 Bethesda Metro Center
Suite 250
Bethesda, MD 20814-5377

703-341-3500
800-372-1033
FAX 800-253-0332
Home Page: www.ioma.com

Covers white-collar exemptions, how to pay employees for rest and overtime periods, legal holidays, how to handle vacation, severance and negotiated termination pay rules, and give managers a concise rundown of new federal and state withholding and minimum wage changes, new rules, rates and requirements.

17289 What's Ahead in Personnel
Remy Publishing Company
1439 W Summerdale Ave
Suite 440
Chicago, IL 60640-2115

773-769-6760
800-542-6670
FAX 773-464-0166
E-Mail: webmaster@passportnewsletter.com
Home Page: www.passportnewsletter.com

Contains information on current HR trends, legal issues and company practices.
Frequency: SemiMonthly

17290 What's Working In Consulting
Kennedy Information
1 Pheonix Mill Lane
Floor 3
Fitzwilliam, NH 03447

603-924-1006
800-531-0007
E-Mail: customerservice@kennedyinfo.com
Home Page: www.kennedyinfo.com

Alan Weiss, Editor

Provides practical guidance on improving consulting skills and managing a consulting practice.
Cost: $197.00
Frequency: Monthly
ISSN: 1535-3036

17291 Women in Business
Business Journal of Portland
851 Sw 6th Ave
Suite 500
Portland, OR 97204-1342

503-274-8733
800-486-3289
FAX 503-219-3450
E-Mail: borben@bizjournals.com
Home Page: www.bizjournals.com/portland

Craig Wessel, Publisher
Dan McMillan, Managing Editor
Rob Smith, Editor
George Vaughan, Advertising Director

Special supplement of The Business Journal that celebrates the achievements of women making a difference in the business world and

community
Cost: $89.00
36 Pages
ISSN: 0742-6550
Printed in 4 colors on newsprint stock

17292 Work and Family Life
230 W 55th Street
Apartment 6B
New York, NY 10019-5212

212-557-3555
FAX 212-557-6555
E-Mail: susan@workandfamilylife.com
Home Page: www.workandfamily.com

Ellen Galinsky, Executive Editor
Susan Ginsberg, Editor/Publisher
Anne Perryman, Editor
Susan Seitel, President

Provides information and practical solutions to
a wide range of family, job and health issues.
Purpose is to help readers find pleasure and sat-
isfaction in their many roles at work, at home,
and in their communities.
Cost: $ 295.00
Frequency: Monthly
Circulation: 50000
Founded in 1984
Printed in 4 colors on matte stock

17293 Working Smart
National Institute of Business Management
1750 Old Meadow Rd
Suite 302
Mc Lean, VA 22102-4304

703-905-8000
800-543-2055
FAX 703-905-8042
E-Mail: customer@nibm.net
Home Page: www.nibm.net

Steve Sturm, President
Morey Stettner, Editor
Phil Ash, Marketing Director

Ready, relevant and reliable advice for manag-
ers on workplace issues.
Cost: $48.00
10 Pages
Frequency: Monthly
ISSN: 1049-4855
Founded in 1937
Printed in 2 colors on matte stock

Magazines & Journals

17294 AFSM: Professional Journal
Assiocation for Services Management
International
11031 Via Frontera
Suite A
San Diego, CA 92127

239-275-7887
800-333-9786
FAX 239-275-0794
E-Mail: info@afsmi.org
Home Page: www.afsmi.org

Jb Wood, President/CEO
John Schoenewald, Executive Director

A journal aimed at management issues.
64 Pages
Frequency: Monthly
Founded in 1975

17295 APICS: The Performance Advantage
APICS Association for Operations
Management

8430 West Bryn Mawr Avenue
Suite 1000
Chicago, IL 60631

773-867-1777
800-444-2742
FAX 773-639-3000
E-Mail: webmaster@apics.org.
Home Page: www.apics.org
Social Media: *Facebook, Twitter, LinkedIn,
Youtube*

Doug Kelly, Editor
Jennifer Procter, Managing Editor
Beth Rennie, Senior Editor

Provides comprehensive articles on enterprise
resources planning, supply chain management,
e-business, materials management and produc-
tion and inventory management.
Cost: $65.00
64 Pages
Frequency: 10/Year
Circulation: 66,000
ISSN: 1056-0017
*Mailing list available for rent: 40,000 names at
$100 per M*
Printed in 4 colors on glossy stock

**17296 American Academy of Medical
Administrators**
American Acadeny of Medical
Administrators
701 Lee St
Suite 600
Des Plaines, IL 60016-4516

847-759-8601
FAX 847-759-8602
E-Mail: info@aameda.org
Home Page: www.aameda.org

Renee Schleichar, CEO
Holly Estal, Director of Education
Guy Snyder, Director of Education
Rhonda Guptill, Chief Financial Officer
24 Pages
Frequency: Quarterly
Founded in 1957
Mailing list available for rent
Printed in 2 colors on glossy stock

17297 American Cemetery
Kates-Boylston Publications
11300 Rockville Pike
Suite 1100
Rockville, MD 20852

800-500-4585
800-500-4585
FAX 301-287-2150
E-Mail: AmericanFD@aol.com
Home Page: www.kates-boylston.com

Adrian F Boylston, Publisher
Thomas Lorge, Executive Director
Thomas Parmalee, Executive Director
Amy Fidalgo, Production Manager

Features articles on cemetery administration,
maintenance, sales and public relations. Also
includes coverage of conventions, new ceme-
teries and new building ideas.
Cost: $39.95
Frequency: Monthly
Circulation: 5800

**17298 American Small Businesses
Association**
206 E College St
Suite 201
Grapevine, TX 76051-5381

817-488-8770
800-801-2722
FAX 817-251-8578

Bill Will Sr, President
Wanda Johnson, Bookkeeper

Represents the interests of small businesses.
Printed in on glossy stock

17299 Association Management Magazine
American Society of Association Executives
1575 I St Nw
Suite 11
Washington, DC 20005-1103

202-626-2700
888-950-2723
FAX 202-371-8315
E-Mail: publicpolicy@asaenet.org
Home Page: www.asaenet.org/

Karl Ely, Publisher
Keith C Skillman, Editor

Serves the field of trade business professional
and philanthropic associations.
Cost: $30.00
Frequency: Monthly
Circulation: 22507
Founded in 1920

**17300 Benchmarking: A Practitioner's
Guide for Becoming & Staying the
Best**
Quality & Productivity Management
Association
300 N Martingale Road
Suite 230
Schaumburg, IL 60173-2407

FAX 847-619-3383

William Ginnodo, Publisher
Lesley Williams, Publications Manager

Promotes benchmarking as a technique for
comparing processes, products or services with
the world's best encouraging ways to do things
faster, better, and less cost.

17301 Bits and Pieces
Economics Press
12 Daniel Road
Fairfield, NJ 07004-2565

973-227-1224
FAX 973-227-9742

Arthur Lenehan, Publisher

Management and common sense plus anecdotes
and quotes.
Cost: $1.00
Circulation: 266,000

17302 Bloomberg Businessweek
Bloomberg
731 Lexington Avenue
New York, NY 10022

212-318-2000
800-955-4003
FAX 212-617-5999
Home Page: www.bloomberg.com

Daniel L. Doctoroff, President/CEO
Peter T. Grauer, Chairman
Beth Mazzeo, Head of Global Data Products
Div.
Thomas F. Secunda, Head of Global Financial
Products
Matthew Winkler, Editor-in-Chief

Offers a global perspective to help senior executives profit from faster, smarter, and more informed decisions. Bloomberg Businessweek
reaches more C-level executives than any other
business magazine.
Cost: $4.95
Frequency: Weekly
Founded in 1981

17303 Building Operating Management
Trade Press Publishing Corporation
2100 W Florist Avenue
Milwaukee, WI 53209-3799

414-228-7701
FAX 414-228-1134

E-Mail: info@tradepress.com
Home Page: www.tradepress.com

Edward Sullivan, Editor
Bobbie Reid, Production Director
Scott Cunningham, Associate Publisher
Eric Muench, Director of Circulation
Robert J Wisniewski, President/CEO

Serves the field of facilities management, encompassing commercial building: office buildings, real estate/property management firms, developers, financial institutions, insurance companies, apartment complexes, civic/convention centers, including members of the Building Owners and Managers Association
Frequency: Monthly
Circulation: 70000
Founded in 1943

17304 Business Facilities

Group C Communications
PO Box 2060
Red Bank, NJ 07701-0901

732-842-7433
800-524-0337
FAX 732-758-6634
E-Mail: webmaster@groupc.com
Home Page: www.groupc.com

Edgar T Coene, President
Ted Coene, Publisher
Karim Khan, Editor
Beth Sicignano, Marketing Manager
Connie Donatantonio, Circulation Manager

Magazine covering the fields of corporation expansion, economic development and real estate.
Cost: $30.00
Frequency: Monthly
Circulation: 30309
Founded in 1969

17305 Business First

Business News
455 S 4th St
Suite 278
Louisville, KY 40202-2551

502-583-1731
FAX 502-587-1703
E-Mail: borben@bizjournals.com
Home Page: www.bizjournals.com

Tom Monahan, President
Carol Brando Timmons, Editor
Judith Berzof, Associate Editor
Rebecca Ray, Assistant Editor
Cost: $83.00
Frequency: Monthly

17306 C2M Consulting to Management

Journal of Management Consulting
858 Longview Road
Burlingame, CA 94010-6974

650-342-1954
FAX 650-344-5005
Home Page: www.c2m.com

E Michael Shays, Publisher
Marsha Lewin, Chairman Editorial

The journal, which is read in over 60 countries, presents methods and processes for management consultants helping them to enlarge and perfect their skills and service to clients.
Cost: $80.00
Frequency: Quarterly
Circulation: 5000
ISSN: 0158-7778
Founded in 1981

17307 CFO: the Magazine for Chief Financial Officers

CFO Publishing Corporation

253 Summer St
Suite 3
Boston, MA 02210-1114

617-345-9700
FAX 617-951-4090
Home Page: www.cfo.com

Frank Quigley, President

Features insurance, cash management, taxes, benefits, accounting, buyers guide.
Circulation: 365,409

17308 COM-SAC, Computer Security, Audit & Control

Management Advisory Services & Publications
PO Box 81151
Wellesley Hills, MA 02481-0001

781-235-2895
FAX 781-235-5446
E-Mail: Info@masp.com
Home Page: www.masp.com

Presents tutorials and articles of current interest in computer security and audit, presents a comprehensive digest of all key articles and books published on the fields of computer security and control.
Cost: $98.00
Frequency: Quarterly
Founded in 1973

17309 Central Penn Business Journal

Journal Publications
101 N 2nd Street
2nd Floor
Harrisburg, PA 17101-1600

717-236-4300
FAX 717-909-6803
E-Mail: webmaster@journalpub.com
Home Page: www.centralpennbusiness.com

David A Schankweiler, Publisher
Gary Nalbandian, CEO/President
Jason Klinger, Editor

Provides comprehensive news for the business community.
Cost: $64.95
56 Pages
Frequency: Weekly
Circulation: 10,500
ISSN: 1058-3599
Founded in 1985

17310 Chain Leader

Raymond Herrmann
2000 Clearwater Drive
Oak Brook, IL 60523

630-288-8242
FAX 630-288-8215
Home Page: www.chainleader.com

Mary Boltz Chapman, Editor-in-Chief
Maya Norris, Managing Editor
Ray Herrmann, Publisher

Targets senior management of chain restaurant companies.
Frequency: Monthly
Circulation: 17323
Founded in 1960

17311 Chief Executive

Chief Executive Group
110 Summit Avenue
Montvale, NJ 07645

201-930-5959
FAX 201-930-5956
E-Mail: contact@chiefexecutive.net
Home Page: www.chiefexecutive.net

Carol Evans, Publisher
Robin Uhl, Circulation Manager
William J. Holstein, Editor-in-Chief
Edward M. Kopko, CEO/Chairman
Chris Chalk, Vice President of Sales

A journal of strategy and analysis by and for chief executives.
75 Pages
Frequency: Monthly
Circulation: 42000
Founded in 1976

17312 Club Management Magazine

Finan Publishing Company
107 W Pacific
Saint Louis, MO 63119

314-961-6644
FAX 314-961-4809
Home Page: www.club-mgmt.com

Thomas J Finan, Publisher/Editor
Dee Kaplan, Publisher
Dianne Dierkes, Circulation Manager

The resource for successful club operations.
Cost: $26.95
Frequency: 3 Issues a year
Founded in 1927
Mailing list available for rent: 21,000 names
Printed in 4 colors on glossy stock

17313 Commitment Plus

Quality & Productivity Management Association
300 N Martingale Road
Suite 230
Schaumburg, IL 60173-2407

FAX 847-619-3383

William Ginnodo, Editor/Author

This monthly newsletter is for managers who want to improve quality, productivity and service through people. It contains brief case studies, written primarily by QPMA staff, showing how operating managers, or their people, went about implementing improvements in their organizations' operating managers, and regularly reinforce the improvement message. This newsletter is free to members.
Cost: $95.00
4 Pages
Frequency: Monthly

17314 Competitive Intelligence Review

John Wiley & Sons
111 River St
Hoboken, NJ 07030-5790

201-748-6000
800-825-7550
FAX 201-748-6088
E-Mail: info@wiley.com
Home Page: www.wiley.com

William J Pesce, CEO

Collection and analysis of business information.
Cost: $68.95
Frequency: Quarterly
Circulation: 3250
Founded in 1807

17315 Consulting Magazine

Kennedy Information
One Phoenix Mill Lane
Floor 3
Peterborough, NH 03458

603-924-1006
800-531-0007
E-Mail: bookstore@kennedyinfo.com
Home Page: www.kennedyinfo.com

Jack Sweeney, Editor-in-Chief
Mina Landrisina, Managing Director

The only magazine written exclusively for management consultants, consulting is dedicated to fostering performance excellence and career success. Consulting serves the information needs of those responsible for shaping the

business strategies of their clients.
Cost: $99.00
Frequency: Monthly
ISSN: 1525-4321
Founded in 1970

17316 Contingency Planning & Management
Witter Publishing Corporation
20 Commerce Street
Flemington, NJ 08822

908-788-0343
FAX 908-788-3782
Home Page: www.witterpublishing.com

Bob Joudanin, Publisher
Paul Kirvan, Editor
Courtney Witter, Print
Circulation/Subscriptions
Andrew Witter, President

Serves the fields of financial/banking, manufacturing industrial, transportation, utilities, telecommunications, health care, government, insurance and other allied fields.
Cost: $195.00
Frequency: Monthly
Founded in 1987

17317 Contingency Planning & Recovery Journal
Management Advisory Services & Publications
PO Box 81151
Wellesley Hills, MA 02481-0001

781-235-2895
FAX 781-235-5446
E-Mail: Info@masp.com
Home Page: www.masp.com

The only independent quarterly that is membership and subscriber supported. It presents current state of affairs in emergency preparedness, contingency planning and business resumption planning and business continuity.
Cost: $ 75.00
16 Pages
Frequency: Quarterly
Founded in 1972
Printed in 2 colors

17318 Corporate Meetings & Incentives
Penton Media Inc
10 Fawcett Street
Suite 500
Cambridge, MA 02138

847-763-9504
866-505-7173
E-Mail: shatch@meetingsnet.com
Home Page: www.meetingsnet.com
Social Media: *Facebook, Twitter, LinkedIn*

Susan Hatch, Editor

Serves those involved in organizing business meetings, conventions, corporate travel agencies, and related fields.
Cost: $87.00
Frequency: Monthly
Circulation: 32200
Founded in 1980
Printed in 4 colors

17319 Corporate Security
Strafford Publications
PO Box 13729
Atlanta, GA 30324-0729

404-881-1141
800-926-7926
FAX 404-881-0074
E-Mail: customerservice@straffordpub.com
Home Page: www.straffordpub.com

Richard Ossoff, Publisher
Joan McKenna, Editor
Marianne Mueller, Marketing

Intelligence briefing on the latest security developments, best practices, the most important trends and new technolgies.
Cost: $330.00
23 Pages
ISSN: 0889-0625
Founded in 1984

17320 Cost Engineering Journal
AACE International
1265 Suncrest Towne Centre Drive
Morgantown, WV 26505-1876

304-296-8444
800-858-2678
FAX 304-291-5728
E-Mail: info@aacei.org
Home Page: www.aacei.org

Marvin Gelhausen, Managing Editor
Noah Kinderknecht, Editor

International hournal of cost estimation, cost/schedule control, and project management read by cost professionals around the world to get the most up-to-date information about the profession.
Frequency: Monthly
Founded in 1956

17321 Crain's New York Business
Crain Communications
711 3rd Ave
New York, NY 10017-4014

212-210-0100
FAX 212-210-0200
E-Mail: customerservice@crainsnewyork.com.
Home Page: www.crainsnewyork.com
Social Media: *Facebook, Twitter, LinkedIn*

Norm Feldman, President

Dedicated to exclusive coverage of business in New York City, Crain's keeps tabs on the people, the companies, the products, the politics and much more.
Frequency: Weekly
Circulation: 61000
Mailing list available for rent

17322 Customer Interaction Solutions
Technology Marketing Corporation
800 Connecticut Ave
1st Floor East
Norwalk, CT 06854-1936

203-852-6800
800-243-6002
FAX 203-866-3326
E-Mail: tmc@tmcnet.com
Home Page: www.tmcnet.com
Social Media: *Twitter*

Rich Tehrani, CEO

Dedicated to teleservices and e-services outsourcing, marketing and customer relationship management issues.
Frequency: Monthly
Founded in 1972

17323 Decision Sciences Journal
Decision Sciences Institute
35 Broad Street
Atlanta, GA 30303

404-651-4000
FAX 404-413-7714
E-Mail: dsi@gsu.edu
Home Page: www.decisionsciences.org

Gary L Ragatz, President
Julie Kendall, Treasurer
Carol J. Latta, Executive Director
Terrell G. Williams, Marketing Director
Vicki Smith-Daniels, Editor

Scientific quantitative, behavioral and computational approaches to decision making.
Cost: $100.00
Frequency: Quarterly
Circulation: 5000
Founded in 1968

17324 Destination KC
Show-Me Publishing
306 E 12th Street
Suite 1014
Kansas City, MO 64106

816-358-8700
FAX 814-474-1111
E-Mail: ingrams@unicom.net

Joe Sweeney, Editor-in-Chief

Kansas City's business relocation and information guide.
Cost: $36.00
984 Pages
Frequency: Monthly
ISSN: 1046-9958
Printed in 4 colors on glossy stock

17325 Direct
Primedia
1166 Avenue of the Americas/10th Fl
New York, NY 10036

212-204-4200
FAX 913-514-6895
E-Mail: sales@rmsreprints.com
Home Page: www.penton.com

Eric Jacobson, Senior VP
Charles Vietri, Managing Editor
Cheryll Richter, Marketing Manager
Andria Gennlauderslager, Circulation Manager
Chris Meyer, Director, Corporate Communications

Serves the marketing and media industries.
Circulation: 46500
ISSN: 1046-4174
Printed in 4 colors

17326 Director
NFDA Publications
13625 Bishops Dr
Brookfield, WI 53005-6607

262-789-1880
800-228-6332
FAX 262-789-6977
E-Mail: nfda@nfda.org
Home Page: www.nfda.org

Christine Pepper, CEO
Chris Raymond, Editor
Benjamin Lund, Assistant Editor
Fay Spano, Director of Public Relations

The Director is specifically designed to inform and educate the funeral service professional in today's world.
Cost: $45.00
114 Pages
Frequency: Monthly
Circulation: 14,761
ISSN: 0199-3186
Founded in 1882
Printed in 4 colors on glossy stock

17327 Discovery
Cooper Group
381 Park Ave S
Suite 801
New York, NY 10016-8822

212-696-2512
FAX 212-696-2517
Home Page: www.cooperdirect.com

Harold Cooper, CEO

Focusing on critical management issues that drive growth, profitability and shareholder

value.
Cost: $10.00
Circulation: 1500
Founded in 1984

17328 Economist
PO Box 58524
Boulder, CO 80322-8524

303-945-1917
800-456-6086
FAX 303-604-7455
E-Mail: ukpressoffice@economist.com
Home Page: www.economist.com

Helen Alexander, CEO
Kate Cooke, Group Communications Manager
David Hanger, Publisher
James Wilson, Founder

The Economist is a news and business publication written for top business decision-makers and opinion leaders who need a wide range of information and views on world events. It explores the close links between domestic and international issues, business, finance, current affairs, science and technology.
160 Pages
Frequency: Weekly
Circulation: 1009759
ISSN: 0013-0613
Founded in 1843
Printed in 4 colors on glossy stock

17329 Executive Update
Greater Washington Society of Assn Executives
1300 Pennsylvania Avenue NW
Washington, DC 20004

202-048-8014
FAX 202-326-0995
Home Page: www.gwsae.org

Liz Whittenmore, Publisher
Scott Briscoe, Editor
Theresa Magner, Director Advertising
Jam Armstrong, Circulation Manager
Susane Sarsati, CEO/President

Association news aimed at the executive level.
120 Pages
Frequency: Monthly
Circulation: 13300
Founded in 1980

17330 Expansion Management
Penton Media
1166 Avenue of the Americas/10th Fl
New York, NY 10036

212-204-4200
FAX 216-696-6662
E-Mail: information@penton.com
Home Page: www.penton.com

Jane Cooper, Marketing
Bill King, Chief Editor
Jodi Svenson, Production Manager
Chris Meyer, Director, Corporate Communications
Mary Abood, Vice President

Employs charts, graphs and art to lead readers through well organized sections, such as regional reviews, state reports, industry news, case studies and international reports. Addresses the key issues that attract executives in companies that need facts on resource management.
Frequency: Monthly
Circulation: 45015
Founded in 1986

17331 Facilities Manager
APPA
1643 Prince St
Alexandria, VA 22314-2818

703-684-1446
FAX 703-549-2772

E-Mail: lander@appa.org
Home Page: www.appa.org

Steve Glazner, Editor
Anita Dosik, Managing Editor
Cost: $120.00
Frequency: Bimonthly
Circulation: 5,500
ISSN: 0882-7249

17332 Financial Management Journal
Financial Management Association International
4202 E Fowler Ave
Suite 3331
Tampa, FL 33620-9951

813-974-2084
FAX 813-974-3318
E-Mail: fma@coba.usf.edu
Home Page: www.fma.org

Jack S Rader, Executive Director
Jeffrey Coles, Advisory Editor

Financial Management serves both academicians and practitioners who are concerned with the financial management of non-financial businesses, financial institutions, and public and private not-for-profit organizations. The journal serves the profession by publishing significant new scholarly research in finance that is of the highest quality.
Frequency: Quarterly

17333 Financial Manager
Broadcast Cable Financial Management Association
550 W Frontage Rd
Suite 3600
Northfield, IL 60093-1243

847-716-7000
FAX 847-716-7004
E-Mail: info@mediafinance.org
Home Page: www.bcfm.com

Mary Collins, President
Jamie Smith, Director of Operations
Rachelle Brooks, BCCA Sales

A bi-monthly magazine published by the Broadcast Cable Financial Management Association.
Cost: $69.00
36 Pages
Circulation: 300
Founded in 1961
Mailing list available for rent: 1100 names at $495 per M

17334 Forbes Magazine
Forbes Media LLC.
60 5th Ave
New York, NY 10011-8868

212-620-2200
FAX 212-620-1857
E-Mail: readers@forbes.com
Home Page: www.forbes.com

Malcolm S Forbes Jr, CEO
Bruce Rogers, VP Marketing
Paul Maidment, Executive Editor
Michael Smith Maidment, VP, GM Operations

A magazine giving detailed information about business and finance.
Frequency: Monthly

17335 Fortune Magazine
Time Inc./Time Warner
1271 Avenue of the Americas
16th Floor
New York, NY 10020-1393

212-522-1212
800-274-6800
FAX 212-522-0602

Home Page: www.timeinc.com
Social Media: *Facebook, Twitter*

Laura Lang, CEO
Howard M. Averill, CFO
Leslie Picard, President
Stephanie George, Chief Marketing Officer
John Huey, Editor-in-Chief

FORTUNE is a global leader in business journalism. The magazine has a great history of providing analysis and news critical to business people.
Cost: $5.00
Frequency: Annual/18
Circulation: 1M
Founded in 1930

17336 Global IT Consulting Report
Kennedy Information
1 Kennedy Place
Route 12 S
Fitzwilliam, NH 03447

212-973-3855

Martin Zook, Editor

The business of information technology consulting, featuring news, analysis, benchmasking data and our exclusive Intelligence Briefing.
Cost: $895.00
16 Pages
Frequency: Monthly

17337 Golf Course Management
Golf Course Superintendents Association of America
1421 Research Park Dr
Lawrence, KS 66049-3859

785-841-2240
800-472-7878
FAX 785-832-4488
E-Mail: hrmail@gcsaa.org
Home Page: www.gcsaa.org

Mark Woodward, CEO
Lacy Stattelman, Marketing Specialist
Carla Sturgeon, Sales Coordinator
Shelly Howard, Publications Coordinator

Golf Course Superintendent, economical, research and commercial interests concerned with golf course management and improvement. Provides information, education and representation for golf course managment profession.
Cost: $ 48.00
Frequency: Monthly
Circulation: 40000
ISSN: 0192-3048
Founded in 1926

17338 HR Magazine
SHRM/Society for Human Resource Management
1800 Duke St
Alexandria, VA 22314-3494

703-535-6000
866-898-4724
FAX 703-535-6474
E-Mail: shrmeducation@shrm.org.
Home Page: www.shrm.org
Social Media: *Facebook, Twitter, LinkedIn, Youtube*

Susan R Meisinger, CEO
Leon Rubis, Editor

The world's leading HR resource, offering perspective and in-depth information to leading HR professionals for over 50 years.
Cost: $70.00
Frequency: Monthly
Circulation: 197000
ISSN: 1047-3149
Founded in 1956

17339 IJCRA
World Assoc for Case Method Research & Application

23 Mackintosh Avenue
Needham, MA 02492-1218

781-444-8982
800-523-6468
FAX 781-444-1548
E-Mail: wacra@rcn.com
Home Page: www.wacra.org

Dr Hans E Klein, President/Executive Director
Dr Charles H Patti, Publications Director

Provides members and case writers and case teachers from around the world the opportunity to share their work with colleagues, to learn from colleagues and to create an international network for ccase writing, case teaching and interactive teaching applications.
Frequency: Quarterly
ISSN: 1554-7752

17340 Information Resources Management Journal

Information Resources Management Association
701 E Chocolate Ave
Suite 200
Hershey, PA 17033-1240

717-533-8845
FAX 717-533-8861
E-Mail: members@irma-international.org
Home Page: www.irma-international.org

Jan Travers, Executive Director

An applied research, refereed, international journal providing coverage of challenges, opportunities, problems, trends, and solutions encountered by both scholars and practitioners in the field of information technology management.
Cost: $95.00
Frequency: Quarterly
ISSN: 1040-1628

17341 Institute of Management & Administration Newsletter

Institute of Management and Administration
3 Bethesda Metro Center
Suite 250
Bethesda, MD 20814-5377

703-341-3500
800-372-1033
FAX 800-253-0332
Home Page: www.ioma.com

Monthly newsletter that offers information for all those involved in international sales, looking for new distribution channels and how to reduce exports costs and risks.
Circulation: 180,000

17342 International Cemetery & Funeral Management

International Cemetery & Funeral Association
1895 Preston White Drive
Suite 220
Reston, VA 20191-5434

703-391-8400
800-645-7700
FAX 703-391-8416
Home Page: www.icfa.org

Susan Loving, Managing Editor
Larry Stuart Jr, General Manager

Serves as the primary communication vehicle for ICFA news, membership activities, legislation, marketing and management, including the financial aspects of cemetery and funeral home operation.
Cost: $25.00
64 Pages
Circulation: 6200
ISSN: 0270-5281
Founded in 1887
Printed in 4 colors on glossy stock

17343 Journal of Corporate Renewal

Turnaround Management Association
150 S Wacker Drive
Suite 900
Chicago, IL 60606

312-578-6900
FAX 312-578-8336
E-Mail: info@turnaround.org
Home Page: www.turnaround.org
Social Media: *Facebook, Twitter, LinkedIn*

Lisa Poulin, President
Patrick Lagrange, Chairman
Linda Delgadillo, Executive Director

The only international nonprofit association dedicated to corporate renewal and turnaround management. TMA's 9,000 members in 46 regional chapters comprise a professional community of turnaround practitioners, attorneys, accountants, investors, lenders, venture capitalists, appraiser, liquidators, executive recruiters and consultants. Three international conferences each year offer networking and educational sessions on the latest trends and best practices in the restructuring field.
Frequency: 9/Year
Circulation: 9000+

17344 Journal of Information Technology Management

Association of Management
920 Battlefield Boulevard
Suite 100
Chesapeake, VA 23322

757-482-2273
FAX 757-482-0325
E-Mail: aomgt@aom-iaom.org
Home Page: www.aom-iaom.org

Dr Al Bento, Editor-in-Chief

A forum for the communication of solutions found by practitioners and academicians to the mulitfaceted problems associated with managing information and information technology as a corporate resource.
Frequency: Quarterly

17345 Journal of Management Systems

Association of Management
920 Battlefield Boulevard
Suite 100
Chesapeake, VA 23322

757-482-2273
FAX 757-482-0325
E-Mail: aomgt@aom-iaom.org
Home Page: www.aom-iaom.org

Dr John Saee, Editor-in-Chief

Promotes the integreation and cross-fertilization of the behavioral/organizational and information sciences and to encourage, sharpen and expand the dialogue between academicians and practitioners from an interdisiplinary perspective

17346 Journal of Quality Technology

American Society for Quality
600 N Plankinton Avenue
PO Box 3005
Milwaukee, WI 53201-3005

414-272-8575
800-248-1946
FAX 414-272-1734
E-Mail: help@asq.org
Home Page: www.asq.org
Social Media: *Facebook, Twitter, LinkedIn*

Roberto M Saco, President
Paul E Borawski, Executive Director
Erica Gumieny, Sales
Fay Spano, Communications/Media Relations

Published by the American Society for Quality, the JQT is a quarterly, peer-reviewed journal that focuses on the subject of quality control

and the related areas of reliability and similar disciplines.
Cost: $30.00
100M Members
Frequency: Quarterly
Founded in 1946

17347 MSI

Reed Business Information
30 Technology Parkway South
Suite 100
Norcross, GA 30092

630-574-0825
800-424-3996
FAX 630-288-8781
E-Mail: webmaster@reedbusiness.com
Home Page: www.reedbusiness.com

Jeff Greisch, President
Kevin Parker, Editorial Director
Jim Casella, CEO
Nancy Bartels, Senior Editor
Eric Roth, Circulation Manager
Frequency: Monthly
Founded in 1977

17348 MWorld: Journal of the American Management Association

American Management Association
1601 Broadway
Suite 7
New York, NY 10019-7420

212-586-8100
FAX 212-903-8168
E-Mail: customerservice@amanet.org
Home Page: www.amanet.org

Edward T Reilly, CEO
Florence M Stone, Senior Vice President
Arthur Levy, Senior Vice President
Roger Kelleher, Manager
Jorge Rubio, Managing Director

Free quarterly management journal for American Management Association's executive and individual members.
48 Pages
Frequency: Quarterly
Circulation: 25,000
Founded in 2002
Printed in 2 colors on glossy stock

17349 Maintenance Technology

Applied Technology Publications
1300 S Grove Ave
Suite 105
Barrington, IL 60010-5246

847-382-8100
FAX 847-304-8603
Home Page: www.mt-online.com

Arthur Rice, President/CEO
Bill Kiesel, Vice President/Publisher
Jane Alexander, Editor-In-Chief
Rick Carter, Executive Editor
Randy Buttstadt, Director of Creative Services

Maintenance Technology magazine serves the business and technical information needs of managers and engineers responsible for assuring availability of plant equipment and systems. It provides readers with articles on advanced technologies, strategies, tools, and services for the life-cycle management of capital assets.
Frequency: Monthly
Circulation: 50,827
Mailing list available for rent: 35,263 names at $$15 per M

17350 Manage

National Management Association

2210 Arbor Blvd
Suite A
Moraine, OH 45439-1580

937-294-0421
FAX 937-294-2374
E-Mail: nma@nma1.org
Home Page: www.nma1.org

Douglas Shaw, Publisher
Richard Hergert, Owner
Steve Bailey, CEO
Mike McCulley, Chief Operations Officer

Association news for executives.
32 Pages
Frequency: Quarterly
Founded in 1925

17351 Management Consultants International

Kennedy Information
37 Beach Rd
Singapore 199597

65 -100-0688
FAX 656-234-0688
E-Mail: corporate@cacmci.com
Home Page: www.cacmci.com

News and business intelligence on management consulting worldwide. Monthly issues feature country by country surveys of local consulting firms.
Cost: $1122.00
16 Pages
Frequency: Monthly
ISSN: 0956-3253

17352 Medical Group Management Journal

Medical Group Management Association
104 Inverness Ter E
Englewood, CO 80112-5313

303-799-1111
FAX 303-643-9599
E-Mail: infocenter@mgma.com
Home Page: www.mgma.com

William Jessee, CEO
Eileen Barker, senior Vice President
Anders Gilberg, senior Vice President
Natalie Jamieson, Administrative Assistant

Encompasses pertinent problems, questions and issues relating to group practice management.
Frequency: Bi-Monthly

17353 New Mobility

PO Box 220
415 Horsham Road
Horsham, PA 19044

215-675-9133
888-850-0344
FAX 215-675-9376
E-Mail: info@newmobility.com
Home Page: www.newmobility.com
Social Media: *Facebook, Twitter, MySpace*

Tim Gilmer, Editor
Jean Dobbs, Editorial Director, VP
Kim Brennan, Circulation/List Manager
Amy Blackmore, VP of Sales
Jeff Leonard, SVP of Marketing + Communication

New Mobility encourages the integration of active-lifestyle wheelchair users into mainstream society, while simultaneously reflecting the vibrant world of disability-related arts, media, advocacy and philosophy. Our stories foster a sense of community.
Cost: $27.95
Frequency: Monthly

17354 Operations & Fulfillment

Primedia

11 River Bend Drive South
PO Box 4242
Stamford, CT 06907-242

203-589-9900
800-775-3777
FAX 203-358-5823
Home Page: www.multichannelmerchant.com

Sherry Chiger, Editorial Director
Melisa Dowling, Executive Editor
Len Roberto, Circulation Manager
Kate Dimarco, Creative Director of Production
Barry Litwin, VP Sales/Marketing

Provides executives information they can't get anywhere else and reach executives and managers with purchasing authority in all areas of operations management. Information on direct to customer fulfillment..
Cost: $85.00
Circulation: 40000
Founded in 1984

17355 Organization Development Journal

Organization Development Institute
11234 Walnut Ridge Road
Chesterland, OH 44026-1240

440-729-7419
FAX 440-729-9319
E-Mail: dian@odinstitute.com
Home Page: www.odinstitute.org/

Dr. Donald W Cole, Publisher
Dr. Donald W Cole, CEO/President
Jenny Maes, Editor

A journal published quarterly for human resource people, managers and organization development people. The most frequently cited OD/OB publication in the world.
Cost: $80.00
100 Pages
Frequency: Quarterly
Circulation: 700
ISSN: 0889-6402
Founded in 1968
Mailing list available for rent: 9M names
Printed in one color on newsprint stock

17356 PM Network

Project Management Institute
14 Campus Blvd
Newtown Square, PA 19073-3299

610-356-4600
FAX 610-356-4647
Home Page: www.pmi.org

Gregory Balestrero, CEO
Louis J Mercken, Chair
Iain Fraser, Vice Chair
James McGeehan, Public Relations
Jane Farley, Secretary

A monthly magazine published by the Project Management Institute.
75 Pages
Frequency: Monthly
Mailing list available for rent

17357 Print Solutions Magazine

Document Management Industries Association
433 E Monroe Avenue
Alexandria, VA 22301-1693

703-836-6232
800-336-4641
FAX 703-549-4966
Home Page: www.printsolutionsmag.com/

Peter L Colaianni, Editor-in-Chief
Darin Painter, Managing Editor
Preeti Vasishtha, Assistant Editor
Andrew Brown, Assistant Editor

Source for marketing, management and product information.
Frequency: Monthly
Circulation: 42000
ISSN: 0532-1700

Founded in 1962
Printed in 4 colors on glossy stock

17358 Professional Journal

AFSM International
11031 Via Frontera
Suite A
San Diego, CA 92127-1709

858-673-3055
800-333-9786
FAX 239-275-0794
E-Mail: info@asfmi.org
Home Page: www.afsmi.org

John Schoenewald, Executive Director
Jb Wood, President/Ceo

A magazine for executives, managers and professionals in the high-technology services industry.
Cost: $90.00
114 Pages
Circulation: 7000
ISSN: 1049-2135
Founded in 1975
Printed in 4 colors on glossy stock

17359 Project Management Journal

Project Management Institute
14 Campus Blvd
Newtown Square, PA 19073-3299

610-356-4600
FAX 610-356-4647
Home Page: www.pmi.org

Gregory Balestrero, CEO
Mark Langley, Managing Director
Gary Boyler, Publisher
Dan Goldfischer, Editor in Chief
Beverly Cook, Production Manager

A quarterly journal published by the Project Management Institute.
65 Pages
Frequency: Quarterly
Mailing list available for rent

17360 Purchasing

Reed Business Information
6 Alfred Circle
Bedford, MA 00173

972-980-8810
FAX 630-288-8686
Home Page: www.designnews.com
Social Media: *Facebook, Twitter, LinkedIn*

Kathy Doyle, Publisher
Lockie Montgomery, Production Manager
Anne Millen Porter, Business Manager
Paul Teague, Chief Editor.

About the purchasing professional in American industry.
Founded in 1920

17361 Quality Engineering

American Society for Quality
600 N Plankinton Avenue
PO Box 3005
Milwaukee, WI 53201-3005

414-272-8575
800-248-1946
FAX 414-272-1734
E-Mail: help@asq.org
Home Page: www.asq.org
Social Media: *Facebook, Twitter, LinkedIn*

Roberto M Saco, President
Paul E Borawski, Executive Director
Erica Gumieny, Sales
Fay Spano, Communications/Media Relations

Co-published with Taylor and Francis, this journal is for professional practitioners and researchers whose goal is quality engineering im-

provements and solutions.
Cost: $34.75
100M Members
Frequency: Quarterly/Members Price
Founded in 1946

17362 Quality Management Journal
American Society for Quality
600 N Plankinton Avenue
PO Box 3005
Milwaukee, WI 53201-3005

414-272-8575
800-248-1946
FAX 414-272-1734
E-Mail: help@asq.org
Home Page: www.asq.org
Social Media: *Facebook, Twitter, LinkedIn*

Roberto M Saco, President
Paul E Borawski, Executive Director
Erica Gumieny, Sales
Fay Spano, Communications/Media Relations

Published by the American Society for Quality,
the QMT is a quarterly, peer-reviewed journal
that focuses on the subject of quality management practice and provides a discussion forum
for both practitioners and academics in the area
of research.
Cost: $50.00
100M Members
Frequency: Quarterly
Founded in 1946

17363 Quality Progress
American Society for Quality
600 N Plankinton Avenue
PO Box 3005
Milwaukee, WI 53201-3005

414-272-8575
800-248-1946
FAX 414-272-1734
E-Mail: help@asq.org
Home Page: www.asq.org
Social Media: *Facebook, Twitter, LinkedIn*

Roberto M Saco, President
Paul E Borawski, Executive Director
Erica Gumieny, Sales
Fay Spano, Communications/Media Relations

Published by the American Society for Quality,
QP is a peer-reviewed journal that focuses on
the subject of quality control, discussing the
usage and implementation of quality principles
including the subject areas of organizational
behavior, knowledge management and process
improvement.
Cost: $55.00
100M Members
Founded in 1946

17364 Recruiting Trends
Kennedy Information
One Phoenix Mill Lane
Floor 3
Peterborough, NH 03458

603-924-1006
800-531-0007
E-Mail: customerservice@kennedyinfo.com
Home Page: www.kennedyinfo.com

Joseph McCool, Editor
Mina Landrisina, Managing Director

Provides strategies and tactics for creating and
maintaining a competitive workforce.
Cost: $99.00
8 Pages
Frequency: Monthly
ISSN: 0034-1827
Founded in 1970

17365 Retail Merchandiser
MacFadden Publishing

233 Park Ave S
6th Floor
New York, NY 10003-1606

212-979-4800
FAX 212-979-7342
Home Page: www.retail-merchandiser.com

Jeff Friedman, Publisher
Greg Masters, Managing Editor
Toni Riggio, Sales Coordinator
Anita M Wise, Production Manager

Serves those in management positions of mass
retail and discount companies.
Cost: $99.00
Frequency: Monthly
Circulation: 34,188
Founded in 1961

17366 Risk Management
Risk & Insurance Management Society
655 3rd Avenue
2nd Floor
New York, NY 10017

212-286-9292
FAX 212-286-9716
E-Mail: chapterservices@RIMS.org
Home Page: www.rims.org

Ted Donovan, Publisher
Bill Coffin, Editor-in-Chief
Jared Wade, Associate Editor
Callie Nelson, Circulation Manager
Todd Lockwood, Advertising Sales Manager
Cost: $64.00
Frequency: Monthly
Circulation: 15000
Founded in 1950

17367 SAM Advanced Management Journal
Society for Advancement of Management
Corpus Christi - College of Business
6300 Ocean Drive - Unit 5807
Corpus Christi, TX 78412-5807

361-825-6045
FAX 361-825-2725
E-Mail: moustafa@cob.tamucc.edu
Home Page: www.samnational.org

Moustafa H. Abdelsamad, President/CEO
R. Clifton Poole, Secretary
S.G. Fletcher, Treasurer
Everette Anderson, VP, Sales & Marketing
Anthony Buono, Director

A quarterly, refereed publication especially de-
signed for general managers.
Cost: $64.00
3000 Members
Frequency: Quarterly
Founded in 1912

17368 SAM Management In Practice
Society for Advancement of Management
Corpus Christi - College of Business
6300 Ocean Drive, Unit 5807
Corpus Christi, TX 78412-5807

361-825-6045
FAX 361-825-2725
E-Mail: moustafa@cob.tamucc.edu
Home Page: www.samnational.org

Moustafa H. Abdelsamad, President/CEO
R. Clifton Poole, Secretary
S.G. Fletcher, Treasurer
Everette Anderson, VP, Sales & Marketing
Anthony Buono, Director

A quarterly, refereed publication especially designed for general managers.
3000 Members
Frequency: Quarterly
Founded in 1912

17369 Shelby Report
Shelby Publishing Company

517 Green St Nw
Gainesville, GA 30501-3300

770-534-8380
FAX 770-535-0110
E-Mail: shelbpub@bellsouth.net
Home Page: www.shelbypublishing.com

Ron Johnston, President
Chuck Gilmer, Editor

Serving the grocery industry in Arizona, Ar-
kansas, Colorado, Kansas, Louisana, Missouri,
New Mexico, Oklahoma, and Texas,
Cost: $36.00
Frequency: Monthly
Circulation: 25201
Founded in 1966

17370 Si Review
Staffing Industry Analysts
881 Fremont Ave
Suite A3
Los Altos, CA 94024-5637

650-948-9303
800-950-9496
FAX 650-232-2360
Home Page: www.sireport.com

Ron Mester, President
Theresa Daly, Production Manager

Tools and techniques for staffing industry professionals. How-to's and survey articles for
branch management, upper management, owners, and sales/service personnel in employment
service companies. Display advertising included.
Cost: $99.00
Frequency: 22 issues per y
Founded in 1989
Printed in 4 colors on glossy stock

17371 Software Quality Professional
American Society for Quality
600 N Plankinton Avenue
PO Box 3005
Milwaukee, WI 53201-3005

414-272-8575
800-248-1946
FAX 414-272-1734
E-Mail: help@asq.org
Home Page: www.asq.org
Social Media: *Facebook, Twitter, LinkedIn*

Roberto M Saco, President
Paul E Borawski, Executive Director
Erica Gumieny, Sales
Fay Spano, Communications/Media Relations

Published by the American Society for Quality,
the SQP is a quarterly, peer-reviewed journal
for software development professionals that focuses on the subject of quality practice principles in the implementation of software and the
development of software systems.
Cost: $45.00
100M Members
Frequency: Quarterly
Founded in 1946

17372 South Florida Business Journal
American City Business Journals
120 W Morehead St
Suite 400
Charlotte, NC 28202-1874

704-973-1000
800-486-3289
FAX 704-973-1001
E-Mail: borben@bizjournals.com
Home Page: www.bizjournals.com

Whitney R Shaw, CEO
Megan Foley, Marketing Director
David Harris, Managing Editor

Covers all aspects of business in South Florida.
Cost: $99.00
Frequency: Weekly
ISSN: 1528-0527

17373 Staffing Management
SHRM/Society for Human Resource
Management
1800 Duke St
Alexandria, VA 22314-3494

703-535-6000
866-898-4724
FAX 703-535-6474
E-Mail: shrmeducation@shrm.org.
Home Page: www.shrm.org
Social Media: *Facebook, Twitter, LinkedIn,
Youtube*

Susan R Meisinger, CEO
Leon Rubis, Editor

Formerly known as Employment Management
Today, this magazine provides information on
the latest techniques and trends in recruiting
and retaining your most important commodity:
your employees.
Cost: $35.00
56 Pages
Frequency: Quarterly
Circulation: 10000
Founded in 1995

17374 Supermarket News - Retail/Financial
Fairchild Publications
7 W 34th St
New York, NY 10001-8100

212-630-3880
800-204-4515
FAX 212-630-3868
E-Mail: custserv@espcomp.com
Home Page: www.supermarketnews.com
Dan Bagan, Publishing Director
David Orgel, Editor-in-Chief
Christina Veiders, Managing Editor
Joy Kulick, Marketing
Cost: $45.00
Frequency: Weekly
ISSN: 0039-5803
Founded in 1892

17375 Supervision Magazine
National Research Bureau
320 Valley St
Burlington, IA 52601-5513

319-752-5415
FAX 319-752-3421
E-Mail: mail@national-research-bureau.com
Home Page:
www.national-research-bureau.com

Diane M Darnall, President
Teresa Levinson, Editor

Dedicated to providing the most timely and rel-
evant information to today's supervisors and
managers.
Frequency: Monthly
Circulation: 1200
Founded in 1930

17376 Supply Chain Management Review
Reed Business Information
225 Wyman St
Suite 3
Waltham, MA 02451-1216

781-734-8000
FAX 781-734-8076
Home Page: www.reedbusiness.com

Mark Finklestein, President
Frank Quinn, Chief Editor
Susan Lacefield, Associate Editor
Mary Ann Gajewski, Production Manager
Stuart Whayman, CFO
Contains in-depth feature articles on various
aspects of Supply Chain Management. SCM is
the science of integrating the flow of goods and
information from initial souring and purchasing, order processing and fulfillment, production planning and scheduling, inventory
management, transportation, distribution and

customer service. Each issue delivers in-depth
feature articles from the thought leaders in the
supply chain community.
Cost: $199.00
Circulation: 12000

17377 Supply Chain Technology News
Penton Media
1166 Avenue of the Americas/10th Fl
New York, NY 10036

212-204-4200
FAX 216-696-6662
E-Mail: information@penton.com
Home Page: www.penton.com

Jane Cooper, Marketing
Chris Meyer, Director, Corporate
Communications

Focuses on the practical application of technology accross a broad range of supply chain
functions.

17378 Tapping the Network Journal
Quality & Productivity Management
Association
300 N Martingale Road
Suite 230
Schaumburg, IL 60173-2407

708-619-2909
FAX 847-619-3383

William Ginnodo, Editor/Author

This quarterly publication is, By and For Organizational Change Agents. Most articles are
written by QPMA members. Its purpose is to
share - in a straightforward, factual and practical manner - what has been learned within the
authors' organization during the course of a
particular change effort. It is provided free to
members, and made available to non-member
subscribers.

17379 Training
50 S 9th Street
Minneapolis, MN 55402

612-333-0471
FAX 612-333-6526
Home Page: www.vnu.com

Rob van den Bergh, CEO
Rob Ruijter, CFO
AC Nielsen, Marketing
Founded in 1960

**17380 WACRA: World Association for Case
Method Research & Application**
23 Mackintosh Avenue
Needham, MA 02492-1218

781-444-8982
FAX 781-444-1548
E-Mail: wacra@rcn.com
Home Page: www.wacra.org

Dr Hans E Klein, President/Executive Director
Denise Smith, Conference Office

Advancing the use of the case method and
other interactive methodologies in teaching,
training and planning.
Cost: $75.00
2000 Members
Circulation: digital
ISSN: 1931-7549
Founded in 1984

17381 Warehousing Management
Reed Business Information
30 Technology Parkway South
Suite 100
Norcross, GA 30092

646-746-6400
800-424-3996
FAX 646-756-7583

E-Mail: webmaster@reedbusiness.com
Home Page: www.reedbusiness.com

John Poulin, CEO
John R Johnson, Editor-in-Chief
James Reed, Owner
Jane Burgess, Marketing Director
Warehousing Management targets warehousing
and distribution center operations managers
with analysis, news, trends, equipment and
events.
Circulation: 47185
Founded in 1977

17382 Workgroup Computing Report
Patricia Seybold Group
Po Box 783
Needham Heights, MA 02492

617-742-5200
800-826-2424
FAX 617-742-1028
E-Mail: feedback@customers.com
Home Page: www.psgroup.com
Social Media: *Twitter*

Patricia Seybold, Founder/CEO

Provides information on implementing
workflow, document management, groupware,
and business process reengineering.
Cost: $440.00
Frequency: Monthly
Mailing list available for rent

17383 World
Economist
111 W 57th Street
The Economist Building
New York, NY 10019

212-541-5730
FAX 212-541-9378
E-Mail: usrights@economist.com

Dudley Fishburn, Editor
David Hanger, Publisher
124 Pages
ISBN: 0-862181-66-6
Printed in 4 colors on glossy stock

**17384 Young Presidents' Organization -
Magazine**
Young Presidents' Organization
451 Decker Drive
Suite 200
Irving, TX 75062-3954

972-504-4600
FAX 972-650-4777
Home Page: www.ypo.org

Thomas Stauffer, Executive Director
Les Ward, Manager
Frequency: BiAnnual
Circulation: 8000
Printed in on glossy stock

Trade Shows

17385 AACE Annual Meeting
AACE International
1265 Suncrest Towne Centre Drive
Morgantown, WV 26505-1876

304-296-8444
800-858-2678
FAX 304-291-5728
E-Mail: info@aacei.org
Home Page: www.aacei.org
Social Media: *Facebook, LinkedIn*

Andrew S Dowd Jr, Executive Director
Jennie Amos, Marketing/Meetings Manager
Frequency: June

17386 AHRA Annual Meeting & Exposition
Association for Medical Imaging
Management
490B Boston Post Road
Suite 200
Sudbury, MA 01776

978-443-7591
800-334-2472
FAX 978-443-8046
E-Mail: info@ahraonline.org
Home Page: www.ahraonline.org
Social Media: *Facebook, Twitter, LinkedIn*

Edward Cronin, Jr., CEO
Sarah Murray, Executive Assistant
Emily Ryan, Membership Coordinator
Debra Murphy, Publications Director

A resource and catalyst for the development of
professional leadership in imaging sciences. A
driving force toward improving the healthcare
environment. Containing 171 booths and 171
exhibits.
5000 Members
*Mailing list available for rent: 4000 names at
$250 per M*

**17387 Administrative Assistants Executive
Secretaries Seminar**
PA Douglas & Associates
644 Strander Boulevard
#411
Seattle, WA 98188

206-244-6441
FAX 780-444-8002
Home Page: www.padouglas.com

Dr. Paul A Douglas MBA, PhD, CMC, Leader

To provide seminars, workshops and educational materials to individuals from the United
States, Canada, and Europe. Includes an intensive three-day workshop for exploring and developing intellectual, organizational and
interpersonal abilities.
Founded in 1975

**17388 American Society of Association
Executives Annual Meeting & Expo**
American Society of Association Executives
The ASAE Building
1575 I Street NW
Washington, DC 20005

202-262-2723
FAX 202-371-8315
E-Mail: publicpolicy@asaenet.org
Home Page: www.asaenet.org

John Graham, Executive Director

Professional service companies that specialize
in providing management services for association on a fee-for-service basis. Exhibits related
to managing associations.
Frequency: Annual

17389 Annual Lean Six Sigma Conference
American Society for Quality
600 N Plankinton Avenue
PO Box 3005
Milwaukee, WI 53201-3005

414-272-8575
800-248-1946
FAX 414-272-1734
E-Mail: help@asq.org
Home Page: www.asq.org
Social Media: *Facebook, Twitter, LinkedIn*

Roberto M Saco, President
Paul E Borawski, Executive Director
Erica Gumieny, Sales
Fay Spano, Communications/Media Relations

An exclusive two-day briefing and networking
event designed by and for the top practitioners
in the Six Sigma community.
100M Members
Frequency: Annual/February
Founded in 1946

17390 Annual Quality Audit Conference
American Society for Quality
600 N Plankinton Avenue
PO Box 3005
Milwaukee, WI 53201-3005

414-272-8575
800-248-1946
FAX 414-272-1734
E-Mail: help@asq.org
Home Page: www.asq.org
Social Media: *Facebook, Twitter, LinkedIn*

Roberto M Saco, President
Paul E Borawski, Executive Director
Erica Gumieny, Sales
Fay Spano, Communications/Media Relations

Topics of interest include: new innovating au-
dit/process approaches, value added involvement, corporate expectations, corporate/social
responsibility, auditing in the overall corporate
scheme.
100M Members
Frequency: October
Founded in 1946

17391 Annual Service Quality Conference
American Society for Quality
600 N Plankinton Avenue
PO Box 3005
Milwaukee, WI 53201-3005

414-272-8575
800-248-1946
FAX 414-272-1734
E-Mail: help@asq.org
Home Page: www.asq.org
Social Media: *Facebook, Twitter, LinkedIn*

Roberto M Saco, President
Paul E Borawski, Executive Director
Erica Gumieny, Sales
Fay Spano, Communications/Media Relations

The sessions we plan will help you to navigate
through unpredictable consumer behavior and
increasing competition to build a strong foundation for reaching superior levels of quality
service.
100M Members
Frequency: September
Founded in 1946

**17392 Annual World Conference on Quality
and Improvement**
American Society for Quality
600 N Plankinton Avenue
PO Box 3005
Milwaukee, WI 53201-3005

414-272-8575
800-248-1946
FAX 414-272-1734
E-Mail: help@asq.org
Home Page: www.asq.org
Social Media: *Facebook, Twitter, LinkedIn*

Roberto M Saco, President
Paul E Borawski, Executive Director
Erica Gumieny, Sales
Fay Spano, Communications/Media Relations

Conference focuses on quality and improvement with more than 2,000 exhibits and attendees. Keynote speakers and sessions discuss
quality tools, techniques and methodologies.
Provides the opportunity for members to meet
and network with colleagues in the industry.
100M Members
Frequency: May
Founded in 1946

17393 Association for Services Management
11031 Via Frontera
Suite A
San Diego, CA 92127

239-275-7887
800-333-9786
FAX 239-275-0794
E-Mail: info@afsmi.org
Home Page: www.afsmi.org

John Schoenwald, Executive Director
Jb Wood, President/Ceo

Management convention and exposition.
Frequency: Fall

**17394 Association for Strategic Planning
Annual Conference**
Association for Strategic Planning
12021 Wilshire Boulevard
Suite 286
Los Angeles, CA 90025-1200

877-816-2080
FAX 323-954-0507
Home Page: www.strategyplus.org
Social Media: *Facebook, Twitter, LinkedIn*

Dr Stanley G Rosen, President
Janice Laureen, Executive Director

Nation's premier forum for professional discussion and exchange of information and experiences among strategic planning practitioners.
Frequency: February

**17395 Association for Worksite Health
Promotion Annual International
Conference**
60 Revere Drive
Suite 500
Northbrook, IL 60062-1577

847-480-9574
FAX 847-480-9282
Home Page: www.awhp.org

Liz Freyn, Conference Manager

122 booths of information and supplies to promote and develop quality programs of health
and fitness in business and industry. Seminar,
workshop, conference, tours and luncheon.
950 Attendees
Founded in 1974

17396 Association of Management Meeting
Association of Management
920 Battlefield Boulevard
Suite 100
Chesapeake, VA 23322

757-482-2273
FAX 757-482-0325
E-Mail: aomgt@aom-iaom.org
Home Page: www.aom-iaom.org

Dr Karin Klenke, Co-Founder/President
Dr WM A Hamel, CEO
T J Mills, VP Comptroller
800 Attendees
Frequency: Annual

**17397 Circulation Managers Association
International**
11600 Sunrise Valley Drive
Reston, VA 20191-1412

703-506-1661

Joseph Forsee, Show Manager

100 booths exhibiting products such as news
racks, rubber products and software.
225 Attendees
Frequency: June

**17398 Coaching and Teambuilding Skills for
Managers and Supervisors**
SkillPath Seminars

6900 Squibb Road
PO Box 2768
Mission, KS 66201-2768

913-623-3900
800-873-7545
FAX 913-362-4241
E-Mail: webmaster@skillpath.com
Home Page: www.skillpath.com

One-day workshop to sharpen your leadership skills and boost your team's productivity. Various locations and dates.

17399 Construction Specifications Institute Annual Show & Convention
110 South Union Street
Suite 100
Alexandria, VA 22314

703-684-0300
800-689-2900
FAX 703-684-8436
E-Mail: csi@csinet.org
Home Page: www.csinet.org
Social Media: *Facebook, Twitter, LinkedIn, Youtube,Slideshare,Flickr*

Eugene A Valentine, President
W Richard Cooper, VP

Education sessions that focus on industry topics such as; Business and Professional Development, Design & Pre-Construction Activities, Facility Management, Formats & Documents, Legal, Public Facilities & Communities, Safety & Security, Specialty Construction, and Specifications.
6,000 Attendees
Frequency: Annual
Founded in 1954

17400 EMA Annual Conference & Exposition
SHRM/Society for Human Resource Management
1800 Duke Street
Alexandria, VA 22314

703-535-6000
866-898-4724
FAX 703-535-6474
E-Mail: shrmeducation@shrm.org.
Home Page: www.shrm.org/
Social Media: *Facebook, Twitter, LinkedIn, Youtube*

Johnny C Taylor Jr, Chairman
Susan Meisinger, President/CEO
Robert O Gonzales, Secretary
Robb E Van Cleave, Treasurer

Conference devoted to employment management issues.
700 Attendees
Frequency: March/April

17401 Financial Management Association International Annual Meeting
University of South Florida
College of Business Administration/BSN 3331
4202 E Fowler Avenue
Tampa, FL 33620-5500

813-974-2084
FAX 813-974-3318
E-Mail: fma@coba.usf.edu
Home Page: www.fma.org/

Jonathan Karpoff, President Director
Jacqueline Garner, Vice President Financial Education
Rawley Thomas, VP Practitioner Services
Kenneth Eades, Vice President Global Services
Anthony Saunders, Vice President Annual Meeting

Annual meeting and exhibits of financial management related equipment, supplies and services.
Frequency: October

17402 Fundamentals of Personnel Law for Managers and Supervisors
Human Resources Council
6900 Squibb Road
PO Box 804441
Kansas City -4441

800-601-4636

Rose Miller, Trainer

One-day seminar covering the legal issues affecting everyday management of employees. Various locations and dates.

17403 Hartford Conference on Leadership Development & Teambuilding
SkillPath Seminars
6900 Squibb Road
PO Box 2768
Mission, KS 66201-2768

913-623-3900
800-873-7545
FAX 913-362-4241
E-Mail: enroll@skillpath.net

Conference teaches practical leadership skills thorough real-life examples, pratical methods and techniques. Suitable for managers, supervisors, team leaders and team members.

17404 IRMA Annual Conference
Information Resources Management Association
701 E Chocolate Avenue
Suite 200
Hershey, PA 17033

717-533-8845
FAX 717-533-8661
E-Mail: member@irma-international.org
Home Page: www.irma-international.org

Mehdi Khosrow-Pour PhD, President
Sherif Kamel PhD, Communications Director
Gerald Grant PhD, IRMA Doctoral Symposium Director
Lech Janczewski PhD, IRMA World Representative Director
Paul Chalekian, IRMA United States Representative

Provides forums for researchers and practitioners to share leading-edge knowledge in the global resource information management area. Various seminars, conventions and conferences, and other training programs are offered by IRMA throughout the year.
Frequency: May

17405 Int'l. Association of Healthcare Central Svc. Material Management
IAHCSMM Annual Conference
213 W Institute Place
Suite 307
Chicago, IL 60610-3195

312-440-0078
800-962-8274
FAX 312-440-9474
E-Mail: mailbox@iahcsmm.com
Home Page: www.iahcsmm.com

Betty Hanna, Executive Director
Marilyn Corida, Secretary/Treasurer
Lisa Huber, President
Bruce T. Bird, President

125 EXHIBITORSlication separates supervisors/directors from technicians.
600+ Attendees
Frequency: Annual

17406 International Public Management Associatio n for Human Resources Trade Show
Int'l Public Management Assoc for Human Resources

1617 Duke St
Alexandria, VA 22314-3406

703-549-7100
FAX 703-684-0948
E-Mail: ipma@pma-hr.org
Home Page: www.ipma-hr.org

Neil Reichenberg, Executive Director
Sima Hassassian, COO
Tina Chiappetta, Sr Director Gov't Affairs/Comm
500 Attendees

17407 Labor-Management Initiative (LMI)
International Association of Fire Chiefs
4025 Fair Ridge Dr
Fairfax, VA 22033-2868

703-273-0911
FAX 703-273-9363
Home Page: www.iafc.org
Social Media: *Facebook, LinkedIn*

Al H. Gillespie, President & Chairman of the Board
Hank Clemmensen, First Vice President
William R. Metcalf, Second Vice President
Richard Carrizzo, Treasurer
Luther L. Fincher, Jr., Director-At-Large

Provides exceptional networking opportunities and dynamic education to foster and enhance cooperative and collaborative labor-management relationships.
12000 Members
Founded in 1873

17408 National Quality Education Conference
American Society for Quality
600 N Plankinton Avenue
PO Box 3005
Milwaukee, WI 53201-3005

414-272-8575
800-248-1946
FAX 414-272-1734
E-Mail: help@asq.org
Home Page: www.asq.org
Social Media: *Facebook, Twitter, LinkedIn*

Roberto M Saco, President
Paul E Borawski, Executive Director
Erica Gumieny, Sales
Fay Spano, Communications/Media Relations

Provides teachers, administrators, and support personnel opportunities to examine continuous improvement principles used in education. It provides resources and best practices to help you address requirements of No Child Left Behind, while helping you increase student achievement and improve overall performance.
100M Members
Frequency: November
Founded in 1946

17409 New York Social Media Marketing Conference
SkillPath Seminars
6900 Sqibb Road
PO Box 2768
Mission, KS 66201-2768

913-623-3900
800-873-7545
FAX 913-362-4241
E-Mail: webmaster@skillpath.com
Home Page: www.skillpath.com

Steve Nichols, Customer Care Representative
Robb Garr, President

This state-of-the-art conference walks through everything needed to start using social media to drive real business results, even for someone who doesn't know the difference between a tweet and a like button. There's no reason to miss out any longer on the proven, bottom-line benefits of marketing with social media.
Frequency: Semi-Annual, April

17410 Project Management for IT Professionals

CompuMaster
6900 Squibb Road
PO Box 2973
Mission, KS 66201-1373

913-362-3900
800-867-4340
FAX 913-432-4930
E-Mail: compumaster@mcimail.com
Home Page: www.compumaster.net

Casey Smith, Customer Service

A two-day workshop that will help you meet complex project deadlines and budgets. Held in various locations in November and December. Customization at your location available for groups of twenty or more.

17411 Society for Advancement of Management, Inc. (SAM)

Society for Advancement of Management
Corpus Christi - College of Business
6300 Ocean Drive, Unit 5808
Corpus Christi, TX 78412-5808

361-825-3045
888-827-6077
FAX 361-825-5609
E-Mail: sam@samnational.org
Home Page: www.samnational.org

Moustafa H. Abdelsamad, President/CEO
Ken E. Byus, Treasurer
Everette Anderson, VP, Sales & Marketing

Featuring speakers, sponsors, presentations, workshops and discussions.
2500 Members
Founded in 1912

17412 Turnaround Management Association Annual Fall Conference

Turnaround Management Association
150 S Wacker Drive
Suite 900
Chicago, IL 60606

312-578-6900
FAX 312-578-8336
E-Mail: info@turnaround.org
Home Page: www.turnaround.org
Social Media: *Facebook, Twitter, LinkedIn*

Lisa Poulin, President
Patrick Lagrange, Chairman
Linda Delgadillo, Executive Director

The only international nonprofit association dedicated to corporate renewal and turnaround management. TMA's 9,000 members in 46 regional chapters comprise a professional community of turnaround practitioners, attorneys, accountants, investors, lenders, venture capitalists, appraiser, liquidators, executive recruiters and consultants. Three international conferences each year offer networking and educational sessions on the latest trends and best practices in the restructuring field.
600 Attendees
Frequency: Annual/Fall

17413 Turnaround Management Association Spring Conference

Turnaround Management Association
150 S Wacker Drive
Suite 900
Chicago, IL 60606

312-578-6900
FAX 312-578-8336
E-Mail: info@turnaround.org
Home Page: www.turnaround.org
Social Media: *Facebook, Twitter, LinkedIn*

Lisa Poulin, President
Patrick Lagrange, Chairman
Linda Delgadillo, Executive Director

The only international nonprofit association dedicated to corporate renewal and turnaround management. TMA's 9,000 members in 46 regional chapters comprise a professional community of turnaround practitioners, attorneys, accountants, investors, lenders, venture capitalists, appraiser, liquidators, executive recruiters and consultants. Three international conferences each year offer networking and educational sessions on the latest trends and best practices in the restructuring field.
600 Attendees
Frequency: Annual/Spring

17414 Volunteer & Combination Officers Section Symposium in the Sun

International Association of Fire Chiefs
4025 Fair Ridge Dr
Fairfax, VA 22033-2868

703-273-0911
FAX 703-273-9363
Home Page: www.iafc.org
Social Media: *Facebook, LinkedIn*

Al H. Gillespie, President & Chairman of the Board
Hank Clemmensen, First Vice President
William R. Metcalf, Second Vice President
Richard Carrizzo, Treasurer
Luther L. Fincher, Jr., Director-At-Large

Addresses the unique needs of volunteer and combination departments including transitioning from a volunteer to a combination department, recruitment and retention, leadership and management, staffing and more.
12000 Members
Founded in 1873

17415 WACRA Annual Conference Research & Application

World Assoc for Case Method Research & Application
23 Mackintosh Avenue
Needham, MA 02492-1218

781-444-8982
FAX 781-444-1548
E-Mail: hans.klein@wacra.org
Home Page: www.wacra.org

Dr Hans E Klein, President/Executive Director
Dr Joelle Piffault, Director/Development/Membership
Dr Pavel Zufan, Director/Business/Economics

Directories & Databases

17416 ABI/INFORM

UMI/Data Courier
620 S 3rd Street
Suite 400
Louisville, KY 40202-2475

800-626-2823
FAX 502-589-5572

This database contains more than 675,000 citations, appearing in over 900 international periodicals covering business and management related areas.

17417 ARMA International's Buyers Guide

ARMA International
11880 College Blvd
Suite 450
Overland Park, KS 66215

913-341-3808
800-422-2762
FAX 913-341-3742
E-Mail: hq@arma.org

Home Page: www.arma.org/conference
Social Media: *Facebook, Twitter, LinkedIn*

Formerly the Association of Record Managers and Administrators, this guide has 75-100 companies listed.

17418 Analysis of Workers' Compensation Laws

Chamber of Commerce of the United States
1615 H St Nw
Washington, DC 20062-0002

202-659-6000
FAX 202-463-5836
Home Page: www.uschamber.org

Thomas J Donohue, CEO
Jean Hunt, Administrative Assistant

Offers a list of workers' compensation administrators.
Cost: $25.00
Frequency: Annual

17419 Association of Management Consulting Firms

AMCF
380 Lexington Avenue
Suite 1700
New York, NY 10168

212-551-7887
FAX 212-551-7934
E-Mail: info@amcf.org
Home Page: www.amcf.org

Elizabeth A Kovacs, President/CEO
Kathleen Fish, Director Programs
Samantha Colon, Executive Administrator

About 50 management consulting firms that are members of ACME.
Cost: $50.00
Frequency: Biennial
Founded in 1929

17420 Business Information Desk Reference: Where to Find Answers to Questions

Palgrave Macmillan
175 5th Ave
New York, NY 10010-7728

212-982-3900
FAX 212-307-5035
Home Page: www.ibtauris.com

Bruce McKenzie, President
Stuart Weir, Production Director
Paul Davighi, Marketing Director
Liz Stuckey, Secretary

Over 1,000 print material, online databases and federal agencies covering over 24 business areas are listed.

17421 Business Information Resources - Online Database

Grey House Publishing
4919 Route 22
PO Box 56
Amenia, NY 12501

518-789-8700
800-562-2139
FAX 518-789-0556
E-Mail: gold@greyhouse.com
Home Page: http://gold.greyhouse.com
Social Media: *Facebook, Twitter*

Leslie Mackenzie, Publisher
Richard Gottlieb, Editor

This one-stop, business building database provides immediate access to the resources you need for success in the industry of your choice. This is the kind of must have information that, before now, could take hours to find. With a subscription to the Directory of Business Information Resources - Online Database, you'll have immediate access to over 17,000 associations, magazines, journals, newsletters, trade

shows, directories, databases, and web sites for 100 industry groups.
Founded in 1981

17422 Business Library

Dow Jones & Company
4300 North Route 1
South Brunswick, NJ 08852

609-520-4000

Covers all types of topics and subjects that are of interest to US business markets.
Frequency: Full-text

17423 Business Opportunities Handbook

Enterprise Magazines
1020 N Broadway
Suite 111
Milwaukee, WI 53202-3157

414-272-9977
FAX 414-272-9973
E-Mail: info@busop1.com
Home Page: www.franchisehandbook.com

Betsy Green, Owner

Over 2,500 listings of franchises, dealers and distributors that offer business opportunities to individuals.
Cost: $5.99
150 Pages
Frequency: Quarterly

17424 Career Guide: Dun's Employment Opportunities Directory

Dun & Bradstreet Information Service
3 Sylvan Way
Parsippany, NJ 07054-3822

973-605-6000
FAX 973-605-9630

Offers information on more than 5,000 companies, leading employers of the United States, that provide career opportunities in sales, marketing and management.
Cost: $385.00
2700 Pages
Frequency: Annual

17425 Company Intelligence

Information Access Company
362 Lakeside Drive
Foster City, CA 94404-1171

650-378-5200
800-227-8431

Offers company news and financial information with an emphasis placed on hard-to-find privately held companies in the United States and worldwide.

17426 Corporate Technology Database

One Source Information Services
300 Baker Ave
Concord, MA 01742-2131

978-318-4300
800-554-5501
FAX 978-318-4690
E-Mail: sales@onesource.com
Home Page: www.onesource.com

Philip J Garlick, President
John Brewer, Vice Chairman
Brad Haigis, VP/Products
Beth Jacaruso, VP/Content

Offers profiles of over 45,000 public and private US corporations and operating units of large corporations that develop or manufacture some 100,000 high-technology products.
Frequency: Directory

17427 Corporate Yellow Book

Leadership Directories
104 5th Ave
New York, NY 10011-6901

212-627-4140
FAX 212-645-0931
E-Mail: corporate@leadershipdirectories.com
Home Page: www.leadershipdirectories.com

David Hurvitz, CEO

Contact information for over 48,000 executives at over 1,000 companies and more than 9,000 board members and their outside affiliations.
Cost: $360.00
1,400 Pages
Frequency: Quarterly
ISSN: 1058-2098
Founded in 1986

17428 Directory of Business Information Resources

Grey House Publishing
4919 Route 22
PO Box 56
Amenia, NY 12501

518-789-8700
800-562-2139
FAX 845-373-6390
E-Mail: books@greyhouse.com
Home Page: www.greyhouse.com
Social Media: *Facebook, Twitter*

Leslie Mackenzie, Publisher
Richard Gottlieb, Editor

The source for contacts in over 98 business areas, from advertising and agriculture to utilities and wholesalers. This carefully researched volume details, for each business industry, the associations representing each industry, the newsletters that keep members current, the magazines and journals that are important to the trade, the top conventions and industry web sites that provide important marketing information. Includes contact names with phone, fax, website and e-mail information.
Cost: $195.00
2300 Pages
Frequency: Annual
ISBN: 1-592371-93-0
Founded in 1981

17429 Directory of Executive Recruiters

Kennedy Information
One Phoenix Mill Lane
Floor 3
Peterboro, NH 03458

603-924-1006
800-531-0007
E-Mail: customerservice@kennedyinfo.com
Home Page: www.kennedyinfo.com

Lists over 8,900 offices of 5,678 executive search firms in the US, Canada and Mexico. Includes key data and contact info on each firm. Directory is indexed by recruiter specialities, function, industry, key principals, and geography. Corporate edition is specially designed for corporate buyers of search services and search providers.
Cost: $179.95
1180 Pages
Frequency: Annual
ISBN: 1-885922-81-7
ISSN: 0090-6484

17430 Directory of Management Consultants

Kennedy Information
1 Phoenix Mill Lane
Floor 3
Peterborough, NH 03458

603-924-1006
800-531-0007
E-Mail: bookstore@kennedyinfo.com
Home Page: www.kennedyinfo.com

The premier directory of management consulting firms, published since 1979. The 10th edi-

tion profiles more than 2,400 firms in North America. Indexed by services, industries, geography, and key contacts.
Cost: $295.00
850 Pages
Frequency: Biennial
ISBN: 1-885922-69-8
ISSN: 0743-6890
Founded in 1919
Mailing list available for rent: 7600 names at $200 per M

17431 Directory of Management Information Systems Faculty

Management Information Systems Research Center
355 Humphrey-271 9th Avenue S
Minneapolis, MN 55455

763-783-7496
FAX 612-626-1316
E-Mail: jdegross@csom.umn.edu
Home Page: www.webfoot.csom.umn.edu

Gordon B Davis, Editor
Janice I DeGross, Manager
Kate Terry, Manager
Abby Pinto, Managing Director

College-level teachers of subjects related to management information systems and technology.
Cost: $25.00

17432 Directory of Outplacement & Career Management Firms

Kennedy Information
One Phoenix Mill Lane
Floor 3
Peterborough, NH 03458

603-924-1006
800-531-0007
E-Mail: customerservice@kennedyinfo.com
Home Page: www.kennedyinfo.com

Profiles 365 firms in 1,351 offices worldwide and identifies 1,875 key principals. Includes key data on revenues, staff sizes, fees & expense policies, and contact information. Indexed by industry specialty, geography and individual outplacement professional.
Cost: $129.00
606 Pages
ISBN: 1-885922-65-5

17433 Directory of US Labor Organizations

BNA Books
3 Bethesda Metro Center
Suite 250
Bethesda, MA 02814-5377

703-341-3500
800-372-1033
FAX 800-253-0332
E-Mail: customercare@bna.com
Home Page: www.bna.com

Gregory C McCaffery, President

Over 200 national unions and professional and state employees associations engaged in labor representation are profiled.
Cost: $55.00
110 Pages
Frequency: Annual

17434 Diversity in Corporate America

Hunt-Scanlon Corporation
700 Fairfield Avenue
Stamford, CT 06902

203-352-2920
FAX 203-352-2930

James A Mueller, Founder
Scott Scanlon, CEO
Smooch S Reynolds, President
A David Brown, Managing Director
John D Delpino, Director - Executive Staffing

2,200 listings of executives responsible for managing corporate diversity in the US.
Cost: $179.00
Frequency: Biennial

17435 Employee Service Management: NESRA Buyers Directory
National Employee Services & Recreation Assn
568 Spring Road
Suite D
Elmhurst, IL 60126

630-559-0020
FAX 630-559-0025
E-Mail: esmahq@esmassn.org
Home Page: www.esmassn.org

Renee Mula, Editor

Includes a list of over 200 member manufacturers and distributors offering products and services for employee discount programs and employee store merchandise to members.
Frequency: Annual

17436 Employment, Hours and Earnings
US Department Of Commerce
200 Constitution Ave Nw
Washington, DC 20210-0001

202-693-5000
FAX 202-219-8822
E-Mail: webmaster@dol.gov
Home Page: www.dol.gov

Hilda L Solis, CEO
Sonya Carrion, Director

This database aimed at employees and management cover US employment, hours and earnings.

17437 Fortune Magazine
Time Inc./Time Warner
1271 Avenue of the Americas
16th Floor
New York, NY 10020-1393

212-522-1212
800-274-6800
FAX 212-522-0602
Home Page: www.timeinc.com
Social Media: *Facebook, Twitter*

Laura Lang, CEO
Howard M. Averill, CFO
Leslie Picard, President
Stephanie George, Chief Marketing Officer
John Huey, Editor-in-Chief

FORTUNE is a global leader in business journalism. The magazine has a great history of providing analysis and news critical to business people.
Founded in 1922

17438 Fortune: Deals of the Year Issue
Time Inc./Time Warner
1271 Avenue of the Americas
16th Floor
New York, NY 10020-1393

212-522-1212
800-274-6800
FAX 212-522-0602
Home Page: www.timeinc.com

Laura Lang, CEO
Howard M. Averill, CFO
Leslie Picard, President
Stephanie George, Chief Marketing Officer
John Huey, Editor-in-Chief

Offers information on 50 of the largest United States corporate financial transactions, including mergers, acquisitions and leveraged buyouts.
Cost: $5.00
Frequency: Annual
Founded in 1922

17439 Gale Group Management Contents®
Gale/Cengage Learning
2250 Perimeter Park Drive
Suite 300
Morrisville, NC 27560

919-804-6400
800-334-2564
FAX 919-804-6410
E-Mail: gale.content@A@cengage.com
Home Page: www.library.dialog.com
Social Media: *Facebook, Twitter, LinkedIn, Youtube*

Patrick C Sommers, President

A specialized database that provides current information on business practices and management techniques from key management journals. The database provides theoretical background and practical how to approaches to key management disciplines.
Frequency: Weekly

17440 International Directory of Executive Recruiters
Kennedy Information
One Phoenix Mill Lane
Floor 3
Peterborough, NH 03458

603-924-1006
800-531-0007
E-Mail: customerservice@kennedyinfo.com
Home Page: www.kennedyinfo.com

A comprehensive source of worldwide executive recruiting firms and consultancies. List full contact information for search firms in 60 countries. Indexed by management function, industry, firm, and search firm principals.
Cost: $149.00
800 Pages
ISBN: 1-885922-53-1

17441 International Registry of OD Professional
Organization Development Institute
11234 Walnut Ridge Road
Chesterland, OH 44026-1240

440-729-7419
E-Mail: donwcole@aol.com

Dr. Donald W Cole RODC, President

A who's who directory of services and supplies to the industry. Includes: The OD Code of Ethics; a Statement on the Knowledge and Skill Necessary for Competence in O.D.; a listing of not just names and addresses, but the credential of all those registered with us; a list of all the OD organizations in the world and all the OD/OB academic programs in the world.
Cost: $25.00
300 Pages
Frequency: Annual

17442 Labor Arbitration Information System
LRP Publications
747 Dresher Road, Suite 500
PO Box 980
Horsham, PA 19044-0980

215-840-0912
FAX 215-784-9639
E-Mail: webmaster@lrp.com
Home Page: www.lrp.com

Sandy Johnson, Director/Manager

Comprehensive indexing system for arbitration awards available. The easy-to-use, one-stop indexing system covers all the major arbitration reporting services including AAA, BNA, and CCH.
Cost: $515.00
Frequency: Monthly
Founded in 1977

17443 Meeting the Needs of Employees with Disabilities
Resources for Rehabilitation
22 Bonad Road
Winchester, MA 01890

781-368-9094
FAX 781-368-9096
Home Page: www.rfr.org

Offers various descriptions of organizations and products that assist those involved in the employment of people with disabilities.
Cost: $42.95
Frequency: Biennial

17444 SHRM Membership Directory Online
SHRM/Society for Human Resource Management
1800 Duke St
Alexandria, VA 22314-3494

703-535-6000
866-898-4724
FAX 703-535-6474
E-Mail: shrmeducation@shrm.org.
Home Page: www.shrm.org
Social Media: *Facebook, Twitter, LinkedIn, Youtube*

Susan R Meisinger, CEO
Robert O Gonzales, Secretary
Robb E Van Cleave, Treasurer

An exclusive benefit for SHRM members, the SHRM Membership Directory Online is a searchable database catagorized by by name, title, company, company size, job function or location.

17445 Small Business Sourcebook
Gale/Cengage Learning
27500 Drake Road
Farmington Hills, MI 48331-3535

248-699-4253
800-877-4253
FAX 877-363-4253
E-Mail: gale.galeord@cengage.com
Home Page: www.gale.cengage.com
Social Media: *Facebook, Twitter, Youtube*

Patrick C Sommers, President

In this two volume annotated guide you'll discover more than 340 specific small business profiles and 99 general small business topics, small business programs and assistance programs in the US, its territories and Canadian provinces and US federal government agencies and offices specializing is small business issues, programs and assistance.
Frequency: Annual/2 Volumes
ISBN: 1-414421-75-3

17446 Small Business or Entrepreneurial Related Newsletter
Prosperity & Profits Unlimited
PO Box 416
Denver, CO 80201-0416

303-573-5564

A Doyle, Editor

A mini directory of listings for small businesses.
Cost: $19.95
8 Pages
Frequency: Every 2 Years
Circulation: 2,500
Founded in 1990
Printed in one color on matte stock

17447 Staffing Industry Sourcebook
Staffing Industry Analysts
881 Fremont Ave
Suite A3
Los Altos, CA 94024-5637

650-948-9303
800-950-9496

FAX 650-232-2360
Home Page: www.sireport.com

Ron Mester, Manager
Jeff Reeder, Mgr Editor/SI Review
Sona Sharma, Mgr Editor/IT Serv Business Report
Linda Hubbard, Director of Marketing
Leslie Austin, Customer/Membership

Source Book, Facts and Figures for Market Research on the staffing industry.
Cost: $285.00
451 Pages
Frequency: BiAnnual
ISBN: 1-883814-10-3

17448 Transnational Corporations and Labor: A Directory of Resources
Third World Resources
1218 E 21st Street
Oakland, CA 94606

510-533-7583
FAX 510-533-0923

Danielle Mahones, Executive Director

This directory is a source for books, periodicals and audiovisuals on transnational corporations and labor issues.
Cost: $14.95
160 Pages

Industry Web Sites

17449 http://gold.greyhouse.com
G.O.L.D Grey House OnLine Databases
Grey House Publishing's online database platform, GOLD, offers Quick Search, Keyword Search and Expert Search for most business sectors including management markets. The GOLD platform makes finding the information you need quick and easy - whether you're a novice searcher or an experienced database user. All of Grey House's directory products are available for subscription on the GOLD platform.

17450 www.aahc.net
AAHC American Association of Healthcare Consultant

17451 www.aaimnhta.com
American Association of Industrial Management
Dedicated to better management and the over-all objective which is the formulation of broad management principles and strategies that will insure sucessful management and promote the principles of free, private and competitive enterprise with individual opportunity and freedom under a constitutional government.

17452 www.aameda.org
American Academy of Medical Administrators
Department heads and administrators in areas of hospital and health administration.

17453 www.afsmi.org
AFSM International
A global organization dedicated to furthering the knowledge, understanding, and career development of executives, managers and professionals in the high-technology service industry.

17454 www.amanet.org
American Management Association
Offers a full range of business education and management development programs for indivudual and organizations in Europe, the Americas and Asia. Learn superior business skills and best management practices through a

variety of seminars, conferences and special events.

17455 www.amcf.org
AMCF
Seeks to unite management consulting firms in order to develop and improve professional standards and practice in the field. Offers information and referral services on management consultants.

17456 www.americanassocofindmgmt.com
American Association of Industrial Management
Dedicated to better management and the formulation of broad management principles and strategies that will ensure sucessful management and promote the principles of free, private and competive enterprise with individual opportunity and freedom under a constitutional government.

17457 www.aom-iaom.org
Association of Management
Formerly the Association of Human Resources Management and Organizational Behavior.

17458 www.apics.org
APICS Association for Operations Management
The primary purpose of this specific industry group is to educate food and beverage manufacturers on effective marketing strategies, market trends and material management.

17459 www.aspanet.org
American Society for Public Administration
The nation's most respected society representing all forums in the public service arena. Advocate for greater effectiveness in government agents of goodwill and professionalism addressing key public service issues by promoting change at both the local and international levels, we can enhance the quality of lives worldwide.

17460 www.awhp.org
Association for Worksite Health Promotion
Exists to advance the profession of worksite health promotion and the career development of its practitioners and to improve the performance of the programs they administer. Represents a variety of disciplines and worksites, for decision-makers in the areas of health promotion/disease prevention and health-care cost management.

17461 www.besthealthplans.com
Best Employers Association
Market and administer medical and dental insurance for large and small groups. Specializes in group insurance and employee benefits.

17462 www.bizintell.com
Business Intelligence Association
Business to business research on a wide variety of industries. Specialize in primary and hard-to-find secondary information.

17463 www.cmaa.org
Club Managers Association of America
Professional association for managers of membership clubs. Members manage country, city, athletic, faculty, yacht, town and military clubs. Objectives to promote and advance friendly relations among persons connected with the management of clubs and other associations of similar character.

17464 www.cmaonline.org
The Christian Management Association
Designed to assist those involved in the management of Christian organizations.

17465 www.cmeinc.org
Center for Management Effectiveness
Conducts management training programs and publishes self-scoring inventories, trainer guides and workbooks on stress management, resolution of conflict, risk taking, decision making and building managerial skills.

17466 www.corptech.com
CORPTECH Information Services
Corporations and operating units of large corporations that develop or manufacture some 100,000 high-technology products.

17467 www.emsnetwork.com/cbt
Center for Breakthrough Thinking
Organized to promote and institutionalize the teaching and application of Breakthrough Thinking in universities, corporations and governments in solving problems, leveraging opportunities, and achieving change.

17468 www.expedia.com
Expedia.com
Internet travel service offers access to airlines, hotels, car rentals, vacation packages, cruises and corporate travel.

17469 www.greyhouse.com
Grey House Publishing
Authoritative reference directories for most business sectors including management markets. Users can search the online databases with varied search criteria allowing for custom searches by product category, geographic area, sales volume, keyword, subject and more. Full Grey House catalog and online ordering also available.

17470 www.iamc.org
Industrial Asset Management Council
Members are companies engaged in the management of two or more organizations on a professional client basis.

17471 www.icmci.org
ICMCI Intn'l Council of Mgnt Consulting Institutes
For national institutes from around the world that certify professional management consultants; promotes professional development and networking between consultants and the highest standards of performance for clients.

17472 www.icsa.com
International Customer Service Association
Dedicated to promoting the development and awareness of the customer service profession through networking, education and research.

17473 www.icsb.org
International Council for Small Business
Management development.

17474 www.imc-ymca.org/join.html
International Management Council
IMC provides individuals with opportunities for continually developing their leadership and management skills through a network of shared experiences and education.

17475 www.imcusa.org/
IMC-USA Institute of Management Consultants-USA
For management consultants in the United States, organized to establish consulting as a self-regulating profession, meriting public confidence and respect. Toward the achievement of this goal IMC awards the international appelation CMC for certified management consultants.

17476 www.ioma.com

Institute of Management & Administration

Organization helps to provides information and guidance to management teams for various businesses.

17477 www.ipma-hr.org

International/Public Management Assn For Human Res

Human resource professionals, representing the interests of over 6,000 individual and 1,300 agency members, at the federal, state and local levels of government. Promotes excellence in human resource management through the ongoing development of professional and ethical standards, and through its publishing and educational training programs.

17478 www.members.aol.com/odinst

Organization Development Institute

Promotes the understanding of organization development and offers three categories of membership: professional consultant, regular and student.

17479 www.mgma.com

Medical Group Management Association

The oldest and largest professional membership association dedicated to medical practice management. Serves their members by offering timely and relevant networking and educational opportunities that keep the members up-to-date on the practice management field.

17480 www.mt-online.com

Applied Technology Publications

MT-online.com is the premier source of capacity assurance and best practice solutions for manufacturing, process and service operations worldwide. Online home of Maintenance Technology magazie, the dynamic MT-online.com portal serves the critical technical, business and professional-development needs of engineers, managers and technicians from across all industrial, institutional and commercial sectors.

17481 www.nacdonline.org

National Association of Corporate Directors

Fosters research, surveys, seminars and director for corporate. Maintains placement service.

17482 www.naesaa.com

National Association of Executive Secretaries and Administrative Assistants

Publishes a newsletter 11 times per year.

17483 www.nsha.biz

National Small Business United

Volunteer-led association. Primary mission is to advocate state and federal policies that are beneficial to small business, the state and the nation and to promote the growth of free enterprise.

17484 www.pmi.org

Project Management Institute

Fosters recognition of the need for project management professionalism. Offers professional certification and bestows awards.

17485 www.promanager.org

Professional Managers Association

A national membership association representing the interests of professional managers, management officials and non-bargaining unit employees in the federal government.

17486 www.rbma.org

Radiology Business Management Association

Promotes management education and study of practice economics, legislative issues and consumer trends.

17487 www.samnational.org

Society for Advancement of Management

SAM members come from a variety of disciplines - productions, finance, marketing, accounting and more who share a common bond of interest in becoming stronger managers.

17488 www.shrm.org

Society for Human Resource Management

17489 www.shrm.org/ema

Society for Human Resources/Employment Mgt Assn

A national association comprised primarily of corporate human resource professionals responsible for hiring and staffing.

17490 www.ssainfo.com

Support Services Alliance

Multi-state membership organization that provides cost-savings services and legislative representation for small businesses and the self-employed. Also offers services to the memberships of more than 100 affiliated state, regional and national associations.

17491 www.wacra.org

World Assn for Case Method Research & Application

Members are professional and academicians with an interest in the use of the case method in teaching, training and planning. Interactive, innovative teaching and learning methods.

17492 www.ypo.org

Young Presidents' Organization

Members are corporate presidents under the age of fifty whose companies employ at least fifty employees.

Associations

17493 APICS: Association for Operations Management

8430 West Bryn Mawr Avenue
Suite 1000
Chicago, IL 60631

773-867-1777
800-444-2742
FAX 773-639-3000
E-Mail: webmaster@apics.org.
Home Page: www.apics.org
Social Media: *Facebook, Twitter, LinkedIn, Youtube*

Robert D Boyle, Chair of the Board
Abe Eshkenazi, CSCP, CPA,, Chief Executive Officer
Sharon Rice, Executive Director
Dean Martinez, Executive Vice President
Jennifer K Daniels, Vice President, Marketing

Provides lifelong learning for lifetime success. APICS certification programs, training tools and networking opportunities increase workplace performance. The society supports 20,000 manufacturing and service industry companies worldwide.
Cost: $110.00
60000 Members
Frequency: Membership/Professional
Founded in 1957

17494 ASM International

9639 Kinsman Rd
Materials Park, OH 44073-0002

440-338-5151
800-336-5152
FAX 440-338-4634
E-Mail: memberservices@asminternational.org
Home Page: www.asminternational.org
Social Media: *Facebook, Twitter, LinkedIn*

Prof. C. Ravi Ravindran, FASM, President
Dr. Sunniva R. Collins, FASM, Vice President
Thomas S Passek, Managing Director & Secretary
Jeane Deatherage, Administrator, Foundation Programs
Virginia Shirk, Foundation Executive Assistant

The society for materials engineers and scientists, a worldwide network dedicated to advancing industry, technology and applications of metals and materials.
35000 Members
Founded in 1913

17495 Adhesive & Sealant Council

7101 Wisconsin Ave
Suite 990
Bethesda, MD 20814-4805

301-986-9700
FAX 301-986-9795
E-Mail: info@ascouncil.org
Home Page: www.ascouncil.org
Social Media: *Twitter, LinkedIn*

Traci Jensen, Chairman
Matt Devine, President
Steve Duren, Senior Director, Member Services
Kate Zando, Director, Finance
Mark Collatz, Director, Government Relations

A North American trade association dedicated to representing the adhesive and sealant industry. ASC is bound by the collective efforts of its members, and strives to improve the industry operating government and strengthen its member companies.
Founded in 1958

17496 American Bearings Manufacturers Association

2025 M St NW
Suite 800
Washington, DC 20036-3309

202-367-1155
FAX 202-367-2155
E-Mail: info@americanbearings.org
Home Page: www.americanbearings.org
Social Media: *Facebook, Twitter*

Brian Lindsay, Chair
Jim Porter, Vice Chair
Scott Lynch, President & Secretary
Kelly Sherrard, AssociationÿCoordinatorÿ
Peter Shapiro, Senior Associate

Promotes bearing standardization. Sponsors Bearing Technical Committee.
36 Members
Founded in 1917

17497 American Brush Manufacturers Association

736 Main Ave, Suite 7
Durango, CO 81301

720-392-2262
FAX 866-837-8450
E-Mail: info@abma.org
Home Page: www.abma.org
Social Media: *Facebook, Twitter, LinkedIn*

David Park, Executive Director

Trade association representing North American manufacturers of brooms, brushes, mops and rollers.
175 Members
Founded in 1917

17498 American Machine Tool Distributors Association

AMTDA
7901 Westpark Drive
McLean, VA 22102-4206

703-893-2900
800-524-0475
FAX 703-893-1151
E-Mail: amt@amtonline.org
Home Page: www.amtonline.org
Social Media: *Facebook, Twitter, LinkedIn, YouTube*

DouglasÿK. Woods, President
Amber L Thomas, Vice President - Advocacy
JefferyÿH Traver, Vice President - Business
PeterÿR. Eelman, Vice President - Exhibitions
LindaÿG Montfort, Vice President-Finance & HR

AMTDA will lead distributors of manufacturing technology by providing essential programs and services that help its members gain global recognition from customers and supplies as the preferred method of distribution.
Cost: $50.00
8-12 Pages
Frequency: Monthly
Circulation: 3400
Founded in 1924

17499 American Society for Quality

American Society for Quality
600 N Plankinton Avenue
PO Box 3005
Milwaukee, WI 53201-3005

414-272-8575
800-248-1946
FAX 414-272-1734
E-Mail: help@asq.org
Home Page: www.asq.org
Social Media: *Facebook, Twitter, LinkedIn, Youtube*

John C. Timmerman, Chairman
Paul E Borawski, Executive Director
Jennifer Janzen, Director, Human Resources
Laurel Nelson-Rowe, Managing Director
Michelle Mason, Managing Director

ASQ's mission is to facilitate continuous improvement and increase customer satisfaction. Promotes quality principles, concepts and technologies. Provides information, contacts and opportunities to make things better in the workplace, in communities and in people's lives.
100M Members
Founded in 1946

17500 American Textile Machinery Association

201 Park Washington Ct
Falls Church, VA 22046-4527

703-538-1789
FAX 703-241-5603
E-Mail: info@atmanet.org
Home Page: www.atmanet.org

Will Motchar, Chairman
Clay D Tyeryar, President/Assistant Treasurer
Harry W. Buzzerd, Jr., ATMA Management Counsel
Susan A. Denston, ATMA Executive Vice President
Carlos F. J. Moore, ATMA International Trade

The American Textile Machinery Association/ATMA's purpose is to advance the common interests of its members, improve business conditions within the US textile machinery industry from a global perspective and market the industry and members' machinery, parts and services.
Founded in 1933

17501 Association for Manufacturing Technology

7901 Westpark Drive
McLean, VA 22102-4206

703-893-2900
800-524-0475
FAX 703-893-1151
E-Mail: amt@amtonline.org
Home Page: www.amtonline.org
Social Media: *Facebook, Twitter, LinkedIn, YouTube*

Douglas K Woods, President
Amber L Thomas, Vice President - Advocacy
JefferyÿH Traver, Vice President - Business
PeterÿR. Eelman, Vice President - Exhibitions
LindaÿG Montfort, Vice President-Finance & HR

Represents American providers of manufacturing machinery and equipment. Its goal is to promote technological advancements and improvements in the design, manufacture and sale of member's products in those markets and act as an industry advocate on trade organizations thoroughout the world.
Founded in 1902

17502 Association of Equipment Manufacturers

6737 W Washington St
Suite 2400
Milwaukee, WI 53214-5650

414-272-0943
866-236-0442
FAX 414-272-1170
E-Mail: aem@aem.org
Home Page: www.aem.org
Social Media: *Twitter*

John Patterson, Chairman
Dennis Slater, President
Al Cervero, Vice President, Marketing
John Nowak, Chief Financial Officer
Anne Forristall Luke, Vice President, Political & Public

Composed of manufacturers of screens and feeders used in aggregates, mining and industrial processing. Promotes and furthers the in-

terests of members in safety, production, engineering, government relations and other industry matters.
8 Members
Founded in 1959

17503 Contract Packaging Association
1833 Centre Point Circle
Suite 123
Naperville, IL 60563-4848

630-544-5053
FAX 630-544-5055
E-Mail: info@contractpackaging.org
Home Page: www.contractpackaging.org
Social Media: *Twitter, LinkedIn*

Vicky Smitley, President
Chris Nutley, Past President
Tim Koers, Vice President
John Mazelin, Executive Director
Mark O' Malley, Treasurer

Formed for contract packaging firms and those businesses related to them. Promotes the growth and welfare of member firms.
155 Members
Founded in 1992

17504 Conveyor Equipment Manufacturers Association (CEMA)
5672 Strand CT
Suite 2
Naples, FL 34110

239-514-3441
FAX 239-514-3470
E-Mail: kim@cemanet.org
Home Page: www.cemanet.org
Social Media: *Facebook, Twitter, LinkedIn*

Warren Chandler, President
Robert Reinfried, Executive Vice President
Jerry Heathman, Vice President
Jim McKnight, Secretary
Garry Abraham, Treasurer

Involved in writing industry standards, the CEMA seeks to promote among its members and the industry standardization of design manufacture and application on a voluntary basis and in such manner as will not impede development of conveying machinery and component parts or lessen competition. CEMA sponsors an annual Engineering Conference that allows Member Company Engineers to meet and develop or improve CEMA Consensus Industry Standards and National Standards that affect the conveyor industry.
96 Members
Founded in 1933

17505 Flexible Packaging Association
185 Admiral Cochrane Drive
Suite 105
Annapolis, MD 21401

410-694-0800
FAX 410-694-0900
E-Mail: fpa@flexpack.org
Home Page: www.flexpack.org

Marla Donahue, President

One of the leading trade associations for converters of flexible packaging and suppliers to the industry. Also provides a wealth of information to its members through focused services and benefits of membership.

17506 Food & Beverage Marketplace Directory
Grey House Publishing
4919 Route 22
PO Box 56
Amenia, NY 12501-0056

518-789-8700
800-562-2139
FAX 518-789-0556
E-Mail: books@greyhouse.com

Home Page: www.greyhouse.com
Social Media: *Facebook, Twitter*

Richard Gottlieb, President
Leslie Mackenzie, Publisher

A three-volume set that is the most comprehensive resource in the food and beverage industry. Available in print, a subscription-based online database, as well as a mailing list and database formats.
Cost: $595.00
2000 Pages
Frequency: Annual
Founded in 1981

17507 Grocery Manufacturers Association
1350 Eye St NW
Suite 300
Washington, DC 20005-3377

202-639-5900
FAX 202-639-5932
E-Mail: info@gmaonline.org
Home Page: www.gmabrands.com
Social Media: *Facebook, Twitter, RSS*

Pamela G Bailey, President
Jim Flannery, Senior Executive Vice President
Dr. Leon Bruner, DVM, Ph.D., Senior Vice President
Louis Finkel, Executive Vice President
Sean Darragh, Executive Vice President, Global

Manufacturers of food and nonfood products sold through the grocery trade. US sales are more than $500 billion, GMA members employ more than 2.5 million workers in the nation.
135 Members
Founded in 1908

17508 International Packaged Ice Association
238 East Davis Blvd
Suite 213
Tampa, FL 33606

813-258-1690
E-Mail: jane@packagedice.com
Home Page: www.packagedice.com
Social Media: *Facebook, YouTube*

Bob Morse, Chairman
Bo Russell, Vice Chairman/Treasurer
John Smibert, Secretary/Assistant Treasurer
Mike Ringstaff, Associate Member

Manufacturers and distributors of ice and their suppliers.
150 Members
Founded in 1917

17509 Manufacturers' Agents National Association
6321 W. Dempster Street
Suite 110
Morton Grove, IL 60053

949-859-4040
877-626-2776
FAX 949-855-2973
E-Mail: MANA@MANAonline.org
Home Page: www.manaonline.org
Social Media: *Facebook, Twitter, LinkedIn, YouTube, Google+*

ken McGregor, Chairman
Charles Cohon, CPMR, President and CEO
Jerry Leth, Vice President and General Manager
Lisa Ball, Member Services Coordinator
Doug Bower, Director of Strategic Alliances

Association for independent agents and firms representing manufacturers and other businesses in specified territories on a commission basis, including consultants and associate member firms interested in the manufacturer/agency method of marketing.
Founded in 1947

17510 Material Handling Institute
8720 Red Oak Blvd # 201
Suite 201
Charlotte, NC 28217-3996

704-676-1190
FAX 704-676-1199
E-Mail: gbaer@mhia.org
Home Page: www.mhi.org
Social Media: *Facebook, Twitter, LinkedIn, Youtube, Blooger, RSS*

Dave Young, Chairman
John Paxton, President
Gregg E. Goodner, Vice President

Industrial steel shelving is loaded by hand and generally stores materials that are small in size, with multiple parts stores on a given shelf separated by dividers, boxes and drawers.
400 Members
Founded in 1945

17511 National Association of Display Industries
4651 Sheridan Street
Suite 470
Hollywood, FL 33021

954-893-7300
FAX 954-893-7500
E-Mail: nadi@nadi-global.com
Home Page: www.nadi-global.com

Klein Merriman, Executive Director
Tracy Dillon, Director Communications

A leading association for the visual merchandising profession. As visual merchandising has evolved over the years into playing an integral role in retail, NADI has always taken the lead in information and educating members. The association's already significant support for the visual design profession has grown with NADI's exclusive sponsorship of GlobalShop's Visual Merchandising Show and StoreXpo.
350 Members
Founded in 1942

17512 National Association of Manufacturers
733 10th Street NW
Suite 700
Washington, DC 20001

202-637-3000
800-814-8468
FAX 202-637-3182
E-Mail: manufacturing@nam.org
Home Page: www.nam.org
Social Media: *Facebook, Twitter, LinkedIn, Youtube, RSS, Flickr*

Gregg M. Lundgren, Chairman
John F. Lundgren, Vice Chairman
Jay Timmons, President
Linda E. Kelly, Senior Vice President, Legal
Richard I. Klein, Senior Vice President

Enhances the competitiveness of manufacturers and improves American living standards by shaping a legislative and regulatory environment conductive to US economic growth and to increase understanding among policy makers, the media and the general public about the importance of manufacturing to America's economic strength.
14000 Members
Founded in 1895

17513 National Automatic Merchandising Association
20 N Wacker Dr # 3500
Suite 3500
Chicago, IL 60606-3102

312-346-0370
FAX 312-704-4140
E-Mail: dmathews@vending.org

Home Page: www.vending.org
Social Media: *Facebook, Twitter, YouTube*

Howard Chapman, NCE, CCS, Chairman
Patrick Hagerty, Chair Elect
Heidi Chico, Vice Chair
Peter A. Tullio, Past Chair
Jeffery R. Smith, Secretary/Treasurer

Serves food and refreshment, vending, contract foodservice management and office coffee service industries.
2500 Members
Founded in 1936

17514 National Cotton Batting Institute

4322 Bloombury St
Southaven, MS 38672

901-218-2393
FAX 662-449-0046
E-Mail: info@natbat.com
Home Page: www.natbat.com

Weston Arnall, President
Greg Windsperger, VP
Fred Middleton, Executive Secretary-Treasurer

NCBI respresents U.S. companies that manufacture and sell batting for use in mattresses, futons, home furnishing, and upholstered products. It provides a range of services to assist its members in expanding markets, monitoring and contributing to legislative and regulatory decisions that affect the industry, and conducting consumer education and information programs.
27 Members
Founded in 1954

17515 North American Punch Manufacturers Association

21 Turquoise Avenue
Naples, FL 34114

239-775-7245
FAX 239-775-7245
E-Mail: bobjanmay@napma.org
Home Page: www.napmaa.org/aboutus.asp

Robert E May, Executive Secretary

Principal program of NAPMA is the standardization of all punches, dies and retainers manufactured by the various member companies.
23 Members
Founded in 1963

17516 Pressure Vessel Manufacturers Association

800 Roosevelt Rd.
Building C,Suite 312
Glen Ellyn, IL 60137

630-942-6590
FAX 630-790-3095
E-Mail: info@pvma.org
Home Page: www.pvma.org/

Rick Fryda, President
Bill Kahl, Vice President
Brooke Cornard, Secretary/Treasurer
GregŸMc Rae, Director
Michael Pischke, Immediate Past President

Members are manufacturers of ASME code pressure vessels and suppliers, components and services to pressure vessel manfacturers.
31 Members
Founded in 1975

17517 Production and Operations Management Society

Dept. of Management-Univ. of Baltimore
1420 N Charles Street
Baltimore, MD 21201-5720

410-837-4727
FAX 410-837-5675
E-Mail: poms@eng.fiu.edu
Home Page: www.poms.org/

Sushil Gupta, PhD, Executive Director
Chelliah Sriskandarajah, Ph.D., Associate

Executive Director
Metin Çakanyildirim, Associate Professor of Operations

Members are professionals and academics with an interest in production and operations management.
1200 Members
Founded in 1989

17518 Refractories Institute

1300 Sumner Avenue
Cleveland, OH 44115

216-241-7333
FAX 216-241-0105
E-Mail: info@refractoriesinstitute.org
Home Page: www.refractoriesinstitute.org

Robert Crolius, President

National trade association for refractory manufacturers, suppliers of equipment and raw materials and installers of refractory products.
80 Members
Founded in 1951

17519 Remanufacturing Industries Council

RICI
4401 Fair Lakes Ct
Suite 210
Fairfax, VA 22033-3848

FAX 703-968-2878
Home Page: www.rici.org
Social Media: *Facebook, LinkedIn, Google+*

Larry Rice, CEO

A coalition of associations and companies in the remanufacturing industry.
Founded in 1997

17520 Remanufacturing Institute

Po Box 48
Lewisburg, PA 17837

570-523-0992
FAX 705-555-5555
E-Mail: rgiuntini@reman.org
Home Page: www.reman.org

Ron Giuntini, Executive Director

A coalition of associations and companies in the entire manufacturing industry. There are over 73,000 companies in this industry. Our goal is to unite them into a powerful organization.
11 Members
Founded in 1997

17521 The Benchmarking Network

4606 Fm 1960 Rd W
Suite #250
Houston, TX 77069-4617

281-440-5044
FAX 281-440-6677
Home Page: www.benchmarkingnetwork.com
Social Media: *Facebook, Twitter*

AMBC is a focused group of manufacturing process improvement professionals that looks to identify the best practices surrounding manufacturing issues for the overall operations of the members.

17522 Ultrasonic Industry Association

PO Box 2307
Dayton, OH 45401-2301

937-586-3725
FAX 937-586-3699
E-Mail: uia@ultrasonics.org
Home Page: www.ultrasonics.org

Mark Hodnett, President
Mark Schafer, VP
Ron Stault, Treasurer
Janet Devine, Secretary

Improving processes, techniques and materials through the application of ultasonic technology.
70 Members
Founded in 1956

17523 United Association of Manufacturers Representatives

P.O. Box 4216
Dana Point, CA 92669

949-481-5214
FAX 417-779-1576
E-Mail: info@uamr.com
Home Page: www.uamr.com/

Karen Kittrell Mazzola, Executive Director

Benefits manufacturers and independent sales representatives and is a national marketing association.
3,000 Members
Founded in 1965

17524 Waste Equipment Technology Association

4301 Connecticut Ave Nw
Suite 300
Washington, DC 20008-2304

202-244-4700
800-424-2869
FAX 202-966-4824
E-Mail: wastecinfo@WASTEC.org
Home Page: www.wasterecycling.org
Social Media: *Facebook, Twitter, LinkedIn, Youtube*

Mike Savage, Chairman
Sharon H. Kneiss, President and CEO
Philip Hagan, Director, Safety
Sheila R. Alkire, Director, Education
Catherine Maimon, Manager, Meetings

Manufacturers of waste handling, collection and processing equipment.
Founded in 1972

Newsletters

17525 Infocus Newsletter

319 SW Washington Street
Suite 710
Portland, OR 97204-2618

503-227-3393
FAX 503-274-7667
Home Page: www.bfma.org

Lea Anne A Fuchs, President
Andy Palatka, Executive Director
Tonya Macalino, Adversiting and Sales

Infocus is a newsletter focused on industry topics and products.
Cost: $75.00
Circulation: 1,100
Founded in 1960
Mailing list available for rent: 1M names at $200 per M

17526 Innovators Digest

InfoTeam
PO Box 15640
Plantation, FL 33318-5640

954-473-9560
FAX 954-473-0544

Merton Allen, Editor

A multidisciplinary publication covering developments in science, engineering, products, markets, business development, manufacturing and other technological developments having industrial or commercial significance.
Frequency: Bi-Annual

17527 Intelligent Manufacturing

Lionheart Publishing

2555 Cumberland Pkwy Se
Suite 299
Atlanta, GA 30339-3921

770-432-2551
FAX 770-432-6969
E-Mail: llewellyn@lionhrtpub.com

John Llewellyn, Publisher
David Blanchard, Editor

Provides expert solutions to manufacturing professionals covering production problems, developments in manufacturing systems.
Cost: $20.00
Circulation: 1,598

17528 Manufacturing Technology
National Technical Information Service
5285 Port Royal Rd
Springfield, VA 22161-0001

703-605-6000
FAX 703-605-6900
E-Mail: info@ntis.gov
Home Page: www.ntis.gov

Linda Davis, VP
Patrik Ekstr"m, Business Development Manager
Reuel Avila, Managing Director

Covers CAD/CAM, robotics, robots, productivity, manufacturing, planning, processing and control, plant design and computer software.

17529 News & Views
American Mold Builders Association
3601 Algonquin Rd
Suite 304
Rolling Meadows, IL 60008-3136

847-222-9402
FAX 630-980-9714
E-Mail: info@amba.org
Home Page: www.amba.org

Melissa Millhuff, Executive Director
Peter Manship, Managing Director
Kym Conis, Managing Director
Frequency: Quarterly
Circulation: 2000
Founded in 1973

17530 Noise Regulation Report
Business Publishers
2222 Sedwick Drive
Durham, NC 27713

800-223-8720
FAX 800-508-2592
E-Mail: custserv@bpinews.com
Home Page: www.bpinews.com

Exclusive coverage of airport, highway, occupational and open space noise, noise control and mitigation issues.
Cost: $511.00
10 Pages
Frequency: 12 per year
Printed in on matte stock

17531 RPA Newsletter
Retail Packaging Association
2205 Warwick Way, Suite 110
Marriottsville, MD 21104

410-925-9809
FAX 513-527-4999
E-Mail: info@retailpackaging.org
Home Page: www.retailpackaging.org

Joel Zaas, President
Frequency: Weekly
Founded in 1989

17532 Service Management
National Association of Service Management

PO Box 250796
Milwaukee, WI 53225

414-466-6060
FAX 414-466-0840
Home Page: www.nasm.com

Don Buelow, Publisher
Caryn Anderson, Editor
Ken Cook, Treasurer

Offers information on manufacturing and service companies.
40 Pages
Frequency: Quarterly
Circulation: 300

17533 Vision
Society of Manufacturing Engineers
1 SME Drive
PO Box 930
Dearborn, MI 48128

313-425-3000
800-733-4763
FAX 313-425-3400
E-Mail: service@sme.org
Home Page: www.sme.org

Mark Tomlinson, Executive Director
Greg Sheremet, Publisher

The newsletter highlights the latest developments in the machine vision industry including applications, techniques and methods.
Cost: $75.00
Frequency: Quarterly
Circulation: 1,100
ISSN: 1544-3531
Founded in 1984

Magazines & Journals

17534 APICS: The Performance Advantage
APICS Association for Operations Management
5301 Shawnee Road
Alexandria, VA 22312-2317

703-548-8851
FAX 703-354-8106
E-Mail: webmaster@apics.org
Home Page: www.apics.org

Doug Kelly, Editor
Jennifer Procter, Managing Editor
Jeffery Raynes, CEO

Provides comprehensive articles on enterprise resources planning, supply chain management, e-business, materials management and production and inventory management.
Cost: $65.00
64 Pages
Circulation: 66000
ISSN: 1056-0017
Mailing list available for rent: 40,000 names at $100 per M
Printed in 4 colors on glossy stock

17535 Adhesives & Sealants
Business News Publishing Company
PO Box 400
Flossmoor, IL 60422

708-922-0761
FAX 708-922-0762
E-Mail: mcphersont@bnpmedia.com
Home Page: www.adhesivesmag.com

Susan Love, Publisher
Teresa Mc Pherson, Editor
Kari Rowe, Circulation Manager
Violeta Ivezaj, Senior Marketing Manager
Cost: $33.00
Frequency: Monthly
Circulation: 15000
Founded in 1926

17536 Adhesives Age
2 Grand Central Tower
140 East 45th Street, 40th Floor
New York, NY 10017

212-884-9528
FAX 212-884-9514
E-Mail: ltattum@chemweek.com
Home Page: www.chemweek.com

Lyn Tattum, Group Vice President/Publisher
Joe Minnella, Global Sales Director

Adhesives Age provides readers with vital information: global industry coverage of the development, manufacture, and application of adhesives, sealants, and related products.
Cost: $75.00
62 Pages
Frequency: Weekly
Circulation: 22994
ISSN: 0001-821X
Founded in 1958
Mailing list available for rent
Printed in 4 colors on glossy stock

17537 Advanced Materials & Processes
ASM International
9639 Kinsman Rd
Materials Park, OH 44073

440-338-5151
800-336-5152
FAX 440-338-4634
E-Mail: memberservices@asminternational.org
Home Page: www.asminternational.org
Social Media: *Facebook, Twitter, LinkedIn*

Joseph M Zion, Publisher
Joanne Miller, Managing Editor
Margaret Hunt, Editor-in-Chief
Jeane Deatherage, Administrator, Foundation Programs
Virginia Shirk, Foundation Executive Assistant

AM&P, the monthly technical magazine from ASM International, is designed to keep readers aware of leading-edge developments and trends in engineering materials - metals and alloys, engineering polymers, advanced ceramics, and composites - and the methods used to select, process, fabricate, test, and characterize them.
Frequency: Monthly
Circulation: 32M
Founded in 1977

17538 American Fastener Journal
Carol McGuire
11305 E. Monument Drive
Scottsdale, AZ 85262-4746

480-488-3500
FAX 480-488-3247
E-Mail: mmcguire@fastenerjournal.com
Home Page: www.fastenerjournal.com

Mike McGuire, Publisher/Editor
Jackie McGuire, Executive Editor
Micki Leopard, Circulation Manager

This journal for the fastener industry covers technical articles, inspections, quality assurance, materials applications, specifications and standards, as well as manufacturer, distributors and supplier profiles. Publishes annual buyers guide - The American Fastener Source Guide
Cost: $45.00
Circulation: 13000
Founded in 1981
Printed in 4 colors on glossy stock

17539 American Funeral Director
Kates-Boylston Publications
11300 Rockville Pike
Suite 1100
Rockville, MD 20852

800-500-4585
800-500-4585

FAX 732-730-2515
Home Page: www.kates-boylston.com

Adrian F Boylston, Publisher
Thomas Parmalee, Executive Director
Amy Fidalgo, Production Manager

Articles on funeral home construction, finance, mortuary law, shipment of human remains by air transportation, sales and display methods, advertising and public relations, new equipment and other association activiies. Also includes personnel news about funeral directors and related supply firms.
Cost: $49.95
Frequency: Monthly
Circulation: 12168
Founded in 1918

17540 Automatic Machining Magazine
Screw Machine Publishing Company
1066 Gravel Rd
Suite 201
Webster, NY 14580-1769

585-787-0820
800-610-6950
FAX 585-787-0868
Home Page: www.automachmag.com

Wayne Wood, President
Linda Iobiondo, Circulation Manager

General industry news for professionals in the metal turning and cold forming fields.
Cost: $55.00
142 Pages
Frequency: Monthly
Circulation: 13000
Founded in 1939
Printed in 4 colors on glossy stock

17541 CNC West
Arnold Publications
14340 Bolsa Chica Avenue E
PO Box 100
Westminster, CA 92684-100

714-899-0733
FAX 714-899-0738
E-Mail: larnold@cnc-west.com
Home Page: www.cnc-west.com

Shawn Arnold, Publisher
Chuck Bush, Editor
Shawn Arnold, CEO/President
Shawn Arnold, Circulation Manager
Shawn Arnold, Marketing Manager

News and trends on western jobshops and manufacturers
Cost: $32.50
Circulation: 22000
Founded in 1981
Printed in 4 colors on glossy stock

17542 Card Manufacturing
International Card Manufacturing Association
PO Box 727
Princeton Junction, NJ 08550-727

609-799-4900
FAX 609-799-7032
E-Mail: info@icma.com
Home Page: www.icma.com

Lynn McCullough, Association Manager
Jeffrey E Barnhart, Communications Manager
Kaitlin Friedmann, Communications Manager
Al Vrancart, Founder

Advertiser supported trade magazine featuring industry news and features on all aspects of the plastic card production worldwide, and the news of the ICMA.
Cost: $75.00
Circulation: 3000

17543 Coatings World
Rodman Publishing

70 Hilltop Rd
Suite 3000
Ramsey, NJ 07446-1150

201-825-2552
FAX 201-825-0553
E-Mail: info@rodpub.com
Home Page: www.nutraceuticalsworld.com
Social Media: *Facebook, Twitter, LinkedIn*

Rodman Zilenziger Jr, President
Matt Montgomery, VP

Coatings World is directed at industry personnel concerned with developing and manufacturing paints, coatings, adhesives and sealants. Feature articles and industry news are directed at chemists, formulators and all levels of management that must keep abreast of technical products and market developments.
Cost: $50.00
136 Pages
Frequency: Monthly
Circulation: 17315
ISSN: 1527-1129
Mailing list available for rent
Printed in 4 colors on glossy stock

17544 Composites Fabrication
Composites Fabricators Association
1010 N Glebe Rd
Suite 450
Arlington, VA 22201-4749

703-525-0714
FAX 703-525-0743
E-Mail: info@acmanet.org
Home Page: www.acmanet.org/

Elly Shariat, Marketing Manager
Andy Rusnak, Editor
Roxanne Fraver, Marketing & Circulation
Sabeena Hickman, Deputy Director
Jessica Howard, Production Manager

Presents information on new technology, trends and techniques for manufacturers in the fiberglass and composites industry.
Cost: $41.00
114 Pages
Circulation: 8000
ISSN: 1084-841X
Printed in 4 colors on glossy stock

17545 Consumer Goods Technology
Edgell Communications
4 Middlebury Boulevard
Randolph, NJ 07869

973-252-0100
FAX 973-252-9020
Home Page: www.consumergoods.com

Andrew Gaffney, Group Publisher
Steve Rosenstock, Publisher
Tim Clark, Editor-in-Chief
Alliston Ackerman, Assistant Editor
Pat Wisser, Production Manager

Provides case histories, technology overviews, new products and industry news to assist corporations and management in the consumer goods industry.
Frequency: Monthly
Circulation: 25000
Founded in 1984

17546 Contingency Planning & Management
Witter Publishing Corporation
20 Commerce Street
Flemington, NJ 08822

908-788-0343
FAX 908-788-3782
Home Page: www.witterpublishing.com

Bob Joudanin, Publisher
Paul Kirvan, Editor In Chief
Courtney Writter, Circulation Manager
Andrew Witter, President

Serves the fields of financial/banking, manufacturing industrial, transportation, utilities, telecommunications, health care, government, insurance and other allied fields.
Frequency: Monthly
Founded in 1987

17547 Contract Management
National Contract Management Association
1912 Woodford Road
Vienna, VA 22182-3728

703-489-9231
800-344-8096
FAX 703-448-0939
E-Mail: memberservices@ncmahq.org
Home Page: www.ncmahq.org

Amy Miedema, Editor-in-Chief
Neal Couture, Executive Director

It covers the myriad aspects of government and commercial contract management. News and features provide information on such topics as procurement policy, on-the-job techniques, regulations, case law, ethics, contract administration, electronic commerce, international and small business matters, education and career development.
Cost: $75.00
80 Pages
Frequency: Monthly
Circulation: 22000
Founded in 1959
Printed in 4 colors on glossy stock

17548 Control Design
Putman Media
555 W Pierce Rd
Suite 301
Itasca, IL 60143-2626

630-467-1300
FAX 630-467-0197
E-Mail: lgoldberg@putman.net
Home Page: www.putman.net

John Cappelletti, President
Mike Bacidore, Editor-in-Chief/Publisher
Anetta Gauthier, Production Manager
Lori Goldberg, Operations Manager

Markets to the manufacturing facilities under the government's standard industry classification (SIC) code 35, which manufacture a broad range of products from turbines, conveyors and machine tools to food processing, printing presses and computers.
Cost: $96.00
Circulation: 50,046
ISSN: 1094-3366
Founded in 1938
Printed in 4 colors

17549 Design News
Reed Business Information
30 Technology Parkway South
Suite 100
Norcross, GA 30092

646-746-6400
800-424-3996
FAX 646-756-7583
E-Mail: webmaster@reedbusiness.com
Home Page: www.reedbusiness.com

John Poulin, CEO
Karen Auguston Field, Editor-in-Chief
James Reed, Owner

Informs professionals in the technology industry of all the latest in new product introductions in fields such as bearings, fastening/joining and new technology.
Circulation: 170000

17550 Distributor's Link
4297 Corporate Sq
Naples, FL 34104-4754

239-643-2713
800-356-1639
FAX 239-643-5220
E-Mail: leojcoar@linkmagazine.com
Home Page: www.linkmagazine.com/

Maryann Marzocchi, President
Tracey Lumia, Director of Sales and Marketing

Information aimed at the fastener distributors nationwide.
Cost: $45.00
Frequency: Quarterly
Circulation: 50000
Founded in 1975

17551 Edplay
Fahy-Williams Publishing
PO Box 1080
Geneva, NY 14456-8080

315-789-0458
800-344-0559
FAX 315-789-4263
Home Page: www.edplay.com

Kevin Fahy, Publisher
Tina Manzer, Editorial Director
Mark Stash, Art Director
Alyssa Lafaro, Associate Editor

Serves toy manufacturers and dealers. Offers product reviews, industry profiles, and reader surveys.
Circulation: 13000
Founded in 1984

17552 Fastener Technology International
Initial Publications
PO Box 5451
Akron, OH 44334-0451

330-864-2122
FAX 330-864-5298
E-Mail: mcnulty@fastenertech.com
Home Page: www.fastenertech.com

Job Lippincott, Publisher
Michael J. McNulty, Vice President and Editor

Contains articles on company profiles, new equipment, literature, products, fastener topics and patents.
Cost: $40.00
Circulation: 13,000
Founded in 1981
Printed in 4 colors on glossy stock

17553 Fastening
Mike McGuire
293 Hopewell Drive
Powell, OH 43065-9350

614-848-3232
800-848-0304
FAX 614-848-5045
Home Page: www.fastening.com

Mike McGuire, Publisher

In-depth and up-to-date information about fastening products, design/applications, people, companies, fastening industry events and specifications.
Cost: $30.00
Frequency: Quarterly
Circulation: 28,000
Founded in 1995
Printed in 4 colors on glossy stock

17554 Forming & Fabricating
Society of Manufacturing Engineers
1 SME Drive
Box 930
Dearborn, MI 48128

313-425-3000
800-733-4763
FAX 313-425-3400

E-Mail: advertising@sme.org
Home Page: www.sme.org

Mark Tomlinson, Executive Director
Greg Sheremet, Publisher

News and features regarding the forming and fabricating industry with the intention of improving process productivity and project quality. Special focus on technology and its applications in manufacturing.
Frequency: Monthly
Circulation: 66616

17555 ITE Solutions
Institute of Industrial Engineers
25 Technology Pkwy S
Suite 150
Norcross, GA 30092-2946

770-449-0461
FAX 770-263-8532
E-Mail: webmaster@iienet.org
Home Page: www.iienet.org

17556 InTech
Instrumentation, Systems, and Automation Society
67 Alexander Drive
Research Triangle Park, NC 27709

919-549-8411
FAX 919-990-9434
E-Mail: info@isa.org
Home Page: www.isa.org

Richard Simpson, Publisher
Greg Hale, Editor
Rob Renner, Executive Officer
Chip Lee, Publication Director

Regular issue features include new product developments, new processes, research updates and general industry news.
Cost: $75.00
Frequency: Monthly
Circulation: 67000
Founded in 1945

17557 Industrial Equipment News
Thomas Publishing Company
5 Penn Plz
Suite 10
New York, NY 10001-1860

212-695-0500
800-733-1127
FAX 212-290-7362
E-Mail: businesslists@thomaspublishing.com
Home Page: www.thomaspublishing.com

Carl Holst-Knudsen, CEO
Joseph Rosta, Editor-in-Chief
Marie Urbanowicz, Marketing Manager

Serves the industrial field including manufacturing, mining, utilities, construction, transportation, governmental establishments, and educational services.
Frequency: Monthly
ISSN: 0019-8258
Founded in 1898

17558 Industrial Maintenance & Plant Operation
Reed Business Information
199 East Badger Road
Suite 201
Madison, WI 53713

973-920-7787
FAX 973-920-7531
E-Mail: hpendrak@reedbusiness.com
Home Page: www.impomag.com

Scott Sward, Publisher
Rick Carter, Editor-in-Chief
R Reed, Owner

Kyle Orr, Circulation Manager
Hank Pendrak, Marketing Director
Circulation: 100000
Founded in 1975

17559 Industrial Market Place
Wineberg Publications
7842 Lincoln Avenue
Skokie, IL 60077

847-676-1900
800-323-1818
FAX 847-676-0063
E-Mail: info@industrialmktpl.com
Home Page: www.industrialmktpl.com

Joel Wineberg, President
Jackie Bitensky, Editor

Has advertisements on machinery, industrial and plant equipment and services and industrial auctions in each issue.
Cost: $175.00
Circulation: 14000
Founded in 1951
Mailing list available for rent: 120 names at $70 per M
Printed in 4 colors on glossy stock

17560 Job Shop Technology
Edward Publishing
16 Waterbury Road
Prospect, CT 06712-1215

203-758-4474
800-317-0474
FAX 203-758-3427
Home Page: www.jobshoptechnology.com

Mark W Shortt, Editor
Cindy Wilkinson, Circulation Director

Published to aid product manufacturers who outsource parts and manufacturing services. Specializes in manufacturing processes for the metals, plastics, rubber, and electronics industries, including virtually any outsourced manufacturing service.
Frequency: Quarterly
Circulation: 100,000
Founded in 1986
Mailing list available for rent: 90875 names at $125 per M
Printed in 4 colors on glossy stock

17561 Journal of Coatings Technology
Federation of Societies for Coatings Technology
527 Plymouth Rd
Suite 415
Plymouth Meetin, PA 19462-1641

610-940-0777
FAX 610-940-0292
Home Page: www.coatingstech.org

Robert F Ziegler, Publisher
Patricia D Ziegler, Administrative Assistant
Shelby Ferguson, Administrative Assistant
Chris Hobson, Communications Manager
Lance Edwards, Director

For the industrial and service organizations in paint and manufacturing plants, raw materials suppliers for coatings, printing inks and sealants.
Cost: $120.00
Frequency: Monthly

17562 Journal of Materials Engineering and Performance
ASM International
9639 Kinsman Road
Materials Park, OH 44073-0002

440-338-5151
800-336-5152
FAX 440-338-4634
E-Mail: memberservice@asminternational.org

Home Page: www.asminternational.org
Social Media: *Facebook, Twitter, LinkedIn*

Jeane Deatherage, Administrator, Foundation Programs
Virginia Shirk, Foundation Executive Assistant

Peer-reviewed journal that publishes contributions on all aspects of materials selection, design, characterization, processing and performance testing. The journal for solving day-to-day engineering challenges - especially those involving components for larger systems.
Cost: $1965.00
Frequency: Bimonthly
Circulation: 305
Founded in 1992

17563 Journal of Phase Equilibria
ASM International
9639 Kinsman Rd
Materials Park, OH 44072

440-338-5151
800-336-5152
FAX 440-338-4634
E-Mail: memberservices@asminternational.org
Home Page: www.asminternational.org
Social Media: *Facebook, Twitter, LinkedIn*

Jeane Deatherage, Administrator, Foundation Programs
Virginia Shirk, Foundation Executive Assistant

Peer-reviewed journal that contains basic and applied research results, evaluated phase diagrams, a survey of current literature, and comments or other material pertinent to the previous three areas. The aim is to provide a broad spectrum of information concerning phase equilibria for the materials community.
Cost: $1965.00
Frequency: Bimonthly
Circulation: 305

17564 Journal of Process Control
Butterworth Heinemann
313 Washington Street
Newton, MA 02458-1626

617-928-5460
FAX 781-933-6333

JD Perkins, Editor
T McAvoy, Regional Editor

Covers the application of control theory, operations research, computer science and engineering principles to the solution of process control problems.

17565 Journal of Quality Technology
American Society for Quality
600 N Plankinton Avenue
PO Box 3005
Milwaukee, WI 53201-3005

414-272-8575
800-248-1946
FAX 414-272-1734
E-Mail: help@asq.org
Home Page: www.asq.org
Social Media: *Facebook, Twitter, LinkedIn*

Roberto M Saco, President
Paul E Borawski, Executive Director
Erica Gumieny, Sales
Fay Spano, Communications/Media Relations

Published by the American Society for Quality, the JQT is a quarterly, peer-reviewed journal that focuses on the subject of quality control and the related areas of reliability and similar disciplines.
Cost: $30.00
100M Members
Frequency: Quarterly
Founded in 1946

17566 Maintenance Technology
Applied Technology Publications

1300 S Grove Ave
Suite 105
Barrington, IL 60010-5246

847-382-8100
FAX 847-304-8603
Home Page: www.mt-online.com

Arthur Rice, President/CEO
Bill Kiesel, Vice President/Publisher
Jane Alexander, Editor-In-Chief
Rick Carter, Executive Editor
Randy Buttstadt, Director of Creative Services

Maintenance Technology magazine serves the business and technical information needs of managers and engineers responsible for assuring availability of plant equipment and systems. It provides readers with articles on advanced technologies, strategies, tools, and services for the life-cycle management of capital assets.
Frequency: Monthly
Circulation: 50,827
Mailing list available for rent: 35,263 names at $$15 per M

17567 Managing Automation
Thomas Publishing Company
5 Penn Plz
Suite 10
New York, NY 10001-1860

212-695-0500
800-733-1127
FAX 212-290-7362
E-Mail: contact@thomaspublishing.com
Home Page: www.thomaspublishing.com

Carl Holst-Knudsen, CEO
Greg MacSweeney, Managing Editor
Kim Vennard, Senior Marketing Manager
Shawn Jacobs, Director of Sales

Serves the needs of those managers and engineers responsible for the planning and implementation of factory automation at both the plant and enterprise levels.
Cost: $60.00
Frequency: Monthly
Circulation: 100246
Founded in 1898

17568 Manufacturers Mart
Philip G Cannon Jr
PO Box 310
Georgetown, MA 01833-0410

978-352-3320
800-835-0017
FAX 401-348-0797
E-Mail: info@manufacturersmart.com
Home Page: www.manufacturersmart.com

Phillip Cannon, Publisher
Linda Smith, Editor

Information and news on manufacturing companies with a regional focus in New England. New product articles, coverage of advances in technology, compliance issues, case studies, announcements and calendar events. Online version includes searchable index of products and services.
32 Pages
Frequency: Monthly
Circulation: 30000
Founded in 1978
Printed in 4 colors on newsprint stock

17569 Manufacturing Engineering
Society of Manufacturing Engineers
1 SME Drive
PO Box 930
Dearborn, MI 48128

313-425-3000
800-733-4763
FAX 313-425-3400

E-Mail: advertising@sme.org
Home Page: www.sme.org

Mark Tomlinson, Executive Director
Greg Sheremet, Publisher
Karen Manardo, Director of Communication
Tom Drozda, Publisher/Advertising

Serves metalworking industry machining, forming, inspection, assembly and processing operations.
Frequency: Monthly
Circulation: 1,11,966
Founded in 1932

17570 Manufacturing News
Publishers & Producers
PO Box 36
Annandale, VA 22003

703-750-2664
FAX 703-750-0064
E-Mail: editor@manufacturingnews.com
Home Page: www.manufacturingnews.com

Richard McCormack, Publisher/Editor

Gives in-depth analysis of critical manufacturing trends, insightful interviews with top players in industry and government and up-to-the-minute business news about issues that directly affect your ability to compete and prosper and takes a look at software and hardware, sucessful manufacturers, and profound technological changes.
Cost: $495.00
12 Pages
Frequency: Fortnightly
Circulation: 30,000
ISSN: 1078-2397
Founded in 1994
Printed in on matte stock

17571 Manufacturing Systems
2000 Clearwater Drive
Oak Brook, IL 60523-8809

630-288-8000
FAX 630-320-7373
Home Page: www.manufacturing.net

Michelle Palmer, Publisher
Mary Ann Brockway, Circulation Manager
David Greenfield, Editor

Information management for increased manufacturing productivity.
Cost: $6.00
Frequency: Monthly
Circulation: 114682

17572 Marketeer
1602 E Glen Avenue
Peoria, IL 61614-5451

VB Cook, Editor

New products for manufacturing.
Cost: $15.00
16 Pages
Frequency: Monthly
Founded in 1952

17573 Marking Industry Magazine
Marking Devices Publishing Company
136 W Vallette St
Suite 6
Elmhurst, IL 60126-4377

630-832-5200
FAX 630-832-5206
Home Page: www.markingdevices.com

David Hachmeister, President

New products, processes and services, MDAI and other association news, shows and seminars, sales and management methods.
Cost: $54.00
Frequency: Monthly
Circulation: 1300
Founded in 1907

17574 Material Handling Equipment Distributors Association
Data Key Communications
201 US Highway 45
Vernon Hills, IL 60061-2398

847-680-3500
FAX 847-362-6989
E-Mail: connect@mheda.org
Home Page: www.mheda.org

Loren Swakow, President
Elizabeth Richard, Editor/Executive VP
Kathy Carter, Marketing Manager

Updates on technology, association news and announcements, industrial perspectives and outlook and new product information.
Cost: $24.00
Frequency: Quarterly
Circulation: 4000
Founded in 1954

17575 Material Handling Network
Network Publishing
252 E Washington Street
East Peoria, IL 61611-338

309-699-4431
800-447-6901
FAX 309-698-0801
Home Page: www.mhnetwork.com

Andra Stephens, Editor
Bob Behrens, General Manager
Andra Stephens, Advertising/Sales
Mindi Mitzelfelt, Graphic Designer

Monthly journal written for material handling distributors/dealers and people who sell racks, bins, conveyors, dock equipment, lift trucks, batteries, and pallet jacks - both power and non-power.
Cost: $65.00
156 Pages
Frequency: Monthly
Circulation: 12058
Founded in 1981
Printed in 4 colors on n stock

17576 Material Handling Product News
Reed Business Information
225 Wyman St
Suite 3
Waltham, MA 02451-1216

781-734-8000
FAX 781-734-8076
Home Page: www.reedbusiness.com

Mark Finklestein, President
Joseph Pagnotta, Editor-in-Chief
Joanna Schumann, Marketing Manager
Michael Holowchuck, Circulation Manager
Steve McCoy, Associate Publisher

Literature reviews, new product listings and new systems and services are featured regularly.
Frequency: Monthly
Founded in 1977

17577 Materials at High Temperatures
Butterworth Heinemann
313 Washington Street
Newton, MA 02458-1626

617-928-5460
FAX 781-933-6333

T Suzuki, Co-Editor
TB Gibbons, Co-Editor

Serves the needs of those developing and using materials for high temperature applications in the power, chemical, engine, processing and furnace industries.

17578 Mid-America Commerce & Industry
Mid-America Commerce & Industry

2432 Sw Pepperwood Rd
Topeka, KS 66614-5293

785-272-5280
FAX 785-272-3729
E-Mail: maci@maci-mag.com
Home Page: www.maci-mag.com/

David Lippe, President

Regional industrial magazine covering manufacturing in Missouri, Kansas, Nebraska, Oklahoma, Arizona and Iowa
Cost: $18.00
Frequency: Monthly

17579 Midrange ERP
MFG Publishing
9 W Street
Beverly, MA 01915-2225

978-927-1419
FAX 978-921-1255
E-Mail: editor@mfg-erp.com
Home Page: www.mfg-erp.com

Deborah A Turbide, Publisher

Planning and scheduling issues, polices and procedures, as well as system improvements.
Circulation: 40000
Founded in 1996

17580 Modern Applications News
Nelson Publishing
2500 Tamiami Trl N
Nokomis, FL 34275-3476

941-966-9521
FAX 941-966-2590
E-Mail: nelpub@ix.netcom.com
Home Page: www.healthmgttech.com
Social Media: Facebook

A Verner Nelson, President
John Mullaly, Editor
Bob Olree, Publisher
Joan Southerland, Marketing
Wyanne Harwell, Circulation Manager

Information includes coverage of abrasives and grinding, automated handling and robotics, CAD/CAM, coatings and finishings, coolants, lubricants and filters, cutting tools, heat treating, ID marking, lasers, machining centers, and shop control software.
Cost: $127.00
Frequency: Monthly
Circulation: 80340
Founded in 1962

17581 NC Shop Owner
Penton Media
1166 Avenue of the Americas/10th Fl
New York, NY 10036

212-204-4200
FAX 216-696-6662
E-Mail: information@penton.com
Home Page: www.penton.com

Jane Cooper, Marketing
Chris Meyer, Director, Corporate Communications

News of industry events, new product information, updates on manufacturing technology and a special technology focus section.
Frequency: Semiannual
Circulation: 120,000

17582 National Association of Relay Manufacturers
2500 Wilson Boulevard
Arlington, VA 22201

703-907-8025
FAX 703-875-8908
E-Mail: narm@ecaus.org
Home Page: www.ecaus.org/narm

Electronical relay and associated switching devices. Engrs. Relay HB - 5th Edition - $60.00 plus $7.00 postage and handling; IRC Proceed-

ing 2002 - $60.00 plus $7.00 postage and handling
Cost: $60.00
Circulation: 1000
Founded in 1947

17583 New Equipment Digest
Penton Media
1166 Avenue of the Americas/10th Fl
New York, NY 10036

212-204-4200
FAX 216-696-6662
E-Mail: information@penton.com
Home Page: www.penton.com

Chris Meyer, Director, Corporate Communications
Robert F King, Editor
Sarah Hughes, Production Manager
Bobbie Macy, Circulation Manager
David B. Nussbaum, CEO

Serves the general industrial field which include manufacturing, processing, engineering services, construction, transportation, mining, public utilities, wholesale distributors, educational services, libraries, and governmental establishments.
Frequency: Monthly
Circulation: 206154
Founded in 1892

17584 Off-Highway Engineering
SAE
400 Commonwealth Dr
Warrendale, PA 15086-7511

724-776-4841
877-606-7323
FAX 724-776-5760
E-Mail: sohe@sae.org
Home Page: www.saesections.org

Richard O Schaum, President

Off-Highway Engineering serves the international off highway design and manufacturing field which consists of producers of construction, lawn and garden, agricultural equipment, and industrial vehicles. Also served are makers of engines and parts and components and others allied to the field.
Cost: $70.00
66 Pages
Circulation: 16308
ISSN: 1074-6919
Founded in 1905
Printed in 4 colors on glossy stock

17585 Planning Guidebook
Reed Business Information
6 Alfred Circle
Bedford, MA 00173

972-980-8810
FAX 617-558-4700
E-Mail: corporatecommunications@reedbusiness.com
Home Page: www.designnews.com

William Shordon, Editor
Jim Casella, CEO

Offers information and news on manufacturing companies.
Frequency: Monthly
Founded in 1946

17586 Plant
Rogers Media Publishing
777 Bay Street
Toronto, Ontario M5W1A

416-596-5729
FAX 416-596-5552
Home Page: www.plant.ca

Joe Terrett, Editor
Kathy Smith, Production Manager
Jessica Jubb, Manager

PLANT serves manufacturing and processing industries in Canada.
Cost: $125.00
Frequency: 18 per year
ISSN: 0845-4213
Founded in 1941

17587 Plant Services
Putman Media
555 W Pierce Rd
Suite 301
Itasca, IL 60143-2626

630-467-1300
FAX 630-467-0197
E-Mail: mbrenner@putman.net
Home Page: www.putman.net

John Cappelletti, CEO
Mike Bacidore, Editor-in-Chief
Mike Brenner, Group Publisher
Keith Larson, VP Content

For maintenance and engineering managers responsible for keeping manufacturing plants running efficiently.
Cost: $96.00
Circulation: 80100
Founded in 1938
Mailing list available for rent: 10,000 names
Printed in 4 colors on glossy stock

17588 Plating and Surface Finishing
1155 Fifteenth Street, NW
Suite 500
Washington, DC 20005

202-457-8401
FAX 407-281-6446
E-Mail: aesf@aesf.org
Home Page: www.aesf.org

Jon Bednerik CAE, Publisher
Tom Urban, Advertising Manager
Donn Berry, Editor
Dan Denston, Executive Director
John Flatley, Senior Advisor and NASF Liaison

AESF is an international society that advances the science of surface finishing to benefit industry and society through education information and social involvement, as well as those who provide services, supplies and support to the industry.
Cost: $125.00
Frequency: Monthly
Circulation: 4000
Founded in 1909

17589 Powder Coating
OSC Publishing
1300 E 66th Street
Minneapolis, MN 55423-2642

612-866-2242
FAX 612-866-1939

Richard R Cress, Publisher
Richard Link, Manager

Our information focuses on the application, pre-treatment, materials, materials handling, and curing processes. Also features case histories.
Frequency: 9 per year
Circulation: 23587

17590 Precision Manufacturing
Minnesota Precision Manufacturing Association
3131 Fernbrook Ln N
Suite 111
Minneapolis, MN 55447-5336

763-473-4090
FAX 763-473-2804
Home Page: www.mpma.com

Dennis A Olson, President
Garry Bultnick, Sales Manager
LuAnn Bartley, Executive Director

Publication for job shop owners, managers and engineers and industrial suppliers, distributors, OEM buyers and purchasing agents, manufacturing representatives and technical colleges.
Circulation: 7900
Founded in 1958
Printed in on glossy stock

17591 Process Cooling & Equipment
Business News Publishing Company
1050 IL Route 83
Suite 200
Bensenville, IL 60106-1096

630-377-5909
FAX 630-694-4002
E-Mail: meaneys@bnpmedia.com
Home Page: www.process-cooling.com

Katie Rotella, President
Linda Becker, Editor
Sean Meaney, Sales Manager

Focuses on temperatures down through cryogenic levels in industrial processes and in equipment cooling.

17592 Process Heating
Business News Publishing Company
155 Pfingsten Road
Suite 205
Deerfield, IL 60015

847-405-4000
FAX 248-502-1001
E-Mail: PHeditors@bnpmedia.com
Home Page: www.process-heating.com
Social Media: *Facebook, Twitter*

Anne Armel, Publisher
Linda Becker, Associate Publisher/Editor
Beth McClelland, Production Manager
Sean Meaney, Sales Manager
Caroline Eychenne, European Sales Representative

Magazine covers heat processing at temperatures up to 1000 degrees F at end user and OEM plants in 9 industries. Follow us at twitter.com/ProcessHeating, www.facebook.com/ProcessHeating
Circulation: 25000
Founded in 1994

17593 Products Finishing
Gardner Publications
6915 Valley Ln
Cincinnati, OH 45244-3153

513-527-8800
800-950-8020
FAX 513-527-8801
E-Mail: narnold@gardnerweb.com
Home Page: www.gardnerweb.com

Rick Kline Sr, CEO
Matthew J Little, Editor
Nancy Eigel-Miller, Marketing Director
Nancy Arnold, Circulation Manager
John Campos, Manager

Covers production, management, engineering, design, etc. in plants where metal and plastic products are eletroplated, anodized, painted, buffed, cleaned or otherwise finished.
Cost: $89.00
Frequency: Monthly
Circulation: 42000
Founded in 1928
Printed in 4 colors on glossy stock

17594 Progressive Distributor
Pfingsten Publishing
730 Madison Avenue
Fort Atkinson, WI 53538

920-563-5225
800-932-7732

FAX 920-563-4269
Home Page: www.progressivedistributor.com

Rich Vurva, Editor
Pat OBrien, Executive Director
Mitch Bouchard, Secretary, Treasurer

Sales and marketing magazines for top manager, salespeople and marketing executives in industrial and construction distribution firms.
Circulation: 24337
Founded in 1996
Printed in 4 colors on glossy stock

17595 Quality
Business News Publishing
1050 IL Route 83
Suite 200
Bensenville, IL 60106-1096

630-377-5909
FAX 630-227-0204
E-Mail: williamst@bnpmedia.com
Home Page: www.qualitymag.com

Katie Rotella, President
Thomas A Williams, Publisher
Christopher Sheehy, Manager

Quality is a monthly business publication serving the quality assurance and process improvement needs of more than 80,000 North American manufacturing professionals.
Cost: $75.00
74 Pages
Frequency: Monthly
Circulation: 64000
ISSN: 0360-9936
Founded in 1962
Printed in 4 colors on glossy stock

17596 Quality Engineering
American Society for Quality
600 N Plankinton Avenue
PO Box 3005
Milwaukee, WI 53201-3005

414-272-8575
800-248-1946
FAX 414-272-1734
E-Mail: help@asq.org
Home Page: www.asq.org
Social Media: *Facebook, Twitter, LinkedIn*

Roberto M Saco, President
Paul E Borawski, Executive Director
Erica Gumieny, Sales
Fay Spano, Communications/Media Relations

Co-published with Taylor and Francis, this journal is for professional practitioners and researchers whose goal is quality engineering improvements and solutions.
Cost: $34.75
100M Members
Frequency: Quarterly/Members Price
Founded in 1946

17597 Quality Management Journal
American Society for Quality
600 N Plankinton Avenue
PO Box 3005
Milwaukee, WI 53201-3005

414-272-8575
800-248-1946
FAX 414-272-1734
E-Mail: help@asq.org
Home Page: www.asq.org
Social Media: *Facebook, Twitter, LinkedIn*

Roberto M Saco, President
Paul E Borawski, Executive Director
Erica Gumieny, Sales
Fay Spano, Communications/Media Relations

Published by the American Society for Quality, the QMT is a quarterly, peer-reviewed journal that focuses on the subject of quality management practice and provides a discussion forum for both practitioners and academics in the area

of research.
Cost: $50.00
100M Members
Frequency: Quarterly
Founded in 1946

17598 Quality Observer: ICSS Journal

Quality University Press
3970 Chain Bridge Road
PO Box 1111
Fairfax, VA 22030-3316

703-691-9496
Home Page: www.thequalityobserver.com

Johnson A Edosomwan, Editor

Case studies, interviews, international and national news and regular colums covering service in manufacturing, high-tech, government agencies and non-profit organizations.
Cost: $139.00
50 Pages
Frequency: 4 per year
Circulation: 15,000
ISSN: 1057-9583
Printed in 4 colors on glossy stock

17599 Quality Progress

American Society for Quality
600 N Plankinton Avenue
PO Box 3005
Milwaukee, WI 53201-3005

414-272-8575
800-248-1946
FAX 414-272-1734
E-Mail: help@asq.org
Home Page: www.asq.org
Social Media: *Facebook, Twitter, LinkedIn*

Roberto M Saco, President
Paul E Borawski, Executive Director
Erica Gumieny, Sales
Fay Spano, Communications/Media Relations

Published by the American Society for Quality, the QP is a peer-reviewed journal that focuses on the subject of quality control, discussing the usage and implementation of quality principles including the subject areas of organizational behavior, knowledge management and process improvement.
Cost: $55.00
100M Members
Founded in 1946

17600 Scan Tech News

Reed Business Information
30 Technology Parkway South
Suite 100
Norcross, GA 30092

630-574-0825
800-424-3996
FAX 630-288-8781
E-Mail: webmaster@reedbusiness.com
Home Page: www.reedbusiness.com

Jeff Greisch, President

Updates in trends in ADC technology and standards, the latest news from leading industry events, and product developments that streamline the flow of essential information in industrial settings.
Frequency: Monthly
Circulation: 82M

17601 Software Quality Professional

American Society for Quality
600 N Plankinton Avenue
PO Box 3005
Milwaukee, WI 53201-3005

414-272-8575
800-248-1946
FAX 414-272-1734
E-Mail: help@asq.org

Home Page: www.asq.org
Social Media: *Facebook, Twitter, LinkedIn*

Roberto M Saco, President
Paul E Borawski, Executive Director
Erica Gumieny, Sales
Fay Spano, Communications/Media Relations

Published by the American Society for Quality, the SQP is a quarterly, peer-reviewed journal for software development professionals that focuses on the subject of quality practice principles in the implementation of software and the development of software systems.
Cost: $45.00
100M Members
Frequency: Quarterly
Founded in 1946

17602 Solid State Technology

PennWell Publishing Company
1421 S. Sheridan Road
Tulsa, OK 74112

918-835-3161
800-331-4463
FAX 603-891-9294
Home Page: www.pennwell.com

Christine Shaw, VP
David Barach, Publisher

Serves firms involved in the manufacturing and testing of semi-conductor materials, equipment, device/circuits manufacturing and OEM manufacturing with in-house IC manufacturing facilities.
Cost: $213.00
Frequency: Monthly
ISSN: 0038-111X
Founded in 1958
Mailing list available for rent

17603 Solid Surface

Cygnus Publishing
PO Box 803
Fort Atkinson, WI 53538-0803

920-000-1111
800-547-7377
FAX 920-563-1699
E-Mail: paul.bowers@cygnuspub.com
Home Page: www.cygnusb2b.com

John French, CEO
Russ Lee, Editor
Paul Bowers, Group VP
Charlie Lillis, Content Licensing
Kathy Scott, Director of Public Relations

Solid surfaces link between fabricator, distributor, supplier, and manufacturer. It is dedicated to providing reliable and timely information, including updates on the latest fabrication trends and techniques, with a fresh perspective and a sense of humor.
Cost: $25.00
Circulation: 4,500
Founded in 1966

17604 Springs Manufacturer Institute

Spring Manufacturers Institute
2001 Midwest Rd
Suite 106
Oak Brook, IL 60523-1378

630-495-8588
FAX 630-495-8595
E-Mail: info@smihq.org
Home Page: www.smihq.org

Lynne Carr, President
Rita Schauer, Editor
Kim Kostecki, Member Services Coordinator
Pashun McNulty, Financial Admin Coordinator
Russ Bryer, Secretary, Treasurer

Provides how-to and technical articles on inspection methods, design, finishes, manufacturing processes, materials and equipment, also contains financial and management articles on

the interests of precision mechanical spring manufacturers.
130 Pages
Frequency: Quarterly
Circulation: 12,000
Printed in 4 colors on glossy stock

17605 Supply Chain e-Business

Keller International Publishing Corporation
150 Great Neck Rd
Suite 400
Great Neck, NY 11021-3309

516-829-9722
FAX 516-829-9306
Home Page: www.supplychainbrain.com

Thomas A Foster, Editor-in-Chief
Russell W Goodman, Managing Editor
Jerry Keller, President
Mary Chavez, Director of Sales

Offers a thorough analysis of on-line solutions designed to help corporations achieve greater supply-chain visiblity and real-time connections with suppliers and customers
Frequency: Bi-Monthly
Circulation: 45M
ISSN: 1525-4887
Printed in 4 colors on glossy stock

17606 Target

Association for Manufacturing Excellence
380 W Palatine Road
Wheeling, IL 60090-5831

847-520-3282
FAX 847-520-0163
E-Mail: info@ame.org
Home Page: www.ame.org

Robert W Hall, Editor-in-Chief
Dick Barton, Director of Advertising

Contains coverage on educational events, opinion columns, a networking section and more, reflecting manufacturing competitiveness, and improvement concepts and activities for the members of the Association for Manufacturing Excellence and interested academia.
Cost: $125.00
Frequency: Quarterly
Circulation: 5000
Founded in 1985

17607 US Industries Today

Postitive Publications
225 Madison Avenue
Morristown, NJ 07960

973-292-2600
FAX 973-292-2696
Home Page: www.usitoday.com

Peter Mercer, Editor
Sabastian Fraser, CEO/President

Provides information on the latest developments across the whole range of the US manufacturing industry, covering stock market analysis, US business leaders, business profiles and industry sector reports, as well as new products and services.
Cost: $15.00
Circulation: 65000
Founded in 1998

Trade Shows

17608 AES/EPA Conference/Exhibit: Environmental Control for Surface Finishing

American Electroplaters and Surface Finishers Soc.

1155 Fifteenth Street, NW
Suite 500
Washington, DC 20005

202-457-8401
FAX 407-281-6446
E-Mail: exhibit@aesf.org
Home Page: www.aesf.org

Kathy Shumacher, Show Manager
Dan Denston, Executive Director
John Flatley, Senior Advisor and NASF
Liaison

One-hundred exhibitors of waste treatment,
pollution control, surface finishing equipment
and surfaces.
600 Attendees
Frequency: June

17609 AESF SUR/FIN Annual Technical Conference and Exhibit of Surface Finishers
American Electroplaters and Surface
Finishers Soc.
1155 Fifteenth Street, NW
Suite 500
Washington, DC 20005

202-457-8401
FAX 407-281-6446
E-Mail: exhibit@aesf.org
Home Page: www.aesf.org

Dan Denston, Executive Director
John Flatley, Senior Advisor and NASF
Liaison

More than 300 suppliers to the industry will attend.
Frequency: June

17610 AESF Week - Society's Annual Winter Meeting
American Electroplaters and Surface
Finishers Soc.
1155 Fifteenth Street, NW
Suite 500
Washington, DC 20005

202-457-8401
FAX 407-281-6446
E-Mail: exhibit@aesf.org
Home Page: www.aesf.org

Dan Denston, Executive Director
John Flatley, Senior Advisor and NASF
Liaison
Frequency: June

17611 AME Annual Conference
Association for Manufacturing Excellence
380 W Palatine Road
Suite 7
Wheeling, IL 60090-5863

847-520-3282
FAX 847-520-0163
E-Mail: info@ame.org
Home Page: www.ame.org

Vivian Bartt, Manager
Dick Barton, Director of Advertising
Frequency: November
Founded in 1985

17612 AMSE International Manufacturing Science & Engineering Conference
American Society of Mechanical Engineers
Three Park Avenue
New York, NY 10016-5990

973-882-1170
800-843-2763
E-Mail: CustomerCare@asme.org
Home Page: www.asme.org

The MSEC highlights cutting edge manufacturing research in technical paper, poster and
panel sessions.
3200 Attendees
Frequency: Annual/Fall

17613 ASM Heat Treating Society Conference & Exposition
ASM International
9639 Kinsman Road
Materials Park, OH 44073

440-385-5151
800-336-5152
FAX 440-338-4634
E-Mail:
pamela.kleinman@asminternational.org
Home Page: www.asminternational.org
Social Media: *Facebook, Twitter, LinkedIn*

Pamela Kleinma, Senior Manager, Events
Kellye Thomas, Exposition Account Manager
Jeane Deatherage, Administrator, Foundation
Programs
Virginia Shirk, Foundation Executive Assistant

Conference and exhibits of heat treating equipment and supplies plus information of interest
to metallurgists, manufacturing, research and
design technical professionals. 300 exhibitors.
3500 Attendees
Frequency: September, Bi-Annual
Founded in 1974

17614 ASM Materials Science & Technology (MS&T)
ASM International
9639 Kinsman Road
Materials Park, OH 44073-0002

440-338-5151
800-336-5152
FAX 440-338-4634
E-Mail:
pamela.kleinman@asminternational.org
Home Page: www.asminternational.org
Social Media: *Facebook, Twitter, LinkedIn*

Pamela Kleinman, Senior Manager, Events
Kelly Thomas, Exposition Account Manager
Jeane Deatherage, Administrator, Foundation
Programs
Virginia Shirk, Foundation Executive Assistant

Annual event focusing on testing, analysis,
characterization and research of materials such
as engineered materials, high performance metals, powdered metals, metal forming, surface
modification, welding and joining. 350
exhibitors.
4,000 Attendees
Frequency: Annual/October
Founded in 2005

17615 Adhesive and Sealant Council Fall Convention
Adhesive & Sealant Council
7101 Wisconsin Avenue
Suite 990
Bethesda, MD 20814

301-986-9700
FAX 301-986-9795
E-Mail: bob.willis@ascouncil.org
Home Page: www.ascouncil.org

Bob Willis, Senior Manager
Conventions/Meetings
Frequency: October

17616 AeroMat Conference and Exposition
ASM International
9639 Kinsman Road
Materials Park, OH 44073-0002

440-385-5151
800-336-5152
FAX 440-338-4634
E-Mail: kim.schaefer@asminternational.org
Home Page: www.asminternational.org
Social Media: *Facebook, Twitter, LinkedIn*

Kim Schaefer, Event Manager
Kelly Thomas, Exposition Account Manager
Jeane Deatherage, Administrator, Foundation
Programs
Virginia Shirk, Foundation Executive Assistant

Conference for Aerospace Meterials Engineers,
Structural Engineers and Designers. The annual
event focuses on affordable structures and
low-cost manufacturing, titanium alloy technology, advanced intermetallics and refractory
metal alloys, materials and processes for space
applications, aging systems, high strength steel,
NDT evaluation, light alloy technology, welding and joining, and engineering technology.
150 exhibitors.
1500 Attendees
Frequency: Annual/June
Founded in 1984

17617 Annual Elevator Convention and Exposition
356 Morgan Avenue
PO Box 6507
Mobile, AL 36660

251-479-4514
800-730-5093
FAX 251-479-7043
E-Mail: naec@mindspring.com
Home Page: www.elevator-world.com

Ricia S Hendrick, President/Publisher
Robert Caporale, Senior VP and Editor
Frequency: Annual

17618 Annual Lean Six Sigma Conference
American Society for Quality
600 N Plankinton Avenue
PO Box 3005
Milwaukee, WI 53201-3005

414-272-8575
800-248-1946
FAX 414-272-1734
E-Mail: help@asq.org
Home Page: www.asq.org
Social Media: *Facebook, Twitter, LinkedIn*

Roberto M Saco, President
Paul E Borawski, Executive Director
Erica Gumieny, Sales
Fay Spano, Communications/Media Relations

An exclusive two-day briefing and networking
event designed by and for the top practitioners
in the Six Sigma community.
100M Members
Frequency: Annual/February
Founded in 1946

17619 Annual Meeting & Leadership Conference
Private Label Manufacturers Association
(PLMA)
630 Third Avenue
New York, NY 10017

212-972-3131
FAX 212-983-1382
E-Mail: info@plma.com
Home Page: www.plma.com

Brian Sharoff, President
Myra Rosen, VP
Tom Prendergast, Director, Research Services

Members look at key issues for the years
ahead.
3200+ Members
Frequency: Annual
Founded in 1979

17620 Annual Quality Audit Conference
American Society for Quality
600 N Plankinton Avenue
PO Box 3005
Milwaukee, WI 53201-3005

414-272-8575
800-248-1946
FAX 414-272-1734
E-Mail: help@asq.org

Home Page: www.asq.org
Social Media: *Facebook, Twitter, LinkedIn*

Roberto M Saco, President
Paul E Borawski, Executive Director
Erica Gumieny, Sales
Fay Spano, Communications/Media Relations

Topics of interest include: new innovating audit/process approaches, value added involvement, corporate expectations, corporate/social responsibility, auditing in the overall corporate scheme.
100M Members
Frequency: October
Founded in 1946

17621 Annual Service Quality Conference

American Society for Quality
600 N Plankinton Avenue
PO Box 3005
Milwaukee, WI 53201-3005

414-272-8575
800-248-1946
FAX 414-272-1734
E-Mail: help@asq.org
Home Page: www.asq.org
Social Media: *Facebook, Twitter, LinkedIn*

Roberto M Saco, President
Paul E Borawski, Executive Director
Erica Gumieny, Sales
Fay Spano, Communications/Media Relations

The sessions we plan will help you to navigate through unpredictable consumer behavior and increasing competition to build a strong foundation for reaching superior levels of quality service.
100M Members
Frequency: September
Founded in 1946

17622 Annual World Conference on Quality and Improvement

American Society for Quality
600 N Plankinton Avenue
PO Box 3005
Milwaukee, WI 53201-3005

414-272-8575
800-248-1946
FAX 414-272-1734
E-Mail: help@asq.org
Home Page: www.asq.org
Social Media: *Facebook, Twitter, LinkedIn*

Roberto M Saco, President
Paul E Borawski, Executive Director
Erica Gumieny, Sales
Fay Spano, Communications/Media Relations

Conference focuses on quality and improvement with more than 2,000 exhibits and attendees. Keynote speakers and sessions discuss quality tools, techniques and methodologies. Provides the opportunity for members to meet and network with colleagues in the industry.
100M Members
Frequency: May
Founded in 1946

17623 Association of Loudspeaker Mfg. & Acoustics (ALMA) Symposium

ALMA International
55 Littleton Road
13B
Ayer, MA 01432

978-772-6977
E-Mail: management@almainternational.org
Home Page: www.almainternational.org

Spiro Iraclianos, President, VP

Unlike other audio-related events, ALMA Symposia focuses exclusively on products, services and technical and business topics relevant to the loudspeaker industry. Invited speakers present technical papers to keep attendees abreast of the latest developments and expert panelists

discuss the latest topics. Training programs are also offered. Exhibit hall features more than 30 industry professionals.
100 Members
Frequency: Annual
Founded in 1962

17624 Atlantic Design Engineering

Canon Communications
11444 W Olympic Boulevard
Suite 900
Los Angeles, CA 90064-1549

310-445-4200
FAX 310-445-4299
Home Page: www.cancom.com/

Shannon Cleghorn, Customer & Media Coordinator
Erwin Laner, Promotional Manager

The Atlantic Design Engineering show serves the East Coast's design, process and manufacturing marketplace. Product classifications include Coatings & Finishes, composites, Computer Aided Design/Computer Aided Manufacturing, Electrical/Electronic, Electro Optical Components & Equipment, Engineered Safety Products, Engineering Management & Tools, Fasteners, Fluid Media, Fluid Power & Control and more. Held at the Jacob K. Javits Convention Center in New York, New York.
1319 Attendees
Frequency: June

17625 CleanRooms East

PennWell Conferences and Exhibitions
1421 S. Sheridan Road
Tulsa, OK 74112

918-835-3161
800-331-4463
FAX 603-891-9200
E-Mail: andrear@pennwell.com
Home Page: www.pennwell.com

Andrea Rollins, Show Manager
Lisa Gowern, Registration Manager
Meg Villeure, Conference Manager

CleanRooms shows, the international forums exclusively serving the contamination control industry, couples exhibits with 100% technology-driver conference programs.
3000 Attendees
Frequency: March
Mailing list available for rent

17626 Close the Loop Technical Symposium

2001 Midwest Road
Suite 106
Oak Brook, IL 60523-1335

630-495-8588
FAX 630-495-8595
E-Mail: info@smihq.org
Home Page: www.smihq.org

Russ Bryer, Secretary, Treasurer
Jim Kobrinetz, Technical Director
Christy Johnson, Manager

Symposium will highlight the latest technolgy and best practice solutions to difficult technical problems that are regularly experienced by the spring designer, spring user and manufacturing personel.

17627 Contract Packaging Association Annual Meeting

Contract Manufacturing & Packaging
1601 Bond Street
Suite 101
Naperville, IL 60563

630-544-5053
FAX 630-544-5055
Home Page: www.contractpackaging.com

John Mazelin, President
John Riley, VP
Frequency: April

17628 Dollar Store Expo

Retail Dollar Store Association
11540 S Eastern Avenue
Suite 100
Henderson, NV 89052

702-893-9090
800-859-9247
FAX 702-893-9227
E-Mail: info@bentleyintl.net
Home Page: www.dollarstoreexpo.com

Kristina Mullen, Show Manager
Wendy Witherspoon, Manager

Four-hundred and fifty booths for products that retail for a dollar or less. Wholesalers, distributors, manufacturers, importers and representatives for surplus, jewelry, hair and beauty, automotive, food items, household goods, gifts, toys, party supplies, seasonal and closeouts.
2,500 Attendees
Frequency: June
Founded in 2002

17629 Int'l Conference on Powder Injection Molding of Metals & Ceramics

Innovative Material Solutions
605 Severn Drive
State College, PA 16803

814-867-1140
FAX 814-867-2813
E-Mail: info@imspowder.com

Frequency: March

17630 International Integrated Manufacturing Technology Trade Exhibition

Reed Exhibition Companies
383 Main Avenue
Norwalk, CT 06851

203-840-4800
FAX 203-840-4801
E-Mail: inquiry@reedexpo.com
Home Page: www.reedexpo.com/app/homepage

Elizabeth Hitchcock, International Sales

Expo and conference dedicated to the products and technology needed by engineering operations and management to automate and integrate manufacturing.
Frequency: June

17631 International Manufacturing Technology Show

7901 Westpark Drive
Mc Lean, VA 22102-4206

703-893-2900
800-828-7469
FAX 703-827-5250
E-Mail: peelman@AMTonline.org
Home Page: www.amtonline.org

Peter Eelman, VP Exhibitions
Michelle Edmonson, Exhibitions Operations Manager

Manufacturing equipment trade show.
85M Attendees
Frequency: Biennial
Founded in 1927

17632 International Symposium for Testing & Failure Analysis

ASM International
9639 Kinsman Road
Materials Park, OH 44073

440-338-5151
800-336-5152
FAX 440-338-4634
E-Mail: kim.schaefer@asminternational.org

Home Page: www.asminternational.org
Social Media: *Facebook, Twitter, LinkedIn*

Kim Schaefer, Event Manager
Kelly Thomas, Exposition Account Manager
Jeane Deatherage, Administrator, Foundation
Programs
Virginia Shirk, Foundation Executive Assistant

Annual event focusing on microelectronic and elcetronic device failure analysis, techniques, EOS/ESD testing and descretes aimed at failure analysis engineers and managers, technicians and new failure analysis engineers. 200 exhibitors.
1100 Attendees
Frequency: Annual/November

**17633 International Thermal Spray
Conference & Exposition**
ASM International
9639 Kinsman Road
Materials Park, OH 44073

440-338-5151
800-336-5152
FAX 440-338-4634
E-Mail: natalie.nemec@asminternational.org
Home Page: www.asminternational.org
Social Media: *Facebook, Twitter, LinkedIn*

Natalie Neme, Event Manager
Kelly Thomas, Exposition Account Manager
Jeane Deatherage, Administrator, Foundation
Programs
Virginia Shirk, Foundation Executive Assistant

Global annual event attracting professional interested in thermal spray technology focusing on advances in HVOF, plasma and detonation gun, flame spray and wire arc spray processes, performance of coatings, and future trends. 150 exhibitors.
1000 Attendees
Frequency: Annual/May

**17634 Lean Management and Solutions
Conference**
Institute of Industrial Engineers
3577 Parkway Lane
Suite 200
Norcross, GA 30092

770-449-0460
800-494-0460
FAX 770-441-3295
E-Mail: cs@iienet.org
Home Page: www.iienet.org

Elaine Fuerst, Marketing Director

The place to find the leaders in lean management and all the tools that you need for success.
300 Attendees
Frequency: September

17635 METALfab
532 Forest Parkway
Suite A
Forest Park, GA 30297-6137

404-363-4009
FAX 404-366-1852
E-Mail: nommainfo@nomma.org
Home Page: www.nomma.org

Martha Pennington, Show Manager
Todd Daniel, Editor
Barbara Cook, Executive Director
Martha Pennington, Meetings Manager

Trade show sponsored by National Ornamental and Miscellaneous Metals Association.
1000 Attendees
Frequency: March

**17636 Medical Design & Manufacturing
Exhibition East/West**
Canon Communications

11444 W Olympic Boulevard
Los Angeles, CA 15494

310-445-4200
FAX 310-996-9499
Home Page: www.cancom.com

Shannon Cleghorn, Customer & Media
Coordinator
Erwin Laner, Promotional Manager

Design, development, and manufacture of medical products, from high-volume, single-use disposables to next-generation diagnostic instruments and advanced imaging systems. Preview the latest advances in medical-grade materials, assembly components, electronics, machinery, software, systems, services, and more.
Frequency: May

**17637 Medical Equipment Design &
Technology Conference**
Canon Communications
11444 W Olympic Boulevard
Los Angeles, CA 90064-1549

310-445-4200
FAX 310-996-9499
Home Page: www.cancom.com

Shannon Cleghorn, Customer & Media
Coordinator
Erwin Laner, Promotional Manager

Design, development, and manufacture of medical products, from high-volume, single-use disposables to next-generation diagnostic instruments and advanced imaging systems. Preview the latest advances in medical-grade materials, assembly components, electronics, machinery, software, systems, services and more.
Frequency: September

17638 Midwest Job Shop Show
Edward Publishing
16 Waterbury Road
Prospect, CT 06712-1215

203-758-4474
FAX 203-758-4476
Home Page: www.jobshoptechnology.com

Jennifer Bryda, Production Manager
Christoper Davis, Manager
Gerald Schmidt, President

A source for forming, fabricating, shaping, and assemblies. The show is designed to attract the highest caliber engineers and buyers from product manufacturers. There will be 170 exhibitors and booths.
1500 Attendees

17639 National Manufacturing Week
Reed Exhibition Companies
383 Main Street
Norwalk, CT 06851

203-840-4800
FAX 203-840-4801
E-Mail: inquiry@reedexpo.com
Home Page:
www.reedexpo.com/app/homepage

Elizabeth Hitchcock, International Sales

The pre-eminent American forum for the display of industrial technology.
1.5M Attendees
Frequency: March

**17640 National Plant Engineering and
Facilities Management Show and
Conference**
Reed Exhibition Companies
383 Main Avenue
Norwalk, CT 06851

203-840-4800
FAX 203-840-4801
E-Mail: inquiry@reedexpo.com

Home Page:
www.reedexpo.com/app/homepage
Frequency: June

**17641 National Quality Education
Conference**
American Society for Quality
600 N Plankinton Avenue
PO Box 3005
Milwaukee, WI 53201-3005

414-272-8575
800-248-1946
FAX 414-272-1734
E-Mail: help@asq.org
Home Page: www.asq.org
Social Media: *Facebook, Twitter, LinkedIn*

Roberto M Saco, President
Paul E Borawski, Executive Director
Erica Gumieny, Sales
Fay Spano, Communications/Media Relations

Provides teachers, administrators, and support personnel opportunities to examine continuous improvement principles used in education. It provides resources and best practices to help you address requirements of No Child Left Behind, while helping you increase student achievement and improve overall performance.
100M Members
Frequency: November
Founded in 1946

17642 Pacific Design Engineering
Canon Communications
11444 W Olympic Boulevard
Los Angeles, CA 90064

310-445-4200
FAX 310-996-9499
Home Page: www.cancom.com

Shannon Cleghorn, Customer & Media
Coordinator
Erwin Laner, Promotional Manager

Serves the West Coast's dynamic design, process, and manufacturing marketplace. Product classifications include: Coatings and Finishes, Composites, Computer Aided Design/Computer Aided Manufacturing, Electrical/Electronic, Electrc Optical Compnents and Equipment, Engineered Safety Products, Engineering Management and Tools, Fasteners, Fluid Media, Fluid Power and Control.
Frequency: January

**17643 Packaging & All That Jazz Trade
Show**
Retail Packaging Association
PO Box 43517
Cincinnati, OH 45243

513-527-4333
FAX 513-527-4999
E-Mail: info@retailpackaging.org
Home Page: www.retailpackaging.org

Joel Zaas, President

Provides exhibitors and attendees opportunities to enjoy the great city of New Orleans and network and conduct business, all without losing valuable days in the office.
600 Attendees
Frequency: Annual

17644 Simulation Solutions Conference
Institute of Industrial Engineers
3577 Parkway Lane
Suite 200
Norcross, GA 30092

770-449-0460
800-494-0460
FAX 770-441-3295
E-Mail: cs@iienet.org
Home Page: www.iienet.org

Elaine Fuerst, Marketing Director

Simulation techniques. Tools and software used in a wide range of industries and applications.
250 Attendees

17645 South-Tec Machine Tool and Manufacturing Show
Society of Manufacturing Engineers
1 SME Drive
#930
Dearborn, MI 48121

313-425-3000
800-733-4763
FAX 313-425-3400
E-Mail: service@sme.org
Home Page: www.sme.org

Mark Tomlinson, Executive Director
Greg Sheremet, Publisher
70M Attendees
Founded in 1932

17646 Southern Job Shop Show
Edward Publishing
16 Waterbury Road
Prospect, CT 06712-1215

203-758-4474
FAX 860-768-4475
Home Page: www.jobshoptechnology.com

Mark W Shortt, Editor
Gerald Schmidt, President
Christopher Davis, Manager

The show is designed to attract the highest caliber engineers and buyers from your major DEM product manufacturers.
1500 Attendees
Frequency: March

17647 Spring World Expo
PO Box 1144
Highland Park, IL 60035

847-433-1335
FAX 847-433-3769
E-Mail: info@casmi-springworld.org
Home Page: www.springworld.org

Gerald H Reese, Executive Director
Tracy Hodge, Director
4500 Attendees
Frequency: October

Directories & Databases

17648 Agricultural & Industrial Manufacturers Membership Directory
Agricultural & Industrial Manufacturers Rep Assn
7500 Flying Cloud Drive
Suite 900
Eden Prairie, MN 55344

952-253-6230
866-759-2467
FAX 952-835-4774
Home Page: www.aimrareps.org

Michael J Kowalczyk, President
Ronald R Reed, VP
Cost: $25.00
Frequency: Annual October

17649 Directory of Manufacturing Research Centers
Manufacturing Technology Information
10 W 35th Street
Chicago, IL 60616-3717

312-431-1442
800-421-0586
FAX 312-567-4736

E-Mail: info@iitri.org
Home Page: www.iitri.org

Paula Marggraf, Editor
Cost: $75.00
Frequency: Irregular

17650 Directory of Waste Equipment Manufacturers and Distributors
WASTEC Equipment Technology Association
4301 Connecticut Ave NW
Suite 300
Washington, DC 20008-2304

202-966-4701
FAX 202-966-4818
Home Page: www.wastec.org

Christine Hutcherson, Director Member Services
Bruce Parker, President
Gary T Satterfield, Executive VP
Sandra Price, Director Member Services

About 250 member manufacturers of waste handling, collection and processing equipment.
Cost: $5.00
Frequency: Annual

17651 Encyclopedia of American Industries
Grey House Publishing
4919 Route 22
PO Box 56
Amenia, NY 12501

518-789-8700
800-562-2139
FAX 845-373-6390
E-Mail: books@greyhouse.com
Home Page: www.greyhouse.com
Social Media: *Facebook, Twitter*

Leslie Mackenzie, Publisher
Richard Gottlieb, Editor

A two volume set, Volume I provides separate coverage of nearly 500 manufacturing industries, while Volume II presents nearly 600 essays covering the vast array of services and other non-manufacturing industries in the United States. Combined, these two volumes provide individual essays on every industry recognized by the U.S. Standard Industrial Classification (SIC) system.
Cost: $650.00
3000 Pages
ISBN: 1-592372-44-9
Founded in 1981

17652 Manufacturers Representatives of America: Yearbook and Directory of Members
Manufacturers Representatives of America
PO Box 150229
Arlington, TX 76015-6229

817-465-5511
FAX 817-561-7275

WR Bess, Executive Director

Several hundred independent manufacturers' representatives in paper, plastic, packaging and sanitary supplies.
Cost: $250.00
Frequency: Annual Fall
Circulation: 1,200

17653 Manufacturing & Distribution USA
Gale/Cengage Learning
27500 Drake Road
Farmington Hills, MI 48331-3535

248-699-4253
800-877-4253
FAX 877-363-4253
E-Mail: gale.galeord@cengage.com
Home Page: www.gale.cengage.com
Social Media: *Facebook, Twitter, Youtube*

Patrick C Sommers, President

This new edition also features enhanced coverage of input-output data by industrial sector when available as well as classifications of leading public and private corporations in each industry.
ISBN: 1-414408-67-6

17654 Rauch Guide to the US Rubber Industry
Grey House Publishing
4919 Route 22
PO Box 56
Amenia, NY 12501

518-789-8700
800-562-2139
FAX 845-373-6390
E-Mail: books@greyhouse.com
Home Page: www.greyhouse.com
Social Media: *Facebook, Twitter*

Leslie Mackenzie, Publisher
Richard Gottlieb, Editor

Provides current market information and trends; industry economics and government regulations; company share data for each of the leading product categories; technology and raw material information; industry sources of further data; and unique profiles of 847 rubber manufacturers, a section which includes all known companies with rubber sales at or over $1 million annually.
Cost: $595.00
500 Pages
ISBN: 1-592371-30-2
Founded in 1981

17655 Small Business Inovation Research
1000 Independence Avenue SW
Washington, DC 20585-1207

202-571-1300
Home Page: www.er.doe.gov/

Lawrence Small, CEO
Frequency: Annual

17656 Sound and Vibration: Buyer's Guide Issue
Acoustical Publications
PO Box 40416
27101 E. Oviatt Road
Bay Village, OH 44140-0416

440-835-0101
FAX 440-835-9303
E-Mail: sv@mindspring.com
Home Page: www.sandv.com.home/htm

Jack Mowry, Editor and Publisher
Scott J Lothes, Assistant Editor/Webmaster

This directory offers a list of manufacturers of products for noise and vibration control.
Frequency: Monthly
Circulation: 19,000
ISBN: 0-038181-09-9
Mailing list available for rent: 21M names
Printed in 4 colors on glossy stock

17657 ThomasNet
Thomas Publishing Company, LLC
User Services Department
5 Penn Plaza
New York, NY 10001

212-695-0500
800-699-9822
FAX 212-290-7362
E-Mail: contact@thomaspublishing.com
Home Page: www.thomasnet.com
Social Media: *Facebook, Twitter, LinkedIn*

Carl Holst-Knudsen, President
Robert Anderson, VP, Planning
Mitchell Peipert, VP, Finance
Ivy Molofsky, VP, Human Resources

A way to reach qualified businesses that list their company information on ThomasNet.com. Detailed profiles promote their products, ser-

vices, capabilities and brands carried. The ThomasNet.com web site is the most up-to-date compilation of 650,000 North American manufacturers, distributors, and service companies in 67,000 industrial categories.
Founded in 1898

17658 Who Audits America
Data Financial Press
PO Box 668
Menlo Park, CA 94026-0668

650-321-4553
FAX 650-321-4427

A who's who directory of services and supplies.
Cost: $133.00
600 Pages
Frequency: SemiAnnual

Industry Web Sites

17659 http://gold.greyhouse.com
G.O.L.D Grey House OnLine Databases
Grey House Publishing's online database platform, GOLD, offers Quick Search, Keyword Search and Expert Search for most business sectors including a wide variety of manufacturing markets. The GOLD platform makes finding the information you need quick and easy - whether you're a novice searcher or an experienced database user. All of Grey House's directory products are available for subscription on the GOLD platform.

17660 www.abrasiveengineering.com
Abrasive Grain Association
Members manufacture natural and artificial grains used in grinding wheels, coated abrasives etc.

17661 www.aesf.org
American Electroplaters and Surface Finishers Soc.
AESF is an international society that advances the science of surface finishing to benefit industry and society through education information and social involvement, as well as those who provide services, supplies and support to the industry.

17662 www.agma.org
American Gear Manufacturers Association
Manufacturers of gears and geared speed changers.

17663 www.ahma.org
American Hardware Manufacturers Association
Over 280 manufacturer representatives in the hardware industry.

17664 www.amba.org
American Mold Builders Association
Promotes the development, welfare, and expansion of businesses engaged in the manufacture of molds and related tooling.

17665 www.amtda.org
American Machine Tool Distributors Association
For distributors of manufacturing technology.

17666 www.ararental.org
American Rental Association
For rental business owners and equipment suppliers.

17667 www.arcat.com
National Association of Relay Manufacturers
NARM is a trade association for the electro-mechanical relay and associated switching devices industry. An affiliate of Electronic Industries Alliance.

17668 www.asphaltinstitute.org
Asphalt Institute
Conducts education, research, and engineering services related to asphalt products; conducts seminars and sells publications and videos on asphalt technology.

17669 www.awci.com/
American Watchmakers-Clockmakers Institute
Examines and certifies master watchmakers and clockmakers. Maintains a placement service. Conducts home study courses.

17670 www.awci.org
Association of the Wall and Ceiling Industries
Offers information on contractors, manufacturers, suppliers and organizations affiliated with the interior design, building and contracting community. Strives to provide services and undertake activities that enhance the members ability to operate a successful business.

17671 www.bia.org
Brick Industry Association
Supports the industry by rendering technical assistance to architects and designers, by providing marketing assistance to the industry, by monitoring and positively influencing governmental actions, by working to assure the long term availability of bricklayers and by providing other member services as appropriate.

17672 www.cancentral.com
Can Manufacturers Institute
Industry, environmental and consumer information.

17673 www.carpet ushion.org
Carpet Cushion Council
Encourages distribution and use of seperate carpet cushions. Works with regulatory agencies at the national, state and local levels.

17674 www.cl2.com
Chlorine Institute
Promotes safe handling of chlorine and caustic materials and sponsors awards.

17675 www.cmit.edi.gatech.edu/
Center for Manufacturing Information
Provides a non-instrusive environment in which manufacturers can objectively evaluate and compare the latest computer-based technologies.

17676 www.cottonseed.com
National Cottonseed Products Association
Services include the administration of trading rules and standards, a research program, information service center and product promotion of cotton seed food and feed products.

17677 www.cti.org
Cooling Technology
Seeks to improve technology, design and performance of water conservation apparatus. Provides inspection services and conducts research.

17678 www.divbusiness.com
Diversified Business Communications
Provides management services for associations and organizations seeking to expand domestically and overseas, as well as direct mail, internet, telemarketing campaigns and market research.

17679 www.fluidcontrolsinstitute.org
Fluid Controls Institute
Manufacturers of devices for fluid control, such as temperature and pressure regulators, strainers, gauges, control valves, solenoid valves, steam traps, etc.

17680 www.fluidsealing.com
Fluid Sealing Association
An international association of manufacturers of mechanical packings, sealing devices, gaskets, rubber expansion joints and allied products.

17681 www.graphicsPor.org
Graphics Products Association
Independent manufacturers and suppliers of paperboard packaging. Purposes are to futher development, use and sale of members product. Compiles statistics and bestows awards.

17682 www.greyhouse.com
Grey House Publishing
Authoritative reference directories for most business sectors including a wide variety of manufacturing markets. Users can search the online databases with varied search criteria allowing for custom searches by product category, geographic area, sales volume, keyword, subject and more. Full Grey House catalog and online ordering also available.

17683 www.housewares.org
National Housewares Manufacturers Association
Links to other associations.

17684 www.iccsafe.org/
International Code Council
Nonprofit membership association with more than 16,000 members who span the building community, from code enforcement officials to materials manufacturers. Dedicated to preserving the public health, safety and welfare in the built environment through the effective use and enforcement of model codes.

17685 www.icea.net
Insulated Cable Engineers Association
Professional organization dedicated to developing cable standards for the electric power, control and telecommunications industries. Ensures safe, economical and efficient cable systems utilizing proven state-of-the-art materials and concepts. ICEA documents are of interest to cable manufacturers, architects and engineers, utility and manufacturing plant personnel, telecommunication engineers, consultants and OEMs.

17686 www.ifai.com
Industrial Fabrics Association International
Provides many products, services and programs to industry members.

17687 www.ilma.org
Independent Lubricant Manufacturers Association
Independent blenders and compounders of lubricants.

17688 www.iopp.org
Institute of Packaging Professionals
Association for packing professionals.

17689 www.ipc.org
IPC-Association Connecting Electronics Industries
Works to develop standards in circuit board assembly equipment. Brings together all players in the electronic interconnection industry, including designers, board manufacturers, assembly companies, suppliers and original

equipment manufacturers. Offers workshops, conferences, meetings and online communications.

17690 www.isri.org
Institute of Scrap Recycling Industries
Members include processors, brokers and consumers of scrap metal, rubber, paper, textiles, plastics and glass.

17691 www.marinecanvas.com
Marine Fabricators Association
Firms and individuals engaged in the design, construction, and installation of marine fabric products. Provides certification and product standards.

17692 www.mechanical.com
Mechanical.Com
Manufacturing industry database.

17693 www.mep.nist.gov
Manufacturing Extension Partnership
A nationwide network of more thatn 70 not-for-profit centers whose sole purpose is to provide small and medium-sized manufacturers with the help they need to succeed.

17694 www.mfgworld.com/index.html
Manufacturing World Online
Manufacturing news, software, industry reports and links.

17695 www.mhia.org/psc/PSC_Products_Racks.cfm
Rack Manufacturers Institute
Makers of steel industrial storage racks.

17696 www.mt-online.com
Applied Technology Publications
MT-online.com is the premier source of capacity assurance and best practice solutions for manufacturing, process and service operations worldwide. Online home of Maintenance Technology magazie, the dynamic MT-online.com portal serves the critical technical, business and professional-development needs of engineers, managers and technicians from across all industrial, institutional and commercial sectors.

17697 www.naima.org
North American Insulation Manufacturers Assn

17698 www.nam.org
National Association of Manufacturers
Represents industry's views on national and international problems to government.

17699 www.naumd.com
North American Assoc. of Uniform Manufacturers
Promotes interests of manufacturers and distributors of uniforms and career wear.

17700 www.ncspa.org
National Corrugated Steel Pipe Association
NCSPA seeks to promote sound public policy relating to the use of corrugated steel drainage structures in private and public construction.

17701 www.nei.org
Nuclear Energy Institute
Members are of utilities, manufacturers of electrical generating equipment, researchers, architects, engineers, labor unions, and others interested in the generation of electricity by nuclear power.

17702 www.nomma.org
National Ornamental and Miscellaneous Metals

Association

Publishes the Ornamental and Miscellaneous Metals Fabricator magazine. Holds annual convention and trade show (METALfab). Membership dues: $275 fabricators, $250 local supplier, $325 regional supplier, $425 nationwide supplier.

17703 www.nwpca.org
National Wooden Pallet & Container Association
Represents manufacturers, recyclers and distributors of pallets, containers and reels.

17704 www.p3-ny.org/
Women in Production
Promotes the interests of women in the production profession.

17705 www.patmi.org
Powder Actuated Tool Manufacturers Institute
Represents manufacturers of construction tools used to fasten to and into steel and concrete.

17706 www.powertoolinstitute.com
Power Tool Institute
Trade association representing manufacturers of power tools.

17707 www.reman.org
Remanufacturing Institute International
A coalition of associations and companies in the entire manufacturing industry. There are over 73,000 companies in this industry. Our goal is to unite them into a powerful organization.

17708 www.sawingassociation.com/
North American Sawing Association

17709 www.smma.org
SMMA: Small Motors & Motion Association
Manufacturing trade association. Members include electric motor and motion control companies, as well as suppliers, users, and associated businesses such as consultants, universities and distributors.

17710 www.steeltubeinstitute.org
Steel Tube Institute of North America
Members produce steel tubes and pipes from carbon, stainless or alloy steel for applications ranging from large structural tubing to small redrawn tubing.

17711 www.sunglassassociation.com
Sunglass Association of America
A nonprofit trade association of manufacturers and import-wholesale sunglasses, sunglass parts, components, materials, and reading glasses.

17712 www.thomasnet.com/index.html
Thomas Register of American Manufacturers
Industrial buying guide of US and Canadian manufacturers.

17713 www.tileusa.com
Tile Council of America
Manufacturers and suppliers of ceramic wall and floor tiles.

17714 www.tpatube.org
Tube & Pipe Association International
TPA is an educational technology association serving the metal tube and pipe producing and fabricating industries.

17715 www.ttmanet.org
Truck Trailer Manufacturers Association
News of interest to trailer manufacturers and suppliers.

17716 www.vending.org
National Automatic Merchandising Association
For makers and operators of automatic vending equipment.

17717 www.westernroofing.net/
Roof Tile Institute
Manufacturers of clay and concrete roof tiles. Emphasis is on technical issues and codes that involve tile. Has annual budget of approximately $300,000 a year. Publications available to members.

Associations

17718 Academy of Marketing Science
PO Box 248012
Coral Gables, FL 33124-8012

305-284-6673
FAX 305-284-3762
Home Page: www.ams-web.org

Dr. Harold W Berkman, Director
Sally Sultan, Coordinator

Fosters education professional standards in marketing science. Sponsers the AMS Foundation which provides grants for the advancement of teaching and research.
1500 Members
Founded in 1971

17719 American Association of Family & Consumer Sciences
400 N Columbus Street
Suite 202
Alexandria, VA 22314-2264

703-706-4600
800-424-8080
FAX 703-706-4663
E-Mail: staff@aafcs.org
Home Page: www.aafcs.org
Social Media: *Facebook, Twitter, LinkedIn, Flickr, Pintrest*

Peggy Wild, CFCS, President
Carolyn Jackson, CFCS, Executive Director
Gwynn Mason, Director of Communications
Beverly Card, CFCS, President-Elect
Victoria Marie Gribschaw, S.C.,, Treasurer

An association dedicated to Family & Consumer Sciences professionals. AAFCS strives to improve the quality and standards of individual and family life by providing educational programs, influencing public policy, and through communication.
10000 Members

17720 American Chamber of Commerce Executives
1330 Braddock Place
Suite 300
Alexandria, VA 22314

703-998-0072
FAX 888-577-9883
E-Mail: webmaster@acce.org
Home Page: www.acce.org
Social Media: *Facebook, Twitter, LinkedIn, RSS*

Betty Nokes, Chairman of the Board
Mick Fleming, President
Tamara Philbin, COO
Chris Mead, Senior VP, Members
Jacqui Cook, Chief Financial Officer
1300+ Members
Founded in 1914

17721 American Marketing Association
American Marketing Association
311 S Wacker Dr # 5800
Suite 5800
Chicago, IL 60606-6629

312-542-9000
800-262-1150
FAX 312-542-9001
Home Page: www.themarketingfoundation.org
Social Media: *Facebook, Twitter, LinkedIn, Blog, Google+*

Jerome D. Williams, Chairperson
Dennis L. Dunlap, Chief Executive Officer
Roger A. Kerin, Vice Chairperson
Donald R. Lehmann, Vice Chairperson
William Cron, Treasurer

A professional association for individuals and organizations involved in the practice, teaching and study of marketing worldwide.
40000 Members
Founded in 1992
Mailing list available for rent

17722 Association for Innovative Marketing
34 Summit Avenue
Sharon, MA 02067-2149

781-784-8283
Home Page: www.manta.com
Social Media: *Facebook, Twitter, Google+*

Facilitates sharing of innovative ideas; bestows awards, maintains library and speaker bureau.
Founded in 1989

17723 Association for Postal Commerce
1800 Diagonal Road
Suite 320
Alexandria, VA 22314-2862

703-524-0096
FAX 703-997-2414
Home Page: www.postcom.org

Gene Del Polito, President

National organization representing those who use, or who support, the use of mail as a medium for communication and commerce. Publishes a weekly newsletter covering postal policy and operational issues.
231 Members
Founded in 1947

17724 Association of Marketing Service Providers
Mailing & Fulfillment Service Association
1800 Diagonal Road
Suite 320
Alexandria, VA 22314-2862

703-836-9200
FAX 703-548-8204
E-Mail: mfsa-mail@mfsanet.org
Home Page: www.epicomm.org
Social Media: *Facebook, Twitter, LinkedIn, Youtube, RSS, Vimeo, Google+*

Ken Garner, President/CEO
Tom Cobery, Vice President
Samantha Lake, Director of Marketing/Communication
Patty Dumas, Director of Accounting
Tyler T. Keeney, Director of Member Satisfaction

The national trade association for the mailing and fulfillment services industry.
Founded in 1920
Mailing list available for rent

17725 Association of Marketing and Communication Professionals
127 Pittsburgh St.
Dallas, TX 75207

214-377-3524
FAX 214-377-3548
E-Mail: info@amcpros.com
Home Page: amcpros.com
Social Media: *Facebook, LinkedIn, YouTube, Google+, RSS*
Founded in 1995

17726 Association of Sale Marketing Companies
1010 Wisconsin Avenue NW
Suite 900
Washington, DC 20007

202-337-9351
FAX 202-337-4508
E-Mail: info@asmc.org
Home Page: www.asmc.org

Mark Baum, President/CEO
Karen Connell, Contact

Provides referral service and other methods of assistance in locating sales and marketing companies.
250 Members
Founded in 1995

17727 Biomedical Marketing Association
10293 N Meridian Street
Suite 175
Indianapolis, IN 46290

317-816-1640
800-278-7886
FAX 317-816-1633
E-Mail: info@bmaonline.org
Home Page: www.bmaonline.org

Michael L Boner, President

Builds diagnostic industry leadership by providing market education, professional development and a forum for fellowship and the exchange of ideas.

17728 Brand Activation Association
650 First Avenue
Suite 2-SW
New York, NY 10016-3207

212-420-1100
FAX 212-533-7622
E-Mail: pma@pmalink.org
Home Page: www.baalink.org/
Social Media: *Facebook, Twitter, LinkedIn*

Bonnie J Carlson, President
Noelle Boddewyn, Executive Assistant
Mike Kaufman, VP of Marketing
Marybeth Petescia, Marketing Manager
Christine Goonan, Director of Membership

Mission is to encourage the highest standards of excellence in promotion marketing. Represents member interests and promotes better understanding promotion in the marketing mix.
700 Members
Founded in 1911

17729 Business Marketing Association
708 Third Avenue
Suite 123
New York, NY 10017

212-697-5950
FAX 212-687-7310
E-Mail: info@marketing.org
Home Page: www.marketing.org
Social Media: *Facebook, Twitter, LinkedIn*

Katherine Button Bell, Chairman
Stephen Liguori, Vice Chair
George Stenitzer, VP, Thought Leadership
Chris Schermer, VP, Marketing
Bob Felsenthal, VP, Membership

The Business Marketing Association/BMA, a preeminent service organization for professionals, provides expertise in business-to-business marketing and communications. The BMA offers an information-packed Website, online skills-building, marketing certification programs, and industry surveys and papers. In addition, members have the opportunity to interact with peers at seminars, chapter training programs and the BMA Annual Conference.
Founded in 1922

17730 Business Marketing Association: Atlanta
2801 Buford Highway
Druid Chase Suite 375
Atlanta, GA 30329

404-641-9417
800-664-4262
FAX 312-822-0054
E-Mail: info@bmaatlanta.com
Home Page: www.bmaatlanta.com

Social Media: *Facebook, Twitter, LinkedIn, Youtube*

Martine Hunter, President
Rory Carlton, Treasurer
Eduardo Esparza, Co-Chair of Marketing
Mark Potter, Membership Chairperson
Nancy Bistritz, Public Relations

The Atlanta chapter of the BMA includes marketing executives from a variety of industries and backgrounds including research, advertising, promotions, events, Web development, printing and more. The BMA offers an information-packed Website, online skills-building, marketing certification programs, and industry surveys and papers. In addition, members have the opportunity to interact with peers at seminars, participate in chapter training programs and the BMA Annual Conference.
Founded in 1922

17731 Business Marketing Association: Boston

246 Hampshire Street
Cambridge, MA 02130

617-418-4000
800-664-4262
FAX 312-822-0054
E-Mail: info@thebmaboston.com
Home Page: www.thebmaboston.com/

Michael Lewis, President
Will Robinson, VP Public Relations
Matthew Mamet, VP Internet Marketing
Larry Perreault, VP Finance
Chris Perkett, VP Programming

BMA Boston helps members improve their ability to manage business-to-business marketing and communications for greater productivity and profitability by providing unique access to information, ideas, and the experience of peers. The BMA offers an information-packed Website, online skills-building, marketing certification programs, and industry surveys and papers. In addition, members have the opportunity to interact with peers at seminars, chapter training programs and the BMA Annual Conference.

17732 Business Marketing Association: Houston

PO Box 710350
Houston, TX 77271-0350

713-723-1325
FAX 713-723-1326
E-Mail: info@bmahouston.com
Home Page: www.bmahouston.org
Social Media: *Facebook, Twitter, LinkedIn, Youtube*

Diana Salerno, President
Linda Ives, Executive Director
Megan Coffing, Vice President
Bob Wallace, Treasurer

Dedicated to serving the needs of business to business Associations worldwide.
Founded in 1922

17733 Business Marketing Association: Hudson Valley

304 Wall Street
Kingston, NY 12401

845-340-4708
800-664-4262
E-Mail: alviankamaly@gmail.com
Home Page: www.bma-hv.org

Bud Clarke, President
Joan Giewat, First Vice President
June Bisel, Second Vice President
Rebecca D Jones, Treasurer
John Bassler, Secretary

Offers ways for its members to expand their business expertise and grow professionally.

17734 Business Marketing Association: Indy

8650 Commerce Park Place
Indianapolis, IN 46268

800-664-4262
FAX 317-285-2068
E-Mail: information@bmaindy.org
Home Page: www.bmaindy.org

John Faust, President
Christine Johnston, Secretary
Judy Knafel, Treasurer

To promote the quality and effectiveness of Indiana-developed business-to-business marketing communications through the continuous learning of its members.

17735 Cable & Telecommunications Association for Marketing

120 Waterfront Street, Suite 200
National Harbor, MD 20745

301-485-8900
FAX 301-560-4964
E-Mail: info@ctam.com
Home Page: www.ctam.com
Social Media: *Facebook, Twitter, LinkedIn, Youtube*

Matrk Greatrex, Chair
Anne Cowan, President and CEO
Angie Britt, Vice President of Advanced Products
Jamia Bigalow, Vice Chair
Jonathan Hargis, Secretary / Treasurer

CTAM is dedicated to the discipline and development of consumer marketing excellence in cable television, new media and telecommunications services.
5500 Members
Founded in 1976

17736 Communications Marketing Association

PO Box 5680
Lago Vista, TX 78645

512-656-7747
E-Mail: CMAExecDirector@aol.com
Home Page: www.cma-cmc.org
Social Media: *Facebook, Twitter, LinkedIn, YouTube*

Rex Reed, President
Larry Weber, Vice President
Karen Hollingsworth, Executive Director
Tony Fulton, Treasurer
Larry Seige, Secretary

17737 Communications Roundtable

1250 24th Street NW
Suite 250
Washington, DC 20037

202-755-5180
FAX 202-466-0544
Home Page: www.roundtable.org

Michael Reichgut, Chairman
Shawn Dolley, CEO

Association of more than 20 public relations, marketing, graphics, advertising, training and other communications organizations with more than 12,000 professional members. The goals include furthering professionalism, cooperation between member organizations, career and employment support, and employer assistance.

17738 Construction Marketing Association

1220 Iroquois Ave.
Ste. #210
Naperville, IL 60563

630-868-5061
Home Page:
www.constructionmarketingassociation.org

Social Media: *Facebook, Twitter, LinkedIn, YouTube, Pinterest, Google+*

Neil M. Brown, Chair/ Founder
Kevin Enke, Board Member, Rick
Kean O'Brien, Board Member
Deborah Hodges, Board Member
Founded in 2009

17739 Construction Marketing Research Council C/O CMPA

4625 South Wendler Drive
Suite 111
Tempe, AZ 85282

602-431-1441
FAX 602-431-0637
E-Mail: info@c-m-r-c.com
Home Page: www.c-m-r-c.com/

Craig Schulz, President
Don Johnson, Director at Large
Jim McMahon, Treasurer

Members are professionals in the construction products industry with responsiblities for their firms' corporate strategic planning and the conduct of marketing research activities. Membership is restricted to the highest level marketing research or planning professional within a company.
25 Members
Founded in 1992

17740 Council for Marketing and Opinion

470 Portage Lakes Dr
Suite 102
Akron, OH 44319

330-564-4211
FAX 330-645-6750
E-Mail: info@cmoresearch.com
Home Page: cmoresearch.com
Social Media: *Facebook, Twitter, LinkedIn*

S. Michelle Henry, President/Co-Founder
Amanda Barna, Vice President/Co-Owner
Anthony Matonis, Senior Dir., Research and Analytics
Ryan Thompson, Research Associate
Brandon Dalo, Research Operations Manager

A non-profit organization which works on behalf of the survery research industry to improve respondent cooperation in research, and to promote positive legislation and prevent restrictive legislation which could impact the survey research industry.
150+ Members
Founded in 1992

17741 Data-Driven Marketing

Direct Marketing Association
1120 Avenue of the Americas
New York, NY 10036-6700

212-768-7277
FAX 212-302-6714
E-Mail: ed_berkowitz@primediabusiness.com
Home Page: www.thedma.org
Social Media: *Facebook, Twitter, LinkedIn*

Gunther Schmachar, Chairman
Eva Reda, Vice Chairman
JoAnne Monfradi Dunn, CEO & President, Direct Marketing
Bruce Bieger, Senior Managing Director
Cathy Butler, SVP, Group Account Director

17742 Destination Marketing Association International

2025 M Street NW
Suite 500
Washington, DC 20036

202-296-7888
FAX 202-296-7889
E-Mail: info@destinationmarketing.org

Home Page: www.destinationmarketing.org
Social Media: *Facebook, Twitter, Google+*

Joseph Marinelli, Chair
Alison Best, CDME, Chair Elect
David Adler, Founder/CEO
Stephanie Pace Brown, Secretary/ Treasurer
Cleo Battle, CDME, Immediate Past Chair

17743 Direct Marketing Association

1120 Avenue of the Americas
New York, NY 10036-6700

212-768-7277
FAX 212-302-6714
E-Mail: customerservice@the-dma.org
Home Page: www.thedma.org
Social Media: *Facebook, Twitter, LinkedIn*

Gunther Schmachar, Chairman
Eva Reda, Vice Chairman
JoAnne Monfradi Dunn, CEO & President,
Direct Marketing
Thomas J. Benton, Chief Operating Officer
Jerry Cerasale, J.D., Senior Vice President

The leading global trade association of businesses and nonprofit organizations using and supporting multichannel direct marketing tools and techniques. DMA advocates standards for responsible marketing, promotes relevance as the key to reaching consumers with desirable offers, and provides cutting edge research, education and networking opportunities to improve results throughout the end to end direct marketing process.
3100 Members
Founded in 1917

17744 Distributive Education Clubs of America

1908 Association Dr # A
Reston, VA 20191-1594

703-860-5000
FAX 703-860-4013
E-Mail: info@deca.org
Home Page: www.deca.org
Social Media: *Facebook, Twitter, LinkedIn, Youtube, RSS*

Jim Brock, President
Edward Davis, Executive Director
Lynore Levenhagen, Secretary
Mary Peres, Treasurer

To enhance the co-curricular education of students with interest in marketing, management, and entrprenuership. Helps students to develop skills and competence for marketing careers, to build self-esteem, to experience leadership and to practice community service.
Founded in 1946

17745 Diving Equipment & Marketing Association

858-616-6408
800-862-3483
FAX 858-616-6495
E-Mail: info@dema.org
Home Page: www.dema.org
Social Media: *Facebook, Twitter, LinkedIn, Google+, YouTube, RSS, Instagr*

Stephen Ashmore, President & Director
William Cline, Director
Jenny Collister, Director
Scott Daley, Director
Stuart Cove, Director
1300 Members

17746 EMarketing Association

40 Blue Ridge Dr.ÿ
Charlestown, RI 02813

800-496-2950
800-496-2950
FAX 408-884-2461
E-Mail: admin@emarketingassociation.com

Home Page: www.emarketingassociation.com
Social Media: *Facebook, Twitter, LinkedIn*

An international association of emarketing professionals. Members include governments, professionals and students involved with the emarketing arena. The eMA provides marketing resources, services, research, certifications, educational programs and events to its members and the marketing community.
2500 Members
Founded in 1997

17747 Electronic Retailing Association

607 14th Street, NW
Suite 530
Washington, DC 20005

703-841-1751
800-987-6462
FAX 425-977-1036
E-Mail: webadmin@retailing.org
Home Page: www.retailing.org
Social Media: *Facebook, Twitter, LinkedIn, Youtube.Flickr*

Gregory Sater, Chairman of the Board
Julie Coons, President & CEO
Kevin Kelly, Chief Financial Officer
Bill McClellan, Vice President, Government Affairs
Dave Martin, Vice President, Marketing

The trade association that represents the leaders of direct response: members who maximize revenues through electronic retailing on television, online and on radio. ERA strives to protect the regulatory and legislative climate of direct response while ensuring a favorable landscape that enhances e-retailers' ability to bring quality products and services to the consumer.
Founded in 1990

17748 Entertainment Resource & Marketing Association

2315 28th Street
Suite 204
Santa Monica, CA 90405

310-452-0426
E-Mail: Tami@erma.org
Home Page: www.erma.org
Social Media: *Facebook, Twitter, LinkedIn, Google+*

Michael Schrager, President
Amy Ferguson, Vice President
Eric Dahlquist, Treasurer
Nikki David, Secretary
Tami Cooper, Ethics Committee

17749 Foodservice Sales & Marketing Association

1810-J York Road #384
Lutherville, MD 21093

800-617-1170
800-617-1170
FAX 888-668-7496
E-Mail: info@fsmaonline.com
Home Page: www.fsmaonline.com
Social Media: *Facebook, Twitter, LinkedIn, Youtube*

Stuart Wolff, Chairman of the Board
Rick Abraham, President & CEO
Sharon Boyle, Vice President
Jessica Muffoletto, Manager, Membership & Meetings
Barry Maloney, General Counsel

Specializes in selling food and related products to foodservice companies.
150 Members
Founded in 2003
Mailing list available for rent

17750 Global Retail Marketing Association

Home Page: www.thegrma.com
Social Media: *Twitter, LinkedIn*

Bill Brand, Advisory Board Member
Brian Beitler, Advisory Board Member
Ron Bonacci, Advisory Board Member
Lily Chang, Advisory Board Member
John Aylward, Advisory Board Member

17751 Healthcare Public Relations & Marketing Association

5406 Hazeltine Ave.
Sherman Oaks, CA 91401

714-647-2430
E-Mail: info@hprma.org
Home Page: www.vnetitclients.com/hprma2
Social Media: *Facebook, Twitter, LinkedIn*

Pamela Westcott, President
Ava Alexander, Sponsorships
Jennifer Heinley, Secretary
Kathleen Curan, Communications
Lisa Killen, Membership

17752 Hospitality Sales and Marketing Association

7918 Jones Branch Drive
Suite 300
McLean, VA 22102

703-506-3280
FAX 703-506-3266
E-Mail: info@hsmai.org
Home Page: www.hsmai.org
Social Media: *Facebook, Twitter, LinkedIn, Flicker*

Rob Torres, Chair
Marina MacDonald, Vice Chair
Robert A. Gilbert, CHME, CHA, President & CEO
Juli Jones, Vice President
Fran Brasseux, CHSE, Executive Vice President
7000 Members
Founded in 1927

17753 Incentive Marketing Association

9700 W. Bryn Mawr Avenue
Suite 210
Rosemont, IL 60018

847-447-1082
FAX 630-369-3773
E-Mail: info@incentivemarketing.org
Home Page: ima.site-ym.com
Social Media: *Facebook, Twitter, LinkedIn, Stumbleupon, Tumblr, Blogger,*

Spencer Toomey, CPIM, President
Sean Roark, CPIM, Executive Vice President
Heidi Chatfield, CPIM, Vice President
Donna Chrobak, Executive Director
John Hornbogen, Treasurer

Members are professional premium/incentive marketing executives.
650 Members
Founded in 1998

17754 Incentive Performance Center

5008 Castle Rock Way
Naples, FL 34112

914-591-7600
FAX 239-775-7537
E-Mail: info@incentivecentral.org
Home Page: www.incentivecentral.org

Howard C Henry, Executive Director/CAE

Your portal to new ways of achieving business goals by capturing the power of your best customers and employees.
150 Members
Founded in 1984

17755 Insurance Marketing & Communications Association

4248 Park Glen Road
Minneapolis, MN 55416

952-928-4644
FAX 952-929-1318
E-Mail: info@imcanet.com
Home Page: imcanet.com
Social Media: *Facebook, Twitter, LinkedIn, YouTube*

Mark Friedlander, President
Gloria Grove, Executive Director
Anna Hargis, Executive Vice President
John Abbott, Member
Emily Hathcoat, Treasurer
Founded in 1923

17756 Internet Marketing Association

10 Mar Del Rey
San Clemente, CA 92673

949-443-9300
FAX 949-443-2215
E-Mail: info@imanetwork.org
Home Page: imanetwork.org
Social Media: *Facebook, Twitter, LinkedIn, RSS, Google+, YouTube*

Sinan Kanatsiz, CIM, Chairman & Founder
Matthew Langie, CIM, Vice Chair of Education
Rachel Reenders, CIM, Executive Director
Vince Walden, Finance Director
David Steinberg, CIM, VP of Business Alliances
90000 Members
Founded in 2001

17757 Legal Marketing Association

330 North Wabash Avenue
Suite 2000
Chicago, IL 60611-4267

312-321-6898
FAX 312-673-6894
E-Mail: membersupport@legalmarketing.org
Home Page: www.legalmarketing.org
Social Media: *Facebook, Twitter, LinkedIn, Youtube*

Betsi Roach, Executive Director
Susan Lane, Director of Operations
Adrianne Watson, Membership Services
Lizzie Duvall, Membership Services
Justine Gershak, Membership Services

LMA is a nonprofit organization dedicated to serving the needs and maintaining the professional standards of the men and women involved in marketing within the legal profession.
2700 Members
Founded in 1985

17758 Life Insurance Direct Marketing Association

3227 S. Cherokee Lane
Suite 1320
Woodstock, GA 30188

770-516-0207
866-890-LEAD
E-Mail: info@lidma.org
Home Page: lidma.org
Social Media: *Facebook, Twitter, LinkedIn*

Pat Wedeking, Chair
Byron Udell, President
Jeff McCauley, Vice President
Staci Birk, Director
Cynthia Farrow, Secretary/ Treasurer

17759 Manufacturers Agents National Association

16-A Journey
Suite 200
Aliso Viejo, CA 92656-3317

949-859-4040
877-626-2776
FAX 949-855-2973
E-Mail: mana@manaonline.org
Home Page: www.manaonline.org

Tom Hayward, CPMR, Chairman
Charles Cohon, CPMR, President and CEO
Jerry Leth, Vice President and General Manager
Lisa Ball, Member Services Coordinator
Doug Bower, Director of Strategic Alliances
6600 Members
Founded in 1947

17760 Marketing Agencies Association Worldwide

60 Peachcroft Drive
Bernardsville, NJ 07924

908-428-4300
FAX 908-766-1277
E-Mail: vincentsottosanti@maaw.org
Home Page: www.maaw.org

Aldo Cundari, President
Aldo Cundari, 1st Vice President
Dan Mortimer, VP On-line Services
John Williams, Executive Director
Rick Shaver, Treasurer

The Marketing Agencies Assocation Worldwide (MAA) is the only global organization dedicated solely to the CEOs, Presidents,Managing Directors and Principals of top marketing services agencies.
75 Members
Founded in 1963

17761 Marketing Education Association

PO Box 27473
Tempe, AZ 85285-7473

602-750-6735
E-Mail: mea@nationalmea.org
Home Page: www.nationalmea.org

Fosters the development and expansion of education for and about marketing as a descrete, clearly defined profession. Members are high school and postsecondary marketing educations as well as university-level teacher educations and collegiate marketing teacher education students.
Founded in 1982

17762 Marketing Research Association

1156 15th Street NW
Suite 302
Washington, DC 20005

202-800-2545
FAX 888-512-1050
E-Mail: membership@marketingresearch.org
Home Page: www.marketingresearch.org
Social Media: *Facebook, Twitter, LinkedIn, Google+*

David Almy, CEO

The Marketing Research Association's Blue Book Research Services Directory is the research industry number one reference source.
Founded in 1957

17763 Marketing Science Institute

Marketing Science Institute
1000 Massachusetts Avenue
Cambridge, MA 02138-5396

617-491-2060
FAX 617-491-2065
E-Mail: msi@msi.org

Home Page: www.msi.org
Social Media: *Facebook, Twitter, LinkedIn*

Katherine N.ÿ Lemon, Executive Director
Marni Zea Clippinger, Chief Operating Officer
Earl Taylor, Chief Marketing Officer
Liza Hostetler-Ingalls, Administrative Assistant
Susan Keane, Editorial Director

MSI publishes research done on a variety of marketing topics, including: E - Commerce, Metrics, Branding, New Products and Innovations, Communications and more. Individual papers and subscriptions are available. We accept proposals and papers for grant consideration.
65 Members
Founded in 1961

17764 Mass Marketing Insurance Institute

3007 Tilden Street, NW
Suite 7M-103
Washington, DC 20008

816-221-7575
FAX 816-772-7765
E-Mail: Jeffrey.M.Collins@MedStar.net
Home Page: www.mi2.org
Social Media: *Twitter, Youtube, Pinterest, RSS, Googl*

Greg Carlile, Executive Director
Laurie Weber, Associate Director

Provides a forum for professionals engaged in marketing, sales and administration of employee benefits such as worksite marketing, payroll deduction and other mass marketed services.

17765 Materials Marketing Associates

136 South Keowee Street
Dayton, OH 45402

937-222-1024
FAX 937-222-5794
E-Mail: email@mma4u.com
Home Page: www.mma4u.com

Kimberley Fantaci, President

Members are chemical distributors representing manufacturers marketing chemical raw material specialties to makers of coatings, inks, pharmaceuticals, adhesives, cosmetics, plastics, soaps, detergents, etc.
19 Members
Founded in 1963

17766 Midwest Direct Marketing Association

P.O. Box 75
Andover, MN 55304

763-607-2943
FAX 763-753-2240
E-Mail: office@mdma.org
Home Page: www.mdma.org

Ben DuBois, Communications Director
Jolee Molitor, Programs Director
Vicki Erickson, Secretary/Treasurer
Jolee Moiltor, Past President

Dedicated to the advancement of professional and ethical practice of direct response marketing by members throughout the Upper Midwest.
600 Members
Founded in 1960

17767 Mobile Marketing Association

41 E 11th St
11th Floor
New York, NY 10003

646-257-4515
E-Mail: northamerica@mmaglobal.com
Home Page: www.mmaglobal.com

Social Media: *Facebook, Twitter, LinkedIn, Google+*

Greg Stuart, Chief Executive Officer
Sheryl Daija, CSO & GM, Global Events
Chris Babayode, Managing Director, EMEA
Fabiano Destri Lobo, Managing Director, Latam
Michael Wis, SVP, Global Finance Administration
800 Members

17768 Multi-Level Marketing International Association
119 Stanford Court
Irvine, CA 92612-1671

949-854-0484
FAX 949-854-7687
E-Mail: info@mlmia.com
Home Page: www.mlmia.com
Social Media: *Facebook, Twitter, LinkedIn*

Doris Wood, Chairman/President Emeritus
Linda Bruno, Secretary

Seeks to strengthen and improve the Direct Sales/Network Marketing/Multi-Level Marketing industry in the United States and abroad.
Founded in 1985

17769 Multicultural Marketing Resources
150 West 28th Street
Suite 1501
New York, NY 10001

212-242-3351
FAX 212-691-5969
E-Mail: lisa@multicultural.com
Home Page: www.multicultural.com
Social Media: *Facebook, Twitter, LinkedIn*

Lisa Skriloff, President
Cassandra Richardson-Coughlin, Marketing/Sales Assistant
Kelleh Jian, Marketing/Sales Assistant
Mukti Ajmeri, Marketing/Sales Assistant
Nadia M, Marketing/Sales Assistant

A place where corporate executives can find diverse resources, experts and information on how to market to multicultural (ethnic and niche) consumer markets.
Founded in 1994

17770 National Association of Display Industries
4651 Sheridan Street
Suite 470
Hollywood, FL 33021

954-893-7300
FAX 954-893-7500
E-Mail: nadi@nadi-global.com
Home Page: www.nadi-global.com

Klein Merriman, Executive Director
Tracy Dillon, Director Communications

A leading association for the visual merchandising profession. As visual merchandising has evolved over the years into playing an integral role in retail, NADI has always taken the lead in informing and educating members. The association's already significant support of the visual design profession has grown with NADI's exclusive sponsorship of GlobalShop's Visual Merchandising Show and StoreXpo.
Founded in 1942

17771 National Energy Marketers Association
3333 K Street, NW
Suite 110
Washington, DC 20007

202-333-3288
FAX 202-333-3266
Home Page: www.energymarketers.com

Dan Verbanac, Chair, Executive Committee
Chris Hendrix, 1st Vice Chair, Executive

Committee
Pierre Koshakji, 2nd Vice Chair, Executive Committee
Craig Goodman, President
Harry Warren, Chair Emeriti

17772 North American Farmers' Direct Marketing Association
62 White Loaf Road
Southampton, MA 1073

FAX 413-233-4285
E-Mail: Charlie @ Whiteloafridge.com
Home Page: www.farmersinspired.com
Social Media: *Facebook, Twitter, Pinterest, YouTube*

Cynthia Chiles, President/ Chair
Charlie Touchette, Executive Director
Becky Walters, VP of Membership
Ben Beaver, VP of Education
Mike Dunn, Treasurer/ Finance Team Chair

17773 Performance Marketing Association
364 East Main St.
Suite 444
Middletown, DE 19709

805-233-7987
Home Page: thepma.org
Social Media: *Facebook, Twitter, LinkedIn, RSS, Google+*

Brian Littleton, President
Tony Pantano, Treasurer
Tricia Meyer, Secretary
Todd Crawford, Board Member
Rachel Honoway, Board Member
20000 Members
Founded in 2008

17774 Petroleum Marketers Association of America
1901 North Fort Myer Drive
Suite 500
Arlington, VA 22209

703-351-8000
FAX 703-351-9160
E-Mail: info@pmaa.org
Home Page: www.pmaa.org
Social Media: *Facebook, Twitter*

Grady Gaubert, Chairman
Mike Bailey, Vice Chair
Mark Whitehead, 2nd Vice Chair
Benny Hodges, Brands Division Director
Greg Benson, West Region Chair
Founded in 1909

17775 Photo Marketing Association International
7918 Jones Branch Drive
Suite 300
McLean, VA 22102

703-665-4416
800-762-9287
FAX 703-506-3266
E-Mail: pma_information_central@pmai.org
Home Page: www.pmai.org
Social Media: *Facebook, Twitter, LinkedIn*

Allen Showalter, President
Robert L. Hanson, Vice President
Jim Esp, Executive Director/Secretary
Bill Eklund, Treasurer
18000 Members
Founded in 1924

17776 Power Marketing Association
E-Mail: pma@powermarketers.com
Home Page: www.powermarketers.com

Ralph E. Beaty III,
Membership/Communications Manager
Carol Ofiesh, Member Services Manager
Phil Ofiesh, Data Services Manager
Scott Spiewak, Publisher

17777 Private Label Manufacturers Association
630 Third Avenue
New York, NY 10017-6770

212-972-3131
FAX 212-983-1382
E-Mail: info@plma.com
Home Page: www.plma.com

Myra Rosen, Vice President
Brian Sharoff, President

Trade Association promoting the Private Label Industry.
3200+ Members
Founded in 1979

17778 Produce Marketing Association
1500 Casho Mill Road
Newark, DE 19711

302-738-7100
FAX 302-731-2409
Home Page: www.pma.com
Social Media: *Facebook, Twitter, Pinterest, Flickr*

Cathy Burns, President
Bryan Silbermann, Chief Executive Officer
Tony Parassio, Chief Operating Officer
Yvonne Bull, Chief Financial Officer
Margi Prueitt, Executive Director

17779 Producers Livestock Marketing Association
PO Box 540477
North Salt Lake, UT 84054-0477

801-936-2424
800-791-BEEF
E-Mail: homeoffice@producerslivestock.com
Home Page: www.producerslivestock.com

Rick O'Brien, General Manager
Brad Jones, Branch Manager
Bob Elliot, Assistant Branch Manager
Vivian Reed, Office Manager
Founded in 1935

17780 Professional Insurance Marketing Association
35 E. Wacker Dr
Suite 850
Chicago, IL 60601-2106

817-569-PIMA
FAX 312-644-8557
E-Mail: mona@pima-assn.org
Home Page: www.pima-assn.org
Social Media: *Twitter, LinkedIn*

Daniel O'Brien, CLU, President
Mona F. Buckley, MPA, Chief Executive Officer
William Suneson, Secretary
Mark Kelsey, Treasurer
Dave Armstrong, Director
120 Members

17781 Promotion Industry Council
1805 N Mill Street
Naperville, IL 60563-1275

630-369-7781
FAX 630-369-3773

Manufacturers, distributors and users of promotion premiums. Increases understanding of incentives and the premium promotion process.
100 Members
Founded in 1940

17782 Re:Gender
11 Hanover Square
24th Floor
New York, NY 10005-2819

212-785-7335
FAX 212-785-7350
E-Mail: info@regender.org

Home Page: www.regender.org
Social Media: *Facebook, Twitter, RSS*

Lucie Lapovsky, Chair
Aine Duggan, President
Andrea Greenblatt, Vice President of Operations
Debbie Kellogg, Vice President for External Rel
Gail Cooper, Vice President for Programs

A network of 120 leading research, policy and advocacy centers committed to improving the lives of women and girls. Provides the latest news, information and strategies needed to ensure fully informed debates, effective policies and inclusive practices.
3,000 Members
Founded in 1981

17783 Restaurant Marketing & Delivery Association

3636 Menaul Blvd.
Ste. 323
Albuquerque, NM 87110

E-Mail: membership@rmda.info
Home Page: www.rmda.info
Social Media: *Facebook, Twitter, LinkedIn*

Paul Birrell, President
David Farmer, Vice President
Wes Garrison, Treasurer
Anu Mehra, Convention
Luke Katuin, Technology
Founded in 1990

17784 Sales and Marketing Executives International

PO Box 1390
Sumas, WA 98295-1390

312-893-0751
FAX 312-893-0751
E-Mail: admin@smei.org
Home Page: www.smei.org
Social Media: *Facebook, Twitter, LinkedIn, Youtube, RSS,Blog*

Clinton J. Schroeder MBA, CME, CS, Chairman
Willis Turner CAE CME CSE, President & Chief Executive Officer
Hans-Benno Mastboom, Senior Vice Chair
Antonio Rios-Ramirez, Senior Vice Chair
Nathalie Roemer CME, Secretary Treasurer

Members are most commonly professionals in the fields of sales and marketing management, market research management, sales training, distribution management and other senior executives in small and medium businesses.
10000 Members
Frequency: Annual Meeting (Fall)
Founded in 1935

17785 Search Engine Marketing Professional Organization

401 Edgewater Pl.
Suite 600
Wakefield, MA 1880

718-876-8866
E-Mail: info@sempo.org
Home Page: www.sempo.org
Social Media: *Facebook, Twitter, LinkedIn, Blogpot, YouTube, Google+,Pint*

Mike Grehan, Chair
Mike Gullaksen, President
Simon Heseltine, VP of Education
Marc Engelsman, VP of Research
Krista LaRiviere, VP of Local Group
Founded in 2002

17786 Society for Marketing Professional Services

123 North Pitt Street
Suite 400
Alexandria, VA 22314

703-549-6117
800-292-7677
FAX 703-549-2498
E-Mail: info@smps.org
Home Page: www.smps.org
Social Media: *Facebook, Twitter, LinkedIn, Youtube,Pinterest*

Ronald D. Worth, CAE, FSMPS, CPS, CEO
Lisa Bowman, Senior Vice President
Mark DellaPietra, Vice President of Education
Tina Myers, CAE, Senior Vice President
Michele Santiago, Director of Marketing

Serving marketing and business development professionals employed by architectural, engineering and construction firms, SMPS provides education and networking opportunities tailored to build your bottom line.
5600 Members
Founded in 1973
Mailing list available for rent: 6000 names at $200 per M

17787 Society of Independent Gasoline Marketers

3930 Pender Drive
Suite 340
Fairfax, VA 22030

703-709-7000
FAX 703-709-7007
E-Mail: sigma@sigma.org
Home Page: www.sigma.org

Tom Gresham, President
Kenneth A. Doyle, CAE, Executive Vice President
Mary Alice Kutyn, Director Meetings
Dennis Cuevas, Director of Education
Mary Alice Kutyn, Director of Meetings

Members are independent gasoline marketers.
270 Members
Founded in 1958

17788 Specialty Equipment Market Association

1575 S. Valley Vista Drive
Diamond Bar, CA 91765-0910

909-610-2030
FAX 909-860-0184
E-Mail: sema@sema.org
Home Page: www.sema.org
Social Media: *Facebook, Twitter, Google+*

Dough Evans, Chairman
Christopher J. Kersting, President and CEO
George Afremow, Vice President
Steve McDonald, Vice President of Government Affair
John Kilroy, Vice President/General Manager, PRI

Represents the automotive aftermarket industry with government agencies and trade and consumer groups.
5200 Members
Founded in 1963

17789 Sport Marketing Association

1972 Clark Ave.
Alliance, OH 44601

330-829-8207
E-Mail: smaoffice@mountunion.edu
Home Page: www.sportmarketingassociation.com
Social Media: *Facebook, Twitter, LinkedIn*

Jim Kadlecek, President
Khalid Ballouli, VP of Academic Affairs
Elizabeth Gregg, VP of Student Affairs

Steven McKelvey, VP of Industry Relations
Beth Grupsmith, Social Media Consultant
Founded in 2002

17790 Strategic Account Management Association

10 N. Dearborn St.
2nd Floor
Chicago, IL 60602

312-251-3131
FAX 312-251-3132
E-Mail: napolitano@strategicaccounts.org
Home Page: www.strategicaccounts.org
Social Media: *Facebook, Twitter, LinkedIn, Pinterest, Google+*

Bernard Quancard, President/CEO
Katherine Gotsick, Chief Operations Officer
Frankie Cusimano, Senior Manager, Membership
Matt Fegley, Chief Business Development Officer
Richard Rottsolk, Senior Manager, Corporate Resource

The Strategic Account Management Association is a non-profit organization devoted to developing and promoting the concept of customer-supplier partnering. SAMA is dedicated to the professional and personal development of the executives charged with managing national, global, and strategic account relationships, and to elevating the status of the profession as a whole. SAMA provides literature, training and research into best practices in large, complex, global customer account management.
2000 Members
Founded in 1964

17791 Thomson Reuters

Thomson Reuters
2395 Midway Rd
Carrollton, TX 75006

646-223-4000
888-885-0206
FAX 888-216-1929
E-Mail: trta.lei-support@thomsonreuters.com
Home Page: www.tax.thomsonreuters.com

David K R Thomson, Chairman
Thomas H Glocer, CEO & Director
Robert D Daleo, Chief Financial Officer
Kelli Crane, Senior Vice President & CIO

A national organization that focuses on marketing and sales intelligence for top level marketing executives.

17792 Trade Show Exhibitors Association

2214 NW 5th St.
Suite 1005
Bend, OR 97701

541-317-8768
FAX 541-317-8749
E-Mail: tsea@tsea.org
Home Page: www.tsea.org
Social Media: *Facebook*

Amanda Helgemoe, President
Michael Mulry, Vice President
Glenda Brundgardt, Treasurer
Chris Griffin, Secretary

Members are companies using exhibits for marketing, advertising or public relations.
1800 Members
Founded in 1966

17793 Transportation Marketing & Sales Association

9382 Oak Avenue
Waconia, MN 55387

952-466-6270
Home Page: www.tmsatoday.org/

Social Media: *Facebook, Twitter, LinkedIn, YouTube*

David Hoppens, Chairman
Dino Moler, President
Beth Carroll, VP-Administration & Finance
Candi Cybator, VP- Content & Strategy
Andy Williams, VP- Membership & Outreach
Founded in 1924

17794 Word of Mouth Marketing Association

200 East Randolph Street
Suite 5100
Chicago, IL 60601

312-577-7610
FAX 312-275-7687
E-Mail: membership@womma.org
Home Page: www.womma.org
Social Media: *Facebook, Twitter, LinkedIn, YouTube, Google+*

Suzanne Fanning, President
Chris Spallino, Director of Marketing
Jennifer Connelly, Events Manager
Chelsea Hickey, Marketing Manager & Editor
The Word of Mouth Association is dedicated to word of mouth and social media marketing. It is the leader in ethical word of mouth marketing practices through eduation including the WOMMA summit, professional marketing opportunities and knowledge sharing.
Founded in 2004

Newsletters

17795 Advanced Selling Power

Thompson Group
6850 Austin Center Blvd
Suite 100
Austin, TX 78731-3201

512-418-8869
FAX 512-418-1209
E-Mail: carol@thompson-group.com
Home Page: www.thompson-group.com

Terry E Thompson, Publisher
Valerie A Canaday, Editor
Carol Thompson, President

Provides sales tactics, strategies and ideas to sales professinals and entrepreneurs. Each issue helps salespeople learn how to put together presentations, develop openings that keep customers interested, use testimonials correctly and more.
Cost: $10.00
Circulation: 1000
Founded in 1993

17796 Airline Financial News

Phillips Business Information
1201 Seven Locks Road
Suite 300
Potomac, MD 20854-2931

301-541-1400
FAX 301-309-3847

Grier Graham, Editor
Newsletter that provides the most timely financial reports and market analysis for the entire airline industry.
Cost: $695.00
Frequency: Weekly

17797 Antin Marketing Letter

Alan Antin/Antin Marketing Group
19888 Sw Monte Vista Dr
Suite 205
Beaverton, OR 97007-5412

503-356-0504
FAX 913-663-5552

E-Mail: AMG@commonsensemarketing.com
Home Page: www.commonsensemarketing.com

Brad Antin, President
Alan Antin, Director of Marketing
William Hammond, Director of Marketing
How-to info on marketing for professionals and entrepreneurs (service businesses, retailers, wholesalers, professional practice).
Cost: $197.00
Frequency: Monthly

17798 Application Servers and Media Servers

Probe Research
3 Wing Drive
Suite 240
Cedar Knolls, NJ 07927-1000

973-285-1500
FAX 973-285-1519
Home Page: www.proberesearch.com

This bulletin describes the market for both applications and media servers; examines key issues and provides a profile of selected players in various product categories.

17799 Art of Self Promotion

Ilise Benun/Creative Marketing and Management
PO Box 23
Hoboken, NJ 07030

201-653-0783
800-737-0783
FAX 201-222-2494
E-Mail: ilise@marketing-mentor.com
Home Page: www.artofselfpromotion.com

Lisa Cyr, Author
Ilise Benun, Marketing Manager
Nuts'n bolts for manageable marketing for small business owners and self employed professionals.
Cost: $100.80
8 Pages
Frequency: Quarterly
Founded in 1995

17800 Association of Incentive Marketing News

Association of Incentive Marketing
1601 North Bond Street, Suite 303
Naperville, IL 60563

603-369-7780
FAX 603-369-3773
E-Mail: karen@incentivemarketing.org
Home Page: www.incentivemarketing.org

George Meredith, Editor
Susan Peterson, Director of Membership
Nicole Sweigart, Administrative Director
Paul Cernohous, Director
Karen Renk, Executive Director

Articles cover promotion industry news and Association information and events.
Frequency: Quarterly
Circulation: 300

17801 Auctioneer

National Auctioneers Association
8880 Ballentine
Overland Park, KS 66214

913-541-8084
FAX 913-894-5281
E-Mail: hcombest@auctioneers.org
Home Page: auctions.auctioneers.org

Robert Shively, CEO
Wendy Dellinger, Advertising Manager
Steve Baska, Publications Editor
Ryan Putnam, Assistant Editor

Keeps members of the National Auctioneers Association informed of trends and legal issues

related to auctioneering. Chronicles activities of the Association and its membership.
Frequency: Monthly
Circulation: 7000
Founded in 1948

17802 Automated and Self-Provisioning Servers

Probe Research
3 Wing Drive
Suite 240
Cedar Knolls, NJ 07927-1000

973-285-1500
FAX 973-285-1519
Home Page: www.proberesearch.com

A look at service provider implementation of automated and self - provisioning software systems. An explanation of the causes of delay and QoS degradation in IP networks.

17803 BDA

BDA News
900 W Sunset Boulevard
Suite 900
Los Angeles, CA 90069

310-712-0040
FAX 310-712-0039
Home Page: www.bda.tv

Jill Masters, VP Member Services
Jim Chabin, President
Newsletter, awards annual, magazine and directory published by BDA for designers in the motion graphics industry.
Cost: $5.00
Frequency: Monthly
Circulation: 2000
Printed in 4 colors on glossy stock

17804 Bandwidth Management: Driving Profitablity to the Botton Line

Probe Research
3 Wing Drive
Suite 240
Cedar Knolls, NJ 07927-1000

973-285-1500
FAX 973-285-1519
Home Page: www.proberesearch.com

Provides an analysis of the type of issues that require Bandwidth Management solutions. Makes a comparison of the types of technical solutions implemented in different parts of the network and the major benefits of each solution. Also analyzes the trends seen in IP traffic and inter - relationship with bandwidth management.

17805 Bulletproof Marketing for Small Businesses

Kay Borden/Franklin-Sarrett Publishers
3761 Vinyard Trce Ne
Marietta, GA 30062-5227

770-578-9410
FAX 770-977-5495

Kay Borden, President
Publicity for small businesses, particularly producing news releases that get printed.
Cost: $15.00
Frequency: SemiAnnual
Founded in 1994

17806 Business Owner

Mailing & Fulfillment Service Association
1421 Prince Street
Suite 410
Alexandria, VA 22314-2806

703-836-9200
FAX 703-548-8204
E-Mail: mfsa-mail@mfsanet.org

Home Page: www.mfsanet.org
Social Media: *Facebook, Twitter, LinkedIn*

David L Perkins Jr, Editor
Leo Raymond, Vice President

Developed specifically to communicate with owners and CEOs on issues unique to them. You'll receive a wealth of knowledge on growing your business, tax issues, insurance, estate planning, management, finance and much more.
Frequency: Bi-Monthly

17807 Business-2-Business Marketer

Business Marketing Association
Ste 123
1833 Centre Point Cir
Naperville, IL 60563-4848

630-544-5054
FAX 630-544-5055
E-Mail: info@marketing.org
Home Page: www.marketing.org
Social Media: *Facebook, Twitter, LinkedIn*

Jeffrey Hayzlett, Chairman
Gary Slack, Vice Chairman
Bob Goranson CBC, Treasurer

Editorial covers all apsects of integrated marketing disciplines, including: sales management, trade show marketing, datbase and direct mail marketing, presentations, telemarketing, public relations, advertising and electronic marketing.
Cost: $150.00
16 Pages
Circulation: 4300
ISSN: 1073-4538
Founded in 1922
Printed in 4 colors on glossy stock

17808 Cable & Wireless

Probe Research
3 Wing Drive
Suite 240
Cedar Knolls, NJ 07927-1000

973-285-1500
FAX 973-285-1519
Home Page: www.proberesearch.com

A look at cable & wireless IP infrastructure, how the company is operating it, and how it is managing services on its network.

17809 Cable Headed Equipment Markets Upstarts

Probe Research
3 Wing Drive
Suite 240
Cedar Knolls, NJ 07927-1000

973-285-1500
FAX 973-285-1519
Home Page: www.proberesearch.com

This bulletin analyses the CMTS market and the role the equipment plays in the plans of the major cable operators to move towards the goal of full service operators. A market forecast is included and the major players profiled.

17810 Cambridge Reports Trends and Forecasts

Cambridge Reports
955 Massachusetts Ave
Suite 8
Cambridge, MA 02139-3178

617-661-0110
FAX 617-661-3575

Gene Pokorny, Publisher
Key changes in consumer and public opinions.

17811 Career News Update

American Marketing Association

311 S Wacker Dr
Suite 5800
Chicago, IL 60606-6629

312-542-9000
800-262-1150
FAX 312-542-9001
Home Page: www.marketingpower.com
Social Media: *Facebook, Twitter, LinkedIn, Youtube*

Dennis Dunlap, CEO

You'll receive the latest career and hiring advice as well as useful job resources and employment listings.
Frequency: Monthly
Mailing list available for rent

17812 Collegiate Trends

Strategic Marketing
550 N Maple Ave
Suite 102
Ridgewood, NJ 07450-1611

201-612-8100
FAX 201-612-1444
E-Mail: weil@studentmonitor.com
Home Page: www.studentmonitor.com

Marketing and media trends for marketers targeting college students.
Cost: $95.00
Frequency: Quarterly
Founded in 1987

17813 Colloquy

Frequency Marketing
PO Box 610
Milford, OH 45150-0610

513-248-2882
FAX 513-248-2672
E-Mail: info_de@epsilon.com
Home Page: www.epsilon.com

Bryan Kennedy, President/CEO
Jill Z. McBride, Chief Operating Officer
Catherine Lang, Chief Operating Officer
Paul Dundon, Chief Financial Officer
Jeanette Fitzgerald, General Counsel

Frequency Marketing, is the publisher of the COLLOQUY newsletter and COLLOQUY.com Web site, which are dedicated tot he discrimination of information about analysis of frequency marketing strategies and programs worldwide. COLLOQUY also provides educational and research services on a global basis to the loyalty marketing industry, and offers substantial news, research libraries and program archives to qualified subscribers at COLLOQUY.com.
Frequency: Quarterly
Circulation: 16,000+
Founded in 1990

17814 Competitive Advantage

Competitive Advantage
PO Box 10828
Portland, OR 97296-0828

503-274-2953
FAX 503-274-4349

Jim Moran, Publisher
Tonya Shrives, Promotional Director

Provides sales, marketing and management tools to make careers and companies more prosperous.
Circulation: 10,000

17815 Conference Board Management Briefing - Marketing

Conference Board
845 3rd Ave
Suite 2
New York, NY 10022-6600

212-759-0900
FAX 212-980-7014

E-Mail: june.shelp@conference-board.org
Home Page: www.conference-board.org

Jonathan Spector, CEO

Trends and practices in marketing.
Frequency: Monthly

17816 Creative Marketing Newsletter

Association of Retail Marketing Services
10 Drs James Parker Boulevard
Suite 103
Red Bank, NJ 07701-1500

732-842-5070
FAX 732-219-1938
E-Mail: info@goarms.com
Home Page: www.goarms.com

Gerri Hopkins, Executive Director
Lisa McCauley, Administrative Director

Retail promotion marketing newsletter for supermarkets, convenience stores, drug chains and suppliers of retail promotions.
Frequency: Quarterly
Printed in 3 colors on matte stock

17817 Creative Selling

Bentley-Hall
120 E Washington St
Suite 913
Syracuse, NY 13202-4003

315-701-0308
FAX 315-471-2138

Contains training material for sales managers and sales training managers.
Cost: $7.00
Circulation: 6,500

17818 Current Global Carrier Market Environment, Global Carrier

Probe Research
3 Wing Drive
Suite 240
Cedar Knolls, NJ 07927-1000

973-285-1500
FAX 973-285-1519
Home Page: www.proberesearch.com

Addresses a sweeping review of current strategic, business, economic, financial, network technology, network operations and service portfolio topics now at work in global and international carriage. Also includes a discussion of the potential risk assessment value of existing and future bandwidth trading and arbitrage exchanges.

17819 Current Thinking on Network Evolution and Its Laws

Probe Research
3 Wing Drive
Suite 240
Cedar Knolls, NJ 07927-1000

973-285-1500
FAX 973-285-1519
Home Page: www.proberesearch.com

This issue focuses on three laws of network evolution used by new entrants and by vendors. These three laws seem to be justified when the stock market rewarded new entrants with enormous valuations simply based on technology and expensive business plans. Now that the stock market no longer rewards such ventures, an analysis of these three laws is warranted and what impact thay have had on the carrier business.

17820 Customers First

Dartnell Corporation

4660 N Ravenswood Avenue
Chicago, IL 60640-4510

773-907-9500
FAX 773-561-3801

Clark Fetridge, Publisher
Jim Nawrocki, Editor

A practical periodical that provides employees with an organized plan of action for building and improving customer relations.
Cost: $62.00

17821 Daily News E-Mail (3D)
Direct Marketing Association
1120 Avenue of the Americas
New York, NY 10036-6700

212-768-7277
FAX 212-302-6714
E-Mail: customerservice@the-dma.org
Home Page: www.the-dma.org

Lawrence M Kimmel, CEO

Delivers the essential news, research, hot trends, and technological developments from the nations leading newspapers, trade publications, and the government all in an easy-to-read, time-saving format.

17822 Dartnell Sales and Marketing Executive Report
Dartnell Corporation
4660 N Ravenswood Avenue
Chicago, IL 60640-4510

773-907-9500
800-341-7874
FAX 773-907-0645
E-Mail: infochicago@insightpd.com
Home Page: www.insightpd.com

Craig Scherer, Senior Partner
Anthony Annibale, General Manager
Cost: $168.00
Frequency: Monthly
Founded in 1917

17823 Data Service: ISDN, Private Lines, Frame Relay and ATM
Probe Research
3 Wing Drive
Suite 240
Cedar Knolls, NJ 07927-1000

973-285-1500
FAX 973-285-1519
Home Page: www.proberesearch.com

We survey and highlight four major data transport technologies detailing the technology's strengths, weakness, specific applications, and basic carrier strategies.

17824 Defining the M-Commerce Value Chain
Probe Research
3 Wing Drive
Suite 240
Cedar Knolls, NJ 07927-1000

973-285-1500
FAX 973-285-1519
Home Page: www.proberesearch.com

Defines and unifies all participants in a mobile commerce transaction using the sentence Selecting, ordering and paying for items using a mobile device in a secure fashion. Examines the m-commerce business models selected carriers, ASPs and other vendors.

17825 Delaney Report
PRIMEDIA Intertec-Marketing & Professional Service

149 5th Avenue
#725
New York, NY 10010-6801

212-979-7881
FAX 212-979-0691
E-Mail: tdrinfo@aol.com
Home Page: http://www.delaneyreport.com

Thomas Delaney, Editor

Provides information on personnel changes, trade literature and indsutry events for advertising, media, media, and public relations executives. Reports on global news and developments.
Cost: $74.00

17826 Digital Subscriber Line Access Multiplexer Upstarts
Probe Research
3 Wing Drive
Suite 240
Cedar Knolls, NJ 07927-1000

973-285-1500
FAX 973-285-1519
Home Page: www.proberesearch.com

This bulletin examines the major DSALM vendors and forecast the market for DSLAM ports and equipment revenue until 2006.

17827 Downtown Promotion Reporter
Alexander Communications Group
1916 Park Ave
Suite 501
New York, NY 10037-3733

212-281-6099
800-232-4317
FAX 212-283-7269
E-Mail: info@downtowndevelopment.com
Home Page: www.downtowndevelopment.com

Romauld Alexander, President
Nadine Harris, Marketing Manager

Tested ideas for promotion, public relations, marketing, increasing business, participation, downtown image building, sales, and events.
Cost: $189.00
Frequency: Monthly
Founded in 1954

17828 Drop Shippng News
Consolidated Marketing Services
PO Box 7838
New York, NY 10150

212-688-8797
FAX 212-688-8797
Home Page: www.drop-shipping-news.com

Nicholas T Scheel, Editor/Publisher

Covers all facets of Drop Shipping; source directory for 300,000 consumer products. Book 'Drop Shipping' marketing methods.
Cost: $25.00
Frequency: Monthly
Founded in 1977

17829 Dynamic Selling
Economics Press
12 Daniel Road
Fairfield, NJ 07004-2565

973-227-1224
FAX 973-227-9742

Covers sales issues and ways to improve sales.

17830 Effective Telephone Techniques
Dartnell Corporation
4660 N Ravenswood Avenue
Chicago, IL 60640-4510

773-907-9500
FAX 773-561-3801

Clark Fetridge, Publisher
Kim Anderson, Editor

Training bulletin helps your team build profitable customer relations with every call.
Cost: $62.00

17831 Empoyment Points
Mailing & Fulfillment Service Association
1421 Prince Street
Suite 410
Alexandria, VA 22314-2806

703-836-9200
FAX 703-548-8204
E-Mail: mfsa-mail@mfsanet.org
Home Page: www.mfsanet.org
Social Media: *Facebook, Twitter, LinkedIn*

Leo Raymond, Vice President

The content is written for business owners and operators who want to stay informed about current employment issues. The editorial is targeted on human resource issues and employment practices in the mailing and fulfillment services industry.
Frequency: 4x/Year
Circulation: 2000

17832 Fiberoptics Market Intelligence
KMI Corporation
98 Spit Brook Rd
Suite 400
Nashua, NH 03062-5737

603-243-8100
FAX 603-891-9172
Home Page: www.kmiresearch.com

Richard Mack, VP/General Manager
David Janoff, President
Kurt A Ruderman, Analyst/Editor

Markets, technologies, strategic planning, issues, standards and competition in the fiber optics industry.
Cost: $595.00
Frequency: Fortnightly
Founded in 1974

17833 Frohlinger's Marketing Report
Marketing Strategist Communications
7 Coppel Drive
Tenafly, NJ 07670-2903

201-569-6088
FAX 201-568-8538

Joseph Frohlinger, Editor/Publisher

Global marketing, advertising and media NL with emphasis on strategic and trend articles.
Cost: $200.00
Frequency: Bi-Monthly
Founded in 1988

17834 Growth Strategies
Growth Strategies
2118 Wilshire Blvd
#826
Santa Monica, CA 90403-5704

310-721-6322
FAX 310-828-0427

Roger Selbert, President

A newsletter published twice a monthly since 1981 has been presciently reporting on economic, social, political, technological, demographic, lifestyle, consumer, business, management, workforce and marketing trends.
Cost: $146.00
Frequency: Monthly
Founded in 1981
Printed in 2 colors on glossy stock

17835 Guerrilla Marketing International
Cascade Seaview Corporation
PO Box 1336
Mill Valley, CA 94942-1336

415-383-5426
FAX 415-381-8361

William Shear, Publisher

Marketing insights, trends and tips for small business.
Cost: $59.00
8 Pages
Frequency: Bi-Monthly
Founded in 1989
Printed in one color on glossy stock

17836 Home Business Idea Possibility Newsletter
Prosperity & Profits Unlimited
PO Box 416
Denver, CO 80201-0416

303-573-5564

A Doyle, Editor
Possibilities for home businesses.
Cost: $7.50
4 Pages
Frequency: Annual
Circulation: 1,000
Founded in 1996
Printed in one color on matte stock

17837 How Long Can Traffic Grow?
Probe Research
3 Wing Drive
Suite 240
Cedar Knolls, NJ 07927-1000

973-285-1500
FAX 973-285-1519
Home Page: www.proberesearch.com

Carrier lack of agreement on standard metrics for traffic measurement allows for any interpretation of data, misleads investors and vendors. Optical networking's future depends on a more rational approach to traffic statistics. An assessment of the three drivers for optical networking are discussed.

17838 INFO Marketing Report
Towers Club Press
9170 NW 11th Avenue
Vancouver, WA 98665

360-574-3084

Jerry Buchanan, Editor
Focuses on marketing of HOW TO information in all its many forms: print, audio, video, public speaking, etc.
Cost: $69.95
Frequency: Monthly
Founded in 1974

17839 Imaging Market Forum
Technology Marketing Corporation
800 Connecticut Ave
1st Floor East
Norwalk, CT 06854-1936

203-852-6800
800-243-6002
FAX 203-866-3326
E-Mail: tmc@tmcnet.com
Home Page: www.tmcnet.com
Social Media: *Twitter*

Rich Tehrani, CEO
Case studies and opinions.

17840 Infomercial Marketing Report
Steven Dworman and Associates
11533 Thurston Circle
Los Angeles, CA 90049-2426

310-472-6360

Steve Dworman, Editor/Publisher
Insider information on the infomercial industry.
Cost: $395.00
Frequency: Monthly

17841 Information Advisor
Information Today

143 Old Marlton Pike
Medford, NJ 08055-8750

609-654-6266
800-300-9868
FAX 609-654-4309
E-Mail: custserv@infotoday.com
Home Page: www.infotoday.com

Thomas H Hogan, President
Roger R Bilboul, Chairman Of The Board

Provides comprehensive evlauation of research tools, timely and specific information you will use, new sources valuable to researchers and head to head analysis of the most popular information services.
Cost: $165.00
Frequency: Monthly
Mailing list available for rent

17842 International Marketing Service Newsletter
IDG Communications
375 Cochituate Road
#9171
Framingham, MA 01701-4653
Frank Cutitta, Publisher

This newsletter concentrates on the overseas advertising and marketing industry.

17843 International Product Alert
Marketing Intelligence Service
482 N Main St
Canandaigua, NY 14424-1049

585-374-6326
800-836-5710
FAX 585-374-5217
Home Page: www.productscan.com

Tom Vierhile, Editor
Reports product introductions from Europe, Asia and throughout the world.
Cost: $795.00
Frequency: Fortnightly
Founded in 1983

17844 JonesReport
PO Box 50038
Indianapolis, IN 46250-7830

317-576-9889
800-878-9024
FAX 317-576-0441
E-Mail: ctrmktg@jonesreport.com
Home Page: www.jonesreport.com

William Willburn, Publisher/President
William Willburn, Editor
Lue Dyar, Circulation Manager

Monthly newsletter for shopping center marketing professionals. Free Resource Guide in September. Salary Survey results in December. Christmas planner issues in April. STEALable marketing ideas in every issue. Sample copies are available.
Cost: $145.00
16 Pages
Frequency: Monthly
Circulation: 1000
Founded in 1980
Mailing list available for rent: 6M names at $110 per M
Printed in 2 colors on matte stock

17845 Levin's Public Relations Report
Levin Public Relations & Marketing
2 East Ave
Suite 201
Larchmont, NY 10538-2419

914-834-2570
FAX 914-834-5919
Home Page: www.saralevin.com

Sara B Levin, President
Sylvia Moss, Editor

Strategies, tactics for the CEO, VP Sales and Marketing seeking new marketing/public relations effectiveness.
Cost: $29.00
Frequency: Quarterly
Founded in 1978

17846 Licensing Journal
PO Box 1169
Stamford, CT 06904-1169

203-358-0848

Charles Grimes, Publisher
A publication directed to leaders in the Intellectual Property, Technology and Entertainment Communities. Accepts advertising.
Cost: $150.00
23 Pages
Frequency: Annual
Circulation: 1,000

17847 Licensing Letter
EPM Communications
19 W. 21st St., #303
New York, NY 10010

212-941-0099
888-852-9467
FAX 212-941-1622
E-Mail: info@epmcom.com
Home Page: www.epmcom.com

Ira Mayer, President
Michele Khan, Marketing

Contains features on licensed properties, market trends and survey analysis.
Cost: $467.00
Frequency: 22x Year
Founded in 1977

17848 Long Haul Market
Probe Research
3 Wing Drive
Suite 240
Cedar Knolls, NJ 07927-1000

973-285-1500
FAX 973-285-1519
Home Page: www.proberesearch.com

In this report, we take a look into the long haul market space and discuss some of the reasons - supply, demand and the resulting prices - that have reversed these service providers fortunes so dramatically over the past year or so. We also discuss long haul product lines, new networking technology and provide a table comparing market participants for convenient reference.

17849 M-Commerce Security
Probe Research
3 Wing Drive
Suite 240
Cedar Knolls, NJ 07927-1000

973-285-1500
FAX 973-285-1519
Home Page: www.proberesearch.com

In this bulletin, we examine the issue of security in the m-commerce transaction and the technologies that are appering to address it. We also create international m-commerce forecasts by region.

17850 Mainly Marketing
Schoonmaker Associates
30150 Telegraph Road
Suite 155
Bringham Farms, MI 48025

248-594-7800
FAX 866-211-5711
E-Mail: info@mainlymkt.com
Home Page: www.mainlymkt.com

WK Schoonmaker, Publisher
Marketing high technology products.

17851 Make It Happen
Action Marketing
3747 NE Sandy Boulevard
Portland, OR 97232-1840

503-287-8321
FAX 503-282-2980

CE Colwell, Publisher
Marketing news for starting a business and marketing products.

17852 Market: Africa/Mid-East
PRS Group
6320 Fly Rd
Suite 102
East Syracuse, NY 13057-9792

315-431-0511
FAX 315-431-0200
E-Mail: custserv@prsgroup.com
Home Page: www.prsgroup.com

Mary Lou Walsh, President
Patti Davis, Chairman
Ben McTernan, Managing Editor
Patty Redhead, Production Manager
Demographic and lifestyle information about consumers in Africa and the Middle East.
Cost: $397.00
Frequency: Monthly
Founded in 1979

17853 Market: Asia Pacific
PRS Group
6320 Fly Rd
Suite 102
East Syracuse, NY 13057-9792

315-431-0511
FAX 315-431-0200
E-Mail: custserv@prsgroup.com
Home Page: www.prsgroup.com

Mary Lou Walsh, President
Patti Davis, Chairman
Ben McTernan, Managing Editor
Patty Redhead, Production Manager
Population and lifestyle trend information about consumers in the Asia-Pacific region.
Cost: $397.00
Frequency: Monthly
Circulation: 225
Founded in 1979
Printed in 2 colors on matte stock

17854 Market: Latin America
PRS Group
6320 Fly Rd
Suite 102
East Syracuse, NY 13057-9792

315-431-0511
FAX 315-431-0200
E-Mail: custserv@prsgroup.com
Home Page: www.prsgroup.com

Mary Lou Walsh, President
Patti Davis, Chairman
Ben McTernan, Managing Editor
Patty Redhead, Production Manager
Population and lifestyle trend information about consumers in the Latin America region.
Frequency: Monthly
Founded in 1979

17855 Marketing Academics Newsletter
American Marketing Association
311 S Wacker Dr
Suite 5800
Chicago, IL 60606-6629

312-542-9000
800-262-1150
FAX 312-542-9001
Home Page: www.marketingpower.com
Social Media: *Facebook, Twitter, LinkedIn, Youtube*

Dennis Dunlap, CEO

This newsletter provides news and information that affect and inform this important constituency. It reviews Academic Council activities, profiles Academic SIGS and highlights upcoming events.
Mailing list available for rent

17856 Marketing Communications Report
14629 SW 104 Street
#272
Miami, FL 33186-4929

305-595-0063
FAX 305-595-0380

Pete Silver, Editor

Highlights prevalent thoughts on successful marketing strategies and reviews new products.
Frequency: Monthly

17857 Marketing Dynamics
Recognition Technologies Users
Association
10 High Street
Suite 630
Boston, MA 02110-1605

FAX 617-426-8911

Franklin Cooper, Publisher

Focuses on strategic marketing and planning in technology and industrial areas including technology commercialization. Also features articles on government programs and how to participate in them. International market and business development also are featured.
Cost: $120.00
Frequency: Bi-Monthly
Circulation: 5,000
Printed in 2 colors on glossy stock

17858 Marketing Insights
WPI Communications
55 Morris Ave
Suite 300
Springfield, NJ 07081-1422

973-467-8700
800-323-4995
FAX 973-467-0368
E-Mail: info@wpicomm.com
Home Page: www.wpicomm.com

Steve Klinghoffer, President
Marilyn Lang, Chairman
Founded in 1952

17859 Marketing Library Services
Information Today
143 Old Marlton Pike
Medford, NJ 08055-8750

609-654-6266
800-300-9868
FAX 609-654-4309
E-Mail: custserv@infotoday.com
Home Page: www.infotoday.com

Thomas H Hogan, President
Roger R Bilboul, Chairman Of The Board

Provides information professional in all types of libraries with specfic ideas for marketing their services.
Cost: $79.95
Frequency: Bi Monthly
ISSN: 0896-3908
Mailing list available for rent

17860 Marketing Matters Newsletter
American Marketing Association
311 S Wacker Dr
Suite 5800
Chicago, IL 60606-6629

312-542-9000
800-262-1150
FAX 312-542-9001
Home Page: www.marketingpower.com

Social Media: *Facebook, Twitter, LinkedIn, Youtube*

Dennis Dunlap, CEO

This e-newsletter updates readers on the latest happenings in the marketing profession through news briefs, indepth features and interviews
Frequency: 2x/Monthly
Mailing list available for rent

17861 Marketing Power Newsletter
American Marketing Association
311 S Wacker Dr
Suite 5800
Chicago, IL 60606-6629

312-542-9000
800-262-1150
FAX 312-542-9001
Home Page: www.marketingpower.com
Social Media: *Facebook, Twitter, LinkedIn, Youtube*

Dennis Dunlap, CEO

This update of the latest news, research and trends in the marketing industry and allied fields.
Frequency: Weekly
Mailing list available for rent

17862 Marketing Pulse
Unlimited Positive Communications
11 N Chestnut Street
New Paltz, NY 12561-1706

845-565-0615
FAX 845-255-2231

Bill Harvey, Editor/Publisher

Focus on all aspects of new electronic media, advertising, entertainment, and marketing.
Cost: $300.00
Frequency: Monthly
Founded in 1979

17863 Marketing Report
Progressive Business Publications
PO Box 3019
Malvern, PA 19355-0719

610-695-0201
800-220-5000
FAX 610-647-8098
E-Mail: customer_service@pbp.com
Home Page: www.pbp.com

Ed Satell, CEO
Christine Wheeler, Marketing Manager
Cost: $264.00
8 Pages
Founded in 1989

17864 Marketing Researchers Newsletter
American Marketing Association
311 S Wacker Dr
Suite 5800
Chicago, IL 60606-6629

312-542-9000
800-262-1150
FAX 312-542-9001
Home Page: www.marketingpower.com
Social Media: *Facebook, Twitter, LinkedIn, Youtube*

Dennis Dunlap, CEO

This e-newsletter provides members with content designed to educate and inform researchers or any member interested in marketing research topics.
Mailing list available for rent

17865 Marketing Science Institute
Newsletter
Marketing Science Institute

1000 Massachusetts Ave
Suite 1
Cambridge, MA 02138-5379

617-491-2060
FAX 617-491-2065
E-Mail: msi@msi.org
Home Page: www.msi.org

Russ Winer, Executive Director
Leana McAlister, CEO

Focuses on people and events of MSI.
Circulation: 8000
Founded in 1968

17866 Marketing Technology
Zhivago Marketing Partners
381 Seaside Dr
Jamestown, RI 02835-2376

401-423-2400
FAX 401-423-2700
E-Mail: kristin@zhivago.com
Home Page: www.zhivago.com

Kristin Zhivago, President
Philip Zhivago, CEO
Thomas Baker, Owner

Solutions to internal political problems encountered by high-tech marketers, critiques marketing campaigns, and discuss what's working.
Cost: $269.00
Frequency: Monthly
Founded in 1970

17867 Marketing Thought Leaders Newsletter
American Marketing Association
311 S Wacker Dr
Suite 5800
Chicago, IL 60606-6629

312-542-9000
800-262-1150
FAX 312-542-9001
Home Page: www.marketingpower.com
Social Media: *Facebook, Twitter, LinkedIn, Youtube*

Dennis Dunlap, CEO

These articles focus on the issues and concepts that shape marketing today and tomorrow.
Frequency: Monthly
Mailing list available for rent

17868 Marketing to Emerging Minorities
EPM Communications
19 W. 21st St., #303
New York, NY 10010

212-941-0099
888-852-9467
FAX 212-941-1622
E-Mail: info@epmcom.com
Home Page: www.epmcom.com

Ira Mayer, President
Michele Khan, Marketing
Melanie Shreffler, Editor

Research, trends and lifestyle coverage of minority markets.
Cost: $377.00
Frequency: Monthly

17869 Marketscan International
Miller Freeman Publications
2655 Seely Avenue
San Jose, CA 95134

408-943-1234
FAX 408-943-0513

Paul W Kelash, Editor/Publisher

PC and Networking news in Europe, Asia, and Latin America.
Cost: $395.00
Frequency: Monthly
Founded in 1987

17870 Master Salesmanship
Clement Communications
10 LaCrue Avenue
PO Box 36
Concordville, PA 19331

610-459-4200
888-358-5858
FAX 610-459-4582
E-Mail: customerservice@clement.com
Home Page: www.clement.com

Andrew B Clancy, Managing Editor
George Clement, President

Newsletter for professional salespeople.
Cost: $156.00
Founded in 1919

17871 Meditation Software Market
Probe Research
3 Wing Drive
Suite 240
Cedar Knolls, NJ 07927-1000

973-285-1500
FAX 973-285-1519
Home Page: www.proberesearch.com

Examines the mediation market, the major and niche players, functionality of the solutions, and service provider deployments.

17872 Multimedia Strategist
Leader Publications
345 Park Avenue S
New York, NY 10010-1707

212-779-9200
800-888-8300
FAX 212-696-1848
E-Mail: reprintscustomerservice@alm.com
Home Page: www.alm.com

Stuart M Wise, Editor
Kerry Kyle, Circulation Director
William L Pollak, CEO/President
Aric Press, Editorial Director
Kevin Vermeulen, Vice President, Group Publisher
Cost: $175.00
Frequency: Monthly
ISSN: 1080-3904
Founded in 1997

17873 New Account Selling
Dartnell Corporation
4660 N Ravenswood Avenue
Chicago, IL 60640-4510

773-907-9500
FAX 773-561-3801

Clark Fetridge, Publisher
Terry Breen, Editor

Timely and effective techniques for building sales and improving profits. Instructive series ideal for training new sales people and for increasing the productivity of your sales veterans.
Cost: $62.00

17874 New Age Marketing Opportunities Newsletter
New Editions International
PO Box 2578
Sedona, AZ 86339-2578

928-282-9574
800-777-4751
FAX 928-282-9730
Home Page: www.newagemarket.com

Sophia Tarila PhD, Production Manager

Focuses on issues dealing with good marketing buys, resources and pertinent marketing programs dealing in the historic, visionary marketplace.
Cost: $24.00
4 Pages
Frequency: Bi-Monthly

Circulation: 450
Mailing list available for rent
Printed in one color on matte stock

17875 Next Generation IAD for SOHO Markets
Probe Research
3 Wing Drive
Suite 240
Cedar Knolls, NJ 07927-1000

973-285-1500
FAX 973-285-1519
Home Page: www.proberesearch.com

Examines the market for VoDSL - comapatible Integrated Access Devices (IAD) targeted toward SOHO customers. Identifies key issues associated with development, analyzes competitive dynamics and market requirements and reviews selected vendor products.

17876 On The Move
Transportation Marketing Communications Assoc
9382 Oak Avenue
Waconia, MN 55387

952-442-5638
FAX 952-442-3941
E-Mail: briano7@tmcatoday.org
Home Page: www.tmcatoday.org

John Ferguson, President
Tom Nightingale, VP
Tracy Robinson, Treasurer
Edward Moritz, Secretary
Brian Everett, Executive Director

Provides regular feature articles on ways to effectively create more impact in transportation marketing, sales and communications strategies.

17877 Online Marketing Letter
Cyberware Media
1005 Terminal Way
Suite 110
Reno, NV 89502

808-874-0089
Home Page: www.cyberware.com

Jonathan Mizel, Editor/Publisher

Reviews the marketing of products and services over commercial online services of the internet.
Cost: $195.00
Frequency: Quarterly
Founded in 1993

17878 Online Marketplace
Jupiter Communications Company
627 Broadway
2nd Floor
New York, NY 10012-2612

212-533-8885
FAX 212-780-6075

Adam Schoenfeld, Editor
Gene DeRose, Publisher

Interactive transaction.
Cost: $545.00
Frequency: Monthly

17879 Organized Executive
Briefings Publishing Group
1101 King St
Suite 110
Alexandria, VA 22314-2944

703-548-3800
800-722-9221
FAX 703-684-2136
Home Page: www.briefings.com

Stephanie Winston, Editor-in-Chief
Lois Willingham, Production Manager

A publication designed to help busy people more effectively master their activities and time

by applying advanced organizational strategies developed by Stephanie Winston.
Cost: $97.00
8 Pages
Frequency: Monthly
Circulation: 30000
Founded in 1981
Mailing list available for rent: 6000 names at $125 per M
Printed in 2 colors on matte stock

17880 Overcoming Objections

Dartnell Corporation
4660 N Ravenswood Avenue
Chicago, IL 60640-4510

773-907-9500
FAX 773-561-3801

Clark Fetridge, Publisher
Christen Heide, Editor

Designed to give sales team practical responses to every objection they're likely to face and imparts proven techniques for turning every type of sales objection into a sales opportunity.
Cost: $62.00

17881 Perspectives

1375 King Avenue
PO 12279
Columbus, OH 43212-2220

614-486-6708
800-448-0398
FAX 614-486-1819
E-Mail: service@mark-ed.com
Home Page: www.mark-ed.org

J Gleason, President
Mary Carlisi, Production Manager

Information on education and marketing. Provides professional support and materials. Primary clients are schools, colleges and educational institutions.
Cost: $25.00
Circulation: 7500
Founded in 1971
Printed in 4 colors on matte stock

17882 Photo Marketing

Photo Marketing Association International
3000 Picture Pl
Jackson, MI 49201-8853

517-788-8100
FAX 517-788-8371
Home Page: www.pmai.org

Ted Fox, CEO
Terri Cameron, Publisher
Cost: $30.00
Frequency: Monthly
Founded in 1980

17883 PostScripts

Mailing & Fulfillment Service Association
1421 Prince Street
Suite 410
Alexandria, VA 22314-2806

703-836-9200
FAX 703-548-8204
E-Mail: mfsa-mail@mfsanet.org
Home Page: www.mfsanet.org
Social Media: *Facebook, Twitter, LinkedIn*

Leo Raymond, Editor
Leo Raymond, Vice President

Each issue of PostScripts highlights a theme relevant to mailing or fulfillment operations, such as production management or information technology.
Frequency: 18x/Year
Circulation: 2800

17884 Postal Points

Mailing & Fulfillment Service Association

1421 Prince Street
Suite 410
Alexandria, VA 22314-2806

703-836-9200
FAX 703-548-8204
E-Mail: mfsa-mail@mfsanet.org
Home Page: www.mfsanet.org
Social Media: *Facebook, Twitter, LinkedIn*

Leo Raymond, Editor
Leo Raymond, Vice President

Deals exclusively with current and pending postal and delivery issues. Here you will find the facts and analysis of developing postal issues.
Frequency: 18x/Year

17885 Premium Marketing Club of New York

Association of Retail Marketing Services
10 Drs James Parker Boulevard
Suite 103
Red Bank, NJ 07701-1500

732-842-5070
FAX 732-219-1938
Home Page: www.goarms.com

Gerri Hopkins, Executive Director
Lisa McCauley, Administrative Director

Provides education and networking information.
Frequency: 10 per year
Founded in 1930
Printed in one color

17886 Pricing Advisor

Pricing Advisor
3535 Roswell Rd
Suite 59
Marietta, GA 30062-8828

770-509-9933
FAX 770-509-1963
E-Mail: info@pricingsociety.com
Home Page: www.pricingsociety.com

Eric Mitchell, President
Michelle Darko, Editor
Sobem Nwoko, COO

Pricing strategy and tactics for marketing and corporate executives.
Cost: $400.00
8 Pages
Frequency: Monthly

17887 Product Alert

Marketing Intelligence Service
482 N Main St
Canandaigua, NY 14424-1049

585-374-6326
800-836-5710
FAX 585-374-5217
Home Page: www.productscan.com

Christine Dengler, Marketing Manager
Tom Vierhile, CEO
Diane Beach, Editor

A twice-monthly briefing on new packaged goods introduced in North America. Featuring product pictures and descriptions with indexing provided in two convenient formats. Also available in a twice monthly, international version.
Cost: $795.00

17888 Promos & Premiums

New World Media
PO Box 95
Newton Centre, MA 02156

781-483-8967
FAX 617-367-9151

Jennifer Sawyer English, Editor/Publisher
Barbara Kalunian, Publisher

Informs consumers, collectors, dealers, and marketing executives about the best special offers available nationwide.
Cost: $19.95
Frequency: Monthly
Founded in 1994

17889 Research Alert

EPM Communications
19 W. 21st St., #303
New York, NY 10010

212-941-0099
888-852-9467
FAX 212-941-1622
E-Mail: info@epmcom.com
Home Page: www.epmcom.com

Ira Mayer, President
Michele Khan, Marketing
Melanie Shreffler, Editor

Analyzes research on consumer behavior and attitudes.
Cost: $389.00
Frequency: 24x Year

17890 Revisiting R&D

Probe Research
3 Wing Drive
Suite 240
Cedar Knolls, NJ 07927-1000

973-285-1500
FAX 973-285-1519
Home Page: www.proberesearch.com

With the collapse of the bull market and the apparent collapse of viable wireline competition, the ILECs must focus on the role of wireless as a major competitor. The new Bush administration appears to be pro-ILEC and this will translate into a series of reglatory initiatives that may in total favor the ILECs R&D agendas have to shift to support innovative solutions in the access domain and in mobile.

17891 Roper's Public Pulse

Roper Starch Worldwide
29 W 35th Street
5th Floor
New York, NY 10001-2299

212-240-5300
FAX 212-564-0465
E-Mail: dcrispell@roper.com
Home Page: www.roper.com

Diane Crispell, Editor

Content includes the latest research on demographic trends, new insights from opinion research experts as to what Americans think, concise, brand-focused data, current consumer attitudes toward dozens of American themes, as well as news updates on special markets and brands.
Cost: $299.00
Frequency: Monthly
Circulation: 2000

17892 SBC

Probe Research
3 Wing Drive
Suite 240
Cedar Knolls, NJ 07927-1000

973-285-1500
FAX 973-285-1519
Home Page: www.proberesearch.com

Discussion and analysis of ILEC/vendor market dynamics; case study of SBC's metro optical architecture; technology evolution; new services offered; incorporation of passive optical networking and metro DWDM rollouts; strategy going forward.

17893 Sales Bullet

Economics Press

12 Daniel Road
Fairfield, NJ 07004-2565

973-227-1224
FAX 973-227-9742

Robert Guder, Editor
Diane Cody, Promotional Director

Covers the fundamental and subtleties of professional selling with methods, principles and ideas all salespoeple will find useful.
Circulation: 9,000

17894 Sales Manager's Bulletin
Bureau of Business Practice
76 Ninth Avenue
7th Floor
New York, NY 10011

212-771-0600
FAX 212-771-0885
Home Page: www.aspenpublishers.com

Robert Becker, CEO
Gustavo Dobles, VP Operations

For front-line sales management. Focus on sales hiring, training, managing, motivation, results. Reports what people in sales management field are doing to produce measurable sales profits.
Cost: $9.00
Circulation: 4,290

17895 Sales Productivity Review
Penoyer Communications
PO Box 2509
Santa Clara, CA 95055-2509

408-248-5458
800-248-5458
FAX 408-296-6917
E-Mail: info@penoyer.com
Home Page: www.penoyer.com

Flyn Penoyer, President

Edited for sales management with an editorial focus that will assist in improving sales productivity and effectiveness.
Cost: $5.00
Frequency: 6 issues per ye

17896 Sales Promotion Monitor
Commerce Communications
418 N 3rd Street
Suite 303
Milwaukee, WI 55410-2444

414-225-9085
FAX 414-225-9095
E-Mail: tom@com-broker.com
Home Page: www.com-broker.com

K Sederberg, Publisher
Tom Millitzer, Contact

News and information concerning all aspects of sales promotion.

17897 Sales Rep's Advisor
Alexander Communications Group
1916 Park Ave
Suite 501
New York, NY 10037-3733

212-281-6099
800-232-4317
FAX 212-283-7269
E-Mail: info@repsadvisor.com
Home Page: www.repsadvisor.com

Romauld Alexander, President
Bill Keenan, Editor
Adam Reis, Marketing

For independent manufacturers sales representatives. Filled with concise advice and ideas for reducing costs and increasing profits.
Cost: $199.00
Frequency: Monthly
ISSN: 0278-5048
Founded in 1954

17898 Sarah Stambler's E-Tactics Letter
E-Tactics
370 Central Park W
#210
New York, NY 10025-6517

212-222-1713
FAX 212-678-6357
E-Mail: info@e-tactics.com
Home Page: www.e-tactics.com

Sarah Stambler, President
Shlomo Bar-Ayal, Circulation Manager

Publication devoted to the creative use of electronic alternative media in the design and implementation of customer driven marketing, research and publication strategies.
Circulation: 5000
ISSN: 1070-809X
Founded in 1984

17899 School Marketing Newsletter
School Market Research Institute
1721 Saybrook Road
PO Box 10
Haddam, CT 06438

860-345-8183
800-838-3444
FAX 860-345-3985
E-Mail: school.market@snet.net
Home Page: www.school-market.com

Bob Stimolo, Publisher
Lynn Stimolo, Account Executive
Sally Chittenden, Account Executive

How to articles, trends, original research, interviews with experts on school marketing Pre-K - 12th.
Cost: $119.00
12 Pages
Frequency: Monthly
Circulation: 500
ISSN: 0882-701X
Founded in 1980
Printed in one color on matte stock

17900 Selling Advantage
Progressive Business Publications
PO Box 3019
Malvern, PA 19355-0719

610-695-0201
800-220-5000
FAX 610-647-8098
E-Mail: webmaster@pbp.com
Home Page: www.pbp.com

Ed Satell, CEO
Phillip Ahr, Editor

Business-to-business sales advice to assist sales staff and sales managers.
Cost: $94.56
Circulation: 60,000
Founded in 1989

17901 Selling To Kids
Phillips Publishing
PO Box 611130
Potomac, MD 20859-2931

301-208-6787
FAX 301-340-1451
Home Page:
www.phillips.com/cgi/catalog/info?m2k

Angela Duff, Associate Publisher

Editorial offers news and practical advice on strategies in successful marketing. Includes information on market research, buying trends, and media opportunities and features news on conferences as well as a look at new products and services.
Cost: $495.00
Frequency: BiWeekly

17902 Selling to Seniors
CD Publications

8204 Fenton St
Silver Spring, MD 20910-4571

301-588-6380
800-666-6380
FAX 301-588-6385
E-Mail: info@cdpublications.com
Home Page: www.cdpublications.com

Michael Gerecht, President
Jean Van Ryzin, Editor

Published as a subscriber driven newsletter targeting marketers and advertisers of products and services for the mature market.
Cost: $294.00
Frequency: Monthly
Founded in 1961
Mailing list available for rent: 2,000 names at $160 per M

17903 Service Level Agreements
Probe Research
3 Wing Drive
Suite 240
Cedar Knolls, NJ 07927-1000

973-285-1500
FAX 973-285-1519
Home Page: www.proberesearch.com

Details service level agreements that are being offered by several major service providers, and examines many of the popular software solutions taht are being used in their networks. Also a briefly discusses XML, and its potential uses.

17904 Siedlecki on Marketing
Richard Siedlecki Business & Marketing
4767 Lake Forrest Drive NE
Atlanta, GA 30342-2539

770-436-8271
FAX 403-303-9939

Richard Siedlecki, Editor

Tips, techniques, and insights on marketing.
Cost: $49.00
6 Pages
Frequency: BiWeekly
Circulation: 500
Printed in one color on matte stock

17905 Strategic Health Care Marketing
Health Care Communications
11 Heritage Lane
PO Box 594
Rye, NY 10580-594

914-967-6741
FAX 914-967-3054
E-Mail: healthcomm@aol.com
Home Page: www.strategichealthcare.com

Michele von Dambrowski, Editor/Publisher
Michele von Dambrowski, CEO

Business development and marketing startegies for health care executives.
Cost: $279.00
12 Pages
Frequency: Monthly
Circulation: 1200
Founded in 1984
Printed in 2 colors on matte stock

17906 Subscribe
PO Box 194
Bryn Mawr, PA 19010-0194
Lynn Kerrigan, Editor
Gail Jennings, Administration

A newsletter offering marketing ideas to help gain new subscribers and retain old ones.
Cost: $49.00
Frequency: Quarterly

17907 Successful Closing Techniques
Dartnell Corporation

4660 N Ravenswood Avenue
Chicago, IL 60640-4510

773-907-9500
FAX 773-561-3801

Clark Fetridge, Publisher
Terry Breen, Editor

Fail-safe techniques for acquiring bigger sales
and more frequent closings.
Cost: $62.00

17908 Target Market News
Target Market News
228 S Wabash Ave
Suite 210
Chicago, IL 60604-2383

312-408-1881
FAX 312-408-1867
E-Mail: TargetMarketNews@aol.com
Home Page: www.targetmarketnews.com
Social Media: *Facebook, Twitter*

Ken Smikle, President
Hallie Mummert, Editor

News and developments in the areas of black
consumer marketing and black-oriented media.
Cost: $40.00
12 Pages
Frequency: Monthly
Founded in 1988

17909 Trends Journal
Trends Research Institute
P.O.Box 3476
Kingston, NY 12402-3476

845-876-6700
FAX 845-758-5252
Home Page: www.trendsresearch.com

Gerald Celente, Editor
Emily Arter, Manager

Offers the inside track on trends affecting your
business, your profession, your life. Forecasts
on over 300 trend categories - consumer, social, economic, political, media, health, family,
education, and other domestic and international
trends.
Cost: $185.00
Frequency: Quarterly
Founded in 1980
Printed in 2 colors on glossy stock

17910 Upline
MLM Publishing
106 W South Street
Charlottesvle, VA 22902-5039

FAX 434-979-1602

John Milton Fogg, Editor
Randolph Byrd, Publisher

Distribution training for network (multilevel)
marketers.
Founded in 1990

17911 Video Marketing Newsletter
Outback Group Productions
PO Box 872
Harrison, AR 72602-0872

FAX 870-741-4727

Dan Reynolds, Editor/Publisher

Information, business opportunities, marketing
tips, product reviews. For people interested in
producing and marketing their own videos.
Cost: $185.00
Frequency: Monhtly
Founded in 1989

**17912 What's Working in Sales
Management**
Progressive Business Publications

PO Box 3019
Malvern, PA 19355-0719

610-695-0201
800-220-5000
FAX 610-647-8098
E-Mail: webmaster@pbp.com
Home Page: www.pbp.com

Ed Satell, CEO
Richard Kern, Editor

Sales management news and issues.
Cost: $264.00
Founded in 1989

17913 Youth Markets Alert
EPM Communications
19 W. 21st St., #303
New York, NY 10010

212-941-0099
888-852-9467
FAX 212-941-1622
E-Mail: info@epmcom.com
Home Page: www.epmcom.com

Ira Mayer, President
Michele Khan, Marketing
Larissa Faw, Editor

Research reports on trends in youth response to
marketing techniques and buying.
Cost: $447.00
Frequency: 24x Year

Magazines & Journals

17914 ADCLIP
National Research Bureau
320 Valley St
Burlington, IA 52601-5513

319-752-5415
FAX 319-752-3421
E-Mail: mail@national-research-bureau.com
Home Page:
www.national-research-bureau.com

Diane M Darnall, President
Nancy Heinzel, Circulation Manager

Individualized adclipping service providing
market intelligence information on various retail operations. Includes full size, pages, market
strategies, advertising promotion ideas, new
store openings and more.

17915 Adage Global
Crain Communications
711 3rd Ave
New York, NY 10017-4014

212-210-0785
FAX 212-210-0200
E-Mail: info@crain.com
Home Page: www.crain.com

Norm Feldman, President
Scott Donaton, Editor
David Klein, Publisher
Philip Scarano, Circulation Director
Vanessa Reed, Marketing Director

Dedicated to being the world's essential adver-
tising, marketing and media publication, with
editors around the world, Adage covers topics
of significance form Times Square to Taiwan.
Cost: $69.95
Frequency: Weekly
Circulation: 57,800
Founded in 1943
Printed in 4 colors

17916 Advertising Age
Ad Age Group/Division of Crain
Communications

711 3rd Ave
New York, NY 10017-4014

212-210-0785
FAX 212-210-0465
E-Mail: jbloom@adage.com
Home Page: www.adage.com

Norm Feldman, President

Editorial insights, exclusive analysis and proprietary data take readers beyond the day's
news giving it context helping our audience understand ongoing and emerging trends.
Frequency: Weekly
Circulation: 56650

17917 Adweek
Prometheus Global Media
770 Broadway
New York, NY 10003-9595

212-493-4100
FAX 646-654-5368
Home Page: www.prometheusgm.com
Social Media: *Facebook, Twitter, RSS*

Richard D. Beckman, CEO
James A. Finkelstein, Chairman
Madeline Krakowsky, Vice President
Circulation
Tracy Brator, Executive Director Creative
Service

Adweek is the source for advertising and
agency news, information and opinion. Covering the industry from an agency perspective
Adweek focuses on the image makersand those
who create the strategy and the ads as well as
those who buy the media and handle client relations.
Cost: $149.00
Frequency: Weekly
Circulation: 36032
Founded in 1978

17918 Agency Sales Magazine
Manufacturers Agents National Association
16-A Journey
Suite 200
Aliso Viejo, CA 92656

949-859-4040
877-626-2776
FAX 949-855-2973
E-Mail: mana@manaonline.org
Home Page: www.manaonline.org

Jack Foster, Editor

Chronicling the changes which continue to take
place nationwide that affect you and your business. Explores the latest tax developments,
sales tips, market data, management aids, legal
bulletins and more.
96 Pages
Frequency: Monthly
Circulation: 50000
Printed in on glossy stock

17919 Agri Marketing Magazine
Henderson Communications LLC
1422 Elbridge Payne Rd
Suite 250
Chesterfield, MO 63017-8544

636-728-1428
FAX 636-777-4178
E-Mail: info@agrimarketing.com
Home Page: www.agrimarketing.com

Lynn Henderson, President

Covers the unique interests of corporate agribusiness executives, their marketing communications agencies, the agricultural media, ag
trade associations and other ag related
professionals.
Circulation: 8000
Founded in 1962

17920 AgriSelling Principles and Practices
Henderson Communications LLC

1422 Elbridge Payne Rd
Suite 250
Chesterfield, MO 63017-8544

636-728-1428
FAX 636-777-4178
E-Mail: info@agrimarketing.com
Home Page: www.agrimarketing.com

Lynn Henderson, President
Marilyn Holschuh, Editor

This 448-page book is utilized by many major agribusiness corporations and academic institutions for training its sales and marketing staff and or students.

17921 American Demographics

Primedia
Customer Service
PO Box 2042
Marion, OH 43306-8142

800-529-7502
FAX 740-389-5574
Home Page: www.demographics.com

Kerry J Smith, Publisher
Seema Nayyar, Editor

Coverage includes regional and national consumer trends, lifestyles, media preferences and purchasing behaviors. Regular features present case histories and in-depth demographic profiles.
Cost: $69.00
Frequency: Monthly
Circulation: 34,304

17922 Brand Marketing

Fairchild Publications
7 W 34th St
New York, NY 10001-8100

212-988-2882
FAX 212-630-3868
E-Mail: info@brandmarketingltd.com
Home Page: www.brandmarketingltd.com

Richard Faul, Publisher
Mary Berner, President

Covers how manufactureres launch and build brands, and how they leverage brand equity in new ways using new techniques. These ways include partnerships with retailers via trade marketing and information technology and a variety of cost-reduction strategies such as everyday low pricing and efficient consumer response.
Cost: $90.00
Frequency: Monthly
Circulation: 18,543

17923 Brandweek

Prometheus Global Media
770 Broadway
New York, NY 10003-9595

212-493-4100
FAX 646-654-5368
Home Page: www.prometheusgm.com

Richard D. Beckman, CEO
James A. Finkelstein, Chairman
Madeline Krakowsky, Vice President Circulation
Tracy Brater, Executive Director Creative Service

Focuses on marketing strategy and services, brand identity, sponsorships, licensing, media usage and distribution and promotions.
Frequency: Weekly
Circulation: 25784
Founded in 1991

17924 Broker News

Broker Publishing

PO Box 20287
Fountain Hills, AZ 85269-0287

480-816-1400
800-475-3565
FAX 480-836-7767
Home Page: www.brokernews-online.com

Joanne Genualdi, Account Executive

Serving insurance producers and financial planners across the country.
Cost: $12.00
32+ Pages
Frequency: Bi-Monthly
Founded in 1990

17925 BtoB Magazine

Ad Age Group/ Division of Crain Communications
711 3rd Ave
New York, NY 10017-4014

212-210-0785
FAX 212-210-0200
E-Mail: info@crain.com
Home Page: www.crain.com

Norm Feldman, President

Dedicated to integrated business to business marketing. Every page is packed with substance news, reports, technologies, benchmarks, best practices served up by the most knowledgeable journalists.
Frequency: Monthly
Circulation: 45000

17926 Business Journal

120 W Morehead Street
Suite 200
Charlotte, NC 28202

704-472-2340
800-948-5323
FAX 704-973-1102
E-Mail: borben@bizjournals.com
Home Page: www.bizjournals.com/charlotte

Robert Morris, Editor
Megan Foley, Marketing Manager
Jeannie Falknor, Publisher

Provides marketing solutions and caring service.
Cost: $82.00
Frequency: Monthly

17927 CRM Magazine

Information Today
143 Old Marlton Pike
Medford, NJ 08055-8750

609-654-6266
800-300-9868
FAX 609-654-4309
E-Mail: custserv@infotoday.com
Home Page: www.infotoday.com

Thomas H Hogan, President
Roger R Bilboul, Chairman Of The Board

Offers vital information that will help you benefit from the experience of others in the industry.
Cost: $23.95
Mailing list available for rent: 4M names
Printed in 4 colors on glossy stock

17928 Catalog Success

North American Publishing Company
1500 Spring Garden St
Suite 1200
Philadelphia, PA 19130-4094

215-238-5300
FAX 215-238-5342
E-Mail: phatch@napco.com
Home Page: www.catalogsuccess.com

Ned S Borowsky, CEO
Matt Griffin, Associate Editor
Peggy Hatch, VP Group Publishing

Putting marketing management to the test.
Frequency: Monthly
Circulation: 20000
ISSN: 1524-2307
Founded in 1999
Printed in 4 colors

17929 Chamber Executive Magazine

American Chamber of Commerce Executives
4875 Eisenhower Ave
Suite 250
Alexandria, VA 22304-4850

703-998-0072
FAX 703-212-9512
E-Mail: webmaster@acce.org
Home Page: www.acce.org
Social Media: *Facebook, Twitter, LinkedIn*

Mick Flemming, President
Frequency: 5X a year

17930 Circulation Management

Primedia
1166 Avenue of the Americas/10th Fl
New York, NY 10036

212-204-4200
FAX 913-514-6895
Home Page: www.penton.com

Eric Jacobson, Senior VP
Ron Wall, Chief Officer
Chris Meyer, Director, Corporate Communications

Serves consumer/special interest and business/trade/association publications.
Frequency: Monthly
ISSN: 0888-8191
Founded in 1986
Printed in 4 colors

17931 Connect

Media-Mark
114 Sansome St
Suite 1224
San Francisco, CA 94104-3803

415-743-6220
FAX 415-421-6225
E-Mail: connect@media-mark.com
Home Page: www.media-mark.com

Art Garcia, Publisher

Features report on news-making agencies and corporate departments making news, as well as the people managing them, and rate/review PR services and products. Regular sections also report on international PR/marketing andmedia, women in marketing, investor relations, internet marketing, senior-level moves and promotions, account changes, trends, case studies and industry chatter.

17932 Consumer Goods Technology

Edgell Communications
4 Middlebury Boulevard
Randolph, NJ 07869

973-252-0100
FAX 973-252-9020
E-Mail: cs@e-circ.net
Home Page: www.edgellcommunications.com

Gabriele A. Edgell, Chairman & CEO
Joe Skorupa, Editor-in-Chief
Andrew Gaffney, Group Publisher
Gerald Ryerson, President

Consumer Goods Technology serves manufacturers of accessories, shoes, apparel, appliances, consumer electronics, office products, automotive aftermarket products, seasonal merchandise, transporters of consumer products, consultants and others allied to the field.
Frequency: Monthly
Circulation: 25035
Founded in 1984
Printed in 4 colors on glossy stock

17933 Currents
Council for Advancement & Support of Education
1307 New York Ave Nw
Suite 1000
Washington, DC 20005-4726

202-393-1301
FAX 202-387-4973
E-Mail: memberservicecenter@case.org
Home Page: www.case.org

John Lippincott, President
Deborah Bongiorno, Editor in chief
Tracy Baird, Marketing
Anne Eigeman, Editor

Offers articles on integrated marketing, technology and other industry related information.
Cost: $115.00
Frequency: Monthly
ISSN: 0748-478X
Founded in 1975

17934 Customer Interaction Solutions
Technology Marketing Corporation
800 Connecticut Ave
1st Floor East
Norwalk, CT 06854-1936

203-852-6800
800-243-6002
FAX 203-866-3326
E-Mail: tmc@tmcnet.com
Home Page: www.tmcnet.com
Social Media: *Twitter*

Rich Tehrani, CEO
Tracey Schelmetic, Editorial Director

Dedicated to teleservices ans e-services outsoucing, marketing and customer relationship management issues.
Frequency: Monthly
Circulation: 13400

17935 CyberDealer
Meister Publishing Company
37733 Euclid Ave
Willoughby, OH 44094-5992

440-942-2000
800-572-7740
FAX 440-975-3447
Home Page: www.meisternet.com

Gary Fitzgerald, President

Helps agricultural dealerships better manage their operations.
Frequency: 6 per year

17936 DECA Dimensions
Distributive Education Clubs of America
1908 Association Dr
Suite A
Reston, VA 20191-1594

703-860-5000
FAX 703-860-4013
E-Mail: info@deca.org
Home Page: www.deca.org

Edward Davis, Executive Director
Cindy Allen, Assistant Director
Christopher Young, Assistant Director

For student members interested in marketing, management, and entrepreneurial careers. Delivered to members in the classroom and integrated into the curriculum. Exhibitors welcome to our national and regional conferences.
Cost: $ 5.00
Circulation: 185,000
ISSN: 1060-6106
Founded in 1948
Printed in 4 colors

17937 Daily Record
11 E Saratoga St
Baltimore, MD 21202-2199

410-752-3849
FAX 410-752-2894
E-Mail: editor@mddailyrecord.com
Home Page: www.mddailyrecord.com

Chris Eddings, Publisher
Mark Chashir, Editor
Susan Hoettner, Marketing
Kris Charddo, Circulation Manager
Cost: $190.00
Frequency: Daily
Circulation: 9000
Founded in 1888

17938 Dealerscope Merchandising
North American Publishing Company
1500 Spring Garden St
Suite 1200
Philadelphia, PA 19130-4094

215-238-5300
800-818-8174
FAX 215-238-5342
E-Mail: gclauser@napco.com
Home Page: www.napco.com

Ned S Borowsky, CEO
Eric Schwartz, President
Grant Clauser, Editorial Director
David Dritsas, Editor-in-Chief
Sean Downey, Managing Editor

Offers news on the marketing of appliances and consumer electronics on a national and regional basis.
Frequency: Monthly
Circulation: 20000
Founded in 1958

17939 Direct
Primedia
3585 Engineering Drive
Suite 100
Norcross, GA 30092

678-421-3000
800-216-1423
FAX 212-206-3622
E-Mail: dkarbowski@primedia.com
Home Page: www.primedia.com

Jack Condon, Chief Operating Officer
Ray Schultz, Editorial Director
Charles Vietri, Managing Editor
Elizabeth O'Connor, Publisher

Magazine of direct marketing management.
Cost: $85.00
Circulation: 46,527
Founded in 1989

17940 Do-It-Yourself Retailing
5822 W 74th St
Indianapolis, IN 46278-1756

317-297-1190
FAX 317-328-4354
Home Page: www.nrha.org

John Hammond, Executive Director

17941 Exhibitor Magazine
206 S Broadway
Suite 745
Rochester, MN 55903-0368

507-289-6556
888-235-6155
FAX 507-289-5253
Home Page: www.exhibitoronline.com
Social Media: *Facebook, Twitter, LinkedIn*

Lee Knight, President
John Pavek, VP of Publishing

Mission is to provide trade show marketing professionals with the tools and education to produce high-performance programs with mea-

surable results.
Cost: $78.00
Frequency: Monthly
ISSN: 0739-6821

17942 Greenville Magazine
303 Haywood Rd
Greenville, SC 29607-3426

864-271-1105
FAX 864-271-1165
Home Page: www.greenvillemagazine.com

Paul Gesimondo, President

Features content summary, web-only extras, advertiser links, and access to reader service forms and various contests and programs.
Frequency: Monthly
Circulation: 10,002

17943 Journal of International Marketing
American Marketing Association
311 S Wacker Dr
Suite 5800
Chicago, IL 60606-6629

312-542-9000
800-262-1150
FAX 312-542-9001
Home Page: www.marketingpower.com
Social Media: *Facebook, Twitter, LinkedIn, Youtube*

Dennis Dunlap, CEO

Presents scholarly and managerially relevant articles on international marketing.
Mailing list available for rent

17944 Journal of Marketing Research
American Marketing Association
311 S Wacker Dr
Suite 5800
Chicago, IL 60606-6629

312-542-9000
800-262-1150
FAX 312-542-9001
Home Page: www.marketingpower.com
Social Media: *Facebook, Twitter, LinkedIn, Youtube*

Dennis Dunlap, CEO

Covers a wide range of marketing research concepts, methods and applications. You'll read about new techniques, contributions to knowledge based on experimental methods and developments in related fields that have a bearing on marketing research.
Mailing list available for rent

17945 Journal of Nonprofit & Public Sector Marketing
Taylor & Francis
325 Chestnut Street
Suite 800
Philadelphia, PA 19106

800-354-1420
FAX 215-625-2940
Home Page: www.tandf.co.uk

Gillian Sullivan Mort, Editor

A peer reviewed journal devoted to the study of the adaption of traditional marketing principles for use by nonprofit organizations and government agencies.
Cost: $186.00
Frequency: Quarterly
Circulation: 500
ISSN: 1049-5142
Founded in 1976

17946 Journal of Public Policy & Marketing
American Marketing Association

311 S Wacker Dr
Suite 5800
Chicago, IL 60606-6629

312-542-9000
800-262-1150
FAX 312-542-9001
Home Page: www.marketingpower.com
Social Media: *Facebook, Twitter, LinkedIn, Youtube*

Dennis Dunlap, CEO

Each issue features a wide ranging forum for the research, findings and discussion of marketing subjects related to business and government.
Mailing list available for rent

17947 Journal of the Academy of Marketing Science

Sage Publications
2455 Teller Rd
Newbury Park, CA 91320-2234

805-499-9774
800-818-7243
FAX 800-583-2665
E-Mail: info@sagepub.com
Home Page: www.sagepub.com

Blaise R Simqu, CEO

Promotes research and the dissemination of research results through the study and improvement of marketing as an economic, ethical and social force.
Cost: $112.00
112 Pages
Frequency: Bi-annually
Circulation: 1100
Founded in 1965

17948 License Magazine

Advanstar Communications
641 Lexington Ave
Suite 8
New York, NY 10022-4503

212-951-6600
FAX 212-951-6793
E-Mail: sekstract@advanstar.com
Home Page: www.licensemag.com

Joseph Loggia, CEO
Tony Lisanti, Editor

Detailed coverage and research on the $177+ billion licensed consumer product business including: retail and merchandising trends; promotional partnerships; available and recently granted property licenses; research reports; and case studies on licensed consumer product categories based on publishing and art, entertainment, brands, sports, fashion, home decor, and interactive media properties
Cost: $59.00
Frequency: Monthly
Circulation: 25000
Founded in 1998
Printed in 4 colors

17949 Magnet Marketing & Sales

Graham Communications
40 Oval Rd
Suite 2
Quincy, MA 02170-3813

617-328-0069
800-659-0069
FAX 617-471-1504
Home Page: www.grahamcomm.com

John R Graham, President
Cynthia Cantrell, Editor
John Graham, CEO
Jonathan Bloom, Marketing manager

A marketing and sales newsletter.
Cost: $18.95
9 Pages
Frequency: Quarterly
Printed in 2 colors on matte stock

17950 Marketing

Mane/Marketing
13901 NE 175th Street
#M
Woodinville, WA 98072-8548

425-487-9111
FAX 425-487-3158
E-Mail: coff@marketings.com

Larry Coffman, Publisher

Features important area events, industry projects, awards and executives of note. Highlights the latest information on marketing trends and pattern analysis. Free subscription.
Frequency: Monthly
Circulation: 11M

17951 Marketing Health Services

American Marketing Association
311 S Wacker Dr
Suite 5800
Chicago, IL 60606-6629

312-542-9000
800-262-1150
FAX 312-542-9001
Home Page: www.marketingpower.com
Social Media: *Facebook, Twitter, LinkedIn, Youtube*

Dennis Dunlap, CEO

Specifically aimed at senior level healthcare marketers and managers, offers targeted information, practical strategies and thought provoking commentary to help achieve your goals and shape your vision
Frequency: Quarterly
Mailing list available for rent

17952 Marketing Management

American Marketing Association
311 S Wacker Dr
Suite 5800
Chicago, IL 60606-6629

312-542-9000
800-262-1150
FAX 312-542-9001
Home Page: www.marketingpower.com
Social Media: *Facebook, Twitter, LinkedIn, Youtube*

Dennis Dunlap, CEO

Focuses on strategic marketing issues that marketing managers face every day.
Frequency: 6x/Year
Mailing list available for rent

17953 Marketing Recreation Classes

Learning Resources Network
1554 Hayes Drive
Manhattan, KS 66502-5068

785-539-5376
FAX 888-234-8633
E-Mail: draves@lern.org
Home Page: www.lern.org/

William Draves, Editor

This magazine offers information on marketing and advertising trends.
8 Pages
Frequency: Monthly
Founded in 1980

17954 Marketing Research

American Marketing Association
311 S Wacker Dr
Suite 5800
Chicago, IL 60606-6629

312-542-9000
800-262-1150
FAX 312-542-9001
Home Page: www.marketingpower.com
Social Media: *Facebook, Twitter, LinkedIn, Youtube*

Dennis Dunlap, CEO

Researchers and managers count on this resource to help stay on top of current methodologies and issues, management concerns and the latest books and software.
Frequency: Quarterly
Mailing list available for rent

17955 Marketing Science: INFORMS

INFORMS
7240 Parkway Dr
Suite 310
Hanover, MD 21076-1344

410-850-0300
800-446-3676
FAX 410-757-3515
E-Mail: informs@informs.org
Home Page: www.informs.org

Mark Doherty, Executive Director
Barry List, Director Marketing
Patricia Shaffer, Director Publications
Richard C Larson, President

Marketing journal offering marketing and advertising articles. Provides help for marketing decision makers and deeper understanding of marketing phenomena.
Cost: $172.00
Frequency: Quarterly
Circulation: 1800
ISSN: 0732-2399
Founded in 1982

17956 Marketing to Women

EPM Communications
19 W. 21st St., #303
New York, NY 10010

212-941-0099
888-852-9467
FAX 212-941-1622
E-Mail: info@epmcom.com
Home Page: www.epmcom.com

Ira Mayer, President
Larissa Faw, Editor

Topics covers attitudes and buying behaviors of the female consumer, market segment demographics, gender gap and health issues, media preferences and the role of technology.
Cost: $35.00
Frequency: Monthly

17957 Marketrac

Marketrac San Diego
4 First American Way
Santa Ana, CA 92707

714-250-6400
800-345-7334
Home Page: www.facorelogic.com

Gerald Schultz, Editor
Jim Lucich, Promotional Manager

Marketing communications: people, places, events, trends, new products, technology, public relations, advertising, broadcast, TV, radio, video production, promotions, market research, direct mail, trademark, copyright law, accounting, employee management printing, graphics, color separations, novelty promotions.
Cost: $15.00
32 Pages
Frequency: Monthly

17958 NAPRA ReView

109 N Beach Road
PO Box 9
Eastsound, WA 98245-9

360-376-2001
800-367-1907
FAX 360-376-2704

E-Mail: marilyn@marilynmcguire.com
Home Page: www.napra.com

Erin Johnson, Advertising Sales
Marilyn McGuire, Editor
Marilyn McGuire, CEO/President
Frequency: 10 issues a year
Circulation: 180000
Founded in 1986

17959 POINT

Direct Marketing Association
1120 Avenue of the Americas
New York, NY 10036-6713

212-768-7277
FAX 212-302-6714
Home Page: www.the-dma.org
Social Media: *Facebook, Twitter, LinkedIn*

John A. Greco Jr, President & CEO

DMA's digital magazine.

17960 POP Design

In-Store Marketing Institute
8550 W. Bryn Mawr
#200
Chicago, IL 60631

773-992-4450
FAX 773-992-4455
E-Mail: info@instoremarketer.org
Home Page: www.p2pi.org/

Peter Hoyt, President

Serves the news and product information needs
of producers and designers of instore displays,
signs and fixtures. Each issue features the latest
trends and technologies vital to building and
designing successful instore merchandising.
Frequency: Monthly
Circulation: 18000
Printed in 4 colors on glossy stock

17961 PSMJ Marketing Tactics

PSMJ Resources
10 Midland Avenue
Newton, MA 02458-1000

617-965-0055
800-537-7765
FAX 617-965-5152
E-Mail: info@psmj.com
Home Page: www.psmj.com

Frank Stasiowski, Production Manager

Provides marketing tactics and techniques for
the design industry.
Cost: $267.00
8 Pages
Frequency: Monthly
Founded in 1975
Mailing list available for rentat $125 per M
Printed in 2 colors on matte stock

17962 Personal Selling Power

1140 International Parkway
PO Box 5467
Fredericksburg, VA 22406-467

540-752-7000
800-752-7355
FAX 540-752-7001
E-Mail: feedback@sellingpower.com
Home Page: www.sellingpower.com

John Nuzzi, VP / Associate Publisher
Laura Gschwandtner, CEO

Sales education/motivation magazine designed
to train, educate, motivate salespeople.
Cost: $33.00
140 Pages
Frequency: 10 times a year
ISSN: 1093-2216
Printed in 4 colors on glossy stock

17963 Point of Purchase Magazine

1115 Northmeadow Parkway
Roswell, GA 30076

847-647-7987
800-241-9034
FAX 847-647-9566
E-Mail: popmag@halldata.com
Home Page: www.popmag.com

Murray Kasmenn, Publisher
Julie Andrews, Sales Manager
Larry Shore, Sales Manager
Ted Eshleman, Account Executive
Alison Medina, Executive Editor

Addresses the industry perspective of the brand
marketer and the retailer and focuses on retail
trends, case studies, statistics and profitability.
Cost: $60.00
Frequency: 9 per year
Circulation: 18,506

17964 Politically Direct

Direct Marketing Association
1120 Avenue of the Americas
New York, NY 10036-6700

212-768-7277
FAX 212-302-6714
E-Mail: customerservice@the-dma.org
Home Page: www.the-dma.org

Lawrence M Kimmel, CEO

Published both in print and digital versions,
this newsletter on DMA advocacy efforts keeps
DMA members informed and involved in the
politics and policies that impact them today and
ahead of the curve on developments that will
affect them tomorrow.

17965 PromaxBDA

PROMAX
1522 Cloverfield Blvd.
Suite E
Santa Monica, CA 90404

310-788-7600
FAX 310-788-7616
Home Page: www.promaxbda.org

Jonathan Black-Verk, President & CEO
Jill Lindeman, General Manager

Magazine, newsletter and directory published
by PROMAX for members only, promotion and
marketing professionals in electronic media.
Frequency: Annual
Circulation: 2500
Founded in 1952
Printed in 4 colors on glossy stock

17966 Quirk's Marketing Research Review

Quirk Enterprises
4662 Slater Rd
Eagan, MN 55122-2362

651-379-6200
FAX 651-379-6205
E-Mail: info@quirks.com
Home Page: www.quirks.com
Social Media: *Facebook, Twitter, LinkedIn*

Steve Quirk, President
Joe Rydholm, Editor
Evan Tweed, Vice President Sales
Alice Davies, Manager

Emphasizes marketing research case histories
and techniques used by researchers in a variety
of industries, from consumer products to advertising, includes directories of research services
and new products and features personnel announcements.
Cost: $70.00
30000 Members
Circulation: 16013
Founded in 1986
Mailing list available for rent: 17000 names
Printed in 4 colors on glossy stock

17967 Recharger Magazine

Recharger Magazine
1050 E Flamingo Rd
Suite N237
Las Vegas, NV 89119-7427

702-438-5557
877-902-9759
FAX 702-873-9671
E-Mail: info@rechargermag.com
Home Page: www.rechargermag.com

Tom Enerson, Publisher
Amy Turner, Manager
Becky Fenton, Manager
Amy Weiss, Director
Nancy Calabrese, Sales Manager

Information including articles that cover busi-
ness and marketing, technical updates, associa-
tion and industry news, and company profiles.
Related features focus on the importance of re-
cycling, government legislation, and product
comparisons.
Cost: $45.00
Frequency: Monthly
Circulation: 8000
Founded in 1997

17968 Response TV

Advanstar Communications
Ste 300
17770 Cartwright Rd
Irvine, CA 92614-5815

714-513-8400
800-527-7008
FAX 714-513-8412
E-Mail: george@directresponsetv.com
Home Page: www.directresponsetv.com

John Yarring, Publisher
Thomas Haire, Editor
Joe Logia, CEO/President
Jodi Dressig, Circulation manager
Gina Cohen, Manager

Addresses industry concerns regarding regula-
tory issues, production, fulfillment and
aftermarketing. Designed for direct marketers,
product owners and related agencies.
Cost: $39.00
Frequency: Monthly
Circulation: 21345
Founded in 1993

17969 Sales Executive

Sales Marketing Executives of Greater New
York
13 E 37th Street
#8
New York, NY 10016-2821

212-685-3613
FAX 212-725-3752

Edward Glanegan, Publisher
Patricia Israel, Editor

For sales executives in New York.
Circulation: 2,500

17970 Sales Upbeat

Economics Press
12 Daniel Road
Fairfield, NJ 07004-2565

973-227-1224
FAX 973-227-9742

John Beckley, Publisher
Robert Guder, Editor

Sales methods and techniques, quotes and an-
ecdotes about selling.
Cost: $2.00
Circulation: 52,000

17971 Salesmanship

LRP Publications/Dartnell Corporation

PO Box 980
Horsham, PA 19044-0980

215-784-0912
800-341-7874
FAX 215-784-9639
E-Mail: webmaster@lrp.com
Home Page: www.lrp.com

Todd Lutz, CFO

Enhances training program with engaging and instructive reminders and shape-up tips that pay off in greater gains from sales force.
Cost: $62.00

17972 Say Yes Marketing Script Presentations
Frieda Carrol Communications
PO Box 416
Denver, CO 80201-0416

303-575-5676

This reference contains marketing presentations for various kinds of businesses.
Cost: $52.95

17973 Security Distributing & Marketing
Reed Business Information
1050 IL Route 83
Suite 200
Bensonville, IL 60106

630-616-0200
FAX 630-227-0214
Home Page: www.sdmmag.com

Bill Zalud, Editorial Director
Susan Whitehurst, Production Manager
Lyn Sopala, Production Manager

Security Distributing and Marketing serves security installing dealers, security installing dealers with central station equipment, central station services, access control system specialists and systems integrators.
Cost: $82.00
104 Pages
Frequency: 19 per year
Circulation: 28,298
ISSN: 0049-0016
Founded in 1971
Printed in 4 colors on glossy stock

17974 Selling Magazine
Selling Magazine
477 Madison Avenue
New York, NY 10022-5802

212-751-0485
FAX 212-224-3592

Marjorie Weiss, Publisher

Selling is targeted to business-to-business salespeople.
Cost: $5.00
Circulation: 155162

17975 Senior Marketwatch
Campbell Associates
185 Martling Ave
Tarrytown, NY 10591-4703

914-332-1177
FAX 914-332-1177

Arnold Thiesfeldt, Publisher

Features research based on tastes, trends, and resources of the senior market, as a means for advertisers and marketers to target and focus their products.
Cost: $242.00
12 Pages
Frequency: Monthly
Founded in 1997

17976 Southern California Marketing Media
Southern California Marketing Media

5 Via Caseta
Rancho Santa Margarita, CA 92688-4947

949-713-3188
FAX 714-713-3188
E-Mail: gklayman@pacbell.net

Gary Klayman, Publisher

Written to report on marketing strategies, techniques and new products for the Southern California area, includes various company, client and media updates, new trends, and guides to developing individualized marketing programs.

17977 Subscription Marketing
Blue Dolphin Communications
526 Boston Post Road
Wayland, MA 01778-1833

978-358-5795
FAX 508-358-5795
E-Mail: subs@bluedolphin.com
Home Page: www.bluedolphin.com

Donald L Nicholas, Publisher

Offers trade strategies for maximizing product profitability. Provides perspective on success and failure stories.
Cost: $195.00
Frequency: Monthly

17978 Supermarket News
Fairchild Publications
750 3rd Ave
New York, NY 10017-2703

212-630-4000
800-204-4515
FAX 212-630-3563
E-Mail: customerservice@fairchildpub.com
Home Page: www.supermarketnews.com

Mary G Berner, CEO
David Merrefield, Editorial Director
Cost: $44.50
40 Pages
Frequency: Weekly
Circulation: 36346
ISSN: 0039-5803
Founded in 1892

17979 TODAY - The Journal of Work Process Improvement
Recognition Technologies Users Association
185 Devonshire Street
Suite 770
Boston, MA 02110-1407

617-426-1167
FAX 617-521-8675
E-Mail: info@tawpi.org
Home Page: www.tawpi.org

Dan Bolita, Editor
Frank Moran, CEO/President
Jason Glass, VP Sales
Cost: $27.69
Circulation: 5000
ISSN: 1073-2233
Founded in 1997
Printed in 2 colors on glossy stock

17980 Target Marketing
North American Publishing Company
1500 Spring Garden St
Suite 1200
Philadelphia, PA 19130-4094

215-238-5300
FAX 215-238-5342
E-Mail: editor.tm@napco.com
Home Page: www.targetmarketingmag.com
Social Media: *Facebook, Twitter, LinkedIn*

Ned S Borowsky, CEO
Lisa Yorgey, Managing Editor
Drew James, Sales Manager

Covers telemarketing, list rental, testing and management, circulation, catalogue and on-

line/web marketing, and direct response advertising.
Cost: $65.00
Frequency: Monthly
Circulation: 42,000
Mailing list available for rent

17981 Telemarketing & Call Center Solutions
Technology Marketing Corporation
800 Connecticut Ave
1st Floor East
Norwalk, CT 06854-1924

203-852-6800
800-243-6002
FAX 203-866-3326
E-Mail: tmc@tmcnet.com
Home Page: www.tmcnet.com
Social Media: *Twitter*

Nadji Tehrani, President
Linda Driscoll, Editor

First and only authoritative guide to effective and profitable marketing through business telecommunications. Provides information on technology and services releases, new techniques and management strategies.
Cost: $7.00
Frequency: 24 times
Circulation: 31419
Founded in 1972

17982 Velocity
Strategic Account Management Association
33 N La Salle Street
Suite 3700
Chicago, IL 60602

312-251-3131
FAX 312-251-3132
Home Page: www.strategicaccounts.org

Greg Bartlett, Editor

Contains exclusive, in-depth articles on topics such as negotiation, customer management, internal alignment and effective team communications.
Cost: $65.00
52 Pages
Frequency: Quarterly
Circulation: 2000
Founded in 1964
Printed in 4 colors

17983 Wireless for the Corporate User
Probe Research
3 Wing Drive
Suite 240
Cedar Knolls, NJ 07927-1000

973-285-1500
FAX 973-285-1519

Jack Killion, Publisher

Edited for the corporate user/decision maker to keep abreast of the growth product and service offerings, the expanding uses and the technological, political and standardization issues of the wireless arena.
Circulation: 43000

17984 World Trade
BNP Media
2401 W. Big Beaver Rd, Suite 700
Troy, MI 48084

248-362-3700
Home Page: www.bnpmedia.com
Social Media: *Facebook, Twitter, LinkedIn*

Katie Rotella, President
Cost: $37.00
58 Pages
Frequency: Monthly

Trade Shows

17985 Annual Conference and Mailing Fulfillment Expo
Mailing & Fulfillment Service Association
1421 Prince Street
Suite 410
Alexandria, VA 22314-2806

703-836-9200
FAX 703-548-8204
E-Mail: mfsa-mail@mfsanet.org
Home Page: www.mfsanet.org
Social Media: *Facebook, Twitter, LinkedIn*

Ken Garner, President
Jennifer Root, Director
Bill Stevenson, Director Marketing
Leo Raymond, Vice President

Quality educational sessions, industry specific exhibit hall, networking and more.
Frequency: Annual

17986 Annual Conference for Catalog & Multichannel Merchants (ACCM)
Direct Marketing Association
1120 Avenue of Americas
New York, NY 10036

212-768-7277
FAX 212-302-6714
Home Page: www.the-dma.org
Social Media: *Facebook, Twitter, LinkedIn*

Julie Hogan, SVP Conference & Events
10M Attendees

17987 Annual Conference on Healthcare Marketing
Alliance for Healthcare Strategy & Marketing
11 S LaSalle Street
Suite 2300
Chicago, IL 60603

312-704-9700
FAX 312-704-9709
Home Page: www.alliancehlth.org/hlthmktg

Workshop and social events plus 50 exhibits of marketing communications, health care information lines, stategic planning and more.
600 Attendees
Frequency: Annual
Founded in 1984

17988 Business Intelligence Conference
The Conference Board
845 Third Avenue
New York, NY 10022

212-339-0345
FAX 212-836-9740
Home Page:
www.conference-board.org/intelligence.htm

Shows how you can utilize business intelligence in your own organization to enhance performace and drive results.
Frequency: June, Chicago

17989 DMA Annual Conference & Exhibition
Direct Marketing Association
1120 Avenue of Americas
New York, NY 10036-6700

212-768-7277
FAX 212-302-6714
E-Mail: dmaconferences@the-dma.org
Home Page: www.the-dma.org

Lawrence M Kimmel, CEO
Julie A Hogan, SVP Conferences/Events

Brings together thousands of practitioners and experts from the entire marketing continuum to discuss solutions and best practices to achieve optimal channel mix and integration that lead to measurable results and increase real-time customer engagement.
12000 Attendees
Frequency: October

17990 DMB: Direct Marketing to Business Conference
Target Conference Corporation
11 Riverbend Drive S
Stamford, CT 06907-0949

203-358-9900
FAX 203-358-5815

Ed Berkowitz
National conference for business to business direct marketers. 75 table tops
1000+ Attendees
Frequency: March
Mailing list available for rent

17991 Direct Marketing Conference National Conference
DMB Miami
Fontainebleau Hilton Resort and Towers
Miami, FL 33152

203-358-3751
800-927-5007
Home Page: www.intertecevents.com

Information on improving R.O.I. and stay ahead of the competition, create customer centric business, synthesize traditional marketing strategies with the internet.

17992 Electronic Retailing Association Annual Convention
Electronid Retailing Association
607 14th Street, NW, Suite 530
Washington, DC 20005

703-841-1751
800-987-6462
FAX 425-977-1036
E-Mail: contact@retailing.org
Home Page: www.retailing.org
Social Media: *Facebook, Twitter, LinkedIn, Youtube.Flickr*

Karla Kelly, VP Meetings/Conventions
Christy Brzonkala Hopkins, Meetings Coordinator

17993 Email Evolution Conference
Direct Marketing Association
1120 Avenue of Americas
New York, NY 10036-6700

212-768-7277
FAX 212-302-6714
E-Mail: dmaconferences@the-dma.org
Home Page: www.the-dma.org

Julie A Hogan, SVP Conference/Events
Lawrence M Kimmel, CEO

Focuses on the ever-changing and evolving world of email marketing, providing you with the best ways to capitalize on the high ROI this low-cost communication tool can provide both on its own, and integrated with social, search, mobile, video and other email enhancers.
10M Attendees
Frequency: Annual/February

17994 Exhibitor Conference
Exhibitor Magazine Group
206 S Broadway
Suite 745
Rochester, MN 55904-6565

507-289-6556
888-235-6155
FAX 507-289-5253
E-Mail: exhibitorshow@heiexpo.com

Home Page: www.exhibitoronline.com
Social Media: *Facebook, Twitter, LinkedIn*

Carol Fojtik, Managing Director/Sr Vice President

Conference program combined with exhibit hall featuring latest products and resources shaping the future of exhibiting and corporate event programs. Anyone responsible for planning, managing or implementing trade show or corporate event marketing functions should attend. Conference is held annually in Las Vegas, NV.
5M Attendees
Frequency: March, Las Vegas
Founded in 1989

17995 FSMA Top 2 Top Conference
1810-J York Road #384
Lutherville, MD 21093

410-715-4084
800-617-1170
FAX 888-668-7496
E-Mail: info@fsmaonline.com
Home Page: www.fsmaonline.com

Bob Watson, Chair
Rick Abraham, President
Frequency: Annual/February
Mailing list available for rent

17996 High Performance Linux on Wall Street
Flagg Management
353 Lexington Avenue
New York, NY 10016

212-286-0333
FAX 212-286-0086
E-Mail: flaggmgmnt@msn.com
Home Page: www.flaggmgmt.com

Russell Flagg, President

Featuring Linux and HPC futures discussions, virtualization, cloud computing and service-driven datacenters, open source meets low latency, VLDB architectures, cost reduction with Linux, and more.
1000 Attendees
Frequency: Annual
Founded in 2001

17997 MBA Research Conclave
MBAResearch and Curriculum Center
1375 King Avenue
PO Box 12279
Columbus, OH 43212

614-486-6708
800-448-0398
FAX 614-486-1819
E-Mail: servic@mbaresearch.org
Home Page: www.mbaresearch.org

Marsha Dyer, Customer Service Manager
Kimberly Holstlaw, Executive Adminstrator
James Gleason, President/CEO

Containing 20 booths and 15 exhibits.
500 Attendees
Frequency: June
Founded in 1971

17998 MDMA's Annual Direct Marketing Conference & Expo
Midwest Direct Marketing Association
P.O. Box 75
Andover, MN 55304

763-607-2943
FAX 763-753-2240
E-Mail: office@mdma.org
Home Page: www.mdma.org

Joan Forde, President
Cindy McCleary, Director

Containing 55 booths and 50 companies exhibiting.
Frequency: April
Mailing list available for rent: 1.1M+ names

17999 MFSA Midwinter Executive Conference

Mailing & Fulfillment Service Association
1421 Prince Street
Suite 410
Alexandria, VA 22314-2806

703-836-9200
FAX 703-548-8204
E-Mail: mfsa-mail@mfsanet.org
Home Page: www.mfsanet.org
Social Media: *Facebook, Twitter, LinkedIn*

Ken Garner, President
Jennifer Root, Director
Bill Stevenson, Director Marketing
Leo Raymond, Vice President

Will address financial operations and business valuation, marketing your own company, the changing world of postal regulations, technology in fulfillment, building a sales team, being strong in digital printing and the landscape of employment law.

18000 MLMIA Annual Corporate Convention and Expo

Multi-Level Marketing International Association
119 Stanford Court
Irvine, CA 92612-1671

949-854-0484
FAX 949-281-2114
E-Mail: info@mlmia.com
Home Page: www.mlmia.com
Social Media: *Facebook, Twitter*

Doris Wood, Chair/President Emeritus
Del Hickman, Executive Director
Eugene Argent, VP Support
Kate Jackson, Treasurer
Linda Bruno, Secretary

Seeks to strengthen and improve the Direct Sales/Network Marketing/Multi-Level Marketing industry in the United States and abroad. Members are companies which market their products and services directly to consumers through independent distributors, suppliers to the industry and distributors who interface with consumers.
Founded in 1985

18001 Mailer Strategies Conference

Mailing & Fulfillment Service Association
1421 Prince Street
Suite 410
Alexandria, VA 22314-2806

703-836-9200
FAX 703-548-8204
E-Mail: mfsa-mail@mfsanet.org
Home Page: www.mfsanet.org
Social Media: *Facebook, Twitter, LinkedIn*

Ken Garner, President
Jennifer Root, Director
Bill Stevenson, Director Marketing
Leo Raymond, Vice President

This conference will focus solely on postal issues that are important to your operations.

18002 Marketing Federation's Annual Conference on Strategic Marketing

Marketing Federation
109 58th Avenue
Saint Petersburg, FL 33706-2203

727-363-7805
FAX 727-367-6545

Greg Stemm

Offers attendees information on how to boost attendance at their seminars, conferences and expositions.

18003 NCDM Conference

Direct Marketing Association
1120 Avenue of Americas
New York, NY 10036-6700

212-768-7277
FAX 212-302-6714
E-Mail: dmaconferences@the-dma.org
Home Page: www.the-dma.org

Julie A Hogan, SVP Conference/Events
Lawrence M Kimmel, CEO

Presents industry experts and hard-hitting case studies from a variety of verticals, such as financial services, retail, automotive, publishing, non-profit and many more, who will share the latest strategies and methodologies in gathering, analyzing, leveraging and protecting your most valuable business asset - customer data.
10M Attendees
Frequency: Annual/December

18004 NCDM Conferences National Center for Database Marketing

Primedia Business Exhibitions
11 River Bend S
PO Box 4254
Stamford, CT 06907

203-358-9900
FAX 203-358-5815
Home Page: www.ncdmsummer.com or www.ncdmwinter.com

Ed Berkowitz, Director Sales

A conference offering a highly qualified audience of database marketing decision-makers from all over the country, including a high concentration of marketers from the Midwest and West coast. Containing 210 booths and 100 exhibits.
2500 Attendees
Frequency: July/December

18005 National Conference on Operations & Fulfillment (NCOF)

Direct Marketing Association
1120 Avenue of Americas
New York, NY 1003-6700

212-768-7277
FAX 312-302-6714
E-Mail: dmaconferences@the-dma.org
Home Page: www.the-dma.org

Julie A Hogan, SVP Conference/Events
Lawrence M Kimmel, CEO

Focus on innovative solutions for warehouse, distribution, operations, and ecommerce needs in the ever-changing world of operations and fulfillment.
10M Attendees
Frequency: Annual/April

18006 National Hispanic Market Trade Show and Media Expo (Se Habla Espanol)

Hispanic Business
5385 Hollister Avenue, Ste. 204
Santa Barbara, CA 93111

805-964-4554
800-806-4268
FAX 805-964-5539
E-Mail: info@hispanstar.com
Home Page: www.hispanicbusiness.com
Social Media: *Facebook, Twitter, LinkedIn*

John Pasini, Cfo/Coo

Annual show of 100 exhibitors of market/research, media, advertising, public relations, information services and recruitment.
1500 Attendees
Mailing list available for rent

18007 National Mail Order Merchandise Show

Expo Accessories
47 Main Avenue
Clifton, NJ 07014-1917

973-661-9681

Martin Deeks, Show Manager
300 booths.
5M Attendees
Frequency: January

18008 New York Nonprofit Conference

Direct Marketing Association
1120 Avenue of Americas
New York, NY 10036-6700

212-768-7277
FAX 212-302-6714
E-Mail: dmaconferences@the-dma.org
Home Page: www.the-dma.org

Julie A Hogan, SVP Conference/Events
Lawrence M Kimmel, CEO

Discover which acknowledgement programs work best-and why, increase the revenue with membership options-as well as traditional fundraising appeals, learn how the Internet and e-mail campaigns can improve fundraising, lower costs and increase advocacy.
10M Attendees

18009 PROMO Live

Prism Business Media
PROMO Live
11 River Bend South
Stamford, CT 06907

508-743-0105
800-927-5007
FAX 508-759-4552
E-Mail: registration@prism2b.com
Home Page: www.thepromoevent.com

Kim Stolfi, Conference/Show Coordinator
Florence Torres, Conference Program Manager
Frequency: Oct Chicago

18010 Photo Marketing Association International

3000 Picture Place
Jackson, MI 49201

517-788-8100
FAX 517-788-8371
E-Mail: pma_education@pmai.org
Home Page: www.pmai.org

Ted Fox, Executive Director
Mary Anne LaMarre, Operations Officer

Containing 3,230 booths and 645 exhibits. Promoting the growth of the photography industry through coorperation.
24M Attendees
Frequency: February

18011 Promo Expo

Promo Expo Sales
The Navy Pier
Chicago, IL 60606

800-927-5007
FAX 203-358-3751
Home Page: www.promoexpo.com

The largest conference and exhibition dedicated to the promotion marketing industry, and the one event where you can meet with over four thousand promotion marketing decision makers.
Frequency: October

18012 Publishers Multinational Direct Conference
1501 3rd Avenue
New York, NY 10028-2101

212-734-7040
FAX 212-986-3757

Alfred Goodloe, President
Offers publishers information and seminars on how to build sales and profits in foreign markets.
Frequency: March

18013 Securities Industry and Financial Markets Association (SIFMA) Annual Meeting
1101 New York Avenue NW
8th Floor
Washington, DC 20005

202-962-7300
FAX 202-962-7305
Home Page: www.sifma.org
Social Media: *Facebook, Twitter, LinkedIn*

T Timothy Ryan Je, President/CEO
Randy Snook, Senior Managing Director/EVP
Donald D Kittell, CFO

The Securities Industry and Financial Markets Association/SIFMA Annual Meeting and Conference program addresses a variety of topics that may include competitiveness of the U.S. capital markets, global exchange consolidation, regulatory and legal initiatives, and trends in the fixed-income and capital markets.
Mailing list available for rent

18014 SourceMedia Conferences & Events
SourceMedia
One State Street Plaza
27th floor
New York, NY 10004

212-803-6093
800-803-3424
FAX 212-803-8515
E-Mail: abconferences@sourcemedia.com
Home Page: www.sourcemedia.com/
Social Media: *Facebook, Twitter, LinkedIn*

James M Malkin, Chairman & CEO
William Johnson, CFO
Steve Andreazza, VP, Sales & Customer Service
Celie Baussan, SVP, Operations
Anne O'Brien, EVP Marketing & Strategic Planning

SourceMedia Conferences & Events attract over 20,000 attendees worldwide. The content embraces a variety of formats, including: conferences, executive roundtables, expositions, Web seminars, custom events and pod casts. With over 70 events annually, participants are provided with premier content as well as access to the industry's top solution providers. Markets served include: accounting; banking; capital markets; financial services; information technology; insurance; and real estate.
Mailing list available for rent

18015 TMCA Annual Conference & Marketing Expo
Transportation Marketing Communications Assoc
9382 Oak Avenue
Waconia, MN 55387

952-442-5638
FAX 952-442-3941
E-Mail: brian07@tmcatoday.org
Home Page: www.tmcatoday.org

John Ferguson, President
Tom Nightingale, VP
Tracy Robinson, Treasurer

Edward Moritz, Secretary
Brian Everett, Executive Director
200 Attendees
Frequency: Annual

Directories & Databases

18016 Adweek Directory
Prometheus Global Media
770 Broadway
New York, NY 10003-9595

212-493-4100
FAX 646-654-5368
Home Page: www.prometheusgm.com

Richard D. Beckmand, CEO
James A. Finkelstein, Chairman
Madeline Krakowsky, Vice President Circulation
Tracy Brater, Executive Director Creative Service

Adweek Directories Online is where you will find searchable databases with comprehensive information on ad Agencies, brand marketers and multicultural media.
Frequency: Annual
Circulation: 800
Founded in 1981

18017 Affluent Markets Alert
EPM Communications
488 E 18th Street
Brooklyn, NY 11226-6702

FAX 718-469-7124

Offers complete coverage on affluent market trends containing complete contact and price information on books, monographs, journals and newspapers.
Frequency: Full-text

18018 AmericanProfile
Donnelley Marketing Information Services
25 Tremont Ave
#10250
Stamford, CT 06906-2330

203-325-9801
800-866-2255
FAX 203-553-7276
Home Page: www.donnellyestates.com

Richard Donnelly, Owner

A database retrieval and reporting system that contains 1980 and 1990 census data, current year updates and 5-year projections of selected demographic characteristics and proprietary statistics.

18019 Annual Directory of Marketing Information Companies
American Demographics
PO Box 4949
Stamford, CT 06907-0949

203-358-9900

Offers a list of firms offering demographic and research services, data retrieval and analysis, market evaluation and forecasting.
Frequency: Annual
Circulation: 5,000

18020 Annual Mail Order Sales Directory & Mail Order 750 Report
Marketing Logistics
1460 Cloverdale Avenue
Highland Park, IL 60035-2817

847-831-1575

Arnold L Fishman, President
This comprehensive directory offers a list of mail order businesses reporting at least 5 million dollars in annual sales. The 750 report

gives mail order companies, businesses and mail order catalogs, 250 listings of each.
Cost: $1095.00
Frequency: Annual

18021 Boomer Report
FIND/SVP
625 Avenue of the Americas
New York, NY 10011-2020

212-807-2656
800-346-3787
FAX 212-645-7681

Andrew P Garvin, President
With over 77 million baby boomers, this report carefully tracks news stories, market surveys, and interviews the experts to help you spot opportunities and position your products.
Cost: $195.00
8 Pages
Frequency: Monthly

18022 Bradford's Directory of Marketing Research Agencies & Consultants
Bradford's Directory of Marketing Research Agency
9991 Caitlin Center
Manassas, VA 20110-4282

703-614-4000

Thomas Bradford, Owner

Over 2,500 companies that are involved in management or market research are listed.
Cost: $90.00
400 Pages
Frequency: Biennial
Circulation: 5,000

18023 Business Marketing Association Membership Directory & Yellow Pages
Business Marketing Association
Ste 123
1833 Centre Point Cir
Naperville, IL 60563-4848

630-544-5054
FAX 630-544-5055
E-Mail: info@marketing.org
Home Page: www.marketing.org
Social Media: *Facebook, Twitter, LinkedIn*

Jeffrey Hayzlett, Chairman
Gary Slack, Vice Chairman
Bob Goranson, Treasurer

Offers information on over 4,500 member business communications professionals in the field of advertising, marketing communications and marketing. Additional benefits of membership include opportunites for networking, professional development seminars, and access to marketing research and studies.
Frequency: Annual

18024 Catalog Connection
Holy B Pasiuk
210 E 5th Street
Greenville, NC 06437-0527

252-758-8612
Home Page: www.catalogconnection.net

Over 400 companies that supply catalogs of their merchandise to consumers and businesses are profiled in this directory.
55 Pages
Frequency: Biennial

18025 Catalog Handbook
Enterprise Magazines

1020 N Broadway
Suite 111
Milwaukee, WI 53202-3157

414-272-9977
FAX 414-272-9973
Home Page: www.franchisehandbook.com

Offers information on companies that offer product catalogs.
Cost: $6.99
106 Pages
Frequency: Quarterly
Circulation: 30,000
Founded in 1989

18026 Complete Directory of Mail Order Catalog Products

Sutton Family Communications & Publishing Company
920 State Route 54 East
Elmitch, KY 42343

270-276-9500
E-Mail: jlsutton@apex.net

Theresa Sutton, Editor
Lee Sutton, General Manager

Print-out from database of wholesalers, manufacturers, distributors, importers and close-out houses. Database is updated daily to guarantee the most current and up-to-date sources available.
Cost: $157.50
100+ Pages

18027 Direct Marketing Marketplace

National Register Publishing
430 Mountain Ave.
Suite 400
New Providence, NJ 07974

800-473-7020
FAX 908-673-1189
E-Mail: nrpeditorial@marquiswhoswho.com
Home Page: www.nationalregisterpub.com

Provides contact information for direct marketers, service firms and suppliers.

18028 Directory Marketplace

Todd Publications
PO Box 635
Nyack, NY 10960-0635

845-358-6213
FAX 845-358-1059
E-Mail: toddpub@aol.com

Barry Klein, Editor

Directories and Reference Books for business, education, and libraries; news of new directories.
Cost: $25.00
Frequency: Bi-Monthly
Founded in 1987

18029 Directory of Franchising Organizations

Pilot Books
127 Sterling Avenue
PO Box 2102
Greenport, NY 11944

631-477-0978
800-797-4568
FAX 631-477-0978

Over 1,300 current franchise opportunities in 45 categories.
Cost: $12.95
Frequency: Annual
Circulation: 0
ISBN: 0-875762-15-8

18030 Directory of Mail Order Catalogs

Grey House Publishing

4919 Route 22
PO Box 56
Amenia, NY 12501

518-789-8700
800-562-2139
FAX 845-373-6390
E-Mail: books@greyhouse.com
Home Page: www.greyhouse.com
Social Media: *Facebook, Twitter*

Leslie Mackenzie, Publisher
Richard Gottlieb, Editor

The premier source of information on the mail order catalog industry. Covers over 13,000 consumer and business catalog companies with 44 different product chapters from Animals to Toys and Games.
Cost: $395.00
1600 Pages
Frequency: Annual
ISBN: 1-592373-96-8
Founded in 1981

18031 Directory of Mail Order Catalogs - Online Database

Grey House Publishing
4919 Route 22
PO Box 56
Amenia, NY 12501

518-789-8700
800-562-2139
FAX 845-373-6390
E-Mail: gold@greyhouse.com
Home Page: http://gold.greyhouse.com
Social Media: *Facebook, Twitter*

Leslie Mackenzie, Publisher
Richard Gottlieb, Editor

Reach over 10,000 consumer catalog companies in one easy-to-use source with The Directory of Mail Order Catalogs - Online Database. Filled with business-building detail, each company profile gives you the information you need to access that organization quickly and easily. Listings provide key contacts, sales volume, employee size, printing information, circulation, list data, product descriptions and much more.
Frequency: Annual
Founded in 1981

18032 Entertainment Marketing Letter

EPM Communications
19 W. 21st St., #303
New York, NY 10010

212-941-0099
888-852-9467
FAX 212-941-1622
E-Mail: info@epmcom.com
Home Page: www.epmcom.com

Ira Mayer, Owner
Terence Keegan, Editor

Database covering marketing techniques used in the entertainment industry.
Cost: $449.00
Frequency: 24 Issues/Year

18033 Food & Beverage Market Place

Grey House Publishing
4919 Route 22
PO Box 56
Amenia, NY 12501

518-789-8700
800-562-2139
FAX 845-373-6390
E-Mail: books@greyhouse.com
Home Page: www.greyhouse.com
Social Media: *Facebook, Twitter*

Leslie Mackenzie, Publisher
Richard Gottlieb, Editor

This information packed three-volume set is the most powerful buying and marketing guide for the US food and beverage industry. Includes thousands of industry freight and transportation listings.
Cost: $595.00
2000 Pages
Frequency: Annual
ISBN: 1-592373-61-5
Founded in 1981

18034 Food & Beverage Marketplace: Online Database

Grey House Publishing
4919 Route 22
PO Box 56
Amenia, NY 12501

518-789-8700
800-562-2139
FAX 518-789-0556
E-Mail: gold@greyhouse.com
Home Page: http://gold.greyhouse.com
Social Media: *Facebook, Twitter*

Richard Gottlieb, President
Leslie Mackenzie, Publisher

This complete updated Food & Beverage Market Place: Online Database is the go-to source for the food and beverage industry. Anyone involved in the food and beverage industry needs this 'industry bible' and the important contacts to develop critical research data that can make for successful business growth.
Frequency: Annual
Founded in 1981

18035 GreenBook: Worldwide of Market Research Companies and Services

NY American Marketing Association
116 East 27th Street
6th Floor
New York, NY 10016-1799

212-687-3280
FAX 212-202-7920
E-Mail: info@greenbook.org
Home Page: www.greenbook.org
Social Media: *Twitter, LinkedIn*

Lucas Pospichal, Managing Director

Comprehensive listings of over 1,500 market research firms in the US and Canada. Listings in over 300 service categories and market industries. The most reliable reference resource for buyers of marketing research services.
Cost: $350.00
880 Pages
Frequency: Yearly
Circulation: 4,500
Founded in 1962

18036 Infomercial Marketing Sourcebook

Prometheus Global Media
770 Broadway
New York, NY 10003-9595

212-493-4100
FAX 646-654-5368
Home Page: www.prometheusgm.com

Richard D. Beckman, CEO
James A. Finkelstein, Chairman
Madeline Krakowsky, Vice President Circulation
Tracy Brater, Executive Director Creative Service

A complete resource guide for everyone involved in the infomercial industry.

18037 International Directory of Marketing Research Companies & Services

New York Chapter/American Marketing Association
310 Madison Avenue
New York, NY 10017-6009

212-986-1418

Offers more than 1,500 marketing research consultants and suppliers of marketing research

data.
Cost: $105.00
600 Pages
Frequency: Annual
Circulation: 6,000

18038 International Network Marketing Reference Book & Resource Directory
MLM Group Publications
12 Rose Center
Norwood, MA 02062-2603

Offers valuable information on over 800 companies in the multi-level marketing industry.
Cost: $15.75
85 Pages

18039 Leadership Library on Internet and CD-ROM
Leadership Directories
104 5th Ave
New York, NY 10011-6901

212-627-4140
FAX 212-645-0931
E-Mail: info@leadershipdirectories.com
Home Page: www.leadershipdirectories.com

David Hurvitz, CEO

Makes all 14 leadership directories available over the Internet and on CD-ROM in one integrated directory. They provide subscribers with complete contact information in one database. Subscription includes Internet access and four CD-ROM editions quarterly.
Cost: $3065.00
Frequency: Updated Daily
ISSN: 1075-3869
Founded in 1999
Mailing list available for rent
Printed in A colors on B stock

18040 MDMA Membership and Resource Directory
Midwest Direct Marketing Association
P.O. Box 75
Andover, MN 55304

763-607-2943
FAX 763-753-2240
E-Mail: office@mdma.org
Home Page: www.mdma.org

Ed Harrington, Manager
Cindy McCleary, Director
400 Pages
Frequency: April
Mailing list available for rent: 1.1M+ names

18041 Mail Order Business Directory
B Klein Publishers
PO Box 8503
Coral Springs, FL 33075-8503
Bernard Klein, Editor

A listing of over 12,000 corporations in the US and 500 international firms doing business by mail order and catalogs.
Cost: $95.00
400 Pages
Frequency: Annual

18042 Mail Order Product Guide
Todd Publications
PO Box 635
Nyack, NY 10960-0635

845-358-6213
800-747-1086

A listing of over 1,500 manufacturers and importers to the mail order industry worldwide.
Cost: $50.00
250 Pages
Frequency: Triennial
Circulation: 5,000

18043 Market Scope
Trade Dimensions

45 Danbury Rd
Wilton, CT 06897-4445

203-563-3000
FAX 203-563-3131
Home Page: www.tradedimensions.com

Lynda Gutierrez, Managing Editor

The definitive source of market share and category sales data for supermarkets. The book configures the information in Trade Dimensions' database to determine market share by Nielsen, DMA, MSA and IRI definitions - over 300 markets in all. Market Scope also provides extensive category sales data as reported by Nielsen and IRI.
Cost: $325.00
Frequency: Annual

18044 Marketing Guidebook
Trade Dimensions
45 Danbury Rd
Wilton, CT 06897-4445

203-563-3000
FAX 860-563-3131
Home Page: www.tradedimensions.com

Lynda Gutierrez, Managing Editor
Jane Sheulin, Editor

The 'blue book' sales and marketing professionals have depended on for 30 years. The directory details the supermarket industry from distribution standpoint, comprising over 800 profiles, organized into 52 market areas. Includes all grocery chains and wholesalers that do a minimum of $30 million in sales. Also includes food brokers, non-food distributors, and small wholesalers in each market.
Cost: $340.00
Frequency: Annual

18045 Marketing Made Easier: Directory of Mailing List Companies
Todd Publications
PO Box 635
Nyack, NY 10960-0635

845-358-6213
800-747-1056
FAX 845-358-3203
E-Mail: toddpubQ@aol.com
Home Page: toddpublications.com

Barry Klein, Editor

Over 1,100 companies that sell mailing lists and the type of lits they handle.
Cost: $55.00
100 Pages
Frequency: Biennial
Circulation: 5,000
ISBN: 0-915344-83-1
Founded in 1972
Mailing list available for rent: 1,000 names at $100 per M
Printed in 2 colors

18046 Marketing Tools Directory
American Demographics
PO Box 4949
Stamford, CT 06907-0949

203-358-9900
800-832-1486
FAX 607-273-3196

List of firms offering demographic and research services, data retrieval, and analysis, market evaluation and forecasting media services.
Frequency: Annual

18047 Marketing on a Shoestring: Low-Cost Tips for Marketing Products & Services
John Wiley & Sons

111 River St
Hoboken, NJ 07030-5790

201-748-6000
800-825-7550
FAX 201-748-6088
E-Mail: info@wiley.com
Home Page: www.wiley.com

William J Pesce, CEO

Business and professional associations that can assist individuals or companies in improving their marketing are profiled.
Cost: $14.95
236 Pages

18048 National Agri-Marketing Association
11020 King St
Suite 205
Overland Park, KS 66210-1201

913-491-6500
FAX 913-491-6502
E-Mail: agrimktg@nama.org
Home Page: www.nama.org
Social Media: *Facebook, Twitter, LinkedIn, Youtube, Flickr*

Jennifer Pickett, CEO
Vicki Henrickson, Vice President
2500 Pages
Frequency: Annual Spring
Founded in 1956

18049 National Directory of Addresses and Telephone Numbers
Omnigraphics
2500 Penobscot Building
Detroit, MI 48226

313-961-1340

This new edition provides the most current names and addresses for businesses and services throughout the United States, arranged alphabetically and by business type.
Cost: $60.00
1,500 Pages
Frequency: Hardcover
ISBN: 0-780800-20-6

18050 National Trade and Professional Associations of the United States
Columbia Books
1212 New York Avenue NW
Suite 330
Washington, DC 20005-3987

202-641-1662
888-265-0600
FAX 202-898-0775
E-Mail: info@columbiabooks.com
Home Page: www.columbiabooks.com

Buck Downs, Senior Editor

Lists 7,600 national trade associations, professional societies and labor unions. Five convenient indexes enable you to look up associations by subject, budget, geographic area, acronym and executive director. Other features include: contract information, serial publications, upcoming convention schedule, membership/staff size, budget figures, and background information.
Cost: $99.00
Frequency: Annual Feburary

18051 New Marketing Opportunities
New Editions International
PO Box 2578
Sedona, AZ 86339-2578

928-282-9574
800-777-4751
FAX 928-282-9730
Home Page: www.newagemarket.com

Sophia Tarila, Author
Pat Bush, CEO

7,000 New Age and Metaphysical publishers, events, retailers, distributors, services, publications, reviewers, catalogers, media connections, internet connections, associations and other resources.
Cost: $139.95
Frequency: Annual
ISBN: 0-944773-18-4
Mailing list available for rent

18052 Procter & Gamble Marketing Alumni Directory
Ward Howell International
300 S Wacker Drive
Suite 2940
Chicago, IL 60606-6703

Membership directory listings.
120 Pages
Frequency: Annual

18053 Quirk's Marketing Research Review
Quirk Enterprises
PO Box 23536
Minneapolis, MN 55423-0536

952-854-5101
FAX 612-854-8191
E-Mail: evan@quirks.com
Home Page: www.quirks.com

Thomas Quirk, Publisher
Evan Tweed, Associate Publisher
Joseph Rydholm, Editor
Alice Davies, Manager

Publishing case histories and discussions of techniques which can be used by purchasers of research products and services. Also directories of research services. Accepts advertising.
Cost: $60.00
64 Pages
Frequency: 11 per year
Circulation: 15,500
Mailing list available for rent: 15.5M names
Printed in 4 colors on glossy stock

18054 Shop-at-Home Directory
Belcaro Group
7100 E Belvue
Suite 305
Greenwood Village, CO 80111
Marc Braunstein, President

This valuable informational source offers information on over 400 companies that offer direct mail order sales.
Cost: $3.00
60 Pages
Frequency: SemiAnnual

18055 Source Book Of Multicultural Experts
Multicultural Marketing Resources
101 5th Ave
Suite 10B
New York, NY 10003-1008

212-242-3351
FAX 212-691-5969
E-Mail: lisa@multicultural.com
Home Page: www.multicultural.com
Social Media: *Facebook, Twitter, LinkedIn*

Lisa Skriloff, President
Agata Porter, Account Executive & Editor
Yartish Bullock-Okeke, Public Relations/Sales Manager
Melanie Eisenberg, Director, Client Services
Annette Chow, Director Sales/Business Development

An annual directory that includes companies with expertise in marketing to different cultural and lifestyle markets. Resources include how to reach ethnic consumers, and contacts and leads for possible business alliances.
Cost: $19.99
Frequency: Annually
Circulation: 4000
Founded in 1994

18056 Sports Market Place Directory
Grey House Publishing
4919 Route 22
PO Box 56
Amenia, NY 12501

518-789-8700
800-562-2139
FAX 518-789-0556
E-Mail: books@greyhouse.com
Home Page: www.greyhouse.ocm
Social Media: *Facebook, Twitter*

Leslie Mackenzie, Publisher
Richard Gottlieb, Editor

For over 20 years, this comprehensive, up-to-date directory has offered direct access to the Who, What, When & Where of the Sports Industry. With this directory on your desk, you have a comprehensive tool providing current key information about the people, organizations and events involving the explosive sports industry at your fingertips.
Cost: $225.00
1800 Pages
Frequency: Annual
ISBN: 1-592373-48-8
Founded in 1981

18057 State and Regional Associations of the United States
Columbia Books
1212 New York Avenue NW
Suite 330
Washington, DC 20005-3987

202-641-1662
888-265-0600
FAX 202-898-0775
E-Mail: info@columbiabooks.com
Home Page: www.columbiabooks.com

Buck Downs, Senior Editor

Lists 7,200 of the largest and most significant state and regional trade and professional organizations in the US Look up associations by subject, budget, state, acronym, or chief executive. Also lists contract information, serial publications, upcoming convention schedule, membership/staff size, budget figures, and background information.
Cost: $79.00
Frequency: Annual March

18058 Who's Who: MASA Buyer's Guide to Blue Ribbon Mailing Services
Mailing & Fulfillment Service Association
1421 Prince Street
Suite 410
Alexandria, VA 22314-2806

703-836-9200
FAX 703-548-8204
E-Mail: mfsa-mail@mfsanet.org
Home Page: www.mfsanet.org
Social Media: *Facebook, Twitter, LinkedIn*

Ken Garner, President
Bill Stevenson, Director Marketing
Leo Raymond, Vice President

Offers a detailed listing of suppliers of equipment, products and services to the direct mail industry, most containing a description of the specific products they provide.
Frequency: Annual

Industry Web Sites

18059 http://gold.greyhouse.com
G.O.L.D Grey House OnLine Databases
Grey House Publishing's online database platform, GOLD, offers Quick Search, Keyword Search and Expert Search for most business sectors including advertising and marketing

markets. The GOLD platform makes finding the information you need quick and easy - whether you're a novice searcher or an experienced database user. All of Grey House's directory products are available for subscription on the GOLD platform.

18060 www.adweek.com
Adweek
Leading decision makers in the advertising and marketing field go to Adweek.Com everyday for breaking news, insight, buzz, opinion, analysis, research and classifieds. The resources of all six regional editions of Adweek, as well as the national edition of Brandweek are combined with the knowledge of our online editors and the multimedia/interactive capabilities of the web to deliver vital information quickly and effectively to our target audience.

18061 www.ama.org
American Marketing Association
Represents marketers and keeps members informed of trends in advertising. Fosters research, sponsors seminars and provides educational placement service.

18062 www.apmaw.org
Assn of Promotion Marketing Agencies Worldwide
A trade association of sales promotion agencies with at least two years experience.

18063 www.assist-intl.com
Assist International
International trade promotion and consulting firm: mailing lists, seminars, conferences, international business expo.

18064 www.awmanet.org
American Wholesale Marketers Association
Government affairs, trade shows, publications, and products.

18065 www.bmahouston.org
Business Marketing Association: Houston
Dedicated to serving the needs of business to business Associations worldwide.

18066 www.choosecherries.org
Cherry Marketing Institute
An organization providing cherry information and promoting material to food manufacturers, food service operators and others.

18067 www.fmi.org
Food Marketing Institute
Events, publications, industry and consumer information and media.

18068 www.greyhouse.com
Grey House Publishing
Authoritative reference directories for most business sectors including advertising and marketing markets. Users can search the online databases with varied search criteria allowing for custom searches by product category, geographic area, sales volume, keyword, subject and more. Full Grey House catalog and online ordering also available.

18069 www.inma.org
International Newspaper Marketing Association
Individuals in marketing, circulation, research and public relations of newspapers.

18070 www.manaonline.org
Manufacturers Agents National Association
A national organization for manufacturer's agents and manufacturers who contract for the services of these representatives.

18071 www.mark-ed.org

Marketing Education Center

Committed to education for and about marketing. Provides professional support and training materials. Primary clients are schools, colleges, and educational institutions.

18072 www.marketing.org

Business Marketing Association

Pre-eminent service organization for professional's in this vital industry.

18073 www.marketingpower.com

American Marketing Association

A professional association for individuals and organizations involved in the practice, teaching and study of marketing worldwide.

18074 www.mfsanet.org

Mailing & Fulfillment Service Association

The national trade association for the mailing and fulfillment services industry.

18075 www.mlmia.com

Multi-Level Marketing International Association

Seeks to strengthen and improve the multi-level marketing industry in the United States and abroad.

18076 www.msi.org

Marketing Science Institute

Seeks to improve marketing practice and education, conducts research.

18077 www.nacda.com

National Assn of Collegiate Marketing Admin.

Members are public relations and marketing professionals in college and university athletic departments. Promotes standards and provides professional support.

18078 www.pdma.org

Product Development and Management Association

International association serving those with a professional interest in improving the management of product innovation.

18079 www.pma.com

Produce Marketing Association

Products and services, issues and information, conventions and expos.

18080 www.pmc-ny.com

Premium Marketing Club of New York

Provides education and networking opportunities for members from all areas of the marketing field

18081 www.printing.org

Graphic Arts Marketing Information Service

A section of Printing Industries of American that provides market research and statistics to its members. Research is member selected and directed.

18082 www.promax.tv

PROMAX

International association of promotion and marketing, professionals in electronic media. Promotes the effectiveness of promotion and marketing within the industry and the academic community.

18083 www.retailing.com

Electronic Retailing Association

Members include infomercial producers, marketers, product developers, broadcasters and other industries serving the infomercial market.

18084 www.riahome

Research Institute of America

A national organization that focuses on marketing and sales intelligence for top level marketing executives.

18085 www.sigma.org

Society of Independent Gasoline Marketers

Members are independent gasoline marketers.

18086 www.smps.org

Society for Marketing Professional Services

Promotes new business development of architectural, engineering, planning, design and construction management firms.

18087 www.strategicaccounts.org

Strategic Account Management Association

Dedicated to the professional and personal development of the executives charged with managing national, global, and strategic account relationships, and to elevating the status of the profession as a whole.

18088 www.teleport.com

International Trade Resources

An overview of the steps required to market abroad. Updated guide to the web's best global business sites and more.

18089 www.the-dma.org

Direct Marketing Association

Leading global trade association of business and nonprofit organizations using and supporting direct marketing tools and techniques.

18090 www.tpnregister.com

TPN Register

Business to business marketplace.

International Trade Resources

18091 Albania Mission to the United Nations

320 E 79th Street
New York, NY 10075

212-249-2059
FAX 212-535-2917
E-Mail: mission.newyork@mfa.gov.al
Home Page: www.albania-un.org

Geronimo Albano, Owner

18092 Antigua and Barbuda Department of Tourism and Trade

25 S.E. 2nd Avenue
Suite 300
Miami, FL 33131

305-381-6762
FAX 305-381-7908
E-Mail: cganuear@bellsouth.net
Home Page: www.antigua-barbuda.org

Byron Spencer, Manager

18093 Austrian Trade Commission

120 West 45th Street
9th Floor
New York, NY 10036

212-421-5250
FAX 212-421-5251
E-Mail: newyork@advantageaustria.org
Home Page: www.advantageaustria.org/us

Peter Athanasiadis, Manager
Sabine Miller, Project Manager
Walter HAfle, Director

18094 Belize Mission to the United Nations

675 Third Avenue
Suite 1911
New York, NY 10017

212-986-1240
FAX 212-593-0932
E-Mail: belize@un.int
Home Page: www.un.int/belize/staff.htm

Janine Coye-Felson, Minister-Counsellor
Dina S. Shoman, Counsellor/Director of Trade
Alfonso Gahona, First Secretary

18095 Botswana Embassy

1531-1533 New Hampshire Avenue NW
Washington, DC 20036

202-244-4990
E-Mail: smautle@botswanaembassy.org
Home Page: www.botswanaembassy.org

H.E. Ms. Tebelelo Seretse, Ambassador
Ms. Sophie Heide Mautle, Deputy Head of Mission

18096 British Trade and Investment Office

845 3rd Avenue
9th Floor
New York, NY 10022

212-745-0495
E-Mail: uktiusa@ukti.gsi.gov.uk
Home Page: www.ukti.gov.uk
Social Media: *Twitter, LinkedIn, YouTube, flickr*

Nick Baird, Chief Executive Officer
Jon Harding, Chief Operating Officer
Crispin Simon, Managing Director, Trade
Michael Boyd, Managing Director
Sandra Rogers, Managing Director, Marketing

18097 Bulgarian General Consulate

121 E 62nd Street
New York, NY 10021

212-935-4646
FAX 212-319-5955
E-Mail: consulate.newyork@mfa.bg
Home Page: www.consulbulgaria-ny.org

18098 Business Council for the United Nations

801 2nd Avenue
2nd Floor
New York, NY 10017

212-907-1300
FAX 212-682-9185
E-Mail: unahq@unausa.org
Home Page: www.unausa.org/bcun
Social Media: *Facebook, Twitter, YouTube, flickr*

Allison B MacEachron, Executive Director

18099 Chile Trade Commission

866 United Nations Plaza
Suite 603
New York, NY 10017

212-207-3266
FAX 212-207-3649

Alejandro Cerda, Trade Commissioner

18100 Colombia Government Trade Bureau

1701 Pennsylvania Avenue, N W
Suite 560
Washington, DC 20006

202-887-9000
FAX 202-223-0526
E-Mail: Fadul@coltrade.org

18101 Consulate General of Bahrain
866 2nd Avenue
14th Floor
New York, NY 10017

212-223-6200
FAX 212-319-0687
Home Page:
www.un.int/bahrain/consulate.html

Jassim Buallay, Manager

18102 Consulate General of Belgium
1065 Avenue of Americas
22nd Floor
New York, NY 10018

212-586-5110
212-586-7472
FAX 212-582-9657
E-Mail: NewYork@diplobel.fed.be
Home Page: www.diplomatie.be/newyork/

Piet Morisse, Manager

18103 Consulate General of Bolivia
211 E 43rd Street
Suite 702
New York, NY 10017

212-599-6767
FAX 212-687-0532

Jorge Heredia Cavero, Manager

18104 Consulate General of Brazil
1185 Avenue of the Americas
21st Floor
New York, NY 10036-2601

917-777-7777
FAX 212-827-0225
E-Mail: cg.novayork@itamaraty.gov.br
Home Page:
http://novayork.itamaraty.gov.br/en-us/

Julio Cesar Gomes Dos Sant, Manager

18105 Consulate General of Costa Rica
14 Penn Plaza, #1202
225 West 34th Street
New York, NY 10122

212-509-3066
212-509-3066
FAX 212-509-3068
FAX 212-509-3068
Home Page: www.costariica-embassy.org

Otto Barcas, Manager

18106 Consulate General of Germany
871 United Nations Plaza
New York, NY 10017

212-610-9700
FAX 212-940-0402

Bernhard Von Der Planit, Manager

18107 Consulate General of Haiti
815 2nd Avenue
6th Floor
New York, NY 10017

212-697-9767
FAX 212-681-6991
Home Page: www.haitianconsulate-nyc.org
Social Media: *Facebook, Twitter*

Marie Therese, Manager

18108 Consulate General of Honduras
255 West 36th Street
First Level
New York, NY 10018

212-714-9451
FAX 212-714-9453

Home Page: www.hondurasemb.org
Social Media: *Facebook, Twitter*

18109 Consulate General of India
3 E 64th Street
New York, NY 10065

212-774-0600
FAX 212-861-3788
E-Mail: info@bls-india-usa.com
Home Page: www.indiacgny.com
Social Media: *Facebook, Twitter, Youtube*

Dnyaneshwar M Mulay, Consul General
Mr. P.K. Bajaj, Consul (Head of Chancery)

18110 Consulate General of Indonesia
5 E 68th Street
New York, NY 10021

212-879-0600

18111 Consulate General of Israel
800 Second Avenue
New York, NY 10017

212-499-5000
E-Mail: info@newyork.mfa.gov.il
Home Page: www.israelfm.org
Social Media: *Facebook, Twitter, YouTube, flickr*

Ido Aharoni, Consul General

18112 Consulate General of Kenya
866 UN Plaza
Suite 4016
New York, NY 10017

212-421-4741
FAX 212-486-1985
Home Page:
www.kenya.embassy-online.net/kenya-consulat
e-general-new-york.php

Rolando Visconti, Manager

18113 Consulate General of Lebanon
9 E 76th Street
New York, NY 10021

212-744-7905
FAX 212-794-1510
E-Mail: lebconsny@aol.com
Home Page: www.lebconsny.org/

Hassan Saad, Manager

18114 Consulate General of Lithuania
420 5th Avenue
3rd Floor
New York, NY 10018

212-354-7840

Rimantas Morkvenas, Manager

18115 Consulate General of Malta
249 E 35th Street
New York, NY 10016

212-425-2345

18116 Consulate General of Morocco
10 East 40th Street
New York, NY 10016

212-758-2625
FAX 646-395-8077
Home Page: www.moroccanconsulate.com/

Ramon Xilotl, Manager

18117 Consulate General of Nicaragua
820, 2nd Avenue, 8th floor.,
Suite 802
New York, NY 10017

212-983-1981
FAX 212-989-5528

E-Mail: info@ConsuladoDeNicaragua.com
Home Page: consuladodenicaragua.com

Jose Flores, Manager
Nohelia Urcuyo, Consul

18118 Consulate General of Nigeria
828 2nd Avenue
New York, NY 10017

212-808-0301
FAX 212-687-1476
E-Mail: cgnny@nigeriahouse.com
Home Page: www.nigeriahouse.com/
Social Media: *Facebook*

18119 Consulate General of Paraguay
801 2nd Avenue
Suite 600
New York, NY 10017

212-682-9441
FAX 212-682-9443
E-Mail: info@consulparny.com
Home Page: www.consulparny.com/ingles/

Juan Baiardi, Manager

18120 Consulate General of Peru
215 Lexington Avenue
21st Floor
New York, NY 10016

212-481-7410
Home Page: www.consuladoperu.com/

18121 Consulate General of Qatar
809 United Nations Plaza
4th Floor
New York, NY 10017

212-486-9335

18122 Consulate General of Russia
2790 Green St
San Francisco, CA 94123

415-928- 687
FAX 415-929-0306
E-Mail: russianlegal@sbcglobal.net
Home Page: www.consulrussia.org/eng

18123 Consulate General of Saudi Arabia
866 Second Avenue
5th Floor
New York, NY 10017

212-752-2740
Home Page:
www.saudiembassy.net/embassy/us_offices.asp
x

Abdulrahman Gdaia, Excellency

18124 Consulate General of Slovenia
600 3rd Avenue
24th Floor
New York, NY 10016

212-370-3007
FAX 212-370-3581
Home Page: www.culturalprofiles.net/slovenia

Reimo Pettai, Manager
Sayed Jahangir, Director of Publications

18125 Consulate General of South Africa
333 E 38th Street
9th Floor
New York, NY 10016

212-213-4880
FAX 212-213-0102
E-Mail: consulate.ny@foreign.gov.za
Home Page:

www.southafrica-newyork.net/consulate/
Social Media: *Facebook*

George Monyemangene, Consul General

18126 Consulate General of St. Lucia
800 2nd Avenue
9th Floor
New York, NY 10017

212-499-5000

Julian Hunte, Manager

18127 Consulate General of Switzerland
633 3rd Avenue
30th Floor
New York, NY 10017

212-599-5700

Raymond Loretan, Excellency

18128 Consulate General of Trinidad & Tobago
125 Maiden Lane
Unit 4A, 4th Floor
New York, NY 10038

212-682-7272
FAX 212-232-0368
E-Mail: consulate@ttcgny.com
Home Page: www.ttcgnewyork.com/
Social Media: *Facebook, Twitter, You Tube*

Hon Harold Robertson, Contact

18129 Consulate General of Ukraine
240 E 49th Street
New York, NY 10017

212-371-6965
FAX 212-371-5547
E-Mail: gc_usn@mfa.gov.ua
Home Page: www.ny.mfa.gov.ua/en

18130 Consulate General of Uruguay
420 Madison Avenue
6th Floor
New York, NY 10017

212-753-8191
FAX 212-753-1603
E-Mail: consulado@consuladouruguaynewyork.com
Home Page: www.consuladouruguaynewyork.com/english-1/

Basil Bryan, Manager

18131 Consulate General of Venezuela
7 E 51st Street
New York, NY 10022

212-826-1660

18132 Consulate General of the Commonwealth of the Bahamas
231 E 46th Street
2nd Floor
New York, NY 10017

212-717-5643

Hon Eldred E Bethel, Contact

18133 Consulate General of the Dominican Republic
1715 22nd Street NW
Washington, DC 20008

202-332-6280
FAX 202-265-8057

18134 Consulate General of the Netherlands
666 Third Avenue
19th Floor
New York, NY 10017

877-388-2443
FAX 212-246-9769
E-Mail: nyc@minbuza.nl
Home Page: http://ny.the-netherlands.org/
Social Media: *Facebook, Twitter*

Wanda Fleck, Manager

18135 Consulate General of the Principality of Monaco
565 5th Avenue
New York, NY 10017

212-286-0500

Magguy Maccario-Doyle, Manager

18136 Consulate General of the Republic of Croatia
369 Lexington Avenue
11th Floor
New York, NY 10017

212-972-2277

Abdul Seraj, Manager

18137 Consulate General of the Republic of Belarus
708 3rd Avenue
21st Floor
New York, NY 10017

212-682-5392

Sergei Kolos, Manager

18138 Consulate of Guyana
866 United Nations Plaza
New York, NY 10017

212-527-3215

Brentnold Evans, Manager

18139 Consulate of the Republic of Uzbekistan
866 United Nations Plaza
Suite 327-A
New York, NY 10017-7671

212-754-6178

18140 Cyprus Embassy Trade Center
13 E 40th Street
New York, NY 10016

212-213-9100
FAX 212-213-2918
E-Mail: ctcny@cyprustradeny.org
Home Page: www.cyprustradeny.org/

Aristos Constantine, Trade Commissioner

The commission's primary role is to further and expand the economic interests of the Republic of Cyprus through promoting, facilitating and attracting foreign investment and fostering the expansion of exports of Cyprus' goods and services, in addition to monitoring related market and policy issues.

18141 Department of Trade- Government of Antigua & Barbuda
610 5th Avenue
Suite 311
New York, NY 10020

212-541-4117

18142 Ecuadorian Consulate
2535 15th Street NW
Washington, DC 20009

202-234-7200
FAX 202-667-3482
E-Mail: consuladodc@ecuador.org
Home Page: www.ecuador.us

Pablo Yanez, Consulate

18143 Egyptian Consulate Economic & Commercial Office
3521 International Ct. NW
Washingotn, DC 20008

202-895-5400
FAX 202-244-4319
E-Mail: embassy@egyptembassy.net
Home Page: www.egyptembassy.net
Social Media: *Facebook*

Ayden Nour, Executive Director

18144 Embassy of Australia
1601 Massachusetts Avenue NW
Washington, DC 20036

202-797-3000
FAX 202-797-3168
Home Page: www.usa.embassy.gov.au
Social Media: *Facebook, Twitter*

Kim Beazley, Ambassador

18145 Embassy of Benin
2124 Kalorama Road NW
Washington, DC 20008

202-232-6656
FAX 202-265-1996
E-Mail: info@beninembassy.us
Home Page: www.beninembassy.us

Cyrille Segbe Oguin, President

18146 Embassy of Bosnia and Herzegovina
2109 E Street NW
Washington, DC 20037

202-337-1500
FAX 202-337-1502
E-Mail: info@bhembassy.org
Home Page: www.bhembassy.org

Mitar Kujundzic, Ambassador Extraordinary

18147 Embassy of Cambodia
4530 16th Street NW
Washington, DC 20011

202-726-7742
202-726-7824
FAX 202-726-8381
E-Mail: camemb.usa@mfa.org.kh
Home Page: www.embassyofcambodia.org
Social Media: *Facebook*

Hem Heng, Ambassador

18148 Embassy of Ethiopia Trade Affairs
3506 International Drive NW
Washington, DC 20008

202-364-1200
FAX 202-587-0195
E-Mail: ethiopia@ethiopianembassy.org
Home Page: www.ethiopianembassy.org

Girma Birru, Ambassador

18149 Embassy of Finland
3301 Massachusetts Avenue NW
Washington, DC 20008

202-298-5800
FAX 202-298-6030
E-Mail: sanomat.was@formin.fi
Home Page: www.finland.org
Social Media: *Facebook, Twitter*

Ritva Koukku-Ronde, Ambassador
Kristiina Vuorenp,,,,, Assistant to the

Ambassador
Tarja Thatcher, Social Secretary

18150 Embassy of Georgia
2209 Massachusettes Avenue, NW
Washington, DC 20008

202-387-2390
FAX 202-387-0864
E-Mail: georgianconsulate1@verizon.net
Home Page: www.embassy.mfa.gov.ge

Temur Yakobashvili, Ambassador

18151 Embassy of Grenada
1701 New Hampshire Ave, NW
Washington, DC 20009-2501

202-265-2561
FAX 292-265-2468
E-Mail: embassy@grenadaembassyusa.org
Home Page: www.grenadaembassyusa.org
Social Media: *Facebook, Twitter, Google Plus*

E. Angus Friday, Ambassador
Patricia D Clarke, Counsellor
Dianne C Perrotteÿ, Administrative Assistant
Lucia Amedee, Receptionist/Office Assistant

18152 Embassy of Jamaica (JAMPRO)
1520 New Hampshire Ave, NW
Washington, DC 20036

202-452-0660
FAX 202-452-0036
E-Mail: firstsec@jamaicaembassy.org
Home Page: www.embassyofjamaica.org

Dr Stephen Vasciannie, Ambassador

18153 Embassy of Mali
2130 R Street NW
Washington, DC 20008

202-332-2249
FAX 202-332-6603
E-Mail: info@maliembassy.us
Home Page: www.maliembassy.us

Al Maamoun Baba Lamine Keita, Ambassador
Muhamed Ouzouna Maiga, The First
Counselor
Ahmadou Barazi Maiga, The Second Counselor
Salif Sanogo, The Third
Counselor-Communication
Colonel Bourama Sangare, Defence Attache

18154 Embassy of Mongolia
2833 M Street NW
Washington, DC 20007

202-333-7117
FAX 202-298-9227
E-Mail: dc@mongolianembassy.us
Home Page: www.mongolianembassy.us
Social Media: *Facebook, Twitter, Youtube*

H.E. Altangerel Bulgaa, Ambassador
Gansukh Damdin, Minister Counsellor, Deputy
Chief
Munkhjargal Byamba, Counsellor
Colonel Boldbat Khasbazar, Defense Attache
Gantulga Chadraabal, Political Affairs/
Counsellor

18155 Embassy of Panama
2862 McGill Terrace NW
Washington, DC 20008

202-483-1407
202-483-8416
FAX 202-483-8413
E-Mail: info@embassyofpanama.org
Home Page: www.embassyofpanama.org
Social Media: *Facebook*

Mario E. Jaramillo, Ambassador

18156 Embassy of Tanzania
1232 22nd St, NW
Washington, DC 20037

202-884-1080
202-939-6125
FAX 202-797-7408
E-Mail: ubalozi@tanzaniaembassy-us.org
Home Page: www.tanzaniaembassy-us.org

H.E. Liberataÿ Mulamula, Ambassador
Lily Munankaÿ, Minister
Paul Mwafongoÿ, Minister Plenipotentiary,
Economics
B. GÿEmmanuel Maganga, Defense Attach,
Edward Masanja, Financial Attache

18157 Embassy of Tunisia
1515 Massachusetts Avenue NW
Washington, DC 20005

202-862-1850
FAX 202-862-1858
Home Page: www.tunconsusa.org/

Gordon Gray, Ambassador

18158 Embassy of Uganda
5911 16th Street NW
Washington, DC 20011

202-726-7100
FAX 202-726-1727
E-Mail: owonekha@ugandaembassyus.org
Home Page: www.ugandaemb.org
Social Media: *Facebook, Twitter*

Oliver Wonekha, Ambassador
Alfred Nnam, Deputy Chief of Mission (DCM)
Dickson Ogwang, Minister Counselor
Patrick Muganda Guma, Counselor
Sam Bhoi Omara, First Secretary

18159 Embassy of Vietnam
1233 20th Street NW
Suite 400
Washington, DC 20036

202-861-0737
FAX 202-861-0917
E-Mail: info@vietnamembassy.us
Home Page: www.vietnamembassy-usa.org

Nguyen Quoc Cuong, Ambassador

18160 Embassy of Zimbabwe
1608 New Hampshire Avenue
Washington, DC 20009

202-332-7100
FAX 202-483-9326
E-Mail: info33@zimbabwe-embassy.us
Home Page: www.zimbabwe-embassy.us

Machivenyika Mapuranga, Ambassador
Richard T Chibuwe, Minister Counselor and
Deputy Chief
R Matsika, Counselor
Whatmore Goora, Counselor (Political)
Col. George Chinoingira, Defence Attache

**18161 Embassy of the Hashemite Kingdom
of Jordan**
3504 International Drive NW
Washington, DC 20008

202-966-2664
FAX 202-966-3110
E-Mail:
HKJEmbassyDC@jordanembassyus.org
Home Page: www.jordanembassyus.org
Social Media: *Facebook, Twitter, Youtube,
Pintrest*

Alia Hatoug Bouran, Ambassador

**18162 Embassy of the Lao People's
Democratic Republic**
2222 S Street NW
Washington, DC 20008

202-332-6416
202-667-0076
FAX 202-332-4923
E-Mail: embasslao@gmail.com
Home Page: www.laoembassy.com

Seng Soukhathivong, Ambassador

**18163 Embassy of the People's Republic of
China**
3505 International Place NW
Washington, DC 20008

202-495-2266
FAX 202-495-2138
E-Mail: chinaembpress_us@mfa.gov.cn
Home Page: www.china-embassy.org

Zhang Yesui, Ambassador

18164 Embassy of the Republic of Angola
2100-2108 16th Street, NW
Washington, DC 20009

202-785-1156
FAX 202-822-9049
E-Mail: angola@angola.org
Home Page: www.angola.org

Alberto do Carmo Bento Ribeiro, Ambassador
Sofia Pegado da Silva, Minister Counselor
Manuel Francisco Lourenͱo, First Secretary -
Head of Consular
Ineclito Lima, First Secretary - Consular
Section
ÿMercedes Quintino, First Secretary - Consular
Section

18165 Embassy of the Republic of Fiji
2000 M Street,NW
Suite 710
Washington, DC 20036

202-466-8320
FAX 202-466-8325
E-Mail: info@fijiembassydc.com
Home Page: www.fijiembassydc.com

Winston Thompson, Ambassador

18166 Embassy of the Republic of Latvia
2306 Massachusettes Ave, NW
Washington, DC 20008

202-328-2840
FAX 202-328-2860
E-Mail: embassy.usa@mfa.gov.lv
Home Page: www.mfa.gov.lv/en/usa/
Social Media: *Facebook, Twitter, Flickr*

Andris Razans, Ambassador
Jurijs Pogrebnaks, Deputy Chief of Mission
and Counsel
Vineta Mekoneÿ, Counsellorÿ
Gita Leitlandeÿ, Defense Counsellorÿ
Valts Vitums, First Secretary

18167 Embassy of the Republic of Liberia
5201 16th Street N. W.
Washington, DC 20011

202-723-0437
FAX 202-723-0436
Home Page: www.liberianembassyus.org/

Charles Minor, President

18168 Embassy of the Republic of Yemen
2319 Wyoming Ave, NW
Washington, DC 20008

202-965-4760
FAX 202-337-2017

E-Mail: ambassador@yemenembassy.org
Home Page: www.yemenembassy.org

Abdulwahab Abdulla Al-Hajjri, Ambassador
Nadia Hashem, Assistant to the Ambassador

18169 Embassy of the Republic of the Marshall Islands
2433 Massachusetts Avenue NW
Washington, DC 20008

202-234-5414
FAX 202-232-3236
E-Mail: info@rmiembassyus.org
Home Page: www.rmiembassyus.org

Charles R. Paul, Ambassador

18170 Estonian Embassy in Washington
2131 Massachusetts Avenue NW
Washington, DC 20008

202-588-0101
FAX 202-588-0108
E-Mail: Embassy.Washington@mfa.ee
Home Page: www.estemb.org

Marina Kaljurand, Ambassador
Tanel Sepp, Deputy Chief of Mission
Indrek Kannik, Counselor (Security Policy)
Oleg Dmitrijev, First Secretary (Political Affairs)
Marju Korts, Third Secretary (Economic Affairs)

18171 Fair Trading Commission
800 2nd Avenue
2nd Floor
New York, NY 10017

246-424-260
FAX 246-424-0300
E-Mail: info@ftc.gov.bb
Home Page: www.ftc.gov.bb

Peggy Griffith, CEO
Founded in 1955

18172 French Trade Commission
1 E Wacker Drive
Suite 3730
Chicago, IL 60601

312-661-1880
FAX 310-843-1700
Home Page: www.ubifrance.com
Social Media: *Facebook, Twitter, LinkedIn*

18173 Gambia Mission to the United Nations
800 2nd Avenue
Suite 400 F
New York, NY 10017

212-949-6640
FAX 212-856-9820
Home Page: www.gambiamissionun.org
Tamsir Jallow, Ambassador

18174 General Consulate of Luxembourg
17 Beekman Place
New York, NY 10022

212-888-6664
FAX 212-888-6116
E-Mail: newyork.cg@mae.etat.lu
Home Page: http://newyork-cg.mae.lu/en/The-Consulate-General

Jean-Claude Knebeler, Consul General
Saba Amroun-Febres, Consular Officer

18175 Gibraltar Information Bureau
1156 15th Street NW
Suite 1100
Washington, DC 20005

202-452-1108
FAX 202-452-1109
Perry Stieglitz, Executive Director

18176 Greek Trade Commission
150 E 58th Street
17th Floor
New York, NY 10155

212-751-2404
FAX 212-593-2278

Yannis Papadimitriou, Manager

18177 Guatemala Trade Office
57 Park Avenue
New York, NY 10017

212-689-1014
FAX 212-689-6414
E-Mail: guatrade@aol.com

Roberto Rosenberg, Manager

18178 Hong Kong Trade Development Council
219 E 46th Street
New York, NY 10017-2951

212-838-8688
FAX 212-838-8941
E-Mail: hktdc@hktdc.org
Home Page: www.tdctrade.com

Jack So Chak Kwong, Chairman
Promotes trade between the United States and Hong Kong.
Founded in 1966

18179 Hungarian Trade Commission
425 Bloor Street, East
Suite 501
Toronto-Ontario M4W 3R4

416-923-3596
FAX 416-923-2097
E-Mail: itdtoronto@hungariantrade.org

Gyula Cseko, Trade Commissioner

18180 Icelandic Consulate General
800 3rd Avenue
36th Floor
New York, NY 10022

212-593-2700
646-282-9360
FAX 646-282-9369
E-Mail: icecon.ny@mfa.is
Home Page: www.iceland.is/us/nyc
Social Media: *Facebook*

Hlynur Gudjonsson, Consul & Trade Commissioner
Berg_¢ra Laxdal, Cultural Representative
Founded in 1939

18181 International Chamber of Commerce (ICC)
1212 Avenue of the Americas
New York, NY 10036-1689

212-703-5065
FAX 212-575-0327
Home Page: www.iccwbo.org
Social Media: *Facebook, Twitter, LinkedIn, Youtube*

Gerard Worms, Chairman
Harold McGraw III, Vice-Chairman
Founded in 1919

18182 Irish Trade Board
345 Park Avenue
17th Floor
New York, NY 10154

212-180-0800

Jean McCluskey, Marketing Executive

18183 Italian Trade Commission
33 East 67th Street
New York, NY 10065-5949

212-980-1500
FAX 212-758-1050

E-Mail: newyork@ice.it
Home Page: www.italtrade.com/countries/americas/usa/new york.htm

Michelle Jones, Editor
Robert Luongo, Executive Director
Developments in the Italian wine industry and market, as well as reviews of imported wines from Italy.

18184 Japanese External Trade Organization
1221 Avenue of the Americas
42nd Floor
New York, NY 10020

212-997-0400
FAX 212-997-0464
E-Mail: jetrony@jetro.go.jp
Home Page: www.jetro.org
Social Media: *Facebook, Twitter*

Masaki Fujiharaÿ, Director, Business Developmentÿ
Daiki Nakajimaÿ, ICT/Environmentÿ

18185 Kazakhstan Mission to the United Nations
305 East 47th Street
3rd Floor
New York, NY 10017

212-230-1900
FAX 212-230-1172
E-Mail: kazakhstan@un.int
Home Page: www.kazakhstanun.org

Byrganym Aitimova, Ambassador
Akan Rakhmetulin, DeputyPermanent Representative
Israil Tilegen, Minister Counsellor
Ruslan Bultrikov, Counsellor
Tluezan Seksenbay, Counsellor

Historic contributions in the field of nuclearÿdisarmamentand non-proliferation by voluntarily eliminating its nuclear arsenal, acceding to the NPT as a non-nuclear state and shutting down the former Semipalatinsk nuclear testing ground, thus ensuring global and regional stability
Founded in 1992

18186 Korea Trade Promotion Center (KOTRA)
460 Park Avenue
14th Floor
New York, NY 10022

212-826-0900
FAX 212-888-4930
E-Mail: kotrany@hotmail.com
Home Page: www.kotrana.org

Sungpil Umo, President
Il Hoon Ko, Deputy Director

18187 Kyrgyzstan Mission to the United Nations
866 United Nations Plaza
Suite 477
New York, NY 10017

212-486-4214
FAX 212-486-5259
Home Page: www.un.int/wcm/content/site/kyrgyzstan

Talaibek Kydyrov, Ambassador
Nuran Niyazaliev, Counsellor
Nurbek Kasymov, First Secretary
Diana Sarygulova, Third Secretary
Asel Davydova, Chief Administrative Specialist

Landlocked republic in the eastern part of Central Asia which is bordered in the north by Kazakhstan, in the east by China, in the south by China and Tajikistan, and in the west by

Uzbekistan. Bishkek is the capital and largest city.
Founded in 1993

18188 Malaysia Trade Commission
313 E 43rd Street
3rd Floor
New York, NY 10017

212-986-6310
FAX 212-490-8576
E-Mail: malnyun@kln.gov.my
Home Page: www.kln.gov.my

Hussein Haniff, Ambassador

18189 Mexico Trade Commission
757 3rd Avenue
Suite 2400
New York, NY 10017-2042

212-826-2978

18190 Moldova Mission to the United Nations
35 East 29th Street
New York, NY 10016

212-447-1867
FAX 212-447-4067
E-Mail: unmoldova@aol.com
Home Page:
www.un.int/wcm/content/site/moldova

Vlad Lupan, Ambassador
Larisa Miculet, Counsellor
Carolina Podoroghin, Third Secretary
Tatianana Dudnicenco, Chief Financial Officer
Litvac Sergiu, Administrator
Founded in 1992

18191 New Zealand Trade Development Board
222 East 41st Street
New York, NY 10017-6739

212-497-0200

18192 Norwegian Trade Council
2720 34th Street NW
Washington, DC 20008

202-333-6000
FAX 202-469-3990
E-Mail: emb.washington@mfa.no
Home Page: www.norway.org
Social Media: *Twitter, LinkedIn, Flickr, Instagram, Tumblr*

Kare R.Aas, Ambassador
Lajla Jakhelin, Minister
Elin Kylvag, Personal Assistant
Berit Enge, Minister Counsellor

Innovation Norway promotes nationwide industrial development profitable to both the business economy and Norways national economy, and helps release the potential of different districts and regions by contributing towards innovation, internationalisation and promotion. Innovation Norway also promotes tourism to Norway

18193 Pakistan Trade Commission
12 E 65th Street
4th Floor
New York, NY 10021

212-879-5800

Abbas Zaidi, Manager

18194 Permanent Mission of Bangladesh to the United Nations
820 East Diplomat Center, 2nd Avenue
4th Floor
New York, NY 10017

212-867-3434
FAX 212-972-4038
E-Mail: bangladesh@un.int
Home Page:
www.un.int/wcm/content/site/bangladesh

A.K.Abdul Momen, Ambassador
Mustafizur Rahman, Permanent Representative
Andalib Elias, Counsellor
Samia Anjum, Counsellor

Peaceful settlement of disputes, promotion of human rights, protection of environment, sustainable development and so on.
Founded in 1990

18195 Permanent Mission of Ghana to the United Nations
19 E 47th Street
New York, NY 10017

212-832-1300
FAX 212-751-6743
E-Mail: ghanaperm@aol.com
Home Page: www.un.int/ghana

Ken Kanda, Ambassador
William Kanyirige, Minister
Henry T.Menson, Minister-Counsellor
J.R Adogla, Minister-Counsellor
N.A Abayena, Counsellor
Founded in 1957

18196 Permanent Mission of Myanmar (Formerly Burma)
10 E 77th Street
New York, NY 10075

212-744-1271
FAX 212-744-1290
E-Mail: mynmarmnission@verizon.net
Home Page: www.myanmarmissionny.org

H.E.U. Kyaw Tin, Ambassador
A.Kyaw Zan, Minister counsellor
Ko Ko Shien, Minister Counsellor

18197 Permanent Mission of Saint Vincent & the Grenadines to the United Nations
800 2nd Avenue
Suite 400-G
New York, NY 10017

212-599-0950
FAX 212-599-1020
E-Mail: mission@svg-un.org
Home Page: www.svg-un.org
Social Media: *Facebook, Twitter, YouTube*

Camillo M. Gonsalves, Ambassador
Nedra Miguel, Minister Counsellor
Mozart Carr, Attache
Maglyn Carrington, Secretary/Accountant

Primary channel for communications between the Vincentian Government and the United Nations in New York City.
Founded in 1998

18198 Permanent Mission of the Czech Republic to the United Nations
1109-1111 Madison Avenue
New York, NY 10028

646-981-4001
FAX 646-981-4099
E-Mail: un.newyork@embassy.mzv.cz
Home Page: www.mzv.cz/un.newyork
Social Media: *Facebook, Twitter, LinkedIn*

Edita Hrda, Amabassador
David Cervanka, Deputy Permanent Representative
Founded in 1945

18199 Permanent Mission of the Kingdom of Bhutan to the United Nations
343 East 43rd Street
New York, NY 10017

212-682-2268
FAX 212-661-0551
E-Mail: bhutan@un.int
Home Page:
www.un.int/wcm/content/site/bhutan

Lhtu Wangchuk, Ambassador

18200 Permanent Mission of the Republic of Sudan to the United Nations
655 3rd Avenue
Suite 500-10
New York, NY 10017

212-593-0999

Jenine Selson, Manager

18201 Permanent Mission of the Republic of Armenia to the United Nations
119 E 36th Street
New York, NY 10016

212-752-3370

Andrezej Towpik, Manager

18202 Permanent Mission of the Solomon Islands to the United Nations
800 2nd Avenue
Suite 400
New York, NY 10017

212-599-6192
FAX 212-661-8925
E-Mail: simun@foreignaffairs-solomons.org
Home Page:
www.un.int/wcm/content/site/solomonislands

Collin Beck, Ambassador
Hellen Beck, Counsellor
Vanessa M.Kenilorea, Third Secretary
B Jagne, Manager

18203 Philippines Commercial Office
556 5th Avenue
New York, NY 10036

212-764-1330

18204 Poland Trade Commission
675 3rd Avenue
19th Floor
New York, NY 10017

212-351-1713

Phyllis Poland, Owner

18205 Portuguese Trade Commission
590 5th Avenue
3rd Floor
New York, NY 10036

212-354-4403
FAX 212-575-4737
E-Mail: chamber@portugal-us.com
Home Page: www.portugal-un.org

18206 Romanian Consulate General
11766 Wilshire Blvd
Suite 560
Los Angeles, CA 90025

310-444-0043
FAX 310-445-0043
Home Page: http://www.romanian.com

Corina Suteu, Manager

The Romanian projects are on hold, as inhouse resources were diverted to more lucrative projects hosted at NetSide. If you have an interst to develop something in Romanian, please let me know and perhaps we can work something out.

18207 Singapore Trade Commission
55 E 59th Street
Suite 21-B
New York, NY 10022

212-421-2869
FAX 212-421-2206
E-Mail: newyork@contactsingapore.org

Kc Yeoh, Executive Director

18208 Slovak Republic Mission to the United Nations
866 United Nations Plaza
Suite 493
New York, NY 10017

212-980-1558

18209 Swedish Trade Council
150 N Michigan Avenue
Chicago, IL 60601

312-781-6222
Social Media: *Facebook, Twitter*

Stefam Bergstrom, Manager

18210 Syrian Arab Republic Embassy
2215 Wyoming Avenue NW
Washington, DC 20008

202-232-6313
FAX 202-265-4585
E-Mail: consular@syrembassay.net

18211 Taiwan Trade Center
5201 Great America Parkway
Suite 306
Santa Clara, CA 95054-112

408-988-5018
FAX 408- 98-5029
E-Mail: office@taiwantradesf.org
Home Page: http://sf.taiwantrade.com.tw/
Founded in 1970

18212 Tajikistan Mission to the United Nations
136 E 67th Street
New York, NY 10021

212-744-2196
FAX 212-472-7645

Khamrokhon Zaripov, President
Abduvokhid Karimov, Minister

18213 Thailand Trade Center- Consulate General of Thailand
401 N Michigan Avenue
Suite 544
Chicago, IL 60611

312-467-0044
FAX 312-467-1690
E-Mail: ttcc@wwa.com

18214 Trade Commission of Denmark
285 Peachtree Road NE
Suite 920
Atlanta, GA 30303

404-588-1588
FAX 678-904-9714
E-Mail: atlhkt@um.dk

Taksoe Jensen, Ambassador
Henrik Bronner, Manager

18215 Trade Commission of Spain
500 N Michigan Avenue
Suite 1500
Chicago, IL 60611

312-644-1154
Home Page: www.spaintechnology.com

18216 Turkish Trade Commission
821 United Nations Plaza
4th Floor
New York, NY 10017

212-687-1530

18217 Turkmenistan Mission to the United Nations
866 United Nations Plaza
Suite 424
New York, NY 10017

212-486-8908
FAX 212-486-2521
E-Mail: turkmenistan@un.int

Aksoltan Ataeva, Manager

18218 United Nations Mission to El Salvador
46 Park Avenue
New York, NY 10016

212-679-1616
FAX 212-725-3467
E-Mail: elsalvador@un.int
Home Page:
www.un.int/wcm/content/site/elsalvador

Antonio Montiero, Manager

Associations

18219 AMT: Association for Manufacturing Technology
7901 Westpark Dr
Mc Lean, VA 22102-4206

703-893-2900
800-524-0475
FAX 703-893-1151
E-Mail: AMT@amtonline.org
Home Page: www.amtonline.org
Social Media: *Facebook, Twitter, LinkedIn, Youtube*

Bob Simpson, President
Douglas K. Woods, First Vice Chairman
John Byrd, President

ÿThe Association For Manufacturing Technology represents and promotes U.S.-based manufacturing technology and its members-those who design, build, sell, and service the continuously evolving technology that lies at the heart of manufacturing
370 Members
Founded in 1902

18220 APMI International Advancement of Powder Metallurgy
105 College Road E
Princeton, NJ 08540-6992

609-452-7700
FAX 609-987-8523
E-Mail: info@mpif.orgÿ
Home Page: www.mpif.org

Dean Howard, President
Michael E Lutheran, Director
C James Trombino CAE, Director

A non-profit professional society which promotes the advancement of powder metallurgy (PM) and particulate materials as a science. Its purpose is to disseminate and exchange information about PM and particulate materials through publications, conferences, and other activities of the society.
Founded in 1959

18221 ASM International
9639 Kinsman Rd
Materials Park, OH 44072

440-338-5151
800-336-5152
FAX 440-338-4634
E-Mail: memberservices@asminternational.org
Home Page: www.asminternational.org
Social Media: *Facebook, Twitter, LinkedIn*

Stanley Theobald, Managing Director
Thomas S Passek, Association Managing Director
Joseph M Zion, Director, Sales & Marketing
Jeane Deatherage, Administrator, Foundation Programs
Virginia Shirk, Foundation Executive Assistant

The society for materials engineers and scientists, a worldwide network dedicated to advancing industry, technology and applications of metals and materials.
35000 Members
Founded in 1913

18222 ASM International Materials Information Society
9639 Kinsman Road
Materials Park, OH 44073-0002

440-338-5151
800-336-5152
E-Mail:
memberservicecenter@asminternational.org
Home Page: www.asminternational.org
Social Media: *Facebook, Twitter, LinkedIn*

Founded in 1913

18223 Aluminum Anodizers Council (AAC)
1000 North Rand Road
Suite 214
Wauconda, IL 60084

847-526-2010
FAX 847-526-3993
E-Mail: mail@anodizing.org
Home Page: www.anodizing.org
Social Media: *LinkedIn*

Todd Hamilton, Chairman
Gregory T Rajsky CAE, President

Represents the interests of aluminum anodizers worldwide and is the principal trade organization for the andozing industry in North America. It promotes the interests of its members through technical exchange, ongoing education, statistical data, market promotion and industry representation.
85 Members
Founded in 1988

18224 Aluminum Association
Aluminum Association
1400 Crystal Drive
Suite 430
Arlington, VA 22209-2444

703-358-2960
FAX 703-358-2961
E-Mail: info@aluminum.org
Home Page: www.aluminum.org
Social Media: *Facebook, Twitter, LinkedIn*

J Stephen Larkin, President
Joe Quinn, VP, Public Affairs
Heidi Biggs Brock, President
Ryan Olsen, Vice President, Business Informatio

Members are manufacturers of aluminum mill products and producers of aluminum.
70 Members

18225 Aluminum Extruders Council
1000 North Rand Road
Suite 214
Wauconda, IL 60084

847-526-2010
FAX 847-526-3993
E-Mail: mail@aec.org
Home Page: www.aec.org
Social Media: *Facebook, Twitter, LinkedIn, Blog*

James Bine, Chairman
Duncan Crowdis, Vice Chairman
Rand A Baldwin CAE, President

An international association dedicated to helping manufacturers, engineers, architects and others to discover why aluminum extrusoin is the preferred material process for better products
135 Members
Founded in 1950

18226 American Association of Professional Farriers
1313 Washington Street
Unit 5
Shelbyville, KY 40065

Home Page: www.professionalfarriers.comÿ

Dave Farley APF CF, President
Steve Prescott APF CJF, Vice President
Roy Bloom APF CJF, Treasurer
Jeff Ridley APF CJF TE, Immediate Past President
Bryan Quinsey, Executive Director
Founded in 2011

18227 American Ceramic Society
600 N. Cleveland Ave.
Suite 210
Westerville, OH 43082

240-646-7054
866-721-3322
FAX 240-396-5637
E-Mail: customerservice@ceramics.org
Home Page: www.ceramics.orgÿ
Social Media: *Facebook, Twitter, LinkedIn, RSS, Google+, YouTube*

18228 American Electroplaters and Surface Finishers Society (AESF)
1155 15th Street NW
Suite 500
Washington, DC 20005

202-457-8401
FAX 202-530-0659
E-Mail: info@aesf.org
Home Page: www.aesf.org
Social Media: *Facebook, Twitter, LinkedIn, RSS, Google+, YouTube*

John Flatley, Executive Director
Courtney Mariette, Bookstore/Education
Holly Wills, Membership
Dan Denston, Executive Director
John Flatley, Senior Advisor and NASF Liaison

AESF is an international society that advances the science of surface finishing to benefit industry and society through education, information and social involvement, as well as those who provide services, supplies and support to the industry.
5000 Members
Founded in 1911

18229 American Farriers Association
4059 Iron Works Pkwy
Suite 1
Lexington, KY 40511-8488

859-233-7411
FAX 859-231-7862
E-Mail: info@americanfarriers.org
Home Page: www.americanfarriers.org
Craig Trnka, President
Bob S.Earle, VP
Bryan Quinsey, Executive Director
Rachel Heighton, Office Manager
Founded in 1971

18230 American Foundry Society
1695 N Penny Ln
Schaumburg, IL 60173-4555

847-824-0181
800-537-4237
FAX 847-824-7848
E-Mail: library@afsinc.org
Home Page: www.afsinc.org
Social Media: *Facebook, Twitter, LinkedIn*

Jerry Call, Executive VP
Ian Kay, VP
David Peterson, Membership Director

Trade association representing the interests of foundry workers across the nation. Offers publications, seminars and networking to promote business in the trade.
10000 Members
Founded in 1896

18231 American Galvanizers Association
6881 S Holly Circle
Suite 108
Centennial, CO 80112

720-554-0900
FAX 720-554-0909
E-Mail: aga@galvanizeit.org
Home Page: www.galvanizeit.org

Social Media: *Facebook, Twitter, LinkedIn, Google+, YouTube*

John Gregor, President
Philip G. Rahrig, Executive Director

Non-profit dedicated to supporting galvanizers and promoting state-of-the-art technological developments in corrosion control.
Founded in 1933

18232 American Galvinizers Association

6881 South Holly Circle,
Suite 108
Centennial, CO 80112

720-554-0900
FAX 720-554-0909
E-Mail: aga@galvanizeit.org
Home Page: www.galvanizeit.orgÿ
Social Media: *Facebook, Twitter, LinkedIn, Google+, YouTube*

Tommy Rose, President
John Gregor, First Vice President
Tim Pendley, Second Vice President
Philip G Rahrig, Executive Director
Dr. Tom Langill, Technical Director
Founded in 1933

18233 American Institute of Mining, Metallurgical & Petroleum Engineers

8307 Shaffer Parkway
Po Box 270728
Littleton, CO 80127-0013

303-948-4255
FAX 303-948-4260
E-Mail: aime@aimehq.org
Home Page: www.aimeny.org

Rick Rolater, Emeny Director
James R Jorden, President

Organized and operated exclusively to advance, record and disseminate significant knowledge of engineering and the arts and sciences involved in the production and use of minerals, metals, energy sources and materials for the benefits of humankind, both directly as AIME and through memeber societies.

18234 American Institute of Steel Construction

One East Wacker Drive
Suite 700
Chicago, IL 60601-1802

312-670-2400
FAX 312-670-5403
E-Mail: solutions@aisc.org
Home Page: www.aisc.org
Social Media: *RSS*

Roger E. Ferch, President

18235 American Iron & Steel Institute

25 Massachusetts Ave., NW, Suite 800
Washington, DC 20001

202-452-7100
FAX 202-496-9702
E-Mail: webmaster@steel.org
Home Page: www.recycle-steel.org
Social Media: *Facebook, Twitter, Youtube, Google+, Blog*

Chip Foley, VP
David Bell, VP/CEO

Works with market development communications programs in automotive, construction and container markets.

18236 American Society for Metals

9639 Kinsman Road
Materials Park, OH 44073-0002

440-338-5151
800-336-5152
E-Mail:
memberservicecenter@asminternational.org

Home Page: www.asminternational.org
Social Media: *Facebook, Twitter, LinkedIn*
Founded in 1913

18237 American Welding Society

8669 Doral Boulevard, Suite 130
Doral, FL 33166

305-443-9353
800-443-9353
FAX 305-443-7559
Home Page: www.aws.org
Social Media: *Facebook, Twitter, Instagram*

Ray Shook, Manager
Andy Cullison, Publisher
Amy Nathan, Public Relations Manager

Involved in writing industry standards.
48000 Members
Founded in 1919

18238 American Wire Cloth Institute

25 North Broadway
Tarrytown, NY 10591

914-332-0040
FAX 914-332-1541
E-Mail: info@hti.org
Home Page: www.hti.org

Richard C Byrne, Executive Director

Formerly the Industrial Wire Cloth Institute (1978)
Founded in 1933

18239 American Wire Producers Association

PO Box 151387
Alexandria, VA 22315

703-299-4434
FAX 703-299-4434
E-Mail: info@awpa.org
Home Page: www.awpa.org

Founded in 1981

18240 American Zinc Association

American Bearing Manufacturers
Association
2025 M St NW
Suite 800
Washington, DC 20036-2422

202-367-1155
FAX 202-367-2232
E-Mail: info@americanbearings.org
Home Page: www.americanbearings.org

Brain Lindsay, Chairman
Jim Porter, Vice Chair
Pete Eich, Past chair
Cheryl Caulfield, President
Chris Coughlin, Treasurer

Washington D.C. based trade organization comprised of primary and secondary producers of zinc metal, zinc oxide and zinc dust marketed in the United States, as well as consumers.
18 Members
Founded in 1990

18241 Artist-Blacksmiths Association of North

259 Muddy Fork Road
Jonesborough, TN 37659

423-913-1022
FAX 423-913-1023
E-Mail: abana@abana.org
Home Page: www.abana.org
Social Media: *Facebook, Twitter*

David Hutchison, President
Amy Pieh, First VP
Peter Renzetti, 2nd Vice President
Bill Clemens, Treasurer
Mark Haddix, Secretary

For the professional and amateur blacksmith.
4500 Members
Founded in 1973
Mailing list available for rent

18242 Association for Iron & Steel Technology (AIST)

186 Thorn Hill Rd
Warrendale, PA 15086-7528

724-814-3000
FAX 724-814-3001
E-Mail: memberservices@aist.org
Home Page: www.aist.org
Social Media: *Facebook, Twitter, LinkedIn, YouTube*

Ronald E Ashburn, Executive Director
Lori Wharrey, Board Administrator
Chris McKelvey, Assistant Board Administrator
Stacy Vermecky, Membership Services Manager
Penny English, Member Administrator

The Association for Iron & Steel Technology (AIST) is an international technical association representing iron and steel producers, their allied suppliers and related academia. The association is dedicated to advancing the technical development, production, processing and application of iron and steel.
12300 Members
Founded in 2004

18243 Association for Manufacturing Technology

7901 Westpark Drive
McLean, VA 22102

703-893-2900
877-578-4000
FAX 703-893-1151
E-Mail: amt@mfgtech.org
Home Page: www.amtonline.org
Social Media: *Facebook, Twitter, LinkedIn, YouTube*

Douglas K. Woods, President
Amber Thomas, First Vice Chairman
John Byrd, President
Rebeeca Stahl, Chief Financial Officer
Ian Stringer, Director

ÿThe Association For Manufacturing Technology represents and promotes U.S.-based manufacturing technology and its members-those who design, build, sell, and service the continuously evolving technology that lies at the heart of manufacturing

18244 Association of Battery Recyclers

PO Box 290286
Tampa, FL 33687

813-626-6151
FAX 813-622-8387
E-Mail: joycemorales@aol.com
Home Page: batteryrecyclers.com

Joyce Morales, Secretary/Treasurer

Investigates means and methods to achieve compliance with OSHA and EPA regulations impacting the secondary lead smelting industry.
Founded in 1976

18245 Association of Industrial Metallizers, Coaters and Laminators (AIMCAL)

201 Springs Street
Fort Mill, SC 29715

803-948-9470
FAX 803-948-9471
E-Mail: aimcal@aimcal.org
Home Page: www.aimcal.org
Social Media: *Facebook, Twitter*

Dan Bemi, President
Danis Roy, VP
Craig Sheppard, Executive Director

Tracey Ingram, Senior Administrator
David Bryant, Treasurer

Nonprofit trade organization for makes of coated, laminated and metalized papers.
Founded in 1970
Mailing list available for rent

18246 Association of Steel Distributors
401 N Michigan Avenue
Chicago, IL 60611

312-673-5793
FAX 312-527-6705
E-Mail: headquarters@steeldistributors.org
Home Page: www.steeldistributors.org
Social Media: *Facebook, Twitter, LinkedIn, Instagram*

Ron Pietrzak, Executive Director
Brain Robbins, President
Andy Gross, Executive Vice President
Mike Sawyer, Vice President
Bill Vitucci, Treasurer

ASD is a nonprofit organization, providing the steel distribution industry a forum for ideas exchange and market information.
Founded in 1943

18247 Association of Women in the Metal Industries
19 Mantua Road
Mt Royal, NJ 08061

856-423-3201
FAX 856-423-3420
E-Mail: awmi@talley.com
Home Page: www.awmi.org
Social Media: *Facebook, Twitter, LinkedIn*

Haley Brust, Executive Director
Donna Peters, President
Carol Chizmar, Vice President
Lauren Lebakken, Secretary
Lauren Kerekes, Treasurer

An international, professional organization dedicated to promoting and supporting the advancement of women in the metal industries.
Founded in 1981

18248 Cast Iron Soil Pipe Institute
2401 Fieldcrest Dr.
Mundelein, IL 60660

224-864-2910
Home Page: www.cispi.org
Founded in 1949

18249 Cast Metals Institute
1695 N Penny Ln
Schaumburg, IL 60173-4555

847-824-0181
800-537-4237
FAX 847-824-7848
E-Mail: library@afsinc.org
Home Page: www.afsinc.org
Social Media: *Facebook, Twitter, LinkedIn*

Mark Nagel, Executive VP
Sandy Salisbury-Linton, Vice Chairman

Supports all those involved in the cast metal industry. Hosts annual trade show.
Founded in 1956

18250 Closure & Container Manufacturers Association
14070 Proton Rd.
Suite 100, LB 9
Dallas, TX 75244-3601

972-333-9107
FAX 972-490-4219
E-Mail: office@bevtech.org
Home Page: www.bevtech.org/
Social Media: *Facebook, Twitter, LinkedIn*

Brain Stegmann, President
Cloeann Durham, 1st Vice President
Sieg Muller, 2nd Vice President

Ron Puvak, Immediate Past President
Larry Hobbs, Executive Director

Conducts public relations for member companies and establishes industry standards.
38 Members
Founded in 1984

18251 Copper Development Association
260 Madison Ave
New York, NY 10016-2403

212-251-7200
800-232-3282
FAX 212-251-7234
E-Mail: questions@cda.copper.org
Home Page: www.copper.org
Social Media: *Facebook, Twitter, LinkedIn, Google+*

Andrew G Kireta, President & CEO
Victoria Prather, Manager Communications
Michels Harold, VP Technaloy Services
Luis Lozano, Technical Consultant
Lorraine Herzing Mills, VP/Finance/Administration

Seeks to expand the uses and applications of copper and copper products. Responsible for industry-wide market statistics and research.
75 Members
Founded in 1963

18252 Copper and Brass Servicenter Association
6734 w. 121st street
Suite 1019
overland park, KS 66209

913-396-0697
FAX 913-345-1006
Home Page: www.copper-brass.org
Social Media: *Facebook, Twitter, LinkedIn, YouTube, Flickr*

Dick Farmer, President
Garret Herringdon, VP
Mark Wolman, Treasurer
Robbert James, Secretary
Cscott F. Immell, Immediate Past President

Distriburors (servicenters) of fabricated copper and copper alloy products (sheet, plate, coil, rod bar, tube, etc) and their brass mill suppliers.
75 Members
Founded in 1951

18253 Ductile Iron Pipe Research Association
P.O. Box 19206
Suite O
Golden, CO 80402

205-402-8700
FAX 205-402-8730
E-Mail: info@dipra.org
Home Page: www.dipra.org
Social Media: *Facebook, Twitter, YouTube*

Jon R. Runge, CAE, President
Richard W Bonds, Technical Director
L. Gregg Horn, VP, Technical Services
Josh Blount, Staff Engineer/Project Manager

Established as the Cast Iron Pipe Publicity Bureau.
7 Members
Founded in 1915

18254 Ductile Iron Society
15400 Pearl Rd
Suite 234
Strongsville, OH 44136-6017

440-665-3686
FAX 440-878-0070
E-Mail: jwood@ductile.org
Home Page: www.ductile.org

Robert O.Rourke, President
MIke Galvin, VP

Pete Guidi, Treasurer
James N.Wood, Executive and Technical Director
Patricio Gil, Past President

A technical society servicing the ductile iron industry. To advance the technology, art, science of ductile iron production and to disseminate all such information to the members.
102 Members
Founded in 1958

18255 Edison Welding Institute
1250 Arthur E Adams Dr
Columbus, OH 43221-3585

614-688-5000
FAX 614-688-5001
E-Mail: info@ewi.org
Home Page: www.ewi.org
Social Media: *Facebook, Twitter*

Henry Cialone, President
Dr Karl Graff, Executive Director
Richard Rogovin, Chair

Companies and organizations with an interest in new developments in welding equipment and technology.

18256 Electrical Manufacturing & Coil Winding Association
PO Box 278
Imperial Beach, CA 91933-0278

619-435-3629
FAX 619-435-3639
E-Mail: cthurman@earthlink.net
Home Page: www.emcwa.org

Richard Duke, President
Charles Thurman, Executive Director
Don Stankiewicz, Vice President

A non-profit voluntary organization dedicated to the furtherance of the conception, research, design, manufacturing, marketing and use of electrical products. The Association provides an array of educational opportunities that enhance the development, knowledge, and use of electrical technology and products. Providing an annual forum to display products, ideas and innovations is a key element in this educational process.
400 Members
Founded in 1973
Mailing list available for rent

18257 Fabricators & Manufacturers Association International
833 Featherstone Road
Rockford, IL 61107

815-399-8700
888-394-4362
E-Mail: info@fmanet.org
Home Page: www.fmanet.org
Social Media: *Facebook, Twitter, LinkedIn, YouTube, Google+*

Ed Youdell, President & CEO

Organization seeking to improve the metal forming and fabricating industry.
2300 Members
Founded in 1970

18258 Fabricators and Manufacturers Association
Fabricators and Manufacturers Association
833 Featherstone Road
Rockford, IL 61107-6302

815-399-8700
FAX 815-484-7700
E-Mail: info@fmanet.org
Home Page: www.fmanet.org
Social Media: *Facebook, Twitter, LinkedIn*

Gerald M Shankel, President/CEO
Jim Warren, Director/Membership + Education
Vicki Webb, Director/Information Technology

Mark Hoper, Director/Expositions
Michael Long, Director/Education
1500 Members
Founded in 1971

18259 Forging Industry Association
1111 Superior Ave.
Suite 615
Cleveland, OH 44114

216-781-6260
FAX 216-781-0102
E-Mail: info@forging.org
Home Page: www.forging.org
Social Media: *Facebook, Twitter, LinkedIn*

Roy W. Hardy, President
Joe Boni, CFO
Don Farley, Director of Marketing
Theresa Ferry, Executive Assistant
Pat Kasik, Executive Assistant

18260 Global Platinum & Gold
5380 S 154th St
Gilbert, AZ 85298-6138

480-946-1242
FAX 480-946-1242
Home Page: www.globalplatinumonline.com

A natural resources mining company engaged
in the processing and commercial extraction of
precious metals from complex ores.

**18261 Gold Prospectors Association of
America**
43445 Business Park Drive
Suite #113
Temecula, CA ÿ92590

951-699-4749
800-551-9707
FAX 951-699-4062
E-Mail: info@goldprospectors.org
Home Page: www.goldprospectors.org
Social Media: *Facebook, Twitter, LinkedIn,
YouTube*

Thomas Massie, CEO

GPAA is the largest recreational gold prospecting club. Owner of The Outdoor Channel, a cable TV channel featuring real outdoors for real
people.
35M Members
Founded in 1985

**18262 Industrial Diamond Association of
America**
P.O. Box 29460ÿ
Columbus, OH 43229

614-797-2265
614-425-0712
FAX 614-797-2264
E-Mail: tkane-ida@insight.rr.com
Home Page: www.superabrasives.org

Terry M. Kane, Executive Director

**18263 Industrial Metal Containers Section
of the Material Handling Institute**
8720 Red Oak Boulevard
Suite 201
Charlotte, NC 28217-3996

704-676-1190
FAX 704-676-1199
E-Mail: gbaer@mhia.org
Home Page: www.mhi.org
Social Media: *Facebook, Twitter, LinkedIn,
YouTube*

Dave Young, Chairman
John Patrox, President
Gregg E.ÿ Goodner, Vice President
Steve Buccella, VP, Corporate Sales/BD
Bryan Carey, President and CEO

Promotes the market and develops a code of
ethics. Serves as liaison among members and
other groups.
9 Members
Founded in 1972

18264 Industrial Perforators Association
6737 W. Washington St
Milwaukee, WI 53214

414-389-8618
FAX 414-276-7704
E-Mail: infof@iperf.org
Home Page: www.iperf.org
Social Media: *Facebook, Twitter*

Delores Morris, Executive Secretary

Members are companies making perforated
metal products.

18265 Innovative Material Solutions
225 Canterbury Drive
State College, PA 16803

814-867-1140
FAX 814-867-2813
E-Mail: info@imspowder.com

Supports all those involved in research in the
materials industry. Hosts annual trade show.

**18266 Institute of Scrap Recycling
Industries**
1615 L St NW
Suite 600
Washington, DC 20036-5664

202-662-8500
FAX 202-626-0900
E-Mail: dennywhite@scrap.org
Home Page: www.isri.org
Social Media: *Facebook, Twitter, LinkedIn,
YouTube*

Robin K.Wiener, President
Sandy Bishop, VP Finance/Administration
Rachel Bookman, Admin Assistant
Thomas Crane, Director of Membership

ISRI provides education, advocacy, and compliance training while promoting public awareness of the role recycling plays in the U.S.
economy, global trade, the environment and
sustainable development.

**18267 International Chromium
Development Association**
43 rue de la Chauss‚e d'Antinÿ
Paris 75009

014-076-0689
FAX 014-076-0687
E-Mail: info@icdacr.com
Home Page: www.icdacr.com

Samancor Chrome, Chairperson
Founded in 1984

18268 International Copper Association
260 Madison Ave
16th Floor
New York, NY 10016-2403

212-251-7240
FAX 212-251-7245
E-Mail: info@copperalliance.org
Home Page: www.copperalliance.org
Social Media: *Facebook, Twitter, LinkedIn,
Google+*

Francis J Kane, President

Promoting the use of copper by communicating
the unique attributes that make this sustainable
element an essential contributor to the formation of life, to advances in science and technology, and to a higher standard of living
worldwide.
Founded in 1989

**18269 International Council on Mining and
Metals**
35/38 Portman Square
London W1H 6LR

207-467-5070
FAX 207-467-5071
E-Mail: info@icmm.com
Home Page: www.icmm.com
Social Media: *Twitter, LinkedIn, YouTube, RSS*

Tom Butler, CEO
Aidan Davy, Deputy President
John Atherton, Director, Materials Stewardship
Ross Hamilton, Director, Environment and
Climate C
Brigid Janssen, Director, Communications
Founded in 2001

18270 International Hard Anondizing
P.O. Box 5
Moorestown, NJ 08054

856-234-0330
FAX 856-727-9504
E-Mail: staff@ihanodizing.com
Home Page: www.ihanodizing.com
Social Media: *Facebook*

Denise Downing, Executive Director

Formed by companies in the hard anodizing
business to provide a forum for the exchange of
technical information and to act as a clearing
house for information about the industry.
Founded in 1989

**18271 International Lead Management
Center**
2525 Meridian Parkway
Suite 100
Durham, NC 27713

919-287-1872
FAX 919-361-1957
E-Mail: info@ilmc.org
Home Page: www.ilmc.orgÿ

**18272 International Lead Zinc Research
Organization**
1822 NC Highway 54 East
Suite 120
Durham, NC 27713-5243

919-361-4647
FAX 919-361-1957
E-Mail: jhendric@ilzro.org
Home Page: www.ilzro.org

Stephen Wilkinson, President
Judith Hendrickson, Corporate Secretary

Members are miners, smelters and refiners of
lead and zinc. Supports research and development of new uses for the metals and refinement
existing uses. Has an annual budget of approximately $5.3 million.
77 Members
Founded in 1958

18273 International Magnesium Association
1000 N Rand Rd
Suite 214
Wauconda, IL 60084-1180

847-526-2010
FAX 847-526-3993
E-Mail: info@intlmag.org
Home Page: www.intlmag.org
Social Media: *LinkedIn*

Greg Patzer, Executive VP
Eileen Hoblit, Administrative Coordinator
Ken White, Chairman
Jan Guy, President
Dr. Karl Kainer, Immediate Past President

IMA is to promote the use of the metal magnesium in material selection and encourage innovative applications of the versatile metal.
125 Members
Founded in 1943

18274 International Platinum GroupÿMetals Association

Schiess-Staett-Strasse 30
Germany, MU 80339

895-199-6770
FAX 895-199-6719
E-Mail: info@ipa-news.com
Home Page: www.ipa-news.com

Deon Carter, President
Steve Phiri, Director
Gabriele Randlshofer, Managing Director
Tania Bossi, Communications Manager
Julian K"hle, Government AffairsÿManager
Founded in 1987

18275 International Precious Metals Institute

5101 N 12th Avenue
Suite C
Pensacola, FL 32504

850-476-1156
FAX 850-476-1548
E-Mail: mail@ipmi.org
Home Page: www.ipmi.org
Social Media: *Facebook, LinkedIn, YouTube*

Robert Ianniello, President

International association of producers, refiners, fabricators, scientists, users, financial institutions, merchants, private and public sector groups and the general precious metals community created to provide a forum for the exchange of information and technology.
Founded in 1987

18276 International Thermal Spray Association

Post Office Box 1638
Painesville, OH 44077

440-357-5400
FAX 440-357-5430
E-Mail: itsa@thermalspray.org
Home Page: www.thermalspray.org
Social Media: *Facebook, LinkedIn*

Kathy M Dusa, Administrative Assistant
Bill Moiser, Chairman
Jim Rayan, Vice Chairman
David Wright, Executive Officer

Strengthens the level of awareness in general industry and government on the increasing capabilities and advantages of thermal spray technology for surface engineering through business opportunities, technical support and a social network. Contributes to growth and education in the thermal spray industry.
70 Members
Founded in 1948

18277 International Titanium Association

11674 Huron Street
Suite 100
Northglenn, CO 80234

303-404-2221
FAX 303-404-9111
E-Mail: ita@titanium.org
Home Page: www.titanium.org
Social Media: *titanium2011.pathable.com*

Brett S.Paddock, President & CEO
Donn S.Hickton, VP
Hunter R.Dalton, Treasurer
Susan M.Abkowitz, Director
Jennifer Simpson, Executive Director

International Titanium Association is an international membership based trade association dedicated to the titanium metal industry. Estab-

lished in 1984, ITA strives to connect the public interested in using titanium with specialists from across the globe who offer sales and technical assistance.
120 Members
Founded in 1984

18278 Lead Industries Association

13 Main Street
Sparta, NJ 07871

973-726-5323
FAX 973-726-4484
E-Mail: miller@leadinfo.com
Home Page: www.leadinfo.com

Jeffrey T Miller, Executive Director

Nonprofit trade association representing the lead industries in the US and abroad. It collects and distributes information about the users of lead products in industry, vehicles, radioactive waste disposal and noise barriers. Its services are availble, generally free of charge, to anyone interested in the uses of lead and lead products.

18279 Machinery Dealers National Association

Machinery Dealers National Association
315 S Patrick St
Alexandria, VA 22314-3532

703-836-9300
800-872-7807
FAX 703-836-9303
E-Mail: office@mdna.org
Home Page: www.mdna.org
Social Media: *Facebook, Twitter, LinkedIn, YouTube*

Ron Shuster, President
Mark Robinson, Executive VP

Supports manufacturers involved in metal working machine tools. Publishes annual directory.

18280 Magnet Distributors and Fabricators Association

8 S Michigan Avenue
Suite 1000
Chicago, IL 60603

312-541-2667
FAX 312-580-0165

August L Sisco, Executive Secretary

Distributors and magnetic materials and fabricators of magnetic components, plus suppliers to the distributor/fabricators.
31 Members
Founded in 1991

18281 Metal Building Contractors and Erectors Association

PO Box 499
Shawnee Mission, KS 66201

913-432-3800
800-866-6722
FAX 913-432-3803
Home Page: www.mbcea.org

Angela M Cruse, Executive Director
Tim Seyler, President

To support the professional advancement of metal building contractors, erectors, and the industry.
235 Members
Founded in 1968

18282 Metal Building Manufacturers Association

1300 Sumner Avenue
Cleveland, OH 44115-2851

216-241-7333
FAX 216-241-0105
E-Mail: mbma@mbma.com

Home Page: www.mbma.com
Social Media: *Twitter, LinkedIn, Google+*

Charles M Stockinger, General Manager
Charles E Praeger, Assistant General Manager
W Lee Shoemaker, Ph.D., P.E., Director of Research & Engineering
Dan J.Walker, Senior Technical Enginner
Jay D.Johnson, Director of Architectural Services

Promotes the design and construction of metal building systems in the low-rise, non-residential building marketplace.
Founded in 1956

18283 Metal Construction Association

8735 W. Higgins Rd.
Suite 300
Chicago, IL 60631

847-375-4718
FAX 847-375-6488
E-Mail: mca@metalconstruction.org
Home Page: www.metalconstruction.org
Social Media: *Facebook, LinkedIn*

Dedicated to promoting the use of metal in construction. Initiative include market development, educational programs, issue and product awareness compaigns and publication of technical guidelines and specifications manuals. Also monitors and confronts challenges affecting the industry such as code restructions.
100 Members
Founded in 1983

18284 Metal Findings Manufacturers

30-R Houghton Street
Providence, RI 02904

401-861-4667
FAX 401-861-0429
E-Mail: info@mfma.net
Home Page: www.mfma.net

John Augustyn, Executive Officer

Makers of metal parts and fittings used in the assembly of jewelry.
Founded in 1930

18285 Metal Injection Molding Associationÿ

105 College Road East
Princeton, NJ 8540

609-452-7700
609-987-8523
FAX 609-987-8523
E-Mail: info@mpif.org
Home Page: www.mimaweb.org

18286 Metal Powder Industries Federation

105 College Rd E
Princeton, NJ 08540-6692

609-452-7700
FAX 609-987-8523
E-Mail: info@mpif.org
Home Page: www.mpif.org

Michael Latheran, President, CEO
Jilliane Regan, VP
Jim Adams, Manager
James R.Dale, VP

As its name states, it is aÿfederation of trade associations-six in all-that are concerned with some aspect of powder metallurgy, metal powders, or particulate materials.
210 Members
Founded in 1944

18287 Metal Service Center Institute

4201 Euclid Ave
Suite 550
Rolling Meadows, IL 60008-2025

847-485-3000
FAX 847-485-3001
E-Mail: info@msci.org

Home Page: www.msci.org
Social Media: *Facebook, Twitter, LinkedIn*

Bob Weidner, President
Jonathan Kalkwarf, VP Finance/Administration
Rose Manfredini, VP Member Information
Services
Chris Marti, VP Technology
375 Members
Founded in 1907

18288 Metals Service Center Institute
4201 Euclid Ave
Rolling Meadows, IL 60008

847-485-3000
FAX 847-485-3001
E-Mail: info@msci.org
Home Page: www.msci.org
Social Media: *Facebook, Twitter, LinkedIn*

Bob Weidner, President/ Chief Executive
Officer
Ann D'Orazio, Vice President,
Marketing-Growth
Ashley DeVecht, Director of Communications
Rose Manfredini, Vice President, Membership
Chris Marti, Vice President, Research
400+ Members

18289 Mineral Information Institute
12999 E. Adam Aircraft Circle
Englewood, CO 80112-4167

303-948-4200
FAX 800-763-3132
E-Mail: MEC@smenet.org
Home Page:
www.MineralsEducationCoalition.org
Social Media: *Facebook, Twitter, YouTube*

Sharon Schonhaut, Director
Rebecca Smith, Curriculum Coordinator
Rachel Grimes, Outreach Coordinator
Carol Kiser, Purchases dept

Nonprofit organization dedicated to educating
youth about the science of minerals and other
natural resources and about their importance in
our everyday lives.

18290 Minerals, Metals & Materials Society
184 Thorn Hill Road
Warrendale, PA 15086-7514

724-769-9000
800-759-4867
FAX 724-776-3770
E-Mail: webmaster@tms.org
Home Page: www.tms.org
Social Media: *Facebook, LinkedIn, YouTube*

James Robinson, Executive Director
Nellie Luther, Professional Affairs Coordinator
Gail Miller, Executive Assistant
Nancy Lesko, Executive & Board
Administrator
Steve Reubi, Controller

Supports all those devoted to exploring the
many aspects of materials science and engineering. Publishes monthly magazine.
Founded in 1993

**18291 Mining and Metallurgical Society of
America**
PO Box 810
Boulder, CO 80306-0810

303-444-6032
FAX 415-897-1380
E-Mail: contactmmsa@mmsa.net
Home Page: www.mmsa.net
Social Media: *Facebook, Twitter, LinkedIn*

Betty L. Gibbs, Executive Director
Matt Bender, President
Barney Guarnera, VP
Paul C. Jones, Treasurer
Michael Blois, Secretary

Concerned with the conservation of the nation's mineral resources and the best interest of
the mining and metallurgical industries.
350 Members
Founded in 1908

**18292 National Association for Surface
Finishing**
1155 15th Street NW
Suite 500
Washington, DC 20005

202-457-8404
FAX 202-530-0659
Home Page: www.nasf.org
Social Media: *Facebook, Twitter*

Erik Welys, President
Paul Brancato, VP
Brain Harrick, Secretary/Treasurer
Jery Wahlin, Executive

The National Association for Surface Finishing
is a trade association whose mission is to promote the advancement of the surface finishing
industry worldwide.

**18293 National Association of Aluminum
Developers**
4201 Euclid Ave
Suite 550
Rolling Meadows, IL 60008-2025

847-485-3000
FAX 847-485-3001
E-Mail: info@msci.org
Home Page: www.msci.org
Social Media: *Facebook, Twitter, LinkedIn*

Bob Weidner, President
Jonathan Kalkwarf, VP Finance/Administration
Rose Manfredini, VP Member Information
Services
Chris Marti, VP Technology
Ann Zastrow, VP

NAAD is the trade association of North American service centers and principal suppliers engaged in marketing aluminum products.
400 Members
Founded in 1914

18294 National Blacksmiths and Welders
PO Box 123
Arnold, NE 69120

308-848-2913
Home Page: www.arcat.com
Social Media: *Facebook, Twitter, Google+*

Dave Christen, President
Jim Lindquist, First Director
Gerry Westhoff, Second VP
James Holman, Executive Director

Blacksmiths, welders and manufacturing machine shops. Organize and offer assistance to
state organizations for the advancement of their
members with education and guiding measures
for the present and future prospects of the
trade.
175 Members
Founded in 1895

18295 National Coil Coating Association
1300 Sumner Ave
Cleveland, OH 44115-2851

216-241-3333
FAX 216-781-0621
E-Mail: ncca@coilcoating.org
Home Page: www.coilcoating.org
Social Media: *Facebook, Twitter*

NCCA is an established trade organization dedicated to the growth of coil coated products. A
unified organization that provides resources
and leadership in order to ensure that coil
coated materials are the product of choice.
Founded in 1962

**18296 National Institute for Metal Working
Skills**
10565 Fairfax Boulevard
Suite 203
Fairfax, VA 22030

703-352-4971
FAX 703-352-4991
E-Mail: kdoyle@nims-skills.com
Home Page: www.nims-skills.org

James Wall, Executive Director
David Morgan, Director of Business
Development
Catherine Ross, Accrediation Incharge

A nonprofit organization formed by metalworking trade associations, national labor organizations, a council of state governors, companies
and educators to support the development of a
skilled workforce for the metalworking
industry.
Founded in 1995
Mailing list available for rent

**18297 National Ornamental &
Miscellaneous Metals Association**
P.O. Box 492167
Ste. 127 #311
Lawrenceville, GA 30049

888-516-8585
FAX 888-279-7994
E-Mail: nommainfo@nomma.org
Home Page: www.nomma.org
Social Media: *Facebook, Twitter, LinkedIn,
YouTube, Vimeo, Flickr*

Allyn Moseley, President
Cathy Vequist, VP/Treasurer
Keith Majka, President-Elect
Mark Koenke, Immediate Past President
Todd Daniel, Executive Director

Supports all those involved in the ornamental
and miscellaneous metal industry. Publishes
bi-monthly magazine.
1000 Members
Founded in 1958

**18298 National Ornamental and
Miscellaneous Metals**
P.O. Box 492167
Ste. 127 #311
Lawrenceville, GA 30049

888-516-8585
FAX 888-279-7994
E-Mail: nommainfo@nomma.org
Home Page: www.nomma.org
Social Media: *Facebook, Twitter, LinkedIn,
YouTube*

Todd Daniel, Executive Director
Liz Harris, Member Care & Operations
Manager
Martha Pennington, Meetings & Exposition
Manager
Allyn Moseley, President
Cathy Vequist, VP/Treasurer
Founded in 1958

**18299 National Tooling & Machining
Association**
National Tooling & Machining Association
1357 Rockside Road
Cleveland, OH 44134

800-248-6862
800-248-6862
FAX 216-264-2840
E-Mail: info@ntma.org
Home Page: www.ntma.org

Rob Akers, CEO
Rich Basalla, Membership Officer
Tiffany Bryson, Sales/Sponsorship Manager
John Capka, Chief Financial Officer

Trade organization representing the precision custom manufacturing industry throughout the US. Has an active safety & education program.
Founded in 1972

18300 National Welding Supply Association
Fernley & Fernley
1900 Arch St
Philadelphia, PA 19103-1404

215-564-3484
FAX 215-564-2175
Home Page: www.nwsa.com
Social Media: *Facebook, Twitter*

William R. Surman, President
William Mehlenbeck, Vice President
R.J Kuhn, Treasurer
Bryan Beck, Immediate Past President
Jay Armstrong, Director
1200 Members
Founded in 1945

18301 Non-Ferrous Founders' Society
1480 Renaissance Drive
Suite 310
Park Ridge, IL 60068

847-299-0950
FAX 847-299-3598
E-Mail: nffstaff@nffs.org
Home Page: www.nffs.org
Social Media: *Facebook, Twitter*

James L Mallory, Executive Director
Jerrod A Weaver, Director Of Education and Training
Ryan J Moore, Member Services Manager
Manufacturers of bronze, brass and aluminum castings.
185 Members
Founded in 1943

18302 North American Die Casting Association
3250 Arlington Heights Rd
Suite 101
Arlington Heights, IL 60004

847-279-0001
FAX 847-279-0002
E-Mail: nadca@diecasting.org
Home Page: www.diecasting.org
Social Media: *Facebook, Twitter, LinkedIn, YouTube, Instagram*

Neal Shapiro, Affairs Committee Chairman

Supports all those involved in the die casting industry. Publishes bi-monthly magazine.
Founded in 1957

18303 Precision Metalforming Association
6363 Oak Tree Blvd
Cleveland, OH 44131-2500

216-901-9667
FAX 216-901-9190
E-Mail: pma@pma.org
Home Page: www.pma.org
Social Media: *Facebook, Twitter, LinkedIn, YouTube*

Nels Leutwiler, Chairman
Dennis J Keat, First Vice Chairman
Bernie Rosselli Jr, Second Vice Chairman/Treasurer
William Gaskin, President

Members include producers of metal stampings, spinnings, washers and precision sheet metal fabrications as well as suppliers of equipment, materials and services.
1300 Members
Founded in 1913

18304 Resistance Welder Manufacturers
8669 NW 36 Street
Suite 130
Miami, FL 33166

305-443-9353
FAX 305-442-7451
E-Mail: rwma@aws.com
Home Page: www.aws.org/rwma/
Social Media: *Facebook, LinkedIn*

Mark Gramelspacher, Chairman
Ed Langhenry, Vice Chairman
Tom Snow, Vice Chairman

Strives to create widespread awareness and use of the various resistance welding processes and equipment, improve relations between individual manufacturers, foster higher ethical standards throughout the industry, develop industry standards to assist users of resistance welding equipment.
82 Members
Founded in 1935

18305 Sheet Metal Workers International Association
1750 New York Avenue, NW
6th Floor
Washington, DC 20006

Home Page: www.smwia.org

18306 Sheet Metal and Air Conditioning Contractors' National Association
4201 Lafayette Center Dr
Chantilly, VA 20151-1219

703-803-2980
FAX 703-803-3732
Home Page: www.smacna.org
Social Media: *Facebook, Twitter, LinkedIn, YouTube*

Vincent Sandusky, CEO

An international trade association representing 4,500 contibuting contractor firms in the sheet metal and air conditioning industry. Develops technical standards and manuals addressing all facets of the sheet metal and air conditioning industry.
1944 Members
Founded in 1943

18307 Silver Institute
1400 I Street, NW
Suite 550
Washington, DC 20005

202-835-0185
FAX 202-835-0155
E-Mail: info@silverinstitute.org
Home Page: www.silverinstitute.org

Fernando Alanis, President
Mitchell Krebs, VP
Thomas Angelos, Treasurer
Michael Dirienzo, Executive Director and Secretary
Mark Spurbeck, Assistant Treasurer

International association of miners, refiners, fabricators and wholesalers of silver and silver products.
Founded in 1971

18308 Silver Users Association
3930 walnut Street
Suite 210
Fairfax, VA 22030

703-934-0219
800-245-6999
FAX 703-359-7562
E-Mail: sas@silversmithing.com
Home Page: www.silverusersassociation.org

Mike Merolla, President
John Gannon, VP

Represents the interests of corporations that make, sell and distribute products and services in which silver is an essential part. SUA membership includes representatives from the photographic, electronic, silverware and jewelry industries; producers of semi-fabricated and industrial products; and, mirror manufacturers.
30 Members
Founded in 1947

18309 Society of American Silversmiths
PO Box 786
West Warwick, RI 02893

401-461-6840
FAX 401-461-0162
E-Mail: sas@silversmithing.com
Home Page: www.silversmithing.com

Jeffrey Herman, Founder/Executive Director

Founded to preserve the art and history of handcrafted holloware and flatware plus provide support, networking and greater access to the market for its artisan members. Artisans are silversmiths both practicing and retired who now or used to smith as a livelihood. Educates the public as to the aesthetic and investment value of this art form and demystifies silversmithing techniques through its literature and national exhibits.
240 Members
Founded in 1989

18310 Society of Manufacturing Engineers
Society of Manufacturing Engineers
One SME Drive
PO Box 930
Dearborn, MI 48121

313-425-3000
800-733-4763
FAX 313-425-3400
E-Mail: advertising@sme.org
Home Page: www.sme.org
Social Media: *Facebook, Twitter, LinkedIn, YouTube, Google+*

Wayne F. Frost, President
Debbie Holton, Managing Director
Mark Tomlinson, Executive Director
Greg Sheremet, Publisher
Jeannine Kunz, Managing Director

Supports all those involved in the metalworking industry, specifically machining, forming, inspection, assembly and processing operations. Publishes magazine.
70M Members
Founded in 1932

18311 Society of North American Goldsmiths
PO Box 1355
Eugene, OR 97440

541-345-5689
FAX 541-345-1123
Home Page: www.snagmetalsmith.org
Social Media: *Facebook, Twitter, LinkedIn*

Nicole Jaquard, President
Peggy Eng, Conferences
Becky Mcdonah, Secretary
Anne Havel, Treasurer
Renee Zettle-Sterling, Past President

Promotes a favorable and enriching environment in which contemporary metalsmiths practice their art. One aspect of this process is educating the public about the quality and rich diversity within the field of metalsmithing. Exhibitions, public forums, lectures, and published documents are our primary methods of reaching out to the public. SNAG sponsors workshops, seminars, audio-visual services and an annual conference.
Founded in 1969

18312 Specialty Steel Industry of North America

3050 K Street, N.W.
Washington, DC 20007

202-342-8630
800-982-0355
FAX 202-342-8451
Home Page: www.ssina.com

18313 Steel Deck Institute

PO Box 25
Fox River Grove, IL 60021-0025

847-458-4647
FAX 412-487-3326
E-Mail: steve@sdi.org
Home Page: www.sdi.org

Steven A Roehrig, Managing Director

Trade association providing uniform industry standards for the engineering, design, manufacture and field usage of steel decks.
29 Members
Founded in 1939

18314 Steel Door Institute

30200 Detroit Rd
Cleveland, OH 44145-1967

440-899-0010
FAX 440-892-1404
E-Mail: info@steeldoor.org
Home Page: www.steeldoor.org

Jeff Wherry, Executive Director

Producers of all metal frames and doors for commercial, industrial and residential construction.

18315 Steel Founders Society of America

780 McArdle Dr
Unit G
Crystal Lake, IL 60014-8155

815-455-8240
FAX 815-455-8241
E-Mail: monroe@sfsa.org
Home Page: www.sfsa.org
Social Media: *Facebook*

Raymond Monroe, Executive VP
Rick Boyd, Vice President of Technology
Kelly DiGiacomo, CPA, Director of Finance
Rob Blair, Manager of Information Services
David Poweleit, Director of Engineering

A technically oriented trade association serving the steel casting industry.
Founded in 1902

18316 Steel Manufacturers Association

1150 Connecticut Ave NW
Suite 715
Washington, DC 20036-4131

202-296-1515
FAX 202-296-2506
E-Mail: cipicchio@steelnet.org
Home Page: www.steelnet.org

Philip K. Bell, President
Eric J. Stuart, VP, Energy & Environment
Adam B. Parr, VP, Policy & Communications
Annie Stefanec, Member Services Coordinator

The majority of SMA members are minimills companies engaged in electric air furnace/continuous caster steel productions as well as hot and cold rolling of steel mill products. A growing number of integrated steel producers are also members.

18317 Steel Plate Fabricators Association

944 Donata Ct
Lake Zurich, IL 60047-5025

847-438-8265
FAX 847-438-8766
E-Mail: info@steeltank.com

Home Page: www.steeltank.com
Social Media: *Facebook, LinkedIn, Youtube*

Anne Kiefer, Director Of Administration
Wayne B. Geyer, President
J Michael Braden, VP
Jerry Stetzler, Treasurer

Protection of the environment and preservation of air and water quality are key concerns for the owners and operators of tanks, pressure vessels, specialty fabrications and piping systems.
Founded in 1916

18318 Steel Service Center Institute

701 West Mason Street
Springfield, OH 44128

217-528-4035
800-252-2516
FAX 847-485-3001
E-Mail: info@ssci.org
Home Page: www.ssoci.org
Social Media: *Facebook*

Thomas Conley, President
S Harbke, Director
570 Members
Founded in 1909

18319 Steel Shipping Container Institute

120 Hatton Drive
Severna Park, MD 21146-4400

410-544-0385
FAX 503-581-2221
E-Mail: snauman@industrialpackaging.org
Home Page: whysteeldrums.org
Social Media: *Facebook, Twitter, LinkedIn, YouTube, Google+*

Kyle R. Stavig, Chairman
Leonard H. Berenfield, Vice Chairman
John McQuaid, Senior Advisor

18320 Steel Tank Institute

944 Donata Ct
Lake Zurich, IL 60047-5025

847-438-8265
FAX 847-438-8766
E-Mail: info@steeltank.com
Home Page: www.steeltank.com
Social Media: *Facebook, LinkedIn, Youtube*

Anne Kiefer, Director Of Administration
Wayne B. Geyer, President
J Michael Braden, VP
Jerry Stetzler, Treasurer

Protection of the environment and preservation of air and water quality are key concerns for the owners and operators of tanks, pressure vessels, specialty fabrications and piping systems.
Founded in 1916

18321 Steel Tube Institute of North America

2516 Waukegan Road, Suite 172
Glenview, IL 60025

847-461-1701
FAX 847-660-7981
E-Mail: sti@apk.net
Home Page: www.steeltubeinstitute.org
Social Media: *Facebook, LinkedIn*

Timothy F Andrassy, Executive Director
Peggy Sams, Executive Assistant
Mary Gregel, Administrative Assistant
Dave Seeger, President

Members produce steel tubes and pipes from carbon, stainless or alloy steel, for applications ranging from large structural tubing to small redrawn tubing.
87 Members
Founded in 1930

18322 The Aluminum Association

1400 Crystal Drive
Suite 430
Arlington, VA 22202

703-358-2960
E-Mail: info@aluminum.org
Home Page: www.aluminum.org
Social Media: *Facebook, Twitter, LinkedIn*

Layle Smith, Chairman
Garney B. Scott, III, Vice Chairman
Michelle O'Neill, Second Vice Chair
Heidi Brock, President
Karen Bowden, Vice President, Administration

18323 The American Institute of Mining, Metallurgical and Petroleum Engineers

12999 East Adam Aircraft Circle
Englewood, CO 80112

303-325-5185
FAX 888-702-0049
E-Mail: aime@aimehq.org
Home Page: www.aimehq.org
Social Media: *Facebook, LinkedIn, YouTube, RSS*

Behrooz Fattahi, President
Garry W. Warren, President Elect
Nikhil C. Trivedi, President-Elect Designate
Dale E. Heinz, Past President
Drew Meyer, Trustee
Founded in 1871

18324 The Fabricators & Manufacturers

833 Featherstone Road
Rockford, IL 61107

815-399-8700
888-394-4362
Home Page: www.fmanet.org
Social Media: *Facebook, Twitter, LinkedIn, YouTube, Google+*

Edwin Stanley, Chair
Al Zelt, First Vice Chairman
Vivek Kumar Gupta, Second Vice Chairman
Lyle Menke, Secretary/ Treasurer
Carlos Borjas, Immediate Past Chair
Founded in 1970

18325 The Minerals, Metals, and Materials Society

184 Thorn Hill Road
Warrendale, PA 15086-7514

800-759-4867
FAX 724-776-3770
E-Mail: webmaster@tms.org
Home Page: www.tms.org
Social Media: *Facebook, LinkedIn, YouTube*

Hani Heneiny, President
Elizabeth A. Holm, Past President
Patrice E. A. Turchi, Vice President
James Robinson, Secretary/ Executive Director
Robert W. Hyers, Financial Planning Officer

18326 The Silver Users Association

3930 walnut Street
Suite 210
Fairfax, VA 22030

703-934-0219
800-245-6999
FAX 703-359-7562
E-Mail: sas@silversmithing.com
Home Page: www.silverusersassociation.org

Bill LeRoy, President
Mike Huber, Vice President
Jack Gannon, Immediate Past President
Bill Hamelin, Treasurer
John King, Secretary
Founded in 1947

18327 Tube and Pipe Association International

833 Featherstone Road
Rockford, IL 61107

815-399-8700
888-394-4362
FAX 815-484-7700
E-Mail: info@tpatube.org
Home Page: www.fmanet.org
Social Media: *Facebook, Twitter, LinkedIn, YouTube, Google+*

Gerald Shankel, President
Mike Hedges, VP Finance/CFO

TPA is an educational technology association serving the metal tube and pipe producing and fabricating industries. It is an affiliate association of the Fabricators and Manufacturers Association International.
Founded in 1970

18328 US Magnetic Materials Association

1120 East 23rd St.
Indianapolis, IN 46206

717-898-2294
Home Page: www.usmagneticmaterials.com

Ed Richardson, Chairman/ President/ Treasurer
Peter Dent, Vice President
Daniel McGroarty, Vice President
Rob Strahs, Secretary/ Vice President
Kerry LaPierre, Board Member

18329 US Pipe and Foundry Company

Two Chase Corporate Drive
Suite 200
Birmingham, AL 35244

866-347-7473
FAX 205-254-7494
E-Mail: info@uspipe.com
Home Page: www.uspipe.com
Social Media: *Facebook, Twitter, LinkedIn, YouTube, Google+*

Paul Ciolino, Chief Executive Officer
Bob Waggoner, SVP, Marketing and Sales
Norb Gross, VP, Supply Chain & Logistics
Brad Overstreet, Chief Financial Officer
Vinod Upadhyay, VP, Information Technology

Supports all those involved with the foundry industry. Publishes semi-monthly newsletter.
Founded in 1899

18330 Unified Abrasives Manufacturers Association

30200 Detroit Road
Cleveland, OH 44145-1967

440-899-0010
FAX 440-892-1404
E-Mail: contact@uama.org
Home Page: www.uama.org

Founded in 1999

18331 United States Cutting Tool Institute

1300 Sumner Ave
Cleveland, OH 44115-2851

216-241-7333
FAX 216-241-0105
E-Mail: uscti@uscti.com
Home Page: www.uscti.com

Charles M Stockinger, Secretary-Treasurer
Thomas Hagg, President
Steve Stokey, Senior Vice President
Philip Kurtz, Vice President

The premier trade association for all manufacturers of any type of cutting tools designed and sold to the metalworking, woodworking, and other industrial and consumer markets.
60 Members
Founded in 1988

18332 Welding Research Council

PO Box 201547
Shaker Heights, OH 44122

216-658-3847
FAX 216-658-3854
E-Mail: mprager@forengineers.org
Home Page: www.forengineers.org/wrc

Coordinates welding research.
Founded in 1935

18333 Welding Research Council, Inc.

PO Box 201547
Shaker Heights, OH 44122

216-658-3847
FAX 216-658-3854
E-Mail: mpc@forengineers.org
Home Page: www.forengineers.org

Martin Prager, PhD, Executive Director

An outgrowth of the ASTM-ASME Joint Committee on the effect of temperature on the properties of metals which was founded in 1925 to meet the apparent need for information on the subject in the construction of central power stations.
600 Members
Founded in 1966

18334 Wire Association International

71 Bradley Rd.
Suite 9
Madison, CT 06443

203-453-2777
FAX 203-453-8384
Home Page: www.wirenet.org
Social Media: *Facebook, Twitter, LinkedIn, YouTube*

Steven J Fetteroll, Executive Director
Phyilis Conon, Technical Information Director

Technical association serving the global wire and cable industry by providing educational materials, sponsoring trade shows and international technical conferences.
Founded in 1930

18335 Wiring Harness Manufacturers Association

15490 101st Ave. N.
Suite 100
Maple Grove, MN 55369

763-235-6467
FAX 763-235-6461
E-Mail: whma@whma.org
Home Page: www.whma.org

Andrew Larsen, Executive Director
Rick Bromn, Chairman
Donnie Hill, Vice Chairman/Secretary
Randy Olson, Treasurer
Lyle Fahning, Immediate Past Chair

To provide the cooperative forum through which members companies can solve both their specific problems and also help resolve industry problems.
4 Pages
Frequency: Quarterly
Circulation: 5,000

Newsletters

18336 Abrasive Users News Fax

Meadowlark Technical Services
144 Moore Rd
Butler, PA 16001-1312

724-282-6210
FAX 724-234-2376
E-Mail: aes@abrasiveengineering.com
Home Page: www.abrasivesmall.com

Ted Giese, Executive Director

Newsletter from the Abrasive Engineering Society.
Cost: $50.00
Circulation: 500
Founded in 1957

18337 American Iron and Steel Institute News

American Iron and Steel Institute
25 Massachusetts Ave., NW, Suite 800
Suite 705
Washington, DC 20001

202-452-7100
FAX 202-496-9702
E-Mail: steelnews@steel.org
Home Page: www.recycle-steel.org
Social Media: *Facebook, Twitter, Youtube*

Chip Foley, VP
Dave James, Marketing

Publication of the nonprofit trade organization representing approximately 65 percent of steel companies in the US, Canada and Mexico.
Circulation: 6000
Founded in 1855

18338 American Metal Market

Michael G Botta
825 7th Avenue
New York, NY 10019-6014

212-887-8510
FAX 212-887-8522
E-Mail: custserv@amm.com
Home Page: www.amm.com

Gloria T LaRue, Editor
Catalino Abrei, Owner

A daily newspaper of the metals industry covering news and pricing information for corporate, purchasing and manufacturing management.
Frequency: Daily
Circulation: 10,500

18339 Anodizing Newsline

Aluminum Anodizers Council (AAC)
1000 North Rand Road
Suite 214
Wauconda, IL 60084

847-526-2010
FAX 847-526-3993
E-Mail: mail@anodizing.org
Home Page: www.andoizing.org

Todd Hamilton, Chairman
Gregory T Rajsky CAE, President
Frequency: Quarterly
Circulation: 250

18340 Building & Architecture News

Copper Development Association
260 Madison Ave
New York, NY 10016-2403

212-251-7200
800-232-3282
FAX 212-251-7234
E-Mail: questions@cda.copper.org
Home Page: www.copper.org

Andrew G Kireta, President & CEO
Victoria Prather, Manager Communications
Michels Harold, VP Technaloy Services
Arnold W Ray, VP Environmental Division
Lorraine Herzing Mills, VP/Finance/Administration

A special-edition newsletter that focuses onthe use of copper and copper alloys in commercial and residential design and construction.
Frequency: Monthly

18341 CBSA Capsules

Copper and Brass Servicenter Association

994 Old Eagle School Road
Suite 1019
Wayne, PA 19087

610-971-4850
FAX 610-971-4859
Home Page: www.cbsa.copper-brass.org

Daniel Erck, President
Robert A Lewis, VP

Content includes information about conventions and seminars, programs and activities sponsored by the CBSA, general business/industry news, legislation information and government regulations.
Cost: $35.00
6 Pages
Frequency: Monthly
Circulation: 200
Founded in 1951

18342 Cables Industry Analyst

CRU International
6305 Ivy Ln
Suite 422
Greenbelt, MD 20770-6339

301-441-8997
FAX 301-441-4726
E-Mail: sales@crugroup.com
Home Page: www.crugroup.com

Florence Kauffman, VP

Written for managers and executives in the wire industry around the globe. Spotlights effective management techniques and superior administrative skills in the industry, profiles industry leaders, notes personnel movements and features general industry news.
Cost: $965.00
12 Pages
Frequency: Monthly
ISSN: 1368-4191

18343 Futuretech

John Wiley & Sons
111 River St
Hoboken, NJ 07030-5790

201-748-6000
800-825-7550
FAX 201-748-6088
E-Mail: info@wiley.com
Home Page: www.wiley.com

William J Pesce, CEO

Edited for product development and technology transfer engineers. Intelligence service that deals with new technologies with demonstrated commercial appeal still in the early stages of development in leading corporate, academic and university labs. Contains analysis and exploitation information.
Cost: $1500.00
24 Pages
Frequency: Monthly

18344 IMA Weekly Updates

1000 N Rand Rd
Suite 214
Wauconda, IL 60084-1180

847-526-2010
FAX 847-526-3993
E-Mail: info@intlmag.org
Home Page: www.intlmag.org

Greg Patzer, Executive Vice-President
Heidi Diederich, Administrative Coordinator

Develops international use and acceptance of magnesium metal and its alloys in all product forms. Members are organizations or individuals engaged in the production, manufacture or marketing of metallic magnesium or those supplying materials, equipment or consulting.
Cost: $90.00
Frequency: Weekly
Circulation: 5000

Founded in 1943
Printed in 2 colors on glossy stock

18345 IMPI Conference

International Precious Metals Institute
5101 N 12th Avenue
Suite C
Pensacola, FL 32504

850-476-1156
FAX 850-476-1548
E-Mail: mail@ipmi.org
Home Page: www.ipmi.org

Robert Ianniello, President

annual conference holds technical sessions, evening social receptions and a golf tournament. Also some product demonstrations.
400 Attendees
Frequency: Annual

18346 MBCEA Newsletter

Metal Building Contractors & Erectors Association
PO Box 499
Shawnee Mission, KS 66201

913-432-3800
FAX 913-432-3803
E-Mail: MBCEA@kc.rr.com
Home Page: www.mbcea.org

Angela M Cruse, Executive Director
Tim Seyler, President
Official newsletter of the Metal Building Contractors and Erectors Association (MBCEA), a trade association, formed in 1968 to provide programs and services, as well as to support the interests of metal building contractors and erectors.

18347 Metal Construction Association

MCA Newsletter
4799 West Lake Street
Glenview, IL 60025

847-375-4718
FAX 877-665-2234
E-Mail: mengle@amctec.com
Home Page: www.metalconstruction.org

Mark Engle, Executive VP
Julie Weldon, Chairman

Dedicated to promoting the use of metal in construction. Initative include market development, educational programs, issue and product awareness campaigns, and publication of technical guidelines and specifications manuals.
100 Pages
Frequency: Quartly
Founded in 1983

18348 Precious Metals News

International Precious Metals Institute
5101 N 12th Avenue
Suite C
Pensacola, FL 32504

850-476-1156
FAX 850-476-1548
E-Mail: mail@ipmi.org
Home Page: www.ipmi.org

Robert Ianniello, President
Cost: $30.00
Frequency: Quarterly
Circulation: 1000
Founded in 1976

18349 R&D Focus

International Lead Zinc Research Organization
2525 Meridian Parkway
PO Box 12036
Research Triangle Park, NC 27709-2036

919-361-4647
FAX 919-361-1957

E-Mail: rputnam@ilzro.org
Home Page: www.ilzro.org

Rob Putnam, Publisher
Doug Zabor, President

Reports on current research and development products in the metal industry.
Frequency: Quarterly
Circulation: 100
Founded in 1958

18350 Steel Industry Weekly Review

2 Uxbridge Road
Scarsdale, NY 10583-2725
Karl Keffer, Publisher

Offers industry news for steel workers.
Cost: $75.00
Frequency: Monthly

18351 Titanium

International Titanium Association
2655 W Midway Blvd
Suite 300
Broomfield, CO 80020-7187

303-404-2221
299-942-5371
FAX 303-404-9111
E-Mail: jsimpson@titanium.org
Home Page: www.titanium.org

Frequency: Quarterly
Circulation: 5000
Founded in 1960

18352 US Piper

US Pipe and Foundry Company
PO Box 10406
James Canada
Birmingham, AL 35202-406

205-547-7254
FAX 205-254-7494
Home Page: www.uspipe.com

George Bogs, Publisher
Ray Torok, President
Walter Knollenberg, VP

Articles deal with advantages of using new products.
16 Pages
Circulation: 9000
Founded in 1899

18353 WRC Bulletin

Welding Research Council
3 Park Avenue
27th Floor
New York, NY 10016-5902

212-591-7956
FAX 212-591-7183
E-Mail: bulletinsales@forengineers.org
Home Page: www.forengineers.org/wrc

CR Felmley Jr, Publisher

Offers information and updates for the welding community.
Cost: $300.00
Frequency: Monthly
Circulation: 900

Magazines & Journals

18354 AISE Steel Technology

Association of Iron & Steel Engineers
186 Thorn Hill Road
Warrendale, PA 15086

724-776-6040
FAX 724-776-1880
E-Mail: info@aist.org
Home Page: www.aise.org

Ronald Ashburn, Managing Director
Marge Baker, Editor

Gerry Kane, Sales Manager
Karen Hadley, Managing Editor
Janet McConnell, Production Editor

Information relating to the design and construction of equipment, machinery and plants for the production and processing of iron and steel.
Cost: $115.00
Frequency: Monthly
Circulation: 8000
Founded in 2004

18355 APMI International

105 College Road E
Princeton, NJ 08540-6622

609-452-7700
FAX 609-987-8523
E-Mail: apmi@mpif.org
Home Page: www.mpif.org

Christopher Adam, President
David L Schaefer, Director
Jim Adams, Manager

Monthly newsletter for all those involved the metal powder producing and consuming industries. Regular editorial features.
Founded in 1965

18356 Abrasives

PO Box 11
Byron Center, MI 49315

616-530-3220
FAX 616-530-6466
Home Page: www.abrasivesmagazine.com

Rose Trevino, Publisher/Editor

Covers research and development in the abrasives field including information about grinding and finishing applications.
Cost: $27.00
Frequency: Annual+
Circulation: 35000

18357 Advanced Materials & Processes

ASM International
9639 Kinsman Rd
Materials Park, OH 44073

440-338-5151
800-336-5152
FAX 440-338-4634
E-Mail: memberservices@asminternational.org
Home Page: www.asminternational.org
Social Media: *Facebook, Twitter, LinkedIn*

Joseph M Zion, Publisher
Joanne Miller, Managing Editor
Margaret Hunt, Editor-in-Chief
Jeane Deatherage, Administrator, Foundation Programs
Virginia Shirk, Foundation Executive Assistant

AM&P, the monthly technical magazine from ASM International, is designed to keep readers aware of leading-edge developments and trends in engineering materials - metals and alloys, engineering polymers, advanced ceramics, and composites - and the methods used to select, process, fabricate, test, and characterize them.
Frequency: Monthly
Circulation: 32M
Founded in 1977

18358 Aluminum Recycling & Processing for Energy Conservation and Sustainability

Aluminum Association

1525 Wilson Blvd
Suite 600
Arlington, VA 22209-2444

703-358-2960
FAX 703-358-2961
Home Page: www.aluminum.org

John Green, Editor
Heidi Biggs Brock, President
Nicholas Adams, Vice President, Business
Frequency: Yearly

18359 American Machinist

Penton Media
1166 Avenue of the Americas/10th Fl
New York, NY 10036

212-204-4200
FAX 216-696-6662
E-Mail: ameditor@penton.com
Home Page: www.penton.com

Jane Cooper, Marketing
Patricia L Smith, Executive Editor
Charles Bates, Senior Editor
Jim Benes, Associate Editor
Chris Meyer, Director, Corporate Communications

Magazine of the manufacturing business. Plays an integral role in educating and informing our readers of the significant developments of manufacturing technology. The intent of every issue is to describe new metalworking technologies that help the readership speed production, cut costs, and stay competitive in the global market.
Frequency: Monthly
Circulation: 80000
Founded in 1892
Printed in 4 colors

18360 American Metal Market

Reed Business Information
225 Park Avenue South
New York, NY 10003

646-274-6257
FAX 630-288-8686
Home Page: www.amm.com
Social Media: *Twitter, LinkedIn*

Lawrence S Reed, President
Gloria LaRue, Editor-in-Chief
Catalino Abrei, Owner

Thoroughly covers the metals industry, from production to distribution to recycling. American Metal Market is comprehensive, timely, reliable and invaluable daily newspaper for today's metal industry professionals.
Cost: $725.00
16 Pages
Frequency: Daily
Circulation: 10000
Printed in on glossy stock

18361 American Tool, Die & Stamping News

Eagle Publications
42060 Grand River Ave
Suite 103
Novi, MI 48375-2572

248-347-3487
800-783-3491
FAX 248-347-3492
E-Mail: info@ameritooldie.com
Home Page: www.ameritooldie.com

Arthur Brown, President
Joan Oakley, CEO

Applications, techniques, equipment and accessories of metal stamping, moldmaking, electric discharge machining; and new product information relating to the tool and die industry. Accepts advertising.
70 Pages
Circulation: 36000
ISSN: 0192-5709

Founded in 1971
Printed in 5 colors on glossy stock

18362 Anvil Magazine

PO Box 1810
Georgetown, CA 95634-1810

530-333-2142
800-942-6845
FAX 530-333-2906
Home Page: www.anvilmag.com

Rob Edwards, Publisher
Timothy Sebastian, Editor-in-Chief
Jody Edwards, Advertising Manager

World-wide coverage of the blacksmithing and farrier trades.
Cost: $29.50
Frequency: Monthly
Circulation: 5000
Founded in 1980

18363 Anvil's Ring

Artist-Blacksmiths' Association of North America
5821 Helias Drive
Jefferson, MO 65101-9316

573-395-3304
FAX 573-395-3201

Jim McCarty, Editor

Covers such topics as architectural iron, decorative design, primitive artifacts, advice, and Association news. Also discusses supply sources, formal blacksmithing instruction and employment opportunities.
Frequency: Monthly
Circulation: 4000

18364 Association of Iron and Steel Engineers Steel Technology

Three Gateway Center
Suite 1900
Pittsburgh, PA 15222-1004

412-281-6323
FAX 412-281-6216
E-Mail: rashburn@aist.org
Home Page: www.aise.org

Ronald E Ashburn, Executive Director
Frank E Farmer, Graphic Designer
Chris Brown, Graphic Designer
Stacy Varmecky, General Manager

AISE Steel Technology is the monthly technical journal of AISE. Highly authorative, it contains exclusive technical information relating to all phases of iron and steelmaking and finishing.
50+ Pages
Frequency: Monthly
Printed in 4 colors

18365 Automatic Machining Magazine

Screw Machine Publishing Company
1066 Gravel Rd
Suite 201
Webster, NY 14580-1769

585-787-0820
800-610-6950
FAX 585-787-0868
Home Page: www.automachmag.com

Wayne Wood, President

General industry news for professionals in the metal turning and cold forming fields.
Cost: $45.00
142 Pages
Frequency: Monthly
Circulation: 13000
Founded in 1941
Printed in 4 colors on glossy stock

18366 Casting World

Continental Communications

104 Florence Ln
Fairfield, CT 06824-2215

203-255-7752
FAX 203-377-7230

Wilburt W Troland, President

In-depth news on all aspects of ferrous and
non-ferrous casting.
Cost: $99.00
Frequency: Quarterly
Circulation: 35000

18367 Coil World

CJL Publishing
8 High Point
Cedar Grove, NJ 07009

973-571-7155
FAX 973-571-7102
E-Mail: philcola@optonline.net
Home Page: www.coilworld.com

Philip E Colaiacovo, Editor-in-Chief/Publisher
Carl Hoffman, Circulation Manager
Shawn A Savage, Creative Director
A L Colaiacovo, Production/Advertising Svcs
Manager

Offers articles on coil coating operations,
fabricatiors, service centers, OEMs which use
prepainted metals, new products, upcoming
events, industry news, personnel announcements and committee updates.
Frequency: Quarterly
Circulation: 10000

18368 Cutting Technology

Penton Media
1166 Avenue of the Americas/10th Fl
New York, NY 10036

212-204-4200
FAX 216-696-6662
E-Mail: information@penton.com
Home Page: www.penton.com

Jane Cooper, Marketing
Patricia Smith, Executive Editor
Gil Apelis, Manager
Chris Meyer, Director, Corporate
Communications

Covers the full gamut of information essential
to the success and productivity of those in-
volved in metalcutting manufacturing.
Cost: $35.00
Circulation: 40000
Founded in 1892
Printed in 4 colors

18369 Cutting Tool Engineering

CTE Publications
40 Skokie Blvd
Suite 450
Northbrook, IL 60062-1698

847-498-9100
866-207-1450
FAX 847-559-4444
E-Mail: alanr@jwr.com
Home Page: www.ctemag.com

John Wm Roberts, CEO
Alan Richter, CEO
Alan Rooks, Director

Cutting Tool Engineering serves manufacturing
plants in the metal working industries.
Cost: $65.00
72 Pages
Frequency: Monthly
Circulation: 34871
ISSN: 0011-4189
Founded in 1955
Printed in 4 colors on glossy stock

18370 Die Casting Engineer Magazine

North American Die Casting Association

241 Holbrook Drive
Wheeling, IL 60090

847-279-0001
FAX 847-279-0002
E-Mail: nadca@diecasting.org
Home Page: www.diecasting.org
Social Media: *Facebook, Twitter, LinkedIn,
youtube, Flickr*

Donna Peterson, Editor
Norwin A Merens, Managing Director

Provides members with the latest industry information, technology innovation and
state-of-the-art developments. Each issue presents readers with up to date die casting news
topics, opinion features of interest, and an editorial theme.
Cost: $150.00
1000 Pages
Frequency: Bi-Monthly
Founded in 1989

18371 Die Casting Management

C-K Publishing
PO Box 247
Wonder Lake, IL 60097-0247

815-728-0912
FAX 815-728-0912
Home Page: www.diecastmgmt.com

Rob Crofts, Publisher

The main content focuses on profitable management, and includes articles on finance, marketing, technology, engineering, industry
developments, and government legislation.
Frequency: Bi-Monthly
Circulation: 4500

18372 Ductile Iron News

Ductile Iron Society
15400 Pearl Rd
Suite 234
Strongsville, OH 44136-6017

440-665-3686
FAX 440-878-0070
E-Mail: jwood@ductile.org
Home Page: www.ductile.org

Scott Gledhill, President
Patricio Gill, VP
Pete Guidi, Treasurer

The main material focuses on the technical data
and applications, production statistics, and profiles of foundries.
Frequency: 3-4x/Year

18373 Engineering and Mining Journal

Mining Media
8751 E Hampden Ave
Suite C1
Denver, CO 80231-4930

303-751-5370
FAX 303-283-0641
E-Mail: info@mining-media.com
Home Page: www.e-mj.com

Peter Johnson, President
Steve Fiscor, Editor-in-Chief
Russ Carter, Managing Editor
Gina Tverdak, Assistant Editor

Serves the field of mining including explora-
tion, development, milling, smelting, refining
of metals and nonmetallics.
Cost: $79.00
Frequency: Monthly
Circulation: 10523
Founded in 1866
Printed in 4 colors on glossy stock

18374 Equip-Mart

116 N Camp Street
Seguin, TX 78155

830-303-3328
800-864-1155

FAX 830-372-3011
E-Mail: story@storycomm.com
Home Page: www.equip-mart.com

James Story, President
Tammy Reilly, Publisher
Kim Wiemann, Circulation Manager

Used metalworking equipment.
Cost: $50.00
Frequency: Monthly
Circulation: 36000
Founded in 1994

18375 Fabricator

Fabricators and Manufacturers Association
833 Featherstone Road
Rockford, IL 61107

815-227-8281
866-879-9144
FAX 815-484-7700
E-Mail: dand@thefabricator.com
Home Page: www.thefabricator.com

Dan Davis, Executive Editor

North America's leading magazine for the
metal forming and fabricating industry that de-
livers the news, technical articles, and case his-
tories that enable fabricators to do their jobs
more efficiently.
Cost: $75.00
Frequency: Monthly
Circulation: 55000
Founded in 1970
Printed in 4 colors on glossy stock

18376 Finishers' Management

Publication Management
4350 Di Paolo Center
Glenview, IL 60025-5212

847-699-1700
FAX 847-699-1703
Home Page: www.finishers-management.com

David Friedman, Publisher
Kristy Judycki, Editor

Our publishing highlights include new product
developments, equipment innovations, new
production methods and reviews of current in-
dustry financial trends in the finishing industry.
Cost: $35.00
50 Pages
Frequency: 10 per year
Circulation: 12000
ISSN: 0015-2358
Founded in 1957
Printed in 4 colors on glossy stock

18377 Forging

Penton Media
1166 Avenue of the Americas/10th Fl
New York, NY 10036

212-204-4200
FAX 216-696-6662
E-Mail: forgeditor@penton.com
Home Page: www.penton.com

Jane Cooper, Marketing
Robert Brooks, Editor
Melody Berendt, Circulation
Chris Meyer, Director, Corporate
Communications

Dedicated to providing industrial part forgers
with current market, product, process and
equipment news and trend analysis.
Cost: $31.50
62 Pages
Circulation: 5000
ISSN: 1054-1756
Founded in 1990
Printed in 4 colors on glossy stock

18378 Foundry Management & Technology

Penton Media

1166 Avenue of the Americas/10th Fl
New York, NY 10036

212-204-4200
FAX 216-696-6662
E-Mail: jwright@penton.com
Home Page: www.penton.com

Jane Cooper, Marketing
Dave Shanks, Publisher
Melody Berendt, Circulation Manager
Chris Meyer, Director, Corporate
Communications

Received by management, production, engineering, research and technical professionals in the foundry industry.
Cost: $54.00
70 Pages
Frequency: Monthly
ISSN: 0360-8999
Printed in 4 colors on glossy stock

18379 Gases & Welding Distributor
Penton Media
1166 Avenue of the Americas/10th Fl
New York, NY 10036

212-204-4200
FAX 216-696-6662
E-Mail: infomation@penton.com
Home Page: www.penton.com

Jane Cooper, Marketing
Patricia L Smith, Executive Editor
Charles Bates, Senior Editor
Jim Benes, Associate Editor
Melody Berendt, Circulation Manager

Marketing, management and technology magazine that aids distributors of welding supplies, industrial/medical/specialty gases, and safety products to sell more effectively to diverse markets.
Cost: $55.00
74 Pages
Frequency: six issues a year
ISSN: 1079-3909
Printed in 4 colors

18380 Heat Treating Progress
ASM International
9639 Kinsman Rd
Novelty, OH 44072-9603

440-338-5151
800-336-5152
FAX 440-338-4634
E-Mail:
MemberServiceCenter@asminternational.org
Home Page: www.asminternational.org

Stanley Theobald, Executive Director
Dean Peters, Editor-in-Chief
Lana Shapowal, Manager
Tina Long, Circulation Manager
Vin LeGendre, Publisher
Frequency: Monthly
Founded in 1913

18381 Industrial Paint & Powder Magazine
Reed Business Information
30 Technology Parkway South
Suite 100
Norcross, GA 30092

630-574-0825
800-424-3996
FAX 630-288-8781
E-Mail: webmaster@reedbusiness.com
Home Page: www.reedbusiness.com

Jeff Greisch, President

Coatings on manufacturing.
Cost: $55.00
Frequency: Monthly
Circulation: 38000
Founded in 1924

18382 Industrial Product Bulletin
Gordon Publications

301 Gibraltar Drive
#650
Morris Plains, NJ 07950-3400

973-292-5100
FAX 973-539-3476

Todd Baker, Publisher
Anita LaFond, Editor

Publication for executives and professionals in the process and metalworking industries.
Cost: $7.00
Circulation: 200,050

18383 Inspection Trends
American Welding Society
550 Nw 42nd Ave
Miami, FL 33126-5699

305-443-9353
800-443-9353
FAX 305-443-7559
E-Mail: info@aws.org
Home Page: www.aws.org

Ray Shook, President
Jeff Hufsey, Deputy Executive Director
Ray Shook, Executive Director
Kristin Campbell, Assistant Editor
Robert Pali, Treasurer

Our information assists inspection personnel through information and reports on new technology and equipment, tips on inspection techniques and interpretation, as well as by giving examples of practical methodology.
Cost: $50.00
Frequency: Quarterly
Circulation: 18000
Founded in 1989

18384 International Journal of Powder Metallurgy
APMI International
105 College Road E
Princeton, NJ 08540-6992

609-452-7700
FAX 609-987-8523
E-Mail: apmi@mpif.org
Home Page: www.apmiinterantional.org

Dr Alan Lawley, Editor-in-Chief
Peter K Johnson, Contributing Editor

Embraces a wide range of materials and processes including classical press and sinter PM and advanced particulate materials.
Cost: $230.00
Frequency: Bi-Monthly
ISSN: 0888-7462

18385 Iron & Steel Technology
Association for Iron & Steel Technolgy (AIST)
186 Thorn Hill Rd
Warrendale, PA 15086-7528

724-814-3000
FAX 724-814-3001
E-Mail: membersevices@aist.org
Home Page: www.aist.org
Social Media: *Facebook, Twitter, LinkedIn*

Karen D Hickey, Managing Editor
Amanda Blyth, Technical Editor
Janet McConnell, Production Editor

The official monthly publication of AIST, this is the premier technical journal for metallurgical, engineering, operating and maintenance personnel in the global iron and steel industry.
Cost: $20.00
Frequency: Monthly
Circulation: 9600

18386 Journal of Materials Engineering and Performance
9639 Kinsman Road
Materials Park, OH 44073-2

440-338-5151
FAX 440-338-4634
E-Mail: cust-srv@asminternational.org
Home Page: www.asm-intl.org

Ash Khare, President
Stanley Theobald, Managing Director

Peer-reviewed journal which publishes contributions on all aspects of materials selection, design, characterization, processing and performance testing. The scope includes all materials used in engineering applications: those that typically result in components for larger systems.
Cost: $1184.00
Circulation: 645
Founded in 1913

18387 Journal of Minerals, Metals & Materials Society
Minerals, Metals & Minerals Society
184 Thorn Hill Road
Warrendale, PA 15086-7511

724-776-9000
FAX 724-776-3770
E-Mail: webmaster@tms.org
Home Page: www.tms.org

Alexander R Scott, Executive Director
Robert Makowski, Communications Director

To promote the global science and engineering profession's concerned with minerals, metals and materials. Founded in 1871. Publishes a monthly magazine.
Cost: $20.00
Frequency: Monthly
Circulation: 10000
Founded in 1880

18388 Journal of Phase Equilibria
ASM International
9639 Kinsman Rd
Materials Park, OH 44072

440-338-5151
800-336-5152
FAX 440-338-4634
E-Mail: memberservices@asminternational.org
Home Page: www.asminternational.org
Social Media: *Facebook, Twitter, LinkedIn*

Jeane Deatherage, Administrator, Foundation Programs
Virginia Shirk, Foundation Executive Assistant

Peer-reviewed journal that contains basic and applied research results, evaluated phase diagrams, a survey of current literature, and comments or other material pertinent to the previous three areas. The aim is to provide a broad spectrum of information concerning phase equilibria for the materials community.
Cost: $1965.00
Frequency: Bimonthly
Circulation: 305

18389 Light Metal Age
Fellom Publishing Company
170 S Spruce Ave
Suite 120
S San Francisco, CA 94080-4557

650-588-8832
FAX 650-588-0901
E-Mail: lma@lightmetalage.com
Home Page: www.buffalowildwings.com

Ann Marie Fellom, Publisher
Cost: $45.00
Frequency: Monthly
Circulation: 5000
ISSN: 0024-3345

Founded in 1944
Printed in 4 colors on glossy stock

18390 Locator Services

Locator Online
315 S Patrick St
Suite 3
Alexandria, VA 22314-3532

703-836-9700
800-537-1446
FAX 703-836-7665
E-Mail: webmaster@locatoronline.com
Home Page: www.locatoronline.com

Terry Pitman, Publisher

Used metalworking equipment.
Frequency: Monthly
Circulation: 225000
Founded in 1969

18391 Machine Shop Guide

Worldwide Communications
401 Worthington Avenue
Harrison, NJ 07029-2039

973-497-7555
FAX 973-497-7556

Robert L Hatschek, Executive Editor

Information on manufacturing technology, new applications for manufacturing technology and new products.
Circulation: 102893

18392 Manufacturers Showcase

Heartland Communications Group
1003 Central Avenue
Po Box 1052
Fort Dodge, IA 50501

515-955-1600
800-203-9960
FAX 515-955-3753
E-Mail: ads@imtproduction.com
Home Page: www.imtgetsresults.com

Natalie Fevold, Operations Manager
Sandy Simonson, Sales Manager

A magazine for new metalworking machinery, tooling and supplies.
Frequency: Monthly

18393 Manufacturing Engineering

Society of Manufacturing Engineers
1 Sme Drive
PO Box 930
Dearborn, MI 48121

313-425-3000
800-733-4763
FAX 313-425-3400
E-Mail: advertising@sme.org
Home Page: www.sme.org

Mark Tomlinson, Executive Director
Greg Sheremet, Publisher
Gene Nelson, President

Serves metalworking industry machining, forming, inspection, assembly and processing operations.
Frequency: Monthly
Circulation: 111966
Founded in 1932

18394 Metal Architecture

Modern Trade Communications
7450 Skokie Blvd
Suite 200
Skokie, IL 60077-3374

847-674-2200
FAX 847-674-3676
Home Page: www.moderntrade.com

John Lawrence, President
Mark Wiebusch, Marketing & Operations
Shawn Zuver, Editorial & Production

Low-rise construction involving architects, engineers and specifiers.
Frequency: Monthly
Circulation: 29513

18395 Metal Center News

Reed Business Information
30 Technology Parkway South
Suite 100
Norcross, GA 30092

630-574-0825
800-424-3996
FAX 630-288-8781
E-Mail: webmaster@reedbusiness.com
Home Page: www.reedbusiness.com

Jeff Greisch, President

Reports on verious phases of metal center operations.

18396 Metal Finishing

Elsevier Science
655 Avenue of the Americas
New York, NY 10010-5107

212-633-3800
FAX 212-633-3850
E-Mail: PressOffice@elsevier.com
Home Page: www.elsevier.com

Young Suk Chi, President
Patti Ann Frost, Managing Editor
Susan Canalizo, Director, Manager
Greg Valero, Manager

Finishes and finishing of metal products.
Cost: $87.00
Frequency: Monthly
Circulation: 19824
Founded in 1903

18397 Metal Mecanica

Gardner Publications
901 poncedeleon blvd
sute 601
Coral Gables, FL 33134-3029

513-527-8977
800-950-8020
FAX 305-448-9942
E-Mail: trivas@metalmecanica.com
Home Page: www.metalmecanica.com

David Ash, President
Eduardo Tovar, Editor
Holgar Hilkinger, Circulation Manager
Alfredo Domador, Publisher
Circulation: 12157
Founded in 1905

18398 MetalForming

Precision Metalforming Association
6363 Oak Tree Blvd
Cleveland, OH 44131-2500

216-901-9667
FAX 216-901-9190
E-Mail: pma@pma.org
Home Page: www.metalformingmagazine.com

Brad Kuvin, Editor
Kathy DeLollis, Publisher
William Gaskin, President
Daniel Ellashek, VP
Lou Kren, Senior Editor

Edited for decision makers in the precision metal forming industry.
Cost: $59.95
100 Pages
Frequency: Monthly
Circulation: 60000
Founded in 1967
Printed in 4 colors on matte stock

18399 Metallurgical and Materials Transactions

Minerals, Metals & Materials Society

184 Thorn Hill Road
Warrendale, PA 15086-7528

724-776-9000
FAX 724-776-3770
E-Mail: webmaster@tms.org
Home Page: www.tms.org

Robert Makowski, Publishing Director
Cost: $1467.00
Frequency: 13 issues
ISSN: 1073-5615

18400 Metalsmith

Society of North American Goldsmiths
5009 Londonderry Drive
Tampa, FL 33647-1336

813-977-5326
FAX 813-977-8462
E-Mail: editor@snagmetalsmith.org
Home Page: www.snagmetalsmith.org

Suzanne Ramljak, Editor
Dana Singer, Executive Director
Ken Bova, President
Jean Savarese, Advertising Director
Ellen Laing, Program Manager

Information which explores new work in the jewelry, holloware, blacksmithing, and sculpture fields. Profiles of master metalsmiths are included.
Cost: $65.00
Circulation: 13,500
Founded in 1969

18401 Metalworking Digest

Reed Business Information
30 Technology Parkway South
Suite 100
Norcross, GA 30092

973-920-7000
800-424-3996
FAX 973-920-7531
E-Mail: webmaster@reedbusiness.com
Home Page: www.reedbusiness.com

Rich Stevancsecz, Editor
Joe May, Publisher
Cloin Ungaro, CEO/President
Steve Koppelman, Circulation Manager
R Reed, Owner
Frequency: Monthly
Circulation: 115000
Founded in 1969

18402 Metalworking Distributor

Penton Media
1166 Avenue of the Americas/10th Fl
New York, NY 10036

212-204-4200
FAX 216-696-6662
E-Mail: information@penton.com
Home Page: www.penton.com

Jane Cooper, Marketing
Thomas Grasson, Editor
Susan Cubranich, Production Manager
Chris Meyer, Director, Corporate Communications

Publication exclusively devoted to distributors and wholesales in the metalworking industry to help improve marketing, management, and technology knowledge as well as provide information on new markets.
Frequency: Quarterly
Circulation: 5,000
Printed in 4 colors

18403 Modern Applications News

Nelson Publishing
2500 Tamiami Trl N
Nokomis, FL 34275-3476

941-966-9521
FAX 941-966-2590
E-Mail: subscriptions@nelsonpub.com

Home Page: www.healthmgttech.com
Social Media: *Facebook*

A Verner Nelson, President

Information includes coverage of abrasives and grinding, automated handling and robotics, CAD/CAM, coatings and finishings, coolants, lubricants and filters, cutting tools, heat treating, ID marking, lasers, machining centers, and shop control software.
Frequency: Monthly
Circulation: 84000
Founded in 1967

18404 Modern Casting

American Foundrymen's Society
1695 N Penny Ln
Schaumburg, IL 60173-4555

847-824-0181
800-537-4237
FAX 847-824-7848
E-Mail: circ@afsinc.org
Home Page: www.afsinc.org

Jerry Call, Executive VP
Sandy Salisbury-Linton, Vice Chairman
Kyle Bauer, Editor
Barbara Jackowski, Circulation Manager
Alfred Spada, Editor-In-Chief

Designed to promote the technological advances in the industry.
Cost: $50.00
Frequency: Monthly
Circulation: 19000
Founded in 1896

18405 Modern Machine Shop

Gardner Publications
6915 Valley Ln
Cincinnati, OH 45244-3153

513-527-8800
800-950-8020
FAX 513-527-8801
E-Mail: mmsmkt@gardnerweb.com
Home Page: www.gardnerweb.com

Rick Kline Sr, CEO
Mark D Albert, Editor-in-Chief
Dianne Hight, Circulation Manager
John Campos, Manager
Brian Wertheimer, Account Manager

Reaches metalworking plants of all sizes - from small job shops to giant aerospace and automotive plants. It is edited for those involved in metalworking operations, particularly those performed on machine tools.
Cost: $89.00
Frequency: Monthly
Circulation: 107000
Founded in 1928
Mailing list available for rent: 106M names
Printed in 4 colors on glossy stock

18406 Occupational Hazards

Penton Media
1166 Avenue of the Americas/10th Fl
New York, NY 10036

212-204-4200
FAX 216-696-6662
E-Mail: information@penton.com
Home Page: www.penton.com

Jane Cooper, Marketing
Bob Marinez, Publisher
David B Nussbaum, CEO
Jennifer Daugherty, Communications Manager
Chris Meyer, Director, Corporate Communications

Analysis of qualified recipients who have indicated that they recommend, select and/or buy the safety equipment, fire protection and other occupational health products.
65 Pages
Frequency: Monthly
Circulation: 65777

ISSN: 0029-7909
Founded in 1892
Printed in 4 colors on glossy stock

18407 Ornamental and Miscellaneous Metals Fabricator

National Ornamental & Miscellaneous Metals Assn
532 Forest Parkway
Suite A
Forest Park, GA 30297-6137

404-363-4009
FAX 404-366-1852
E-Mail: nommainfo@nomma.org
Home Page: www.nomma.org

Curt Witter, CEO/President
Todd Daniel, Editor

Magazine published by National Ornamental and Miscellaneous Metals Association.
Cost: $30.00
Circulation: 10000
Founded in 1958

18408 Platt's Metals Week

McGraw Hill
3333 Walnut Street
Boulder, CO 80301

720-548-5000
800-752-8878
FAX 720-548-5701
E-Mail: metals@platts.com
Home Page: www.mcgraw-hill.com

Jackie Roche, Editor-in-Chief
Terry McGraw, CEO
Harry Sachinsis, President
Jackie Roche, Publisher

Extensive price listings in four currencies.
Frequency: Weekly

18409 Powder Coating

OSC Publishing
1300 E 66th Street
Minneapolis, MN 55423-2642

612-866-2242
FAX 612-866-1939

Richard R Cress, Publisher
Richard Link, Manager

Our information focuses on the application, pre-treatment, materials, materials handling, and curing processes. Also features case histories.
Cost: $95.00
Frequency: Monthly
Circulation: 23587

18410 Practical Welding Today

Fabricators and Manufacturers Association
833 Featherstone Road
Rockford, IL 61107-6302

815-399-8700
FAX 815-484-7700
E-Mail: info@fmanet.org
Home Page: www.fmanet.org

Gerald M Shankel, President/CEO
Michael Hedges, VP Finance/CFO
Scott Stevens, Publisher
Kim Clothier, Director of Circulation
Jim Gorzek, Marketing

Practical Welding Today is the only hands on, down-to-earth magazine with information that welders can use in the shop or out in the field. Published six times per year with more than 40,000 subcribers, it covers topics such as systems and equipment, safety, consumables, cutting and welding prep, welding inspection and more. In addition, Practical Welding Today has a regular lineup of application articles, welder profiles, product highlights and valuable buyers' guides.
Circulation: 40000
Printed in 4 colors on glossy stock

18411 Products Finishing

Gardner Publications
6915 Valley Ln
Cincinnati, OH 45244-3153

513-527-8800
FAX 513-527-8801
E-Mail: narnold@gardnerweb.com
Home Page: www.gardnerweb.com

Rick Kline Sr, CEO
Beverly Graves, Manager
John Campos, Manager
Brian Wertheimer, Account Manager
Eddie Kania, Sales Manager

Covers production, management, engineering, design, etc. in plants where metal and plastic products are eletroplated, anodized, painted, buffed, cleaned or otherwise finished.
Cost: $89.00
Frequency: Monthly
Circulation: 45552
Founded in 1928
Printed in 4 colors on glossy stock

18412 Projects in Metal

Village Press
2779 Aero Park Drive
PO Box 629
Traverse City, MI 49686-9101

231-463-3712
FAX 231-946-3289
E-Mail: villagepre@aol.com
Home Page:
www.members.aol.com/vpshop/pim/htm

Robert Goff, Publisher

In each issue you will find plans for valuable tools and accessories, and challenging hobby projects. Every project is complete in one issue.
Frequency: Bi-Monthly
Circulation: 15000

18413 Recycling Today

GIE Media
4012 Bridge Avenue
Cleveland, OH 44113-3320

216-961-4130
800-456-0707
FAX 216-961-0364
E-Mail: btaylor@gie.net
Home Page: www.recyclingtoday.com

Jim Keefe, Group Publisher
Brian Taylor, Editor
Richard Foster, CEO
Helen Duerr, Director of Production
Megan Ries, Advertising Coordinatior

Published for the secondary commodity processing/recycling market.
Cost: $30.00
Frequency: Monthly
Founded in 1980

18414 SCRAP

Institute of Scrap Recycling Industries
1615 L Street NW
Suite 600
Washington, DC 20036-5664

202-662-8500
FAX 202-626-0900
E-Mail: kentkiser@scrap.org
Home Page: www.scrap.org

Kent Kiser, Publisher
Marian Weiss, Production Manager
Rachel H Pollack, Editor-In-Chief
Valerie Hillyer, Circulation/Advertising Associate

A bi-monthly magazine that covers all aspects of the international scrap recycling industry, including market trends, business management, personnel issues, equipment and technology,

regulations and legislation, and more.
Cost: $36.00
16 Pages
Frequency: 6 per year
Circulation: 7400
ISSN: 1092-8618
Founded in 1928

18415 Secondary Marketing Executive
LDJ Corporation
P.O.Box 2180
Waterbury, CT 06722-2180

203-755-0158
800-325-6745
FAX 203-755-3480

John Florian, Editorial Director
Linda Herrmann, Account Executive

Delivers news, analysis and how-to advice to people involved in the buying and selling of mortgage loans and servicing rights nationwide.
Cost: $48.00
44 Pages
Frequency: Monthly
Circulation: 21,000
Founded in 1986

18416 Shop Owner
Penton Media
1166 Avenue of the Americas/10th Fl
New York, NY 10036

212-204-4200
FAX 216-696-6662
E-Mail: information@penton.com
Home Page: www.penton.com

Jane Cooper, Marketing
Thomas J Grasson, Editorial Director
Charles Bates, Senior Editor
Melody Berendt, Circulation Manager
Janet Marioneaux, Administrative Assistant

Digest-sized publication covering information essential to the success of the small to medium manufacturing shop.
Frequency: Quarterly
Circulation: 120000
Founded in 1998
Printed in 4 colors

18417 Stamping Journal
Fabricators and Manufacturers Association
833 Featherstone Road
Rockford, IL 61107-6302

815-399-8700
FAX 815-484-7700
E-Mail: info@fmanet.org
Home Page: www.fmanet.org

Gerald Shankel, President/CEO
Michael Hedges, CFO
Scot Stevens, Publisher
Jim Gorzek, Sales Manager
Kim Clothier, Circulation Manager

Stamping Journal, the only North American magazine devoted exclusively to metal stamping, has been delivering the industry's latest techniques, news and ideas to subscribers worldwide for 13 years. Published six times per year, with more than 35,000 subscribers, Stamping Journal focuses on metal stamping technology including, tool and die, material handling, coil processing, stamping presses, press feeding, quick die change and more.
Cost: $65.00
Frequency: Monthly
Circulation: 35000
Founded in 1970
Printed in 4 colors on glossy stock

18418 Tooling & Production
NP Communications, LLC

2500 Tamiami Trail N
Nokomis, FL 34275

941-966-9521
FAX 941-966-2590
E-Mail: vnelson@nelsonpub.com
Home Page: www.toolingandproduction.com

Vern Nelson, Publisher/Editorial Director
Bob West, Managing Editor/Associate Publisher

Provides information to metalworking professionals working in large, high-throughput plants. Original editorial delivers technology, products, and processes applying to aerospace, automotive, medical equipment, mold, tool & die manufacturing, and much more.
100 Pages
Frequency: Monthly
Circulation: 70000
ISSN: 0040-9243
Founded in 1934
Printed in 4 colors on glossy stock

18419 Tube & Pipe Journal
Fabricators and Manufacturers Association
833 Featherstone Road
Rockford, IL 61107-6302

815-998-8700
FAX 815-484-7701
E-Mail: info@fmanet.org
Home Page: www.fmanet.org

Gerald Shankel, President/CEO
Michael Hedges, CFO

The Tube and Pipe Journal is North America's only magazine devoted exclusively to metal tube and pipe manufacturing. Published 8 times per year and with more than 30,000 subscribers, TPJ covers topics such as tube producing, bending and forming, cutting and sawing, welding, tooling, coil and material handling, and more. TPJ also provides expanded coverage of hydroforming technology in the Hydroforming Journal, a separate supplement published four time per year alongside TPJ.
Cost: $200.00
Circulation: 30000
Founded in 1970
Printed in 4 colors on glossy stock

18420 US Glass, Metal & Glazing
Key Communications
PO Box 569
Garrisonville, VA 22463

540-577-7174
FAX 540-720-5687
E-Mail: info@glass.com
Home Page: www.glass.com

Debra Levy, Publisher
Ellen Giard Chilcoat, Editor
Penny Stacey, Advertising Coordinator

Serves manufactures/fabricators, contract glaziers, distributors and wholesalers, retailors/dealers of glass/metal and or glass/metal products and other allied to the field.
Frequency: Monthly
Circulation: 15000
ISSN: 0041-7661
Founded in 1995
Printed in 4 colors on glossy stock

18421 Welding Design & Fabrication
Penton Media
1166 Avenue of the Americas/10th Fl
New York, NY 10036

212-204-4200
FAX 216-696-6662
E-Mail: information@penton.com
Home Page: www.penton.com

Jane Cooper, Marketing
Dean Peters, Editor
David Nussbaum, CEO

Chris Meyer, Director, Corporate Communications

Reaches designers, engineers, managers, superviisors, and buyers in plants and field sites in the US and Canada who conduct welding and fabricating operations. Reports on processes and equipment, materials, safety, testing and inspection in the manufacturing of fabricated metal products, structural projects and equipment maintenance.
Frequency: Monthly
Circulation: 40000
Founded in 1892
Printed in 4 colors

18422 Welding Innovation
James F Lincoln Arc Welding Foundation
22801 Saint Clair Ave
Cleveland, OH 44117-2524

216-481-4300
FAX 216-383-8220
Home Page: www.jflf.org/

Roy Morrow, President
Richard D Seif, Chairman
Vicki Wilson, Administrative Assistant
Dave Manning, Executive Director

Informative articles related to welding steel structures such as bridges and buildings, as well as notices of related conferences.
Circulation: 40000
Founded in 1936

18423 Welding Journal
American Welding Society
550 Nw 42nd Ave
Miami, FL 33126-5699

305-443-9353
800-443-9353
FAX 305-443-7559
E-Mail: info@aws.org
Home Page: www.aws.org

Ray Shook, President
Jefferey Weber, Publisher
Cecilia Barbier, Senior Coordinator Market
Robert Pali, Treasurer

Our feature articles include new product listings, book reviews and the application of new operating procedures.
Frequency: Monthly
Circulation: 46000
Founded in 1919

18424 Wire Rope News & Sling Technology
Wire Rope News
PO Box 871
Clark, NJ 07066-871

908-486-3221
FAX 732-396-4215
E-Mail: vsent@aol.com
Home Page: www.wireropenews.com

Edward J Bluvias, Publisher
Conrad Miller, Editor

Wire Rope News & Sling Technology is edited for manufacturers and distributors of wire rope, chain, cordage, related hardware, and sling fabricators. Content includes technical articles, news, and reports describing the manufacture and use of wire rope in marine, construction, mining, aircraft and offshore drilling operations. Cordage, slings, chain and fittings are also covered. Editorial content contains articles about fabricating companies, new products and people in the news.
Cost: $20.00
Circulation: 4400
ISSN: 0740-1809
Founded in 1979
Printed in 4 colors on glossy stock

Trade Shows

18425 AFS/CMI Advanced Foundry Operations Conference
American Foundrymen's Society
1695 N Penny Ln
Schaumburg, IL 60173-4555

847-824-0181
800-537-4237
FAX 847-824-7848
Home Page: www.afsinc.org

Frequency: March

18426 AISTech Conference & Exposition
Association for Iron & Steel Technology
186 Thorn Hill Rd
Warrendale, PA 15086-7528

724-814-3000
FAX 724-814-3001
E-Mail: memberservices@aist.org
Home Page: www.aist.org
Social Media: *Facebook, Twitter, LinkedIn*

Ronald E Ashburn, Executive Director
William A Albaugh, Technology Programs Manager
Joann Cantrell, Publications Manager/Editor
Mark Didiano, Finance & Administration Manager
Stacy Varmecky, Membership Communications Manager

Featuring technologies from across the globe, allowing steel producers to compete in today's global market. Submit technical papers for presentation at the event. 300 exhibitors. Registration starts at $425.
4500 Attendees
Frequency: Annual/Spring

18427 ASM Heat Treating Society Conference & Exposition
ASM International
9639 Kinsman Road
Materials Park, OH 44073

440-385-5151
800-336-5152
FAX 440-338-4634
E-Mail: pamela.kleinman@asminternational.org
Home Page: www.asminternational.org
Social Media: *Facebook, Twitter, LinkedIn*

Pamela Kleinma, Senior Manager, Events
Kellye Thomas, Exposition Account Manager
Jeane Deatherage, Administrator, Foundation Programs
Virginia Shirk, Foundation Executive Assistant

Conference and exhibits of heat treating equipment and supplies plus information of interest to metallurgists, manufacturing, research and design technical professionals. 300 exhibitors.
3500 Attendees
Frequency: September, Bi-Annual
Founded in 1974

18428 ASM Materials Science & Technology (MS&T)
ASM International
9639 Kinsman Road
Materials Park, OH 44073-0002

440-338-5151
800-336-5152
FAX 440-338-4634
E-Mail: pamela.kleinman@asminternational.org
Home Page: www.asminternational.org
Social Media: *Facebook, Twitter, LinkedIn*

Pamela Kleinman, Senior Manager, Events
Kelly Thomas, Exposition Account Manager

Jeane Deatherage, Administrator, Foundation Programs
Virginia Shirk, Foundation Executive Assistant

Annual event focusing on testing, analysis, characterization and research of materials such as engineered materials, high performance metals, powdered metals, metal forming, surface modification, welding and joining. 350 exhibitors.
4,000 Attendees
Frequency: Annual/October
Founded in 2005

18429 Advanced Productivity Conference and Expo- Cleveland
Society of Manufacturing Engineers
1 SME Drive
PO Box 930
Dearborn, MI 48121

313-425-3000
800-733-4763
FAX 313-425-3400
E-Mail: advertising@sme.org
Home Page: www.sme.org

Mark Tomlinson, Executive Director
Greg Sheremet, Publisher

200 Exhibits of equipment, supplies and services for the tool and manufacturing engineering fields.
13800 Attendees
Frequency: Biennial
Founded in 1984

18430 AeroMat Conference and Exposition
ASM International
9639 Kinsman Road
Materials Park, OH 44073-0002

440-385-5151
800-336-5152
FAX 440-338-4634
E-Mail: kim.schaefer@asminternational.org
Home Page: www.asminternational.org
Social Media: *Facebook, Twitter, LinkedIn*

Kim Schaefer, Event Manager
Kelly Thomas, Exposition Account Manager
Jeane Deatherage, Administrator, Foundation Programs
Virginia Shirk, Foundation Executive Assistant

Conference for Aerospace Meterials Engineers, Structural Engineers and Designers. The annual event focuses on affordable structures and low-cost manufacturing, titanium alloy technology, advanced intermetallics and refractory metal alloys, materials and processes for space applications, aging systems, high strength steel, NDT evaluation, light alloy technology, welding and joining, and engineering technology. 150 exhibitors.
1500 Attendees
Frequency: Annual/June
Founded in 1984

18431 American Foundrymen's Society Castings Congress and Cast Expo
505 State St
Des Plaines, IL 60016-2267

847-824-0181
FAX 847-824-7845

Kristy Glass, Show Manager

300 booths including technical papers and panel sessions for the metal casting industry.
12000 Attendees
Frequency: Annual

18432 American Society Engineers: Design International
Systems and Design Group

3 Park Avenue
Floor 27
New York, NY 10016-5902

212-903-4160

Fred Goldfarb, Program Manager
Virgil Carter, CEO

150 booths.
2.5M Attendees
Frequency: August

18433 American Welding Show
American Welding Society
8669 Doral Boulevard, Suite 130
Doral, FL 33166

305-443-9353
800-443-9353
FAX 305-443-7559
Home Page: www.aws.org

Ray Shook, Executive Director
Jefferey Weber, Publisher
Amy Nathan, Public Relations Manager

350 booths of welding and allied industries held in conjunction with metal form.
Frequency: Annual

18434 American Zinc Association
1112 16th Street NW
Suite 240
Washington, DC 20036-4818

202-478-8200
FAX 202-835-0155
E-Mail: info@zinc.org
Home Page: www.zinc.org

George Vary, Executive Director
David Adkins, Secretary
Frequency: February

18435 Annual International Titanium Conference
International Titanium Association
1871 Folsom Street
Suite 200
Boulder, CO 80302-5714

303-443-7515
FAX 303-443-4406
Home Page: www.titanium.org

Amy Fitzgerald, Manager
800 Attendees
Frequency: October
Founded in 1984

18436 Artist-Blacksmiths Association of North America
PO Box 206
Washington, MO 63090

636-390-2133
FAX 423-913-1023
Home Page: www.abasna.otg

Marcus Vickery, Conference Coordinator

Meeting and exhibitions, workshops, demonstrations and artistic metalwork for the professional and amateur blacksmith.

18437 Association of Industrial Metallizers, Coaters and Laminators Conference
201 Springs Street
Fort Mill, SC 29708

803-802-7820
FAX 803-802-7821
E-Mail: aimcal@aimcal.org
Home Page: www.aimcal.org

Craig Sheppard, Executive Director
Erin Davis, Communications Manager

Displays relating to coaters and laminators, metallizers and producers of metallized film

and or paper on continuous rolls, suppliers of plastic films, papers and adhesives.
Frequency: Annual
Founded in 1970

18438 Cast Expo
Cast Metals Institute
1695 N Penny Ln
Schaumburg, IL 60173-4555

847-824-0181
800-537-4237
FAX 847-824-7848
Home Page: www.castmetals.com
Social Media: *Facebook, Twitter, LinkedIn*

CastExpo attracts thousands of decision-making metalcasters from around the world, all of whom are looking for the latest advancements in equipment, technology and services to use in their own facilities.
Frequency: May

18439 Electrical Manufacturing & Coil Winding Expo
PO Box 278
Imperial Beach, CA 91933-0278

619-435-3629
FAX 619-435-3639
E-Mail: cthurman@earthlink.net
Home Page: www.emcwa.org

Richard Duke, President
Charles Thurman, Executive Director
Don Stankiewicz, Vice President

An annual technical conference and exhibition related to the manufacture of electrical products. Exhibitors include suppliers of materials and process equipment used in manufacturing electric motors, trnasformers, and other electrical devices. 150 exhibitors, free admission.
2000 Attendees

18440 FABTECH International
Fabricators and Manufacturers Association
833 Featherstone Road
Rockford, IL 61107-6302

815-399-8700
FAX 815-399-7279
E-Mail: info@fmametalfab.org
Home Page: www.fmametalfab.org

Mark Hoper, Director

Metal forming, fabricating, finishing and welding event that gives all the tools neded to improve productivity, increase profits and find new ways to survive in today's competitive business environment.
25000 Attendees
Frequency: Annual/November

18441 Furnaces North America
Metal Treating Institute
504 Osceola Ave
Jacksonville Beach, FL 32250

904-249-0448
FAX 904-249-0459
Home Page: www.heattreat.net

Tom Morrison, Show Manager

North America's Premier Heat Treat Only Event, Furnaces North America 2012, will be held October 1-3, 2012 in Nashville, TN.
340 Members
1200 Attendees
Frequency: September
Founded in 1933

18442 International Anodizing Conference & Exposition
Aluminum Anodizers Council (AAC)

1000 North Rand Road
Suite 214
Wauconda, IL 60084

847-526-2010
FAX 847-526-3993
E-Mail: mail@anodizing.org
Home Page: www.andoizing.org

Terry D Snell, Chairman
Todd Hamilton, Vice Chairman
Gregory T Rajsky CAE, President
120 Attendees
Frequency: Annual

18443 International Symposium for Testing and Failure Analysis
ASM International
9639 Kinsman Road
Materials Park, OH 44073-0002

440-385-5151
FAX 440-338-4634

Jan DiRosa, Expositions Sales

Annual event focusing on microelectronic and electronic device failure analysis, techniques, EOS/ESD testing and discretes aimed at failure analysis engineers and managers, technicians and new failure analysis engineers. Santa Clara Convention Center, Santa Clara, California.
1,100 Attendees
Frequency: November

18444 International Thermal Spray Conference & Exposition
ASM International
9639 Kinsman Road
Materials Park, OH 44073

440-338-5151
800-336-5152
FAX 440-338-4634
E-Mail: natalie.nemec@asminternational.org
Home Page: www.asminternational.org
Social Media: *Facebook, Twitter, LinkedIn*

Natalie Neme, Event Manager
Kelly Thomas, Exposition Account Manager
Jeane Deatherage, Administrator, Foundation Programs
Virginia Shirk, Foundation Executive Assistant

Global annual event attracting professional interested in thermal spray technology focusing on advances in HVOF, plasma and detonation gun, flame spray and wire arc spray processes, performance of coatings, and future trends. 150 exhibitors.
1000 Attendees
Frequency: Annual/May

18445 Iron & Steel Exposition
Association of Iron & Steel Engineers
3 Gateway Center
Suite 1900
Pittsburgh, PA 15222-1000

412-281-6323
FAX 412-281-4657
Home Page: www.aise.org

Ronald E Ashiurn, Managing Director
Chris Brown, Graphic Designer
Stacy Varmecky, General Manager

Includes technical sessions and exhibits of equipment, supplies and services for the metals producing industry.
25M Attendees

18446 MBCEA Annual Conference
Metal Building Contractors & Erectors Association
PO Box 499
Shawnee Mission, KS 66201

913-432-3800
FAX 913-432-3803

E-Mail: MBCEA@kc.rr.com
Home Page: www.mbcea.org

Angela M Cruse, Executive Director
Tim Seyler, President

Annual conference with the mission to support the professional advancement of metal building contractors, erectors and our industry.
Frequency: February

18447 METALFORM
Precision Metalforming Association
6363 Oak Tree Boulevard
Independence, OH 44131

216-901-8800
FAX 216-901-9190
E-Mail: rjudson@pma.org
Home Page: www.metalform.com

Amy Primiano, Director Expositions
William Gaskin, President

A regional networking and educational event that brings buyers and sellers from metal stamping and fabricating markets together in a dynamic and interactive environment.
5,000 Attendees
Frequency: March

18448 Metalworking Machine Tool Expo
Marketing International Corporation
200 N Glebe Road
Suite 900
Arlington, VA 22203-3728

703-527-8000
FAX 703-527-8006

Annual show of 100 machine tools suppliers.
8000 Attendees

18449 NFFS Summit Conference
Non-Ferrous Founders' Society
1480 Renaissance Drive
Suite 310
Park Ridge, IL 60068

847-299-0950
FAX 847-299-3598
E-Mail: staff@nffs.org
Home Page: www.nffs.org

Frequency: February

18450 National Ornamental and Miscellaneous Metals Association
532 Forest Parkway
Suite A
Forest Park, GA 30297-6137

404-363-4009
FAX 888-279-7994
E-Mail: nommainfo@nomma.org
Home Page: www.nomma.org

Barbara Cook, Executive Director
Todd Daniel, Editor
Cyndi Smith, Office Manager
Martha Pennington, Meetings/Exposition Manager

This annual convention and trade show — METALfab — is for all those involved in the ornamental and metallury industries.
900 Attendees
Founded in 1958

18451 PowderMet
APMI International
105 College Road E
Princeton, NJ 08540-6992

609-452-7700
FAX 609-987-8523
E-Mail: info@mpif.org
Home Page: www.mpif.org

Nicholas T Mares, President
Michael E Lutheran, Director
C James Trombino CAE, Director

An annual international conference serving the powder metallurgy industry with a standalone exhibit featuring industry service providers and equipment suppliers.
1000 Attendees
Frequency: Annual

18452 SMACNA Annual Convention
Sheet Metal and Air Conditioning
Contractor's Natl
4201 Lafayette Center Drive
Chantilly, VA 20151-1219

703-803-2980
FAX 703-803-3732
E-Mail: info@smacna.org
Home Page: www.smacna.org

Vincent R Sandusky, CEO

Sheet metal and air conditioning contractors explore the newest ideas, technologies, and trends in the construction industry.
Frequency: October

18453 TMS Annual Meeting Exhibition
Minerals, Metals & Materials Society
184 Thorn Hill Road
Warrendale, PA 15086

724-776-9000
FAX 724-776-3770
E-Mail: webmaster@tms.org
Home Page: www.tms.org

Cindy Wilson, Show Manager
Alexander Scott, Executive Director

International metals and materials exhibition. Production, processing, engineering and research. Held in Charlotte, North Carolina.
3,500 Attendees
Frequency: March

18454 WESTEC-Advanced Productivity Expo
Society of Manufacturing Engineers
1 SME Drive
PO Box 930
Dearborn, MI 48121

313-425-3000
800-733-4763
FAX 313-425-3400
E-Mail: advertising@sme.org
Home Page: www.sme.org

Mark Tomlinson, Executive Director
Greg Sheremet, Publisher

600 booths displaying machine tools and metalworking products and services.
40M Attendees
Frequency: Annual

Directories & Databases

18455 Aluminum Association Aluminum Standards & Data
Aluminum Association
900 19th Street NW
Washington, DC 20006-2105

202-862-5100

Contains the nominal composition and composition limits, typical mechanical and physical properties and tensile properties limits for US wrought aluminum alloys. Updated periodically.

18456 Aluminum Extruders Council Buyer's Guide
1000 North Rand Road
Suite 214
Wauconda, IL 60084

847-526-2010
FAX 847-526-3993

E-Mail: mail@aec.org
Home Page: www.aec.org
Social Media: *LinkedIn*

Thomas J Schabel, Chairman
Duncan Crowdis, Vice Chairman
Rand A Baldwin CAE, President
135 Members
Frequency: Annual
Founded in 1950

18457 DRI Steel Forecast
DRI/McGraw-Hill
24 Hartwell Ave
Lexington, MA 02421-3103

781-860-6060
FAX 781-860-6002
E-Mail: support@construction.com
Home Page: www.construction.com

Walt Arvin, President

This comprehensive database offers over 500 quarterly and annual forecasts on production, shipment, and consumption of raw steel and steel products in the United States.

18458 Directory Iron and Steel Plants
Association for Iron & Steel Technology
186 Thorn Hill Rd
Warrendale, PA 15086-7528

724-814-3000
FAX 724-814-3001
E-Mail: memberservices@aist.org
Home Page: www.aist.org
Social Media: *Facebook, Twitter, LinkedIn*

Ronald E Ashburn, Executive Director
William A Albaugh, Technology Programs
Manager
Joann Cantrell, Publications Manager/Editor
Mark Didiano, Finance & Administration
Manager
Stacy Varmecky, Membership Communications
Manager

The Directory lists more than 2,000 companies and 17,500 individuals. Featuring data on essentially ever steel producer in the USA, Canada and Mexico, including names and titles of executive, enginnering, maintenance and operating personnel. Also includes an alpha listing of all major equipment, product and service providers to the international iron and steel industry, and a listing of associations affiliated with the industry, with complete geo-indexing. Softbound book with CD.
Cost: $95.00
Frequency: M-$95/NM-$135
ISBN: 1-935117-00-1

18459 Dun's Industrial Guide: Metalworking Directory
Dun & Bradstreet Information Service
3 Sylvan Way
Parsippany, NJ 07054-3822

973-605-6000
800-526-0651
FAX 973-605-9630

Over 78,000 original equipment manufacturers, metal distributors, and machine tools/metalworking machinery distributors.
Cost: $775.00
Frequency: Annual

18460 EDM Today Yearbook
EDM Publications
230 W Parkway
Suite 3-1
Pompton Plains, NJ 07444-1065

973-831-1334
FAX 973-831-1195

Jack Sebzda, Editor
Frequency: Annual

18461 Economic Handbook of the Machine Tool Industry
AMT - The Association for Manufacturing
Technology
7901 Westpark Dr
Mc Lean, VA 22102-4206

703-893-2900
FAX 703-893-1151
E-Mail: amt@amtonline.org
Home Page: www.amtonline.org

Bob Simpson, President

Complete statistics for the US machine tool industry, including exports and imports.
Cost: $295.00
Frequency: Annual
Printed in one color on matte stock

18462 Equip-Mart
116 N Camp Street
Seguin, TX 78155

830-303-3328
800-864-1155
FAX 830-372-3011
Home Page: www.equip-mart.com

Directory of available used metalworking equipment.
Frequency: Weekly

18463 Foundry Management & Technology: Where to Buy Directory Issue
Penton Publishing Company
1166 Avenue of the Americas/10th Fl
New York, NY 10036

212-204-4200
FAX 216-696-1752
E-Mail: information@penton.com
Home Page: www.penton.com

Dean Peters, Editor
Chris Meyer, Director, Corporate
Communications

Listing of about 1,700 manufacturers of foundry products.
Cost: $15.00
Frequency: Annual, September
Circulation: 22,000

18464 Fundamentals of Steel Product Physical Metallurgy
Association for Iron & Steel Technology
(AIST)
186 Thorn Hill Road
Warrendale, PA 15086-7528

724-814-3000
FAX 724-814-3001
E-Mail: memberservices@aist.org
Home Page: www.steellibrary.com

Bruno C De Cooman, Author
John G Speer, Author

This directory is an introduction to steel products for industry professionals. With its readily accessible style, the book allows the reader to easily grasp important scientific topics that play an essential role in current steel research, product development and applications. ISBN: 978-1-935117-16-2
Cost: $110.00
Frequency: Annual

18465 Industrial Laser Review: Buyers' Guide of Companies & Products
PennWell Publishing Company
10 Tara Boulevard
5th Floor
Nashua, NH 03062-2800

603-891-0123
FAX 603-891-0574

Home Page:
www.industrial-lasers.com/index.html

David Belforte, Editor
Frequency: Annual July

18466 Industrial Machine Trader
Heartland Industrial Group
1003 Central Avenue
PO Box 1415
Fort Dodge, IA 50501

515-955-1600
800-247-2000
FAX 515-955-3753
E-Mail: igproduction@industrialgroup.com
Home Page: www.industrialgroup.com
Social Media: Facebook, Twitter, LinkedIn

Virginia Rodriguez, Publisher

Printed directory of available used metalworking equipment.
150+ Members
Frequency: Weekly
Founded in 1966

18467 International Lead and Zinc
WEFA Group
800 Baldwin Tower Boulevard
Eddystone, PA 19022-1368

610-490-4000
FAX 610-490-2770
E-Mail: info@wefa.com
Home Page: www.wefa.com

This database contains quarterly and annual time series on lead and zinc.

18468 International Powder Metallurgy Directory
Metal Powder Industries Federation
105 College Rd East
Princeton, NJ 08540-6692

609-452-7700
FAX 609-987-8523
E-Mail: info@mpif.org
Home Page: www.mpif.org

Michael Lutheran, President
Jim Adams, Director, Technical Services
C. James Trombino, Executive Director, CEO
Jillaine K. Regan, VP, Finance & Administration
Jessica Tamasi, Advertising & Exhibit Manager

Leading reference source for powder metallurgy parts producers and industry suppliers worldwide.
Cost: $30.00
210 Members
504 Pages
Frequency: Annual, Paperback
Founded in 1944

18469 Iron and Manganese Ore Databook
Metal Bulletin
220 5th Avenue
New York, NY 10001-7708

212-136-6202
800-MET-L 25
FAX 212-213-6273

John Bailey, Editor
Iron and manganese ore producers and traders worldwide.
Cost: $179.00
Frequency: Quadrennial

18470 Iron and Steel Works of the World
Metal Bulletin
220 5th Avenue
19th Floor
New York, NY 10001-7781

212-213-6202
FAX 202-213-1870
Home Page: www.metalbulleton.com

Henry Cooke, Editor

Lists over 1,500 major iron and steel plants worldwide.
Cost: $439.00
730 Pages

18471 Locator Services
315 S Patrick St
Alexandria, VA 22314-3532

703-836-9700
800-537-1446
FAX 703-836-7665
E-Mail: sales@locatoronline.com
Home Page: www.locatoronline.com

Terry Pitman, Publisher
Printed directory of available used metalworking equipment.
Frequency: Monthly
Circulation: 225,000

18472 Metal Bulletin's Prices and Data Book
Metal Bulletin
220 5th Avenue
19th Floor
New York, NY 10001-7781

212-213-6202
FAX 212-213-1870
E-Mail: help@metalbulletin.com
Home Page: www.metalbulletin.com

Richard ODonoghue, Manager
Ania Tumm, Marketing Manager
Julius Pike, Account Manager

A list of national and international associations and trading organizations concerned with iron, steel and nonferrous ores and metals.
Cost: $165.00
Frequency: Annual

18473 Metal Casting Industry Directory
Penton Media
1166 Avenue of the Americas/10th Fl
New York, NY 10036

212-204-4200
FAX 216-696-6662
E-Mail: information@penton.com
Home Page: www.penton.com

Jane Cooper, Marketing
Chris Meyer, Director, Corporate Communications
Directory of services and supplies to the industry.
Cost: $425.00
300 Pages

18474 Metal Center News: Metal Distribution Issue
Hitchcock Publishing Company
191 S Gary Avenue
Carol Stream, IL 60188-2095

630-690-5600

Joseph Marino, Editor
Offers a list of producers and industrial metals and metal products, manufacturers of metal processing and handling equipment.
Cost: $25.00
Frequency: Annual
Circulation: 14,000

18475 Metal Finishing Guidebook Directory
Metal Finishing/Elsevier Science
360 Park Ave S
New York, NY 10010-1736

212-633-3980
FAX 212-633-3913
E-Mail: metalfinishing@elsevier.com
Home Page: www.elsevier.com

Ys Chi, President
Patti Ann Frost, Managing Editor
Matthew Smaldon, Circulation Manager

Bill Godfrey, Chief Information Officer
Cost: $87.00
Founded in 1962

18476 Metal Finishing: Guidebook Directory
Metal Finishing/Elsevier Science
650 Avenue of Americas
New York, NY 10011

212-633-5100
FAX 212-633-5140
Home Page: www.metalfinishing.com

Eugene Nadel, Publisher
Don Walsh, Director of operations
Enthone Taps, Communications Manager
Jonathan Timms, Director of Marketing
Frequency: Annual January

18477 Metal Statistics
American Metal Market
350 Hudson Street
4th Floor
New York, NY 10014-4504

212-666-2420
800-662-4445
FAX 212-519-7522
E-Mail: custserv@amm.com
Home Page: www.amm.com

Gloria Larme, Editor-in-Chief

The statistical guide to North American metals.
Hardcover $265.00, Softcover $185.00.
404 Pages
Frequency: Annual
ISBN: 0-910094-01-2
Founded in 1908

18478 Metal Statistics: Ferrous Edition
American Metal Market
350 Hudson Street
4th Floor
New York, NY 10014-4504

212-662-2420
800-662-4445
FAX 818-487-4550
E-Mail: custserv@amm.com
Home Page: www.amm.com

Machael Botta, Publisher
Gloria LaRue, Editor-in-Chief

Statistics for North American metals, also Canadian and Mexican statistucs, International tables and graphs, International trade labor contractsand recycling and scrap alternatives.
Cost: $265.00
Frequency: Annual
ISBN: 0-910094-00-4

18479 Metals Datafile
Materials Information
ASM International
Materials Park, OH 44073

440-930-4888
FAX 440-338-4634

This database contains designation and specification numbers for ferrous and non-ferrous metals and alloys.
Frequency: Full-text

18480 Metalworking Machinery Mailer
Tade Publishing Group
29501 Greenfield Road
Suite 120
Southfield, MI 48076

248-552-8583
800-966-8233
FAX 248-552-0466
Home Page: www.tadesite.com

Tom Lynch, Editor

Printed directory of available used metalworking equipment.
Frequency: Monthly

18481 Mineral and Energy Information
Mineral Information Institute
505 Violet St
Golden, CO 80401-6714

303-277-9190
FAX 303-277-9198
E-Mail: mii@mii.org
Home Page: www.mii.org

Profiles of associations, government agencies
and special interest groups in North America
that are sources of publications and products on
mineral related subjects.
Cost: $15.00

**18482 Modern Machine Shop: CNC &
Software Guide Software Issue**
Gardner Publications
6915 Valley Ln
Cincinnati, OH 45244-3153

513-527-8800
FAX 513-527-8801
Home Page: www.gardnerweb.com

Rick Kline Sr, CEO
Richard Kline, Manager
John Campos, Manager
Brian Wertheimer, Account Manager
Eddie Kania, Sales Manager
Frequency: Annual April

**18483 Parts Cleaning: Master Source
Buyer's Guide**
Witter Publishing Corporation
84 Park Avenue
Suite 32
Flemington, NJ 08822-1172

908-788-0343
FAX 908-788-3782
Home Page: www.partscleaningweb.com

Andrew Witter, Owner
Frequency: Annual July

**18484 Pipe and Tube Mills of the World with
Global Technical Data**
Preston Publishing Company
715 S Sheridan Rd
Tulsa, OK 74112-3139

918-834-2356
FAX 918-299-4795
E-Mail: preston@webzone.net
Home Page: www.prestonpipe.com

Richard Preston, Owner
LaSondra L O'Farrell, President

We also have a monthly trade journal The Pres-
ton Pipe and Tube Report.
Cost: $245.00
842 Pages
Frequency: BiAnnual
Founded in 1995
Printed in one color on matte stock

**18485 Powder Metallurgy Suppliers
Directory**
Metal Powder Industries Federation
105 College Rd East
Princeton, NJ 08540-6692

609-452-7700
FAX 609-987-8523
E-Mail: info@mpif.org
Home Page: www.mpif.org

Michael Lutheran, President
Jim Adams, Director, Technical Services
C. James Trombino, Executive Director, CEO
Jillaine K. Regan, VP, Finance &
Administration
Jessica Tamasi, Advertising & Exhibit Manager

Over 50 producers and suppliers of metal pow-
der who belong to the Metal Powder Producers
Association or Refractory Metals Association.
210 Members
Frequency: Paperback
Founded in 1944

**18486 Precision Cleaning: Master Source
Buyer's Guide**
Witter Publishing Corporation
84 Park Avenue
Suite 32
Flemington, NJ 08822-1172

908-788-0343
FAX 908-788-3782
Home Page: www.precisioncleaningweb.com

Andrew Witter, Owner
Frequency: Annual

18487 Purchasing Magazine
Reed Business Information
275 Washington St
Newton, MA 02458-1611

617-964-3030
FAX 617-558-4327
E-Mail: support@designnews.com
Home Page: www.designnews.com

About 1,800 metal producers, distributors, die
casters, foundries, forgers, coil coaters and
powder metals.
Cost: $15.00
Frequency: Annual

**18488 Reference Book for Metal Working
Machinery**
Machinery Dealers National Association
1110 Spring St
Silver Spring, MD 20910-4019

301-585-9496
800-872-7807
FAX 301-588-7830

Nearly 1,000 metal working machine tool manufacturers; international coverage.
Cost: $75.00

18489 Serial Number Reference Book
Machinery Dealers National Association
315 S Patrick St
Alexandria, VA 22314-3532

703-836-9300
800-872-7807
FAX 703-836-9303
E-Mail: office@mdna.org
Home Page: www.mdna.org

Mark Robinson, Executive VP
Richard Levy CEA, President

Sourcebook for metalworking machinery has
been designed to lead the reader as quickly as
possible to the specific serial number/age information he is seeking.
Cost: $29.95
778 Pages

**18490 Silver Refiners of the World and their
Identifying Ingot Marks**
Silver Institute
1112 16th St Nw
Suite 240
Washington, DC 20036-4818

202-347-8200
Home Page: www.silverinstitute.org

Over 80 refiners in over 18 countries are profiled.
Cost: $33.00
85 Pages

18491 Welding Design & Fabrication
Penton Media

1166 Avenue of the Americas/10th Fl
New York, NY 10036

212-204-4200
FAX 216-696-6662
E-Mail: information@penton.com
Home Page: www.penton.com

Jane Cooper, Marketing
Chris Meyer, Director, Corporate
Communications

For owner operators and managers of professional welding shops.
Frequency: Annual, December

**18492 Who's Who in Powder Metallurgy
Membership Directory**
Metal Powder Industries Federation
105 College Rd East
Princeton, NJ 08540-6692

609-452-7700
FAX 609-987-8523
E-Mail: info@mpif.org
Home Page: www.mpif.org

Michael Lutheran, President
Jim Adams, Director, Technical Services
C. James Trombino, Executive Director, CEO
Jillaine K. Regan, VP, Finance &
Administration
Jessica Tamasi, Advertising & Exhibit Manager

An annual listing of the members of the APMI
International and the Metal Powder Industries
Federation.
Cost: $105.00
210 Members
88 Pages
Frequency: Annual
ISSN: 0361-6304
Founded in 1944

Industry Web Sites

18493 http://gold.greyhouse.com
G.O.L.D Grey House OnLine Databases

Grey House Publishing's online database platform, GOLD, offers Quick Search, Keyword
Search and Expert Search for most business
sectors including metals and metalworking
markets. The GOLD platform makes finding
the information you need quick and easy -
whether you're a novice searcher or an experienced database user. All of Grey House's directory products are available for subscription on
the GOLD platform.

18494 www.ace.org
Aluminum Extruders Council

An international trade association representing
aluminum extruders.

18495 www.aimcal.org
Association of Industrial Metallizers,
Coaters
and Laminators

Packaging equipment.

18496 www.aisc.org
American Institute of Steel Construction

Nonprofit trade association and technical institute established to serve the structural steel industry in the US. Our purpose is to promote the
use of structural steel through research activities, market development, education, codes and
specifacations, technical assistance, quality
certifacation and standardization.

18497 www.aise.org
Association of Iron & Steel Engineers

Production and processing of iron and steel.

18498 www.amea.org
Association of Machinery and Equipment Appraisers
Members are appraisers of the metalworking industry.

18499 www.asminternational.org
ASM International provides information and networking for metals and materials professionals through its website.

18500 www.aws.org
American Welding Society

18501 www.cbsa.copper-brass.org
Copper and Brass Servicenter Association
Distributors of fabricated copper and copperalloy products, Sheets,plate, coil, rod, bar, pipe, tubing, etc.

18502 www.cmadc.org
Closure Manufacturers Association
Conducts public relations for member companies and establishes idustry standards.

18503 www.coilcoaters.org
National Coil Coaters Association

18504 www.construction.com
McGraw-Hill Construction
McGraw-Hill Construction (MHC), part of The McGraw-Hill Companies, connects people and projects across the design and construction industry, serving owners, architects, engineers, general contractors, subcontractors, building product manufacturers, suppliers, dealers, distributors and adjacent markets.

18505 www.copper.org
Copper Development Association
Seeks to expand the uses and applications of copper and copper products. Responsible for industry-wide market statistics and research.

18506 www.ductile.org
Ductile Iron Society
A technical society servicing the ductile iron industry. To advance the technology, art, science of ductile iron production and to disseminate all such information to the members.

18507 www.emcw.org
Electrical Manufacturing & Coil Winding Assn
Promotes welfare of the motor and coil industry. Offers courses and workshops.

18508 www.fmanet.org
Fabricators and Manufacturers Association
FMA is an educational association serving the metal forming and fabricating industry. Technology areas include sheet metal fabrucating, stamping, roll forming, coil processing, punching, and plate structural fabricating.

18509 www.forengineers.org/wrc
Welding Research Council
Coordinates welding research.

18510 www.greyhouse.com
Grey House Publishing
Authoritative reference directories for most business sectors, incluidng metal and metalworking markets. Users can search the online databases with varied search criteria allowing for custom searches by product category, geographic area, sales volume, keyword, subject and more. Full Grey House catalog and online ordering also available.

18511 www.ilzro.org
International Lead Zinc Research Organization
For miners, smelters and refiners of lead and zinc. Supports research and developement of new uses for the metals and refinement existing uses.

18512 www.intlmag.org
International Magnesium Association
Develops international use and acceptance of magnesium metal and its alloys in all product forms. Members are organizations or individuals engaged in the production, manufacture or marketing of metallic magnesium or those supplying materials, equipment or consulting.

18513 www.ipmi.org
International Precious Metals Institute
Miners, refiners, producers and users of precious metals, as well as research scientists and mercantilists.

18514 www.iss.org
Iron & Steel Society
Seeks to be the premier professional and technical society serving its members and advancing knowledge exchange in the global iron and steel industry. Publishes a monthly magazine.

18515 www.mbcea.org
Metal Building Contractors & Erectors Association
To support the professional advancement of metal building contractors, erectors, and the industry.

18516 www.mdna.org
Machinery Dealers National Association

18517 www.metalforming.com
Precision Metalforming Association
For producers of metal stampings, spinnings, washers and precision sheet metal fabrications as well as suppliers of equipment, materials and services.

18518 www.mfgtech.org
Association for Manufacturing Technology

18519 www.mhia.org
Material Handling Institute
Promotes the market and develops a code of ethics. Serves as liaison among members and other groups.

18520 www.mmsa.net
Mining and Metallurgical Society of America
A professional organization dedicated to increasing public awareness and understanding about mining and why mined materials are essential to modern society and human well being.

18521 www.mpif.org
Metal Powder Industries Federation
Promotes the science and industry of powder metallurgy through technical meetings, seminars, conferences, and publications.

18522 www.naad.org
National Association of Aluminum Distributors
NAAD is the trade association of North American service centers and principal suppliers engaged in marketing aluminum products.

18523 www.nffs.org
Non-Ferrous Founder's Society
Manufacturers of bronze, brass and aluminum castings.

18524 www.nwsa.com
Fernley & Fernley

18525 www.powdercoating.org
Powder Coating Institute

18526 www.scra.org/amc/tfa
Ferroalloys Association
Promotes the ferroalloy industry in the areas of technology, international trade, environment and health, safety and government relations.

18527 www.sdi.org
Steel Deck Institute
Trade association providing uniform industry standards for the engineering, design, manufacture and field usage of steel decks.

18528 www.silversmithing.com
Society of American Silversmiths
Founded to preserve the art and history of handcrafted holloware and flatware plus provide support, networking and greater access to the market forsilversmiths. Educates the public as to the aesthetic and investment value of this art form.

18529 www.smacna.org
Sheet Metal and Air Conditioning Contactor's Natl
An international trade association representing 4,500 contibuting contractor firms in the sheet metal and air conditioning industry. Develops technical standards and manuals addressing all facets of the sheet metal and air conditioning industry.

18530 www.spfa.org
Steel Plate Fabricators Association

18531 www.ssci.org
Steel Service Center Institute

18532 www.steel.org
American Iron and Steel Institute
Works to protect interests of manufacturers in the steel industry.

18533 www.steeldistributors.org/asd
Association of Steel Distributors
Bestows Steel Distributor of The Year Award and the Presidents Award of Merit.

18534 www.steelnews.com
Association for Iron and Steel Technology (AIST)
SteelNews.com is a publication created by the Association for Iron and Steel Technology (AIST) for the steel community. The site features daily updates of the latest global headlines.

18535 www.steeltubeinstitute.org
Steel Tube Institute of North America
Members produce steel tubes and pipes from carbon, stainless or alloy steel, for applications ranging from large structural tubing to small re-drawn tubing.

18536 www.sweets.construction.com
McGraw Hill Construction
In depth product information that lets you find, compare, select, specify and make purchase decisions in the industrial product marketplace.

18537 www.taol.com/uscti
United States Cutting Tool Institute
For those in the domestic cutting tool market.

18538 www.thermalspray.org
International Thermal Spray Association
Strengthens the level of awareness in general industry and government on the increasing capabilities and advantages of thermal spray technology for surface engineering through business opportunities, technical support and a

social network. Contributes to growth and education in the thermal spray industry.

18539 www.titanium.org
International Titanium Association
Contact ITA for mailing list price.

18540 www.uschamber.org/chamber/mall
Silver Users Association

Represents the interests of corporations that make, sell and distribute products and services in which silver is an essential part. SUA membership includes representatives from the photographic, electronic, silverware and jewelry industries; producers of semi-fabricated and industrial products; and, mirror manufacturers.

18541 www.wirenet.org
Wire Association International

Technical association serving the global wire and cable industry by providing educational materials, sponsoring trade shows and international technical conferences.

18542 www.zinc.org
American Zinc Association

Provides information on the zinc industry and hosts international conference on zinc.

Associations

18543 Alabama Surface Mining Commission
PO Box 2390
Jasper, AL 35502

205-221-4130
FAX 205-221-5077
E-Mail: asmc@asmc.alabama.gov
Home Page: www.surface-mining.state.al.us

Dr. Randall C. Johnson, Director
Ann Miles, Executive Secretary
Carla D.Lightsey, Chief Divison of SMCR
Milton McCarthy, Legal Division

Doing its part to balance civilization's demands for natural resources and environmental conservation in the state of Alabama.
Founded in 1972

18544 Alaska Miners Association
121 W. Fireweed
Suite 120
Anchorage, AK 99503-4575

907-563-9229
FAX 907-563-9225
E-Mail: ama@alaskaminers.org
Home Page: www.alaskaminers.org
Social Media: *Facebook, Twitter, LinkedIn, Google+*

Jason Brune, President
Lorna Shaw, First Vice President
Mike Satre, SecondÿVice President
Kim Aasand, Treasurer
James Fueg, Past President

Works to promote the mining industry in Alaska. It advocates the development and use of Alaska's mineral resources to provide an economic base for the State. AMA monitors the activities of State and Federal Government, Congress and the Legislature that affect mineral development.

18545 American Association for Crystal Growth
6986 S. Wadsworth Court
Litteton, CO 80128

303-539-6907
FAX 303-482-2775
E-Mail: AACG@comcast.net
Home Page: www.crystalgrowth.org

Anthony L Gentile, Executive Administrator
David Bliss, Chairman
Russ Dupuis, Chair

AACG is a nonprofit technical membership organization where the primary function is a organic conference in the fall of crystal growth and characterization. A newsletter is published 3 times per year and distributed to members.
600 Members
Founded in 1966

18546 American Coal Ash Association
38800 Country Club Drive
Suite 3050
Farmington Hills, MI 48331

720-870-7897
FAX 720-870-7889
E-Mail: info@acaa-usa.org
Home Page: www.acaa-usa.org

Thomas H Adams, Executive Director

To advance the management and use of coal combustion products in ways that are environmentally responsible, technically sound, commercially competitive, and supportive of a sustainable global community
126 Members
Founded in 1968

18547 American Exploration and Mining Association
10 N Post St
Suite 305
Spokane, WA 99201-0722

509-624-1158
FAX 509-623-1241
E-Mail: info@miningamerica.org
Home Page: www.miningamerica.org

Mari-Ann Green, President
Ron Parratt, 1st Vice President
Steve Alfers, 2nd Vice President
Shelia Bush, Secretary
Laura Skaer, Executive Director

Provides liaison between mining, industry and government. Offers short course on current technology.
2000 Members
Founded in 1890

18548 American Geosciences Institute
4220 King St
Alexandria, VA 22302-1502

703-379-2480
FAX 703-379-7563
E-Mail: webmaster@agiweb.org.
Home Page: www.agiweb.org
Social Media: *Facebook, Twitter*

P.Patrick Leahy, Executive Director
Dr. Wayne D. Pennington, President
Dr. Sharon Mosher, President Elect
Ann Benow, Outreach and Development Director
Walter R.Sisson, Finance and administrator Director

A nonprofit federation of 45 geoscientific and professional associations that represents more than 120,000 geologists, geophysicists, and other earth scientists.
45 Members
Founded in 1948

18549 American Institute of Mining, Metallurgical & Petroleum Engineers
12999 East Adam Aircraft Circle
Eglewood, CO 80112-5991

303-325-5185
FAX 888-702-0049
E-Mail: aime@aimehq.org
Home Page: www.aimehq.org
Social Media: *Facebook, LinkedIn, YouTube, RSS*

Brajendra Fattahi, President
Garry W. Warren, President-Elect
Nikhil C. Trivedi, President-Elect Designate
Dale E. Heinz, Past President
Drew Meyer, Trustee

Supporting member societies by exercising fiscal responsibility, distributing funds, facilitating interaction with the larger scientific and engineering community, enhancing collaboration among the member societies, and honoring the legacy and traditions of AIME.
130M Members
Founded in 1871

18550 American Institute of Professional Geologists
1200 Washington St.
Thornton, CO 80241-3134

303-412-6205
FAX 303-253-9220
E-Mail: aipg@aipg.org
Home Page: www.aipg.org
Social Media: *Facebook, LinkedIn*

William J Siok, Executive Director
Wendy J.Davidson, Assistant Director
Cathy L.Duran, Professional Services
Cristie J.Valero, Office Assistant
Vickie Hill, Membership Services

Founded to certify the credentials of practicing geologists and to advocate on behalf of the profession.
5000 Members
Founded in 1963

18551 Arizona Mining Association
916 W Adams St
Suite B-134
Phoenix, AZ 85007

602-266-4416
FAX 602-230-8413
Home Page: www.azmining.org

Sydney Hay, President
June Castelhano, Administrative Assistant

Recognizes the importance of educating Arizona's citizens about the critical role the mining industry plays not only in our state and nation, but also in the world.
Founded in 1965

18552 Arizona State Mine Inspectors
1700 West Washington
4th Floor
Phoenix, AZ 85007-4655

602-542-5971
FAX 602-542-5335
E-Mail: admin@mi.state.az.us
Home Page: www.asmi.az.gov

John Stanford, Sr.Deputy Mine Inspector
Tim Evans, Assistant State Mine Inspector
Jack Speer, Deputy Mine Inspector Reclamation
Wiiliam Schifferns, Deputy Mine Inspector

Priority mission is to enforce state mining laws which protect mine employees, residents, and the Arizona environment. Focused on providing the best customer service to Arizona residents and mining enterprises.
330 Members
Founded in 1912

18553 Association for Mineral Exploration British Columbia
889 W Pender Street
Suite 800
Vancouver, BC V6C-3B2

604-689-5271
FAX 604-681-2363
E-Mail: info@amebc.ca
Home Page: www.amebc.ca
Social Media: *Facebook, Twitter*

Gavin C Dirom, President/CEO
Rick Conte, Vice President
David McLelland, Chair
Diane Nicolson, Vice Chair
Sam Adkins, Director

AME BC is the predominant voice of mineral exploration and development in British Columbia.
5400 Members
Founded in 1912

18554 Association of Bituminous Contractors
1250 Eye St NW
Suite 620
Washington, DC 20005-5976

202-296-5745
FAX 202-331-8049

William H Howe, President

Members are general and independent contractors constructing coal mines and coal mine facilities and also bargains with the United Mine Workers.
150 Members
Frequency: Annual/March

18555 Association of Equipment Manufacturers

6737 West Washington Street
Suite 2400
Milwaukee, WI 53214-5647

414-272-0943
FAX 414-212-1170
E-Mail: aem@aem.org
Home Page: www.aem.org

James Ebbinghaus, VP

Representing manufacturers of architectural, construction, forestry, materials handling and liabilty equipment.

18556 Bureau of Land Management

1849 C Street NW
Room 5665
Washington, DC 20240

202-208-3801
FAX 202-208-5242
Home Page: www.blm.gov
Social Media: *Facebook, Twitter, LinkedIn, YouTube*

Ted Bingham, President
Robert C Bruce, VP

18557 California Mining Association

1029 J Street
Suite 420
Sacramento, CA 95814

916-554-1000
FAX 916-554-1042
E-Mail: spridmore@calcima.org
Home Page: www.calcima.org

Adam Harper, Association Manager
Stephanie Pridmore, Association Administrator
Gary W. Hambly, President/CEO

Represents the breadth and depth of California's mining industry including producers of precious metals (such as gold and silver), industrial minerals (including borates, limestone, rare earth elements, clays, gypsum and tungsten) and rock, sand and gravel.

18558 Canadian Institute of Mining, Metallurgy and Petroleum

3500 de Maisonneuve Blvd. W.
Suite 1250
Westmount, QC H3Z-3CI

514-939-2710
FAX 514-939-2714
E-Mail: cim@cim.org
Home Page: www.cim.org
Social Media: *Facebook, Twitter, LinkedIn, YouTube*

Russell E Hallbauer, CIM President
Jean Vavrek, CIM Executive Director
Danielle Langlois, Director
Benoit Sawyer, Controller
Jasen Coady, Web Developer

The leading technical society of professionals in the Canadian minerals, metals, materials and energy industries.
12000 Members
Founded in 1898

18559 China Clay Producers Association CCPA

113 Arkwright Landing
Macon, GA 31210

478-757-1211
FAX 478-757-1949
E-Mail: info@georgiamining.org
Home Page: www.kaolin.com/

Lee Lemke, Executive VP

The mission of the China Clay Producers Association is to promote the common business interest of producers of china clay and the development of coordinated policies, which as-

sure the industry will continue to provide jobs and contribute to the Georgia economy. In addition, objectives also include informing members of proposed legislation, regulatory actions and other matters affecting the kaolin industry, and to maintain the industry's strong community commitment.
Founded in 1978

18560 Colorado Mining Association

216 16th St
Suite 1250
Denver, CO 80202-5161

303-575-9199
FAX 303-575-9194
E-Mail: colomine@coloradomining.org
Home Page: www.coloradomining.org
Social Media: *Facebook, Twitter*

Stuart Sanderson, President
Fred J. Menzer, Chairman
William Zisch, Chairman-Elect
Stephen A. Onorofskie, Treasurer

Composed of both small and large enterprises engaged in the exploration for, production and refining of, metals, coal, oil shale, and industrial minerals; firms that manufacture and distribute mining and mineral processing equipment and supplies; and other institutions providing services and supplies to the mineral industry.
Founded in 1876

18561 Copper Development Association

260 Madison Ave
New York, NY 10016-2403

212-251-7200
FAX 212-251-7234
E-Mail: questions@cda.copper.org
Home Page: www.copper.org
Social Media: *Facebook, Twitter, LinkedIn, Google+*

Thomas S. Passek, President & CEO
Victoria Prather, Manager Communications
Michels Harold, VP Technaloy Services
Luis Lozano, Technical Consultant
Lorraine Herzing Mills, VP/Finance/Administration

Promoting the use of copper by communicating the unique attributes that make this sustainable element an essential contributor to the formation of life, to advances in science and technology, and to a higher standard of living worldwide.
75 Members
Founded in 1963

18562 Desert Research Institute

2215 Raggio Pkwy
Reno, NV 89512-1095

775-673-7300
FAX 775-673-7421
Home Page: www.dri.edu
Social Media: *Facebook, Twitter*

Stephen G Wells, President
Ellen Oppenheim, SVP, Finance & Admin/COO
Dr. Alan Gertler, VP, Research/Chief Science Officer
Chris Fritsen, VP, Academic and Faculty Affairs
Chris Ipsen, Assistant VP IT/CIO

A nonprofit statewide division of the university and community college system of Nevada, DRI pursues a full-time program of basic and applied environmental research on a local, national, and international scale. DRI employees nearly 400 full and part-time staff scientists, technicians, and support personnel.
Founded in 1959

18563 Environmental Information Association

6935 Wisconsin Avenue
Suite 306
Chevy Chase, MD 20815-6112

301-961-4999
888-343-4342
FAX 301-961-3094
E-Mail: info@eia-usa.org
Home Page: www.eia-usa.org

Brent Kynoch, Managing Director
Kim Goodman, Membership and marketing Manager
Kelly Rut, Development Manager
Nehmesah Israel, Admin Assistant
Chris Gates, Treasurer

Providing the environmental industry with the information needed to remain knowledgeable, responsible, and competitive in the environmental health and safety industry.

18564 Excavation Engineering Associates

1352 SW 175th Street
Seattle, WA 98166

206-248-7388
FAX 206-244-7994
Home Page: www.expeditionsonline.org
Social Media: *Facebook, Twitter, LinkedIn, Google+*

Estelle Friant, Secretary
James E.Friant, President

Underground excavation.

18565 Federal Mine Safety and Health Review Commission

1331 Pennsylvania Avenue, NW, Suite 520N
Suite 520N
Washington, DC 20004-1710

202-434-9900
FAX 202-434-9906
E-Mail: fmshrc@fmshrc.gov
Home Page: www.fmshrc.gov

Richard Baker, Executive Director

Independent adjudicative agency that provides administrative trial and apellate review of legal disputes arising under the Federal Mine Safety and Health Amendments Act of 1977 (mine act).

18566 Geological Society of America

PO Box 9140
Boulder, CO 80301-9140

303-357-1000
800-472-1988
FAX 303-357-1070
E-Mail: web@geosociety.org
Home Page: www.geosociety.org
Social Media: *Facebook, Twitter, LinkedIn, YouTube*

Jonathan G. Price, President
Claudia I. Mora, Vice President
Bruce R. Clark, Treasurer
Vicki McConnell, Executive Director/Secretary
Nancy L. Wright, Technical Program Manager

Provides access to elements that are essential to the professional growth of earth scientists at all levels of expertise and from all sectors, academic, government, business, and industry. Membership unites thousands of earth scientists from every corner of the globe in a common purpose to study the mysteries of our planet and share scientific findings.
16000 Members
Founded in 1888

18567 Gold Prospectors Association of America

43445 Business Park Drive
Suite #113
Temecula, CA 92590

951-699-4749
800-551-9707
FAX 951-699-4062
E-Mail: info@goldprospectors.org
Home Page: www.goldprospectors.org
Social Media: *Facebook, Twitter, LinkedIn, YouTube*

Thomas Massie, CEO

GPAA is the largest recreational gold prospecting club. Owner of The Outdoor Channel, a cable TV channel featuring real outdoors for real people.
35M Members
Founded in 1968

18568 Idaho Mining Association

802 W Bannock St
Suite 301
Boise, ID 83702-5840

208-342-0031
FAX 208-345-4210
E-Mail: ima@mineidaho.com
Home Page: www.mineidaho.com/
Social Media: *Twitter*

Randy Vranes, President
Corey Millard, 1st Vice President
Dennis Facer, 2nd Vice President
Jack Lyman, Executive Vice President

Founded to further the interests of Idaho's mining industry and minerals production. Mission is to act as the unified voice for its members to ensure the long-term health and well being of Idaho's mining industry.
Founded in 1903

18569 International Lead Association

2 Bravingtons Walk
London N1 9AF

44 (0)20 7833 8090
FAX 44 (0)20 7833 1611
E-Mail: enq@ila-lead.org
Home Page: www.ila-lead.org
Social Media: *Twitter, LinkedIn*

Nonprofit trade association representing the lead industries in the US and abroad. It collects and distributes information about the users of lead products in industry, vehicles, radioactive waste disposal and noise barriers. Its services are availble, generally free of charge, to anyone interested in the uses of lead and lead products.

18570 Lignite Energy Council

1016 E. Owens Avenue
PO Box 2277
Bismarck, ND 58502-2277

701-258-7117
800-932-7117
FAX 701-258-2755
E-Mail: lec@lignite.com
Home Page: www.lignite.com
Social Media: *Facebook, Twitter, LinkedIn, YouTube*

Jason Bohrer, President/CEO
Alan Hodnik, Chairman
Robert McLennan, Chairman-Elect
Mike Jones, Ph. D., VP, Research and Development
Steve Van Dyke, VP, Communications

Regional Trade Association - promotes policies and activities that maintain a viable lignite industry and enhance development of our regions' lignite resources.
355 Members
Founded in 1974

18571 Mine Safety Institue of America

319 Paintersville Road
Hunker, PA 15139

724-925-5150
E-Mail: sikora.lisa@dol.gov
Home Page: www.miningorganizations.org/msia.htm

Frank Linkous, President
Ronnie Biggerstaff, 1st VP
Joseph Sbaffoni, 2nd VP
William Gerringer, 3rd VP
Gerald E. Davis, Secretary/Treasurer

The objectives of the Mine Safety Institute of America is to provide successful educational programs, safer and healthier working conditions, more productivity in the mining industry, and support of good legislature pertaining to mining.
Founded in 1908

18572 Mine Safety and Health Administration

1100 Wilson Blvd
21st Floor
Arlington, VA 22209-3939

202-693-9400
800-746-1553
FAX 202-693-9401
Home Page: www.msha.gov

David G Dye, Executive Director

Administers the Federal Mine Safety and Health Act of 1977 (Mine Act) and enforces compliance with mandatory safety and health standards as a means to eliminate fatal accidents; to reduce the frequency and severity of nonfatal accidents, to minimize health hazards and to promote mineral processing operations in the US, regardless of size, employees, commodity mined or method of extraction.

18573 Mineral Economics and Management Society

Colorado School Of Mines
Golden, CO 49931

303-273-3150
FAX 906-487-2944
Home Page: www.outreach.mines.edu

Patricia Dillon, President

A society for mineral, energy, and natural resource professionals who apply economics, finance and policy analysis to the issues facing the minerals and materials industries. These issues include supply and demand of mineral commodities, international trade in mineral and energy raw materials, environmental issues, natural resource, mineral and energy conservation, and related government policies.
200 Members
Founded in 1991

18574 Mineral Information Institute

12999 E. Adam Aircraft Circle
Englewood, CO 80112

303-948-4236
FAX 303-948-4265
E-Mail: mii@mii.org
Home Page: www.mineralseducationcoalition.org/
Social Media: *Facebook, Twitter, LinkedIn, YouTube*

Jaqueline S. Dorr, Manager

Nonprofit organization dedicated to educating youth about the science of minerals and other natural resources and about their importance in our everyday lives.

18575 Minerals, Metals & Materials Society

184 Thorn Hill Road
Warrendale, PA 15086-7514

800-759-4867
800-759-4867
FAX 724-776-3770
E-Mail: webmaster@tms.org
Home Page: www.tms.org
Social Media: *Facebook, LinkedIn*

James Robinson, Executive Director
Adrianne Carolla, Deputy Executive Director
Peter DeLuca, Accountant

Dedicated to the development and dissemination of the scientific and engineering knowledge bases for materials-centered technologies.

18576 Mining Foundation of the Southwest

PO Box 42317
Tucson, AZ 85733

520-577-7519
FAX 520-577-7073
E-Mail: admin@miningfoundationsw.org
Home Page: www.miningfoundationsw.org

Advances the science of mining and related industries by educating members and the public. Annual American Mining Hall of Fame First Saturday in December. A newsletter is published.
92 Members
Founded in 1982

18577 Mining and Metallurgical Society of America

PO Box 810
PO Box 810
Boulder, CO 80306-0810

303-444-6032
FAX 415-897-1380
E-Mail: contactmmsa@mmsa.net
Home Page: www.mmsa.net
Social Media: *Facebook, Twitter, LinkedIn*

Alan K Burton, Business Manager
Mark leVier, President
Robert Schafer, VP
Kenneth Brunk, Treasurer

Concerned with the conservation of the nation's mineral resources and the best interest of the mining and metallurgical industries.
350 Members
Founded in 1908

18578 National Association of State Land Reclamationists

Coal Research Center/Southern Illinois University
47 School Street
Suite 301
Philippi, WV 26416

304-940-0271
FAX 618-453-7346
E-Mail: aharrington@crc.siu.edu
Home Page: naslr.org

Sam Faith, President
Janet Yates, Vice President
Derek Giebell, Secretary/Treasurer
Jennifer Keese, Chairman

The National Association of State and Land Reclamationists advocates the use of research, innovative technology and professional discourse to foster the restoration of lands and waters affected by mining related activities.
140 Members
Founded in 1972

18579 National Lime Association

200 N Glebe Rd
Suite 800
Arlington, VA 22203-3728

703-243-5463
FAX 703-243-5489
Home Page: www.lime.org

William C.Herz, Executive Director
Arline Seeger, General Counsel
Hunter Prillaman, Director Of Government
Affairs
Robert Hirsch, Director of Environment
Lori D.Oney, Admin Director

Trade association for US and Canadian manufacturers of high calcium quicklime, dolomitic quicklime and hydrated lime, collectively referred to as lime. NLA represents the interests of its members in Washington, provides input on standards and specifications for lime, and funds and manages research on current and new uses for lime.
63 Members
Founded in 1902

18580 National Mining Association

101 Constitution Ave Nw
Suite 500 East
Washington, DC 20001-2133

202-463-2600
FAX 202-463-2666
E-Mail: webmaster@nma.org
Home Page: www.nma.org
Social Media: *YouTube*

Harry M. Conger, Chairman
Kevin Cruntchfield, Vice Chairman
Rich Nolan, Senior VP
Hal Quinn, President & CEO
Bruce Watzman, SVP, Regulatory Affairs

The voice of U.S. mining in Washington.
325 Members
Founded in 1995

18581 National Ocean Industries Association

1120 G St NW
Suite 900
Washington, DC 20005-3801

202-347-6900
FAX 202-347-8650
E-Mail: jwilliams@noia.org
Home Page: www.noia.org
Social Media: *Facebook, Twitter, LinkedIn, YouTube*

Randall Luthi, President
Franki Stuntz, Sr.VP
Anna Chapman, VP, Conferences & Special
Events
Nicoltte Nye, VP, Comm. &ÿIndustry Affairs
Jeff Vorberger, VP, Policy & Government
Affairs

National organization engaged in offshore construction, drilling and petroleum production, geophysical exploration, ship building and repair, deep-sea mining and related activities in the development and use of marine resources.
300 Members
Founded in 1972

18582 National Ready Mixed Concrete Association

900 Spring St
Silver Spring, MD 20910-4015

240-485-1139
FAX 301-585-4219
E-Mail: info@nrmca.org
Home Page: www.nrmca.org
Social Media: *Facebook, Twitter, LinkedIn, YouTube*

Robert Garbini, President
Deana Angelastro, Executive Administrator
Allen Hamblen, Chairman
Ted Chandler, Vice Chairman
Scott Parson, Secretary/Treasurer

The mission of the National Ready Mixed Concrete Association is to provide exceptional value for our members by responsibly representing and serving the entire ready mixed concrete industry through leadership, promotion, education, and partnering to ensure ready mixed concrete is the building material of choice.
1200 Members
Founded in 1930

18583 National Stone, Sand & Gravel Association

1605 King St
Alexandria, VA 22314-2726

703-525-8788
800-342-1415
FAX 703-525-7782
E-Mail: jwilson@nssga.org
Home Page: www.nssga.org
Social Media: *Facebook, Twitter, LinkedIn, YouTube*

Jennifer Joy Wilson, President & CEO
Gus Edwards, Executive Vice President
Janice B. Springs, Executive Assistant
Charles S. Luck IV, Chairman
Hal F.ÿ Williford Jr., First Vice Chairman

Represents the stone, sand and gravel — or aggregate — industries. Our members account for 90 percent of the crushed stone and 70 percent of the sand and gravel produced annually in the US.
25 Members
Founded in 1916

18584 Nevada Mining Association

201 W. Liberty Street
Suite 300
Reno, NV 89501

775-829-2121
FAX 775-852-2631
Home Page: www.nevadamining.org
Social Media: *Facebook, Twitter, YouTube*

Tim Crowley, President
Dylan Shaver, Public Affairs
Lauren Arends, Office Manager
Joseph Riney, Information System
Administrator

Represents all aspects of the mining industry. Provides representation for the broad mining industry in public outreach activities such as public relations, media relations, and community relations.

18585 North American Insulation Manufacturers Association

11 Canal Center Plaza
Suite 103
Alexandria, VA 22314

703-684-0084
FAX 703-684-0427
Home Page: www.naima.org

Mark Andrews, Chairman
Jeffrey Brisley, Vice Chairman
Cut Rich, President & CEO/ Treasurer
Angus Crane, Executive Vice President

An authoritative resource on energy-efficiency, sustainable performance, and the application and safety of fiber glass, rock wool, and slag wool insulation products. The voice of the insulation industry for architects and builders, design, process and maintenance engineers, contractors, code groups and standards organizations, government agencies, public interest, energy and environmental groups, and homeowners.

18586 Perlite Institute

2207 Forest Hills Drive
Suite A
Harrisburg, PA 17112

717-238-9723
FAX 717-238-9985
E-Mail: info@perlite.org
Home Page: www.perlite.org
Social Media: *Facebook, Twitter*

Matt Goecker, President
Matthew Malaghan, Vice President
Paul Dunlavey, Secretary/Treasurer
Denise Calabrese, Executive Director

An international association which establishes product standards and specifications, and which encourages the development of new product uses through research.
183 Members
Founded in 1949

18587 Rocky Mountain Association of Geologists

910 16th Stÿ
Ste 1214
Denver, CO 80202-2997

303-573-8621
FAX 303-628-0546
E-Mail: staff@rmag.org
Home Page: www.rmag.org

Donna Anderson, President
Mark Sonnenfeld, First VP
Jewel Wellborn, Second VP
Sandi Pillissier, Executive Director
2200 Members
Founded in 1922

18588 Silver Institute

1400 I Street, NW
Suite 550
Washington, DC 20005

202-835-0185
FAX 202-835-0155
E-Mail: info@silverinstitute.org
Home Page: www.silverinstitute.org

Robert Quartermain, President
Michael Dirienzo, Executive Director

International association of miners, refiners, fabricators and wholesalers of silver and silver products.

18589 Silver Users Association

3930 walnut Street
Suite 210
Fairfax, VA 22030

703-930-7790
800-245-6999
FAX 703-359-7562
E-Mail: sas@silversmithing.com
Home Page: www.silverusersassociation.org

Bill Le Roy, President
Mike Huber, VP
John King, Secretary
Bill Hamelin, Treasurer
29 Members
Founded in 1947

18590 Silver Valley Mining Association

604 Bank St.
Wallace, ID 83873

208-556-1621
Home Page: www.silverminers.org

Dedicated to promoting the Silver Valley of northern Idaho and its mining industry. Informs the public of the history and merits of the region, serving various beneficiary needs of the mining industry, and serving those who work in the industry and the investing public.

18591 Society for Mining, Metallurgy & Exploration
12999 E. Adam Aircraft Circle
Englewood, CO 80112

303-948-4200
800-763-3132
FAX 303-973-3845
E-Mail: sme@smenet.org
Home Page: www.smenet.org
Social Media: *Facebook, Twitter, LinkedIn, YouTube, Google+*

John N. Murphy, President
Drew A. Meyer, President-Elect

Advances the worldwide mining and minerals community through information exchange and professional development.
13000 Members
Founded in 1957

18592 Society of Economic Geologists
7811 Shaffer Pkwy
Littleton, CO 80127-3732

720-981-7874
FAX 720-981-7874
E-Mail: seg@segweb.org
Home Page: www.segweb.org
Social Media: *Facebook, Twitter, LinkedIn, YouTube*

Fran‡ois Robert, President
Robert P. Foster, President-Elect
A. Jamesÿ Macdonald, Vice President for Regional Affairs
Regina M. Baumgartner, VP, Student Affairs
Brian G Hoal, Executive Director

International organization of individual members with interests in the field of economic geology. Membership includes representatives from the industry, academia and government institutions. Annual meetings, publications, field conferences and short courses ensure active communication of economic geology related concepts with the membership and the economic geology profession at large.
3400 Members
Founded in 1920

18593 Society of Exploration Geophysicists
8801 South Yale
Suite 500
Tulsa, OK 74137-3575

918-497-5500
FAX 918-497-5557
E-Mail: web@seg.org
Home Page: www.seg.org/index.shtml
Social Media: *Facebook, Twitter, LinkedIn, YouTube, Google+*

Dr. Bob A. Hardage, President
Dr. David James Monk, President-Elect
Dr. Wafik Bulind Beydoun, Vice-President
Nancy Jo House, Secretary/ Treasurer
Dr. Tamas Nemeth, Editor

The Society of Exploration Geophysicists/SEG is a not-for-profit organization that promotes the science of geophysics and the education of applied geophysicists. SEG fosters the expert and ethical practice of geophysics in the exploration and development of natural resources, in characterizing the near surface, and in mitigating earth hazards.
Founded in 1930

18594 Society of Mineral Analysts
PO Box 50085
Sparks, NV 89435-0085

562-467-8980
E-Mail: services@sma-online.org
Home Page: www.sma-online.org
Social Media: *Facebook, Twitter, LinkedIn*

Patrick Brown, Director

The Society of Mineral Analysts is a non-profit organization, whose members are assayers, chemists, laboratory managers, geologists, suppliers and vendors both in and serving the mineral analysis industry.
250 Members
Founded in 1986

18595 Solution Mining Research Institute
105 Apple Valley Circle
Clarks Summit, PA 18411

570-585-8092
FAX 570-585-8091
E-Mail: info@solutionmining.org
Home Page: www.solutionmining.org

John O Voight, Executive Director
Carolyn L Diamond, Assistant Executive Director

Members are companies interested in the production of salt brine and solution mining of potash and soda ash, as well as production of slt covers, used for storage of oil, gas, chemicals, compressed air and waste.
100 Members
Founded in 1958

18596 Sorptive Minerals Institute
1155 15th St NW
Suite 500
Washington, DC 20005-2725

202-289-2760
FAX 202-530-0659
E-Mail: lcoogan@navista.net
Home Page: www.sorptive.org

Lee Coogan, Executive Director

The Sorptive Minerals Institute represents the absorbent clay industry and is a not-for-profit industry trade association that would serve as the marketing, promotion and research arm of the absorbent clay indsutry with the goal of enhancing long-range growth and profitability.
Founded in 1970

18597 Sulphur Institute
1020 19th Street NW, Suite 520
Washington, DC 20036

202-331-9660
FAX 202-293-2940
E-Mail: sulphur@sulphurinstitute.org
Home Page: www.sulphurinstitute.org

Robert J Morris, President
Thomas W.Dunn, Director
Joshua C.Maak, Communications Manager
Donald S.Messik, VP,Communications

The Sulphur Institute (TSI) is an international, non-profit organization established in 1960. The Institute is the global advocate for sulphur, representing all stakeholders engaged in producing, consuming, trading, handling or adding value to sulphur. We seek to provide a common voice for all stakeholders to promote the uninterrupted, efficient and safe handling and transportation of all sulphur products while protecting the best interests of the environment
Founded in 1960

18598 US Geological Survey
950 National Ctr
Reston, VA 20192-0001

703-648-4302
FAX 703-648-6373
E-Mail: dc_va@usgs.gov
Home Page: www.usgs.gov

Founded in 1879

18599 United Mine Workers of America International Union
18354 Quantico Gateway Drive
Suite 200
Triangle, VA 22172

703-291-2400
FAX 703-208-7227
Home Page: www.umwa.org

Cecil E Roberts, President
Daniel J Kane, Secretary/Treasurer

The United Mine Workers of America International Union is an organization with a diverse membership that includes coal miners, clean coal technicians, health care workers, truck drivers, manufacturing workers and public employees throughout the United States and Canada. The Union works to fight for safe workplaces, good wages and benefits, and fair representation.
120M Members
Founded in 1890

18600 Utah Mining Association
136 S Main St
Suite 709
Salt Lake City, UT 84101-1683

801-364-1874
FAX 801-364-2640
E-Mail: mining@utahmining.org
Home Page: www.utahmining.org
Social Media: *Facebook, Twitter*

Mark Karll, Chairman
Greg Gergory, Vice Chairman
Mark Compton, President
Mike Brown, 1st Vice President
Chadd Baker, 2nd Vice President

Provides its members with full-time professional industry representation before the State Legislature; various government regulatory agencies on the federal, state and local levels; other associations, and business and industry groups. Helps to promote and protect the mining industry.
Founded in 1915

18601 Vibrating Screen Manufacturers Association
6737 W Washington Street
Suite 2400
Milwaukee, WI 53214-5650

414-272-0943
866-236-0442
FAX 414-272-1170
E-Mail: aem@aem.org
Home Page: www.aem.org
Social Media: *Twitter*

Dennis Slater, President
Al Cervero, Senior VP

AEM is teh international trade and business development resource for companies that manufacture equipment, products andservices used worldwide in the construction, agricultural, minimg, forestry, and utility industries.
8 Members
Founded in 1959

18602 Women in Mining National Organization
PO Box 260246
Lakewood, CO 80226-0246

303-298-1535
866-537-9697
E-Mail: wim@womeninmining.org
Home Page: www.womeninmining.org/aboutwim.htm

Betty Mahaffey, President
Christine Ballard, Vice President
Stephen Tibbals, Treasurer
Hannah McNally, Secretary

Women in Mining/WIM was founded in 1972 in Denver, Colorado, by several women whose intent was to facilitate education about the mining industry for themselves and for those not acquainted with the role the industry plays in their lives. In addition to providing valuable educations benefits, the WIM organization offers members an opportunity to become acquainted and work with others involved in the mining industry and thereby acquire new personal and professional contacts.
600 Members

18603 World Gold Council

510 Madison Ave
9th Floor
New York, NY 10022

212-317-3800
FAX 212-688-0410
Home Page: www.gold.org
Social Media: *Facebook, Twitter, Google+*

Organization formed and funded by the world's leading gold mining companies with the aim of stimulating and maximizing the demand for, and holding of gold by consumers, investors, industry and the official sector.
Founded in 1987

Newsletters

18604 AME BC News

Assoc for Mineral Exploration British Columbia
889 W Pender Street
Suite 800
Vancouver, BC V6C-3B2

604-689-5271
FAX 604-681-2363
E-Mail: info@amebc.ca
Home Page: www.amebc.ca

Gavin C Dirom, President/CEO

A member e-newsletter that captures essential mineral exploration and mining news, announces important upcoming events, gives an inside look at what is happening within AME BC, announces new and renewed members and more.
5400 Members
Frequency: Bi-Weekly
Founded in 1912

18605 Alaska Geology Survey News

Alaska Division of Geological Survey
3354 College Rd
Fairbanks, AK 99709-3707

907-451-5000
FAX 907-451-5050
E-Mail: dggsnews@dnr.state.ak.us
Home Page: www.dggs.dnr.state.ak.us

Robert Swenson, Executive Director
Trudy Wassel, Business Manager
John Parrott, Manager

Alaska miners and earth scientists.
4 Pages
Frequency: Monthly
Printed in on glossy stock

18606 Ash at Work

American Coal Ash Association
15200 E Girard Ave
Suite 3050
Aurora, CO 80014-3955

720-870-7897
FAX 720-870-7889
E-Mail: info@acaa-usa.org
Home Page: www.acaa-usa.org

Thomas Adams, Executive Director

Association news. non-profit trade association.
160 Members
Frequency: 2x/Year
Founded in 1968
Printed in 4 colors on glossy stock

18607 Bulletin

Northwest Mining Association
10 N Post St
Suite 220
Spokane, WA 99201-0722

509-624-1158
FAX 509-623-1241
E-Mail: nwma_info@nwma.org
Home Page: www.nwma.org

Laura Skaer, Executive Director
Mike Heywood, Marketing Director

Published every six weeks. 12-16 page newsletter covering issues relevant to the hardrock mining industry.
Circulation: 1500
Founded in 1895

18608 Coal Week International

McGraw Hill
PO Box 182604
Columbus, CO 43272

877-833-5524
800-752-8878
FAX 614-759-3749
E-Mail: customer.service@mcgraw-hill.com
Home Page: www.mcgraw-hill.com

John Slater, Publisher

Offers information and news to and of the mining industry in North America.
Cost: $467.00
Frequency: Monthly
Founded in 1884

18609 Coaldat Productivity Report

Pasha Publications
1600 Wilson Boulevard
Suite 600
Arlington, VA 22209-2510

703-528-1244
800-424-2908
FAX 703-528-1253

Harry Baisden, Group Publisher
Michael Hopps, Editor
Kathy Thorne, Circulatin Manager

Shows quarterly and year-to-date total coal production in tons, productivity in tons per miner per day, average number of employees for each mine, mining methods used, controlling company, mine location, district number, union affiliation and whether the mine is surface or underground. Both a controlling company and a state/country format are available.
Cost: $545.00
60 Pages
Frequency: Quarterly

18610 Control

Putman Media Company
555 W Pierce Rd
Suite 301,Pierce Road
Itasca, IL 60143-2626

630-467-1300
FAX 630-467-0197
E-Mail: jcappelletti@putman.net
Home Page: www.putman.net

John Cappelletti, President
Walter Boies, Circulation Manager

Designed for instrumentation and control systems professionals.
Frequency: Fortnightly
Circulation: 35000
Founded in 1945

18611 Legal Quarterly Digest of Mine Safety and Health Decisions

Legal Publication Services
888 Pittsford Mendon Center Road
Pittsford, NY 14534

585-582-3211
FAX 585-582-2879
E-Mail: MineSafety@aol.com
Home Page: www.minesafety.com

Ellen Smith, Owner/publisher
Melanie Aclander, Editor

Covers legal decisions on health and safety law in the mining industry.
Cost: $525.00
100 Pages
Frequency: Annual+
Founded in 1991

18612 Machinery Outlook

Manfredi & Associates
20934 W Lakeview Pkwy
Mundelein, IL 60060-9502

847-949-9080
FAX 847-949-9910
E-Mail: frank@manfredi.com
Home Page: www.machineryoutlook.com

Frank Manfredi, President

A newsletter about and for the construction and mining machinery industry.
Cost: $365.00
14 Pages
Frequency: Monthly
Founded in 1984
Printed in one color on matte stock

18613 Mine Regulation Reporter

Pasha Publications
1600 Wilson Boulevard
Suite 600
Arlington, VA 22209-2509

703-528-1244
800-424-2908
FAX 703-528-1253

Harry Baisden, Group Publisher
Michael Hopps, Editor
Kathy Thorne, Circulation Manager

The only biweekly newsletter and document service in the US for mine safety and environmental managers and attorneys. It covers mine safety, health and environmental regulations, legislation and court decisions that affect mine operations.
Cost: $785.00
Frequency: BiWeekly

18614 Mining Foundation of the Southwest

PO Box 42317
Tucson, AZ 85733

520-577-7519
FAX 520-577-7073
E-Mail: admin@miningfoundationsw.org
Home Page: www.miningfoundationsw.org

William Dresher, President
Jean Austin, Office Manager

Advances the science of mining and related industries by educating members and the public. Annual American Mining Hall of Fame First Saturday in December.
90 Pages
Founded in 1973

18615 Mining and Metallurgical Society of America Newsletter

476 Wilson Avenue
Novato, CA 94947-4236

415-897-1380
FAX 415-899-0262

E-Mail: contactmmsa@mmsa.net
Home Page: www.mmsa.net

Alan K Burton, Executive Director

Society news and information for professionals in the mining industry.
6 Pages
Founded in 1908

18616 Reclamation Matters
American Society of Mining and Reclamation
3134 Montevesta Road
Lexington, KY 40502-3548

859-351-9032
FAX 859-335-6529
E-Mail: asmr@insightbb.com
Home Page: www.asmr.us
Social Media: *Facebook*

Dennis Neuman, President
Richard Bamhisel, Executive Secretary

Newsletter of the ASMA. Free to members or $10/year.
500 Members
Founded in 1983

18617 Utah Mining Association Newsletter
Utah Mining Association
136 South Main Street
Suite 709
Salt Lake City, UT 84101-1683

801-364-1874
FAX 801-364-2640
E-Mail: mining@utahmining.org
Home Page: www.utahmining.org

Todd Bingham, President
Bryan Nielson, Chairman
Marilyn Tuttle, Office Manager

Provides updates on the mining industry.

18618 e-DIGEST & Washington Watch Newsletter
National Stone, Sand & Gravel Association
1605 King St
Alexandria, VA 22314-2726

703-525-8788
800-342-1415
FAX 703-525-7782
E-Mail: jwilson@nssga.org
Home Page: www.nssga.org

Jennifer Joy Wilson, President & CEO
Gus Edwards, Executive Vice President
Janice B. Springs, Executive Assistant

Member benefit of the NSSGA. Available online only.
25 Members
Frequency: Weekly
Founded in 1916

Magazines & Journals

18619 ASH at Work
American Coal Ash Association
15200 E Girard Ave
Suite 3050
Aurora, CO 80014-3955

720-870-7897
FAX 720-870-7889
E-Mail: info@acaa-usa.org
Home Page: www.acaa-usa.org

Thomas H Adams, Executive Director

The only magazine covering all facets of the coal combustion products industry. Read by ACAA members and others interested in the use and management of coal combustion products.
126 Members
Frequency: Bi-Annually

Circulation: 10000
Founded in 1968

18620 Alaska Miner
Alaska Miners Association
3305 Arctic Blvd
Suite 105
Anchorage, AK 99503-4575

907-563-9229
FAX 907-563-9225
E-Mail: ama@alaskaminers.org
Home Page: www.alaskaminers.org

Steven Borell, Executive Director

News and developments regarding Alaskan mining efforts.

18621 Alaska Miners Association Journal
Alaska Miners Association
3305 Arctic Boulevard
Suite 105
Anchorage, AK 99503-4575

907-563-9229
FAX 907-563-9225
E-Mail: ama@alaskaminers.org
Home Page: www.alaskaminers.org

Steven Borell, Executive Director

18622 CIM Magazine
Canadian Inst of Mining, Metallurgy & Petroleum
3400 de Maisonneuve Boulevard W
Suite 855
Montreal, QC H3Z-3B8

514-939-2710
FAX 514-939-2714
Home Page: www.cim.org

Dawn Nelley, Publications

Provides important information on mine developments, new technologies, safety, HR, products and services, and business issues.
Frequency: 8x's a Year
Circulation: 11,289

18623 Coal
MacLean Hunter
29 N Wacker Drive
Floor 9
Chicago, IL 60606-3298

312-726-2802
FAX 312-726-4103

Art Sanda, Editor
Elisabeth O'Grady, Executive Director

Articles cover maintenance and production of coal mines.
Cost: $62.50
Frequency: Monthly
Circulation: 22,000
Founded in 1964

18624 Coal Age
Primedia
29 N Wacker Avenue
10th Floor
Chicago, IL 60606

312-726-2802
FAX 312-726-2574
Home Page: www.coalage.com

Peter Johnson, Publisher
Stever P Fiscor, Editor-in-Chief
Ben Fromenthal, Production Manager

Geared primarily toward professionals in the coal mining and processing industries. Coal Age focuses on news, with in-depth features on coal mining operations and changing technologies.
Cost: $49.00
54 Pages
Frequency: Monthly
Circulation: 17900
ISSN: 1040-7820

Founded in 1911
Printed in 4 colors on glossy stock

18625 Coal Journal
PO Box 3068
Pikeville, KY 41502-3068

606-432-0206
FAX 606-432-2162

Terry L May, Publisher

Information concentrating on government regulations, emerging technologies and trade literature, and analyzes governmental actions and their impact on the coal industry.
Frequency: Quarterly
Circulation: 10000

18626 Coal People
Al Skinner Enterprises
PO Box 6247
Charleston, WV 25362-247

304-342-4129
800-235-5188
FAX 304-343-3124
E-Mail: cpm@newwave.net
Home Page: www.coalpeople.com

Al Skinner, Editor
Christina Karaum, Managing Editor
Beth Terranova, Sales Manager
Angela McNealy, Circulation Manager

Features special news and product sections for the coal industry. Home interest, historical pices, coal industry personalities.
Cost: $25.00
60 Pages
Frequency: 10 times ayear
Circulation: 11500
Founded in 1976
Printed in 4 colors on glossy stock

18627 EARTH Magazine
American Geosciences Institute
4220 King St
Alexandria, VA 22302-1502

703-379-2480
FAX 703-379-7563
E-Mail: agi@agiweb.org
Home Page: www.earthmagazine.org
Social Media: *Facebook, Twitter*

Patrick Leahy, Executive Director
Dr. Wayne D. Pennington, President
Dr. Sharon Mosher, President Elect
Michael D. Lawless, Treasurer
Dr. Berry H. Tew, Jr., Secretary

The science behind the headlines.
Frequency: Monthly
Founded in 1948

18628 Engineering & Mining Journal
Primedia Publishing
330 N Wabash Avenue
Suite 2300
Chicago, IL 60611

312-595-1080
FAX 312-595-0295
E-Mail: info@mining-media.com
Home Page: www.e-mj.com

Peter Johnson, Publisher
Steve Fiscor, Editor

Serves the field of mining including exploration, development, milling, smelting, refining of metals and nonmetallics
108 Pages
Frequency: Monthly
Circulation: 20589
ISSN: 0095-8948
Founded in 1866
Printed in 4 colors on glossy stock

18629 Environmental & Engineering Geoscience
Geological Society of America

PO Box 9140
Boulder, CO 80301-9140

303-357-1019
800-472-1988
FAX 303-357-1070
E-Mail: gsa@geosociety.org
Home Page: www.geosociety.org
Social Media: *Facebook, Twitter, LinkedIn,
YouTube*

John W. Geissman, President
George H. Davis, Vice President
Jonathan G. Price, Treasurer
John W. Hess, Executive Director/ Secretary

Contains new theory, applications, and case
histories illustrating the dynamics of the
fast-growing environmental and applied
disciplines.
16000 Members
Frequency: Quarterly
Founded in 1888

18630 GSA Today

Geological Society of America
PO Box 9140
Boulder, CO 80301-9140

303-357-1019
800-472-1988
FAX 303-357-1070
E-Mail: gsa@geosociety.org
Home Page: www.geosociety.org
Social Media: *Facebook, Twitter, LinkedIn,
YouTube*

John W. Geissman, President
George H. Davis, Vice President
Jonathan G. Price, Treasurer
John W. Hess, Executive Director/ Secretary

Lead science articles are refereed and should
present the results of exciting new research or
summarize and synthesize important problems
or issues.
16000 Members
Frequency: Monthly
Founded in 1888

18631 Geology

Geological Society of America
PO Box 9140
Boulder, CO 80301-9140

303-357-1019
800-472-1988
FAX 303-357-1070
E-Mail: gsa@geosociety.org
Home Page: www.geosociety.org
Social Media: *Facebook, Twitter, LinkedIn,
YouTube*

John W. Geissman, President
George H. Davis, Vice President
Jonathan G. Price, Treasurer
John W. Hess, Executive Director/ Secretary

Articles cover all earth-science disciplines and
include new investigations and provocative
topics. Professional geologists and university-level students in the earth sciences use this
widely read journal to keep up with scientific
research trends.
16000 Members
Frequency: Monthly
Founded in 1888

18632 Geophysics

Society of Exploration Geophysicists
8801 South Yale
Suite 500
Tulsa, OK 74137-3575

918-497-5500
FAX 918-497-5557
E-Mail: web@seg.org
Home Page: www.seg.org/index.shtml
Social Media: *Facebook, Twitter, LinkedIn*

Dr. Bob A. Hardage, President
Dr. David James Monk, President-Elect

Dr. Wafik Bulind Beydoun, Vice-President
Nancy Jo House, Secretary/ Treasurer
Dr. Tamas Nemeth, Editor

Encompasses all aspects of research, exploration, and education in applied geophysics.
Founded in 1930

18633 Geosphere

Geological Society of America
PO Box 9140
Boulder, CO 80301-9140

303-357-1019
800-472-1988
FAX 303-357-1070
E-Mail: gsa@geosociety.org
Home Page: www.geosociety.org
Social Media: *Facebook, Twitter, LinkedIn,
YouTube*

John W. Geissman, President
George H. Davis, Vice President
Jonathan G. Price, Treasurer
John W. Hess, Executive Director/ Secretary

Electronic journal, peer-reviewed covering all
geoscience disciplines in a medium that accom-
modates animations, sound, and movie files.
16000 Members
Frequency: Bimonthly
Founded in 1888

18634 Geotimes

American Geological Institute
4220 King St
Alexandria, VA 22302-1502

703-379-2480
FAX 703-379-7563
Home Page: www.agiweb.org/
Social Media: *Facebook, Twitter*

Dr. Wayne D. Pennington, President
Dr. Sharon Mosher, President Elect
Michael D. Lawless, Treasurer
Dr. Berry H. Tew, Jr., Secretary

Nonprofit federation of 40 geoscientific and
professional associations that represents more
than 100,000 geologists, geophysicsts, and
other earth scientists. AGI provides information services to geoscientists, serves as a voice
of shared interests in our profession, plays a
major role in strengthening geoscience education, and strives to increase public awareness of
the vital role the geosciences play in society's
use of resources and interaction with the environment.
Cost: $42.95
250M Members
40 Pages
Frequency: Monthly
Circulation: 100000
Founded in 1948

18635 Hydrogeology Journal

Geological Society of America
PO Box 9140
Boulder, CO 80301-9140

303-357-1019
800-472-1988
FAX 303-357-1070
E-Mail: gsa@geosociety.org
Home Page: www.geosociety.org
Social Media: *Facebook, Twitter, LinkedIn,
YouTube*

John W. Geissman, President
George H. Davis, Vice President
Jonathan G. Price, Treasurer
John W. Hess, Executive Director/ Secretary

Features peer-reviewed papers on theoretical
and applied hydrogeology. Describes worldwide progress in the science integrating
subsurface hydrology and geology with supporting disciplines.
16000 Members
Frequency: Bi-Monthly
Founded in 1888

18636 JOM: The Member Journal of TMS

Minerals, Metals & Minerals Society
184 Thorn Hill Road
Warrendale, PA 15086-7514

724-776-9000
800-759-4867
724-776-9000
FAX 724-776-3770
E-Mail: tmsgeneral@tms.org
Home Page: www.tms.org
Social Media: *Facebook, LinkedIn*

Garry W. Warren, President
Wolfgang A. Schneider, Vice President
Warren Hunt, Jr., Secretary/ Executive Director
Adrian C. Deneys, Director/ Chair

A technical journal devoted to exploring the
many aspects of materials science and engineering. Reports scholarly work that explores
the state-of-the-art processing, fabrication, design, and application of metals, ceramics, plastics, composites, and other materials.
Cost: $131.00
Frequency: Monthly
Circulation: 10000
Founded in 1948

18637 Journal of Electronic Materials

Minerals, Metals & Materials Society
184 Thorn Hill Road
Warrendale, PA 15086-7514

800-759-4867
FAX 724-776-3770
E-Mail: webmaster@tms.org
Home Page: www.tms.org
Social Media: *Facebook, LinkedIn*

Reports on the science and technology of electronic materials while examining new applications for semiconductors, magnetic alloys,
insulators, and optical and display materials.
Frequency: Monthly

18638 Lithosphere

Geological Society of America
PO Box 9140
Boulder, CO 80301-9140

303-357-1019
800-472-1988
FAX 303-357-1070
E-Mail: gsa@geosociety.org
Home Page: www.geosociety.org
Social Media: *Facebook, Twitter, LinkedIn,
YouTube*

John W. Geissman, President
George H. Davis, Vice President
Jonathan G. Price, Treasurer
John W. Hess, Executive Director/ Secretary

Peer-reviewed journal focusing on processes
that affect the crust, upper mantle, landscapes,
and/or sedimentary systems at all spatial and
temporal scales.
16000 Members
Frequency: Bimonthly
Founded in 1888

18639 Metallurgical and Materials Transactions

Minerals, Metals & Materials Society
184 Thorn Hill Road
Warrendale, PA 15086-7514

800-759-4867
FAX 724-776-3770
E-Mail: webmaster@tms.org
Home Page: www.tms.org
Social Media: *Facebook, LinkedIn*

Highly respected, peer-reviewed journals for
metallurgy and materials science.
Frequency: Monthly

18640 Mine Safety and Health News

Legal Publication Services

888 Pittsford Mendon Center Road
Pittsford, NY 14534

585-582-3211
FAX 585-582-2879
E-Mail: MineSafety@aol.com
Home Page: www.minesafety.com

Ellen Smith, Owner
Melanie Aclander, Editor
Cost: $525.00
Founded in 1991

18641 Mine and Quarry Trader

Primedia
7355 N Woodland Drive
PO Box 603
Indianapolis, IN 46206

317-991-1350
800-827-7468
FAX 317-299-1356
Home Page: www.mineandquarry.com

John Owen, Production Manager
Colleen Leath, Circulation Director
Kyle Agert, Publisher
Laura Larahaag, Marketing
Ellen Rolett, Manager

Equipment and services geared to the mining, aggregate and heavy construction industries.
Cost: $21.00
76 Pages
Frequency: Monthly
Circulation: 34406
Founded in 1976
Printed in 4 colors on matte stock

18642 Miners News

Miners News
9792 W Glen Ellyn Street
PO Box 4965
Boise, ID 83711

800-624-7212
FAX 208-658-4901
E-Mail: minersnews@msn.com
Home Page: www.minersnews.com

Gary White, Publisher
Shirley White, Public Relations

Information on mining history and provides insight into new technology and products used in mining.
Cost: $25.00
Circulation: 6512
ISSN: 0890-6157
Founded in 1985

18643 Mines Magazine

Colorado School of Mines Alumni Association
1600 Arapahoe Street
PO Box 1410
Golden, CO 80402

303-733-3143
FAX 303-273-3583
E-Mail: magazine@mines.edu
Home Page: www.minesmagazine.com
Social Media: *Facebook, Twitter, LinkedIn*

Nick Sutcliffe, Editor
Anita Pariseau, CEO/President
Amie Chitwood, Manager
Heidi Boersma, Administrative Assistant

Mines magazine is a critical communication serving the Colorado School of Mines community. Its mission is to keep readers informed about the school, to further the goals of the school and the alumni association, and to foster connectedness.
Cost: $35.00
Frequency: Quarterly
Circulation: 20000
Founded in 1910
Printed in 4 colors on glossy stock

18644 Mining Record

Mining Record Company
PO Box 1630
Castle Rock, CO 80104-6130

303-888-8871
800-441-4708
FAX 303-663-7823
E-Mail: customerservice@miningrecord.com
Home Page: www.miningrecord.com

Don E Howell, Editor
Dale Howell, Marketing

Has been in continuous publication for 115 years and is recognized as the industry's leading newspaper. Focuses on timely and credible news reporting on exploration, discovery, development, production, joint ventures, acquisitions, operating results, legislation, government reports and metals prices. Its readership is concentrated in the mining industry proper; mining companies and all individuals engaged in large or small mine production.
Cost: $45.00
16 Pages
Frequency: Monthly
Circulation: 5100
ISSN: 0026-5241
Founded in 1889
Printed in on newsprint stock

18645 New Equipment Digest

Penton Media
1300 E 9th St
Suite 316
Cleveland, OH 44114-1503

216-696-7000
FAX 216-696-6662
E-Mail: information@penton.com
Home Page: www.pentonmsc.com

Jane Cooper, Marketing
Jennifer Daugherty, Communications Manager
John DiPaola, Group Publisher
Robert F King, Editor
Bobbie Macy, Circulation Manager

Serves the general industrial field which includes manufacturing, processing, engineering services, construction, transportation, mining, public utilities, wholesale distributors, educational services, libraries, and governmental establishments.
Cost: $65.00
Frequency: Monthly
Circulation: 206000
Founded in 1892

18646 North American Mining

Mining Media
1005 Terminal Way
#140
Reno, NV 89502-2179

775-323-1553
FAX 775-323-1553

Dorothy Y Kosich, Editor

Information broken into departments which include environment, finance, government, management, new product news, profiles, safety issues and development technology updates.
Frequency: Bi-Monthly
Circulation: 7000

18647 Northern Miner

Southam Magazine Group
950 Wadsworth Boulevard
Suite 308
Lakewood, CO 80215

303-607-0853
800-459-8314
FAX 303-607-0862
E-Mail: northernminer2@northernminer.com
Home Page: www.northernminer.com

John Cumming, Editor
Brian Warriner, Sales Representatives

News and information for the mining industry.
Cost: $89.00
Frequency: Weekly
Founded in 1915
Printed in 4 colors on glossy stock

18648 Pay Dirt

Copper Queen Publishing Company
Copper Queen Plaza
PO Drawer 48
Bisbee, AZ 85603-48

520-432-2244
FAX 520-432-2247

Gary Dillard, Editor
Caryl Larkins, CEO
Frank Barco, Publisher
Gruce Rubin, Marketing

Keeps readers informed on current mining developments, changes in policies and decisions by state and federal agencies affecting mining. Accepts advertising.
Cost: $30.00
34 Pages
Frequency: Monthly
Circulation: 2200
ISSN: 0886-0920
Founded in 1938

18649 Pit & Quarry Magazine

The Aggregates Authority
1360 E. Ninth St.
Suite 1070
Cleveland, OH 44114

216-706-3700
800-669-1668
FAX 216-706-3711
E-Mail: scarr@questex.com
Home Page: www.pitandquarry.com

Sean Carr, Publisher

Exclusively for nonmetallic minerals producers.

18650 Professional Geologist

American Institute of Professional Geologists
1200 N Washington St
Suite 285
Thornton, CO 80241-3134

303-412-6205
FAX 303-253-9220
E-Mail: aipg@aipg.org
Home Page: www.aipg.org

William J Siok, Executive Director
Wendy Davidson, Assistant Director
Frequency: Bi-Monthly

18651 Reclamation Matters

American Society of Mining and Reclamation
3134 Montevesta Road
Lexington, KY 40502-3548

859-351-9032
FAX 859-335-6529
E-Mail: asmr@insightbb.com
Home Page: www.asmr.us

Dennis Neuman, President
Richard Bamhisel, Executive Secretary

Dissemination of technical information relating to the reclamation of lands disturbed by mineral extraction. Members yearly issue is paid out of proceeding.
500 Members
Founded in 1973

18652 Silver Valley Mining Journal
414 Sixth Street
Wallace, ID 83873

208-556-1621
E-Mail: silverminers@usamedia.tv
Home Page: www.silverminers.com

Provides information about silver mining.

18653 Skillings Mining Review
WestmorelandFlint
11 E Superior St
Suite 514
Duluth, MN 55802-3015

218-727-1552
FAX 218-733-0463
Home Page: www.westmorelandflint.com

John Hyduke, President
Ivan Hohnstadt, General Manager
Holly Olson, Circulation Manager

Skillings Mining Review covers breaking news
about mining companies and their suppliers,
dynamics of the global marketplace, technical
aspects of mining and processing, people in the
industry and their contributions to it. Also production and shipping reports, and the latest
news from coal and power industries.
Cost: $69.00
28 Pages
Frequency: Monthly
Circulation: 1500
ISSN: 0037-6329
Founded in 1912
Printed in 4 colors on glossy stock

18654 The Leading Edge
Society of Exploration Geophysicists
8801 South Yale
Suite 500
Tulsa, OK 74137-3575

918-497-5500
FAX 918-497-5557
E-Mail: web@seg.org
Home Page: www.seg.org/index.shtml
Social Media: *Facebook, Twitter, LinkedIn*

Dr. Bob A. Hardage, President
Dr. David James Monk, President-Elect
Dr. Wafik Bulind Beydoun, Vice-President
Nancy Jo House, Secretary/ Treasurer
Dr. Tamas Nemeth, Editor

Gateway publication introducing new geophysical theory, instrumentation, and established
practices to scientists in a wide range of
geoscience disciplines. Most material is presented in a semitechnical manner that minimizes mathematical theory and emphasizes
practical applications.
Frequency: Monthly
Founded in 1930

18655 United Mine Workers Journal
United Mine Workers of America
900 15th Street NW
Washington, DC 20005-2585

202-842-7200
FAX 202-842-7227
E-Mail: sales@wmwa.net
Home Page: www.wmwa.net

Doug Gibson, Editor

Information sent to members of the United
Mine Workers of America, retirees, other labor
unions, politicians and opinion makers in the
United States and abroad. Reports on issues inside and outside the UMWA that are of interest
to its members. Also contains features on politics, the arts, media and the culture of US
workers.
Frequency: Monthly
Circulation: 200000

18656 Valley Gazette
Hometown Publications

1000 Bridgeport Ave
Suite 3-2
Shelton, CT 06484-4676

203-926-2080
FAX 203-926-2091
Home Page: www.zwire.com

Gina Burkhart, CEO
Susane Hunter, Editor
Sharon Sakal, Circulation Manager
John Schneider, Marketing Manager
Frequency: Weekly
Circulation: 12322

18657 World Dredging, Mining & Construction
Placer Corporation
PO Box 17479
Irvine, CA 92623-7479

949-474-1120
FAX 949-863-9261
E-Mail: info@worlddredging.com
Home Page: www.worlddredging.com

MJ Richardson, Publisher
Steve Richardson, Editor
Robert Lindaur, Circulation Manager

International and national news for the dredg-
ing.
Cost: $40.00
100 Pages
Frequency: Monthly
Circulation: 3400
ISSN: 1045-0343
Founded in 1965
Printed in 4 colors on glossy stock

18658 World Mining Equipment
13544 Eads Road
Prairieville, LA 70769

225-673-9400
FAX 225-677-8277
E-Mail: info@mining-media.com
Home Page: www.mining-media.com

Steve Fiscor, Editor in chief
Richard Johnson, Managing Editor
Russ Carter, Managing Editor
Victor Matteucci, National Sales Manager
Cost: $29.95
Frequency: Monthly
Circulation: 10,523
Founded in 1866

Trade Shows

18659 ACAA Annual Meeting
American Coal Ash Association
38800 Country Club Drive
Farmington Hills, MI 48331-3439

720-870-7897
FAX 720-870-7889
E-Mail: info@acaa-usa.org
Home Page: www.acaa-usa.org

Thomas Adams, Executive Director
150 Attendees

18660 ASMA Annual Meeting
American Society of Mining and
Reclamation
3134 Montevesta Road
Lexington, KY 40502-3548

859-351-9032
FAX 859-335-6529
E-Mail: asmr@insightbb.com
Home Page: www.asmr.us
Social Media: *Facebook*

Dennis Neuman, President
Richard Bamhisel, Executive Secretary

Approximately 30 exhibitors.
300 Attendees
Frequency: Annual

18661 Alaska Miners Association Convention
Alaska Miners Association
3305 Arctic Boulevard
Suite 105
Anchorage, AK 99503-4575

907-563-9229
FAX 907-563-9225
E-Mail: ama@alaskaminers.org
Home Page: www.alaskaminers.org

Steven Borell, Executive Director

Forty booths supporting businesses of the mining industry and state and federal agencies involved with regulating the industry.
500 Attendees
Frequency: Annual/March

18662 American Federation Mineralogical Society Rocky Mountain
816 Whipporwhill Sourt
Bartlesville, OK 74006

918-827-6405

T Alf, President

One hundred tables of gems, minerals and fossils for wholesale and retail dealers.
4M Attendees
Frequency: September

18663 American Gem & Mineral Suppliers Association
PO Box 741
Patton, CA 92369-0741

760-241-3191

Renata Williams, Executive Chairman

Ten booths.
100 Attendees
Frequency: February

18664 Arminera
Marketing International
200 N Glebe Road
Suite 900
Arlington, VA 22203

703-527-8000
FAX 703-527-8006

Seminar, banquet and 400 exhibits of supplies,
equipment and services for the mining industry.
8500 Attendees
Frequency: Biennial

18665 Ash at Work Transportation Research Board
American Coal Ash Association
15200 E Girard Ave
Suite 3050
Aurora, CO 80014-3955

720-870-7897
FAX 720-870-7889
E-Mail: info@acaa-usa.org
Home Page: www.acaa-usa.org

Thomas Adams, Executive Director

Non-profit trade association.
160 Members
Frequency: 2x/Year
Founded in 1968
Printed in 4 colors on glossy stock

18666 EIA National Conference & Exposition
Environmental Information Association

6935 Wisconsin Avenue
Suite 306
Chevy Chase, MD 20815-6112

301-961-4999
888-343-4342
FAX 301-961-3094
E-Mail: info@eia-usa.org
Home Page: www.eia-usa.org

Dana Hudson, President
Mike Schrum, President Elect
Kevin Cannan, Vice President
Joy Finch, Secretary
Chris Gates, Treasurer

Providing the environmental industry with the information needed to remain knowledgeable, responsible, and competitive in the environmental health and safety industry.
Frequency: Annual/March

18667 MIACON Construction, Mining & Waste Management Show

Finocchiaro Enterprises
2921 Coral Way
Miami, FL 33145-3053

305-441-2865
FAX 305-529-9217
Home Page: www.miacon.com

Michael Finocchiaro, President
Jose Garcia, VP
Justine Finocchiaro, Chief Operations

Annual show of 650 manufacturers, suppliers, distributors and exporters of equipment, machinery, supplies and services for the construction, mining and waste managment industries. There will be 600 booths.
10M Attendees
Frequency: December
Founded in 1994

18668 MINExpo International

National Mining Association
101 Constitution Avenue NW
Suite 500 East
Washington, DC 20001-2133

202-463-2600
FAX 202-463-2666
Home Page: www.minexpo.com

Harold P. Quinn, Jr., President & CEO

MINExpo is the mining industry's premier showcase for companies specializing in every facet of mining: open pit, underground, processing and preparation, mine site development, exploration and surveying, smelting and refining, and reclamation.
30000 Attendees
Frequency: Annual/September

18669 Mineral Exploration Roundup

Assoc for Mineral Exploration British Columbia
889 W Pender Street
Suite 800
Vancouver, BC V6C 3B2

604-689-5271
FAX 604-681-2363
E-Mail: info@amebc.ca
Home Page: www.amebc.ca
Social Media: *Facebook, Twitter*

Simone Hill, Acting Dir., Member Relations
Morgen Andoff, Acting Manager, Special Events
Roxanne Finnie, Manager, Member Relations

AME BC is the predominant voice of mineral exploration and development in British Columbia. AME BC represents members including geoscientists, prospectors, engineers, students, exploration and mining companies and suppliers who are engaged in mineral exploration and develoment in BC and throughout the world. AME BC annually hosts international guests from around the world during the annual Min-

eral Exploration Roundup conference that takes place every January.
5000 Members
Frequency: Annual/January
Founded in 1912

18670 National Western Mining Conference & Exhibition

Colorado Mining Association
216 16th Street
Suite 1250
Denver, CO 80202-5161

303-575-9199
FAX 303-575-9194
E-Mail: colomine@coloradomining.org
Home Page: www.coloradomining.org

Stuart Sanderson, President

Annual show of 90 exhibitors of equipment and support services for the mining industry.
1000 Attendees

18671 Northwest Mining Association Annual Meeting and Exposition

Northwest Mining Association
10 N Post Street
Suite 220
Spokane, WA 99201

509-624-1158
FAX 509-623-1241
Home Page: www.nwma.com

Pat Nelsen, Operations Director

Annual mining convention in the US. Containing 335 booths, 280 exhibits and more than 20 technical sessions. The second largest annual mining convention in the USA. Founded in 1895.
2.5M Attendees
Frequency: December

18672 Randol Gold Forum

Randol International Limited
18301 W Colfax Avenue
#T1B
Golden, CO 80401-4834

303-526-7618
FAX 303-271-0334
Home Page: http://www.randol.com

Hans Von Michaelis, President
Patti Hamilton, Sales Coordinator

Mining companies exposition.
350 Attendees
Frequency: September

18673 Rapid Excavation Tunneling Conference Expo

PO Box 625002
Littleton, CO 80162-5002

303-973-9550

DD Daley, Meeting Manager

75 booths.
1M Attendees
Frequency: June

18674 SME Annual Meeting

Society of Mining, Metallurgy, and Exploration
12999 E. Adam Aircraft Circle
Englewood, CO 80112

303-948-4200
800-763-3132
FAX 303-973-3845
E-Mail: sme@smenet.org
Home Page: www.smenet.org
Social Media: *Facebook, Twitter, LinkedIn*

John N. Murphy, President
Drew A. Meyer, President-Elect
David L. Kanagy, Executive Director

Mine to Market: Now It's Global.
4M Attendees
Frequency: Annual/February

18675 UMA Annual Convention

Utah Mining Association
136 S Main St
Suite 709
Salt Lake City, UT 84101-1683

801-364-1874
FAX 801-364-2640
E-Mail: mining@utahmining.org
Home Page: www.utahmining.org

Todd Bingham, President
Terry Maio, Chairman
Marilyn Tuttle, Administrator
Frequency: August

Directories & Databases

18676 Coal Data

National Coal Association
100 Independence Ave, SW
Washington, DC 20585

202-586-8800

Offers important data on the 50 largest coal mines in the country.
Cost: $50.00

18677 Coal Mine Directory

Primedia
29 N Wacker Drive
10th Floor
Chicago, IL 60606-3203

312-726-2802
800-621-9907
FAX 312-726-2574
Home Page: www.primediabusiness.com

Art Sanda, Editor
Patricia L Yos, Editor

Over 2,000 coal mines are profiled that are based in the United States and Canada.
Cost: $149.00
Frequency: Annual January
Circulation: 700

18678 DRI Coal Forecast

DRI/McGraw-Hill
24 Hartwell Ave
Lexington, MA 02421-3103

781-860-6060
FAX 781-860-6002
E-Mail: support@construction.com
Home Page: www.construction.com

Walt Arvin, President

Offers valuable information on the mining of coal by supply region and producing state; total coal by demand region; cost and demand by the consumer sector.

18679 Engineering and Mining Journal: Buying Directory Issue

Primedia
29 N Wacker Drive
10th Floor
Chicago, IL 60606

312-726-2802
800-621-9907
FAX 312-726-2574
Home Page: www.primediabusiness.com

Robert Wyllie, Editor

List of manufacturers and suppliers of mining equipment.
Cost: $35.00
Frequency: Annual November
Circulation: 23,000

18680 Expanded Shale, Clay and Slate Institute Roster of Members

Expanded Shale, Clay and Slate Institute
35 East Wacker Dr.
Suite 850
Chicago, IL 60601

801-272-7070
FAX 312-644-8557
E-Mail: info@escsi.org
Home Page: www.escsi.org

John Riese, President

About 15 producers by the rotary kiln method of lightweight aggregates of expanded shales, clays, and slates; international coverage.

18681 Geophysical Directory

Geophysical Directory
PO Box 130508
Houston, TX 77219-0508

713-291-1922
800-929-2462
FAX 713-529-3646
Home Page: www.geophysicaldirectory.com

Claudia LaCalli, Editor
Stewart Schafer, Owner

About 4,500 companies that provide geophysical equipment, supplies or services and mining and petroleum companies that use geophysical techniques.
Cost: $135.00
400 Pages
Frequency: Annual March
Circulation: 2,000
Founded in 1946
Mailing list available for rent: 2500 names
Printed in 4 colors on glossy stock

18682 Iron and Manganese Ore Databook

Metal Bulletin
220 5th Avenue
#Enus-19T
New York, NY 10001-7708

212-136-6202
800-MET-L 25
FAX 212-213-6273

John Bailey, Editor

Iron and manganese ore producers and traders worldwide.
Cost: $179.00
Frequency: Quadrennial

18683 Keystone Coal Industry Manual

Primedia
29 N Wacker Drive
10th Floor
Chicago, IL 60611

312-726-2802
800-621-9907
FAX 312-726-2574
Home Page: www.primediabusiness.com

Art Sanda, Editor
Patricia L Yos, Editor

Coal companies and mines, coke plants, coal preparation plants, domestic and export coal sales companies.
Cost: $260.00
Frequency: Annual January
Circulation: 1,400

18684 Landmen's Directory and Guidebook

American Association of Professional Landmen
4100 Fossil Creek Boulevard
Fort Worth, TX 76137-2723

817-847-7700
FAX 817-847-7704

E-Mail: aapl@landman.org
Home Page: www.landman.org

Le'ann Callihan, Editor/Publications Department

About 7,500 member specialists in assembling or disposing of land or rights required for oil, gas, coal andmineral exploration and exploitation in the US and Canada.
Cost: $100.00
Frequency: Annual November
Circulation: 7,500
ISSN: 0272-8370

18685 Minerals Yearbook

US Geological Survey
1730 E Parham Rd
Richmond, VA 23228-2202

804-261-2600
FAX 804-261-2659
E-Mail: dc_va@usgs.gov
Home Page: www.usgs.gov

Charles G Groats, Director

The Minerals Yearbook discusses the performance of the worldwide minerals and materials industry and provides background information to assist in interpreting that performance. Contents of the individual Minerals Yearbook volumes are, Volume I, Metals and Minerals, Volume II, Area Reports:Domestic, and Volume III, Area Reports: International.
200+ Pages
Frequency: Annual
Founded in 1935

18686 Mining Directory

Metal Bulletin
220 5th Avenue
10th Floor
New York, NY 10001-7708

212-213-6202
800-MET-L 25
FAX 212-213-6273
E-Mail: 72610.3721@compuserve.com
Home Page: www.metbul.com/metbul/mbhome

Don Nelson, Editor

Offers valuable information on mines, mining equipment manufacturers, suppliers of equipment and services to the industry and industry consultants.
Cost: $158.00

18687 Mining Engineering: SME Membership Directory

Society of Mining, Metallurgy & Exploration
12999 E. Adam Aircraft Circle
Englewood, CO 80112

303-948-4200
800-763-3132
FAX 303-973-3845
E-Mail: sme@smenet.org
Home Page: www.smenet.org
Social Media: *Facebook, Twitter, LinkedIn*

John N. Murphy, President
Drew A. Meyer, President-Elect

A list of over 18,000 persons engaged in the location, exploration,treatment and marketing of all classes of minerals except petroleum.
Cost: $150.00
Frequency: Annual
Circulation: 20,000
ISSN: 0026-5187

18688 National Ocean Industries Association: Directory of Membership

National Ocean Industries Association

1120 G St NW
Suite 900
Washington, DC 20005-3801

202-347-6900
FAX 202-347-8650
Home Page: www.noia.org

Tom Fry, President

Over 300 firms engaged in offshore construction, drilling and petroleum production, geophysical exploration, ship building and repair, deep-sea mining and related activities in the development and use of marine resources.
Frequency: Annual

18689 Pit & Quarry: Reference Manual & Buyers' Guide Issue

Advanstar Communications
2501 Colorado Avenue
Suite 280
Santa Monica, CA 90404-4503

310-857-7500
FAX 310-857-7510
E-Mail: info@advanstar.com
Home Page: www.advanstar.com

List of approximately 1,000 manufacturers and other suppliers of equipment, products and services to the nonmetallic mining and quarrying industry.
Cost: $25.00
Frequency: Annual
Circulation: 25,000

18690 Randol Buyer's Guide

Randol International Limited
18301 W Colfax Avenue
#T-2
Golden, CO 80401-4834

303-526-7618
800-726-3652
FAX 303-278-9229
Home Page: http://www.randol.com

Hans Von Michaelis, Editor

Approximately 10,000 companies that offer equipment and services used in the mining industry.
Cost: $35.00
Frequency: Annual
Circulation: 10,000

18691 Randol Mining Directory

Randol International Limited
18301 W Colfax Avenue
#T1B
Golden, CO 80401-4834

303-526-7618
FAX 303-271-0334
Home Page: http://www.randol.com

Hans Von Michaelis, President
Patti Hamilton, Sales Coordinator

The most comprehensive source of information on all mines in the USA. Used for systematic marketing to mines and exploration companies, statistical research and more, offering 10,000 industry contacts.

18692 Rock Products: Buyer's Guide Issue

Primedia
29 N Wacker Drive
10th Floor
Chicago, IL 60606

312-726-2802
FAX 312-726-2574
Home Page: www.primediabusiness.com

Rick Marley, Editor
Scot Bieda, Publisher
David Pistello, Classified

List of about 1,500 providers worldwide of equipment and services for the nonmetallic

mineral mining and processing industry.
Cost: $100.00
Frequency: Annual November
Circulation: 23,000

18693 Silver Refiners of the World and their Identifying Ingot Marks
Silver Institute
1112 16th St NW
Suite 240
Washington, DC 20036-4818

202-347-8200
Home Page: www.silverinstitute.org

Over 80 refiners in over 18 countries are profiled.
Cost: $33.00
85 Pages

18694 Western Mining Directory
Howell Publishing Company
1758 Blake St
Denver, CO 80202-1226

303-296-8000
800-441-4748
FAX 303-296-1123
E-Mail: howell@rmi.net

Dave Howell, Owner

Directory of mining companies and mines nationwide.
Cost: $49.00
Circulation: 5,000
Founded in 1968

18695 World Aluminum: A Metal Bulletin Databook
Metal Bulletin
220 5th Avenue
19th Floor
New York, NY 10001-7781

212-213-6202
FAX 212-213-1870
E-Mail: help@metalbulletin.com
Home Page: www.metalbulletin.com

Richard ODonoghue, Manager
Ania Tumm, Marketing Manager
Julius Pike, Account Manager

Offers information on producers and traders of aluminum and aluminum alloys.
Cost: $247.00
540 Pages
ISSN: 0951-2233

18696 World Mining Equipment
Metal Bulletin
220 5th Avenue
New York, NY 10001

212-213-6202
FAX 212-213-6619
Home Page: www.wme.com

Mike Woof, Editor

Manufacturers of mining equipment.
Cost: $246.00
66 Pages
Circulation: 13M
ISSN: 0746-729X
Printed in 4 colors on glossy stock

Industry Web Sites

18697 ca.uky.edu/assmr
American Society of Mining and Reclamation

18698 http://gold.greyhouse.com
G.O.L.D Grey House OnLine Databases
Grey House Publishing's online database platform, GOLD, offers Quick Search, Keyword

Search and Expert Search for most business sectors including mining markets. The GOLD platform makes finding the information you need quick and easy - whether you're a novice searcher or an experienced database user. All of Grey House's directory products are available for subscription on the GOLD platform.

18699 www.acaa-usa.org
American Coal Ash Association
Promotes the beneficial use of coal cumbustion products.

18700 www.aem.org
Vibrating Screen Manufacturers Association

18701 www.agiweb.org
American Geological Institute
Provides information services to geoscientists, serves as a voice of shared interests in our profession.

18702 www.aimeny.org
American Institute of Mining & Petroleum Engineers
Organization was founded to further the arts and sciences employed to recover the earth's minerals and convert them to useful products.

18703 www.aipg.org
American Institute of Professional Geologists
Founded to certify the credentials of practicing geologists and to advocate on behalf of the profession.

18704 www.alaskaminers.org
Alaska Miners Association
Encourage and support responsible mineral production in Alaska.

18705 www.amebc.ca
Assn for Mineral Exploration British Columbia
Supports and promotes the mineral exploration community and related services by disseminating information to the public and governments, thereby assisting in the creation of wealth and jobs through sustainable mineral developement.

18706 www.asmi.state.az.us
State Mine Inspector

18707 www.azcu.org
Arizona Mining Association
Provides information about mining, specifically copper mining and the impact it has on our lives.

18708 www.blm.org
Bureau of Land Management

18709 www.calmining.org
California Mining Association
Represents the breadth and depth of California's mining industry.

18710 www.ces.ca.uky.edu/assmr
American Society for Surface Mining & Reclamation
Dissemination of Technical information relating to the reclamation of lands disturbed by mineral extraction. Members yearly issue is paid out of proceedings. Membership dues - $50/regular; $10/students.

18711 www.chamberofmines.bc.ca
BC & Yukon Chamber of Mines
A list of mines in the Unites States.

18712 www.cim.org
Canadian Inst of Mining, Metallurgy & Petroleum

Strives to be the association of choice for professionals in the minerals industries.

18713 www.coloradomining.org
Colorado Mining Association
Serves as a spokesman for the mining industry in Colorado.

18714 www.copper.org
Copper Development Association

18715 www.crc.siu.edu/nasir.htm
National Association of State Land Reclamationists

18716 www.crystalgrowth.org
American Association for Crystal Growth
For those interested in organic crystal growth.

18717 www.dri.edu
Desert Research Institute
Information on basic and applied environmental research on a local, national, and international scale. For scientists, technicians, and support personnel.

18718 www.fmshre.gov
Federal Mine Safety and Health Review Commission

18719 www.geosociety.org
Geological Society of America

18720 www.gold.org
World Gold Council

18721 www.goldprospecters.org
Gold Prospectors Association

18722 www.greyhouse.com
Grey House Publishing
Authoritative reference directories for most business sectors, including mining markets. Users can search the online databases with varied search criteria allowing for custom searches by product category, geographic area, sales volume, keyword, subject and more. Full Grey House catalog and online ordering also available.

18723 www.idahomining.org
Idaho Mining Association
Founded to further the interests of Idaho's mining industry and minerals production.

18724 www.kaolin.com
China Clay Producers Association

18725 www.leadinfo.com
Lead Industries Association

18726 www.lignite.com
Lignite Energy Council
Promotes policies and directs activities that maintain a viable lignite industry and enhance the development of our regions lignite resources.

18727 www.lime.org
National Lime Association
Trade association for US and Canadian manufacturers of high calcium quicklime, dolomitic quicklime and hydrated lime, collectively referred to as lime.

18728 www.minecon.com/index.html
Mineral Economics and Management Society

18729 www.miningfoundationsw.org
Mining Foundation of the Southwest

18730 www.miningorganizations.org/msia.htm
Mine Safety Institute of America

18731 www.miningusa.com
Mining Associations-National

A list of associations throughout the United States.

18732 www.mmsa.net
Mining and Metallurgical Society of America

A professional organization dedicated to increasing public awareness and understanding about mining and why mined materials are essential to modern society and human well being.

18733 www.msha.gov
Mine Safety and Health Administration

18734 www.naima.org
Mineral Insulation Manufacturers Association

Trade association of North American manufacturwers of fiberglass, rock wool, and slag wool insulation products.

18735 www.nevadamining.org
Nevada Mining Association

Represents all aspects of the mining industry in the state of Nevada.

18736 www.nma.org
National Mining Association

The only national trade organization represents the interests of mining before Congress, the Administration, federal agencies, the judiciary and the media.

18737 www.noia.org
National Ocean Industries Association

National organization engaged in offshore construction, drilling and petroleum production, geophysical exploration, ship building and repair.

18738 www.nssga.org
National Stone, Sand & Gravel Association

18739 www.nwma.org
Northwest Mining Association

Provides liaison between mining industry and government. Offers short course on current technology.

18740 www.perlite.org
Perlite Institute

18741 www.pitandquarry.com
The Aggregates Authority-Pit and Quarry

A magazine exclusively for nonmetallic minerals producers.

18742 www.rheology.org
Society of Rheology

18743 www.rmag.org
Rocky Mountain Association of Geologists

18744 www.seg.org
Society of Exploration Geophysicists

18745 www.segweb.org
Society of Economic Geologists

The society of economic geologists is an international organization of individual members with interest in the field of economic geology.

18746 www.silverinstitute.org
Silver Institute

18747 www.silverminers.org
Silver Valley Mining Association

dedicated to promoting the Silver Valley of northern Idaho and its mining industry.

18748 www.smenet.org
Society for Mining, Metallurgy & Exploration

Advances the worldwide mining and minerals community through information exchange and professional development.

18749 www.solutionmining.org
Solution Mining Research Institute

18750 www.sorptive.org
Sorptive Minerals Institute

18751 www.sulphurinstitute.org
Sulphur Institute

18752 www.surface-mining.state.al.us
Alabama Surface Mining Commission

Balance civilization's demands for natural resources and environmental conservation in the state of Alabama.

18753 www.tmra.com
Texas Mining & Reclamation Association

18754 www.tms.org
Minerals, Metals & Materials Society

Dedicated to the development and dissemination of the scientific and engineering knowledge bases for materials-centered technologies.

18755 www.umwa.org
United Mine Workers of America

18756 www.usgs.gov
US Geological Survey

18757 www.utahmining.org
Utah Mining Association

Helps to promote and protect the mining industry. Provides its members with full-time professional industry representation before the State Legislature; various government regularoty agencies on the federal, state and local levels, other associations, and business and industry groups.

18758 www.womeninmining.org
Women in Mining

Associations

18759 Academy of Motion Picture Arts and Sciences
8949 Wilshire Blvd
Beverly Hills, CA 90211-1972

310-247-3000
FAX 310-271-3395
Home Page: www.oscars.org
Social Media: *Facebook, Twitter, LinkedIn, Youtube*

The Academy was founded to advance the arts and sciences of motion pictures; foster cooperation among creative leaders for cultural, educational and technological progress; recognize outstanding achievments; cooperate on technical research and improvement of methods and equipment; provide a common forum and meeting ground for various branches and crafts; represent the viewpoint of actual creators of the motion picture. Hosts annual Academy Awards.
6000 Members
Founded in 1927

18760 Academy of Science Fiction Fantasy and Horror Films
334 W 54th St
Los Angeles, CA 90037-3806

323-752-5811
FAX 323-752-5811
E-Mail: saturn.awards@ca.rr.com
Home Page: www.saturnawards.org
Social Media: *Facebook, Twitter*

Robert Holguin, President
Roger Fenton, VP
Michael Laster, Director

Culminated from the Count Dracula Society, the Academy hosts the annual Science Fiction Film Awards, called the Saturn Awards.
Founded in 1972

18761 American Cinema Editors
100 Universal City Plaza
Verna Fields Building 2282 Room 190
Universal City, CA 91608

818-777-2900
FAX 818-733-5023
E-Mail: americancinema@earthlink.net
Home Page: www.americancinemaeditors.org
Social Media: *Facebook, Twitter*

Alan Heim, President
Stephen Rivkin, VP
Lillian Bennson, Secretary
Ed Abroms, Treasurer
Jan Ambler, A.C.E

A non-profit corporation committed to the encouragement of mutually-beneficial dialogue with other members of the motion picture industry and to educating the general public. Holds the annual ACE Eddie Awards honoring the nominees for the Film Editing Award given by the Academy of Motion Pictures Arts and Sciences.
Founded in 1950

18762 American Film Institute
2021 North Western Ave.
Los Angeles, CA 90027-1657

323-856-7600
FAX 323-467-4578
E-Mail: information@afi.com
Home Page: www.afi.com
Social Media: *Facebook, Twitter, YouTube, Tumblr, Instagram*

Bob Gazzale, President & CEO

The AFI is a nonprofit educational and cultural organization dedicated to preserving and honoring America's film heritage and educating its next generation of filmmakers.

18763 American Society of Cinematographers
1782 N Orange Drive
PO Box 2230
Hollywood, CA 90028

323-969-4333
800-448-0145
FAX 323-882-6391
E-Mail: office@theasc.com
Home Page: www.theasc.com
Social Media: *Facebook, Twitter, YouTube, Instagram, Vimeo*

Daryn Okadaan, President
Michael Negrin, Secretary
Victor J Kemper, Treasurer
Rachael K. Bosley, Managing Director

The ASC is not a labor union or guild, but is an educational, cultural and professional organization. Membership is possible by invitation and is extended only to directors of photography with distinguished credits in the industry. Publishes 'American Cinematographer' magazine.
Founded in 1919

18764 Art Directors Guild
11969 Ventura Blvd
Suite 200
Studio City, CA 91604-2619

818-762-9995
FAX 818-762-9997
E-Mail: lydia@artdirectors.org
Home Page: www.adg.org
Social Media: *Facebook, Twitter, Instagram, Vimeo*

Scott Roth, Executive Director
Lisa Frazza, Secretary
Michael Baugh, Treasurer
Sasha Aronson, Executive Assistant to Scott Roth
Alexandra Schaaf, Manager Membership Department

The creative talents that concieve and manage the background and settings for most films and television projects are members of the Art Directors Guild, Local 800. They and most other crafts of the entertainment industry are members of the International Alliance of Theatrical Stage Employees, Moving Picture Technicians, Artists and Allied Crafts of the United States, its Territories and Canada.
935 Members
Founded in 1937

18765 Assistant Directors Training Program
15301 Ventura Blvd.
Bldg E #1075
Sherman Oaks, CA 91403

818-386-2545
FAX 818-386-2876
E-Mail: mail@dgptp.org
Home Page: www.trainingplan.org

Tom Joyner, Chair

Provides motion picture and television industry training as directed by the Alliance of Motion Picture and Television Producers and the Directors Guild of America.
Founded in 1965

18766 Association of Cinema and Video Laboratories
Bev Wood C/O Deluxe Laboratories
1377 North Serrano Avenue
Hollywood, CA 90027

323-462-6171
FAX 206-682-6649
E-Mail: beverly.wood@bydeluxe.com
Home Page: www.acvl.org

Bev Wood, President
Chip Wilkenson, First VP
John Carlson, Second VP

Kevin Dillon, Treasurer
Bob Olson, Secretary

Provides opportunities for discussion and exchange of ideas in connection with administrative, technical and managerial problems in the motion picture and video industry. The Association is concerned with improvements in technical practices and procedures, public and industry relations, product specifications to vendors, the impact of current and impending governmental regulations, and any and all other areas of interest to the laboratory industry.
80 Members
Founded in 1953

18767 Association of Talent Agents
9255 Sunset Blvd
Suite 930
Los Angeles, CA 90069-3317

310-274-0628
FAX 310-274-5063
E-Mail: shellie@agentassociation.com
Home Page: www.agentassociation.com

Sandy Bresler, President
Sheldon Sroloff, VP
Jim Gosnell, Secretary/Treasurer
Karen Stuart, Executive Director
Shellie Jetton, Administrative Director

A non-profit trade association representing talent agencies in the industry. ATA is the voice of unified talent and literary agencies. ATA agencies represent the vast majority of working artists, including actors, directors, writers, and other artists in film, stage, television, radio, commercial, literary work, and other entertainment enterprises.
Founded in 1937

18768 Casting Society of America
1149 N. Gower Street
Suite 110
Los Angeles, CA 90038

323-785-1011
FAX 323-463-4753
E-Mail: info@castingsociety.com
Home Page: www.castingsociety.com

Richard Hicks, President
Matthew Lessall, Vice President
Sharon Bialy, Secretary
Mark Simon, Treasurer

CSA is the largest professional association of Casting Directors in the world. They work in all areas of entertainment in film, television and theatre. CSA continually seeks to expand their standing in the industry by providing information and opportunities that support is members.
500+ Members
Founded in 1982

18769 Children in Film
11271 Ventura Blvd.
Studio City, CA 91604

818-432-7400
800-902-9001
E-Mail: contact@childreninfilm.com
Home Page: www.childreninfilm.com

Toni Casala, President
Trisha Noble, Director, Permit Services
Heather Broeker, Director, Marketing

To provide tools and information needed to successfully employ a child in the entertainment industry while also lending a healthy, positive view into the world of child actors.
Founded in 2000

18770 Directors Guild of America
7920 W Sunset Blvd
Los Angeles, CA 90046-3347

310-289-2000
800-421-4173

FAX 310-289-2029
E-Mail: LDavis@dga.org
Home Page: www.dga.org

Jay Roth, President
Steven Soderbergh, National VP
Gilbert Cates, Secretary/Treasurer

The DGA represents Film and Television Directors, Unit Production Managers, First Assistant Directors, Second Assistant Directors, Technical Coordinators and Tape Associate Directors, Stage Managers and Production Assistants.

18771 Film Society of Lincoln Center

70 Lincoln Center Plz
New York, NY 10023-6595

212-875-5601
FAX 212-875-5636
E-Mail: webmaster@filmlinc.com
Home Page: www.filmlinc.com
Social Media: *Facebook, Twitter, YouTube*

Serge Joseph, Manager
Daniel H Stern, President
Wendy Keys, Secreatry
James Bouras, Treasurer
Lesli Klainberg, Executive Director

Celebrates American and international cinema, recognizes and supports new filmmakers, and enhances awareness, accessibility and understanding of the art among a broad and diverse film going audience. The Film Society is best known for two international festivals - the New York Film Festival and the New Directors/New Films festival.
Founded in 1969

18772 Greek Americans in the Arts and Entertainment

3916 Sepulveda Blvd
Suite 107
Culver City, CA 90230

323-651-3507
FAX 310-933-0250
E-Mail: info@americanhellenic.org
Home Page: www.americanhellenic.org
Social Media: *Facebook, Twitter, LinkedIn*

Dr. Menas Kafatos, Chairman
Eleftheria Polychronis, Vice President
Aris Anagnos, Vice President of Political Action
Dr. Tasos Chassiakos, VP, Culture & Education, Secretary
Alexander Mizan, Treasurer

Follows the legacy of Greek-Americans in the arts and entertainment field.

18773 Historians Film Committee

711 E. Boldt Way
Box 80
Appleton, WI 54911

920-832-6649
FAX 202-544-8307
E-Mail: center@filmandhistory.org
Home Page: www.filmandhistory.org

Peter C Rollins, Editor-in-Chief

The Committee exists to further the use of film sources in teaching and research, to disseminate information about film and film use to historians and other social scientists, to work for an effective system of film preservation so that scholars may have ready access to film archives, and to organize periodic conferences dealing with film.
Founded in 1970

18774 Hollywood Arts Council

PO Box 931056
Hollywood, CA 90093

323-462-2355
FAX 323-465-9240
E-Mail: admin@hollywoodartscouncil.org

Home Page: www.hollywoodartscouncil.org
Social Media: *Facebook, LinkedIn, YouTube*

David Warren, Chairman
Matthew Leum, Vice Chair
Patti Negri, Secretary
Steven P. Tronson, Treasurer
Joni Labaqui, Director

Promotes, nurtures and supports the arts in Hollywood. Has served the community through advocacy, coalition building, free public arts events and after school programs.
400 Members
Founded in 1978

18775 Independent Film & Television Alliance

10850 Wilshire Blvd
9th Floor
Los Angeles, CA 90024-4628

310-446-1000
FAX 310-446-1600
E-Mail: info@ ifta-online.org
Home Page: www.ifta-online.org
Social Media: *Facebook, LinkedIn, YouTube*

Michael Ryan, Chairman
Nicolas Chartier, Vice Chairperson
Kirk D' Amico, General Vice Chairperson
Charlotte Mickie, Vice Chairperson, Non-Californian
Lise Romanoff, Vice Chairperson/Secretary

A non-profit association whose mission is to provide the independent film and television industry with high-quality marketplace-oriented services and worldwide representation. The Alliance actively lobbies the United States and Eurpoean governments and the international organizations on measures that impact production and distribution.
Founded in 1980

18776 International Animated Film Society

2114 W Burbank Blvd
Burbank, CA 91506-1232

818-842-8330
FAX 613-232-6315
E-Mail: info@asifa-hollywood.org
Home Page: www.animationarchive.org

Amtran Manoogian, President

A California nonprofit organization established to promote and encourage the art and craft of animation. They support and encourage animation education, supports the preservation and critical evaluation of animation history, recognize achievement of excellence in the art and field of animation, strive to increase the public awareness of animation, act as a liaison to encourage the free exchange of ideas within the animation community, as well as a variety of other goals.
350 Members
Founded in 1974

18777 International Cinematographers Guild

7755 W Sunset Boulevard
Hollywood, CA 90046

323-876-0160
FAX 323-876-6383
E-Mail: admin@camerguild.com
Home Page: www.cameraguild.com
Social Media: *Facebook, Twitter*

Steven Poster, President
Lewis Rothenberg, National VP
Alan M. Gitlin, Secretary/Treasurer
Bruce C Doering, Executive Director

The International Cinematographers Guild welcomes camera professionals from across the United States and around the world.

18778 International Documentary Association

3470 Wilshire Blvd
Suite 980
Los Angeles, CA 90010

213-232-1660
FAX 213-232-1669
E-Mail: michael@documentary.org
Home Page: www.documentary.org
Social Media: *Facebook, Twitter, LinkedIn, Youtube*

Michael Lumpkin, Executive Director
Cindy Chyr, Development Director
Andrew Kaiser, Development Associate
Jina Chung, Associate
Amy Halpin, Manager

A nonprofit membership organization dedicated to supporting the efforts of nonfiction film and video makers throughout the United States and the world; promoting the documentary form; and expanding opportunities for the production, distribution, and exhibition of documentary.
2800+ Members
Founded in 1982

18779 International Stunt Association

11331 Ventura Boulevard
Suite 100
Studio City, CA 91604

818-760-2072
FAX 818-501-5656
E-Mail: info@isastunts.com
Home Page: www.isastunts.com
Social Media: *Facebook, Twitter*

Leading the industry in exciting action while holding safety above all else, ISA is a fraternal organization whose membership is by invitation only. It is comprised of the top stuntment, stunt coordinators and second unit directors that Hollywood has to offer and a safety record that is second to none.
Founded in 1980

18780 Motion Picture Association of America

15301 Ventura Boulevard
Building E
Sherman Oaks, CA 91403

818-995-6600
FAX 818-285-4403
Home Page: www.mpaa.org

Christopher J Dodd, President/CEO

Serves as the voice and advocate of the American motion picture, home video and television industries. The association advocates for strong protection of the creative works produced and distributed by the industry, fights copyright theft around the world, and provides leadership in meeting new and emerging industry challenges.
7 Members
Founded in 1922

18781 Motion Picture Editors Guild

7715 Sunset Boulevard
Suite 200
Hollywood, CA 90046

323-876-4770
800-705-8700
FAX 323-876-0861
E-Mail: webmester@editorsguild.com
Home Page: www.editorsguild.com
Social Media: *Facebook*

Alan Heim, President
Gregg Rudloff, VP
Louis Bertini, Second Vice Presdient
Diane Adler, Secretary
Rachel B Igel, Treasurer

A national labor organization representing free-lance and staff post-production professionals. MPED negotiates new collective bargaining agreements and enfoces existing agreements with employers involved in post-production. They provide assistance for securing better conditions, including but not limted to financial, medical, safety and artistic concerns.
6000 Members
Founded in 1937

18782 Motion Picture Pilots Association

7435 Valjean Avenue
Van Nuys, CA 91406

818-947-5454
E-Mail: moviepilots@cox.net
Home Page: www.moviepilots.com

Cliff Fleming, Board Director
Dirk Vahle, Board Director
Rick Shuster, Board Director
Neil Looy, Board Director
Kevin LaRosa, Board Director

The MPPA promotes aviation safety and the interest of aviators working in the motion picture, television and entertainment industries; establishes, conducts and maintains such activities which promote higher aviation standards and better business methods as may assist in the advancement of aviation in the Entertainment Aviation Profession; cooperates with those government agencies, industry organizations, entities or association whose objective is the betterment or advancement of the industry.
Founded in 1997

18783 Motion Picture Sound Editors

10061 Riverside Dr.
PMB Box 751
Toluca Lake, CA 91602-2550

818-506-7731
FAX 818-506-7732
E-Mail: info@mpse.org
Home Page: mpse.org
Social Media: *Facebook, Twitter, LinkedIn, YouTube*

Frank Morrone, President
Mark Lanza, Vice President

Organization for the improvement of the professional status of sound editors.

18784 National Association of Theatre Owners

1705 N St. NW
Washington, DC 20036

202-962-0054
E-Mail: nato@natodc.com
Home Page: natoonline.org

John Fithian, President & CEO

Exhibition trade organization that helps its members influence federal policy-making on issues of concern.

18785 Producers Guild of America

8530 Wilshire Blvd
Suite 450
Beverly Hills, CA 90211-3115

310-358-9020
FAX 310-358-9520
E-Mail: info@producersguild.org
Home Page: www.producersguild.com

Marshall Herskovitz, President
Vance Van Paten, Executive Director
Grant Stoner, Director Membership
Courtney Cowan, Treasurer
Gale Ann Hurd, Secretary

The PGA represents, protects and promotes the interests of all members of the producing team by providing employment opportunities and health and welfare benefits for all members of the producing team; combating deceptive or uneraned credits within the producing team;

and representing the interests of the entire producing team. The producing team consists of all those whose interdependency and support of each other are necessary for the creation of motion pictures and television programs.
500 Members
Founded in 1950

18786 Society for Cinema & Media Studies

640 Parrington Oval
Wallace Old Science Hall Room 300
Norman, OK 73019

405-325-8075
FAX 405-325-7135
E-Mail: office@cmstudies.org
Home Page: www.cmstudies.org
Social Media: *Facebook, Twitter*

Steven Cohan, President
Victoria E.ÿ Johnson, Secretary
Amanda Klein, Treasurer
Jane Dye, Administrative Coordinator
Pamela Wojcik, President-Elect

A professional organization of college and university educators, filmmakers, historians, critics, scholars, and others devoted to the study of the moving image. The gaols of SCMS are to promote all areas of media studies within universities and two- and four-year colleges; to encourage and reward excellence in scholarship and writing; to facilitate and improve the teaching of media studies as disciplines and to advance multi-cultural awareness and interaction.
1M Members
Founded in 1959

18787 Society of Camera Operators

PO Box 2006
Toluca Lake, CA 91610

818-382-7070
FAX 323-856-9155
E-Mail: info@soc.org
Home Page: www.soc.org
Social Media: *Facebook, Twitter*

Dan Dodd, Director
Mark August, President
Michael Scott, First VP
Mitch Dubin, Second VP
Lisa Stacilauskas, Third Vice Presidentÿ

Non-profit organization which advances the art and creative contribution of the operating cameraman in the Motion Picture and Television Industries.
Founded in 1979
Mailing list available for rent

18788 Society of Motion Picture & Television Engineers

3 Barker Ave
5th Floor
White Plains, NY 10601-1509

914-761-1100
FAX 914-761-3115
Home Page: www.smpte.org
Social Media: *Facebook, Twitter, LinkedIn, Youtube*

Barbara Lange, Executive Director
Sally-Ann D'Amato, Director Operations
Roberta Gorman, Manager
Peter Symes, Director Engineering
Amiee Ricca, Marketing and Communications

The SMPTE is the leading technical society for the motion imaging industry. It was founded to advance theory and development in the motion imaging field. Today, it publishes ANSI-approved Standards, Recommended Practices, and Engineering Guidelines. SMPTE holds conferences and local Section meetings to bring people and ides together, allowing for useful interaction and information exchange.
100 Members
Founded in 1916

18789 Stuntmen's Association of Motion Pictures

5200 Lankershim Blvd.
Suite 190
North Hollywood, CA 91601

818-766-4334
FAX 818-766-5943
E-Mail: hq@stuntmen.com
Home Page: www.stuntmen.com

Chris Doyle, Manager
Alex Daniels, First VP
John Moio, Second VP
Oliver Keller, Secretary
Hugh Aodh O'Brien, Treasurer

Seeks to improve working conditions for stuntmen. Encourages members to uphold high professional standards.
135 Members
Founded in 1961

18790 Stuntwomen's Association of Motion Pictures

3760 Cahuenga Blvd
Suite 104
Studio City, CA 91604-2411

818-588-8888
888-817-9267
FAX 818-762-0907
E-Mail: INFO@STUNTWOMEN.COM
Home Page: www.stuntwomen.com
Social Media: *Facebook*

Jane Austin, President

A professional association for stuntwomen and stunt coordinators which seeks to uphold professional standards and improve working conditions.
Founded in 1967

18791 Sundance Institute

1825 Three Kings Drive
PO Box 684429
Park City, UT 84060

435-658-3456
FAX 435-658-3457
E-Mail: Institute@sundance.org
Home Page: www.sundance.org
Social Media: *Twitter, LinkedIn, Instagram*

Robert Redford, President
Keri Putnam, Executive Director
Geoffrey Gilmore, Director Sundance Film Festival
Brooke McAffee, Director Finance
Ellen Oh, Associate Director Marketing

Non-profit organization dedicated to the discovery and development of independent artists and audiences. The Institute seeks to discover, support, and inspire independent film and theatre artists from the United States and around the world, and to introduce audiences to their new work. The Institutes programs include the annual Sundance Film Festival, held in Park City, Utah each January.
Founded in 1981

18792 United Stuntwomen's Association

26893 Bouquet Canyon Rd.
Suite C, Box 218
Saugus, CA 91350

818-508-4651
E-Mail: usastunts@usastunts.com
Home Page: www.usastunts.com

Bonnie Happy, President
Debbie Evans, Vice President

Trade association of professional stuntwomen, co-ordinators and second unit directors.
Founded in 1984

18793 University Film and Video Association
UFVA Membership Office C/O Cheryl Jestis
University of Illinois Press
1325 South Oak Street
Champaign, IL 61820-6903

217-244-0626
866-244-0626
FAX 217-244-9910
E-Mail: ufvahome@gmail.com
Home Page: www.ufva.org
Social Media: *Facebook, Twitter, LinkedIn, Instagram, YouTube*

Francisco Menendez, President
Jennifer Machiorlatti, Executive VP
Brett Levner, Secretary
Tom Sanny, Treasurer
Cheryl Jestis, Membership Coordinator

Supports those interested in the fields of film and video production, history, criticism, and aesthetics. Provides training, education, and a quarterly magazine.
Cost: $75.00
Founded in 1947

18794 Women in Film
6100 Wilshire Blvd
Suite 710
Los Angeles, CA 90048-5107

323-935-2211
FAX 323-935-2212
E-Mail: info@wif.org
Home Page: www.wif.org
Social Media: *Facebook, Twitter, YouTube*

Tichi Wilkerson-Kassel, Founder
Cathy Schulman, President
Glen Alpert, VP Membership
Nicole Katz, CFO
Gayle Nachlis, Executive Director

WIFs purpose is to empower, promote, nurture, and mentor women in the industry through a network of valuable contacts, events, and programs.
10000 Members
Founded in 1974

Newsletters

18795 American Academy of Arts & Sciences Bulletin
American Academy of Arts & Sciences
136 Irving Street
Cambridge, MA 02138

617-576-5000
FAX 617-576-5050
E-Mail: vsp@amacad.org
Home Page: www.amacad.org

Leslie Berkowitz, President
Mark Robinson, Director, Operations
Paul Karoff, Director, Communications

Features the following departments: Academy News; Around the Country; Noteworthy; and Remembrance.
Frequency: 2x/year

18796 Festival Rag
541 Main Street
Union, WV 24983

FAX 888-813-5457
E-Mail: markus@kemek.com
Home Page:
www.kemek.com/independent-film/the-festival-rag

Markus Varjo, Publisher
Cil Ripley, Editor-In-Chief

Dave Roberts, Managing Editor
Carl Merrick, Content & Development

Dedicated to true independent filmmaking and filmmakers, and broadcast to thousands of media-industry subscribers. Provides information on film festivals worldwide, including interviews with filmmakers and programmers.

18797 Film Advisory Board Monthly
Film Advisory Board
263 W Olive Avenue
#377
Burbank, CA 91502

323-461-6541
FAX 323-469-8541
Home Page: www.filmadvisoryboard.org
Social Media: *Facebook, Twitter, LinkedIn*

Janet Stokes, President

Information and news on the entertainment industry.
Frequency: Monthly
Founded in 1975
Printed in one color on glossy stock

18798 Hollywood Arts Council
PO Box 931056
Hollywood, CA 90093

323-462-2355
FAX 323-465-9240
E-Mail: bianca@hollywoodartcouncil.org
Home Page: www.hollywoodartscouncil.org

Promotes, nurtures and supports the arts field in Hollywood. Newsletter is included with membership.
Founded in 1978
Printed in 4 colors on glossy stock

18799 Preview Family Movie & TV Review
Movie Morality Ministries
6302 Riverside Dr
Irving, TX 75039

972-409-9960
800-807-8071
FAX 785-255-4316
E-Mail: preview@fni.com
Home Page: www.merchantcircle.com

Dave Haverty, President
Greg Shull, Editor
Susan Haverty, Desktop Publisher/Office Manager

Reviews current films and TV series from a Christian and family values perspective.
Cost: $34.00
Frequency: Monthly
ISSN: 0892-6468
Printed in 2 colors on matte stock

Magazines & Journals

18800 Advanstar
Advanstar Communications
641 Lexington Ave
Suite 8
New York, NY 10022-4503

212-951-6600
FAX 212-951-6793
E-Mail: info@advanstar.com
Home Page: www.advanstar.com

Joseph Loggia, CEO

News and features emphasize innovation in equipment technology and creative technique for editing, graphics, and special effects. Covers all budget levels from desktop post to feature films.
130 Pages
Frequency: Monthly
Circulation: 31464
Founded in 1986

18801 American Cinematographer
American Society of Cinematographers
1782 North Orange Drive
PO Box 2230
Hollywood, CA 90078-2230

323-969-4333
800-448-0145
FAX 323-876-4973
E-Mail: office@theasc.com
Home Page: www.theasc.com

Covers feature films, television, commercials, music videos, digital video, new equipment, DVD and book releases and much more. An exploration and a reflection of today's cinematography. A publication of the American Society of Cinematographers.
Cost: $29.95
Frequency: Monthly
Circulation: 42000
Founded in 1919
Mailing list available for rent

18802 Animation Magazine
Animation Magazine
26500 W.Agoura Rd
Suite 102
Calabasas, CA 91302

818-883-2884
FAX 818-883-3773
E-Mail: info@animationmagazine.net
Home Page: www.animationmagazine.net

Jean Thoren, President

Promotes the art and business of animation and gives recognition to those animators and technicians who make the world of animation what it is today.
Cost: $50.00
Frequency: Monthly
Circulation: 30000
ISSN: 1041-617X
Founded in 1986
Printed in 4 colors on glossy stock

18803 Celebrity Service
8833 W Sunset Boulevard
Suite 401
Los Angeles, CA 90069-2171

213-883-3671
FAX 310-652-9244

Robert Dean, Manager/Director

A listing of celebrities names and addresses. Publisher of the Celebrity Bulletin informing the entertainment and news industry of which celebrities are traveling to Hollywood and New York
Frequency: Bi-Monthly

18804 Cineaste
Cineaste Magazine
243 5th Ave
Suite 706
New York, NY 10016

212-366-5720
FAX 212-366-5724
E-Mail: cineaste@cineaste.com
Home Page: www.cineaste.com

Gary Crowdus, Editor-in-Chief
Cynthia Lucia, Editor
Richard Porton, Editor
Dan Georgakas, Consulting Editor
Vicki Robinson, Production Assistant

An internationally recognized independent film magazine. Features contributions from many of America's most articulate and outspoken writers, critics and scholars. Focussing on both the art and politics of the cinema.
Cost: $ 20.00
Frequency: Quarterly
Circulation: 11000
ISSN: 0009-7004

Founded in 1967
Mailing list available for rent

18805 Cinefantastique
CFQ Media
PO Box 34425
Los Angeles, CA 90034-0425

310-204-0825
FAX 310-204-5882
E-Mail: info@cfq.com
Home Page: www.cfq.com

Frederick Clarke, Editor

Provides coverage of genre entertainment. Each issue features in-depth coverage of sci-fi, fantasy and horror films, TV, DVDs, games, toys, books, comics and more.
Cost: $34.95
Frequency: Monthly
Circulation: 40,000

18806 Cinefex
79 Daily Drive
#309
Camarillo, CA 93010

805-383-0800
FAX 805-383-0803
E-Mail: advertising@cinefex.com
Home Page: www.cinefex.com

A quarterly magazine devoted to motion picture special effects.
Cost: $32.00
180 Pages
Frequency: Quarterly
Circulation: 30000
ISSN: 0198-1056
Founded in 1980
Printed in 4 colors

18807 Cinema Journal
University of Texas Press
2100 Comal
PO Box 7819
Austin, TX 78713-7819

512-471-7233
800-252-3206
FAX 512-232-7178
E-Mail: utpress@uts.cc.utexas.edu
Home Page: www.utexas.edu/utpress

Sponsored by the Society for Cinema and Media Studies. The journal presents recent scholarship by SCMS members. It publishes essays on a wide variety of subjects from diverse methodological perspectives. A 'Professional Notes' section informs Society of Cinema and Media Studies readers about upcoming events, research opportunities, and the latest published research. Cinema Journal is a member of the CELJ, the Conference of Editors of Learned Journals.
Cost: $42.00
144 Pages
Frequency: Quarterly
Circulation: 2800
ISSN: 0009-7101
Founded in 1950
Printed in on matte stock

18808 Daily Variety/Gotham
360 Park Avenue South
New York, NY 10010-3659

646-746-7001
FAX 646-746-6977
E-Mail: vtccustserv@cdsfulfillment.com
Home Page: www.variety.com

Peter Bart, Editor-in-Chief
Timothy M Gray, Editor
Ted Johnson, Managing Editor
Kathy Lyford, Managing Editor
Phil Gallo, Associate Editor

Focus is on Broadway theater, network television headquarters, regional music business, and

local film production. Explores the role of New York City in relation to the national and global entertainment industries.
Cost: $259.00
Frequency: Daily
Founded in 1905

18809 Daily Variety/LA
5900 Wilshire Boulevard
Suite 3100
Los Angeles, CA 90036-3659

323-617-9100
FAX 323-857-0494
E-Mail: vtcustserv@cdsfulfillment.com
Home Page: www.variety.com

Peter Bart, Editor-in-Chief
Timothy M Gray, Editor
Ted Johnson, Managing Editor
Kathy Lyford, Managing Editor
Phil Gallo, Associate Editor

Focus is on Hollywood, network television headquarters, regional music business, and local film production. Explores the role of Hollywood in relation to the national and global entertainment industries.
Cost: $259.00
Frequency: Daily
Founded in 1905

18810 Film & History
Historians Film Committee
Lawrence University, Memorial Hall B5
711 E Boldt Way
Appleton, WI 54911

920-832-6649
E-Mail: centre@filmandhistory.org
Home Page: www.h-net.org/~filmhis

Peter C Rollins, Director
Deborah Carmichael, Editor-in-Chief
Cynthia Miller, Associate Editor-in-Chief

An Interdisciplinary Journal of Film and Television Studies concerned with the impact of motion pictures on our society. Film and History focuses on how feature films and documentary films both represent and interpret history. Types of articles include: Analysis of individual films and/or television programs from a historical perspective, survey of documents related to the production of films, or analysis of history as explored through film.
Cost: $50.00
Frequency: Bi-annually
Circulation: 1000
ISSN: 0360-3695
Founded in 1970

18811 Film & Video Magazine
110 William Street
11th Floor
New York, NY 10038

212-621-4900
FAX 212-621-4635
Home Page:
www.studiodaily.com/filmandvideo

Bryant Frazer, Editor-in-Chief
Pete Putman, Senior Editor
Alison Johns, Editor-in-Chief
Scott Gentry, Group Publisher
Jarrett Cory, Classified Sales

Covers new ideas in creating entertainment by focusing on technique in the production and finishing of features, TV programming, music videos and commercials. No longer publishes print copies, magazine is 100% digital
Frequency: Monthly
Founded in 1983
Printed in 4 colors

18812 Film Journal International
VNU Business Media

770 Broadway, 7th Floor
New York, NY 10003-9595

212-493-4097
FAX 646-654-7694
E-Mail: subscriptions@filmjournal.com
Home Page: www.filmjournal.com

Penny Vane, President
Sid Holt, Editorial Director
Robert Sunshine, Publisher/Editor
Robin Klamfoth, Advertising Director
Kevin Lally, Executive Editor

A trade publication covering the motion picture industry, including theatrical exhibition, production, distribution, and allied activities. Articles report on US and international news, with features on current production, industry trends, theatre design, equipment, concessions, sound, digital cinema, screen advertising, and other industry-related news. Each issue also includes the Buying and Booking Guide, with comprehensive feature film reviews.
Cost: $65.00
Frequency: Monthly
Founded in 1934
Mailing list available for rent

18813 Film Threat
Film Threat International Headquarters
5042 Wilshire Boulevard
PMB 1500
Los Angeles, CA 90036

FAX 310-274-7985
E-Mail: advertise@filmthreat.com
Home Page: www.filmthreat.com
Social Media: *Facebook, Twitter*

Mark Bell, Editor-in-Chief
Eric Campos, Senior Contributing Editor
Chris Gore, Founder/Publishjer

The print edition of Film Threat retired in 1997, but the legend has lived on as an internet journalism mainstay. FilmThreat.com delivers film reviews, film festival coverage, exclusive filmmaker interviews and original video content.
Cost: $10.50
Frequency: Bi-Monthly
Circulation: 100,000
Founded in 1985

18814 Hollywood Life
Movieline Magazine
10537 Santa Monica Blvd
Suite 250
Los Angeles, CA 90025-4952

310-234-9501
FAX 310-234-0332
E-Mail: hollywoodlife@pcspublink.com
Home Page: www.hollywoodlive.net

Anne Volokh, President

Formerly called Movieline, an entertainment lifestyle featuring interviews with stars, directors and producers; as well as information on celebrity shopping, up and coming talent, soundtracks, electronics and fashion associated with hollywood style and trends.
Cost: $13.75
Frequency: Monthly
Founded in 1989
Printed in 4 colors on glossy stock

18815 Hollywood Reporter
Prometheus Global Media
770 Broadway
New York, NY 10003-9595

212-493-4100
FAX 646-654-5368
Home Page: www.prometheusgm.com
Social Media: *Facebook, Twitter, YouTube*

Richard D. Beckman, CEO
James A. Finkelstein, Chairman
Madeline Krakowsky, Vice President

Circulation
Tracy Brater, Executive Director Crative Service

Gives fresh ideas for film and TV. Covers the full spectrum of craft and commerce in the entertainment industry.
Cost: $199.00
Frequency: Weekly
Circulation: 34770

18816 International Cinematographers Guild Magazine

7755 W Sunset Blvd
Suite 300
Los Angeles, CA 90046-3911

323-876-0160
FAX 323-876-6383
E-Mail: info@icgmagazine.com
Home Page: www.cameraguild.com

Steven Poster, President
John McCarthy, Marketing

Serves as the journal of 'how to' for film and digital techniques. It incorporates a wide range of editorial for specific job categories in relation to cinematography for Film/Hi-Def/Digital production and defines the tools and technology necessary for advancement in this field. The magazine is written for members of the International Cinematographers Guild, including cinematographers, camera operators, camera assistants, still photographers, publicists, film loaders, and others in the field.
Cost: $48.00
Frequency: Monthly
Founded in 1929

18817 International Documentary Magazine

International Documentary Association
Ste M270
1201 W 5th St
Los Angeles, CA 90017-1476

213-534-3600
FAX 213-534-3610
E-Mail: tom@documentary.org
Home Page: www.documentary.org

Thomas White, Editor
Tamara Krinsky, Associate Editor
Jodi Pais Montgomery, Manager Advertising Sales
Michael Lumpkin, Executive Director

Devoted exclusively to nonfiction media.
Frequency: Monthly
Founded in 1982
Printed in 4 colors on glossy stock

18818 Journal of Film and Video

University Film and Video Association
University of Illinois Press
1325 S Oak Street
Champaign, IL 61820

217-244-0626
866-244-0626
FAX 217-244-9910
E-Mail: journals@uiuc.edu
Home Page: www.ufva.org

Stephen Tropiano, Editor
Cheryl Jestis, Membership

Focuses on scholarship in the fields of film and video production, history, criticism, and aesthetics. Topics include film and related media, education in these fields, and the function of film and video in society.
Cost: $40.00
Frequency: Quarterly
Circulation: 1200

18819 Journal of Popular Film and Television

Heldref Publications

1319 18th St Nw
Suite 2
Washington, DC 20036-1802

202-296-6267
800-365-9753
FAX 202-296-5149
E-Mail: subscribe@heldref.org
Home Page: www.heldref.org

James Denton, Executive Director
Gary Edgerton, Co-Executive Editor

Articles discuss networks, genres, series and audiences, as well as celebrity stars, directors and studios. Regular features include essays on the social and cultural background of films and television programs, filmographies, bibliographies, and commisioned book and video reviews.
Cost: $51.00
Frequency: Quarterly
ISSN: 0195-6051
Founded in 1956

18820 Keyframe Magazine

DMG Publishing
2756 N Green Valley Pkwy
Suite 261
Henderson, NV 89014-2120

702-990-8656
FAX 702-992-0471
E-Mail: info@dmgpublishing.com
Home Page: www.dmgpublishing.com

Dariush Derakhshani, Editor-in-Chief
Cheri Madison, Managing Editor
Charles Edgin, Editorial Director
Alice Edgin, Executive Editor

In response to reader requests, Keyframe is adding to its LightWave and Photoshop tutorials and content additional bonus pages covering other tools used by digital artists. As Keyframe evolves into this larger, better magazine, its new title with be HDRI 3D.
Cost: $54.00
Circulation: 9000
Founded in 1997

18821 Millimeter Magazine

PO Box 2100
Skokie, IL 60076-7800

847-763-9504
866-505-7173
FAX 847-763-9682
E-Mail: millimeter@pbinews.com
Home Page: www.millimeter.com

Cynthia Wisehart, Editor

In a fast-changing and challenging industry, Millimeter anticipates the future. Its early coverage of important technology-driven trends such as 24p production, desktop post, and digital cinema has helped readers remain competitive and plan their business investments. Millimeter is an authoritative resource for professionals in production, postproduction, animation, streaming, and visual effects for motion pictures, television and commercials.
Cost: $70.00
Frequency: Monthly

18822 Movie Collectors World

Arena Publishing
PO BOX 309
Fraser, MI 48026

586-774-4311
FAX 703-940-4566
E-Mail: mail@mcwonline.com
Home Page: www.mcwonline.com

Brian Bukantis, Editor

Leading collector's publication for collectors of movie memorabilia, with an emphasis on collectible movie posters. Each issue is filled with ads from dealers and collectors all over the world. In any monthly issue, you will find movie posters common and rare - everything from the 'Golden Age' to today's blockbusters.
Cost: $36.00
36-44 Pages
Frequency: Monthly
Circulation: 6000

18823 MovieMaker

MovieMaker Magazine
8328 De Soto Ave.
Canoga Park, CA 91304

310-742-7214
888-881-5861
FAX 818-349-9922
Home Page: www.moviemaker.com

Timothy Rhys, Publisher/Editor-in-Chief
Jennifer M Wood, Editor
Phillip Williams, Editor at Large
Ian Bage, New Marketing Services
Liza Kelley, Production Manager

MovieMaker is the world's most widely - read independent movie magazine that focuses on the art and business of making movies. Its editorial mix is a progressive mix of in depth interviews and criticism combined by practical techniques and advice on financing, distribution and production strategies.
Cost: $18.00
Frequency: Quarterly
Circulation: 54000
Founded in 1993
Mailing list available for rentat $175 per M

18824 Premiere Magazine

Hachette Filipacchi Media US Inc
1633 Broadway
Suite 41
New York, NY 10019-6708

212-767-6000
FAX 212-481-6428
Home Page: www.premiere.com

Jessica Letkemann, Editor
Jennifer Cooper, Producer

A magazine for young adults, which focuses on the art and commerce of the film industry. Premiere's feature articles, profiles and monthly columns include original photography, interviews with Hollywood's A-list and up-and-coming talent, studio heads and producers.

18825 Produced By

The Producers Guild of America
8530 Wilshire Blvd
Suite 450
Beverly Hills, CA 90211-3115

310-358-9020
FAX 310-358-9520
E-Mail: info@producersguild.org
Home Page: www.producersguild.com

Vance Van Petter, Executive Director
Audra Whaley, Director Operations
Kyle Katz, Director Member Benefits
Chris Greenr, Director Communications
Dan Dodd, Advertising

Provided as a benefit with membership to the Producers Guild of America.
Frequency: Quarterly
Circulation: 325
Founded in 1962

18826 Producer

Testa Communications
25 Willowdale Avenue
Port Washington, NY 11050-3779

516-767-2500
FAX 516-767-9335
Home Page: avvproducersguide.com

Randi Altman, Editor
Sande Seidman, Advertising Manager

Magazine aimed at producers, directors and creative people in the image and sound realms, with production stories on feature films, television, commercials, documentary, and corporate video projects. Accent is on the creative application of technology, following producers into the field and onto the studio set.
Cost: $15.00
Frequency: Bi-Monthly
Circulation: 18,300

18827 SMPTE Journal

Society of Motion Picture & Television Engineers
3 Barker Ave
Sute 5
White Plains, NY 10601-1509

914-761-1100
FAX 914-761-3115
E-Mail: smpte@smpte.org
Home Page: www.smpte.org
Social Media: *Facebook, Twitter*

Kimberly Maki, Executive Director
Charlie Barone, Administrative Assistant

Featuring industry-leading papers and standards, each month the Journal keeps its members on the cutting edge of the industry. Each issue provides the latest research and papers, ranging in style from technical, scientific, and tutorial, to applications/practices. Readers are kept up-to-date on events and meetings, the latest publications and brochures, and new products and developments.
Cost: $140.00
Frequency: Monthly
Circulation: 10000
Founded in 1916
Printed in on glossy stock

18828 San Francisco Cinematheque

San Francisco Cinematheque
145 Ninth Street
Suite 240
San Francisco, CA 94103

415-552-1990
FAX 415-552-2067
E-Mail: sfc@sfcinematheque.org
Home Page: www.sfcinematheque.org

Stephen Anker, Executive Director
Alfonso Alvarez, Board Director
Gina Basso, Board Director
Aimee Friberg, Board Director
Jeff Lambert, Board Director

Supports risk-taking art, cutting edge artists and the boundless potential of creative expression.
Cost: $15.00
Frequency: Monthly
Founded in 1961

18829 Script

Forum
5638 Sweet Air Road
Baldwin, MD 21013-9009

410-592-3466
888-245-2228
FAX 410-592-8062
E-Mail: scriptmag@fwmedia.com
Home Page: www.scriptmag.com
Social Media: *Facebook, YouTube, RSS*

Mark Madnick, Publisher
David Geatty, Founding Publisher
Shelly Mellot, Editor-in-Chief
Andrew Schneider, Managing Editor
Maureen Green, Editor

A leading source of information on the crage and business of writing for film and television. Each issues delivers informative articles on writing, developing and marketing screenplays and television scripts. Most articles are written by working writers. Additionally, development executives, agents, managers and entertainment

attorneys contribute regularly.
Cost: $24.95
Frequency: Bi-Monthly
Circulation: 12000

18830 Starlog

1372 Broadway
2nd Floor
New York, NY 10018

212-689-2830
800-934-6788
E-Mail: rita@starloggroup.com
Home Page: www.starlog.com

David McDonnel, Editor
Norman Jacobs, Founder

Information on science fiction happenings in the movies and television industries.
Cost: $56.97
Frequency: Monthly
Circulation: 350000

18831 The Independent

Home Page: independent-magazine.org
Social Media: *Facebook, Twitter*

Online source of information and inspiration for independent, grassroots and activist media makers.
Founded in 2007

18832 Variety

Reed Business Information
5700 Wilshire Boulevard
Suite 120
Los Angeles, CA 90036-3659

323-857-6600
866-698-2743
FAX 323-857-0494
E-Mail: VTCCustserv@cdsfulfillment.com
Home Page: www.variety.com

Charles C Koones, Publisher
Peter Bart, Editor-in-Chief
Timothy Gray, Editor
Kathy Lyford, Managing Editor
Christopher Wessel, Circulation Director

Variety covers all aspects of film, television and cable, homevideo, music, new media and technolgy, theater and finance. Topics run from people, companies, products and performances, to development, financing, distribution, regulation and marketing.
Cost: $259.00
Frequency: Weekly
Circulation: 35168
Founded in 1905

Trade Shows

18833 American Film Institute Festival: AFI Fest

American Film Institute
2021 N Western Avenue
Los Angeles, CA 90027-1657

323-856-7896
866-234-3378
FAX 323-856-9118
E-Mail: AFIFEST@AFI.com
Home Page: www.afifest.com

Jennifer Morgerman, Publicity Director
Stacey Leinson, Publicity Manager
Lagan Sebert, Publicity Coordinator
John Wildman, Filmmaker Press Liaison
Alison Deknatel, Director Communications

A 10-day event held each November, the festival features a rich slate of films from emerging filmmakers, nightly red-carpet gala premieres and global showcases of the latest work from the great film masters. AFI runs concurrently with the American Film Market. Together, AFT

Fest and AFM provide the film industry with the only concurrent festival/market event in North America.
60000 Attendees
Frequency: November
Founded in 1986

18834 International Cinema Equipment (ICECO) Showest

Magna-Tech Electronic Company
5600 NW 32nd Avenue
Miami, FL 33142

305-573-7339
FAX 305-573-8101
E-Mail: www.iceco@iceco.com
Home Page: www.showest.com

Steven H Krams, President
Dara Reusch, VP
Julio Urbay, VP International Sales/Marketing
Fancisco Blanco, VP Technical Services
Arturo Quintero, Architectural Design/Development

Annual convention for the Motion Picture industry. It is an international gathering devoted exclusively to the movie business. It is also the single largest international gathering of motion picture professionals and theatre owners in the world, with delegates from more than 50 countries in attendance each year.
Frequency: March
Founded in 1975

18835 International Cinema Equipment Company ICECO Show East

Magna-Tech Electronic Company,Inc.
1998 NE 150th Street
North Miami, FL 33181

305-573-7339
FAX 305-573-8101
E-Mail: iceco@aol.com
Home Page: www.iceco.com

Steven H Krams, President
Dara Reusch, VP
Julio Urbay, VP International Sales/Marketing
Francisco Blanco, VP/Technical Services
Arturo Quintero, Architectural Design & Development

This annual convention brings together over 1300 colleagues from the motion picture industry in the United States, Latin America and the Caribbean. The convention provides information on industry trends, screen films and product reels, state-of-the-art theatre equipment along with services and technologies vital to the industry.
1300 Attendees
Founded in 1975

18836 Moondance Film Festival

970 9th Street
Boulder, CO 80302

303-545-0202
E-Mail: director@moondancefilmfestival.com
Home Page: www.moondancefilmfestival.com

Elizabeth English, Festival Founder/Executive Director
Kyle/Erica Saylors, Festival Director/Event Coordinator
Karina Pyudik, Registration Coordinator
Douglis C Garvin, Special Events Coordinator
Roy Bodner, Publicist/Media Relations

The Festival's primary goal is to present films and scripts which have the power to raise awareness about vital social issues, educating writers and filmmakers, as well as festival audiences, and inspiring them to take positive action. The Festival's objective is to promote and encourage independent filmmakers, screenwriters and playwrights, and the best works in films, screenplays, stageplays, TV scripts,

radioplays, film scores, lyrics, librettos, music videos, and short stories.
Frequency: Annual

18837 New York Film Festival
Film Society of Lincoln Center
70 Lincoln Center Plaza
New York, NY 10023

212-875-5610
888-313-6085
E-Mail: filminfo@filmlinc.com
Home Page: www.filmlinc.com
Social Media: *Facebook, Twitter*

Rose Kuo, Executive Director
Richard Pena, Program Director
Lesli Klainberg, Managing Director

Celebrates American and international cinema and recognizes and supports new filmmakers.
Frequency: Annual

18838 Sundance Film Festival
Sundance Institute
1825 Three Kings Drive
PO Box 684426
Park City, UT 84060

435-658-3456
FAX 435-658-3457
E-Mail: Institute@sundance.org
Home Page: www.sundance.org

Robert Redford, Founder
Keri Putnam, Executive Director
Jill Miller, Managing Director

Annual festival held in Park City, Utah as a US showcase for American and International independent film. The Institute is dedicated to the development of artists of independent vision and the exhibition of their new work. Since its inception, the Institute has grown into an internationally recognized resource for thousands of independent artists.
Frequency: January
Founded in 1981

18839 Telluride Film Festival
National Film Preserve
800 Jones Street
Berkeley, CA 94710

510-665-9494
FAX 510-665-9589
E-Mail: mail@telluridefilmfestival.org
Home Page: www.telluridefilmfestival.org

Bill Pence, Founder
Stella Pence, Founder

Well situated on the international film festival calendar, Terruride takes place in Telluride, Colorado, and is defined by sense of purity and commitment.
Founded in 1974

18840 Toronto International Film Festival
TIFF Bell Lightbox
350 King Street West
Toronto

888-599-8433
Home Page: www.tiff.net

William Marshall, Founder
Piers Handling, Director & CEO
Noah Cowan, Artistic Director, Bell Lightbox
Cameron Bailey, Co-Director

Publicly attended film festival that takes place each September in Toronto, Ontario, Canada, showing upwards of 400 films from more than 60 countries. The festival is currently headquartered at TIFF Bell Lightbox, which opened in 2010.
Founded in 1976
Mailing list available for rent

Directories & Databases

18841 Annual Index to Motion Picture Credits
Academy of Motion Picture Arts and Sciences
8949 Wilshire Blvd
Beverly Hills, CA 90211-1972

310-247-3000
FAX 310-271-3395
Home Page: www.oscars.org

The Index is closely tied to the annual Academy Awards presentation. As part of the Academy Awards process, the Academy of Motion Picture Arts and Sciences gathers credits for each film hoping to qualify for awards. These credits, compiled and verified by the film's producer or distributor, are the core of the Annual Index and IMPC database. In addition to personal credits, IMPC also records index production and releasing dates, MPAA ratings, running times, color, language, and more.
Frequency: Annual
ISBN: 0-942102-37-1
ISSN: 0163-5123
Founded in 1934

18842 Blu-Book Production Directory
Hollywood Creative Directory
5055 Wilshire Blvd
Los Angeles, CA 90036-6103

323-525-2369
800-815-0503
FAX 323-525-2398
E-Mail: hcdcustomerservice@hcdonline.com
Home Page: www.hcdonline.com

Valencia McKinley, Manager

A comprehensive directory for professionals in the production and post-production industries. Provides current contact information needed to produce a film, TV program, commercial, or music video. The directory contains a special tabbed section on premier below-the-line craft professionals, along with selective credits, and has been expanded to include New York production facilities and services, making it one of the only bi-coastal resources of its kind.
Cost: $39.95
450 Pages
Frequency: Annual
ISBN: 1-928936-44-X

18843 Boxoffice: Circuit Giants
Boxoffice
PO Box 1634
Des Plains, IL 60019

212-627-7000
Home Page: www.boxoffice.com

Peter Cane, Publisher
Joe Policy, CEO
Annlee Ellingson, Editor
Francesca Dinglasan, Senior Editor
Bob Vale, VP Advertising and Sales

Directory of the largest exhibition chains. Available to subscribers of Boxoffice magazine
Cost: $59.95
Frequency: Annual
Founded in 1990

18844 Boxoffice: Distributor Directory
Boxoffice
PO Box 1634
Des Plains, IL 60019

212-627-7000
Home Page: www.boxoffice.com

Peter Cane, Publisher
Joe Policy, CEO

Annlee Ellingson, Editor
Francesca Dinglasan, Senior Editor
Bob Vale, VP Advertising and Sales

Listings of studio and independent film suppliers. Available to subscribers of Boxoffice magazine
Cost: $59.95
Frequency: Annual
Founded in 1990

18845 Directors Guild of America Directory of Members
Directors Guild of America
7920 W Sunset Blvd
Los Angeles, CA 90046-3347

310-289-2000
800-421-4173
FAX 310-289-2029
Home Page: www.dga.org

Jay Roth, President
Morgan Rumpf, Director Communications
Paul Zepp, Membership Administrator
Darrell L Hop, Editor DGA Monthly/Website
Michael Apted, Secretary

The DGA represents Film and Television Directors, Unit Production Managers, First Assistant Directors, Second Assistant Directors, Technical Coordinators and Tape Associate Directors, Stage Managers and Production Associates. The Directory is available in print and on-line
Cost: $25.00
Frequency: Annual

18846 Editors Guild Directory
Motion Picture Editors Guild
7715 Sunset Boulevard
Suite 200
Hollywood, CA 90046

323-876-4770
800-705-8700
FAX 323-876-0861
E-Mail: info@editorsguild.com
Home Page: www.editorsguild.com

Ron Kutak, Executive Director
Tomm Carroll, Publications Director
Serena Kungr, Director Membership Services
Adriana Iglesias-Dietl, Membership Administrator
Tris Carpenter, Manager

An invaluable resource for producers, directors and post production professionals alike. It lists contact, credit, award and classification information for all of the Guild's active members at the time of publication, as well as a list of Oscar and Emmy winners for every year since the awards began. It also includes a retirees section.
Cost: $25.00
Frequency: Bi-Annual
Founded in 1994

18847 Fame Index
Hollywood Madison Group
11684 Ventura Boulevard
#258
Studio City, CA 91604-2499

818-762-8008
FAX 818-762-8089
Home Page: holllywood-madison.com

Jonathan Holiff, Founder/President/CEO

Search over 10,000 celebrities from actors to athletes to find every performer who meets your needs. The Index has more than 250 searchable criteria including: age, sex, children, birthplace, genre, fees, ethnicity/heritage, biography, statistics, interests, hobbies, sports, personality attributes, charity affiliations, medical conditions, and endorsement histories. Contact information includes agent, manager, publicist,

business manager, attorney, and personal assistant.
Founded in 1996

18848 Film Journal: Distribution Guide Issue
Film Journal International
770 Broadway
5th Floor
New York, NY 10003-9595

646-654-7680
FAX 646-654-7694
Home Page: www.filmjournal.com

Robert Sunshine, Publisher/Editor
Kevin Lally, Executive Editor
Rex Roberts, Associate Editor
Andrew Sunshine, Advertising Director
Katey Rich, Editorial Assistant

The International Distribution and subdistribution Guide supplements the regular monthly Buying and Booking Guide. It is designed to furnish ready reference information on the who, what, where and how of theatrical sales. It lists the names, addresses, personnel, telephone numbers and product of domestic and international distributors, both major and independent, along with similar information on regional exchanges together with national companies they handle.
Frequency: Annual

18849 Film Journal: Equipment Guide
Film Journal International
770 Broadway
5th Floor
New York, NY 10003-9595

646-654-7680
FAX 646-654-7694
Home Page: www.filmjournal.com

Robert Sunshine, Publisher/Editor
Kevin Lally, Executive Editor
Robin Klamfoth, Advertising Director
Rex Roberts, Associate Editor
Katey Rich, Editorial Assistant

The Equipment, Concessions and Services Guide is designed to provide ready reference information on the theatrical equipment and concessions industry. It lists in detail the company names, addresses, telephone numbers, personnel, affiliations and products of equipment and concession manufacturers and service companies, along with similar information on US and foreign service dealers and suppliers, arranged in alphabetical order according to state or country.
Frequency: Annual

18850 Film Journal: Exhibition Guide
Film Journal International
770 Broadway
5th Floor
New York, NY 10003-9595

212-493-4097
FAX 646-654-7694
E-Mail: subscriptions@filmjournal.com
Home Page: www.filmjournal.com

Robert Sunshine, Publisher/Editor
Kevin Lally, Executive Editor
Robin Klamfoth, Advertising Director
Rex Roberts, Associate Editor
Sarah Sluis, Editorial Assistant

The exhibition Guide is an alphabetical listing designed to provide ready reference information on the leading theatrical motion picture circuits. It lists in comprehensive detail such data as company names, addresses and phone numbers, total screens and new screens projected, division office locations, top personnel,

recent circuit acquisitions, and a state-by-state breakdown of screens.
Frequency: Annual
Founded in 1934
Mailing list available for rent

18851 Film Superlist: Motion Pictures in the Public Domain
Hollywood Film Archive
8391 Beverly Blvd
Ste. 321
Los Angeles, CA 90048-2633

323-655-4968

Richard Baer, Executive Director
Created by Walter E. Hurst and updated by Richard Baer. 1992-1994. Three volumes to date, covering 50,000 films from the years 1894-1939, 1940-1949 and 1950-1959.

18852 Grey House Performing Arts Directory
Grey House Publishing
4919 Route 22
PO Box 56
Amenia, NY 12501

518-789-8700
800-562-2139
FAX 845-373-6390
E-Mail: books@greyhouse.com
Home Page: www.greyhouse.com
Social Media: *Facebook, Twitter*

Leslie Mackenzie, Publisher
Richard Gottlieb, Editor

The most comprehensive resource covering the Performing Arts. This directory covers current information on over 8,500 Dance Companies, Instrumental Music Programs, Opera Companies, Choral Groups, Theater Companies, Performing Arts Series, Performing Arts Facilities and Artist Management Groups.
Cost: $185.00
1200 Pages
Frequency: Annual
ISBN: 1-592373-76-3
Founded in 1981

18853 Grey House Performing Arts Directory - Online Database
Grey House Publishing
4919 Route 22
PO Box 56
Amenia, NY 12501

518-789-8700
800-562-2139
FAX 518-789-0556
E-Mail: gold@greyhouse.com
Home Page: www.gold.greyhouse.com
Social Media: *Facebook, Twitter*

Leslie Mackenzie, Publisher
Richard Gottlieb, Editor

The Grey House Performing Arts Directory - Online Database provides immediate access to dance companies, orchestras, opera companies, choral groups, theater companies, series, festivals and perfoming arts facilities across the country, or in their region, state, or in your own backyard. It offers unequaled coverage of the Performing Arts - over 8,500 listings - of the major performance organization, facilities, and information resources.
Frequency: Annual
Founded in 1981

18854 International Motion Picture Alamanc
Quigley Publishing Company
64 Wintergreen Lane
Groton, MA 01450

860-228-0247
800-231-8239
FAX 860-228-0157

E-Mail: quigleypub@aol.com
Home Page: www.quigleypublishing.com

William J Quigley, President/Publisher
Eileen Quigley, Editor

Contains over 400 pages of biographies and 500 pages of reference material. From 1928 to the present day, the complete set contains the biography of everyone who has ever been of importance to the Industry. Each edition includes thousands of company listings, credits for current films and films released in the prior ten years, statistics and awards and complete coverage of all aspects of the industry, including production, distribution and exhibition.
Cost: $175.00
Frequency: Annual

18855 International Television and Video Almanac
Quigley Publishing Company
64 Wintergreen Lane
Groton, MA 01450

860-228-0247
800-231-8239
FAX 860-228-0157
E-Mail: quigleypub@aol.com
Home Page: www.quigleypublishing.com

William J Quigley, President/Publisher
Eileen Quigley, Editor

Each edition contains over 400 pages of biographies and an additional 500 pages of reference material on television programs, broadcast, cable and satellite, production services, the video industry, statistics and awards. Included are detailed listings for thousands of companies, as well as coverage outside the United States.
Cost: $175.00
Frequency: Annual
Founded in 1955

18856 Mini Reviews
Cineman Syndicate
31 Purchase St
Suite 203
Rye, NY 10580-3013

914-967-5353
Home Page: www.minireviews.com

John P McCarthy, Editor

An easy to read, easy to use guide for movie watchers updated weekly.
Frequency: Weekly
Founded in 2000

18857 Motion Picture TV and Theatre Directory
Motion Picture Enterprises
PO Box 276
Tarrytown, NY 10591-0276

212-245-0969
FAX 212-245-0974
Home Page: www.mpe.net

Neal R Pilzer, Publisher

The Guide is mailed to members of 59 trade associations, unions and professional societies; decision-makers at advertising agencies, production companies, TV stations, and government agencies; faculty and students of nearly 200 film schools; and other prime purchasers of film and TV equipment and services nationwide. Companies are listed both by category and company name. Listings include company name, address and telephone number as well as fax numbers, e-mail addresses, and web site URLs.
Cost: $18.80
335 Pages
Frequency: Annual
Circulation: 82500
Founded in 1963

18858 Movie World Almanac
Hollywood Film Archive
8391 Beverly Blvd
PMB 321
Los Angeles, CA 90048-2633

323-655-4968

Richard Baer, Executive Director
Lists over 200 major American and foreign
film distributors who handle old and contemporary films.

18859 Reel Directory
Lynetta Freeman
PO Box 1910
Boyes Hot Springs, CA 95416

415-531-9760
FAX 707-581-1725
E-Mail: info@reeldirectory.com
Home Page: www.reeldirectory.com

Lynetta Freeman, Manager
Keith Marsalis, Director
Katie Carney, Director of Marketing
Source for Film, Video and Multimedia in
Northern California.
Cost: $25.00
700 Pages
Frequency: Annual
Circulation: 5,000
Founded in 1979

18860 Studio Report: Film Development
Hollywood Creative Directory
5055 Wilshire Blvd
Los Angeles, CA 90036-6103

323-525-2369
800-815-0503
FAX 323-525-2398
E-Mail: hcdcustomerservice@hcdonline.com
Home Page: www.hcdonline.com

Valencia McKinley, Manager
The only directory of its kind, in print for the
first time. A complete breakdown of film development project tracking. A-Z listings by title,
spec screenplays sold, hot studio projects,
cross-referenced by studio, production company and genre. The directory's main body
consists of an alphabetical listing of all in-de-
velopment projects that have achieved a for-
ward-moving milestone some time in the last
five months. Subsequent sections sort and
cross-reference the information to highlight aspects
Cost: $19.95
190 Pages
ISBN: 1-928936-49-0

Industry Web Sites

18861 http://gold.greyhouse.com
G.O.L.D Grey House OnLine Databases
Grey House Publishing's online database platform, GOLD, offers Quick Search, Keyword
Search and Expert Search for most business
sectors including motion picture and entertainment markets. The GOLD platform makes finding the information you need quick and easy -
whether you're a novice searcher or an experienced database user. All of Grey House's directory products are available for subscription on
the GOLD platform.

18862 www.actioncutprint.com
Action-Cut-Print
Website for filmmakers. filmmaking resources,
free ezine for directors, film and TV bookstore.
The Director's Chair magazine by director Pe-
ter D. Marshall.

18863 www.artdirectors.org
Art Directors Guild
Conceive and manage the background and set-
tings for most films and television projects.

18864 www.asatalent.com
ASA/Affordable Services
Entertainment services are brought to you as
you need them and when you need them at the
best price available. Security services, studio
teachers, and medical services.

18865 www.castingsociety.com
Casting Society of America
An organization representing casting directors.

18866 www.discoverhollywood.com
Hollywood Arts Council
Promotes, nurtures and supports the arts field
in Hollywood. Discover Hollywood on line.

18867 www.documentary.org
International Documentary Association
A nonprofit association founded to promote
non-fiction film and video, to support the efforts of documentary film and video makers
around the world, and to increase public appreciation and demand for the documentary.

18868 www.greyhouse.com
Grey House Publishing
Authoritative reference directories for most
business sectors including motion picure and
entertainment markets. Users can search the online databases with varied search criteria allowing for custom searches by product category,
geographic area, sales volume, keyword, subject and more. Full Grey House catalog and
online ordering also available.

18869 www.iqfilm.org
International Quorum of Film and Video
Producers
Fosters the exchange of information and ideas.
Seeks to raise professional standards. Dissemi-
nates information on new concepts and
technology.

18870 www.millimeter.com
Millimeter Magazine
Authoritative resource for more than 33,000
qualified professionals in production,
postproduction, animation, streaming and visual effects for motion pictures, television and
commercials.

18871 www.mpaa.org
Motion Picture Association of America
Promotes high moral and artistic standards in
motion picture production. Maintains Motion
Picture Association Political Action
Committee.

18872 www.nyfa.com
New York Film Academy
Educational institution devoted to providing focused filmmaking and acting instructions.
Geared to offer an intensive, hands-on experience which gives students the opportunity to
develop their creative skills to the fullest extent
possible.

18873 www.oscars.org
Academy of Motion Picture Arts and
Sciences
Current information on motion pictures, the
arts and sciences, events and screenings.

18874 www.producersguild.com
Producers Guild of America
Members are producers of motion pictures and
television shows mainly in the Los Angeles
area.

18875 www.resumegenie.com
Motion Pictures job listings, salary information
and job search tips.

18876 www.smpte.org
Society of Motion Picture & Television
Engineers
Advances the practice and theory of engineer-
ing in television and film industry.

18877 www.stuntnet.com
International Stunt Association
Represents those involved in stunt work for the
entertainment industry.

18878 www.stuntwomen.com
Stuntwomen's Association of Motion
Pictures
A professional association for stuntwomen and
stunt coordinators which seeks to uphold professional standards and improve working
conditions.

18879 www.sundance.org
Sundance Institute
Nonprofit corporation dedicated to the support
and development of emerging screenwriters
and directors of vision. Hosts the Sundance
Film Festival.

18880 www.wif.org
Women in Film
For global entertainment,communication and
media industries. Focuses on contemporary issues facing women and provides an extensive
network of valuable contacts, educational programs, scholars, film finishing funds, grants,
community outreach, advocacy and practical
services that promote, nurture and mentor
women to achieve their highest potential.

Associations

18881 American Historic Racing Motorcycle Association
309 Buffalo Run
Goodlettsville, TN 37072

615-420-6435
FAX 615-420-6438
E-Mail: dlamberth@comcast.net
Home Page: www.ahrma.org
Social Media: *Facebook*

Mark Hatten, Chairman
Matthew Benson, Communications Director
Mark Hatten, Treasurer
Rob Poole, Secretary
Carl Anderson, Treasurer

For individuals interested in vintage racing motorcycles.
5M Members
Founded in 1989

18882 American Motorcyclist Association
13515 Yarmouth Dr
Pickerington, OH 43147-8273

614-856-1900
800-AMA-JOIN
FAX 614-856-1920
E-Mail: tlindsay@ama-cycle.org
Home Page: www.americanmotorcyclist.com
Social Media: *Facebook, YouTube*

Rob Dingman, President
Maggie McNally, Chair
Perry King, Vice Chairman
Scott Papenfus, Marketing Director
Ken Ford, Assistant Treasurer

The association's purpose is to pursue, protect and promote the interests of motorcyclists, while serving the needs of its members.
270M Members
Founded in 1924

18883 Antique Motorcycle Club of America
PO Box 663
Huntsville, AL 35804

256-509-9095
E-Mail: amcaExecutiveDirector@gmail.com
Home Page: antiquemotorcycle.org
Social Media: *Facebook, Instagram*

Keith S. Kizer, Executive Director

The AMCA is the largest club of its kind in the United States.
11000 Members

18884 Breakdown & Legal Assistance for Motorcyclists
13047 Ventura Blvd
Suite 100
Studio City, CA 91604-2250

818-377-6280
800-424-5377
FAX 818-377-6290
E-Mail: russbrown@russbrown.com
Home Page: www.russbrown.com
Social Media: *Facebook, Twitter*

J Russell Brown II, President

A support group for motorcyclists. Offers roadside assistance for emergencies and breakdowns. Attorney referral service specializing in motorcycle accident cases. Brochures and guest speakers available upon request, also offers a twenty-four hour toll-free hotline.
100M Members
Founded in 1983

18885 Christian Motorcyclists Association
PO Box 9
Hatfield, AR 71945

Home Page: www.cmausa.org

John Ogden Sr., Chairman & CEO

Interdenominational and evangelistic Christian ministry dedicated to reaching people for Christ through motorcycling.
Founded in 1975

18886 Combat Veterans Motorcycle Association

Home Page: www.combatvet.org

Non-profit organization of veteran motorcycle hobbyists whose charitable events raise money for veteran care facilities.
Founded in 2001

18887 Harley Owners Group
National H.O.G. Office
PO Box 453
Milwaukee, WI 53201

800-258-2464
FAX 414-343-4515
Home Page: www.harleydavidson.com
Social Media: *Facebook, YouTube*

James L Ziemer, President/CEO

Harley Davidson established the Harley Owners Group in response to a growing desire by Harley riders for an organized way to share their passion and show their pride.
60000 Members
Founded in 1983

18888 Motorcycle & Moped Industry Council
716 Gordon Baker Road
Suite 100
North York, M2H 3B4, ON

416-491-4449
877-470-6642
FAX 416-493-1985
E-Mail: info@mmic.ca
Home Page: www.mmic.ca

Robert Ramsay, President

National nonprofit trade association which represents the responsible interest of the major motorcycle distributors, as well as the manufacturers, distributors and the retail outlets of motorcycle-related products and services, and individual owners and riders of motorcycles in Canada.
140 Members
Founded in 1971

18889 Motorcycle Industry Council
2 Jenner Street
Suite 150
Irvine, CA 92618-3806

949-727-4211
FAX 949-727-3313
E-Mail: dkopf@mic.org
Home Page: www.mic.org

Robert Moffit, Chairman
Tim Buche, President
David Kopf, Manager

A nonprofit national trade association created to represent the motorcycle industry.
Cost: $25.00
300 Members
Frequency: Annual
ISSN: 0149-3027
Founded in 1914

18890 Motorcycle Riders Foundation
1325 G Street NW
Suite 500
Washington, DC 20005

202-546-0983
FAX 202-546-0986
E-Mail: jeff@mrf.org
Home Page: www.mrf.org

Kirk Willard, President
Mike Kerr, Vice President
Paulette Pinkham, Secretary
Chuc Coulter, Treasurer
Tiffany Latimer, Office Manager

To continue developing an aggressive, independent national advocate for the advancement of motorcycling and its associated lifestyle which is financially stable and exceeds the needs of motorcycling enthusiasts.
Founded in 1987

18891 Motorcycle Safety Foundation
2 Jenner
Suite 150
Irvine, CA 92618-3812

949-727-3227
800-446-9227
FAX 949-727-4217
E-Mail: MSF@msf-usa.org
Home Page: www.msf-usa.org
Social Media: *Facebook, Twitter, YouTube*

Tim Buche, President

Founded by the five leading manufacturers and distributors of motorcycles for the purpose of public safety education.
7 Members
Founded in 1972

18892 Women in the Wind
PO Box 8392
Toledo, OH 43605-0392

E-Mail: becky@womeninthewind.org
Home Page: www.womeninthewind.org

Becky Brown, Founder/Treasurer
Gale Collins, President
Lauranne Bailey, VP
Peggy Zeeb, Secretary

Seeks to promote a positive image for women motorcyclists. Educates members on maintenance and safety.
1000 Members
Founded in 1979

Newsletters

18893 AHRMA Newsletter
American Historic Racing Motorcycle Association
PO Box 882
Wausau, WI 54402-0882

715-842-9699
FAX 715-842-9545
Home Page: www.ahrma.org

Jeff Smith, Director
Matt Benson, Executive Director
David Lamberth, Executive Director

For individuals interested in vintage motorcycles.
Cost: $2.00
Circulation: 5,000

18894 MRF Reports
Motorcycle Riders Foundation
236 Massachusetts Ave Ne
Suite 204
Washington, DC 20002-4980

202-546-0983
FAX 202-546-0986

E-Mail: jeff@mrf.org
Home Page: www.mrf.org

Eric Hampton, Editor/Publisher
Frequency: Bi-Monthly

Magazines & Journals

18895 American Motorcyclist
American Motorcyclist Association
13515 Yarmouth Dr
Pickerington, OH 43147-8273

614-856-1900
800-262-5646
FAX 614-856-1920
E-Mail: membership@ama-cycle.org
Home Page:
http://www.americanmotorcyclist.com

Rob Dingman, President
Bill Wood, Editor-in-Chief
Grant Parsons, Managing Editor
John Holliday, Circulation

Magazine covers every facet of motorcycling.
Each monthly issue details the people, places
and events - from road rallies to road races -
that make up the American motorcycling experience.
Cost: $39.00
Frequency: Monthly
Circulation: 260000
Founded in 1924
Printed in 4 colors on glossy stock

18896 Biker
Paisano Publishers
PO Box 3075
Agoura Hills, CA 91376-3075

818-898-8740
800-962-985
FAX 818-889-1252
Home Page: easyridersevents.com

Joe Teresi, Publisher
Dean Shawier, Editor

Events and charity events for the motorcycle
enthusiast.
Cost: $15.00
96 Pages
Founded in 1971

18897 Cycle World
Hachette Filipacchi Media US
1499 Monrovia Ave
Newport Beach, CA 92663-2752

949-720-5300
FAX 949-631-2374
Home Page: www.hfmus.com

Nancy Laporte, Executive Director
David Edwards, Editor-in-Chief

Publication for motorcycle enthusiasts.
Cost: $16.00
136 Pages
Frequency: Monthly
Circulation: 325000

18898 Cycling USA
United States Cycling Federation
1 Olympic Plz
Colorado Spring, CO 80909-5775

719-866-4581
FAX 719-866-4628
E-Mail: web@usacycling.org
Home Page: www.usacycling.org

Gerard Bisceglia, CEO
Sean Petty, Chief of Staff

Bike racing magazine.
Cost: $10.00
24 Pages
Circulation: 3000
Founded in 1920

18899 Dealernews Magazine
Advanstar Communications
New York
New York, NY 10016-5778

212-951-6600
800-854-3112
FAX 212-951-6793
E-Mail: info@advanstar.com
Home Page: www.dealernews.com

Mike Vaughan, Publisher
Mary Slepicka, Associate Publisher
Arlo Redwine, Managing Editor

Written for and read by a qualified power
sports dealer network and related industry associates. It features articles on merchandising,
sales techniques and profiles of successful retailers. Industry trends and business conditions
are monitored through exclusive industry
research.
Frequency: Monthly
Circulation: 17535
Founded in 1965
Printed in 4 colors on glossy stock

18900 Easyriders
Paisano Publishers
3547 Old Conejo Rd
Suite 106
Newbury Park, CA 91320

800-962-9857
800-825-7294
FAX 805-375-4591
E-Mail: info@easyridersevents.com
Home Page: easyridersevents.com

Joe Teresi, Publisher
Keith Ball, Editor
John Green, President

Motorcycle magazine.
Cost: $39.95
136 Pages
Frequency: Monthly
Founded in 1971

18901 Motorcycle Dealer News
Edgell Communications
4500 Campus Drive
Suite 100
Santa Ana, CA 92705

FAX 949-252-0499

Don Emde, Publisher

For dealers of power sports equipment and supplies.
Cost: $25.00

18902 Motorcycle Industry Magazine
Industry Shopper Publishing
PO Box 160
Gardnerville, NV 89410-160

775-782-0222
800-576-4624
FAX 775-782-0266
Home Page: www.mimag.com

Rick Campbell, Publisher
Rick Campbell, Editor
Caroline Carr, Sales Manager

Provides information to the motorcycle and accessory dealer and or retailer on products, services, events and people aiming to maximize
profitablity and growth, also includes personal
watercraft vehicles, ATV's and snowmobiles.
Frequency: Monthly
Circulation: 14000
ISSN: 0884-626X
Founded in 1976
Printed in 4 colors on glossy stock

18903 Shootin the Breeze
Women in the Wind
PO Box 8392
Toledo, OH 43605-0392

Home Page: www.womeninthewind.org

Becky Brown, Founder
Gale Collins, President
Lauranne Bailey, VP
Peggy Zeeb, Secretary

Available to all Women in the Wind members.
Frequency: 6x/year

18904 The Antique Motorcycle
Antique Motorcycle Club of America
PO Box 3004
Westerville, OH 43086

740-803-2584
Home Page: antiquemotorcycle.org

Greg Harrison, Editor
Paul Holdsworth, Director of Advertising

Official publication of The Antique Motorcycle
Club of America, Inc.
Frequency: Bimonthly
Founded in 2010

18905 Upshift Magazine
Motorcycle & Moped Industry Council
3000 Steeles Avenue East
Suite 201
Markham, Ontario L3R 4T9

416-491-4449
877-470-6642
FAX 416-493-1985
E-Mail: info@mmic.ca
Home Page: www.mmic.ca

Steve Thornton, Producer

Features articles and information on motorcycles.
Frequency: Quarterly

Trade Shows

18906 AMA Members Tour
American Motorcyclist Association
13515 Yarmouth Drive
Pickerington, OH 43147

614-856-1900
FAX 614-856-1920
E-Mail: tlindsay@ama-cycle.org
Home Page:
http://www.americanmotorcyclist.com

Will Stoner, Director Special Events

The goal is to spread awareness of the benefits
of membership and the importance of the work
of the AMA does in protecting all motorcyclists' right to ride.
Frequency: Semi-Annual, June

18907 AMA Vintage Motorcycle Days
American Motorcyclist Association
13515 Yarmouth Drive
Pickerington, OH 43147

614-856-1900
FAX 614-856-1920
E-Mail: tlindsay@ama-cycle.org
Home Page: www.amadirectlink.com

Will Stoner, Director Special Events

Will benefit the Motorcycle Hall of Fame Museum and will feature an exhibit of classic motorcycles and memorabilia.
Frequency: July

18908 Annual Meeting of the Minds
Motorcycle Riders Foundation

236 Massachusetts Avenue NE
Suite 510
Washington, DC 20002-4980

202-546-0983
FAX 202-546-0986
E-Mail: downs@mrf.org
Home Page: www.mrf.org

Carol Downs, Conference Director

Designed to educate and motivate those in the motorcyclists' rights community. The premier leadership conference that boasts an audience from across the nation and around the world.
Frequency: September

18909 Beast of the East
Motorcycle Riders Foundation
236 Massachusetts Avenue NE
Suite 510
Washington, DC 20002-4980

202-546-0983
FAX 202-546-0986
E-Mail: downs@mrf.org
Home Page: www.mrf.org

Carol Downs, Conference Director

Designed to educate and motivate those in the motorcyclists' rights community. These events are a great chance to meet other people who are as passionate about motorcyclists' rights as you are.
Frequency: April

18910 Best of the West
Motorcycle Riders Foundation
236 Massachusetts Avenue NE
Suite 510
Washington, DC 20002-4980

202-546-0983
FAX 202-546-0986
E-Mail: downs@mrf.org
Home Page: www.mrf.org

Carol Downs, Conference Director

Designed to educate and motivate those in the motorcyclists' rights community. These events are a great chance to meet other people who are as passionate about motorcyclists' rights as you are.
Frequency: June

18911 International Motorcycle Show
Advanstar Communications
201 E Sandpointe
Suite 600
Santa Ana, CA 92707

714-138-8400
FAX 714-513-8481
Home Page: www.motorcycleshows.com

Jeff D'Entremont, Show Director
Leah Stevens, Account Manager
Chris Alonzo, Account Manager
Exposition for motorcyclists and enthusiasts.

18912 Los Angeles Calendar Motorcycle Show
Breakdown & Legal Assistance for Motorcyclists
13047 Ventura Boulevard
Suite 100
Studio City, CA 91604

323-321-1483
800-424-5377
FAX 818-377-6290
E-Mail: russbrown@russbrown.com
Home Page: www.russbrown.com

Russ Brown, President

Biggest custom and performance streetbike event.
Frequency: July
Founded in 1983

18913 Motocross American Reunion and Exhibit Grand Opening
American Motorcyclist Association
13515 Yarmouth Drive
Pickerington, OH 43147

614-856-1900
800-262-5646
FAX 614-856-1920
Home Page: americanmotorcyclist.com

Since 1924, the AMA has protected the future of motorcycling and promoted the cotorcycle lifestyle. As the world's largest motorcycling rights organization, the AMA advocates for motorcyclists' interests in the halls of local, state and federal government, the committees of international governing organizations, and the court of pulic opinion.
Frequency: July
Founded in 1924

18914 Motorcycle and Parts
Glahe International
PO Box 2460
Germantown, MD 20875-2460

301-515-0012
FAX 301-515-0016
Home Page: www.glahe.com

Exhibits of motorcycle equipment, supplies and services.

18915 Summer Nationals
Women in the Wind
PO Box 8392
Toledo, OH 43605-0392

Home Page: www.womeninthewind.org

Becky Brown, Founder/Treasurer
Gale Collins, President
Lauranne Bailey, VP
Peggy Zeeb, Secretary
Frequency: July

Directories & Databases

18916 MSF Guide to Motorcycling Excellence
Motorcycle Safety Foundation
2 Jenner
Irvine, CA 92618-3812

949-727-3227
FAX 949-727-4217
Home Page: www.msf-usa.org

Tim Buche, President

Covering the skills, knowledge and strategies for riding right. Subjects include: preparing yourself and your bike, developing street strategies, and advanced theory for experienced riders.
Cost: $24.95
176 Pages

18917 MilitaryBikers.org
Home Page: www.militarybikers.org
Social Media: *Facebook*

Directory and discussion boards of military motorcycle clubs.

18918 Motorcycle Statistical Annual
Motorcycle Industry Council
2 Jenner Street
Suite 150
Irvine, CA 92618-3806

949-727-4211
FAX 949-727-3313

This industry-related directory offers statistical information on US motorcycle manufacturers and distributors, as well as national and state motorcycle associations.
Cost: $25.00
Frequency: Annual
ISSN: 0149-3027

Industry Web Sites

18919 http://gold.greyhouse.com
G.O.L.D Grey House OnLine Databases
Grey House Publishing's online database platform, GOLD, offers Quick Search, Keyword Search and Expert Search for most business sectors including motorcycle and biking markets. The GOLD platform makes finding the information you need quick and easy - whether you're a novice searcher or an experienced database user. All of Grey House's directory products are available for subscription on the GOLD platform.

18920 www.ahrma.org
American Historic Racing Motorcycle Association
For individuals interested in vintage racing motorcycles.

18921 www.amadirectlink.com
American Motorcyclist Association
Covers every facet of motorcycling: the people, places and events that make up the American motorcycling experience. In addition, this award winning website offers profiles of issues affecting everyone who rides, and provides tools that help motorcyclists communicate directly with legislators, business leaders and the news media.

18922 www.greyhouse.com
Grey House Publishing
Authoritative reference directories for most business sectors including motocycle and biking markets. Users can search the online databases with varied search criteria allowing for custom searches by product category, geographic area, sales volume, keyword, subject and more. Full Grey House catalog and online ordering also available.

18923 www.mic.org
Motorcycle Industry Council
Nonprofit national trade association created to represent the motorcycle industry.

18924 www.mmic.ca
Motorcycle & Moped Industry Council
National nonprofit trade association which represents the responsible interest of the major motorcycle distributors, as well as the manufacturers, distributors and the retail outlets of motorcycle related products and services, and individual owners and riders of motorcycles in Canada.

18925 www.msf-usa.org
Motorcycle Safety Foundation
Founded by the five leading manufacturers and distributors of motorcycles for the purpose of public safety education.

18926 www.russbrown.com
Breakdown & Legal Assistance for Motorcyclists
A support group for motorcyclists. Offers roadside assistance for emergencies and breakdowns. Attorney referral service specializing in motorcycle accident cases. Brochures and guest speakers available upon request, also offers a twenty-four hour toll-free hotline.

Associations

18927 Academy of Country Music
5500 Balboa Blvd
Suite 200
Encino, CA 91316-1505

818-788-8000
FAX 818-788-0999
E-Mail: info@acmcountry.com
Home Page: www.acmcountry.com

Drain Murphy, Chairman
David Young, Director Operations
Tiffany Moon, Secretary
Brandi Brammer, Project Manager
Tree Paine, Director Marketing

Involved in numerous events and activities promoting country music. Presents annual awards.
4M Members
Founded in 1964

18928 Accordian Federation of North America
14126 E Rosencrans Boulevard
Santa Fe Springs, CA 90670

562-921-5058
E-Mail: afna@musician.org
Home Page: www.afnafestival.org
Social Media: *Facebook, Twitter, Google+*

Madeleine D'Ablaing, President
Debbie Gray, VP
Oakley Yale, Secretary
Prisscilla Martinez, Treasurer
Larry Demian, Parliamentarian

Members are primarily teachers and music school owners with the primary purpose to encourage young people to pursue their music study. Holds festivals and competitions
75 Members
Founded in 1972

18929 Accordion Teachers Guild
10349 Century,Lane
Overland Park, KS 66215

913-722-5625
E-Mail: Betty@BettyJoSimon.com
Home Page: www.accordions.com/atg

Betty Jo Simon, President
Liz Finch, First VP
Amy Jo Sawyer, Second VP
Joan C. Sommers, Executive Secretary
John Neu, Treasurer

ATG members are accordion teachers and professionals committed to furthering the progress of the accordion by improving teaching standards, music and all phases of music education.
Founded in 1940

18930 Acoustical Society of America
1305 Walt Whitman Road
Suite 300
Melville, NY 11747-4300

516-576-2360
FAX 631-923-2875
E-Mail: asa@acousticalsociety.org
Home Page: www.acousticalsociety.org

Christy K. Holland, President
Lily M. Wang, Vice President
David Feit, Treasurer
Christopher J. Struck, Standards Director
Susan E. Fox, Executive Director

Premier international scientific society in acoustics, dedicated to increasing and diffusing the knowledge of acoustics and its practical applications.

18931 American Choral Directors Association
545 Couch Drive
PO Box 2720
Oklahoma City, OK 73101-2720

405-232-8161
FAX 405-232-8162
Home Page: www.acdaonline.org

Timothy Sharp, Executive Director
Jerry Mccoy, President
Haiary Aphelstadt, VP
Jo-Ann Miller, Treasurer

Nonprofit music-education organization whose central purpose is to promote excellence in choral music through performance, composition, publication, research and teaching. In addition, ACDA strives to elevate choral music's position in American society through arts advocacy. Holds annual convention.
Cost: $90.00
19500 Members
Founded in 1959

18932 American College of Musicians
PO Box 1807
Austin, TX 78767

512-478-5775
FAX 512-478-5843
E-Mail: ngpt@pianoguild.com
Home Page: www.pianoguild.com

Richard Allison, President
Julia Kruger, VP

Provides student awards and teachers benefits.
Founded in 1931

18933 American Composers Alliance
PO Box 1108
New York, NY 10040

212-568-0036
E-Mail: info@composers.com
Home Page: composers.com
Social Media: *Facebook, Twitter, YouTube*

Gina Genova, Director

Music publisher and licensor representing Americans composing in the classical style.
Founded in 1937

18934 American Federation of Musicians of the United States and Canada
1501 Broadway
Suite 600
New York, NY 10036-5501

212-869-1330
FAX 212-764-6134
E-Mail: info@afm.org
Home Page: www.afm.org
Social Media: *Facebook, Twitter, YouTube*

Thomas Lee, President
Linda Patterson, Executive Secreatry to President

AFM is an association of professional musicians united through their locals so that they can live and work in dignity; produce work that will be fulfilling and compensated fairly; have a meaningful voice in decisions that affect them; have the opportunity to develop their talents and skills; whose collective voice and power will be realized in a democratic and progressive union; and who oppose the forces of exploitation through their union solidarity.
10K Members
Founded in 1896

18935 American Federation of Violin and Bow Makers
1035 S. Josephine Avenue
Rosalia, WA 99170-9551

507-396-3411
E-Mail: info@afvbm.org
Home Page: www.afvbm.com

Yung Chin, President
David Bonsey, Vice President
William Scott, Treasurer
Peg Baumgartel, Secretary

Members are those with recognized professional abilities and experience in either making or repairing violins and bows. They are elected to the Federation and are entitled to all privileges and duties of membership. The Federation has designed programs to held develop the technical skills and knowledge of the membership through seminars and regular meeting events. The Federation sponsors exhibitions as a forum for makers,musicians and the general public.
Cost: $300.00
Founded in 1980

18936 American Gamelan Institute
603-448-6060
FAX 603-448-6060
E-Mail: agi@gamelan.org
Home Page: www.gamelan.org

Founded in 1983

18937 American Guild of Music
PO Box 599
Warren, MI 48090

248-686-1975
E-Mail: agm@americanguild.org
Home Page: www.americanguild.org

Barry Carr, President
Joanne Darby, Treasurer
Lorelei Eccleston Dart, First VP
Steve Petrunak, Second VP

The world's oldest international music organization. Its membership is open to independent music teachers, music store owners and their teaching staffs, music publishers and instrument manufacturers and music students.
6000 Members

18938 American Guild of Musical Artists
1430 Broadway
14th Floor
New York, NY 10018-3308

212-265-3687
FAX 212-262-9088
E-Mail: agma@musicalartists.org
Home Page: www.musicalartists.org
Social Media: *Facebook, Twitter*

Alan S.Gordon, Executive Director
Gerry Angel, Director of Operations
Deborah A.Maher, Associate Executive Director
Gerry Angel, Director of Operations

AGMA is a labor union. It negotiates collective bargaining agreements for its members that provide them with these vital benefits: guaranteed salaries; rehearsal and overtime pay; regulated work hours; vacation and sick pay; access to low-cost health benefits; good-faith resolution of disputes; and protection of their legal and contractual rights.
5700 Members
Founded in 1936

18939 American Guild of Organists
475 Riverside Drive
Suite 1260
New York, NY 10115-0055

212-870-2310
FAX 212-870-2163

E-Mail: info@agohq.org
Home Page: www.agohq.org
Social Media: *Facebook, Twitter, LinkedIn, Google+*

James Thomashower, Executive Director
Marcia Van Oyen, Director

Membership in the American Guild of Organists is primarily through local chapters, which hold regular meetings featuring performances, lectures, seminars, and discussions on a wide variety of topics. Many chapters also offer monthly newsletters, scholarship programs, musician placement services, and substitute referrals to employing institutions. Membership can also be without chapter affiliation.
20000 Members
Founded in 1896

18940 American Harp Society
PO Box 278
Greenfield Center, NY 12833

518-893-7495
E-Mail: elizabetharp@juno.com
Home Page: www.harpsociety.org

Ann Yeung, President
Barbara Lepke Sims, 1st VP
Carolyn Munford, 2nd VP
Erin Wood, Secretary
Ashanti Pretlow, Executive Secretary

Promotes and fosters the appreciation of the harp as a musical instrument, to encourage the composition of music for the harp and to improve the quality of performance of harpists.
Cost: $50.00
3000 Members
Founded in 1962

18941 American Music Therapy Association
8455 Colesville Rd
Suite 1000
Silver Spring, MD 20910-3392

301-589-3300
FAX 301-589-5175
E-Mail: info@musictherapy.org
Home Page: www.musictherapy.org
Social Media: *Facebook, Twitter, YouTube*

Andrea Farbman, Executive Director
Brian Abrams, Mid Atlantic Region President

The mission of the American Music Therapy Association is to advance public awareness of the benefits of music therapy and increase access to quality music therapy services in a rapidly changing world.
3800 Members
Founded in 1998

18942 American Musical Instrument Society
1106 Garden Street
Hoboken, NJ 07030

201-656-0107
E-Mail: amis@guildassoc.com
Home Page: www.amis.org
Social Media: *Facebook*

Albert R Rice, President
Carolyn Bryant, Vice-President
Deborah Check Reeves, Secretary
Joanne Kopp, Treasurer

Promotes better understanding of all aspects of history, design, construction, restoration, and usage of musical instruments in all cultures and from all periods. The membership of AMIS includes collectors, historians, curators, performers, instrument makers, restorers, dealers, conservators, teachers, students, and many institutional members.
Founded in 1971

18943 American Musicological Society
6010 College Station
Brunswick, ME 04011-8451

207-798-4243
877-679-7648
FAX 877-679-7648
E-Mail: ams@ams-net.org
Home Page: www.ams-net.org
Social Media: *Facebook, Twitter, YouTube*

Robert Judd, Executive Director
Al Hipkins, Office Manger
Melissa Kapocius, Secretary

Advances research in the various fields of music as a branch of learning and scholarship.
3600 Members
Founded in 1934

18944 American Orff-Schulwerk Association
PO Box 391089
Cleveland, OH 44139-8089

440-543-5366
FAX 440-600-7332
E-Mail: info@aosa.org
Home Page: www.aosa2.org

Katharine P. Johnson, Executive Director
Jo Ella Hug, President
Julie Scott, VP
Jennifer Hartman, Treasurer

Professional organization of music and movement educators dedicated to the creative teaching approach developed by Carl Orff and Gunild Keetman.
Cost: $70.00

18945 American School Band Directors Association
227 N 1st Street
PO Box 696
Guttenberg, IA 52052-0696

563-252-2500
FAX 563-252-2500
E-Mail: asbda@alpinecom.net
Home Page: www.asbda.com
Social Media: *Facebook*

Blair Callaway, President
Susan Barrett, Secretary
Blair Callaway, Treasurer
Dennis Hanna, Manager
Russ Hilton, Treasurer

Nationwide organization dedicated to the support of professional and college band conductors. Membership by invitation only.
1200 Members
Founded in 1953

18946 American Society of Composers, Authors and Publishers (ASCAP)
1 Lincoln Plaza
New York, NY 10023-7097

212-621-6000
FAX 212-621-8453
E-Mail: info@ascap.com
Home Page: www.ascap.com
Social Media: *Facebook, Twitter, LinkedIn, YouTube*

Paul Williams, President/Chairman
James M Kendrick, Treasurer
Caroline Bienstock, Secretary
John Lofrumento, CEO

Performing rights organization created and controlled by composers, songwriters and music publishers. Protects the rights of its members by licensing and distributing royalties for the non-dramatic public performances of their copyrighted works. An online newsletter is also available filled with the most up-to-date information about professional opportunities, legislative issues, member benefits and more.
26000 Members
Founded in 1914

18947 American Society of Music Arrangers and Composers
5903 Noble Ave
Van Nuys, CA 91411-3026

818-994-4661
FAX 818-994-6181
E-Mail: asmac@theproperimageevents.com
Home Page: www.asmac.org
Social Media: *Facebook, Twitter, LinkedIn, Youtube*

Scherr Lillico, Executive Director
Duane L Tatro, Vice President
Ray Charles, Vice President

Professional society for arrangers, composers, orchestrators, and musicians. Monthly meetings with great speakers from the music industry.
500 Members
Founded in 1938

18948 American Song Writers Association
205-815-8180
E-Mail:
info@americansongwritersassociation.com
Home Page:
www.americansongwritersassociation.com
Social Media: *Facebook, Twitter, Pinterest*

18949 American String Teachers Association
4155 Chain Bridge Rd
Fairfax, VA 22030-4102

703-279-2113
FAX 703-279-2114
E-Mail: asta@astaweb.com
Home Page: www.astaweb.com

Donna Hale, Executive Director
Beth Danner-Knight, Deputy Director
Mary Jane Dye, Deputy Director

A membership organization for string and orchestra teachers and players, helping them to develop and refine their careers. Members range from budding student teachers to artist-status performers, businesses who supply goods and services to the string and orchestra world plus colleges, universities, music programs and conservatories.
11300 Members
Founded in 1946

18950 American Union of Swedish Singers
E-Mail: president@auss.org
Home Page: www.auss.org

500+ Members

18951 American Viola Society
14070 Proton Rd
Suite 100
Dallas, TX 75244-3601

972-233-9107
FAX 972-490-4219
E-Mail: info@avsnationaloffice.org
Home Page: www.americanviolasociety.org
Social Media: *Facebook, Twitter*

Nokunthula Ngwenyama, President
Madeline Crouch, General Manager
Karin Brown, Secretary
Michelle Sayles, Treasurer

An association for the promotion of viola performance and research. AVS membership is accompanied by two print issues of the Journal of the American Viola Society (JAVS) each year.
1000 Members

18952 Americana Music Association
The Factory at Franklin
PO Box 628
Franklin, TN 37065

615-386-6936
FAX 615-386-6937
E-Mail: press@americanamusic.org

Home Page: www.americanamusic.org
Social Media: *Facebook, Twitter, Pinterest, YouTube*

Jed Hilly, Executive Director
Danna Strong, Director
Michelle Aquilato, Director of Marketing
Sarah Comardelle, Manager of Marketingÿ
Whitney Holmes, Manager of Member Relations

18953 Association for Electronic Music

Home Page:
www.associationforelectronicmusic.orgÿ
Social Media: *Twitter*

Mark Lawrence, CEO

18954 Association of Concert Bands

6613 Cheryl Ann Drive
Independence, OH 44131-3718

800-726-8720
FAX 216-524-1897
Home Page: www.acbands.org
Social Media: *Facebook*

Allen Beck, President
Nada Vencl, Secretary
Mike Montgomery, CIO
Howard Habenicht, Treasurer

The purpose of ACB is to encourage and foster adult concert community, municipal, and civic bands and to promote the performance of the highest quality traditional and contemporary literature for band.
750 Members
Founded in 1977

18955 Blues Foundation

421 S.Main St
Memphis, TN 38103-4464

901-527-2583
FAX 901-529-4030
E-Mail: jay@blues.org
Home Page: www.blues.org
Social Media: *Facebook, Twitter, LinkedIn, YouTube, RSS*

Jay Sieleman, President
Joey Whitmer, DeputuDirector
Cindy James, Membership
Chadd Webb, Treasurer

A nonprofit corporation which serves as the hub for the worldwide passion for Blues Music.
Founded in 1980

18956 Carnatic Music Association of North America

P O Box 234
Fords, NJ 8863

908-521-0500
800-362-6137
E-Mail: webmaster@cmana.org
Home Page: www.cmana.orgÿ

Aravind Narasimhan, President
Chithra Krishnan, Vice President
Rajesh Nathan, Secretary
Rhama Narayanan, Treasurer

18957 Chamber Music America

99 Madison Avenue
5th Floor
New York, NY 10016

212-242-2022
FAX 646-430-5667
Home Page: www.chamber-music.org

Susan Dadian, Program Director
Margaret M Lioi, CEO
Louise Smith, Chair

Promotes artistic excellence and economic stability within the profession and to ensure that chamber music is a vital part of American life. Their vision is that chamber music serves as a model of cooperation and collaboration, that audiences become more committed to supporting chamber music and the professionals who devote their lives to this art form, and that opportunities for the performance of chamber music increase in traditional concert venues and beyond.
Founded in 1977

18958 Chinese Arts and Music Association

P.O. Box 50531
Seattle, WA 98015-0531

206-817-6888
E-Mail: chinamusic@comcast.net
Home Page: www.uschinamusic.org

Warren Chang, President
Angel Yan, Board Member
Janelle Yeung, Board Member
Minghwa Chiem, Board Member
Buyun Zhao, Director

18959 Chorus America

1156 15th St NW
Suite 310
Washington, DC 20005-1747

202-331-7577
FAX 202-331-7599
E-Mail: service@chorusamerica.org
Home Page: www.chorusamerica.org
Social Media: *Facebook, Twitter, Youtube*

Ann Meier Baker, President & Chief Executive Officer
Rollo Dilworth, Chairman
David C. Howse, Treasurer
Mary Lou Lyons, Secretary
Gayle M. Ober, Immediate Past Chair

Chorus America's mission is to build a dynamic and inclusive choral community so that more people are enriched by the beauty and power of choral singing.
2100 Members
Founded in 1977

18960 Church Music Association of America

P.O. Box 4344
Roswell, NM 88202-4344

505-263-6298
E-Mail: contact@musicasacra.com
Home Page: www.musicasacra.comÿ
Social Media: *Facebook, Twitter, Google+*

Founded in 1964

18961 College Music Society

312 E Pine St
Missoula, MT 59802-4624

406-721-9616
FAX 406-721-9419
E-Mail: cms@music.org
Home Page: www.music.org
Social Media: *Facebook, Twitter, LinkedIn, YouTube, Google+*

Robby D Gunstream, Executive Director
David B. Williams, President

A consortium of college, conservatory, university and independent musicians and scholars interested in all disciplines of music. Its mission is to promote music teaching and learning, musical creativity and expression, research and dialogue, and diversity and interdisciplinary interaction.
9500 Attendees
Founded in 1958

18962 Conductors Guild

719 Twinridge Ln
Richmond, VA 23235

804-553-1378
FAX 804-553-1876
E-Mail: guild@conductorsguild.org

Home Page: www.conductorsguild.org
Social Media: *Facebook, Twitter, LinkedIn*

Amanda Burton Winger, Executive Director
Scott Winger, Assistant Director
David Leibowitz, Editor
Rufus Jones Jr, Editor

The Conductors Guild is the only music service organization devoted exclusively to the advancement of the art of conducting and to serving the artistic and professional needs of conductors.
1850+ Members
Founded in 1975

18963 Contemporary Record Society

724 Winchester Road
Broomall, PA 19008

610-544-5920
FAX 610-544-5920
E-Mail: crsnews@verizon.net
Home Page:
www.mysite.verizon.net/vzeeewvp/contemporaryrecordsociety/

Caroline Hunt, Contact

Promotes both a fellowship in the musical arts between artists, composers and presenters and commercial recordingsa and participants in this endeavor. The intent of the Society is to advance the cause of music in the United States and throughout the world, promoting an association among its constituents. The scope of the Society's repertoire includes the musical masterworks of both well-known and relatively unknown composers of all periods.
Cost: $45.00
Founded in 1981

18964 Country Music Association

One Music Circle S
Nashville, TN 37203

615-244-2840
FAX 615-242-4783
Home Page: www.cmaworld.com
Social Media: *Facebook, Twitter, YouTube, Instagram*

Gary Overton, Chairman
Troy Tomlison, President
Jessie Schmidt, Secretary/Treasurer
Steve Moore, CEO

CMA is dedicated to bringing the poetry and emotion of Country Music to the World. They will continue a tradition of leadership and professionalism, promotoing the music and recognizing excellence in all its forms. They foster a spirit of community and sharing, and respect and encourage creativity and the unique contributions of everyone. It is a place to have fun and celebrate success.
5000+ Members
Founded in 1958

18965 Country Radio Broadcasters

1009 16th Avenue South
Nashville, TN 37212

615-327-4487
FAX 615-329-4492
E-Mail: news@crb.org
Home Page: www.countryradioseminar.com/
Social Media: *Facebook, Twitter*

Ed Salamon, Executive Director
Chasity Crouch, Business Manager
Bill Mayne, VP
Carole Bowen, Secretary
Jeff Walker, Treasurer

A nonprofit eductional organization. It is the principal entity that brings Country radio together with the Country music industry for learning opportunities that promote growth.
Founded in 1969

18966 Creative Musicians Coalition
PO Box 6205
Peoria, IL 61601-6205

309-685-4843
800-882-4262
FAX 309-685-4879
E-Mail: aimcmc@aol.com
Home Page:
www.creativemusicianscoalition.com

Ronald Wallace, Founder/President

An international organization dedicated to the advancement of new music and the success of independent musicians.
1000 Members
Founded in 1984

18967 East-2-West Marketing & Promotion
559 Wanamaker Road
Jenkintown, PA 19046-2219

215-884-3308
FAX 215-884-1083
Home Page: www.musiciansnetwork.com

Jackie Paul, President/CEO

Marketing and promotion.
Mailing list available for rent

18968 Folk Alliance International
509 Delaware
#101
Kansas City, MO 64105

901-522-1170
FAX 816-221-3658
E-Mail: fa@folk.org
Home Page: www.folk.org/
Social Media: *Facebook, Twitter, YouTube, Instagram*

Lewis Meyers, Executive Director
Mary Sue Twohy, VP
Alan Korolenko, Secretary
Donald Davidoff, Treasurer
Lisa Schwartz, Secretary

The service association for the field, working on behalf of the folk music and dance industry year round. They offer a business directory of contacts for members, and a non-profit group exemption program for US-based organizations.
Cost: $70.00
Founded in 1989

18969 Folklife Center Of International House
3701 Chestnut Street
Philadelphia, PA 19104

215-387-5125
FAX 215-895-6550

Osagie Imasogie, President
Tanya Steinberg, Executive Director
William Parker, Director Of Communications Events

To present the highest caliber of traditional arts.

18970 Freelance Musicians' Association
E-Mail: info@freelancemusicians.org
Home Page: www.freelancemusicians.org

18971 Gospel Music Association
741 cool Springs Blvd.
Franklin, TN 37067

615-242-0303
FAX 615-254-9755
E-Mail: service@gospelmusic.org
Home Page: www.gospelmusic.org
Social Media: *Facebook, Twitter, LinkedIn, Youtube*

John Styll, President
Scott Brickell, Director

Charles Dorris, Founder/Chairman
Ed Harper, Director
Ed Leonard, Director

Our mission is to expose, promote and celebrate the gospel through music. GMA serves as a voice for the Christian music community. It provides an atmosphere in which artists, industry leaders, retail stores, radio stations, concert promoters and local churches can coordinate their efforts for the purpose of benefitting the industry as a whole, while remaining true to the purpose of communicating the gospel message.
Cost: $85.00
5000 Members
Founded in 1964

18972 Guitar Accessory and Marketing Association (GAMA)
Po Box 757
New York, NY 10033

212-795-3630
FAX 212-795-3630
E-Mail: assnhdqs@earthlink.net
Home Page: www.discoverguitar.com

Membership is comprised of guitar and guitar accessory manufacturers and various consumer magazines.
Founded in 1933

18973 Guitar Foundation of America
PO Box 2900
Palos Verdes Peninsula, CA 78717

877-570-1651
FAX 877-570-3409
E-Mail: info@guitarfoundation.org
Home Page: www.guitarfoundation.org
Social Media: *Facebook, Twitter*

Dr. Martha Masters, President
Jill Winchell, Operations Manager
Martha Masters, Executive VP
Jeff Cogan, VP
Robert Lane, Vice President/Secretary

Provides its members the combined advantages of a guitar society, a library, a publisher, a continuing education resource, and an artis council. The GFA is a non-profit educational and literacy organization devoted to furthering the knowledge of and interest in the guitar and its music.
Cost: $40.00
Founded in 1973

18974 International Association for the Study of Popular Music
Home Page: www.iaspm.net
Founded in 1981

18975 International Association of Electronic Keyboard Manufacturers
305 Maple Avenue
Wyncote, PA 19095-3228

617-747-2816
Home Page: www.iaekm.org

An association that comprises the global manufacturers of electronic keyboards and affiliated software and publications.

18976 International Association of Jazz Education
PO Box 724
Manhattan, KS 66505

785-776-8744
FAX 785-776-6190
E-Mail: bill@iage.org
Home Page: www.iaje.org

Bill McFarlin, Executive Director
Chuck Owen, President
Ronald Carter, VP
Laura Johnson, Treasurer
Brian Coyle, Secretary

To ensure the continued development and growth of jazz through education and outreach.
Cost: $70.00
8000 Members
Founded in 1989

18977 International Bluegrass Music Association
608 West, Irish Drive
Nashville, TN 37204

615-256-3222
888-438-4262
FAX 615-256-0450
E-Mail: info@ibma.org
Home Page: www.ibma.org
Social Media: *Facebook, Twitter, LinkedIn, Youtube*

Dan Hayes, Executive Director
Stan Zdonik, Vice Chair/Associations
Peter D'Addario, Treasurer
Lee Michael Demsey, Secretary

IBMA works together for high standards of professionalism, a greater appreciation for our music, and the success of the worldwide bluegrass community.

18978 International Clarinet Association
14070 Proton Rd
Suite 100 LB9
Dallas, TX 75244

972-233-9107
FAX 972-490-4219
E-Mail: membership@clarinet.org
Home Page: www.clarinet.org
Social Media: *Twitter*

John Cipolla, President
Tod Kerstetter, Treasurer
Caroline Hartig, Secretary
So Rhee, Executive Director

A community of clarinetists and clarinet enthusiasts that supports projects that will benefit clarinet performance; provides opportunities for the exchange of ideas, materials and information among its members; fosters the composition, publication, recording, and distribution of music for the clarinet; encourages the research and manufacture of a more definitive clarinet; and encourages and promotes the perfomance and teaching of a wide variety of repertoire for the clarinet.
4000 Members
Founded in 1990

18979 International Computer Music Association
1819 Polk St.
Suite 330
San Francisco, CA 94109

FAX 734-878-3031
E-Mail: icma@umich.edu
Home Page: www.computermusic.org

Tom Erbe, President
Michael Gurevitchÿ, VP, Membership
Margaret Schedel, VP, Conferences
Chryssie Nanou, Treasurer, Secretary
Christopher Haworth, Array Editor
Founded in 1974

18980 International Horn Society
E-Mail: exec-secretary@hornsociety.org
Home Page: www.hornsociety.org

Frank Lloyd, President
Joseph Ognibene, VP
Marian Hesse, Secretary/Treasurer
Heidi Vogal, Executive Secretary
Cost: $35.00
3500 Members
Founded in 1970

18981 International Music Products Association NAMM

5790 Armada Drive
Carlsbad, CA 92008-4608

760-438-8001
800-767-6266
FAX 760-438-7327
E-Mail: info@namm.org
Home Page: www.namm.org
Social Media: *Facebook, Twitter, YouTube, Pinterest*

Larry Morton, President
Mark Goff, President/Owner
Joe Lamond, President/CEO
Chris Martin, Chairman/CEO
Robin Walenta, President/CEO

An association whose mission is to unify, lead and strengthen the international music products industry and increase active participation in music making.
9000 Members
Founded in 1901

18982 International Piano Guild

PO Box 1807
Austin, TX 78767

512-478-5775
E-Mail: ngpt@pianoguild.com
Home Page: www.pianoguild.com

Richard Allison, President

A division of the American College of Musicians Professional society of piano teachers and music faculty members. Its primary function is to establish definite goals and awards for students of all levels, from the earliest beginner to the gifted prodigy. Its purpose is to encourage growth and enjoyment through the study of piano.
118m Members
Founded in 1929

18983 International Polka Association

4608 S Archer Ave
Chicago, IL 60632-2932

773-254-7771
800-867-6552
E-Mail: ipa@internationalpolka.com
Home Page: www.internationalpolka.com
Social Media: *Facebook, YouTube*

Dave Ulczycki, President
Rick Rzeszutko, First VP
Fred Kenzierski, Second VP
Marlene Gill, Secretary
Linda Niewierowski, Treasurer

An educational and charitable organization for the preservation, promulgation and advancement of polka music and to promote, maintain and advance public interest in polka entertainment; to advance mutual interests and encourage greater cooperation among its members who are engaged in polka entertainment; and to encourage and pursue the study of polka music, dancing and traditional folklore. Responsible for the continued operation and growth of the Polka Music Hall of Fame and Museum.
Cost: $15.00
8M Members
Founded in 1968

18984 International Society of Folk Harpers and Craftsmen

1614 Pittman Drive
Missoula, Mt 59803

406-542-1976
E-Mail: harps@thorharp.com
Home Page: www.folkharpsociety.org

Dave Kolacny, President
Timothy Habinski, First VP
Verlene Schermer, Second VP

Alice Williams, Secretary
Barbra Bailey Bradley, Treasurer

The mission of the ISFHC is: to promote the playing and enjoyment of the folk harp by all; to promote education, creation and development in the building of the folk harp; to increase awareness of professional folk harpers; and to increase public awareness of the music and joys of the folk harp.
Cost: $30.00
Founded in 1985

18985 Keyboard Teachers Association International

361 Pin Oak Lane
Westbury, NY 11590-1941

516-333-3236
FAX 516-997-9531
Home Page: www.musiciansnetwork.com

Dr. Albert DeVito, President

18986 League of American Ochestras

33 W 60th Street
New York, NY 10023-7905

212-262-5161
FAX 212-262-5198
E-Mail: league@symphony.org
Home Page: www.americanorchestras.org

Henry Fogel, CEO
Jesse Rosen, President/CEO
Aja Stephens, Assistant to President
Steven C. Parrish, Vice Chair
Heather Noonan, Vice Chair

Provides leadership and service to American orchestras while communicating to the public the value and importance of orchestras and the music they perform. The League links a national network of thousands of musicians, conductors, managers, board members, volunteers, staff members and business partners, providing a wealth of services, information, and educational opportunities to its members.
1200 Members
Founded in 1942
Mailing list available for rent

18987 Metropolitan Opera Guild

70 Lincoln Center Plz
New York, NY 10023-6593

212-769-7000
FAX 212-769-7007
E-Mail: info@metguild.org
Home Page: www.metoperafamily.org/guild/
Social Media: *Facebook, Twitter, LinkedIn, YouTube, Instagram*

David Dik, Manager

Seeks to encourage the appreciation of opera and to support the Metorpolitan Opera. The guild provides programs and services in many areas designed to further these goals. Publishes monthly magazine and organizes special events throughout the year to raise funds.
100M Members
Founded in 1935

18988 Midland Center For The Arts Midland Music And Concert Series

1801 W. St Andrews Road
Midland, MI 48640

989-631-8250
FAX 989-631-7890
E-Mail: hohmeyer@mcfta.org
Home Page: www.mcfta.org
Social Media: *Facebook, Twitter, LinkedIn, Youtube*

Michael Tiknis, President
James Hohmeyer, Artistic Director
Robb Wouose, Managing Director
Mark Bachman, Director
David Blakemore, Director

encourage concert audiences; Providing students with opportunities to experience professional performances.

18989 Music Business Association

1 Eves Drive
Suite 138
Marlton, NJ 8053

856-596-2221
FAX 856-596-7299
Home Page: www.musicbiz.org
Social Media: *Facebook, Twitter, RSS*

Fred Beteille, Chairman
Steve Harkins, Vice Chairman
John Trickett, Treasurer
Ryan Redington, Secretary
James Donio, President

Membership organization promoting music commerce.

18990 Music Critics Association of North America

722 Dulaney Valley Rd.
#259
Baltimore, MD 21204

410-435-3881
E-Mail: info@mcana.org
Home Page: www.mcana.org

Barbara Jepson, President
John Fleming, Vice President
James Bash, Treasurer
Roy C. Dicks, Secretary
Robert Leininger, Managing Director

An association for the promotion of high standards in classical music criticism.

18991 Music Distributors Association

14070 Proton Rd
Suite 100 LB9
Dallas, TX 75244-3601

972-233-9107
FAX 972-490-4219
E-Mail: office@musicdistributors.org
Home Page: www.musicdistributors.org

International, nonprofit trade association representing and serving manufacturers, wholesalers, importers and exporters of musical instruments and accessories, sound reinforcement products and published music.
Cost: $675.00
Founded in 1939

18992 Music Library Association

1600 Aspen Commons
Suite 100
Middleton, WI 53562

608-836-5825
FAX 608-831-8200
E-Mail: mla@areditions.com
Home Page: www.musiclibraryassoc.org
Social Media: *Facebook, Twitter*

Michael Colby, President
Pamela Bristah, Secretary
Paul Cary, Admin Officer
Linda W.Blair, Admin Officer

Provides a forum for issues surrounding music, music in libraries, and music librarianship.
Cost: $90.00
Founded in 1931

18993 Music Performance Fund

1501 Broadway
Suite 600
New York, NY 10036

212-391-3950
FAX 212-221-2604
E-Mail: sramos@musicpf.org

Home Page: www.musicpf.org
Social Media: *Facebook*

Den Beck, Trustee
Al Elvin, Director of Finance
Linda Williamson, Manager

A nonprofit public service organization head-quartered in New York City. MPF is the world's largest sponsor of live, admission-free musical programs.
Founded in 1948

18994 Music Performance Trust Funds
1501 Broadway
Suite 600
New York, NY 10036

212-391-3950
FAX 212-221-2604
E-Mail: sramos@musicpf.org
Home Page: www.musicpf.org
Social Media: *Facebook*

Dan Beck, Trustee
Vidrey Blackburn, Grant Review Process
Al Elvin, Director of Finance
Samantha Ramos, Team Member
Founded in 1948

18995 Music Publishers Association
243 5th Ave
Suite 236
New York, NY 10016-8728

212-675-7354
FAX 212-675-7381
E-Mail: mpa-admin@mpa.org
Home Page: www.mpa.org

Kathleen Marsh, President
Bryndon Bay, Treasurer
Todd Vunderink, Secretary
Lauren Keiser, Second VP
75 Members
Founded in 1895

18996 Music Publishers Association of the United States
243 5th Ave.
Suite 236
New York, NY 10016

212-675-7354
FAX 212-675-7381
E-Mail: admin@mpa.org
Home Page: www.mpa.org

Kathleen Marsh, President
Sean Patrick Flahaven, Vice President
Lauren Keiser, Second Vice President
Sonya Kim, Secretary
Erin Rogers, Treasurer

The MPA fosters communication among publishers, dealers, music educators, and all ultimate users of music. It is a nonprofit association which addresses itself to issues pertaining to every area of music publishing with an emphasis on the issues relevant to the publishers of print music for concert and educational purposes.
75 Members
Founded in 1895

18997 Music Teachers National Association
1 W. 4th St.
Ste. 1550
Cincinnati, OH 45202-3004

513-421-1420
888-512-5278
FAX 513-421-2503
E-Mail: mtnanet@mtna.org
Home Page: www.mtna.org
Social Media: *Facebook, Twitter*

Gary L Ingle, Executive Director
Rebecca Grooms Johnson, NCTM, President
Karen Thickstun, NCTM, VP
Scott McBride Smith, NCTM, President-Elect
Sylvia Coats, NCTM, Secretary-Treasurer

The mission of the MTNA is to advance the value of music study and music making to society and to support the professionalism of music teachers.
24000 Members
Founded in 1876
Mailing list available for rent: 23,000 names at $85 per M

18998 Music Video Production Associationÿ

E-Mail: infomvpa@gmail.com
Home Page: www.mvpa.com

Coleen Haynes, President
Missy Galanadia, Vice President
Kim Dellara, Vice President
Grant Cihlar, Treasurer
Amanda Fox, Board of Director

18999 Music for All Foundation
39 W Jackson Place
Suite 150
Indianapolis, IN 46225

317-636-2263
FAX 317-524-6200
E-Mail: info@music-for-all.org
Home Page: www.musicforall.org

Eric Martin, President/CEO
Nancy H.Carlson, Executive VP/CFO
Carolyn Ealy, Education and Office Manager
Tonya Bullock, Accounting manager
Gayle W. Doster, Chairman

Committed to expanding the role of music and the arts in education, to heightening the public's appreciation of the value of music and arts education, and to creating a positive environment for the arts through societal changes.
Founded in 1975
Mailing list available for rent

19000 Musical Box Society International
MBSI Member Registration
PO Box 10196
Springfield, MO 65808-0196

FAX 417-886-8839
Home Page: www.mbsi.org
Social Media: *Facebook, Twitter, Digg, Yahoo, Reddit, StumbleUp*

A nonprofit organization dedicated to the enjoyment, sstudy and preservation of all automatic musical instruments. Members receive the bimonthly scholarly journal, Mechanical Music, covering educational articles, relevant events, activities, news, information, and advertisements and the biennial, Directory of Members, Museums and Dealers. Hosts annual convention.
Cost: $55.00
2.8M Members
Founded in 1949

19001 Musicians Foundation
875 Sixth Avenue
Suite 2303
New York, NY 10001-3507

212-239-9137
FAX 212-239-9138
E-Mail: info@musiciansfoundation.org
Home Page: www.musiciansfoundation.org
Social Media: *Facebook, Twitter*

BC Vermeersch, Executive Director
Hans E Tausig, President
Joseph Hertzberg, Treasurer

Representing interests on the condition and social welfare of professional musicians and their families. Provides emergency financial assistance to meet current living, medical and allied expenses.
Founded in 1914

19002 National Academy of Recording Arts and Sciences
3030 Olympic Blvd.ÿ
Santa Monica, CA 90404

310-392-3777
FAX 310-392-2188
Home Page: www.grammy.org
Social Media: *Facebook, Twitter, YouTube, Instagram*

Ryan Seacrest, Honorary Chair
Tim Bucher, Chair
Geoff Cottrillÿ, Vice Chair
Rachna Bhasin, Secretary/Treasurer
Rusty Rueff, Chair Emeritus
Founded in 1988

19003 National Association for Music Education MENC
1806 Robert Fulton Drive
Reston, VA 20191

703-860-4000
800-336-3768
FAX 703-860-1531
Home Page: www.menc.org
Social Media: *Facebook, Twitter, LinkedIn, Google+, Pinterest*

John J Mahlmann, Executive Director
Lynn Brinckmeyer, President

Mission is to advance music education by encouraging the study and making of music by all.
Founded in 1907

19004 National Association of Band Instrument Manufacturers
2026 Eagle Road
PO Box 51
Normal, IL 61761

309-452-4257
FAX 309-452-4825
E-Mail: napbirt@napbirt.org
Home Page: www.napbirt.org
Social Media: *Facebook*

Jerome Hershman, Contact
Bill Mathwes, Executive Director
Ross, Watkins

A trade association of band instrument manufacturers, importers and distributors including accessories selling to the trade only.
34 Members
Founded in 1976

19005 National Association of College Wind and Percussion Instructor
Division of Fine Arts
Truman State University
Kirksville, MO 63501

660-785-4442
FAX 660-785-7463
E-Mail: cmoore@fsu.edu
Home Page: www.nacwpi.org
Social Media: *Facebook*

Chris Moore, President
Michael Dean, VP
Richard K Weerts, Executive Secretary/Treasurer

A forum for communication within the profession of applied music on the college campus. The Association is composed of university, college, and conservatory teachers.
Cost: $35.00
600 Members
Founded in 1951

19006 National Association of Composers

P.O. Box 49256
Barrington Station
Los Angeles, CA 90049

Home Page: www.music-usa.org/nacusa

Greg A. Steinke, Ph.D., President/ Chair
Wieslaw V Rentowski ỹ, Vice President
Sylvia ỹ Constantinidis, M.M., Secretary
Joe L. Alexander, Treasurer
Daniel Kessner, Past President
Founded in 1933

19007 National Association of Negro Musicians Inc

931 Monroe Drive NE
Suite A102-159
Atlanta, GA 30308

404-647-7217
FAX 404-745-0128
E-Mail: info@nanm.org
Home Page: www.nanm.org
Social Media: *Facebook, Twitter*

Byron J. Smith, President
Geraldine Boone, First VP
Sylvia Turner Hollified, Second VP
Marydith Lawson, Executive Secretary
Daniel.J Long, Treasurer

Dedicated to the preservation, encouragement and advocacy of all genres of the music of African Americans. Holds a national convention in a different city eac year, offering a chance to participate in workshops, seminars, lectures and performances. NANM invites the professional artists, the educator, the student, the amateur, the lover of music to become a part of this organization's 'Pride in a Cultural Heritage.'
2.5M Members
Founded in 1919

19008 National Association of Pastoral Musicians

962 Wayne Ave
Suite 210
Silver Spring, MD 20910-4461

240-247-3000
FAX 240-247-3001
E-Mail: npmsing@npm.org
Home Page: www.npm.org

Richard B. Rev.Msgr, President
Kathleen Haley, Director Membership Services
Lowell Hickman, Office Manager/Executive Assistant
Joseph Lively, Comptroller
Paul Lagoy, Secretary & Mil Clerk

Fosters the art of musical liturgy. The members of NPM serve the Catholic Church in the United States as musicians, clergy, liturgists, and other leaders of prayer.
9000 Members
Founded in 1976

19009 National Association of Professional Band Instrument Repair Technicians

2026 Eagle Road
PO Box 51
Normal, IL 61761

309-452-4257
FAX 309-452-4825
E-Mail: napbirt@napbirt.org
Home Page: www.napbirt.org
Social Media: *Facebook*

Bill Mathews, Executive Director
Ross Watkins, Admin. Manager

A nonprofit international educational association dedicated to the advancement of the craft of band instrument repair. Their mission is to promote the highest possible standards of band instrument repair, restoration and maintenance by providing members with multi-level profes-

sional development by offering technical training, continuing education and the publication of their bi-monthky trade journal.
Cost: $95.00
1300 Members
Founded in 1976

19010 National Association of Recording Merchandisers

1 Eves Drive
Suite 138
Marlton, NJ 08053-3130

856-596-2221
FAX 856-596-7299
E-Mail: donio@narm.com
Home Page: www.musicbiz.org/
Social Media: *Facebook, Twitter, RSS*

Fred Beteille, Chair
Steve Harkins, Vice Chairman
John Trickett, Treasurer
Ryan Redington, Secretary
Jim Donio, President

A not-for-profit trade association that serves the music retailing community in the areas of networking, advocacy, information, education and promotion. Membership includes music and other entertainment retailers, wholesalers, distributorsm record labels, multimedia suppliers, and suppliers of related products and services, as well as individual professionals and educators in the music business field.
Founded in 1958

19011 National Association of Schools of Music

11250 Roger Bacon Drive
Suite 21
Reston, VA 20190-5248

703-437-0700
FAX 703-437-6312
E-Mail: info@arts-accredit.org
Home Page: www.arts-accredit.org

Don Gibson, President
Mark Wait, VP
Mellasenah Y Morris, Treasurer

An organization of schools, conservatories, colleges and universities. NASM provides information to potential students and parents, consultations, stastistical information, professional development and policy analysis. It is the national accrediting agency for music and music-related disciplines.
635 Members
Founded in 1924

19012 National Association of Teachers of Singing

9957 Moorings Drive
Suite 401
Jacksonville, FL 32257-2416

904-992-9101
FAX 904-262-2587
E-Mail: info@nats.org
Home Page: www.nats.org
Social Media: *Facebook, Twitter, LinkedIn, YouTube, Pintrest, Flickr*

Allen Henderson, Executive Director
Deborah Guess, Director of Operations
Amanda Wood, Membership & Program Coordinator
Margie Patterson, Bookkeeper/Executive Assistant
Tina Hooks, AdministrativeỹAssistant

To encourage the highest standards of the vocal art and of ethical principles in the teaching of singing; and to promote vocal education and research at all levels, both for the enrichment of the general public and for the professional advancement of the talented.
7000 Members
Founded in 1944

19013 National Ballroom and Entertainment Association

PO Box 274
Decorah, IA 52101-7600

563-382-3871
E-Mail: nbea@q.com
Home Page: www.nbea.com
Social Media: *Facebook*

Larry Bowers, President
Pat Brannon, Vice President
John Matter, Executive Director
Ken Paulsen, Treasurer

National nonprofit association which advocates that social dancing is a life-long activity that contributes to the physical, mantal, and social well-being of an individual. They believe that social dancing should be preserved for current and future generations and introduced to to-day's youth as an alternate form of social interaction.
450 Members
Founded in 1947

19014 National Band Association

Membership Office
745 Chastain Road-Ste 1140
PO Box 102
Kennesaw, GA 30144

601-297-8168
FAX 601-266-6185
E-Mail: info@nationalbandassociation.org
Home Page: www.nationalbandassociation.org
Social Media: *Facebook, Twitter, RSS*

Richard Good, President
Scott Casagrande, First VP
Scott Tobias, Second VP
Linda Moorehouse, Secretary/Treasurer
David Gregory, Advisor to the President

The purpose of the NBA is to promote the musical and educational significance of bands and is dedicated to the attainment of a high level of excellence for bands and band music. It is open to anyone and everyone interested in bands, regardless of the length if his/her experience, type of position held, or the specific area at which he/she works. The membership roster includes men and women from every facet of the band world.
3M Members
Founded in 1960

19015 National Endowment for the Arts

400 7th Street, SW
Washington, DC 20506-0001

202-682-5400
E-Mail: webmgr@arts.gov
Home Page: www.arts.govỹ

Jane Chu, Chairman
Laura Callanan, Senior Deputy Chairman
Beth Bienvenu, Accessibility Director
Wendy Clark, Director of Museums
Ayanna N. Hudson, Arts Education Director

Independent federal agency that works with state arts agencies, local leaders, philanthropists and other federal agencies to give Americans opportunities to participate in the arts.

19016 National Federation of Music Clubs

1646 W Smith Valley Rd
Greenwood, IN 46142-1550

317-882-4003
FAX 317-882-4019
E-Mail: info@nfmc-music.org
Home Page: www.nfmc-music.org
Social Media: *Facebook, Twitter, LinkedIn, Youtube*

Carolyn Nelson, President
Michael Edwards, First VP
Kay Hawthorne, Secretary
Barbara Hildebrand, Treasurer
Jennifer Keller, Administrative Manager

NFMC provides opportunities for musical study, performance and appreciation to more than 200,000 senior, student and junior members in 6,500 music-related clubs and organizations nationwide. Members are professional and amateur musicians, vocalists, composers, dancers, performing artists, arts and music educators, music students, generous music patrons and benefactors, and music lovers of all ages.
170M Members
Founded in 1898

19017 National Music Council of the United States

425 Park Street
Montclair, NJ 07043ÿ

973-655-7974
E-Mail: sandersd@mail.montclair.edu
Home Page: www.musiccouncil.org

Michael Butera, President
Carolyn Nelson, First Vice President
Paul Williams, Second Vice President
Del R. Bryant, Third VP
Linda Lorence, Treasurer
Founded in 1940

19018 National Opera Association

PO Box 60869
Canyon, TX 79016-0869

806-651-2857
FAX 806-651-2958
Home Page: www.noa.org
Social Media: *Facebook*

David Holley, President
Ruth Dobson, Vice President for Conventions
Paul Houghtaling, Vice President for Regions
Carol Ann Modesitt, Treasurer
Robert Hansen, Executive Director

The NOA seeks to promote a greater appreciation of opera and music theatre, to enhance pedagogy and performing activities, and to increase performance opportunities by supporting projects that improve the scope and quality of opera. Members in the United States, Canada, Europe, Asia and Australia participate in a wide array of activities in support of this mission.
775 Members
Founded in 1955
Mailing list available for rent

19019 Nationalÿ Associationÿ ofÿ Musicÿ Merchants

5790 Armada Drive
Carlsbad, CA 92008ÿ

760-438-8001
800-767-6266
FAX 760-438-7327
E-Mail: info@namm.org
Home Page: www.namm.org
Social Media: *Facebook, Twitter, Pinterest, YouTube*

Larry Morton, Chairman
Mark Goff, Vice Chairman
Robin Walenta, Treasurer
Chris Martin, Secretary
Joe Lamond, President/ CEO

19020 North American Basque Organizations

E-Mail: info@naBASQUE.org
Home Page: www.nabasque.org

Valerie Arrechea, President
Mary Gaztambide, Vice President
Grace Mainvil, Treasurer
Marisa Espinalÿ, Secretary
Kate Camino, Administrator
Founded in 1973

19021 Opera America

330 7th Ave
16th Floor
New York, NY 10001-5248

212-796-8620
FAX 212-796-8621
E-Mail: Info@operaamerica.org
Home Page: www.operaamerica.org

Marc A Scorca, President
Frayda B. Lindemann, Chairman
Timothy O'Leary, Treasurer
James W Wright, Secretary
Rebecca Ackerman, Membership Manager

Opera America serves and strengthens the field of opera by providing a variety of informational, technical, and administrative resources to the greater opera community. Its fundamental mission is to promote opera as exciting and accessible to individuals from all walks of life.

19022 Organization of American Kodaly Educators

10801 National Blvd.
Suite 405
Los Angeles, CA 90064

310-441-3555
FAX 310-441-3577
E-Mail: info@oake.org
Home Page: www.oake.org
Social Media: *Facebook, Twitter, Google+*

Joan Dahlin, Manager
Kevin Pearson, VP
Mary Neeley Stevens, Secretary
Kathy Hickey, Treasurer
Gary Shields, Administrative Director

The purpose of this organization is to promote Zoltan Kodaly's concept of Music for Everyone, through the improvment of music education in schools.
Founded in 1973

19023 Pedal Steel Guitar Association

PO Box 20248
Floral Park, NY 11002-0248

516-616-9214
FAX 516-616-9214
E-Mail: bobpsga@optonline.net
Home Page: www.psga.org

Kelly Foster Griffin, President
Jane Smith, VP
Kathy Hickey, Treasurer
David Gadberry, Secretary
Doug Mack, Newsletter Editor

A nonprofit organization whose primary purpose is to share information on playing the steel guitar and in particular the pedal steel guitar. Publishes the Pedal Steel Newsletter ten times per year
1540 Members
Founded in 1973

19024 Percussive Arts Society

110 W Washington Street
Suite A
Indianapolis, IN 46204

317-974-4488
FAX 317-974-4499
E-Mail: percarts@pas.org
Home Page: www.pas.org
Social Media: *Facebook, Twitter, Instagram*

Julie Hill, President
Georgr Barrett, VP
Dr. Chris Hanning, Secretary
Michael Balter, Treasurer
Jeffery Hartsough, Executive Director

A music service organization promoting percussion education, research, performance and appreciation throughout the world. Offers two print publications, the Percussive Arts Society International Headquarters/Museum and the an-

nual Percussive Arts Society International Convention.
Cost: $85.00
7000 Members
Founded in 1961

19025 Piano Technicians Guild

4444 Forest Ave
Kansas City, KS 66106

913-432-9975
FAX 913-432-9986
E-Mail: ptg@ptg.org
Home Page: www.ptg.org
Social Media: *Facebook, Twitter, YouTube*

Barbara Cassaday, Executive Director
Phil Bondi, RPT, President
Paul Brown, RPT, VP
Paul Adams, RPT, Secretary-Treasurer

A nonprofit organization serving piano tuners, technicians, and craftsmen throughout the world, organized to promote the highest possible service and technical standards among piano tuners and technicians.
4100 Members
Founded in 1957

19026 Positive Music Association

Home Page:
www.positivemusicassociation.comÿ

Sambodhiÿ Prem, Composer/ Guitarist
400 Members
Founded in 2003

19027 Production Music Association

9220 Sunset Blvd.
Suite 220
Los Angeles, CA 90069

E-Mail: hunter@pmamusic.com
Home Page: www.pmamusic.com
Social Media: *Facebook, Twitter, YouTube*

Randy Thornton, Chairman
Adam Taylor, Vice Chairman
Ivy Tombak, Treasurer
Ron Mendelsohn, Secretary
Joel Goodman, Board Member
Founded in 1997

19028 Recording Industry Association of America

1025 F ST N.W.
10th Floor
Washington, DC 20004

202-775-0101
Home Page: www.riaa.com

Mitch Glazier, Sr. Executive Vice President
Steven M. Marks, Chief, Digital Business

19029 Retail Print Music Dealers Association

2650 Midway Rd
Suite 230
Carrolton, TX 75006

972-818-1333
FAX 214-483-7004
E-Mail: cwilbur@penders.com
Home Page: www.printmusic.org

Madeleine Crouch, Owner
Myrna Sislen, VP/Secretary
Christie Smith, VP/Treasurer

A professional trade organization founded to address the special needs and interests of the print music industry. RPMDA provides a common meeting ground for the congenial interchange of ideas among print music dealers; promotes ethical standards and policies in dealing with music publishers; promotes better dealer/publisher relations; serves the public and encourages music education; provides associa-

tion-sponsored activities and publications that help its members prepare for future trends.
275 Members
Founded in 1976

19030 Rhythm and Blues Foundation
P.O.Box 22438
Philadelphia, PA 19101

215-985-4822
FAX 215-985-1195
E-Mail: info@rhythmblues.org
Home Page: www.rhythm-n-blues.org

Patricia Wilson Aden, Executive Director
Jim Fifield, Vice Chairman
Jeff Harleston, Treasurer
Kenneth Gamble, Secretary

Nonprofit service organization dedicated to the historical and cultural preservation of Rhythm and Blues music. The Foundation provides financial support, medical assistance and educational outreach through various grants and programs to support R&B amd Motown artists of the 40s, 50s, 60s and 70s.
Founded in 1988

19031 Society of Professional Audio Recording Services
9 Music Square S
Suite 222
Nashville, TN 37203

800-771-7727
FAX 214-722-1422
E-Mail: spars@spars.com
Home Page: www.spars.com
Social Media: *Facebook, Twitter, YouTube*

Avatar Studios, President
Eric W Johnson, Secretary
Jessica Dally, Treasurer
Sherri Tantleff, Director

SPARS is dedicated to excellence through innovation, education and communication.
200 Members
Founded in 1979
Mailing list available for rent

19032 Songwriters Guild of America
5120 Virginia Way
Suite C22
Brentwood, TN 37027

615-742-9945
800-524-6742
FAX 615-630-7501
E-Mail: corporate@songwritersguild.com
Home Page: www.songwritersguild.com
Social Media: *Facebook, Twitter, LinkedIn, RSS*

Joe Whitt, Manager

Provides agreements between songwriters, composers and publishers. The SGA will take such lawful actions as will advance, promote and benefit the profession.
4000 Members
Founded in 1931

19033 Sweet Adelines International
9110 S. Toledo
Tulsa, OK 74147-0168

918-622-1444
800-992-7464
FAX 918-665-0894
E-Mail: admin@sweetadelineintl.org
Home Page: www.sweetadelineintl.org
Social Media: *Facebook, Twitter, YouTube, Pinterest*

Donna Kerley, Dicector Finance/Administration
Kelly Kirchoff, Director Communications
Jane Hanson, Marketing/Membership Coordinator
Kelly Bailey, Chief Executive Officer
Tammy Talbot, Chief Operating Officer

A worldwide organization of women singers committed to advancing the musical art form of barbershop harmony through education and performances. Their motto is to 'Harmonize the World.'
27000 Members
Founded in 1945

19034 The Society for American Music
Stephen Foster Memorial
University of Pittsburgh
Pittsburgh, PA 15260

412-624-3031
E-Mail: sam@american-music.org
Home Page: www.american-music.org
Social Media: *Facebook*

Judy Tsouŷ, Board of Trustee/ President
Kay Norton, Board of Trustee, VP
Sabine Feisst, Treasurer
Mariana Whitmer, Executive Director
Neil Lerner, Secretary
Founded in 1975

19035 United States Germanic Music Association
E-Mail: mikesurrattmusic@gmail.com
Home Page: www.usgma.us

19036 World Piano Competition/AMSA
441 Vine St
Suite 1030
Cincinnati, OH 45202-2832

513-421-5342
FAX 513-421-2672
E-Mail: info@amsa-wpc.orgm
Home Page: www.amsa-wpc.org

Gloria Ackerman, Founder, CEO
William Selnick, Treasurer
Stanley Aronoff, Event Chair
Leon Fleisher, President

Provides an continuum of services and role models to assist youth in need. Their task is to provide a venue of excitement and compassion to teach them to do their best to prepare for the enormous challenges they will face as they approach adulthood.
2.5M Members
Founded in 1956

Newsletters

19037 American Guild Associate News Newsletter
American Guild of Music
PO Box 599
Warren, MI 48090-4905

248-686-1975
FAX 630-968-0197
E-Mail: agm@americanguild.org
Home Page: www.americanguild.org

Richard Chizmadia, Editor-in-Chief

Offers information and news for professionals in the music profession.
Cost: $25.00
5000 Members
Frequency: Quarterly
Founded in 1901

19038 American Music Center Opportunity Update
American Music Center
322 8th Ave
Suite 1001
New York, NY 10001-6774

212-366-5263
FAX 212-366-5265

E-Mail: center@amc.net
Home Page: www.amc.net

Joanne Cossa, Executive Director

A listing of composition competitions, calls for scores, workshops, and other opportunities delivered every month via e-mail to members of the American Music Center.
Frequency: Monthly
Founded in 1939

19039 American Musical Instrument Society Newsletter
AMIS
1106 Garden Street
Hoboken, NJ 07030

201-656-0107
E-Mail: amis@guildassoc.com
Home Page: www.amis.org

Albert R Rice, President
Carolyn Bryant, Vice-President
Deborah Check Reeves, Secretary
Joanne Kopp, Treasurer

Official notices and news of the Society's activites; short articles and communications; recent acquisition lists from member institutions; news of members; and classified ads.
Frequency: 2x/Year

19040 American Musicological Society Inc
University of Iowa
6010 College Station
Brunswick, ME 04011-8451

207-798-4243
877-679-7648
FAX 207-798-4254
E-Mail: ams@ams-net.org
Home Page: www.ams-net.org

Peter Alexander, Editor
Robert Judd, Executive Director
Al Hipkins, Office Manager
Melissa Kapocius, Secretary

The AMS Newsletter is published simiannually in February and August. The February Newsletter is mailed with the new Directory and Ballot each year. The August Newsletter is mailed with the Annual Meeting information and registration form each year.
Frequency: Semi-Annually
Founded in 1934

19041 American School Band Directors Association Newsletter
American School Band Directors Association
227 N 1st Street
PO Box 696
Guttenberg, IA 52052-0696

563-252-2500
FAX 563-252-2500
E-Mail: asbda@alpinecom.net
Home Page: www.asbda.com

Monte Dunnum, President
Valerie Gaffney, Secretary
Blair Callaway, Treasurer

Reports and information for members of the ASBDA
Frequency: Quarterly
Founded in 1953
Printed in 2 colors on matte stock

19042 American Viola Society Newsletter
American Viola Society
14070 Proton Rd
Suite 100
Dallas, TX 75244-3601

972-233-9107
FAX 972-490-4219
E-Mail: stemple@comcast.net
Home Page: www.madcrouch.com

Madeleine Crouch, President

A monthly e-newsletter. It contains announcements from the AVS, upcoming local chapter events, and other important items.
Frequency: Monthly

19043 Banjo Newsletter
PO Box 3418
Annapolis, MD 21403-0418

800-759-7425
FAX 410-263-6503
E-Mail: bnl@infionline.net
Home Page: www.banjonews.com

Newletter focusing on Bluegrass banjo music.
Mailing list available for rent

19044 Bluegrass Music Profiles
Bluegrass Publications
PO Box 850
Nicholasville, KY 40340-0850

859-333-6456
E-Mail: info@bluegrassmusicprofiles.com
Home Page: www.bluegrassmusicprofiles.com
Social Media: *Facebook, Twitter*

Information on Bluegrass music.

19045 Bluegrass Now
PO Box 2020
Rolla, MO 65402

573-341-7335
E-Mail: Bgn@fidnet.com
Home Page: www.bluegrassnow.com

Information on Bluegrass music.

19046 Bluegrass Unlimited
PO Box 771
Warrenton, VA 20188-0771

540-349-8181
800-258-4727
E-Mail: info@bluegrassmusic.com
Home Page: www.bluegrassmusic.com

Information on Bluegrass music.
Mailing list available for rent

19047 Brooklyn Institute for Studies in American Music
Brooklyn College
2900 Bedford Ave
Brooklyn, NY 11210-2889

718-951-5000
Home Page:
www.brooklyn.cuny.edu/bb/fac/american.htm

Karen L Gould, President

Music news and Academy activities.
Frequency: Semi-Annual
Founded in 1861

19048 CMS Newsletter
College Music Society
312 E Pine Street
Missoula, MT 59802

406-721-9616
FAX 406-721-9419
E-Mail: cms@music.org
Home Page: www.music.org

Robby D Gunstream, Executive Director

19049 Dirty Linen
PO Box 6660
Baltimore, MD 21239-6600

410-583-7973
E-Mail: office@dirtylinen.com
Home Page: www.dirtylinen.com

Information on Bluegrass music.

19050 Early Music Newsletter
New York Recorder Guild

145 W 93 Street
New York, NY 10025-7559

212-662-2946
E-Mail: mzumoff@nyc.rr.com
Home Page:
www.priceclan.com/nyrecorderguild/

Michael Zumoff, Executive Director

A publication of the New York Recorder Guild
10 Pages
Frequency: Monthly

19051 Flatpicking Guitar
High View Publications
PO Box 2160
Pulaski, VA 24301

540-980-0338
800-413-8296
FAX 540-980-0557
E-Mail: info@flatpickingmercantile.com
Home Page: www.flatpick.com

Information on Bluegrass music and the Flatpick guitar.
Mailing list available for rent

19052 GMA Update
Gospel Music Association
PO Box 22697
Nashville, TN 37202

615-242-0303
FAX 615-254-9755
E-Mail: info@gospelmusic.org
Home Page: www.gospelmusic.org

John Styll, President
Jackie Patillo, Executive Director

GMA's industry e-newsletter available to any non-GMA member who wishes to receive it. Sent out once a month, GMA Update contains the latest news about the Christian music industry and valuable information about the GMA.
Frequency: Monthly
Mailing list available for rent

19053 GMAil
Gospel Music Association
PO Box 22697
Nashville, TN 37202

615-242-0303
FAX 615-254-9755
Home Page: www.gospelmusic.org

John Styll, President

E-newsletter sent weekly to GMA members. Includes weekly music sales, charts, news, links to valuable resources, and information about upcoming GMA and industry events.
Frequency: Weekly
Founded in 1964

19054 Girl Groups Gazette
PO Box 69A04
Department HSND
West Hollywood, CA 90069-0066
Louis Wendruck, Editor/Publisher

For fans of girl groups and female singers of the 1960's and 70's including photos, discographies, records, t-shirts, postcards, and videos.
Cost: $20.00
Frequency: Quarterly
Founded in 1988

19055 In the Groove
Michigan Antique Phonograph Society
60 Central St
Battle Creek, MI 49017-3704

269-968-1299
E-Mail:
ITG@michiganantiquephonographsociety.org

Home Page:
www.michiganantiquephonographsociety.org

Phil Stewart, Editor
Eileen Stewart, Editor

The Newsletter of the Michigan Antique Phonograph Society. Includes show, sales and auction announcements, MAPS chapter news, President's message, monthly feature articles, letters to the editor, and swap shop.
Cost: $25.00
24 Pages
Frequency: Monthly
Founded in 1976

19056 International Bluegrass Music Association
IBMA
2 Music Cir S
Suite 100
Nashville, TN 37203-4381

615-256-3222
888-438-4262
FAX 615-256-0450
E-Mail: info@ibma.org
Home Page: www.ibma.org

Dan Hays, Executive Director

Information on Bluegrass music from the IBMA

19057 Music for the Love of It
67 Parkside Drive
Berkeley, CA 94705-2409

510-654-9134
FAX 510-654-4656
E-Mail: tedrust@musicfortheloveofit.com
Home Page: www.musicfortheloveofit.com

Edgar Rust, Publisher/Editor
Janet Telford, Co-Editor

A newsletter for people everywhere who love making music. Every issues brings new enthusiasm, new ideas and new opportunities for making music.
Frequency: Bi-Monthly
ISSN: 0898-8757
Founded in 1988
Printed in on matte stock

19058 National Music Museum Newsletter
National Music Museum
414 E Clark St
Vermillion, SD 57069-2307

605-677-5306
FAX 605-677-6995
E-Mail: smm@usd.edu
Home Page: www.usd.edu/smm/

Andre Larson, Director

Quarterly Newletter which includes feature articles written by the curatorial staff and lists recent acquisitions. Published in February, May, August and November. It is available with basic museum membership.
Cost: $35.00
Printed in 4 colors

19059 No Depression
908 Halcyon Avenue
Nashville, TN 37204

615-292-7084
Home Page: www.nodepression.net

Information on Bluegrass music
Founded in 1995

19060 Notes a Tempo
West Virginia University
Fairmount State University
1201 Locust Avenue
Fairmont, WV 26554

304-293-4841
Home Page:

www.wvmea.tripod.com/Notes_a_Tempo_Winter_10.pdf

David Bess, Co-Editor
Becky Terry, Co-Editor

The official publication of the West Virginia Music Educators. Published Fall, Winter and Spring
20-32 Pages
Frequency: 3 per year
Circulation: 1115

19061 Old Time Herald
P.O.Box 61679
Durham, NC 27715-1679

919-286-2041
E-Mail: info@oldtimeherald.org
Home Page: www.oldtimeherald.org

Sarah Bryan, Editor-in-chief
Peter Honig, Business Director

Information on Bluegrass music
Mailing list available for rent

19062 Pedal Steel Newsletter
Pedal Steel Guitar Association
PO Box 20248
Floral Park, NY 11002-0248

516-616-9214
FAX 516-616-9214
E-Mail: bobpsga@optonline.net
Home Page: www.psga.org

Doug Mack, Editor
Bob Maickel, President

Dedicated to the art of playing pedal steel guitar. Every issue contains tablature arrangements of songs for the steel guitar as well as coming events, record reviews, product reports and news concerning the instrument.
Frequency: 10 x Per Year
ISSN: 1088-7954
Founded in 1973
Mailing list available for rent

19063 Percussion News
Percussive Arts Society
110 W Washington Street
Suite A
Indianapolis, IN 46204

317-974-4488
FAX 317-974-4499
E-Mail: percarts@pas.org
Home Page: www.pas.org

Rick Mattingly, Editor
Hillary Henry, Art Director
Lisa Rogers, President

Newsletter devoted to membership activities. This colorful newsletter also features a Classified Advertising section. Percussion News is published in January, March, May, July, September and November.
Frequency: 6 Editions Per Year
Founded in 1961
Mailing list available for rent

19064 Rolling Stone
Rolling Stone Magazine
1290 Ave of the Americas
2nd Floor
New York, NY 10104-0298

212-484-1616
800-283-1549
FAX 212-484-1771
E-Mail: rollingstone@real.com
Home Page: www.rssoundingboard.com
Social Media: *Facebook, Twitter, YouTube, RSS, Foursqare*

Jann Wenner, President

A monthly newsletter geared for marketing, advertising and music exexecutives. It includes information on such matters as rock tours and musician endorsements, ad campaigns and rock

contests.
Cost: $50.00
Frequency: Monthly
Founded in 1967
Mailing list available for rent

19065 Roots and Rhythm Newsletter
Roots and Rhythm
PO Box 837
El Cerrito, CA 94530

510-526-8373
888-766-8766
FAX 510-526-9001
E-Mail: roots@toast.net
Home Page: www.rootsandrhythm.com

Frank Scott, Owner
Nancy Scott-Noennig, Co-Owner

Lists, reviews and makes available for sale, recordings of blues, rhythm and blues, rockabilly, country, folk, ethnic, nostalgia and jazz music. Each newsletter reviews about 400 items and lists another 500 without reviews.
Frequency: Bi-Monthly
Circulation: 10000
Founded in 1974
Printed in 2 colors on newsprint stock

19066 Sing Out!
PO Box 5460
Bethlehem, PA 18015-0460

610-865-5366
FAX 215-895-3052
E-Mail: info@singout.org
Home Page: www.singout.org

Information on Bluegrass music
Mailing list available for rent

19067 Tempo
Academy of Country Music
5500 Balboa Blvd
Suite 200
Encino, CA 91316-1505

818-788-8000
FAX 818-788-0999
E-Mail: info@acmcountry.com
Home Page: www.acmcountry.com

Butch Waugh, Chairman

Devoted exclusively to the country music industry.
12 Pages
Frequency: Quarterly
Circulation: 4500
Founded in 1964

19068 The Voice
1156 15th St NW
Suite 310
Washington, DC 20005-1747

202-331-7577
FAX 202-331-7599
E-Mail: service@chorusamerica.org
Home Page: www.chorusamerica.org

Ann Meier Baker, President & Chief Executive Officer
1600 Members
Frequency: Quarterly
Circulation: 5000
ISSN: 1074-0805
Founded in 1977

19069 Westfield Center
Westfield Center for Early Keyboard Studies

726 University Ave,Room 102
Cornell University
Ithaca, NY 14850-3914

607-255-3065
E-Mail: info@westfield.org
Home Page: www.westfield.org

Annette Richards, Executive Director
Maja Anderson, Program Coordinator
Evan Cortens, Administrative Assistant

E-newsletter providing information to professional keyboard musicians.
12 Pages
Frequency: Monthly
Founded in 1979

19070 Women in Bluegrass Newsletter
PO Box 2498
Winchester, VA 22604

800-227-2357
E-Mail: Nmhentry@visuallink.com
Home Page:
www.murphymethod.com/womeninbluegrass.cfm

Information on women in bluegass music

Magazines & Journals

19071 AfterTouch: New Music Discoveries
Music Discovery Network
PO Box 6205
Peoria, IL 61601-6205

309-685-4843
800-882-4262
FAX 309-685-4878
E-Mail: aimcmc@aol.com
Home Page: www.musicdiscoveries.com

Ronald Wallace, Editor

A magazine for music lovers who would like to experience new sights and sounds and would like to keep their fingers on the pulse of the music industry.
Frequency: Annual
Circulation: 10,000
Founded in 1984
Printed in on glossy stock

19072 American Music
University of Illinois Press
1325 South Oak Street
MC-566
Champaign, IL 61820-6903

217-244-0626
866-244-0626
FAX 217-244-8082
E-Mail: journals@uillinois.edu
Home Page: www.press.uillinois.edu

Michael Pisani, Editor
Jeff McArdle, Journals Marketing/Advertising Mgr.

Publishes articles on American composers, performers, publishers, institutions, events, and the music industry as well as book and recording reviews, bibliographies, and discographies.
Cost: $45.00
Frequency: Quarterly
Circulation: 1650
ISSN: 0734-4392
Founded in 1981
Mailing list available for rent: 1,650 names at $100 per M
Printed in 2 colors on glossy stock

19073 American Music Teacher
Music Teachers National Association

441 Vine St
Suite 505
Cincinnati, OH 45202-2813

513-421-1420
888-512-5278
FAX 513-421-2503
E-Mail: mtnanet@mtna.org
Home Page: www.mtna.org

Gary L Ingle, Executive Director
Gail Berenson, President
Janice Wenger, VP

Provides articles, reviews and regular columns that inform, educate and challenge music teachers and foster excellence in the music teaching profession.
Cost: $30.00
Circulation: 35000
Founded in 1876
Mailing list available for rent: 24000 names at $85 per M
Printed in 4 colors on glossy stock

19074 American Organist
American Guild of Organists
475 Riverside Dr
Suite 1260
New York, NY 10115-0055

212-870-2310
800-246-5115
FAX 212-870-2163
E-Mail: info@agohq.org
Home Page: www.agohq.org
Social Media: *Facebook*

James Thomashower, Executive Director

Most widely read journal devoted to organ and choral music in the world. Official journal of the American Guild of Organists, the Royal Canadian College of Organists, and the Associated Pipe Organ Builders of America.
Cost: $ 52.00
Frequency: Monthly
Circulation: 24000
ISSN: 0164-3150
Founded in 1967

19075 American String Teachers Journal
American String Teachers Association
4155 Chain Bridge Rd
Fairfax, VA 22030-4102

703-279-2113
FAX 703-279-2114
E-Mail: asta@astaweb.com
Home Page: www.astaweb.com

Donna Hale, Executive Director
Beth Danner-Knight, Deputy Director

Available to members. Provides an overview of current articles featured in the journal. Also answers questions about content, advertising, and contact information.
Cost: $90.00
Frequency: Quarterly
Circulation: 11,300
Mailing list available for rent: 10M+ names

19076 American Viola Society Journal
American Viola Society
14070 Proton Rd
Suite 100LB
Dallas, TX 75244-3601

972-233-9107
FAX 972-490-4219
E-Mail: info@avsnationaloffice.org
Home Page: www.americanviolasociety.org

Nokuthula Ngwenyama, President
Karin Brown, Secretary
Michelle Sayles, Treasurer
Kathryn Steely, Webmaster

Peer reviewed journal which promotes interest in the viola.
Cost: $42.00
Frequency: Annually
Circulation: 1500
Founded in 1984

19077 BMI Musicworld
Broadcast Music
7 World Trade Center
250 Greenwich Street
New York, NY 10007-0030

212-220-3000
FAX 212-246-2163
Home Page: www.bmi.com

Del Bryant, CEO
John E Cody, COO/EVP

Performing rights organization. Articles of interest to the songwriting community.
Founded in 1985

19078 Billboard Magazine
Prometheus Global Media
770 Broadwaye Blvd.
New York, NY 10003-9595

212-493-4100
FAX 646-654-5368
Home Page: www.prometheusgm.com
Social Media: *Facebook, Twitter*

Richard D. Beckman, CEO
James A. Finkelstein, Chairman
Madeline Krakowsky, Vice President Circualtion
Tracy Brater, Executive Director Creative Service

Packed with in-depth music and entertainment features including the latest in new media and digital music, global coverage, music and money, touring, new artists, radio news and retail reports.
Cost: $149.00
Frequency: Weekly
Founded in 1894

19079 CCM Magazine
Salem Publishing
402 BNA Drive
Suite 400
Nashville, TN 37217

615-386-3011
FAX 615-386-3380
E-Mail: info@ccmcom.com
Home Page: www.ccmmagazine.com
Social Media: *Facebook, Twitter, RSS*

Jim Cumbee, President

The voice of Contemporary Christian Music. Each monthly issue features music news, exclusive interviews, and an in-depth look at the spiritual lives of today's leading Christian music artists.
Cost: $19.95
Frequency: Monthly
Founded in 1978
Printed in 4 colors on glossy stock

19080 Callboard
Theatre Bay Area
1663 Mission St
Suite 525
San Francisco, CA 94103-2487

415-430-1140
FAX 415-430-1145
E-Mail: tba@theatrebayarea.org
Home Page: www.theatrebayarea.org
Social Media: *Facebook, Twitter, YouTube*

Karen Mc Kevitt, Manager

Provides trade information for professionals in the Bay Area. The magazine contains the following departments: Letterbox, Inside the Industry, Community News, How Did They Do That, Keep An Eye On, Editors' Picks and En-

core.
Cost: $65.00
Frequency: Monthly
ISSN: 1064-0703
Founded in 1976
Printed in 2 colors on matte stock

19081 Chamber Music Magazine
Chamber Music America
UPS Box 458
243 Fifth Avenue
New York, NY 10016

212-242-2022
FAX 212-242-7955
Home Page: www.chamber-music.org

Susan Dadian, Program Director
Margaret M Lioi, CEO
Louise Smith, Chair
Cost: $5.95
Frequency: Bi-Monthly
Circulation: 6000
Founded in 1977

19082 Choral Journal
American Choral Directors Association
545 Couch Drive
Oklahoma City, OK 73102

405-232-8161
FAX 405-232-8162
Home Page: www.acdaonline.org

Carroll Gonzo, Editor
Ron Granger, Managing Editor

Contains articles and columns of a scholarly and practical nature in addition to reviews of newly released CD recordings, books, and printed music.
Frequency: Monthly

19083 Clarinet Journal
International Clarinet Society
PO Box 5039
Wheaton, IL 60189-5039

630-665-3602
FAX 630-665-3848
E-Mail: info@clarinet.org
Home Page: www.clarinet.org

James Gillespie, Editor
So Rhee, Executive Director
Maxine Ramey, President
Caroline Hartig, Secretary
Tod Kerstetter, Treasurer

Contains articles in wide variety of areas written by performers and scholars.
Cost: $25.00
Frequency: Quarterly
Circulation: 3000

19084 Clavier
Instrumentalist Publishing Company
200 Northfield Road
Northfield, IL 60093-3390

847-446-5000
888-446-6888
FAX 847-446-6263
E-Mail: editor@theinstrumentalist.com
Home Page: www.instrumentalistmagazine.com
Social Media: *Facebook*

James Rohner, Publisher
Judy Nelson, Editor

Provides new ideas and advice for piano teachers from leading educators. The focus of each issue is to offer practical advice for teachers. Articles include interviews with prominent performers, teachers and composers, the latest teaching methods, tributes to great artists of the past, and reviews of newly publshed music, educational software and videos.
Cost: $17.00
Frequency: 10X Per Year
Circulation: 16000

Founded in 1965
Mailing list available for rent

19085 Close Up Magazine

Country Music Association
One Music Circle S
Nashville, TN 37203

615-244-2840
FAX 615-242-4783
E-Mail: international@cmaworld.com
Home Page: www.cmaworld.com

Profiles of country music artists, various
songwriters and industry news. Members of the
Association receive the magazine as a benefit
of their membership.
Circulation: 8000
Founded in 1958

19086 Country Weekly Magazine

American Media Inc
1000 American Media Way
T-Rex Technology Center
Boca Raton, FL 33464-1000

561-997-7733
FAX 561-989-1298
Home Page: www.nationalenquirer.com

David J Pecker, CEO

Devoted to country music and entertainment.
Packed with feature articles and photos of
country music personalities, music and video
reviews, tour dates and late breaking news
from the world of country music.
Cost: $34.95
Frequency: Bi-Weekly

19087 DJ Times

Testa Communications
25 Willowdale Avenue
Port Washington, NY 11050-3779

516-767-2500
800-937-7678
FAX 516-767-9335
E-Mail: djtimes@testa.com
Home Page: www.djtimes.com

Jim Tremayne, Editor-in-Chief
Steve Thorakos, Production Manager

Colorful tabloid magazine dedicated to professional mobile and club DJs. Specialized music
sections, new product departments for sound
and lighting, record reviews, business columns,
informative entertainer profiles and more.
Cost: $19.40
Frequency: Monthly
Circulation: 30000
Founded in 1988

19088 Diapason

Scranton Gillette Communications
3030 W Salt Creek Lane
Suite 201
Arlington Heights, IL 60005-5025

847-391-1000
FAX 847-390-0408
E-Mail: jbutera@sgcmail.com
Home Page: www.thediapason.com

Jerome Butera, Editor/Publisher
Joyce Robinson, Associate Editor

Devoted to the organ, the harpsichord, the car-
illon, and church music. Includes feature articles, reviews, reports, news, organ
specifications, and a calendar, as well as classified advertisements.
Cost: $35.00
Frequency: Monthly
ISSN: 0012-2378
Founded in 1909

19089 Discoveries

700 East State Street
Ioal, WI 54990-0001

715-445-2214
800-258-0929
FAX 715-445-4087
E-Mail: wayne.youngblood@fwpubs.com
Home Page: www.discoveriesmag.com

Mark Willliams, Publisher
Wayne Youngblood, Editorial Director
Cathy Bernardy, Associate Editor
Todd Whitesel, Associate Editor
Trevor Lauber, Advertising Sales Manager

Keeps close watch on market trends for collectible records, CDs and memorabilia. The Market
Watch pages serve to interpret the mass of information available online and break it down to
the most useful data collectors need. Each
monthly issue is full of personality and opinion, with many reviews to help you determine
where to spend your money. Coverage includes
rock 'n' roll, rhythm &'blues, pop, doo-wop,
classic jazz and country western recordings.
Cost: $28.00
Frequency: Monthly
Circulation: 10,859
Founded in 1988

19090 Downbeat

102 N Haven Road
PO Box 906
Elmhurst, IL 60126

630-941-2030
800-554-7470
FAX 630-941-3210
E-Mail: service@downbeat.com
Home Page: www.downbeat.com

Kevin Maher, CEO

Monthly magazine includes such features as
Readers Poll results, festival reviews, CD re-
views, feature articles and more.
Cost: $29.95
Frequency: Monthly
Mailing list available for rent

19091 Electronic Musician

PRIMEDIA
6400 Hollis Street
Suite 12
Emeryville, CA 94608-1086

510-653-3307
E-Mail: emeditorial@prismb2b.com
Home Page: www.emusician.com
Social Media: *Facebook, Twitter*

Steve Oppenheimer, Editor-in-Chief
Joe Perry, Associate Publisher
Marie Briganti, List Manager

Magazine for musicians recording and produc-
ing music in a home or personal studio envi-
ronment. They are a source of user-friendly
technical information for musicans. Features
include: Tech Page, ProFile, Working Musi-
cian, Sound Design Workshop, Making Tracks,
Square One, Reviews, What's New, Master
Class, Final Mix, and Editors Choice Awards.
Cost: $23.97
Frequency: Monthly
Circulation: 61102
Founded in 1986
Mailing list available for rent

19092 Flute Talk

Instrumentalist Company
200 Northfield Road
Northfield, IL 60093-3390

847-446-5000
888-446-6888
FAX 847-446-6263
E-Mail: fteditor@instrumentalistmagazine.com
Home Page:

www.instrumentalistmagazine.com
Social Media: *Facebook*

Flute Talk is written for professional flute players, teachers, and advanced students. Frequent
topics include performance analyses of flute
repertoire, current teaching techniques, piccolo
articles, interviews with prominent performers
and teachers, and reviews of new music, recordings, and books for flutists.
Cost: $13.00
Frequency: 10 x Per Year
Circulation: 12000
Founded in 1981

19093 Goldmine

700 E State Street
Iola, WI 54990-0001

715-445-2214
800-258-0929
FAX 715-445-4087
E-Mail: susan.sliwicki@fwmedia.com
Home Page: www.goldminemag.com
Social Media: *Facebook, YouTube, RSS,
Pinterest*

Jeff Pozorski, Publisher
Brian Earnest, Editorial Director
Peter Lindblad, Associate Editor
Tim Neely, Research Director
Trevor Lauber, Advertising Sales Manager

The world's largest marketplace for collectible
records, CDs, and music memorabilia covering
Rock N' Roll, Blues, Country, Folk, and Jazz.
Large volumes of For Sale and Wanted ads are
placed by collectors and dealers. Includes arti-
cles on recording stars of the past and present
with discographies listing all known releases, a
listing of upcoming record-and-CD-collector
conventions, album reviews, hobby and music
news, a collecting column, a letters section, and
Collector Mania (Q&A).
Cost: $39.95
Frequency: Bi-Weekly
Circulation: 17026
Founded in 1974
Mailing list available for rent

19094 Guitar One

Cherry Lane Magazines
6 E 32nd St
Suite 11
New York, NY 10016-5422

212-561-3000
800-825-4942
FAX 212-447-6885
E-Mail: guitarshop@worldnet.att.net
Home Page: www.guitarmag.com

Peter W Primont, CEO
Jonathan Simpson-Bint, President
Holly Klingel, VP Circulation
Steve Aaron, Publishing Director
Greg Di Benedetto, Publisher

Information on everything from the guitar
equipment evaluations to news on the latest
trends and technological developments to special insider pieces covering the sound secrets of
today's top players.
Cost: $24.95
Frequency: Monthly
Circulation: 105,000
Founded in 1985

19095 Guitar Review

Albert Augustine Limited
151 W 26th St
Suite 4
New York, NY 10001-6810

917-661-0220
FAX 917-661-0223
E-Mail: mail@guitarreview.com
Home Page: www.albertaugustine.com

Steven Griesgraber, President
Eliot Fisk, Associate Editor

David Starobin, Associate Editor
Ian Gallagher, Music Editor
Matthew Hough, Circulation

Scholarly articles related to the classical guitar.
Cost: $28.00
48 Pages
Frequency: Quarterly
Circulation: 4000
Founded in 1946

19096 HipHop Weekly

Z & M Media
401 Broadway
New York, NY

212-696-0831
Home Page: www.hiphopweekly.com
Social Media: *Facebook, Twitter*

Covers the entire hip hop culture.

19097 Instrumentalist

Instrumentalist Company
200 Northfield Road
Northfield, IL 60093-3390

847-446-5000
888-446-6888
FAX 847-446-6263
E-Mail:
insteditor@instrumentalistmagazine.com
Home Page:
www.instrumentalistmagazine.com
Social Media: *Facebook*

A magazine school band and orchestra directors
can depend on for practical information to use
for then ensembles. The articles written by veteran directors and performers cover a wide
range of topics, including rehearsal techniques,
conducting tips, programming ideas, instrument clinics, repertoire analyses, and much
more. Monthly new music reviews guide directors to selecting the best music for their students.
Cost: $21.00
Frequency: Monthly
Circulation: 16,000
Founded in 1945
Printed in 4 colors

19098 International Musician

American Federation of Musicians
1501 Broadway
Suite 600
New York, NY 10036-5501

212-869-1330
FAX 212-764-6134
E-Mail: info@afm.org
Home Page: www.afm.org

Thomas Lee, President

Delivers the latest happenings in music. Focuses on the overall well-being of all musicians. Provides news pertaining to symphonic,
rock, freelance, recording and touring musicians. IM features articles on pressing issues
sich as piracy, legislation, on-the-job struggles,
and the effects of technology.
Cost: $25.00
Frequency: Monthly
Circulation: 110000
Founded in 1896
Printed in on n stock

19099 JAMIA

American Musical Instrument Society
389 Main Street
Suite 202
Malden, MA 02148

781-397-8870
FAX 781-397-8887
E-Mail: amis@guildassoc.com
Home Page: www.amis.org

Stewart Carter, President
Joanne Kopp, Treasurer

Presents peer-reviewed articles that assist in
both professionals and students to develop and
apply biomedical and health informatics to patient care, teaching, research, and health care
administration.
Frequency: Bi-Monthly
Founded in 1971

19100 Jazz Education Journal

JazzTimes Magazine,Madavor Media
85 Quincy Ave
Suite 2
Quincy, MA 02169

617-706-9110
FAX 617-536-0102
E-Mail: karen@iage.org
Home Page: www.jazztimes.com

Leslie M Sabina, Editor
Karen Mayse, Advertising

Provides news and information in the field of
jazz education. Contains information of today's
top jazz artists, reviews, transcriptions, industry news, and articles on improvisation, teaching techniques, history, performance,
composition, arranging and music business.
Cost: $23.95
100 Pages
Circulation: 10,000
Founded in 1968
Mailing list available for rent
Printed in on glossy stock

19101 Journal of American Organbuilding

American Institute of Organ Builders
PO Box 35306
Canton, OH 44735

330-806-9011
E-Mail: robertsullivan@pipeorgan.org
Home Page: www.pipeorgan.org

Jeffrey L Weiler, Editor

Features technical articles, product and book
reviews, and a forum for the exchange of building and service information and techniques. Subscriptions are provided free to AIO members,
and are available to non-members for $24.00
per year.
Cost: $24.00
Frequency: Quarterly
Founded in 1974
*Mailing list available for rent: 350 names at
$250 per M*
Printed in on glossy stock

19102 Journal of Music Theory

Yale University
Department of Music
PO Box 208310
New Haven, CT 06520-8310

203-432-2985
FAX 203-432-2983
E-Mail: jmt.editor@yale.edu
Home Page: www.yale.edu/jmt/

Ian Quinn, Editor
David Clampitt, Associate Editor
Richard Cohn, Associate Editor
Daniel Harrison, Associate Editor
Patrick McCreless, Associate Editor

Publishes peer-reviewed reseach in Music The-
ory.
Cost: $30.00
Frequency: Annual
Founded in 1957

19103 Journal of Music Therapy

American Music Therapy Association
8455 Colesville Rd
Suite 1000
Silver Spring, MD 20910-3392

301-589-3300
FAX 301-589-5175

E-Mail: info@musictherapy.org
Home Page: www.musictherapy.org

Andrea Farbman, Executive Director

Research in the area of music therapy and reha-
bilitation, a forum for authoratative articles of
current music therapy research and theory, use
of music in the behavioral sciences, book re-
views, and guest editorials.
Cost: $120.00
Frequency: Quarterly
Circulation: 6000
ISSN: 0022-2917
Founded in 1998

19104 Journal of Research in Music Education

MENC Subscription Office
PO Box 1584
Birmingham, AL 35201

800-633-4931
E-Mail: menc@ebsco.com
Home Page: www.menc.org
Social Media: *Facebook, Twitter*

Keeps members informed of the latest music
education research. Offers a collection of reports that includes thorough analyses of theories and projects by respected music
researchers. Issued four times yearly.
Frequency: Quarterly
Founded in 1907
Printed in on matte stock

19105 Journal of Singing

National Association of Teachers of Singing
9957 Moorings Dr
Suite 401
Jacksonville, FL 32257-2416

904-992-9101
FAX 904-262-2587
E-Mail: info@nats.org
Home Page: www.nats.org

Richard Dale Sjoerdsma, Editor-in-Chief

Provides current information regarding the
teaching of singing as well as results of recent
research in the field. The Journal serves as a
historical record and a venue for teachers of
singing and other scholars to share the resilts of
their work in areas such as history, diction,
voice science, medicine, and voice pedagogy.
Frequency: 5x times/year

19106 Journal of the American Musicological Society

University of California Press, Journals
Division
2000 Center Street Way
Suite 203
Berkeley, CA 94704-1223

510-643-7154
FAX 510-642-9917
E-Mail: journals@ucpress.edu
Home Page: www.ucpressjournals.com

Bruce Alan Brown, Editor
Louise Goldberg, Assistant Editor
Julie Cumming, Book Review Editor

The JAMS publishes scholarship from all fields
of musical inquiry: from historical musicology,
critical theory, music analysis, iconography and
organology, to performance practice, aesthetics
and hermeneutics, ethnomusicology, gender
and sexuality, popular music and cultural studies. Each issue includes articles, book reviews,
and communications.
Cost: $42.00
Frequency: Tri-Annual
Circulation: 5000
ISSN: 0003-0139
Founded in 1893

19107 Jukebox Collector Magazine
2545 SE 60th Court
Pleasant Hill, IA 50327-5099

515-265-8324
FAX 515-265-1980
E-Mail: JukeboxCollector@att.net
Home Page: www.jukeboxmagazine.com

Rick Botts, Editor

Focuses on collectors of jukeboxes from the
40's, 50's, and 60's. There are approximately
150 jukeboxes for sale each month, along with
show events information. Accepts advertising.
Cost: $33.00
36 Pages
Frequency: Monthly
Circulation: 1800
Founded in 1977

19108 Live Sound International
111 Speen Street
Framingham, MA 01701

415-387-4009
800-375-8015
FAX 866-449-3761
E-Mail: amclean@livesoundint.com
Home Page: www.livesoundint.com

Mark Herman, Publisher
Jeff MacKay, Editor
Mitch Gallagher, Associate Editor
Sara Elliott, Advertising

The editorial focus is performance audio and
event sound. Contains audio production tech-
niques, new products, equipment applications
and associated commercial concerns.
Cost: $60.00
Frequency: Monthly
Circulation: 20,000
Mailing list available for rent
Printed in on glossy stock

19109 Mix
Prism Business Media
6400 Hollis St
Suite 9
Emeryville, CA 94608-1052

510-658-3793
866-860-7087
FAX 510-653-5142
E-Mail: mixeditorial@prismb2b.com
Home Page: www.mixonline.com

Melinda Paras, Owner
Erika Lopez, Associate Publisher
Tom Kenny, Editor
John Pledger, Publisher
Christen Pocock, Marketing Director

Mix covers a wide range of topics including:
recording, live sound and production, broadcast
production, audio for film and video, and music technology. In addition, Mix includes coverage of facility design and construction,
location recording, tape/disc manufacturing,
education, and other topics of importance to audio professionals. Distributed in 94 countries.
Cost: $35.97
Frequency: Monthly
Circulation: 45244
Founded in 1977

19110 Modern Drummer
Modern Drummer Publications
12 Old Bridge Rd
Cedar Grove, NJ 07009-1288

973-239-4140
FAX 973-239-7139
E-Mail: mdinfo@moderndrummer.com
Home Page: www.moderndrummer.com

Isabel Spagnardi, Owner
Tracy A Kearns, Associate Publisher
Bill Miller, Editor-in-Chief
Rick Van Horn, Senior Editor
Adam Budofsky, Managing Editor

Every issue of Modern Drummer includes in-
terviews with the world's leading drummers, a
full roster of columns on all facets of drum-
ming, complete drum charts, solos and patterns
performed by your favorite players, insightful
reviews on the hottest new geat, the best in
CDs, books, and DVDs for drummers, and
giveaways worth thousands of dollars.
Cost: $29.97
Frequency: Monthly
Circulation: 6000
ISSN: 1078-1757
Founded in 1993
Mailing list available for rent
Printed in 4 colors on glossy stock

19111 Music
102 N Haven Road
PO Box 906
Elmhurst, IL 60126-2932

630-941-2030
FAX 630-941-3210
E-Mail: subscriptions@musicincmag.com
Home Page: www.musicincmag.com

Zach Phillip, Editor
Kevin Maher, CEO
John Cahill, Eastern Advertising
Tom Burns, Western Advertising
Chris Maher, Classified Ads

Offered free to those involved in music products retailing. Delivers news you can use for
the musical products industry. Geared toward
store owners and managers in musical product
retail and repair shops in the United States and
Canada.
Frequency: 11 Per Year
Circulation: 8,949
Founded in 1934

19112 Music & Sound Retailer
Testa Communications
25 Willowdale Avenue
Port Washington, NY 11050

516-767-2500
800-937-7678
FAX 516-767-9335
E-Mail: testa@testa.com
Home Page: www.testa.com

Brian Berk, Editor

News magazine serving owners, managers and
sales personnel in retail musical-instument and
sound-product dealershops. The magazine's
emphasis is on full-line and combo dealerships
offering guitars, drums, electronic keyboards
and digital pianos, recording and sound-rein-
forcement products, lighting, DJ equipment,
software, print and accessories. Recurring features include 'MI Spy,' 'Top Ten,'
'Veddatorial,' 'Selling Points,' and editor's letter
Cost: $18.00
Frequency: Monthly
Circulation: 11000
Founded in 1985

19113 Music Row
1231 17th Avenue S
PO Box 158542
Nashville, TN 37215-8542

615-321-3617
FAX 615-329-0852
E-Mail: sales@musicrow.com
Home Page: www.musicrow.com

David M Ross, CEO/President

Written for people who work in the music business. Contents include record reviews, current
news items, timely interviews or discovering
hot talent first. Music Row subscriptions include six print issues per year, daily Afternoon
News updates via e-mail and @Musicrow reports every Tuesday, Thursday and Friday via

e-mail.
Cost: $159.00
Frequency: Six Per Year
Circulation: 14000
Founded in 1981
Printed in 4 colors on glossy stock

19114 Music Trades Magazine
Music Trades
80 West Street
Englewood, NJ 07631-0432

201-871-1965
800-423-6530
FAX 201-871-0455
E-Mail: music@musictrades.com
Home Page: www.musictrades.com

Brian Majeski, Publisher
Richard T Watson, Managing Editor
Juanita Hampton, Circulation Manager

A blend of industry news, hard sales and marketing data, trend analysis and management
tips in every issue. Target audience is retailers,
distributors, and manufacturers of musical instruments, professional audio equipment and
related products, worldwide.
Cost: $16.00
Frequency: Monthly
Circulation: 7500
Founded in 1890
Mailing list available for rent

19115 Music and Sound Journal
912 Carlton Road
Tarpon Spring, FL 34689

727-938-0571
E-Mail: sound@masj.com
Home Page: www.masj.com

Don Kulak, Founder/Owner

Brings readers the future of sound today, with
new music, experimental sound, cutting edge
audio and acoustics and alternative media. MSJ
is written for people who are discriminating
about music, audio, and sound - people who
want to improve their sonic environments on
all levels, without having to study pages of data
- people who want to more fully understand the
profound impact sound has on every aspect of
their daily lives.
ISSN: 1541-8545
Founded in 1988

19116 Musical Merchandise Review
21 Highland Circle
Suite One
Needham, MA 02494

781-453-9310
800-964-5150
FAX 781-453-9389
E-Mail: mprescott@symphonypublishing.com
Home Page: www.mmrmagazine.com

Lee Zapis, President
Sidney L Davis, Group Publisher
Richard E Kessel, Publisher/Advertising Sales
Maureen Johan, Classified Sales

Serves retailers of musical instruments, accessories, and related services as well as wholesalers, importers/exporters and manufacturers of
related products. Its purpose is to communicate
facts and ideas that will benefit musical merchandisers and their daily business operations
as well as help them enhance their growth. Its
editorial approach includes features on industry
trends and innovations, new product promotion, in-store display techniques, financing,
planning and dealer surveys.
Cost: $32.00
Frequency: Monthly
Founded in 1879
Mailing list available for rentat $100 per M
Printed in 4 colors

19117 New on the Charts
Music Business Reference
70 Laurel Place
New Rochelle, NY 10801-7105

914-632-3349
FAX 914-633-7690
E-Mail: lenny@notc.com
Home Page: www.notc.com

Leonard Kalikow, Publisher/Editor

Circulation limited to professionals only, provides major signings, contracts and directories.
Cost: $365.00
Frequency: Monthly
Circulation: 5,000
ISSN: 0276-7031
Founded in 1976

19118 Notes
Music Library Association
8551 Research Way
Suite 180
Middleton, WI 53562

608-836-5825
FAX 608-831-8200
E-Mail: mla@areditions.com
Home Page: www.musiclibraryassoc.org

Michael Colby, President
Jane Gottlieb, Editor

19119 Opera America Newsline
Opera America
330 7th Ave
Suite 1600
New York, NY 10001-5248

212-796-8620
FAX 212-796-8631
E-Mail: info@operaamerica.org
Home Page: www.operaamerica.org

Marc Scorca, President

Provides company news from around the world, articles on issues affecting the field, professional opportunities, and updates on OPERA America programs and activities. Complimentary subscription with all membership levels, excluding stand-alone professional subscriptions.
Frequency: 10X Per Year
Founded in 1970

19120 Opera News
Metropolitan Opera Guild
70 Lincoln Center Plz
New York, NY 10023-6577

212-769-7000
FAX 212-769-7007
E-Mail: info@metguild.org
Home Page: www.metoperafamily.org

David Dik, Manager

Monthly magazine that reports on opera around the world. Issues include reviews of commercial recordings and live performances, profiles of artists and articles by eminent writers on the music scene.
Cost: $29.95
Frequency: Monthly
Circulation: 60000
Founded in 1883

19121 Percussive Notes
Percussive Arts Society
110 W Washington Street
Suite A
Indianapolis, IN 46204

317-974-4488
FAX 317-974-4499
E-Mail: percarts@pas.org
Home Page: www.pas.org

Rick Mattingly, Editor
Hillary Henry, Managing Editor

The official journal of the Percussive Arts Society. Published in February, April, June, August, October and December, this magazine features a variety of articles and advertising aimed at professional and student percussionists. Regular sections are devoted to drumset, marching percussion, world percussion, symphonic percussion, technology, keyboard, health and wellness, research and reviews.
Cost: $85.00
Frequency: 6 Times Per Year
Circulation: 8000
Founded in 1961
Mailing list available for rent

19122 Piano Guild Notes
Piano Guild Publications
PO Box 1807
Austin, TX 78767-1807

512-478-5775
FAX 512-478-5843
E-Mail: ngpt@pianoguild.com
Home Page: www.pianoguild.com

Richard Allison, President

Music industry publication focusing on Piano Guild members and activities.
Cost: $16.00
Frequency: Quarterly
Circulation: 11000
Founded in 1929
Printed in 2 colors

19123 Piano Technicians Journal
Piano Technicians Guild
4444 Forest Avenue
Kansas City, KS 66106

913-432-9975
FAX 913-432-9986
E-Mail: ptg@ptg.org
Home Page: www.ptg.org

Barbara Cassaday, Executive Director
Jim Coleman Jr RPT, President
Norman R Cantrell RPT, VP

Monthly technical magazine covering all phases of working on pianos. Articles explore new tools, industry news and organizational issues. Feature articles range from setting up a repair shop to rebuilding techniques.
Cost: $ 150.00
Frequency: Monthly
Circulation: 4300
ISSN: 0031-9562

19124 Pitch Pipe
Sweet Adelines International
9110 S Toledo
PO Box 470168
Tulsa, OK 74137-0168

918-622-1444
800-992-7464
FAX 918-665-0894
E-Mail: Joey@sweetadelineintl.org
Home Page: www.sweetadelineintl.org

Pat LeVezu, President
Joey Mechell Stenner, Editor
Kelly Kirchhoff, Director Communications

Official publication of Sweet Adelines International, the world's largest singing performance and music education organization for women. The Pitch Pipe informs, educates and recognizes the members who have made the organization a success. The subscription price for members is included in the annual per capita fee.
Cost: $12.00
Frequency: Quarterly
Circulation: 30,000
Founded in 1947
Mailing list available for rent: 30M names
Printed in 4 colors on glossy stock

19125 Playback
American Society of Composers, Authors & Publisher
1 Lincoln Plz
New York, NY 10023-7097

212-621-6027
800-952-7227
FAX 212-362-7328
E-Mail: Playback@ascap.com
Home Page: www.ascap.com

Marilyn Bergman, President
Phil Crossland, Executive Editor
Jin Moon, Deputy Editor
Mike Barsky, Advertising
David Pollard, Design

The Society's magazine is loaded with full-color photos, features the latest news on ASCAP events, new member listings, legislative updates, feature articles on members, distribution info, upcoming workshops and showcases and much more.
Cost: $12.00
Frequency: Annual
Circulation: 100,000
ISSN: 1080-1391

19126 Pro Audio Review
IMAS Publishing
28 East 28th Street
12th Floor
New York, NY 22041

212-378-0400
FAX 212-378-0470
E-Mail: letters@proaudioreview.com
Home Page: www.proaudioreview.com

John Gatski, Publisher/Executive Editor
Brett Moss, Managing Editor
Claudia Van Veen, Advertising

Reviews of the latest new equipment written by audio professionals in the field, from bench tests checking the specs, to new product announcements.
Cost: $24.95
Frequency: Monthly
Circulation: 26000
ISSN: 1083-6241
Founded in 1995
Mailing list available for rent: 30,000 names at $145 per M
Printed in 4 colors on glossy stock

19127 Pro Sound News
United Business Media
28 East 28th Street
12th Floor
New York, NY 10019

212-378-0400
FAX 212-378-2160
E-Mail: sedorusa@optonline.net
Home Page: www.governmentvideo.com

Gary Rhodes, International Sales Manager

Provides timely and accurate news, industry analysis, features and technology updates to the expanded professional audio community.
Cost: $30.00
Frequency: Monthly
Circulation: 250003
Printed in 4 colors

19128 RePlay Magazine
PO Box 572829
Tarzana, CA 91357-7004

818-776-2880
FAX 818-776-2888
E-Mail: editor@replaymag.com
Home Page: www.replaymag.com

Edward Adlum, President
Barry Zweben, Marketing

A trade publication for those within the coin-operated amusement machine industry,

primarily distributors, manufacturers and operators of jukeboxes and games.
Cost: $65.00
Frequency: Monthly
Circulation: 36000
ISSN: 1534-2328
Founded in 1975
Mailing list available for rent
Printed in 4 colors on glossy stock

19129 Rolling Stone Magazine

1290 Ave of the Americas
Floor 2
New York, NY 10104-0295

212-484-1616
FAX 212-484-1771
Home Page: www.rssoundingboard.com
Social Media: *Facebook, Twitter*

Jann Wenner, President

Covers pop culture, politics etc in a massive amount of music articles, interviews, news, reviews, photos, and sound clips.

19130 Sheet Music Magazine

PO Box 58629
Boulder, CO 80323

914-244-8500
800-759-3036
FAX 914-244-8560
Home Page: www.sheetmusicmagazine.com

Ed Shanaphy, Publisher

Features actual reproduction of popular songs, both words and music, articles on various aspects of musical performance and interest for many types of musicians, and self improvement features for keyboard and fretter instrument players. A single year's subscription brings you at least 66 great songs best-loved standards and today's most lyrical hits.
Cost: $22.97
Frequency: Bi-Monthly
Circulation: 50,000

19131 Society News

Contemporary Record Society
724 Winchester Road
Broomall, PA 19008

610-544-5920
FAX 915-808-4232
E-Mail: crsnews@verizon.net
Home Page:
www.mysite.verizon.net/vzeeewvp/contemporaryrecordsociety/id3.

Jack M Shusterman, Advertising

Offers opportunities to CRS consitituents, progress notes on its associates, various awards and performance possibilities. The Society News offers feature articles of renowned composers/performers and reviews of music, recordings and music books.
Founded in 1983

19132 Southwestern Musician

Texas Music Educators Association
7900 Centre Park
PO Box 140465
Austin, TX 78714-0465

512-452-0710
888-318-8632
FAX 512-451-9213
E-Mail: rfloyd@tmea.org
Home Page: www.tmea.org

Robert Floyd, Executive Director
Karen Kneten, Communications Manager
Tesa Harding, Advertising/Exhibit Manager
Laura Kocian, Financial Manager
Rita Ellinger, Membership Assistant

The official magazine of the TMEA. Publsihed monthly August through May. Included with membership. A President's newsletter is published each June when necessary to provide an update on TMEA activities. The purposed of this publication is to serve the music educators of Texas as a means of communication or professional philosophy and action and to promote the field of music education within the state.
Circulation: 14000
Founded in 1938
Mailing list available for rent: 10,000 names
Printed in 4 colors on glossy stock

19133 Symphony Magazine

American Symphony Orchestra League
33 W 60th St
Suite 5
New York, NY 10023-7905

212-262-0638
FAX 212-262-5198
E-Mail: editor@symphony.org
Home Page: www.symphony.org

Henry Fogel, CEO
Stephen Alter, Advertising Manager
Michael Rush, Production Manager

Bimonthly magazine of the American Symphony Orchestra League. Discusses issues critical to the orchestra community and communicates the value and importance of orchestras and the music they perform. Publishes articles on compelling issues and trends relevant to the entire orchestra field. Its readers include professional staff, musicians, and board members in the orchestra industry and related fields; orchestra patrons and volunteers; and music critics and arts and media professionals.
Cost: $22.00
Frequency: Bi-Monthly
Circulation: 18000
Founded in 1942
Mailing list available for rent
Printed in 4 colors

19134 Symposium

312 E Pine Street
Missoula, MT 59802

406-721-9616
800-729-0235
FAX 406-721-9419
E-Mail: cms@music.org
Home Page: www.music.org

Robby D Gunstream, Executive Director
Cynthia Taggart, President
Glenn Stanley, Editor

Serves as a vehicle for the dissemination of information and ideas on music in higher education. The content of the publication highlights concerns of general interest and reflects the work of the Society in the areas of music represented on its Board of Directors.
Frequency: One Per Year
Circulation: 8000
Founded in 1968
Printed in one color on matte stock

19135 Vibe

E-Mail: vbecustserv@cdsfulfillment.com
Home Page: www.vibe.com

Mimi Valdez, Editor-In-Chief

Covers the trends, the events, and culture of the urban scene. Film, fashion and art to politics and music-pop, jazz, R&B, dance, hip hop, rap, house and more.
Cost: $11.95
Frequency: Monthly

Trade Shows

19136 ASTA National Conference

American String Teachers Association

4155 Chain Bridge Road
Fairfax, VA 22030

703-279-2113
FAX 703-279-2114
E-Mail: asta@astaweb.com
Home Page: www.astaweb.com

Donna Sizemore Hale, Executive Director
Beth Danner-Knight, Deputy Director
Jody McNamara, Deputy Director

Recognizing the wealth of our rich traditions as well as offer members new horizons in teaching and performing strings. Cost of attendance begins at $255. 150 exhibitors.
2000 Attendees
Frequency: Annual/March

19137 American Choral Directors Association National Conference

American Choral Directors Association
545 Couch Drive
Oklahoma City, OK 73102

405-232-8161
FAX 405-232-8162
Home Page: www.acdaonline.org

Dr Tim Sharp, Executive Director

4 full days of concerts, interest sessions, exhibits, and networking.
Frequency: Annual/March

19138 American Guild of Organists, National Conference

475 Riverside Drive
Suite 1260
New York, NY 10115

212-870-2310
FAX 212-870-2163
E-Mail: info@agohq.org
Home Page: www.agohq.org

James Thomashower, Executive Director
Jennifer Madden, Manager Membership
Harold Calhoun, Mgr Competitions

Over 20 exhibits and a workshop for professional, amatuer and student organists.
Frequency: Biennial

19139 American Harp Society National Conference

3416 Primm Lane
Birmingham, AL 35216

205-795-7130
FAX 205-823-2760
E-Mail: execsecretary@harpsociety.org
Home Page: www.harpsociety.org

Christa Grix, National Conference Chair
Lynne Aspnes, Conference Program Advisory Chair
Delaine Fedson, President

Conference will explore the mind-body-music connection, the creative process, and the connection between creativity and learning. The conference will include multiple disciplines including educators, composers, performers, therapists and practioners.
300 Attendees
Frequency: Annual
Founded in 1962

19140 American Institute of Organbuilders Annual Convention

American Institute of Organ Builders
PO Box 130982
Houston, TX 77219

713-529-2212
FAX 713-529-2212
E-Mail: pipes@pipeorgan.org
Home Page: www.convention.pipeorgan.org

Rene Marceau, Convention Committee Chairman

Annual convention includes supplier exhibits, technical lectures, sight-seeing tours, professional examinations, lectures and organ demonstrations.
Frequency: October
Founded in 1974
Mailing list available for rent: 350 names at $250 per M

19141 American Music Therapy Conference
National Music Therapy Association
8445 Colesville Road
Suite 1000
Silver Spring, MD 20910

301-589-3300
FAX 301-589-5175
Home Page: www.musictherapy.org

Seminar and exhibits of publications, musical instruments, books, learning aids and recordings.
Frequency: November

19142 American Musical Instrument Society
1106 Garden Street
Hoboken, NJ 07030

202-656-0107
E-Mail: amis@guildassoc.com
Home Page: www.amis.org

Susan Thompson, Program Co-Chair
Kathryn Libin, Program Co-Chair

A broad range of topics include the history, design, use, care and acoustics of musical instruments in all cultures and from all periods.
Frequency: Annual

19143 American Musicological Society Annual Meeting
American Musicological Society
6010 College Station
Brunswick, ME 04011-8451

207-798-4243
877-679-7648
FAX 877-679-7648
E-Mail: ams@ams-net.org
Home Page: www.ams-net.org

Robert Judd, Executive Director

A society of professional musicologists and university educators. The annual meetings are held in the fall each year; 2007- Quebec; 2008- Nashville; 2009- Philadelphia.
2000 Attendees
Frequency: Annual
Founded in 1948
Mailing list available for rent: 3515 names at $100 per M

19144 American Orff-Schulwerk Association National Conference
American Orff-Schulwerk Association
PO Box 391089
Cleveland, OH 44139-8089

440-543-5366
FAX 440-600-7332
E-Mail: info@aosa.org
Home Page: www.aosa2.org

Karen Medley, Conference Chair

One hundred exhibits of music, music books, software, insturments, and gifts in addition to National Conference of 2000+ music educators.
2400 Attendees
Frequency: November
Founded in 1969

19145 American Symphony Orchestra League National Conference
33 W 60th Street
5th Floor
New York, NY 10023

212-262-5161
FAX 212-262-5198

E-Mail: league@symphony.org
Home Page: www.symphony.org

Stephen Alter, Advertising and Meetings Manager
Meghan Whitbeck, Advertising/Meetings Coordinator
Henry Fogel, President/CEO

Ninety booths incorporating all facets of classical music industries including industry suppliers, music publishers and computer technology.
1200 Attendees
Frequency: June

19146 CMS National Conference
College Music Society
312 E Pine Street
Missoula, MT 59802

406-721-9616
FAX 406-721-9419
E-Mail: cms@music.org
Home Page: www.music.org

Robby D Gunstream, Executive Director

Presents higher education's broadest array of topics dealing with music. Attendees are faculty, administrators, graduate students, independent scholars, composers, publishers, and music business personnel who share a common interest and dedication to the improvement of music and its relationship to the other academic disciplines of higher education.
450 Attendees
Frequency: Annual/October

19147 Chamber Music America National Conference
Chamber Music America
305 7th Avenue
5th Floor
New York, NY 10001

212-242-2022
FAX 212-242-7955
Home Page: www.chamber-music.org

Susan Dadian, Program Director
Margaret M Lioi, CEO
Louise Smith, Chair
700 Attendees
Frequency: Annual

19148 Chorus America Annual Conference
910 17th Street NW
Washington, DC 20006

202-776-0215
FAX 202-776-0224
E-Mail: service@chorusamerica.org
Home Page: www.chorusamerica.org

Ann Meier Baker, President/CEO
Melanie Garrett, Membership Services Manager

This four day conference offers seminars, workshops, concerts, expert consultations and peer-group meetings in a friendly, dynamic environment.
500 Attendees
Frequency: June
Printed in 2 colors on matte stock

19149 Country Radio Seminar
Country Radio Broadcasters
819 18th Avenue S
Nashville, TN 37203

615-327-4487
FAX 615-329-4492
E-Mail: info@crb.org
Home Page: www.crb.org

Ed Salamon, Executive Director
Chasity Crouch, Business Manager
Carole Bowen, Secretary

Conference attendees include major radio groups and record labels as well as independ-

ents, Features include exhibits, seminars and shows.
2300 Attendees
Frequency: Annual
Founded in 1969

19150 Folk Alliance Annual Meeting
Folk Alliance
510 South Main
1st Floor
Memphis, TN 38103

901-522-1170
FAX 816-221-3658
E-Mail: fa@folk.org
Home Page: www.folkalliance.org

200+ artists, 4 nights of show cases, four days of feature concerts, exhibit hall parties, panels, workshops, clinics and much more all under one roof.
3000 Attendees

19151 Gospel Music Week
Gospel Music Association
PO Box 22697
Nashville, TN 37202

615-242-0303
FAX 615-254-9755
E-Mail: info@gospelmusic.org
Home Page: www.gospelmusic.org

Jackie Patillo, Executive Director

Listen to new music as you experience over 100 eclectic performances throughout the week from today's top artists and tomorrow's hit-makers, invent new waysof enhancing your ministry through educational opportunities found in over 100 seminars and panels and through the sharing of your ideas with colleagues. Connect with your industry peers and friends at various networking opportunities including receptions, roundtables and more.
3,000 Attendees
Frequency: April
Founded in 1964

19152 Gospel Music Workshop America
PO Box 34635
Detroit, MI 48208

313-898-6900
FAX 313-898-4520
E-Mail: manager@gmwnational.org
Home Page: www.gmwnational.org

Rev Albert L Jamison, Sr, Chair, Board of Directors
Sheila Smith, Director Operations
Mark Smith, Convention Manager

Conferences open with a highly spirited service including Sacraments, music from choirs within the GMWA, Psalmists and the preached Word. This is followed by lectures, speakers, preachers and over 100 courses offered during the week. Nightly musicals include chapter choirs and national recording artists. Midnight services are held which include music, preaching and various recordings by the Women's Division, Men's Division, Youth/Young Adult division and a service by Bishop Richard White.
16M Attendees
Frequency: August
Founded in 1967

19153 Horns Over the Sea
Central Washington University Music Department
400 E University Way
Ellensburg, WA 98926-7458

509-963-1226
FAX 509-963-1239

E-Mail: gross@music.ucsb.edu
Home Page: www.hornsociety.org

Jeffrey Snedeker, President
Steven Gross, Conference Coordinator
Heidi Vogel, Membership Coordinator

Features renowned hornists, guest ensembles, recitals and master classes
450 Attendees
Frequency: August

19154 International Association of Jazz Educators Conference

International Association of Jazz Education
PO Box 724
Manhattan, KS 66505

785-776-8744
FAX 785-776-6190
E-Mail: info@iage.org
Home Page: www.iaje.org

Bill McFarlin, Executive Director

This four-day conference fatures a 75,000 square-food music industry exposition, commission premieres, technology presentations, research papers, award ceremonies, and performances by over 500 of the world's most respected professional jazz groups and musicians.
8000 Attendees
Frequency: Annual

19155 International Computer Music Conference

International Computer Music Association
1819 Polk Street
Suite 330
San Francisco, CA 94109

FAX 734-878-3031
E-Mail: icma@umich.edu
Home Page: www.computermusic.org
Social Media: *Facebook*

Tae Hong Park, President
Margaret Schedel, VP of Conference
Chryssie Nanou, Treasurer/Secretary
Tom Erbe, VP, Membership
Sandra Neal, Administrative Assistant

The International Computer Music Association is an international affiliation of individuals and institutions involved in the technical, creative, and performance aspects of computer music. It serves composers, engineers, researchers and musicians who are interested in the integration of music and technology.
Founded in 1974

19156 International Horn Competition of America

BGSU Continuing and Extended Education
14 College Park
Bowling Green, OH 43403-0200

509-963-1226
FAX 509-963-1239
Home Page: www.ihcamerica.org

Jeffrey Snedeker, President
Andrew Pelletier, Host

International competition specifically for the horn as a solo instrument.
450 Attendees
Frequency: July

19157 International Steel Guitar Convention

College Music Society
312 East Pine Street
Missoula, MT 59802

406-721-9616
FAX 406-721-9419
E-Mail: cms@music.org
Home Page: www.music.org

Social Media: *Facebook, Twitter, YouTube, RSS*

Dewitt Scott Sr, President
Mary Scott, Secretary

Sixty-five booths that provide entertainment from steel guitarists and various instruments including the bass guitar.
3M Attendees
Frequency: August

19158 Mid-South Horn Conference

Central Washington University Music Department
400 E University Way
Ellensburg, WA 98926-7458

509-963-1226
FAX 509-963-1239
E-Mail: campbellel@umkc.edu
Home Page: www.hornsociety.org

Jeffrey Snedeker, President
Ellen Campbell, Event Host
Heidi Vogel, Membership Coordinator

Features renowned hornists, guest ensembles, recitals and master classes
450 Attendees
Frequency: March

19159 Midwest International Band & Orchestra Clinic

Midwest International Band & Orchestra Clinic
111 E Touhy Ave
Suite 250
Des Plaines, IL 60018

847-424-4163
FAX 773-321-1509
E-Mail: info@midwestclinic.org
Home Page: www.midwestclinic.org

The purpose to the clinic is to raise the standards of music education, to develop new teaching techniqes, to examine, analyze, analyze and appraise literature dealing with music, demonstrations for the betterment of music education. 350 exhibitors, 565 booths, 30 concerts, and 50 instructional clinics.
12000 Attendees
Frequency: December

19160 Music Teachers National Association Convention

441 Vine Street
Suite 3100
Cincinnati, OH 45202

513-421-1420
888-512-5278
FAX 513-421-2503
E-Mail: mtnanet@mtna.org
Home Page: www.mtna.org

Gary L Ingle, Executive Director
Gail Berenson, President
Janice Wenger, VP

Atendees include independent music teachers, college faculty, students and parents from all over North America.
2500 Attendees
Frequency: Annual
Founded in 1876
Mailing list available for rent: 23000 names at $85 per M

19161 NAMM: International Music Products Association

5790 Armada Drive
Carlsbad, CA 92008-4608

760-438-8001
800-767-6266
FAX 760-438-7327
E-Mail: tradeshow@namm.com
Home Page: www.thenammshow.com

Joe Lamond, President

NAMM's trade shows are all about the experience. The experience of checking out the latest gear, of networking with other music product professionals, of attending free business-boosting classes. From the cook exhibits to the sizzling hot nightlife, music and music making always take center stage.
80000 Attendees
Frequency: January

19162 NATS National Conference

National Association of Teachers of Singing
9957 Moorings Dr
Suite 401
Jacksonville, FL 32257-2416

904-992-9101
FAX 904-262-2587
E-Mail: info@nats.org
Home Page: www.nats.org

Allen Henderson, Executive Director
Deborah L Guess, Director of Operations
Frequency: June/July

19163 National Association for Music Education Conference

1806 Robert Fulton Drive
Reston, VA 20191-4348

703-860-4000
800-336-3768
FAX 703-860-1531
Home Page: www.menc.org
Social Media: *Facebook, Twitter, LinkedIn*

John J Mahlmann, Executive Director
Margaret Jamborsky, Director Meetings/Conventions
Elizabeth Lasko, Director Public Relations/Marketing
Amanda Kidwell, Membership Director

To advance music education by encouraging the study and making of music by all.
5M Attendees
Frequency: April

19164 National Association of Pastoral Musicians Convention

National Association of Pastoral Musicians
962 Wayne Avenue
Suite 210
Silver Spring, MD 20910-4461

240-247-3000
FAX 240-247-3001
E-Mail: npmsing@npm.org
Home Page: www.npm.org

J Michael McMahon, President
Kathleen Haley, Membership Services Director
Paul H Colloton, Continuing Education Director
Lowell Hickman, Executive Assistant/Office Manager

200 workshop sessions, 5 major addresses, music education classes, clinics, new music showcases and exhibits, musical performances, prayer and songs, adult and children's choirs, handbells, youth gatherings, Liturgical Space Tour.
4000 Attendees
Frequency: July

19165 National Association of Recording Merchandising Trade Show

9 Eves Drive
Suite 120
Marlton, NJ 08053-3130

856-596-2221
FAX 859-596-3268
E-Mail: still@narm.com
Home Page: www.narm.com
Social Media: *Facebook, Twitter, RSS*

Jim Donio, President
Pat Daly, Meeting Planner
Evelyn Dichter, Membership Coordinator

Susan L'Ecuyer, VP
Communications/Marketing

One-on-One meeting opportunities, welcome
reception, keynote speakers, marketplace exhibits, live performances, forums, receptions
and awards dinner
3M Attendees
Frequency: April/May

19166 National Association of Schools of Music Annual Meeting

National Association of Schools of Music
11250 Roger Bacon Drive
Suite 21
Reston, VA 20190-5248

703-437-0700
FAX 703-437-6312
E-Mail: info@arts-accredit.org
Home Page: www.arts-accredit.org

Don Gibson, President
Mark Wait, VP
Mellasenah Y Morris, Treasurer
Frequency: November

19167 National Opera Association Conference

National Opera Association
PO Box 60869
Canyon, TX 79016

806-651-2857
FAX 806-651-2958
E-Mail: rhansen@mail.wtamu.edu
Home Page: www.noa.org
Social Media: *Facebook, RSS*

Robert Hansen, Executive Director
Robert Thieme, Editor

Annual conference and exhibits of opera related equipment, supplies and services.
775 Attendees
Frequency: Annual
Founded in 1954

19168 Northeast Horn Workshop

Central Washington University Music
Department
400 E University Way
Ellensburg, WA 98926-7458

509-963-1226
FAX 509-963-1239
E-Mail: rdodsonw@mansfield.edu
Home Page: www.hornsociety.org

Jeffrey Snedeker, President
Rebecca Dodson, Workshop Host
Heidi Vogel, Membership Coordinator

Features renowned hornists, guest ensembles,
recitals and master classes
450 Attendees
Frequency: February

19169 Opera America Conference

Opera America
330 7th Avenue
16th Floor
New York, NY 10001-5248

212-796-8620
FAX 212-796-8631
Home Page: www.operaamerica.org
Social Media: *RSS*

Session topics include identifying ways to harness the power of the best new technologies,
how to reach current and prospective audiences, how to gain support from donors, and
how to enrich the lives of children and adults
who are now downloading podcasts, reading
blogs, and designing their own multimedia
communications.
275 Attendees
Frequency: April

19170 Piano Technicians Guild Annual Convention

Piano Technicians Guild
4444 Forest Avenue
Kansas City, KS 66106

913-432-9975
FAX 913-432-9986
E-Mail: ptg@ptg.org
Home Page: www.ptg.org

Barbara J Cassaday, Executive Director
Jim Coleman Jr RPT, President
Norman R Cantrell RPT, VP

Come for the learning: find a hands-on class
for your skill level; pick from sessions covering every type of piano service; squeeze in a
mini-tech; prepare for the RPT exams; see the
latest and greatest piano products.
650 Attendees
Frequency: June

19171 Sweet Adelines International Convention

Sweet Adelines International
PO Box 470168
Tulsa, OK 74147-0168

918-622-1444
800-992-7464
FAX 918-665-0894
Home Page: www.sweetadelineintl.org

Kathy Hayes, Director Meetings/Corporate
Service
Ruth Cameron, Meetings/Exhibits Coordinator
Jane Hanson, Marketing Coordinator
Connie Heyer, Membership Registrar
Kellye Kirchhoff, Director Communications

Heart-pounding chorus competitions, the rush
and excitement of the quartet competition, education classes, shopping in the Harmony Ba-
zaars and good times with old friends and new
are all included in the International
Convention.
8M Attendees
Frequency: October

19172 Winter Music Conference

3450 NE
12th Terrace
Fort Lauderdale, FL 33334

954-563-4444
FAX 954-563-1599
E-Mail: info@wintermusicconference.com
Home Page: www.wintermusicconference.com

Regarded as the singular networking event in
the dance music industry, attracting professionals from over 60 different countries.

19173 World of Bluegrass

International Bluegrass Music Association
2 Music Circle South
Suite 100
Nashville, TN 37203

615-256-3222
888-438-4262
FAX 615-256-0450
E-Mail: info@ibma.org
Home Page: www.ibma.org

Dan Hays, Executive Director
Nancy Cardwell, Special Projects Coordinator
Jill Snider, Member/Convention Services

Build relationships with event producers, record label reps, agents and managers, broadcasters, association leaders, educators, the
media, instrument builders, artists and composers. Educational and networking events like
seminars, facilitated discussions and workshops are the primary focus of the conference.
Browse through 100+ booths in the Exhibit
Hall. You will hear bluegrass music around the
clock for seven days. The Highpoint of the

Conference is the International Bluegrass
Music Awards.
1,800 Attendees
Frequency: October

Directories & Databases

19174 American Music Center Directory

American Music Center
90 John Street
Suite 312
New York, NY 10038

212-645-6949
FAX 212-366-5265
E-Mail: library@newmusicusa.org
Home Page: www.amc.net

Joanne Cossa, Executive Director
Lyn Liston, Director New Music Information
Peter Shavitz, Director Development
Lisa Taliano, Director Information Technology
Carlos Camposeco, Director Finance and
Administration

Mailing lists include all United States members; all International and United States members; Composer Members in the United States;
Members in the New York City Metropolitan
area; and Members in the United States and
Canada.

19175 American Society of Composers, Authors and Publishers

American Soc. of Composers, Authors &
Publishers
1 Lincoln Plz
New York, NY 10023-7097

212-621-6027
FAX 212-621-8453
E-Mail: ACE@ascap.com
Home Page: www.ascap.com

Marilyn Bergman, President
Johnny Mandel, Writer Vice Chairman
Jay Morgenstern, Publisher Vice Chairman
Arnold Broido, Treasurer
Kathy Spanberger, Secretary

ASCAP created the dial-up ACE system as a
useful tool for music professionals. An enhanced World Wide Web version of this database is now available. The database contains
information on all compositions in the ASCAP
repertory which have appeared in any of
ASCAP's domestic surveys, including foreign
compositions licensed by the ASCAP in the
United States.
Frequency: Annual
Founded in 1993

19176 AudArena International Guide

Billboard Directories
PO Box 15158
North Hollywood, CA 91615

818-487-4582
800-562-2706
E-Mail: info@billboard.com
Home Page: www.orderbillboard.com

Arkady Fridman, Inside Sales Manager

Complete data on over 4,400 venues worldwide, including Amphitheaters, Arenas, Stadiums, Sports Facilities, Concert Halls and New
Constructions. Also includes complete listings
of companies offering services to the touring
industry in the Facilty Buyer's Guide. The
guide features contact names, phone and fax
numbers, e-mail and web site addresses, market
population, facility capacities and staging con-
figurations, and rental fees and ticketing rights.
Cost: $99.00
325 Pages
Frequency: Annual

19177 Billboard Subscriber File
Edith Roman Associates
PO Box 1556
Pearl River, NY 10965

845-620-9000
800-223-2194
FAX 845-620-9035
E-Mail: john.logiudice@edithroman.com
Home Page: www.edithroman.com

Steve Roberts, President
Wayne Nagrowski, E-Mail List Info Contact

Directory listees include booking agencies and agents, clubs, music publishers, promoters, radio stations, record labels, sound and lighting services, retailers, video, venues, wholesalers, equipment and manufacturing and general services.
Frequency: Annual

19178 Bluegrass Resource Directory
International Bluegrass Music Association
2 Music Cir S
Suite 100
Nashville, TN 37203-4381

615-256-3222
888-438-4262
FAX 615-256-0450
E-Mail: info@ibma.org
Home Page: www.ibma.org

Member Directory can only be accessed by IBMA members.
Cost: $25.00
88 Pages
Frequency: Annual

19179 Gospel Music Industry Directory
Gospel Music Association
P.O Box 22697
Nashville, TN 37202

615-242-0303
FAX 615-254-9755
E-Mail: info@gospelmusic.org
Home Page: www.gospelmusic.org
Social Media: *Facebook, YouTube*

John Styll, President
Scott Brickell, Director
Ed Harper, Director

Formerly called the Networking Guide, the GMA Music Industry Directory is a comprehensive listing of Christian and Gospel music artists, managers, booking agents, record companies, publishing companies and more. Active GMA Professional members get a copy of the directory free. Associate and Student GMA members can purchase one for a discounted rate.

19180 Grey House Performing Arts Directory
Grey House Publishing
4919 Route 22
PO Box 56
Amenia, NY 12501

518-789-8700
800-562-2139
FAX 845-373-6390
E-Mail: books@greyhouse.com
Home Page: www.greyhouse.com
Social Media: *Facebook, Twitter*

Leslie Mackenzie, Publisher
Richard Gottlieb, Editor

The most comprehensive resource covering the Performing Arts. This directory provides current information on over 8,500 Dance Companies, Instrumental Music Programs, Opera Companies, Choral Groups, Theater Companies, Performing Arts Series, Performing Arts Facilities and Artist Management Groups.
Cost: $185.00
1200 Pages
Frequency: Annual

ISBN: 1-592373-76-3
Founded in 1981

19181 Grey House Performing Arts Directory - Online Database
Grey House Publishing
4919 Route 22
PO Box 56
Amenia, NY 12501-0556

518-789-8700
800-562-2139
FAX 518-789-0556
E-Mail: gold@greyhouse.com
Home Page: www.gold.greyhouse.com
Social Media: *Facebook, Twitter*

Leslie Mackenzie, Publisher
Richard Gottlieb, Editor

The Grey House Performing Arts Directory - Online Database provides immediate access to dance companies, orchestras, opera companies, choral groups, theater companies, series, festivals and perfoming arts facilities across the country, or in their region, state, or in your own backyard. It offers unequaled coverage of the Performing Arts - over 8,500 listings - of the major performance organization, facilities, and information resources.
Frequency: Annual
Founded in 1981

19182 International Buyers Guide
Billboard Directories
PO Box 15158
North Hollywood, CA 91615

818-487-4582
800-562-2706
E-Mail: info@billboard.com
Home Page: www.billboard.com/directories

Arkady Fridman, Inside Sales Manager

A must-have resource for doing business in the music industry, covers every aspect of the recording business worldwide. The latest edition includes contact information on: record labels, video and digital music companies, distributors and importers/exporters; music publishers and rights organizations - blank media manufacturers, pressing plants and services; manufacturers of jewel boxes and other packaging and equipment services; and suppliers of store fixtures, security and accessories.
Cost: $179.00
340 Pages
Frequency: Annual

19183 International Talent and Touring Guide
Billboard Directories
PO Box 15158
North Hollywood, CA 91615

818-487-4582
800-562-2706
E-Mail: info@billboard.com
Home Page: www.billboard.com/directories

Arkady Fridman, Inside Sales Manager

A reference guide for anyone who books, promotes or manages talent. Features over 30,000 listings, including 12,900 artists, managers and agents worldwide, including the USA and Canada. The guide includes contact names, phone and fax numbers, e-mail and website addresses, artists and their record labels, managers and agents, tour services and merchandise, sound and lighting vendors, equipment and instrument rentals, limo rentals, security services, plus national promoters and their key personnel
Cost: $139.00
242 Pages
Frequency: Annual

19184 Keyboard Teachers Association International
Dr. Albert DeVito
361 Pin Oak Lane
Westbury, NY 11590-1941

516-333-3236
FAX 516-997-9531

Albert DeVito, President

Music teachers and those related to keeping members updated as to activity going on in music world.
Frequency: Quarterly
Founded in 1963

19185 MLA Membership Handbook
Music Library Association
8551 Research Way
Suite 180
Middleton, WI 53562

608-836-5825
FAX 608-831-8200
E-Mail: mla.areditions.org
Home Page: www.musiclibraryassoc.org

Philip Vandermeer, President

A mailing list that is available for rental in a variety of formats.
Cost: $25.00
Founded in 1931

19186 Music Library Association Membership Directory
Music Library Association
8551 Research Way
Suite 180
Middleton, WI 53562

608-836-5825
FAX 608-831-8200
E-Mail: mla@areditions.com
Home Page: www.musiclibraryassoc.org

Jerry L. McBride, President

The MLA mailing list is available for rental in a variety of formats. Members include music librarians, librarians who work with music as part of their responsibilities, composers and music scholars, and others interested in the program of the association.

19187 Musical America Directory
Musical America
PO Box 1330
Highstown, NJ 08520

609-448- 334
800-221-5488
FAX 609-371-7879
E-Mail: info@musicalamerica.com
Home Page: www.musicalamerica.com
Social Media: *Facebook, Twitter, YouTube*

Joyce Wasserman, Subscription Information
Bob Hudoba, Contact

Provides thousands of names, phone numbers, addresses, and Email and Web site addresses for manangers, orchestras, opera companies, festivals, presenters, venues and more around the world.
Cost: $125.00
Mailing list available for rent

19188 Musician's Guide
Billboard Directories
PO Box 15158
North Hollywood, CA 91615

818-487-4582
800-562-2706
E-Mail: info@billboard.com
Home Page: www.billboard.com/directories

Arkady Fridman, Inside Sales Manager

Everything the working musician needs to book gigs, contact record labels, find a manager, and locate tour services. The latest edition

includes A & R Directory, Music Business Services, and City by City listings.
Cost: $15.95
170 Pages
Frequency: Annual

19189 National Opera Association Membership Directory
PO Box 60869
Canyon, TX 79016-0869

806-651-2857
FAX 806-651-2958
E-Mail: rhansen@mail.wtamu.edu
Home Page: www.noa.org
Social Media: *Facebook, RSS*

Robert Hansen, Executive Director
JoElyn Wakefield Wright, President
Edith Kirkpatrick Vrenios, VP Resources
Philip Hageman, Treasurer
Carol Notestine, Recording Secretary

Members of the National Opera Association are entitled to receive the NOA Freelance Artists and Production Resources databases, the NOA membership directory, and access to the NOA e-mail listserve.
Frequency: Annual
Mailing list available for rent

19190 Orion Blue Book: Guitars and Musical Instruments
Orion Research Corporation
14555 N Scottsdale Rd
Suite 330
Scottsdale, AZ 85254-3487

480-951-1114
FAX 480-951-1117
E-Mail: sales@UsedPrice.com
Home Page: www.orionbluebook.com

Roger Rohrs, Owner

77,834 products listed; products listed from 1970s to present; over 450 manufacturers listed; 2 volumes - hardbound or on CD-ROM. Lists musical instruments from Accordians to Xylophones
Cost: $195.00
Frequency: Annual
Founded in 1981

19191 Orion Blue Book: Professional Sound
Orion Research Corporation
14555 N Scottsdale Rd
Suite 330
Scottsdale, AZ 85254-3487

480-951-1114
800-844-0759
FAX 480-951-1117
E-Mail: sales@UsedPrice.com
Home Page: www.orionbluebook.com

Roger Rohrs, Owner

Features over 48,964 products from the 1950's to present. Over 350 manufacturers listed. Comes in hardbound or on CD-ROM. Lists products from Cartridge Players to Wireless Microphone Systems.
Cost: $150.00
970 Pages
Frequency: Annual
Founded in 1973

19192 Orion Blue Book: Vintage Guitar
Orion Research Corporation
14555 N Scottsdale Rd
Suite 330
Scottsdale, AZ 85254-3487

480-951-1114
800-844-0759
FAX 480-951-1117
E-Mail: sales@UsedPrice.com
Home Page: www.orionbluebook.com

Roger Rohrs, Owner

Features more than 11,413 products from the 1800's to present. Over 30 manufacturers listed. Comes in hardbound or CD-ROM, Lists products from Banjos to Ukuleles.
Cost: $50.00
Frequency: Quarterly
Founded in 1990

19193 Record Retailing Directory
Billboard Directories
PO Box 15158
North Hollywood, CA 91615

818-487-4582
800-562-2706
E-Mail: info@billboard.com
Home Page: www.billboard.com/directories

Arkady Fridman, Inside Sales Manager

Over 5,500 listings covering the entire retailing community. Provides access to major chain headquarters and local outlets; complete coverage of independent retailers; hard-to-find audiobook retailers; and the booming world of online record retailing, plus store genre or specialization; executives, owners, buyers and planners; address, phone, fax, email and web.
Cost: $215.00
Frequency: Annual

19194 Source Directory of Books, Records and Tapes
Sutton's Super Marketplace
153 Sutton Lane
Fordsville, KY 42343

270-276-9880
E-Mail: mtsutton32@earthlink.net
Home Page: www.pubdisco.com

Jerry Sutton, Owner/Founder

Publishers, recording studios, wholesalers, distributors, manifacturers and importers. Approximatley 450 records. Changes daily as updated.
Cost: $55.20

19195 Source Directory of Musical Instruments
Sutton's Super Marketplace
153 Sutton Lane
Fordsville, KY 42343

270-276-9880
E-Mail: mtsutton32@earthlink.net
Home Page: www.pubdisco.com

Jerry Sutton, Owner/Founder

Listings in directory include names, addresses, phone and fax numbers, and product descriptions from wholesale distributors, Importers, Manufacturers, Close-out houses and Liquidators. Updated daily.
Cost: $55.20

Industry Web Sites

19196 http://gold.greyhouse.com
G.O.L.D Grey House OnLine Databases

Grey House Publishing's online database platform, GOLD, offers Quick Search, Keyword Search and Expert Search for most business sectors including music and performance markets. The GOLD platform makes finding the information you need quick and easy - whether you're a novice searcher or an experienced database user. All of Grey House's directory products are available for subscription on the GOLD platform.

19197 www.acdaonline.org
American Choral Directors Association

Nonprofit music-education organization whose central purpose is to promote excellence in

choral music through performance, composition, publication, research and teaching.

19198 www.acmcountry.com
Academy of Country Music

Involved in numerous events and activities promoting country music. Presents annual awards.

19199 www.afm.org
American Federation of Musicians of the United
States and Canada

Union representing over 100,000 professional musicians, performing in all genres of music.

19200 www.afvbm.com
American Federation of Violin and Bow Makers

Strives to elevate professional standards of craftmanship and ethical conduct among members. Helps members develop technical skills and knowledge.Research and study organization.

19201 www.agohq.org
American Guild of Organists

Promotes the organ in its historic and evolving roles and provides a forum for mutual support, inspiration, education and certification.

19202 www.ascap.com
American Society of Composers Authors & Publishers

Membership association of more than 260,000 US composers, song writers, lyricists and music publishers.

19203 www.asmac.org
American Society of Music Arrangers and Composers

Professional society for arrangers, composers, orchestrators, and musicians. Monthly meetings with great speakers from the music industry.

19204 www.billboard.com

The ultimate music industry research tool and information source. The Member Service database is state-of-the-art electronic information service, enabling users to efficiently access information from a variety of music industry databases via the World Wide Web.

19205 www.chorusamerica.org
Chorus America

National service for orchestral choruses, independent choruses and professional choruses.

19206 www.clarinet.org
International Clarinet Association

Seeks to focus attention on the importance of the clarinet and to foster communication of the fellowship between clarinetists.

19207 www.cmaworld.com
Country Music Association

Promotes and publicizes country music.

19208 www.creativemusicalcoalition.com
Creative Musician Coalition

A national organization that brings the world of new music to its readers. Includes in depth music reviews, informative artist interviews, interesting articles and feature columns, and valuable resource material.

19209 www.flmusiced.org
Florida Music Educators Association

Florida Music Educators Association and Florida School Music Association.

19210 www.folkharpsociety.org
International Society of Folk Harpers and Craftsmen

Conducts technical and artistic programs and promotes craft exchange.

19211 www.gospelmusic.org
Gospel Music Association

Dedicated to providing leadership, direction and unity for all facets of the gospel music industry. Through education, communication, information, promotion and recognition, the GMA is striving to help those involved in gospel music.

19212 www.greyhouse.com
Grey House Publishing

Authoritative reference directories for most business sectors including music and performance markets. Users can search the online databases with varied search criteria allowing for custom searches by product category, geographic area, sales volume, keyword, subject and more. Full Grey House catalog and online ordering also available.

19213 www.guitarfoundation.org
Guitar Foundation of America

Supports the serious studies of the guitar.

19214 www.harpsociety.org
American Harp Society

Improves the quality of the instrument and performance.

19215 www.horndoggie.com/horn
International Horn Society

A national organization that focuses on music industry news and information.

19216 www.iaekm.org
International Association of Electronic Keyboard Manufacturers

Global manufacturers of electronic kayboards and affiliated software and publications.

19217 www.ibma.org
World of Bluegrass

IBMA: working together for high standards of professionalism, a greater appreciation for our music, and the success of the world-wide bluegrass community.

19218 www.imeamusic.org
Indiana Music Educators Association

Supports and advances music education in Indiana.

19219 www.internationalpolka.com
International Polka Association

Educational organization concerned with the preservation and advancement of polka music. Operates the Polka Music Hall of Fame and Museum, and presents the International Polka Fesitval every year during the complete first weekend of August.

19220 www.metguild.org
Metropolitan Opera Guild

Seeks to promote greater understanding and interest in opera.

19221 www.mpa.org
Music Publishers Association of the United States

Encourages understanding of the copyright laws and works to protect musical works against infringements and piracy.

19222 www.mtna.org
Music Teachers National Association

This is a nonprofit organization of independent and collegiate music teachers committed to furthering the art of music through teaching, performance, composition and scholarly research.

19223 www.music.org
College Music Society

The Society is a national service organization for college conservatory and university music teachers.

19224 www.musicalartists.org
American Guild of Musical Artists

Exclusive bargaining agent for all concert musical artists.

19225 www.musicdistributors.org
Music Distributor Association

A trade association of 160 manufactures, importers, wholesalers of musical instruments and accessories, domestic and international selling to the trade only

19226 www.musiclibraryassoc.org
Music Library Association

Promotes growth and establishment in the use of music libraries, musical instruments and musical literature.

19227 www.nacwpi.org
National Association of College Wind and Percussion Instructors

Teachers of wind and percussion instruments in American colleges and universities.

19228 www.napbirt.org
National Association of Professional Band Instrument Repair Technicians

Promotes technical integrity in the craft. Surveys tools and procedures to improve work quality. Makes available emergency repair of band instruments. Provides placement services.

19229 www.narm.com
National Association of Recording Merchandisers

Not-for-profit trade association that represents the retailers, wholesalers, and distributors of prerecorded music in the United States.

19230 www.nats.org
National Association of Teachers of Singing

To encourage the highest standards of the vocal art and of ethical principals in the teaching of singing; and to promote vocal education and research at all levels, both for the enrichment of the general public and for the professional advancement of the talented.

19231 www.nbea.com
National Ballroom and Entertainment Association

Provides exchange for owners and operators of ballrooms.

19232 www.noa.org
National Opera Association

To advance the appreciation, composition and production of opera.

19233 www.npm.org
National Association of Pastoral Musicians

Membership organization primarily composed of musicians, musician-liturgist, clergy, and other leaders of prayer devoted to serving the life and mission of the Church through fostering the art of musical liturgy in Roman Catholic worshiping communities in the United States.

19234 www.nyssma.org
New York State School Music Association

Advocates and improves the education in music of all people in New York State.

19235 www.pas.org
Percussive Arts Society

Promotes drums and percussion through a viable network of performers, teachers, students, enthusiasts and sustaining members. Offers publications, a worldwide network of the World Percussion Network, the Percussive Arts Society International Headquarters/Museum and the annual Percussive Arts Society International Convention.

19236 www.pianoguild.com
International Piano Guild

A division of the American College of Musicians Professional society of piano teachers and music faculty members. Sponsers national examinations.

19237 www.printmusic.org
Retail Print Music Dealers Association

The voice of the print music industry.

19238 www.ptg.org
Piano Technicians Guild

Conducts technical institutes at conventions and seminars. Promotes public education in piano care. Bestows awards. Publishes monthly technical journal by subscriptions.

19239 www.spars.com
Society of Professional Audio Recording Services

Members are individuals, companies and studios connected with the professional recording industry.

19240 www.symphony.org
American Symphony Orchestra League

The national nonprofit service and educational organization dedicated to strengthening symphony and chamber orchestras. It provides artistic, organizational and financial leadership and service to orchestral conductors, managers, volunteers and staff.

19241 www.tmea.org
Texas Music Educators Association

Promoting excellence in music education.

Associations

19242 ARMA International

11880 College Blvd
Suite 450
Overland Park, KS 66210

913-341-3808
800-422-2762
FAX 913-341-3742
E-Mail: hq@arma.org
Home Page: www.arma.org
Social Media: *Facebook, Twitter, LinkedIn*

Marilyn Bier, Executive Director
Peter Kurilecz, IGP, CRM, CA, President
Tera Ladner, J.D., IGP, CRM, President-Elect
Brenda Prowse, CRMÿ, Treasurer
Fred Pulzello, IGP, CRM, Immediate Past
President

A not-for-profit professional association and
the authority on managing records and information.
11000 Members
Founded in 1955

19243 Business and Institutional Furniture Manufacturers Association

678 Front Ave NW
Suite 150
Grand Rapids, MI 49504-5368

616-285-3963
FAX 616-285-3765
E-Mail: email@bifma.org
Home Page: www.bifma.org
Social Media: *Facebook, Twitter, LinkedIn*

Dan Tuoghy, President
Thomas Reardon, Executive Director
Sylvain Garneau, Vice President
Franco Bianchi, Treasurer

BIFMA is a not-for-profit trade association of
furniture manufacturers and suppliers, addressing issues of common concern.
245+ Members
Founded in 1973

19244 Graphic Arts Information Network

200 Deer Run Road
Sewickley, PA 15143

412-741-6860
800-910-4283
FAX 412-741-2311
E-Mail: printing@printing.org
Home Page: www.printing.org/
Social Media: *Facebook, Twitter, LinkedIn, RSS*

Michael F Makin, President

Members are companies printing labels for
food or consumer products.
40 Members

19245 Independent Office Products & Furniture Dealers Association

3601 E. Joppa Road
Baltimore, MD 21234

410-931-8100
FAX 410-931-8111
E-Mail: info@iopfda.org
Home Page: www.nopanet.org/
Social Media: *Twitter, LinkedIn*

Mike Tucker, President
Paul Miller, Director Government Affairs
Paula Kreuzburg, M.D
Alicia Ellis, Director, Marketing

Association for independent office product and
office furniture dealers. IOPFDA is comprised
of the National Office Products Alliance
(NOPA) and the Office Furniture Dealers
Alliance (OFDA).
1500 Members
Founded in 1904

19246 National Office Products Alliance

3601 E Joppa Rd.
Baltimore, MD 21234

410-931-8100
FAX 410-931-8111
Home Page: www.nopanet.org

Paula Kreuzburg, Executive Director

Information and resources to promote the success of member dealers.

19247 Office Furniture Dealers Alliance

3601 E Joppa Rd.
Baltimore, MD 21234

410-931-8100
FAX 410-931-8111
E-Mail: info@ofda.org
Home Page: www.ofdanet.org
Social Media: *LinkedIn*

Rod Manson, Chair
Paula Kreuzburg, Executive Director

The Alliance's mission is to provide independent dealers with information and tools to help
them succeed in a changing industry.
1200 Members

19248 Office Furniture Distribution Association

P.O. Box 2548
Secaucus, NJ 07096

517-467-9355
FAX 517-467-9056
E-Mail: theofda@yahoo.com
Home Page: www.theofda.org

75 Members
Founded in 1923

19249 Office Products Representatives

3131 Elbee Road
Dayton, OH 45439

937-297-2250
800-447-1684
FAX 937-297-2254
E-Mail: info@oprareps.org
Home Page: www.oprareps.org

Carol Hinton, Owner
100 Members
Founded in 1974

19250 Office Products Wholesalers Association

5024 Campbell Boulevard
Baltimore, MD 21236

410-931-8100
FAX 410-931-8111
E-Mail:
info@BusinessSolutionsAssociation.com
Home Page: www.opwa.org

Cal Clemons, Executive Vice President
Paula Kreuzberg, Associate Director

Members are chief executives of office product
wholesalers and manufacturers.
165 Members
Founded in 1995

19251 Society for Service Professionals in Printing

433 E Monroe Ave
Alexandria, VA 22301-1645

703-684-0044
866-600-8820
FAX 703-548-9137
E-Mail: ssppsupport@sspp.org
Home Page: www.sspp.org

Peter Colaianni, Executive Director
Marj Green, Director

Individual membership society dedicated to the
needs of customer service professionals in the
printing industry.
8 Members
Founded in 1993

Newsletters

19252 BTA Hotline Online

Business Technology Association
12411 Wornall Rd
Suite 200
Kansas City, MO 64145-1212

816-941-3100
800-325-7219
FAX 816-941-2829
E-Mail: info@bta.org
Home Page: www.bta.org

Brent Hoskins, Executive Director
Terry Chapman, President

Current copier/printer and network systems industry news.
Founded in 1926

19253 Digital Image Review

Buyers Laboratory
20 Railroad Avenue
Hackensack, NJ 07601-3309

201-896-6439
FAX 201-488-0461
E-Mail: info@buyerslab.com
Home Page: www.buyerslab.com

Daria Hoffman, Managing Editor
Michael Danziger, CEO

Devoted to digital topics, all types of digital office products, industry news and trends, trade
show, pricing changes and much more.
Cost: $305.00
16 Pages
Frequency: Monthly
Founded in 1961

19254 Executary

National Association of Executive
Secretaries
900 S Washington Street
Suite G13
Falls Church, VA 22046-4009

703-237-8616
FAX 703-533-1153
E-Mail: headquarters@theaeap.com
Home Page: www.theaeap.com
Social Media: *LinkedIn*

Ruth Ludeman, Director

Packed with practical advice on various issues
of interest to administrative professionals.
Seeks to support AEAP's mission to assist
members in achieving their career goals by
keeping you informed of advances and changes
in the administrative profession.
Frequency: 10x/Year
Mailing list available for rent: 5000 names

19255 Form & Document Industry Newsletter

319 SW Washington Street
Suite 710
Portland, OR 97204-2618

503-227-3393
FAX 503-274-7667
E-Mail: bfma@bfma.org
Home Page: www.bfma.org

Andy Palatka, Executive Director
Tonya Macalino, Editor
Tonya Macalino, Marketing

Industry newsletter containing educational articles and rules on the latest processes, tech-

niques, and products in the form and document industry. Library rate is $35.00 per year.
Cost: $50.00
38574 Pages
Circulation: 700
Founded in 1958
Mailing list available for rent: 1000 names at $400 per M

19256 Jot and Jolts
Economics Press
12 Daniel Road
Fairfield, NJ 07004-2565

973-227-1224
800-526-2554
FAX 973-227-8360
Home Page: www.epinc.com

Monthly planner for supervisors to the office products industry.
Cost: $16.20
26 Pages
Frequency: Monthly
Printed in on glossy stock

19257 MFP Report
Bissett Communications
Apt 44
20919 Bloomfield Ave
Lakewood, CA 90715-1840

562-809-8917
FAX 562-809-1627
Home Page: http://www.mfpreport.com

Brian R Bissett, Publisher

A newsletter providing information on manufacturers, suppliers, sellers, and managers of multifunction peripherals and connected office equipment of the latest MFP business, market and technology issues and their impact.
Frequency: Monthly

19258 Scanner
Private Label Manufacturers Association (PLMA)
630 Third Avenue
New York, NY 10017-6506

212-972-3131
FAX 212-983-1382
E-Mail: info@plma.com
Home Page: www.plma.com

Brian Sharoff, President
Myra Rosen, VP
Tom Prendergast, Director, Research Services

News and information for the private label industry.
3200+ Members
6 Pages
Frequency: Quarterly
Circulation: 12000
Founded in 1979

Magazines & Journals

19259 Better Buys for Business
Progressive Business Publications
PO Box 3019
Malvern, PA 19355-0719

610-695-0201
800-247-2185
FAX 610-647-8098
E-Mail: webmaster@pbp.com
Home Page: www.pbp.com

Ed Satell, CEO
Steve Hannaford, Editor

Publishes 10 non-advertising buyer's guides for office equipment (copiers, printers, fax machines and scanners), with objective, unbiased information and evaluations. Each issue includes in-depth write-ups on all manufacturers

and their models, easy to read specifications and price charts to compare models and Editor's Choice selections - awarded to the best machines in each product category
Cost: $149.00
Circulation: 4,000
ISSN: 1084-2055
Founded in 1980
Printed in 4 colors on matte stock

19260 Business Documents
North American Publishing Company
1500 Spring Garden St
Suite 1200
Philadelphia, PA 19130-4094

215-238-5300
800-627-2689
FAX 215-238-5342
E-Mail: tbay@napco.com
Home Page: www.napco.com

Ned S Borowsky, CEO
Brian C Ludwick, Publisher

For professional buyers of forms, labels and electronic systems. Emphasizes internal and external design, production and management of business documents either as traditionally printed forms or electronically generated documents.
Cost: $24.00
42 Pages
Frequency: Monthly
Founded in 1958
Mailing list available for rent
Printed in 2 colors on matte stock

19261 Business Forms, Labels & Systems
North American Publishing Company
1500 Spring Garden St
Suite 1200
Philadelphia, PA 19130-4094

215-238-5300
800-627-2689
FAX 215-238-5342
E-Mail: webmaster@napco.com
Home Page: www.napco.com/

Ned S Borowsky, CEO
Judith Cavaliere, Publisher
Maggie DeWitt, Senior Editor
Cynthia Graham, Associate Editor
Jennifer Hans, Associate Editor

For independent manufacturers and distributors in the forms and systems industry. Emphasizes product applications, marketing and sales ideas and new technology.
Cost: $49.00
Frequency: Monthly
Circulation: 12000
Founded in 1958
Mailing list available for rent
Printed in 4 colors on glossy stock

19262 Business Solutions
Corry Publishing
5539 Peach Street
Erie, PA 16506

814-380-0025
800-290-5460
FAX 814-864-2037
E-Mail: editor@corrypub.com
Home Page: www.corrypub.com

John Clifton, Group Publisher
Melinda Reed-Fadden, Circulation Manager
Dan Schell, Editor
Carrie Brocious, Marketing Director
Jim Roddy, President

Informative magazine including analysis of technological and marketing developments.
Frequency: Monthly
Circulation: 43000
Founded in 1980

19263 Business Technology Association
Buiness Technology Association
12411 Wornall Rd
Suite 200
Kansas City, MO 64145-1212

816-941-3100
800-325-7219
FAX 816-941-2829
E-Mail: info@bta.org
Home Page: www.bta.org
Social Media: *Facebook, Twitter, LinkedIn*

Brent Hoskins, Executive Director
Ron Hulett, Vice President

An international trade organization serving dealers, value added resellers, systems integrators, manufacturers and distributors in the network computing and office automation industries. The association provides educational programs, professional forums, discount services and other benefits designed to help members be more profitable and competitive. BTA members provide business solutions in local area networks, wide area networks, document management and a wide variety of office technologies.
Cost: $30.00
Frequency: Monthly
Circulation: 3500
ISBN: 1-092916-9 -
Founded in 1927
Mailing list available for rent: 1200 names

19264 Digital Information Network
Buyers Laboratory
20 Railroad Avenue
Hackensack, NJ 07601-3309

201-587-0828
FAX 201-488-0461
E-Mail: info@buyerslab.com
Home Page: www.buyerslab.com

Daria Hoffman, Managing Editor

A comprehensive test report service which provides test reports on all the office products BLI evaluates. Subscribers will also get a sixteen page monthly newsletter called Digital Imaging Review, and will recieve a copy of BLI's Multifunctional Specification Guide, Facsimile-Based Products, Copier-Based Products and the Printer Specification Guide, as well as updated specifications throughout the term of their subscription.
Cost: $755.00

19265 Hard Copy Supplies Journal
Lyra Research
PO Box 9143
Newtonville, MA 02640-9143

617-454-2600
FAX 617-454-2601
Home Page: www.lyra.com

Charles LeCompte, Publisher
Frank Stefansson, CEO/President
Jim Forrest, Managing Editor
Jennifer Sprague, Vice President of Sales
Andre Rebelo, Marketing Manager

In-depth coverage of current innovations in marketing materials and media, including ink jet cartridges, toner, paper and film, and monitors the fast-moving corporate developments, such as lawsuits, mergers, distribution, tactics, and marketing campaigns.
Cost: $550.00
Frequency: Monthly
Circulation: 2,000
Founded in 1991

19266 Information Management Magazine
ARMA International

11880 College Blvd
Suite 450
Overland Park, KS 66210

913-341-3808
800-422-2762
FAX 913-341-3742
E-Mail: hq@arma.org
Home Page: www.arma.org

Marilyn Bier, Executive Director
Jody Becker, Associate Editor
Brenda Prowse, Treasurer

The leading source of information on topics and issues central to the management of records and information worldwide. Each issue features insightful articles written by experts in the management of records and information.
Cost: $115.00
Frequency: Bi-monthly
Circulation: 11000
ISSN: 1535-2897
Mailing list available for rent: 9000 names
Printed in 4 colors on glossy stock

19267 Mail: Journal of Communication Distribution
Excelsior Publications
One Millstone Road
Gold Key Box 2425
Milford, PA 18337

570-861-1969
FAX 570-686-3495

Francis P Ruggiero, Publsher
Circulation: 43000

19268 Office Dealer
Quality Publishing
252 N Main Street
Suite 200
Mount Airy, NC 27030-3810

336-783-0000
FAX 336-783-0045
E-Mail: bcomer@os-od.com
Home Page: www.os-od.com/

Richard Kunkel, Publisher
Simon DeGroot, Editorial Director
Bessie Comer, Sales/Advertising Coor
Scott Cullen, Managing Editor
Debbie Hooker, Director of Publishing Services

Information including the latest industry news pertaining to resellers, plus office dealer conventions and other newsworthy events.
Circulation: 17020

19269 Office Solutions
Quality Publishing
252 N Main Street #200
PO Box 1028
Mount Airy, NC 27030-3810

336-783-0000
FAX 336-783-0045
E-Mail: osod@os-od.com
Home Page: www.os-od.com

Richard Kunkel, Publisher
Simon Degroot, Editorial Director
Debbey Hooker, Circulation Manager
Bill Middleton, Marketing Manager
Scott Cullen, Managing Editor

Information on state of the art, survey and overview of articles and product offerings. Emphasis on personal computing, software, telecommunications, personnel and financial management.
Cost: $36.00
Circulation: 81250
Founded in 2003

19270 Office Systems Research Journal
SW Missouri Council of Governments

901 S National Avenue
Springfield, MO 65804

417-836-5000
FAX 417-836-4146
Home Page: www.smsu.edu

Diane May, Executive Director

A journal offering research and news of the office supplies and products industry.
Cost: $35.00
Circulation: 400

19271 Print Solutions Magazine
Document Management Industries Association
433 E Monroe Avenue
Alexandria, VA 22301-1693

703-836-6232
FAX 703-549-4966
Home Page: www.printsolutionsmag.com

Peter L Colaianni CAE, Editor-in-Chief

Source for marketing, management and product information.
Cost: $49.00
276 Pages
Frequency: Monthly
ISSN: 0532-1700
Printed in 4 colors on glossy stock

19272 Recharger Magazine
Recharger Magazine
1050 E Flamingo Rd
Suite N237
Las Vegas, NV 89119-7427

702-438-5557
877-902-9759
FAX 702-873-9671
E-Mail: info@rechargermag.com
Home Page: www.rechargermag.com

Phyllis Gurgevich, Publisher
Amy Turner, Managing Editor
Michael MacDonald, Graphics Director
Sara Feest, Sales Assistant
Monica Miceli, Associate Editor

Information including articles that cover business and marketing, technical updates, association and industry news, and company profiles. Related features focus on the importance of recycling, government legislation, and product comparisons.
Cost: $45.00
Frequency: Monthly
Circulation: 8000

Trade Shows

19273 ARMA International Conference & Expo
ARMA International
11880 College Blvd
Suite 450
Overland Park, KS 66215

913-341-3808
800-422-2762
FAX 913-341-3742
E-Mail: hq@arma.org
Home Page: www.arma.org/conference
Social Media: *Facebook, Twitter, iConference*

Carol Jorgenson, Meetings/Education Coordinator
Wanda Wilson, Senior Manager, Conferences
Elizabeth Zlitni, Exposition Manager

Conference, seminar, workshop, banquet, award ceremony and 175 exhibits of micrographics, optical disk, automated document storage and retrieval systems and more

technology of interest to information professionals.
3500 Attendees
Frequency: Annual
Founded in 1956

19274 American Business Women's Association Convention
9100 Ward Parkway
PO Box 8728
Kansas City, MO 64114

816-361-6621
800-228-0007
FAX 816-361-4991
E-Mail: abwa@abwa.org
Home Page: www.abwa.org

Wendy Mabrey, Corporate Sponsorship Coordinator
Carolyn Elman, Executive Director

One-hundred exhibits of equipment, supplies and services for women in business, seminar and banquet.
2000 Attendees
Frequency: November

19275 American Society for Training & Development Conference & Exposition
American Society for Training & Development
1640 King Street
PO Box 1443
Alexandria, VA 22313-2043

703-683-8100
FAX 703-683-8103
E-Mail: customercare@astd.org
Home Page: www.astd.org

Michael Neff, Executive Director
2000 Attendees

19276 Business Show
INPEX
217 9th Street
Pittsburgh, PA 15222-3506

412-881-1300
800-544-6739
FAX 412-288-4546
E-Mail: info@inventionshow.com
Home Page: www.inventionshow.com/

Nevin Arora, Product Manager

Annual show of 150 exhibits of office furniture, supplies and machines; computers; media; specialty items; financial services; printing services; security systems; entertainment; cellular phones and pagers; sinage; travel agencies; audio-visual equipment and car rental agencies.
5000 Attendees

19277 Business Technology Association
Business Technology Association
12411 Wornall Road
Suite 200
Kansas City, MO 64145-1212

816-941-3100
800-325-7219
FAX 816-941-4838
E-Mail: info@bta.org
Home Page: www.bta.org
Social Media: *Facebook, Twitter, LinkedIn*

Brent Hoskins, Executive Director
Ron Hulett, Vice President
Founded in 1926
Mailing list available for rent: 1200 names

19278 Document World/American Business Equipment and Computer Show
Key Productions

116 Murphy Road
Hartford, CT 06114-2121

860-247-8363

Eldred Codling, Show Manager

Features exhibits of computer software, hardware, supplies and services.
6M Attendees
Frequency: April

19279 National Stationery Show
George Little Management
10 Bank Street
White Plains, NY 10606-1954

914-486-6070
800-272-7469
FAX 914-948-6180
Home Page: www.

Lori Robinson, VP
Kelly Bristol, Assistant Show Manager
George Little II, President

A show for greeting cards and social stationery, writing instruments and home office products, party ware and giftwrap, scrapbooking and craft supplies, albums, frames and much more.
14000 Attendees
Frequency: May

Directories & Databases

19280 ARMA International's Buyers Guide
ARMA International
11880 College Blvd
Suite 450
Overland Park, KS 66215

913-341-3808
800-422-2762
FAX 913-341-3742
E-Mail: hq@arma.org
Home Page: www.arma.org/conference

75-100 companies listed. Free.

19281 Directory of Mail Order Catalogs
Grey House Publishing
4919 Route 22
PO Box 56
Amenia, NY 12501

518-789-8700
800-562-2139
FAX 845-373-6390
E-Mail: books@greyhouse.com
Home Page: www.greyhouse.com
Social Media: *Facebook, Twitter*

Leslie Mackenzie, Publisher
Richard Gottlieb, Editor

The premier source of information on the mail order catalog industry. Covers over 13,000 consumer and business catalog companies with 44 different product chapters including office supplies, stationery and more.
Cost: $395.00
1900 Pages
Frequency: Annual
ISBN: 1-592373-96-8
Founded in 1981

19282 Directory of Mail Order Catalogs - Online Database
Grey House Publishing
4919 Route 22
PO Box 56
Amenia, NY 12501

518-789-8700
800-562-2139
FAX 845-373-6390
E-Mail: gold@greyhouse.com

Home Page: http://gold.greyhouse.com
Social Media: *Facebook, Twitter*

Leslie Mackenzie, Publisher
Richard Gottlieb, Editor

Reach over 10,000 consumer catalog companies in one easy-to-use source with The Directory of Mail Order Catalogs - Online Database. Filled with business-building detail, each company profile gives you the information you need to access that organization quickly and easily. Listings provide key contacts, sales volume, employee size, printing information, circulation, list data, product descriptions and much more.
Frequency: Annual
Founded in 1981

19283 Orion Blue Book: Copier
Orion Research Corporation
14555 N Scottsdale Rd
Suite 330
Scottsdale, AZ 85254-3487

480-951-1114
800-844-0759
FAX 480-951-1117
E-Mail: support@orionbluebook.com
Home Page: www.orionbluebook.com/

Roger Rohrs, Owner

List of manufacturers of copiers and other office equipment.
Cost: $39.00
Frequency: Annual

Industry Web Sites

19284 http://gold.greyhouse.com
G.O.L.D Grey House OnLine Databases

Grey House Publishing's online database platform, GOLD, offers Quick Search, Keyword Search and Expert Search for most business sectors, including office supplies and services makrets. The GOLD platform makes finding the information you need quick and easy - whether you're a novice searcher or an experienced database user. All of Grey House's directory products are available for subscription on the GOLD platform.

19285 www.americanpayroll.org
American Payroll Association

Association of payroll and human resource professionals. Website furthers information exchange and meeting announcements.

19286 www.bfma.org
Business Forms Management Association

For form systems professionals interested in the effective capture distribution and management of information in electronic and paper forms.

19287 www.bifma.org
Business and Institutional Furniture Manufacturers
Association

The voice of the office furniture industry, BIFMA members are manufacturers and suppliers of goods and services to the industry.

19288 www.dmia.org
Document Management Industries
Association

19289 www.greyhouse.com
Grey House Publishing

Authoritative reference directories for most business sectors including office products and services markets. Users can search the online

databases with varied search criteria allowing for custom searches by product category, geographic area, sales volume, keyword, subject and more. Full Grey House catalog and online ordering also available.

19290 www.iopfda.org
Independent Office Products & Furniture
Dealers
Association

Association for independent office product and office furniture dealers. IOPFDA is comprised of the National Office Products Alliance (NOPA) and the Office Furniture Dealers Alliance (OFDA).

19291 www.oprareps.org
Office Products Representatives Association

Provides programs and services that promote the role of the independant manufactures' representative in the various distribution channels within the entire office products industry.

19292 www.sspp.org
Society for Service Professionals in Printing

Individual membership society dedicated to the needs of customer service professionals in the printing industry.

19293 www.theofda.org
Office Furniture Distribution Association

Associations

19294 American Forest & Paper Association
1111 19th St NW
Suite 800
Washington, DC 20036-3652

202-463-2700
800-878-8878
FAX 202-463-2785
E-Mail: info@afandpa.org
Home Page: www.afandpa.org
Social Media: *Facebook, Twitter, LinkedIn, YouTube*

James B. Hannan, Chairman
Doyle R. Simons, 1st Vice Chairman
Alexander Toeldte, 2nd Vice Chairman
Donna A. Harman, President & CEO
Jan A. Poling, Vice President & Secretary

To provide significant value to member companies through outstanding performance in those areas that are key to members' success and where an association can be more effective than individual companies.
Founded in 1993

19295 American Paper Machinery Association
201 Park Washington Ct
Falls Church, VA 22046-4527

703-538-1787
FAX 703-241-5603
E-Mail: apmahq@aol.com
Home Page: www.papermachinery.org

Clay D Tyeryar, Chief Administrative Executive
Judith O Buzzerd, Manager Meetings
Sharon Kelly, Coordinator Member Services

To promote the global common interests, image and business relations of the membership.
35 Members
Founded in 1971

19296 Association of Independent Corrugated Converters
113 S. West Street
3rd floor
Alexandria, VA 22314

703-836-2422
877-836-2422
FAX 703-836-2795
E-Mail: info@aiccbox.org
Home Page: www.aiccbox.org
Social Media: *Facebook, Twitter, LinkedIn, YouTube*

A Steven Young, President
Maria Frustaci, Administrative Director
David Core, CAE, Director Education
Taryn Pyle, Director Meetings
Chris Richards, Webmaster/Systems Manager

Represents and protects, the business interests of the independent sector of the corrugated packaging industry. Dedicated to strengthening the independent's position in the marketplace through programs and publications that empower our members to compete successfully in a rapidly changing industry and an increasingly competitive and global business environment.
750 Members
Founded in 1974

19297 Fibre Box Association
500 Park Boulevard
Suite 985
Itasca, IL 60143

847-364-9600
FAX 847-364-9639
E-Mail: fba@fibrebox.org

Home Page: www.fibrebox.org
Social Media: *LinkedIn*

Bill Hoel, Chairman
Peter Watson, First Vice Chairman
Douglas Bonsik, Second Vice-Chairman
Dennis J. Colley, President
Mike Waite, Immediate Past Chairman

A non-profit association that represents and serves the corrugated industry. It also brings together the North American manufacturers to improve the overall well being of the industry and to provide an array of services that enable member companies to conduct their business more effectively , responsibly and efficiently.
170 Members
Founded in 1940

19298 Foodservice/Packaging Institute
7700 Leesburg Pike
Suite 421
Falls Church, VA 22043

703-592-9889
FAX 703-592-9864
E-Mail: fpi@fpi.org
Home Page: www.fpi.org
Social Media: *Facebook, Twitter, LinkedIn, Blog*

Lynn Dyer, President
Natha Dempsey, VP
Caron Mason, Communications Manager
Jennifer Goldman, Manager

A national association comprised of manufacturers and suppliers of single-use foodservice packaging products.
25 Members
Founded in 1933

19299 Forest Resources Association, Inc.
1901 Pennsylvania Ave. NW
Suite 303
Washington, DC 20006

202-296-3937
FAX 202-296-0562
Home Page: www.forestresources.org
Social Media: *Facebook, Twitter, YouTube*

Deb Hawkinson, President
Neil Ward, Vice President

Promotes sustainable use of forest resources in the interests of its members.

19300 International Corrugated Packaging Foundation
113 S West Street
Alexandria, VA 22314-2858

703-549-8580
FAX 703-549-8670
E-Mail: info@icpfbox.org
Home Page: www.icpfbox.org
Social Media: *Twitter*

Steven Landal, Chairman
Richard M Flaherty, President
Thomas W.H. Walton, Vice Chairman
A Steven Young, Treasurer
Paul Vishny, Secretary

An industry led philantrophic organization dedicated to building a knowledgeable workforce for the corrugated packaging industry.
Founded in 1985

19301 International Council of Forest and Paper Associations

E-Mail: info@icfpa.org
Home Page: www.icfpa.org

Elizabeth de Carvalhaes, President

Worldwide network of forest and paper associations advocates for industry at international level.

19302 International Molded Fiber Association
355 Lexington Avenue
Floor 15
New York, NY 10017ÿ

262-241-0522
FAX 262-241-3766
E-Mail: Alan@IMFA.org
Home Page: www.imfa.org
Social Media: *Facebook, Twitter, LinkedIn*

Cassandra Niesing, Asst. Director
Joseph Grygny, Chairman

Acts as an information center for the molded fiber industry with worldwide membership of users and manufacturers of molded fiber producs. Promotes use of natural and recycled fibers.
Founded in 1996

19303 National Council for Air and Stream Improvement
PO Box 133138
Research Triangle Park, NC 27709-3318

919-941-6400
FAX 919-941-6401
E-Mail: ryeske@ncasi.org
Home Page: www.ncasi.org

NCASI's mission is to serve the forest products industry as a center of excellence for providing technical information and scientific research needed to achieve the industry's environmental goals and principles.
Founded in 1943

19304 National Paper Trade Association
330 North Wabash Avenue
Suite 2000
Chicago, IL 60611

312-321-4092
800-355-6782
FAX 312-673-6736
E-Mail: NPTA@goNPTA.com
Home Page: www.gonpta.com
Social Media: *Facebook, Twitter, YouTube*

Greg Savage, Chairman
Donald C Clampitt, First Vice Chairman
Travis M. Mlakar, Second Vice Chairman
William Frohlich, President
Hilton Maze, Treasurer

Supports all those professionals in the paper, packaging and allied products distribution industries. Publishes monthly magazine.
2000 Members
Founded in 1903

19305 National Paperbox Association
1901 Pennsylvania Avenue NW
Suite 1508
Washington, DC 20006

202-466-7252
FAX 413-747-7777
E-Mail: npahq@paperbox.org
Home Page: www.paperbox.org
Social Media: *Facebook, Twitter, LinkedIn, YouTube*

Ben Markens, President
Lou Kornet, Vice President
Kim Guarnaccia, Director of Marketing
Brian Chaisson, Director of Industry Benchmarking
Jennie Markens, Director of General Leaders

Serves as the voice of the paperbox and packaging industry. Also represents the concerns of boxmaker nationally, internationally and at the local level through its Regional Divisions. Publishes bi-monthly magazine and holds an annual convention.
100 Members
Founded in 1839

19306 Paper Distribution Council
National Paper Trade Association
330 North Wabash Avenue
Suite 2000
Chicago, IL 60611

312-321-4092
FAX 312-673-4092
E-Mail: NPTA@goNPTA.com
Home Page: www.gonpta.com
Social Media: *Facebook, Twitter, YouTube*

Greg Savage, Chairman
Donald C Clampitt, First Vice Chairman
Travis M. Mlakar, Second Vice Chairman
William Frohlich, President
Hilton Maze, Treasurer

Association for paper, packaging and applied
products distribution channels.
35 Members
ISBN: 1-092807-3 -
Founded in 1958

**19307 Paper Industry Management
Association**
15 Technology Parkway South
Norcross, GA 30092

770-209-7230
FAX 770-209-7359
E-Mail: mcornell@pimaweb.org
Home Page: www.pimaweb.com
Social Media: *Facebook, Twitter, Youtube*

Ralph W Feck, President
Terry M Gallagher, Regional VP
Jim Weir, Executive VP/COO
Julie Weldon, Senior Manager
Patrick Andrus, Marketing Coordinator

Contributes to the strength of the international
pulp and paper community by providing the
means for our members to address relevant industry issues and to develop their management
and leadership skills.
4500 Members
Founded in 1919

**19308 Paper Shipping Sack Manufacturers
Association**
5050 Blue Church Road
Coopersburg, PA 18036

610-282-6845
FAX 610-282-1577
E-Mail: admin@pssma.org
Home Page: www.pssma.com

Richard E. Storat, President
Ross Barett, Chairman
Donald P Belmont, Vice Chairman

Provides its member companies with programs
and services which further the industry's objectives and in doing so promote and enhance the
welfare of the industry.
45 Members
Founded in 1933

19309 Paperboard Packaging Council
1350 Main Street
Suite 1508
Springfield, MA 01103-1670

413-686-9191
FAX 413-747-7777
E-Mail: paperboardpackaging@ppcnet.org
Home Page: www.ppcnet.org
Social Media: *Facebook, Twitter, LinkedIn,
YouTube*

Ben Markens, President
Lou Kornet, Vice President

Members are companies making folding cartons. Provides publications and instructional
materials on the paper industry and recycling.
92 Members
Founded in 1929

**19310 Technical Association of the Pulp &
Paper Industry**
15 Technology Parkway South
Norcross, GA 30092

770-446-1400
800-322-8686
FAX 770-446-6947
E-Mail: webmaster@tappi.org
Home Page: www.tappi.org

Larry N Montague, CEO
Chris Luettgen, Chair
Paul R. Durocher, Vice Chair

To engage the people and resources of our association in providing technically sound solutions to the workplace problems and
opportunities that challenge our current and
future members.
12000 Members
ISSN: 0734-1415
Founded in 1915

**19311 United Paperworkers International
Union**
33 Gilmer Street SE
PO Box 3967
Atlanta, GA 30303-3202

404-413-2000
FAX 404-651-4314
E-Mail: libdgg@langate.gsu.edu
Home Page: www.library.gsu.edu
Social Media: *Facebook, Twitter, LinkedIn,
YouTube, Instagram, Flickr, Vi*

Mike Dees, President

Bestows awards and conducts training seminars.
Founded in 1972

Newsletters

**19312 American Forest & Paper Association
Report**
American Forest & Paper Association
1111 19th St NW
Suite 800
Washington, DC 20036-3652

202-463-2700
FAX 202-463-2785
E-Mail: info@afandpa.org
Home Page: www.afandpa.org

Covers events of the paper, wood and forest industry. Distribution is limited to association
members only.
Cost: $1200.00
4 Pages
Frequency: Weekly
Founded in 1993

19313 Conservatree Greenline
Greenline Publications
PO Box 590780
San Francisco, CA 94159-780

415-386-8646
FAX 415-391-7890
Home Page: www.conservatree.com

Alan Davis, Founder/Publisher
Susan Kinsella, Editor

Reports on efforts and achievements by busi-
nesses on the environmental front.
Cost: $59.00
Circulation: 25000
Founded in 1976

19314 Essential Resources, LLC
45 S Park Pl
Suite 330
Morristown, NJ 07960-3924

908-832-6979
FAX 908-832-6970

Newsletters for plastic, chemical, pharmaceutical, and packaging industries.
5-15 Pages

19315 Official Board Markets
Advanstar Communications
2835 N Sheffield Avenue
Suite 226
Chicago, IL 60657-9213

312-553-8922
FAX 312-553-8929
Home Page: www.packaging-online.com

Mark Arzoumanian, Editor-in-Chief
Esther Durkalski, Managing Editor

Covers the corrugated container and folding
carton converting industries.
Cost: $180.00
24 Pages
Frequency: Weekly
Circulation: 5900
Founded in 1915
Printed in on glossy stock

19316 Seaboard Bulletin
International Paper
PO Box 1200
Bucksport, ME 04416-1200

207-469-1700
FAX 207-469-1705

David Bailey, President
Paper industry news.

Magazines & Journals

19317 Asia Pacific PaperMaker
Paper Industry Management Association
4700 West Lake Avenue
Glenview, IL 60025-1485

847-375-6860
FAX 877-527-5973
E-Mail: info@pimaweb.org
Home Page: www.pima-online.org

Jim Weir, Executive VP/CEO
Patrick Andrus, Marketing Coordinator
Patrick Filippelli, Sales Manager
Sarah Walsh, Administrative Assistant
Mary Cornell, Account Manager
Founded in 1919

19318 Board Converting News
NV Business Publishers Corporation
43 Main St
Avon By the Sea, NJ 07717-1051

732-502-0500
FAX 732-502-9606
E-Mail: tvilardi@NVPublications.com
Home Page: www.nvpublications.com

Ted Vilardi, Owner
Jim Curley, Editor-in-Chief
Robyn Smith, Executive Publisher
Gail Kalina, Production Manager
Dan Brunton, Managing Director

News for the corrugated box and folding carton
industry along with box and carton transacted
prices.
Cost: $180.00
140 Pages
Frequency: Weekly

19319 Converting Magazine
Reed Business Information

2000 Clearwater Dr
Oak Brook, IL 60523-8809

630-574-0825
FAX 630-288-8781
E-Mail: psaran@reedbusiness.com
Home Page: www.reedbusiness.com

Jeff Greisch, President
Mark Spaulding, Editor-in-Chief
Steve Reiss, VP
Frequency: Monthly
Circulation: 4000

19320 Distribution Sales & Management

National Paper Trade Association
500 B1 - County Boulevard
Suite 200E
Farmingdale, NY 11735-5402

631-777-2223
FAX 631-777-2224
Home Page: www.goNPTA.com

Debra Ray, Editor
Bill Fronlinch, Publisher

The business magazine for the paper, packaging and allied products distribution channel.
Cost: $49.00
48 Pages
Frequency: Monthly
Circulation: 17000
ISSN: 1092-8073
Founded in 1959
Printed in on matte stock

19321 European PaperMaker

Paper Industry Management Association
1699 Wall Street
Suite 212
Mount Prospect, IL 60056

847-699-1706
FAX 847-956-0520
Home Page: www.pima-online.org

Mary Cornell, Account Manager

19322 International Paper Board Industry

Brunton Publications & NV Public
43 Main Street
Avon By The Sea, NJ 07717-1051

732-502-0500
FAX 732-502-9606
E-Mail: jcurley@NVPublications.com
Home Page: www.nvpublications.com

Mike Brunton, Publisher
Jim Curley, Editor-in-Chief
Gail Kalina, Production Manager
Tom Vilardi, President
Dan Brunton, Managing Director

Information on corrugated paper and converting industry, encompassing news and production worldwide.
Cost: $60.00
Frequency: Monthly
Circulation: 10021

19323 Latin American PaperMaker

Paper Industry Management Association
1699 Wall Street
Suite 212
Mount Prospect, IL 60056

847-956-0250
FAX 847-956-0520
E-Mail: info@pima-online.org
Home Page: www.pima-online.org

Ralph W. Feck, President
Jim Weir, COO/Executive VP
Patrick Andrus, Marketing Coordinator
Patrick Filippelli, Sales Manager
Sarah Walsh, Administrative Assistant
Founded in 1919

19324 Mill Trade Journal's Recycling Markets

NV Business Publishers Corporation
43 Main St
Avon By the Sea, NJ 07717-1051

732-502-0500
800-962-3001
FAX 732-502-9606
E-Mail: advertising@NVPublications.com
Home Page: www.nvpublications.com

Ted Vilardi, Owner
Roy Bradbrook, Editor
Jim Curley, Editor-in-Chief
Gail Kalina, Production Manager
Robyn Smith, Executive Publisher

Information on recycling mills paper stock, scrap metal and plastics brokers and dealers used by the municipal governments and private organizations as a basis for letting contracts.
Cost: $130.00
Frequency: Fortnightly
Circulation: 3625
Founded in 1984
Printed in 2 colors on matte stock

19325 NPTA Distribution Sales & Management

111 Great Neck Road
Suite 418
Great Neck, NY 11021-5402

516-829-3070
FAX 516-829-3074

19326 North American PaperMaker

Paper Industry Management Association
4700 West Lake Avenue
Glenview, IL 60025-1485

847-375-6860
FAX 877-527-5973
E-Mail: info@pimaweb.org
Home Page: www.pima-online.org

Jim Weir, Executive VP/COO
Pam Oddi, Administrative Assistant
Patrick Filippelli, Sales Manager
Patrick Andrus, Marketing Coordinator
Julie Weldon, Senior Manager
Founded in 1919

19327 Paper Age Magazine

O'Brien Publications
20 Schofield Rd
Suite 200B
Cohasset, MA 02025-1922

781-749-5255
FAX 781-749-5896
E-Mail: info@paperage.com
Home Page: www.paperage.com

John O'Brien, Owner
John O'Brien, Managing Editor
Michael O'Brien, Publisher

For management and supervisory personnel of pulp, paper and paperboard mills. Tabloid-sized magazine covering the pulp, paper and converting industry, with a unique mix of timely and insightful coverage of corporate strategies, mill operations, technological innovations, industry issues, as well as analysis of the latest production and marketing trends.
Cost: $90.00
Circulation: 36156
Founded in 1884

19328 Paper Industry Equipment Magazine

PO Box 5675
Montgomery, AL 36103

604-264-1158
888-224-6611
FAX 604-264-1367

E-Mail: info@paperindustrymag.com
Home Page: www.paperindustrymag.com

Tim Shaddick, Publisher
Peter N Williamson, Editor

Services and equipment for the pulp/paper industry.
Cost: $12.00
32 Pages
Circulation: 1900
Founded in 1984
Printed in 4 colors on glossy stock

19329 Paper Stock Report: News and Trends of the Paper Recycling Markets

McEntee Media Corporation
13727 Holland Road
Brook Park, OH 44142

216-362-7979
FAX 216-362-6553
Home Page: www.recycle.cc

Ken McEntee, President

Covers news and trends of the scrap paper markets.
Cost: $115.00
Frequency: BiWeekly
Founded in 1990

19330 Paper, Paperboard and Wood Pulp Monthly Statistical Summary

American Forest & Paper Association
1111 19th St NW
Suite 800
Washington, DC 20036-3652

202-463-2700
800-878-8878
FAX 202-463-2700
E-Mail: info@afandpa.org
Home Page: www.afandpa.org

Donna Harman, CEO
Henson Moore, President

For the pulp and paper industry.
Cost: $435.00
Frequency: Monthly
Founded in 1878

19331 Recycled Paper News

McEntee Media Corporation
9815 Hazelwood Ave
Strongsville, OH 44149-2305

440-238-6603
FAX 440-238-6712
E-Mail: info@recycle.cc
Home Page: www.recycle.cc

Ken Mc Entee, Owner

Coverage of markets and environmental issues related to recycled paper and evironmentally friendly paper making process.
Cost: $235.00
Frequency: Monthly
Founded in 1990

19332 Solutions! for People, Processes and Paper

TAPPI and PIMA
15 Technology Parkway S
Norcross, GA 30092

770-446-1400
800-322-8686
FAX 770-446-6947
E-Mail: webmaster@tappi.org
Home Page: www.tappi.org

Larry N Montague, CEO
Thomas J Garland, Vice Chairman

19333 TAPPI Journal

Technical Association of the Pulp & Paper Industry

15 Technology Parkway S
Norcross, GA 30092

770-446-1400
800-322-8686
FAX 770-446-6947
E-Mail: webmaster@tappi.org
Home Page: www.tappi.org

Larry N Montague, CEO
Thomas J Garland, Vice Chairman

Serves domestic and international pulp, paper, paperboard, packaging and converting industries; manufacturers and suppliers of machinery, equipment, chemicals and other material.
Cost: $350.00
130 Pages
Frequency: Monthly
Circulation: 40637
ISSN: 0734-1415
Founded in 1915
Printed in 4 colors on glossy stock

19334 Walden's Paper Report

Walden-Mott Corporation
225 N Franklin Tpke
Ramsey, NJ 07446-1600

201-818-8630
888-292-5336
FAX 201-818-8720
E-Mail: editorial@walden-mott.com
Home Page: www.waldenmott.com

Alfred F Walden, President
Linda Colhen, Director of Operations
Kirk Hardy, Director of Operations

Reports on company expansions and general financial notes on the manufacturers, as well as personnel changes and appointments. Concise review of news on the North American paper industry.
Cost: $240.00
8 Pages
Circulation: 500
Founded in 1884

Trade Shows

19335 Annual Information Technology Conference

PIMA-Paper Industry Management Association
4700 West Lake Avenue
Glenview, IL 60025-1485

847-375-6860
FAX 877-527-5973
E-Mail: info@pimaweb.org
Home Page: www.pimaweb.org

Carol Waugh, Meetings Manager

Three-day conference to bring together IT and process control professionals from around the world to share their knowledge of information technology in the pulp and paper industry and to promote systems applications. The only IT conference planned for and by IT professionals.
500 Attendees
Frequency: Annual, April

19336 International Bioenergy and Bioproducts Conference (IBBC)

Technical Association of the Pulp & Paper Industry
15 Technology Parkway S
Norcross, GA 30092

770-446-1400
800-322-8686
FAX 770-446-6947

E-Mail: webmaster@tappi.org
Home Page: www.tappi.org

Norman F. Marsolan, Chair
Thomas J. Garland, Vice Chair
Larry N. Montague, President & CEO

Focusing on technical advancements and commercialization of bioconversion technologies that leverage the forest products manufacturing infrastructure and will include technical presentations, expert panels, case studies, and reports from projects that address feedstock and harvesting improvements to increase yield and quality of biomass, and much more.
500 Attendees
Frequency: Annual/October

19337 National Paper Trade Association Convention Expo

National Paper Trade Association
111 Great Neck Road
Suite 418
Great Neck, NY 11021-5497

516-829-3070
FAX 312-673-6736
E-Mail: bill@goNPTA.com
Home Page: www.gonpta.com

William Frohlich, President

Annual convention of 135 manufacturers, suppliers and distributors of paper products, including packaging materials, health care disposables, industrial and retail packaging supplies, sanitary supplies and computer equipment.
3000 Attendees
Frequency: Annual September
Founded in 1903

19338 National Stationery Show

George Little Management
10 Bank Street
White Plains, NY 10606-1954

914-486-6070
800-272-7469
FAX 914-948-6180
Home Page: www.

Lori Robinson, VP
Kelly Bristol, Assistant Show Manager
George Little II, President

A show for greeting cards and social stationery, writing instruments and home office products, party ware and giftwrap, scrapbooking and craft supplies, albums, frames and much more.
14000 Attendees
Frequency: May

19339 National Trade Association Paper Plastics Allied Products Exposition

National Paper Trade Association
111 Great Neck Road
Suite 418
Great Neck, NY 11021-5402

516-829-3070
E-Mail: bill@goNPTA.com
Home Page: www.gonpta.com

William Frohlich, President

Industrial and retail packaging, computer products and supplies and equipment. 30 booths.
7M Attendees
Frequency: October

19340 Paper, Plastics and Allied Products Exposition

National Paper Trade Association
111 Great Neck Road
Suite 418
Great Neck, NY 11021-5497

516-829-3070
FAX 516-829-3074
Home Page: www.gonpta.com

William Frohlich, President

Annual show and exhibits of industrial papers, plastics and plastic products allied to the paper industry.
7000 Attendees

19341 Pulp and Paper

Glahe International
PO Box 2460
Germantown, MD 20875-2460

301-515-0012
FAX 301-515-0016

Exhibits of equipment, supplies and services for the pulp and paper industries.

Directories & Databases

19342 Directory of Corrugated Plants

Fibre Box Association
2850 Golf Road
Suite 412
Rolling Meadows, IL 60008

847-364-9600
FAX 847-364-9639
E-Mail: shuske@fibrebox.org
Home Page: www.fibrebox.org

Sharlene Huske

Lists companies and their related plant facilities that manufacture corrugated and solid fiber paperboard products in North America.
Cost: $200.00

19343 Grade Finder's Competitive Grade Finder

Grade Finders
622 Exton Commons
Exton, PA 19341

610-524-7070
FAX 610-524-8912
E-Mail: info@gradefinders.com
Home Page: www.gradefinders.com

Mark A Subers, President
Phyllis Subers, Office Manager

List of about 5500 manufacturers and distributors of paper. Also lists 6,000 grades of paper competitive classification.
Cost: $60.00
700 Pages
Frequency: Annual April
Circulation: 13,000
ISBN: 0-929502-14-0
Founded in 1967
Printed in one color on matte stock

19344 Grade Finder's Paper Buyers Encyclopedia

Grade Finders
622 Exton Commons
Exton, PA 19341

610-524-7070
FAX 610-524-8912
E-Mail: info@gradefinders.com
Home Page: www.gradefinders.com

Mark Subers, President

A list of about 6,700 manufacturers, converters and suppliers to the paper industry. In addition, it lists over 4,000 grades of paper categorized into competitive classifications showing each grades rating, opacity, color availability, etc. Also contains an extensive how-to buy paper section.
Cost: $150.00
530 Pages
Frequency: Annual
Circulation: 7000

19345 National Institute of Packaging and Handling Logistics Engineers

5903 Ridgeway Drive
Grand Prairie, TX 75052

817-466-7490
866-464-7453
FAX 570-523-0606
E-Mail: admin@niphle.com
Home Page: www.niphle.com
Social Media: *Facebook, Twitter, LinkedIn*

Richard D Owen, Executive Director

An assemblage of professionals whose interest in the complex and diverse practice of distribution and logistics is a common bond.

19346 PIMA Buyers Guide

Paper Industry Management Association
4700 W Lake Avenue
Glenview, IL 60025-1485

847-375-6860
FAX 877-527-5973
E-Mail: info@pimaweb.org
Home Page: www.pimaweb.org

Jospeh Agnew, Editor
Pam Oddi, Editorial Support

Directory aimed at the paper and pulp industry offering various information on manufacturers of chemicals and supplies used in the manufacturing of paper.
Cost: $120.00
60 Pages
Frequency: Annual
Circulation: 2,000
Printed in on matte stock

19347 Rauch Guide to the US and Canadian Pulp & Paper Industry

Grey House Publishing
4919 Route 22
PO Box 56
Amenia, NY 12501

518-789-8700
800-562-2139
FAX 845-373-6390
E-Mail: books@greyhouse.com
Home Page: www.greyhouse.com
Social Media: *Facebook, Twitter*

Leslie Mackenzie, Publisher
Richard Gottlieb, Editor

Provides current market information and trends; industry economics and government regulations; company share data for each of the leading product categories; technology and raw material information; industry sources of further data; and unique profiles of 500+ pulp and paper manufacturers, a section which includes all known companies with pulp and paper sales at or over $15 million annually.
Cost: $595.00
400 Pages
ISBN: 1-592371-31-0
Founded in 1981

19348 TAPPI Membership Directory and Company Guide

Technical Association of the Pulp & Paper Industry
15 Technology Parkway S
Norcross, GA 30092

770-446-1400
800-322-8686
FAX 770-446-6947
E-Mail: webmaster@tappi.org
Home Page: www.tappi.org

Larry N Montague, CEO
Thomas J Garland, Vice Chairman

About 35,000 member executives, managers, engineers, technologists and superintendents in the pulp, paper, packaging, converting,

non-wovens and allied industries.
Cost: $140.00
Frequency: October

19349 Walden's ABC Guide and Paper Production Yearbook

Walden-Mott Corporation
225 N Franklin Tpke
Ramsey, NJ 07446-1600

201-818-8630
FAX 201-818-8720
Home Page: www.waldenmott.com

Alfred F Walden, President
Kirk Hardy, Director of Operations

Offers a large list of manufacturers and suppliers of printing papers.
Cost: $117.50
300 Pages
Frequency: Annual January

Industry Web Sites

19350 http://gold.greyhouse.com

G.O.L.D Grey House OnLine Databases

Grey House Publishing's online database platform, GOLD, offers Quick Search, Keyword Search and Expert Search for most business sectors including paper and allied products markets. The GOLD platform makes finding the information you need quick and easy - whether you're a novice searcher or an experienced database user. All of Grey House's directory products are available for subscription on the GOLD platform.

19351 www.afandpa.org

American Forest and Paper Association

Serves forest, paper, paperboard and wood products packaging industry

19352 www.fibrebox.org

Fibre Box Association

For national corrigated manufacturers.

19353 www.fpi.org

Foodservice & Packaging Institute

Manufacturers, suppliers and distributors of one-time use products used for food service, as well as packaging products made from paper, plastic, aluminum and other materials. Membership dues based on sales.

19354 www.gonpta.com

National Paper Trade Association

Association for paper, packaging and applied products distribution channel.

19355 www.greyhouse.com

Grey House Publishing

Authoritative reference directories for most business sectors including paper and allied products markets. Users can search the online databases with varied search criteria allowing for custom searches by product category, geographic area, sales volume, keyword, subject and more. Full Grey House catalog and online ordering also available.

19356 www.tappi.org

Technical Association of the Pulp & Paper Industry

Associations

19357 Actors Equity Association
165 W 46th St
New York, NY 10036-2500

212-869-8530
FAX 212-719-9815
Home Page: www.actorsequity.org

Alan Eisenberg, CEO
Mark Zimmerman, President
David Lotz, National Director of
Communications
Mary Lou Westerfield, Natioanl Director
Policy
Flora Stamatiades, National Director
Organizing

A labor union that represents Actors and Stage
Managers in the United States. Seeks to advance, promote and foster the art of live theatre
as an essential component of our society. Negotiates wages and working conditions and provides a wide range of benefits, including health
and pension plans.
45000 Members
Founded in 1913

19358 African Performing Arts Association
PO Box 660573
Atlanta, GA 30366

E-Mail: info@africanperformingarts.org
Home Page: www.africanperformingarts.org

Founded in 2001

19359 Alternate ROOTS
115 Martin Luther King Jr Dr
Suite 200
Atlanta, GA 30303

404-577-1079
FAX 404-577-7991
E-Mail: ennis@alternateroots.org
Home Page: www.alternateroots.org
Social Media: *Facebook, Twitter, Flickr*

**19360 American Alliance for Theatre and
Education**
4908 Auburn Avenue
Bethesda, MD 20814-3474

301-200-1944
FAX 301-280-1682
E-Mail: info@aate.com
Home Page: www.aate.com
Social Media: *Facebook, Twitter, LinkedIn,
RSS*

Gary Minyard, President
Kelly Prestel, Treasurer
Amy P.Jenson, Advocacy Director
Jeremy Kisling, Communications Director
Mitch Mattson, Planning Director

The national voice for theatre and education,
representing artists and educators serving
young people in theatre and education. Its
members play a vital role in advocating for the
interests of children who benefit from theatre
in their communities and classrooms. AATE
embraces diversity and encourages inclusion of
all races, social classes, ages, genders, religions, sexual orientations, national
organizations and abilities.
700 Members
Founded in 1986

**19361 American Association of Community
Theatre**
1300 Gendy St Forth Worth
Lago Vista, TX 76107

817-732-3177
866-687-2228
FAX 817-732-3178
E-Mail: info@aact.org

Home Page: www.aact.org
Social Media: *Facebook, Twitter, LinkedIn*

Julie Crawford, Executive Director
Linda Lee, President
Gary Walker, Executive VP
Frank Peot, Secretary
Tim Jebsen, Treasurer

The national voice of community theatre, representing the interests of its members and over
7,000 theatres across the US and with the
armed services overseas. Its mission is to foster
the encouragement and development of, and
commitment to, the highest standards by community theatres, including standards of excellence for production, management, governance,
community relations and service.
1800 Members
Founded in 1986

19362 American Composers Forum
75 West 5th Street
Suite 522
Saint Paul, MN 55102-1439

651-228-1407
FAX 651-291-7978
E-Mail: lhoeschler@gmail.com
Home Page: www.composersforum.org
Social Media: *Facebook, Twitter*

Mary Ellen Childs, Chair
Patrick Castillo, Vice Chair
Dan Thomas, Vice Chair
David Ranheim, Secretary
Sam Hsu, Treasurer
2000 Members
Founded in 1973

19363 American Dance Therapy Association
10632 Little Patuxent Pkwy
Suite 108
Columbia, MD 21044-3263

410-997-4040
FAX 410-997-4048
E-Mail: info@adta.org
Home Page: www.adta.org
Social Media: *Facebook, Twitter, Pinterest,
YouTube*

Gloria Farrow, Manager
Jody Wager, President
Gloria J Farrow, Operations Director
Meghan Dempsey, Treasurer
Gail Wood, Secretary

Professional organization of dance movement
therapists, with members both nationally and
internationally; offers training, research findings, and a newsletter. Holds annual
conference.
1.1M Members
Founded in 1966

19364 American Disc Jockey Association
20118 N 67th Avenue
Suite 300-605
Glendale, AZ 85308

888-723-5776
888-723-5776
FAX 866-310-4676
E-Mail: office@adja.org
Home Page: www.adja.org
Social Media: *Facebook, Twitter, YouTube*

Rob Snyder, Director

An association of professional mobile entertainers. Encourages success for its members
through continuous education, camaraderie,
and networking. The primary goal is to educate
Disc Jockeys so that each member acts
ethically and responsibly.

**19365 American Federation of Musicians of
the United States and Canada**
1501 Broadway
Suite 600
New York, NY 10036-5501

212-869-1330
FAX 212-764-6134
E-Mail: info@afm.org
Home Page: www.afm.org
Social Media: *Facebook, Twitter, YouTube*

Thomas Lee, President
Linda Patterson, Executive Secreatry to
President

AFM is an association of professional musicians united through their locals so that they
can live and work in dignity; produce work that
will be fulfilling and compensated fairly; have
a meaningful voice in decisions that affect
them; have the opportunity to develop their talents and skills; whose collective voice and
power will be realized in a democratic and progressive union; and who oppose the forces of
exploitation through their union solidarity.
10K Members
Founded in 1896

**19366 American Indian Registry for the
Performing Arts**
1717 N Highland
Suite 614
Los Angeles, CA 90028

213-962-6574
Home Page:
www.afn.org/~native/orgnztns.htm

Organization of American Indian performers
and technical personnel in the entertainment
field.

19367 American Institute of Organ Builders
PO Box 35306
Canton, OH 44735

330-806-9011
E-Mail: robert_sullivan@pipeorgan.org
Home Page: www.pipeorgan.org
Social Media: *Twitter*

Philip Parkey, President
Michael Lauffer, Vice President
Louis E Patterson, Secretary
Charles R Eames, Treasurer
Joseph O'Donnell, Secretary

Sponsors training seminars, quarterly journal
and annual convention for pipe organ builders
and service technicians.
385 Members
Founded in 1974
*Mailing list available for rent: 350 names at
$250 per M*

19368 American Institute of Organbuilders
PO Box 35306
Canton, OH 44735

330-806-9011
E-Mail: robert_sullivan@pipeorgan.org
Home Page: www.pipeorgan.org
Social Media: *Facebook*

Philip Parkey, President
Michael Lauffer, Vice President
Robert Sullivan, Executive Secretary
Joseph O'Donnell, Secretary
Charles R. Eames, Treasurer
Founded in 1974

19369 Americans for the Arts
1000 Vermont Avenue, NW
6th Floor
Washington, DC 20005

202-371-2830
FAX 202-371-0424
Home Page: www.americansforthearts.org

Social Media: *Facebook, Twitter, LinkedIn, YouTube, Pinterest*

Abel Lopez, Chair
Ramona Baker, Vice Chair
C. Kendric Fergeson, Immediate Past Chair
Michael Spring, Secretary
Julie Muraco, Treasurer
Founded in 1960

19370 Associated Pipe Organ Builders of America

P.O. Box 8268
Erie, PA 8268

800-473-5270
800-473-5270
Home Page: www.apoba.com

Bob Rusczyk, Executive Director
Richard Parsons, President
Paul Lytle, Vice President
Randall Dyer, Secretary
Seth Marshall, Treasurer

A professional association of North American firms engaged in building traditional pipe organs. Members are a select group of organbuilders who have passed stringent membership requirements which include commitment to principles regarding the use of electronic technology in organ building.
27 Members

19371 Association for Theatre in Higher Education

1000 Westgate Dr.
Ste. 252
St. Paul, MN 55114

651-288-3430
800-918-9216
FAX 651-290-2266
E-Mail: info@athe.org
Home Page: www.athe.org
Social Media: *Facebook*

Patricia Ybarra, President
Terry Brino Dean, Secretary
Nina Lenoir, Treasurer

ATHE serves the interests of its diverse individual and organization members. Its vision is to advocate for the field of theatre and performance in higher education. It serves as an intellectual and artistic center for producing new knowledge about theatre and performance-related disciplines. cultivating vital alliances with other scholarly and creative disciplines, linking with professional and community-based theatres, and promoting access and equity.
1700 Members
Founded in 1986

19372 Association of Arts Administration Educators

Bolz Center for Arts Administration
188 Hanford Street
Columbus, OH 43206

312-469-0795
FAX 608-265-2735
E-Mail: info@artsadministration.org
Home Page: www.artsadministration.org
Social Media: *Facebook, Twitter, RSS*

Andrew Taylor, President/Director
John McCann, VP
Phyllis Johnson, Treasurer
Stephen Boyle, Secretary

The Association of Administration Educators (AAAE) is an international organization incorporated as a nonprofit institution within the United States. Its mission is to represent college and university graduate and undergraduate programs in the arts administration, encompassing training in the management of visual, performing, literary, media, cultural and arts service organizations.
Founded in 1975

19373 Association of Hispanic Arts

P.O.Box 1169
El Barrio, NY 10029

212-876-1242
888-876-1240
FAX 212-876-1285
E-Mail: informacion@latinoarts.org
Home Page: www.latinoarts.org

Nicholas L Arture, Executive Director
Julia L Gutierrez-Rivera, Program Officer/Arts Service Coord.
Crystal Chaparro, Office Assistant
Gregory Castro, Comptroller
Brenda L Jiminez, Board Chair

A nonprofit arts service organization serving the Latino arts and cultural community. AHA was established out of the need to create funding and presenting opportunities for individual Latino artists and cultural organizations whose contributions were unrecognized and whose efforts were underserved by mainstream public and private institutions.
Founded in 1975

19374 Association of Performing Arts Presenters

1211 Connecticut Ave NW
Suite 200
Washington, DC 20036-2716

202-833-2787
888-820-2787
FAX 202-833-1543
E-Mail: info@artspresenters.org
Home Page: www.apap365.org/
Social Media: *Facebook, Twitter, YouTube*

Sandra Gibson, President
Dr. Michael Blachly, Chair
Brain Jose, Vice Chairman
Nicole Borrelli Hearn, Vice Chair
Todd Wetzel, Treasurer

A national membership and advocacy organization dedicated to bringing performing artists and audiences together.
1900 Members
Founded in 1957

19375 Broadcast Music Incorporated BMI

7 World Trade Center
250 Greenwich Street
New York, NY 10007-0030

212-220-3000
FAX 212-246-2163
E-Mail: newyork@bmi.com
Home Page: www.bmi.com
Social Media: *Facebook, Twitter, LinkedIn, YouTube, Pinterest, RSS, Insta*

Del Bryant, CEO
John E Cody, COO/Executive VP

American performing rights organization that represents approximately 300,000 songwriters, composers and music publishers in all genres of music. The nonprofit company collects license fees on behalf of those American creators it represents, as well as thousands of creators from around the world who chose BMI for representation in the US. These fees are then distributed as royalties to the writers, composers and copyright holders it represents.
300m Members
Founded in 1939

19376 Chinese Music Society of North America

PO Box 5275
Woodridge, IL 60517-0275

630-910-1551
FAX 630-910-1561
Home Page: www.chinesemusic.net

Sin-Yan Shen, President
Kok-Koon Ng, VP

Yuan-Yuan Lee, Executive Director
Billie Jefferson, Artistic Administrator
Der-Tung Yuan, Membership

A national nonprofit organization founded to increase and diffuse the knowledge of Chinese music and performing arts. Today it has grown to become the national association of Chinese musicians and scholars and National and International organization specializing in Research and Educational Material in English concerning Music/Theater/Dance and Musical Instruments from China and Non-Western Cultures.
Founded in 1969

19377 Chorus America

P.O. Box 2646
Suite 310
Arlington, VA 22202-0646

202-331-7577
FAX 202-331-7599
E-Mail: webmaster@chorusamerica.org
Home Page: www.chorusamerica.org
Social Media: *Facebook, Twitter, YouTube, Google+*

Rollo Dilworth, Chairman
Gayle. M Ober, Immediate Past Chairman
Mitch Menchaca, Interim CEO
Michael McCarthy, Treasurer
Mary Lyons, Secretary
2000 Members
Founded in 1977

19378 Classical Action

165 W 46th St
Suite 1300
New York, NY 10036-2514

212-997-7717
FAX 212-840-0551
E-Mail: classicalaction@broadwaycares.org
Home Page: www.classicalaction.org
Social Media: *Facebook, Twitter*

Charles Hamlen, Founding Director
Chris Kenney, Associate Director

Since 1993, Classical Action has provided a unified voice for all those within the performing arts community to help combat HIV/AIDS and the devastating effects of this epidemic.
Founded in 1993

19379 Conductors Guild

719 Twinridge Ln
Richmond, VA 23235

804-553-1378
FAX 804-553-1876
E-Mail: guild@conductorsguild.org
Home Page: www.conductorsguild.org
Social Media: *Facebook, Twitter, LinkedIn*

Gordon Johnson, President
Amanda Burton Winger, Executive Director
Erin Freeman, VP
Christopher Blair, Treasurer
David Leibowitz, Secretary

The Conductors Guild is the only music service organization devoted exclusively to the advancement of the art of conducting and to serving the artistic and professional needs of conductors.
1850+ Members
Founded in 1975

19380 Congress on Research in Dance

SUNY College of Brockport
257 Charles Street
Cambridge, MA 02141-2022

205-823-5517
FAX 205-823-2760
E-Mail: info@cordance.org
Home Page: www.cordance.org

Anne Flynn, President
Helen Thomas, Chair, Editorial Board
Petri Hoppu, PhD, Vice President

Hannah Kosstrin, PhD, Treasurer
Bridget Cauthery, Treasurer-Elect

A not-for-profit, interdisciplinary organization with an open, international membership. Its purposes are: to encourage research in all aspects of dance, including related fields; to foster the exchange of ideas, resources, and methodology, through publication, international and regional conferences and workshops; to promote the accessibility of research materials.
Cost: $35.00
750 Members
Founded in 1965
Mailing list available for rent

19381 Costume Society of America

Home Page: www.costumesocietyamerica.com
Social Media: *Facebook, Twitter, LinkedIn, YouTube*

19382 Country Dance & Song Society

116 Pleasant St
Suite 345
Easthampton, MA 01027-2759

413-203-5467
FAX 413-203-5471
E-Mail: office@cdss.org
Home Page: www.cdss.org
Social Media: *Facebook, Twitter, Instagram, YouTube, Flickr*

Rima Dael, Executive/Artistic Director
Carol Compton, Financial Manager
Christine Dadmun, Membership Admin
Bob Blondin, Business Manager
Robin Hayden, Development Director

A national organization dedicated to the preservation and promotion of English and Anglo-American traditional and historical folk dance, music and song. Composed of individual members and affiliate groups, it functions both as an international service bureau and as a facilitator in building and maintaining local and regional dance, music and song communities. It exists to meed needs for community-based activity, for active participation, and for sharing and keeping historical and folk
3400 Members
Founded in 1915

19383 Dance Critics Association

Old Chelsea Station
PO Box 1882
New York, NY 10011

732-643-4008
E-Mail: dancecritics@hotmail.com
Home Page: www.dancecritics.org

Kena Herod, Co-Chair
Linda Traiger, Co-Chair

Encourages excellence in dance criticism through education, research and the exchange of ideas. Produces quarterly newsletter.
Cost: $50.00
300 Members
Founded in 1973

19384 Dance Educators of America

PO Box 740387
Suite262
Boynton Beach, FL 33474

914-636-3200
800-329-3868
FAX 914-636-5895
E-Mail: info@dancedea.com
Home Page: www.usadance.dancedea.com/
Social Media: *Facebook, Twitter, Youtube*

Vickie Sheer, Executive Director
Fran Peters, President
Charles Kelley, Treasurer
Robyn Bourdeau, Chief Financial Officer
Stephen Ball, Events and DEA Coordinator

Dedicated to improving the quality and teaching abilities of its member teachers and enhancing their education of students, as well as furthering the professional and ethical standards in the performing arts and of dance in all its form. Membership is limited to qualified teachers.
Cost: $150.00
1800 Members
Founded in 1932

19385 Dance Films Association

252 Java Street
Suit 333
Brooklyn, NY 11222

347-505-8649
FAX 212-727-0765
E-Mail: info@dancefilms.org
Home Page: www.dancefilms.org
Social Media: *Facebook, Twitter, Vimeo*

Deidra Towers, Executive Director
Latika Young, Education Director
Anna Brady Nuse, Festival Coordinator
Julian Barnett, Research/Development

Supports all those professionals in both the dance and the film community. Publishes bi-monthly magazine.
Cost: $50.00
Founded in 1956

19386 Dance Masters of America

PO Box 610533
Bayside, NY 11361

718-255-4013
FAX 718-225-4293
E-Mail: dmamann@aol.com
Home Page: www.dma-national.org

Shely Pack Manning, National President
Robert Mann, National Executive Secretary
Charleen Locascio, National Treasurer

An international organization of dance educators who have been certified by test to teach whose main focus is advancing the art of dance and improving the practice of its teaching.
2.5M Members
Founded in 1884

19387 Dance USA

1111 16th St NW
Suite 300
Washington, DC 20036-4830

202-833-1717
FAX 202-833-2686
E-Mail: danceusa@danceusa.org
Home Page: www.danceusa.org
Social Media: *Facebook, Twitter, YouTube, Vimeo*

Amy Fitterer, Executive Director
Tom Thielen, Director Finance/Operations
Katherine Fabian, Membership Manager
Dough Singleton, Chair
Andrea Clark-Smith, Vice Chair

Provides a forum for the discussion of issues of concern to members and a support network for exchange of information.
400 Members
Founded in 1982

19388 Dance/USA

1111 16th Street NW Ste. 300
Washington, DC 20036

202-833-1717
Home Page: www.danceusa.org
Social Media: *Facebook, Twitter, YouTube, Vimeo*

Dough Singleton, Chair
Charlotte Ballet, Chair Elect
Andrea Clark-Smith, Vice Chair
Sarah Thompson, Secretary
Robert Dorf, Treasurer

19389 Dramatists Guild of America

1501 Broadway
Suite 701
New York, NY 10036-5505

212-398-9366
FAX 212-944-0420
E-Mail: igor@dramaguild.com
Home Page: www.dramatistsguild.com

Ralph Sevush, Executive Director Business Affairs
Gary Garrison, Executive Director Creative Affairs
Abby Marcus, Managing Director
Roland Tec, Director of Membership

The Dramatists Guild of America was established over eighty years ago, and is the only professional association that advances the interests of playwrights, composers, lyricists and librettists writing for the living stage.
6000+ Members
Founded in 1964

19390 Educational Theatre Association

2343 Auburn Ave
Cincinnati, OH 45219-2819

513-421-3900
FAX 513-421-7077
Home Page: www.schooltheatre.org
Social Media: *Facebook, Twitter, Instagram, YouTube*

Jay Seller, President
Frank Pruet, VP
Julie Woffington, Executive Director
Jim Flanagan, Director of Operations
Ginny Butsch, Community Manager

EdTA is a professional organization for theatre educators. In addition to providing professional development, advocacy, and networking support to its members, Edta oprtates the International Society, an honorary organization for high school and middle school theatre students.
4600+ Members
Founded in 1929

19391 Esperanza Performing Arts Association

Po Box 502591
San Diego, CA 92150

858-391-1311
E-Mail: info@esperanzaarts.org
Home Page: www.esperanzaarts.org

Alan Cox, Executive Director
Adam Stout, Assistant Director

19392 Fractured Atlas

248 W. 35th Street, 10th Fl.
New York, NY 10001

888-692-7878
FAX 212-277-8025
E-Mail: support@fracturedatlas.orgÿ
Home Page: www.fracturedatlas.orgÿ
Social Media: *Facebook, Twitter, LinkedIn*

Holly Sidford, Chair
Russell Wills Taylor, Vice Chair
Adam Forest Huttler, Executive Director
Adam Huttler, Secretary
Alanna Weifenbach, Treasurer
Founded in 1998

19393 Fritz and Lavinia Jensen Foundation

Foundation for the Carolinas
220 N Tryon Street
Charlotte, NC 28202

704-641-4691
FAX 704-973-4599
E-Mail: info@jensenfoundation.org
Home Page: www.jensenfoundation.org

Ann Todd, Competition Coordinator
Jane W. Pardue, President
R. Benjamin Leaptrott, Jr., Vice Presidentÿ

Oliver Worthington, Vice President
Gene Hoots, Trustee

Sponsors voice competitions supporting opera and other classical singers.

19394 Gina Bachauer International Piano Foundation

138 W Broadway
Suite 220
Salt Lake City, UT 84101-1913

801-297-4250
FAX 801-521-9202
E-Mail: info@bachauer.com
Home Page: www.bachauer.com
Social Media: *Facebook, Twitter, Flickr, Google+, YouTube*

Thomas Holst, Manager
Kimi Kawashima, Manager
Arlo McGinn, Secretary
Nathan Morgan, Treasurer
Kary Billings, Chairman

The mission of the Foundation is to further the pianistic art, foster excellence in performance and teaching, develop opportunities for pianists beyond the scope of the organization and offer leadership in developing a musically-educated community.
Founded in 1976

19395 Guild of American Luthiers

8222 S Park Ave
Tacoma, WA 98408-5226

253-472-7853
FAX 253-472-7853
E-Mail: orders@luth.org
Home Page: www.luth.org
Social Media: *Facebook*

Debra G Olsen, Executive Director
Tim Olsen, Editor
Kurt Kendall, Membership

Manufacturers and repairs stringed instruments; offers quarterly journal and triennial meeting.
Cost: $45.00
3000 Members
Founded in 1972

19396 Institute of Outdoor Drama

201 Erwin Building
Mail Stop 528
Greenville, NC 27858-4353

252-328-5363
FAX 252-328-0968
Home Page: www.outdoor-theatre.org
Social Media: *Facebook, Twitter, RSS*

Michael C. Hardy, Director
Susan D. Phillips, Business Manager
Founded in 1963

19397 International Association of Round Dance Teachers

2803 Louisiana St
Longview, WA 98632-3536

360-423-7423
877-943-2623
FAX 208-377-1236
E-Mail: roundalab@roundalab.org
Home Page: www.roundalab.org
Social Media: *Facebook*

Gil & Judy Martin, General Chairman
Jeanne & Warren Shane, Vice Chairman
Chuck & Becky Jaworski, Marketing Membership

Supports all those involved in the field of square dancing. Publishes quarterly magazine.
Founded in 1974
Mailing list available for rent

19398 International Computer Music Association

1819 Polk Street
Suite 330
San Francisco, CA 94109

FAX 734-878-3031
E-Mail: icma@umich.edu
Home Page: www.computermusic.org
Social Media: *Facebook*

Tae Hong Park, President
Margaret Schedel, VP Of Conference
Michael Gurevich, Vice President for Membership
Tae Hong Park, Vice President for Preservation
Chryssie Nanou, Treasurer/Secretary

The International Computer Music Association is an international affiliaton of individuals and institutions involved in the technical, creative, and performance aspects of computer music. It serves composers, engineers, researchers and musicians who are interested in the integration of music and technology.
Cost: $63.52
450 Members

19399 International Festivals and Events Association

2603 W Eastover Ter
Boise, ID 83706-2800

208-433-0950
FAX 208-433-9812
E-Mail: nia@ifea.com
Home Page: www.ifea.com
Social Media: *Facebook, Twitter, LinkedIn, YouTube*

Steven Schmader, President
Nia Hovde, VP/Marketing

A voluntary association of events, event producers, event suppliers, and related professionals and organizations whose common purpose is the production and presentation of festivals, events, and civic and private celebrations.
2000 Members
Founded in 1956

19400 International Performing Arts for Youth

1315 Walnut Street
Suite 320
Philadelphia, PA 19107

267-690-1325
FAX 267-519-3343
Home Page: www.ipayweb.org

Ms. Peg Schuler-Armstrong, President
Ms. Pamela K. Lieberman, Vice President
Ms. Mary Kate Barley-Jenkins, Immediate Past President
Jeremy Boomer Stacey, Executive Director
Ms. Nadine Carew, Treasurer
Founded in 2001

19401 International Planned Music Association

5900 S Salina Street
Syracuse, NY 13205

315-469-7711
FAX 315-469-8842
Home Page: www.ipmanet.com

Bob Bobuk, President
Gary Alshouse, VP
Barb Cowsert, Secretary
Jon Baker, Treasurer
Jack Carroll, General Counsel

IPMA is a trade organization made up of providers of planned and programmed music services and key vendors. The Associatin exists to provide members with a common ground on which to share informatio about running exciting, profitable franchises and to provide associ-

ate members with opportunities to expand their sales in markets all over the world.
200 Members

19402 International Society for the Performing Arts

630 9th Avenue
Suite 213
New York, NY 10036-4752

212-206-8490
FAX 212-206-8603
E-Mail: info@ispa.org
Home Page: www.ispa.org
Social Media: *Facebook, Twitter, Pinterest*

Anthony Sargent, Chair
Jeff Daniel, Treasurer
Margia Claudia, Secretary
Johann Zietsman, CEO
Lynne Caruso, Membership Manager

A nonprofit organization of executives and directors of concert and performance halls, festivals, performing companies, and artists competitions; government cultural officials; artists' managers; and other interested parties with a professional involvement in the performing arts around the world, and in every arts disciplie. The purpose of ISPA is to develop, nurture, energize and educate an international network of arts leaders and professionals who are dedicated to advancing its field.
600 Members
Founded in 1949

19403 International Theatre Equipment Association

770 Broadway
5th Floor
New York, NY 10003-9595

646-654-7680
FAX 212-257-6428
E-Mail: info@itea.com
Home Page: www.itea.com

Robert Sunshine, Executive Director
Barry Ferrell, President
Jack Panzeca, VP
Joe DeMeo, Treasurer
Sarah Fuller, Secretary

Fosters and maintains professional, business and social relationships among its members within all segments of the motion picture industry. Bestows annual Teddy Award to manufacturer of the year and the annual Rodney Award to dealer of the year.
Cost: $375.00
180 Members
Founded in 1971

19404 International Ticketing Association

10401 N Meridian St
Suite 300
Indianapolis, IN 46290

212-629-4036
FAX 212-629-8532
E-Mail: info@intix.org
Home Page: www.intix.org
Social Media: *Facebook, Twitter, LinkedIn*

Jennifer Aprea, Board Chair
Gary Lustig, Chair-Elect
Mardi S Dilger, Past Chair
Jena L Hoffman, President
Amber E Kinney, Treasurer

Non-profit association committed to the improvement, progress and advancement of ticket management. Provides educational programs, trade shows, conducts surveys, conference proceedings, and its valuable membership directory.
Founded in 1982

19405 Jazz Education

3303 South Rice, Suite 107
PO Box 8031
Houston, TX 77056

713-839-7000
FAX 715-839-8266
E-Mail: jazzed@jazzedcation.org
Home Page: www.jazzeducation.org
Social Media: *Facebook, LinkedIn*

Tracy Scott, Executive Director

Nonprofit music organization providing worthwhile educational activities for school-aged youth in the field of music. Includes many subjects not covered by school systems. Promotes appreciation and understanding of Jazz.
Founded in 1970

19406 League of American Orchestras

33 West 60th Street
New York, NY 10023

212-262-5161
FAX 212-262-5198
E-Mail: member@americanorchestras.org
Home Page: www.americanorchestras.org
Social Media: *Facebook, Twitter, YouTube*

Patricia A Richards, Chair
Steven C. Parrish, Vice Chair
Jesse Rosen, President/ CEO
Barry A Sanders, Secretary
Robert A Peiser, Treasurer
800 Members
Founded in 1942

19407 League of American Theatres and Producers

729 Seventh Avenue
5th Floor
New York, NY 10019

212-764-1122
FAX 212-944-2136
E-Mail: league@broadway.org
Home Page: www.broadwayleague.com
Social Media: *Facebook, Twitter, LinkedIn, Pinterest, Instagram, YouTube*

Charolette St Martin, Executive Director
Colin Gibson, Director Finance
Jane Svendsen, Director Marketing
Ed Sandler, Director Membership Services

National trade association for the commercial theatre industry whose principal activity is negotiation of labor contracts and government relations.
400 Members
Founded in 1930

19408 League of Historic American Theatres

9 Newport Drive
Suite 200
Forest Hillÿ, MD 21050

443-640-1058
877-627-0833
FAX 443-640-1031
E-Mail: info@lhat.org
Home Page: www.network.lhat.org/

Frances Holden, Executive Director
Thomas Johnson, VP
Alice North, Treasurer
John Bell, Chair
Don Telford, Immediate Past Chair

The League of Historic American Theatres, a nonprofit membership association, promotes the rescue, rehabilitation and sustainable operation of historic theatres throughout North America. Founded in 1976, the League serves its members through educational programs, publications, specialized services and an annual conference and theatre tour.
500+ Members
Founded in 1976

19409 Literary Managers and Dramaturgs of the Americas

PO Box 36
New York, NY 10129

212-561-0315
800-680-2148
E-Mail: lmdanyc@hotmail.com
Home Page: www.lmda.org
Social Media: *Facebook, Twitter*

Brain Quirt, Chair
Beth Blickers, President
Danielle Carroll, Administrative Director
Nichole Gantshar, Treasurer
Richard Wolfe, VP

The mission of the LMDA is to affirm the role of dramaturg, to expand the possibilities of the field to other media and institutions and to cultivate, develop and promote the function of dramaturgy and literary management.
500 Members

19410 Mid-Atlantic Arts Foundation

201 N Charles Street
Suite 401
Baltimore, MD 21201-4102

410-539-6656
FAX 410-837-5517
E-Mail: info@midatlanticarts.org
Home Page: www.midatlanticarts.org
Social Media: *Facebook, Twitter, YouTube, Pinterest*

Alan Cooper, Executive Director
E Scott Johnson, Secretary

MAAF celebrates, promotes and supports the richness and diversity of the region's art resources and works to increase access to the arts and other cultures of the region and the world.
40000 Members
Founded in 1979
Mailing list available for rent: 30,000 names

19411 Music Distributors Association

14070 Proton Road
Suite 100 LB 9
Dallas, TX 75244-3601

972-233-9107
FAX 972-490-4219
E-Mail: office@musicdistributors.org
Home Page: www.musicdistributors.org

An international nonprofit trade association representing and serving manufacturers, wholesalers, importers and exporters of musical instruments and accessories, sound reinforcement products and published music.
Cost: $675.00
Founded in 1939

19412 National Alliance for Musical Theatre

520 Eighth Avenue
Suite 301
New York, NY 10018

212-714-6668
FAX 212-714-0469
E-Mail: info@namt.org
Home Page: www.namt.orgÿ
Social Media: *Facebook, Twitter, RSS, YouTube*

Donna Lynn Hilton, President
Kevin Moriarty, Vice President
Betsy King Militelo, Executive Director
Peter Rothstein, Secretary
Jeff Loeb, Treasurer

Not-for-profit working for the advance of musical theatre.
30000 Members
Founded in 1985

19413 National Association for Drama Therapy

Suite 101
Suite 220
Albany, NY 12203

888-416-7167
FAX 518-463-8656
E-Mail: office@nadta.org
Home Page: www.nadta.org
Social Media: *Facebook, Twitter, YouTube, Instagram*

Nadya Trytan, President
Jeremy Segall, MA, RDT, LCAT, VP
Whitney Sullivan, RDT, LCSW, Secretary
Dani York, RDT, LCAT, Treasurer
Nancy Sondag, Membership

A nonprofit association which establishes and upholds high standards of professional competence and ethics among drama therapists; to develop criteria for training and registration; to sponsor publications and conferences; and to promote the profession of drama therapy through information and advocacy.
Founded in 1979

19414 National Association for Music Education

1806 Robert Fulton Drive
Reston, VA 20191

703-860-4000
800-336-3768
FAX 703-860-1531
Home Page: www.nafme.org
Social Media: *Facebook, Twitter, LinkedIn, Google+, Pinterest*

Lynn M Brinckmeyer, President

The mission of MENC is to advance music education by encouraging the study and making of music by all. MENC offers more than 100 books, videos and compact discs, as well as two general-interest magazines on music education and four more closely targeted journals.
Founded in 1907
Mailing list available for rent: 60,000 names

19415 National Association of Latino Arts and Cultures

1208 Buena Vista
San Antonio, TX 78207

210-432-3982
FAX 210-432-3934
E-Mail: info@nalac.org
Home Page: www.nalac.org
Social Media: *Facebook, Twitter*

Maria Lÿpez De L,on, Executive Director

A nonprofit dedicated exclusively to serving Latino arts communities.
Founded in 1989

19416 National Association of Performing Arts Managers and Agents

459 Columbus Avenue
#133
New York, NY 10024

E-Mail: tuluck@fairpoint.net
Home Page: www.napama.org

Jerry Ross, President
David Wannen, Vice President
Jeff Laramie, Vice President
Laurelle Favreau, Secretary
Robin Pomerance, Treasurer
Founded in 1979

19417 National Corporate Theatre Fundÿ

505 Eighth Avenue
Suite 2303
New York, NY 10018

212-750-6895
FAX 212-750-6977

Home Page: www.theatreforward.org
Social Media: *Facebook, Twitter, YouTube*

Richard Thomas, Honorary Chair
James S Turley, Chairman
Gretchen Shugart, President
Bruce R Ewing, Secretary
Frank Orlowski, Treasurer

19418 National Costumers Association

6000 E. Evans Ave.
#3-205
Denver, CO 80222ÿ

317-351-1940
800-622-1321
FAX 317-351-1941
E-Mail: office@costumers.org
Home Page: www.costumers.org

Janie Westendorf, President
Deborah Meredith, First Vive President
Linda Adams Foat, Second VP
Jennifer Skarstedt, Secretary/Treasurer

The objectives on the NCA are to establish and maintain professional and ethical standards of business in the costume industry. They encourage and promote a greater and more diversified use of costumes in all fields of human activity. They provide trade information, cooperation and friendship among its members together with a sound public relations policy.
400 Members
Founded in 1923

19419 National Dance Association

1900 Association Dr
Reston, VA 20191-1502

703-476-3400
800-213-7193
FAX 703-476-9527
E-Mail: nda@aahperd.org
Home Page: www.aahperd.org/nda
Social Media: *Facebook, Twitter*

Colleen Dean, Manager
Marcey E Siegel, VP Dance Education
Mary Ann Laverty, VP Dance Performance

A nonprofit service organization dedicated to increasing knowledge, improving skills and encouraging sound professional practices in dance education while promoting and supporting creative and healthy lifestyles through high quality dance programs.
2000 Members
Founded in 1932

19420 National Dance Education Organization

8609 2nd Avenue
Suite 203 B
Silver Spring, MD 20910

301-585-2880
FAX 301-585-2888
E-Mail: info@ndeo.org
Home Page: www.ndeo.org

Susan McGreevy-Nichols, Executive Director
Patricia Cohen, Treasurer

A nonprofit organization dedicated to promoting standards of excellence in dance education.
2000 Members
Founded in 1998

19421 National Endowment for the Arts

1100 Pennsylvania Ave NW
Washington, DC 20506

202-682-5400
FAX 202-682-5611
E-Mail: webmgr@arts.gov
Home Page: www.arts.endow.gov
Social Media: *Facebook, Twitter*

Dana Gioia, CEO
Guilomar Barbi, Scheduler
Sarah Cook, Executive Assistant

Jon P Peede, Counselor to the Chairman
Sydney Smith, Administrative Specialist

The National Endowment for the Arts, an investment in America's living heritage, serves the public good by nurturing the expression of human creativity, supporting the cultivation of community spirit, and fostering the recognition and appreciation of the excellence and diversity of our nation's artistic accomplishments.

19422 National Music Publishers Association

101 Constitution Avenue NW
Suite 705 East
Washington, DC 20001

202-742-4375
FAX 202-393-6673
E-Mail: pr@nmpa.org
Home Page: www.nmpa.org
Social Media: *Facebook, Twitter, YouTube, Instagram*

Martin Bandier, President/CEO
John Eastman, Director

The NMPA is committed to promoting and advancing the interests of music publishers and their songwriting partners. Their goal is to foster a business climate that allows its members to thrive creatively and financially.
800 Members
Founded in 1917

19423 National Performance Network

1024 Elysian Fields Avenue
New Orleans, LA 70117

504-595-8008
FAX 504-595-8006
E-Mail: info@npnweb.org
Home Page: www.npnweb.org
Social Media: *Facebook, Twitter*

Abe Rybeck, Chair
Yolanda Cesta Cursach, Vice Chair
MK Wegmann, President/ CEO
Meena Natarajan, Secretary
Shannon Daut, Treasurer
Founded in 1985

19424 National Piano Travelers Association

401 Sawkill Road
PO Box 2264
Kingston, NY 12401-2264

845-338-1464
FAX 845-338-5751
Home Page: www.pianotravelers.com

Roy Chandler, President
Bob dove, VP
Dawn Demars, Secretary/Treasurer

Buys and sells pianos.
110 Members

19425 Network of Ensemble Theaters

PO Box 83526
Portland, OR 97283

E-Mail: info@ensembletheaters.net
Home Page: www.ensembletheaters.net

Laurie McCants, President
August Schulenburg, Vice President
Mark Valdez, Executive Director
Cynthia Ling Lee, Secretary
Bruce Allardice, Treasurer
Founded in 1995

19426 New England Theatre Conference

215 Knob Hill Drive
Hamden, CT 06518

617-851-8535
FAX 203-288-5938
E-Mail: mail@netconline.org
Home Page: www.netconline.org

James Fergudon, President
Jeffrey Watts, Executive VP

Jamie Taylor, VP Administration/Finance
Chris Crossen-sills, Executive Secretary
Jim Quinn, Clerk of the Corporation

Non-profit corporation, composed of individuals and organizations in the six-State region of New England, who are active and interested in the performing arts. The NETC promotes excellence in theatre for their region, and supports quality theatre and performance in all of its diversity.
500 Members
Founded in 1952

19427 New Music USA

90 Broad St.
Suite 1902
New York, NY 10004

212-645-6949
E-Mail: info@newmusicusa.org
Home Page: www.newmusicusa.org
Social Media: *Facebook, Twitter, Vimeo*

Ed Harsh, President & CEO
Frederick Peters, Chair

Part of the Performing Arts Alliance, New Music USA advocates for the creation and performance of new music.

19428 North American Drama Therapy Association

Suite 101
Suite 220
Albany, NY 12203

888-416-7167
888-416-7167
FAX 518-463-8656
E-Mail: office@nadt.org
Home Page: www.nadta.org
Social Media: *Facebook, Twitter, YouTube, Instagram*

Nadya Trytan, President
Jason Butler, President-Elect
Jeremy Segall, Vice President
Whitney Sullivan, Secretary
Dani York, Treasurer
Founded in 1979

19429 North American Performing Arts Managers and Agents

459 Columbus Ave
Suite 133
New York, NY 10024-5129

212-362-8304
800-867-3281
E-Mail: info@napama.org
Home Page: www.napama.org

Richard Baird, Owner
David Wannen, VP
Jerry Ross, VP
Susan Endrizzi Moris, Secretary
Robin Pomerance, Treasurer

National nonprofit trade association dedicated to promoting the professionalism of its members and the vitality of the performing arts. NAPAMA promotes the mutual advancement and the best interests of performing arts managers and agents; promotes open discourse among members and within the larger field; gives active consideration and expression of opinion on questions affecting the industry and develops and encourages ethical and sound business practices.
Cost: $150.00
Founded in 1979

19430 OPERA America

330 Seventh Avenue
New York, NY 10001

212-796-8620
FAX 212-796-8621
E-Mail: Info@operaamerica.org
Home Page: www.operaamerica.orgÿ

Social Media: *Facebook, Twitter, Google+, YouTube*

Dr. Frayda B. Lindemann, Chairman
Susan F. Morris, Vice Chairman
Marc A. Scorca, President/ CEO
William Florescu, Secretary
Timothy O'Leary, Treasurer
Founded in 1973

19431 Oratorio Society of New York
1440 Broadway
23rd Floor
New York, NY 10018-9759

212-400-7255
E-Mail: president@oratoriosocietyofny.org
Home Page: www.oratoriosocietyofny.org
Social Media: *Facebook, Twitter, Youtube*

Richard A Pace, Chairman & Presidentÿ
Mary J.Knight, Vice President
Marie Gangemi, Treasurer
Jay Jacobson, Secretary
Kent Tritle, Music Director

New York City's second oldest cultural organization. On December 25, 1874 the society began what has become an unbroken tradition of annual performances of Handel's Messiah (at Carnegie Hall since its opening in 1891).
Founded in 1873

19432 Performing Arts Alliance
1211 Connecticut Ave. NW
Suite 200
Washington, DC 20036

202-207-3850
FAX 202-833-1543
E-Mail: info@theperformingartsalliance.org
Home Page:
www.theperformingartsalliance.org
Social Media: *Facebook, Twitter*

Mario Garcia Durham, Chair

The Alliance advocates for federal policy that fosters the contributions to society of America's professional nonprofit arts organizations and artists.
30K Members
Founded in 1977

19433 Performing Arts Association
719 Edmond St
St Joseph, MO 64501-2268

816-279-1225
E-Mail: info@paastjo.org
Home Page:
www.saintjosephperformingarts.org
Social Media: *Facebook, Twitter*

David Cripe, President
Elaine Smith, VP
Debbie Demuth, Secretary
Kim Lueger, Treasurer
Beth Sharp, Director

Mission is to provide a diverse selection of performing arts in the St. Joseph area by presenting programs that foster, increase and promote public knowledge and appreciation of music, theatre and dance and lectures on subjects of cultural interests.
Founded in 1979

19434 Performing Arts Medicine Association
PO Box 117
Englewood, CO 80151

303-808-5643
FAX 866-408-7069
E-Mail: webmaster@artsmed.org
Home Page: www.artsmed.org
Social Media: *Facebook, Twitter, LinkedIn*

Julie Massaro, Executive Director
Mary Fletcher, Consultant

John Chong, President
Dorry Allen, Manager of Member Services

Organization for physicians and other professionsl persons who are involved in treatment and/or research in the field of Performing Arts Medicine.
Founded in 1989

19435 Piano Manufacturers Association
14070 Proton Road
Suite 100
Dallas, TX 75244

972-233-9107
FAX 972-490-4219
Home Page: www.pianonet.com

Donald W Dillon, Executive Director

Piano industry trade association.
Founded in 1991

19436 Piano Technicians Guild
4444 Forest Avenue
Kansas City, KS 66106

913-432-9975
FAX 913-432-9986
E-Mail: ptg@ptg.org
Home Page: www.ptg.org
Social Media: *Facebook, Twitter, YouTube*

Barbara Cassaday, Executive Director
Jim Coleman, President
Norman R. Cantrell, VP
Phil A Bondi, Secretary/Treasurer

A nonprofit organization serving piano tuners, technicians, and craftsman throughout the world, organized to promote the highest possible service and technical standards among piano tuners and technicians.
4100 Members
Founded in 1957

19437 Production Music Library Association
1600 Aspen Commons
Suite 100
Middleton, WI 53562

608-836-5825
FAX 608-831-8200
E-Mail: mla@areditions.com
Home Page: www.musiclibraryassoc.org
Social Media: *Facebook, Twitter*

Jerry L McBride, President
Michael Colby, VP
Pamela Bristah, Secretary

Provides a forum for issues surrounding music, music in libraries, and music librarianship. Members include music librarians, librarians who work with music as part of their responsibilities, composers and music scholars, and others interested in the program of the association.
20 Members
Founded in 1931

19438 Professional Women Singers Association
P.O. Box 29
Deer Park, NY 11729

212-969-0590
FAX 928-395-2560
E-Mail: professionalwomensingers@gmail.com
Home Page: www.womensingers.org
Social Media: *Facebook*

Elissa Weiss, President
Allison Atteberry, First VP
Sarah Downs, Second VP
Ruth Ann Cunningham, Secretary
Mary Lou Zobel, Treasurer

Non-profit networking organization for professional women singers. The group sponsors con-

certs, master classes and seminars for both singers and the community at large.
40 Members
Founded in 1982

19439 Screen Actors Guild
5757 Wilshire Blvd
7th Floor
Los Angeles, CA 90036-3600

323-954-1600
855-724-2387
FAX 323-549-6792
Home Page: www.sagaftra.org

Allen Rosenburg, President
Kent McCord, First VP
Paul Christie, Second VP
Steve Fried, Third Vice President
Connie Stevens, Secretary/Treasurer

Labor union affiliated with AFL-CIO which represents actors in film, television and commercials. The Guild exists to enhance actors' working conditions, compensation and benefits and to be a powerful, unifed voice on behalf of artists' rights.
120M Members
Founded in 1933

19440 Society of American Magicians
PO Box 510260
Saint Louis, MO 63151-0260

314-846-5659
FAX 314-846-5659
E-Mail: rmblowers@aol.com
Home Page: www.magicsam.com
Social Media: *Facebook, Twitter*

J.Christopher Bontjes, President
Bruce Kalver, First VP
Mike Miller, Second VP
Chuck Lehr, Secretary
Mary Ann Blowers, Treasurer

Founded to promote and maintain harmonious fellowship among those interested in magic as an art, to improve ethics of the magical profession, and to foster, promote and improve the advancement of magical arts in the field of amusement and entertainment. Membership includes professional and amateur magicians, manufacturers of magical apparatus and collectors.
5.5M Members
Founded in 1902

19441 Society of Stage Directors & Choreograhers
321 W. 44th Street
Suite 804
New York, NY 10036

212-391-1070
FAX 212-302-6195
E-Mail: Info@SDCweb.org
Home Page: www.sdcweb.org
Social Media: *Facebook, Twitter, LinkedIn, Google+, Instagram*

Susan H Schulman, President
John Rando, Executive Vice President
Leigh Silverman, Vice President
Oz Scott, Secretary
Ethan McSweeny, Treasurer
Founded in 1965

19442 Society of Stage Directors and Choreographers
321 W. 44th Street
Suite 804
New York, NY 10036-5653

212-391-1070
800-541-5204
FAX 212-302-6195
E-Mail: Info@SDCweb.org
Home Page: www.sdcweb.org

Social Media: *Facebook, Twitter, LinkedIn, Google+, Instagram*

Susan H Schulman, President
John Rando, Executive Vice President
Leigh Silverman, Vice President
Oz Scott, Secretary
Ethan McSweeny, Treasurer

An independent labor union representing directors and choreographers in American theatre.
1700 Members
Founded in 1965
Mailing list available for rent

19443 Southern Arts Federation

1800 Peachtree St NW
Suite 808
Atlanta, GA 30309-2512

404-874-7244
FAX 404-873-2148
Home Page: www.southarts.org
Social Media: *Facebook, Twitter, LinkedIn*

Susie Surkamer, Executive Director
Stephanie Conner, Secretary
Ken May, Treasurer
David Batley, Marketing/Communications Director

In partnership with nine state arts agencies: promotes and supports arts regionally, nationally and internationally; enhances the artistic excellence and professionalism of Southern Arts Organizations and artists; serves the diverse population of the south.
Founded in 1975

19444 Stage Directors and Choreographers Foundation

321 W. 44th Street
Suite 804
New York, NY 10036

212-391-1070
FAX 212-302-6195
E-Mail: Info@SDCweb.org
Home Page: www.sdcfoundation.org
Social Media: *Facebook, Twitter, LinkedIn, Google+, Instagram*

Susan H Schulman, President
John Rando, Executive Vice President
Leigh Silverman, Vice President
Oz Scott, Secretary
Ethan McSweeny, Treasurer
Founded in 1965

19445 The Actors' Fund

729 Seventh Avenue, 10th floor
New York, NY 10019

212-221-7300
E-Mail: info@actorsfund.org
Home Page: www.actorsfund.org
Social Media: *Facebook, Twitter, LinkedIn, YouTube*

Brian Stokes Mitchell, Chairmen
Philip S. Birsh, Vice Chair
Marc Grodman, Secretary
Abby Schroeder, Assistant Secretary
Steve Kalafer, Treasurer
Founded in 1882

19446 The United States Disc Jockey Association

Post Office Box 43252
Nottingham, ML 21236

443-903-2013
E-Mail: support@usdja.com
Home Page: www.usdja.com
Social Media: *Facebook, Twitter, Vimeo*

Jason Walsh, President

19447 Theatre Authority

165 West 46th Street
New York, NY 10036

212-869-8530
FAX 212-719-9815
Home Page:
www.actorsequity.org/benefits/theatreauthority.asp

Presides over theatrical agencies and performing arts organizations.

19448 Theatre Bay Area

1119 Market Street
2nd Floor
San Francisco, CA 94103

415-430-1140
FAX 415-430-1145
E-Mail: tba@theatrebayarea.org
Home Page: www.theatrebayarea.org
Social Media: *Facebook, Twitter, Pinterest, YouTube*

Karen Mc Kevitt, Executive Director
Dale Albright, Director, Member Services
Clayton Lord, Director, Audience Development

Theatre Bay Area's mission is to unite, strengthen and promote the theatre community in the San Francisco Bay Area, working on behalf of their conviction that the performing arts are an essential public good, critical to a healthy and truly democratic society, and invaluable as a source of personal enrichment and growth.
3,000 Members
Founded in 1976

19449 Theatre Communications Group

520 8th Ave
24th Floor
New York, NY 10018-8666

212-609-5900
FAX 212-609-5901
E-Mail: tcg@tcg.org
Home Page: www.tcg.org
Social Media: *Facebook, Twitter, Instagram*

Theresa Eyring, Executive Director
Jennifer Cleary, Director of Membership

The mission of the TCG is to strengthen, nurture and promote the professional not-for-profit American theatre. TCG believes that their diversity as a field is their greatest strength. They celebrate differences in aesthetic, culture, organizational structure, and geography. They believe that every theatre makes a contribution to the greater field as a whole, that every performance expands the artistic vocabulary for us all, and that we all benefit from one another's presence.
Cost: $39.95
14000 Members
Frequency: Monthly
Founded in 1961

19450 Theatre Development Fund

520 Eight Avenue
Suite 801
New York, NY 10018-6507

212-912-9770
E-Mail: info@tdf.org
Home Page: www.tdf.org
Social Media: *Facebook, Twitter, YouTube, Google+*

Earl D. Weiner, Chairman
Sandra Kresch, Vice Chairman
Robert T. Goldm Treasurer, Deborah
Hartnett Secretary

Not-for-profit service organization for the performing arts. TDF administers a wide range of audience development and financial assistance programs that encourage production of new plays and musicals and enable more New Yorkers and visitors to enjoy the riches and variety

of the city's theatre, dance and music.
Cost: $25.00
Founded in 1968

19451 US Institute for Theatre Technology

315 S Crouse Ave
Suite 200
Syracuse, NY 13210-1835

315-463-6463
800-938-7488
FAX 315-463-6525
E-Mail: info@.usitt.org
Home Page: www.usitt.org
Social Media: *Facebook, Twitter, LinkedIn, Instagram, Pinterest*

Carol Carrigan, Manager
Patricia Dennis, Secretary
Travis DeCastro, Treasurer

Association of design, production and technology professionals in the performing arts and entertainment industry whose mission is to promote the knowledge and skills of its members. International in scope, USITT draws its board of directors from across the US and Canada. Sponsors projects, programs, research, symposia, exhibits and annual conference. Disseminates information on aesthetic and technical developments.
3700 Members
Founded in 1960

19452 USA Dance Inc

PO Box 152988
Cape Coral, FL 33915-2988

800-447-9047
FAX 239-573-0946
E-Mail: central-office@usadance.org
Home Page: usadance.org
Social Media: *Facebook, Twitter, LinkedIn, YouTube*

Lydia Scardina, National President
Bill Rose, Sr.Vice President
Greg Warner, National Secretary
Esther Freeman, National Treasurer
Ken Richards, VP, Dance Sports

Nonprofit organization working to promote ballroom dancing, both as a recreational activity and as a competitive sport, and to educate the public about the mental, physical and social benefits of dance.
23000 Members
Founded in 1965

19453 United Square Dancers of America

E-Mail: usda@usda.org
Home Page: www.usda.org
Social Media: *Facebook*

Mike Matsko, President
L Paul Schmidt, Vice President
Jim Maczko, Past President
Milene McCall, Secretary
Jim Taylor, Treasurer
Founded in 1981

19454 United States Association of Fringe Festivals

Home Page: www.fringefestivals.us

Association of alternative performing arts festivals.

19455 United States Institute for Theatre Technology

315 South Crouse Avenue
Suite 200
Syracuse, NY 13210

315-463-6463
800-938-7488
FAX 800-938-7488
E-Mail: info@usitt.org
Home Page: www.usitt.org

Social Media: *Facebook, Twitter, LinkedIn, Instagram, Pinterest*

Lea Asbell Swanger, President
Carolyn Satter, Vice President
David Grindle, Executive Director
Jimmie Byrd, Secretary
Dan Culhane, Treasurer
Founded in 1960

19456 Voice and Speech Trainers Association

773-888-2782
E-Mail: president@vasta.org
Home Page: www.vasta.org

Lynn Watson, President
Betty Moulton, President Elect
Mandy Rees, Past President
Melanie Julian, Secretary
Artemis Preeshl, Treasurer
Founded in 2005

19457 Women in the Arts Foundation

C/O E Butler
245 Broome Street
New York, NY 10002ÿ

212-941-0130
E-Mail: info@nyartistsequity.org
Home Page: www.nyartistsequity.org/
Social Media: *Twitter, Instagram*

Regina Stewart, Executive Director
Eric Butler, Executive Coordinator
Linda Butti, Executive Coordinator
Sari Menna, Financial Coordinator

WIA works to overcome discrimination against women artists. They provide information to help women function effectively as professional artists. WIA is open to all women interested in the arts.
150 Members
Founded in 1971

19458 Writers Guild of America

7000 West Third Street
Los Angeles, CA 90048

323-951-4000
FAX 323-782-4800
Home Page: www.wga.org
Social Media: *Facebook, Twitter, YouTube, RSS*

Chris Keyser, President
Howard A. Rodman, Vice President
Carl Gottlieb, Secretary/ Treasurer
Billy Ray, Board of Directors
Shawn Ryan, Board of Directors
Founded in 1921

Newsletters

19459 American Dance

240 West 14th Street
New York, NY 10011

212-932-2789
E-Mail: info@americandanceguild.org
Home Page: www.americandanceguild.org
Social Media: *Facebook*

Gloria McLean, President
Tina Croll, VP

Contains articles on member news, dance, and education.
Frequency: 4 per year
Founded in 1956

19460 Artsearch

Theatre Communications Group

520 8th Ave
Suite 305
New York, NY 10018-4156

212-609-5900
FAX 212-609-5901
E-Mail: tcg@tcg.org
Home Page: www.tcg.org

Theresa Eyring, Executive Director
Artsearch is divided into five main categories: Administration, Artistic, Production/Design, Career Development, and Education.
Cost: $75.00
Frequency: Bi-Monthly
ISSN: 0730-9023
Founded in 1961
Printed in on newsprint stock

19461 Broadside

Theatre Library Association
New York Public Library for Performing Arts
40 Lincoln Center Plaza
New York, NY 10023

E-Mail: info@tla-online.org
Home Page:
www.tla-online.org/publications/broadside.html

Nancy Friedland, President
Angela Weaver, VP
Rebecca Lord, Executive Secretary
Collen Reilly, Treasurer

Features articles and news items related to exhibitions and collections, information about TLA-sponsored events, book reviews, and other items of interest in the fields of theatre, film, and dance.
ISSN: 0068-2748
Founded in 1937

19462 Country Dance and Song Society News

Country Dance and Song Society
116 Pleasant St
Suite 345
Easthampton, MA 01027-2759

413-203-5467
FAX 413-203-5471
E-Mail: news@cdss.org
Home Page: www.cdss.org

Caroline Batson, Editor
Rima Dael, Executive Director
Bob Blondin, Business Manager

A selection of articles, letters and poems. CDSS News is available as a benefit of membership in the Country Dance and Song Society.
ISSN: 1070-8251
Founded in 1915

19463 DNBulletin

151 W 30th Street
Suite 202
New York, NY 10001

212-564-0985
FAX 212-216-9027
E-Mail: dnbinfo@dancenotation.org
Home Page: www.dancenotation.org

Senta Driver, Editor

Dance news for consumers and professionals.
Founded in 1940
Printed in 2 colors on matte stock

19464 Dancedrill

3101 Poplarwood Court
Suite 310
Raleigh, NC 27604-1010

919-872-7888
FAX 919-872-6888

Susan Wershing, Publisher
Kay Crawford, Editor

Publication informs members of dance drill teams and their directors.
Frequency: 4 per year

19465 Dramatists Guild Newsletter

Dramatists Guild of America
1501 Broadway
Suite 701
New York, NY 10036-5505

212-398-9366
FAX 212-944-0420
Home Page: www.dramaguild.com

Ralph Sevush, Executive Director

Supplement to 'The Dramatist,' available only to Guild members, includes bi-monthly reports from New York and Los Angeles, advice from the Business Affairs Department, the latest information on submission and career development opportunities, and reminders of approaching deadlines.

19466 INTIX Bulletin

International Ticketing Association
One College Park, 8910 Purdue Road
Suite 480
Indianapolis, IN 46268

212-629-4036
FAX 212-628-8532
E-Mail: info@intix.org
Home Page: www.intix.org

Jena L Hoffman, President
Kathleen O'Donnell, Director

E-bulletin provides news from the International Ticketing Association including information about upcoming events, conferences and exhibitions, industry news.
1200 Members
Frequency: Monthly
ISSN: 1071-6254
Founded in 1979
Printed in 4 colors on glossy stock

19467 In Focus

National Association of Theatre Owners
13190 SW 68th Parkway
Suite 200
Portland, OR 97223-8368

503-207-4700
877-388-8385
FAX 503-207-1937
Home Page: http://www.infocus.com

19468 In Theater

Parker Publishing & Communications
214 Sullivan St
Suite 2C
New York, NY 10012-1354

212-228-1225
FAX 212-719-4477
E-Mail: intheater@aol.com
Home Page: www.parkerhodges.com

Emily Parker, President

Offers the reader a behind-the-scenes perspective of how a show is technically conceived, rehearsed and staged. Regular departments center on drama and musical reviews, listings of shows in major cities and columnist options.
Cost: $78.00
Frequency: Weekly
Circulation: 71,068

19469 InLEAGUE

League of Historic American Theatres
2105 Laurel Bush Rd
Suite 201
Bel Air, MD 21015

443-640-1058
877-627-0833
FAX 443-640-1031

E-Mail: info@lhat.org
Home Page: www.lhat.org

Frances Holden, Executive Director
John Bell, VP
Darlene Smolik, Treasurer
Edward Kelsey, Secretary

Quarterly newsletter which reports news from historic theatre progects around the country and features articles on all facets of historic theatre restoration and operation. The newsletter solicits articles and information from the membership.
Frequency: Quarterly
Founded in 1976

19470 Job Contact Bulletin

Southeastern Theatre Conference
1175 Revolution Mill Dr.
Studio 14
Greensboro, NC 27405

336-272-3645
FAX 336-272-8810
E-Mail: arpil@setc.org
Home Page: www.setc.org

April J'C Marshall, Contact
Jack Benjamin, President
H. Duke Guthrie, Treasurer

On-line employment listing of Classified Ads for theatrical positions, auditions, and more.
Founded in 1949

19471 Performing Arts Insider

PAI C/O Total Theater
PO Box 31
Greeley, CO 80632

970-405-3077
E-Mail: totalpost@totaltheater.com
Home Page: performingartsinsider.com

A leading source of information about the perfoming arts in New York City and around the country. Each issue includes day-by-day calendar listings of shows on broadway, off and off-broadway, plus dance, opera, cabaret and special events. Also includes comprehensive theatre guides, listing the author, director, cast, designers, synopsis, theater and box office details, as well as contact information for producers, press agents, general managers and casting directors.
Cost: $275.00
Frequency: Monthly+9 Mid-Month Updat
Founded in 1944
Printed in on matte stock

19472 SETC News

Southeastern Theatre Conference
1175 Revolution Mill Dr.
Studio 14
Greensboro, NC 27405

336-272-3645
FAX 336-272-8810
E-Mail: deanna@setc.org.net
Home Page: www.setc.org

Deanna Thompson, Editor
Jack Benjamin, President
H. Duke Guthrie, Treasurer

Provides news and important information to members of the Southeaster Theatre Conference on upcoming SETC events, advocacy efforts, awards and competitions as well as items of special interest to the various divisions and interest areas. In addition, SETC News publishes news about people and organizations based in the Southeast.
Circulation: 4000
Founded in 1949

19473 Spotlight

American Association of Community Theatre

1300 Gendy St Forth Worth
Forth Worth, TX 76107

817-732-3177
866-687-2228
FAX 817-732-3178
E-Mail: info@aact.org
Home Page: www.aact.org
Social Media: *Facebook, Twitter*

Julie Angelo, Executive Director
John Sullivan, President

News and updates on issues pertinent to community theatre.
Cost: $2.00
24 Pages
Circulation: 2000
Founded in 1958
Mailing list available for rent: 9,500 names at $180 per M
Printed in on matte stock

19474 Technical Brief

Yale School of Drama
222 York Street
PO Box 208244
New Haven, CT 06520

203-432-8188
FAX 203-432-8129
E-Mail: bronislaw.sammler@yale.edu
Home Page: www.technicalbrief.org

Ben Sammler, Editor
Dan Harvey, Editor

Produced for technical managers in theater. Written by professionals for professionals, its purpose is simple: communication. Technical Brief provides a dailogue between technical practitioners from the several performing arts who all share similar problems.
Cost: $15.00
Frequency: 3 X Year
Founded in 1924

19475 Women in the Arts Bulletin

Women in the Arts Foundation
32-35 30th Street
D24
Long Island City, NY 11106

212-941-0130
E-Mail: reginas@anny.org
Home Page:
www.womenintheartsfoundation.org

Erin Butler, Editor
Regina Stewart, Executir Director
Sandra Cockerham, President

Gallery information and reviews. Women in the Arts Foundation works to overcome discrimination against women artists.
Frequency: Monthly
Founded in 1971

Magazines & Journals

19476 American Dancer

USA Dance
PO Box 152988
Cape Coral, FL 33915-2988

800-447-9047
FAX 239-573-0946
Home Page: www.usadance.org

Shawn Fisher, Editor

News of interests to dance enthusiasts.
Cost: $25.00
Frequency: Bi-Monthly
Circulation: 23000

19477 American Theatre Magazine

Theatre Communications Group

520 8th Ave
Suite 305
New York, NY 10018-8666

212-609-5900
FAX 212-609-5901
E-Mail: custserve@tcg.org
Home Page: www.tcg.org

Jim O'Quinn, Editor in Chief
Nicole Estvanik Taylor, Managing Editor
Cost: $35.00

19478 Applause Magazine

Denver Center for Performing Arts
1101 13th St
Denver, CO 80204-5319

303-893-3272
800-641-1222
FAX 303-893-3206
Home Page: www.denvercenter.org

Randy Weeks, President
Daniel L. Ritchie, Chairman &CEO

A publication of the Denver Center Theatre Company and Dever Center Attractions
Frequency: 8-10 per year
Founded in 1988
Printed in 4 colors on glossy stock

19479 Asian Pacific American Journal

Asian American Writers Workshop
16 W 32nd St
Suite 10A
New York, NY 10001-1093

212-494-0061
FAX 212-494-0062
E-Mail: desk@aaww.org
Home Page: www.aaww.org

Ken Chen, Executive Director
Jeannie L Wong, Adminstrative Director
Anjali Goyal, Programs Assistant
Jeffrey Lin, Designer
Hanya Yanagihara, Journal Editor

Features include short fiction, poems, essays, stage scripts, translations and artwork.
Frequency: Semi-Annual
ISSN: 1067-778X
Founded in 1992

19480 Back Stage

770 Broadway 7th Floor
New York, NY 10003

212-493-4420
800-658-8372
E-Mail: advertising@backstage.com
Home Page: www.backstage.com

Charles Weiss, Manager
Jamie Painter Young, Editor-in-Chief
Jenelle Riley, Film/TV Editor
Leonard Jacobs, Theatre Editor
Sherry Eaker, Editor-at-Large

Four print, four interactive and two face-to-face publications. Provides casting, news, articles and other resources for working actors, cingers, dancers and behind-the-scenes staff and crew.
Cost: $84.00
Circulation: 30,000
Founded in 1960
Mailing list available for rent

19481 Bomb Magazine

New Art Publications
80 Hanson Pl
Suite 703
Brooklyn, NY 11217-1506

718-636-9100
866-354-0334
FAX 718-636-9200
E-Mail: info@bombsite.com

Home Page: www.bombsite.com
Social Media: *Facebook, Twitter, YouTube*

Betsy Sussler, Publisher/Editor
Mary-Ann Monforton, Associate Publisher
Nell McClister, Senior Editor
Lucy Raven, Managing Editor
Paul W Morris, Director Marketing/Special Projects

Focuses on contemporary art, literature, theater, film, music.
Cost: $495.00
Frequency: Quarterly
Circulation: 60,000
Founded in 1981
Mailing list available for rent
Printed in 4 colors on matte stock

19482 BoxOffice Magazine

BoxOffice Media
9107 Wilshire Blvd.
Suite 450
Beverly Hills, CA 90210-4241

310-876-9090
Home Page: www.boxoffice.com

Peter Crane, Publisher
Kenneth James Bacon, Creative Director
Phil Contrino, Editor
Amy Nicholson, Editor

The premier trade magazine covering the latest developments in the movie industry, from films in production to digital cinema and everything in between.
Founded in 1948

19483 Callaloo

Johns Hopkins University Press
2715 N Charles St
Baltimore, MD 21218-4363

410-516-6900
800-537-5487
FAX 410-516-6998
Home Page:
www.press.jhu.edu/journals/callaloo

William Brody, President
Kyle G Dargan, Managing Editor

Journal of African and African-American issues. Content includes original works by, and critical studies of, black writers worldwide. Offers a rich mixture of fiction, poetry, plays, critical essays, cultural studies, interviews, and visual art, as well as special thematic issues.
Frequency: Quarterly
Circulation: 2,500
ISSN: 0161-2492
Founded in 1976

19484 Canadian Theatre Review

University of Toronto Press
5201 Dufferin Street
Toronto, ON M3H-5T8

416-667-7810
800-221-9985
FAX 416-667-7881
E-Mail: journals@utpress.utoronto.ca
Home Page: www.utpjournals.com
Social Media: *Facebook, Twitter, Blog*

Anne Marie Corrigan, VP
Audrey Greenwood, Advertising/Marketing Coordinator

Provides critical analysis and innovative coverage of current developments in Canadian theatre. Advocates new issues and artists. Publishes at least one significant new playscript per issue. Each issue includes at least one complete playscript related to the issue theme, insightful articles, and informative reviews.
Cost: $40.00
Frequency: Quarterly
ISSN: 0315-0836
Founded in 1974
Mailing list available for rentat $250 per M

19485 Confrontation

CW Post Campus English Department
720 Northern Blvd
Greenvale, NY 11548-1300

516-626-0099
FAX 516-299-3566
E-Mail: confrontation@liu.edu
Home Page: www.liunet.bkstore.com

Jayne Mo, Manager

Brings new talent to light in the shadows cast by well-known authors. Each issue contains orignal work by famous and by lesser known writers.
Cost: $10.00
Frequency: Twice Yearly
Founded in 1968

19486 Contact Quarterly Journal of Dance and Improvisation

Contact Collaborations
PO Box 603
Northampton, MA 01061

413-586-1181
FAX 413-586-9055
E-Mail: info@contactquarterly.com
Home Page: www.contactquarterly.com

Lisa Nelson, Co-Editor
Nancy Stark Smith, Co-Editor
Melinda Buckwalter, Associate Editor
Kristin Horrigan, Operations Manager/Advertising
Bill McCully, Development/Marketing

A journal of dance, improvisation, performance and contemporary movement arts. Presents materials that spring from the experience of doing. Encourages articulation and dialogue and stimulates activity and exploration within the field of movement and its performance.
Cost: $22.00
Frequency: BiAnnual
Founded in 1978

19487 Cue Magazine

PO Box 2027
Burlingame, CA 94011-2027

415-348-8004
FAX 650-348-7781
Home Page: www.cuemagazines.com

Devoted to the Northern California, Seattle and Portland commercial film, video and multimedia industries and locations that support production.
Frequency: Monthly

19488 Dance Chronicle

Taylor & Francis Group
270 Madison Ave
Floor 4
New York, NY 10016-0601

212-679-3853
FAX 212-564-7854
Home Page: www.summitcom.com

George Dorris, Co-Editor
Jack Anderson, Co-Editor
Edwin Bayrn, Associate Editor

Covers a wide variety of topics, including dance and music, theater, film, literature, painting and aesthetics.
Cost: $465.00
Frequency: TriAnnual
ISSN: 0147-2526

19489 Dance Magazine

Macfadden Performing Arts Media

333 7th Avenue
11th Floor
New York, NY 10001

212-979-4800
Home Page: www.dancemagazine.com

Amy Cogan, VP/Group Publisher
Karen Hildebrand, VP Editorial
Jessi Petrov, Publishing/Marketing Director
Wendy Perron, Editor-in-Chief

The must read magazine for professional and aspiring dancers. From Broadway to ballet and tap to hip hop, not other magazine keeps you in touch with what is going on in all disciplines of dance.
Cost: $34.95
Frequency: Monthly
Circulation: 300,000
ISSN: 0011-6009
Founded in 1927
Printed in 4 colors on glossy stock

19490 Dance Research Journal

Congress on Research in dance
3416 Primm Lane
Birmingham, AL 24702-6170

205-823-5517
FAX 205-823-2760
E-Mail: ashanti@cordance.org
Home Page: www.cordance.org

Ann Dils, Co-Editor
Jill Green, Co-Editor

Published twice a year by the Congress on Research in Dance, this journal carries scholarly articles, book reviews, lists of books and journals received, and reports of scholarly conferences, archives and other projects of interest to the field.
Cost: $65.00
Frequency: Bi-annually
ISSN: 0149-7677
Founded in 1965
Mailing list available for rent: 750+ names at $75 per M

19491 Dance Spirit

Macfadden Performing Arts Media, LLC
333 7th Avenue
11th Floor
New York, NY 10001

212-979-4800
Home Page: www.dancespirit.com

Amy Cogan, VP/Group Publisher
Karen Hildebrand, VP Editorial
Jessi Petrov, Publishing/Marekting Director
Kayte Lydon, Editor-in-Chief

Dedicated to inspiring the next generation of dancers. Packed with expert advice on dance techniques and performing, health and nutrition tips and the latest styles to keep you looking your best from studio to stage to school.
Cost: $16.95
Frequency: 10 Per Year
Founded in 1980

19492 Dance Teacher Magazine

Macfadden Performing Arts Media
333 7th Avenue
11th Floor
New York, NY 10001

212-979-4800
FAX 646-459-4900
Home Page: www.dance-teacher.com

Amy Cogan, VP/Group Publisher
Karen Hildebrand, VP Editorial/Editor-in-Chief
Jessie Petrov, Publishing/Marketing Director

The only magazine written just for dance professionals. Packed with useful ideas that will help you and your students become better danc-

ers.
Cost: $24.95
Frequency: Monthly
Circulation: 60000
Founded in 1979
Printed in 4 colors

19493 Dance on Camera Journal
Dance Films Association
48 W 21st St
Suite 907
New York, NY 10010-6989

212-727-0764
FAX 212-727-0764
E-Mail: info@dancefilms.org
Home Page: www.dancefilms.org
Social Media: *Facebook, Twitter*

Deidra Towers, Executive Director
Marta Renzi, President
Harry Streep, VP
Amy Meharg, Treasurer
Nolini Barretto, Secretary

Subjects range from reviews and essays, news
items regarding dance films, festivals,
opportunites, and issues facing artists
Frequency: Bi-Monthly
Founded in 1956

19494 Dance/USA Journal
Dance/USA
1111 16th St Nw
Suite 300
Washington, DC 20036-4830

202-833-1717
FAX 202-833-2686
E-Mail: danceusa@danceusa.org
Home Page: www.danceusa.org

Andrea Snyder, Executive Director
Tom Thielen, Director Finance/Operations
Katherine Fabian, Membership Manager

The journal features articles on issues of importance to the dance community; news stories
relating to arts and dance; essays from leaders
in the dance field; notes on changes, transitions
and opportunities in the field; calendar of up
coming events; and highlights of Dance/USA
sponsored events. Subscription is free to members of Dance/USA.
Cost: $40.00
28-36 Pages
Frequency: Quarterly
Founded in 1982
Printed in 2 colors on glossy stock

19495 Descant
50 Baldwin Street
PO Box 314 Station P
Toronto, ON M5S-2S8

416-593-2557
FAX 416-593-9362
E-Mail: info@descant.ca
Home Page: www.descant.on.ca
Social Media: *Facebook*

Karen Mulhallen, Editor-in-Chief
Vera DeWaard, Managing Editor
Mary Newberry, Project Manager
Stacey May Fowles, Circulation Manager
Pasha Malla, Director of Outreach

A quarterly journal publishing new and estab-
lished contemporary writers and visual artists
from Canada and around the world. Devoted to
the discovery and development of new writers,
and places their work in the company of cele-
brated writers.
Cost: $28.00
Frequency: Quarterly
Circulation: 1200
ISSN: 0382-909X
Founded in 1970
Mailing list available for rent

19496 Drama Review
MIT Press
55 Hayward Street
Cambridge, MA 02142-1493

617-253-5646
800-207-8354
FAX 617-258-6779
E-Mail: journals-info@mit.edu
Home Page: www.mitpress.mit.edu
Social Media: *Facebook, Twitter, RSS*

Rebbecca Mc Leod, Owner

TDR focuses on performances in their social,
economic, and political contexts. It emphasizes experimental, avant-garde, intercultural
and interdisciplinary performance. TDR covers
dance, theatre, performance art, visual art, popular entertainment, media, sports, rituals, and
performance in politics and everyday life.
Frequency: Quarterly
Founded in 1955

19497 Dramatics Magazine
Educational Theatre Association
2343 Auburn Ave
Cincinnati, OH 45219-2819

513-421-3900
FAX 513-421-7077
E-Mail: jpalmarini@schooltheatre.org
Home Page: schooltheatre.org
Social Media: *Facebook, Twitter*

Donald A Corathers, Publications Director
James Palmarini, Editor

Dramatics is the only magazine that is edited
exclusively for students and teachers of theatre.
Contents include practical articles about acting,
directing, playwriting, design, and technical
theatre; interviews with working professionals
that illuminate the process of becoming a theatre artist; options for higher education and
training in theatre; playscripts; reports on new
shows and other important events in the theatre
world; book, video, and CD-ROM reviews, and
more.
Cost: $27.00
4000 Members
Frequency: 9x/ A Year
Circulation: 34100
ISSN: 0012-5989
Founded in 1929

19498 Encore Performance Publishing
PO Box 95567
South Jordan, UT 84095-0567

801-282-8159
E-Mail: encoreplay@aol.com
Home Page: www.encoreplay.com

Michael C Perry, President

Publishes a variety of publications for those
professionals in the performing arts industry.

19499 Gospel Today
Gospel Today
PO Box 800
Fairburn, GA 30213

770-719-4825
FAX 770-716-2660
E-Mail: admin@gospeltoday.com
Home Page: www.gospeltoday.com

Dr Teresa Hairston, Publisher

To provide a quality publication to inspire, edu-
cate, inform, and empower readers towards
standards of Godly excellence.
Cost: $17.97
Frequency: 8 Per Year
Circulation: 250000
Founded in 1989
Printed in 4 colors on glossy stock

19500 Hispanic Arts News
Association of Hispanic Arts

1025 Connecticut Ave
Suite 1000
Washington, DC 20036

202-657-5158
888-876-1240
FAX 202-478-2767
E-Mail: informacion@latinoarts.org
Home Page: www.hispanics.einnews.com
Social Media: *Facebook, Twitter*

Features in depth articles on the local and national arts community, including artist profiles
and a calendar of events.
Frequency: 9 Per Year
*Mailing list available for rent: 5000 names at
$80 per M*

19501 JazzTimes
JazzTimes Magazine
Madavor Media,85 Quincy Ave
Suite 2
Quincy, MA 02169

617-706-9110
800-437-5828
FAX 617-536-0102
Home Page: www.jazztimes.com

Glen Sabin, CEO
Eric Wynne, Consumer Advertising Director

JazzTimes contains extensive news coverage,
award winning jazz journalism, hundreds of
CD, Book and Video reviews, World class photography and award winning graphics, informative features and columns, special theme issues,
special directories, readers poll and critic pics,
and sound$weeps giveaways and prizes.
Cost: $23.95
Frequency: 10 Issues per y
Circulation: 86000
Founded in 1980

**19502 Journal of Arts Management, Law,
Society**
Heldref Publishers
325 Chestnut Street
Suite 800
Philadelphia, PA 19106

215-625-8900
800-354-1420
FAX 202-296-5149
E-Mail:
customer.service@taylorandfrancis.com
Home Page: www.heldref.org

James Denton, Executive Director

A resource for arts policymakers and analysts,
sociologists, arts and cultural administrators,
educators, trusteed, artists, lawyers, and citizens concerned with the performing, visual,
and media arts as well as cultural affairs. Articles, commentaries, and reviews of publications address marketing, intellectual property,
arts policy, arts law, governance, and cultural
production and dissemination, from a variety of
philosophical, disciplinary, and national and international perspectives.
Cost: $79.00
Frequency: Monthly
ISSN: 1063-2921
Founded in 1956

19503 Journal of Dance Education
National Dance Education Organization
8609 2nd Avenue
Suite 203 B
Silver Spring, MD 20910

301-585-2880
FAX 301-585-2888
E-Mail: info@ndeo.org
Home Page: www.ndeo.org
Social Media: *Facebook, Twitter*

Susan McGreevy-Nichols, Executive Director
Jane Bonbright EdD, Executive Director

Patricia Cohen, Treasurer
Cost: $90.00
Frequency: Quarterly
Circulation: 2000
ISSN: 1529-0824

19504 Lighting Dimensions

Primedia Business
249 W 17th St
New York, NY 10011-5382

212-206-1894
800-827-3322
FAX 212-514-3719
Home Page: lightingdimensions.com

Doug MacDonald, Group Publisher
David Johnson, Associate Publisher/Editorial
Marian Sandberg-Dierson, Editor
Mark Newman, Managing Editor
Jennifer Hirst, Director

Trade publication for lighting professionals in film, theatre, television, concerts, clubs, themed environments, architecctural, commercial, and industrial lighting. Sponsors of the LDI Trade Show and the Broadway Lighting Master Classes.
Cost: $34.97
Frequency: 12/year
Circulation: 14,177
Founded in 1989

19505 Mid-Atlantic Events Magazine

1800 Byberry Road
Suite 901
Huntingdon Valley, PA 19006

215-947-8600
800-521-8588
FAX 215-947-8650
E-Mail: editor@eventsmagazine.com
Home Page: www.eventsmagazine.com
Social Media: *Facebook, Twitter, YouTube*

Jim Cohn, Publisher
Rich Kupka, Editor
Fred Cohn, VP Sales
Katie O'Connell, Director Sales/Marketing
Dana Kurtbek, Production

Focused on Hospitality in the Mid-Atlantic area. It assists the Associations, Corporations, Government, Group and Independent Meeting, Event and Travel Planners who are responsible for arranging Conventions, Trade Shows, Hotel Accommodations, Corporate/Group Travel, Meetings, Seminars, Conferences, Symposiums, Site Selections, Special Events, Banquets, Entertainment, Corporate Golf Outings and Golf Tournaments, Company Picnics, Team Building, Retreats, Board Meetings, Training & Development.
Circulation: 26000
ISSN: 0896-3967
Founded in 1987
Mailing list available for rent
Printed in 8 colors on glossy stock

19506 National Squares

National Square Dance Convention
C/O Gene and Connie Triplett
2760 Polo Club Boulevard
Matthews, NC 28105

704-847-1265
E-Mail: Richp27890@aol.com
Home Page:
www.nationalsquaredanceconvention.com

Dick/Linda Peterson, Editors
Gene/Connie Triplett, Circulation Managers
Dick/Linda Peterson, Public Relations

A national square dance magazine published by the National Executive Committee of the National Square Dance Convention.
Cost: $7.00
Frequency: Quarterly

19507 New England Theatre Journal

New England Theatre Conference
215 Knob Hill Drive
Hamden, CT 06518

617-851-8535
FAX 203-288-5938
E-Mail: mail@netconline.org
Home Page: www.netconline.org

Sabine Klein, President
Jeffrey Watts, Executive VP
Charles Emmons, VP Administration/Finance

Scholarly publication produced once per year. Includes book and theatre reviews, historical analyses, and other well-written articles by noted authors. Free to NETC members. Specifically designed to provide members, and others interested in live theatre arts, with the information and resources they need to enhance their careers, promote their groups, and sharpen their theatre skills.
Cost: $10.00
Frequency: Annual
Founded in 1952

19508 Nouveau Magazine

Barbara Tompkins
5933 Stoney Hill Rd
New Hope, PA 18938-9602

215-794-5996
FAX 215-794-8305
E-Mail: info@nouveaumagazine.com
Home Page: www.nouveaumagazine.com

Barbara Tompkins, Publisher

Features theater reviews.
Frequency: Monthly
Founded in 1981
Printed in 4 colors on glossy stock

19509 OffBeat

OffBeat
421 Frenchmen St
Suite 200
New Orleans, LA 70116-2039

504-944-4300
877-944-4300
FAX 504-944-4306
E-Mail: offbeat@offbeat.com
Home Page: www.offbeat.com
Social Media: *Facebook, Twitter, Flickr*

Jan Ramsy, Publisher
Joseph L Irrera, Managing Editor
Bunny Matthews, Senior Editor
Michael Jastroch, Magazine Design/Production
Doug Jackson, Distribution Manager

Consumer-oriented music magazine focusing on New Orleans and Louisiana music. Regular columns on Cajun music, zydeco, traditional and contemporary jazz, brass band (Mardi Gras second-line music), New Orleans R & B, Louisiana and delta blues, Gospel, modern and roots rock and our internationally-appreciated culture and cusine. Information on music fairs and festivals in the region is given.
Cost: $29.00
Frequency: Monthly
Circulation: 50000
ISBN: 1-090081-0-
Founded in 1985
Mailing list available for rent: 15000 names
Printed in 4 colors on newsprint stock

19510 Performing Arts Insider Magazine

PAI C/O Total Theater
PO Box 31
Greeley, CO 80632

970-405-3077
E-Mail: paipress@aol.com
Home Page: www.performingartsinsider.com

David Lefkowitz, Publisher/Editor
Richmond Shepard, Publisher
J. Weil, Advertising Sales

Includes day-by-day calendar listings of shows on Broadway, Off and Off-Off Broadway, plus dance, opera, cabaret and special events. Also included are comprehensive theater guides, listing the author, director, cast, designers, synopsis, theater and box office details, as well as contact information for producers, press agents, general managers and casting directors.
Cost: $275.00
Frequency: Monthly+9 Updates
Circulation: 2000
Founded in 1944

19511 Performing Arts Resources

Theatre Library Association
New York Public Library for Performing Arts
40 Lincoln Center Plaza
New York, NY 10023

E-Mail: info@tla-online.org
Home Page:
www.tla-online.org/publications/par.html

Nancy Friedland, President
Angela Weaver, VP
Rebecca Lord, Executive Secretary
Colleen Reilly, Treasurer

Features articles on resource materials in the fields of theatre, popular entertainment, film, television and radio, information on public and private collections, and essays on conservation and collection management of theatre arts materials.
Cost: $30.00
Frequency: Irregular
Circulation: 500
ISSN: 0360-3814
Founded in 1974

19512 Playbill

34-15 61st Street
Woodside, NY 11377

212-557-5757
FAX 212-682-2932
E-Mail: agans@playbill.com
Home Page: www.playbill.com

Andrew Gans, Editor

The exclusive magazine for Broadway and Off-Broadway theatregoers, providing the information necessary for the understanding and enjoyment of each show, including features articles and columns by and about theatre personalities, entertainment, travel, fashion, dining and other editorial pieces geared to the lifestyle of the upscale, active theatre attendee. Playbill also serves New York's three most prominent performing arts venues - the Metropolitan Opera House, Lincoln Center and Carnegie Hall
Cost: $24.00
Frequency: Monthly
Founded in 1884

19513 Plays: Drama Magazine for Young People

Plays Magazine
PO Box 600160
Newton, MA 02460

617-630-9100
800-630-5755
FAX 617-630-9101
E-Mail: lpreston@playsmag.com
Home Page: www.playsmag.com

Elizabeth Preston, Editor

Includes eight to ten royalty-free one-act plays, arranged by age level. Modern and traditional plays for the celebration of all important holidays and occasions. Adaptable to all cast sizes with easy to follow instructions for settings and costumes. A complete source of original plays and programs for school-age actors and audiences.
Cost: $39.00
Frequency: 7 X Per Year
Circulation: 6000

Founded in 1940
Printed in on matte stock

19514 Pointe Magazine
Macfadden Performing Arts Media LLC
333 7th Avenue
11th Floor
New York, NY 10001

212-979-4800
Home Page: www.pointemagazine.com

Amy Cogan, VP/Group Publisher
Karen Hildebrand, VP Editorial
Jessie Petrov, Publishing/Marketing Director

Dedicated exclusively to the world of ballet.
Frequency: Bi-Monthly
Circulation: 120000

19515 Pollstar: Concert Hotwire
Pollstar
4697 W Jacquelyn Ave
Fresno, CA 93722-6443

559-271-7900
FAX 559-271-7979
E-Mail: info@pollstar.com
Home Page: www.pollstar.com

Gary Smith, COO
Shari Rice, VP
Gary Bongiovanni, CEO

Trade publication for the concert industry offering global coverage and information including concert tour schedules, ticket sales information and more.
Cost: $449.00
Frequency: Weekly
Circulation: 20000
Printed in 4 colors

19516 Shakespeare Bulletin
University of North Carolina
Department of English
9201 University City Boulevard
Charlotte, NC 28223

E-Mail: sbeditor@email.uncc.edu
Home Page: www.shakespeare-bulletin.org

Seymour Isenberg, Founding Editor
Andrew James Hartley, Editor
Jeremy Lopez, Theatre Review Editor
Genevieve Love, Book Review Editor
Kirk Melnikoff, Shakespeare on Film Editor

A peer-reviewed journal of performance and criticism and scholarship which provides commentary on Shakespeare and Renaissance drama through feature articles, thatre and film reviews, and book reviews. The journal is a member of the Conference of Editors of Learned Journals.
Cost: $35.00
Frequency: Quarterly
ISSN: 0748-2558
Founded in 1982
Mailing list available for rent
Printed in on matte stock

19517 Show Music
Po Box A
East Haddam, CT 06423-0466

860-873-8664
FAX 860-873-2329
E-Mail: rklink@goodspeed.org
Home Page: www.showmusic.org

Ryan Klink, Managing Editor
Maz O Preeo, Editor-In-Chief

Internationally acclaimed by professionals and fans as the premier magazine covering musical theatre around the world. Show music combines insightful interviews and reviews of productions, recordings, videos and books.

19518 Sondheim Review
PO Box 11213
Chicago, IL 60611-0213

773-275-4254
800-584-1020
FAX 773-275-4254
E-Mail: info@sondheimreview.com
Home Page: www.sondheimreview.com

Dedicated to the work of the musical theater and Broadway's foremost composer and lyricist, Stephen Sondheim. Each issue contains news, interviews, upcoming productions in the area, puzzles and more.
Cost: $19.95
Frequency: Quarterly
Circulation: 40000
ISSN: 1076-450X
Founded in 1994
Mailing list available for rent: 6,000 names at $105 per M
Printed in on glossy stock

19519 Southern Theatre
Southeastern Theatre Conference
1175 Revolution Mill Dr.
Studio 14
Greensboro, NC 27405

336-272-3645
FAX 336-272-8810
E-Mail: setc@setc.org
Home Page: www.setc.org

Elizabeth Baun, Executive Director
April J'Callahan Marshall, Professional Theatre Services Mgr
Hardy Koenig, Educational Services Manager

Spotlights people, places and organizations within the region that are paving new paths in theatre. Includes low-cost strategies for design success, tips on hot markets for playwrights, new books of special interest, innovative ideas for marketing theatre, inside track on new trends and some of the region's up-and-coming theatre stars. Subscription is free with SETC membership.
Cost: $18.75
Frequency: Quarterly
Circulation: 4000+
Founded in 1949

19520 Spectrum
110 S Jefferson Street
Dayton, OH 45402-3412

937-220-1600
800-247-1614
FAX 937-220-1642
E-Mail: comments@thinktv.org
Home Page: www.thinktv.org
Social Media: *Facebook, Twitter, YouTube*

Jerry Kathman, President&CEO
Brad Mays, Treasurer
Alisa Poe, Secretary

ThinkTV's monthly member magazine. Contains program listings for both ThinkTV 16 and ThinkTV14 as well as interesting feature stories, station news and more.
Frequency: Weekly
Circulation: 18000
Founded in 1959

19521 Stage of the Art
American Alliance for Theatre and Education
4908 Auburn Avenue
Bethesda, MD 20814-3474

301-200-1944
FAX 301-280-1682
E-Mail: info@aate.com.edu
Home Page: www.aate.com
Social Media: *Facebook, Twitter, RSS*

David Young, Editor
JoBeth Gonzalez, Director Publications/Research

Published by the American Alliance for Theatre and Education.
Mailing list available for rent: 700 names at $150 per M

19522 Stagebill
Stagebill
144 E 44th Street
New York, NY 10017

212-476-0640
FAX 212-983-5976
E-Mail: bmattison@stagebill.com
Home Page: www.avant-rus.com/stagebill

Fred B Tarter, Chairman/President/CEO
Gerry Byrne, Chairman/President/CEO
Ben Mattison, Editorial Contact

Publisher of the program magazines for the leading, theaters, symphonies, dance companies and performing arts centers in the United States. A national performing arts magazine.
Frequency: Monthly
Founded in 1924

19523 Stages
Curtains
301 W 45th Street
Apartment 5A
New York, NY 10036-3825

FAX 201-836-4107

Frank Scheck, Editor
Cost: $20.00
Frequency: Monthly
Circulation: 35,000

19524 TD & T: Theatre Design & Technology
US Institute for Theatre Technology
315 South Crouse Avenue
Suite 200
Syracuse, NY 13210

315-463-6525
FAX 315-463-6525
E-Mail: info@.usitt.org
Home Page: www.usitt.org
Social Media: *Facebook, Twitter*

David Roger, Editor
Arnold Wengrow, Book Review Editor
Michelle Smith, Membership/Advertising Manager
N Deborah Hazlett, Art Director

Published by United States Institute for Theatre Technology. Focuses on USITT's ten interest areas: architecture, costume design and technology, education, engineering, health and safety, lighting, management, scene design, sound design, and technical production.
3700 Members
Frequency: Quarterly

19525 Teaching Theatre Journal
Educational Theatre Association
2343 Auburn Ave
Cincinnati, OH 45219-2819

513-421-3900
FAX 513-421-7077
E-Mail: jpalmarini@schooltheatre.org
Home Page: schooltheatre.org
Social Media: *Facebook, Twitter*

Donald A Corathers, Publications Director
James Palmarini, Editor

For professional theatre educators. A typical issue includes an article on acting, directing, playwriting, or technical theatre; a profile of an outstanding educationl theatre program; a piece on curriculum design, assessment, or teaching

methodology; and reports on current trends or issues in the field, such as funding, standards, or certification.
4000 Members
Frequency: Quarterly
Circulation: 4000
ISSN: 1077-2561
Founded in 1929

19526 Technical Brief
Yale School of Drama
222 York Street
PO Box 208244
New Haven, CT 06520

203-432-8188
FAX 203-432-8129
E-Mail: bronislaw.sammler@yale.edu
Home Page: www.technicalbrief.org

Ben Sammler, Co-Editor
Don Harvey, Co-Editor

Written by professionals for professionals, providing a dialogue between technical practitioners from the several performing arts. The succinct articles, complete with mechanical drawings, represent the best solutions to recurring technical problems. Published October, January and April.
Cost: $15.00
Frequency: 3X Per Year
Founded in 1924

19527 Theater Magazine
Yale School of Drama
1120 Chapel Street
P.O Box 1257
New Haven, CT 06505

203-432-1234
FAX 203-432-6423
E-Mail: yalerep@yale.edu
Home Page: www.yale.edu/drama

Tom Sellar, Editor
Laraine Sammler, Business Manager
Alex Grennan, Director of Business/Comm

Periodicals, essays and articles of the Yale School of Drama.
Cost: $22.00
Frequency: Annual+
Circulation: 2500
Founded in 1924
Mailing list available for rent: 1.5M names
Printed in one color on matte stock

19528 Theatre Bay Area Magazine
1663 Mission Street
Suite 525
San Francisco, CA 94103

415-430-1140
FAX 415-430-1145
E-Mail: tba@theatrebayarea.org
Home Page: www.theatrebayarea.org
Social Media: *Facebook, Twitter, YouTube*

Karen Mc Kevitt, Executive Director
Dale Albright, Director, Member Services
Clayton Lord, Director, Audience Development
Cost: $5.95
Frequency: Monthly
Circulation: 4500

19529 Theatre Bill
Jerome Press
332 Congress St
Suite 2
Boston, MA 02210-1217

617-423-3400
FAX 617-423-7108
Home Page: www.showofthemonthtravel.com

Jerome Rosenfeld, Owner

19530 Theatre Journal
Johns Hopkins University Press

2715 N Charles St
Baltimore, MD 21218-4363

410-516-6900
800-537-5487
FAX 410-516-6968
E-Mail: webmaster@jhupress.jhu.edu
Home Page: www.press.jhu.edu

William Brody, President
David Z Saltz, Co-Editor
Sonja Arsham Kuftinec, Performance Review Editor
James Peck, Book Review Editor
Bob Kowkabany, Managing Editor

One of the most authoritative and useful publications of theatre studies available today. Theatre Journal features social and historical studies, production reviews, and theoretical inquiries that analize dramatic texts and production. Official journal of the Association for Theatre in Higher Education.
Cost: $40.00
Frequency: Quarterly
Circulation: 2492
ISSN: 0192-2882
Founded in 1878
Mailing list available for rent

19531 Theatre Symposium
Auburn University
1175 Revolution Mill Dr.
Studio 14
Greensboro, NC 27405

336-272-3645
FAX 336-272-8810
E-Mail: setc@setc.org
Home Page: www.setc.org

M Scott Phillips, Editor

An annual publication of works of scholarship resulting from a single topic meeting held on a southeastern university campus each year. Available to adult members only. A copublication of the Southeaster Theatre Conference and the University of Alabama Press.

19532 Theatre Topics
Johns Hopkins University Press
2715 N Charles St
Baltimore, MD 21218-4363

410-516-6900
800-537-5487
FAX 410-516-6998
E-Mail: webmaster@jhupress.jhu.edu
Home Page: www.press.jhu.edu

William Brody, President
Sandra G Shannon, Co-Editor
DeAnna Toten Beard, Book Review Editor
Elanore Lampners, Managing Editor
Beverley Pevitts, Founding Editor

Focuses on performance studies, dramaturgy, and theatre pedagogy. Concise and timely articles on a broad array of practical, performance-oriented subjects, with special attention to topics of current interest to the profession. Keeps readers informed of the latest developments on the stage and in the classroom. The official journal of the Association for Theatre in Higher Education. Published in March and September.
Cost: $32.00
Frequency: Semi-Annually
Circulation: 1528
ISSN: 1054-8378
Founded in 1878
Mailing list available for rent

19533 Youth Theatre Journal
American Alliance for Theatre and Education

4908 Auburn Ave
Bethesda, MD 20814

301-200-1944
FAX 301-235-7108
E-Mail: info@aate.com
Home Page: www.aate.com

A scholarly journal dedicated to advancing the study and practice of theatre and drama with, for, and by the people of all ages. It is concerned with all forms of scholarship of the highest quality that inform the fields of theatre for young audiences and drama/theatre education.
Cost: $25.00
Frequency: 2x/Year
Circulation: 1000
ISSN: 0892-9092
Mailing list available for rent: 700 names at $150 per M

Trade Shows

19534 CinemaCon
National Association of Theatre Owners
750 1st St NE
Suite 1130
Washington, DC 20002-4241

202-962-0054
FAX 202-962-0370
E-Mail: nato@natodc.com
Home Page: www.natoonline.org

John Fithian, President
Gary Klein, VP
Kathy Conroy, Executive Director

A gathering of cinema owners and operators.
4000 Members
Frequency: Annual/March

19535 EXPO
Theatre Bay Area
870 Market Street
Suite 375
San Francisco, CA 94102-3002

415-430-1140
FAX 415-430-1145
E-Mail: dale@theatrebayarea.org
Home Page: www.theatrebayarea.org

Dale Albright, Director of Individual Services

Theatre Bay Area's EXPO is where attendees can meet those kinds of businesses that might offer services to the theatre community: theatre companies, actors, etc. There are also break-out sessions discussing issues of interest to the theatre community.
500+ Attendees
Frequency: May

19536 EdTA Thespian Festival
Educational Theatre Association
2343 Auburn Ave
Cincinnati, OH 45219-2819

513-421-3900
FAX 513-421-7077
Home Page: www.schooltheatre.org
Social Media: *Facebook, Twitter*

Michael Peitz, Executive Director
Gloria McIntyre, President
Jay Seller VP

The premiere showcase for high school theatre, drawing students and teachers from throughout the United States and abroad.
3000 Attendees

19537 Educational Theatre Association Conference
Educational Theatre Association

2343 Auburn Ave
Cincinnati, OH 45219-2819

513-421-3900
FAX 513-421-7077
Home Page: www.schooltheatre.org
Social Media: *Facebook, Twitter*

Michael Peitz, Executive Director
Gloria McIntyre, President
Jay Seller VP
400 Attendees
Frequency: Annual

19538 International Association of Venue Managers
International Association of Assembly Managers
635 Fritz Drive
Suite 100
Coppell, TX 75019-4442

972-906-7441
800-935-4226
FAX 972-906-7418
E-Mail: mike.meyers@iaam.org
Home Page: www.iaam.org

Steven Peters, President
Robyn Williams, First Vice President
Frequency: Annual

19539 NDEO National Conference
National Dance Education Organization
8609 2nd Avenue
Suite 203 B
Silver Spring, MD 20910

301-585-2880
FAX 301-585-2888
E-Mail: info@ndeo.org
Home Page: www.ndeo.org

Susan McGreevy-Nichols, Executive Director
Jane Bonbright EdD, Executive Director
Patricia Cohen, Treasurer

Provides 200+ professional development sessions for artists, educators and administrators teaching or supporting dance education programs in PreK-12, colleges/universities, private studio/schools of dance, community centers and performing arts organizations.
800 Attendees
Frequency: Annual

19540 National Black Theatre Festival
610 Coliseum Drive
Suite 1
Winston-Salem, NC 27106

336-723-2266
E-Mail: nbtf@bellsouth.net
Home Page: www.nbtf.org

Patrice Toney, President
Frequency: Annual, Winston-Salem

19541 National Square Dance Convention
PO Box 5790
Topeka, KS 66605-5790

317-635-4455
Home Page: www.57nsdc.com

Ernie Stone, Executive Committee
Barbara Stone, Executive Committee
250 booths and 250 exhibitors.
20M+ Attendees
Frequency: June

19542 New England Theatre Conference
215 Knob Hill Drive
Hamden, CT 06518

617-851-8535
FAX 203-288-5938

E-Mail: mail@netconline.org
Home Page: www.netconline.org

Sabine Klein, President
Jeffrey Watts, Executive VP
Charles Emmons, VP Administration/Finance

Promoting excellence in theatre, a conference of New England's oldest, largest regional theatre association.
800+ Attendees
Frequency: November
Founded in 1952

19543 North Carolina Southeastern Theatre Conference
1175 Revolution Mill Drive
Suite 14
Greensboro, NC 27405-0868

336-272-3645
FAX 336-272-8810
E-Mail: info@setc.org
Home Page: www.setc.org

Betsey Baun, Executive Director
April Marshall, Contact/Pro. Theatre Services

Join over 4,000 Theatre Artists for education, exchanges, ideas, products, networking and great theatre. Convention activities include keynote speakers, auditions, guest speakers, festivals, design competition, commercial and educational expo exhibits, scholarship awards, social events and workshops.
4000+ Attendees

19544 Prescott Park Arts Festival
105 Marcy Street
PO Box 4370
Portsmouth, NH 03802-4370

603-436-2848
FAX 603-436-1034
E-Mail: info@prescottpark.org
Home Page: www.prescottpark.org
Social Media: *Facebook*

Ben Anderson, Executive Director
John Moynihan, General Manager
Catherine Wejchert, Development Coordinator

Provide a financially accessible, quality multi-arts festival to a diverse audience.

19545 TCG National Conference
Theatre Communications Group
520 8th Ave
24th Floor
New York, NY 10018-4156

212-609-5900
FAX 212-609-5901
E-Mail: tcg@tcg.org
Home Page: www.tcg.org

Theresa Eyring, Executive Director
Jennifer Cleary, Membership Director

19546 US Institute for Theatre Technology Annual Conference & Stage Expo
USITT
315 S Crouse Avenue
Suite 200
Syracuse, NY 13210

315-463-6463
800-938-7488
FAX 315-463-6525
E-Mail: info@usitt.org
Home Page: www.usitt.org
Social Media: *Facebook, Twitter, LinkedIn*

Carl Lefko, President
Patricia Dennis, Secretary
Travis DeCastro, Treasurer

The Conference offers over 175 sessions featuring design, technology, costume, sound, architecture, management, engineering, and production. The Stage Expo showcases businesses, products, services, and eductional opportunities in the performing arts and

entertainment industry. With over 150 exhibitors, Stage Expo provides conference attendees with the opportunity to see the newest and best products and services on the market today.
3700 Members
3800 Attendees
Frequency: March
Founded in 1960

Directories & Databases

19547 Academy Players Directory
2210 W Olive Avenue
Suite 320
Burbank, CA 91506

310-247-3058
FAX 310-550-5034
E-Mail: info@playersdirectory.com
Home Page: www.playersdirectory.com

The Players Directory appeared in 1937 as the first reliable casting directory that listed both featured stars and extras. Today, more than 16,000 actors are included.
Cost: $75.00
Founded in 1937

19548 American Association of Community Theatre Membership Directory
1300 Gendy St Forth Worth
St Forth Worth, TX 76107

817-732-3177
866-687-2228
FAX 817-732-3178
E-Mail: info@aact.org
Home Page: www.aact.org

Julie Angelo, Executive Director
Linda Lee, President
Carole Ries, VP Public Relations
Frank Peot, Secretary
Tim Jebsen, Treasurer

The database includes addresses for over 7,000 community theatre organizations in the USA. Only available to members.
Mailing list available for rent: 10000 names at $180 per M

19549 Americans for the Arts Field Directory
Americans for the Arts
1 E 53rd St
2nd Floor
New York, NY 10022-4242

212-223-2787
FAX 212-980-4857
Home Page: www.artsactionfund.org
Social Media: *Facebook, Twitter, RSS, You Tube*

Suzanne Niemeyer, Editor
Robert L Lynch, President/CEO
Liz Bartolomeo, Public Relations/Marketing Coord
Chad Bauman, Director Print/Multimedia
Graham Dunstan, Assoc Director Publication Sales

A must-have resource for anyone working in the arts and community development. The directory provides contact information for local, state, regional, and national arts service organizations-more than 4,000 entries broken down by state and region. Also includes contact information for professional consultants working in the nonprofit arts field. A great networking tool.
Cost: $35.00
262 Pages

19550 Association of Performing Arts Presenters Membership Directory
APAP

1211 Connecticut Ave NW
Suite 200
Washington, DC 20036-2716

202-833-2787
888-820-2787
FAX 202-833-1543
E-Mail: info@artspresenters.org
Home Page: www.artspresenters.org

Sandra Gibson, President
Sean Handerhan, Marketing

An invaluable resource for keeping in touch
with colleagues. Puts more than 1,450 presenters, service organizations, artists, management
companies, consultants, and vendors at your
fingertips. An excellent networking tool for
everyone on your staff.
1900 Members
Frequency: Annual
Founded in 1957

19551 Complete Catalogue of Plays

Dramatists Play Service
440 Park Ave S
New York, NY 10016-8012

212-683-8960
FAX 212-213-1539
E-Mail: webmasters@dramatists.com
Home Page: www.dramatists.com
Social Media: *Facebook*

Stephen Fultan, President
Rafael J Rivera, VP Finance/Administration
Michael Q Fellmeth, VP Publications/IT
Tamra Feifer, Director Operations

The Complete Catalogue is published in odd
years and the Supplement of New Plays in even
years. Both books are distributed, without
charge, to current customers in the Fall of each
year.
412 Pages
Founded in 1936

19552 Costume Designers Guild Directory

Costumer Designers Guild
4730 Woodman Avenue
Suite 430
Sherman Oaks, CA 91423-2400

818-905-1557
FAX 818-905-1560
E-Mail: cdgia@earthlink.net
Home Page: www.costumedesignersguild.com

Cheryl Downey, Executive Director
Deborah N Landis, President

Directory includes members' names, classification, and other statistical information.
Frequency: Annual

19553 Dance Annual Directory

Dance Magazine
333 7th Ave
11th Floor
New York, NY 10001-5109

212-979-4800
FAX 212-979-4817
E-Mail: emacel@dancemagazine.com
Home Page: www.dancemagazine.com

Karla Johnson, Publisher
Emily Macel, Editor
Karen Hildebrand, Editorial Director
Wendy Perron, Editor-in-Chief
Hanna Rubin, Managing Editor

Reach 300,000+ dancers, dance teachers, and
dance professionals in the dance world.
Cost: $100.00
Frequency: Annual

19554 Dance Magazine College Guide

Dance Magazine

333 7th Ave
11th Floor
New York, NY 10038-3900

212-979-4800
FAX 212-979-4817
E-Mail: subscriptions@dancemagazine.com
Home Page: www.dancemagazine.com

Karla Johnson, President
Karen Hildebrand, Editorial Director
Wendy Perron, Editor-in-Chief
Hanna Rubin, Managing Editor
Kate Lydon, Education Editor

With over 500+ listings, Dance Magazine College Guide is a comprehensive source for dance
degree programs in higher education. Find application deadlines and audition dates. Get student perspectives and career advice. Online
database offers the ability to identify programs
that match an individual's personal criteria for
degree, type of dance, location, department
size, tuition and more.
Cost: $29.95
Frequency: Annual

19555 Dance Magazine: Summer Dance Calendar Issue

Dance Magazine
33 W 60th Street
Floor 10
New York, NY 10023-7905

212-245-9050
800-331-1750
Home Page: www.dancemagazine.com

A list of dance workshops and special programs
for students are listed.
Cost: $3.95
Frequency: Annual
Circulation: 100,000

19556 Dance/USA Annual Directory and List-Serv

Dance/USA
1111 16th St NW
Suite 300
Washington, DC 20036-4830

202-833-1717
FAX 202-833-2686
E-Mail: danceusa@danceusa.org
Home Page: www.danceusa.org

Andrea Snyder, Executive Director
Tom Thielen, Director Finance/Operations
Katherine Fabian, Membership Manager

On-going list-servs keep many peer councils in
touch throughout the year, by providing a quick
and easy connection to peer counseling when
members have an immediate question or problem. Information about dance companies,
schools, presenters, service organizations and
commercial suppliers is included in the annual
copy of Dance Annual Directory.
Frequency: Annual
Circulation: 400+

19557 Directory of Theatre Training Programs

Theatre Directories
P.O.Box 2409
Manchester Center, VT 05255-2409

802-867-9333
FAX 802-867-2297
E-Mail: info@theatredirectories.com
Home Page: www.theatredirectories.com

Peg Lyons, Editor
PJ Tumielewicz, Editor

Profiles admissions, tuition, faculty, curriculum, facilities, productions and philosophy of
training at 475 programs in the US, Canada and
abroad: Colleges, Universities, Conservatories,
Undergraduate and Graduate degrees. Includes
Combined Auditions information. Indexed by

degrees offered in each program.
Cost: $39.50
ISBN: 0-933919-61-1

19558 Dramatics College Theatre Directory

Educational Theatre Association
2343 Auburn Ave
Cincinnati, OH 45219-2815

513-421-3900
FAX 513-421-7077
Home Page: www.edta.org
Social Media: *Facebook, Twitter*

Michael Peitz, Executive Director
Gloria McIntyre, President
Jay Seller, VP

Lists more than 250 college, university, and
conservatory theatre programs, offering a
sketch of each based on information provided
by the schools. The listings can be used to measure each school against one's own criteria for
location, setting, courses of study, admission
requirements, and cost. Find out which programs offer merit scholarships and grants and
how those funds are awarded. Use the contact
information to get in touch with the programs
that seem to offer the best fit for your needs
Cost: $9.00
Frequency: Annual

19559 Dramatics Magazine: Summer Theatre Directory

Educational Theatre Association
2343 Auburn Ave
Cincinnati, OH 45219-2815

513-421-3900
FAX 513-421-7077
Home Page: www.edta.org
Social Media: *Facebook, Twitter*

Michael Peitz, Executive Director
Gloria McIntyre, President
Jay Seller, VP

Lists nearly 200 summer theatre programs and
stock companies, offering a sketch of each
based on factual information provided by the
schools, camps, and theatre companies. The
listings can be used to measure each program
against one's own criteria for location, setting,
housing, courses of study, admission requirements and fees.
Cost: $9.00
Frequency: Annual

19560 Dramatist's Sourcebook

Theatre Communications Group
520 8th Ave
24th Floor
New York, NY 10018-4156

212-609-5900
FAX 212-609-5901
E-Mail: tcg@tcg.org
Home Page: www.tcg.org

Theresa Eyring, Executive Director
Kelly Haydon, Database Manager
Jennifer Cleary, Director Membership
Terence Nemeth, Publisher
Kathy Sova, Editorial Director

Completely revised, with more than 900 opportunities for playwrights, translators, composers,
lyricists, and librettists, as well as opportunities
for screen, radio, and television writers. Thoroughly indexed, with a calendar of deadlines.
The Sourcebook contains scrip-submission procedures for more than 350 theatres seeking new
plays; guidelines for more than 150 prizes; and
sections on agents, fellowships and residencies.
Cost: $22.95
Frequency: Annual
ISBN: 1-559362-94-4
Founded in 1980

19561 Dramatists Guild Annual Resource Directory
Dramatists Guild of America
1501 Broadway
Suite 701
New York, NY 10036-5505

212-398-9366
FAX 212-944-0420
Home Page: www.dramaguild.com

Ralph Sevush, Executive Director

The Resource Directory is an annual sourcebook available only to Guild members, sent automatically as one of the privileges of Guild members. It includes lists of conferences and festivals, contests, producers, publishers, agents and attorneys, fellowships and grants, and workshops throughout the US and the world.
Frequency: Annual

19562 Encyclopedia of Exhibition
National Association of Theatre Owners
750 1st St Ne
Suite 1130
Washington, DC 20002-4241

202-962-0054
FAX 202-962-0370
E-Mail: nato@natodc.com
Home Page: www.natoonline.org

John Fithian, President
Gary Klein, VP
Kathy Conroy, Executive Director

Packed with information on film grosses, upcoming releases, and filmgoer demographics. Also features a directory of international and domestic exhibitors and distributors, cinema companies ranked by screen count, trade publications and more
Cost: $500.00
Frequency: Annual

19563 Feedback Theatrebooks and Prospero Press
Feedback Theatrebooks & Prospero Press
PO Box 174
Brooklin, ME 04616

207-359-2781
FAX 207-359-5532

Publishes theatre histories, cookbooks, directories, anthologies of plays, plays published before WWII, and format guidelines for playwrights.

19564 Grey House Performing Arts Directory
Grey House Publishing
4919 Route 22
PO Box 56
Amenia, NY 12501

518-789-8700
800-562-2139
FAX 845-373-6390
E-Mail: books@greyhouse.com
Home Page: www.greyhouse.com
Social Media: *Facebook, Twitter*

Leslie Mackenzie, Publisher
Richard Gottlieb, Editor

The most comprehensive resource covering the Performing Arts. This directory provides current information on over 8,500 Dance Companies, Instrumental Music Programs, Opera Companies, Choral Groups, Theater Companies, Performing Arts Series, Performing Arts Facilities and Artist Management Groups.
Cost: $185.00
1200 Pages
Frequency: Annual
ISBN: 1-592373-76-3
Founded in 1981

19565 Grey House Performing Arts Directory - Online Database
Grey House Publishing
4919 Route 22
PO Box 56
Amenia, NY 12501-0056

518-789-8700
800-562-2139
FAX 518-789-0556
E-Mail: gold@greyhouse.com
Home Page: www.gold.greyhouse.com
Social Media: *Facebook, Twitter*

Leslie Mackenzie, Publisher
Richard Gottlieb, Editor

The Grey House Performing Arts Directory - Online Database provides immediate access to dance companies, orchestras, opera companies, choral groups, theater companies, series, festivals and perfoming arts facilities across the country, or in their region, state, or in your own backyard. It offers unequaled coverage of the Performing Arts - over 8,500 listings - of the major performance organization, facilities, and information resources.
Frequency: Annual
Founded in 1981

19566 Money for Film and Video Artists
Americans for the Arts
1 E 53rd St
2nd Floor
New York, NY 10022-4242

212-223-2787
FAX 212-980-4857
Home Page: www.artsactionfund.org
Social Media: *Facebook, Twitter, RSS, You Tube*

Suzanne Niemeyer, Editor
Robert L Lynch, President/CEO
Liz Bartolomeo, Public Relations/Marketing Coord
Chad Bauman, Director Print/Multimedia
Graham Dunstan, Assoc Director Publication Sales

A comprehensive resource guide to fellowships, grants, awards, low-cost facilities, emergency assistance programs, technical assistance, and support services. Entries include contact information; type of award and/or scope of service; eligibility requirements; application procedures; deadlines and more.
Cost: $14.95
317 Pages
ISBN: 1-879903-09-1

19567 Money for International Exchange in the Arts
Americans for the Arts
1 E 53rd St
2nd Floor
New York, NY 10022-4242

212-223-2787
FAX 212-980-4857
Home Page: www.artsactionfund.org
Social Media: *Facebook, Twitter, RSS, You Tube*

Suzanne Niemeyer, Editor
Robert L Lynch, President/CEO
Liz Bartolomeo, Public Relations/Marketing Coord
Chad Bauman, Director Print/Multimedia
Graham Dunstan, Assoc Director Publication Sales

This resource includes grants, fellowships and awards for travel and work abroad; support and technical assistance for international touring and exchange; international artists' residencies; programs that support artists' professional development, and more. Indexed by region, disci-

pline and type of support.
Cost: $14.95
122 Pages
ISBN: 1-879903-01-6

19568 Money for Performing Artists
Americans for the Arts
1 E 53rd St
2nd Floor
New York, NY 10022-4242

212-223-2787
FAX 212-980-4857
Home Page: www.artsactionfund.org
Social Media: *Facebook, Twitter, RSS, You Tube*

Suzanne Niemeyer, Editor
Robert L Lynch, President/CEO
Liz Bartolomeo, Public Relations/Marketing Coord
Chad Bauman, Director Print/Multimedia
Graham Dunstan, Assoc Director Publication Sales

Lists awards, grants, fellowships, competitions, auditions, workshops, and artists' colonies, as well as emergency and technical assistance programs.
Cost: $12.00
240 Pages
ISBN: 0-915400-96-0
Founded in 1991

19569 Money for Visual Arts
Americans for the Arts
1 E 53rd St
2nd Floor
New York, NY 10022-4242

212-223-2787
FAX 212-980-4857
Home Page: www.artsactionfund.org
Social Media: *Facebook, Twitter, RSS, You Tube*

Suzanne Niemeyer, Editor
Robert L Lynch, President/CEO
Liz Bartolomeo, Public Relations/Marketing Coord
Chad Bauman, Director Print/Multimedia
Graham Dunstan, Assoc Director Publication Sales

A guide to grants, fellowships, awards, artist colonies, emergency and technical assistance, and support services. Entries include contact information; type of award and/or scope of service; eligibility requirements; application procedures; deadlines, and more.
Cost: $14.95
340 Pages

19570 Musical America International Directory of the Performing Arts
Commonwealth Business Media
50 Millstone Rd
Suite 200
East Windsor, NJ 08520-1418

609-371-7700
800-221-5488
FAX 609-371-7879
E-Mail: info@musicalamerica.com
Home Page: www.cbizmedia.com

Stephanie Challener, Publisher
Sedgwick Clark, Editor
Susan Elliot, News Editor
Bob Hudoba, Data Editor

Features over 14,000 detailed listings of worldwide arts organizations, including key contact information such as name, address, phone, fax, Web site and E-mail addresses, budget category, type of event and seating capacity. In addition, through advertising, over 10,000 artists are indexed in the alphabetical and categorical indexes. Categories include artist managers, orchestras, opera companies, concert series, festi-

vals, competitions, music schools and departments, record companies, and more.
Founded in 1898

19571 NYC/On Stage
Theatre Development Fund
520 Eight Avenue
Suite 801
New York, NY 10018-6507

212-912-9770
E-Mail: info@tdf.org
Home Page: www.tdf.org
Social Media: *Facebook*

Earl D. Weiner, Chair
Sandra Kresch, Vice Chairman
Robert T. Goldman, Treasurer
Deborah Hartnett, Secretary

Theater, dance, and music companies and performing arts centers in New York City.
Founded in 1995

19572 National Network For Artist Placement
National Network for Artist Placement
935 W Avenue 37
Los Angeles, CA 90065

323-222-4035
800-354-5348
E-Mail: NNAPnow@aol.com
Home Page: www.artistplacement.com

Warren Christensen, Consultant

Internship opportunities in dance, music, theatre, art and film.
Cost: $85.00
375 Pages
Frequency: Bi-Annual
ISBN: 0-945941-13-7

19573 Opera America Membership Directory
Opera America
330 7th Ave
16th Floor
New York, NY 10001-5248

212-796-8620
FAX 212-796-8631
E-Mail: info@operaamerica.org
Home Page: www.operaamerica.org
Social Media: *YouTube*

Marc Scorca, President

Directory of Opera America's Company, Business, Library, and Affilliate Members, indexed alphabetically and geographically. Includes the Annual Report to Members, a description of Opera America's programs and services, and a list of individual members.
Cost: $25.00
Frequency: Annual

19574 Plays and Playwrights
International Society of Dramatists
1638 Euclid Avenue
Miami Beach, FL 33139-7744

305-882-1864
Home Page: http://blog.nytesmallpress.com/

Offers valuable information on over 1,000 dramatists producing works in English.
Cost: $29.95
200 Pages
Frequency: Annual
Circulation: 10,000

19575 Regional Theatre Directory
Theatre Directories

P.O.Box 2409
Manchester Center, VT 05255-2409

802-867-9333
FAX 802-867-2297
Home Page: www.theatredirectories.com

Peg Lyons, Editor
PJ Tumielewicz, Editor

Profiles over 400 theatres including dinner theatres, equity and non-equity. Find out when/where auditions are held, when resumes shoul be sent, housing and transportation policy, and general description of company. If you want to find a job or an internship as an actor, designer, technician or staff in a professional regional or dinner theatre anywhere in the country, this directory can help you.
Cost: $29.50
Frequency: Annual
ISBN: 0-933919-63-8
Founded in 1984

19576 ShowBiz Bookkeeper
Theatre Directories
P.O.Box 2409
Manchester Center, VT 05255-2409

802-867-9333
FAX 802-867-2297
E-Mail: info@theatredirectories.com
Home Page: www.theatredirectories.com

The tax record-keeping system for professionals working in the arts.
Cost: $22.95

19577 Stars in Your Eyes...Feet on the Ground
Theatre Directories
P.O.Box 2409
Manchester Center, VT 05255-2409

802-867-9333
FAX 802-867-2297
E-Mail: info@theatredirectories.com
Home Page: www.theatredirectories.com

PJ Tumielewicz, Editor
Peg Lyons, Editor

For teens who want to act...Practical advice for young actors: learning how show business works; agents and managers; local cable shows and television commercials; auditioning for stage, student films and TV; choosing a school; dealing with rejection; parental support and more. Written by a 19-year old professional actress.
Cost: $16.95
ISBN: 0-933919-42-5

19578 Student's Guide to Playwriting Opportunities
Theatre Directories
P.O.Box 2409
Manchester Center, VT 05255-2409

802-867-9333
FAX 802-867-2297
E-Mail: info@theatredirectories.com
Home Page: www.theatredirectories.com

Michael Write, Directory Editor
Christi Pyland, Directory Editor
PJ Tumielewicz, Theatre Directories, Inc Editor
Peg Lyons, Theatre Directories, Inc Editor

An essential tool for every high shool or college student with an interest in playwriting. Comprehensive listings of 79 academic programs and another 80 professional development programs geared for the young writer. New essays on the art, process and business of playwriting.
Cost: $23.95
128 Pages
ISBN: 0-933919-53-0

19579 Summer Theatre Directory
Theatre Directories

P.O.Box 2409
Manchester Center, VT 05255-2409

802-867-9333
FAX 802-867-2297
E-Mail: info@theatredirectories.com
Home Page: www.theatredirectories.com

Opportunities at over 350 summer theatres, theme parks, and summer training programs.
Cost: $29.50

19580 Theatre Profiles Database
Theatre Communications Group
520 8th Ave
24th Floor
New York, NY 10018-4156

212-609-5900
FAX 212-609-5901
E-Mail: tcg@tcg.org
Home Page: www.tcg.org

Theresa Eyring, Executive Director
Kelly Haydon, Database Manager
Jennifer Cleary, Director Membership
Terence Nemeth, Publisher
Kathy Sova, Editorial Director

Online database of more than 400 theatre members in 47 states, 17,000 individual members, 100 Trustee Leadership Network members and a growing number of University, Funder and Business Affiliates.
Frequency: Annual

19581 Whole Arts Directory
Midmarch Arts Press
300 Riverside Dr
Apartment 8A
New York, NY 10025-5279

212-666-6990
FAX 212-865-5510
E-Mail: info@midmarchpress.org
Home Page: www.midmarchartspress.org

Cynthia Navaregga, Manager

Directory to arts resources, organiztions, museums, galleries, colonies, retreats, art therapy, information services, and much more. Highly useful material for all artists, students, organizations and institutions.
Cost: $12.95
175 Pages
ISBN: 0-960247-67-x
Founded in 1987
Printed in on matte stock

Industry Web Sites

19582 http://gold.greyhouse.com
G.O.L.D Grey House OnLine Databases

Grey House Publishing's online database platform, GOLD, offers Quick Search, Keyword Search and Expert Search for most business sectors including performing arts markets. The GOLD platform makes finding the information you need quick and easy - whether you're a novice searcher or an experienced database user. All of Grey House's directory products are available for subscription on the GOLD platform.

19583 www.aact.org
American Association of Community Theatre

Non-profit corporation fostering excellence in community theatre productions and governance through community theatre festivals, educational opportunity publications, network, resources, and website.

19584 www.aahperd.org/nda
National Dance Association

A nonprofit service organization dedicated to increasing knowledge, improving skills and encouraging sound professional practices in dance education while promoting and supporting creative and healthy lifestyles through high quality dance programs.

19585 www.aate.com
American Alliance for Theatre and Education
Members are artists, teachers and professionals who serve youth theatres and theatre educational programs.

19586 www.absolutewrite.com
Absolute Write
Advice for writers, including playwrights.

19587 www.actorsequity.org
Actors Equity Association
Labor union affiliated with AFL-CIO which represents actors in film, television and commercials.

19588 www.actorsite.com
Actor Site
Audition and other information.

19589 www.actorsource.com
Actorsource
Extensive information and resources for actors.

19590 www.actorstheatre.org
Actors Theatre of Louisville
Supports new playwrights. For information on entering a play, click Humana Festival.

19591 www.adta.org
American Dance Therapy Association
Founded in 1966; professional organization of dance movement therapists, with members both nationally and internationally; offers training, research findings, and a newsletter.

19592 www.aislesay.com
Aislesay
Internet magazine of stage reviews and opinions.

19593 www.americandanceguild.org
American Dance Guild
Non-profit membership organization; sponsors professional seminars, workshops, a student scholarship and other projects and institutes programs of national significance in the field of dance.

19594 www.americantheaterweb.com
American Theater Web
Find theaters, Broadway shows and musicals.

19595 www.answers4dancers.com
Answers for Dancers
Dance Magazine sponsors this site.

19596 www.artsmed.org
Performing Arts Medicine Association
Organization for physicians and professionals interested in the research of Performing Arts Medicine.

19597 www.artspresenters.org
Association of Performing Arts Presenters
Celebrates rich and diverse performing arts to the public.

19598 www.artstabilization.org
National Arts Strategies
Offers training and technical assistance to arts organizations.

19599 www.bachauer.com
Gina Bachauer International Piano Foundation
Produce a yearly piano international competition

19600 www.backstage.com
Backstage.com
Information for actors, casting calls, film reviews, auditions and acting jobs.

19601 www.backstagejobs.com
Theatre Design and Technical Jobs Page
Employment opportunities.

19602 www.backstageworld.com
Backstage World
Post your resume and search for design and technical job opportunities worldwide.

19603 www.bmi.com
BMI
Secures the rights of songwriters/composers. Collects license fees for the public performance of music and pays royalties to its copyright owners.

19604 www.catf.org
Contemporary American Theater Festival
Dedicated to providing and developing new American Theater.

19605 www.cincinnatiarts.org
Cincinnati Arts Association
Dedicated to supporting performing and visual arts.

19606 www.classicalaction.org
Classical Action
Provides a unified voice for all those within the performing arts community to help combat HIV/AIDS.

19607 www.computermusic.org
International Computer Music Association
Supports the performance aspects of computer music; publishes newsletter and holds annual conferance.

19608 www.conductorsguild.org
Conductors Guild
Dedicated to encouraging the highest standards in the art and profession of conducting. Founded in 1975.

19609 www.contactimprov.net
Contact Improv
Improvisation for dancers.

19610 www.costume-con.org
Costume Connections
Costume conferences.

19611 www.costume.org
International Costumers' Guild
An affiliation of amateur hobbyist and professional costumers.

19612 www.costumegallery.com
Costume Gallery
A central location on the web for fashion and costume since 1996.

19613 www.costumers.org
National Costumers Association
Seeks to establish and maintain professional and ethical standards of business in the costume industry.

19614 www.costumes.org
Costumer's Manifesto
Online book, information and links.

19615 www.costumesocietyamerica.com
Costume Society of America
Education, research, presentation and design.

19616 www.creativedir.com
Creative Directory Services
Directory of suppliers for costumes, sets, special effects and stunts.

19617 www.criticaldance.com
Dance Critics Association
Critical dance forum and ballet dance magazine

19618 www.csulb.edu/~jvancamp/copyrigh.html
Csulb.edu
Copyrighting choreographic works.

19619 www.csusa.org/face/index.htm
Friends of Active Copyright Education
Playwrights should click on Words, then Copyright Basics.

19620 www.cyberdance.org
Cyber Dance
Collection of links to modern dance and classical ballet resources.

19621 www.danceart.com/edancing
Danceart.com
Ballet and dance art, features, chat and more.

19622 www.dancenotation.org
Dance Notation Bureau
Notation basics, Notated Theatrical Dances Catalogue and links.

19623 www.dancepages.com
Dance Pages.com
Offers resources to dance teachers.

19624 www.dancer.com/dance-links
Dance Links
Links to many dance sites.

19625 www.danceusa.org
Dance/USA
Provides a forum for the discussion of issues of concern to membersand a support network for exchange of information; also bestows awards.

19626 www.deadance.com
Dance Educators of America
Promotes the education of teachers in the performing arts.

19627 www.dma-national.org
Dance Masters of America
An organization of dance teachers.

19628 www.dramaguild.com
Dramatists Guild
Comprehensive organization that deals solely with Broadway and off-Broadway producers, off-off-Broadway groups, agents, theatres and sources of grants.

19629 www.dramaleague.org
Drama League
Seeks to strengthen American theatre through the nurturing of stage directors.

19630 www.dtw.org
Dance Theater Workshop
Identifies, presents and supports independent contemporary artists and dance companies to advance dance and live performances in New York and worldwide.

19631 www.edta.org
Educational Theater Association

Theater educators working to increase support for theater programs in the educational system.

19632 www.esperanzaarts.org
Esperanza Performing Arts Association

19633 www.etecnyc.net
Entertainment Technology Online
For employment in design and technical theatre, click on Classifieds. Also offers resources and buyers guides for theatrical lighting.

19634 www.gmn.com
Global Music Network
Go backstage, watch rehearsals, listen to performances of classical and jazz artists.

19635 www.goldmime.com
Goldston Mime Foundation: School for Mime
Holds summer seminars and workshops.

19636 www.greyhouse.com
Grey House Publishing
Authoritative reference directories for most business sectors including performing arts markets. Users can search the online databases with varied search criteria allowing for custom searches by product category, geographic area, sales volume, keyword, subject and more. Full Grey House catalog and online ordering also available.

19637 www.harada-sound.com/sound/handbook
Kai's Sound Handbook
Information for sound designers.

19638 www.hawaii.edu
Association for Theatre in Higher Education
Promotes quality in theatre education.

19639 www.heniford.net/1234
Small Cast One-Act Guide Online
List of short plays.

19640 www.ifea.com
International Festivals and Events Association
Network for planning events and exchange programs; publishes quarterly magazine.

19641 www.intix.org
International Ticketing Association
Not-for-profit association representing 22 countries worldwide and more than 1,200 members. Committed to the improvement, progress and advancement of ticket management, and to reach this goal provides educational programs, trade shows, conducts surveys and conference proceedings and produces a membership directory.

19642 www.ispa.org
International Society for the Performing Arts
Foundation

Supports international cooperation, facilitates networking and enhances professional dialogue.

19643 www.jensenfoundation.org
Fritz and Lavinia Jensen Foundation
Sponsors competitions.

19644 www.latinoarts.org
Association of Hispanic Arts
A multidisciplary organization which supports Hispanic arts organizations and individual artists with technical assistance. The organization facilitates projects and programs designed to

foster the appreciation, growth, and well being of the Latino cultural community. It's quarter publication, AHA; Hispanic Arts News, features in depth articles on the local and national arts community, including artist profiles and a calendar of events.

19645 www.lib.colum.edu/costwais.html
Costume Image Database
Access costume images.

19646 www.light-link.com
Lightsearch.com
Lists of lighting equipment suppliers.

19647 www.livebroadway.com
League of American Theatres and Producers
National trade association for the commercial theatre industry whose principal activity is negotiation of labor contracts and government relations.

19648 www.lmda.org
Literary Managers and Dramaturgs of the Americas
Voluntary membership organization.

19649 www.luth.org
Guild of American Luthiers
Manufacturers and repairs stringed instruments; offers quarterly journal and triennial meeting.

19650 www.lycos.com
Lycos
Click Arts and Entertainment, then Dance, Theatre or Performing Arts.

19651 www.magicsam.com
Society of American Magicians
Founded to promote and maintain harmonious fellowship among those interested in magic as an art, to improve ethics of the magical profession, and to foster, promote and improve the advancement of magical arts in the field of amusement and entertainment. Membership includes professional and amateur magicians, manufacturers of magical apparatus, and collectors.

19652 www.makeupmag.com
Make-Up Artist Magazine
Make-up artist magazine online.

19653 www.members.aol.com/thegoop/gaff.html
Gaff Tape Webring
Tech theatre.

19654 www.midatlanticarts.org
Mid Atlantic Arts Foundation
Provides leadership and support for artists and arts organizations in the Mid-Atlantic region and beyond.

19655 www.milieux.com/costume
Costume Source
Provides online sources for materials, costumes, accessories and books.

19656 www.mtishows.com
Music Theatre International
Scripts, cast recordings, study guides, production slides and other resources.

19657 www.musicalamerica.com
Musicalamerica.com
Late-breaking industry news, full search capabilities, immediate interaction between Presenter and Artist Manager/Artist.

19658 www.musicianshealth.com
Chiropractic Performing Arts Association
To educate amateur and professional entertainers, musicians and dancers about reaching optimum health potential through natural, drug-free, conservative chiropractic care.

19659 www.nadt.org
National Association for Drama Therapy
Promotes the profession of Drama Therapy.

19660 www.namm.org
NAMM-International Music Products Association
Offers professional development seminars; sells musical instruments and allied products.

19661 www.napama.org
North American Performing Arts Managers and Agents
A cooperative voice in a competitive business.

19662 www.natoonline.org
National Association of Theatre Owners
Exhibition trade organization, representing more than 30,000 movie screens in all 50 states, and additional cinemas in 50 countries worldwide.

19663 www.nbtf.org
National Black Theatre Festival

19664 www.netconline.org
New England Theatre Conference
Non-profit educational corporation founded to develop, expand and assist theatre activity in community, educational and professional levels in New England. Holds annual auditions.

19665 www.netsword.com/stagecombat.html
Netsword
Lessons on stage combat.

19666 www.newplaysforchildren.com
New Plays Online
Plays for children and young adults.

19667 www.nmpa.org
National Music Publishers' Association
Publishes a quarterly newsletter and holds an annual meeting.

19668 www.ntcp.org
Non-Traditional Casting Project
Promotes inclusive practices in television, theatre and film.

19669 www.nyfa.org
New York Foundation for the Arts
Employment openings in the arts.

19670 www.nypl.org/reseach/lpa/lpa.html
New York Public Library for the Performing Arts
Primary research collection.

19671 www.nytimes.com
New York Times on the Web
Arts and Theatre contains play reviews.

19672 www.oobr.com
Off-Off-Broadway Review
Lists information on off-off broadway shows such as: title of show, author, director, producing company, theatre, address, box-office phone number, dates and times, admission price and contact info.

19673 www.opencasting.com
Open Casting
Bulletin board containing auditions, crew calls, casting notices and links.

19674 www.paastjo.org
Performing Arts Association
Provides a diverse selection of performing arts.

19675 www.pen.org
PEN: American Center
Site of the international literary community organization.

19676 www.performingarts.net
Performing Arts Online
Dedicated to the perpetuation of quality performing arts.

19677 www.pianonet.com
Piano Manufacturers Association International
Manufacturers and suppliers of pianos and parts; holds annual trade show.

19678 www.pipeorgan.org
American Institute of Organ Builders
Sponsers training seminars, quarterly journal and annual convention for pipe organ builders and service technicians.

19679 www.plasa.org
Professional Lighting and Sound Association
Web site for PLASA, a leading trade body for Lighting and Sound Professionals.

19680 www.playbill.com
Playbill Online
Listings for Broadway and off Broadway theatre productions. Also guides for sites, including summer stock, national touring shows and regional theatres worldwide.

19681 www.playwrights.org
Playwrights Center of San Francisco
Playwrites directory.

19682 www.playwrightshorizons.org
Playwrights Horizon
At home page click arrow. On next page click working with PH. You will see Writing Submissions.

19683 www.playwrightsproject.com
Playwrights Project
Promotes literacy, creativity and communication skills in young people through drama-based activities.

19684 www.press.jhu.edu/press/journals/paj
Johns Hopkins University Press
A journal of performance and art.

19685 www.press.jhu.edu/press/journals/tj
Johns Hopkins University Press
Theatre Journal

19686 www.press.jhu.edu/press/journals/tt
Johns Hopkins University Press
Theatre Topics

19687 www.proppeople.com
Proppeople.com
Online home for props professionals.

19688 www.renfaire.com/Language/index.html
Renfaire.com
Lessons on proper Elizabethan accents.

19689 www.rigging.net
Rigger's Page
Technical information on stage rigging equipment.

19690 www.roundalab.org
Roundalab
A professional international society of individuals who teach round dancing at any phase.

19691 www.safd.org
Society of American Fight Directors
Promotes safety in directing staged combat and theatrical violence.

19692 www.sag.org
Screen Actors Guild
Labor union affiliated with AFL-CIO which represents actors in film, television and commercials.

19693 www.sapphireswan.com/dance
Dance Directory
Dance resources.

19694 www.setc.org
Southeastern Theatre Conference
Annual conventions include auditions.

19695 www.sfballet.org
San Francisco Ballet Association
Provides a repertoire of classical and contemporary ballet; to provide educational opportunities for professional dancers and choreographers; to excel in ballet, artistic direction and administration.

19696 www.southarts.org
Southern Arts Federation
Serves as the leadership voice to increase the regional, national and international awareness and prominence of Southern arts. Creates mechanisms and partnerships to expand local, regional, national and international markets for Southern arts.

19697 www.spolin.com
Spolin Center
Information on improvisational theatre.

19698 www.ssdc.org
Society of Stage Directors and Choreographers
An independent labor union representing directors and choreographers in American theatre.

19699 www.stage-directions.com
Stage Directions Magazine
The practical and technical side of theatrical operations.

19700 www.stageplays.com/markets.htm
Playwrights Noticeboard
Information on contests, publishing and production opportunities.

19701 www.stetson.edu/csata/thr_guid.html
McCoy's Guide to Theatre and Performance Studies
A brief guide to internet resources in theatre and performance studies put out by Stetson University.

19702 www.summertheater.com
Directory of Summer Theater in the United States
Search for summer theater opportunities by alphabetized listings or geographic region.

19703 www.talkinbroadway.com
Talkin' Broadway
Theatrical events and information on and off Broadway and other selected geographical locations.

19704 www.tcg.org
Theatre Communications Group
Supports alliances among playwrights, theatres and communities. Promotes not-for-profit theatre and offers resources to jobseekers. Offers financial support to designers and directors through its Career Development Program.

19705 www.tdf.org
Theatre Development Fund
Not-for-profit service organization. Provides support for every area of the dance, music and professional theatre field. Founded 1968.

19706 www.teleport.com/~bjscript/index.htm
Essays on the Craft of Dramatic Writing
Essays on writing a screenplay, play or novel.

19707 www.theatre-resource.com
Theatre Resource
Career and employment information.

19708 www.theatrebayarea.org
Theatre Bay Area
Serving more than 400 member theatre companies and 3,000 individual members in the San Francisco Bay Area and Northern California, Theatre Bay Area provides monthly classes, workshops, events, information and publications.

19709 www.theatrecrafts.com
Theatrecrafts.com
Practical information about technical theatre techniques for theatre folk at any level.

19710 www.theatrejobs.com
Theatrejobs.com
Online job placement. Festival listings, summer stock, assistantships, apprenticeships, fellowships and internships.

19711 www.theatrelibrary.org/links
Performing Arts Links
General resources including applied and interactive theatre, performing arts data service and art sites. Digital librarian includes glossary of technical theatre terms.

19712 www.theatrelibrary.org/links/index.html
Theatrelibrary.org
Master categories are Theatre, Dance, Cinema and Reviews.

19713 www.thecastingnetwork.com/webring.html
Casting Network.com
By and for actors.

19714 www.theplays.org
Electronic Literature Foundation
William Shakespeare's plays online.

19715 www.top20performingarts.com
Top 20 Performing Arts
Online directory for Perfoming Arts education.

19716 www.towson.edu/worldmusiccongresses
World Music Congresses
1997-2010 World Cello Congress' II-V, 2004 The First World Guitar Congress and 2008 World Guitar Congress II. Celebrations of music with international gatherings of the world's greatest musicians, composers, conductors, instrument manufacturers students, and music lovers from around the globe.

19717 www.unc.edu/depts/outdoor
Institute of Outdoor Drama
Summer jobs for all theatrical personnel.

19718 www.ups.edu/professionalorgs/dramat urgy
Dramaturgy Northwest
Relevant information for all dramaturgs.

19719 www.urta.com
University/Resident Theatre Association
Coalition of theatre training programs. Sponsors unified auditions.

19720 www.usabda.org
USA Dance
Non-profit organization working to promote ballroom dancing, both as a recreational activity and as a competetive sport.

19721 www.usitt.org
United States Institute for Theatre Technology
The association of design, production and technology professionals in the performing arts and entertainment industry whose mission is to promote the knowledge and skills of its members. International in scope, USITT draws its board of directors from across the US and Canada. Sponsors projects, programs, research, symposia, exhibits, and annual conference. Disseminates information on aesthetic and technical developments.

19722 www.variety.org
Variety
e-version of the show business newspaper.

19723 www.vcu.edu/artweb/playwriting
Playwriting Seminars
An opinioned web companion on the art and craft of playwriting for theatre and dance.

19724 www.vl-theatre.com
WWW Virtual Library
Links to theatre and drama resources. Updated daily.

19725 www.writersguild.com
Writers Guild of America
List of Agents and information on Mentor program.

19726 www.wwar.com
World Wide Arts Resources
Links to Theatre and Dance.

19727 www2.sundance.org
Sundance Institute
Information on the Sundance Theatre Laboratory summer workshop for directors, playwrights, choreographers, solo performers and composers. For information on submitting a play, click Theatre Program on home page.

Associations

19728 AAPG Foundation
PO Box 979
Tulsa, OK 74101-0979

918-560-2644
855-302-2743
FAX 918-560-2642
Home Page: foundation.aapg.org
Social Media: *Facebook, Twitter*

David Curtiss, Executive Director

The Foundation supports the geosciences by providing funding for educational and research programs.
Founded in 1967

19729 ADSC International Association of Foundation Drilling
8445 Freeport Parkway Suite 325
Irving, TX

469-359-6000
FAX 469-359-6007
E-Mail: adsc@adsc-iafd.com
Home Page: www.adsc-iafd.com
Social Media: *Facebook, Twitter, LinkedIn*

Al Rasband, President
Martin McDermott, Vice President
Lance Kitchens, Treasurer
Rick Marshall, Director
Greg Sullivan, Director

19730 American Association of Drilling Engineers
P.O. Box 107
Houston, TX 77001

281-293-9800
E-Mail: info@aade.org
Home Page: www.aade.org
Social Media: *Facebook*

Geree Wald Morton, President
Randy Thomas, Vice President
Duane Halverson, Treasurer
Jannie Snelson, Secretary
Bob Vaughn, Executive Director
Founded in 1978

19731 American Association of Petroleum Geologists
1444 S. Boulder
PO Box 979
Tulsa, OK 74119

918-584-2555
800-364-2274
FAX 918-560-2665
E-Mail: bulletin@aapg.org
Home Page: www.aapg.org
Social Media: *Facebook, Twitter, LinkedIn, YouTube*

Paul Weimer, President
Denise M. Cox, Secretary
Edward Beaumont, President-Elect
James S. McGhay, Treasurer
Stephen E. Laubach, Editor

Supports those professionals involved in the field of geology as it relates to petroleum, natural gas, and other energy products. Publishes monthly journal of peer-reviewed articles.
30000 Members
Founded in 1917

19732 American Association of Petroleum Geologis
P.O. Box 979
Tulsa, OK 74101-0979

918-560-2644
855-302-2743
FAX 918-560-2642

Home Page: foundation.aapg.org
Social Media: *Facebook, Twitter, Stumbleupon*

David Curtiss, Executive Director
David E. Lange, Deputy Executive Director
April Stuart, Program Coordinator
Tamra Campbell, Administrative Assistant
Karen Piqune, Librarian
Founded in 1967

19733 American Association of Professional Landmen
800 Fournier Street ÿ
Fort Worth, TX 76102

817-847-7700
FAX 817-847-7704
E-Mail: aapl@landman.org
Home Page: www.landman.org
Social Media: *Facebook, Twitter, LinkedIn, YouTube*

Jack C. Richards, President
Jim R. Dewbre, 1st Vice President
Melanie Bell,CPL, Executive VP
Bernard J. Ulicy, 2nd Vice President
C.Craig Young, Sr.Director

AAPL's mission is to promote the highest standards of performance for all land professionals, to advance their stature and to encourage sound stewardship of energy and mineral resources.
7000 Members
Founded in 1955

19734 American Fuel & Petrochemical Manufacturer s
1667 K Street NW
Ste. 700
Washington, DC 20006

202-457-0480
FAX 202-457-0486
Home Page: www.afpm.org
Social Media: *Facebook, Twitter, RSS*

David Lamp, Chairman
Gregory J. Goff, Vice Chair
Charles T. Drevna, Executive Assistant
Rich Moskowitz, General Counsel
Diana Cronan, Communications Director
450 Members
Founded in 1902

19735 American Gas Association
400 N Capitol Street NW
Washington, DC 20001

202-824-7000
FAX 202-824-7092
E-Mail: ykorolevich@aga.org
Home Page: www.aga.org
Social Media: *Facebook, Twitter, LinkedIn, Myspace, Flickr*

Terry D. McCallister, Chairman
Dave McCurdy, President & CEO
Ralph A. LaRossa, 1st Vice Chair
Pierce H. Norton II, 2nd Vice Chair
Gregg S. Kantor, Immediate Past Chairman

The American Gas Association advocates the interests of its members and their customers, and provides information and services promoting efficient demand and supply growth and operational excellence in the safe, reliable and efficient delivery of natural gas.
Founded in 1918

19736 American Institute of Mining Metallurgical & Petroleum Engineers
12999 East Adam Aircraft Circle
Englewood, CO 80112

303-325-5185
FAX 888-702-0049
E-Mail: aime@aimehq.org
Home Page: www.aimehq.org

Social Media: *Facebook, LinkedIn, YouTube, RSS*

Brajendra Fattahi, President
Garry W. Warren, President-Elect
Nikhil C. Trivedi, President-Elect Designate
Dale E. Heinz, Past President
Drew Meyer, Trustee

AIME is and shall be a New York State Nonprofit Corporation organized and operated to advance and disseminate, through the programs of the Member Societies, knowledge of engineering and the arts and sciences involved in the production and use of minerals, metals, energy sources and materials for the benefit of humankind, and to represent AIME and the Member Societies within the larger engineering community.
90000 Members
Founded in 1871

19737 American Oil & Gas Historical Society
1201 15th Street
Ste 300
Washington, DC 20005

Home Page: aoghs.org
Social Media: *Facebook, Twitter, LinkedIn, Google+*

Bruce A. Wells, Executive Director
Founded in 2003

19738 American Petroleum Institute
1220 L St NW
Washington, DC 20005-4070

202-682-8000
FAX 202-682-8232
Home Page: www.api.org
Social Media: *Facebook, Twitter, YouTube, Flickr*

Jack N.Gerard, President & CEO

The only national trade association that represents all aspects of America's oil and natural gas industry. Members are producers, refiners, suppliers, pipeline operators and marine transporters, as well as service and supply companies that support all segments of the industry.
400+ Members
Founded in 1919

19739 Association of Desk and Derrick Clubs
5321 South Sheridan Road
Suite 24
Tulsa, OK 74145

918-622-1749
FAX 918-622-1675
E-Mail: ado@addc.org
Home Page: www.addc.org
Social Media: *Facebook, Twitter, YouTube*

Linda Rodgers, President
Connie Harrison, Vice President
Maggi Franks, Treasurer
Babara Ann Pappas, Secretary
Sheryl Minear, RP, Parliamentarian
Founded in 1949

19740 Association of Drilled Shaft Contractors
8445 Freeport Parkway
Suite 325
Irving, TX 75063

469-359-6000
FAX 469-359-6007
E-Mail: adsc@adsc-iafd.com
Home Page: www.adsc-iafd.com
Social Media: *Facebook, LinkedIn*

Tom Witherspoon, President
Tom Tuozzolo, Vice President
Luke Schuler, Treasurer
Tom Bird, Chairman

A professional, internationa, nonprofit trade association representing the anchored earth retention, drilled shaft, micropile, and other heavy civil construction/design industries. Members include specialty subcontractors, manufacturers and suppliers, academicians and design engineers in the private and public sectors.
Founded in 1972

19741 Association of Energy Service Companies

14531 FM 529
Suite 250
Houston, TX 77095-3528

713-781-0758
800-672-0771
FAX 713-781-7542
E-Mail: pjordan@aesc.net
Home Page: www.aesc.net
Social Media: *Facebook, Twitter, LinkedIn*

Kenny Jordan, Executive Director
Patty Jordan, Publisher/Sales Manager
Angla Fails, Administrative Manager
Roni Ashley, Director Accounting Services

Professional trade association for well-site service contractors and businesses providing goods and services to well-site contractors. Develops and sells training and safety materials.
600 Members
Founded in 1956

19742 Association of International Petroleum Negotiators

11767 Katy Freeway
Suite 412
Houston, TX 77079

281-558-7715
FAX 281-558-7073
E-Mail: president@aipn.org
Home Page: www.aipn.org

John Bowman, President
Judith Kim, VP - Communication
Steven Otillar, VP - Education
Kimberly Reeder, VP - Membership
Joseph Wesley, VP - Planning
Founded in 1982

19743 Association of Oil Pipe Lines

1808 Eye St NW
Suite 300
Washington, DC 20006-5423

202-408-7970
FAX 202-280-1949
E-Mail: aopl@aopl.org
Home Page: www.aopl.org
Social Media: *Facebook, Twitter*

Andrew J.Black, President
Steven M.Kramer, General Counsel
John Stoody, Director
Heather Keith, Director
Rekha Chandrasekher, Industry Analyst

Acts as an information clearinghouse for the public, the media and the pipeline industry; provides coordination and leaderships for the industry's ongoing joint Environmental Safety Initiative; and represents common carrier crude and product petroleum pipleines in Congress, before regulatory agencies, and in the federal courts.
47 Members
Founded in 1947

19744 Association of Petroleum Industry Cooperative Managers

Home Page: www.apicom.org
Founded in 1972

19745 Association of Petroleum Surveying & Geomatics

Home Page: www.apsg.info
Social Media: *Facebook, Twitter, LinkedIn*

Jackie Portsmouth, Chairman
Ashok Wadwani, Vice Chair
Kevin Crozier, Nominations Chair
Alma Alling, Communications Chair
Robert Edwards, Secretary/ Treasurer
Founded in 1998

19746 Concrete Sawing & Drilling Association

100 2nd Ave South
Ste 240N
St. Petersburg, FL 33701

727-577-5004
E-Mail: info@CSDA.org
Home Page: www.csda.org
Social Media: *Facebook, Twitter, YouTube, Instagram*

Judith O'Day, President
Kevin Baron, Vice President
Patrick O'Brien, Executive Director
Jim Dvoratchek, Past President
Mike Orzechowski, Secretary/ Treasurer

19747 Coordinating Research Council

5755 North Point Parkway
Suite 265
Alpharetta, GA 30022-3067

678-795-0506
FAX 678-795-0509
E-Mail: jantucker@crcao.com
Home Page: www.crcao.org

Brent Bailey, Executive Director
Christopher Tennant, Deputy Director
Debra Carter, Controller
Betty Taylor, Administrative Assistant
Jan Beck, Committee Coordinator and Webmaster

A nonprofit organization that directs, through committee action, engineering and environmental studies on the interaction between automotive/other mobility equipment and petroleum products.
1M Members
Founded in 1942

19748 Council of Petroleum Accountants Societies

445 Union Blvd.
Suite 207
Lakewood, CO 80228

303-300-1311
877-992-6727
FAX 303-300-3733
Home Page: www.copas.org
Social Media: *Facebook, Twitter, LinkedIn*

Tom Wierman, Executive Director
Cheri McCallister, Administrator
Anita Hartz, Creative Specialist
Rich Moring III, President
Jeff Wright, Vice President

Members are accountants involved in, or closely related to, the oil and gas industry. Also provides ethical standards for energy accountants and is the certification organization for the Accredited Petroleum Accountant program.
3200 Members
Founded in 1961

19749 Domestic Petroleum Council

101 Constitution Avenue NW
Suite 800
Washington, DC 20001-2133

202-742-4300
Home Page: www.dpcusa.org/

William F Whitsitt, President

To work constructively for sound energy, environmental and related public policies that encourage responsible exploration, development, and production of natural gas and crude oil to meet consumer needs and fuel our economy.
24 Members
Founded in 1975

19750 Drilling Engineering Association

10370 Richmond Ave, Suite 760
Houston, TX 77042

713-292-1945
FAX 713-292-1946
E-Mail: scott.maddox@iadc.org
Home Page: dea-global.org

Ben Bloys, Chairman
David Dowell, Advisory Board Member
Glenda Wylie, Advisory Board Member
Robert Estes, Advisory Board Member
Scott Maddox, Secretary/ Treasurer

19751 Energy Security Council

9720 Cypresswood Dr.
Suite 206
Houston, TX 77070ỹ

281-587-2700
FAX 281-807-6000
E-Mail: mindy@energysecuritycouncil.org
Home Page: www.energysecuritycouncil.org

Rob Ream, Chairman
Rick Powers, Vice-Chairman
Butch Brazell, Director of Global Security
Clete Buckaloo, Director of Law Enforcement
Kent Chrisman, Director of Corp. Security & Admin.

Founded as Petroleum Industry Security Council and assumed its current name in 1999. Provides support to security professionals and business developers in the energy industry.
450 Members
Founded in 1976

19752 Energy Telecommunications and Electrical Association

5005 Royal Lane
Suite 116
Irving, TX 75063

888-503-8700
FAX 972-915-6040
Home Page: www.entelec.org
Social Media: *LinkedIn*

Dan Mueller, President
Michael Burt, 1st Vice President
James Coulter, 2nd Vice President
Becky Holland, 3rd Vice President
Richard Nation, Secretary/ Treasurer

A user association that focuses on communications and control technologies used by petroleum, natural gas, pipeline and electric utility companies. Primary goal is to provide education for its members.
Founded in 1928

19753 Energy Traffic Association

3303 Main Street Corridor
Houston, TX 77002

713-528-2868
FAX 713-464-0702
E-Mail: russell@energytraffic.org
Home Page: www.energytraffic.org

Ralph Lopez, President
Renee Ahmed, Vice President/ Secretary
Russell Powell, Executive Director
Roger Rood, Immediate Past President
Tonya Svoboda, Board member

A nonprofit educational association of logistics professionals in the energy industry. Membership consists of managers of energy industry

logistics departments and those logistics providers serving the energy industry.
100 Members
Founded in 1941

19754 Fiberglass Tank and Pipe Institute
14323 Heatherfield
Suite 101
Houston, TX 77079-7407

713-690-7777
FAX 713-690-2842
E-Mail: info@fiberglasstankandpipe.com
Home Page: www.fiberglasstankandpipe.com

Bobby Jin, President

The fiberglass-reinforced, thermosetting, plastic tank and pipe manufacturing industry. Members are domestic manufacturers.
5 Members
Founded in 1987

19755 Foundation Drilling Magazine
Association of Drilled Shaft Contractors
8445 Freeport Parkway
Suite 325
Irving, TX 75063

469-359-6000
FAX 469-359-6007
E-Mail: adsc@adsc-iafd.com
Home Page: www.adsc-iafd.com
Social Media: *Facebook, Twitter, LinkedIn*

Tom Witherspoon, President
Tom Tuozzolo, Vice President
Luke Schuler, Treasurer
Tom Bird, Chairman

The best news source within our industry. Filled with information about design, projects and updates on what's going on where, Foundation Drilling Magazine is devoted to reporting on the drilled shaft, anchored retention, and other related industries.
Frequency: 8x Yearly
Founded in 1972

19756 Gas Research Machinery Council
3030 LBJ Freeway
Suite 1300
Dallas, TX 75234

972-620-4026
FAX 972-620-1613
E-Mail: memberservices@southerngas.org
Home Page: www.gmrc.org

Craig Linn, Chairman
Roland Trevino, Vice Chairman
Mike Grubb, President & CEO
Jane Butler, Vice President
Scott Schubring, Project Supervisory Committee

Members are companies in the natural gas, oil and petrochemical industries in mechanical and fluid systems design.
75 Members
Founded in 1952

19757 Independent Liquid Terminals Association
1005 North Glebe Road
Suite 600
Arlington, VA 22201

703-875-2011
FAX 703-875-2018
E-Mail: info@ilta.org
Home Page: www.ilta.org

E David Doane, President
Melinda Whitney, Director/Government Affairs
Eric W. Thomas, Chairman
John G. McGrossin, Treasurer
Seph E. Shotwell, Secretary

Supports all those bulk, liquid terminal owners/operators and establishments supplying equipment, goods and services to the bulk liquid terminaling industry. Publishes monthly newsletter.
Founded in 1974

19758 Independent Lubricant Manufacturers
400 N Columbus St
Suite 201
Alexandria, VA 22314-2264

703-684-5574
FAX 703-836-8503
E-Mail: ilma@ilma.org
Home Page: www.ilma.org
Social Media: *Facebook, Twitter*

Celeste Powers, Executive Director
Martha Jolkovski, Director Publications/Advertising
Glenn Boyle, Second Vice President
Dixon W Benz II, Executive Sales Manager

Independent blenders and compounders of lubricants.
Founded in 1976

19759 Independent Terminal Operators Association
1150 Connecticut Avenue NW
9th Floor
Washington, DC 20036-4129

202-828-4100
FAX 202-828-4130
E-Mail: wbode@bode.com

William H Bode, Secretary & General Counsel

Represents indepedent petroleum distributors.
15 Members
Founded in 1970

19760 Institute of Gas Technology
1700 S Mount Prospect Rd
Des Plaines, IL 60018-1804

847-768-0500
FAX 847-768-0501
E-Mail: publicrelations@gastechnology.org
Home Page: www.gastechnology.org
Social Media: *Facebook, Twitter, LinkedIn, YouTube*

David Carroll, President & CEO
Chris Herman, Treasurer & CFO
Paul Chromek, General Counsel & Secretary

An independent, not-for-profit center for energy and environmental research, development, education and information. Main function is to perform sponsored and in-house research, development and demonstration, provide educational programs and services, and disseminate scientific and technical information.
Founded in 1941

19761 International Association for Energy Economics
28790 Chagrin Blvd.,
Ste 350
Clevelend, OH 44122

216-464-5365
E-Mail: iaee@iaee.org
Home Page: www.iaee.org

Peter R. Hartley, President
Anne Neumann, VP - Publication
Jurgis Vilemas, VP -Finance
Lori Smith Dschell, VP -Communications
Ponald D. Ripple, VP -Conferences

19762 International Association of Directional Drilling

281-288-6484
Home Page: www.iadd-intl.org

Jim Oberkircher, Founder/ CEO
Arstrong Lee Agbaji, Assistant Director
Bill Bailey, Board Member
Ed Dew, Board Member
Chris McCartney, Board Member

19763 International Association of Drilling Contractors
10370 Richmond Ave
Suite 760
Houston, TX 77042-9687

713-292-1945
FAX 713-292-1946
E-Mail: info@iadc.org
Home Page: www.iadc.org
Social Media: *Facebook, Twitter, LinkedIn, RSS*

Stephen Colville, President and CEO
Tap Powell, Executive VP
Mike Killalea, Group VP
Jason McFarland, Corporate Development
Mike Dubose, VP-Interantional Dept

Dedicated to enhancing the interests of the oil-and-gas and geothermal drilling and completion industry worldwide
1239 Members
Founded in 1940

19764 International Coiled Tubing Association
PO Box 1082
Montgomery, TX 77356

936-520-1549
FAX 832-201-9977
E-Mail: ababin@icota.com
Home Page: www.icota.com

Alan Turner, Sr.Co-Chair
Jason Skufca, Executive Director
David Larimore, Treasurer
Allison Babin, Secretary
Federico Botero, Board Member
7 Members
Founded in 1994

19765 International Energy Credit Association
1120 Route 73
Suite C
Mt. Laurel, NJ 08054

856-380-6854
FAX 856-439-0525
E-Mail: ieca@ahint.com
Home Page: www.ieca.net
Social Media: *Facebook, Twitter, LinkedIn*

Zachary Starbird, President
James Hawkins, 1st VP
John Early, Treasurer
Jamie Swartz, VP Education
Steve Harwitz, Director-Environment Regulations

Members are credit and financial executives with companies whose product is a petroleum derivative.
800 Members
Founded in 1923

19766 International Geophysical Association
1225 North Loop West
Suite 220
Houston, TX 77008

713-957-8080
FAX 713-957-0008
E-Mail: info@iagc.org
Home Page: www.iagc.org
Social Media: *Facebook, Twitter, Youtube*

Nikki Martin, President
Walt Rosenbusch, VP
Gail Adams, VP of Communications
Dr.Robert Gisiner, Director of Marine Environment
Criss Rennie, Director-Membership

Represents the industry that provides geophysical services to the oil and gas industry.
203 Members
Founded in 1971

19767 International Oil Scouts Association

PO Box 940310
Houston, TX 77094-7310

512-472-8138
Home Page: www.oilscouts.com
Social Media: *Facebook*

Pam Florek, President
Christi Sarat, Executive VP
Don Grimm, Second VP
Lisa Bonin, Secretary
Ty Cline, VP Finance

Compiles statistics on exploration and development wells in the United States. Offers professional development and scholarship programs.
175 Members
Founded in 1924

19768 International Slurry Surfacing Association

3 Church Cir
PMB 250
Annapolis, MD 21401

410-267-0023
FAX 410-267-7546
E-Mail: krissoff@slurry.org
Home Page: www.slurry.org
Social Media: *Facebook, Twitter*

Rusty Price, President
Carter Dabney, Vice President
Rex Eberly, Secretary
Eric Reimschiissel, Treasurer
Bob Jerman, Technical Director

A non profit association dedicated to the interests, education, and success of slurry surfacing professionals and corporations around the world.
200 Members
Founded in 1963

19769 International Union of Petroleum and Industrial Workers

8131 E Rosecrans Avenue
Paramount, CA 90723

562-630-6232
800-624-5842
FAX 562-408-1073
E-Mail: petroleumworkers@aol.com
Social Media: *Facebook*

George R Beltz, International President
Pamela Parlow, Internat'l Secretary/Tresurer
5000 Members
Founded in 1951

19770 Interstate Natural Gas Association of America

20 F Street, NW
Suite 450
Washington, DC 20001

202-216-5900
FAX 202-216-0870
Home Page: www.ingaa.org

Donald F. Santa, Jr., President & CEO
Richard R Hoffmann, Executive Director
Catherine J Landry, Director of Communications
James O'Bryant, Researcher & Comm Assistant
Martin E. Edwards, VP, Legislative Affairs

Trade association of natural gas pipelines in the United States, Canada, Mexico and Europe.
25 Members
Founded in 1944

19771 Interstate Oil and Gas Compact Commission

900 NE 23rd Street
Oklahoma City, OK 73105

405-525-3556
FAX 405-525-3592

E-Mail: communications@iogcc.ok.gov
Home Page: www.iogcc.state.ok.us

Mary Fallin, Chairman
David Porter, Vice Chairman
Michael Teague, 2nd Vice Chairman
Mike Smith, Executive Director
Gerry Baker, AssociateExecutive Director

The members are states that produce oil or gas; associate states support the conservation of America's energy resources. Also establishes rules andguidelines for the proper maintenance of wells.
700 Members
Founded in 1935

19772 Liaison Committee of Cooperating Oil and Gas Association

1718 Columbus Road SW
PO Box 535
Granville, OH 13023-0535

740-587-0444
FAX 202-857-4799
E-Mail: stewart@ooga.org
Home Page: www.energyconnect.com/liason

Thomas E Stewart, Secretary/Treasurer

Established to facilitate communication among state and regional oil and gas associations.
25 Members
Founded in 1957

19773 Mid-Continent Oil and Gas Association

730 North Blvd.
Baton Rouge, LA 70802

225-387-3205
FAX 225-344-5502
Home Page: www.lmoga.com
Social Media: *Facebook, Twitter, Flickr*

Chris John, President
Tyler Gray, General Counsel
Brent Golleher, Director of Government
Richard Metcalf, Director of Environmental Affairs
Ashley Cain, Manager of Communications

At the forefront of the continually changing legal, legislative and regulatory issues facing a growing and diverse membership.
7.5M Members
Founded in 1917

19774 NLGI

249 SW Noel
Suite 249
Lee's Summit, MO 64063

816-524-2500
FAX 816-524-2504
E-Mail: nlgi@nlgi.org
Home Page: www.nlgi.org
Social Media: *LinkedIn*

David J Como, Vice President
Kim Smallwood, Secretary
Joe Kaperick, Treasurer
Kimberly Hartley, Executive Director
Marilyn Brohm, Manager, Membership & Market

Members are companies that manufacture and market all types of lubricating greases, additive or equipment suppliers, and research and educational groups whose interests are primarily technical.
280 Members
Founded in 1933

19775 NORA Association of Responsible Recyclers

7250 Heritage Village Plaza
Suite 201
Gainesville, VA 20155

703-753-4277
FAX 703-753-2445

E-Mail: sparker@noranews.org
Home Page: www.noranews.org

Bill Hinton, President
Chirs Bergstrom, Executive Vice President
Roy Schumacher, Vice President
Scott D Parker, Executive Director
Casey Parker, Associate Director

Members are companies that reprocess used antifreeze, wastewater, oil filters, chemicals and companies that provide products or services to the industry.
211 Members
Founded in 1985

19776 National Association of Convenience Stores

1600 Duke Street
Alexandria, VA 22314

703-684-3600
FAX 703-836-4564
E-Mail: panderson@nacsonline.com
Home Page: www.nacsonline.com
Social Media: *Facebook, Twitter, LinkedIn, YouTube, Instagram*

Henry Armour, President and CEO
Paige Anderson, Director, Government Relations
Amy Ashley-Burke, Director
Laura Beck, Marketing Specialist
Reed Armstrong, Products & Services Manager
Founded in 1961

19777 National Association of Division Order Analysts

PO Box 2300
Lee's Summit, MO 64063

972-715-4489
E-Mail: administrator@nadoa.org
Home Page: www.nadoa.org
Social Media: *Facebook, Twitter, LinkedIn, RSS*

Nancy Cemino, President
Brenda Pirrozzolo, 1st VP/Finance
Sandi Rupprecht, 2nd VP/Site Selection
Jean Hinton, Treasurer
Michele Lawton, Recording Secretary
900 Members
Founded in 1974

19778 National Association of Oil and Energy Services Professionals

PO Box 67
East Petersburg, PA 17520

717-625-3076
888-552-0900
FAX 717-625-3077
E-Mail: jgarber@thinkoesp.org
Home Page: www.naohsm.org
Social Media: *Facebook, Twitter, LinkedIn, YouTube*

Al Breda, President
Ralph Adams, Vice-President
Mike Hodge, Treasurer
Paul Cuprewich, Secretary
George Fantacone, Vice President

Members are oil heat service managers and small business owners. Also provides members with technical tapes, books and speakers to train thei employee technicians.
1500 Members
Founded in 1952

19779 National Association of Petroleum Investment Analysts

415 Hayward Mill Road
Concord, MA 01742-4604

978-369-0084
FAX 978-369-0086

E-Mail: dbm@napia.org
Home Page: www.napia.org

Gregory B. Barnett, Membership Chairman
Michael D. Smolinski, President
D. Barry McKennitt, Executive Director
Tyler Dann II, Board Member
Nancy J. F. Prue, Board Member
Founded in 1974

19780 National Association of Royalty Owners

15 W 6th St
Suite 2626
Tulsa, OK 74119

918-794-1660
800-558-0557
FAX 918-794-1662
E-Mail: NARO@NARO-us.org
Home Page: www.naro-us.org
Social Media: *Facebook, Twitter*

Candice Brewer, President
James Elder, Vice President
Emily Wagner, Corporate Secretary
JIm Leonard, Treasurer

Assists mineral and royalty owners in the effective management of their mineral properties. Provides information on tax, regulatory, and legislative matters. Conducts seminars and bestows awards.
5M Members
Founded in 1980

19781 National Drilling Association

4036 Center Rd
Suite B
Brunswick, OH 44212

877-632-4748
877-632-4748
FAX 216-803-9900
E-Mail: info@nda4u.com
Home Page: www.nda4u.com
Social Media: *Facebook, LinkedIn*

Dan Dunn, President
Michael Willey, Vice President
Larry Gibel, Secretary/ Treasurer
Timothy Augustine, Director

A non-profit trade association of contractors, manufacturers and affiliated members from the drilling industry representing the geotechnical, environmental and mineral exploration sectors of this industry.
250+ Members
Founded in 1972

19782 National Ocean Industries Association

1120 G St NW
Suite 900
Washington, DC 20005

202-347-6900
FAX 202-347-8650
E-Mail: jwilliams@noia.org
Home Page: www.noia.org
Social Media: *Facebook, Twitter, LinkedIn, YouTube, Google+*

Randall Luthi, President
Franki Stunz, Sr.Vice President
Ann Chapman, VP Conferences and Events
Megan Bel Miller, VP Government Relations
Nicoltte Nye, VP Communications

Represents all facets of the domestic offshore and related industries. Member companies are dedicated to the development of offshore oil and natural gas for the continued growth and security of the US.
320+ Members
Founded in 1972

19783 National Petrochemical & Refiners Association

1667 K Street, NW
Suite 700
Washington, DC 20006

202-457-0480
FAX 202-457-0486
E-Mail: info@afpm.org
Home Page: www.afpm.org
Social Media: *Facebook, Twitter*

Gregory J Goff, Chairman
Lawrence M Ziemba, Vice Chair
Chet Thompson, President
Brandon E Williams, Executive Vice President
Rebecca H Adler, Senior director, Communications

Association that represents the petrochemical and refining industries, sponsors periodic conferences, and seeks to inform policymakers and the public. Issues include the recycling of used oils and other liquid wastes.
450 Members
Founded in 1902

19784 National Petroleum Council

1625 K St NW
Suite 600
Washington, DC 20006

202-393-6100
FAX 202-331-8539
E-Mail: info@npc.org
Home Page: www.npc.org

Charles D. Davidson, Chair
Rex W. Tillerson, Vice Chair
Marshall W. Nichols, Executive Director
Ernest J. Moniz, Secretary

Self-supporting, federal advisory body to the Secretary of Energy established in 1946 at the request of President Truman.
191 Members
Founded in 1946

19785 National Petroleum Energy Credit Association

1302 Clayton Nolen Drive
Horseshoe Bay, TX 78657

830-220-3797
FAX 817-796-1080
E-Mail: ContactUs@npeca.org
Home Page: www.npeca.org

Mike Swillo, President
Mark L. Macha, 1st Vice President
Della White, 2nd Vice President
Laura Roussel, 3rd Vice President
Terry Faber, Secretary
Founded in 1935

19786 National Propane Gas Association

1899 L St NW
Suite 350
Washington, DC 20036

202-466-7200
FAX 202-466-7205
E-Mail: info@npga.org
Home Page: www.npga.org

Charlie Ory, Chairman
Stuart Weidie, Chairman-Elect
Jerry Brick, Vice-Chairman
Richard Roldan, President & CEO
Chris Earhart, Treasurer

Members are producers and distributors of liquified petroleum gas and equipment manufacturers.
3500 Members
Founded in 1931

19787 National Stripper Well Association

1201 15th St NW
Suite 300
Washington, DC 20005

202-857-4722
FAX 202-857-4799
E-Mail: webmaster@ipaa.org
Home Page: www.ipaa.org
Social Media: *Facebook, Twitter, LinkedIn, Youtube*

Michael Watford, Chairman
Mark K.Miller, Vice Chair
Diemer True, Treasurer
Barry Russell, President & CEO

This operates under the Independent Petroleum Association, which is an informed voice for the exloration and production segment of the industry. It provides economic and statistical information, and develops investment symposia and other opportunities for its members.
1600+ Members
Founded in 1929

19788 Natural Gas Supply Association

1620 Eye St., NW
Suite 700
Washington, DC 20006

202-326-9300
FAX 202-326-9330
E-Mail: NaturalGas.org
Home Page: www.ngsa.org
Social Media: *Twitter*

Bill Green, Chairman
Frans Everts, Vice Chair
Dean E. Wiggins, President
A.Scott Moore, Secretary-Treasurer

Represents U.S.-based producers and marketers of natural gas on issues that affect the natural gas industry, including the residential and industrial consumers who rely on the fuel for a myriad of purposes.
14 Members
Founded in 1965

19789 Newport Associates

7400 E Orchard Road
Suite 320
Englewood, CO 80111-2528

FAX 303-779-0908

Association for over 450 oil companies in over 20 world regions.

19790 Nuclear Energy Institute

1201 F St., NW
Suite 1100
Washington, DC 20004-1218

202-739-8000
FAX 202-785-4019
E-Mail: webmaster@nei.org
Home Page: www.nei.org
Social Media: *Facebook, Twitter, LinkedIn, Google+, YouTube, Pinterest, F*

Donald E. Brandt, Chairman
Christopher M. Crane, President & CEO
Marvin S. Fertel, President & CEO
Alexande W. Flint, Senior Vice President
Maria G. Korsnick, Chief Operating Officer

Members are of utilities, manufacturers of electrical generating equipment, researchers, architects, engineers, labor unions, and others interested in the generation of electricity by nuclear power.
350 Members
Founded in 1984

19791 Paper, Allied-Industrial, Chemical and Energy Workers International Union

3340 Perimeter Hill Drive
Nashville, TN 37211

615-834-8590
FAX 615-731-6362
E-Mail: jhill@isdn.net
Home Page: www.paceunion.org

Jim Pannell, VP
Lynne Baker, Associate Director Communications
Joan Hill, Director Research & Education
Elaine Piper, Owner

Work to make life better for the workers and their families.
320M Members
Founded in 1884

19792 Petroleum Equipment & Services Association

2500 Citywest Blvd
Suite 1110
Houston, TX 77042-3049

713-932-0168
E-Mail: info@pesa.org
Home Page: pesa.org
Social Media: *Facebook, Twitter, LinkedIn, Google+, YouTube*

Gary Halverson, Chairman
Saeid Rahimian, Vice Chairman
Burk L. Ellison, First VP
Leslie Shockley Beyer, President
Molly Smart, Vice President of Communications
200 Members
Founded in 1933

19793 Petroleum Equipment Institute

PO Box 2380
Tulsa, OK 74101-2380

918-494-9696
FAX 918-491-9895
E-Mail: dooley@pei.org
Home Page: www.pei.org
Social Media: *Facebook, Twitter, LinkedIn, Google+*

Kevin McKinney, President
Steve Trabilsy, Vice President
Robert Renkes, Executive Vice President
Robert Peavey, Treasurer

Members are makers and distributors of equipment used in service stations, bulk plants and other petroleum marketing facilities.
1600+ Members
Founded in 1951
Mailing list available for rent: 1600 names at $275 per M

19794 Petroleum Investor Relations Association

2800 Post Oak Boulevard
Suite 5450
Houston, TX 77056

713-621-7800
FAX 978-369-0086
E-Mail: chris.pitre@rowancompanies.com
Home Page: www.rowancompanies.com

Thomas P. Burke, President
W.Matt Ralls, Executive Chairman
Stephen Butz, Executive VP & Treasurer
Mark A. Keller, Executive Vice President
Melanie M. Trent, Company Secretary

Represents investor communications professional in the peroleum and natural gas industry
100 Members
Founded in 1923

19795 Petroleum Marketers Association

1901 Fort Myer Dr
Suite 1200
Arlington, VA 22209-1609

703-351-8000
FAX 703-351-9160
Home Page: www.pmaa.org

Daniel F Gilligan, President
Nancy Kniher, Director Member Service
Cost: $50.00
700 Members

19796 Petroleum Marketers Association of America

1901 North Fort Myer Drive
Suite 500
Arlington, VA 22209

703-351-8000
FAX 703-351-9160
E-Mail: info@pmaa.org
Home Page: www.pmaa.org
Social Media: *Facebook, Twitter*

Grady Gaubert, Chairman
Mike Bailey, Vice Chair
Mark Whitehead, 2nd Vice Chair
Rob Underwood, President
Sherri Stone, Vice President
Founded in 1909

19797 Petroleum Retailers & Auto Repair Association

1051 Brinton Road
Suite 304
Pittsburgh, PA 15221

412-241-2380
FAX 412-241-2815
E-Mail: web-email-2010@prara.com
Home Page: www.prara.com

Jeff Decker, President
Dennis Budzynski, 1st Vice President
Gauttam Patel, 2nd Vice President
Nancy Maricondi, Executive Director
Ray Moore, Treasurer
Founded in 1937

19798 Petroleum Technology Transfer Council

PO Box 710942
Oak Hill, VA 20171

703-620-4797
FAX 571-485-8255
E-Mail: hq@pttc.org
Home Page: www.pttc.org
Social Media: *Facebook*

J.C. Hall, Chairman
Barry Tew, Vice Chairman
Mary Carr, Executive Director
Jeremy Viscomi, Executive Director
Kathy Chapman, Director of Operations

Fosters the effective transfer of exploration and production technology to US petroleum producers through regional resource centers, workshops, websites, publications, etc.
Founded in 1993

19799 Pipeline Research Council International

3141 Fairview Park Drive
Suite 525
Falls Church, VA 22042

703-205-1600
FAX 703-205-1607
E-Mail: gtenely@prci.com
Home Page: www.prci.org

Phillip DePriest, Chairman
Jeff Whiworth, Vice Chairman
Cliff Johnson, President
Michael P. Whelan, Director
Gary Choquette, Senior Program Manager

Sponsors research on technical issues facing the natural gas transmission industry. Members are companies operating pipeline systems.
78 Members
Founded in 1952
Mailing list available for rent

19800 Rocky Mountain Oil and Gas Association

1900 Grant Street
Denver, CO 80203

303-860-0099
FAX 303-861-0373

Jess D Cooper, General Manager
Linda Swain, Manager

A trade association, representing oil and gas industries.
600 Members
Founded in 1920

19801 Service Station Dealers of America

1532 Pointer Ridge Place
Suite G
Bowie, MD 20716

301-390-4405
FAX 301-390-3161
E-Mail: mgates@wmda.net
Home Page: www.ssda-at.com
Social Media: *Facebook, Twitter*

Peter S Kischak, President
Fred Bordoff, 1st Vice President
Billy Hillmuth, 2nd Vice President
Hugh Campbell, Treasurer

Service Station Dealers of America/National Coalition of Petroleum Retailers and Allied Trades is a national association composed of individual and state affiliate associations representing service station dealers, repair facilities, car washes and convenience stores.
Founded in 1947

19802 Society of Independent Gasoline Marketers

3930 Pender Drive
Suite 340
Fairfax, VA 22030

703-709-7000
E-Mail: sigma@sigma.org
Home Page: www.sigma.org

Tom Gresham, President
David Baker, 1st Vice President
William Bradford, 2nd Vice President
Liz Menz, Education Director
Nancy Muskett, Marketing Director
260 Members
Founded in 1958

19803 Society of Petroleum Engineers

222 Palisades Creek Drive
Richardson, TX 75080

972-952-9393
800-456-6863
FAX 972-952-9435
E-Mail: spedal@spe.org
Home Page: www.spe.org
Social Media: *Facebook, Twitter, LinkedIn, YouTube, Instagram*

Nathan Meehan, President
Janeen Judah, VP Finance
Mark A. Rubin, CEO & Executive VP
Stephen Graham, Chief Operations Officer
Cordella Wong, Managing Director

Supports those professionals involved in the field of exploration, drilling, production, and reservoir management, as well as related manufacturing and service organizations. Publishes monthly magazine.
12400 Members
Founded in 1957

19804 Society of Petroleum Evaluation Engineers
5535 Memorial Drive
Houston, TX 77007

713-651-1639
FAX 713-951-9659
E-Mail: info@spee.org
Home Page: www.spee.org

Gary Gonzenbach, President
Dee Patterson, Vice President
Floyd Siegle, Secretary/Treasurer
Brad DeWitt, Director

Members are engineers specializing in the fields of petroleum and natural gas properties.
495 Members
Founded in 1962

19805 Society of Petrophysicists and Well Log Analysts
8866 Gulf Freeway
Suite 320
Houston, TX 77017

713-947-8727
FAX 713-947-7181
E-Mail: info@spwla.org
Home Page: www.spwla.org
Social Media: *Facebook, Twitter, LinkedIn*

Thaimar Ramirez, President
Luiz Quintero, President-Elect
Brett L.Wendt, VP Technology
Oliver Mullin, VP Publications

Provides information services to scientists in the petroleum and mineral industries, serves as a voice of shared interests in our profession, plays a major role in strengthening petrophysical education, and strives to increase the awareness of the role petrophysics has in the Oil and Gas Industry and the scientific community.
3300 Members
Founded in 1959

19806 Solution Mining Research Institute
105 Apple Valley Circle
Clarks Summit, PA 18411

570-585-8092
FAX 570-585-8091
E-Mail: info@solutionmining.org
Home Page: www.solutionmining.org
Social Media: *LinkedIn*

Dr. Benoit Brouard, President
Kerry L. DeVries, Vice President
Dr. Fritz Wilke, Secretary-Treasurer
Klaus Buschbom, Program Chairman
John O. Voigt, Executive Director

Members are companies interested in the production of salt brine and solution mining of potash and soda ash, as well as production of salt covers, used for storage of oil, gas, chemicals, compressed air and waste.
100 Members
Founded in 1965

19807 Southern Gas Association
3030 LBJ Freeway
Suite 1500
Dallas, TX 75234

972-620-8505
FAX 972-620-1613
E-Mail: memberservices@southerngas.org
Home Page: www.southerngas.org
Social Media: *Facebook, Twitter, YouTube, RSS*

Henry P. Linginfelter, Chairman
Frank Yoho, 1st Vice Chair
Jerry L. Morris, 2nd Vice Chair
Mike Grubb, President & CEO
Kimberly Watson, Secretary - Treasurer
116 Members
Founded in 1908

19808 Spill Control Association of America
103 Oronoco Street
Suite 200
Alexandria, VA 22314

571-451-0433
FAX 443-640-1086
E-Mail: info@scaa-spill.org
Home Page: www.scaa-spill.org

Rick Lewis, President
Devon Grennan, VP
Nelson Fetgatter, Treasurer
Robert Chambers, Secretary
John Allen, Executive Director

Members are companies concerned with cleaning up spills of oil and hazardous products and manufacturers of specialized products for spill control.
Founded in 1973

19809 The Independent Petroleum Association of America
1201 15th St NW
Suite 300
Washington, DC 20005

202-857-4722
FAX 202-857-4799
Home Page: www.ipaa.org
Social Media: *Facebook, Twitter, LinkedIn, YouTube*

Michael Watford, Chairman
Mark Miller, Vice Chairman
Barry Russell, President & CEO
Diemer TRUE, Treasurer
Lee O. Fuller, Executive Vice President

Members are small producers of oil and natural gas and their suppliers.
5500 Members
Founded in 1929

19810 The National Petroleum Management Association
10908 Courthouse Rd
Ste 102-301
Fredericksburg, VA 22408

540-507-4371
FAX 540-507-4372
Home Page: www.npma-fuelnet.org

Jack Lavin, President
Alan Reynolds, VP - Communication
Ruth Lavin, Marketing Officer
Erin Creese, San Antonio Office Manager
Al Pond, Board Member

19811 The Society of Exploration Geophysicists
8801 South Yale
Suite 500
Tulsa, OK 74137-3575

918-497-5500
FAX 918-497-5557
Home Page: www.seg.org/seg
Social Media: *Facebook, Twitter, LinkedIn, YouTube, Google+, Instagram*

Michael C. Forrest, Chair
Dr. John Holloway, President
Alison W. Small, Treasurer
William L. Abriel, President-Elect
Dr. Eve S. Sprunt, First Vice President

19812 Tubular Exchanger Manufacturers Association, Inc.
25 North Broadway
Tarrytown, NY 10591

914-332-0040
FAX 914-332-1541
E-Mail: tema@tema.org
Home Page: www.tema.org

Richard C Byrne, Secretary

Sets standards for the industry, known as TEMA Standards, which are sold to the chemical processing and petroleum refining industries
18 Members
Founded in 1939

19813 US Oil & Gas Association
1101 K Street NW
Suite 425
Washington, DC 20005

202-638-4400
Home Page: www.usoga.org
Social Media: *Facebook, Twitter*

Walter G. Mayfield, Chairman
Albert L. Modiano, President
Tim Stewart, Vice President
Founded in 1917

19814 Western Petroleum Marketers Association
PO Box 571500
Salt Lake City, UT 84157-1500

801-263-9762
888-252-5550
FAX 801-262-9413
E-Mail: info@wpma.com
Home Page: www.wpma.com
Social Media: *Facebook, Twitter, LinkedIn, YouTube*

Brad Bell, President
Rick Reese, 1st Vice President
Ron Berry, 2nd Vice President
Mark Lytle, 3rd Vice President
Gregg Benson, Senior PMAA Director

Trade magazine for petroleum marketers, c-store owners, and businesses associated with petroleum marketing.
700 Members
Founded in 1953

19815 Western States Petroleum Association
1415 L St
Suite 600
Sacramento, CA 95814

916-498-9203
FAX 916-444-5745
Home Page: www.wspa.org
Social Media: *Facebook, Twitter*

Catherine Reheis-Boyd, President
Tupper Hull, Vice President
Steven Arita, Senior Environmental Coordinator
Barbara Chichester, Bookkeeper

Trade association that represents the full spectrum of those companies that refine, produce, transport, and market petroleum and petroleum products in six western states: Arizona, California, Oregon, Nevada, Hawaii and Washington.
35 Members
Founded in 1907

Newsletters

19816 Butane-Propane News
PO Box 660698
Arcadia, CA 91066-698

626-357-2168
800-214-4386
FAX 626-303-2854
Home Page: www.bpnews.com

Natalie Peal, Publisher
Ann Rey, Editorial Director

Petroleum and propane industry news.
Cost: $32.00
Frequency: Monthly
Founded in 1939

19817 Clean-Coal/Synfuels Letter

McGraw Hill
PO Box 182604
Columbus, OH 43272

614-304-4000
877-833-5524
FAX 614-759-3749
E-Mail: customer.service@mcgraw-hill.com
Home Page: www.mcgraw-hill.com
Social Media: *Facebook, Twitter, You Tube*

John Higgins, Publisher

Provides worldwide coverage of the development of clean-coal technologies.
Cost: $840.00
6 Pages
Frequency: Monthly
Founded in 1899

19818 Cold Water Oil Spills

Cutter Information Corporation
37 Broadway
Suite 1
Arlington, MA 02474-5500

781-648-1950
800-888-8939
FAX 781-648-1950
E-Mail: service@cutter.com
Home Page: www.cutter.com

Kim Leonard, Editor
Karen Coburn, Senior Consultant
Hillel Glazer, Senior Consultant
Ron Blitstein, Director

Clean up and control of oil spills in cold and icy waters.
Cost: $175.00
Founded in 1986

19819 Fuel Line

National Petrochemical & Refiners
Association
1667 K Street, NW
Suite 700
Washington, DC 20006-1654

202-457-0480
FAX 202-457-0486
E-Mail: info@npra.org
Home Page: www.npra.org

Charles Drevna, President
Gerald R. Van De Velde, CFO
Rebbie J. Riley, Executive Assistant

Addresses motor fuels regulations, policy and related issues. Available online only for NPRA members.
450 Members
Frequency: Weekly

19820 Gas Daily

1200 G Street NW
#1000
Washington, DC 20005

202-383-2100
800-752-8878
FAX 202-383-2125
E-Mail: support@platts.com
Home Page: www.gasdaily.com

Mark Davidson, Publisher
Bill Loveless, Director
Larry Foster, Director
Dixie Barrett, Vice President

Information on spot prices cash markets and regulatory developments for the natural gas industry.
Cost: $2255.00
Frequency: Daily

19821 Gas Storage Report

Pasha Publications

1600 Wilson Boulevard
#600
Arlington, VA 22209-2510

703-528-1244
FAX 703-528-7821
Home Page: www.pasha.com

Jeff Pruzan, Editor

Detailed charts that list monthly storage activity of all interstate pipelines and covers all phases of the underground storage of natural gas.
Cost: $495.00
Frequency: Monthly

19822 Golob's Oil Pollution Bulletin

World Information Systems
PO Box 535
Cambridge, MA 02238-0535

FAX 617-492-3312

Richard S Golob, Publisher
Roger B Wilson Jr, Editor

Provides news analysis on oil pollution prevention, control and cleanup. Covers oil spills worldwide, regulations, legislation and court decisions, technical reports, new equipment and products, contract opportunities and awards, and conference notices.
Cost: $335.00
Frequency: BiWeekly
Circulation: 20,000

19823 Green Room Report

National Petrochemical & Refiners
Association
1667 K Street, NW
Suite 700
Washington, DC 20006-1654

202-457-0480
FAX 202-457-0486
E-Mail: info@npra.org
Home Page: www.npra.org

Charles Drevna, President
Gerald R. Van De Velde, CFO
Rebbie J. Riley, Executive Assistant

Addresses current environmental and safety events, including regulation and policy issues of EPA and OSHA. Available only online to NPRA members.
450 Members
Frequency: Weekly

19824 Gulf of Mexico Newsletter

Offshore Data Services
3200 Wilcrest Dr
Suite 170
Houston, TX 77042-3366

832-463-3000
FAX 832-463-3100
Home Page: www.ods-petrodata.com

Thomas E Marsh, President
Hannah Hartland, Chairman

Aimed at the supply and service people of the off-shore oil and gas industry in the Gulf of Mexico, covers all significant industry news and events, and summarizes construction and field development activities.
Cost: $259.00
Frequency: Weekly
Circulation: 2150
Founded in 2002

19825 Hart's Renewable Fuel News

Hart Evepy Publishing LP

1201 Seven Locks Road
#300
Potomac, MD 20854

301-354-2100
FAX 301-424-7260
Home Page: www.worldfuels.com

Rachel Gantz, Editor
Robert Gaph, Executive Editor
Jack Peckham, Executive Editor
Theresa Ward, Managing Editor

Refinery updates, oxygenation schemes, capital spending, strategic alliances and essential business intelligence on corporate moves.
Cost: $1495.00
Frequency: Weekly
Founded in 1973

19826 ILMA Compoundings

Independent Lubricant Manufacturers
Association
400 N Columbus St
Suite 201
Alexandria, VA 22314-2264

703-684-5574
FAX 703-836-8503
E-Mail: ilma@ilma.org
Home Page: www.ilma.org

Celeste Powers, Executive Director
Martha Jolkovski, Director
Publications/Advertising

Focuses on legislative, regulatory, marketing and industry news of concern to independent blenders and compounders of high-quality lubricants. Accepts advertising.
Cost: $150.00
20 Pages
Frequency: Monthly
Circulation: 1800
Founded in 1948

19827 Independent Liquid Terminals Association Newsletter

Independent Liquid Terminals Association
1444 I St Nw
Suite 400
Washington, DC 20005-6538

202-842-9200
FAX 703-875-2018
E-Mail: info@ilta.org
Home Page: www.ilta.org

E David Doane, President
Gwen Butler, Office Manager

Monthly publication detailing federal, state and local legislative and regulatory action, ILTA response and ILTA events. Geared specifically to bulk liquid terminal owners/operators and establishments supplying equipment, goods and services to the bulk liquid terminaling industry.
8 Pages
Frequency: Monthly
Printed in 2 colors

19828 Institute of Gas Technology

Institute of Gas Technology
1700 S Mount Prospect Rd
Des Plaines, IL 60018-1804

847-768-0500
FAX 847-768-0501
E-Mail: publicrelations@gastechnology.org
Home Page: www.gastechnology.org

David Carroll, President/CEO
Edward Johnston, Managing Director
Carol Worster, Manager
Newsletter
Cost: $495.00
Founded in 1945

19829 International Directory of Oil Spills and Control Products and Services

Cutter Information Corporation

37 Broadway
Suite 1
Arlington, MA 02474-5500

781-648-8700
FAX 781-648-8707
E-Mail: consortium@cutter.com
Home Page: www.cutter.com
Social Media: *Facebook, Twitter, LinkedIn, RSS*

Verna Allee, Senior Consultant

Products and services listed by category.
Cost: $75.00

19830 International Gas Technology Highlights

Institute of Gas Technology
1700 S Mount Prospect Rd
Des Plaines, IL 60018-1804

847-768-0664
FAX 847-768-0669
E-Mail: gtiadmin@gastechnology.org
Home Page: www.gastechnology.org

David Carroll, President/CEO
Edward Johnston, Managing Director

A biweekly newsletter covering international developments in energy with a focus on natural gas.
Cost: $100.00
4 Pages
Circulation: 1600
Founded in 1946
Printed in 2 colors on matte stock

19831 International Oil News

William F Bland
709 Turmeric Ln
Durham, NC 27713-3103

919-544-1717
FAX 919-544-1999
E-Mail: mbs@PetroChemical-News.com
Home Page:
www.petrochemical-news.com/pcn.htm

Susan Kensil, President
Mollie B Sandor, Circulation Director

A weekly report of current news about all areas of the international petroleum industry, exploration, production, processing, transportation and marketing.
Cost: $857.00
Frequency: Weekly
Founded in 1963

19832 International Summary and Review of Oil Spills

Cutter Information Corporation
37 Broadway
Suite 1
Arlington, MA 02474-5500

781-648-8700
FAX 781-648-8707
Home Page: www.cutter.com

Verna Allee, Senior Consultant

International coverage of the gas and oil industry.
Cost: $100.00
Frequency: Monthly
Founded in 1986

19833 LNG Observer

Institute of Gas Technology
1700 S Mount Prospect Rd
Des Plaines, IL 60018-1804

847-768-0664
FAX 847-768-0669
Home Page: www.gastechnology.org

David Carroll, President/CEO

A bimonthly publication covering the worldwide liquefied natural gas industry, including political developments, technology, economics,

statistics and interviews with industry leaders.
Cost: $395.00
24 Pages
Frequency: Bi-Monthly
Circulation: 2,000
ISBN: 1-053694-9 -

19834 Leading Edge

Society of Exploration Geophysicists
PO Box 702740
Tulsa, OK 74170-2740

918-497-5500
FAX 918-497-5557
E-Mail: web@seg.org
Home Page: www.seg.org
Social Media: *Facebook, Twitter, LinkedIn*

Mary Fleming, Executive Director
Vladimir Grechka, Editor
David J Monk, President
Richard D Miller, First V.P
Dennis A Cooke, Second V.P.

19835 Lundberg Letter

Lundberg Survey
911 Via Alondra
Camarillo, CA 93012-8048

805-383-2400
800-660-4574
FAX 805-383-2424
E-Mail: lsi@lundbergsurvey.com
Home Page: www.lundbergsurvey.com

Trilby Lundberg, President

News on the US gasoline and diesel market. Retail and wholesale prices, market shares, consumption, taxes, station populations and consumer trends.
Cost: $399.00
Founded in 1950

19836 NGI's Daily Gas Price Index

Intelligence Press
PO Box 70587
Washington, DC 20024

202-583-2596
800-427-5747
FAX 202-318-0597
E-Mail: subscriptions@intelligencepress.com
Home Page: intelligencepress.com

Ellen Beswick, Publisher
Mike Nazzaro, Managing Editor
Alexander Steis, Managing Editor

Gas industry news, reports and statistics.
Cost: $1045.00
Frequency: Daily

19837 National Association of Royalty Owners

12316 Andrews Drive
Suite B
Oklahoma City, OK 73120-5779

405-573-2972
800-558-0557
FAX 405-286-9402
E-Mail: naro@naro-us.org
Home Page: www.naro-us.org

Paul Covert, VP
Wana Box, President
David Guest, Manager

Newsletter for members. Also a book is available Look Before You Lease.
Cost: $6.50
Frequency: Monthly
Founded in 1980

19838 Natural Gas Intelligence/Gas Price Index

Intelligence Press

PO Box 70587
Washington, DC 20024

202-583-2596
800-427-5747
FAX 202-318-0597
E-Mail: ellen@intelligencepress.com
Home Page: www.intelligencepress.com

Ellen Beswick, Publisher
Alexander Steis, Managing Editor

Statistics and research for the gas and petroleum industry.
Cost: $1195.00
Frequency: Weekly
Founded in 1981

19839 Natural Gas Week

Energy Intelligence Group
1401 New York Ave Nw
Suite 500
Washington, DC 20005-2102

202-393-5113
FAX 202-393-5115
E-Mail: info@accion.org
Home Page: www.accion.org

Maria Otero, President
Mike Sultan, Managing Director
John Lwande, Managing Director
Melissa Baez, Project Manager

Economics news covering the gas industry.
Cost: $1860.00
20 Pages
Frequency: Weekly
Founded in 1985
Printed in 2 colors on matte stock

19840 News Fuel & Vehicles Report

Inside Washington Publishers
1919 S Eads St
Suite 201
Arlington, VA 22202-3028

703-418-3981
800-424-9068
FAX 703-416-8543
E-Mail: support@iwpnews.com
Home Page: www.iwpnews.com

Latest news, research and reports on alternative fuels and vehicles development aimed toward the program managers, lobbyists, policy makers, and auto, oil and corn chemical industries.
Cost: $985.00
Founded in 1980

19841 Ocean News & Technology

Technology Systems Corporation
PO Box 1096
Palm City, FL 34991-7174

772-221-7720
FAX 772-221-7715
E-Mail: techsystems@sprintmail.com
Home Page: www.ocean-news.com

Dan White, Editor
Sharon White, Circulation Manager

Magazine focusing on the major business areas of the ocean industry. News articles and technology developments are covered in areas including defense, offshore oil, diving, science, environment and marine.
Cost: $45.00
Founded in 1981

19842 Offshore Rig Newsletter

Offshore Data Services
3200 Wilcrest Dr
Suite 170
Houston, TX 77042-3366

832-463-3000
FAX 832-463-3100
Home Page: www.ods-petrodata.com

Thomas E Marsh, President
Barry Young, Chairman

Emerging markets, accidents, new technology, financing schemes, insurance trends, rig construction, moves, sales, and rates, labor problems, attrition, marketing strategies, and the corporate activities of drilling contractors.
Cost: $220.00
Frequency: Monthly
Circulation: 900
Founded in 1973

19843 Oil Daily

Energy Intelligence Group
1401 New York Ave Nw
Suite 500
Washington, DC 20005-2102

202-393-5113
FAX 202-393-5115
E-Mail: info@accion.org
Home Page: www.accion.org

Maria Otero, President
John Lwande, Managing Director
Melissa Baez, Project Manager

Magazine on the petroleum and oil industry, available on line.
Cost: $1880.00
Frequency: Daily
Circulation: 60000
Founded in 1951

19844 Oil Express

United Communications Group
11300 Rockville Pike
Street 1100
Rockville, MD 20852-3030

301-287-2700
FAX 301-816-8945
E-Mail: webmaster@ucg.com
Home Page: www.ucg.com

Benny Dicecca, President

Information for gasoline marketers.
Cost: $447.00
8 Pages
Frequency: Monthly
Founded in 1977

19845 Oil Spill Intelligence Report

Aspen Publishers
111 8th Ave
Suite 700
New York, NY 10011-5207

212-771-0600
800-234-1660
FAX 212-771-0885
Home Page: www.aspenpublishers.com

Richard Kravits, Executive VP
Gerry Centrowitz, Marketing/Communications Manager

Provides timely coverage of oil spills worldwide.
Cost: $695.00
6 Pages
Frequency: Weekly
Founded in 1978

19846 Oil Spill United States Law Report

Aspen Publishers
76 Ninth Avenue
7th Floor
New York, NY 10011

212-771-0600
800-638-8437
Home Page: www.aspenpublishers.com

Mark Dorman, CEO
Gustavo Dobles, VP Operations

Professionals who need to stay abreast of US federal and state regulations.
Cost: $7.67
12 Pages
Frequency: Monthly

19847 Oil, Gas and Petrochem Equipment

PennWell Publishing Company
1421 S Sheridan Rd
Tulsa, OK 74112-6619

918-835-3161
800-331-4463
FAX 918-831-9476
E-Mail: headquarters@penwell.com
Home Page: www.pennwell.com

Robert Biolchini, President
Tim L Tobeck, Group Publisher
J B Avants, Publisher & Editor

The petroleum industry's only all new products and services magazine. Each month it announces the newest developments in equipment, products, systems and services for drilling, production, refining, petrochemical manufacturing, pipeline/storage and gas processing.
Cost: $35.00
Frequency: Monthly
Circulation: 32000
Founded in 1955
Mailing list available for rent; 32,000 names
Printed in 4 colors on glossy stock

19848 PIW's Oil Market Intelligence

286 Madison Ave
Suite 14
New York, NY 10017-6368

212-557-3000
FAX 212-557-5051
Home Page: www.piw.pubs.com

Offers information on oil and gas stocks and bonds.
Frequency: Monthly

19849 PTTC Network News

Petroleum Technology Transfer Council
16010 Barkers Point Lane
Suite 220
Houston, TX 77079

281-921-1720
FAX 281-921-1723
E-Mail: hq@pttc.org
Home Page: www.pttc.org

Kristi Lovendahl, Webmaster/Newsletter Editor
Norma Gutierrez, Circulation Director
Donald Duttlinger, Executive Director
Russell Lindsay, Advertising Sales Director

16 page newsletter with east to read summaries of new oil and natural gas technologies.
Frequency: Quarterly
Circulation: 17000
Founded in 1994

19850 PetroChemical News

William F Bland
PO Box 16666
Chapel Hill, NC 27516-6666

919-490-0700
FAX 919-490-3002

Susan D Kensil, Editor

A fast, accurate report of significant world petrochemical developments.
Cost: $739.00
4 Pages
Frequency: Weekly

19851 Petroleum Intelligence Weekly

5 E 37th St
Suite 5
New York, NY 10016-2807

212-532-1112
FAX 212-532-4479
E-Mail: info@energyintel.com
Home Page: www.energyintel.com

Tom Wallin, President
Peter Kemp, Editor

Raja W. Sidawi, Chairman
Sarah Miller, Editor-at-Large

News of the oil and gas industries worldwide.
Cost: $3340.00
Frequency: Weekly
Founded in 1961

19852 Platt's Oilgram News

McGraw Hill
3333 Walnut Street
Boulder, CO 80301-2525

720-485-5000
800-752-8878
FAX 720-548-5701
E-Mail: support@platts.com
Home Page: www.platts.com
Social Media: *Facebook, Twitter, LinkedIn, YouTube,LinkedIn,RSS,Blog*

O Marashian, Publisher
James Keener, Marketing
Harry Sachinsis, President

News of the oil and gas industries worldwide.
Frequency: Daily
Founded in 1888
Mailing list available for rent

19853 Public Gas News

American Public Gas Association
201 Massachusetts Ave Ne
Suite C-4
Washington, DC 20002-4957

202-464-0240
FAX 202-464-0246
E-Mail: website@apga.org
Home Page: www.apga.org

Bert Kalisch, President
Bob Beauregard, Marketing
Chuck Warrington, Managing Director

Written for public gas managers to keep them apprised of industry news.
Cost: $50.00
Circulation: 1000
Founded in 1961
Printed in on matte stock

19854 Security Watch

National Petrochemical & Refiners Association
1667 K Street, NW
Suite 700
Washington, DC 20006-1654

202-457-0480
FAX 202-457-0486
E-Mail: info@npra.org
Home Page: www.npra.org

Charles Drevna, President
Gerald R. Van De Velde, CFO
Rebbie J. Riley, Executive Assistant

Important security-related events, announcements, and background stories from government and industry. Written for members of the refining and petrochemical industries who have facility security responsibilities.
450 Members
Frequency: Weekly

19855 Tech Update

National Petrochemical & Refiners Association
1667 K Street, NW
Suite 700
Washington, DC 20006-1654

202-457-0480
FAX 202-457-0486
E-Mail: info@npra.org
Home Page: www.npra.org

Charles Drevna, President
Gerald R. Van De Velde, CFO
Rebbie J. Riley, Executive Assistant

Highlights developments in safety, plant security, technology, government regulations, and NPRA technical meetings for the petroleum refining and petrochemical industries.
450 Members
Frequency: Bi-Weekly

19856 WPMA Weekly Update
Western Petroleum Marketers Association
PO Box 571500
Murray, UT 84157

801-263-9762
888-252-5550
FAX 801-262-9413
E-Mail: info@wpma.com
Home Page: www.wpma.com

Gene Inglesby, Executive Director
Rob Franklin, President
Bob Ogan, VP

E-newsletter.
Frequency: Weekly
Founded in 1953

19857 Washington Report
Interstate Natural Gas Association of America
555 13th St Nw
Suite 300W
Washington, DC 20004-1109

202-637-8600
FAX 202-637-8615
Home Page:
www.stonebridge-international.com

Anthony S Harrington, CEO
Samuel Berger, Manager

Natural gas newsletter places a special emphasis on developments that affect the interstate pipeline industry. It covers Congress, the Federal Energy Regulatory Commission and other federal agencies, state and Canadian regulatory boards and company news.

19858 Weekly Propane Newsletter
Butane-Propane News
PO Box 660698
Arcadia, CA 91066-0698

626-357-2168
FAX 626-303-2854
Home Page: www.bpnews.com

Natalie Peal, Publisher
Kurt Ruhl, National Sales Manager

Weekly updates and rates on the propane and gas industry.
Cost: $205.00
8 Pages
Frequency: Weekly
Circulation: 2000
Founded in 1939
Printed in one color on matte stock

19859 Western Petroleum Marketers Association
PO Box 571500
Salt Lake, UT 84157-1500

801-263-9762
FAX 801-262-9413
E-Mail: info@wpma.com
Home Page: www.wpma.com
Social Media: *Facebook, Twitter*

Gene Inglesby, Executive Director
Sandra Peterson, Editor
Brett Adams, President
Robert Fung, First V.P.
Lary Poulton, Second V.P.

Accepts advertising.
Founded in 1953

19860 World Gas Intelligence
575 Broadway
New York, NY 10012-3230

212-941-5500
FAX 212-941-5509
Home Page: www.piw.pubs.com

Edward L Morse, Publisher
Jocelyn Strauber, Circulation Director

International coverage of the oil and gas industry.
Cost: $985.00
Frequency: SemiMonthly
Mailing list available for rent

Magazines & Journals

19861 AAPG Bulletin
American Association of Petroleum Geologists
PO Box 979
Tulsa, OK 74101-979

918-584-2555
FAX 918-560-2632
E-Mail: bulletin@aapg.org
Home Page: www.aapg.org

Beverly Molyneux, Managing Editor
David Curtiss, CEO/President
Larry Nations, Marketing

Peer reviewed articles that cover major extent and detailed geologic data. Information on petroleum, natural gas, and other energy products.
Cost: $305.00
Frequency: Monthly
Circulation: 30000
ISSN: 0149-1423
Founded in 1917

19862 AAPG Explorer
American Association of Petroleum Geologists
1444 S Boulder Avenue
PO Box 979
Tulsa, OK 74101-979

918-584-2555
800-288-7636
FAX 918-560-2665
E-Mail: postmaster@aapg.org
Home Page: www.aapg.org

Patrick J F Gratton, President
Ernest A Mancini, Editor
Brenda Merideth, Advertising Sales Manager

News for explorationists of oil, gas and minerals as well as for geologists with environmental and water well concerns.
Cost: $50.00
Frequency: Monthly
Circulation: 30000
ISBN: 0-195298-6 -
Founded in 1917
Printed in 4 colors on matte stock

19863 American Gas Magazine
American Gas Association
400 N Capitol Street NW
Suite 450
Washington, DC 20001

202-824-7000
FAX 202-824-7092
Home Page: www.aga.org
Social Media: *Facebook, Twitter, YouTube,RSS,Flickr*

Dave McCurdy, CEO
Kevin Hardardt, CFO/CAO
Ysabel Korolevich, Membership Services
Frequency: 10x/Year
Founded in 1918

19864 American Oil and Gas Reporter
National Publishers Group
PO Box 343
Derby, KS 67037

316-788-6271
800-847-8301
FAX 316-788-7568
E-Mail: reporter@feist.com
Home Page: www.fiest.com

Charlie Cookson, Publisher
Bill Campbell, Managing Editor

The American Oil & Gas Reporter serves the exploration, drilling and production segments of the oil and gas industry.
Cost: $65.07
Frequency: Monthly
Circulation: 7384
Founded in 1958

19865 BIC - Business & Industry Connection
BIC Alliance
Po Box 3502
Covington, LA 70434

985-893-8692
FAX 985-893-8693
E-Mail: bic@bicalliance.com
Home Page: www.bicalliance.com

Jamie Craig, Editor
Earl Heard, CEO/President
Kathy Dugas, Administrator
Joe Storer, Manager

Information on oil and gas, refining, petrochemical, environmental, construction, engineering, pulp and paper, state agencies and municipalities business.
Cost: $45.00
Circulation: 75000

19866 Bloomberg Natural Gas Report
Bloomberg Financial Markets
100 Business Park Drive
Princeton, NJ 08542-840

609-279-3000
800-395-9403
FAX 917-369-7000
E-Mail: munis@bloomberg.com
Home Page: www.bloomberg.com/energy

Michael Bloomberg, Publisher
Ronald Henkoff, Editor

News, interviews, and analysis of topics of importance to all levels of the natural gas market.
12 Pages
Frequency: Weekly
Circulation: 1700
Founded in 1980

19867 Butane-Propane News
Butane-Propane News
PO Box 660698
Arcadia, CA 91006

626-357-2168
800-214-4386
FAX 626-303-2854
Home Page: www.bpnews.com

Natalie Peal, Publisher
Ann Rey, Editorial Director
Kurt Ruhl, Sales Manager

Petroleum and propane industry news.
Cost: $32.00
56 Pages
Frequency: Monthly
Circulation: 16500
Founded in 1939
Printed in 4 colors on glossy stock

19868 Coal People
Al Skinner Enterprises

PO Box 6247
Charleston, WV 25362-0247

304-342-4129
800-235-5188
FAX 304-343-3124
E-Mail: cpm@newwave.net
Home Page: www.coalpeople.com

A Skinner, Owner
Christina Karawan, Managing Editor
Beth Terranova, Sales Manager
Angela McNealy, Circulation Manager
C K Lane, Senior Vice President

Features special news and product sections for the coal industry.
Cost: $25.00
60 Pages
Circulation: 11500
Founded in 1976
Printed in 4 colors on glossy stock

19869 Compressor Tech Two
Diesel & Gas Turbine Publications
20855 Watertown Rd
Suite 220
Waukesha, WI 53186-1873

262-754-4100
FAX 262-754-4175
E-Mail: slizdas@dieselpub.com
Home Page: www.dieselspec.com

Michael Osenga, President
Brent Haight, Managing Editor
Kara Kane, Advertising Manager
Christa Johnson, Production Manager
Sheila Lizdas, Circulation Manager

Covers oil and gas exploration, drilling, oilfield contracting, gas and petrochemical pipeline and storage, as well as petrochemical, hydrocarbon and gas processing industries.
Circulation: 12000

19870 Diesel Progress: North American Edition
Diesel & Gas Turbine Publications
20855 Watertown
Suite 220
Waukesha, WI 53186-1873

262-754-4100
800-558-4322
FAX 262-832-5075
E-Mail: mosenga@dieselpub.com
Home Page: www.dieselspec.com

Michael Osenga, President
Sheila Lizdas, Circulation Manager
Lynne Diefenbach, Advertising Manager
Christa Johnson, Production Manager

Geared towards readers interested in state-of-the-art systems technology. Features include new product listings, systems design, research amd product testing as well as systems maintenance and rebuilding.
Frequency: Monthly
Circulation: 26011
Founded in 1969

19871 Drill Bits
National Drilling Association
1545 W 130th St
Suite A2
Hinckley, OH 44233-9121

330-273-5756
877-632-4748
FAX 216-803-9900
E-Mail: info@nda4u.com
Home Page: www.nda4u.com

Peggy McGee, President
Dan Dunn, VP
Jim Howe, Secretary/Treasurer
Tim Cleary, Board of Directors
R. Alan Garrard, Board of Directors

A non-profit trade association of contractors, manufacturers and affiliated members from the drilling industry representing the geotechnical, environmental and mineral exploration sectors of this industry.
250+ Members
Frequency: 2 X/Year
Founded in 1972

19872 Drilling Contractor
International Association of Drilling Contractors
10370 Richmond Ave
Suite 760
Houston, TX 77042-9687

713-292-1945
FAX 713-292-1946
E-Mail: info@iadc.org
Home Page: www.iadc.org

Lee Hunt, President
Tom Terrell, Senior VP Business Development

All drilling, all completing, all the time.
Cost: $50.00
40 Pages
Frequency: 6x/Year
Circulation: 34500
Printed in 4 colors

19873 Energy Markets
Hart Publications
4545 Post Oak Place
#210
Houston, TX 77027

713-993-9320
FAX 713-840-8585

Linda K Rader, Editor
Robert C Jarvis, Publisher

Energy Markets serves the following energy industry business classifications: utilities, municipalities, consultants and financial services, regulators, and other companies allied to or supportive of the energy industry.
Frequency: Monthly
Circulation: 25,751
Founded in 1993

19874 Energy Network
Gulf Publishing Company
PO Box 2608
Houston, TX 77252

713-529-4301
800-231-6275
FAX 713-520-4433
E-Mail: store@gulfpub.com
Home Page: www.gulfpub.com
Social Media: *Twitter, LinkedIn, RSS, YouTube*

John D Royall, President/CEO
Ron Higgins, VP Sales/Publisher

Edited for companies that sell products to the oil and gas industry.
Founded in 1916
Mailing list available for rent

19875 Fuel Oil News
Hunter Publishing Limited
3100 S King Dr
Suite 1004
Chicago, IL 60616-3483

312-567-9981
FAX 312-846-4632
Home Page: www.fueloilnews.com

Luke Hunter, Partner
Joanne Juda, Circulation Director
Kate Kenny, Publisher
Keith Reid, Senior Editor
Patricia McCartney, Associate Editor

For home heating oil retailers.
Cost: $28.00
70 Pages
Frequency: Monthly
Circulation: 18000
Founded in 1935
Printed in 4 colors on glossy stock

19876 Gas Turbine World
Pequot Publishing
PO Box 447
Southport, CT 36490

203-259-1812
FAX 203-254-3431
Home Page: http://www.gtwbooks.com

Robert Farmer, Editor
Victor Debiasi, Publisher
Janes Janson, Marketing
Peg Walker, Circulation Manager

Serves the electric, utility and non-untility power generation, oil/gas production and processing industries.
Cost: $135.00
Frequency: Weekly
Circulation: 11000
Founded in 1979

19877 Gas Utility Manager
James Informational Media
6301 Gaston Avenue
#541
Dallas, TX 75214-6204

214-827-4630
FAX 847-391-9058
E-Mail: ruth@BetterRoads.com
Home Page: www.betterroads.com

Mike Porcaro, Publisher
Mike Porcaro, CEO/President
Carole Spohr, Marketing Manager
Stacy Stiglic, Circulation Manager
Ruth Stidger, Editor

Federal and international regulations, new supply projects, research and development projects and gas industry news.
Cost: $95.00
40 Pages
Frequency: Annual+
Circulation: 40000
Founded in 1931

19878 Georgia Petroleum Marketer
Georgia Oilmen Association
1775 Spectrum Drive
Suite 100
Lawrenceville, GA 30043

770-995-7570
FAX 770-995-9757
E-Mail: rlane@gaoilassoc.com
Home Page: www.georgiaoilmenassoc.com

Roger T Lane, President/Editor
Mary R Franklin, Associate Editor
100 Pages
Frequency: Annual
Circulation: 800

19879 Hart's E & P
Hart Publications
1616 S Voss Rd
Suite 1000
Houston, TX 77057-2641

713-993-9320
FAX 713-840-8585
E-Mail: directoryeditor@hartenergy.com
Home Page: www.hartenergy.com

Rich Eichler, CEO
Joe Fisher, Senior Vice President
Kristine Klavers, Senior Vice President
Frederick Potter, Executive Vice President

Technical approaches and improvements related to both offshore and land drilling and extraction of petroleum products, also new product information and personality profiles.
Cost: $59.00
Frequency: Monthly
Circulation: 25000

19880 Hart's Gas/LPG Markets
Hart Publications

6011 Executive Drive
#200
Rockville, MD 20852-3804

301-468-1039
FAX 301-468-1039
Home Page: www.hartpub.com

Robert Gough, Editor

Financial reports on individual natural gas and liquid gasoline companies, their stock analysis, value and future mergers or acquisitions that may affect the pricing of gasoline or companies involved in the industry.
Cost: $ 1497.00
Frequency: Monthly

19881 Hart's Oil & Gas Interests
Hart Publications
6011 Executive Boulevard
#200
Rockville, MD 20852-3804

301-468-1039
FAX 301-468-1039
Home Page: www.hartpub.com

Brian Crotty, Group Publisher

Designed to keep readers abreast of developments and investment ideas in the petroleum and natural gas industry.
Frequency: Monthly

19882 Hart's Oil & Gas Investor
Hart Publications
1616 S Voss Rd
Suite 1000
Houston, TX 77057-2641

713-993-9320
800-874-2544
FAX 713-840-8585
E-Mail: directoryeditor@hartenergy.com
Home Page: www.hartenergy.com

Rich Eichler, CEO
Leslie Haines, Editor-in-Chief
Nissa Darbonne, Executive Editor
Kristine Klavers, Senior Vice President
Frederick Potter, Executive Vice President

Company performance, investment forecasts, economic outlooks, management strategy reports, focusing on the financial aspects of the petroleum and natural gas industry.
Cost: $297.00
Frequency: Monthly
Circulation: 5100
Printed in 4 colors

19883 Hart's World Refining
Hart Publications
4545 Post Oak Place
Suite 210
Houston, TX 77027-3105

713-993-9320
800-874-2544
FAX 713-840-8585
Home Page: www.hartpub.com

David Coates, Publisher
Jeremy Grunt, Executive Editor
Terry Higgins, Executive Publisher
Robert Gough, Editorial Director
Rich Eichler, President

Covers projects, financing and market developments, along with feedstock and product supply, demand, pricing information, technical and regulatory events associated with the manufacture, supply, and use of transportation fuels refining technologies, business strategies and fuel policy legislation.
Cost: $149.00
Circulation: 15,693
Founded in 1980

19884 Hydrocarbon Processing
Gulf Publishing Company

PO Box 2608
Houston, TX 77252-2608

713-529-4301
800-231-6275
FAX 713-520-4433
E-Mail: store@gulfpub.com
Home Page: www.gulfpub.com
Social Media: *Twitter, LinkedIn, RSS, YouTube*

John D Royall, President/CEO
Ron Higgins, VP Sales/Publisher

Concentrates on the problems facing management and technical personnel in the worldwide hydrocarbon processing industry. Accepts advertising.
Cost: $120.00
Frequency: Monthly
Circulation: 30000
Founded in 1916
Mailing list available for rent
Printed in on glossy stock

19885 Journal of Geophysical Research
American Geophysical Union
2000 Florida Ave Nw
Washington, DC 20009-1277

202-462-6900
800-966-2481
FAX 202-328-0566
E-Mail: usaha@usaha.org
Home Page: www.agu.org
Social Media: *Facebook, Twitter, LinkedIn, YouTube, RSS, Flickr, Blog*

Christine McEntee, Executive Director
John Orcutt, Publisher

There are five sections covering soid earth, oceans, atmosphere, planets, and space physics.
Cost: $20.00
Frequency: Monthly
Circulation: 10,000
Founded in 1919

19886 Journal of Petroleum Technology
Society of Petroleum Engineers
PO Box 833836
Richardson, TX 75083-3836

972-952-9300
800-456-6863
FAX 972-952-9435
E-Mail: service@spe.org
Home Page: www.spe.org

Mark Rubin, Executive Director
Giovanni Paccaloni, President
Paul Thone, Senior Manager of Sales
Niki Bradbury, Managing Director

Journal of Petroleum Technology serves the field of exploration, drilling, production, and reservoir management as well as related manufacturing and service organizations.
98 Pages
Frequency: Monthly
Circulation: 51205
Founded in 1949
Printed in 4 colors on glossy stock

19887 LP/Gas
Advanstar Communications
131 W 1st St
Duluth, MN 55802-2065

218-740-7200
800-346-0085
FAX 218-740-7079
E-Mail: info@advanstar.com
Home Page: www.advanstar.com

Kent Akervik, Manager
Sean Carr, Publisher
Joseph Loggia, CEO
Kris Meyer, Circulation Manager
Brian Kanaba, National Sales Manager

The propane industry's premier information source.
Cost: $30.00
36 Pages
Frequency: Monthly
Circulation: 15320
ISSN: 0024-7103
Printed in 4 colors on glossy stock

19888 Landman
American Association of Professional Landmen
4100 Fossil Creek Boulevard
Fort Worth, TX 76137-2723

817-847-7700
FAX 817-847-7704
E-Mail: aapl@landman.org
Home Page: www.landman.org

Le'ann Callihan, Editor
Robin Forte, President

Accepts advertising.
Cost: $50.00
76 Pages
Founded in 1955

19889 Lubricants World
4545 Post Oak Place
Suite 230
Houston, TX 77027

713-840-0378
FAX 713-840-0379

Kathryn B Carnes, Editor

19890 NLGI Spokesman
National Lubricating Grease Institute
4635 Wyandotte St
Suite 202
Kansas City, MO 64112-1537

816-931-9480
FAX 816-753-5026
E-Mail: nlgi@nlgi.org
Home Page: www.nlgi.org

Kim Bott, Executive Director
Kim Bott, Administrative Assistant

About 50% of technical or scientific information amied at the manufacturers, users and suppliers of lubricating grease.
Cost: $53.00
Frequency: Monthly
Circulation: 2500
Founded in 1933

19891 National Petroleum News
Bel-Av Communications
359 Galahad Rd
Bolingbrook, IL 60440-2108

E-Mail: kreid@m2media360.com
Home Page: www.npnweb.com

Keith Reid, Editor-in-Chief
Debra Reschke, Managing/Research Editor

The independent voice of the petroleum industry, content is aimed at the owner, operator or senior manager-the people who make the big decisions that require capital, time and resources.
Cost: $64.00
90 Pages
Frequency: Monthly
Circulation: 38000
Founded in 1909

19892 Natural Gas Fuels
RP Publishing
2696 S Colorado Blvd
Suite 595
Denver, CO 80222-5944

303-863-0521
FAX 303-863-1722

E-Mail: info@rppublishing.com
Home Page: www.rppublishing.com

Frank Rowe, President

Technological advances, marketing strategies, legislative activities, successful applications, and corporate and government initiatives to promote natural gas-powered vehicles
Circulation: 7000
Founded in 1992

19893 O&A Marketing News
KAL Publications
559 S Harbor Blvd
Suite A
Anaheim, CA 92805-4547

714-563-9300
FAX 714-563-9310
Home Page: www.kalpub.com

Kathy Laderman, President
Doreen Philbin, Advertising Sales Manager
Jim Penn, Circulation Manager
Linda Squeo, Marketing Manager

Coverage of industry events and related shows for wholesale and retail marketers of gasoline, oil and automotive service replacement products in the thirteen Pacific-Western states.
Cost: $20.00
Circulation: 7000
Founded in 1966

19894 Offshore
PennWell Publishing Company
1421 S Sheridan Rd
Tulsa, OK 74112-6619

918-835-3161
800-331-4463
FAX 918-831-9476
E-Mail: Headquarters@PennWell.com
Home Page: www.pennwell.com

Robert Biolchini, President
Biol Chini, CEO
Tommie Grigg, Circulation Manager
Elbon Ball, Editor
Jayne Gilfinger, Marketing Manager

Offshore serves the international oil and gas industry in its marine/offshore operations.
Cost: $75.00
186 Pages
Frequency: Monthly
Circulation: 40000
ISSN: 0030-0608
Founded in 1910
Mailing list available for rent
Printed in 4 colors on glossy stock

19895 Oil & Gas Journal
PennWell Publishing Company
1700 West Loop S
#1000
Houston, TX 77027-3005

713-621-9720
FAX 713-963-6285
E-Mail: sales@pennwell.com
Home Page: www.ogjonline.com

Tom T Terrell, Publisher
Tim Sullivant, Regional Sales Manager
Mike Moss, Regional Sales Manager

Detailed interpreation and information of the world developments in the oil and gas industry
Cost: $79.00
Frequency: Weekly
Circulation: 36090
Founded in 1990
Printed in 4 colors on glossy stock

19896 Oil Spill Contingency Planning: A Global Perspective
Aspen Publishers

76 Ninth Avenue
7th Floor
New York, NY 10011

212-771-0600
800-638-8437
Home Page: www.aspenpublishers.com

Mark Dorman, CEO
Gustavo Dobles, VP Operations

Hands-on guidebook to contingency planning for oil spills.
Cost: $195.00

19897 Oilheating
Industry Publications
3621 Hill Rd
Parsippany, NJ 07054-1001

973-331-9545
FAX 973-331-9547
E-Mail: info@oilheating.com
Home Page: www.spraytechnology.com
Social Media: *Facebook*

Cynthia Hundley, Publisher

Addresses issues on dispatching and delivery efficiency, residential and commercial fuel oil use, as well as sales and services of oilfired equipment.
Cost: $42.00
Frequency: Monthly
Circulation: 13280
ISSN: 1092-6003
Founded in 1922
Mailing list available for rent

19898 Petroleo International
Keller International Publishing Corporation
150 Great Neck Rd
Suite 400
Great Neck, NY 11021-3309

516-829-9722
FAX 516-829-9306
Home Page: www.supplychainbrain.com

Victor Prieto, Editor
Sean Noble, Publisher
Steve Kann, Circulation Manager
Jerry Keller, President
Mary Chavez, Director of Sales

Spanish language petroleum/petrochemical magazine.
100 Pages
Circulation: 10,314
Founded in 1943

19899 SPE Drilling & Completion
Society of Petroleum Engineers
PO Box 833836
Richardson, TX 75083-3836

972-529-9300
800-456-6863
FAX 972-952-9435
E-Mail: service@spe.org
Home Page: www.spe.org

Giovanni Paccaloni, President
Shashana Pearson, Editor
Mary Jane, Advertising Manager
Georgeann Bilich, Publisher
Niki Bradbury, Managing Director

Technical papers selected for the drilling profession reviewed by peers on topics such as casing, instrumentation, bit technology, fluids, measurment, deviation control, telemetry, completion and well control.
Cost: $60.00
Frequency: Quarterly
Circulation: 3588
Founded in 1984

19900 Sea Technology Magazine
Compass Publications, Inc.

1501 Wilson Blvd
Suite 1001
Arlington, VA 22209-2403

703-524-3136
FAX 703-841-0852
E-Mail: oceanbiz@sea-technology.com
Home Page: www.sea-technology.com
Social Media: *Twitter*

Amos Bussmann, President/Publisher
Joy Carter, Circulation Manager
Meghan Ventura, Managing Editor

Worldwide information leader for marine/offshore business, science and engineering. Read in more than 110 countries by management, engineers, scientists and technical personnel working in industry, government and education.
Cost: $40.00
Frequency: Monthly
Circulation: 16304
ISSN: 0093-3651
Founded in 1960
Mailing list available for rentat $80 per M
Printed in 4 colors

19901 Today's Refinery
Chemical Week Associates
2 Grand Central Tower,140 East 45th Street
40th floor
New York, NY 10017

212-884-9528
FAX 212-884-9514
E-Mail: ltattum@chemweek.com
Home Page: www.chemweek.com
Social Media: *Twitter, RSS,Blog*

John Rockwell, VP
Joe Minnella, Global Sales Director
LYN TATTUM, Publisher
Robert Westervelt, Editor-in-Chief

Editorials from industry leaders focusing on current problems facing the industry. Highlights on legistation, activity, government regulations,and reports on major industry meetings.
Frequency: Monthly
Circulation: 10,000
Mailing list available for rent

19902 Utility & Pipeline Industries
WMO DannHausen Corporation
330 North Wabash
Suite 3201
Chicago, IL 60611

312-628-5870
FAX 312-628-5878
E-Mail: wod@dannhausen.com
Home Page: www.gasinindustries.com

Bob Higgins, Publisher
Heidi Liddle, Production Manager
Karen Ebbesmeyer, Circulation Manager
Ruth W. Stidger, Editor-in-Chief
Cory Sekine Pettite, Managing Editor

Market to federal agencies, bureaus, government departments and toll authorities. Accepts advertising.
Cost: $20.00
62 Pages
Frequency: Monthly
Circulation: 10680

19903 Washington Report
National Ocean Industries Association
1120 G St Nw
Suite 900
Washington, DC 20005-3801

202-347-6900
FAX 202-347-8650

Home Page: www.noia.org
Social Media: *Facebook, Twitter, YouTube*

Tom Fry, President
Franki K Stuntz, Director Administration
Nolty J Thuriot, Director Congressional Affairs
Frequency: Bi-Weekly

19904 Well Servicing
Workover Well Servicing Publications
10200 Richmond Avenue
Suite 275
Houston, TX 77042

713-781-0758
800-692-0771
FAX 713-781-7542
E-Mail: kjordan@aesc.net
Home Page: www.aesc.net

Kenny Jordan, Executive DIrector
Polly Fisk, Editor
Patty Jordan, Circulation

New products listing and reviews, field reports, and information on companies in the industry. Written and edited for energy service company professionals, and oil & gas operations.
40 Pages
Circulation: 11000
ISSN: 0043-2393
Founded in 1956

19905 Western Petroleum Marketers News Magazine
Western Petroleum Marketers Association
PO Box 571500
Murray, UT 84157

801-263-9762
888-252-5550
FAX 801-262-9413
E-Mail: info@wpma.com
Home Page: www.wpma.com

Gene Inglesby, Executive Director
Rob Franklin, President
Bob Ogan, VP
Frequency: Quarterly

19906 World Oil
Gulf Publishing Company
PO Box 2608
Houston, TX 77252

713-529-4301
800-231-6275
FAX 713-520-4433
E-Mail: store@gulfpub.com
Home Page: www.gulfpub.com
Social Media: *Twitter, LinkedIn, RSS, YouTube*

John D Royall, President/CEO
Ron Higgins, VP Sales/Publisher

Reaches the exploration, drilling, producing, and well servicing segments of the oil and gas industry.
Cost: $34.00
100 Pages
Frequency: Monthly
Circulation: 36000
ISSN: 0043-8790
Founded in 1916
Mailing list available for rent
Printed in 4 colors on glossy stock

Trade Shows

19907 American Association of Petroleum Geologists Annual Convention/Expo
American Association of Petroleum Geologists
PO Box 979
Tulsa, OK 74119

918-584-2555
800-364-2274

FAX 918-560-2665
E-Mail: convene@aapg.org
Home Page: www.aapg.org
Social Media: *Facebook, Twitter, LinkedIn, YouTube*

Randa Reeder-Briggs, Annual Meeting Manager
Melissa Howerton, Annual Meeting Assistant
Steph Benton, Exhibit Manager
Rick Fritz, Executive Director
Edward 'Ted' Beaumont, President

Exhibits of instrumentation, equipment, supplies, services and publications for petroleum geologists, geophysicists and engineers.
7000 Attendees
Frequency: Annual/April

19908 American School of Gas Measurement Technology Meeting
PO Box 3991
Houston, TX 77253-3991

903-486-7875
FAX 512-267-9243
Home Page: www.asgmt.com

Seminar, workshop, and tours, plus 95 exhibits of gas measurement, equipment, supplies and services.
600 Attendees
Frequency: Annual
Founded in 1927

19909 Asia Pacific Improved Oil Recovery Conference
Society of Petroleum Engineers-Texas
222 Palisades Creek Drive
PO Box 833836
Richardson, TX 75083-3868

972-952-9300
FAX 972-952-9435
Home Page: www.spe.org

Oil recovery exhibition.
Mailing list available for rent

19910 Beaumont Industrial Petrochemical Trade Show
Lobos Services
16016 Perkins Road
Baton Rouge, LA 70810-3631

225-751-5626

Debbie Balough, Show Manager

Informs local industry of the full array of industrial equipment for the chemical industries.
5M Attendees
Frequency: January

19911 Circum-Pacific Council Energy Mineral Resources
5100 Westheimer Road
Houston, TX 77056-5596

713-709-9071
FAX 713-622-5360

Mary Stewart, Show Manager
Napoleon Carcamo, Owner

50 booths.
1.2M Attendees
Frequency: November

19912 Eastern Oil and Gas Equipment Show
Pennsylvania Oil and Gas Association
412 N 2nd Street
Harrisburg, PA 17101-1342

717-939-9551

Stephen Rhoads, Show Manager
175 booths displaying new technologies, products and services relating to the oil and gas industries.
1M Attendees
Frequency: June

19913 Entelec Conference & Expo
Energy Telecommunications and Electrical Assoc
5005 W Royal Lane
Suite 116
Irving, TX 75063

972-929-3169
888-503-8700
FAX 972-915-6040
E-Mail: blaine@entelec.org
Home Page: www.entelec.org

Blaine Siske, Executive Manager
Susan Joiner, Exhibits Manager
Michael Blurt, President
James C Coulter, First V.P
Kenneth Clouse, Second V.P.

To bring together communications and control technology professionals from the petroleum, natural gas, pipeline, and electric utility companies for three days of quality training, seminars, exhibits and networking.
Frequency: Annual/May
Founded in 1928

19914 Europe International Offshore Exchange
222 Palisades Creek Drive
Richardson, TX 75080-2040
Donna Anderson, Show Manager

1,100 booths.
21M Attendees
Frequency: September

19915 International Thermal Spray Conference & Exposition
ASM International
9639 Kinsman Road
Materials Park, OH 44073

440-338-5151
800-336-5152
FAX 440-338-4634
E-Mail: natalie.nemec@asminternational.org
Home Page: www.asminternational.org
Social Media: *Facebook, Twitter, LinkedIn*

Natalie Neme, Event Manager
Kelly Thomas, Exposition Account Manager

Global annual event attracting professional interested in thermal spray technology focusing on advances in HVOF, plasma and detonation gun, flame spray and wire arc spray processes, performance of coatings, and future trends. 150 exhibitors.
1000 Attendees
Frequency: Annual/May

19916 Landman
American Association of Petroleum Landmen
4100 Fossil Creek Boulevard
Fort Worth, TX 76137-2723

817-847-7700
FAX 817-847-7704
Home Page: http://www.landman.org

Carolyn Stephens, Editor
Le Ann Pembroke, Advertising Manager
50 booths.
1.5M Attendees
Frequency: June

19917 Liquified Gas Association Southwest
PO Box 9925
Austin, TX 78766-0925

FAX 512-834-0758

Cheryl Tomanetz, Show Manager
125 booths.
1.8M Attendees
Frequency: September

19918 Liquified Natural Gas
Reed Exhibition Companies

255 Washington Street
Newton, MA 02458-1637

617-584-4900
FAX 617-630-2222

Elizabeth Hitchcock, International Sales

Presentation for the liquefied natural gas industry.
2.5M Attendees
Frequency: May

19919 Liquified Petroleum Gas Exposition Midwest

4100 Country Club Drive
Jefferson City, MO 65109-0302

573-634-5345
FAX 573-893-2623

Emma Krommel, Show Manager

100 booths of large transport and bobtail delivery trucks.
1M Attendees
Frequency: June

19920 Midwest Petroleum & Convenience Tradeshow

Illinois Petroleum Marketers Association
PO Box 12020
Springfield, IL 62791-2020

217-544-4609
FAX 217-789-0222

Bill Fleischli, Executive VP, Managing Editor

Suppliers and manufacturers to petroleum marketing and convenience store trades, including pumps, computers, trucks, safety devices, canopies, car washes and tank testing. 300 booths.
4M Attendees
Frequency: June

19921 National Petro Refiners Association Refinery Petrochemical Plant

1899 L Street NW
Suite 1000
Washington, DC 20036-3810

202-457-0480
Home Page: http://www.npra.org

Robert Dzuiban, Show Manager
Robert Slaughter, President

A forum for the exchange of technical information and services to the petroleum industry.
1.3M Attendees
Frequency: May

19922 Offshore Technology Conference

222 Palisades Creek Drive, Richardson
Richardson, TX 75080-2040

972-952-9494
866-229-2386
FAX 972-952-9435
E-Mail: service@spe.org
Home Page: www.spe.org

Alan Wegener, Show Manager
Niki Bradbury, Managing Director

Consisting of a forum to disseminate technical information for the advancement of engineering.
30M Attendees
Frequency: May

19923 Petroleum Computer Conference

Society of Petroleum Engineers
222 Palisades Creek Drive
Richardson, TX 75080-2040

972-952-9300
FAX 972-952-9435
E-Mail: service@spe.org
Home Page: www.spe.org

Niki Bradbury, Managing Director

Annual show of 50 microcomputer manufacturers and suppliers who provide hardware and software to the petroleum industry.
650 Attendees

19924 Petroleum Equipment Institute (CONVEX) and Exhibits

Petroleum Equipment Institute
PO Box 2380
Tulsa, OK 74101-2380

918-494-9696
FAX 918-491-9895
E-Mail: cdooley@pei.org
Home Page: www.pei.org

Connie Dooley, Administrative Director
Robert Renkes, Marketing Director
Sarah West, Marketing Director
Rick Long, General Manager

Annual show of manufacturers of petroleum marketing equipment. There are 215 exhibiting companies with 675 booths.
4500 Attendees
Frequency: October
Founded in 1951

19925 Society Petro Engineers Annual Meeting

PO Box 833836
Richardson, TX 75083-3836

972-952-9300
FAX 972-952-9435

Lois Woods, Show Manager
Mark Rubin, Executive Director

Conference with exhibits of drilling and production equipment and materials.
10M Attendees
Frequency: September

19926 Society Petro Engineers Permian Basin Oil Gas Recovery Conference and Expo

PO Box 833836
Richardson, TX 75083-3836

972-952-9300

Susan Bell, Event Manager

70 booths.
400 Attendees
Frequency: March

19927 Society Petro Engineers Petroleum Computer Conference and Expo

PO Box 833836
Richardson, TX 75083-3836

972-952-9300

Georgie Cumiskey, Event Manager

30 booths of microcomputer hardware and software for the petroleum industry.
300 Attendees
Frequency: July

19928 Society Petro Engineers Production Operations Symposium

PO Box 833836
Richardson, TX 75083-3836

972-952-9300

Karen Rodgers, Event Manager
Mark Rubin, Executive Director

70 booths of oil and gas industry related products and services.
1M Attendees
Frequency: March

19929 Society Petro Engineers Rocky Mountain

PO Box 833836
Richardson, TX 75083-3836

972-952-9300

Georgie Cumiskey, Event Manager

60 booths.
300 Attendees
Frequency: April

19930 Society Petro Engineers Western Regional Meeting

PO Box 833836
Richardson, TX 75083-3836

972-952-9300

Lois Woods, Exchange Manager
Mark Rubin, Executive Director

65 booths.
700 Attendees
Frequency: May

19931 Society of Petro Engineers Eastern Regional Meeting

PO Box 833836
Richardson, TX 75083-3836

972-952-9300

Susan Bell, Event Manager
Mark Rubin, Executive Director

Offers a forum for the exchange of ideas between petroleum and gas engineers.
500 Attendees
Frequency: October

19932 Society of Petro Engineers Enhanced Oil Recovery Symposium and Exchange

PO Box 833836
Richardson, TX 75083-3836

972-952-9300

Georgie Cumiskey, Event Manager
Mark Rubin, Executive Director

100 booths.
1.6M Attendees
Frequency: April

19933 Southeast Petro Food Marketing Expo

7300 Glenwood Avenue
Raleigh, NC 27612

919-782-4411
FAX 919-782-4414
E-Mail: svinson@ncpma.org
Home Page: www.sepetro.org

Sharon Vinson, Show Manager

550 booths and 400+ exhibitors serving the petroleum and convenience store industries in the southeast.
2,000 Attendees
Frequency: March

19934 WPMA Convention & Convenience Store Expo

Western Petroleum Marketers Association
Po Box 571500
Salt Lake, UT 84157-1500

801-263-9762
FAX 801-262-9413
E-Mail: info@wpma.com
Home Page: www.wpma.com
Social Media: *Facebook, Twitter*

Gene Inglesby, Executive Director
Jan Roothoff, Administration Director

In addition to Las Vegas entertainment and special events, the convention offers keynote speakers around current issues and topics, as well as workshops. Over 400 exhibits. Registration costs vary.
3750 Attendees
Frequency: Annual/Winter

19935 Western Petroleum Marketers Convention & Convenience Store Expo

Western Petroleum Marketers Association

PO Box 571500
Salt Lake, UT 84157-1500

801-263-9762
888-252-5550
FAX 801-262-9413
E-Mail: info@wpma.com
Home Page: www.wpma.com
Social Media: *Facebook, Twitter*

Gene Inglesby, Executive Director
Jan Roothoff, Administration Director
Bob Ogan, VP

430 booths.
3500 Attendees
Frequency: February

19936 World Gas Conference

American Gas Association
400 N Capitol Street NW
Washington, DC 20001

202-824-7000
FAX 202-824-7092
E-Mail: ykorolevich@aga.org
Home Page: www.aga.org
Social Media: *Facebook, Twitter, LinkedIn, Myspace, Flickr*

John W. Somerhalder, II, Chairman
Dave McCurdy, President & CEO
Lawrence T. Borgard, 1st Vice Chair
Ronald W. Jibson, 2nd Vice Chair

Information towards building a sustainable future for the gas industry.
Frequency: Quadrennial
Founded in 1918

Directories & Databases

19937 APILIT

American Petroleum Institute
275 7th Avenue
9th Floor
New York, NY 10001-6708

212-989-9001
FAX 212-366-4298

Over 500,000 citations are offered from 1978, to the literature related to the oil refining and petrochemical industries.

19938 Africa-Middle East Petroleum Directory

PennWell Directories
1700 West Loop S
Suite 1000
Houston, TX 77027-3005

713-621-9720
800-752-9764
FAX 281-499-6310
E-Mail: susana@penwell.com
Home Page: www.petroleumdirectories.com

Jonelle Moore, Editor
Tim Sullivant, Manager

A directory for: associations, government agencies, drilling, exploration and production of natural gas, petrochemicals, pipeline operators etc.
Cost: $125.00
156 Pages

19939 American Oil and Gas Reporter Directory

Domestic Petroleum Publishers
PO Box 343
Derby, KS 67037-0343

316-788-6271
FAX 316-788-7568

Bill Campbell, Editor
Charlie Cookson, Publisher

State oil and natural gas regulatory agencies.
Cost: $25.00
Frequency: Annual March
Circulation: 13,540

19940 American Oil and Gas Reporter: American Drilling Rig Directory Issues

National Publishers Group
PO Box 343
Derby, KS 67037-0343

316-788-6271
FAX 316-788-7568

Bill Campbell, Editor
Charlie Cookson, Publisher

List of contractors engaged in onshore drilling for petroleum and gas.
Cost: $25.00
Frequency: SemiAnnual
Circulation: 13,540

19941 American Oil and Gas Reporter: Directory of Crude Oil Purchasers Issue

Domestic Petroleum Publishers
PO Box 343
Derby, KS 67037-0343

316-788-6271
FAX 316-788-7568

Bill Campbell, Editor
Charlie Cookson, Publisher

List of companies buying crude oil in the US.
Cost: $25.00
Frequency: Annual July
Circulation: 13,540

19942 Armstrong Oil Directories

Armstrong Oil
Po Box 52106
Amarillo, TX 79159-2106

806-457-9300
FAX 806-457-9301
E-Mail: support@armstrongoil.com
Home Page: www.armstrongoil.com

Alan Armstrong, Owner

Directory of services and supplies to the industry.
Cost: $53.50
300 Pages
Frequency: Annual

19943 Brown's Directory of North American and International Gas Companies

Advanstar Communications
131 W 1st St
Duluth, MN 55802-2065

218-740-7200
800-346-0085
FAX 218-740-7079
E-Mail: info@advanstar.com
Home Page: www.advanstar.com

Kent Akervik, Manager
Joseph Loggia, CEO

Operating gas companies, brokers and refineries are listed in this comprehensive directory with worldwide coverage.
Cost: $265.00
350 Pages
Frequency: Annual
Circulation: 1,000

19944 Canadian Oil Industry Directory

PennWell Directories
1700 West Loop S
Suite 1000
Houston, TX 77027-3005

713-621-9720
800-752-9764
FAX 281-499-6310

E-Mail: susana@penwell.com
Home Page: www.petroleumdirectories.com

Susan Anderson, Editor
Tim Sullivant, Manager

A directory for: associations, government agencies, drilling contractors, engineering, construction, exploration, production, petrochemicals, pipeline operators, etc.
Cost: $135.00

19945 Congress Legislative Directory

American Gas Association
1515 Wilson Boulevard
Suite 100
Arlington, VA 22209-2469

703-841-8400

Offers information on members of both houses of the United States Congress, federal government agencies relevant to the natural gas industry.
Cost: $10.00
220 Pages
Frequency: Annual

19946 Contracts for Field Projects & Supporting Research on Enhanced Oil Recovery

US Department of Energy
PO Box 1398
Bartlesville, OK 74005

918-336-0307
FAX 918-337-4418

Herbert A Tiedemann, Editor

Energy Department technical project officers and contractors.
97 Pages
Frequency: Quarterly
Founded in 1997

19947 Crude Oil Analysis Data Bank

PO Box 2565
Bartlesville, OK 74005-2565

918-336-2400

Contains over 9,000 analyses, obtained from the Bureau of Mines, of worldwide crude oil deposits.
Frequency: Full-text

19948 DRI/Platt's Oil Prices

DRI/McGraw-Hill
24 Hartwell Ave
Lexington, MA 02421-3103

781-860-6060
FAX 781-860-6002
E-Mail: support@construction.com
Home Page: www.construction.com

Walt Arvin, President

Database provides weekly, monthly and daily time series of worldwide petroleum product prices.

19949 Drilling & Well Servicing Contractors

Midwest Publishing Company
2230 E 49th Ste E
Tulsa, OK 74105-8771

918-582-2000
800-829-2002
FAX 918-587-9349
E-Mail: info@midwestpub.com
Home Page: www.midwestpub.com

Will L Hammack, Owner

Approximately 4,000 drilling and well servicing contractors, equipment suppliers, manufacturers and service companies.
Cost: $150.00
Frequency: Annual, September
Founded in 1943

19950 Dwight's Offshore and Bid Data
Dwight's Energydata
1633 Firman Drive
Suite 100
Richardson, TX 75081-6790

972-783-8002
800-468-3381
FAX 972-783-0058

This large database offers the most current information on bids, lease ownership data, and competitive intelligence data on the petroleum industry.

19951 Fuel Oil News-Source Book Issue
Fuel Oil News
3496 E Lake Lansing Road
Suite 150
East Lansing, MI 48823-6223

517-337-4040
Home Page:
http://fueloilnews.com/Media/MediaManager/2010%20FON%20Media%20Ki

Offers a list of over 600 manufacturers and suppliers of oil handling, heating and delivering companies.
Cost: $10.00
Frequency: Annual
Circulation: 17,000

19952 GOA Membership Directory
Georgia Oilmen Association
1775 Spectrum Drive
Suite 100
Lawrenceville, GA 30043-5745

770-995-7570
FAX 770-995-9757
E-Mail: kcarter@gaoilassoc.com
Home Page: www.georgiaoilmensassoc.com

Roger T Lane, President/Editor
Mary R Franklin, Associate Editor
Karen Carter, Executive Assitant

Directory of active and associate members and other valuable information.
Cost: $250.00
42 Pages
Frequency: Monthly
Circulation: 1,300
Printed in on glossy stock

19953 Gas and Oil Equipment Directory
Underwriters Laboratories
2600 N.W.Lake Rd
Camas, WA 98607-8542

847-412-0136
877-854-3577
FAX 847-272-8129
E-Mail: cec.@us.ul.com
Home Page: www.ul.com
Social Media: *Facebook, Twitter, YouTube*

Keith E Williams, CEO
John Drengenberg, Manager Consumer Affairs

Companies that have qualified to use the UL listing mark or classification marking on or in connection with products that have been found to be in compliance with UL's requirements.
Cost: $9.00
Frequency: Annual October

19954 Hart Energy Publishing
4545 Post Oak Place Drive
Suite 210
Houston, TX 77027-3105

713-993-9320
800-874-2544
FAX 713-840-8585
E-Mail: jeff@grainnet.com
Home Page: www.hartenergy.com

Jeff Miller, Director Marketing
Matt Beltz, Marketing Associate
Rich Eichler, President

Kristine Klavers, Senior Vice President
Frederick Potter, Executive Vice President

Hart Energy Publishing is the worldwide leader in energy industry publishing. With fiver energy magazines, E & P, Oil and Gas investors, Pipeline gas technology, energy markets and world refining. Hart Energy Publishing also has a range of newsletters and centers devoted to the downstream Energy industry.
15 Pages
Frequency: Monthly

19955 Hart Publications
4545 Post Oak Place Drive
Houston, TX 77027-3105

713-993-9320
800-874-2544
FAX 713-840-8585
Home Page: www.hartpub.com

Gina Acosta, Fulfillment
Rich Eichler, President

Directories, magazines and newsletters of the oil and gas industry
15 Pages
Frequency: Annually

19956 International Oil Spill Control Directory
Cutter Information Corporation
37 Broadway
Suite 1
Arlington, MA 02474-5500

781-648-8700
FAX 781-648-8707
E-Mail: consortium@cutter.com
Home Page: www.cutter.com
Social Media: *Facebook, Twitter, LinkedIn, RSS*

Verna Allee, Senior Consultant
Karen Coburn, President & CEO
Paul Bergeron, CFO & COO
Anne Mullaney, Vice-President

Offers valuable information on more than 1,000 suppliers of more than 3,500 oil spill cleanup, prevention and control products and services.
Cost: $95.00
225 Pages
Frequency: Annual

19957 Marketers, Purchasers & Trading Companies
Midwest Publishing Company
2230 E 49th Ste E
Tulsa, OK 74105-8771

918-582-2000
800-829-2002
FAX 918-587-9349
E-Mail: info@midwestdirectories.com
Home Page: www.midwestdirectories.com

Will Hammack, Editor

Over 5,300 purchasers, marketers and traders of refined products, crude oil and natural gas.
Cost: $145.00
Frequency: Annual October

19958 McGraw-Hill GasWire
DRI/McGraw-Hill
24 Hartwell Ave
Lexington, MA 02421-3103

781-860-6060
FAX 781-860-6002
E-Mail: support@construction.com
Home Page: www.construction.com

Walt Arvin, President

Contains news and analyses of the US natural gas market.
Frequency: Full-text

19959 Member Directory and Oil & Gas Agencies
Interstate Oil and Gas Compact Commission
PO Box 53127
Oklahoma City, OK 73152-3127

405-525-3556
800-822-4015
FAX 405-525-3592
E-Mail: iogcc@iogcc.state.ok.us
Home Page: www.iogcc.state.ok.us

Christine Hansen, Executive Director
Alesha Leemaster, Communications Manager

About 600 state representatives to the commission from 29 oil and gas producing states and seven associate states and committee members from related industries and government agencies.
Cost: $11.00
Frequency: Annual

19960 NOIA Leaders
National Ocean Industries Association
1120 G St NW
Suite 900
Washington, DC 20005-3801

202-347-6900
FAX 202-347-8650
Home Page: www.noia.org
Social Media: *Facebook, Twitter, YouTube*

Tom Fry, President
Franki K Stuntz, Director Administration
Nolty J Thuriot, Director Congressional Affairs
Frequency: Annual
Founded in 1972

19961 National Petroleum News: Buyer's Guide Issue
2101 S Arlington Heights Road
Arlington Heights, IL 60005-4185

847-427-9512
FAX 847-427-2041

Jim Bursch, Publisher
Don Smith, Editor

A comprehensive listing of products and services for the petroleum industry.
Cost: $30.00
Frequency: Annual
Circulation: 18,000

19962 National Petroleum News: Market Facts Issue
2101 S Arlington Heights Road
Arlington Heights, IL 60005-4185

847-427-9512
FAX 847-427-2041

Jim Bursch, Publisher
Don Smith, Editor

Offers the industry's most up-to-date compilation of petroleum/convenience store facts, figures and trends.
Cost: $75.00
Frequency: Annual
Circulation: 18,000

19963 Natural Gas Industry Directory
PennWell Directories
1700 West Loop S
Suite 1000
Houston, TX 77027-3005

713-621-9720
800-752-9764
FAX 281-499-6310
E-Mail: susana@penwell.com
Home Page: www.petroleumdirectories.com

Susan Anderson, Editor
Tim Sullivant, Manager

Major divisions of the natural gas industry worldwide.
Cost: $165.00

19964 Offshore Services and Equipment Directory

Greene Dot
11686 Jocatal Center
San Diego, CA 92127-1147

858-485-0189
FAX 858-485-5139

Renee Garza, Editor

About 5,000 suppliers of equipment and services to the offshore petroleum exploration and production industry worldwide.
Cost: $235.00
Frequency: Annual May
Circulation: 4,000

19965 Oil and Gas Directory

Geophysical Directory
Po Box 130508
Houston, TX 77219-0508

713-529-1922
800-929-2462
FAX 713-529-3646
Home Page: www.geophysicaldirectory.com

Stewart Schafer, Owner

Valuable information is listed on over 5,000 companies worldwide that are involved in petroleum exploration and drilling.
Cost: $130.00
700 Pages
Frequency: Annual, October
Circulation: 2,000
Founded in 1970

19966 Oil and Gas Field Code Master List

US Energy Information Administration
1000 Independence Av SW
#E1-231
Washington, DC 20585-0001

202-586-8800
FAX 202-586-0727
Home Page: www.eia.doe.gov

John H Weiner, Executive Director

All identified oil and gas fields in the US.
Cost: $27.00
Frequency: Annual December

19967 Permit Data On-Line

Petroleum Information Corporation
PO Box 2612
Denver, CO 80201-2612

303-595-7500
800-645-3282

Oil well drilling permits granted by regional governmental agencies.
Frequency: Weekly

19968 PetroProcess HSE Directory

Atlantic Communications LLC
1635 W Alabama St
Houston, TX 77006-4101

713-831-1768
FAX 713-523-7804
E-Mail: info@oilonline.com
Home Page: www.oilonline.com

Shaun Wymes, President
Rob Garza, General Manager
Graham Thomson, General Manager
Ray Vanegas, Manager
Doug Duguid, Managing Director
Cost: $79.00
650 Pages
Frequency: Annual
Founded in 1990

19969 Petroleum Equipment Directory

Petroleum Equipment Institute

6514 E 69th St
Tulsa, OK 74133-1729

918-494-9696
FAX 918-491-9895
E-Mail: rrenkes@pei.org
Home Page: www.pei.org

Robert N Renkes, Executive VP
Sarah West, Marketing Director
Rick Long, General Manager

Member manufacturers, distributors and installers of petroleum marketing equipment worldwide are offered.
Cost: $50.00
395 Pages
Frequency: Annual
Circulation: 3,000

19970 Petroleum Marketers Association of America Directory

Petroleum Marketers Association of America
1901 Fort Myer Dr
Suite 500
Arlington, VA 22209-1609

703-351-8000
800-300-7622
FAX 703-351-9160
Home Page: http://www.pmaa.org

Daniel F Gilligan, President
Sarah Dodge, Director/Legislative Affairs
Patricia Murrey, Director/Administration
Holly Tuminello, VP
Izua Yang, Manager/Communications/Conferences

About 45 state and regional member associations. A national organization representing the nation's independent petroleum marketers.
Cost: $50.00
Frequency: Annual February
Circulation: 2,000

19971 Petroleum Marketing Management Buyers Guide

Graphic Concepts
1801 Rockville Pike
Suite 330
Rockville, MD 20852-1633

A list of suppliers of products, equipment and services to combination gas station owners and convenience stores.
Frequency: Annual
Circulation: 20,000

19972 Petroleum Software Directory

PennWell Publishing Company
3050 Post Oak Boulevard
Suite 200
Houston, TX 77056-6570

713-219-9720
800-752-9764
FAX 713-963-6228
E-Mail: susana@pennwell.com

More than 800 companies that produce over 1,800 micro-, mini- and mainframe computer software packages designed for petroleum industry applications.
Cost: $195.00
Frequency: Annual June
Circulation: 1,000

19973 Petroleum Supply Annual

Superintendent of Documents
1000 Independence Ave SW
Washington, DC 20585

202-586-8800
Home Page:
http://www.eia.doe.gov/oil_gas/petroleum/data
_publications/petrol

Contains information on the supply and disposition of crude oil and petroleum products. Reflects data collected by the petroleum industry

during 1998 through annual and monthly surveys, it is divided in to two volumes. The first volume contains three sections, Summary Statistics, Detailed Statistics, and Refinery Capacity, each with final annual data. Volume 1 cost is $17.00, volume 2 $51.00
175 Pages
Frequency: Annual
Founded in 1999

19974 Pipeline & Gas Journal: Buyer's Guide Issue

Oildom Publishing Company of Texas
PO Box 941669
Houston, TX 77094-8669

281-558-6930
FAX 281-558-7029
Home Page: www.oildompublishing.com

Jeff Share, Editor

List of over 700 companies supplying products and services used in construction and operation of cross country pipeline and gas distribution systems.
Cost: $75.00
Frequency: May

19975 Pipeline & Gas Journal: Directory of Pipeline Operating Companies

Oildom Publishing Company of Texas
PO Box 941669
Houston, TX 77218-9368

281-558-6930
FAX 281-558-7029
Home Page: www.oildompublishing.com

Jeff Share, Editor
Oliver Klinger, Editor

List of companies operating oil and gas transmission pipelines worldwide.
Cost: $80.00
Frequency: September
Circulation: 27,000

19976 Platts Insight

The McGraw-Hill Companies
1221 Avenue of the Americas
New York, NY 10020

212-904-2000
E-Mail: power@platts.com
Home Page: www.platts.com

Glenn Goldberg, President, Information & Media

A comprehensive look at the energy industry, with year end outlook editions on global energy, sustainability, electric power, nuclear and more.

19977 SPE: Annual Membership Directory

Society of Petroleum Engineers
PO Box 833836
Richardson, TX 75083-3836

972-952-9300
800-456-6863
FAX 972-952-9435

Georgeann Bilich, Editor

List of 52,000 member petroleum engineers.
Cost: $150.00
Frequency: Annual May
Circulation: 5,000

19978 Supply, Distribution, Manufacturing and Service

Midwest Publishing Company
2230 E 49th Ste E
Tulsa, OK 74105-8771

918-582-2000
800-829-2002
FAX 918-587-9349

E-Mail: info@midwestdirectories.com
Home Page: www.midwestdirectories.com

Will Hammack, Editor

8,000 oil well supply stores, service companies and equipment manufacturers.
Cost: $165.00
Frequency: Annual, September
Founded in 1943

19979 TULSA Database

Petroleum Abstracts
101 Harwell
Tulsa, OK 74104-3189

918-631-2297
800-247-8678
FAX 918-599-9361
Home Page: www.pa.utulsa.edu

Pam Weaver, Assistant Director
David Brown, Assistant Director of Marketing
Pam Jenni, Managing Editor

Contains more than 700,000 citations, with abstracts, to the worldwide literature and patents on the exploration, development and production of petroleum resources.
Frequency: Weekly Updates

19980 US Non-Utility Power Directory on CD-ROM

PennWell Publishing Company
PO Box 1260
Tulsa, OK 74101-1260

918-835-3161
800-752-9764
FAX 918-831-9555

Gockel Delma, Sales

Offers a unique source of information to industry professionals including a listing of over 1,423 plant locations including project names, site addresses, plant types, fuels, installed capacity, power contract information, operating control systems, ownership and more.
Cost: $695.00
Frequency: Annual

19981 US Offshore Oil Company Contact List

Offshore Data Services
PO Box 19909
Houston, TX 77224-1909

713-781-7094
FAX 713-781-9594

Marie Sheffer, Editor
Linda Parino, Circulation Director

Approximately 265 oil companies with US offshore leases.
Cost: $135.00
Frequency: Annual
Circulation: 800
ISBN: 1-058587-7 -
Mailing list available for rent

19982 USA Oil Industry Directory

PennWell Publishing Company
3050 Post Oak Boulevard
Suite 200
Houston, TX 77056-6570

713-219-9720
800-752-9764
FAX 713-963-6228
E-Mail: susana@pennwell.com

Laura Bell, Editor
Susan Anderson, Publisher

Over 3,600 independent oil producers, fund companies, petroleum marketing companies, crude oil brokers and integrated oil firms.
Cost: $165.00
Frequency: Annual October
Circulation: 5,000

19983 USA Oilfield Service, Supply and Manufacturers Directory

PennWell Publishing Company
3050 Post Oak Boulevard
Suite 200
Houston, TX 77056-6570

713-219-9720
800-752-9764
FAX 713-963-6228
E-Mail: susana@pennwell.com

Guntis Moritis, Editor

About 3,600 companies that provide oilfield equipment, supplies and services to the oil industry.
Cost: $145.00
Frequency: Annual October
Circulation: 2,500

19984 West Coast Petroleum Industry Directory

Economic Insight
3004 Sw 1st Ave
Portland, OR 97201-4708

503-222-2425
FAX 503-242-2968
E-Mail: info@econ.com
Home Page: www.econ.com

Sam Van Vactor, President

Individuals and companies that refine, buy and sell oil and petroleum products are listed.
Cost: $85.00
204 Pages
Frequency: Quarterly

19985 World Oil-Marine Drilling Rigs

Gulf Publishing Company
3301 Allen Parkway
Houston, TX 77019-1896

713-294-4301

Offers information on over 600 mobile and self-contained drilling rigs including submersibles, drillships and barges.
Cost: $11.00
Frequency: Annual
Circulation: 30,000

Industry Web Sites

19986 http://gold.greyhouse.com

G.O.L.D Grey House OnLine Databases

Grey House Publishing's online database platform, GOLD, offers Quick Search, Keyword Search and Expert Search for most business sectors including petroleum and allied services markets. The GOLD platform makes finding the information you need quick and easy - whether you're a novice searcher or an experienced database user. All of Grey House's directory products are available for subscription on the GOLD platform.

19987 www.aesc.net

Association of Energy Service Companies

Professional trade association for well-site service contractors and businesses providing goods and services to well-site contractors. Develops and sells training and safety materials.

19988 www.aopl.org

Association of Oil Pipe Lines

Assembles statistics and other data relating to the pipeline industry for presentation to Congress, government departments, trade associations, and the public.

19989 www.api.org

American Petroleum Institute

Seeks to maintain cooperation between government and industry, fosters foreign and domestic trade in American petroleum products, conducts research.

19990 www.bpnews.com

Butane-Propane News

Petroleum and propane industry news.

19991 www.entelec.org

Energy Telecommunications and Electrical Assoc

A user association focusing on communications and control technologies used by petroleum, natural gas, pipeline and electric utility companies.

19992 www.greyhouse.com

Grey House Publishing

Authoritative reference directories for most business sectors including petroleum and allied products marktes. Users can search the online databases with varied search criteria allowing for custom searches by product category, geographic area, sales volume, keyword, subject and more. Full Grey House catalog and online ordering also available.

19993 www.iadc.org

International Association of Drilling Contractors

Conducts educational and training programs. Sponsors safety contest and bestows awards.

19994 www.igt.org

Institute of Gas Technology

An independent not-for-profit center for energy and environmental research, development, education and information. Main function is to perform sponsored and in-house research, development and demonstration, provide educational programs and services, and disseminate scientific and technical information.

19995 www.iosc.org

Oil Spill Conference

Strives to create a global colloquim for public, government and business ideas addressing all aspects of oil spills impacting the environment. International exchange of information and ideas dealing with spill prevention, planning, response and restoration processes, protocols and technology.

19996 www.liquidrecyclers.org

NORA, An Association of Responsible Recyclers

Members are companies that reprocess used antifreeze, wastewater, oil filters, chemicals and companies that provide products or services to the industry.

19997 www.naro-us.org

National Association of Royalty Owners

Assists mineral and royalty owners in the effective management of their mineral properties. Provides information on tax, regulatory, and legislative matters. Conducts seminars and bestows awards.

19998 www.noraoil.com

National Oil Recyclers Association

Members are companies that reprocess used oil into fuel oil or recycle antifreeze, wastewater, oil filters and companies that provide products or services to the industry.

19999 www.npc.org

National Petroleum Council

Self-supporting federal advisory body to the Secretary of Energy established in 1946 at the request of President Truman.

20000 www.npga.org

National Propane Gas Association

Members are producers and distributors of liquefied petroleum gas and equipment manufacturers.

20001 www.npradc.org

National PetroChemical & Refiners Association

Members are petroleum, petrochemical and refining companies.

20002 www.oilscouts.org

International Oil Scouts Association

Compiles statistics on exploration and development wells in the US. Offers professional development and scholarship programs.

20003 www.pei.org

Petroleum Equipment Institute

Members are makers and distributors of equipment used in service stations, bulk plants and other petroleum marketing facilities.

20004 www.pttc.org

Petroleum Technology Transfer Council

Fosters the effective transfer of exploration and production technology to US petroleum producers through regional resource centers, workshops, websites, publications, etc.

20005 www.spwla.org

Society of Professional Well Log Analysts

Promotes the evaluation of formations, through well logging techniques, in order to locate gas, oil and other minerals.

20006 www.wspa.org

Western States Petroleum Association

For companies that refine, produce, transport, and market petroleum and petroleum products in six western states: Arizona, California, Oregon, Nevada, Hawaii and Washington.

Associations

20007 ASPCA
424 E 92nd St
New York, NY 10128-6804

212-876-7566
FAX 212-876-0014
E-Mail: publicinformation@aspca.org
Home Page: www.aspca.org
Social Media: *Facebook, Twitter, Pinterest, YouTube, Google+*

Tim F. Wray, Chair
Frederick Tanne, Vice- Chair
Frederik Gradin, Treasurer
Sally Spooner, Secretary
Matthew Bershadker, President & CEO

Society for the humane treatment of animals, established in 1866.
300+ Members
Founded in 1866

20008 American Animal Hospital Association
12575 W Bayaud Ave
Lakewood, CO 80228-2021

303-986-2800
FAX 303-986-1700
E-Mail: info@aahanet.org
Home Page: www.aahanet.org
Social Media: *Facebook, Twitter, LinkedIn, Youtube*

John Albers, Executive Director
Ellin Davis, Secretary

A group of hospitals and animal practitioners serving the industry.
33000 Members
Founded in 1933

20009 American Boarding Kennels Association
1702 E Pikes Peak Avenue
Colorado Springs, CO 80909

719-667-1600
FAX 719-667-0116
E-Mail: info@abka.com
Home Page: www.abka.com

James Krack, Executive Manager

Information about the pet industry products, including pet foods, supplements, retail supplies, construction materials, cages, computers and software.
Founded in 1977

20010 American Cat Fanciers Association
PO Box 1949
Nixa, MO 65714-1949

417-725-1530
FAX 417-725-1533
E-Mail: ACFA@aol.com
Home Page: www.acfacat.com

Doug Blackmore, President
Alan Lanners, First VP
Donald Finger, Second VP
Cindy Skeen, Executive Director

Central registry for cats. Sanctions shows, publishes a bimonthly newsletter, offers a yearbook and maintains pedigree records.
800 Members
Founded in 1955

20011 American Farriers Association
4059 Iron Works Pkwy
Suite 1
Lexington, KY 40511

859-233-7411
877-268-4505
FAX 859-231-7862
E-Mail: info@americanfarriers.org

Home Page: www.americanfarriers.org
Social Media: *Facebook*

Thomas Dubois, President
Jon Johnson, President-Elect
Dave Johnson, Vice President
Bruce Worman, Treasurer
Donnie Perkinson, Secretary

To further the professional development of farriers, to provide leadership and resource for the benefit of the farrier industry, and to improve the welfare of the horse through continuing farrier education.
2.4M Members
Founded in 1971

20012 American Federation of Aviculture
STAT Marketing
11240 Waples Mill Road
Suite 200
Fairfax, VA 22030

703-281-4043
FAX 703-359-7562
E-Mail: info@aaham.org
Home Page: www.aaham.org
Social Media: *Facebook, Twitter, LinkedIn, YouTube, Google+, Pinterest*

Christine Stottlemyer, Chair
Victoria Di Tomaso, President
John Currier, First VP
Lori Sickelbaugh, Second VP
Amy Mitchell, Treasurer

Information for manufacturers, suppliers, distributors and retailers of exotic birds and related products, including feed, seeds, cages, toys, vitamins and minerals.
Founded in 1968

20013 American Humane Association
1400 16th Street NW
Suite 360
Washington, DC 20036

818-501-0123
800-227-4645
FAX 818-762-0908
E-Mail: info@americanhumane.org
Home Page: www.americanhumane.org
Social Media: *Facebook, Twitter, LinkedIn, YouTube, RSS, Pinterest*

Robin R. Ganzert, President & CEO
Audrey Lang, Sr. Vice President
Cliffard Rose, Chief Financial Officer
Stephanie Carmody, General Counsel
Kwane Stewart, National Director

Protects children and animals from cruelty, neglect, abuse, and exploitation.
Founded in 1877

20014 American Kennel Club
260 Madison Ave
New York, NY 10016

212-696-8200
FAX 212-696-8239
E-Mail: info@akc.org
Home Page: www.akc.org
Social Media: *Facebook, Twitter, YouTube, Pinterest, Google+, I*

Ronald Menaker, Chairman
Carl C. Ashby, Vice Chairman
Dennis B. Sprung, President
James P. Crowley, Executive Secretary
Joseph V. Baffuto Jr., Chief Financial Officer

The prinicipal registry of pure-bred dogs in the United States. More ways to enjoy your dog.
15000 Members
Founded in 1884

20015 American Morgan Horse Association
4066 Shelburne Rd
Suite 5
Shelburne, VT 05482

802-985-4944
FAX 802-985-8897
E-Mail: info@morganhorse.com
Home Page: morganhorse.com
Social Media: *Facebook, Twitter, Youtube, Pinterest*

Jeff Gove, President
Kris Breyer, Vice President
Carol Fletcher, Vice President of Finance
Julie Broadway, Executive Director

Information for Morgan horse breeders and owners.
7000 Members
Founded in 1909

20016 American Paint Horse Association
2800 Meacham Boulevard
Fort Worth, TX 76137

817-834-2742
FAX 817-834-3152
E-Mail: askapha@apha.com
Home Page: www.apha.com
Social Media: *Facebook, Twitter, YouTube*

Ron Shelly, President
Susie Shaw, President-Elect
George Ready, Vice President
Dr. Craig Wood, Senior Committee Member
Billy L. Smith, Executive Director

Information for owners and riders of American Paint Horses.
55000 Members
Founded in 1960

20017 American Pet Products Association
255 Glenville Rd.
Greenwich, CT 06831

203-532-0000
800-452-1225
FAX 203-532-0551
Home Page: www.americanpetproducts.org

Bob Vetere, President & CEO
Andrew Darmohraj, EVP & COO

Trade association of manufacturers, manufacturers' representatives, importers and livestock suppliers.
1200 Members
Founded in 1958

20018 American Pet Products Manufacturers Association
255 Glenville Road
Greenwich, CT 06831

203-532-0000
800-452-1225
FAX 203-532-0551
E-Mail: andy@appma.org
Home Page: www.americanpetproducts.org

Robert Merar, Chairman
Bob Vetere, President & CEO
Andrew Darmohraj, Executive Vice President & COO
Steve Ware, Treasurer
Edith Martingnetti, General Mgr/Exhibitor Registration

Information for manufacturers of pet products and service providers in the pet industry.
Frequency: Annual
Founded in 1958

20019 American Rabbit Breeders Association
PO Box 5667
Bloomington, IL 61702

309-664-7500
FAX 309-664-0941

E-Mail: info@arba.net
Home Page: arba.net

Josh Humphries, President
Randy Shumaker, VP
Eric Stewart, Executive Director
David Freeman, Treasurer
Roger Hassenpflug, Director

Information for rabbit breeders and owners.
23000 Members
Founded in 1910

20020 American Veterinary Medical Association

1931 N Meacham Rd
Suite 100
Schaumburg, IL 60173-4360

847-303-6142
800-248-2862
FAX 847-925-1329
E-Mail: sgranskog@avma.org
Home Page: www.avma.org
Social Media: *Facebook, Twitter, LinkedIn, YouTube, Flickr*

Tim Frey, Manager
Michael Walters, Director Communications Division
Dr. Gail Golab, Assistant Director

Publishes various journals and information for members. Acts as a clearinghouse for veterinarians.
86500 Members
Founded in 1863

20021 Animal Health Institute

1325 G St NW
Suite 700
Washington, DC 20005-3127

202-637-2440
FAX 202-393-1667
E-Mail: rphillips@ahi.org
Home Page: www.ahi.org
Social Media: *Facebook, Twitter, Flickr, YouTube*

Alexander S.Mathews, President & CEO
Ron Phillips, VP Legislative/Public Affairs
Dr Richard A A.Carnevale, VP, Regulator
Dr Kent McClure, General Counsel
Carolyn S Ayers, VP, Admin. & Finance

Represents manufacturers of animal health care products.
24 Members
Founded in 1941

20022 Animal Legal Defense Fund

170 East Cotati Avenue
Cotati, CA 94931

707-795-2533
FAX 707-795-7280
E-Mail: info@aldf.org
Home Page: www.aldf.org
Social Media: *Facebook, Twitter, YouTube, Pinterest*

Sarah Luick, Chair
Marilyn Forbes, Vice- Chair
Lisa Brewer, Secretary
Jim Rockenbach, Treasurer
Stephen Wells, Executive Director

Information on animal protection, wildlife conservation and animal rights.
10000 Members
Founded in 1979

20023 Association of Pet Dog Trainers

The Association of Pet Dog Trainers
2365 Harrodsburg Road A325
Lexington, KY 40504

800-738-3647
FAX 864-331-0767
E-Mail: education@apdt.com

Home Page: www.apdt.com
Social Media: *Facebook, Twitter, LinkedIn*

Amber Burckhalter, Board Chair
Jill-Marie O'Brien, Board Vice-Chair
Robin Bennet, Board Treasurer
Casey Lomanaco, Board Secretary
Megan Armstrong, Board Member

Enhancing the human/dog relationship by educating trainers, other animal professionals and the public and advocating dog friendly training.
6000 Members
Founded in 1993

20024 Delta Society

875 124th Ave NW
Suite 101
Bellevue, WA 98005

425-679-5500
800-869-6898
FAX 425-679-5539
E-Mail: info@deltasociety.org
Home Page: petpartners.org
Social Media: *Facebook, Twitter, LinkedIn, YouTube, Pinterest, Instagram*

C. Annie Magnant, President & CEO
David E. Williams, Chief Medical Officer
Linda Dicus, Executive Assistant
Chris Calabro, Director of Technology
Mary M. Callahan, Senior National Director

Information on human-animal interactions. Service Dog Center provides information and advocacy for dogs trained to assist people with disabilities. Pet Partners Program trains volunteers, health professionals, animals for animal-assisted therapy and activities.
4.6M Members
Founded in 1977

20025 International Association of Pet Cemeteries & Crematories

4991 Peachtree Road
Atlanta, GA 30341

518-594-3000
800-952-5541
FAX 770-457-8160
E-Mail: info@iaopc.com
Home Page: www.iaopc.com

Angie Hansen, President
Robert Blosser, Vice President
Debra Bjorling, Treasurer
Scott Hunter, Advisory Council
Donna Bethune, Executive Administrator

Educates the public on pet burials and the disposal of sick and diseased animals to eliminate contamination of ground and water. Conducts workshops and research projects.
175 Members
Founded in 1971

20026 International Professional Groomers

6475 Wallace Rd NW
Salem, OR 97304

503-551-2397
FAX 503-581-1220
E-Mail: info@ipgicmg.com
Home Page: www.ipgicmg.com
Social Media: *Facebook, Twitter*

Linda Easton, President

Represents the professional pet grooming industry, providing continuing education to members and public information on the proper care treatment. also publishes a quarterly newsletter.
500 Members
Founded in 1988

20027 National Association of Professional Pet Care

1120 Route 73
Suite 200
Mt. Laurel, NJ 08054

856-439-0324
FAX 856-439-0525
E-Mail: napps@petsitters.org
Home Page: www.petsitters.org
Social Media: *Facebook, Twitter, LinkedIn, Google+, Pinterest*

Yvette Gonzales, President
Jessica Abernathy, President Elect
Cyndy Lippert, Secretary-Treasurer
Cathleen Delaney, Administrative Director
Kara Jenkins, Director

Nonprofit organization dedicated to serving the needs of professional pet care providers. Promotes ethical standards and fosters cooperation among members in the pet care industry.
2200+ Members
Founded in 1989

20028 National Congress of Animal Trainers

23675 W Chardon Rd
Grayslake, IL 60030-9584

847-546-0717
FAX 847-546-3454

John F Cuneo, President

For trainers and breeders of rare animals.
300 Members

20029 National Dog Groomers Association of American

PO Box 101
Clark, PA 16113

724-962-2711
FAX 724-962-1919
E-Mail: ndga@nationaldoggroomers.com
Home Page: www.nationaldoggroomers.com
Social Media: *Facebook*

Jeffrey Reynolds, Executive Director
Wendy Booth, Certification Coordinator
Sue Zecco, Contest Coordinator

To unite groomers through membership and offer optional certification testing throughout the United States.
2.4M Members
Founded in 1969

20030 National Humane Education Society

PO Box 340
Charles Town, WV 25414-0340

304-725-0506
FAX 304-725-1523
E-Mail: information@nhes.org
Home Page: www.nhes.org
Social Media: *Facebook, Twitter, YouTube*

Anna C Briggs, Founder
James D Taylor, President
Cynthia L Taylor, Vice President
Virginia Dungan, Treasurer
Christina B Fernandez, Secretary

Mission to foster a sentiment of kindness to animals.
400M+ Members
Founded in 1948

20031 National Pigeon Association

17128 Colima Drive Unit 603
Hacienda Heights, CA 91745

626-820-8080
E-Mail: npasecretary@yahoo.com
Home Page: www.npausa.org
Social Media: *Facebook, Twitter*

Jerry Gagne, President
Lennie Mefferd, Secretary/Treasurer
Tim Stajkowski, Eastern Vise President
Roger Hansen, Western Vice President

Special information for members.
Founded in 1920

20032 National Taxidermists Association
PO Box 384
Pocahontas, IL 62275

618-669-2929
FAX 618-669-2909
E-Mail: nationaltaxidermistassoc@frontier.com
Home Page: www.nationaltaxidermists.com
Social Media: *Facebook, Twitter, YouTube, Google+, Pinterest*

Michelle Burkholder, President
Russell Knight, Vice President
Harry Whitehead, Treasurer
Tim Thacker, Secretary
Garvice Thomas, Board of Directors

Preserving animals to their natural form.
2500 Members
Founded in 1972

20033 PETCO Foundation
654 Richland Hills Dr.
San Antonio, TX 78245

858-453-7845
888-824-7257
FAX 858-909-2618
Home Page: www.petco.com
Social Media: *Facebook, Twitter, Instagram*

Brian Devine, Chairman
Charlie Piscitello, President
Judith Munoz, Vice President
Susanne Kogut, Executive Director
Rana Smith, Director

We put animals first. The Petco Foundation supports community organization and efforts that enhance the lives of companion animals.
Founded in 1999

20034 People for the Ethical Treatment of Animals (PETA)
501 Front Street
Norfolk, VA 23510

757-622-7382
FAX 757-622-0457
E-Mail: info@peta.org
Home Page: www.peta.org
Social Media: *Facebook, Twitter, Pinterest, Google+*

Ingrid Newkirk, President

Opposes all forms of animal exploitation. Seeks to educate the public on what the group sees as the three major institutionalized cruelty issues: the exploitation and abuse of animals in experimentation, the manufacturing of fur apparel, and slaughtering for human consumption.
80000 Members
Founded in 1980

20035 Pet Care Services Association
2760 N Academy Boulevard
Suite 120
Colorado Springs, CO 80917

719-667-1600
877-570-7788
FAX 719-667-0116
E-Mail: info@petcareservices.org
Home Page: www.petcareservices.org

Joan Saunders, CEO

Seeks to upgrade the industry through educational programs and conventions. Promotes code of ethics and accreditation programs for kennel operators.
2400 Members
Founded in 1977

20036 Pet Food Institute
2025 M St NW
Suite 800
Washington, DC 20036

202-367-1120
FAX 202-367-2120
E-Mail: info@petfoodinstitute.org
Home Page: www.petfoodinstitute.org

Duane H Ekedahl, Executive Director

Represents dog and cat food manufacturers. Supporting initiative to advance the quality of dog and cat food. Supporting research in pet nutrition and the important role of pets in our society. Promoting the overall care and well-being of pets.
100 Members
Founded in 1958

20037 Pet Industry Distributors Association
3465 Box Hill Corporate Center Dr.
Suite H
Abingdon, MD 21009

443-640-1060
FAX 443-640-1086
E-Mail: pida@kingmgmt.org
Home Page: www.pida.org
Social Media: *LinkedIn*

Scott Rath, Chairman
Mark Smith, Vice Chairman
Jeff Boyd, Secretary/Treasurer
Steven T. King, President
Marci Hickey, Director of Meetings

Represents wholesaler-distributors of pet products, providing training and education to members.
190 Members
Founded in 1968

20038 Pet Industry Joint Advisory Council
1615 Duke Street
Suite 100
Alexandria, VA 22314

202-452-1525
800-553-7387
FAX 202-452-1516
E-Mail: info@pijac.org
Home Page: www.pijac.org
Social Media: *Facebook, Twitter*

Ken Oh, Chair
Andy Ponte, First Vice-Chair
Marcie Whichard, Second Vice-chair
Laura Reid, Secretary/Treasurer
Edwin Sayres, President & CEO

Monitors federal and state regulations and legislation affecting industry. Sponsors research and educational projects including certification programs in veterinary care and husbandry for companion animals, in-store training videos, etc.
1500 Members
Founded in 1971

20039 Pet Lovers Association
PO Box 145
Joppa, MD 21085

410-679-0978

Elden Harrison, President

Advises pet owners of their responsibilities.
Founded in 1983

20040 Pet Pride
P.O. Box 1055
Pacific Palisades, CA 90272

310-836-5427
Home Page: www.petpride.org

Ruth Argust, President

Public education programs for proper cat care.
50000 Members
Founded in 1965

20041 Pet Sitters International
201 East King Street
King, NC 27021-9163

336-983-9222
FAX 336-983-5266
E-Mail: info@petsit.com
Home Page: www.petsit.com
Social Media: *Facebook, Twitter, LinkedIn, YouTube, Google+*

Terry Chance, Marketing Director
Beth Stultz, Marketing Manager
Chris Sutphin, Member Services Manager
Patti Moran, President
Mike Moran, Vice President

Society of professional pet sitters. Membership provides valuable benefits - educational resources for those engaged in the pet-sitting industry. Also provides a forum to network with peers who share a common vision of excellence in at-home pet care.
7000 Members
Founded in 1994

20042 PetCenter.Com: Internet Animal Hospital PetFoodDirect.com
189 Main Street
Harleysville, PA 19438

215-513-1999
FAX 215-513-7286
Home Page: www.the petcenter.com

T J Dunn, Jr DVM, Director

Award winning virtual animal hospital for dog and cat love. Mission of providing dog and cat caretakers with a better understanding of the medical and surgical treatment of pets. Created by veterinarians under the direction of Dr T.J. Dunn, all articles are presented in non-medical terms, just as if the veterinarian was speaking to you personally in a real exam room. Associated with PetFoodDirect.com

20043 PetFoodDirect.com
189 Main St
Harleysville, PA 19438

215-513-1999
877-738-3663
FAX 215-513-7286
Home Page: www.petfooddirect.com
Social Media: *Facebook, Twitter*

Brock Weatherup, CEO
Jon Roska, Jr, Founder & VP of Merchandising
Rose Hamilton, Chief Marketing Officer
Matthew Murray, VP, Finance
Joe Falkenstein, CFO & VP of Operations

Largest pure play entailer for premium pet food, supplies and accessories on the internet. Our customers can order from a huge selection of pet products, have access to value-added services, including information on pet healthcare and nutrition.
Founded in 1997

20044 US Animal Health Association
4221 Mitchell Ave
Saint Joseph, MO 64507

816-671-1144
FAX 816-671-1201
E-Mail: usaha@usaha.org
Home Page: www.usaha.org

Dr. Bruce King, President
Dr. David Schmitt, President-Elect
Dr. Boyd Parr, First Vice President
Barbara Determan, Second Vice President
Dr. Kristin Haas, Third Vice President

Science-based, non-profit, voluntary organization. Concerning disease eradication, animal health, emerging diseases, food safety, public health, animal welfare, and international trade.
1400 Members
Founded in 1897

20045 United Kennel Club
100 E Kilgore Rd
Kalamazoo, MI 49002-5584

269-343-9020
FAX 269-343-7037
E-Mail: conformation@ukcdogs.com
Home Page: www.ukcdogs.com

Tanya Raab, President
Todd Kellam, Senior Vice President
Angela Smith, Senior Director of Research &
Dev
Taylor Armstrong, Customer Service Manager
Allen Gingerich, Senior Director of Hunting
Events

Responsible for dog pedigrees and transfer of
ownership of pedigree dogs. Best registry of
pure-bred dogs.
50 Members
Founded in 1898

**20046 Western and English Sales
Association**
451 E 58th Avenue
Suite 4128
Denver, CO 80216

303-295-1040
800-295-1041
FAX 303-295-0941
E-Mail: info@denver-wesa.com
Home Page: www.denver-wesa.com
Social Media: *Facebook*

Mark Broughton, Chairperson
Scott Piper, President
Gerald Adame, Vice President
Tracy Patterson, Secretary
Jay Phillips, Treasurer

Trade association
1200 Members
Founded in 1921

20047 World Pet Association
135 West Lemon Ave.
Monrovia, CA 91016

626-447-2222
FAX 626-447-8350
E-Mail: info@wpamail.org
Home Page: worldpetassociation.org

Jim Boschee, Chairman
Michael Twain, CFO
Vic Mason, 1st Vice Chair
Barry Berman, 2nd Vice Chair
Pete Risano, Secretary

A non-profit, membership-controlled trade association organized to represent its members
and the interests of the companion animal and
product industry. America's oldest pet industry
trade association. Our mission is to promote responsible pet care worldwide.

**20048 World Society for the Protection of
Animals**
89 South Street
2nd Floor
Boston, MA 02111

508-879-8350
800-833-9772
FAX 212-564-4250
E-Mail: wspa@wspausa.com
Home Page: www.wspa.usa.org
Social Media: *Facebook, Twitter, YouTube*

Laura Simpson, USA Director
Peter Davies, Director General
Robert S Cummings, President
John Bowen, Secretary
Carter Luke, Treasurer

International animal protection news reports.
Lobbies for effective animal welfare laws and
provides educational material.
12 Members

Newsletters

20049 ASPCA Report
424 E 92nd St
New York, NY 10128-6804

212-876-7566
Home Page: www.aspca.com
Janice Borzendowski, Publisher
Ed Sayres, Director
Kathryn Investigations, Director
Bonnie Shelter, Operations Manager

Pet care news, issues, features and reviews.
Frequency: Weekly
Founded in 1866

20050 Animals International
World Society for the Protection of Animals
34 Deloss Street
Framingham, MA 01702

508-879-8350
FAX 508-620-0786
E-Mail: wspa@wspausa.com
Home Page: www.wspa-international.org/

Laura Salter, USA Director
Susan Sherwin, Press Contact

International animal protection news reports.
Cost: $10.00
12 Pages
Frequency: Quarterly
Founded in 1981

20051 Animals' Advocate
Animal Legal Defense Fund
170 E Cotati Avenue
Cotati, CA 94931-4474

707-795-2533
FAX 707-795-7280
E-Mail: info@aldf.org
Home Page: www.aldf.org/action.htm

Stephen Wells, Executive Director

A newsletter offering information on animal
protection, wildlife conservation and animal
rights.
4 Pages
Frequency: Monthly

20052 Anthrozoos
Delta Society
875 124th Ave Ne
Suite 101
Bellevue, WA 98005-2531

425-226-7357
FAX 425-235-1076
E-Mail: info@deltasociety.org
Home Page: www.deltasociety.org

Lawrence Norvell, CEO
Robert T Franklin, Secretary
Stephanie LaFarge, Secretary
David BellRetired, Treasurer

Scientific journal on the interactions of people,
animals and nature.
Cost: $40.00
72 Pages
Frequency: Quarterly
Circulation: 800
Founded in 1977

**20053 Association of Pet Dog Trainers
Newsletter**
750 Executive Center Dr
Box 35
Greenville, SC 29615

864-331-0764
800-738-3647
FAX 856-439-0525

E-Mail: information@apdt.com
Home Page: www.apdt.com

Richard Spencer, Executive Director
Pat Miller, Treasurer
Sue Pearson, Treasurer
Kellyann Conway-Payne, Vice President
Pia Silvani, Secretary

Building better trainers through education.
Founded in 1993

20054 Cat Industry Newsletter
Good Communications
PO Box 10069
Austin, TX 78766-1069

512-454-9062
800-968-1738
FAX 512-454-3420
Home Page: www.petfoodnews.com

Ross Becker, Editor

Business newsletter for catfood, cat products
and cat litter industries. Covers business news,
marketing, new products in the pipeline, indus-
try data.
Cost: $295.00
6 Pages
Frequency: Monthly
ISSN: 1074-7788
Founded in 1992
Printed in on matte stock

20055 Dog Industry Newsletter
Good Communications
PO Box 10069
Austin, TX 78766-1069

512-454-9062
800-968-1738
FAX 512-454-3420
Home Page: www.petfoodnews.com

Ross Becker, Editor

Business newsletter for petfood,and pet prod-
ucts industries.Covers business news, market-
ing, new products in the pipeline, industry data.
Cost: $295.00
10 Pages
Frequency: Monthly
ISSN: 1074-777X
Founded in 1990
Printed in on matte stock

20056 Humane News
Associated Humane Societies
124 Evergreen Ave
Newark, NJ 07114-2133

973-824-7080
FAX 973-824-5937
E-Mail: associatedhumane@aol.com
Home Page:
www.associatedhumanesocieties.org

Roseann Trezza, Executive Director

News concerning animal welfare.
24 Pages
Frequency: Monthly
Circulation: 75000
Founded in 1906

20057 IPG Newsletter
International Professional Groomers
6475 Wallace Rd NW
Salem, OR 97304-9743

847-758-1938
800-258-4765
FAX 847-758-8031
E-Mail: jkurpiel@aol.com
Home Page: www.ipgcmb.com

Judy Kurpiel, President

A quarterly newsletter published by the International Professional Groomers.
6 Pages
Frequency: Quarterly

Circulation: 500
Founded in 1988

20058 International Pet Industry News
Good Communications
PO Box 10069
Austin, TX 78766-1069

512-454-9062
800-968-1738
FAX 512-454-3420
Home Page: www.petfoods.com

Ross Becker, Editor

Business newsletter for international petfood, pet products industries. Covers business news, marketing, new products in the pipeline, industry data.
Cost: $295.00
8 Pages
Frequency: Monthly
ISSN: 1074-780X
Founded in 1993
Printed in on matte stock

20059 K-9 Courier
PO Box 49
Jerico Springs, MO 64756

Monthly newsletter for breeders.
Frequency: Monthly

20060 Pet Gazette
Gazette Publishing
1309 N Halifax Avenue
Daytona Beach, FL 32118-3658

E-Mail: editor@petgazette.net
Home Page: www.petgazette.net

Robin Nudd, Advertising Coordinator
Amy McWilliams, Circulation

Pictures, anecdotes, cartoons and more for the pet industry.
Cost: $12.50
24 Pages
Frequency: Quarterly
Circulation: 300

20061 Pet Partners Newsletter
Delta Society
875 124th Ave Ne
Suite 101
Bellevue, WA 98005-2531

425-226-7357
FAX 425-235-1076
E-Mail: info@deltasociety.org
Home Page: www.deltasociety.org

Lawrence Norvell, CEO
Stephanie LaFarge, Secretary
David BellRetired, Treasurer

How-to newsletter for pet owners who volunteer in animal-assisted therapy and activity programs.
Cost: $6.00
2 Pages
Frequency: Monthly
Circulation: 2500
Founded in 1977

20062 Pet Planet Newsletter
PO Box 150899
Denver, CO 80215-0899

303-986-2800
FAX 303-986-1700
Home Page: www.healthypet.com

John W Albers, Executive Director
Gregg Takashima, Vice President

A group of hospitals and animal practitioners serving the industry.
Cost: $60.00
64 Pages
Frequency: Bi-Monthly
Circulation: 14,000

Founded in 1985
Printed in on glossy stock

20063 Pet Stuff
Pet Stuff
608 Tumbleweed Lane
Fall Brook, CA 92028-9446

760-728-9306
FAX 760-728-9735

Robert Tanner, Publisher

A direct co-op mailing service to the pet industry. Accepts advertising.
Frequency: BiWeekly

20064 PetLetter
Pet Industry Joint Advisory Council
1146 19th St NW
Suite 350
Washington, DC 20036-2438

202-452-1525
800-553-7387
FAX 202-452-1516
E-Mail: info@pijac.org
Home Page: www.pijac.org

Michael Addox, VP & General Counsel
Michael Canning, President

Contains a breadth of information on the current status of pending state and federal legislation, science and educational program news, the release of PIJAC publications, other PIJAC news, and a list of the newest Certified Anical Specialists

20065 Veterinary Industry Newsletter
Good Communications
PO Box 10069
Austin, TX 78766-1069

512-454-9062
800-968-1738
FAX 512-454-3420
Home Page: www.petfoodsnews.com

Ross Becker, Editor

Business newsletter for petfood, animal health and veterinary industries.Covers business news, marketing, new products in the pipeline, industry data.
Cost: $295.00
10 Pages
Frequency: Monthly
ISSN: 1074-7796
Founded in 1993
Printed in one color on matte stock

20066 Watchbird
PO Box 56218
Phoenix, AZ 85079

602-484-0931
FAX 602-484-0109
E-Mail: webmaster@afabirds.org
Home Page: www.afabirds.org/

Jerry Crowley, Executive VP
S Rosenbeltt, Circulation Director
Benny Gallaway, President

Journal on conservation, education, bird keeping and breeding.
Circulation: 6000
Founded in 1974

Magazines & Journals

20067 Animal Fair
7 Penn Plaza
11th Floor
New York, NY 10001

212-629-0392
FAX 212-988-7486

E-Mail: editor@animalfair.com
Home Page: www.animalfair.com

Wendy Diamond, Editorial Director
Wendy Diamond, CEO/President
Cost: $19.95
Frequency: Bi-annually
Founded in 1999

20068 Aquarium Fish Magazine
Fancy Publications
PO Box 6050
Mission Viejo, CA 92690

949-855-8822
FAX 949-855-3045
E-Mail: aquariumfish@fancypubs.com
Home Page: www.animalnetwork.com

Devoted to pet stores and readers who keep freshwater and saltwater species of tropical fish.
Cost: $15.97
Frequency: Monthly
Circulation: 49,700
Founded in 1905

20069 Bird Talk
Fancy Publications
3 Burroughs
Irvine, CA 92618

949-855-8822
FAX 949-855-3045
E-Mail: ibt@bowtieinc.com
Home Page: www.birdtalkmagazine.com

Edward Bauman, Editor

Pet news.
Cost: $13.99
64 Pages
Frequency: Monthly
Founded in 1983

20070 BirdTimes
Pet Publishing
7-L Dundas Circle
Greensboro, NC 27407

336-292-4047
FAX 336-292-4272
Home Page: www.petpublishing.com

Mike Hammond, Publisher
Cost: $17.97
Circulation: 50000
ISSN: 1096-7923
Founded in 1992
Printed in 4 colors on glossy stock

20071 Bloodlines
United Kennel Club
100 E Kilgore Rd
Portage, MI 49002-5584

269-343-9020
FAX 269-343-7037
E-Mail: webmaster@ukcdogs.com
Home Page: www.ukcdogs.com

Wayne Cavanaugh, President
Rosie Reeds, Advertising

A comprehensive publication covering breeding, showing and registering of animals.
Cost: $24.00
Frequency: Monthly
Founded in 1898

20072 Cat Fancy Magazine
Fancy Publications
3 Burroughs
Irvine, CA 92618

949-855-8822
FAX 949-855-3045
Home Page: www.animalnetwork.com

Susan Logan, Editor
Sandy Meyer, Managing Editor

Offers information to cat owners and pet shop owners regarding cats.
Cost: $14.99
Frequency: Monthly
Founded in 1965

20073 Cats & Kittens

Pet Publishing
7-L Dundas Circle
Greensboro, NC 27407

336-292-4047
FAX 336-292-4272
Home Page: www.petpublishing.com

Mike Hammond, Publisher
Rita Davis, Editor

Cat enthusiast magazine.
Cost: $19.97
52 Pages
Circulation: 50000
ISSN: 1079-8285
Founded in 1998
Printed in 4 colors on glossy stock

20074 Cats Magazine

PRIMEDIA Enthusiast Group
3585 Engineering Drive
Suite 100
Norcross, GA 30092

678-421-3000
800-216-1423
FAX 212-745-0121
E-Mail: information@primedia.com
Home Page: www.primedia.com

Mike Carney, Publisher
Doug Stange, Editor
Kelly P Conlin, CEO

For cat owners.
Founded in 1989

20075 Dog & Kennel

Pet Publishing
7-L Dundas Circle
Greensboro, NC 27407

336-292-4047
FAX 336-292-4272
Home Page: www.petpublishing.com

Mike Hammond, Publisher
Rita Davis, Editor

Dog enthusiast magazine.
Cost: $4.99
64 Pages
Circulation: 50000
ISSN: 1079-8277
Founded in 1996
Printed in 4 colors on glossy stock

20076 Dog Fancy Magazine

Fancy Publications
3 Burroughs
Irvine, CA 92618

949-855-8822
800-546-7730
FAX 949-855-3045
E-Mail: bowtiepress@bowtieinc.com
Home Page: www.animalnetwork.com

Susane Chney, Editor
Scott Montey, Publisher
Dock Style, CEO/President
Christy Chism, Circulation Manager
Steven Sapoher, Marketing Manager

A magazine covering the world of dogs.
Cost: $96.00
Frequency: Monthly

20077 Dog World Magazine

Charels A Tupta
3 Burroughs
Irvine, CA 92618

949-855-8822
800-361-8056

FAX 949-855-3045
E-Mail: letters@dogworld.com
Home Page: www.dogworldmag.com/

Charels A Tupta, Publisher
Donna Marcel, Chairman

Written for the serious dog enthusiast, Dog World is the authority on dog care. Special editorial on behavior, nutrition, health care and training, plus thousands of classified and display listings in every issue.
Cost: $14.99
132 Pages
Frequency: Monthly
Circulation: 64876
Founded in 1916

20078 Dogs USA

Fancy Publications
3 Burroughs
Irvine, CA 92618

949-855-8822
FAX 949-855-3045
Home Page: www.animalnetwork.com

Edward Bauman, Editor

Registration, breeding, pedigree news, bloodlines, etc. for dogs.
Cost: $5.95
Frequency: Annual

20079 Equestrian Retailer

Morris Communications
PO Box 7980
Colorado Springs, CO 80907-5339

719-633-5524
FAX 719-633-1392
Home Page: www.equestrianretailer.com

Rick Swan, Associate Publisher
Kathy Swan, Executive Editor
William S Morris, President
Karen Ficklin, Circulation Manager
Rob Fulkerson, General Manager

Serves to promote profitablity in the equine industry.
60 Pages
Circulation: 11000
Founded in 1998
Printed in 4 colors on matte stock

20080 Freshwater and Marine Aquarium Magazine

RC Modeler Corporation
PO Box 487
Sierra Madre, CA 91025-0487

626-355-1476
800-523-1736
FAX 626-355-6415
Home Page: www.mag-web.com

Patricia Crews, President

A magazine aimed at aquarium pertaining to fish and marine life, hobboyists.
Cost: $22.00
200 Pages
Frequency: Monthly
Circulation: 65000
Founded in 1978
Printed in 4 colors on glossy stock

20081 Good Dog!

PO Box 10069
Austin, TX 78766-1069

512-454-9062
800-968-1738
FAX 512-454-3420
E-Mail: help@gooddogmagazine.com
Home Page: www.gooddogmagazine.com

Judith Becker, Editor
Ross Becker, Publisher

Consumer magazine for dog owners. Nationally known for its test reports on dog food and products for dogs. Also publishes books on dog

food, puppy selection and genetics.
Cost: $12.00
36 Pages
Circulation: 40000
ISSN: 0899-6024
Founded in 1988
Printed in 4 colors

20082 NAPPS Network

Association of Professional Pet Sitters
15000 Commerce Parkway
Suite C
Mt Laurel, NJ 08054

856-439-0324
FAX 856-439-0525
E-Mail: napps@ahint.com
Home Page: www.petsitters.org

Sally Liddick, Co-Director
Charlotte Reed, Editor/Publisher
Jerry Wentz, President
Caitlin Dougherty, Manager
Kimberly Libucki, Administrative Assistant

Official publication of the Association of Professional Pet Sitters.
Frequency: Quarterly
Circulation: 1500
Founded in 1989

20083 Pet Age Magazine

HH Backer Associates
18 S Michigan Ave
Suite 1100
Chicago, IL 60603-3233

312-578-1818
FAX 312-578-1819
E-Mail: hhbacker@hhbacker.com
Home Page: www.hhbacker.com

Patty Backer, President
Karen MacLeod, Editor in Chief
Mark Mitera, VP
Beth Morrissey, Production Coordinator
Cathy Foster, Senior Editor

Pet AGE helps pet/pet suppliers ratailers suceed in today competive marketplace. Editorial features emphasize progressive management and trends and issues. Accepts advertising.
Cost: $70.00
80 Pages
Frequency: Monthly
Circulation: 23076
ISSN: 0098-5406
Founded in 1965
Printed in on glossy stock

20084 Pet Business Magazine

Pet Business
333 7th Ave
11th Floor
New York, NY 10001-5004

212-979-4861
FAX 646-674-0102
E-Mail: emckiernan@petbusiness.com
Home Page: www.petbusiness.com

Craig Rexford, VP
Mike Burnette, Founder
Jerry Thom, Founder
David Litwak, Editor In Chief
Nisa Cirulnick, Sales & Marketing Coordinator

Trade magazine for the pet industry. News, new products, animal care and legislative topics. Accepts advertising.
Cost: $49.97
Circulation: 24,000
Founded in 1973
Mailing list available for rent: 19.5M names
Printed in 4 colors on glossy stock

20085 Pet Product News Magazine

Fancy Publications

3 Burroughs
PO Box 6040
Irvine, CA 92618

949-855-8822
FAX 949-855-3045
Home Page: www.animalnetwork.com

Edward Bauman, Editor
Journal focusing on new products and other industry news.

20086 Pet Sitter's World

Pet Sitters International
201 E King St
King, NC 27021-9161

336-983-9222
FAX 336-983-5266
E-Mail: info@petsit.com
Home Page: www.petsit.com

Patti Moran, President
Designed to educate pet sitters and affiliated firms on pet-sitting industry buiness practices, ideas, products, field-tested consumer tips and trends
Cost: $36.00
56 Pages
Frequency: Bimonthly
Circulation: 8500
Founded in 1985
Printed in on glossy stock

20087 Petfood Industry

WATT Publishing Company
303 N Main Street
Suite 500
Rockford, IL 61101

815-966-5400
FAX 815-966-6416
Home Page: www.wattnet.com

James Watt, Chairman/CEO
Greg Watt, President/COO
Jeff Swanson, Publishing Director
The leading global information source for the petfood manufacturing industry, connecting manufacturing organizations with their supplier counterparts.
Cost: $48.00
46 Pages
Frequency: Monthly
Circulation: 9795
ISSN: 0031-6245
Founded in 1959
Printed in 4 colors on glossy stock

Trade Shows

20088 AVMA Annual Convention

American Veterinary Medical Association
1931 N Meacham Road
Suite 100
Schaumburg, IL 60173-4360

847-036-6142
800-248-2862
FAX 847-925-1329
E-Mail: avmainfo@avma.org
Home Page: www.avma.org
Social Media: *Facebook, Twitter, LinkedIn, YouTube*

Larry Corry DVM, 2009-10 President
Larry Kornegay DVM, 2009-10 President-Elect
Seminar and more than 300 exhibits of products, materials, equipment, data, and services for veterinary medicine. Education and hands-on labs, exhibit hall, charitable events and networking
10000 Attendees
Frequency: Annual/July

20089 America's Family Pet Expo

World Wide Pet Supply Association
406 S 1st Avenue
Arcadia, CA 91006-3829

626-447-2222
800-999-7295
FAX 626-447-8350
Home Page: www.wwpsa.com

Rick Newman, President
Lewis M Sutton, CFO
Steve Segner, First VP
Russ Feller, Second Vice President
Dr. Robert Bray, Equine Outreach

Brings together all elements of the companion animal world and promotes responsible pet ownership. Demonstrations, speakers, product exhibits, hobbyist shows, rides for the children, contests and more. 500 booths. April, Orange County, CA
80M Attendees
Frequency: April/September
Founded in 1990

20090 American Animal Hospital Association Annual Meeting

American Animal Hospital Association
12575 W Bayaud Avenue
Lakewood, CO 80228

303-986-2800
FAX 303-986-1700
E-Mail: donna.johnson@aahanet.org
Home Page: www.aahanet.org

Donna Johnson, Exhibit Coordinator
Chuck Potter, Annual Meeting Manager
John Albers, Executive Director
250 scientific displays related to small animal veterinary care, computer software, marketing consulting services and pet care products.
3000 Attendees
Frequency: Annual
Founded in 1933

20091 American Boarding Kennels Association Annual Convention & Trade Show

1702 E Pikes Peak Avenue
Colorado Springs, CO 80909

719-667-1600
FAX 719-667-0116
E-Mail: info@abka.com
Home Page: www.abka.com

James Krack, Executive Manager
Kathryn Eddy, Show Manager
Annual show and exhibit of pet industry products, including pet foods, supplements, retail supplies, construction materials, cages, computers and software.
300 Attendees
Frequency: October
Founded in 1977

20092 American College of Veterinary Opthalmologists Confernce

2316 West Northern Avenue
Phoenix, AZ 85021

602-995-2871
FAX 602-995-1770

Lisa Schultz, Practice Manager
Meeting and 30 exhibits of opthamology equipment and information.
400 Attendees
Frequency: Annual

20093 American College of Veterinary Surgeons - Veterinary Symposium

American College of Veterinary Surgeons

19785 Crystal Rock Dr,
Suite 305
Germantown, MD 20874

301-916-0200
FAX 301-916-2287
E-Mail: acvs@acvs.org
Home Page: www.acvs.org

Ann T Loew, Executive Director
William B Henry, VP
Mark Markel, Chair
Marvin L Olmstead, ACVS President
Ann Loew, Executive Director
Over 150 exhibits featuring veterinary equipment, supplies and services.
1500 Attendees
Frequency: October 5-7
Founded in 1965

20094 American Federation of Aviculture Inc

STAT Marketing
PO Box 91717
Austin, TX 78709

512-585-9800
FAX 512-858-7029
E-Mail: afaoffice@afabirds.org
Home Page: www.afabirds.org
Social Media: *Facebook, Twitter*

Nancy Speed, National President
Linda Sheaffer, Chair
Jamie Whittaker, First VP
Brent Gattis, Second VP
Brent Andrus, CFO
Annual convention for manufacturers, suppliers, distributors and retailers of exotic birds and related products, including feed, seeds, cages, toys, vitamins and minerals. 65 booths.
750 Attendees
Founded in 1974

20095 American Humane Association Annual Meeting and Training Conference

American Humane Association
1400 16th Street NW
Suite 360
Washington, DC 20036

303-792-9900
800-227-4645
FAX 818-762-0908
E-Mail: info@americanhumane.org
Home Page: www.americanhumane.org
Social Media: *Facebook, Twitter, RSS, YouTube, Pinterest*

Robert R Ganzert, President/CEO
Clifford Rose, CFO
Over 50 exhibits of animal welfare equipment, including pet food, cages, trucks, id programs and veterinary services. Breakfast, luncheon, reception.
700 Attendees
Frequency: Annual
Founded in 1982

20096 American Morgan Horse Association Grand National Show

3 Bostwick Road
PO Box 960
Shelburne, VT 05482-0960

802-985-4944
FAX 802-985-8897
E-Mail: info@morganhorse.com
Home Page: morganhorse.com

Raymond Gifford, Show Manager
Fred Braden, Executive Director
Offers you a way to enjoy your Morgan in a competitive setting, while enjoying the company of other Morgan exhibitors. 30 booths.
8M Attendees
Frequency: October

20097 American Paint Horse Association World Championship Horse Shows
PO Box 961023
Fort Worth, TX 76161-0023

817-834-2742
FAX 817-834-3152
Home Page: http://www.apha.com

Carl Parker, President
Richard Cox, VP
Alice Singleton, Senior Committee Member
Ed Robert, Executive Secretary

A 14 day annual event that has become the proving ground for competitors striving to show that they ride or own the best American Paint Horses in the world. 100 booths.
5M Attendees
Frequency: July

20098 American Pet Products Manufacturers Association National Tradeshow
255 Glenville Road
Greenwich, CT 06831

203-532-0000
800-452-1225
FAX 203-532-0551
E-Mail: andy@appma.org
Home Page: www.appma.org

Bob Vetere, COO/Managing Director
Jennifer Bilbao, Marketing/PR Administrator
Andrew Darmohraj, VP/Deputy Managing Director
Jamie Cavanaugh, Trade Show Coordinator
Edith Martingnetti, General Mgr/Exhibitor Registration

Breakfast, reception, and 1400 pet products manufacturers exhibits.
Frequency: Annual
Founded in 1959

20099 American Rabbit Breeders Association National Convention
8 Westport Court
Bloomington, IL 61704

309-664-7500
FAX 309-664-0941
Home Page: arba.net

Glen Carr, Executive Director

Seminar, banquet, luncheon and 1500 rabbit breeders exhibits.
3000 Attendees
Frequency: Annual
Founded in 1910

20100 American Veterinary Medical Association Annual Convention
American Veterinary Medical Association
1931 N Meacham Road
Suite 100
Schaumburg, IL 60173

847-036-6142
FAX 847-925-1329
E-Mail: convention@avma.org
Home Page: www.avma.org

Dr Bonnie Beaver, President
David Little, Director

Seminar and 310 exhibits of products, materials, equipment, data, and services for veterinary medicine.
10000 Attendees
Frequency: Annual

20101 Annual Pet Industry Trade Show
World Wide Pet Supply Association

406 S 1st Avenue
Arcadia, CA 91006-3829

626-447-2222
FAX 626-447-8350
Home Page: www.wwpsa.com

Doug Poindexter, Executive VP

A comprehensive collection of exhibits and educational events unparalleled in the industry.

20102 Global Pet Expo
American Pet Products Association
255 Glenville Rd.
Greenwich, CT 06831

203-532-0000
800-452-1225
FAX 203-532-0551
E-Mail:
globalpetexpo@americanpetproducts.org
Home Page: globalpetexpo.org
Social Media: *Facebook, Twitter, Flickr, YouTube*

Andrew Darmohraj, Executive Vice President & COO
Tracey Wilson, Show Manager
Sarah Bopp, Associate Manager

Pet industry's largest annual trade show featuring buyers from more than 80 countries.
Frequency: Annual

20103 HH Backer Pet Industry Christmas Trade Show
HH Backer Associates
200 S Michigan Avenue
Suite 840
Chicago, IL 60604

312-663-4040
FAX 312-663-5676
E-Mail: hhbacker@hhbacker.com
Home Page: www.hhbacker.com

Patty Backer, President/Publisher
Karen Long MacLeod, Assoc Publisher/Editor in Chief
M Christopher Mitera, VP
Colette Fairchild, CMP, Trade Show Director
Julie Wichert, Sales Manager

Containing 1000 plus booths and 550 plus exhibits consisting of pet supplies, products and services.
9M Attendees
Frequency: October
Founded in 1967

20104 HH Backer Pet Industry Spring Trade Show
HH Backer Associates
200 S Michigan Avenue
Suite 840
Chicago, IL 60604

312-663-4040
FAX 312-663-5676
E-Mail: hhbacker@hhbacker.com
Home Page: www.hhbacker.com

Patty Backer, President/Publisher
Karen Long MacLeod, Assoc Publisher/Editor in Chief
M Christopher Mitera, VP
Collette Fairchild, CMP, Trade Show Director
Julie Wichert, Sales Manager

Containing 1000 plus booths and 550 plus exhibits consisting of pet supplies, products and services.
10M Attendees
Frequency: April
Founded in 1967

20105 NAPPS Annual Convention: National Assoc. of Professional Pet Sitters
17000 Commerce Parkway
Suite C
Mt. Laurel, NJ 08054

856-439-0324
FAX 856-439-0525
E-Mail: napps@ahint.com
Home Page: www.petsitters.org

Felicia Lembesis, Administrative Director
Rebecca Haines, Registration Coordinator
Kelly Calzaretta, Meeting/Exhibit Manager
Cathe Delaney, Membership Coordinator
Caitlin Dougherty, Manager

Exhibits, business sessions and networking opportunities. Provide tools and support to foster the success of members' businesses. To promote the value of pet sitting to the public and the advocate the welfare of animals.
Frequency: September

20106 National Pet Products Controlled Marketing Conference
Controlled Marketing Conferences
PO Box 1771
Monument, CO 80132

719-488-0226
888-316-0226
FAX 719-488-8168
E-Mail: nlginfo@nlgshow.com
Home Page: www.nlgshow.com

Robert Mikulas, President
Chris Wolf, VP

This event is run in conjunction with the National Lawn and Garden Show.
3000 Attendees
Frequency: June

20107 National Pigeon Association
1717 SE 43rd Terrace
Topeka, KS 66609-1728

785-267-5732
FAX 785-783-2846
E-Mail: secretary@npausa.com
Home Page: www.npausa.com

Frank Barrachina, President
Pat Avery, Secretary, Treasurer
James Avery, Secretary/Treasurer
Jerry McCalmon, Show Manager

Special information and exhibits about our members and the hobby of pigeon raising.
500 Attendees
Frequency: January
Founded in 1920

20108 Pet Exposition Trade Show
Pet Industry Distributors Association
2105 Laurel Bush Road
Suite 200
Bel Air, MD 21015

443-640-1060
FAX 443-640-1086
E-Mail: pida@kingmgmt.org
Home Page: www.pida.org

Steven T King CAE, President
Fred Schober, Chairman
Perry Parks, 2nd Vice Chairman
Randy Reber, Secretary/Treasurer
Steven T King, President

Containing 500 booths and 300 exhibits.
3000 Attendees
Frequency: March
Founded in 1968

20109 Pet Food Institute Meeting and Trade Show
Pet Food Institute

2025 M Street NW
Washington, DC 20036

202-367-1120
FAX 202-367-2120
E-Mail: info@petfoodinstitute.org
Home Page: www.petfoodinstitute.org

Stephen Payne, Public Relations Manager
Duane Ekedahl, Executive Director

Annual exhibits of equipment, supplies and
services for manufacturers of commercially
prepared dry, semi-moist and canned pet foods.
250 Attendees
Frequency: October

20110 Petfood Forum

WATT Publishing Company
303 N Main Street
Suite 500
Rockford, IL 61101

815-966-5400
FAX 815-966-6416
E-Mail: blentine@wattmm.com
Home Page: www.wattnet.com

Tim Phillips, Editor
Clay Schreiber, Publisher
James Watt, Owner

A technical trade show and symposium for the
pet food industry including manufacturers, suppliers to the industry as well as other pet food
professsionals. Containing 143 booths.
850 Attendees
Frequency: April
Founded in 1993
Mailing list available for rent

20111 Quest for Excellence

Pet Sitters International
201 East King Street
King, NC 27021-9163

336-983-9222
FAX 336-983-3755
E-Mail: info@petsit.com
Home Page: www.petsit.com

Kay Calzemari, Operating Manager
Beth Stoltz, Member Service Coordinator
Amy Woodleaf, Manager/Membership
John Long, Public Relations Coordinator
Dotty Shantz, Member Service

Containing 20+ exhibits.
250 Attendees
Frequency: September
Founded in 1994

**20112 Super Zoo Annual WWPSA Pet
Industry Trade Show**

World Wide Pet Supply Association
406 S 1st Avenue
Arcadia, CA 91006-3829

626-447-2222
FAX 626-447-8350
Home Page: www.wwpsa.com

Caryn Cohan-Bates, Manager

America's oldest pet industry trade show offering over 450 exhibitors with 850 booths. Seminars, workshops, grooming events and more are
held for retailers and wholesalers.
9000 Attendees
Frequency: July
Founded in 1951

20113 Tufts Animal Expo

Hynes Convention Center
900 Boylston Street
Boston, MA 02115

617-954-2000
800-845-8800
FAX 617-954-2125

E-Mail: info@mccahome.com
Home Page: www.mccahome.com

Animal care professionals addressed the social
and medical impact pets have on human lives.
7000 Attendees
Frequency: October

**20114 World of Private Label International
Trade Show**

Private Label Manufacturers Association
(PLMA)
630 Third Avenue
New York, NY 10017

212-972-3131
FAX 212-983-1382
E-Mail: info@plma.com
Home Page: www.plma.com

Brian Sharoff, President
Myra Rosen, VP
Tom Prendergast, Director, Research Services

This show has brought retailers together with
manufacturers to help them find new products,
make new contacts, and discover new ideas that
will help their private label programmers succeed and grow.

Directories & Databases

**20115 American Humane Association
Directory**

American Humane Association
1400 16th Street NW
Suite 360
Washington, DC 20036

303-792-9900
800-227-4645
FAX 818-762-0908
E-Mail: info@americanhumane.org
Home Page: www.americanhumane.org
Social Media: *Facebook, Twitter,
RSS,YouTube,Pinterest*

Robert R Ganzert, President
Clifford Rose, CFO

Animal protection agencies; Canadian and
some other foreign agencies are available; national and individual state editions are
available.

**20116 Directory of Animal Care and Control
Agencies**

American Humane Association
63 Inverness Dr E
Englewood, CO 80112-5117

303-792-9900
800-227-4645
FAX 303-792-5333
E-Mail: info@americanhumane.org
Home Page: www.americanhumane.org

Marie Wheatley, President

Over 6,000 animal protection agencies; Canadian and some other foreign agencies are available; national and individual state editions are
available.
Cost: $75.00

20117 Market Research Report

Animal Health Institute
1325 G St NW
Suite 700
Washington, DC 20005-3127

202-637-2440
FAX 202-393-1667
E-Mail: amathews@ahi.org
Home Page: www.ahi.org

Alexander Mathews, President
Dr Richard A Carnevale, VP Regulatory,
Scientific, Int'l

Ron Phillips, VP/Legislative/Public Affairs
Sandra L Phelan, Director Regulatory Affairs
Carolyn S Ayers, VP Administration/Finance

An annual directory published by the Animal
Health Institute.
Cost: $150.00
50 Pages
Frequency: Annual
Founded in 1941

20118 Pets/Animals Forum

CompuServe Information Service
5000 Arlington Centre Blvd
Columbus, OH 43220-5439

614-326-1002
800-848-8199

This database provides a forum for the discussion of typical house and exotic pets.
Frequency: Bulletin Board

20119 Veterinary Economics

Veterinary Healthcare Communications
8033 Flint
Lenexa, KS 66214

913-492-4300
800-255-6864
FAX 913-492-4157
Home Page: www.vetmedpub.com

Daniel R. Verdon Chapman, Executive Director
Ray Click, VP/General Manager

Publishes two monthly magazines, a full drug
list resource, and business books; conducts the
Central Veterinary Conference trade show;
rents its mail lists and does custom communi-
cation projects.
Frequency: Monthly
Circulation: 52,000
Mailing list available for rent: 48M+ names
Printed in 4 colors on matte stock

Industry Web Sites

20120 http://gold.greyhouse.com

G.O.L.D Grey House OnLine Databases

Grey House Publishing's online database platform, GOLD, offers Quick Search, Keyword
Search and Expert Search for most business
sectors including pet and pet supply markets.
The GOLD platform makes finding the information you need quick and easy - whether
you're a novice searcher or an experienced database user. All of Grey House's directory
products are available for subscription on the
GOLD platform.

20121 www.aahanet.org

American Animal Hospital Association

A group of hospitals and animal practitioners
serving the industry.

20122 www.abka.com

American Boarding Kennels Association

Seeks to upgrade the industry through educational programs and conventions. Promotes
code of ethics and accreditation programs for
kennel operators.

20123 www.ahi.org

Animal Health Institute

Resource for you to learn more about how animals health products work, how they are used
and their many benefits.

20124 www.akc.org

American Kennel Club

The principal registry of pure-bred dogs in the
US.

20125 www.allpets.com

Dog.com

Best selection of dog supplies and prices, news and forum about dogs, health issues, grooming and the well-being for our four-legged friends.

20126 www.apdt.com

Association of Pet Dog Trainers

Official web site of the association. Includes members in the news, training events, industry news, trainer search engine, conference news and merchandise.

20127 www.aspca.org

ASPCA

Society for the humane treatment of animals, established in 1866.

20128 www.avma.org

American Veterinary Medical Association

Publishes various journals and information for members. Acts as a clearinghouse for veterinarians.

20129 www.deltasociety.org

Delta Society

Information on human-animal interactions. Service Dog Center provides information and advocacy for dogs trained to assist people with disabilities. Pet Partners Program trains volunteers, health professionals, animals for animal-assisted therapy and activities.

20130 www.greyhouse.com

Grey House Publishing

Authoritative reference directories for most business sectors including pet and pet supply markets. Users can search the online databases with varied search criteria allowing for custom searches by product category, geographic area, sales volume, keyword, subject and more. Full Grey House catalog and online ordering also available.

20131 www.nhes.org

National Humane Education Society

Fights for the prevention of cruelty to animals in any form. Fostering a sentiment of kindness since 1948.

20132 www.npausa.com

National Pigeon Association

Special information for members and for the hobby of pigeon raising.

20133 www.peta.org

People for the Ethical Treatment of Animals (PETA)

Opposes all forms of animal exploitation. Seeks to educate the public on what the group sees as the three major institutionalized cruelty issues: the exploitation and abuse of animals in experimentation, the manufacturing of fur apparel, and slaughtering for human consumption.

20134 www.petfoodinstitute.org

Pet Food Institute

Represents the manufacturer of 97% of all dog and cat food produced in the US. Dedicated to promoting the overall care and well-being of pets. Research in pet nutrition, proper feedings and pet care.

20135 www.petpride.org

Pet Pride

Operates a no kill free shelter for the lifetime of homeless cats.

20136 www.petsit.com

Pet Sitters International

Society of professional pet sitters. Membership provides valuable benefits - educational resources for those engaged in the pet-sitting industry. Also provides a forum to network with peers who share a common vision of excellence in at-home pet care.

20137 www.petsitters.org

National Association of Professional Pet Sitters

The only non-profit organization dedicated to serving the needs of professional pet care providers. Promotes ethical standards and fosters cooperation among members in the pet care industry.

20138 www.pida.org

Pet Industry Distributors Association

Represents wholesaler-distributors of pet products, providing training and education to members.

20139 www.pijac.org

Pet Industry Joint Advisory Council

Monitors federal and state regulations and legislation affecting the industry. Sponsors research and educational projects including certification programs in veterinary care and husbandry for companion animals, in-store training videos, etc.

20140 www.usaha.org

United States Animal Health Association

Science-based, non-profit, voluntary organization. Members are state and federal animal health officials, universities, veterinarians, livestock producers, research scientists, and extension services all to control livestock diseases in the US.

20141 www.wspa.americas.org

The Resource Center of the Americas

International animal protection news reports. Informs, educates and organizes economic justice and cross-cultural understanding in the Americas.

20142 www.wwpsa.com

World Wide Pet Supply Association

Seeks to advance the economic interests of members. Promotes responsible pet ownership. Sponsors consumer and trade shows for the pet industry.

Associations

20143 Advertising Photographers of America
419 Lafayette St,2nd Floor
New York, NY 10003

212-807-0399
FAX 212-727-8120
E-Mail: jocelyn@apany.com
Home Page: www.apanational.com

Martin Trailer, President
Matthew Klein, VP
Julia Graham, Director

Our goal is to establish, endorse and promote professional practices, standards and ethics in the photographic and advertising community.
650 Members
Founded in 1981

20144 American Photographic Artists Guild
568 Main Street
Wilbraham, MA 01095

785-883-4166
E-Mail: katfalls@tdi.net
Home Page: www.useassociations.com

D John McCarthy, President
Joanie Ford, Historian/Merits/Degrees
Miles Andonov, Education
Lori Smith, Membership/Public Relations
Joanie Ford, Chairman

Encourages a better understanding between the photographer, the color artist and the retoucher. Conducts educational programs, sponsors competitions and bestows awards.
Founded in 1966

20145 American Photography Association

407-536-4611
877-627-2360
E-Mail:
images@americanphotographyassociation.or
Home Page:
www.americanphotographyassociation.org
Social Media: *Facebook, Twitter*

To promote the interest, appreciation and participation in photography by all levels of photographers.

20146 American Photograpic Artists
5042 Wilshire Blvd
#321
Los Angeles, CA 90036

Home Page: apanational.org
Social Media: *Facebook, Twitter, LinkedIn, Vimeo*

Tony Gale, National Board President
Michael Grecco, National Board EVP
John Durant, National Board SVP
Lee White, National Board Vice President
Andrew Strauss, National Board Treasurer

A not-for-profit organization for professional photographers.
Founded in 1981

20147 American Society for Photobiology
1313 Dolley Madison Blvd
Suite 402
McLean, VA 22101

785-865-9405
800-627-0326
FAX 785-843-6153
E-Mail: headquarters@photobiology.org
Home Page: www.photobiology.org
Social Media: *Facebook, LinkedIn*

Keith Cengel, President
Georg Wondrak, President-Elect
David Drupa, Executive Secretariat

Don Forbes, Secretary
Teresa Busch, Treasurer

Founded to further the scientific study of the effects of light on all living organisms.
1600 Members
Founded in 1972

20148 American Society for Photogrammetry and Remote Sensing
5410 Grosvenor Lane
Suite 210
Bethesda, MD 20814-2160

301-493-0290
FAX 301-493-0208
Home Page: www.asprs.org
Social Media: *Facebook, Twitter*

Dr. E. Lynn Usery, President
Dr. Charles K. Toth, President Elect
Rebecca A. Morton, Vice President
Roberta E. Lenczowski, National Director
Dr. Donald T.ÿ Lauer, Treasurer

A professional scientific association to advance the knowledge of and improve mapping sciences.
7000 Members
Founded in 1934

20149 American Society of Media Photographers
150 North 2nd Street
Philadelphia, PA 19106

215-451-2767
E-Mail: info@asmp.org
Home Page: asmp.org
Social Media: *Facebook, Twitter, LinkedIn*

Jenna Close, Chair
Luke Copping, Vice-Chair
Mark Green, Treasurer
Irene Owsley, Secretary
Tom Kennedy, Executive Director

A trade association which protects and promotes the interests of photographers whose work is for publication.
Founded in 1942

20150 American Society of Photographers
3120 N. Argonne Dr.
Milwaukee, WI 53222

414-871-6600
FAX 978-272-5201
E-Mail: jonallyn@aol.com
Home Page: www.asofp.com
Social Media: *Facebook, Twitter, Instagram*

Randy McNeilly, Chairman of the Board
Kalen Henderson, President
Jessica Vogel, President Elect
Dennis Hammon, Vice President
Gabriel I. Alonso, Secretary Treasurer

Membership requirements include membership in Professional Photographers of America and either a Master of Photography, a Photographic Craftsmen, or a photographic specialist. Publishes a quarterly newsletter.
850 Members
Founded in 1937

20151 American Society of Picture Professionals
201 E 25th St.,
Suite 11c
New York, NY 10010

516-500-3686
FAX 424-247-9844
E-Mail: aspp-ny@aspp.com
Home Page: www.aspp.com
Social Media: *Facebook, Twitter, LinkedIn, YouTube, RSS*

Sam Merrell, Executive Director
Cecilia de Querol, National President
Steve Spelman, Secretary

Mary F Loftus, Treasurer
Anita Dunca, Membership Co-Chair

Members are image producers, stock photo agencies, and image users.Provides networking and educational opportunities in the image transaction industry.
800 Members
Founded in 1969

20152 Antique and Amusement Photographers International
P.O.Box 3094
McDonough, GA 30253

860-578-2274
FAX 877-865-1052
E-Mail: info@oldtimephotos.org
Home Page: www.oldtimephotos.org
Social Media: *Facebook, Twitter, LinkedIn, Pinterest*

Derrick Gillikin, President
Susan K. Crutchfield, Executive Director
Michele Powers, Secretary
Sarana Rogers, Treasurer
Trent Edwards, Vice President

Members are photography studies and photographers, primarliy in the US and Canada, specializing in costume photography and suppliers to the industry.
200 Members
Founded in 1990

20153 Association of International Photography Art Dealers
2025 M Street NW
Suite 800
Washington, DC 20036

202-367-1158
FAX 202-367-2158
E-Mail: info@aipad.com
Home Page: www.aipad.com
Social Media: *Facebook, Twitter, Instagram, Flickr, Vimeo*

Catherine Edelman, President
Kraige Block, Vice President
Susan Herzig, Treasurer
Richard Moore, Secretary
Meredith Y. Robertson, Executive Director

Galleries and private dealers in fine photography who have been in business for at least three years.
125 Members
Founded in 1979

20154 BioCommunications Association
220 Southwind Lane
Hillsborough, NC 27278

919-245-0906
E-Mail: office@bca.org
Home Page: www.bca.org
Social Media: *Facebook, Twitter, LinkedIn, YouTube*

Nancy Hurtgen, Executive Director
Connie Johansen, President
James Koepfler, Secretary/ Treasurer
Susanne Loomis, Vice President
Karen M. Hensley, Dir. Of Communications

Made up of professionals who create and use the highest quality images and presentations in visual communications media for teaching and documentation in the life sciences and medicine.
140 Members
Founded in 1931

20155 Center for Photography at Woodstock
59 Tinker St
Woodstock, NY 12498

845-679-9957
FAX 845-679-6337
E-Mail: info@cpw.org
Home Page: www.cpw.org

Social Media: *Facebook, Twitter, Flickr, Vimeo, Instagram*

Howard Greenberg, Founder, Chair
Clinton Cargill, Vice President
Jed Root, Treasurer
Andy Young, Secretary
Ariel Shanberg, Executive Director

The Center for Photography at Woodstock is a not-for-profit, artist-centered organization dedicated to supporting artists working in photography and related media and engaging audiences through opportunities in which creation, discovery, and education are made possible.
Founded in 1977

20156 Council on Fine Art Photography

5613 Johnson Ave
Bethesda, MD 20817-3503

301-897-0083

Lowell Anson Kenyon, Executive Director

Members are fine art photographers employing silver processes.
50 Members
Founded in 1982

20157 Digital Media Licensing Association

3165 S. Alma School Road
#29-261
Chandler, AZ 85248-3760

714-815-8427
E-Mail: cathy@digitalmedialicensing.org
Home Page: www.pacaoffice.org
Social Media: *Facebook, Twitter, LinkedIn, RSS, Skype*

Sarah Fix, President
Elena Flanagan-Eister, Vice President
Chris Carey, Treasurer
Julie Zentmaier, Secretary
Cathy Aron, Executive Director

A community of visual media licensing professionals.
100+ Members
Founded in 1951

20158 Evidence Photographers International Council

229 Peachtree St. NE
#2200
Atlanta, GA 30303

570-253-5450
800-356-3742
FAX 404-614-6406
E-Mail: csc@evidencephotographers.com
Home Page: www.evidencephotographers.com
Social Media: *Facebook*

Claire White, Association Director

A non profit educational and scientific organization with the primary purpose is the advancement of forensic photography/videography in civil evidence and law enforcement.
2000 Members
Founded in 1968

20159 IEEE Standards Association

445 Hoes Lane
Piscataway, NJ 08854-4141

732-981-0060
FAX 732-562-1571
E-Mail: i3amembership@i3a.org
Home Page: standards.ieee.org
Social Media: *Facebook, Twitter, LinkedIn*

Bruce Kraemer, President
John Kulick, Chairman
Yatin Trivedi, Treasurer
Konstantinos Karachalios, Secretary
Phil Wennblom, Corporate Advisory Group

Formerly (1997) National Association of Photographic Manufacturers and (2001) Photographic and Imaging Maufacturers Association. The Silver Council is a program sponsored by

I3A that monitors environmental regulation of commercial silver use. Membership fee varies,based on annual sales.
81 Members
Founded in 1946

20160 Independent Photo Imagers

2518 Anthem Village Drive
Suite 104
Henderson, NV 89052

702-617-1141
FAX 702-617-1181
E-Mail: info@ipiphoto.com
Home Page: www.ipiphoto.com
Social Media: *Facebook, Twitter, LinkedIn, YouTube, Pinterest, Instagram*

Joel Miller, Chairman
Ron Mohney, Executive Director
T.K. Broecker, Treasurer
Koby Marowelli, Secretary
Larry Steiner, Vice Chairman

An association of independent photographers, who use various means of developing their pictures.
45 Members
Founded in 1982

20161 International Color Consortium

1899 Preston White Driveÿ
Reston, VA 20191ÿ

703-264-7200
Home Page: www.color.org

Max Derhak, Co-Chair
William Li, Co-Chair
Ray Cheydleur, Vice Chair
Deborah Orf, Secretary
Phil Green, Technical Secretary

An association to promote the use and adoption of open, vendor-neutral, cross-platform color management.
Founded in 1993

20162 International Fire Photographers Association

143 40th Street
New Orleans, LA 70124

504-482-9616
FAX 504-486-4946
E-Mail: president@ifpaonline.com
Home Page: ifpafirephotos.org/
Social Media: *Facebook, Twitter, Google+, Yahoo*

Chris E Mickal, President
Michael Heller, VP

Promote professionalism in all aspects of fire photography, specifically in the fields of fire, educational, and investigative photography and the recognition of all fire photography organizations as an important tool in the fire service and law enforcement
200 Members
Founded in 1964

20163 International Graphic Arts Education Association

1899 Preston White Drive
Reston, VA 20191

703-758-0595
Home Page: www.igaea.org

Monika Zarzycka, President
Kelly Glentz Brush, Secretary
Dr. Jerry Waite, Treasurer
Tony Cimaglia, First Vice-President (Publications)
Michael Williams, President-Elect

An association of educators in partnership with industry, dedicated to sharing theories, princi-

ples, techniques, and processes relating to graphic communications and imaging theory.
800 Members
Founded in 1923

20164 Naples Art Association

The von Liebig Art Center
585 Park St.
Naples, FL 34102

239-262-6517
Home Page: www.naplesart.org
Social Media: *Facebook, Twitter, LinkedIn, Pinterest, YouTube*

Andrew Sroka, Board President
Aimee Schlehr, Executive Director
Shea Lindner, Programs Manager
Maureen Christensen, Development Director
Callie Spilane, Education Director

A nonprofit organization to promote and advance education, interest and participation in the visual arts.
Founded in 1956

20165 National Association of Photo Equipment Technicians

300 Picture Place
Jackson, MI 49201

517-788-8100
FAX 517-788-8371
E-Mail: bcovey@pmai.org
Home Page: www.arcat.com

William Covey, Executive Liaison

Provides information on the photogrpahic industry to those engaged in the photographic repair.
250 Members
Founded in 1973

20166 National Association of Quick Printers (NAQP)

One Meadowlands Plaza
Suite 1511
East Rutherford, NJ 07073

201-634-9600
800-642-6275
FAX 201-634-0324
E-Mail: webmaster@napl.org
Home Page: www.naqp.com
Social Media: *Facebook, Twitter, LinkedIn, YouTube,RSS, Pinterest, Google*

Joseph Truncale, President & CEO
Nigel Worme, Chairman
Willam Gavigan, Treasurer/ Secretary
Niels Winther, Vice Chairman
Mike Philie, Senior Vice President

Furthers the business of quick printers, copy shops, and small format commercial printers. Also welcomes manufacturers and suppliers of equipment and consumables, trade publications, and consultants to the quick print industry.
900 Members
Founded in 1975

20167 National Photograpic Society

15 Woodbine Farm Business Park
Threemilestone, UK

843-289-0615
Home Page: www.thenps.com
Social Media: *Facebook, Twitter, Google+, RSS*

Rod Pascoe, Chairman
Stu Cooper, Mentor and Trainer
Sarah Fitzgerald, Liaison Manager
Paul Spiers, Head of marketing
Susan Hurren, Social Media and Press

A society for both professional as well as enthusiast photographers.

20168 National Press Photographers Association

120 Hooper Street
Athens, GA 30602-3018

706-542-2506
FAX 919-383-7261
E-Mail: Cdeale@nppa.org
Home Page: nppa.org
Social Media: *Facebook, Twitter, LinkedIn, Vimeo*

Mark Dolan, President
Melissa Lyttle, Vice President
Carolyn Hall, Treasurer
Michael King, Secretary
Michael Borland, Immediate Past President

Sponsors numerous, annual television and print media workshops. Conducts annual competition for news photos and television news film. Monthly magazine job information bank given to all members.
6500+ Members
Founded in 1946

20169 National Stereoscopic Association

Portland, OR

503-771-4440
E-Mail: strwld@teleport.com
Home Page: stereoworld.org
Social Media: *Facebook*

Lawrence Kaufman, Chairman
Lee Pratt, President
John Bueche, Vice President
Carl Bowers, Treasurer
Ronald Gold, Vice President, Marketing

A nonprofit organization to promote research, practice, collection and use of vintage and contemporary stereoviews, stereo cameras and equipment.
Founded in 1974

20170 North American Nature Photography Association

6382 Charleston Road
Alma, IL 62807

618-547-7616
FAX 618-547-7438
E-Mail: info@nanpa.org
Home Page: www.nanpa.org
Social Media: *RSS*

Gabby Salazar, President
Sean Fitzgerald, President-Elect
Susan Day, Executive Director
Bruce Haley, Treasurer
Clay Bolt, Board Member

Committed solely to serving the field of nature photography. Provides education, information develops standards and promotes nature photography as an art form and teaching medium.
Founded in 1993

20171 North American Nature Photography Associat ion

6382 Charleston Road
Alma, IL 62807

618-547-7616
FAX 618-547-7438
E-Mail: info@nanpa.org
Home Page: www.nanpa.org
Social Media: *Facebook, Twitter, LinkedIn, RSS, Google+*

Gabby Salazar, President
Sean Fitzgerald, President Elect
Bruce Haley, Past-President, Treasurer
Clay Bolt, Board Member
Gary Farber, Board Member

An organization dedicated to photography of nature.

20172 PERA

Pera Innovation Park, Nottingham Rd.
Melton Mowbray
Leicestershire, UK LE13 0PB

166-450-1501
800-776-8616
FAX 408-512-5254
E-Mail: enquiries@peraconsulting.com
Home Page: www.pera.com
Social Media: *Facebook, Twitter*

Glyn Goddard, Non-Executive Director
Dean Hallam, Chief Financial Officer
Alan Baxter, Non Executive Director
John Hill, Executive Chairman
Paul Trantor, Chief Executive Officer

An association for production equipment rental personnel and organizations.
75 Members
Founded in 1973

20173 Photo Chemical Machining Institute

11 Robert Toner Blvd
234
North Attleboro, MA 02763

508-385-0085
FAX 508-232-6005
E-Mail: cflaherty@pcmi.org
Home Page: www.pcmi.org

Catherine Flaherty, Executive Director
William Fox, President
Mike Lynch, Vice-President
Eric Kemperman, Treasurer
Philip Greiner, Secretary

Members are companies producing metal products through photo chemical machining. In addition the Institute includes companies that service the PCM industry and supply its needs.
210 Members
Founded in 1967

20174 Photo Marketing Association International

718 Jones Branch Drive
Suite 300
McLean, VA 22102

703-665-4416
800-762-9287
FAX 703-506-3266
E-Mail: pma_advertising@pmai.org
Home Page: www.pmai.org
Social Media: *Facebook, Twitter, LinkedIn*

Gabrielle Mullinax, President
Georgia McCabe, CEO/ Executive Director
Jerry Sullivan, Vice-President
Lisa Otto, Treasurer
Mark Klostermeyer, Sr. Vice President

A national organization of associations and manufacturers and suppliers of photographic equipment; also members of the National Association of Photo Equipment Technicians and of the Professional School Photographers of America.
18000 Members
Founded in 1924

20175 Photographic Society of America

8241 S Walker Avenue
Suite 104
Oklahoma City, OK 73139

405-843-1437
855-772-4636
Home Page: www.psa-photo.org

Charlie Burke, President
Elena McTighe, Executive Vice President
Dana Cohoon, Treasurer
Stan Bormann, Secretary
Ralph Durham, Conference Vice President

Worldwide interactive organization for anyone interested in photography, professional or serious amateur. Offers a wide variety of activities, monthly magazine, photo and digital competitions, study groups via mail and Internet, how-to programs, an annal conference, and many other activites and services.
Founded in 1934

20176 Photoimaging Manufacturers and Distributor s Association

7600 Jericho Turnpike
Suite 301
Woodbury, NY 11797

516-802-0895
FAX 516-364-0140
E-Mail: jackie@pmda.com
Home Page: www.pmda.com
Social Media: *Facebook, Twitter, LinkedIn*

Dan Unger, President
Michelle Fernandez, VP
Jay Kelbley, VP
Jim Malcolm, VP
Jerry Grossman, Executive Director

Contributes to the progress and welfare of the photoimaging industry.
Founded in 1939

20177 Picture Agency Council of America

23046 Avenida De La Carlota
Suite 600
Laguna Hills, CA 92653

714-815-8427
FAX 949-679-8224
E-Mail: execdirector@pacaoffice.org
Home Page: www.stockindustry.org

Cathy Aron, Executive Director
Maria Kessler, President

Trade association for stock picture companies in North America. Serves member agencies, their clients and their contributing photographers by promoting communication among photo agencies and other professional groups.
150 Members
Founded in 1951

20178 Professional Aerial Photographers' Association

12069 Cessna Place
Brookshire, TX 77423

703-887-8703
FAX 703-281-6700
E-Mail: cboyle@boyleconsulting.com
Home Page:
professionalaerialphotographers.com

Chuck Boyleÿ, President
Laura Boyko, VP, Programs
Kent Larson, VP, Membership
John Mooney, Treasurer, Secretary
Julie Belanger, ExecutiveÿDirector

A professional trade organization for aerial photographers.
Founded in 1974

20179 Professional Photographer Magazine

229 Peachtree St NE
Suite 2200
Atlanta, GA 30303

404-522-8600
800-742-7468
FAX 404-614-6406
E-Mail: ppmag@omeda.com
Home Page: www.ppmag.com
Social Media: *Facebook, Twitter, Pinterest*

David Trust, CEO
Bob Lloyd, President
Dana Groves, Marketing Executive

Portrait, commercial, wedding, industrial and specialized photographers and photographic artists.
28000 Members
Founded in 1869

20180 Professional Photographers Association

Professional Photographers Assoc. of New England
PO Box 568
Durham, NH 3824

603-868-2970
FAX 860-423-9402
E-Mail: exsec@ppane.com
Home Page: www.ppane.com
Social Media: *Facebook, YouTube*

Lorraine Bedell, President
Steve Lourenco, President Elect
Madonna Lovett, Vice President of Programs
Fred Stiteler, Executive Secretary
Alison Miniter, Vice President of Comm
1000 Attendees
Frequency: September
Founded in 1860

20181 Professional Photographers of America

229 Peachtree St. NE
Suite 2200
Atlanta, GA 30303

404-522-8600
FAX 404-614-6400
Home Page: www.ppa.com
Social Media: *Facebook, Twitter, LinkedIn, Google+, Instagram, YouTube*

Susan Michal, Chairman
Michael Timmons, President
Lori Craft, Vice President
Rob Behm, Treasurer
Stephen Thetford, Director

A nonprofit trade association for photographers.
Founded in 1869

20182 Professional Picture Framers Association

83 South Street Unit
#303
Freehold, NJ 7728

732-536-5160
800-762-9287
FAX 517-788-8371
E-Mail: info@ppfadirectory.com
Home Page: www.ppfa.com
Social Media: *Facebook, Twitter, LinkedIn*

John Pruitt CPF, President
Fran Gray MCPF, VP

A trade association of manufacturers, wholesalers, print publishers, importers and retailers selling art, framing and related supplies.
3000 Members
Founded in 1971

20183 Professional Travelogue Sponsors

El Camino College Foundation
16007 Crenshaw Boulevard
Torrance, CA 90506

310-329-5345
800-832-5345
FAX 310-715-7875
E-Mail: artstickets@elcamino.edu
Home Page:
www.elcamino.edu/centerforthearts
Social Media: *Facebook, Twitter, YouTube, Instagram, Flickr*

Thomas Fallow, President
Bruce Spain, Executive Director
Rick Christophersen, Director
Sara Hamilton, Administrative Assistant
Nancy Adler, Production Manager

Currently the largest documentary Travel Film Program Sponsor and Presenter.
55 Members
Founded in 1967

20184 Professional Women Photographers

Metropolitan Opera Guild
119 W. 72nd St.
#223
New York, NY 10023

212-867-7745
E-Mail: pwp@pwponline.org
Home Page: www.pwponline.org
Social Media: *Facebook, Twitter, LinkedIn, Amazon, RSS*

Beth Shaw, President
Fredda Gordon, Vice President
Francoise Jeanpierre, Treasurer
Joann Frechette, Secretary
Elizabeth Currier, Membership

To support and promote the work of women photographers through the sharing of ideas, resources and experience, to provide educational forums to enogurage artistic growth and photographic development, and to stimulate public interst in and support for the art of photography
170 Members
Founded in 1975
Mailing list available for rent

20185 SPIE, the international society for optics and photonics

1000 20th Street
Bellingham, WA 98225-6705

360-676-3290
888-504-8171
FAX 360-647-1445
E-Mail: customerservice@spie.org
Home Page: www.SPIE.org
Social Media: *Facebook, Twitter, LinkedIn, RSS, YouTube, Blogspot*

Prof. Toyohiko Yatagai, President
Dr. Eugene G. Arthurs, CEO
Dr. Glenn D. Boreman, Vice President
Gary Spiegel, Secretary/ Treasurer
Dr. Robert A. Lieberman, President-Elect

Members are scientists, engineers, researchers and companies interested in technology and applications of optical, electro-optical, fiber-optic, laser, and photonic systems.
14000 Members
Founded in 1955

20186 Silver Users Association

3930 Walnut St.
Suite 210
Fairfax, VA 22030

703-930-7790
FAX 703-359-7562
E-Mail: pmiller@mwcapitol.com
Home Page: www.silverusersassociation.org
Social Media: *Facebook*

Paul A Miller, Executive Director
Bill LeRoy, President
Mike Huber, VP
John King, Secretary
Bill Hammerle, Treasury

Represents manufacturers and distributors of products in which silver is an essential element. Works for the recognition of silver as a commodity and the removal of governmental regulations which retard its free exchange in commerce both foreign and domestic. Also helps provide a stable trading climate in the metal, it monitors the silver market to insure that silver information available to the industry and public is accurate.
45 Members
Founded in 1947

20187 Society for Photographic Education

2530 Superior Avenue
Suite 403
Cleveland, OH 44114

216-622-2733
FAX 216-622-2712

E-Mail: membership@spenational.org
Home Page: www.spenational.org
Social Media: *Facebook, Twitter, Instagram*

Jeff Curto, National Board Chair
Anne Massoni, Vice-Chair
James Wyman, Executive Director
Lupita Murillo Tinnen, Treasurer
Robin Germany, Secretary

The Society for Photographic Education is a non-profit membership organization that provides a forum for the discussion of photogrphy and related media as a means of creative expression and cultural insight. Through its interdisciplinary porgrams, services and publications, the society seeks to promote a broader understanding of the medium in all its forms, and to foster the development of its practice, teaching, scholarship and criticism.
1800 Members
Founded in 1963

20188 Society of American Travel Writers

One Parkview Plaza
Suite 800
Oakbrook Terrace, IL 60181

312-420-6846
FAX 414-359-1671
E-Mail: info@satw.org
Home Page: www.satw.org
Social Media: *Facebook, Twitter, LinkedIn*

Paul Lasley, President
Barbara Orr, Vice President
Peggy Bendel, Secretary
Tom Adkinson, Treasurer
Catherine Hamm, President-Elect

Photographers and 35 associate member representatives of airlines, hotels, resorts, tourist agencies and public relations firms.
Founded in 1955

20189 Student Photographic Society

229 Peachtree St. NE
Suite 2200
Atlanta, GA 30303

888-722-1334
E-Mail: info@studentphoto.com
Home Page: studentphoto.com
Social Media: *Facebook, Twitter, Google+*

Susan Michal, Chairman
Michael Timmons, President
Lori Craft, Vice President
Rob Behm, Treasurer
Stephen Thetford, Director

Provides career building resources, networking opportunities and information for photography students.
Founded in 1999

20190 Take Great Pictures

109 White Oak Lane
Suite 72F
Old Bridge, NJ 08857

732-679-3460
FAX 516-364-0140
E-Mail: webmaster@TakeGreatPictures.com
Home Page: www.takegreatpictures.com
Social Media: *RSS*

Willard Clark, Executive Director

Founded as Photographic Merchandising and Distributing Association and became Photographic Manufacturers and Distributors Association before assuming its present name in 1999. Membership is $500/year for associate members and $1,000/year for voting members.
20000 Members
Founded in 1939

20191 The Association of Independent Architectural Photographers

4531 Cambridge Court
Bountiful, UT 84010

801-738-8786
E-Mail: aiap@photographer.org
Home Page: www.aiap.net

A professional organization for architectural photographers.

20192 The Society for Photographic Education

2530 Superior Avenue
Suite 403
Cleveland, OH 44114

216-622-2733
FAX 216-622-2712
E-Mail: membership@spenational.org
Home Page: www.spenational.org
Social Media: *Facebook, Twitter, Instagram*

Jeff Curto, National Board Chair
Anne Massoni, Vice-Chair
James Wyman, Executive Director
Lupita Murillo Tinnen, Treasurer
Robin Germany, Secretary

A nonprofit ogranization for the advancement of education in photography.
1800 Members
Founded in 1963

20193 University Photographers Association of America

SUNY Brockport
350 New Campus Drive
Brockport, NY 14420-2931

716-395-2133
FAX 662-915-1298
E-Mail: jdusen@brockport.edu
Home Page: www.upaa.org

Glenn Carpenter, President
Robert Jordan, VP
Nick Romanenko, Treasurer
Mark Carriveau, Secretary
Bill Bitzinger, Board Member

Members are college and university photographers who are concerned with the application and practice of photography.
250 Members
Founded in 1961

20194 Wedding & Portrait Photographers International (WPPI)

85 Broad St.
11th Floor
New York, NY 10004

646-654-4500
FAX 310-846-4770
Home Page: www.wppionline.com
Social Media: *Facebook, Twitter, YouTube, Instagram*

Stephen Sheanin, CEO/President
John McGeary, Senior Vice President
Lauren Wendle, VP, Publisher
Neeta Lakhani, Operations Manager
Jason Groupp, Director

Promotes high artistic and technical standards. Serves as a forum for an exchange of technical knowledge. Members are offered the opportunity to purchase special products and services.
2.8M Members
Founded in 1978

20195 Wedding Photojournalist Association

Home Page: www.wpja.com

A resource of photojournalists and candid wedding photographers.
Founded in 2002

20196 White House News Photographers Association

7119 Ben Franklin Station
Washington, DC 20044-7119

202-785-5230
E-Mail: info@whnpa.org
Home Page: www.whnpa.org
Social Media: *Facebook, Twitter*

Whitney Shefte, President
Jim Bourg, Vice President
Jon Elswick, Treasurer
Joshua Roberts, Secretary
Dennis Brack, Ex Officio

Volunteer association of professional photographers covering the Washington political venue. Activities include educational seminars, work with high school students and an annual awards contest. Our work is seen in newspapers, magazines, television and on the Internet.
500 Members
Founded in 1941

20197 Worldwide Community of Imaging Association

2282 Springport Road
Suite F
Jackson, MI 49202ÿ

517-788-8100
800-762-9287
FAX 517-788-8371
Home Page: www.pmai.org
Social Media: *Facebook, Twitter, LinkedIn*

Bill Eklund, President
Gabrielleÿ Mullinax, Senior Vice President
Jerry Sullivan, Vice President
Mark Klostermeyer, MCPF, Treasurer
Jim Esp, Secretary, Executive Director

United diverse professionals in the imaging industry worldwide.
Founded in 1924

Newsletters

20198 American Society of Media Photgraphers Bulletin

Photo District News
150 North Second Street
Philadelphia, PA 19106

215-451-2767
FAX 215-451-0880
E-Mail: info@asmp.org
Home Page: www.asmp.org
Social Media: *Facebook, Twitter, LinkedIn*

Holly Hughes, Editor
Jeffery Roberts, President

Member publication that addresses the news and preoccupations of the photography industry.
Frequency: Quarterly
Circulation: 5500
Founded in 1944

20199 BCA News

BioCommunications Association
220 Southwind Lane
Hillsborough, NC 27278-7907

919-245-0906
FAX 919-245-0906
E-Mail: khensley@mdanderson.org
Home Page: www.bca.org
Social Media: *Facebook, Twitter, LinkedIn, Blog,Tumblr*

Karen Hensley, Editor
Susanne Loomis, President
Joseph Kane, Vice-President
James Koepfler, Secretary-Treasurer

Keeps members informed about such things as annual meetings, chapter activities, awards and member updates.
Frequency: 2-3x/Year

20200 Dance on Camera Journal

Dance Films Association
48 W 21st St
Suite 907
New York, NY 10010-6989

212-727-0764
FAX 212-727-0764
E-Mail: info@dancefilmsassn.org
Home Page: www.dancefilms.org

Deidra Towers, Executive Director
Louise Spain, CEO

The only service organization in the world dedicated to both the dance and the film community.
Cost: $45.00
Circulation: 350
Founded in 1956

20201 Future Image Report

Future Image
520 South EI Camino Real
Suite 206A
San Mateo, CA 94402

650-579-0493
800-749-3572
FAX 650-579-0566
E-Mail: hbravo@futureimage.com
Home Page: www.futureimage.com

Alexis J Gerard, Editor/Publisher
Paul Worthington, Managing Editor
Heidy Bravo, Circulaion Manager

News and analysis of technology and market developments in photo-digital imaging, for management-level industry professionals.
Cost: $500.00
Founded in 1991

20202 Light Impressions Review

PO Box 940
Rochester, NY 14603-0940

716-271-8960

William Edwards, Publisher
Lance Speer, Director

Photography notes and news.
Cost: $15.00
16 Pages
Frequency: Monthly

20203 NTIS Alert- Photography & Recording Devices

National Technical Information Service
5285 Port Royal Rd
US Department of Commerce
Alexandria, VA 22312

703-605-6000
800-553-6847
FAX 703-605-6900
E-Mail: info@ntis.gov
Home Page: www.ntis.gov

Linda Davis, VP
Cost: $140.00
Founded in 1955

20204 Photo Marketing

Photo Marketing Association International
2282 Springport Road
Suite F
Jackson, MI 49202

517-788-8100
800-762-9287
FAX 517-788-8371
E-Mail: gpageau@pmai.org

Home Page: www.pmai.org
Social Media: *Facebook, Twitter, LinkedIn*

Ted Fox, CEO
Allen Showalter, President
Mark Klostermeyer, Vice-President
Robert L Hanson, Treasurer

News of interest to the photo business on both a national and international basis.
Cost: $5.00
4 Pages
Frequency: Monthly
Circulation: 12,141
Founded in 1925

20205 PhotoDaily
PhotoSource International
1910 35th Ave
Pine Lake Farm
Osceola, WI 54020-5602

715-248-3800
800-624-0266
FAX 715-248-7394
E-Mail: info@photosource.com
Home Page: www.photosource.com

Rohn Engh, President
Bruce Swenson, Production Manager
Jonna Zehma, Editor

Pairs photographers with the picture needs of magazine and book editors.
Cost: $330.00
Frequency: Daily
Founded in 1976

20206 Photobulletin
PhotoSource International
1910 35th Ave
Osceola, WI 54020-5602

715-248-3800
800-624-0266
FAX 715-248-7394
E-Mail: info@photosource.com
Home Page: www.photosource.com

Rohn Engh, President

Lists photographic needs of photobuyers buying in the top-notch markets.
Frequency: Daily
Founded in 1980
Printed in one color

20207 Photofinishing News
Photofinishing News
219 Lafeyette Avenue
Westwood, NJ 07675-904

201-819-2533
E-Mail: hans@photo-news.com
Home Page: www.photo-news.com

Hans Kuhlman, Editor

Technical / marketing coverage of worldwide photography / photo-imaging industry, reviews of new products, tradeshows and market statistics.
Cost: $150.00
12 Pages
ISBN: 0-889239-3 -
ISSN: 1536-6553
Founded in 1970
Printed in one color on matte stock

20208 Photograph Collector
140 East Richardson Avenue
Suite 301
Langhorne, PA 19047-2824

215-891-0214
E-Mail: info@photoreview.org
Home Page: www.photoreview.org

Stephen Perloff, Editor

News and analysis for collectors, curators and dealers. Current coverage of the auction market, trends, discoveries, museums and trade

shows. Accepts advertising.
Cost: $149.95
8 Pages
Frequency: Monthly
ISBN: 0-271083-8 -
Founded in 1980
Printed in one color on matte stock

20209 Professional Photographers Association of New England
98 Windham Street
PO Box 316
Willimantic, CT 06226-316

203-488-2334
860-423-1402
FAX 860-423-9402
E-Mail: info@ppane.com
Home Page: www.ppane.com

Harvey Goldstein, Editor
Ruth Clegg, CEO/President
Circulation: 1000
Founded in 1961
Printed in on glossy stock

Magazines & Journals

20210 Advanced Imaging
Cygnus Publishing
102 Wilmont Road
Suite 470
Deerfield, IL 60015-3601

847-405-0257
E-Mail: larry.adams@cygnusb2b.com
Home Page: www.cygnusb2b.com

Dave Brambert, Group Publisher
Larry Adams, Editor-in-Chief
Richard Reiff, President
Hank Russell, Managing Editor

Contains information on professional photographic techniques and new approaches in all forms of media.
Cost: $60.00
Frequency: Monthly
Circulation: 44009
Founded in 1966

20211 Afterimage
Visual Studies Workshop
31 Prince Street
Rochester, NY 14607-1405

585-442-8676
FAX 585-442-1992
E-Mail: info@vsw.org
Home Page:
www.vsw.org/afterimage/index.html

Karen VanMeenen, Editor
Joanna Heatwole, Managing Editor

Geared toward media arts and photography artists, curators, academics, administrators and students. Features photography, independent film and video coverage, artist's books, alternative publishing and cultural studies issues. Also highlights conference and festival reports and scholarly feature articles.
Cost: $33.00
Circulation: 10000
Founded in 1980

20212 American Photo
1633 Broadway
43rd Floor
New York, NY 10019

212-676-6000
800-274-4514
FAX 212-489-4217

E-Mail: jiannello@hfmus.com
Home Page: www.hfmus.com/

David Schonauer, Editor-in-Chief
Krissa Cavouras, Associate Editor
Richard Rabinowitz, Publisher

Profiles of professional photographers and other photographic topics.
Cost: $4.99
Frequency: 6 Issues per year
Circulation: 27,733
Founded in 1888

20213 Aperture
Aperture Foundation
547 W 27th St
Suite 4
New York, NY 10001-5511

212-505-5555
800-825-0061
FAX 212-979-7759
E-Mail: info@aperture.org
Home Page: www.aperture.org

Michael Culloso, President
Cathy Kaplan, Vice-Chairman
Frederick Smith, Treasurer

Dedicates itself to celebrating the finest in creative photography. Through the periodicals exquisitely reproduced images, rivaling the quality of the photographers' original prints, subscribers experience a wealth of challenging, beautiful pictures on a series of significant topics. Accepts advertising.
Cost: $40.00
80 Pages
Frequency: Quarterly
Founded in 1952
Mailing list available for rent

20214 Exposure
Society for Photographic Education
2530 Superior Avenue
Suite 403
Cleveland, OH 44114

216-622-2733
FAX 216-622-2712
E-Mail: membership@spenational.org
Home Page: www.spenational.org

Virginia Morrison, Executive Director
Nina Barcellona, Advertising & Publications
Meghan Borato, Registrar
Carla Pasquale, Office/Accounts Manager
Cost: $15.00
Frequency: Biannual
Mailing list available for rent: 700 names

20215 History of Photography
Routledge Publishing
7625 Empire Drive
Florence, KS 41042-2919

800-354-1420
E-Mail: orders@taylorandfrancis.com
Home Page: www.taylorandfrancis.com

Graham Smith, Editor
Ann Haddrell, Advertising Manager

An international publication devoted to the history and criticism of the basic sematic unit of all modern media.
Cost: $396.00
92 Pages
Frequency: Annual+
ISSN: 0308-7298
Founded in 1977

20216 Imaging Business
Cygnus Business Media
3 Huntington Quadrangle
Suite 301N
Melville, NY 11747-4618

631-845-2700
800-308-6397
FAX 631-845-7109

E-Mail: bill.schiffner@cygnuspub.com
Home Page: www.labsonline.com

Bill Schiffner, Associate Publisher

Formerly called Photographic Processing. Covers photographic equipment, processing, suppliers and dealers. No longer in publication, but last six years of issues available in online archive.
Cost: $66.00
Frequency: Monthly
Circulation: 21000
ISSN: 0031-8744
Founded in 1936
Printed in 4 colors

20217 News Photographer
National Press Photographers Association
3200 Croasdaile Dr
Suite 306
Durham, NC 27705-2588

919-383-7246
FAX 919-383-7261
E-Mail: info@nppa.org
Home Page: www.nppa.org
Social Media: *Facebook, Twitter, LinkedIn, Vimeo*

Mindy Hutchison, Executive Director
Robert Gould, President

Features articles, news and profiles about still and television news photography.
Cost: $38.00
Frequency: Monthly
Circulation: 10500
ISSN: 0199-2422
Founded in 1946
Printed in 4 colors

20218 Outdoor Photographer
Werner Publishing Corporation
12121 Wilshire Blvd
Suite 1200
Los Angeles, CA 90025-1168

310-820-1500
FAX 310-826-5008
E-Mail: editors@outdoorphotographer.com
Home Page: www.outdoorphotographer.com
Social Media: *Facebook, Twitter*

Steve Warner, Owner
Ibarionex Perello, Associate Editor
Cost: $14.97
Founded in 1965
Mailing list available for rent

20219 PC Photo
Werner Publishing
12121 Wilshire Blvd # 1200
12th Floor
Los Angeles, CA 90025-1168

310-820-1500
FAX 310-826-5008
E-Mail: editors@pcphotomag.com
Home Page: www.wernerpublishing.com

Steve Werner, Owner
Rob Shepherd, Editor

Covers the new desktop darkroom or home photo lab technologies, trends and methods. Designed to stimulate desktop photographers through the listing of new products and technologies.
Cost: $11.97
Founded in 1965

20220 PCPhoto Magazine
Werner Publishing Corporation
12121 Wilshire Blvd
Suite 1200
Los Angeles, CA 90025-1176

310-820-1500
FAX 310-826-5008

E-Mail: rjones@wernerpublishing.com
Home Page: www.wernerpublishing.com

Steve Werner, Owner

Shows you how to enjy the exciting and affordable new world of computers and photography. Features step-by-step instructions, evaluations of the latest equipment, tips from the pros, and more!
Cost: $11.97
Frequency: 9 Issues
Mailing list available for rent

20221 PHOTO Techniques
Preston Publications
6600 W Touhy Ave
Niles, IL 60714-4516

847-647-2900
FAX 847-647-1155
E-Mail: jwhite@phototechmag.com
Home Page: www.prestonpub.com

Tinsley Preston, Owner
Joe White, Editor
Connie Turgon, Marketplace Advertising

PHOTO Techniques offers practical articles that help solve shooting, processing, lighting and printing problems. This is the one magazine that walks you step by step through new techniques. Every other issue contains a digital section. Departments you can rely on include; Master Printing Class, David Vestal's commentary, Photochemistry and more. There are valuable guides to cameras, papers, films, useful accessories and darkroom suppliers.
Cost: $27.99
Founded in 1979
Mailing list available for rent: 30,000 names at $145 per M

20222 Photo District News
Prometheus Global Media
770 Broadway
New York, NY 10003-9595

212-493-4100
FAX 646-654-5368
Home Page: www.prometheusgm.com

Richard D. Beckman, CEO
James A. Finkelstein, Chairman
Madeline Krakowsky, Vice President Circulation
Tracy Brator, Executive Director Creative Service

Delivers the information photographers need to survive in a competitive business from marketing and business advice to legal issues, photographic techniques, new technologies and more.
Frequency: Monthly
Founded in 1980

20223 Photo Insider
123 US Hwy 46 (West)
Fairfield, NJ 07004

973-377-2007
800-631-0300
E-Mail: editor@photoinsider.com
Home Page: www.photoinsider.com
Social Media: *Facebook, Twitter, LinkedIn, YouTube,Foursquare,Flickr,Pint*

Founded in 1947

20224 Photo Lab Management
PLM Publishing
1312 Lincoln Boulevard
Santa Monica, CA 90401-1706

310-451-1344
FAX 310-395-9058
E-Mail: info@plmpublishing.co.uk

Home Page:
www.plmpublishing.co.uk/home.htm

Claire F Irwin, Editor
Paula L McCulloch, Publishing Director
John DH Colley, Marketing Manager

Specifically for those who work in the photo lab business. Contains articles on personnel and technical information.
Cost: $15.00
52 Pages
Frequency: Monthly
Founded in 1979

20225 Photo Marketing
Photo Marketing Association International
2282 Springport Road
Suite F
Jackson, MI 49202

517-788-8100
800-762-9287
FAX 517-788-8371
E-Mail: PMA_Publications@pmai.org
Home Page: www.pmai.org
Social Media: *Facebook, Twitter, LinkedIn*

Ted Fox, CEO
Allen Showalter, President
Mark Klostermeyer, Vice-President
Robert L Hanson, Treasurer

Directed to the marketing and advertising professionals, offers information on marketing photography nationally and internationally.
Cost: $50.00
80 Pages
Frequency: Monthly
Circulation: 12141
Founded in 1924

20226 Photo Metro
1590 Golden Gate Avenue
San Francisco, CA 94115

415-243-9917
FAX 415-243-9919
Home Page: www.photometro.com

Henry Brimmer, Publisher

Image-oriented magazine dedicated to photography, features portfolios, interviews and book reviews. Accepts advertising.
Cost: $20.00
32 Pages
Frequency: Monthly
Founded in 1982

20227 Photo Stock News
1910 35th Road
Pine Lake Farm
Osceola, WI 54020

715-248-3800
FAX 715-248-7394
E-Mail: info@photosource.com
Home Page: www.photosource.com
Social Media: *Facebook, Twitter*

Ron Engh, Editor
Angela Dober, Managing Editor

Contains information of interest to freelance stock photographers, includes the latest industry trends and strategies. Regular issue features include Electronic Highway.
Frequency: 12 per year

20228 PhotoStockNotes
PhotoSource International
1910 35th Ave
Osceola, WI 54020-5602

715-248-3800
800-624-0266
FAX 715-248-7394
E-Mail: info@photosource.com
Home Page: www.photosource.com

Rohn Engh, Owner
Angela Dober, Managing Editor

Trends in the editorial stock photo industry.
Cost: $36.00
3 Pages
Frequency: Monthly
Founded in 1976

20229 Photography Quarterly

Center for Photography at Woodstock
59 Tinker St
Woodstock, NY 12498-1236

845-679-9957
FAX 845-679-6337
E-Mail: info@cpw.org
Home Page: www.cpw.org
Social Media: *Facebook, Twitter*

Ariel Shanberg, Executive Director
Akemi Hiatt, Program Associate
Lawrence Lewis, Operations Manager
Lindsay Stern, Education Coordinator

Founded in 1977, tthe Center for Photography
at Woodstock is a not-for-profit 501 (c)3 artist-centered organization dedicated to supporting artists working in photography and related
media and engaging audiences through opportunities in which creation, discovery and education are made possible.
Cost: $25.00
Frequency: Quarterly
Circulation: 2500
ISSN: 0890-4639
Founded in 1977
Printed in one color on glossy stock

20230 Photoletter

PhotoSource International
1910 35th Ave
Osceola, WI 54020-5602

715-248-3800
800-624-0266
FAX 715-248-7394
E-Mail: info@photosource.com
Home Page: www.photosource.com

Rohn Engh, Owner

A publication covering the world of photography.
Cost: $264.00
4 Pages
Frequency: Weekly

20231 Photopro Magazine

Patch Communications
5211 S Washington Avenue
Titusville, FL 32780-7315

321-268-5010
FAX 321-267-1894

Christi Ashby, Publisher
Suzanne Odistro, Advertising Manager

A professional trade publication covering pho-
tography nationally and internationally.
Cost: $16.95
80 Pages
Frequency: Monthly
Founded in 1990

20232 Picture Magazine

319 Lafayette Street
No 135
New York, NY 10012

212-352-2700
FAX 212-352-2155
E-Mail: picmag@aol.com
Home Page: www.picturemagazine.com

Brock Wylan, Pulisher
Katherine Nguyen, Associate Editor

Phot industry trade publication.

20233 Popular Photography

Hachette Filipacchi Magazines

1633 Broadway
43rd Floor
New York, NY 10019-6708

212-767-6000
800-876-6636
FAX 212-767-5600
E-Mail: popphoto@neodata.com
Home Page: www.popularphotography.com

Alain Lemarchand, CEO
Tami Kelly, Founder
Nate Silver, Founder

A publication offering information and updates
to the photography world.
Cost: $12.00
80 Pages
Frequency: Monthly
ISSN: 0032-4582

20234 Popular Photography & Imaging American PHOTO Magazine

Bonnier Corp
1633 Broadway
Suite 4200
New York, NY 10019-6708

212-767-6000
FAX 212-767-5600
E-Mail: popphoto@hfnm.com
Home Page: www.popphoto.com
Social Media: *Facebook, Twitter, RSS*

Jeffrey Roberts, Publisher
Russell Brock, Associate Editor

Comprehensive coverage of the latest equipment, inspiring images by leading photographers, in-depth how-to articles and
wuthoritative reports. Draws upon top professionals in the field to inform committed readers
who are passionate about pictures.
Mailing list available for rent

20235 Professional Photographer

PPA Publications
229 Peachtree Street NE
International Tower, Suite 2200
Atlanta, GA 30303-1608

404-522-8600
800-786-6277
FAX 404-614-6405
E-Mail: ppa@bframe.com
Home Page: www.ppmag.com

Cameron Bishopp, Senior Manager
Publications
Jeff Kent, Senior Editor
Dana Groves, Marketing Executive

Business magazine for professional photographers. Delivers valuable articles packed with
money making ideas to improve photography
techniques and business skills. Accepts advertising.
Cost: $27.00
80 Pages
Frequency: Monthly
Circulation: 30000
Founded in 1910

20236 Rangefinder Magazine

Rangefinder Publishing
6255 W Sunset Blvd
Los Angeles, CA 90028

323-817-3500
FAX 323-817-1994
Home Page: www.rangefindermag.com

Steve Sheanin, CEO
Bill Hurter, Editor

Includes product and new equipment reviews,
lighting and technical pieces, how-to's, promotion and marketing stories, portraiture tips, accessories and system round-ups, computer
technology, black-and-white shooting, lens reviews, processing techniques
Frequency: Monthly

20237 Select Magazine

Select Worldwide
18-20 Farringdon Lane
1st Floor Clerks Court
London UK EC1R 3AU

4.40207E+12
FAX 4.40207E+12
E-Mail: info@select-magazine.com
Home Page: www.select-magazine.com
Social Media: *Twitter, Blog*

Joe Carbonara, Managing Editor

Select is used worldwide by creative decision
makers in the advertising, graphic design, fashion and retail world.
Frequency: 2x/Year
Circulation: 7500

20238 Shutterbug

1415 Chaffee Drive
Suite #10
Titusville, FL 32780

321-269-3212
FAX 321-225-3146
E-Mail: editorial@shutterbug.com
Home Page: www.shutterbug.net

Ron Leach, Publisher
Eileen Meister, Advertising Sales Manager
Josh Heitsenrether, Marketing Coordinator
George Schaub, Editor
Cost: $17.95
Frequency: Monthly
Founded in 1989

20239 Studio Photography

Cygnus Business Media
1233 Janesville Avenue
Fort Atkinson, WI 53538

631-963-6200
800-547-7377
E-Mail: circulation@spdonline.com
Home Page: www.imaginginfo.com/spd/
Social Media: *RSS*

Liz Vickers, Group Publisher
Alice B Miller, Editor
Jackie Dandoy, Circulation Manager
Ashley Birkholz, Classified Sales
Barry Ancona, List Rental Manager

Formerly Studio Photography & Design. Showcases the hottest portrait, wedding, commercial,
digital, and travel photographers every month.
It is also supported by a selection of supple-
mentary guides, tech tips, tutorials, and product
round-ups.
Frequency: Monthly
Circulation: 50000
Founded in 1936

Trade Shows

20240 ASPRS Annual Conference

American Society for
Photogammetry/Remote Sensing
5410 Grosvenor Lane
Suite 210
Bethesda, MD 20814-2160

301-493-0290
FAX 301-493-0208
E-Mail: asprs@asprs.org
Home Page: www.asprs.org
Social Media: *Facebook, Twitter*

James Plasker, Executive Director
Kimberly A Tiley, Assistant Executive Director
Jesse Winch, Program Manager

Educational sessions and exhibits committed to
advancing knowledge in the mapping sciences
and promoting the responsible application of
photogrammetry, remote sensing and related
technologies.

20241 BIOCOMM
BioCommunications Association
220 Southwind Lane
Hillsborough, NC 27278-7907

919-245-0906
FAX 919-245-0906
E-Mail: office@bca.org
Home Page: www.bca.org
Social Media: *Facebook, Twitter, LinkedIn*

Nancy Hurtgen, Manager Central Office
Susanne Loomis, President
Joseph Kane, Vice-President
James Koepfler, Secretary-Treasurer

Includes a packed program of seminars, workshops, a juried media salon, and commercial exhibits to provide attendees with inspiration and the latest information on visual media in the life sciences.
Frequency: Annual

20242 PMA Annual Convention and Trade Show
3000 Picture Place
Jackson, MI 49201

517-885-5980
FAX 517-788-8371
E-Mail: pma_trade_exhibits@pmai.org
Home Page: www.pmai.org

Rod Folland, Trade Exhibit Sevices Executive
Mary Anne LaMarre, Operations Officer
Ted Fox, Executive Director

Formerly the Photo Marketing Association, PMA is a global forum for photo imaging industry education, networking and introductions of new products and technologies. Includes conferences and meetings of the Association of Professional Color Imagers, the Digital Imaging Marketing Association, the Photo Imaging Education Association, the Professional Picture Framers Association, the Professional Scrapbook Retailers Organization and the Professional School Photographers Association.
24M Attendees
Frequency: February/March

20243 Photohistory
Photographic Historical Society
PO Box 39563
Rochester, NY 14604-9563

585-461-4545

Triennial show and exhibits of cameras and photographic images.
Frequency: October, Rochester

20244 Photovision
Glahe International
PO Box 2460
Germantown, MD 20875-2460

301-515-0012
FAX 301-515-0016

Exhibits of photography equipment, supplies and services.

20245 Professional Photographer American Expo
Professional Photographers of America
229 Peachtree Street NE
International Tower, Suite 2200
Atlanta, GA 30303-1608

404-522-8600
FAX 404-614-6401
Home Page: http://www.ppa.com

Dana Groves, Advertising Director

Devoted to new technologies in the photography field. 300 booths.
5M Attendees
Frequency: July

20246 SPE Regional & National Conference
Society for Photographic Education
2530 Superior Avenue
Suite 403
Cleveland, OH 44114

216-622-2733
FAX 216-622-2712
E-Mail: membership@spenational.org
Home Page: www.spenational.org

Virginia Morrison, Executive Director
Nina Barcellona, Advertising & Publications
Meghan Borato, Registrar
Carla Pasquale, Office/Accounts Manager
1000 Attendees
Frequency: Annual

20247 SPIE Photonics West
1000 20th Street
PO Box 10
Bellingham, WA 38227-0010

360-676-3290
888-504-8171
FAX 360-647-1445
E-Mail: help@spie.org
Home Page: www.SPIE.org
Social Media: *Facebook, Twitter, LinkedIn*

Eugene G Arthurs, Executive Director

Conference proceedings, and SPIE digital library.
14000 Members
Founded in 1955

20248 WPPI Conference & Expo
Wedding & Portrait Photographers International
85 Broad St.
11th Fl.
New York, NY 10004

646-846-4500
FAX 310-846-4770
Home Page:
www.wppionline.com/wppi-show.shtml

Industry event for wedding and portrait photographers and filmmakers.
13000 Attendees

Directories & Databases

20249 Complete Directory of Film & Photo Products
Sutton Family Communications & Publishing Company
920 State Route 54 East
Elmitch, KY 42343

270-276-9500
E-Mail: jlsutton@apex.net

Theresa Sutton, Publisher
Lee Sutton, Editor

Print-out from database of wholesalers, manufacturers, distributors, importers and close-out houses. Database is updated daily to guarantee the most current and up-to-date sources available.
Cost: $34.50
100 Pages

20250 Directory of Free Stock Photography
Infosource Publishing
10 E 39th Street
6th Floor
New York, NY 10016-0111

212-683-8905

Offers valuable information on federal, state and local governments which will provide pho-tographs free of charge for commercial use.
Cost: $14.50
150 Pages
Frequency: Biennial

20251 Green Book: Directory of Natural History and General Stock Photography
AG Editions
41 Union Sq W
Suite 525
New York, NY 10003-3230

212-929-0959
FAX 212-924-4796
E-Mail: info@agpix.com
Home Page: www.ag-editions.com

Ann Guifoyle, Editor
Sharon Powers, Manager

Over 400 photographers and photo agencies that provide stock photography.
Cost: $28.00
368 Pages
Frequency: Biennial
Circulation: 6500
Founded in 1986

20252 Guide to Photography Workshops
Shaw Guides
P.O. Box 231295
New York, NY 10023

212-799-6464
FAX 212-724-9287
E-Mail: info@shawguides.com
Home Page:
http://photoworkshops.shawguides.com

Workshops are profiled that are aimed at amateurs and professionals, including photo tours, studio intensives and specialized instruction.
Cost: $19.95
300 Pages
Frequency: Biennial

20253 Hemingway's Glamour Photographer's Resource Directory
Looking Glass Photography
5975 Keller Road
Saint Louis, MO 63128-3359

314-849-8952

Buyers of glamour photography, including film and video producers are profiled.
Cost: $40.00
200 Pages
Frequency: Biennial
Circulation: 1,000

20254 Industrial Photography: Gold Book Issue
PTN Publishing Company
445 Broadhollow Road
Melville, NY 11747-3669

516-465-7684

Steve Shaw, Editor

A list of manufacturers of photographic equipment and supplies, motion picture laboratories, videotape production facilities, equipment rental services, custom developing services and photographic repair services.
Cost: $5.75
Frequency: Annual December
Circulation: 40,000

20255 Orion Blue Book: Camera
Orion Research Corporation
14555 N Scottsdale Rd
Suite 330
Scottsdale, AZ 85254-3487

480-951-1114
800-844-0759

FAX 480-951-1117
Home Page: www.bluebook.com

Roger Rohrs, Owner

List of manufacturers of cameras.
Frequency: Annual

20256 Photographer's Complete Guide to Exhibition & Sales Spaces
Consultant Press
13 Laight St
#201
New York, NY 10013-2119

212-431-3130

Bob Speirs, Owner

Directory of services and supplies to the industry.
Cost: $24.95
280 Pages

20257 Photographic Trade News: Master Buying Guide
Cygnus Business Media
445 Broad Hollow Road
Melville, NY 11747-3669

631-845-2700
FAX 631-845-2723
Home Page: www.cynuspub.com

Offers a list of manufacturers and distributors of photographic equipment and photography associations.
Frequency: Annual

20258 Photography Forum
CompuServe Information Service
5000 Arlington Centre Blvd
Columbus, OH 43220-5439

614-326-1002
800-848-8199

Offers a forum for the discussion of photography on both the amateur and professional levels.
Frequency: Bulletin Board

20259 Photography RoundTable
GE Information Services
401 N Washington Street
Rockville, MD 20850-1707

301-388-8284

Cathy Ge, Owner

Provides a forum for the exchange of photography tips and information.
Frequency: Bulletin Board

20260 Who's Who in Photographic Management
Photo Marketing Association International
2282 Springport Road
Suite F
Jackson, MI 49202

517-788-8100
800-762-9287
FAX 517-788-8371
Home Page: www.pmai.org
Social Media: *Facebook, Twitter, LinkedIn*

Ted Fox, CEO
Allen Showalter, President
Mark Klostermeyer, Vice-President
Robert L Hanson, Treasurer

Over 15,500 members of the association and manufacturers and suppliers of photographic equipment; also members of the National Association of Photo Equipment Technicians and of the Professional School Photographers of America.
Cost: $75.00
Frequency: Annual

Industry Web Sites

20261 http://gold.greyhouse.com
G.O.L.D Grey House OnLine Databases

Grey House Publishing's online database platform, GOLD, offers Quick Search, Keyword Search and Expert Search for most business sectors including photography markets. The GOLD platform makes finding the information you need quick and easy - whether you're a novice searcher or an experienced database user. All of Grey House's directory products are available for subscription on the GOLD platform.

20262 www.aspp.com
American Society of Picture Professionals

Members are image producers, stock photo agencies, and image users.Provides networking and educational opportunities in the image transaction industry.

20263 www.bca.org
BioCommunications Association

Made up of professionals who create and use the highest quality images and presentations in visual communications media for teaching and documentation in the life sciences and medicine.

20264 www.cpw.org
Center for Photography at Woodstock

Founded in 1977, the Center for Photography at Woodstock is a not-for-profit 501(c)3 artist-centered organization dedicated to supporting artists working in photography and related media and engaging audiences through opportunities in which creation, discovery and education are made possible.

20265 www.editorialphoto.com
Editorial Photographers

Internet discussion forum on business issues with more than 3000 subscribers participating from over 30 countries around the globe. Via the forum photographers exchange information on business practices, copyright and contract concerns. Useful resources such as sample business forms, publisher contract reviews and more can be found here.

20266 www.greyhouse.com
Grey House Publishing

Authoritative reference directories for most business sectors including photography markets. Users can search the online databases with varied search criteria allowing for custom searches by product category, geographic area, sales volume, keyword, subject and more. Full Grey House catalog and online ordering also available.

20267 www.nppa.org
National Press Photographers Association

Sponsors numerous annual television and print media workshops. Conducts annual competition for newsphotos and television newsfilm. Monthly magazine job information bank given to all members.

20268 www.ppa.com
Professional Photographers of America

Portrait, commercial, wedding, industrial and specialized photo- graphers and photographic artists.

20269 www.stockindustry.org
Picture Agency Council of America

The trade association for stock picture agencies in North America.

Associations

20270 ASM International
9639 Kinsman Rd
Materials Park, OH 44073-0002

440-338-5151
800-336-5152
FAX 440-338-4634
E-Mail: memberservices@asminternational.org
Home Page: www.asminternational.org
Social Media: *Facebook, Twitter, LinkedIn*

Nichol Campana, Director of Devlpt &
Operations
Jeane Deatherage, Administrator
Mary A. Jerson, Administrative Assistant
Virginia Shirk, Foundation Ex Assistant
Terry F. Mosier, Managing Director

The society for materials engineers and scientists, a worldwide network dedicated to advancing industry, technology and applications of metals and materials.
35000 Members
Founded in 1913

20271 American Chemistry Council
American Chemistry Council
700 Second St.,NE
Washington, DC 20002

202-249-7000
FAX 202-249-6100
E-Mail: api@plastics.org
Home Page: www.polyurethane.org
Social Media: *Facebook, Twitter, LinkedIn, RSS*

Anne Womack Koltan, VP of Communications
Nacole B. Hinton, Managing Dir. Of Human
Resources
Calvin M. Dooley, President and CEO
Dell Perelman, Chief of staff and General
Counsel
Raymond O'Bryan, CFO & Chief
Administration Officer

API is composed of companies that supply polyurethane resins or chemicals used in polyurethane resins, manufacture polyurethanes, produce machinery used in the manufacture or processing polyurethane, or engage in the business of applying polyurethane products in end use applications. API consists of several groups that focus on critical industry issues such as product stewardship, recycling, communications.
80 Members
Founded in 1977

20272 American Composites Manufacturers Association
3033 Wilson Blvd
Suite 420
Arlington, VA 22201

703-525-0511
FAX 703-525-0743
E-Mail: info@acmanet.org
Home Page: www.acmanet.org
Social Media: *Facebook, Twitter, LinkedIn, RSS*

Tom Dobbins, President
Jeff Craney, Chairman
Kevin Barnett, Chairman-Elect/ Treasurer
Kimberly Howard, Secretary
Leon Garoufalis, Vice Chairman

Presents information on new technology, trends and techniques for manufacturers in the fiberglass and composites industry.
600 Members
Founded in 1979

20273 American Electroplaters and Surface Finishers Society (AESF)
1155 15th Street NW
Suite 500
Washington, DC 20005

202-457-8404
FAX 202-530-0659
E-Mail: info@aesf.org
Home Page: www.aesf.org
Social Media: *Facebook, Twitter, LinkedIn, RSS, Google+*

John Flatley, Executive Director
Courtney Mariette, Bookstore/Education
Melissa Walker, Membership
Carrie Hoffman, Deputy Executive Director

AESF is an international society that advances the science of surface finishing to benefit industry and society through education, information and social involvement, as well as those who provide services, supplies and support to the industry.
5000 Members
Founded in 1909

20274 American Plastics Council
American Chemistry Council
700 Second St.,NE
Washington, DC 20002

202-249-7000
800-243-5790
FAX 202-249-6100
Home Page: www.plastics.org
Social Media: *Facebook, Twitter, LinkedIn, RSS*

Calvin M Dooley, President
Anne Womack Koltan, VP of Communications
Nacole B. Hinton, Managing Dir. Of Human
Resources
Dell Perelman, Chief of staff and General
Counsel
Raymond O'Bryan, CFO & Chief
Administration Officer

Major trade association for the US plastics industry. We demonstrate that plastics are a responsible choice and promote the countless ways that plastics make lives better, healthier and safer.
24 Members

20275 American Society for Plasticulture
526 Brittany Drive
State College, PA 16803

814-238-7045
FAX 814-238-7051
E-Mail: contact@plasticulture.org
Home Page: www.plasticulture.org

Henry Taber, President
William Tietjen, Chairman
Patricia Heuser, Executive Director
Jodi Fleck-Arnold, VP

Promotes research, education and technology application for plastics used in agricultural and horticultural production systems. Hosts a congress every year or so; published proceedings of research presentations.
100 Members
Founded in 1962

20276 Association of Industrial Metallizers, Coaters and Laminators
201 Springs Street
Fort Mill, SC 29715

803-948-9470
FAX 803-948-9471
E-Mail: aimcal@aimcal.org
Home Page: www.aimcal.org

Dan Bemi, President
Danis Roy, Vice President
David Bryant, Treasurer

Craig Sheppard, Executive Director
Dante Ferrari, Directors at Large

Nonprofit trade organization for makers of coated, laminated and metalized papers. AIMCAL serves as the global forum for the flexible metallizing, coating and laminating industry by providing resources, services and information. AIMCAL collects and distributes information to increase industry knowledge, while fostering an environment that builds relationships and a spirit of cooperation between member companies worldwide.
260 Members
Founded in 1970

20277 Association of Postconsumer Plastic Recyclers
1001 G Street, NW
Suite 500 West
Washington, DC 20001

202-316-3046
Home Page: www.plasticsrecycling.org
Social Media: *Facebook, Twitter, LinkedIn*

Steve Alexander, Executive Director
Josh Standish, Technical Director
Dave Cornell, Technical Consultant
Kara Pochiro, Communications Director
Liz Bedard, Rigids Program Director

Represents companies that acquire, reprocess and sell the output of more than 90 percent of the post-consumer plastic processing capacity in North America.
Founded in 1992

20278 Association of Rotational Molders International
800 Roosevelt Rd
Suite C-312
Glen Ellyn, IL 60137

630-942-6589
FAX 630-790-3095
E-Mail: info@rotomolding.org
Home Page: www.rotomolding.org
Social Media: *Facebook, LinkedIn*

Adam Webb, Managing Director
Corey Claussen, President
Dru Laws, Treasurer/Secretary
Conchita Miranda, Vice President
Rick Church, Executive Dircetor

Seeks to increase awareness of roto-molding, exchange technical information, provide education, and standardize production guidelines.
425 Members
Founded in 1976

20279 Berkshire Plastics Network
Downtown Pittsfield Office
66 Allen Street
Pittsfield, MA 01201

413-499-4000
800-438-9572
FAX 413-447-9641
E-Mail: info@berkshirechamber.com
Home Page: www.berkshirechamber.com
Social Media: *Facebook, Twitter, LinkedIn, YouTube*

Linda Gaspardi Febles, Chair
Jonathan Butler, President & CEO
June Roy-Martin, VP Member Services
Lori Gazzillo, Chair-Elect
Chip Moore, Treasurer

A consortium of more than 40 independent companies, representing virtually every discipline in the design and production of molds, components and plastic products.

20280 International Association of Plastics Distribution
6734 W 121st St
Overland Park, KS 66209

913-345-1005
FAX 913-345-1006
E-Mail: iapd@iapd.org
Home Page: www.iapd.org
Social Media: *Facebook, Twitter, LinkedIn, YouTube, Flickr*

Susan E. Avery, Chief Executive Officer
Kevin Short, President
Mitch Opalich, Vice-President
Wayne Gono, Executive Committee Member
Tyler Booth, Member

The International Association of Plastics Distribution, founded in 1956, is an international trade association comprised of companies engaged in the distribution and manufacture of plastics materials. Represented are materials in semi-finished stock shapes, such as sheet, rod, tube, pipe, valves, fittings, film and related products. Members' materials are produced and distributed for a wide variety of engineering and high performance applications.
Founded in 1956

20281 International Molded Fiber Association
355 Lexington Avenue, Floor 15
New York, NY 10017

262-241-0522
FAX 262-241-3766
E-Mail: Alan@IMFA.org
Home Page: www.imfa.org
Social Media: *Facebook, Twitter, LinkedIn*

Cassandra Niesing, Asst. Director
Joseph Grygny, Chairman/ Founder
Hubert Ranger, Founder

Acts as an information center for the molded fiber industry with worldwide membership of users and manufacturers of molded fiber producs. Promotes use of natural and recycled fibers.
Founded in 1997

20282 National Association for PET Container Resources
7310 Turfway Road
Suite 550
Florence, KY 41042

859-372-6635
FAX 707-935-1998
E-Mail: n4mayshun@napcor.com
Home Page: www.napcor.com
Social Media: *Facebook*

Rick Moore, Executive Director
Resa Dimino, Director of Public Policy
Kate Eagles, Project Director

National association for the PET plastic industry. Promotes the use of PET plastic packaging and facilitates the recycling of PET containers.
13 Members
Frequency: Bi-Monthly
Founded in 1987

20283 National Certification In Plastics (NCP)
Society of the Plastics Industry
1667 K St NW
Suite 1000
Washington, DC 20006-1620

202-496-4400
888-627-3660
FAX 202-496-4444
E-Mail: ncp@socplas.org
Home Page: www.certifyme.org

Barbara Darby, Manager Plastics Learning Network
Barry Eisenberg, Director Communications/Marketing

The National Certification in Plastics (NCP) program is a national, voluntary certification examination that tests plastics operations employees' skills and knowledge. The National Certification in Plastics exam tests the knowledge and skill level of plastics operations employees in one of the four major plastics processes - injection molding, extrusion, thermoforming or blow molding.The NCP program is sponsored by the Society of the Plastics Industry.

20284 Plastic Pipe and Fittings Association
800 Roosevelt Rd
Building C, Suite 312
Glen Ellyn, IL 60137

630-858-6540
FAX 630-790-3095
Home Page: www.ppfahome.org
Social Media: *Facebook, RSS*

Richard W Church, Executive Director

The Plastic Pipe and Fittings Association (PPFA) is a national trade association comprised of member companies that manufacture plastic piping, fittings and solvent cements for plumbing and related applications, or supply raw materials, ingredients or machinery for the manufacturing process.
Founded in 1978

20285 Plastic Shipping Container Institute
5614 Connecticut Avenue, N.W
#284
Washington, DC 20015

202-253-4347
FAX 202-330-5092
E-Mail: info@psconline.org
Home Page: www.pscionline.org

David H Baker, General Counsel

The Plastic Shipping Container Institute (PSCI) is an international organization of producers of plastic pails (rigid, plastic shipping containers). The Institute's mission is to promote the common interests of, and the general well being of, the plastic shipping container industry, including consideration of local, state and federal regulatory and legislative issues and international trade issues impacting customers, suppliers and consumers.
Founded in 1967

20286 Plastics Institute of America
University of Massachusetts Lowell, Plastics Engin
Ball Hall Room 204
One University Avenue
Lowell, MA 01854

978-934-2575
FAX 978-934-3089
E-Mail: contactus@plasticsinstitute.org
Home Page: www.plasticsinstitute.org

Aldo Crugnola, Executive Director
Angelo Sabatalo, Chair Elect
Dan Mielcarek, Chair
Nick R. Schott, Secretary/ Director of Training
Marlene Gosling, Treasurer

The Plastics Institute of America is a not-for-profit educational and research organization dedicated to providing service to the plastics industries. We support, foster and guide plastics education and research at all levels to ensure the continued growth of the industry. Since our founding the Institute has held to this mission with ongoing educational programs and resources for skilled workers, professionals and industry executives.
Founded in 1961

20287 Plastics Learning Network
Society of the Plastics Industry

7 North Laurens Street
Greenville, SC 29601

864-239-2939
FAX 864-239-0549
E-Mail: bdarby@socplas.org
Home Page: www.plasticslearning.org

Barbara Darby, Manager Plastics Learning Network
Barry Eisenberg, Director Communications/Marketing

Training opportunities are available for plastics employers and employees through the Plastics Learning Network (PLN) which is sponsored by the Society of the Plastics Industry's (SPI). Courses from qualified instructors are presented as on-site courses tailored to individual work schedules. Courses currently available are Operator Training in Injection Molding and Extrusion. Financial aid is available.
Founded in 2001

20288 Plastics Pipe Institute
105 Decker Court
Suite 825
Irving, TX 75062

469-499-1044
FAX 469-499-1063
E-Mail: info@plasticpipe.org
Home Page: www.plasticpipe.org
Social Media: *Facebook, LinkedIn, YouTube*

Tony Radoszewski, President
Lance MacNevin, Director of Engineering
Sarah Patterson, Technical Director
Dana gecker, Marketing Communications Manager
Vicki Hackett, Office Manager/Executive Assistant

The major trade association representing all segments of the plastics piping industry. As an association, PPI focuses collaborative efforts to accumulate data, concentrate facts and target resources toward advancements in applications and increases in widespread usage.
300 Members
Founded in 1950

20289 Plastics USA
1667 K St.NW.
Suite 1000
Washington, DC 20006

202-974-5200
FAX 202-296-7005
E-Mail: tradeshows@socplas.org
Home Page: www.socplas.org
Social Media: *Facebook, Twitter, LinkedIn*

Adam Krumhans, Trade Show Coordinator
Donald Duncan, President

Plastics USA, sponsored by The Society of the Plastics Industry/SPI, is held once every three years. The three-day trade show and educational program, which is sponsored by the Society of Plastics Engineers, has proven to be an ideal business forum for the North American plastics industry. Last held in Chicago in 2001, Plastics USA attracted over 15,000 attendees and the show featured 435 exhibiting companies occupying 95,000 square feet of exhibit space.
12M Members

20290 Polymer Processing Institute
New Jersey Institute Of Technology
University Heig
Guttenberg Information Technologies Center
Suite 3901
Newark, NJ 07102-1982

973-596-5256
FAX 973-642-4594

E-Mail: info@polymers-ppi.org
Home Page: www.polymers-ppi.com

Ming-Wan Young, Ph.D, President
Costas G. Gogos, Ph.D, Senior
Advisor/President Emeritus
Mariann Pappagallo, Administrative
Consultant
Niloufar Faridi, Ph.D, Senior Technical
Consultant
Linjie Zhu, Ph.D., Technical Director

The Polymer Processing Institute is an independent research corporation headquartered at New Jersey Institute of Technology, Newark, New Jersey. Its mission is to assist industry by implementing the advanced knowledge in the field of polymer technology and related areas through sponsored research, development and education, and to disseminate information via technology transfer.
Founded in 1999

20291 Polystyrene Packaging Council (PSPC)
American Chemistry Council
700 Second St.,NE
Washington, DC 20002

202-249-7000
FAX 202-249-6100
Home Page:
www.polystrenerecyclingnetwork.com
Social Media: *Facebook, Twitter, RSS*

Michael H. Levy, Senior Director
Annie F. Walton, Administrative Assistant
Calvin M. Dooley, President and CEO
Dell Perelman, Chief of staff and General Counsel

PSPC, a business unit of the American Plastics Council, is a nonprofit trade association dedicated to providing accurate information on the environmental impact of polystyrene packaging, including polystyrene recycling programs. PSPC's membership includes manufacturers of polystyrene resin, polystyrene foam and rigid food service packaging.

20292 Polyurethane Manufacturers Association
6737 W Washington Avenue
Suite 1300
Milwaukee, WI 53214

414-431-3094
FAX 414-276-7704
E-Mail: info@pmahome.org
Home Page: www.pmahome.org
Social Media: *Facebook, Twitter, LinkedIn*

Phil Green, President
R. Bruce DeMent, Director
Robert Adkins, Director
Linda Katz, Vice President/ Treasurer
Mike Kochak, Past President

The Polyurethane Manufacturers Association is the trade association of the cast polyurethane elastomer industry, serving processors of polyurethane products, materials and equipment suppliers and independent agents. PMA exchanges and disseminates information on standards, materials, processes and technical matters, in addition to monitoring regulatory and legislative activity affecting the urethane industry.
90 Members
Founded in 1971

20293 SPI
1667 K St NW
Suite 1000
Washington, DC 20006

202-974-5200
888-627-3660
FAX 202-296-7005

Home Page: www.plasticbag.com
Social Media: *Facebook, Twitter, LinkedIn*

Donna Dempsey, Executive Director
Betsy Coleman, Assistant Director
Yvonne Wade, Assistant Manager
Jack Riopelle, Chairman
John Wilhite, Vice Chairman

Members are US and Canadian manufacturers of plastic retail bags. A business unite of the Society of the Plastics Industry, Inc. that actively promotes the growth of the plastic film and bag industry. FBF membership includes companies that are in the plastic bag segment of the industry as well as those in the film sector.
50 Members
Founded in 1937

20294 Society of Plastics Engineers
6 Berskshire Blvd
Suite 306
Bethel, CT 6801

203-775-0471
FAX 203-775-8490
E-Mail: info@4spe.org
Home Page: www.4spe.org
Social Media: *Facebook, Twitter, LinkedIn, RSS*

Susan Oderwald, Executive Director
Dick Cameron, President
Dr. Jaime A. Gomez, Vice President/Treasurer
Monica Verheij, Vice President/Secretary
William De Vos, Chief Executive Officer

The premier source of peer-reviewed technical information for plastics professionals. SPE takes action every day to help individuals and companies in the plastics industry succeed by spreading knowledge, strengthening skills, and promoting plastics.
15000 Members
Founded in 1942

20295 Society of the Plastics Industry
1425 K Street NW
Suite 500
Washington, DC 20005

202-974-5200
FAX 202-296-7005
E-Mail: feedback@plasticindustry.org
Home Page: www.plasticsindustry.org
Social Media: *Facebook, Twitter, LinkedIn, YouTube*

William Cartuaex, President
Fred Daniell, Chair
James Murphy, Vice Chair
Wylie Royce, Treasurer
Tad McGwire, Secretary

Trade association representing one of the largest manufacturing industries in the US. Members represent the entire plastics industry supply chain, including processors, machinery and equipment manufacturers and raw material suppliers. The US plastics industry employs 1.5 million workers and provides $304 billon in annual shipment.
1100 Members
Founded in 1937

20296 Thermoforming Institute
1667 K St NW
Suite 240
Washington, DC 20006-1620

202-974-5200
FAX 202-296-7005
E-Mail: feedback@plasticindustry.org
Home Page: www.thermoforminginstitute.org
Social Media: *Facebook, Twitter, LinkedIn*

William Cartuaex, President
Gene Janders, VP Trade Shows

A business unit of the Society of the Plastics Industry, Incorporated,the Thermoforming In-

stitute is comprised of principal officers of companies or divisions significantly engaged in the manufacture of custom thermoformed products.
1200 Members
Founded in 1937

Newsletters

20297 ACM Monthly
Composite Market Reports
PO Box 137
Gilbert, AZ 85299-0137

480-507-6882
FAX 480-507-6986
E-Mail: info@compositemarketreports.com
Home Page:
www.compositemarketreports.com/

John R. White, Executive Director/CEO
Patricia Ryan, Operations/COO
Russell Harris, Director Financial Services
Wayne Graves, Director Information Systems
Brian Hebert, Marketing/Communications Manager

Reports on market and technology intelligence for materials suppliers.

20298 Additives for Polymers
Reed Elsevier Science Direct
9555 Springboro Pike
Miamisburg, OH 45342

937-865-6800
FAX 937-865-1349
E-Mail: s.barrett@elsevier.com
Home Page: www.elsevier.com

Guy Kitteringhem, Publisher
A Weawer, Editor
S. Barrett, Program Editor
Marike Westra, Director Corporate Relations
Ylann Schemm, Communications Executive

Each issue identifies and details relevant materials and products, new applications, new research and technical developments, newly issued US and British patents.
Frequency: Monthly
Founded in 1887
Printed in on matte stock

20299 Advanced Materials & Composites News
Composites Worldwide
991 C Lomas Santa Fe Drive
PMB469
Solana Beach, CA 92075-2141

858-755-1372
FAX 858-755-5271
E-Mail: compositesnews@adelphia.net
Home Page: www.compositesnews.com

Steve Loud, Editor
Susan Loud, Managing Editor

Focuses on the processes, applications markets, design, international activities and more related to composites and other advanced materials, particularly for civil engineering and construction, but for all markets and structural applications, including aerospace, transportation, and industrial.
Cost: $598.00
Circulation: 1000

20300 Composite Industry Monthly
Composite Market Reports
PO Box 137
Gilbert, AZ 85299

480-507-6882
FAX 480-507-6986

E-Mail: info@compositemarketreports.com
Home Page: www.compositemarketreports.com

William Benjamin, Publisher
John R. White, Executive Director/CEO
Patricia Ryan, Operations/COO
Wayne Graves, Director Information Systems
Russell Harris, Director Financial Services

Market and technology intelligence for users, prime and sub-contractors, universities, government and others.
Cost: $1495.00
Frequency: Monthly
Circulation: 8177
Founded in 1971

20301 Modern Plastics Worldwide

Canon Communications
11444 W Olympic Blvd
Suite 900
Los Angeles, CA 90064-1555

310-445-4200
FAX 310-445-4299
E-Mail: info@modplas.com
Home Page: www.modplas.com/

Charlie Mc Curdy, President
Kevin O'Grady, Publisher

Industry trends and developments. Accepts advertising.
Cost: $150.00
125 Pages
Frequency: Monthly

20302 POF Newsletter

Information Gatekeepers
PO Box 35880
Brighton, MA 02135-1000

617-782-5033
800-323-1088
FAX 617-782-5735
E-Mail: info@igigroup.com
Home Page: www.igigroup.com

Paul Polishuk, CEO
Bev Wilson, Managing Editor
Will Ashley, IT Director/Media Manager

Covers recent developments in the plastic optical fiber industry. Also provides updates on components, systems, applications, standards and a calendar of related events.
Cost: $395.00
Founded in 1977

20303 Plastic Focus

Plastics Connection
PO Box 814
Amherst, MA 01004-0814

413-549-5020
FAX 413-549-9955
Home Page: www.trplastics.com

Michael L Berins, Publisher
Armando Honegger, CEO

Newsletter for buyers, sellers, and users of plastic.
Cost: $275.00
Frequency: Bi-Weekly

20304 Plastics Brief Newsletter

Plastic Marketing News Brief Market Search
2727 North Holland Sylvania Road
Suite A
Toledo, OH 43615-1800

419-535-7899
FAX 419-535-1243
Home Page: www.sagepub.com

James Best, Publisher

For plastic sales and marketing executives. Covers new materials, new applications, market trends, price changes.
Cost: $249.00
Frequency: Monthly

20305 Plastics Machinery & Auxiliaries

Canon Communications
Ste 370
3300 E 1st Ave
Denver, CO 80206-5806

303-321-2322
FAX 303-321-3552
E-Mail: msnyder@pma-magazine.com
Home Page: www.pma-magazine.com/

Merle R. Snyder, Editor
Jamie Quanbeck, Online Editor
Heidi Hill, Managing Editor
Kate Hunley, Associate Editor

Plastics Machinery & Auxiliaries provides readers with a forum for learning about new products and services used in a wide range of plastics processes. Plastics Machinery & Auxiliaries is distributed free of charge to qualified professionals in the plastics processing industry, in the USA and Canada.

20306 Plastics News

Crain Communications
1725 Merriman Rd
Suite 300
Akron, OH 44313-5283

330-836-9180
FAX 330-836-2831
E-Mail: info@crain.com
Home Page: www.crain.com

Robert S Simmons, VP
Linda Whelan, Marketing Manager

Delivers breaking news, features, detailed rankings, economic data and materials pricing to readers around the world.
Frequency: Weekly
Circulation: 60054
Founded in 1989

20307 Plastics Recycling Update

PO Box 42270
Portland, OR 97242-0270

503-233-1305
FAX 503-233-1356
E-Mail: info@resource-recycling.com
Home Page:
www.resource-recycling.com/rr.html
Social Media: Facebook, Twitter, RSS

Jerry Powell, Editor/Publisher
Rick Downing, Advertising Director
Dylan de Thomas, Managing Editor
Mary Lynch, Assistant Publisher
Chad Powell, Director of Research

Resource Recycling is the journal of recycling and composting professionals. Each month, the latest information is provided about post-consumer waste recovery efforts including: collection system assessments; processing developments; markets analyses, and legislative and regulatory reviews. Additional features includes special commodity and regular departments on equipment, recycling and composting programs, association and state activities.
Cost: $58.00
Frequency: Monthly
ISSN: 0147-2429
Founded in 1981
Printed in 2 colors

20308 Plastics Week

Market Search
Laguna Beach, CA

949-212-7400
Home Page: www.plasticsweek.com

James R Best, Publisher
Linda Best, Production Manager
Jim Best, Editor
Jim Best, CEO

Weekly newletters on plastics. Focusing on strategies, markets, technology, recycling and

environmental issues.
Cost: $480.00
6 Pages
Founded in 1961

20309 Polymer Blends, Alloys, and Interpenetrating Polymer Networks

Sage Publications
2455 Teller Rd
Newbury Park, CA 91320-2234

805-499-9774
800-818-7243
FAX 805-499-0871
E-Mail: info@sagepub.com
Home Page: www.sagepub.com

Blaise R Simqu, CEO
David P McCune, Director

Survey and summary of the growing literature and patents in the promising area of plastics technology. Each issue provides new information on chemistry, properties and performance, testing, processing, and application.
Cost: $ 455.00
40 Pages
Frequency: Monthly
ISSN: 0893-6684
Printed in 2 colors on matte stock

20310 Polyurethane Newsletter

Polyurethane Manufacturers Association
1155 Gratiot Ave
Detroit, MI 48207-2732

313-446-6000
E-Mail: info@pmahome.org
Home Page: www.pmahome.org

Mike Katz, President
Jane Sviniski, Executive Director
Jennifer Rzepka, Assoc. Executive Director
Frequency: Quarterly

20311 Rubber and Plastics News

Crain Communications
1725 Merriman Rd
Suite 300
Akron, OH 44313-5283

330-836-9180
FAX 330-836-2831
E-Mail: info@crain.com
Home Page: www.crain.com

Robert S Simmons, VP

It provides news, features, technical and marketing information in print and daily on the Internet to rubber manufacturers, suppliers, consultants and laboratories worldwide.
Frequency: Bi-Weekly
Circulation: 16387

Magazines & Journals

20312 Advanced Composites Monthly

Composite Market Reports
PO Box 137
Gilbert, AZ 85299-0137

480-507-6882
FAX 480-507-6986
E-Mail: info@compositemarketreports.com
Home Page: www.compositemarketreports.com

William Benjamin, President/Editor
Chris Red, Market Research
Cher Benjamin, VP
Joe Benjamin, Office Manager

Provides information to personnel at all levels in the advanced composite manufacturing industry.
10 Pages
Frequency: Monthly
Founded in 1975

20313 Advanced Materials & Processes
ASM International
9639 Kinsman Rd
Materials Park, OH 44073

440-338-5151
800-336-5152
FAX 440-338-4634
E-Mail: memberservices@asminternational.org
Home Page: www.asminternational.org

Joseph M Zion, Publisher
Thomas S. Passek, Managing Editor
Margaret Hunt, Editor-in-Chief

AM&P, the monthly technical magazine from ASM International, is designed to keep readers aware of leading-edge developments and trends in engineering materials - metals and alloys, engineering polymers, advanced ceramics, and composites - and the methods used to select, process, fabricate, test, and characterize them.
Frequency: Monthly
Circulation: 32M
Founded in 1977

20314 Digest of Polymer Developments
STR-Specialized Technology Resources
10 Springborn Ctr
Enfield, CT 06082-4814

860-749-8371
FAX 860-749-8234
E-Mail: strnet@strus.com
Home Page: www.strlab.com

Dennis Jilot, CEO

Covers domestic and international information on new plastics applications, potential growth and market performance, as well as current events in the plastics and allied chemicals industries. Contains a cumulative index by market and another by plastics materials for quick reference.
Cost: $625.00

20315 GraFiber News
Composite Market Reports
PO Box 137
Gilbert, AZ 85299-0137

480-507-6882
FAX 602-507-6986
E-Mail: info@compositemarketreports.com
Home Page: www.compositemarketreports.com

William Benjamin,
President/Publisher/Editor/CEO
Cher Benjamin, VP
Chris Red, Market Research
Joe Benjamin, Office Manager

Provides global coverage of the aerospace industry for advanced material suppliers.
Cost: $2556.25
10 Pages
Frequency: Monthly
ISSN: 1058-9023
Founded in 1973
Printed in 4 colors on matte stock

20316 IAPD Magazine
International Association of Plastics Distribution
6734 W 121st St
Leawood, KS 66209-2002

913-345-1007
FAX 913-345-1006
E-Mail: iapd@iapd.org
Home Page: www.iapd.org

Deborah Hamlin, Manager
Patrick M Foose, Board President
Howard J Natal, VP Board of Directors

Published by the International Association of Plastics Distributors/IAPD, the magazine provides information on the plastics industry with special emphasis on profitability and advances in technology. IAPD fosters the development of the plastics industry through the collection,

production and dissemination of quality information and education, and by being a catalyst in assuring proactive representation in the governmental and public arenas.
Cost: $90.00
68 Pages
Frequency: Monthly
Circulation: 10000
Founded in 1956
Printed in 4 colors on glossy stock

20317 Injection Molding Magazine
Canon Communications
11444 W Olympic Blvd
Ste.900
Los Angeles, CA 90064

310-445-4200
E-Mail: cburke@immnet.com
Home Page: www.immnet.com
Social Media: Facebook, Twitter, LinkedIn

Paul Miller, President/CEO
Stephen Corrick, Publisher/VP/Sales & Marketing
Jeff Tade, Publications Production Manager
Willy Bruijns-Miller, VP Circulation

Custom and captive molding operations, product design, moldmaking, processing information, new materials and equipment, and management issues are the editorial focus.
Cost: $168.57
Frequency: Monthly
Circulation: 37500
Founded in 1999

20318 Journal of Cellular Plastics
Sage Publications
2455 Teller Rd
Newbury Park, CA 91320-2234

805-499-9774
800-818-7243
FAX 805-499-0871
E-Mail: journals@sagepub.com
Home Page: www.sagepub.com

Blaise R Simqu, CEO

A permanent record for international achievements in the science, technology, and economics of cellular plastics. It has been a major source of information on this topic for 35 years. Each issue presents outstanding technical advances in chemistry, formulation, processing, testing, properties, performance, and applications.
Cost: $901.00
96 Pages
Frequency: Bi-Monthly
ISSN: 0021-955X
Printed in 2 colors on matte stock

20319 Journal of Composite Materials
Sage Publications
2455 Teller Rd
Newbury Park, CA 91320-2234

805-499-9774
800-818-7243
FAX 805-499-0871
E-Mail: journals@sagepub.com
Home Page: www.sagepub.com

Blaise R Simqu, CEO
Thomas Hahn, Editor

The leading medium for composite materials technology transfer. Featuring original studies from international material scientists, the journal seeks to emphasize practical applications with no compromise in technical integrity.
Cost: $4576.00
96 Pages
Frequency: Bi-Monthly
ISSN: 0021-9983
Founded in 1965
Printed in 2 colors on matte stock

20320 Journal of Elastomers and Plastics
Sage Publications
2455 Teller Rd
Newbury Park, CA 91320-2234

805-499-9774
800-818-7243
FAX 805-499-0871
E-Mail: journals@sagepub.com
Home Page: www.sagepub.com

Blaise R Simqu, CEO
S. Qutubuddin, Editorial Board

The latest contributions to the technology and properties of elastomers and related polymeric products. Major emphasis is placed on specialty and high performance elastomers. The journal regularly presents current information on the chemistry, processing, properties, and applications of recently developed and improved elastomeric materials.
Cost: $867.00
96 Pages
Frequency: Quarterly
ISSN: 0095-2443
Printed in 2 colors on matte stock

20321 Journal of Materials Engineering and Performance
American Society for Metals
9639 Kinsman Road
Materials Park, OH 44073-0002

440-338-5151
800-336-5152
FAX 440-338-4634
E-Mail: memberservices@asminternational.org
Home Page: www.asminternational.org

Gernant E. Maurer, President
Thomas S. Passek, Managing Director

Peer-reviewed journal that publishes contributions on all aspects of materials selection, design, characterization, processing and performance testing. The scope includes all materials used in engineering applications, those that typically result in components for larger systems.
Cost: $1397.00
Frequency: Bimonthly
Circulation: 645

20322 Journal of Materials Processing
Elsevier ScienceDirect
360 Park Ave S
New York, NY 10010-1736

212-989-5800
888-437-4636
FAX 212-633-3990
E-Mail: journals@sagepub.com
Home Page: www.elsevier.com

Erik Engstrom, CEO
J. Gunasekera, Regional Editor North America

Original papers developments in traditional and innovative processing technologies for metals, polymers, composites, ceramics, and specialty materials. The scope is international and interdisciplinary.
Cost: $5208.00
96 Pages
Frequency: 42 Issues Per Year
ISSN: 0924-0136
Printed in 2 colors on matte stock

20323 Journal of Phase Equilibria
ASM International
9639 Kinsman Rd
Materials Park, OH 44073-0002

440-338-5151
800-336-5152
FAX 440-338-4634
E-Mail: memberservices@asminternational.org
Home Page: www.asminternational.org

Gernant E. Maurer, President
Thomas S. Passek, Managing Director

Peer-reviewed journal that contains basic and applied research results, evaluated phase diagrams, a survey of current literature, and comments or other material pertinent to the previous three areas. The aim is to provide a broad spectrum of information concerning phase equilibria for the materials community.
Cost: $1965.00
Frequency: Bimonthly
Circulation: 305
Mailing list available for rent

20324 Journal of Plastic Film & Sheeting

Sage Publications
2455 Teller Rd
Newbury Park, CA 91320-2234

805-499-9774
800-818-7243
FAX 805-499-0871
E-Mail: journals@sagepub.com
Home Page: www.sagepub.com

Blaise R Simqu, CEO

The Journal of Plastic Film and Sheeting improves communication concerning plastic film and sheeting with major emphasis on the propagation of knowledge which will serve to advance the science and technology of these products and thus better serve industry and the ultimate consumer. The journal reports on the wide variety of advances that are rapidly taking place in the technology of plastic film and sheeting.
Cost: $795.00
88 Pages
Frequency: Quarterly
ISSN: 8756-0879
Printed in 2 colors on matte stock

20325 Journal of Polymer Science

John Wiley & Sons
111 River St
Hoboken, NJ 07030-5790

201-748-6000
FAX 201-748-6088
E-Mail: info@wiley.com
Home Page: www.wiley.com

William J Pesce, CEO

The Journal of Polymer Science provides a continuous forum for the dissemination of thoroughly peer-reviewed, fundamental, international research into the preparation and properties of macromolecules. Part A: Polymer Chemistry is devoted to studies in fundamental organic polymer chemistry and physical organic chemistry. Polymer Physics (Part B) details contemporary research on all aspects of polymer physics.
200 Pages
Frequency: 48 Issues Per Year
ISSN: 0887-624X

20326 Journal of Reinforced Plastics and Composites

Sage Publications
2455 Teller Rd
Newbury Park, CA 91320-2234

805-499-9774
800-818-7243
FAX 805-499-0871
E-Mail: journals@sagepub.com
Home Page: www.sagepub.com

Blaise R Simqu, CEO
Christos C. Chamis, Editorial Board

The Journal of Reinforced Plastics and Composites presents research studies on a broad range of today's reinforced plastics and composites. The journal provides a permanent record of achievements in the science, technology, and economics of reinforced plastics and composites. Reports on special topics are regularly included such as recycling, environmental effects, novel materials, com-

puter-aided design, predictive modelling, and composite materials.
Cost: $4509.00
Frequency: 18 Times Per Year
ISSN: 0731-6844
Founded in 1962

20327 Journal of Thermoplastic Composite Materials

Sage Publications
2455 Teller Rd
Newbury Park, CA 91320-2234

805-499-9774
800-818-7243
FAX 805-499-0871
E-Mail: journals@sagepub.com
Home Page: www.sagepub.com

Blaise R Simqu, CEO
M.N. Ghasemi Jejhad, Associate Editor

An international forum for the presentation of new advances in the technology of this class of materials. Emphasis is given to the fundamental areas of new material development and characterization, design, rheological behavior in short, discontinuous, and continuous fiber systems; process development, manufacturing science, matrix-fiber interphase charaterization; short and long-term performance prediction; and engineering data base assistance for thermoplastic composites.
Cost: $1186.00
96 Pages
Frequency: Bi-Monthly
ISSN: 0892-7057
Printed in 2 colors on matte stock

20328 Journal of Vinyl and Additive Technology

John Wiley & Sons
111 River St
Hoboken, NJ 07030-5790

201-748-6000
FAX 201-748-6088
E-Mail: subinfo@wiley.com
Home Page: www.wiley.com

William J Pesce, CEO
Elliot L. Weinberg, Associate Editor

Journal of Vinyl and Additive Technology is a peer-reviewed technical publication for new work in the fields of polymer modifiers and additives, vinyl polymers and selected review papers. Over half of all papers in JVAT are based on technology of additives and modifiers for all classes of polymers: thermoset polymers and both condensation and addition thermoplastics. Papers on vinyl technology include PVC additives.
Cost: $336.00
Frequency: Quarterly
Circulation: 625
ISSN: 1083-5601
Founded in 1942

20329 Journal of Wide Bandgap Materials

Sage Publications
2455 Teller Rd
Newbury Park, CA 91320-2234

805-499-9774
800-818-7243
FAX 805-499-0871
E-Mail: journals@sagepub.com
Home Page: www.sagepub.com

Blaise R Simqu, CEO
Shojiro Komatsu, Editorial Advisory Board

The Journal of Wide Bandgap Materials is an international journal publishing original peer-reviewed papers on fundamental, experimental and theoretical developments in the science and engineering of wide bandgap materials. The Journal provides a broad-based forum for the publication and sharing of ongoing research and development efforts in the

field of wide bandgap materials.
Cost: $245.00
96 Pages
Frequency: Quarterly
ISSN: 1524-511X
Printed in 2 colors on matte stock

20330 Medical Plastics & Biomaterials

Canon Communications
11444 W Olympic Blvd
Suite 900
Los Angeles, CA 90064-1555

310-445-4200
800-243-9696
FAX 310-445-4299
E-Mail: feedback@cancom.com
Home Page: www.cancom.com

Charlie Mc Curdy, President
Tonna Anuligo, Technical Editor
Kevin O'Grady, Group Publisher

Technical information on the full range of plastics and biomaterials used in manufacturing and packaging medical products.
Cost: $59.00
Frequency: Monthly
Circulation: 61200
Founded in 1978

20331 Modern Plastics

Canon Communications
11444 W Olympic Blvd
Suite 900
Los Angeles, CA 90064-1555

310-445-4200
FAX 310-445-4299
E-Mail: info@modplas.com
Home Page: www.modplas.com/
Social Media: *Facebook, Twitter, LinkedIn*

Charlie Mc Curdy, President
Kevin O'Grady, Publisher

Serves companies utilizing plastics. Developments in resin technology, machinery/processing techniques and additive innovation.
Cost: $59.00
Frequency: Monthly
Circulation: 50300
Founded in 1978

20332 PM/USA Green Sheet

Marketing Handbook
PO Box 243687
Boynton Beach, FL 33424-3687

561-732-5858
FAX 561-732-2607
E-Mail: results@greensheetads.com
Home Page: www.greensheetads.com

Lee Noe, Publisher/Editor
Bob Miller, Technical Director

For those responsible for manufacturing operations.
Cost: $45.00
Frequency: Monthly
Founded in 1972

20333 PMA Polytopics

Polyurethane Manufacturers Association
6737 W Washington Avenue
Suite 1300
Milwaukee, WI 53214

414-431-3094
FAX 414-276-7704
E-Mail: info@pmahome.org
Home Page: www.pmahome.org

Mike Katz, President

The Polyurethane Manufacturers Association is the trade association of the cast polyurethane elastomer industry, serving processors of polyurethane products, materials and equipment suppliers and independent agents. PMA exchanges and disseminates information on standards, materials, processes and technical

matters, in addition to monitoring regulatory and legislative activity affecting the urethane industry.
90 Members
Frequency: Quarterly
Circulation: 250
Founded in 1971

20334 Plastics Business News
Plastics Universe
2727 Holland Sylvania Road
Suite A
Toledo, OH 43615

419-535-7899
FAX 419-535-1243
E-Mail: mberins@javanet.com
Home Page:
www.plasticx.com/pub/plast_11.html

Michael L. Berins, Publisher

A weekly newsletter published for the professionals in the plastic industry. Covers advances in materials and processes, pricing, new applications and markets, international competition, etc.
Cost: $327.00
Frequency: Weekly
Founded in 1972

20335 Plastics Distributor and Fabricator Magazine
KLW Enterprises
PO Box 669
LaGrange, IL 60525-0669

708-588-1845
FAX 708-588-1846
E-Mail: pdfm@plasticsmag.com
Home Page: www.plasticsmag.com

David Whelan, Editor/Publisher
Riia O'Donnell, Associate Editor
Lynette Zeitler, Art Director

Contains industry and products news relevant to the manufacture, distribution and fabrication of plastic rod, sheet and tube.
Founded in 1983
Printed in 4 colors on glossy stock

20336 Plastics Engineering
Society of Plastics Engineers
13 Church Hill Rd
Newtown, CT 06470

203-775-0471
FAX 203-775-8490
E-Mail: info@4spe.org
Home Page: www.4spe.org

Susan Oderwald, Executive Director

Communication to SPE's global audience of plastics professionals about current developments in the industry, technology, and activities of the Society.
Frequency: Monthly
Circulation: 35000

20337 Plastics Focus
Plastics Universe
2727 Holland Sylvania Road
Suite A
Toledo, OH 43615

419-535-7899
FAX 419-535-1243

James Best, CEO

Bi-Monthly updates on new applications and markets for plastics, new polymers, alloys and blends as well as machinery, processing developments, and international competitions and opportunities.
Cost: $295.00

20338 Plastics Hotline
Industry Marketing Solutions

809 Central Avenue
PO Box 893, 2nd Floor
Fort Dodge, IA 50501-1052

888-247-2006
FAX 515-574-2237
E-Mail: steve@plasticshotline.com
Home Page: www.plasticshotline.com
Social Media: *Facebook, Twitter, LinkedIn, YouTube*

Steve Scanlan, Publisher
Jim Rykhus, List Marketing Specialist
Cara Jondle, Tradeshow & Marketing Manager
Jody Kirchoff, Operations

Plastics Hotline has been published since 1983. This weekly periodical continues to be the National Marketplace for Plastic Processors to buy and sell equipment, parts and services.
Cost: $69.00
Frequency: Weekly
Founded in 1990

20339 Plastics Machining & Fabricating
Onsrud Cutter
800 Liberty Dr
Libertyville, IL 60048-2374

847-362-1560
FAX 847-362-5028
E-Mail: info@plasticsmachining.com
Home Page: www.plasticsmachining.com

Harry Urban, Publisher

Plastics Molding & Fabricating is an online technical and management magazine dedicated to the secondary plastics processing industry. It is edited for qualified professionals whose operations include: machining, milling, fabricating, forming, bending, bonding, molding, printing and finishing of plastics. Editorial subjects include case studies, technology updates, trends & news and opinion pieces.
Frequency: Bi-Monthly
Circulation: 15,015

20340 Plastics Technology
Gardner Publications
6915 Valley Ln
Cincinnati, OH 45244-3153

513-527-8800
800-950-8020
FAX 513-527-8801
E-Mail: cnorman@gardnerweb.com
Home Page: www.gardnerweb.com

Rick Kline Sr, CEO
Sherry Fuchs, Managing Editor
Theresa Basso, Production Editor
Joe Grande, Senior Editor

A premier source of technical and business information for plastics processors, each issue reports on technological innovations and developments in the plastics processing market and reaches more than 47,000 processors who depend on authoritative coverage on applying new technology, evaluating products and practical manufacturing.
Frequency: Monthly
Circulation: 47559
Founded in 1928

20341 Polymer Engineering & Science
John Wiley & Sons
111 River St
Hoboken, NJ 07030-5790

201-748-6000
FAX 201-748-6088
E-Mail: subinfo@wiley.com
Home Page: www.wiley.com

William J Pesce, CEO
Alan J Lesser, Associate Editor
Laura Espinet, Journal Production
Kim Thompkins, Advertising/Media

Presents papers of fundamental significance to engineers and scientists interested in polmeric

materials.
Cost: $545.00
Frequency: Monthly
Circulation: 86000
Founded in 1945

Trade Shows

20342 ANTEC
Society of Plastics Engineering
13 Church Hill Road
Newtown, CT 06470

203-775-0471
FAX 203-775-8490
E-Mail: info@4spe.org
Home Page: www.4spe.org

Susan Oderwald, Executive Director

The largest technical conference for the plastics industry

20343 ASM Heat Treating Society Conference & Exposition
ASM International
9639 Kinsman Road
Materials Park, OH 44073

440-385-5151
800-336-5152
FAX 440-338-4634
E-Mail:
pamela.kleinman@asminternational.org
Home Page: www.asminternational.org

Pamela Kleinma, Senior Manager, Events
Kellye Thomas, Exposition Account Manager

Conference and exhibits of heat treating equipment and supplies plus information of interest to metallurgists, manufacturing, research and design technical professionals. 300 exhibitors.
3500 Attendees
Frequency: September, Bi-Annual
Founded in 1974

20344 ASM Materials Science & Technology (MS&T)
ASM International
9639 Kinsman Road
Materials Park, OH 44073-0002

440-338-5151
800-336-5152
FAX 440-338-4634
E-Mail:
pamela.kleinman@asminternational.org
Home Page: www.asminternational.org

Pamela Kleinman, Senior Manager, Events
Kelly Thomas, Exposition Account Manager

Annual event focusing on testing, analysis, characterization and research of materials such as engineered materials, high performance metals, powdered metals, metal forming, surface modification, welding and joining. 350 exhibitors.
4,000 Attendees
Frequency: Annual/October
Founded in 2005

20345 AeroMat Conference and Exposition
ASM International
9639 Kinsman Road
Materials Park, OH 44073-0002

440-385-5151
800-336-5152
FAX 440-338-4634
E-Mail: kim.schaefer@asminternational.org
Home Page: www.asminternational.org

Kim Schaefer, Event Manager
Kelly Thomas, Exposition Account Manager

Conference for Aerospace Meterials Engineers, Structural Engineers and Designers. The annual

event focuses on affordable structures and low-cost manufacturing, titanium alloy technology, advanced intermetallics and refractory metal alloys, materials and processes for space applications, aging systems, high strength steel, NDT evaluation, light alloy technology, welding and joining, and engineering technology. 150 exhibitors.
1500 Attendees
Frequency: Annual/June
Founded in 1984

20346 Association of Industrial Metallizers, Coaters and Laminators
201 Springs Street
Fort Mill, SC 29715

803-948-9470
FAX 803-948-9471
E-Mail: aimcal@aimcal.org
Home Page: www.aimcal.org

Craig Sheppard, Executive Director
Caleb Howe, Communications Manager
Ed Cohen, Technical Consultant
Norma Bryant, Office Manager

Displays relating to coaters and laminators, metallizers and producers of metallized film and or paper on continuous rolls, suppliers of plastic films, papers and adhesives.
Frequency: Annual
Founded in 1970

20347 Health Pack Innovative Technology Conference
1833 Centre Point Circle
Suite 123
Naperville, IL 60563

630-544-5051
FAX 630-544-5055
E-Mail: info@healthpack.net
Home Page: www.healthpack.net

Heather Jayson, Show Coordinator
Steve Bunell, Operations Manager
Curtis Larson, Program Coordinator
John Spitzley, Program Co-Chairman
Angela Holty, Owner

Unique annual conference focuses exclusively on medical device packaging, bringing together medical device manufacturers, packaging materials suppliers and converters, contract packagers, test labs, and other service providers. Food and beverage functions served in the exhibition area provide repeated opportunities for networking between exhibitors, attendees, and conference speakers. Conference location in St. Petersburg, Florida, 20 booths.
100 Attendees
Frequency: March

20348 International Association of Plastics Distributors Convention
6734 W 121st Street
Overland Park, KS 66209

913-345-1005
FAX 913-345-1006
E-Mail: iapd@iapd.org
Home Page: www.iapd.org

Susan E Avery, Executive Director
Patrick M Foose, Board President
Howard J Natal, VP Board of Directors

IAPD is an international trade association comprised of companies engaged in the distribution and manufacture of plastics materials. The annual convention features numerous exhibits that represent a variety of materials in the plastics industry including semi-finished stock shapes, such as sheet, rod, tube, pipe, valves, fittings, film and related products. 76 booths.
450 Attendees
Frequency: September
Founded in 1956

20349 International Plastics Show
1801 K Street NW
Suite 1000
Washington, DC 20006

202-974-5200
FAX 202-296-7005
E-Mail: tradeshows@socplas.org
Home Page: www.socplas.org or www.npe.org

Ken Rietz, President
Brigid Hughes, Director Trade Show Promotions
Adam Krumhansl, Trade Show Coordinator

Containing 2,000 exhibits.
85M+ Attendees
Frequency: June

20350 National Agricultural Plastics Congress
American Society for Plasticulture
526 Brittany Drive
State College, PA 16803

814-238-7045
FAX 814-238-7051
E-Mail: info@plasticulture.org
Home Page: www.plasticulture.org

William Tietjen, Chairman Plastics Congress
Henry Taber, President
Jodi Fleck-Arnold, VP
Edward Carey, Secretary/Treasurer
Patricia Heuser, Executive Director

Plastic products used in agriculture. 15-25 booths.
150 Attendees
Frequency: March/November

20351 National Plastics Exposition
Society of the Plastics Industry
1667 K Street NW
Suite 1000
Washington, DC 20006

202-974-5200
FAX 202-296-7005
E-Mail: feedback@plasticsindustry.org
Home Page: www.plasticsindustry.org
Social Media: *Facebook, Twitter, LinkedIn*

William R Carteaux, President/CEO
Jon Kurrie, VP Government Affairs/Public Policy
Al Damico, Executive VP

This expo features exhibits of molded, extruded, fabricated, laminated and calendered plastics, raw materials, machinery and laboratory equipment for the industry.
75M Attendees
Frequency: June

20352 PLASTEC East Trade Show
Canon Communications
11444 West Olympic Boulevard
Los Angeles, CA 90064-1549

310-445-4200
FAX 310-996-9499
E-Mail: register@cancom.com
Home Page: www.plasteceast.com

Diane O'Connor, Trade Show Director
Shannon Cleghorn, Customer & Media Coordinator

Five co-located shows, 1,750 plastic exhibitors. The Trade Show takes place every 2 years, in odd years.
32000 Attendees

20353 PLASTEC West Trade Show
Canon Communications
2901 28th Street
Suite 100
Santa Monica, CA 90405

310-445-4200
FAX 310-996-9499
E-Mail: Tssalesadmin@ubm.com

Home Page: www.plastecwest.com
Social Media: *Twitter*

Diane O'Connor, Trade Show Director
Jane Sullivan, Exhibit Contact

Five co-located shows, 3,000 exhibitors, trade show features plastics, packaging and manufacturing industries.
45000 Attendees
Frequency: January/February

20354 PMA Annual Meeting
Polyurethane Manufacturers Association
6737 W Washington Avenue
Suite 1300
Milwaukee, WI 53214

414-431-3094
FAX 414-276-7704
E-Mail: info@pmahome.org
Home Page: www.pmahome.org

Mike Katz, President

The Polyurethane Manufacturers Association is the trade association of the cast polyurethane elastomer industry, serving processors of polyurethane products, materials and equipment suppliers and independent agents. PMA exchanges and disseminates information on standards, materials, processes and technical matters, in addition to monitoring regulatory and legislative activity affecting the urethane industry.

20355 POLYCON
International Cast Polymer Association
3033 Wilson Blvd
Suite 4200
Arlington, VA 22201

703-525-0511
FAX 703-525-0743
E-Mail: icpa@icpa-hq-org
Home Page: www.icpa-hq.org

Jeanne McCormack, Director Conferences & Meetings
Elizabeth Cookson, Mgr Conferences & Program Dvlpmt
Debbie Cannon, President

The program includes three days of in-depth educational programming, exhibits, a product showcase, and more. Sponsored annually by the International Cast Polymer Association/ICPA, POLYCON is the largest convention and trade show for the cast polymer industry. Over 800 industry professionals attend the convention to network, attend educational sessions, and visit with over 70 exhibitors.
Frequency: Annual

20356 PPI Annual Meeting
Plastics Pipe Institute
105 Decker Court
Suite 2
Irving, TX 75062

469-499-1044
FAX 469-499-1063
E-Mail: info@plasticpipe.org
Home Page: www.plasticpipe.org

Tony Radoszewski, Executive Director
Camille Rubeiz, Director Engineering
Stephen Boros, Technical Director
Frequency: May

20357 Polyurethane Manufacturers Association Meeting
Polyurethane Manufacturers Association
6737 W Washington Avenue
Suite 1300
Milwaukee, WI 53214

414-431-3094
FAX 414-276-7704

E-Mail: info@pmahome.org
Home Page: www.pmahome.org

Payam Towfigh, President
Jane Sviniski, Executive Director
Jennifer Rzepka, Assoc. Executive Director
150 Attendees
Frequency: Annual/April

20358 Polyurethanes Technical Conference
Alliance for the Polyurethanes Industry
700 Second St.,NE
Arlington, VA 22209

703-741-5103
FAX 703-741-5655
E-Mail: api@plastics.org
Home Page: www.polyurethane.org

Richard E Mericle, Executive Director
Kaye Robinson, Conference Planning
Committee

Semi-annual trade show for the polyurethanes
industry in North America. International technical conference and exposition will feature
technical and industry issues sessions, poster
session and exhibits.
Frequency: September/October
Founded in 1977

20359 World Adhesive Conference & Expo
Adhesive & Sealant Council
7101 Wisconsin Avenue
Suite 990
Bethesda, MD 20814

301-986-9700
FAX 301-986-9795
E-Mail: bob.willis@ascouncil.org
Home Page: www.ascouncil.org
Social Media: *Twitter, LinkedIn, RSS*

Bob Willis, Senior Manager
Conventions/Meetings
Glenn E Frommer, President
C.Russell Thompson Jr, President and CEO
Christine A Byrant, Director
Frequency: April

Directories & Databases

**20360 American Mold Builders
Association/AMBA Membership
Directory**
American Mold Builders Association
3601 Algonquin Rd
Suite 207
Rolling Meadows, IL 60008-3136

847-222-9402
FAX 630-980-9714
E-Mail: info@amba.org
Home Page: www.amba.org or
amba.org/adOppGrid.php

Melissa Millhuff, Executive Director

AMBA represents nearly 325 member companies comprised of approximately 9,000 employees and representing just over $2 billion in
annual tooling sales. Members span 35 states
with 12 chapter affiliations. AMBA member
companies serve original equipment manufacturers in every industry including automotive,
medical, electronics/electrical, toys, recreation
and sporting goods, building and construction,
lawn and garden, consumer, and industrial.
Free to members and available to others for
$50.00.
Cost: $50.00
Frequency: Annual
Circulation: 2,200
Founded in 1973

**20361 Handbook of Plastic Compounds,
Elastomers and Resins**
John Wiley & Sons
10475 Crosspoint Blvd
Indianapolis, IN 46256-3386

317-572-3000
FAX 317-572-4000
Home Page: www.wiley.com

Lou Peragallo, Manager
Michael Ash, Editor

Directory of services and supplies to the industry. A complete, accurate, and current data
source on primary material tradename products
for the rubber and plastic industries. This handbook gives short, easy-to-find information on
over 15,000 chemical trademark products currently sold throughout the world.
Cost: $385.00
ISBN: 0-471188-30-1

20362 IAPD Membership Directory
International Association of Plastics
Distribution
6734 W 121st St
Overland Park, KS 66209-2002

913-345-1005
FAX 913-345-1006
E-Mail: iapd@iapd.org
Home Page: www.iapd.org

Susan Avery, Executive Director

The IAPD Membership Directory lists almost
400 companies by membership category with
their locations, phone and fax numbers, key
personnel and plastics products. There is also a
listing of companies by geographical location,
as well as an alphabetical listing of individuals
from the various companies.
Cost: $150.00
Frequency: Annual May

20363 Plastics Business News
Plastics Universe
2727 Holland Sylvania Road
Suite A
Toledo, OH 43615

419-535-7899
FAX 419-535-1243
E-Mail: mberins@javanet.com
Home Page:
www.plasticx.com/pub/plast_11.html

Michael L. Berins, Publisher

Offers information on the plastics industry,
forecasts, mergers, and new product develop-
ments.
Cost: $327.00
Frequency: Weekly
Founded in 1972

20364 Plastics Compounding Redbook
Advanstar Communications
2501 Colorado Avenue
Suite 280
Santa Monica, CA 90404

310-857-7500
FAX 310-857-7510
E-Mail: info@advanstar.com
Home Page: www.advanstar.com

Joseph Loggia, CEO
Chris DeMoulin, VP
Susannah George, Marketing Director

List of suppliers — over 1,000 — of resin, additives, fillers and other materials compounding equipment and services to the plastic
industry.
Cost: $150.00
280 Pages
Frequency: Annual
Circulation: 12,000

20365 Plastics Digest/PA Index
IHS/Information Handling Services
15 Inverness Way E
Englewood, CO 80112-5710

303-736-3000
800-525-7052
FAX 303-736-3150
Home Page: www.ihsenergy.com
Social Media: *Facebook, Twitter, LinkedIn*

Jerre Stead, CEO
Michael Armstrong, Director

A list of over 200 manufacturers and suppliers
of plastics materials are listed in this comprehensive directory. CD format only.
Cost: $768.00

**20366 Plastics Engineering Handbook of the
Society of the Plastics Industry**
Society of the Plastics Industry
1667 K St NW
Suite 1000
Washington, DC 20006-1620

202-974-5200
800-541-0736
FAX 202-296-7005
E-Mail: feedback@plasticsindustry.org
Home Page: www.plasticsindustry.org
Social Media: *Facebook, Twitter, LinkedIn*

William Cartuaex, President
Jon Kurrie, VP Government Affairs/Public
Policy
Al Damico, Executive VP

Educational groups, associations, consultants
and providers of technical data, literature and
materials to the reinforced plastics industry.
Cost: $175.00

20367 Plastics News Datebook Online
Crain Communications
1725 Merriman Rd
Suite 300
Akron, OH 44313-5283

330-836-9180
FAX 330-836-2831
E-Mail: info@crain.com
Home Page: www.crain.com

Robert S Simmons, VP
Linda Whelan, Marketing Manager

This business to business buyers guide highlights products and services such as extruders,
sheet manufacturers, film, rod and sheet suppliers, processors, roto-molding equipment, injection molding, polyurethane machinery, resin
producers and compounders. The Plastics News
Online Directory helps you, as a BtoB buyer,
research products and make smart buying
decisions.

20368 Plastics News Web Watch Directory
Crain Communications
1725 Merriman Rd
Suite 300
Akron, OH 44313-9006

330-836-9180
800-678-9595
FAX 330-836-2831
E-Mail: editorial@plasticsnews.com
Home Page: www.crain.com

Robert S Simmons, VP
Anthony Eagan, Publisher

Contains processors, primary equipment, auxiliary equipment, resin suppliers, compounders,
recyclers, tooling and molds, design and
prototyping, trade associations, industry
services and more.
154 Pages
ISSN: 1042-802X
Printed in 4 colors on glossy stock

20369 Rauch Guide to the US Adhesives & Sealants Industry

Grey House Publishing
4919 Route 22
PO Box 56
Amenia, NY 12501

518-789-8700
800-562-2139
FAX 845-373-6390
E-Mail: books@greyhouse.com
Home Page: www.greyhouse.com
Social Media: *Facebook, Twitter*

Leslie Mackenzie, Publisher
Richard Gottlieb, Editor

Contains information providing data on industry economics, government regulations, technology, raw materials, products and markets in addition to industry activities, organizations and sources of information on trade shows, exhibits, professional associations and societies. Provides unique profiles of more than 700 suppliers.
Cost: $595.00
361 Pages
ISBN: 1-592371-29-9
Founded in 1981

20370 Rauch Guide to the US Plastics Industry

Grey House Publishing
4919 Route 22
PO Box 56
Amenia, NY 12501-0056

518-789-8700
800-562-2139
FAX 518-789-0556
E-Mail: books@greyhouse.com
Home Page: www.greyhouse.com
Social Media: *Facebook, Twitter*

Leslie Mackenzie, Publisher
Richard Gottlieb, Editor

Offers comprehensive data on the $182 billion industry, the Guide is a highly valued industry resource covering the economics, processes, materials, sales and activities of leading U.S. plastics producers. Additional features include a personnel index with key industry executives and an enhanced company listing containing detailed information indicating subsidiary, division or parent information, Internet site addresses, E-mail addresses, and key contacts.
Cost: $595.00
646 Pages
ISBN: 1-592371-28-0
Founded in 1981

20371 Who's Who in World Petrochemicals and Plastics

Reed Business Information
3355 West Alabama
Suite 700
Houston, TX 77098

713-523-2613
888-525-3255
FAX 713-525-2659
E-Mail: csc@icis.com
Home Page: www.icis.com/

Jamie Reed, Owner
Andy Soloman, Global Editorial Director
Chrissy Salisbury, Manager

More than 9,600 individuals from 3,700 petrochemical and plastic companies worldwide.
Cost: $276.00
Frequency: Annual November
Circulation: 1,500

20372 Worldwide Petrochemical Directory
PennWell Directories

1455 West Loop South
Suite 400
Houston, TX 77027-3005

713-621-9720
800-736-6935
FAX 713-963-6285
E-Mail: billw@pennwell.com
Home Page: www.pennwell.com

Bob Tippee, Editor
David Nakamura, Refining/Petrochemical Editor
Guntis Moritis, Production Editor
Tim Sullivant, Manager

2,980 operative petrochemical plants with 8,675 personnel in 4,320 locations are listed with their parent companies, plant locations, products produced, capacities, and current production volumes if available. Approximately 9,340 locations having 13,145 Email and 4,330 Website addresses are listed for engineering, construction, manufacturing, supply and service companies with a description of products and services provided. Included are 350 cross-references reflecting mergers and acquisitions.
Cost: $150.00
Frequency: Annual November
Circulation: 3,500
Mailing list available for rent

Industry Web Sites

20373 http://gold.greyhouse.com
G.O.L.D Grey House OnLine Databases

Grey House Publishing's online database platform, GOLD, offers Quick Search, Keyword Search and Expert Search for most business sectors including plastics markets. The GOLD platform makes finding the information you need quick and easy - whether you're a novice searcher or an experienced database user. All of Grey House's directory products are available for subscription on the GOLD platform.

20374 www.aimcal.org
Association of Industrial Metallizers, Coaters
and Laminators

Packaging equipment.

20375 www.americanmanufacturers.com
AmericanManufacturers.com

Product exchanges and electronic requests for quotes.

20376 www.apexq.com
American Plastics Exchange

Molders and extruders can review data sheets and bid for prime virgin resin.

20377 www.ariba.com
Ariba

Allows buyers and sellers to find trading partners and negotiate prices.

20378 www.assettrade.com
AssetTrade.com

Used equipment and machinery.

20379 www.berkshireplastics.org
Berkshire Plastics Network

Consortium of more than 40 independent companies, representing virtually every discipline in the design and production of molds, components and plastics products.

20380 www.chematch.com
CheMatch.com

Buyers and sellers exchange for plastic materials.

20381 www.chemconnect.com
ChemConnect

Buyers and sellers can find partners and negotiate price.

20382 www.chemcross.com
ChemCross

Online trading offered by Asian producers of plastics and chemicals.

20383 www.commerxplasticsnet.com
Commerx

Online training.

20384 www.dovebid.com
DoveBid

Bidding on used equipment, as well as capital assets.

20385 www.e-resin.com
e-Resin.com

Direct negotiation with suppliers for additives, materials and finished products.

20386 www.efodia.com
eFodia

Online purchasing of chemical processing, compounding and additives, other materials.

20387 www.elastomersolutions.com
ElastomerSolutions

Online trading for the elastomers industry.

20388 www.ewinwin.com
eWinWin

Associations, cooperatives, buyers and suppliers can employ an aggregation system for lower priced purchases.

20389 www.freemarkets.com
FreeMarkets

Reverse auction in which suppliers submit online bids for commodities, services, parts and materials.

20390 www.getplastic.com
GetPlastic.com

Materials designed for those who purchase resins.

20391 www.greyhouse.com
Grey House Publishing

Authoritative reference directories for most business sectors including plastics markets. Users can search the online databases with varied search criteria allowing for custom searches by product category, geographic area, sales volume, keyword, subject and more. Full Grey House catalog and online ordering also available.

20392 www.i2i.com
Industry to Industry

Buying and selling of plastics.

20393 www.justforplastics.com
Justforplastics.com

Marketplace for plastic services, tooling, equipment and products.

20394 www.mfgconnect.com
Mfgconnect.com

Exchange product development information and CAD files prior to bidding on contracts.

20395 www.napcor.com
National Association for Pet Container Resources

National trade association which promotes the recycling of pet con-tainers and the usage of pet plastic.

20396 www.omnexus.com
Omnexus Corporation
Trading in equipment, services, materials and tooling for central injection and blow molders.

20397 www.onechem.com
OneChem
Software applications and transactional store-front for global commercial transactions in plastics and chemicals.

20398 www.packagingexchange.com
PackagingExchange.Com
Storefront transactions and online auction for packaging products, equipment and materials.

20399 www.packexpo.com
Packexpo.com
Source for packaging materials, machinery, parts and services.

20400 www.packtion.com
Packtion Corporation
Informational tools and exchange opportunites for packaging services.

20401 www.plasticlink.com
PlasticLink.Com
Materials, equipment and products for thermoformers, extruders and semifinished shape processors.

20402 www.plasticpipe.org
Plastics Pipe Institute
The major trade association representing all segments of the plastics piping industry. As an association, PPI focuses collaborative efforts to accumulate data, concentrate facts and target resources toward advancements in applications and increases in widespread usage.

20403 www.plastics.org
American Plastics Council
Gateway to plastics on the internet.

20404 www.plasticsandchemicals.com
Plasticsandchemicals.com
Bid-based marketplace.

20405 www.plasticsbin.com
NetVendor
Trading in scrap resin and surplus plastic inventory.

20406 www.plasticsindustry.org
Society of the Plastics Industry
The Society of the Plastics Industry is the trade association representing one of the largest manufacturing industries in the US. SPI's 1,500 members represent the entire plastics industry supply chain, including processors, machinery and equipment manufacturers and raw material suppliers. The US plastics industry employs 1.5 million workers and provides $304 billon in annual shipment.

20407 www.plasticsrecycling.org
AssociationOd Postconsumer Plastic Recyclers
Represents companies that acquire, reprocess and sell the output of more than 90 percent of the post-consumer plastic processing capacity in North America.

20408 www.plasticulture.com
American Society for Plasticulture
Promotes research, education, and technology application for plastics used in agricultural and horticultural production systems. Hosts a con-gress every year or so; published proceedings of research presentations.

20409 www.pmahome.org
Polyurethane Manufacturers Association
The Polyurethane Manufacturers Association is the trade association of the cast polyurethane elastomer industry, serving processors of polyurethane products, materials and equipment suppliers and independent agents. PMA exchanges and disseminates information on standards, materials, processes and technical matters, in addition to monitoring regulatory and legislative activity affecting the urethane industry.

20410 www.polymeradditives.com
PolymerAdditives.com
Purchase brand-name polymer additives online.

20411 www.polymersite.com
PolymerSite.com/PolySort
Exchange site for resins and compounds. Flexible negotiations in a sealed bid environment.

20412 www.polyurethane.org
Alliance for the Polyurethanes Industry
For companies that supply polyurethane resins or chemicals used in polyurethane resins, manufacture polyurethanes, produce machinery used in the manufacture or processing polyurethane, or engage in the business of applying polyurethane products in end use applications.

20413 www.primeadvantage.com
Prime Advantage Corporation
Buying consortium offers volume discounts on resins and components.

20414 www.sorcity.com
Sorcity.com
Reverse auction in which buyer files request for quote and supplier bids.

20415 www.supplierone.com
SupplierOne.com
Supply chain management and e-marketplace for manufactured components.

20416 www.thedock.com
The Dock Exchange
Buying and selling of equipment online.

20417 www.theplasticsexchange.com
ThePlasticsExchange.com
Trading in commodity prime resins.

20418 www.worldwideplastics.com
TheBuyersNet.com
Catalog of semifinished materials.

Associations

20419 American Society of Plumbing Engineers
6400 Shafer Ct.
Suite 350
Rosemont, IL 60018-4914

847-296-0002
FAX 847-296-2963
E-Mail: info@aspe.org
Home Page: www.aspe.org

Billy Smith, Executive Director/CEO, Secretary
Mitch Clemente, President
David E. DeBord, Vice President, Education
Chris Graham, Treasurer
Scott Steindler, Vice President, Technical

The American Society of Plumbing Engineers (ASPE) is a professional organization dedicated to the advancement of the science of plumbing engineering, to the professional growth and advancement of its members and the health, welfare and safety of the public. The Society disseminates technical data and information, sponsors activities that facilitate interaction with fellow professionals, and, through research and education, expands the base of knowledge of the plumbing engineering industry.
6000+ Members
Founded in 1964

20420 American Society of Sanitary Engineering
18927 Hickory Creek Dr.
Suite 220
Mokena, IL 60448

708-995-3019
FAX 708-479-6139
Home Page: www.asse-plumbing.org

John F. Flader, Treasurer
Douglas A. Marian, International President
Scott Hamilton, Executive Director
Michele Kilpatrick, Administrative asst.
Dana Colombo, Vice President

Members are from all segments of the plumbing industry, including contractors, engineers, inspectors, journeymen, apprentices and others who are involved in various segments of the industry. Provides information, an opportunity to exchange ideas, solve problems and offers a forum where all sides can express their views.
300 Members
Founded in 1906

20421 American Supply Association
1200 N. Arlington Heights Rd.
Suite 150
Itasca, IL 60143

630-467-0000
FAX 630-467-0001
E-Mail: info@asa.net
Home Page: www.asa.net
Social Media: *Facebook, Twitter, LinkedIn*

Michael Adelizzi, Executive VP, Secretary
John Strong, Chairman
Rick Fantham, President
Steve Cook, Treasurer
Tim Milford, President-Elect

ASA is a not-for-profit national organization serving wholesale distributors and their suppliers in the plumbing, heating, cooling and industrial pipe, valves, and fittings industries. ASA provides a forum for trading partners from around the country to discuss critical issues facing them, and offers a menu of products and services uniquely geared to their needs.
800 Members
Founded in 1969

20422 International Association of Plumbing and Mechanical Officials (IAPMO)
4755 E Philadelphia Street
Ontario, CA 91761

909-472-4100
800-854-2676
FAX 909-472-4150
E-Mail: info@iapmo.org
Home Page: www.iapmo.org
Social Media: *Facebook, Twitter, LinkedIn*

Bruce Pfeiffer, President
DJ Nunez, Vice Pesident
Russ Chaney, CEO
David Straub, Treasurer/ Secretary
Neil Bogatz, General counsel

IAPMO has been protecting the public's health and safety for more than eighty years by working in concert with government and industry to implement comprehensive plumbing and mechanical systems around the world.
5000 Members
Founded in 1926

20423 Manufacturers Standardization Society
127 Park St NE
Vienna, VA 22180-4602

703-281-6613
FAX 703-281-6671
E-Mail: info@msshq.org
Home Page: www.mss-hq.org

Robert O'Neill, Executive Director

The Manufacturers Standardization Society (MSS) of the Valve and Fittings Industry is a non-profit technical association organized for development and improvement of industry, national and international codes and standards for valves, valve actuators, valve modifications, pipe fittings, pipe hangers, flanges, and associated seals.
Cost: $1800.00
Founded in 1924

20424 Midwest Distributors Association (MWDA)
1200 N. Arlington Heights Rd.
Suite 150
Itasca, IL 60143

630-467-0000
FAX 312-464-0091
E-Mail: info@mwda.net
Home Page: www.mwda.net

Dave Poteete, President
Ryan Curry, Secretary/ Treasurer
Todd Restel, President-Elect
Chris Murin, Executive Director
John Bennerotte, Director

The mission of the MWDA is to professionally promote the improvement of the industry by providing quality programs, educational and training opportunities to improve operational efficiency and marketing effectiveness, and by facilitating the exchange of ideas and information throughout the distribution channel. The MWDA serves the states of Illinois, Iowa, Kansas, Minnesota, Missouri, Nebraska, North Dakota, South Dakota, Upper Michigan and Wisconsin.
110 Members
Founded in 1942

20425 National Kitchen and Bath Association
687 Willow Grove St
Hackettstown, NJ 07840

908-850-1206
800-843-6522
FAX 908-852-1695
E-Mail: feedback@nkba.org
Home Page: www.nkba.org

Social Media: *Facebook, Twitter, LinkedIn, Pinterest*

Maria Stapperfenne, President
Mark Kovich, President-Elect
Denise M. Dick, Vice President
Blue Arnold, Secretary
Lorenzo Marquez, Treasurer

The NKBA enhances the success of its members in the kitchen and bath industry through networking, education, certification, marketing and business tools, leadership opportunities, and the annual Kitchen/Bath Industry Show.
40000 Members
Founded in 1963

20426 North Central Wholesalers Association/NCWA
7107 Crossroads Blvd
Suite 106
Brentwood, TN 37027

615-371-5004
FAX 615-371-5444
E-Mail: terry@northcentralwholesalers.org
Home Page: www.northcentralwholesalers.org

Howard Wolff, President
Jock Castoldi, Treasurer
Russ Visner, Director

The NCWA serves wholesale distributors of plumbing, heating, cooling and piping products in Indiana, Michigan, Ohio, Western Pennsylvania and West Virginia, sponsoring educational conferences and offering networking opportunities. During the year NCWA offers its members seminars, workshops, newsletters, industry statistics, an annual regional convention and other traditional trade association programs.
75 Members
Founded in 2003

20427 Pacific Southwest Distributors Association
7345 E Evans Rd
No. 7
Scottsdale, AZ 85260

480-991-5703
FAX 480-991-5704
E-Mail: rbluth@qwestoffice.net
Home Page: www.thepsda.info

Bob Bluth, Owner
Michael Adelizzi, Executive Vice President

Made up of distributors of heating, cooling and plumbing supplies.
Founded in 1946

20428 Plastic Pipe and Fittings Association
800 Roosevelt Rd
Building C, Suite 312
Glen Ellyn, IL 60137

630-858-6540
FAX 630-790-3095
Home Page: www.ppfahome.org
Social Media: *Facebook, RSS*

Richard W Church, Executive Director

The Plastic Pipe and Fittings Association (PPFA) is a national trade association of member companies that manufacture plastic piping, fittings and solvent cements for plumbing and related applications, and supply raw materials, ingredients or machinery for the manufacturing process. The PPFA provides relevant information needed to properly design, specify and install plastic piping systems, promoting an understanding of the environmental impact and benefits of thermoplastic piping products.
78 Members
Founded in 1978

20429 Plumbing Heating Cooling Contractors Association
180 South Washington Street
Suite 100
Falls Church, VA 22046

703-237-8100
800-533-7694
FAX 703-237-7442
E-Mail: naphcc@naphcc.org
Home Page: www.phccweb.org
Social Media: *Facebook, Twitter, LinkedIn, RSS*

Kevin Tindall, President-Elect
Elicia Magruder, Vice President of Communications
Michael Copp, Executive Vice President
Steven A. Rivers, President
Laurie Crigler, Secretary

National organization designed for suppliers of equipment, supplies and services for the plumbing, heating and cooling industries.
3700 Members
Founded in 1883

20430 Plumbing Manufacturers International
1921 Rohlwing Rd
Unit G
Rolling Meadows, IL 60008

847-481-5500
FAX 847-481-5501
E-Mail: bhiggens@pmihome.org
Home Page: www.pmihome.org
Social Media: *Facebook, Twitter, LinkedIn, YouTube, Google+*

Fernando Fernandez, President
Paul Patton, Vice- President
Barbara C. Higgens, CEO/Executive Director
Peter Jahrling, Treasurer
Tim Kilbane, Immediate Past President

The Plumbing Manufacturers Institute (PMI) is the trade association of plumbing products manufacturers. The Institute functions as a sounding board for its members, a source for industry and market information, and as a coordinating and decision-making body for dealing with industry issues. It is active in many arenas as it helps develop and maintain standards and codes, and works closely with government agencies at all levels - federal, state and local.
44 Members
Founded in 1975

20431 Plumbing and Drainage Institute
800 Turnpike Street
Suite 300
North Andover, MA 01845

978-557-0720
800-589-8956
FAX 978-557-0721
E-Mail: pdi@PDIonline.org
Home Page: www.pdionline.org

William Whitehead, Executive Director

An association of manufacturers of engineered plumbing products. Our members and licensees make products such as; flood drains, roof drains, sanitary floor drains, cleanouts, water hammer arresters, swimming pool drains, backwater valves, grease interceptors, fixture supports and other drainage specialties.
14 Members

20432 Plumbing and Mechanical Contractors Association of Oregon
14695 SW Millikan Way
Beaverton, OR 97006

503-626-6666
FAX 503-626-6630

E-Mail: fwall@pmcaoregon.com
Home Page: www.pmcaoregon.com

Frank Wall, Executive Director
250 Members
Founded in 1980

20433 Southern Wholesalers Association
201 Seaboard Lane
7107 Crossroads Blvd
Suite 106
Brentwood, TN 37027

615-371-5004
FAX 615-371-5444
E-Mail: terry@southernwholesalers.org
Home Page: www.southernwholesalers.org
Social Media: *Facebook*

Travis Elrod, President
Brendan Donahue, First VP/ Treasurer
John Simmons, Second VP
Harry Hays, Chairman Ex-Officio
Coley Herin, Chairman of the Board

The Southern Wholesalers Association is a regional association composed of leading Wholesalers of plumbing, heating, and cooling equipment and supplies; pipe, valves and fittings; and water systems throughout the southeast, as well as, Associate Member suppliers and reps to the phcp, pvf and water systems industry.
850 Members
Founded in 1928

20434 United Association
Three Park Place
Annapolis, MD 21401

410-269-2000
FAX 410-267-0382
Home Page: www.ua.org
Social Media: *Facebook, Twitter, YouTube*

William P. Hite, General President
Mark McManus, General Secretary-Treasurer
Union of plumbers, fitters, welders and service techs.
370K Members
Founded in 1889

20435 Valve Manufacturers Association of America
1050 17th Street NW
Suite 280
Washington, DC 20036-5521

202-331-8105
FAX 202-296-0378
E-Mail: wsandler@vma.org
Home Page: www.vma.org

Greg Rogowski, Chairman
Bob Kemple, Vice Chairman
William S. Sandler, President
Marc Pasternak, Vice President
Judy Tibbs, Director of Education

VMA represents the interests of nearly 100 U.S. and Canadian valve actuator, and control manufacturers who account for approximately 80% of the total industrial valve shipments out of U.S. and Canadian facilities. The American valve industry supplies approximately 35% of worldwide valve demand. VMA member companies employ 20,000 men and women directly in supporting jobs. VMA is the only organization exclusively serving U.S. and Canadian manufacturers of industrial valves, controls and actuator
100 Members
Founded in 1938

20436 Western Suppliers Association
3423 Investment Blvd
Suite 204
Hayward, CA 94545

510-670-0962
800-752-8833

FAX 510-670-9081
E-Mail: info@wsagroup.org
Home Page:
www.westernsuppliersassociation.com
Richard Amaro, President
Frank Nisonger, Vice President
Ted Green, Treasurer
Glenn Kunishige, Director
Frank Mullin, Advisory Director

A regional office that represents various wholesalers in the heating, plumbing and piping fields.
Founded in 1952

Newsletters

20437 Plumbing Systems & Design
2980 River Rd
Des Plaines, IL 60018

847-296-0002
FAX 773-695-9007
E-Mail: info@aspe.org
Home Page: www.psdmagazine.com

Gretchen Pienta, Managing Editor
David Jern, Executive Publisher
Rachel Boger, Graphic Designer
Richard Albrecht, Website

Industry leading technical publication with ASPE news and features. Free to ASPE members and subscribers.
Frequency: Monthly
Circulation: 27000
Founded in 1965
Printed in on glossy stock

Magazines & Journals

20438 Directory of Listed Plumbing Products Official Magazine
Int'l Assn of Plumbing & Mechanical Officials
4755 E Philadelphia St
Ontario, CA 91761-2816

909-472-4100
FAX 909-472-4150
Home Page: www.iapmo.org
Social Media: *Facebook, Twitter, LinkedIn, YouTube*

Gary Hice, VP
Dan Daniels, President
Russ Chancy, CEO
Dwight Perkins, Senior Director
Cost: $75.00
7000 Members
1300 Pages
Frequency: 6x Yearly
Circulation: 26,000
Founded in 1926

20439 OFFICIAL Magazine
Int'l Assn of Plumbing & Mechanical Officials
4755 E Philadelphia St
Ontario, CA 91761-2816

909-472-4100
800-854-2676
FAX 909-472-4150
E-Mail: info@iapmo.org
Home Page: www.iapmo.org

Gary Hile, President
Bruce Pfeiffer, VP
Russ Chancy, CEO
The nation's leading source for information about plumbing and mechanical safety codes. This publication is geared toward plumbers,

mechanical contractors, manufacturers and government safety officials who need to know safety code information
Cost: $75.00
9000 Members
Frequency: Bi-Monthly
Circulation: 26000
Founded in 1958

20440 PM Engineer
Business News Publishing Company
155 N Pfingsten Rd
#205
Deerfield, IL 60015

630-377-5909
FAX 248-502-1023
E-Mail: privacy@BNPMedia.com
Home Page: www.pmengineer.com

Bob Miondonski, Group Publisher & Editor
Mike Miazga, Ednior Editor
Julius Ballanco, Editorial Director
Suzette Rubio, Online Editor
John Siegenthaler, Hydronics Editor

Provides technical sheets, manufacturer product brochures, news features and analysis of useful industry information on the engineering and design of plumbing, piping, hydronics, cooling/heating, and fire protection/sprinkler systems. Free to trade engineers.
80 Pages
Circulation: 25000
Printed in 4 colors on glossy stock

20441 PM Plumbing & Mechanical
Business News Publishing Company
155 N Pfingsten Rd
#205
Deerfield, IL 60015

630-377-5909
FAX 248-502-1023
E-Mail: privacy@BNPMedia.com
Home Page: www.pmmag.com/

Bob Miondonski, Group Publisher & Editor
Mike Miazga, Ednior Editor
Julius Ballanco, Editorial Director
Suzette Rubio, Online Editor
John Siegenthaler, Hydronics Editor

Serves plumbing, hydronic heating and mechanical contractors.
Frequency: Monthly
Circulation: 45091

20442 Plumbing Engineer
TMB Publishing
2165 Shermer Rd
Suite A
Northbrook, IL 60062-5474

847-564-1127
FAX 847-564-1264
E-Mail: editor@plumbingengineer.com
Home Page: www.plumbingengineer.com

John Mesenbrink, Chief Editor
Marilyn Cunningham, Assistant Editor
Cate Brown, Production Manager
Sadie Bechtold, Production Assistant
Mark Bruno, Art Director

Offers news and updates to plumbing engineers and manufacturers.
Cost: $35.00
Frequency: Monthly
Founded in 1973

20443 Plumbing Standards
American Society of Sanitary Engineering

901 Canterbury Rd
Suite A
Cleveland, OH 44145-1480

440-835-3040
FAX 440-835-3488
Home Page: www.asse-plumbing.org

James Bickford, President
Donald R Jr. Summers, First VP
Steve Silber, Second VP
Scott Hamilton, Third VP
Ron Murray, Immiate Past President

Topics include standards information, updates, water, wastewater, plumbing design guidelines, and technical information pertaining to the water industry.
Cost: $12.00
Frequency: Quarterly
Circulation: 15000
Founded in 1906

20444 Reeves Journal
23421 South Pointe Drive
Suite 280
Laguna Hills, CA 92653

949-830-0881
FAX 949-859-7845
E-Mail: hendersont@bnpmedia.com
Home Page: www.reevesjournal.com

Ellyn Fishman, Publisher
Kati Larson, Advertising Sales
Jack Sweet, Editor
Souzan Azar, Production

Reeves Journal, one of the oldest publications in the plumbing industry, addresses the regional opportunities and challenges facing plumbing/heating/cooling-phc contractors, wholesalers and engineers in the 14 western United States, focusing on the products, issues, codes and regulations relevant to the phc industry.
Frequency: Monthly
Founded in 1926

20445 Supply House Times
American Supply Association
155 N Pfingsten Rd
#205
Deerfield, IL 60015

312-464-0090
FAX 312-464-0091
E-Mail: info@asa.net
Home Page: www.supplyht.com

Bob Miondonski, Group Publisher & Editor
Mike Miazga, Ednior Editor
Julius Ballanco, Editorial Director
Suzette Rubio, Online Editor
John Siegenthaler, Hydronics Editor

Articles on plumbing, heating, cooling, and piping products.
50 Pages
Frequency: 6x Yearly
Circulation: 2,500
Mailing list available for rent: 4,000 names
Printed in 4 colors on matte stock

20446 United Association Journal
United Association
Three Park Place
Annapolis, MD 21401

410-269-2000
FAX 410-267-0382
Home Page: www.ua.org

William P. Hite, President
Mark McManus, General Secretary/Treasurer

Official publication of the United Association of Journeymen and Apprentices of the Plumbing and Pipe Fitting Industry.
Frequency: Monthly
Circulation: 315000
ISSN: 0095-7763
Founded in 1889

20447 Valve Magazine
Valve Manufacturers Association of America
1050 17th Street NW
Suite 280
Washington, DC 20036-5521

202-331-8105
FAX 202-296-0378
E-Mail: wsandler@vma.org
Home Page: www.valvemagazine.com

William S Sandler, President
Judy Tibbs, Associate Publisher/Editor-in-Chief
Sue Partyke, Advertising Director
Chris Guy, New Products, Media & Industry News
Michelle Wandres, Art Director/Production Manager

Promotion of significance and application of US and Canadian manufactured industrial valves and actuators.
Frequency: Quarterly
Circulation: 2600

Trade Shows

20448 ASPE Engineered Plumbing Exposition
National Trade Show Productions
313 South Patrick Street
Alexandria, VA 22314-1117

703-683-8500
800-687-7469
FAX 703-836-4486
Home Page: www.ntpshow.com/ or www.aspe.org

Robert E Harar, Chairman and CEO
Karin Frendrich, Chief Operating Officer
Jennifer Hoff, Executive Director

A biennial exhibits trade show for the plumbing and engineering industry, the Engineered Plumbing Exposition, sponsored by the American Society of Plumbing Engineers/ASPE, is a gathering of plumbing, engineering and design products, equipment and services. Everything from pipes to pumps to fixtures, from compressors to computers and consulting services, is on display to allow engineers and specifiers to view the newest and most innovative design materials available to them.
7000 Attendees
Founded in 1964

20449 Business and Education Conference
Int'l Assoc of Plumbing and Mechanical Officials
4755 E Philadelphia Street
Ontario, CA 91761

909-472-4100
800-854-2676
FAX 909-472-4150
E-Mail: info@iapmo.org
Home Page: www.iapmo.org

GP Russ Chaney, Chief Executive Officer
Gaby Davis, Director of Worldwide Operations
Neil Bogatz, General Counsel
Monte Bogatz, Associate General Counsel
Tricia Schwenke, Executive Assistant

IAPMO's annual conference brings together the public health and safety officials dedicated to plumbing and mechanical systems. for more than eighty years this venue allows for the free flow of information about changes in these necessary systems and provides technical education allowing these professionals hig

competency in the associated cides and standards.
9000 Members
600 Attendees
Frequency: Annual/September
Founded in 1923

20450 Directory of Listed Plumbing Products Annual Conference
Int'l Assn of Plumbing & Mechanical Officials
4755 E Philadelphia St
Ontario, CA 91761-2816

909-472-4100
FAX 909-472-4150
Home Page: www.iapmo.org
Social Media: *Facebook, Twitter, LinkedIn, YouTube*

Gary Hice, VP
Dan Daniels, President
Russ Chancy, CEO
Dwight Perkins, Senior Director
7000 Members
450 Attendees
Founded in 1926

20451 MSS Annual Meeting
Manufacturers Standardization Society
127 Park St NE
Vienna, VA 22180-4602

703-281-6613
FAX 703-281-6671
E-Mail: orders@mss-hq.org
Home Page: www.mss-hq.org

Robert O'Neill, Executive Director
Frequency: Annual/May
Founded in 1924

20452 Mid-Atlantic Plumbing Heating Cooling Expo
Reber-Friel Company
221 King Manor Drive
Suite A
King Of Prussia, PA 19406-2500

610-272-4020
FAX 610-272-5190

Richard Retzback, Show Manager
350 booths featuring products and services used by the plumbing, heating and cooling industries.
4.3M Attendees
Frequency: Annual/November

20453 National Plumbing, Heating, Cooling and Piping Products Exposition
American Supply Association
222 Merchandise Mart Plaza
Suite 1400
Chicago, IL 60654

312-464-0090
FAX 312-464-0091
E-Mail: info@asa.net
Home Page: www.asa.net/

Karen Weeks, Show Manager
Bob Higgason, Owner
George Conyngham Jr., President
Colin Perry, Treasurer
Inge Calderon, Secretary

Offers information and a forum for the exchange of ideas among plumbing, heating and cooling engineers.
11M Attendees

20454 NetworkASA
American Supply Association
222 Merchandise Mart
Suite 1400
Chicago, IL 60654

312-464-0090
FAX 312-464-0091

E-Mail: info@asa.net
Home Page: www.asa.net

Ruth Mitchell, Meetings/Conventions Director

For distributors and manufacturers in the PHCP/PVF industry. Provides information and opportunities that cannot be found with other organizations or events.
Frequency: Annual

20455 Spring Septic System Conference
Granite State Designers & Installers Association
53 Regional Drive
Concord, NH 03301-3520

603-228-1231
FAX 603-228-2118
E-Mail: info@gsdia.org
Home Page: www.gsdia.org

Carl Hagstrom, Director
Randy Orvis, Director

Conference and trade show with 30 exhibitors and booths for septic system professionals and other allied industries.
400 Attendees
Frequency: Annual/March

Directories & Databases

20456 Complete Directory of Plumbing Products
Sutton Family Communications & Publishing Company
National Fleamarketeer
155 Sutton Lane
Fordsville, KY 42343

270-740-0870
E-Mail: jlsutton@apex.net
Home Page: www.fleamarketeer.net

Theresa Sutton, Editor
Lee Sutton, General Manager

Print-out from database of wholesalers, manufacturers, distributors, importers and close-out houses. Database is updated daily to guarantee the most current and up-to-date sources available.
Cost: $55.20
100+ Pages

20457 Directory of Custom Compounders
Delphi Marketing Services
400 E 89th Street
Apartment 2J
New York, NY 10128-6728
Dr. Newman Giragosian, Editor

Offers information on manufacturers of custom mixtures of plastics and resins.
Cost: $295.00
115 Pages
Frequency: Annual

20458 Directory of Listed Plumbing Products
Int'l Assn of Plumbing & Mechanical Officials
4755 E Philadelphia St
Ontario, CA 91761-2816

909-472-4100
FAX 909-472-4150
Home Page: www.iapmo.org

Leticia Wilson, Manager
Dan Daniels, VP
Russ Chancy, Executive Director

Directory of products and supplies to the plumbing industry.
Cost: $93.00
1300 Pages
Frequency: Monthly

20459 Plumbing Engineer: Product Directory Issue
TMB Publishing
2165 Shermer Rd
Suite A
Northbrook, IL 60062-5474

847-564-1127
FAX 847-564-1264
E-Mail: editor@plumbingengineer.com
Home Page: www.tmbpublishing.com

John Mesenbrink, Chief Editor
Marilyn Cunningham, Assistant Editor
Cate Brown, Production Manager
Sadie Bechtold, Production Assistant
Mark Bruno, Art Director

Over 400 plumbing products from approximately 250 manufacturers.
Frequency: Annual/January
Circulation: 2,6104

20460 Who's Who in the Plumbing-Heating-Cooling Contracting Business
Nat'l Assn of Plumbing-Heating-Cooling Contractors
180 South Washington Street
PO Box 6808
Falls Church, VA 22046-2900

703-237-8100
800-533-7694
FAX 703-237-7442
E-Mail: naphcc@naphcc.org
Home Page: www.phccweb.org

Frank Maddalon, President
Keith Bienvenu, President-Elect
David Dugger, VP
Kevin Tindall, Secretary
Gerry Kennedy, Executive VP

About 6,000 professional plumbing/heating/cooling contractors and member firms.
Cost: $75.00
Frequency: Annual
Circulation: 15,000
Founded in 1883

Industry Web Sites

20461 http://gold.greyhouse.com
G.O.L.D Grey House OnLine Databases

Grey House Publishing's online database platform, GOLD, offers Quick Search, Keyword Search and Expert Search for most business sectors including plumbing and heating markets. The GOLD platform makes finding the information you need quick and easy - whether you're a novice searcher or an experienced database user. All of Grey House's directory products are available for subscription on the GOLD platform.

20462 www.asa.net
American Supply Association
For industry wholesale distributors and manufacturers.

20463 www.aspe.org
American Society of Plumbing Engineers
Seeks to resolve professional problems in plumbing engineering. Operates a certification program.

20464 www.asse-plumbing.org
American Society of Sanitary Engineering
Members are from all segments of the plumbing industry, including contractors, engineers, inspectors, journeymen, apprentices and others involved in the industry. Provides information, the opportunity to exchange ideas, solve prob-

lems and offers forum where all sides can express their views.

20465 www.construction.com
McGraw-Hill Construction

McGraw-Hill Construction (MHC), part of The McGraw-Hill Companies, connects people and projects across the design and construction industry, serving owners, architects, engineers, general contractors, subcontractors, building product manufacturers, suppliers, dealers, distributors and adjacent markets.

20466 www.greyhouse.com
Grey House Publishing

Authoritative reference directories for most business sectors including plumbing and heating markets. Users can search the online databases with varied search criteria allowing for custom searches by product category, geographic area, sales volume, keyword, subject and more. Full Grey House catalog and online ordering also available.

20467 www.iapmo.org
Int'l Assoc of Plumbing and Mechanical Officers

IAPMO has been protecting the public's health and safety for more than eighty years by working in concert with government and industry to implement comprehensive plumbing and mechanical systems around the world.

20468 www.pdionline.org
Plumbing and Drainage Institute

For manufacturers of engineered plumbing products, flood drains, roof drains, sanitary floor drains, cleanouts, water hammer arresters, swimming pool drains, backwater valves, grease interceptors, fixture supports, and other drainage specialties.

20469 www.sweets.construction.com
McGraw Hill Construction

In depth product information that lets you find, compare, select, specify and make purchase decisions in the industrial product marketplace.

20470 www.uboiler.com
Uniform Boiler and Pressure Vessel Laws Society

Established to promote uniformity in rules, laws and regulations for boiler and pressure vessel safety based on the requirements of the American Society of Mechanical Engineers Boiler and Pressure Vessel Code and other related national standards.

20471 www.vma.org
Valve Manufacturers Association of America

Associations

20472 Amalgamated Printers Association
3019 Elm Lane
Middleton, WI 53562

406-928-4757
E-Mail: TWOEMPRESS@aol.com
Home Page: apa-letterpress.com
Social Media: *Facebook, Twitter, LinkedIn, Google+, Pinterest*

Sky Shipley, President
Joe Warren, VP
Cindy Iverson, Secretary/Treasurer
Howard Gelbert, Director
David Kent, Archivist

The Amalgamated Printers' Association was organized in 1958 as a hobby printers group so that members could improve their skills, expand their knowledge, and exchange samples of their letterpress work in addition to encouraging excellence of printing content, design, and techniques.
150 Members
Founded in 1958

20473 American Printing History Association
PO Box 4519
Grand Central Station
New York, NY 10163

E-Mail: secretary@printinghistory.org
Home Page: printinghistory.org

Robert McCamant, President

Membership organization promoting the study of the history of printing and related arts such as calligraphy and typography.

20474 Assoc. Suppliers of Printing, Publishing & Converting Technologies
1899 Preston White Drive
Reston, VA 20191

703-264-7200
FAX 703-620-0994
E-Mail: npes@npes.org
Home Page: www.npes.org

Ralph J. Nappi, President
Michael Ring, Chairman
Mal Baboyian, Treasurer
Mark J. Nuzzaco, Secretary
Marc Olin, Vice President & General Manager

The Association for Suppliers of Printing, Publishing and Converting Technologies is a trade association that represents manufacturers, importers and distributors of equipment, supplies, systems and software used in every printing, publishing and converting process from design to distribution. Virtually all industry products and processes are represented by the member companies, which range in size from under $1 million in annual sales revenue to more than $1 billion.
600 Members
Founded in 1933

20475 Binding Industries of America
Printing Industry of Illinois
200 Deer Run Road
Sewickley, PA 15143

412-741-6860
800-910-4283
FAX 412-741-2311
E-Mail: printing@printing.org
Home Page: www.bindingindustries.org
Social Media: *Facebook, Twitter, LinkedIn, Google+, Pinterest*

Frederick A. Hartwig, Manager, Environment ane Health
Gary A. Jones, Assistant Vice President

Chris Eckhart, Chairman
Chris Webbert, Vice-Chairman

A trade association representing bindery and looseleaf manufacturers, graphic finishers, and supplies to those industries
350 Members
Founded in 1955

20476 Book Manufacturers' Institute (BMI)
2 Armand Beach Drive
Suite 1B
Palm Coast, FL 32137-2612

386-986-4552
FAX 386-986-4553
E-Mail: info@bmibook.com
Home Page: www.bmibook.org

Daniel N Bach, Executive VP & Secretary
Jac B. Garner, President
Kent H. Larson, President-Elect/ Vice President
Paul Genovesse, Treasurer
Robert J. Boyd, General counsel

Since 1933, the Book Manufacturers' Institute, Inc. (BMI) has been the leading nationally recognized trade association of the book manufacturing industry. BMI member companies annually produce the great majority of books ordered by the U. S. book publishing industry. Today, BMI is a vital part of the industry, playing a leading role by providing an intra-industry communications link among book manufacturers, publishers, suppliers and governmental bodies.
90 Members
Founded in 1933

20477 Center for Book Arts
28 W 27th St
3rd Floor
New York, NY 10001

212-481-0295
FAX 212-481-9853
E-Mail: info@centerforbookarts.org
Home Page: www.centerforbookarts.org
Social Media: *Facebook, Twitter, YouTube, Flickr, Instagram*

Andrew W Mellon, Chair
Brian Hannon, Vice Chair
Robert J. Ruben, MD & Co Chair
Nancy Macomber, Treasurer
David W. Lowden, Secretary

The Center for Book Arts is dedicated to preserving the traditional crafts of book-making, as well as exploring and encouraging contemporary interpretations of the book as an art object. Each year the Center offers three terms of courses, workshops and seminars taught by experienced book artists, and providing hands-on training in all aspects of traditional and contemporary bookmaking, including bookbinding, letterpress printing, papermaking, and other associated arts.
Founded in 1974

20478 Flexographic Technical Association Inc.
3920 Veterans Memorial Highway
Suite 9
Bohemia, NY 11716-1074

631-737-6020
FAX 631-737-6813
E-Mail: memberinfo@flexography.org
Home Page: www.flexography.org
Social Media: *Twitter, LinkedIn*

Allen J. Marquardt, Chair
Jack Fulton, Vice Chair
Howard B. Vreeland, Chair-elect
Mark Cisternino, President
Dan Doherty, Treasurer

Technical society devoted exclusively to the flexographic printing industry.
1500 Members
Founded in 1958

20479 Gravure Association of the Americas
8281 Pink Lake Rd.
Denver, NC 28037

201-523-6042
FAX 201-523-6048
E-Mail: gaa@gaa.org
Home Page: www.gaa.org
Social Media: *Facebook, LinkedIn*

Philip Pimlott, Executive Director

The Association promotes gravure printing, a high-tech process that runs on the fastest and widest presses in the world.
Founded in 2013

20480 In-Plant Printing and Mailing Association
455 S. Sam Barr Drive
Suite 203
Keaney, MO 64060

816-919-1691
FAX 816-902-4766
E-Mail: ipmainfo@ipma.org
Home Page: www.ipma.org
Social Media: *Facebook, Twitter, LinkedIn, YouTube, Google+*

Carma Goin, Executive Director
Rob Lingard, President
Tammy Golden, Secretary/Treasurer
Mike Lincoln, President-Elect
Dwayne Magee, Membership Representative

The professional association for all segments of the in-house corporate printing and mailing professionals who work for educational institutions, the government, and private industry.
600 Members
Founded in 1964

20481 International Waterless Printing Association
International Waterless Printing Association
5 Southside Dr Unit 11-328
Clifton Park, NY 12065

518-387-9321
800-850-0660
FAX 518-310-2383
E-Mail: info@waterless.org
Home Page: www.waterless.org

John O'Rourke, Vice president
Brian Amos, Secretary
Julie Leonhard, Treasurer
Joel Friedman, Executive Director
Ruud Kempers, Director European Operations

Dedicated to the informational and educational needs of its printer and sponsor members. Seeks to inform designers and print buyers about the many benefits the process offers.
Founded in 1993

20482 Printing Brokerage Buyers Association
1530 Locust Street
Mezanine 124
Philadelphia, PA 19102

215-821-6581
866-586-9391
FAX 561-845-7130
E-Mail: info@ pbbai.net
Home Page: www.pbba.org
Social Media: *RSS*

Vincent Mallardi, Chairman

Promotes business relationships among brokers, buying groups, manufacturers and related companies. Sets standards, codes and supplies information and referrals.

20483 Printing Impressions
North American Publishing Company
(NAPCO)
1500 Spring Garden St
12th Floor
Philadelphia, PA 19130

215-238-5338
888-889-9491
FAX 212-238-5280
E-Mail: webmaster@napco.com
Home Page: www.piworld.com
Social Media: *Facebook, Twitter, LinkedIn,
Yahoo,Windows Live*

Rosemary Sirico, President
Diane Pesce, VP
Mark T. Michelson, Editor-in-Chief
Erik Cagle, Senior Editor, PI Weekly Editor
Alex Schwartz, Senior Editor, PI Weekly Editor
Promotes the interests of women in the produc-
tion profession.
Founded in 1966

20484 Printing Industries of America
301 Brush Creek Road
Warrendale, PA 15086-7529

412-741-6860
800-910-4283
FAX 412-741-2311
E-Mail: info@printing.org
Home Page: www.printing.org
Social Media: *Facebook, Twitter, LinkedIn,
Pinterest*

Michael F. Makin, Ex-Officio
Mr Michael S Wurst, Treasurer
Paul L Cousineau, Chairman, Research
Committee
David A. Olberding, Chairman of the Board of
Directors
Bradley L. Thompson, 1st Vice Chairman
A graphic arts trade association representing
our members in this industry. Printing Indus-
tries of America, along with its affiliates, deliv-
ers products and services that enhance the
growth, efficiency and profitability of its mem-
bers and the industry through advocacy, educa-
tion, research and technical information
10000 Members
Founded in 1887

20485 Printing Industries of New England
5 Crystal Pond Road
Southborough, MA 01772

508-804-4100
800-365-7463
FAX 508-804-4119
E-Mail: webmaster@pine.org
Home Page: www.pine.org
Social Media: *Facebook, Twitter, LinkedIn*

Tad Parker, President
Kurt Peterson, Chairman
Bob Clement, Secretary/Treasurer
Justin Pallis, Vice Chairman
Mike Peluso, Member at Large

Serves more than 450 commercial printing and
graphic communications companies throughout
five New England states. Provides products and
services on an ongoing basis to help member
companies operate more profitably.
450 Members
Founded in 1887

**20486 Printing Industries of Northern
California**
665 3rd St
Suite 500
San Francisco, CA 94107

415-495-8242
800-659-3363
FAX 800-824-1911
E-Mail: info@vma.bz
Home Page: main.vma.bz

Social Media: *Facebook, Twitter, LinkedIn,
Google+, Pinterest, YouTube, V*

Frank Parks, Chairman
John Crammer, 1st Vice Chairman
Arnold Greenfield, Ex Officio
Dan Nelson, President
David Katz, Vice President

The Printing Industries of Northern California
(PINC) is a non-profit trade association serving
several industry segments in Northern California, primarily the print production and print
buying segments.

**20487 Printing Industry Association of the
South**
305 Plus Park Blvd
Nashville, TN 37217

615-366-1094
FAX 615-366-4192
E-Mail: info@pias.org
Home Page: www.pias.org

Ed Chalifoux, President

The Printing Industry Association of the South
(PIAS), a non-profit trade association, is dedicated to assisting the entire industry to continue
to expand in the region and help the industry
prosper across the seven-state region of Alabama, Arkansas, Kentucky, Louisiana, Mississippi, Tennessee and West Virginia.
520 Members

**20488 Printing and Graphic
Communications Association**
6411 Ivy Lane
Suite 700
Greenbelt, MD 20770

Home Page: www.pgca.org

Serves the graphic communications community
in the Washington, D.C. metropolitan area.
Founded in 1914

**20489 Society for Service Professionals in
Printing (SSPP)**
Document Management Industries
Association
433 E Monroe Ave
Alexandria, VA 22301-1645

703-684-0044
877-777-7398
FAX 703-548-9137
E-Mail: ssppinfo@sspp.org
Home Page: www.sspp.org

Peter Colainni, Executive Director
Marj Green, Director
Kevin Cooper, Billing Coordinator
Pam Decker, Webmaster

A national organization that focuses on rates,
service and trends in the printing industry for
consumers. SSPP provides information about
both printing and customer service to its members through three monthly newsletters and
special interest bulletins. SSPP sponsors the national Certification Examination for Printing
Service Specialists (CPSS), which recognizes
those printing service specialists who have attained a proscribed body of knowledge about
both printing and customer service.
Cost: $150.00

**20490 Specialty Graphic Imaging
Association**
10015 Main St
Fairfax, VA 22031

703-385-1335
888-385-3588
FAX 703-273-0456
E-Mail: sgia@sgia.org, webmaster@sgia.org
Home Page: www.sgia.org

Social Media: *Facebook, Twitter, LinkedIn,
Wordpress*

Michael Robertson, President
James Gill, Associate Vice Chairman
Hoddy Peck, Chairman
Lynn Krinsky, Treasurer
Scott Crosby, Secretary

Participants include corporations, institutions
and individuals interested in screen printing
and digital imaging. Conducts technical research and training workshops.
Founded in 1986

20491 The 3D Printing Association
Silicon Valley Center
2570 N First St.
San Jose, CA 95131

408-600-2647
Home Page: www.the3dprintingassociation.org

The Association supports and represents all interests in the 3D printing industry.
Founded in 2013

Newsletters

20492 Binding Edge
Printing Industry of Illinois
200 Deer Run Road
Sewickley, PA 15143

412-741-6860
800-910-4283
FAX 412-741-2311
E-Mail: gain@piagatf.org
Home Page: www.bindingindustries.org
Social Media: *Facebook, Twitter, LinkedIn*

Michael Makin, President/CEO
Justin Goldstein, Manager

Includes articles designed to help bindery and
loose leaf facilities improve their processes and
keep up on the latest technologies.
Frequency: Quarterly
Circulation: 12000

**20493 Business Printing Technologies
Report**
DMIA
433 East Monroe Avenue
Alexandria, VA 22301-1645

703-836-6232
FAX 703-836-2241
E-Mail: dmia@dmia.org
Home Page: www.dmia.org

Timothy J Mehl, President
Peter L Colaianni, Executive VP
Brad Holt, VP Media/Publications
Robert O'Connell, Treasurer
Marj Green, VP Operations

Offers a complete overview of the printing in-
dustry.
Frequency: Annual
Circulation: 5600
Founded in 1955

20494 Economic Edge
National Association for Printing
Leadership
One Meadowlands Plaza
Suite 1511
East Rutherford, NJ 07073

201-634-9600
800-642-6275
FAX 201-634-0324
E-Mail: webmaster@napl.org
Home Page: www.napl.org

Social Media: *Facebook, Twitter, LinkedIn, YouTube, RSS*

Joseph Truncale, President
Timothy Fischer, Executive VP/COO

Economic analysis of the graphic arts industry.
Cost: $150.00
12 Pages
Frequency: Quarterly
Founded in 1933

20495 Footprints

Footprint Communications
1339 Massachusetts Street
Lawrence, KS 66044

800-488-8316
FAX 785-832-0087
E-Mail: mike@footcom.com
Home Page: www.footprints.com

Dick Vinocur, Publisher

A newsletter for the printing industry reporting news, management, marketing and financial data (including industry stock indexes), product introductions, personnel changes, association affairs and recent acquisitions and mergers. Footprints also reports on exhibits, shows, meetings and conferences in the graphic arts industry.
Cost: $327.00
Frequency: Fortnightly

20496 Graphic Arts Monthly Online

Reed Business Information
4709 Golf Road
Skokie, IL 60076

800-217-7874
FAX 630-288-8781
E-Mail: psaran@reedbusiness.com
Home Page: www.reedbusiness.com

Jeff Greisch, President
Bill Esler, Editor-in-Chief
Lisa Cross, Web Site Editor
Stephanie Kauffman, Reprint Management Services
Mark Kelsey, CEO

Graphic Arts Monthly Online is a subscriber-based Web portal for printing professionals and print buyers featuring current and archived news, research and business tools, online classifieds, used equipment marketplace and online training and education.
Cost: $159.00
Frequency: Monthly

20497 Graphic Communicator

Graphic Communications International Union
25 Louisiana Avenue N.W
Washington, DC 20001

202-624-6800
FAX 202-721-0600
E-Mail: webmessenger@gciu.org
Home Page: www.gciu.org
Social Media: *Facebook, Twitter*

James P Hoffa, President
Ken Hall, Secretary-Treasurer

Tabloid size newspaper for and about members of the GCIU. The international union represents workers in the printing/publishing industry. Members range from desktop operators to paper handler.
Cost: $12.00
Circulation: 100000
Founded in 1983

20498 NAQP Network

National Association for Printing Leadership

One Meadowlands Plaza
Suite 1511
East Rutherford, NJ 07073

201-634-9600
800-642-6275
FAX 201-634-0324
E-Mail: webmaster@napl.org
Home Page: www.naqp.com
Social Media: *Facebook, Twitter, LinkedIn, YouTube, RSS*

Joseph P Truncale, President & CEO
Dean D' Ambrosi, Vice President
Carol Rocke, Marketing Coordinator

Editorial content covers technologial advances, product news, profiles on industry leaders, and club events.
Frequency: Monthly
Circulation: 900

20499 Printing News

Cygnus Publishing
3 Huntington Quadrangle
Suite 301N
Melville, NY 11747-3601

631-845-2700
800-308-6397
FAX 631-249-5774
E-Mail: editor@printingnews.com
Home Page: www.printingnews.com
Social Media: *Facebook, Twitter, LinkedIn*

David Kastriner, Publisher
Michael Zerner, Associate Publisher
David Lindsay, Editor-in-Chief
Rachel Frank, Editor

Includes timely news and information on a variety of subjects including technological breakthroughs, industry trends, marketing, finance, as well as industry leader and corporate profiles.
Cost: $39.95
Frequency: Weekly
Circulation: 9000
Founded in 1928
Mailing list available for rent

20500 SGIA Journal

Specialty Graphic Imaging Association
10015 Main St
Fairfax, VA 22031-3489

703-385-1335
888-385-3588
FAX 703-273-0456
E-Mail: sgia@sgia.org
Home Page: www.sgia.org
Social Media: *Facebook, Twitter, LinkedIn*

Michael Robertson, President
Sondra Fry Benoudiz, VP Membership
Lynn Krinsky, Chairman
Pete Gallo, First Vice Chairman
Tim Markley, Second Vice Chairman

Provides members with access to information relative to industry trends and the latest news such as emerging markets, government regulations, and technological developments.
Cost: $149.00
Frequency: Bi-Monthly
Circulation: 3800
Founded in 1948
Printed in 2 colors on glossy stock

20501 Signature Service

Signature Service Real Estate Rainier
302 Binghampton Street W
PO Box 8
Rainier, WA 98576

360-446-4646
877-446-4647
FAX 360-446-2400

E-Mail: ssppinfo@sspp.org
Home Page: www.signatureservice.com

Peter Colaianni, Executive Director
Marj Green, Director
Kevin Cooper, Billing Coordinator
Pam Decker, Webmaster

Newsletter covering rates, service and trends in the printing industry for consumers.
Cost: $115.00
8 Pages
Frequency: Monthly
Circulation: 2000

Magazines & Journals

20502 American InkMaker

Cygnus Publishing
PO Box 803
Fort Atkinson, WI 53538-0803

920-000-1111
800-547-7377
FAX 920-563-1699
E-Mail: Rich.Reiff@CygnusPub.com
Home Page: www.cygnusb2b.com

John French, CEO
Robert Stange, Senior VP Marketing

Offers information to the professional ink manufacturer. The editorial content consists of contributed technical papers and nontechnical features about trends, technology and global happenings to help our readers to improve their profitability in addition to featuring a monthly interview with printers.
Cost: $46.00
Circulation: 3800
Founded in 1923

20503 American Printer

American Printer
2100 West Loop South
Suite 900
Houston, TX 77027-3515

713-300-0674
E-Mail: info@AmericanPrinter.com
Home Page: www.americanprinter.com
Social Media: *Facebook, Twitter, RSS*

Katherine O'Brien, Editor
Michael P Koch, Senior Art Director
Denise Kapel, Managing Editor
Carrie Cleaveland, Assistant Editor
Jill Roth, Director Brand Development

Regular issue features include new products listings, new equipment technology and reports on system developments.
Frequency: Monthly
Circulation: 86037
Founded in 1883
Mailing list available for rent

20504 Awards & Engraving Magazine

National Business Media
PO Box 1416
Broomfield, CO 80038-1416

303-469-0424
800-669-0424
FAX 303-469-5730
E-Mail: steve@nbm.com
Home Page: www.nbm.com
Social Media: *Facebook, Twitter, LinkedIn*

Bob Wieber, President
Dave Pomeroy, Publisher

Content includes a special focus, and regular articles on signage, the glass market, business management, people profiles, and advances in technology.
Cost: $38.00
Frequency: Monthly
Founded in 1985

20505 Big Picture
325 Public Street
Providence, RI 02905

401-752-3442
800-421-1321
FAX 401-752-3528
E-Mail: webmaster@bigpicturelearning.org
Home Page: www.bigpicture.org

Tedd Swormstedt, CEO
Ronald A. Wolk, Chairman

This publication reports on digital printing of
visual communications with coverage of digital
printing from image capture and processing to
finishing and display.
Frequency: Monthly
Circulation: 48000
Founded in 1996

20506 Dealer Communicator
Fichera Communications
441 South State Road 7
Suite 14
Margate, FL 33068-2823

954-971-4360
800-327-8999
FAX 954-971-4362
E-Mail: omike@dealercommunicator.com
Home Page: www.dealercommunicator.com

Orazio Fichera, Publisher/President
Particia Leavitt, VP

Provides national and international coverage
for the graphic arts and printing industries.
Cost: $30.00
32 Pages
Frequency: Monthly
Circulation: 13619
Founded in 1982
Printed in 4 colors on glossy stock

20507 Digital Graphics
National Business Media
PO Box 1416
Broomfield, CO 80038-1416

303-469-0424
800-669-0424
FAX 303-465-3424
E-Mail: kmergent@nbm.com
Home Page: www.nbm.com
Social Media: *Facebook, Twitter, LinkedIn*

Bob Wieber, President
Ken Mergentime, Editor

Regular departments track public stock
comapnies of interest to the industry, report on
international graphics news and highlight recent technological advances.
64 Pages
Frequency: Monthly
Circulation: 18583
Founded in 1985
Printed in 4 colors

20508 Digital Output
Rockport Custom Publishing
100 Cummings Ctr
Suite 321E
Beverly, MA 01915-6101

978-921-7850
FAX 978-921-7870
E-Mail: edit@rockportpubs.com
Home Page: www.rockportpubs.com

Thomas Tetreault, CEO
Lynn Weese, Account Executive

Provides case studies and trend updates, as well
as discussing how and why companies integrate
and coordinate their marketing strategies.
Frequency: 12 + 2 Buyers Guides

20509 Document Processing Technology
RB Publishing Company

2424 American Lane
PO Box 259906
Madison, WI 53725-9906

608-277-8785
800-536-1992
FAX 608-241-8666
E-Mail: rbpub@rbpub.com
Home Page: www.rbpub.com

Ron Brent, Publisher/President
Allison Lloyd, Managing Editor
Marll Thiede, Executive Editor/VP
Rachel Spahr, Circulation Manager
Tonjia Weber, Production Manager

Covers digital printing, publishing and distribution. Feature and special topic articles focus
on industry trends, technology and strategies
for high-volume document processors.
Frequency: Monthly
Circulation: 10000
Founded in 1988

20510 Electronic Publishing
PennWell Publishing Company
1421 S Sheridan Rd
Tulsa, OK 74112-6619

918-835-3161
800-331-4463
FAX 918-831-9476
E-Mail: Headquarters@PennWell.com
Home Page: www.pennwell.com

Robert Biolchini, President
Courtney E Howard, Managing Editor
Frank J Romano, Sr Contributing & Founding
Editor
Nancy A Hitchcock, Senior Associate Editor

For those who communicate in print, including
service bureaus, printers, prepress houses and
desktop publishers, it provides latest products,
news and related developments.
Cost: $59.00
Frequency: Monthly
Circulation: 68441
Founded in 1910
Mailing list available for rent

20511 Flash Magazine
BlackLighting
252 Riddle Pond Road
West Topsham, VT 05086

800-252-2599
800-252-2599
FAX 802-439-6462
E-Mail: salesBL@BlackLightning.com
Home Page: www.flashweb.com

Walter Vose Jeffries, Publisher

Flash Magazine was started in 1989 and is all
about desktop publishing, book-on-demand
binding, inkjet & laser printinting, heat transfers and other topics of interest to the small
time publisher and graphic artist. The Flash is
filled with great how-to articles that will help
you take care of your printer, do maintenance
& repairs yourself, teach you about graphics,
digital photography, scanning and laser etching
glass and book-on-demand publishing, binding
and so much more.
Cost: $20.00
Frequency: Monthly
Circulation: 112000

20512 Flexo Magazine
Flexographic Technical Association
3920 Veterans Memorial Highway
Suite 9
Bohemia, NY 11716

631-737-6020
FAX 631-737-6813
E-Mail: membership@flexography.org

Home Page: www.flexography.org
Social Media: *Facebook, LinkedIn*

Robert Moran, Publisher
Christian Bonawandt, Editor

Trade publication for the flexographic printing
industry.
1300 Members
Frequency: Monthly

**20513 Forms & Direct Mail Manufacturer's
Marketplace**
Bulls-Eye Communications
211 Champion Avenue
Webster, NY 14580

585-265-3045
E-Mail: waterford@waterfordweb.com

Marsha A Thompson, Editor

The resource magazine of business forms and
direct mail printers. Spotlights news and prod-
ucts in the industry.
Cost: $49.00
Frequency: Bi-Monthly
Circulation: 4,870

20514 Graphic Communications World
Hayzlett & Associates
3313 South Western Avenue
Sioux Falls, SD 57106

605-355-5531
FAX 605-275-2087
Home Page: www.hayzlett.com/index.htm

Jeanette Clinkunbroomer, Editor
Jeff Hayzlett, Owner

Offers a comprehensive overview of the
graphic arts and communications industry.
Cost: $347.00
Frequency: Monthly
Founded in 1968

20515 Gravure
Gravure Association of America
1200A Scottsville Road
Rochester, NY 14624-5703

585-436-2150
FAX 585-436-7689
E-Mail: lwshatch@gaa.org
Home Page: www.gaa.org

Laura Wayland-Smith Hatch, Editor
William Martin, President/CEO

Editorial coverage focuses on the technical de-
velopments in gravure printing, the financial
performance of the industry and association
member activities.
Cost: $67.00
Circulation: 3500
ISSN: 0894-4946
Founded in 1987
Printed in 4 colors on matte stock

20516 High Volume Printing (HVP)
Innes Publishing Company
28100 North Ashley Circle
PO Box 7280
Libertyville, IL 60048

847-816-7900
800-247-3306
FAX 847-247-8855
E-Mail: meinnes@innespub.com
Home Page: www.innespub.com

Mary Ellen Innes, Publisher
Ray Roth, Editor
Barb Pettersen, Circulation Manager
Mary Ellin Innes, President
Judy Abbott, Administrative Assistant

HVP offers a strategic mix of management and
production-oriented editorial content, and has
consistently led in coverage of new technologies and regulatory issues. It focuses on the
bottom-line realities involved in merging tomorrow's technologies with today's operating

environment. Subjects include prepress, press, and postpress equipment and technology, sales and marketing management, training, regulatory issues and more.
Circulation: 39057
Founded in 1982

20517 IPA Bulletin

IPA: Association of Graphic Solutions Providers
7200 France Ave S
Suite 223
Edina, MN 55435-4309

952-896-1908
800-255-8141
FAX 708-596-5112
E-Mail: bessie@ipa.org
Home Page: www.ipa.org

Steven Bonnoff, Executive Director
Becky Walroth, Editorial Assistant
Steven Bonoff, President

Association news offering information on prepress and graphic arts.
Cost: $20.00
6 Pages
Circulation: 2,100
ISSN: 1539-137X
Founded in 1911
Printed in 4 colors on glossy stock

20518 In Plant Graphics

North American Publishing Company
1500 Spring Garden St
Suite 1200
Philadelphia, PA 19130-4094

215-238-5300
FAX 215-238-5342
E-Mail: editor.ipg@napco.com
Home Page: www.ipgonline.com

Ned S Borowsky, CEO
Glen Reynolds, Publisher
Dorlissa Goodrich, Production Manager
Maggie Tajack, Advertising Promotion Manager
Brian Ludwig, Group Publisher

Articles include management advice, technical information, industry news and reader profiles.
Cost: $65.00
60 Pages
Frequency: Monthly
Circulation: 20,000
ISSN: 1087-2817
Founded in 1996
Printed in 4 colors on glossy stock

20519 In Plant Printer

Innes Publishing Company
28100 North Ashley Circle
Suite 101
Libertyville, IL 60048

847-816-7900
800-247-3306
FAX 847-247-8855
E-Mail: meinnes@innespub.com
Home Page: www.innespub.com

Mary Ellin Innes, President
Jack Klasnic, Editor
Barbara Pettersen, Circulation Manager
Teri Saeed, Production Manager
Judy Abbott, Administrative Assistant

Serves printing, graphics and typesetting facilities located in business, industry, education, government, hospitals, associations, and non-profit organizations.
Cost: $110.00
70 Pages
Frequency: Monthly
Circulation: 247637
ISSN: 0891-8996
Founded in 1977
Printed in 4 colors on glossy stock

20520 Ink World

Ink World Direct Limited
108 Queens Road
Nuneaton, WI 07446-1150

800-011-2011
E-Mail: info@rodpub.com
Home Page: www.ink-world.com

Rodman Zilenziger Jr, President
Matt Montgomery, VP

Covers the printing inks, coatings and allied industries.
64 Pages
Frequency: Monthly
Circulation: 6187
Founded in 1994
Printed in 4 colors on glossy stock

20521 Inside Finishing Magazine

Foil & Speciality Effects Association
2150 Southwest Wesport Drive
Suite 101
Topeka, KS 66614

785-271-5816
FAX 785-271-6404
E-Mail: fseamail@fsea.com
Home Page: www.fsea.com

Jeff Peterson, Executive Director
Gayla Peterson, Sales Director
Kym Conis, Assistant Director
Eric.J Carter, Art Director & Webmaster

A quarterly magazine published by the Foil Stamping and Embossing Association, Inside Finishing has a targeted circulation of 6,000 graphic finishing decision makers. These include trade finishers, folding carton companies, greeting card manufacturers, and commercial printers with finishing/bindery operations. It also includes a small percentage of graphic designers involved in the foil stamping and embossing industry, and, of course, industry suppliers to the graphic finishing industry.
56 Pages
Frequency: 4 issues
Founded in 1994

20522 Instant and Small Commercial Printer ISCP

Innes Publishing Company
28100 North Ashley Circle
PO Box 7280
Libertyville, IL 60048-7280

847-816-7900
800-247-3306
FAX 847-247-8855
E-Mail: daninnes@innespub.com
Home Page: www.innespub.com

Dan Innes, Publisher
Linda Casey, Editor
Barb Pettersen, Circualtion MAnager
Mary Ellin Innes, President

ISCP magazine publishes how-to articles and case histories on printing and photocopy reproduction. Emphasis on desktop publishing and short-run digital technologies reflects the growth of this service in instant printing operations. Management stories are aimed at helping the publication's largely entrepreneurial audience grapple successfully with everyday problems and spot new opportunities for growth.
Frequency: Monthly
Circulation: 413671
Founded in 1982

20523 Label & Narrow Web Industry

Rodman Publishing
70 Hilltop Rd
Suite 3000
Ramsey, NJ 07446-1150

201-825-2552
FAX 201-825-0553
E-Mail: label@rodpub.com

Home Page: www.labelandnarrowweb.com
Social Media: *Facebook, Twitter, LinkedIn, RSS*

Rodman J. Zilenziger Jr, President
Matthew Montgomery, VP
Kathleen Scully, Publisher
Steve Katz, Editor
Catherine Diamond, Associate Editor

Label and Narrow Web serves manufacturers of label and narrow web including labels, tags, tape, materials, substrates, machinery, and equipment and others allied to the field.
80 Pages
Circulation: 11000
ISSN: 1095-3248
Founded in 1996
Mailing list available for rent
Printed in 4 colors on glossy stock

20524 New England Printer and Publisher

Printing Industries of New England
5 Crystal Pond Rd
Southborough, MA 01772-1758

508-804-4100
800-365-7463
FAX 508-804-4119
E-Mail: jtepper04@pine.org
Home Page: www.pine.org

John Scibelli, Manager
Joe La Valla, Chairman
Brie Drummond, Production Manager
Kurt Peterson, Vice-Chairman
Bob Clement, Secretary-Treasurer

Trade magazine for printers and publishers.
Cost: $2.40
48 Pages
Frequency: Monthly
Circulation: 4000
Founded in 1938
Printed in 4 colors on matte stock

20525 New Pages: Alternatives in Print and Media

New Pages Press
PO Box 1580
Bay City, MI 48706

989-671-0081
FAX 313-743-2730
E-Mail: newpagesonline@hotmail.com
Home Page: www.newpages.com

Casey Hill, Publisher
Denise Hill, Editor

News and information for bookstores and libraries.
Cost: $12.00
64 Pages
Frequency: Quarterly

20526 Newspapers & Technology

Conley Magazines
1623 Blake Street
Suite 250
Denver, CO 80202

303-575-9595
FAX 303-575-9555
Home Page: www.newsandtech.com/

Mary Van Meter, Publisher
Chuck Moozakis, Editor-in-Chief
Tara McKeekin, Editor
Hays Goodman, Associate Editor/Webmaster

Newspapers & Technology is a monthly trade publication for newspaper publishers and department managers involved in applying and integrating technology. Written by industry experts, News & Tech provides regular coverage of the following departments: prepress, press, postpress and new media.
Circulation: 16,874

20527 PC Presentations Productions

Pisces Publishing Group

1400 South Nova Road
Suite 303
Daytona Beach, FL 32114-5851

203-877-1927
FAX 203-877-1927
Home Page: www.piscespub.com

Don Johnson, Editor/Publisher
Douglas Finlay, Managing Editor

PC Presentations Productions is a free online
magazine intended for both the high-end professional and the student. Graphic and video tutorials for intermediate and advanced content
producers are regular features as are HTML
and Javascript tutorials and Website design tutorials intended for students and others wishing
to add these skills.
Frequency: Weekly
ISSN: 1065-9699

20528 Package Printing
North American Publishing Company
1500 Spring Garden St
Suite 1200
Philadelphia, PA 19130-4094

215-238-5300
800-627-2689
FAX 215-238-5342
E-Mail: customerservice@napco.com
Home Page: www.packageprinting.com
Social Media: *Facebook, Twitter, LinkedIn,*
Yahoo, Windows Live

Ned S Borowsky, CEO
Brian Ludwick, Publisher
Robert Margulies, Sales Manager
Megan Wolf, Assistant Editor
Sean Sams, Advertising Account Manager

Trade publication serving the business and
technology needs of presidents and CEOs of
flexible packaging, tag and label, folding rigid
boxes and directing operations.
Cost: $99.50
75 Pages
Frequency: Monthly
Circulation: 24000
Founded in 1958
Mailing list available for rent

20529 Paper Magazine
365 Broadway
6th Floor
New York, NY 10013

212-226-4405
800-829-9160
FAX 212-226-0062
E-Mail: edit@papermag.com
Home Page: www.papermag.com

Sharon Phair, Advertising & Marketing
Kim Hastreiter, Publisher
Alexis Swerdloff, Executive Editor
Nobu Massiah, Editor
Carol Lee, Creative Director

PAPER Magazine focuses on the latest trends
in pop culture, style, music and film, including
information on New York art exhibits, club list-
ings, literary events, movie reviews and shows.
Includes night-life guide.
Cost: $9.97
Frequency: 10 Issues Per Year
Circulation: 90,000
Founded in 1984

20530 Print Business Register
Cygnus Business Media
3 Huntington Quadrangle
Suite 301 North
Melville, NY 11747

631-845-2700
800-308-6397
FAX 631-845-2741

Home Page: www.cygnusb2b.com
Social Media: *Facebook*

Michael Zerner, Publisher
Rachel Frank, Editor

Editorial material reports on mergers, acquisitions, reorganizations and major issues affecting the marketplace of the commercial printing
industry.
Frequency: Weekly
Circulation: 650
Mailing list available for rent

20531 Print Magazine
RC Publications
38 east 29th street, 4th floor
New York, NY 10016

212-447-1400
FAX 212-447-5231
E-Mail: info@printmag.com
Home Page: www.printmag.com
Social Media: *Facebook, Twitter, Flickr*

Joel Toner, Publisher

Regular highlights include advertising and promotion design, corporate identity, design education and film/TV production. Also covered
are creative trends and technological advances
in photography, printing, web design, illustration, motion graphics and packaging. Includes
profiles of visual artists, ad agencies and
graphic design firms.
Cost: $37.00
Frequency: Monthly
Circulation: 54149
Mailing list available for rent

20532 Print Solutions Magazine
Document Management Industries
Association
330 N Wabash Ave
Suite 2000
Chicago, IL 60611

800-230-0175
FAX 312-673-6880
Home Page: www.psda.org

Peter L Colaianni CAE, Editor-in-Chief
Preeti Vasishtha, Assistant Editor
Lashell Stratton, Assistant Editor
Rebecca Trela, Assistant Editor

The independent's source for marketing, man-
agement and product information.
Cost: $49.00
276 Pages
Frequency: Monthly
Circulation: 42000
ISSN: 0532-1700
Founded in 1962
Printed in 4 colors on glossy stock

20533 Print on Demand Business
Cygnus Business Media
1233 Janesville Avenue
Fort Atkinson, WI 53538

631-845-2700
800-547-7377
FAX 631-845-2741
E-Mail: info@cygnus.com
Home Page: www.cygnusb2b.com/

Bob Hall, Executive Editor
Denise Gustavson, Managing Editor
Paul Bonaiuto, CFO
John French, CEO

Editorial includes a look at new products, industry news, updated technology, tips on the
best equipment and a look ahead with an upcoming calendar of events.
Frequency: Bi-Monthly

20534 Printing Impressions
North American Publishing Company

1500 Spring Garden St
Suite 1200
Philadelphia, PA 19130-4094

215-238-5300
800-627-2689
FAX 215-238-5342
E-Mail: mmichelson@napco.com
Home Page: www.napco.com

Ned S Borowsky, CEO
Chris Bauer, Managing Editor
Tunisia Bey, Circulation Manager

Offers news, articles, updates, statistics, re-
search reports and more for the printing indus-
try including printers involved in commercial
and newspaper printing and trades.
Frequency: Weekly
Circulation: 83035
Founded in 1958
Mailing list available for rent

20535 Printing Industry Association of the
South - Magazine
Printing Industry Association of the South
PO Box 290249
Nashville, TN 37229-0249

615-366-1094
FAX 615-366-4192
E-Mail: info@pias.org
Home Page: www.pias.org

Ed Chalifoux, President
James Tepper, Board Member

Print industry information. Free with member-
ship.
Frequency: Monthly
Circulation: 5000
Printed in 4 colors on glossy stock

20536 Printing Manager
National Association of Printing Leadership
One Meadowlands Plaza
Suite 1511
East Rutherford, NJ 07073

201-634-9600
800-642-6275
FAX 201-634-0324
E-Mail: webmaster@napl.org
Home Page: www.napl.org

Joseph P Truncale, President/CEO
Timothy Fischer, Executive Vp/COO

Provides current news for printing executives
including the latest industry, marketing and
management news.
40 Pages
Frequency: Quarterly
Circulation: 6000
Founded in 1933
Mailing list available for rent
Printed in 4 colors

20537 Printing News Magazine
Cygnus Business Media
3 Huntington Quadrangle
Suite 301N
Melville, NY 11747

631-845-2700
FAX 631-845-2741
E-Mail: editor@printingnews.com
Home Page: www.printingnews.com
Social Media: *Facebook, Twitter, LinkedIn,*
RSS

David Nathenson, Publisher
Michael Zerner, Associate Publisher
David Lindsay, Editor-in-Chief
Rachel Frank, Editor

News and information on the graphic arts industry in New York, Connecticut, New Jersey
and Pennsylvania.
Cost: $39.95
44 Pages
Circulation: 7000
Founded in 1937

20538 Printing News Online
Cygnus Business Media
3 Huntingon Quadrangle
Suite 301N
Melville, NY 11747

631-845-2700
800-308-6397
FAX 631-845-2741
E-Mail: editor@printingnews.com
Home Page: www.printingnews.com
Social Media: *Facebook, Twitter, LinkedIn, RSS*

David Nathenson, Publisher
Michael Zerner, Associate Publisher
David Lindsay, Editor-in-Chief
Rachel Frank, Editor

Includes timely news and information on a variety of subjects including technological breakthroughs, industry trends, marketing, finance, as well as industry leader and corporate profiles.

20539 Publishing Executive
North American Publishing Company
1500 Spring Garden St
Suite 1200
Philadelphia, PA 19130-4094

215-238-5300
FAX 215-238-5342
E-Mail: nskodzinski@napco.com
Home Page: www.printmediamag.com/

Ned S Borowsky, CEO
Noelle Skodzinski, Editor-in-Chief
Matt Steinmetz, Associate Editor
Rhoda Dixon, Circulation Manager
Candas Carmen, Associate Publisher

Publishing Executive (formerly PrintMedia) delivers information to magazine publishers, associations, corporate publishers, advertising and marketing agencies.
Circulation: 17500

20540 Quick Printing
Cygnus Business Media
3 Huntington Quadrangle
Suite 301 North
Melville, NY 11747-803

631-845-2700
800-308-6397
FAX 631-845-2741
E-Mail: Bob@quickprinting.com
Home Page: www.quickprinting.com
Social Media: *Facebook*

Jann Levesque, Group Publisher
Kelley Holmes, Publisher
Bob Hall, Editor
Denise Gustavson, Managing Editor

Business journal for those in the printing business.
Cost: $66.00
Frequency: Monthly
Circulation: 48000
Founded in 1937
Mailing list available for rent

20541 SGIA Journal
Specialty Graphic Imaging Association
10015 Main St
Fairfax, VA 22031-3489

703-385-1335
888-385-3588
FAX 703-273-0456
E-Mail: sgia@sgia.org
Home Page: www.sgia.org
Social Media: *Facebook, Twitter, LinkedIn*

Michael Robertson, President
Sondra Fry Benoudiz, VP Membership

Published quarterly in January, April, July and October.
Circulation: 14000
Founded in 1948

20542 Screen Printing
ST Media Group International
11262 Cornell Park Dr
Cincinnati, OH 45242-1812

513-421-2050
800-421-1321
FAX 513-421-5144
E-Mail: customer@stmediagroup.com
Home Page: www.stmediagroup.com

Tedd Swormstedt, CEO
Brian Foos, CFO
Mark Kissling, Director

Screen printing professionals have relied on Screen Printing for landmark coverage of the latest techniques and technologies that save time, energy and money.
Frequency: Monthly
Circulation: 17000
Founded in 1953
Mailing list available for rent: 17,000 names at $200 per M

20543 Signs of the Times & Screen Printing en Espanol
ST Media Group International
11262 Cornell Park Dr
Cincinnati, OH 45242-1812

513-421-2050
800-421-1321
FAX 513-421-5144
E-Mail: customer@stmediagroup.com
Home Page: www.stmediagroup.com

Tedd Swormstedt, CEO
Brian Foos, CFO
Mark Kissling, Director

Covering the industries of signmaking, screen printing and digital imaging for Spanish speaking visual communications markets.
Frequency: Monthly
Circulation: 17000
Founded in 1906
Mailing list available for rent

20544 Wide Format Imaging Magazine
Cygnus Publishing
3 Huntington Quadrangle
Suite 301 North
Melville, NY 11747

631-845-2700
800-308-6397
FAX 631-845-2741
E-Mail: davis@wide-formatimaging.com
Home Page: www.wide-formatimaging.com
Social Media: *Facebook, Twitter, LinkedIn, RSS*

David Nathenson, Publisher
Karen Lowry-Hall, Editor
Denise M Gustavson, Managing Editor/Web Editor
Charlie Lillis, Director Content Licensing
Katie Brennan, Vice President

Wide Format Imaginging Magazine provides information on new technologies, analysis of new products, business management tips, and profiles of significant people in the industry. The magazine is a monthly business publication serving 18,000 wide-format professionals. These mostly small business owners are responsible for wide- and large-format drawings, blueprints, soft signage, outdoor signage, posters, POP displays, digital fine art printmaking, and large trade show graphics.
Cost: $25.00
Frequency: Monthly
Mailing list available for rent

20545 BIA Mid Management Conference
Printing Industry of Illinois
200 Deer Run Road
Sewickley, PA 15143

412-741-6860
800-910-4283
FAX 412-741-2311
E-Mail: printing@printing.org
Home Page: www.bindingindustries.org
Social Media: *Facebook, Twitter, LinkedIn*

Michael Makin, President/CEO
Justin Goldstein, Manager

Brings together mid-managers from trade binderies, graphic finishing, information packaging, custom loose leaf manufacturing, and the suppliers to those industries.
600 Attendees
Frequency: Annual/May

20546 CMM International
Romeland house
Romeland Hill
St Albans
Herdfordshire

212-268-4160
FAX 212-268-4178
E-Mail: info@mackbrooks.co.uk
Home Page: www.cmmshow.com

The premier converting and package printing event for thousands of professionals.
Frequency: June4-7 Chicago
Founded in 1978

20547 Graphic Arts
Graphic Arts Show Company
1899 Preston White Drive
Reston, VA 20191-5468

703-264-7200
FAX 703-620-9187
E-Mail: info@gasc.org
Home Page: www.gasc.org

Chris Price, VP
Kelly Kilga, Director Operations
Ralph Nappi, President

One of America's foremost regional prepress, printing, publishing, and converting trade shows. 300 booths, 70,000 square feet.
18000 Attendees
Frequency: March
Founded in 1982

20548 Graphics of the Americas
Printing Association of Florida
6275 Hazeltine National Drive
Orlando, FL 32822

407-240-8009
800-331-0461
FAX 407-240-8333
E-Mail: gain@piagatf.org
Home Page: www.goa.2013.com

Bill Maguire, Chairman
Larry Kudeviz, Treasurer
Rob Hasson, First Vice Chairman
Art Abbott, Second Vice Chairman
George Ryan, CEO

We are the second largest Graphic Arts and Converting show in America. We give you two vital markets, Southeast US and Latin America: Mexico, South America, Central America and the Caribbean. Our 28 year track record reflects our success with both exhibitors and show visitors.
20000 Attendees

20549 Gutenberg Festival
American Printer
2100 West Loop South
Suite 900
Houston, TX 77027-3515

713-300-0674
E-Mail: info@AmericanPrinter.com
Home Page: www.americanprinter.com
Social Media: *Facebook, Twitter, RSS*

Kelly Kilga, Conference/Show Operations
Director
Lilly Kinney, Conference Manager
Tina Scott, Exhibit Sales Director
Chrissie Hahn, Exhibit Sales Manager

The top printing event on the west coast and
the only place to see live running equipment
both traditional and digital.
15000 Attendees
Frequency: April
Mailing list available for rent

20550 Interquest
Interquest Ltd.
513-D Stewart Street
Charlottesville, VA 22902

434-979-9945
FAX 434-979-9959
E-Mail: iquest@inter-quest.com
Home Page: www.inter-quest.com

David Davis, Director

Interquest analysts will present key results
from the company's latest research in the field.
Frequency: March

20551 Labelexpo America
Tarsus Group Plc

E-Mail: sales@labelexpo.com
Home Page: www.labelexpo-americas.com

Label, printing, decoration, web printing and
converting industry's largest expo.
Frequency: Sept, Chicago

**20552 National Association of Professional
Print Buyers**
15050 Northeast 20th Avenue
Suite A
North Miami, FL 33181-1123

305-956-9563

Vincent Mallardi, Executive Director
400 booths.
2.5M Attendees
Frequency: April
Founded in 1969

**20553 Non-Impact Printing Conference and
Exhibit**
IS&T-The Society for Imaging Science &
Technology
7003 Kilworth Lane
Springfield, VA 22151-4008

703-642-9090
FAX 703-642-9094
E-Mail: info@imaging.org
Home Page: www.imaging.org

Robert R Buckley, President
Ingeborg Tastl, Secretary
Scott Silence, Treasurer

Annual conference and exhibits of non-impact
printing equipment, supplies and services, including printer components, printer
consumables, paper and document handling devices and display units.
620 Attendees

20554 Print
Graphic Arts Show Company

1899 Preston White Drive
Reston, VA 20191-5435

703-264-7200
FAX 703-620-9187
E-Mail: info@gasc.org
Home Page: www.gasc.org

Ralph Nappi, President
Chris Price, Vice President
Kelly Kilga, Director Communications
Lilly Kinney, Conference Manager

This is the largest, most comprehensive event
for the commercial, package printing and converting industry in the world in 2013. This
huge international event held every four years
offers you more running machinery under one
roof than any other event anywhere.
40000 Attendees
Frequency: September/Annual
Founded in 1968
Mailing list available for rent

20555 Print Media Conference & Expo
c/o North American Publishing Company
1500 Spring Garden St, Suite 1200
Philadelphia, PA 19130-4094

888-627-2630
FAX 215-409-0100
E-Mail: printmediaexpo@napco.com
Home Page: www.pubxpo.com

20556 SGIA Technology Show
Specialty Graphic Imaging Association
10015 Main Street
Fairfax, VA 22031-3489

703-385-1335
888-385-3588
FAX 703-273-0456
E-Mail: sgia@sgia.org
Home Page: www.sgia.org
Social Media: *Facebook, Twitter, LinkedIn*

Michael Robertson, President/CEO
Sondra Fry Benoudiz, VP Membership

Technologies showcased include: embossing,
printing, graphics, digital imaging, screen
printing and embroidering.
14000 Attendees
Frequency: September
Founded in 1948

**20557 Tools of Change for Publishing
Conference**
O'Reilly Media, Inc.
1005 Gravenstein Highway North
Sebastopol, CA 95472

707-827-7019
800-889-8969
FAX 707-824-8268
E-Mail: orders@oreilly.com
Home Page: www.oreilly.com
Social Media: *Facebook, Twitter, YouTube,RSS*

Gina Blaber, Vice President, Conferences
Suzanne Axtell, Communications Manager
Shirley Bailes, Speaker Manager

Expect coverage with a range of practical,
in-depth sessions that cover the innovations
rocking every aspect of the art, craft, and business of publishing in the 21st century.
Frequency: February

20558 Vue/Point Conference
Graphic Arts Show Company
1189 Preston White Drive
Reston, VA 22091-4367

703-264-7200
FAX 703-620-9187
E-Mail: info@gasc.org
Home Page: www.gasc.org

David Poulos, Conference Coordinator

Presents topics via panel discussions composed
of printing professionals who are willing to
share their experiences.

Directories & Databases

20559 Coldset Web Offset Directory
Printing Industries of America/Graphic Arts
200 Deer Run Rd
Sewickley, PA 15143-2600

412-741-6860
800-910-4283
FAX 412-741-2311
E-Mail: printing@printing.org
Home Page: www.printing.org
Social Media: *Facebook, Twitter, LinkedIn*

Michael F Makin, President
Eric Delzer, Chairman

Over 600 printing firms with more than 1,000
presses in the US, Puerto Rico and Canada are
profiled.
Cost: $120.00
Frequency: BiAnnual

20560 Corporate and Incentive Travel
Coastal Communications Corporation
2700 N Military Trail
Suite 120
Boca Raton, FL 33431-6394

561-989-0600
FAX 561-989-9509
E-Mail: ccceditor@att.net
Home Page: www.themeetingmagazines.com

Harvey Grotsky, Publisher/Editor-In-Chief
Susan Wycoff Fell, Managing Editor
Susan S Gregg, Managing Editor
Mitch D Miller, Creative Director

Read by over 40,000 ABC audited meeting and
incentive travel planners and key executives responsible for meeting decisions. Articles range
monthly from in-depth how-to's, to issue oriented features, examinations of professional
concerns, thoroughly researched destination reports, and columns by industry experts
Cost: $50.00
Frequency: Annual
Circulation: 60,000
Founded in 1983
Mailing list available for rent

**20561 Directory International
Suppliers/Printing
Publishing/Converting Technologies**
Association for Suppliers of Printing,
Publishing
& Converting Technologies
1899 Preston White Drive
Reston, VA 20191-4367

703-264-7200
FAX 703-620-0994
E-Mail: npes@npes.org
Home Page: www.npes.org

Ralph J Nappi, President
Douglas Sprei, Director
Marketing/Communications
Jesus A Romero, Database Manager
Steve Prejsner, Manager of Technology

An online, freely accessible, association database of NPES member companies and more
than 500 products, searchable by product category, keyword or company name.
220 Pages
Frequency: Biennial

20562 Heatset Web Offset Directory
Printing Industries of America/Graphic Arts

200 Deer Run Rd
Sewickley, PA 15143-2600

412-741-6860
800-910-4283
FAX 412-741-2311
E-Mail: gain@piagatf.org
Home Page: www.printing.org
Social Media: *Facebook, Twitter, LinkedIn*

Michael Makin, President
Eric Delzer, Chairman

Offers information on nearly 500 heatset web
printing firms in the United States, Puerto Rico
and Canada including products produced.
Cost: $50.00
110 Pages
Frequency: BiAnnually

20563 In Plant Reproductions: Buyer's Guide Issue

North American Publishing Company
1500 Spring Garden St
Suite 1200
Philadelphia, PA 19130-4094

215-238-5300
800-627-2689
FAX 215-238-5342

Ned S Borowsky, CEO

Firms that manufacture or supply equipment,
materials and services to printing facilities of
firms or organizations, including art, paste-up
and copy preparation, mailing systems, darkroom equipment, presses, paper, word processing, computerized composition and electronic
publishing.
Cost: $35.00
Frequency: Annual December
Circulation: 41,000

20564 International Directory of Private Presses

Educators Research Service
2443 Fair Oaks Boulevard
Suite 316
Sacramento, CA 95825-7684

Home Page: www.briarpress.org

Offers valuable information on over 1,200 private presses and hobbyist printers worldwide.
Cost: $50.00
300 Pages
Frequency: Annual

20565 Print Image International

401 N Michigan Avenue
Suite 2100
Chicago, IL 60611-4245

312-268-8015
800-234-0640
FAX 312-321-6869
Home Page: www.printimage.org

John Giles, Editor
Steve Johnson, President
300 Pages

20566 Rauch Guide to the US Ink Industry

Grey House Publishing
4919 Route 22
PO Box 56
Amenia, NY 12501-0056

518-789-8700
800-562-2139
FAX 518-789-0556
E-Mail: books@greyhouse.com
Home Page: www.greyhouse.com
Social Media: *Facebook, Twitter*

Leslie Mackenzie, Publisher
Richard Gottlieb, Editor

The Guide to this complex and diffuse $4.2 bil-
lion ink industry provides market facts and figures in a highly organized format, ideal for
today's busy personnel. The report serves as a

ready-reference for top executives as well as
the industry newcomer.
Cost: $595.00
700 Pages
ISBN: 1-592371-26-4
Founded in 1981

20567 Rauch Guide to the US and Canadian Pulp & Paper Industry

Grey House Publishing
4919 Route 22
PO Box 56
Amenia, NY 12501-0056

518-789-8700
800-562-2139
FAX 518-789-0556
E-Mail: books@greyhouse.com
Home Page: www.greyhouse.com
Social Media: *Facebook, Twitter*

Leslie Mackenzie, Publisher
Richard Gottlieb, Editor

Provides current market information and trends
to; industry economics and government regulations; company share data for each of the leading product categories; technology and raw
material information; industry sources of further data; and unique profiles of 500+ pulp and
paper manufacturers, a section which includes
all known companies with pulp and paper sales
at or over $15 million annually.
Cost: $595.00
400 Pages
ISBN: 1-592371-31-0
Founded in 1981

20568 Who's Who SGIA

Specialty Graphic Imaging Association
10015 Main St
Fairfax, VA 22031-3489

703-385-1335
888-385-3588
FAX 703-273-0456
E-Mail: sgia@sgia.org
Home Page: www.sgia.org
Social Media: *Facebook, Twitter, LinkedIn*

Michael Robertson, President
Sondra Fry Benoudiz, VP Membership
Circulation: 3,800
Founded in 1948

Industry Web Sites

20569 http://gold.greyhouse.com

G.O.L.D Grey House OnLine Databases
Grey House Publishing's online database platform, GOLD, offers Quick Search, Keyword
Search and Expert Search for most business
sectors including printing and allied markets.
The GOLD platform makes finding the information you need quick and easy - whether
you're a novice searcher or an experienced database user. All of Grey House's directory
products are available for subscription on the
GOLD platform.

20570 www.fsea.com

Foil Stamping and Embossing Association
For companies engaged in the process of hot
stamping or embossing in the graphics industry
and companies that manufacture, distribute or
provide services to the hot stamping/embossing
industry.

20571 www.gaa.org

Gravure Association of America
Members are gravure printers, converters, suppliers and users.

20572 www.greyhouse.com

Grey House Publishing
Authoritative reference directories for most
business sectors including printing and allied
markets. Users can search the online databases
with varied search criteria allowing for custom
searches by product category, geographic area,
sales volume, keyword, subject and more. Full
Grey House catalog and online ordering also
available.

20573 www.iaphc.org

International Assn of Printing House
Craftsmen
A voluntary graphic arts organization in which
many people share their knowledge and their
skill with one another. Open to anyone in any
part of the graphic arts community who wish
technical information.

20574 www.ipa.org

International Prepress Association
Members produce pre-press material for the
graphics industry.

20575 www.magazine.org

Magazine Publishers of America
Promotes magazines as an advertising medium.
Provides information services and assistance to
members in areas of circulation marketing.

20576 www.napim.org

National Association of Printing Ink
Manufacturers
Purpose is to represent the printing ink industry
in the U.S.A.

20577 www.napl.org

National Association for Printing
Leadership
Promotes the interests in leadership for
priniting professionals.

20578 www.npes.org

NPES-Association for Suppliers of Printing
&
Publishing Technology

Members are manufacturers and distributors of
graphic arts equipment, systems, software and
supplies. Promotes marketing, safety and industry standards, international trade and government relations.

20579 www.pbbai.net

Printing Brokerage Buyers Assoc
International
Promotes business relationships among brokers, buying groups, manufacturers and related
companies. Sets standards and codes and supplies information and referrals.

20580 www.pgca.org

Printing and Graphic Communications
Association
Serving the graphic communications commu-
nity in the Washington, D.C. metropolitan area.

20581 www.pias.org

Printing Industry Association of the South
Represents the print industry.

20582 www.pinc.org

Print Buyers Association
For professionals in print buying.

20583 www.pine.org

Printing Institute of New England

20584 www.polymers.com

Polymers DotCom

20585 www.printing.org
Printing Industries of America (PIA)
The largest graphic arts organization founded over 100 years ago.

20586 www.teched.Vt.edu/gcc
Graphic Comm Central
Web portal for education in the graphic communications industry.

20587 www.waterless.org
Waterless Printing Association
Dedicated to the informational and educational needs of its printer and sponsor members.

Associations

20588 American Society of Health Care Marketing
1 N Franklin Street
Chicago, IL 60606-3421

773-327-1064
FAX 312-422-4579

20589 Arthur W Page Society
230 Park Avenue
Suite 455
New York, NY 10169

212-400-7959
FAX 347-474-7399
E-Mail: rbolton@awpagesociety.com
Home Page: www.awpagesociety.com
Social Media: *Twitter, LinkedIn, YouTube, RSS*

Roger Bolton, President
Gary Sheffer, Chairman
Valerie Di Maria, Secretary
Robert De Fillippo, Treasurer
Sally Benjamin Young, Vice Chair

Professional public relations organization with
a single mission, to strengthen the management
policy role of the chief public relations officer.
Conducts seminars and conferences.
397 Members
Founded in 1983

20590 Association of Women in Communications
3337 Duke Street
Alexandria, VA 22314

703-370-7436
FAX 703-342-4311
E-Mail: info@womcom.org
Home Page: www.womcom.org
Social Media: *Facebook, Twitter, LinkedIn, YouTube, Google+*

Mitzie Zerr, Chair
Linda Timm Hankmeier, Director
Lisa Angle, Secretary
Missy Kruse, Vice Chair
Pat Meads, Treasurer

Professional organization that champions the
advancement of women across all communications disciplines by recognizing excellence,
promoting leadership and positioning its members at the forefront of the evolving communications era. Hosts a bi-annual conference.
3500 Members
Founded in 1909

20591 Baptist Communicators Association
1519 Menlo Drive
Kennesaw, GA 30152

770-425-3728
E-Mail: webmaster@baptistcommunicators.org
Home Page: www.baptistcommunicators.org
Social Media: *Facebook, Twitter, Vimeo, Wordpress*

Ian Richardson, President
Joe Westbury, Treasurer
Shawn Hendricks, President-Elect
Barbara L. Denman, Program Chair-Elect
Brian Hobbs, Program Chairs

PR and Journalism professionals.
300 Members
Founded in 1953

20592 Business Marketing Association: Atlanta
2801 Buford Highway, Druid Chase
Suite 375
Atlanta, GA 30329

404-641-9417
800-664-4262
FAX 312-822-0054
E-Mail: info@bmaatlanta.org
Home Page: bmaatlanta.org
Social Media: *Facebook, Twitter, LinkedIn, Google+*

Moira Vetter, President
Mark Towery, President Elect
Subodh Singh, VP Member Services
Khoi Ta, VP Young Professionals
Mark Miranda, VP Sponsorship

The Atlanta chapter of the BMA includes marketing executives from a variety of industries
and backgrounds including research, advertising, promotions, events, Web development,
printing and more. The BMA offers an information-packed Website, online skills-building,
marketing certification programs, and industry
surveys and papers. In addition, members have
the opportunity to interact with peers at seminars, participate in chapter training programs
and the BMA Annual Conference.
Founded in 1922

20593 Business Marketing Association: Boston
246 Hampshire Street
Cambridge, MA 02130

617-418-4000
800-664-4262
FAX 312-822-0054
E-Mail: info@thebmaboston.com
Home Page: www.thebmaboston.com

Michael Lewis, President
Will Robinson, VP Public Relations
Matthew Mamet, VP Internet Marketing
Larry Perreault, VP Finance
Chris Perkett, VP Programming

BMA Boston helps members improve their
ability to manage business-to-business marketing and communications for greater productivity and profitability by providing unique access
to information, ideas, and the experience of
peers. The BMA offers an information-packed
Website, online skills-building, marketing certification programs, and industry surveys and
papers. In addition, members have the opportunity to interact with peers at seminars, chapter
training programs and the BMA Annual
Conference.

20594 Communications Roundtable
1250 24th Street NW
Suite 250
Washington, DC 20037

202-755-5180
FAX 202-466-0544
Home Page: www.roundtable.org

Michael Reichgut, Chairman
Shawn Dolley, CEO

Association of more than 20 public relations,
marketing, graphics, advertising, training and
other communications organizations with more
than 12,000 professional members. The goals
include furthering professionalism, cooperation
between member organizations, career and employment support, and employer assistance.

20595 Consultants in Public Relations SA
4200 Massachusetts Avenue NW
Washington, DC 20016

202-244-2580
FAX 202-224-2581
E-Mail: jreed94680@ad.com

John M Reed, Chairman
Founded in 1970

20596 Council of Communications Management
65 Enterprise
Aliso Viejo, CA 92656

866-463-6226
FAX 303-850-6819
E-Mail: info@thecommunicationexchange.org
Home Page: www.ccmconnection.com
Social Media: *Facebook, LinkedIn*

Becky Healy, President
Barry Mike, Past President
Kerrin Nally, Secretary
Jeff Kosiorek, Vice President
Michael Rudnick, Treasurer

Established more than 40 years ago as a forum
for seasoned professionals to share best practices in organizational communications.
Founded in 1955

20597 Council of Public Relations Firms
32 East 31st Street
9th Floor
New York, NY 10016

646-588-0139
FAX 646-651-4770
E-Mail: kcripps@prcouncil.net
Home Page: www.prfirms.org
Social Media: *Twitter, LinkedIn, YouTube,RSS, Pinterest, Flickr*

Kathy Cripps, President
Matt Shaw, Senior Vice President
Bryan Harris, Treasury
Aaron Schoenherr, Secretary
Chris Graves, Chairman
100+ Members

20598 Entertainment Publicists Professional Society
PO Box 5841
Beverly Hills, CA 90209

E-Mail: info@eppsonline.org
Home Page: www.eppsonline.org

Rick Markovitz, President

The Society has chapters in Los Angeles and
New York. Members work in publicity, promo-
tions and marketing.
Founded in 1991

20599 Hispanic Public Relations Association
PO Box 86760
Los Angeles, CA 90086-0760

E-Mail: info@hpra-usa.org
Home Page: www.hpra-usa.org
Social Media: *Facebook, Twitter*

Andy Checo, President

The HPRA's mission is the professional development and advancement of its members and
the practice of Hispanic public relations.
Founded in 1984

20600 Institute for Public Relations
University of Florida
PO Box 118400
2096 Weimer Hall
Gainesville, FL 32611-8400

352-392-0280
FAX 352-846-1122
E-Mail: ace@ifas.ufl.edu
Home Page: www.instituteforpr.org

Social Media: *Facebook, Twitter, LinkedIn, YouTube, RSS*

Dr. Tina McCorkindale, President & CEO
Kenneth Makovsky, Co-Chairs
Jenn Moyer, Foundations Operations Manager
Gary Sheffer, Treasurer
Dr. Sarab Kochhar, Director of Research

Improving the effectiveness of organizations by advancing the professional knowledge and practice of public relations through research and education.
Founded in 1956
Mailing list available for rent

20601 International Association of Business Communicators
601 Montgomery Street
Suite 1900
San Francisco, CA 94111

415-544-4700
800-776-4222
FAX 415-544-4747
E-Mail: member_relations@iabc.com
Home Page: www.iabc.com
Social Media: *Facebook, Twitter, LinkedIn, YouTube, Pinterest, Google+, I*

Michael Ambjorn, Chair
Dianne Chase, Vice Chair
Sharon L. Hunter, Director
Ginger D. Homan, Secretary/ Treasurer
Carlos Fulcher, Executive Director

International knowledge network for professionals engaged in strategic business communication management.
12000 Members
Founded in 1970

20602 Original Equipment Suppliers Association
Original Equipment Suppliers Association
25925 Telegraph Rd
Suite 350
Southfield, MI 48033-2553

248-952-6401
FAX 248-952-6404
E-Mail: info@oesa.org
Home Page: www.autopr.org
Social Media: *Facebook, Twitter, LinkedIn, RSS, Tumblr*

Daniel E. Sceli, Chair
Samir Salman, Vice Chairman
Julie A Fream, President & CEO
Joseph B. Anderson Jr., Director
Jacqui Dedo, Senior Advisor

Provides a forum for information exchange among communication professionals with the automotive industry. Two conferences are held every year, topics are integrated marketing, communications and the automotive industry.
450 Members
Founded in 1998

Newsletters

20603 Bulldog Reporter
InfoCom Group
5900 Hollis Street
Suite L
Emeryville, CA 94608-2008

510-653-3035
800-959-1059
FAX 510-596-9331
Home Page: www.infocomgroup.com

James Sinkinson, Publisher
Tim Gray, President

Emphasis on placement opportunities and media profiles, as well as personnel changes at

media outlets throughout the US.
Cost: $599.00
Frequency: Fortnightly
Circulation: 5000
Founded in 1980

20604 Contacts: Media Pipeline for PR People
Larimi Communications Association
500 Executive Boulevard
Ossining on Hudson, NY 10562-1114

914-923-9400
FAX 914-923-9484
E-Mail: info@mercommawards.com
Home Page: www.mercommawards.com/

Michael M Smith, Publisher
Madeleine Gillis, Editor

Provides pipeline of communications between what an editor needs and a public relations person can supply.
Cost: $287.00
1 Pages
Frequency: Weekly
Founded in 1975
Printed in one color

20605 Downtown Promotion Reporter
Alexander Communications Group
1916 Park Ave
Suite 501
New York, NY 10037-3733

212-281-6099
800-232-4317
FAX 212-283-7269
E-Mail: info@downtowndevelopment.com
Home Page: www.downtowndevelopment.com/

Romauld Alexander, President

Tested ideas for promotion, public relations, marketing, increasing business, participation, downtown image building, sales, and events.
Cost: $189.00
Frequency: Monthly
ISSN: 0363-2830

20606 Healthcare PR & Marketing News
Phillips Business Information
1201 Seven Locks Road
Suite 300
Potomac, MD 20854-2931

301-354-1400
FAX 301-340-1451

Sharmi Banik, Editor
Kismet Toksu Gould, Publisher

Issues faced by health care executives in PR firms and hospitals. Regular features include industry surveys, case studies and executive profiles.
Cost: $397.00
Frequency: Bi-Monthly
Founded in 1992

20607 High-Tech Hot Sheet
Hot Sheet Publishing
114 Sansome Street
Suite 1224
San Francisco, CA 94104

415-421-6225
FAX 415-421-6225

Art Gracia, Editor/Publisher

Reporting updates and changes in staff, beat assignments, new publications, suspension of publishing in high-tech media.
Cost: $395.00
Frequency: Monthly
Founded in 1987

20608 Holmes Report
Holmes Group

271 W 47th St
Suite 23A
New York, NY 10036-1447

212-333-2300
FAX 212-333-2624
E-Mail: gdrury@holmesreport.com
Home Page: www.holmesreport.com

Paul Holmes, President
Greg Drury, Managing Editor
Arun Sudhaman, Managing Editor

Source of information for public relations and corporate communications professionals.
Cost: $290.00
Frequency: Weekly
Circulation: 15,000
ISBN: 0-972364-50-1
Founded in 2001
Printed in 4 colors on glossy stock

20609 Interactive PR & Marketing News
Phillips Publishing
1201 Seven Locks Road
#300
Potomac, MD 20854-2931

301-354-1400
FAX 301-424-8602
E-Mail: editor@interactivepr.com
Home Page: www.phillips.com

Angela Duff, Publisher

Covers the latest trends and news on the World Wide Web and Internet markets and looks at their users.
Cost: $347.00
Frequency: 23 per year
Circulation: 5M

20610 Interactive Public Relations
Ragan Communications
316 N Michigan Ave
Suite 400
Chicago, IL 60601-3773

312-960-4100
800-493-4867
FAX 312-960-4106
E-Mail: cservice@ragan.com
Home Page: www.ragan.com

Jim Ylisela, Publisher
Mark ragan, CEO
Kasia Chalko, Marketing Director

Includes targeted newsletters in the areas of employment communication, Web PR, organizational writing and editing, sales and marketing, media relations, motivational management, and investor relations.
Cost: $279.00
Founded in 1970

20611 Jack O'Dwyer's Newsletter
JR O'Dwyer Company
271 Madison Ave
Suite 600
New York, NY 10016-1013

212-683-2750
FAX 212-683-2750
E-Mail: jack@odwyerpr.com
Home Page: www.odwyerpr.com

Jack O'Dwyer, President
Fay Shapiro, Publisher
Eileen Kelly, Sales Manager
John ODwyer, Advertising Sales Manager

Covers current happenings in both electronic and print media, including new PR products and accounts, PR campaigns, and books about public relations.
Cost: $295.00
Frequency: Weekly
Founded in 1970

20612 Levin's Public Relations Report
Levin Public Relations & Marketing

2 East Ave
Suite 201
Larchmont, NY 10538-2419

914-834-2570
FAX 914-834-5919
Home Page: www.saralevin.com

Sara B Levin, President
Sylvia Moss, Editor

Strategies, tactics for the CEO, VP Sales and
Marketing seeking new marketing/public rela-
tions effectiveness.
Cost: $29.00
Frequency: Monthly
Founded in 1984

20613 Media Relations Insider
InfoCom Group
124 Linden Street
Oakland, CA 94607

510-596-9300
800-959-1059
Home Page: www.infocomgroup.com
Social Media: *Facebook, Twitter, LinkedIn,
RSS*

Eastern and Western editions give you media
news and exclusive interviews with top busi-
ness journalists in your region.
Cost: $399.00
Frequency: Monthly
Mailing list available for rent

20614 Media Relations Report
Ragan Communications
316 N Michigan Ave
Suite 400
Chicago, IL 60601-3773

312-960-4100
800-493-4867
FAX 312-960-4106
E-Mail: cservice@ragan.com
Home Page: www.ragan.com

Jim Ylisela, Publisher
Mark Ragan, CEO
Cost: $28.92
Frequency: Monthly
Circulation: 1000
Founded in 1975
Mailing list available for rent
Printed in 2 colors on matte stock

20615 MediaQuest
MediaQuest Publishing
PO Box 9222
Boston, MA 02114-0996

617-536-5353
FAX 617-367-9151

Barbara Kalunian, Editor/Publisher

Media placement becomes easier for PR professionals through behind the scenes interviews
with leading journalists at top broadcast and
print outlets.
Cost: $295.00
Frequency: Bi-Monthly
Founded in 1990

20616 Memo to the President
American Association State Colleges &
Universities
1307 New York Ave Nw
Suite 5
Washington, DC 20005-4723

202-293-7070
800-542-2062
FAX 202-296-5819

E-Mail: chilcotts@aascu.org
Home Page: www.aascu.org

Edward Elnendorf, President
Susan M Chilcott, Editor
Cost: $100.00
6 Pages
Frequency: Monthly
Circulation: 1200
ISSN: 0047-6692
Founded in 1961
Printed in 2 colors on matte stock

20617 O'Dwyers Washington Report
JR O'Dwyer Company
271 Madison Ave
#600
New York, NY 10016-1013

212-683-2750
FAX 212-683-2750
E-Mail: jack@odwyerpr.com
Home Page: www.odwyerpr.com

Jack O'Dwyer, President
Kevin McCowley, Advertising Sales Manager
John ODwyer, Advertising Sales Manager
Covers Washington public relations and public
affairs lobbying news.
Cost: $95.00
8 Pages

20618 Opportunity
Career Skills Press/Brody Communications
815 Greenwood Ave
Suite 8
Jenkintown, PA 19046-2800

215-886-1688
800-726-7936
FAX 215-886-1699
E-Mail: info@brodypro.com
Home Page: www.brodypro.com

Marjorie Brody, President
Miryam S Raddy, Marketing Manager

Feature products published by Career Skills
Press unit.
4 Pages
Frequency: Quarterly
Circulation: 10000
Founded in 1983
Printed in 4 colors on glossy stock

20619 PR Intelligence Report
Lawrence Ragan Communications
316 N Michigan Ave
Suite 400
Chicago, IL 60601-3773

312-960-4100
FAX 312-960-4106
E-Mail: cservice@ragan.com
Home Page: www.ragan.com

Jim Ylisela, Publisher
Mark Regan, CEO

Digs below the surface to provide the details,
insights and information you need to improve
your career, make your next campaign a success, or avoid costly mistakes.
Cost: $279.00
8 Pages
Circulation: 1000
Founded in 1970
Printed in 2 colors on matte stock

20620 PR News
Phillips Business Information
4 Choke Cherry Rd
Fl 2
Rockville, MD 20850-4024

301-450-0035
FAX 301-340-3169
Home Page: www.prandmarketing.com

Matthew Schwartz, Editor
Diane Schwartz, Publisher

Briefing on the latest PR trends, what's working and what's not. We feature case studies of
successful PR campaigns.
Cost: $697.00
10 Pages
Frequency: Weekly
Founded in 1944

20621 PR Reporter
Lawrence Ragan Communications
316 N Michigan Ave
Suite 400
Chicago, IL 60601-3773

312-960-4100
800-493-4867
FAX 312-960-4106
E-Mail: cservice@ragan.com
Home Page: www.ragan.com

Jim Ylisela, Publisher
Mark Ragan, President
Rebecca Anderson, Managing Editor

Weekly publication dedicated to the behavioral
aspects of public relations, public affairs and
communication strategies. Its quick read format
keeps you up to date on the latest theories, research, public opinions, case studies and successful public relations techniques.
Frequency: Weekly
Founded in 1970

20622 PR Tactics
Public Relations Society of America
33 Maiden Ln
Suite 11
New York, NY 10038-5150

212-460-1400
FAX 212-995-0757
E-Mail: helpdesk@prsa.org
Home Page: www.prsa.org

Catherine Bolton, President
Philip Bonaventura, Chief Financial Officer
Cost: $75.00
32 Pages
Frequency: Monthly
Circulation: 25000
Founded in 1947
Printed in 4 colors on newsprint stock

20623 PR Watch
Center for Media and Democracy
520 University Ave
Suite 227
Madison, WI 53703-4929

608-260-9713
FAX 608-260-9714
E-Mail: editor@prwatch.org
Home Page: www.prwatch.org

Lisa Graves, Executive Director
Dave Ross, Secretary
Sheldon Rampton, Research Director
Kristian Knutsen, Administrative Assistant

Investigates and exposes how the public relations industry and other professional propagan-
dists manipulate public information,
perceptions and opinion on behalf of governments and special interests.
Frequency: Quarterly
Founded in 1993

20624 PR Week
114 W 26th Street
3rd Floor
New York, NY 10001

646-638-6000
FAX 646-638-6115
E-Mail: letters@prweek.com
Home Page: www.prweek.com

Lisa Kirk, Publishing Director
Julia Hood, Editor-in-Chief

Cutting-edge newsletter of public relations.
Frequency: Weekly

20625 Partyline Publishing
PartyLine Publishing Company
35 Sutton Place
New York, NY 10022-2464

212-755-3487
FAX 212-755-4859
E-Mail: byermon@ix.netcom.com
Home Page: www.partylinepublishing.com

Morton Yarmon, Editor
Betty Yarmon, Publisher/Editor-in-chief

Weekly media newsletter, delivered by E-mail,
that informs their readers of the latest happenings in the media world...new editors, new publications, new networks, new shows on existing
networks, new producers, any and all media
news.
Cost: $139.50
Frequency: Weekly
Circulation: 1,400
Founded in 1960

20626 Pro Motion
Beyond the Byte
PO Box 388
Fallston, MD 21047

410-877-3524
800-861-1235
FAX 410-877-7064
Home Page: www.pro-motionsnetwork.com

Emily Laisy, President

News of interest to Media Escort and publi-
cists.
Cost: $12.00
4 Pages
Frequency: Quarterly
Circulation: 325
ISSN: 0886-6104
Founded in 1985
Printed in one color on matte stock

20627 Public Relations Career
Opportunities
CEO Update
1575 I Street NW
#1190
Washington, DC 20005-1105

202-408-7900
FAX 202-408-7907

James Zaniello, Editor

Public relations and publis affairs job opportu-
nities compensating $35,000 plus nationwide.
Cost: $217.00
Frequency: Bi-Monthly
Founded in 1986

20628 Ragan's Interactive Public Relations
Lawrence Ragan Communications
316 N Michigan Ave
Suite 400
Chicago, IL 60601-3773

312-960-4100
800-878-5331
FAX 312-960-4106
E-Mail: cservice@ragan.com
Home Page: www.ragan.com

Jim Ylisela, Publisher

Dedicated to helping PR people navigate
cyberspace.
Cost: $269.00
8 Pages
Frequency: Monthly
Circulation: 800
Founded in 1970
Printed in 2 colors on matte stock

20629 Ragan's Media Relations Report
Lawrence Ragan Communications

316 N Michigan Ave
Chicago, IL 60601-3773

312-960-4100
800-493-4867
FAX 312-960-4106
E-Mail: cservice@ragan.com
Home Page: www.ragan.com

Jim Ylisela, Publisher
David Murray, Editor
Diane Tillman, Marketing Manager

Content focuses on personal changes, moves
and additions in various media, including television, radio and print. Offers tips on angles to
take, interviews top journalists on what type of
information they prefer, and continuously updates contact numbers and addresses.
Cost: $317.00
Frequency: Monthly
Founded in 1970
Printed in 2 colors on matte stock

20630 West Coast PR Newsletter
West Coast MediaNet
5928 Lindley Avenue
Encino, CA 91316-1047

818-893-3449
FAX 818-776-1930
Home Page: www.westcoastprjobs.com

Darren Shuster, Publisher
Ken West, Manager

Delivers in-depth inteviews and features, new
media contacts and personnel updates, tips
from experts in various fields, and listings of
new PR markets. Regular coverage includes
media web site and book reviews, as well as
how-to articles, all with a West Coast angle.
Cost: $75.00
16 Pages
Frequency: 12 issues
Circulation: 1M

Magazines & Journals

20631 ACH Product & Marketing
Handbook for Financial Institutions
& Companies
NACHA: The Electronic Payments
Association
13450 Sunrise Valley Drive
Suite 100
Herndon, VA 20171

703-561-1100
FAX 703-787-0996
E-Mail: info@nacha.org
Home Page: www.nacha.org

Janet O Estep, CEO
Marcie Haitema, Chairperson

Designed for full financial institutions and
companies to assist them in understanding
ACH products and services-their benefits, risk
management considerations, marketing techniques and FAQs from both corporate and consumer perspectives.
Cost: $70.00
Frequency: Annual+

20632 Communication World
Int'l Association of Business
Communicators
601 Montgomery Street
Suite 1900
San Francisco, CA 94111

415-544-4700
FAX 415-544-4747

E-Mail: cwmagazine@iabc.com
Home Page: www.iabc.com

Natasha Nicholson, Executive Editor
Sue Khodarahmi, Managing Editor
Sue Cavallaro, Production Editor

Covers the latest in communication research,
technology and trends through in-depth reports
and insightful interviews.
Cost: $150.00
Frequency: Bi-Monthly
Founded in 1970

20633 Currents
Council for Advancement & Support of
Education
1307 New York Ave Nw
Suite 1000
Washington, DC 20005-4726

202-393-1301
FAX 202-387-4973
E-Mail: memberservicecenter@case.org
Home Page: www.case.org

Deborah Bangiorno, Editor
Donald Falkenstein, Vice President of Finance
Will Hayden, Production Coordinator
John Lippincott, President
Marla Misek, Senior Editor

Offers information on campus fund raising,
public relations,and alumni administration.
Cost: $115.00
Circulation: 15000
Founded in 1974

20634 International Public Relations Review
18 W Church Street
Saint Frederick, MD 31701

229-567-8074
FAX 912-845-2991

John Reed, Publisher

Public relations international communications
issues for senior level PR professionals.

20635 Jack O'Dwyer's Services Report
JR O'Dwyer Company
271 Madison Ave
Suite 600
New York, NY 10016-1013

212-683-2750
FAX 212-683-2750
E-Mail: jack@odwyerpr.com
Home Page: www.odwyerpr.com

Jack O'Dwyer, Owner
John ODwyer, Advertising Sales Manager
Eileen Kelly, Sales Manager

Information on film, videotape, database and
release distribution industries which serve pub-
lic relations professionals.
Cost: $45.00
Frequency: Monthly
Circulation: 4500
Founded in 1980

20636 Jack O'Dwyers Washington Report
JR O'Dwyer Company
271 Madison Ave
Suite 600
New York, NY 10016-1013

212-683-2750
FAX 212-683-2750
E-Mail: jack@odwyerpr.com
Home Page: www.odwyerpr.com

Jack O'Dwyer, Owner
John ODwyer, Advertising Sales Manager
Cost: $60.00
Frequency: Weekly
Founded in 1970

20637 Managing Media Relations in a Crisis
NACHA: The Electronic Payments
Association

13450 Sunrise Valley Drive
Suite 100
Herndon, VA 20171

703-561-1100
FAX 703-787-0996
E-Mail: info@nacha.org
Home Page: www.nacha.org

Janet O Estep, CEO
Marcie B Haitema, Chairperson

This guide is designed to assist your organization to develop, test and execute a crisis communication plan. Understand how to address the issues, know whom to call and in what order to alert them, which vendors you can count on to help, and how to develop a means to track the crisis as it grows or abates.
Cost: $30.00

20638 Public Relations Quarterly
Howard Penn Hudson
44 W Market Street
PO Box 311
Rhinebeck, NY 12572-311

845-876-2081
800-572-3451
FAX 845-876-2561
Home Page: www.hudsonsdirectory.com

Howard Penn Hudson, Editor/Publisher
Elaine F Newman, Executive Editor
Berecah Sullivan, Circulation Manager
Nichole Latierre, Marketing Manager

Independent public relations magazine, now 48 years old, presenting articles and columns on the theory and process of public relations and communications.
Cost: $65.00
Frequency: Quarterly
ISSN: 0033-3700
Founded in 1955
Printed in on matte stock

20639 Public Relations Review
Elsevier
6277 Seaharbor Drive
Orlando, FL 32887

877-839-7126
Home Page: www.elsevier.com

Jan D Achenbach, Editor-In-Chief
Bill Godfrey, Chief Information Officer
David Clark, Senior Vice President

Covers public relations, education, government, survey research, public policy, history and bibliographies.
Cost: $110.00
Frequency: 12 issues
Circulation: 1M
ISSN: 0363-0111

20640 Public Relations Strategist
Public Relations Society of America
33 Maiden Ln
Suite 11
New York, NY 10038-5150

212-460-1400
FAX 212-995-0757
E-Mail: william.murray@prsa.org
Home Page: www.prsa.org

Gary McCormick, Chairman/CEO
William Murray, President & COO
Philip Bonaventura, CFO
Jeneen Garcia, Vice President

With emphasis on the issues and trends affecting public relations management, it examines the changing concepts and challenges current practices with relevant, original and thought-provoking articles.
Cost: $100.00
Frequency: 4 issues per ye
Circulation: 20538
Founded in 1947

20641 Public Relations Tactics
Public Relations Society of America
33 Maiden Ln
Suite 11
New York, NY 10038-5150

212-460-1400
FAX 212-995-0757
E-Mail: helpdesk@prsa.org
Home Page: www.prsa.org

Gary McCormick, Chairman/CEO
Gale Spreter, Marketing Manager
Alison Stateman, Managing Editor
Catherine A Bolton, Executive Director
Philip Bonaventura, Chief Financial Officer

News, trends and how-to information for public relations people.
Cost: $75.00
Frequency: Monthly
Circulation: 20538
Founded in 1947

20642 Reputation Management
Editorial Media & Marketing International
708 3rd Avenue
Frnt 2
New York, NY 10017-4201

212-687-5260
E-Mail: kingraham@prcentral.com
Home Page: www.prcentral.com

Kara T Ingraham, Publisher/COO

Editorial focuses on finance, marketing, human resources, government and society. Highlights domestic and international corporate news presenting observations and perspectives vital to the industry.
Cost: $52.00
Frequency: Bi-Monthly
Circulation: 12M
Founded in 1995

Trade Shows

20643 American Society of Health Care Marketing and Public Relations Trade Show
1 N Franklin Street
31st Floor
Chicago, IL 60606-3421

773-327-1064
FAX 312-422-4579

Lauren Barnett, Executive Director

Sixty booths of communications, printing, computer equipment, public relations and fund raising consultants in the health care profession.
600 Attendees
Frequency: September

20644 Arthur W Page Society
Arthur W Page Society
317 Madison Ave
Suite 1607
New York, NY 10017-5201

212-400-7959
FAX 347-474-7399
Home Page: www.awpagesociety.com
Social Media: *Facebook, Twitter, YouTube, RSS*

Roger Bolton, President
Gary Shepper, Chairman
Valerie Di Maria, Secretary
Frequency: Annual/September
Founded in 1986

20645 National Hispanic Market Trade Show and Media Expo (Se Habla Espanol)
Hispanic Business Inc

5385 Hollister Avenue
Suite 204
Santa Barbara, CA 93111

800-806-4268
FAX 805-964-5539
E-Mail: info@hispanstar.com
Home Page: www.hispanstar.com
Social Media: *Facebook, Twitter, LinkedIn*

John Pasini, Cfo/Coo

Annual show of 100 exhibitors of market/research, media, advertising, public relations, information services and recruitment.
1500 Attendees

20646 National School for Public Relations
15948 Derwood Rd
Rockville, MD 20855

301-519-0496
FAX 301-519-0494
E-Mail: info@nspra.org
Home Page: www.nspra.org

Mildred Wainger, Administration Services

Offers information and news for professionals in the field of public relations.
600 Attendees
Frequency: July

20647 Strategic Media Relations Conference
Ragan Communications
316 N Michigan Avenue
Chicago, IL 60601

312-960-4100
800-878-5331
FAX 312-960-4106
E-Mail: cservice@ragan.com
Home Page: www.raganinstitute.com

Showcase of best practices for winning top media coverage in a new era. Learn how peers have garnered more ink, managed crises, built their brands and gone global. Attend pre- and post-conference sessions that provide career-boosting skills in crisis survival, media training, online media relations, PR writing, persuasive communications, PR management, digital PR and pitching stories.
Frequency: March

Directories & Databases

20648 Adweek Directory
Prometheus Global Media
770 Broadway
New York, NY 10003-9595

212-493-4100
FAX 646-654-5368
Home Page: www.prometheusgm.com

Richard D. Beckman, CEO
James A. Finkelstein, Chairman
Madeline Krakowsky, Vice President Circulation
Tracy Brater, Executive Director Creative Service

Adweek Directories Online is where you will find searchable databases with comprehensive information on ad agencies, brand marketers and multicultural media.
Frequency: Annual
Circulation: 800
Founded in 1981

20649 Bacon's Newspaper & Magazine Directories
Cision U.S., Inc.

322 South Michigan Avenue
Suite 900
Chicago, IL 60604

312-263-0070
866-639-5087
E-Mail: info.us@cision.com
Home Page: us.cision.com

Joe Bernardo, President & CEO
Heidi Sullivan, VP & Publisher
Valerie Lopez, Research Director
Jessica White, Research Director
Rachel Farrell, Research Manager

Two volume set listing all daily and community newspapers, magazines and newsletters, news service and syndicates, syndicated columnists, complete editorial staff listings of each publication provided, covers U.S., Canada, Mexico, and Carribean.
Cost: $350.00
4,700 Pages
Frequency: Annual
ISSN: 1088-9639
Founded in 1951
Printed in one color on matte stock

20650 Bacon's Radio/TV/Cable Directory
Cision U.S., Inc.
332 South Michigan Avenue
Suite 900
Chicago, IL 60604

312-263-0070
866-639-5087
E-Mail: info.us@cision.com
Home Page: www.us.cision.com

Joe Bernardo, President & CEO
Heidi Sullivan, VP & Publisher
Valerie Lopez, Research Director
Jessica White, Research Director
Rachel Farrell, Research Manager

Includes comprehensive coverage for contact and programming information for more than 3,500 television networks, cable networks, television syndicators, television stations, and cable systems in the United States and Canada.
Cost: $350.00
Frequency: Annual
ISSN: 1088-9639
Printed in one color on matte stock

20651 Burrelle's Media Directory
BurrellesLuce
75 E Northfield Rd
Livingston, NJ 07039-4532

973-992-6600
800-631-1160
FAX 973-992-7675
E-Mail: inquiry@burrellesluce.com
Home Page: www.burrellesluce.com
Social Media: *Facebook, Twitter, LinkedIn, RSS*

Robert C Waggoner, CEO

Approximately 60,000 media listings in North America. Listings cover newspapers, magazines (trades and consumer), broadcast, and internet outlets.
Cost: $795.00
Frequency: Annual

20652 Corporate Yellow Book
Leadership Directories
104 5th Ave
New York, NY 10011-6901

212-627-4140
FAX 212-645-0931
E-Mail: corporate@leadershipdirectories.com
Home Page: www.leadershipdirectories.com

David Hurvitz, CEO

Contact information for over 48,000 executives at over 1,000 companies and more than 9,000

board members and their outside affiliations.
Cost: $360.00
1,400 Pages
Frequency: Quarterly
ISSN: 1058-2098
Founded in 1986

20653 Leadership Library in Print
Leadership Directories
104 5th Ave
New York, NY 10011-6901

212-627-4140
FAX 212-645-0931
E-Mail: info@leadershipdirectories.com
Home Page: www.leadershipdirectories.com

David Hurvitz, CEO

Complete set of all 14 leadership directories. Provides subscribers with complete contact information for the 400,000 individuals who constitute the institutional leadership of the US.
Cost: $2300.00
Frequency: Semiannually
Founded in 1996

20654 O'Dwyer's Directory of Corporate Communications
JR O'Dwyer Company
271 Madison Ave
Suite 600
New York, NY 10016-1013

212-683-2750
FAX 212-683-2750
E-Mail: jack@odwyerpr.com
Home Page: www.odwyerpr.com

Jack O'Dwyer, Owner
John ODwyer, Advertising Sales Manager

Public relations departments are profiled that represent the United States companies that are listed on the New York Stock Exchange.
Cost: $110.00
400 Pages
Frequency: Annual

20655 PR News
Phillips Business Information
7811 Montrose Road
Potomac, MD 20854

301-340-2100
E-Mail: feedback@healthydirections.com
Home Page: www.healthydirections.com

This database offers information on public relations issues.
Cost: $597.00
Frequency: 48 issues

20656 PR Newswire
150 E 58th Street
31st Floor
New York, NY 10155-0002

212-355-0090
FAX 212-832-9406

This comprehensive database offers current news, financial news, earnings statements, mergers, acquisitions, proxy contests and general features pertaining to the public relations industry.
Frequency: Directory

20657 Public Relations Tactics
Public Relations Society of America
33 Maiden Ln
New York, NY 10038-5150

212-460-1400
FAX 212-995-0757
E-Mail: william.murray@prsa.org
Home Page: www.prsa.org

Catherine Bolton, Manager

List of products and services used by public relations professionals worldwide.
Frequency: Annual June

20658 Public Relations Tactics: Register Issue/The Blue Book
Public Relations Society of America
33 Maiden Ln
New York, NY 10038-5150

212-460-1400
FAX 212-995-0757
E-Mail: william.murray@prsa.org
Home Page: www.prsa.org

Catherine Bolton, Manager

About 17,000 public relations practitioners in business government education etc., who are members.
Cost: $100.00
Frequency: Annual July

20659 Publicity at Your Finger Tips
Federal Systems
PO Box 298-L
Oliver Springs, TN 37840-0298

865-483-3579

Offers a comprehensive list of magazines, newspapers and other publications in the United States that provide publicity for businesses, churches and charitable organizations.
Cost: $24.95

20660 Staffing Industry Supplier Directory and Buyers Guide
Staffing Industry Analysts
881 Fremont Ave
Suite A3
Los Altos, CA 94024-5637

650-948-9303
800-950-9496
FAX 650-232-2360
Home Page: www.sireport.com

Ron Mester, Manager

Complete listing of suppliers and products for temporary help, placement and recruiting firms in the staffing industry.
Cost: $89.50
295 Pages
Frequency: Annual
ISBN: 1-883814-11-1

Industry Web Sites

20661 http://gold.greyhouse.com
G.O.L.D Grey House OnLine Databases

Grey House Pubishing's online database platform, GOLD, offers Quick Search, Keyword Search and Expert Search for most business sectors including public relations and media markets. The GOLD platform makes finding the information you need quick and easy - whether you're a novice searcher or an experienced database user. All of Grey House's directory products are available for subscription on the GOLD platform.

20662 www.absolutelypr.com
Absolutely Public Relations
Results-driven media relations - local, trade, national.

20663 www.achieva.info
ACHIEVA

20664 www.aem.org
Construction Equipment Advertisers and Public
Relations Council

A council of AEM that works to promote marketing, sales and advertising of construction equipment.

20665 www.afgcan.org
AFHCAN Project

20666 www.aprc-online.org
Automotive Public Relations Council
Provides a forum for information exchange among communication professionals with the automotive industry.

20667 www.bloomgross.com
Bloom Gross & Associates
Executive recruitment firm with corporate communications, public relations, marketing/branding/market research, and direct marketing/sales promotion practice areas.

20668 www.case.org
Council for the Advancement and Support of Ed.
Offers information on campus fund raising, public relations and alumni administration.

20669 www.cof.org
Council on Foundations
Non profit trade association for foundations

20670 www.greyhouse.com
Grey House Publishing
Authoritative reference directories for most business sectors including public relations and media markets. Users can search the online databases with varied search criteria allowing for custom searches by product category, geographic area, sales volume, keyword, subject and more. Full Grey House catalog and online ordering also available.

20671 www.iabc.com
International Association of Business Communicators

An international association for members who are professionals in organizational communications and public relations. Accepts advertising.

20672 www.instituteforpr.com
Institute for Public Relations
To improve the effectiveness of organizations by advancing the professional knowledge and practice of public relations through research and education.

20673 www.kscpublivrelations.com
KSC Public Relations
Full-service advertising, public relations and marketing firm serving real estate developers, health care automotive, and manufacturers.

20674 www.magnetcom.com
Magnet - Communications
Public relations firm.

20675 www.mediaaccessgroup.com
Media Access Group

20676 www.multicultural.com
Multicultural Marketing Resources Asian American
Advertising Federation

A public relations/marketing firm where corporate executives will find diverse resources, experts and information on how to market to multicultural (ethnic and niche) consumer markets.

20677 www.niri.org
National Investor Relations Institute
Professional association of corporate officers and investors relations consultants.

20678 www.petersgrouppr.com
PetersGroup Public Relations
Provides a full range of marketing and public relations programs to national and international businesses. The agency works closely with technology clients ranging from Funded start-ups to Fortune 500 companies, to integrate the right mix of research, strategy, positioning and media to help customers meet their ongoing business and communication goals.

20679 www.pinnacleww.com
Pinnacle Worldwide
For independent public relations firms in major markets around the globe.

20680 www.progressivepr.com
PPR Communications

20681 www.prpublishing.com
Public Relations Publishing Company
Case studies, research and trends in public relations and information on issues of importance to PR professionals.

20682 www.prsa.org
Public Relations Society of America
A major professional association of public relations practitioners.

20683 www.prweek.com
PR Week

20684 www.silveranvil.org
Silver Anvil Resource Center
Online database of public relations campaigns.

20685 www.washingtonpost.com
Washington Post

20686 www.wepr.org
Women Executives in Public Relations
Provides a support network for women in public relations. Offers grants and scholarships for courses in public relations and for college students studying communications.

Associations

20687 Alliance for Audited Media
48 W Seegers Road
Arlington Heights, IL 60005-3913

224-366-6939
FAX 224-366-6949
E-Mail: service@accessabc.com
Home Page: www.accessabc.com
Social Media: *Facebook, Twitter, LinkedIn, YouTube, Instagram*

Christina Meringolo, Chairwoman
Scott Kruse, Vice Chair
Tom Drouillard, President/Managing Director
Edward Boyd, Secretary
Liberta Abbondante, Treasurer

The world's largest circulation-auditing organization, ABC provides circulation data on 1,400+ newspapers and more than 1,100 periodicals to ABC-member publications, advertisers and advertising agencies.
4.1M+ Members
Founded in 1914

20688 Alliance of Area Business Publications
2512 Artesia Blvd
Suite 200
Redondo Beach, CA 90278

310-379-8261
FAX 310-379-8283
E-Mail: aabpstaff@gmail.com
Home Page: www.bizpubs.org
Social Media: *RSS*

C James Dowden, Executive Director
Jeff Nutall, President
Lisa Jones, Vice President
Joel Zwiebel, Secretary-Treasurer
Shelly Elmore, Director

Represents metropolitan area and state wide business to business publications with conventions, newsletters, and other services.
1.2M Members
Founded in 1979

20689 American Black Book Writers' Association
269 S Beverly Drive Street 2600
Beverly Hills, CA 90212

310-306-4042

Will Gibson, President

Members include all African Americans who are involved with any aspects of the publishing industry.
4M Members

20690 American Book Producers Association
31 W 8th Street
2nd Floor
New York, NY 10011

917-741-1919
800-209-4575
FAX 212-675-1364
E-Mail: office@ABPAonline.org
Home Page: www.abpaonline.org
Social Media: *Facebook*

Richard Rothschild, President
David Katz, Manager
Nancy Hall, Vice President
Valerie Tomaselli, Treasurer
Michael Centore, ABPA Administrator

Increases the book industry's awareness of members capabilities and exchanges information on improving business. Develops concepts for books and other publications.
Founded in 1980

20691 American Booksellers Association
333 Westchester Avenue
Suite S202
White Plains, NY 10604

914-406-7500
800-637-0037
FAX 914-417-4013
E-Mail: info@bookweb.org
Home Page: www.bookweb.org
Social Media: *Facebook, Twitter, YouTube*

Oren Teicher, CEO
Betsy Burton, President
Robyn DesHotel, Chief Financial Officer
Robert Sindelar, Vice President/ Secretary
Joy Dallangra-Sanger, Senior Program Officer

Trade organization pledge to protecting the well-being of book retailers and promoting the availability of books.
2000 Members
Founded in 1900

20692 American Library Association
50 E Huron St
Chicago, IL 60611-2795

312-944-6780
800-545-2433
FAX 312-440-9374
E-Mail: ala@ala.org
Home Page: www.ala.org
Social Media: *Facebook, Twitter, LinkedIn, Stumbleupon, Friendfeed, Reddi*

Robert E. Banks, Executive Board Member
Keith Michael Fiels, Executive Director
Sari Feldman, President
Mario Gonzalez, Treasurer
Dr. Julie B. Todaro, President-Elect

To provide leadership for the development, promotion, and improvement of library and information services and the profession of librarianship in order to enhance learning and ensure access to information for all.
65000 Members
Founded in 1876

20693 American Society of Journalists & Authors
355 Lexington Avenue
15th Floor
New York, NY 10017-6603

212-997-0947
FAX 212-937-2315
E-Mail: staff@asja.org
Home Page: www.asja.org
Social Media: *Facebook, Twitter, LinkedIn, Google+, Instagram*

Alexandra Canto Owens, Executive Director
Neil O'Hara, Treasurer
Randy Dotinga, President
Sherry Beck Paprocki, Vice-President
Sandra Lamb, Secretary
1200 Members
Founded in 1948

20694 Antiquarian Booksellers Association of America
20 W 44th St
Suite 507
New York, NY 10036

212-944-8291
FAX 212-944-8293
E-Mail: sbenne@abaa.org
Home Page: www.abaa.org
Social Media: *Facebook, Twitter, RSS*

Susan Benne, Executive Director
Thomas Goldwasser, President
Mary Gilliam, Vice-President/ Secretary
Charles Kutcher, Treasurer

A trade association of rare book dealers.
480 Members
Founded in 1949

20695 Arizona Book Publishing Association
6340 South Rural Road
#118-152
Tempe, AZ 85283

602-274-6264
E-Mail: info@azbookpub.com
Home Page: www.azbookpub.com

Sam Henrie, President
Mike Wentz, Managing Editor

20696 Associated Church Press
924 Woodcrest Way
Oviedo, FL 32762

407-341-6615
FAX 407-386-3236
E-Mail: AssociatedChurchPress@gmail.com
Home Page: www.theacp.org
Social Media: *Facebook, Twitter, RSS*

Joe Thoma, Executive Director
Cynthia Martens, President
Carlos Medley, Treasurer
Terri Lackey, Associate Director
Charlotte Indico, Associate Director

Aims to share ideas and concerns in religious publishing and to stimulate higher standards of religious journalism to exert a more positive influence.
240 Members
Founded in 1916

20697 Association for Information and Image Management
1100 Wayne Avenue
Suite 1100
Silver Spring, MD 20910

301-587-8202
800-477-2446
FAX 301-587-2711
E-Mail: aiim@aiim.org
Home Page: www.aiim.org
Social Media: *Facebook, Twitter, LinkedIn, RSS, YouTube, Google+*

Paul Engel, Chairman
Anthony Peleska, Vice Chair
Timothy Elmore, Immediate Past Chair
Mark Patrick, Executive Committee Member at Large
Daniel Antion, Treasurer

Members are users and manufacturers of equipment and supplies of the information and image industry.
10M Members
Founded in 1943

20698 Association of American Publishers (AAP)
455 Massachusetts Avenue NW
Suite 700
Washington, DC 20001

202-347-3375
FAX 202-347-3690
E-Mail: info@publishers.org
Home Page: www.publishers.org
Social Media: *Facebook, Twitter, LinkedIn, RSS*

Tom Allen, President & CEO
Brian Murray, Chair
Y.S. Chi, Vice Chair
W.Drake McFeely, Treasurer
Bert Ramlow, Executive Assistant & CEO

AAP is the trade association for the US book publishers, providing advocacy and communications on behalf of the industry. AAP represents the industry's priorities on policy, legislative and regulatory issues regionally, nationally and worldwide. These include protection of intellectual property rights and worldwide copyright enforcement, digital and new technology issues, funding for education

and libraries, tax and trade, censorship and
literacy.
400+ Members
Founded in 1970

20699 Association of American University Presses

28 West 36th Street
Suite 602
New York, NY 10018

212-989-1010
FAX 212-989-0275
E-Mail: info@aaupnet.org
Home Page: www.aaupnet.org
Social Media: *Facebook, Twitter, RSS*

Peter Berkery, Executive Director
Tim Muench, Assistant Director
Meredith Babb, President
Susan Doerr, Treasurer
David Hamrick, President Elect

Members are university presses and a limited
number of presses of non-degree-granting
scholarly institutions.
125 Members
Founded in 1937
Mailing list available for rent: 2.2M names

20700 Association of Catholic Publishers

4725 Dorsey Hall Dr.
Suite 1, PMB 709
Ellicott City, MD 21042

410-988-2926
FAX 410-571-4946
Home Page: www.catholicpublishers.org

Therese Brown, Executive Director

Catholic publishers and content producers.

20701 Association of Directory Publishers

116 Cass Street
PO Box 1929
Traverse City, MI 49684

800-267-9002
FAX 231-486-2182
E-Mail: hq@adp.org
Home Page: www.adp.org
Social Media: *Facebook, Twitter, LinkedIn, YouTube*

Laura Hill, Chairman
Todd McKnight, First Vice Chairman
Jim Hail, Treasurer
Danny Bills, Secretary
Cindi A. Aldrich, President/CEO
240 Members
Founded in 1898

20702 Association of Directory Publishers (ADP)

116 Cass St.
Traverse City, MI 49684

800-267-9002
FAX 231-486-2182
E-Mail: hq@adp.org
Home Page: www.adp.org
Social Media: *Facebook, Twitter, LinkedIn, YouTube*

Cindi A. Aldrich, President & CEO
Laura Hill, Chairman

The association is the communication link to
the Telephone Directory industry. It provides a
forum for the exchange of ideas and information among publishers of telephone, city and
special interest directories and provides continuous training to assist in the enhancement of
the publisher's operation.
240 Members
Founded in 1898

20703 Association of Free Community Papers

135 Old Cove Rd
Suite 210
Liverpool, NY 13090

877-203-2327
FAX 781-459-7770
E-Mail: loren@afcp.org
Home Page: www.afcp.org
Social Media: *Facebook, Twitter, LinkedIn, YouTube, Instagram*

Loren Colburn, Executive Director
Carol Toomey, President
Karen Sawicz, Secretary / Treasurer
Greg Birkett, 1st Vice President
Shane Goodman, 2nd Vice President

Offers national classified advertising placement
services; conducts charitable programs, sponsors competition, compiles statistics.
250 Members
Founded in 1951

20704 Association of Medical Media

1120 Route 73
Suite 200
Mount Laurel, NJ 08054

856-380-6814
FAX 856-439-0525
E-Mail: info@ammonline.org
Home Page: www.ammonline.org
Social Media: *Facebook, Twitter, LinkedIn*

Lisa Trofe, Executive Director

Members of this nonprofit are medical publishing firms, content providers and others in the
medical communications field.

20705 Author's Coalition of America

P.O. Box 929
Pentwater, MI 49449

231-869-2011
FAX 313-882-3047
E-Mail: dkelly@authorscoalition.org
Home Page: www.authorscoalition.org

Dorien Kelly, Assistant Administrator

An organization of U.S. based authors and creators united to receive and distribute non-title
specific reprographic royalties to member organizations, assist in further development of collective licensing programs and act for the
general benefit of authors. The ACA is an association of twenty independent authors' organizations representing text writers, songwriters,
visual artists, illustrators and photographers.
80000 Members
Founded in 1994

20706 Book Industry Study Group (BISG)

145 W. 45th Street
Suite 601
New York, NY 10036

646-336-7141
FAX 646-336-6214
E-Mail: info@bisg.org
Home Page: www.bisg.org
Social Media: *Twitter, RSS*

Mark Kuyper, Executive Director
Tara Catogge, Chair
Andrew Savikas, Vice-Chair
Fran Toolan, Secretary
Muareen McMahon, Treasurer

BISG is the leading US book trade association
for standardized best practices, research and
education.
170 Members
Founded in 1975

20707 Book Manufacturers' Institute

2 Armand Beach Drive
Suite 1B
Palm Coast, FL 32137-2612

386-986-4552
FAX 386-986-4553
E-Mail: info@bmibook.com
Home Page: www.bmibook.org

Daniel N Bach, Executive VP
Kent H Larson, Vice President/ President- Elect
Jac B Garner, President
Paul Genovese, Treasurer
Jackie Murray, Conference Coordinator

Since 1933, the Book Manufacturers' Institute,
Inc (BMI) has been the leading nationally recognized trade association of the book manufacturing industry. BMI member companies
annually produce the great majority of books
ordered by the U.S. book publishing industry.
Today, BMI is a vital part of the industry, playing a leading role by providing an intra-industry communications link among book
manufacturers, publishers, suppliers and
governmental bodies.
94 Members
Founded in 1933

20708 Community of Literary Magazines and Presses

154 Christopher St.
Suite 3C
New York, NY 10014-9110

212-741-9110
FAX 212-741-9112
E-Mail: info@clmp.org
Home Page: www.clmp.org
Social Media: *Facebook, Twitter*

Jeffrey Lependorf, Executive Director

Organization serving independent literary publishers.
Founded in 1967

20709 Guild of Book Workers

521 5th Avenue
New York, NY 10175

212-292-4444
E-Mail: secretary@guildofbookworkers.org
Home Page: www.guildofbookworkers.org

Jennifer Evers, Membership Chair
Mark Andersson, President
Bexx Caswell, Vice President
Catherine Burkhard, Secretary
Alicia Bailey, Treasurer

To broaden public awareness of the hand book
arts, to stimulate commissions of fine bindings,
and to stress the need for sound book conservation and restoration.
900+ Members
Founded in 1906

20710 Impact Publishers, Inc.

Impact Publishers
5674 Shattuck Avenue
Oakland, CA 94609

805-466-5917
800-748-6273
FAX 800-652-1613
E-Mail: customerservice@newharbinger.com
Home Page: www.newharbinger.com
Social Media: *Facebook, Twitter, Pinterest*

Offers the finest in practical, reader-friendly
help on a wide variety of personal interpersonal
matters: relationships, divorce recovery,
parenting, stress, personal growth, and mental
health.
Founded in 1973

20711 Independent Book Publishers Association
1020 Manhattan Beach Blvd
Suite 204
Manhattan Beach, CA 90266

310-546-1818
FAX 310-546-3939
E-Mail: info@ibpa-online.org
Home Page: www.ibpa-online.org
Social Media: *Facebook, Twitter, LinkedIn, Flickr, RSS*

Angela Bole, Executive Director
Rana DiOrio, Secretary
Florrie Binford-Kichler, President
Rob Price, Treasurer
Peter Goodman, Chair

Provides cooperative marketing programs, education and advocacy within the publishing industry.
4000+ Members
Founded in 1983

20712 Independent Free Papers of America
104 Westland Drive
Columbia, TN 38401

931-922-4171
800-441-4372
Home Page: www.ifpa.com
Social Media: *Facebook, Twitter, LinkedIn*

Doug Fabian, President
Jane Means, Vice President
Danielle Burnett, CADNET Director
Douglas Fry, Executive Director
Mark Helmer, Treasurer

Bestows awards and compiles statistics.
300 Members
Founded in 1980

20713 International Digital Enterprise Alliance
1600 Duke Street
Suite 420
Alexandria, VA 22314

703-837-1070
FAX 703-837-1072
E-Mail: info@idealliance.org
Home Page: www.idealliance.org

David Steinhardt, CEO
Steve Bonoff, Executive Vice President
Joe Duncan, Chairman
Marriott Winchester, Vice-Chairman
Neil Johnson, Treasurer

Founded as The Graphic Communications Association , was formed to help member companies apply the latest computer-related technologies to all forms of print and electronic publishing
Founded in 1966

20714 Jenkins Independent Publishers
Jenkins Group
1129 Woodmere Ave.
Suite B
Traverse City, MI 49686

231-330-0445
800-706-4636
FAX 231-933-0448
Home Page: www.bookpublishing.com

Jerrold R. Jenkins, Chairman And CEO

Provides comprehensive marketing and custom book publishing services for independent and small press book publishers.
160 Members
Founded in 1996

20715 Magazine Publishers of America
757 Third Avenue
11th Floor
New York, NY 10017

212-872-3700
FAX 212-888-4217
E-Mail: mpa@magazine.org
Home Page: www.magazine.org
Social Media: *Facebook, Twitter, LinkedIn, YouTube,Pinterest*

Nancr Telliho, Interim President & CEO
Andrew Clurman, Executive Assistant
Stephen M. Lacy, Chairman
Thomas Harty, Treasurer
Eric Zinczenko, Secretary

Promotes magazines as an advertising medium. Provides information services and assistance to members in areas of circulation marketing.
240 Members
Founded in 1919

20716 National Association of Hispanic Publications, Inc.
529 14th St. NW
Suite 923
Washington, DC 20045

202-662-7250
Home Page: www.nahp.org
Social Media: *Facebook, Twitter*

Martha Montoya, President

Trade advocacy organization promoting Spanish-language newspapers, magazines and related media.

20717 National Association of Desktop Publishers
462 Old Boston Road
Topsfield, MA 01983-1232

978-876-6855
800-874-4113
E-Mail: nadtp@aol.com

Barry Harrigan, Owner

Trade organization which serves the desk top publishing industry and offers information resources.
5M Members
Founded in 1987

20718 National Association of Hispanic Publications
National Press Building
529 14th Street NW
Suite 923
Washington, DC 20045

202-662-7250
FAX 703-610-9005
E-Mail: directory@nahp.org
Home Page: www.nahp.org
Social Media: *Facebook, Twitter*

Clara Escobedo, President
Martha Montoya, Vice President, Membership
Christina Monte Scott, Treasurer
Norma Condreay, Secretary
Jesus Cobian, Membership Chair

Promotes the Hispanic print media as a valuable means of communication. Works to ensure that member publications are listed in National Media Directories.
200 Members
Founded in 1982

20719 National Association of Independent
PO Box 430
Highland City, FL 33846-0430

863-648-4420
E-Mail: naip@aol.com
Home Page: www.publishersreport.com

Betty A Lampe, Executive Director

Assists and educates small publishing companies. Conducts seminars on marketing strategies, target audience, and techniques of book distribution. Especially helpful for the beginning or self-publisher.
500 Members
Founded in 1979

20720 National Association of Publishers' Representatives
2800 W. Higgins Road
Suite 440
Hoffman Estates, IL 60169

877-263-9640
FAX 847-885-8393
E-Mail: info@naproline.org
Home Page: www.naproline.org
Social Media: *Facebook, LinkedIn*

Darren Dunay, President
Everett Knapp III, Chairman
Craig Pitcher, Vice President
Jan Zeman, Secretary/Treasurer
David Bayard, Board of Directors

Provides information for publishers' representatives selling advertising space.
250 Members
Founded in 1950

20721 National Music Publishers Association
975 F Street, NW
Suite 375
Washington, DC 20004

202-393-6672
FAX 202-393-6673
E-Mail: admin@mpa.org
Home Page: www.nmpa.org
Social Media: *Facebook, Twitter, YouTube, Instagram*

David Israelite, President/CEO
Chris Clyde, Senior Vice President
Todd Vunderink, Secretary
Caroline Bienstock, Treasurer
Irwin Robinson, Chairman

An advocate for the protection of music copyrights.
800 Members
Founded in 1917

20722 National Newspaper Association
PO Box 7540
Columbia, MO 65205-7540

573-777-4980
800-829-4662
FAX 703-237-9808
E-Mail: membership@nna.org
Home Page: nnaweb.org
Social Media: *Facebook, Twitter, RSS Feeds*

Dave Bordewyk, Executive Director
Tonda F. Rush, Chief Operating Officer
Chip Hutcheson, President
Susan Rowell, Treasurer
Matthew Paxton, Vice President

Industry trade newspaper. Accepts advertising.
2000 Members
Founded in 1885

20723 National Paper Trade Association
330 North Wabash Avenue
Suite 2000
Chicago, IL 60611

312-321-4092
800-355-6782
FAX 312-673-6736
E-Mail: gerri@goNPTA.com
Home Page: www.gonpta.com
Social Media: *Twitter, LinkedIn, YouTube*

William Frohlich, President
Sean Samet, Executive Vice President
Hilton Maze, Chairman

Don Clampitt, Treasurer
Kevin Gammonley, CEO

An Association for the paper, packaging, and supplies distribution industry.
2000 Members
Founded in 1903

20724 Newspaper Association of America

4401 Wilson Blvd
Suite 900
Arlington, VA 22203

571-366-1000
FAX 571-366-1195
E-Mail: joan.mills@naa.org
Home Page: www.naa.org
Social Media: *Facebook, Twitter, LinkedIn, YouTube, RSS, Google+*

Robert J. Dickey, Past Chairman
Stephen P. Hills, Vice Chairman
Tony W. Hunter, Secretary
Donna Bareett, Chairman
Michael J. Klingensmith, Treasurer

Founded by the merger of seven associations serving the newspaper industry. Focuses on the major issues that affect today's newspaper industry public policy and legal matters, advertising revenue growth and audience development across the medium's broad portfolio of products and digital platforms.
2000 Members
Founded in 1992

20725 Online Publishers Association (OPA)

1350 Broadway
Suite 606
New York, NY 10018

646-473-1000
FAX 646-473-0200
E-Mail: info@digitalcontentnext.org
Home Page: digitalcontentnext.org
Social Media: *Facebook, Twitter, LinkedIn, Google+*

Michael Zimbalist, Chairman
Krishan Bhatia, Vice Chairman
Drew Schutte, Treasurer
David Payne, Secretary
Marty Moe, President

The Online Publishers Association (OPA) is a not-for-profit trade organization dedicated to representing high-quality online content providers before the advertising community, the press, the government and the public.
Founded in 2001

20726 PSP American Medical Publishers Committee

Association of America Publishers, Inc
71 Fifth Avenue
2nd Floor
New York, NY 10003-3004

212-255-0200
FAX 212-255-7007
E-Mail: jtagler@publishers.org
Home Page: www.PSPcentral.org

Patrick J. Kelly, Chair
Susan King, Vice Chair
Jennifer Crewe, Editorial Director
H. Frederick Dylla, Executive Director & CEO
Thomas Easley, Senior Vice President

The primary goals of the PSP/AMPC are to educate, advocate, engage in outreach and philanthropy and frame issues of relevance to medical publishers, including promoting a positive image of scientific and medical publishing.
300 Members
Founded in 1960

20727 Science Fiction & Fantasy Writers of America

PO Box 3238
Enfield, CT 06083-3238

Home Page: www.swfa.org
Social Media: *Facebook, Twitter*

Cat Rambo, President
Kate Baker, Operations Manager

Professional organization for writers of fantasy, science fiction and related genres. Host of the Nebula Awards.

20728 Society for Collegiate Journalists

1584 Wesleyan Drive
Virginia Inesleyan College
Norfolk, VA 23502-5599

757-455-3419
FAX 757-461-5025
E-Mail: wjruehlmann@vwc.edu
Home Page: www.scj.us
Social Media: *Facebook*

Mary Beth Earnheardt, Executive Director
Frank Barnas, President
Vivian Wagner, Second VP
Martha Collins, Third V.P
Rick Stewart, First Vice President

A collegiate journalism organization.
800 Members
Founded in 1909

20729 Society for Scholarly Publishing

10200 W 44th Ave
Suite 304
Wheat Ridge, CO 80033

303-422-3914
FAX 720-881-6101
E-Mail: info@sspnet.org
Home Page: www.sspnet.org
Social Media: *Facebook, Twitter, LinkedIn, RSS*

Howard Ratner, Past President
Melanie Dolechek, Executive Director
Ann Michael, President
Byron Laws, Secretary/Treasurer
Rick Anderson, President-Elect

A group that represents scholarly publications, such as journals, university publications and magazines.
800 Members
Founded in 1978

20730 Society of National Association Publications

12100 Sunset Hills Road
Suite 130
Reston, VA 20190

703-234-4063
FAX 703-435-4390
E-Mail:
info@associationmediaandpublishing.org
Home Page:
associationmediaandpublishing.org
Social Media: *Facebook, Twitter, LinkedIn, Flickr*

John T. Adams, Executive Director
Angel Alvarez-Mapp, President
John Falcioni, Vice President
Joe Vallina, Treasurer
Carla Kalogeridis, Editorial Director

Develops standards for editorial and advertising content of association and professional society magazines.
1045 Members
Founded in 1963

20731 Software & Information Industry Association

1090 Vermont Ave NW
6th Floor
Washington, DC 20005-4905

202-289-7442
800-388-7478
FAX 202-289-7097
E-Mail: piracy@siia.net
Home Page: www.siia.net
Social Media: *Facebook, Twitter, LinkedIn*

Ken Wasch, President
Tom Davin, Senior Vice President & MD
Tom Meldrum, Vice President
Heather Farley, COO
David Foster, CEO

Members are microcomputer software firms. Services include data collection program, software protection, contracts reference disk, conferences and lobbying.
1200 Members
Founded in 1984

20732 Special Libraries Association

331 S Patrick St
Alexandria, VA 22314-3501

703-647-4900
FAX 703-647-4901
E-Mail: sla@sla.org
Home Page: www.sla.org
Social Media: *Facebook, Twitter, LinkedIn, Youtube, RSS*

Tom Rink, President-Elect
Jill Strand, President
John DiGilio, Treasurer
Linda Broussard, Chief Financial Officer
Doug Newcomb, Chief Executive Officer

International association of information professionals who work in special libraries serving business, research, government and institutions that produce specialized information.
7000 Members
Founded in 1856

20733 Specialized Information Publishers Association

1090 Vermont Ave NW
Sixth Floor
Washington, DC 20005-4095

202-289-7442
800-356-9302
FAX 202-289-7097
Home Page: www.sipaonline.com
Social Media: *Facebook, Twitter, LinkedIn, Digg, Google+*

Henry Greene, Executive Director
Ken Wasch, President
Keith Kupferschmid, General Counsel and SVP
Tom Davin, Senior Vice President
Tom Meldrum, Vice President, Finance

International trade association serving the interests of publishers of newsletters and specialized information services.
450 Members
Founded in 1977
Mailing list available for rentat $65 per M

20734 The Association of Publishers for Special Sales

PO Box 9725
Colorado Springs, CO 80932-0725

719-924-5534
FAX 719-213-2602
E-Mail: kaye@bookpass.org
Home Page: community.bookapss.org
Social Media: *Facebook, Twitter, Google+, Yahoo*

Scott Flora, Consultant
Brian Jud, Executive Director
June Hyjek, Manager

Sarah Tufano, Administrative Assistant
Kim Tuttle, Executive Assistant

A nonprofit trade association for independent presses and self-publishers who want to produce better books and market them successfully. SPAN offers a monthly newsletter with information-rich articles and great benefits.
1300 Members
Founded in 1996

20735 University of Denver
Sturm Hall
2000 East Astbury Ave
Denver, CO 80208

303-871-2570
FAX 303-871-2501
E-Mail: pi-info@du.edu
Home Page: www.du.edu/publishinginstitute
Social Media: *Facebook, Twitter, YouTube, Flickr*

Jill Smith, Director
Jennifer Conder, Associate Director
Margaret Shaheen, Program Administrator

A certificate program that combines workshops in editing and marketing with lecture/teaching sessions conducted by leading experts from all areas of publishing.
Founded in 1864

20736 Western Publications Association
823 Rim Crest Dr
Westlake Village, CA 91361

805-495-1863
888-735-1545
FAX 866-735-1545
E-Mail: wpa@wpa-online.org
Home Page: www.wpa-online.org
Social Media: *Facebook, Twitter, LinkedIn, RSS*

Jane Silbering, Executive Director
Jennifer Hamilton Bingo, Vice President
Norb Garrett, President
John Brooks, Treasurer/ Secretary
Darren Buford, Director

Represents magazine publishing companies and companies related to publishing industry, in the western United States.
200 Members
Founded in 1951

20737 Women in Production
276 Bowery
New York, NY 10012

212-334-2106
FAX 212-431-5786
E-Mail: admin@p3-ny.org
Home Page: www.p3-ny.org

Rosemary Sirico, President
Diane Pesce, VP

Nonprofit profesional and educational association whose mission is to facilitate career growth and education through peer support and the exchange of information.
500 Members
Founded in 2003

20738 Women's National Book Association
PO Box 237
FDR Station
New York, NY 10150

212-208-4629
FAX 212-208-4629
E-Mail: info@wnba-books.org
Home Page: www.wnba-books.org
Social Media: *Facebook, Twitter, LinkedIn, RSS*

Carin Siegfried, President
Jane Kinney-Denning, Vice President
Shannon Janeczek, Secretary
Gloria Toler, Treasurer
Valeri Tomaselli, Past President

An organization of women and men in all occupations allied to the book industry.
800 Members
Founded in 1917

20739 Yellow Pages Publishers Association
Connell Corporate Park
400 Connell Drive
Suite 1100
Berkeley Heights, NJ 07922-2747

908-286-2380
FAX 908-286-0620
E-Mail: KimberlyEnik@ypassociation.org
Home Page: www.yellowpageblues.com
Social Media: *Facebook, Twitter, LinkedIn, YouTube,Blog*

George Burnett, Chairman
Dennis Payne, Vice Chairman
Neg Norton, President

Trade association which represents the Yellow Pages industry. YPPA's publisher members collectively produce over 96 percent of all directories published in the United States and account for 99 percent of the revenues generated by Yellow Pages advertising.
340 Members
Founded in 1988

Newsletters

20740 AAP Monthly Report
Association of American Publishers
71 5th Ave
Suite 2
New York, NY 10003-3004

212-255-1407
FAX 212-255-7007
E-Mail: jtagler@publishers.org
Home Page: www.pspcentral.org

John Tagler, VP/Executive Director
Sara Pinto, Director
Kate Kolendo, Project Manager

A report offering information and news to the publishing community.
Cost: $800.00

20741 American Book Producers Association Newsletter
American Book Producers Association
151 W 19th Street
3rd Floor
New York, NY 10011

917-741-1919
800-209-4575
FAX 212-675-1364
E-Mail: office@abpaonline.org
Home Page: www.abpaonline.org

David Rubel, Publisher
Dan Tucker, Co-President
David Katz, Manager
Richard Rothschild, President
Kirsten Hall, Administrator

Trade association of independent book producers in the United States and Canada.
6 Pages
Frequency: Monthly
Circulation: 2500
Founded in 1980
Printed in 2 colors on matte stock

20742 Augsburg Fortress Newsletter for Church Leaders
Augsburg Fortress
PO Box 1209
Minneapolis, MN 55440-1209

612-330-3300
800-328-4648

FAX 800-722-7766
Home Page: www.augsburgfortress.org

Roderick Olson, Publisher

Monthly newsletter designed to equip pastors, church leaders, Christian leaders, Christian Educators and volunteers with valuable and timely resources, promotions, and ministry ideas.
Frequency: Monthly eNewsletter

20743 BISG Bulletin
BISG Book Industry Study Group
145 W 45th Street
Suite 601
New York, NY 10017-6588

646-336-7141
FAX 646-336-6214
E-Mail: info@bisg.org
Home Page: www.bisg.org
Social Media: *Twitter, RSS*

Len Vlahos, Executive Director
Dominique Raccah, Co-Chair
Kelley Maier, Vice-Chair
Judith Appelbaum, Secretary
George Tattersfield, Treasurer

News and information from the Book Industry Study Group regarding book industry technologies, conferences, opinions, policy development, supply chain and more.
Founded in 1976

20744 Book Arts
Center for Book Arts
28 W 27th St
Suite 3
New York, NY 10001-6906

212-481-0295
FAX 212-481-9853
E-Mail: info@centerforbookarts.org
Home Page: www.centerforbookarts.org
Social Media: *Facebook, Twitter, YouTube,Flickr*

Alexander Campos, Executive Director

Center news and activities.
Founded in 1974

20745 Book News
American Book Producers Association
151 W 19th Street
3rd Floor
New York, NY 10011

917-741-1919
800-209-4575
FAX 212-675-1364
E-Mail: office@abpaonline.org
Home Page: www.abpaonline.org

Richard Rothschild, President
Bok Hee, Manager
Bill Raggio, Contact

Monthly newsletter is part of the membership benefits; provides a transcript of the monthly member luncheon's speaker, as well as association and member news.
Frequency: Benefit of Membership
Founded in 1980

20746 Bookselling This Week
American Booksellers Association
200 White Plains Rd
Suite 600
Tarrytown, NY 10591

800-637-0037
FAX 914-591-2720
E-Mail: info@bookweb.org
Home Page: www.bookweb.org

Oren Teicher, CEO
Len Viahos, COO
Ellie Chang, CFO
Frequency: Weekly
Circulation: 10000

20747 Educational Marketer
Simba Information
60 Long Ridge Rd
Suite 300
Stamford, CT 06902-1841

203-325-8193
888-297-4622
FAX 203-325-8975
E-Mail:
customerservice@simbainformation.com
Home Page: www.simbanet.com/

Linda Kopp, Publisher

Reports on the entire educational publishing
spectrum from el-hi to College. It covers the
complete range of print and electronic tools including software, and multimedia materials. It
details mergers, acquisitions, financial reports,
distribution, adoption and enrollment trends,
legislative issues
Cost: $650.00
8 Pages
Founded in 1989
Printed in 4 colors

20748 Exchange
Association of American University Presses
Rm 602
30 W 36th St
New York, NY 10018-8063

212-989-1010
FAX 212-989-0275
E-Mail: aaupny@netcom.com
Home Page: aaupnet.org/

Hollis Holmes, Publisher
Peter J Givler, Executive Director
Rachel Weiss, Marketing Manager
Latasha Watters, Marketing Coordinator

Reports on issues relevant to scholarly publishing.
Cost: $10.00
16 Pages
Frequency: Quarterly

20749 Footprints Newsletter
Evangelical Christian Publishers
Association
4816 S Ash Ave
Suite 101
Tempe, AZ 85282-7735

480-966-3998
FAX 480-966-1944
E-Mail: info@ecpa.org
Home Page: www.ecpa.org

Mark Kuyper, President
Kelly Gallagher, VP
Dave Bird, Marketing

An international, not-for-profit, trade organization serving its industry by promoting excellence and professionalism, sharing relevant
data, stimulating Christian fellowship, raising
the effectiveness of member houses, and equipping them to meet the needs of the changing
marketplace.
Frequency: Monthly
Circulation: 280

20750 Fusion Magazine
Newspaper Association of America
4401 Wilson Blvd
Suite 900
Arlington, VA 22203-4195

571-366-1000
FAX 571-366-1195
E-Mail: joan.mills@naa.org
Home Page: www.naa.org
Social Media: *Facebook, Twitter, LinkedIn,
YouTube,RSS*

Reggie Hall, Senior VP
James M Moroney, Chairman
Robert Dickey, Secretary

Donna Barrett, Treasurer
Robert M Nutting, Vice Chairman

This newsletter focuses on the business of diversity within the newspaper industry. In it you
will find new strategies for making diversity
work in advertising, news and editorial, circulation, marketing, production, human resources
and the business office.
Frequency: Quarterly
Mailing list available for rent

20751 Guild of Book Workers-Newsletter
Guild of Book Workers
521 5th Avenue
17th Floor
New York, NY 10175-1799

212-285-5581
Home Page:
palimpsest.stanford.edu/byorg/gbw

Margaret Johnson, Publisher
Bernadette Callery, Membership Secretary

Information for the book arts field.
Circulation: 800

20752 Hotline
1825 Ponce de Leon
Suite 429
Coral Gables, FL 33133

703-992-9339
800-356-9302
FAX 703-992-7512
E-Mail: sipa@online.com
Home Page: www.hotline.com

Henry Greene, Executive Director

Furthers the professional and economic interests of members. Future plans include seminars, research and representing members before
federal agencies. Available only to members.
Founded in 1977
Printed in one color on matte stock

**20753 Independent Book Publishers
Association Newsletter**
Independent Book Publishers Association
1020 Manhattan Beach Blvd
Suite 204
Manhattan Beach, CA 90266

310-546-1818
FAX 310-546-3939
E-Mail: info@ibpa-online.org
Home Page: www.ibpa-online.org
Social Media: *Facebook, Twitter, LinkedIn,
Flickr,RSS*

Terry Nathan, Executive Director
Lisa Krebs, Assistant Director
Steve Mettee, Board Chair
Roy M Carlisle, Treasurer
Florrie Kichler, President

Publicity, sales, legal, and marketing opportunities and news articles for independent book
publishers.
Frequency: Monthly
Circulation: 6000

20754 Independent Publishers Trade Report
PO Box 176
Southport, CT 06490-176

860-669-5848
FAX 203-332-7629

Henry Berry, Publisher

News and information for independent publishers, monthly column in the COSMEP Newsletter.

20755 Independent Small Press Review
WHW Publishing

930 Via Fruteria
Santa Barbara, CA 93110-2322

609-408-8000
Home Page: www.ifpa.com

Gary Rudy, Executive Director

Offers a comprehensive look at the concerns
and issues of the small business publisher.

**20756 John Kremer's Book Marketing Tip
of the Week**
Open Horizons Publishing
PO Box 2887
Taos, NM 87571

575-751-3398
800-796-6130
FAX 575-751-3100
E-Mail: info@bookmarket.com
Home Page: www.bookmarket.com

John Kremer, Editor
Robert Sanny, Advertising/Sales Manager

Email newletter offering new PR and sales
leads and tips every week.
Frequency: Weekly
Founded in 1982
Mailing list available for rent

20757 Lifelong Learning Market Report
Simba Information
60 Long Ridge Rd
Suite 300
Stamford, CT 06902-1841

203-325-8193
888-297-4622
FAX 203-325-8975
E-Mail:
customerservice@simbainformation.com
Home Page: www.simbanet.com

Linda Kopp, Publisher

News and analysis for content and service providers of corporate training and professional
development materials. Includes news on
merger and aczuisitions, industry financial performance and trends, product development and
distribution.
Cost: $625.00
Founded in 1989

20758 MBR Bookwatch
Midwest Book Review
278 Orchard Drive
Oregon, WI 53575-1129

608-835-7937
E-Mail: mbr@execpc.com
Home Page: www.midwestbookreview.com

James A Cox, Editor-in-Chief

A monthly online book review publication that
will showcase the reviews and commentaries of
those MBR editors and specialized reviewers
who've demonstrated expertise in their field.
Bookwatch will also feature author interviews
and editorial observations of various aspects of
the publishing world, offered by knowledgeable and articulate participants.
140 Pages
Frequency: Monthly
Circulation: 30,000
Founded in 1976

**20759 National Association of Professional
Print Buyers**
15050 NE 20th Avenue
Suite A
North Miami, FL 33181-1123

305-956-9563

Vincent Millardi, Publisher

Accepts advertising.
Cost: $315.00
296 Pages
Frequency: Monthly

20760 NewsInc.
Cole Group
PO Box 719
Pacifica, CA 94044-719

650-557-9595
FAX 650-475-8479
E-Mail: admin@colegroup.com
Home Page: www.colegroup.com

David M Cole, Publisher/Editor
Marge Wetmore, Circulation Manager

The weekly newsletter about the business of
the newspaper business, written for media executives and the investments community. subscriptions available in digital or print formats,
as well as for archive access.
Cost: $99.00
Frequency: 48/Yr, for Digital Access
Founded in 1989

20761 Newsletter on Newsletters
Newsletter on Newsletters
PO Box 348
Rhinebeck, NY 12572-0348

845-876-5222
FAX 845-876-4943
E-Mail: newsonnews@newsletterbiz.com
Home Page: www.newsletterbiz.com

Paul Swift, Editor

Graphics, editorial, promotions, management
and reports on the entire newsletter industry.
Cost: $275.00
Founded in 1970

**20762 Online Publishing Update
E-Newsletter**
Newspaper Association of America
4401 Wilson Blvd
Suite 900
Arlington, VA 22203-4195

571-366-1000
FAX 571-366-1195
E-Mail: joan.mills@naa.org
Home Page: www.naa.org
Social Media: *Facebook, Twitter, LinkedIn,
YouTube,RSS*

Reggie Hall, Senior VP
James M Moroney, Chairman
Robert Dickey, Secretary
Donna Barrett, Treasurer

A round-up of news, research, industry trends,
best practices and more, focusing on items of
interest to newspaper and digital media executives. Online Publishing Update e-newsletter is
published every Monday, Wednesday and
Friday.
Frequency: 3x/Weekly

20763 PMA Newsletter
Publishers Marketing Association
627 Aviation Way
Manhattan Beach, CA 90266-7107

310-372-2732
FAX 310-374-3342
E-Mail: info@ibpa-online.org
Home Page: www.pma-online.org

Terry Nathan, Executive Director

Publishing law, copyrighting, marketing, busi-
ness management all directed toward the inde-
pendent book publishing community.
Frequency: Monthly
Circulation: 10000
Founded in 1983

20764 Personal Composition Report
Graphic Dimensions
134 Caversham Woods
Pittsford, NY 14534-2834

585-381-3428

Michael Kleper, Publisher

Covers all aspects of electronic publishing and
imaging including news, reviews and in-depth
analysis. Begun in 1979 by Professor Michael
Kleper of RIT, the newsletter has provided consistent, valuable information for its readers.
Cost: $100.00
16 Pages
Frequency: Annual
Printed in one color on matte stock

20765 Pleasures of Publishing
Columbia University
2960 Broadway
New York, NY 10027-6900

212-854-1754
FAX 212-749-0397
Home Page: www.columbia.edu

Robert Kasdin, Executive VP
Mathew Martg, Marketing

Industry news.

20766 Professional Publishing Report
Simba Information
60 Long Ridge Rd
Suite 300
Stamford, CT 06902-1841

203-325-8193
FAX 203-325-8915
E-Mail:
customerservice@simbainformation.com
Home Page: www.simbanet.com

Linda Kopp, Publisher
Charlie Friscia, Marketing
John Fuller, Executive Editor

Newletter focuses on the $10 billion profes-
sional publishing industry. Features in-depth
analysis of each of the four major professional
publishing categories: scientific/technical,
medical, legal and business. Provides revenue
breakdowns by media and market, merger and
acquisition news, and analysis of market
trends.
Cost: $715.00
Founded in 1989

20767 Publishers Monthly Domestic Sales
Association of American Publishers
50 F St Nw
Suite 400
Washington, DC 20001-1565

202-347-3375
FAX 202-347-3690
E-Mail: info@publishers.org
Home Page: www.publishers.org

Tom Allen, CEO
Katie Blough, Editor
Patricia Schroeder, President
Tina Jordan, Vice President
Kate Kolendo, Project Manager

Sales charts, index and rates for the publishing
community.
Frequency: Monthly
Founded in 1970

20768 Publishers Multinational Direct
Direct International
1501 Third Avenue
New York, NY 10028-2101

212-861-4188
FAX 212-628-5070
E-Mail: directin@ix.netcom.com
Home Page: www.publishersmultinational.com

Alfred Goodloe, Editor

National and international coverage of the publishing community including printing, prepress
and direct marketing.
Cost: $195.00
Frequency: Monthly

20769 Publishers Report
National Association of Independent
Publishers
PO Box 430
Highland City, FL 33846-430

863-648-4420
FAX 836-648-4420
E-Mail: naip@aol.com
Home Page: www.publishersreport.com

Betsy A Lampe, Publisher

Provides a clearinghouse of information on
small/independent publishing for its members.
Accepts advertising. Departments include:
'New Books, Audios & Videos,' It's a Date,'
'NAIP Book Review,' 'New Media Sources,'
'Wanted,' 'In the Know,' 'F41,' and various
others helpful for new publishers and
self-publishers.

20770 Publishers' Auxiliary
National Newspaper Association
1010 N Glebe Road
Suite 450
Arlington, VA 22201

703-658-8808
FAX 703-907-7901
E-Mail: info@nna.org
Home Page: www.nna.org

Stan Schwartz, Managing Editor
Lynn Ediger, Marketing Manager

Providing personnel announcements, new tech-
nology, economic trends, and new publicaiton
and distribution methods for executives in the
newpaper industry.
Cost: $85.00
Frequency: Monthly
Circulation: 8102
Founded in 1885

20771 Publishing Markets
Reed Business Information
275 Washington St
Newton, MA 02458-1611

617-964-3030
FAX 617-558-4327
Home Page: www.designnews.com

Deborah Selsky, Publisher
San Buchan, Editor

Economic and demographic trends that affect
the book publishing market.
Cost: $129.00

20772 Publishing Poynters
Para Publishing
PO Box 8206-240
Santa Barbara, CA 93118-8206

805-968-7277
800-727-2782
FAX 805-968-1379
E-Mail: danpoynter@parapublishing.com
Home Page: www.parapublishing.com
Social Media: *Facebook, Twitter*

Dan Poynter, Editor
Becky Carbone, Production Manager

Book publishing news and ideas: marketing,
promotion and distribution.
Cost: $9.95
20 Pages
Frequency: Monthly
Circulation: 16000
ISSN: 1530-5694
Founded in 1969
Printed in one color

20773 Report on Preschool Programs
Business Publishers,Inc
2222 Sedwick Drive
Durham, NC 27713

800-223-8720
FAX 800-508-2592

E-Mail: custserv@bpinews.com
Home Page: www.bpinews.com

The one source to turn to for timely, accurate coverage of important developments in Head Start, child care, health care, special education and much more.
Cost: $357.00
8 Pages
Founded in 1963

20774 SPAN

Small Publishers Association of North America
1618 W Colorado Avenue
Colorado Springs, CO 80904-4029

719-475-1726
FAX 719-471-2182
E-Mail: span@spannet.org
Home Page: www.spannet.org

Marilyn Ross, Editor
Cathy Bowman, Production Manager

Includes money-making articles and book industry information.
24 Pages
Frequency: Monthly
Circulation: 4000
Founded in 1996

20775 SPAN Internet Newsletter

Small Publishers Association of North America
PO Box 9725
Colorado Springs, CO 80932-0725

719-924-5534
FAX 719-213-2602
E-Mail: brad@spannet.org
Home Page: www.spannet.org
Social Media: *Facebook, Twitter*

Marilyn Ross, Executive Director/Editor
Tom Ross, VP

The SPAN Internet Newsletter features timely and useful information on many aspects of writing and the publishing industry, including articles on book marketing and publicity in addition to providing links to industry related Websites.
Frequency: Monthly
Circulation: 4000
Founded in 1996

20776 Small Publisher Co-Op

Nigel Maxey
1521 SE Palm Court
PO Box 1620
Stuart, FL 34994-1620

772-287-8117
E-Mail: spcoop@hotmail.com
Home Page: www.spco-op.com

Niyel Maxey, President/Editor
Kevin Hawken, Member Service Manager

This monthly newsletter offers a guide to publishing and marketing books, reports, periodicals, etc.
Cost: $15.00
Circulation: 5900

20777 Span Connection

Small Publishers Association of North America
PO Box 1306
Buena Vista, CO 81211-1306

719-395-4790
FAX 719-395-8374
E-Mail: span@spannet.org
Home Page: www.spannet.org

Scoot Flora, Editor
Scoot Flora, CEO

Wide variety of news and information about small-scale and individual publishing.
Cost: $105.00
Frequency: Monthly
Circulation: 4000
Founded in 1996

20778 Specialty Directory Publishing Market Forecast

Simba Information
60 Long Ridge Rd
Suite 300
Stamford, CT 06902-1841

203-325-8193
888-297-4622
FAX 203-325-8975
E-Mail: info@simbanet.com
Home Page: www.simbanet.com

Kathy Mickey, Managing Editor/Analyst
David Goddard, Senior Editor/Analyst
Michael Norris, Senior Editor/Analyst

Complete market size, revenue and growth figures and forecasts including revenues driven by electronic products and exclusive reanking of leading publishers by revenue.
Cost: $495.00
Frequency: Anually
Founded in 1989

20779 The Bookwoman

Women's National Book Association
PO Box 237
FDR Station
New York, NY 10150

212-208-4629
FAX 212-208-4629
Home Page: www.wnba-books.org
Social Media: *Facebook, Twitter, LinkedIn, RSS*

Joan Gelfand, President
Mary Grey James, Vice President/President-Elect
Ruth Light, Secretary
Margaret E Auer, Treasurer
Shannon Janeczek, The Bookwoman, Managing Editor

Bi-annual journal for members of the Women's National Book Association. Stories of interest for people in the world of books. Book review are includes, how-to information and chapter news from across the United States. Ad space available.
2 Pages
Frequency: Biennial
Circulation: 1000
Founded in 1917

Magazines & Journals

20780 AP Special Edition

Associated Press
450 W 33rd St
New York, NY 10001-2647

212-621-1849
FAX 212-833-7574
E-Mail: info@ap.org
Home Page: www.apme.com

Collins Munro, Manager
Kathelene Carroll, Editor
Laure Morris, Marketing Manager
Alan Miller, Managing Editor
Debra Simmons, Secretary
Frequency: Monthly
Circulation: 7000
Founded in 1848

20781 American Libraries Magazine

50 East Huron Street
Chicago, IL 60611

800-545-2433
FAX 312-944-7841
E-Mail: membership@ala.org
Home Page: www.ala.org

Keith Fields, Publisher, ALA Executive Director
Mary Mackay, Marketing & Sales Director
Camila Alire, ALA President

News and information on legislation concerning libraries, new publications and technology issues
Cost: $70.00
Frequency: 10x/Yr $ incl in ALA dues
Circulation: 60,000
ISSN: 0002-9769
Founded in 1876

20782 Book Dealers World

North American Bookdealers Exchange
PO Box 606
Cottage Grove, OR 97424

541-942-7455
FAX 541-942-7455
Home Page: www.bookmarketingprofits.com

Al Galasso, Editorial Director
Steve Sherman, Publisher

The book marketing magazine for independent publishers and mail order entrepreneurs. A publication of the North American Book Dealers Exchange, an international book marketing organization, specializing in cooperative opportunities at trade shows, in mail order, press releases and more.
Cost: $45.00
32 Pages
Frequency: Quarterly
Circulation: 10000
ISSN: 1098-8521
Founded in 1980
Printed in on newsprint stock

20783 Book Promotion Hotline

Ad-Lib Publications
51 1/2 W Adam
PO Box 1102
Fairfield, IA 52556-3226

515-472-6617
800-669-0773
FAX 641-472-3186

Marie Kiefer, Editor/Publisher

Provides media contacts and other marketing sources of interest to the publisher/marketing trade.
Cost: $150.00
4 Pages
Frequency: Weekly
Circulation: 1,000

20784 Booklist

American Library Association
50 E Huron St
Chicago, IL 60611-2788

312-280-2518
800-545-2433
E-Mail: kfiels@ala.org
Home Page: www.ala.org

Keith Michael Fiels, Executive Director
Mary Ellen Quinn, Editor

The purpose of this guide is to provide information on materials worthy of consideration for purchase by small and medium sized public libraries.
Cost: $79.95
Founded in 1876

20785 CBA Marketplace

Association for Christian Retail

9240 Explorer Drive
Suite 200
Colorado Spring, CO 80920

719-265-9895
800-252-1950
FAX 719-272-3510
E-Mail: info@cbaonline.org
Home Page: www.cbaonline.org

Bill Anderson, President/CEO
Cliff Goins, Treasurer
Greg Thornton, Director of Publications
George Thomsen, Chairman
Robin Hogan, Secretary

Resource for Christian retailers & suppliers.
Cost: $59.95
Frequency: Monthly
Circulation: 8000
Mailing list available for rent

20786 Christian Retailing
Strang Communications Company
600 Rinehart Rd
Lake Mary, FL 32746-4868

407-333-0600
FAX 407-333-7100
Home Page: www.strang.com

Stephen Strang, CEO
Tircia Stafford, Circulation Director

A trade journal designed to inform Christian
bookstore owners about books, music and gifts,
videos, etc. Also it features topics to help retailers run a successful business.
Cost: $75.00
72 Pages
Frequency: Monthly
Circulation: 10000
Founded in 1975

20787 Circulation Management
PRIMEDIA Intertec-Marketing &
Professional Service
PO Box 4235
Stamford, CT 06907-0235

212-475-2212
FAX 203-358-5823
Home Page: www.circman.com

Roberta Thomas, Publisher

Subscriptions, renewals, direct mail, list selec-
tion, circulation planning, data management,
fulfillment and list management.
Cost: $39.00
Frequency: Monthly
Circulation: 10,000

20788 Collegiate Journalist
Society for Collegiate Journalists
1584 Wesleyan Drive
Virginia Wesleyan College
Virginia Beach, VA 23502-5599

757-455-3419
FAX 757-461-5025
E-Mail: wjruehlmann@vwc.edu
Home Page: www.scj.us

J D Tarpley, Publisher
William Ruehlmann, CEO/President
Adam Earnheardt, Editor

For editors of yearbooks, magazines and newspapers.
Cost: $5.00
28 Pages
Frequency: Monthly

20789 Complete Guide to Self-Publishing
Communication Creativity

425 Cedar
Buena Vista, CO 81211-0909

719-395-8659
800-331-8355
FAX 719-395-8374

Marilyn Ross, Publisher
Matthew Sullivan, Editor

The most comprehensive resource available
about the business of publishing. Offers everything you need to know to write, publish, promote and sell books.
Cost: $19.99
521 Pages
ISBN: 1-582970-91-2

20790 Desktop Publishers Journal
462 Boston Street
Topsfield, MA 01983

FAX 800-492-1014
Home Page: www.dtpjournal.com

Barry Harrigan, Contact

Offers a comprehensive array of news, analysis, features and reviews on the latest products
and services on the market today.
Cost: $15.00
Frequency: 12 issues

20791 Editor & Publisher
Editor & Publisher International Yearbook
11 W 19th Street
10th Floor
New York, NY 10011-4234

212-291-1259
FAX 212-691-7287
Home Page: www.mediainfo.com

Michael Parker, President

Covers all facets of the newspaper business to-
day and is regarded as the bible of the newspa-
per industry.
Cost: $184.00
Frequency: 46 issues
Founded in 1884

20792 Editorial Eye
EEI Communications
66 Canal Center Plz
Suite 200
Alexandria, VA 22314-5507

703-683-0683
FAX 703-683-4915
E-Mail: info@eeicommunications.com
Home Page: www.eeicom.com

James T Degrafferei, CEO
Robin Cormier, VP
Candee Wilson, Director
Linda B. Jorgensen, Editor

Offering information on written excellence, ed-
itorial information and communication skills
for readers.
Cost: $125.00
Frequency: Monthly
Founded in 1972

20793 Electronic Publishing
PennWell Publishing Company
10 Tara Boulevard
5th Floor
Nashua, NH 03062-2880

603-891-0123
FAX 603-891-0539
E-Mail: genepri@pennwell.com
Home Page: www.electronic-publishing.com

Gene Pritchard, Publisher

For those who communicate in print, including
service bureaus, printers, prepress houses and
desktop publishers, it provides latest products,
news and related developments.
Cost: $45.00
Frequency: Monthly
Circulation: 68,441

20794 F&W Publications
1507 Dana Avenue
Cincinnati, OH 45207

513-396-6160
FAX 513-531-1025
Home Page: www.writersdigest.com

Jeff Lapin, President

Articles that reflect the current state of Ameri-
can freelance writing.
72 Pages
Frequency: 8 per year
Circulation: 85,000
ISBN: 7-148602-50-8
Founded in 1930

20795 FLEXO Magazine
Flexographic Technical Association Inc
900 Marconi Avenue
Ronkonkoma, NY 11779-7212

631-737-6020
FAX 631-737-6813
Home Page: www.flexography.org

Robert Moran, President
Christian Bonawandt, Editor

Up-to-date on the changes and advances in the
rapidly-expanding flexographic industry.
Cost: $55.00
Frequency: Monthly

**20796 Folio: Magazine for Magazine
Management**
Red 7 Media, LLC
10 Norden Place
Norwalk, CT 06855

203-854-6730
FAX 203-854-6735
E-Mail: tsilber@red7media.com
Home Page: www.foliomag.com

Stefanie Botelho, Associate Editor
Kerry Smith, President /CEO
Dan Trombetto, Group Creative Director
Tony Silber, General Manager
John Ellertson, Director Advertising Sales
Manager

Written for the people who run the nation's
magazines. Offers authoritative intelligence on
the magazine market to enable industry professionals to navigate the widening range of strategic options. Every issue delivers features on
the people and technologies that are transforming the magazine business, along with useful
columns and departments, thought-provoking
analysis and tactical advice for building successful magazines.
Cost: $96.00
Frequency: Monthly
Circulation: 11550
Founded in 1971

20797 ForeWord Reviews
ForeWord Magazine
425 Boardman Avenue
Traverse City, MI 49684

231-933-3699
FAX 231-933-3899
Home Page: www.forewordreviews.com

Victoria Sutherland, Owner
Stacy Price, Director Advertising Sales

Review books and other servies for authors and
small publishers.
Cost: $40.00
Frequency: Monthly
Circulation: 20000
Founded in 1998
Printed in 4 colors on 6 stock

20798 INFO FLEX
Flexographic Technical Association Inc

3920 Veterans Memorial Highway
Suite 9
Bohemia, NY 11716

631-737-6020
FAX 631-737-6813
E-Mail: memberinfo@flexography.org
Home Page: www.flexography.org

Mark Cisternino, President
Greg Platt, Chairman
Dan Doherty, Treasurer
Jason Barrier, Director

The show floor boasts 200+ booths manned by
flexography's leading suppliers, as well as a
presentation theater, and educational pavilion, a
social event and more
Frequency: Annual/May

20799 Independent Publisher Magazine

Jenkins Group
1129 Woodmere Avenue
Suite B
Traverse City, MI 49686-4275

231-933-0445
800-706-4636
FAX 231-933-0448
Home Page: www.bookpublishing.com

Jerrold R Jenkins, President
Jim Barmes, Editor
Andrew Pargel, Marketing Manager

Trade journal for the independent publishing,
community, university presses, librarians,
bookstores and professionals.
Cost: $40.00
Frequency: Monthly
Circulation: 8000
Founded in 1988
Mailing list available for rent: 42M names
Printed in 4 colors on glossy stock

20800 Information Publishing: Business/ Professional Markets & Media

Simba Information
60 Long Ridge Rd
Suite 300
Stamford, CT 06902-1841

203-325-8193
FAX 203-325-8915
E-Mail: simbainfo@simbanet.com
Home Page: www.simbanet.com

Linda Kopp, Publisher
Donna Devall, Marketing Director
Charlie Friscia, Director of Advertising

Demonstrates how publishers are profiting
from media. Discover the opportunities in
newsletters, directories, books, magazines,
journals and electronic information services.
More than 300 pages of information and analysis, 100 tables and charts, financial and operating information on more than 50 key
publishing companies, 16 principal information
markets reviewed in-depth, with five year forecasts by market and by media.
Cost: $1995.00
Founded in 1989

20801 Inside Edge

International Publishing Management
Association
1205 W College Street
Liberty, MO 64068

816-781-1111
FAX 660-781-2790
E-Mail: ipmainfo@ipma.org
Home Page: www.ipma.org

Larry Aaron, Executive Director
Susan Murphy, Editor
Jack Welch, CEO
Lea Holt, Director

Offers information on the association's activities, industry trends, and corporate publishing

facility profiles.
Cost: $50.00
24 Pages
Frequency: Monthly
Circulation: 1500
Mailing list available for rent: 2M names

20802 MultiMedia & Internet @Schools

Information Today
143 Old Marlton Pike
Medford, NJ 08055-8750

609-654-6266
800-300-9868
FAX 609-654-4309
E-Mail: custserv@infotoday.com
Home Page: www.infotoday.com

Thomas H Hogan, President
Roger R Bilboul, Chairman Of The Board
John C Yersak, Vice President
Sue Hogan, Director
John Brokenshire, CFO

A practical guide for K-12 library media specialists, technology coordinators and other educators with information on how to get
high-performance learning from technology-based school products, services and resources.
Cost: $ 39.95
Frequency: 6 issues/yr
Mailing list available for rent: 4M names
Printed in 4 colors on glossy stock

20803 New Age Publishing and Retailing Alliance Trade Journal

PO Box 9
Eastsound, WA 98245-0009

360-376-2702
FAX 360-376-2704

Marilyn McGuire, Executive Director
Carole Scarfuto, Administrative Director

Covers the publishing and retailing trades.
Frequency: Bi-Monthly
Circulation: 10,000

20804 NewsInc

PO Box 719
Pacifica, CA 94044-719

650-557-9595
FAX 650-557-9696
E-Mail: news@newsinc.net
Home Page: www.newsinc.net

David Cole, Publisher/Editor
Cost: $147.00
Frequency: Weekly
Founded in 1989

20805 Newspapers & Technology

Conley Magazines
1623 Blake Street
Suite 250
Denver, CO 80202

303-575-9595
FAX 303-575-9555
E-Mail: letters@newsandtech.com
Home Page: www.newsandtech.com/

Mary Van Meter, Publisher
Chuck Moozakis, Editor-in-Chief
Tara McMeekin, Editor
Hays Goodman, Associate Editor/Webmaster

Newspapers & Technology is a monthly trade
publication for newspaper publishers and department managers involved in applying and
integrating technology. Written by industry experts, News & Tech provides regular coverage
of the following departments: prepress, press,
postpress and new media.
Circulation: 16,874
Mailing list available for rent

20806 Poets & Writer's Magazine

Poets & Writers

150 Broadway
New York, NY 10038-4381

212-566-2424
FAX 212-587-9673
E-Mail: editor@pw.org
Home Page: www.pettuswilliams.com

Marvin K Pettus, President
Christine Cassidy, Marketing Director
William Hayes, Finance Executive

Interviews, essays, grants and awards, practical
information for poets and writers.
Cost: $19.95
Circulation: 60000

20807 Progressive Review

1312 18th Street NW
5th Floor
Washington, DC 20036

202-835-0770
FAX 202-835-0779
E-Mail: news@prorev.com
Home Page: www.prorev.com

Sam Smith, Editor
Frequency: Monthly
Founded in 1964

20808 Publish

462 Boston Street
Suite 310
Topsfield, MA 01983

978-887-6855
FAX 978-887-9245

Barry Harrigan, Owner

20809 Publishers Weekly

PO Box 51593
Harlan, IA 51593

800-278-2991
FAX 712-733-8019
E-Mail: pwycustserv@cdsfulfillment.com
Home Page: www.publishersweekly.com
Social Media: *Facebook, Twitter, LinkedIn,
RSS*

Jim Milliot, Co-Editorial Director
Michael Coffey, Co-Editorial Director
Diane Roback, Children's Book Editor
Louisa Ermelino, Reviews Director
Calvin Reid, News Editor

PW is the international journal of book publishing and bookselling including business
news, reviews and bestseller lists targeted at
publishers, booksellers, librarians and literary
agents.
Frequency: Weekly
Founded in 1872

20810 Publishing & Production Executive

Mark Hertzog
1500 Spring Garden Street
Suite 1200
Philadelphia, PA 19130

215-238-5300
FAX 215-238-5457
Home Page: www.ppe-online.com

Allison Schill Eckel, Managing Editor
Gretchen Kirby, Editor

Addresses technological trends and issues relevant to print production managers specializing
in books, magazines, catalogs, agency or corporate communications.
Frequency: 12 per year
Circulation: 30,000

20811 Quill

PO Box 94080
Palatine, IL 60094-v

765-653-3333
800-789-1331

FAX 800-789-8955
Home Page: www.quill.com

20812 Searcher: Magazine for the Database Professional
Information Today
143 Old Marlton Pike
Medford, NJ 08055-8750

609-654-6266
800-300-9868
FAX 609-654-4309
E-Mail: custserv@infotoday.com
Home Page: www.infotoday.com
Social Media: *Facebook, Twitter*

Thomas H Hogan, President
Roger R Bilboul, Chairman Of The Board

Explores and deliberates on a comprehensive range of issues important to the professional database researcher. Combines evaluations of data content with discussions of delivery media.
Cost: $86.95
Frequency: 10 issues/yr
Mailing list available for rent: 4M names
Printed in 4 colors on glossy stock

20813 Student Press Review
Columbia University
2960 Broadway
New York, NY 10027-6900

212-854-1754
FAX 212-749-0397
E-Mail: cspa@columbia.edu
Home Page: www.columbia.edu

Robert Kasdin, Executive VP
Helen F Smith, Editor
Edmund J Sullivan, Publisher

Reports and advises on high school and college student media. Offers how-to articles and features to improve student newspapers, magazines and yearbooks in schools, colleges, and universities.
Frequency: Quarterly
Circulation: 2200
Founded in 1925

20814 Volt Report on Directory Publishing
Volt Directory Marketing
1800 Byberry Road
Suite 800
Huntingdon Valley, PA 19006-3520

800-677-3839
FAX 215-938-5549

Kathy Wolden, Editor

As the monitor of the directory publishing industry, the Morgan report provides news on the people, companies, products and opportunities shaping the industry today. Includes practical how-to guidance on key facets of the directory publishing process as well as strategic overviews.
Cost: $95.00
12 Pages
Frequency: Monthly

20815 Writer Magazine
21027 Crossroads Circle
PO Box 1612
Waukesha, WI 53187-1612

262-796-8776
800-533-6644
FAX 262-796-1615
Home Page: corporate.kalmbach.com

Sylvia Burack, Publisher
Elfrieda Abbe, Executive Vice President
Chuck Croft, Executive Vice President

Practical guide to instruct, inform, and inspire writers as they work toward the goal of publication. Writers of short stories, novels, poetry,

plays or science fiction, readers will find straightforward advice, up-to-date market lists and tips on manuscript submission.
Cost: $29.00
Frequency: Monthly
Circulation: 43000
Founded in 1987

20816 Writer's Digest
F&W Publications
4700 E Galbraith Rd
Cincinnati, OH 45236-2726

513-531-2690
800-258-0929
FAX 513-531-1843
E-Mail: WritersDig@fwpubs.com
Home Page: www.fwpublications.com

David Nussbaum, CEO
Jim Ogle, Chief Financial Officer
Kate Rados, Marketing Director
Stacie Berger, Communications Director

Information and how to tips for freelance writers.
Cost: $19.96
Frequency: Monthly
Founded in 1920

Trade Shows

20817 AAP General Annual Meeting
Association of American Publishers (AAP)
455 Massachusetts Avenue NW
Suite 700
Washington, DC 20001-2777

202-347-3375
FAX 202-347-3690
E-Mail: info@publishers.org
Home Page: www.publishers.org
Social Media: *Twitter*

Karen Abramson, President & CEO
Tina Jordan, Vice President
Allan R Adler, VP for Legal & Government Affairs
Jay Diskey, Executive Director, School Division
Gail Kump, Director, Membership Marketing

Discussion topics include the state of digital content, distribution channels and copyright protection as seen through the prism of publishers and their historic partners.
200 Members
Frequency: Annual

20818 ADP Annual Convention and Partners Trade Show
Association of Directory Publishers
116 Cass St.
Traverse City, MI 49684

800-267-9002
FAX 231-486-2182
Home Page: adp.org/node/669
Social Media: *Facebook, Twitter, LinkedIn, YouTube*

Cindi A. Aldrich, President & CEO
Valerie Donn, Director of Meetings & Events
Frequency: Annual

20819 American Library Association Annual Conference
American Library Association
50 E Huron Street
Chicago, IL 60611

800-545-2433
E-Mail: customerservice@ala.org
Home Page: www.ala.org

Loriene Roy, President
Keith Michael Fiels, Executive Director

Annual meeting and exhibits of books, periodicals, reference works, audio visual equipment, films, data processing services, computer hardware and software, library equipment and supplies.

20820 American Medical Publishers' Association Annual Meeting
71 Fifth Avenue
2nd Floor
New York, NY 10003

212-255-0200
FAX 212-255-7007
E-Mail: jtagler@publishers.org
Home Page: www.pspcentral.org
Social Media: *LinkedIn*

John Tagler, VP/Executive Director
Sara Pinto, Director
Kate Kolendo, Project Manager

Information provided to medical publishing field.
Frequency: Annual
Founded in 1960

20821 Association of American University Presses Conference
Association of American University Presses
71 W 23rd Street
Suite 901
New York, NY 10010-3264

212-989-1010
FAX 212-989-0275
E-Mail: annualmeeting@aaupnet.org
Home Page:
www.aaup.uchicago.edu/aaup_home.html

Peter Givler, Executive Director
Timothy Muench, Assistant Director

Annual conference and exhibits of equipment, supplies and services for scholarly publishing divisions of colleges and universities.
125 Attendees
Frequency: Annual

20822 Association of College and Research Libraries
American Library Association
50 E Huron Street
Chicago, IL 60611-5295

312-280-2511
800-545-2433
FAX 312-280-2520
E-Mail: customerservice@ala.org
Home Page: www.ala.org/acrl

Mary Ellen Davis, Executive Director

Two hundred exhibitors with computers and web products, audiovisual products, furniture and library equipment.
3000 Attendees
Frequency: Biennial
ISSN: 0099-0086
Founded in 1978
Mailing list available for rent

20823 Association of Free Community Papers
1630 Miner Street
Suite 204, Box 1989
Idaho Springs, CO 80452

877-203-2327
FAX 781-459-7770
Home Page: www.afcp.org

Craig Mullin, Executive Director
Brianne Janes, Graphic Designer

Exhibits for publishers of free circulation papers and shopping/advertising guides.
Frequency: Annual
Founded in 1951

20824 Book Expo America
Reed Exhibitions

383 Main Avenue
Norwalk, CT 06851

203-404-4800
800-840-5614
E-Mail: cmuller@reedexpo.com
Home Page: www.bookexpoamerica.com
Social Media: *Facebook, Twitter, LinkedIn, YouTube, Pinterest*

Courtney Muller, Event Manager
Cathy Glickstein, Registration
Lisa Montanaro, Sales Executive

Sponsored by American Booksellers Association and Association of American Publishers. More than 2,000 exhibits, 500 authors, over 60 conference sessions as well as a special area for rights business, all the latest titles across genres, uncover hidden gems, network, and meet the industry contacts to put you instantly on top of what you need to know for your business and job.
Frequency: May/June
Founded in 2000

20825 Christian Booksellers Association
9240 Explorer Drive
Colorado Springs, CO 80920

800-252-1950
FAX 719-272-3510
E-Mail: info@cbaonline.org
Home Page: www.cbaonline.org

Bill Anderson, President
Mike Regennitter, Executive Director
Scott Graham, Director

Exhibition and sales of Christian oriented products to include categories of books and Bibles, music, framed art, jewelry, videos, clothing gifts, cards, stationary, children products, computer software, church supplies, curriculum and store supplies.
12M Attendees
Frequency: July

20826 Digital Book Printing Forum
Interquest Ltd.
513-D Stewart Street
Charlottesville, VA 22902

434-979-9945
FAX 434-979-9959
E-Mail: iquest@inter-quest.com
Home Page: www.inter-quest.com

David Davis, Director

Interquest analysts will present key results from the company's latest research in the field.
Frequency: March

20827 Digital Book World
FAX new

Jeremy Greenfield, Editorial Director
Raymond Kyle, Business Development Manager
Gary Lynch, Group Publisher
Amanda Malek, Online Product Development

A year-round platform offering educational and networking resources for consumer publishing professionals and their partners - including agents, booksellers and technology vendors - online and in person

20828 FFTA Annual Forum & INFO FLEX Exhibition
Flexographic Technical Association Inc
3920 Veterans Memorial Highway
Suite 9
Bohemia, NY 11716

631-737-6020
FAX 631-737-6813
E-Mail: memberinfo@flexography.org
Home Page: www.flexography.org

Mark Cisternino, President
Joe Tuccitto, Director of Education

Doreen Monteleone, Director Environmental Affairs
Sharon Cox, Director of Marketing
Katie Dubois, Creative Services Manager

Presents the most promising technological advances and emerging market opportunities to keep you and your company up to date.
1600+ Attendees

20829 FOLIO Show
Red 7 Media, LLC
10 Norden Place
Norwalk, CT 06855

203-854-6730
FAX 203-854-6735
Home Page: www.folioshow.com/
Social Media: *Facebook, Twitter, LinkedIn*

Tony Silberg, Publisher/General Manager
John Ellertson, Group Sales Director
Magan Sprenger, Account Executive
Tania Babiuk, Account Executive
Kerry Smith, President

Biennial show and exhibits of publishing supplies, paper, printing equipment, color separators, fulfillment houses, lists and related equipment, supplies and services to the magazine and book publishing trades.
7,000 Attendees

20830 InfoCommerce
InfoCommerce Group Inc
2 Bala Plaza
Suite 300
Bala Cynwyd, PA 19004

610-649-1200
FAX 610-471-0515
E-Mail: rchristensen@infocommercegroup.com
Home Page: www.infocommercegroup.com

Roxanne Christensen, Dir Awards Conferences & Consulting

Convenes all kinds of publishers who are bound only by their ability and willingness to take risks.
Frequency: Oct, Philadelphia

20831 NCRW Annual Conference
National Council for Research on Women
11 Hanover Square
24th Floor
New York, NY 10005-2819

212-785-7335
FAX 212-785-7350
E-Mail: ncrw@ncrw.org
Home Page: www.ncrw.org

Mariam K Chamberlain, Founding President
Linda G Basch, President
Frequency: June

20832 New England Booksellers Association Annual Trade Show
1770 Massachusetts Avenue
#332
Cambridge, MA 02140

617-576-3070
800-466-8711
FAX 617-576-3091
Home Page: www.newenglandbooks.org/

Allan Schmid, President
Dale Szczeblowski, VP

Offers the opportunity for publishers to get their products in the hands of the booksellers in an area with one of the highest concentrations of readers in the country. This traditional multi-media exhibition is the largest of the regional conference in bookseller attendance.
2M+ Attendees
Frequency: September/October

20833 Publishing Institute
Publishing Institute

University of Denver
2000 E. Asbury Ave
Denver, CO 80208

303-832-5280
FAX 303-871-2501
E-Mail: pi-info@du.edu
Home Page: www.du.edu/publishinginstitute

Elizabeth Geiser, Director
Joyce Meskis, Director

A certificate program that combines workshops in editing and marketing with lecture/teaching sessions conducted by leading experts from all areas of publishing.
90 Attendees
Frequency: July-August

20834 Publishing University
Independent Book Publishers Association
1020 Manhattan Beach Blvd
Suite 204
Manhattan Beach, CA 90266

310-546-1818
FAX 310-546-3939
E-Mail: info@ibpa-online.org
Home Page: www.ibpa-online.org

Terry Nathan, Executive Director
Lisa Krebs, Assistant Director
Steve Mettee, Board Chair
Roy M Carlisle, Treasurer
Florrie B Kichler, President

A 2-day publishing conference focusing on education and networking. 40 exhibitors.
300 Attendees
Frequency: Annual

20835 Small Press Book Fair
Small Press Center
20 W 44th Street
New York, NY 10036-6604

212-764-7021
FAX 212-354-5365
E-Mail: smallpress@aol.com
Home Page: www.smallpress.org

Mary Bertschmann, Chair
Lloyd Jassin, Vice Chair
Mashala Solammi, Owner

One of the major book fairs for small press. Containing 100 booths and 100 exhibits.
2,500 Attendees
Frequency: March

20836 Tools of Change for Publishing Conference
O'Reilly Media, Inc.
1005 Gravenstein Highway North
Sebastopol, CA 95472

707-827-7000
800-998-9938
FAX 707-829-0104
E-Mail: conf-webmaster@oreilly.com
Home Page: www.oreilly.com
Social Media: *Facebook, Twitter, LinkedIn, RSS*

Gina Blaber, Vice President, Conferences
Suzanne Axtell, Communications Manager
Shirley Bailes, Speaker Manager

Expect coverage with a range of practical, in-depth sessions that cover the innovations rocking every aspect of the art, craft, and business of publishing in the 21st century.
Frequency: February
Mailing list available for rent

20837 Writing Academy Seminar
Writing Academy

4010 Singleton Road
Rockford, IL 61114

815-877-9675
Home Page: www.wams.org/indexhtm

Annual seminar and exhibits by Christian writers.

20838 Yellow Pages Publishers Association Convention

Yellow Pages Publishers Association
116 Cass Street
Traverse City, MI 49684

800-267-9002
FAX 231-486-2182
E-Mail: hq@adp.org
Home Page: www.adp.org/

R. Lawrence Angove, President
Bonnie Pintozzi, COO
Vernon Smith, Treasurer

Annual convention and exhibits of equipment, supplies and services for the publication of Yellow Pages telephone directories.

Directories & Databases

20839 2,224 Public Libraries Data Files

Open Horizons Publishing
PO Box 2887
Taos, NM 87571

575-751-3398
800-796-6130
FAX 575-751-3100
E-Mail: info@bookmarket.com
Home Page: www.bookmarket.com

John Kremer, Editor
Robert Sanny, Advertising/Sales Manager

Database features 2,224 general public libraries, with name and address; no phone, fax, or email. Download in your choice of formats along with an information sheet.
Cost: $40.00
Frequency: Database
Founded in 1982

20840 Advertising and Publicity Resources for Scholarly Books

Association of American University Presses
Rm 602
30 W 36th St
New York, NY 10018-8063

212-989-1010
FAX 212-989-0275
E-Mail: info@aaupnet.org
Home Page: www.aaupnet.org

Peter Givler, Executive Director
Timothy Muench, Marketing Coordinator
Latasha Watters, Marketing Coordinator

This comprehensive directory lists periodicals which accept advertising or review copies of scholarly publications.
Cost: $189.00
425 Pages

20841 Alternative Publications: A Guide to Directories and Other Sources

Mcfarland & Company
Po Box 611
Jefferson, NC 28640-0611

336-246-4460
FAX 336-246-5018
E-Mail: info@mcfarlandpub.com
Home Page: www.mcfarlandpub.com
Social Media: *Facebook, Twitter, LinkedIn*

Robert Franklin, President

Offers indexes and abstracts, review sources and bibliographies dealing with alternative

publications.
Cost: $18.95
96 Pages

20842 American Book Producers Directory

American Book Producers Association
160 5th Avenue
New York, NY 10010-7003

212-645-2368
800-209-4575
FAX 212-242-6799
E-Mail: office@ABPAonline.org
Home Page: www.abpaonline.org

David Rubel, President
David Katz, Treasurer
Valerie Tomaselli, Treasurer
Nancy Hall, Vice President
40 Pages
Circulation: 2,000
Founded in 1980
Printed in 2 colors on matte stock

20843 American Book Trade Directory

Information Today
143 Old Marlton Pike
Medford, NJ 08055-8750

609-654-6266
800-300-9868
FAX 609-654-4309
E-Mail: custserv@infotoday.com
Home Page: www.infotoday.com
Social Media: *Facebook, Twitter*

Thomas H Hogan, President
Roger R Bilboul, Chairman Of The Board

A US book trade community. Profiles 25,500 retail and antiquarian book dealers, plus 1,200 book and magazine wholesalers, distributors, and jobbers in all 50 states and US territories.
Cost: $299.00
1800 Pages
ISBN: 1-573872-12-1

20844 American Directory of Writer's Guidelines

Dustbooks
PO Box 100
Paradise, CA 95967-0100

530-877-6110
800-477-6110
FAX 530-877-0222
E-Mail: directories@dustbooks.com
Home Page: www.dustbooks.com

Brigitte M Phillips, Editor
Susan D Klassen, Editor
Doris Hall, Editor

These guidelines help writers target their submissions to the exact needs of the individual publisher. A compilation of information for freelancers from more than 1,500 magazine editors and book publishers.
Cost: $29.95
752 Pages
ISBN: 1-884956-40-8

20845 Association of American University Presses Directory

Association of American University Presses
Rm 602
30 W 36th St
New York, NY 10018-8063

212-989-1010
FAX 212-989-0275
E-Mail: info@aaupnet.org
Home Page:
www.aaup.uchicago.edu/aaup_home.html

Peter Givler, Executive Director
Timothy Muench, Assistant Director

114 presses and affiliates worldwide.
Cost: $14.95
Frequency: Annual November

20846 Bacon's Newspaper & Magazine Directories

Cision U.S., Inc.
322 South Michigan Avenue
Suite 900
Chicago, IL 60604

312-263-0070
866-639-5087
E-Mail: info.us@cision.com
Home Page: us.cision.com

Joe Bernardo, President & CEO
Heidi Sullivan, VP & Publisher
Valerie Lopez, Research Director
Jessica White, Research Director
Rachel Farrell, Research Manager

Two volume set listing all daily and community newspapers, magazines and newsletters, news service and syndicates, syndicated columnists, complete editorial staff listings of each publication provided, covers U.S., Canada, Mexico, and Carribean.
Cost: $350.00
4,700 Pages
Frequency: Annual
ISSN: 1088-9639
Founded in 1951
Printed in one color on matte stock

20847 Bacon's Radio/TV/Cable Directory

Cision U.S., Inc.
332 South Michigan Avenue
Suite 900
Chicago, IL 60604

312-263-0070
866-639-5087
E-Mail: info.us@cision.com
Home Page: www.us.cision.com

Joe Bernardo, President & CEO
Heidi Sullivan, VP & Publisher
Valerie Lopez, Research Director
Jessica White, Research Director
Rachel Farrell, Research Manager

Includes comprehensive coverage for contact and programming information for more than 3,500 televsion networks, cable networks, television syndicators, television stations, and cable systems in the United States and Canada.
Cost: $350.00
Frequency: Annual
ISSN: 1088-9639
Printed in one color on matte stock

20848 Book Marketing 105: Choosing a Book Distribution System

Open Horizons Publishing
PO Box 2887
Taos, NM 87571

575-751-3398
800-796-6130
FAX 575-751-3100
E-Mail: info@bookmarket.com
Home Page: www.bookmarket.com

John Kremer, Editor
Robert Sanny, Advertising/Sales Manager

A mini-guide including criteria for deciding how to distribute books. Also includes complete information on 30 distributors, 4 library distributors, 89 book publishers who also distribute for other publishers, 3 sales reps to the chains, 27 bookstore wholesalers, 34 library wholesalers, and 23 Spanish-launguage wholesalers. Plus a sample distribution contract.
Cost: $30.00
Frequency: Ebook Download
Founded in 1982

20849 BookStats

Association of American Publishers (AAP)

455 Massachusetts Avenue NW
Suite 700
Washington, DC 20001-2777

202-347-3375
FAX 202-347-3690
E-Mail: info@publishers.org
Home Page: www.publishers.org
Social Media: *Twitter*

Karen Abramson, President & CEO
Tina Jordan, Vice President
Allan R Adler, VP for Legal & Government
Affairs
Jay Diskey, Executive Director, School
Division
Gail Kump, Director, Membership Marketing

Provides a comprehensive view of the size and
shape of the US book publishing industry measured by publisher net unit and dollar sales.
Frequency: Annual

20850 Books and Periodicals Online
Literary Technology Alliance
264 Lexington Avenue
Room 4C
New York, NY 10016-4182

212-686-8816
FAX 212-686-8776
E-Mail: info@booksandperiodicals.com
Home Page: www.booksandperiodicals.com/

Nuchine Nobari MLS, MBA, Editor

BPO is an international directory of periodicals
included in onlinedatabases. Arranged alphabetically, entries include Publication title, dates
covered in each database, whether coverage is
in Full text, Abstract, or Index, ISSN, and title
changes. Online hosts and addresses for producers and vendors are given in separate list.
Lists over 97,000 sources and includes an ap-
pendix of newspapers and their URL, in alphabetical and geographic order.
Cost: $399.00
3400 Pages
Frequency: 4 issues
Circulation: 1400
ISBN: 0-963027-78-X
Founded in 1987
Printed in 2 colors

20851 Business Info USA
InfoUSA
5711 S 86th Cir
Omaha, NE 68127-4146

402-593-4500
888-260-7943
FAX 402-331-6287
E-Mail: karen.peters@infousa.com
Home Page: www.infousa.com

Vinod Gupta, CEO
Karen Peters, Account Executive
Cost: $2750.00
Frequency: Monthly
Circulation: 4000000
Founded in 1972

20852 Business Periodicals Index
HW Wilson Company
950 Dr Martin L King Jr Blvd
Bronx, NY 10452-4297

718-588-8405
800-367-6770
FAX 718-590-1617
Home Page: www.hwwilson.com

Harold Regan, CEO
Kathleen McEvoy, Director of Public Relations

Designed for businesses, business schools and
libraries, business periodicals index covers
English-language business periodicals and
trade journals. Users enjoy quick access to feature articles, product reviews, interviews, biographical sketches, corporate profiles,
obituaries, surveys, book reviews, reports from

associations, societies, trade shows and conferences, and more. The database also provides
SIC codes for industries and names of
corporations used as subject headings.

20853 Catalog Sales Data Files
Open Horizons Publishing
PO Box 2887
Taos, NM 87571

575-751-3398
800-796-6130
FAX 575-751-3100
E-Mail: info@bookmarket.com
Home Page: www.bookmarket.com

John Kremer, Editor
Robert Sanny, Advertising/Sales Manager

Database features the top 1,350 catalogs,
internet bookstore sites, chain store outlets,
wholesalers, distributors, and other special
sales outlets. Includes catalog names, buyers,
addresses, phone and fax numbers, emails,
website, types of books carried, and other important details.
Cost: $30.00
Frequency: Database
Founded in 1982

20854 Celebrate Today
Open Horizons Publishing
PO Box 2887
Taos, NM 87571

575-751-3398
800-796-6130
FAX 575-751-3100
E-Mail: info@bookmarket.com
Home Page: www.bookmarket.com

John Kremer, Editor
Robert Sanny, Advertising/Sales Manager

Database with 18,290 holidays, special days,
weeks, months and historical anniversaries.
Searchable by subject interest. Includes contact
info and websites in most cases. Useful for set-
ting pub dates and doing PR tie-ins.
Cost: $30.00
Frequency: Database
Founded in 1982

**20855 Complete Directory of Large Print
Books and Serials**
4919 Route 22
PO Box 56
Amenia, NY 12546

518-789-8700
800-562-2139
FAX 518-789-0556
E-Mail: customerservice@greyhouse.com
Home Page: www.greyhouse.com

R R Bowker

Provides nine easy to use indexes including Title, Author, General Reading Subject, Textbook
Subject, Children's Subject, Serials Subject,
and Serials Title. For easy acquisition, full contact information on publishers, wholesalers and
distributors is provided in a separate index.
Frequency: Annual
ISBN: 0-835249-41-6

20856 Corporate Yellow Book
Leadership Directories
398 RXR Plaza
Uniondale, NY 11556

516-730-1900
E-Mail: corporate@leadershipdirectories.com
Home Page: www.corporate.yellowbook.com

David Hurvitz, CEO
Bryan Turner, CFO
Jim McCusker, President

Contact information for over 48,000 executives
at over 1,000 companies and more than 9,000

board members and their outside affiliations.
Cost: $400.00
1,400 Pages
Frequency: Quarterly
ISSN: 1058-2098
Founded in 1986

20857 Directories in Print
Gale/Cengage Learning
10650 Toebben Drive
Independence, KY 41051

800-824-5179
800-354-9706
FAX 800-487-8488
E-Mail: higheredcs@cengage.com
Home Page: www.gale.com

Patrick C Sommers, President

Describes more than 16,000 active rosters,
guides and other print and nonprint address
lists published in the United States and worldwide.
Frequency: Annual
ISBN: 1-414421-75-3

20858 Directory of Poetry Publishers
Dustbooks
PO Box 100
Paradise, CA 95967-0100

530-877-6110
800-477-6110
FAX 530-877-0222
E-Mail: directories@dustbooks.com
Home Page: www.dustbooks.com

Len Fulton, Editor

Over 2,100 magazines, small and commercial
presses and university presses that accept po-
etry for publication.
Cost: $25.95
300 Pages
Frequency: Annual
Circulation: 2,000
ISBN: 0-916685-47-0

**20859 Directory of Small Magazines Press
Magazine Editors & Publishers**
Dustbooks
PO Box 100
Paradise, CA 95967-0100

530-877-6110
800-477-6110
FAX 530-877-0222
E-Mail: directories@dustbooks.com
Home Page: www.dustbooks.com

Len Fulton, Editor

This directory contains more than 7,500 listings of editors and publishers in alphabetical
order, along with their associated publishing
companies, their addresses, phones, e-mail addresses and Web pages. Includes self publishers.
Cost: $25.95
460 Pages
Frequency: Annual
Circulation: 1,000
ISBN: 0-913218-28-6
Founded in 1967
Mailing list available for rent

**20860 Editor & Publisher International
Yearbook**
Editor & Publisher Company
770 Broadway
New York, NY 10003-9595

212-291-1259
800-336-4380
FAX 646-654-5370
Home Page: www.editorandpublisher.com

Sid Holt, Editor-in-Chief
Greg Mitchell, Editor
Michael Parker, President

Daily and Sunday newspapers in the US and Canada; weekly newspapers; foreign daily newspapers; special service newspapers; newspaper syndicates; news servides; journalism schools; foreign language and Black newspapers in the US; news, picture and press services; feature and news syndicates; comic and magazine services; advertising clubs; trade associations; clipping bureaus; house organs; journalism awards; manufacturers of equipment and supplies.
Cost: $230.00
Frequency: Annual March

20861 Editor & Publisher Market Guide
Editor & Publisher Company
770 Broadway
New York, NY 10003-9595

212-291-1259
800-336-4380
FAX 646-654-5370
Home Page: www.editorandpublisher.com
Sid Holt, Editor-in-Chief
Greg Mitchell, Editor
Michael Parker, President
More than 1,700 newspaper markets in the US and Canada.
Cost: $100.00
Frequency: Annual November
Circulation: 4,500

20862 Editor & Publisher: Journalism Awards and Fellowships Directory Issue
Editor & Publisher Company
770 Broadway
New York, NY 10003-9595

212-291-1259
800-336-4380
FAX 646-654-5370
Home Page: www.editorandpublisher.com
Sid Holt, Editor-in-Chief
Greg Mitchell, Editor
Michael Parker, President
Over 500 cash prizes, scholarships, fellowships and grants available to journalists and students for work on special subjects or in specific fields.
Cost: $4.00
Frequency: Annual December
Circulation: 28,500

20863 Grey House Publishing
4919 Route 22
PO Box 56
Amenia, NY 12546

518-789-8700
800-562-2139
FAX 518-789-0556
E-Mail: customerservice@greyhouse.com
Home Page: www.greyhouse.com
Leslie Mackenzie, Publisher
Richard Gottlieb, Editor
Publishes over 100 titles including reference directories in the areas of business, education, health, statistics and demographics, as well as educational encyclopedias and business handbooks. All titles offer detailed information in well-organized formats. Many titles available online.
Founded in 1981

20864 IBPA Directory
Independent Book Publishers Association
627 Aviation Way
Manhattan Beach, CA 90266

310-318-2270
FAX 310-374-3342

E-Mail: info@ibpa-online.org
Home Page: www.ibpa-online.org
Terry Nathan, Executive Director
Lisa Krebs, Assistant Director
A directory of members and one of regional affiliates is available online with multi-level search options.

20865 International Directory of Little Magazines & Small Presses
Dustbooks
PO Box 100
Paradise, CA 95967-0100

530-877-6110
FAX 530-877-0222
E-Mail: directories@dustbooks.com
Home Page: www.dustbooks.com
Len Fulton, Editor
Lists more than 4,000 book and magazine publishers of literary, avant garde, cutting-edge contemporary, left wing, right wing and radical chic fiction to non-fiction essays, reviews, artwork, music, satire, criticism, commentary, letters, parts of novels, longpoems, concrete art, collages, plays, news items and more.
Cost: $55.00
Frequency: Annual/Cloth
Circulation: 1,000
ISBN: 0-916685-49-7

20866 International Literary Market Place
Information Today
143 Old Marlton Pike
Medford, NJ 08055-8750

609-654-6266
800-300-9868
FAX 609-654-4309
E-Mail: custserv@infotoday.com
Home Page: www.infotoday.com
Social Media: *Facebook, Twitter*
Thomas H Hogan, President
Roger R Bilboul, Chairman of the Board
John C Yersak, Vice President
John Brokenshire, CFO
The directory of the international book publishing industry with 16,500 up to date profiles with book related concerns, including trade organizations, distributors, dealers, literary associations, trade publications, book trade events, and other resources conveniently organzied in a country by counrty format
Cost: $240.00
1800 Pages
ISBN: 1-573871-75-3

20867 Livestock Publications Council Membership Directory
Livestock Publications
910 Currie Street
Fort Worth, TX 76107

817-336-1130
FAX 817-232-4820
E-Mail: dianej@flash.net
Home Page: www.livestockpublications.com
Offers information on over 100 US and Canadian LPC-member livestock magazines, newspapers and newsletters.
40 Pages

20868 Magazines for Libraries
R R Bowker LLC
630 Central Ave
New Providence, NJ 07974-1506

908-286-0288
888-269-5372
FAX 908-219-0098
E-Mail: info@bowker.com
Home Page: www.bowker.com
R R Bowker

Magazines for Libraries provides the serials information you need to build and maintain a quality collection that best meets the needs of your library's users.
Frequency: Triennial
ISBN: 1-600301-16-2

20869 National Journal
National Journal
600 New Hampshire Ave NW
Washington, DC 20037-2403

202-739-8400
800-207-8001
FAX 202-833-8069
E-Mail: service@nationaljournal.com
Home Page: www.nationaljournal.com
John Fox Sullivan, President
Steve Hull, Senior VP
Timothy B Clark, VP
Publishes directories in the area of government.

20870 Progressive Periodicals Directory
Progressive Education
PO Box 120574
Nashville, TN 37212-0574

615-367-1874
Craig T Canan, Editor
About 600 social-concerns periodicals.
Cost: $16.00

20871 Publishers, Distributors and Wholesalers of the United States
R R Bowker LLC
630 Central Ave
New Providence, NJ 07974-1506

908-286-0288
888-269-5372
FAX 908-219-0098
E-Mail: info@bowker.com
Home Page: www.bowker.com
R R Bowker
In this 2 volume set locate publishers, museum and association imprint and trade organizations that publish, software firms, audio-cassette producers and even publishers that have gone out of business.
Frequency: 2 Volumes
ISBN: 0-835249-66-9

20872 Publishing & Production Executive: Who's Who of Suppliers and Services
North American Publishing Company
1500 Spring Garden St
Suite 1200
Philadelphia, PA 19130-4094

215-238-5300
800-777-8074
FAX 215-238-5342
E-Mail: customerservice@napco.com
Home Page: www.napco.com
Ned S Borowsky, CEO
Directory of services and supplies to the industry.
Circulation: 30,000
Mailing list available for rent

20873 Single Unit Supermarkets Operators
Chain Store Guide
3922 Coconut Palm Dr
Tampa, FL 33619-1389

813-627-6700
800-778-9794
FAX 813-627-7094
E-Mail: info@csgis.com
Home Page: www.csgis.com
Mike Jarvis, Publisher
Shami Choon, Manager
Discover more than 7,100 single-unit supermarkets with annual sales topping $500,000

dollars. This comprehensive desktop reference makes it easy to reach our compiled list of 21,000 key executives and buyers, plus their primary wholesalers.
Cost: $335.00
725 Pages
Frequency: Annual

20874 Small Publishers Association of North America (SPAN)
PO Box 1306
Buena Vista, CO 81211-1306

719-395-4790
FAX 719-395-8374
Home Page: www.spannet.org

Marilyn Ross, Executive Director/Editor
Tom Ross, VP
Cathy Bowman, Production Manager

Online resource for book publishing know-how. Works to advance the image and profits of self publishers and independent publishers through education and marketing opportunities.

20875 Something About the Author
Gale/Cengage Learning
Po Box 09187
Detroit, MI 48209-0187

248-699-4253
800-877-4253
FAX 248-699-8049
E-Mail: gale.galeord@cengage.com
Home Page: www.gale.com

Patrick C Sommers, President

An easy to use source for librarians, students and other researchers each volume in this series provides illustrated biographical profiles of approximately 75 children's authors and artists. This critically acclaimed series covers more than 12,000 individuals, ranging from established award winners to authors and illustrators who are just beginning their careers.
ISBN: 1-414442-17-3

20876 Standard Periodical Directory
Oxbridge Communications
39 W. 29 St.
301
New York, NY 10001

212-741-0231
800-955-0231
FAX 212-633-2938
E-Mail: custserv@mediafinder.com
Home Page: www.mediafinder.com

Patricia Hagood, President

Circulation, advertising and list rental info for more than 75,000 North American periodicals.
Cost: $1495.00
2,326 Pages
Frequency: Annual
Circulation: 3,500
ISBN: 1-891783-23-8
ISSN: 0085-6630
Founded in 1964
Printed in 4 colors

20877 Top 700 Independent Bookstores
Open Horizons Publishing
PO Box 2887
Taos, NM 87571

641-472-6130
800-796-6130
FAX 641-472-1560
E-Mail: info@bookmarket.com
Home Page: www.bookmarket.com

John Kremer, Editor
Robert Sanny, Advertising/Sales Manager

Database of 790 stores with address, book buyer, owner, event coordinator, phone, fax, email, website and more. Lists the largest bookstores that work with authors and that buy

from indy book publishers. Compiled from industry news, author and publisher recommendations, and research. The report comes as a data file download in your choice of Access, Excel, comma- or tab-delimited ASCII, d-Base or rich text format.
Cost: $40.00
Frequency: Database
Founded in 1982

20878 Ulrich's Periodicals Directory
R R Bowker LLC
630 Central Ave
New Providence, NJ 07974-1506

908-286-1090
888-269-5372
FAX 908-219-0098
E-Mail: info@bowker.com
Home Page: www.bowker.com

Michael Cairns, CEO
Annie Callanan, COO

An essential reference tool for any serials librarian the Ulrich's Periodicals Directory™ is overflowing with the latest international bibliographic information on journals, magazines and newspapers.

Industry Web Sites

20879 http://gold.greyhouse.com
G.O.L.D Grey House OnLine Databases
Grey House Publishing's online database platform, GOLD, offers Quick Search, Keyword Search and Expert Search for most business sectors including publishing and allied markets. The GOLD platform makes finding the information you need quick and easy - whether you're a novice searcher or an experienced database user. All of Grey House's directory products are available for subscription on the GOLD platform.

20880 www.aaup.princetou.edu
Exchange
Reports on issues relevant to scholarly publishing.

20881 www.aaupnet.org/membership/directory
Association of American University Presses
Members are university presses and a limited number of presses of non-degree-granting scholarly institutions.

20882 www.abaa.org
Antiquarian Booksellers Association of America
A trade association of rare book dealers.

20883 www.abpaonline.org
American Book Producers Association
Increases the book industry's awareness of members capabilities and exchanges information on improving business. Develops concepts for books and other publications.

20884 www.accessabc.com
Audit Bureau of Circulations
The world's largest circulation-auditing organization, ABC provides circulation data on 1,400+ newspapers and more than 1,100 periodicals to ABC-member publications, advertisers and advertising agencies.

20885 www.ampaonline.org
American Medical Publishers' Association
Information provided to the medical publishing field.

20886 www.bisg.org
Book Industry Study Group
Promotes and supports research, enabling various sectors of the industry to develop and expand their professional and business plans. Book Industry Study Group has various paperback publications.

20887 www.bizpubs.org
Alliance of Area Business Publications
Represents metropolitan area and state-wide business to business publications with conventions, newsletters, and other services.

20888 www.bookbuilders.org
Bookbuilders West
A nonprofit organization that provides a forum for publishers and suppliers to share experiences via dinners, social events and educational seminars.

20889 www.bookmarketingprofits.com
North American Bookdealers Exchange
Independent publishers and mail order entrepreneurs. An international book marketing organization specializing in cooperative opportunities at trade shows, in mail order, press releases, and more.

20890 www.bookpublishing.com
Jenkins Independent Publishers

20891 www.catholicpress.org
Catholic Press Association of the US and Canada

20892 www.clmp.org
Council of Literary Magazines and Presses
Membership is open to any noncommercial literary magazine or press that publishes at least one or more books per year.

20893 www.columbia.edu/eu/cspa
Columbia Scholastic Press Association
International student press association composed of writing students, journalists and faculty advisers in schools and colleges through educational conferences, idea exchanges and recognition programs.

20894 www.du.edu/pi
Publishing Institute
A national organization that combines workshops in editing and marketing with lecture/teaching sessions conducted by leading experts from all areas of publishing.

20895 www.ecpa.org
Evangelical Christian Publishers Association
Promotes excellence and professionalism, shares relevant data, and equips Christian publishers to meet the needs of the changing marketplace.

20896 www.flexography.org
Flexographic Technical Association

20897 www.flexography.org/flexsys/index.cfm
Flexographic Technical Assn Education & Training
Magazine publishing.

20898 www.greyhouse.com
Grey House Publishing
Authoritative reference directories for most business sectors including publishing and allied markets. Users can search the online databases with varied search criteria allowing for custom searches by product category, geographic area, sales volume, keyword, subject and more. Full

Grey House catalog and online ordering also available.

20899 www.interquest.Com

FAX new

A market and technology research and consulting firm in the field of digital printing and publishing that produces studies on topics such as digital printing, transactional printing, variable imaging, etc.

20900 www.ipma.org

International Publishing Management Association

The professional association for in-house corporate publishing professionals who work for educational institutions, governments and private industry.

20901 www.naa.org

Newspaper Association of America

Founded by the merger of seven associations serving the newspaper industry. Focuses on the major issues that affect today's newspaper industry public policy and legal matters, advertising revenue growth and audience development across the medium's broad portfolio of products and digital platforms.

20902 www.ncrw.org

National Council for Research on Women

A network of 120 leading research, policy and advocacy centers dedicated to improving the lives of women and girls. Provides the latest news, analysis and strategies needed to ensure fully informed debates, effective policies and inclusive practices.

20903 www.newsletters.org

Newsletter & Electronic Publishers Association

International trade association serving the interests of publishers of newsletters and specialized information services.

20904 www.nmpa.org

National Music Publishers' Association

20905 www.p3-ny.org/

Partnership in Print Production

Promotes the interests of women.

20906 www.pacificpress.com

Pacific Press Publishing Association

Promotes the interests of publishing, press, and media professionals.

20907 www.papertrade.com

National Paper Trade Association

20908 www.publishers.org

Association of American Publishers

Principal trade association for the US book publishing industry members comprise most of the major commerical book publishers in the US, as well as smaller and medium-sized houses, not-for-profit publishers, university presses, and scholarly societies.

20909 www.publishersreport.com

National Association of Independent Publishers

Assists and educates small publishing companies. Conducts seminars on marketing strategies, target audience, and techniques of book distribution. Especially helpful for the beginning or self-publisher.

20910 www.snaponline.org

Society of National Association Publications

Develops standards for editorial and advertising content of association and professional society magazines.

20911 www.spannet.org

Small Publishers Association of North America

For independent presses and self-publishers who want to produce better books and market them more successfully.

20912 www.sspnet.org

Society for Scholarly Publishing

A group that represents scholarly publications, such as journals, university publications and magazines.

20913 www.theacp.org

Associated Church Press

Aims to share ideas and concerns in religious publishing and to stimulate higher standards of religious journalism to exert a more positive influence.

20914 www.thomson.com

Thomson.Com

A shared Web service that provides critical tools for more than 35 publishers.

20915 www.wpa-online.org

Western Publications Association

Represents magazine publishing companies and companies related to publishing industry, in the western United States.

Associations

20916 Accredited Review Appraisers Council
ARAC
303 W Cypress Street
San Antonio, TX 78212

800-486-3676
Home Page: www.arac.lincoln-grad.org

Provides education and designation in appraisal and real estate review.

20917 American Association of Certified Wedding Planners
210 W College St
Suite 400
Grapevine, TX 76051

214-342-2378
E-Mail: president@aacwp.org
Home Page: www.aacwp.org
Social Media: *Facebook, Twitter, Instagram*

Trudy Baade, President
Wendy Kidd, Vice-President
Micki Novak, Treasurer
Jenny Cline, Secretary
Jennifer Ashford, Education

A national organization that offers designations to qualified appraisers, teaches courses on latest appraisal information and offers courses on home inspection.

20918 American College of Real Estate Lawyers
11300 Rockville Pike
Suite 903
Rockville, MD 20852

301-816-9811
FAX 301-816-9786
E-Mail: webmaster@acrel.org
Home Page: www.acrel.org

Kenneth M. Jacobson, President
Roger D. Winston, Vice President
Jay A. Epstien, Treasurer
Steven A. Waters, Secretary
Kathryn C. Murphy, President-Elect

Members are CPAs working in the real estate field.

20919 American Homeowners Foundation
6776 Little Falls Rd
Arlington, VA 22213-1213

703-536-7776
800-489-7776
FAX 703-536-7079
E-Mail: ahga@amricanhomeowners.org
Home Page: www.americanhomeowners.org

Bruce Itahn, President

A national consumer organization representing the nation's 75 million homeowners.
Founded in 1984

20920 American Industrial Real Estate
Pacific Financial Center
500 North Brand
Suite 900
Glendale, CA 91203

213-687-8777
FAX 213-687-8616
E-Mail: jcruz@airea.com
Home Page: www.airea.com
Social Media: *Facebook, Twitter*

Joy D'La Cruz, Chief Operations Officer
Tim Hayes, Executive Director
Joseph T. Faulkner, President
Louis J. Tomaselli, Vice-President
Joseph Lin, President Elect

Encourages high professional standards. Has developed industrial multiple listing system and standard lease form. Publishes a quarterly newsletter.
1600 Members
Founded in 1960

20921 American Land Title Association
1800 M Street, NW
Suite 300S
Washington, DC 20036-5828

202-296-3671
800-787-ALTA
FAX 202-223-5843
E-Mail: service@alta.org
Home Page: www.alta.org
Social Media: *Facebook, Twitter, LinkedIn, YouTube, Google+*

Michelle L. Korsmo, CEO
Jack Rattikin, Chair, Finance Committee
John M. Hollenbeck, President
Steven G. Day, Treasurer
Daniel D. Mennenoh, President-Elect

Trade organization for title insurers, abstractors and agents.
4600+ Members
Founded in 1907
Mailing list available for rent: 3000 names at $500 per M

20922 American Planning Association
205 N. Michigan Ave
Suite 1200
Chicago, IL 60601

312-431-9100
FAX 312-786-6700
E-Mail: CustomerService@planning.org
Home Page: www.planning.org
Social Media: *Facebook, Twitter, LinkedIn, YouTube, Flickr, RSS*

James Drinan, Executive Director/CEO
Caroline Rhea, President
Ann Simms, Chief Operating Officer
Harriet Bogdanowicz, Chief Communications Officer
Mark Ferguson, Chief Information Officer

A public interest and research organization representing practicing planners, officials, and citizens involved with urban and rural planning issues. APA's objective is to encourage planning that will meet the needs of people and society more effectively.
Founded in 1978

20923 American Rental Association
1900 19th St
Moline, IL 61265

309-764-2475
800-334-2177
FAX 309-764-1533
E-Mail: ara@ararental.org
Home Page: www.ararental.org

Christine Wehrman, CEO/ Executive Vice-President
Terry Turner, President
Paul Phelon, Chairman
Roger Vajgrt, President-Elect
Mark Gilbertson, SIG Chair

Benefits members (rental business owners and equipment suppliers) by promoting, representing and enhancing the rental industry, resulting in improved rental services to the public.
8600 Members
Founded in 1955

20924 American Resort Development Association
1201 15th St Nw
Suite 400
Washington, DC 20005-2842

202-371-6700
FAX 202-289-8544
E-Mail: customerservice@arda.org,
webmaster@arda
Home Page: www.ardafoundation.org

Howard C. Nusbaum, President & CEO
Darla Zanini, Executive Vice President
Robert A. Miller, Chairman
Lan Wang, Research Director
Randall Upchurch, Vice Chairman

International trade association composed of resort developers and resort industry suppliers.
1000 Members
Founded in 1982

20925 American Society of Appraisers
11107 Sunset Hills Rd
Suite 310
Reston, VA 20190

703-478-2228
800-272-8258
FAX 703-742-8471
E-Mail: asainfo@appraisers.org
Home Page: www.appraisers.org
Social Media: *Facebook, Twitter, LinkedIn, YouTube*

Jim Hirt, Chief Executive Officer
Susan Fischer, Governance Manager
Linda B. Trugman, International President
Sharon A. Desfor, International Secretary/ Treasurer
Susan Golashovsky, International Vice President

Professional association of appraisers of all disciplines.
5000 Members
Founded in 1936

20926 American Society of Farm Managers and Rural Appraisers
950 S Cherry St
Suite 508
Denver, CO 80246-2664

303-758-3513
FAX 303-758-0190
Home Page: www.asfmra.org
Social Media: *Facebook, Twitter, LinkedIn*

Douglas W Slothower, Executive VP
LeeAnn E. Moss, Academic Vice President
Michael J. Krause, First Vice President
Fred L. Hepler, President
Merrill E. Swanson, President-Elect

Premier professional organization for professionals who provide management, consultation and valuation services on rural and agricultural assets. Provides members with the resources, information and leadership that enables them to provide valuable services to the agricultural community.
Founded in 1929

20927 Asian Real Estate Association of America
3990 Old Town Ave.
C304
San Diego, CA 92110

619-795-7873
FAX 619-795-7822
E-Mail: contact@areaa.org
Home Page: www.areaa.org
Social Media: *Facebook, Twitter, LinkedIn, Instagram*

Carmen Chong, Chairwoman

Represents the interests of the Asian real estate market.

20928 Building Owners and Managers Association International

1101 15th Street., NW
Suite 800
Washington, DC 20005

202-408-2662
FAX 202-326-6377
E-Mail: info@boma.org
Home Page: www.boma.org
Social Media: *Facebook, Twitter, LinkedIn, YouTube, Pinterest*

Brian M. Hartnetiaux, Chair-Elect
Kent C. Gibson, Chair & Chief Elected Officer
Henry Chamberlain, Presdent & COO
Robert M. Brierley, Vice Chair
Daniel W. Chasney, Secretary/Treasurer

Owners and managers of commercial office buildings.
7.5M Members
Founded in 1907

20929 Commercial Real Estate Women

655 15th Street NW
Washington, DC 20005

202-737-3262
E-Mail: jennyw@crewnetwork.org
Home Page: www.crewdc.org
Social Media: *LinkedIn*

Pam Zandy, Director of Special Events
Bari Nichols, President
Nancy Petrash, Treasurer
Susan Denner, Director of Communications
Michelle Kilby, President-Elect

Provides a forum for women who are involved in commercial real estate and wish to network as well as reap the benefits of their courses.
9000 Members
Founded in 1989

20930 Commercial-Investment Real Estate Institute

430 N Michigan Avenue
Suite 800
Chicago, IL 60611

312-321-4460
Home Page: www.ccim.com
Social Media: *Facebook, Twitter, Google+, RSS*

Walter S. Clements, Executive VP
Mark Macek, President
Steven W. Moreira, President-Elect
Robin L. Webb, First Vice-President
Charles C. Connely, Treasurer

Functions as a professional association of real estate practitioners who have successfully completed its certification program or are striving toward it.
4M Members

20931 Community Associations Institute

6402 Arlington Blvd
Suite 500
Falls Church, VA 22042

703-970-9220
888-224-4321
FAX 703-970-9558
E-Mail: CAI-INFO@CAIonline.org
Home Page: www.caionline.org
Social Media: *Facebook, Twitter, LinkedIn, Vimeo*

Composed of community and condominium associations managers, management companies and other business partners.
33500 Members
Founded in 1973

20932 CoreNet Global

CoreNet Global Inc

133 Peachtree ST NE
Suite 3000
Atlanta, GA 30303

404-589-3200
800-726-8111
FAX 404-589-3201
E-Mail: registeration@corenetglobal.org
Home Page: www.corenetglobal.org
Social Media: *Facebook, Twitter, LinkedIn, YouTube, Google+, RSS*

Angela Cain, CEO
Jim Scannell, Chairman
John Davis, Controller
Larry Bazrod, COO
Damion Daubon, Office Manager

Formerly NACORE International.
9000 Members

20933 Council of Real Estate Brokerage Managers

Country Radio Broadcaster's Inc
430 N. Michigan Ave.
Chicago, IL 60611

615-327-4487
800-621-8738
FAX 312-329-8882
E-Mail: info@crb.com
Home Page: www.crb.com
Social Media: *Facebook, Twitter, LinkedIn*

Bette McTamney, President
Ginny Shipe, CEO
Tara Maric, Director of Member services
Michael Bindman, Finance Vice President
Adorna Carroll, President-Elect

Members are real estate firm owners and managers.
7000 Members
Founded in 1968

20934 Council of Residential Specialists

430 N Michigan Ave
3rd Floor
Chicago, IL 60611

312-321-4400
800-462-8841
FAX 312-329-8551
E-Mail: crshelp@crs.com
Home Page: www.crs.com
Social Media: *Facebook, Twitter, LinkedIn, YouTube, Google+, RSS*

Lana Vukovljak, CEO
Dale Carlton, Chair
Janelle Pfleiger, Vice Chair
Mary McCall, Chair of Nominating
Leigh Brown, 1st VP

Seeks to establish cooperation among brokers engaged in buying, selling, trading and leasing of real estate.
40000 Members
Founded in 1976

20935 Council of Residential Specialties

430 N Michigan Ave
3rd Floor
Chicago, IL 60611

312-321-4400
800-462-8841
FAX 312-329-8551
E-Mail: crshelp@crs.com
Home Page: www.crs.com
Social Media: *Facebook, Twitter, LinkedIn, YouTube, Google+, RSS*

Lana Vukovljak, CEO
Dale Carlton, Chair
Janelle Pfleiger, Vice Chair
Mary McCall, Chair of Nominating
Leigh Brown, 1st VP

A council of the Realtors National Marketing Institute.
40000 Members
Founded in 1976

20936 Counselors of Real Estate

430 N Michigan Ave
Chicago, IL 60611

312-329-8427
FAX 312-329-8881
E-Mail: info@cre.org
Home Page: www.cre.org

Mary Walker Fleischmann, President & CEO
Noah D. Shlaes, Chair of the Board
James S. Lee, First Vice Chair
Brent A. Palmer, Second Vice Chair
John J. Hentschel, Liaison Viice Chair

Association members provide the public with expert, objective advice on property and land related matters. Individuals invited to join are awarded the CRE designation.
1100 Members
Founded in 1953

20937 Institute for Responsible Housing Preservation

799 9th Street NW
Suite 500
Washington, DC 20001-4501

202-585-8000
FAX 202-585-8080
E-Mail: jlesk@nixonpeabody.com
Home Page: www.nixonpeabody.com
Social Media: *Facebook, Twitter, LinkedIn, YouTube, RSS*

Margaret Wagner, Vice president
Greg Gossard, Treasurer
Alex Viorst, President
Brian Poulin, Chairman
Steve Whyte, Secretary

IRHP members are owners and managers of Low Income Housing Preservation and Resident Housing Act housing and ELIHPA housing and concerned professionals.
Founded in 1989

20938 Institute of Real Estate Management

430 N Michigan Ave
Chicago, IL 60611

800-837-0706
FAX 800-338-4736
E-Mail: getinfo@irem.org
Home Page: www.irem.org
Social Media: *Facebook, Twitter, LinkedIn, YouTube*

Alfred Ojejinmi, Senior Vice President
J. Benjamin McGrew, Secretary/ Treasurer
Cheryl Ann Gray, Senior Vice President
Christopher Mellen, President
Michael T. Lanning, President-Elect

Awards property manager certificate to qualifying individuals and accreditates management organizations and management firms. Offers management courses.
40000 Members
Founded in 1976

20939 International Council of Shopping Centers

1221 Ave of the Americas
41st Floor
New York, NY 10020-1099

646-728-3800
FAX 732-694-1690
E-Mail: membership@icsc.org
Home Page: www.icsc.org
Social Media: *Facebook, Twitter, LinkedIn, YouTube, Google+, Pinterest, I*

Michael P Kercheval, CEO
Jennifer Collin, Manager, Membership Development
Glen Hale, CFO
Sheri Pupello, Member Communications
Michelle Anderson, Education Coordinator

Fosters professional standards of performance in the development, construction, financing, leasing, management and operation of shopping centers throughout the world.
70000 Members
Founded in 1957

20940 International Exchangers Association

PO Box L
Rancho Santa Fe, CA 92067-0560

973-496-5784
FAX 973-496-5784

Works to standardize procedures and establish professional ethics.
3.2M Members
Founded in 1978

20941 International Real Estate Federation

1050 Connecticut Ave NW
Suite 500
Washington, DC 20036

202-772-3308
E-Mail: bill@fiabci-usa.com
Home Page: www.fiabci-usa.com

Ruth Kruger, President
Bill Endsley, Secretary General
Susan Greenfield, Treasurer
Lance Fulford, Vice President
Maire Rosol, President-Elect

Encourages private ownership of real property and understanding of property rights and obligations.

20942 International Real Estate Institute

810 N Farrell Drive
Palm Springs, CA 92262

760-327-5284
877-743-6799
FAX 760-327-5631
E-Mail: support@assoc-hdqts.org
Home Page: www.irei-assoc.org

Ross Ford III, President & CEO
Bill Merrell, Executive Director

An organization comprised of thousands of real estate professionals from over 98 countries around the world. Acts as a voting member of, and property advisor to, the United Nations. Members specialize in real estate and property management. Arranges and promotes international educational real estate seminars.
2000 Members
Founded in 1975

20943 Maine Apartment Owners and Managers Association, Inc.

P.O. Box 282
Bath, ME 04530

207-623-3480
800-204-4311
E-Mail: maoma@maoma.org
Home Page: www.maineapartmentowners.com

A national organization that presents the facts and information builder/developer/owners/manager members need to keep abreast of in the world of multi-family housing. Monthly issue will bring the reader timely insight on real estate, tax news, financing techniques, and effective management procedures, and keeps readers aware of the new developments in the condominium market.

20944 Mortgage Bankers Association of America

Mortgage Bankers Association
1919 M Street NW
5th Floor
Washington, DC 20036

202-557-2700
800-793-6222
E-Mail: membership@mortgagebankers.org

Home Page: www.mortgagebankers.org
Social Media: *Facebook, Twitter, LinkedIn, YouTube*

Bill Emerson, Chairman
David H. Stevens, President/CEO
Rodrigo Lopez, Chairman-Elect
J. David Motley, Vice-Chairman
Marcia Davies, Chief Operating Officer

Seeks to improve methods of originating, servicing and marketing loans.
2.8M Members
Founded in 1914

20945 National Affordable Housing Management

400 N Columbus Street
Suite 203
Alexandria, VA 22314

703-683-8630
FAX 703-683-8634
Home Page: www.nahma.org
Social Media: *Facebook, Twitter, LinkedIn, YouTube*

Kris Cook, Executive Director
Brenda Moser, Director, Meetings & Membership
Larry Keys, Director, Govt. Affairs
Rajni Agarwal, Director, Finance & Administration
Scott McMillen, Coordinator, Govt. Affairs

Trade association representing individuals involved in the management of affordable multi-family housing.
Founded in 1990

20946 National Apartment Association

4300 Wilson Blvd
Suite 400
Arlington, VA 22203

703-518-6141
FAX 703-248-9440
E-Mail: webmaster@naahq.org
Home Page: www.naahq.org
Social Media: *Facebook, Twitter, LinkedIn, YouTube, Google+, Pinterest, F*

Doug Culkin, President &CEO
Chanal Thomas, Office Manager
Judy Reynolds, Senior Manger, Governance
Bob Pinnegar, EVP & COO
Lynn Miller, Administrator

The largest organization dedicated solely to rental housing-serves 26,000 rental housing professionals representing 3.4 million apartments nationwide. NAA lobbies for the industry, provides education programs, publishes Units Magazine, and conducts an annual Education Conference and Trade Show.
68000 Members
Founded in 1939

20947 National Association of Home Builders

1201 15th St NW
Washington, DC 20005

202-266-8200
800-368-5242
FAX 202-266-8400
E-Mail: info@nahb.org
Home Page: www.nahb.org
Social Media: *Facebook, Twitter, LinkedIn, Pinterest, Google+*

Gerald M Howard, CEO
Tom Woods, Chairman
Ed Brady, 1st Vice Chairman of the Board
Granger MacDonald, 2nd Vice Chairman of the Board
Randy Noel, 3rd Vice Chairman

Represents the building industry by serving its members and affiliated state and local builders associations.
1.4M Members
Founded in 1942

20948 National Association of Housing Cooperatives

1444 I Street NW
Suite 700
Washington, DC 20005-6542

202-737-0797
FAX 202-216-9646
E-Mail: info@nahc.coop
Home Page: www.coophousing.org
Social Media: *Facebook, Twitter*

Linda Brockway, Treasurer
Ralph J. Marcus, Chairman
Gregory J. Carlson, President
Fred Gibbs, Vice President
Anne Hills, Secretary

A nonprofit national federation of housing cooperatives, professionals, organizations and individuals promoting the interests of cooperative housing communities. Housing cooperatives are a form of multi family home ownership.
1000 Members
Founded in 1952

20949 National Association of Master Appraisers

303 W Cypress St
San Antonio, TX 78212-5512

210-271-0781
800-229-6262
FAX 210-225-8450
E-Mail: djd@masterappraisers.org
Home Page: www.masterappraisers.org

Del Martinez, Manager
Christopher Deane, Marketing And Production Manager

Provides basic and advanced courses in techniques, management practices and marketing strategies. Offers designations in real estate appraisal MRA (Master Residential Appraisers), MFLA (Master Farm & Land Appraiser) and MSA (Master Senior Appraiser).

20950 National Association of Real Estate Investment Trusts

1875 I St NW
Suite 600
Washington, DC 20006

202-739-9400
800-3 N-REIT
FAX 202-739-9401
E-Mail: info@nareit.org
Home Page: www.reit.com
Social Media: *Facebook, Twitter, LinkedIn, Google+, YouTube, RSS*

Steven A. Wechsler, President &CEO
David B. Henry, 1st Vice Chair
Edward J. Fritsch, 2nd Vice Chair
Timothy J. Naughton, Treasurer
David J. Neithercut, Chairman

NAREIT is the representative voice for U.S. REITs and publicly traded real estate companies worldwide. Members are real estate investment trusts and other businesses that own, operate and finance income-producing real estate, as well as those firms and individuals who advise, study and service these businesses.

20951 National Association of Realtors

430 N Michigan Ave
Chicago, IL 60611-4087

312-645-7730
800-874-6500
FAX 312-329-8576
Home Page: www.realtor.org

Social Media: *Facebook, Twitter, LinkedIn, Skype, Google+*

Dale Stinton, CEO
Tom Salomone, President-Elect
Chris Polychron, President
Mike McGrew, Treasurer
Bill Brown, First Vice President

Promotes education, high professional standards and modern techniques of real estate work.
1.1M Members
Founded in 1908

20952 National Association of Residential Property Managers
638 Independence Parkway
Suite 100
Chesapeake, VA 23320

757-466-3336
800-782-3452
FAX 866-466-2776
E-Mail: info@narpm.org
Home Page: www.narpm.org
Social Media: *Facebook, Twitter, LinkedIn, RSS*

Andrew Propst, President
Gail S. Phillips, Executive Director
Bart Sturzl, President-Elect
Leeann Ghiglione, Treasurer
Stephen D. Foster, Past President

Provides education and publications for the single-family residential property manager.
Founded in 1987

20953 National Association of Review Appraisers and Mortgage Underwriters
810 N. Farrell Drive
Palm Springs, CA 92262

760-327-5284
877-743-6805
FAX 760-327-5631
E-Mail: support@assoc-hdqts.org
Home Page: www.naramu.org

Robert G Johnson, Executive Director
Fred Simon, Production Manager

Conducts educational seminars. Maintains library, speakers bureau and operates a placement service.
6.5M Members
Founded in 1976

20954 National Council of Exchangors
11 West Main Street
Suite 223
Belgrade, MT 59714

858-222-1608
FAX 928-771-2323
E-Mail: admin@ncexchangors.com
Home Page: www.ncexchangors.com

Michael Libster, President & Chair
Kenneth L Kisner, Ex. President
Alex Ruggieri, Secretary
William Jones, Treasurer

A non-profit association and is a nationwide network of real estate professionals who specilize in marketing real estate equities primarily through the medium of the real estate exchange. This network is comprised of local groups organized into regional chapters.
400+ Members

20955 National Low Income Housing Coalition
1000 Vermont Ave
Suite 500
Washington, DC 20005

202-662-1530
FAX 202-393-1973
E-Mail: info@nlihc.org

Home Page: www.nlihc.org
Social Media: *Facebook, Twitter, LinkedIn, Blog*

Sheila Crowley, President &CEO
Malik Siraj Akbar, Communications Specialist
Khara Norris, Director of Administration
Andrew Aurand, Vice President for Research
Josephine Clarke, Executive Assistant

A national nonprofit organization representing housing advocates, organizers, tenants and professionals in the housing field. The Coalition advocates, represents and educates for decent housing and neighborhoods for all low-income people. It works with Congress and the executive branch to obtain adequate Federal support for low-income housing and related programs.
Founded in 1974

20956 National Property Management Association
3525 Piedmont Road, Building 5
Suite 300
Atlanta, GA 30305

404-477-5811
FAX 404-240-0998
E-Mail: hq@nmpa.org
Home Page: www.npma.org
Social Media: *Facebook, LinkedIn*

Cinda Brockman, Executive Vice President
Marcia Whitson, National President
Ivonne Bachar, Vice President of Administration
Rosanne Green, Vice President of Certification
Jessica Dzara, Vice President of Comm & Marketing

Nonprofit professional association dedicated to the cost effective management of personal property and fixed assets.
3700 Members
Founded in 1970

20957 National Real Estate Investors Association
7265 Kenwood Rd.
Suite 368
Cincinnati, OH 45236

859-261-3335
888-762-7342
FAX 859-422-4916
E-Mail: info@nationalreia.com
Home Page: www.nationalreia.com
Social Media: *Facebook, Twitter*

Rebecca Mc Lean, Executive Director
Scott Whaley, VP
Anna Mills, Treasurer
Lisa Kay Hansen, Secretary
Charles Tassell, Director of Governmental Affairs

Coalition of trade associations serving real estate investors, landlords and owners. Provides education and product services for officers and members.
115 Members
Founded in 1985

20958 National Residential Appraisers Institute
Registered Financial Planners Institute
2001 Cooper Foster Park Rd
Amherst, OH 44001

440-935-1698
FAX 888-254-5314
E-Mail: info@repi.com
Home Page: www.nraiappraisers.com

Brian Schreiber, President
Jack Braman, Vice President/Education Director
Adrian Fredrick, Secretary
Rich Farina, Director

Promotes professionalism in the evaluation of residential real estate and requires demonstra-

tion appraisals and testing for professional certification.
451 Members
Founded in 1977

20959 National Society of Environmental Consultants
Po Box 12528
San Antonio, TX 78212-0528

210-225-2897
800-486-3676
FAX 210-225-8450
Home Page: www.nsec.lincoln-grad.org

Deborah Deane, President

Provides standards, education and a forum for real estate environmental site consultants. Provides a designation program for individuals doing environmental assessments and promotes education and further information about real estate environmental problems.

20960 National Society of Professional Surveyors
National Society of Professional Surveyors
5119 Pegasus Court
Suite Q
Frederick, MD 21704

240-439-4615
FAX 240-439-4952
E-Mail: curtis.sumner@nsps.us.com
Home Page: www.acsm.net
Social Media: *Facebook, Twitter, YouTube*

Curt Sumner, Executive Director
Jon Warren, President
Rick Howard, Chairman
Jan Fokens, Vice President
Robert Miller, Treasurer

Organization of professionals for networking and education in the topographical field.
5500 Members
Frequency: Annual
Founded in 1942

20961 National Trust for Historic Preservation
2600 Virginia Avenue
Suite 1100
Washington, DC 20037

202-588-6000
800-944-6847
FAX 202-588-6038
E-Mail: info@savingplaces.org
Home Page: savingplaces.org
Social Media: *Facebook, Twitter, Pinterest, Instagram, YouTube*

Stephanie K. Meeks, President &CEO
Tabitha Almquist, Chief of Staff
Carla Washinko, Chief Financial & Admin Officer
Paul Edmondson, Chief Legal Officer
Amy Maniatis, Chief Marketing officer

A private, nonprofit membership organization dedicated to saving historic places and revitlizing America's communities. Also provides leadership, education, advocacy, and resources to save America's diverse historic places and revitalize the communities.
270k Members
Founded in 1949
Mailing list available for rent

20962 Neighborhood Reinvestment Corporation
92 Argonaut
Suite 255
Aliso Viejo, CA 92656-3100

949-770-2000
800-808-3372
FAX 949-770-2157

E-Mail: sales@federalregister.com
Home Page: www.federalregister.com

Supplies training, grants, developmental assistance, and a range of other technical services designed to help the local partnerships achieve substantially self-reliant neighborhoods. The goal is to improve a neighborhood's housing and physical conditions, build a positive community image, and establish a healthy real estate market and a core of neighbors capable of managing the continued health of their neighborhood.
Founded in 1978

20963 Professional Certification Board

Po Box 12528
San Antonio, TX 78212-0528

210-225-2897
800-486-3676
FAX 210-225-8450
Home Page: www.nsec.lincoln-grad.org

Deborah Deane, President

Provides education and board certificates for the real estate appraisal specialties of manufactured housing valuation, business valuation and litigation management.

20964 Professional Housing Management Association

154 Fort Evans Road NE
Leesburg, VA 201176

703-771-1888
FAX 703-771-1888
E-Mail: mkcooper@earthlink.net
Home Page: www.phma.com
Social Media: *Facebook, Twitter, LinkedIn, Flickr*

Barry Scribner, Treasurer
Del Eulberg, President
Elijah A. Wilki Wilkerson, Executive Vice President
Jon R. Moore, Exective Director
Chris Cole, Secretary

Members are federal government employees, civilian or military, who are directly involved in housing management or provides direct support to the field.
3,120 Members
Founded in 1973

20965 Property Owners Association

1072 Madison Ave
Lakewood, NJ 08701

732-780-1966
FAX 732-780-1611
E-Mail: info@poanj.org
Home Page: www.poanj.org
Social Media: *Facebook, Twitter*

Jeffery Feld, Sergeant-At-Arms
Marc Tunis, Treasurer
Larry Rosen, President
Derek Reed, Vice President
Jerry Cheslow, Secretary

The Property Owners Association of New Jersey, Inc. brings together owners and operators of residential real estate, interested persons, and related industry personnel for educational and information sharing purposes.
550 Members
Founded in 1949

20966 Real Estate Buyers Agent Council

430 N Michigan Avenue
Chicago, IL 60611

800-648-6224
800-648-6224
FAX 312-329-8632
E-Mail: REBAC@realtors.org
Home Page: www.rebac.net

Social Media: *Facebook, Twitter, LinkedIn, YouTube*

Walter T McDonald, President
Larry Von Feldt, VP/Liaison to Gov Affairs
Pat Kaplan, VP Liaison to Committees
Amy Gunaka, Marketing Manager

Represents professional real estate agents who act as buyers' agents.
50000 Members
Founded in 1988
Mailing list available for rent

20967 Real Estate Capital Resources Association

1350 I Street NW
Washington, DC 20005-3305

202-663-3740
FAX 202-371-0069

G David Fensterheim, Executive Director

Represents firms that provide third party workout and capital recovery services in connection with distressed real estate and real estate related assets.
100 Members
Founded in 1989

20968 Real Estate Educators Association

7739 E Broadway
Suite 337
Tuscon, AZ 85710

520-690-2380
FAX 856-423-3420
E-Mail: MemberCare@reea.org
Home Page: www.reea.org
Social Media: *Facebook, Twitter*

Michael McAllister, President
Melissa Kleeman-Moy, Secretary
Bill Aaron, Treasurer
Tina Lapp, President-Elect
Kris Inman, Executive Director

Individuals involved in training and education.
1,400 Members
Founded in 1979

20969 Real Estate Information Providers Association

1420 16th Street NW
Washington, DC 20036-2218

202-298-8169
FAX 202-332-2301
E-Mail: reipa@aol.com
Home Page: www.reipa.com

Randy Dyer, Executive Director

Supports professional information providers in the real estate industry.
Founded in 1995

20970 Real Estate Roundtable

801 Pennsylvania Ave NW
Suite 720
Washington, DC 20004

202-639-8400
FAX 202-639-8442
E-Mail: info@rer.org
Home Page: www.rer.org

William C. Rudin, Chairman
Jeffrey D DeBoer, President/CEO
Jeanne Kane, Chairman-Elect
Debra A. Cafaro, Secretary
Thomas M. Flexner, Treasurer

Actively involves public and private real estate owners, advisors, builders, investors, lenders and managers on key tax, capital and credit, energy, environmental and homeland security policy issues in Washington. Its members are senior principals from every spectrum of the commercial real estate industry and leaders of major national real estate trade associations.
230 Members
Founded in 1999

20971 Realtors Land Institute

430 N Michigan Ave
Floor 11
Chicago, IL 60611

312-329-8440
800-441-5263
FAX 312-329-8633
E-Mail: rli@realtors.org
Home Page: www.rliland.com
Social Media: *Facebook, Twitter, LinkedIn, Google+*

Michele Cohen, Executive VP
Teri Jensen, President
Bob Turner, President-Elect
Brandon Rogillio, Vice President
George Clift, Immediate Past President

Promotes competence and accredits members. Maintains educational programs for real estate brokers.
1.9M Members
Founded in 1944

20972 Society of Industrial and Office Realtors

1201 New York Ave NW
Suite 350
Washington, DC 20005-6126

202-449-8200
FAX 202-216-9325
E-Mail: membership@sior.com
Home Page: www.sior.com
Social Media: *Facebook, Twitter, LinkedIn, Pinterest, Google+, Youtube*

Richard Hollander, Executive VP
Allen Gump, President
Geoffrey Kasselman, President-Elect
Del Markward, Vice-President
Jack Whalen, Treasurer

Active members are brokers, consultants and appraisers.
3100 Members
Founded in 1939

20973 SourceMedia

One State Street Plaza
27th floor
New York, NY 10004

212-803-8200
800-803-3424
FAX 212-843-9608
E-Mail: custserv@sourcemedia.com
Home Page: www.sourcemedia.com

Douglas J. Manoni, CEO
Michael P. Caruso, CFO
David Longobardi, EVP & Chief Content Officer
Minna Rhee, Chief Digital Officer
Marianne Collins, Chief Revenue Officer

SourceMedia provides market information, including news, analysis, and insight to the financial services and related industries such as accounting and technology, through its publications, industry-standard data applications, seminars and conferences. The informational services that SourceMedia delivers are available in print or online, including newspapers and magazines, reference directories, database products, software, web seminars and live events.

20974 The American Real Estate & Urban Economics Association

821 Academic Way,223 RBB
Tallahassee, FL 32306-1110

850-644-7898
FAX 850-644-4077
E-Mail: elaffitte@fsu.edu
Home Page: www.areuea.org

Stuart Rosenthal, President
Edward Coulson, First VP

Marsha J. Courchane, Executive Vice President
Liz Laffitte, Executive Director
David H. Downs, Treasurer

Addresses academic and commercial concerns in real estate and commercial economics.
1200 Members
ISSN: 1080-8620
Founded in 1964

20975 Women's Council of Realtors
430 N Michigan Ave
Chicago, IL 60611

312-329-8483
800-245-8512
FAX 312-329-3290
E-Mail: wcr@wcr.org
Home Page: www.wcr.org
Social Media: *Facebook, Twitter, LinkedIn, Pinterest, Instagram*

Jeff Hornberger, Executive Vice President
Carol Raabe, VP Operations
Sindy Ready, President
Jo Ann Stevens, Financial Secretary
Melissa Zimbelman, President-elect

Provides opportunities for women in real estate at the local, state and national level. Offers courses in leadership training and referral and relocation buisness.
40000 Members
Founded in 1938

20976 Worldwide ERC
4401 Wilson Blvd
Suite 510
Arlington, VA 22203

703-842-3400
FAX 703-527-1552
E-Mail: CustomerCare@WorldwideERC.org
Home Page: www.erc.org
Social Media: *Facebook, Twitter, LinkedIn, Pinterest*

Peggy Smith, President & CEO
Robert J. Horsley, Vice Chair- Finance
Dale L. Collins, Chair-Elect
Cindy Salter, Chairman
Sharon Byrnes, Vice Chair-Talent Community

A national organization that examines key issues affecting the relocation industry for the benefit of corporations, government agencies, and firms or individuals providing specific services to relocated employees and their families. Accepts advertising.
1600 Members
Founded in 1964

Newsletters

20977 ACREL News
American College of Real Estate Lawyers
11300 Rockville Pike
Suite 903
Rockville, MD 20852-3034

301-816-9811
FAX 301-816-9786
E-Mail: webmaster@acrel.org
Home Page: www.acrel.org

Jill Pace, Executive Director
Frequency: Monthly

20978 AOMA Newsletter
Apartment Owners & Managers Assn of America
65 Cherry Avenue
Cherry Plaza
Watertown, CT 06795

FAX 860-274-2580

Robert J McGough, Editor
Pietro

Each month the AOMA newsletter presents the facts and information builder/developer/owners/manager members need to keep abreast of in the world of Multi-Family housing. Every monthly issue will bring the reader timely insight on Real Estate, tax news, financing techniques, and effective management procedures, and keeps readers aware of the new developments in the condominium market.
Cost: $125.00
Frequency: 12 issues
Circulation: 6,200
Mailing list available for rent
Printed in one color

20979 ASFMRA News
Amer. Society of Farm Managers & Rural Appraisers
950 S Cherry St
Suite 508
Denver, CO 80246-2664

303-758-3513
FAX 303-758-0190
E-Mail: asfmra@agri-associations.org
Home Page: www.asfmra.org

Cheryl L Cooley, Manager Communications
Thomas V. Boyer, President

Informs ASFMRA members of education, member, event, meeting and government issues.
Cost: $24.00
Founded in 1929
Mailing list available for rent: 2500 names at $1M per M

20980 Accredited Review Appraiser
Accredited Review Appraisers Council
303 W Cypress Street
San Antonio, TX 78212-5512

800-486-3676
FAX 210-225-8450
E-Mail: rlp@lincoln-grad.org
Home Page: arac.lincoln-grad.org

Deborah J Deane, Publisher
Rachel L Phelps, Marketing Manager

Offers information on appraisals and real estate reviews.
8 Pages
Frequency: Quarterly
Founded in 1987
Printed in one color on matte stock

20981 Advise and Counsel
National Association of Counselors
303 W Cypress St
San Antonio, TX 78212-5512

210-271-0781
800-229-6262
FAX 210-225-8450
E-Mail: djd@masterappraisers.org
Home Page: www.masterappraisers.org

Offers information on real estate and appriasal counseling services.
Cost: $45.00
8 Pages
Frequency: Quarterly
Circulation: 4000

20982 American Chapter News
American Chapter International Real Estate Assn
30700 Russell Ranch Road
Westlake Village, CA 91362

805-557-2300
FAX 805-557-2680
Home Page: www.realtors.com

Teresa Salmon, Publisher

International real estate news and information.
Cost: $110.00
8 Pages
Frequency: Monthly

20983 American Industrial Real Estate Association Newsletter
American Industrial Real Estate Association
700 S Flowers Street
Suite 600
Los Angeles, CA 90017

213-687-8777
FAX 213-687-8616
E-Mail: support@airea.com
Home Page: www.airea.com

Ron Surace, COO
6 Pages
Frequency: Quarterly
Founded in 1964
Printed in 3 colors on glossy stock

20984 American Society of Farm Managers and Rural Appraisers Newsletter
Amer. Society of Farm Managers & Rural Appraisers
950 S Cherry St
Suite 508
Denver, CO 80246-2664

303-758-3513
FAX 303-758-0190
E-Mail: asfmra@agri-associations.org
Home Page: www.asfmra.org

Cheryl L Cooley, Manager Communications/ IT/PR
Hope S. Evans, Membership Coordinator

Provides professionals involved in rural property issues such as management and appraisal, with information on the industry as well as educational opportunities. Includes membership and information from the American Society of Farm Manager and Rural Appraisers.
Cost: $30.00
Frequency: Annual+
ISSN: 1076-3856
Founded in 1929
Mailing list available for rent: 2500 names at $1M per M
Printed in 2 colors on glossy stock

20985 Andrews Report
Report Publications
9595 Whitney Drive
#100
Indianapolis, IN 46280
William Woburn, Publisher

For owners and operators of small shopping centers.
Cost: $147.00
12 Pages
Frequency: Monthly

20986 Apartment Management Newsletter
AMN Publishing
PO BOX 352
Massapequa, NY 11758

516-551-5343
E-Mail: amnpub@aol.com
Home Page: amnpub.tripod.com/id4.html

Helene Mandelbaum, Editor
Vera West, Circulation Manager

News and information for apartment owners and managers, including tips and techniques for marketing, maintenance, personnel and compliance with national laws and requirements.
Cost: $6.00
Founded in 2001

20987 Apartment Management Report
Apartment Owners & Managers Assn of America

65 Cherry Avenue
Cherry Plaza
Watertown, CT 06795-238

FAX 860-274-2580

Robert J McGough, Editor
Janet Pietro, Circulation Manager

Researched and written for the owner/manager, overall property manager, and for the on site managers. Typical in depth subjects cover the nuts and bolts of every day management. Research reports on tenant renting strategies, model apartments, security, outside maintenance, how to avoid and handle tenant complaints, and more.
Cost: $72.85
6 Pages
Frequency: Monthly
Circulation: 6200
Mailing list available for rent: 6000 names
Printed in one color

20988 Asset Watch
LDI Publishing
1401 16th Street NW
Washington, DC 20036-2201

202-232-2144
FAX 202-232-4757

Steve Sullivan, Publisher

News and analysis of federal asset sales RDIC, LRTC, HUD, etc., contracting and resolutions.
Cost: $475.00
6 Pages
Frequency: 5 per year

20989 Asset-Backed Alert
Harrison Scott Publications
5 Marine View Plz
Suite 301
Hoboken, NJ 07030-5722

201-386-1491
800-283-9363
FAX 201-659-4141
E-Mail: info@hspnews.com
Home Page: www.hspnews.com

Andy Albert, Chairman/Publisher
Thomas J Ferris, Director
Michelle Lebowitz, Director

A weekly update on global securitization
Cost: $2297.00
20 Pages
Frequency: Weekly
Circulation: 500
Founded in 1990
Mailing list available for rent: 900 names at $400 per M
Printed in one color on matte stock

20990 Bulletin
Property Management Association
7508 Wisconsin Ave
Suite 4
Bethesda, MD 20814-3561

301-657-9200
FAX 301-907-9326
E-Mail: info@pma-dc.org
Home Page: www.pma-dc.org

Tom Cohn, Executive Director

News and events surrounding the real estate industry.
Cost: $100.00
24 Pages
Frequency: Monthly

20991 Commercial Lease Law Insider
Brownstone Publishers
149 5th Ave
Suite 10
New York, NY 10010-6832

212-473-8200
FAX 212-473-8786

E-Mail: vendomecs@qualitycustomercare.com
Home Page: www.brownstone.com

John M Striker Esq, Publisher
Nicole Lefton Esq, Editor

Commercial leasing strategies, techniques and insights with practical aids such as model lease clauses, checklists, do's and dont's, as well as coverage of new court decisions affecting commercial leases. Readership consists of commercial property owners, managers and real estate attorneys.
Cost: $337.00
Frequency: Monthly
Mailing list available for rental $110 per M
Printed in 2 colors on matte stock

20992 Commercial Property News
Miller Freeman Publications
600 Harrison Street
Suite 400
San Francisco, CA 94107-1391

FAX 415-905-2239

David Nussbaum, Publisher
Maxine Jaffe, Editor

Tabloid newspaper edited for commercial property professionals.
Cost: $4.00
Circulation: 34,000

20993 Commercial Real Estate Digest
Vestal Communications
334 Humphrey Drive
Evergreen, CO 80439-9655
Robert Vestal, Publisher

Master copy newsletter allowing unlimited copy additions before subscriber prints and distributes to clients.
Cost: $495.00
2 Pages
Frequency: Quarterly

20994 Community Association Law Reporter
Community Associations Institute
6402 Arlington Blvd
Suite 500
Falls Church, VA Falls Chur

Fal-s C-urch
888-224-4321
FAX 703-970-9558
E-Mail: caidirect@caionline.org
Home Page: www.caionline.org

Daniel Brannigan, Editor

Information on legal cases and court decisions concerning condominum, cooperative and homeowner associations.
Cost: $208.00
8 Pages
Frequency: Monthly
Founded in 1973

20995 Community Associations Institute News
Community Associations Institute
6402 Arlington Blvd
Suite 500
Falls Church, VA Falls Chur

Fal-s C-urch
888-224-4321
FAX 703-970-9558
E-Mail: caidirect@caionline.org
Home Page: www.caionline.org

Daniel Brannigan, Editor

Real estate news and reports.
Frequency: Monthly
Founded in 1973

20996 Community Management
Community Associations Institute

6402 Arlington Blvd
Suite 500
Falls Church, VA Falls Chur

Fal-s C-urch
888-224-4321
FAX 703-970-9558
E-Mail: caidirect@caionline.org
Home Page: www.ciaonline.org

Daniel Brannigan, Editor

Bimonthly newsletter of news, strategies and trends written especially for managers of condominium and homeowner associations. This easy to read, award-winning newsletter comes packed with how-to information on such subjects as cutting expenses, complying with federal laws, working effectively with boards of directors, ensuring community safety and resolving disputes. It often features case studies of succcessful new approaches in community association management and operations.
Cost: $59.00
8 Pages
Founded in 1973

20997 Daily Commerce
Daily Journal Corporation
PO Box 54026
Los Angeles, CA 90054-0026

213-229-5300
FAX 213-229-5481
Home Page: www.dailyjournal.com

Gerald L Salzman, CEO
Ray Chagolla, Circulation Manager
Lisa Churchill, Editor

personnel announcements, datebook information, consumer news, and the internet, information on government foreclosers, default notices, lending reports and probate estate sales.
Cost: $237.00
Frequency: Monthly
Circulation: 10000

20998 Environmental Consultant
National Society of Environmental Consultants
PO Box 12528
San Antonio, TX 78212-0528

210-225-2897
800-486-3676
FAX 210-225-8450
Home Page: nsec.lincoln-grad.org/

Deborah Deane, President

Offers information, articles and news of interest to real estate environmental site consultants.
Cost: $50.00
16 Pages
Frequency: Quarterly
Circulation: 4000
Founded in 1992

20999 Housing Affairs Letter
CD Publications
8204 Fenton St
Silver Spring, MD 20910-4571

301-588-6380
800-666-6380
FAX 301-588-6385
E-Mail: info@cdpublications.com
Home Page: www.cdpublications.com

Michael Gerecht, President
Tom Edwards, Editor

The latest news on housing activity nationwide, including private, public and subsidized housing, legislation and regulations.
Cost: $559.00
Frequency: Weekly
Founded in 1961
Mailing list available for rent: 2,000 names at $160 per M

21000 Housing the Elderly Report
CD Publications
8204 Fenton St
Silver Spring, MD 20910-4571

301-588-6380
800-666-6380
FAX 301-588-6385
E-Mail: info@cdpublications.com
Home Page: www.cdpublications.com

Michael Gerecht, President
Jeff Pines, Editor

News and advice for owners and managers of
long-term care facilities on marketing and managing all types of elderly housing, with profiles
of new senior housing projects, business reports and an exclusive annual salary survey.
Cost: $294.00
Frequency: Monthly
Founded in 1961
*Mailing list available for rent: 2,000 names at
$160 per M*

21001 Inside IREM
Institute of Real Estate Management
430 N Michigan Ave
Suite 7
Chicago, IL 60611-4011

312-329-6000
FAX 312-661-0217
E-Mail: info@crs.com
Home Page: www.irem.org

Russell Salzman, CEO

Membership newsletter for members of the Institute of Real Estate Management. It includes
news on IREM policies, programs and new
products. Federal, state and local legislative developments affecting real estate and asset management are also reported.
40000 Pages
Founded in 1976

21002 Inspector
American Society of Home Inspectors
932 Lee Street
Suite 101
Des Plaines, IL 60016-3520

847-759-2820
800-248-2744
FAX 847-759-1620
E-Mail: webmaster@ashi.org
Home Page: www.ashi.org

Richard Clough, Executive Director
Paul Christensen, President

Newsletter for members of New England chap-
ter of American Society of Home Inspectors.
Cost: $250.00
Frequency: Monthly
Circulation: 6000
Founded in 1976

21003 International Real Estate Newsletter
1224 N Nokomis NE
Alexandria, MN 56308-5072

320-763-4648
FAX 320-763-9290
E-Mail: iami@iami.org
Home Page: www.iami.org/

David Held, Production Manager
Robert Johnson, CEO

A compilation of international real estate information which is disseminated to the International Real Estate Institute's membership and
to other subscribers. This publication also reviews the latest accomplishments of the Institute and those of its high quality professional
members.
Cost: $29.50
4 Pages
Frequency: Monthly

Founded in 1975
Printed in one color on newsprint stock

21004 Ledger Quarterly
Community Associations Institute
6402 Arlington Blvd
Suite 500
Falls Church, VA Falls Chur

Fal-s C-urch
888-224-4321
FAX 703-970-9558
E-Mail: caidirect@caionline.org
Home Page: www.caionline.org

Quarterly newsletter of financial news for condominium, cooperative and homeowner associations. If you participate in any way in the
financial management of an association, this
eight-page newsletter is a resource you should
have. It's absolutely vital for keeping
up-to-date on trends in asssociation accounting
practices, calculating the best strategies to minimize association taxes, and advising the board
on investments.
Cost: $67.00
Frequency: Quarterly
Circulation: 12000+
Founded in 1973

21005 Mac News
Mid-Atlantic Council of Shopping Centers
8811 Colesville Road
Silver Spring, MD 20910-4343

301-890-1467

Tom Cohn, Publisher
News of the council.
Cost: $100.00
20 Pages
Frequency: Monthly

21006 Managing Housing Letter
CD Publications
8204 Fenton St
Silver Spring, MD 20910-4571

301-588-6380
800-666-6380
FAX 301-588-6385
E-Mail: info@cdpublications.com
Home Page: www.cdpublications.com

Michael Gerecht, President
Charles Wisniowski, Editor

News and advice for owners, managers and
professionals dealing with apartments and the
real estate industry.
Cost: $269.00
Frequency: Monthly
Founded in 1978
*Mailing list available for rent: 2,000 names at
$160 per M*

21007 Mobilehome Parks Report
Thomas P Kerr
3807 Pasadena Ave
Suite 100
Sacramento, CA 95821-2880

916-971-0489
800-392-5180
FAX 916-971-1849
E-Mail: tkerr@aol.com
Home Page: www.aol.com

Reports on trends, issues, court decisions, legislation, financing and other matters of concern
to owners and developers of manufactured
housing communities. Valuable to attorneys
and others who specialize in this segment of
the Housing Industry.
Cost: $125.00
8 Pages
Frequency: Monthly
Circulation: 350
Founded in 1998
Printed in one color on matte stock

**21008 National Association of
Neighborhoods Newsletter**
1300 Pennsylvania Avenue
NW Suite 700
Washington, DC 20004

202-332-7766
FAX 202-332-2314
E-Mail: staff@nanworld.org
Home Page: www.nanworld.org

C Y Doyd, Editor
Ricardo C Byrd, President

Offers news and information to the community
real estate industry.
Frequency: Quarterly
Circulation: 10,000
Founded in 1975

21009 New England Real Estate Journal
East Coast Publications
PO Box 55
Accord, MA 02018

781-878-4540
800-654-4993
FAX 781-871-1853
E-Mail: nerej@rejournal.com
Home Page: www.rejournal.com

Tom Murray, Publisher
David Denelle, Editor

Business publication for the commercial-indus-
trial-investment real estate industries.
Cost: $2.00
Frequency: Weekly
Circulation: 13000
Founded in 1961
Printed in on newsprint stock

21010 Professional Apartment Management
Brownstone Publishers
149 5th Ave
Suite 10
New York, NY 10010-6832

212-473-8200
800-643-8095
FAX 212-473-8786
E-Mail: custserv@brownstone.com
Home Page: www.brownstone.com

Mary Lopez, Production Manager
Michael Koplin, Circulation Director

Strategies, techniques and suggestions for attracting and retaining paying tenants, and
avoiding legal disputes. Includes model language for leases, sample ads, plus coverage of
legal issues, recent court decisions and the like.
Cost: $217.00
Frequency: Monthly
Founded in 1972
Printed in 2 colors on matte stock

21011 Real Estate Alert
Harrison Scott Publications
5 Marine View Plz
Suite 301
Hoboken, NJ 07030-5722

201-386-1491
FAX 201-659-4141
E-Mail: info@hspnews.com
Home Page: www.hspnews.com

Andy Albert, Chairman/President
Michelle Lebowitz, Director

Contains information for real estate and finan-
cial professionals looking for opportunities to
buy or manage assets.
Cost: $1397.00
8 Pages
Frequency: Weekly
Circulation: 300+
Founded in 1989
Printed in 4 colors

21012 Real Estate Asset Manager
Lincoln Graduate Center - Executive Offices
PO Box 12528
San Antonio, TX 78212-0528

210-225-2897
800-531-5333
FAX 210-225-8450
E-Mail: ms@lincoln-grad.org
Home Page: www.lincoln-grad.org

Debroah Deane, President
Rachel Phelps, Marketing Manager

Offers news and information on environmental
concerns, real estate and appraisals.
8 Pages

21013 Real Estate Brokers Insider
Alexander Communications Group
1916 Park Ave
Suite 501
New York, NY 10037-3733

212-281-6099
800-232-4317
FAX 212-283-7269
E-Mail: info@brokersinsider.com
Home Page: www.brokersinsider.com/

Romauld Alexander, President
Nadine Harris, Marketing Manager

Provides agency broker/owners with in depth
information on how to run their businesses
better.
Cost: $247.00
8 Pages
Frequency: Fortnightly
ISSN: 1086-2935
Founded in 1978

21014 Real Estate Economics
AREUEA
PO Box 9958
Richmond, VA 23228-1148

866-273-8321
FAX 877-273-8323
E-Mail: areuea@areuea.org
Home Page: www.areuea.org

Susan Watcher, Publisher
David C. Ling, Editor

Discussions on topics such as housing prices,
office markets, real estate valuation and ap-
praisal.
Cost: $100.00
Frequency: Quarterly
Founded in 1964

21015 Real Estate Investor's Monthly
John T Reed Publishing
342 Bryan Dr
Alamo, CA 94507-2858

925-820-6292
FAX 925-820-1259
E-Mail: johnreed@johntreed.com
Home Page: www.johntreed.com

John T Reed, President

Information for owners who manage and own
their own property, suggestions for increasing
their investment returns.
Cost: $125.00
8 Pages
Frequency: Monthly
Circulation: 500
Founded in 1980

21016 Tax Credit Advisor
1400 16th St Nw
Suite 420A
Washington, DC 20036-2216

202-939-1790
FAX 202-265-4435

E-Mail: info@housingonline.com
Home Page: www.housingonline.com

Peter Bell, President
Glenn Petherick, Executive Director
Thom Amdur, Executive Director
David Abromowitz, Secretary

Monthly newsletter providing comprehensive
coverage of all aspects of the federal low-income housing tax credit program, the primary
incentive for low-income apartment development. Covers legislation, IRS rules, equity and
debt programs, and market trends.
Cost: $269.00
12 Pages
Frequency: Monthly
Circulation: 750

21017 Upward Directions
Community Associations Institute
6402 Arlington Blvd.
Suite 500
Falls Church, VA 22042

703-970-9220
888-224-4321
FAX 703-970-6558
Home Page: www.caionline.org

Tom Skiba, CEO

NBBC-CAM's quarterly newsletter for the further education and professional development of
CMCA Certificants. Program news, updates on
state credentialing activities, legislation and
regulation and continuing education opportunities make this newsletter required reading for
Certified Managers of Community Associations (CMCA's. Everything you need to know
to earn, maintain and optimize the benefits
from manager certification from the National
Board of Certification.
Frequency: Quarterly

Magazines & Journals

21018 ALQ Real Estate Intelligence Report
Common Communications
PO Box 5702
Portsmouth, NH 03802-5702

800-299-9961
800-299-9961
FAX 603-436-5202
E-Mail: IRexec@REintel.com
Home Page: www.reintel.com

Pat Remick, Editor
Frank Cook, Publisher

A close examination of buyer agency movement, services rendered by brokerages, the impact of technology on real estate and success
stories.
Cost: $200.00
Frequency: Quarterly
Founded in 1989

21019 Affordable Housing Finance
Alexander & Edwards Publishing
33 New Montgomery St
Suite 290
San Francisco, CA 94105-4520

415-315-1241
800-989-7255
FAX 415-315-1248
Home Page: www.hanleywood.com

Rob Britt, Manager
Andre Shashaty, President
Susan Piel, Conference Director
Michael Premsrirat, Circulation Manager
Carol Yee, Office Manager

Offers practical information on obtaining debt
and equality financing from federal, state, and
local governments as well as private resources.

In-depth coverage on the federal low-income
housing tax credit program, tax-exempt bond
financing, corporate tax credit investigation.
Cost: $119.00
Frequency: Monthly
Circulation: 9000

21020 Alliance
John W Yopp Publications
6540 Julian Road
Gainesville, GA 30506-5550

800-849-9677
FAX 800-849-8418
E-Mail: info@jwyopp.com
Home Page: www.jwyopp.com

Mary Y Cronley, Associate Pubisher/Editor
Natalie Gilmer, Accounts Manager

Articles provide news and information on topics of interest, including marketing and sales,
pre-need campaigns and other operational
topics.
Frequency: Monthly
Circulation: 8000
Founded in 1919

21021 American Cemetery
Kates-Boylston Publications
11300 Rockville Pike
Suite 1100
Rockville, MD 20852

800-500-4585
800-500-4585
FAX 301-287-2150
E-Mail: AmericanFD@aol.com
Home Page: www.kates-boylston.com

Adrian F Boylston, Publisher
Thomas Lorge, Executive Director
Thomas Parmalee, Executive Director
Amy Fidalgo, Production Manager

Features articles on cemetery administration,
maintenance, sales and public relations. Also
includes coverage of conventions, new ceme-
teries and new building ideas.
Cost: $39.95
Frequency: Monthly
Circulation: 5800

21022 Apartment Age Magazine
Apartment Association of Greater Los
Angeles
621 S Westmoreland Ave
Los Angeles, CA 90005-3962

310-536-0281
FAX 213-382-3970
E-Mail: webmaster@aagla.org
Home Page: www.aagla.org

Charles Isham, VP
Kevin Postema, Editor/Advertising Director
Larry Cannizzaro, President

Serving the interests of residential rental prop-
erty owners.
Cost: $48.00
80 Pages
Frequency: Monthly
Circulation: 40000
ISSN: 0192-0030

21023 Apartment Finance Today Magazine
Hanley Wood LLC
One Thomas Circle, NW
Suite 600
Washington, DC 20005

202-452-0800
FAX 202-785-1974
Home Page: www.hanleywood.com

John McManus, Editorial Director
Shabnam Mogharabi, Editor-In-Chief

Provides in-depth and inbiased reporting and
insightful alaysis for owners, developers and

asset managers.
Cost: $29.00
80 Pages
Circulation: 11784
ISSN: 1097-4059
Founded in 1995
Printed in 4 colors on glossy stock

21024 Apartment News
Arizona Multi-Housing Consulting
Corporation
5110 N 44th Street
Suite L160
Phoenix, AZ 85018-2107

602-224-0135
800-316-6403
FAX 602-224-0657
E-Mail: info@azama.org
Home Page: www.azama.org

Terry Feinberg, President
Mitchell McBay, Marketing Manager
Erick Richard, Editor
Wayne Kaplan, Director of Community
Relations
Marilyn Everroad, Events Manager
Articles on state and national government af-
fairs, education, marketing, crime prevention,
maintenance and legal issues relating to the Ar-
izona multihousing industry.
Cost: $50.00
Frequency: Monthly
Circulation: 2500
Founded in 1964
Printed in on glossy stock

21025 Area Development
Halcyon Business Publications
400 Post Avenue
Westbury, NY 11590-2267

516-338-0900
FAX 516-338-0100
Home Page: www.areadevelopment.com

Dennis Shea, Publisher/CEO
Geraldie Gambale, Editor
Gertrude Staudt, Circulation Manager
Focuses on the factors necessary for a success-
ful corporate expansion or relocation, labor,
taxes, incentives, quality of life, market access,
and transportation.
Cost: $75.00
Circulation: 45000
Founded in 1970

21026 Brownfield Renewal
Brownfield Renewal
2200 E Devon Ave
Suite 354
Des Plains, IL 60018

312-488-4830
FAX 312-488-4220
E-Mail: editorial@brownfieldrenewal.com
Home Page: www.brownfieldrenewal.com

Steve Dwyer, Editorial Director
Monica Acuna, Circulation Director
Dedicated to the remediation, redevelopment
and reuse of brownfields.
Cost: $79.95
Frequency: Bimonthly
ISSN: 1554-8791
Founded in 1999

21027 Building Operating Management
Trade Press Publishing Corporation
2100 West Florist Avenue
Milwaukee, WI 53209-3799

414-228-7701
FAX 414-228-1134
E-Mail: info@tradepress.com
Home Page: www.tradepress.com

Scott G Holverson, Regional Sales Manager
Edward Sullivan, Editor

Eric Muench, Director of Circulation
Bobbie Reid, Production Director
Robert Wisniewski, President/CEO
Serves the field of facilities management, en-
compassing commercial building: office build-
ings, real estate/property management firms,
developers, financial institutions, insurance
companies, apartment complexes, civic/con-
vention centers, including members of the
Building Owners and Managers Association
Frequency: Monthly
Circulation: 70000
Founded in 1915

21028 Business Facilities
Group C Communications
PO Box 2060
Red Bank, NJ 07701-0901

732-842-7433
800-524-0337
FAX 732-758-6634
E-Mail: jsemple@groupc.com
Home Page: www.groupc.com

Edgar T Coene, President
Jim Semple, Production Manager
Mary McCandless, Production Manager
Bill MacRae, Marketing Director
Magazine covering the fields of corporation ex-
pansion, economic development and real estate.
Cost: $30.00
Frequency: Monthly
Circulation: 43500
Founded in 1968

21029 Business Journal
120 W Morehead Street
Suite 200
Charlotte, NC 28202

704-347-2340
800-948-5323
FAX 704-973-1102
E-Mail: borben@bizjournals.com
Home Page: www.bizjournals.com/charlotte

Robert Morris, Editor
David Harris, Managing Editor
Kim Moser, Advertising Assistant
Megan Foley, Marketing Director
Jeannie Falknor, Publisher
Provides marketing solutions and caring ser-
vice.
Cost: $82.00
Frequency: Daily

21030 CF Apartment Reporter
PO Box 480894
Denver, CO 80248-894

303-663-0606
FAX 303-663-1616
Home Page: www.clayfil.com

Peggy Berg, President
Cost: $199.00
Frequency: Quarterly
Founded in 1984

21031 CF Industrial Reporter
Clayton-Fillmore
PO Box 480894
Denver, CO 80248-894

303-663-0606
FAX 303-663-1616
Home Page: www.clayfil.com

Howard Treibitz, Editor
Briefs of the markets broken down into specific
cities, includes briefs of the economy and aver-
age manufacturing.
Cost: $189.00
Frequency: Monthly

21032 Commercial
Oakland Press

28 W Huron St
Pontiac, MI 48342-2100

248-745-4794
248-332-1988
FAX 248-332-3003

Edward Moss, Owner
A showcase of available commercial properties
in the region.
Cost: $18.00
Frequency: Monthly
Circulation: 30,000

21033 Common Ground
Community Associations Institute
6402 Arlington Blvd
Suite 500
Falls Church, VA Falls Chur

Fal-s C-urch
888-224-4321
FAX 703-970-9558
E-Mail: caidirect@caionline.org
Home Page: www.caionline.org

Dori Meinert, Editor
CAL's award-winning bimonthly magazine for
condominium and homeowner associations,
managers and other industry professionals.
Would you like to learn how a Web site can
help your community association? Or peruse
tips on cutting your budget? Or find out about
the New Urbanism and other community development trends? Stay informed and involved via
features and departments on the legal, political
mechanical, personal, and day-to-day realities
of community association life.
Cost: $69.00
Frequency: Monthly
Founded in 1978

21034 Comparative Statistics of Industrial and Office Real Estate Markets
Society of Industrial & Office Realtors
1201 New York Ave NW
Suite 350
Washington, DC 20005-6126

202-449-8200
FAX 202-216-9325
E-Mail: admin@sior.com
Home Page: www.sior.com

Richard Hollander, Executive VP
Craig S Meyer, President
A comprehensive publication that summarizes
the results of a nationwide survey of industrial
and office real estate market activity.
Cost: $135.00
300 Pages
Frequency: Annual+
Circulation: 3000

21035 Condo Management
Papers
342 Hathaway Boulevard
Suite 26
New Bedford, MA 02740

978-524-1758
888-412-6636
FAX 508-993-2329
E-Mail: editor@condomgmt.com
Home Page: www.condomgmt.com

Melanie L Lange, Publisher
Lisa Zimmerer, Marketing Manager
Ken Sheldon, Editorial Support
News and features on condominium manage-
ment issues throughout these regions, regular
features on financial services, product services
and other related topics.
Cost: $50.00
Circulation: 10000

21036 Connections
Women's Council of Realtors

430 N Michigan Ave
Chicago, IL 60611-4011

312-329-8483
800-462-8841
FAX 312-329-3290
E-Mail: info@crs.com
Home Page: www.wcr.org

Gary Krysler, Executive Director
Carol Raabe, VP Operations

Top producers in the real estate industry share
their strategies for success.
32 Pages
Circulation: 14000
Founded in 1966
Printed in 4 colors on matte stock

21037 Cooperative Housing Journal
National Association of Housing
Cooperatives
630 Eye St NW
Washington, DC 20001-3736

202-289-3500
FAX 202-289-8181
E-Mail: nahro@nahro.org
Home Page: www.nahro.org

Saul Ramirez, Executive Director
Deniz Tunder, Editor

Articles of lasting value to leaders in coopera-
tive housing.
Cost: $25.00
Circulation: 3000
Founded in 1933

21038 Cooperator
Yale Robbins Publications
102 Madison Ave
5th Floor
New York, NY 10016-7417

212-683-5700
FAX 212-545-0764
E-Mail: mrsales@mrofficespace.com
Home Page: www.mrofficespace.com

Yale Robbins, Owner
Pam Liebman, CEO/President
Judith C Grover, Managing Editor
George Rubin, Circulation Manager
Ellen Levy, Advertising Manager

Articles covering management, maintenance
business, finance, law, interior design and re-
lated topics.
Cost: $30.00
Frequency: Monthly
Circulation: 75000
Founded in 1985
Printed in 4 colors

21039 Daily Record
11 E Saratoga St
Baltimore, MD 21202-2199

410-752-3849
FAX 410-752-2894
E-Mail: editor@mddailyrecord.com
Home Page: www.mddailyrecord.com

Chris Eddings, Publisher
Suzanne Fischer-Huettner, VP Sales
Christopher J Chardo, Circulation Director
Mark R Cheshire, Editor-in-Chief
Jeffrey Raymond, Editor
Cost: $190.00
Frequency: Daily
Founded in 1888

21040 Development
National Assn of Industrial & Office
Properties
2201 Cooperative Way
3rd floor
Herndon, VA 20171-4583

703-904-7100
800-666-6780

FAX 703-904-7942
E-Mail: feedback@naiop.org
Home Page: www.naiop.org

Thomas Bisacquino, President
Shirley A Maloney, Publisher

Articles pertaining to industrial and office real
estate - development, ownership, management,
investment, financing, leasing, etc.
Cost: $65.00
72 Pages
Frequency: Quarterly
Circulation: 14000
ISSN: 0888-6067
Founded in 2000
Printed in 4 colors on glossy stock

21041 Developments
American Resort Development Association
1201 15th St NW
Suite 400
Washington, DC 20005-2842

202-371-6700
FAX 202-289-8544
E-Mail: hnusbaum@arda.org
Home Page: www.ardafoundation.org

Howard Nusbaum, President

Serves the timeshare industry.
Frequency: Monthly
Circulation: 1,000
Founded in 1978

21042 Financial Freedom Report
2450 Fort Union Boulevard
Salt Lake City, UT 84121-3337

FAX 801-944-4334

Carolyn Tice, Editor

An investor's information services company
which specializes in home business start-up,
analysis, acquisition and maintenance of real
property.
Cost: $119.00
72 Pages
Frequency: 4 issues
Founded in 1976

21043 First Tuesday
Realty Publications
PO Box 20069
Riverside, CA 92516-69

909-781-7300
FAX 909-781-4721

Fred Crane, Publisher

Provides practical assistance to real estate professional. Includes legal and economic updates
affecting the commercial and residential
developments.
Frequency: Monthly
Circulation: 5000

21044 Global Property Investor
Alexander & Edwards Publishing
220 Sansome Street
11th Floor
San Francisco, CA 94104-2326

415-151-1241
800-989-7255
FAX 415-249-1595
Home Page: www.housingfinance.com

Shabnam Mogharabi, Director
Christine Serlin, Executive Editor

Objective, independent journal covering commercial property investment and development
trends with readership in Europe, Asia and
North America.

21045 Hotel Journal
Stacey Horowitz

45 Research Way
Suite 106
East Setauket, NY 11733

631-246-9300
FAX 631-246-9496
E-Mail: Info@hoteljournal.com
Home Page: www.hoteljournal.com

Stacey Silver, Group Publisher
Stefani C O'Connor, Executive News Editor
Cathy Urell, Senior Desk Editor
Barbara Jordan, Production Manager
Hope Rosenzweig, Advertising Manager
Cost: $85.00
Frequency: Monthly

21046 In Business
Business Information
2718 Dryden Drive
Madison, WI 53704

608-246-3599
FAX 608-246-3597

Jody Glynn Patrick, Publisher
Joseph Vanden Plas, Editor

The business magazine for the Greater Madison
Market.
48 Pages
Frequency: Monthly
Circulation: 15,000
ISSN: 0192-7450

21047 Ingram's
Show-Me Publishing, Inc
PO Box 411356
Kansas City, MO 64141-1356

816-842-9994
FAX 816-474-1111
E-Mail: editorial@ingramsonline.com
Home Page: www.ingramsonline.com

Joe Sweeney, Editor-in-Chief/Publisher
Jack Cashill, Executive Editor

Kansas City's business magazine.
Cost: $36.00
114 Pages
Frequency: Monthly
ISSN: 1046-9958
Printed in 4 colors on glossy stock

21048 Institutional Real Estate Letter
Institutional Real Estate
2274 Camino Ramon
San Ramon, CA 94583

925-244-0500
FAX 925-244-0520
Home Page: www.irei.com

H Lawrence Hull Jr, Chairman
Geoffrey Dohrmann CRE,
Founder/President/CEO
Larry Gray, Editorial Director

Offers analysis of market trends related to pen-
sion fund investment in real estate.
Cost: $2495.00
Frequency: Monthly
Founded in 1987

21049 International Real Estate Journal
International Real Estate Institute
810 N Farrell Drive
Palm Springs, CA 92262

760-327-5284
877-743-6799
FAX 760-327-5631
E-Mail: info@irei-assoc.org
Home Page: www.irei-assoc.org

Roger Wood, Production Manager
James Held, Production Manager
Robert Johnson, CEO

A full color magazine dedicated to discussing
and promoting real estate opportunities all over
the world. The articles cover a wide array of in-

ternational Real Estate topics and are written by top international professionals.
Frequency: Monthly
Circulation: 10,000
Founded in 1977

21050 Journal of Property Management
Institute of Real Estate Management
430 N Michigan Ave
Suite 7
Chicago, IL 60611-4011

312-329-6000
FAX 312-661-0217
E-Mail: custserv@irem.org
Home Page: www.irem.org

Russell Salzman, CEO
Anthony Smith, President

Features articles on management, leasing and development of all property types.
Cost: $69.95
Circulation: 18000
Founded in 1976

21051 Journal of Real Estate Taxation
Thomson Reuters
195 Broadway
New York, NY 10007

817-332-3709
800-431-9025
FAX 888-216-1929
Home Page: ria.thomsonreuters.com

Paul D Carman, Editor-in-Chief
Robert J Murdich JD, Managing Editor

Complete, ongoing coverage of all aspects of real estate tax planning. In-depth articles by leading attorneys, accountants, and real estate authorities keep you abreast of the latest developments and how they affect real estate tax planning.
Cost: $315.00
Frequency: Quarterly

21052 MB News
Monument Builders of North America
401 N Michigan Avenue
Suite 2200
Chicago, IL 60611-4267

800-233-4472
FAX 312-673-6732
Home Page: www.monumentbuilders.org

Greg Patzer, Executive VP
Marty Kraslen, Manager

The Monument Builders of North America represent the leading retail, wholesale and manufacturing and supply firms of the monument industry. Articles promote public interest, knowledge and appreciation of memorialization.
Cost: $70.00
Frequency: 12 issues
Circulation: 1400

21053 Midwest Real Estate News
The Law Bulletin Publishing Company
415 N State St
Suite 1
Chicago, IL 60654-8116

312-644-7800
FAX 312-644-4255
E-Mail: dwalsh@lbpc.com
Home Page: www.lawbulletin.com

Lanning Macfarland Jr, President
Tricia Haddon, Associate Publisher
Bob Craig, Editor
Robert Carr, Associate editor

The Midwest's only commercial real estate source.
Cost: $60.00
Frequency: Monthly
Circulation: 16914

Founded in 1854
Printed in 4 colors on glossy stock

21054 Mobility Magazine
Worldwide ERC
4401 Wilson Boulevard
Suite 510
Arlington, VA 22203

703-842-3400
FAX 703-527-1552
E-Mail: webmaster@worldwideerc.org
Home Page: www.worldwideerc.org

Anita Brienza GMS, SVP
Communications/Marketing
Frank Mauck, Managing Editor

Relocation leaders share experiences, offer new solutions to age-old challenges, set industry trends, describe best practices and policies, as well as comment on key issues affecting the relocation profession.
Cost: $48.00
68 Pages
Frequency: Monthly
Circulation: 12500
Founded in 1960

21055 Mortgage and Real Estate Executives Report
PO Box 64833
Saint Paul, MN 55164-0833

212-929-7500
800-950-1205
FAX 212-367-6718

21056 Multifamily Executive
MGI Publications
1 Thomas Cir NW
Suite 600
Washington, DC 20005-5803

202-452-0800
FAX 202-785-1974
E-Mail: arice@hanleywood.com
Home Page: www.hanleywood.com

Ed McNeill, President
Stephanie Davis, Production Manager
Alison Rice, Editor
Nicola Pellegrini, Marketing
J Michael Boyle, Publisher

Software and technology innovations, legislation, property development, management and renovation topics. Subscription free to qualified individuals.
Frequency: Monthly
Circulation: 25000
ISSN: 1089-4721
Founded in 1976
Printed in 4 colors on glossy stock

21057 National Real Estate Investor
Penton Media
249 W 17th Street
New York, NY 10011

212-204-4200
E-Mail: david.bodamer@penton.com
Home Page: www.nreionline.com

Marianne Rivera, Publisher
David Bodamer, Editorial Director
Susan Piperato, Managing Editor

The leading authority on commercial real estate trends. Readers represent a cross-section of disciplines-brokerage, construction, owner/development, finance/investment, property managment, corporate real estate, and real estate services.
Circulation: 33000
Founded in 1939

21058 National Relocation & Real Estate Magazine
RISMedia, Inc

69 E Avenue
Norwalk, CT 06851

203-855-1234
800-724-6000
E-Mail:
realestatemagazinefeedback@rismedia.com
Home Page: rismedia.com

John Featherston, Publisher
Steve Empey, CEO

Information on emerging trends and important issues affecting the various industries that are involved in relocating people and the home buying process.
Cost: $42.84
Frequency: Monthly
Circulation: 34,500
Founded in 1985

21059 New Homes Guide
4902 Eisenhower Boulevard
Suite 216
Tampa, FL 33634

813-823-3535
FAX 813-290-7380

Emily Boyd, Manager
Sharon Kirkbride, Contact

21060 Office & Industrial Properties
MGI Publications
301 Oxford Valley Road
#1301
Yardley, PA 19067-7706

215-321-5112
FAX 215-321-5122

Edward McNeill Jr, President/Editor-in-Chief

Contains business, technology, design and financial aspects concerning large private properties.
Cost: $36.00
Frequency: Bi-Monthly
Circulation: 15,000

21061 Office Buildings Magazine
Yale Robbins Publications
102 Madison Ave
5 Floor
New York, NY 10016-7417

212-683-5700
800-411-2229
FAX 212-545-0764
E-Mail: mrosales@mrofficespace.com
Home Page: www.mrofficespace.com

Yale Robbins, Owner
Henry Robbins, Marketing
Debbie Estock, Editor
Dane Pedupo, Circulation

Offers information on appraising and betterment of the real estate community in major markets in the Northeast.
Cost: $675.00
Frequency: Annual+
Founded in 1982
Printed in 4 colors

21062 Pest Control
Questex Media
600 Superior Ave E
Suite 1100
Cleveland, OH 44114-2614

216-706-3620
800-669-1668
FAX 216-706-3711
E-Mail: pestcon@questex.com
Home Page: www.questex.com

Tony Davino, Executive VP
Matt Waddell, Publisher
Matt Simoni, Sales Manager
Frank Andorka, Editorial Director

Serves the structural pest control industry.
Frequency: Monthly
Circulation: 21600
ISSN: 0031-6121
Founded in 1933
Printed in 4 colors on glossy stock

21063 Plants, Sites & Parks
12350 NW 39th Street
Suite 101
Coral Springs, FL 33065

954-753-2660
800-753-2660
FAX 954-755-7048

Kevin Castellani, Group Publisher
Steve Chaffin, Publisher/Editor-in-Chief
Lisa M Bouchey, Managing Editor

Industrial office and economic development, facility planning and site selection for manufacturing and service industries.
Circulation: 44,500

21064 Professional Report
Society of Industrial & Office Realtors
1201 New York Ave NW
Suite 350
Washington, DC 20005-6126

202-449-8200
FAX 202-216-9325
E-Mail: admin@sior.com
Home Page: www.sior.com

Richard Hollander, Executive VP
Craig S Meyer, President

Articles by industry experts focusing on new paradigm in the practice of commercial real estate.
Cost: $295.00
Frequency: Quarterly
Circulation: 2,200
Founded in 1991

21065 RCI Timeshare Business
RCI
PO Box 80229
Indianapolis, IN 46280-0229

317-805-9000
FAX 317-805-9618
E-Mail: alyssa.chase@rci.com
Home Page: www.rci.com

Alyssa Chase, Editor
Katherine Jones, Publisher
David Tontius, CEO/President

Serves timeshare resorts/developers, hoteliers, operations and others allied to the field.
42 Pages
Frequency: Monthly
Circulation: 9000
Founded in 1974
Printed in 4 colors on glossy stock

21066 RCI Ventures Magazine
RCI
9998 N Michigan Road
Carmel, IN 46032

317-059-9584
FAX 317-805-9507
E-Mail: alyssa.chase@rci.com
Home Page: www.rciventures.com

Alyssa Chase, Editor
Nicole Keller, Senior Editor

Gathering of more than 4,000 of timesharing's best and brightest executives.
Frequency: April
Circulation: 35000
ISSN: 1099-6753
Printed in 4 colors on 6 stock

21067 Real Estate Business
Realtors National Marketing Institute

430 N Michigan Avenue
#300
Chicago, IL 60611-4002

312-321-4400
FAX 312-329-8882
E-Mail: spatterson@crs.com
Home Page: www.crs.com

Sara Patterson, Editor-in-Chief
Eric Berkland, Marketing
Nina Cottrell, CEO
Ron Canning, Vice President

Information for real estate agents and brokers engaged in US residential sales activities.
Cost: $24.00
64 Pages
Circulation: 48000
Founded in 1976

21068 Real Estate Executive
Sunshine Media
735 Broad Street
Suite 708
Chattanooga, TN 37402

423-266-3234
800-624-7496
FAX 423-266-7960
E-Mail: info@sunshinemedia.com
Home Page: www.sunshinemedia.com

Tony Young, President
Jim Martin, President/CEO
David McDonald, Publisher

About real estate professionals from real estate professionals. Reaches 100 percent of the professional real estate audience in each market it serves. Each issue profiles a leading realty executive or agency within your local real estate market, as well as an assortment of new products, services and innovations.
Cost: $36.00
Frequency: Monthly
Circulation: 3000
Founded in 1996

21069 Real Estate Finance Journal
Thomson Reuters
610 Opperman Drive
Eagan, MN 55123

652-168-7700
Home Page: www.west.thomson.com

Examines the opportunities and pitfalls facing real estate owners, developers, investors and lenders. Focuses on financing, liability, investments, taxes and asset management.
Cost: $558.00
Frequency: Quarterly

21070 Real Estate Finance Today
Mortgage Bankers Association of America
1919 Pennsylvania Avenue NW
Washington, DC 20006-3404

202-557-2700
E-Mail: membership@mortgagebankers.org
Home Page: www.mortgagebankers.org

Features inside news reports on events and trends affecting the residential and commercial mortgage markets.

21071 Real Estate Forum
Real Estate Media
120 Broadway
Suite 5
New York, NY 10271

212-929-6976
Home Page: www.reforum.com

Michael G Desiato, VP/Group Publisher
Sule Aygoren Carranza, Editor
Paul Bubny, Managing Editor
Alexa Faulkner, Circulation

The one source for market intelligence and business generation.
Frequency: Monthly
Circulation: 53821
Founded in 1940

21072 Real Estate Review
Thomson Reuters
195 Broadway
Suite 4
New York, NY 10007-3124

646-822-2000
800-231-1860
FAX 646-822-2800
E-Mail: trta.lei-support@thomsonreuters.com
Home Page: www.ria.thomsonreuters.com

Elaine Yadlon, Plant Manager
Thomas H Glocer, CEO & Director
Robert D Daleo, Chief Financial Officer
Kelli Crane, Senior Vice President & CIO

Information on financing, mortgage banking, investments, and related legal and tax issues, also covers US commercial, indiustrial and residential development.
Frequency: Quarterly
Circulation: 5,500

21073 Real Property, Property and Trust Journal
American Bar Association
321 N Clark St
Chicago, IL 60654-7598

312-988-5000
800-285-2221
FAX 312-988-6281
E-Mail: askaba@abanet.org
Home Page: www.abanet.org

Tommy H Wells Jr, President
Jennifer Collins, Advertising Sales Coordinator

Scholarly articles in the fields of estate planning, trust law and real property law.
Cost: $60.00
Frequency: Quarterly
Founded in 1878

21074 Realtor Magazine
New York State Association of Realtors
430 N Michigan Avenue
Suite 430
Chicago, IL 60611-4087

800-874-6500
FAX 312-329-5978
E-Mail: narpubs@realtors.org
Home Page: realtormag.realtor.org

Stacey Mancrieff, Editor
Frank Sibley, Senior VP/Publisher
Christina H Spira, Managing Editor
Wanda Clark, Publications Assistant
Pamela G Kabati, Vice President / Editorial Director

The business tool for real estate professionals. The New York Report is given after page 8.
Cost: $56.00
70 Pages
Frequency: Monthly
ISSN: 1522-0842
Founded in 1908
Printed in 4 colors on glossy stock

21075 Rental Management
1900 19th Street
Moline, IL 61265-4179

309-764-2475
800-334-2177
FAX 309-764-1533
Home Page: www.ararental.org

Chris Wehrman, Executive VP
Joe Lynch, Deputy Executive VP

A monthly magazine published by the American Rental Association
Frequency: Monthly
Circulation: 18000

21076 Residential Specialist

430 N Michigan Ave
Suite 3
Chicago, IL 60611-4011

312-828-9129
FAX 312-329-8882
E-Mail: info@crs.com
Home Page: www.crs.com

Nina Cottrell, CEO
Eric Berkland, Director Marketing
Carol Raabe, Vice President of Operations
Carlee Londo, Marketing Manager
Richard Lawson, Director of Products

Published by the Council of Residential Specialists.
Cost: $29.95
64 Pages
Circulation: 40000
Founded in 1976

21077 Site Selection Magazine

Conway Data
6625 the Corners Pkwy
Suite 200
Peachtree Corners, GA 30092-3334

770-446-6996
FAX 770-263-8825
Home Page: www.conway.com

Adam Jones-Kelley, Managing Director
Loura Lyne, President
Julie Clark, Circulation Manager

Focus is on political, international and quality of life issues, also provides development groups, business parks, labor factors, relevant technology, real estate and finance information.
Cost: $90.00
Frequency: Monthly
Circulation: 45000
Founded in 1954

21078 Timeshare Business

RCI
PO Box 80229
Indianapolis, IN 46280-0229

317-805-9000
FAX 317-805-9618
E-Mail: alyssa.chase@rci.com
Home Page: www.rci.com

Alyssa Chase, Editor
Nicole keller, Senior Associate Editor
Rita Corea, Circulation Manager

Magazine for resort developers, property managers, sales and marketing professionals, homeowners association boards, and other key personnel in the timeshare industry.
42 Pages
Frequency: Monthly
Circulation: 35000
ISSN: 1099-6753
Founded in 1974
Printed in 4 colors on 6 stock

21079 US Sites & Development

Vulcan Publications
PO Box 12846
Birmingham, AL 35202-2846

205-328-6198
Home Page: www.vulcanpub.com

Val Carrier, Publisher

Includes tax laws, real estate trends, as well as labor and work force issues.

21080 Unique Homes

327 Wall St
Princeton, NJ 08540-1518

609-688-1110
877-688-1110
FAX 609-688-0201
E-Mail: krussell@uniquehomes.com
Home Page: www.uniquehomes.com

Kathleen Carlin-Russell, Manager
Lauren Baier Kim, Managing Editor
Cheryl Jock, Production Manager
Robert Burke, Custom Publishing Manager
Cost: $24.97
Circulation: 54,856
Founded in 1978

21081 Units Magazine

National Apartment Association
4300 Wilson Boulevard
Siote 400
Arlington, VA 22203

703-518-6141
FAX 703-248-9440
E-Mail: webmaster@naahq.org
Home Page: www.naahq.org

Doug Culkin, President
Paul Bergeron, Communications Director

Contains news and information essential to all facets of the apartment industry-with a focus eacho month on managemetn, marketing, maintenance and politics.
Cost: $99.00
80 Pages
Frequency: Monthly
Circulation: 80,000
Printed in on glossy stock

21082 Vacation Industry Review

Interval International
PO Box 431920
Miami, FL 33243-1920

305-666-1861
FAX 305-663-2227
Home Page: www.resortdeveloper.com

Craig M Nash, CEO
Alina Betancourt, Account Executive
Ximena Villegas, Account Executive

Vacation Industry Review is a quarterly trade publication covering the global timeshare, fractional, vacation ownership resort industry. It discusses industry issues and trends and showcases new resort developments and key markets. It also covers products and services of interest to the industry, and the activities of prominent individuals and companies.
48/64 Pages
Frequency: Quarterly
Circulation: 28,000
Founded in 1984
Printed in 4 colors on glossy stock

21083 Vacation Ownership World

CHB Company
8701 Collins Ave Ph
Miami, Fl 33154

305-864-6083
FAX 305-864-6085
E-Mail: resort@nas.com
Home Page: www.vomagazine.com

Jon Paulisin, Publisher/President
Lou Skidmore, Editor
Howard White, Circulation Manager

News and feature stories, in depth analysis of the issues and trends affecting the industry of global timesharing.
Founded in 1984

21084 Valuation Insights & Perspectives

Appraisal Institute

550 W Van Buren St
Suite 1000
Chicago, IL 60607-3850

312-335-4100
FAX 312-335-4400
E-Mail: puborders@appraisalinstitute.org
Home Page: www.appraisalinstitute.org

Fred Grubbe, CEO
Larisa Phillips, President

Offers a collection of high interest articles, and features industry and institute news section and columns on legal matters, technology, marketing and timely appraisal issues.
Cost: $48.00
18 Pages
Frequency: Quarterly
Circulation: 82000
Founded in 1996
Printed in 4 colors on glossy stock

Trade Shows

21085 American Congress on Surveying & Mapping Annual Conference

6 Montgomery Village Avenue
Suite 403
Gaithersburg, MD 20879

240-680-0765
FAX 240-632-1321
E-Mail: curtis.sumner@acsm.net
Home Page: www.acsm.net

Curt Sumner, Executive Director
Ilse Genovese, Communications Director
Bob Jupin, Accounting Manager

One hundred and thirty exhibits of industry related equipment, supplies and services plus workshop and conference.
2000 Attendees
Frequency: Annual
Founded in 1934

21086 American Land Tree Association Annual Convention

1828 L Street NW
Suite 705
Washington, DC 20036-5104

202-296-3671
Home Page: http://www.alta.org

James Maher, VP
1M Attendees
Frequency: October

21087 American Real Estate Society Annual Meeting

American Real Estate Society
Cleveland State University-BU327
Dept. Finance, Business College
Cleveland, OH 44114

216-687-4732
FAX 216-687-9331
Home Page: www.aresnet.org

Annual meeting and 10 exhibitors that are publishers, data providers, technical foundtions. Exhibits relate to decision-making within real estate finance, real estate market analysis, investment, valuation, development and other areas related to real estate.
300 Attendees
Frequency: April

21088 American Society of Appraisers International Appraisal Conference

11107 Sunset Hills Rd
Suite 310
Reston, VA 20190

703-478-2228
800-272-8258

FAX 703-742-8471
E-Mail: asainfo@appraisers.org
Home Page: www.appraisers.org
Social Media: *Facebook, Twitter, LinkedIn, YouTube*

Jane Grimm, Executive VP
Susan Fischer, Governance Manager
Jack Washbourn, President

Exhibits for professional appraisers.
5000 Members
Frequency: Annual
Founded in 1936

21089 Apartment Association of Greater Dallas Annual Trade Show
4230 LBJ Freeway
Suite 140
Dallas, TX 75244

972-385-9091
FAX 972-385-9412
E-Mail: pkelley@aagdallas.com
Home Page: www.aagdallas.com

Paula Kelley CMP, Director of Events
Gerry Henigsman, Executive Assistant
Marsha Stephenson, Executive Assistant
Bradley Elliott, Director of Communications
Donna Derden, Vice President

Tours and 240 displays of industry related supplies and services.
3000 Attendees
Frequency: April
Founded in 1963

21090 Apartment Association of Metro Denver Educational Expo and Trade Show
650 S Cherry Street
Suite 635
Denver, CO 80246

303-290-0403
FAX 303-329-0403

Mark Williams, Executive Director

Seminar, reception and 142 exhibits of property management equipment, supplies, services and information.
1500 Attendees
Frequency: Annual

21091 BOMA Winter Business Meeting & Leadership Conference
Building Owners & Managers Association Int'l
1201 New York Avenue NW
Suite 300
Washington, DC 20005

202-408-2662
FAX 202-371-0181
E-Mail: info@boma.org
Home Page: www.boma.org

Henry Chamberlain, President/CEO
Laura Best, Conference Director

Opportunity for business professionals to discuss problems, security, exchange ideas and share experience and knowledge.
Frequency: January

21092 BUILDINGS-New York
Reed Exhibition Companies
383 Main Avenue
Norwalk, CT 06851-1543

203-840-4800
FAX 203-840-9570

Annual show of 425 exhibitors of products and services for the building owner, developer, manager, co-ops and superintendents in the commercial and residential real estate market, including asbestos abatement, waterproofing, restoration, financial services, utilities, laundry equipment, cleaning services, computer software, elevators, heating and air conditioning,

light safety/security, renovation and restoration.
9,000 Attendees

21093 Coldwell Bankers Annual National Show
27271 Las Ramblas
Mission Viejo, CA 92691-6386

949-673-3650
FAX 973-496-5784

Sandra Deering, Manager
Seventy-five booths.
4.5M Attendees

21094 MIPIM
Reed Exhibition Companies
255 Washington Street
Newton, MA 02458-1637

617-584-4900
FAX 617-630-2222

Elizabeth Hitchcock, International Sales
International property market conference.
4M Attendees
Frequency: March

21095 National Association of Realtors Meetings and Trade Show
430 N Michigan Avenue
Chicago, IL 60611-4087

312-645-7730
800-874-6500
E-Mail: infocentral@realtors.org
Home Page: www.realtor.org

Karen Crafton, Convention Executive Secretary
Sue Gourley, Conventions VP
Terrence McDermott, CEO
Bill Armstrong, Treasurer

Seminars and networking, plus updates in the industry. More than 200 exhibiting companies.
6500 Attendees
Frequency: May

21096 National Association of Realtors Trade Exposition
National Association of Realtors
430 N Michigan Avenue
Chicago, IL 60611-4002

312-645-7730
FAX 312-329-8882
E-Mail: info@crs.com
Home Page: www.crs.com

Sara Patterson, Director Communications
Terrence McDermott, Vice President
Ron Canning, Vice President

Spring show of 250 exhibitors of real estate industry equipment, supplies and services, including hardware and software, marketing programs, office products, mortgage and financial services and insurance.
40000 Attendees
Founded in 1976

21097 Old House New House Home Show
4051 E Main Street
St Charles, IL

630-515-1160
E-Mail: kp@corecomm.net
Home Page: www.kennedyproductions.com
Social Media: *Facebook*

Beth Wall, Contact

Discover the latest innovations, seeing creative solutions and gathering the motivation to tackle home improvement projects.
Frequency: Sept/Oct Illinois

21098 Real Show
Journal of Property Management

430 N Michigan Avenue
Chicago, IL 60611-4002

312-329-6064
FAX 312-329-8882
E-Mail: info@crs.com
Home Page: www.crs.com

Sara Patterson, Director Communications
Ron Canning, Vice President

A trade show with 275 exhibitors and 450 booths, for professional owners and managers of investment residential and commercial property.
40000 Attendees
Founded in 1976

21099 Realmart
National Association of Industrial & Office Prop.
Woodlyn Park-2201 Coop. Way
Herndon, VA 22071

703-267-6665
FAX 703-904-7974
E-Mail: garvin@naiop.org

Annual show of 100 suppliers of companies catering to the commercial real estate industry.
1,000 Attendees

21100 Realtors Conference & Expo
National Association of Realtors
430 North Michigan Ave.
Chicago, IL 60611

800-874-6500
E-Mail: convinfo@realtors.org
Home Page: www.realtor.org/convention.nsf
Social Media: *Facebook, Twitter, LinkedIn, YouTube*

Dale Stinton, Chief Executive Officer
Chris Polychron, President

Networking, educational sessions on timely topics and a vendor expo.
Frequency: Annual

21101 SourceMedia Conferences & Events
SourceMedia
One State Street Plaza
27th floor
New York, NY 10004

212-803-6093
800-803-3424
FAX 212-803-8515
E-Mail: abconferences@sourcemedia.com
Home Page: www.sourcemedia.com/

James M Malkin, Chairman & CEO
William Johnson, CFO
Steve Andreazza, VP, Sales & Customer Service
Celie Baussan, SVP, Operations
Anne O'Brien, EVP Marketing & Strategic Planning

SourceMedia Conferences & Events attract over 20,000 attendees worldwide. The content embraces a variety of formats, including: conferences, executive roundtables, expositions, Web seminars, custom events and pod casts. With over 70 events annually, participants are provided with premier content as well as access to the industry's top solution providers. Markets served include: accounting; banking; capital markets; financial services; information technology; insurance; and real estate.
Mailing list available for rent

21102 Trade Expo
Professional Housing Management
PO Box 4251
Leesburg, VA 20177

703-327-6873
800-543-7188
FAX 703-327-4005

E-Mail: phmainfo@earthlink.net
Home Page: www.phma.com

Jon Moore, Director
Mona Pearson, Trade Expo Coordinator

At the expo there will be 230 booths with 150 exhibitors.
1,200 Attendees
Frequency: January

Directories & Databases

21103 America's Top-Rated Cities
Grey House Publishing
4919 Route 22
PO Box 56
Amenia, NY 12501

518-789-8700
800-562-2139
FAX 518-789-0556
E-Mail: books@greyhouse.com
Home Page: www.greyhouse.com
Social Media: *Facebook, Twitter*

Leslie Mackenzie, Publisher
Richard Gottlieb, Editor

Provides current, comprehensive statistical information in one easy-to-use source on the 100 top cities that have been cited as the best for business and living in the US. Available as a four volume set or individual volumes (Southern, Western, Central and Eastern)
Cost: $225.00
2000 Pages
ISBN: 1-592373-49-6
Founded in 1981

21104 America's Top-Rated Smaller Cities
Grey House Publishing
4919 Route 22
PO Box 56
Amenia, NY 12501

518-789-8700
800-562-2139
FAX 845-373-6390
E-Mail: books@greyhouse.com
Home Page: www.greyhouse.com
Social Media: *Facebook, Twitter*

Leslie Mackenzie, Publisher
Richard Gottlieb, Editor

America's Top-Rated Smaller Cities provides current, comprehensive data on 110 US cities, all top-ranked by population growth, median income, unemployment rate and crime rate. This informative handbook allows readers to see, at a glance, a concise social, business, economic, demographic and environmental profile of each city, including brief evaluative comments.
Cost: $195.00
1800 Pages
ISBN: 1-592372-84-8
Founded in 1981

21105 American Resort Development Association: Membership Directory
American Resort Development Association
1201 15th St Nw
Suite 400
Washington, DC 20005-2842

202-371-6700
FAX 202-289-8544
E-Mail: hnusbaum@arda.org
Home Page: www.ardafoundation.org

Howard Nusbaum, President
Lou Ann Burney, VP
Rob Dumm, Finance
Alexa Antonuk, Communications Manager

Over 800 member firms in the resort development industry, including developers, finance

companies, architectural firms, audiovisual companies, direct mail companies, rental and vacation exchange companies and law firms.
Frequency: Annual Winter

21106 American Society of Appraisers Directory
American Society of Appraisers
11107 Sunset Hills Rd
Suite 310
Reston, VA 20190

703-478-2228
800-272-8258
FAX 703-742-8471
E-Mail: asainfo@appraisers.org
Home Page: www.appraisers.org
Social Media: *Facebook, Twitter, LinkedIn, YouTube*

Jane Grimm, Executive VP
Susan Fischer, Governance Manager
Jack Washbourn, President

Directory of association members who are accredited appraisers.
Cost: $12.50
5000 Members
Circulation: 8,000
Founded in 1936

21107 Buyers Broker Registry
Who's Who in Creative Real Estate
PO Box 23275
Ventura, CA 93002-3275

Offers valuable information on over 650 real estate agents in the United States who have met performance requirements set by the publisher.
Cost: $25.00
136 Pages
Frequency: Annual

21108 CRB/CRS Referral Directory
Realtors National Marketing Institute
430 N Michigan Avenue
Suite 300
Chicago, IL 60611-4002

FAX 312-329-8882
Home Page: http://www.crs.com

Gwen Voelker, Editor

Aimed at the real estate industry, this directory lists over 32,000 real estate brokerage managers and residential sales specialists.
Cost: $45.00
776 Pages
Frequency: Annual
Circulation: 32,000

21109 CRE Member Directory
Counselors of Real Estate
430 N Michigan Ave
Chicago, IL 60611-4019

312-329-8427
FAX 312-329-8881
Home Page: www.cre.org

Mary Fleischmann, President
Frequency: Annual March

21110 Commercial Investment Real Estate
CCIM Institute
430 N Michigan Ave
Chicago, IL 60611-4011

312-321-4460
FAX 312-321-4530
E-Mail: magazine@ccim.com
Home Page: www.ccim.com

Jonathan Falk, Manager
Ken Setlak, Chief Financial Officer
Sara Drummond, Executive Editor

Directory of services and supplies to the industry.
40000 Pages
Founded in 1976

21111 Comparative Guide to American Suburbs
Grey House Publishing
4919 Route 22
PO Box 56
Amenia, NY 12501

518-789-8700
800-562-2139
FAX 845-373-6390
E-Mail: books@greyhouse.com
Home Page: www.greyhouse.com
Social Media: *Facebook, Twitter*

Leslie Mackenzie, Publisher
Richard Gottlieb, Editor

Covers statistics on the 2,000+ suburban communities surrounding the 60 largest metropolitan areas - their population characteristics, income levels, economy, school systems and important data on how they compare to one another.
Cost: $150.00
1000 Pages
ISBN: 1-592371-80-9
Founded in 1981

21112 Crime in America's Top-Rated Cities
Grey House Publishing
4919 Route 22
PO Box 56
Amenia, NY 12501

518-789-8700
800-562-2139
FAX 845-373-6390
E-Mail: books@greyhouse.com
Home Page: www.greyhouse.com
Social Media: *Facebook, Twitter*

Leslie Mackenzie, Publisher
Richard Gottlieb, Editor

Details over twenty years of crime statistics in all major crime categories: violent crimes, property crimes and total crime. Conveniently arranged by city, it offers details that compare the number of crimes and crime rates for the city, suburbs and metro area with national crime trends for violent, property and total crimes. Statistics on anti-crime programs, crime risk, hate crimes, illegal drugs, law enforcement, correctional facilities, death penalty, laws and much more.
Cost: $155.00
839 Pages
ISBN: 1-891482-84-X
Founded in 1981

21113 Crittenden's Real Estate Buyers Directory
Crittendon Research
250 Bel Marin Keys Boulevard
Novato, CA 94949-5727

415-382-2400
800-421-3483
FAX 415-382-2476
Home Page: www.crittendenonline.com

John Goodwin, Editor/Publisher
Vitalario Laeson, Marketing Director
Pati Bess, Customer Service Director

A list of over 500 real estate buyers, including private institutional investors, banks, pension funds and real estate investment trusts.

21114 Crittendon Directory of Real Estate Financing
Crittendon Research
250 Bel Marin Keys Boulevard
Novato, CA 94949-5727

415-382-7790
FAX 415-382-2476

Listing of over 400 major lenders, investors and joint ventures enagged in commercial and

residential real estate financing and investing.
Cost: $387.00
500 Pages
Frequency: Semiannual

21115 DAMAR Real Estate Information Service Online Database
3550 W Temple Street
Los Angeles, CA 90004-3620

800-873-2627

This comprehensive database offers real estate information, with an emphasis on California.
Frequency: Full-text

21116 Directory of 2,500 Active Real Estate Lenders
International Wealth Success
PO Box 186
Merrick, NY 11566-0186

516-766-5850
800-323-0548
FAX 516-766-5919
E-Mail: admin@iwsmoney.com
Home Page: www.iwsmoney.com

Tyler G Hicks, President

Lists 2,500 names and addresses of direct lenders or sources of information on possible lenders for real estate.
Cost: $25.00
197 Pages
Frequency: Annually
ISBN: 1-561503-37-1
Founded in 1985

21117 Directory of Accredited Real Property Appraisers
American Society of Appraisers
PO Box 17265
Washington, DC 20041-7265

202-337-0037
800-272-8258
FAX 202-742-8471

Rebecca Ewing, Publication Manager

Approximately 1,700 urban, residential, rural, ad valorem and timberland appraisers; limited international coverage.
Frequency: Annual January

21118 Directory of Professional Appraisal Services
American Society of Appraisers
PO Box 17265
Washington, DC 20041-7265

202-337-0037
800-272-8258
FAX 202-742-8471
E-Mail: asainfo@appraisers.org
Home Page: www.appraisers.org

Rebecca Ewing, Publisher/Editor

Over 3,000 tested and accredited members appraisers of real and personal property, businesses, machinery and equipment are listed.
Cost: $10.00
275 Pages
Frequency: Annual
Circulation: 8,000

21119 Directory of Real Estate Development and Related Education Programs
Urban Land Institute
625 Indiana Avenue NW
Suite 400
Washington, DC 20004-2923

202-247-7116

Over 60 programs are profiled that are currently being offered at colleges and universities

in the area of real estate.
Cost: $19.00
132 Pages
Frequency: Biennial

21120 ERC Directory of Real Estate Appraisers and Brokers
Employee Relocation Council
1720 N Street NW
Washington, DC 20036-2900

202-857-0857

Tina Lung, Editor
Cost: $35.00
1,100 Pages
Frequency: Annual

21121 European Investment in United States Real Estate
Mead Ventures
PO Box 44952
Phoenix, AZ 85064-4952

Investors, developers and brokers located in Europe are the focus of this valuable directory.
Cost: $195.00
406 Pages
Frequency: Annual

21122 Executive Guide to Specialists in Industrial and Office Real Estate
Society of Industrial & Office Realtors
1201 New York Ave NW
Suite 350
Washington, DC 20005-6126

202-449-8200
FAX 202-216-9325
E-Mail: admin@sior.com
Home Page: www.sior.com

Richard Hollander, Executive VP
Craig S Meyer, President

Thousands of specialists are listed that are integrated with industrial real estate and related industries.
Cost: $60.00
210 Pages
Frequency: Annual

21123 FDIC: Investment Properties Publication
Federal Deposit Insurance Corporation
550 17th St Nw
Washington, DC 20429-0002

202-000-1111
FAX 202-898-8595

Mitchell L Glassman, Plant Manager

Offers information on properties owned by the Federal Deposit Insurance Corporation, including land, commercial real estate, multifamily dwellings and hotels and motels.
200 Pages
Frequency: Quarterly

21124 Guide to Real Estate and Mortgage Banking Software
Real Estate Solutions
2609 Klingle Road NW
Washington, DC 20008-1202

202-362-9854

Lists approximately 500 real estate and mortgage banking computer software, hardware and products.
Cost: $49.95
640 Pages
Frequency: Biennial

21125 Income & Cost for Organization & Servicing of 1-4 Unit Residential Loans
Mortgage Bankers Association of America

1919 Pennsylvania Avenue NW
Washington, DC 20006-3404

202-557-2700
E-Mail: membership@mortgagebankers.org
Home Page: www.mortgagebankers.org

Annual report provides data and analysis on the income and expenses associated with the organization, warehousing, marketing and servicing or one-to-four-unit residential marketing loans.
80 Pages
Frequency: $150 Member/$300 Non

21126 Japanese Investment in US Real Estate Review
Mead Ventures
PO Box 44952
Phoenix, AZ 85064-4952

FAX 602-234-0076

This is a complete database listing documenting Japanese purchases of US golf courses, houses, office buildings and industrial properties.
Frequency: Full-text

21127 Journal of the American Society of Farm Managers and Rural Appraisers
ASFMRA
950 S Cherry St
Suite 508
Denver, CO 80246-2664

303-758-3513
FAX 303-758-0190
E-Mail: asfmra@agri-associations.org
Home Page: www.asfmra.org

Cheryl L Cooley, Manager
Communications/PR
Mailing list available for rent: 2500 names at $1M per M

21128 Major Cities Canada
Grey House Publishing
4919 Route 22
PO Box 56
Amenia, NY 12501

800-562-2139
FAX 845-373-6390
FAX new
Home Page: www.greyhouse.ca

Richard Gottlieb, President

Provides an in-depth comparison and analysis of the 50 most populated cities in Canada. Split into 4 major categories; background, study rankings, development offices, and statistical tables
Cost: $180.00
793 Pages

21129 Million Dollar Guide to Business and Real Estate Loan Sources
International Wealth Success
PO Box 186
Merrick, NY 11566-0186

516-766-5850
800-323-0548
FAX 516-766-5919
E-Mail: admin@iwsmoney.com
Home Page: www.iwsmoney.com

Tyler G Hicks, President

Lists hundreds of business and real estate lenders, giving their lending data in very brief form.
Cost: $25.00
201 Pages
Frequency: Annually
Founded in 1990

21130 Monthly Resort Real Estate Property Index
MDR Telecom
4742 La Villa Marina
Unit A
Marina Del Rey, CA 90292-7086
Mario Collura, Editor

Offers information on resort timeshares and resort condominiums for rent or sale.
Cost: $10.00
80 Pages
Frequency: Monthly

21131 Mortgage Banking Performance Report
Mortgage Bankers Association of America
1919 Pennsylvania Avenue NW
Washington, DC 20006-3404

202-557-2700
E-Mail: membership@mortgagebankers.org
Home Page: www.mortgagebankers.org

The report includes an annual summary, is a financial statement analysis of mortgage banking company performance.
80 Pages
Frequency: $125 Member/$175 Non
Founded in 1992

21132 Mortgage Banking Sourcebook
Mortgage Bankers Association of America
1919 Pennsylvania Avenue NW
Washington, DC 20006-3404

202-557-2700
E-Mail: membership@mortgagebankers.org
Home Page: www.mortgagebankers.org

Comprehensive directory to federal and state government agencies, industry trade associations colleges and universities, and other organizations and sources of information on mortgage lending, Includes an entire network of industry contact complete with addresses, telephone and fax numbers and internet website addresses.
Cost: $40.00
144 Pages
Founded in 1997

21133 Mortgage Finance Database
Mortgage Bankers Association of America
1919 Pennsylvania Avenue NW
Washington, DC 20006-3404

202-557-2700
Home Page: www.mortgagebankers.com

This database contains the most comprehensive and up-to-date collection of mortgage-related variables currently available.

21134 National Association of Independent Fee Appraisers: Membership Directory
National Association of Independent Fee Appraisers
7501 Murdoch Avenue
Saint Louis, MO 63119-2810

314-645-7583
FAX 314-781-2872

Donna Walters, Publications

Five thousand and five hundred independent real estate appraisers.
Frequency: Annual January

21135 National Association of Master Appraisers Membership Directory
National Association of Master Appraisers
303 W Cypress St
San Antonio, TX 78212-5512

210-271-0781
800-229-6262
FAX 210-225-8450

E-Mail: djd@masterappraisers.org
Home Page: www.masterappraisers.org

Del Martinez, Manager
Christopher Deane, Marketing And Production Manager

Approximately 3,500 real estate appraisers.
Frequency: Annual January
Circulation: 3,500

21136 National Association of Real Estate Appraisers
P.O. Box 879
Palm Springs, CA 92263

76- 32- 528
877-815-4172
FAX 760-327-5631
E-Mail: info@narea-assoc.org
Home Page: www.narea-assoc.org

Dallas Martin, President

A complete guide to the REIT industry with approximately 240 real estate investment trusts, and over 1,000 associate members listed.
Cost: $695.00
600 Pages
Frequency: Annual

21137 National Association of Real Estate Companies: Membership Directory
National Association of Real Estate Companies
216 W Jackson Blvd
Suite 625
Chicago, IL 60606-6945

312-263-1755
FAX 312-750-1203
E-Mail: info@narec.org
Home Page: www.narec.org

Kim Klein, Administrator

About 200 real estate development companies.
Frequency: Quarterly

21138 National Directory of Exchange Groups
Creative Real Estate Magazine
PO Box L
Rancho Santa Fe, CA 92067-0560

858-756-1441
FAX 818-156-1111

Lists over 125 professional real estate marketing groups practicing tax-deferred real estate exchanges.
Cost: $72.00
48 Pages
Frequency: Monthly
Circulation: 51,000
ISBN: 0-194722-2 -

21139 National Real Estate Directory
Real Estate Publishing Company
P.O. Box 180635
Coronado, CA 92118

866-431-5223
FAX 619-615-2350
Home Page:
www.national-real-estate-directory.com

Over 22,000 federal and state agencies, offices and departments related to the regulation of real estate, real estate associations and publications are listed.
Cost: $29.95
110 Pages
Frequency: Biennial

21140 National Real Estate Investor Sourcebook
Primedia

5680 Greenwood Plaza Boulevard
Suite 300
Greenwood Village, CO 80111

303-741-2901
FAX 720-489-3101
Home Page: www.primediabusiness.com

Barbara Katinsky, Editor

List of about 7,000 companies and individuals in 18 real estate fields.
Cost: $78.95
Frequency: Annual, September
Circulation: 33,000

21141 National Referral Roster
Candy Holub
615 5th Street SE
Cedar Rapids, IA 52401-2158

319-364-6167
800-553-8878
FAX 319-369-0029
Home Page: www.roster.com

Candy Holub, Publisher
Mary Richeson, Business Developer
Joey Grim, Business Developer

Approximately 90,000 Real Estate offices nationwide. Provides an effective, comprehensive and easy-to-use tool for realtors to make successful referrals to other relators nationwide.
Cost: $95.00
936 Pages
Frequency: Annual
Circulation: 18,000
ISSN: 1075-1084
Founded in 1923
Printed in 2 colors on newsprint stock

21142 National Toll-Free 800 Guide to Real Estate Publications and Publishers
Real Estate Publishing Company
4580 Brookside Rd
Cameron Park, CA 95682-9619

530-677-3864

Joe Wgle, President

Directory of publications to the industry.
Cost: $15.95
82 Pages
Frequency: Biennial

21143 Nelson's Directory of Institutional Real Estate
Nelson Publications
2500 Tamiami Trl N
Nokomis, FL 34275-3476

941-966-9521
FAX 941-966-2590
E-Mail: webmaster@nelsonpub.com
Home Page: www.healthmgttech.com

A Verner Nelson, Owner
Marcia Boysen, Editor

Institutional investors who invest in real estate: investment managers, real estate service firms, insurance companies, plan sponsors, corporations and REIT's.
Cost: $335.00
Frequency: Annual August

21144 One List Directory
MRH Associates
365 Willard Avenue
Suite 2K
Newington, CT 06111-2373

800-727-5478

Over 700 companies and 6,000 company divisions are involved as listees in this comprehensive directory. Included is a section of over 12,000 contact personnel in the real estate and

construction industry.
Cost: $545.00
750 Pages
Frequency: Annual

21145 Professional Relocation and Real Estate Services Directory
Relocation Information Service
113 Post Road E
2nd Floor
Westport, CT 06880-3410

203-256-1079
FAX 203-227-3800

Offers over 6,000 real estate brokerage companies, appraisal firms, home inspectors and services companies.
Cost: $95.00
800 Pages
Frequency: Annual
Circulation: 35,000

21146 Profiles of America
Grey House Publishing
4919 Route 22
PO Box 56
Amenia, NY 12501

518-789-8700
800-562-2139
FAX 845-373-6390
E-Mail: books@greyhouse.com
Home Page: www.greyhouse.com
Social Media: *Facebook, Twitter*

Leslie Mackenzie, Publisher
Richard Gottlieb, Editor

This four volume set details over 40,000 places, from the biggest metropolis to the smallest unicorporated hamlet and provides statistical details and information on over 50 different topics including: geography, climate, population, economy, income, taxes, education, housing, health and environment, public safety, transportation, presidential election results and more.
Cost: $795.00
10000 Pages
ISBN: 1-891482-80-7

21147 Profiles of...Series - State Handbooks
Grey House Publishing
4919 Route 22
PO Box 56
Amenia, NY 12501

518-789-8700
800-562-2139
FAX 845-373-6390
E-Mail: books@greyhouse.com
Home Page: www.greyhouse.com
Social Media: *Facebook, Twitter*

Leslie Mackenzie, Publisher
Richard Gottlieb, Editor

Each state-by-state volume in this new series provides at-a-glance detailed demographic and statistical data on every populated place in the state, along with easy-to-use comparative rankings. Series includes 20 states. Additional states added each year.
Founded in 1981

21148 Real Estate & Land Use Regulation in Eastern and Central Europe
WorldTrade Executive
PO Box 761
Concord, MA 01742-0761

978-287-0301
FAX 978-287-0302
E-Mail: info@wtexec.com
Home Page: www.wtexec.com

Alison French, Production Manager

Topics covered include: leasing in Russia: helpful hints for tenants; a guide to government agencies regulating development in Moscow

and St. Petersburg; current law and practice for the Russian real estate market; the real estate lease in the Czech Republic; environmental considerations for acquisition of property in Hungary.
Cost: $135.00

21149 Real Estate Applications Software Directory
Real Estate Center
Texas A and M University
College Station, TX 77843-0001

979-845-2031
800-244-2144
FAX 713-845-0460
E-Mail: info@recenter.tamu.edu
Home Page: www.recenter.tamu.edu

David S Jones, Senior Editor
Ted C Jones, Director
Gary Maler, Director

About 300 suppliers of several hundred software packages with applications related to the real estate industry.
Cost: $30.00
Frequency: Annual October

21150 Real Estate Books and Periodicals in Print
Real Estate Publishing Company
PO Box 41177
Sacramento, CA 95841-0177

530-677-3864

John Johnsich, Publisher

Over 400 publishers of real estate books and periodicals and their product lines are profiled in this directory.
Cost: $29.95
256 Pages
Frequency: Annual
ISBN: 0-914256-33-5
Founded in 1975

21151 Real Estate Data
DataQuick Information Systems
9620 Towne Centre Dr
San Diego, CA 92121-1963

858-455-6900
800-863-INFO
FAX 858-455-7848
E-Mail: customercare@dataquick.com
Home Page: www.dataquick.com

Sara Stephenson, Marketing

More than 12 million developed and undeveloped real properties in California, Arizona, Nevada, Oregon and Washington.
Frequency: Daily

21152 Real Estate RoundTable
GE Information Services
801 Pennsylvania Ave
NW Suite 720
Washing, DC 20004

202-639-8400
FAX 202-639-8442
E-Mail: info@rer.org
Home Page: www.rer.org

Cathy Ge, Owner
Clifton Rodgers, Senior Vice President

This database provides a forum for discussions between professional realtors and individuals interested in the buying and selling of residential and commercial property.
Frequency: Bulletin Board

21153 Real Estate Software Directory and Catalog
Z-Law Software

PO Box 40602
Providence, RI 02940-0602

401-273-5588
800-526-5588
FAX 401-421-5334
Home Page: www.z-law.com
Social Media: *Facebook*

Gary L Sherman, President

A comprehensive guide to real estate and mortgage banking software. Includes IBM and MAC applications for realtors, landlords, property managers, investors, developers, attorneys, contractors, appraisers, loan agents, and anyone in real estate.
Frequency: SemiAnnual

21154 Timeshare Multiple Listing Service
MDR Telecom
11965 Venice Boulevard
Suite 204
Los Angeles, CA 90066-3954

323-539-9701
800-423-6377
FAX 310-915-7212
E-Mail: triwest@att.net
Home Page: www.triwest-timeshare.com

Mario A Collura, Production Manager
Mario A Collura, Author

Approximately 6,000 pieces of timeshare real estate in the US, Mexico, and Carribean.
Cost: $10.00
60 Pages
Frequency: Monthly
ISBN: 1-888176-11-3
Founded in 1984

21155 Timeshare Vacation Owners HIP Resort Directory
TRI Publishing
11965 Venice Boulevard
Suite 204
Los Angeles, CA 90066-3954

800-423-6377
FAX 310-915-7212
Home Page: www.triwest-timeshare.com

Mario A Collura, President
Viccie Mac, Managing Editor

This is the only combined resort directory for buyers, owners and industry professionals. Over 3,000 resorts.
Cost: $18.95
111 Pages
Frequency: Every 2 Years
ISBN: 1-888176-12-1
Founded in 1995

21156 US Real Estate Register
Barry
312 Main St
Wilmington, MA 01887-2791

978-658-7174

Joe Barry, Owner

Offers information on real estate departments of large national companies, industrial organizations and chambers of commerce involved in real estate development.
Cost: $58.00
575 Pages
Frequency: Annual

21157 United National Real Estate Catalog
United National Real Estate
4700 Belleview Avenue
Kansas City, MO 64112-1315

816-561-1115
800-999-1020
FAX 816-231-5599

James Marinovich

Offers information on several thousand farms, ranches and country estates.
Cost: $4.95
200 Pages
Frequency: Semiannual

21158 Who's Who in Luxury Real Estate
JBL
2110 Western Avenue
Seattle, WA 98121-2110

206-441-7900
800-488-4066
FAX 206-441-5297

Approximately 500 international luxury real estate brokers.
Cost: $19.95
Frequency: Annual

Industry Web Sites

21159 http://gold.greyhouse.com
G.O.L.D Grey House OnLine Databases
Grey House Publishing's online database platform, GOLD, offers Quick Search, Keyword Search and Expert Search for most business sectors including real estate and allied markets. The GOLD platform makes finding the information you need quick and easy - whether you're a novice searcher or an experienced database user. All of Grey House's directory products are available for subscription on the GOLD platform.

21160 www.aagdallas.com
Apartment Association of Greater Dallas

21161 www.airea.com
American Industrial Real Estate Association
Encourages high professional standards. Has developed industrial multiple listing system and standard lease form. Publishes a quarterly newsletter

21162 www.americanhomeowners.org
American Homeowners Foundation
Serves as an educational and research consumer group offering books, model contracts, special studies, home buying, selling,investing, building, financing and remodeling.

21163 www.appraisalinstitute.org
Appraisal Institute
Promotes a code of ethics and uniform standards of the real estate appraisal practice. Publishes periodicals, books and appraisal-related materials, and sponsors courses and seminars.

21164 www.appraisers.org
American Society of Appraisers
Professional association of appraisers of all kinds.

21165 www.areuea.org
American Real Estate and Urban Economics Assoc
Addresses academic and commercial concerns in real estate and commercial economics.

21166 www.asfmra.org
American Soc of Farm Managers and Rural Appraisers
Provides professionals involved in rural property issues such as management and appraisal, with information on the industry as well as educational opportunities. Includes membership and information from the American Society of Farm Manager and Rural Appraisers.

21167 www.commercialsources.com
The official commercial real state site of the National Association Of Realtors.

21168 www.crb.com
Council of Real Estate Brokerage Managers
Members are real estate firm owners and managers.

21169 www.cre.org
Couselors of Real Estate
Association members provide the public with expert, objective advice on property and land related matters. Individuals invited to join are awarded the CRE designation.

21170 www.creonline.com
6440 Sky Pointe Dr.
Suite 140-187
Las Vegas, NV 89131

810-793-0261
Home Page: www.creonline.com
Social Media: *Facebook, Twitter, LinkedIn*

Jeanne Ekhaml, Operations
State-by-state and county-by-county listing of real estate investment clubs.

21171 www.erc.org
Employee Relocation Council
A national organization that examines key issues affecting the relocation industry for the benefit of corporations, government agencies, and firms or individuals providing specific services to relocated employees and their families. Accepts advertising.

21172 www.fiabci-usa.com
FIABCI-USA
Encourages private ownership of real property and understanding of property rights and obligations.

21173 www.greyhouse.com
Grey House Publishing
Authoritative reference directories for most business sectors including real estate and allied markets. Users can search the online databases with varied search criteria allowing for custom searches by product category, geographic area, sales volume, keyword, subject and more. Full Grey House catalog and online ordering also available.

21174 www.homestore.com
Homestore.com's family of sites is the leading destination for the home and the real estate- related information on the Internet. Provides informatin on Finance and Insurance, Home Improvement, Decorating, Lawn and garden, Home Electronics amd more.

21175 www.iaia.org
International Association for Impact Assessment
IAIA provides a forum for the exchange of the ideas and experiences to stimulate innovation in assessing, managing and mitigating the consequences of development.

21176 www.icsc.org
International Council of Shopping Centers
Fosters professional standards of performance in the development, construction, financing, leasing, management and operation of shopping centers throughout the world.

21177 www.nahma.org
National Affordable Housing Management Association
Trade association representing companies and individuals involved in the management of affordable multifamily housing.

21178 www.npma.org
National Property Management Association
Represents asset management professionals and keeps members a breast of trends in asset accountability technologies. Sponsors seminars, training courses: certification program.

21179 www.realtor.com
National Association of Realtors
Seeks to establish cooperation among brokers engaged in buying, selling, trading and leasing for realestate.

21180 www.realtylocator.com
Realty Locator
Over 100,000 real estate links nationwide in 10,000 cities and towns in all 50 states.

21181 www.reea.org
Real Estate Educators Association
Individuals involved in training and education.

21182 www.reipa.com
Real Estate Information Providers Association
Supports professional information providers in the real estate industry.

21183 www.relibrary.com/index.html
Real Estate Library
Contains essential resources for buyers, sellers, home owners and real estate professionals.

21184 www.rfpi.com/wrai.htm
National Residential Appraisers Institute
Promotes professionalism in the evaluation of residential real estate and requires demonstration appraisals and testing for professional certification.

Associations

21185 American Bakers Association

601 Pennsylvania Ave., NW
Suite 230
Washington, DC 20004

202-789-0300
FAX 202-898-1164
E-Mail: info@americanbakers.org
Home Page: americanbakers.org
Social Media: *Twitter, LinkedIn, YouTube, RSS*

Rich Scalise, Chairman
Fred Penny, First Vice Chairman
Bradley K. Alexander, Second Vice Chairman
Robb MacKie, President/ CEO
Erin Sharp, Treasurer

Represents the interests of bakers.
Founded in 1897

21186 American Bakers Institute

1300 I St Nw
Suite 700W
Washington, DC 20005

202-789-0300
FAX 202-898-1164
E-Mail: info@americanbakers.org
Home Page: www.americanbakers.org
Social Media: *Twitter, LinkedIn, YouTube, RSS*

Robb Mac Kie, President & CEO
James Hamilton, Counsel
Howard R. Alton, Chairman
Lee Sanders, Secretary
Albert Lepage, Treasurer

Association comprised of wholesale bakers.
300 Members
Founded in 1897

21187 American Culinary Federation

180 Center Place Way
St. Augustine, FL 32095

800-624-9458
FAX 904-940-0741
E-Mail: acf@acfchefs.net
Home Page: www.acfchefs.org
Social Media: *Facebook, Twitter, LinkedIn, RSS, Flickr*

Thomas J. Macrina, President
Michael Ty, Immediate Past President
William Tillinghast, Treasurer
Kyle Richardson, Secretary
Brian A. Hardy, Vice President, Central Region

Professional chefs' organization.
Founded in 1929

21188 American Culinary Federation: Chef & Child Foundation

180 Center Place Way
St Augustine, FL 32095

904-824-4468
800-624-9458
FAX 904-825-4758
E-Mail: acf@acfchefs.net
Home Page: www.acfchefs.org
Social Media: *Facebook, Twitter, Flickr, RSS*

Heidi Cramb, Executive Director
Thomas J. Macrina, Presiednt
James Taylor, Secretary
William Tillinghast, Treasurer
Michael Ty, Immediate Past President

Seeks to teach children proper nutrition and feed hungry children in the US.
20000 Members
Founded in 1929

21189 American Edged Products Manufacturers Association

30200 DetroitRd.
Westlake, OH 44145

440-899-0010
FAX 440-892-1404
E-Mail: info@aepma.org
Home Page: www.aepma.org
Social Media: *Facebook, Twitter, LinkedIn, You Tube*

J. Jeffery Wherry, Executive Director
Rick Joswick, VP
Alan Peppel, Treasurer
Bob Clemence, President
Gregory Borrosch, Associate Member Representative

Serves the marketing and manufacturing of the cutlery industry.
23 Members
Founded in 1951

21190 American Hotel and Lodging Association

1250 I Street, NW
Suite 1100
Washington, DC 20005

202-289-3100
FAX 202-289-3199
E-Mail: eiinfo@ahla.com
Home Page: www.ahla.com
Social Media: *Facebook, Twitter, LinkedIn*

Jim Abrahamson, Chair
Mark Carrier, Vice Chair
Geoff Ballotti, Secretary/ Treasurer
Katherine Lugar, President/ CEO
Joori Jeon, Executive Vice President & CFO

Organization focused on the needs of every aspect of the lodging industry.

21191 American Institute of Baking

1213 Bakers Way
Manhattan, KS 66505-3999

785-537-4750
800-633-5137
FAX 785-537-1493
E-Mail: sales@aibonline.org
Home Page: www.aibonline.org
Social Media: *Facebook, Twitter, LinkedIn*

Andrew Biane, President, CEO
Susan Hancock, Vice President, Innovation
Maureen Olewnik, Senior Vice President
Doug Markham, Director, People Processes
Tom Ogle, Chief Financial Officer

Committed to protecting the safety of the food supply chain worldwide and providing high value technical programs.
Founded in 1919

21192 American Institute of Wine and Food

P.O. Box 4961
Louisville, KY 40204

502-456-1851
800-274-2493
FAX 502-456-1821
E-Mail: info@aiwf.org
Home Page: www.aiwf.org
Social Media: *Facebook*

Frank Giaimo, National Chair
Mary Chamberlin, National Vice Chair
Drew Jaglom, National Secretary
George Linn, National Treasurer
Shannon Madison, Executive Committee Member

A nonprofit organization dedicated to advancing the understanding, appreciation and quality of wine and food.
Founded in 1981

21193 American Personal & Private Chef Associati on

4572 Delaware Streetÿ
San Diego, CA 92116

619-294-2436
800-644-8389
E-Mail: webmaster@personalchef.com
Home Page: www.personalchef.com
Social Media: *Facebook, Twitter, LinkedIn, Pinterest*

Candy Wallace, Founder, Executive Director

Organization for professional chefs.

21194 American Restaurant Association

PO Box 51482
Sarasota, FL 34232

941-379-2228
E-Mail:
info@americanrestaurantassociation.com
Home Page:
www.americanrestaurantassociation.com

Jerry Dalton, Vice President of Commodities

An organization for the entire restaurant business.
Founded in 1996

21195 American Society of Baking

7809 N Chestnut Avenue
Kansas City, MO 64119

800-713-0462
FAX 888-315-2612
E-Mail: info@asbe.org
Home Page: www.asbe.org
Social Media: *Facebook, Twitter, Google+*

Ramon Rivera, Chairman
Mario Somoza, 1st Vice Chairman
Wendi Ebbing, 2nd Vice Chairman
Bill Zimmerman, 3rd Vice Chairman
Teresa Ruder, Secretary/ Treasurer

Promoting the advancement of baking science and technology through the exchange of information and interaction among baking industry professionals.
Founded in 1924

21196 Association of Correctional Food Service Affiliates

PO Box 10065
Burbank, CA 91510

818-843-6608
FAX 818-843-7423
Home Page: www.acfsa.org
Social Media: *Facebook, Twitter, LinkedIn, Shutterfly*

Laurie Maurino, President
Robin Sherman, Past President
Timothy Thielman, Vice President
Carlos Salazar Jr., VP Elect / Treasurer
Linda Mills, Secretary

An organization dedicated to advancing all aspects of food service in correctional facilities.
Founded in 1969

21197 Commercial Food Equipment Service Association

3605 Centre Circle
Fort Mill, SC 29715

336-346-4700
336-346-4745
FAX 336-346-4745
E-Mail: pault@cfesa.com
Home Page: www.cfesa.com
Social Media: *Facebook, LinkedIn, YouTube*

Paul Toukatly, President
John Schwindt, Vice President
Gary Potvin, Vice President
Wayne Stoutner, Treasurer
David Hahn, Secretary

An organization for certified technicians servicing food equipment.
Founded in 1963

21198 Cookie and Snack Bakers Association
7517 Winton Drive
Indianapolis, IN 46268

888-789-3090
Home Page: casba.us

William H. Bennett, President
Kevin Boyle, Immediate Past President
Tom Lugar, Treasurer
Mike Kriegermeiery, Secretary
Craig S. Parrish, Executive Director
An organization for cookie and snack bakers.
Founded in 1970

21199 Cookware Manufacturers Association
PO Box 531335
Birmingham, AL 35253-1335

205-592-0389
FAX 205-599-5598
E-Mail: hrushing@usit.net
Home Page: www.cookware.org
Social Media: *Facebook, Twitter, LinkedIn, Pinterest*

Jay Zalinskas, President
Gene Karlson, VP
Hugh J Rushing, Executive VP
Represents manufactures of cookware and bakeware in the US and Canada. Publishes consumer guides to cookware and engineering standards for industry.
21 Members
Founded in 1920

21200 Council of State Restaurant Associations
2055 L St. NW
Washington, DC 20036

202-973-5377
E-Mail: admin@staterestaurantassociations.org
Home Page: staterestaurantassociations.org

Stan Harris, President
The Council works to promote the success of State Restaurant Associations.

21201 Foodservice Consultants Society International
P.O. Box 4961
Louisville, KY 40204

502-379-4122
E-Mail: Info@fcsi.org
Home Page: www.fcsi.org
Social Media: *Facebook, Twitter*

Jonathan Doughty, President
James Petersen, FCSI, Treasurer/ Secretary
Toni Clarke, FCSI, Board of Director
William Taunton, FCSI, Board of Director
Martin Rahmann, FCSI, Board of Director
A foodservice association with members in over 30 countries.
1000+ Members
Founded in 1955

21202 Green Restaurant Association
89 South Streety
Suite 802
Boston, MA 2111

617-737-3344
E-Mail: info@dinegreen.com
Home Page: www.dinegreen.com
Social Media: *Facebook, Twitter*

Nonprofit organization that provides information and resources for making aspects of restaurants more eco-friendly.
Founded in 1990

21203 Home Baking Association
2931 SW Gainsboro Road
Topeka, KS

785-478-3283
FAX 785-478-3024
E-Mail: hbapatton@aol.com
Home Page: www.homebaking.org
Social Media: *Facebook, Twitter, Flickr*

Sam Garlow, President
Tom Payne, 1st Vice President
Eric Wall, 2nd Vice President

National organization promoting scratch baking education and practice.
Founded in 1951

21204 International Association of Culinary Professionals
1221 Avenue of the Americas
42nd floor
New York, NY 10020

646-358-4957
866-358-4951
FAX 866-358-2524
E-Mail: membership@iacp.com
Home Page: www.iacp.com
Social Media: *Facebook, Twitter, LinkedIn, Vimeo, YouTube*

Martha Holmberg, Chief Executive Officer
Shani Phelan, Member Programs & Operations
Jeremy Mitchell, President
Raghavan Iyer, Past Chair
Margaret Bradley-Foley, Chair of the Board

A not for profit organization whose members represent virtually every profession in the culinary universe: teachers, cooking school owners, caterers, writers, chefs, media cooking personalities, editors, publishers, food stylists, food photographers, restauranteurs, leaders of major food corporations and vintners. Literally a who's who of the food world. Founded in 1978.
3000 Members
Founded in 1978

21205 International Caterers Association
3601 East Joppa Road
Baltimore, MD 21234

410-931-8100
FAX 410-931-8111
E-Mail: paulak@clemonsmgmt.com
Home Page: internationalcaterers.org
Social Media: *Facebook, Twitter, Instagram*

Jennifer Perna, President
Pat Christofolo, Immediate Past President
Jen Delaye, President's Council Chairy
Robin Selden, Treasurer
Jim Calato, Secretary

Organization for catering professionals.

21206 International Food Service Executives Association Headquarters
4955 Miller Street
Suite 107
Wheat Ridge, CO 80033

702-838-8821
800-893-5499
FAX 303-420-9579
E-Mail: ifseahqoffice@gmail.com
Home Page: www.ifsea.com
Social Media: *Facebook, Twitter, LinkedIn*

Grant Thompson, Chairman of the Board
Edward Manley, President/COO
David Orosz, International Chairman of the Board
Gina Vance, International Chairman of the Board

Provides education and community service to the foodservice industry.
3,000 Members
Founded in 1901

21207 James Beard Foundation
167 W 12th St
New York, NY 10011

212-675-4984
800-362-3273
FAX 212-645-1438
E-Mail: info@jamesbeard.org
Home Page: www.jamesbeard.org
Social Media: *Facebook, Twitter*

Susan Ungaro, President
Mitchell Davis, Executive Vice President
Marilyn Platzer, Chief Financial & Operating Officer
Nancy Kull, Executive Asst. to the President
Anna Mowry, Special Projects Manager
Nonprofit organization dedicated to preserving the country's culinary heritage and fostering the appreciation and development of gastronomy by recognizing and promoting excellence in all aspects of the culinary arts.
Founded in 1986

21208 Mobile Industrial Caterers' Association
7300 Artesia Boulevard
Buena Park, CA 90621-1804

714-632-6800
FAX 714-632-5405
Home Page: www.mobilecaterers.com

Kelly Ramirez, Executive Director

Aids with problems common within the industry through exchange of ideas, advice on legal problems, safety standards and licensing regulations.
185 Members
Founded in 1964

21209 National Association for Catering and Events
10440 Little Patuxent Parkway
Suite 300
Columbia, MD 21044

410-290-5410
FAX 410-630-5768
E-Mail: INFO@NACE.NET
Home Page: www.nace.net
Social Media: *Facebook, Twitter, LinkedIn, Pinterest, YouTube*

Joe Mahoney, President
Bonnie Fedchock, Executive Director
Donnell Bayot, Second Vice President
Kate Patay, CPCE, Secretary/ Treasurer
Lisa Hopkins Barry, Immediate Past President

Serves catering professionals and the vendors and suppliers that support them.
4000+ Members
Founded in 1950

21210 National Bar & Restaurant Management Association
307 Jackson Avenue W
Oxford, MS 38655

662-236-5510
800-247-3881
FAX 662-236-5541
E-Mail: jrobinson@oxpub.com
Home Page: www.nightclub.com
Social Media: *Facebook, Twitter, LinkedIn, Instagram, Vimeo*

Jon Taffer, President
Leo J. Squatrito, VP, Sale & Marketing
Erica Walsh, Marketing Manager
Greg Goulski, Director of Sales, Digital Media
Kristen Santoro, Content & Conference Dircetor

21211 National Council of Chain Restaurants

1101 New York Ave NW
Washington, DC 20005

202-783-7971
800-673-4692
FAX 202-737-2849
E-Mail: purviss@nrf.com
Home Page: nrf.com
Social Media: *Facebook, Twitter, LinkedIn, YouTube, Instagram, Flickr*

Matthew R. Shay, President
Kip Tindell, Chairman
Cicely Simpson, Treasurer
Mindy F. Grossman, Secretary
Mary Schell, Vice Chairman

A division of the National Retail Federation, NCCR was formed by a group of foodservice and restaurant executives who felt that they were not receiving adequate government relations representation from existing organizations. The NCCR helps shape federal legislative and regulatory issues that are of uniform significance to our member companies. Comprised of nearly 40 of the largest chain restaurant companies in the country.
Frequency: Inquire For Membership
Founded in 1965

21212 National Restaurant Association

2055 L Street NW
Suite 700
Washington, DC 20036

202-331-5900
800-424-5156
FAX 202-331-2429
Home Page: www.restaurant.org
Social Media: *Facebook, Twitter, YouTube*

Jack Crawford, Chair
Joe Kadow, Vice Chair
Jeff Davis, Treasurer
Dawn Sweeney, President/ Chief Executive Officer
Ed Beck, SVP, Technology

Striving to help members build customer loyalty, find financial success and provide rewarding careers in foodservice.
Founded in 1919

21213 North American Association of Food Equipment Manufacturers

161 North Clark Street
Suite 2020
Chicago, IL 60601

312-821-0201
FAX 312-821-0202
E-Mail: info@nafem.org
Home Page: www.nafem.org
Social Media: *Facebook, Twitter, LinkedIn*

Deirdre Flynn, Executive Vice President
Michael L. Whiteley, President
Joseph Carlson, Secretary/ Treasurer
Kevin Fink, President-Elect
Marianne Byrne, Marketing Manager

Dealers and distributors of foodservice equipment and supplies.
700 Members
Founded in 1979

21214 North American Association of Foodservice Equipment Manufacturers

161 North Clark Street
Suite 2020
Chicago, IL 60601

312-821-0201
FAX 312-821-0202
E-Mail: info@nafem.org

Home Page: www.nafem.org
Social Media: *Facebook*

Michael L. Whiteley, CFSP, President
Kevin Fink, CFSP, President-Elect
Joseph Carlson, CFSP, Secretary/Treasurer
Deirdre Flynn, CFSP, Executive Vice President
Charlie Souhrada, CFSP, Director, Member Services

Trade association for foodservice and food equipment manufacturers.

21215 Professional Chef's Association

P.O. Box 453
Frederick, CO 80530

720-379-8759
E-Mail: info@ProfessionalChef.com
Home Page: professionalchef.com
Social Media: *Facebook, Twitter, LinkedIn*

Organization for professional chefs.
Founded in 1997

21216 Restaurant Facility Management Association

5600 Tennyson Parkway
Suite 265
Plano, TX 75024

972-805-0905
FAX 972-805-0906
Home Page: www.rfmaonline.com

Kevin Carringer, Chair
Annaji Sailer, Board Vendor Representative
Roger Goldstein, Immediate Past Chair
John F. Getha, Treasurer
Nic Mclaughlin, Secretary

Association for restaurant facility management professionals.

21217 United States Personal Chef Association

7680 Universal Blvd.
Suite 550
Orlando, FL 32819

800-995-2138
E-Mail: info@uspca.com
Home Page: www.uspca.com
Social Media: *Facebook, Twitter, LinkedIn, RSS, Google+, YouTube*

Larry Lynch, President
Robert Lynch, Vice President
Vince Likar, Director of Member Service
Annise Jackson, Manager of Membership
Dan Chancellor, Marketing Manager

Organization offering all the necessary resources for those interested in starting their own personal chef business.
Founded in 1991

Newsletters

21218 AEPMA News & Views

American Edged Products Manufacturers Association
21165 Whitfield Pl
Suite 105
Sterling, VA 20165

703-433-9281
FAX 703-433-0369
E-Mail: info@aepma.org
Home Page: www.aepma.org

David Barrack, Executive Director
Robert Clemence, VP
Tom Arrowsmith, Treasurer

Serves the marketing and manufacturing of the cutlery industry.
Frequency: Twice/Year

21219 American Culinary Federation Newsletter

American Culinary Federation
180 Center Place Way
St Augustine, FL 32095-8859

904-824-4468
800-624-9458
FAX 904-825-4758
Home Page: www.acfchefs.org

Heidi Cramb, Executive Director
Edward G Leonard, President
Brent T. Frei, Director of Marketing
Kay Orde, Editor
Michael Feierstein, Administrative Assistant

The official membership newsletter of the American Culinary Federation.
Frequency: Monthly
Circulation: 21000
Founded in 1929
Printed in 2 colors on matte stock

21220 Baker's Math

American Bakers Institute
1300 I St Nw
Suite 700W
Washington, DC 20005-7203

202-789-0300
FAX 202-898-1164
Home Page: www.americanbakers.org

Robb Mac Kie, President

21221 CHRIE Communique

Int'l Council on Hotel, Restaurant Institute Edu.
2810 North Parham Road
suite 230
Richmond, VA 23294-3006

804-747-4971
FAX 804-346-5009
E-Mail: publications@chrie.org
Home Page: www.chrie.org

Dale Gaddy, Publisher
Mike Zema, President
Kathy McCarty, CEO
Joseph Bradley, Treasurer

Monthly newsletter offering information on industry, significant hospitality and tourism education job listings.
Cost: $65.00
Frequency: Monthly
Circulation: 1800
Founded in 1946

21222 Cameron's Foodservice Marketing Reporter

Cameron's Publications
5423 Sheridan Drive
PO Box 676
Williamsville, NY 14231

519-586-8785
FAX 519-586-8816
E-Mail: products@cameronpub.com
Home Page: www.cameronpub.com

Nina T Cameron, Editor
Bob McClelland, Publisher
Peggy Kelly, Circulation Manager

Successful promotion and advertising case histories for the restaurant and hotel industry.
Cost: $197.00
Frequency: Fortnightly
Founded in 1970

21223 Center of the Plate

American Culinary Federation
180 Center Place Way
St Augustine, FL 32095-8859

904-824-4468
800-624-9458
FAX 904-825-4758

E-Mail: acf@acfchefs.net
Home Page: www.acfchefs.org

Heidi Cramb, Executive Director
Edward Leonard, Administrative Assistant
Michael Feierstein, Administrative Assistant
Bryan Hunt, Graphic Designer
Patricia Carroll, Director of Communications

Official membership newsletter of the American Culinary Federation.
Cost: $50.00
Frequency: Monthly
Circulation: 25000+
Founded in 1929

21224 Wine on Line Food and Wine Review
Enterprise Publishing
PO Box 328
Blair, NE 68008-0328

402-426-2121
FAX 402-426-2227
E-Mail: news@enterprisepub.com
Home Page: www.enterprisepub.com

Mark Rhoades, President
Dough Barber, Editor
Lynette Hansen, Sales Manager
Bill Smutko, Circulation Manager
Dave Smith, Production Manager

Reviews, feature articles and information on all areas of food and wine, including restaurants, hotels, trains and airlines. Accepts advertising.
Cost: $36.00
10 Pages
Circulation: 13150
Founded in 1800

Magazines & Journals

21225 Chain Store Information Guide
3922 Coconut Palm Dr
Tampa, FL 33619

800-778-9794
FAX 813-627-6888
Home Page: www.chainstoreguide.com

A national organization that serves the commercial and institutional food and lodging industry.
Founded in 1967

21226 Cheers
257 Park Avenue S
3rd Floor, Suite 303
New York, NY 10010

212-967-1551
FAX 646-654-2099

John Eastman, Owner

Every issue is designed to help on-premise operators enhance the profitability of their beverage operations.

21227 Chef
Talcott Communications Corporation
20 N Wacker Dr
Suite 3900
Chicago, IL 60606-3188

312-726-2410
FAX 312-726-2554
Home Page: www.ucco.com/tc.htm

Laura Herold, President
Rob Benes, Senior Editor
Morgan Holzman, Contributing Editor
David Pizzimenti, Circulation Manager

Information on food production and presentation, includes chef profiles, trend studies, marketing information and restaurant profiles.
Cost: $32.00
Frequency: Monthly
Circulation: 38769

ISSN: 1087-061X
Founded in 1956
Printed in 4 colors on glossy stock

21228 Coffee & Cuisine
Coffee Talk
1218 3rd Avenue
#1315
Seattle, WA 98101-3021

206-521-7247
FAX 206-623-0446
Home Page: www.coffeecuisine.com

Kerri Goodman, Publisher

Covers new products, personnel moves, industry news, how to articles, education, and techniques to increase sales growth for the coffee, cold beverage and foodservice industry.
Cost: $36.00
Frequency: Monthly
Circulation: 30000

21229 Cooking for Profit
CP Publishing
PO Box 267
Fond du Lac, WI 54936-267

920-923-3700
FAX 920-923-6805
E-Mail: comments@cookingforprofit.com
Home Page: www.cookingforprofit.com

Colleen Phalen, Editor-in-Chief

Paid subscription trade magazine targeted to foodservice owners, managers and chefs. Each month features current trends in food preparation with step-by-step recipes and photographs; effective management techniques; and the latest in foodservice equipment — all written by industry experts. Also features in-depth profiles of a successful foodservice operation.
Cost: $26.00
28 Pages
Frequency: Monthly
Founded in 1932
Printed in 4 colors on glossy stock

21230 Cornell Hotel & Restaurant Administration Quarterly
Elsevier Science Publishing Company
537 Statler Hall
Ithaca, NY 14853-6902

607-255-9780
FAX 607-254-2922
E-Mail: hosp_research@cornell.edu
Home Page: www.hotelschool.cornell.edu

Dr. Michael Sturman, Editor
Glenn Withiam, Executive Editor
Nicole Roach, Marketing

A journal devoted to the development and exchange of management ideas for the hospitality industry.
Cost: $113.00
Frequency: Quarterly
Circulation: 4500
Founded in 1963

21231 Culinary Trends
Culinary Trends Publications
6285 E Spring Street
#107
Long Beach, CA 90808-4000

310-496-2558
FAX 310-421-8993
Home Page: www.culinarytrends.com

Fred Mensigna, Publisher
Linda Mensinga, Editor

Information for food and beverage managers along with managers of hotels and restaurants.
Cost: $21.60
Frequency: Quarterly
Circulation: 10000

21232 El Restaurante Mexicano
Maiden Name Press
1010 Lake St
Suite 604
Oak Park, IL 60301-1136

708-848-3200
800-407-5845
FAX 708-445-9477
E-Mail: kfurore@restmex.com
Home Page: www.restmex.com

Joe Madden, President
Kathleen Furore, Managing Director
Jessica Pantanini, Managing Director

A bilingual magazine featuring industry specific food news, features restaurant profiles and new product information for personnel of restaurants serving mexican/southwestern menu items nationwide.
Cost: $18.00
Circulation: 27000
Founded in 1997

21233 FEDA News & Views
Foodservice Equipment Distributors Association
223 W Jackson Boulevard
#620
Chicago, IL 60606-6911

312-427-9605
FAX 312-427-9607
E-Mail: feda@feda.com
Home Page: www.feda.com

Stacy Ward, Managing Editor
Ray Herrick, Executive VP
Adela Ramos, Administration Director, Manager
Bruce Gulbas, President

Focus is on sales, technology, new products and other areas of benefit to dealers, as well as industry trends and news.
Cost: $150.00
Circulation: 1200
Founded in 1933

21234 Food & Beverage News
Food & Beverage News
1886 W Bay Drive
#E6
Largo, FL 33770-3017

727-585-7745
FAX 727-585-7245
Home Page: www.fbnews.com

Dennis J Regan, Publisher

News on the latest liquor law, new products, and government legislation.
Cost: $28.00
Frequency: Monthly
Circulation: 16,880

21235 Food Arts Magazine
M Shanken Communications
387 Park Ave S
Suite 8
New York, NY 10016-8872

212-684-4224
FAX 212-684-5424
Home Page: www.cigaraficionado.com

Marvin Shanken, Publisher

A magazine devoted to the restaurant industry.
Cost: $40.00
Frequency: Monthly
Founded in 1988

21236 Foodservice Equipment & Supplies Specialist
Reed Business Information

1350 E Touhy Avenue
Des Plaines, IL 60018-3358

630-320-7000
FAX 630-288-8686
Home Page: www.reedbusiness.com

Mitchell Schechter, Editor-in-Chief
Niles Crum, Publisher

Magazine for professionals who specify, sell
and distribute foodservice equipment, supplies
and furnishings.
Cost: $69.95
64+ Pages
Frequency: Monthly
Circulation: 27M
Founded in 1947
Printed in 4 colors on glossy stock

21237 Foodservice Equipment Reports
Robin Ashton
2000 Clearwater Drive
Oak Brook, IL 60523-3358

630-288-8000
800-446-6551
FAX 630-288-8265
E-Mail: webmaster@reedbusiness.com
Home Page: www.reedbusiness.com

Josph Carbonara, Editor-in-Chief
Maureen Slocum, Publisher
Keithy Mcnamara, Marketing
katy Tucker, Circulation Manager
Jeff Greisph, CEO

Geared toward manufacturers of foodservice
equipment and their agencies.
Cost: $106.90
Frequency: Monthly
Circulation: 22719
Founded in 1947

21238 Franchise Times
2808 Anthony Lane S
Minneapolis, MN 55418

612-767-3200
800-528-3296
FAX 612-767-3230
E-Mail: info@franchisetimes.com
Home Page: www.franchisetimes.com

Mary Jo Larson, Publisher
Nancy Weingartner, Executive Editor
Beth Ewen, Managing Editor

Investigative pieces, analysis and profiles to
help franchisors, franchisees and vendors improve their businesses.
Frequency: 10x/year

21239 Fresh Cup Magazine
Fresh Cup Publishing Company
537 SE Ash Street Suite 300
PO Box 14827
Portland, OR 97293-827

503-236-2587
800-868-5866
FAX 503-236-3165
E-Mail: jan@freshcup.com
Home Page: www.freshcup.com

Julie Beals, Editor
Nicole Maas, Sales/Marketing Associate
Bill Berninger, Circulation Director
Ward Barbee, Publisher
Jan Gibson, Owner
Cost: $57.00
68 Pages
Frequency: Monthly
Circulation: 14000
Founded in 1992
Printed in 4 colors on glossy stock

21240 Full-Service Restaurant
Home Page: www.fsrmagazine.com
Social Media: *Facebook, Twitter*

Greg Sanders, Group Publisher
Connie Gentry, Editor

Ideas and insights for decision-makers in
full-service restaurant industry.
Founded in 2012

21241 Gourmet News
Oser Communications Group
1877 N Kolb Road
Tucson, AZ 85715

520-721-1300
Home Page: www.gourmetnews.com

Rocelle Aragon, Editor
Kate Seymour, Senior Associate Publisher

The business newspaper for the gourmet indus-
try.
40 Pages
Frequency: Monthly
Circulation: 23381
ISSN: 1052-4630
Founded in 1991
Printed in 4 colors on glossy stock

**21242 Journal of Foodservice Business
Research**
Taylor & Francis
325 Chestnut Street
Suite 800
Philadelphia, PA 19106

800-354-1420
FAX 215-625-2940
Home Page: www.tandf.co.uk

David A Cranage, Editor

Features articles from international experts in
various disciplines, including management,
marketing, finance, law, food technology, nutrition, psychology, information systems, anthropology, human resources, and more.
Cost: $ 92.00
Frequency: Quarterly
ISSN: 1537-8020
Founded in 1978

21243 Midsouthwest Restaurant
3800 North Portland Avenue
Oklahoma City, OK 73112-2982

405-942-8181
800-375-8181
FAX 405-942-0541
Home Page: www.okrestaurants.com

Jim Hopper, President/CEO
Shannon Moad, Editor
Debra Bailey, Deputy Director
Frequency: Quarterly
Circulation: 2500
Founded in 1933

21244 Nation's Restaurant News
Lebhar-Friedman Publications
425 Park Ave
Suite 6
New York, NY 10022-3526

212-756-5220
FAX 212-756-5250
E-Mail: info@lf.com

Lebhar Friedman, Publisher
Michael Cardillo, VP Sales
Leslie Wolowitz, Advertising

Serves commercial and onsite food service and
lodging establishments including restaurants,
schools, universities, hospitals, nursing homes
and other health and welfare facilities, hotels
and motels with food service, government installations, clubs and other related firms.
Cost: $44.95
Frequency: Weekly
Circulation: 85999

Founded in 1925
*Mailing list available for rent: 100,000 names
at $100 per M*
Printed in 4 colors on matte stock

21245 National Culinary Review
American Culinary Federation
180 Center Place Way
St Augustine, FL 32095-8859

904-824-4468
800-624-9458
FAX 904-825-4758
Home Page: www.acfchefs.org

Heidi Cramb, Executive Director
Edward G Leonard, Administrative Assistant
Michael Feierstein, Administrative Assistant
Bryan Hunt, Graphic Designer
Patricia Carroll, Director of Communications

Accepts advertising.
Cost: $50.00
Frequency: Monthly
Founded in 1929

21246 National Dipper
US Exposition Corporation
1028 W. Devon Avenue
Elk Grove Village, IL 60007

847-301-8400
FAX 847-301-8402
E-Mail: lynda@nationaldipper.com
Home Page: www.nationaldipper.com

Lynda Utterback, Publisher

Information for retail ice cream and frozen yo-
gurt owners and operators, includes changes
and developments in the business.
Cost: $55.00
Circulation: 17000
Founded in 1985
Printed in 4 colors on glossy stock

21247 Quick Service Restaurant
Home Page: www.qsrmagazine.com
Social Media: *Facebook, Twitter*

Greg Sanders, Group Publisher
Sam Oches, Editor

Leading source of news about "limited-service"
restaurant industry.

21248 Restaurant Digest
Panagos Publishing
3930 Knowles Avenue
#305
Kensington, MD 20895-2428

301-929-6200
FAX 301-929-6550
Home Page: www.foodservicedepot.com

Bruce Panagos, Publisher

Developments and news of interest to owners,
managers, and operators of dining and entertainment establishments in the region.

21249 Restaurant Hospitality
Donohue/Meehan Publishing
1801 E 9th St
Suite 920
Cleveland, OH 44114-3103

216-931-7258
FAX 216-696-1752
E-Mail: rheditor@penton.com
Home Page: www.restaurant-hospitality.com

Jeff Donohoe, President
Jess Grossberg, Publisher
Gail Bellamy, Managing Editor
Sue Apple, Production Manager
Frequency: Monthly
Circulation: 117,721
Founded in 1892

21250 Restaurant Marketing
Oxford Publishing

Ste 1
1903b University Ave
Oxford, MS 38655-4150

662-236-5510
800-247-3881
FAX 662-281-0104
Home Page: www.restaurant-marketing.net
Frequency: Bi-Monthly

21251 Restaurant Wine
Wine Profits
PO Box 222
Napa, CA 94559-222

707-224-4777
FAX 707-224-6740
Home Page: www.restaurantwine.com
Ronn Wiegand, Publisher
Paul Grieco, Co-Owner

Information on the marketing of wine in restaurants, hotels and clubs, wine and food pairing ideas and review of wines.
Cost: $99.00
Frequency: Monthly
Circulation: 3000
ISSN: 1040-7030
Printed in 2 colors on matte stock

21252 Restaurants & Institutions
Reed Business Information
2000 Clearwater Dr
Oak Brook, IL 60523-8809

630-574-0825
FAX 630-288-8781
E-Mail: jamie.popp@reedbusiness.com
Home Page: www.reedbusiness.com
Jeff Greisch, President
Scott Hume, Managing Editor

Commercial and noncommercial foodservice establishments including restaurant, hotels, motels, fast-food chains,coffee shops, food stores with foodservice
Frequency: Monthly
Circulation: 155512
Founded in 1937
Printed in 4 colors on glossy stock

21253 Restaurants USA
National Restaurant Association
1200 17th St NW
Washington, DC 20036-3006

202-331-5900
800-424-5156
FAX 202-331-2429
Home Page: www.restaurant.org
Dawn M Sweeney, CEO
Sarah Hamaker, Treasurer
Phil Hickey, Treasurer

A trade magazine offering information for restaurant owners and managers, including industry trends, operational pointers, management principles and association activities.
Cost: $125.00
48 Pages
Frequency: Monthly
Circulation: 44000
Founded in 1980
Printed in 4 colors

21254 Restaurants, Resorts & Hotels
Publishing Group
PO Box 318
Trumbull, CT 06611-0318

860-279-0149
FAX 203-254-7104

James Martone, Publisher

Information on new products, supplies, food and equipment for those executives and manag-

ers who have responsibility for the food.
Cost: $24.00
Frequency: Monthly
Circulation: 97,000

21255 Southeast Food Service News
8805 Tamiami Trail N #301
Naples, FL 34108

239-514-1258
E-Mail: efischer@sfsn.com
Home Page: www.sfsn.com
Social Media: *Y*

Elliott R Fischer, Marketing Director
John P Hayward, Account Executive
Elsie Olson, Production Manager
Frequency: Monthly
Founded in 1977

21256 Southwest Food Service News
4011 W Plano Pkwy
Suite 121
Plano, TX 75093-5620

972-943-1254
FAX 972-943-1258
Home Page: www.southwestfoodservice.com

Sam Ballard, Publisher

21257 Total Food Service
PO Box 2507
Greenwich, CT 06836-2507

203-661-9090
FAX 203-661-9325
Home Page: www.totalfood.com

Fred Klashman, President

21258 Yankee Food Service
Griffin Publishing Company
201 Oak St
Suite A
Pembroke, MA 02359

781-294-4700
866-677-4700
FAX 781-829-0134
E-Mail: info@griffinpublishing.net
Home Page: www.griffinpublishing.net
Kevin Griffin, President
Lynda Bassett, Editor
Henry Zacchini, Associate Publisher
Karen Harty, Vice President
Julie Mignosa, Office Manager

Reports news and happenings of the food service industry in New England.
Cost: $47.00
48 Pages
Frequency: Monthly
Circulation: 26110
Founded in 1979

Trade Shows

21259 AEPMA Annual Meeting
American Edged Products Manufacturers Association
21165 Whitfield Pl
Suite 105
Sterling, VA 20165

703-433-9281
FAX 703-433-0369
E-Mail: info@aepma.org
Home Page: www.aepma.org

David Barrack, Executive Director
Robert Clemence, VP
Tom Arrowsmith, Treasurer

Offering training and certificate programs, and management courses.
Frequency: Annual

21260 American Culinary Federation Central Regional Conference
American Culinary Federation
10 San Bartola Drive
Saint Augustine, FL 32085

904-824-4468
800-624-9458
FAX 904-825-4758
E-Mail: acf@acfchefs.net
Home Page: www.acfchefs.org

Brent Frei, Director Marketing
Michael Baskette, Administrative Assistant
Michael Feierstein, Administrative Assistant
Bryan Hunt, Graphic Designer
Patricia Carroll, Director of Communications

Culinary equipment, supplies and services. Seminars, workshops, cooking demos, more.

21261 American Culinary Federation National Convention
10 San Bartola Drive
Saint Augustine, FL 32086

904-824-4468
800-624-9458
FAX 904-825-4758
E-Mail: acf@acfchefs.net
Home Page: www.acfchefs.org

Brent Frei, Director Marketing
Michael Baskette, Administrative Assistant
Michael Feierstein, Administrative Assistant
Bryan Hunt, Graphic Designer
Patricia Carroll, Director of Communications

200 booths of products and foodstuffs for the food service industry. Seminars, workshops, cooking demos, more.

21262 American Culinary Federation Northeast Regional Conference
American Culinary Federation
10 San Bartola Drive
Saint Augustine, FL 32086

904-824-4468
800-624-9458
FAX 904-825-4758
E-Mail: acf@acfchefs.net
Home Page: www.acfchefs.org

Brent Frei, Director Marketing
Michael Baskette, Administrative Assistant
Michael Feierstein, Administrative Assistant
Bryan Hunt, Graphic Designer
Patricia Carroll, Director of Communications

Culinary equipment, supplies and services. Seminars, workshops, cooking demos, more.

21263 American Culinary Federation Southeast Regional Conference
American Culinary Federation
10 San Bartola Drive
Saint Augustine, FL 32086

904-824-4468
800-624-9458
FAX 904-825-4758
E-Mail: acf@acfchefs.net
Home Page: www.acfchefs.org

Brent Frei, Director Marketing
Michael Baskette, Administrative Assistant
Michael Feierstein, Administrative Assistant
Bryan Hunt, Graphic Designer
Patricia Carroll, Director of Communications

Culinary equipment, supplies and services. Seminars, workshops, cooking demos, more.

21264 American Culinary Federation Western Regional Conference
American Culinary Federation
10 San Bartola Drive
Saint Augustine, FL 32086

904-824-4468
800-624-9458

FAX 904-825-4758
E-Mail: acf@acfchefs.net
Home Page: www.acfchefs.org

Brent Frei, Director Marketing
Michael Baskette, Administrative Assistant
Michael Feierstein, Administrative Assistant
Bryan Hunt, Graphic Designer
Patricia Carroll, Director of Communications

Culinary equipment, supplies and services.
Seminars, workshops, cooking demos, more.

21265 Annual Hotel, Motel and Restaurant Supply Show of the Southeast

Leisure Time Unlimited
708 Main Street
PO Box 332
Myrtle Beach, SC 29577

843-448-9483
800-261-5991
FAX 843-626-1513
E-Mail: hmrss@sc.rr.com
Home Page: www.hmrsss.com

Brooke P Baker, Show Director

Trade show for the hospitality industry.
23000 Attendees
Frequency: January
Founded in 1975

21266 Fancy Food Show

Specialty Food Association, Inc.
136 Madison Avenue
12th Floor
New York, NY 10016

212-482-6440
FAX new
Home Page: www.specialtyfood.com

Mike Silver, Chair
Becky Renfro Borbolla, Treasurer
Dennis Deschaine, Past Chairperson
Shawn McBride, Vice Chair
Matt Nielsen, Secretary

Over 80,000 on-trend and best-in-class products, including confections, cheese, coffee, snacks, spices, ethnic, natural, organic and more. 1,300 exhibitors representing specialty foods and beverages from across the United States and 35 countries and regions.

21267 Hospitality Food Service Expo Southeast and Atlanta International Wine

Reed Business Information
275 Washington Street
Boston, MA 02458

617-261-1166
FAX 617-558-4327
Home Page: www.cahners.com

Patrick Paleno, Show Manager
Barry Reed Jr, CFO
Stuart Whayman, CFO

400 booths featuring educational seminars, culinary salon, and exhibits of products and services.
12M Attendees
Frequency: October

21268 National Restaurant Association: Restaurant, Hotel-Motel Show

1200 17th Street NW
Washington, DC 20036-3006

202-331-5900
Home Page: http://www.nraef.org

Reed Hayes, President, Chief Operating Officer
Steven Anderson, President

1,800 booths for the food service industry exhibiting food and beverages.
105M Attendees
Frequency: May

21269 Restaurant Innovation Summit

National Restaurant Association
2055 L St. NW
Suite 700
Washington, DC 20036

202-331-5900
800-424-5156
FAX 202-331-2429
Home Page:
www.restaurant.org/Events-Networking/Events
Social Media: *Facebook, Twitter*

Jack Crawford, Chairman

Innovations in technology and how they may be applied to the restaurant industry.
Frequency: Annual

21270 Year of Enchantment

Int'l Council on Hotel, Restaurant Institute Edu.
1200 17th Street NW
Washington, DC 20036-3006

202-467-6300
E-Mail: publications@chrie.org
Home Page: www.chrie.org

Susan Gould, Manager
Joseph Bradley, Treasurer

Containing 70+ booths and 50+ exhibits.
750 Attendees
Frequency: August
Founded in 1946

Directories & Databases

21271 Chain Restaurant Operators Directory

Chain Store Guide
3922 Coconut Palm Dr
Tampa, FL 33619-1389

813-627-6700
800-972-9202
FAX 813-627-7094
E-Mail: info@csgis.com
Home Page: www.csgis.com

Mike Jarvis, Publisher
Arthur Sciarrotta, Senior VP

Discover more than 5,600 listings and more than 26,000 unique personnel within the Restaurant Chain, Foodservice Management, and Hotel/Motel Operator markets in the U.S. and Canada. Each company must have at least $1 million in annual sales either system wide or industry and have two or more units/accounts.
Cost: $335.00
Frequency: Annual

21272 Culinary Collection Directory

International Association/Culinary Professionals
304 W Liberty Street
Suite 201
Louisville, KY 40202

502-587-7953
800-928-4227
FAX 502-589-3602
E-Mail: info@iacp.com
Home Page: www.iacp.com

Kerry Edwards, Sr Member Services Representative
Trina Gribbins, Manager

Teachers, cooking school owners, caterers, writers, chefs, media cooking personalities, editors, publishers, food stylists, food photographers, restauranteurs, leaders of major food corporations and vintners. Literally a who's who of the food world.

21273 Food & Beverage Market Place

Grey House Publishing
4919 Route 22
PO Box 56
Amenia, NY 12501

518-789-8700
800-562-2139
FAX 845-373-6390
E-Mail: books@greyhouse.com
Home Page: www.greyhouse.com
Social Media: *Facebook, Twitter*

Leslie Mackenzie, Publisher
Richard Gottlieb, Editor

This information packed three-volume set is the most powerful buying and marketing guide for the US food and beverage industry. Includes thousands of industry freight and transportation listings.
Cost: $595.00
2000 Pages
Frequency: Annual
ISBN: 1-592373-61-5
Founded in 1981

21274 Food & Beverage Marketplace: Online Database

Grey House Publishing
4919 Route 22
PO Box 56
Amenia, NY 12501

518-789-8700
800-562-2139
FAX 845-373-6390
E-Mail: gold@greyhouse.com
Home Page: http://gold.greyhouse.com
Social Media: *Facebook, Twitter*

Richard Gottlieb, President
Leslie Mackenzie, Publisher

This complete updated Food & Beverage Market Place: Online Database is the go-to source for the food and beverage industry. Anyone involved in the food and beverage industry needs this 'industry bible' and the important contacts to develop critical research data that can make for successful business growth.
Frequency: Annual
Founded in 1981

21275 Getaways for Gourmets in the Northeast

Wood Pond Press
365 Ridgewood Rd
West Hartford, CT 06107-3517

860-521-0389
FAX 860-313-0185
Home Page: www.green-cuisine.com

Richard M Woodworth, Owner

Directory of services and supplies to the industry.
Cost: $14.95
514 Pages

21276 High Volume Independent Restaurants Database

Chain Store Guide
3922 Coconut Palm Dr
Tampa, FL 33619-1389

813-627-6700
800-778-9794
FAX 813-627-7094
E-Mail: info@csgis.com
Home Page: www.csgis.com

Mike Jarvis, Publisher
Shami Choon, Manager

Covers this growing niche through its nearly 5,900 listings featuring casual dining, family restaurants and fine dining establishments. Plus, access to over 15,000 key personnel names puts you in contact with key decision

makers.
Cost: $335.00
1,000 Pages
Frequency: Annual

21277 International Association of Culinary Professionals
304 W Liberty Street
Suite 201
Louisville, KY 40202

502-587-7953
800-928-4227
FAX 502-589-3602
E-Mail: info@iacp.com
Home Page: www.iacp.com

Kerry Edwards, Sr Member Services Representative
Trina Gribbins, Manager

A not for profit organization whose members represent virtually every profession in the culinary universe: teachers, cooking school owners, caterers, writers, chefs, media cooking personalities, editors, publishers, food stylists, food photographers, restauranteurs, leaders of major food corporations and vintners. Literally a who's who of the food world. Founded in 1978.

21278 Restaurant Hospitality: Hospitality 500 Issue
Penton Media
1166 Avenue of the Americas
New York, NY 10036

212-204-4200
FAX 216-696-6662
E-Mail: information@penton.com
Home Page: www.penton.com
Social Media: *Facebook, Twitter, LinkedIn*

Jane Cooper, Marketing
Chris Meyer, Director
Bev Walter, Service Manager

500 independent restaurants selected on basis of sales.
Cost: $25.00
Frequency: Annual, June
Circulation: 123,000

21279 Restaurants and Institutions: Annual 400 Issues
Reed Business Information
1350 E Touhy Avenue
Suite 200E
Des Plaines, IL 60018-3358

847-962-2200
FAX 630-288-8686
Home Page: www.reedbusiness.com

Roland Dietz, CEO
Stuart Whayman, CFO
Cost: $25.00
Frequency: Annual
Circulation: 16,000

21280 Zagat.com Restaurant Guides
Zagat Survey
4 Columbus Cir
New York, NY 10019-1180

212-977-6000
FAX 212-977-9760
E-Mail: customerservice@zagat.com
Home Page: www.zagat.com

Tim Zagat, CEO

Zagat.com was launched in May of 1999 and contains the most trusted and authoritive dining information online for over 20,000 restaurants in twenty eight cities worldwide, with 17 more cities to be added shortly. Based in New York City, the Zagat survey was founded in 1979 by Tim and Nina Zagat.

Industry Web Sites

21281 http://gold.greyhouse.com
G.O.L.D Grey House OnLine Databases

Grey House Publishing's online database platform, GOLD, offers Quick Search, Keyword Search and Expert Search for most business sectors including restaurant markets. The GOLD platform makes finding the information you need quick and easy - whether you're a novice searcher or an experienced database user. All of Grey House's directory products are available for subscription on the GOLD platform.

21282 www.acfchefs.org
American Culinary Federation

Member organization of professional chefs and cooks. Certifies chefs, accredits culinary programs and promotes culinary arts.

21283 www.chefcertification.com
American Culinary Federation

Offers the required courses for ACF certification online.

21284 www.chowbaby.com

This web site is search engine for restaurants.It makes finding the perfect eatery close to your home or travel destination. Online reservations, maps, menus and more. You can search by Internatinal Location, US Location, US Map, or Cuisine type.

21285 www.chrie.org
Int'l Council on Hotel, Restaurant Institute Edu.

To enhance professionalism at all levels of the hospitality and tourism industry through education and training.

21286 www.greyhouse.com
Grey House Publishing

Authoritative reference directories for most business sectors including restaruant markets. Users can search the online databases with varied search criteria allowing for custom searches by product category, geographic area, sales volume, keyword, subject and more. Full Grey House catalog and online ordering also available.

21287 www.iacp.com
International Association of Culinary Professionals

A not for profit organization whose members represent virtually every profession in the culinary universe: teachers, cooking school owners, caterers, writers, chefs, media cooking personalities, editors, publishers, food stylists, food photographers, restauranteurs, leaders of major food corporations and vintners. Literally a who's who of the food world. Founded in 1978.

21288 www.ifsea.org
International Food Service Executives

Provides education and community service to the foodservice industry.

21289 www.restaurant.org
National Restaurant Association

Trends, government affairs, training, research, dining guides and links.

21290 www.therestaurantfinder.com

This search engine help to find restaurants by type or location.

Associations

21291 American Beverage Licensees
5101 River Rd
Suite 108
Bethesda, MD 20816-1560

301-656-1494
FAX 301-656-7539
E-Mail: info@ablusa.org
Home Page: www.ablusa.org
Social Media: *Facebook, Twitter, RSS*

John D. Bodnovich, Executive Director
Warren Scheidt, President
Raymond Cox, Treasurer
Terry Harvath, Vice President
John Moran, Vice President

Supports all those involved with the retailing of beverages.
20000 Members

21292 American Booksellers Association
333 Westchester Avenue
Suite S202
White Plains, NY 10604

914-406-7500
800-637-0037
FAX 914-417-4013
E-Mail: info@bookweb.org
Home Page: www.bookweb.org
Social Media: *Facebook, Twitter, YouTube*

Oren Teicher, CEO
Dan Cullen, Content Officer
Eleanor Chang, CFO
Betsy Burton, President
Robert Sindelar, Vice President/Secretary

Trade organization pledge to protecting the well-being of book retailers and promoting the availability of books.
2000 Members
Founded in 1900

21293 American Collegiate Retailing Association
Loyola University/Department of Marketing
6363 Saint Charles Avenue
New Orleans, LA 70118-6195

504-865-2011
FAX 504-865-3496
Home Page: www.acraretail.org

Rodney Runyan, President
Jane Swinney, Vice President
Robert Paul Jones, Secretary
Susan S. Fiorito, Treasurer
Leigh Sparks, Member-at-Large

Organization of faculty from colleges with a background in retailing.
400 Members
Founded in 1950

21294 American Mobile Retail Association
213-785-4783
E-Mail: info@americanmra.com
Home Page:
americanmobileretailassociation.blogspot.ca
Social Media: *Facebook, Twitter*

Stacey Jischke-Steffe, Co-Founder/President
Jeanine Romo, Co-Founder/Vice President

Support and assistance for mobile retailers.

21295 Associated Surplus Dealers/Associated Merchandise Dealers
ASD/AMD Merchandise Group
2950 31st Street
Suite 100
Santa Monica, CA 90405-3037

310-396-6006
800-421-4511

FAX 310-399-2662
Home Page: www.merchandisegroup.com

Leading producer of trade shows and publications in the variety and general merchandise industry.
15000 Members
Founded in 1961

21296 Association for Retail Technology
1101 New York Ave NW
Washington, DC 20005

202-783-7971
800-673-4692
FAX 202-737-2849
E-Mail: arts@nrf.com
Home Page: www.nrf.com
Social Media: *Facebook, Twitter, LinkedIn, YouTube, Instagram, Flickr*

Matthew Shay, President and CEO
Carleen Kohut, COO
Mallory Duncan, SVP& General Counsel
David French, SVP, Govt. Relations
Mike Gatti, SVP, Member Relations

Subsidiary of the National Retail Federation, this is a retailer-driven membership organization dedicated to creating an international, barrier-free technology environment for retailers. ARTS was established to ensure that technology works to enhance a retailer's ability to develop store level business solutions and avoid situations that limit a retailer's ability to implement change while providing industry standards designed to provide greater value at lower costs.
175 Members
Founded in 1993

21297 Association of Retail Marketing Services
10 Drs James Parker Boulevard
Suite 103
Red Bank, NJ 07701-1500

732-842-5070
866-231-6310
FAX 732-219-1938
E-Mail: info@goarms.com
Home Page: www.goarms.com

Gerri Hopkins, Executive Director
Lisa McCauley, Administrative Director

Supports all those involved with the marketing of all aspects of the retail industry, manufacturing, distribution, representation.
100 Members
Founded in 1957

21298 Black Retail Action Group
68 East 131st Street
Suite 704
New York, NY 10037

212-234-3050
FAX 212-234-3053
E-Mail: info@bragusa.org
Home Page: bragusa.org
Social Media: *Instagram*

Nicole Cokley-Dunlap, Co-President
Shawn R.Outler, Co-President
Regina Gwynn, Vice President-Operations
Leslie Smith, Vice President-Finance
Juanita Fields, Secretary
500 Members
Founded in 1970

21299 Christian Booksellers Association (CBA)
1365 Garden of the Gods Rd
Suite 105
Colorado Spring, CO 80907

719-265-9895
800-252-1950
FAX 719-272-3508
E-Mail: info@cbaonline.org

Home Page: www.cbaonline.org
Social Media: *Facebook, Twitter*

Curtis Riskey, President
Sue Smith, Chairman
Bob Hawkins. Jr, Secretary
Bill Couey, Treasurer
Robin Hogan, Vice Chairman

Provides products and services to assist and support Christian retail stores.
3.4M Members
Founded in 1950

21300 Comics Professional Retail Organization
PO Box 16804
Irvine, CA 92623-6804

714-446-8871
Home Page: www.comicspro.org
Social Media: *Facebook, Twitter*

Peter Dolan, President

The voice of direct-market comic book retailers.

21301 Electronic Retailing Association
607 14th Street, NW
Suite 530
Washington, DC 20005

703-841-1751
800-987-6462
FAX 425-977-1036
E-Mail: webadmin@retailing.org
Home Page: www.retailing.org
Social Media: *Facebook, Twitter, LinkedIn, YouTube, Flickr*

Julie Coons, President and CEO
Gregory Sater, Chairman
Chris Reinmuth, Secretary
Christopher Hearing, Treasurer
Poonam Khubani, Chairman-Elect

To foster growth, development and acceptance of the rapidly growing direct response industry worldwide for the companies who use the power of electronic media to sell goods and services to the public.
Founded in 1990
Mailing list available for rent

21302 Franchise Consultants International Association
5147 S Angela Road
Memphis, TN 38117-3454

901-368-3881
FAX 202-628-0812
E-Mail: franmark@msn.com
Social Media: *Facebook, Twitter, LinkedIn*

William Richey, Executive Director

Seeks to coordinate effective and professional franchise consulting, serves as a clearinghouse and operates a library.
800 Members
Founded in 1980

21303 Institute of Store Planners
25 N Broadway
Tarrytown, NY 10591-3221

914-332-1806
FAX 914-332-1541
E-Mail: adminisp@ispo.org
Home Page: www.ispo.org

Richard C Byrne, Manager
Kenneth Nisch, VP
Ronald Kline, Chairman
Richard Byrne, Manager

Provides a forum for debate and discussion by store design experts and retailers. Sponsors student design programs.
1300 Members
Founded in 1961

21304 International Center for Companies of Food

Shuwaikh Industrial Area. Block 143
Street 111
Shuwaikh, KU 70655

965-483-8750
FAX 965-484-0125
E-Mail: info@internationa-center.com
Home Page: www.international-center.com
Social Media: *Facebook, Twitter, LinkedIn*

Shaker Al-Samman, MD

Provides management research on problems related to food distribution and serves as an international forum where food chain store executives can meet to exchange ideas and information.
500 Members
Founded in 1960

21305 International Council of Shopping Centers

1221 Ave of the Americas
41 St. Fl.
New York, NY 10020-1099

646-728-3800
FAX 732-694-1690
E-Mail: membership@icsc.org
Home Page: www.icsc.org
Social Media: *Facebook, Twitter, LinkedIn, YouTube, Pinterest, Google+, I*

Sheri Pupello, Member Communcations Representative
Cecilia Perrino, Customer Service/ InfoCenter
Glen Hale, CFO
Jesse Tron, Director, Communications
Jennifer Collin, Manager, Membership Development

Supports all those involved with any aspect of shopping centers.
70000 Members
Founded in 1957

21306 International Franchise Association

1900 K Street, NW
Suite 700
Washington, DC 20006

202-628-8000
FAX 202-628-0812
Home Page: www.franchise.org
Social Media: *Facebook, Twitter, LinkedIn, YouTube, Instagram*

Robert Cresanti, President
Melanie Bergeron, Chair of the Board
Aziz Hashim, Vice Chairman
Shelly Sun, Treasurer
Liam Brown, Secretary

Membership consists of companies franchising the distribution of goods or services.
Founded in 1997

21307 International Map Trade Association

2629 Manhattan Avenue
PMB 281
Hermosa Beach, CA 90254

310-376-7731
FAX 949-458-0300
E-Mail: imta@maptrade.org
Home Page: www.maptrade.org

Chris Knoebel, President
Sanford J Hill, Executive Director

Membership comprised of retail stores featuring maps, travel books, globes, and travel products, plus publishers and manufacturers producing these products. Publishes a monthly newsletter.
800 Members
Founded in 1981

21308 International Premium Cigar & Pipe Retailers Association

4 Bradley Park Ct
Suite 2H
Columbus, GA 31904-3637

706-494-1143
FAX 706-494-1893
E-Mail: info@rtda.org
Home Page: www.ipcpr.org
Social Media: *Facebook, Twitter, LinkedIn, YouTube*

Finnie Helmuth, President
Craig Cass, 1st Vice President
Ken P. Neumann, 2nd Vice President
John Anderson, Treasurer
Greg Zimmerman, Secretary

Trade association of high quality tobacconists.
2,350 Members
Founded in 1933

21309 Marine Retailers Association of America

8401 73rd Ave. N.
Suite 71
Minneapolis, MN 55428

763-315-8043
FAX 708-763-9236
E-Mail: matt@mraa.com
Home Page: www.mraa.com
Social Media: *Facebook, Twitter, LinkedIn, RSS*

Matt Gruhn, President
Liz Walz, Vice President
Randy Wattenbarger, Chairman
Joe Lewis, Vice Chairman
Joe Hoffmaster, Secretary/ Treasurer

Raising the standards of retailing within the industry. Promotes activities for the recreational boating industry and holds seminars to improve management.
2.5M Members
Founded in 1972

21310 Museum Store Association

3773 E Cherry Creek North Dr
Suite 755
Denver, CO 80209

303-504-9223
FAX 303-504-9585
E-Mail: info@museumstoreassociation.org
Home Page: www.museumdistrict.com
Social Media: *Facebook, Twitter, LinkedIn, Pinterest*

Stuart Hata, First Vice President
David Duddy, President
Alice McAuliffe, Treasurer
Jama Rice, Executive Director/ CEO
Julie Steiner, Second Vice President
2500 Members
Frequency: April, Annually
Founded in 1955

21311 National Advisory Group

2063 Oak Street
Jacksonville, FL 32204

904-845-5989
E-Mail: info@nagconvinience.com
Home Page: nagconvenience.com
Social Media: *Facebook*

Joseph Howton, Executive VP
Mary Banmiller, President
Bill Donahe, Publisher
Ben Jatlow, Chairman

This association represents senior level management of retail companies organized to enhance buying power, merchandising programs and an exchange of ideas. Membership dues: Retail Average $300, Associations $350.
500 Members
Founded in 1983

21312 National Association General Merchandise Representatives

1037 Us Highway 46
Suite C102
Clifton, NJ 07013-2461

973-614-9211
FAX 973-916-1986
E-Mail: frankp@performancesales.com
Home Page: www.nagmr.com
Social Media: *Facebook, Twitter, Pinterest, RSS*

David Perrone, President
Jordan Stone, Vice President
Ronald Ross, Treasurer
Rich Siporin, Secretary
Bruce Funk, Director

A professional association of consumer product brokers representing leading manufacturers to the drug, mass merchandise and food trade.

21313 National Association of Catalog Showrooms

PO Box 736
Northport, NY 11768-0736

631-754-4364
FAX 631-754-4364
Home Page: www.businessfinance.com
Social Media: *Facebook, Twitter, LinkedIn*

Members are catalog showroom operators and catalog publishers & associate members are suppliers.
350 Members
Founded in 1972

21314 National Association of Chain Drug Stores

1776 Wilson Blvd
Suite 200
Arlington, VA 22209

703-549-3001
FAX 703-836-4869
E-Mail: contactus@nacds.org
Home Page: www.nacds.org
Social Media: *Facebook, Twitter, LinkedIn, YouTube, Flickr*

Steven C Anderson, President/CEO
Randy Edeker, Chairman
Juna Ortiz, Treasurer
Martin Otto, Vice Chairman
Jose Barra, Director

The chief purpose of NACDS is to represent the views and policy positions of member chain drug companies.
105 Members
Founded in 1933

21315 National Association of College Stores

528 E Lorain St
Oberlin, OH 44074-1298

440-775-7777
800-622-7498
FAX 440-774-5315
E-Mail: service@nacscorp.com
Home Page: www.nacscorp.com

Kurt K. Schoen, President & COO
Marc Fleischaker, Secretary/ Legal Counsel
Brian E Cartier, CEO
Frank Sulen, CFO & Treasurer
Steve Alb, Chairperson

Provides educational and support services and products to college stores. Promotes business methods and ethics. Conducts manager certification, educational services and research.
3.9M Members
Founded in 1963

21316 National Association of Convenience Stores

1600 Duke Street
Alexandria, VA 22314

703-684-3600
877-684-3600
FAX 703-836-4564
Home Page: www.nacsonline.com
Social Media: *Facebook, Twitter, LinkedIn, YouTube, Instagram*

Henry Armour, Staff Liason
R. Timothy Columbus, Legal Counsel
Kathy LeBeouf, Executive Director
Brian E Cartier, CEO
Jack Kofdarali, Chairman

Association supporting key industry trends and innovative practices of convenience store companies.
2.3M Members
Founded in 1961
Mailing list available for rent

21317 National Association of Music Merchants

5790 Armada Dr
Carlsbad, CA 92008

760-438-8001
800-767-6266
FAX 760-438-7327
E-Mail: info@namm.org
Home Page: www.namm.org
Social Media: *Facebook, Twitter, YouTube, Pinterest*

Joe Lamond, President
Chris Martin, Treasurer
Joel Menchey, Secretary
Mark Goff, Chairman
Robin Valenta, Vice Chairman

Retailers of musical instruments.
3.6M Members

21318 National Association of Resale Professionals

PO BOX 190
St Clair Shores, MI 48080

586-294-6700
800-544-0751
FAX 586-588-7018
E-Mail: info@narts.org
Home Page: www.narts.org

Adele R. Meyer, Executive Director
Gail A. Seigel, Director of Membership Services

A national trade association for owners and managers of resale thrift shops. Purpose is to provide educational networking to promote the industry.
1100+ Members
Founded in 1984

21319 National Automatic Merchandising Association

20 N Wacker Dr
Suite 3500
Chicago, IL 60606

312-346-0370
800-331-8816
FAX 312-704-4140
E-Mail: jbradshaw@vending.org
Home Page: www.vending.org
Social Media: *Facebook, Twitter, x, YouTube*

Howard Chapman, Chairman
Peter A. Tullio, Past Chair
Heidi Chico, Vice Chairman
Patrick Hagerty, Chair-Elect
Carla Balakgie, President & CEO

Collectively advancing and promoting the automatic merchandising and coffee service industries, members include service companies, equipment manufacturers and suppliers of products and services to operating service companies.
1250+ Members
Founded in 1936

21320 National Council of Chain Restaurants

325 7th St NW
Suite 1100
Washington, DC 20004

202-783-7971
800-673-4692
FAX 202-737-2849
E-Mail: info@nrf.com
Home Page: www.nccr.net

Chip Kunde, Chairman
Rob Green, Executive Director
Scott Vinson, Vice President
Cicely Simpson, Treasurer
Lynn Liddle, Secretary

The leading trade association exclusively representing chain restaurant companies. Working to advance sound public policy that best serves the interests of restaurant businesses and the millions of people they employ.
Founded in 1965

21321 National Grocers Association

1005 N Glebe Rd
Suite 250
Arlington, VA 22201-5758

703-516-0700
FAX 703-516-0115
E-Mail: amamone@nationalgrocers.org
Home Page: www.nationalgrocers.org
Social Media: *Facebook, Twitter, LinkedIn*

Peter J. Larkin, President & CEO
Charlie Bray, Executive Vice President
Rich Niemann, Chairman
Cheryl Sommer, Treasurer
Rich McMenamin, Secretary

Works to advance understanding, trade, and cooperation in the food industry. Represents members interests before the government. Offers store planning, and engineering, training and advertising.
1.5M Members
Founded in 1982

21322 National Ice Cream Retailers Association

1028 West Devon Ave.
Elk Grove Village, IL 60007

847-301-7500
866-303-6960
FAX 847-301-8402
E-Mail: info@nicra.org
Home Page: www.nicra.org
Social Media: *Facebook*

Lynda Utterback, Executive Director
Carl Chaney, President
Neil McWilliams, Vice President
Jim Oden, President-Elect
Nanette Frey, Past President

Members are in retail frozen dessert businesses. Some offer food services either full of limited and some operate convenience stores. The common denominator is that all members offer frozen desserts for take home or on site consumption.
350 Members
Founded in 1933

21323 National Restaurant Association

2055 L St. NW
Suite 700
Washington, DC 20036

202-331-5900
800-424-5156
FAX 202-331-2429

Home Page: www.restaurant.org
Social Media: *Facebook, Twitter, YouTube*

Jack Crawford, Chair
Joe Kadow, Vice Chair
Jeff Davis, Treasurer
Dawn Sweeney, President & CEO
Ed Beck, Chief Information Officer & SVP
60000 Members
Founded in 1917

21324 National Restaurant Association Education Foundation

2055 L St. NW
Washington, DC 200036

312-715-1010
800-424-5156
FAX 312-583-9767
E-Mail: rgifford@restaurant.org
Home Page: www.nraef.org
Social Media: *Facebook, Twitter, YouTube, Tumblr, Pinterest*

Michael A. Hickey, Chair
Gregory J. Hamer, Treasurer
Lorna C. Donatone, Vice-Chairman
Dawn Sweeney, President & CEO
Rob Gifford, Executive Vice President

NRAEF is the philanthropic foundation of the National Restaurant Association. Committed to enhancing the restaurant industry's service to the public through education, community engagement and promotion of career opportunities.
Founded in 1987

21325 National Retail Federation

1101 New York Ave NW
Washington, DC 20005

202-783-7971
800-673-4692
FAX 202-737-2849
Home Page: www.nrf.com
Social Media: *Facebook, Twitter, LinkedIn, YouTube, Instagram, Flickr*

Matthew R. Shay, President/CEO
Mindy F. Grossman, Vice Chair
Autor Erik, Vice President
Kip Tindell, Chairman
Kip Tindell, Treasurer & Chairman of Finance

Retail trade association with membership that comprises all retail formats and channels of distribution including department, specialty, discount, catalog, Internet and independent stores. NRF members represent an industry that encompasses more than 1.4 million US retail establishments which employ more than 23 million people — about one in five American workers — and registered 2002 sales of $3.6 trillion. NRF's international members operate stores in more than 50 nations.
55M Members
Founded in 1990

21326 National Shoe Retailers Association

7386 N. La Cholla Blvd
Tucson, AZ 85741

520-209-1710
800-673-8446
FAX 410-381-1167
E-Mail: info@nsra.org
Home Page: www.nsra.org
Social Media: *Facebook, Twitter, LinkedIn, Google+, Pinterest*

Jeff Greenberg, Board Chairman
Chuck Schuyler, President
Lenny Comeras, Vice Chairman
Rick Ravel, Past Chairman
Jeanette Riechers, Vice Chairman

Membership association for independent shoe retailers. Provides business services such as credit-card processing and shipping at special low members only prices. Also provides educa-

tional and training programs, consulting and other services.
1400 Members
Founded in 1912

21327 National Ski & Snowboard Retailers Association
1601 Feehanville Drive
Suite 300
Mount Prospect, IL 60056

847-391-9825
888-527-1168
FAX 847-391-9827
E-Mail: info@nssra.com
Home Page: www.nssra.com

Larry Weindruch, President
Paul Prutzman, Chairman

The retail voice for the ski and snowboard industries and provides information and services you need to operate more successfully.
250 Members
Founded in 1987

21328 National Sporting Goods Association
1601 Feehanville Drive
Suite 300
Mount Prospect, IL 60056

847-296-6742
800-815-5422
FAX 847-391-9827
E-Mail: info@nsga.org
Home Page: www.nsga.org

Ken Meehan, Chairman of the Board
Matt Carlson, President/CEO
Dan Wiersma, CFO
Randy Nill, Treasurer/ Chairman-Elect
Jeff Rosenthal, Past chairman

Association of retailers, manufacturers and suppliers of sports equipment, footwear and apparel.
2000+ Members
Founded in 1929

21329 North American Equipment Dealers Association
1195 Smizer Mill Rd
Fenton, MO 63026

636-349-5000
FAX 636-349-5443
E-Mail: naeda@naeda.com
Home Page: www.naeda.com
Social Media: *Facebook, Twitter*

Richard Lawhun, President
Joe Nash, Immediate Past President
Mark Foster, 2nd Vice Chair & Secretary
Brian Carpenter, First Vice Chair & Treasurer
Blaine Bingham, Chairman

NAEDA and its affiliates provides a variety of educational, financial, legislative and legal services to equipment dealers in the United States and Canada.
5000 Members
Founded in 1900

21330 North American Retail Dealers Association
222 South Riverside Plaza
Suite 2100
Chicago, IL 60606

312-648-0649
800-621-0298
FAX 312-648-1212
E-Mail: nardasvc@narda.com
Home Page: www.narda.com
Social Media: *Facebook, LinkedIn*

Leon Barbachano, Chairman
Timothy W. Seavey, First Vice Chairman
Leon Barbachano, Second Vice Chairman
Michael Fischer, Past Chairman & Treasurer
Otto Papasadero, Executive Director

A national organization of association members, independent retailers selling and servicing major appliances, consumer electronics products, furniture and computers. Emphasis is placed on ideas that help readers become better, more profitable businesses. Articles are featured regularly on displays, salesmanship, financial analysis and service management.
1000 Members
Founded in 1943

21331 Oriental Rug Importers Association
400 Tenafly Road
Suite 699
Tenafly, NJ 7670

201-866-5054
FAX 201-866-6169
E-Mail: llaufer@oria.org
Home Page: www.oria.org

Lucille Laufer, Executive Director
Reza Momeni, President
Kami Navid, Vice-President
Behrooz Hakimian, Treasurer
Ramin Kalaty, Secretary

Membership is concentrated in the New York area.
Founded in 1958

21332 Point-of-Purchase Advertising Internationa l
440 N. Wells Street
Suite 740
Chicago, IL 60654

312-863-2900
FAX 312-229-1152
E-Mail: todddittman@retailenvuronments.org
Home Page: www.popai.com
Social Media: *Facebook, Twitter, LinkedIn, Pinterest*

Michelle Adams, Chairman
Keith Arndt, Co-Vice Chair
Scott Eisen, Treasurer
Bob Zanotti, Co-Vice Chair
Madeline Baumgartner, Market Research Manager

Supports all those involved with in-store promotional programs — and research on marketing and retail trends.
1400 Members
Founded in 1936

21333 Professional Audio-Video Retailers Association
10 E 22nd Street
Suite 310
Lombard, IL 60148-6191

630-268-1500
800-621-0298
FAX 630-953-8957

Debra Smith, Executive Director

Supports owners and operators of independently owned, audio/video stores. Members includes manufacturers of high-end audio/video equipment.
204 Members
Founded in 1979

21334 Professional Sales Association
5045 Park Ave West
Suite 1B
Seville, OH 44273

330-299-7343
FAX 300-408-0075
Home Page: www.profsales.com

Jim Mcgonical, President
Charlie Martin, Central Regional Manager
Alex Marsden, Eastern Regional Manager

An organization of manufacturers' representative firms which sell hardware, housewares,

lawn and garden products and traffic appliances to the retail trade.
25 Members
Founded in 1969

21335 Retail Advertising & Marketing Association
328 7th St Nw
Suite 1100
Washington, DC 20004

202-626-8181
800-673-4692
FAX 202-737-2849
E-Mail: gattim@nrf.com
Home Page: www.rama-nrf.org
Social Media: *Facebook, Twitter, LinkedIn, Google+*

Libby Landen, VP, Strategic Marketing
Mike Gatti, Executive Director
Kelly Gilmore, Senior Vice president
Kathy Grannis, Manager, Media Relations
Marcia Tabler, RAMA Consultant

Provides visionary leadership that promotes creativity, innovation and excellence within all marketing disciplines that strategically elevates our members and our industry.
1600 Members
Founded in 1952

21336 Retail Industry Leaders Association
1700 N Moore St
Suite 2250
Arlington, VA 22209

703-841-2300
FAX 703-841-1184
E-Mail: suzie.squier@rila.org
Home Page: www.rila.org
Social Media: *Facebook, Twitter, LinkedIn*

Hubert Joly, Director At- Large
Richard Dreiling, Chairman
Eric Wiseman, Treasurer
William Rhodes III, Vice Chairman
Robert Niblock, Secretary

Retail Industry Leaders Association is a trade association of the lasgest and fastest growing companies in the retail industry, its members include over 400 retailers, product manufacturers, and service suppliers.
400+ Members
Founded in 1969

21337 Retail Merchants Association
5101 Monument Ave.
Richmond, VA 23230

804-662-5500
866-750-2532
FAX 804-662-5507
E-Mail: info@retailmerchants.com
Home Page: www.retailmerchants.com
Social Media: *Facebook, Twitter, LinkedIn*

Nancy C. Thomas, President & CEO

The Association is dedicated to helping local retailers and small businesses grow.
Founded in 1906

21338 Retail Packaging Association
105 Eastern Avenue
Suite 104
Annapolis, MD 21403

410-940-6459
FAX 410-263-1659
E-Mail: info@retailpackaging.org
Home Page: www.retailpackaging.org

Tony Van Belkom, President
Bob Gant, VP
Jatin Patel, Treasurer~
Denise Cabera, Secretary

Serves its members and the entire retail packaging industry. Also organizes the largest trade show and conference of its kind in the US. A self-governed not-for-profit organization com-

prised of professionals involved in all facets of production and distribution of retail packaging products.
Founded in 1989

21339 Retail Systems Alert Group
377 Elliot Street Po Box 332
Newton Upper Falls, MA 02464

617-527-4626
FAX 617-527-8102
E-Mail: info@retailsystems.com
Home Page: www.retailsystems.com

Brian Kilcourse, President
Tom Friedman, Chairman
Karen Moss, Editor
Lisa Gayle, Advertising Manager

Retail Systems Alert Group has helped companies reach a highly qualified audience of Extened Retail Industry professionals through advertising, sponsorship, research, and exhibiting opportunities.
Founded in 1870

21340 Scuba Retailers Association
4 Florence Street
Somerville, MA 02145

617-623-7722
Social Media: *Facebook, Twitter, LinkedIn*

James Estabrook, Executive Director
Members are stores selling scuba and association underwater equipment.
500 Members
Founded in 1989

21341 Small Business Technology Council
National Small Business Association
1156 15th St Nw
Suite 1100
Washington, DC 20005

202-662-9700
800-835-6728
E-Mail: alec@sbtc.org
Home Page: www.sbtc.org
Social Media: *Facebook, Twitter, RSS*

James Morrison, President
Robert Schmidt, Co-Chair
Heidi Jacobus, Co-Chair
Jere Glover, Executive Director
Larry Nannis, Treasurer

Working with and providing web sites for the very small business.
120 Members
Founded in 2000

21342 Vacuum and Sewing Dealers Trade Association
2724 2nd Ave
Des Moines, IA 50313-4933

515-282-9101
800-367-5651
FAX 515-282-4483
E-Mail: mail@vdta.com, ads@vdta.com
Home Page: www.vdta.com

Craig Dorman, Sales
Charley Dunham, Chairman
Judy Patterson, President
Marlin Graham, Vice-President
Beth Vitiritto, Managing Editor

Seeks to increase the independent vacuum cleaner and sewing machine dealer market share.
20,00 Members
Founded in 1981

21343 Wine and Spirits Guild of America
3530 Vinings Ridge Court
Atlanta, GA 30339

770-956-8808
FAX 770-988-8634

E-Mail: info@wineandspiritsguild.com
Home Page: www.wineandspiritsguild.com

Barbara Owen, Conference Manager
Brad Feuerbacher, President
Cedric Matin, Ex-Officio President & Director
David Jabour, 2nd Vice President and Treasurer
Gary Fisch, 1st Vice President

Promotes the exchange of information on merchandising, marketing and buying of wines and spirits.
40 Members
Founded in 1948

Newsletters

21344 American Collegiate Retailing Association Newsletter
Loyola University/Department of Marketing
PO Box 121
New Orleans, LA 70118

504-865-2011
FAX 504-865-3851
E-Mail: admit@loyno.edu
Home Page: www.loyno.edu

Kevin Wildes, President
Alice Glenn, Secretary
Cynthia Tucker, Editor
Mary Degnan, Marketing Manager
Janice Long, Circulation Manager

Educational retailing news and information.
Frequency: Quarterly
Founded in 1923

21345 Bookselling This Week
American Booksellers Association
200 White Plains Rd
Suite 600
Tarrytown, NY 10591

800-637-0037
FAX 914-591-2720
E-Mail: info@bookweb.org
Home Page: www.bookweb.org

Oren Teicher, CEO
Len Viahos, COO
Ellie Chang, CFO
Frequency: Weekly
Circulation: 10000

21346 Campus Marketplace
National Association of College Stores
500 E Lorain St
Oberlin, OH 44074-1238

440-775-0120
800-622-7498
FAX 440-775-4769
E-Mail: webteam@nacs.org
Home Page: www.nacs.org

Brian Cartier, CEO
Carrie Tompkins, Editor

Weekly newsletter covering college store industry: sales, trends, news, personnel and address changes for stores as well as vendors.
Frequency: Monthly
Circulation: 4000
Founded in 1982

21347 For the President's Eyes Only
Bureau of Business Practice
76 Ninth Avenue
7th Floor
New York, NY 10011

212-771-0600
FAX 212-771-0885
Home Page: www.aspenpublishers.com

Robert Becker, CEO
Gustavo Dobles, VP Operations

Provides the latest information on areas of vital interest to the head of the company.
12 Pages
Frequency: 2 per year

21348 Insider
Trade Dimensions
45 Danbury Rd
Wilton, CT 06897-4445

203-563-3000
FAX 203-563-3131
Home Page: www.tradedimensions.com

Brain Thomas, Editor
Kristina Castle, Circulation Coordina

Shopping center weekly newsletter that profiles the latest retailer expansion plans, giving - in addition to the numbers of stores operated and planned, the areas targeted, and the type of locations sought - a thumbnail sketch of what makes the concept unique, and what the company specifically looks for in a site.
Cost: $299.00
Frequency: Weekly
Founded in 1970

21349 International Map Trade Association
2629 Manhattan Avenue
PMB 281
Hermosa Beach, CA 90254-2447

310-376-7731
FAX 949-458-0300
Home Page: www.maptrade.org

Sandy Hill, Executive Director
Linda Hill, Editor

Membership comprised of retail stores featuring maps, travel books, globes, and travel products, plus publishers and manufacturers producing these products. Publishes a monthly newsletter
Cost: $60.00
20 Pages
Frequency: Monthly
ISSN: 1065-6324
Founded in 1981
Printed in on matte stock

21350 Mouser Report
CAMCO
124 E Carolina Avenue
Crewe, VA 23930-1802

434-645-1993
800-448-8595
FAX 434-645-8232

Charles Mouser, Publisher
Brend DeLuca, Circulation Director

Newsletter covers the latest trends in retail and advertising.
Cost: $96.00
16 Pages
Frequency: Monthly

21351 NRF-BTM Retail Executive Opinion Survey
National Retail Federation
325 7th St
Suite 1101
Washington, DC 20004-2808

202-783-7971
800-673-4692
FAX 202-737-2849
Home Page: www.nrf.com
Social Media: *Facebook, Twitter, LinkedIn*

Matthew Shay, President
Scott Krugman, Publisher
Mader Richard, Executive Director
Michael Gatti, VP/Marketing
David French, VP

Gathers the opinions of the industry's top executives on trends in merchandising, hiring, sales

expectations, customer traffic and special seasonal related developments.
Frequency: Monthly

21352 NRF/BIGresearch Consumer Intentions and Actions Survey
National Retail Federation
325 7th St Nw
Suite 1101
Washington, DC 20004-2808

202-783-7971
800-673-4693
FAX 202-737-2849
Home Page: www.nrf.com

Matthew Shay, President
Scott Krugman, Publisher
Mader Richard, Executive Director
Michael Gatti, VP/Marketing
David French, VP

Index on consumer shopping behavior. The survey also gauges consumer spending during holidays.
Frequency: Weekly

21353 NSSRA Newsletter
National Ski and Snowboard Retailers Association
1604 Feehanville Drive
Suite 300
Mount Prospect, IL 60056-6213

847-228-8277
FAX 847-439-0111
E-Mail: info@nssra.com
Home Page: www.nssra.com

Larry Weindruch, President
Paul Prutzman, Chairman

Keeps members informed on critical industry issues, such as guidelines, litigation exposure and marketing
Frequency: Quarterly
Circulation: 1000

21354 National Research Bureau Newsletter
National Research Bureau
320 Valley St
Burlington, IA 52601-5513

319-752-5415
FAX 319-752-3421
E-Mail: contactus@supervisionmagazine.com
Home Page:
www.national-research-bureau.com

Diane M Darnall, President
William H. Wood, Founder

A newsletter is created for a company by combining a customized masthead with a four page, monthly issue of helpful information on a business field selected by the company.
4 Pages
Frequency: Daily
Founded in 1933
Printed in 3 colors

21355 Retail CEO Insider
National Retail Federation
325 7th St Nw
Suite 1100
Washington, DC 20004-2808

202-783-7971
800-673-4693
FAX 202-737-2849
Home Page: www.nrf.com
Social Media: *Facebook, Twitter, LinkedIn, You Tube*

Matthew Shay, President
Scott Krugman, Publisher
Mader Richard, Executive Director
Michael Gatti, VP/Marketing
David French, VP

Two-page private news briefing for CEOs, chairpersons and presidents of National Retail Federation member companies. Provides con-

cise, bullet-point coverage of issues facing the industry in the style of the Kiplinger Washington Letter, with a heavy emphasis on government affairs and public policy. Distributed to approximately 650 C-level executives.
Frequency: Monthly

21356 Retail Sales Outlook
National Retail Federation
325 7th St Nw
Suite 1101
Washington, DC 20004-2808

202-783-7971
800-673-4693
FAX 202-737-2849
Home Page: www.nrf.com
Social Media: *Facebook, Twitter, LinkedIn*

Matthew Shay, President
Scott Krugman, Publisher
Mader Richard, Executive Director
Michael Gatti, VP/Marketing
David French, VP

Economic analysis of the retail industry.
Frequency: Quarterly

21357 Shopping Center Management Insider
6 East 32nd St
8th Floor
New York, NY 10016

212-812-8420
800-519-3692
E-Mail: info@vendomegrp.com
Home Page: www.vendomegrp.com

Steven Gordon Esq, Editor

Tested management techniques, legal insights and how-to guidelines for running a shopping center or mall. Includes model notices to tenants, letters, agreements, rules, etc.
Cost: $297.00
Frequency: Monthly
Founded in 1985
Printed in 2 colors on matte stock

21358 T-Shirt Business Info Mapping Newsletter
Prosperity & Profits Unlimited
PO Box 416
Denver, CO 80201-0416

303-575-5676

A Doyle, Editor

How-to T-shirt business and information.
Cost: $8.00
8 Pages
Frequency: Annual
Circulation: 1,450
Founded in 1989
Printed in one color on matte stock

Magazines & Journals

21359 Accessory Merchandising
Vance Publishing
400 Knightsbridge Pkwy
Lincolnshire, IL 60069-3628

847-634-2600
FAX 847-634-4379
E-Mail: mreckling@vancepublishing.com
Home Page: www.vancepublishing.com

Peggy Walker, President
Chandra Palermo, Editor
Michael R. Reckling, Group Publisher
Steven J. Kulikowski, Marketing Manager
Douglas Riemer, Circulation Director

21360 Army/Navy Store & Outdoor Merchandiser
445 Broad Hollow Road
Suite 21
Melville, NY 11747

631-845-2700
FAX 631-845-2797

Military surplus, workwear, casual apparel, camping, hunting and sporting goods, and outdoor clothing industries.
Cost: $25.00
Frequency: Monthly
Circulation: 12M

21361 Barnard's Retail Trend Report
Barnard Enterprises
17 Kenneth Road
Upper Montclair, NJ 07043-2541

973-655-8888
Home Page: www.retailtrends.com

Kurt Barnard, Publisher/Editor
Jim Adamson, CEO

Forecasts market trends in the retailing industry and on consumer spending.
Cost: $179.00
10 Pages
Circulation: 1200
Founded in 1984
Printed in 2 colors on newsprint stock

21362 Casual Living
Reed Business Information
2000 Clearwater Dr
Oak Brook, IL 60523-8809

630-574-0825
FAX 630-288-8781
Home Page: www.reedbusiness.com

Jeff Greisch, President
Mark Kelsey, MD
Jeremy Knibbs, Chief Executive

21363 Chain Merchandiser
Merchandising Publications Company
PO Box 95C
Baker City, OR 97814-0095

FAX 541-523-2063

Ruth Sanders, Business Manager
Henry Von Morpurgo, Editor/Publisher

A national service and promotion program incorporating Specialty Foods and Beverages and Deli-Dairy World. Devoted to improved merchandising methods at every level of the marketing and distributing processes - from the field and factory and warehouse to retail sales persons - to provide better customer values, lower costs and greater profits.

21364 Chain Store Age
Lebhar-Friedman
425 Park Ave
Suite 6
New York, NY 10022-3526

212-756-5088
800-216-7117
FAX 212-838-9487
E-Mail: info@lf.com
Home Page: www.lf.com

Heather Martin, Manager
John Rapuzzi, Group Publisher
Antonia Peterson, Desk Editor
J Roger Friedman, President

Offers a full overview of chain stores, including management, operation, construction and modernization, store equipment, real estate and advertising.
Frequency: Monthly
Circulation: 35551
Founded in 1925

21365 College Store
Executive Business Media
PO Box 1500
Westbury, NY 11590-0812

516-334-3030
FAX 516-334-3059
E-Mail: webteam@nacs.org
Home Page: www.nacs.org

Cynthia D'Angelo, President
Ron Stevens, Editor

Covers the college bookstore market retail industry.
Cost: $40.00
40 Pages
Frequency: Bi-Monthly
Circulation: 6,800

21366 College Store Executive
Executive Business Media
825 Old Country Road
PO Box 1500
Westbury, NY 11590-812

516-334-3030
FAX 516-334-3059
E-Mail: ebm-mail@ebmpubs.com
Home Page: www.ebmpubs.com

Ken Baglino, Editor
Nancy Wilderwith, Advertising Manager

A merchandising and news magazine edited for those responsible for buying and merchandising products for college retail stores.
Cost: $35.00
36 Pages
Circulation: 8547
ISSN: 0010-1141
Founded in 1970
Printed in 4 colors on glossy stock

21367 College Store Magazine
National Association of College Stores
500 E Lorain St
Oberlin, OH 44074-1238

440-775-0120
800-622-7498
FAX 440-775-4769
E-Mail: webteam@nacs.org
Home Page: www.nacs.org

Brian Cartier, CEO
Keith Galestock, Editor
Tara Ellis, Associate Editor

Covers the college store industry's long term issues and trends, focusing on retailing, technology and serving campus communities.
Cost: $66.00
Mailing list available for rent

21368 DSN Retailing Today
Lebhar-Friedman
425 Park Ave
Suite 6
New York, NY 10022-3526

212-756-5088
800-216-7117
FAX 212-838-9487
E-Mail: info@lf.com
Home Page: www.dsnretailingtoday.com

Heather Martin, Manager
Tim Craig, Editor-in-Chief
Tony Lisanti, Editorial Director
Roger Friedman, CEO

Leading international newspaper serving the growing mass market.
Frequency: Monthly
Circulation: 34000
Founded in 1925

21369 Dealerscope
North American Publishing Company

1500 Spring Garden St
Suite 1200
Philadelphia, PA 19130-4094

215-238-5300
800-818-8174
FAX 215-238-5342
E-Mail: sdowney@napco.com
Home Page: www.dealerscope.com
Social Media: *Facebook, Twitter, LinkedIn*

Ned S Borowsky, CEO
David Dritsas, Editor-in-Chief
Eric Schwartz, President/Publishing
Rhoda Dixon, Circulation Manager
Suzanne DeFruscio, Advertising Promotion Manager

Dedicated to delivering peer-based knowledge and experience, Dealerscope is the ultimate vehicle for presenting product and service solutions to the consumer.
Founded in 1958

21370 Display & Design Ideas
Shore Varrone
6255 Barfield Road
#200
Atlanta, GA 30328-4332

404-848-0077
FAX 404-252-4436
Home Page: www.svi-atl.com

Doug Hope, Publisher
Steve Kaufman, Editor
Lee Pritcher, Owner

Product news and design solutions for those in the retail chain indusrty.
Cost: $60.00
Frequency: Monthly
Circulation: 18,039

21371 Do-It-Yourself Retailing
5822 W 74th St
Indianapolis, IN 46278-1756

317-297-1190
FAX 317-328-4354
E-Mail: vecchie@sbcglobal.net
Home Page: www.nrha.org

John Hammond, Executive Director
Kevin Hohman, Publisher
Frequency: Monthly
Circulation: 44333

21372 Drug Store News
Lebhar-Friedman
425 Park Ave
Suite 6
New York, NY 10022-3526

212-756-5088
FAX 212-838-9487
E-Mail: tlisanti@lf.com
Home Page: www.drugstorenews.com

Heather Martin, Manager
Tony Lisanti, Editor

Publication consists of merchandising trends and pharmacy developments. Provides extensive coverage of every major segment of chain drug retailing and combination stores.
Cost: $189.00
Frequency: Weekly
Circulation: 40000
Founded in 1925

21373 Edplay
Fahy-Williams Publishing
PO Box 1080
Geneva, NY 14456-2137

315-789-0458
800-344-0559
FAX 315-789-4263
Home Page: www.fwpi.com

J Kevin Fahy, Publisher
Tina Manzer, Editorial Director

Jason Hagerman, Advertising Account Rep
Bradley G Gordner, Senior Editor
Tricia King, Office Manager

Serves toy manufacturers and dealers. Offers product reviews, industry profiles, and reader surveys.
Cost: $22.00
Frequency: Quarterly
Circulation: 7684

21374 Flea Markets Magazine
FleaMarkets.com
1156 15th St NW
Suite 1100
Washington, DC 20005-1755

202-293-8830
800-835-6728
Home Page: www.fleamarkets.com

Todd McCracken, President
A quarterly magazine published by FleaMarkets.com.
Cost: $15.00
Frequency: Quarterly
Circulation: 3000
Founded in 1989

21375 Gacs Today
Naylor Publications
PO Box 855
Snellville, GA 30078-855

770-736-9723
FAX 770-736-9725
Home Page: www.gacs.com

Jim Tudor, CEO
Frequency: Quarterly
Circulation: 2500
Founded in 1973

21376 Garden Center Merchandising & Management
Branch-Smith Publishing
PO Box 1868
Fort Worth, TX 76101-1868

817-882-4110
800-433-5612
FAX 817-882-4121
E-Mail: webmaster@branchsmith.com
Home Page: www.branchsmith.com

David Branch, President
Terri Smith, Director Circulation
Carol Miller, Editor
Frequency: Monthly
Circulation: 15143
Founded in 1915

21377 Garden Center Products & Supplies
Branch-Smith Publishing
PO Box 1868
Fort Worth, TX 76101-1868

817-882-4110
800-433-5612
FAX 817-882-4121
E-Mail: dbranch@branchsmith.com
Home Page: www.branchsmith.com

David Branch, President
Patrice Kuhl, Publisher/Sales Director
Frequency: Monthly
Founded in 1910

21378 Hearth & Home
Village West Publishing
PO Box 1288
Laconia, NH 03247-2008

603-528-4285
800-258-3772
FAX 603-524-0643
Home Page: www.homehearth.com

Richard Wright, Editor
Jackie Avignone, Sales Manager

Information for retailers and others selling hearth products, patio furnishing, barbecues, spas, garden accessories, and other outdoor products.
Cost: $11.95
Circulation: 18000
ISSN: 0273-5695
Founded in 1980

21379 International Gaming and Wagering Business
BNP Media
PO Box 1080
Skokie, IL 60076-9785

847-763-9534
FAX 847-763-9538
E-Mail: igwb@halldata.com
Home Page: www.igwb.com
Social Media: Facebook, Twitter, LinkedIn

James Rutherford, Editor
Lynn Davidson, Marketing
Tammie Gizicki, Director

Focuses on business strategy, legislative information, food service and promotional concerns.
Frequency: Monthly
Circulation: 25000

21380 Kitchenware News
United Publications
PO Box 1056
Yarmouth, ME 04096-2056

207-846-0600
FAX 207-846-0657
Home Page: www.kitchenwares.com

Brooke Taliaferro, President
Jim McNeil, Publisher

News and information on the latest products and equipment for the retail kitchenware industry.
Cost: $45.00
Frequency: Monthly
Circulation: 12,117

21381 MMR/Mass Market Retailers
Racher Press
220 5th Avenue
New York, NY 10001-7798

212-213-6000
FAX 212-725-4594
E-Mail: info@racherpress.com
Home Page: www.massmarketretailers.com

Susan Schinitsky, Publisher
David Pinto, Editor
John Dioguardi, Director Sales/Marketing
Kevin Burke, Group Advertising Director
Pam Vandernoth, Circulation Director

News, analysis, trends, and events for drug, discount, and supermarket chain executives.
Cost: $185.00
Circulation: 21645
Founded in 1984

21382 Magazine Retailer
MetaMedia
124 W 24th Street
#3-D
New York, NY 1011-1920

212-989-6978
FAX 212-255-7143

David Orlow, Publisher
Djalal Mohammadi, President

Merchandising tips, new tiles, publication changes, consumer purchasing trends, industry news and media impact on sales.
Cost: $19.00
Frequency: Quarterly
Circulation: 10,326

21383 Mass Market Retailer
Racher Press

220 5th Avenue
New York, NY 10001-7708

212-213-6000
FAX 212-725-3961
E-Mail: info@racherpress.com
Home Page: www.massmarketretailers.com

Susan Schinitsky, Publisher
David Pinto, Editor
Susan Schinitsky, CEO/President
John Dioguardi, Marketing
Pam Vandernoth, Circulation Manager

News and information on the drug store chain industry.
Cost: $35.00
30 Pages
Founded in 1984

21384 Military Market
Gannet Company
6883 Commercial Dr
Springfield, VA 22151-4202

703-750-8643
FAX 703-750-8717
E-Mail: rhynema@atpco.com
Home Page: www.gannettoffset.com

Dennis V Washburn, CEO
David Craig, Managing Editor

Provides trade information, trends, and news for military commisionary and post/base exchange managers.
Cost: $84.00
Frequency: Monthly
Circulation: 12000
Founded in 1940

21385 Museum Store Magazine
Museum Store Association
4100 E Mississippi Ave
Suite 800
Denver, CO 80246-3055

303-504-9223
FAX 303-504-9585
E-Mail: membership@museumdistrict.com
Home Page: www.museumdistrict.com

Beverly J Barsook, Executive Director
Amy Nicholas, Editor
Cost: $34.00
Frequency: Quarterly
Circulation: 3000
Founded in 1955
Printed in 4 colors on glossy stock

21386 Museums & More Specialty Shops Product News
Museums & More Specialty Product News
PO Box 128
Sparta, Mi 49345-2122

616-887-9008
FAX 616-887-2666
Home Page: www.museumsandmore.com

Julie McCallum, Editor
Jon Kaufman, Publisher

Product highlights and marketing strategies for the owners and oporators of gift shops in museums and other public attractions.
Cost: $35.00
Frequency: Quarterly
Circulation: 28014

21387 NACS SCAN
National Association of Convenience Stores
1600 Duke St
Suite 700
Alexandria, VA 22314-3436

703-684-3600
FAX 703-836-4564
E-Mail: webmaster@nacsonline.com
Home Page: www.nacsonline.com

Hank Armour, President

A bi-monthly magazine offering information on key industry trends and innovative practices of convenience store companies.
Cost: $840.00
Frequency: Monthly
Circulation: 3000
Founded in 1961

21388 NAEDA Equipment Dealer
North American Equipment Dealers Association
1195 Smizer Mill Rd
Fenton, MO 63026-3480

636-349-5000
FAX 636-349-5443
E-Mail: naeda@naeda.com
Home Page: www.naeda.com
Social Media: Twitter, LinkedIn

Paul Kindinger, President/CEO
Michael Williams, VP, Government Relations/Treasurer
Terry Leath, Executive Assistant
Roger Gjellstad, First Vice Chair
Lester Killebrew, Chairman

Monthly management and merchandising magazine featuring articles about successful dealers, new products, new technology, industry news and much more.
Cost: $40.00
5000 Members
Frequency: Monthly
Circulation: 9,500
ISSN: 1074-5017
Founded in 1900
Printed in 4 colors on glossy stock

21389 NARDA Independent Retailer
North American Retail Dealers Association
10 E 22nd Street
Suite 310
Lombard, IL 60148-6191

630-953-8950
800-621-0298
FAX 630-953-8957
Home Page: www.narda.com

Tom Drake, CEO/President
Gennifer Michalek, Chairman

Emphasis is placed on ideas that help readers become better, more profitable businesses. Articles are featured regularly on displays, salesmanship, financial analysis and service management.
Cost: $78.00
36 Pages
Frequency: Monthly
Circulation: 2000
ISSN: 1098-9714
Founded in 1943
Mailing list available for rent: 2,000 names
Printed in 4 colors on glossy stock

21390 New Age Retailer
Continuity Publishing
2183 Alpine Way
Bellingham, WA 98226-8045

360-676-0789
800-463-9243
FAX 360-676-0932
E-Mail: info@newageretailer.com
Home Page: www.newageretailer.com

Molly Trimble, CEO
Ray Hemachandra, Editor-in-Chief
Laurel Leigh, Editor
Stephanie R Hager, Circulation Manager
Ellen Koolen, Production Manager

Provides information on new products and business to business trade magazine that supports store owners by providing independent product reviews, retail advice and coverage of

the new age and spirtual lviing industry.
Cost: $ 85.00
192 Pages
Circulation: 10000
Founded in 1987
Mailing list available for rent: 6,000 names at $150 per M

21391 POP Design
In-Store Marketing Institute
7400 Skokie Blvd
Skokie, IL 60077-3339

847-675-7400
FAX 847-675-7494
E-Mail: info@instoremarketer.org
Home Page: www.instoremarketer.org
Social Media: *Facebook, Twitter, LinkedIn*

Peter Hoyt, President

Serves the news and product information needs of producers and designers of instore displays, signs and fixtures. Each issue features the latest trends and technologies vital to building and designing successful instore merchandising.
Frequency: Monthly
Circulation: 18000
Printed in 4 colors on glossy stock

21392 POPAI News
Point-of-Purchase Advertising Institute
1600 Duke Street
Suite 400
Alexandria, VA 22314

703-373-8815
FAX 703-373-8801
E-Mail: bcotter@popai.com
Home Page: www.popai.com
Social Media: *Facebook, Twitter, LinkedIn*

Berk Cotter, Director Member Services
Richard Blatt, CEO/President
Stephen Morant, Manager Production Services
Sean Simmons, General Manager

Provides the point-of-purchase industry with coverage of marketing and retail trends, with an emphasis on in-store promotional programs. Editorial offers coverage of marketing programs, display case histories, preview of new promotional campaigns, sales volume and trends. Accepts advertising.
Cost: $40.00
Frequency: Monthly
Founded in 1940

21393 Pollution Engineering
Reed Business Information
2000 Clearwater Dr
Oak Brook, IL 60523-8809

630-574-0825
FAX 630-288-8781
E-Mail: greenr@bnpmedia.com
Home Page: www.reedbusiness.com
Social Media: *Facebook, Twitter, LinkedIn*

Jeff Greisch, President
Erin Puranananda, Marketing Manager
Seth Fisher, Products Editor
Mark Kelsey, Chief Executive Officer

Serves the field of pollution control in manufacturing industries, utilities, consulting engineers and constructors. Also serves government agencies including administration of federal, state and local environmental programs.
Frequency: Monthly
ISSN: 0032-3640
Founded in 1977

21394 Publishers Weekly
PO Box 51593
Harlan, IA 51593

800-278-2991
FAX 712-733-8019
E-Mail: pwycustserv@cdsfulfillment.com

Home Page: www.publishersweekly.com
Social Media: *Facebook, Twitter, LinkedIn*

George Slovik, President
Michael Coffey, Co-Editorial Director
Diane Roback, Children's Book Editor
Louisa Ermelino, Reviews Director
Calvin Reid, News Editor

PW is the international journal of book publishing and bookselling including business news, reviews and bestseller lists targeted at publishers, booksellers, librarians and literary agents.
Frequency: Weekly
Founded in 1872

21395 Retail Cost of Doing Business
American Floorcovering Association
2211 E Howell Avenue
Anaheim, CA 92806-6009

714-572-8370

Offers an overview of the retail trade.
Frequency: Annual

21396 Retail Focus
National Sporting Goods Association
1601 Feehanville Drive
Suite 300
Mount Prospect, IL 60056

847-296-6742
800-815-5422
FAX 847-391-9827
E-Mail: info@nsga.org
Home Page: www.nsga.org

Bob Dickman, Chairman of the Board
Matt Carlson, President/CEO
Dan Kasen, Director of Information Services

Magazine for members only
Frequency: Bi-Monthly
Mailing list available for rent

21397 Retail Observer
Retail Observer
1442 Sierra Creek Way
San Jose, CA 95132-3618

408-272-8974
800-393-0509
FAX 408-272-3344
E-Mail: info@retailobserver.com
Home Page: www.retailobserver.com/

Chuck Edmonds, Publisher
Lee Boucher, Editor

Edited for owners, managers and retail sales personnel of appliance stores, home entertainment stores and kitchen and bath dealers.
Frequency: Monthly
Circulation: 11750

21398 Retail Systems Alert
Retail Systems Alert Group
PO Box 332
Newton Upper Falls, MA 02464-02

617-527-4626
FAX 617-527-8102
Home Page: www.retailsystems.com

Thomas H Friedman, Publisher

Provides updated information on automation news and trends, including decision systems, information systems implementation, in-store merchandise management, and case studies of retailers.
Cost: $295.00
8 Pages
Frequency: Monthly
Founded in 1988

21399 Retail Systems Reseller
Edgell Communications

4 Middlebury Boulevard
Suite 107
Randolph, NJ 07869-1111

973-252-0100
FAX 973-252-9020
Home Page: www.edgellcommunications.com

Michael Kachmar, Publisher
Joseph S King, Editor-in-Chief
Gabriele A Edgell, CEO
Dan Ligorner, Director of Marketing

Offers information to retailers, dealers, systems integraters, VARs, VADs, etc., on retail technology for small to mid-size retailers.

21400 RetailTech
770 Broadway
New York, NY 10003-9522

646-654-7480
FAX 646-654-7568
Home Page: www.retail-merchandiser.com

21401 STORES Magazine
National Retail Federation
325 7th St NW
Suite 1101
Washington, DC 20004-2808

202-783-7971
800-673-4693
FAX 202-737-2849
E-Mail: pennw@nrf.com
Home Page: www.nrf.com
Social Media: *Facebook, Twitter, LinkedIn*

Matthew Shay, President
Scott Krugman, Publisher
Mader Richard, Executive Director
Michael Gatti, VP/Marketing
David French, VP

Magazine of the National Retail Federation. Provides timely information of importance to senior retail headquarters executives. Every issue reports on trends in retail technology, credit and payment systems, logistics and supply chain and other vital store operations.
Cost: $120.00
Frequency: Monthly
Circulation: 35000

21402 Succe$$ful $ource$
Sutton Family Communications & Publishing Company
155 Sutton Lane
Fordsville, KY 42343

270-740-0870
E-Mail: jlsutton@apex.net
Home Page: www.fleamarketeer.net

Theresa Sutton, Publisher

The #1 trade magazine for multi-billion dollar flea market industry.
Cost: $5.00
Circulation: 100000
Founded in 1977

21403 Supermarket News
Fairchild Publications
750 3rd Ave
New York, NY 10017-2703

212-630-4000
800-204-4515
FAX 212-630-3563
E-Mail: customerservice@fairchildpub.com
Home Page: www.supermarketnews.com

Mary G Berner, CEO
David Merrefield, Editorial Director
Dan Bagan, Publishing Director
David Orgel, Editor-in-Chief
Cost: $44.50
40 Pages
Frequency: Weekly
Circulation: 36346

ISSN: 0039-5803
Founded in 1892

21404 Today's Grocers

Florida Grocer Publications
PO Box 430760
S Miami, FL 33246

305-661-0792
800-440-3067
FAX 305-661-6720

Jack Nobles, Publisher
Dennis Kane, Editor

Provides the latest food industry news and
trends to Florida, Georgia, Alabama, Louisiana,
Mississippi and the Carolinas.
Cost: $29.00
24 Pages
Frequency: Monthly
Circulation: 19,000
ISSN: 1529-4420
Founded in 1956
Printed in on newsprint stock

Trade Shows

21405 ASD/AMD Houston Variety Merchandise Show

ASD/AMD Merchandise Group
2950 31st Street
Suite 100
Santa Monica, CA 90405

310-396-6006
800-421-4511
FAX 310-399-2662
Home Page: www.merchandisegroup.com

Julie Ichiba, Show Director

Our newest variety and general merchandise
trade show offers buyers in the southwestern
US and Mexico terrific product sourcing opportunities for all types of popular consumer
goods.
12000 Attendees

21406 ASD/AMD Las Vegas Trade Show

ASD/AMD Merchandise Group
2950 31st Street
Suite 100
Santa Monica, CA 90405

310-396-6006
800-421-4511
FAX 310-399-2662
Home Page: www.merchandisegroup.com

Julie Ichiba, Show Director

The summer edition of the largest variety merchandise event in the US attracts over 50,000
buyers to Las Vegas. Tens of thousands of
unique products in hundreds of popular consumer product categories are on display at this
even
50000 Attendees
Frequency: August

21407 ASD/AMD's Atlantic City Variety Merchandise Show

ASD/AMD Merchandise Group
2950 31st Street
Suite 100
Santa Monica, CA 90405

310-396-6006
800-421-4511
FAX 310-399-2662
Home Page: www.merchandisegroup.com

Julie Ichiba, Show Director

Held in Atlantic City, New Jersey, this event is
a popular destination for east coast retailers to
make deals and place orders for variety and
general merchandise in hundreds of popular

consumer categories before the summer selling
season begins.
10000 Attendees
Frequency: May

21408 ASD/AMD's Fall Variety Merchandise Show

ASD/AMD Merchandise Group
2950 31st Street
Suite 100
Santa Monica, CA 90405

310-396-6006
800-421-4511
FAX 310-399-2662
Home Page: www.merchandisegroup.com

Julie Ichiba, Show Director

The fall edition of the general merchandise
event on the east coast takes place in New York
City. It's the last opportunity of the year for retailers to place orders for goods before the busy
holiday buying season.
12000 Attendees
Frequency: September

21409 ASD/AMD's Las Vegas Merchandise Expo

ASD/AMD Merchandise Group
2950 31st Street
Suite 100
Santa Monica, CA 90405

310-396-6006
800-421-4511
FAX 310-399-2662
Home Page: www.merchandisegroup.com

Julie Ichiba, Show Director

Held in Las Vegas, Nevada, this event is strategically timed for western US retailers to stock
their shelves with quality, value-priced variety
and general merchandise in between our larger
Las Vegas Trade Shows in March and Agust.
5,000 Attendees
Frequency: June

21410 ASD/AMD's New York Variety Merchandise Show

ASD/AMD Merchandise Group
2950 31st Street
Suite 100
Santa Monica, CA 90405

310-396-6006
800-421-4511
FAX 310-399-2662
Home Page: www.merchandisegroup.com

Julie Ichiba, Show Director

Held in New York City, this event is the first
opportunity of the New Year for variety and
general merchandise retailers to stock their
shelves after the holidays with popular,
value-priced consumer goods in hundreds of
product categories.
12500 Attendees
Frequency: January

21411 ASD/AMD's Orlando Variety Merchandise Show

ASD/AMD Merchandise Group
2950 31st Street
Suite 100
Santa Monica, CA 90405

310-396-6006
800-421-4511
FAX 310-399-2662
Home Page: www.merchandisegroup.com

Julie Ichiba, Show Director

Held in Orlando, Florida, this event is a popular destination for southeastern US retailers to
make deals and place orders for variety and

general merchandise in hundreds of popular
consumer categories.
5,500 Attendees
Frequency: April

21412 Accent on Design

George Little Management
10 Bank Street
Suite 1200
White Plains, NY 10606-1954

914-486-6070
800-272-7469
FAX 914-948-2867
Home Page: www.nyigf.com

Elizabeth Murphy, Manager
George Little II, President

370 booths of the latest and most innovative
gift lines such as decorative accessories and
home furnishings.
50M Attendees
Frequency: August
Founded in 1984

21413 American Beverage Licensees Annual Convention & Trade Show

National Association of Beverage Retailers
5101 River Road
Suite 108
Bethesda, MD 20816-1560

301-656-1494
FAX 301-656-7539
Home Page: www.nabronline.org

Harry Wiles, Executive Director
Shawn Ross, Office Manager

Annual show of 75 manufacturers, suppliers
and distributors of alcoholic beverages.
1,000 Attendees

21414 Associated Surplus Dealers/Associated Merchandise Dealers Trade Show

ASD/AMD Merchandise Group
2950 31st Street
Suite 100
Santa Monica, CA 90405

310-255-4633
800-421-4511
FAX 310-399-3662
Home Page: www.merchandisegroup.com

Sam Bundy, Group President

Gifts, souvenirs and assorted merchandise for
professional buyers.
15000 Attendees
Frequency: Annual/March

21415 Book Expo America

Reed Exhibitions
383 Main Avenue
Norwalk, CT 06851

203-404-4800
800-840-5614
E-Mail: cmuller@reedexpo.com
Home Page: www.bookexpoamerica.com
Social Media: *Facebook, Twitter, LinkedIn*

Courtney Muller, Event Manager
Cathy Glickstein, Registration

Sponsored by American Booksellers Association and Association of American Publishers.
More than 2,000 exhibits, 500 authors, over 60
conference sessions as well as a special area for
rights business, all the latest titles across genres, uncover hidden gems, network, and meet
the industry contacts to put you instantly on top
of what you need to know for your business
and job.
Frequency: May/June
Founded in 2000

21416 CMM International: FLEX Expo

Bruno Blenheim

Fort Lee Executive Park
Fort Lee, FL 07024

800-829-3976
FAX 201-346-1602

Nick Helyer, President

Exhibits by franchisers and sellers to the franchise industry. 125 booths.
5M Attendees
Frequency: June

21417 Customer Relationship Management Course: C RMretail

National Retail Federation
325 7th Street NW
Suite 1101
Washington, DC 20004

202-783-7971
FAX 202-737-2849
E-Mail: exhibit@nrf.com
Home Page: www.nrf.com
Social Media: *Facebook, Twitter, LinkedIn*

Michael Tuttle, Director Exhibits
Cindy Shin, Director Sales

CRMretail is a cross-industry conference, bringing together retail business leaders and the leading technology companies, solutions providers, consultants and academicians in the field of customer relationship management. Annual CRMretail research conducted by Gartner Dataquest is also released at this conference.
200 Attendees
Frequency: Late Spring
Founded in 1993

21418 Green Profit's Retail Experience

Green Profit Magazine
335 N River Street
Batavia, IL 60510

630-208-9080
888-888-0013
FAX 630-208-9350
E-Mail: info@ballpublishing.com
Home Page:
www.ballpublishing.com/conferences

Michelle Mazza, Show Manager

Educational event and tradeshow dedicated exclusively to garden center retailing. Covers topics from store layout and design to merchandising strategies and business management. 20 booths
300 Attendees
Frequency: September
Founded in 2006

21419 International Council of Shopping Centers Fall Convention Trade & Exposition

International Council of Shopping Centers
1221 Ave Of The Americas
41st Fl
New York, NY 10020-1099

646-728-3800
FAX 732-694-1755
E-Mail: icsc@icsc.org
Home Page: www.icsc.org

Michael Kercheval, President/CEO
Denise Adrian, Director Of Marketing

21420 International Franchise Association Expo

1501 K St NW
Suite 350
Washington, DC 20005-1412

202-628-8000
FAX 202-628-0812

Matthew Shay, President
Patricia Langfeld, VP

75 booths.
1M Attendees
Frequency: February

21421 Internet Retailer Conference & Exhibition

Internet Retailer
300 S Wacker Drive
Suite 602
Chicago, IL 60606

FAX 312-362-9532
Home Page: www.internetretailer.com
Social Media: *Facebook, Twitter, LinkedIn*

Learn the strategies, practices and tools to lift your site into e-retailing's second decade of growth. Network with your peers in the only show serving e-retailers from all merchant channels.
Frequency: Annual

21422 Logistics

Retail Industry Leaders Association
1700 N Moore Street
Suite 2250
Arlington, VA 22209

703-841-2300
FAX 703-841-1184
Home Page: www.imra.org

Britt Wood, VP
Sean Nodland, Manager

This event brings together retailers, consumer product companies, and suppliers of goods and service logistics side of business
400 Attendees
Frequency: February

21423 Loss Prevention Conference & Exhibition

National Retail Federation
325 7th Street NW
Suite 1100
Washington, DC 20004

202-783-7971
FAX 202-737-2849
E-Mail: exhibit@nrf.com
Home Page: www.nrf.com
Social Media: *Facebook, Twitter, LinkedIn*

Michael Tuttle, Director Exhibits
Scott Krugman, Publisher
Mader Richard, Executive Director
Michael Gatti, VP/Marketing
David French, VP

Major conference for Loss Prevention, Internal Audit and Risk Management professionals in the retail industry.
1500 Attendees
Frequency: June
Founded in 1993

21424 Loss Prevention, Auditing & Safety Conference

Retail Industry Leaders Association
1700 N Moore Street
Suite 2250
Arlington, VA 22209

703-841-2300
FAX 703-841-1184
E-Mail: rhett.asher@retail-leaders.org
Home Page: www.retail-leaders.org
Social Media: *Facebook, Twitter, LinkedIn*

Rhett Asher

Annual information exchange.
325 Attendees
Frequency: April

21425 Marketing Conference

International Mass Retail Association

1700 N Moore Street
Suite 2250
Arlington, VA 22209

703-841-2300
FAX 703-841-1184
Home Page: www.imra.org

Peter Kim, Owner

21426 NACS Show Annual Meeting and Exposition

National Association of Convenience Stores
1600 Duke Street
Alexandria, VA 22314

703-684-3600
FAX 703-836-4564
E-Mail: nacs@nacs.com
Home Page: www.nacsshow.com

Jane Berzan, VP Events/Mktg/Supplier Relations
Sherry Romello, Director Meetings and Conventions
24000 Attendees
Frequency: October

21427 National Lawn & Garden Controlled Marketing Conference

Controlled Marketing Conferences
PO Box 1771
Monument, CO 80132

719-488-0226
888-316-0226
FAX 719-488-8168
Home Page: www.nlgshow.com /
www.marketingconferences.com

Robert Mikulas, President
Chris Wolf, VP

This year CMC events will be linked to the National Lawn ans Garden Show - The Expo Division. Don't miss out on the industries most important lawn and garden headlines event.
3000 Attendees
Frequency: June

21428 National Retail Federation Annual Conference and Expo

National Retail Federation
325 7th Street NW
Suite 1100
Washington, DC 20004-2808

202-783-7971
FAX 202-783-0581
E-Mail: webmaster@nrf.com
Home Page: www.nrf.com

Michael Tuttle, Director Exhibits
Cindy Shin, Director Sales
Tracy Mullin, President

600 booths exhibiting the latest in retail technology, new developments in credit validation, security and materials handling.
12M Attendees
Frequency: January

21429 Retail Advertising Conference: RAC

Retail Advertising & Marketing International
325 7th Street NW
Suite 1100
Washington, DC 20004

202-626-8183
FAX 202-737-2849
Home Page: www.rama-nrf.org

Mike Gatti, VP Marketing

Definitive event for retail advertising and marketing professionals each year featuring the RAC Awards gala dinner and Retail Hall of Fame induction annually.
1000 Attendees
Frequency: February

21430 Retail Promotion Show
Association of Retail Marketing Services
10 Drs James Parker Boulevard
Suite 103
Red Bank, NJ 07701-1500

732-842-5070
866-331-6310
FAX 732-219-1938
E-Mail: info@goarms.com
Home Page: www.goarms.com

Gerri Hopkins, Executive Director

Annual show of 65 manufacturers, suppliers, distributors and representatives of dinnerware, glassware, housewares, books, videos, games, sweepstakes, dolls and plush toys suppliers used as retail promotions.
1200 Attendees
Frequency: March, Annual

21431 Shop.org Annual Summit
Shop.org
325 7th Street NW
Suite 1100
Washington, DC 20004

202-626-8183
FAX 202-626-8191
Home Page: www.shop.org

Diane Furstenberg, COO
Lane Bryant, VP Marketing

Provides a unique opportunity for Internet and multi-channel retail industry leaders to exchange ideas, perspectives, opportunities and challenges in an intimate and comfortable setting. The Summit features dialogues with distinguished keynote speakers, provocative panels and debates on timely issues, and important original research.
600 Attendees
Frequency: September

21432 Shop.org Members' Forum
Shop.org
325 7th Street NW
Suite 1100
Washington, DC 20004

202-626-8183
FAX 202-626-8191
Home Page: www.shop.org

Diane Furstenberg, COO
Lane Bryant, VP Marketing

Attendees see presentations for an online holiday recap and new multichannel retail research sessions as well as roundtable discussions and other networking events.
350 Attendees
Frequency: January

21433 Southern Convenience Store & Petroleum Show
PO Box 855
Snellville, GA 30078

770-736-9723
FAX 770-736-9725
E-Mail: jtudor@aol.com
Home Page: www.gacs.com

Jim Tudor, President

Contains 250 exhibits.
3,000 Attendees
Founded in 2003

21434 Store Fixturing Show
Shore Varrone

6255 Barfield Road NE
Suite 200
Atlanta, GA 30328-4332

404-848-0077
800-241-9034
FAX 770-252-4436

Russ Eisenhardt, VP Trade Shows
Lee Pritcher, Owner

The largest annual store design event in the world. The event also includes The Visual Merchandising Show, the Retail Operations & Construction Expo, the POPAI Expo and the Exhibit Ideas Show. 800 exhibitors in total.
15M Attendees
Frequency: April

21435 Store Operations & Human Resources Conference
International Mass Retail Association
1700 N Moore Street
Suite 2250
Arlington, VA 22209

703-841-2300
FAX 703-841-1184
Home Page: www.imra.org

This educational event provides attendees with an opportunity to learn from experts in their fields on the most pressing topics of the day

Directories & Databases

21436 Annual Trade Show Directory
Forum Publishing Company
383 E Main St
Centerport, NY 11721-1538

631-754-5000
FAX 631-754-0630
Home Page: www.forum123.com

Martin Stevens, Owner

Over 1,800 merchandise trade shows throughout the United States and Canada.
Cost: $39.95
312 Pages
Frequency: Annual

21437 Association of Retail Marketing Services Membership Directory
Association of Retail Marketing Services
10 Drs James Parker Boulevard
Suite 103
Red Bank, NJ 07701-1500

732-842-5070
FAX 732-219-1938
Home Page: www.goarms.com

Gerri Hopkins, Executive Director
Lisa McCauley, Administrative Director

Membership directory.
Cost: $25.00
Frequency: Annual

21438 Directory of Convenience Stores
Trade Dimensions
45 Danbury Rd
Wilton, CT 06897-4445

203-563-3000
FAX 860-563-3131
Home Page: www.tradedimensions.com

Jennifer Gillbert, Editor
Lynda Guticulez, Managing Editor

The directory comprises nearly 1,500 detailed profiles on the companies you need to do business with - extensive dependable information on the grocery industry's most volatile segment.
Cost: $245.00
Frequency: Annual

21439 Directory of High Discount Merchandise Sources
B Klein Publishers
Po Box 6578
Delray Beach, FL 33482-6578

561-496-3316
FAX 561-496-5546

Bernard Klein, Owner

Approximately 1,200 sources of products offered at high discounts.
Cost: $35.00
Frequency: Annual

21440 Directory of Mail Order Catalogs
Grey House Publishing
4919 Route 22
PO Box 56
Amenia, NY 12501

518-789-8700
800-562-2139
FAX 845-373-6390
E-Mail: books@greyhouse.com
Home Page: www.greyhouse.com
Social Media: *Facebook, Twitter*

Leslie Mackenzie, Publisher
Richard Gottlieb, Editor

The premier source of information on the mail order catalog industry. Covers over 13,000 consumer and business catalog companies with 44 different product chapters from Animals to Toys and Games.
Cost: $395.00
1900 Pages
Frequency: Annual
ISBN: 1-592373-96-8
Founded in 1981

21441 Directory of Mail Order Catalogs - Online Database
Grey House Publishing
4919 Route 22
PO Box 56
Amenia, NY 12501

518-789-8700
800-562-2139
FAX 845-373-6390
E-Mail: gold@greyhouse.com
Home Page: http://gold.greyhouse.com
Social Media: *Facebook, Twitter*

Leslie Mackenzie, Publisher
Richard Gottlieb, Editor

Reach over 10,000 consumer catalog companies in one easy-to-use source with The Directory of Mail Order Catalogs - Online Database. Filled with business-building detail, each company profile gives you the information you need to access that organization quickly and easily. Listings provide key contacts, sales volume, employee size, printing information, circulation, list data, product descriptions and much more.
Frequency: Annual
Founded in 1981

21442 Directory of Major Malls
PO Box 837
Nyack, NY 10960-0837

845-348-7000
FAX 845-426-0802

Tama J Shor, Editor/Publisher
Murray Shor, Consulting Publisher

Contains 2865 listings with over 1800 leasing/site plans of major malls, with many showing the anchors, design layout, intersecting streets, peripheral land, and major highways.
ISBN: 0-932599-13-3

21443 Directory of Mass Merchandisers
Trade Dimensions

45 Danbury Rd
Wilton, CT 06897-4445

203-563-3000
FAX 860-563-3131
Home Page: www.tradedimensions.com

Lynda Gutierrez, Managing Editor
Jennifer Gilbert, Editor

This directory defines this complex class of retail trade. Includes profiles of the chains and
leading mass merchandisers by market area.
Also includes HBC suppliers and store type
breakdowns by state/region.
Cost: $245.00
Frequency: Annual

**21444 Discount & General Merchandising
Stores**
Chain Store Guide
3922 Coconut Palm Dr
Tampa, FL 33619-1389

813-627-6700
800-972-9292
FAX 813-627-7094
E-Mail: info@csgis.com
Home Page: www.csgis.com

Mike Jarvis, Publisher
Shami Choon, Manager

This database is an in-depth look at the
mass-merchandising segment, bringing you access to more than 7,000 listings along with
over 23,000 key personnel. This report includes
targeted research from sectors such as Discount
Department Stores, General Merchandise
Stores, Dollar Stores, Automotive Aftermarket
Retailers and Computer & Consumer Electronics Chains.
Cost: $335.00
720 Pages
Frequency: Annual

21445 Discount Merchandiser
McFadden Publishing Company
233 Park Ave S
6th Floor
New York, NY 10003-1606

212-979-4800
FAX 212-979-7342

Steven Jacober, Editor

Profiles of the top 55 chains and list of top 85
discount merchandising companies.
Cost: $40.00
Frequency: Annual June

**21446 International Franchise Association -
Franchise Opportunities Guide**
1501 K St NW
Suite 350
Washington, DC 20005-1412

202-628-8000
FAX 202-628-0812
Home Page: www.franchise.org

Matthew Shay, President

This directory lists over 3,000 companies offering franchises.
Cost: $21.00
300 Pages
Frequency: SemiAnnual

21447 Leading Chain Tenants Database
Chain Store Guide
3922 Coconut Palm Dr
Tampa, FL 33619-1389

813-627-6700
800-778-9794
FAX 813-627-7094
E-Mail: info@csgis.com
Home Page: www.csgis.com

Mike Jarvis, Publisher
Arthur Sciarrotta, Senior VP

Information on more than 8,600 retailers in the
U.S. and Canada with over 32,000 personnel
contacts. This database will lead you to new
real estate prospects across a vast range of industries. Whether you are in real estate development, leasing or sales, the opportunities are
endless.
Cost: $365.00

21448 NRB Shopping Center Directory
Trade Dimensions
45 Danbury Rd
Wilton, CT 06897-4445

203-563-3000
FAX 860-563-3131
Home Page: www.nrbonline.com

Patricia Kelly, Managing Editor
Stephanie Strano, Circulation Director

The most comprehensive book on shopping
centers available. Encompassing over 37,000
centers from neighborhood to super regional,
the Directory is organized into four volumes:
East, Midwest, South, West. A fifth volume is
dedicated exclusively to the industry's top contacts, comprising the names and contact information for anyone who owns, leases, or
manages three or more centers.
Cost: $325.00
Frequency: Annual

21449 Outlet Project Directory
Value Retail News
29399 Us Highway 19 N
Suite 370
Clearwater, FL 33761-2138

727-781-7557
800-669-1020
FAX 727-536-4389
Home Page: www.valueretailnews.com

Cher Russell-Street, Editor

Factory outlet projects.
Cost: $179.00
Frequency: SemiAnnual

21450 Outlet Retail Directory
Off-Price Specialists, Value Retail News
14250 49th St N
Clearwater, FL 33762-2800

727-464-6460
FAX 727-453-7419

James Pierce, Manager

Over 500 outlet retail chains are profiled.
280 Pages
Frequency: Semiannual

21451 Products & Services Directory
Value Retail News
29399 Us Highway 19 N
Suite 370
Clearwater, FL 33761-2138

727-781-7557
800-669-1020
FAX 727-536-4389
Home Page: www.valueretailnews.com

Cher Russell-Street, Editor

More than 2,000 service companies specializing in outlet or off-price retailing and development industries.
Cost: $49.00
Frequency: Annual

21452 Productscan Online
Marketing Intelligence Service
6473 State Route 64
Naples, NY 14512-9726

585-374-6326
FAX 585-374-5217
Home Page: www.productscan.com

Tom Vierhile, Manager
Julie Fox, Finance Executive

This database is dedicated solely to new
launches of consumer packaged goods. Includes label copy, in-depth reports on innovations, and product pictures capable of statistical
analysis and manufacturer history reports.
Cost: $3995.00

**21453 Retail Industry Buying Guide:
STORES Magazine**
National Retail Federation
325 7th St NW
Suite 1100
Washington, DC 20004-2808

202-783-7971
800-673-4693
FAX 202-737-2849
E-Mail: pennw@nrf.com
Home Page: www.nrf.com
Social Media: *Facebook, Twitter, LinkedIn*

Matthew Shay, President
Scott Krugman, Publisher
Mader Richard, Executive Director
Michael Gatti, VP/Marketing
David French, VP

Capital spending in the products and services
that are imperitive to running a smooth and efficient retail operation were particularly hard
hit in the past year. In the face of continued un-
certainty, it's essential that retailers make informed decisions on how to best invest their
limited capital to ensure a positive return on
their investment. This directory is that source
of information.
Frequency: Monthly
Circulation: 35000

21454 Retail Tenant Directory
Trade Dimensions
45 Danbury Rd
Wilton, CT 06897-4445

203-563-3000
FAX 860-563-3131
Home Page: www.tradedimensions.com

Garrett Van Siclen, Publisher
Thomas Donato, Editor

Complete and accurate details for 5,000+ growing retailers that are looking for space. Holding
company section lists corporate profiles for
major parent companies which own two or
more major retail chains in the US. Individual
company profiles include retail classifications,
total number of stores, operating names, sales
volume, who to contact, extensive site selection
criteria including demographic preferences, expansion plans, acquisitions, format changes and
more.
Cost: $345.00
1500 Pages
Frequency: Annual
ISBN: 0-911790-29-2

**21455 Shippers Guide to Department &
Chain Stores Nationwide**
Shippers Guides
PO Box 112
Duarte, CA 91009-0112

626-357-6430
FAX 626-357-6366

Profiles over 1,000 department stores and chain
stores and information about routing and
freight movement.
Cost: $349.00
350 Pages
Frequency: Annual
*Mailing list available for rent: 1,000 names at
$299 per M*

21456 Shopping Center Directory
National Research Bureau

333 W Wacker Drive
Suite 900
Chicago, IL 60606-1284

312-346-3900

This large directory offers information on over 30,000 shopping centers in four regional volumes.
Cost: $225.00
3,200 Pages
Frequency: Annual

21457 Single Unit Supermarkets Operators
Chain Store Guide
3922 Coconut Palm Dr
Tampa, FL 33619-1389

813-627-6700
800-778-9794
FAX 813-627-7094
E-Mail: info@csgis.com
Home Page: www.csgis.com

Mike Jarvis, Publisher
Shami Choon, Manager

Discover more than 7,100 single-unit supermarkets with annual sales topping $500,000 dollars. This comprehensive desktop reference makes it easy to reach our compiled list of 21,000 key executives and buyers, plus their primary wholesalers.
Cost: $335.00
725 Pages
Frequency: Annual

21458 Stores: Top 100 Retailers Issue
National Retail Federation
325 7th St NW
Suite 1100
Washington, DC 20004-2808

202-783-7971
800-673-4694
FAX 202-737-2849
E-Mail: pennw@nrf.com
Home Page: www.nrf.com
Social Media: *Facebook, Twitter, LinkedIn*

Matthew Shay, President
Scott Krugman, Publisher
Mader Richard, Executive Director
Michael Gatti, VP/Marketing
David French, VP

100 US retail companies having largest estimated sales during preceding year.
Cost: $75.00
Frequency: Annual July
Circulation: 35,000

21459 Supermarket, Grocery & Convenience Stores
Chain Store Guide
3922 Coconut Palm Dr
Tampa, FL 33619-1389

813-627-6700
800-778-9794
FAX 813-627-7094
E-Mail: info@csgis.com
Home Page: www.csgis.com

Mike Jarvis, Publisher
Shami Choon, Manager

Contains information on close to 3,400 U.S. and Canadian supermarket chains, each with at least $2 million in annual sales - one of the most profitable segments in this sector of the economy. The companies in this database operate over 41,000 individual supermarket, superstore, club store, gourmet supermarkets and combo-store units. A special convenience store section profiles 1,700 convenience store chains operating over 85,000 stores.
Cost: $335.00
Frequency: Annual

21460 Top Shopping Centers: Major Markets 1-50
National Research Bureau
333 W Wacker Drive
Suite 900
Chicago, IL 60606-1284

312-346-3900
Cost: $895.00

21461 US Trade Pages
Global Source
1511 K Street NW
Washington, DC 20005-1403
Kara Kent, Editor

These directories including a volume on Brazil, Chile, Canada, Mexico, Venezuela, and Argentina list trade associations and professional services that provide information on imports and exports between the US and the above listed companies.
Cost: $59.95
Frequency: 6 Volumes

21462 World Federation of Direct Selling Associations Directory
WFDSA
1776 K St Nw
Washington, DC 20006-2304

202-546-5330
FAX 202-453-9010
Home Page: www.wfdsa.org
Social Media: *Facebook, Twitter, LinkedIn*

A Harold, President
Founded in 1789

Industry Web Sites

21463 http://gold.greyhouse.com
G.O.L.D Grey House OnLine Databases
Grey House Publishing's online database platform, GOLD, offers Quick Search, Keyword Search and Expert Search for most business sectors including retailing markets. The GOLD platform makes finding the information you need quick and easy - whether you're a novice searcher or an experienced database user. All of Grey House's directory products are available for subscription on the GOLD platform.

21464 www.aamp.com
American Association of Meat Processors
The membership consists of small to medium sized meat, poultry and food businesses including: packers, processors, wholesalers, home food service businesses, retailers, deli and catering operators. AAMP is also affiliated with 34 state, regional and provincial organizations which represent meat and poultry businesses.

21465 www.bookweb.org
American Booksellers Association
Trade association for retail booksellers. Not for profit.

21466 www.fdi.org
International Center for Companies of Food Trade
and Industry/North America

Provides management research on problems related to food distribution and serves as an international forum where food chain store executives can meet to exchange ideas and information.

21467 www.fleamarkets.org
National Flea Market Association

Represents Flea Market and Swap Meet owners and managers and disseminates information to the general public and media regarding the flea market industry worldwide.

21468 www.goarms.com
Association of Retail Marketing Services
Approximately 60 retailers involved in the ARMS retail promotion show, held annually.

21469 www.greyhouse.com
Grey House Publishing
Authoritative reference directories for most business sectors including retail markets. Users can search the online databases with varied search criteria allowing for custom searches by product category, geographic area, sales volume, keyword, subject and more. Full Grey House catalog and online ordering also available.

21470 www.ispo.org
Institute of Store Planners
Provides a forum for debate and discussion by store design experts and retailers. Sponsors student design programs.

21471 www.maptrade.org
International Map Trade Association
Membership comprised of retail stores featuring maps, travel books, globes, and travel products, plus publishers and manufacturers producing these products. Publishes a monthly newsletter

21472 www.mraa.com
Marine Retailers Association of America
Promotes activities for the recreational boating industry and holds seminars to improve management.

21473 www.nacs.org
National Association of College Stores
Provides educational and support services and products to college stores. Promotes business methods and ethics. Conducts manager certification, educational services and research.

21474 www.nag-net.com
Convenience Stores/Petroleum Marketers Association
This association represents senior level management of retail companies organized to enhance buying power, merchandising programs and an exchange of ideas. C-Stores/Petroleum Marketers membership dues: Retail Av. $300, Assoc. $500

21475 www.nagmr.org
National Association General Merchandise Repr
A professional association of consumer product brokers representing leading manufacturers to the retail trade.

21476 www.narda.com
North American Retail Dealers Association
A national organization of association members, independent retailers selling and servicing major appliances, consumer electronics products, furniture and computers. Emphasis is placed on ideas that help readers become better, more profitable businesses. Articles are featured regularly on displays, salesmanship, financial analysis and service management.

21477 www.nationalPawnbrokers.org
National Pawnbrokers Association
Nonprofits organization that supports all those involved with the retail pawnbrokers.

21478 www.nationalgrocers.org
National Grocers Association

Works to advance understanding, trade, and co-operation in the food industry. Represents members interests before the government. Offers store planning, and engineering, training and advertising.

21479 www.nicyra.org
National Ice Cream & Yogurt Retailers Association

Members are in retail frozen dessert businesses. Some offer food services either full of limited and some operate convenience stores. The common denominator is that all members offer frozen desserts for take-home or on-site consumption.

21480 www.nrf.com
National Retail Federation

Retail trade association with membership that comprises all retail formats and channels of distribution including department, specialty, discount, catalog, Internet and independent stores. NRF members represent an industry that encompasses more than 1.4 million US retail establishments which employ more than 23 million people — about one in five American workers — and registered 2002 sales of $3.6 trillion. NRF's international members operate stores in more than 50 nations.

21481 www.nsgachicagoshow.com
National Sporting Goods Association

Members consist of retailers, wholesalers, suppliers, sales agents and media. Sponsor of NSGA World Sports EXPO, held annually in Chicago, and the NSGA Management Conference. Has an annual budget of approximately $8 million.

21482 www.nssra.com
National Ski & Snowboard Retailers Association

The retail voice for the ski and snowboard industries and provides information and services you need to operate more successfully.

21483 www.retailsystems.com
Retail Systems Alert Group

For retail and supply chain professionals. Access to community centers, newsletter information, and online ordering information is also available.

21484 www.rtda.org
Retail Tobacco Dealers of America
Trade association of high quality tobacconists.

21485 www.shop.org
Shop.org

Association for retailers online. It's where professional retailerscome together to garner the insight, knowledge and intellegence to make better decisions in the evolving world of the Internet and multi-channel retailing.

21486 www.smallbusinesslocator.com
Small Business Association

Providing information to mom and pop businesses.

Associations

21487 Acrylonitrile Group
1250 Connecticut Ave Nw
Suite 700
Washington, DC 20036

202-419-1500
FAX 202-659-8037
E-Mail: angroup@regnet.com
Home Page: www.angroup.org

Robert J Fensterheim, Executive Director

Represents producers and users of the industrial chemical used to make plastics, fibers and synthetic rubber products.
Founded in 1981

21488 American Chemical Society: Rubber Division
411 Wolf Ledges
Suite 201
Akron, OH 44311

330-972-7814
FAX 330-972-5269
Home Page: www.rubber.org

John Long, Councilor
Leo Goss, Chair-Elect
Terry DeLapa, Chair
William Stahl, Treasurer
Jerry McCall, Secretary

The Rubber Division of the American Chemical Society is a professional organization dedicated to providing educational programs, technical resources and other vital services for the people associated with rubber and affiliated industries.
Founded in 1909

21489 Association for Rubber Products Manufacturers
7321 Shadeland Station Way
Suite 285
Indianapolis, IN 46256

317-863-4072
FAX 317-913-2445
Home Page: www.arpminc.com

Association dedicated to helping industry executives improve their businesses.
Founded in 2010

21490 Engineering with Rubber: How to Design Rubber Components
American Chemical Society: Rubber Division
411 Wolf Ledges
Suite 201
Akron, OH 44311

330-972-7814
FAX 330-972-5269
Home Page: www.rubber.org

John Long, Councilor
Leo Goss, Chair-Elect
Terry DeLapa, Chair
William Stahl, Treasurer
Jerry McCall, Secretary

Teaches the beginning engineer the principles of rubber science and technology-what rubber is, how it behaves, and how to design simple engineering components.
Founded in 1909

21491 International Institute of Synthetic Rubber Producers, Inc.
3535 Briapark Drive
Suite 250
Houston, TX 77042

713-783-7511
FAX 713-783-7253

E-Mail: info@iisrp.com
Home Page: www.iisrp.com

Juan Ramon Salinas, Managing Director/CEO
Roxanna Bauza-Petrovic, General Director of Programs
Sue Flynn, Executive Assistant/ Event Coor
Robin Boyd, Manager of Accounts
Mary O'Connor, European Section Secretariat

International trade association for synthetic rubber producers to receive and benefit from statistical, environmental, and technical information in order to keep abreast of the world's market growth and events.
50 Members
Founded in 1960

21492 North American Recycled Rubber Association
1621 Mcewen Drive
Unit 24
Whitby Ontario, CA L1N-9A5

905-433-7669
FAX 905-433-0905
E-Mail: narra@oix.com
Home Page: www.recycle.net

Diane Sarracini, Contact

Created to bring together the various stakeholders affiliated with the recycled rubber industry.
Founded in 1994

21493 Polyurethane Foam Association
9724 Kingston Pike
334 Lakeside Plaza
Loudon, TN 37774

865-657-9840
FAX 865-381-1292
E-Mail: rluedeka@pfa.org
Home Page: www.pfa.org

Robert Luedeka, Executive Director

The mission of the Polyurethane Foam Association (PFA) is to educate customers and other groups about flexible polyurethane foam (FPF) and to promote its use in manufactured and industrial products.
Founded in 1980

21494 Polyurethane Manufacturers Association
6737 W Washington Avenue
Suite 1300
Milwaukee, WI 53214

414-431-3094
FAX 414-276-7704
E-Mail: info@pmahome.org
Home Page: www.pmahome.org
Social Media: *Facebook, Twitter, LinkedIn*

Phil Green, President
Robert Adkins, Director
R. Bruce DeMent, Director
Linda Katz, VP/Treasurer/Secretary
Mike Kocak, Past President

The Polyurethane Manufacturers Association is the trade association of the cast polyurethane elastomer industry, serving processors of polyurethane products, materials and equipment suppliers and independent agents. PMA exchanges and disseminates information on standards, materials, processes and technical matters, in addition to monitoring regulatory and legislative activity affecting the urethane industry.
90 Members
Founded in 1971

21495 Rubber & Plastics News
1725 Merriman Rd.
Akron, OH 44313-5251

330-836-9180
FAX 330-836-2831

Home Page: www.rubbernews.com
Social Media: *Facebook, Twitter, LinkedIn*

Domestic and international rubber industry news as well as new technology and products.
Frequency: 25x/year
Founded in 1971

21496 Rubber Division, American Chemical Society
411 Wolf Ledges
Suite 201
Akron, OH 44311

330-972-7814
FAX 330-972-5269
Home Page: www.rubber.org

John Long, Councilor
Leo Goss, Chair-Elect
Terry DeLapa, Chair
William Stahl, Treasurer
Jerry McCall, Secretary

Rubber division of the American Chemical Society is a professional association dedicated to providing educational programs, technical resources and other vital services for the people associated with rubber and affiliated industries. Serves as a global resource for networking and partnerships with academics and industry.
Founded in 1909

21497 Rubber Manufacturers Association
1400 K St Nw
Suite 900
Washington, DC 20005

202-682-4800
FAX 202-682-4854
E-Mail: info@rma.org
Home Page: www.rma.org
Social Media: *Facebook, Twitter, YouTube*

Charlie Cannon, President & CEO
Tracey Norberg, Senior Vice President, General Coun
Daniel Zielinski, Senior Vice President, Public Affai

National trade association for makers of tires and other rubber products.
100 Members
Founded in 1915

21498 Rubber Pavements Association
10000 N. 31st Ave
Suite D-408
Phoenix, AZ 85051

480-517-9944
877-517-9944
FAX 480-517-9959
E-Mail: dougc@rubberpavements.org
Home Page: www.rubberpavements.org

Mark Belshe, Executive Director
Guadalupe Dickerson, Office Manager
Cliff Ashcroft, President

Dedicated to encouraging greater usage of high quality, cost effective asphalt pavements containing recycled tire rubber.
Founded in 1985

21499 Single Ply Roofing Institute
465 Waverley Oaks Road
Suite 421
Waltham, MA 02452

781-647-7026
FAX 781-647-7222
E-Mail: info@spri.org
Home Page: www.spri.org

SPRI represents sheet membrane and related component suppliers in the commercial roofing industry.
Founded in 1981

21500 Society of the Plastics Industry
1425 K Street NW
Suite 500
Washington, DC 20005

202-974-5200
202-296-7005
FAX 202-296-7005
Home Page: www.plasticsindustry.org
Social Media: *Facebook, Twitter, LinkedIn, YouTube*

William Cartuaex, President

Represents the entire plastics industry in a manner that promotes development of the industry and enhances public understanding of its contributions while meeting the needs of society and providing value to members.
Founded in 1937

21501 Tire Industry Association
1532 Pointer Ridge Place
Suite G
Bowie, MD 20716-1883

301-430-7280
800-876-8372
FAX 301-430-7283
E-Mail: info@tireindustry.org
Home Page: www.tireindustry.org
Social Media: *Facebook, Twitter, LinkedIn*

Roy Littlefield, Executive VP
Mike Wolfe, Treasurer
Tom Formanek, Secretary
Freda0 Pratt-Boyer, President
Ken Brown, Past President

TIA is an international association representing all segments of the tire industry, including those that manufacture, repair, recycle, sell, service or use new or retreaded tires, and also those suppliers or individuals who furnish equipment, material or services to the industry. TIA was formed by the July 2002 merger of the International Tire & Rubber Association (ITRA) and the Tire Association of North America (TANA).
7000+ Members
Founded in 2002

21502 Tire Retread and Repair Information Bureau
1013 Birch St.
Falls Church, VA 22046

703-533-7677
877-394-6811
FAX 703-533-7678
E-Mail: info@retread.org
Home Page: www.retread.org
Social Media: *Facebook, Twitter, YouTube*

David Stevens, Managing Director
Brian Hayes, President
Phil Boarts, Secretary/ Treasurer
Eddie Burleson, Vice President
Mike Berra, Director

Our goal is to provide the motoring public (both in the private and public sectors) with the most up-to-date information about the economic and environmental benefits of tire retreading and tire repairing.
Founded in 1974

21503 Tread Rubber Manufacturers Group
Piper and Marbury
1200 19th Street NW
Washington, DC 20036-2430

202-614-4171

Works to improve tire retreading techniques and to safeguard the public interest in retreading.

Newsletters

21504 Rubber Chemistry and Technology
Rubber Division, American Chemical Society
PO Box 499
Akron, OH 44325-3801

330-972-7883
FAX 330-972-5269

Lu Ann Blazeff, Publisher

Information on materials and equipment pertaining to the rubber industry. Accepts advertising.
Cost: $487.50
Frequency: 5 Times per Year

21505 Rubber and Plastics News
Crain Communications
1725 Merriman Rd
Suite 300
Akron, OH 44313-5283

330-836-9180
800-678-9595
FAX 330-836-2831
E-Mail: editorials@rubbernews.com
Home Page: www.crain.com

Robert S Simmons, VP
Edward Noga, Editor

Discusses production, research and development, management, sales and marketing.
Cost: $79.00
24 Pages
Frequency: Monthly
Circulation: 16258
Founded in 1971
Printed in 4 colors on glossy stock

21506 Worldwide Rubber Statistics
Int'l Institute of Synthetic Rubber Producers
2077 S Gessner Rd
Suite 133
Houston, TX 77063-1150

713-783-7511
FAX 713-783-7253
E-Mail: orderfs@iisrp.com
Home Page: www.iisrp.com
Social Media: *Facebook, Twitter, LinkedIn*

Jim Mc Graw, CEO
Dr K Leon Loh Sr, Senior Director of Programs
Sue Flynn, Executive Assistant
Robin Boyd, Manager of Accounts

Guide to the synthetic and natural rubber industry, including Centrally Planned Economy Countries.
Cost: $1050.00
40 Members
Founded in 1960

Magazines & Journals

21507 Global Tire News.com
Rubber & Plastic News
1725 Merriman Rd
Suite 300
Akron, OH 44313-5283

330-836-9180
330-836-9180
FAX 330-836-1005
E-Mail: dsector@crain.com
Home Page: www.rubbernews.com
Social Media: *Facebook, Twitter, LinkedIn*

Dave Cielasko, Publisher
Don Sector, Advertising Coordinator
Mike McNulty, Rubber & Plastics News Staff

Writer
Brent Weaver, Classified Coordinator

Provides rubber industry information relative to tire manufacturers; top tire company managers; plant listings and other data. Subscription to annual publication includes access to Global Tire News.com.
Cost: $79.00
Frequency: Annual

21508 PMA Polytopics
Polyurethane Manufacturers Association
6737 W Washington Avenue
Suite 1300
Milwaukee, WI 53214

414-431-3094
FAX 414-276-7704
E-Mail: info@pmahome.org
Home Page: www.pmahome.org

Mike Katz, President
Mike Cocak, VP
Mike Cocak, Secretary
Paul Blasco, Director Public Relations

The Polyurethane Manufacturers Association is the trade association of the cast polyurethane elastomer industry, serving processors of polyurethane products, materials and equipment suppliers and independent agents. PMA exchanges and disseminates information on standards, materials, processes and technical matters, in addition to monitoring regulatory and legislative activity affecting the urethane industry.
90 Members
Frequency: Quarterly
Circulation: 250
Founded in 1971

21509 Rubber World
Lippincott & Peto
PO Box 5451
Akron, OH 44334-0451

330-864-2122
FAX 330-864-5298
E-Mail: jhl@rubberworld.com
Home Page: www.rubberworld.com

Job Lippincott, President
Dennis Kennelly, VP Sales
Don R Smith, Editor
Darlene Ballard, Director of Marketing Services
Jill Rohrer, Managing Editor

Provides complete technical coverage to the rubber industry.
Cost: $34.00

Trade Shows

21510 International Latex Conference
Crain Communications
1725 Merriman Road
Suite 300
Akron, OH 44313-5283

330-836-9180
FAX 330-836-1005
E-Mail: cstevens@crain.com
Home Page: www.rubbernews.com

Twelve exhibitors with 12 booths.
Frequency: July

21511 International Tire Exhibition and Conference
Crain Communications
1725 Merriman Road
Suite 300
Akron, OH 44313-5283

330-836-9180
FAX 330-836-1005

E-Mail: cstevens@crain.com
Home Page: www.rubbernews.com

One-hundred and thirty exhibitors with 110 booths.
Frequency: September

21512 PMA Annual Meeting

Polyurethane Manufacturers Association
6737 W Washington Avenue
Suite 1300
Milwaukee, WI 53214

414-431-3094
FAX 414-276-7704
E-Mail: info@pmahome.org
Home Page: www.pmahome.org

Mike Katz, President
Mike Cocak, VP
Mike Cocak, Secretary
Paul Blasco, Director Public Relations

The Polyurethane Manufacturers Association is the trade association of the cast polyurethane elastomer industry, serving processors of polyurethane products, materials and equipment suppliers and independent agents. PMA exchanges and disseminates information on standards, materials, processes and technical matters, in addition to monitoring regulatory and legislative activity affecting the urethane industry.

21513 Rubber Expo

American Chemical Society-Rubber Division
PO Box 499
Akron, OH 44309-0499

330-972-7814
800-227-5558
FAX 330-972-5269
E-Mail: help@acs.org
Home Page: www.chemistry.org

Sherri L Poorman, Exhibition Manager

Biennial show of 300 manufacturers and suppliers of equipment, supplies and services for the rubber industry, including machinery, chemicals, raw rubber, finished rubber products, quality control equipment and related equipment.
8,000 Attendees
Frequency: October, Cleveland

21514 Rubber Mini Expo

American Chemical Society-Rubber Division
PO Box 499
Akron, OH 44309-0499

330-972-7814
FAX 330-972-5269
E-Mail: shbarr@rubber.org
Home Page: www.rubber.org

Sue Barr, Exposition & Future Sites Manager

Biennial show of 150 manufacturers, suppliers and custom services for the rubber industry, including machinery, chemicals, raw rubber, finished rubber products, quality control equipment and related equipment.
3000 Attendees
Frequency: October

21515 Rubber and Plastics Industry Conference of the United Steelworkers of America

5 Gateway Center
Pittsburgh, PA 15220

412-562-6971
FAX 412-562-6963

John Sellers, Executive VP
90M Attendees
Founded in 1935

Directories & Databases

21516 Rauch Guide to the US Rubber Industry

Grey House Publishing
4919 Route 22
PO Box 56
Amenia, NY 12501

518-789-8700
800-562-2139
FAX 845-373-6390
E-Mail: books@greyhouse.com
Home Page: www.greyhouse.com
Social Media: *Facebook, Twitter*

Leslie Mackenzie, Publisher
Richard Gottlieb, Editor

Provides industry structure and current market information about the $39 billion US rubber industry which faces intense inter-material competition and severe government regulation. The report contains a wealth of marketing and related technical information about the busines.
Cost: $595.00
500 Pages
ISBN: 1-592371-30-2
Founded in 1981

21517 Rubber World Blue Book: Materials, Compounding and Machinery

Lippincott & Peto
Po Box 5451
Akron, OH 44334-0451

330-864-2122
FAX 330-864-5298
Home Page: www.rubberworld.com

Job Lippincott, Owner

Over 850 suppliers of over 8,000 chemicals, materials and compounding ingredients for rubber manufacturers.
Cost: $103.00
Frequency: Annual
Circulation: 4,000

21518 Rubber World: Custom Mixers Directory

Lippincott & Peto
Po Box 5451
Akron, OH 44334-0451

330-864-2122
FAX 330-864-5298
Home Page: www.rubberworld.com

Job Lippincott, Owner

A list of rubber manufacturers providing custom mixes.
Cost: $3.00
Frequency: Annual

21519 Rubber World: Machinery Suppliers Issue

Lippincott & Peto
Po Box 5451
Akron, OH 44334-0451

330-864-2122
FAX 330-864-5298
Home Page: www.rubberworld.com

Job Lippincott, Owner

Lists suppliers of used and rebuilt machinery and instrumentation and test equipment to the rubber industry.
Cost: $3.00
Frequency: Annual
ISBN: 0-035957-2

21520 Rubber and Plastics News: Rubicana Issue

Crain Communications

1725 Merriman Rd
Suite 300
Akron, OH 44313-5283

330-836-9180
800-678-9595
FAX 330-836-2831
Home Page: www.crain.com

Robert S Simmons, VP

A list of over 1,000 rubber product manufacturers and suppliers of equipment, services and materials.
Cost: $85.00
Frequency: Annual
Circulation: 15,000

Industry Web Sites

21521 http://gold.greyhouse.com

G.O.L.D Grey House OnLine Databases

Grey House Publishing's online database platform, GOLD, offers Quick Search, Keyword Search and Expert Search for most business sectors including rubber markets. The GOLD platform makes finding the information you need quick and easy - whether you're a novice searcher or an experienced database user. All of Grey House's directory products are available for subscription on the GOLD platform.

21522 www.greyhouse.com

Grey House Publishing

Authoritative reference directories for most business sectors including rubber markets. Users can search the online databases with varied search criteria allowing for custom searches by product category, geographic area, sales volume, keyword, subject and more. Full Grey House catalog and online ordering also available.

21523 www.iisrp.com

Int'l Institute of Synthetic Rubber Producers

For manufacturers of synthetic rubber.

21524 www.itra.com

International Tire and Rubber Association

Information on tire retreading and repairing, new tires, scrap tire reduction and removal equipment, rubber recycling technologies, recycled rubber products and allied services including brake equipment, wheel alignment, tire balancers, tire changers, service trucks, marketing/sales and management programs and computer systems.

21525 www.rma.org

Scrap Tire Management Council

For tire manufacturers marketers of scrap tires.

21526 www.rubbernews.com

Rubber & Plastics News
1725 Merriman Rd.
Akron, OH 44313-5251

330-836-9180
FAX 330-836-2831
Home Page: www.rubbernews.com

Website of Rubber & Plastics News magazine. Updated daily with an online archive, statistics and rankings.

Associations

21527 AAA Foundation for Traffic Safety

607 14th Street NW
Suite 201
Washington, DC 20005

202-638-5944
FAX 202-638-5943
E-Mail: info@aaafoundation.org
Home Page: www.aaafoundation.org
Social Media: *Facebook, Twitter, RSS*

Peter Kissinger, President/CEO
Kenneth Johnson, Treasurer
Laura Dunn, Manager of Research &
Communication
Paul C. Petrillo, Chairman
John Tomlin, Secretary

AAA Foundation for Traffic Safety is dedicated to saving lives and reducing injuries on the roads. It is a not-for-profit, publicly-supported charitable educational and research organization.
Founded in 1947

21528 ASIS International

1625 Prince St
Alexandria, VA 22314-2818

703-519-6200
888-968-1968
FAX 703-519-6299
E-Mail: asis@asisonline.org
Home Page: www.asisonline.org
Social Media: *Facebook, Twitter, LinkedIn, You Tube*

David C. Davis, President-Elect
Dave N. Tyson, President
Thomas J. Langer, Treasurer
Richard E. Chase, Secretary
Richard E. Widup, Chairman

The largest organization for security professionals. ASIS is dedicated to increasing the effectiveness and productivity of security professionals by developing educational programs and materials that cover broad security interests, such as the ASIS Annual Seminar and Exhibits, as well as specific topics. ASIS also advocates the role and value of the security management profession to the media, governmental entities, and the public.
Founded in 1955

21529 Academy of Security Educators & Trainers

16 Penn Plaza
Suite 1570
New York, NY 10001

212-268-4555
800-947-5827
FAX 212-563-4783
Home Page: www.academyofsecurity.org

Dr Richard W Kobetz, Executive Director
Jerry Heying, President
Mary E Kobetz, Secretary-Treasurer

Non-profit organization of security professionals dedicated to exploring the large spectrum of issues confronting the security field. Meetings are held to discuss, design, develop, and exchange thoughts and ideas in an open forum. Awards the CST (certified security trainer) designation.
300 Members
Founded in 1980

21530 Advanced Medical Technology Association: AdvaMed

701 Pennsylvania Ave Nw
Suite 800
Washington, DC 20004-2654

202-783-8700
FAX 202-783-8750
E-Mail: info@advamed.org
Home Page: www.advamed.org
Social Media: *Facebook, Twitter, LinkedIn, You Tube*

Stephen J Ubl, President/CEO
David Nexon, Senior Executive VP
Kenneth Mendez, Sr. Executive Vice President
Vincent Forlenza, Chairman
Jason Rupp, Vice President

Dedicated to providing members with the advocacy, information, education and tangible solutions necessary for success in a world of increasingly complex medical regulations.
1300 Members
Founded in 1975

21531 Advocates for Highway and Auto Safety

750 1st St NE
Suite 1130
Washington, DC 20002

202-408-1711
FAX 202-408-1699
E-Mail: advocates@saferoads.org
Home Page: www.saferoads.org
Social Media: *Facebook, Twitter*

Judith Lee Stone, President
Jacqueline Gillan, VP
Judie Pasquini, Director
Peter Kurdock, Advocates' State Coordinator

An organization whose members advocate the support and advancement of highway and auto safety through the implementation of state and federal laws, programs and policies.
Founded in 1989

21532 American Association for Aerosol Research (AAAR)

12100 Sunset Hills Road
Suite 130
Reston, VA 20190

703-437-4377
FAX 800-485-3106
E-Mail: info@aaar.org
Home Page: www.aaar.org

Jay Turner, President
Allen Robinson, Vice President Elect
Sheryl Ehrman, Vice President
Linsey Marr, Treasurer
Suresh Dhaniyala, Secretary

AAAR is a nonprofit professional organization for scientists and engineers who wish to promote and communicate technical advances in the field of aerosol research. The Association fosters the exchange of information among members and with other disciplines through conferences, symposia and publication of a professional journal. Committed to the development of aerosol and its application to important social issues, AAAR offers an international forum for education, communication and networking.
1000 Members
Founded in 1982

21533 American Association of Occupational Health Nurses

2920 Brandywine Rd # 100
Suite 100
Chamblee, GA 30341-5539

770-455-7271
FAX 850-484-8762

Home Page: www.gonursing.org
Social Media: *Facebook, Twitter, LinkedIn*

Ann Cox, Executive Director

AAOHN is a principal force in developing and promoting the profession of occupational and environmental health nursing by providing education, resources, and advocacy.
Founded in 1942

21534 American Association of Poison Control Centers

3201 New Mexico Ave
Suite 310
Washington, DC 200016

202-362-3867
800-222-1222
FAX 202-362-8377
E-Mail: pc@posion.org
Home Page: www.poison.org
Social Media: *Facebook*

Toby Litovitz, Executive Director

Nonprofit nationwide organization of poison centers and others interested in the prevention and treatment of poisoning. Promotes the reduction of injury, illness and death from poisonings through public and professional education and scientific research. Promotes universal access to certified regional poison centers.
Founded in 1980

21535 American Bio-Recovery Association

39 St.Mary Street
Norwalk, OH 44857

419-663-2819
888-979-2272
FAX 440-499-9959
Home Page: www.americanbiorecovery.org

Andrew Yurchuck, President
Eric Morse, Vice President
Robert O'Connor, Secretary
Barbara Jones, Treasurer

A nationwide non-profit association of crime and trauma scene recovery professionals who are dedicated to upholding the highest technical, ethical and educational guidelines of the biohazard remediation industry.

21536 American Biological Safety Association

1200 Allanson Rd
Mundelein, IL 60060-3808

847-949-1517
866-425-1385
FAX 847-566-4580
E-Mail: info@absa.org
Home Page: www.absa.org

Edward Stygar III, Executive Director
Marian Downing, President
Melissa Moreland, President-Elect
Carol McGhan, Treasurer
Scott Alderman, Councilor

ABSA's goals are to provide a professional association that represents the interest and needs of practitioners of biological safety, and to provide a forum for the continued and timely exchange of biosafety information.
Founded in 1984

21537 American Chemical Society

1155 16th St NW
Washington, DC 200036

202-872-4600
800-333-9511
FAX 202-872-4615
E-Mail: help@acs.org
Home Page: www.acs.org

Social Media: *Facebook, Twitter, LinkedIn, Google+*

Thomas M. Connelly, CEO
Madeleine Jacobs, Executive Director
Diane Grob Schmidt, President
Pat N. Confalone, Chair
George M. Bodner, Director Publications

Supports chemists and companies who work with chemicals and their by-products.
158 M Members
Founded in 1876

21538 American College of Occupational and Environmental Medicine

25 Northwest Point Blvd
Suite 700
Elk Grove Village, IL 60007-1030
847-818-1800
FAX 847-818-9266
E-Mail: acoeminfo@acoem.org
Home Page: www.acoem.org
Social Media: *Twitter, YouTube*

Kathryn L. Mueller, Past President
Charles M. Yarborough III, Vice President
Mark A. Roberts, President
James A. Tacci, President-Elect
Jeffery S. Harris, Secretary-Treasurer

Occupational and environmental medicine is devoted to the prevention and management of occupational and injury, illness and disability, and promotion of health and productivity of workers, thier families and communities.
5000 Members
Founded in 1916

21539 American Conference of Governmental Industrial Hygienists

1330 Kemper Meadow Drive
Cincinnati, OH 45240
513-742-2020
FAX 513-742-3355
E-Mail: mail@acgih.org
Home Page: www.acgih.org
Social Media: *Facebook, Twitter, LinkedIn, Google+*

J. Torey Nalbone, Chair
Shannon Henshaw Gaffney, Vice Chair
John S. Morawetz, Secretary/ Treasurer
A. Anthony Rizzuto, Executive Director
Susan Arnold, Director

A member-based organization and community of professionals that advances worker health and safety through education and the development and dissemination of scientific and technical knowledge.
Founded in 1938

21540 American Correctional Association

206 N. Washington Street
Alexandria, VA 22314
703-224-0000
FAX 703-224-0179
E-Mail: IndiaV@aca.org
Home Page: www.aca.org
Social Media: *Facebook, Twitter, LinkedIn, YouTube*

Mary L. Livers, President
Lanette C. Linthicum, President-Elect
Daron Hall, Past President
James A Gondles, Secretary
Gary C. Mohr, Treasurer

Formerly known as the National Prison Association.
Founded in 1870

21541 American Fire Safety Council

1909 K St Nw
Suite 400
Washington, DC 20006-1168
202-338-0022
FAX 202-955-6215
E-Mail: info@fire-safety.net
Home Page: www.fire-safety.net
Social Media: *Facebook, Twitter, LinkedIn*

Mike Heimowitz, President

Improving fire safety through enhancement of fire codes and standards and promoting responsible use of flame retardants and flame retardant products. AFSC was created to provide a stronger and broader voice on advocacy and safety issues.
Founded in 2003

21542 American Fire Sprinkler Association

12750 Merit Drive
Suite 350
Dallas, TX 75251
214-349-5965
FAX 214-343-8898
E-Mail: afsainfo@firesprinkler.org
Home Page: www.firesprinkler.org
Social Media: *Facebook, Twitter, LinkedIn, YouTube, Flickr*

Steve Muncy, President
Frank Mortl III, Executive Vice President
Joseph A. Heinrich, Chairman
Michael F. Meehan, First Vice-Chairman
Thomas J. McKinnon, Treasurer

Nonprofit international association representing open shop fire sprinkler contractors, dedicated to the educational advancement of its members and promotion of the use of automatic sprinkler systems. Offers a convention and exhibition, correspondence course, monthly magazine and a monthly newsletter.
900 Members
Founded in 1981

21543 American Gas Association

400 N Capitol Street NW
Suite 450
Washington, DC 20001
202-824-7000
FAX 202-824-7092
E-Mail: ykorolevich@aga.org
Home Page: www.aga.org
Social Media: *Facebook, Twitter, LinkedIn, YouTube, Wordpress, Instagram*

Dave McCurdy, President/CEO
Gregg S. Kantor, Immediate Past Chairman
Pierce H. Norton II, 2nd Vice Chairman
Terry D. McCallister, Chairman
Ralph A. LaRossa, 1st Vice Chairman

The American Gas Association advocates the interests of its members and their customers, and provides information and services promoting efficient demand and supply growth and operational excellence in the safe, reliable and efficient delivery of natural gas.
200 Members
Founded in 1918

21544 American Industrial Hygiene Association

3141 Fairview Park Drive
Suite 777
Falls Church, VA 22042
703-849-8888
FAX 703-207-3561
E-Mail: infonet@aiha.org
Home Page: www.aiha.org
Social Media: *Facebook, Twitter, LinkedIn, YouTube, RSS*

Deborah Imel Nelson, Vice President
Daniel H. Anna, President
Steven E. Lacey, President-Elect

Cynthia A. Ostrowski, Treasurer
Kathleen S. Murphy, Secretary

AIHA promotes healthy and safe environments by advancing the science, principles, practice, and value of industrial hygiene and occupational and environmental health and safety.
10400 Members
Founded in 1939

21545 American Insurance Association

2101 L Street, NW
Suite 400
Washington, DC 200037
202-828-7100
FAX 202-293-1219
E-Mail: info@aiadc.org
Home Page: www.aiadc.org
Social Media: *Facebook, Twitter, LinkedIn, YouTube, RSS*

Leigh Ann Pusey, President/CEO
J. Stephen Zielezienski, SVP & General Counsel
Joseph Digiovanni, SVP, State Affairs
David S. Lauer, VP/ Treasurer
Peter R. Foley, VP, Claims Administration

A property, casualty insurance trade organization representing more than 40,000 insurers that write more than $120 billion in premiums each year. AIA member companies offer all types of property-casualty insurance, including personal and commercial auto insurance, commercial property and liability coverage for small businesses, worker's compensation, medical malpractice coverage, and product liability insurance.
40000 Members
Founded in 1866

21546 American National Standards Institute ANSI

1899 L Street, NW
11th Floor
Washington, DC 20036
202-293-8020
FAX 202-293-9287
E-Mail: info@ansi.org
Home Page: www.ansi.org
Social Media: *Facebook, Twitter, LinkedIn, YouTube, Google+*

Joe Bhatia, President/CEO
Susan Bose, Manager Membership Services
Tricia Power, Manager, Corporate Governance
James T. Pauley, Chairman
Patricia A. Griffin, Vice President and General Counsel

To enhance the global competition of business and quality of life by promoting and facilitating voluntary consensus standards and conformity assessment systems, and safeguarding their integrity.
1000 Members
Founded in 1916

21547 American Polygraph Association

PO Box 8037
Chattanooga, TN 37414-0037
423-892-3992
800-272-8037
FAX 423-894-5435
E-Mail: manager@polygraph.org
Home Page: www.polygraph.org
Social Media: *Facebook, Twitter*

Lisa Jacocks, National Office Manager
Walt Goodson, President
Raymond Nelson, Chairman
Gordon L. Vaughan, General Counsel
Darryl Starks, Vice-President Government

Representing experienced polygraph examiners in private business; law enforcement and government. Professional APA polygraph examiners administer hundreds of thousands of

polygraph exams each year worldwide. The APA establishes standards of ethical practices, techniques, instrumentation and research, as well as provides advanced training and continuing education programs.
2700+ Members
Founded in 1966

21548 American Public Health Association

800 I Street NW
Washington, DC 20001

202-777-2742
FAX 202-777-2534
E-Mail: comments@apha.org
Home Page: www.apha.org
Social Media: *Facebook, Twitter*

Dr Georges C Benjamin, Executive Director
Shiriki Kumanyika, President
Richard J. Cohen, Treasurer
Jose Fernandez-Pena, Vice Chair
Camara P. Jones, President Elect

Influencing policies and setting priorities for over 125 years. Thoughout its history it has been in the forefront of numerous efforts to prevent disease and promote health.
Founded in 1872

21549 American Red Cross

2025 E. St.,NW
Washington, DC 20006

202-303-5214
800-733-2767
FAX 202-639-3021
E-Mail: info@usa.redcross.org
Home Page: www.redcross.org
Social Media: *Facebook, Twitter, Flickr, YouTube*

Gail J McGovern, President/CEO
Bonnie McElveen-Hunter, Chairman
Brian J. Rhoa, CFO
David Meltzer, General Counsel
Jennifer L. Hawkins, Corporate Secretary

The American Red Cross is where people mobilize to help their neighbors across the street, across the country and across the world, in emergencies. Each year, in communities large and small, victims of some 70,000 disasters turn to the nearly one million volunteers and 35,000 employees of the Red Cross.
31000 Members
Founded in 1881

21550 American Safety & Health Institute

4148 Louis Avenue
Holiday, FL 34691

727-437-7560
800-682-5067
E-Mail: info@ashinstitute.org
Home Page: www.ashinstitute.org
Social Media: *Facebook, Twitter, LinkedIn*

Frank Swiger, Manager

Nonprofit association of professional safety & health educators providing nationally recognized training programs through more than 5000 approved training centers across the US and in several foreign countries.
30000 Members
Founded in 1996

21551 American Society for Industrial Security

1625 Prince Street
Alexandria, VA 22314-2882

703-519-6200
FAX 703-519-6299
E-Mail: asis@asisonline.org
Home Page: www.asisonline.org
Social Media: *Facebook, Twitter, LinkedIn, YouTube*

Dave N. Tyson, President
Michael J Stack, CEO

Thomas J. Langer, Treasurer
Richard E. Chase, Secretary
Richard E. Widup, Chairman

ASIS International (ASIS) is the largest organization for security professionals, with more than 33,000 members worldwide. ASIS is dedicated to increasing the effectiveness and productivity of security professionals by developing educational programs and materials that address broad security interests, such as the ASIS Annual Seminar and Exhibits, as well as specific security topics.
33000 Members
Founded in 1955

21552 American Society for Nondestructive Testing

1711 Arlingate Lane
PO Box 28518
Columbus, OH 43228-0518

614-274-6003
800-222-2768
FAX 614-274-6899
Home Page: www.asnt.org
Social Media: *Facebook, Twitter, LinkedIn, YouTube*

Arnold Bereson, Executive Director
Roger Engelbart, Vice- President
David Mandina, Secreatry/ Treasurer
Robert J. Potter, Chair
Raymond G. Morasse, President

ASNT is the world's largest technical society for nondestructive tests (NDT) professionals.
15000 Members
Founded in 1941

21553 American Society of Crime Laboratory Directors (ASCLD)

139A Technology Drive
Garner, NC 27529

919-773-2044
FAX 919-861-9930
E-Mail: president@ascld.org
Home Page: www.ascld.org
Social Media: *Facebook, Twitter, LinkedIn, RSS*

Jody Wolf, President
Cicilia Doyle, Secretary
Jeremy Triplett, President-Elect
Jean Stover, Executive Director
Ramona Robertson, Administrative Assistant

The American Society of Crime Laboratory Directors (ASCLD) is a nonprofit professional society of crime laboratory directors and forensic science managers dedicated to providing excellence in forensic science through leadership and innovation.
Founded in 1973

21554 American Society of Criminology

1314 Kinnear Rd
Suite 212
Columbus, OH 43212-1156

614-292-9207
FAX 614-292-6767
E-Mail: asc@asc41.com
Home Page: www.asc41.com
Social Media: *Facebook, Twitter*

Ruth Peterson, President-Elect
Chris Eskridge, Executive Director
Candace Kruttscnitt, President
Eric Baumer, Vice President
Bonnie Fisher, Treasurer

The American Society of Criminology is an international organization concerned with criminology, embracing scholary, scientific and profesional knowledge concerning the etiology, prevention, control, and treatment of crime and delinquency.

21555 American Society of Industrial Security

1625 Prince St
Alexandria, VA 22314-2882

703-519-6200
FAX 703-519-6299
E-Mail: asis@asisonline.org
Home Page: www.asisonline.org
Social Media: *Facebook, Twitter, LinkedIn, YouTube*

Richard E. Widup, Chairman
Dave N. Tyson, President
Michael J. Stack, CEO
Thomas J. Langer, Treasurer
Richard E. Chase, Secretary

The largest international organization for professionals who are responsible for security, including managers and directors of security.
33000 Members
Founded in 1955

21556 American Society of Mechanical Engineers

Two Park Ave
New York, NY 10016-5990

800-843-2763
800-843-2763
973-882-1170
FAX 202-429-9417
E-Mail: CustomerCare@asme.org
Home Page: www.asme.org
Social Media: *Facebook, Twitter, LinkedIn*

K.Keith Roe, President- Nominee
Julio Guerrero, President
J.Robert Sims, Immediate Past President
James W. Coaker, Secretary/ Treasurer
Thomas G. Loughlin, Executive Director

Through its initiatives in education, advocacy and public policy, the ASME. Foundation impacts all aspects of the mechanical engineering community.
1.4M Members
Founded in 1880

21557 American Society of Safety Engineers

520 N. Northwest Hwy
Park Ridge, IL 60068

847-699-2929
FAX 847-768-3434
E-Mail: customerservice@asse.org
Home Page: www.asse.org
Social Media: *Facebook, Twitter, LinkedIn, Instagram*

Michael Belcher, President
Fred J. Fortman, Secretary & Executive Treasurer
Thomas F. Cecich, President-Elect
James D. Smith, Senior Vice President
Stephanie A. Helgerman, VP, Finance

The oldest and largest professional safety organization. Its members manage, supervise and consult on safety, health, and environmental issues in industry, insurance, government and education.
36000 Members
Founded in 1911

21558 American Traffic Safety Services Association

15 Riverside Parkway
Suite 100
Fredericksburg, VA 22406-1022

540-368-1701
800-272-8772
FAX 540-368-1717
E-Mail: memberservices@atssa.com
Home Page: www.atssa.com
Social Media: *Facebook, Twitter, YouTube*

Scott Seeley, Chairman
Debra Ricker, Chairman Elect

Juan Arvizu, At-large-Director
Sue Reiss, Foundation President (Non-Voting)
Craig Sliter, Guardrail Services Div Director

The American Traffic Safety Services Association, is an international trade association founded in 1969. It has has represented companies and individuals in the traffic control and roadway safety industry.
11630 Members
Founded in 1969

21559 American Welding Society

8669 NW 36 St.
Suite 130
Miami, FL 33126-6672

305-443-9353
800-443-9353
FAX 305-443-7559
E-Mail: info@aws.org
Home Page: awsnow.org
Social Media: *Facebook, Twitter, Instagram*

David J. Landon, President
David L. McQuaid, Vice President
John R. Bray, Vice President
Dale Flood, Vice President
Robert G. Pali, Treasurer

The mission of the American Welding Society is to advance the science, technology and application of welding and allied joining and cutting processes, including brazing, soldering and thermal spraying.
70000 Members
Founded in 1919

21560 Associated Locksmiths of America

3500 Easy St
Dallas, TX 75247

214-819-9733
800-532-2562
FAX 214-819-9736
E-Mail: jim@aloa.org
Home Page: www.aloa.org
Social Media: *Facebook, Twitter, LinkedIn*

David Lowell, Executive Director
Charles Gibson, Secretary

ALOA is an international professional organization of highly qualified security professionals engaged in consulting, sales, installation and maintenance of locks, keys safes, premises security, access controls, alarms, and other security related endeavors.
10M Members
Founded in 1956

21561 Association of Air Medical Services

909 N. Washington St.
Suite 410
Alexandria, VA 22314

703-836-8732
FAX 703-836-8920
E-Mail: information@aams.org
Home Page: www.aams.org

Dawn Mancuso, Executive Director
Dave Evans, Chair
Graeme Field, Vice Chair
Rick Sherlock, CEO & President
Douglas A. Garretson, Treasurer

AAMS is built on the idea that representation from a variety of medical transport services and businesses can be brought together to share information, collectively resolve problems and provide leadership in the medical transport community.
581 Members
Founded in 1980

21562 Association of Certified Fraud Examiners

716 West Ave
Austin, TX 78701-2727

512-478-9000
800-245-3321
FAX 512-478-9297
E-Mail: MemberServices@acfe.com
Home Page: www.acfe.com
Social Media: *Facebook, Twitter, LinkedIn*

John D. Gill, VP- Education
James D. Ratley, President/CEO
Joseph T. Wells, Chairman
Bruce Dorris, Program Director & Vice President
Jeanette LeVie, Vice President- Administration

The mission of the Association of Certified Fraud Examiners is to reduce the incidence of fraud and white-collar crime and to assist its members in its dectection and prevention.
75000 Members
Founded in 1988

21563 Association of Christian Investigators

2553 Jackson Keller
Suite 200
San Antonio, TX 78230

210-342-0509
FAX 210-342-0731
E-Mail: kelmar@kelmarpi.com
Home Page: www.a-c-i.org

Kelly E Riddle, President
Hugo Briseno, Director, Georgia
Timothy Friend, Director, California (Northern)
Andrew Smart, Director, Alabama
Paul Jacob, Director, Alaska

Provides a spirit-filled organization that promote the investigative profession in a non-competitive atmosphere. Provides an environment in which investigators can create meaningful and long-term relationships with other investigators outside the professional bonds.
1000+ Members
Founded in 1996

21564 Association of Contingency Planners

136 Everett Road
Albany, NY 12205

414-908-4945
800-445-4227
FAX 414-768-8001
E-Mail: staff@acp-international.com
Home Page: www.acp-international.com
Social Media: *Facebook, Twitter, LinkedIn*

Leo A Wrobel, President
Bonnie Canal, Chairman
Michael Carver, Treasurer
Steve Elliot, Board Member
Michael J. Morganti, Secretary

Nonprofit trade association dedicated to fostering continued professional growth and development in effective contingency and business resumption planning.
2300 Members
Founded in 1983

21565 Association of Professional Industrial Hygienists

2288 Gunbarrel Rd
Ste 154/364
Chattanooga, TN 37421

888-481-3006
E-Mail: APIH@epbfi.com
Home Page: www.apih.usÿ

Offers credentialing to industrial hygienists.
Founded in 1994

21566 Association of Public Safety Communication Officials-International

351 N Williamson Boulevard
Daytona Beach, FL 32114-1112

386-322-2500
888-272-6911
FAX 386-322-2501
E-Mail: apco@apcointl.org
Home Page: www.apcointl.org
Social Media: *Facebook, Twitter, LinkedIn, psconnect*

John W. Wright, Immediate Past President
Brent Lee, President
Cheryl J. Greathouse, 1st VP
Martha K. Carter, 2nd VP
Derek Poarch, Ex-Officio

The Association of Public-Safety Communications Officials International (APCO) is a member driven association of communications professionals that provides leadership; influences public safety communications decisions of government and industry; promotes professional development; and, fosters the development and use of technology for the benefit of the public.
16000 Members
Founded in 1932

21567 Association of State Dam Safety Officials

239 S. Limestone
Lexington, KY 40508

859-550-2788
E-Mail: info@damsafety.org
Home Page: www.damsafety.orgÿ
Social Media: *Facebook, Twitter, LinkedIn, YouTube*

Jim Pawloski, President
Dusty Myers, President Elect
Tom Woosley, Past President
Roger Adams, Secretary
Jon Garton, Treasurer

Organization for safety officials overseeing state dams.
3000 Members
Founded in 1983

21568 Association of State Floodplain Managers

575 D'Onoforio Drive
Suite 200
Madison, WI 53719

608-828-3000
FAX 608-828-6319
E-Mail: asfpm@floods.org
Home Page: www.floods.org
Social Media: *Facebook, Twitter, LinkedIn, Tumblr*

Larry A Larson, DirectorEmeritus, Sr. Policy Adviso
Maria Cox Lamm, Vice Chair
Karen McHugh, Treasurer
Leslie Durham, Secretary
Ceil C. Strauss, Chair

It is the mission of the Association to mitigate the losses, costs and human suffering caused by flooding and to promote wise use of the natural and beneficial functions of floodplains.
6500 Members
Founded in 1976

21569 Automatic Fire Alarm Association

81 Mill Street
Suite 300
Gahanna, OH 43230

614-416-8076
844-438-2322
FAX 614-453-8744
E-Mail: fire-alarm@afaa.org

Home Page: www.afaa.org
Social Media: *Facebook, Twitter, LinkedIn, Yahoo*

Jack McNamara, President/Executive Director
Rick Heffernan, Secretary
Randall L. Hormann, Administrative Director
William Koffel, Vice President
Rodger Reiswig, Treasurer

Striving to be the foremost industry advocate organization dedicated to improving the quality, reliability and value of fire and life safety systems.
Founded in 1953

21570 Aviation Safety Institute

PO Box 2480
Carlingford, NS 2118

128-819-2455
FAX 128-572-5248
E-Mail: enquiry@asi.net.au
Home Page: www.asi.net.au
Social Media: *Twitter, LinkedIn*

Edward H Wachs, President/Chair
Thomas Clevinger, VP/Treasurer
Richard Davies, Managing Director
Melinda Brennan, Manager-WHS
Kevin Mulholland, Manager-Audit

An aviation safety research center established in 1973. Studying the most overlooked, most important area of aviation safety.
Founded in 2008

21571 Board of Certified Safety Professionals

2301 W. Bradley Avenue
Champaign, IL 61821

217-359-9263
FAX 217-359-0055
E-Mail: bcsp@bcsp.org
Home Page: www.bcsp.org
Social Media: *Facebook, Twitter, LinkedIn, Google+*

Cece M Weldon, President
John E. Hodges, Vice President
Jack H. Dobson, Treasurer
Teresa M. Turnbeaugh, CEO, Secretary
Guy Snyder, CFO

Operating solely as a peer certification board with the purpose of certifying practitioners in the safety profession.
Founded in 1969
Mailing list available for rent: 20,000 names

21572 Business Disaster Preparedness Council

Lee County Emergency Management
PO Box 398
Ft. Meyers, FL 33902-398

239-399-9779
FAX 941-477-3636
E-Mail: board@leegov.com

Bob Lee, Owner

Public and private partnership whose goal it is to assist business in planning for and recovering from natural disasters and emergencies.
Founded in 1998

21573 CPWR: Center for Construction Research and Training

8484 Georgia Ave
Suite 1000
Silver Spring, MD 20910

301-578-8500
FAX 301-578-8572
E-Mail: cpwrwebsite@cpwr.com
Home Page: www.cpwr.com
Social Media: *Facebook, Twitter, RSS, YouTube*

Sean McGarvey, President
Richard Resnick, Vice President/ General

Counsel
Chris Trahan, Deputy Director
Erich J. Stafford, Executive Director
Brent Booker, Secretary/ Treasurer

CPWR is committed to preventing illness, injury, and death in the construction industry through its safety and health research, broad network of trainers, and on-going outreach to workers and employers.
Founded in 1990

21574 Canada Safety Council

1020 Thomas Spratt Place
Ottawa, ON K1G 5L5

613-739-1535
FAX 613-739-1566
E-Mail: cs@safety-council.org
Home Page: canadasafetycouncil.org
Social Media: *Facebook, Twitter*

Jack Smith, President
Raynald Marchand, General Manager, Programs
Judy Lavergne, Secretary
Peter Slivar, Manager, Finance & Administration
Lewis Smith, Communications

The Canada Safety Counil is a national, non-government, charitable organization dedicated to safety. Mission is to lead in the national effort to reduce preventable deaths, injuries and economic loss in public and private places throughout Canada.
Founded in 1968

21575 Canadian Alarm & Security Association

50 Acadia Avenue
Suite 201
Markham, ON L3R 0B3

905-513-0622
800-538-9919
FAX 905-513-0624
E-Mail: staff@canasa.org
Home Page: www.canasa.org
Social Media: *Facebook, Twitter, LinkedIn*

JF Champagne, Ex-Officio
Carl Jorgensen, Vice president
Carol Cairns, Treasurer
Kevin Hincks, Secretary
Philippe Bouchard, President

A national non-profit organization dedicated to promoting the interests of its members and the safety and security of all Canadians.
Founded in 1977

21576 Central Station Alarm Association

8150 Leesburg Pike
Suite 700
Vienna, VA 22182

703-242-4670
FAX 703-242-4675
E-Mail: techadmin@csaaintl.org
Home Page: csaaintl.org
Social Media: *Facebook, Twitter, LinkedIn, RSS*

Jay Hauhn, Executive Director
Joe Nuccio, First Vice President
Pamela Petrow, President
Graham Westphal, Secretary
Ivan Spector, Treasurer

Represents companies offering security (alarm) monitoring systems through a central station. It also represents companies that provide services and products to the industry.
300+ Members
Founded in 1950

21577 Clery Center

110 Gallagher Road
Wayne, PA 19087

484-580-8754
888-251-7959
FAX 484-580-8759
Home Page: clerycenter.org
Social Media: *Facebook, Twitter, LinkedIn, YouTube*

Constance B. Clery, Co-Founder & Chairwoman
Howard K. Clery, Co-Founder
Benjamin F. Clery, Treasurer
Roger Carolin, Chairman
Christopher F. McConnell, Vice Chairman

A non-profit organization whose mission is to prevent violence, substance abuse and other crimes in college and university campus commumities across the United States, and to compassionately assist the vicitims of these crimes.
Founded in 1987

21578 Commercial Vehicle Safety Alliance

6303 Ivy Lane
Suite 310
Greenbelt, MD 20770-6319

301-830-6143
FAX 301-830-6144
E-Mail: cvsahq@cvsa.org
Home Page: www.cvsa.org
Social Media: *Facebook, Twitter, LinkedIn, YouTube*

Collin B. Mooney, Executive Director
Maj. Jay Thompson, President
Julius Debuschewitz, Vice President
Capt. Christoph Turner, Secretary

The Commercial Vehicle Safety Alliance (CVSA) is a nonprofit organization, established to promote an environment free of commercial vehicle accidents and incidents. Our mission is to promote commercial motor vehicle safty and security by providing leadership to enforcement, industry and policy makers.
540 Members
Founded in 1980

21579 Computer Security Institute

350 Hudson St.
Suite 300
New York, NY 10014

415-947-6320
FAX 415-947-6023
E-Mail: csi@ubm.com
Home Page: www.gocsi.com
Social Media: *Facebook, Twitter, LinkedIn*

Jody Nurre, Sales Director
Mary Griffin, Membership Director
Robert Richardson, Director
Terri Curran, Director
Cheryl Jackson, Information Systems

Computer Security Institute serves the needs of information security professionals through membership, educational events, security surveys and awareness tools.
Founded in 1974

21580 Consumer Data Industry Association

1090 Vermont Ave NW
Suite 200
Washington, DC 20005-4964

202-371-0910
FAX 202-371-0134
E-Mail: cdia@cdiaonline.org
Home Page: www.cdiaonline.org

Norm Magnuson, VP
Betty Byrnes, Member Services

The Consumer Data Industry Association is an international trade association, founded in 1906, that represents consumer information

companies that provide fraud prevention and risk management products, credit and mortgage reports, tenant and employment screening services, check fraud and verification services, and collection services.
140 Members
Founded in 1906

21581 Conveyor Equipment Manufacturers Association (CEMA)

5672 Strand CT
Suite 2
Naples, FL 34110

239-514-3441
FAX 239-514-3470
E-Mail: phil@cemanet.org
Home Page: www.cemanet.org
Social Media: *Facebook, Twitter, LinkedIn*

Jerry Heathman, President
Garry Abraham, Vice President
Robert Reinfried, Executive VP
Paul Ross, Secretary
E.A. Thompson, Treasurer

Involved in writing industry standards, the CEMA seeks to promote among its members and the industry standardization of design manufacture and application on a voluntary basis and in such manner as will not impede development of conveying machinery and component parts or lessen competition. CEMA sponsors an annual Engineering Conference that allows Member Company Engineers to meet and develop or improve CEMA Consensus Industry Standards and National Standards that affect the conveyor industry.
96 Members
Founded in 1933

21582 Council of International Investigators

PO Box 565
Elmhurst, IL 60126-0565

630-501-1880
888-759-8884
FAX 206-367-8777
E-Mail: office@cii2.org
Home Page: www.cii2.org
Social Media: *Facebook, LinkedIn*

Galen Clements, Executive Regional Director
Sheila Ponnosamy, President
Eduard Sigrist, Past president/ Treasurer
Anne Styren, Secretary
Bert Falbaum, VP/ Executive Regional Director

The Council of International Investigators was formed to encourage a greater association among owners and operators of investigation agencies while developing mutual trust and respect.
Founded in 1955

21583 Council on Certification of Health, Environmental & Technologists

2301 W. Bradley Avenue
Champaign, IL 61821

217-359-9263
FAX 217-359-0055
E-Mail: cchest@cchest.org
Home Page: www.cchest.org
Social Media: *Facebook, Twitter, LinkedIn, Google+*

Angie Kluth, Chief accounting Officer
Andrea Kamradt, Examination Manager
Treasa Turnbeaugh, CEO
Robert Schneller, COO
Teresa Hasken, CFO

CCHEST is recognized as the leader in high-quality, third-party accredited health, safety, and environmental credentialing for technologists, technicians, supervisors, and workers.
3000 Members
Founded in 1969

21584 Dangerous Goods Advisory Council

7501 Greenway Center Drive
Suite 760
Greenbelt, MD 20770

202-289-4550
FAX 202-289-4074
E-Mail: info@dgac.org
Home Page: www.dgac.org
Social Media: *Facebook, Twitter*

Del Billings, Technical director
Vaughn Arthur, Secretary & President
Barbara Lantry-Miller, Treasurer
Ben Barrett, Chair
Greg Allen, Vice Chair

DGAC fulfills its mission by providing education, technical assistance and information to the private and public sectors. Members incude shippers in the chemical, petroleum, and pharmaceutical industries, manufacturers, carriers, container manufacturers and reconditioners, emergency/waste clean-up companies, trade associations, and others involved in the transport of dangerous goods.
Founded in 1978

21585 Electrical Safety Foundation International

1300 N 17th Street
Suite 900
Rosslyn, VA 22209

703-841-5935
FAX 703-841-3329
E-Mail: info@esfi.org
Home Page: www.esfi.org
Social Media: *Facebook, Twitter, LinkedIn, YouTube*

Stephen Sokolow, Chairman
John Engel, Vice Chairman
Brett Brenner, President
Kevin Cosgriff, Treasurer
Patrick Davin, Secretary

The mission of the Electrical Safety Foundation International (ESFI) is to advocate electrical safety in the home and in the workplace in order to reduce electrically-related fatalities, injuries and property loss. ESFI is committed to: Being the unbiased authority in electrical safety issues for consumers, the workforce, and the media; Identifying and addressing evolving electrical safety needs; Advocating safety technology, compliance with codes and standards, and risk-reducing behaviors.
Founded in 1994

21586 Electronic Security Association

6333 North State Highway 161
Suite 350
Irving, TX 75038

972-807-6800
888-447-1689
FAX 972-807-6883
Home Page: www.esaweb.org
Social Media: *Facebook, Twitter, LinkedIn*

Marshall Marinace, President
Dee Ann Harn, Vice President
Merlin Guilbeau, Executive Director
Jon Sargent, Secretary
Steve Paley, Treasurer

Trade association representing the electronic security industry.
Founded in 1948

21587 Environmental Information Association

6935 Wisconsin Ave
Suite 306
Chevy Chase, MD 20815-6112

301-961-4999
888-343-4342
FAX 301-961-3094
E-Mail: info@eia-usa.org

Home Page: www.eia-usa.org
Social Media: *Twitter, Google+*

Kevin Cannan, President
Chris Gates, President-Elect
Mike Schrum, Past President
Robert De Malo, Secretary
Kyle Burroughs, Treasurer

Nonprofit organization dedicated to providing environmental information to individuals, members and industry. Disseminates information on the abatement of asbestos and lead-based paint, indoor air quality, safety and health issues, analytical issues and environmental site assessments.

21588 Executive Protein Institute

Executive Protection Institute
16 Penn Plaza
Suite 1130
New York, NY 10001

212-268-4555
FAX 212-563-4783
E-Mail: info@personalprotection.com
Home Page: www.personalprotection.com
Social Media: *Facebook, LinkedIn*

John Negus, Asst. Executive Director
Jerry Heying, Executive Director
Eugene R. Ferrara, Chief Instructor
John F. Musser, Chief to Staff
Ana Paula Alfonso, Operations Director

A non-profit professional society whose members include academics, trainers, students, law enforcement and government officials, self-employed professionals, security officers, directors from major intenational corporations, security service organizations, and communications, energy, retail, chemicals, insurance, petroleum and utility companies.
2800 Members
Founded in 1978

21589 False Alarm Reduction Association

10024 Vanderbilt Circle
Unit 4
Rockville, MD 20850

301-519-9237
FAX 301-519-9508
E-Mail: info@faraonline.org
Home Page: www.faraonline.org

Brad Shipp, Executive Director
Kerri McDonald, President
Nadya Morgan, Vice President-Electronics Security
Tammy Foxworth, Vice President-Fire
Steven Heggemann, Treasurer

Primarily made up of persons employed by government and public safety agencies in charge of, or working in, False Alarm Reduction Units. The goal is to assist these individuals in reducing false alarms for their jurisdiction.
Founded in 1997

21590 Federal Law Enforcement Officers Association

7945 MacArthur Blvd.
Suite 201
Cabin John, MD 20818

202-870-5503
866-553-5362
FAX 717-932-2262
E-Mail: fleoa@fleoa.org
Home Page: www.fleoa.org
Social Media: *Facebook, Twitter*

Jon Adler, National President
Nate Catura, National Executive VP
Chris Schoppmeyer, Vice President-Agency Affairs
Lazaro Cosme, Vice President-Operations
Frank Terreri, Vice President-Legislative Affairs

Founded by a group of concerned federal agents from Customs, the IRS, FBI and INS, its goal is to assure that legal assistance and representation are a phone call away.
24000 Members
Founded in 1977

21591 Financial & Security Products Association (FSPA)
1024 Mebane Oaks Rd.
Suite 273
Mebane, NC 27302

919-648-0664
800-843-6082
FAX 919-648-0670
E-Mail: info@fspa1.com
Home Page: www.fspa1.com
Social Media: *LinkedIn*

Linda Abell, Chairman
L.A Smith, President
Fred Wheeler, Director
Gene Polito, Vice President
Kevin Callahan, Secretary/ Treasurer

Independent dealers, manufacturers and associates whose outstanding products and services give financial institutions a crucial edge in performance, efficiency and economy.
Founded in 1973

21592 Fire Apparatus Manufacturers' Association (FAMA)
PO Box 3065
Ocala, FL 34478

352-843-3404
FAX 781-334-2911
E-Mail: office@fama.org
Home Page: www.fama.org

Harold Boer, President
Bruce Whitehouse, VP

Membership association for manufacturers of emergency vehicles and components affixed to or carried upon the vehicle.
125 Members
Founded in 1946

21593 Fire Equipment Manufacturers' Association
1300 Sumner Avenue
Cleveland, OH 44115

216-241-7333
FAX 216-241-0105
E-Mail: fema@femalifesafety.org
Home Page: www.femalifesafety.org
Social Media: *LinkedIn, YouTube, Wordpress, Slideshare*

The premier trade association representing leading brands, and spanning dozens of product categories, related to fire protection.
27 Members
Founded in 1925

21594 Fire Suppression Systems Association
3601 East Joppa Road
Baltimore, MD 21234

410-931-8100
FAX 410-931-8111
E-Mail: fssa@clemonsmgmt.com
Home Page: www.fssa.net
Social Media: *Facebook, Twitter, LinkedIn*

Scott Bailey, Director
Eric Burkland, Immediate Past President
Ray Aldridge, Vice President
Helen Lowery, Secretary/ Treasurer
Tim Carman, President

An organization of manufacturers, suppliers, and design-installers, dedicated to providing a higher level of fire protection. Members are specialists in protecting high value special hazardareas from fire.
Founded in 1982

21595 Flight Safety Foundation
801 N. Fairfax Street
Suite 400
Alexandria, VA 22314-1774

703-739-6700
FAX 703-739-6708
E-Mail: wahdan@flightsafety.org
Home Page: www.flightsafety.org
Social Media: *Facebook, Twitter, LinkedIn*

Jon Beatty, President/CEO
Stephanie Mackin, Support Services Manager
David Barger, Treasurer
Ken Hylander, Chair
Kenneth P. Quinn, General Counsel & Secretary

Flight Safety Foundation is an independent, nonprofit, international organization engaged in research, auditing, education, advocacy and publishing to improve aviation safety. The Foundation's mission is to pursue the continuous improvement of global aviation safety and the prevention of accidents.
1000+ Members
Founded in 1947

21596 Homeland Security Industries Association
666 11th Street NW
Suite 315
Washington, DC 20001

202-386-6471
FAX 202-331-8191
E-Mail: info@hsianet.org
Home Page: www.hsianet.org

Brenda Boone, Owner

Nonprofit group providing a mechanism for government and the private sector to coordinate on a wide range of homeland security issues. Monitors legislation, regulations and hearings, provides training, and develops position papers reflecting industry concerns.
200+ Members
Founded in 2002

21597 Institute for Health & Productivity Management
17470 N. Pacesetter Way
Scottsdale, AZ 85255

480-305-2100
FAX 480-305-2189
E-Mail: sean@ihpm.org
Home Page: www.ihpm.org

Sean Sullivan, President/CEO
Bill Williams, Senior VP & Co-Founder
Pamella Thomas, Chief Medical Officer
Steve Priddy, Executive Director
Deborah Love, EVP & COO

Nonprofit organization making employee health an investment in corporate success through enhanced workplace performance.
Founded in 1997

21598 Institute for Intergovernmental Research
PO Box 12729
Tallahassee, FL 32317-2729

850-385-0600
FAX 850-422-3529
E-Mail: nygc@iir.com
Home Page: www.iir.com

Keith G Burt, Advisory Board
Emory B. Williams, Chairman
John Czernis, President
Meena Harris, Executive Vice President
R. Clay Jester, Senior Vice President

21599 Insurance Institute for Highway Safety
1005 N Glebe Rd
Suite 800
Arlington, VA 22201

703-247-1500
FAX 703-247-1588
E-Mail: rrader@iihs.org
Home Page: www.iihs.org
Social Media: *Twitter, YouTube, RSS*

Adrian Lund, President
Russ Rader, SVP, Communications
Eric Williams, Counsel
Shelly Shelton, Senior Legal Administrator
Brenda O'Donnell, VP, Insurer Relations

The Insurance Institute for Highway Safety is a nonprofit research and communications organization funded by auto insurers.
Founded in 1959

21600 Int'l Association for Counterterrorism & Security Professionals
PO Box 10265
Arlington, VA 22210

201-461-5422
E-Mail: acsp@aol.com
Home Page: www.iacsp.com

Steven Fustero, Executive Director

Our goals include creating a center of information and educational services for those concerned about the challenges now facing all free societies, and promoting professional ethics in the counter terrorism field.
Founded in 1992

21601 International Association For Healthcare Security and Safety
PO Box 5038
Glendale Heights, IL 60139

630-529-3913
888-353-0990
FAX 630-529-4139
E-Mail: info@iahss.org
Home Page: www.iahss.org
Social Media: *Facebook, Twitter, LinkedIn*

David LaRose, President
Jeff A. Young, President Elect
Ben Scaglione, Vice President/Secretary
Colleen Kucera, Executive Director
Nancy Felesena, Executive Assistant

An association dedicated to professionals involved in managing and directing security and safety in healthcare establishments.
Founded in 1968

21602 International Association for Identification
2131 Hollywood Blvd.
Suite 403
Hollywood, FL 33020

954-589-0628
FAX 954-589-0657
Home Page: www.theiai.org
Social Media: *Facebook*

Bridget Lewis, President
Harold Ruslander, 1st Vice President
Steve Johnson, Board Chair/Past President
Phyllis Karasov, legal Counsel
Glen Calhoun, COO

This is a forum where forensic specialists worldwide can interact as a whole. The main focus of any forensic organization is training and research to ensure all specialists maintain the highest levels of integrity and professionalism in order to meet the constant challenges to our individual disciplines.
Founded in 1915

21603 International Association for Computer Systems

6 Swarthmore Lane
Dix Hills, NY 11746

631-499-1616
FAX 631-462-9178
E-Mail: iacssjalex@aol.com
Home Page: www.iacss.com

Robert J Wilk, President
Promotes the security of computer information systems. Certifies individuals as Computer Systems Security Professionals.
Founded in 1981

21604 International Association for Healthcare Security and Safety

PO Box 5038
Glendale Heights, IL 60139

630-529-3913
888-353-0990
FAX 630-529-4139
E-Mail: info@iahss.org
Home Page: www.iahss.org
Social Media: *Facebook, Twitter, LinkedIn*

David LaRose, President
Richardy Dufresne, Sr., Member-at-Large
Jeff A. Young, President-Elect
Dana Frentz, VP/Treasurer
Ben Scaglione, VP/Secretary
Nonprofit professional organization of healthcare security and safety executives around the world. Works to improve and professionalize security and safety in healthcare facilities through the exchange of information and experiences among members. A magazine, newsletter and an annual meeting are benefits of membership.
1700 Members
Founded in 1968

21605 International Association of Arson Investigators

2111 Baldwin Ave
Suite 203
Crofton, MD 21114

410-451-3473
800-468-4224
FAX 410-451-9049
Home Page: www.firearson.com
Social Media: *Facebook, Twitter, LinkedIn, YouTube*

Daniel Heenan, President
George Codding, 1st VP
Soctt Bennett, 2nd VP
Peter Mansi, Immediate Past President
Kevin Crawford, Director
Dedicated to improving the professional development of fire and explosion investigators by being the global resource for fire investigation, technology and research
7500 Members
Founded in 1949

21606 International Association of Black Professional Firefighters

1200 G St. nW
Suite 800
Washington, DC 20005

202-434-4526
877-213-2170
FAX 202-434-8707
E-Mail: evpiabpff@yahoo.com
Home Page: www.iabpff.org
Social Media: *Facebook, Twitter, LinkedIn*

James Hill, President
Sam Aubrey Jr., Treasurer
Kenyatta Smith, EVP
Melanie Anderson, Financial Secreatry
Freddie Jackson, Sergeant at Arms

Promotes interracial progress throughout the fire service and encourages African American firefighters to seek elevated ranks. Offers an annual convention, education courses an an online resource page.
Founded in 1970

21607 International Association of Bomb Technicians and Investigators

1120 International Parkway
Suite 129
Fredericksburg, VA 22406

540-752-4533
FAX 540-752-2796
E-Mail: admin@iabti.org
Home Page: www.iabti.org
Social Media: *Facebook, Twitter, LinkedIn*

James T. Wooten, International Director
The IABTI is an independent, non-profit, professional association formed for countering the criminal use of explosives. This is accomplished through the exchange of training, expertise and information among personnel employed in the fields of law enforcement, emergency services, the military, forensic science and other related fields.
Founded in 1973

21608 International Association of Campus Law Enforcement Administrators

342 N Main Street
West Hartford, CT 06117-2507

860-586-7517
FAX 860-586-7550
E-Mail: info@iaclea.org
Home Page: www.iaclea.org
Social Media: *Facebook*

Patricia Patton, Director
David L Perry, Immediate Past President
Willaim F Taylor, President
Randy A Burba, President- Elect
Jasper Cooke, VP for Finance
Advances public safety for educational institutions by providing educational resources, advocacy and professional development.
Founded in 1958

21609 International Association of Chiefs of Police

44 Canal Center Plaza
Suite 200
Alexandria, VA 22314

703-836-6767
800-THE-IACP
FAX 703-836-4543
E-Mail: information@theiacp.org
Home Page: www.theiacp.org
Social Media: *Facebook, Twitter, LinkedIn, RSS, YouTube*

Rechard Beary, President
Vincent Talucci, Executive Director/CEO
Gwen Boniface, Deputy Executive Director
John Firman, Director of Strategic Partnerships
Paul Santiago, Director of Intl. Policing Division
The association's goals are to advance the science and art of police services; to develop and disseminate improved administrative, technical and opreration practices and promote their use in police work; to foster police cooperation and the exchange of information and experience among police administrators throughout the world; to bring about recruitment and training in the police profession of qualified person.
15000 Members
Founded in 1893

21610 International Association of Crime Analysts

9218 Metcalf Ave.
Suite 364
Overland Park, KS 66212

919-940-3883
800-609-3419
E-Mail: iaca@iaca.net
Home Page: www.iaca.net
Social Media: *Facebook, Twitter, LinkedIn, RSS*

Ericka Jackson, VP, Membership
Carolyn Cassidy, President
Tony Berger, VP, Administration
Eric Drifmeyer, Treasurer
Dawn Clausius, Secretary
The International Association of Crime Analysts was formed in 1990 to help crime analysts around the world improve their skills and make valuable contacts, to help law enforcement agencies make the best use of crime analysis, and to advocate for standards of performance and technique within the profession itself. This is accomplished through training, networking, and publications.
Founded in 1990

21611 International Association of Dive Rescue Specialists

8103 East US Highway
36, Box 171 Avon
INDIANA, US 46123

317-464-9787
800-423-7911
FAX 317-641-0730
E-Mail: dowens@iadrs.org
Home Page: www.iadrs.org
Social Media: *Twitter*

Blades Robinson, Executive Director
Steven Orusa, Operations Director
David Owens, Dir. Of communications
Fred Jackson, Advisory Board
Steve Fleming, Board of Directors
IADRS is dedicated to helping water rescue professionals stay informed about advances in training, equipment, and life saving techniques.
Founded in 1977

21612 International Association of Fire Chiefs

4025 Fair Ridge Dr
Suite 300
Fairfax, VA 22033-2868

703-273-0911
FAX 703-273-9363
E-Mail: thicks@iafc.org
Home Page: www.iafc.org
Social Media: *Facebook, Twitter, LinkedIn, RSS*

Mark W. Light, Executive Director
Chief Thomas Jenkins, 2nd VP
Chief Rhoda Mae Kerr, President and Chairman of the Board
Chief G. Keith Bryant, President 2014-2015
Chief Richard R Carrizzo, Treasurer
Provides leadership to career and volunteer chief, chief fire officers and managers of emergency service organization throughout the inernational community through vision, information, education, services and representation to enhance their professionalsim and capabilities.
12000 Members
Founded in 1873

21613 International Association of Firefighters

1750 New York Ave
Nw Suite 300
Washington, DC 20006-5395

202-737-8484
FAX 202-737-8418
E-Mail: pr@iaff.org
Home Page: www.iaff.org
Social Media: *Facebook, Twitter, Youtube, Flickr, Pinterest*

Harold Schaitberger, President
Jim Lee, Chief of Operations
Peter L. Gorman, Chief of Staff
Thomas H. Miller, Secretary/ Treasurer
William Romaka, 1st VP

Represents city and county firefighters and state and federal workers such as forestry firefighters and emergency medical workers at certain industrial facilities. Addressed are health and safety, labor relations, training, hazardous materials and burn injuries and education.
240k Members
Founded in 1903

21614 International Association of Personal Protection Agents

PO Box 266
Arlington Heights, IL 60006-0266

847-870-8007
FAX 847-870-8990
E-Mail: proproserv@aol.com
Home Page: www.iappa.net
Social Media: *Facebook*

Stephen R. Barnhart, Executive Director
Charles Mallice, Operations & Training Director
Nikolai Ehlers, CCPA, Senior Security Consultant
James A. King, Chief Advisor
Arnaldo B. Merli, CCPA, International Security Consultant

Professional, nonprofit membership body open to military and civilian law enforcement personnel and people from the public and private sector who are engaged in the protection of royalty, presidential, state and diplomatic officials, government, military and corporate executives, personalities from the entertainment world and those involved in witness and prisoner protection.
Founded in 1989

21615 International Association of Professional Security Consultants

575 Market St.
Suite 2125
San Francisco, CA 94105

415-536-0288
FAX 415-764-4915
E-Mail: iapsc@iapsc.org
Home Page: www.iapsc.org
Social Media: *LinkedIn*

Harold Gillens, President
Alan Brockbank, Vice President
Kerry Parker, Executive Director
Ken Wheatley, Secretary
Lynda Buel, Treasurer

The International Association of Professional Security Consultants (IAPSC) is a widely recognized consulting association in the security industry. Its rigid membership requirements ensure that potential clients may select from the most elite group of professional, ethical and competent security consultants available to them.
Founded in 1984

21616 International Biometrics & Identification Association

1090 Vermant Avenue
NW, 6th Floor
Washington, DC 20005

202-789-4452
FAX 202-289-7097
E-Mail: ibia@ibia.org
Home Page: www.ibia.org
Social Media: *Facebook, Twitter, RSS*

Raffie Beroukhim, Director
Christer Bergman, Secretary
Robert Harbour, President and Chairman of the Board
Walter Hamilton, Vice Chairman
Mike DePasquale, Treasurer
IBIA provides strong and growing value to its members, expanding business opportunities for the industry, advocating government support for the useof biometrics in leading commercial and public-sector applications, and reporting on key issues of strategic importance to the membership.
Founded in 1998

21617 International Biometrics Industry Association

1090 Vermont Avenue,
NW, 6th Floor
Washington, DC 20005

202-789-4452
FAX 202-289-7097
E-Mail: ibia@ibia.org
Home Page: www.ibia.org
Social Media: *Facebook, Twitter, RSS*

Robert Harbour, Chairman/ President
Walter Hamilton, Vice Chairman
Raffie Beroukhim, Director
Christer Bergman, Secretary
Mike DePasquale, Treasurer

Trade association representing developers, manufacturers and integrators of biometric hardware and software.
Founded in 1998

21618 International Centre for the Prevention of Crime

465 rue St-Jean Street
Bureau 803
Montreal, QU H2Y-2R6

514-288-6731
FAX 514-288-8763
E-Mail: cipc@cipc-icpc.org
Home Page:
www.crime-prevention-intl.org/english
Social Media: *Facebook, Twitter, LinkedIn*

Vincenzo Castelli, Administrator
Erich Marks, VP
Chantal Bernier, President
Elizabeth Johnston, Secretary
Paul Girard, Treasurer

The ICPC is an international forum for national government local authorities, public agencies, specialized institutions, and non-government organisations of exchange experience, consider emerging knowledge, and improve policies and programs in crime prevention and community safety. ICPC staff monitors developments, provides direct assistance to members, and contributes to public knowledge and understanding in the field.
Founded in 1994

21619 International Consumer Product Health & Safety Organization

7044 S. 13th Street
Oak Creek, WI 53154

414-908-4930
FAX 301-601-3543
E-Mail: customercare@icphso.org

Home Page: www.icphso.org
Social Media: *Twitter, LinkedIn*

Rick Brenner, Vice President
Alan Kaufman, President
Nancy Cowles, President-Elect
D Fenton, Executive Director
Ann Weeks, Past President

ICPHSO holds a unique position in its ability to attract the interest of a broad range of health and safety professionals and interested consumers, world-wide.
Founded in 1993

21620 International Fire Service Training Association

930 N Willis
Stillwater, OK 74078

405-744-5723
FAX 405-744-8204
E-Mail: customer.service@osufpp.org
Home Page: www.ifsta.org
Social Media: *Facebook, Twitter, LinkedIn*

Robert Moore, State Fire Organization
Steve Ashbrock, Fire Dept.
Steve Austin, Fire Service Affiliate
Mike Wieder, Fire Organisation
Scott D. Kerwood, Fire Department

Nonprofit organization associated with Fire Protection Publications, a department of the College of Engineering, Architecture and Technology at Oklahoma State University.
Founded in 1934

21621 International Foundation for Protection Officers

1250 Tamiami
Tr. N Ste.206
Naples, FL 34102

239-430-0534
FAX 239-430-0533
E-Mail: adminifpo@earthlink.net
Home Page: www.ifpo.org
Social Media: *Facebook, Twitter, LinkedIn*

Sandi J Davies, Executive Director
Michael Stroberger, Secretary/Treasurer
Rck Daniels, Chairman
Karl Poulin, Director
Tom M. Conley, Past Chairman

Nonprofit organization for the purpose of facilitating the training and certification needs of protection officers and security supervisors from both the commercial and proprietary sectors.
Founded in 1988

21622 International High Technology Crime Investigation Association

3288 Goldstone Drive
Roseville, CA 95747

916-408-1751
FAX 916-384-2232
E-Mail: info@htcia.org
Home Page: www.htcia.org
Social Media: *Facebook, Twitter, LinkedIn*

Shadiÿ Hayden, President
Tom Quilty, Past President
Peter Morin, 1st Vice President
Steve Branigan, Secretary
Matt Samuelson, Treasurer

Designed to encourage, promote, aid and effect the voluntary interchange of data, information, experience, ideas and knowledge about methods, processes, and techniques relating to investigations and security in advanced technologies among its membership.
3500 Members
Founded in 1984

21623 International Hologram Association
2149 Cascade Ave
Suite 106
Hood River, OR 97031-1087

541-386-9449
FAX 541-386-1564
Home Page: www.hairmasterssalon.com

More than 60 of the worlds leading hologram manufacturers are members. Dedicated to promoting the interests of those quality hologram manufacturers worldwide and to helping our customers to achieve their security, packaging graphic and other objectives through the effective use of holography.
Founded in 1993

21624 International Hologram Manufacturers Association
4 Windmill Business Village
Brooklands Close, SU TW167DY

193-278-5680
FAX 193-278-0790
E-Mail: info@ihma.org
Home Page: www.ihma.orgÿ

Mike Messmer, Chairman
Nuray Yilmaz, Board Member
Umendra Gupta, ASPA Representative
Diana Newcomb, Board Member
Rajan Thomas, Asian Representative

A not for profit organization serving the hologram manufacturing industry.
Founded in 1993

21625 International Locksmiths Association
PO Box 9560
Naperville, IL 60567-0560

866-745-5625
E-Mail: keys150@juno.com
Home Page: www.ilanational.org

Tom Ripp, Director/Co-Chair
Larry Bowman, Vice President
Kurt Kloeckner, Treasurer
Kevin T. Piiper, National President
John Rendle, Secretary

Members are locksmiths, carpenters and building engineers who are employed by colleges, universities, hospitals, companies and government facilities. Dedicated to the education of members and the benefit of our institutions.

21626 International Municipal Signal Association
597 Haverty Court
Suite 100
Rockledge, FL 32955

321-392-0500
800-723-4672
FAX 321-806-1400
E-Mail: info@imsasafety.org
Home Page: www.imsasafety.org
Social Media: *Facebook, Twitter, LinkedIn*

Douglas M. Aiken, Deputy Executive Director
Mike Flanigan, Past President
Hans Kristensen, President
Kan Balltrip, President-Elect
Leonard Addair, Director-at-Large

Basic purpose of the organization is to keep its members and others in the profession, up-to-date on proper procedures of construction and maintenance of signal systems and informed on new products and equipment developments.
10000 Members
Founded in 1896

21627 International Photoluminescent Safety
2001 Jefferson Davis Highway
Suite 1004
Arlington, VA 22202-3617

703-416-0060
FAX 703-416-0014
E-Mail: info@plsafety.org
Home Page: www.plsafety.org

Tom Thompson, Executive Director

A leader in the marine safety and implementation of the highest possible performance, manufacturing maintenance, service and training standards, for all lifesaving, survival and emergency rescue equipment.
131 Members
Founded in 1986

21628 International Process Servers Association
2854 Larimer St
Denver, CO 80205

585-232-8590
800-611-2774
FAX 877-824-2482
E-Mail: richard@processservers.com
Home Page: www.iprocessservers.com

Unifies process servers in the United States and throughout the world, as the single greatest resource for all process servers and private investigators.

21629 International Safety Equipment Association
1901 N Moore Street
Suite 808
Arlington, VA 22209-1762

703-525-1695
FAX 703-528-2148
E-Mail: isea@safetyequipment.org
Home Page: www.safetyequipment.org
Social Media: *Facebook, Twitter, LinkedIn*

Daniel K Shipp, President
Nate Kogler, Public Affairs Director
Craig Wallentine, Office Services Manager
Eric Beck, Chairman
Brian Lyons, Past Chairman

Trade association in the US for companies that manufacture safety equipment. Member companies are world leaders in the design and manufacture of clothing and equipment used in factories, construction sites, hospitals and clinics, farms, schools, laboratories, and in the home — anywhere people are doing work. Our common goal is to protect the health and safety of people exposed to hazardous and potentially harmful environments.
Founded in 1933

21630 International Security Management Association
PO Box 623
Buffalo, IA 52728-0623

563-381-4008
800-368-1894
FAX 563-381-4283
E-Mail: susan.pohlmann@isma.com
Home Page: isma.com/

Tim Janes, President
Mike Howard, Executive Director
Damin Memeekin, Second VP
Mary Welsh, Deputy Executive Director

ISMA's mission is to provide and support an international forum of selected security executives whose combined expertise wil be utilized in a synergistic manner in developing, assimilating, sharing knowledge within security disciplines for the ultimate purpose of enhancing professional and business standards.
400 Members
Founded in 1983

21631 International System Safety Society
PO Box 70
Unionville, VA 22567-0070

540-854-8630
FAX 540-854-4561
E-Mail: syssafe@ns.gemlink.com
Home Page: www.system-safety.org
Social Media: *Facebook, LinkedIn*

Dr. Rod Simmons, President
Bob Schmedake, Immediate Past President
Pam Kniess, Executive Secretary
Chuick Muniak, Executive Vice President
Clif Ericson, Treasurer

The System Safety Society is a non-profit organization dedicated to supporting the safety professional in the application of system engineering and systems management to risk analysis. The Society is international in scope and draws members throughout the world.
4500 Members
Founded in 1962

21632 International of Personal Protection Agents
PO Box 266
Arlington Heights, IL 60006-0266

847-870-8007
FAX 847-870-8990
E-Mail: proproserv@aol.com
Home Page: www.iappa.net
Social Media: *Facebook*

Dr. Stephen Barnhart, Executive Director
Charles Mallice, Operations &Training Director
Mr Nikolai Ehlers, Senior Security Consultant
Mr James A King, Chief Advisor
Mr Chris Menary, National Director

Professional, nonprofit membership body open to military and civilian law enforcement personnel and people from the public and private sector who are engaged in the protection of royalty, presidential, state and diplomatic officials, government, military and corporate executives, personalities from the entertainment world and those involved in witness and prisoner protection.
Founded in 1989

21633 Investigators of America
PO Box 4243
Downey, CA 90241

562-869-2535
877-393-7792
FAX 562-869-5268
E-Mail: dkalepi@earthlink.net
Home Page: www.investigatorsofamerica.com

John R. Spencer, Director
Dave Blair, Director
Roberto A. Rivera, Director
Edwin C. Hodges, Director
Steven Rambam, Director

Investigators of America is a rapidly growing association comprised of elite private investigators, insurance adjusters, and expert witnesses across the United States with affiliates in other countries.

21634 Laser Institute of America
13501 Ingenuity Dr
Suite 128
Orlando, FL 32826

407-380-1553
800-345-2737
FAX 407-380-5588
E-Mail: lia@lia.org
Home Page: www.lia.org

Social Media: *Facebook, Twitter, LinkedIn, Google+*

Yongfeng Lu, Past President
Lin Li, President Elect
Rodert Thomas, President
Stephen Capp, Treasurer
Paul Denney, Secretary

The Laser Institute of America is the professional membership society dedicated to fostering lasers, laser applications and safety worldwide. Its mission is to foster lasers, laser applications, and laser safety worldwide. Serving the industrial, medical, research and government communities, LIA offers technical information and networking opportunities to laser users from around the globe.
1200 Members
Founded in 1968

21635 Mine Safety and Health Administration

1100 Wilson Blvd
21st Floor
Arlington, VA 22209-3939

202-693-9400
800-746-1553
FAX 202-693-9401
Home Page: www.msha.gov
Social Media: *Facebook, Twitter*

David G Dye, Executive Director

Mission is to enforce compliance with mandatory safety and health standards as a means to eliminate fatal accidents, reduce the frequency and severity of nonfatal accidents, minimnize health hazards, and to promote improved safety and health conditions in national mines.
Founded in 1978

21636 Motorcycle Safety Foundation

2 Jenner
Suite 150
Irvine, CA 92618

800-446-9227
E-Mail: msf@msf-usa.org
Home Page: www.msf-usa.orgÿ
Social Media: *Facebook, Twitter, YouTube*

Russ Brenan, Chair
Joseph Dagley, Vice Chair
Tim Buche, President & CEO
Robert Gladden, Vice President
Steve Piehl, Secretary/ Treasurer

Provides information on rider training, licensing, and goverment relations.

21637 National Alarm Association of America

PO Box 3409
Dayton, OH 45401

937-461-2208
800-283-6285
FAX 937-461-4759
E-Mail: info@naaa.org
Home Page: www.naaa.org

Gene Riddlebaugh, President
Grant Angell, Senior VP Associate Affairs
Ricardo Gonzales, Vice President

Mission is to advance the welfare of members through the free exchange, among members of ideas and the dissemination of information concerning trade practices, business conditions, technical developments, within the industry, and any related subject of concern to the security industry.
Founded in 1984

21638 National Association of Elevator Safety Authorities

PO Box 640
Rochester, WA 98579

360-292-4968
800-746-2372
FAX 360-292-4973
E-Mail: dotty@naesai.org
Home Page: www.naesai.org

George W. Gibson, Advisor
Douglas S Warne, President
Dean G Mclellan, VP
Fredick C Slater, Treasurer
Michael Stewart, Secretary

Elevator inspector certification and continuing education.
2500 Members
Founded in 1969

21639 National Association of Fire Equipment Distributors

180 N. Wabash Avenue
Suite 401
Chicago, IL 60601

312-461-9600
FAX 312-461-0777
E-Mail: dharris@nafed.org
Home Page: www.nafed.org
Social Media: *Facebook, LinkedIn, YouTube*

Ed Hugill, President
Danny Harris, Ex Officio
Tim Krulan, Treasurer
George Seymour, President Elect
Bill Johnson, Director

Mission is to improve the economic environment, business performance, and technical competence in the fire protection industry.
Founded in 1963

21640 National Association of Fraud Investigators

2519 NW 23rd St.
Suite 204
Oklahoma City, Ok 73107

405-833-2327
E-Mail: RBrown2150@aol.com
Home Page: www.nafraud.com

Established to improve communications and expand the network of professional fraud investigators.

21641 National Association of Legal Investigators

235N Pine Street
Lansing, MI 48933

517-702-9835
866-520-NALI
FAX 517-372-1501
E-Mail: val@julianvail.com,
larry@julianvail.co
Home Page: www.nalionline.org
Social Media: *Facebook, Twitter*

Don C. Johnson, National Director
Jayne McElfnesh, Assistant National Director
Andi Murphy, National Secretary
Julian Vail, Association Management
Nicole Bocra Gray, Regional Director-Northeast Region

Membership in NAL is open to all professional legal investigators who are actively engaged in negligence investigations for plaintiff and/or criminal defense, and who are employed by investigative firms, law firms or public defender agencies.
Founded in 1967

21642 National Association of Safety Professionals

1531 South
Post Road
Shelby, NC 28152

800-922-2219
FAX 704-487-1579
E-Mail: info@naspweb.com
Home Page: www.naspweb.com
Social Media: *Facebook, Twitter*

Eric Gislason, Executive Director
Jon Beard, IT Analyst

A nonprofit membership organization providing training, consultative services as well as certifications.
10000 Members

21643 National Association of Security Companies

444 North Capitol Street, NW
Suite 345
Washington, DC 20001

202-347-3257
FAX 202-393-7006
E-Mail: information@nasco.org
Home Page: www.nasco.org

Jim McNulty, Chair
Stephen Kasloff, 1st Vice Chair
Julie Payne, 2nd Vice Chair
Lynn Oliver, Secretary
David Buckman, Treasurer

To promote standards and professionalism for private security officers and within contract security.

21644 National Burglar & Fire Alarm Association

2300 Valley View Lane
Suite 230
Irving, TX 75062

214-260-5970
888-447-1689
FAX 214-260-5979
E-Mail: MerlinG@alarm.org
Home Page: www.alarm.org
Social Media: *Facebook, Twitter, YouTubee*

Merlin Guilbeau, Executive Director
Georgia Calaway, Communications/PR Director
Founded in 1948

21645 National Classification Management Society

994 Old Eagle School Rd
Suite 1019
Wayne, PA 19087-1866

610-971-4856
FAX 610-971-4859
E-Mail: info@classmgmt.com
Home Page: www.classmgmt.com
Social Media: *Facebook, Twitter, LinkedIn*

Sharon K. Tannahill, Executive Director
Mr. Dennis Arriage, President
Mrs. Aprilli Abbott, Vice President
Dean Young, Treasurer
Ms. Debbie Young, Secretary

Advancing the practice of classification management in the disiplines of industrial security, information security, government designated unclassified information, and intellectual property, and to foster the highest qualities of security professionalism among its members.
1,300 Members
Founded in 1964

21646 National Council of Investigation & Security Services

7501 Sparrows Point Boulevard
Baltimore, MD 21219-1927

800-445-8408
FAX 410-388-9746
E-Mail: nciss@comcast.net
Home Page: www.nciss.org

Carolyn Ward, Executive Director
Francie Koehler, Past President
Debbie Anderson, Secretary
Don C. Johnson, CLI
Bill Fletcher, Treasurer

A cooperative of those companies and associations responsible for providing private security and investigation services to the legal profession, business community, government and the public.
1300 Members
Founded in 1975

21647 National Counterterrorism Center

National Counterterrorism Center
Washington, DC 20511

703-733-8600
E-Mail: nctcpao@nctc.gov
Home Page: www.nctc.govÿ
Social Media: *Facebook, Twitter, YouTube, RSS, Tumblr, Flickr*

Nicholas J. Rasmussen, Director
John J. Mulligan, Deputy Director

The primary organization in the United States Government for integrating and analyzing all intelligence pertaining to counterterrorism.

21648 National Crime Justice Association

720 7th Street NW
Third Floor
Washington, DC 20001

202-628-8550
FAX 202-448-1723
E-Mail: info@ncja.org
Home Page: www.ncja.org
Social Media: *Facebook, Twitter, LinkedIn, Pinterest, RSS*

Cabell C. Cropper, Executive Director
Lisa Nine Accordini, Senior Staff Associate
Bethany Broida, Director of Communications
Robert Greeves, Senior Policy Adviser
Janene Scelza, Web Manager

Exists to promote the developemtn of justice systems in states, tribal nations, and units of local government that enhance public saftety ; prevent and reduce the harmful effects of criminal and delinquent behavior on victims, individuals and communities; adjudicate defendants and sanction offenders fairly and justly; and that are effective and efficient.
Founded in 1971

21649 National Crime Prevention Council

1201 Connecticut Avenue, NW
Suite 200
Washington, DC 20036

202-466-6272
FAX 202-296-1356
E-Mail: webmaster@ncpc.org
Home Page: www.ncpc.org

David A. Dean, Chairman
Ann M. Harnkins, President & CEO
Jean Adnopoz, Secretary
John p. Box, Treasurer
Robert F. Diegelman, Vice Chair

Aids people in keeping themselves, their families, and their communities safe from crime. NCPC produces tools that communities can use to learn crime prevention strategies, engage

community members, and coordinate with local agencies.
136 Members
Founded in 1979

21650 National Defense Industrial Association

2111 Wilson Blvd
Suite 400
Arlington, VA 22201-3061

703-522-1820
FAX 703-522-1885
E-Mail: info@ndia.org
Home Page: www.ndia.org
Social Media: *Facebook, Twitter, LinkedIn, YouTube, Pinterest, Google+*

Mckinley Craig, President & CEO
O'Connell Cyndi, Web Operations
Barry D. Bates, VP, Operations
Goodman Will, VP, Government Policy
Dino Pignotti, VP, Advertising

A leading defense idustry association whose mission is to promote national security through a variety of means, including education, training and advocacy.
28100 Members
Founded in 1919

21651 National Electrical Manufacturers

1300 17th St N
Suite 900
Arlington, VA 22209

703-841-3200
FAX 703-841-5900
E-Mail: webmaster@nema.org
Home Page: www.nema.org
Social Media: *Facebook, Twitter, LinkedIn, RSS, YouTube, Google+*

Kevin J. Cosgriff, President
Donald J. Hendler, Chairman
Maryrose Sylvester, Vice Chair
David G. Nord, Treasurer
John W. Estey, Board Committee Chairman

NEMA's mission is to promote the competitiveness of its member companies by providing quality services that will impact positively on standrds, government regulation and market economics.
400 Members
Founded in 1926

21652 National Emergency Equipment Dealers Association

8421 Frost Way
Annandale, VA 22003

703-280-4622
FAX 703-280-0942
E-Mail: KentonP1@aol.com
Home Page: www.femsa.org
Social Media: *Facebook, Twitter, LinkedIn, Pinterest, Google+, Tumblr*

Kenton Pattie, Executive Director

Serves dealers who sell and service fire, rescue, and emergency rescue systems equipment and apparatus. Preserves and strengthens the free market system for dealers through advocacy, information and training. Assists dealers profitably deliver high quality products and support to the nation's emergency services.
Founded in 1915

21653 National Fire Protection Association

1 Batterymarch Park
Quincy, MA 02169-7471

617-770-3000
800-344-3555
FAX 617-770-0700
E-Mail: publicaffairs@nfpa.org
Home Page: www.nfpa.org

Social Media: *Facebook, Twitter, LinkedIn, YouTube, Google+, RSS, Pintere*

Jim Pauley, President/CEO
Randolph W. Tucker, 1st VP
Ernest J. Grant, Chairman
Amy R. Action, Secretary
Thomas A. Lawson, Treasurer

The mission of the NFPA is to reduce the worldwide burden of fire and other hazards on the quality of life by providing and advocating consensus codes and standards, research, training and education.
75000 Members
Founded in 1896

21654 National Fire Sprinkler Association

40 Jon Barrett Rd.
Patterson, NY 12563

845-878-4200
FAX 845-878-4215
E-Mail: info@nfsa.org
Home Page: www.nfsa.org
Social Media: *Facebook, Twitter, LinkedIn, YouTube, Google+*

Russell P. Fleming, Executive Vice President
Alan Wiginton, Director
Dennis Coleman, Chairman
James Boulanger, Treasurer
Larry Thau, Vice Chair

The goal is to create a market for the widespread acceptance of competently installed automatic fire sprinkler systems in new and existing construction. Members are makers and installers of automatic fire sprinklers and related equipment.
Founded in 1905

21655 National Floor Safety Institute (NFSI)

PO Box 92607
Southlake, TX 76092

817-749-1700
FAX 817-749-1702
E-Mail: info@nfsi.org
Home Page: www.nfsi.org
Social Media: *Facebook, Twitter, LinkedIn*

Richard Bing, Senior Marketing Manager
Russell Kendzior, President & Chairman
Howard W. Harris, Treasurer
Steven C. Spencer, Vice President
Beth B Risinger, CEO/Executive Director

Mission is to aid in the prevention of slip-and-fall accidents through education, training and recearch. The NFSI is led by a fifteen-member Board of Directors representing product manufacturers, insurance underwriters, trade associations, and independent consultants.
Founded in 1997

21656 National Institute for Occupational Safety & Health

1600 Clifton Rd
Atlanta, GA 30329-4027

404-639-3385
800-232-4636
FAX 513-533-8573
E-Mail: eidtechinfo@cdc.gov
Home Page:
www.cdc.gov/niosh/homepage.html
Social Media: *Facebook, Twitter, RSS, MySpace, YouTube, Flickr*

John Howard MD, Director
Hubert H Humphrey, Chief of Staff
Max Lum EdD, Assoc Director Health

To promote health and quality of life by preventing and controlling disease, injury, and disability.

21657 National Institute of Standards and Technology (NIST)
100 Bureau Dr
Stop 1070
Gaithersburg, MD 20899-1070

301-975-6478
800-877-8339
FAX 301-948-6107
E-Mail: inquiries@nist.gov
Home Page: www.nist.gov
Social Media: *Facebook, Twitter, LinkedIn, RSS, YouTube, Flickr*

W. Watt Starnes, CEO
Dr. William E. May, Director
Kevin Kimball, Chief of Staff
George Jenkins, Chief Financial Officer
Heather Mayton, Executive Officer

Promotes US innovation and industrial competitiveness by advancing measurement science, standards, and technology in ways that enhance economic security and improve quality of life. It's four cooperative programs are NIST Laboratories, Baldrige National Quality Program, Manufacturing Extension Partnership, and Advanced Technology Program.
Founded in 1901

21658 National Nuclear Security Administration
1000 Independence Ave.,
S.W.
Washington, DC 20585

202-586-5000
800-342-5363
FAX 202-586-7371
Home Page: www.nnsa.energy.gov
Social Media: *Facebook, Twitter, YouTube, Flickr, RSS*

Frank G. Klotz, Administrator
Madelyn Creedon, Principal Deputy Administrator
Annie Harrington, Deputy Administrator
Bruce Diamond, General Counsel
Deborah Wilbar, Associate Administrator

Organization for advancing nuclear sciences, technologies and engineering.
Founded in 2000

21659 National Safety Council
1121 SpringLake Dr.
Itasca, IL 60143-3201

630-285-1121
800-621-7619
FAX 630-285-1434
E-Mail: customerservice@nsc.org
Home Page: www.nsc.org
Social Media: *Facebook, Twitter, LinkedIn, YouTube, Google+*

Deborah Hersman, CEO
John P. Surma, Chairman
Patrick Phelan, Chief Financial Officer
Shay Gallagher, Vice President
Jeane Wrenn, Senior Director/General Counsel

Nonprofit, nongovernmental, international public service organization dedicated to protecting life and promoting health.
48000 Members
Founded in 1913

21660 National Safety Management Society
PO Box 4460
Walnut Creek, CA 94596-0460

800-321-2910
E-Mail: nsmsinc@yahoo.com
Home Page: www.nsms.us
Social Media: *Facebook, Twitter, LinkedIn, RSS*

Roosevelt Smith, President
John H Bridges III, Director
Jeffery Chung, Board Member

Marilyn Clark Alston, Board Member
Charles W. McGlothlin, Board Member

Mission is to support managers and their employees in their responsibility to assure the safety of all employees.
Founded in 1966

21661 National Sheriffs' Association
1450 Duke Street
Alexandria, VA 22314

800-424-7827
FAX 703-838-5349
E-Mail: mkendall@sheriffs.org
Home Page: www.sheriffs.org
Social Media: *Facebook, Twitter, LinkedIn, Google+*

John E. Aubrey, Immediate Past President
John Thompson, Interim Executive Director
Linda Foldvik, Director of Finance
Miriam Kendall, Executive Secretary
Fred G. Wilson, Director of Outreach & Law

An organization to promote criminal justice, homeland security and public safety.
Founded in 1940

21662 National Society of Professional Insurance Investigators
PO Box 88
Delaware, OH 43015

888-677-4498
FAX 740-369-7155
E-Mail: nspii@nspii.com
Home Page: www.nspii.com
Social Media: *LinkedIn, RSS*

Micheal E. Jacobs, President
Jeffrey W. Ferrand, First VP
Michall Beagle, Secretary/Membership Chairman

A professional society for research and education.
590 Members
Founded in 1983

21663 National Tooling & Machining Association
1357 Rockside Road
Cleveland, OH 44134

301-248-6200
800-248-6862
FAX 216-264-2840
E-Mail: info@ntma.org
Home Page: www.ntma.org
Social Media: *Twitter, LinkedIn*

Jeff Kelly, CEO
John Belza, President

Supports its members through education, training and resources.
2700 Members
Founded in 1943

21664 Nationalÿ Associationÿof Schoolÿ Safetyÿ and Law Enforcement Officials
19411 S. W.
308thÿ Street
Homestead, FL 33030

305-905-1323
FAX 305-247-9915
Home Page: www.nassleo.org
Social Media: *Facebook, Twitter*

Augustine Pescatore, Chairman
Larry D. Johnson, President
Chief Ian Moffett, President Elect
Hector Garcia, Secretary
Rudy Perez, Treasurer

Provides levels of resources for school law enforcement and safety officials.

21665 Professional Investigators & Security Association
PO Box 3307
Fairfax, VA 22038-3307

703-818-0552
FAX 703-818-0551
E-Mail: kbreenpi@yahoo.com
Home Page: www.vapisa.com
Social Media: *Facebook, Twitter*

Kristopher W. Wilgus, 1st, Vice President
Susan Spofford, 2nd Vice President
Nicole Bocra Grray, President
Vacant T.B.A., Secretary
Narma J. Duncan, Treasurer

PISA is recognized as the preeminent professional organization representing members of the Private Security Services.
Founded in 1984

21666 Professional Records & Information Service s Management
8735 W Higgins Rd
Suite 300
Chicago, IL 60631

847-375-6344
800-336-9793
FAX 847-375-6343
E-Mail: info@prismintl.org
Home Page: www.prismintl.org
Social Media: *Facebook, Twitter, LinkedIn*

Dave Bergeson, Executive Director
Chad Sorrell, President
Chris Kelly, Vice President
Michael Fruchter, Secretary/ Treasurer
Chris Pearson, Asst. Secretary

A nonprofit trade association for the commercial information management industry whose vision is to be the primary global resource for commercial information management outsourcing providers.
Founded in 1930

21667 SAFE Association
PO Box 130
Creswell, OR 97426-0130

541-895-3012
FAX 541-895-3014
E-Mail: safe@peak.org
Home Page: www.safeassociation.com
Social Media: *Facebook*

Barr Shope, President
Joe Spinosa, President-Elect
Mathew Wawrowski, Vice President
Jerry Ride, Treasurer
Alex Mc Gill, Secretary

Dedicated to the preservation of human life. Provides a common meeting ground for the sharing of problems, ideas and information.
Founded in 1956

21668 Safe & Vault Technicians Association
3500 Easy St
Dallas, TX 75247

214-819-9733
800-532-2562
FAX 214-819-9736
Home Page: www.savta.org

Charles Gibson, President

Provides a host of benefits to help its members stay informed, solving day to day problems, and out-performing the competition. Has helped thousands of safe and vault techicians achieve personal and professional success.
Founded in 1986

21669 Safety Equipment Distributors Association

1901 North Moore Street
Suite 808
Arlington, VA 22209-1762

703-525-1695
FAX 703-528-2148
E-Mail: jackie@ksgroup.org
Home Page: www.safetycentral.org
Social Media: *Facebook, Twitter, LinkedIn*

Eric Beck, Chairman
Brian Lyons, Past Chairman
Daniel K. Shipp, President
Sheila Eads, Vice Chairman
Jim Johnson, General Manager

The Saftey Equipment Distributor's Association is the trade association comprised of companies that distribute safety equipmant and related products and services. Its member companies are leaders in the distribution of personal protective equipment to a broad spectrum of users, including general industry, construction, municipalities, utilities, schools and laboratories.
175 Members
Founded in 1933

21670 Safety Glazing Certification Council

P.O. Box 730
100 W. Main St.
Sackets Harbor, NY 13685

315-646-2234
FAX 315-646-2297
E-Mail: staff@amscert.com
Home Page: www.sgcc.org

John Kent, Administrative Staff
Peter Weismantle, President
Richard Paschel, Vice President
June Willcott, Secretary
Elaine S. Rodmanÿ, Treasurer

Nonprofit corporation that provides for the certifacation of safety glazing materials, comprised of safety glazing manufacturers and other parties concerned with public safety. SGCC is managed by a board of directors comprised of representatives from the safety glazing industry and the public interest sector.
105 Members
Founded in 1971

21671 Scaffold & Access Industry Association

400 Admiral Blvd
Kansas City, MO 64106

816-595-4860
866-687-7115
FAX 602-257-1166
E-Mail: rjm@scaffold.org
Home Page: www.scaffold.org
Social Media: *Facebook, Twitter, LinkedIn, RSS*

Paula Manning, President Elect
Mike Russell, President
Frankÿ Frietsch, Treasurer
Ted Beville, Vice President
Colby Hubler, Secretary

Nonprofit organization which promotes scaffold safety and education through its publications, conventions, tradeshows and training programs.
Founded in 1972

21672 Scaffold and Access Industry Association

400 Admiral Blvd
Kansas City, MO 64106

816-595-4860
FAX 816-472-7765
E-Mail: info@saiaonline.org
Home Page: www.saiaonline.org

Social Media: *Facebook, Twitter, LinkedIn, RSS*

Mike Russell, President
Paula Manning, President Elect
Ted Beville, Vice President
Colby Hubler, Secretary
Frank Frietsch, Treasurer

To promote, represent and enhance the access, scaffolding and forming industry for the benefit of its members.
Founded in 1972

21673 Security Hardware Distributors Association

105 Eastern Avenue
Suite 104
Annapolis, MD 21403

410-940-6346
FAX 410-263-1659
E-Mail: info@shda.org
Home Page: www.shda.org

Sean Steinmann, President
Rob Justen, Director
Karen Hoffman-Kahl, Immediate Past President
John Burke, Vice President
David Swartz, Treasurer

Offers education and services to its members.
150 Members
Founded in 1940

21674 Security Industry Association

8405 Colesville Road
Suite 500
Silver Spring, MD 20910

301-804-4700
866-817-8888
FAX 301-804-4701
E-Mail: info@siaonline.org
Home Page: www.siaonline.org
Social Media: *Facebook, Twitter, LinkedIn, YouTube*

Denis Hebert, Chairman Elect
Herve Fages, Vice Chairman
Scott Schafer, Treasurer
V. John Storia, Chairman
John Romanowich, Secretary

SIA is dedicated to promoting growth, advancement, and professionalism within the security industry. Its activities fall into four core concentrations: government relations, research & technology, education & training, and standards.
510 Members
Founded in 1969

21675 Semiconductor Environmental Safety & Health Association

1313 Dolley Madison Boulevard
Suite 402
McLean, VA 22101

703-790-1745
FAX 703-790-2672
E-Mail: BBurk@Burkinc.com
Home Page: www.seshaonline.org
Social Media: *Facebook, Twitter, LinkedIn*

Hilary Matthews, President
Brett J Burk, Executive Director
Steven Roberge, Treasurer
Raymond Mvdaid, Secretary
Paul M Connor, President-Elect

SESHA is the premier association serving the global semiconductor and associated technology industries by providing education and professional development.
1500 Members
Founded in 1978

21676 Society for Occupational & Environmental Health

1010 Vermont Ave., NW
Suite 513
Washington, DC 20005

202-347-4976
FAX 202-347-4950
E-Mail: kkirkland@aoec.org
Home Page: www.soeh.org

Ronald Denny Dobbin CIH, President
Katherine H. Kirrkland, Executive Director
Sarah Shiffert, Association Director
Mark Catlin, Governing Board

The Society plays a unique, integrating role by bringing together professionals in government, and academia. It reduces occupational and environmental hazards through the presentation of scientific data and the dynamic exchange of information across institutions and disciplines.
Founded in 1972

21677 Society of Fire Protection Engineers

9711 Washingtonian Blvd
Suite 380
Gaithersburg, MD 20878

301-718-2910
FAX 240-328-6225
E-Mail: sfpehqtrs@sfpe.org
Home Page: www.sfpe.org
Social Media: *Facebook, Twitter, LinkedIn, YouTube, RSS*

Milosh Puchovsky, President-Elect
Michael Madden, President
Carl F. Baldassarra, President-Elect
Jack Poole, Secretary
Peter Willse, Vice President

The purpose of the Society is to advance the science and practice of fire protection engineering and its allied fields, to maintain a high ethical standard among its members and to foster fire protection engineering education. The Society provides a program of educational offerings and provides technical publications.
4500 Members
Founded in 1950

21678 The American Association of Safety Council s

Home Page: www.safetycouncils.orgÿ

Jim Meade, President
Darby Vorce, Vice President
Dianna Braud, Past President
Lynndee Riley, Secretary
Toni Burrows, Treasurer

An international association of safety professionals

21679 The Association of State Floodplain Managers

575 D'Onofrio Drive
Suite 200
Madison, WI 53719

608-828-3000
FAX 608-828-6319
E-Mail: memberhelp@floods.org
Home Page: www.floods.orgÿ
Social Media: *Facebook, Twitter, LinkedIn, Google+, Tumblr*

Maria Cox Lamm, Vice Chair
Ceil Strauss, Chair
Chad Berginnis, Executive Director
Leslie Durham, Secretary
Karen McHugh, Treasurer

To promote education, policies and activities that mitigate current and future losses, costs and human suffering caused by flooding.

21680 The International Biometric Society

1444 I Street, NW
Suite 700
Washington, DC 20005

202-712-9049
FAX 202-216-9646
E-Mail: ibs@biometricsociety.org
Home Page: www.biometricsociety.org
Social Media: *Facebook, Twitter, LinkedIn*

John Hinde, President
Elizabeth Thompson, President Elect
Dee Ann Walker, Executive Director
Jose Pinheiro, Director
James Carpenter, Secretary/ Treasurer

21681 The National Burglar & Fire Alarm

440 North Broad Street
Suite 130
Philadelphia, PA 19130

215-400-6428
FAX 215-400-4717
E-Mail: secretary@nassleo.org
Home Page: www.alarm.org
Social Media: *Facebook, Twitter, YouTube*

21682 The World Institute for Security Enhancement

702-722-7779
E-Mail: training@worldinstitute.org
Home Page: www.worldinstitute.org

G.F. Bryant, Executive Director
Henry D Infante, Director of Operations
Rubern Bala, Director of International Marketing
M Gregory Scott, Director of Intnl. Investigations
Lisa A Kane, Director of Health

21683 Transportation Security Administration

866-289-9673
E-Mail: TSA-ContactCenter@tsa.dhs.gov
Home Page: www.tsa.govÿ
Social Media: *Facebook, Twitter, LinkedIn, YouTube*

Peter Neffenger, Administrator
Kenneth Fletcher, Chief Risk Officer
Thomas McDaniels, Chief of Staffs
Francine Kerner, Chief Counsel
Pat Rose, Finance
Founded in 2001

21684 U.S. Fire Administration

16825 S. Seton Ave.
Emmitsburg, MD 21727

301-447-1000
888-382-3827
FAX 301-447-1441
E-Mail: netcadmissions@fema.dhs.gov
Home Page: www.usfa.fema.gov
Social Media: *Facebook, Twitter, YouTube*

Ernest Mitchell, US Fire Administrator
Kyle Blackman, Executive Officer
Vanetta Huff, Secretary
Angela Cunningham, Administrative Specialist
Elizabeth Miller, Budget Analysis

21685 U.S. Security Associatesÿ

200 Mansell Court Fifth Floor
Roswell, GA 30076

770-625-1500
800-730-9599
Home Page: www.ussecurityassociates.com
Social Media: *Facebook, Twitter, LinkedIn, YouTube, Google+*

Founded in 1993

21686 Underwriters Laboratories

333 Pfingsten Rd
Northbrook, IL 60062-2096

847-412-0136
FAX 847-272-8129
E-Mail: northbrook@us.ul.com
Home Page: www.ul.com
Social Media: *Facebook, Twitter, LinkedIn, YouTube, Google+, Pinterest*

Christian Anschuetz, SVP & Chief Information Officer
Terry Brady, SVP & Chief Legal Officer
Adrian Groom, SVP & Chief Human Resources Officer
Michael Saltzman, SVP & CFO
Barbara Guthrie, SVP & Public Safety Officer

Underwriters Labdoratories Inc. is an independent, not-for-profit product-safty testing and certification organization, that has been testing products for safety for more than a century.
Founded in 1894

21687 United States Association of Professional Investigators

175 Hutton Ranch Rd
Ste 103-165
Kalispell, MO 59901

877-894-0615
FAX 877-851-0794
E-Mail: infor@usapi.org
Home Page: www.usapi.orgÿ
Social Media: *Twitter*

Randy Torgerson, President
fred Ritz, Vice President
Leah Ritz, Executive Director
Stephane Juneau, CFO

21688 United States Marine Safety Association

5050 Industrial Road
Suite 2
Wall Township, NJ 07727

732-751-0102
FAX 732-751-0508
E-Mail: fhornig@vanebrothers.com
Home Page: www.usmsa.orgÿ

Frank Hornig, President
Karen Hansen, Vice President
Tom Thompson, Executive Director
Maureen Fackenthal, Administrative Director
Dan Connor, Treasurer

21689 United States Society on Damsÿ

1616 Seventeenth Street
Suite 483
Denver, CO 80202

303-628-5430
FAX 303-628-5431
E-Mail: stephens@ussdams.org
Home Page: www.ussdams.org

John S. Wolfhope, President
Dean B. Durkee, Secretary-Treasurer
Daniel L. Wade, Vice President
Larry D. Stephens, Executive Director
John D. Rice, Board of Director

21690 Veterans of Safety

22 Logan Street
New Bedford, MA 02740

660-543-4281
E-Mail: info@vetsofsafety.org
Home Page: www.vetsofsafety.org

Warren K Brown, Past President
Dr Nigel Ellis, VP
Dianna Bryant, Executive Director
Wendell W. Wahlstedt, President
Christopher M Gates, Counsil of Ambassadors

Our mission is the promotion of safety, health, and environmental awareness by using and making available the lifetime experience of professionals throughout the world.
Founded in 1941

21691 Western States Auto Theft Investigators Association Southern Chapter

6 Hutton Centre Drive
Suite 1040
Santa Ana, CA 92707

714-434-9600
E-Mail: webmaster@wsati.org
Home Page: www.wsati.org
Social Media: *Facebook, Twitter*

Heather Roberts, Secretary
Brian Yori, VP
Aristeed Powell, President
Jeff Enfield, Treasurer
Richard O. Knapp, Legal Counsel

A non-profit organization that is comprised of professionals representing law enforcement, rental car and insurance companies, and other individuals whose goal is to reduce vehicle theft.
Founded in 1965

21692 Women Investigators Association

PO Box 18305
Encino, CA 91416

800-603-3524
E-Mail: womeninvas@aol.com
Home Page: www.w-i-a.org

Debra J Burdette, Executive Director
Robinette Desrochers, VP/Membership Director

Offering education and training, certification, networking, group discounts and represents women in our industry to the media.

Newsletters

21693 ACP Sentinel
Association of Contingency Planners

7044 S 13th St
Oak Creek, WI 53154-1429

414-768-8000
800-445-4227
FAX 414-768-8001
E-Mail: Membership@techenterprises.net
Home Page: www.naspa.com

Scott Sherer, Executive Director
Shirley Runnels, Membership

News and event information for national and local chapters dedicated to fostering continued professional growth and development in effective contingency and business planning.
Cost: $75.00
Frequency: Quarterly
Founded in 1983

21694 American Society of Crime Laboratory Directors

139K Technology Drive
Garner, NC 27529

919-773-2044
FAX 919-773-2602
E-Mail: info@nfstc.org
Home Page: www.ascld.org

William E Marbaker, President
Susan C Scholl, Membership

Contains useful information and news to maintain and improve communications among crime laboratory directors and their staff.
Cost: $100.00
Frequency: Quarterly
Founded in 1973

21695 CGAA Signals
Central Station Alarm Association
8150 Leesburg Pike
Suite 700
Vienna, VA 22182-2721

703-242-4670
FAX 703-242-4675
E-Mail: communications@csaaul.org
Home Page: www.csaaul.org

Stephen P Doyle, Executive VP/CEO
Celia Besore, VP Marketing & Programs
300+ Members
Frequency: Quarterly
Circulation: 1200
Founded in 1950

21696 Councilor
Safety & Health Council of Northern New
England
57 Regional Dr
Suite 6
Concord, NH 03301-8518

603-228-1401
800-834-6472
FAX 603-224-0998
E-Mail: safety@shcnne.org
Home Page: www.shcnne.org

Lyman Cousens, Executive Director

Covers current regulatory issues as well as
health and safety information. Free to members.
16 Pages
Frequency: Monthly
Founded in 2004
Printed in 2 colors on matte stock

21697 Emergency Preparedness News
Business Publishers
2601 University Boulevard W
#200
Silver Spring, MD 20902

301-929-5700
800-274-6737
FAX 301-949-8844
E-Mail: custserv@bpinews.com
Home Page: www.bpinews.com

Adam P Goldstein, Publisher
Deborah Eby, Editor
David Henderson, Director
Melissa Worcester, Service

Dedicated solely to disaster management: from
securing pre-disaster mitigation and counter
terrorism funds, to staying prepared for hurricanes, terrorist threats, fires, floods and other
natural disasters. Only available online now.
Cost: $357.00
Frequency: Monthly
ISSN: 0275-3782

21698 FAMA Flyer
Fire Apparatus Manufacturers' Association
PO Box 397
Lynnfield, MA 01940-0397

781-334-2911
FAX 781-334-2911
E-Mail: info@fama.org
Home Page: www.fama.org

Grady North, President
Greg Kozey, VP

A newsletter that is written specifically for Fire
Apparatus Manufactures and Fire Associations
across the United States.
Frequency: 3x/Yr
Circulation: 500

21699 HTCIA Newsletter
3288 Goldstone Drive
Roseville, CA 95747

916-408-1751
FAX 916-408-7543
Home Page: www.htcia.org

Carol Hutchings, Executive Director
For members only
Frequency: Quarterly

21700 Homeland Security & Defense
McGraw Hill
1200 G St Nw
Suite 900
Washington, DC 20005-3821

202-383-2377
FAX 202-383-2438
Home Page: www.aviationnow.com

Jennifer Michels, President
Paul Hoversten, Managing Editor
Mark Lipowicz, Publisher
Iain Blackhall, Managing Director

News items for defense and homeland security
professionals. Available in print or electroni-
cally.
Cost: $595.00
Frequency: Weekly
Founded in 1920

21701 Nine Lives Associates: Newsletter
Executive Protection Institute
PO Box 802
Berryville, VA 22611

540-554-2540
FAX 540-554-2558
E-Mail: info@personalprotection.com
Home Page: www.personalprotection.com

Ronald J. Wilczynski, President
Tom Quilty, VP
Peter Morin, Tresurer
Jose Soltero, Secretary

Personal protection news and announcements
for member graduates of Executive Protection
Institute.
Founded in 1980

21702 Progress
National Association of Elevator Safety
6957 Littlerock Road SW
Suite A
Tumwater, WA 98512

360-292-4968
800-746-2372
FAX 360-292-4973
E-Mail: dotty@naesai.org
Home Page: www.naesai.org
Social Media: *Facebook, Twitter, LinkedIn*

Dotty Stanlaske, Executive Director
Dean McLellan, President
Bill Snyder, VP

Informs members of the newest developments
in the elevator industry; listings of all cur-
rently-scheduled seminars, updated classes and
workshops; a message from the Executive Director with news from the main office; articles
addressing code questions and issues; news
from around the globe and advertising
opportunities.
Frequency: Monthly

**21703 Progress Report: The Foundation
Newsletter**
AAA Foundation for Traffic Safety

14th Street NW
Suite 201
Washington, DC 20005

202-638-5944
FAX 202-638-5943
Home Page: www.aaafoundation.org

Fairley Mahlum, Communications Director
Frequency: Monthly

21704 Protection News
International Foundation for Protection
Officers
PO Box 771329
Naples, FL 34107-1329

239-430-0534
FAX 239-430-0533
E-Mail: sandi@ifpo.com
Home Page: www.ifpo.org

Sandi J Davies, Executive Director
Michael Stroberger, Secretary/Treasurer

Circulation to all IFPO members and candidates in associated programs. Publication is designed to keep professionals current on trends
within the security industry and is full of valuable information and commentary pertinent to
the enhancement of life, safety and property
protection.
Cost: $18.00
Frequency: Quarterly
Founded in 1988

21705 SAFE Symposium News
SAFE Association
PO Box 130
Creswell, OR 97426

541-895-3012
FAX 541-895-3014
E-Mail: safe@peak.org
Home Page: www.safeassociation.com
Social Media: *Facebook*

Al Loving, President
John Fair, President-Elect

The SAFE Association is dedicated to the preservation of human life. It provides a common
meeting ground for the sharing of problems,
ideas and information. SAFE is a non-profit international association headquartered in Oregon, with chapters located throughout the
world. SAFE publishes a quarterly Newsletter
and Proceedings of the Annual SAFE Symposium. These publications are valuable reference
sources for the professional involved in all
forms of safety and survival.
1100+ Attendees
Frequency: Quarterly
Founded in 1954

21706 SIA News
Security Industry Association
8405 Colesville Road
Suite 500
Alexandria, MD 20109

301-804-4700
866-817-8888
FAX 301-804-4701
E-Mail: info@siaonline.org
Home Page: www.siaonline.org

Richard Chace, CEO
Rand Price CAE, COO
Donald Erickson, Government Relations
Director

Informs and educates members and prospective
members of SIA activities, news, and informa-
tion. Available online only.
Frequency: 2 X'S Monthly
ISSN: 1071-6713
Founded in 1969

21707 Safety Compliance Letter
Bureau of Business Practice

111 Eight Avenue
New York, NY 10011

800-638-8437
Home Page: www.aspenpublishers.com

Alicia Pierce, Publisher
Michele Rubin, Editor

Monitors and reports on the regulatory environment and provides subscribers with up-to-date information in a concise and easy-to-read format, with references and resources (including internet addresses) to get additional help on particular topics.
Cost: $289.00
Frequency: Monthly
ISBN: 9-900003-20-0
Founded in 1920

21708 Salt & Highway Deicing

Salt Institute
700 N Fairfax St
Suite 600
Alexandria, VA 22314-2085

703-549-4648
FAX 703-548-2194
E-Mail: info@saltinstitute.org
Home Page: www.saltinstitute.org

Richard L Hanneman, President
Tammy Goodwin, Administrative Director

A quarterly e-newsletter published by the Salt Institute.
Frequency: Quarterly
Circulation: 8000
Founded in 1914
Printed in on glossy stock

21709 Security Director's Report

Institute of Management and Administration
1 Washington Park
Suite 1300
Newark, NJ 07102

212-244-0360
FAX 973-622-0595
Home Page: www.ioma.com

Designed to help security directors keep pace with the rapidly evolving world of corporate security. Alerts to critical news, import new security products, and up-to-date advice that you need to know to effectively manager your security department.
Cost: $419.00
Frequency: Monthly

21710 Signal

American Traffic Safety Services
Association
15 Riverside Parkway
Suite 100
Fredericksburg, VA 22406-1022

540-368-1701
800-272-8772
FAX 540-368-1717
Home Page: www.atssa.com
Social Media: *Facebook, Twitter*

James Baron, Communications Director

Covers legislative updates, industry news and meeting information, as well as other items of interest to the roadway safety industry as is a full-color publication.
Frequency: Quarterly

21711 Society Update

American Society of Safety Engineers
1800 E Oakton Street
Des Plaines, IL 60018

847-699-2929
FAX 847-768-3434
E-Mail: customerservice@asse.org

Home Page: www.asse.org
Social Media: *Facebook*

Fred J Fortman, Executive Director
Jim Drzewiecki, Finance/Controller Director
Diane Hurns, Manager Public Relations
Department

Membership benefit via e-mail with news, information on training, plus happenings in the 150 chapters throughout the US.
Cost: $60.00
Founded in 1911

21712 Workplace Substance Abuse Advisor

LRP Publications
PO Box 24668
West Palm Beach, FL 33416-4668

561-622-6520
800-341-7874
FAX 561-622-0757
E-Mail: custserve@lrp.com
Home Page: www.lrp.com

Kenneth Kahn, President

Current developments affecting how your workplace deals with alcohol and drug abusing employees. Comprehensive overview of all the areas you need to know to create and maintain an effective substance abuse program in your company.
Cost: $377.00
Frequency: 2 X'S Month
Founded in 1977

Magazines & Journals

21713 Access Control & Security Systems

PRIMEDIA Business Magazines & Media
1166 Avenue of the Americas
Shawnee Mission, NY 10036

212-204-4200
FAX 913-514-6895
E-Mail: prothman@primediabusiness.com
Home Page: www.penton.com

Eric Jacobson, Senior VP
Gregg Herring, Publisher
Paul Rothman, Associate Editor
Brenda Wiley, Advertising Production Manager
Marty McCallen, National Sales Manager

Product overview articles and columns cover topics on door entry, CCTV, operators and gates, sensors and perimeter security.
Frequency: Monthly
Circulation: 38000+
Founded in 1905

21714 American Industrial Hygiene Association Journal

American Industrial Hygiene Association
2700 Prosperity Ave
Suite 250
Fairfax, VA 22031-4321

703-849-8888
FAX 703-207-3561
E-Mail: infonet@aiha.org
Home Page: www.aiha.org
Social Media: *Facebook, Twitter, LinkedIn*

Lisa Junker, Senior Editor
Michael Brandt, President
Dave Bentley, Marketing Manager
Sheila Brown,, Associate Editor
Peter Oneil, Executive Director

Essential source of information on occupational health and evironmental health and safety issues. Available in print and online.
780 Pages
Frequency: Monthly
Founded in 1982

21715 Business & Legal Reports

Business & Legal Reports
PO Box 6001
Old Saybrook, CT 06475-6001

860-510-0100
800-727-5257
FAX 860-510-7225
E-Mail: service@blr.com
Home Page: www.blr.com

Robert L Brady, CEO
Peggy Carter-Ward, Editor-in-Chief

Provides essential tools for safety and environmental compliance and training needs.
32 Pages

21716 Campus Safety Journal

Bricepac
12228 Venice Boulevard Suite 541
PO Box 66515
Los Angeles, CA 90066

310-390-5277
FAX 310-390-4777
E-Mail: tnelson@campusjournal.com
Home Page: www.campusjournal.com

Pat Restivo, Circualtion
John Horn, President

Provides a vehicle for communicating campus safety and security issues to all interested parties at the middle, secondary, college and university levels.
40 Pages
Frequency: Monthly
Circulation: 20000
Founded in 1992
Printed in 4 colors on glossy stock

21717 Compliance Magazine

Briefings Media Group
PO Box 787
Williamsport, PA 17703

800-791-8699
FAX 570-320-2079
Home Page: www.compliancemag.com

Betty Hintch, Editor
Laura Daugherity, Production Coordinator

Compliance Magazine offers the latest in government regulations, including the materials and information needed to stay in compliance, safety trends, and a complete Safety Buyers' Guide.
Frequency: Annual
Founded in 1985

21718 Computer Fraud & Security

Elsevier Science
360 Park Ave S
New York, NY 10010-1736

212-633-3980
FAX 212-633-3913
Home Page: www.elsevier.com

Provides practical, usable information to effectively manage and control computer and information security within commercial organizations.
Frequency: Monthly
ISSN: 1361-3723
Founded in 1979

21719 Computer Security Journal

Computer Security Institute
600 Harrison Street
San Francisco, CA 94107

415-947-6320
FAX 415-947-6023
E-Mail: csi@cmp.com
Home Page: www.gocsi.com
Social Media: *Facebook, Twitter, LinkedIn*

Russell Kay, Publisher

Keeps you informed with comprehensive, practical articles, case studies, reviews and com-

mentaries written by knowledgeable computer security professionals.
Cost: $224.00
Frequency: Quarterly
Circulation: 3000
Founded in 1974

21720 Computers & Security

Elsevier Science
360 Park Ave S
New York, NY 10010-1736

212-633-3980
FAX 212-633-3913
Home Page: www.elsevier.com
Social Media: *Facebook, Twitter, LinkedIn*

Provides a blend of leading edge research and sound practical management advice.
Frequency: Monthly
ISSN: 0167-4048
Founded in 1997

21721 Corporate Security

Strafford Publications
PO Box 13729
Atlanta, GA 30324-0729

404-881-1141
800-926-7926
FAX 404-881-0074
E-Mail: custserv@straffordpub.com
Home Page: www.straffordpub.com

Richard Ossoff, President
George Coleman, Manager

Intelligence briefing on the latest security developments, best practices, the most important trends and new technolgies.
Cost: $330.00
Frequency: Bi-Monthly
ISSN: 0889-0625
Founded in 1984

21722 EMS Product News

Cygnus Publishing
PO Box 803
Fort Atkinson, WI 53538-0803

920-000-1111
800-547-7377
FAX 920-563-1699
E-Mail: Ronnie.Garret@cygnuspub.com
Home Page: www.cygnusb2b.com
Social Media: *Facebook, Twitter, LinkedIn*

John French, CEO
Nancy Perry, Editor

Product information written with the emergency medical service professional in mind.
Cost: $53.00
Frequency: 6 Issues
Circulation: 20000

21723 Emergency Medical Product News

Cygnus Business Media
PO Box 803
Fort Atkinson, WI 53538-0803

920-000-1111
800-547-7377
FAX 920-563-1699
Home Page: www.cygnusb2b.com

John French, CEO
Ronnie Garrett, Director of Public Relations
Kathy Scott, Director of Public Relations
Paul Bonaiuto, CFO

A bi-monthly tabloid-sized magazine showcasing new products in the Emergengy Medical Technician's scope of use.

21724 Emergency Medical Services

Cygnus Business Media
PO Box 803
Fort Atkinson, WI 53538-0803

920-000-1111
FAX 920-563-1699
E-Mail: scott.cravens@cygnusb2b.com

Home Page: www.cygnusb2b.com
Social Media: *Facebook, Twitter, LinkedIn*

John French, CEO
Nancy Perry, Associate Publisher

A magazine designed for both career and volunteer EMS professionals. This magazine has been rated number one for editorial quality, reader interest and advertising pages.
Frequency: Monthly

21725 Fire & Arson Investigator Magazine

International Association of Arson Investigators
2111 Baldwin Ave
Suite 203
Crofton, MD 21114

410-451-3473
FAX 410-451-9049
Home Page: www.firearson.com

David Nichols, President
Cost: $75.00
Frequency: Quarterly

21726 Fire EMS

PennWell
PO Box 1260
Tulsa, OK 74101-1260

918-835-3161
800-331-4463
FAX 918-831-9497
E-Mail: headquarters@pennwell.com
Home Page: www.pennwell.com
Social Media: *Facebook, Twitter*

Robert F Biolchini, CEO
Junior Isles, Publisher/Editor

News, product information and feature articles of interest to paramedics.
Cost: $30.00
Frequency: Monthly
Printed in 4 colors on glossy stock

21727 Fire Engineering

PennWell
PO Box 1260
Tulsa, OK 74101-1260

918-835-3161
800-962-6484
FAX 918-831-9497
E-Mail: dianef@pennwell.com
Home Page: www.pennwell.com
Social Media: *Facebook, Twitter*

Robert F Biolchini, CEO
Diane Feldman, Executive Editor
Bobby Halton, Editor-in-Chief

Provides education and training to the fire service through a hands-on, technically oriented editorial package.
Cost: $29.95
106 Pages
Frequency: Monthly
Circulation: 44824
ISSN: 0015-2587
Printed in 4 colors on glossy stock

21728 Fire Protection Engineering

Society of Fire Protection Engineers
7315 Wisconsin Ave
Suite 620E
Bethesda, MD 20814-3234

301-718-2910
FAX 301-718-2242
E-Mail: sfpehqtrs@sfpe.org
Home Page: www.sfpe.org

David D Evans, Executive Director
Rebecca Salzman, Membership Coordinator
Samuel Dannaway, Publisher
James D Mike, President

Technical magazine advancing the science and practice of fire protection and its allied fields.
Cost: $145.00
Frequency: Quarterly
Circulation: 4500
Founded in 1950

21729 IMSA Journal

International Municipal Signal Association
165 E Union Street
PO Box 539
Newark, NY 14513-0539

315-331-2182
800-723-4672
FAX 315-331-8205
E-Mail: info@imsasafety.org
Home Page: www.imsasafety.org

Marilyn Lawrence, Publisher & Executive Director
Sharon Earl, Editor

Each issue focuses on different topics, including Dispatch/Public Safety Telecommunications, Fire Alarm Interior, Fire Alarm Municipal, FCC Licensing, Flagging, Roadway Lighting, Signs & Markings, Traffic Signal Systems, Two-Way Radios, Wireless Data, Wireless Traffic Control, and Work Zone Safety.
Cost: $700.00
Frequency: Bimonthly
Circulation: 12,000
ISSN: 1064-2560

21730 Industrial Hygiene News

Rimbach Publishing
8650 Babcock Blvd
Suite 1
Pittsburgh, PA 15237-5010

412-364-5366
800-245-3182
FAX 412-369-9720
E-Mail: info@rimbach.com
Home Page: www.rimbach.com

Norberta Rimbach, President
Karen Galante, Circulation Manager

Articles, news and product information for professionals in Occupational Health and Industrial Hygiene.
Circulation: 60,111
Founded in 1978

21731 Industrial Safety & Hygiene News

Business News Publishing
2401 W Big Beaver RD
Suite 700
Troy, MI 48084

248-244-6498
800-837-7370
FAX 248-244-6439
E-Mail: bradfordd@bnpmedia.com
Home Page: www.ishn.com
Social Media: *Facebook, Twitter, LinkedIn*

Katie Rotella, President
Dave Johnson, Editor
Randy Green, Advertising Manager

Feature articles and product information for safety, health and environmental professionals. Free subscription to qualified professionals.
Cost: $58.00
Frequency: Monthly
Founded in 1926

21732 Infection Control Today

Virgo Publishing LLC
3300 N Central Ave
Suite 300
Phoenix, AZ 85012-2532

480-675-9925
FAX 480-990-0819

E-Mail: peggyj@vpico.com
Home Page: www.vpico.com

Jenny Bolton, President
Kelly Ridley, VP
Jennifer Janos, Controller

Infection Control Today provides science based articles for the general ward, operating room, sterile processing and environmental services departments of healthcare facilities as well as for the public health community.
Mailing list available for rent: 30000+ names

21733 Journal of Fire Sciences

Sage Publications
2455 Teller Rd
Newbury Park, CA 91320-2234

805-499-9774
800-818-7243
FAX 805-499-0871
E-Mail: info@sagepub.com
Home Page: www.sagepub.com
Social Media: *LinkedIn*

Blaise R Simqu, CEO

Reporting new developments in related technology. Peer-reviewed articles by recognized specialists from around the world. In-depth articles provide new science based information useful in materials research and product development.
Cost: $1281.00
88 Pages
Frequency: Bi-Monthly
ISSN: 0734-9041
Founded in 1965
Printed in 2 colors on matte stock

21734 Journal of Occupational and Environmental Medicine (JOEM)

American College of
Occupational/Environmental Med
25 Northwest Point Blvd
Suite 700
Elk Grove Village, IL 60007

847-818-1800
FAX 847-818-9266
E-Mail: acoeminfo@acoem.org
Home Page: www.acoem.org

Barry Eisenberg, Executive Director
Marianne Dreger, Communications Director

The official publication of the ACOEM, the Journal provides the latest data on reseach, as well as practical information for use in everyday practice. Readers find articles, case reviews, news and calendar of events, book reciews, and information about new product offerings.
Cost: $338.00
Frequency: Monthly/Free for Members
ISSN: 1076-2752
Founded in 1916

21735 Journal of Security Education

Academy of Security Educators & Trainers
PO Box 802
Berryville, VA 22611

540-554-2540
FAX 540-554-2558
Home Page: www.asetcse.org

Dr Richard W Kobetz, Executive Director
Dr HHA Cooper, President
Mary E Kobetz, Secretary-Treasurer

21736 Law and Order Magazine

Hendon Publications
130 Waukegan Rd
Suite 202, 2nd Floor
Deerfield, IL 60015-4912

847-444-3300
800-843-9764
FAX 847-444-3333

E-Mail: info@hendonpub.com
Home Page: www.hendonpub.com

Henry Kingwill, President
Henry Kingwill, Publisher
Kathryn Murnik, Director

Latest news of interest to police and law enforcement professionals. New product and service information, available in print and online.
Cost: $24.95
Frequency: Monthly
Circulation: 32304
Founded in 1953

21737 Materials Evaluation

American Society for Nondestructive Testing
1711 Arlingate Lane
PO Box 28518
Columbus, OH 43228-518

614-274-6003
800-222-2768
FAX 614-274-6899
E-Mail: kwie@asnt.org
Home Page: www.asnt.org

Paul McIntire, Publication Manager
Betsy Blazar, Marketing Manager
Shelby Reeves, Owner
Wayne Hollile, Executive Director

Research, reviews and information of nondestructive testing materials. Provides members and subscribers the latest news and technical information concerning this industry.
Cost: $10.00
Frequency: Monthly

21738 National Defense Magazine

National Defense Industrial Association
2111 Wilson Blvd
Suite 400
Arlington, VA 22201-3061

703-522-1820
703-247-9469
FAX 703-522-1885
E-Mail: info@ndia.org
Home Page: www.ndia.org

Lawrence Farrell, President
Sandra I Erwin, Editor
Sharon Foster, Circulation Manager

Places main focus on issues concerning the U.S. defense industry. Provides the trends in national security, including technology advancement, acquisition policy, critical industry sectors, and marketing are editorial staples.
Cost: $40.00
Frequency: Monthly
Circulation: 30000
ISSN: 0092-1491
Founded in 1946

21739 National Fire Protection Association Newsletter

National Fire Protection Association
1 Batterymarch Park
Quincy, MA 02169-7471

617-770-3000
800-344-3555
FAX 617-770-0700
E-Mail: publicaffairs@nfpa.org
Home Page: www.nfpa.org

James M. Shannon, President/CEO
Peg O'Brien, Administrator - Public Affairs
Sharon Gamache, Executive Director
Bruce Mullen, CFO
Paul Crossman, VP, Marketing

Written for various fire safety professionals and covers major topics in fire protection and suppression. The Journal carries investigation reports written by NFPA specialists, special NFPA statistical studies on large-loss fires, multiple deaths, fire fighter deaths and injuries and others annually and articles on fire protec-

tion advances, public education and information of interest to NFPA members.
75000 Members
Frequency: Monthly
Founded in 1896

21740 National Locksmith

National Publishing Company
1533 Burgundy Pkwy
Streamwood, IL 60107-1811

630-837-1250
FAX 630-837-1210
E-Mail: natllock@aol.com
Home Page: www.locksmithledger.net

Marc Goldberg, Publisher
Greg Mango, Editor

New products, marketing, sales, merchandising, and the array of factors involved in successful locksmith enterprises and services. Informs professionals about the latest news and techniques in security.
Cost: $46.00
Frequency: Monthly
Circulation: 17000
Founded in 1983

21741 Occupational Hazards

Penton Media
1166 Avenue of the Americas
Suite 316
Cleveland, NY 10036

212-204-4200
FAX 216-696-6662
E-Mail: information@penton.com
Home Page: www.penton.com

Jane Cooper, Marketing
Bob Marinez, Publisher
Rob Howlette, Advertising Manager
Chris Meyer, Director
Bev Walter, Customer Service

Analysis of qualified recipients who have indicated that they recommend, select and/or buy the safety equipment, fire protection and other occupational health products.
Cost: $50.00
65 Pages
Frequency: Monthly
Circulation: 71,000
ISSN: 0029-7909
Founded in 1892
Printed in 4 colors on glossy stock

21742 Oregon Investigator

PO Box 2705
Portland, OR 97208

866-584-8645
E-Mail: webmaster@oali.org
Home Page: www.oali.org

Ted J Tolliver, Executive Director
Patricia Vollbrect, President

Official journal of the organization setting a standard of excellence among investigators. Legislative issues and news of upcoming seminars.
Founded in 1983

21743 Pest Control Technology

GIE Media
4012 Bridge Avenue
Cleveland, OH 44113

216-961-4130
800-456-0707
FAX 216-961-0364
Home Page: www.pctonline.com

Dan Moreland, Publisher
Jodi Dorsch, CEO

Directed towards technological and educational advancement in the pest control industry.
Cost: $35.00
76 Pages
Frequency: Monthly

ISSN: 0730-7608
Founded in 1972
Printed in 4 colors on glossy stock

21744 Pollution Equipment News

Rimbach Publishing
8650 Babcock Blvd
Suite 1
Pittsburgh, PA 15237-5010

412-364-5366
800-245-3182
FAX 412-369-9720
E-Mail: info@rimbach.com
Home Page: www.rimbach.com

Norberta Rimbach, President
Karen Galante, Circulation Manager
Paul Henderson, VP of Sales and Marketing
Richard Rimbach, Owner

Provides information to those responsible for
selecting products and services for air, water,
wastewater and hazardous waste pollution
abatement.
Frequency: Bi-Annually
Circulation: 91000
Founded in 1968

21745 Process Safety Progress

John Wiley & Sons
1475 Crosspoint Boulevard
Indianapolis, IN 46256

877-762-2974
FAX 800-597-3299
Home Page: www.wiley.com
Social Media: *LinkedIn*

D A Crowl, Editor
Joseph F Louvar, Editor

Practical information for engineering profes-
sionals. Focuses on chemical and hydrocarbon
safety, loss prevention and health.
Cost: $345.00
Frequency: Quarterly
ISSN: 1066-8527
Founded in 1908

21746 Professional Safety

American Society of Safety Engineers
1800 E Oakton Street
Des Plaines, IL 60018

847-699-2929
FAX 847-768-3434
E-Mail: customerservice@asse.org
Home Page: www.asse.org
Social Media: *Facebook, Twitter*

Fred Fortman, Executive Director
Jim Drzewiecki, Finance/Controller Director
Diane Hurns, Manager Public Relations
Department

Journal of the well known professional safety,
health and environmental organization. Articles
provide in-depth examination of health and
safety concerns.
Cost: $60.00
Frequency: Monthly
Founded in 1990

21747 Public Safety Communications/APCO Bulletin

Association of Public-Safety Comm
Officials Int'l
351 N Williamson Boulevard
Daytona Beach, FL 32114-1112

386-322-2500
888-272-6911
FAX 386-322-2501
E-Mail: apco@apcointl.org
Home Page: www.apcointl.org/
Social Media: *Facebook, Twitter, LinkedIn, You Tube*

Toni Edwards, Managing Editor
George S Rice Jr, Executive Director
Susan Stowell, Member Services Director

Garry Mendez, Marketing/Communications
Director
Robert Gurss Esq., Legal/Government Affairs
Director

Newsletter dedicated to the enhancement of
public safety communications and to serving its
more than 15,000 members, the people who use
public safety communications systems and services. Subscription is a member benefit.
Frequency: Monthly
Circulation: 13000
ISSN: 1526-1646
Founded in 1935

21748 Quality Digest

Quality Control International
555 East Avenue
P.O. Box 1769
Chico, CA 95926

530-893-4095
FAX 530-893-0395
E-Mail: qualitydigest@qualitydigest.com
Home Page: www.qualitydigest.com
Social Media: *Facebook*

Michael Richman, Managing Editor
Dirk Dusharme, Technical Editor
Scott Papon, Publisher
April Johnson, Circulation Manager

Serves the field of quality-related activites in
manufacturing, financial services, communications, utilities, transportation, government, military, retail, educational institutions, health
care, consulting, aerospace, software, agricultural, forestry, fishing, mining, construction
and other industries. Available in print and free
online.
Cost: $59.00
Frequency: Monthly
ISSN: 1049-8699
Founded in 1981

21749 SAFE Newsletter

SAFE Association
PO Box 130
Creswell, OR 97426

541-895-3012
FAX 541-895-3014
E-Mail: safe@peak.org
Home Page: www.safeassociation.com

Marcia Baldwin, President
Bryan Billings, President-Elect
Frequency: 4-6x/Year
Circulation: 1000
Founded in 1957

21750 SC Magazine

Haymarket Media
161 Worcester Road
Suite 201
Framingham, MA 01701

508-879-9792
FAX 508-879-2755
E-Mail: iarmstrong@westcoast.com
Home Page: www.scmagazine.com
Social Media: *Facebook, Twitter, LinkedIn*

Illena Armstrong, Editor-in-Chief
Gil Torren, Sales Director
Sherry Oommen, Circulation Director

Covers all industries that use information secu-
rity systems. Provides data on information se-
curity products, services, market trends and
industry developments.
Cost: $60.00
133 Pages
Frequency: Monthly
Circulation: 40,000
ISSN: 1096-7974
Founded in 1999
Printed in 4 colors

21751 Safe & Vault Technology

Safe & Vault Technicians Association

3500 Easy St
Dallas, TX 75247-6416

214-819-9771
FAX 214-819-9736
Home Page: www.savta.org

Charles Gibson, President
Mike Oelert, Editor

Industry news, reviews, announcements and
new products of paticular interest to readers.
Cost: $45.00
Frequency: Monthly
Circulation: 3000
Founded in 1986

21752 Safety & Health

National Safety Council
PO Box 558
Itasca, IL 60143-0558

630-775-2213
800-621-7615
FAX 630-285-1315
E-Mail: info@nsc.org
Home Page: www.nsc.org

Alan C McMillan, CEO
Melissa J Ruminski, Managing Editor
Suzanne Powills, Publisher

Coverage of safety news and changes, trade
shows and training courses.
Cost: $58.50
Frequency: Monthly
Founded in 1954
Mailing list available for rent

21753 Security Dealer

Cygnus Publishing
PO Box 803
Fort Atkinson, WI 53538-0803

920-000-1111
800-547-7377
FAX 920-563-1699
Home Page: www.cygnusb2b.com

John French, CEO
Susan Brady, Editor-in-Chief
Susan Whitehurst, Group Publisher

Trade publication for those in the electronic
burglary and fire alarm system business.
Cost: $112.00
Frequency: Monthly
Circulation: 25500
Founded in 1966

21754 Security Distributing and Marketing

Business News Publishing
1050 IL Route 83
Suite 200
Bensenville, IL 60106-1096

630-377-5909
FAX 630-227-0214
E-Mail: zaludb@bnpmedia.com
Home Page: www.sdmmag.com

Katie Rotella, President
Laura Stepanek, Editor
Russ Gager, Senior Editor

Information source for the electronic security,
life safety and home systems industries. Subscription free to professionals.
Frequency: Monthly
Circulation: 28000

21755 Security Industry Buyers Guide

ASIS International

21756 Security Magazine

Business News Publishing
2401 W Big Beaver Rd
Suite 700
Troy, MI 48084-3333

248-362-3700
FAX 248-362-0317

E-Mail: zalud@bnpmedia.com
Home Page: www.bnpmedia.com

Mitchell Henderson, CEO
Mark McCourt, Publisher
Russ Gager, Senior Editor
Laura Stepanek, Editor
Mark McCourt, Pulisher

Covers all types of businesses, including industrial manufacturing, service companies, institutions and government, as well as consulting, design, and integrator firms that specify security. News, columns and security product information. No charge to professionals.
Frequency: Monthly
Circulation: 40590
Founded in 1964
Printed in 4 colors on glossy stock

21757 Security Management
American Society for Industrial Security
1625 Prince Street
Alexandria, VA 22314-2818

703-519-6200
800-368-5685
FAX 703-519-6299
E-Mail: sharowitz@asisonline.org
Home Page: www.securitymanagement.com

Denny White, Publisher
Sherry Harowitz, Editor-in-Chief
Carlton Purvis, Associate Editor

Features, news and trends in the security world. In print and online.
Cost: $48.00
Frequency: Monthly
Founded in 1955

21758 Security Products
Stevens Publishing Corporation
5151 Belt Line Rd
10th Floor
Dallas, TX 75254-7507

972-687-6700
FAX 972-687-6767
Home Page: www.stevenspublishing.com

Craig S Stevens, President
Margaret Perry, Circulation Director
Russell Lindsay, Publisher
Ralph Jensen, Editor
Karina Sanchez, Managing Editor

Offers examples of security solutions set by such facilities as casinos and hospitals, and explores such issues as false alarm reduction and personnel training, it also highlights new technologies.
Cost: $75.00
Frequency: Monthly
Circulation: 65000
Founded in 1925

21759 Security Sales & Integration
Bobit Publishing Company
3520 Challenger St
Torrance, CA 90503-1640

310-533-2400
FAX 310-533-2500
E-Mail: info@securitysales.com
Home Page: www.bobit.com

Edward J Bobit, CEO
Scott Goldfine, Editor-in-chief
Michael Zawinski, Publisher

News, feature articles, columnists and new products in the field of electronic security.
Cost: $15.00
Frequency: Monthly
Founded in 1981

21760 Security and Privacy
IEEE Computer Society

10662 Los Vaqueros Drive
PO Box 3014
Los Alamitos, CA 90720-1314

714-821-8380
800-272-6657
FAX 714-821-4010
E-Mail: help@computer.org
Home Page: www.computer.org/security

Angela Burgess, Publisher
Kathy Clark-Fisher, Lead Editor
Georgann Carter, Circulation Manager
George Cybenko, Editor-in-Chief

Trans-border data flow issues, protocols, database management and security. Available online to members and in print to others.
Cost: $29.00
Frequency: 6 Issues/Year
Circulation: 1600
Founded in 1979

21761 Sound & Video Contractor
Primedia
PO Box 12914
Overland Park, KS 66282

913-341-1300
FAX 913-967-1903
E-Mail: mjohnson@primediabusiness.com
Home Page: www.svconline.com

Michael Goldman, Editor
Cynthia Wisehart, Editorial Director
Charissa Young, Associate Editor

Contains information on sound systems, video display, security, CCTV, home theater, and automation. Delivers in depth instruction and examples of successful installations, fundamental acoustical and video theory and news on new technologies affecting the systems contracting business.
Cost: $35.00
Frequency: Monthly
Circulation: 21000
Founded in 1983
Mailing list available for rent: 20,500 names at $110 per M

21762 The Poison Line
American Association of Poison Control Centers
3201 New Mexico Ave NW
Suite 310
Washington, DC 20016-2739

202-895-4259
800-222-1222
FAX 202-362-8377
E-Mail: info@aapcc.org
Home Page: www.poison.org

M Litovitz, Executive Director
Frequency: Biannual
Founded in 1958

21763 Underground Focus
Planet Underground
411 South Evergreen
Manteno, IL 60950

815-468-7814
FAX 815-468-7644
E-Mail: ufmagazine@underspace.com
Home Page: www.underspace.com
Social Media: *Facebook, Twitter, LinkedIn*

Ron Rosencrans, Founder
Amy Chmura, Editor

Documents the importance of careful excavation and helps them get the budgets to do the job. Powerfully dramatizes the need for underground damage prevention, excavation safety, and the hazards of not protecting the subsurface infrastructure.
Cost: $25.00
46 Pages
Circulation: 21800
ISSN: 1090-400X

Founded in 1986
Printed in 4 colors on glossy stock

Trade Shows

21764 AAAR Annual Meeting
American Association for Aerosol Research
15000 Commerce Parkway
Suite C
Mount Laurel, NJ 08054

856-439-9080
FAX 856-439-0525
E-Mail: dbright@ahint.com
Home Page: www.aaar.org

Lynn Russell, Program Chair
Melissa Baldwin, Executive Director

Exibits related to aerosol research in areas including industrial process, air pollution, and industrial hygiene. Over 600 professionals attend.
600 Attendees
Frequency: Annual, October

21765 ASFPM Annual Conference
Association of State Floodplain Managers
2809 Fish Hatchery Road
Suite 204
Madison, WI 53713

608-274-0123
FAX 608-274-0696
E-Mail: asfpm@floods.org
Home Page: www.floods.org

Larry Larson, Executive Director
Becky Head, Member Services Coordinator

Focus on floodproofing techniques, materials, floodproofing and elevation contractors, current issues and programs, new federal tax impications and the various means of funding floodproofing projects. implications. Held June in Norfolk, VA.
Frequency: Annual
Founded in 1951

21766 ASIS International
1625 Prince Street
Alexandria, VA 22314-2818

703-519-6200
FAX 703-519-6299
E-Mail: asis@asisonline.org
Home Page: www.asisonline.org

Shannon Burch, Exhibits Manager
Michael Stack, Executive Director

Exhibits related to loss prevention and security for public and private organizations. Held September 24-26, 2007 at the Las Vegas Convention Center in Las Vegas, Nevada.
Frequency: September
Founded in 1955

21767 America's Fire & Security Expo
ROC Exhibitions
1963 University Lane
Lisle, IL 60532

630-271-8210
FAX 630-271-8234
E-Mail: info@rocexhibitions.com
Home Page: www.americassecurity.com

Jerry Carter, Marketing Director

Annual 3 day marketplace featuring state-of-the-art security products, systems and services. Over 50 free educational sessions. Emphasis on the markets of Latin America, the Caribbean and the Southeastern US.
Frequency: July

21768 American Biological Safety Association Conference
1200 Allanson Road
Mundelein, IL 60060-3808

847-949-1517
847-566-4580
FAX 847-566-4580
E-Mail: absa@covad.net
Home Page: www.absa.org

LouAnn Burnett, Chair

Exhibits of biological safety equipment, supplies and services. Held October at the Opryland Hotel in Nashville, Tennessee.
300 Attendees
Frequency: October
Founded in 1984

21769 American Fire Sprinkler Association Annual Convention & Exhibition
American Fire Sprinkler Association
12750 Merit Drive
Suite 350
Dallas, TX 75251

214-349-5965
847-949-1517
FAX 214-343-8898
E-Mail: afsainfo@firesprinkler.org
Home Page: www.firesprinkler.org

Steve Muncy, President
Janet Knowles, VP/Makreting & Communications

120 exhibits of sprinkler heads, pipe, hangers, tools and other equipment. Seminar, workshop and tours. Held September in Phoenix, Arizona.
1000 Attendees
Frequency: September
Founded in 1981

21770 American Industrial Hygiene Association Conference and Exposition
American Industrial Hygiene Association
2700 Prosperity Avenue
Suite 250
Fairfax, VA 22031

703-849-8888
FAX 703-207-3561
E-Mail: infonet@aiha.org
Home Page: www.aiha.org
Social Media: *Facebook, Twitter, LinkedIn*

Caroline Lacey, Expo Manager
Carol Tobin, Director
Peter Oneil, Executive Director
Michael Brandt, President

Conference for occupational and environmental health and safety professionals around the globe. Held June in Philadelphia, Pennsylvania.
10400 Members
4,000 Attendees
Frequency: Annual

21771 American Society for Nondestructive Testing Conference
1711 Arlingate Lane
PO Box 28518
Columbus, OH 43228-0518

614-274-6003
800-222-2768
FAX 614-274-6899
E-Mail: kwie@asnt.org
Home Page: www.asnt.org

Michael O'Toole, Senior Manager Conferences
Jacquie Giunta, Meeting Coordinator
Ruth Staat, Exhibit/Event Supervisor

Seminar, conference and 150 exhibits of nondestructive testing equipment, services, supplies and laboratory representatives. Holds a smaller

conference in the spring. Held November in Las Vegas, Nevada.
3000 Attendees
Frequency: Fall

21772 American Society of Crime Laboratory Directors Annual Symposium
139 Technology Drive
Suite K
Garner, NC 27529-7970

919-773-2044
FAX 919-773-2602
E-Mail: rkahn@ag.state.oh.us
Home Page: www.ascld.org

Bill Marbaker, President

Devoted to providing training in leadership and management techniques in the field of forensic science. Also offers membership the opportunity to network with other laboratory directors.
Frequency: October

21773 American Society of Safety Engineers Professional Development Conference
American Society of Safety Engineers
1800 E Oakton Street
Des Plaines, IL 60018

847-699-2929
FAX 847-768-3434
E-Mail: customerservice@asse.org
Home Page: www.asse.org

Fred Fortman, Executive Director
Jim Drzewiecki, Finance/Controller Director
Diane Hurns, Manager Public Relations Department

Annual conference and expo of 250 manufacturers and suppliers of safety equipment and health products. Held June
3500 Attendees
Frequency: June

21774 Annual American Occupational Health Conference
American College of Occupational/Environmental Med
25 Northwest Point Blvd
Suite 700
Elk Grove Village, IL 60007

847-818-1800
FAX 847-818-9266
E-Mail: acoeminfo@acoem.org
Home Page: www.acoem.org
Social Media: *Facebook, Twitter, LinkedIn, You Tube*

Barry Eisenberg, Executive Director
Marianne Dreger, Communications Director
AOHC
Frequency: Annual/Spring

21775 Applied Ergonomics Conference
Institute of Industrial Engineers
3577 Parkway Lane
Suite 200
Norcross, GA 30092

770-449-0461
800-494-0460
FAX 770-263-8532
E-Mail: cs@iienet.org
Home Page: www.iienet.org/annual

Carol LeBlanc, Conference Manager

An exclusive event for ergonomists, engineers, and safety professionals. The conference focuses on how companies have successfully implemented programs that provide excellent return on their ergonomics investment. Held May Nashville, Tennessee.
800 Attendees
Frequency: March
Founded in 1998

21776 Associated Locksmiths of America & Safe and Vault Tech Security Expo
Associated Locksmiths of America
3500 Easy Street
Dallas, TX 75247-6416

214-819-9733
800-532-2562
E-Mail: convention@aloa.org
Home Page: www.aloa.org
Social Media: *Facebook*

Karen Lyons, Conventions/Meetings
Kim Hammond, Exhibits/Sales

Features industry innovation, training, networking and education in the security world. Over 350 exhibitors with cash and carry merchandise. Held July, in Charlotte, North Carolina.
4000 Attendees
Frequency: July
Founded in 1956

21777 BOMA Annual Convention
Building Owners & Managers Association Int'l
1201 New York Avenue NW
Suite 300
Washington, DC 20005

202-408-2662
FAX 202-326-6377
E-Mail: info@boma.org
Home Page: www.boma.org
Social Media: *Facebook, Twitter, LinkedIn*

Henry Chamberlain, President/COO
Kurt R Padavano, Chairman & CEO
Richard Gringer, Chair
Ray Mackry, Circulation Manager

Opportunity for business professionals to discuss problems, security, exchange ideas and share experience and knowledge. Held July 21-24, 2007 at the Jacob K Javits Convention Center in New York City.
Frequency: July

21778 Bomb Technicians & Investigators Annual Conference
PO Box 160
Goldvein, VA 22720-0160

540-752-4533
FAX 540-752-2796
E-Mail: admin@iabti.org
Home Page: www.iabti.org

Ralph Way PhD, Executive Director

Speakers on the latest information on bomb and bio threats. Attendes are in the fields of law enforcement, fire and emergency services, the military, forensic science and other related fields.
Founded in 1973

21779 CSAA Electronic Security Forum & Exposition
Central Station Alarm Association
440 Maple Avenue E
Suite 201
Vienna, VA 22180

703-242-4670
FAX 703-242-4675
E-Mail: meetings@csaaul.org
Home Page: www.csaaul.org

John McDonald, Meetings/Conferences

Exhibitors, speakers and workshops for the alarm and security professional. Held May
Frequency: May

21780 California Alarm Association Winter Convention

3401 Pacific Avenue
Suite 1C
Marina del Rey, CA 90292

310-305-1277
800-437-7658
FAX 310-305-2077
E-Mail: info@caaonline.org
Home Page: www.caaonline.org

Jon Sargent, President
Jerry Lenander, Executive Director
George DeMarco, Southern VP
Ron Galippo, Secretary

Annual meeting of state trade association comprised of licensed alarm company operators and suppliers of products and services. Nearly 200 alarm companies and 50 suppliers are members. Alarm companies represent 70% of the electronic security industry in California. Held December in San Francisco, California.
Frequency: December

21781 Campus Law Enforcement Administrators Annual Conference

342 N Main Street
Hartford, CT 06117-2507

860-586-7517
FAX 860-586-7550
E-Mail: info@iaclea.org
Home Page: www.iaclea.org

Delores Stafford, President
Carol Ewing, Professional Development

Presentations on sucessful or new programs and current trends.
Frequency: June

21782 Campus Safety Conference

Bricepac
12228 Venice Boulevard
PO Box 66515
Los Angeles, CA 90066

310-390-5277
FAX 800-758-0935
Home Page: www.campusjournal.com

Sandra Watson, Conferences/Training

Training conference designed especially for campus safety professionals at both the secondary school and higher education levels. Features more than 13 seminars of critical importance to campus safety decision makers and staff.
Frequency: 2 Days/November

21783 Card Tech/Secur Tech: CTST Conference & Exhibition

SourceMedia
One State Street Plaza
27th Floor
New York, NY 10004

212-258-6093
800-803-3424
FAX 212-803-8515
E-Mail: abconference@sourcemedia.com
Home Page: www.ctst.com
Social Media: *Facebook, Twitter, LinkedIn*

Nicoal Crawford, Director of Operations
Nikole Tenbrink, Custom Events

250 booth exhibit hall, seminars, luncheons and keynote speakers in the advanced card and biometric technology field. Explores real world applications in several industries including financial services, goverment and security. Held May in San Francisco, California.
50000 Attendees
Frequency: April

21784 Computer Security Conference & Expo

Computer Security Institute

600 Harrison Street
San Francisco, CA 94107

415-947-6320
FAX 415-947-6023
E-Mail: csi@cmp.com
Home Page: www.gocsi.com
Social Media: *Facebook, Twitter*

Jennifer Stevens, Conference Director

Annual event with over 150 educational sessions and exhibitor hall. Held October in Orlando, Florida.
Frequency: November

21785 Contingency Planning & Management

WPC Expositions
84 Park Avenue
Flemington, NJ 08822

908-788-0343
FAX 908-788-0316
Home Page:
www.contingencyplanningexpo.com

Greg Sgroi, Events Director
Brad Lewis, Sales/Exhibits
Courtney Witter, Expo Manager

Serves the fields of financial/banking, manufacturing industrial, transportation, utilities, telecommunications, health care, government, security, assurance, insurance and other allied fields. Shows held in both the east and west coasts.
Frequency: May/November
Founded in 1996

21786 Convention & Traffic Expo

American Traffic Safety Services Association
15 Riverside Parkway
Suite 100
Fredericksburg, VA 22406-1022

540-368-1701
800-272-8772
FAX 540-368-1717
Home Page: www.atssa.com

Joe Jeffrey, Chairman

The premier meeting place for roadway professionals around the world. The program and exhibits are dedicated to issues and products related to all aspects of temporary traffic control and roadway safety.
Frequency: Annual/February

21787 Counterterrorism & Security Professionals Annual Conference

PO Box 10265
Arlington, VA 22210

201-461-5422
Home Page: www.iacsp.com

Steven Fustero, Executive Director

We believe that all elements of the world's societies must become better educated about the threats of terrorism as a first step toward developing innovative and effective countermeasures to combat these ongoing threats. A better informed society will result in a freer one.
Frequency: May
Founded in 1992

21788 Crime Analysts Annual Conference

9218 Metcalf
PMB 364
Overland Park, KS 66212

919-940-3883
E-Mail: nfritz@du.edu
Home Page: www.iaca.net

Noah Fritz, Director
Christopher Bruce, VP Administration

Annual themed conference helping crime analysts around the world improve their skills and

make valuable contacts. Aids law enforcement agencies in making the best use of crime analysis and advocates for standards of performance and technique within the profession itself.
Frequency: October
Founded in 1990

21789 Disaster Response & Recovery Exposition NDMS Conference

J Spargo & Associates
11208 Waples Mill Road
Suite 112
Fairfax, VA 22030

703-631-6200
800-564-4220
FAX 703-654-6931
E-Mail: drre@jspargo.com
Home Page: www.drrexpo.com
Social Media: *Facebook, Twitter, LinkedIn*

Nathan Wills, Account Manager

Held in conjunction with the NDMS Conference; it is an opportunity for local, State and Federal public health practitioners and policy makers to discover the latest equipment, technologies and services available.
2700 Attendees
Frequency: August

21790 Eastern Ergonomics Conference & Exposition

Continental Exhibitions
370 Lexington Avenue
New York, NY 10017

212-370-5005
800-222-2596
FAX 212-370-5699
E-Mail: information@ergoexpo.com
Home Page: www.ergoexpo.com

Lenore Kolb, Vice President of Sales
Walter Chamizon, President

Learn how to use ergonomics to increase productivity and safety at over 80 educational sessions. Try new products from over 100 companies, in over 2,000 square feet of floor space.
Frequency: June

21791 Emergency Preparedness & Response Conference & Exposition: READY

National Trade Productions
313 S Patrick Street
Alexandria, VA 22314

703-683-8500
800-687-7469
FAX 703-706-8234
E-Mail: ready@ntpshow.com
Home Page: www.readyinfousa.com

Janie Bridgeman, Sales Director
Maria Chaloux, Industry Relations

Annual symposium and trade show for personnel from federal, state and local agencies to learn about the latest emergency response equipment, technology, strategies and applications.
Frequency: July

21792 Emergency Response Conference & Expo

PBI Media
1201 Seven Locks Road
Suite 300
Potomac, MD 20854

301-541-1400
FAX 301-309-3847
Home Page: www.pbimedia.com

Robert Lewis, Conference Coordinator

Annual event for first responders and the companies who support them, working together on

land, air and sea to save lives and property. Conference and exhibitors.
Frequency: November

21793 Energy Security Expo
EJ Krause & Associates
6550 Rock Spring Drive
Suite 500
Bethesda, MD 20817-1126

301-493-5500
FAX 301-493-5705
Home Page: www.pipelinesecurity.com

Michael Rosenburg, Show Manager
Edward Krause, President

Intensive conference with workshops led by leading international experts from government and industry. Exhibit area featuring technologies, products and services for pipeline and energy infrastructure including oil, gas, electric grids, power plants and dams.
Frequency: May

21794 Fire-Rescue International
International Association of Fire Chiefs
4025 Fair Ridge Dr
Fairfax, VA 22033-2868

703-273-0911
FAX 703-273-9363
Home Page: www.iafc.org
Social Media: *Facebook, LinkedIn*

Al H. Gillespie, President & Chairman of the Board
Hank Clemmensen, First Vice President
William R. Metcalf, Second Vice President
Richard Carrizzo, Treasurer
Luther L. Fincher, Jr., Director-At-Large

FRI education covers all areas of the emergency service: navigating the political environment, managing change, ethical leadership, EMS issues, career development and moor. Exhibitors showcase the newest fire service innovations in apparatus, technology, equipment, gear and more.
12000 Members
Founded in 1873

21795 Fire-Rescue Med (FRM)
International Association of Fire Chiefs
4025 Fair Ridge Dr
Fairfax, VA 22033-2868

703-273-0911
FAX 703-273-9363
Home Page: www.iafc.org
Social Media: *Facebook, LinkedIn*

Al H. Gillespie, President & Chairman of the Board
Hank Clemmensen, First Vice President
William R. Metcalf, Second Vice President
Richard Carrizzo, Treasurer
Luther L. Fincher, Jr., Director-At-Large

Each spring, Fire-Rescue Med is the conference for fire-based EMS leaders, providing education and training on hiring and retaining EMTs, public and private integration challenges, embracing technology, billing for services, illness prevention programs and more.
12000 Members
Founded in 1873

21796 Global Fire Service Leadership Summit
International Association of Fire Chiefs
4025 Fair Ridge Dr
Fairfax, VA 22033-2868

703-273-0911
FAX 703-273-9363
Home Page: www.iafc.org
Social Media: *Facebook, LinkedIn*

Al H. Gillespie, President & Chairman of the Board
Hank Clemmensen, First Vice President

William R. Metcalf, Second Vice President
Richard Carrizzo, Treasurer
Luther L. Fincher, Jr., Director-At-Large

Discuss important issues, share experiences and learn from one another. In turn, summit participants will generate new ideas to strengthen and advance the cause of the fire service worldwide.
12000 Members
Founded in 1873

21797 Gov't Convention on Emerging Technologies Partnerships for Homeland Security
National Conference Services
6440-C Dobbin Road
Columbia, MD 21045

301-596-8899
888-603-8899
FAX 301-596-6274
Home Page: www.federalevents.com

Fredrick Martin, Director
Anne Slobodien, Chief Executive Officer

Forum for representatives from federal, state and local governments, along with the private sector to collaborate on and experiment with information technology that addresses mission needs critical to homeland security. Exhibits, workshops and simulation exercises.
Frequency: January

21798 GovSec
National Trade Productions
313 S Patrick Street
Alexandria, VA 22314

703-838-8500
FAX 703-836-4486
Home Page: www.govsecinfo.com

Denise Medved, General Manager

Provides a full spectrum of security solutions for federal, state, and local governments tasked with developing comprehensive strategies that address physical security, information security and cyber security needs. Educational programs held in conjunction with displays of a wide variety of security products and services designed specifically for government users.
Frequency: Annual/May

21799 HTCIA International Training Conference & Expo
Int'l High Technnology Crime Investigation Assoc
3288 Goldstone Drive
Roseville, CA 95747

916-408-1751
FAX 916-408-7543
Home Page: www.htcia.org

Carol Hutchings, Executive Director
Ronald J Wilczysnki, First VP/Conference Chair

Intended to attract participants from all over the world to take advantage of the training and networking opportunities that is offered.
Frequency: Annual

21800 Homeland Security Expo & Conference
E-Gov Conferences
3141 Fairview Park Drive
Suite 777
Falls Church, VA 22042-4507

703-876-5060
800-746-0099
FAX 703-876-5059
E-Mail: info@e-gov.com
Home Page: www.e-gov.com

Mike Smoyer, General Manager

Keynote presentations, conference sessions, plenary session and exhibition of solutions and

technologies to enhance homeland security efforts.
Frequency: November/December

21801 IMSA Conference
International Municipal Signal Association
165 E Union Street
PO Box 539
Newark, NY 14513-0539

315-331-2182
800-723-4672
FAX 315-331-8205
E-Mail: info@imsasafety.org
Home Page: www.imsasafety.org
Social Media: *Facebook, Twitter, LinkedIn*

Marilyn Lawrence, Executive Director/Publisher
Sharon Earl, Executive Assistant/Assitant Editor

Schools, technical sessions, exhibit floor and product demos.
1300 Attendees

21802 ISC Expo International Security Conference and Expo-Las Vegas
Reed Exhibition Companies
383 Main Avenue
Norwalk, CT 06851

203-840-4800
FAX 203-840-9322
E-Mail: inquiry@isc.reedexpo.com
Home Page: www.iscwest.com
Social Media: *Facebook, Twitter, LinkedIn*

Amie Cangelosi, Marketing Coordinator
Kara Buonanno, Marketing/Conference Manager

From around the globe, every relevant manufacturer, product, service and industry expert will be on hand for three days under one roof.
Frequency: March/April

21803 ISC: International Security Conference & Expo
Reed Exhibitions
383 Main Avenue
Norwalk, CT 06851

203-840-4800
FAX 203-840-9322
E-Mail: inquiry@isc.reedexpo.com
Home Page: www.isceast.com
Social Media: *Facebook, Twitter, LinkedIn*

Amie Cangelosi, Marketing Coordinator
Kara Buonanno, Marketing/Conference Manager

From around the globe, relevant manufacturers, products, services and industry experts will be on hand under one roof.
Frequency: November

21804 Inside ID: Identification Solutions Mega Show
Inside ID
8900 Saunders Lane
Bethesda, MD 20817

301-365-0186
FAX 301-365-2519
Home Page: www.insideid.com

Ben Miller, President
Liz Wenchel, CEO

Helps define and center the evolution of the emerging disipline of Identity Management. Education and displays of new products and technologies in identification. Facilitates the marketplace of buyers and sellers, provides a broad-based forum, and gathering place for standards groups and associations around the world.

21805 International Cargo Security Council
1400 I Street NW
Suite 1050
Washington, DC 20005-2209

202-821-1787
FAX 410-956-0679
E-Mail: icsc@cargosecurity.com
Home Page: www.cargosecurity.com

Joe Baker Jr, Executive Director
Ellen Parkereman, Meeting Director

Workshops and 60 booth exposition for cargo transportation and security professionals from the entire spectrum of cargo security: air, truck, rail maritime and intermodal.
450 Attendees
Frequency: Annual
Founded in 1973

21806 International Consumer Product Health & Safety Organization Annual Meeting
PO Box 1785
Germantown, MD 20875-1785

301-601-3240
FAX 301-601-3543
E-Mail: icphso@aol.com
Home Page: www.icphso.org

Dedicated to the health and safety issues related to consumer products manufactured and marketed in the global marketplace. Serving both health and safety professionals and consumers by sponsoring national and regional workshops. Annual meeting and training syposium.
Frequency: March
Founded in 1993

21807 NAESA Annual Workshop
National Association of Elevator Safety
6957 Littlerock Road SW
Suite A
Tumwater, WA 98512

360-292-4968
800-746-2372
FAX 360-292-4973
E-Mail: dotty@naesai.org
Home Page: www.naesai.org
Social Media: *Facebook, Twitter, LinkedIn*

Dotty Stanlaske, Executive Director
Dean McLellan, President
Bill Snyder, VP
Frequency: August

21808 National Council of Investigation & Security Annual Conference
7501 Sparrows Point Boulevard
Baltimore, MD 21219-1927

800-445-8408
FAX 410-388-9746
E-Mail: nciss@comcast.net
Home Page: www.nciss.org

Carolyn Ward, Executive Director
Francie Koehler, President
Bruce Hulme, Legislative Director

State associations and firms providing contract security services and investigative services. Our cooperative effort includes a legislative watch and providing accurate information reguarding our profession.
Frequency: March

21809 National Ergonomics Conference & Exposition
Continental Exhibitions
370 Lexington Avenue
New York, NY 10017

212-370-5005
800-222-2596
FAX 212-370-5699

E-Mail: lkolb@ergoexpo.com
Home Page: www.ergoexpo.com

Lenore Kolb, Vice President of Sales
Walter Chamizon, President

Learn how to use ergonomics to increase productivity and safety at over 80 educational sessions. Try new products from over 100 companies, in over 2,000 square feet of floor space.
Frequency: December

21810 National Fire Protection World Safety Conference & Exposition
National Fire Protection Association
1 Batterymarch Park
Quincy, MA 02169-7471

617-770-3000
800-344-3555
FAX 617-770-0700
E-Mail: publicaffairs@nfpa.org
Home Page: www.nfpa.org

James M. Shannon, President/CEO
Peg O'Brien, Administrator - Public Affairs
Sharon Gamache, Executive Director
Bruce Mullen, CFO
Paul Crossman, VP, Marketing

Professional development, networking and hundreds of booths from key industry suppliers.
75000 Members
Frequency: May
Founded in 1896

21811 National Safety Council Congress Expo
National Safety Council
1121 Spring Lake Drive
Itasca, IL 60143

630-775-2213
800-621-7619
FAX 630-285-0798
E-Mail: customerservice@nsc.org
Home Page: http://congress.nsc.org

Nancy Gavin, Expo Manager
Christine Paplaczyk, Exhibit Sales
Alan McMillan, CEO

Annual event for safety, health and the environment.
16000 Attendees
Frequency: September

21812 Police and Security Expo
PO Box 20068
Sarasota, FL 34276-0368

609-466-2111
800-323-1927
FAX 609-466-2675
E-Mail: webmaster@police-security.com
Home Page: www.police-security.com

Displaying goods, products and services for law enforcement and security professionals.
Frequency: June

21813 Professional Security Consultants Annual Conference
525 SW 5th Street
Suite A
Des Moines, IA 50309-4501

515-282-8192
FAX 515-282-9117
E-Mail: iapsc@iapsc.org
Home Page: www.iapsc.org

David G Aggleton, President
Robert A Schultheiss, VP
Dick Goodson, Executive Director
Harold Gillens, Secretary
Frank Pisciotta, Treasurer

Seeks to enhance members knowledge through seminars, training programs, and educational

materials. Works to foster public awareness of the security consulting industry.
Frequency: April
Founded in 1984

21814 Professional Security Alliance Conference & Exhibits
PSA Security Network
12011 N Tejon Street
Denver, CO 80234

303-520-0137
FAX 303-252-1741
E-Mail: lisa@psasecurity.com
Home Page: www.psasecurity.com

Lisa Speyer, Conference/Marketing
Shelley Binder, Customer/Vendor Service
Michelle Medina, Membership

For corporate management, salespeople, project managers and other technicians for PSA member companies. Educational sessions and pavillion featuring video surveillance, access control and biometrics.

21815 Prove It! Measuring Safety Performance Symposium
American Society of Safety Engineers
1800 E Oakton Street
Des Plaines, IL 60018

847-699-2929
FAX 847-768-3434
E-Mail: customerservice@asse.org
Home Page: www.asse.org
Social Media: *Facebook*

Terrie S. Norris, President
Richard A. Pollock, President Elect
Kathy Seabrook, Senior Vice President
Fred J. Fortman, Jr., Secretary & Executive Director
James D. Smith, Vice President, Finance

Demonstrate the performance of your safety program and the value of safety. This symposium will show you how and the rewards are great. Develop leading indicators specific to safety, learn what and how to measure, and learn to use metrics to improve safety performance.
30000 Members
Founded in 1911

21816 Rocky Mountain Health & Safety Conference
Colorado Safety Association
4730 Oakland Street
Suite 500
Denver, CO 80239

303-373-1937
FAX 303-373-1955
E-Mail: info@coloradosafety.org
Home Page: www.coloradosafety.org

Melodye Turek, President
Jan Harris, Finance Manager
Judy Sapp, Manager

Over 100 exhibitors of safety products, regulatory compliance updates and networking. Educational sessions are offered on various safety topics.
Frequency: April
Founded in 1968

21817 SAFE Association Annual Symposium
SAFE Association
PO Box 130
Creswell, OR 97426

541-895-3012
FAX 541-895-3014
E-Mail: safe@peak.org
Home Page: www.safeassociation.com
Social Media: *Facebook*

Marcia Baldwin, President
Bryan Bailey, President-Elect

Presentation topics range from desert survival to the latest aircraft passenger egress aids, cockpit design, restraint systems, and school bus design to international symbols related to transportation and safety, and crew training. Attended by an international group of professionals who are there to share problems and solutions in the field of safety and survival.
1200+ Attendees

21818 SAFE Symposium
SAFE Association
PO Box 130
Creswell, OR 97426

541-895-3012
FAX 541-895-3014
E-Mail: safe@peak.org
Home Page: www.safeassociation.com
Social Media: *Facebook*

Al Loving, President
John Fair, President-Elect

The SAFE Association is dedicated to the preservation of human life. It provides a common meeting ground for the sharing of problems, ideas and information. SAFE is a non-profit international association headquartered in Oregon, with chapters located throughout the world. SAFE publishes a quarterly Newsletter and Proceedings of the Annual SAFE Symposium. These publications are valuable reference sources for the professional involved in all forms of safety and survival.
1100+ Attendees
Frequency: Quarterly
Founded in 1954

21819 Safetech
Safe & Vault Technicians Association
3003 Live Oak Street
Dallas, TX 75204-6128

214-199-9771
FAX 214-827-1810
Home Page: www.savta.org

Joanne Mims, Conventions/Meetings Manager
Annual symposium and trade show for professionals in the valuables protection industry.
Frequency: March

21820 Securing New Ground
Securing New Ground
10100 Sherman Road
Chardon, OH 44024

440-286-4900
FAX 440-286-9169
E-Mail: info@securingnewground.com
Home Page: www.securingnewground.com

Dini Jones, Conference Coordinator
Rebecca Reed, Manager

Annual 2 day conference with influential people impacting the security industry. Learn about financing, new trends and opportunities for the security industry. Breakfast, lunch and reception included.
Frequency: October

21821 Security Canada Trade Shows
Canadian Alarm & Security Association
610 Alden Road
Suite 100
Markam, ON L3R-9Z1

905-513-0622
FAX 905-513-0624
E-Mail: hewitson@canasa.org
Home Page: www.canasa.org

Tracy Cannata, Executive Director
Joyce Everton, Administrative Manager
Lynne Hewiston, Trade Show Manager

Offering four shows annually. Security Canada East is in April, Security Canada Atlantic is in September, Security Canada West is in June and Security Canada Central is in October.

These gaterings offer professional development, information, networking and new products to dealers, distributors, manufacturers and monitoring companies across Canada.
Founded in 1977

21822 Sensors Expo & Conference
Advanstar Communications
1 Phoenix Mill Lane
Peterborough, NH 03458

603-924-5400
FAX 603-924-5401
Home Page: www.sensorsexpo.com

Cathy Walters, Show Director
Jeanne DuVal, Sales Manager

Informative, sensor related sessions, exhibits and special events for thousands of professionals who will help shape the future of sensing technology.
Frequency: June

21823 Texas Association of Fire Educators Annual Instructors Conference
13492 Research Boulevard
Suite 120, PMB 262
Austin, TX 78750-2254

Home Page: www.tx-tafe.org

Alan Storck, President
Tim Sendelbach, VP
Jim Lee, Secretary
Patricia Clinton, Treasurer

Annual gathering for state fire safety instructors to network and learn the latest in the industry.
Frequency: January

21824 Texas Burglar & Fire Alarm Assn. Annual Meeting, Trade Show & Golf Classic
PO Box 59982
Dallas, TX 75229-1982

877-908-2322
FAX 877-908-2522
E-Mail: president@tbfaa.org
Home Page: www.tbfaa.org

Rex Adams, President
JD Benfer, VP
Jan Wilson, Secretary
Malcolm Reed, Treasurer

Annual gathering of a large number of professional security and fire alarm companies that operate in the state of Texas.
Frequency: October

21825 US Maritime Security Expo
EJ Krause & Associates
6550 Rock Spring Drive
Suite 500
Bethesda, MD 20817-1126

301-493-5500
FAX 301-493-5705
Home Page: www.maritimesecurityexpo.com

Lindsey Field, Show Manager
Edward Krause, President

Annual conference and exhibitor hall attended by those who protect ports, harbors, bridges, cargo containers, power plants, off shore oil rigs, railroads, cargo and passenger ships.
Frequency: September

21826 Wildland Urban Interface Conference
International Association of Fire Chiefs
4025 Fair Ridge Dr
Fairfax, VA 22033-2868

703-273-0911
FAX 703-273-9363

Home Page: www.iafc.org
Social Media: *Facebook, LinkedIn*

Al H. Gillespie, President & Chairman of the Board
Hank Clemmensen, First Vice President
William R. Metcalf, Second Vice President
Richard Carrizzo, Treasurer
Luther L. Fincher, Jr., Director-At-Large

Brings together leaders from the local, state and federal levels to collaborate against the fastest growing fire threat in the world. From education and mitigation, suppression strategies, high-hazard operations to policy, WUI addresses the toughest challenges facing the wildland firefighting community.
12000 Members
Founded in 1873

Directories & Databases

21827 American Society for Industrial Security: Annual Membership Directory
American Society for Industrial Security
1625 Prince Street
Alexandria, VA 22314-2818

703-519-6200
800-368-5685
FAX 703-519-6299
E-Mail: asis@asisonline.org
Home Page: www.asisonline.org

Keith Goins, Membership Manager
Michael Stack, Executive Director

25,000 member management specialists in the private and public sectors who formulate security policy and direct security programs to prevent terrorism, dcoument piracy. Available as a membership benefit only.

21828 BCSP Directory and International Registry of Certified Safety Professionals
Board of Certified Safety Professionals
2301 W. Bradley Avenue
Champaign, IL 61874-9571

217-359-9263
FAX 217-359-0055
E-Mail: bcsp@bcsp.org
Home Page: www.bcsp.org

Thomas L Adams, Executive Director

Directory includes over 10,000 safety professionals holding the Certified Safety Professional (CSP) or Associate Safety Professional (ASP) designation.
Circulation: 20000
Founded in 1969
Mailing list available for rent: 20,000 names
Printed in on matte stock

21829 Business Insurance Directory of Safety Consultants & Rehabilitation Mgt.
Crain Communications
360 N Michigan Ave
Chicago, IL 60601-3800

312-649-5200
FAX 312-649-7937
E-Mail: KCrain@crain.com
Home Page: www.crain.com

Keith Crain, CEO
Ronnie Drachman, Director Communications

List of more than 150 employee safety consultants and over 70 employee rehabilitation management providers.
Cost: $4.00
Frequency: Annual
Circulation: 53,000

21830 Central Station Alarm Association Directory
8150 Leesburg Pike
Suite 201
Vienna, VA 22182-2721

703-242-4670
FAX 703-242-4675
Home Page: www.csaaul.org

Steve Doyle, Executive Director
Celia Besore, Director Marketing/Communications
Cost: $195.00
94 Pages
Frequency: Annual
Circulation: 1,000

21831 Computer Security Buyers Guide
Computer Security Institute
600 Harrison Street
San Francisco, CA 94107-1387

415-947-6320
800-227-4675
FAX 415-905-2218
E-Mail: wwilson@infi.com
Home Page: www.gocsi.com/csi

Patrice Rapalus, Editor

About 650 suppliers and consultants of computer security products, including communications and network security, disaster recovery, media security, personnel security and security training.
Cost: $197.00
Frequency: Annual
Circulation: 4,500

21832 Directory of Mail Drop Addresses and Zip Codes
Fraud & Theft Information Bureau
8400 96th Ct S
Boynton Beach, FL 33472-4400

561-732-3653
FAX 561-732-4928
E-Mail: sales@fraudandtheftinfo.com
Home Page: www.fraudandtheftinfo.com

Pat Ford, Owner
Pearl Say, Editor/VP

Identifies every one of the 35,000 mail drops used by credit card thieves to steal your merchandise. Thousands of credit card thieves use thse address, which sound like residential addresses, to hide their identity and true address while stealing from you with stolen credit card numbers.
Cost: $605.50
Frequency: Annual
ISBN: 0-914801-07-4
Founded in 1982

21833 Disaster Resource Guide
Disaster Resource Guide
PO Box 15243
Santa Ana, CA 92735

FAX 714-558-8901
Home Page: www.disaster-resource.com

Articles, business resources and product information for public and private emergency preparedness. Free of charge if subscriber is registered annually.
Frequency: Annual

21834 Fire Protection Equipment Directory
Underwriters Laboratories
333 Pfingsten Rd
Northbrook, IL 60062-2096

847-412-0136
877-854-3577
FAX 847-272-8129
E-Mail: cec@us.ul.com
Home Page: www.ul.com

Social Media: *Facebook, Twitter, LinkedIn, You Tube*

Keith E Williams, CEO
John Drengenberg, Manager Consumer Affairs

Companies that have qualified to use the UL listing mark or classification marking on or in connection with products that have been found to be in compliance with UL's requirements.
Cost: $35.00
Frequency: February

21835 Fire Resistance Directory
Underwriters Laboratories
333 Pfingsten Rd
Northbrook, IL 60062-2096

847-412-0136
877-854-3577
FAX 847-272-8129
E-Mail: cec@us.ul.com
Home Page: www.ul.com
Social Media: *Facebook, Twitter, LinkedIn, You Tube*

Keith E Williams, CEO
John Drengenberg, Manager Consumer Affairs

Companies that have qualified to use the UL listing mark or classification marking on or in connection with products that have been found to be in compliance with UL's requirements. 4 book set.
Cost: $110.00
Frequency: February

21836 Fire Retardant Chemicals Association: Membership Directory
Fire Retardant Chemicals Association
851 New Holland Avenue
Lancaster, PA 17601-5644

202-530-4590
FAX 717-295-4538
E-Mail: frca@fireretardants.org
Home Page: www.fireretardants.org

Approximately 35 member manufacturers and distributors of chemical fire retardants and related supplies.

21837 Fire Suppression Systems Association: Membership Directory
Fire Suppression Systems Association
5024 Campbell Boulevard
Suite R
Baltimore, MD 21236

410-931-2374
FAX 410-931-8111

Approximately 120 member companies that design, manufacture, distribute, install or repair and maintain fire suppression systems.
Frequency: Annual

21838 Grey House Homeland Security Directory
Grey House Publishing
4919 Route 22
PO Box 56
Amenia, NY 12501

518-789-8700
800-562-2139
FAX 845-373-6390
E-Mail: books@greyhouse.com
Home Page: www.greyhouse.com
Social Media: *Facebook, Twitter*

Leslie Mackenzie, Publisher
Richard Gottlieb, Editor

Features the latest contact information for government and private organizations involved with Homeland Security along with the latest product information. The directory provides detailed profiles of nearly 1,500 Federal & State Organizations & Agencies and over 3,000 Officials and Key Executives involved with Homeland Security.
Cost: $195.00
800 Pages
ISBN: 1-592371-96-5
Founded in 1981

21839 Grey House Homeland Security Directory - Online Database
Grey House Publishing
4919 Route 22
PO Box 56
Amenia, NY 12501

518-789-8700
800-562-2139
FAX 845-373-6390
E-Mail: gold@greyhouse.com
Home Page: www.gold.greyhouse.com
Social Media: *Facebook, Twitter*

Leslie Mackenzie, Publisher
Richard Gottlieb, Editor

This comprehensive database presents a wide range of information that is scattered and hard to find elsewhere, providing subscribers with access to the most comprehensive, up-to-date and detailed information on the nation's homeland security contacts and services. This online database contains over 1,100 profiles of Federal and State agencies and companies along with the names of 11,000 key contacts.
Founded in 1981

21840 Grey House Safety & Security Directory
Grey House Publishing
4919 Route 22
PO Box 56
Amenia, NY 12501

518-789-8700
800-562-2139
FAX 845-373-6390
E-Mail: books@greyhouse.com
Home Page: www.greyhouse.com
Social Media: *Facebook, Twitter*

Leslie Mackenzie, Publisher
Richard Gottlieb, Editor

Comprehensive guide to the safety and security industry, including articles, checklists, OSHA regulations and product listings. Focuses on creating and maintaing a safe and secure enviroment, and dealing specifically with hazardous materials, noise and vibration, workplace preparation and maintenance, electrical and lighting safety, fire and rescue and more.
Cost: $165.00
1600 Pages
ISBN: 1-592373-75-5
Founded in 1981

21841 Grey House Transportation Security Directory
Grey House Publishing
4919 Route 22
PO Box 56
Amenia, NY 12501

518-789-8700
800-562-2139
FAX 845-373-6390
E-Mail: books@greyhouse.com
Home Page: www.greyhouse.com
Social Media: *Facebook, Twitter*

Leslie Mackenzie, Publisher
Richard Gottlieb, Editor

Information on everything from Regulatory Authorities to Security Equipment, this top-flight database brings together the relevant information necessary for creating and maintaining a security plan for a wide range of

transportation facilities.
Cost: $195.00
800 Pages
ISBN: 1-592370-75-6
Founded in 1981

21842 Kodex Security Equipment/Systems Database

Security Defense Systems
139 Chestnut Street
#626
Nutley, NJ 07110-2311

973-235-0606
800-325-6339
FAX 973-235-0132
Home Page: www.securitydefense.com

More than 32,000 manufacturers and distributors worldwide of home and office security equipment and systems.
Cost: $295.00
Frequency: Biennial

21843 Material Safety Data Sheet Reference

C&P Press
565 5th Ave
5th Floor
New York, NY 10017-2413

212-587-8620
FAX 646-733-6010
Home Page: www.cppress.com

Regulatory and product safety requirements. Contains full text MSDS's for products listed in the Crop Protection Reference plus additional safety information such as DOT shipping information, SARA Title III regulations, Hazardous Chemical inventory reporting information plus much more. Available in print, database, continually updated electronic version or CD-ROM.

21844 NFPA Journal: Buyers' Guide

National Fire Protection Association
1 Batterymarch Park
Quincy, MA 02169-7471

617-770-3000
800-344-3555
FAX 617-770-0700
E-Mail: publicaffairs@nfpa.org
Home Page: www.nfpa.org

James M. Shannon, President/CEO
Peg O'Brien, Administrator - Public Affairs
Sharon Gamache, Executive Director
Bruce Mullen, CFO
Paul Crossman, VP, Marketing

List of manufacturers and consultants of fire protection, fire safety and fire service products.
Cost: $30.00
75000 Members
Frequency: February
Circulation: 95,000
Founded in 1896

21845 National Directory of Fire Chiefs & EMS Administrators

National Public Safety Information Bureau
2173 Church Street, Suite 201
PO Box 365
Stevens Point, WI 54481-0365

715-345-2772
800-647-7579
FAX 715-345-7288
E-Mail: info@safetysource.com
Home Page: www.safetysource.com

Laura Gross, Vice President of Procurement
Steve Cywinski, Account Manager
John Diser, Account Manager
Christina Scott, Business Development Manager

Vital contact resource for busy professionals. Contact nearly every fire and emergency de-

partment in the US, nearly 35,000 departments.
Cost: $129.00
Frequency: June
Circulation: 10000
Founded in 1964

21846 National Directory of Law Enforcement Administrators

National Public Safety Information Bureau
2173 Church Street, Suite 201
PO Box 365
Stevens Point, WI 54481-0365

715-345-2772
800-647-7579
FAX 715-345-7288
E-Mail: info@safetysource.com
Home Page: www.safetysource.com

Laura Gross, Vice President of Procurement
Steve Cywinski, Account Manager
John Diser, Account Manager
Christina Scott, Business Development Manager

Listing of police departments, sheriffs, criminal prosecutors, state law enforcement, criminal investigation and homeland security agencies.
Cost: $129.00
Frequency: June
Circulation: 10000
ISBN: 1-880245-22-1
Founded in 1964

21847 National Work Zone Safety Information Clearinghouse

Texas Transportation Institute
3135 Tamu
College Station, TX 77843-0001

979-845-1715
888-447-5556
E-Mail: workzone@tamu.edu
Home Page: www.wzsafety.tamu.edu

Cooperative partnership between the American Road and Transportation Builders Association and the Texas Transportation Institute. Offers information traffic accidents and crashes, equipment and technology, legislation, research projects and training.

21848 Occupational Safety & Health Database

American Industrial Hygiene Association
2700 Prosperity Ave
Suite 250
Fairfax, VA 22031-4321

703-849-8267
FAX 703-207-3561
E-Mail: infonet@aiha.org
Home Page: www.aiha.org

Steven Davis, Executive Director
Wanda Barbour, Chairman
Paul DeBiase, Secretary

Web accessible database with over 22,000 original abstracts covering virtually all aspects of the occupational safety and health field. Records contain original abstracts as well as complete bibliographic information. Documents represented are from sources dating back to the early 1970s as well as important articles from earlier literature.
Cost: $240.00
Frequency: Individual Subscription

21849 Security Industry Sourcebook

PRIMEDIA Business Magazines & Media
1166 Avenue of the Americas
Shawnee Mission, NY 66282-2901

212-204-4200
FAX 913-514-6895
E-Mail: landerson@primediabusiness.com
Home Page: www.penton.com

Eric Jacobson, Senior VP

Listings of over 600 manufacturers and distributors of security and safety products.
Frequency: Annual
Circulation: 28,400

21850 Society of Fire Protection Engineers: Membership Roster

Society of Fire Protection Engineers
7315 Wisconsin Ave
Suite 1225W
Bethesda, MD 20814-3234

301-718-2910
FAX 301-718-2242
E-Mail: info@aiia-sfpe.org
Home Page: www.sfpe.org

Pamela A Powell, Editor
Kathleen Almond, Executive Director
Allan Freedman, Executive Director
Frequency: Annual February

Industry Web Sites

21851 http://gold.greyhouse.com

G.O.L.D Grey House OnLine Databases

Grey House Publishing's online database platform, GOLD, offers Quick Search, Keyword Search and Expert Search for most business sectors including safety and security markets. The GOLD platform makes finding the information you need quick and easy - whether you're a novice searcher or an experienced database user. All of Grey House's directory products are be available for subscription on the GOLD platform.

21852 www.abih.org

American Board of Industrial Hygiene

Information on credentials for Certified Industrial Hygienist status.

21853 www.afaa.org

Automatic Fire Alarm Association

Members are made up of manufacturers, installers and others interested in fire alarm and detection equipment. Seminars are conducted on a national basis.

21854 www.allbounty.com

North American Recovery Network

Worldwide portal for agents of collateral repossesion and bail bonds. Chats, forums and industry news.

21855 www.aloa.org

Associated Locksmiths of America

News and event information for the locksmith industry. Maintains referral service and offers insurance and bonding programs.

21856 www.alw.nih.gov/Security/security

Center for Information Technology
Computer security information and links.

21857 www.apco911.org

Association of Public-Safety Communications
Officials International

Dedicated to the enhancement of public safety communications and to serving its more than 15,000 members, the people who use public safety communications systems and services.

21858 www.asisonline.org

American Society for Industrial Security

Organization which features ideas and practices for business and industrial security managers.

21859 www.asse.org
American Society of Safety Engineers
Information for members on upcoming meetings, training and local chapters.

21860 www.atssa.org
American Traffic Safety Services Association
Promotes uniform use of lights, signs, pavement markings and barricades. Distributes technical information and sponsors training courses for worksite traffic supervisors.

21861 www.bioxs.com
Bio XS
Biometrics newsletter updated weekly. Features company profiles and new products.

21862 www.buildershardware.com
Builders Hardware Manufacturers Association
Code & life safety regulation information concerning locks and builders hardware.

21863 www.businesssecuritytips.com
Security Industry Association
Provides businesses with technology specific information and helps business owners and managers understand how available technology can be be better utilized.

21864 www.ccohs.ca
Canadian Centre for Occupational Safety & Health
Information on safety and industrial health topics in Canada.

21865 www.cdc.gov/niosh/homepage.html
National Institute for Occupational Safety/Health
Information on chemical safety, emergency response, injuries, construction, mining, agriculture concerns, respirators and much more.

21866 www.cert.org
Carnegie Mellon Software Engineering Institute
News, statistics and helpful articles relating to computer security.

21867 www.chemsafety.gov
US Chemical Safety & Hazard Investigation Board
Investigative reports of chemical safety incidents and an archive of completed investigations and recommendations made to regulators.

21868 www.cisecurity.org
Center for Internet Security
Helps organizations around the world effectively manage the risks related to internet security.

21869 www.csrc.nist.gov
National Institute of Standards & Technology
Information, links and white papers from the Information Technology Laboratory, the Computer Security Division and the Computer Security Resource Center.

21870 www.disaster-resource.com
Disaster Resource Guide
News, articles, business resources and product highlights for security and business managers as well as contingency planners who are in charge of emergency business recovery.

21871 www.eia-usa.org
Environmental Information Association
Nonprofit organization dedicated to providing environmental information to individuals, members and the industry. Disseminates information on the abatement of asbestos and lead-based paint, indoor air quality, safety and health issues, analytical issues and environmental site assessments.

21872 www.fama.org
Fire Apparatus Manufacturers' Association
Membership association for manufacturers of emergency vehicles and components affixed to or carried upon the vehicle.

21873 www.findbiometrics.com
Topickz
Showcases new technologies in biometric security and provides links to companies providing them.

21874 www.first.org
Forum of Incident Response and Security Teams
Brings together a variety of computer security incident response teams from government, commercial and academic organizations. This site encourages cooperation in incident prevention, rapid reaction to incidents and to promote information sharing.

21875 www.fraud.org
National Consumers League
Your source for Internet and telemarketing fraud information.

21876 www.fraudandtheftinfo.com
Fraud and Theft Information Bureau
Provides problem solving, crime prevention, money saving manuals and fraud blocker databases.

21877 www.fssa.net
Fire Suppression Systems Association
Association news and events for designers, suppliers and installers of special hazard fire suppression equipment, gases and detectors.

21878 www.ginetwork.com
Global Investigators Network
Worldwide internet based organization for private investigators.

21879 www.gocsi.org
Computer Security Institute
Information on computer and network security.

21880 www.greyhouse.com
Grey House Publishing
Authoritative reference directories for most business sectors including safety and security markets. Users can search the online databases with varied search criteria allowing for custom searches by product category, geographic area, sales volume, keyword, subject and more. Full Grey House catalog and online ordering also available.

21881 www.highwaysafety.org
Insurance Institute for Highway Safety
Vehicle safety news and statistics from traffic and motor vehicle safety organization supported by auto insurers.

21882 www.htcia.org
Int'l High Technology Crime Investigation Assoc
Designed to encourage, promote, aid and effect the voluntary interchange of data, information, experience, ideas and knowledge about methods, processes, and techniques relating to investigations and security in advanced technologies among its membership.

21883 www.imsasafety.org
International Municipal Signal Association
Basic purpose of the organization is to keep its members and others in the profession, up-to-date on proper procedures of construction and maintenance of signal systems and informed on new products and equipment developments.

21884 www.infoguys.com
Spyville
Process servers associations, articles and certification information, forensic experts and a searchable database for private investigators or those seeking to hire one.

21885 www.infosecuritymag.techtarget.com
Tech Target
Online information technology magazine.

21886 www.intsi.org
International Security Industry Organization
Dedicated to improving effcient communication to all stakeholders in the security industries and provides them with the necessary information to be more effective in their daily tasks.

21887 www.investigativeprofessionals.com
Investigative Professionals
Consult with a professional investigator, accomplish a people locator search, do a background check, conduct your own investigation or get information on becoming a private investigator.

21888 www.issa.org
Information Systems Security Association
International computer system information from an organization of security professionals and practitioners.

21889 www.museum-security.org
Museum Security Network
Free internet service and mailing list for museum security professionals, curators, librarians, registrar and specialized police.

21890 www.naaa.org
National Alarm Association of America
Alarm dealers association offers training, tips, an online newsletter and other member benefits.

21891 www.ndia.org
National Defense Industrial Association
To provide legal and ethical forum for the interchange of ideas between the government and industry to resolve industrial problems of joint concern.

21892 www.net-security.org
Help Net Security
Daily updated security related site.

21893 www.nfpa.org
National Fire Protection Association
The mission of the NFPA is to reduce the worldwide burden of fire and other hazards on the quality of life by providing and advocating consensus codes and standards, research, training and education.

21894 www.nnsa.doe.gov
National Nuclear Security Administration
Increasing public awareness of nuclear security and current energy issues. Links to website of supporting offices.

21895 www.nsi.org
National Security Institute
Features industry and product news, computer alerts, travel advisories, a calender of events, a directory of products and services and access to a virtual security library.

21896 www.ope.ed.gov/security
Campus Security Statistics

Direct link to reported criminal offenses for over 6000 colleges and universities in the US. If you are considering a college in a large urban city, a small liberal arts college, a specialized college or a community college you can find their security statistics here.

21897 www.osh.net
Workcare

Links to health and safety news. Offers online newsletter free to subscribers.

21898 www.osha.gov
Occupational Safety & Health Administration

Regulations and standards for worker safety in the US. Also included are a searchable database of recent safety violation citations, electronic safety lessons for many industries, a spot where workers can report safety concerns, safety tipsheets and a section for Spanish speaking workers.

21899 www.osha.gov/dop/nacosh.html
Nat'l Advisory Comm. on Occupational Safety/Health

News releases, federal register notices, reports, meeting agendas and contact information for the 12 members representing management, labor, occupational health and safety and the public. This group advises the secretaries of labor and health and human services on occupational safety and health programs and policies.

21900 www.pavnet.org
Partnership Against Violence Network

Virtual library of information about violence and youth-at-risk, representing data from seven different Federal agencies.

21901 www.personalprotection.com
Nine Lives Associates

Information on programs which emphasize personal survival skills and techniques for the protection of others. Information on training and list of protective agents and consultants.

21902 www.picoffeshop.com
PI Coffee Shop

Articles and a national forum of interest to private investigators.

21903 www.pimall.com
PI Mall

Information for private investigator contacts, products, training and services.

21904 www.processservers.com
International Process Servers Association

Resource for process servers and private investigators. Message board and searchable database by zipcode to locate a local process server.

21905 www.ready.gov
US Government

Updates and information on how the Department of Homeland Security is working to keep America safe.

21906 www.rims.org
Risk & Insurance Management Society

Information on worker's compensation, enterprise risk, risk management and financing, corporate governance and risk management.

21907 www.rmsecgroup.com
Risk Management Security Group

Addresses general aviation and cargo security concerns, training for professional transportation personnel, provides threat vulnerability assessments and literature.

21908 www.safeassociation.com
SAFE Association

Website of the nonprofit organization dedicated to the preservation of human life. It provides a common meeting ground for the sharing of problems, ideas and information.

21909 www.saferoads.org
Advocates for Highway and Auto Safety

Information on road safety issues, federal programs, polls, reports and helpful links for consumers, safety and law enforcement agencies, insurance agents and organizations.

21910 www.safetycentral.org
Safety Equipment Distributors Association

Represents wholesale-distributors of safety equipment and works to enhance and improve distribution through excellence in communications, training, education and services.

21911 www.safetyhealthmanager.org
National Safety Management Society

A professional society dedicated to the advancement of new concepts of accident prevention and loss control, promoting safety management.

21912 www.safetysmart.com
Bongarde Holdings

Safety education products and information.

21913 www.safetysource.com
National Public Safety Information Bureau

News, events, web guide and public safety shopping for professionals in corrections, EMS, fire and police departments.

21914 www.securityfocus.com
Symantec

Offers a forum for objective reporting by security experts on the latest computer security threats and prevention.

21915 www.securitysales.com
Security Sales & Integration

Breaking news of electronic security concerns and articles from the current issue of Security Sales & Integration.

21916 www.siaonline.org
Security Industry Association

Promotes growth, expansion and professionalism within the security industry. Online newsletter has the daily top ten headlines in security.

21917 www.stats.bls.gov
Bureau of Labor Statistics

Data on workplace injuries, illnesses and fatalities.

21918 www.terrorismcentral.com
Terrorism Central

Responding to the need for a single, trusted source of information about terrorism and related security issues, this central information repository comprises original and secondary sources spanning decades of research.

21919 www.ul.com/auth/tca
Underwriters Laboratories

Code Authority — online newsletter for the code community.

21920 www.vpppa.org
Voluntary Protection Program Participant's Assoc.

Information on the Occupational Safety and Health Administration's Voluntary Protection Participant program for companies.

21921 www.whitehouse.gov/homeland
Whitehouse

Updates of Homeland Security department and staff activities, list of state homeland security officers and contact information.

21922 www1.blr.com
Business & Legal Reports

Provides essential tools for safety and environmental compliance and training needs.

Associations

21923 American Apparel & Footwear Association

1601 N Kent Street
Suite 1200
Arlington, VA 22209

703-524-1864
800-520-2262
FAX 703-522-6741
E-Mail: nherman@wewear.org
Home Page: www.apparelandfootwear.org
Social Media: *Facebook, Twitter, LinkedIn, YouTube*

Aaron M. Albert, President
Thomas Glaser, Treasurer
Katherine Gold, Secretary
Rick Helfenbein, Chairman
Rob DeMartini, Vice Chairman

The national trade association representing apparel, footwear and other swen products companies and their suppliers which compete in the global market.
400 Members
Founded in 1960

21924 Association of Footwear Distributors

1319 F St Nw
Suite 700
Washington, DC 20004

202-737-5660
FAX 202-645-0789
E-Mail: info@fdra.org
Home Page: fdra.org
Social Media: *Facebook, Twitter, LinkedIn, Flickr, Instagram*

Matt Priest, President
Andy Polk, Vice President
Thomas Crockett, Director of Gov. & Reg. Affairs
Christie Horan, Marketing & Comm. Coordinator
Sue Myrick, Strategic Policy Advisor

Major distributors of footwear.
130+ Members
Founded in 1944

21925 Fashion Footwear Association of New York

274 Madison Avenue
Suite 1701
New York, NY 10016

212-751-6422
FAX 212-751-6404
E-Mail: info@ffany.org
Home Page: www.ffany.org
Social Media: *Facebook, Twitter, Pinterest, Youtube*

Ronald Fromm, President
Diane Sullivan, Secretary
Debbie King, Vice Chairman
Jim Issler, Chairman
Wayne Kulkin, Treasurer

4 International Trade Shows per year.
300 Members
Founded in 1980

21926 Footwear Distributors and Retailers of America

1319 F St Nw
Suite 700
Washington, DC 20004

202-737-5660
FAX 202-645-0789
E-Mail: info@fdra.org
Home Page: www.fdra.org

Social Media: *Facebook, Twitter, LinkedIn, Flickr, Instagram*

Andy Polk, Vice President
Rick Muskat, Chairman
Edward Rosenfeld, Vice Chair
Mike Jeppesen, Treasurer
Matt Priest, President

Trade association for footwear distributors and volume retailers.
130+ Members
Founded in 1944

21927 Pedorthic Footwear Association

1610 East Forsyth Street
Suite D
Americus, GA 31709

229-389-3440
FAX 888-563-0945
E-Mail: pedorthicsusa@gmail.com
Home Page: www.pedorthics.org
Social Media: *Facebook, Twitter, LinkedIn, Google+, Pinterest*

Matt Almeida, Secretary
Jay Zaffater, Past President
Robert Sobel, President
Dean Mason, Vice President
Christopher J. Costantini, Treasurer

Membership organization for individuals and companies involved in the design, manufacture, modification and fit of therapeutic footwear. Provides educational programs, publications, legislative monitoring, marketing materials, professional liason and business operations services.
Cost: $55.00
2000 Members
Founded in 1958

21928 Sports and Fitness Industry Association

8505 Fenton Street
Suite 211
Silver Spring, MD 20910

301-495-6321
FAX 301-495-6322
E-Mail: info@sfia.com
Home Page: www.sfia.org
Social Media: *Facebook, Twitter, LinkedIn*

Tom Cove, President & CEO
Cameron Jacobs, Manager,Business Operations
Chip Baldwin, CFO
Bill Sells, VP of Government Relations
Lauren Wallace, Director

Our purpose is to support our member companies and promote a healthy environment for the sporting goods industry. SGMA enhances industry vitality and fosters sports, fitness and active lifestyle participation.
1000 Members
Founded in 1906

21929 Two Ten Footwear Foundation

1466 Main St
Waltham, MA 02451

800-346-3210
FAX 781-736-1555
E-Mail: info@twoten.org
Home Page: www.twoten.org
Social Media: *Facebook, Twitter, LinkedIn, Flickr, YouTube*

Michael Atmore, Editorial Director
Robert McHugh, Treasurer
Blake Krueger, Chairman
Diane Sullivan, Vice Chair
Lawrence Siff, Secretary

Mission is to take action and create change for those in need. Built upon a foundation of caring, serving our community through social services and educational programs.
Founded in 1939

21930 United Shoe Retailers Association

PO Box 4931
West Hills, CA 91308

818-703-6062
FAX 866-929-6068
Home Page: usraonline.org

Linda Hauss, Executive Director

The Association helps independent shoe retailers be profitable.
Founded in 1977

Newsletters

21931 Footwear News

Fairchild Publications
750 3rd Ave
Suite 7
New York, NY 10017-2700

212-630-4320
800-360-1700
Home Page: www.wwd.com/footwear-news

Jay Spaleta, Publisher
Katie Abel, Editor

Weekly publication covering the international footwear industry's fashion trends, news developments, finances and market data.
Cost: $72.00
Frequency: Weekly
Circulation: 17892
Founded in 1892

21932 WSA Today

Show Dailies International
460 Richmond Street West
Suite 701
Toronto, ON 90049-5103

416-730-8488
800-360-3234
FAX 416-730-1878
Home Page: www.ingle-international.com

Rich DiGiacomo, Publisher
Robin Ingle, Chairman/CEO

Features products and industry news, conference information and interviews. Published daily during the semiannual Western Shoe Show.
Founded in 1946

Magazines & Journals

21933 Current Pedorthics

Pedorthic Footwear Association
7150 Columbia Gateway Drive
Suite G
Columbia, MD 21046-1151

410-381-8282
800-673-8447
FAX 410-381-1167
E-Mail: info@pedothrics.org
Home Page: www.pedorthics.org

Ed Habre, Board Chairman
Chuck Schuyler, President
Tanya Allain, Communicaton Coordinator

Covers pedorthics; the design, manufacture, modification and fit of shoes and foot orthoses to alleviate foot problems caused by disease, overuse or injury.
Cost: $35.00
44 Pages
Frequency: Quarterly
Circulation: 5000
Founded in 1958

21934 Footwear Market Guide
307 West 38th Street
Suite 1005
New York, NY 10018

212-398-5505
FAX 212-398-5504
E-Mail: customercare@infomat.com
Home Page: www.infomat.com
Social Media: *Facebook, Twitter, LinkedIn*

Provides a broad industry overview, including key press, manufacturing and sales contacts in one superb, value-priced package.
Cost: $165.00

21935 National Shoe Retailers Magazine
7150 Columbia Gateway Drive
Suite G
Columbia, MD 21046-1151

410-381-8282
800-673-8446
FAX 410-381-1167
E-Mail: info@nsra.org
Home Page: www.nsra.org

Nancy Hultquist, Director Communications
Bill Boettge, President

Provides businesses information such as credit-card processing and shipping at special features for the industry.
36 Pages
Founded in 1912
Printed in 2 colors on glossy stock

21936 Pedorthic Footwear Magazine
7150 Columbia Gateway Drive
Suite G
Columbia, MD 21046-1151

410-381-7278
800-673-8447
FAX 410-381-1167
E-Mail: info@pedorthics.org
Home Page: www.pedorthics.org

Nancy Hultquist, Director Communications
Brian Lagana, Executive Director
Kalin Wilburn, Sales Coordinator
Mike Forgrave, Publisher
Amy Bloom, Membership Manager

Provides educational articles, marketing materials and professional information.
Cost: $55.00
44 Pages
Circulation: 5000
Founded in 1958
Printed in 2 colors on glossy stock

21937 Runner's World
Runner's World Magazine Company
135 N 6th Street
Emmaus, PA 18098

610-967-5171
800-845-8050
FAX 610-967-8883
E-Mail: rwforums@rodale.com
Home Page: www.runnersworld.com

Andrew R Hersam, Publisher
David Willey, Editor
Steven Pleshette Murphy, CEO/President
Charles DeLana, Marketing
Richard Alleger, Vice President of Finance

A magazine dedicated to the lifestyle fitness activity of running. Aims to inform, advise, educate and motivate runners of all ages and abilities.
Cost: $21.00
Frequency: Monthly
Circulation: 530511
Founded in 1966
Mailing list available for rent: 370,000 names
Printed in on glossy stock

21938 Shoe Retailing Today
National Shoe Retailers Association

7150 Columbia Gateway Drive
Suite G
Columbia, MD 21046-1151

410-381-8282
800-673-8446
FAX 410-381-1167
E-Mail: info@nsra.org
Home Page: www.nsra.org

Bill Boettge, Managing Director
Nancy Hultquist, Editor

Offers information to independent shoe retailers across the country.
Cost: $35.00
Circulation: 4000
Founded in 1912

21939 Shoestats
Footwear Industries of America
1420 K St NW
Suite 600
Washington, DC 20005-2506

202-962-0380
FAX 202-789-7257
E-Mail: shoes@shoeinfonet.com
Home Page: www.shoeinfonet.com

Maria L Abrantes, President
Ivo Geidl, office Manager

Complete statistical coverage of the footwear industry.
Cost: $40.00
210 Pages
Frequency: Bi-annually

Trade Shows

21940 Annual Symposium
Pedorthic Footwear Association
7150 Columbia Gateway Drive
Columbia, MD 21046-2972

800-673-8447
FAX 410-381-1167
E-Mail: info@pedorthics.org
Home Page: www.pedorthics.org

Jeanne Williams, Manager
Brian Lagana, Executive Director

The Annual Symposium is a combination education event and trade show expo. Containing 100+ booths and exhibits.
600+ Attendees
Frequency: November
Founded in 1958

21941 Global Leather
American Apparel & Footwear Association
1601 N Kent Street
Suite 1200
Arlington, VA 22205

703-524-1864
800-520-2262
FAX 847-522-6741
Home Page: www.apparelandfootwear.org

Kevin M Burke, President
Stephen E Lamar, VP
Scott Elmore, Marketing

Showcases the best in new leather materials and components for the footwear leather, needle and allied trades of North America. Brings together hundreds of exhibitors from the major sourcing cities around the world, showcasing thousands of products.
400 Members
1500 Attendees
Frequency: February/August
Founded in 2000

21942 Metropolitan Shoe Show New York
50 W 34th Street
Apartment 8A6
New York, NY 10001-3057

212-564-1069

Mary Stanton, Show Manager

225 booths.
2M Attendees
Frequency: March/September

21943 Northwest Show Travelers Buying Show Market
2720 W 43rd Street
Minneapolis, MN 55410-1643

612-920-5005

Dona Merchant, Show Manager

100 booths of shoe retailers and specialty store personnel from Minnesota, Iowa, North Dakota, Maryland and South Dakota.
1.5M Attendees
Frequency: January

21944 PFA Annual Symposium & Exhibition
Pedorthic Footwear Association
1610 E Forsyth St.
Suite D
Americus, GA 31709

229-389-3440
FAX 888-563-0945
E-Mail: pedorthicsusa@gmail.com
Home Page: www.pedorthics.org

Jeanne Williams, Show Manager
Brian Lagana, Executive Director
Nancy Hultquist, Director Communications

One hundred fifty booths plus educational sessions regarding the design, manufacture or modification and fit of shoes and foot orthoses to alleviate foot problems caused by disease, congenital condition, overuse or injury.
1000 Attendees
Frequency: November

21945 University of Shoe Retailing Conference
National Shoe Retailers Association
7386 N. La Cholla Blvd
Tucson
Arizona 85741

520-209-1710
800-673-8446
Home Page: www.nsra.org

Rob Kaufman, Conference Chairman
Tricia Keane, Conference Co-Chair
Chuck Schuyler, President
Mark Denkler, Chair
Frequency: July, Las Vegas

21946 World Shoe Associates: Shoe Show
15821 Ventura Boulevard
Suite 415
Encino, CA 91436-2974

818-799-9400
FAX 949-851-8523
Home Page: www.wsashow.com

Chris Aiken, Show Manager

One million square feet of exhibition space. Features thousands of footwear styles, accesories, handbags and foot care products.
12M Attendees
Frequency: August/February

Directories & Databases

21947 American Shoemaking
Shoe Trades Publishing Company

61 Massachusetts Avenue
PO Box 1530
East Arlington, MA 02174-8160

781-648-8160
FAX 781-646-9832
Home Page: www.shoetrades.com

John J Moynihan, Publisher

Brings the shoe manufacturer the news he
needs to know.
Cost: $55.00
30 Pages
Frequency: Monthly

21948 Business Performance Report
National Shoe Retailers Association
7387 N. La Cholla Blvd
Tucson
Arizona 85741

520-209-1711
800-673-8446
E-Mail: info@nsra.org
Home Page: www.nsra.org

Rob Kaufman, Conference Chairman
Tricia Keane, Conference Co-Chair
Chuck Schuyler, President
Mark Denkler, Chair

Comprehensive, in-depth, financial account of
retail shoe stores. Benchmark for retailers to
compare their own operations.

21949 Complete Directory of Socks & Shoes
Sutton Family Communications &
Publishing Company
155 Sutton Lane
Fordsville, KY 42343

270-740-0870
E-Mail: jlsutton@apex.net
Home Page: www.fleamarketeer.net

Theresa Sutton, Editor
Lee Sutton, General Manager

Print-out from database of wholesalers, manufacturers, distributors, importers and close-out
houses. Database is updated daily to guarantee
the most current and up-to-date sources available.
Cost: $44.50
100+ Pages

21950 Directory of Mail Order Catalogs
Grey House Publishing
4919 Route 22
PO Box 56
Amenia, NY 12501

518-789-8700
800-562-2139
FAX 845-373-6390
E-Mail: books@greyhouse.com
Home Page: www.greyhouse.com
Social Media: *Facebook, Twitter*

Leslie Mackenzie, Publisher
Richard Gottlieb, Editor

The premier source of information on the mail
order catalog industry. Covers over 13,000 con-
sumer and business catalog companies with 44
different product chapters from Animals to
Toys and Games.
Cost: $395.00
1900 Pages
Frequency: Annual
ISBN: 1-592373-96-8
Founded in 1981

**21951 Directory of Mail Order Catalogs -
Online Database**
Grey House Publishing
4919 Route 22
PO Box 56
Amenia, NY 12501

518-789-8700
800-562-2139

FAX 845-373-6390
E-Mail: gold@greyhouse.com
Home Page: http://gold.greyhouse.com
Social Media: *Facebook, Twitter*

Leslie Mackenzie, Publisher
Richard Gottlieb, Editor

Reach over 10,000 consumer catalog companies in one easy-to-use source with The Directory of Mail Order Catalogs - Online Database.
Filled with business-building detail, each company profile gives you the information you
need to access that organization quickly and
easily. Listings provide key contacts, sales volume, employee size, printing information, circulation, list data, product descriptions and
much more.
Frequency: Annual
Founded in 1981

**21952 Financial Performance Profile of
Public Consumer Products
Manufacturers**
Kurt Salmon Associates
1355 Peachtree St NE
Suite 900
Atlanta, GA 30309-3257

404-892-0321
FAX 404-898-9590
E-Mail: services@kurtsalmon.com
Home Page: www.kurtsalmon.com

William B Pace, CEO

About 23 publicly held footwear manufacturers.
Frequency: Annual June

**21953 Footwear Distributors and Retailers
of America: Membership Directory**
Footwear Distributors and Retailers of
America
1319 F Street NW
Washington, DC 20004-1106

202-628-1838
FAX 202-638-2615
Home Page: http://www.fdra.org

Peter Mangione, President

About 65 American footwear importers and retailers.

21954 Shoe Factory Buyer's Guide
Shoe Trades Publishing Company
323 Cornelia Street
Suite 274
Plattsburgh, NY 12901

514-457-8787
FAX 514-457-5832
E-Mail: sfbg@shoetrades.com
Home Page: www.shoetrades.com

George McLeash, Publisher

Over 750 suppliers and their representatives to
the shoe manufacturing industries in the US
and Canada.
Cost: $59.00
Frequency: Annual
Circulation: 1,000

Industry Web Sites

21955 http://gold.greyhouse.com
G.O.L.D Grey House OnLine Databases

Grey House Publishing's online database platform, GOLD, offers Quick Search, Keyword
Search and Expert Search for most business
sectors including shoe and accessory markets.
The GOLD platform makes finding the information you need quick and easy - whether
you're a novice searcher or an experienced database user. All of Grey House's directory

products are available for subscription on the
GOLD platform.

21956 www.apparelandfootwear.org
American Apparel & Footwear Association

National trade association representing apparel,
footwear and other sewn products companies
and their suppliers. Our mission is to promote
and enhance our members competitiveness,
productivity and profitability in the global
market.

21957 www.greyhouse.com
Grey House Publishing

Authoritative reference directories for most
business sectors including shoe and accessory
makrets. Users can search the online databases
with varied search criteria allowing for custom
searches by product category, geographic area,
sales volume, keyword, subject and more. Full
Grey House catalog and online ordering also
available.

21958 www.sgma.com
Sporting Goods Manufacturers Association

For manufacturers, producers, and distributers
of sports apparel, athletic footwear, fitness,and
sporting goods equipment.

21959 www.ssia.info
Shoe Service Institute of America

Shop to shop chat room, links and listings of
manufacturers and wholesalers plus shoe care
tips.

Associations

21960 International Network for Social Network Analysis
1404 1/2 Adams Avenue
Huntington, WV 25704

304-208-8001
FAX 304-523-9701
E-Mail: support@insna.org
Home Page: www.insna.org
Social Media: *Facebook, Twitter*

Laura Skvoretz, Chair/ Treasurer
John Skvoretz, President
Katherine Fraust, Vice President
Yanjie Bian, Board Member
Ulrik Brandes, Board Member

The International Network for Social Network Analysis was developed for researchers interested in social network theory and understanding the online world. Members discuss the virtual community, the virtual workplace and social support.
Founded in 1977

21961 Social Media Association
Home Page: socialmediaassoc.com
Social Media: *Facebook, Twitter, LinkedIn, RSS, Google+, Pinterest*

Paul Rubell, President
Hilary Topper, Founder
Paul Biedermann, Creative Director/Owner
Beth Granger, Board Member
Donna Rivera-Downey, Chief Marketing & Communications

Social Media Association brings together the media community both online and offline. Members are interested in business and innovation through social, digital and future media.

21962 Social Media Club
Post Office Box 14881
San Francisco, CA 94114-0881

Home Page: socialmediaclub.org
Social Media: *Facebook, Twitter, LinkedIn, YouTube, Google+, Pinterest*

Golden Ashby, President
Ali Sabkar, Founder
Cynthia Johnson, Editorial Director
Naomi Assaraf, Sponsorship Director
Anders Abrahamsson, International Web Editorial

Social Media Club was founded to host conversations around the world that explore key issues facing society as technologies transform the way we connect, communicate, collaborate and relate to each other.
300 Members
Founded in 2006

21963 Social Media Professional Association
530 Lytton Avenue
Palo Alto, CA 94301

650-600-3844
800-123-4567
E-Mail: info@smpa.us
Home Page:
www.socialmediaprofessionalassociation.com
Social Media: *Facebook, Twitter, LinkedIn, YouTube, Google+, Pinterest*

The Social Media Professional Association provides training, education, and advocacy for its members. It also offers a Social Media Marketing Certification program that aids existing business owners and entrepreneurs as they grow or start new businesses in the social media and mobile web marketing fields.

21964 The Internet Association
Washington, DC

E-Mail: news@internetassociation.org
Home Page: internetassociation.org
Social Media: *Facebook, Twitter, LinkedIn, RSS, Google+, Flickr, YouTube,*

Michael Beckerman, President
Oisin Hanrahan, CEO and Co-founder

The Internet Association represents America's leading internet companies and their global community of users. They are dedicated to policy solutions that protect internet innovations and empowers users.

21965 The Social Network Association
E-Mail: info@thesocialnetworkassociation.com
Home Page: thesocialnetworkassociation.com
Social Media: *Facebook, Twitter, Google+, RSS*

Jim Nico, Founder and CEO
Dr. Jane Bellan Karwoski, PhD, MSW, Chief Science Officer
Terry Monoson-Nico, Program Director
Daniel Goodsell, General Counsel
Gian Brown, Member, Advisory Board

The Social Network Association is a collaborative industry forum enabling social networking businesses and users to collectively identify and resolce common issues in a productive environment. It provides a comprehensive suite of applications and services to all its members.
Founded in 2011

21966 Word of Mouth Marketing Association
200 East Randolph Street
Suite 5100
Chicago, IL 60601

312-577-7610
FAX 312-275-7687
E-Mail: membership@womma.org
Home Page: www.womma.org
Social Media: *Facebook, Twitter, LinkedIn, YouTube, Google+, RSS*

Suzanne Fanning, President
Harvey Morris, Vice President
Jennifer Connelly, Events Manager
Leah Marshall, Director of Development
Pam Smith, Editorial Director
Founded in 2004

21967 eMarketing Association
40 Blue Ridge Dr.
Charlestown, RI 02813

800-496-2950
FAX 408-884-2461
E-Mail: ema@emarketingassociation.com
Home Page: emarketingassociation.com
Social Media: *Facebook, Twitter, LinkedIn, RSS*

eMarketing Association is the world's largest association of online marketers. Members meet and network with the top leaders in the eMarketing arena, through its Power Networking Party which helps businesses with new and significant marketing efforts.

Newsletters

21968 A Formula for Fueling Ad Agency New Business Through Social Media
American Association of Advertising Agencies

1065 Avenue of the Americas
16th Floor
New York, NY 10018

212-682-2500
FAX 212-682-8391
Home Page: www.aaaa.org
Social Media: *Facebook, Twitter, LinkedIn*

Nancy Hill, President
Michael D. Donahue, Executive Vice President
Laura J. Bartlett, CFO & COO
Michele Adams, Board Secretary

Designed to focus and kick-start your agency's understanding, participation, credibility and leadership in social media with less expense, time and frustration. Created for C level and senior executives charged with the responsibility of new business development.

21969 NRB Today
National Religious Broadcasters
9510 Technology Dr
Manassas, VA 20110-4149

703-330-7100
FAX 703-330-7100
E-Mail: info@nrb.org
Home Page: www.nrb.org
Social Media: *Facebook*

Frank Wright, President/CEO
Linda Smith, EVP/COO
Kenneth Chan, Director of Communications

This weekly newsletter by National Religious Broadcasters covers the latest news from the association and NRB's member organizations. The newsletter also serves as a source for tips, trends, and insights relevant to Christian communicators across the spectrum. Topics include audience building, branding, business strategy, innovation, job hunting, leadership, management, marketing, social media, and web strategy. NRB Today also features occasional columns, movie reviews, and product reviews.
Founded in 1944

Magazines & Journals

21970 The Social Media Monthly
Home Page: www.thesocialmediamonthly.com

A monthly magazine for all things involving social media.

Trade Shows

21971 ANA Digital & Social Media Conference
Association of National Advertisers
708 Third Avenue
33 Floor
New York, NY 10017

212-697-5950
FAX 212-661-8057
E-Mail: info@ana.net
Home Page: www.ana.net
Social Media: *Facebook, Twitter, LinkedIn, YouTube*

Bob Liodice, President & CEO
Christine Manna, COO
William Zengel, EVP

Discussing how to use social media to impact the consumer decision journey and how to effectively partner with other companies to maximize social media reach and more.

21972 International Network for Social Network Analysis

1404 1/2 Adams Avenue
Huntington, WV 25704

304-208-8001
FAX 304-523-9701
Home Page: www.insna.org
Social Media: *Facebook, Twitter*

Laura Skvoretz, Chair/ Treasurer
John Skvoretz, President
Katherine Fraust, Vice President
Yanjie Bian, Board Member
Ulrik Brandes, Board Member

The International Network for Social Network Analysis was developed for researchers interested in social network theory and understanding the online world. Members discuss the virtual community, the virtual workplace and social support.
Founded in 1977

21973 New York Social Media Marketing Conference

SkillPath Seminars
6900 Sqibb Road
PO Box 2768
Mission, KS 66201-2768

913-623-3900
800-873-7545
FAX 913-362-4241
E-Mail: webmaster@skillpath.com
Home Page: www.skillpath.com

Steve Nichols, Customer Care Representative
Robb Garr, President

This state-of-the-art conference walks through everything needed to start using social media to drive real business results, even for someone who doesn't know the difference between a tweet and a like button. There's no reason to miss out any longer on the proven, bottom-line benefits of marketing with social media.
Frequency: Semi-Annual, April

21974 Response Expo

201 Sandpointe Ave
Suite 500
Santa Ana, CA 92707-8700

714-338-6700
800-854-3112
FAX 714-513-8482
E-Mail: thaire@questex.com
Home Page: www.responsemagazine.com
Social Media: *Facebook, Twitter, LinkedIn, YouTube*

Thomas Haire, Editor
Don Rosenberg, VP
Kristina Kronenberg, Marketing Director

Focuses on the evolution of consumers from passive watchers to active and empowered brand evangelists. Technology and social media have enabled and encouraged consumers to engage and interact with content. Learn how to take DR marketing from traditional campaign management to the future of customer engagement.
Frequency: Monthly
Circulation: 12000
Founded in 1987

21975 Social Media Association

Home Page: socialmediaassoc.com/events
Social Media: *Facebook, Twitter, LinkedIn, RSS, Google+, Pinterest*

Paul Rubell, President
Hilary Topper, Founder
Paul Biedermann, Board Member
Beth Granger, Board Member
Donna Rivera-Downey, Board Member

Social Media Association brings together the media community both online and offline.

Members are interested in business and innovation through social, digital and future media.

21976 Social Media Club

Post Office Box 14881
San Francisco, CA 94114-0881

Home Page: socialmediaclub.org/events
Social Media: *Facebook, Twitter, LinkedIn, YouTube, Google+, Pinterest*

Golden Ashby, President
Ali Sabkar, New Chapter MD
Cynthia Johnson, Editorial Director
Naomi Assaraf, Sponsorship Director
Anders Abrahamsson, International Web Editorial

Social Media Club was founded to host conversations around the world that explore key issues facing society as technologies transform the way we connect, communicate, collaborate and relate to each other.
300 Members
Founded in 2006

21977 Transformation LA

American Association of Advertising Agencies
1065 Avenue of the Americas
16th Floor
New York, NY 10018

212-682-2500
FAX 212-682-8391
E-Mail: kipp@aaaa.org
Home Page: www.aaaa.org
Social Media: *Facebook, Twitter, LinkedIn*

Nancy Hill, President
Chris Weil, Chair
Andrew Bennett, Director at Large
Sharon Napier, Secretary/Treasurer

Talent recruitment and retention; regulatory updates; mobility; social media; and growing your business are a few of the sessions scheduled. Tour some of the entertainment capital's most creative facilities, including innovative 4A's member agencies.

21978 Word of Mouth Marketing Association

65 E. Wacker Place
Suite #500
Chicago, IL 60601

312-853-4400
FAX 312-275-7687
E-Mail: membership@womma.org
Home Page:
www.womma.org/events-education/events
Social Media: *Facebook, Twitter, LinkedIn, YouTube, Google+*

Suzanne Fanning, President
Chris Spallino, Director of Marketing
Jennifer Connelly, Events Manager
Chelsea Hickey, Marketing Manager & Editor
Founded in 2004

Associations

21979 ADMA Annual Meeting
Alaskan Dog Mushers Association
PO Box 70662
Fairbanks, AK 99707-0662

907-457-6874
FAX 907-479-3516
E-Mail: adma@sleddog.org
Home Page: www.sleddog.org
Social Media: *Facebook*

Dawn Brown, Secretary
Shannon Erhart, Trustee
Paula Ciniero, President
Casey Thompson, Vice President

Alaskan Dog Mushers Association annual
meeting

21980 ATP Tour
Association of Tennis Professionals
201 ATP Tour Boulevard
Ponte Vedra Beach, FL

904-856-6400
800-527-4811
FAX 904-285-5966
Home Page: www.atptennis.com
Social Media: *Facebook, Twitter, Instagram,
Google+,Youtube*

Giorgio di Palermo, Player Representative
Mark Young, Vice Chairman
Flip Galloway, Chief Operating Officer
Chris Kermode, Executive Chairman &
President
Mark Webster, Tournament Representative

Operates the official tennis computer ranking
system. Administers entry system for international tennis circuit and tennis system. Membership restricted to male, touring, professional
tennis players.
Founded in 1972

21981 Academy for Sports Dentistry
P.O. Box 364
Farmersville, IL 62533

800-273-1788
217-227-3431ÿ
FAX 217-227-3438
E-Mail: sportsdentistry@consolidated.net
Home Page:
www.academyforsportsdentistry.org
Social Media: *Facebook, Twitter*

Shelly Lott, Executive Secretary
James Lovelace, President
Wayne Nakamura, President-Ellet
E. Jan Chithalen, Treasurer
W Robert Howarth, Immediate Past President
Founded in 1983

21982 Adventure Cycling Association
150 East Pine Street
PO Box 8308
Missoula, MT 59807

406-721-1776
800-755-2453
FAX 406-721-8754
E-Mail: info@adventurecycling.org
Home Page: www.adventurecycling.org
Social Media: *Facebook, Twitter, Flickr,
YouTube, Instagram, Pi*

Leigh Carter, General Manager
Andy baur, Secretary
Andrew Huppert, Treasurer
Donna O'Neal, Vice- President
Wally Werner, President

Their mission is to inspire people of all ages to
travel by bicycle for fitness, fun and self-dis-
covery. A non-profit organization, it is a resource offering many programs for cyclists,

including a national network of bicycle touring
routes and organized trips.
42000 Members
Founded in 1972

**21983 Aerobics and Fitness Association of
America**
15250 Ventura Blvd
Suite 200
Sherman Oaks, CA 91403-3297

818-905-0040
877-968-7263
FAX 818-788-6301
E-Mail: contactafaa@afaa.com
Home Page: www.afaa.com
Social Media: *Facebook, Twitter, LinkedIn,
Google+, Pinterest, Youtube, I*

Linda Pfeffer, President

Association for the education, certification and
training of exercise instructors; information resource center for consumers.
Founded in 1983

**21984 Amateur Athletic Union of the United
States**
PO Box 22409
Lake Buena Vista, FL 32830

407-934-7200
800-AAU-4USA
FAX 407-934-7242
Home Page: www.aausports.org
Social Media: *Facebook, Twitter, YouTube,
Pinterest, Instagram*

Dr. Roger Goudy, President/CEO
James Parker, Director Sports
Rachel D'Orazio, Director Marketing/Websites
Pam Marshall, Director Sponsorship
Cynthia Diaz, Director Finance

The AAU hosts the Junior Olympic Games, 30
youth sports programs, 25 adult sports programs, awards over 200,000 championship
medals annually, partnered with Walt Disney
World to host events at Disney's Wide World of
Sports Complex, and presents an annual James
E. Sullivan memorial award.
500M Members
Founded in 1888

21985 Amateur Softball Association
2801 NE 50th St.ÿ
Oklahoma City, OK 73111ÿ

405-424-5266
Home Page: www.asasoftball.com
Social Media: *Facebook, Twitter, YouTube,
Instagram*

Craig Cress, Executive Director
Shirley Adkins, Executive Secretary
Mark Loehrs, Chief Financial Officer
Steve Walker, Director of Operations
Savannah Edwards, Director of I.T
Founded in 1933

**21986 American Academy of Podiatric
Sports Medicine**
109 Greenwich Dr
Walkersville, MD 21793-9121

352-620-8562
888-854-3338
301-845-9887
FAX 352-620-8765
E-Mail: info@aapsm.org
Home Page: www.aapsm.org
Social Media: *Facebook*

Rita J. Yates, Executive Director
David Jenkins, President
Maggie Fournier, Secretary-Treasurer
Alex Kor, Vice-President
Amol Saxena, Director

Serves to advance the understanding, prevention and management of lower extremity sports
and fitness injuries. They believe that provid-

ing such knowledge to the profession and the
public will optimize enjoyment and safe participation in sports and fitness activities. They accomplish this mission through professional
education, scientific research, public awareness
and membership support.
800 Members
Founded in 1970

**21987 American Alliance for Health,
Physical Education, Recreation and
Dance**
1900 Association Dr
Reston, VA 20191-1598

703-476-3400
800-213-7193
FAX 703-476-9527
Home Page: www.aahperd.org
Social Media: *Facebook, Twitter, LinkedIn,
Pinterest, Instagram*

Steve Jefferies, President
Charlene Burgeson, Executive Director
Hans Van Der Mars, Program Director
E. Paul Roetert, CEO
Dolly D. Lambdin, President-Elect

Organization that provides educational programs, resources and support for professionals
within the fields of health, physical education,
recreation and dance.
25000 Members
Founded in 1885

21988 American Amateur Baseball Congress
100 W Broadway
Farmington, NM 87401

505-327-3120
800-557-3120
FAX 505-327-3132
E-Mail: info@aabc.us
Home Page: www.aabc.us

Richard Neely, President
Mike Diamond, Executive VP
Tedra Liessmann, Secretary/Treasurer
Rusty Hill, Legal Advisor

Provides profressive and continuous organized
competition for sub teens through adults.bers.
250M Members
Founded in 1935

**21989 American Association of Collegiate
Registrars and Admissions Officers**
One Dupont Circle NW
Suite 520
Washington, DC ÿ20036ÿ

202-293-9161
202-296-3359
FAX 202-872-8857
E-Mail: iec@aacrao.org
Home Page: www.aacrao.org
Social Media: *Facebook, Twitter, LinkedIn,
Google+*

Michael Reilly, Executive Director
Melanie Gottlieb, Deputy Director
Gene Parker, Administrative Assistant
Charles Han, Asst Director, IT
Martha Henebry, Director of Operations

**21990 American Baseball Coaches
Association**
4101 Piedmont Parkway
Suite C
Greensboro, NC 27410

336-821-3140
FAX 336-886-0000
E-Mail: abca@abca.org
Home Page: www.abca.org
Social Media: *Facebook, Twitter, LinkedIn,
Google+*

Bill Arce, Director
Dave Keilitz, Executive Director
Scott Berry, Immediate Past President

Mark Johnson,, Chair
Ed BlankMeyer, President

Association of Baseball Coaches in the United States.
6500 Members
Founded in 1945

21991 American Camp Association

5000 State Road 67 N
Martinsville, IN 46151-7902

765-342-8456
800-428-2267
FAX 765-342-2065
E-Mail: pr@acacamps.org
Home Page: www.acacamps.org
Social Media: *Facebook, Twitter, LinkedIn, Google+, RSS, YouTube, Pintere*

Tom Holland, CEO
Tisha Bolger, Chair
Craig whiting, Treasurer
Rue Mapp, Vice-Chair
Steve Baskin, Board Members

Formerly known as the American Camping Association, is a community of camp professionals who have joined together to share their knowledge and experience and to ensure the quality of camp programs.
6700 Members
Founded in 1910

21992 American Canoe Association

503 Sophia St.
Ste 100
Fredericksburg, VA 22401

540-907-4460
FAX 888-229-3792
E-Mail: aca@americancanoe.org
Home Page: www.americancanoe.org/
Social Media: *Facebook, Twitter, LinkedIn, Google+, YouTube, Pinterest, I*

Judge Charles, At-Large
Robin Pope, Secretary
Peter Sloan, Treasurer
Anne Maleady, President
Roby Hackney, Board Member

A nationwide not for profit organization that is in service to the broader paddling public by providing education on matters related to paddling, supporting stewardship of the paddling environment, and enabling programs and events to support paddlesport recreation.
Cost: $18.00
50000 Members
Frequency: 6 Per Year
Circulation: 35000
Founded in 1880

21993 American College of Sports Medicine

401 W Michigan St
Indianapolis, IN 46202-3233

317-637-9200
FAX 317-634-7817
E-Mail: publicinfo@acsm.org
Home Page: www.acsm.org
Social Media: *Facebook, Twitter, YouTube, Pinterest, Instagram*

Asker Jeukendrup, Corporate Representative
Henry S. Miller, Director
Carol Ewing Garber, President-Elect
Dave Hillery, Treasurer
James Pivarnik, Foundation President

The ACSM promotes and integrates scientific research, education, and practical applications of sports medicine and exercise science to maintain and enhance physical performance, fitness, health, and quality of life.
20000 Members
ISBN: 0-195913-1
Founded in 1954

21994 American Council on Exercise

4851 Paramount Dr
San Diego, CA 92123

858-576-6500
888-825-3636
FAX 858-576-6564
E-Mail: support@acefitness.org
Home Page: www.acefitness.org
Social Media: *Facebook, Twitter, LinkedIn, Google+, Pinterest, Youtube, R*

Scott Goudeseune, President & CEO
Nancy Travanian, Chair
John Ellis, Vice Chair
Ariane Amiri, Treasurer
Michele Stanten, Secretary

A nonprofit organization committed to enriching quality of life through safe and effective physical activity. ACE protects all segments of society against ineffective fitness products, programs and trends through its ongoing public education, outreach and research. ACE further protects the public by setting certification and continuing education standards for fitness professionals.
Founded in 1985

21995 American Cutting Horse Association

P.O. Box 2443ÿ
Brenham, TX 77834ÿ

979-836-3370
FAX 979-251-9971
E-Mail: achacutting@yahoo.com
Home Page: www.achacutting.orgÿ
Social Media: *Facebook*

Ryan Combs, Board Member
Jason Borchardtÿ, President
David Wilson, Vice-President
Cary Sims, Treasurer
Trent Bell, Board Member

21996 American Fastpitch Association

2536 Greenacre Avenue
Anaheim, CA 92801

714-952-9311
FAX 714-952-9786
E-Mail: info@afasoftball.com
Home Page: www.afasoftball.com

Terry Fullmer, Director
Ron Gossmer, Director

Represents those individuals engaged in amateur softball.
250M Members

21997 American Football Coaches Association

100 Legends Lane
Waco, TX 76706

254-754-9900
FAX 254-754-7373
E-Mail: info@afca.com
Home Page: www.afca.com

Grant Teaffÿ, Executive Director
Gary Darnell, Associate Executive Director
Vince Thompson, Director of Media Relations
Adam Guess, Managing Director of Finance
Janet Robertson, Director of Conferences & Events
11,00 Members
Founded in 1921

21998 American Greyhound Track Operators Association

Palm Beach Kennel Club
1111 North Congress Avenue
West Palm Beach, FL 33409

561-688-5799
FAX 801-751-2404
Home Page: www.agtoa.com

Juan Fra, President
Dennis Bicsak, Office Coordinator

Sally Briggs, 1st VP
Michael Corbin, Treasurer
Harold Purnell, Counsel
Founded in 1946

21999 American Hockey Coaches Association

7 Concord Street
Gloucester, MA 01930

781-245-4177
FAX 781-245-2492
E-Mail: ahcahockey@comcast.net
Home Page: www.ahcahockey.com
Social Media: *Facebook, Twitter, LinkedIn, YouTube, RSS*

Joe Bertagna, Executive Director
Brian Riley, President
Kathy Bertagna, Membership Administrator
Bruce Delventhal, Treasurer
Brett Peterson, Past President

Maintains the highest possible standards in hockey and the hockey profession
Founded in 1947

22000 American Orthopaedic Society for Sports Medicine

9400 W. Higgind Rd
Suite 300
Rosemont, IL 60018

847-292-4900
877-321-3500
FAX 847-292-4905
E-Mail: aossm@aossm.org
Home Page: www.sportsmed.org
Social Media: *Facebook, Twitter*

Susan Serpico, Executice Asst.
Charles A. Bush-Joseph MD, VP
Bruce Reider MD, Journal Editor
Irvin E Bomberger, Executive Director
Camille Petrick, Managing Director

A national organization of orthopaedic surgeons specializing in sports medicine, including national and international sports medicine leaders.
2000 Members
Founded in 1972

22001 American Recreation Coalition

1225 G St. NW
Suite 650
Washington, DC 20005-3832

202-682-9530
FAX 202-682-9529
E-Mail: bnasta@funoutdoors.com
Home Page: www.funoutdoors.com
Social Media: *Facebook, Twitter*

Derrick Crandall, President & CEO
Catherine Ahern, VP, Member Services
Melinda Meade, Director of Communications
Tom Georgevits, Dir. Of Partner Projects

A non-profit Washington based federation that provides a unified voice for recreation interests to conserve their full and active participation in government policy making on issues such as public land management. ARC works to build public-private partnerships to enhance and protect outdoor recreation opportunities and resources.
100+ Members
Founded in 1979

22002 American Running Association

4405 East West Hwy
Suite 405
Bethesda, MD 20814

301-913-9517
800-776-2732
FAX 301-913-9520

Home Page: www.americanrunning.org
Social Media: *LinkedIn*

David Watt, Executive Director
Maria Kolanowsk, Project Coordinator
Barb Baldwin, Project Consultant

A leading voice and center for information on sports' running medicine. The 'ARA Clinic' provides personal feedback from a select cadre of physicians and sports medicine personnel.
10000 Members
Founded in 1968

22003 American Society of Golf Course Architects

125 N Executive Dr
Suite 302
Brookfield, WI 53005

262-786-5960
FAX 262-786-5919
E-Mail: info@asgca.org
Home Page: www.asgca.org
Social Media: *Facebook, Twitter, LinkedIn*

Rick Robbins, Immediate Past President
Lee Schmidt, President
Steve Smyers, Vice President
Greg Martin, Treasurer
John Sanford, Secretary

A non-profit organization comprised of leading golf course designers in North America. ASGCA is actively involved in many issues realted to the game of golf, including responsible environmental designs.
185 Members
Founded in 1946

22004 American Spa and Health Resort

PO Box 585
Lake Forest, IL 60045

847-234-8851
FAX 847-295-7790
Social Media: *Facebook*

Melanie Ruehle, Contact

Seeks to establish and maintain high standards of quality in US health spas.
Founded in 1982

22005 American Volleyball Coaches Association

2365 Harrodsburg Road
Suite A325
Lexington, KY 40504

859-226-4315
866-544-2822
FAX 859-226-4338
E-Mail: members@avca.org
Home Page: www.avca.org
Social Media: *Facebook, Twitter, YouTube, Pinterest*

Kathy Deboer, Executive Director
Ross Brown, Assistant Executive Director
Anne Kordes, President
Kevin Hambly, President Elect
Kim Norman, NAIA Rep

To advance the development of the sport of volleyball by providing all coaches with educational programs, a forum for opinion exchange and recognition opportunities.
4900 Members
Founded in 1981

22006 Aquatic Exercise Association

PO Box 1609
Nokomis, FL 34274-1609

941-486-8600
888-232-9283
FAX 941-486-8820
E-Mail: aea@ix.netcom.com

Home Page: www.aeawave.com
Social Media: *Facebook*

Julie See, President/ Education Director
Angie Proctor, Executive Director
Dan Yeats, Event Operations Coordinator
Troy Nelson, Administrative Services Coordinator
Donna Blackmon, Operations Administrator

A not-for-profit educational organization dedicated to the growth and development of the aquatic fitness industry and the safety of the public served.
6,000 Members
Founded in 1984
Mailing list available for rent: 85,000 names

22007 Archery Range and Retailers Organization

156 N Main St
Suite D
Oregon, WI 53575

608-835-9060
800-234-7499
FAX 608-835-9360
Home Page: www.archeryretailers.com

Kent Colgrove, Secretary
Martin Stubstad, President
Ervin Wagner, Treasurer
Ron Pelkey, Director
Will Moulton, Vice President

A national organization of porfessional full time archery ranges and pro shops.
140 Members
Founded in 1968

22008 Archery Trade Association

PO Box 70
New Ulm, MN 56073-0070

507-233-8130
866-266-2776
FAX 507-233-8140
E-Mail: info@archerytrade.org
Home Page: www.archerytrade.org
Social Media: *Facebook, Twitter*

Scoff Henrikson, President/CEO
Mark Copeland, Director of Marketing
Jeff Adee, Executive Asst. to the President
Peter Gussie, Communiactions coordinator
Benjamin Summers, Dir. Of finance & Operations

Formerly the Archery Manufacturers and Merchants Organization, provides the core funding and direction for two foundations critical to the future of archery and bowhunting.
Founded in 1947

22009 Association for the Advancement of Applied Sports Psychology

8365 Keystone Crossing
Suite 107
Indianapolis, IN 46240

317-205-9225
FAX 317-205-9481
E-Mail: info@appliedsportpsych.org
Home Page: www.appliedsportpsych.org
Social Media: *Facebook, Twitter, YouTube*

Robert Schinke, Ed.D., President
Brent Walker, Ph.D., President-Elect
Jonathan Metzler, Ph.D., CC-AAS, Past-President Elect
Rebecca Concepcion, Ph.D., Secretary-Treasurerÿ
Kent Lindeman, CMP, Executive Director
Founded in 1986

22010 Association of Diving Contractors International

5206 Fm 1960 Rd W
Suite 202
Houston, TX 77069

281-893-8388
FAX 281-893-5118
E-Mail: rroberts@adc-int.org
Home Page: www.adc-int.org
Social Media: *Facebook, Twitter, LinkedIn*

Phil Newsum, Executive Director
Claudio Castro, At Large Executive Committee Member
Robbie Mistretta, Treasurer
Jay Crofton, 1st VP
Craig Fortenbery, President

The Association of Diving Contractors International, Inc. was founded in 1968 by a small group of diving companies. Their goal was to create a non-profit organization to cultivate and promote the art and science of commercial diving, establish uniform safe standards for commercial divers, and encourage industry-wide observance of these standards.
500 Members
Founded in 1968

22011 Association of Volleyball Professionalsÿ

2183 Fairview Road
Suite 222
Costa Mesa, CA 92627

949-646-4600
E-Mail: contact@avp.com
Home Page: www.avp.com
Social Media: *Facebook, Twitter, LinkedIn, Instagram, YouTube*

Founded in 1983

22012 Athletic Equipment Managers Association

207 E, Bodman
Bement, IL 61813

217-678-1004
FAX 217-678-1005
E-Mail: aema@frontiernet.nen
Home Page: www.equipmentmanagers.org
Social Media: *Facebook, Twitter, LinkedIn*

Kelly Jones, Certification Steering Committee
Mike Royster, Executive Director
Matthew Althoff, Associate Executive Director
Dan Siermine, President
Meli Resendiz, VicePresident

The purpose of the AEMA is to promote, advance, and improve the Equipment Managers Profession in all of its many phases.
700 Members
Founded in 1973
Mailing list available for rent

22013 Billiard and Bowling Institute of America

PO Box 6363
West Palm Beach, FL 33405

561-835-0077
FAX 561-659-1824
E-Mail: bbia@billiardandbowling.org
Home Page: www.billiardandbowling.org

Jeff Mraz, President
Corey Dykstra, VP
Hank Boomershine, Secretary/ Treasurer/ Con. Chairman
Skip Nemecek, Director
Mike Judy, Director

A not-for-profit association formed to service the billiard and bowling industries. The BBIA network is uniquely structured to open channels of communication between manufacturers and distributors in order to assist and improve members' business operations. BBIA provides

an innovative forum for billiard and bowling businesses to share ideas, gain information, gather feedback and explore the dynamics of the product pipeline between manufacturer and end user.
150 Members
Founded in 1940

22014 Bowling Proprietors' Association of America

621 Six Flags Drive
Arlington, TX 76011

817-649-5105
800-343-1329
FAX 817-633-2940
E-Mail: answer@bpaa.com
Home Page: www.bpaamax.com

Vladmir Wapensky, Executive Director

Supports the Bowling Proprietors' Association of American Political Action Committee.
3.6M Members
Founded in 1932

22015 College Swimming Coaches Association of America

1640 Maple
#803
Evanston, IL 60201

847-833-3478
E-Mail: r-groseth@northwestern.edu
Home Page: www.cscaa.org/
Social Media: *Twitter, LinkedIn, YouTube*

Joel Shinofield, Executive Director
Bill Wadley, President
Maureen Travers, Secretary
Chuck Knoles, Treasurer
Bob Pearson, Sergeant-At-Arms

The oldest organization of college coaches in America; a professional organization of college swimming and diving coaches dedicated to serving and providing leadership for the advancement of the sport of swimming at the collegiate level.
Founded in 1922

22016 Cross Country Ski Areas Association

259 Bolton Rd
Winchester, NH 03470

603-239-4341
877-779-2754
FAX 603-239-6387
E-Mail: ccsaa@xcski.org
Home Page: www.xcski.org
Social Media: *Facebook, Twitter*

Chris Frado, President/Executive Director

A non-profit organization representing member ski service providers. The association's purpose is to promote the growth and improve the quality of cross country ski operations in North America.
Cost: $25.00
350 Members
Frequency: Quarterly
Circulation: 350
Founded in 1977

22017 Disabled Sports USA

451 Hungerford Dr.
Suite 100
Rockville, MD 20850

301-217-0960
Home Page: www.disabledsportsusa.org
Social Media: *Facebook, Twitter, YouTube*

Kirk Bauer, Executive Director

Providing opportunities to participate in sports, regardless of ability.
Founded in 1967

22018 Football Writers Association of America (FWAA)

18652 Vista Del Sol Dr
Dallas, TX 75287-4021

972-713-6198
E-Mail: tigerfwaa@aol.com
Home Page: www.sportswriters.net/fwaa
Social Media: *Twitter*

Leeÿ Barfknecht, President
Steve Richardson, Executive director
George Schroeder, Board of Director
Mark Anderson, 1st VP
David Jones, 2nd VP

Established to improve working conditions in college press boxes.
900 Members
Founded in 1941
Mailing list available for rent: 800 names at $50 per M

22019 Golf Coaches Association of America

1225 West Main Street
Suite 110
Norman, OK 73069

405-329-4222
866-422-2669
FAX 405-573-7888
E-Mail: info@collegiategolf.com
Home Page: www.collegiategolf.com
Social Media: *Facebook, Twitter*

Conrad Ray, President
Andrew Sapp, 1st Vice President
Ryan Klatt, Director of Operations
Gregg Grost, CEO
Todd Sattefield, Past President
Founded in 1958

22020 Golf Superintendents Association of America

1421 Research Park Dr
Lawrence, KS 66049

785-841-2240
800-472-7878
FAX 785-832-3643
E-Mail: mbrhelp@gcsaa.org
Home Page: www.gcsaa.org
Social Media: *Facebook, Twitter*

J. Rhett Evans, CEO
Keith A. Ihms, Immediate Past President
William H. Maynard, Secretary /Treasurer
Peter J Grass, Vice President
John J. O'Keefe, President

Provides education programs in formal settings and at home through videotapes and correspondence courses. Administers professional certification programs, publishes magazines and multiple newsletters, conducts and supports research, provides scholarship opportunities, offers employment assistance and career development support, promotes the image of the golf course superintendent through cable TV program 'Par For The Course' and other vehicles. Provides leadership in governmental issues.
22000 Members
Founded in 1926

22021 Harness Tracks of America

4640 E Sunrise Dr
Suite 200
Tucson, AZ 85718-4576

520-529-2525
FAX 520-529-3235
E-Mail: info@harnesstracks.com
Home Page: www.harnesstracks.com
Social Media: *Facebook, Twitter*

Paul J. Estok, Executive VP &General Counsel
Paul Fontaine, President
Hugh Mitchell, Chairman
Christopher Mcerlean, Treasurer
Jason Settlemoir, VP

Mission is to help members obtain their economic objectives by promoting live racing, enhancing and preserving the integrity and image of the sport, and providing information to members and the general public about the sport and the significant economic impact of the industry.
35 Members

22022 Ice Skating Institute

6000 Custer Rd
Bldg 9
Plano, TX 75023

972-735-8800
FAX 972-735-8815
E-Mail: isi@skateisi.org
Home Page: www.skateisi.org
Social Media: *Facebook, Twitter, LinkedIn, Pinterest, Google+*

Peter Martell, Executive Director
Elizabeth Kibat, Controller
Jeff Anderson, Administrative Service Manager
Sandey Carlsen, Membership Coordinator
Angela Tooley, Administrative Assistant

Industry trade association dedicated to providing leadership, education and services to the ice skating industry.
64500 Members
Founded in 1959

22023 International Federation of American Football

79 Rateau Street
La Courneuve 93120

E-Mail: info@ifaf.org
Home Page: www.ifaf.org
Social Media: *Twitter, YouTube*

Makato Keneuji, Senior Vice President
Scotty Hallenbeck, Treasurer
Elesa Zehndorfer, Secretary
Founded in 1896

22024 International Light Transportation Vehicle Association

2 Ravinia Drive
Suite 1200
Atlanta, GA 30346

E-Mail: membership@ILTVA.org
Home Page: www.iltva.org

Caleb Chesser, President
John Rupp, Associate General Counsel
Founded in 1984

22025 International Professional Rodeo Association

1412 S Agnew Ave
Oklahoma City, OK 73108

405-235-6540
FAX 405-235-6577
E-Mail: info@ipraradio.com
Home Page: www.iprarodeo.com

Ronnie Williams, Chief Field Representative
Tom Schick, Chairman
Lindsay Whelchel, Membership/Receptionist
Dale Yerigan, General manager
Tammie Hiatt, IFR Tradshow Coordinator

Governing body for professional rodeo. 500 rodeos across USA and Canada, $5 million prize money per year, 5 million fans.
3500 Members
Founded in 1960

22026 International Sports Heritage Association

PO Box 2384
Florence, OR 97439

541-991-7315
FAX 541-997-3871
E-Mail: info@sportsheritage.org

Home Page: www.sportsheritage.org
Social Media: *Facebook, Twitter*

Karen Bednarski, Executive Director
Marjorie Snyder, President
Susan Wasser, First Vice President
Paula Homan, Second Vice President
Megan Gardner, Treasurer

The mission of ISHA is to educate, promote
and support organizations and individuals engaged in the celebration of sports heritage.
140+ Members
Founded in 1971

22027 Ladies Professional Golf Association
100 International Golf Dr
Daytona Beach, FL 32124-1092

386-274-6200
FAX 386-274-1099
Home Page: www.lpga.com
Social Media: *Facebook, Twitter, RSS,*
YouTube, Instagram, Pinte

Carolyn Bivens, CEO
Karen Durkin, EVP/Chief Marketing Officer
Christopher Higgs, Senior VP/COO
Ken Wooten, VP Finance
Micahael Whan, Commissioner

The LPGA is a non-profit organization involved in every facet of golf. In addition to
staging the LPGA Tour, the LPGA is also committed to advancing women, youth and the
sport of golf through expanding the programs
of the LPGA Teaching and Club Professional
Division, as well as increasing contributions of
the organization and its tournaments to charity.
Founded in 1959

22028 League of American Bicyclists
1612 K St Nw
Suite 308
Washington, DC 20006-2850

202-822-1333
FAX 202-822-1334
E-Mail: bikeleague@bikeleague.org
Home Page: www.bikeleague.org
Social Media: *Facebook, Twitter, LinkedIn,*
Google+

Alex Dotty, Executive Director
Steve Clark, Program Specialist
Alison Dewey, National Summit Director
Lorna Green, Director of Operations
Bill Nesper, Vice President, Programs

Founded in 1880, the League is the only national membership organization of bicyclists in
the United States. The League works to promote and encourage bicycling for recreation
and transportation, and to protect and defend
the rights of bicyclists through advocacy and
education.
Founded in 1880

22029 Melbourne Greyhound Park
1100 N Wickham Rd
Melbourne, FL 32935

321-259-9800
FAX 321-259-3437
Home Page: www.mgpark.com
Social Media: *Facebook, Twitter, YouTube,*
RSS

James J O'Brien, General Manager

Trade association representing the interest of
and providing services to greyhound racetrack
owners and operators via government advocacy, information sharing, annual conference
and trade shows.
35 Members
Founded in 1971
Mailing list available for rent

22030 National Aeronautic Association
1 Reagan National Airport
Suite 202
Washington, DC 20001-6015

703-416-4888
800-644-9777
FAX 703-416-4877
E-Mail: naa@naa.aero
Home Page: www.naa-usa.org

Jonathan Gaffney, President
George Carneal, General Counsel
Walter J. Boyne, Chairman
Roy Kiefer, Treasurer
Elizabeth Matarese, Secretary

A non-profit association dedicated to the advancement of the art, sport and science of aviation in the United States. The official
record-keeper for United States aviation.
3000 Members
Founded in 1922

22031 National Amateur Baseball
Association
PO Box 705
Bowie, MD 20718

410-721-4727
FAX 410-721-4940
E-Mail: nabf1914@aol.com
Home Page: www.nabf.com
Social Media: *Facebook*

Thomas Stout, Director
Derel J Topik, First VP
Glenn McNish, Second VP
Connie Brown, Third VP
Charles Blackburn Jr, Executive Director

The oldest continually operated national
basesball organization in the country.
10M Members
Founded in 1914

22032 National Archery Association (USA
Archery)
4065 Sinton Road
Suite 110
Colorado Springs, CO 80907

719-866-4576
FAX 719-632-4733
E-Mail: membership@usarchery.org
Home Page: www.usarchery.org
Social Media: *Facebook, Twitter, YouTube,*
Instagram, Google+, P

Denise Parker, CEO
Sheri Rhodes, Chairman
Denise Parker, Chief Executive Officer
Amber Hildebrand, Accounting Assistant
Cindy Clark, Office/Finance Manager

Formed to develop and promote the sport of archery. Recognized by the US Olympic committee as the national governing body for the
olympic sport of archery. The NAA selects and
trains mens and womens archery teams to represent the US in international, pan american
and olympic competitions.
8500 Members
Founded in 1894

22033 National Association of Basketball
Coaches
1111 Main St
Suite 1000
Kansas City, MO 64105-2136

816-878-6222
FAX 816-878-6223
Home Page: www.nabc.com
Social Media: *Facebook, Twitter*

Paul Hewitt, 4th VP
Jeff Jones, 3rd VP
Ron Hunter, 2nd VP
Page Moir, 1st VP
Phil Martelli, President

Promotes the advancement and opportunities
for coaches and teachers in the sport of basketball.
5000 Members
Founded in 1927

22034 National Association of Collegiate
Directors of Athletics
24651 Detroit Rd
Cleveland, OH 44145

440-892-4000
FAX 440-892-4007
Home Page: www.nacda.com
Social Media: *Facebook, Twitter*

Erin Dengler, Manager-Communications
Ryan Virtue, Manager- Affiliate Associations
Jason Galaska, Asst. Executive Director
Bob Vecchione, Executive Director
Noreen Byrne, Business Manger

Professional association for college atheltics
directors, assistants and conference administrators. Provides educational opportunities and
serves as a vehicle for networking and the exchange of information to others in the college
sports profession.
1.5M Members
Founded in 1965

22035 National Association of Collegiate
Women Athletic Administrators
2024 Main Street
#1W
Kansas City, MO 64108

816-389-8200
FAX 816-389-8220
Home Page: www.nacwaa.org
Social Media: *Facebook, Twitter, LinkedIn,*
YouTube, Pinterest

Joan McDermott, President
Lynn Hickey, President Elect
Chris Plonsky, Past President
Erin McDermott, Treasurer
Lori Mazza, Secretary

22036 National Association of Professional
Baseball Leagues
1325 Franklin Ave.
Suite 160
Garden City, NY 11530

727-822-6937
FAX 727-821-5819
E-Mail: inquire@napw.com
Home Page: www.napw.com
Social Media: *Facebook, Twitter, LinkedIn,*
Pinteresr

Mike Moore, President
RJ Sparks, Promotional Director

Two hundred and seventy booths.
2.5M Members

22037 National Association of Sporting
Goods Wholesalers
1 Parkview Plaza
Suite 123
Oakbrook Terrace, IL 60181

630-596-9006
FAX 630-544-5055
E-Mail: info@nasgw.org
Home Page: www.nasgw.org
Social Media: *Facebook, Twitter, Flickr*

Kenyon Gleason, President
Peter Brownell, Chairman
Brad Burney, Vice Chair & Director
Mike Halleron, Treasurer
Maurice Desmarais, President & Secretary

Serves as a liaison with other sporting goods
associations. The NASGW is the organizer and

sponsor of the industry's annual meeting/expo event.
400 Members
Founded in 1953

22038 National Association of Sports Commissions
9916 Carver Rd.
Suite 100
Cincinnati, OH 45242

513-281-3888
FAX 513-281-1765
E-Mail: info@SportsCommissions.org
Home Page: www.sportscommissions.orgÿ
Social Media: *Facebook, Twitter, LinkedIn, Pinterest, YouTube, WordPress*

Kevin Smith, CSEE, Chairman
Greg Ayers, CSEE, Vice Chairman/Chair-Elect
Ralph Morton, CSEE, Treasurer
Mike Anderson, CSEE, Secretary
Terry Hasseltine, CSEE, Immediate Past Chair
Founded in 1992

22039 National Association of Sports Officials
2017 Lathrop Ave
Racine, WI 53405

262-632-5448
800-733-6100
FAX 262-632-5460
E-Mail: naso@naso.org
Home Page: www.referee.com
Social Media: *Facebook, Twitter*

Barry Mano, President
Marc Ratner, Chair
Anita Ortega, Vice Chair
Henry Zaborniak, Treasurer

Nonprofit 501(c)(3), educational association providing individual benefits such as training materials, liability and assault protection insurance and more to sports officials of all sports and every level.
16000 Members
Founded in 1976

22040 National Association of Student Financial Aid Administrators
1101 Connecticut AvenueÿNW
Suite 1100
Washington, DC 20036-4303

202-785-0453
FAX 202-785-1487
Home Page: www.nasfaa.org
Social Media: *Facebook, Twitter, LinkedIn, YouTube, Google+*

Eileen O'Leary, National Chair
Dan Mann, National Chair-Elect
Craig Munier, Past National Chair
Justin Draeger, President
Lori Vedder, Treasurer

22041 National Athletic Trainers Association
1620 Valwood Parkway
Suite 115
Carrollton, TX 75006

214-637-6282
860-437-5700
FAX 214-637-2206
E-Mail: webmaster@nata.org
Home Page: www.nata.org
Social Media: *Facebook, Twitter, LinkedIn*

Eve Becker-Doyle, Executive Director
Teresa Foster Welch, Assistant Executive Director
Karen Peterson, Manager Executive Operations
Ellen Satlof, Public Relations Manager
Cynthia Nadel, Marketing Coordinator

Association for professionals in athletic training.
28000 Members
Founded in 1950

22042 National Athletics Trainers' Associationÿ
1620 Valwood Parkway
Suite 115
Carrolltonÿ, TX 75006

214-637-6282
860-437-5700
FAX 214-637-2206
Home Page: www.nata.org
Social Media: *Facebook, Twitter, LinkedIn*

Jim Thornton, MS, ATC, CES, President
MaryBeth Horodyski, EdD, Vice President
Marjorie Albohm, Past President
Tim Weston, MEd, ATC, Board of Director, District 1
Michael Goldenberg, MS, ATC, Board of Director, District 2
35,00 Members
Founded in 1950

22043 National Basketball Athletic Trainers Association
400 Colony Square
Suite 1750
Atlanta, GA 30361

404-892-8919
FAX 404-892-8560
E-Mail: rmallernee@mallernee-branch.com
Home Page: www.nbata.com

Tom Badenour, Chairman

A satelite of the National Athletic Trainers Association. Members are athletic trainers in the NBA.
60 Members
Founded in 1974

22044 National Bicycle Dealers Association
3176 Pullman St.
Suite 117
Costa Mesa, CA 92626

949-722-6909
FAX 949-722-1747
E-Mail: info@nbda.com
Home Page: www.nbda.com

Dan Thornton, Chairman
James Moore, President
Jim Carveth, First VP
Jeff Koenig, Second VP
Chris Kegel, Secretary

The mission of the NBDA is to inspire and serve the specialty bicycle retailer through communicating the value and needs of the specialty bicycle retailer, enhancing the specialty bicycle retailer's profitability, and promoting the passion for cycling. The NBDA is a non-profit association promoting the interests of every specialty bicycle retailer in the United States.
2M Members
Founded in 1946

22045 National Collegiate Athletic Associationÿ
700 W. Washington Street
P.O. Box 6222
Indianapolis, IN 46206-6222

317-917-6222
FAX 317-917-6888
Home Page: www.ncaa.org
Social Media: *Facebook, Twitter, YouTube, Instagram*

Mark Emmert, President

22046 National Cutting Horse Association
260 Bailey Avenue
Fort Worth, TX 76107

817-244-6188
FAX 817-244-2015
E-Mail: info@nchacutting.com

Home Page: www.nchacutting.com
Social Media: *Facebook, Twitter, RSS*

Keith Deaville, President
Ernie Beutenmiller, VP
Jeff Hooper, Executive Director

Members are individuals and organizations interested in the development of superior horses and the refinement of the cutting horse competition.
20500 Members
Founded in 1946

22047 National Fastpitch Coaches Association
2641 Grinstead Drive
Louisville, KY 40206

502-409-4600
FAX 502-409-4622
E-Mail: nfca@nfca.org
Home Page: www.nfca.org
Social Media: *Facebook, Twitter, LinkedIn*

Rhonda Revelle, President
Kathryn Gleason, First VP
Kate Drohan, Second VP

The professional growth organization for fastpitch softball coaches from all competitives levels of play.
4100 Members
Founded in 1983

22048 National Golf Cart Manufacturers Association
NGCMA Attn: Fred Somers, Jr.
2 Ravinia Drive
Suite 1200
Atlanta, GA 30346

770-394-7200
FAX 770-454-0138
E-Mail: membership@ngcma.org
Home Page: www.ngcma.org

Fred L Somers, Jr, Secretary & General Counsel

Non-profit national trade association comprised of the leading golf car and personal transport vehicle manufacturers. NGCMA sponsors the development and maintenance of ANSI sanctioned standards to establish safety specifications for the design and operation of golf cars and PTVs driven by electric motors and internal combustion engines for golf cars.
Founded in 1984

22049 National Golf Foundation
501 N Highway A1A
Suite 401
Jupiter, FL 33477-4577

561-744-6006
888-275-4643
FAX 561-744-6107
E-Mail: general@ngf.org
Home Page: www.ngf.org
Social Media: *Facebook, Twitter, LinkedIn*

Joseph Beditz, President/CEO
Greg Nathan, Sr. Vice President/ Membership

The National Golf Foundation, founded in 1936 and based in Jupiter, Fla., is the industry's knowledge leader on the U.S. golf economy and leading provider of golf industry databases. NGF delivers independent and objective narket intelligence, insights and trends to fulfill its mission: To Keep Golf Businesses Ahead of the Game.
4000 Members
Founded in 1936

22050 National High School Baseball Coaches Association
PO Box 12843
Tempe, AZ 85284

602-615-0571
FAX 480-838-7133
E-Mail: rdavini@cox.net
Home Page: www.baseballcoaches.org

Ron Davini, Executive Director

Provides services and recognition for baseball coaches and to help promote and represent high school baseball across this country.
1600 Members
Founded in 1991

22051 National Hockey League
1185 Avenue of the Americas
Floor 15
New York, NY 10036

212-789-2000
FAX 212-789-2020
Home Page: www.nhl.com
Social Media: *Facebook, Twitter, LinkedIn*

Gary Bettman, Commissioner
William Daly, Deputy Commissioner
John Collins, COO

The NHL is one of the four major professional sports associations in North America, with 30 professional ice hockey franchises in the US and Canada.

22052 National Junior College Athletic Association
1631 Mesa Ave
Suite B
Colorado Springs, CO 80906

719-590-9788
FAX 719-590-7324
E-Mail: meleicht@njcaa.org
Home Page: www.njcaa.org
Social Media: *Facebook, Twitter, Pinterest*

Mary Ellen Leicht, Executive Director
Mark Krug, Ass. Executive Director
Bryce Roderick, President

The purpose of the NJCAA is to promote and foster junior college athletics on intersectional and national levels so that results will be consistent with the total educational program of its members.
525 Members
Founded in 1938

22053 National Pro Fastpitch
3350 Hobson Pike
Hermitage, TN 37076

615-232-2900
FAX 615-232-8880
E-Mail: info@profastpitch.com
Home Page: www.profastpitch.com
Social Media: *Facebook, Twitter, YouTube, Instagram*

Cheri Kempf, Commissioner
Gaye Lynn Wilson, Vice President
Ed Whipple, Supervisor of Officials
Cynthia Gerken, NPF Travel Agent
Nikki Worthman, NPF Intern

22054 National Recreation and Park Association
22377 Belmont Ridge Road
Ashburn, VA 20148-4501

703-858-0784
800-626-6772
FAX 703-858-0794
E-Mail: info@nrpa.org
Home Page: www.nrpa.org

Social Media: *Facebook, Twitter, LinkedIn, YouTube, Pinterest*

Jodie H Adams, President
John Crosby, Marketing
Jessica Lytle, Director

Advancing parks, recreation and environmental conservation efforts that enhance the quality of life for all people.
Founded in 1965

22055 National Rifle Association of America
11250 Waples Mill Rd
Fairfax, VA 22030-7400

703-267-1400
FAX 703-267-3970
E-Mail: membership@nrahq.org
Home Page: www.home.nra.org
Social Media: *Facebook, Twitter*

Oldest sportsmen's organization in the US. Maintains the NRA Political Victory Fund and supports the Institute for Legislative Action. Has an annual budget over $140 million.
4 Members
Founded in 1871

22056 National Soccer Coaches Association of America
30 W. Pershing Rd.
Suite 350
Kansas City, MO 64108

816-471-1941
FAX 816-474-7408
E-Mail: info@nscaa.com
Home Page: www.nscaa.com

George Perry, President
Mike Jacobs, VP, Events
Amanda Vandervort, VP, Marketing
Charlie Slagle, VP, Education
Lesle Gallimore, VP, Membership
Founded in 1941

22057 National Sporting Goods Association
1601 Feehanville Dr
Suite 300
Mt Prospect, IL 60056

847-296-6742
800-815-5422
FAX 847-391-9827
E-Mail: info@nsga.org
Home Page: www.nsga.org
Social Media: *Facebook, Twitter, LinkedIn, Flickr, YouTube*

Ken Meehan, Chairman
Randy Nill, Treasurer/Chairman Elect
Matt Carlson, President

Association of retailers, manufacturers and suppliers of sports equipment, footwear, and apparel.
2000+ Members
Founded in 1929

22058 National Strength and Conditioning Association
1885 Bob Johnson Dr.
Colorado Springs, CO 80906

719-632-6722
800-815-6826
FAX 719-632-6367
Home Page: www.nsca.com

Steven J. Fleck, PhD, President
Todd Miller, PhD, Vice President
Colin Wilborn, PhD, Treasurer-Secretary
Michael Embree, Executive Director
Levi Boren, PhD, Sr. Director of Certification
Founded in 1978

22059 National Youth Sports Coaches Association
2050 Vista Parkway
West Palm Beach, FL 33411

636-797-5334
800-688-5437
FAX 561-684-2546
E-Mail: nysca@nays.org
Home Page: www.nays.org
Social Media: *Facebook, Twitter, LinkedIn, YouTube, RSS, Pinterest, Googl*

Represents coaches involved in youth athletics.
Founded in 1981

22060 Pop Warner Little Scholars
586 Middletown Boulevard
Suite C-100
Langhorne, PA 19047-1867

215-752-2691
FAX 215-752-2879
E-Mail: webmaster@popwarner.com
Home Page: www.popwarner.com
Social Media: *Facebook, Twitter, LinkedIn, YouTube, Rss*

Jon Butler, Executive Director
Mary Fitzgerald, COO
Lisa Moroski, National Cheer/Dance Commissioner

A national youth football and cheerleading organization that provides assistance to its various chapters.
400M Members
Founded in 1929

22061 Professional Association of Diving
30151 Tomas
Rcho Sta Marg, CA 92688-2125

949-858-7234
800-729-7234
FAX 949-267-1267
E-Mail: webmaster@padi.com
Home Page: www.padi.com
Social Media: *Facebook, Twitter, YouTube*

Brian Cronin, CEO

Certifies scuba diving instructors. Provides education/training materials and retail support to its members.
67M Members
Founded in 1966

22062 Professional Association of Volleyball Officials
PO Box 780
Oxford, KS 67119

888-791-2074
FAX 620-455-3800
E-Mail: pavo@pavo.org
Home Page: www.pavo.org

Julie Voeck, President
Joan Powell, President
Crystal Lewis, Board Delegate
Ben Jordan, Director Examinations
Karen Gee, Director Finance

The Professional Association of Volleyball Officials is dedicated to improving the quality of volleyball officiating for all rules codes and skill levels. PAVO strives to increase the number of competent officials through education and mentoring and promotes involvement in the governing bodies of other volleyball officiating groups.
2M Members

22063 Professional Baseball Athletic Trainers Society
1201 Peachtree St Ne
Suite 1750
Atlanta, GA 30361-6320

404-875-7990
FAX 410-730-2219

E-Mail: questions@pbats.com
Home Page: www.pbats.com
Social Media: *Facebook, Twitter, RSS*

Jamie Reed, President
Jim Carroll, Director Public Relations

Serve as an educational resource for the Major League and Minor League baseball athletic trainers. Serves its members by providing for the continued education of the athletic trainer as it relates to the profession, helping improve his understanding of sports medicine so as to better promote the health of his constituency - professional baseball players.
60 Members
Founded in 1983

22064 Professional Bowlers Association

615 Second Ave
Seattle, WA 98104

206-332-9688
FAX 206-332-9722
E-Mail: info@pba.com
Home Page: www.pba.com
Social Media: *Facebook, Twitter, Youtube, RSS*

Fred Schreyer, CEO
Steve Miller, Board Member
Lisa Gil, VP Brand Communications

Acts on behalf of professional bowlers.
3800 Members
Founded in 1958

22065 Professional Football Athletic Trainer Society

1201 Peachtree St Ne
Suite 1750
Atlanta, GA 30361-6320

404-875-7990
FAX 404-892-8560
E-Mail: contact@pfats.com
Home Page: www.pfats.com
Social Media: *Facebook, Twitter, Youtube, RSS*

Rollin E Mallernee II, President

Professional association whose members are the athletic trainers of the NFL. They provide, lead and manage helathcare for the NFL athletes, club employees and members of the NFL community. Dedicated to insuring the highest quality health care is practiced. Guided by the profesional integrity and ethical standards of its members and by the unity they share.
650 Members
Founded in 1982

22066 Professional Golfers Association (PGA)

100 Ave of the Champions
Palm Beach Gdns, FL 33418

561-624-8400
FAX 561-624-8448
E-Mail: webmaster@pga.com
Home Page: www.pga.com
Social Media: *Facebook, Twitter, Google+*

Ted Bishop, President
Derek Sprague, Vice President
Paul Levy, Secretary
Peter Bevacqua, CEO

The world's largest working sports organization comprised of more than 25,000 men and women PGA professionals to promote the game of golf to everyone, and to promote its members as leaders in the golf industry.
28000 Members
Founded in 1916

22067 Professional Inline Hockey Association

1733 East Harrisburg Pike
Middletown, PA 17057

719-200-4208
E-Mail: info@thepiha.com
Home Page: www.thepiha.com

Charles Yoder, Founder
CJ Yoder, President
Jami Yoder, VP
Jim Vanhorn, Chief Financial Officer
Denis Jelcic, Commissioner

22068 Professional Skaters Association

3006 Allegro Park Ln Sw
Rochester, MN 55902

507-281-5122
FAX 507-281-5491
E-Mail: office@skatepsa.com
Home Page: www.skatepsa.com
Social Media: *Facebook, Twitter, LinkedIn, Pinterest, YouTube*

Jimmie Santee, Executive Director
Kelley Morris, First VP
Jackie Brenner, Third VP
Donna Wells, Administrative Assistant
Barb Yackel, Marketing & Events

An international organization responsible for the education of skating coaches. Membership is offered to coaches in every discipline and at all levels, as well as to performing professionals, judges, eligible skaters and friends or patrons of the sport of figure skating.
6000 Members
Founded in 1938

22069 Roller Skating Association

6905 Corporate Dr
Indianapolis, IN 46278

317-347-2626
FAX 317-347-2636
E-Mail: rsa@rollerskating.com
Home Page: www.rollerskating.org
Social Media: *Facebook, Twitter, LinkedIn, YouTube, Pinterest, Google+*

Robert Bentley, President
Michael Jacques, VP
Brian Molony, Treasurer
Jim McMahon, Executive Director

A trade association representing skating center owners and operators; teachers, coaches and judges of roller skating; and manufacturers and suppliers of roller skating equipment.
1000 Members
Founded in 1937

22070 SHAPE America

1900 Association Dr.
Reston, VA 20191

800-213-7193
FAX 703-476-9527
Home Page: www.shapeamerica.org
Social Media: *Facebook, Twitter, Instagram, Pinterest*

Steve Jefferies, President
E. Paul Roetert, Chief Executive Officer

The Society of Health and Physical Educators is a national membership organization for committed to youth fitness and excellence in physical education.
Founded in 1885

22071 Society for American Baseball Research

555 N. Central Ave.
#416
Phoenix, AZ 85004

602-496-1460
800-969-7227
FAX 602-595-5690

E-Mail: info@sabr.org
Home Page: www.sabr.org
Social Media: *Facebook, Twitter, Youtube*

Vince Gennaro, President
Bill Nowlin, VP
Todd Lebowitz, Secretary
F X Flinn, Treasurer
Emily Hawks, Director

Foisters the study of baseball past and present and provides an outlet for educational, historical and research information about the game.
6700 Members
Founded in 1971
Mailing list available for rent: 25000 names at $85 per M

22072 Sporting Arms and Ammunition Manufacturers Institute

11 Mile Hill Rd
Newtown, CT 06470-2359

203-426-4358
FAX 203-426-3592
Home Page: www.saami.org

Steve Sanetti, President
Rick Patterson, Managing Director

SAAMI is an association of the nation's leading manufacturers of sporting firearms, ammunition, and components.
Founded in 1926

22073 Sporting Goods Agents Association (SGAA)

PO Box 998
Morton Grove, IL 60053

847-296-3670
FAX 847-827-0196
E-Mail: sgaa998@aol.com
Home Page: www.sgaaonline.org
Social Media: *LinkedIn*

Skip Nipper, President
Lois Halinton, Chief Operating Officer

International trade association of independent and established sporting goods agents.
500 Members
Founded in 1934

22074 Sporting Goods Manufacturers Association

8505 Fenton Street
Suite 211
Silver Spring, MD 20910

301-495-6321
FAX 301-495-6322
E-Mail: info@sfia.org
Home Page: www.sfia.org

Tom Cove, President & CEO
Chip Baldwin, CFO
Bill Sells, VP, Government Relations
Ron Rosenbaum, SVP, Marketing & Business Dev
Jan Ciambor, Office Manager

SGMA is the trade association of North American manufacturers, producers, and distributers of sports apparel, athletic footwear, fitness, and sporting goods equipment. SGMA represents and supports its members through programs and strategies for sports participation, market intelligence, and public policy.
1000 Members
Founded in 1906

22075 Sports Turf Managers Association

805 New Hampshire St
Suite E
Lawrence, KS 66044

785-843-2549
800-323-3875
FAX 785-843-2977

Home Page: www.stma.org
Social Media: *Facebook, LinkedIn*

Tom Cove, President
David Pinsonneault, President Elect
Rene Aspiron, VP
Allen Johnson, Secretary/Treasurer
Chip Baldwin, CFO

Grounds care for golf and athletic fields.
2500 Members
Founded in 1981

22076 Sportsplex Operators and Developers

Westgate Station
PO Box 24263
Rochester, NY 14624-0263

585-426-2215
FAX 585-247-3112
E-Mail: info@sportsplexoperators.com
Home Page: www.sportsplexoperators.com

John Fitzgerald, President
Diane Aselin, Executive VP
Don Aselin, Executive Director
Norm Rice, Treasurer
Kelly Tharp, Secretary

SODA was formed to meet the needs of the private concerns, public agencies, and other organizations that own or maintain sports complex facilities.
300 Members
Founded in 1981

22077 Tennis Industry Association

117 Executive Center
1 Corpus Christie Place
Hilton Head Island, SC 29928

843-686-3036
FAX 843-686-3078
E-Mail: info@tennisindustry.org
Home Page: www.tennisindustry.org
Social Media: *Facebook, Twitter, LinkedIn, YouTube, Google+, RSS, Pintere*

Jon Muir, President
Jolyn DeBoer, Executive Director
Brian O'Donnell, National Coordinator

To educate the marketplace, fund research and market intelligence and supply this reliable industry data to our member companies. The TIA is the Information source and clearing house for positive tennis news that we supply to TIA members, tennis publications and to the mainstream media in cooperation with the USTA.
800 Members
Founded in 1974

22078 The College Golf Foundation

1225 West Main Street
Suite 110
Norman, OK 73069

405-329-4222
FAX 405-573-7888
E-Mail: info@collegiategolf.com
Home Page: www.collegiategolf.com
Social Media: *Facebook, Twitter*

Conrad Ray, President
Andrew Sapp, 1st Vice President
Greg Sands, 2nd Vice President
Mark Crabtree, 3rd Vice President
Todd Sattefield, Past President
Founded in 1958

22079 The United States Association of Blind Athletes

1 Olympic Plaza
Colorado Springs, CO 80909

719-866-3224
FAX 719-866-3400
Home Page: www.usaba.org
Social Media: *Facebook, Twitter*

Dave Bushland, President
Tracie Foster, Vice President

Gary Remensnyyder, Treasurer
Trishca Zorn-Hudson, Secretary
Mark A. Lucas, MS, Executive Director

22080 U.S. Track & Field and Cross Country Coaches Association

1100 Poydras Street
Suite 1750
New Orleans, LA 70163

504-599-8900
FAX 504-599-8909
E-Mail: sam@ustfccca.org
Home Page: www.ustfccca.org
Social Media: *Twitter, RSS*

Sam Seemes, CEO
Damon Martin, President
Sandra Ford-Centonze, Secretary
Larry Cole, Treasurer
Dave Svoboda, Director of Operations

A non-profit professional organization that represents men's and women's cross country and track & field coaches in the United States.
8000 Members

22081 U.S. Track & Field and Cross Country Coach es Association

1100 Poydras Street
Suite 1750
New Orleans, LA 70163

504-599-8900
FAX 504-599-8909
Home Page: www.ustfccca.org
Social Media: *Facebook, RSS*

Damon Martin, President
Larry Cole, Treasurer
Sandra Ford-Centonze, Secretary
Sam Seemes, Chief Executive Officer
Dave Svoboda, Director of Operations
8,000 Members

22082 US Field Hockey Association

1 Olympic Plaza
Colorado Springs, CO 80909

719-866-4567
FAX 719-632-0979
E-Mail: usfha@usfieldhockey.com
Home Page: www.usfieldhockey.com
Social Media: *Facebook, Twitter, LinkedIn, YouTube, Pinterest, Google+*

Steve Looke, Executive Director
Simon Hoskins, Marketing Director

Represents field hockey, professional and amateur sports.
14000 Members
Founded in 1928

22083 US Handball Association

2333 N Tucson Blvd
Tucson, AZ 85716

520-795-0434
800-289-8742
FAX 520-795-0465
E-Mail: handball@ushandball.org
Home Page: www.ushandball.org
Social Media: *Facebook, Twitter, Vimeo*

Mike Steele, President
LeaAnn Martin, VP
Tom Sove, VP
Mike Driscoll, Treasurer - Southwest Region
Vern Roberts, Executive Director

Organization that runs all the tournaments for the professional and amateur players. Home of the Handball Hall of Fame.

22084 US Lacrosse

113 W University Pkwy
Baltimore, MD 21210

410-235-6882
FAX 410-366-6735
E-Mail: info@uslacrosse.org

Home Page: www.uslacrosse.org
Social Media: *Facebook, Twitter, Youtube, Google+, Instagram*

Steve Stenersen, President & CEO
Bill Schoonmaker, VP, Strategy & Business Development
Cara Morris, VP, Finance & Administration
Ann Kitt Carpenetti, VP, Lacrosse Operations
Mark Hogan, VP, Brand Marketing & Membership

The national governing body of men's and women's lacrosse. Through responsive and effective leadership, the organization provides programs and services to inspire participation while protecting the integrity of the sport. Known as the resource center for the sport, US Lacrosse is devoted to growing the game responsibly, providing programs and services to develop the game nationally, publishing Lacrosse Magazine & LaxMagazine.com, hosting events, and preserving the history of the game.
300M Members
Founded in 1998

22085 US Olympic Committee

One Olympic Plaza
Colorado Springs, CO 80909

719-632-5551
888-222-2313
FAX 719-632-0250
E-Mail: customerservice@donorssupportusoc.org
Home Page: www.teamusa.com
Social Media: *Facebook, Twitter, Youtube, Instagram*

Scott Blackmun, CEO
Lawrence Probst, Chairman
Walter Glover, CFO
Lisa Baird, Chief Marketing Officer
Larry Buendorf, Chief Security Officer

The national committee for the US handles the preparation of the US Olympic, Paralympic and Pan American Games teams.
Founded in 1978

22086 US Professional Tennis Association

3535 Briarpark Drive
Suite One
Houston, TX 77042

713-978-7782
800-877-8248
FAX 713-978-7780
E-Mail: uspta@uspta.com
Home Page: www.uspta.com
Social Media: *Facebook, Twitter, LinkedIn, YouTube, Pinterest, Google+, I*

John Embree, CEO
Fred Viancos, Director of Professional Dev.
Kathy Buchanan, Director of Computer Services
Julie Myers, Director of Creative Services
Ellen Weatherford, Controller

A nonprofit association for professional tennis teachers.
14000 Members
Founded in 1927

22087 US Raquetball Association

AARA National Office
1685 W Uintah Street
Ste. 103
Colorado Springs, CO 80904-2906

719-635-5396
FAX 719-635-0685
E-Mail: sczarnecki@usra.org
Home Page: www.usra.org
Social Media: *Facebook, Twitter, YouTube, Instagram*

Larry Haemmerle, President
Jason Thoerner, VP
Steve Czarnecki, Executive Director
Peggine Tellez, Manager, Sport Development

Myles Hayes, Coordinator, Membership Services

A nonprofit corporation designed to promote the development of competitive and recreational racquetball in the United States. The association offers a 'competitive license' membership for a one year term at $30.00 annually. A lifetime membership is also offered.
40M Members
Frequency: 6 Per Year
Circulation: 25,000
Founded in 1968
Mailing list available for rent

22088 US Ski & Snowboard Association
1 Victory Lane
PO Box 100
Park City, UT 84060

435-649-9090
FAX 435-649-3613
E-Mail: info@ussa.org
Home Page: usskiteam.com
Social Media: *Facebook, Twitter, YouTube, Instagram*

Tiger Shaw, President/CEO
Calum Clark, Vice President, Events
Luke Bodensteiner, EVP, Athletics
Brooke McAffee, VP/CFO
Michael Jaquet, VP, Chief Marketing Officer

The national governing body for Olympic skiing and snowboarding.
30000 Members
Founded in 1904

22089 US Soccer Federation
1801 S Prairie Ave
Chicago, IL 60616

312-808-1300
FAX 312-808-1301
E-Mail: centercircle@ussoccer.org
Home Page: www.ussoccer.org
Social Media: *Facebook, Twitter, YouTube, Google+, Instgram, Vi*

Sunil K Gulati, President
Mike Edwards, EVP
Dan Flynn, CEO/Secretary General

The governing body of soccer in all its form in the United States. US Soccer has helped chart the course for the sport in the USA for 90 years.
Founded in 1913

22090 US Speedskating
5662 Cougar Lane
Kearns, UT 84118

801-417-5360
FAX 801-417-5361
E-Mail: tmorris@usspeedskating.org
Home Page: www.usspeedskating.org
Social Media: *Facebook, Twitter, Youtube*

Ted Morris, Executive Director
Dale Schoon, Director of Finance
Matt Whewell, Communications Director
Angela Bond, Membership Coordinator
Shane Domer, Sports Science Director

Devoted to speedskating and its participants on the national and international levels.
2000 Members
Founded in 1966

22091 US Squash Racquet Association
555 Eighth Ave
Suite 1102
New York, NY 10018-4311

212-268-4090
FAX 212-268-4091
E-Mail: membership@ussquash.com
Home Page: www.ussquash.org

Social Media: *Facebook, Twitter, LinkedIn, Youtube, Flickr*

John A Fry, Chair
David Keating, District Associations
F. Gilpin Lane, Athlete Representative
Michelle Quibell, Athlete Representative
Tim Wyant, Ex Officio

The USSRA is the national governing body for the sport of squash racquets in the United States. A nonprofit, service organization whose primary function is that of management and maintenance of all squash related activities for a growing membership- driven organization.
8000 Members
Founded in 1907

22092 US Synchronized Swimming
132 E Washington Street
Suite 820
Indianapolis, IN 46204

317-237-5700
FAX 317-237-5705
E-Mail: marketing@usasynchro.org
Home Page: www.usasynchro.org
Social Media: *Facebook, Twitter, YouTube, Pinterest, Instagarm*

Judy McGowan, President
Sheila McNabb, VP Competitive Operations
Krista Bessinger, VP, Education & Certification
Nancy Rosengard, VP, Marketing & Member Services
Britt Rooney, Treasurer

Dedicated to the promotion of synchronized swimming. Sanctions and governs all synchronized swimming in the US and selects and trains National and Olympic Teams to represent the US in international competitions.
6000 Members

22093 US Track and Field
132 East Washington Street,
Suite 800
Indianapolis, IN 46204

317-261-0500
FAX 317-261-0481
Home Page: www.usatf.org
Social Media: *Facebook, Twitter, You Tube*

Max Siegel, CEO
Renee Washington, COO
Jill Geer, CPAO
Norman Wain, General Counsel
Carmen Triplet, Special Event Manager

The national governing body for track and field, long-distance running and race waling in the United States.
Founded in 1878

22094 US Volleyball Association
Suite 700
Los Gatos, CA 95031

E-Mail: volleyballorg@hotmail.com
Home Page: www.volleyball.org

Promotes volleyball in the US trains the USA men's and women's teams promotes beach and grassroots volleyball in the United States.
140M Members
Founded in 1928

22095 USA Basketball
5465 Mark Dabling Boulevard
Colorado Springs, CO 80918-3842

719-590-4800
FAX 719-590-4811
Home Page: www.usab.com
Social Media: *Facebook, Twitter, Google+, YouTube*

Jerry Colangelo, Chairman
Chauncey Billups, Athlete Representative
Kim Bohuny, NBA Representative

Jim Carr, National Organizations Rep.
Bob Gardner, NFHS Representative
Founded in 1934

22096 USA Deaf Sports Federation
PO Box 22011
Santa Fe, NM 87502

605-367-5760
FAX 605-782-8441
E-Mail: support@usdeafsports.org
Home Page: www.usdeafsports.org
Social Media: *Facebook, Twitter, RSS, YouTube*

Jack C. Lamberton, President
Jeffrey L.ÿ Salit, Vice President
Mark Apodaca, Chief Financial Officer
Danny Lacey, Chief Development Officer
Brianne Burger, Secretary
Founded in 1945

22097 USA Gymnastics
132 E Washington Street
Suite 700
Indianapolis, IN 46204

317-237-5050
800-345-4719
FAX 317-237-5069
E-Mail: membership@usagym.org
Home Page: www.usa-gymnastics.org
Social Media: *Facebook, Twitter, LinkedIn, YouTube, Instagram*

Peter Vidmar, Chairman
Steve Penny, President
Paul Parilla, Vice Chair
Jim Morris, Treasurer
Gary Anderson, Secretary

The sole national governing body for the sport of gymnastics in the United States. USA Gymnastics creates, organizes and conducts clinics, training camps, team competitions and other aspects of athlete, coach and official selection and development.
13000 Members
Founded in 1963

22098 USA Hockey
1775 Bob Johnson Dr
Colorado Spring, CO 80906-4090

719-576-8724
FAX 719-538-1160
E-Mail: usah@usahockey.org
Home Page: www.usahockey.com
Social Media: *Facebook, Twitter, LinkedIn*

Dave Ogrean, Executive Director
Mike Bertsch, Marketing & Communications
Kim Folsom, Executive Assistant
Rae Briggle, Member Services
Casey Jorgensen, General Counsel

Promotes the sport of hockey. USA Hockey is the national governing body for the sport of ice hockey in the US.
600K Members
Founded in 1937

22099 USA Roller Sports
PO Box 6579
Lincoln, NE 68506

402-483-7551
FAX 402-483-1465
Home Page: www.usarollersports.org
Social Media: *Facebook, Twitter, You Tube*

George Kolibaba, Chairman/President
David Adamy, VP

The national governing body for all amateur skating sports including artistic, roller, and speed skating.
15K Members
Founded in 1937

22100 USA Swimming
One Olympic Plaza
Colorado Springs, CO 80909

719-866-4578
Home Page: www.usaswimming.org

Chuck Wielgus, Executive Director
Pat Hogan, Club Development Managing Director
Mike Unger, Assistant Executive Director
Jim Harvey, Chief Financial Officer
Frank Busch, National Team Director

Devoted to the sport of swimming and its enjoyment nationwide. Governing body for the sport of swimming.
400,0 Members
Founded in 1844

22101 USA Table Tennis
4065 Sinton Road
Suite 120
Colorado Springs, CO 80907

719-866-4583
FAX 719-632-6071
E-Mail: admin@usatt.org
Home Page: www.usatt.org
Social Media: *Facebook, Twitter, LinkedIn, YouTube, Pinterest, Instagarm,*

Gordon Kaye, CEO
Doru Gheorghe, COO/High Performance Director
Teresa Benavides, Financial Director
Andy Horn, Membership Director
Tiffany Oldland, Sanctioning & Ratings Manager

Dedicated to the promotion of the sport of table tennis and sponsors the US team. Membership dues are $40 per year for adults and $20 for those 17 years old and under.
9000+ Members
Founded in 1933

22102 USA Track & Field
USA Track & Field
132 East Washington Street, Suite 8
Indianapolis, IN 46204

317-261-0500
FAX 317-261-0481
Home Page: www.usatf.org

Max Siegel, CEO
Renee Washington, COO
Jill Geer, CPAO
Norman Wain, General Counsel
Carmen Triplet, Special Event Manager
Founded in 1878

22103 USA Water Ski Association
1251 Holy Cow Rd
Polk City, FL 33868

863-324-4341
FAX 863-325-8259
E-Mail: usawaterski@usawaterski.org
Home Page: www.usawaterski.org

The national governing body for organized water skiing in the United States. A member of the International Water Ski Federation (World Governing Body), the Pan American Sports Association and the United States Olympic Committee.
37500 Members
Founded in 1939

22104 USA Weightlifting
1 Olympic Plz
Colorado Spring, CO 80909-5764

719-866-4508
FAX 719-866-4741
E-Mail: usaw@usaweightlifting.org
Home Page: www.usaweightlifting.org

Michael Masik, CEO, General Secretary
Laurie Lopez, Director, Operations

Carissa Gump, Director, Corp. Services
Phil Andrews, Director, Events & Programs

USA Weightlifting is the National Governing Body (NGB) for the Olympic sport of weightlifting in the United States. USA weightlifting is a member of the United States Olympic Committee and a member of the International Weightlifting Federation. As the NGB, USA Weightlifting is responsible for conducting Olympic weightlifting programs throughout the country. The organization conducts a variety of programs that will ultimately develop Olympic, World Championship and Pan American Games' winners.
Cost: $20.00
4000 Members
Frequency: Quarterly
Circulation: 4500
Founded in 1981

22105 United States Amateur Boxing
1 Olympic Plz
Colorado Spring, CO 80909

719-866-2300
FAX 719-866-2132
E-Mail: media@usoc.org
Home Page: www.usaboxing.org

Anthony Bartkowski, Executive Director
Betsy McCallister, Executive Assistant
Brian Lawrence, CFO
Lynette Smith, Director, Membership Services

The national governing body for Olympic-style boxing. It is responsible for the administration, development and promotion of Olympic-style boxing in the United State.
7000 Members
Founded in 1981

22106 United States Bowling Congress
621 Six Flags Dr
Arlington, TX 76011

817-385-8200
800-514-2695
FAX 817-385-8260
E-Mail: abcpr@bowinginc.com
Home Page: www.bowl.com
Social Media: *Facebook, Twitter, LinkedIn, You Tube*

Andrew Cain, President
Frank Wilkinson, VP
Tamoria Adams, Director
Tim Payne, Chief Information Officer
Kevin Dornberger, Director, Team USA

Established in 2005 as the organization to serve amateur adult and youth bowlers of the United States. It resulted from the merger of the American Bowling Congress, Young American Bowling Alliance and USA Bowling. USBC is the national governing body for bowling as recognized by the United States Olympic Committee.
3 M Members
Founded in 2005

22107 United States Canoe Association
509 S Bishop Ave
Secane, PA 19018

610-405-5008
Home Page: www.uscanoe.com

Susan Williams, President
Joan Theiss, Insurance Coordinator

22108 United States Extreme Sports Association
6350 Lake Oconee Parkway
Suite 102-128
Greensboro, GA 30642

877-900-8737
E-Mail: info@usesa.org
Home Page: www.usesa.orgy

22109 United States Fencing Association
1 Olympic Plz
Colorado Spring, CO 80909-5760

719-866-4444
FAX 719-866-4645
E-Mail: info@usfencing.org
Home Page: www.usfencing.org
Social Media: *Facebook, Twitter, LinkedIn, You Tube*

Donald Anthony Jr., Chairman
Sam Cheris, Treasurer
Nathan Anderson, Secretary

National Governing Body for the sport of fencing in the United States. Their mission is to develop fencers to achieve international success and to administer and promote the sport in the USA.
9M Members
Founded in 1891

22110 United States Golf Association
PO Box 708
Far Hills, NJ 07931

908-234-2300
FAX 908-234-9687
E-Mail: mediarelations@usga.org
Home Page: www.usga.org
Social Media: *Facebook, Twitter, LinkedIn, You Tube*

Walter W Driver Jr, President
James E Reinhart, VP
David Fay, Executive Director

An association of member clubs and courses. Conducts the US Open and Women's Open Championships, the Walker and Curtis Cup matches and ten national amateur championships.
7.5M Members
Founded in 1894

22111 United States Harness Writers Association
PO Box 1314
Mechanicsburg, PA 17055

717-766-3219
E-Mail: ushwa@paonline.com
Home Page: www.ushwa.org

Steve Wolf, President
Chris Tully, First VP
Tim Bojarski, Second VP
Judy Davis-Wilson, Treasurer
Jerry Connors, Secretary

Members are media members who cover the sport of harness racing.
300 Members
Founded in 1947

22112 United States Parachute Association
5401 Southpoint Centre Boulevard
Fredricksburg, VA 22407

540-604-9740
FAX 540-604-9741
E-Mail: uspa@uspa.org
Home Page: www.uspa.org
Social Media: *Facebook, Twitter, LinkedIn, YouTube, RSS*

Jay Stokes, President
Randy Allison, Vice President
Sherry Butcher, Secretary
Lee Schlichtemeier, Treasurer
BJ Worth, Chairman

The USPA is a voluntary membership organization of individuals who enjoy and support the sport of skydiving. The purpose of USPA is three-fold: to promote safe skydiving through training, licensing, and instructor qualification programs; to ensure skydiving's rightful place on airports and in the airspace system; and to

promote competition and record-setting programs.
33000 Members
Founded in 1946

22113 United States Racquet Stringers
PO Box 3392
Duluth, GA 92084

760-536-1177
FAX 760-536-1171
E-Mail: usra@racquettech.com
Home Page: www.racquettech.com

David Bone, Executive Director
Dianne Pray, Membership Coordinator
Crawford Lindsey, Editor/Webmaster
Kristine Thom, Production Manager

Educates constituencies to better understand, service, perform with, and enjoy the technological wonders known as racquets, strings, balls, courts, shoes, and stringing machines.
7000 Members
Founded in 1975

22114 United States Tennis Association
70 West Red Oak Lane
White Plains, NY 10604

914-696-7000
Home Page: www.usta.com
Social Media: *Facebook, Twitter, YouTube*

Katrina Adams, Chairman, CEO & President
Andy Andrews, First Vice President
Tommy Ho, Vice President
Don Tisdel, Vice President
Patrick Galbraith, Secretary-Treasurer
Founded in 1881

22115 United States Trotting Association
750 Michigan Ave
Columbus, OH 43215

614-224-2291
877-800-8782
FAX 614-224-4575
E-Mail: stats@ustrotting.com
Home Page: www.ustrotting.com
Social Media: *Facebook, Twitter, LinkedIn, You Tube*

Ivan L Axelrod, Chairman
E Phillip Langley, President
Russell C Williams, Vice Chair
Mike Tanner, VP
Richard Brandt Jr., Treasurer

The USTA licenses owners, trainers, drivers and officials; formulates the rules of racing; maintains and disseminates racing information and records; serves as the registry for the Standardbred breed; endeavors to ensure the integrity of harness racing; insists on the humane treatment of Standardbreds; and promotes the sport of harness racing and the Standardbred breed.
Founded in 1939

22116 United States Water Fitness Association
P.O. Box 243279
Boynton Beach, FL 33424-3279

561-732-9908
FAX 561-732-0950
E-Mail: info@uswfa.org
Home Page: www.uswfa.com

John R Spannuth, President/CEO
Marion Frega, Assistant to President

Nonprofit educational organization that promotes aquatics throughout the US and other countries. Publishes the National Aquatics Newsletter, names the 100 top programs and aquatics in the country, by state and in 25+ categories. Conducts a wide variety of national aquatics certifications including Water Fitness Instructors (primary and masters), aquatic directors, coordinators of water fitness programs.

Conducts annual international aquatics conference.
Founded in 1988

22117 United States of America Cricket Association
8461 Lake Worth Road
Suite B-1-185
Lake Worth, FL 33467

561-839-1888
E-Mail: lbrulport@usaca.org
Home Page: www.usaca.org
Social Media: *Facebook, Twitter*

Gladstone Dainty, President
Michael Gale, 1st Vice President
Rafey Syed, 2nd Vice President
John Thickett, Treasurer
Mascelles Bailey, Secretary

22118 Western Fairs Association
1776 Tribute Rd
Suite 210
Sacramento, CA 95815-4495

916-927-3100
FAX 916-927-6397
E-Mail: stephenc@fairsnet.org
Home Page: www.fairsnet.org

Stephen J Chambers, Executive Director
Jon Baker, VP
Carrie Wright, Marketing
Nichole Farley, Marketing
Lori Hanley, Communications Manager

A non-profit association with members throughout the Western United States and Canada that strives to promote industry standards. Membership includes access to conventions and trade shows, educational training programs as well as legislative advocacy support.
2000 Members
Founded in 1922

22119 Women's Basketball Coaches Association
4646 Lawrenceville Hwy.
Lilburn, GA 30047

770-279-8027
FAX 770-279-8473
E-Mail: membership@wbca.org
Home Page: www.wbca.org
Social Media: *Facebook, Twitter, RSS*

Sue Semrau, President
Coquese Washington, VP
Charli Turner Thorne, Past President
Matthew Mitchell, Secretary
Danielle Donehew, Executive Director
Founded in 1981

22120 Women's National Basketball Associationÿ
645 Fifth Avenue
New York, NY 10022

Home Page: www.wnba.com
Social Media: *Facebook, Twitter, YouTube, Instagram*

22121 Women's Sports Foundation
Eisenhower Park
East Meadow, NY 11554

516-542-4700
800-227-3988
FAX 516-542-4716
E-Mail: info@womenssportsfoundation.org
Home Page:
www.womenssportsfoundation.org
Social Media: *Facebook, Twitter*

Billie Jean King, Founder
Donna Lopiano, CEO
Allison Sawyer, Senior Communications Coordinator

Disseminates information as well as encourages girls and women in sports and physical activity. Organization offers free access to quarterly electronic newsletter, Women's Sports Experience, that provides general updates on the world of girls'and women's sports as well as the Foundation's work.
4000 Members
Circulation: 15000
Founded in 1974

22122 YMCA of the USA
101 N Wacker Dr
Suite 1400
Chicago, IL 60606-1784

312-977-0031
800-872-9622
Home Page: www.ymca.net
Social Media: *Facebook*

Neil Nicoll, CEO

Provides national and state branch divisions.
20.1M Members

22123 ational Federation of State High School Associations
PO BOX 690
Indianapolis, IN 46206

317-972-6900
FAX 317-822-5700
Home Page: www.nfhs.org
Social Media: *Twitter*

Tom Welter, President
Gary Musselman, President-Elect
Gary Ray, B.O.D., Section 2
Jerome Singleton, B.O.D., Section 3
Marty Hickman, B.O.D., Section 4
Founded in 1920

Newsletters

22124 AAPSM Newsletter
American Academy of Podiatric Sports Medicine
109 Greenwich Dr
Walkersville, MD 21793-9121

352-620-8562
888-854-3338
FAX 352-620-8765
E-Mail: info@aapsm.org
Home Page: www.aapsm.org
Social Media: *Facebook*

Rita Yates, Executive Director
David M Davidson, Director

A quarterly newsletter published by the American Academy of Podiatric Sports Medicine.
12 Pages
Frequency: Quarterly
Circulation: 700
Founded in 1970
Mailing list available for rent: 600 names at $125 per M

22125 ARC e-Newsletter
American Recreation Coalition
1225 New York Ave NW
Suite 450
Washington, DC 20005

202-682-9530
FAX 202-682-9529
E-Mail: jmitchelle@funoutdoors.com
Home Page: www.funoutdoors.com

Derrick Crandall, President
Catherine Ahern, VP
Julia Mitchell, Director of Partnership Programs

A monthly e-newsletter distributed via e-mail.
Frequency: Monthly, e-Newsletter
Circulation: Variable

22126 BCA Newsletter
National High School Baseball Coaches Association
PO Box 12843
Tempe, AZ 85284

602-615-0571
FAX 480-838-7133
E-Mail: rdavini@cox.net
Home Page: www.baseballcoaches.org

Ron Davini, Executive Director

22127 Behind the Seams
National Amateur Baseball Federation
PO Box 705
Bowie, MD 20715

301-625-5005
FAX 301-352-0214
E-Mail: NABF1914@aol.com
Home Page: www.nabf.com
Social Media: *Facebook*

J Patrick Eaken, Editor
Charles M Blackburn, Executive Director

The official newsletter of the National Amateur Baseball Federation. Sent to NABF league members.
Frequency: Quarterly
Founded in 1914

22128 CSCAA Newsletter
College Swimming Coaches Association of America
1640 Maple
#803
Evanston, IL 60201

847-833-3478
E-Mail: r-groseth@northwestern.edu
Home Page: www.collegecoaches.org

Bob Groseth, Executive Director
George Kennedy, President

22129 Field Hockey News
US Field Hockey Association
1 Olympic Plaza
Colorado Springs, CO 80909

719-866-4567
FAX 719-632-0979
E-Mail: usfha@usfieldhockey.com
Home Page: www.usfieldhockey.com
Social Media: *Facebook, Twitter, LinkedIn, You Tube*

Steve Looke, Executive Director
Simon Hoskins, Marketing Director
Frequency: Seasonally

22130 Hunting Report for Big Game Hunters
Oxpecker Enterprises
Ste 523
9200 S Dadeland Blvd
Miami, FL 33156-2713

305-670-1361
800-272-5656
FAX 305-716-1376
E-Mail: Subscriptions@HuntingReport.com
Home Page: www.huntingreport.com
Social Media: *Facebook, Twitter, LinkedIn*

Don Causey, President/Publisher
Nick Titus, Production Manager
Provides information on hunting opportunities and conditions in the US, Africa and other parts of the world.
Cost: $60.00
Frequency: Monthly
ISSN: 1052-4746
Founded in 1980

22131 Hunting Report: Birdshooters and Water
Oxpecker Enterprises

Ste 523
9200 S Dadeland Blvd
Miami, FL 33156-2713

305-670-1361
FAX 954-370-1376
E-Mail: subscriptions@huntingreport.com
Home Page: www.huntingreport.com
Social Media: *Facebook, Twitter, LinkedIn*

Don Causey, Publisher

Serving the Sportsman who travels.
Cost: $45.00
14 Pages
Frequency: Monthly
Circulation: 1850
Founded in 1983
Printed in 2 colors on matte stock

22132 InBrief
Sporting Goods Manufacturers Association
8505 Fenton Street
Silver Spring, MD 20910

301-495-6321
FAX 301-495-6322
E-Mail: info@sgma.com
Home Page: www.sgma.com

Tom Cove, President & CEO
Bill Sells, VP Government Relations
Chip Baldwin, CFO
Mike May, Director Communications
Newsletter with information about and for manufacturers in the sporting goods industry.
Frequency: Bi-weekly

22133 International Sports Heritage Association
PO Box 2384
Florence, OR 97439

541-991-7315
FAX 541-997-3871
E-Mail: info@sportsheritage.org
Home Page: www.sportsheritage.org
Social Media: *Facebook, Twitter*

Karen Bednarski, Executive Director
Mike Gibbons, President
Rick Wells, First Vice President
Meg Snyder, Second Vice President
Ben Sopp, Treasurer
E-Newsletter
140+ Members
Frequency: Quarterly
Founded in 1971

22134 Leader Board
Golf Course Superintendents Association of America
1421 Research Park Dr
Lawrence, KS 66049-3859

785-841-2240
800-472-7878
FAX 785-832-4488
E-Mail: infobox@gcsaa.org
Home Page: www.gcsaa.org
Social Media: *Facebook, Twitter*

Mark Woodward, CEO
Melissa Householder, Communications Coordinator
Ed Hiscock, Editor-In-Chief

Bi-monthly newsletter for golf facility decision makers, including superintendents and their employers, presenting timely and useful informaiton about golf course management in a quick easy-to-read format.
Frequency: Monthly
Circulation: 40000
Founded in 1926

22135 Media Sports Business
Kagan Research

1 Lower Ragsdale Dr
Building One Suite 130
Monterey, CA 93940-5749

831-624-1536
800-307-2529
FAX 831-625-3225
E-Mail: info@kagan.com
Home Page: www.kagan.com

Tim Baskerville, President
Tom Johnson, Marketing Manager

Statistics of a different kind. How much media pay to carry sports events, the impact of media on pro sports franchises, and more. Scores big with major league and media players. Three month trial available.
Cost: $945.00
Frequency: Monthly
Founded in 1969

22136 NASGW Newsletter
National Association of Sporting Goods Wholesalers
1833 Centre Point Circle
Suite 123
Naperville, IL 60563

630-596-9006
FAX 630-544-5055
E-Mail: nasgw@nasgw.org
Home Page: www.nasgw.org
Social Media: *Facebook, LinkedIn*

Maurice Desmarais, President
Jack Baumler, Chairman
Kent Williams, Vice Chair
Peter Brownell, Treasurer

Non-profit trade association of wholesalers, distributors and manufacturers. Serves as a liason with other sporting goods associations. The NASGW is the organizer and sponser of the industry's annual meeting/expo event.
400 Members
Founded in 1953

22137 NSGA Sporting Goods Alert
National Sporting Goods Association
1601 Feehanville Dr
Suite 300
Mt Prospect, IL 60056-6035

847-296-6742
FAX 847-391-9827
E-Mail: info@nsga.org
Home Page: www.nsga.org

Jeff Rosenthal, Chairman of the Board
Matt Carlson, President/CEO
Dan Kasen, Director of Information Services
News and rule changes affecting team dealers. Newsletter is free to members.

22138 NSGA Team Line-Up
National Sporting Goods Association
1601 Feehanville Dr
Suite 300
Mt Prospect, IL 60056-6035

847-296-6742
FAX 847-391-9827
E-Mail: info@nsga.org
Home Page: www.nsga.org

Ken Meehan, Chairman of the Board
Matt Carlson, President/CEO
Dustin Dobrin, Director of Information Services

News and rule changes affecting team dealers. Newsletter is free to members.
Frequency: Weekly

22139 National High School Baseball Coaches Association
PO Box 12843
Tempe, AZ 85284

602-615-0571
FAX 480-838-7133

E-Mail: rdavini@cox.net
Home Page: www.baseballcoaches.org

Ron Davini, Executive Director

Association news, information, coaching articles.
Frequency: 2x/Year
Circulation: 1500+
Founded in 1991

22140 Newsline
Golf Course Superintendents Association of America
1421 Research Park Dr
Lawrence, KS 66049-3859

785-841-2240
800-472-7878
FAX 785-832-4488
E-Mail: infobox@gcsaa.org
Home Page: www.gcsaa.org
Social Media: *Facebook*

Mark Woodward, CEO

Membership newsletter highlighting programs and services, and featuring news about the association, its members, the golf course management profession and industry.
Founded in 1926

22141 Parachutist
United States Parachute Association
5401 Southpoint Centre Boulevard
Fredricksburg, VA 22407

540-604-9740
FAX 540-604-9740
E-Mail: uspa@uspa.org
Home Page: www.uspa.org
Social Media: *Facebook, Twitter, LinkedIn, YouTube, RSS*

Elijah Florio, Editor in Chief
Laura Sharp, Managing Editor
Guilherme Cunha, Advertising Manager, Web Developer
David Cherry, Graphic Designer

The official newsletter of the USPA.
33000 Members
Founded in 1946

22142 Running & FitNews
American Running Association
4405 East-West Highway
Suite 405
Bethesda, MD 20814

800-776-2732
800-776-2732
FAX 301-913-9520
E-Mail: milerun@americanrunning.org
Home Page: www.americanrunning.org
Social Media: *Facebook, LinkedIn*

David Watt, Executive Director
Barbara Baldwin, Projects Consultant
Jeff Venables, Editor
Jeff Harbison, President
Bill Young, Secretary/Treasurer

running, health and sports medicine e-newsletter.
Founded in 1968

22143 Sport Scene
North American Youth Sport Institute
4985 Oak Garden Drive
PO Box 957
Kernersville, NC 27285

336-784-4926
800-767-4916
FAX 336-784-5546
E-Mail: jack@naysi.com
Home Page: www.naysi.com
Social Media: *Facebook*

Jack Hutslar, Publisher/Editor

News, features, tips, reviews, statistics, and summaries for people who work with tots, children and teens in fitness, recreation, education, sport and health with the focus on management, resources latest coaching and teaching methods, do's and dont's, safety, program ideas, legal issues, and training programs for leaders. Goal is to provide current information to improve learning while making activities more safe and positive so children can have more fun.
Cost: $ 16.00
Frequency: 6X/yr
ISBN: 0-270181-2 -
Founded in 1979

22144 Team Marketing Report
Team Marketing Report
1653 North Wells St
Suite 2F
Chicago, IL 60614-3962

312-280-2311
847-256-2564
FAX 312-280-2322
E-Mail: info@teammarketing.com
Home Page: www.teammarketing.com
Social Media: *Facebook, Twitter, LinkedIn*

Becky Vallett, Executive Editor
Dan Bulla, Editor-at-Large / Director of Sales

Information on rates, ticket prices, and consumer attitudes, new ideas to help increase sales and exposure through the sports market.
Cost: $195.00
Frequency: Monthly
Founded in 1988

22145 Winning Edge Newsletter
1001 Diamond Ridge
Suite 800
Jefferson City, MO 65109

573-635-1660
FAX 573-635-8233
E-Mail: hq@somo.org
Home Page: www.somo.org
Social Media: *Facebook, Twitter, LinkedIn, YouTube, RSS*

Mark Musso, President
Mandi Steward Mueller, Public Relations Coordinator
Diannah White, Chief Communications Officer
Randy Bohem, Chair
Don Spear, Member

Publication produced for the athletes, volunteers and supports of the Special Olympics.
Frequency: Quarterly
Founded in 1983

Magazines & Journals

22146 ADDvantage
US Professional Tennis Association
3535 Briarpark Drive
Suite 1
Houston, TX 77042-5245

713-978-7782
800-877-8248
FAX 713-978-7780
E-Mail: uspta@uspta.org
Home Page: www.uspta.com

Shawna Riley, Editor
Kim Forrester, Managing Editor

A monthly magazine published by the US Professional Tennis Association. Available through membership only.
36 Pages
Frequency: Monthly
Circulation: 13,000
Founded in 1927
Printed in 4 colors on glossy stock

22147 AKWA Magazine
Aquatic Exercise Association
201 Tamiami Trail
PO Box 1609
Nokomis, FL 34274-1609

941-486-8600
888-232-9283
FAX 941-486-8820
E-Mail: register@aeawave.com
Home Page: www.aeawave.com

Angie Nelson, Executive Director
Julie See, President
Kim Huff, Director of Marketing

The aqautics fitness industry's leading magazine. Brings professionals the most up to date and innovative ideas in programming, management, safety and nutrition for group exercise and personal training in the pool. Available to AEA members with their $65.00 membership.
Circulation: 6000
Founded in 1987
Mailing list available for rent: 90M names
Printed in 4 colors on glossy stock

22148 American Bicyclist Magazine
League of American Bicyclists
1612 K St NW
Suite 800
Washington, DC 20006-2850

202-822-1333
FAX 202-822-1334
E-Mail: elizabeth@bikeleague.org
Home Page: www.bikeleague.org
Social Media: *Facebook, Twitter, LinkedIn, YouTube, RSS*

Andy Clarke, Executive Director

Contains cycling stories; how-to articles; health; legal and safety columns; legislative updates, fitness, cycling technique and travel.
Cost: $35.00
Frequency: Quarterly
Circulation: 40000
Founded in 1880
Printed in 4 colors on glossy stock

22149 American Firearms Industry
AFI Communications
2400 E Las Olas Boulevard
#397
Fort Lauderdale, FL 33301

954-467-9994
FAX 954-463-2501
E-Mail: webmaster@amfire.com
Home Page: www.amfire.com
Social Media: *Facebook, Twitter, LinkedIn*

Andrew Molchan, Editor
Alexandra Molchan, Circulation Manager
Kathleen Molchan, Sales Manager

A business-to-business trade magazine containing articles and information centered on the retailing of firearms and shooting products. Areas covered are: handguns, revolvers, pistols, rifles, shotguns, ammunition, rifle scopes, reloading, holsters, hunting accessories, gun parts, cutlery, knives, archery, bows, crossbows, camping, camouflage, black powder, smokeless powder, binoculars, safes, gunlocks, air guns, used gun news and political news and views relatingto firearms and the industry.
Cost: $18.00
Frequency: Monthly
Circulation: 34
Founded in 1973

22150 American Fitness
Aerobics and Fitness Association of America

15250 Ventura Blvd
Suite 200
Sherman Oaks, CA 91403-3297

818-905-0040
877-968-7263
FAX 818-990-5468
E-Mail: contactafaa@afaa.com
Home Page: www.afaa.com

Linda Pfeffer, President
Roscoe K Fawcett Jr, Publisher

The official publication of the Aerobics and Fitness Association of America. Known for reporting health-related fitness research, current trends, advances in equipment and training applications.
Cost: $27.00
Frequency: Bi-annually
Circulation: 100,000
Founded in 1983

22151 American Hunter
National Rifle Association
11250 Waples Mill Rd
Fairfax, VA 22030-7400

703-267-1400
877-672-2000
Home Page: americanhunter.org
Social Media: *Facebook, Twitter, LinkedIn, YouTube, RSS*

Mark A Keefe IV, Editor

American Hunter offers expertise on how and where to hunt all types of North American game and encourages readers to take advantage of the rich opportunities and to pass along the tradition to the next generation.

22152 American Paddler
American Canoe Association
7432 Alban Station Boulevard
Suite B-232
Springfield, VA 22150

703-451-0141
FAX 703-451-2245
E-Mail: aca@americancanoe.org
Home Page: www.acanet.org

Marty Bartels, Publisher

22153 American Quarter Horse Journal
American Quarter Horse Association
1600 Quarter Horse Drive
PO Box 200
Amarillo, TX 79104

806-764-4888
FAX 806-349-6400
Home Page: www.aqha.com

Bill Brewer, Executive VP
Jim Jennings, Publisher

Industry magazine for Quarter Horse breeders, farm managers and owners.
Cost: $25.00
550 Pages
Frequency: Monthly
Circulation: 66575
Founded in 1948
Printed in 4 colors on glossy stock

22154 American Rifleman
National Rifle Association
11250 Waples Mill Rd
Fairfax, VA 22030-7400

703-267-1400
800-672-3888
FAX 703-267-3971
E-Mail: publications@nrahq.org
Home Page: www.nrapublications.org
Social Media: *Facebook, Twitter, LinkedIn, YouTube, RSS*

Mark Keefe IV, Editor-In-Chief

Premier magazine for shooting and firearms enthusiasts. Coverage is devoted to rifles, shot-

guns, handguns, ammunition, reloading, optics and shooting accessories.
Cost: $35.00
Frequency: Monthly
Circulation: 100000
Founded in 1975

22155 Americas 1st Freedom
National Rifle Association
11250 Waples Mill Rd
Fairfax, VA 22030-7400

703-267-1400
877-672-2000
FAX 703-267-3971
E-Mail: publications@nrahq.org
Home Page: www.nrapublications.org
Social Media: *Facebook, Twitter, LinkedIn, YouTube, RSS*

Mark Keefe IV, Editor-In-Chief

NRA's pure news magazine. Its mission is to deliver professional, compelling, accurate, timely and hard-hitting journalism that tells the truth about the threats to our Second Amendment rights. Subscription complementary with membership in NRA. Otherwise $9.95
Founded in 1975

22156 Aquatic Therapy and Fitness Research
Aquatic Exercise Association
PO Box 1609
Nokomis, FL 34274-1609

941-486-8600
888-232-9283
FAX 941-486-8820
E-Mail: info@aeawave.com
Home Page: www.aeawave.com
Social Media: *Facebook, Twitter, LinkedIn, YouTube, RSS*

Angie Proctor, CEO
Julie See, President
Kim Huff, Director of Marketing

Journal. Peer-reviewed publication providing documented opinions of industry leaders. A multidisciplinary publication, each issue includes two focus areas. Subscription included with AEA membership.
Cost: $65.00
Frequency: Monthly
Circulation: 6000
Founded in 1984

22157 Aquatics International
Leisure Publications
6222 Wilshire Blvd.
Los Angeles, CA 90020-4244

323-644-4801
888-269-8410
FAX 323-964-4842
E-Mail: aquaticsintl@earthlink.com
Home Page: www.aquaticsintl.com
Social Media: *Facebook, Twitter, LinkedIn, YouTube, RSS*

Garry Carter, Sales Manager
Steve Honum, Account Executive
Theresa Wrong, Sales Manager

Articles of interest to colleges and schools; municipal, county and state pool facilities; hotels, resorts and country clubs; fitness clubs; rehab centers; YMCAs; military facilities; and waterparks.
Cost: $30.00
Frequency: 11X/Yr
Circulation: 30000
Mailing list available for rent

22158 Arabian Horse World
Arabian Horse World

1316 Tamsen St
Suite 101
Cambria, CA 93428-3328

805-771-2300
800-955-9423
FAX 805-927-6522
E-Mail: info@ahwmagazine.com
Home Page: www.ahwmagazine.com

Denise Hearst, Publisher

Our philosophy at Arabian Horse World is to promote the Arabian - through education and entertainment - to new levels of appreciation and usefullness. Show results and breeding farms are featured.
Cost: $40.00
Frequency: Monthly
Circulation: 15000
Founded in 1990
Printed in 4 colors on glossy stock

22159 Archery Business Magazine
Grand View Media Group
14505 21st Ave N
Suite 202
Plymouth, MN 55447

763-473-5800
800-766-0039
FAX 763-473-5801
E-Mail: pbrady@affinitygroup.com
Home Page: www.bowhuntingworld.com
Social Media: *Facebook*

Steve Schiffman, Publisher
Mark Melotik, Editor
Patty Brady, Advertising
Steven Hedlund, President

Controlled circulation trade magazine covering the business side of bowhunting and archery: trade news, industry statistics, marketing and product trends, new product research and development, tips for better business management and effective training.
Frequency: Monthly
Circulation: 11000+
Founded in 1975

22160 Arrow Trade Magazine
3479 409th Ave NW
Braham, MN 55006-3340

320-396-3473
888-796-2083
FAX 320-396-3206
E-Mail: timdehn@arrowtrademag.com
Home Page: www.arrowtrademag.com

Tim Dehn, Publisher
Matt Granger, Advertising

A business magazine published for retailers, distributors, sales representatives and manufacturers of bowhunting equipment and camouflage clothing.
Founded in 1997

22161 Athletic Management
MAG
2488 N Triphammer Road
Ithaca, NY 14850

607-257-6970
FAX 607-257-7328
E-Mail: info@athleticbid.com
Home Page: www.momentummedia.com

Mark Goldberg, President
Eleanor Frankel, Editor

Free to college athletic administrators and high school athletic directors in the US and Canada. The editorial mission of Athletic Management is to help Athletic Directors enhance their operations, to share new ideas, and cover pertinent news topics. Feature stories and regular sections address the various facets of managing an

athletic department.
Cost: $25.00
Frequency: Weekly
Circulation: 30200
Founded in 1988
Printed in 4 colors on glossy stock

22162 Bass Times
ESPN

334-272-9530
E-Mail: customerservice@bassmaster.com
Home Page:
sports.espn.go.com/outdoors/bassmaster

Bass Times is packed with news and information for serious bass fishermen. The perfect compliment to Bassmaster Magazine.
Cost: $12.00
Frequency: Monthly

22163 Bassmaster
ESPN

334-272-9530
E-Mail: advertising@basmaster.com
Home Page: sports.espn.go.com/bassmaster
Social Media: *Facebook, Twitter, LinkedIn, YouTube, RSS*

Bassmaster Magazine monthly.
Frequency: Monthly

22164 Black's Buyers Directory
PO Box 2029
Red Bank, NJ 07701

732-224-8700
800-224-9464
FAX 732-741-2827
E-Mail: ms-blacks@attglobal.net
Home Page: www.fieldandstream.com
Social Media: *Facebook, Twitter, LinkedIn, YouTube, RSS*

James F Black Jr, Publisher
Lois Re, Editor
Christopher Pluck, Owner

The complete buyer's guide to equipment. A one-stop source of information on anything and everything that's archery/bowhunting.
Founded in 2001

22165 Bowlers Journal International
Luby Publishing Company
122 S Michigan Ave
Suite 1506
Chicago, IL 60603-6148

312-341-1110
FAX 312-341-1469
E-Mail: email@bowlersjournal.com
Home Page: www.lubypublishing.com

Keith Hamilton, President
Mason King, Editor
Emily Kupper, Circulation Director
Bob Nieman, Editor

Information geared toward all levels of industry personnel. Regular issue features include new products listings, tournament reviews, personality profiles and proprietor workshops.
Cost: $24.00
Frequency: Monthly
Circulation: 22319
Founded in 1913

22166 Bowling Center Management
Bowling Proprietors Association of America
122 S Michigan Avenue
Suite 1506
Chicago, IL 60603-6107

312-341-1110
FAX 312-341-1180
E-Mail: bowlctrman@aol.com

Home Page: www.bcmmag.com
Social Media: *Facebook, Twitter, LinkedIn*

Mike Panozzo, Publisher
Bob Nieman, Editor
Emily Kupper, Circulation Director
Mason King, Editor

Information designed for bowling center owners to help them in the operation and management of their centers.
Cost: $60.00
Frequency: Monthly
Circulation: 5000
Founded in 1995

22167 By Design
American Society of Golf Course Architects
125 N Executive Dr
Suite 302
Brookfield, WI 53005-6035

262-786-5960
FAX 262-786-5919
E-Mail: info@asgca.org
Home Page: www.asgca.org
Social Media: *Facebook, Twitter*

Chad Ritterbusch, Executive Director

E-Magazine highlighting the work of ASGCA golf course architects worldwide. Subscribe at no charge at www.asgca.org
185 Members
Frequency: Quarterly
Circulation: 6000
Founded in 1946

22168 Camping Magazine
American Camp Association
5000 State Road 67 N
Martinsville, IN 46151-7902

765-342-8456
800-428-2267
FAX 765-342-2065
E-Mail: pr@acacamps.org
Home Page: www.acacamps.org
Social Media: *Facebook, Twitter, LinkedIn*

Peg Smith, CEO
Kim Bruno, Communication/Development Head
Terrie Nicodemus, Manager

The official publication of the American Camp Association. Experts in the camp field contribute informative articles and essays on current advances in camp management, staffing and human resources, programming, risk management, special populations and diversity, health and wellness, and more.
Cost: $24.95
Founded in 1920
Mailing list available for rent

22169 Coaching Management
MAG
2488 N Triphammer Road
Ithaca, NY 14850-5220

607-257-6970
FAX 607-257-7328
E-Mail: info@athleticbid.com
Home Page: www.momentummedia.com
Social Media: *Facebook, Twitter, LinkedIn*

Mark Goldberg, Publisher/CEO
Eleanor Frankel, Editor
Dave Dubin, Circulation Director

Information including team equipment, apparel, injury prevention, conditioning, as well as field, stadium and court maintenance and improvement. Primary feature articles cover a wide range of coaching tools and techniques.
Frequency: Bi-annually
Circulation: 20556
Founded in 1988
Mailing list available for rent

22170 Coaching Volleyball
American Volleyball Coaches Association
2365 Harrodsburg Road
Suite A325
Lexington, KY 40504

859-226-4315
866-544-2822
FAX 859-226-4338
E-Mail: members@avca.org
Home Page: www.avca.org
Social Media: *Facebook, Twitter, LinkedIn, YouTube, RSS*

Leah DeBoer, Executive Director
Leah Brock, Communications Manager
Frequency: Bi-Monthly

22171 Cross Country Skier
PO Box 550
Cable, WI 54821

715-798-5500
800-827-0607
FAX 715-798-3599
E-Mail: info@crosscountryskier.com
Home Page: www.crosscountryskier.com
Social Media: *Facebook, Twitter, LinkedIn*

Ron Bergin, Owner

The journal of nordic skiing - destinations, news, training and technique, waxing, competition, equipment and new products, and great features on all facets of the sport of cross country skiing.

22172 Cutting Horse Chatter
National Cutting Horse Association
260 Bailey Avenue
Fort Worth, TX 76107

817-244-6188
FAX 817-244-2015
E-Mail: info@nchacutting.com
Home Page: www.nchacutting.com

Chubby Turner, President
Chris Benedict, VP
Jeff Hooper, Executive Director
Rick Ivey, Tresurer
Alan Gold, Director Marketing
Frequency: Monthly
Circulation: 20500

22173 Deer & Deer Hunting
F+W Media
38 E. 29th Street
New York, NY 10016

212-447-1400
FAX 212-447-5231
E-Mail: contact_us@fwmedia.com
Home Page: www.fwpublications.com

Hugh McAloon, Publisher

Edited for serious, year-round whitetail hunting enthusiasts and focuses on hunting techniques, deer biology and behavior, deer management, habitat requirements, the natural history of deer, and hunting ethics. Contains how-to articles designed to help hunters be successful. Regular columns and departments include book reviews, Deer Browse (unusual observations by hunters), new products, an editor's column, letters from readers, Deer Behavior, Can You Outsmart This Deer? and Q&A.
Cost: $19.99
Circulation: 212500
Founded in 1977
Mailing list available for rent

22174 Fantasy Sports
F+W Media
38 E. 29th Street
New York, NY 10016

212-447-1400
FAX 212-447-5231

E-Mail: contact_us@fwmedia.com
Home Page: www.fwpublications.com

Tom Kessenich, Editor
David Nussbaum, Chair
Jim Ogle, Finance/Administration
Sara Domville, President
Phil Graham, VP

The essential manual for those who participate in Rotisserie and other fantasy sports leagues. Reports extensive statistics to help managers in making personnel moves. Also includes recommendations on who to draft or trade. The April and May issues focus on baseball. The August and September issues focus on football. An up-to-the-minute, online version is also available fo a small fee at www.fantasysportsmag.com
Cost: $9.97
132 Pages
Frequency: 4 Per Year
Circulation: 78,767
Founded in 1989
Mailing list available for rent

22175 Fastpitch Delivery

National Fastpitch Coaches Association
2641 Grinstead Drive,
Suite D
Louisville, KY 42046

502-409-4600
FAX 502-409-4622
E-Mail: nfca@nfca.org
Home Page: www.nfca.org
Social Media: *Facebook, Twitter, LinkedIn, YouTube, RSS*

Lacy Lee Baker, Executive Director
Hildred Deese, Senior Director of Events
Frequency: Monthly
Founded in 1982

22176 Fishermen's News

Philip's Publishing Group
2201 W Commodore Way
Seattle, WA 98199-1298

206-284-8285
800-258-8609
FAX 206-284-0391
E-Mail: circulation@rhppublishing.com
Home Page: www.pacmar.com

Peter Philips, Publisher
Lisa Albers, Managing Editor
Bill Forslund, Advertising Manager
Maggie Cheung, Circulation Manager
Sharon Adjiri, Production Manager

In addition to important fisheries news, every month they bring readers important information and lessons on Safety, entertaining pieces about commercial fishing history, a commercial listing of fishing vessels and equipment in their classified section, updated information on seafood market trends and important notices about all the meetings and conferences occurring on the West Coast.
Cost: $21.00
Frequency: Monthly
Circulation: 14,933
Founded in 1945
Printed in 4 colors on newsprint stock

22177 Fishing Tackle Retailer

ESPN Productions
3500 Blue Lake Drive
Birmingham, AL 35243

407-566-2277
FAX 334-279-7148
E-Mail: customerservice@bassmaster.com
Home Page: www.bassmaster.com
Social Media: *Facebook, Twitter, LinkedIn, YouTube, RSS*

Clem Dippel, Publisher
Scott Wall, Advertising Sales

Information to inform and instruct America's fishing tackle retailers, merchandisers, and distributors on merchandise and sales techniques used to sell fishing tackle.
Cost: $4.00
Frequency: 11X/yr
Circulation: 17720
Founded in 1980
Printed in 4 colors

22178 Funworld

Int'l Association of Amusement Parks & Attractions
1448 Duke St
Alexandria, VA 22314-3403

703-836-3677
FAX 703-836-2824
E-Mail: alee@IAAPA.org
Home Page: www.iaapa.org
Social Media: *Facebook, Twitter, LinkedIn, YouTube*

Charlie Bray, President/CEO
Susan Mosedale, Executive VP
Jan McCool, Executive
Roxanne Pope, Assistant to the President

Funworld Magazine is a service for IAAPA members and provides discussion and illustrative examinations of the amusement and attractions industry form members to stay current and connected. The magazine contains features that analyze various aspects of the amusement business including safety, thrill rides, financial issues, event coverage and profiles of member and nonmember facilities from around the world.
Cost: $45.00
Circulation: 8,500
Founded in 1917

22179 Golf Business

National Golf Course Owners Association
291 Seven Farms Dr
Suite 2
Daniel Island, SC 29492-8000

843-881-9956
800-933-4262
FAX 843-856-3288
E-Mail: golfbusiness@ngcoa.org
Home Page: www.ngcoa.org
Social Media: *Facebook, Twitter, YouTube*

Michael Hughes, CEO
Joe Rice, Publisher
Frank Santangelo, Manager

The official publication of the National Golf Course Owners Association. The editorial content is designed to promote the exchange of information and ideas among course owners and senior industry executives to improve the profitability of their operations. Golf Business is dedicated to serving the entire interest of the golf course operation.
Cost: $35.00
Frequency: Monthly
Circulation: 20000
Founded in 1971
Printed in 4 colors on glossy stock

22180 Golf Course Management

Golf Course Superintendents Association of America
1421 Research Park Dr
Lawrence, KS 66049-3859

785-841-2240
800-472-7878
FAX 785-832-4488
E-Mail: ehiscock@gcsaa.org
Home Page: www.gcsaa.org
Social Media: *Facebook, Twitter*

Mark Woodward, CEO
Scott Hollistor, Editor
Bunny Smith, Managing Editor

Mark Gabrick, Sr Manager Corp Sales/Marketing

Official monthly magazine of Golf Course Superintendents Association of America and golf course management industry's leading professional journal. Includes scientific, technical and practical management articles.
Cost: $60.00
Frequency: Monthly
Circulation: 40,000
Founded in 1932

22181 Golf Course News

4012 Bridge Avenue
Cleveland, OH 44113

216-961-4130
FAX 216-961-0364
Home Page: www.golfcoursenews.com

Kevin Gilbride, Publisher
John Walsh, Editor
Richard Foster, CEO
Chris Foster, President/COO
Doug Adams, Director Marketing

Focuses on course maintenance and management, new course openings, and awards and promotions. New products related to the industry and environment and government issues.
Cost: $45.00
Circulation: 30000

22182 Golf Inc Magazine

Cypress Manazines
250 Bei Marin Key Boulevard, #A
PO Box 1150
Novato, CA 94949-5727

415-382-2400
800-436-6149
FAX 415-382-2416
E-Mail: mikeb@cypressmagazines.com
Home Page: www.cyspressmagazines.com

Jack Crittenden, President
Kim Boalick, Advertising
Mindy Heral, Marketing
Jim Dunlap, Editor-in-Chief

Provides news, success stories and benchmark data for all aspects of the golf course industry - including development, operations, marketing, retail, turf, sales and driving range.
Cost: $65.00
Frequency: Monthly
Circulation: 15000

22183 Golf Range Times

Forecast Golf Group
P.O.Box 3106
Glen Allen, VA 23058-3106

804-379-5760
FAX 804-378-5780
E-Mail: info@forecastgolf.com
Home Page: www.forecastgolf.com

James E Turner, Publisher/Editor
Betty Jo Bass, Advertising Manager

Information on Golf Range industry changes and closings, new ranges, and development information and services.
Cost: $49.95
Frequency: Monthly
Circulation: 6000
Founded in 1990

22184 Golfdom

Questex Medica Group
PO Bo 5057
Brentwood, TN 37024

615-377-3322
866-344-1315
FAX 615-377-3322
E-Mail: questex@sunbeltfs.com
Home Page: www.golfdom.com

Patrick Jones, Publisher
Larry Aylward, Editor

Publication is written for golf course architects, superintendents, management companies, owners, developers, consultants and others in the industry with an interest in golf course design, construction, remodeling and related business and management topics. Subscription is free to Golf course superintendents, owners and managers. Individuals who are not qualified as superintendents, owners and managers can subscribe at the current subscription rate.
Cost: $30.00
Circulation: 3000
Founded in 1927

22185 Government Recreation & Fitness

Executive Business Media
825 Old Country Road
PO Box 1500
Westbury, NY 11590

516-334-3030
FAX 516-334-3059
E-Mail: ebm-mail@ebmpubs.com
Home Page: www.ebmpubs.com

Murry Greenwald, Publisher
Paul Ragnoz, Managing Editor

Government Recreation and Fitness reaches recreation and fitness professionals in every department and agency of the federal government, goes directly to the people who purchase your products, and covers both appropriated and nonappropriated fund budgets. Subscription is free to managers and operators of fitness centers and recreation facilities at US military bases, federal agencies and offices as well as procurement agents for these facilities and others allied to the field
Cost: $35.00
Frequency: 15 issues per year
Circulation: 9974
ISSN: 1086-7899
Founded in 1994
Printed in 4 colors on glossy stock

22186 Gun & Knife Show Calendar

F+W Media
38 E. 29th Street
New York, NY 10016

212-447-1400
FAX 212-447-5231
E-Mail: contact_us@fwmedia.com
Home Page: www.fwpublications.com
Social Media: *Twitter*

Hugh McAloon, Publisher
Bruce Wolberg, Ad Manager
John Koenig, Editor'

A compilation of gun shows and knife shows held throughout the country, and is intended to be used as a complete guide for anyone who attends or displays at these shows. Regular listings include the dates of the show, the address, the city, state, number of tables, and the cost of tables. For attendees, the show hours and the cost of admission are listed. Shows are listed for a full year ahead and there is no charge to list a show.
Cost: $15.95
88 Pages
Frequency: Quarterly
Circulation: 5758
Founded in 1952

22187 Hockey Business News

Straight Line Communications
12327 Santa Monica Boulevard
#202
Los Angeles, CA 90025-2552

310-207-9916
FAX 310-442-6663
E-Mail: hbn@artnet.net

Mark Brown, Publisher

Features articles on ice hockey news and events, Canadian and international news, industry trends and forecasts and new products.
Cost: $60.00
Frequency: 9 per year
Circulation: 5,000

22188 Horseman's Journal

National Horsemen's Administration Corporation
870 Corporate Drive
Suite 300
Lexington, KY 40503

859-259-0451
866-245-1711
FAX 859-259-0452
E-Mail: racing@hpba.org
Home Page: www.hbpa.org

Richard E Glover, Editor
Sandy Erreguin, Advertising Director

Official magazine of the National Horsemen's Benevolent and Protective Association. Designed to give owners and trainers of racehorses information helpful for the running of their horse related businesses.
56 Pages
Circulation: 32,000
Founded in 1942
Printed in 4 colors on glossy stock

22189 ISI EDGE

Ice Skating Institute
600 Custer Rd
Bldg 9
Plano, TX 75023

972-735-8800
FAX 972-735-8815
E-Mail: isi@skateisi.org
Home Page: www.skateisi.org

Peter Martell, Executive Director

Professional journal for the ice skating industry. Focuses on the needs and interests of the industry's managers, skating and hockey directors, instructors, and builders/suppliers.
Frequency: Bi-Monthly

22190 Inside Archery

2960 N Academy Boulevard
Suite 101
Colorado Springs, CO 80917

719-495-9999
FAX 719-495-8899
E-Mail: info@insidearchery.com
Home Page: www.fieldandstream.com
Social Media: *Twitter, LinkedIn*

Bill Krenz, President/Editor
Sherry Krenz, VP/Publisher

The Archery Industry Authority
Founded in 1997

22191 International Bowling Industry

13245 Riverside Drive
Suite 501
Sherman Oaks, CA 91423

818-789-2695
FAX 818-789-2812
E-Mail: info@bowlingindustry.com
Home Page: www.bowlingindustry.com
Social Media: *Twitter, LinkedIn*

Scott Frager, Publisher & Editor
Nick West, Associate Publisher
Fred Groh, Managing Editor
Patty Heath, Office Manager

Information on customer services, new products, industry trends, new concepts in management and marketing techniques, and employee motivation.
Cost: $32.00
Frequency: Monthly
Circulation: 10,205

22192 International Gaming and Wagering Business

BNP Media
PO Box 1080
Skokie, IL 60076-9785

847-763-9534
FAX 847-763-9538
E-Mail: igwb@halldata.com
Home Page: www.igwb.com

James Rutherford, Editor
Lynn Davidson, Marketing
Tammie Gizicki, Director

Focuses on business strategy, legislative information, food service and promotional concerns.
Frequency: Monthly
Circulation: 25000

22193 Journal of Sport and Social Issues

Sage Publications
2455 Teller Road
Newbury Park, CA 91320

800-818-7243
FAX 800-583-2665
E-Mail: journals@sagepub.com
Home Page: www.sagepublications.com
Social Media: *Facebook*

CL Cole, Editor

Brings together the latest research, discussion and analysis on contemporary sport issues.
Cost: $552.00
Frequency: Quarterly
ISSN: 0193-7235

22194 Lacrosse Magazine

113 W University Pkwy
Baltimore, MD 21210-3301

410-235-6882
FAX 410-366-6735
E-Mail: info@uslacrosse.org
Home Page: www.laxmagazine.com
Social Media: *Facebook, Twitter, LinkedIn, Live Blogs*

Steve Stenersen, President
Bill Schoonmaker, COO
Bill Rubacky, Managing Director of Marketing
Kira Muller, Director of Advertising Sales

The most widely circulated publication for the sport of lacrosse, Lacrosse Magazine connects the sport's community, educates players, coaches and officials, entertains fans and keeps the membership of US Lacrosse informed.
Frequency: Monthly
Circulation: 300M
ISSN: 1069-5893
Founded in 1982

22195 Master Skier

PO Box 187
Escabana, MI 49829

906-789-1139
E-Mail: mskier@chartermi.net
Home Page: www.masterskier.com

Journal dedicated to the skiing industry. Delivered to 51,000 readers in 19 countries.
Founded in 1986
Mailing list available for rent

22196 Medicine and Science in Sports and Exercise

American College of Sports Medicine
401 W Michigan Street
PO Box 1440
Indianapolis, IN 46206

317-347-7817
FAX 317-634-7817
E-Mail: msse@acsm.org
Home Page: www.acsm.org

Kent B Pandolf, Editor-in-Chief
Gay Smith, Editor

Scientific research, education, and practical applications of sports medicine and exercise science to maintain and enhance physical performance, fitness, health and quality of life.
Cost: $300.00
Frequency: Monthly
Circulation: 14842
ISSN: 0195-9131
Founded in 1968
Printed in 4 colors on matte stock

22197 Military Trader
F+W Media
38 E. 29th Street
New York, NY 10016

212-447-1400
FAX 212-447-5231
E-Mail: contact_us@fwmedia.com
Home Page: www.fwpublications.com
Social Media: *Facebook, Twitter, LinkedIn, Live Blogs*

Rick Groth, Publisher
John Adams-Graf, Editor
David Nussbaum, Chair
Jim Ogle, Finance
David Blansfield, President

For military collectors, the best monthly source of news, features, collecting advice, shows, and events. Each issue offers thousands of 'For Sale' and 'Wanted' mlitary collectibles from hundreds of dealers and collectors. This is where to go when you are trying to buy or sell vintage military uniforms, pins, medals, helmets, ammunition, firearms, flags, and other militaria.
Cost: $19.00
56 Pages
Frequency: Monthly
Circulation: 9414
Founded in 1975

22198 Military Vehicles
F+W Media
38 E. 29th Street
New York, NY 10016

212-447-1400
FAX 212-447-5231
E-Mail: contact_us@fwmedia.com
Home Page: www.fwpublications.com
Social Media: *Facebook, Twitter, LinkedIn, Live Blogs*

Bill Reed, President
John Adams-Graf, Editor
David Nussbaum, Chair
Jim Ogle, Finance
David Blansfield, President

Each issue includes news, vintage military photos, collecting advice, market information, show listings, and extensive display and classified advertising sections offering to buy and sell hundreds of jeeps, tanks, trucks, vehicle parts, and accessories from dealers and enthusiasts all over the world. Other regular features include book and media reviews, letters to the editor, tech topics, weapons & replicas, models & toys, and internet sightings.
Cost: $23.98
176 Pages
Circulation: 19,000
Founded in 1952

22199 NJCAA Review
National Junior College Athletic Association
1631 Mesa Ave Suite B
Suite 103
Colorado Springs, CO 80920

719-590-9788
FAX 719-590-7324
E-Mail: meleicht@njcaa.org

Home Page: www.njcaa.org
Social Media: *Facebook, Twitter*

Mary Ellen Leicht, Executive Director
Mark Krug, Director Sports Information/Media
Marry Elen, Director
Dee Dorus, Administrative Assistant
Cost: $30.00
Frequency: 10x/Year
Circulation: 2500
Founded in 1989

22200 NRA InSights
National Rifle Association
11250 Waples Mill Rd
Fairfax, VA 22030-7400

703-267-1400
800-672-3888
Home Page: www.nrapublilcations.org
Social Media: *Twitter, LinkedIn*

NRAs official publication for its Junior members. Designed to motivate its readers to participate in all aspects of the shooting sports. Features personality profiles on top junior shooters, hunting stories, how-to pieces, program announcements, product surveys, safety features and educational information about firearms. Subscription included in membership dues.

22201 Online Magazine
Information Today
143 Old Marlton Pike
Medford, NJ 08055-8750

609-654-6266
800-300-9868
FAX 609-654-4309
E-Mail: custserv@infotoday.com
Home Page: www.infotoday.com

Thomas H Hogan, President
Roger R Bilboul, Chairman Of The Board

Online is written for information professionals and provides articles, product reviews, case studies, evaluation and informed opinion about selecting, using and managing electronic information products, plus industry and professional information about onlline database systems.
Cost: $115.00
Frequency: Monthly
Founded in 1976

22202 Outdoors Magazine
Elk Publishing
531 Main St
Colchester, VT 05446-7222

802-879-2013
800-499-0447
FAX 802-860-0005
E-Mail: info@outdoorsmagazine.net
Home Page: www.elkpublishing.com

James Austin, Publisher

A monthly publication covering hunting, fishing and wildlife issues in Vermont, New York, Maine, Massachusetts and Connecticut.
Cost: $18.95
Frequency: Monthly
Circulation: 10000
ISSN: 1096-1976
Founded in 1996
Printed in 4 colors on matte stock

22203 PGA TOUR Partners Magazine
North American Media Group
12301 Whitewater Dr
Suite 260
Minnetonka, MN 55343-4103

952-936-9333
800-688-7611
FAX 952-936-9169
E-Mail: NAMGhq@namginc.com
Home Page: www.namginc.com

Seth Hoyt, Publisher

An exclusive, members-only publication filled with tips and techniques that can be used to improve your game, from the first tee to the 18th green.
Frequency: Bi-Monthly
Circulation: 1.3 m
Founded in 1978

22204 PTR International Tennis Symposium
Professional Tennis Registry
PO Box 4739
Hilton Head Island, SC 29938

843-785-7244
800-421-6289
FAX 843-686-2033
E-Mail: ptr@ptrtennis.org
Home Page: www.ptrtennis.org
Social Media: *Facebook, Twitter*

Dan Santoruk, CEO
Julie Jilly, VP/Operations

To provide education and information for PTR members.
14m Members
Frequency: 6x Annually
Circulation: 15,000
Founded in 1976

22205 Paddler
Paddle Sport Publishing
122 South Orange Av.
Steamboat Springs, CO 80477-5450

970-879-1450
888-774-7554
FAX 970-870-1404
E-Mail: circulation@paddlermagazine.com
Home Page: www.paddlermagazine.com

Eugene Buchanan, Publisher/Editor
Tom Bie, Managing Editor

Each issues is filled with stories on places to paddle, skill enhancement, gear reviews, environmental issues, industry updats and profiles of leading paddlers.
Cost: $18.00
Frequency: Monthly
Circulation: 5527
Printed in 4 colors on glossy stock

22206 Parachutist Magazine
United States Parachute Association
5401 Southpoint Centre Blvd
Fredericksburg, VA 22407-2612

540-604-9740
FAX 540-604-9741
E-Mail: uspa@uspa.org
Home Page: www.uspa.org
Social Media: *Facebook, Twitter*

Jay Stokes, President
Randy Allison, VP
Sherry Butcher, Secretary & National Director
Lee Schlichtemeier, Treasurer
Jan Meyer, National Director

Supporting safe skydiving and those individuals who practice the sport. The magazine discusses issues dealing with training, safety, equipment, and networking the worldwide community of skydivers.
Cost: $4.50
112 Pages
Frequency: Monthly
Circulation: 35000
Founded in 1946

22207 Pool and Spa News
Leisure Publications
6222 Wilshire Blvd
Los Angeles, CA 90020-4244

323-644-4801
888-269-8410
FAX 323-801-4986
E-Mail: poolspanews@hanleywood.com

Home Page: www.poolspanews.com
Social Media: *Facebook, Twitter, LinkedIn*

Dick Coleman, Publisher
Erika Taylor, Editor
Steve Schlange, Marketing Manager
Scot Christ, Accountant

Pool and Spa News goals are: to furnish information to help pool and spa professionals function better in their businesses; to showcase products that can be sold or used in the industry; to help make their business life easier and more rewarding.
Cost: $16.50
Frequency: Semi-Monthly
Founded in 1960
Mailing list available for rent

22208 Powersports Business
Ehlert Publishing Group
3300 Fernbrook Lane N
Suite 200
Plymouth, MN 55447

763-383-4400
800-848-6247
FAX 763-383-4499
E-Mail:
customerservice@powersportsbusiness.com
Home Page: www.powersportsbusiness.com
Social Media: *Facebook, Twitter, LinkedIn*

Mark Adams, CEO
Dave McMahon, Editor

Gives dealers, distributors, and manufacturers timely business news and analysis every three weeks.
Frequency: Weekly
Circulation: 18000
Founded in 1969

22209 Pro Football Weekly
302 Saunders Rd
Suite 100
Riverwoods, IL 60015-3897

847-940-1100
800-331-7529
FAX 847-940-1108
E-Mail: editors@pfwmedia.com
Home Page: www.profootballweekly.com
Social Media: *Facebook, Twitter, LinkedIn*

Hub Arkush, President

Seeks to bring the best coverage in the NFL to its readers.
Cost: $49.95
Frequency: Weekly
Founded in 1967

22210 Professional Skater
Professional Skaters Association
3006 Allegro Park Ln SW
Rochester, MN 55902-4159

507-280-6812
FAX 507-281-5491
E-Mail: office@skatepsa.com
Home Page: www.skatepsa.com

Jimmie Santee, Executive Director

A bi-monthly magazine published by the Professional Skater Association.
Cost: $19.95
40 Pages
Frequency: Bi-Monthly
Founded in 1984

22211 QUAD Off-Road Magazine
Transworld Publishing
Ste 150
2052 Corte Del Nogal
Carlsbad, CA 92011-1491

760-722-7777
FAX 760-722-0653

E-Mail: jasonyoung@twsnet.com
Home Page: www.neodata.com

Jason Young, Publication Contact

Quad off-road magazine delivers all things ATV: Breathtaking photography, tons of practical tips, the hottest nwe products, Quad comparison tests, ARV adventure stories, and much more.
Cost: $9.97
Frequency: Monthly

22212 Quarter Horse Racing Journal
American Quarter Horse Association
PO Box 200
Amarillo, TX 79168-0001

806-376-4811
FAX 806-349-6411
Home Page: www.aqha.com
Social Media: *Facebook, Twitter, LinkedIn, You Tube*

Jim Helzer, President

News and races, health and management, business and industry, winner's circle, the handicapper, horse health, quarter paths, sports medicine, finish line and others are featured articles.
Frequency: Monthly

22213 Racquetball Magazine
USA Racquetball
4244 Russet Court
Lilburn, GA 80904-2906

770-972-2303
FAX 719-635-0685
E-Mail: rjohn@usra.org
Home Page: www.racqmag.com

Jim Hiser, Executive Director
Kevin Joyce, Director Membership
Melody Weiss, Director Finance
Heather Fender, Executive Assistant/Event Coord
Ed Mazur, President

Geared toward a readership of informed, active enthusiasts who seek entertainment, instruction and accurate reporting of events. Available by subscription through the US Racquetball Association National Office.
Cost: $20.00
64 Pages
Frequency: Bi-Monthly
Circulation: 16,000
ISSN: 1060-877X
Founded in 1990
Printed in 4 colors on glossy stock

22214 Recreational Ice Skating
Ice Skating Institute
6000 Custer Rd
Bldg 9
Plano, TX 75023

972-735-8800
FAX 972-735-8815
E-Mail: editor@skateisi.org
Home Page: www.skateisi.org

Peter Martell, Executive Director

Distributed to ISI individual skater members, skating coaches, and rinks and pro shops worldwide. Written for and about ice skating enthusiasts and focuses on promoting ice skating as recreation and sport.
Frequency: Quarterly

22215 Referee
National Association of Sports Officials
2017 Lathrop Ave
Racine, WI 53405-3758

262-632-5448
800-733-6100
FAX 262-632-5460
E-Mail: questions@referee.com

Home Page: www.referee.com
Social Media: *Facebook, Twitter, LinkedIn*

Barry Mano, President

Monthly magazine published by the National Association of Sports Officials. Containes interviews, feature articles, late-breaking news, personality profiles, investigative reports, health, legal and tax tips, and a wide range of technical information for many sports.
Cost: $44.95
80 Pages
Frequency: Monthly
Circulation: 77000
Founded in 1976
Printed in 4 colors on glossy stock

22216 Ride BMX
Transworld Magazines
353 Airport Road
Oceanside, CA 92054

760-722-7777
FAX 760-722-0653
E-Mail: jasonyoung@twsnet.com
Home Page: www.neodata.com
Social Media: *Facebook, Twitter, LinkedIn*

Jason Young, Publication Contact

Publication with information for BMX riders.
Cost: $15.97
Frequency: Monthly

22217 Rodale's Scuba Diving
F+W Media
38 E. 29th Street
New York, NY 10016

212-447-1400
FAX 212-447-5231
E-Mail: contact_us@fwmedia.com
Home Page: www.fwpublications.com
Social Media: *Facebook, Twitter, LinkedIn*

Edited to provide information about the practice of diving, dive travel opportunities, the marine environment, the reader's health and safety and the dive equipment on which they depend. Travel editorial focuses on both domestic and international dive travel and equipment editorial offers readers comparative product reviews.
Cost: $16.97
Frequency: 11 Per Year
Circulation: 187,059
Founded in 1992

22218 Shooting Illustrated
National Rifle Association
11250 Waples Mill Rd
Fairfax, VA 22030-7400

703-267-1400
877-672-2000
Home Page: www.nrapublications.org
Social Media: *Facebook, Twitter, LinkedIn*

Aaron Carter, Associate Editor

Comprehensive, timely and all-inclusive. In its pages you will find the best gun writers in the world, assembled to bring you the latest information on rifles, pistols or shotguns. From handloading to gunsmithing to highpower competition; from varmint rifles to rifles for the world's biggest game; from competition pistols to heavy field revolvers.
Cost: $9.95

22219 Shooting Industry
12345 World Trade Drive
San Diego, CA 92128-3102

858-674-4898
858-605-0254
FAX 619-297-5353
E-Mail: subs@shootingindustry.com

Home Page: www.shootingindustry.com
Social Media: *Facebook, Twitter, LinkedIn*

Russ Thurman, Editor
Brian Friesen, Sales Manager

A trade publication covering the hunting and shooting industries. This publication is available to select dealers and select police personnel only. Dealers must have a current Federal Firearms License and no less than two additional credentials. Police personnel must have a letter from their Police Chief or Range Officer requesting a subscription (on department letterhead).
Cost: $25.00
Frequency: Monthly
Founded in 1955

22220 Shooting Sports Retailer

SSR Communications
200 Croft Street
Suite 1
Birmingham, AL 35242

205-408-3766
FAX 212-944-1884
E-Mail: stuart@grandviewmedia.com
Home Page: www.shootingsportsretailer.com

Glenn Karaban, President

Features articles on shooting sports equipment, sales techniques, new products, sales aids, and potential problems for the wholesale seller of shooting equipment.
Frequency: Monthly
Circulation: 17463
Founded in 1980

22221 Shooting Sports USA

National Rifle Association
11250 Waples Mill Rd
Fairfax, VA 22030-7400

703-267-1400
877-672-2000
Home Page: www.nrapublications.org
Social Media: *Facebook, Twitter*

Information for the competitive shooter, from smallbore to high power, air action pistol and everything in between.
Cost: $9.95

22222 Single Shot Rifle Journal

American Single Shot Rifle Association
PO Box 1162
Niles, MI 49120

269-687-9550
E-Mail: journaleditor@assra.com
Home Page: www.assra.com

Gary Staup, President
John Merz, VP
D. Wayne Stiles, Editor

The official magazine of The American Single Shot Rifle Association. Susbscription is included with membership in the ASSRA.
Cost: $35.00
60 Pages
Frequency: Bi-Monthly
Circulation: 2400
Founded in 1948
Printed in on matte stock

22223 Ski Area Management

Beardsley Publishing Corporation
45 Main Street North
PO Box 644
Woodbury, CT 06798

203-263-0888
FAX 203-266-0452
E-Mail: news@saminfo.com
Home Page: www.saminfo.com

Jennifer Rowan, Publisher
Olivia Rowan, Marketing/Associate Publisher
Donna Jacobs, V.P./Administration

Rick Kahl, Editor
Ann Hasper, Senior Editor

SAM magazine is the professional trade publication for the mountain resort market. It is a bi-monthly, all-paid publication.
Cost: $48.00
Frequency: Monthly
Circulation: 3992
Founded in 1962
Printed in 4 colors on glossy stock

22224 Ski Magazine

929 Pearl Street
5720 Flatiron Parkway
Boulder, CO 80301

303-448-7600
800-678-0817
FAX 303-442-6321
E-Mail: subsvcs@ski.customersvc.com
Home Page: www.skimag.com
Social Media: *Facebook, Twitter, LinkedIn, You Tube*

Kendall Hamilton, Editor-In-Chief
Greg Ditrinco, Executive Editor
Kim Beekman, Managing Editor
Samantha Berman, Senior Editor

Includes information on travel, gear, instruction, snow reports, mountain cams, and gift shops.
Cost: $11.00
Frequency: 8X/year

22225 SkiTrax Magazine

260 Spadina Avenue
Suite 200
Toronto, Canada M5V1P9, ON

416-977-2100
866-754-8729
FAX 416-977-9200
E-Mail: skitrax@passport.ca
Home Page: www.skitrax.com
Social Media: *Facebook, Twitter, LinkedIn, You Tube*

North America's premier nordic publication is the official magazine of the USSA and CCC and offers the broadest coverage of nordic skiing available. Coverage includes comprehensive Annual North American Buyer's Guide; local touring centers and exotic backcountry hide-a-ways; complete North American and international competition coverage; regular tips on products; training, technique, telemark, masters, and waxing; extensive calendar of events; plus much more.

22226 Soccer Journal

National Soccer Coaches Association of America
6700 Squibb Road
Suite 215
Mission, KS 66202

913-362-1747
800-458-0678
FAX 913-362-3439
E-Mail: info@nscca.com
Home Page: www.nscaa.com

The official publication of the National Soccer Coaches of America. Produced exclusively for soccer coaches. Each issue contains technical and tactical articles, news and updates on important events, thoughts from opinion leaders in the sport and features on the interesting people and issues of the game. Subscription included in NSCAA membership.
Cost: $50.00
Frequency: 8X/Year
Circulation: 18000
Founded in 1941

22227 Speedway Illustrated

Speedway Illustrated

107 Elm St
Salisbury, MA 01952-1803

978-465-9099
888-837-3684
FAX 978-465-9033
E-Mail: editorial@speedwayillustrated.com
Home Page: www.speedwayillustrated.com

Dick Berggren, VP
Steve Chryssos, Advertising Manager
Lynne Henry, Advertising Sales

They'll show you how to build and race your own car, and take you inside at NASCAR's hottest teams and stars.
Cost: $19.94
Frequency: Monthly
Circulation: 150000
Founded in 2000

22228 Sporting Goods Business

VNU Business Publications
2900 Veterans Hwy
Bristol, PA 19007-1606

847-763-9050
800-464- 759
FAX 847-763-9037
E-Mail: info@sgdealer.com
Home Page: www.sportinggoodsbusiness.com
Social Media: *Facebook, Twitter*

Michael Marchesano, President
Derek Irwin, CFO
Sid Holt, Editorial Director

Covers information on all facets of sporting goods, including industry news, sales volume analysis, market events coverage, and other statistics, also covers store operation, merchandising, pricing, promotion, cost control, and sales training.
Cost: $75.00
Frequency: Monthly
Circulation: 27,374
Founded in 1905

22229 Sporting Goods Dealer

VNU Publications
PO Box 1184
Skokie, IL 60076-8194

847-763-9050
800-464- 759
FAX 847-763-9037
E-Mail: info@sgdealer.com
Home Page: www.sgdealer.com
Social Media: *Facebook, Twitter*

Michael Marchesano, President/CEO
Sid Holt, Editorial Director
Derek Irwin, CFO

Sporting Goods Dealer offers reporting on industry insiders, new products, and merchandising trends affecting team dealers and retailers that service schools, colleges, and pro and local teams.
Cost: $75.00
Circulation: 10000
Founded in 1905

22230 Sporting News

Sporting News Publishing Company
PO Vox 51570
Boulder, CO 80322-1510

314-997-7111
800-777-6785
FAX 314-993-7798
Home Page: www.sportingnews.com

Pete Spina, Publisher
Kathy Kinkeade, VP

A comprehensive publication covering sporting goods manufacturers, retailers, wholesalers and distributors.
Cost: $15.97
Frequency: Bi-Monthly

22231 Sports Illustrated
Time Life Building
New York, NY 10020-1393

212-229-9797
FAX 212-467-4049
Home Page: www.sportsillustrated.cnn.com

John Huey, Editor-in-Chief
Terry McDonell, Editor, Time Inc. Sports Group
Paul Fichtenbaum, Managing Editor, SI.com

Sports Illustrated is the most respected voice in sports journalism, which reaches a weekly audience of nearly 21 million adults, and SI.com, the 24/7 sports news website that delivers up to the minute news, scores, statistics and in-depth analysis.
Cost: $39.95
Frequency: 56 Issues/Year

22232 Sports Illustrated for Kids
Sports Illustrated
1271 Ave of the Americas
Suite 32
New York, NY 10020-1401

212-522-1212
212-467-4049
FAX 212-522-0318
Home Page: www.sikids.com
Social Media: *Facebook*

Bob Der, Managing Editor & Publisher
Beth Power Bugler, Creative Director
Justin Tejada, Assistant Managing Editor
Paul Ulane, Senior Producer, sikids.com

Great action photos, easy-to-read stories about star athletes, helpful instructional tips from the pros, humor, comics and activities.
Cost: $24.95
Frequency: Monthly

22233 SportsTravel Magazine
Schneider Publishing Company
11835 W Olympic Blvd
Suite 1265
Los Angeles, CA 90064-5814

310-577-3700
877-577-3700
FAX 310-577-3715
E-Mail: info@schneiderpublishing.com
Home Page: www.schneiderpublishing.com
Social Media: *Facebook, Twitter, LinkedIn*

Tim Schneider, President
Lisa Furfine, Associate Publisher
Jason Gewirtz, Managing Editor/SportsTravel

SportsTravel magazine is the event organizer's guide to successfully creating and staging sports events. SportsTravel provides information on sports destinations and venues, transportation and accommodations, bidding for events, sponsorships, and marketing. SportsTravel facilitates relationships among sports governing bodies, host destinations, sponsors, and suppliers.
Cost: $48.00
Circulation: 14,000
ISSN: 1091-5354
Founded in 1997
Printed in 4 colors on glossy stock

22234 Sportsbusiness Journal
Business Journals Inc
120 W Morehead St
Suite 420
Charlotte, NC 28202-1874

704-973-1200
800-829-9389
FAX 704-973-1201
E-Mail: citybiz@bizjournals.com
Home Page: www.citybiznetwork.com

George Conley, President

Provides important news information sports industry executives need to be successful in the fast paced world of sports business
Cost: $249.00
Frequency: 49X/Year
Circulation: 17,000
Founded in 1998

22235 Squash Magazine
23 Cynwyd Road
PO Box 1216
Bala Cynwyd, PA 19004-5216

610-667-4006
FAX 610-667-6539
Home Page: www.us-squash.org
Social Media: *Facebook, Twitter*

Craig W Brand, Executive Director
Keith Klipstein, Executive Director

Articles on the sport of squash racquets in the United States.
Cost: $35.00
Frequency: 10 per year

22236 Synchro Swimming USA
US Synchronized Swimming
132 E Washington Street
Suite 800
Indianapolis, IN 46204-3674

317-237-5700
FAX 317-237-5705
E-Mail: marketing@usasynchro.org
Home Page: www.usasynchro.org

Terry Harper, Executive Director
Taylor Payne, Media Relations Director
Jordan Dillon, Business Development Director
Judy McGowan, President
Frequency: Quarterly
Circulation: 6000

22237 TEE Time Magazine
PO Box 225
Whitman, MA 02382

781-447-2299
FAX 781-447-7773
Home Page: www.teetime-mag.com
Social Media: *Facebook, Twitter*

Mary Porter, Editor
Karen Christoforo, Sales

The Mid-Atlantics region's most comprehensive golf magazine. Each issue includes golf instruction, profiles of Mid-Atlantic personalities, course reviews and more.
Cost: $12.95
64 Pages

22238 Training & Conditioning
MAG
20 East Lake Rd.
Ithaca, NY 14850-5220

607-257-6970
FAX 607-257-7328
E-Mail: info@athleticbid.com
Home Page: www.momentummedia.com

Mark Goldberg, Publisher
Diedra Harkenrider, East and Southeast US Sales Rep
Pennie Small, Manager

Articles on injury protection and treatment, rehabilitation, strength and speed training, as well as cardiovascular equipment for competitive athletes.
Frequency: BiMonthly
Circulation: 27,400

22239 Transworld Motocross
Transworld Publications

353 Airport Road
Oceanside, CA 92054

760-722-7777
FAX 760-722-0653
Home Page: www.neodata.com

Jason Young, Publications Contact
Al Crolius, Manager

Magazine designed for the motocross enthusiast.
Cost: $16.97
Frequency: Monthly

22240 Transworld Skateboarding Business
Transworld Business Subscriptions
2052 Corte del Nogal
Suite 100
Carlsbad, CA 92011

760-722-7777
850-682-7644
FAX 760-722-0653
E-Mail: subsvcs@skate.cusomtersvc.com
Home Page: www.twsbiz.com
Social Media: *Facebook, Twitter, LinkedIn*

Larry Balma, Publisher
Brad McDonald, Manager

Geared toward skateboard retailers, apparel chain buyers, and manufacturers of skateboard products, includes new product information, industry news, and technical innovations.
Cost: $16.97
Frequency: Monthly
Circulation: 14500

22241 Transworld Snowboarding
Transworld Business
Ste 150
2052 Corte Del Nogal
Carlsbad, CA 92011-1491

760-722-7777
850-682-7644
FAX 760-722-0653
E-Mail: twsnowbiz@aol.com
Home Page: www.twsnow.com
Social Media: *Facebook, Twitter, LinkedIn*

Larry Balma, Publisher
Brad McDonald, Manager

Articles on industry news, retailer surveys, new products, and technical studies.
Cost: $14.97
Frequency: 9/Year
Circulation: 20000

22242 Transworld Surf
Transworld Publishing
Ste 150
2052 Corte Del Nogal
Carlsbad, CA 92011-1491

760-722-7777
850-682-7644
FAX 760-722-0653
E-Mail: jasonyoung@twsnet.com
Home Page: www.neodata.com
Social Media: *Facebook, Twitter, LinkedIn*

Jason Young, Publications Contact
Brad McDonald, Manager

Magazine for surfing enthusiasts.
Cost: $12.00
Frequency: Monthly

22243 Trapper & Predator
F+W Media
38 E. 29th Street
New York, NY 10016

212-447-1400
FAX 212-447-5231
E-Mail: contact_us@fwmedia.com
Home Page: www.fwpublications.com

Hugh McAloon, Publisher
Paul Wait, Editor

Contains news, in-depth features, and how-to tips on trapping, the art of predator calling, and animal damage control. Contributors include the top names in the business. Regular columns and departments include The Fur Shed, Let's Swap Ideas, Q&A, and news from state trapping associations nationwide.
Cost: $18.95
Frequency: 10 Per Year
Circulation: 38,260
Founded in 1975

22244 Turkey & Turkey Hunting
F+W Media
38 E. 29th Street
New York, NY 10016

212-447-1400
FAX 212-447-5231
E-Mail: contact_us@fwmedia.com
Home Page: www.fwpublications.com

Hugh McAloon, Publisher
Paul Wait, Editor

Edited for serious, technical, year-round, gun and bow turkey hunters. Features emphasize success and enjoyment of the sport. Articles focus on hunting, scouting, turkey behavior and biology, hunting ethics, new equipment, methodologies, turkey management, and current research. Columns include Tree Call, Mail Pouch, Turkey Biology, a Q&A column, Hunter's Library, Turkey Gear, and Last Call.
Cost: $15.95
Frequency: 6 Per Year
Circulation: 68,962
Founded in 1991

22245 USA Table Tennis
USA Table Tennis
1 Olympic Plaza
Colorado Springs, CO 80909-5746

719-866-4583
FAX 719-632-6071
E-Mail: magazine@usatt.org
Home Page: www.usatt.org
Social Media: *Facebook, Twitter*

Michael Cavanaugh, CEO

Dedicated to providing readers with all of the tools and information necessary to follow or participate in this life-long sport.
9000 Members
Frequency: 6x/Year
Circulation: 8000
Founded in 1935

22246 Velobusiness
Inside Communications
1830 55th St
Boulder, CO 80301-2700

303-440-0601
FAX 303-444-6788

Felix Magowan, President

Trends in the market, new product develoment updates and spot news reports, also includes testing and performance evaluations, as well as marketing, merchandising and sales techniques.
Cost: $35.00
Frequency: Monthly
Circulation: 10,560

22247 Woman's Outlook
National Rifle Association
9582 Hamilton Ave
Huntington Beach, CA 92646

800-565-6651
877-672-2000
Home Page: www.womenoutlook.com

Created especially for women. Covers topics from personal protection and home security to general firearms safety and recreation. Subscription complimentary with membership in NRA. Otherwise $9.95

22248 Woodall's Campground Management
Woodall Publishing Company
PO Box 8600
Ventura, CA 93002-8600

805-667-2001
877-680-6155
FAX 805-667-4122
E-Mail: info@woodallpub.com
Home Page: www.affinitygroup.com

Michael A Schneider, CEO
Kristopher Bunker, Editor
Terry Thompson, Advertising

Information for campground owners and managers, provides methods of management and industry trends along with reports from independent and franchise campgrounds, public parks and state associations.
Cost: $24.95
Frequency: Monthly
Circulation: 10,000
Founded in 1935

Trade Shows

22249 AACCA Spirit Coaches Conference
American Association of Cheerleading Coaches
6745 Lenox Center Court
Suite 318
Memphis, TN 38115

800-533-6583
FAX 901-251-5851
Home Page: www.aacca.org

Jim Lord, Executive Director
Michle Ziegler, Instructor

The official NFHS Sprit Coaches Education Program.
Frequency: Annual
Founded in 1988

22250 AAU Annual Convention
Amateur Athletic Union
1910 Hotel Plaza Boulevard
PO Box 22409
Lake Buena Vista, FL 32830

407-934-7200
FAX 407-934-7242
E-Mail: pam@aausports.org
Home Page: www.aausports.org
Social Media: *Facebook, Twitter*

Pam Marshall, Convention Contact
John Hodges, Exhibitor Information
Bobby Dodd, President/CEO

National Convention of the Amateur Athletic Union.

22251 ASA Sportfishing Summit
American Sportfishing Association
225 Reinekers Lane
Suite 420
Alexandria, VA 22314

703-519-9691
FAX 703-519-1872
E-Mail: mjwilliamson@asafishing.org
Home Page: www.asafishing.org
Social Media: *Facebook, Twitter*

Mary Jane Williamson, Communications Director
Amy Yohanes, Administrative Services Manager
Gordon Robertson, VP
Patrick Egan, Manager

ASA's membership meeting and premier networking event. From special sessions, to business workshops tp association committee meeting, the Summit provides a wide-range of opportunities to gain information on the most relevant issues facing the sportfishing industry.
Frequency: October

22252 ASGCA Meeting
American Society of Golf Course Architects
125 N Executive Dr
Suite 302
Brookfield, WI 53005-6035

262-786-5960
FAX 262-786-5919
E-Mail: info@asgca.org
Home Page: www.asgca.org
Social Media: *Facebook, Twitter*

Chad Ritterbusch, Executive Director
Bob ~ Cupp, President
Rick Robbin, VP
Lee Schmidt, Treasurer
Steve Smyers, Secretary

Combines golfing experiences with informational seminars and social engagements to form a trulyuniqie atmosphere that makes for both an enjoyable and educational meeting experience.
185 Members
Founded in 1946

22253 AVCA Annual Convention
American Volleyball Coaches Association
2365 Harrodsburg Road
Suite A325
Lexington, KY 40504

859-226-4315
866-544-2822
FAX 859-226-4338
E-Mail: members@avca.org
Home Page: www.avca.org
Social Media: *Facebook, Twitter, LinkedIn*

Kathy DeBoer, Executive Director
Will Engle, Assistant Director, Events

A gathering of volleyball coaches and vendors
1700 Members
Frequency: Annual

22254 Action Sports Retailer Trade Exhibit West Fall and Spring
ASR Trade Expo
31910 Del Obispo
Suite 200
San Juan Capistrano, CA 92675

949-226-5744
FAX 949-226-5659
Home Page: www.asrbiz.com

Tina Middleton, Marketing Director
Lisha Steinkoenig, Registration Coordinator
Megan Lara, Expo Coordinator

Provides the ultimate showcase of the action sports and youth lifestyle market by attracting the world's largest and most powerful brands and buyers representing such diverse markets as surf, skate, swim, snow, footwear and fashion.
10M Attendees
Frequency: September/February

22255 Allegheny Sport, Travel and Outdoor Show
Expositions
PO Box 550
Edgewater Branch
Cleveland, OH 44107-0550

216-529-1300
800-600-0307
FAX 216-529-0311
Home Page: www.sportandtravel.com

Chris Fassnacht, Show Producer

Dedicated to hunting, shiftin and camping. Features hundreds of state-of-the-art exhibitors,

dozens of live demonstrations, and a top notch line-up of seminar experts.
Frequency: Annual
Founded in 1985

22256 Amateur Softball Association of America
2801 NE 50th Street
Oklahoma City, OK 73111

405-424-5266
FAX 405-424-3855
E-Mail: bplummer@softball.org
Home Page: www.asasoftball.com

Bill Plummer III, Hall of Fame/Trade Show Manager
Ron Radigonda, Executive Director

Annual meeting of the Amateur Softball Association.
1000+ Attendees
Frequency: Annual/November
Founded in 1933

22257 American Alliance for Health, Physical Education, Recreation & Dance Expo
1900 Association Drive
Reston, VA 20191

703-476-3400
800-213-7193
FAX 703-476-9527
E-Mail: conv@aahperd.org
Home Page: www.aahperd.org
Social Media: *Twitter*

Danny Ballard, President
Judith C Young, VP
Paula Kun, Marketing
Shannon Mueller, Director

National convention and exposition that features many exhibits focusing on products, services and equipment within the fields of health, physical education, recreation and dance.
5000 Attendees
Frequency: Annual/April
Founded in 1879

22258 American Baseball Coaches Association Convention
108 S University Avenue
Suite 3
Mount Pleasant, MI 48858-2327

989-775-3300
FAX 989-775-3600
E-Mail: abca@abca.org
Home Page: www.abca.org
Social Media: *Facebook, Twitter*

Nick Phillips, Membership/Convention Coordinator
4000 Attendees
Frequency: Annual

22259 American Bowling Congress Annual Convention
United States Bowling Congress
5301 South 76th Street
Greendale, WI 53129

414-216-6400
800-514-2695
FAX 414-421-8560
E-Mail: bowlinfo@bowl.com
Home Page: www.bowl.com

Annual conference of the United States Bowling Congress whose mission is to ensure the integrity and protect the future of the sport by providing programs and services and enhancing the bowling experience.

22260 American Camp Association Conference & Exhibits
American Camp Association

5000 State Road 67 N
Martinsville, IN 46151-7902

765-342-8456
800-428-2267
FAX 765-342-2065
Home Page: www.aca-camps.org
Social Media: *Facebook, Twitter, LinkedIn*

Tisher Bolger, President
Scott Brody, VP
Steve Baskin, Treasurer Board of Directors
Peg Smith, CEO

One hundred and forty to one hundred and fifty booths of arts and crafts, computer software, sporting goods, waterfront equipment and more plus a seminar and workshop.
1,200 Attendees
Frequency: Annual
Founded in 1943

22261 American College of Sports Medicine Annual Meeting
401 W Michigan Street
Indianapolis, IN 46202

317-637-9200
FAX 317-634-7817
E-Mail: acsm@acsm.org
Home Page: www.acsm.org
Social Media: *Facebook, Twitter, LinkedIn, You Tube*

James R Whitehead, Executive VP
Janet Walberg Rankin, President

One hundred and eighty-five exhibits of sports equipment, publications, supplies and services, conference and banquet. CME credits available for a nominal fee at time of registration.
5000 Attendees
Frequency: Annual
Founded in 1954

22262 American Football Coaches Association Convention
American Football Coaches Association
100 Legends Lane
Waco, TX 76706

254-754-9900
FAX 254-754-7373
E-Mail: info@acfa.com
Home Page: www.afca.com
Social Media: *Facebook, Twitter*

Grant Teaff, Executive Director

120 booths of equipment, supplies and services relevant to the game of football. Three-day event includees coaching clinic, awards luncheon and Coach of the Year dinner.
6000 Attendees
Frequency: Annual/January
Founded in 1921

22263 American Greyhound Track Operators Association
Palm Beach Kennel Club
1111 North Congress Avenue
West Palm Beach, FL 33409

561-688-5799
FAX 801-754-2404
Home Page: www.agtoa.com
Social Media: *Facebook, Twitter*

Richard Winning, President
Dennis Bicsak, Managing Coordinator
Dennis Bicsak, Managing Coordinator
Michael Corbin~, Treasurer

A forum for all those affiliated with the sport to exchange ideas and to develop new techniques for the improvement and growth of the greyhound industry.
400 Attendees
Frequency: Annual/March

22264 American Hockey Coaches Association Convention
American Hockey Coaches Association
7 Concord Street
Gloucester, MA 01930

781-245-4177
FAX 781-245-2492
E-Mail: ahcahockey@comcast.net
Home Page: www.ahcahockey.com
Social Media: *Facebook, Twitter, LinkedIn*

Joe Bertagna, Executive Director
George Gwozdecky, President
Kevin Sneddon, VP/Convention Planning

70 exhibits of ice hockey equipment and supplies plus worksop and banquet.
500 Attendees
Frequency: Annual/April
Founded in 1960

22265 American Orthopaedic Society for Sports Medicine Annual Meeting
American Orthopaedic Society for Sports Medicine
6300 N River Road
Suite 500
Rosemont, IL 60018-4229

847-292-4900
877-321-3500
FAX 847-292-4905
E-Mail: aossm@aossm.org
Home Page: www.sportsmed.org

Michelle Schaffer, Exhibits Coordinator
Camille Petrick, Manager

130 exhibits of equipment supplies and services for sports medicine and related fields. Banquet and tours available.
1,500 Attendees
Frequency: June/July
Founded in 1972

22266 American Swimming Coaches Association
5101 NW 21st Avenue
Suite 200
Fort Lauderdale, FL 33309

954-563-4930
800-356-2722
FAX 954-563-9813
Home Page: www.swimmmingcoach.org
Social Media: *Facebook*

John Leonard, Executive Director
Lori Klatt, Marketing

Annual convention
1.5M Attendees
Frequency: September

22267 American Youth Soccer Organization
12501 S Isis Avenue
Hawthorne, CA 90250

310-643-6455
800-872-2976
FAX 310-643-5310
Home Page: www.soccer.org

Rick Smith, Executive Director

The AYSO annual general meeting is your opportunity to represent your region, area or section on a national level.
800 Attendees
Frequency: Annual

22268 Archery Trade Show
Archery Trade Association
PO Box 70
Suite 310
Minnesota, UT 84107

507-233-8130
866-266-2776
FAX 507-233-8140
E-Mail: info@archerytrade.org

Home Page: www.archerytrade.org
Social Media: *Facebook, Twitter*

Jay McAnich, President/CEO
Denise Parker, VP/Director Marketing
Cindy Brophy, Manager
Tradeshow/Membership Svces
Kelly A. Kelly, Executive Assistant
Kurt Weber, Director of Marketing

Formerly the Archery Manufacturers and Merchants Organization (AMO), the ATA provides the core funding and direction critical to the future of archery and bowhunting. The trade show features 499 exhibitors cover 155,500 square feet.
8000 Attendees
Frequency: Annual

22269 Arnold Sports Festival
Arnold Sports Festival
1215 Worthington Woods Blvd.
Worthington, OH 43805

614-431-2600
FAX 516-625-1023
E-Mail: lpinney@arnoldexpo.com
Home Page: www.arnoldsportsfestival.com
Social Media: *Facebook, Twitter*

Lucy Pinneyr, Event Chair
Brent LaLonda, Media Contact

Five days of fitness equipment, sports entertainment, supplements, apparel and athletic stars, with more than 17,000 competitive athletes in 40 sporting events. Over 500 exhibitors and 150,000 visitors; takes place during the Arnold Sports Festival
150M+ Attendees
Frequency: March
Founded in 1976

22270 Athletic Equipment Managers Association Convention
723 Keil Ct
Bowling Green, OH 43402-2235

Home Page: www.aema1.com

Sporting goods equipment manufacturers.
300 Attendees
Frequency: June

22271 BCA Convention
National High School Baseball Coaches Association
PO Box 12843
Tempe, AZ 85284

602-615-0571
FAX 480-838-7133
E-Mail: rdavini@cox.net
Home Page: www.baseballcoaches.org

Ron Davini, Executive Director

22272 Bowling Proprieters Association of America International Bowl Expo
615 Six Flags Drive
PO Box 5802
Arlington, TX 76011-6347

800-343-1329
888-649-5585
FAX 817-633-2940
Home Page: www.bpaa.com
Social Media: *Facebook, Twitter, LinkedIn*

Lee Ann Norton, Director Meetings/Events
Laurie Clower, Executive Assistant~
Judy King, Director of Finance

The bowling industry's premier event. Brings together thousands of bowling industry professionals in one place. You can find the latest trends, bowling-related products and services, marketing ideas, profit center opportunities, and tools to help you spread the excitement of bowling throughout your communities. Trade show showcases the latest products and ser-

vices from more than 300 companies in over 900 exhibit booths.
5000 Attendees
Frequency: June
Founded in 1932

22273 CMAA Annual Conference
Club Managers Association of America
1733 King Street
Alexandria, VA 22314

703-739-9500
FAX 703-739-0124
E-Mail: cmaa@cmaa.org
Home Page: www.smaa.org
Social Media: *Facebook, Twitter, LinkedIn, You Tube*

Jim Singerling, Executive VP

Club Managers Association of America Annual World Conference. This International Conference brings together club industry professionals from around the world for five days of challenging education, entertaining social events and an industry trade show.
Founded in 1990

22274 CSCAA National Convention & Clinic
College Swimming Coaches Association of America
1640 Maple
#803
Evanston, IL 60201

847-833-3478
E-Mail: r-groseth@northwestern.edu
Home Page: www.collegecoaches.org
Social Media: *Facebook, Twitter, LinkedIn*

Bob Groseth, Executive Director
George Kennedy, President
Founded in 1990

22275 Colorado RV Adventure Travel Show
Industrial Expositions
1675 Larimer, Suite 700
PO Box 480084
Denver, CO 80248-0084

303-892-6800
800-457-2434
FAX 303-892-6322
E-Mail: info@iei-expos.com
Home Page: www.bigasalloutdoors.com
Social Media: *Facebook, Twitter, LinkedIn*

Jeff Haughton, President
Dianne Seymour, Expo Manager

Recreational vehicles, accessories and travel.
18000 Attendees
Frequency: Annual/January
Founded in 1990

22276 Colorado RV, Sports, Boat and Travel Show
Industrial Expositions
1675 Larimer Street
Suite 700
Denver, CO 80202

303-892-6800
800-457-2434
FAX 303-892-6322
E-Mail: dseymour@iei-expos.com
Home Page: www.bigasalloutdoors.com
Social Media: *Facebook, Twitter, LinkedIn*

Jeff Haughton, President
Dianne Seymour, Expo Manager

Annual trade show of recreational vehicles, sports, boats and travel.
Founded in 1990

22277 Crescent Ski Council
PO Box 17944
Greenville, SC 29606-8944

864-229-7488
FAX 864-235-2504

Home Page: www.crescentskicouncil.org
Social Media: *Facebook, Twitter, LinkedIn, You Tube*

Michelle Shuford, Contact

Exhibits of snow ski resorts and related lodging services. 50 booths.
500 Attendees
Frequency: April
Founded in 1969

22278 DEMA/Diving Equipment & Marketing Association Trade Show
3750 Convoy Street
Suite 310
San Diego, CA 92111-3741

858-616-6408
800-862-3483
FAX 858-616-6495
E-Mail: info@dema.org
Home Page: www.dema.org
Social Media: *Facebook, Twitter, LinkedIn, You Tube*

Christine Von Steiger, Exhibit Space Sales
Tom Markusson, Sponsorship Sales
Tom Ingram, Executive Director
Stephen Ashmore, President

Annual trade show produced by the Diving Equipment & Marketing Association.
10M Attendees
Frequency: Annual

22279 Eastern Fishing and Outdoor Exposition
International Sport Show Producers Association
PO Box 4720
Portsmouth, NH 03802-4720

603-431-4315
FAX 603-431-1971
E-Mail: info@sportshows.com
Home Page: www.sportshows.com
Social Media: *Facebook, Twitter, LinkedIn, You Tube*

Paul Fuller, President

Over 450 exhibitors representing the entire world of fishing and hunting.
45k Attendees
Frequency: Annual/February
Founded in 1996
Mailing list available for rent

22280 Eastern Iowa Sportshow
Iowa Show Productions
PO Box 2460
Waterloo, IA 50704

319-232-0218
FAX 319-235-8932
E-Mail: info@iowashows.com
Home Page: www.iowashows.com
Social Media: *Facebook, Twitter, LinkedIn*

See a huge display of fishing boats, family sport boats, personal watercraft, pontoons, tent campers, travel trailers, fifth wheels, vans, and motorhomes. Plus boat accessories, truck toppers, motorcycles, ATVs, fishing camps, fly-ins, outposts, Lake Erie Walleye charters, family resorts, Lake Michigan sportfishing, houseboat rentals, Golf vacations, canoe outfitters, big game outfitters, tourism associations, campgrounds, camping gear, fishing tackle, archery equipment, targets, decoys, calls.

22281 Fall RV & Van Show
O'Loughlin Trade Shows
PO Box 80750
Portland, OR 97280-1750

503-246-8291
FAX 503-246-1066
E-Mail: otssport@earthlink.net

Home Page: www.oloughlintradeshows.com
Social Media: *Facebook, Twitter, LinkedIn*

Peter O'Loughlin, Show Manager

Portland, OR. Recreational vehicles and vans
Frequency: September

22282 Fly Fishing Show - Denver
854 Opossum Lake Road
Carlisle, PA 17013

717-243-6733
800-420-7582
FAX 717-243-8603
E-Mail: flyfishingshow@aol.com
Home Page: www.flyfishingshow.com
Social Media: *Facebook, Twitter*

Barry Serviente, Executive Director
Annual fly fishing show.

22283 Football Officials Association Southwest Convention
Dallas Football Officials Association
2005 Fairmeadow
Richardson, TX 75080

972-235-9110
FAX 972-235-7675
E-Mail: dfoasecretary@aol.com
Home Page: www.dfoa.com

David Tucker, Registration
Mike Woodard, President

Texas Association of Sports Officials annual convention.
1.8M Attendees
Frequency: Annual

22284 Fred Hall's Western Fishing Tackle & Boat Show: Delmar
Fred Hall & Associates
PO Box 2925
Camarillo, CA 93011

805-389-3339
FAX 805-389-1219

Bart Hall, Show Manager

Featuring all forms of outdoor recreation including boats, fishing tackle, adventure travel and recreational vehicles.

22285 Golf Course Superintendents Association of America
GCSAA
1421 Research Park Drive
Lawrence, KS 66049-3858

785-841-2240
800-472-7878
FAX 785-832-4455
Home Page: www.golfindustryshow.com
Social Media: *Facebook, Twitter, LinkedIn, You Tube*

Julia Ozark, Sr Trade Show Manager
Caroline Gollier, Trade Show Project Manager
Scotti Corley, Meeting/Trade Show Coordinator
Kelly Jo Springirth, Director Exhibit Services
Steve Mona, CEO

Trade show designed for the owners/operators of golf facilities and the professional members of the golf course and club management industries. The event combines education, networking and solutions for golf course superintendents, owners/operators, general managers, chief operating officers, architects and builders.
25M Attendees
Frequency: February

22286 Grand Center Boat Show
Show Span

2121 Celebration Drive NE
Grand Rapids, MI 49525

616-447-2860
800-328-6550
FAX 616-447-2861
E-Mail: events@showspan.com
Home Page: www.showspan.com
Social Media: *Facebook, Twitter, LinkedIn*

Carolyn Alt, Manager

Held at the Grand Center in Grand Rapids, Michigan. Every kind of boat under the sun. Over 400 boats.
82000 Attendees
Frequency: February

22287 Great Lakes Athletic Trainers
8015 Kersey Drive
Indianapolis, IN 46236

815-455-3860
FAX 815-477-6907
Home Page: www.glata.org
Social Media: *Facebook, Twitter, LinkedIn*

Mark Schauer, Co Coordinator
Kevin Gerlach, Co Coordinator

Annual meeting and symposium.
1M Attendees
Frequency: March

22288 Greater Cincinnati Golf Show
North Coast Golf Productions
PO Box 372
Twinsburg, OH 44087-0372

330-963-6963
800-939-0040
FAX 330-487-0352
E-Mail: consumer@northcoastgolfshows.com
Home Page: www.northboastgolfshows.com
Social Media: *Facebook, Twitter, LinkedIn*

America's favorite consumer golf show.

22289 ICAST
American Sportfishing Association
1001 North Fairfax Street
Suite 501
Alexandria, VA 22314

703-519-9691
FAX 703-519-1872
E-Mail: mdelvalle@asafishing.org
Home Page: www.asafishing.org
Social Media: *Facebook, Twitter, LinkedIn*

Maria del Valle, ICAST Director
Kenneth Andres, ICAST Associate
Gordon Robertson, VP
Mary Jane Williamson, Communications Director

The sportfishing industry's largest trade event is a major catalyst for sales and a terrific networking opportunity for the sportfishing community
Frequency: July

22290 ISHA Annual Conference
International Sports Heritage Association
PO Box 2384
Florence, OR 97439

541-991-7315
FAX 541-997-3871
E-Mail: info@sportsheritage.org
Home Page: www.sportsheritage.org
Social Media: *Facebook, Twitter, LinkedIn*

Karen Bednarski, Executive Director
Sheila Kelly, President
Mike Gibbons, First Vice President
Pete Fierle, Second Vice President
Ed Harris, Treasurer

Session discussions, educational sessions and speakers
140+ Members
Founded in 1971

22291 Ice Skating Institute
6000 Custe Rd.
Bldg. 9
Plano, TX 75023

972-735-8800
FAX 972-735-8815
E-Mail: isi@skateisi.org
Home Page: www.skateisi.org
Social Media: *Facebook*

Peter Martell, Executive Director

The industry's leading trade show where you're sure to find the technical information, products and suppliers you need to run your business every day. Who should attend: Arena owners and managers; Hockey and figure skating coaches and instructors; Ice arena programming directors; Operations personnel; builders and suppliers to the industry.
Frequency: Annual/May

22292 International Billiard and Home Recreation Expo
Billiard Congress of America
4345 Beverly Street
Suite D
Colorado Springs, CO 80918

719-264-8300
FAX 719-264-0900
Home Page: www.bca-pool.com
Social Media: *Facebook, Twitter, LinkedIn*

Stephen Ducoff, Executive Director
Carolyn Lewis, Director Trade Services
Amy Long, Director Marketing
Linda Mojer, Director Communications
Kathy Simmons, Member Services Administrator

This show hosts nearly 300 companies in 1400 booths, featuring every product line in the home recreation industry, from billiard and game tables, cues and cue accessories, cloth, balls and apparel, to spas, bowling, darts, foosball, art, home furnishings, novelty items, outdoor living, books, publications, video games, coin-op, pinball, jukeboxes, gaming and much more.
Founded in 1984

22293 International Pool & Spa Expo
PO Box 612128
Dallas, TX 75261-2128

972-536-6350
888-869-8522
FAX 972-536-6364
Home Page: www.poolandspaexpo.com

Tina Brinkley, Operations Coordinator
Kathy Ruff, Operations Manager
Tracy Beaulieu, Conference Manager
Vila Snider, Registration Manager
Donna Bellantone, Assoc Show Director

Latest trends, newest products, and innovative ways to increase sales and add profits to your business.
16M Attendees
Frequency: November

22294 Kansas Sports, Boat and Travel Show
Industrial Expositions
PO Box 480084
Denver, CO 80248

303-892-6800
800-457-2434
FAX 303-892-6322
E-Mail: dseymour@iei-expos.com
Home Page: www.bigasalloutdoors.com

Jeff Haughton, President
Dianne Seymour, Expo Manager

Annual show produced by Industrial Expositions.
Frequency: Annual

22295 Let's Play Hockey International Expo
Let's Play Hockey
2721 East 42nd Street
Minneapolis, MN 55406

612-729-0023
FAX 612-729-0259
E-Mail: letsplay@letsplayhockey.com
Home Page: www.letsplayhockey.com

Doug Johnson, Contact
Doug Johnson, Publisher
Kevin Kurtt, Editor

Hockey Industry Trade Show. Five days of
events. Seminars, races, tournaments, awards
banquet, expo demo day, Hall of Fame display,
buying group meetings and more.
Founded in 1999

22296 Lincoln Boat, Sport and Travel Show
Egan Enterprises
4100 North 84th Street
Lincoln, NE 68505-5465

402-466-8102
FAX 402-467-5630
Home Page: www.nebraskasportshow.com

Pat Egan, Contact Person

Equipment and supplies for the outdoor life.
Frequency: Annual

**22297 Management Conference & Team
Dealer Summit**
National Sporting Goods Association
1601 Feehanville Drive
Suite 300
Mount Prospect, IL 60056

847-966-6742
800-815-5422
FAX 847-391-9827
E-Mail: conference@nsga.org
Home Page: www.nsga.org

Jeff Rosenthal, Chairman of the Board
Matt Carlson, President/CEO
Dan Kasen, Director of Information Services

The Sporting Goods industry's premier educational and networking event, featuring programming aimed at ensuring business' success,
brings together leaders and industry insiders
for engaging conversations and stimulating
presentations.

22298 NABC Convention & MarketPlace
National Association of Basketball Coaches
1111 Main St
Suite 1000
Kansas City, MO 64105-2116

816-878-6222
FAX 816-878-6223
Home Page: www.nabc.com

Jim Haney, Executive Director
Reggie Minton, Deputy Executive Director
Kevin Henderson, Associate Executive
Director
Dottie Yearout, Director of Membership
Services
Janelle Guidry, Convention Manager

The Convention offers Professional Development Clinics
Frequency: Annual/Spring

22299 NACDA Convention
Nat'l Assoc of Collegiate Directors of
Athletics
24651 Detroit Road
Westlake, OH 44145

440-892-4000
FAX 440-892-4007
Home Page: www.nacda.com
Social Media: *Facebook, Twitter, LinkedIn*

Michael Cleary, Executive Director

Devoted to examining contemporary problems
facing today's athletics administrator. Caters to
administrators in all levels of intercollegiate
athletics with general sessions for the entire
membership and breakout sessions which are
geared to the specific needs of administrators at
all levels of the NCAA, NAIA, and NJCAA

22300 NASC Sports Event Symposium
9916 Carver Road
Suite 100
Cincinnati, OH 45242

513-281-3888
FAX 513-281-1765
E-Mail: info@nascsymposium.com
Home Page: www.nascsymposium.com
Social Media: *Facebook, Twitter, LinkedIn*

Don Schumacher, Executive Director
Beth Hecquet, Director of Meetings and Events

National Association of Sports Commissions.
Representing more than 550 organizations. Attendees are provided with new ideas, practical
tips and the hottest trends.
550 Members
Founded in 1992

22301 NASGW Annual Meeting and Expo
National Association of Sporting Goods
Wholesalers
1833 Centre Point Circle
Suite 123
Naperville, IL 60563

630-596-9006
FAX 630-544-5055
E-Mail: nasgw@nasgw.org
Home Page: www.nasgw.org
Social Media: *Facebook, Twitter, LinkedIn*

Maurice Desmarais, President
Jack Baumler, Chairman
Kent Williams, Vice Chair
Peter Brownell, Treasurer

Educational, marketing and communications
opportunity for the hunting and shooting sports
wholesaler, manufacturer and sales
professional.
400 Members
Founded in 1954

22302 NCAA Annual Convention

317-917-6222
FAX 317-917-6888
E-Mail: feedback@ncaasports.com
Home Page: www.ncaasports.com
Social Media: *Facebook, Twitter, LinkedIn*

Trade show and convention
Frequency: January
Founded in 1915

22303 NFCA National Convention
National Fastpitch Coaches Association
100 G T Thames Drive
Suite D
Starkville, MS 39759

662-320-2155
FAX 662-320-2283
E-Mail: nfca@nfca.org
Home Page: www.nfca.org
Social Media: *Facebook, Twitter, LinkedIn*

Lacy Lee Baker, Executive Director
Hildred Deese, Senior Director of Events
Frequency: Annual, December

**22304 NSAA National Convention and
Trade Show**
National Ski Areas Association
133 S Van Gordon Street
Suite 300
Lakewood, CO 80228

303-987-1111
FAX 303-986-2345
E-Mail: nsaa@nsaa.org

Home Page: www.nsaa.org
Social Media: *Facebook, Twitter, LinkedIn*

Michael Berry, President
Keri Hone, Director Events/Projects
Tom Moore, Director Conventions/Meetings
Kate Powers, Director Member Services
Amy Steele, Director Sponsorships

Annual convention of the National Ski Areas
Association

**22305 National Association of Basketball
Coaches Annual Convention**
1111 Main Street
Suite 1000
Kansas City, MO 64105-2136

816-878-6222
FAX 816-878-6223
Home Page: www.nabc.org
Social Media: *Facebook, Twitter, LinkedIn*

James Haney, Executive Director
Reggie Minton, Deputy Executive Director
Kevin Henderson, Associate Executive
Director

Approximately 150 booths offering services
and resources for Basketball Coaches.
3M Attendees
Frequency: March/April

**22306 National Institute for Golf
Management**
National Golf Foundation
1150 South US Highway One
Suite 401
Jupiter, FL 33477

561-744-6006
888-275-4643
FAX 561-744-6107
E-Mail: general@ngf.org
Home Page: www.ngf.org
Social Media: *Facebook, Twitter, LinkedIn*

Annual golf institute sponsored by the National
Golf Foundation.
Frequency: Annual

**22307 National Intramural Recreational
Sports Association**
4185 SW Research Way
Corvallis, OR 97333-1067

541-766-8211
FAX 541-766-8284
E-Mail: nirsa@nirsa.org
Home Page: www.nirsa.org
Social Media: *Facebook, Twitter, LinkedIn*

Kent Blumenthal, Executive Director
Dr. William N. Wasson, Owner

This show provides an annual marketplace for
athletic and recreational equipment, supplies
and services.
1.6M Attendees
Frequency: Annual/April
Founded in 1950

**22308 National Recreation and Park
Association's Conference and
Exposition**
National Recreation and Park Association
22377 Belmont Ridge Road
Ashburn, VA 20148

703-858-0784
FAX 703-858-0794
E-Mail: info@nrpa.org
Home Page: www.nrpa.org

Britt Esen, Director
Jodie H Adams, President
John Crosby, Marketing

Provides targeted learning opportunities specifically for parks and recreation directors, supervisors and managers, community center
directors, recreation programmers, natural re-

sources personnel, therapeutic recreation specialists, citizen advocates and students.
4000 Attendees
Founded in 1965

22309 National Soccer Coaches Association of America

800 Ann Avenue
Kansas City, KS 66101

913-362-1747
800-458-0676
FAX 913-362-3439
Home Page: nscaa.com
Social Media: *Facebook, Twitter, LinkedIn*

Joe Cummings, CEO and Executive Director
Tommy Reder, CFO

Every coach who attends will find something new to add to their soccer reperoire. The trade show consists of more than 300 companies. Attendees can examine the latest soccer-related technology and equipment.
30m Members
9000 Attendees
Frequency: Annual/January
Founded in 1941

22310 National Trappers Association Sports Show

2815 Washington Avenue
Bedford, IN 47421

812-277-9670
866-680-8727
FAX 812-277-9672
E-Mail: ntaheadquarters@nationaltrappers.com
Home Page: www.nationaltrappers.com

Kraig Kaatz, President
Chris Flynn, VP
Kraig Kaatz, General Organizer

300 booths including outdoor sports supplies and dealers.
6M Attendees
Frequency: Annual/August

22311 New York National Boat Show

National Marine Manufacturers Association
148 West 37th Street
11th Floor
New York, NY 10018

212-984-7007
FAX 212-564-2728
Home Page: www.nyboatshow.com
Social Media: *Facebook, Twitter*

Jonathon Pritko, Show Manager
Bob MkAlpine, Exhibitor Relationship Manager
Dan Castellano, Exhibitor Relationships Manager
Elba-Rosales Rise, Show Administrator
Josh Rosales, Operation Coordinator

Annual boat show held at Jacob Javitz Convention Center in New York
Frequency: January

22312 North American Society for Sport Management Conference

North American Society for Sport Management
Slippery Rock University
West Gym 014
Slippery Rock, PA 16057

724-738-4812
FAX 724-738-4858
E-Mail: nassm@sru.edu
Home Page: www.nassm.com
Social Media: *Facebook, Twitter*

North American Society for Sport Management annual convention and trade show.

22313 Northwest Sportshow

General Sports Shows

3539 Hennepin Avenue
Minneapolis, MN 55408-3830

612-827-5833
800-777-4766
FAX 612-827-1424

David Perkins, President

Public show offering the finest presentation of outdoor recreation and marine products and services.
205M Attendees
Frequency: March

22314 Outdoorama Family Sport and Travel Show

Michigan United Conservation Clubs
2101 Wood Street
PO Box 30235
Lansing, MI 48909

517-371-1041
800-777-6720
FAX 517-371-1505
E-Mail: membership@mucc.org
Home Page: www.mucc.org
Social Media: *Facebook, Twitter, LinkedIn*

Sam Washington, Executive Director
Kelly Snyder, Event/Fundraising Assistant
Evan Steiner, Events/Fundraising Specialist

Michigan's favorite outdoor show featuring over 200,000 square feet of exhibit space dedicated to the latest in fishing and hunting equipment, fishing and power boats, recreational vehicles, outdoor gear and vacationing destinations throughout North America. Four-hundred plus booths.
42000 Attendees
Frequency: February
Founded in 1974

22315 PTR International Tennis Symposium

Professional Tennis Registry
PO Box 4739
Hilton Head Island, SC 29938

843-785-7244
800-421-6289
FAX 843-686-2033
E-Mail: ptr@ptrtennis.org
Home Page: www.ptrtennis.org
Social Media: *Facebook, Twitter*

Dan Santoruk, CEO
Julie Jilly, VP/Operations

Symposium of professional tennis teachers and coaches. PTR has excellent relationships and partnerships with industry leaders such as the USTA, Tennis Industry Association, the ITF and many National Tennis Federations.
14m Members
800+ Attendees
Frequency: 2x Per Year
Founded in 1976

22316 Pop Warner Little Scholars Convention

586 Middletown Boulevard
Suite C-100
Langhorne, PA 19047-1867

215-752-2691
FAX 215-752-2879
E-Mail: webmaster@popwarner.com
Home Page: www.popwarner.com
Social Media: *Facebook, Twitter*

Jon Butler, Executive Director
Mary Fitzgerald, COO
Lisa Moroski, National Cheer/Dance Commissioner
1000 Attendees
Frequency: Bi-Annual

22317 Professional Golfers Association Merchandise Show

Reed Exhibitions

383 Main Avenue
Norwalk, CT 06851

203-404-4800
800-840-5628
FAX 203-840-9628
E-Mail: inquiry@pga.reedexpo.com
Home Page: www.pgamerchandiseshow.com
Social Media: *Facebook, Twitter*

Kara Codio, Marketing/Conference Manager
Sherry Major, Media Relations Manager
Jay Andronaco, Event Marketing Manager

The PGA Merchandise Show provides a snap-shot of the industry as a whole and access to products and services that pertain to every aspect of the game. It is the focal point for new product introductions, professional development programs, business meetings and more.
30M Attendees
Frequency: January

22318 Professional Golfers Association Golf Show

Sydney Convention and Exhibition Centre
Darling Harbour
Sydney
Australia NSW 2000

Home Page: www.pgaexpo.com
Social Media: *Facebook, Twitter, LinkedIn*

International PGA Golf Show. 2006 Show held in Australia
50000 Attendees
Frequency: Annual

22319 RSA Convention and Trade Show

Roller Skating Association International
6905 Corporate Drive
Indianapolis, IN 46278

317-347-2626
FAX 317-347-2636
E-Mail: rsa@rollerskating.com
Home Page: www.rollerskating.org
Social Media: *Facebook, Twitter, LinkedIn, You Tube*

Bobby Braun, President
Ron Liette, VP
John Purcell, Executive Director

Helping roller skating industry professionals discover ways to build strong foundations for their businesses.
1000 Members
Frequency: annual
Founded in 1937

22320 Rocky Mountain Snowmobile Expo

Industrial Expositions
1675 Larimer Street
Suite 700
Denver, CO 80202

303-892-6800
800-457-2434
FAX 303-892-6322
E-Mail: dseymour@iei-expos.com
Home Page: www.bigasalloutdoors.com
Social Media: *Facebook, Twitter*

Jeff Haughton, President
Diane Seymour, Expo Manager

Large display of snowmobiles and accessories, meet performance experts, resorts and lodges, winter clothing, ice fishing, winter travel destinations, snowmobile adventure theatre, avalanche awareness, swap meet and more.

22321 SHOT Show: Shooting Hunting Outdoor Trade Show

Reed Exhibition Companies
28 The Quadrant
Richmond 6851

203-404-4800
800-840-5628

FAX 203-840-9628
Home Page: www.reedexpo.com

Worldwide annual gathering that unites manufacturer and retailer and all other industry stakeholders to trade, source and learn about the latest products, innovations and trends in the shooting sports industry.
15M Attendees
Frequency: January

22322 SIA Snow Show
SnowSports Industries America
8377-b Greensboro Drive
McLean, VA 22102-3587

703-556-9020
FAX 703-821-8276
E-Mail: siamail@snowsports.org
Home Page: www.siasnowshow.com
Social Media: *Facebook, Twitter, LinkedIn, YouTube, Wikipedia, Vimeo*

From fashion to skis and snowboards to Nordic, snowshoes, outdoor and basic essentials, the SIA Snow Show previews the entire winter sports market and then deads to the on-snow demo to try it all out on snow.
700+ Members
19M Attendees
Frequency: Annual/January
Founded in 1954

22323 Saltwater Fishing Expo
Eastern Fishing and Outdoor Exposition
PO Box 4720
Portsmouth, NH 03802

603-431-4315
FAX 603-431-1971
Home Page: www.sportshows.com

The Saltwater Fishing Expo is expecting over 300 exhibitors representing the entire spectrum of saltwater sportfishing. There will be dozens of seminars throughout the three days of the show, which will be presented by experts who are at the top of their game.

22324 San Mateo Inernational Sportsmen's Expo
International Sportsmen's Exposition
PO Box 2569
Vancouver, WA 98668-2569

360-693-3700
800-545-6100
FAX 360-693-3352
Home Page: www.sportsexpos.com

Brian Layng, President/CEO
Rick Flattum, Director Operations
Heidi Crannell, Marketing Coordinator
Bruce Tarbet, Sponsorship/Advertising
Brent Layng, Sales Manager
Fishing, hunting, outdoor sports and destination travel show. Connect with new dealers and network with other exhibitors.

22325 Ski Dazzle Ski Show and Snowboard Expo: Chicago
Ski Dazzle
P.O. Box 1839
Laguna Beach, CA 92651

949-497-4977
FAX 949-497-4123
E-Mail: snowdog@skidazzle.com
Home Page: www.skidazzle.com
Social Media: *Facebook, Twitter, LinkedIn, You Tube*

Judy Gray, Owner
Jim Foster, Owner
Hundreds of local, national and international exhibitors including over 85 resorts, ski and snowboard retailers, manufacturers, a huge ski and snowboard sale, and lots of surprises. Over 250 exhibit booths showcasing core companies of skiing and snowboarding.

22326 Ski Dazzle: The Los Angeles Ski Show & Snowboard Expo
P.O. Box 1840
Laguna Beach, CA 92651-1839

949-497-4977
FAX 949-497-4123
E-Mail: snowdog@skidazzle.com
Home Page: www.skidazzle.com
Social Media: *Facebook, Twitter, LinkedIn, You Tube*

Judy Gray, Co-Owner
Jim Foster, Owner
Consumer ski show and snowboard expo at the Los Angeles Convention Center offering 350 ski and snowboard related exhibits. Excellent sponsor and promotional opportunities for 18-49 demographic audience.
90000 Attendees
Frequency: November

22327 Soaring Society of America Annual Convention
5425 West Jack Gomez Boulevard
P.O. Box 2100
Hobbs, NM 88241

575-392-1177
FAX 575-392-8154
E-Mail: feedback@ssa.org
Home Page: www.ssa.org

C Wright, Executive Director
Annual convetion of the Soaring Society of America.

22328 Sporting Goods Manufacturers Markets
1150 17th Street NW
8th Floor
Washington, DC 20036-1604

202-775-1762
FAX 202-296-7462
E-Mail: info@sgma.com
Home Page: www.sgma.com

Tom Cove, President/CEO
Gregg Harrlety, VP
Kalinda Mathis, Director Marketing
Retailers, distributors, wholesalers, importers/exporters and other buyers of sports related products come for 10,000 exhibits of sports apparel, footwear, accessories and e-commerce products and services.
80000 Attendees
Frequency: Spring/Fall

22329 Sports Licensing & Entertainment Marketplace Tailgate Picnic Show
Showproco, LLC
1450 NE 123rd Street
North Miami, FL 33161

305-893-8771
800-327-3736
FAX 305-893-8783
E-Mail: showproco@csnipicom
Home Page: www.showproco.com
Social Media: *Facebook, Twitter, LinkedIn*

Tom Cove, President
Stanley Schwartz, Director
A show dedicated to sports licensed apparel & products with participation from major sports licensors and their licensees. In conjunction will be the Tailgate & Picnic Show, which will bring together all of the products sports fans want to buy. Attendees will represent everything from sporting goods stores to fan shops, grocery to gift shops, drug stores to convenience stores and more.
Frequency: November

22330 Strictly Sail Pacific
Jack London Square
Oakland, CA

800-817-7245
FAX 401-847-2044
E-Mail: info@sailamerica.com
Home Page: www.strictlysail.com
Social Media: *Facebook, Twitter, LinkedIn*

Cynthia Goss, Contact
Annual Boat Show. A mix of boats and gear, seminars and special events. It will feature over 300 exhibitors from 25 states and over 90 seminars.

22331 Surf Expo
Surf Expo Offices
990 Hammond Drive
Suite 325
Atlanta, GA 30328

678-817-7970
800-947-7873
FAX 404-220-3030
E-Mail: rturner@surfexpo.com
Home Page: www.surfexpo.com

Where manufacturers and retailers in the boardsports, and swim and resort industries have come together in a business-first buying and selling environment.
8M Attendees
Frequency: Twice Annually

22332 US Gymnastics Federation
US Gymnastics Congress
Pam American Plaza
201 South Capitol, Suite 300
Indianapolis, IN 46225

317-237-5050
FAX 317-692-5212
Home Page: www.usagym.org

Steve Penny, President
Three days of eduction with over 135 sessions offered. Lectures given by recognized top people in the field. Sessions on coaching, judging, business, preschool, recreational, sports science, fitness, Group Gymnastics and cheerleading. The Trade Show exhibit hall will feature 200 booths of products and information from over 85 different Industry Member vendors.
2M Attendees
Frequency: Annual

22333 US Lacrosse National Convention
113 W University Pkwy
Baltimore, MD 21210-3301

410-235-6882
FAX 410-366-6735
E-Mail: info@uslacrosse.org
Home Page: www.uslacrosse.org
Social Media: *Facebook, Twitter*

Steve Stenersen, President
Bill Schoonmaker, COO
Bill Rubacky, Managing Director of Marketing
Kira Muller, Director of Advertising Sales
Billed as the unofficial start to lacrosse season, the event gathers the best the sport has to offer; providing the largest educational opportunity with over 5,000 coaches, officials, vendors and administrators in attendance. Over 100 exhibitors
5000 Attendees
Frequency: Annual

22334 USA Track and Field Annual Meeting
One RCA Dome
Suite 140
Indianapolis, IN 46225

317-261-0500
FAX 317-261-0481
E-Mail: membership@usatf.org

Home Page: www.usatf.org

Social Media: *Facebook, Twitter, LinkedIn*

Jill Geer, Public Relations

Annual meeting of the USA Track and Field organization.

Frequency: Annual

22335 USTFCCCA Annual Coaches Convention
U.S. Track & Field and Cross Country Coaches Assoc
1100 Poydras Street
Suite 1750
New Orleans, LA 70163

504-599-8900
FAX 504-599-8909
E-Mail: sam@ustfccca.org
Home Page: www.ustfccca.org
Social Media: *Facebook, Twitter, LinkedIn*

Sam Seemes, CEO
Mike Corn, Assistant Director
Sylvia Kamp, Administrator
Tom Lewis, Director of Communications

22336 Underwater Intervention
5206 FM 1960 West
Suite 202
Houston, TX 77069

281-893-8539
800-316-2188
FAX 281-893-5118
E-Mail: rroberts@adc-int.org
Home Page: www.underwaterintervention.com/
Social Media: *Facebook, Twitter, LinkedIn*

Rebecca Roberts, Show Manager
Roff Saxon, Executive Director

Conference covering all aspects of underwater operations. Next trade show is scheduled for 2007 with 200+ booths, sponsored by both the Marine Technology Society and the Association of Diving Contractors International.
2500 Attendees
Founded in 1991

22337 WBCA National Convention
Women's Basketball Coaches Association
4646 Lawrenceville Highway
Lilburn, GA 30047

770-279-8027
FAX 770-279-8473
E-Mail: wbca@wbca.org
Home Page: www.wbca.org
Social Media: *Facebook, Twitter*

Beth Bass, CEO
Shannon Reynolds, COO
Seana Peck, Manager Marketing
Stephanie S Baron, Director Events
Dorinda Schremmer, Director Membership/Conventions

Women's Basketball Coaches Association national convention. Held annually.
Founded in 1981

22338 Water Ski and Wakeboard Expo
1251 Holy Cow Road
Polk City, FL 33868

863-324-4341
FAX 863-325-8529
E-Mail: usawaterski@usawaterski.org
Home Page: www.usawaterski.org
Social Media: *Facebook, Twitter, LinkedIn*

Annual event of the USA Water Ski Organization.
Frequency: Annual

22339 Western Fairs Association Annual Trade Show
Western Fairs Association

1776 Tribute Road
Suite 210
Sacramento, CA 95815-4495

916-927-3100
FAX 916-927-6397
E-Mail: stephenc@fairsnet.org
Home Page: www.fairsnet.org
Social Media: *Facebook, Twitter, YouTube*

Rick Pickering, President
Jon Baker, VP
Stephen J Chambers, Executive Director
Nichole Farley, Marketing

Meet face to face with buyers from the Fair and Festival Industry across the Western United States. Acts, attractions, services, supplies, commericial exhibitors and more.
2000 Members
Frequency: Annual/Jan
Founded in 1922

22340 Western States Toy and Hobby Show
Western Toy and Hobby Representative Association
PO Box 2250
Pomona, CA 91786

909-899-3753
FAX 951-277-1599
E-Mail: toyshow@wthra.com
Home Page: www.wthra.com
Social Media: *Facebook, Twitter*

Phylis St John, Show Director

If it's for kids, it's here. Show is for trade members only, not open to the public.
3000 Attendees
Frequency: March

22341 World Fishing and Outdoor Exposition
Eastern Fishing and Outdoor Exposition
PO Box 4720
Portsmouth, NH 03802-4720

603-431-4315
FAX 603-431-1971
E-Mail: info@sportshows.com
Home Page: www.sportshows.com
Social Media: *Facebook*

You'll find the entire world of fishing and hunting and much more.
Frequency: Annual
Founded in 1978

22342 World Fly Fishing Expo
Eastern Fishing and Outdoor Exposition
PO Box 4720
Portsmouth, NH 03802-4720

603-431-4315
FAX 603-431-1971
E-Mail: info@sportshows.com
Home Page: www.sportshows.com
Social Media: *Facebook*

This expo has all the major manufacturers of fly rods and reels, fly fishing accessories, fly tying materials, guides and lodges.
Frequency: Annual

Directories & Databases

22343 Amusement Park Guide
Globe Pequot Press
246 Goose Ln
Suite 200
Guilford, CT 06437-2186

203-458-4500
FAX 203-458-4601
Home Page: www.globepequot.com

James Joseph, President

The complete guide to the amusement parks in the United States and Canada gives the latest details about new rides at each park, with a special focus on roller coasters.
Cost: $14.95
ISBN: 0-762725-37-0

22344 Athlete and Celebrity Address Directory/Autograph Hunter's Guide
Global Sports Productions
16810 Crystal Drive East
Suite 101
Santa Monica, CA 90404-2702

310-454-9480
FAX 310-454-6590
E-Mail: globalnw@earthlink.net
Home Page: www.sportsbookempire.com
Social Media: *Facebook*

Ed Kobak, Owner
Greg Andrews, VP Operations

Complete source of athlete and sports personality addresses from baseball, basketball, football, hockey, golf, tennis, soccer, boxing and autosports. Also included are television, movie and other celebrities' addresses.
Cost: $ 29.95
198 Pages
Frequency: Annual
ISBN: 0-966796-17-9
Founded in 2005

22345 Baseball Bluebook
8373 N Cedar Hills Lane
Fair Grove, MD 65648

417-833-6550
FAX 417-833-9911
E-Mail: dj@baseballbluebook.com
Home Page: www.baseballbluebook.com

Dennis Wubbena, Owner
Eric Wubbena, President

Directory of baseball club personnel at all levels of play. Spiral bound directory contains Major Leagues, Minor Leagues and Independent League Personnel, contact information and schedules
Cost: $55.00
500 Pages
Frequency: Annual
Founded in 1909

22346 Complete Directory of Fishing Tackle
Sutton Family Communications & Publishing Company
155 Sutton Lane
Fordsville, KY 42343

270-740-0870
E-Mail: jlsutton@apex.net
Home Page: www.fleamarketeer.net

Jerry Sutton, Contact

Listings in directory include names, addresses, phone and fax numbers, and product descriptions from wholesale distributors, Importers, Manufacturers, Close-out houses and liquidators.
Cost: $72.20
100+ Pages

22347 Complete Directory of Outdoor Products
Sutton Family Communications & Publishing Company
155 Sutton Lane
Fordsville, KY 42343

270-740-0870
E-Mail: jlsutton@apex.net
Home Page: www.fleamarketeer.net

Jerry Sutton, Manager

Print-out from database of wholesalers, manufacturers, distributors, importers and close-out houses. Database is updated daily to guarantee

the most current and up-to-date sources available.
Cost: $95.20
100+ Pages

22348 Complete Directory of Sporting Goods

Sutton Family Communications &
Publishing Company
155 Sutton Lane
Fordsville, KY 42343

270-740-0870
E-Mail: jlsutton@apex.net
Home Page: www.fleamarketeer.net

Jerry Sutton, Manager

Print-out from database of wholesalers, manufacturers, distributors, importers and close-out houses. Database is updated daily to guarantee the most current and up-to-date sources available.
Cost: $139.00
100+ Pages

22349 Computer Sports World

675 Grier Drive
Las Vegas, NV 89119-3738

702-735-0101
800-321-5562
FAX 702-294-1322
E-Mail: dandros@vegasinsider.com
Home Page: www.cswstats.com

Statistical information on all aspects of the sports industry.
Frequency: Full-text
Founded in 1983

22350 Encyclopedia of Sports Business Contacts

Global Sports Productions
1223 Broadway
Suite 101
Santa Monica, CA 90404-2702

310-395-6533
FAX 310-454-6590
E-Mail: globalnw@earthlink.net
Home Page: www.sportsbooksempire.com
Social Media: *Facebook, Twitter*

Ed Kobak, President

This huge book covers the business side of sports with addresses, telephone and fax numbers, emails, websites and entire contact personnel from sports organizations, teams, leagues, publications, lawyers and agents, corporate sponsors, sports marketing and management firms and others.
Cost: $79.95
600 Pages
Frequency: Annual
Founded in 2005

22351 Golf Traveler

Affinity Group
64 Inverness Dr E
Englewood, CO 80112-5114

303-728-7428
800-234-3450
FAX 303-728-7257
Home Page: www.affinitygroup.com

Bruce Hoster, Manager

Golf courses and affiliated resorts are listed.
Cost: $2.50
88 Pages
Frequency: BiMonthly
Circulation: 75,000

22352 International Sports Directory

Global Sports Productions

1223 Broadway
Suite 101
Santa Monica, CA 90404-2702

310-395-6533
FAX 310-454-6590
E-Mail: globalnw@earthlink.net
Home Page: www.sportsbooksempire.com

Ed Kobak, Owner

This all-in-one directory covers the entire world of sports from A to Z. Included are addresses, e-mails, websites, telephone and fax numbers and contact personnel from sports organizations, clubs, teams and publications. The most comprehensive sports directory available, covering both national and international listings.
Cost: $29.95
500 Pages
Frequency: Annual
ISBN: 1-891655-02-7
Founded in 1980

22353 Motor Sports Forum

Racing Information Systems
2314 Harriman Ln
Unit A
Redondo Beach, CA 90278-4426

310-374-3750
E-Mail: racing@motorsportsforum.com
Home Page: www.motorsportsforum.com

Michael F Hollander, Editor-in-Chief
Bab Karambelas, Senior Editor

This database contains information on auto racing in the United States and Canada.
Frequency: Bulletin Board

22354 News/Retrieval Sports Report

Dow Jones & Company
1155 Avenue of the Americas
New York, NY 10036-2717

212-597-5756
FAX 212-416-4348
Home Page: www.dowjones.com

Offers information on sports news stories and statistics from United Press International.
Frequency: Full-text

22355 Orion Blue Book: Guns and Scopes

Orion Research Corporation
14555 N Scottsdale Rd
Suite 330
Scottsdale, AZ 85254-3487

480-951-1114
800-844-0759
FAX 480-951-1117
Home Page: www.orionbluebook.com

Roger Rohrs, Owner

List of manufacturers of guns. Current issue contains 18,543 products. Lists products from 1800's to present. Over 300 manufacturers listed.
Cost: $45.00
480 Pages
Frequency: Annual
Founded in 1992

22356 Parks Directory of the United States

Omnigraphics
615 Griswold Street
Detroit, MI 48226

313-961-1340
800-234-1340
FAX 313-961-1383
E-Mail: editorial@omnigraphics.com
Home Page: www.omnigraphics.com

Darren L Smith, Editor

Covers nearly 5,000 national and state parks, and other designated recreational, scenic, and historic areas in the United States and Canada. It provides up-to-date contact and descriptive

information for every national and state park in the U.S.
Cost: $185.00
1,100 Pages
Frequency: Biennial
ISBN: 0-780806-63-8

22357 Q&A Booklets

Sporting Goods Agents Association
14555~N~Scottsdale~Rd
Scottsdale~, AZ 60053

847-296-3670
FAX 847-827-0196
E-Mail: sgaa998@aol.com
Home Page: www.sgaaonline.org

Skip Nipper, President
Lois Halinton, Chief Operating Officer

Sporting Goods Agents Association booklets for manufacturers and agents. Answers questions such as: Why should I use an independent agent rather than hire my own salespeople? What are the most important aspects to examine when I interview an agency? What are independent sporting goods agents and what do they do? What factors should be considered when forming a territory to cover. And more.
Cost: $15.00

22358 Recreation Facilities Products & Services

Sutton Family Communications &
Publishing Company
155 Sutton Lane
Fordsville, KY 42343

270-740-0870
E-Mail: jlsutton@apex.net
Home Page: www.fleamarketeer.net

Jerry Sutton, Manager

Print-out from database of wholesalers, manufacturers, distributors, importers and close-out houses. Database is updated daily to guarantee the most current and up-to-date sources available. Accepts advertising.
Cost: $97.20
100+ Pages

22359 Recreational Sports Directory

National Intramural Recreational Sports Assn
4185 Sw Research Way
Corvallis, OR 97333-1067

541-766-8211
FAX 541-766-8284
E-Mail: nirsa@nirsa.org
Home Page: www.nirsa.org

Kent Blumenthal, Executive Director

Directory of services and supplies to the industry.
Cost: $20.00
400 Pages
Frequency: Annual
Circulation: 1,500

22360 Sporting News Baseball Guide

Sporting News Publishing Company
10176 Corporate Square Drive
Suite 200
Saint Louis, MO 63132-2924

314-997-7111
FAX 314-993-7798
Home Page: www.sportingnews.com

Jim Nuckols, CEO

A list of National and American League and their affiliate minor leagues.
Cost: $12.95
Frequency: Annual

22361 Sporting News Football Register

Sporting News Publishing Company

10176 Corporate Square Drive
Suite 200
Saint Louis, MO 63132-2924

314-997-7111
FAX 314-993-7798
Home Page: www.sportingnews.com

Jim Nuckols, CEO

Directory of services and supplies to the industry.
Cost: $12.95
430 Pages
Frequency: Annual

22362 Sports Address Bible and Almanac
Global Sports Productions
1223 Broadway
Suite 101
Santa Monica, CA 90404-2702

310-395-6533
FAX 310-454-6590
E-Mail: globalnw@earthlink.net
Home Page: www.sportsbooksempire.com

Ed Kobak, Owner
Greg Andrews, VP Operations

Over 7,500 sports listings from professional, semi-pro, Olympic and amateur, collegiate and interscholastic sports organizations, leagues, teams, halls of fame, media outlets and more.
Cost: $34.95
505 Pages
Frequency: Biennial
ISBN: 1-891655-11-6
ISSN: 0743-4561
Founded in 1998

22363 Sports Market Place Directory
Grey House Publishing
4919 Route 22
PO Box 56
Amenia, NY 12501

518-789-8700
800-562-2139
FAX 845-373-6390
E-Mail: books@greyhouse.com
Home Page: www.greyhouse.ocm
Social Media: *Facebook, Twitter*

Leslie Mackenzie, Publisher
Richard Gottlieb, Editor

For over 20 years, this comprehensive, up-to-date directory has offered direct access to the Who, What, When & Where of the Sports Industry. With this directory on your desk, you have a comprehensive tool providing current key information about the people, organizations and events involving the explosive sports industry at your fingertips.
Cost: $225.00
1800 Pages
Frequency: Annual
ISBN: 1-592373-48-8
Founded in 1981

22364 Sports Market Place Directory - Online Database
Grey House Publishing
4919 Route 22
PO Box 56
Amenia, NY 12501

518-789-8700
800-562-2139
FAX 845-373-6390
E-Mail: gold@greyhouse.com
Home Page: www.gold.greyhouse.com
Social Media: *Facebook, Twitter*

Leslie Mackenzie, Publisher
Richard Gottlieb, Editor

For over 20 years, this comprehensive, up-to-date directory provides current key information about the people, organizations and events involving the sports industry including,

contact information and key executives for single sports organizations, multi-sport organizations, media, sponsors, college sports, manufacturers, trade shows and more.
Founded in 1981

22365 Sports RoundTable
GE Information Services
401 N Washington Street
Rockville, MD 20850-1707

301-388-8284
Cathy Ge, Owner

This database provides coverage of major professional, amateur and collegiate sports including football, basketball, baseball, and hockey.
Frequency: Full-text

22366 SportsAlert
Comtex Scientific Corporation
911 Hope Street
#4838
Stamford, CT 06907-2318

FAX 203-358-0236
Home Page: www.sportsalert.net

This database contains sports news and statistics providing real-time coverage of US and international professional, collegiate and amateur athletic events.
Frequency: Full-text

22367 Tennis-Places to Play: Camps and Clinics Issue
Golf Digest Tennis NY Times Magazine Group
5520 Park Avenue
Trumbull, CT 06611-3400

203-373-7000
FAX 203-371-2162

Directory of services and supplies to the industry.
Cost: $2.50
Frequency: Annual
Circulation: 800,000

Industry Web Sites

22368 http://gold.greyhouse.com
G.O.L.D Grey House OnLine Databases
Grey House Publishing's online database platform, GOLD, offers Quick Search, Keyword Search and Expert Search for most business sectors including sports and recreation markets. The GOLD platform makes finding the information you need quick and easy - whether you're a novice searcher or an experienced database user. All of Grey House's directory products are available for subscription on the GOLD platform.

22369 www.aahperd.org
American Alliance for Hlth, Phys. Edu. Rec. Dance

22370 www.aahperd.org/uawgs
National Association for Girls and Women in Sports
A non-profit organization serving the needs of teachers, coaches and participants of sports programs for girls and women.

22371 www.aapsm.org
American Academy of Podiatric Sports Medicine
The American Academy of Podiatric Sports Medicine was founded in San Francisco by a group of podiatric sports physicians who had the insight to realize the need for a podiatric sports medicine association devoted to the

treatment of athletic injuries. Today the AAPSM has over 500 members.

22372 www.aausports.org
Amateur Athletic Union of the United States

22373 www.abca.org
American Baseball Coaches Association
Formerly called the American Association of College Baseball Coaches.

22374 www.aca-camps.org
American Camping Association
Educational programs. Legislative monitoring, child and youth development.

22375 www.acanet.org
American Canoe Association
Promotes the sport of canoeing and its safety, recreational and conservation

22376 www.acsm.org
American College of Sports Medicine
The ACSM promotes and integrates scientific research, education, and practical applications of sports medicine and exercise science to maintain and enhance physical performance, fitness, health, and quality of life.

22377 www.adventurecycling.org
Adventure Cycling Association
Developes road and mountain bike routes, runs bike tours and eventsand also acts as information resource for bicyclists planning trips.

22378 www.aeawave.com
Aquatic Exercise Association
Covers topics relating to aquatic fitness and therapy including industry trends, research, programs, exercises and products.

22379 www.afaa.com
Aerobics and Fitness Association of America
Association for the education, certification and training of exercise instructors; information resource center for consumers.

22380 www.ahcahockey.com
American Hockey Coaches Association
Helps maintain the highest possible standards in hockey and the hockey profession.

22381 www.americanrunning.org
American Running Association
To encourage all people, from youth to adults, to improve their health and fitness by walking and running, and maintaining an active and healthy lifestyle.

22382 www.asgca.org
American Society of Golf Course Architects
A non-profit organization comprised of leading golf course designers in North America. ASGCA is actively involved in many issues realted to the game of golf, including responsible environmental designs.

22383 www.athleticclubs.com
Athletic Net
Click on links to find fitness, sports medicine, general health and wellness, government sites, directories, nutrition and newsgroups.

22384 www.avca.org
American Volleyball Coaches Association
To develop and grow the sport of volleyball

22385 www.baseballcoaches.org
National High School Baseball Coaches Association

Provides services and recognition for baseball coaches and to help promote and represent high school baseball across the country.

22386 www.bikeleague.org
League of American Bicyclists

Founded in 1880, the League is the only national membership organization of bicyclists in the United States. The League works to promote and encourage bicycling for recreation and transportation, and to protect and defend the rights of bicyclists through advocacy and education.

22387 www.collegecoaches.org
College Swimming Coaches Association of America

The oldest organization of college coaches in America; a professional organization of college swimming and diving coaches dedicated to serving and providing leadership for the advancement of the sport of swimming at the collegiate level.

22388 www.greyhouse.com
Grey House Publishing

Authoritative reference directories for most business sectors including sports and recreation markets. Users can search the online databases with varied search criteria allowing for custom searches by product category, geographic area, sales volume, keyword, subject and more. Full Grey House catalog and online ordering also available.

22389 www.iasv.net
International Academy of Sports Vision

Promotes education, research and development of sports visions. Publishes Sportsvision Magazine and annual scientific journal. Mission is to prevent eye injuries and imprrove visual performance in sports.

22390 www.instituteofdiving.com
Institute of Diving

Membership includes sports, commercial and military divers with the purpose being to operate the Museum of Man in the Sea, publish a newsletter, provide a technical library, offer an information exchange, and promote programs and projects for the improvement of knowledge about the underwater world.

22391 www.iprarodeo.com
International Professional Rodeo Association

Governing body for professional rodeo. 500 rodeos across USA and Canada, $5 million prize money per year, 5 million fans.

22392 www.lpga.com
Ladies Professional Golf Association

For women and youth golfers.

22393 www.naa-usa.org
National Aeronautic Association

Members include aerospace corporations, aero clubs, affiliates and major national sporting aviation organizations.

22394 www.nabc.com
National Association of Basketball Coaches

Promotes the advancement and opportunities for coaches and teachers in the sport of basketball.

22395 www.nabf.com
National Amateur Baseball Association

Promotes amateur baseball and the industry in general.

22396 www.nacola.com
Nat'l Assoc of Collegiate Directors of Athletics

Professional association for college athletics directors, assistants and conference administrators. Provides educational opportunities and serves as a vehicle for networking and the exchange of information to others in the college sports profession.

22397 www.nasgw.org
National Association of Sporting Goods

Non-profit trade association of wholesalers, distributors and manufacturers. Serves as a liason with other sporting goods associations.

22398 www.naso.org
National Association of Sports Officials

Not-for-profit 501(c)(3) educational association providing individual benefits such as training materials, liability and assault protection insurance and more to sports officials of all sports and every level.

22399 www.nauticalworld.com
Nautical World

Dedicated to bringing all related web sites within easy access to watersports enthusiasts. This search engine has been designed to locate advertiser's information within Nautical World but will also offer access to other watersport related web sites as well. Offers sections on marine electronics and hardware, sailing, boats, dock supplies, fishing accessories, diving accessories, industry news, watersports, weather forecasting and more.

22400 www.nays.org
National Youth Sports Coaches Association

Represents coaches involved in youth athletics.

22401 www.nfca.org
National Fastpitch Coaches Association

The professional growth organization for fastpitch softball coaches from all competitives levels of play.

22402 www.nflalumni.org
National Football League Alumni

Provides a forum for those individuals retired from the NFL but still playing an active role.

22403 www.ngf.org
National Golf Foundation

Provides market research and serves as an information clearinghouse for the industry. Conducts seminars for golf teachers, coaches and professionals. Conducts golf course development feasibility studies for developers.

22404 www.njcaa.org
National Junior College Athletic Association

NJCAA members are two year institutions recognized by the American Association of Community and Junior Colleges.

22405 www.nra.org
National Rifle Association

Oldest sportsmen's organization in the US. Maintains the NRA Political Victory Fund and supports the Institute for Legislative Action.

22406 www.nsga.org
National Sporting Goods Association

Association of retailers, manufacturers and suppliers of sports equipment, footwear, and apparel.

22407 www.nsgachicagoshow.com
Athletic Goods Team Distributors

Strives to keep athletic team dealers informed of rule changes that affect equipment sales.

22408 www.pga.com
Professional Golfers Association of America

The world's largest working sports organization comprised of more than 25,000 men and women PGA professionals to promote the game of golf to everyone, and to promote its members as leaders in the golf industry.

22409 www.popwarner.com
Pop Warner Little Scholars

A national youth football and cheerleading organization that provides assistance to its various chapters.

22410 www.r-sports.com
Sporting Goods Agents Association

International trade association of independent and established sporting goods agents.

22411 www.restaurantreport.com/top100
Resturant Report On-Line

Includes top 100 food sites, feature stories, newsletters, buyer's guide, marketplace, hospitality jobs.

22412 www.rollerskating.com
Roller Skating Association

Exists for private businessmen and women engaged in the enterprise of roller skating.

22413 www.rollerskating.org
Roller Skating Association International

A trade association representing skating center owners, operators; teachers, coaches and judges of roller skating; and manufacturers and suppliers of roller skating equipment.

22414 www.sabr.org
Society for American Baseball Research

Membership association whose purpose is to facilitate and disseminate baseball research.

22415 www.sgma.com
Sporting Goods Manufacturers Association

For manufacturers, producers, and distributers of sports apparel, athletic footwear, fitness, and sporting goods equipment.

22416 www.skateisi.org
Ice Skating Institute

Industry trade association dedicated to providing leadership, education and services to the ice skating industry.

22417 www.sportsheritage.org
International Sports Heritage Association

The mission of ISHA is to educate, promote and support organizations and individuals engaged in the celebration of sports heritage.

22418 www.sportsmarketplce.com
Grey House Publishing

Provides organizations' contact information with detailed descriptions including: key contacts, physical, mailing, email and web addresses plus phone and fax numbers.

22419 www.sportsmed.org
American Orthopaedic Society for Sports Medicine

Promotes the prevention, recognition and orthopedic treatment of sports injuries.

22420 www.sportsplexoperators.com
Sportsplex Operators and Developers of Association

SODA was formed to meet the needs of the private concerns, public agencies, and other organizations that own or maintain sports complex facilities.

22421 www.teamusa.org
US Olympic Committee

The national committee for the US. Handles the preparation of the US Olympic, Paralympic and Pan American Games teams.

22422 www.tennisindustry.org
Tennis Industry Association

To educate the marketplace, fund research and market intelligence and supply this reliable industry data to our member companies. The TIA is the Information source and clearing house for positive tennis news that we supply to TIA members, tennis publications and to the mainstream media in cooperation with the USTA.

22423 www.usa-swimming.org
USA Swimming

Devoted to the sport of swimming and its enjoyment nationwide.

22424 www.usahockey.com
USA Hockey

Promotes the sport of hockey.

22425 www.usarchery.org
National Archery Association

Supports archers while aiming to advance the sport of archery in the US. Monthly newsletter, Nock-Nock, provides communication among the NAA office, NAA clubs, state associations and the individual members of the NAA. Provides members with news and tournament results ranging from the local and state level to international competition.

22426 www.usatt.org
USA Table Tennis

Dedicated to the promotion of the sport of table tennis and sponsors the US team. Membership dues are $30 per year for adults and $20 for those 18 years old and under.

22427 www.usawaterski.org
USA Water Ski Association

Encourages interest in the sport as well as training and safety.

22428 www.usaweightlifting.org
USA Weightlifting

USA Weightlifting is the National Governing Body (NGB) for the Olympic sport of weightlifting in the United States. USA weightlifting is a member of the United States Olympic Committee and a member of the International Weightlifting Federation. As the NGB, USA Weightlifting is responsible for conducting Olympic weightlifting programs throughout the country. The organization conducts a variety of programs that will ultimately develop Olympic, World Championship and Pan American Games' winners.

22429 www.usfencing.org
United States Fencing Association

Promotes the sport of fencing in the US.

22430 www.usfieldhockey.com
US Field Hockey Association

Represents field hockey, professional and amateur sports.

22431 www.ushandball.org
US Handball Association

Organization that runs all the tournaments for the professional and amateur players. Home of the Handball Hall of Fame.

22432 www.usolimplc.com
United States Amateur Boxing

Promotes the sport of boxing nationwide.

22433 www.uspa.org
United States Parachute Association

A not-for-profit membership association dedicated to the promotion of safe skydiving and the support of those who enjoy it. Sponsors Instructor Rating Program to train and certify instructors, jump masters and examiners.

22434 www.usra.org
US Raquetball Association

A nonprofit corporation designed to promote the development of competitive and recreational racquetball in the United States. The association offers a 'competitive license' membership for a one year term at $15.00 annually, or at discounted longer term rates. A lifetime membership is also offered. A 'Club Recreational Membership' program is offered for an annual fee of $150.00 with a reduced AARA recreational membership available to club members for $3.00 per player.

22435 www.usskiteam.com,
www.ussnowboardteam.com
US Ski & Snowboard Association

Association for skiing and snowboarding nationwide.

22436 www.usspeedskating.org
US Speedskating

Devoted to speedskating and its participants on the national and international levels.

22437 www.ustfccca.org
U.S. Track & Field and Cross Country Coaches Assoc

A non-profit professional organization that represents men's and women's cross country and track & field coaches in the United States.

22438 www.uswfa.com
United States Water Fitness Association

Nonprofit educational organization that promotes aquatics throughout the United States and other countries. Publishes the National Aquatics Newsletter, names the 100 top US water fitness programs and aquatics 5 aquatics in the country, by state and in 25+ categories. Conducts a wide variety of national aquatics certifications including Water Fitness Instructors (primary and masters), aquatic directors, coordinators of water fitness programs. Conducts annual international aquatics conference.

22439 www.volleyball.org
US Volleyball Association

Promotes volleyball in the US trains the USA men's and women's teams promotes beach and grassroots voleyball in the United States.

22440 www.voyager.net/aabc
American Amateur Baseball Congress

Provides administrative services for amateur baseball youth through adults. 250,000 members.

22441 www.ymca.net
YMCA of the USA

Provides national and state branch divisions.

Associations

22442 Allied Stone Industries

PO Box 288145
Chicago, IL 60628-8145

773-928-4800
FAX 773-928-4129
Home Page: www.alliedstone.com
Social Media: *Facebook, Twitter*

Gary Ballerini, President
Pam Pine, VP
Brundene Van Ness, President-Elect
Butch Coleman, Treasurer
Bill Halquist, Secretary

Quarries, fabricators and dealers in stone and concrete.
55 Members
Founded in 1950

22443 American Concrete Institute

38800 Country Club Drive
PO Box 9094
Farmington Hills, MI 48331

248-848-3700
FAX 248-848-3701
E-Mail: ron.burg@concrete.org
Home Page: www.concrete.org
Social Media: *Facebook, Twitter, LinkedIn, Youtube*

Anne M Ellis, President
William B Rushing, VP
Sharon L Wood, VP
Ronald G Burg, Executive VP

ACI is a scientific and educational society representing the interests of concrete users concerned with the design, construction, or maintenance of concrete structures. Conventions and meetings, monthly periodicals and special publications; chapter activities; and technical committees all provide a forum for concrete interests to discuss problems relating to concrete.
20000 Members
Founded in 1904

22444 American Concrete Pavement Association

9450 W Bryn Mawr Ave.
Suite 150
Rosemont, IL 60018

847-966-2272
FAX 847-966-9970
E-Mail: acpa@acpa.org
Home Page: www.pavement.com
Social Media: *Facebook, Twitter, LinkedIn, Youtube*

Jerry Voigt, CEO & President
Mike Lipps, Chairman
Steve Jackson, Vice Chairman
Lori Tiefenthaler, 2nd Vice Chair
Glenn Eder, Treasurer

ACPA is committed to promoting the quality and superiority of concrete pavements. It leads and assists its members in market development, technical expertise, design innovation, research, and public relations. ACPA's membership includes contractors, cement companies, material suppliers, equipment manufacturers and suppliers, ready mix producers, allied associations, bonding and insurance companies, and consulting firms.
Founded in 1963

22445 American Concrete Pipe Association

8445 Freeport Parkway
Suite 350
Irving, TX 75063-2595

972-506-7216
FAX 972-506-7682

E-Mail: info@concrete-pipe.org
Home Page: www.concrete-pipe.org
Social Media: *Facebook, Twitter, LinkedIn, Youtube, Pinterest*

Michael D. Kusch, Chairman
A. C. Gossett, III, Vice Chairman
Darren Wise, Secretary
Brian Rhees, Treasurer
Matt Childs, P.E., President

The American Concrete Pipe Association (ACPA) is a nonprofit organization, composed primarily of manufacturers of concrete pipe and related conveyance products located throughout the United States, Canada and in over 40 foreign countries.
145 Members
Founded in 1907

22446 American Natural Soda Ash Corporation

15 Riverside Avenue
2nd Floor
Westport, CT 06880

203-226-9056
FAX 203-227-1484
E-Mail: contact@ansac.org
Home Page: www.ansac.com
Social Media: *Facebook, Twitter*

Donna McSwain-Santos, Marketing

ANSAC markets, sells and distributes high quality soda ash to over 40 countries around the world.
Founded in 1984

22447 American Society of Concrete Contractors

2025 S Brentwood Blvd
Suite 105
St Louis, MO 63144-1850

314-962-0210
866-788-2722
FAX 314-968-4367
E-Mail: questions@ascconline.org
Home Page: www.ascconline.org
Social Media: *Facebook, Twitter, LinkedIn, Pinterest*

Scott M. Anderson, President
Anthony R. DeCarlo, Jr., VP
Chris Forster, VP
Mario Garza, VP
Keith Wayne, Treasurer/Secretary

The American Society of Concrete Contractors/ASCC seeks to continually advance the qualifications of concrete constructors and encourage greater interaction between designer and constructor. Publishes the Contactor's Guide to Quality Concrete Construction jointly with ACI. Issues Safety Alerts, Safety Bulletins, and a Safety Manual as well as a troubleshooting newsletter, management reports, and a members bulletin.

22448 Concrete Employers Association

900 Spring Street
Silver Spring, MD 20910

240-485-1139
888-846-7622
FAX 301-585-4219
E-Mail: rgarbini@nrmca.org
Home Page: www.nrmca.org
Social Media: *Facebook, Twitter, LinkedIn, Youtube*

Robert Garbini, President
Deana Angelastro, Executive Administrator
Allen Hamblen, Chairman
Ted Chandler, Vice Chairman
Scott Parson, Secretary/Treasurer

Concrete plant manufacturers.
Founded in 1930

22449 Concrete Foundations Association

113 W First Street
PO Box 204
Mount Vernon, IA 52314

319-895-6940
FAX 320-213-5556
E-Mail: info@cfawalls.org
Home Page: www.cfawalls.org

David Martinson, President
Dennis Purinton, Vice-President
Phillip Marone, Secretary
Doug Herbert, Treasurer
Jim Bartley, Past-President

Members are residential foundation contractors and their suppliers. The association produces promotional, marketing and technical materials for members' potential customers; provides its members with newsletters, industry publications, and seminar and trade show opportunities; develops specifications, technical information, and safety programs; and represents its members on national code bodies.
300 Members
Founded in 1975

22450 Concrete Polishing Association of America

38800 Country Club Dr.
Farmington Hills, MI 48331

443-249-7919
E-Mail: info@cpaa-us.org
Home Page:
www.concretepolishingassociation.org
Social Media: *Facebook, Twitter*

Chad Gill, President

Supporting and shaping the concrete polishing industry.
Founded in 2009

22451 Concrete Promotion Council of Northern California

6966 Sunrise Boulevard
Suite 329
Citrus Heights, CA 95610

916-952-0437
888-633-0393
FAX 831-302-7330
E-Mail: Paulette.Salisbury@cncement.org
Home Page: www.cpcnc.org

Paulette Salisbury, Interim Director
Bill Albanese, President Board of Directors
Jeff Nehmens, Treasurer Board of Directors
Dave Bearden, Member Board of Directors
Curt Higgins, Member Board of Directors

A member of the Pacific Southwest Concrete Alliance, composed of companies from all parts of the Northern Californian concrete industry including ready mix suppliers, cement producers, admixture manufacturers, concrete contractors as well as members of the public and private design committees. Their mission is to increase the quantity and diversity of quality concrete projects in Northern California through providing educational opportunities to the Professional Design Community.

22452 Concrete Reinforcing Steel Institute

933 N Plum Grove Road
Schaumburg, IL 60173-4758

847-517-1200
FAX 847-517-1206
E-Mail: brisser@crsi.org
Home Page: www.crsi.org
Social Media: *Facebook, Twitter, LinkedIn*

David McDonald, President
Joe Culligan, Chief Financial Officer
Steven Hawkins, Sr., VP, Marketing
David McDonald, Managing Director
Barbara Burchett, Government Affairs

Conducts research and provides technical information on reinforced concrete design and construction practices.
1600 Members
Founded in 1924

22453 Concrete Sawing and Drilling Association

100 2nd Ave S
Suite 402N
St Petersburg, FL 33701

727-577-5004
FAX 727-577-5012
E-Mail: info@csda.org
Home Page: www.csda.org
Social Media: *Facebook, LinkedIn, Youtube*

Kevin Baron, President
Jack Sondergard, VP
Mike Orzechowski, Secretary/Treasurer
Patrick O'Brien, Executive Director

To promote the use of professional specialty sawing and drilling contractors and their methods.
525 Members
Founded in 1972

22454 Expanded Shale Clay and Slate Institute

35 E Wacker Drive
Suite 850
Chicago, IL 60601

801-272-7070
FAX 312-644-8557
E-Mail: info@escsi.org
Home Page: www.escsi.org
Social Media: *LinkedIn, Youtube*

John Riese, President

Sponsors research at engineering schools, educational seminars and develops industry standards.
Founded in 1908

22455 Flexicore Manufacturers Association

7941 New Carlisle Pike
Huber Heights, OH 45424

937-879-5775
FAX 937-879-0826
Home Page: www.flexicore.com

Strives to protect industry from trade abuses and develop good business practices and quality of product.
11 Members
Founded in 1952

22456 Indiana Limestone Institute of America

1502 I Street
Suite 400
Bedford, IN 47421

812-275-4426
FAX 812-279-8682
E-Mail: jim@iliai.com
Home Page: www.iliai.com

Jim Owens, Technical Director
Todd Schnatzmeyer, Executive Director
Dave Morthland, Office Manager

The trade association which represents quarries and fabricators of Indiana Limestone, as well as associate members who supply goods or services to the industry, ILIA's charte is to eductate and promote
90 Members
Founded in 1928

22457 International Cast Polymer Alliance

3033 Wilson Blvd
Suite 420
Arlington, VA 22201

703-525-0511
FAX 703-525-0743

E-Mail: icpa@icpa-hq.org
Home Page: www.icpa-hq.org

Debbie Cannon, President
John Webster, President Elect
Jack Simmons, Secretary
Jamie Myers, Immediate Past President

Formerly known as the Cultured Marble Institute, is a nonprofit organization representing over 300 members including manufacturers, suppliers, fabricators, and installers of cultured marble, cultured granite, cultured onyx, and solid surface kitchen and bath products.

22458 Marble Institute of America

380 E. Lorain Street
Suite 100
Oberlin, OH 44074

440-250-9222
FAX 440-774-9222
E-Mail: miainfo@marble-institute.com
Home Page: www.marble-institute.com
Social Media: *Facebook, Twitter, LinkedIn, Youtube*

Jonathan Zanger, President
Tony Malisani, VP
Dan Rea, Secretary
David Castelucci, Treasurer

The Marble Institute of America (MIA) is the authoritative source of information on standards of natural stone workmanship and practice and the suitable application of natural stone products.
2000 Members
Founded in 1907

22459 Masonry Society

105 South Sunset Street
Suite Q
Longmont, CO 80501-6172

303-939-9700
FAX 303-541-9215
E-Mail: info@masonrysociety.org
Home Page: www.masonrysociety.org
Social Media: *LinkedIn*

Dr. Russell Brown, President
Scott Walkowicz, President-Elect
Jerry Painter, Vice President
Philip Samblanet, Executive Director
Susan Scheurer, TMS Meeting Planner

Dedicated to the advancement of scientific, engineering, architectual and construction knowledge of masonry. Promotes research and education and disseminates information on masonry materials, design, construction. Publishes newsletters, codes & specifications and material on masonry design.
700 Members
Founded in 1977

22460 National Concrete Burial Vault Association

136 South Keowee Street
Dayton, OH 45402

407-788-1996
888-88 -NCBV
FAX 937-222-5794
E-Mail: info@ncbva.org
Home Page: www.ncbva.org

Jerry Russell, President
Mark Bates, President Elect
Steve Handley, Secretary/Treasurer
Michael Crummitt, Immediate Past President
Ed Bruns, Director

A voluntary nonprofit organization of concrete burial vault manufacturers throughtout the United States and Canada. The purpose of the organization is to provide a unified voice for the concrete burial vault industry regardless of

product affiliation, brand recognition or location.
350 Members
Founded in 1930

22461 National Concrete Masonry Association

13750 Sunrise Valley Dr
Herndon, VA 20171-4662

703-713-1900
FAX 703-713-1910
E-Mail: info@ncma.org
Home Page: www.ncma.org
Social Media: *Facebook, Twitter, LinkedIn, Pinterest*

Robert Thomas, President
Ron Churchill, Director of Sales
Joseph Bowen, Chairman
Patrick Sauter, Chairman-Elect
Dale Puskas, Past Chairman

The national trade association representing the concrete masonry industry. The association is involved in a broad range of technical, research, marketing, government relations and community activities.
Founded in 1918

22462 National Lime Association

200 N Glebe Rd
Suite 800
Arlington, VA 22203-3728

703-243-5463
FAX 703-243-5489
E-Mail: wcherz@lime.org
Home Page: www.lime.org
Social Media: *Facebook*

William C Herz, Executive Director
Jonathan De'Ath, Director
Hunter L. Prillaman, Director, Govt. Affairs
Lori D Oney, Director, Finance, Administration
Robert A. Hirsch, Director, Environment

Trade association for US and Canadian manufacturers of high calcium quicklime, dolomitic quicklime and hydrated lime, collectively referred to as lime. NLA represents the interests of its members in Washington, provides input on standards and specifacations for lime, and funds and manages research on current and new uses for lime.
Founded in 1902

22463 National Precast Concrete Association

200 North Glebe
Suite 200
Arlington, IN 46032

317-571-9500
800-366-7731
FAX 317-571-0041
E-Mail: npca@precast.org
Home Page: www.precast.org
Social Media: *Facebook, Twitter, LinkedIn, Youtube, RSS, Flickr*

William C. Herz, MPH, Executive Director
Phillip Cutler, VP, Technical Services
Lori D. Oney, VP, Finance & Administration
Brenda Ibitz, VP, Development & Member Services
Bob Whitmore, VP, Communications & Public Affairs

An international trade organization, NPCA represents manufacturers of plant produced precast concrete products and companies that provide the equipment, supplies and services to make these products. NPCA also provides technical information throught nine product committees, which consist of members who concentrate on specific product lines within the precast industry.
1100 Members
Founded in 1965

22464 National Ready Mixed Concrete Association
900 Spring St
Silver Spring, MD 20910-4015

301-587-1400
888-846-7622
FAX 301-585-4219
E-Mail: info@nrmca.org
Home Page: www.nrmca.org
Social Media: *Facebook, Twitter, LinkedIn, Youtube*

Robert Garbini, President
Deana Angelastro, Executive Administrator
Allen Hamblen, Chairman
Ted Chandler, Vice Chairman
Scott Parson, Secretary/Treasurer

NRMCA represents its membership of ready mixed concrete producrs in market development, technical research, engineering advances, government relations, and regulatory issues. In addition to conducting educational seminars, workshops, conferences and trade shows, NRMCA disseminates a wide variety of publications for its members, ranging from Congressional digests and promotion pointers to driver education.
Founded in 1930

22465 Ornamental Concrete Producers Association
759 Phelps Johnson Rd
Leitchfield, KY 42754

270-879-6319
FAX 218-751-2186
E-Mail: delpreus@paulbunyan.net
Home Page: www.ornamentalconcrete.org

Del Preuss, Executive Director
Robert Garbini, President
Shawnita Dickens, Manager

An international nonprofit educational association comprised of producers and suppliers.
Cost: $50.00
500 Members
Founded in 1991

22466 Portland Cement Association
5420 Old Orchard Road
Skokie, IL 60077-1083

847-966-6200
FAX 847-966-9781
E-Mail: info@cement.org
Home Page: www.cement.org
Social Media: *Facebook, Twitter, LinkedIn, YouTube*

James Toscasÿ, President/CEO
John Stull, Chair
Karl Watson Jr., Vice-Chair
Tom Beck, President
Steve Ambrose, Vice President

The Portland Cement Association represents cement companies in the United States and Canada. It conducts market development, engineering, research, education, and public affairs programs.
Founded in 1916

22467 Post-Tensioning Institute
Bldg Main
38800 Country Club Dr
Farmington Hills, MI 48331-3439

248-848-3180
FAX 248-848-3181
E-Mail: info@post-tensioning.org
Home Page: www.post-tensioning.org
Social Media: *Facebook, Twitter, LinkedIn*

Theodore L Neff, Executive Director
Robert Sward, President
David Martin, VP
Guy Cloutier, Secretary
Marc Khoury, Past President

Provides research, technical development, marketing and promotional activities for companies engaged in post-tensioned prestressed construction. Members include fabricators and manufacturers.
900 Members
Founded in 1976

22468 Refractories Institute
1300 Sumner Avenue
PO Box 8439
Cleveland, OH 44115

216-241-7333
FAX 216-241-0105
E-Mail: info@refractoriesinstitute.org
Home Page: www.refractoriesinstitute.org

Robert Crolius, President

A trade association which promotes the interests of the refractories industry. TRI has a long tradition of providing support and services to manufacturers of refractory materials and products and suppliers of raw materials, equipment, and services to the refractories industry.
80 Members
Founded in 1951

22469 Specialty Minerals
Minerals Technology
405 Lexington Ave
New York, NY 10174-0002

212-986-2486
800-801-1031
FAX 610-882-8726
E-Mail:
smi.productinfo@specialtyminerals.com
Home Page: www.mineralstech.com

Joseph C Muscari, Executive Chairman
Robert S Wetherbee, President & CEO
Douglas T Dietrich, Senior VP/CFO
D J Monagle III, Senior VP/Managing Director
Thomas J Meek, Senior VP/General Counsel/Secretary

A subsidiary of Minerals Technology, Inc., a resource and technology based organization that develops and produces performance-enhancing minerals, mineral-based and synthetic mineral products for the paper, steel, polymer, healthcare and other manufacturing industries on a worldwide basis.
Founded in 1992

22470 Tilt-Up Concrete Association
113 First Street W
PO Box 204
Mount Vernon, IA 52314-0204

319-895-6911
FAX 320-213-5555
E-Mail: info@tilt-up.org
Home Page: www.tilt-up.org
Social Media: *Facebook, Twitter, LinkedIn, You Tube*

Kimberley Corwin, President
Shane Miller, President Elect
Andrew S McPherson, Treasurer
James M Williams, Secretary

TCA members include contractors, suppliers, architects, and engineers dedicated to the advancement of quality tilt-up concrete construction. Activities include a national promotional program, information clearinghouse, educational seminars, referral service, achievement awards program, development of codes and standards, and a quarterly magazine.
Founded in 1986

Newsletters

22471 Concrete Openings
Concrete Sawing and Drilling Association

13577 Feather Sound Drive
Suite 560
Clearwater, FL 33762

727-577-5004
FAX 727-577-5012
E-Mail: info@csda.org
Home Page: www.csda.org
Social Media: *Facebook, LinkedIn*

Patrick O'Brien, Executive Director
500 Members
300 Attendees
Frequency: Quarterly
Circulation: 17000
Founded in 1972

22472 Cutting Edge
Marble Institute of America
28901 Clemens Road
Suite 100
Cleveland, OH 44145

440-250-9222
FAX 440-250-9223
E-Mail: miainfo@marble-institute.com
Home Page: www.marble-institute.com

Gary Distelhorst, Executive VP/CEO
Helen Distelhorst, Director Meetings/Special Events
Jim Hieb, VP
Frequency: Monthly
Circulation: 1500

22473 Refractory News
Refractories Institute
630 Smithfield Street
Suite 1160
Pittsburgh, PA 15222-3907

412-281-6787
FAX 412-281-6881
E-Mail: triassn@aol.com
Home Page: www.refractoriesinstitute.org
Social Media: *Facebook, Twitter*

Flo Story, Editor

A monthly newsletter featuring timely industry news, information on federal regulations, member updates, announcements on seminars, and the latest refractory information and statistics.
Cost: $24.00
4 Pages
Frequency: Monthly
Circulation: 700
Founded in 1951
Mailing list available for rent
Printed in 2 colors on matte stock

Magazines & Journals

22474 ACI Materials Journal
American Concrete Institute
38800 Country Club Drive
PO Box 9094
Farmington Hills, MI 48333-9094

248-848-3700
FAX 248-848-3701
E-Mail: shannon.hale@concrete.org
Home Page:
www.concrete.org/pubs/journals/mjhome.asp

Shannon M Hale, Technical Editor
Carl R Bischof, Senior Editor Publishing Services
Renee J Lewis, Publishing & Event Services
Douglas J Sordyl, Marketing/Sales/Industry Relations
Donna G Halstead, Finance & Administration

ACI Materials Journal contains individually authored papers as well as papers developed for convention sessions. These papers address structural research, materials research, design

theory, structural analysis, and state-of-the-art reviews.
Founded in 1904
Mailing list available for rent

22475 ACI Structural Journal
American Concrete Institute
38800 Country Club Drive
PO Box 9094
Farmington Hills, MI 48333-9094

248-848-3700
FAX 248-848-3701
E-Mail: shannon.hale@concrete.org
Home Page:
www.concrete.org/pubs/journals/sjhome.asp

Shannon M Hale, Technical Editor
Carl R Bischof, Senior Editor Publishing Services
Renee J Lewis, Publishing & Event Services
Douglas J Sordyl, Marketing/Sales/Industry Relations
Donna G Halstead, Finance & Administration

ACI Structural Journal contains individually authored papers as well as papers developed for convention sessions. These papers address structural research, materials research, design theory, structural analysis, and state-of-the-art reviews.
Founded in 1904
Mailing list available for rent

22476 Cement Americas
Primedia
11555 Central Parkway
10th Floor
Chicago, IL 60606

312-726-2802
FAX 312-726-2574
Home Page: www.cementamericas.com

Steven Prokopy, Editor
Norm Rose, Sales

Cement Americas provides comprehensive coverage of the North and South American cement markets from raw materials extraction to delivery and transportation to the end user. Production-oriented articles focus on areas where the market activity is at its greatest. Coverage of new ideas, technological improvements, industry trends, and views from leading figures in the cement industry ensure that Cement Americas remains the cement industry journal of the Americas.
ISSN: 0035-7464
Printed in 4 colors on glossy stock

22477 Concrete InFocus
Naylor Publications
5950 NW 1st Pl
Gainesville, FL 32607-6018

352-332-1252
800-369-6220
FAX 352-331-3525
E-Mail: chodges@naylor.com
Home Page: www.naylor.com
Social Media: *Facebook, Twitter, LinkedIn, You Tube*

Michael Moss, President

Magazine that's mailed to 5,000+ industry personnel.

22478 Concrete International
American Concrete Institute
38800 Country Club Drive
PO Box 9094
Farmington Hills, MI 48333-9094

248-848-3700
FAX 248-848-3701
E-Mail: ron.burg@concrete.org
Home Page: www.concrete.org

Carl R Bischof, Senior Editor
Ronald G Burg, Executive Vice President

The circulation is concentrated among the most important professionals in the concrete field; the engineers, architects, contractors, manufacturers, and technicians largely responsible for the advancement of concrete technology and practice.
Frequency: Monthly
Circulation: 20000

22479 Concrete Masonry Designs
NCMA
13750 Sunrise Valley Dr
Herndon, VA 20171-4662

703-713-1900
FAX 703-713-1910
E-Mail: ncma@ncma.org
Home Page: www.ncma.org

Robert Thomas, President
Ron Churchill, Director Of Sales

Highlights concrete masonry applications, best practice tips, specifications and details. Also showcases concrete masonry landscape products.
Cost: $1.00
Frequency: Monthly
Circulation: 25000
Founded in 1918
Printed in 4 colors on glossy stock

22480 Concrete Openings
Concrete Sawing and Drilling Association
13577 Feather Sound Drive
Suite 560
St Petersburg, FL 33762

727-577-5004
FAX 727-577-5012
E-Mail: info@csda.org
Home Page: www.concreteopenings.com
Social Media: *Facebook*

Cherryl O'Brien, Editor
Russell Hitchen, Associate Editor
Patrick O'Brien, Publisher

The official magazine of the Concrete Sawing & Drilling Association. Editorial contributions are welcomed and advertisements are encouraged.
Frequency: Quarterly
Circulation: 16000
ISSN: 1093-6483

22481 Concrete Producer
Hanley Wood
426 S Westgate
Addison, IL 60101

630-543-0870
FAX 847-564-9287
E-Mail: ryelton@hanleywood.com
Home Page: www.theconcreteproducer.com

Richard Yelton, Editor-in-Chief
Tom Bagsarian, Managing Editor
Chari O'Rourke, Circulation Manager

Written for decision-making professionals who buy and specify materials, plant equipment, accessories, trucks, and related products used in the major concrete-producing market segments. Each issue offers money saving operational tips, management advice, new products and technology, and solutions to complex concrete-production questions.

22482 Contemporary Stone & Tile Design
Business News Publishing Company
299 Market Street
Suite 320
Saddle Brook, NJ 07663

201-845-5035
FAX 201-291-9002
E-Mail: cstd@bnp.com
Home Page: www.stoneworld.com

Alex Backrach, Publisher
Michael Reis, Editor

Promotes the benefits of natural stone and ceramic tile to a readership of architects, interior designers, specifiers and consumers. Practical tips and commentary on stone and tile design are included, featuring interviews with architects and designers from the world's leading firms.
Cost: $125.00
Frequency: Quarterly
Circulation: 21000
Founded in 1987

22483 MC
National Precast Concrete Association
10333 N Meridian St
Suite 272
Indianapolis, IN 46290-1081

317-571-9500
800-366-7731
FAX 317-571-0041
E-Mail: rhyink@precast.org
Home Page: www.precast.org

Ty Gable, President
Brenda Ibitz, Manager Advertising

MC magazine features detailed articles about the latest industry technologies and developments, perspectives on current industry events, profiles on leading precast concrete companies and case studies of various manufactured concrete applications.
Frequency: Bi-Monthly

22484 Masonry Construction
Hanley Wood
426 S Westgate
Addison, IL 60101

630-543-0870
FAX 847-564-9287
E-Mail: ryelton@hanleywood.com
Home Page: www.masonryconstruction.com
Social Media: *Facebook, Twitter*

Richard Yelton, Editor-in-Chief
Ron Holzhauer, Deputy Editor
Kari Moosman, Associate Editor
Ted Worthington, Managing Editor
Chari O'Rourke, Circulation Manager

Masonry Construction brings together the complex and fragmented components of the masonry industry—contractors, general contractors, architects, engineers, and producers—providing technical advice, innovative methods and materials, state-of-the-art projects, and essential product information.

22485 Precast
National Precast Concrete Association
1320 City Center Drive
Suite 200
Carmel, IN 46032

317-571-9500
800-366-7731
FAX 317-571-0041
E-Mail: npca@precast.org
Home Page: www.precast.org

Ty Gable, President
Brenda Ibitz, VP Development and Member Services
Frequency: Bi-Monthly
Circulation: 5000

22486 Professional Builder
Reed Business Information
8878 Barrons Blvd
Littleton, CO 80129-2345

303-470-4000
800-446-6551
FAX 303-470-4691

E-Mail: subsmail@reedbusiness.com
Home Page: www.reedbusiness.com

Tim Myers, Executive
Stuart Whayman, Finance
Nathan Cahill, HR

The magazine for professionals within the residential building industry. Articles cover industry news, company profiles, market reports, construction technology and merchandising information needed to successfully complete each job.
Frequency: Monthly
Founded in 1977

22487 Rock Products
Primedia
29 N Wacker Drive
10th Floor
Chicago, IL 60606

312-726-2802
FAX 312-726-2574
E-Mail: rmarkley@primediabusiness.com
Home Page: www.rockproducts.com

Rick Markley, Editor
Scott Bieda, Publisher
Sean ~ Carr, Sales Manager

The aggregate industry's journal of applied technology.
Frequency: Monthly
ISSN: 0035-7464
Founded in 1905

22488 Stone World
BNP Media
210 E State Rt 4
Suite 203
Paramus, NJ 07652-5103

201-291-9001
FAX 201-291-9002
E-Mail: info@stoneworld.com
Home Page: www.stoneworld.com

Alex Bachrach, Publisher

A source of information on stone use in architecture and interior design as well as stone production, distribution, installationm and maintenance.

Trade Shows

22489 CSDA Convention and Tech Fair
Concrete Sawing and Drilling Association
13577 Feather Sound Drive
Suite 560
Clearwater, FL 33762

727-577-5004
FAX 727-577-5012
E-Mail: info@csda.org
Home Page: www.csda.org
Social Media: *Facebook, LinkedIn*

Patrick O'Brien, Executive Director
500 Members
300 Attendees
Frequency: Annual
Founded in 1972

22490 Composites and Polycon Convention
American Composites Manufacturers Association
1010 North Glebe Road
Suite 450
Arlington, VA 22201

703-525-0511
FAX 703-525-0743
E-Mail: info@acmanet.org
Home Page: www.icpashow.org

Three-day convention. Attendees will have the opportunity to choose from 100 presentations,

live demonstrations and technical papers. Covering every level of expertise from beginer to advanced, industry experts will address dozens of subject areas in the most striking detail, from technical to production to regulatory to management and more.
Frequency: Annual

22491 Manufactured Concrete Products Exposition
National Concrete Masonry Association
13750 Sunrise Valley Drive
Herndon, VA 20171-4662

703-713-1900
FAX 703-713-1910
E-Mail: ncma@ncma.org
Home Page: www.ncma.org

Mark Hogan, President
Ron Churchill, Director Of Sales

The Manufactured Concrete Products Exposition is brought to you by a partnership between the National Concrete Masonry Association, the Interlocking Concrete Paving Institute and the American Concrete Pipe Association.
Frequency: Annual

22492 National Concrete Burial Vault Association Convention
NCBVA
195 Wekiva Springs Road
Suite 200
Longwood, FL 32779

407-788-1996
FAX 407-774-6751
Home Page: www.ncbva.org

Thomas A Monahan, Executive Director
Heather Jones, Conventions/Event Planning

Convention held annually. Includes awards banquet, installation of officers and more.
Frequency: Annual

22493 PTI Technical Conference and Exhibition
Post-Tensioning Institute
38800 Country Club Drive~
Farmington Hills, MI 48331

248-848-3180
FAX 248-848-3181
E-Mail: info@post-tensioning.org
Home Page: www.post-tensioning.org

Ted Neff, Executive Director
Larry Krauser, President
Marc Khoury, VP
Robert Sward, Secretary

Earn CEUs, attend technical sessions, awards events, exhibits, and ask-the-expert forum.
Frequency: May

22494 Precast Show
National Precast Concrete Association
1320 City Center Drive
Suite 200
Carmel, IN 46032-1074

317-571-9500
800-366-7731
FAX 317-571-0041
E-Mail: npca@precast.org
Home Page: www.precast.org
Social Media: *Facebook, Twitter, LinkedIn, You Tube*

Ty Gable, President
Erica Wells, Director Meetings

Trade show for the precast concrete industry, containing 300 booths and 300 exhibits.
3000 Attendees
Frequency: Annual

22495 StonExpo
Marble Institute of America

28901 Clemens Road
Suite 100
Cleveland, OH 44145

440-250-9222
FAX 440-250-9223
Home Page: www.marble-institute.com

Gary Distelhorst, EVP/CEO
Helen Distelhorst, Meetings/Special Events Director

Where fabricators, installers and distributors can experience everything from natural stone extracted from quarries around the world, to the most technologically advanced fabricating machinery, to the beautiful finished product: exquisite countertops that are installed in both residential and commercial properties today.
Frequency: Annual/January

22496 World of Concrete Exposition
Post Tensioning Institute
8601 North Black Canyon Highway
Suite 103
Phoenix, AZ 85021

602-870-7540
FAX 602-870-7541
E-Mail: info@post-tensioning.org
Home Page: www.post-tensioning.org

Seminars, exhibits and trade shows. Sponsored by the Post-Tensioning Institute.
36M Attendees
Frequency: January/Febuary

Directories & Databases

22497 CSDA Resource Guide & Membership Directory
Concrete Sawing and Drilling Association
100 2nd Avenue S
Suite 402N
St. Petersburg, FL 33701

727-577-5004
FAX 727-577-5012
E-Mail: info@csda.org
Home Page: www.csda.org

Patrick O'Brien, Executive Director
Cost: $12.00
500 Members
97 Pages
Founded in 1972

22498 Dimension Stone Design Manual
Marble Institute of America
28901 Clemens Rd
Suite 100
Cleveland, OH 44145-1166

440-250-9222
FAX 440-250-9223
E-Mail: mia@marble-institute.com
Home Page: www.marble-institute.com

Gary Distelhorst, Executive VP
Helen Distelhorst, Director Meetings/Special Events
Jim Hieb, VP
Michael A. Twiss, President

An authoritative source for guidelines on using natural stone in architectural designs. Contents include sections on granite, marble, limestone, serpentine, travertine, quartz-based stone and slate with product descriptions and technical data; general installation guidelines; guidelines and typical detailing for horizontal surfaces, vertical surfaces, wet areas, furniture and countertops; maintenance of exterior/ interior stone installations; and a glossary of terms relating to dimension stone.
Cost: $90.00
350 Pages
Founded in 1960

22499 Dimension Stones of the World: Book of Color Plates
Marble Institute of America
28901 Clemens Rd
Suite 100
Cleveland, OH 44145-1166

440-250-9222
FAX 440-250-9223
E-Mail: mia@marble-institute.com
Home Page: www.marble-institute.com

Gary Distelhorst, Executive VP
Helen Distelhorst, Director Meetings/Special Events
Jim Hieb, VP
Michael A. Twiss, President

This set contains over 600 full color reproductions of granites, limestones, marbles, onyx, quartz based stone, slate and travertine. On the reverse side of each page are the ASTM test values for absorbption, density, compressive strength, hardness and flexural strength. Also listed for each stone are primary name, country of origin, quarry location, geological age, color range, recommended usage and available sizes.
Cost: $330.00
Founded in 1960

22500 Online MCP
American Concrete Institute
38800 Country Club Drive
PO Box 9094
Farmington Hills, MI 48333-9094

248-483-3700
FAX 248-848-3801
E-Mail: shannon.hale@concrete.org
Home Page: www.concrete.org

William R Tolley, Executive VP
Douglas J Sordyl, Marketing/Sales/Industry Relations
Donna G Halstead, Finance/Administration
Shannon M Hale, Technical Editor
Carl R Bischof, Senior Editor Publishing Services

Contains all of the ACI documents you need to answer your questions about code requirements, specifications, tolerance, concrete proportions, construction methods, evaluations of test results, and many more topics.
Founded in 1994
Mailing list available for rent

22501 Stone World Annual Buyer's Guide
Stone World Magazine
210 Route 4 East
Suite 311
Paramus, NJ 90001

201-291-9001
FAX 201-291-2002
E-Mail: info@stoneworld.com
Home Page: www.stoneworld.com
Social Media: *Facebook, Twitter*

Alex Bachrach, Publisher
Michael Reis, Senior Editor/Associate Publisher

Comprised of six sections covering: stone suppliers, fabricating equipment and suppliers, installation and stone care materials and supplies, associations, services, trade shows and organizers.
Cost: $6.00
Frequency: Annual
Circulation: 22,000
Founded in 1984

Industry Web Sites

22502 http://gold.greyhouse.com
G.O.L.D Grey House OnLine Databases

Grey House Publishing's online database platform, GOLD, offers Quick Search, Keyword Search and Expert Search for most business sectors including stone and concrete markets. The GOLD platform makes finding the information you need quick and easy - whether you're a novice searcher or an experienced database user. All of Grey House's directory products are available for subscription on the GOLD platform.

22503 www.construction.com
McGraw-Hill Construction

McGraw-Hill Construction (MHC), part of The McGraw-Hill Companies, connects people and projects across the design and construction industry, serving owners, architects, engineers, general contractors, subcontractors, building product manufacturers, suppliers, dealers, distributors and adjacent markets.

22504 www.crsi.org
Concrete Reinforcing Steel Institute

Conducts research and provides technical information on reinforced concrete design and construction practices.

22505 www.csda.org
Concrete Sawing and Drilling Association

To promote the use of professional specialty sawing and drilling contractors and their methods.

22506 www.greyhouse.com
Grey House Publishing

Authoritative reference directories for most business sectors including stone and concrete markets. Users can search the online databases with varied search criteria allowing for custom searches by product category, geographic area, sales volume, keyword, subject and more. Full Grey House catalog and online ordering also available.

22507 www.icri.org
International Concrete Repair Institute

To improve the quality of repair, restoration, and protection of concrete and other structures.

22508 www.marble-institute.com
Marble Institute of America

Importers, finishers, wholesalers, fabricators, quarriers and exporters of stone for both interior and exterior application as well as suppliers of machines, tools and services.

22509 www.masonryinstitute.org
1315 Storm Pkwy.
Torrance, CA 90501-5041

310-257-9000
FAX 310-257-1942
Home Page: www.masonryinstitute.org

Source for contacts and publications in the masonry industry.
Founded in 1957

22510 www.post-tensioning.org
Post-Tensioning Institute

Provides research, technical development, marketing and promotional activities for companies engaged in post-tensioned prestressed construction. Members include fabricators and manufacturers.

22511 www.precast.org
National Precast Concrete Association

22512 www.sweets.construction.com
McGraw Hill Construction

In depth product information that lets you find, compare, select, specify and make purchase decisions in the industrial product marketplace.

Associations

22513 4G Americas
1750 - 112th Avenue NE, Suite B220
Bellevue, WA 98004

425-372-8922
FAX 425-372-8923
E-Mail: vicki.livingston@4gamericas.org
Home Page: www.4gamericas.org
Social Media: *Facebook, Twitter, LinkedIn*

Chris Pearson, President
Vicki Livingston, Head of Comm./Analyst
Relations
Jose Otero, Director
Paul Mankiewich, Director
Bob Suffern, Director

**22514 Advanced Television Systems
Committee**
1776 K St. NW
8th Floor
Washington, Dc 20006-2340

202-872-9160
FAX 202-872-9161
Home Page: www.atsc.org
Social Media: *Facebook, Twitter*

Founded in 1982

22515 American Radio Relay League
225 Main St
Newington, CT 06111-1494

860-594-0200
888-277-5289
FAX 860-594-0259
E-Mail: hq@arrl.org
Home Page: www.arrl.org
Social Media: *Facebook, Twitter, Youtube, RSS*

David Sumner, CEO
Joel Harrison, President
Barry Shelley, CFO
Harold Kramer, COO

National membership association for amateur
radio operators.
170m Members
Founded in 1914

**22516 Antenna Measurement Techniques
Association**
6065 Roswell Road
Atlanta, GA 30328

770-864-3488
FAX 770-864-3491
E-Mail: president@amta.org
Home Page: www.amta.org
Social Media: *LinkedIn, RSS*

Peter Collins, President
John Demas, VP
Dennis Lewis, Secretary
Dave Pinnell, Treasurer

Nonprofit professional organization open to individuals with an interest in antenna measurements. Areas of interest include: measurement
facilities, unique or innovative measurement
techniques, test instrumentation and systems,
RCS measurements, compact range design and
evaluation, near-field techniques and their applications, and the practical aspects of
measurement problems and their solutions.
400 Members
Founded in 1979

**22517 Armed Forces Communications and
Electronics Association**
AFCEA International Headquarters

4400 Fair Lakes Ct
Suite 100
Fairfax, VA 22033-3899

703-631-6100
800-336-4583
FAX 703-631-6169
E-Mail: service@afcea.org
Home Page: www.afcea.org
Social Media: *Facebook, Twitter, LinkedIn,
Google+, YouTube, Slideshare,*

LtGen Robert M. Shea, USMC (Ret.),
President/CEO
Linda Gooden, Chair
Brig Gen John Meincke, Vice Chairman
Patrick Miorin, Treasurer/EVP/CFO
James L. Griggs Jr., VP/CIO/CTO

A non-profit international association dedicated
to supporting global security by providing an
ethical environment that encourages a close cooperative relationship among civil government
agencies, the military and industry.
Cost: $35.00
31000 Members
Founded in 1946

**22518 Assn. of Public-Safety
Communications Officials
International**
351 N Williamson Boulevard
Daytona Beach, FL 32114-1112

386-322-2500
888-272-6911
FAX 386-322-2501
E-Mail: apco@apcointl.org
Home Page: www.apcointl.org
Social Media: *Facebook, Twitter, LinkedIn,
Youtube*

Brent Lee, President
Cheryl J. Greathouse, 1St VP
Martha K. Carter, 2nd VP
Doreen Geary, Accounting
Meghan Architect, Publications

A not-for-profit professional organization dedicated to the enhancement of public safety communications. Exists to serve the people who
manage, operate, maintain, and supply the communications systems used to safeguard the
lives and property of citizens everywhere.
16000 Members
Founded in 1935

**22519 Association for Local
Telecommunications Services**
900 17th St NW
Suite 400
Washington, DC 20006-2507

202-296-6650
FAX 202-296-7585
E-Mail: membership@alts.org
Home Page: www.comptelascent.org

Earl Comstock, CEO

COMPTEL is the leading industry accociation
representing communications service providers
and their supplier partners.

**22520 Association of Teleservices
International**
222 S Westmonte Drive
Suite 101
Altamonte Springs, FL 32714

603-362-9489
866-896-2874
FAX 407-774-6440
E-Mail: admin@atsi.org
Home Page: www.atsi.org
Social Media: *Facebook, Twitter, LinkedIn*

Jeff Zindel, President
Doug Robbins, VP
Josue Leon, VP, Secretary

JoAnn Fussell, VP, Treasurer
Gary Edwards, Chairman

Promotes fair competition through appropriate
regulation and legislation; provides research
and development provides support services and
educational opportunities to address challenges
in operating environments; in encourages and
maintains the high standards of ethics and
service.
800+ Members
Founded in 1942

**22521 Broadcast Designers' Association
International**
5700 Wilshire Blvd
Suite 275
Los Angeles, CA 90036

310-788-7600
FAX 310-788-7616
Home Page: www.promaxbda.org
Social Media: *Facebook, Twitter, LinkedIn,
RSS*

Steve Kazanjian, President
Stacy LA Cotera, General Manager
Randy Smith, CFO
Lucian Cojescu, Chief Information Officer

Association for manufacturers or suppliers of
broadcast design equipment, supplies and
services.

22522 CDMA Development Group
575 Anton Blvd.
Suite 440
Costa Mesa, CA 92626

714-545-5211
888-800-CDMA
FAX 714-545-4601
E-Mail: cdg@cdg.org
Home Page: www.cdg.org
Social Media: *Facebook, Twitter, RSS*

Mark S. Richer, President
Jerry Whitaker, Vice President
Lindsy Shelton Gross, Director of
Communications
Daro Bruno, Office Manager
Founded in 1993

**22523 Carnegie Mellon University:
Information Networking Institute**
Electrical & Computer Engineering
Department
4616 Henry Street
Pittsburgh, PA 15213

412-268-7195
FAX 412-268-7196
E-Mail: ini@cmu.edu
Home Page: www.ini.cmu.edu
Social Media: *Facebook, Twitter, LinkedIn,
Youtube, Flickr, Google+*

Dena Haritos Tsamitis, Director
Lynn Carroll, Assistant Director
Andrew Pueschel, Project
Manager/Events/Marketing
Chriss Swaney, Director Public Relations
Sean O'Leary, Manager

The Information Networking Institute was established by Carnegie Mellon as the nation's
first research and education center devoted to
Information Networking.
Founded in 1989

**22524 Cellular Telecommunications
Industry**
CTIA
1400 16th St NW
Suite 600
Washington, DC 20036-2225

202-785-0081
FAX 202-785-0721
Home Page: www.ctia.org

Social Media: *Facebook, Twitter, LinkedIn, Youtube, Flickr, Google+*

Meredith Attwell Baker, President & CEO
Tom Power, Senior VP, General Counsel
Scott Bergmann, VP, Regulatory Affairs
Jot Carpenter, VP, Govt. Affairs
Rocco Carlitti, SVP/CFO

An international organization representing all sectors of wireless communications. As a non-profit membership organization, they represent service providers, manufacturers, wireless data and Internet companies and other contributors to the wireless universe.
Founded in 1984

22525 Center for Strategic and International Studies

1616 Rhode Island Avenue, NW
Washington, DC 20036

202-887-0200
FAX 202-775-3199
Home Page: www.csis.org
Social Media: *RSS*

John J. Hamre, President and CEO
Carig Cohen, Executive Vice President
Jon B. Alterman, SVP
David J. Berteau, SVP & Director
Alice Blevins, SVP for Operations
Founded in 1962

22526 Competitive Telecommunications Association

1200 G St. NW, Suite 350
Washington, DC 20005

202-296-6650
FAX 202-296-7585
Home Page: www.comptel.org
Social Media: *Facebook, Twitter, LinkedIn*

Deborah Ward, Chairwoman
Chris Murray, Vice Chairman
Jim Butman, Treasurer
Ron Beaumont, Director
Bill Barloon, Director
Founded in 1981

22527 Enterprise Wireless Alliance

2121 Cooperative Way
Suite 225
Herndon, VA 20171

703-528-5115
800-482-8282
FAX 703-524-1074
E-Mail: Info@EnterpriseWireless.org
Home Page: www.enterprisewireless.org

Catherine Leonard, Chairman
David Reeves, Vice Chairman
Mark E Crosby, President/CEO
Gordon Day, Treasurer
Sarah Beerbower, Director, Sales and Services

Formerly ITA and AMTA, works to preserve spectrum rights and access for enterprise wireless customers.
400 Members
Founded in 1985

22528 Geospatial Information & Technology Association

1360 University Ave. West
Suite 455
St. Paul, MN 55104-4086

E-Mail: president@gita.org
Home Page: www.gita.org
Social Media: *Facebook, Twitter, LinkedIn, YouTube*

Mark Limbruner, President
Elizabeth Bialek, Treasurer
Eric Hoogenraad, Secretary
Matthew Thomas, President Elect
Rebecca Shumate, At-Large Board Member

22529 Kagan Research

1 Lower Ragsdale Dr
Building One Suite 130
Monterey, CA 93940-5749

831-624-1536
800-307-2529
FAX 831-625-3225
E-Mail: info@kagan.com
Home Page: www.kagan.com
Social Media: *Facebook, Twitter, LinkedIn, Youtube, Google+*

Mike Chinn, President
Tom Corbitt, Chief Administration Officer
Dan Oakey, Chief Contracts Officer

Provides knowledge, insight and industry perspectives, anticipates trends, projects revenues, tracks financing and values the debt and equity of hundreds of privately held and publicly traded media and communications companies.
Founded in 1969

22530 National Association of Broadcastersÿ

1771 N St. NW
Washington, DC 20036

202-429-5300
800-NAB-EXPO
E-Mail: nan@nab.org
Home Page: www.nab.org
Social Media: *Facebook, Twitter, LinkedIn, YouTube*

David Lougee, President
Elizabeth Neuhoff, CEO
Gordon H. Smith, CEO & President
Brian Lawlor, Member, Executive Committee
Don Benson, Member, Executive Committee

22531 National Cable & Telecommunications Association

25 Massachusetts Ave. NW
Suite 100
Washington, DC 20001

202-222-2300
E-Mail: info@ncta.com
Home Page: www.ncta.com
Social Media: *Facebook, Twitter, LinkedIn*

Michael Powell, President & CEO
Neil Smit, Chairman

Trade association for U.S. cable industry.
200 Members

22532 National Cable andÿTelecommunications

25 Massachusetts Avenue, NW
Suite 100
Washington, DC 20001

202-222-2300
FAX 202-222-2514
E-Mail: webmaster@ncta.com
Home Page: www.ncta.com
Social Media: *Facebook, Twitter, LinkedIn*

Michael Powell, President & CEO
James M. Assey, Executive Vice President
K. Dane Snowden, Chief of Staff
Bruce Carnes, SVP, Finance & Administration
William Check, SVP, Science & Technology
200 Members

22533 National Exchange Carrier Association

80 S Jefferson Rd
Suite 1
Whippany, NJ 07981-1009

973-599-0580
800-228-8597
FAX 973-884-8469
E-Mail: webmastr@neca.org
Home Page: www.neca.org
Social Media: *Facebook, Twitter*

William Hegman, CEO
Peter A Dunbar, VP/CFO

James W Frame, VP Operations
Regina McNeil, VP/General Counsel/Corp Secretary
Ed Buchanan, Chair

NECA administer's the FCCs access charge plan. They file access charge tariffs with the FCC, collect and validate cost and revenue data, ensure compliance with FCC rules, distribute revenues from access charges among pool members, process FCC regulatory fees, and offer training and education on a wide variety of telecom topics.
1500 Members
Founded in 1983

22534 National Telephone Cooperative Association

4121 Wilson Blvd
Suite 1000
Arlington, VA 22203-4145

703-351-2000
FAX 703-351-2001
E-Mail: contact@ntca.org
Home Page: www.ntca.org
Social Media: *Facebook, Twitter, LinkedIn, YouTube*

Shirley Bloomfield, CEO
James M. Dauby, President
Doug Boone, VP
William P. Hegmann, Secretary/Treasurer
Don Richards, General Counsel

Non-profit association offering a wide array of member services including a government affairs program; expert legal and industry representation; a broad range of educational services; a comprehensive assortment of regular and special publications and public relations programs; and a well-rounded complement of national and regional meetings.
900 Members
Founded in 1954

22535 Organization for the Promotion and Adv. of Small Telecommunications

4121 Wilson Boulevard
Suite 1000
Arlington, VA 22203

703-351-2000
FAX 703-351-2001
Home Page: www.ntca.org
Social Media: *Facebook, Twitter, LinkedIn, YouTube*

James M. Dauby, President
Shirley Bloomfield, CEO
Doug Boone, VP
William P. Hegmann, Secretary/Treasurer
Don Richards, General Counsel

Protects the interests of small, rural, independent commercial telephone companies and cooperatives that have less than 50,000 access lines.
900 Members
Founded in 1963

22536 Personal Communications Industry

500 Montgomery Street
Suite 700
Alexandria, VA 22314

703-390-0300
800-759-0300
FAX 703-836-1608
E-Mail: webmaster@pcia.com
Home Page: www.pcia.com
Social Media: *Facebook, Twitter, LinkedIn*

Thomas A Murray, Chairman
Steven Marshall, Vice Chairman
David E. Weisman, Treasurer
Jonathan S Adelstein, President & CEO
Tim House, VP, External Relations

Represents companies that develop, own, manage and operate towers, commercial rooftops and other facilities for the provision of all types

of wireless, broadcasting and telecommunication services. PCIA is dedicated to advancing an understanding of the benefits of wireless services and required infrastructure to local and federal government officials and communities at large.
3000 Members
Founded in 1949

22537 Power and Communication Contractors Association
1908 Mt. Vernon Ave.
2nd Floor
Alexandria, VA 22301

703-212-7734
800-542-7222
FAX 703-548-3733
E-Mail: info@pccaweb.org
Home Page: www.pccaweb.org

Timothy Killoren, President
Todd Myers, President-Elect
James Dillahunty, 1st Vice President
Larry Pribyl, 2nd Vice President
John Fluharty, II, Secretary

A national trade association for companies constructing electric power facilities, including transmission and distribution lines and substations and telephone, fiber optic, and cable television systems.
300 Members
Founded in 1945

22538 Satellite Broadcasting and Communications Association
1100 17th St. NW
Ste. 1150
Washington, DC 20036

202-349-3620
800-541-5981
FAX 202-318-2618
E-Mail: info@sbca.org
Home Page: www.sbca.org
Social Media: *Facebook, Twitter, LinkedIn, YouTube*

Andrew Reinsdorf, Chairman
Jeffery Blum, Vice Chairman
Joseph Widoff, Executive Director
Benjamin Rowan, Education Manager
Abdul Salam, Sr. Director of Finance & HR
Founded in 1994

22539 Satellite Industry Association
Home Page: www.sia.org
Social Media: *LinkedIn*

Bill Weller, Chairman
Stacy Fuller, Vice Chairman
Sam Black, Acting President
Dean Hirasawa, Communications Manager
Jennifer Williams, Office Manager
Founded in 1995

22540 Society for Technical Communication
9401 Lee Highway
Suite 300
Fairfax, VA 22031

703-522-4114
FAX 703-522-2075
Home Page: www.stc.org
Social Media: *Facebook, Twitter, LinkedIn, YouTube*

Katherine Brown-Hoekstra, President
Bernard Aschwanden, Vice President
Chris Lyons, Chief Executive Officer
Kimberly Kelly, Education Manager
Molly Jin, Director of Meetings and Education
Founded in 1957

22541 Society of Broadcast Engineers
9102 N Meridian St
Suite 150
Indianapolis, IN 46260-1896

317-846-9000
FAX 317-846-9120
E-Mail: mclappe@sbe.org
Home Page: www.sbe.org
Social Media: *Facebook, Twitter, LinkedIn, YouTube*

Jerry Massey, President
James E. Leifer, VP
Andrea Cummins, Treasurer
Ted Hand, Secretary
John Poray, CAE, Executive Director

SBE provides members with the opportunity to network and share ideas and information in keeping current with the ongoing changes within the industry. Members can attend annual conferences and expositions, have access to educational opportunities and obtain professional certification.
5100+ Members
Founded in 1964
Mailing list available for rent: 5700 names at $170 per M

22542 Society of Cable Telecommunications Engineers
140 Philips Rd
Exton, PA 19341-1318

610-363-6888
800-542-5040
FAX 610-363-5898
E-Mail: information@scte.org
Home Page: www.scte.org
Social Media: *Facebook, Twitter*

Tony Werner, Chairman
Bill Warga, Vice Chairman
Steve Williams, Secretary
Christine Whittaker, Treasurer
Mark Dzuban, President/CEO

A nonprofit, professional organization committed to advancing the careers of cable telecommunications professionals and serving their industry through excellence in professional development, information and standards.
15000 Members
Founded in 1969

22543 Society of Satellite Professionals
New York Information Technology Center
250 Park Ave
7th Floor
New York, NY 10177

212-809-5199
FAX 212-825-0075
Home Page: www.sspi.org
Social Media: *Facebook, Twitter, LinkedIn, YouTube*

Chris Stott, Chairman & CEO
Bryan McGuirk, President
Doug Boone, VP
William P. Hegmann, Secretary/Treasurer
Don Richards, General Counsel

A nonprofit association that serves people working in the satellite industry in countries arount the world. Professional development society of the global satellite industry.
1000 Members
Founded in 1983

22544 Society of Telecommunications Consultants
13275 State Highway 89
PO Box 70
Old Station, CA 96071

530-335-7313
800-782-7670
FAX 530-335-7360
E-Mail: stchdg@stcconsultants.org

Home Page: www.stcconsultants.org
Social Media: *Facebook, Twitter, Pinterest*

Cathy Cimaglia, Administration Manager
The STC is an international organization of independent telecommunications and information technology consultants who serve clients in business and government.
180 Members
Founded in 1976

22545 Telecom Association
31500 Grape Street #3-307
Lake Elsinore, CA 92532

Home Page: www.telecomassociation.com
Social Media: *Facebook, Twitter, LinkedIn, YouTube*

Nancy Hagen Baldwin, President
Dan Baldwin, Executive Director
Kathleen Brown, Administrator
3800 Members
Founded in 1995

22546 Telecom Pioneers
1801 California Street
Suite 225
Denver, CO 80202-2932

303-571-1200
800-872-5995
FAX 303-572-0520
E-Mail: info@telecompioneers.org
Home Page: www.telecompioneers.org

Gloria Pazel, Chairman
Ann Smalley, Vice Chairman
Charlene Hill, Executive Director
Michael Sears, Past Chairman

Formerly known as the Telephone Pioneers of America, TelecomPioneers is comprised of nearly 620,000 current and retired telecommunications employees who have joined together to make their communities better places in which to live and work
Founded in 1911

22547 Telecommunications Industry Association (TIA)
1320 N Courthouse Rd
Suite 200
Arlington, VA 22201-3834

703-907-7700
FAX 703-907-7727
E-Mail: tia@tiaonline.org
Home Page: www.tiaonline.org
Social Media: *Facebook, Twitter*

Grant Seiffert, President
Jennifer Pentecost Sims, Treasurer
Scott Belcher, CEO
Ed Mikoski, Standards/Business Development
Mark Walker, Chair

The Telecommunications Industry Association/TIA represents providers of information, communications and entertainment technology products and services for the global marketplace through its core competencies in standards development, domestic and international policy advocacy, and facilitating member business opportunities. The association facilitates the convergence of new communications networks while working for a competitive and innovative market environment.

22548 Telework Coalition
204 E St Ne
Washington, DC 20002-4923

202-266-0046
E-Mail: info@telcoa.org
Home Page: www.telcoa.org
Social Media: *Facebook, Twitter, LinkedIn*

Chuck Wilsker, President
Jack Heacock, Senior VP & Co-Founder

Enabling virtual, mobile and distributed work through education, technology and legislation.

22549 The National Communication Association

1765 N Street NW
Washington, DC 20036

202-464-4622
FAX 202-464-4600
E-Mail: inbox@natcom.org
Home Page: www.natcom.org
Social Media: *Facebook, Twitter, YouTube, Blog*

Carole Blair, President
Christina S. Beck, First Vice President
Stephen J. Hartnett, Second Vice President
Nancy Kidd, Executive Director
Mark Fernando, Chief Of Staff
Founded in 1914

22550 United Communications Group

9737 Washingtonian Blvd
Suite 200
Gaithersburg, MD 20878-7364

301-287-2700
FAX 301-287-2039
E-Mail: info@ucg.com
Home Page: www.ucg.com

Todd Foreman, Partner-CEO
Nancy Becker, Partner-President
Steve McVearry, General Counsel
Jon Slabaugh, Managing Director, Business Dev
Chris Dingee, CFO

A portfolio of highly focused business and professional publishing companies providing guidance, information, analysis, data and solutions to over two million clients worldwide.
Founded in 1977

22551 United States International Telecommunication Union Association

E-Mail: cherie.mills@pillsburylaw.com
Home Page: www.usitua.org

Audrey Allison, Chair

The USITUA is a U.S. industry forum on International Telecommunication Union policy matters.

22552 United States Telecom Association

607 14th St Nw
Suite 400
Washington, DC 20005-2000

202-326-7300
FAX 202-315-3603
E-Mail: membership@ustelecom.org
Home Page: www.ustelecom.org
Social Media: *Facebook, Twitter, LinkedIn, YouTube*

Walter B McCormick Jr, President/CEO
Robert A. Hunt, Chairman
Alan J. Roth, SEVP
Jonathan Banks, SVP, Law & Policy
Mark Kulish, SVP, Administration & CFO

Trade association representing service providers and suppliers for the telecom industry.
1200 Members

22553 Wireless Communications Alliance

1510 Page Mill Rd.
Palo Alto, CA 94304

E-Mail: promote@wca.org
Home Page: www.wca.org
Social Media: *Facebook, Twitter, LinkedIn*

Founded in 1994

22554 Wireless Internet Service Providers Association

1095 Hilltop Drive #317
Redding, CA 96003

260-622-5776
866-317-2851
E-Mail: tcoffey@wispa.org
Home Page: www.wispa.org
Social Media: *Facebook, Twitter, LinkedIn, Google+, Tumblr*

Alex Phillips, President
Chuck Hogg, Vice President
Mark Radabaugh, Treasurer
Dennis Burgess, Secretary
Trina Coffey, Dir., Operations/Event Management
800 Members

Newsletters

22555 Broadband

IGI Group
1340 Soldiers Field Road
Suite 2
Brighton, MA 02135

617-782-5033
800-323-1088
FAX 617-782-5735
E-Mail: info@igigroup.com
Home Page: www.igigroup.com

Paul Polishuk, President/CEO
Hui Pan, Conference Director
Bev Wilson, Managing Editor
Will Ashley, IT Director/Media Manager

The Broadband Newsletter covers such subjects as: growth in broadband access such as ADSL, cable modems, satellite and fixed wireless; spending plans of the telcos and MSOs for broadband access; important applications that will drive the market; and growth of the internet based on fast internet access.
Cost: $695.00
Frequency: Monthly
Circulation: 1500
Founded in 1977
Mailing list available for rent

22556 Broadband Advertising

Kagan World Media
1 Lower Ragsdale Dr
Building One, Suite 130
Monterey, CA 93940-5749

831-624-1536
800-307-2529
FAX 831-625-3225
E-Mail: info@kagan.com
Home Page: www.kagan.com

Tim Baskerville, President
Tom Johnson, Marketing Manager

Provides critical information about how and where advertising sales will intersect across all broadband platforms. Includes data and analysis previously published in Internet Advertising and Cable TV advertising
Cost: $1095.00
Frequency: Monthly
Founded in 1969

22557 Broadband Technology

Kagan World Media
1 Lower Ragsdale Dr
Building One Suite 130
Monterey, CA 93940-5749

831-624-1536
800-307-2529
FAX 831-625-3225

E-Mail: info@kagan.com
Home Page: www.kagan.com

Tim Baskerville, President
Tom Johnson, Marketing Manager
Michael Schroeder, Manager

Incisive, thorough reports on deployments of bundled services, high-spped data, digital video and telephony. Analyzes and projects growth of set-top boxes, modems, switches, routers and other infrastructure. Provides data and stats on services offered and plant construction by cable, DSL, satellite, wireless and wired phone providers.
Cost: $1045.00
Frequency: Monthly
Founded in 1969

22558 Broadcast Investor

Kagan World Media
1 Lower Ragsdale Dr
Building One Suite 130
Monterey, CA 93940-5749

831-624-1536
800-307-2529
FAX 831-625-3225
E-Mail: info@kagan.com
Home Page: www.kagan.com

Tim Baskerville, President
Tom Johnson, Marketing Manager

The market's most comprehensive sourve of current and historical data on valuations, deals and finance. Trends, forecasts, data.
Cost: $1295.00
Frequency: Monthly
Founded in 1969

22559 CBQ-Communication Booknotes Quarterly

Lawrence Erlbaum Associates
10 Industrial Avenue
Mahwah, NJ 07430

201-258-2200
FAX 201-760-3735
E-Mail: journals@erlbaum.com
Home Page: www.leaonline.com/loi/cbq

Christopher Sterling, Editor
James K Bracken, Assistant Editor

Descriptive reviews of new publications and websites.
Cost: $350.00
Frequency: Quarterly
ISSN: 1094-8007
Founded in 1969

22560 Cable Program Investor

Kagan World Media
1 Lower Ragsdale Dr
Building One, Suite 130
Monterey, CA 93940-5749

831-624-1536
800-307-2529
FAX 831-625-3225
E-Mail: info@kagan.com
Home Page: www.kagan.com

Tim Baskerville, President
Tom Johnson, Marketing Manager

Provides exclusive data and analysis, deal benchmarks and balance sheet assessments. It covers home shopping networks, programming trends, multichannel penetration by platform and ratings data.
Cost: $1045.00
Frequency: Monthly
Founded in 1969

22561 Cable TV Investor

Kagan World Media

1 Lower Ragsdale Dr
Building One,Suite 130
Monterey, CA 93940-5749

831-624-1536
800-307-2529
FAX 831-625-3225
E-Mail: info@kagan.com
Home Page: www.kagan.com

Tim Baskerville, President
Tom Johnson, Marketing Manager

Provides information on the data, the deals, the
valuation metrics, the distillation of information into intelligence. The information you
want and need to remain competitive
Cost: $1295.00
Frequency: Monthly
Founded in 1969

22562 Cable TV Law Reporter
Kagan World Media
1 Lower Ragsdale Dr
Building One Suite 130
Monterey, CA 93940-5749

831-624-1536
800-307-2529
FAX 831-625-3225
E-Mail: info@kagan.com
Home Page: www.kagan.com

Tim Baskerville, President
Tom Johnson, Marketing Manager

The quintessential library of cable court cases,
arbitrations, legal precedents. Labeled and catalogued for easy reference. Required reading for
attorneys, government regulators and top executives. Three month trial available.
Cost: $995.00
Frequency: Monthly
Founded in 1969

22563 Communication
National Technical Information Service
5285 Port Royal Rd
Springfield, VA 22161-0001

703-605-6000
FAX 703-605-6900
E-Mail: customerservice@ntis.gov
Home Page: www.ntis.gov

Linda Davis, VP
Bruce Borzino, Director

Covers common carrier and satellite communications, information theory, graphics, policies,
regulations, studies, radio and television.
Founded in 1991

22564 Communications Daily
Warren Publishing
2115 Ward Ct Nw
Washington, DC 20037-1209

202-872-9200
800-771-9202
FAX 202-318-8350
E-Mail: info@warren-news.com
Home Page: www.warren-news.com

Brig Easley, Executive VP/Controller
Paul Warren, Chair/Publisher
Daniel Warren, President/Editor

Daily publication for the entire telecommunica-
tions indusrty.
Frequency: Daily
Circulation: 70000+
Founded in 1945

22565 Fiber Optic Sensors and Systems
IGI Group
1340 Soldiers Field Road
Suite 2
Brighton, MA 02135

617-782-5033
800-323-1088
FAX 617-782-5735

E-Mail: info@igigroup.com
Home Page: www.igigroup.com

Paul Polishuk, CEO
Hui Pan, Conference Director
Bev Wilson, Managing Editor

Covers procurements, contract awards, requests
for qualifications and proposals, reports on
market studies, patents filed and awarded, new
product announcements, new technology, market forecasts, reviews of important contracts,
important conferences and trade shows, and
Japanese and European developments.
Cost: $695.00
Frequency: Monthly
Founded in 1977

22566 Fiber Optics News
Phillips Business Information
1201 Seven Locks Road
Potomac, MD 20854-2931

301-354-1400
FAX 301-340-0542
E-Mail: stephenh@pennwell.com
Home Page: www.lightwaveonline.com

Ellen Hamm, Publisher
Mark Mikolas, Editor
Stephen Hardy, Editorial Director

Fiber optics in the telecommunications fields.
Cost: $37.00

22567 Fiber Optics Weekly Update
IGI Group
1340 Soldiers Field Road
Suite 2
Brighton, MA 02135

617-782-5033
800-323-1088
FAX 617-782-5735
E-Mail: info@igigroup.com
Home Page: www.igigroup.com

Paul Polishuk, CEO
Hui Pan, Conference Director
Bev Wilson, Managing Editor
Yesim Taskor, Controller

Covers procurements, new contracts, company
buyouts, new products, important publications,
latest news, planned projects, financial reports,
market forecasts, conference and trade show reviews, joint ventures, contract awards, impact
of technology, and international developments.
Cost: $695.00
Frequency: Weekly
Founded in 1977

22568 Fiber Optics and Communications
IGI Group
1340 Soldiers Field Road
Suite 2
Brighton, MA 02135

617-782-5033
800-323-1088
FAX 617-783-5735
E-Mail: editor@igigroup.com
Home Page: www.igigroup.com

Paul Polishuk, Publisher
Hui Pan, Conference Director
Bev Wilson, Managing Editor
Yesim Taskor, Controller

Fiber optics is spreading rapidly into all major
high and low tech fields. This newsletter helps
relieve the pressure on busy executives by reviewing over 300 sources on a regular basis
and providing only the most relevant information.
Cost: $695.00
Frequency: Monthly
Founded in 1977

22569 Fixed Wireless
IGI Group

1340 Soldiers Field Road
Suite 2
Brighton, MA 02135

617-782-5033
800-323-1088
FAX 617-782-5735
E-Mail: editor@igigroup.com
Home Page: www.igigroup.com

Paul Polishuk, CEO
Hui Pan, Conference Director
Bev Wilson, Managing Editor
Yesim Taskor, Controller

Tracks technological breakthroughs, network
developments, market trends, contacts and examines who the players are in this re-emerging
market.
Cost: $695.00
Frequency: Monthly
Founded in 1977

22570 Home Networks
IGI Group
1340 Soldiers Field Road
Suite 2
Brighton, MA 02135

617-782-5033
800-323-1088
FAX 617-782-5735
E-Mail: info@igigroup.com
Home Page: www.igigroup.com

Paul Polishuk, Publisher/CEO
Hui Pan, Conference Director
Bev Wilson, Managing Editor
Yesim Taskor, Controller

The market for home networks is driven by the
15 million homes with two or more PCs requiring interconnection and new housing units being built for tomorrow's home network
environment. This newsletter keeps you connected to this rapidly developing arena of opportunities.
Cost: $695.00
Frequency: Monthly
Founded in 1977

22571 Interval
Society of Cable Telecommunications
Engineers
140 Philips Road
Exton, PA 19341-1318

610-363-6888
800-542-5040
FAX 610-363-5898
E-Mail: scte@scte.org
Home Page: www.scte.org

Mark Durbaz, President/CEO
Catty Oaks, VP

Serving the members of SCTE, Interval high-
lights the events of the Society and it's Chap-
ters.
Cost: $40.00
Circulation: 15000
Founded in 1969

22572 Kagan Media Money
Kagan World Media
1 Lower Ragsdale Dr
Building One, Suite 130
Monterey, CA 93940-5749

831-624-1536
800-307-2529
FAX 831-625-3225
E-Mail: info@kagan.com
Home Page: www.kagan.com

Tim Baskerville, President
Tom Johnson, Marketing Manager
Sandie Borthwick, Executive Director

Designed to continually focus on the essential
trends and hottest topics. Each issue is jammed
with leading media indicators, media merger
and acquisition data, handy benchmarks and

reference charts and the most thought-provoking and insightful analysis.
Cost: $1245.00
Frequency: 48 issues per y
Founded in 1969

22573 LAN Newsletter

IGI Group
1340 Soldiers Field Road
Suite 2
Brighton, MA 02135

617-782-5033
800-323-1088
FAX 617-782-5735
E-Mail: editor@igigroup.com
Home Page: www.igigroup.com

Paul Polishuk, President/CEO
Hui Pan, Conference Director
Bev Wilson, Managing Editor
Yesim Taskor, Controller

Provides information on new developments and products in the LAN-local area network-industry. Discusses both foreign and domestic markets, including new LAN purchases and installation and management changes.
Cost: $695.00
Frequency: Monthly
Circulation: 12000
Founded in 1977

22574 LAN Product News

Worldwide Videotex
Po Box 3273
Boynton Beach, FL 33424

561-738-2276
E-Mail: markedit@juno.com
Home Page: www.wvpubs.com

Provides news and information on the computer Local Area Network (LAN) industry. Covers new hardware and software products, as well as research and development.
Cost: $25.00
Frequency: Monthly

22575 MIC/TECH Data Communications

1111 Marlkress Road
Cherry Hill, NJ 08003-2334

856-489-4310
800-678-4642
FAX 856-424-1999

Lawrence Feidelman, Publisher
Michael Smith, Editor
Carol Bell, Advertising/Sales

Complete performance and pricing of modems, multiplexus, networks and processing.
Cost: $920.00
Frequency: Daily

22576 Microcell Report

150 E 2nd Street
New York, NY 10009-8400

800-883-8989
FAX 212-366-9798

Roger Newell, Publisher

A monthly report on personal communication services including advanced digital mobile telephone applications. Covers regulatory, technical and communication aspects of PCS which includes wireless LANS and PBX.
Cost: $397.00
10 Pages
Frequency: Monthly

22577 Microwave News

Microwave News
PO Box 1799
New York, NY 10163-1799

212-517-2800
FAX 212-734-0316

E-Mail: info@microwavenews.com
Home Page: www.microwavenews.com

Louis Slesin, President

Issues relating to non-ionizing radiation.
Cost: $325.00
Frequency: 6 issues per ye
Founded in 1981

22578 Modem Users News

Worldwide Videotex
Po Box 3273
Boynton Beach, FL 33424

561-738-2276
E-Mail: markedit@juno.com
Home Page: www.wvpubs.com

Provides the latest news and information on software, hardware, supplies and services for individuals and companies who communicate via modems in computer and/or facsimile applications. Contains detailed information, prices, and evaluations of products ranging from protable laptop PC and fax boards, to a wide range of accessible services.
Cost: $25.00
Frequency: Monthly

22579 Newsletter

United Communications Group
11300 Rockville Pike
#1100
Rockville, MD 20852-3012

301-816-8950
FAX 301-816-8945
E-Mail: ccmi@ucg.com
Home Page: www.ucg.com

Sean Oberle, Publisher
Todd Foreman, CEO
Jon Slabaugh, MD
Stephanie Tamburello, HR

Editorial content provides hands-on advice on how to improve their services and reduce their overall operating expenses.
Cost: $379.00
Frequency: BiMonthly

22580 North American Telecom Newswatch

United Communications Group
11300 Rockville Pike
Street 1100
Rockville, MD 20852-3012

301-287-2700
FAX 301-816-8945
E-Mail: webmaster@ucg.com
Home Page: www.ucg.com

Benny Dicecca, President
Todd Foreman, CEO
Jon Slabaugh, MD
Stephanie Tamburello, HR

The news that impacts daily business operations, including equipment updates, regulation issues, long distance and internet useage, and wireless financials.
Founded in 1977

22581 Online Newsletter

Information Intelligence
PO Box 31098
Phoenix, AZ 85046-1098

602-996-2283
Home Page: www.infointelligence.com

Richard Huleatt, Publisher/Editor

Covers all on-line services, suppliers, vendors, CD-ROM data bases, microcomputers and associated equipment.
Cost: $6.25
9 Pages
Frequency: 10 per year
Founded in 1980
Printed in on newsprint stock

22582 Optical Networks and WDM

IGI Group
1340 Soldiers Field Road
Suite 2
Brighton, MA 02135

617-782-5033
800-323-1088
FAX 617-782-5735
E-Mail: info@igigroup.com
Home Page: www.igigroup.com

Paul Polishuk, CEO
Hui Pan, Conference Director
Bev Wilson, Managing Editor
Yesim Taskor, Controller

The WDM newsletter provides worldwide coverage of technology, markets and applications. Covers such subjects as: WDM systems, MAN applications, Gigabit networks, ATM, financials reports, premise wiring, optical amplifiers, optical networks, new products, network management, standards, optical cross connects, frame relay, competitive analysis, manufacturers strategies, optical access, regulations, tariffs, technology, broadband servies, WANs, market forecasts, BOC strategies and more.
Cost: $695.00
Frequency: Monthly
Founded in 1977

22583 Photonics Components/Subsystems

IGI group
1340 Soldiers Field Road
Suite 2
Brighton, MA 02135

617-782-5033
800-323-1088
FAX 617-782-5735
E-Mail: info@igigroup.com
Home Page: www.igigroup.com

Paul Polishuk, Publisher
Hui Pan, Conference Director
Bev Wilson, Managing Editor
Yesim Taskor, Controller

Provides worldwide coverage of technology, markets, and applications. Some subjects covered include: market forecasts, product comparisons, new products, contract awards, new technologies, start-up funding, customer requirements, standards, industry trends, photonics automation, systems developments, licensing, competitive assessments, mergers and acquisitions, and pricing trends.
Cost: $695.00
Frequency: Monthly
Founded in 1977

22584 Plastic Optical Fiber (POF)

IGI Group
1340 Soldiers Field Road
Suite 2
Brighton, MA 02135

617-782-5033
800-323-1088
FAX 617-782-5735
E-Mail: editor@igigroup.com
Home Page: www.igigroup.com

Paul Polishuk, CEO
Hui Pan, Conference Director
Bev Wilson, Managing Editor
Yesim Taskor, Controller

Some of the subjects covered are: applications, products, imaging, patents, technology, market research, suppliers, publications, standards, sensors, cost analyses, mergers, audio systems, lighting/illuminations, medical acquisitions, medical, market opportunities, contracts awarded, automotive, licensing opportunities, RFPs, component costs, investments and signs.
Cost: $395.00
Frequency: 6 issues per yr
Founded in 1977

22585 SCTE Interval
Society of Cable Telecommunications
Engineers
140 Philips Road
Exton, PA 19341-1318

610-363-6888
800-542-5040
FAX 610-363-5898
E-Mail: scte@scte.org
Home Page: www.scte.org

Mark Durbaz, President/CEO
Catty Oaks, VP

SCTE's monthly newsletter keeps members
abreast of association events, activities and
member accomplishments.
Cost: $40.00
Circulation: 15,000
Founded in 1969

22586 Satellite News
Phillips Publishing
7811 Montrose Road
Potomac, MD 20854

301-340-2100
866-599-9491
E-Mail: feedback@healthydirections.com
Home Page: www.healthydirections.com

Satellite telecommunications.
Frequency: Monthly
Founded in 1985

**22587 Society of Telecommunications
Consultants Newsletter**
Society of Telecommunications Consultants
13275 State Highway 89
PO Box 70
Old Station, CA 96071

530-335-7313
800-782-7670
FAX 530-335-7360
E-Mail: stchdq@stcconsultants.org
Home Page: www.stcconsultants.org

Cathy Cimaglia, Administrative Manager
Mark Durbaz, President/CEO
Catty Oaks, VP

A newsletter for update and informational pur-
poses.
Frequency: Quarterly
Founded in 1969

**22588 State & Local Communications
Report**
BRP Publications
1333 H Street NW
Suite 100 E
Washington, DC 20005-4746

202-312-6060
800-822-6338
FAX 202-842-3047

Lynn Stanton, Editor
Victoria Mason, Publisher

Premier biweekly news service covering state
and local communications issues. The in-depth
reporting includes regular coverage of such
timely topics as legislation and regulation, new
state regulatory activities and important business and industry developments in the areas of
telephone, data and enhanced services.
Cost: $599.00
8 Pages
Frequency: BiWeekly

22589 State Telephone Regulation Report
Telecom Publishing Group

1101 King Street
Suite 444
Alexandria, VA 22314-2944

703-683-4100
800-327-7205
FAX 703-739-6490

Chris Vestal, Publisher
Herbert Kirchoff, Editor

Analysis of state telecommunications legisla-
tion.
Cost: $535.00
12 Pages
Frequency: BiWeekly
Printed in 2 colors on matte stock

**22590 Submarine Fiber Optic
Communications Systems**
IGI Group
1340 Soldiers Field Road
Suite 2
Brighton, MA 02135

617-782-5033
800-323-1088
FAX 617-782-5735
E-Mail: editor@igigroup.com
Home Page: www.igigroup.com

Paul Polishuk, Publisher
Hui Pan, Conference Director
Bev Wilson
Yesim Taskor, Controller

Provides a monthly market intelligence report
on new developments in markets, technology
and applications. Of special interest will be developments in optical amplifier technology, solutions, Wavelength Division Multiplexing and
how these are having an impact on the Submarine Fiber Optic business
Cost: $695.00
Frequency: Monthly
Founded in 1977

22591 TR Wireless News
BRP Publications
1333 H Street NW
Suite 100 E
Washington, DC 20005-4707

202-312-6060
800-822-6338
FAX 202-842-3047

Victoria Mason, Publisher
Andrew Kreig, President

Montiors regulatory, technological and market
developments in the rapidly expanding wireless
communications industry. It covers new services, corporate activity, and licensing and
specturm allocation in the areas of personal
communication services.
Cost: $597.00
Frequency: BiWeekly

22592 TV Program Investor
Kagan World Media
1 Lower Ragsdale Dr
Building One, Suite 130
Monterey, CA 93940-5749

831-624-1536
800-307-2529
FAX 831-625-3225
E-Mail: info@kagan.com
Home Page: www.kagan.com

Tim Baskerville, President
Tom Johnson, Marketing Manager

More than just a newsletter, practically a semi-
nar on how much programs cost and what they
are worth. Exclusive spreadsheets with esti-
mates of what goes between the commercials.
Three month trial available.
Cost: $895.00
Frequency: Monthly
Founded in 1969

22593 Telco Competition Report
BRP Publications
1333 H Street NW
Suite 100 E
Washington, DC 20005-4746

202-312-6060
800-822-6338
FAX 202-842-3047

Victoria Mason, Publisher
Brian Hammond, Editor

Provides important information on events and
issues surrounding the $90 billion local ex-
change markets. Each issues covers the continuing regulatory, financial, strategic and
technological ramifications of local exchange
competition, including the second and third-tier
cities being targeted by competitions and strategies for success.
Cost: $596.00
20 Pages
Frequency: BiWeekly

22594 Tele-Service News
Worldwide Videotex
Po Box 3273
Boynton Beach, FL 33424

561-738-2276
E-Mail: markedit@juno.com
Home Page: www.wvpubs.com

Provides news and information on the telephone industry. Covers services, products, research and development and business plans of
RBOCs (Regional Bell Operating Companies),
long distance carriers, and independent vendors.
Cost: $25.00
Frequency: Monthly

**22595 Telecom Daily Lead from US Telecom
Association**
SmartBrief
1401 H Street
N.W, Suite 600
Washington, DC 20005

202-326-7300
FAX 202-326-7333
E-Mail: webmaster@smartbrief.com
Home Page: www.dailylead.com/usta

Portia Krebs, VP Communications
Jason Ross, Lead Editor
Eric Hoffman, Sales Account Director

Free daily newsbriefing, delivered by e-mail,
that covers the telecom industry's top news stories.
Frequency: Daily
Circulation: 11000

22596 Telecom Outlook
Market Intelligence Research Company
2525 Charleston Road
Mountain View, CA 94043-1626
Wyman Bravard, Publisher

Reports on the telecommunications industry.
Frequency: Monthly

22597 Telecom Standards
IGI Group
1340 Soldiers Field Road
Suite 2
Brighton, MA 02135

617-782-5033
800-323-1088
FAX 617-782-5735
E-Mail: editor@igigroup.com
Home Page: www.igigroup.com

Paul Polishuk, President/CEO
Hui Pan, Conference Director
Bev Wilson, Managing Editor
Yesim Taskor, Controller

Provides coverage of standards activities around the world, schedules of standards meetings, the availablity of standards, and how to obtain standards, minutes of standards meetings and drafts of standards.
Cost: $695.00
Frequency: Monthly
Founded in 1977

22598 Telecommunications Mergers and Acquisitions

IGI group
1340 Soldiers Field Road
Suite 2
Brighton, MA 02135

617-782-5033
800-323-1088
FAX 617-782-5735
E-Mail: editor@igigroup.com
Home Page: www.igigroup.com

Paul Polishuk, President/CEO
Hui Pan, Conference Director
Bev Wilson, Managing Editor
Yesim Taskor, Controller

Covers worldwide developments in the telecommunications mergers and acquisitions. In addition to reporting to these activities, the newsletter analyzes potential merger and acquisition candidates, summarizes in an easy-to-read form trends by different companies and industry requirements.
Cost: $695.00
Frequency: Monthly
Founded in 1977

22599 Telecommunications Reports International

BRP Publications
111 Eighth Avenue
7th Floor
New York, NY 10011-4707

212-771-0600
800-234-1660
FAX 212-771-0885
E-Mail: jrohaly@aspenpublishers.com
Home Page: www.aspenpublishers.com

Andrew Jacobson, Publisher
George Brandon, Editor
Jim Monahan, President
Richard H Kravitz, Execitive VP

International telecom policy and trade issues, global services, satellites, tariffs and financial developments.
Cost: $1789.00
Frequency: 24 issues per y

22600 Telemarketing Update

Prosperity & Profits Unlimited
PO Box 416
Denver, CO 80201-0416

303-573-5564

AC Doyle, Publisher

Telemarketing script presentation suggestions and ideas.
Cost: $200.00
8 Pages
Frequency: Annual
Circulation: 2,000
Printed in on matte stock

22601 Telemarketing Update-Catering Service Business Script Presentations

Prosperity & Profits Unlimited
PO Box 416
Denver, CO 80201-0416

303-573-5564

A Doyle, Editor

Catering service telemarketing script presentations.
Cost: $19.95
10 Pages
Frequency: Irregular
Circulation: 2,100
Founded in 1990
Printed in one color on matte stock

22602 VoiceNews

Stoneridge Technical Services
PO Box 1891
Rockville, MD 20849-1891

301-424-0114
FAX 301-424-8971

William Creitz, Publisher/Editor

Covers voice technology for telecommunications and office automation: voice messaging, voice response, speech recognition, speech synthesis.
Cost: $25.00

22603 Why Not An Answering Service?

Prosperity & Profits Unlimited
PO Box 416
Denver, CO 80201-0416

303-573-5564

A Doyle, Editor

Offers information and ideas on telephone answering service possibilities.
Cost: $29.95
73 Pages
Frequency: Every Five Years
Circulation: 5,000
Founded in 1989
Printed in on matte stock

22604 Wireless Market Stats

Kagan World Media
1 Lower Ragsdale Dr
Building One Suite 130
Monterey, CA 93940-5749

831-624-1536
800-307-2529
FAX 831-625-3225
E-Mail: info@kagan.com
Home Page: www.kagan.com

Tim Baskerville, President
Tom Johnson, Marketing Manager

In-depth analysis of metropolitan and rural cellular market efficiency, plus operating statistics, private deal market data, economic and demographic data for narrowband and broadband PCS, ESMR, paging and more.
Cost: $1095.00
Frequency: Monthly
Founded in 1969

22605 Wireless Satellite and Broadcasting

IGI Group
1340 Soldiers Field Road
Suite 2
Brighton, MA 02135

617-782-5033
800-323-1088
FAX 617-782-5735
E-Mail: editor@igigroup.com
Home Page: www.igigroup.com

Paul Polishuk, Publisher
Hui Pan, Conference Director
Bev Wilson, Managing Editor

Subjects covered include: market opportunities, technology, international developments, regulation/policy, standards, applications, procurements, PCN, market forecasts, new products, mergers/acquisitions, joint ventures and more.
Cost: $695.00
Frequency: Monthly
Founded in 1977

22606 Wireless Telecom Investor

Kagan World Media
1 Lower Ragsdale Dr
Building One, Suite 130
Monterey, CA 93940-5749

831-624-1536
800-307-2529
FAX 831-625-3225
E-Mail: info@kagan.com
Home Page: www.kagan.com

Tim Baskerville, President
Tom Johnson, Marketing Manager

Exclusive analysis of private and public values of wireless telecommunications companies, including cellular telephone, ESMR and PCS. Exclusive databases of subscribers, market penetrations, market potential, industry growth. Catching super-fast growth in a capsule.
Cost: $1095.00
Frequency: Monthly
Founded in 1969

22607 Wireless Week

Chilton Company
600 S Cherry Street
Suite 400
Denver, CO 80246-1706

303-393-7449
FAX 303-399-2034

Tom Brooksher, Publisher
Judith Lockwood, Editor

Covers the wireless telecommunications industry.
Circulation: 32,000

22608 Worldwide Videotex Update

Worldwide Videotex
Po Box 3273
Boynton Beach, FL 33424

561-738-2276
E-Mail: markedit@juno.com
Home Page: www.wvpubs.com

Reports news and information on videotex, The Internet, online services, electronic mail, satellite communications and television related technologies, such as teleconferencing and teletext.
Cost: $25.00
Frequency: Monthly

22609 XDSL

IGI Group
1340 Soldiers Field Road
Suite 2
Boston, MA 02135

617-782-5033
800-323-1088
FAX 617-782-5735
E-Mail: bmark@igigroup.com
Home Page: www.igigroup.com

Paul Polishuk, President/CEO
Hui Panb, Conference Director
Bev Wilson, Managing Editor

Subjects covered include: field trials, applicatins, competition ffrom cable and satellite, new products, Telco plans, fiber optics, market forecasts, techology developments, wireless, major player strategies, cable modems, ISDN and more.
Cost: $695.00
Frequency: Monthly
Founded in 1977

Magazines & Journals

22610 ACUTA Journal of Communications Technology in Higher Education
ACUTA
152 W Zandale Drive
Suite 200
Lexington, KY 40503-2486

859-278-3338
FAX 859-278-3268
E-Mail: pscott@acuta.org
Home Page: www.acuta.org
Social Media: *Facebook*

Pat Scott, Editor
Tamara Closs, President
Jerry A Simmer, Director
Corinne Harrison, Executive Officer
Tom Chappel, Finance & Administration

Journal is distributed to telecom, information management professionals at colleges and universities, along with industry professionals with products and services for the higher education vertical market.
Cost: $80.00
48 Pages
Frequency: Quarterly
Circulation: 2320
ISSN: 1097-8658
Founded in 1997
Mailing list available for rent: 2,300 names
Printed in 4 colors on matte stock

22611 ARRL The National Association for Amateur Radio
American Radio Relay League
225 Main St
Newington, CT 06111

860-594-0200
888-277-5289
FAX 860-594-0259
E-Mail: webmaster@arrl.org
Home Page: www.arrl.org

David Sumner, CEO
Kay Craigie, President
Bob Inderbitzen, Marketing Manager

Geared at the IRF and amatuer radio operators industry, provides information on communications theory and technical advances in design and construction. The official journal of the American Radio Relay League.
Cost: $24.00
156M Members
Frequency: Monthly
Circulation: 146000
Founded in 1914

22612 America's Network
Questex Media Group
201 Sandpointe Ave
Suite 500
Santa Ana, CA 92707-8716

714-338-6700
800-854-3112
FAX 714-513-8481
E-Mail: psemple@advanstar.com
Home Page: www.americasnetwork.com

Paul Semple, Publisher
Bill Pettit, National Sales Director

Independent reporting and business analysis of telecommunications technologies for today's public network.
Cost: $100.00
Frequency: Monthly
Circulation: 60,006

22613 Audiotex Update
Worldwide Videotex

PO Box 3273
Boynton Beach, FL 33424-3273

561-738-2276
E-Mail: markedit@juno.com
Home Page: www.wvpubs.com

Mark E Wright, Editor

Provides the latest news and infromation about the audiotex industry, including voice processing information, products, services, as well as research and development.
Cost: $165.00
Frequency: Monthly
Founded in 1981

22614 B/OSS
Virgo Publishing LLC
3300 N Central Ave
Suite 300
Phoenix, AZ 85012-2532

480-675-9925
FAX 480-990-0819
E-Mail: mikes@vpico.com
Home Page: www.vpico.com
Social Media: *Facebook, Twitter, LinkedIn*

Jenny Bolton, President
John Siefert, CEO
Kelly Ridley, VP
Troy Bix, Publisher

Source for news and analysis for telecommunications support systems as they take a leading role in creating and supporting service differentiation in the communications marketplace.
Circulation: 20000
Founded in 1986
Printed in on glossy stock

22615 Business Communications Review
BCR Enterprises
Ste 200
3025 Highland Pkwy
Downers Grove, IL 60515-5668

630-986-1432
800-227-1234
FAX 630-323-5324
Home Page: www.bcr.com

Fred Knight, Publisher

Offers a complete package of the latest information for persons associated with the communications industry.
Cost: $45.00
80 Pages
Frequency: Monthly
Founded in 1971

22616 CTI the Authority on Computer, Internet, & Network Telephony
Technology Marketing Corporation
1 Technology Plz
Norwalk, CT 06854-1936

203-852-6800
800-243-6002
FAX 203-853-2845
E-Mail: ctipress@tmcnet.com
Home Page: www.tmcnet.com
Social Media: *Facebook, Twitter*

Rich Tehrani, CEO
Anthony Graffeo, National Advertising Sales Manager
Greg Galitzine, Editorial Director

Provides tutorials, application stories, and new product listings and reviews, as well as service information. Emphasizes furthering the development, implementation and use of CTI technology.
Frequency: Monthly
Circulation: 50256
Founded in 1998

22617 Cabling Business
Cabling Publications

12035 Shiloh Rd
Suite 350
Dallas, TX 75228-1549

214-322-8171
FAX 214-319-6077
E-Mail: russell@cablingbusiness.com
Home Page: www.cablingbusiness.com
Social Media: *Facebook, Twitter*

Stephen Paulov, President
Christy Sheeran, Business Manager
Rita Paulov, Senior Sales Associate
David Deal, Webmaster
Margaret Patterson, Managing Editor

New product information, troubleshooting hints, and information on installation and repair.
Frequency: Monthly
Circulation: 24070
Mailing list available for rent

22618 Cabling Installation & Maintenance
PennWell Publishing Company
1421 S Sheridan Rd
Tulsa, OK 74112-6619

918-831-9421
800-331-4483
FAX 918-831-9476
E-Mail: patrick@pennwell.com
Home Page: www.pennwell.com

Robert Biolchini, President
Steve Smith, Executive Editor

Emphasizes the problem solving aspects of cable installation in telecommunications, data, and video systems.
Frequency: Monthly
Circulation: 23604
Founded in 1993

22619 Call Center Magazine
Miller Freeman Publications
11 Est 19th Street
3rd Floor
New York, NY 10011

212-600-3000
800-672-6111
FAX 212-691-1191
E-Mail: msteiger@cmp.com
Home Page: www.callcentermagazine.com

Keith Dawson, Editor
Max Steiger, Sales Manager

Dedicated to providing in-depth and unbiased product and strategic information for call center executives.
Frequency: Monthly
Circulation: 32904

22620 Communication Theory
International Communication Association
U de Montreal, Department de Communication
1500 21st Street
Washington, DC 20026

202-955-1444
FAX 202-955-1448
E-Mail: communicationtheory@umontreal.ca.
Home Page: www.icahdq.org
Social Media: *Facebook, Twitter, LinkedIn*

Francois Cooren, Editor

Publishes research articles, theoretical essays, and reviews on topics of broad theoretical interest from across the range of communication studies. Recognizes that approaches to theory develpment and explication are diverse.
Mailing list available for rent

22621 Communication Yearbook
International Communication Association

Ohio University, School of Communication
Study
1501 21st Street
Washington, DC 20026

202-955-1445
FAX 202-955-1449
E-Mail: communicationtheory@umontreal.ca.
Home Page: www.icahdq.org
Social Media: *Facebook, Twitter, LinkedIn*

Dr Christina S. Beck, Editor

Features state-of-the discipline literature reviews of communication research. Highlights reviews of research exploring communication concepts that span traditional 'division' divides, issues of central importance to the accomplishment of communication in a variety of contexts and for diverse communicators throughout the world.
Founded in 1913
Mailing list available for rent

22622 Communications Billing Report
Telecommunications Reports International
76 9th Ave. 7th fl
#100-E
Washington, NY 10011

21- 77- 071
FAX 212-771-0732
E-Mail: joseph.rohaly@wolterskluwer.com
Home Page: www.tr.com
Social Media: *Facebook, Twitter, LinkedIn*

Victoria Mason, Editor-in-Chief

Content provides hard-to-find facts on such issues as developing internet electronic payment systems, keeping on top of new outsourcing opportunities, enhancing customer care and back office functions and making the most of new software developments.
Cost: $765.00
Frequency: BiWeekly

22623 Communications Crossroads
United States Telecom Association
1401 H St NW
Suite 600
Washington, DC 20005-2110

202-326-7300
FAX 202-326-7333
E-Mail: editor@usta.org
Home Page: www.usta.org
Social Media: *Facebook, Twitter, LinkedIn, You Tube*

Walter Mc Kormick, President
James Cooconi, VP
Robert Curry, Tresurer
Robert Hunt, Secretary

Dedicated to the success stories, investment opportunities and industry events that herald the future of small and rural carriers.
Cost: $60.00
Circulation: 3500
Founded in 2006

22624 Enterprise Wireless Magazine
Enterprise Wireless Association
8484 Westpark Drive
Suite 630
McLean, VA 22102-5117

703-528-5115
800-482-8282
FAX 703-524-1074
E-Mail:
customerservice@enterprisewireless.org
Home Page: www.enterprisewireless.org
Social Media: *Facebook, Twitter*

Mark Crosby, President/CEO
Andre Cote, Senior VP
Ila Dudley, VP Spectrum Management
Ron Franklin, VP Membership/Business
Development

Covers how wireless meets the operational needs of business and industrial enterprise users. Used extensivley throughout the year by your prospects to stay informed of technical, industry and association information, and as a comprehensive buyers' guide for the products and services they use most often.
Frequency: Quarterly

22625 Global Telephony
Primedia
3585 Engineering Drive
Suite 100
Norcross,, GA 30092

678-421-3000
800-216-1423
FAX 312-595-0295
E-Mail: mallen@primedia.com
Home Page: www.primediabusiness.com
Social Media: *Facebook, Twitter, LinkedIn, You Tube*

Larry Lannon, Publisher
Carol Wilson, Editor

Telephony delivers timely and intelligent coverage of the news, technologies and business strategies driving the industry.
Frequency: 24/Yr
Circulation: 63,500

22626 Handbooks of Communication Series
International Communication Association
Dept of Comm, University of Colorado at Boulder
1500 21st Street
Washington, DC 20026

202-955-1444
FAX 202-955-1448
E-Mail: communicationtheory@umontreal.ca.
Home Page: www.icahdq.org
Social Media: *Facebook, Twitter, LinkedIn*

Robert T Craig, Editor
Linda Bathgate, Senior Editor

Publishes research articles, theoretical essays, and reviews on topics of broad theoretical interest from across the range of communication studies. Recognizes that approaches to theory devlopment and explication are diverse.
Mailing list available for rent

22627 Human Communication Research
International Communication Association
Dept of Communication Arts & Science,234
Sparks
1500 21st Street
Washington, DC 20026

202-955-1444
FAX 202-955-1448
E-Mail: communicationtheory@umontreal.ca.
Home Page: www.icahdq.org
Social Media: *Facebook, Twitter, LinkedIn*

James P Dillard, Editor

Publishes research articles, theoretical essays, and reviews on topics of broad theoretical interest from across the range of communication studies. Recognizes that approaches to theory devlopment and explication are diverse.
Frequency: Quarterly
Mailing list available for rent

22628 ICA Communique
International Communications Association
1500 21st St NW
1500 21st Street
Washington, DC 20026

202-955-1444
FAX 202-955-1448
E-Mail: communicationtheory@umontreal.ca.
Home Page: www.icahdq.org
Social Media: *Facebook, Twitter, LinkedIn*

M Haley, Executive Director

Publishes research articles, theoretical essays, and reviews on topics of broad theoretical interest from across the range of communication studies. Recognizes that approaches to theory devlopment and explication are diverse.
Cost: $135.00
Frequency: 10/Year
Mailing list available for rent

22629 IEEE Communications Magazine
Institute of Electrical & Electronics
Engineers
3 Park Ave
Suite 17
New York, NY 10016-5997

212-419-7900
FAX 212-752-4929
E-Mail: publications@comsoc.org
Home Page: www.ieee.org
Social Media: *Facebook, Twitter, LinkedIn, You Tube*

Daniel J Senese, CEO
Jack Howell, Executive Director

Written in tutorial applications-driven style by the industry's leading experts. IEEE Communications Magazine delivers usable information on the latest international coverage of current issues and advances in key areas.
Cost: $ 20.00
Frequency: Monthly
Circulation: 43832

22630 IEEE Network
IEEE Operations Center
PO Box 1331
Piscataway, NJ 08855-1331

732-981-0060
FAX 732-981-1721
E-Mail: publications@comsoc.org
Home Page: www.cosmoc.org

John Vig, CEO

The magazine of Global Internetworking provides the most current information for communications professionals involved with the interconnection of computing systems.
Frequency: Bi-Monthly

22631 Intele-Card News
Quality Publishing
523 N Sam Houston Parkway E
Suite 300
Houston, TX 77060

281-272-2744
800-792-6397
FAX 281-847-5752
E-Mail: info@intelecard.com
Home Page: www.intelecard.com

Theresa Ward, Editor-in-Chief
Jo Ann Davy, Managing Editor
Laurette Veres, Owner

Reports on news and events impacting the business of telephone cards, identifies significant trends and profiles industry newsmakers.
Frequency: Monthly
Circulation: 12000
Founded in 1995

22632 Journal of Communication
International Communication Association
Department of Communication-101 Burton
Hall
University of Oklahoma
Norman, OK 73019

405-325-9503
E-Mail: joc@ou.edu
Home Page: www.icahdq.org

Michael Pfau, Editor

A general forum for communication scholarship and publishes articles and book reviews examining a broad range of issues in communication theory and research. Publishes the best available scholarship on all aspects of communication.

22633 Journal of Computer-Mediated Communication

International Communication Association
1500 21st Street
Washington, DC 20026

202-955-1444
FAX 202-955-1448
E-Mail: communicationtheory@umontreal.ca.
Home Page: jcmc.indiana.edu
Social Media: *Facebook, Twitter, LinkedIn*

Susan C Herring, Editor

Publishes research articles, theoretical essays, and reviews on topics of broad theoretical interest from across the range of communication studies. Recognizes that approaches to theory develment and explication are diverse.
Mailing list available for rent

22634 Lightwave

PennWell Publishing Company
1421 S Sheridan Rd
Tulsa, OK 74112-6619

918-831-9421
800-331-4483
FAX 918-831-9476
E-Mail: stephenh@pennwell.com
Home Page: www.pennwell.com

Robert Biolchini, President
Carrie Meadows, Managing Editor
Meghan Fuller, Senior News Editor
Matt Vincent, Associate Editor/Web Editor

An international journal of fiber optics that covers all applications of the technology in telecommunications, data communications, broadcast and cable TV and specialized military applications.
Cost: $137.00
224 Pages
Frequency: Monthly
ISSN: 0741-5834
Founded in 1910
Printed in 4 colors on matte stock

22635 Locating, Testing and Repairing

Stober Research and Communications
PO Box 517
McHenry, IL 60051

815-385-6123
FAX 815-385-7151
Home Page: www.ltrmag.com
Social Media: *Facebook, Twitter*

L Jack Stober, Publisher

Information on copper and fiber optic sets available for telecommunication applications, as well as listings of companies and categories of this equipment. Regular departments contain fault locating and test equipment tips, a new product showcase and a look at new industry literature.
Cost: $100.00
Frequency: Quarterly
Circulation: 27355
Founded in 1998

22636 Mobile Communication Business

Phillips Business Information
7811 Montrose Road
Potomac, MD 20854

301-340-2100
E-Mail: feedback@healthydirections.com
Home Page: www.healthydirections.com
Social Media: *Facebook, Twitter*

Don Steele, Editor

Offers information and the latest technological advances in telecommunications.
Frequency: Monthly
Founded in 1985

22637 Multimedia Telecommunication News

Stoneridge Technical Services
PO Box 1891
Rockville, MD 20849-1891

301-424-0114
FAX 301-424-8971
E-Mail: techwriter@stoneridgetech.com
Home Page: www.stoneridgetech.com

William W Creitz, Editor

Focuses on new products, applications, technological developments, markets and company activites.
Frequency: Monthly

22638 NTCA Exchange

National Telephone Cooperative Association
4121 Wilson Blvd
Suite 1000
Arlington, VA 22203-4145

703-351-2000
FAX 703-351-2001
Home Page: www.ntca.org

Michael E Brunner, CEO

Bi-monthly newsletter examining association and member news, including profiles, business tips and member updates.
Cost: $15.00
Frequency: Bi-Monthly
Circulation: 5100
Founded in 1980

22639 Network Magazine

CMP Media
245 Blackfriars Road
Manhasset, NY 11030

516-562-5000
866-880-8219
FAX 516-562-7013
E-Mail: cmp@cmp.com
Home Page: www.cmp.com

Art Wittmann, Editor
Paula McGinlinchey, Publisher

Network Magazine serves communications carriers, communications service providers including interexchange/PTT's/long distance carriers, business services (non-computer) and other industry organizations.
Cost: $175.00
162 Pages
Frequency: Monthly
Circulation: 125000
ISSN: 1093-8001
Founded in 1986
Printed in 4 colors on matte stock

22640 Networks Update

Worldwide Videotex
Po Box 3273
Boynton Beach, FL 33424

561-738-2276
E-Mail: markedit@juno.com
Home Page: www.wvpubs.com
Social Media: *Facebook, Twitter*

Provides the latest news and information about the computer network industry. This includes national, international, public, private, and military network products, services, companies, marketing strategies, and research and development.
Cost: $25.00
Frequency: Monthly

22641 Opastco Roundtable

OPASTCO
2020 K Street
Suite 700
Washington, DC 20006

202-659-5990
FAX 202-659-4619

E-Mail: roundtable@opastco.org
Home Page: www.opastco.org

John Rose, President
Caurey Watson, Administrative Services Manager

Provides practical, how-to information that small local exchange carriers can use in their day-to-day operations, as well as plain English explanations of industry issues and technologies.
Frequency: BiMonthly

22642 Outside Plant

Practical Communications
220 N Smith St
Suite 228
Palatine, IL 60067-2488

847-202-4683
FAX 847-639-9542
E-Mail: sharon@ospmag.com
Home Page: www.ospmag.com

Sharon Stober, VP/Editorial Director
Karen Adolphson, Managing Editor
Mary Beth Koelling, Executive Director Sales/Marketing

Magazine for telecom outside plant professionals. Reaches ASP engineers, planners, managers and technicians in Bell and independent phone companies.
Cost: $30.00
100 Pages
Frequency: Monthly
Circulation: 25000
Founded in 1983

22643 POINT

Direct Marketing Association
1120 Avenue of the Americas
New York, NY 10036-6713

212-768-7277
FAX 212-768-4547
Home Page: www.the-dma.org
Social Media: *Facebook, Twitter*

John A. Greco Jr, President & CEO

DMA's digital magazine.

22644 Pen Computing Magazine

Pen Computing Publishing Office
120 Bethpage Road
Suite 300
Hicksville, NY 11801

516-433-8725
FAX 516-433-8724
E-Mail: cb@pencomputing.com
Home Page: www.pencomputing.com

Howard Borgen, Publisher
Lisa Krebs, VP Advertising
Wayne Laslo, Advertising Manager
Conrad H Blickenstorfer, Editor-in-Chief
David MacNeill, Executive Editor

Bi-Monthly print journal of pen-based and mobile computing. Hardware and software reviews, expert opinions, feature articles, case studies, how-to, industry news, technical primers and more.
Cost: $18.00
Frequency: Bi-Monthly
Circulation: 79515
Founded in 1993

22645 Politically Direct

Direct Marketing Association
1120 Avenue of the Americas
New York, NY 10036-6700

212-768-7277
FAX 212-302-6714
E-Mail: customerservice@the-dma.org
Home Page: www.the-dma.org

Lawrence M Kimmel, CEO

Published both in print and digital, this newsletter on DMA advocacy efforts keeps DMA members informed and involved in the politics and policies that impact them today and ahead of the curve on developments that will affect them tomorrow.
Frequency: Quarterly

22646 RCR Wireless News

Crain Communications
1746 Cole Blvd
Suite 150
Lakewood, CO 80401-3208

303-733-2500
888-909-9111
FAX 303-733-9941
E-Mail: subs@crain.com
Home Page: www.crain.com

Mary Pemberton, Marketing
Tracy Ford, Associate Publisher/Editor
Dan Meyer, Managing Editor
Pete Racelis, President

News and analysis of the wireless communications industry.
Cost: $69.00
Frequency: Weekly
Circulation: 65000
Founded in 1981
Printed in on matte stock

22647 Satellite Business News

Satellite Business News
1990 M Street NW
Suite 510
Washington, DC 20036-3102

202-785-0505
FAX 202-785-9291
E-Mail: general.mail@satbiznews.com
Home Page: www.satbiznews.com

Bob Scherman, Publisher
Jeffrey Williams, Managing Editor
Charlie Ergen, CEO/President

Up-to-date news on satellite television industry, upcoming events, and new technology for the industry.
Cost: $44.75
Frequency: Bi-annually
Circulation: 565700
Founded in 1983

22648 Satellite News

Phillips Business Information
6181 Executive Blvd
Rockville, MD 20852-3901

301-881-7516
866-279-1930
FAX 301-424-2709
E-Mail: information@phillips.com
Home Page: www.phillips.com

Donald Phelps, President
Robert Phillips, CEO

Information on satellite launches, companies rebounding from losses, blows to competitors and regulatory issues.
Frequency: Weekly
Circulation: 18000
Founded in 1974

22649 Satellite Week

Warren Publishing
2115 Ward Ct NW
Washington, DC 20037-1209

202-872-9200
800-771-9202
FAX 202-318-8350
E-Mail: info@warren-news.com
Home Page: www.warren-news.com

Brig Easley, Executive VP
Paul Warren, Chair/Publisher
Daniel Warren, President/Editor

The definitive weekly source for fast-breaking, international news on space communications policy, regularion, technology and business. Offers up-to-date, comprehensive reports on new technologies, notices of international advances, details about regulation and deregularion, satellite marketplace intelligence, news of DBS developments, and continuous coverage of what industry leaders are doing and saying.
Frequency: Weekly
Founded in 1945

22650 Sound & Communications

Testa Communications
25 Willowdale Avenue
Port Washington, NY 11050-3779

516-767-2500
800-937-7678
FAX 516-767-9335
E-Mail: testa@testa.com
Home Page: www.testacommunications.com
Social Media: *Facebook, Twitter*

Vincent P Testa, President
David A. Silverman, Editor

Covers sound, display, security and multimedia systems, also theory and applications.
Frequency: Monthly
Circulation: 22500
Founded in 1955

22651 Sound & Video Contractor

Primedia
PO Box 12914
Overland Park, KS 66282

913-341-1300
FAX 913-967-1903
E-Mail: mjohnson@premediabusiness.com
Home Page: www.svconline.com

Mark Johnson, Editor
Trevor Boyer, Associate Editor
Trevor Boyer, Associate Editor

Contains information on sound systems, video display, security, CCTV, home theater, and automation. Delivers in depth instruction and examples of successful installations, fundamental acoustical and video theory and news on new technologies eaffecting the systems contracting business.
Cost: $35.00
Frequency: Monthly
Circulation: 21,000
Founded in 1983
Mailing list available for rent: 20,500 names at $110 per M

22652 Sys Admin

CMP Media
303 Second Street
Suite 200
Lawrence, KS 94107

415-947-6000
FAX 785-841-2047
E-Mail: aankerholz@cmp.com
Home Page: www.sysadminmag.com

Amber Ankerhola
Deirdre Blake, MD

SYS ADMIN serves the Unix and Linux system administration market.
Cost: $39.00
100 Pages
Frequency: Monthly
Founded in 1992
Printed in on glossy stock

22653 TELEconference Magazine

Applied Business Telecommunications

201 Sandpoint Ave
Suite 600
Santa Ana, CA 92707-8700

714-513-8400
800-854-3112
FAX 714-513-8680
Home Page: www.advanstar.com

Keith Gallagher, Publisher
Paul DeVeaux, Editor

Devoted to the field of teleconferencing and contains in-depth articles to provide updates on audio/graphic and video teleconferencing applications, trends and developments.
Cost: $10.00
Circulation: 15000
Founded in 1992

22654 Telecommunications

Horizon House Publications
685 Canton St
Norwood, MA 02062-2608

781-762-1319
FAX 781-769-5037
E-Mail: editorial@telecommagazine.com
Home Page: www.horizonhouse.com

Charles A Ayotte, CEO
Robert Bass, Production Manager
Bob Wallace, Editor
William Harrison, Manager
William Bassy, President

Communication technology and market developments for users, service providers and manufacturers worldwide.
Frequency: Monthly
Circulation: 80854
Founded in 1960

22655 Telephone IP News

Worldwide Videotex
Po Box 3273
Boynton Beach, FL 33424

561-738-2276
E-Mail: markedit@juno.com
Home Page: www.wvpubs.com

Provides news and information concerning the information provider (IP) industry for telephone services and two-way paging and wireless information services. Reports on new products available to providers and monitors public service commission rulings as they aplly to information services.
Cost: $25.00
Frequency: Monthly

22656 Telephony

Telephony Division
One IBM Plaza
Suite 2300
Chicago, IL 10151

312-595-1080
FAX 312-595-0296
E-Mail: telephony@prismb2b.com
Home Page: www.primedia.com

Mark Hickey, Publisher
Dan O'Shea, Editor-in-Chief
Kim Brower, Marketing Manager

Written for professionals involved in management, construction, maintenance and marketing of modern telecommunication systems. Focus is on new, technical advances, filed applications and management techniques.
Cost: $3.00
Frequency: Weekly
Circulation: 59000
Founded in 1989

22657 VON

Virgo Publishing LLC

3300 N Central Ave
Suite 300
Phoenix, AZ 85012-2532

480-675-9925
FAX 480-990-0819
E-Mail: mikes@vpico.com
Home Page: www.vpico.com
Social Media: *Facebook, Twitter*

Jenny Bolton, President

Global information on IP Communications strategy.
Mailing list available for rent: 22000+ names at $var per M

22658 Wire Journal International
Wire Association International
1570 Boston Post Road
PO Box 578
Guilford, CT 06437

203-453-2777
FAX 203-453-8384
E-Mail: mmarselli@wirenet.org
Home Page: www.wirenet.org
Social Media: *Facebook, Twitter*

Brian A Bouvier, President
Steven J Fetteroll, Executive Director
Mark A Marselli, Editor-in-Chief
Janice E Swindells, Director of Marketing Services
Robert J Xeller, Director Sales

The leading technical publication for the wire and cable industry. Written for executives, engineers, technical and sales professionals, and purchasing agents engaged in the manufacture of ferrous and nonferrous wire and cable; electrical wire and cable; fiber optic cable; and formed and fabricated wire products.
Frequency: Monthly
Circulation: 13434
Founded in 1930
Printed in 4 colors on glossy stock

22659 Worldwide Telecom
Worldwide Videotex
Po Box 3273
Boynton Beach, FL 33424

561-738-2276
E-Mail: markedit@juno.com
Home Page: www.wvpubs.com
Social Media: *Facebook, Twitter*

Provides the latest news and information on international telecommunication products, services, and contracts. The emphasis is on U.S. telecommunications companies doing business in foreign markets and on products with a potential market overseas.
Cost: $25.00
Frequency: Monthly

22660 Yellow Pages Industry Sourcebook
SIMBA Information
60 Long Ridge Rd
Suite 300
Stamford, CT 06902-1841

203-325-8193
FAX 203-325-8915
E-Mail: info@simbanet.com
Home Page: www.simbanet.com

Linda Kopp, Publisher
Kathy Mickey, Managing Editor

Lists key officers, revenues, leading books, major accounts, sales offices and suppliers for more than 1500 firms involved in yellow pages publishing.
Cost: $99.00

22661 xchange
Virgo Publishing LLC

3300 N Central Ave
Suite 300
Phoenix, AZ 85012-2532

480-675-9925
FAX 480-990-0819
E-Mail: mikes@vpico.com
Home Page: www.vpico.com

Jenny Bolton, President
John Siefert, CEO
Kelly Ridley, VP
Katherine Clements, Publisher

Provides in-depth, executive-level news and analysis regarding strategy, technology and regulation to help communications service providers create new revenue, lower costs and achieve sustainable business models.
Frequency: Annual+
Circulation: 35,003
Founded in 1996

Trade Shows

22662 AFCEA TechNet Asia-Pacific
Armed Forces Communications and Electronics Assn
4400 Fair Lakes Court
Fairfax, VA 22033

703-631-6200
800-564-4220
FAX 703-654-6931
E-Mail: technet@jspargo.com
Home Page: www.afcea.org

Paul doCarmo, Assistant Director/Exhibit Sales
Connie Shaw, Exhibit Sales Account Manager
Herbert Browne, President

Military, government and industry communications and electronics professionals gather to see exhibits of communications and electronics equipment, supplies and services.
2000 Attendees
Frequency: November/Annual
Founded in 1985

22663 AFCEA Technical Committee Tech Forum TechNet International
AFCEA Headquarters
4400 Fair Lakes Court
Fairfax, VA 22033-3899

703-631-6100
800-336-4583
FAX 703-631-6169
E-Mail: service@afcea.org
Home Page: www.afcea.org

Herbert Browne, President
Paul doCarmo, Assistant Director/Exhibit Sales
Connie Shaw, Exhibit Sales Account Manager

One of the nation's largest C4I conventions and expositions and features numerous professional development opportunities and tremendous networking opportunies.
Founded in 1985

22664 AFCEA/USNI West Conference & Exposition
Armed Forces Communications and Electronics Assn
4400 Fair Lakes Court
Fairfax, VA 22033

703-631-6200
800-564-4220
FAX 703-654-6931
E-Mail: west@jspargo.org
Home Page: www.afcea.org

Paul doCarmo, Assistant Director/Exhibit Sales
Connie Shaw, Exhibit Sales Account Manager
Herbert Browne, President

Over 350 of the industry's most recognized defense and technology organizations showcase their technology products and services to top decision-makers from the US Pacific Fleet, Naval Station San Diego, Space & Warfare Command, Naval Base Coronado, Camp Pendleton Marine Corps Base and many other west coast military and government facilities.
6000 Attendees
Frequency: January/Annual
Founded in 1985

22665 AIIM Annual Conference and Expo
Association for Information and Image Management
1100 Wayne Avenue
Suite 1100
Silver Spring, MD 20910-5603

301-587-8202
800-477-2446
FAX 301-587-2711
E-Mail: aiim@aiim.org
Home Page: www.aiim.org
Social Media: *Facebook, Twitter*

Jan Andersson, Chair
Robert Zagami, Vice Chair

The leading industry event for Enterprise Content and Document Management, which encompasses the technologies and strategies used to capture, manage, share, and store documents and digital content.
Frequency: April

22666 APCO Annual Conference & Expo
Assoc of Public-Safety Commun Officials Intl
351 N Williamson Boulevard
Daytona Beach, FL 32114-1112

386-322-2500
888-272-6911
FAX 386-322-2501
E-Mail: apco@apcointl.org
Home Page: www.apcointl.org/
Social Media: *Facebook*

George S Rice Jr, Executive Director
Barbara Myers, Conference Services Director
Brigid Blaschak, Tradeshow Manager
Patricia Giannini, Senior Meeting Coordinator
Garry Mendez, Marketing/Communications Director

The Association of Public-Safety Communications Officials International/APCO 's Annual Conference brings together more than 300 vendors to give you hands-on demonstrations of new technologies you might use in your agency or call centers. The Conference also offers sessions on personal and professional development and a variety of technical skills. Banquet, breakfast and exhibitors of radio, computer, and supporting equipment companies.
6000 Attendees
Frequency: Annual
Founded in 1935

22667 Annual Conference for Catalog & Multichannel Merchants (ACCM)
Direct Marketing Association
1120 Avenue of Americas
New York, NY 10036

212-768-7277
FAX 212-768-4547
Home Page: www.the-dma.org

Julie Hogan, SVP Conference & Events
10M Attendees

22668 Antenna Measurement Techniques Association Show
6065 Roswell Road
Suite 2252
Atlanta, GA 30328

770-864-3488
FAX 770-864-3491
Home Page: www.amta.org
Social Media: *Facebook, Twitter*

Janet O'Neil, Contact

Antenna test equipment, supplies and services for government, private and institutional laboratories involved in design and development.

22669 Association for Communications Technology Professionals in Higher Education
ACUTA
152 W Zandale Drive
Suite 200
Lexington, KY 40503-2486

859-278-3338
FAX 859-278-3268
E-Mail: kbowman@acuta.org
Home Page: www.acuta.org
Social Media: *Facebook, Twitter, LinkedIn, You Tube*

Kellie Bowman, Registration
Jeri Semer, Executive Director

Annual conference and exhibits of educational telecommunications equipment, supplies and services. Containing 95 booths.
600 Attendees
Frequency: Annual
Founded in 1971

22670 Association of Teleservices International Conference
ATSI
12 Academy Avenue
Atkinson, NH 03811

866-896-2874
FAX 703-435-4390
E-Mail: admin@atsi.org
Home Page: www.atsi.org
Social Media: *Facebook, Twitter, LinkedIn, You Tube*

Lori Jenkins, President
Marcy Hewlett, Convention Chair

Exhibits of interest to telephone answering and voice message providers.
800+ Attendees
Founded in 1942

22671 Cable-Tec Expo
Society of Cable Telecommunications Engineers
140 Philips Road
Exton, PA 19341-1318

610-524-1725
800-542-5040
FAX 610-363-5898
E-Mail: info@scte.org
Home Page: expo.scte.org
Social Media: *Facebook, Twitter, LinkedIn, You Tube*

Heather Gosciniak, Director

The Society's Cable-Tec Expo is the premier industry hardware exhibition that also offers an engineering conference, workshops and meetings. Expo contains more than 500 booths and 400 exhibits.
12M Attendees
Frequency: Annual

22672 Call Center Conference and Exposition
CMP Media

11 West 19th Street
New York, NY 10011

888-428-3976
FAX 212-600-3080
E-Mail: CCEventInfo@cmp.com
Home Page: www.cmpevents.com
Social Media: *Facebook, Twitter, LinkedIn, You Tube*

Joni Mitchell, Marketing Manager
Joy Cerequas, Director Events

125 booths, plus conference covering all applications of new technologies and services in call processing, transaction processing and telemarketing.
2.5M Attendees
Frequency: February

22673 Email Evolution Conference
Direct Marketing Association
1120 Avenue of Americas
New York, NY 10036-6700

212-768-7277
FAX 212-302-6714
E-Mail: dmaconferences@the-dma.org
Home Page: www.the-dma.org

Julie A Hogan, SVP Conference/Events
Lawrence M Kimmel, CEO

Focuses on the ever-changing and evolving world of email marketing, providing you with the best ways to capitalize on the high ROI this low-cost communication tool can provide both on its own, and integrated with social, search, mobile, video and other email enhancers.
10M Attendees
Frequency: Annual/February

22674 Entelec Conference & Expo
Energy Telecommunications and Electrical Assoc
5005 Royal Lane
Suite 116
Irving, TX 75063

888-503-8700
FAX 972-915-6040
E-Mail: info@entelec.org
Home Page: www.entelec.org
Social Media: *Facebook, Twitter, LinkedIn*

Blaine Siske, Executive Manager
Amanda Prudden, Association Manager

22675 Enterprise Wireless
Enterprise Wireless Alliance
8484 Westpark Drive
Suite 630
McLean, VA 22102-5117

703-528-5115
FAX 703-524-1074
E-Mail: customerservice@enterprisewireless.org
Home Page: www.enterprisewireless.org
Social Media: *Facebook, Twitter, LinkedIn*

Mark Crosby, President/CEO
Andre Cote, Senior VP
Ila Dudley, VP Spectrum Management
Ron Franklin, VP Membership/Business Development

Co-hosted by AAPC and USMSS, this trade show and conference is for wireless service providers, manufacturers, systems integrators an denterprise users to showcase innovative new wireless products.

22676 IEEE Communications Expo IEEE Globecom
J Spargo & Associates
11208 Waples Mill Road
Suite 112
Fairfax, VA 22030

703-631-6200
800-564-4220

FAX 703-654-6931
E-Mail: ieee@jspargo.com
Home Page: www.ieee.org

Connie Shaw, Exhibit Sales Account Manager

In addition to targeting IEEE Communications Society members, also draws companies from Silicon Valley, Northern California, and the Pacific Rim, who manufacture or distribute products or services to support wireless technologies, optical networking, the Internet, or the telecom marketplace.
2000 Attendees
Frequency: November

22677 INTX
National Cable & Telecommunications Association
25 Massachusetts Ave. NW
Suite 100
Washington, DC 20001

202-222-2300
E-Mail: webmaster@ncta.com
Home Page: www.ncta.com
Social Media: *Facebook, Twitter, LinkedIn*

Michael Powell, President & CEO

The Internet & Television Expo
Frequency: Annual/Spring
Founded in 2015

22678 International Wireless Communication Expo
6300 S Syracuse Way
Suite 650
Englewood, CO 80111-6726

303-904-0407
E-Mail: rugianskis@prismb2b.com
Home Page: www.iwceexpo.com
Social Media: *Facebook, Twitter, LinkedIn*

Rita Ugianskis, Group Show Director
Laura Magliola, Marketing Manager
Stacey Orlick, Director
Catherine E. Campfield, Co-ordinator
Angela Wood, Conference Program Manager

The one place where all industries and communications professionals come together to share thoughts and ideas on wireless communications technologies.
6.5M Attendees
Frequency: March

22679 NATOA Annual Conference
Nat'l Assn of Telecommunication Officer & Advisors
3213 Duke Street
Suite 695
Alexandria, VA 22314

703-519-8035
FAX 703-519-7080
E-Mail: info@natoa.org
Home Page: www.natoa.org
Social Media: *Facebook, Twitter*

Elizabeth Beaty, Executive Director
Jennifer Harman, Manager
Tonya Rideout, Deputy

Containing 30 booths featuring telecommunications equipment and supplies. Cable operators and local governments. Educational sessions topics include technology, competitive markets, programming, and cable franchise administration.
700 Attendees
Frequency: September

22680 NCDM Conference
Direct Marketing Association
1120 Avenue of Americas
New York, NY 10036-6700

212-768-7277
FAX 212-302-6714

E-Mail: dmaconferences@the-dma.org
Home Page: www.the-dma.org

Julie A Hogan, SVP Conferences/Events
Lawrence M Kimmel, CEO

Presents industry experts and hard-hitting case studies from a variety of verticals, such as financial services, retail, automotive, publishing, non-profit and many more, who will share the latest strategies and methodologies in gathering, analyzing, leveraging and protecting your most valuable business asset - customer data.
10M Attendees
Frequency: Annual/December

22681 NEAX 2400 IMS Users Group

40 Marsh Wall
Columbia, CT 29221-0886

803-798-4800
Home Page: www.necusergroup.com
Social Media: *Facebook, Twitter*

Carlisle Reames, Contact

15 booths of educational sessions for NEC 2400 DBX systems users.
350 Attendees
Frequency: April

22682 NXTcomm

Telecommunications Industry Association/TIA
2500 Wilson Boulevard
Suite 300
Arlington, VA 22201-3834

703-907-7700
FAX 703-907-7727
E-Mail: gseiffert@tiaonline.org
Home Page:
www.tiaonline.org/business/events/TIATradeshows.cfm
Social Media: *Facebook, Twitter, LinkedIn*

Grant Seiffert, President
Mike Nunes, Government Relations Director
Lora Magruder, Member Relations Director
Daniel J. Pigott, Chairman of the Board
Thomas Stanton, Vice Chair

NXTcomm is an industry event uniting the premier information and communications technology suppliers with the world's leading communications and entertainment companies. Connect with 450+ exhibitors and 20,000+ attendees. Soak up essential knowledge during insider-led conferences. The global forces that are driving communications-based innovation are here.

22683 National Conference on Operations & Fulfillment (NCOF)

Direct Marketing Association
1120 Avenue of Americas
New York, NY 10036-6700

212-768-7277
FAX 212-302-6714
E-Mail: dmaconferences@the-dma.org
Home Page: www.the-dma.org

Julie A Hogan, SVP Conference/Educational Services
Lawrence M Kimmel, CEO

Focuses on innovative solutions for warehouse, distribution, operations, and ecommerce needs in the ever-changing world of operations and fulfillment.
10M Attendees
Frequency: Annual/April

22684 New York Nonprofit Conference

Direct Marketing Association
1120 Avenue of Americas
New York, NY 10036-6700

212-768-7277
FAX 212-302-6714

E-Mail: dmaconferences@the-dma.org
Home Page: www.the-dma.org

Julie A Hogan, SVP Conference/Events
Lawrence M Kimmel, CEO

Discover which acknowledgement programs work best-and why, increase revenue with membership options-as well as traditional fundraising appeals, learn how the internet and e-mail campaigng can improve fundraising, lower costs and increase advocac
10M Attendees

22685 PCCA Annual Convention

Power and Communication Contractors
1908 Mt. Vernon Ave
Suite 200
Alexandria, VA 22314

703-212-7734
800-542-7222
FAX 703-548-3733
E-Mail: info@pccaweb.org
Home Page: www.pccaweb.org
Social Media: *Facebook, Twitter*

Kevin Mason, President
Larry Libla, President-Elect
Frequency: March

22686 TechNet North 2006

AFCEA Canada & AFCEA International
102 Centrepointe Drive
Ottawa, ON K2G-6B1

613-786-2619
FAX 613-230-1554
E-Mail: kevin@expocorpinc.com
Home Page: www.technetnorth.com
Social Media: *Facebook, Twitter*

Kevin d'Entremont, Exhibit Director
Rick Tachuk, Marketing & Communications Director

Delivers an inovative professional development conference and a major trade exhibition focused on the latest C4ISR solutions, products and technologies for the North American defense and security sectors.

22687 Telecom

607 14th Street
Suite 600
Washington, DC 20005-2164

202-547-2680
FAX 202-326-7333
Home Page: www.usta.org
Social Media: *Facebook, Twitter, LinkedIn, You Tube*

Walter B McCormick Jr, President/CEO
Jaonne Hovis, Chair
Tony Prez, Director

Conference and exhibition offers a variety of educational sessions, special interest seminars and keynote speakers. The show features an estimated 160 exhibitors.
1300 Attendees
Frequency: Annual

22688 Utilities Telecommunications Council Annual Conference and Exhibition

Utilities Telecommunications Council
1129 20th St.NW
Suite 350
Washington, DC 20036

202-872-0030
FAX 202-872-1331
E-Mail: marketing@utc.org
Home Page: www.utc.org
Social Media: *Facebook, Twitter, LinkedIn*

Connie Durcsase, President
Mike Oldak, VP & General Counsel
Karnel Thomas, VM- Member Services
Kathleen Fitzpatric, VP- Operations

Annual conference and exhibits of telecommunications equipment and services.
1,000 Attendees
Founded in 1948

22689 Wire Expo

Wire Association International
1570 Boston Post Road
PO Box 578
Guilford, CT 06437-0578

203-453-2777
FAX 203-453-8384
Home Page: www.wirenet.org
Social Media: *Facebook, Twitter*

Livia Jacobs, Manager Convention/Events
Nicholas Nickoletopoulos, President
Steven J. Fetteroll~, Executive Director
Robert J. Xeller, Sales

Wire Expo provides you with ready-made opportunities—including meeting with more than 450 suppliers on the show floor. You'll gain manufacturing and technical information by attending short courses and listening to some of the 75+ paper that will be presented at WCTS. Social events also provide oppertunities to make conections with other professionals in the wire industry.
4000 Attendees
Frequency: May/June
Founded in 1930

Directories & Databases

22690 Audiotex Directory

ADBG Publishing
PO Box 25929
Los Angeles, CA 90025-0929

310-914-9000
FAX 310-479-0654
Home Page: www.krango.com
Social Media: *Facebook, Twitter*

Larry Podell, Editor

Over 1,200 product and service suppliers in the voice processing fax, and audiotex fields, including hardware, software, vendors, telephone companies, service bureaus, audio programmers, and consultants
Cost: $50.00
Frequency: Annual

22691 Bacon's Radio/TV/Cable Directory

Cision U.S., Inc.
332 South Michigan Avenue
Suite 900
Chicago, IL 60604

312-263-0070
866-639-5087
E-Mail: info.us@cision.com
Home Page: www.us.cision.com

Joe Bernardo, President & CEO
Heidi Sullivan, VP & Publisher
Valerie Lopez, Research Director
Jessica White, Research Director
Rachel Farrell, Research Manager

Includes comprehensive coverage for contact and programming information for more than 3,500 televsion networks, cable networks, television syndicators, television stations, and cable systems in the United States and Canada.
Cost: $350.00
Frequency: Annual
ISSN: 1088-9639
Printed in one color on matte stock

22692 Communication News: Network Access Directory

Nelson Publishing

2500 Tamiami Trl N
Nokomis, FL 34275-3476

941-966-9521
FAX 941-966-2590
Home Page: www.healthmgttech.com
Social Media: *Facebook, Twitter, LinkedIn*

A Verner Nelson, Owner
Cost: $7.00
Frequency: Annual, June
Circulation: 71,000
Mailing list available for rent

22693 Communications News: Broadband Directory

Nelson Publishing
2500 Tamiami Trl N
Nokomis, FL 34275-3476

941-966-9521
FAX 941-966-2590
Home Page: www.healthmgttech.com
Social Media: *Facebook, Twitter, LinkedIn*

A Verner Nelson, Owner
Cost: $7.00
Frequency: Annual, December
Circulation: 71,000
Mailing list available for rent

22694 Communications News: PBX/CTI Directory

Nelson Publishing
2500 Tamiami Trl N
Nokomis, FL 34275-3476

941-966-9521
FAX 941-966-2590
Home Page: www.healthmgttech.com
Social Media: *Facebook, Twitter, LinkedIn*

A Verner Nelson, Owner
Cost: $7.00
Frequency: Annual, April
Circulation: 71,000
Mailing list available for rent

22695 Communications News: Test Directory

Nelson Publishing
2500 Tamiami Trl N
Nokomis, FL 34275-3476

941-966-9521
FAX 941-966-2590
Home Page: www.healthmgttech.com
Social Media: *Facebook, Twitter, LinkedIn*

A Verner Nelson, Owner
Cost: $7.00
Frequency: Annual, February
Circulation: 71,000
Mailing list available for rent

22696 Communications News: Video/ Audioconferencing Directory

Nelson Publishing
2500 Tamiami Trl N
Nokomis, FL 34275-3476

941-966-9521
FAX 941-966-2590
Home Page: www.healthmgttech.com
Social Media: *Facebook, Twitter, LinkedIn*

A Verner Nelson, Owner
Cost: $7.00
Frequency: Annual, October
Circulation: 71,000
Mailing list available for rent

22697 Communications News: Wireless Directory

Nelson Publishing
2500 Tamiami Trl N
Nokomis, FL 34275-3476

941-966-9521
FAX 941-966-2590

Home Page: www.healthmgttech.com
Social Media: *Facebook, Twitter, LinkedIn*

A Verner Nelson, Owner
Cost: $7.00
Frequency: Annual, August
Circulation: 71,000
Mailing list available for rent

22698 Complete Directory of Telephones & Accessories

Sutton Family Communications &
Publishing Company
155 Sutton Lane
Fordsville, KY 42343

270-740-0870
E-Mail: jlsutton@apex.net
Home Page: www.fleamarketeer.net
Social Media: *Facebook, Twitter*

Theresa Sutton, Editor
Lee Sutton, General Manager

Print-out from database of wholesalers, manufacturers, distributors, importers and close-out houses. Database is updated daily to guarantee the most current and up-to-date sources available.
Cost: $55.20
100+ Pages

22699 Corporate Yellow Book

Leadership Directories
104 5th Ave
New York, NY 10011-6901

212-627-4140
FAX 212-645-0931
E-Mail: info@leadershipdirectories.com
Home Page: www.leadershipdirectories.com
Social Media: *Facebook, Twitter*

David Hurvitz, CEO

Contact information for over 48,000 executives at over 1,000 companies and more than 9,000 board members and their outside affiliations.
Cost: $420.00
1,400 Pages
Frequency: Quarterly
ISSN: 1058-2098
Founded in 1986

22700 Directory of Communications Professionals

National Assn of Regulatory Utility
Commissioners
1101 Vermont Ave NW
Suite 200
Washington, DC 20005-3553

202-898-2200
FAX 202-898-2213
Home Page: www.naruc.org
Social Media: *Facebook, Twitter*

Charles Gray, Executive Director
Philip Jones, President

Offers information on consultants and other professionals active in regulated telecommunications.
Cost: $33.00
240 Pages
Frequency: Annual

22701 International Fiber Optics Yellow Pages

Information Gatekeepers
214 Harvard Avenue
Suite 200
Allston, MA 02134-4641

617-232-3111
800-323-1088
FAX 617-734-8562
E-Mail: webmaster@igigroup.com
Home Page: www.fiberopticsyp.com
Social Media: *Facebook, Twitter*

Will Ashley, Contact

The most extensive Fiber Optics reference volume available anywhere. This directory is still the world's only source book devoted exclusively to Fiber Optics.
Cost: $89.95
Frequency: Annual
Founded in 1977

22702 LATA Directory

Center for Communications Management
11300 Rockville Pike
Suite 1100
Rockville, MD 20852-3003

301-770-7490
FAX 301-287-2445
Home Page: www.lataweb.com
Social Media: *Facebook, Twitter*

Ronald Canter, Owner

Offers information on local access transport areas by states.
Cost: $195.00
220 Pages
Frequency: Annual

22703 Local Calling Area Directory

Center for Communications Management
11300 Rockville Pike
Suite 1100
Rockville, MD 20852-3003

301-770-7490
FAX 301-287-2445
Home Page: www.lataweb.com
Social Media: *Facebook, Twitter*

Ronald Canter, Owner

Offers area codes and their zones or exchanges in cities of 100,000 or more in population.
Cost: $795.00
1,050 Pages
Frequency: Annual

22704 Lynx Global Telecom Database

Lynx Technologies
710 Route 46 East
PO Box 368
Little Falls, NJ 07424-0368

973-256-7200
FAX 973-882-3583
E-Mail: msalerno@lynxtech.com
Home Page: www.lynxtech.com
Social Media: *Facebook, Twitter*

Kathleen Elsayed, Production Manager
Mike Salerno, Circulation Director

350 telecommunications carriers services in approximately 200 countries, territories and other political divisions.

22705 Network Management Guidelines and Contact Directory

Network Operations Forum
1200 G Street NW
Washington, DC 20005-3814

202-347-1228
FAX 202-393-5453

Over 25 telecommunications companies.

22706 North American Telecommunications Association - Sourcebook

2000 P St NW
Suite 550
Washington, DC 20036-6921

202-419-0412
Home Page: www.naaee.org

Brian Day, Executive Director
Sue Bumpous, Communications Manager

Offers a wide array of information on manufacturers and suppliers of non-utility telephone terminal equipment.
Cost: $53.00
208 Pages

22707 Outside Plant: Directory of Outside Plant Contractors Issue
Practical Communications
PO Box 183
Cary, IL 60013-0183

847-639-2200
FAX 847-639-7598

John Saxtan, Editor

Offers a list of over 800 contractors in the telecommunications industry that specialize in outside plant projects.
Cost: $30.00
Frequency: Annual
Circulation: 20,000

22708 Phillips Satellite Industry Directory
Phillips Business Information
1201 Seven Locks Road
Potomac, MD 20854-2931

301-354-1400
800-777-5006
FAX 301-309-9473

Minica Kenny, Editor
Don Pazour, CEO

Over 6,000 contacts and more than 3,800 hardware and technical service companies, transponder brokers and resellers, consultants, communications attorneys, publishers, uplinks and downlinks, video conference suppliers, related trade associations, government agencies and satellite telecommunications carriers.
Cost: $257.00
Frequency: Annual January

22709 Phillips Who's Who in Electronic Commerce
Phillips Business Information
1201 Seven Locks Road
Potomac, MD 20854-2931

301-354-1400
800-777-5006
FAX 301-309-9473

Jennifer O Newman, Editor
Don Pazour, CEO

Service providers, value-added banks and networks, software vendors, associations, user groups, consultants, business and technical services for electronic commerce industry.
Cost: $199.00
Frequency: Annual

22710 Pocket Guides to the Internet: Terminal Connections
Information Today
143 Old Marlton Pike
Medford, NJ 08055-8750

609-654-6266
800-300-9868
FAX 609-654-4309
E-Mail: custserv@infotoday.com
Home Page: www.infotoday.com
Social Media: *Facebook, Twitter*

Thomas H Hogan, President
Roger R Bilboul, Chairman Of The Board

Unix/VMS systems and other basic terminal applications and telecommunications programs.
Cost: $9.95

22711 Q-TEL 1000
United Communications Group
11300 Rockville Pike
P.O Box: 217
Rockville, MD 20852-3030

301-816-8950
800-526-5307
FAX 858-674-5491
E-Mail: media@qtel.com.qa

Home Page: www.qtel.qa
Social Media: *Facebook, Twitter*

This database offers information on telecommunications charges.
Frequency: Full-text
Mailing list available for rent

22712 RCR Publications
RCR Publications
1746 Cole Boulevard
Suite 150
Golden, CO 80401

303-733-2500
800-678-9696
FAX 303-733-9941
E-Mail: mbush@crain.com
Home Page: www.rcrnews.com

Melodye Bush, Database Coordinator

Offers a wide variety of information on cellular and personal communications industries. Includes detailed information on carriers and vendors around the world.
Cost: $950.00
Frequency: Annual
Founded in 1991

22713 RCR's Cellular Database
RCR Publications
1746 Cole Boulevard
Suite 150
Golden, CO 80401

303-733-2500
800-678-9696
FAX 303-733-9941
E-Mail: mbush@crain.com
Home Page: www.rcrnews.com

Melodye Bush, Database Coordinator

Offers a wide variety of information on cellular communications industry. Includes detailed information on cellular carriers and vendors.
Cost: $300.00
Frequency: Annual
Founded in 1991

22714 RCR's PCS Database
RCR Publications
1746 Cole Boulevard
Suite 150
Golden, CO 80401

303-733-2500
800-678-9696
FAX 303-733-9941
E-Mail: mbush@crain.com
Home Page: www.rcrnews.com

Melodye Bush, Database Coordinator

Offers a wide variety of information on the personal communications industry. Includes detailed information on PCS carriers and vendors.
Cost: $300.00
Frequency: Annual
Founded in 1991

22715 Satellite Industry Directory
Phillips Business Information
1201 Seven Locks Road
Suite 300
Potomac, MD 20854-2931

301-354-1400
FAX 301-309-9473

Monica Kenny, Editor

Profiles operational and planned satellite systems, equipment and service providers, satellite brokers, uplinkers/downlinkers and more.
Cost: $247.00
750 Pages
Frequency: Annual

22716 Sbusiness
AFSM International

17065 Camino San Bernardo
Suite 200
San Diego, CA 92127-1709

858-673-3055
800-333-9786
FAX 239-275-0794
E-Mail: info@afsmi.org
Home Page: www.afsmi.org
Social Media: *Facebook, Twitter*

John Shoenewald, Executive Director
Jb Wood, President/CEO

The professional journal for customer service and support managers.
Cost: $60.00
100 Pages
Frequency: Bi-Monthly
Circulation: 10000
Founded in 1975
Mailing list available for rent

22717 TCP/IP for the Internet
Mecklermedia Corporation
20 Ketchum Street
Westport, CT 06880-5908

203-341-2806
FAX 203-454-5840

Marshall Breeding, Editor

Standard network protocol for data transmission over the global internet - products and packages for Unix, DOS, Windows and Macintosh platforms.
Cost: $24.95

22718 Telecommunications Directory
Gale/Cengage Learning
10650 Toebben Drive
Detroit, KY 41051

248-699-4253
800-877-4253
FAX 248-699-8049
E-Mail: gale.galeord@cengage.com
Home Page: www.gale.com
Social Media: *Facebook, Twitter*

Patrick C Sommers, President

Provides detailed information on telecommunications companies providing a range of products and services from cellular communications and local exchange carriers to satellite services and Internet service providers.
ISBN: 1-414419-80-5

22719 Telecommunications Export Guide
North American Telecommunications Association
2000 P St NW
Suite 550
Washington, DC 20036-6921

202-419-0412
Home Page: www.naaee.org

Brian Day, Executive Director
Sue Bumpous, Communications Manager

Offers a list of over 135 foreign telecommunications agencies, and federal and state government agencies concerned with exports in the United States.
Cost: $103.00

22720 Telemarketing and Call Center Solutions Buyer's Guide and Directory Issue
Technology Marketing Corporation
800 Connecticut Ave
1st Floor East
Norwalk, CT 06854-1936

203-852-6800
800-243-6002
FAX 203-853-2845
E-Mail: tmc@tmcnet.com
Home Page: www.tmcnet.com

Social Media: *Facebook, Twitter, LinkedIn, You Tube*

Rich Tehrani, CEO
Nanji Tehrani, Chair
David Rodriguez, President/Assistant Treasurer
Michael Genaro, VP

Over 1100 domestic and foreign suppliers of equipment products and services to the telecommunications/telemarketing industry.
Cost: $25.00
Frequency: Annual December
Founded in 1972

22721 Telephone Industry Directory
Phillips Business Information
1201 Seven Locks Road
Suite 300
Potomac, MD 20854-2931

301-354-1400
FAX 301-349-9473

Jennifer Newman, Assistant Managing Editor

Offers valuable information on over 4,800 manufacturers, distributors and suppliers to the telecommunications industry.
Cost: $249.00
750 Pages
Frequency: Annual

22722 Voice Mail Reference Manual and Buyer's Guide
Robins Press
2675 Henry Hudson Parkway W
Apartment 6J
Bronx, NY 10463-7741

718-548-7245
800-238-7130
FAX 718-548-7237
E-Mail: robinspr@ix.netcom.com
Home Page: www.mmdimensions.com/telstore

Marc Robins, Publisher

Offers information on over 60 suppliers of about 90 voice mail systems and service bureaus.
Cost: $65.00
384 Pages
Frequency: Annual
Mailing list available for rent: 10M names
Printed in 2 colors on matte stock

22723 Voice Processing Printed Circuit Cards: A Sourcebook of Suppliers & Products
Robins Press
2675 Henry Hudson Parkway W
Apartment 6J
Bronx, NY 10463-7741

718-548-7245

Offers a list of over 50 vendors of voice processing circuit cards and related technology worldwide.
Cost: $150.00
Frequency: Annual

22724 World Satellite Almanac
Phillips Business Information
1201 Seven Locks Road
Suite 300
Potomac, MD 20854-2931

301-354-1400
FAX 301-340-1520

Monica Kenny, Editor

All commercial satellite systems and operators are profiled.
Cost: $247.00
700 Pages
Frequency: Annual

22725 World Telecommunications Tariff Directory
Lynx Technologies

PO Box 368
Little Falls, NJ 07424-0368

973-256-7200

A comprehensive directory of over 1,200 Local Exchange Carriers and other telecom companies make up this directory. Includes a detailed index for easy cross-referencing by company name, contacts, titles, geographical region, services provided, email and more.
Cost: $699.00
9,000 Pages

Industry Web Sites

22726 http://gold.greyhouse.com
G.O.L.D Grey House OnLine Databases

Grey House Publishing's online database platform, GOLD, offers Quick Search, Keyword Search and Expert Search for most business sectors including telecommunications and media markets. The GOLD platform makes finding the information you need quick and easy - whether you're a novice searcher or an experienced database user. All of Grey House's directory products are available for subscription on the GOLD platform.

22727 www.adweek.com
ADWEEK

Leading decision makers in the advertising and marketing field go to Adweek.Com every day for breaking news, insight, buzz, opinion, analysis, research and classifieds. The resources of all six regional editions of Adweek, as well as the national edition of Brandweek are combined with the knowledge of our online editors and the multimedia-interactive capabilities of the web to deliver vital information quickly and effectively to our target audience.

22728 www.alts.org
Association of Local Telecommunications Services

Represents state and local telecommunications offices.

22729 www.amtausa.org
American Mobile Telecommunications Association

Membership is made up of operators in the 220 MHz, 450 MHz, 800 MHz and 900 MHz bands, as well as product and service providers for the industry. Many members are exploring other areas of the mobile telecommunications industry — digital SMR, Personal Communications Services, data communications, mobile satellite, cable telephony and international wireless interests. AMTA is working with its members and with government to insure that those areas can be pursued successfully.

22730 www.arrl.org
American Radio Relay League

National membership association for amateur radio operators.

22731 www.atis.org
Alliance for Telecommunications Industry Solutions

Membership organization that provides the tools necessary for the industry to identify standards, guidelines and operating procedures that make the interoperability of existing and emerging telecommunications proiducts and services possible.

22732 www.atsi.org
Association of Telemessaging Services

International

Promotes fair competition through appropriate regulation and legislation; provides research and development provides support services and educational opportunities to address challenges in operating environments; in encourages and maintains the high standards of ethics and service.

22733 www.floridapsc.com
Telecommunications Cooperative Network

Offers group purchasing discounts on long-distance telephone services, equipment counseling, and analysis of communications needs.

22734 www.greyhouse.com
Grey House Publishing

Authoritative reference directories for most business sectors including telecommunications and media markets. Users can search the online databases with varied search criteria allowing for custom searches by product category, geographic area, sales volume, keyword, subject and more. Full Grey House catalog and online ordering also available.

22735 www.icea.net
Insulated Cable Engineers Association

Professional organization dedicated to developing cable standards for the electric power, control and telecommunications industries. Ensures safe, economical and efficient cable systems utilizing proven state-of-the-art materials and concepts. ICEA documents are of interest to cable manufacturers, architects and engineers, utility and manufacturing plant personnel, telecommunication engineers, consultants and OEMs.

22736 www.igigroup.com
Information Gatekeepers

Provides worldwide coverage of wireless LAN's, LAN interconnection, wireless in-building and major applications such as point-of-sales, portable computer interconnections and remote data collection.

22737 www.imc.org
Internet Email Consortium

Information about IMC and its members, all the internet email standards and more.

22738 www.isoc.org
Internet Society

International, professional membership organization focusing on standards, education and policy issues.

22739 www.kagan.com
Wireless/Private Cable Investor

The original bible of the wireless cable, multipoint distribution pay TV industry. Published continuously since 1972, this newsletter is the window on cable competition. Three month trial available.

22740 www.ntca.org
National Telephone Cooperative Association

Represents both cooperative and commercial, independent rural phone companies.

22741 www.pcca.org
Power and Communication Contractors

A national trade association for companies constructing electric power facilities, including transmission and distribution lines and substations and telephone, fiber optic, and cable television systems.

22742 www.scte.org

Society of Cable Telecommunications Engineers

For people engaged in engineering, construction, installation, manufacture, technical direction, management, regulation, or administration of broad band communications technologies.

22743 www.steconsulting.org

Society of Telecommunications Consultants

The Society of Telecommunications Consultants is a professional association of Independent telecommunications consultants who provide expert, non based councel to business industry service organizations and government, worldwide. It serves its constituency by providing educational business and networking opportunities and by negotiating tangible and intangible benefits. The STC also serves as a resource, connecting end users to consultants to business, educational and promotrional opportunities.

22744 www.telecommagazine.com

Telecommunications Industry Association

This magazine reports on carrier class and wide area communications technologies for service providers and their corporate network customers worldwide. Coverage includes technology, product, market and application information for serious communications professionals, interexchange, cellular/wireless/satellite carriers, cable companies as well as commercial users and government agencies in the communications industry.

22745 www.telecommute.org

Telecommuting Advisory Council

A comprehensive monthly digest of news about employer-sponsored telecommuting programs for employers working at home or elsewhere off-site. Contains case studies, international news, technology updates, legal and regulatory news, and managerial topics.

22746 www.usta.org

United States Telecom Association

Broad based association for the local exchange carrier industry worldwide.

Associations

22747 Acrylic Council
1285 Avenue of the Americas
35th Floor
New York, NY 10019

212-397-4600
FAX 212-554-4042
E-Mail: info@fabriclink.com
Home Page: www.fabriclink.com
Social Media: *Facebook, Twitter*

Lynn Misiak, Executive Director

A business league created to provide products in facilities maintained in the US. Educates the retailer and consumer of the benefits of acrylic fiber.

22748 Amalgamated Clothing and Textile Workers Union
1710 Broadway
New York, NY 10019-5254

212-255-9655
Home Page: www.acronymfinder.com
Social Media: *Facebook, Twitter*

Jack Sheinkman, President
William Towne, Manager

Sponsors and supports the Political Action Committee in this field.
249M Members
Founded in 1976

22749 American Flock Association
PO Box 1090
Suite C
Cherryville, NC 28021

617-303-6288
FAX 704-671-2366
E-Mail: info@flocking.org
Home Page: www.flocking.org
Social Media: *LinkedIn, YouTube, Pinterest*

Karl Spilhaus, President
Steve Rosenthal, Managing Director

Provides positive leadership to foster a strong flock industry in North America.
60 Members
Founded in 1984

22750 American Home Sewing & Craft Association
PO Box 369
Monroeville, PA 15146

412-372-5950
FAX 412-372-5953
E-Mail: info@sewing.org
Home Page: www.sewing.org

Handicraft and collectibles forum

22751 American Sheep Industry Association
9785 Maroon Circle
Suite 360
Englewood, CO 80112

303-771-3500
FAX 303-771-8200
Home Page: www.sheepusa.org
Social Media: *Facebook*

Burton Pfliger, President
Mike Corn, VP
Benny Cox, Secretary/Treasurer

A federation of state associations dedicated to the welfare and profitability of the sheep industry.
8000+ Members
Founded in 1865

22752 American Textile Machinery Association
201 Park Washington Ct
Falls Church, VA 22046-4527

703-538-1789
FAX 703-241-5603
E-Mail: info@atmanet.org
Home Page: www.atmanet.org
Social Media: *Facebook, Twitter*

Will Motchar, Chairman
Mike Viniconis, Vice Chairman
Clay D Tyeryar, President & Assistant Treasurer
Allen Moore, Vice Chairman/Treasurer
Susan A Denston, Executive VP & Secretary

The American Textile Machinery Association/ATMA's purpose is to improve business conditions within the textile machinery industry of the United States within a global context; to encourage the use of the products of the industry; and to protect, promote, foster and advance the common interests of the members as manufacturers and distributors of textile machinery and parts and machinery accessory to textile machinery on a worldwide basis.
1.5M Members
Founded in 1933

22753 American Yarn Spinners Association
PO Box 99
Gastonia, NC 28053

704-824-3522
FAX 704-824-0630
Home Page: www.aysa.org
Social Media: *Facebook, Twitter*

Michael Hubbard, Executive Director

Provides full service to the sales yarn industry.
100 Members
Founded in 1967

22754 Association of Georgia's Textile, Carpet, & Consumer Products Manufacturers
50 Hurt Plz Se
Suite 985
Atlanta, GA 30303-2941

404-688-0555
FAX 404-584-0720
E-Mail: info@gamfg.org
Home Page: www.gamfg.org
Social Media: *Facebook, Twitter*

Lee Bryan, Chairman
Del Land, Vice Chairman
G L Bowen III, President
Kevin Thieneman, Treasurer
Charles B Jones III, VP & General Counsel
Founded in 1900

22755 Association of Knitted Fabrics
1001 Connecticut Ave NW
Suite 315
Washington, DC 20036

202-822-8028
FAX 202-822-8029
Home Page: www.nationaltextile.org
Social Media: *Facebook, Twitter*

William L Jasper, Chairman
James C Self III, Vice Chairman
Augustine Tantillo, President
Sarah Pierce, Senior VP
Mike Hubbard, VP

Manufacturers of knitted cotton and wool products.
6 Members
Founded in 1935

22756 Carpet & Rug Institute: West
100 South Hamilton Street
Suite 3
Dalton, CA 30720

706-278-3176
FAX 706-278-8835
Home Page: www.carpet-rug.com
Social Media: *Facebook, Twitter, LinkedIn, Youtube, Google+*

Terri Caputo, President
Founded in 1791
Mailing list available for rent

22757 Cotton Council International
1521 New Hampshire Avenue NW
Washington, DC 20036

202-745-7805
FAX 202-483-4040
E-Mail: cottonuse@cotton.org
Home Page: www.cottonusa.org
Social Media: *Facebook, Twitter, YouTube, Pinterest*

James L Webb, Chairman
John A Burch, President
T Jordan Lea, First VP
Dahlen K Hancock, Second VP
Keith T Lucas, Treasurer

22758 Craft Yarn Council
3740 N. Josey Lane
Suite 102
Carrollton, TX 75007

972-325-7232
FAX 972-215-7333
Home Page: www.craftyarncouncil.com
Social Media: *Facebook, Youtube, Google+*

Michael Hubbard, Secretary/Treasurer
Mary Colucci, Executive Director

The Craft Yarn Council represents the leading yarn companies, accessory manufacturers, magazine, book publishers, and consultants in the yarn industry.
Founded in 1981

22759 Durene Association of America
194 S South St
Gastonia, NC 28052-4125

704-865-1651
FAX 704-824-0638

Russell Duren, President

Develops and uses tests to determine quality. Licenses manufacturers to use Durene identification on products.
4 Members
Founded in 1929

22760 Elastic Fabric Manufacturers Council
230 Congress Street
Boston, MA 02110

617-542-8220
FAX 617-542-2199
Home Page: www.textilenta.org

Provides exchange and management services, trade promotions, statistical programs and information bulletins.
32 Members
Founded in 1915

22761 Electrostatic Discharge Association
7900 Turin Road
Building 3
Rome, NY 13440-2069

315-339-6937
FAX 315-339-6793
E-Mail: info@esda.org
Home Page: www.esda.org
Social Media: *Facebook, Twitter, LinkedIn*

Donn Bellmore, President
Leo G Henry, Senior VP

Professional voluntary association dedicated to advancing the theory and practice of electrostatic discharge avoidance. Initial emphasis on the effects of ESD on electronic components has broadened to include textiles, plastics, web processing, explosives, clean rooms and graphic arts. Expands ESD awareness through educational programs, development of standards, tutorials, publications, local chapters, symposia and certification.
Founded in 1982

22762 Hard Fibers Association
120 Genesee Street
Suite 601
Auburn, NY 13021-3603

315-520-0871
FAX 315-255-3292

John Hurd, President

Importers and distributors of sisal, abaca and other hard fibers.

22763 Home Sewing Association
PO Box 369
Monroeville, PA 15146

412-725-5950
FAX 412-372-5953
E-Mail: info@sewing.org
Home Page: www.sewing.org

Joyce Perhac, Manager

Represents most facets of the home sewing industry. National trade association for independent sewing machine dealers and distributors.
1.5M Members
Founded in 1912

22764 INDA Association of Nonwoven Fabrics
1100 Crescent Green
Suite 115
Cary, NC 27518

919-459-3700
FAX 919-459-3701
E-Mail: info@inda.org
Home Page: www.inda.org
Social Media: *Facebook, Twitter, LinkedIn, RSS*

Robert Lovegrove, Chairman
Karen Castle, Vice Chairperson Planning
Renita Jones Anderson, Vice Chairperson Finance
Todd Bassett, Past INDA Chairman
Joan Izzo, Director of Marketing

Mission is to promote the value and profitability of the global nonwovens/engineered fabrics industry to benefit the members.
300 Members
Founded in 1968

22765 Industrial Fabrics Association International
1801 County Road BW
Roseville, MN 55413-4061

651-222-2508
800-225-4324
FAX 651-631-9334
E-Mail: generalinfo@ifai.com
Home Page: www.ifai.com
Social Media: *Facebook, Twitter, LinkedIn, YouTube*

Stephen M Warner, President

A not-for-profit trade association that represent the international specialty fabrics marketplace that facilitates the development, application and promotion of products manufactured by the diverse membership.
2000 Members

22766 Institute of Textile Technology
North Carolina State University

3426 College of Textiles
NSCU Centennial Campus
Raleigh, NC 27695-8301

919-513-7704
888-348-3512
FAX 919-882-9410
E-Mail: wgoneal@itt.edu
Home Page: www.itt.edu
Social Media: *Facebook, Twitter*

W Gilbert O'Neal, President & CEO
George Edmunds, VP

A graduate school supported in part by member companies. Publishes the Textile Technology Digest.

22767 International Society of Industrial Fabric
1801 County Road B W
Roseville, MN 55113-4061

651-222-2508
800-225-4324
FAX 651-631-9334
E-Mail: generalinfo@ifai.com
Home Page: www.ifai.com
Social Media: *Facebook, Twitter, LinkedIn, Youtube*

Mark J Hennessy, President & CEO
Todd V Lindemann, VP, Conference Management
Pam Egan-Blahna, Director, Human Resource
Dan McCarthy, VP, Finance/CFO
Andrew M Aho, Director, Membership & Divisions

A not-for profit trade association whose more than 2,000 member companies represent the international specialty fabrics marketplace. Members range in size from one-person shops to multinational corporations; member products span the entire spectrum of the specialty fabrics industry from fiber and fabric suppliers to manufacturers of end products, equipment and hardware.
350 Members
Founded in 1912

22768 International Textile & Apparel Association
PO Box 70687
Knoxville, TN 37938-0687

865-992-1535
E-Mail: executivedirector@itaaonline.org
Home Page: www.itaaonline.org
Social Media: *Facebook, Twitter, RSS*

Nancy Rutherford, Executive Director

Professional association for 1,000 college professors of clothing and textile studies.
Founded in 1935

22769 Knitted Textile Association
1701 K St. NW
Suite 625
Washington, DC 20006

202-822-8028
FAX 202-822-8029
E-Mail: spierce@ncto.org
Home Page: www.ncto.org
Social Media: *Facebook, Twitter, LinkedIn, YouTube*

Jeffrey Price, Chairman
Rob Chapman, Vice Chairman
Augustine Tantillo, President
Sara Beatty, Secretary
Robin Haynes, Treasurer

The KTA is an active participant in the International Mechinery and Equipment exhibition that takes place in Textile Hall in Greenville, South Carolina and highlights the latest in knitting and related dying and finishing equipment.

22770 Narrow Fabrics Institute
1801 County Road BW
Roseville, MN 55113-4061

651-225-6920
FAX 651-631-9334
E-Mail: generalinfo@ifai.com
Home Page: www.narrowfabrics.org
Social Media: *Facebook, Twitter, LinkedIn, Youtube*

Mary J Hennessy, President & CEO
Todd V Lindemann, VP, Conference Management
Pam Egan-Blahna, Director, Human Resource
Dan McCarthy, VP, Finance/CFO
Andrew M Aho, Director, Membership & Divisions

Conducts research, sells abrasior rods, and compiles statistics on narrow fabrics
40 Members
Founded in 1956

22771 National Cotton Batting Institute
4322 Bloombury St
Southaven, MS 38672

901-218-2393
FAX 662-449-0046
E-Mail: info@natbat.com
Home Page: www.natbat.com
Social Media: *Facebook, Twitter*

Weston Arnall, President
Greg Windsperger, VP
Fred Middleton, Executive Secretary-Treasurer

NCBI represents U.S. companies that manufacture and sell batting for use in mattresses, futons, home furnishing, and upholstered products. It provides a range of services to assist its members in expanding markets, monitoring and contributing to legislative and regulatory decisions that affect the industry, and conducting consumer education and information programs.
27 Members
Founded in 1954

22772 National Cotton Council of America
1918 N Parkway
Memphis, TN 38112-5000

901-274-9030
FAX 901-725-0510
Home Page: www.cotton.org
Social Media: *Facebook, Twitter*

Sledge Taylor, Chairman
Shane Stephens, Vice Chairman
Meredith B Allen, VP
Sid Brough, VP
John C Fricke, VP

The council serves as the central forum for consensus-building among producers, ginners, warehousers, merchants, cottonseed processors/dealers, cooperatives and textile manufacturers.

22773 National Council for Textile Education
Georgia Institute of Technology
1701 K St. NW
Suite 625
Washington, DC 20006

202-822-8028
FAX 202-822-8029
E-Mail: spierce@ncto.org
Home Page: www.ncto.org
Social Media: *Facebook, Twitter, LinkedIn, YouTube*

Jeffrey Price, Chairman
Augustine Tantillo, President
Sara Beatty, Secretary
Robin Haynes, Treasurer
Rob Chapman, Vice Chairman

Members are administrators of college textile departments whose curriculum comprise science-based programs with substantial laboratory and plant experience.

22774 National Council of Textile Organizations
1701 K St. NW
Suite 625
Washington, DC 20006

202-822-8028
FAX 202-822-8029
Home Page: www.ncto.org
Social Media: *Facebook, Twitter, LinkedIn, YouTube*

Augustine Tantillo, President & CEO
Jeffrey Price, Chairman

The voice of the U.S. textile industry.

22775 National Knitwear & Sportswear Association
1701 K St. NW
Suite 625
Washington, DC 20006

202-822-8028
FAX 202-822-8029
E-Mail: spierce@ncto.org
Home Page: www.ncto.org
Social Media: *Facebook, Twitter, LinkedIn, YouTube*

Jeffrey Price, Chairman
Rob Chapman, Vice Chairman
Augustine Tantillo, President
Sara Beatty, Secretary
Robin Haynes, Treasurer

Represents U.S. manufacturers and contractors, designing studios and related business engaged in the production of knitted sportswear and knitted products of all types.

22776 Northern Textile Association
1701 K St. NW
Suite 625
Washington, DC 20006

202-822-8028
FAX 202-822-8029
E-Mail: spierce@ncto.org
Home Page: www.ncto.org
Social Media: *Facebook, Twitter, LinkedIn, YouTube*

Jeffrey Price, Chairman
Rob Chapman, Vice Chairman
Augustine Tantillo, President
Sara Beatty, Secretary
Robin Haynes, Treasurer

The KTA is an active participant in the International Mechinery and Equipment exhibition that takes place in Textile Hall in Greenville, South Carolina and highlights the latest in knitting and related dying and finishing equipment.

22777 Restoration Industry Association
2025 M Street, NW
Suite 800
Rockville, MD 20852

202-367-1180
800-272-7012
FAX 202-367-2180
E-Mail: info@restorationindustry.org
Home Page: www.restorationindustry.org
Social Media: *Facebook, Twitter, LinkedIn*

Scott Stamper, President
Chuck Violand, First Vice President
Mark Springer, Vice President
Jack A. White, Secretary
Larry Holder, Treasurer

A trade association for cleaning and restoration professionals worldwide, and the foremost authority, trainer and educator in the industry.
1100 Members
Founded in 1946

22778 Schiffi Lace & Embroidery Manufacturers Association
26 Industrial Ave
Suite 2
Fairview, NJ 07022-1600

201-840-7611
FAX 201-943-7793
E-Mail: info@schiffli.org
Home Page: www.schiffli.org
Social Media: *Facebook, Twitter*

August Bischoff, President
Vincent Mesiano, VP

Crafted lace, and embroidery that adorns lingerie and dresses t towels, sheets, curtains, tablecloths, patches, logos and much more.
Founded in 1848

22779 Secondary Materials and Recycled Textiles Association
3465 Box Hill Corp. Center Drive
Suite H
Abingdon, MD 21009

443-640-1050
FAX 443-640-1086
E-Mail: Heather@KINGmgmt.org
Home Page: www.smartasn.org
Social Media: *Facebook, Twitter, LinkedIn, Youtube*

Jeff Pearl, President
Eric Stubin, Vice President
David Bloovman, 2nd Vice President
E. Carle Shotwell, Treasurer
Lou Buty, Immediate Past President

A dynamic international association which seeks to strengthen the economic opportunities of its members. Promotes the interdependence of all its industry segments by providing a common forum for networking, education, and trade.
Founded in 1932

22780 Shippers of Recycled Textiles
7910 Woodmont Ave # 1405
Bethesda, MD 20814-3082

301-907-0001
FAX 301-656-1079
E-Mail: smartinfo@kingmgmt.org
Home Page: www.sorti.org
Social Media: *Facebook, Twitter*

Eric Stubin, President
Robert Goode, Treasurer
Lou Buty, VP
75 Members
Founded in 1988

22781 Southern Textile Association
PO Box 66
Gastonia, NC 28053-0066

704-215-4543
FAX 704-215-4160
Home Page: www.southerntextile.org
Social Media: *Facebook, Twitter*

Judson L. Boehmer, Chairman
Todd Wemyss, President
Mike Kingsmore, First VP
Carson Copeland, Second VP
Lillian G. Link, Secretary/Treasurer

Represents the textile and clothing industry in the South.
Founded in 1908

22782 Surface Design Association
PO Box 20430
Albuquerque, NM 87154

707-829-3110
FAX 707-829-3285
E-Mail: info@surfacedesign.org

Home Page: www.surfacedesign.org
Social Media: *Facebook, Twitter, LinkedIn*

Astrid Bennett, President
Jennifer Reis, VP
Joyce Martelli, Treasurer
Tedd Milder, Secretary
Danielle Kelly, Executive Director

Aims to stimulate, promote and improve education in the area of surface design, to encourage the surface designer as an individual artist and to provide a forum for exchange of ideas through conferences and publications.
Founded in 1977
Mailing list available for rentat $75 per M

22783 TRI/Princeton
601 Prospect Ave
PO Box 625
Princeton, NJ 08540

609-430-4820
FAX 609-683-7836
E-Mail: info@triprinceton.org
Home Page: www.triprinceton.org
Social Media: *Facebook, Twitter, LinkedIn*

Kurl L Adams, Chair
David Graham, Vice Chairman
Yash K Kamath, Research Director
Robert J. Bianchin, Chairman of the Board
Kurt L. Adams, Vice Chair

Provides advanced research and education in polymers, fibers, films, personal care and porous materials.
40 Members
Founded in 1930

22784 Textile Care Allied Trades Association
271 Us Highway 46
Suite C205
Fairfield, NJ 07004-2432

973-244-1790
FAX 973-244-4455
E-Mail: info@tcata.org
Home Page: www.tcata.org
Social Media: *Facebook, Twitter, LinkedIn*

David Cotter, CEO
Cheryl Paglia, Office Manager

Represents the interests of distributors and manufacturers of equipment and supplies for the cleaning industry.

22785 Textile Rental Services Association
1800 Diagonal Rd
Suite 200
Alexandria, VA 22314-2842

703-519-0029
877-770-9274
FAX 703-519-0026
E-Mail: trsa@trsa.org
Home Page: www.trsa.org
Social Media: *Facebook, Twitter, LinkedIn, Youtube, RSS*

Greg Jelpema, Chairman
Robert Doud, Executive Director
Joseph Ricci, President & CEO
Tom Newell, Vice President of Operations
Kevin Schwalb, Vp of Government Relations

Covers the uniform, linen supply, health care and dust control service markets.
Founded in 1912

22786 The Knitting Guild Association (TKGA)
1100-H Brandywine Boulevard
Zanesville, OH 43701-7303

740-452-4541
FAX 740-452-2552
E-Mail: tkga@tkga.com
Home Page: www.tkga.com
Social Media: *Facebook, Twitter, Pinterest*

Penny Sitler, Executive Director

Membership organization for knitters with focus on knitting education and enhancing knitters skills.
11000 Members
Founded in 1984

Newsletters

22787 Embroidery News
Schiffi Lace & Embroidery Manufacturers Assn
596 Anderson Avenue
Suite 203
Cliffside Park, NJ 07010-1831

201-943-7757
FAX 201-943-7793

Leonard Seiler, Editor
Eugene Schrouzol, Publisher

Newsletter for the embroidery industry.
Frequency: BiMonthly
Circulation: 500

22788 Marine Textiles
RCM Enterprises
12 Oaks Center #922
Wayzata, MN 55391

800-451-9278

Mara Sidney, Publisher
Jim Penningroth, Editor

Serves firms in the boating market who use fabrics and furnishings. Accepts advertising.
Cost: $28.00

Magazines & Journals

22789 AATCC Review
American Assoc Textile Chemists and Colorists
1 Davis Dr
Research Triangle Park, NC 27709-2215

919-549-8141
800-360-5380
FAX 919-549-8933
E-Mail: danielsj@aatcc.org
Home Page: www.aatcc.org
Social Media: *Facebook, Twitter, LinkedIn*

John Daniels, Executive VP
Debra Hibbard, Executive Assistant
Charles E Gavin, Treasurer
Brenda Jones, Production Manager

Covers all aspects of design, dyeing, printing, finishing, and testing as they relate to textile manufacturing, including fibers, fabrics of all types, garments, carpets, home textiles, and industrial products.
Frequency: Monthly
ISSN: 1532-8813
Founded in 1997
Mailing list available for rent
Printed in 4 colors on glossy stock

22790 Cleaning & Restoration Magazine
Restoration Industry Association
12339 Carroll Avenue~
Suite K
Rockville, MD 20852

301-231-6505
800-272-7012
FAX 301-231-6569
E-Mail: info@restorationindustry.org
Home Page: www.restorationindustry.org

Donald E Manger, Executive Director
Patricia L Harman, Communications Director
Valorie D. Seely, Accountant

Trade journal covering fire and water damage restoration, rug and textile cleaning, indoor air quality and business issues.
Frequency: Monthly
Circulation: 6000

22791 Fabric Architecture
Industrial Fabrics Association International
1801 County Road B W
Roseville, MN 55113-4061

651-222-2508
800-225-4324
FAX 651-631-9334
E-Mail: bnwhite@ifai.org
Home Page: www.ifai.com

Stephen Warner, CEO

Strives to inform architects, designers, landscape architects, engineers and other specifiers about architectural fabric structutres, the fibers and fabrics used to make them, their design possibilities, their construction, and issues regarding their applicability and acceptance.
Cost: $39.00
Frequency: Bi-Monthly

22792 Geotechnical Fabrics Report
Industrial Fabrics Association International
1801 County Road B W
Roseville, MN 55113-4061

651-222-2508
800-225-4324
FAX 651-631-9334
E-Mail: generalinfo@ifai.com
Home Page: www.ifai.com

Stephen Warner, CEO
James Dankert, Managing Editor
Stephen B Duerk, Chairman
Beth L Hungiville, Managing Director
Miller Weldmaster, Director

Peer reviewed technical journal for civil engineers using geosynthetics in road construction, errosion control, hazardous waste, drainage, containment and reinforcement.
Cost: $49.00
Circulation: 16,000
ISSN: 0882-4983
Founded in 1988
Printed in 4 colors on glossy stock

22793 Home Textiles Today
Reed Business Information
360 Park Ave S
New York, NY 10010-1737

646-746-6400
800-446-6551
FAX 646-756-7583
E-Mail:
corporatecommunications@reedbusiness.com
Home Page: www.reedbusiness.com

John Poulin, CEO
Mark Fraser, Publisher

Textile industry news, reports, research and summaries for the professional.
Circulation: 8000
Founded in 1979

22794 IFAI'S Marine Fabricator
Industrial Fabrics Association International
1801 County Road B W
Roseville, MN 55113-4061

651-222-2508
800-225-4324
FAX 651-631-9334
E-Mail: generalinfo@ifai.com
Home Page: www.ifai.com

Stephen Warner, CEO
George K Ochs, Chairman
Jeffrey W Kirk, Vice Chairman

Publication contains articles designed for beginning to intermediate level fabricators, advanced techniques and technology, profiles,

business tips, industry news, new products and publications, and showcases of fabricators' craftmanship.
Frequency: Quarterly
Circulation: 5000
Founded in 1964

22795 Impressions Magazine
Miller Freeman Publications
13760 Noel Rd
Suite 500
Dallas, TX 75240-7336

972-239-3060
800-527-0207
FAX 972-419-7825

Carl Piazza, Publisher
Laura Gonz, Editor

Covers the textile screen printing imprinted sportswear retailing, and commercial embroidery industry. Accepts advertising.
Cost: $36.00
250 Pages
Frequency: Annual

22796 Industrial Fabric Products Review
Industrial Fabrics Association International
1801 County Road B W
Roseville, MN 55113-4061

651-222-2508
800-225-4324
FAX 651-631-9334
E-Mail: generalinfo@ifai.com
Home Page: www.ifai.com

Stephen Warner, CEO

Keeps individuals up to date on the information needed to keep their business growing, including reports on traditional or emerging markets and end products worldwide; forecasts and analyses of industry trends, announcements of new technologies in fibers, fabrics, equipment and treatments, and profiles of growth-oriented businesses and prodcuts.
Cost: $69.00
Frequency: Monthly
Founded in 1915

22797 Journal of Engineered Fibers & Fabrics
INDA Association of Nonwoven Fabrics
1100 Crescent Green
Suite 115
Cary, NC 27511

919-233-1210
FAX 919-233-1282
Home Page: www.inda.org
Social Media: *Facebook, Twitter, LinkedIn*

Rory Holmes, President
Peggy Blake, Director of Marketing
Ian Butler, Director Market Research
Todd~ Bassett, Managing Director
Monica Moretti, Tresurer

International peer reviewed scientific eJournal that publishes original R&D on all aspects o ffabric technologies and their value chain from raw materials to end-use products.
Frequency: Quarterly
Circulation: 3000
Founded in 1968

22798 Journal of Industrial Textiles
851 New Holland Avenue
Suite 3535
Lancaster, PA 17604

717-291-5609
800-233-9936
FAX 717-295-4538
Home Page: www.jit.sagepub.com

22799 Marine Fabricator
Industrial Fabrics Association International

1801 County Road BW,
Roseville, MN 55413

651-222-2508
800-225-4324
FAX 651-631-9334
E-Mail: cptschida@ifai.com
Home Page: www.ifai.com
Social Media: *Facebook, Twitter, LinkedIn*

Galynn Nordstrom, Senior Editor

Educates and informs 5,000 marine shop professionals and also provides reportage that reflects the innovations and trends of the industry.
Cost: $34.00
Frequency: Bi-Monthly

22800 Nonwovens Industry
Rodman Publishing
70 Hilltop Rd
Suite 3000
Ramsey, NJ 07446-1150

201-825-2552
FAX 201-825-0553
E-Mail: info@rodpub.com
Home Page: www.nutraceuticalsworld.com
Social Media: *Facebook, Twitter, LinkedIn*

Rodman Zilenziger Jr, President
Matt Montgomery, VP

Written for nonwoven roll goods producers, converters and end-use manufacturers.
70 Pages
Frequency: Monthly
Circulation: 11000
Founded in 1970

22801 Nonwovens World
MTS Publications
4100 S 7th Street
Kalamazoo, MI 49009-8461

269-375-1236
FAX 269-375-6710
E-Mail:
admin@marketingtechnologyservice.com
Home Page:
www.marketingtechnologyservice.com

James P Hanson, Editor
Cindy Costello, Circulation Manager
Wayne C Carter, Advertising Sales Director

Covers new products, as well as production and marketing strategies.
Circulation: 10384
Founded in 1986

22802 Sheep Industry News
9785 Maroon Circle
Suite 360
Englewood, CO 80112

303-771-3500
FAX 303-771-8200
Home Page: www.sheepusa.org
Social Media: *Facebook*

Clint Krebs, President
Peter Orwick, Executive Director
Rita Kourlis Samuelson, Wool Marketing Director

A federation of state associations dedicated to the welfare and profitability of the sheep industry.
Cost: $25.00
8000+ Members
Frequency: Monthly
Circulation: 8000
Founded in 1865

22803 Surface Design Journal
PO Box 360
Sebastopol, CA 95473-360

707-829-3110
FAX 707-829-3285
E-Mail: info@40surfacedesign.org

Home Page: www.surfacedesign.org
Social Media: *Facebook, Twitter, LinkedIn*

Jason Pollen, President

Professional organization of more than 2,000 textile artists, designers for industry, and academicians.
Cost: $8.00
52 Pages
Frequency: Quarterly
Circulation: 6000
Founded in 1977

22804 Textile Rental Magazine
Textile Rental Services Association
1800 Diagonal Rd
Suite 200
Alexandria, VA 22314-2842

703-519-0029
877-770-9274
FAX 703-519-0026
E-Mail: trsa@trsa.org
Home Page: www.trsa.org
Social Media: *Facebook, Twitter, LinkedIn, You Tube*

Roger Cocivera, President/CEO
Jack Morgan, Editor

Packed with valuable tips and ideas.
Frequency: Monthly

22805 Textile Research Journal
TRI Princeton
PO Box 625
Princeton, NJ 08542

609-924-3150
FAX 609-683-7836
Home Page: www.triprinceton.com

Dr. Gail R Eaton, President

Provides advanced research and education in polymers, fibers, films, personel care and porous materials.
Frequency: Monthly
Founded in 1930

Trade Shows

22806 American Home Sewing & Craft Association Sewing & Craft Show: AHSCA
American Home Sewing and Craft Association
1350 Broadway
Suite 1601
New York, NY 10018

212-714-1633
FAX 212-714-1655
E-Mail: info@sewing.org
Home Page: www.sewing.org

200 exhibits of fabric, notions, patterns, sewing and knitting machines, crafts and trimmings. Attended by professionals from major chain stores, independent retailers, wholesalers and manufacturers.
3000 Attendees
Frequency: Semiannual

22807 American Textile Machinery Exhibition International
Textile Hall Corporation
PO Box 5823
Greenville, SC 29606

864-331-2277
FAX 864-331-2282

Butler Mullins, Director

Exhibition of machinery, supplies and services required for manufacture of yarn and fiber, for the weaving, knitting and dying/printing/finish-

ing processes, for manufacture of non-wovens and for plant maintenance.
10000 Attendees
Frequency: September

22808 Apparel Printing and Embroidery Expo
Primedia
3585 Engineering Drive
Suite 100
Norcross, GA 30092

678-421-3000
FAX 913-967-1898
Home Page: www.primediabusiness.com

Joanie Forsythe, Sales Manager
Arlene Mayfield, President
Scott Asher, VP

Semi-annual show of 200 manufacturers, suppliers and distributors of commercial screen printing and embroidery equipment and supplies, computer graphic systems and softgoods such as T-shirts, sweats, jackets and caps.
3000 Attendees

22809 Apparel Show of the Americas
Bobbin Publishing/Miller Freeman
PO Box 279
Euless, TX 76039

817-215-1600
800-693-1363
FAX 817-215-1666
E-Mail: bobbin.expoinfo@mfi.com
Home Page: wwwmfi.com

Betty Webb, Trade Show Director

Conference, seminar and 329 exhibits of equipment, fabrics, accessories and services for sewn products and apparel.
5790 Attendees
Frequency: Annual
Founded in 1992

22810 Association of Specialists in Cleaning & Restoration Convention
Restoration Industry Association
9810 Patuxent Woods Drive
Suite K
Columbia, MD 21046-1595

443-878-1000
800-272-7012
FAX 443-878-1010
E-Mail: info@restorationindustry.org
Home Page: www.restorationindustry.org
Social Media: *Facebook, Twitter, LinkedIn, You Tube*

Donald E Manger, Executive Director
Patricia L Harman, Communications Director

Annual convention and exhibits of carpet, upholstery and draperies cleaning and restoration equipment, duct cleaning supplies and services, 100+ booths.
600 Attendees
Frequency: Annual
Founded in 1945

22811 Filtration: International Conference & Exposition
INDA Association of Nonwoven Fabrics
1100 Crescent Green
Suite 115
Cary, NC 27511

919-233-1210
FAX 919-233-1282
Home Page: www.inda.org
Social Media: *Facebook, Twitter, LinkedIn*

Rory Holmes, President
Peggy Blake, Director of Marketing
Ian Butler, Director Market Research/Stats

The North American Show for all aspects of filter media. One-stop shopping where you can compare products and prices. See

state-of-the-art products. Great networking experience.
1400 Attendees
Frequency: Annual

22812 Geosynthetics

Industrial Fabrics Association International
1801 County Road BW
Roseville, MN 55113

651-222-2508
800-225-4324
FAX 651-631-9334
E-Mail: confmgmt@ifai.com
Home Page: www.ifaiexpo.info
Social Media: *Facebook, Twitter, LinkedIn*

Beth Wistrcill, Conference Manager

Features design, engineering strategies and cost-saving geosynthetics solutions.
Frequency: February

22813 IDEA, International Engineered Fabrics Con ference + Expositions

INDA Association of Nonwoven Fabrics
1100 Crescent Green
Suite 115
Cary, NC 27518

919-233-1210
FAX 919-233-1282
Home Page: www.inda.org
Social Media: *Facebook, Twitter, LinkedIn*

Dave Rousse, President
Joan Izzo, Director of Marketing
Brad Kalil, Director Market Research/Stats

See, touch and buy state-of-the-art engineered fabrics. Compare all the components used to make first class fabrics-raw materials, chemicals, machinery and converting and finishind services.
5200 Attendees
Frequency: Triennial

22814 IFAI Annual Expo

Industrial Fabrics Association International
1801 County Road BW
Roseville, MN 55113

651-222-2508
800-225-4324
FAX 651-631-9334
Home Page: http://www.ifaiexpo.com

Beth Wistrcill, Conference Manager
Miller Weldmaster, Director
JoAnne Ferris, Director of Marketing

A trade event on the America's for the technical textiles and specialty fabrics industry.
Frequency: Annual/September

22815 International Engineered Fabrics

INDA Association of Nonwoven Fabrics
1100 Crescent Green
Suite 115
Cary, NC 27511

919-233-1210
FAX 919-233-1282
Home Page: www.inda.org
Social Media: *Facebook, Twitter, LinkedIn*

Rory Holmes, President
Peggy Blake, Director of Marketing
Ian Butler, Director Market Research/Stats

See, touch and buy state-of-the-art engineered fabrics. Compare all the components used to make first class fabrics-raw materials, chemicals, machinery and converting and finishind services.

22816 International Fashion and Boutique Shows

100 Wells Avenue
#9103
Newton, MA 02459-3210

617-731-8316

Samuel Starr, Show Manager

1,800 booths.
30M Attendees
Frequency: January

22817 International Fastener Exposition

PEMCO
383 Main Avenue
Norwalk, CT 06851-1543

203-840-7700
FAX 630-260-0395

Barbara Silverman, VP, Show Manager
Laura Rezek, Advertising

450 booths developed specifically for the fastener manufacturing and precision formed parts industry.
4.8M Attendees
Frequency: March

22818 International Hosiery Exposition

Hosiery Association
7421 Carmel Executive Park
Charlotte, NC 28226

704-365-0913
FAX 704-362-2056
E-Mail: thainfo@hosieryassociation.com
Home Page: www.hosieryassociation.com
Social Media: *Facebook, Twitter, LinkedIn*

Sally Kay, President
Sheila Simpson, Director of Finance
Vicki Camp, Office Manager

225 booths.
10M Attendees
Frequency: May
Founded in 1905

Directories & Databases

22819 ATI's Textile Red Book: America's Textile Industries

Billian Publishing Company
2100 Powers Ferry Rd SE
Suite 300
Atlanta, GA 30339-5055

770-955-5656
800-533-8484
FAX 770-952-0669
Home Page: www.billian.com

Jim Borneman, President
Dave Ramsays, Database Sales
Douglas Billian, Owner

Comprehensive reference guide for the textile industry. Includes over 6,000 mills in the US, Canada and Mexico. In addition to providing the complete contact information for the plant, each listing gives key personnel, products produced, fibers processed and mill equipment used.
Cost: $160.00
Frequency: Annual
ISSN: 1047-6903

22820 America's Textiles International

Billian Publishing Company

2100 Powers Ferry Rd SE
Suite 300
Atlanta, GA 30339-5055

770-955-5656
FAX 770-952-0669
Home Page: www.billian.com

Annual directory provides the complete contact information - including Web sites and e-mail addresses for over 2,400 equipment, technology and service providers to the textile industry.
Frequency: Annual
Circulation: 32,000
ISSN: 0890-9970
Founded in 1887

22821 Davison's Textile Blue Book

Davison Publishing Company
PO Box 1289
Concord, NC 28026-1289

704-785-8700
800-328-4766
FAX 704-785-8701
Home Page: www.davisonbluebook.com

Carol Nealy, Advertising Manager

5,400 mills, dryers, finishers, in the United States, Canada, and Mexico.
Cost: $165.00
800 Pages
Frequency: Annual
ISBN: 0-875150-69-1
Founded in 1866

22822 Interior Textiles Fabric Resource Directory

Wool Bureau/Atlanta Merchandise Mart
240 Peachtree Street NW
Suite 6F11
Atlanta, GA 30303-1361

404-577-4320

Approximately 108 manufacturers and suppliers of wool and wool blend upholsteries, wallcoverings and draperies.
45 Pages

22823 International Textile & Apparel Association Membership Directory

PO Box 1360
Monument, CO 80132-1360

719-488-3716
E-Mail: info@itaaonline.org
Home Page: www.itaaonline.org

Sandra S Hutton, Executive Director

Professional association for 1,000 college professors of clothing and textile studies.
8-12 Pages
Frequency: 6 per year
Circulation: Members
Founded in 1944

22824 Knitted Textile Association: Official Resource Guide and Fact Book

Knitted Textile Association
386 Park Avenue
New York, NY 10016-8804

212-545-9014
FAX 212-889-6160

Peter Adelman, Editor

A list of over 150 member manufacturers, suppliers and distributors of knitted fabric products and services.
Cost: $10.00
Frequency: Annual

22825 Knitting Times: Buyers' Guide Issue

National Knitwear & Sportswear Association

386 Park Avenue S
New York, NY 10016-8804

212-545-9014
FAX 212-532-0766
Dawne G Shink, Editor

List of about 4,500 suppliers and manufacturers of chemicals, contract, management and computer services, cutting room equipment, dyeing, finishing and printing equipment, knitted and woven fabrics, fibers and yarn, interfacing, pressing and steaming, knitting, sewing and trimming equipment, materials handling and plant control services.
Cost: $25.00
Frequency: Annual, September
Circulation: 10,000

22826 LDB Interior Textiles Buyers' Guide

EW Williams Publications
342 Madison Avenue
Room 1901
New York, NY 10173-1999

212-697-1122
FAX 212-661-1713
E-Mail: ldb342@aol.com

Renee Bennett, Editor-in-Chief
Aleksandra Kazimierska, Directory Manager
Janys Kuznier, Circulation Director

Over 2,000 manufacturers, importers and suppliers of home fashions products and services, decorative fabric converters and alternative window coverings, fabricators, manufacturer's representatives and others allied to the home fashions trade.
Cost: $40.00
Frequency: Annual June
Circulation: 12,000

22827 Narrow Fabrics Institute: Buyer's Guide

Narrow Fabrics Institute
345 Cedar Street
Suite 800
Saint Paul, MN 55101-1004

800-225-4324
FAX 651-222-8215

Approximately 34 producers of narrow fabrics for use in automotive medical, lifting, environmental safety, recreational, military, air cargo, trucks, and other fields, requiring industrial fabrics.
Frequency: Annual fall

22828 Textile Chemist and Colorist Buyers Guide

American Assoc Textile Chemists and Colorists
PO Box 12215
Research Triangle Park, NC 27709-2215

919-549-8141
800-360-5380
FAX 919-549-8933
E-Mail: danielsj@aatcc.org
Home Page: www.aatcc.org

John Daniels, Executive VP
Debra Hibbard, Executive Assistant
Charles E Gavin, Treasurer
Brenda Jones, Product Orders

Over 500 dye, pigments, machinery and equipment manufacturers are profiled.
ISBN: 0-040490-0 -
Founded in 1921
Mailing list available for rent

22829 Textile Technology Digest

2551 Ivy Road
Charlottesville, VA 22903

434-296-5511
FAX 434-296-2957

E-Mail: webmaster@itt.edu
Home Page: www.itt.edu

Offers abstracts to worldwide literature from more than 1,300 sources annually such as proceedings, trade literature and other sources collected by the institutes library. The CD-ROM quarterly is available for $1,710 plus shipping. Network licenses begin at $500 for up to 10 simultaneous users.
Cost: $545.00
Frequency: Monthly
Founded in 1944

22830 Wool Source List

Kairalla Agency
27 Raymond Street
Manchester, MA 01944-1614
Eleanor Kairalla, Executive Director

Conducts trade and consumer polls on woolen apparel.
360 Pages
Founded in 1939

Industry Web Sites

22831 http://gold.greyhouse.com

G.O.L.D Grey House OnLine Databases

Grey House Publishing's online database platform, GOLD, offers Quick Search, Keyword Search and Expert Search for most business sectors including textile markets. The GOLD platform makes finding the information you need quick and easy - whether you're a novice searcher or an experienced database user. All of Grey House's directory products are available for subscription on the GOLD platform.

22832 www.aatcc.org

American Association of Textile Chemists & Colorists

22833 www.atmanet.org

American Textile Machinery Association

Advances the common interests of its members, works to improve business conditions within the US textile machinery industry from a global perspective and markets the industry and members' machinery, parts and services.

22834 www.carpet-rug.com

Carpet & Rug Institute

22835 www.cottoninc.com

Cotton

22836 www.fibersource.com

American Fiber Manufacturers Association

Trade association for US companies that manufacture synthetic and cellulostic fibers. The industry employs 30,000 people and produces over 9 billion pounds of fiber in the US. The association maintains close ties to other manufactured fiber trade associations worldwide.

22837 www.flocking.org

American Flock Association

Fosters the use of flocked products. Strives to improve and advance flocking technology.

22838 www.greyhouse.com

Grey House Publishing

Authoritative reference directories for most business sectors including textile markets. Users can search the online databases with varied search criteria allowing for custom searches by product category, geographic area, sales volume, keyword, subject and more. Full Grey House catalog and online ordering also available.

22839 www.ifai.com

Industrial Fabrics Association International

Association of geosynthetics, fabricators, installers, equipment manufacturers, suppliers, testing firms, consultants, and educators, who produce textiles, nets, mats, grids, and other products. Industrial Fabrics Association International is the industry's first source for technical fabric resources and information.

22840 www.inda.org

INDA Association of Nonwoven Fabrics Industries

22841 www.itt.edu

Institute of Textile Technology

A graduate school supported in part by member companies. Publishes the Textile Technology Digest.

22842 www.sewing.org

Home Sewing Association

Represents most facets of the home sewing industry. National trade association for independent sewing machine dealers and distributors.

22843 www.sleepproducts.org

International Sleep Products Association

Maintains a strong organization to influence government actions, inform and educate the membership and act on industry issues to enhance the growth, profitability and stature of the sleep products industry. Provides members with information and services to manage their business more effectively and efficiently. Publishes a magazine devoted exclusively to the mattress industry, BEDtimes covers a broad range of issue and news important to the industry.

22844 www.smartasn.org

Shippers of Recycled Textiles

22845 www.textilenta.org

Northern Textile Association

Textile manufacturing trade association.

22846 www.triprinceton.org

TRI Princeton

TRI/Princeton provides advanced research and education in polymers, fibers, films, personel care, and porous materials.

Associations

22847 American Wholesale Marketers Association

11311 Sunset Hills Road
Suite 530
Reston, VA 20190

703-208-3358
800-482-2962
FAX 703-573-5738
E-Mail: info@cdaweb.net
Home Page: www.awmanet.org
Social Media: *Facebook, Twitter, LinkedIn*

Scott Ramminger, President & CEO
Chad Owen, First Vice Chairman
Susie Douglas Munson, Second Vice Chairman
Meredith Kimbrell, Director, Education
Robert Sincavich, Chairman

A trade association supporting the confectionary, tobacco and allied products industries through programs and services. members include wholesale distributors, manufacturers, and other allieds to the industry.
1000 Members
Founded in 1942

22848 Association of Dark Leaf Tobacco Dealers

2500 S Main St
Springfield, TN 37172-0638

615-384-9576
FAX 615-384-6461
E-Mail: info@hailcotton.com
Home Page: www.hailcotton.com

Mike De la Fargue, President & CEO
Tom Wilks, Executive VP
Roderick Roe, CFO
Andy Spies, Executive VP Sales
Eric Van Der Linden, Executive VP

An affiliate of Burley and Dark Leaf Tobacco Export Association.
Founded in 1902

22849 Bright Belt Warehouse Association

PO Box 120004
Raleigh, NC 27606

919-828-8988
FAX 919-821-2092
E-Mail: donaf@clemson.edu

Association of flue-cured tobacco warehousemen.

22850 Burley Stabilization Corporation

835 Bill Jones Industrial Dr.
Springfield, TN 37172

615-212-0508
FAX 866-828-6501
E-Mail: burleytobacco@aol.com
Home Page: www.burleystabilization.com

George Marks, President
Joe K Thomas III, VP
Charlie C Finch, Managing Director

Association of Burley tobacco warehouses in Kentucky, Tennessee, Ohio, Missouri, Indiana, Virginia, West Virginia and North Carolina.

22851 Burley Tobacco Growers Cooperative Association

620 S Broadway
Lexington, KY 40508-3149

859-252-3561
FAX 859-231-9804
E-Mail: stephanie@burleytobacco.com
Home Page: www.burleytobacco.com

Pat Raines, President
Eddie Warren, VP
Robert Reed Bush Sr., Secretary

Al Pedigo, Treasurer
Steve Pratt, General Manager
Burley tobacco grower cooperative

22852 Cigar Association of America

1100 G Street NW
Suite 1050
Washington, DC 20005-7405

202-223-8204
866-482-3570
FAX 202-833-0379
Home Page: www.cigarassociation.org
Social Media: *Facebook, Twitter, LinkedIn, Pinterest*

Dan Carr, Chairman
Craig Williamson, President

Consists of cigar manufacturers, importers and major industry suppliers. Provides government relations and statistical services to the industry and promotes the image of the cigar.
60 Members
Founded in 1937

22853 Eastern Dark-Fired Tobacco

1109 S Main St
Springfield, TN 37172-3509

615-384-4543
FAX 615-384-4545

Dan Borthick, President

Association of North Central Tennessee and South Central Kentucky growers that produce Type 22 Dark fire-cured and Type 35 Dark air-cured (one sucker) tobacco.

22854 Flue-Cured Tobacco Cooperative

1304 Annapolis Dr
Raleigh, NC 27608-2130

919-821-4560
FAX 919-821-4564
E-Mail: arnoldh3151@ipass.net
Home Page: www.ustobaccofarmer.com

Tommy Bunn, President/CEO
Stuart Thompson, CEO
Edward Kacsuta, Chief Financial Officer
Mike Lynch, Senior VP, Global Sales & Marekting
Sam Tie, Manager, Human Resource

Marketing cooperative which administers price support and provides %100 US flue-cured tobacco direct to purchasers.
Founded in 1946

22855 Friends of Tobacco

403 B East New Bern Road
Kinston, NC 20501

919-522-4769
FAX 919-522-4769
E-Mail: fot@fujipub.com
Home Page: fujipub.com/fot

Gary Corbett, President

Nonprofit organization promoting the economic importance of tobacco and freedom of choice in using tobacco products.
16000 Members
Founded in 1991

22856 Retail Tobacco Dealers of America

14611 Goodrich Dr NW
Suite 2H
Gig Harbor, WA 98329

253-857-8934
FAX 253-857-0143
E-Mail: info@fujipub.com
Home Page: www.rtda.org
Social Media: *Facebook, Twitter, LinkedIn, Youtube*

Joe Row, Executive Director

Represents and assists retail tobacconists.
Founded in 1993

22857 Specialty Tobacco Council

102 W Third Street
Suite 200-B
Winston-Salem, NC 27101

336-723-4311
FAX 336-759-0965
E-Mail: hroemer@specialtytobacco.org
Home Page: specialtytobacco.org

Henry C Roemer III, Executive Director

Represents manufacturers and importers of specialty tobacco products.
Founded in 1984

22858 Tobacco Associates

1306 Annapolis Drive
Suite 102
Raleigh, NC 27608-2136

919-821-7670
FAX 919-821-7674
E-Mail: tar@tobaccoassociatesinc.org
Home Page: www.tobaccoassociatesinc.org

Kirk Wayne, President
Hank Mozingo, VP
Veronica Martins, Office Manager

Mission is to enhance understanding of US flue-cured tobacco and assist manufacturers interested in adding quality US leaf to their products.
Founded in 1947
Mailing list available for rent

22859 Tobacco Association of the United States

PO Box 8019
Princeton, NC 08543-8019

609-275-4900
FAX 609-275-8379
E-Mail: tma@tma.org
Home Page: www.tma.org

Tommy Bunn, Executive VP

Promotes market for US leaf tobacco.
100 Members
Founded in 1915

22860 Tobacco Growers Association of North Carolina

3901 Barrett Dr
Suite 202
Raleigh, NC 27609-6611

919-781-0066
FAX 919-781-0066
E-Mail: grahamboyd@nc.rr.com
Home Page: www.tganc.org

Graham Boyd, Executive VP

Commodity association for North Carolina tobacco growers.
10000 Members
Founded in 1981

22861 Tobacco Merchants Association

PO Box 8019
Princeton, NJ 08543-8019

609-275-4900
FAX 609-275-8379
E-Mail: tma@tma.org
Home Page: www.tma.org
Social Media: *Facebook, Twitter*

Farrell Delman, President
Mark Schoenseld, Editor
Roberta Crosdy, Marketing Manager
Mark Schoenseld, Publisher

Tobacco trade association and source of current information on the tobacco industry.
170 Members
Founded in 1915

Newsletters

22862 Tobacco Barometer
Tobacco Merchants Association of the
United States
PO Box 8019
Princeton, NJ 08543-8019

609-275-4900
FAX 609-275-8379
E-Mail: tma@tma.org
Home Page: www.tma.org
Social Media: *Facebook, Twitter*

Mark Schoenseld, Editor
Roberta Crosdy, Marketing Manager
Mark Schoenseld, Farrell
Delman President

Tobacco industry news.
Frequency: Monthly
Founded in 1915

22863 Tobacco Products Litigation Reporter
TPLR
PO Box 1162
Back Bay Annex
Boston, MA 02117-1162

617-373-2026
FAX 617-437-3672
E-Mail: info@tplr.com
Home Page: www.tplr.com/

Richard Daynard, Publisher
Lissy Friedman, Publication Director
Mark Gottlieb, Legal Editor

Tobacco industry news.
Cost: $995.00
Frequency: 8 issues per year
Founded in 1950

22864 Tobacco on Trial
Tobacco Products Liability Project
102 The Fenway
Cushing Hall, Suite 117
Boston, MA 02115-5098

617-373-2026
FAX 617-373-3672
Home Page: www.tobacco-on-trial.com

Richard A Daynard, Publisher
Susan L Frank, Editor
Mark Gottlieb, Executive Director
Richard A Daynard, President

Tobacco industry news.
Cost: $95.00
Founded in 1979

Magazines & Journals

22865 Smokeshop
Lockwood Trade Journal
26 Broadway
Suite 9M2
New York, NY 10004-1777

212-391-2060
800-766-2633
FAX 212-827-0945
E-Mail: sales@smokeshopmag.com
Home Page: www.lockwoodpublications.com

Robert Lockwood, CEO
Edward Hoyt III, Editor
Bob Olesen, Advertising Sales Manager

Retail tobacco dealer's prevailing source for industry news designed to help readers operate their business more successfully.
Cost: $24.00
Founded in 1970

22866 Tobacco International
Lockwood Trade Journal
26 Broadway
Suite 9M2
New York, NY 10004-1777

212-391-2060
FAX 212-827-0945
E-Mail: sales@smokeshopmag.com
Home Page: www.lockwoodpublications.com

Robert Lockwood, CEO
Edward Hoyt III, Editor
Bob Olesen, Advertising Sales Manager

This trade publication offers information and news on the importing and exporting of tobacco.
Cost: $25.00
Frequency: Monthly
Founded in 1970

22867 Tobacco Reporter
SpecComm International
3000 Highwoods Boulevard
Suite 300
Raleigh, NC 27604-1029

919-878-0540
FAX 919-876-8531
E-Mail: customerservice@tobaccoreporter.com
Home Page: www.tobaccoreporter.com
Cost: $36.00

ISSN: 0361-5593

22868 Tobacco Retailer
Bel-Av Communications
359 Galahad Rd
Bolingbrook, IL 60440-2108

E-Mail: cforman@m2media360.com
Home Page: www.tobaccoretailer.com

Charlie Forman, Group Publisher
Richard Brandes, Editor-in-Chief

Features sales, marketing and operations articles, news and new products, personnel advice, cigar reviews, updates on the National Association of Tobacco Outlets and profiles of leading retailers.
Cost: $29.00
Frequency: Bi-Monthly
Circulation: 15000
Founded in 1998

22869 Tobacco Science
2016 Fanning Bridge Road
Fletcher, NC 28732

828-684-3562
FAX 828-684-8715
E-Mail: pam_puryear@ncsu.edu
Home Page: www.tobaccoscience.com

Dr David Shew, Editor
Pam Puryear, Managing Editor

Scientific journal containing technical reports on tobacco and tobacco smoke.

22870 Tobacconist
SpecComm International
3101 Poplarwood Court
Suite 115
Raleigh, NC 27604-1029

919-872-5040
FAX 919-876-6531
E-Mail: mjackson@speccomm.com
Home Page: www.tobacconistmagazine.com

Dayton Matlick, Publisher
Ed O'Connor, Advertising/Sales Manager
Dayton Matlick, Editor
Dayton Matlick, CEO

A business publication for retail tobacconists in the United States that includes information ranging from critical issues to new products and business advice.
Cost: $28.00
Frequency: Quarterly

Trade Shows

22871 AWMA Expo
American Wholesale Marketers Association
1128 16th Street NW
Washington, DC 20036-4808

202-463-2124
800-642-2962
FAX 202-467-0559
E-Mail: robertp@awmanet.org
Home Page: www.awmanet.org

Robert Pignato, VP Marketing/Industry Affairs

Annual show of 4500 manufacturers and suppliers of confectionery, tobacco, snack foods, juice, novelties and related products.

22872 Retail Tobacco Dealers of America Trade Show
4 Bradley Park Court
Suite 2H
Columbus, GA 31904-3637

706-494-1143
FAX 706-494-1893
E-Mail: rtda@msn.com
Home Page: www.rtda.org

Ira Fader Jr, Show Manager

Trade show for premium tobacco products. Not open to the public. For the benefit of association members only. Containing 950 booths and 6,400 exhibits.
5,500 Attendees
Frequency: July

Directories & Databases

22873 Tobacco Barometer: Cigarettes and Cigars/ Smoking, Chewing and Snuff
Tobacco Merchants Association of the
United States
Po Box 8019
Princeton, NJ 08543-8019

609-275-4900
FAX 609-275-8379
Home Page: www.tma.org

Farrell Delman, President

These two databases offers information on every aspect of the tobacco industry.
Frequency: Full-text

22874 Tobacco Reporter's Global Tobacco Industry Guide
SpecComm International
3000 Highwoods Boulevard
Suite 300
Raleigh, NC 27604-1029

919-878-0540
FAX 919-876-8531
E-Mail: sales@tobaccoreporter.com
Home Page: www.tobaccoreporter.com

Noel Morris, Publisher
Taco Tuinstra, Managing Editor

Directory of tobacco suppliers, leaf dealers, processors, manufacturers, brokers, marketing boards and associations.
Cost: $78.00
Frequency: Annual

Industry Web Sites

22875 http://gold.greyhouse.com

G.O.L.D Grey House OnLine Databases

Grey House Publishing's online database platform, GOLD, offers Quick Search, Keyword Search and Expert Search for most business sectors including tobacco markets. The GOLD platform makes finding the information you need quick and easy - whether you're a novice searcher or an experienced database user. All of Grey House's directory products are available for subscription on the GOLD platform.

22876 www.awmanet.org

American Wholesale Marketers Association

A trade association representing corporations in the wholesale tobacco industries.

22877 www.buycheapcigarettes.com

We offer discount cigarettes and tobacco products. Cigarettes and tobacco products are for consumer use only. Minimum order is 3 Cartons.

22878 www.freedomnet.org/tobacco.html

Pipe Tobacco Council

Consists of manufacturers and importers of smoking tobacco in the United States. Provides government relations and statistical services to the industry.

22879 www.greyhouse.com

Grey House Publishing

Authoritative reference directories for most business sectors including tobacco markets. Users can search the online databases with varied search criteria allowing for custom searches by product category, geographic area, sales volume, keyword, subject and more. Full Grey House catalog and online ordering also available.

22880 www.paylesscigarettes.com

Sells dicount cigarettes and tobacco products.

22881 www.taxfreetobacco.com

Sells dicount cigarettess.

22882 www.thetobaccoshop.com

Offers discount cigarettes and tobacco products.

22883 www.tobaccoassociatesinc.org

Website of the association representing US flue-cured tobacco producers.

22884 www.ustobaccofarmer.com

Information of interest to tobacco farmers.

Associations

22885 AIT Worldwide Logistics
701 N Rohlwing Rd
Itasca, IL 60143-1348

815-229-7700
800-669-4248
FAX 630-766-0205
E-Mail: info@aitworldwide.com
Home Page: www.aitworldwide.com
Social Media: *Facebook, Twitter, LinkedIn, You Tube*

Vaughn Moore, President & CEO
Keith Tholan, Executive VP, Sales
Joe Kayser, Executive VP, Finance
Ray Fennelly, Executive VP, Global Development
Chris Jostes, Ocean Transport Coordinator

AIT Worldwide Logistics provides customers with inovative high-tech support and customization that enhances every shipment by tailoring the technology to the systems of each individual customer. AIT distinguishes itself by offering customers a variety of value-added services to enhance supply chain efficiencies: custom-built IT solutions, flexible worldwide service offerings by ground, air, ocean and rail, an extensive global network, competitive price structure, and superior customer service.

22886 APL Logistics
16220 N Scottsdale Rd
Suite 400
Scottsdale, AZ 85254-1720

602-586-4800
800-666-2723
FAX 602-586-4585
E-Mail: michael_zampa@apl.com
Home Page:
www.apllogistics.com/wps/portal/apll

Beat Simon, President
Kurt Breinlinger, Chief Commercial Officer
Danny Goh, Chief Operations Officer
David Frentzel, VP, Contract Logistics
David Howland, VP, Land Transport Services

APL provides customers around the world with container transportation services through a network combining high-quality intermodal operations with state-of-the-art information technology.

22887 Advanced Transit Association
9019 Hamilton Drive
Fairfax, VA 22031-3075

703-591-8328
Home Page: www.advancedtransit.org

Tom Richert, Chairman
Catherine G Burke, President
Bob Dunning, VP
Jerry Kieffer, Manager

Supports the transportation association.
100 Members

22888 Air Courier Conference of America
Express Delivery & Logistics Association
400 Admiral Blvd
Kansas City, MO 64106

703-998-7121
816-221-0254
FAX 703-998-7123
E-Mail: jmorris@aircour.org
Home Page: www.expressassociation.org
Social Media: *LinkedIn*

George Trapp, President
Jim Conway, Executive Director
Ken Bowman, Dir of Strategic Initiatives
Jennifer Crane, Associate Director

Air courier and air package delivery companies.

22889 Air Line Pilots Association, International
1625 Massachusetts Ave NW
Washington, DC 20036

703-689-2270
Home Page: www.alpa.org
Social Media: *Facebook, Twitter, YouTube*

Tim Canoll, President
Joe DePete, First Vice-President
Bill Couette, Vice President-Administration
W. Randolph Helling, Vice-President-Finance
Rick Dominguez, Executive Administrator

International association for airline pilots
Founded in 1931

22890 Air Transport Research Societyÿ
3433 Van Munching Hall
University of Maryland
College Park, MD 20742

301-405-2204
FAX 301-314-1023
E-Mail: atrs@rhsmith.umd.edu
Home Page: www.atrsworld.org

Tae H. Oum, Founder, Chair
Martin Dresner, President, CEO
Anming Zhang, VP, Research
Sveinÿ Gudmundsson, VP, External
Christian Hofer, VP, Programs

A Society for researchers in the field of air transportation
Founded in 1995

22891 Aircraft Owners and Pilots Association (AOPA)
421 Aviation Way
Frederick, MD 21701

301-695-2000
800-872-2672
FAX 301-695-2375
Home Page: www.aopa.org
Social Media: *Facebook, Twitter, LinkedIn, Pinterest, Google+*

Mark Baker, President & CEO
James W. Minow, Executive Director
Bruce Landsberg, Senior Safety Advisor

For pilots and aircraft owners
Founded in 1939

22892 Airlines for America (A4A)
1301 Pennsylvania Ave. NW
Suite 1100
Washington, DC 20004

202-626-4000
E-Mail: ata@airlines.org
Home Page: www.airlines.org
Social Media: *Facebook, Twitter, LinkedIn, YouTube*

Nicholas E. Calio, President & CEO
Paul R. Archambeault, SVP, CFO & COO
David A. Berg, SVP, General Counsel & Secretary
Christine M. Burgeson, SVP, Global Govt. Affairs
Jean Medina, SVP, Communications

Airlines for America advocates for a safe, secure and healthy U.S. airline industry.
Founded in 1936

22893 American Association of Airport Executives
601 Madison Street
Suite 400
Alexandria, VA 22314

703-824-0504
FAX 703-820-1395
E-Mail: member.services@aaae.org
Home Page: www.aaae.org

Social Media: *Facebook, Twitter, LinkedIn, RSS, Pinterest, YouTube*

Jeffrey A. Mulder, Chair
Carl D. Newman, 1st Vice Chair
Scott A. Brockman, 2nd Vice Chair
Janne M. Olivier, Secretary/Treasurer
Brad Van Dam, Senior VP, Federal Affairs

The professional association that represents airport management personnel at public-use commercialand general aviation airports in the US
Founded in 1928

22894 American Association of Motor Vehicle Administrators
4401 Wilson Boulevard
Suite 700
Alexandria, VA 22203

703-522-4200
Home Page: www.aamva.org
Social Media: *Facebook, Twitter, LinkedIn, Flickr, YouTube*

Anne Ferro, President & CEOÿ
Whitney Brewster, Executive Directorÿ
Terri L. Coombesÿ, Deputy Chief of Staff
Stephen Campbell, Commissioner
Heidi Francis, Assistant Deputy Ministerÿ

Non-governmental, voluntary organization who strives to develop model programs in motor vehicle administration
Founded in 1933

22895 American Association of Port Authorities
1010 Duke Street
Alexandria, VA 22314-3589

703-684-5700
FAX 703-684-6321
E-Mail: info@aapa-ports.org
Home Page: www.aapa-ports.org
Social Media: *Facebook, Twitter, LinkedIn*

Kristin Decas, Chairman
Kurt J. Nagle, President & CEO
Jean C. Godwin, Executive Vice President
Colleen O'sullivan, Finance & Human Resources
Maria Estevez, Administrative Assistant

Trade association founded in 1912 that represents over 130 port authorities in the western hemisphere
Founded in 1912

22896 American Association of Railroad Superintendents
425 Third Street SW
Washington, DC 20024

202-639-2100
FAX 630-762-0755
E-Mail: media@aar.org
Home Page: www.aar.org
Social Media: *Facebook, Twitter, LinkedIn, Youtube*

Edward R. Hamberger, President
John Gray, SVP, Policy and Economics
Ian Jefferies, SVP, Government Affairs
Jeffrey Marsh, SVP, Finance and Administration
Patricia M. Reilly, SVP, Communications

Operating department officers of railroads.
500 Members
Founded in 1881

22897 American Association of State Highway & Transportation
444 N Capitol St NW
Suite 249
Washington, DC 20001-1539

202-624-5800
FAX 202-624-5806
E-Mail: info@aashto.org

Home Page: www.transportation.org
Social Media: *Facebook, Twitter, LinkedIn, You Tube*

Bud Wright, Executive Director
Jenet Adem, Director, Finance & Administration
Clarisse Bernardes Coble, Human Resources Manager
Tony Bianchi, Associate Project Director
Belinda Bates, Senior Graphic Designer

Representing highway and transportation departments in the 50 states, the District of Columbia, and Puerto Rico. It represents all five transportation modes: air, highways, public transportation, rail ,and water. Its primary goal is to foster the development, operation, and maintenance of an integrated national transportation system.
Founded in 1981

22898 American Association of State Highway and Transportation Officials

444 North Capitol Street N.W.
Suite 249
Washington, DC 20001

202-624-5800
FAX 202-624-5806
E-Mail: info@aashto.org
Home Page: www.transportation.org
Social Media: *Facebook, Twitter, LinkedIn, YouTube*

Bud Wright, Executive Director
Jenet Adem, Director of Finance
Tony Bianchi, Associate Project Director
John Boyd, Senior Communications Editor
Lloyd Brown, Director of Communications

A standards-setting body which publishes specifications, test protocols anf guidelines used in highway design and construction across the United States

22899 American Automobile Association

1000 AAA Drive
Heathrow, FL 32746-5062

407-444-7966
FAX 800-222-4357
Home Page: www.aaany.com

22900 American Bus Association

111 K Street NE
9th Floor
Washington, DC 20002

202-842-1645
800-283-2877
FAX 202-842-0850
E-Mail: abainfo@buses.org
Home Page: www.buses.org
Social Media: *Facebook, Twitter, LinkedIn*

Peter J Pantuso, President & CEO
Brandon Buchanan, Director, Operations
Clyde J Hart Jr., Senior VP, Govt. Affairs & Policy
Norm Litter, VP, Regulatory & Industry Affairs
Eric Braendel, CFO

ABA supports 3,800 members consisting of motorcoach and tour companies in addition to organizations that represent the tourism and travel industry. ABA strives to educate consumers on the importance of highway and motorcoach safety.
Founded in 1926

22901 American Commodity and Shipping

2102-D Gallows Rd.
Vienna, VA 22182

703-848-9422
FAX 703-848-9424
E-Mail: info@americancommodity.com

Home Page: www.americancommodity.com
Social Media: *Facebook, Twitter, LinkedIn*

22902 American Concrete Pavement Association

9450 W Bryn Mawr Ave.
Suite 150
Rosemont, IL 60018

847-966-2272
E-Mail: acpa@acpa.org
Home Page: www.pavement.com
Social Media: *Facebook, Twitter, LinkedIn, YouTube*

Mike Lipps, Chairman
Steve Jackson, Vice Chairman
Lori Tiefenthaler, 2nd Vice Chair
Jerry Voigt, President, CEO
Glenn Eder, Treasurer

Trade association that exclusively represents the interests of those involved with the design, construction and preservation of concrete pavements.
Founded in 1963

22903 American Council of Highway Advertisers

PO Box 809
North Beach, MD 20714

301-386-3330

22904 American Moving and Storage Association

1611 Duke St
Alexandria, VA 22314-3406

703-683-7410
FAX 703-683-7527
Home Page: www.moving.org
Social Media: *Facebook, Twitter, LinkedIn, Pinterest*

Linda Bauer Darr, CEO
Sandy Lynch, SVP

Represents members including interstate moving and storage companies, local movers, international movers plus industry suppliers and state association members. AMSA's chief goals include strong support for effective government regulations and policies that protect consumers while allowing members to provide quality service at compensatory prices, and ensuring that consumers understand the value of professional moving and storage services.
3200 Members
Founded in 1936

22905 American Public Transportation Association

1300 I Street NW
Suite 1200 East
Washington, DC 20005

202-496-4800
FAX 202-496-4324
E-Mail: meetings2@apta.com
Home Page: www.apta.com
Social Media: *Facebook, Twitter, LinkedIn, Youtube, Flickr, Blog*

Michael P Melaniphy, President & CEO
Petra Mollet, Chief Of Staff
Pamela L Boswell, VP, Workforce Development
Mary Childress, CFO
Art Guzzetti, VP, Policy

APTA is an international organization that supports and represents the transportation industry. Membership benefits include an annual association meeting, an international expo, membership directory, access to online publications, newsletters and electronic news service.
Founded in 1882

22906 American Railroads Association

425 3rd St SW
Siute 114
Washington, DC 20024-3217

202-639-2100
FAX 202-639-2558
E-Mail: media@aar.org
Home Page: www.aar.org
Social Media: *Facebook, Twitter, LinkedIn, YouTube*

Edward R Hamberger, CEO
Jeffrey Marsh, VP Finance/Administration
Ian Jefferies, SVP, Government Affairs
Patricia M. Reilly, SVP, Communications
Michael Rush, SVP, Safety and Operations
Founded in 1934

22907 American Railway Development Association

500 New Jersey Avenue, NW
Suite 400
Washington, DC 20001

202-715-1259
FAX 952-828-9751
E-Mail: info@amraildev.com
Home Page: www.amraildev.com/
Social Media: *Facebook, Twitter, LinkedIn*

Stephanie Johnson, President
Alan Sisk, First VP
Gary Rozmus, Second VP
Mark Holder, Secretary/Treasurer

Members are marketing, real estate and industrial development officers of railroads. Objectives are to foster the industrial, real estate, natural resources and market development activities of North American railroads and through the advancement of ideas and education of its members, further promote the effectiveness of railway development and related work.
200 Members
Founded in 1906

22908 American Railway Engineering and Maintenance-of-Way Association

4501 Forbes Blvd
Suite 130
Lanham, MD 20706-4362

301-459-3200
FAX 301-459-8077
E-Mail: bcaruso@arema.org
Home Page: www.arema.org

Beth Caruso, Executive Director & CEO
Vickie Fisher, Director Finance
Stacy Spaulding, Director of Committees
Janice Clements, Director, membership & Information
Christy Thomas, Events Manager

Fosters concern for design, construction and maintenance of bridges, buildings, water service facilities and other railway structures.
5400 Members
Founded in 1891

22909 American Road and Transportation Builders

1219 28th St NW
Washington, DC 20007-3389

202-289-4434
FAX 202-289-4435
E-Mail: general@artba.org
Home Page: www.artba.org

David S. Zachry, Chairman
Bob Alger, Senior Vice Chair
Matt Cummings, First Vice Chair
Tom Hill, Treasurer
Pete Ruane, Secretary

Offers information and resources for members associated with the transporation building industry.
Founded in 1902

22910 American Short Line & Regional Railroad Association
50 F Street, N.W.
Suite 7020
Washington, DC 20001

202-628-4500
FAX 202-628-6430
E-Mail: lbdarr@aslrra.org
Home Page: www.aslrra.org

Linda Bauer Darr, President & Treasurer
Keith T. Borman, VP, General Counsel
Kathleen M. Cassidy, VP, Member Services
Jo E. Strang, VP, Regulatory Affairs
Jenny M. Bourque, Director

An association of North American short line and regional railroads

22911 American Short Line Railroad Association
50 F Street NW
Suite 7020
Washington, DC 20001-1536

202-628-4500
FAX 202-628-6430
E-Mail: aslrra@aslrra.org
Home Page: www.aslrra.org

Linda Bauer Darr, President & Treasurer
Keith T Borman, VP, General Counsel
Jenny M Bourque, Director, Marketing
Kathleen M Cassidy, VP, Meetings & Member Services
Jenny M. Bourque, Director

Monitors and reports legislative and regulatory activities.
750 Members
Founded in 1913

22912 American Society of Transportation & Logistics
8430 W Bryn Mawr Ave
Suite 1000
Chicago, IL 60631

773-867-1777
FAX 773-639-3000
E-Mail: Info@astl.org
Home Page: www.astl.org
Social Media: *Facebook, Twitter, LinkedIn*

George Yarusavage, CTL C.P.M., Chairman
William J. Ferreira, Vice Chairman
Laurie Denham, PLS, President
Mike A. Regan, DLP, Treasurer
Evelyn Thomchick, CTL, Secretary

Professional organization for transportation and logistics professionals.
Founded in 1946

22913 American Space Transportation Association
General Dynamics
1801 Alexander Bell Drive
Reston, VA 20191-4400

703-548-2723
800-548-2723
FAX 703-295-6222
Home Page: www.asce.org
Social Media: *Facebook, Twitter, LinkedIn, YouTube, Google+*

Patrick J Natale, Executive Director
Pete Shavalay, CFO
Thomas Smith, Deputy Executive Director

The successor organization to the Ad Hoc Industry Group promoting the development of commercial space transportation in the United States.
25 Members
Founded in 1852

22914 American Traffic Safety Services Association
15 Riverside Parkway
Suite 100
Fredericksburg, VA 22406-1022

540-368-1701
800-272-8772
FAX 540-368-1717
Home Page: www.atssa.com
Social Media: *Facebook, Twitter, YouTube*

Scott Seeley, Chairman
Debra Ricker, Chairman Elect
Kathleen Holst, Past President
Henry Ross, Past President
Peter Speer, Past President

An international trade association with the core purpose to advance roadway safety.
Founded in 1969

22915 American Truck Historical Society
10380 N Ambassador Dr.
Suite 101, P.O. Box 901611
Kansas City, MO 64153

816-891-9900
FAX 816-891-9903
E-Mail: don@aths.org
Home Page: www.aths.org
Social Media: *Facebook, Twitter, YouTube*

Don Bretthauer, Executive Director
Shelley Ruhlman, Managing Director
Melinda Hunsberger, Director of Finance
Courtney Dery, Library Director
Jan Martin, Support Systems Specialist

Collects and preserves the history of antique trucks and the industry.
Founded in 1971

22916 American Trucking Associations
950 North Glebe Road
Suite 210
Arlington, VA 22203-4181

703-838-1700
E-Mail: atamembership@trucking.org
Home Page: www.trucking.org
Social Media: *Facebook, Twitter, YouTube*

Bill Graves, President & CEO
Kevin W. Burch, First Vice Chairman
John M Smith, Secretary
David Manning, Vice Chairman
Barry Pottle, Vice Chairman

The largest national trade association for the trucking industry.
Founded in 1933

22917 American Underground Space Association
12999 E. Adam Aircraft Circle
Englewood, CO 80112

303-948-4200
800-763-3132
FAX 303-973-3845
E-Mail: cs@smenet.org
Home Page: www.auca.org
Social Media: *Facebook, Twitter, LinkedIn*

William W Edgerton, Chair
Arthur D Silber, Vice Chairman
700 Members
Founded in 1976

22918 American Waterways Operators
801 N Quincy St
Suite 200
Arlington, VA 22203-1708

703-841-9300
FAX 703-841-0389
Home Page: www.americanwaterways.com
Social Media: *Facebook, Twitter, LinkedIn*

Buckley McAllister, Chairman
Frank Morton, Vice Chairman
George Foster, Treasurer
Thomas A. Allegretti, President & CEO
Mary J. Anastacio, Manager - Finance

Members include domestic carriers transporting commodities by water, shipyards, terminals and affiliated, business.
375 Members

22919 Association for Commuter Transportation
1330 Braddock Place
Suite 350
Alexandria, VA 22314-6405

571-699-3064
888-719-5772
E-Mail: info@actweb.org
Home Page: www.actweb.org
Social Media: *Facebook, Twitter*

Caryn Souza, Director
Marlon Powell, Adminstrative Assistant
Kevin Oliff, Marketing & Outreach Specialist
Jason Pavluchuk, Govt. Relations Specialist

ACT provides you with the resources of an international organization and the support of a regional affiliate of experienced Transportation Demand Management professionals.
810 Members
Founded in 1991

22920 Association for Women in Aviation Maintenance
2330 Kenlee Drive
Cincinnati, OH 45230

386-416-0248
FAX 386-236-0517
E-Mail: whq@awam.com
Home Page: www.awam.org
Social Media: *Facebook, LinkedIn*

Lynette Ashland, President
Jane Shelton, Vice President
Teressa Stark, Treasurer
Laura Gordon, Secretary
Anna Romer, Director | Scholarship Co-Chair

An organization formed for the purpose of championing women's professional growth and enrichment in the aviation maintenance fields.

22921 Association of Air Medical Services
909 N. Washington Street
Suite 410
Alexandria, VA 22314-3143

703-836-8732
FAX 703-836-8920
E-Mail: information@aams.org
Home Page: www.aams.org

Dawn Mancuso, Executive Director
Shirley Scholz, VP
Rick Sherlock, President
Yogendra Sheth, Finance & Accounting Manager

Voluntary nonprofit organization, encourages and supports its members in maintaining a standard of performance reflecting safe operations and efficient, high quality patient care. Built on the idea that representation from a variety of medical transport services and businesses can be brought together to share information, collectively resolve problems and provide leadership in the medical transport community.

22922 Association of American Railroads
425 3rd St Sw
Suite 114
Washington, DC 20024-3217

202-639-2100
FAX 202-639-2558

E-Mail: pubsrvcs@aar.org
Home Page: www.aar.org
Social Media: *Facebook, Twitter, LinkedIn, You Tube*

Edward R Hamberger, CEO
Patricia M. Reilly, SVP Communications
Jeffrey Marsh, SVP, Finance & Administration
Ian Jefferies, SVP, Government Affairs
John Gray, svp, Policy and Economics

Presently serves a joint agency of its individual railroad members to ensure an efficient nation-wide rail system.
80 Members
Founded in 1934

22923 Association of Metropolitan Planning Organizations
444 North Capitol Street, NW
Suite 345
Washington, DC 20000

202-624-3680
FAX 202-624-3685
Home Page: www.ampo.org

Richard Perrin, President
Elaine Clegg, Vice President
R. Todd Ashby, Executive Director
Rich Denbow, Director of Technical Programs
Levon Boyagian, Policy Consultant

A nonprofit organization serving metropolitan planning organizations.
Founded in 1994

22924 Association of Railway Museums
PO Box 370
Tujunga, CA 91043-0370

818-951-9151
FAX 818-951-9151
Home Page: www.railway.museums.org

Ellen Fishburn, Secretary
Paul Hamond, President

The association of railway museums is for the preservation of railway equipment, artifacts and history.
125 Members
Founded in 1961

22925 BAX Global
440 Exchange
Irvine, CA 92602

602-458-6200
800-225-5229
Home Page: www.dbschenkarusa.org
Social Media: *Twitter*

Joseph L Carnes, President
Jay Arnold, VP Human Resources

Specializes in managing the movement of heavyweight packages and cargo of all shapes and sizes.

22926 Boat Owners Association of the United States
880 South Pickett Street
Alexandria, VA 22304-4606

703-461-2878
E-Mail: membership@boatus.com
Home Page: www.boatus.com
Social Media: *Facebook, Twitter, YouTube, Google+*

Richard Schwartz, Chairman, Founder
Margaret Podlich, President
Adam Wheeler, VP and Director of Towing
Heather Lougheed, VP, Membership
John Condon, AVP, Towing Operations

Association of boat owners offering various services, supporting recreational boat and trailer towing activities.
Founded in 1966

22927 Brotherhood of Locomotive Engineers and Trainmen
Standard Building
1370 Ontario St.
Mezzanine, OH 44113-1702

216-241-2630
FAX 216-241-6516
E-Mail: PresStaff@ble-t.org
Home Page: www.ble-t.org

Dennis R. Pierce, National President
E. Lee Pruitt, First Vice President
Marcus J. Ruef, VP, Director of Arbitration
Gil L. Gore, Michael D., Vice President

A trade organization for railroad workers.

22928 Brotherhood of Maintenance of Way Employee s
41475 Gardenbrook Road
Novi, MI 48375-1328

248-662-2660
FAX 248-662-2659
Home Page: www.bmwe.org

Freddie N. Simpson, National Division President
Perry Geller, National Div. Secretary-Treasurer
David R. Scoville, Vice President- Western Region
Roger Sanchez, Vice President- South Region
David D. Joynt, Vice President at Large

A national union representing the workers who build and maintain the tracks, bridges, building and other structures of the railroads.

22929 Brotherhood of Railroad Signalmen
917 Shenandoah Shores Rd
Front Royal, VA 22630-6418

540-622-6522
FAX 540-622-6532
E-Mail: kelly@brs.org
Home Page: www.brs.org
Social Media: *Facebook, Twitter, RSS*

W Dan Pickett, President
Walter A Barrows, Treasurer
Floyd Mason, VP
Mike S. Baldwin, Research

National organization representing the men and women who install and maintain signal systems for most of the nation's railroads.
ISSN: 0037-5020
Founded in 1901

22930 Center for Transportation and the Environment (CTE)
730 Peachtree Street
Suite 760
Atlanta, GA 30308

678-244-4150
FAX 678-244-4151
Home Page: www.cte.tv

Eric Sonnichsen, Chairman
Joe Beno, Treasurer
John Sleconich, Secretary
James B. Martin, M.C.E., P.E., Associate Director
Eugene Murray, B.A., Distance Learning Specialist

A nonprofit organization to improve the efficiency and sustainability of the energy ad transportation systems.
Founded in 1991

22931 Committee for Better Transit
38 W Cliff Street
Somerville, NJ 08876

E-Mail: brooklynbus@hotmail.com
Home Page: www.brooklynbus.tripod.com

The Committee for Better Transit is a forty-one year old New York Metropolitan independent transit advocacy organization comprised of transit experts and users, which seeks cost effective user-friendly solutions to transit challenges.

22932 Energy Traffic Association
935 Eldridge Road
Suite 604
Sugar Land, TX 77478

832-474-3564
Home Page: www.energytraffic.org

Ralph Lopez, President
Renee Ahmed, VP & Secretary
Russell Powell, Executive Director

Formed by the merger of the Oilfield Supply Traffic Association and the Shippers Oil Field Traffic Association, ETA serves the oil and gas industry in transportation, distribution and logistics. Members are energy industry transportation, distribution, purchasing and logistics managers, and transportation and logistics providers.
Founded in 1997

22933 Expediting Management Association
Livingston, TN

931-823-1122
FAX 403-201-6402
Home Page: www.expedite.org

Katherine Rench, C.E.M, President
Glenda Warman, VP
Linda Strauss, Secretary
David Kern, Treasurer
Patricia Murphy, Executive Administrator

The Expediting Management Association, Inc. will maintain a certification program for it's memebers giving them the opportunity to achieve recognition from their peers in the association and industry.
200 Members
Founded in 1972

22934 Express Carriers Association
9532 Liberia Avenue
Suite 752
Manassas, VA 20110

703-361-1058
FAX 703-361-5274
E-Mail: eca@expresscarriers.com
Home Page: www.expresscarriers.com

Paul Steffes, President
Jim Luciani, 1st VP
Mike Coyle, Second VP
Jim King, Treasurer
Jim Bernecker, Secretary

The missio of the ECA is to develop business between carriers, shippers and vendors of products and services to the transportation industry.

22935 Fleet Management Institute (NAFA)
125 Village Boulevard
Suite 200
Princeton, NJ 08540

609-720-0882
FAX 609-452-8004
E-Mail: info@nafa.org
Home Page: www.nafa.org
Social Media: *Facebook, Twitter, LinkedIn, YouTube*

Patricia Murtaugh, Assistant Executive Director
Joanne Marsh, Manager

22936 Flight Safety Foundation
801 N. Fairfax Street
Suite 400
Alexandria, VA 22314-1774

703-739-6700
FAX 703-739-6708
E-Mail: wahdan@flightsafety.org

Home Page: flightsafety.org
Social Media: *Facebook, Twitter, LinkedIn*

Ken Hylander, Chair
David McMillan, Past Chair
Jon Beatty, President and CEO
David Barger, Treasurer
Kenneth P. Quinn, General Counsel and Secretary

Independent, nonprofit international organization engaged in research, auditing, education, advocacy and publishing to improove flight safety.
Founded in 1947

22937 High Speed Grand Transportation
1010 Massachusetts Avenue NW
Washington, DC 20001

202-789-8107
Home Page: www.hsgt.org

22938 Highway Users Federation for Safety and
PO Box 6285
Olympia, WA 98507-1904

253-376-8492
Home Page: www.acronymfinder.com
Social Media: *Facebook*

Diane Steed, President

The Highway Users Federation (WHUF) is an association concerned ith increasing capacity and safer on Highways.

22939 Institute of Transportation Engineers
1627 Eye St NW
Suite 600
Washington, DC 20006

202-785-0060
FAX 202-785-0609
E-Mail: ite_staff@ite.org
Home Page: www.ite.org
Social Media: *Facebook, Twitter, LinkedIn, YouTube, Google+, Pinterest*

Zaki Mustafa, President
W Hibbett Neel Jr., VP
16000 Members
Founded in 1930

22940 Insurance Institute for Highway Safety
988 Dairy Road
Ruckersville, VA 22968

434-985-4600
FAX 434-985-2202
E-Mail: rrader@iihs.org
Home Page: www.iihs.org
Social Media: *Twitter, RSS, YouTube*

Adrian Lund, President
Russ Rader, SVP, Communications
Shelley Shelton, Sr. Legal Associate
Brenda O'Donnell, VP, Insurer Relations
Chamelle Matthew, Sr. Communications Specialist

Independent, nonprofit research and communications organization dedicated to reducing highway crash death, injuries and property damage losses.
Founded in 1959

22941 Intermodal Association of North America
11785 Beltsville Dr
Suite 1100
Calverton, MD 20705-4049

301-982-3400
FAX 301-982-4815

E-Mail: iana@intermodal.org
Home Page: www.intermodal.org

Katie Farmer, Chairman
Adriene Bailey, Vice Chairman
Kevin Lhotak, Treasurer
Kristian Blust, Program Manager
Stacie Fagan, Manager, Info Services HD

Members are motor, rail and water transportation companies. Promotes the benefits and growth of the intermodal freight transportation.
600 Members

22942 International Association of Structural Movers
PO Box 2104
Neenah, WI 54956-2104

803-951-9304
FAX 920-486-1519
E-Mail: info@iasm.org
Home Page: www.iasm.org
Social Media: *Facebook, LinkedIn, YouTube, Google+*

Jim Herman, President
Don Toothman, Jr., VP
Natalie Hammer, Secretaty/Treasurer

Members are movers of heavy structural products, trusses, houses, machinery and masonry structures.
385 Members
Founded in 1983

22943 International Brotherhood of Teamsters
25 Louisiana Ave Nw
Washington, DC 20001-2130

202-624-6800
FAX 202-624-6918
Home Page: www.teamster.org
Social Media: *Facebook, Twitter, Google+*

James P Hoffa, President
Ken Hall, Secretary/Treasurer

Affiliated with the AFL-CIO.
1.3MM Members
Founded in 1954

22944 International Council of Cruise Lines
910 SE 17th Street
Suite 400
Fort Lauderdale, FL 33316

754-224-2200
FAX 754-224-2250
E-Mail: info@cruising.org
Home Page: www.cruising.org
Social Media: *Facebook, Twitter, LinkedIn, Pinterest*

Cindy D'Aoust, CEO
Tom Fischetti, CFO
Bud Darr, SVP Tech & Regulatory Affairs
Lorri Christou, SVP Marketing & Communications
Mike McGarry, SVP, Public Affairs

Dedicated to the promotion and growth of the cruise industry.
Founded in 1975

22945 International Furniture Transportation and Logistics Council
PO Box 889
Gardner, MA 01440-0889

978-632-1913
FAX 978-630-2917
E-Mail: jsears@iftlc.org
Home Page: www.iftlc.org
Social Media: *Twitter*

Raynard F Bohman Jr, Managing Director

Members are furniture manufacturers, retrilers, carriers, wholesalers and warehouses of allied products.
300 Members

22946 International Marine Transit Association
34 Otis Hill Road
Hingham, MA 02043

781-749-0078
FAX 781-749-0078
E-Mail: terryboots@cs.com
Home Page: www.interferry.com
Social Media: *Twitter, RSS*

Mike Grainger, Chairman
John Steen-Mikkelsen, President
Mike Corrigan, Treasurer
Len Roueche, Secretary

Membership includes ferry operators, naval architects, manufacturers, suppliers, and others in the ferry industry around the world.
400 Members
Founded in 1976

22947 International Parking Institute
1330 Braddock Place
Suite 350
Alexandria, VA 22314

571-699-3011
FAX 703-566-2267
E-Mail: ipi@parking.org
Home Page: www.parking.org
Social Media: *Facebook, Twitter, LinkedIn, YouTube, Pinterest, Instagram*

Liliana Rambo, CAPP, Chair of the BOD
Kim Jackson, CAPP, Chair-elect
Cindy Campbell, Past Chair
Rick Decker, CAPP, Treasurer
Shawn D. Conrad, CAE, Executive Director

Organization that provides educational and technical services to parking professionals and to the public.
Founded in 1962

22948 International Road Federation
500 Montgomery Street
Fifth Floor
Alexandria, VA

703-535-1001
FAX 703-535-1007
E-Mail: info@IRFnews.org
Home Page: www.irfnet.org
Social Media: *Facebook, Twitter, LinkedIn, Flickr*

A service organization for better road transportation systems.
Founded in 1948

22949 International Safe Transit Association
1400 Abbot Rd
Suite 160
East Lansing, MI 48823-1900

517-333-3437
888-367-4782
FAX 517-333-3813
E-Mail: ista@ista.org
Home Page: www.ista.org
Social Media: *Facebook, Twitter, LinkedIn*

Edward A Church, President
A J Gruber, VP, Technical Services
Lisa Bonsignore, VP, Special Events
Larry Dull, VP, Sustainable Solutions
Kathy A Joneson, VP, Communications

Members are shippers, carriers, manufacturers, packagers, package designers and testing laboratories, included in transport packaging.
750 Members
Founded in 1948
Mailing list available for rent: 4000 names at $500 per M

22950 Interstate Trucking Association
Express Carriers Association

9532 Liberia Avenue
#752
Manassas, VA 20110

703-361-1058
866-322-7447
FAX 703-361-5274
E-Mail: eca@expresscarriers.com
Home Page: www.expresscarriers.com

Paul Steffes, President
Jim Luciani, First VP
Mike Coyle, Second VP
Jim King, Treasurer
Jim Bernecker, Secretary

Organization of newly enacted state legislation regulations having direct impact on vehicle operations, fuel taxes, registration size and weight.

22951 Landstar Global Logistics

13410 Sutton Park Drive S
Jacksonville, FL 32224

904-398-9400
800-872-9400
E-Mail: corpcomm@landstar.com
Home Page: www.landstar.com
Social Media: *Facebook, LinkedIn*

Henry H Gerkens, Chairman, President & CEO
Jim B Gattoni, Executive VP, CFO
Joe Beacorn, VP & Chief Safety Operations Office
Larry S Thomas, VP/Chief Information Officer
Michael Kneller, VP, General Counsel & Secretary

Mission is to be the leading non-asset based provider of transportation capacity delivering safe, sepcialized transportation services to customers worldwide utilizing a network of agents, third-party capacity owners and employees.

22952 Mid-West Truckers Association

2727 N Dirksen Pkwy
Springfield, IL 62702-1490

217-525-0310
FAX 217-525-0342
E-Mail: info@midwesttruckshow.com
Home Page: www.midwesttruckshow.com
Social Media: *Facebook*

Don Schaefer, President

Serves trucking industry by lobbying on their behalf, assisting with registration, license plate procurement and group insurance programs. Conducts educational programs, has own self-funded workers compensation insurance program. Trade association represents truck owners in 14 states.
2700 Members
Founded in 1962

22953 Motor Transport Management Group

PO Box 605
Rillito, AZ 85654

520-616-0175
FAX 208-561-2980
Home Page: www.transportationmg.com
Social Media: *Facebook*

22954 National Air Carrier Association

1000 Wilson Boulevard
Suite 1700
Arlington, VA 22209-3928

703-358-8060
FAX 703-358-8070
Home Page: www.naca.cc

Oakley Brooks, President
Paul H Doell, Director, Govt. Affairs
George R Paul, Director Technical Services
Paul H Doell, Director Government Affairs
7 Members
Founded in 1962

22955 National Air Traffic Controllers Association

1325 Massachusetts Avenue N.W.
Washington, DC 20005

202-628-5451
800-266-0895
FAX 202-628-5767
Home Page: www.natca.org
Social Media: *Facebook, Twitter, LinkedIn, YouTube, Instagram*

Paul Rinaldi, President
Trish Gilbert, Executive Vice President
Mike MacDonald, Regional VP
Kevin Peterson, Regional VP
Jim Ullmann, Regional VP

Members are controllers in public and private sectors and Federal Aviation Administration engineers.

22956 National Air Transportation Association

818 Connecticut Avenue, NW
Suite 900
Washington, DC 22302-1507

202-774-1535
800-808-6282
FAX 703-845-8176
Home Page: www.nata.aero
Social Media: *Facebook, Twitter, LinkedIn, RSS*

Andy Priester Scheeringa, Chairman
Marty Hiller, Vice Chairman
Thomas L Hendricks, President
Greg Schmidt, Treasurer
Guy Hill, Jr., Secretary

Aggressively promotes safety and the success of aviation service businesses through its advocacy efforts before government, the media and the public as well as by providing valuable programs and forums to further its members' prosperity.
1800 Members
Founded in 1940

22957 National Asphalt Pavement Association

5100 Forbes Blvd
Lanham, MD 20708

301-731-4748
888-468-6499
FAX 301-731-4621
Home Page: www.asphaltpavement.org

A trade association that exclusively represents the interests of the asphalt pavment matieral producer and paving contractor on the national level with Congress, government agenices and other national trade and business organizations.

22958 National Association of Freight & Logistics

P.O.Box 60944
Dubai

714-343-1112
FAX 714-343-1105
Home Page: www.nafl.ae

David Phillips, President
Kevin Ennis, VP
Nadia Abdul Aziz, Secretary General
Suman Chakrabarti, Treasurer

Previously the National Committee of Freight Forwarders, the NAFL brings together in one body all the major players in the freight fowarding, logistics, and shipping industries.
Founded in 1992

22959 National Association of Rail Shippers

77 K Street NE
8th Floor
Washington, DC 20002-4681

202-650-6500
800-432-2250
FAX 972-644-8208
E-Mail: nars@onramp.net
Home Page: www.rollcall.com
Social Media: *Facebook, Twitter, LinkedIn, You Tube*

Charlie Mitchell, VP
Laurie Battaglia, Publisher

Strives to provide a sound transportation system. Bestows annual Award of Excellence.
2M Members
Founded in 1937

22960 National Association of Railroad Passengers

505 Capitol Court NE
Suite 300
Washington, DC 20002-7706

202-408-8362
FAX 202-408-8287
E-Mail: narp@narprail.org
Home Page: www.narprail.org
Social Media: *Facebook, Twitter, Google+*

Jim Mathews, President & CEO
Sean Jeans-Gail, VP
Robert J. Stewart, Chairman
Carol Haslett, Vice Chair
Stephen J. Salatti, Secretary

Seeks to increase public awareness of rail passenger service and its benefits. Works for a national transportation policy.
12M Members
Founded in 1967

22961 National Association of State Aviation Officials

8400 Westpark Dr.
2nd Floor
McLean, VA 22102

703-454-0649
E-Mail: info@nasao.org
Home Page: www.nasao.org
Social Media: *Facebook, Twitter, LinkedIn*

Gary Cathey, Chairman
Brad Brandt, Vice Chairman
Ronnie Mitchell, Treasurer
Carol L. Comer, Immediate Past Chairman
Greg Principato, President/ CEO

Established to ensure uniformity of safety measures and to standardize airport regulations.
Founded in 1931

22962 National Business Aviation Association

1200 G Street NW
Suite 1100
Washington, DC 20005ÿ

202-783-9000
FAX 202-331-8364
E-Mail: info@nbaa.org
Home Page: www.nbaa.org

Edward M. Bolen, President, CEO
Dan Hubbard, SVP, Communications
Chris Strong, SVP, Conventions & Membership
Steve Brown, Chief Operating Officer
Marc Freeman, Chief Financial Officer

Promotes the aviation interests of organizations utilizing general aviation aircraft for business purposes.
Founded in 1947

22963 National Business Travel Association
123 North Pitt Street
Alexandria, VA 22314-3234

703-684-0836
FAX 703-342-4324
E-Mail: info@nbta.org
Home Page: www.gbta.org
Social Media: *Facebook, Twitter, LinkedIn, You Tube*

Christle Johnson, President & CEO
Mark Ziegler, Vice President
Hema Shah, Chief Financial Officer
Hayford Mensah, CPA, Director, Finance
Getnesh Made, Manager, Finance

Offers over 1,300 corporate travel managers and allied members in the United States and Canada.
7000+ Members
Founded in 1968

22964 National Center for Bicycling and Walking
1612 K Street, NW
Suite 802
Washington, DC 20006

202-223-3621
E-Mail: info@bikewalk.org
Home Page: www.bikewalk.org

Mark Plotz, Senior Associate / Program Manager
John Williams, CenterlinesÿEditor
Jim Johnston, Web/Systems Administrator

A resident program at the Project for Public Spaces, Inc.
Founded in 1977

22965 National Child Transport Association
Hall of States
444 N Capitol St Nw
Suite 438
Washington, DC 20001-1505

202-624-7710
FAX 202-624-5899
E-Mail: bthompson@ncsha.org
Home Page: www.ncsha.org
Social Media: *Facebook, Twitter*

Barbara J Thompson, Executive Director
Cary D Knox, Executive Office Admin
Thomas R. Gleason, President
Grant S. Whitaker, Vice President
Ralph M. Perrey, Secretary/Treasurer

Thirty booths.
1.2M Members

22966 National Customs Brokers and Forwarders
1200 18th St Nw
Suite 901
Washington, DC 20036-2572

202-466-0222
FAX 202-466-0226
E-Mail: staff@ncbfaa.org
Home Page: www.ncbfaa.org
Social Media: *Facebook, Twitter, LinkedIn*

Darrell Sekin, Jr., Chairman
Geoffrey Powell, President
Amy Magnus, VP
Scott E. Larson, Treasurer
William S. App, Jr., Secretary

Learn about new business leads, stay on top of Customs Service and other agency regulations that will impact your operations and provide invaluable professional development resources for your employees.
600+ Members
Founded in 1897

22967 National Defense Transportation Association (NDTA)
50 S Pickett Street
Suite 220
Alexandria, VA 22304

703-751-5011
FAX 703-823-8761
E-Mail: info@ndtahq.com
Home Page: www.ndtahq.com
Social Media: *Facebook, Twitter, LinkedIn*

Mark H. Buzby RADM, USN (Ret.), President & COO
Jim Veditz COL, USA (Ret.), Senior VP Operations
Lee Matthews, VP, Marketing & Corp. Development
Patty Casidy, VP, Finance
Rebecca Jones, Executive Asst. To President

Intended as a liasion between government, military and private transportation officials.
7800 Members
Founded in 1944

22968 National Highway Carriers
PO Box 6099
Buffalo Grove, IL 60089

847-634-0606
FAX 847-634-1026
E-Mail: nhcdg@aol.com
Home Page: www.national-highway.com

Founded in 1942

22969 National Industrial Transportation League
1700 N Moore St
Suite 1900
Arlington, VA 22209-1931

703-524-5011
FAX 703-524-5017
E-Mail: info@nitl.org
Home Page: www.nitl.org
Social Media: *Twitter*

Bruce J Carlton, President & CEO
Ellie Gilanshah, VP, Finance, Admin & Membership
Doug J. Kratzberg, Chairman
Mary Pileggi, 1st Vice Chairman
Gary A. Palmer, 2nd Vice Chairman

Provides information to the industrial transportation industry, including computer services software and innovations for transportation operations.
600 Members
Founded in 1907

22970 National Institute of Certified Moving Consultants
1420 King Street
Alexandria, VA 22314-2794

703-683-7410
800-538-6672
FAX 703-683-7527
E-Mail: cert@nicet.org
Home Page: www.nicet.org
Social Media: *Facebook, LinkedIn*

Michael A Clark, Chief Operating Executive
Ahmed Farouki, Senior Director, Technical Services
Regina L. Stevenson, Director, Administrative Services
Brian Gifford, Director, Quality Management
Paul L. Stockman, Manager, Certification Services

Awards the certified moving consultant designation to those who have passed an exam testing their liability.
Founded in 1961

22971 National Institute of Packaging and Handling Logistics Engineers
5903 Ridgeway Drive
Grand Prairie, TX 75052

817-466-7490
866-464-7453
FAX 570-523-0606
E-Mail: admin@niphle.com
Home Page: www.niphle.com
Social Media: *Facebook, Twitter, LinkedIn*

Sean Kerins, President

An assemblage of professionals whose interest in the complex and diverse practice of distribution and logistics is a common bond.
600 Members
Founded in 1956

22972 National Marine Representatives Associatio n
PO Box 360
Gurnee, IL 60031

847-662-3167
FAX 847-336-7126
E-Mail: info@nmraonline.org
Home Page: www.nmraonline.org

Rob Gueterman, President
Brandon Flack, Past President
Keith LaMarr, Vice President
Neal Tombley, Treasurer
Clayton Smith, Secretary

A national organization serving marine industry sales representatives and the manufacturers who sell marine products.
Founded in 1960

22973 National Motor Freight Traffic Association
1001 North Fairfax Street
Suite 600
Alexandria, VA 22314-1798

703-838-1810
866-411-6632
FAX 703-683-6296
E-Mail: customerservice@nmfta.org
Home Page: www.nmfta.org
Social Media: *LinkedIn*

Paul Levine, Executive Director
Joel Ringer, Chairman, CCSB
Urban Jonson, Chief Technology Officer
Leslie Tate, Finance & HR Manager
Urban Jonson, Chief Technology Officer

Provides expertise in freight classification, packaging, and transportation codes.

22974 National Motorcoach Network
PO Box 1088
Mount Jackson, VA 22842

540-477-3202
800-469-0062
FAX 540-477-3858
E-Mail: smk@motorcoach.com
Home Page: www.motorcoach.com/byways

Founded in 1983

22975 National Parking Association
1112 16th St Nw
Suite 840
Washington, DC 20036-4880

202-296-4336
800-647-7275
FAX 202-296-3102
E-Mail: info@npapark.org
Home Page: www.npapark.org
Social Media: *Facebook, Twitter, LinkedIn, YouTube*

Mark Muglich, Chairman
Alan B. Lazowski, Chair Elect
Nicolle Judge, Vice Chair

David Damus, Secretary
Robert A Zuritsky, Treasurer

Proudly serving the nation's parking industry since 1951. Our members are comprised of parking professionals in both the public and private sectors from across the country and around the world. NPA members are private operators, parking consultants, colleges and universities, municipalities, parking authorities, hospitals and medical centers and industry vendors.
2500+ Members
Founded in 1951
Mailing list available for rent

22976 National Private Truck Council
950 N. Glebe Road
Suite 2300
Arlington, VA 22203-4183

703-683-1300
FAX 703-683-1217
Home Page: www.nptc.org
Social Media: *Facebook, Twitter, LinkedIn, Flickr, YouTube, RSS*

Tom Moore, CTP, Senior Vice President
George Mundell, Executive Vice President & COO
Gary F. Petty, President & CEO
Serena Porter, Membership Manager
Rick Schweitzer, General Counsel & Gov. Affairs

National trade association dedicated exclusively to representing private motor carrier fleets.
Founded in 1939

22977 National School Transportation Association
122 South Royal Street
Alexandria, VA 22314

703-684-3200
800-222-6782
FAX 703-684-3212
E-Mail: info@yellowbuses.com
Home Page: www.yellowbuses.org
Social Media: *Facebook, Twitter, LinkedIn, YouTube*

Todd Monteferrario, President
Steve Hey, President Elect
Blake Krapf, Secretary/Treasurer
Ronna Weber, Executive Director
Meaghan Allain, Membership & Ops Coor.

Strives to provide safe transportation, foster safety, and an atmosphere conducive to private enterprise.
3M Members
Founded in 1964

22978 National Small Shipments Traffic
330 N Wabash Avenue
Suite 2000
Chicago, IL 60611

202-367-1174
FAX 202-686-2877
E-Mail: info@nasstrac.org
Home Page: www.nasstrac.org
Social Media: *Facebook, Twitter, LinkedIn*

Doug Easley, Chairperson
Chris Norek, Ph.D., President
Terri Reid, 1st VP
Marc Feeser, 2nd VP
Tom Wenzinger, Treasurer

Members are truck, air, rail and sea shippers of freight weighing less than 10,000 pounds.
250 Members
Founded in 1952

22979 National Waterways Conference
110 N Glebe Rd.
Suite 1010
Arlington, VA 22201

703-224-8007
FAX 866-371-1390
E-Mail: amy@waterways.org
Home Page: www.waterways.org

Jim Oliver, Chairman
Jamie McCurry, Vice Chairman
Amy W. Larson, Esq.,, President
Randy Richardson, VP
Carole Wright, Director of Internal Operations

Dedicated to a greater understanding of the widespread public benefits of the American waterways system.
350 Members
Founded in 1960

22980 National/International Safe Transit Association
200 E Randolph
Suite 4120
Chicago, IL 60601-7683

312-552-6300
FAX 312-552-6302
E-Mail: Rich.Jernstedt@porternovelli.com
Home Page: www.porternovelli.com
Social Media: *Facebook, Twitter, LinkedIn, YouTube, Google+*

Karen Van Bergen, CEO
Rich Cline, President/Senior Partner
Brad MacAfee, President, NA/Senior Partner
Patrick Resk, CFO/Senior Partner
Joseph Russo, COO/Partner

22981 Natural Gas Vehicles for America
400 N Capitol St Nw
Washington, DC 20001-1511

202-824-7360
FAX 202-824-7087
E-Mail: rkolodziej@ngvamerica.org
Home Page: www.ngvamerica.org
Social Media: *Facebook, Twitter, LinkedIn, YouTube*

Matthew Godlewski, President
Jeffrey Clarke, Gen. Counsel & Dir., Reg. Affairs
Paul Kerkhoven, Director, Government Affairs
Lucas Blanchard, Dir., Ops, Membership & Planning
Dan Bowerson, Director, Technology & Dev.

Members are organizations with an interest in encouraging the development of natural gas powered vehicles.
250 Members
Founded in 1988

22982 Network of Employers for Traffic Safety
344 Maple Avenue, West
#357
Vienna, VA 22180-5162

703-755-5350
888-221-0045
E-Mail: sgillies@trafficsafety.org
Home Page: trafficsafety.org

Jack Hanley, Executive Director
Susan Gillies, Administrative Lead
Joseph L. McKillips, CSP, Chair

Focused on improving traffic safety.

22983 North American Shippers Association
1600 St. Georges Ave
PO Box 249
Rahway, NJ 07065

732-680-4540
FAX 732-388-6580

E-Mail: nasaships@hillebrandgroup.com
Home Page: www.nasaships.com

Case Pieterman, Executive Director
Stephen Ballas, President

Members are shippers of wine and alcoholic beverages.
430 Members
Founded in 1987

22984 North American Transportation Council
427 Garrison Rd.
Unit 3 & 4
Fort Erie, ON L2A 6E6

800-559-7421
FAX 905-994-0117
E-Mail: info@fca-natc.org
Home Page: www.natc.com

Dave Sirgey, President
Mary Anne Vehrs, Sales & Marketing
Julie Gauthier, Administrative Assistant
Diane Sheppard, Accounting Supervisor
Jon Ainsworth, Manager, IT & Dev

Represents Canadian and US based motor carriers engaged in for-hire trucking in the North American transborder market.

22985 Passenger Vessel Association
103 Oronoco Street
Suite 200
Alexandria, VA 22314-1549

703-518-5005
800-807-8360
FAX 703-518-5151
E-Mail: pvainfo@passengervessel.com
Home Page: www.passengervessel.com
Social Media: *Facebook*

Dave Anderson, President
Margo Marks, Vice President
Jeff Whitaker, Secretary/Treasurer
John Groundwater, Executive Director
Edmund Welch, Legislative Director

Represents operators of tours, excursions, ferries, charter vessels, dinner boats and other small passenger vessels.
600 Members
Founded in 1971

22986 Railway Industrial Clearance Association
8900 Eastloch Dr.
Suite 215
Spring, TX 77379

281-826-0009
Home Page: www.rica.org

Rick Ford, Chairman
Kelli Collins, President
Justin Gilmet, VP
Mike Scott, Treasurer
Mark Lockwood, Secretary

Representation includes all aspects of logistics associated with the movement of dimensional cargo via rail.
400+ Members
Founded in 1969

22987 Railway Supply Institute
425 Third Street, S.W.
Suite 920
Washington, DC 20024

202-347-4664
FAX 202-347-0047
E-Mail: simpson@rsiweb.org
Home Page: www.rsiweb.org
Social Media: *Twitter, LinkedIn*

Thomas D Simpson, President
Nicole B Brewin, VP, Govt. Affairs
Robyn M. Leach, VP, Administration
Amanda T. Patrick, CEM, Trade Shows & Marketing

Brian M. Kellman, Membership & Grassroots Coordinator

The railway equipment and supply industry.
300 Members
Founded in 1908

22988 Railway Systems Suppliers
13133 Professional Drive
Suite 100
Jacksonville, FL 32225

904-379-3366
FAX 904-379-3941
E-Mail: rssi@rssi.org
Home Page: www.rssi.org

N. Michael Choat, President
Walter Winzen, Executive VP
Franklin Brown, 1st VP
Phil Hess, 2nd VP
Michael A. Drudy, Exe. Director/Secretary/Treasurer

A trade association serving the communication and signal segment of the rail transportation industry. Manages an annual trade show.
260+ Members
Founded in 1966

22989 Regional Airline Association
2025 M Street NW
Washington, DC 20036-3309

202-367-1170
FAX 202-367-2170
E-Mail: registration@raa.org
Home Page: www.raa.org
Social Media: *Facebook, Twitter, YouTube*

Faye Malarkey Black, President
Stacey Bechdolt, Senior VP, Operations & Safety
Allie Cortes, Associate
Liam Connolly, Senior Director- Regulatory Affairs
Staci Morgan, Operations Manager

Membership consists of more than 70 airlines and 350 associate members that provide goods and services.
300 Members
Founded in 1975

22990 Roadmasters and Maintenance of Way Association of America
4501 Forbes Blvd
Suite 130
Lanham, MD 20706

301-459-3200
FAX 301-459-8077
E-Mail: bcaruso@arema.org
Home Page: www.arema.org
Social Media: *Facebook, LinkedIn*

Beth Caruso, CAE, Executive Director & CEO
Vickie Fisher, CAE, Director, Finance
Stacy Spaulding, CAE, Dir., Committees & Tech Services
Lindsay Hamilton, Director, Marketing & Communication
Janice Clements, Director, Membership & IS

Railroad executives concerned with track and roadway management.
2.1M Members
Founded in 1997

22991 Shippers Oil Field Traffic Association
907 Kiowa Drive E
Gainesville, TX 76240-9575

940-668-7735
FAX 940-668-7212
Home Page: www.all-acronyms.com
Social Media: *Facebook, Twitter*

50 Members
Founded in 1941

22992 Society of Automotive Engineers
400 Commonwealth Dr
Warrendale, PA 15096

724-776-4841
877-606-7323
FAX 724-776-0790
E-Mail: customerservice@sae.org
Home Page: www.sae.org
Social Media: *Facebook, Twitter, LinkedIn, Google+*

David L. Schutt, PhD, Chief Executive Officer
Gregory L. Bradley, Esq., General Counsel
Sandra L. Dillner, Director of Human Resources
Brian Kaleida, Chief Information Officer
Frank Menchaca, Chief Product Officer

Offers automotive engineers the technical information and expertise used in building, maintaining and operating self propelled vehicles for use on land, sea, air or space.

22993 Space Transportation Association
4305 Underwood Street
University Park, MD 20782

703-855-3917
E-Mail: rich@spacetransportation.us
Home Page: www.spacetransportation.us

Richard Coleman, President
Ty McCoy, Chairman

Represents the interests of organizations which intend to develop, build, operate and use space transportation vehicles and systems in order to provide reliable, economical, safe and routine access to space for public and private entities.
20 Members
Founded in 1989

22994 Taxicab, Limousine & Paratransit Association
3200 Tower Oaks Boulevard
Suite 220
Rockville, MD 20852

301-984-5700
FAX 301-984-5703
E-Mail: info@tlpa.com
Home Page: www.tlpa.org

Alfred La Gasse III, CEO
Harold Morgan, Executive VP
Leah New, Manager, Communications
Michelle A Jasper, Manager, Meetings
Ayesha Plaskett, Office Assistant

Members include owners of taxicab, limousine, airport shuttle, paratransit and nonemergency medical transportation fleets.
1107 Members
Founded in 1917
Mailing list available for rent: 6,000 names at $100 per M

22995 The American Road & Transportation Builders Association
1219 28th Street, N.W.ÿ
Washington, DC 20007ÿ

202-289-4434
E-Mail: info@artba.org
Home Page: www.artba.org
Social Media: *Facebook, Twitter, LinkedIn, YouTube, Google+*

David S. Zachry, Chairman
Bob Alger, Senior Vice Chairman
Matt Cummings, First Vice Chairman
Rob Charter, Vice Chairman At-Large
Tom Hill, Treasurer

National transportation construction trade group.
Founded in 1902

22996 The Associated General Contractors of America
2300 Wilson Blvd.
Suite 300
Arlington, VA 22201

703-548-3118
800-242-1767
FAX 703-548-3119
E-Mail: info@agc.org
Home Page: www.agc.org
Social Media: *Facebook, Twitter, LinkedIn, YouTube*

Charles L. Greco, President
Mark Knight, Senior Vice President
Art Daniel, Vice Presidentÿ
Joseph Stella, Treasurer
Stephen E. Sandherr, CEO

Trade association for the construction industry.
26000 Members
Founded in 1918

22997 The Institute of Navigation
8551 Rixlew Ln.
STE 360
Manassas, VA 20109

703-366-2723
FAX 703-366-2724
E-Mail: membership@ion.org
Home Page: www.ion.org
Social Media: *Facebook, Twitter, LinkedIn, YouTube*

Lisa Beaty, Executive Director
Rick Buongiovanni, IT Director
Ken Esthus, Marketing Director
Miriam Lewis, Program/Author Liaison
Megan Andrews, Senior Meeting Manager

Nonprofit professional society dedicated to the advancement of the art and sciece of positioning, radar and navigation.
Founded in 1945

22998 The Intelligent Transportation Society of America (ITS America)
1100 New Jersey Ave. SE
Suite 850
Washington, DC 20003

202-484-4847
800-374-8472
E-Mail: info@itsa.org
Home Page: www.itsa.org
Social Media: *Facebook, Twitter, LinkedIn, YouTube, Flickr*

Jill M. Ingrassia, Chair
Chris Murray, Vice Chair
Dana Christensen, Treasurer
Regina Hopper, President and CEO
Michael Eason, Chief Financial Officer

Organization dedicated to advancing the research, development and design of surface transportation systems.
1200+ Members
Founded in 1991

22999 The National Customs Brokers & Forwarders Association of America
1200 18th Street, NW
#901
Washington, DC 20036

202-466-0222
FAX 202-466-0226
Home Page: www.ncbfaa.org
Social Media: *Facebook, Twitter, LinkedIn*

Darrell Sekin, Jr., Chairman, Board
Geoffrey Powell, President
Scott E. Larson, Treasurer
William S. App, Jr., Secretary
Amy Magnus, VP

Represents and supports members of the US freight forwarding industry providing education and publications.
970+ Members
Founded in 1987

23000 Transport Workers Union of America
501 3rd Street NW
9th Floor
Washington, DC 20001

202-719-3900
FAX 202-347-0454
Home Page: www.twu.org
Social Media: *Facebook, Twitter, Youtube, Flickr*

Harry Lombardo, President
John Samuelson, Executive VP
Alex Garcia, Secretary/Treasurer

Chartered by the Congress of Industrial Organizations.
110M Members
ISBN: 0-039865-9 -
Founded in 1934

23001 Transportation Clubs International
P.O. Box 426
Union, WA 98592

877-858-8627
E-Mail:
info@transportationclubcinternational.co
Home Page:
www.transportationclubsinternational.com

Members are individuals in all phases of transportation, traffic management and physical distribution.
10M Members

23002 Transportation Institute
5201 Auth Way
Camp Springs, MD 20746-4211

301-423-3335
FAX 301-423-0634
E-Mail: info@trans-inst.org
Home Page: www.trans-inst.org

James L Henry, Chairman & President
Jerome K Welsch Jr, COO
Robert E Johnston, Executive VP

Members are US flag shipping, towing and dredging companies.
100 Members
Founded in 1967

23003 Transportation Intermediaries Association
3601 Eisenhower Avenue
Suite 110
Alexandria, VA 22304

703-299-5700
888-910-4747
FAX 703-836-0123
E-Mail: info@tianet.org
Home Page: www.tianet.org
Social Media: *Facebook, Twitter, LinkedIn*

Robert Voltmann, President/CEO
Cindy Amos, Dir. Education & Meeting
Nancy O'Liddy, Dir. Policy & TIA Services
Valerie Sumner, Meetings Manager
Roberta Sumner, Meetings Manager

Education and policy organization for North American transportation intermediaries. TIA is the only national association representing the interests of all third party transportation service providers. The members of TIA include logistics management firms, property brokers, perishable commodities brokers, freight forwarders, intermodal marketers, ocean and air forwarders, and NVOCC's.
1200 Members
Founded in 1978

23004 Transportation Loss Prevention & Security Association
155 Polifly Road
Hackensack, NJ 07601

732-350-3776
E-Mail: eloughman@nakblaw.com
Home Page: www.tlpsa.org

William D Bierman, Executive Director
Edward M Loughman, Assistant to Executive Director

Originally a combination of the National Freight Claim Council and the Transportation Loss Prevention and Security Council, this independent association supports all persons who have an interest in loss and damage claims and security issues. Members include carriers, shippers, vendors, law enforcement, attorneys, insurance carriers, third-party logistics, etc.
Founded in 2000

23005 Transportation Research Board
500 Fifth Street NW
Washington, DC 20001

202-334-2934
FAX 202-334-2527
E-Mail: rallen@nas.edu
Home Page: www.trb.org
Social Media: *Facebook, Twitter, LinkedIn*

Janet M. McNaughton, Senior Editor
Rosa P Allen, Administrative Coordinator
Cynthia M Baker, Executive Assistant
Anthony T Bailey, Financial Associate
Thomas R. Menzies, Senior Program Officer

23006 Transportation Research Forum
Department 2880
PO Box 6050
Fargo, ND 58108-6050

701-231-7766
FAX 701-231-1945
E-Mail: info@trforum.org
Home Page: www.trforum.org
Social Media: *Facebook, LinkedIn*

Pat McCarthy, Executive VP
David Ripplinger, President
P.S. Sriraj, VP, Membership
Marla Westervelt, VP, Public Relations
Joe Schwieterman, VP, Chapter Relations

An independent organization of transportation professionals.
300 Members
Founded in 1958

23007 Truck Renting and Leasing Corporation
675 N Washington Street
Suite 410
Alexandria, VA 22314

703-299-9120
800-426-1420
FAX 703-299-9115
Home Page: www.trala.org

Jack Jacoby, President & CEO
Peter Einisman, Manager of Government Relations
Shannon Davison, Director of Communications & Events
Tonya Gibbs, VP, Finance & Business Operations
Andrew Stasiowski, Director, Govt. Relations

A multi-national technology company, NRLC monitors legislation and other issues affecting the truck/trailer leasing and rental industry. It also manufacturers heavy-duty, on-and-off-road trucks worldwide.
275 Members
Founded in 1978

23008 Truck Trailer Manufacturers Association
7001 Heritage Village Plaza
Suite 220
Gainesville, VA 20155

703-549-3010
FAX 703-549-3014
E-Mail: ttma@erols.com
Home Page: www.ttmanet.org

Jeff Sims, President
John Freller, Engineering Manager
Nancy Livingston, Administration

News of interest to trailer manufacturers and suppliers.

23009 United Bus Owners of America
113 S West Street
4th Floor
Alexandria, VA 22314-2824

703-838-8262
800-424-8262
FAX 703-838-2950
E-Mail: info@uma.org
Home Page: www.uma.org
Social Media: *Facebook, Twitter, LinkedIn, Youtube*

Victor S Parra, President & CEO
Ken Presley, VP, Industry Relations & COO
Maggie Masterson, Meetings & Operations Director
Terri Tackett, Marketing & Membership Director
Brian Annett, Chairman

Serves the bus industry, with particular emphasis on group travel and tourism.
800 Members
Founded in 1971

23010 United States Telecom Association
607 14th St Nw
Suite 400
Washington, DC 20005-2000

202-326-7300
FAX 202-315-3603
E-Mail: membership@ustelecom.org
Home Page: www.ustelecom.org
Social Media: *Facebook, Twitter, LinkedIn, Youtube*

Walter B. McCormick, Jr., President/CEO
Robert A. Hunt, Chairman of the Board
Alan J. Roth, Senior Executive Vice President
Mark Kulish, SVP, Admin & CFO
Anne Veigle, SVP, Communications

Trade association representing service provides and suppliers for the telecom industry.
Cost: $699.00

23011 Wine and Spirits Shippers Association
11800 Sunrise Valley Dr
Suite 332
Reston, VA 20191-5302

207-805-1664
800-368-3167
FAX 703-860-2422
E-Mail: info@wssa.com
Home Page: www.wssa.com
Social Media: *Facebook, Twitter, LinkedIn, RSS*

Alison Leavitt, Managing Director
Gretchen Veevaert, Program Coordinator
Cecilia Borruso, Contract Supervisor/Pricing Analyst
Heather Randolph, Director of Operations
Louis Healey, President

Provides members with services that allow for the efficient and economical transportation of alcoholic beverages.
320 Members
Founded in 1976

23012 Women's Transportation Seminar: National
1701 K St Nw
Suite 800
Washington, DC 20006-1504

202-955-5085
FAX 202-955-5088
E-Mail: membership@wtsinternational.org
Home Page: www.wtsinternational.org
Social Media: *Facebook, Twitter, LinkedIn, Pinterest, Instagram*

Beverley Swaim-Staley, Chair
Diane Woodend Jones, Vice Chairman
Felicia Boyd, Secretary
Rina Cutler, Treasurer
Marcia Ferranto, President/CEO
5000+ Members
Founded in 1977

23013 Womens Transportation Seminar
1701 K St Nw
Suite 800
Washington, DC 20006-1504

202-955-5085
FAX 202-955-5088
E-Mail: membership@wtsinternational.org
Home Page: www.wtsinternational.org
Social Media: *Facebook, Twitter, LinkedIn, Pinterest, Instagram*

Beverley Swaim-Staley, Chair
Diane Woodend Jones, Vice Chairman
Felicia Boyd, Secretary
Rina Cutler, Treasurer
Marcia Ferranto, President/CEO
5000+ Members
Founded in 1977

23014 World Organization of Dredging
Post Office Box 2035
Spotsylvania, VA 22553

619-839-9474
FAX 360-750-1445
E-Mail: tmverna@westerndredging.org
Home Page: www.woda.org

Anders Jensen, President
Dr A Csiti, General Manager
Rashyan Allays, Secretary
Thomas M. Verna, Executive Director

Develops professionalism in individuals involved in the dredging industry.
2700 Members
Founded in 1981

Newsletters

23015 ABA Insider
American Bus Association
111 K Street NE
Suite 575
Washington, DC 20005-5923

202-842-1645
FAX 202-842-0850
E-Mail: abainfo@buses.org
Home Page: www.buses.org

Peter J Pantuso, CEO
Eron Shosteck, Marketing

ABA's biweekly newsletter that keeps members informed on the travel, tourism and motorcoach industry.
Frequency: Biweekly
Founded in 1926

23016 Advanced Transit News
Advanced Transit Association

PO Box 162
Palo Alto, CA 94302

800-779-0544
800-779-0544
FAX 800-779-0544
E-Mail: jpaskry@davinciglobal.com
Home Page: www.advancedtransit.org

Catherine G. Burke, President
Bob Dunning, VP
Lawrence Fabian, Publisher

Offers information on the American transit system.
100 Pages
Frequency: Quarterly
Founded in 1953
Printed in one color on matte stock

23017 Center for Microcomputers in Transportation
512 Weil Hall
PO Box 116585
Gainesville, FL 32611

352-392-7575
800-226-1013
FAX 352-389-2324
E-Mail: mctrans@ce.ufl.edu
Home Page: www.mctrans.ce.ufl.edu

Mark Newman, Associate Director
Max Crumit, Executive Vice President
Kirk Hatfield, Director
Founded in 1986

23018 Dispatch & Division Newsletters
Taxicab, Limousine & Paratransit Association
3200 Tower Oaks Blvd
Suite 220
Rockville, MD 20852

301-984-5700
FAX 301-984-5703
E-Mail: info@tlpa.org
Home Page: www.tlpa.org

Alfred LaGasse, CEO
Victor Dizengoff, President

Dispatch features articles on industry business issues, provides advice on running a transportation company, and comes with division specific bi-monthly newsletters.
Frequency: Bimonthly
Circulation: 6000

23019 Dual News
Driving School Association of America
11 W Pomona Boulevard
Monterey Park, CA 91754

FAX 626-722-0485

George Hensel, Publisher

Association news for student driving instructors and educational personnel.
Frequency: BiWeekly
Circulation: 5,000

23020 Fleet Street
Greenwich Consulting
15821 Fetlock Lane
Chino Hills, CA 91709

909-606-2271
FAX 909-597-7759

Karen Edward, Publisher

Consulting newsletter geared toward Distribution and Fleet Management Executives - Provides transportation managers with cost-cutting methodologies.
Circulation: 15500

23021 HazMat Transport News
Business Publishers

8737 Colesville Road
Suite 1100
Silver Spring, MD 20910-3925

301-876-6300
800-274-6737
FAX 301-587-4530
E-Mail: custserv@bpinews.com
Home Page: www.bpinews.com

Leonard A Eiserer, Publisher
Beth Early, Operations Director

Regulatory and legislative development affecting hazardous materials transportation. In-depth coverage on research and special programs administration, hazmat regulation programs and enforcement actions.
Cost: $447.00
Founded in 1963

23022 Inside DOT and Transportation Week
King of Communications Group
1325 Massachusetts Ave Nw
Suite 310
Washington, DC 20005-4194

240-455-6801
800-926-5464
FAX 240-628-5774
Home Page: www.kingpublishing.com

F King, President
Dave Ahearn, Editor
Wenita Lhill-waddell, Marketing
Linda Gasparello, General Manager

Offers information to persons working in the transportation profession.
Cost: $1300.00
12 Pages
Frequency: Daily
Founded in 1973
Printed in one color on newsprint stock

23023 Interstate Information Report
Express Carriers Association
9532 Liberia Avenue,
Suite 130
Manassas, VA 20190-3233

703-361-1058
866-322-7447
FAX 704-435-4390
E-Mail: eca@expresscarriers.com
Home Page: www.expresscarriers.com

Carrie Ehlers, President
Stuart Hyden, First Vice President

Compilation of newly enacted state legislation regulations having direct impact on vehicle operations, fuel taxes, registration size and weight.

23024 Legislative Alert
Taxicab, Limousine & Paratransit Association
3200 Tower Oaks Blvd
Suite 220
Rockville, MD 20852

301-984-5700
FAX 301-984-5703
E-Mail: info@tlpa.org
Home Page: www.tlpa.org

Alfred LaGasse, CEO
Victor Dizengoff, President

TLPA's members-only bulletin of early alerts to critical changes in the industry, announcing threats and opportunities on issues that are before Congress and federal agencies. Organizes operators to take action, and provides knowledge and awareness.
Circulation: 6000

23025 McTrans
Center for Microcomputers in Transportation

512 Weil Hall
PO Box 116585
Gainesville, FL 32611

352-392-7575
800-226-1013
FAX 352-389-2324
E-Mail: mctrans@ce.ufl.edu
Home Page: www.mctrans.ce.ufl.edu

CE Wallace, Publisher
Mark Newman, Associate Director
Max Crumit, Executive Vice President
Kirk Hatfield, Director

Information about microcomputer software and resources in transportation.
Circulation: 8,000
Founded in 1986

23026 Passenger Transport

American Public Transit Association
1666 K St Nw
Suite 1100
Washington, DC 20006-1215

202-496-4800
FAX 202-496-4324
E-Mail: hbrett@apta.com
Home Page: www.apta.com

Karol J Popkin, CEO
Petra Mollet, VP
Rosemary Sherid, Marketing

Information on federal legislative, administrative and regulatory developments, management and operations, new technology, and state and local developments in public transit.
Cost: $75.00
Frequency: B-Weekly
Circulation: 5000
Founded in 1882

23027 Proclaim

Slesia Companies
619 Broad Creek Dr
Fort Washington, MD 20744-5800

301-292-1970
FAX 301-292-1787
Home Page: fdrs.ag.utk.edu

Dale L Anderson, President

Covers transportation freight claims.
Frequency: Monthly

23028 Rider's Digest

Metropolitan Atlanta Road Transit
2424 Piedmont Rd Ne
Atlanta, GA 30324-3311

404-848-5000
FAX 404-848-5098
E-Mail: schedinfo@itsmarta.com
Home Page: www.itsmarta.com

Nathaniel P Ford Sr, CEO

Public transportation news.
Frequency: Monthly

23029 TransitPulse

Trans 21
55 Virginia St
Dorchester, MA 02125-2352

617-825-9687
FAX 617-482-7417

Lawrence J Fabin, Publisher

Newsletters and faxed advisory service on worldwide developments in Automated People Movers.
Cost: $75.00
4 Pages
Frequency: BiMonthly
Circulation: 500
Printed in one color on matte stock

23030 Transport Workers Union of America

Transport Workers Union of America

1700 Broadway
Suite 2
New York, NY 10019-5905

212-259-4900
FAX 202-347-0454
E-Mail: mailbox@twu.org
Home Page: www.twu.org

James Little, President
David Rosen, General Counsel
Alex Garcia, Director

Chartered by the Congress of Industrial Organizations.
Frequency: Monthly
ISBN: 0-039865-9
Founded in 1934

23031 Transportation Intermediaries Association

3601 Eisenhower Avenue
Suite 110
Alexandria, VA 22304

703-299-5700
FAX 703-836-0123
E-Mail: info@tianet.org
Home Page: www.tianet.org

Robert Voltmann, President/CEO
Larry Fisher, Contact

Education and policy organization for North American transportation intermediaries. TIA is the only national association representing the interests of all third party transportation service providers. The members of TIA include logistics management firms, property brokers, perishable commodities brokers, freight forwarders, intermodal marketers, ocean and air forwarders, and NVOCC's.
700 Pages
Frequency: Monthly

23032 US Rail News

Business Publishers
222 Sedwick Dr
Suite 101
Durham, NC 27713

800-223-8720
FAX 800-508-2592
E-Mail: custserv@bpinews.com
Home Page: www.bpinews.com

Reports on the trends, legislation, regulations, acquisitions, business opportunities and technological developments that directly affect the rail industry.
Cost: $437.00
Frequency: 25 per year
Founded in 1963

23033 Urban Transport News

Business Publishers
8737 Colesville Road
Suite 1100
Silver Spring, MD 20910-3928

301-876-6300
800-274-6737
FAX 301-587-4530
E-Mail: custserv@bpinews.com
Home Page: www.bpinews.com

Leonard A Eiserer, Publisher
Beth Early, Operations Director

Comprehensive briefings on trends, regulations, legislation, business and technological developments in the mass transit area.
Cost: $437.00
Founded in 1963

Magazines & Journals

23034 Air Medical Journal

526 King Street
Suite 415
Alexandria, VA 22314-3143

703-836-8732
800-525-3712
FAX 703-836-8920
E-Mail: information@aams.org
Home Page: www.aams.org

Renee Holleran, Editor
Dawn M Mancuso, Director
John Fiegel, Director

An association of health care entities operating helicopter transport services. Magazine is published, price included in membership.
375 Pages
Founded in 1980
Printed in on glossy stock

23035 American Journal of Transportation

Fleur de Lis Publishing
1354 Hancock Street
Suite 300
Quincy, MA 02169

617-328-5005
800-599-6358
FAX 617-328-5999
E-Mail: editorial@ajot.com
Home Page: www.ajot.com/

George Lauriat, Editor
Ann Radwan, Associate Editor
William Bourbon, Publisher
Bob Kirk, Production Manager
Kristen Davis, Graphic Designer

Newspaper serving the shipping, trucking, air freight and railroad industries in the US and Canada.
Cost: $98.00
Frequency: Weekly
Circulation: 8115
ISSN: 1529-1820
Founded in 1994
Printed in on newsprint stock

23036 American Mover

American Movers Conference
1611 Duke St
Alexandria, VA 22314-3406

703-683-7410
FAX 703-683-7527
E-Mail: info@moving.org
Home Page: www.moving.org

Linda Bauer Darr, CEO
Joseph M Harrison, President
Carol Laird, Production Manager
Norma Gyovai, Advertising Manager

This publication covers the moving and storage industry.
Cost: $60.00
24 Pages
Frequency: Monthly
Circulation: 3700
Founded in 1958

23037 American Shipper

Howard Publications
300 W Adams Street Suite 600
PO Box 4728
Jacksonville, FL 32201-4728

904-355-2601
800-874-6422
FAX 904-791-8836
Home Page: www.americanshipper.com

Nancy Barry, Production Manager
Hayes Howard, Publisher

Kerry Cowart, Circulation Manager
James Blaeser, Sales Associate

Provides those involved in domestic and global supply chain management with news and information of a strategic nature, useful in the formation of logistics polices and partnerships.
Cost: $36.00
104 Pages
Frequency: Monthly
Circulation: 13705
ISSN: 1074-8350
Founded in 1951
Printed in 4 colors on glossy stock

23038 American Trucker

Primedia
7355 Woodland Drive
Indianapolis, IN 46278-1769

317-991-1350
800-827-7468
FAX 317-299-1356
Home Page: www.trucker.com

Dallas Nauert, Production Manager
Diana Starks, Circulation Director

A trade publication featuring new and used trucks, trailors,parts and services for the heavy duty trucking industry.
Cost: $21.00
Frequency: Monthly
Circulation: 930338
Founded in 1975
Printed in 4 colors on matte stock

23039 Analysis of Class I Railroads

Association of American Railroads
50 F Street NW
Floor 3
Washington, DC 20001-1564

202-392-2334
877-999-8824
FAX 202-639-5546
E-Mail: kdonley@aar.org
Home Page: www.aar.org

Kelly Donley, Marketing
Tom White, Editor
Edward Hamberger, CEO/President
Joyce Koeneman, Manager

Offers information on the railroad travel industry.
Cost: $250.00
Founded in 1934

23040 Atlantic Northeast Rails & Ports

162 main street
Yarmouth, ME 04096

207-846-3549
FAX 603-215-4482
Home Page: www.atlanticnortheast.com

Chop Hardenbergh, CEO/President
Cost: $375.00
Frequency: Monthly
Circulation: 300
Founded in 1994

23041 Better Roads

WMO DannHausen Corporation
PO Box 558
Park Ridge, IL 60068

847-696-2391
FAX 847-696-3445
E-Mail: wod@dannhausen.com

Wm O Dannhausen, Publisher

Market to federal agencies, bureaus, government departments, states, counties township road and city public works.
Cost: $26.96
Frequency: Monthly
Circulation: 38406
Founded in 1769

23042 Brotherhood of Locomotive Engineers

Brotherhood of Locomotive Engineers
1370 Ontario St
Cleveland, OH 44113-1701

216-241-2630
FAX 216-241-6516
E-Mail: policy@ble.org
Home Page: www.ble.org

Ed Rodzwicz, CEO
John Bentley, Editor

23043 Bus Conversions Magazine

MAK Publishing
7246 Garden Grove Boulevard
Westminster, CA 92683

714-799-0062
FAX 714-799-0042
E-Mail: editor@busconversions.com
Home Page: www.busconversions.com

Michael A Kadletz, Publisher
Rikki Gee, Publication Manager

how-to, full color, monthly magazine that includes photos, floor plans, helpful hints and guides for buying, selling, selecting, and converting a bus to an RV or executive entertainer's coach. Features pages of classified ads and valuable info on maintaining, operating and updating your coach.
Cost: $38.00
72 Pages
Circulation: 8000
ISSN: 1070-6526
Founded in 1992
Printed in 4 colors on glossy stock

23044 Bus Ride

Friendship Publications
4742 N 24th St
Suite 340
Phoenix, AZ 85016-4884

602-265-7600
800-541-2670
FAX 602-277-7588
E-Mail: steve@busride.com
Home Page: www.busride.com

Steve Kane, Publisher/Editor-in-Chief
Wayne Bryan, Editor
Donna Arnseth, Circulation Administrator
Maria Jolly, Assistant Editor
Valerie Valtierra, Production Director

Bus industry trade journal with articles about bus companies, training agencies and manufacturers and suppliers to the bus industry.
Cost: $39.00
120 Pages
Frequency: Monthly
Circulation: 16000
Founded in 1965
Printed in 4 colors on glossy stock

23045 Chief Logistics Officer

Penton Media
1166 Avenue of the Americas/10th
Suite 316
Cleveland, NY 10036

212-204-4200
FAX 216-696-6662
E-Mail: information@penton.com
Home Page: www.penton.com

Jane Cooper, Marketing
Perry A Trunick, Editor
Maryann Jovorek, Production Manager
Chris Meyer, Director

Magazine for supply chain leaders, supplement to Transportation and Distribution.
Cost: $50.00
48 Pages
Frequency: Quarterly
Circulation: 12M
Founded in 1960
Printed in 4 colors on glossy stock

23046 Classic Trains

James Folcum
21027 Crossroads Circle
Waukesha, WI 53187

262-796-8776
FAX 262-796-1615
Home Page: www.classictrain.com

Rob McGornigal, Editor
Mike Yuhaf, Advertising Manager

Publication features stories on antique and old trains.

23047 Commercial Carrier Journal

Chilton Company
3200 Rice Mine Road NE
Tuscaloosa, AL 35406

800-633-5953
FAX 610-964-4647
E-Mail: prichards@randallpub.com
Home Page: www.ccjmagazine.com

Chip Magner, Publisher
F Michael Reilly, CEO
Catherine J Randall, Chairman
Avery Vise, Editorial Director
Paul Richards, Editor

For fleet management.
Frequency: Monthly
Circulation: 101176
Founded in 1934

23048 Contracting for Transportation & Logistics Services

120 Main Street
Huntington, NY 11743-6906

631-270-0100
FAX 516-549-8962
E-Mail: tcpc@transportlaw.com
Home Page: www.transportlaw.com

William J Augello, Executive Director

Published by the Transportation Consumer Protection Council.
Cost: $48.00
Founded in 2001

23049 Corporate Procedures for Shipping & Receiving

120 Main Street
Huntington, NY 11743-6906

631-270-0100
FAX 516-549-8962
E-Mail: tcpc@transportlaw.com
Home Page: www.transportlaw.com

William J Augello, Executive Director

Published by the Transportation Consumer Protection Council.
Cost: $95.00
Founded in 1998

23050 Defense Transportation Journal

National Defense Transportation Association
50 S Pickett Street
Suite 220
Alexandria, VA 22304-7206

703-751-5011
FAX 703-823-8761
E-Mail: info@ndtahq.com
Home Page: www.ndtahq.com

LTG Kenneth Wykle, President
Karen Schmitt, Managing Editor

The official publication of the National Defense Transportation Association and the only publication for the government and military transportation industry.
Cost: $35.00
Frequency: Bi-Monthly
Circulation: 8500

23051 Destinations
American Bus Association
700 13th St NW
Suite 575
Washington, DC 20005-5923

202-842-1645
800-283-2877
FAX 202-842-0850
E-Mail: abainfo@buses.org
Home Page: www.buses.org

Peter J Pantuso, CEO
Eron Shosteck, Marketing

Motorcoach travel across North America and
Association news.
80 Pages
Frequency: Monthly
Circulation: 6000
Founded in 1926
Printed in 4 colors on glossy stock

23052 Digest
American Bus Association
700 13th St NW
Suite 575
Washington, DC 20005-5923

202-842-1645
800-283-2877
FAX 202-842-0850
E-Mail: abainfo@buses.org
Home Page: www.buses.org

Peter J Pantuso, CEO
Judi Bredemeier, Editor
Chrystal Farmer, Marketing Manager
Michael Hayes, Publisher

Legislation news.
Cost: $150.00
Circulation: 3200
Founded in 1996
Printed in 2 colors on matte stock

23053 Direction
American Moving and Storage Association
1611 Duke St
Alexandria, VA 22314-3406

703-683-7410
FAX 703-683-7527
Home Page: www.moving.org

Matthew Hicks, Advertising
John Parkinson, Editorial
Allison Bresky, Production

Provides news and in-depth feature articles to
provide members with vital information to help
operate their companies more profitably.
Cost: $35.00
Frequency: Bi-Monthly
Circulation: 4000

23054 Fleet Equipment Magazine
Maple Publishing Company
3550 Embassy Parkway
Akron, OH 44333-8318

330-670-1234
FAX 330-670-0874
Home Page: www.truklink.com

Tom Gelinas, Editor
Bill Babcox, President
Robert Dorn, Publisher
Kelly McAleese, Ad Services Manager
Lindsey Fritz, Circulation Manager

Edited for fleet equipment managers of truck
fleets.
Cost: $82.00
Frequency: Monthly
Circulation: 61,571
Founded in 1974

23055 Freight Claims in Plain English
120 Main Street
Huntington, NY 11743-6906

631-270-0100
FAX 516-549-8962
E-Mail: tcpc@transportlaw.com
Home Page: www.transportlaw.com

William J Augello, Executive Director

Published by the Transportation Consumer Pro-
tection Council.
Cost: $100.00
Founded in 1995

23056 Freight Claims: Filing & Recovery
120 Main Street
Huntington, NY 11743-6906

631-270-0100
FAX 516-549-8962
E-Mail: tcpc@transportlaw.com
Home Page: www.transportlaw.com

William J Augello, Executive Director

Published by the Transportation Consumer Pro-
tection Council.
Cost: $48.00
Founded in 2001

23057 Go-West Magazine
Motor Transport Management Group
3251 Beacon Road
West Sacramento, CA 95691-3475

916-373-3630
FAX 916-852-5707

Jim Beach, Editor

Complete overview of the transportation industry.
Frequency: Monthly

23058 Guide to Transportation After the Sunsetting of the ICC
120 Main Street
Huntington, NY 11743-6906

631-270-0100
FAX 516-549-8962
E-Mail: tcpc@transportlaw.com
Home Page: www.transportlaw.com

William J Augello, Executive Director

Published by the Transportation Consumer Pro-
tection Council.
Cost: $75.00
Founded in 1997

23059 Heavy Duty Trucking
Newport Communications
38 Executive Park
Suite 300
Irvine, CA 92614-6755

949-261-1636
FAX 949-261-2904
E-Mail: webmaster@truckinginfo.com
Home Page: www.truckinginfo.com

Doug Condra, President
Susan Condra, Circulation Manager
Susan Patterson, Marketing
Marty Mc Collan, Publisher

National business magazine for managers of
medium and heavy duty truck fleets, and manu-
facturers and dealers of those trucks and the
components used to build them.
Cost: $65.00
Frequency: Monthly
Circulation: 90000
Founded in 1922
Printed in 4 colors on glossy stock

23060 Hemispheres
Pace Communications

PO Box 13607
Greensboro, NC 27415-3607

336-378-6065
800-346-1336
FAX 336-275-2864
Home Page: www.pacecommunications.com

Bonnie McElveen, CEO
Leigh Klee, Chief Financial Officer
Ed Calfo, Executive Vice President

Children's magazine for US airline fliers.
Frequency: Monthly
Circulation: 60000
Founded in 1973

23061 High Performance Composites
Ray Publishing
P.O.Box 992
Morrison, CO 80465-0992

303-467-1776
FAX 303-467-1777
Home Page: www.compositeworld.com

Approach is technical, offering cutting-edge
design, engineering, prototyping, and manufacturing solutions for aerospace and other traditional and emerging structural applications
for advanced composites.

23062 ITE Journal
Institute of Transportation Engineers
1099 14th St NW
Suite 300E
Washington, DC 20005-5924

202-289-0222
FAX 202-289-7722
E-Mail: ite_staff@ite.org
Home Page: www.it.org

Thomas Brahms, CEO
Shannon Gore Peters, Editor
Christina Denekas, Circulation Manager
Richard T Romer, International President

Provides timely news and information on sub-
jects of interest to professionals responsible for
traffic engineering, transportation planning,
ITS, transit, safety, demand management, edu-
cation etc.
Cost: $100.00
300 Pages
Frequency: Monthly
Circulation: 7500
Founded in 1930

23063 Inbound Logistics Magazine
Thomas Publishing Company
5 Penn Plaza
New York, NY 10001-1810

212-950-0500
FAX 212-629-1565
E-Mail: editor@inboundlogistics.com
Home Page: www.inboundlogistics.com

Keith Biondo, Publisher
Felecia Stratton, Editor
Carolyn Smolin, Circulation Manager
Robert Malone, Executive Editor

Accepts advertising.
Frequency: Monthly
Circulation: 55050
Founded in 1981

23064 Institute of Transportation Engineering Journal
Institute of Transportation Engineering
1627 Eye St. NW
Suite 600
Washington, DC 20006

202-785-0060
FAX 202-785-0609
E-Mail: ite_staff@ite.org
Home Page: www.ite.org

Thomas Brahms, CEO
Christina Denekas, Marketing Manager

Marianne Saglam, Communications & Media Sr. Director

Dedicated to the transportation engineering field. A journal is published for members only.
Cost: $65.00
Frequency: Monthly
Circulation: 17000
Founded in 1930

23065 International Rail Journal
Simmons-Boardman Publishing Corporation
345 Hudson St
Suite 1201
New York, NY 10014-7123

212-620-7200
FAX 212-633-1165
E-Mail: db@railjournal.co.uk
Home Page: www.simmonsboardman.com

Arthur J McGinnis Jr, President

Covers the rapidly developing railway marketplace for railway and rail transit managers and engineers, suppliers and consultants worldwide.
Frequency: Monthly
Circulation: 100960
Founded in 1960

23066 Journal of the Transportation Research Forum
Transportation Research Forum
Department 2880
PO Box 6050
Fargo, ND 58108-6050

701-231-7766
FAX 701-231-1945
E-Mail: info@trforum.org
Home Page: www.trforum.org

Richard Gritta, President
Starr McMullen, VP

Contains original manuscripts which are timely in scope and germane to transportation
300 Members
Frequency: 3x/Year
Founded in 1958

23067 Lifting & Transportation International
7249 Dorset Avenue
Saint Louis, MO 63130

314-863-8979
FAX 314-863-8786
E-Mail: adwyer@douglaspublications.com

Eugene Brymer, Publisher
Andrew Dwyer, Editor

Covers trucking overdimensional loads, heavy crane, and ridging work.
Cost: $8.00

23068 Locomotive Engineers Journal
Brotherhood of Locomotive Engineers
1370 Ontario St
Standard Building
Cleveland, OH 44113-1701

216-241-2630
FAX 216-241-6516
E-Mail: execstaff@ble.org
Home Page: www.ble.org

Ed Rodzwicz, CEO
Kathleen Policy, Associate Editor
Don M Hahs, President

Designed to meet the information needs of professional engineers throughout North America, also for railroad enthusiasts.
Cost: $10.00
Frequency: Quarterly
Circulation: 54000
Founded in 1863

23069 Logistics Management & Distribution Report
Reed Business Information
225 Wyman St
Suite 3
Waltham, MA 02451-1216

781-734-8000
800-662-7776
FAX 781-734-8076
E-Mail: lm@reedbusiness.com
Home Page: www.reedbusiness.com

Mark Finklestein, President
Peter Bradley, CFO
Stuart Whayman, CFO

Logistics Management and Distribution Report is written for managers and professionals in charge of traffic, transportation, purchasing, inventory control, containerization and warehousing the functions of physical distribution and business logistics. Covers marketing and operating strategies, cost reduction opportunities and governmental regulation and law.
Frequency: Monthly
Circulation: 30,000
Founded in 1977

23070 Marine Digest & Transportation News
Marine Publishing
1710 South Norman Street
Seattle, WA 98144-1234

206-709-1840
FAX 206-324-8939
Home Page: www.marinedigest.com

Peter Hurme, Publisher/Senior Editor
Gary Greenewald, Circulation Manager
Tom Henning, Sales/Marketing Manager
M Daigle, Owner

Serves the maritime shipping community primarily in the western United States. Updates on new products, suppliers, legislation and insurance are featured.
Cost: $28.00
Frequency: Monthly
Circulation: 7200
Founded in 1922

23071 Mass Transit Magazine
Cygnus Publishing
PO Box 803
Fort Atkinson, WI 53538-0803

920-000-1111
FAX 920-563-1699
Home Page: www.cygnusb2b.com

John French, CEO
Carie Grall, Associate Publisher
Paul Bowers, Group VP
Debbie Dumke, Manager
Deb Krause, National Accounts Manager
Cost: $120.00
Frequency: Monthly
Founded in 1966

23072 Movers News
New York State Movers & Warehousemen's Association
125 Maiden Lane
11th Floor
New York, NY 10038

212-635-0510
FAX 212-635-0511
E-Mail: nymovers@msn.com
Home Page: www.movernet.com/nysmwa

David Blake, Editor
John Palisand, President

Association news.
Cost: $24.00
Frequency: BiMonthly
ISSN: 8750-1155
Founded in 1937

23073 National Bus Trader
National Bus Trader
9698 W Judson Rd
Polo, IL 61064-9015

815-946-2341
FAX 815-946-2347
Home Page: www.busmag.com

Larry Plachno, CEO

Equipment magazine for over-the-road and integral buses in the United States and Canada.
Cost: $25.00
Frequency: Monthly
Circulation: 7000
ISSN: 0194-939X
Founded in 1977
Printed in on glossy stock

23074 New Equipment Digest
Penton Media
1166 Avenue of the Americas/10th
Suite 316
New York, NY 10036

212-204-4200
FAX 216-696-6662
E-Mail: information@penton.com
Home Page: www.penton.com

Jane Cooper, Marketing
Tom Sockel, Associate Editor
Robert King, Editor
Sarah Hughes, Production Manager
Bobbie Macy, Circulation Manager

Serves the general industrial field which includes manufacturing, processing, engineering services, construction, transportation, mining, public utilities, wholesale distributors, educational services, libraries and governmental establishments.
Frequency: Monthly
Circulation: 206154
Founded in 1936

23075 P&D Magazine
Motor Transport Management Group
3251 Beacon Road
West Sacramento, CA 95691-3475

916-373-3630
FAX 916-852-5707

Robert L Titus, Publisher

Edited for the needs of pick up and delivery.
Cost: $5.00
Circulation: 33,571

23076 PC-Trans
University of Kansas
2011 Learned Hall
Lawrence, KS 66044-7526

785-864-2700
FAX 785-864-5655
E-Mail: mgivechi@ku.edu
Home Page: www.ku.edu

Lisa Harris, Editor
Mehrdad Givechi, Manager
Alice Kuo, Advertising
Pat Weaver, Director

Software reviews and miscellaneous computer information for transportation professionals.
Circulation: 13000
Founded in 1872

23077 Progressive Railroading
Trade Press Publishing Corporation
PO Box 694
Milwaukee, WI 53201-694

414-271-5011
FAX 414-228-1134
Home Page: www.facilities.com

Steve Bolte, Publisher
Pat Foran, Editor
Tim Rowe, Marketing

Wendy Melnick, Production Manager
Robert J Wisniewski, CEO

Feature includes management techniques, purchasing developments, engineering innovations and general industry news.
Cost: $55.00
Frequency: Monthly
Circulation: 25,207
Founded in 1994

23078 Protecting Shippers' Interests
120 Main Street
Huntington, NY 11743-6906

631-270-0100
FAX 516-549-8962
E-Mail: tcpc@transportlaw.com
Home Page: www.transportlaw.com

William J Augello, Executive Director

Published by the Transportation Consumer Protection Council.
Cost: $75.00
Founded in 1997

23079 RV Business
TL Enterprises
3601 Calle Tecate
Camarillo, CA 93012-5056

805-987-1800
FAX 805-389-0484
E-Mail: tlecs@magserv.com
Home Page: www.rvbusiness.com

Katherine Sharma, Editor
Denielle Sternburg, Business Manager
Sherman Goldenberg, Publisher

Reports on various aspects of the recreational vehicle industry, including forecasting trends, new technologies, marketing and business concepts.
Cost: $12.00
Frequency: Monthly

23080 Rail News Update
Association of American Railroads
50 F Street NW
Floor 3
Washington, DC 20001-1564

202-392-2334
FAX 202-639-5546

Publishes pertinent new in the railroad industry especially covering Washington news. Covers Department of Transportation and Interstate Commerce activities.
Frequency: BiWeekly

23081 Railroad Facts
Association of American Railroads
50 F Street NW
Floor 3
Washington, DC 20001-1564

202-392-2334
FAX 202-639-5546
E-Mail: pubsrvcs@aar.org
Home Page: www.aar.org

Kelly Donley, Marketing
Tom White, Editor
Edward R Hamberger, CEO/President

Offers statistical information and research reports on railroad travel.
Cost: $15.00
Frequency: Annual+
Founded in 1934

23082 Railroad Ten-Year Trends
Association of American Railroads
50 F Street NW
Floor 3
Washington, DC 20001-1564

202-392-2334
FAX 202-639-5546

E-Mail: pubsrvcs@aar.org
Home Page: www.aar.org

Offers historical facts and perspectives on America's railroad industry.
Cost: $100.00
Frequency: Annual+
Founded in 1934

23083 Railway Age
Simmons-Boardman Publishing Corporation
345 Hudson St
Suite 1201
New York, NY 10014-7123

212-620-7200
FAX 212-633-1165
E-Mail: wvantuono@sbpub.com
Home Page: www.simmonsboardman.com

Arthur J McGinnis Jr, President

Emphasis is placed on technology, operations, strategic planning, marketing and other issues such as legislative, labor and management developments.
Frequency: Monthly
Circulation: 260030
Founded in 1876

23084 Railway Track and Structures
Simmons-Boardman Publishing Corporation
345 Hudson St
Suite 1201
New York, NY 10014-7123

212-620-7200
FAX 212-633-1165
E-Mail: tjudge@sbpub-chicago.com
Home Page: www.simmonsboardman.com

Arthur J McGinnis Jr, President

A technical magazine designed to meet the information needs of the roadway and other civil engineering related departments of North American rail freight and passenger operators.
Frequency: Monthly
Circulation: 8541

23085 Refrigerated Transporter
Penton Media
1166 Avenue of the Americas/10th
Suite 316
New York, NY 10036

212-204-4200
800-441-0294
FAX 913-514-6895
Home Page: www.penton.com

Eric Jacobson, Senior VP

23086 School Bus Fleet
Bobit Publishing Company
3520 Challenger St
Torrance, CA 90503-1640

310-533-2400
FAX 310-533-2500
Home Page: www.bobit.com

Edward J Bobit, CEO
Cliff Henke, Editor

A magazine that serves the field of pupil transportation, to public and private schools and to independent contract operators transporting students.
Cost: $42.00
Frequency: Monthly
Circulation: 24000
Founded in 1961

23087 Shippers' Domestic Truck Bill of Lading & Common Carrier Rate Agreement Kit
Transportation & Logistics Council
120 Main Street
Huntington, NY 11743

631-549-8988
FAX 631-549-8962

E-Mail: tlc@transportlaw.org
Home Page: www.tlccouncil.org

Diane Smid, Membership Secretary
Judy Selvaggio, Administrative Secretary
George Pezold, Executive Director

Published by the Transportation Consumer Protection Council.
Cost: $50.00
Frequency: Monthly
Founded in 1974

23088 Signalman's Journal
Brotherhood of Railroad Signalmen
601 W Golf Road
Box U
Mount Prospect, IL 60056-4276

847-439-3732
FAX 847-439-3743
E-Mail: signalman@brs.org
Home Page: www.brs.org

W Dan Pickett, President
Walter A Barrows, Treasurer

Information concerning railroad signaling devices, equipment and apparatus, also includes current events and items pertaining to railroad signalmen.
40 Pages
Frequency: Quarterly
Circulation: 10700
ISSN: 0037-5020
Founded in 1901
Printed in 4 colors on glossy stock

23089 Southern Motor Cargo
477 S Shady Grove Road
Memphis, TN 38120-2512

901-346-5943
FAX 901-276-5400

Wallace Witmer Jr, Editor

Offers information on shipping.
Cost: $30.00
66 Pages
Frequency: Monthly
Founded in 1945

23090 Speedlines
High Speed Grand Transportation Association
1010 Massachusetts Avenue NW, #110
Washington, DC 20001-5402

202-789-8107
FAX 212-789-8109
Home Page: www.hsgt.org

Mark Dysart, Editor

Exclusively devoted to the High Speed Ground Transportation Association covering broad policy debates, state activity reports, federal developments and technological papers.
Frequency: Quarterly
Circulation: 3,200

23091 Structural Mover
International Association of Structural Movers
PO Box 2637
Lexington, SC 29071-2637

803-951-9304
FAX 803-951-9314
E-Mail: gbrymer@alltel.net
Home Page: www.iasm.org

N Eugene Brymer, Staff Executive

A magazine written specifically for members of the International Association of Structural Movers. Subcription to quarterly magazine included in price of membership to IASM.
Frequency: Quarterly
Circulation: 500

23092 Teamster Magazine
International Brotherhood of Teamsters

25 Louisiana Ave NW
Washington, DC 20001-2130

202-624-6800
FAX 202-624-6918
E-Mail: communications@teamster.org
Home Page: www.teamster.org

James P Hoffa Jr, President
Per Bernstein, Editor-in-Chief

Affiliated with the AFL-CIO. Magazine is published for members only of 30 pages.
Cost: $12.00
Circulation: 1.4 mill
Founded in 1903

23093 Traffic Management
Reed Business Information
275 Washington St
Newton, MA 02458-1611

617-964-3030
FAX 617-630-3730
E-Mail: webmaster@reedbusiness.com
Home Page: www.designnews.com

Mitch MacDonald, Editor
Ron Bondlow, Publisher

Accepts advertising.
100 Pages
Frequency: Monthly
Circulation: 73000
Founded in 1982

23094 Traffic World
Journal of Commerce
33 Washington Street
13th Floor
Newark, NJ 07102

973-848-7000
800-255-1341
FAX 973-848-7068
Home Page: www.trafficworld.com

William B Cassidy, Managing Editor

Discusses all facets of the transportation industry. Also online at www.joc.com.
Cost: $174.00
Frequency: Weekly
Founded in 1907

23095 Trailer/Body Builders
Tunnell Publications
PO Box 66010
Houston, TX 77266

713-523-8124
800-880-0368
FAX 713-523-8384
Home Page:
advertisers.trailer-bodybuilders.com

Paul Schenck, Editor
Ray Anderson, Publisher
Bruce Sauer, Editorial Director
Wanda Tunnell, Advertising Director
Diana Smith, Advertising Sales

Serves the truck trailer and truck body manufacturing industry. Accepts advertising.
Cost: $38.00
Frequency: Monthly

23096 Transport Fleet News
Transport Publishing
1962 N Bissell Street
#3
Chicago, IL 60614-5015

773-058-8540

Lillana Rogala, Publisher

Industry news and product for fleet supervisors.
Circulation: 10,500

23097 Transportation & Distribution
Penton Media

1166 Avenue of the Americas/10th
Suite 316
New York, NY 10036

212-204-4200
FAX 216-696-6662
E-Mail: editor@logisticstoday.com
Home Page: www.penton.com

Jane Cooper, Marketing
Antoinette Sanchez-Perkins, Circulation Manager
Newt Barret, Publisher
Dave Blanchard, Editor
David Nussbaum, CEO

Serves the information needs of logistics professionals, identifying trends and providing expert views on strategic, management and operational subjects affecting logistics. Accepts advertising.
Cost: $60.00
78 Pages
Frequency: Monthly
Circulation: 85000
Founded in 1960
Printed in 4 colors on glossy stock

23098 Transportation Leader
Taxicab, Limousine & Paratransit Association
3200 Tower Oaks Blvd
Suite 220
Rockville, MD 20852

301-984-5700
FAX 301-984-5703
E-Mail: info@tlpa.org
Home Page: www.tlpa.org

Alfred LaGasse, CEO
Victor Dizengoff, President

Leading resource for news and information on issues, trends, and people in the private, for-hire passenger transportation industry. Provides readers with an array of features, articles, and columns that include information on managing a transportation company, industry trends, driver's tips, an industry calendar of events, coverage of TLPA events, and advertisements from the industry's leading suppliers.
Cost: $4.00
48 Pages
Frequency: Quarterly
Circulation: 6000
Founded in 1920
Mailing list available for rent: 6,000 names at $100 per M
Printed in 4 colors on glossy stock

23099 Trucker's Connection
Megan Cullingford
5960 Crooked Creek Road
Suite 15
Norcross, GA 30092

770-416-0927
FAX 770-416-1734
Home Page: www.truckersconnection.com

Dan Barnhill, Editor
Reid Ramsay, Production Manager
Megan Cullingford, General Manager
David Guthrie, Advertising Sales

Published for the use of long haul, over-the-road truck drivers, owner operators, small trucking company fleet owners, safety and recruiting of personnel for trucking companies in the US and Canada.
Frequency: Monthly
Circulation: 16,5,000
Founded in 1986
Printed in 4 colors on glossy stock

Trade Shows

23100 AAR Annual Convention and Exhibit
Railway Systems Suppliers
9306 New Lagrange Road
Suite 100
Louisville, KY 40242

502-327-7774
FAX 502-327-0541
E-Mail: rssi@rssi.org
Home Page: www.rssi.org

Donald Remaley, Executive Director
Franklin Brown, President

Railroad signal and communication equipment displays, annual meeting & banquet.
Frequency: Annual
Founded in 1960

23101 AREMA Annual Conference & Exposition
American Railway Engineering & Maintenance-of-Way
10003 Derekwood Ln
Suite 210
Lanham, MD 20706-4362

301-459-3200
FAX 301-459-8077
E-Mail: dknight@arema.org
Home Page: www.arema.org/meetings

Desiree Knight, Director, Conferences & Seminars

Approximately 198 exhibitors from all segments of the railway engineering and maintenance industry, in addition to the conference talks, seminars, and events. Advanced registration for non-members starts at $760.
1600 Attendees
Frequency: Annual

23102 ARTBA National Convention
American Road and Transportation Builders Assn
1219 28th St NW
Washington, DC 20007-3389

202-289-4434
FAX 202-289-4435
E-Mail: general@artba.org
Home Page: www.artba.org

Pete Ruane, President
Matt Jeanneret, Sr. VP, Communications/Marketing
Jaime Mahoney, Publications Manager
Liz Cavallaro, Sales Manager
Tom Hill, Treasurer
Frequency: Annual/Fall

23103 American Bus Marketplace
1015 15th Street NW
Washington, DC 20005-2605

202-842-9100
800-283-2877
FAX 202-842-0850

Katie Robbins

Sales and marketing event for the North American group travel industry. 350 booths.
2M Attendees
Frequency: December

23104 American Car Rental Association Convention
11250 Roger Bacon Drive
#8
Reston, VA 20190

703-787-7718
FAX 703-435-4390
Home Page: www.acra.org
Gwendolyn Hogan

One hundred exhibits of cars, vans, buses, computers, equipment and services for car rental company owners and officers. Conference, reception and dinner.
600 Attendees
Frequency: Annual
Founded in 1978

23105 American Public Transportation Association Expo
1666 K Street NW
Suite 1100
Washington, DC 20006

202-496-4800
FAX 202-496-4324
E-Mail: meetings2@apta.com
Home Page: www.apta.com

William W Millar, President
Petra Mollet, VP
Rosemary Sherid, Marketing

Seminar, workshop, conference, luncheon, banquet, tours and 800 exhibits for the planning designing and finance and operation of public transportation.
15000 Attendees
Frequency: October 2008/2011
Founded in 1882

23106 American Railroads Association Communication and Signal Division
50 F Street NW
Washington, DC 20001-1530

202-392-2334

William Peters, Show Manager
Joyce Koeneman, Manager

Transportation equipment and services.
1.5M Attendees

23107 Association for Commuter Transportation Convention
808 17th Street NW
Suite 200
Washington, DC 20006-3910

202-393-3497
Home Page: tmi.cob.fsu.edu/act

Elizabeth Stutts, President
Kenneth M Sufka, Executive Director
Shamus Misek, VP
Kim Tabah, Director of Development
Barbara Ash, Communications Manager

Thirty booths.
300 Attendees
Frequency: September

23108 Association of Railway Museums Convention
Association of Railway Museums
PO Box 370
Tujunga, CA 91043-0370

818-951-9151
FAX 818-951-9151

Paul Hammond, President ARM

Annual show and exhibits for the preservation of railway equipment, artifacts and history. Seminar, tours, banquet and dinner.
125 Attendees
Frequency: October
Founded in 1961

23109 Biodiesel Investor Conference
Platts
24 Hartwell Avenue
Lexington, MA 02421

781-860-6100
866-355-2930
E-Mail: registration@platts.com
Home Page: www.platts.com

Frequency: June Houston

23110 Education Conference & Expo
American Moving and Storage Association
1611 Duke St
Alexandria, VA 22314-3406

703-683-7410
FAX 703-683-7527
Home Page: www.moving.org

Linda Bauer Darr, CEO
Sandy Lynch, SVP

The largest gathering of moving and storage industry professionals in the country. With more than 30 education sessions and over 10 hours of dedicated network time, the conference & expo offers countless opportunities to further your career while making new business contacts.
Frequency: Annual/March

23111 Fleet Management Institute (NAFA) Convention
100 Wood Avenue S
Suite 310
Iselin, NJ 08830

732-494-8100
FAX 732-494-6789
E-Mail: info@nafa.org
Home Page: www.nafa.org

Patricia Murtaugh, Assistant Executive Director
Joanne Marsh, Manager

Fleet management education and automobile parts and services, as well as maintenance for business and public service vehicles. 250 booths
2M Attendees
Frequency: April/May

23112 Institute of Transportation Engineers Annual Meeting
Institute of Transportation Engineers
525 School Street SW
Suite 410
Washington, DC 20024-2729

202-548-8050
FAX 202-863-5486
Home Page: www.ite.org

Marianne Wool, Manager
Shannon Gore Peters, Editor

Annual meeting of 100 exhibitors of transportation equipment, supplies and services.
2,000 Attendees
Frequency: Las Vegas

23113 International Association of Structural Movers Annual Convention
PO Box 600
Oakton, VA 22124

703-648-3225
FAX 503-543-6697
Home Page: www.iasm.org

Containing 20 booths and 15 exhibits.

23114 International Public Transit Expo
Pemco/Professional Expo Management Company

191 S Gary Avenue
Carol Stream, IL 60188-2092

630-690-5600
FAX 203-840-9662

Barbara Silverman, VP

The world's largest transit industry event offering a chance for top transit officials to meet with manufacturers from around the world.
16M Attendees
Frequency: October

23115 International Truck and Bus Expo
Society of Automotive Engineers
400 Commonwealth Drive
Warrendale, PA 15096-0001

724-772-8548
FAX 724-776-0790
Home Page: www.sae.org

Andrew Brown, Treasurer

23116 Link
R&D Associates
16607 Blanco Road
Suite 305
San Antonio, TX 78232-1940

210-682-4302
FAX 830-493-8036

David Dee, Editor

Articles of interest to the food, food packaging, food processing and foodservice industry. 50 booths.
300 Attendees
Frequency: Spring/Fall

23117 NDTA Forum & Expo
National Defense Transportation Association
50 S Pickett Street
Suite 220
Alexandria, VA 22304-7206

703-751-5011
FAX 703-823-8761
E-Mail: info@ndtahq.com
Home Page: www.ndtahq.com

LTG Kenneth Wykle, President
COL Dennis Edwards, VP Marketing

A key element in the Association's fulfillment of its educational and professional development missions and it also offers outstanding opportunities for networking and mentoring.
1200 Attendees
Frequency: Annual/September

23118 NPA
National Parking Association
1112 16th Street NW
Suite 840
Washington, DC 20036

202-296-4336
800-647-7275
FAX 202-296-3102
E-Mail: info@npapark.org
Home Page: www.npapark.org

Herb Anderson, VP Advertising & Exposition
Frequency: Oct Washington

23119 National Industrial Transportation League Trade Show
1700 N Moore St
Suite 1900
Arlington, VA 22209-1931

703-524-5011
FAX 703-524-5017
E-Mail: info@nitl.org
Home Page: www.nitl.org

Arthur E. Cole, President
Michael J Barr, First Vice Chairman
Peter Gatti, Executive VP

Annual show of 250 exhibitors of computer services software and innovations for transportation operations.
600 Members
Founded in 1907

23120 National Private Truck Council Management/ Education Conference
National Private Truck Council
66 Canal Center Plaza
Alexandria, VA 22314-1591

703-683-1300
FAX 703-683-1217

Gary Petty, CEO
Annual conference and exhibits of equipment, supplies and services for processors, shippers, distributors and retailers who operate their own truck fleets to advance their primary nontransportation business enterprises.

23121 North American Truck Show
North American Expositions Company
33 Rutherford Avenue
Boston, MA 02129-3795

617-242-6092
800-225-1577
FAX 617-242-1817
Home Page: www.truckingexpo.com

Gregory Soughlin, Show Manager
Six hundred booths.
25M Attendees
Frequency: May

23122 TLPA Annual Convention & Trade Show
Taxicab, Limousine & Paratransit Association
3200 Tower Oaks Boulevard
Suite 220
Rockville, MD 20852

301-984-5700
FAX 301-984-5703
E-Mail: info@tlpa.com
Home Page: www.tlpa.org

Alfred La Gasse III, Executive VP
Victor Dizengoff, President
Shares information vital to owners or taxicab, limousine, airport shuttle, paratransit and nonemergency medical transportation fleets. 100 suppliers and exhibitors of the newest products available to the industry.
1000 Attendees
Frequency: Annual

23123 TransComp Exhibition
National Industrial Transportation League
1700 N Moore Street
Suite 1900
Arlington, VA 22209-1931

703-524-5011
FAX 703-524-5017
E-Mail: info@nitl.org
Home Page: www.nitl.org

Ellie Gilanshah, VP Finance and Membership
3000 Attendees
Frequency: November
Founded in 1907

23124 Transportation Intermediaries Annual Convention & Trade Show
Transportation Intermediaries Association
3601 Eisenhower Avenue
Suite 110
Alexandria, VA 22304

703-299-5700
FAX 703-836-0123
E-Mail: info@tianet.org
Home Page: www.tianet.org

Robert Voltmann, President/CEO
Larry Fisher, Contact

Education and policy organization for North American transportation intermediaries. TIA is the only national association representing the interests of all third party transportation service providers. The members of TIA include logistics management firms, property brokers, perishable commodities brokers, freight forwarders, intermodal marketers, ocean and air forwarders, and NVOCC's.
700 Attendees
Founded in 1978

23125 Transportation Research Forum Annual Meeting
Transportation Research Forum
Department 2880
PO Box 6050
Fargo, ND 58108-6050

701-231-7766
FAX 701-231-1945
E-Mail: info@trforum.org
Home Page: www.trforum.org

Richard Gritta, President
Starr McMullen, VP
300 Members
Founded in 1958

23126 Women's Transportation Seminar
Women's Transportation Seminar
1 Walnut Street
Boston, MA 02108-3616

617-367-3273
FAX 617-227-6783

Annual seminar and exhibits of transportation equipment, supplies and services.

Directories & Databases

23127 AAA Bridge and Ferry Directory
American Automobile Association
1000 AAA Drive
Heathrow, FL 32746-5062

407-444-7966

Melanie Fuller, Highway Infoformation Coordinator
Offers information on over 500 toll facilities in the US, Canada and Mexico that enable automobiles and passengers to complete toll non-highway portions of their journey.
Cost: $12.50
103 Pages
Frequency: Annual

23128 AREMA Membership Directory & REMSA Buyer's Guide
American Railway Engineering & Maintenance-of-Way
10003 Derekwood Ln
Suite 210
Lanham, MD 20706-4362

301-459-3200
FAX 301-459-8077
E-Mail: jclement@arema.org
Home Page: www.arema.org/meetings

Janice Clements, Director, Membership & IS
A full listing of AREMA members and REMSA companies. Free for members; $50 for additional member copy; $200 for non-members
Cost: $200.00
400 Pages

23129 ARTBA Transportation Officials & Engineers Directory
American Road and Transportation Builders Assn

1219 28th St NW
Washington, DC 20007-3389

202-289-4434
FAX 202-289-4435
E-Mail: general@artba.org
Home Page: www.artba.org

Pete Ruane, President
Matt Jeanneret, Sr. VP, Communications/Marketing
Jaime Mahoney, Publications Manager
Liz Cavallaro, Sales Manager
Tom Hill, Treasurer
An annual survey of local, state and federal transportation agencies offered as a pocket-sized publication and as a mergeable Excel spreadsheet. The TO&E Directory includes key information about more than 6,000 state and local transportation departments and authorities, including URLs and e-mail addresses. From $195 for members to get the pocket edition to $475 for non-members to get the Excel version.
6300 Members
Frequency: Annual
Founded in 1902

23130 Affiliated Warehouse Companies Directory
Affiliated Warehouse Companies, Inc
PO Box 295
Hazlet, NJ 07730-0295

732-739-2323
FAX 732-739-4154
E-Mail: sales@awco.com
Home Page: www.awco.com

Jim McBride, President
Patrick McBride, Vice President
Third party logistics and public warehousing, marketing and sales company. Directory is free.
Founded in 1953
Mailing list available for rent: 8,500 names at $100 per M
Printed in 4 colors

23131 Air CargoWorld & Traffic World
Knight-Ridder Financial
75 Wall Street
Floor 23
New York, NY 10005-2833

212-429-2307
FAX 212-372-7148

Offers valuable information on cash, futures and options markets.

23132 Airline, Ship & Catering: Onboard Service Buyer's Guide & Directory
International Publishing Company of America
664 La Villa Dr
Miami Springs, FL 33166-6030

305-887-1700
FAX 305-885-1923

Alexander Morton, Owner
Offers information on over 6,000 airlines, railroads, ship lines and termianl restaurants.
Cost: $125.00
Frequency: Annual
Circulation: 6,000

23133 American Bus Association's Motorcoach Marketer
American Bus Association
700 13th St NW
Suite 575
Washington, DC 20005-5923

202-842-1645
FAX 202-842-0850

E-Mail: abainfo@buses.org
Home Page: www.buses.org

Peter J Pantuso, CEO
Eron Shosteck, Marketing

This directory is a comprehensive guide of the bus and travel industry offering information on hotels and sightseeing services, attractions, museums, restaurants and more.
500 Pages
Frequency: Annual
Founded in 1926

23134 American Public Transit Association Membership Directory

American Public Transit Association
1666 K St NW
Suite 1100
Washington, DC 20006-1215

202-496-4800
FAX 202-496-4324
E-Mail: hbrett@apta.com
Home Page: www.apta.com

Karol J Popkin, CEO
Petra Mollet, VP
Rosemary Sherid, Marketing

A who's who directory of services and supplies within the public transportation industry.
Founded in 1882

23135 American Shortline Railway Guide

Kalmbach Publishing Company
Po Box 1612
Waukesha, WI 53187-1612

262-796-8776
FAX 262-796-1615
Home Page: www.trains.com

Gerald Boettcher, President

Directory of services and supplies to the industry.
Cost: $18.95
320 Pages

23136 Bus Garage Index

Friendship Publications
PO Box 1472
Spokane, WA 99210-1472

800-541-2670
FAX 509-325-0405

Bruce Sankey, President
Leslie Maris, VP Marketing
Linda Metler, Production Manager

Offers information on over 900 garages and service centers in the United States and Canada offering services to buses on charter service and tours.
Cost: $28.00
140 Pages
Circulation: 3,000
Mailing list available for rent: 14M names
Printed in 4 colors on glossy stock

23137 Bus Industry Directory

Friendship Publications
PO Box 1472
Spokane, WA 99210-1472

800-541-2670
FAX 509-325-0405

Bruce Sankey, President/Publisher
Leslie Maris, VP Marketing

A comprehensive list of over 4,500 intercity and charter bus companies and local transit authorities in the United States and Canada.
Cost: $78.00
500 Pages
Frequency: Annual
Mailing list available for rent: 14M names
Printed in 4 colors on glossy stock

23138 Carrier Routing Director

Transportation Technical Services

500 Lafayette Boulevard
Fredericksburg, VA 22401-6070

540-899-9872
800-666-4887
FAX 888-665-9887
Home Page: www.ttstrucks.com

Thomas R Fugee, Executive VP

Two thousand six hundred top common and contract carriers, toll-free faxes, states served + Canadian provinces and Mexico, equipment types, commodities.
Cost: $145.00
Frequency: Annual
Founded in 1992

23139 DRI Transportation Detail

DRI/McGraw-Hill
24 Hartwell Ave
Lexington, MA 02421-3103

781-860-6060
FAX 781-860-6002
E-Mail: support@construction.com
Home Page: www.construction.com

Walt Arvin, President

This time series contains annual and quarterly data describing aspects of the transportation industry.

23140 Defense Transportation Journal NDTA Almanac

National Defense Transportation Association
50 S Pickett Street
Suite 220
Alexandria, VA 22304-7206

703-751-5011
FAX 703-823-8761
E-Mail: info@ndtahq.com
Home Page: www.ndtahq.com
Social Media: *Facebook, Twitter, LinkedIn, You Tube*

LTG Kenneth Wykle, President
COL Dennis Edwards, VP Marketing

Reference book of Military/Government/Transportation industry companies and executives
128 Pages

23141 Directory of Shippers

Transportation Technical Services
500 Lafayette Boulevard
Fredericksburg, VA 22401-6070

540-899-9872
800-666-4887
FAX 888-665-9887
Home Page: www.ttstrucks.com

Thomas R Fugee, Executive VP

Compilateion of 14,000 logistics executives. Key information on 13,500 companies, phone, fax-e-mail, addresses, SIC's, revenue. Great marketing sales and research tool.
Cost: $170.00
Frequency: Annual
Founded in 1992

23142 Directory of Transportation Professionals

National Assn of Regulatory Utility Commissioners
PO Box 684
Washington, DC 20044-0684

202-898-2200

Offers valuable information on over 100 regulated transportation firms and professionals.
Cost: $20.00
150 Pages
Frequency: Annual

23143 Directory of Truck Dealers

Transportation Technical Services

500 Lafayette Boulevard
Fredericksburg, VA 22401-6070

540-899-9872
800-666-4887
FAX 888-665-9887
Home Page: www.ttstrucks.com

Thomas R Fugee, Executive VP

Unique, extensive list of 2,700 of the nation's kmid-size/heavy truck dealers. Address, brands sold, serviced, keky contacts, phone and fax.
Cost: $95.00
Frequency: Annual
Founded in 1992

23144 Foreign Flag Merchant Ships Owned by US Parent Companies

US Department of Transportation
400 7th Street SW
Room 8117
Washington, DC 20590-0001

202-366-4000

Directory of services and supplies to the industry.
20 Pages
Frequency: SemiAnnual

23145 Greenwood's Guide to Great Lakes Shipping

Freshwater Press
1700 E 13th Street
Suite 3-R
Cleveland, OH 44114-3213

216-241-0373
FAX 216-781-6344
Home Page: www.lakeboats.com

Michael Dills, VP/General Manager

Offers companies that ship water-carried commodities and service firms on the Great Lakes Seaway systems. Details of vessels, dock facilities, shipyards, etc.
Cost: $71.00
650 Pages
Frequency: Annual
Circulation: 2,500
Founded in 1960
Printed in on glossy stock

23146 Grey House Transportation Security Directory

Grey House Publishing
4919 Route 22
PO Box 56
Amenia, NY 12501

518-789-8700
800-562-2139
FAX 845-373-6390
E-Mail: books@greyhouse.com
Home Page: www.greyhouse.com
Social Media: *Facebook, Twitter*

Leslie Mackenzie, Publisher
Richard Gottlieb, Editor

Provides information on everything from Regulatory Authorities to Security Equipment, this top-flight directory brings together the relevant information necessary for creating and maintaining a security plan for a wide range of transportation facilities.
Cost: $195.00
800 Pages
ISBN: 1-592370-75-6
Founded in 1981

23147 Inland River Guide

Waterways Journal
319 N 4th St
Suite 650
St Louis, MO 63102-1994

314-241-7354
FAX 314-241-4207

E-Mail: info@waterwaysjournal.net
Home Page: www.waterwaysjournal.net

H Nelson Spencer Iii, Publisher
John S Shoulberg, Editor/Associate Publisher
Ed Rahe, Advertising Sales
Alan Bates, Manager
Marie Rausch, Advertising Sales Director

The only directory published specifically for
the benefit of the companies doing business
along the inland and intracoastal waterways. It
contains vital information about companies servicing all industry segments.
Cost: $65.00
600+ Pages
Frequency: Annual
Circulation: 3,000
Founded in 1972

23148 Inland River Record

Waterways Journal
319 N 4th St
Suite 650
St Louis, MO 63102-1994

314-241-7354
FAX 314-241-4207
E-Mail: hnspencer@waterwaysjournal.net
Home Page: www.waterwaysjournal.net

H Nelson Spencer III, Publisher
John S Shoulberg, Manager
Alan Bates, Manager
Marie Rausch, Advertising Sales Director

Lists in detail more than 3,500 commercial
towboats and tugs, U.S. engineer vessels and
Coast Guard vessels navigating the Mississippi
and Ohio, their tributaries and the Gulf
Intracoastal Waterway.
Cost: $37.50
475 Pages
Frequency: Annual
Circulation: 3,000

23149 Leonard's Guide National Third Party Logistics Directory

GR Leonard & Company
49 E Huntington Dr
Arcadia, CA 91006-3210

626-574-1800
800-574-5250
E-Mail: grico@ix.netcom.com
Home Page: www.leonardsguide.com

David Ercolani, President

Approximately 2,000 transportation brokers
and third party logistics firms and brokerages
in the US and Canada.
Cost: $75.00
Frequency: Annual Spring

23150 Light List

United States Coast Guard
2100 2nd Street SW
Washington, DC 20593-0002

202-488-8157
FAX 202-366-5063

Offers information to the shipping industry in
the form of lights. This comprehensive directory offers a list of lights, fog signals,
daybeacons, radiobeacons and LORAN stations
operated or authorized by the US Coast Guard.
Various volumes are offered.
Cost: $25.00
200+ Pages
Frequency: Volumes

23151 Mass Transit: Consultants Issue

Cygnus Publishing

Po Box 803
Fort Atkinson, WI 53538-0803

920-000-1111
FAX 920-563-1699
Home Page: www.cygnusb2b.com

John French, CEO
Kathy Scott, Director of Public Relations
Paul Bonaiuto, CFO

Offers listings of over 300 urban transportation
architects, designers, engineers and other specialists serving the urban transportation
industry.
Frequency: BiMonthly

23152 Mexican Motor Carrier Directory

Transportation Technical Services
500 Lafayette Boulevard
Fredericksburg, VA 22401-6070

540-899-9872
800-666-4887
FAX 888-665-9887
Home Page: www.ttstrucks.com

Thomas R Fugee, Executive VP

Unique, extensive and key information on 500
Mexican carriers.
Cost: $145.00
Frequency: Annual

23153 NARUC Compilation of Transportation Regulatory Policy

National Assn of Regulatory Utility
Commissioners
PO Box 684
Washington, DC 20044-0684

202-898-2200
Home Page: http://www.naruc.org

Offers a list of over 100 regulatory agencies in
the United States and Canada for the transportation industry.
Cost: $33.00

23154 National Customs Brokers and Forwarders Association of America

National Customs Brokers & Forwarders
Association
1200 18th St NW
Suite 901
Washington, DC 20036-2572

202-466-0222
FAX 202-466-0226
E-Mail: staff@ncbfaa.org
Home Page: www.ncbfaa.org

Barbara Reilly, Executive VP

About 600 customs brokers, international air
cargo agents, and freight forwarders in the
United States.
Cost: $24.00
Frequency: Annual

23155 National Highway Carriers Directory

National Highway Carriers Directory
PO Box 6099
Buffalo Grove, IL 60089-6099

847-634-0606
FAX 847-634-1026
Home Page: www.national-highway.com

Pam W Ferreira, President/Editor

Offers information on over 700 motor carriers,
LTL carriers, truckload companies, warehousing companies, transportation brokers, freight
forwarders, Canadian carriers, over 250,000
points and terminals for LTL carriers, refrigerated carries, and more. Now also on CD-ROM:
$399.00 with free book.
Cost: $195.00
1,400 Pages
Frequency: Spring & Fall
Founded in 1948
Printed in 2 colors on newsprint stock

23156 National Industrial Transportation League Reference Manual

National Industrial Transportation League
1700 N Moore St
Suite 1900
Arlington, VA 22209-1931

703-524-5011
FAX 703-524-5017
E-Mail: info@nitl.org
Home Page: www.nitl.org

Bruce J Carlton, President
Frequency: SemiAnnual

23157 National Institute of Packaging, Handling and Logistic Engineers

NIPHLE
5903 Ridgeway Drive
Grand Prairie, TX 75052

817-466-7490
866-464-7453
FAX 570-523-0606
E-Mail: ninphle@dejazzd.com
Home Page: www.niphle.org

Richard D Owen, Executive Director
Founded in 1956

23158 National Motor Carrier Directory

Transportation Technical Services
500 Lafayette Boulevard
Fredericksburg, VA 22401-6070

540-899-9872
800-666-4887
FAX 888-665-9887
Home Page: www.ttstrucks.com

Thomas R Fugee, Executive VP

CEO, fleet size, toll-free/fax number, revenue,
SCAC, trailer type, TK or LTL, trucks plus
tractors owned and leased and more.
Cost: $395.00
1982 Pages
Frequency: Annual
Founded in 1992

23159 Official Railway Guide: North American Freight Service Edition

Commonwealth Business Media
50 Millstone Rd
Suite 200
East Windsor, NJ 08520-1418

609-371-7700
800-221-5488
FAX 609-371-7879
Home Page: www.cbizmedia.com

Alan Glass, CEO

Directory of services and supplies to the indus-
try.
Cost: $245.00
Frequency: BiMonthly

23160 Pacific Shipper's Transportation Services Directory

PRIMEDIA Information
10 Lake Drive
Hightstown, NJ 08520-5321

609-371-7700
800-224-5488
Home Page: www.primediainfo.com

Amy Middlebrook, Editor
John Capers III, Publisher
John Murphy, Circulation Director

Offers valuable information on coastal transportation operations and support services on
the Pacific Coast.
Cost: $202.00
730 Pages
Frequency: Annual
Printed in 4 colors on newsprint stock

23161 Private Fleet Directory
Transportation Technical Services
500 Lafayette Boulevard
Fredericksburg, VA 22401-6070

540-899-9872
800-666-4887
FAX 888-665-9887
Home Page: www.ttstrucks.com

Thomas R Fugee, Executive VP

Over 26,000 private fleets in the US that transport their own freight (Wal-Mart, Ace Hardware, Toys R Us).
Cost: $295.00
1,900 Pages
Frequency: Annual July
Founded in 1992

23162 Railway Line Clearances
Commonwealth Business Media
10 Lake Drive
Hightstown, NJ 08520-5321

609-371-7703
800-224-5488
FAX 609-371-7830
Home Page: www.cbizmedia.com

Alan Glass, Chairman/CEO
Susan Murray, Publisher
Kathy Keeney, Associate Publisher

This directory offers weight limitations, heights and widths of clearances for railroads in North America and Canada, parts of the United States, clearance contacts and AAR rules and regulation.
Cost: $200.00
Frequency: Annual
Printed in 2 colors on matte stock

23163 Refrigerated Transporter: Warehouse Directory Issue
Tunnell Publications
PO Box 66010
Houston, TX 77266

713-523-8124
FAX 713-523-8384
Home Page: http://www.refrigeratedtrans.com

Gary Macklin, Editor

Listing of approximately 265 refrigerated warehouses in the US and Canada.

23164 Survey of State Travel Offices
United States Travel Data Center
1100 New York Avenue NW
Washington, DC 20005-3934

202-326-7300
FAX 202-408-1255

Patrick Thompson, Editor

State and territorial government agencies responsible for travel and travel promotion in their states.
Cost: $475.00
Frequency: Annual March

23165 Transportation Management Association Directory
Association for Commuter Transportation
1518 K St NW
Suite 503
Washington, DC 20005-1203

202-737-2926
FAX 202-347-8847
E-Mail: info@nadca.com
Home Page: www.nadca.com

Kenneth Sufka, Executive Vice President

Over 50 established transportation management associations in the United States are the focus of this comprehensive directory.
123 Pages
Circulation: 400

23166 Transportation Research Board Directory
Transportation Research Board
2101 Constitution Ave Nw
Washington, DC 20418-0007

202-334-2933
FAX 202-334-2527
E-Mail: TABSales@nas.edu
Home Page: www.nationalacademies.org/trb

Robert Skinner, CEO

Directory lists organizations and committee members with an interest in transportation. Individual affiliate information is no longer available in print or in electronic format.
Frequency: Annual

23167 USTA Industry Directory
United States Telecom Association
1401 H St NW
Suite 600
Washington, DC 20005-2110

202-326-7300
FAX 202-326-7333
Home Page: www.usta.org

Walter McKormick, President
Joan Johnson, Secretary

Comprehensive directory of over 1200 local exchange carriers and other telecom companies make up this directory. Includes a detailed index for easy cross-referencing by company name, contacts, titles, geographical region, services provided, e-mail and more. USTA's directory is your gateway to the telecom industry.
Cost: $699.00
Frequency: Annual

23168 WESTLAW Transportation Library
West Publishing Company
610 Opperman Drive
Eagan, MN 55123-1340

651-687-7327
Home Page: www.westgroup.com

This database offers information on US transportation laws.
Frequency: Full-text

Industry Web Sites

23169 http://gold.greyhouse.com
G.O.L.D Grey House OnLine Databases

Grey House Publishing's online database platform, GOLD, offers Quick Search, Keyword Search and Expert Search for most business sectors including transportation markets. The GOLD platform makes finding the information you need quick and easy - whether you're a novice searcher or an experienced database user. All of Grey House's directory products are available for subscription on the GOLD platform.

23170 www.apta.com
American Public Transit Association

Maintains biographical archives and operates a placement service.

23171 www.ar.org
Association of American Railroads

Seeks to advance knowledge of scientific and economic location, construction, maintenance and operation of railroad.

23172 www.buses.org
American Bus Association

Trade association for the North American bus industry.

23173 www.expedia.com
Expedia.com

Internet travel service offers access to airlines, hotels, car rentals, vacation packages, cruises and corporate travel.

23174 www.expresscarriers.com
Interstate Trucking Association

Organization of newly enacted state legislation regulations having direct impact on vehicle operations, fuel taxes, registration size and weight.

23175 www.gams.org
Association of Air Medical Services

An association of health care entities operating helicopter transport services.

23176 www.greyhouse.com
Grey House Publishing

Authoritative reference directories for most business markets including transportation markets. Users can search the online databases with varied search criteria allowing for custom searches by product category, geographic area, sales volume, keyword, subject and more. Full Grey House catalog and online ordering also available.

23177 www.hotwire.com
Hotwire.com

Internet travel service offering discounts on flights, hotels, car rentals, packages and cruises.

23178 www.iasm.org
International Association of Structural Movers

Members are movers of heavy structural products, trusses, houses and machinery and masonry structures.

23179 www.iccl.org
Internhational Council of Cruise Lines

For North American oceangoing, overnight major cruise line companies.

23180 www.intermodal.org
Intermodal Association of North America

Members are motor, rail and water transportation companies. Promotes the benefits and growth of intermodal freight transportation.

23181 www.ista.org
International Safe Transit Association

Members are shippers, carriers, manufacturers, packagers, package designers and testing laboratories, included in transport packaging.

23182 www.ite.org
Institute for Transportation Engineering

Dedicated to the transportation engineering field.

23183 www.moving.org
American Moving and Storage Association

Represents members including interstate moving and storage companies, local movers, international movers plus industry suppliers and state association members. AMSA's chief goals include strong support for effective government regulations and policies that protect consumers while allowing members to provide quality service at compensatory prices, and ensuring that consumers understand the value of professional moving and storage services.

23184 www.narprail.org
National Association of Railroad Passengers

Seeks to increase public awareness of rail passenger service and its benefits. Works for a national transportation policy.

23185 www.nbta.org
National Business Travel Association
Offers over 1,300 corporate travel managers and allied members in the United States and Canada.

23186 www.ndtahq.com
National Defense Transportation Association
Intended as a liasion between government, military and private transportation officials.

23187 www.nitl.org
National Industrial Transportation League
Annual show of 250 exhibitors of computer services software and innovations for transportation operations.

23188 www.npapark.org
National Parking Association
For operators of public and private parking facilities, including government, hospitals, colleges, universities and others.

23189 www.raa.org
Regional Airline Association
Membership consists of more than 70 airlines, plus 350 Associate members provide goods and services.

23190 www.railway.museums.org
Association of Railway Museums
The association of railway museums is for the preservation of railway equipment, artifacts and history.

23191 www.rampages.onramp.net/~nars/
National Association of Rail Shippers
Strives to provide a sound transporation system. Bestows annual Award of Excellence.

23192 www.rpi.org
Railway Progress Institute
The railway equipment and supply industry.

23193 www.rssi.org
Railway Systems Suppliers
A trade association serving the communication and signal segment of the rail transportation industry. Manages an annual trade show.

23194 www.scooltrans.com
National School Transportation Association
Strives to provide safe transportation, foster safety, and an atmosphere conducive to private enterprise.

23195 www.teamster.org
International Brotherhood of Teamsters
Affiliated with the AFL-CIO.

23196 www.terry.org
International Marine Transit Association
Membership includes ferry operators, naval architects, manufacturers, suppliers, and others in the terry industry around the world.

23197 www.tianet.org
Transportation Intermediaries Association
For North American transportation intermediaries including logistics management firms, property brokers, perishable commodities brokers, freight forwarders, intermodal marketers, ocean and air forwarders.

23198 www.travel.yahoo.com
Yahoo.com
Internet travel service providing access to flights, hotels, car rentals, vacation packages and cruises.

23199 www.travelocity.com
Sabre Holdings
Travel service offering consumers access to hundreds of airlines and thousands of hotels, as well as cruise, last-minute and vacation packages and best-in-class car rental companies.

23200 www.tww.org
Transport Workers Union of America
Chartered by the Congress of Industrial Organizations.

23201 www.waterways.org
National Waterways Conference
For shippers, barge lines and local port authorities working to promote a better understanding of the public value of the American waterways system.

23202 www.woda.org
World Organization of Dredging Associations
Develops professionalism in individuals involved in the dredging industry.

Associations

23203 American Bus Association
111 K Street NE
9th Floor
Washington, DC 20002

202-877-2208
800-283-2877
FAX 202-842-0850
E-Mail: abainfo@buses.org
Home Page: www.buses.org
Social Media: *Facebook, Twitter, LinkedIn, YouTube*

Peter J Pantuso, President & CEO
Roderick Lewis, Director, Membership & BD
Suzanne Te Beau Rohde, VP, Govt. Affairs & Policy
Brandon Buchanan, Director of Regulatory Affairs
Daniel Hoff, Director, Gov Affairs & Policy

ABA supports 3,800 members consisting of motorcoach and tour companies in addition to organizations that represent the tourism and travel industry. ABA strives to educate consumers on the importance of highway and motorcoach safety.
Founded in 1926

23204 American Council of Highway Advertisers
1101 14th St., NW
Suite 1030
Washington, DC 20005-5635

202-857-0044
FAX 202-857-7809
E-Mail: info@crp.org
Home Page: www.opensecrets.org
Social Media: *Facebook, Twitter, LinkedIn, RSS, YouTube*

Sheila Krumholz, Executive Director
Jacob Hileman, IT Director
Sarah Bryner, Research Director
Viveca Novak, Editorial & Communications Director
Dan Auble, Senior Researcher
Founded in 1983

23205 American Society of Travel Agents (ASTA)
675 N. Washington Street
Suite 490
Alexandria, VA 22314

703-739-2782
800-275-2782
FAX 703-684-8319
E-Mail: askasta@asta.org
Home Page: www.asta.org
Social Media: *Facebook, Twitter, LinkedIn*

Zane Kerby, President & CEO
Paul Ruden, EVP, Legal & Industry Affairs
Eben Peck, SVP, Government & Industry Affairs
Mark Meader, VP, Industry Affairs
Sue Sheats, VP, Business Development

Promotes and encourages travel among people of all nations. Serves as an information resource for the travel industry.
21M Members
Founded in 1931

23206 Association of Corporate Travel Executives
510 King Street
Suite 220
Alexandria, VA 22314-2964

262-763-1902
800-375-2283
FAX 613-836-0619
E-Mail: info@acte.org
Home Page: www.acte.org
Social Media: *Facebook, Twitter, LinkedIn, YouTube, RSS*

Kurt Knackstedt, President
Greeley Koch, Executive Director
Jeff Kurn, Treasurer
Greeley Koch, Chief Staff Officer
Amber Kelleher, Global Engagement

Provides a forum for the discussion of ideas and information related to the corporate travel industry. Conducts educational programs and conferences.
700 Members
Founded in 1988
Mailing list available for rent

23207 Association of Group Travel Executives
AH Light Company
510 King Street
Suite 220
Alexandria, VA 22314

262-763-1902
800-375-2283
FAX 908-273-2344
E-Mail: info@acte.org
Home Page: www.acte.org
Social Media: *Facebook, Twitter, LinkedIn, YouTube, RSS*

Kurt Knackstedt, President
Greeley Koch, Executive Director
Jeff Kurn, Treasurer
Greeley Koch, Chief Staff Officer
Amber Kelleher, Global Engagement

Affiliated with the Travel Industry Association of America.
675 Members
Founded in 1988

23208 Association of Retail Travel Agents
4320 North Miller Road
Scottsdale, AZ 85251

800-969-6069
FAX 866-743-2087
E-Mail: info@artonline.com
Home Page: www.artaonline.com
Social Media: *Facebook, Twitter, LinkedIn, You Tube*

Nancy Linares, Board of Director

Promotes the interests of retail travel agents through representation on industry councils and testimony before Congress. Conducts joint marketing and educational programs.
2800 Members
Founded in 1963

23209 Association of Travel Marketing Executives
PO Box 3176
West Tisbury, MA 02575

508-693-0550
FAX 508-693-0115
E-Mail: kzern@atme.org
Home Page: www.atme.org
Social Media: *Facebook, Twitter, LinkedIn, Flickr*

Kristin Zern, Executive Director
Henry Harteveldt, Chairman
Susan Black, Vice Chairman
Jeffrey DeKorte, Secretary
Jacqueline Johnson, Treasurer
Founded in 1980

23210 Association of Travel Marketing Executives
PO Box 3176
West Tisbury, MA 02575

508-693-0550
FAX 508-693-0115
E-Mail: kzern@atme.org
Home Page: www.atme.org
Social Media: *Facebook, Twitter, LinkedIn, Flickr*

Kristin Zern, Executive Director
Henry Harteveldt, Chairman
Susan Black, Vice Chairman
Jeffrey DeKorte, Secretary
Jacqueline Johnson, Treasurer

Travel and tourism reports.
Founded in 1980

23211 Caribbean Hotel Association
2655 Le Jeune Rd
Suite 910
Coral Gables, FL 33134

305-443-3040
FAX 305-675-7977
E-Mail: membership@caribbeanhotelandtourism.com
Home Page: www.caribbeanhotelandtourism.com
Social Media: *Facebook, Twitter, LinkedIn*

Richard Doumeng, Chairman
Emil Lee, President
Karolin Troubetzkoy, 1st VP
Stuart Bowe, 2nd VP
Karen Whitt, 3rd VP

Mission is to optimize the full potential of the Caribbean hotel and tourism industry by serving member needs and building partnerships. It's a LLC registered in the Cayman Islands, with offices in San Juan, Puerto Rico and Miami, FL.
Founded in 1959

23212 Greater Independent Association of National Travel Services
915 Broadway
20th Floor
New York, NY 10010-7130

212-627-0001
FAX 212-627-1110
E-Mail: info@fullpic.com
Home Page: www.fullpic.com
Social Media: *Twitter, Youtube*

Desiree Gruber, President
Susan Shapiro, Executive Director

Aims to establish a travel industry marketing cooperative. Holds regional workshops and seminars.
1.8M Members
Founded in 1968

23213 Hospitality Sales & Marketing Association International
1760 Old Meadow Road
Suite 500
McLean, VA 22102

703-506-3280
FAX 703-506-3266
E-Mail: info@hsmai.org
Home Page: www.hsmai.org
Social Media: *Facebook, Twitter, LinkedIn, Flickr*

Rob Torres, Chairman
Jeff Senior, Chair Elect
Mark Thompson, Secretary/Treasurer
Marina MacDonald, Vice Chair
Robert A. Gilbert, CHME, CHA, President & CEO

The hospitality indutry's source for knowledge, community, and recognition for leaders committed to professional development, sales growth, revenue optimization, marketing and branding.
7000 Members
Founded in 1927

23214 International Association of Convention and Visitor Bureaus
2025 M St Nw
Suite 500
Washington, DC 20036-3349

202-296-7888
FAX 202-296-7889
E-Mail: info@destinationmarketing.org
Home Page: www.destinationmarketing.org
Social Media: *Facebook, Twitter, LinkedIn, Google+, YouTube, Flickr, Slid*

Charles Jeffers II, Interim CEO & COO
Valencia Bembry, SVP
Stephanie Ann Russell, Executive Assistant
Christine Shimasaki, CDME, CMP, Managing Director
Elaine Rosquist, CMP, Director of Services

Promotes sound professional practices in the solicitation and servicing of meetings and conventions. Members represent travel/tourism related businesses. Publications include an electronic newsletter and online directory.
Founded in 1914
Mailing list available for rent: 1200 names at $400 per M

23215 International Association of Travel
PO Box D
Hurleyville, NY 12747

845-434-7777

Promotes accurate reporting on fields of aviation, travel, tourism and airports.
50+ Members
Founded in 1988

23216 National Association of Business Travel Agents
National Association of Business Travel Agents
1920 L St. NW
Suite 300
Washington, DC 20036-2365

202-463-6223
FAX 202-463-6239
E-Mail: nabe@nabe.com
Home Page: www.nabe.com
Social Media: *Twitter*

Tom Beers, Executive Director
Colette Brissett, Administrative Director
Chris Jonas, Director, Comm. and Programs
Suzanne Clegg, Events Coordinator
Robert Crow, Editor, Business Economics

NBTA is a forum bringing together business travel buyer and supplier professionals from around the world. Membership includes access to the industry's premier network of corporate and government travel decision-makers and purchasers, a monthly e-newsletter as well as a quarterly publication, world-wide and local events, CTE opportunities and professional certificate programs.
Founded in 1959

23217 National Association of RV Parks and Campgrounds
9085 E. Mineral Circle
Suite 200
Centennial, CO 80112

303-681-0401
800-395-2267
FAX 303-681-0426
E-Mail: info@arvc.org
Home Page: www.arvc.org
Social Media: *Facebook, Twitter, LinkedIn, Youtube*

Paul Bambei, President/CEO
Candra Talley, Membership Program Manager
Barb Youmans, Senior Director of Education
Jennifer Schwartz, Vice President, Marketing
Molly Martin, Marketing Coordinator

The association actively protects the best interests of its members on a federal level and provides awareness and assistance against government legislation & regulations at all levels(national, state and local).
3100 Members
Founded in 1966
Mailing list available for rent: 3,200 names

23218 National Motorcoach Network
PO Box 1088
Mount Jackson, VA 22842

540-477-3202
800-469-0062
FAX 540-477-3858
E-Mail: smk@motorcoach.com
Home Page: www.motorcoach.com/byways

Founded in 1983

23219 National Tour Association
101 Prosperous Place
Suite 350
Lexington, KY 40509

859-264-6540
800-682-8886
FAX 859-264-6570
E-Mail: pam.inman@ntastaff.com
Home Page: www.ntaonline.com
Social Media: *Facebook, Twitter, LinkedIn, Youtube, Google+, Instagram*

Pam Inman, President
Jackie Burchett, Controller, Director, HR
Amanda Martino, Office Manager
Doug Rentz, Director, Marketing & Comm.
Catherine Prather, Executive Vice President

The National Tour Association is an organization of nearly 4,000 international tourism professionals focused on the development, promotion and increased use of tour operators packaged travel.
4000 Members
Founded in 1951
Mailing list available for rentat $500 per M

23220 Office of General Supply and Services
1800 F Street, NW
Washington, DC 20405

202-564-2480
866-606-8220
E-Mail: NCSCcustomer.service@gsa.gov
Home Page: www.gsa.gov
Social Media: *Facebook, Twitter, Youtube, RSS*

Adam Neufeld, Deputy Administrator
Denise Turner Roth, Administrator
Katy Kale, Chief Of Staff
Reginald Cardozo, Deputy Chief of Staff
Norman Dong, Public Buildings Service

The Office of General Supplies and Services (GSS) is responsible for acquisition services and comprehensive supply chain management, including excess/surplus federal property.
Founded in 1949

23221 Passenger Vessel Association
103 Oronoco Street
Suite 200
Alexandria, VA 22314-1549

703-518-5005
800-807-8360
FAX 703-518-5151
E-Mail: pvainfo@passengervessel.com
Home Page: www.passengervessel.com
Social Media: *Facebook*

John Groundwater, Executive Director
Margo Marks, Vice President
Leslie Kagarise, Director of Finance
Lee Hill, Chief Financial Officer
Edmund Welch, Legislative Director

Represents operators of tours, excursions, ferries, charter vessels, dinner boats and other small passenger vessels.
600 Members
Founded in 1971

23222 Receptive Services Association
2365 Harrodsburg Road
Suite A325
Lexington, KY 40504

859-219-3545
866-939-0934
FAX 859-226-4404
E-Mail: headquarters@rsaa.com
Home Page: www.rsana.com
Social Media: *Facebook, Youtube*

Matt Grayson, Executive Director
Rachel Gates, Member Services Administrator
Toby Bishop, Sales Manager
Jonathan Zuk, Chairman
Veronique Hubert, Vice Chairman

Helping receptive operators serve international tour companies through partnerships with North American suppliers.
570 Members

23223 Recreational Vehicle Industry Association
1896 Preston White Drive
Reston, VA 20191

703-620-6003
FAX 703-620-5071
Home Page: www.rvia.org

David Humphreys, President

The national trade association representing recreation vehicle manufacturers and their component parts suppliers who build more than 98% of all RVsproduced in the U.S.
Founded in 1963

23224 Society of American Travel Writers
One Parkview Plaza
Suite 800
Oakbrook Terrace, IL 60181

414-359-1671
FAX 414-359-1671
E-Mail: info@satw.org
Home Page: www.satw.org
Social Media: *Facebook, Twitter, LinkedIn*

Paul Lasley, President
Annette Thompson, Immediate Past President
Barbara Orr, Vice President, Membership
Tom Adkinson, Treasurer
Peggy Bendel, Secretary

Photographers and 35 associate member representatives of airlines, hotels, resorts, tourist agencies and public relations firms.
Founded in 1955

23225 Society of Incentive and Travel Executives
330 N Wabash Ave
Chicago, IL 60611

312-321-5148
FAX 312-527-6783
E-Mail: site@siteglobal.com
Home Page: www.siteglobal.com
Social Media: *Facebook, Twitter, LinkedIn, Youtube*

Kevin M. Hinton, CEO
Ashley Mayrisch, Marketing Coordinator
Maggie Vaulman, Membership Associate
Adrianne Stokes, Operations Associate
Murphy Goodworth, Global Conference Director

An individual membership society covering 70 countries. Members are corporate users, airlines, Tourist Boards, cruise lines, destination management companies, consultants, hotels/re-

sorts, travel agents, incentive travel houses and publications.
2000 Members
Founded in 1973

23226 Travel Industry Association of America
1100 New York Ave Nw
Suite 450
Washington, DC 20005-3934

202-408-8422
FAX 202-408-1255
Home Page: www.tia.org

Roger J Dow, President & CEO
Todd Davidson, Treasurer & Director
Bonnie L Carlson, Secretary & Director

Members are hotels, airlines and travel agencies interested in promoting increased travel to and within the US.
2100 Members
Founded in 1941

23227 Travel and Tourism Research Association
5300 Lakewood Road
Whitehall, MI 49461

248-708-8872
FAX 248-814-7150
E-Mail: info@ttra.com
Home Page: www.ttra.com

Dan Mishell, Chairman
Jeffrey Eslinger, President
Susan Bruinzeel, 1st VP/Conference Chair
Dr. Marion Joppe, 2nd VP/Membership Chair
John Markham, Treasurer
Founded in 1970

23228 U.S. Travel Association
1100 New York Ave. NW
Suite 450
Washington, DC 20005

202-408-8422
FAX 202-408-1255
E-Mail: feedback@ustravel.org
Home Page: www.ustravel.org

Todd Davidson, Chair
Roger J. Dow, President

The Association advocates for the importance of travel, and the freedom to travel, to a healthy U.S. economy.

23229 Volunteers for Peace
7 Kilburn Street
Suite 316
Belmont, VT 05401

802-540-3060
FAX 802-540-3061
E-Mail: info@vfp.org
Home Page: www.vfp.org
Social Media: *Facebook, Twitter*

Megan Brook, Executive Director
Alexandra Smith, International Placement Coordinator
Scott Simpson, LICSW, President
Jamena Grant, Secretary, Treasurer

A Vermont nonprofit membership organization promoting over 3000 international voluntary service projects in 100 countries. Workcamps are an affordable way to travel, live and work abroad.
2000 Members
Founded in 1982

Newsletters

23230 AAA World
2040 Market Street
Philadelphia, PA 19103

215-851-0291
800-763-9900
FAX 215-851-0297
E-Mail: letters@aaaworld.com
Home Page: www.aaaworld.com

Allen EeWalle, CEO
Sandy Kaden, Circulation Manager

Promotes travel destinations, gives advice on traveling and helpful automobile information.
Cost: $71.00
Circulation: 2.1 mill
Founded in 1900

23231 ABA Insider
American Bus Association
111 K Street NE
9th Floor
Washington, DC 20002

202-842-1645
FAX 202-842-0850
E-Mail: abainfo@buses.org
Home Page: www.buses.org

Peter J Pantuso, CEO
Buchcannon Brandon, Director of Operations
Hart Clyde, Senior VP of Government Affairs
Hoff Daniel, Director of ABA Foundation & Policy
Jones Patrick, Legislative & Communications Coordi

ABA's biweekly newsletter that keeps members informed on the travel, tourism and motorcoach industry.
Frequency: Biweekly
Founded in 1926

23232 Caribbean Reporter
Caribbean Hotel Association
18 Calle Marseilles
San Juan, PR 907-1682

787-725-2901
FAX 787-725-9180
Home Page: www.chahotels.com

Beverly Telemague, Publisher
Membership news.
Cost: $4.99
Frequency: Monthly
Founded in 1959

23233 Entree Travel Newsletter
Entree Publishing
PO Box 5148
Santa Barbara, CA 93150-5148

805-969-5848
FAX 805-969-5849
E-Mail: wtomicki@aol.com
Home Page: www.entreenews.com

William Tomicki, Editor/Publisher

Travel, fashion and beauty ideas, sports and photography, wines and restaurants reviews new literature, music and film of interest to the travel and food enthusiast.
Cost: $75.00
Frequency: Monthly
Circulation: 8000
Printed in one color on matte stock

23234 IACVB e-News
Int'l Association of Convention & Visitor Bureaus

2025 M St Nw
Suite 500
Washington, DC 20036-3349

202-296-7888
FAX 202-296-7889
Home Page: www.destinationmarketing.org

Michael D Gehrisch, CEO
Kristen Clemens, Editor

An electronic newsletter published by the International Association of Convention and Visitor Bureaus. Available with membership.
Frequency: Weekly
Circulation: 1300
Founded in 1914
Mailing list available for rent: 1200 names at $400 per M

23235 Ocean and Cruise News
PO Box 329
Northport, NY 11768

203-329-2787
FAX 203-329-2767
E-Mail: news@wocls.org
Home Page: www.wocls.org/

Tom Cassidy, VP
Geroge Devol, President

Complete news on cruises.
Cost: $30.00
Frequency: Monthly
Circulation: 7000
Founded in 1980

23236 Travel Industry Association of America Newsletter
Travel Industry Association of America
1100 New York Ave Nw
Suite 450 W
Washington, DC 20005-6130

202-408-8422
FAX 202-408-1255
Home Page: www.tia.org

Roger J Dow, CEO
C Betsi, Marketing Manager
Kathy Keefe, Editor

Travel information.
Cost: $1350.00
Frequency: Monthly
Circulation: 3500
Founded in 1941
Printed in 3 colors on glossy stock

23237 Travel Management Newsletter
Reed Travel Group
500 Plaza Dr
Secaucus, NJ 07094-3619

201-902-1800
FAX 202-902-2053
Home Page: www.tmdaily.com

Steve Bailey, Publisher

Discusses the news and views of the travel professional.
Cost: $735.00
Frequency: Weekly

23238 Travel Manager's Executive Briefing
Health Resources Publishing
1913 Atlantic Ave
Suite 200
Manasquan, NJ 08736-1067

732-292-1100
800-516-4343
FAX 732-292-1111
E-Mail: info@themcic.com
Home Page: www.healthresourcesonline.com

Robert K Jenkins, Publisher
Lisa Mansfield, Marketing Assistant

Read by travel managers of major corporations, Fortune 500 companies and corporate travel agencies twice a month to get up to the minute

developments in the important field of travel and expense cost control.
Cost: $447.00
ISSN: 0272-569x

23239 Travel Weekly
500 Plaza Drive
Secaucus, NJ 07094-3685

201-902-1696
FAX 201-902-2053
Home Page: www.travelweekly.com

William D Scott, Publisher

Industry news, articles and stories on the travel industry.
Cost: $26.00
Frequency: BiWeekly

23240 Travel and Tourism Executive Report
10200 W 44th Avenue
Suite 304
Wheat Ridge, CO 80033-2840

303-463-2887

Francine Butler, Executive Director

Established as the Travel Research Association as the result of a merger.
750 Pages

23241 Travelwriter Marketletter
21553 Center Point Circle
Ashburn, VA 20147

571-214-9086
FAX 208-988-7672
Home Page: www.travelwriterml.com

Mimi Backhausen, Editor & Publisher

A monthly newsletter for travel writers and travel photographers. It's mainly about marketing travel articles, photography and travel books; also describes free trips for professional travel writers.
Cost: $75.00
10 Pages
Frequency: Monthly
Circulation: 1000
ISSN: 0738-9093

23242 Tuesday Newsletter
National Tour Association
101 Prosperours Place
Suite 350
Lexington, KY 40509

859-264-6540
800-682-8886
FAX 859-264-6570
E-Mail: questions@ntastaff.com
Home Page: ntaonline.com

Lisa Simon, President

The National Tour Association is an organization of nearly 4,000 North American tourism professionals focused on the development, promotion and increased use of tour operators packaged travel.
Cost: $36.00
100 Pages
Frequency: Monthly
Circulation: 5000
Founded in 1998
Mailing list available for rent: 3,800 names

Magazines & Journals

23243 ABC Preferred Flight Planner: Europe- Middle East-Africa
ABC Corporate Services/Reed Travel Group

500 Plaza Drive
Secaucus, NJ 07094-3619

201-678-8775
FAX 201-902-2053
Home Page: www.infotec-travel.com

Luis Murcia, Owner

Offers information on properties and locations of interest to corporate business travelers.
250 Pages
Frequency: SemiAnnual
Circulation: 65,000

23244 ASTA Agency Management
Miller Freeman Publications
2655 Seely Avenue
San Jose, CA 95134

408-943-1234
FAX 408-943-0513

Mary Pat Sullivan, Publisher

Provides concise and useful information on trends in the industry and practical ideas regarding the profitable administration of travel agencies.
Cost: $36.00
Frequency: Monthly
Circulation: 35,182

23245 ASU Travel Guide
448 Ignacio Boulevard
Suite 333
San Rafael, CA 94949-5539

415-898-9500
866-459-0300
FAX 415-898-9501
Home Page: www.asutravelguide.com

Christopher Gil, Managing Editor
Hank Sousa, VP

Provides information concerning worldwide travel destinations and other locales of interest to travelers and the bargains and discounts available to airline employees.
352 Pages
Frequency: Quarterly
Circulation: 700000
Founded in 1971
Printed in 4 colors on glossy stock

23246 Bank Travel Management
Group Travel Leader
301 East High Street
Lexington, KY 40507

859-253-0455
FAX 859-253-0499
E-Mail: info@grouptravelleader.com
Home Page: www.banktravelmanagement.com

Mac Lacy, President & Publisher
Herb Sparrow, Executive Editor
Brian Jewell, Associate Editor
Kelly Tyner, Director of Sales & Marketing
Stacey Bowman, National Account Manager

Regular sections include: The Banker's Box, managing your senior program, and marketing your trips, with special features on personal travel accounts, trends in travel and banking clubs. Subscriptions are complimentary for qualified travel planners.
Cost: $49.00
Frequency: 6/Year
Circulation: 4100
Founded in 1994

23247 Bus Tours Magazine
National Bus Trader
9698 W Judson Rd
Polo, IL 61064-9015

815-946-2341
FAX 815-946-2347

E-Mail: nbt@busmag.com
Home Page: www.busmag.com

Larry Plachno, President
Shaye Hall, Assistant Editor
Nancy Ann Plachno, Business Manager

Focuses on the operations, arrangements and marketing techniques used to plan these excursions as well as what's new in the industry.
Cost: $10.00
Frequency: Monthly
Circulation: 7,200
Founded in 1979

23248 Byways
National Motorcoach Network
42 Cabin Hill Lane
Mt Jackson, VA 22842

540-773-3323
800-469-0062
FAX 540-477-3858
E-Mail: nmn@motorcoach.com
Home Page: www.motorcoach.com/byways
Social Media: *Facebook, Twitter, LinkedIn*

Stephen M Kirchner, Publisher/Editor

Featuring North America's leading travel destinations. Includes riverboat gambling updates and special reports on the top 50 motorcoach destinations.
48 Pages
Frequency: Bi-Monthly
Circulation: 20000
Founded in 1983

23249 City Visitor
Travelhost
5755 Granger Road
Independence, OH 44131

972-556-0541
FAX 972-432-8729
Home Page: www.travelhost.com

James E Buerger, President

Travelhost is an in room publisher edited for the business and vacation traveler, with news features and general information relating to travel, recreation, business, new products and services and leisure activities.
Cost: $33.00
Frequency: Monthly
Founded in 1967

23250 Conde Nast Traveler Business Extra
Conde Nast
4 Times Sq
14th Floor
New York, NY 10036-6561

212-286-2860
FAX 212-286-5960
Home Page: www.condenast.com

Charles H Townsend, CEO

Relates to gathering information for tourism.

23251 Corporate & Incentive Travel
Coastal Communications Corporation
2700 N Military Trail
Suite 120
Boca Raton, FL 33431

561-989-0600
FAX 561-989-9509
E-Mail: ccceditor1@att.net
Home Page: www.themeetingmagazines.com

Harvey Grotsky, Publisher/Editor-In-Chief
Susan Wyckoff Fell, Managing Editor
Susan Gregg, Managing Editor

The magazine for corporate meetings and incentive travel planners. In-depth editorial focus on site selection, accommodations and transportation, current legislation, conference, seminar and training facilities, budget and cost controls, and destination reports. Regular features highlight industry news and develop-

ments, trends and personalities, meeting values, facilities, and destinations.
Frequency: Monthly
Circulation: 40,000
Founded in 1983

23252 Corporate and Incentive Travel

Coastal Communications Corporation
2700 N Military Trail
Suite 120
Boca Raton, FL 33431-6394

561-989-0600
FAX 561-989-9509
Home Page: www.themeetingmagazines.com

Harvey Grotsky, President & CEO
Susan Wyckoff Fell, Managing Editor
Susan S Gregg, Managing Editor

This magazine is edited for corporate meeting planners with the responsibility for staging and planning meetings, incentive travel programs, conferences and conventions.
Frequency: Monthly
Founded in 1983

23253 Country Discoveries

5400 S 60th Street
Greendale, WI 53129-1404

414-423-0100
800-344-6913
FAX 414-423-8463
Home Page: www.reimanpub.com

Focuses on backwoods travel in both the United States and Canada.
Cost: $14.98
Founded in 1965

23254 Courier

National Tour Association
546 E Main St
Lexington, KY 40508-2342

859-226-4444
800-682-8886
FAX 859-226-4447
E-Mail: questions@ntastaff.com
Home Page: ntaonline.com

Lisa Simon, President

Courier Magazine helps readers to meet their responsibilities involved with their jobs.
Cost: $36.00
110 Pages
Frequency: Monthly
Circulation: 6000
ISSN: 0279-4489
Founded in 1955
Printed in 4 colors on glossy stock

23255 Cruise Industry News - Annual

Nissel-Lie Communications
441 Lexington Avenue
Room 809
New York, NY 10017-3910

212-986-1025
FAX 212-986-1033
E-Mail: info2@cruiseindustrynews.com
Home Page: www.cruiseindustrynews.com

Oivind Mathisen, Editor/Publisher
Angela Mathisen, Advertising
Director/Publisher
Monty Mathisen, Reporter/Web Editor

The only book of its kind, and often rated the most comprehensive information source on the industry by cruise line executives.
Cost: $575.00
Frequency: Annual+
Founded in 1988

23256 Cruise Industry News Quarterly Magazine

Nissel-Lie Communications

441 Lexington Avenue
Room 809
New York, NY 10017-3910

212-986-1025
FAX 212-986-1033
E-Mail: info2@cruiseindustrynews.com
Home Page: www.cruiseindustrynews.com

Oivind Mathisen, Editor/Publisher
Angela Mathisen, Advertising
Director/Publsher
Monty Mathisen, Reporter/Web Editor

The magazine covers all aspects of cruise operations, shipbuilding, new ships, cruise companies, ship reviews, onboard services, food and beverage, and ports and destinations.
Cost: $495.00
Frequency: Quarterly
Circulation: 50000
Founded in 1991
Printed in 4 colors

23257 Destinations

American Bus Association
700 13th St NW
Suite 575
Washington, DC 20005-5923

202-842-1645
800-283-2877
FAX 202-842-0850
E-Mail: abainfo@buses.org
Home Page: www.buses.org

Peter J Pantuso, CEO
Eron Shosteck, Marketing

Motorcoach travel across North America and Association news.
80 Pages
Frequency: Monthly
Circulation: 6000
Founded in 1926
Printed in 4 colors on glossy stock

23258 Digital Travel

Jupiter Communications Company
475 Park Ave S
Suite 4
New York, NY 10016-6901

212-547-7900
800-481-1212
FAX 212-953-1733
Home Page: www.jup.com

Alan Meckler, CEO
Marla Kammer, Managing Editor

Editorial includes the latest information and technology in agencies, airlines, lodging, ticketing, mapping, Web advertising, transaction processing, revenue models, demographics, and full-service sites.
Cost: $595.00
Frequency: Monthly

23259 Family Motor Coaching Magazine

Family Motor Coach Association
8291 Clough Pike
Cincinnati, OH 45244-2796

513-474-3622
800-543-3622
FAX 513-474-2332
E-Mail: jyeatts@fmca.com
Home Page: www.fmca.com

Don Eversman, Executive Director
Ranita Jones, Sales Manager
Cost: $3.99
Frequency: Monthly
Circulation: 140000

23260 Frequent Flyer Magazine

2000 Clearwater Drive
Oak Brook, IL 60523

630-574-6000
800-342-5674
FAX 630-574-6565

23261 Going on Faith

Group Traveler Leader
301 E High Street
Lexington, KY 40507

859-253-0455
888-253-0455
FAX 859-253-0499
E-Mail: circmanager@grouptravelleader.com
Home Page: www.grouptravelleader.com

Mac Lacy, Publisher
Herb Sparrow, Executive Editor
Brian Jewell, Associate Editor
Kelly Tyner, Director of Sales & Marketing
Stacey Bowman, National Account Manager

The national travel newspaper for churches, synagogues and Religious organizations. The official newspaper for the Going on Faith Conference. Online.
Frequency: 6/Year
Circulation: 5500
Founded in 1997

23262 Group Travel Leader

Group Travel Leader
301 E High St
Lexington, KY 40507-1509

859-253-0455
FAX 859-253-0499
E-Mail: maclacy@grouptravelleader.com
Home Page: www.grouptravelleader.com

Mac Lacy, President
Herb Sparrow, Executive Editor
Brian Jewell, Associate Editor
Kelly Tyner, Director of Sales & Marketing
Stacey Bowman, National Account Manager

Supplies the senior travel planner with new destinations, unique points of interest and historical venues for their group, club or organization.
Cost: $39.00
Frequency: Monthly
Circulation: 30000
Founded in 1991

23263 HSMAI Marketing Review

Hospitality Sales & Marketing Association Int'l
1760 Old Meadow Road
Suite 500
McLean, VA 22102

703-506-3280
FAX 703-506-3266
E-Mail: info@hsmai.org
Home Page: www.hsmai.org

Kathleen Tindell, Editor

Features in-depth information and columns on best practices, web marekting, international affairs and future forecasting.
Cost: $65.00
7000 Pages
Frequency: Quarterly
Circulation: 10000
Founded in 1927

23264 Inside Flyer

Flight Plan
1930 Frequent Flyer Point
Colorado Springs, CO 80915

719-597-8889
800-767-8896
FAX 719-597-6855

E-Mail: editor@insideflyer.com
Home Page: www.insideflyer.com/

Randy Petersen, Editor/publ/CEO
Karen Heldt, Advertising Coordinator
Linda Hanwella, Managing Editor

Leading publication of information for and
about frequent traveler programs.
Cost: $45.00
Frequency: Monthly
Founded in 1986
Mailing list available for rent
Printed in 4 colors on matte stock

23265 Jax Fax Travel Marketing
Jax Fax
52 West Main Street
Milford, CT 06460-3310

203-301-0255
FAX 203-301-0250
Home Page: www.jaxfax.com

Doug Cooke, President
Marc Spac, Publishing Director
Theresa Seanlon, Editor
Marjorie Vincent, Circulation Manager
Peter Badeau, Associate Publisher

Monthly travel trade magazine featuring desti-
nation information and listings of discounted
airfares and tour packages.
Cost: $15.00
Frequency: Monthly
Circulation: 25000
Founded in 1973
Printed in 4 colors on glossy stock

23266 Mexico Today
2009 S 10th Street
McAllen, TX 78503-5405

956-686-0711
800-222-0158
FAX 956-686-0732
E-Mail: info@sanbornsinsurance.com
Home Page: www.sanbornsinsurance.com

Pete Castillo, Marketing Director
Frequency: Quarterly
Circulation: 5000
Printed in 4 colors on glossy stock

23267 Mid-Atlantic Group Tour Magazine
Shoreline Creations
PO Box 638
Yarmouth Port, MA 02675-638

508-398-0400
FAX 616-393-0085
E-Mail: travel@grouptour.com
Home Page: www.grouptour.com

Carl Wassink, Publisher
Carol Smith, Editor
Katie Weller, Circulation Manager
Jamie Cannon, Marketing Manager
Ruth Wassink, Vice President

Material looks at the latest offerings in tour
travel including restaurants, theater, shopping,
hotels, festivals, and events and activities.
Frequency: Quarterly
Circulation: 10000
Founded in 1980

23268 Midwest Traveler
12901 N Forty Drive
Saint Louis, MO 63141

314-523-6981
800-222-7623
FAX 314-523-6982
Home Page: www.aaatravelermags.com

Mike Right, Editor
Cost: $3.00
Circulation: 45000
Founded in 1902

23269 Mobility
1717 Pennsylvania Avenue NW
8th Floor
Washington, DC 20006

202-293-7744
FAX 202-659-8631
Home Page: www.erc.org/MOBILITY_Online

23270 NBTA Travel Quarterly
National Association of Business Travel
Agents
123~North~Pitt Street
4th Floor
Alexandria, VA 22314

703-684-0836
FAX 703-342-4324
E-Mail: info@nbta.org
Home Page: www.nbta.org

Caleb Tiller, Sr Dir, Marketing &
Communications
Wendy Santiago, Marketing Manager
Nicole Hayes, Assistant Manager,
Communications
Jack Machlum, CEO
Kevin Maguire, VP/Chief Information Officer

This publication provides valuable information
on NBTA, its members and the corporate travel
industry, to help the professional stay connected to the industry.
Frequency: Quarterly/Members Only

23271 New England Tour Magazine
Shoreline Creations
PO Box 638
Yarmouth Port, MA 02675-638

508-398-0400
FAX 508-398-4703
E-Mail: travel@grouptour.com
Home Page: www.grouptour.com

Carol Smith, Editor
Carl Wassink, President
Katie Weller, Circulation Manager
Jamie Cannon, Marketing
Ruth Wassink, Executive Vice President

Promotes and covers the attractions, lodging,
dining, events and other highlights of popular
and less-famous travel destinations in the
region.
Frequency: Quarterly
Circulation: 10000
Founded in 1925

23272 Onboard Services
International Publishing Company of
America
50 Millstone Road
Building 300 Suite 110
East Windsor, NJ 08520

609-945-8000
800-280-8591
FAX 609-945-8080
E-Mail: general@obcc.net
Home Page: www.onboard-services.com

Alexander Morton, President
George Hulcher, Contributing Editor

Keeps airline, cruise ships, railroad, and terminal concessions management and purchasing
departments up-to-date on all phases of passenger services.
Cost: $25.00
24 Pages
ISSN: 0892-4236
Founded in 1968
Printed in 4 colors on glossy stock

23273 Ozark Mountain Visitor
200 Industrial Park Drive
Hollister, MO 65672-5327

417-334-3161
FAX 417-335-3933

23274 Pacific Asia Travel News
Americas Publishing Company
3657 Harriet Road
Victoria, Can, BC V8Z-3T1

250-260-1883
FAX 250-953-5250

Malcolm Scott, Publisher

Issues include a news dateline with features on
travel trends and outlooks, a special destination
focus, and updates from the Pacific Asia Travel
Association.
Cost: $30.00
Frequency: BiMonthly
Circulation: 24,000

23275 Practical Gourmet
Linick Group
PO Box 102
Middle Island, NY 11953-0102

631-924-3888
FAX 631-924-3890
E-Mail: linickgrp@att.net
Home Page: www.lgroup.addr.com

Andrew S Linick, CEO
Roger Dextor, Production
Barbara Deal, Marketing Manager

The focus of this publication is light, healthy
gourmet dining; includes reports on wine tast-
ing, food festivals, contests, celebrations, cook-
ing schools and other events.
Cost: $48.00
36 Pages
Frequency: Monthly
Circulation: 210,000
Founded in 1975
*Mailing list available for rent: 210 M names at
$110 per M*
Printed in 4 colors on glossy stock

23276 Recommend
Worth International Communication Corp
PO Box 171070
Hialeah, FL 33017-1070

305-828-0123
800-447-0123
FAX 305-826-6950
Home Page: www.recommend.com

Laurel A Herman, Publisher
Lorri Robbins, National Director

Contains colorful information on worldwide
destinations, resorts, hotels, transportation and
tour operators, as well as marketing angles to
help travel agents sell travel.
Cost: $48.00
Frequency: Monthly
Circulation: 60000
Founded in 1967
Printed in on glossy stock

**23277 Runzheimer Reports on Travel
Management**
Runzheimer Park
Rochester, WI 53167-9999

262-712-2200
800-558-1702
FAX 262-971-2254

Rex Runzheimer, President

23278 Sea Mass Traveler
PO Box 3189
Newport, RI 02840-0322

401-848-2922

23279 Southwest Airlines Spirit
Pace Communications
2811 McKinney Avenue
Suite 360
Dallas, TX 75204

214-580-2491
FAX 214-580-8070
Home Page: www.spiritmag.com

Jay Heinrichs, Editorial Director
John McAlley, Executive Editor
Frequency: Monthly
Circulation: 400088
Founded in 1971

23280 Specialty Travel Index
PO Box 458
San Anselmo, CA 94979

415-594-4900
888-624-4030
FAX 415-455-1648
E-Mail: info@specialtytravel.com
Home Page: www.specialtytravel.com

Karin Kinsey, Art Director
Stean Hansen, Circulation Manager
Andy Alpine, Marketing Manager
Risa Weinreb, Editor
Judith Alpine, Advertising Manager

Directory/magazine of adventure and specialty travel.
Cost: $10.00
Circulation: 32000
ISSN: 0889-7085
Founded in 1980
Printed in 4 colors on glossy stock

23281 SportsTravel Magazine
Schneider Publishing Company
11835 W Olympic Blvd
Suite 1265
Los Angeles, CA 90064-5814

310-577-3700
FAX 310-577-3715
E-Mail: info@schneiderpublishing.com
Home Page: www.schneiderpublishing.com
Social Media: *Facebook, Twitter, LinkedIn*

Tim Schneider, President
Jason Gewirtz, Managing Editor/Sports Travel
Lisa Furfine, Associate Publisher
Chad Starbuck, Marketing Manager

Includes articles on travel training, sports law, event spotlights, and vital information on sites, hotels, transportation, trade shows and upcomiong events for team travel planners and event organizers.
Cost: $48.00
Frequency: Monthly
Circulation: 1400
ISSN: 1091-5354
Founded in 1997
Printed in on glossy stock

23282 Sun Valley Magazine
Mandala Media LLC
111 1st Avenue North #1M
Meriwether Building
Hailey, ID 83333

208-788-0770
FAX 208-788-3881
Home Page: www.sunvalleymag.com

Laurie C Sammis, Publisher/Editor-in-Chief
Mike McKenna, Editor
Julie Molema, Production Director

Articles on the arts, community, recreation, dining, shopping and real estate in the Sun Val-

ley, Idaho area.
Cost: $22.00
Frequency: Quarterly
Circulation: 20000

23283 Sundancer's West
1108 Meadowview Drive
Euless, TX 76039

817-545-5265
FAX 817-571-6481
E-Mail: gwat/@swbell.net
Home Page: www.sundancerswest.com

Gerry Watkins,
Webmaster/Editor/Photographer

23284 Travel & Leisure
American Express Publishing Corporation
1120 Avenue of the Americas
Suite 9
New York, NY 10036-6700

212-382-5600
800-888-8728
FAX 212-382-5878
Home Page: www.tlexplorer.com

Ed Kelly, CEO
Nancy Novogrod, Editor-in-Chief
Antonia LoPresti, Senior Marketing Manager
Cost: $19.95
Frequency: Monthly
Circulation: 950000

23285 Travel & Leisure Golf
American Express Publishing Corporation
1120 Avenue of the Americas
Suite 9
New York, NY 10036-6700

212-382-5600
800-947-7961
FAX 212-382-5878
Home Page: www.amexpub.com

Ed Kelly, CEO
Antonia LoPresti, Senior Marketing Manager
Maura Smale, Project Manager
John Rodenburg, Publisher
Rashmi George, Advertising Coordinator
Cost: $19.95
Frequency: Monthly
Circulation: 950000

23286 Travel Agent International
Universal Media
PO Box 5386
Bloomington, IL 61702-5386

309-663-6327
FAX 212-883-1244
E-Mail: tai@taitravelbmi.com
Home Page: www.taitravelbmi.com

Richard P Friese, Publisher

Provides profiles on resorts and attractions for each given season.
Cost: $250.00
Frequency: 10 per year
Circulation: 19,100

23287 Travel Counselor
Miller Freeman Publications
600 Harrison Street
6th Fl
San Francisco, CA 94107

415-947-6000
800-764-759
FAX 415-947-6055
E-Mail: email@travel-counselors.com
Home Page: www.travel-counselors.com

Contains business information and analysis appropriate to the retail agency profession
Frequency: 7 per year
Circulation: 28,000

23288 Travel Trends
Meredith Corporation

125 Park Ave
New York, NY 10017-5529

212-557-6600
FAX 212-551-7161

Peter Mason, Publisher/Editor
Information on the trends of the travel industry.
Frequency: Quarterly
Circulation: 5,000

23289 Travel World
East - West News Bureau
16051 W. Tampa Palms Blvd
Tampa, FL 33647

813-978-0877
800-494-3279
FAX 310-836-8769
E-Mail: debbie@travelworld1.com
Home Page: www.travelworld1.com

Elizabeth Barnes, Executive Director
Debbie Stewart, Manager

23290 Travel World News
Travel Industry Network
Ste 8
28 Knight St
Norwalk, CT 06851-4719

203-286-6679
FAX 203-286-6681
E-Mail: editor@travelworldnews.com
Home Page: www.travelworldnews.com

Charles Gatt Jr, Publisher
Peter Gatt, Associate Publisher

Monthly trade publication covering the retail travel industry. Each issue contains industry information and coverage for agents who are making recommendations and booking for their clients, including comprehensive, up to date, and worldwide product news and destination editorial coverage. Available online and in print.
Frequency: Monthly
Circulation: 22000
Founded in 1988

23291 Travel, Food & Wine
Punch-In-Syndicate
400 E 59th Street
Floor 9
New York, NY 10022-2342

212-755-4363
E-Mail: punchin@usa.net
Home Page: www.punchin.com

J Walman, Editor

A magazine featuring articles and reviews on travel, food and wine, columns on airlines, hotels, cruise ships, railroads, resorts, restaurants, and spas. Also theater reviews, cinema, radio and all forms of entertainment.
Cost: $300.00
Frequency: Monthly

23292 TravelBound!
Group Traveler Leader
301 E High Street
Lexington, KY 40507

859-253-0455
888-253-0455
FAX 859-253-0499
E-Mail: circmanager@grouptravelleader.com
Home Page: www.grouptravelleader.com
Social Media: *Facebook, Twitter, LinkedIn, You Tube*

Mac Lacy, Publisher
Herb Sparrow, Executive Editor
Brian Jewell, Associate Editor
Kelly Tyner, Director of Sales & Marketing
Stacey Bowman, National Account Manager

The national magazine for African American Group Traveling, and the official magazine for

the African American Travel Conference (AATC).
Circulation: 4500
Founded in 2001

23293 Travelhost Magazine
Travelhost
10701 N Stemmons Fwy
Dallas, TX 75220-2419

972-556-0541
FAX 972-432-8729
E-Mail: editor@travelhostps.com
Home Page: www.travelhost.com

James E Buerger, CEO
David B Portener, Associate Publisher
Frequency: Monthly
Circulation: 60000
Founded in 1967

23294 Trip
Charlotte Trip
2424 N Davidson St
Suite 106 B
Charlotte, NC 28205-2382

704-376-7800
FAX 704-376-7802
Home Page: www.charlottetrip.com

Marie Margaret, CEO/President/Publisher
Dana Jorden, Editor
Jenifer Krupa, Marketing Manager
Angie Jones, Circulation Manager
Cost: $18.00
Frequency: Monthly
Circulation: 35000
Founded in 1990

23295 Vermont Green Mountain Guide
44 Country Road
North Springfield, VT 05150-9738

802-886-3333
Home Page:
www.vtliving.com/newspapers/vtgreenmtnguid

Cindy Thiel, President

Trade Shows

23296 Adventure Travel and Outdoor Show
McRand International
1 Westminster Place
Suite 300
Lake Forest, IL 60045-1867

FAX 847-295-4419

Richard Dux, VP
Sue Wildman, VP
Exhibits by tour operators, outfitters and others geared toward soft and hard adventure travel vacations and outdoor activities.
15M Attendees
Frequency: January

23297 American Society of Travel Agents Conference
1101 King Street
Ste. 200
Alexandria, VA 22314-2944

703-739-2782
FAX 703-684-8319
E-Mail: bdaniels@asta.org
Home Page: www.asta.org

Chris Vranas, VP
Brooke Daniels, Event Manager
Gathering of travel agents, airlines, hotels and tour operators that provides the opportunity to view and discuss new products, services and trends in the industry. 700 booths.
6M Attendees
Frequency: November

23298 American Travel Market Exhibition Company
Reed Exhibition Companies
383 Main Avenue
Norwalk, CT 06851-1543

203-840-4800
FAX 203-840-9628
Home Page: www.reedexpo.com

Gregg Vautrin, CEO

The national event for all US travel buyers, including tour operators, travel agents, corporate travel buyers and meeting/conference planners. One of a global series of Travel Market events.
Frequency: September

23299 Annual American and Canadian Sport, Travel and Outdoor Show
Expositions
Edgewater Branch
PO Box 550
Cleveland, OH 44107-0550

216-529-1300
FAX 216-529-0311
Home Page: ech.case.edu

John Grabowskie, Online Editor
John Bedan, Associate Online Editor
Nathan Delany, Associate Online Editor

975 exhibits of hunting and fishing equipment, travel services, boats, recreational vehicles and related equipment, supplies and services.
300k Attendees
Frequency: Annual
Founded in 1935

23300 Annual Boat, Vacation and Outdoor Show
Showtime Productions
PO Box 4372
Rockford, IL 61110

815-877-8043
FAX 815-877-9037
E-Mail: brenda@showtimeproduction.net
Home Page: showtimeproduction.net

Duane Nichols, President
Brenda Rotoco, Event Coordinator

Boat, travel, outdoor equipment, supplies, and services plus demonstrations.
28000 Attendees
Frequency: February
Founded in 1970

23301 Annual Capital Sport Fishing, Travel and Outdoor Show
International Sport Show Producers Association
PO Box 4720
Portsmouth, NH 03802-4720

603-431-4315
FAX 603-431-1971
E-Mail: info@sportshows.com
Home Page: www.sportshows.com

Paul Fuller, President

Over 350 exhibits of sports, fishing, recreation and travel equipment, supplies and services.
45k Attendees
Frequency: Annual
Founded in 1996

23302 Arabian Travel Market
Reed Exhibition Companies

383 Main Avenue
PO Box 6059
Norwalk, CT 06851

203-840-4800
FAX 203-840-9628
Home Page: www.arabiantravelmarket.com

Three hundred exhibitors with travel related information, supplies and services.
5915 Attendees
Frequency: Annual

23303 Corporate and Incentive Travel
685 S. Washington Street
Alexandira, VA 22314

703-683-0123
FAX 703-683-4545
E-Mail: info@corporateincentivetravel.net
Home Page: www.corporateincentivetravel.net

Corporate travel forum.

23304 Destinations Showcase
Intl. Association of Convention/Visitors Bureaus
2025 M Street
Suite 500
Washington, DC 20036

202-296-7888
FAX 202-296-7889
E-Mail: info@destinationmarketing.org
Home Page: www.destinationsshowcase.com
Social Media: *Facebook, Twitter*

Michael D Gehrisch, President/CEO

Containing 100-200 exhibits at tradeshows.
575 Attendees
Founded in 1914
Mailing list available for rent: 1200+ names at $400 per M

23305 Discover America International Pow Wow
Travel Industry Association of America
1100 New York Avenue NW
Suite 450
Washington, DC 20005-3934

202-408-8422
FAX 202-408-1255
E-Mail: feedback@ustravel.org
Home Page:
www.ustravel.org/events/international-pow-wo
w

Rodger Dow, President & CEO
Siming Cao, Coordinator
Geoff Freeman, Executive Vice President and COO
Rebecca Shafer, Director of Executive Operations

Annual show of 1050 suppliers of travel products and services.
5,600 Attendees

23306 Euro Travel Forum
Reed Exhibition Companies
255 Washington Street
Newton, MA 02458-1637

617-584-4900
FAX 617-630-2222

Elizabeth Hitchcock, International Sales

A mobile, multi-product and multi-destination travel trade exhibition bringing travel products from all over the world into direct contact with travel agents and travel buyers from the leisure, business and incentive products industries.
27M Attendees
Frequency: April

23307 Family Motor Coach Association Convention
8291 Clough Pike
Cincinnati, OH 45244-2756

513-474-3622
800-543-3622
FAX 513-388-5286
E-Mail: jyeatts@fmca.com
Home Page: www.fmca.com

Jerry Yeatts, Convention Director
Ranita Jones, Sales Manager
Shawna Grubbs, Sales Assistant

Convention for Motorhome enthusiasts. Includes hundreds of motorhome displays, supplier displays and component displays.
15M Attendees
Frequency: Mar/Apr/July/Aug
Founded in 1963

23308 Heartland Travel Showcase
Hart Productions
130 E Chestnut Street
Suite 301
Columbus, OH 43215

513-281-0022
800-896-4682
FAX 513-281-3322
Home Page:
www.heartlandtravelshowcase.com

Annual show and exhibits of information from 10 midwest states and the province of Ontario on travel destinations, attractions, accommodations, activities and restaurants.
Frequency: February

23309 Incentive Travel and Meeting Executives Show
Hall-Erickson
98 E Naperville Road
Westmont, IL 60559-1559

630-963-9185
800-752-6312
FAX 630-434-1216
E-Mail: moti@heiexpo.com
Home Page: www.motivationshow.com

Nancy A Petitti, Show Director
20M Attendees
Frequency: October
Founded in 1972

23310 Motivation Show
Hall-Erickson
98 E Naperville Road
Westmont, IL 60559-1559

630-963-9185
800-752-6312
FAX 630-434-1216
E-Mail: moti@heiexpo.com
Home Page: www.motivationshow.com

Nancy A Petitti, Exhibit Show Manager
25M Attendees
Frequency: September
Founded in 1929

23311 NTA Convention
National Tour Association
546 E Main St
Lexington, KY 40508

859-226-4444
800-682-8886
FAX 859-226-4414
E-Mail: questions@ntastaff.com
Home Page: ntaonline.com

Lisa Simon, President
Cathy Greteman, Chair & CEO
Matt Grayson, Director, Industry & Govt Relations
Erin Turner, Event Manager

The National Tour Association is an organization of nearly 4,000 international tourism professionals focused on the development, promotion and increased use of tour operators packaged travel.
Mailing list available for rental $500 per M

23312 National Camping Industry Expo
3700 W Flamingo Rd
Las Vegas, NV 22182-2240

703-932-2342
FAX 703-734-3004
Home Page: www.gocampingamerica.com

Rick Carbo, Manager
Chandana Karmarkar, Manager

National camping industry expo, only trade expo for RV parks and campground owners/operators. Containing 120 booths and 100 exhibitors.
850+ Attendees
Frequency: November
Founded in 1966
Mailing list available for rent: 3,200 names

23313 Recreational Vehicle Industry Association National RV Trade Show
1896 Preston White Drive
Reston, VA 20191-4325

703-206-6003

David Humphreys, President
Mary Hutya, VP

Six hundred and thirty booths.
10M Attendees
Frequency: November

23314 Seatrade Cruise Convention
Miller Freeman Publications
13760 Noel Road
Suite 500
Dallas, TX 75240

800-527-0207
FAX 214-419-8855

23315 Sport Travel Outdoor Show
Expositions
PO Box 550
Cleveland, OH 44107-0550

216-529-1300
FAX 330-529-0311

Judy Fassnacht, Show Manager

475 booths of products and services related to the outdoor travel industry.
93M Attendees
Frequency: February

23316 Sports Travel and Adventure
Show Productions
800 Roosevelt Road
Suite 407
Glen Ellyn, IL 60137-5839

630-694-4611
FAX 630-790-0209

Sandra Lewis, Show Manager

Two hundred and fifty six booths geared toward outdoor enthusiasts.
15M Attendees
Frequency: February

23317 Travel Industry Association American Pow Wow Marketing
1100 New York Avenue NW
Suite 450W
Washington, DC 20005

202-408-8422

Sue Elms, Show Manager
Roger Dow, CEO

Seven hundred booths where providers of US travel products promote these products.
3M Attendees
Frequency: April

23318 Travel and Tourism Research Association Show
546 E Main Street
Lexington, KY 40508-2342

859-226-4355
FAX 859-226-4355
E-Mail: lisalcarey@aol.com
Home Page: www.ttra.com

Twenty booths exhibiting information of interest to members of the Tourism Research Association.
400 Attendees
Frequency: June

23319 TravelAge Tradeshows
11400 West Olympic Blvd
Suite 325
Los Angeles, CA 90064

310-954-2510
FAX 212-237-3007
Home Page: www.travelagewest.com/Magazine

Nancy Montella, Show Manager

Four hundred booths of educational and business-oriented tradeshow that provides a vehicle for various people within the travel industry to meet and exchange information on products, services and trends.
2.5M Attendees
Frequency: March

23320 World Travel Market
Reed Exhibition Companies
255 Washington Street
Newton, MA 02458-1637

617-584-4900
FAX 617-630-2222
Home Page: www.wtmlondon.com

Elizabeth Hitchcock, International Sales

Premium travel show.
43M Attendees
Frequency: November

Directories & Databases

23321 ABC Cruise and Ferry Guide
Reed Travel Group
Church Street
Hertfordshire, England, LU 5 4HB

Offers information on international shipping companies operating passenger services and cruises.
320 Pages
Frequency: Quarterly
ISBN: 0-001048-0 -

23322 ABC Guide to International Travel
Reed Travel Group
Church Street
Hertfordshire, England, LU 5 4HB

Offers a list of foreign consulates in London, England that offer travel information to tourists.
Frequency: Quarterly

23323 Access Travel: Airports
Airport Operators Council International

1220 19th Street NW
Suite 200
Washington, DC 20036-2463

202-293-8500
FAX 202-331-1362

Information is given on over 500 airports
worldwide that offer handicapped facilities.
50 Pages

23324 Airport Hotel Directory

3255 Wilshire Boulevard
Suite 1514
Los Angeles, CA 90010-1418

213-739-1956

Restaurants and hotels are listed that are a close
proximity to major airports.
Cost: $12.00
170 Pages

23325 American Bus Association's Motorcoach Marketer

American Bus Association
111 K Street NE
9th Floor
Washington, DC 20002

202-842-1645
FAX 202-842-0850
E-Mail: abainfo@buses.org
Home Page:
www.buses.org/Member-Resources/Motorcoach-Marketer

Peter J Pantuso, CEO
Eron Shosteck, Marketing

This directory is a comprehensive guide of the
bus and travel industry offering information on
hotels and sightseeing services, attractions, museums, restaurants and more.
500 Pages
Frequency: Annual
Founded in 1926

23326 American Society of Travel Agents Membership Directory

NACTA
1101 King St
Alexandria, VA 22314-2963

703-739-2782
FAX 703-684-8319
Home Page: www.nacta.com

Bill Maloney, Manager

Travel agents that represent over 17,000 agencies in the United States, Canada and overseas
are the focus of this comprehensive directory.
Cost: $125.00
600 Pages
Frequency: Annual

23327 CMP Publications Travel File

CMP Publications
600 Community Dr
Manhasset, NY 11030-3810

516-562-5000
FAX 516-562-5718

This large database covers the travel industry,
with emphasis on news for travel agents and
business travelers.
Frequency: Full-text

23328 Club Metro

Metro Online
1358 Hooper Avenue
Ste. 293
Toms River, NJ 08752

212-794-2664
Home Page: www.clubmetrousa.com

This database contains information on travel,
entertainment, and metropolitan services.
Frequency: Bulletin Board

23329 Condo Vacations: the Complete Guide

Lanier Publishing International
PO Box 20429
Oakland, CA 94620-0429

Condominiums that are available for vacation
rentals are listed.
Cost: $14.95
320 Pages
Frequency: Annual

23330 Cruise Industry News Annual

Nissel-Lie Communications
441 Lexington Avenue
Suite 809
New York, NY 10017-3910

212-986-1025
FAX 212-986-1033
E-Mail: info2@cruiseindustrynews.com
Home Page: www.cruiseindustrynews.com

Oivind Mathisen, Editor/Publisher
Angela Mathisen, Publisher/Advertising
Director
Monty Mathisen, Reporter/Web Editor

This book presents the entire worldwide cruise
industry from new ships on order to supply/de-
mand scenarios; plus reports on relevant issues,
financial results, newbuilding and second-hand
ship values, shipbuilding, new technology and
on board services; plus exclusive reports on
each sailing region, and a comprehensive directory of all cruised lines, shipyards, ports and
other suppliers.
Cost: $450.00
300 Pages
Frequency: Annual
Founded in 1988

23331 Environmental Vacations: Volunteer Projects to Save the Planet

John Muir Publications
PO Box 613
Santa Fe, NM 87504-0613

505-466-6360
FAX 505-988-1680

Information is given on vacations that provide
opportunities to assist environmental projects.
Cost: $16.95
250 Pages

23332 Federal Travel Directory

Office of Federal Supply & Services
4 Crystal Mall Building
Washington, DC 20406-0001

202-564-2480

A list of airlines is offered in this directory that
are under contract to the federal government.
Cost: $77.00
Frequency: Monthly

23333 Ford's Travel Guides

Ford's Travel Guides
19448 Londelius Street
Northridge, CA 91324-3511

818-987-1413

Offers valuable information on cruise ships and
their planned cruises for one year ahead.
Cost: $14.95
200 Pages
Frequency: Quarterly
Circulation: 5,000

23334 Foster Travel Publishing Website

Foster Travel Publishing
Po Box 5715
Berkeley, CA 94705-0715

510-549-2202
FAX 510-549-1131
E-Mail: lee@fostertravel.com
Home Page: www.fostertravel.com

Lee Foster, Owner

award winning travel writing and photography
on 200 worldwide locations, presented to the
consumer and to the content buyer on the web
or in print looking for travel writing or travel
photography.
Frequency: Full-text

23335 Free US Tourist Attractions

Pilot Books
127 Sterling Avenue
PO Box 2102
Greenport, NY 11944

631-477-0978
800-797-4568
FAX 631-477-0978

A directory of free family entertainment in ev-
ery state of the union.
Cost: $12.95
ISBN: 0-875762-04-2

23336 International Workcamp Directory

VFP International Voluntary Service
7 Kilburn Street
Suite 31
Burlington, VT 05401

802-540-3060
FAX 802-540-3061
E-Mail: vfp@vfp.org
Home Page: www.vfp.org

Meg Brook, President
Chelsea Frisbee, Outgoing Volunteer
Coordinator
Peter Coldwell, Treasurer/Founder
Scott Simpson, Board Chair
Matt Messier, Secretary

An annual booklet listing over 2400 opportuni-
ties for meaningful travel throughout Western
and Easter Europe, Russia, Africa, Asia, Aus-
tralia and Latin America. 2-3 week programs
are $200 including room and board.
Cost: $20.00
2000 Members
289 Pages
Frequency: Annual
Circulation: 2,000
ISBN: 0-945617-20-8
ISSN: 0896-565X
Founded in 1982
Printed in 4 colors

23337 National Bed and Breakfast Association Guide

National Bed & Breakfast Association
2009 Family Circle
Lexington, KY 50505

859-255-0076
FAX 859-255-0938
Home Page: www.bbinnsofamerica.com

Phyllis Featherston, Executive Director
Cost: $17.95
600 Pages
Frequency: Every 2-3 Years
ISBN: 0-961129-86-7
Founded in 1982
Printed in 2 colors on matte stock

23338 OAG Flights2Go

UBM Aviation
3025 Highland Parkway
Suite 200
Downers Grove, IL 60515-5561

630-515-5300
FAX 630-515-3251
Home Page: www.oagtravel.com

Anthony Smith, Group Publisher
Jason Holland, Editor
Simon Barker, Publisher

Flights2Go provides mobile access to worldwide flight schedules in an instance direct to
your mobile device. No matter where you are,

you can look up flight schedules from across the globe and even check flight status.

23339 OAG Travel Planner Pro
UBM Aviation
3025 Highland Parkway
Suite 200
Downers Grove, IL 60515-5561

630-515-5300
FAX 630-515-3251
Home Page: www.oagtravel.com

Anthony Smith, Group Publisher
Jason Holland, Editor
Simon Barker, Publisher

OAG Travel Planner Pro is the premier online tool for travel arrangers who need to create, manage, and save complex travel plans quickly and easily.

23340 Official Bus Guide
Russell's Guides
834 3rd Avenue SE
Cedar Rapids, IA 52403-2408

319-364-6138
FAX 319-364-4853

A list of 475 intercity bus companies in the United States, Canada and Mexico.
Cost: $9.90
Frequency: Monthly
Circulation: 14,000

23341 Official Handbook of Travel Brochures
Vacation Publications
1502 Augusta Drive
Suite 415
Houston, TX 77057-2484

713-974-6903

16 Pages
Frequency: Quarterly
Circulation: 38,000

23342 Real Guides
Farmers Trip & Travel
PO Box 473
Mount Morris, IL 61054-0473

FAX 815-734-1223

A series of guidebooks that list sites, attractions and events in a city or country.
Cost: $8.00
300 Pages
Frequency: Per Edition

23343 Reed's Travel Group's Travel Agent Database
Reed Travel Group
2000 Clearwater Dr
Oak Brook, IL 60523-8809

630-574-0825
800-424-3996
FAX 630-288-8781
Home Page: www.reedbusiness.com

Jeff Greisch, President

About 65,000 wholesale, retail and cooperative travel agencies worldwide, including tour operators.
Cost: $270.00

23344 Society of American Travel Writers: Membership Directory
Society of American Travel Writers
4101 Lake Boone Trail
Suite 201
Raleigh, NC 27607-7506

FAX 919-787-4916

Sarah Haw, Member Services

About 550 newspaper and magazine travel editors, writers, columnists and photo journalists and

broadcasters in the US and Canada.
Cost: $95.00
Frequency: Annual February

23345 Thomas Cook Airports Guide Europe
Thomas Cook
Unit 11, Coningsby Road
Peterborough, England, PE 3 85B

Offers valuable information on over 75 public airports in Europe.
255 Pages
Frequency: Biennial

23346 Thomas Cook Airports Guide International
Thomas Cook
Unit 11, Coningsby Road
Peterborough, England, PE 3 85B

Offers valuable information on over 90 airport facilities outside of the United Kingdom.
255 Pages
Frequency: Biennial

23347 Tours.com
490 Post St
Suite 1701-A
San Francisco, CA 94102-1308

415-956-0111
FAX 415-956-0117
E-Mail: info@tours.com
Home Page: www.tours.com

Maria Polk, President/CEO/Co-Founder
Karin Wacaster, Public Relations
Marijo Douglass, Finance Executive

Home of the Worldwide Directory of Tours and Vacation Packages.
Founded in 1995

23348 Travel Agent: Focus 500 Directory Issue
Universal Media
801 2nd Ave
New York, NY 10017-8638

212-986-5100
FAX 212-883-1244

Lists of attractions, restaurants, convention and visitor bureaus, hotel chains and management companies, cruise lines, state tourism offices, travel trade associations, tourist railways.
Frequency: Annual October
Circulation: 50,000

23349 Travel Editors: US Consumer & Inflight Magazines
Rocky Point Press
4830 Ranchito Avenue
Sherman Oaks, CA 91423-1927

FAX 818-763-4818

Listings of travel editors of US consumer and in-flight magazines.
Frequency: Annual

23350 Travel Forum
CompuServe Information Service
5000 Arlington Centre Blvd
Columbus, OH 43220-5439

614-326-1002
800-848-8199
Home Page: www.travelforum.org

This database contains information on travel and related topics of interest, including travel planning.
Frequency: Bulletin Board

23351 Travel Industry Association of America: Travel Media Directory
Travel Industry Association of America

1100 New York Ave NW
Suite 450
Washington, DC 20005-6130

202-408-8422
FAX 202-408-1255
E-Mail: feedback@tia.org
Home Page: www.tia.org

Roger J Dow, CEO
Peter Strebel, Secretary

Travel editors of major newspapers, magazines and broadcast outlets.
Cost: $40.00
Frequency: Annual
Circulation: 3,000

23352 Travel Insider's Guide to Alternative Accommodations
Travel Insider
PO Box 14
Streamwood, IL 60107-0014

206-338-3381
FAX 206-338-3381

John E Sullivan, Editor

Over 400 sources for alternative accommodations worldwide, such as farmhouses, castles, universities and country inns.
Cost: $9.95
Frequency: Annual October

23353 Travel Photo Source Book
Society of American Travel Writers
4101 Lake Boone Trail
Suite 201
Raleigh, NC 27607-7506

715-248-3800
FAX 919-787-4916
Home Page: www.photosource.com

Nancy Belcher, Editor

Nearly 100 member photographers and 35 associate member representatives of airlines, hotels, tourist agencies and public relations firms.
Frequency: Biennial

23354 Travel Tips USA
Renaissance Publications
7950 Jones Branch Drive
McLean, VA 22108-0605

614-777-1227
E-Mail: accuracy@usatoday.com
Home Page: www.usatourist.com

Michelle Leco
Mike Leco

Amusement parks, attractions and festivals are among some of the categories listed in this travel directory.
Cost: $17.95
320 Pages

23355 Travel World News Resource Directory
Travel Industry Network
28 Knight Street
Norwalk, CT 06851

203-286-6679
FAX 203-286-6681
E-Mail: editor@travelworldnews.com
Home Page: www.travelworldnews.com

Charles Gatt Jr, Publisher
Peter Gatt, Associate Publisher

A directory by continent/region/locale of local vendors, tour operators, railways, cruise lines, and travel links.
Founded in 1988

23356 Travel and Tourism Research Association: Membership Directory
Travel and Tourism Research Association

546 E Main Street
Lexington, KY 40508-2342

859-226-4355
FAX 859-226-4355
E-Mail: lisalcarey@aol.com

Lisa Carey, Executive Director

Over 750 state and local tourism bureaus and
other federal and provincial government agencies, airlines, media, hotels, university bureaus
of business research and other university departments and research and consulting firms
concerned with travel research, marketing and
promotion.
Cost: $50.00
Frequency: Annual June

**23357 Travel, Leisure and Entertainment
News Media**
Larriston Communications
PO Box 20229
New York, NY 10025-1518

212-864-0150
FAX 212-662-8103

Sheila Gordon, Editor

Over 350 travel and leisure magazines and
daily newspapers with circulations of over
50,000 that have special leisure or entertainment sections.
Cost: $89.00
Frequency: Annual May

23358 Traveler's Hotline Directory
Forte Travel Lodge
Po Box 270469
San Diego, CA 92198-2469

858-487-9596
800-578-7878
FAX 858-487-9658

Victor Ferrette, Partner

Approximately 12,000 travel services such as
air couriers, auto rental agencies, campgrounds,
resorts, hotels, spas, travel groups and airlines
that offer toll-free domestic or international
telephone numbers.
Cost: $15.95

23359 Travelers Information RoundTable
GE Information Services
401 N Washington Street
Rockville, MD 20850-1707

301-388-8284

Cathy Ge, Owner

Provides a forum enabling users to share information on a range of travel topics.
Frequency: Bulletin Board

23360 West Coast Travel
Foster Travel Publishing
Po Box 5715
Berkeley, CA 94705-0715

510-549-2202
FAX 510-549-1131
E-Mail: lee@fostertravel.com
Home Page: www.westcoasttravels.com

Lee Foster, Owner

This database offers information for travelers
and tourists on approximately 150 locations in
the western United States, Canada and Mexico.
Frequency: Full-text

23361 Worldspan TravelShopper
WORLDSPAN
300 Galleria Parkway
Atlanta, GA 30339

770-637-7400
FAX 770-563-7004
Home Page: www.worldspan.com

Rakesh Gangwal, CEO

This database offers travel information, including 5 million domestic and international flights
for every airline in the world for more than
100,000 cities.
Frequency: Directory

Industry Web Sites

23362 http://gold.greyhouse.com
G.O.L.D Grey House OnLine Databases

Grey House Publishing's online database platform, GOLD, offers Quick Search, Keyword
Search and Expert Search for most business
sectors including travel markets. The GOLD
platform makes finding the information you
need quick and easy - whether you're a novice
searcher or an experienced database user. All of
Grey House's directory products are available
for subscription on the GOLD platform.

23363 www.biztravel.com
Biztravel.com

Internet travel service offering discounts on
flights, hotels, car rentals, packages and
cruises.

23364 www.buses.org
American Bus Association

Trade association for the North American bus
industry.

23365 www.expedia.com
Expedia.com

Internet travel service offers access to airlines,
hotels, car rentals, vacation packages, cruises
and corporate travel.

23366 www.gocampingamerica.com
National Association of RV Parks and
Campgrounds

Nat ARVC serves the business and legislative
needs of more than 3,200 member RV parks
and campgrounds.

23367 www.goworldnet.com/cgi-bin
Worldnet USA

States and their hotels, theaters and museums.

23368 www.greyhouse.com
Grey House Publishing

Authoritative reference directories for most
business markets including travel markets. Users can search the online databases with varied
search criteria allowing for custom searches by
product category, geographic area, sales volume, keyword, subject and more. Full Grey
House catalog and online ordering also
available.

23369 www.hotwire.com
Hotwire.com

Internet travel service offering discounts on
flights, hotels, car rentals, packages and
cruises.

23370 www.hsmai.org
Hospitality Sales and Marketing Association

To provide resources to sales and marketing
professionals at all levels of thier career in
travel, hospitality, and tourism.

23371 www.iacvb.org
International Association of Convention and
Visitor Bureaus

Promotes sound professional practices in the
solicitation and servicing of meetings and conventions. Members represent travel/tourism-re-

lated businesses. Publications include a electronic newsletter and on-line directory.

23372 www.info.now.com/site
Society of Incentive and Travel Executives

An individual membership society covering 70
countries. Members are corporate users, airlines, Tourist Boards, cruise lines, destination
management companies, consultants, hotels/re-
sorts, travel agents, incentive travel houses and
publications.

23373 www.nbba.com
National Bed & Breakfast Association

Innkeepers of bed and breakfast lodgings.

23374 www.ntaonline.com
National Tour Association

For North American tourism professionals focused on the development, promotion and increased use of tour operators packaged travel.

23375 www.orbitz.com
Orbitz.com

Internet travel service offering discounts on
flights, hotels, car rentals, packages and
cruises.

23376 www.rsana.com
Receptive Services Association

Helping receptive operators serve international
tour companies through partnerships with
North American suppliers.

23377 www.tia.org
Travel Industry Association of America

For hotels, airlines and travel agencies interested in promoting increased travel to and
within the US

23378 www.travel.com
Travel.com

Internet travel service providing access to
flights, hotels, car rentals, vacation packages
and cruises.

23379 www.travel.lycos.com
Lycos.com

Internet travel service offering discounts on
flights, hotels, car rentals, packages and
cruises.

23380 www.travel.yahoo.com
Yahoo.com

Internet travel service providing access to
flights, hotels, car rentals, vacation packages
and cruises.

23381 www.travelocity.com
Sabre Holdings

Travel service offering consumers access to
hundreds of airlines and thousands of hotels, as
well as cruise, last-minute and vacation packages and best-in-class car rental companies.

23382 www.waveconcepts.com/arta
Association of Retail Travel Agents

Promotes the interests of retail travel agents
through representation on industry councils and
testimony before Congress. Conducts joint
marketing and educational programs.

Associations

23383 ABF Freight Systems
3801 Old Greenwood Road
PO Box 10048
Fort Smith, AR 72917-0048

479-785-8700
800-610-5544
FAX 479-785-8701
E-Mail: customercare@abf.com
Home Page: www.abfs.com
Social Media: *Facebook, Twitter, LinkedIn, Google+*

Robert A Davidson, CEO
Shannon Lively, Vive President of Transportation

Concentrates on national and regional transportation of general commodities freight, involving primarily LTL shipments. Mission is to provide reliable transportation services in a responsible manner to meet customers' unique needs.

23384 America's Independent Truckers' Association
P.O. Box 1250
Clinton, MS 39060

601-924-9606
844-464-2482
Home Page: www.aitaonline.com
Social Media: *Facebook, Twitter*

Larry Daniel, Founder

Created to serve independent owner operators and small to medium sized fleet owners.
Founded in 1997

23385 American Towman Network
7 West Street
Warwick, NY 10990

201-722-3000
800-732-3869
FAX 201-722-3010
E-Mail: towcrazy@wrecker.com
Home Page: www.towman.com
Social Media: *Facebook, RSS*

Jim Sorrenti, Editor
Steven Calitri, Editor in Chief
Henry Calitri, Exhibit Sales

23386 American Truck Historical Society
10380 N. Ambassador Drive
Suite 101
Kansas City, MO 64153

816-891-9900
FAX 816-891-9903
Home Page: www.aths.org
Social Media: *Facebook, Twitter, YouTube*

Collects and preserves the history of antique trucks and the industry.
Founded in 1971

23387 American Trucking Association
950 North Glebe Road
Suite 210
Arlington, VA 22203-4181

703-838-1700
866-821-3468
FAX 703-838-8884
E-Mail: atamembership@trucking.org
Home Page: www.trucking.org
Social Media: *Twitter*

Pat Thomas, Chairman
Bill Graves, President & CEO
Kevin W. Burch, ATA First Vice Chairman
David Manning, ATA Second Vice Chairman
John M Smith, Secretary
Founded in 1933

23388 American Trucking Associations
950 North Glebe Road
Suite 210
Arlington, VA 22203-4181

703-838-1700
866-821-3468
E-Mail: atamembership@trucking.org
Home Page: www.trucking.org
Social Media: *Facebook, Twitter, YouTube*

Pat Thomas, ATA Chairman
Bill Graves, ATA President/CEO
Kevin W. Burch, ATA First Vice Chairman
David Manning, ATA Second Vice Chairman
Barry Pottle, ATA Vice Chairman

The largest national trade association for the trucking industry that promotes safety on America's highways, improves the industry's image, efficiency, and competitiveness, educates the public about the critical role trucking plays in the economy, and researches significant industry issues.
Founded in 1933

23389 Association of American Railroads
425 3rd Street SW
Washington, DC 20024

202-639-2100
E-Mail: media@aar.org
Home Page: www.aar.org
Social Media: *Facebook, Twitter, LinkedIn, YouTube*

Edward R. Hemberger, President & CEO
John Gray, SVP, Policy and Economics
Ian Jefferies, SVP, Government Affairs
Jefferey Marsh, SVP, Finance and Administration
Patricia M. Reilly, SVP, Communications

Represents North America's freight railroads and Amtrak.

23390 Association of Independent Corrugated Packaging
113 S. West Street
3rd Floor
Alexandria, VA 22314

703-836-2422
877-836-2422
FAX 703-836-2795
E-Mail: info@aiccbox.org
Home Page: www.aiccbox.org
Social Media: *Facebook, Twitter, LinkedIn, YouTube*

A. Steven Young, President
Taryn Pyle, Director, Marketing & Communication
Cindy Guarino-Huber, Director, Meetings
Virginia Humphrey, Director, Membership
Ralph Young, Technical Advisor

Provides a forum for discussion of problems and offers educational programs and seminars.
1100 Members
Founded in 1974

23391 Automotive Parts Remanufacturers Association
4460 Brookfield Corporate Drive
Suite H
Chantilly, VA 20151-1671

703-968-2772
FAX 703-968-2878
Home Page: www.apra.org
Social Media: *Facebook, Twitter, LinkedIn, YouTube*

Tim Roth, Chairman
Omar Cueto, Vice Chairman
Jay Robie, Treasurer
Dean Conner, Secretary
Nick Staub, Past Chairman

Association for remanufacturers of automotive parts.
Founded in 1941

23392 Carrier Information Exchange
4601 N Fairfax Drive
Suite 1160
Arlington, VA 22203

703-841-6374
FAX 703-841-6370
E-Mail: mcinfosupport@egov.com
Home Page: www.mcinfo.org

23393 Commercial Vehicle Safety Alliance
6303 Ivy Lane
Suite 310
Greenbelt, MD 20770-631

301-830-6144
E-Mail: cvsahq@cvsa.org
Home Page: www.cvsa.org
Social Media: *Facebook, Twitter, LinkedIn, YouTube*

A nonprofit organization dedicated to improving the safety of commercial vehicles.

23394 Council of Fleet Specialists
315 Delaware Street
Kansas City, MO 64105-1256

816-421-2600
FAX 816-421-0515

UJ Reese, Executive VP

Members are distributors of parts and services for heavy-duty trucks.
210 Members
Founded in 1967

23395 Driver Employee Council of America
1001 G St Nw
Suite 500-W
Washington, DC 20001-4564

202-434-4100
FAX 202-842-0011
E-Mail: info@khlaw.com
Home Page: www.khlaw.com
Social Media: *LinkedIn, RSS*

Jerome H Heckman, Partner

Members are companies leasing truck drivers to private carriers.
43 Members
Founded in 1992

23396 Express Carriers Association
9532 Liberia Avenue
#752
Manassas, VA 20110

703-361-1058
FAX 703-361-5274
E-Mail: eca@expresscarriers.org
Home Page: www.expresscarriers.org

Paul Steffes, President
Jim Luciani, First VP
Mike Coyle, 2nd VP
Jim King, Treasurer, Marketing Chair
Jim Bernecker, Secretary

The mission of the ECA is to develop business between carriers, shippers and vendors of products and services to the transportation industry.

23397 Gemini Shippers Group
137 West 25th Street
3rd Floor
New York, NY 10001

212-947-3424
FAX 212-629-0361
E-Mail: info@geminishippers.com
Home Page: www.geminishippers.com

Social Media: *Facebook, Twitter, LinkedIn, Google+*

Sara L. Mayes, CEO and President
Kenneth O'Brien, Chief Operating Officer
Nicole Uchrin, Managing Director
Rich Moore, Sales Director
Arlene L. Blocker, Membership Director

Shippers association with global contracts for all commodities.
200 Members
Founded in 1916

23398 Heavy Duty Representatives Association
160 Symphony Way
Elgin, IL 847-760-00

330-725-7160
800-763-5717
FAX 330-725-7160
E-Mail: trucksvc@aol.com
Home Page: www.hdra.org

Larry Rossenthal, President
Walt Sirman, Vice President
John Stojak, Secretary

Independent sales agencies which sell heavy-duty components to the trucking and aftermarket industries.

23399 Independent Truck Owner-Operators
1 NW OOIDA Drive
Grain Valley, MI 64029

816-229-5791
800-444-5791
E-Mail: Jim_Johnston@ooida.com
Home Page: www.ooida.com
Social Media: *Facebook, Twitter, YouTube*

Jim Johnston, President
Todd Spencer, EVP
Woody Chambers, General VP
Robert Esler, Secretary
Bill Rode, Treasurer

Trade association for business and human resources equipment financing.
15000 Members
Founded in 1973

23400 Intermodal Association of North America
11785 Beltsville Drive
Suite 1100
Calverton, MD 20705

301-982-3400
FAX 301-982-4815
Home Page: www.intermodal.org/

Joanne F. Casey, President & CEO
Debbie Sasko, AVP, Information Services
James R. Morrow, AVP, Membership
Maggie Miller, Director, Member Services
Angie Mogensen, Director, Conferences & Events

A trade association serving the combined interests of the intermodal freight industry.
Founded in 1991

23401 Lake Carriers Association
20325 Center Ridge Road
Suite 720
Rocky River, OH 44116-3508

440-333-4444
FAX 440-333-9993
E-Mail: info@lcaships.com
Home Page: www.lcaships.com
Social Media: *Twitter*

James H I Weakley, President
Glen G Nekvasil, VP
Harold W Henderson, General Counsel
Thomas G. Rayburn, Director of Env.& Reg. Affairs
Katherine A. Gumeny, Secretary/Treasurer

Members are US- Flag Great Lakes vessel operators engaged in transporting iron ore, coal, grain, limestone, cement and petroleum products.
Founded in 1880

23402 Light Truck Assessory Alliance
SEMA
1575 S.Valley Vista Drive
Diamond Bar, CA 91765-0910

909-396-0289
E-Mail: info@sema.org
Home Page: www.sema.org
Social Media: *Facebook, Twitter, Google+*

Nate Shelton, Chairman
Doug Evans, Chair-Elect
Christopher J Kersting, President & CEO
George Afremow, VP, CFO
Tom Myroniak, VP, Marketing & Market Research

A national organization with 150 manufacturers of truck caps and light truck accessories.

23403 Mid-West Truckers Association
2727 N Dirksen Pkwy
Springfield, IL 62702-1490

217-525-0310
FAX 217-525-0342
E-Mail: info@mid-westtruckers.com
Home Page: www.mid-westtruckers.com
Social Media: *Facebook, YouTube*

Don Schaefer, Executive Vice President
Matt Wells, Associate Director
Jeanne Campo, Secretary/Treasurer
Candy Wendt, Drug & Alcohol Supervisor
Diana McMahan, Membership Coordinator

Serves the trucking industry by lobbying on their behalf, assisting with registration, license plate procurement and group insurance programs. Conducts educational programs, has own self-funded workers compensation insurance program. Trade association represents truck owners in 14 states.
3000 Members
Founded in 1962

23404 National Association of Small Trucking Companies
2054 Nashville Pike
Gallatin, TN 37066

615-451-4555
800-264-8580
FAX 615-451-0041
E-Mail: david.owen@nastc.com
Home Page: www.nastc.com
Social Media: *Twitter*

David Owen, President
Buster Anderson, Executive Vice President
Dana Campbell, Vice President Of Operations
Hunter Owen, VP, Sales and Marketing
Angel Clark, Director of Safety & Compliance

Association for small trucking fleets and companies.
Founded in 1989

23405 National Association of Truck Stop Operators
1330 Braddock Place
#501
Alexandria, VA 22314-1483

703-549-2100
800-956-9160
FAX 703-684-4525
E-Mail: editor@natso.com
Home Page: www.natso.com
Social Media: *Facebook, Twitter, Youtube, RSS*

Tom Heinz, Chairman
Thomas M O'Brien, Secretary/Treasurer
Lisa J Mullings, President & CEO
Taryn Brice-Rowland, Director of Member

Engagement
Roger Cole, Editor, Biz Brief

NATSO is the professional association of America's $42 billion travel plaza and truckstop industry. NATSO represents the industry on legislative and regulatory matters; serves as the official source of information on the diverse travel plaza and truckstop industry; provides education to its members; conducts an annual convention and trade show; and supports efforts to generally improve the business climate in which its members operate.
1230+ Members
Founded in 1990

23406 National Automobile Dealers Association
8400 Westpark Dr
Mc Lean, VA 22102-3591

703-821-7000
800-252-6232
FAX 703-821-7234
E-Mail: help@nada.org
Home Page: www.nada.org
Social Media: *Facebook, Twitter, LinkedIn, Flickr, Youtube*

Bill Fox, Chairman
Jeff Carlson, Vice Chairman
Peter Welch, President
Joe Cowden, EVP/COO/CFO
David Regan, EVP, Legislative Affairs

Manufacturers, suppliers and distributors of products and services designed to control dealership expenses, help merchandising or improve profitability.
19700 Members
Founded in 1917

23407 National Food Distributors Association
401 N. MIchigan Avenue
Suite 2200
Chicago, IL 60611-4267

312-644-6610
FAX 212-482-6459
E-Mail: info@allfoodbusiness.com
Home Page: www.allfoodbusiness.com

An organization comprised of independent store-to-door service distributors and suppliers of specialty food items.
2100 Members
Founded in 1952

23408 National Motor Freight Traffic Association Inc.
1001 North Fairfax Stree
Suite 600
Alexandria, VA 22314

703-838-1810
866-411-6632
FAX 703-683-6296
E-Mail: customerservice@nmfta.org
Home Page: www.nmfta.org
Social Media: *LinkedIn*

Paul Levine, Executive Director
Urban Jonson, Chief Technology Officer
Leslie Tate, Finance/HR Manager
Joel Ringer, Chairman, CCSB
Patricia Haddad, Senior Software Engineer

To serve as a research and development organization providing the transportation industry with the necessary information to advance and improve their interests and welfare.
950 Members
Founded in 1956

23409 National Private Truck Council
950 N Glebe Rd
Suite 530
Arlington, VA 22203-4183

703-683-1300
FAX 703-683-1217
E-Mail: tmoore@nptc.org
Home Page: www.nptc.org
Social Media: *Facebook, Twitter, LinkedIn, Youtube, Flickr, RSS*

Gary S Petty, President & CEO
Tom Moore, CTP, SVP
Serena Porter, Membership Manager
George Mundell, EVP & COO
Rick Schweiter, General Counsel & Govt. Affairs

Distributors, shippers, processors, jobbers and manufacturers who transport their own goods and are owners of their own truck fleets. Sponsors national safety contests, safety seminars, management workshops, fleet management certification.
650 Members
Founded in 1939

23410 National Truck Equipment Association
37400 Hills Tech Dr
Farmington Hill, MI 48331-3414

248-489-7090
800-441-6832
FAX 248-489-8590
E-Mail: info@ntea.com
Home Page: www.ntea.com
Social Media: *Facebook, Twitter, LinkedIn, Flickr, YouTube, Instagram*

Steve Carey, Executive Director
Carole Vartanian, Accounting Manager
Derek Eng, Director of Information Technology
Sheree Campbell, Executive Assistant
Michelle Kubitz, Director of Events

NTEA currently represents nearly 1,600 small to mid sized companies that manufacture, distribute, install, buy, sell and repair commercial trucks, truck bodies, truck equipment, trailers and accessories. The major commercial truck chassis manufacturers also belong to the NTEA as associate members.
1800 Members
Founded in 1964

23411 National Truck Leasing System
2651 Warrenville Road
Suite 560
Oakbrook Terrace, IL 60515

630-538-8878
800-729-6857
FAX 630-953-0040
E-Mail: eventsadmin@nationalease.com
Home Page: www.nationalease.com
Social Media: *Facebook, Twitter, LinkedIn, Google+*

John Grainger, President
Members are independent truck leasing companies.
Founded in 1944

23412 National Truck and Heavy Equipment Claims Council (NTHECC)
PO Box 5928
Fresno, CA 93755-5928

559-431-3774
FAX 559-436-4755
Home Page: www.nthecc.org

Betty Clayton, President
Ed Williams, President Elect
Kelly R. Reich, Past President
Shane Carder, Secretary
Darrell W. Bickley, Treasurer

Repair and manufacturing facilities, insurance companies and adjusters concerned with insuring of heavy equipment and trucks. Promotes safety.
125 Members
Founded in 1961

23413 National Truckers Association, Inc.

E-Mail: info@nationaltruckers.com
Home Page: www.nationaltruckers.com

Information and services for independent owner operators and small fleets.

23414 National Trucking Industrial Relations
908 King Street
Alexandria, VA 22314-3067

703-836-5506
Home Page: www.all-acronyms.com
Social Media: *Facebook*

Trucking executives and lawyers concerned with personnel and labor relations issues.
128 Members
Founded in 1987

23415 NorthAmerican Transportation Association
9120 Double Diamond Parkway
Ste 346
Reno, NV 89521-4842

800-805-0040
Home Page: www.ntassoc.com
Social Media: *Facebook, Twitter, LinkedIn, YouTube*

Association of transportation safety and compliance professionals serving the motor carrier industry.
Founded in 1989

23416 Owner Operator Independent Drivers
1 NW OOIDA Drive
Grain Valley, MI 64029-1000

816-229-5791
800-444-5791
FAX 816-229-0518
E-Mail: webmaster@ooida.com
Home Page: www.ooida.com
Social Media: *Facebook, Twitter, Youtube*

Jim Johnston, President
Todd Spencer, EVP
Woody Chambers, General VP
Robert Esler, Secretary
Bill Rode, Treasurer

National association for owner-operators, professional drivers and small fleet owners. Lobbies federal and state government and advises on all legislation affecting the trucking industry. Provides insurance, financial products and business services.
15000 Members
Frequency: Monthly
Circulation: 200000
Founded in 1973

23417 Owner Operators of America
PO Box 582
Orchard Park, NY 14127-0582

Merchants providing goods and services to truck drivers, operators and owners. Seeks to protect the status, interests and image of truck drivers. Offers discounts on fuel, tires, food, repairs, parts and insurance. Provides tax filing assistance. Sponsors trade shows, conferences and public relations programs.
250 Members
Founded in 1982

23418 Professional Truck Driver Institute
Express Carriers Association

555 E Barddock Road
Alexandria, VA 22314

703-647-7015
866-322-7447
FAX 703-836-6610
E-Mail: dheller@truckload.org
Home Page: www.ptdi.org

David Money, Chairman
Kevin Bursch, Vice Chair
Mary Beth McCollum, Secretary
David Heller, Director
Marlene Dakita, Certification Coordinator

The nation's foremost advocate of optimum standards and professionalism for entry level truck driver training.
60 Members
Founded in 1986

23419 Professional Truck Driving Institute
555 E. Braddock Road
Alexandria, VA 22314

703-647-7015
FAX 703-846-6610
E-Mail: dheller@truckload.org
Home Page: www.ptdi.org

David Money, Chairman
Kevin Bursch, Vice Chair
Mary Beth McCollum, Secretary
David Heller, Director
Marlene Dakita, Certification Coordinator

Advocates of truck-driver training standards, driver professionalism and safety.
Founded in 1986

23420 Professional Trucking Services Association
United Truckers Service
1001 Bayhill Drive
Suite 300
San Bruno, CA 94066

650-260-3170
FAX 770-929-3201
Home Page: www.allbusiness.com
Social Media: *Facebook, Twitter, Youtube, RSS, Google+*

Members are service bureaus which assist trucking companies in obtaining licensing and permits.
52 Members
Founded in 1984

23421 Specialized Carriers and Rigging
5870 Trinity Parkway
Suite 200
Centreville, VA 20120

703-698-0291
FAX 571-722-1698
E-Mail: info@scranet.org
Home Page: www.scranet.org
Social Media: *Facebook, Twitter, LinkedIn*

Alan Barnhart, Chairman
Bruce Forster, President
John McTyre, VP
Delynn Burkhalter, Treasurer
Terry Young, Assistant Treasurer

Members are carriers, crane and rigging operators and millwrights engaged in the transport of heavy goods.
1300 Members
Founded in 1959

23422 The Association Of American Truckers
P.O. Box 230369
Montgomery, AL 36123-0369

800-426-6221
FAX 334-269-1352

E-Mail: will@americantruckersonline.com
Home Page: www.americantruckersonline.com

Provides insurance and other trucking related products for the American Trucking Associations.

23423 The Trucking Industry Defense Association

3601 E. Joppa Road
Baltimore, MD 21234

410-931-8100
FAX 410-931-8111
E-Mail: info@tida.org
Home Page: www.tida.org
Social Media: *LinkedIn*

Joel B. Schechter, President
Dana Hoffman, Secretary
William Schrank, General Counsel
Tim Sullivan, Treasurer
Ren,e Theragood, Executive Director

A nonprofit assocation devoted to sharing knowledge and resources for defense of the trucking industry.

23424 Transportation Intermediaries Association

1625 Prince St
Suite 200
Alexandria, VA 22314-2883

703-299-5700
888-910-4747
FAX 703-836-0123
E-Mail: info@tianet.org
Home Page: www.tianet.org
Social Media: *Facebook, Twitter, LinkedIn*

Robert Voltmann, President/CEO
Cindy Amos, Dir. Education & Meeting
Nancy O'Liddy, Dir. Policy & TIA Services
Valerie Sumner, Meetings Manager
Roberta Sumner, Meetings Manager

Education and policy organization for North American transportation intermediaries. The only national association representing the interests of all third party transportation service providers. Members include logistics management firms, property brokers, perishable commodities brokers, freight forwarders, intermodal marketers and ocean and air forwarders.
700 Members
Founded in 1977

23425 Transportation Loss Claim and Security

120 Main Street
Huntington, NY 11743-6906

631-549-8988
FAX 631-549-8962
Home Page: www.tlcouncil.org

Reed Tepper, Chairman
Nadia Martin, CCP, President
Phillip Lamb, Secretary/Treasurer
Curtis Hart, Vice President
Kristen Walberg, CCP, Regional Director

A nonprofit trade association dedicated to the prevention of freight loss, damage and delay, the promulgation of reasonable liability rules, laws and claim policies.
660 Members
Founded in 1974

23426 Truck Frame and Axle Repair Association

3741 Enterprise Drive SW
Rochester, MN 55902-0122

800-232-8272
FAX 813-626-5385
E-Mail: w.g.reich@att.net

Home Page: www.taraassociation.com
Social Media: *Facebook*

Paul Jones, President
Ken Dias, Consultant
Bill Hinchcliffe, Secretary/Treasurer

For operators and owners of heavy duty truck repair facilities, fleet managers, truckers and insurance damage appraisers.
110 Members
Founded in 1966

23427 Truck Trailer Manufacturers Association

7001 Heritage Village Plaza
Suite 220
Gainesville, VA 20155

703-549-3010
FAX 703-549-3014
E-Mail: ttma@erols.com
Home Page: www.ttmanet.org

Jeff Sims, President
John Freiler, Engineering Manager
Nancy Livingston, Administration

A national organization of truck and tank trailer manufacturers and 120 suppliers to the industry.
Founded in 1941

23428 Truck and Heavy Equipment Claims Council

PO Box 5928
Fresno, CA 93755-5928

559-431-3774
FAX 559-436-4755
Home Page: www.nthecc.org

Betty Clayton, President
Ed Williams, President Elect
Kelly R. Reich, Past President
Shane Carder, Secretary
Darrell W. Bickley, Treasurer

Repair and manufacturing facilities, insurance companies and adjusters concerned with insuring of heavy equipment and trucks. Promotes safety.
45 Members
Founded in 1961

23429 Truck-Frame Axle Repair Association

Home Page: www.taraassociation.com
Social Media: *Facebook*

Paul Jones, President
Ken Dias, Consultant
Bill Hinchcliffe, Secretary/Treasurer

Association for truck frame and axle repairers.

23430 Trucker Buddy International

3200 Rice Mine Rd
Tuscaloosa, A 35406

05 -48 -261
800-692-8339
E-Mail: info@truckerbuddy.org
Home Page: www.truckerbuddy.org
Social Media: *Facebook, Twitter*

K.C. Brau, President
Elizabeth Barna, Vice President
Brad Williamson, Secretary
Steve Sichterman, Treasurer
Randy Schwartzenburg, Executive Director

A nonprofit organization for educating and mentoring schoolchildren via trucker penpals.
Founded in 1992

23431 Truckload Carriers Association

555 E Braddock Rd
Alexandria, VA 22314-2182

703-838-1950
FAX 703-836-6610
E-Mail: tca@truckload.org
Home Page: www.truckload.org

Social Media: *Facebook, Twitter, LinkedIn, Youtube, Flickr*

Keith Tuttle, Chairman
Russell Stubbs, 1st Vice Chair
Daniel I. Doran, 2nd Vice Chair
Rob Penner, Treasurer
Aaron Tennant, Secretary

Dedicated to representing the interests of truckload carriers. TCA is a proud member-driven organization, providing benefits and services to the members regardless of size.
800 Members
Founded in 1938

23432 United Truckers Association

9090 FM 1026
Gouldbusk, TX 76845

484-681-9283
FAX 956-425-9350
E-Mail: info@utatruckers.com
Home Page:
www.unitedtruckersassociation.com

Assocation for truck drivers.
Founded in 1995

23433 Used Truck Association

325 County Club Drive
Suite A
Stockbridge, GA 30281

817-439-3900
877-438-7882
FAX 817-439-3609
E-Mail: contact@uta.org
Home Page: www.uta.org
Social Media: *Facebook, LinkedIn*

Rick Clark, President
Craig Kendall, VP
Angelique Pierce, Secretary
Brock Frederick, Treasurer
Marty Crawford, President Emeritus

Used truck manufacturers and dealerships.
800 Members
Founded in 1988

Newsletters

23434 American Trucker

PRIMEDIA Intertec-Technology & Transportation
PO Box 12901
Shawnee Mission, KS 66282-2901

913-341-1300
800-827-7468
FAX 913-514-6895
Home Page: www.trucker.com

Eric Jacobson, Senior VP
Coleen Liatch, Supervisor

Information for those interested in the truck industry. Contains articles on new and used trucks, supplies, equipment, financing, pricing, and other truck related services.
Cost: $21.00
Frequency: Monthly
Circulation: 600000
Founded in 1926

23435 Owner Operator News

PO Box 582
Orchard Park, NY 14127-0582

FAX 716-941-5582

Charles DeVaul, Publisher

Trucking news and information.
Frequency: Monthly

23436 TCA Newsletter

Truckload Carriers Association

555 E Braddock Road
Suite CS-4
Alexandria, VA 22314-2182

703-838-1960
FAX 703-836-6610
E-Mail: tca@truckload.org
Home Page: www.truckload.org
Social Media: *Twitter, TCA News*

Chris Burruss, President
Deborah Sparks, VP
Gary Salisbury, Chairman

Load carriers association is a non profit trucking association founded in 1938.
850 Members
Frequency: Weekly
Founded in 1938

23437 Transportation Intermediaries Update

Transportation Intermediaries Association
1625 Prince St
Suite 200
Alexandria, VA 22314-2883

703-299-5700
FAX 703-836-0123
E-Mail: voltmann@tianet.org
Home Page: www.tianet.org

Robert Voltmann, President

Education and policy organization for North
American transportation intermediaries. TIA is
the only national association representing the
interests of all third party transportation service
providers. The members of TIA include logistics management firms, property brokers, perishable commodities brokers, freight
forwarders, intermodal marketers, ocean and
air forwarders, and NVOCC's.
700 Pages
Frequency: Monthly

23438 Truck Equipment News

National Truck Equipment Association
37400 Hills Tech Dr
Farmington Hill, MI 48331-3414

248-489-7090
800-441-6832
FAX 248-489-8590
E-Mail: info@ntea.com
Home Page: www.ntea.com

James Carney, Executive Director
Dennis Jones, First Vice President

Covers NTEA and member/industry activities,
business management issues, technical topics,
excise tax applications, sales/marketing management topics, legislative and regulatory
news, monthly new truck retail sales figures,
NTEA/industry events calendar, and other current topics of interest to industry members.
Cost: $72.00
150 Pages
Frequency: Monthly
Circulation: 1600
Founded in 1964

23439 Trucker Publications

Trucker Publications
PO Box 3413
Little Rock, AR 72203-3413

501-666-0500
FAX 501-666-0700
Home Page: www.thetrucker.com

Ray Wittenberg, Publisher

Up to date, comprehensive coverage of news
affecting both drivers and management, including regulatory issues, road conditions, fuel, and
current trends in technology.
Cost: $21.50
Frequency: BiWeekly
Circulation: 27,500

23440 Truckload Carriers Report

Truckload Carriers Association
555 E Braddock Road
Suite CS-4
Alexandria, VA 22314-2182

703-838-1950
FAX 703-836-6610
E-Mail: tca@truckload.org
Home Page: www.truckload.org

Chris Burruss, President
Deborah Sparks, VP
Kevin Burch, Chairman

A newsletter for truckload carriers executives.
Free to association members.
Frequency: Weekly
Founded in 1938

Magazines & Journals

23441 American Shipper

Howard Publications
300 W Adams Street Suite 600
PO Box 4728
Jacksonville, FL 32201-4728

904-355-2601
800-874-6422
FAX 904-791-8836
Home Page: www.americanshipper.com

Hayes H Howard, Publisher
Gary G. Burrows, Managing Editor

Provides those involved in domestic and global
supply chain management with news and infor-
mation of a strategic nature, useful in the for-
mation of logistics polices and partnerships.
Cost: $30.00
100 Pages
Frequency: Monthly
Circulation: 13487
ISSN: 1074-8350
Founded in 1951
Printed in 4 colors on glossy stock

23442 Commercial Carrier Journal

Reed Business Information
2000 Clearwater Dr
Oak Brook, IL 60523-8809

630-574-0825
FAX 630-288-8781
Home Page: www.reedbusiness.com

Jeff Greisch, President

For executives who manage, operate and main-
tain United States utility and specialty fleets.
Cost: $45.00
Frequency: Monthly

23443 Diesel Equipment Superintendent

Business Journals
50 Day Street
Norwalk, CT 06854-3100

203-853-6015
FAX 203-852-8175

James Jones, Editor

Maintenance management in areas of selection,
of heavy duty trucks and trailers.
Cost: $25.00
100 Pages
Frequency: Monthly
Founded in 1923

23444 Fastline Productions

PO Box 248
Buckner, KY 40010-248

502-222-0146
800-626-6409
FAX 502-222-0615

E-Mail: helpdesk@fastline.com
Home Page: www.fastlinepub.com

William Howard, Editor
Crysten Minzenberger, Marketing Director
Gail Olszewski, Owner

Nationwide and regional picture buying guides
for the trucking industry.
Circulation: 4900
Founded in 1978

23445 Fleet Owner Magazine

Primedia
11 River Bend Drive South
PO Box 4949
Stamford, CT 06907-949

203-358-9900
FAX 203-358-5811
E-Mail: frcs@pbsub.com
Home Page: www.fleetowner.com

Thomas Duncan, Vice President
Jim Mele, Editor-in-Chief
David Cullen, Executive Editor

Monthly business magazine serving executives
and managers in commercial trucking fleets.
Cost: $40.00
Frequency: Monthly
Founded in 1928

23446 Journal of HazMat Transportation

Packaging Research International
404 Price St
West Chester, PA 19382-3531

610-436-8292
877-429-7447
FAX 610-436-9422
Home Page: www.hazmatship.com

Vincent A Vitollo, Owner

A professionally prepared technical reporting
system, focused exlusively on explaining
changes to the hazardous materials transporta-
tion regulations. Thoroughly covers and pro-
vides technical reviews of the US 49CFR,
International Civil Aviation Organization Tech-
nical Instructions, the International Maritime
Dangerous Goods Code, and the European
Road and Rail Regulations.
Cost: $209.00
Circulation: 1000
Founded in 1990
Printed in 4 colors on matte stock

23447 Keep on Truckin' News

Mid-West Truckers Association
2727 N Dirksen Pkwy
Springfield, IL 62702-1490

217-525-0310
FAX 217-525-0342
E-Mail: info@mid-westtruckers.com
Home Page: www.keepontruckinptc.info

Don Schaefer, President

For members of Mid-West Association.
64 Pages
Frequency: Monthly
Circulation: 4000
Founded in 1964
Printed in 4 colors on glossy stock

23448 Land Line Magazine

1 NW OOIDA Drive
Grain Valley, MO 64029-712

816-229-5791
800-444-5791
FAX 816-443-2227
E-Mail: info@landlinemag.com
Home Page: www.landlinemag.com

Todd Spencer, Editor-in-Chief
Sandi Soendker, Publisher
Jim Johnson, CEO/President
Mike Schermoly, Marketing
Pam Perry, Circulation Manager

Edited for the owner/operator and independent trucker and small fleet operator who drive heavy duty trucks.
13 Pages
Frequency: Monthly
Circulation: 200000+
Founded in 1973
Printed in 4 colors on glossy stock

23449 Lifting & Transportation International
2895 Chad Drive
Eugene, Or 97408

800-493-2295
FAX 541-342-3307
E-Mail: adwyer@douglaspublications.com
Home Page: www.liftandtransport.com/

Eugene Brymer, Publisher
Andrew Dwyer, Editor
Jason Pierce, VP

Covers trucking overdimensional loads, heavy crane, and ridging work.
Cost: $110.00
Founded in 1958

23450 Light & Medium Truck
TT Publishing
2200 Mill Road
Alexandria, VA 22314-4654

703-838-1770
FAX 703-548-3662
E-Mail: bharmon@trucking.org
Home Page: www.lmtruck.com

Bruce Harmon, Managing Editor
Debra Devine, Production Coordinator
Stanford Erickson, Associate Publisher
Scott Smith, Circulation Manager
Paul Rosenthal, Marketing Manager

Provides information for day to day management of a company using light to medium duty trucks, such as equipment safety, alternative fuels, maintenance and government regulations.
Frequency: Monthly
Circulation: 50509
Founded in 1945

23451 Mid-West Truck Trader
Heartland Communications
15400 Knoll #500
Dallas, TX 75248

800-247-2000
FAX 515-574-2213

Bruce Foval, Editor

Trucking industry news and views.
Cost: $59.00
56 Pages
Frequency: Monthly
Founded in 1976

23452 Milk & Liquid Food Transporter
Brady Company
N80w12878 Fond Du Lac Ave
Menomonee Falls, WI 53051-4410

262-255-0100
FAX 262-255-3388
Home Page: www.bradymg.com

Kathy Wall, President

Information for owners, operators and managers of companies that haul milk or other liquid foods in sanitary or food grade tankers. Publication covers maintenance, association news, state of the industry, business management, and activities of independent haulers.
Cost: $12.00
Frequency: Monthly
Circulation: 4,100

23453 Modern Bulk Transporter
Tunnell Publications

PO Box 66010
Houston, TX 77266

713-523-8124
FAX 713-523-8384

Charles Wilson, Editor
Robin Anderson, Advertising Director

Serves the truck industry that transports petroleum and petroleum products. Accepts advertising.
Cost: $25.00
Frequency: Monthly

23454 NATSO Truckers News
Newport Communications
PO Box W
Newport Beach, CA 92658-8910

949-261-1636
FAX 949-261-2904
Home Page: www.heavytruck.com

W Dewey Clower, Publisher

Provides industry news, legislation affecting drivers, product developments, and on road service.
Cost: $20.00
Frequency: Monthly
Circulation: 182,716

23455 Newport's Road Star
Newport Communications
38 Executive Park
Suite 300
Irvine, CA 92614-6755

949-261-1636
800-233-1911
FAX 949-261-2904
E-Mail: ssturgess@truckinginfo.com
Home Page: www.truckinginfo.com

Doug Condra, President
Faye Solem, Circulation Manager
Steve Sturgess, Editor

Monthly magazine for professional long-distance tractor-trailer drivers, who either own their own trucks or drive for trucking companies.
Frequency: Monthly
Circulation: 153000
Founded in 1898

23456 Oklahoma Motor Carrier
Okalahoma Trucking Association
7201 N Classen Boulevard
Suite 106
Oklahoma City, OK 73116-620

405-843-9488
800-368-9576
FAX 405-843-7310
Home Page: www.oktrucking.org

Dan Case, Executive Director
Craig Schneithorst, Chairman

Official publication of Associated Motor Carriers of Oklahoma, the state trade association for the trucking industry.
30 Pages
Frequency: Quarterly
Circulation: 3000
Founded in 1932
Printed in 4 colors

23457 Over the Road
Ramp Publishing Group
PO Box 549
Roswell, GA 30077

770-587-0311
FAX 770-642-8874
Home Page: www.ramppub.com

Marvin Shefsky, Publisher

Information for professional truck drivers, owners, operators, and fleet drivers on current events, industry news, driver profiles, and em-

ployment opportunities.
Cost: $30.00
Frequency: Monthly
Circulation: 116624

23458 Overdrive Magazine
Randall Publishing Company
PO Box 2155
Tuscaloosa, AL 35403-2155

205-758-2585
800-633-5953
FAX 205-758-2593
E-Mail: editors@overdriveonline.com
Home Page: www.randallpub.com

Wayne Randall, President
Brad Holthaus, Publisher
Linda Longton, Editor

For the owner/operator and small fleet operator.
Cost: $30.00
Frequency: Monthly
Circulation: 104753
Founded in 1934
Printed in 4 colors on glossy stock

23459 Owner Operator
Reed Business Information
2000 Clearwater Dr
Oak Brook, IL 60523-8809

630-574-0825
FAX 630-288-8781
Home Page: www.reedbusiness.com

Jeff Greisch, President

For independent truckers and small fleet owners.
Frequency: Monthly

23460 Pro Trucker
Ramp Publishing Group
PO Box 549
Roswell, GA 30077-549

770-587-0311
800-878-0311
FAX 770-642-8874
Home Page: www.protruckeronline.com

Greg McClendon, Sales Manager
Marvin Shefsky, Publisher

Professional truck drivers, owners, operators, and fleet drivers, information on interviews, industry news, employment information, distribution locations and leasing options for the professional drivers.
Frequency: Monthly
Circulation: 116000
Founded in 1981

23461 Refrigerated Transporter
Tunnell Publications
PO Box 66010
Suite 200
Houston, TX 77266

713-523-8124
FAX 713-523-8384
E-Mail: ray.anderson@penton.com
Home Page: www.refrigeratedtrans.com

Raymond Anderson, Publisher
Gary Macklin, Editor-in-Chief
Jay Miller, Editorial
Mary Singlletary, Directories

Serves transportation and distribution companies concerned with the handling of temperature controlled commodities. Accepts advertising. Free to qualified subscribers.
Cost: $45.00
103 Pages
Frequency: Monthly
Printed in 4 colors on glossy stock

23462 Road King
Hammock Publishing

28 White Bridge Road
Suite 209
Nashville, TN 37205

615-385-9745
FAX 615-386-9349
Home Page: www.roadking.com

Rex Hammock, President

Focuses on trucking lifestyles, achievements and interests. Offers articles on equipment and driver success.
Cost: $15.00
Frequency: BiMonthly
Circulation: 222,590

23463 Successful Dealer

Kona Communications
707 Lake Cook Road
Deerfield, IL 60015

847-498-3180
800-767-5662
FAX 847-498-3197
E-Mail:
truckbooks@konacommunications.com
Home Page: www.successfuldealer.com

Denise Rondini, Editorial Director
James D Moss, Publisher
James D Moss, President
Tom Cory, Circulation Manager
John S Dickson, National Sales Manager

Edited for the dealer organization covering dealerships, selling and servicing medium to heavy-duty trucks, trailers and construction equipment. Accepts advertising.
Cost: $50.00
52 Pages
Frequency: bi-monthly
Circulation: 23000
ISSN: 0161-6080
Founded in 1918
Printed in g colors on 4 stock

23464 Trailer/Body Builders

Tunnell Publications
PO Box 66010
Houston, TX 77266

713-523-8124
800-880-0368
FAX 713-523-8384
E-Mail: ray.anderson@penton.com
Home Page: www.trailer-bodybuilders.com

Ray Anderson, Publisher
Bruce Sauer, Editor
Rick Weber, Associate Editor

Serves the truck trailer and truck body manufacturing industry. Accepts advertising.
Cost: $25.00
Frequency: Monthly
Circulation: 15500
Founded in 1960

23465 Transport Topics

Express Carriers Association
950 N. Glebe Road
Suite 210
Arlington, VA 22203

703-838-1770
866-322-7447
FAX 703-838-7916
E-Mail: habramso@ttnews.com
Home Page: www.ttnews.com

Bruce harmon, Managing Editor
Neil Abt, News Editor
Nancy Baily, Copy Editor

Trucking industry news, features and analysis.

23466 Transportation Equipment News

Vulcan Publications

PO Box 55886
Birmingham, AL 35255

205-328-6198
FAX 205-987-2882
Home Page: www.vulcanpub.com

Ian Greenspan, Publisher

Extensive coverage of government regulations, recruiting and training issues as well as buying and leasing, maintenance and industry trade shows.

23467 Truck Accessory News

Bobit Publishing
3520 Challenger St
Torrance, CA 90503-1640

310-533-2400
FAX 310-533-2500
Home Page: www.bobit.com

Edward J Bobit, CEO
Travis Weeks, Publisher
Jerry Martin, Circulation Manager

Provides information on product and merchandise trends, covers industry news on retail activities, and interviews top executives and buyers.
Cost: $37.00
Frequency: Monthly
Circulation: 10000
Founded in 1961

23468 Trucker's Connection

Megan Cullingford
5960 Crooked Creek Road
Suite 15
Norcross, GA 30092

770-416-0927
FAX 770-416-1734
Home Page: www.truckersconnection.com

David Guthrie, Advertising Sales
Dan Barnhill, Editor
Megan Cullingford, General Manager
Reid Ramsay, Production Manager
Jamie Adcock, Advertising Sales

Published for the use of long haul, over-the-road truck drivers, owner operators, small trucking company fleet owners, safety and recruiting of personnel for trucking companies in the US and Canada.
Frequency: Monthly
Circulation: 165000
Founded in 1986
Printed in 4 colors on glossy stock

23469 Truckin'

McMullen Argus Publishing
2400 E Katella Avenue
11th Floor
Anaheim, CA 92806-6832

714-939-2559
FAX 714-978-6390
E-Mail: info@primedia.com
Home Page: www.primediaautomotive.com

Steve Parr, CEO
Susan Brocett, Marketing Manager
Brad Christopher, Publisher
Steve Warner, Editor
Jerome Dziechiasz, Sales Manager

Provides information on testing new trucks, reviewing accessories and trucking' activities.
Cost: $24.95
Frequency: Monthly
Circulation: 180000

23470 Trucking Technology

167 Cherry Street
Suite 430
Milford, CT 06460-3466

203-882-9485

23471 World Wide Shipping (WWS)

World Wide Shipping Guide
16302 Byrnwyck Ln
Odessa, FL 33556-2807

813-920-4788
FAX 813-920-8268
E-Mail: info@wwship.com
Home Page: www.wwship.com

Lee Di Paci, Publisher
Barbara Edwards, Marketing Manager
Bob Susor, Marketing Manager

Dedicated to the interests of North American exporters, importers, distributors, freight forwarders, NVOCC's and customs brokers requiring freight tranportation services and equipment.
Cost: $32.00
32 Pages
Frequency: Fortnightly
Circulation: 9000
ISSN: 1060-7900
Founded in 1919
Printed in 4 colors on glossy stock

Trade Shows

23472 American Truck Dealers Convention and Equipment Exposition

National Automobile Dealers Association
8400 Westpark Drive
Mc Lean, VA 22102-3522

703-217-7000
FAX 703-821-7075
Home Page: www.nada.org

Gary Heimes

Annual show of 100 manufacturers, suppliers and distributors of products and services designed to control dealership expenses, help merchandising or improve profitability.
2,500 Attendees
Founded in 1963

23473 American Trucking Association Management Conference and Exhibition

American Trucking Association
2200 Mill Road
Alexandria, VA 22314-4677

703-838-1700
800-282-5463
FAX 703-838-5720
E-Mail: trucking@cais.com
Home Page: www.cais.com/ata

Bill Graves, President

Annual show of 168 exhibitors of equipment, supplies and services related to the trucking industry.
1,500 Attendees
Frequency: Annual
Founded in 1984

23474 ECA Shipper: Carrier Marketplace

Express Carriers Association
9532 Liberia Avenue
Manassas, VA 20110

703-361-1058
866-322-7447
FAX 703-361-5274
E-Mail: eca@expresscarriers.com
Home Page: www.expresscarriers.com

Carrie Ehlers, President
Stuart Hyden, First Vice President

Premier business to business event featuring one on one interviews between shippers, carri-

ers and vendors of products/services to the transportation industry.
300+ Attendees
Frequency: April
Founded in 1997

23475 International Truck and Bus Expo
Society of Automotive Engineers
400 Commonwealth Drive
Warrendale, PA 15096-0001

724-772-8548
FAX 724-776-0790
Home Page: www.sae.org

23476 Light Truck Accessory Expo
Truck Cap and Accessory Association
6564 Loisdale Court
Suite 430
Springfield, VA 22150-1812

703-822-0707
800-283-8242
FAX 703-922-7806

Kendra Moore, Director Meetings/Marketing
Annual show of 150 manufacturers of truck caps and light truck accessories.
2,500 Attendees

23477 Midwest Truck Show
Mid-West Truckers Association
2727 N Dirksen Parkway
Springfield, IL 62702

217-525-0310
FAX 217-525-0342
E-Mail: info@mid-westtruckers.com
Home Page: www.mid-westtruckers.com

Don Schaefer, Executive VP

Annual show and exhibits of trucks, trailers, financing information, computers, insurance information and related equipment, supplies and services. Containing 200 booths and 150 exhibitors.
6,000 Attendees
Frequency: February

23478 TCA Annual Convention
Truckload Carriers Association
555 E Braddock Road
Suite CS-4
Alexandria, VA 22314-2182

703-838-1960
FAX 703-836-6610
E-Mail: tca@truckload.org
Home Page: www.truckload.org
Social Media: *Facebook, Twitter, TCA News*

Chris Burruss, President
William Giroux, EVP Conventions/Marketing
Casey Bloyer, Senior Manager
Conventions/Mktg
Mackenzie Tolliver, Coordinator
Conventions/Marketing

Truckload carriers is a trade association that represents the truckload segment of the motor carrier industry, affiliated with the american trucking association.
900 Members
1800 Attendees
Frequency: Annual/March
Founded in 1938

23479 TCA Newsletter Annual Convention
Truckload Carriers Association
555 E Braddock Road
Suite CS-4
Alexandria, VA 22314-2182

703-838-1960
FAX 703-836-6610
E-Mail: tca@truckload.org

Home Page: www.truckload.org
Social Media: *Twitter, TCA News*

Chris Burruss, President
Deborah Sparks, VP
Tom Kretsinger, Chairman

Load carriers association is a non profit trucking association founded in 1938.
850 Members
1200 Attendees
Frequency: Weekly
Founded in 1938

23480 Truck Show Las Vegas
Independent Trade Show Management
1155 Chess Drive
Suite 102
Foster City, CA 94404-1117

650-349-4876
800-227-5992
FAX 650-349-5169
E-Mail: rsherrard@truckshow.com
Home Page: www.truckshow.com

Sue K Fena, Sr. Show Coordinator
Roger Sherrard, President

The premier commercial truck and equipment show in the USA. Containing 2,500 booths and 350 exhibits, also offers seminars and workshops on current topics in the trucking industry.
20M Attendees
Frequency: June
Founded in 1961
Mailing list available for rent

23481 Truckerfest
Newport Communications
38 Executive Park
Suite 300
Irvine, CA 92614-6755

949-261-1636
800-233-1911
FAX 949-261-2904
Home Page: www.truckerfest.com

Bud Farquhar, Show Manager
BJ Iverson, Events Coordinator

Trucker appreciation event at Alamo Travel Plaza, Reno, NV. Truck Parade, trucker games, music, free dinners, truck beauty contest, and fireworks. Containing 75 booths and 60 exhibits.
10M Attendees
Frequency: August

23482 Trucking Show Mid-America
1404 Browns Lane
Suite E
Louisville, KY 40207

Home Page: www.truckingshow.com

Timothy Young, Show Manager

Four hundred and fifty booths displaying the latest in trucking.
35M Attendees
Frequency: March

23483 Work Truck Show
National Truck Equipment Association
37400 Hills Tech Drive
Farmington Hills, MI 48331-3414

248-489-7090
800-441-6832
FAX 248-489-8590
E-Mail: info@ntea.com
Home Page: www.ntea.com

Tom Rawson, President
Dennis Jones, First Vice President

Annual business to business event designed to bring together distributors, upfitters, manufacturers, buyers and users of work trucks in all

industries including delivery, government, construction and landscaping.
7,000 Attendees
Frequency: March

Directories & Databases

23484 Fleet Owner-Specs and Buyers' Directory Issue
Primedia
1166 Avenue of the Americas/10th Fl
Shawnee Mission, NY 10036

212-204-4200
FAX 913-514-6895
Home Page: www.penton.com

Eric Jacobson, Senior VP
Tom Moore, Editor
Chris Meyer, Director

Lists of manufacturers of equipment and materials used in the operation, management and maintenance of truck and bus fleets.
Cost: $5.00
Frequency: Annual October
Circulation: 100,250

23485 Grey House Transportation Security Directory
Grey House Publishing
4919 Route 22
PO Box 56
Amenia, NY 12501

518-789-8700
800-562-2139
FAX 845-373-6390
E-Mail: books@greyhouse.com
Home Page: www.greyhouse.com
Social Media: *Facebook, Twitter*

Leslie Mackenzie, Publisher
Richard Gottlieb, Editor

Provides information on everything from Regulatory Authorities to Security Equipment, this top-flight directory brings together the relevant information necessary for creating and maintaining a security plan for a wide range of transportation facilities.
Cost: $195.00
800 Pages
ISBN: 1-592370-75-6
Founded in 1981

23486 Heavy Duty Representatives Profile Directory
Heavy Duty Representatives Association
160 Symphony Way
Elgin, IL 60120

847-760-0067
800-763-5717
FAX 330-722-5638
E-Mail: trucksvc@aol.com
Home Page: hdra.org

Larry Rosenthal, President
Walt Sirman, Vice President
John Stojack, Secretary

About 60 independent sales agencies which sell heavy-duty components to the trucking and aftermarket industries.
Frequency: Annual January

23487 Heavy Duty Trucking: CFS Buyers Guide
Newport Communications Div.-HIC Corporation

38 Executive Park
Suite 300
Irvine, CA 92614-6755

949-261-1636
FAX 949-261-2904

Doug Condra, Publisher

Five hundred Council of Fleet Specialists member manufacturers and wholesalers specializing in heavy-duty truck parts and repairs.
Cost: $45.00
Frequency: Annual January
Circulation: 98,502

23488 NTEA Membership Roster & Product Directory

National Truck Equipment Association
37400 Hills Tech Dr
Farmington Hill, MI 48331-3414

248-489-7090
800-441-6832
FAX 248-489-8590
E-Mail: info@ntea.com
Home Page: www.ntea.com

James Carney, Executive Director
Dennis Jones, First Vice President

Over 1,600 manufacturers and distributors of commercial trucks, bodies, trailers and related equipment. Information includes: product info, membership category, affiliate membership, join date, address, phone and fax numbers, e-mail address, Web site address.
Cost: $50.00
Frequency: Annual
Founded in 1964

23489 National Private Truck Council: Official Membership Directory

2200 Mill Road
Suite 350
Alexandria, VA 22314

703-683-1300
FAX 703-683-1217
Home Page: www.nptc.org

Gary Petty, President/CEO
Richard LaRoche, Director Membership

The only organization that represents the interests and concerns of private fleets — companies that use in-house or dedicated truck fleets to support distribution of their products. The directory includes members listed by: company, individual and industry. Both private fleet and supplier members are listed.
Cost: $145.00
100 Pages
Frequency: Annual
Printed in 4 colors on glossy stock

23490 Truck Trailer Manufacturers Association: Membership Directory

Truck Trailer Manufacturers Association
8506 Wellington Road
Suite 101
Alexandria, VA 20109

703-549-3010
FAX 703-549-3014
E-Mail: ttma@erols.com
Home Page: www.ttmanet.org

Richard Bowling, President

About 100 truck and tank trailer manufacturers and 120 suppliers to the industry.
Cost: $135.00
Frequency: Annual

23491 Trucksource: Sources of Trucking Industry Information

Express Carriers Association

9532 Liberia Avenue
Suite 130
Manassas, VA 20110

703-361-1058
866-322-7447
FAX 703-361-5274
E-Mail: eca@expresscarriers.org
Home Page: www.expresscarriers.com

Carrie Ehlers, President
Stuart Hyden, First Vice President

Features over 1,000 sources of information on the trucking industry, including industry reports, videos, periodicals and databases about the motor carrier industry.

23492 Vocational Equipment Directory for GMC Truck Dealers

Verbiest Publishing Company
1155 Henrietta Street
Birmingham, MI 48009-1906

Directory of services and supplies to the industry.
Cost: $25.00
200 Pages
Frequency: Annual
Circulation: 6,000

Industry Web Sites

23493 http://gold.greyhouse.com
G.O.L.D Grey House OnLine Databases

Grey House Publishing's online database platform, GOLD, offers Quick Search, Keyword Search and Expert Search for most business sectors including trucking and transportation markets. The GOLD platform makes finding the information you need quick and easy - whether you're a novice searcher or an experienced database user. All of Grey House's directory products are available for subscription on the GOLD platform.

23494 www.expresscarriers.com
National Tank Truck Carriers

Conducts research, promotes federal standards of construction, design, use and operation of tank trucks.

23495 www.greyhouse.com
Grey House Publishing

Authoritative reference directories for most business sectors including trucking and transportation markets. Users can search the online databases with varied search criteria allowing for custom searches by product category, geographic area, sales volume, keyword, subject and more. Full Grey House catalog and online ordering also available.

23496 www.natso.com
NATSO

NATSO is the professional association of America's $42 billion travel plaza and truckstop industry. NATSO represents the industry on legislative and regulatory matters; serves as the official source of information on the diverse travel plaza and truckstop industry; provides education to its members; conducts an annual convention and trade show; and supports efforts to generally improve the business climate in which its members operate.

23497 www.nptc.org
National Private Truck Council

Distributors, shippers, processors, jobbers and manufacturers who transport their own goods and are owners of their own truck fleets.

23498 www.ntea.com
National Truck Equipment Association

For small to mid-sized companies that manufacture, distribute, install, sell and repair commercial trucks, truck bodies, truck equipment, trailers and accessories.

23499 www.ooida.com
Owner Operator Independent Drivers Association

For owner-operators, professional drivers and small fleet owners.

23500 www.ptdi.org
Professional Truck Driver Institute

Advocate of optimum standards and professionalism for entry-level truck driver training.

23501 www.scranet.org
Specialized Carriers and Rigging Association

Members are carriers, crane and rigging operators and millwrights engaged in the transport of heavy goods.

23502 www.specialtyfoods.org
National Food Distributors Association

An organization comprised of independent store-to-door service distributors and suppliers of specialty food items.

23503 www.truckline.com
American Trucking Association

23504 www.ttmanet.org
Truck Trailer Manufacturers Association

A national organization of truck and tank trailer manufacturers and 120 suppliers to the industry.

Associations

23505 Action Committee for Rural Electrification

11640 73rd Avenue North
Maple Grove, MN 55369

763-424-1020
FAX 763-424-5820
Home Page: www.mrea.org
Social Media: *Facebook, Twitter, LinkedIn*

Wesley Waller, Chair
Thomas Woinarowicz, 1st Vice Chair
Butch Lindenfelser, 2nd Vice Chair
Linda Laitala, Secretary
Philip Nestande, Treasurer

Political action committee that advocates support for rural electrification.
18M Members
Founded in 1967

23506 Air Conditioning Contractors of America

2800 S Shirlington Rd
Ste 300
Arlington, VA 22206

703-575-4477
888-290-2220
E-Mail: paul.stalknecht@acca.org
Home Page: www.acca.org
Social Media: *Facebook, Twitter, LinkedIn, YouTube, Google+*

Phil London, Chairman
Jerry Bosworth, Vice Chairman
Don Langston, Secretary/Treasurer
Paul T. Stalknecht, President/ Chief Executive Officer
Kevin Holland, SVP, Business Operations

An association of HVAC contractors.
Founded in 1968

23507 Air and Waste Management Association

One Gateway Center, 3rd Floor
420 Fort Duquesne Blvd
Pittsburgh, PA 15222-1435

412-232-3444
800-270-3444
FAX 412-232-3450
E-Mail: info@awma.org
Home Page: www.awma.org
Social Media: *Facebook, Twitter, LinkedIn*

Dallas Baker, President
Diane Freemanÿ, Vice President
Stephanie Glyptis, Secretary/Executive Director
Nancy Meilahn Fowler, Treasure
Kim Marcus, Vice President

Association for air and waste management.
Founded in 1907

23508 Alliance to Save Energy

1850 M Street, NW
Suite 610
Washington, DC 20036

202-857-0666
Home Page: www.ase.org
Social Media: *Facebook, Twitter, LinkedIn, YouTube, Google+, Flickr*

Mark Warner, Chairman
Jane Palmieri, Co-Chairman
Kateri Callahan, President
William Von Hoene, 1st Vice Chair
Frank Murray, Secretary

Promotes energy efficiency to acheive a healthier economy and a cleaner environment.
Founded in 1977

23509 American Coal Ash Association

38800 Country Club Drive
Farmington Hills, MI 48331

720-870-7897
FAX 720-870-7889
E-Mail: info@acaa-usa.org
Home Page: www.acaa-usa.org

Thomas Adams, Executive Director
Alyssa Barto, Member Liaison
John Ward, Communications Coordinator

A nonprofit trade association devoted to recycling the materials created from burning coal.
Founded in 1968

23510 American Gas Association

400 North Capitol Street, NW
Suite 450
Washington, DC 20001

202-824-7000
Home Page: www.aga.org
Social Media: *Facebook, Twitter, LinkedIn, You Tube*

Terry D. McCallister, Chairman
Dave McCurdy, President/ CEO
Ralph A. LaRossa, First Vice Chairman
Pierce H. Norton II, Second Vice Chairman
Gregg S. Kantor, Immediate Past Chairman

The American Gas Association advocates the interests of its members and their customers, and provides information and services promoting efficient demand and supply growth and operational excellence in the safe, reliable and efficient delivery of natural gas.
Founded in 1918

23511 American National Standards Institute

1899 L Street, NW
11th Floor
Washington, DC 20036

202-293-8020
FAX 202-293-9287
E-Mail: info@ansi.org
Home Page: www.ansi.org
Social Media: *Facebook, Twitter, LinkedIn, YouTube, Google+*

Kevan P. Lawlor, Chair of the Board
S. Joe Bhatia, President and CEO
Patricia A. Griffin, Staff Liaison
Kemi Allston, Program Administrator
Louis Almodovar, Senior Business Analyst

A private nonprofit organization that oversees the development of coluntary consesus standards for products.
Founded in 1918

23512 American Nuclear Society

555 North Kensington Avenue
La Grange Park, IL 60526

708-352-6611
800-323-3044
FAX 708-352-0499
Home Page: www.ans.org
Social Media: *Facebook, Twitter, LinkedIn*

Robert C. Fine, Executive Director
Valerie Vasilievas, Staff Liaison
Jeff Mosses, Sales Manager
Susan Gallier, Editor
Ed Du Temple, Department Director

For personnel involved in nuclear power operation and development. Coverage includes power, plant operations and maintenance, fuel cycle, legislation, international employment and more.
Founded in 1954

23513 American Petroleum Institute

1220 L Street, NW
Washington, DC 20005-4070

202-682-8000
E-Mail: certification@api.org
Home Page: www.api.org
Social Media: *Facebook, Twitter, Pinteresr, YouTube, RSS*

Linda Rozett, VP, Comm.
Jack N. Gerard, President/ CEO
Kyle Isakower, Vice President
Robert Greco, Group Director
Louis Finkel, EVP, Gov. Affairs

The largest US trade association for the oil and natrual gas industry.
Founded in 1919

23514 American Public Energy Agency

233 South 13th Street
Suite 1500
Lincoln, NE 68508

402-438-1177
800-476-3749
FAX 402-742-0022
E-Mail: rmock@apea.org
Home Page: www.apea.org
Social Media: *Facebook*

Roger W. Mock, President/ CEO
Denise Barnhill, Executive Assistant

Purpose is to provide energy acquisition and energy-related services for its members and other public agencies, and to assist such agencies in acquiring stable energy supplies, reducing energy costs through group purchases, and developing enhanced energy acquisition mechanisms.
40 Members
Founded in 1995

23515 American Public Power Association

2451 Crystal Drive
Suite 1000
Arlington, VA 22202-4804

202-467-2900
E-Mail: info@PublicPower.org
Home Page: www.publicpower.org
Social Media: *Facebook, Twitter, LinkedIn, You Tube, Instagram, Pinterest*

Douglas Hunter, Chairman
Walter Haase, Vice Chairman
Andrew M. Boatright, Chair Elect
Paula DiFonzo, Immediate Past Chair
Paul McElroy, Treasurer

Service association for community-owned eletric utilities.
Founded in 1940

23516 American Public Works Association

2345 Grand Boulevard
Suite 700
Kansas City, MO 64108-2625

816-472-6100
800-848-APWA
FAX 816-472-1610
Home Page: www.apwa.net
Social Media: *Facebook, Twitter, LinkedIn, YouTube*

Brian R. Usher, PWLF, President
Ann Daniels, Director of Accreditation
Larry Frevert, Interim Executive Director
Brian Van Norman, Director of Chapter Relations
Mary Coleman, Senior Finance Manager

International educational and professional association of public agencies, private sector companies, and individuals dedicated to providing high quality public works goods and services. AWA provides a forum in which public works professionals competency, increase the performance of their agencies and companies, and

bring important public works-related topics to public attention in local, state, and federal areas. Mailing list for members only.
Founded in 1984

23517 American Society of Appraisers

11107 Sunset Hills Rd
Suite 310
Reston, VA 20190

703-478-2228
800-272-8258
FAX 703-742-8471
E-Mail: asainfo@appraisers.org
Home Page: www.appraisers.org
Social Media: *Facebook, Twitter, LinkedIn, YouTube*

Bonny Price, Chief Operations Officer
Joseph Noselli, MBA, CPA, Chief Financial Officer
Jim Hirt, Chief Executive Officer
Sharlyne Tsai, Director of Information Technology
John Russell, Director of Government Relations

Multi-discipline organization for appraisers.
Founded in 1939

23518 American Solar Energy Society

2525 Arapahoe Ave
Ste E4-253
Boulder, CO 80302

303-443-3130
FAX 303-443-3212
E-Mail: info@ases.org
Home Page: www.ases.org
Social Media: *Facebook, Twitter, LinkedIn, digg*

David Panich, Chairman
Francis de Winter, Vice-Chairman
Richard Behlmann, Secretary
Kris Brettingen, Treasurer
Lauren Harrower, Membership Manager/Data Analyst

Individuals and professionals working in the field of solar energy and conservation.
Founded in 1954

23519 American Water Works Association

6666 W. Quincy Ave.
Denver, CO 80235ÿ

303-794-7711
800-926-7337
FAX 303-347-0804
Home Page: www.awwa.org
Social Media: *Facebook, Twitter, LinkedIn, You Tube, RSS*

Gene C. Koontz, President
Jeanne M. Bennett-Bailey, President Elect
John J. Donahue, Immediate Past President
Jon Eaton, VP/Minnesota Section Director
David E. Rager, Treasurer

An international nonprofit scientific and educational association to improve water quality and supply.
Founded in 1881

23520 American Wind Energy Association

1501 M Street NW
Suite 1000
Washington, DC 20005

202-383-2500
FAX 202-383-2505
E-Mail: windmail@awea.org
Home Page: www.awea.org
Social Media: *Facebook, Twitter, LinkedIn*

Mike Garland, Chair
Pam Poisson, SVP Operations/CFO
Matthew Fuller, Director, Finance
Chi Wei, Director, Information Technology
Tom Kiernan, Chief Executive Officer

A national trade association representing wind power project developers, equipment suppliers, services providers, parts manufacturers, utilities, researchers, and others involved in the wind industry. Promotes wind energy as a clean source of electricity for consumers around the world.
2400 Members

23521 Association of Energy Engineers

3168 Mercer University Drive
Atlanta, GA 30341

770-447-5083
Home Page: www.aeecenter.org

Dr. Scott Dunning, President
Asit Patel, President Elect
Paul Goodman, Treasurer
Ron Slossburg, Region 1 Vice President
Albert Thumann, Executive Director

Promotes energy certification, management and education.
17500 Members
Founded in 1977

23522 Association of Financial Guranty Insurers

139 Lancaster Street
Albany, NY 12210-1903

518-449-4698
E-Mail: tcasey@mackinco.com
Home Page: www.afgi.org

Bruce E. Stern, Chairman
Adam Bergonzi, Vice Chair
Cathleen Matanle, Secretary
Susan Comparato, Treasurer

Insure and reinsure municipal bonds and asset-backed securities.
Founded in 1971

23523 Association of Home Appliance Manufacturers

1111 19th Street NW
Suite 402
Washington, DC 20036

202-872-5955
E-Mail: info@ahem.org
Home Page: www.aham.org

Joseph McGuireÿ, President
Wayne Morris, Vice President

Represents the manufacturers of household appliances and products and services associated with them.
Founded in 1915

23524 Association of Home Appliance Manufacturer

1111 19th Street NW
Suite 402
Washington, DC 20036

202-872-5955
E-Mail: info@ahem.org
Home Page: www.aham.org

Joseph M. McGuireÿ, President
Wayne Morris, VP, Technical Ops & Standards
Jill Notini, VP, Comm. & Marketing
Charlotte Skidmore, Dir, Energy & Environmental Policy
Matt Williams, Director, Standards
Founded in 1915

23525 Automatic Meter Reading Association

60 Revere Dr # 500
Suite 500
Northbrook, IL 60062-1591

847-480-9628
888-612-2672
FAX 847-480-9282
E-Mail: amra@amra-intl.org

Home Page: www.amra-intl.org
Social Media: *Facebook, Twitter, LinkedIn*

John Waxman, Manager
John Waxman, Manager
Founded in 1986

23526 Buliding Owners and Managers Association

1101 15th St., NW
Suite 800
Washington, DC 20005

202-408-2662
FAX 202-326-6377
E-Mail: info@boma.org
Home Page: www.boma.org
Social Media: *Facebook, Twitter, LinkedIn, YouTube, Pinterest*

Kent C. Gibson, Chair/Chief Elected Officer??
Robert M. Brierley, BOMA Fellow, Vice Chair
Henry Chamberlain, President/ COO
Daniel W. Chancey, RPA, Secretary/Treasurer
Patricia M. Areno, CAE, Senior Vice President

Association for building managers and owners.
Founded in 1907

23527 Edison Electric Institute

701 Pennsylvania Ave Nw
Washington, DC 20004-2608

202-508-5000
E-Mail: feedback@eei.org
Home Page: www.eei.org
Social Media: *Facebook, Twitter, LinkedIn, Youtube*

Nick Akins, Chairman
Tom Fanning, Vice Chair
Chris Crane, Vice Chair
Pat Vincent-Collawn, Vice Chair
Thomas R Kuhn, President

Advocates public policy, expands market opportunities and provides strategic business information for the shareholder-owned electric utility industry.
180 Members
Founded in 1930

23528 Electric Power Research Institute

3420 Hillview Avenue
Palo Alto, CA 94304

650-855-2000
800-313-3774
FAX 704-595-2871
E-Mail: askepri@epri.com
Home Page: www.epri.com
Social Media: *Facebook, Twitter, LinkedIn*

Michael W. Howard, President/CEO
Gil C. Quiniones, Chairman
Robin (Rob) E. Manning, Vice President, Transmission
Pamela J. Keefe, SVP/CFO/Treasurer
Tom Alley, Vice President, Generation

Nonprofit energy research consortium for the benefit of utility members, their customers and society. Mission is to provide science and technology-based solutions of indispensable value to our global energy customers by managing a far-reaching program of scientific research, technology development and product implementation.
660 Members
Founded in 1973

23529 Electric Power Supply Association

1401 New York Ave Nw
Suite 1230
Washington, DC 20005-2110

202-628-8200
FAX 202-628-8260

Home Page: www.epsa.org
Social Media: *Facebook, Twitter, LinkedIn*

John E Shelk, President/CEO
Nancy E Bagot, Senior Vice President
William S Burlew, VP, Govt. Affairs

23530 Energy Engineering
Association of Energy Engineers
3168 Mercer University Drive
Atlanta, GA 30341

770-447-5083
FAX 770-446-3969
E-Mail: info@aeecenter.org
Home Page: www.aeecenter.org
Social Media: *Facebook, Twitter, LinkedIn*

Dr. Scott Dunning, President
Ruth Whitlock, Executive Admin
Jennifer Vendola, Controller
Angie Quarles, Executive Director's Assistant
Albert Thumann, Executive Director

Engineering solutions to cost efficiency problems and mechanical contractors who design, specify, install, maintain, and purchase non-residential heating, ventilating, air conditioning and refrigeration equipment and components.
17500 Members
Founded in 1977

23531 Energy Information Administration
National Energy Information Center
1000 Independence Av Sw
Suite 1E-238
Washington, DC 20585-0001

202-586-8800
FAX 202-586-0727
E-Mail: InfoCtr@eia.gov
Home Page: www.eia.gov
Social Media: *Facebook, Twitter, LinkedIn, YouTube, Flickr, RSS*

John H Weiner, Executive Director

Government agency that provides statistical energy data, information and referral assistance to the government and private sectors, academia and the public. NEIC also provides Government Printing Office ordering information. Single copies of blank data collection forms, directories and EIA press releases are free of charge to all users. Ordering information on EIA machine readable files available through the National Technical Information Service and the Government Printing Office.
Founded in 1977

23532 Environment and Energy Study Institute
1112 16th Street, NW
Suite 300
Washington, DC 20036

202-628-1400
FAX 202-204-5244
E-Mail: info@eesi.org
Home Page: www.eesi.org
Social Media: *Facebook, Twitter, YouTube, Google+*

Jared Blum, Chairman
Carol Werner, Executive Director
David Robison, Director of Finance & Admin
Susan Williams, Director of Development
Alison Alford, Programs & Administrative Assistant

Educating Congress on energy efficiency and renewable energy, advancing innovating policy solutions.
Founded in 1984

23533 Gas Research Institute
1700 S Mount Prospect Road
Des Plaines, IL 60018-1804

847-768-0500
FAX 847-768-0501
E-Mail:

businessdevelopmentinfo@gastechnology.or
Home Page: www.gri.org
Social Media: *Facebook, Twitter*

John Riordan, President/CEO

23534 Geothermal Energy Association
209 Pennsylvania Avenue SE
Washington, DC 20003

202-454-5261
FAX 202-454-5265
Home Page: www.geo-energy.org
Social Media: *Facebook, Twitter, LinkedIn, YouTube, Wordpress*

Joe Greco, Chairman
Yoram Bronicki, President
Doug Glaspey, Vice President
Terryÿ Page, Secretary-Treasurer
Mihaela-Daniela Lobontiu, Business Manager

A US trade organization that supports the expanded use of geothermal energy.
Founded in 1988

23535 Government Finance Officers Association
203 N. LaSalle Street
Suite 2700
Chicago, IL 60601-1210

312-977-9700
FAX 312-977-4806
Home Page: www.gfoa.org
Social Media: *Facebook, Twitter, LinkedIn, YouTube*

Heather A. Johnston, President
Marc Gonzales, President Elect
Jeffrey Esser, Executive Director/CEO
John Jurkash, Chief Financial Officer
Tami Garrett, Secretary

A professional association of finance officers.
Founded in 1906

23536 Independent Petroleum Association of America
1201 15th Street NW
Suite 300
Washington, DC 20005

202-857-4722
FAX 202-857-4799
Home Page: www.ipaa.org
Social Media: *Facebook, Twitter, LinkedIn, YouTube*

Michael Watford, Chairman
Mark Miller, Vice Chairman
Barry Russell, President/CEO
Lee O. Fuller, Executive Vice President
Dan Naatz, SVP, Gov. Relations

Membership organization ensuring a strong, viable domestic oil and natural gas industry.
Founded in 1929

23537 Institute of Industrial Engineers
3577 Parkway Lane
Suite 200
Norcross, GA 30092

770-449-0460
800-494-0460
FAX 770-441-3295
E-Mail: chapters@iienet.org
Home Page: www.iienet.org
Social Media: *Facebook, Twitter, LinkedIn*

Don Greene, CEO
Donna Calvert, COO
Monica Elliott, Director, Communications

Dedicated to supporting engineers involved in all industrial applications.

23538 Institute of Public Utilities
Owen Graduate Hall
735 East Shaw Lane, Room W157
East Lansing, MI 48825-1109

517-355-1876
FAX 517-355-1854
E-Mail: ipu@msu.edu
Home Page: ipu.msu.edu/
Social Media: *Facebook, Twitter, LinkedIn*

Janice A Beecher, Director
Ligita Nelson, Administrative Assistant
Kenneth Rose, Ph.D., Senior Fellow
Steven Kihm, Senior Fellow (Finance)
Joydeep Mitra, Senior Faculty Associate

Research and training center at Michigan State University. Program focuses on regulation and management of energy, telecommunications and water companies.
Founded in 1965

23539 International District Energy Association (IDEA)
24 Lyman Street
Suite 230
Westborough, MA 01581

508-366-9339
FAX 508-366-0019
E-Mail: idea@districtenergy.org
Home Page: www.districtenergy.org
Social Media: *Facebook, Twitter, YouTube, Flickr, RSS*

Bruce Ander, Chair
Tim Griffin, Vice Chair
Chris Lyons, 2nd Vice Chair
James Adams, Secretary/Treasurer
Ken Smith, Past Chair

IDEA fosters the success of its members as leaders in providing reliable, economical, and environmentally sound district energy services.
1780 Members
Founded in 1909

23540 International Gas Turbine Institute
6525 The Corners Pkwy
Ste. 115
Norcross, GA 30092

404-847-0072
FAX 404-847-0151
E-Mail: igti@asme.org
Home Page: igti.asme.org

Madiha Kotb, President
Thomas G Loughlin, Executive Director
Founded in 1880

23541 International Ground Source Heat Pump Association
1201 S. Innovation Way Dr.
Suite 400'
Stillwater, OK 74074

405-744-5175
800-626-4747
FAX 405-744-5283
E-Mail: igshpa@okstate.edu
Home Page: www.igshpa.okstate.edu
Social Media: *Facebook, Twitter, YouTube, Google+*

Robert Ingersoll, Director
John Turley, President
Garen Ewbank, Vice President
Jeromy Cotton, Secretary
Allan Skouby, Treasurer

A nonprofit organization to advance ground source heat pumps.
Founded in 1987

23542 International Right of Way Association

19210 South Vermont Avenue
Building A Suite 100
Gardena, CA 90248

310-538-0233
888-340-4792
FAX 310-538-1471
E-Mail: info@irwaonline.org
Home Page: www.irwaonline.org
Social Media: *Facebook, Twitter, LinkedIn, YouTube*

Mark Rieck, EVP
Fred Nasri, VP, CFO
Deidre C Alves, VP, Professional Development
Barbara Billitzer, VP, Publisher & Editor
Daniel M. Stekol, VP, Field Operations

Members are responsible for acquiring land over which to run utility lines, pipelines and roads.
10,00 Members
Founded in 1934

23543 Municipal Waste Management Association

PO Box 1894
Guelph, ON N1H 4E9

519-823-1990
FAX 519-823-0084
E-Mail: ben@municipalwaste.ca
Home Page: www.municipalwaste.ca

Ben Bennett, Executive Director
Melissa Campbell, Membership Co-ordinator
Karyn Hogan, Chair
Stephanie Sidler, Treasurer
Brad Whitelaw, Secretary

Concerned with the processing of municipal solid waste for the production of recyclable materials, heat, and energy. Members are local government organizations; associate members are from the private sector.
200 Members
Founded in 1987

23544 National Association of Counties

25 Massachusetts Avenue, NW
Suite 500
Washington, DC 20001ÿ

202-393-6226
888-407-6226
FAX 202-393-2630
E-Mail: nacomeetings@naco.org
Home Page: www.naco.org
Social Media: *Facebook, Twitter, LinkedIn, YouTube*

Sallie Clark, President
Bryan Desloge, First Vice President
Matthew D. Chase, Executive Director
Kathy Nothstine, Program Director
Bert Jarreau, Chief Innovation Officer

The only national organization that represents county governments of the US.
Founded in 1935

23545 National Association of Energy Service Companies

1615 M St Nw
Suite 800
Washington, DC 20036-3213

202-822-0950
FAX 202-822-0955
E-Mail: info@naesco.org
Home Page: www.naesco.org
Social Media: *Facebook, LinkedIn*

David Weiss, Chairman
Mike Kearney, Vice Chair
Scott Ririe, Secretary
Natasha Shah, Treasurer
Terry E. Singer, Executive Director

23546 National Association of Regulatory Utility Commissioners (NARUC)

1101 Vermont Avenue, NW
Suite 200
Washington, DC 20005

202-898-2200
FAX 202-898-2213
E-Mail: admin@naruc.org
Home Page: www.naruc.org
Social Media: *Facebook*

Lisa Edgarÿ, Chairman/President
Travis Kavullaÿ, First Vice President
Robertÿ Powelson, Second Vice President
Charles Gray, Executive Director
David E. Ziegner, Treasurer

A trade association representing the state public service commissioners who regulate utility services, such as electricity, gas, telecommunication, water, and transportation throughout the country.
Founded in 1889

23547 National Association of State Energy Officials

2107 Wilson Boulevard
Suite 850
Arlington, VA 22201

703-299-8800
FAX 703-299-6208
E-Mail: energy@naseo.org
Home Page: www.naseo.org
Social Media: *Facebook, Twitter, LinkedIn, Youtube, Flickr*

David Terry, Executive Director
Jeffrey C. Genzer, General Counsel
Melissa Savage, Senior Program Director
Rodney Sobin, Senior Program Director
Sandy Fazeli, Senior Program Director

The only non-profit organization that represents the Governor-designated energy officials from each state and territory. The organization was established to improve the effectiveness and quality of state energy programs and policies, provide policy input and analysis of federal energy issues and be a repository of information on energy issues of concern to the states.
56 Members
Founded in 1986

23548 National Association of State Utility

8380 Colesville Road
Suite 101
Silver Spring, MD 20910

301-589-6313
FAX 301-589-6380
E-Mail: nasuca@nasuca.org
Home Page: www.nasuca.org

Bill Levis, Interim Executive Director
Nicole Haslup, Deputy Director

Members are state appointed individuals that represent rate-payers in their state.
44 Members
Founded in 1979

23549 National Electrical Contractors Associatio n

3 Bethesda Metro Center
Suite 1100
Bethesda, MD 20814

301-657-3110
FAX 301-215-4500
Home Page: www.necanet.org
Social Media: *Facebook, Twitter, LinkedIn, YouTube, Flickr*

Traci Pickus, Secretary/Treasurer
John M. Grau, CEO
Daniel G. Walter, Vice President/COO
Beth Ellis, Executive Director
Geary Higgins, Vice President, Labor Relations

A trade association representing electrical contractors.
Founded in 1901

23550 National Energy Marketers Association

3333 K Street NW
Suite 110
Washington, DC 20007

202-333-3288
FAX 202-333-3266
Home Page: www.energymarketers.com
Social Media: *Facebook, LinkedIn*

A nonprofit trade association representing suppliers and consumers of natural energy.

23551 National Hydropower Association

25 Massachusetts Ave NW
Suite 450
Washington, DC 20001

202-682-1700
FAX 202-682-9478
E-Mail: help@hydro.org
Home Page: www.hydro.org
Social Media: *Facebook, Twitter*

Linda Church Ciocci, Executive Director
Steve Wenke, Vice President
John McCormick, President
Debbie Mursch, Treasurer
John Suloway, Secretary

A nonprofit national association dedicated exclusively to advancing the interests of the hydropower industry. Seeks to secure hydropower's place as a climate-friendly, renewable and reliable energy source that serves national environmental and energy policy objectives.
140 Members
Founded in 1983

23552 National Mining Association

101 Constitution Ave. NW
Suite 500
Washington, DC 20001

202-463-2600
FAX 202-463-2666
Home Page: www.nma.org
Social Media: *Facebook, Twitter, LinkedIn, YouTube*

Harry M. Red Conger, Chairman
Kevin Crutchfield, Vice Chairman
Hal Quinn, President & CEO
Rich Nolan, SVP, Government & Political Affairs
Bruce Watzman, SVP, Regulatory Affairs

Association for the mining industry in the US.

23553 National Rural Electric Cooperative Association

4301 Wilson Blvd
Suite 1
Arlington, VA 22203-1860

703-907-5500
FAX 703-907-5526
E-Mail: veronica.franco@nreca.coop
Home Page: www.nreca.coop
Social Media: *Facebook, Twitter, LinkedIn, Youtube*

Jo Ann Emerson, CEO
Peter Baxter, SVP, Insurance & Financial Services
Jim Bausell, SVP, Communications
Jeffrey Connor, COO/Chief of Staff
Kirk Johnson, SVP, Government Relations

Membership consists of cooperative systems, public power and public utility districts. Annual budget of approximately $94 million. Sponsors and supports the Action for Rural Electrification Political Action Committee.
1000 Members
Founded in 1942

23554 North American Association of Utility Distributors
3105 Corporate Exchange Court
Bridgeton, MO 63044

314-506-0724
FAX 314-506-0790
E-Mail: director@naaud.org
Home Page: www.naaud.org

Ralphÿ Knobbe, President
Patrickÿ Novak, Vice President
Linda Coker, Executive Director
Jimÿ Reinhardt, Treasurer

A member of the National Association of Wholesler-Distributors.

23555 North American Electric Reliability
3353 Peachtree Road, N.E
Suite 600, North Tower
Atlanta, GA 30326

404-446-2560
FAX 404-467-0474
E-Mail: communications@nerc.net
Home Page: www.nerc.com

Gerry W. Cauley, President/CEO
Mark Lauby, SVP/Chief Reliability Officer
Charles A. Berardesco, SVP/General Counsel/Corp Secretary
Michael Walker, SVP/CFO/CAO/Treasurer
Stan Hoptroff, VP/CTO

Principal organization for coordinating and promoting North America's electrical supplies, demands and reliability issues.
11 Members
Founded in 1968

23556 Northwest Public Power Association
9817 Ne 54th St
Suite 200
Vancouver, WA 98662-6064

360-254-0109
FAX 360-254-5731
E-Mail: nwppa@nwppa.org
Home Page: www.nwppa.org
Social Media: *Facebook, Twitter*

Anita J Decker, Executive Director
Debbie Kuraspediani, Communication Director
Brenda Dunn, Associate Editor/Advertising
Glenda Waite, Graphic Artist
Greg Blank, Web/IT Technician

A international training organization for electric utilities in 10 western states and 4 western Canadian provinces.
Cost: $75.00
200 Members
Frequency: Monthly/Annual
Founded in 1940

23557 Power Transmission Distributors Association
230 W Monroe St
Suite 1410
Chicago, IL 60606-4703

312-516-2100
FAX 312-516-2101
E-Mail: ptda@ptda.org
Home Page: www.ptda.org
Social Media: *Twitter, LinkedIn*

Ajay Bajaj, President
LeRoy Burcroff, 1st VP
Thomas Clawser, 2nd VP
Chris Bursack, Treasurer
Ann Arnott, Executive Vice President/CEO

Members are industrial power transmission/motion control distributor firms representing locations throughout North America and several other countries and manufacturing firms.
Founded in 1960

23558 Public Utilities Risk Management Association
1900 West Park Drive
Suite 150
Westborough, MA 1581

508-983-1457
FAX 508-599-3427
Home Page: www.purma.org
Social Media: *Facebook*

Wayne Doerpholz, President
Jeannine Millett, Vice President
Jeffrey Dobbins, Secretary
Gail Cohen, Treasurer
Paul Heanue, Director

Founded to provide risk management and insurance services to municipal utilities.
Founded in 1996

23559 The Association of Businesses Advocating Tariff Equality
151 S. Old Woodward Avenue
Suiteÿ200
Birmingham, MI 48009ÿ

248-988-5861
E-Mail: rstrong@clarkhill.com
Home Page: abate-energy.org

Robert Strong, Legal Counsel

An organization for protecting the interests on industrial customers in energy and related matters.
Founded in 1981

23560 US Energy Information Administration
1000 Independence Ave Sw
Suite 1E-238
Washington, DC 20585-0001

202-586-8800
FAX 202-586-0727
E-Mail: InfoCtr@eia.gov
Home Page: www.eia.doe.gov
Social Media: *Facebook, Twitter, Youtube, RSS*

Adam Sieminski, Administrator
Howard K. Gruenspecht, Deputy Administrator
John Conti, Assistant Admin for Energy Analysis
Stephen Harvey, Assistant Admin, Energy Statistics
Gina Pearson, Assistant Administrator, Comm.

23561 United States Energy Association
1300 Pennsylvania Avenue, NW
Suite 550
Washington, DC 20004

202-312-1230
FAX 202-682-1682
E-Mail: reply@usea.org
Home Page: www.usea.in
Social Media: *Facebook, Twitter, Google+*

Vickey A. Bailey, Chairman
Barry K. Worthington, Executive Director
Will Polan, Senior Director
Brain Kearns, Chief Financial Officer
Sheila Slocum Hollis, Treasurer

The US Member Committee of the World Energy Council (WEC).

23562 Water Environment Federation
601 Wythe St
Alexandria, VA 22314-1994

703-684-2400
800-666-0206
FAX 703-684-2492
E-Mail: inquiry@wef.org
Home Page: www.wef.org
Social Media: *Facebook, Twitter*

Eileen O'Neill, Executive Director
Barry Liner, Director
Lisa McFadden, Sr. Program Manager

Steve Harrison, Manager-Technical Programs
Elizabeth Conway, Committee Coordinator
34000 Members
Founded in 1928

Newsletters

23563 Clearing Up
Energy NewsData
PO Box 900928
Seattle, WA 98109-9228

206-285-4848
FAX 206-281-8035
E-Mail: newsdata@newsdata.com
Home Page: www.newsdata.com

Steve Ernst, Managing Editor
Daniel Sackett, Circulation Director

Covers energy policy, resource development, public utility and energy litigation and energy marketing financing in the Pacific Northwestern United States and Western Canada.
Cost: $1199.00
14 Pages
Frequency: Weekly
ISSN: 0738-2332
Founded in 1982
Printed in one color on matte stock

23564 Electric Utility Week
McGraw Hill
PO Box 182604
Columbus, OH 43272

877-833-5524
800-752-8878
FAX 614-759-3749
E-Mail: customer.service@mcgraw-hill.com
Home Page: www.mcgraw-hill.com

Dan Tanz, Chief Editor
Paul Carlsen, Senior Editor
Harold McGraw, III, President

Provides news of significant developments affecting the electric utility industry focusing on state and federal regulation, management and bulk power markets. Publishes charts of prices utilities pay for fuels.
Cost: $2165.00
Frequency: Weekly
Founded in 1909

23565 Energy Daily
King Publishing Group
1325 Massachusetts Ave Nw
Suite 310
Washington, DC 20005-4194

240-455-6801
800-926-5464
FAX 240-628-5774
Home Page: www.energy-daily.com

F King, President
George Lobsenz, Editor

Information regarding energy use, supply and demand, power and heat generation, energy sources, conversion and storage, and energy and fuel conversion processes.
Cost: $1900.00
Frequency: Daily
Founded in 1974

23566 Energy Report
Pasha Publications
101 Second St
Suite 110
Petaluma, CA 94952

707-981-8999
800-424-2908

FAX 707-981-8998
Home Page: www.theenergyreport.com

Harry Baisden, Group Publisher
Barry Cassell, Editor

Coverage includes comprehensive policies and
issues affecting oil, natural gas, electricity,
cogeneration, power markets, nuclear energy,
taxation, global warming and energy business
opportunities.
Cost: $872.00
20 Pages
Frequency: Weekly
Founded in 1978

23567 HydroWorld Alert

HCI Publications
410 Archibald St
Kansas City, MO 64111-3288

816-931-1311
FAX 816-931-2015
Home Page: www.hcipub.com

Leslie Eden, President

Bi-weekly fax report on international hydroelectric project developments, business trends,
and news relevant to organizations seeking
business developments.
Cost: $635.00
Frequency: Weekly
Founded in 1970

23568 Hydrowire

HCI Publications
410 Archibald St
Kansas City, MO 64111-3288

816-931-1311
FAX 816-931-2015
E-Mail: hci@aol.com
Home Page: www.hcipub.com

Leslie Eden, President

Concise, bi-weekly report on major news in the
hydroelectric industry. Includes timely listings
of licensing for hydroelectric power projects.
Also covers news and business opportunities in
the North American hydroelectric industry.
Cost: $425.00
Circulation: 500
Founded in 1994

23569 IE News: Utilities

Institute of Industrial Engineers
3577 Parkway Lane
Suite 200
Norcross, GA 30092

770-449-0460
800-494-0460
FAX 770-441-3295
E-Mail: cs@iienet.org
Home Page: www.iienet.org
Social Media: *Facebook, Twitter, LinkedIn*

Elaine Fuerst, Marketing Director
Monica Erikson, Communicaton
David Gatton, Managing Director

Association news.
4 Pages
Frequency: Quarterly
Circulation: 400
Founded in 1948

23570 Inside Energy

Platts, McGraw Hill Companies
1200 G St Nw
Suite 1000
Washington, DC 20005-3814

202-942-8788
800-752-8878
FAX 202-383-2025
E-Mail: support@platts.com
Home Page: www.platts.com

Bill Loveless, Editor
Georgia Safos, Circulation Director

Covers the Department of Energy including energy, science/technology, and environmental
management programs as well as energy programs at the Interior Department.
Cost: $1810.00
16 Pages
Frequency: Weekly
Founded in 1888

23571 NARUC Bulletin

Nat'l Assn of Regulatory Utility
Commissioners
1101 Vermont Ave Nw
Suite 200
Washington, DC 20005-3553

202-898-2200
FAX 202-898-2213
E-Mail: admin@naruc.org
Home Page: www.naruc.org

Charles Gray, Executive Director
Jaclyn Wintle, Publications Coordinator
Diane Munns, Publisher

A quasi-governmental nonprofit corporation
composed of governmental agencies engaged in
the regulation of public utilities and carriers. Its
primary mission is to serve the consumer interest by seeking to improve the quality and effectiveness of public regulation in America.
Cost: $110.00
16 Pages
Frequency: Weekly
Circulation: 2000
Founded in 1889
Mailing list available for rent
Printed in one color on matte stock

23572 National Association of Regulatory Utility Commissioners Newsletter

Natl Assoc of Regulatory Utility
Commissioners
1101 Vermont Ave Nw
Suite 200
Washington, DC 20005-3553

202-898-2200
FAX 202-898-2213
E-Mail: admin@naruc.org
Home Page: www.naruc.org

Charles Gray, Executive Director
Jaclyn Wintle, Publications Coordinator
Judi Sord, Circulation Manager

A national organization that offers valuable information on over 150 consultants and other
professionals active in regulated water, sewer
and related industries.
Cost: $125.00
Circulation: 1800
Founded in 1889

23573 Northeast Power Report

McGraw Hill
PO Box 182604
Columbus, OH 43272

877-833-5524
800-752-8878
FAX 614-759-3749
E-Mail: customer.service@mcgraw-hill.com
Home Page: www.mcgraw-hill.com
Social Media: *Facebook, Twitter, LinkedIn*

Ron Dionne, Publisher
Rob Ingraham, Publisher
Harold McGraw, III, President
Steven H. Weiss, VP

Provides news of significant developments affecting the electric utility industry focusing on
state and federal regulation, management and
bulk power markets. Publishes charts of prices
utilities pay for fuels.
Cost: $745.00
16 Pages
Frequency: BiWeekly
Founded in 1909

23574 Nuclear Waste News

Business Publishers
222 Sedwick Dr
Suite 101
Durham, NC 27713

800-223-8720
FAX 800-508-2592
E-Mail: custserv@bpinews.com
Home Page: www.bpinews.com

Worldwide coverage of the nuclear waste man-
agement industry including waste generation,
packaging, transport, processing and disposal.
Cost: $697.00
10 Pages
Frequency: 25 per year
Founded in 1963
Mailing list available for rent
Printed in 2 colors on matte stock

23575 NuclearFuel

McGraw Hill
PO Box 182605
Columbus, OH 43273

877-833-5525
800-752-8879
FAX 614-759-3750
E-Mail: customer.service@mcgraw-hill.com
Home Page: www.mcgraw-hill.com

Michael Knapik, Editor
Rob Ingraham, Publisher
Harold McGraw, III, President
Steven H. Weiss, VP

Provides news of significant developments affecting the electric utility industry focusing on
state and federal regulation, management and
bulk power markets. Publishes charts of prices
utilities pay for fuels.
14 Pages
Founded in 1910

23576 Nucleonics Week

McGraw Hill
PO Box 182604
Columbus, OH 43272

877-833-5524
800-752-8878
FAX 614-759-3749
E-Mail: support@platts.com
Home Page: www.mcgraw-hill.com

Margaret Ryan, Editor

Covers all aspects of commercial nuclear
power.
Cost: $2265.00
12 Pages
Frequency: Monthly
Founded in 1888

23577 Public Gas News

American Public Gas Association
11094 Lee Hwy
Suite 102
Fairfax, VA 22030-5034

703-352-3890
FAX 703-352-1271
E-Mail: info@apga.org
Home Page: www.apga.org

Robert S Cave, Executive Director

Written for public gas managers to keep them
apprised of industry news.
Cost: $50.00
Circulation: 1000
Printed in 2 colors

23578 Public Utilities

State Capitals Newsletters
PO Box 7376
Alexandria, VA 22307-7376

703-768-9600
FAX 703-768-9690

Home Page: statecapitals.com
Cost: $345.00

Frequency: Weekly

23579 Public Utilities: From the State Capitals
Wakeman Walworth
300 N Washington Street
Suite 204
Alexandria, VA 22314-2530

703-689-9600
FAX 703-549-1372
Home Page:
www.publicworks.houstontx.gov/utilities/

Keyes Walworth, Publisher

Covers state regulations of all forms of public utilities across the nation. It reports on new rate structures, allowable profit margins, special taxes, consumer relations, environmental legislation, nuclear plant regulations, deregulation programs and programs for low-income customers.

23580 Utility Environment Report
McGraw Hill
PO Box 182604
Columbus, OH 43272

877-833-5524
800-752-8878
FAX 614-759-3749
E-Mail: customer.service@mcgraw-hill.com
Home Page: www.mcgraw-hill.com

Rob Ingraham, Publisher
Harold McGraw, III, President
Steven H. Weiss, VP

Provides news of significant developments affecting the electric utility industry focusing on state and federal regulation, management and bulk power markets. Publishes charts of prices utilities pay for fuels.
Cost: $695.00
18 Pages
Founded in 1899

23581 Utility Executive
Water Environment Federation
601 Wythe St
Alexandria, VA 22314-1994

800-666-0206
FAX 703-684-2492
Home Page: www.wef.org
Social Media: Facebook, Twitter

Matt Bond, President
Cordell Samuels, President-Elect
Sandra Ralston, Vice President
Chris Browning, Treasurer
Jeff Eger, Secretary and Executive Director

For managers and executives at water & wastewater treatment plants, consultants, and others interested in utility management. Focuses on such pertinent business issues as public private partnerships, capital financing options, strategic planning methods, public outreach approaches, and staff development.
79 Members
ISSN: 1044-9943
Founded in 1928

23582 Utility Reporter: Fuels, Energy and Power
InfoTeam
PO Box 15640
Plantation, FL 33318-5640

954-473-9560
FAX 954-473-0544

Randy M Allen CPA, Editor

Focuses on activities involving: power generation, combustion, delivery and transmission; alternative energy devices and systems; heat transfer, storage and utilization; and myriad of

related topics.
Cost: $289.00
20 Pages
Frequency: Monthly
ISBN: 0-890298-4 -
Printed in one color on matte stock

23583 Wind Energy Smart Brief
American Wind Energy Association
1501 M Street NW
Suite 1000
Washington, DC 20005

202-383-2500
FAX 202-383-2505
E-Mail: windmail@awea.org
Home Page: www.awea.org
Social Media: Facebook, Twitter, LinkedIn, You Tube

Denise Bode, CEO

This newsletter delivers quickly digestible summaries of the day's wind energy-related stories from across the media, as well as links to those stories.
Frequency: Weekly

23584 Wind Energy Weekly
American Wind Energy Association
1501 M Street NW
Suite 1000
Washington, DC 20005

202-383-2500
FAX 202-383-2505
E-Mail: windmail@awea.org
Home Page: www.awea.org

Denise Bode, CEO

Packed with detailed and up-to-date information on the world of wind energy that simply can't be obtained elsewhere.
Frequency: Weekly

23585 WindLetter
American Wind Energy Association
1501 M Street NW
Suite 1000
Washington, DC 20005

202-383-2500
FAX 202-383-2505
E-Mail: windmail@awea.org
Home Page: www.awea.org
Social Media: Facebook, Twitter, LinkedIn, You Tube

Denise Bode, CEO

Recap's the month's most significant wind energy news and includes interesting for wind energy enthusiasts.
Frequency: Monthly

Magazines & Journals

23586 APWA Reporter
American Public Works Association
2345 Grand Blvd
Suite 700
Kansas City, MO 64108-2625

816-472-6100
800-848-2792
FAX 816-472-1610
E-Mail: ddancy@apwa.net
Home Page: www.apwa.net
Social Media: Facebook, Twitter, LinkedIn

Kaye Sullivan, Executive Director
David Dancy, Director Marketing

Circulation to entire membership of American Public Works Association.
Cost: $100.00
Frequency: Monthly
Circulation: 25000
ISBN: 0-092487-3 -

Founded in 1937
Mailing list available for rent

23587 Alternative Energy
PWG
205 S Beverly Drive
#208
Beverly Hills, CA 90212-3827

310-273-3486
FAX 310-858-8272
Home Page: www.bp.com

Irwin Stambler, Publisher
Ahmad Taleban, President

Reports on future economic and technological trends.
Cost: $95.00
12 Pages
Frequency: Monthly
Printed in 2 colors on matte stock

23588 Alternative Energy Retailer
Zackin Publications
PO Box 2180
Waterbury, CT 06722-2180

203-755-0158
800-325-6745
FAX 203-755-3480
E-Mail: info@aer-online.com
Home Page: www.aer-online.com

Paul Zackin, Publisher
Michael Griffin, Editor
Arlene Sorrentino, Production Coordinator
Jeanette Laliberte, Marketing Manager
June Han, Subscription Manager

Covers solid fuel burning, marketing, technology, and sales.
Frequency: Monthly
Circulation: 14,000

23589 American Gas Magazine
American Gas Association
400 N Capitol Street NW
Suite 450
Washington, DC 20001

202-824-7000
FAX 202-824-7092
Home Page: www.aga.org
Social Media: Facebook, Twitter, LinkedIn

David N Parker, CEO
Kevin Hardardt, CFO/CAO
Ysabel Korolevich, Membership Services
Frequency: 10x/Year
Founded in 1918

23590 American Public Works Association
American Public Works Association
2345 Grand Blvd
Suite 700
Kansas City, MO 64108-2625

816-472-6100
800-848-2792
FAX 816-472-1610
E-Mail: ddancy@apwa.net
Home Page: www.apwa.net

Kaye Sullivan, Executive Director
David Dancy, Marketing Director

International educational and professional association of public agencies, private sector companies, and individuals dedicated to providing high quality public works goods and services. AWA provides a forum in which public works professionals competency, increase the performance of their agencies and companies, and bring important public works-related topics to public attention in local, state, and federal areas. Mailing list for members only.
Cost: $100.00
40 Pages
Frequency: Monthly
ISSN: 0092-4873
Founded in 1937

23591 American Water Works Association Journal
American Water Works Association
6666 W Quincy Ave
Denver, CO 80235-3098

303-794-7711
800-926-7337
FAX 303-347-0804
E-Mail: journal@awwa.org
Home Page: www.awwa.org

Andrew Richardson, President
Jack W. Hoffbuhr, Executive Director

Journal of the professional society of North American drinking water experts. Dues cover subscription for members.
Cost: $120.00
152 Pages
Frequency: Monthly
ISSN: 0003-150X
Founded in 1935

23592 Bulletin
NW Public Power Association
9817 Ne 54th St
Suite 200
Vancouver, WA 98662-6064

360-254-0109
FAX 360-254-5731
E-Mail: nwppa@nwppa.org
Home Page: www.nwppa.org

Will Lutgen, Executive Director

Readership consists of directors, chairmen and managers of electric utilities in the ten Western States and four Canadian provinces. Provides news and events of the public power industry in the Pacific Northwest Region.
Cost: $ 32.00
32 Pages
Circulation: 6200
Printed in 4 colors

23593 Chief Engineer
Chief Engineers Association of Chicagoland
4701 Midlothian Turnpike
Crestwood, IL 60445

708-293-1720
FAX 708-633-7008
Home Page: www.chiefengineer.org

Ernest K Wulff, Editor

Covers building maintenance issues, laws and rulings relative to chief engineers, as well as mechanical and general HVAC equipment.
Frequency: Monthly
Circulation: 2000
Founded in 1935
Mailing list available for rent: 2K names

23594 Cogeneration Monthly Letter
Cogeneration Publications Company
509 Tennessee Avenue
Alexandria, VA 22305-1336

703-683-1868
FAX 703-683-1878
Home Page: www.powermarketers.com

Scott Spiewak, Publisher

Discusses new technology and legislation governing power generating facilities. Includes listings of planned projects.
Frequency: 5 per year
Circulation: 5000

23595 Diesel & Gas Turbine Worldwide
Diesel & Gas Turbine Publications
20855 Watertown Rd
Suite 220
Waukesha, WI 53186-1873

262-754-4100
800-558-4322
FAX 262-832-5075

E-Mail: slizdas@dieselpub.com
Home Page: www.dieselpub.com

Michael Osenga, President
Mark McNeely, Editor
Lynne Diefenbach, Advertising Manager
Christa Johnson, Production Manager

Focuses on the design, production, installation, operation, and maintenance of engines in the global marine, power generation, oil and gas, or railroad industries.
Frequency: bi-Monthly
Circulation: 20100
Founded in 1935

23596 Diesel Progress: International Edition
Diesel & Gas Turbine Publications
20855 Watertown Rd
Suite 220
Waukesha, WI 53186-1873

262-754-4100
FAX 262-832-5075
E-Mail: slizdas@dieselpub.com
Home Page: www.dieselspec.com

Michael Osenga, President
Sue Bollwahn, Circulation Manager
Katie Evans, Sales Manager
Michael J Brezonick, Editor-in-Chief

Focuses on new products and technology that serves engineering, marketing, service and equipment, purchasing, administrative, and others allied to the field.
Circulation: 10273
Founded in 1935

23597 District Energy
International District Enery Association (IDEA)
24 Lyman Streetad
Suite 230
Westborough, MA 01581

508-366-9339
FAX 508-366-0019
E-Mail: idea@districtenergy.org
Home Page: www.districtenergy.org

Peter Myers, Editor
Rob Thornton, President

Journal of district heating and cooling industry, congeneration, physical plants and energy efficiency. Accepts advertising.
Cost: $40.00
Frequency: Quarterly

23598 Electric Light & Power
Technical Publishing
1421 S. Sheridan Road
Tulsa, OK 74112

981-831-9884
FAX 918-831-9834
E-Mail: candiced@pennwell.com
Home Page: www.elp.com

Wayne Beaty, Editor
Candice Doctor, Sales Director
Michael Grossman, Publisher
Teresa Hansen, Editor in Chief

Offers articles on the electric utility industry.
Cost: $38.00
84 Pages
Frequency: Monthly
Founded in 1922

23599 Electric Perspectives
Edison Electric Institute
701 Pennsylvania Avenue NW
Washington, DC 20004-2696

202-508-5000
800-344-5453
FAX 202-508-5794

E-Mail: feedback@eei.org
Home Page: www.eei.org

Thomas R Kuhn, President
Brian Farrell, Member Relations Director

The magazine for management in America's investor-owned electric utilities. Covers all areas of utility operations and concerns, providing detailed analyses and farsighted commentary on how issues and trends are shaping the industry today and the future impact.
Cost: $50.00
Frequency: Bi-Monthly
Circulation: 10000
ISSN: 0364-474X
Founded in 1981

23600 Energy Efficiency Journal
NAESCO
1615 M St NW
Suite 800
Washington, DC 20036-3213

202-822-0950
FAX 202-822-0955
Home Page: www.eceee.org/ee_journal

Terry E Singer, Executive Editor
Nina Lockhart, Senior Program Manager
Donald Gilligan, Publisher

Targets energy service companies, electric and gas utilities and other energy providers. Highlights industry news and features energy conservation.
Frequency: Quarterly
Circulation: 200

23601 Energy Manager
Primedia
3585 Engineering Drive
Suite 100
Norcross, GA 30092

678-421-3000
FAX 913-514-6895
Home Page: www.primedia.com

Eric Jacobson, Senior VP
Charles Stubs, President
Kim Payne, VP
Mike Barber, Accountant

Subjects include energy management systems, HVAC, automated building systems, plant and facilities control, and negotiating supplier contracts. Features include legislative news from Washington, analysis of rare updates, relevant news from around the world and new product reviews.
Frequency: 5 per year
Circulation: 50,000
Founded in 1998

23602 Energy Today
Trend Publishing
529 14th St NW
Suite 954
Washington, DC 20045-1925

202-662-8827
FAX 202-662-8829

Arthur Kranish, Editor

Includes news and analysis, new regulatory and technical developments, grant and contract opportunities, investigative reports, and market studies.
Frequency: Monthly

23603 Energy and Housing Report
Alan L Frank Associates
9124 Bradford Road
Silverspring, MD 20901-4918

703-866-4397
FAX 301-565-3298
Home Page: homeenergy.org

Mary James, Publisher
Iain Walker, Executive Editor

Cass Duggan, Circulation Manager
Carol A. Markell, Marketing Manager
Alan Meier, President

Research in consumption with the goal of increasing energy conservation at the residential level. Follows trends in consumption and the effects of conservation efforts on energy use.
Founded in 1994

23604 Energy in the News
New York Mercantile Exchange
1 N End Ave
New York, NY 10282-1101

212-299-2000
FAX 212-301-4700
E-Mail: marketing@nymex.com
Home Page: www.nymex.com

Samuel Gaer, Executive VP

Covers market fundamentals, trading strategies and market conditions. Provides information that keeps future commission merchants, industry executives, options and cash market traders up-to-date with trends affecting the energy industry.
Frequency: Quarterly
Circulation: 35000

23605 Gas Turbine World
Pequot Publishing
PO Box 447
Southport, CT 06490-447

203-259-1812
FAX 203-259-0532
Home Page: www.business-magazines.com

Victor Debiasi, Publisher

Focuses on implementing policy, specification, design, maintenance, and modernization of the systems and equipment of electric power generation.
Cost: $135.00
Frequency: Monthly
Circulation: 10000

23606 Generation Week
Pasha Publications
1600 Wilson Boulevard
#600
Arlington, VA 22209-2509

703-528-1244
800-424-2908
FAX 703-816-7821
Home Page: www.pasha.com

Tod Sedgwick, Publisher

On new technology and innovative operation of power plants.
Frequency: Weekly

23607 HRW: Hydro Review Worldwide
HCI Publications
410 Archibald St
Kansas City, MO 64111-3288

816-931-1311
FAX 816-931-2015
E-Mail: hci@aol.com
Home Page: www.hcipub.com

Leslie Eden, President
Marla Barness, Editor
Bob Merrigan, Marketing

Magazine serving information needs of people associated with hydro throughout the world. Managing and improving plant operations, solving problems, financing and essential business news are covered extensively.
Cost: $44.00
Circulation: 4673
Founded in 1982

23608 Hart's Energy Markets
Hart Publications

4545 Post Oak Place
#210
Houston, TX 77027-3105

713-993-9320
FAX 713-840-0983
E-Mail: dgriffin@hartenergy.com
Home Page: www.hartenergy.com

Dana Griffin Smith, Publisher
Joe Fisher, Editor
Richard Eichler, President

Keeps readers abreast of trends and opportunities in the marketplace. Covers such topics as electricity deregulation, gas unbundling, rebundling of services, nuclear and renewable energy, technological developments and regulatory issues.
Frequency: Monthly
Circulation: 14000
Founded in 1973

23609 Home Power
PO Box 520
Ashland, OR 97520-18

541-512-0201
800-707-6585
FAX 530-475-0836
E-Mail: info@homepower.com
Home Page: www.homepower.com

Karen Perez, Publisher
Joe Schwartz, Manager

Covers photovoltaics, wind turbines, solar heating, methane, batteries, inverters, water pumping, electric vehicles, controls, and instruments. Examines the design and installation of balanced renewable energy systems in the home, while also reviewing products ranging from solar pumps to refrigerators.
Cost: $22.50
Circulation: 19200
Founded in 1987

23610 Hydro Review
HCI Publications
410 Archibald St
Kansas City, MO 64111-3288

816-931-1311
FAX 816-931-2015
Home Page: www.hcipub.com

Leslie Eden, President

Magazine providing in-depth coverage of the North American hydroelectric industry. Rehab, redevelopment, dam safety and the environment are explored.
Cost: $65.00
Circulation: 500
Founded in 1980

23611 Independent Energy
PennWell Publishing Company
1421 S Sheridan Rd
Tulsa, OK 74112-6619

918-831-9421
800-331-4463
FAX 918-831-9476
Home Page: www.pennwell.com

Robert Biolchini, President

Focuses on analysis and views aimed at doing business more successfully. Reports important market information, trends and equipment advances affecting power project development, financing, construction, operation and management.
Frequency: Monthly
Circulation: 10962
Founded in 1961

23612 New Equipment Digest
Penton Media

1300 E 9th St
Suite 316
Cleveland, OH 44114-1503

216-696-7000
FAX 216-696-6662
E-Mail: information@penton.com
Home Page: www.newequipment.com

Jane Cooper, Marketing
Tom Sockel, Associate Editor
Robert King, Editor
Sarah Hughes, Production Manager
Bobbie Macy, Circulation Manager

Serves the general industrial field which includes manufacturing, processing, engineering services, construction, transportation, mining, public utilities, wholesale distributors, educational services, libraries and governmental establishments.
Frequency: Monthly
Founded in 1936

23613 Northeast Sun
NE Sustainable Energy Association
50 Miles St
Suite 3
Greenfield, MA 01301-3255

413-774-6051
FAX 413-774-6053
E-Mail: nesea@nesea.org
Home Page: www.nesea.org

David Barclay, Executive Director

Addresses the current issues of solar energy and natural gas power. Also provides an exchange of ideas for those seeking other environmentally sound energy sources.
Frequency: Monthly
Circulation: 5000
Founded in 1974

23614 Northwest Public Power Bulletin
Northwest Public Power Association
9817 NE 54th St
Suite 200
Vancouver, WA 98662-6064

360-254-0109
FAX 360-254-5731
E-Mail: nwppa@nwppa.org
Home Page: www.nwppa.org

Will Lutgen, President
Brenda Dunn, Associate Editor
Debbie Kuraspediani, Director Communications

Trade publication for consumer-owned electric utilities managers, directors, commissioners and management staff.
Cost: $25.00
28 Pages
Frequency: Monthly
Circulation: 6000
Founded in 1947

23615 Nuclear News
American Nuclear Society
555 N Kensington Ave
La Grange Park, IL 60526-5592

708-352-6611
FAX 708-352-0499
E-Mail: advertising@ans.org
Home Page: www.nuclear-news.net

Jack Tuohy, Executive Director
Mike Diekman, Information Department Head
Sarah Wells, Editor
Gloria Nawrocki, Marketing Manager

For personnel involved in nuclear power operation and development. Coverage includes power, plant operations and maintenance, fuel cycle, legislation, international employment and more.
Cost: $290.00
Frequency: Monthly
Circulation: 12000

Founded in 1954
Printed in on glossy stock

23616 Nuclear Plant Journal

EQES
1400 Opus Place
Suite 904
Downers Grove, IL 60515

630-858-6161
FAX 630-858-8787
E-Mail: michelle@goinfo.com
Home Page: www.nuclearplantjournal.com

Newal Agnihotri, Publisher

Nuclear Plant Journal includes technical papers, informative articles and departments aimed at developing better methods, systems, products and services in the nuclear power industry. The Journal is compiled through the research efforts of professional engineers who are specialists in their respective fields.
Circulation: 14000
ISSN: 0892-2055
Founded in 1983
Printed in on glossy stock

23617 Power Engineering International

PennWell Publishing Company
1421 S Sheridan Rd
Tulsa, OK 74112-6619

918-831-9421
800-331-4463
FAX 918-831-9476
E-Mail: Headquarters@PennWell.com
Home Page: www.pennwell.com

Robert Biolchini, President
Candice Doctor, Regional Sales Manager
Rick Huntzicker, National Sales Manager
Junior Isles, Publisher & Editorial Director
Rafael A Junquera, Editor

A variety of topics including plant design, operations, management and applications. New products are also reviewed.
Frequency: Monthly
Circulation: 34000
Founded in 1910

23618 Private Power Executive

Pequot Publishing
PO Box 447
Southport, CT 06490-0447

203-259-1812
FAX 203-259-0532

Victor de Biasi, Publisher

Written for cogenerators and developers involved in planning, design, financing, installation and operation of cogeneration plants for industrial, municipal, hospitals, and commercial district heating and cooling.
Frequency: BiMonthly
Circulation: ll,500

23619 Public Power Magazine

American Public Power Association
1875 Connecticut Ave NW
Suite 1200
Washington, DC 20009-5715

202-467-2900
800-515-2772
FAX 202-467-2910
E-Mail: mrufe@appanet.org
Home Page: www.publicpower.org

Alan Richardson, Executive Director
Michael L Kurtz, Publisher

The only national magazine published especially for policymaking and managerial personnel of local publicly owned electric systems. Public Power keeps readers abreast of policy developments, managerial techniques, new technologies, research and development and

legislative issues. Subscription, $50.00
Cost: $10.00
72 Pages
Circulation: 11100
ISSN: 0033-3654
Founded in 1942

23620 Public Utilities Fortnightly

Public Utilities Reports
8229 Boone Blvd
Suite 400
Vienna, VA 22182-2623

703-847-7720
800-368-5001
FAX 703-917-6964
E-Mail: pur@pur.com
Home Page: www.pur.com
Social Media: *Twitter*

Bruce Radford, Publisher
Michael Burr, Editor-In-Chief
Philip Cross, Vice President/ Legal Editor
Joseph Paparello, Director of Sales
Jean Cole, Marketing Manager

Independent publisher for the energy industry.
Cost: $459.00
Frequency: Weekly
Founded in 1929

23621 Public Utility Weekly

Public Utilities Reports
8229 Boone Blvd
Suite 400
Vienna, VA 22182-2623

703-847-7720
800-368-5001
FAX 703-917-6964
Home Page: www.pur.com

Bruce Radford, President
Richard Stavros, Executive Editor
Joseph Paparello, Marketing Manager
Phillip Cross, Legal Publisher

Designed to serve as a communication forum for the utility industry covering state commission rulings and federal regulatory issues.
Founded in 1915

23622 Solar Today

American Solar Energy Society
4760 Walnut Street
Suite 106
Boulder, CO 80301-2843

303-443-3130
FAX 303-443-3212
E-Mail: info@solartoday.org
Home Page: www.ases.org

Regina Thompson, Editor/Associate Publisher
Seth Masia, Deputy Editor
Brooke Simmons, Manager of Online Publishing

Provides information, case histories and reviews of a variety of renewable energy technologies, including solar, wind, biomass and geothermal.
Cost: $29.00
90 Pages
Circulation: 7000
Founded in 1987

23623 SolarToday

American Solar Energy Society
2400 Central Avenue
Sutie A
Boulder, CO 80301

303-443-3130
FAX 303-443-3212
E-Mail: ases@ases.org
Home Page: www.ases.org
Social Media: *Facebook, Twitter*

Bradley D Collins, Publisher
Gina Johnson, Editor

Brings together ASES' professional members as contributors and readers, amid the community of ASES chapters nationwide, to publish industry-leading editorial for more than 23 years. The leading renewable energy magazine for consumers and professionals.

23624 Transmission & Distribution World

Primedia
PO Box 12901
Shawnee Mission, KS 66282-2901

913-341-1300
800-441-0294
FAX 913-514-6895
E-Mail: rbush@primediabusiness.com
Home Page: www.tdworld.com
Social Media: *Facebook, Twitter*

Eric Jacobson, Senior VP
Rick Bush, Editor
Frequency: Monthly
Circulation: 49000
Founded in 1996

23625 Turbomachinery International

Business Journals
PO Box 5550
Norwalk, CT 06856-5550

203-663-7814
FAX 203-852-8175
Home Page: www.turbomachinerymag.com

Richard Zanetti, Publisher

Includes updates of new approaches to energy conservation, new equipment listings and business/financial news.
Frequency: BiMonthly
Circulation: 11,100
Founded in 1959

23626 Utilities Law Review

John Wiley & Sons
Office A10 Spinners Court
55 West End
Witney, OX OX8 6

199-370-6183
800-825-7550
FAX 199-370-9410
Home Page: www.lawtext.com/

Nicholas Gingell, Publisher
Cosmo Graham, Editor
William J Pesce, CEO/President
Charlotte Villiers, Assistant Editor
Peter Crowther, Current Survey Editor

Edited by a team of specialist UK and European lawyers, it is the leading journal in this fast-changing field. Providing detailed coverage of electricity, gas, telecommunications, transport, water and broadcasting.
Cost: $4920.00
Frequency: Bi-Monthly
Circulation: 250
Founded in 1807

23627 Utility & Telephone Fleets

Practical Communications
482 Holly Ave
Saint Paul, MN 55102

651-91 -997
FAX 651-224-2347
Home Page: www.utfleets.com/

Judith F Chance, Group Publisher
Mike Domke, Publisher
Carol Birkland, Editor
Tom Gelinas, Editorial Director

The equipment, accessory and information resource for fleet professionals.
Circulation: 18,000
Founded in 1980

23628 Utility Automation

PennWell Publishing Company

1421 S Sheridan
PO Box 1260
Tulsa, OK 74112

918-835-3161
FAX 918-831-9497
E-Mail: ua@pennwell.com
Home Page: www.utility-automation.com
Social Media: *Facebook, Twitter*

Shirley Wilson, Marketing Manager
Steven M Brown, Editor
Michael Grossman, Publisher
Robert F Biolchini, CEO/President
Janet Orteon, Circulation Manager

Innovative energy solutions.
Cost: $74.00
50 Pages
Circulation: 32200
ISSN: 1085-2328
Founded in 1996

23629 Utility Automation International
PennWell Publishing Company
1421 S Sheridan Rd
Tulsa, OK 74112-6619

918-831-9421
800-331-4463
FAX 918-831-9476
E-Mail: headquarters@pennwell.com
Home Page: www.pennwell.com
Social Media: *Facebook, Twitter*

Robert Biolchini, President
Tina Jackson, Circulation Manager
Doug Pryor, Editor
Brad Dillman, Marketing
Circulation: 24002
Founded in 1910

23630 Utility Business
PRIMEDIA Intertec-Technology &
Transportation
PO Box 12901
Shawnee Mission, KS 66282-2901

913-341-1300
FAX 913-514-6895
E-Mail: barry-lecerf@intertec.com
Home Page: www.primedia.com
Social Media: *Facebook, Twitter, LinkedIn*

Eric Jacobson, Senior VP

Editorial emphasis is on providing the reader
with solutions and commentary for identifying
and developing company assets, realizing the
impact technology has on the business, and responding to the evolving demands of the
marketplace.
Frequency: 8 per year
Circulation: 50,000

23631 Utility Contractor
3925 Chain Bridge Road
Suite 300
Fairfax, VA 22030

703-358-9300
FAX 703-358-9307
E-Mail: bill@nuca.com
Home Page: www.nuca.com

Bill Hillman, CEO

Serves the underground utility construction industry, including contractors, manufacturers,
suppliers, engineering firms, municipal/pub-
lic/private utilities, and others allied to the
field.
Frequency: Monthly
Circulation: 59329
ISSN: 1098-0342
Founded in 1963

23632 Utility Executive
Water Environment Federation

601 Wythe St
Alexandria, VA 22314-1994

703-684-2400
800-666-0206
FAX 703-684-2492
E-Mail: csc@wef.org
Home Page: www.wef.org

Bill Bertera, Executive Director
Jack Benson, Marketing Manager

Editorial focuses on issues such as continuous
improvement, privatization, financial and risk
management, as well as benchmarking and
leadership. Problem solving strategies are included for everything from wastewater treatment efficiency to negotiation contracts and
proposal evaluations, and address relevant, current issues facing utility managers today.
Cost: $33.00
Frequency: Monthly
Founded in 1928

23633 Utility Fleet Management
TT Publishing
2200 Mill Road
Alexandria, VA 22314-1994

703-838-1770
FAX 703-838-6259
Home Page: www.ttnews.com

Bob Raft, Publisher

Focuses on fleet management issues and new
equipment.
Cost: $25.00
Frequency: Monthly
Circulation: 15,000

23634 Western Energy
Magellan
827 NE Oregon Street
Suite 200
Portland, OR 97232-2172

503-231-1994
FAX 503-231-2595
Home Page: www.westernenergy.org

Chuck Meyer, President
Jody Brassfield-English, Controller
Karen Himes, Webmaster

Contains technical features designed to inform
and educate workers and technicians in the energy production field.
Frequency: BiMonthly
Circulation: 5,058

Trade Shows

23635 AMRA Symposium
Automatic Meter Reading Association
60 Revere Drive
Suite 500
Northbrook, IL 60062

847-480-9628
888-612-2672
FAX 847-480-9282
Home Page: www.amra-intl.org

Joyce Paschall, Executive Director

Gas, water and electric utilities, telephone companies and installation companies equipment
and supplies for meter reading .
1600 Attendees
Frequency: Annual
Founded in 1986

23636 APWA International Public Works
Congress & Expo
American Public Works Association

2345 Grand Boulevard
Suite 700
Kansas City, MO 64108-2625

816-472-6100
800-848-2792
FAX 816-472-1610
E-Mail: ddancy@apwa.net
Home Page: www.apwa.net
Social Media: *Facebook, Twitter, LinkedIn*

Peter King, Executive Director
David Dancy, Marketing Director

Offers the benefit of a variety of educational
sessions, depth of the exhibit program and endless opportunities for networking. The latest
cutting-edge technologies, managerial techniques and regulatory trends designed to keep
you focused on the right solutions at the right
time.
6500 Attendees
Frequency: Annual/September
ISSN: 0092-4873
Founded in 1894

23637 American Public Power Association of
Engineers Operations Workshop
2301 M Street NW
Floor 3
Washington, DC 20037-1427

202-467-2900

Barbara Opicka, Marketing Assistant
Alan Richardson, President/CEO

50 booths.
1.3M Attendees
Frequency: February/March

23638 Buscon East/West
Conference Management Company
200 Connecticut Avenue
Norwalk, CT 06854-1940

203-866-4400

David Caplin, Show Manager

Principal industry event for systems builders
and electronics engineers.
5M Attendees

23639 EEI Convention & Expo
Edison Electric Institute
701 Pennsylvania Avenue NW
Washington, DC 20004-2696

202-508-5000
800-344-5453
FAX 202-508-5794
E-Mail: feedback@eei.org
Home Page: www.eei.org
Social Media: *Facebook, Twitter, LinkedIn*

Thomas R Kuhn, President
Brian Farrell, Member Relations Director

Meeting of Senior executives in the power industry
750 Attendees
Frequency: Annual

23640 Northwest Public Power Engineering
& Operations Show
9817 NE 54th Street
Suite 200
Vancouver, WA 98662-6064

360-254-0109
FAX 360-254-5731
E-Mail: nwppa@nwppa.org
Home Page: www.nwppa.org

Scott Lowry, Training Manager
Debbie Kuraspediani, Director
Communications
900 Attendees
Frequency: May

23641 Smart Energy Summitt
Parks Associates

15950 N. Dallas Parkway
Suite 575
Dallas, TX 75248

972-490-1113
800-727-5711
FAX 972-490-1133
E-Mail: info@parksassociates.com
Home Page: www.parksassociates.com

Tricia Parks, Founder and CEO
Stuart Sikes, President
Farhan Abid, Research Analyst
Bill Ablondi, Director, Home Systems
Research
John Barrett, Director of Research

Smart Energy Summit is an annual three-day event that examines the opportunities and technical business requirements inherent in the consumer programs and advanced systems and services made possible by Smart Grids and Residential Energy Management solutions.
Frequency: Annual
Founded in 1986

23642 WINDPOWER Conference and Exhibition

American Wind Energy Association
(AWEA)
1501 M Street NW
Suite 1000
Washington, DC 20005

202-383-2500
FAX 202-383-2505
E-Mail: windmail@awea.org
Home Page: www.windpowerexpo.org
Social Media: *Facebook, Twitter*

Denise Bode, Chief Executive Officer
Pam Poisson, Chief Financial Officer
Britt Theismann, Chief Operating Officer
Rob Gramlich, Senior VP, Public Policy
Peter Kelley, VP, Public Affairs

The WINDPOWER Conference & Exhibition is produced by the American Wind Energy Association to provide a venue for the wind industry to network, do business, and solve problems. Recognized as one of the fastest-growing trade shows in the U.S., WINDPOWER includes nearly 1,400 exhibiting companies, thousands of qualified wind energy professionals, engaging educational information and unmatched networking opportunities and special events.
2500 Members
20000 Attendees
Frequency: Annual

Directories & Databases

23643 DRI Utility Cost Forecasting

DRI/McGraw-Hill
24 Hartwell Ave
Lexington, MA 02421-3103

781-860-6060
FAX 781-860-6002
Home Page: www.construction.com

Walt Arvin, President

This large database covers the US public utility industry, including cost inputs for pumps, gas compressors, steam pipes and gas and electric meters.

23644 Directory of Electric Power Producers and Distributors

McGraw Hill

2 Penn Plz
5th Floor
New York, NY 10121-2298

212-760-8589
FAX 212-904-2723
Home Page: www.mcgraw-hill.com

Offers information on over 3,500 investor-owned, municipal, rural cooperative and government electric utility systems in the United States and Canada.
Cost: $395.00
1,200 Pages
Frequency: Annual

23645 Directory of Electric Utility Company Libraries in the United States

Library Services Committee/Edison Electric Inst
701 Pennsylvania Avenue NW
Washington, DC 20004-2608

202-347-2693

Over 90 investor-owned electric utility company libraries throughout the country are profiled.
Cost: $10.00
149 Pages
Frequency: Annual

23646 Directory of Energy Professionals

Assn of Regulatory Utility Commissioners
PO Box 684
Washington, DC 20044-0684

202-898-2200

Offers information on consultants and other professionals active in regulated energy utility industries.
Cost: $44.00
450 Pages
Frequency: Annual

23647 Directory of Publicly Owned Natural Gas Systems

American Public Gas Association
11094 Lee Hwy
Suite 102
Fairfax, VA 22030-5034

703-352-3890
FAX 703-352-1271
E-Mail: info@apga.org
Home Page: www.apga.org

Robert S Cave, Executive Director

A listing of all publicly owned natural gas systems in the US.
Cost: $50.00
80 Pages
Frequency: Annual
Circulation: 1,000
Printed in on matte stock

23648 Electric Utility Cost Forecast

WEFA Group
800 Baldwin Tower Boulevard
Eddystone, PA 19022-1368

610-490-4000
FAX 610-490-2770
E-Mail: info@wefa.com
Home Page: www.wefa.com

Mary Novak

This time series covers prices, construction and operating costs pertinent to the electric utilities industry.

23649 Electric Utility Industry

Midwest Publishing Company
2230 E 49th Ste E
Tulsa, OK 74105-8771

918-582-2000
800-829-2002
FAX 918-587-9349

E-Mail: info@midwestdirectories.com
Home Page: www.midwestdirectories.com

Will Hammack, Editor

Approximately 6,000 utility companies, contractors, engineering firms, equipment manufacturers and supply companies.
Cost: $155.00
Frequency: Annual February
Founded in 1943

23650 Financial Statistics of Major Investor-Owned Electric Utilities

US Energy Information Administration
1000 Independence Ave SW
Washington, DC 20585-0001

202-586-8800
FAX 202-586-0727
Home Page: www.eia.doe.gov

John H Weiner, Executive Director

Offers data from over 180 major investor-owned electric utilities in the United States.
Cost: $33.00
Frequency: Annual

23651 Gas Industry Training Directory

American Gas Association
1515 Wilson Boulevard
Suite 100
Arlington, VA 22209-2469

703-841-8400
FAX 703-841-8406
Home Page: www.ihrdc.com

David F Sullivan, Industry Training

Over 600 programs are available in this directory from gas transmission and distribution companies, manufacturers of gas-fired equipment, consultants, etc., and from gas associations.
Frequency: Annual February

23652 Guide to Hydropower Mechanical Design

HCI Publications
410 Archibald St
Kansas City, MO 64111-3288

816-931-1311
FAX 816-931-2015
E-Mail: hci@aol.com
Home Page: www.hcipub.com

Leslie Eden, President

Developed by the Hydropower Technical Committee of the American Society of Mechanical Engineers. A ready reference for individuals who design hydropower facilities and producers and distributors of electricity.
Cost: $125.00
Circulation: 4673

23653 Handy-Whitman Index of Public Utility Construction Costs

Whitman, Requardt and Associates
801 S Caroline St
Baltimore, MD 21231-3311

410-235-3450
FAX 410-243-5716
Home Page: www.wrallp.com

Jenny Miller, Human Resources

This database covers indexes of building costs for construction of public utilities in the United States.

23654 International Directory of Electric Power Producers and Distributors

McGraw Hill

1200 G St NW
Suite 250
Washington, DC 20005-3821

202-383-2377
FAX 202-383-2438
Home Page: www.aviationnow.com

Jennifer Michels, Manager

Offers valuable information on over 3,000 power generating and distribution systems in over 200 countries overseas.
Cost: $345.00

23655 International Directory of Nuclear Utilities
Nuexco
950 17th Street
Suite 2500
Denver, CO 80202-2825

303-534-3100

This comprehensive directory offers information on over 120 utilities in 30 countries that operate nuclear plants with a capacity of at least 100 megawatts.
Cost: $220.00
264 Pages
Frequency: Annual
Founded in 1968

23656 Inventory of Power Plants in the United States
US Energy Information Administration
1000 Independence Ave SW
Washington, DC 20585-0001

202-586-8800
FAX 202-586-0727
Home Page: www.eia.doe.gov

John H Weiner, Executive Director

Information is given on existing and projected and jointly-owned power plants within electric utility systems.
Cost: $23.00
393 Pages
Frequency: Annual

23657 LEXIS Public Utilities Law Library
Mead Data Central
9443 Springboro Pike
Dayton, OH 45401

888-223-6337
FAX 518-487-3584
Home Page: www.lexis-nexis.com

Andrew Prozes, CEO

This database contains information on public utilities-related case decisions from all state supreme courts and most state appellate courts.
Frequency: Full-text

23658 Northwest Electric Utility Directory
Northwest Public Power Association
9817 Ne 54th St
Suite 4576
Vancouver, WA 98662-6064

360-254-0109
FAX 360-254-5731
Home Page: www.nwppa.org

Will Lutgen, President
Randy Shipley, Project Manager

Annual directory for electric utilities in 10 western states and 4 western Canadian provinces.
Frequency: Annually

23659 PUR Analysis of Investor-Owned Electric & Gas Utilities
Public Utilities Reports
2111 Wilson Boulevard
Suite 200
Arlington, VA 22201-3001

Covers over 200 investor-owned electric and gas operating and holding companies.
Cost: $395.00
Frequency: Annual

23660 Pipeline & Utilities Construction: Contractors Issue
Oildom Publishing Company of Texas
PO Box 219368
Houston, TX 77218-9368

281-558-6930

Offers a comprehensive list of over 5,000 individual contracting firms concerned with the construction of oil and gas pipelines, water and sewer lines and gas distribution systems.
Cost: $80.00
Frequency: Annual
Circulation: 25,000

23661 Platts UDI
1200 G St NW
Suite 1000
Washington, DC 20005-3814

202-383-2144
800-752-8878
FAX 202-942-8789
E-Mail: udi@platts.com
Home Page: www.marketing.platts.com

Liane Kucher, Manager

Publisher of directories for world-wide electric power industry.

23662 Power Engineering
PennWell Publishing Company
1421 S Sheridan Rd
Tulsa, OK 74112-6619

918-831-9421
800-331-4463
FAX 918-831-9476
E-Mail: headquarters@pennwell.com
Home Page: www.power-eng.com

Rick Huntzicker, National Brand Manager
Dan Idoine, Regional Brand Manager

List of manufacturers and suppliers of products and services to the power plant and utility engineering industries.
Cost: $10.00
Frequency: Annual, September

23663 Public Power Directory of Local Publicly Owned Electric Utilities
American Public Power Association
2301 M St Nw
Suite 300
Washington, DC 20037-1427

202-467-2900
FAX 202-467-2910
Home Page: www.appanet.org

Alan Richardson, Executive Director
Cost: $90.00
Frequency: Annual
Circulation: 13,000

23664 Rural Electrification: Directory Issue
National Rural Electric Cooperative Association
4301 Wilson Blvd
Arlington, VA 22203-1860

703-907-5500
FAX 703-907-5526
Home Page: www.nreca.org

Glenn English, CEO

Over 1,000 electric cooperatives.
Frequency: Annual July
Circulation: 35,000

23665 The Utility Connection
Home Page: www.utilityconnection.com

Links to more than 4,000 utilities, industry associations and organizations, news outlets and state and federal regulatory and information sites.
Founded in 1995

23666 UDI Who's Who at Electric Power Plants
Utility Data Institute
1200 G St NW
Suite 250
Washington, DC 20005-3814

202-942-8788

Offers valuable information on over 6,000 key personnel at over 1,200 electric utility plants.
Cost: $195.00
Frequency: Annual

23667 US Electric Utility Industry Software Directory
PennWell Publishing Company
PO Box 1260
Tulsa, OK 74101-1260

918-835-3161
800-752-9764
FAX 918-831-9555
Home Page: www.utilityconnection.com

Wayne Beaty, Editor
Steve Hall, Advertising/Sales

An amazing reference directory offering information on over 400 programs in 75 applications categories covering all aspects of the electric power industry.
Cost: $175.00
140 Pages
Frequency: Annual

Industry Web Sites

23668 http://gold.greyhouse.com
G.O.L.D Grey House OnLine Databases
Grey House Publishing's online database platform, GOLD, offers Quick Search, Keyword Search and Expert Search for most business sectors including utility markets. The GOLD platform makes finding the information you need quick and easy - whether you're a novice searcher or an experienced database user. All of Grey House's directory products are available for subscription on the GOLD platform.

23669 www.aeecenter.org
Association of Energy Engineers
Source of information on the field of energy efficiency, utility deregulation, plant engineering, facility management and environmental compliance. Membership includes more than 8,000 professionals and certification programs. Offers seminars, conferences, job listings and certification programs.

23670 www.apea.org
American Public Energy Agency
Purpose is to provide energy acquisition and management services for public agencies.

23671 www.apga.org
American Public Gas Association
Association of municipal gas systems.

23672 www.apwa.net
American Public Works Association
For public agencies, private sector companies, and individuals dedicated to providing high quality public works goods and services.

23673 www.awwa.org
American Water Works Association

The professional society of North American drinking water experts. Develop standards and support research programs in waterworks design, construction, operation, and management. Conducts in-service training schools and offers placement service.

23674 www.bus.msu.edu/ipu
Institute of Public Utilities

Research and training center at Michigan State University. Program focuses on regulation and management of energy, telecommunications and water companies.

23675 www.eei.org
Edison Electric Institute

Advocates public policy, expands market opportunities and provides strategic business information for the shareholder-owned electric utility industry. Find out more about EEI's members, upcoming meetings, career opportunities and products and services.

23676 www.eia.doe.gov/
Energy Information Administration

23677 www.electricity-online.com
Electricity-Online

23678 www.electricity-online.com/
Electricity Journal and Daily

23679 www.energycentral.com
Energy Central

23680 www.energymarketers.com
National Energy Marketers Association

23681 www.energyonline.com
EnergyOnLine

23682 www.energysearch.com
EPRI Energysearch

Provides fast, accurate search results on global energy topics, and science and technolgoy R&D for the electricity industy.

23683 www.energyusernews.com
Energy User News Magazine

23684 www.epri.com
Electric Power Research Institute

Nonprofit organization providing science and technology-based solutions to its global energy customers. Manages a far-reaching program of research, technology development and product implementation.

23685 www.epsa.org
Electric Power Supply Association

23686 www.greyhouse.com
Grey House Publishing

Authoritative reference directories for most business sectors including utility markets. Users can search the online databases with varied search criteria allowing for custom searches by product category, geographic area, sales volume, keyword, subject and more. Full Grey House catalog and online ordering also available.

23687 www.gri.org
Gas Research Institute

23688 www.hydro.org
National Hydropower Association

For public and private utilities, developers, equipment manufacturers, engineering and design firms, environmental and hydro liscensing consultants, and legal and financial firms. Membership dues: $1,000 - $18,000.

23689 www.icea.net
Insulated Cable Engineers Association

Professional organization dedicated to developing cable standards for the electric power, control and telecommunications industries. Ensures safe, economical and efficient cable systems utilizing proven state-of-the-art materials and concepts. ICEA documents are of interest to cable manufacturers, architects and engineers, utility and manufacturing plant personnel, telecommunication engineers, consultants and OEMs.

23690 www.mcgraw-hill.com
McGraw Hill

Provides news of significant developments affecting the electric utility industry focusing on state and federal regulation, management and bulk power markets.

23691 www.naesco.org
National Association of Energy Service Companies

23692 www.naruc.org
National Association of Regulatory Utility Commissioners

A national organization that offers valuable information on over 150 consultants and other professionals active in regulated water, sewer and related industries.

23693 www.naseo.org
National Association of State Energy Officials

23694 www.nerc.com
North American Electric Reliability Council

Voluntary organization promoting bulk electric system reliability and security.

23695 www.nreca.org
Action Committee for Rural Electrification

Political action committee that advocates support for rural electrification.

23696 www.oilonline.com
OilOnLine

23697 www.platts.com
Electrical World

The latest trends in utility engineering and IT, equipment and services, best business practices and critical industry thinking. For managers, engineers and technicians who plan, design, build, maintain and upgrade electric T&D systems around the world.

23698 www.ptda.org
Power Transmission Distributors Association

Members are power transmission/motion control distributor throughout manufacturing firms.

23699 www.publicworks.com
Public Works Online

For professionals in the public works industry.

23700 www.wateronline.com
Water Online

Associations

23701 1394 Trade Association
23117 39th Ave SE
Bothell, WA 98021

425-870-6574
FAX 425-320-3897
E-Mail: info@1394ta.com
Home Page: www.1394ta.org

Richard Mourn, Chair
Morten Lave, Vice Chairman
Dave Thompson, Secretary/Editor
Richard Davies, Financial Officer

A trade association devoted to IEEE 1394 communications product furtherance.

23702 Adult Video Association
8033 Sunset Boulevard
PMB 851
Los Angeles, CA 90046-5323

323-436-0060
FAX 818-501-7502
E-Mail: bmargold@aol.com

William Margold, Director

Trade association primarily concerned with opposing legislative initiatives to restrict the sale of sexually explicit film and video.
400 Members
Founded in 1987

23703 American Rhetoric
Home Page: www.americanrhetoric.com

An association dedicated to rhetoric and public communication in the US.

23704 Association for Recorded Sound Collections
c/o Nathan Georgitis
Knoght Library, 1299 University of
Eugene, OR 97403-1299

E-Mail: execdir@arsc-audio.org
Home Page: www.arsc-audio.orgÿ
Social Media: *Facebook, Twitter, YouTube*

Nathan Georgitis, Executive Director

A nonprofit organization dedicated to the preservation and study of sound recordings in all genres.
Founded in 1966

23705 Association of Visual Communicators
8130 La Mesa Boulevard
#406
La Mesa, CA 91941-6437

619-427-7524
Home Page: www.ivca.org
Social Media: *Facebook, Twitter, LinkedIn,
You Tube*

Marco Forgione, CEO
David Cambridge, Head, Finance &
Administration
Janet Cambridge, Administration
Dave Comley, Commercial Director

Sponsors seminars and competitions. Presents CINDY awards annually for 16mm films, videotapes, 35mm filmstrips, and video disc production.
500 Members
Founded in 1957

23706 Audio Engineering Society
551 Fifth Ave.
Suite 1225
New York, NY 10176

212-661-8528
FAX 212-682-0477
Home Page: www.aes.org

Social Media: *Facebook, Twitter, LinkedIn,
YouTube, RSS, Google+*

Andre Mayo, President
David W. Scheirman, Vice President, Western
Region
Michael Fleming, Vice President, Central
Region
Ron Streicher, Secretary
Garry Margolis, Treasurer

Worldwide professional association for professionals and students involved in the audio industry.
14000 Members
Founded in 1948

23707 Audio Publishers Association
100 North 20th Street, Suite 400
Philadelphia, PA 19103

215-564-2729
E-Mail: info@otrpr.com
Home Page: www.audiopub.org

Linda Lee, President
Anthony Goff, Vice President
Beth Anderson, Director
Janet Benson, Secretary
Sean McManus, Treasurer

Association for audio publishers.
Founded in 1987

23708 BICSI
Building Industry Consulting Service
International
8610 Hidden River Pkwy
Tampa, FL 33637-1000

813-979-1991
800-242-7405
FAX 813-971-4311
E-Mail: bicsi@bicsi.org
Home Page: www.bicsi.org
Social Media: *Facebook, Twitter, LinkedIn,
Youtube*

Michael Collins, President
Brian Ensign, President Elect
Robert Erickson, Secretary
Mel Lesperance, RCDD, Treasurer
John D. Clark Jr., CAE, Executive
Director/CEO

BICSI members include cabling contractors, manufacturers, systems integrators and other telecom professionals.
Founded in 1977

23709 Bay Area Video Coalition
2727 Mariposa St
2nd Floor
San Francisco, CA 94110-1468

415-861-3282
FAX 415-861-4316
E-Mail: edu@bavc.org
Home Page: www.bavc.org
Social Media: *Facebook, Twitter, LinkedIn,
YouTube, Flickr, Instagram*

Angela Jones, President
Dawn Valadez, VP
Andy Wasklewicz, Treasurer
Carol Varney, Executive Director
Mindy Aronoff, Director of Training

A national organization for independent video producers and artists. Advanced, noncommercial, media arts center dedicated to providing access to media, education and technology.
Founded in 1976

23710 Central Station Alarm Association
8150 Leesburg Pike
Suite 700
Vienna, VA 22182-2721

703-242-4670
FAX 703-242-4675
E-Mail: techadmin@csaaintl.org
Home Page: www.csaaul.org

Social Media: *Facebook, Twitter, LinkedIn,
RSS*

Jay Hauhn, Executive Director
Madeline Fullerton McMahon, SVP, Finance &
Admin
Pamela Petrow, President
John McDonald, VP, Meetings and
Conventions
Becky Lane, VP, Membership and Programs

Trade association representing companies offering security/alarm monitoring systems through a central station.
Founded in 1950

23711 Church Music Association of America
12421 New Point Drive
Richmond, VA 23233

505-263-6298
E-Mail: contact@musicasacra.com
Home Page: musicasacra.com/music/recordings
Social Media: *Facebook, Twitter, Google+*

William P. Mahrt, President
Horst Buchholz, Vice President
Jeffrey Tucker, Director of Publications
Mary Jane Ballou, Secretary
Adam Wright, Treasurer

A nonprofit association for Catholic church musicians.
Founded in 1964

23712 Cinema Audio Society
827 Hollywood Way #632
Burbank, CA 91505

818-752-8624
FAX 818-752-8624
E-Mail:
CASAwards@CinemaAudioSociety.org
Home Page: cinemaaudiosociety.org
Social Media: *Facebook, Twitter, YouTube*

Mark Ulano, CAS, President
Phillip Palmer, CAS, Vice President
Deb Adair, Director
David J. Bondelevitch, CAS, Secretary
Peter R. Damski, CAS, Treasurer

An association celebrating the scores of movies and films.
Founded in 1964

23713 CompTIA
3500 Lacey Road
Suite 100
Downers Grove, IL 60515

630-678-8300
866-835- 80
FAX 630-678-8384
E-Mail: techvoice@comptia.org
Home Page: www.comptia.org
Social Media: *Facebook, Twitter, LinkedIn,
YouTube, Google+, Pinterest*

MJ Shoer, Chairman
Mont Phelps, Vice Chair
Todd Thibodeaux, President/CEO
Nancy Hammervik, SVP, Industry Relations
Brian Laffey, Chief Financial Officer

CompTIA is a trade association representing the international technology community. Its goal is to provide a unified voice, global advocacy, and leadership, and to advance industry growth through standards professional competence, education, and business solutions.

**23714 Consumer Electronics Association
(CEA)**
1919 S Eads Street
Arlington, VA 22202

703-907-7600
866-858-1555
301-631-3983
FAX 703-907-7675
E-Mail: cea@ce.org
Home Page: www.ce.org

Social Media: *Facebook, Twitter, LinkedIn, Flickr, Google+*

Daniel Pidgeon, Chair
David Hagan, Vice Chair
Gary Shapiro, President/CEO
Glenda MacMullin, Treasurer
Karen Chupka, Secretary

Consumer Electronics Association (CEA) provides valuable and innovative member-only resources including: exclusive information and unparalleled market research, networking opportunities with business advocates and leaders, up-to-date educational programs and technical training, exposure in extensive promotional programs, and representation from the voice of the industry.

23715 Entertainment Merchants Association

16530 Ventura Blvd, Suite 400
Encino, CA 91436-4551

818-385-1500
FAX 818-933-0911
E-Mail: info@entmerch.org
Home Page: www.entmerch.org
Social Media: *Facebook, Twitter*

Marty Graham Rentrak, Chairman
Jonathan Zepp, Vice Chairman
Mark Fisher, President & CEO
Sean Bersell, SVP, Public Affairs
Carla Immordino, VP, Finance & Administration

A nonprofit international trade association dedicated to advancing the interests of the home entertainment industry.
45,00 Members
Founded in 2006

23716 Entertainment Software Association

575 7th Street NW, Suite 300
Washington, DC 20004

E-Mail: esa@theESA.com
Home Page: www.theesa.com
Social Media: *Facebook, Twitter*

Michael D. Gallagher, President and CEO

The trade association of the video game industry.
Founded in 2000

23717 IFPI-Representing the Recording Industry Worldwide

3470 NW 82nd Avenue
Suite 680
Doral, FL 33122

305-567-0861
FAX 305-567-0871
Home Page: www.ifpi.org
Social Media: *Twitter*

Frances Moore, Chief Executive Officer
Lauri Rechardt, Legal
Ang Kwee Tiang, Regional Director, Asia
Javier Asensio, Regional Director, Latin America
Jeremy Banks, Director, Anti-Piracy

Promoting the value of recorded music, safeguarding record producers' rights and expanding the commercial uses of recoded music in all markets.
1300 Members

23718 International Society of Videographers

8499 S. Tamiami Trail
Suite 208
Sarasota, FL 34238

941-923-5334
FAX 941-921-3836
E-Mail: info@weva.com
Home Page: www.weva.com

Social Media: *Facebook, Twitter, LinkedIn, You Tube*

Exchanges information on technologies, techniques, and equipment, sponsors Hall of Fame and an international convention.
Founded in 1981

23719 National Association of Record Industry Professionals

P.O. Box 2446
Los Angeles, CA 91610-2446

818-769-7007
Home Page: www.narip.com
Social Media: *Facebook, Twitter, YouTube, Vimeo*

Association for all professionals in the music business.
130,0 Members
Founded in 1998

23720 Production Equipment Rental Association

14661 Tustin St.
PO Box 55515
Sherman Oaks, CA 91413-0515

407-629-4122
877-629-4122
FAX 407-629-8884
Home Page: www.productionhub.com
Social Media: *Facebook, Twitter, LinkedIn, YouTube, Google+, Pinterest, V*

Pat Patin, President
Mark Beasley, VP/Marketing
John Johnston, Executive Director

A worldwide trade organization that supplies production equipment to the entertainment industry. PERA promotes the commercial advancement of new technologies available from member companies to meet the ever-changing requirements of their client's artistic challenges.
180 Members
Founded in 1998

23721 Professional Audio-Video Retailers Association

10 E 22nd Street
Suite 301
Lombard, IL 60148-6191

630-268-1500
800-621-0298
FAX 630-953-8957
E-Mail: webmaster@paralink.org
Home Page: www.paralink.org

Rosemary Wenstrom

An organization formed to assist the owners and operators of independently owned, high-end audio/video stores to work toward the mutually compatible goal of providing services to members which would be unattainable by retailers working separately.
204 Members

23722 Professional Lighting and Sound Assoiciation

630 Ninth Avenue, Suite 609
New York, NY 10036

212-244-1505
FAX 212-244-1502
E-Mail: info@plasa.org
Home Page: www.plasa.org
Social Media: *Facebook, Twitter*

Matthew Griffiths, Chief Executive Officer
Shane McGreevy, Chief Finance Officer
Lori Rubinstein, Director of International Programs
Jackie Tien, Group Publisher
Christopher Toulmin, Director of Events

A trade association for the lighting and sounds of the entertainment industry.
1200+ Members

23723 Recording Industry Association of America

1025 F ST N.W., 10th Floor
Washington, DC 20004

202-775-0101
Home Page: www.riaa.com

Cary Sherman, Chairman & CEO
Mitch Glazier, Senior Executive Vice President
Steven M. Marks, Chief/ General Counsel, Director
Bill Hearn, Director

A trade group that represents the U.S. recording industry whose mission is to foster a business and legal climate that supports and promotes our members' creative and financial vitality.

23724 Special Interests

590 Knox Run Road
PO Box 193
Lanse, PA 16849-0193

814-345-6845
800-735-6997
FAX 814-345-5566
E-Mail: verasi@verizon.net

Vera A Lockey, Owner

Health and safety sales DVD and videos.
Founded in 1997

23725 University Film and Video Association

E-Mail: ufvahome@gmail.com
Home Page: www.ufva.org
Social Media: *Facebook, Twitter, LinkedIn, Vimeo, Instagram, YouTube*

Francisco Menendez, President
Jennifer Machiorlatti, Executive Vice President
Heather Addison, Conference Vice President
Joseph Brown, Editorial Vice President
Tom Sanny, Treasurer

Association for videography and film making at universities.

23726 Video Software Dealers Association

16530 Ventura Blvd
Suite 400
Encino, CA 91436-4554

818-385-0567
800-955-8732
FAX 818-385-0567
E-Mail: servicecenter@vsda.org
Home Page: www.vsda.org

Crossan Andersen, President
Carrie Dieterich, VP Marketing
Mark Fisher, VP Membership/Strategic Initiatives
Sean Bersell, VP Public Affairs
Nancy Gordon, iDEA Manager Ops & Special Projects

Nonprofit international trade association with a membership exceeding 4,500 member companies, representing more than 25,000 locations. Members include retailers, as well as manufacturers, distributors and related businesses that constitute the home video industry. Acts as a spokesperson for home video industry both internally and legislatively.
4.5M Members
Founded in 1981

23727 Wedding and Event Videographers Association International

8499 S. Tamiami Trail, #208
Sarasota, FL 34238

941-923-5334
FAX 941-921-3836

E-Mail: info@weva.com, admin@weva.com
Home Page: www.weva.com

International association for wedding and event videographers.

Newsletters

23728 Consumer Multimedia Report
Warren Publishing
2115 Ward Ct Nw
Washington, DC 20037-1209

202-872-9200
800-771-9202
FAX 202-318-8350
E-Mail: info@warren-news.com
Home Page: www.warren-news.com

Brig Easley, Manager
Daniel Warren, President/Editor
Paul Warren, Chair/Publisher

Emphasizes on emerging technologies, marketing strategies, and industry events and news.
Cost: $462.00
Frequency: BiWeekly

23729 DVD: Laser Disc Newsletter
PO Box 420
East Rockaway, NY 11518-420

516-594-9304
FAX 516-594-9307
E-Mail: doug@dvdlaser.com
Home Page: www.dvdlaser.com

Douglas Pratt, Publisher

A consumer guide to DVD's with news, reviews, ads and more.
Cost: $47.50
24 Pages
Frequency: Monthly
Circulation: 5000
ISSN: 0749-5250
Founded in 1984
Mailing list available for rent: 5000 names at $100 per M

23730 PRC News
Corbell Publishing Company
201 S Alvarado St
Suite 410
Los Angeles, CA 90057-2353

213-483-4559
FAX 310-258-8096
E-Mail: info@corbell.com
Home Page: www.corbell.com

Gabriel Carabello, President
Joseph Daneshrad, Circulation Manager

A weekly newsletter for the home video industry. Covers pre-recorded video statistics, people, calendar, etc.
Cost: $577.00
8 Pages
Frequency: Monthly
Circulation: 2000
ISSN: 0898-302X
Founded in 1988
Mailing list available for rent: 7000 names at $75 per M
Printed in on newsprint stock

23731 Production Equipment Rental Association
1806 Hammerlin Ave
Winter Park, FL 32789

407-629-4122
877-629-4122
FAX 407-629-8884
E-Mail: info@peraonline.org
Home Page: www.productionhub.com

Social Media: *Facebook, Twitter, LinkedIn, You Tube*

Pat Patin, President
Mark Beasley, VP/Marketing
John Johnston, Executive Director

A worldwide trade organization that supplies production equipment to the entertainment industry. PERA promotes the commercial advancement of new technologies available from member companies to meet the ever-changing requirements of their client's artistic challenges.
180 Members

23732 Video Business
Reed Business Information
2000 Clearwater Dr
Oak Brook, IL 60523-8809

630-574-0825
FAX 630-288-8781
E-Mail: kevin.davis@reedbusiness.com
Home Page: www.reedbusiness.com

Jeff Greisch, President
Paul Sweeting, Editor-at-Large
Charles Tanner, Circulation Manager

Publication includes the retail marketplace, probes business trends and issues, reviews new and upcoming video titles, and contains information and advice for running a successful retail business, and charts top video titles.
Cost: $70.00
Frequency: Weekly
Circulation: 47807
Founded in 1983

23733 Video Investor
Kagan Research
1 Lower Ragsdale Dr
Building One Suite 130
Monterey, CA 93940-5749

831-624-1536
800-307-2529
FAX 831-625-3225
E-Mail: info@kagan.com
Home Page: www.kagan.com
Social Media: *Facebook, Twitter, LinkedIn*

Tim Baskerville, President
Tom Johnson, Marketing Manager

Authoritative look inside the business of renting and selling video cassettes. Exclusive estimates of retail and wholesale transactions and inventories. Tracking movies into the home. Three month trial is available.
Cost: $ 795.00
Frequency: Monthly

Magazines & Journals

23734 AudioVideo International
Dempa Publications
275 Madison Avenue
New York, NY 10016-1101

212-682-3755
FAX 212-682-2730
Home Page: www.dempa.net/

Harry Iguchi, General Manager

Articles cover systems of home entertainment.
Cost: $48.00
100 Pages
Frequency: Quarterly
Founded in 1950

23735 CE Pro
EH Publishing
PO Box 989
Framingham, MA 01701-0989

508-820-1515
FAX 508-663-1599

E-Mail: ehpubinc@ionet.net
Home Page: www.electronichouse.com

Kenneth D. Moyes, President
Jason Knott, Editor

Provides timely, top quality business, industry and product information, technical how-to articles, product comparisons, dealer profiles and marketing and management tips.
Frequency: Monthly
Circulation: 30,000

23736 CE Vision Magazine
Consumer Electronics Association
1919 S Eads Street
Arlington, VA 22202

703-907-7600
866-858-1555
301-631-3983
FAX 703-907-7675
E-Mail: cea@ce.org
Home Page: www.ce.org

Gary Shapiro, President/CEO
Pat Lavelle, Chairman
Peter Lesser, Industry Executive Advisor
Jason Oxman, VP Communications
Jenny Pareti, Public Policy Director

Features valuable and innovative articles that address market research, networking opportunities with business advocates and leaders, up-to-date educational programs and technical training, exposure in extensive promotional programs, and representation from the voice of the industry.

23737 CVC Report
Creative Video Consulting
PO Box 5195
Saratoga Springs, NY 12866-8038

212-533-9870
FAX 212-473-3772
E-Mail: cvcreort@aol.com
Home Page: www.cvc.nic.in

Mitchell Rowen, Publisher

Information for music video programming and production fields, contains charts, reviews, play lists, industry dialogue and news.
Cost: $225.00
Frequency: BiMonthly
Circulation: 800

23738 Digital Content Producer
Prism Business Media
9800 Metcalf Avenue
Overland Park, KS 66212-2216

913-341-1300
FAX 913-967-1905
E-Mail: subs@prismb2b.com
Home Page: www.digitalcontentproducer.com

Scott Schwadron, Publisher
Cynthia Wisehart, Editoral Director
Kerby Asplund, Marketing
Laury Reeves, Circulation Manager

Features new product listings, updates on state of the art technology applied to new production techniques, and business industry news.
Cost: $70.00
Frequency: Monthly
Circulation: 50000
Founded in 1975

23739 Markee
HJK Publications
1018 Rosetta Dr
Deltona, FL 770-341-08

386-774-8881
FAX 386-774-8908
E-Mail: markee@markeemag.com

Home Page: www.markeemag.com/
Social Media: *Facebook, Twitter, LinkedIn*

Janet Karcher, Publisher
Jonathan T Hutchinson, Editor-In-Chief
Shirley Boone, Circulation
Shirley Boone, Circulation

For the Southeast and Southwest film industry.
Cost: $24.00
Frequency: Monthly
Circulation: 12200
Founded in 1986

23740 PRC News
Corbell Publishing Company
201 S Alvarado St
Suite 410
Los Angeles, CA 90057-2353

213-483-4559
FAX 310-312-4551
E-Mail: info@corbell.com
Home Page: www.corbell.com
Social Media: *Facebook, Twitter, LinkedIn*

Gabriel Carabello, President
Eric Jacobson, Senior VP
Maria Arnone, Publisher
Kelly Conlin, CEO
Lori Reeves, Circulation Manager

Contains information on pre-recorded videos,
software, hardware and blank cassettes, in-
cludes industry news, pricing and distribution
updates, and reviews videos soon to be re-
leased.
Cost: $577.00
8 Pages
Frequency: Monthly
Circulation: 2000
ISSN: 0898-302X
Founded in 1988
Printed in one color

23741 Professional Audio-Video Retailers
10 E 22nd Street
Suite 301
Lombard, IL 60148-6191

630-268-1500
800-621-0298
FAX 630-953-8957
E-Mail: webmaster@paralink.org
Home Page: www.paralink.org

Rosemary Wenstrom

An organization formed to assist the owners
and operators of independently owned,
high-end audio/video stores to work toward the
mutually compatible goal of providing services
to members which would be unattainable by retailers working separately.
204 Members

23742 Prosound News
United Entertainment Media
28 East 28th Street
27th Fl
New York, NY 10016

212-378-0400
FAX 212-378-2170
E-Mail: sedorusa@optonline.net
Home Page: www.governmentvideo.com
Social Media: *Facebook, Twitter, LinkedIn*

Gary Rhodes, International Ssales Manager
Frequency: Monthly
Circulation: 25500
Founded in 1978

23743 Sound & Video Contractor
Primedia
PO Box 12901
Shawnee Mission, KS 66282-2901

913-341-1300
866-505-7173
FAX 913-514-6895
E-Mail: svcs@primedia.com

Home Page: www.primedia.com
Social Media: *Facebook, Twitter, LinkedIn*

Eric Jacobson, Senior VP
Maria Arnone, Publisher
Kelly Conlin, CEO
Lori Reeves, Circulation Manager
Kiby Asplund, Marketing Manager

Contains information on sound systems, video
display, security, CCTV, home theater, and automation. Delivers in depth instruction and examples of successful installations, fundamental
acoustical and video theory and news on new
technologies affecting the systems contracting
business.
Cost: $35.00
Frequency: Monthly
Circulation: 21000
Founded in 1895
*Mailing list available for rent: 20,500 names at
$110 per M*

23744 Television Broadcast
Miller Freeman Publications
28 East 28th Street
Suite 4
New York, NY 10016

212-636-2700
FAX 212-378-2170
E-Mail: sedorusa2optonline.net
Home Page: www.governmentvideo.com
Social Media: *Facebook, Twitter, LinkedIn*

Gary Rhodes, International Sales Manager

Television Broadcast primarily serves TV stations including commercial, public, educational, religious military TV stations or
networks; teleproduction facilities including
production, post-production, tape duplication,
effects, audio production or independent
program producer.
Frequency: Monthly
Circulation: 30,374
Founded in 1978
Printed in 4 colors on glossy stock

23745 Video & Entertainment
Fairchild Publications
2407 Timberloch Place
Suite B
New York, NY 77380

281-419-5725
877-652-5295
FAX 281-419-5712
Home Page: www.supermarketnews.com

Dan Bagan, President
David Orgal, Editor

23746 Video Age International
Video Age International
216 E 75th St
Suite PW
New York, NY 10021-2921

212-288-3933
FAX 212-734-9033
E-Mail: sales@videoageinternational.com
Home Page: www.videoageinternational.com
Social Media: *Facebook, Twitter, LinkedIn*

Dom Serafini, Publisher

Offers information on program sales and distri-
bution of videocassettes, discs and allied me-
dia.
Cost: $30.00
Frequency: 7x/Year
Circulation: 12000

23747 Video Librarian
Video Librarian
3435 NE Nine Boulder Dr
Poulsbo
Seabeck, WA 98370

360-626-1259
800-692-2270

FAX 360-830-9346
E-Mail: vidlib@videolibrarian.com
Home Page: www.videolibrarian.com

Randy Pitman, President
Anne Williams, Marketing Director
Jazza Williams, Associate Editor

Offers video reviews and news for public,
school, academic and special libraries.
Cost: $64.00
56 Pages
Circulation: 2000
ISSN: 0887-6851
Founded in 1986

23748 Video Store Magazine
201 Sandpointe Ave
Suite 600
Santa Ana, CA 92707-8700

714-338-6700
800-854-3112
FAX 714-513-8402
E-Mail: selliott@advanstar.com
Home Page: www.homemediaretailing.com

Thomas Arnold, Editor
Don Rosenberg, Publisher
Susan Elliott, Publications Coordinator
Steven J. Apple, Director, Business
Development
Renee Rosado, Online Manager

Offers market research and buying information
for industry people.
Cost: $48.00
Frequency: Weekly
Circulation: 44257

23749 Videomaker Magazine
Videomaker
1350 East 9th Street
PO Box 4591
Chico, CA 95927-4591

530-891-8410
FAX 530-891-8443
Home Page: www.videomaker.com

Stephen Muratore, Editor-in-Chief
Jennifer O'Rourke, Managing Editor

Information about the world of camcorders,
computers, tools and techniques for making
video in a way that is timely, applicable, pertinent, engaging and understandable. Each
month we teach production techniques, explain
technology and include no less than two informative buyer's guides of products central to
video. In addition, we are committed to objective analysis of videomaking products so our
audience can rely on us for unbiased reporting.
Cost: $3.99
Frequency: Monthly
Circulation: 90,000
ISSN: 0889-4973
Printed in 4 colors on glossy stock

Trade Shows

**23750 International Consumer Electronics
Show (C ES)**
Las Vegas Hotel & Casino
3000 S. Paradise
Las Vegas, VA 22202

866-539-8430
Home Page: www.ceweb.org
Social Media: *Facebook, Twitter, LinkedIn*

Gary Shapiro, President/CEO
Pat Lavelle, Chairman
Peter Lesser, Industry Executive Advisor
Jason Oxman, VP Communications
Jenny Pareti, Public Policy Director

The CES reaches across global markets, connects the industry and enables consumer elec-

tronics to grow and thrive. International CES is owned and prroduced by the Consumer Electronics Association (CEA).
2000 Members
Frequency: January

23751 International Society of Videographers
PO Box 296
Sparkill, NY 10976-0296

859-624-5429
FAX 845-359-8527

Steve Jambeck, Executive Director

Exchanges information on technologies, techniques, and equipment, sponsors Hall of Fame and an international convention.
Founded in 1981

Directories & Databases

23752 AV Market Place
Information Today
143 Old Marlton Pike
Medford, NJ 08055-8750

609-654-6266
800-300-9868
FAX 609-654-4309
E-Mail: custserv@infotoday.com
Home Page: www.infotoday.com

Thomas H Hogan, President
Roger R Bilboul, Chairman Of The Board

The complete business directory of audio, audio visual, computer systems, film, video, and programming with industry yellow pages. The only guide needed to find more than 7,500 companies that create, apply or distribute AV equipment and services for business, education, science, and government.
Cost: $199.95
1700 Pages
Frequency: February
ISBN: 1-573871-87-7

23753 Orion Blue Book: Computer
Orion Research Corporation
14555 N Scottsdale Rd
Suite 330
Scottsdale, AZ 85254-3487

480-951-1114
FAX 480-951-1117

Roger Rohrs, Owner

A list of manufacturers of data processing hardware and products for the computer industry.
Cost: $200.00
Frequency: Annual

23754 Orion Blue Book: Video and Television
Orion Research Corporation
14555 N Scottsdale Rd
Suite 330
Scottsdale, AZ 85254-3487

480-951-1114
800-844-0759
FAX 480-951-1117
Home Page: www.bluebook.com

Roger Rohrs, Owner

List of more than 450 manufacturers of video and television products such as cameras, recorders, disc players, projectors, extenders, microphones, mixers, processors and color monitors.
Cost: $144.00
Frequency: Annual January

23755 Video Networks
Bay Area Video Coalition

1111 17th Street
San Francisco, CA 94107-2406

415-613-3282
FAX 415-861-4316
Home Page: www.bavc.com

List of over 100 film festivals for independent video producers and artists.
Cost: $3.00
Frequency: Annual

23756 Video Source Book
Gale/Cengage Learning
Po Box 09187
Detroit, MI 48209-0187

248-699-4253
800-877-4253
FAX 248-699-8049
E-Mail: gale.galeord@cengage.com
Home Page: www.gale.com
Social Media: *Facebook, Twitter, LinkedIn, You Tube*

Patrick C Sommers, President

The Video Source Book continues its comprehensive coverage of the wide universe of video offerings with listing for more than 130,000 complete program listings, encompassing over 160,000 videos.
Frequency: Annual
ISBN: 1-414435-09-6
Mailing list available for rent

Industry Web Sites

23757 http://gold.greyhouse.com
G.O.L.D Grey House OnLine Databases
Grey House Publishing's online database platform, GOLD, offers Quick Search, Keyword Search and Expert Search for most business sectors including video and audio markets. The GOLD platform makes finding the information you need quick and easy - whether you're a novice searcher or an experienced database user. All of Grey House's directory products are available for subscription on the GOLD platform.

23758 www.1394ta.org
1394 Trade Association

23759 www.asid.org
American Society of Interior Designers (ASID)

23760 www.avreps.org
Independent Professional Representatives Org

23761 www.bavc.org
Bay Area Video Collection

23762 www.bicsi.org
BICSI

23763 www.caba.org
Continental Automated Buildings Association (CABA)

23764 www.ce.org
Consumer Electronics Association (CEA)

23765 www.cedia.org
Custom Electronic Design & Installation Associatio

23766 www.comptia.org
CompTIA

23767 www.copper.org
Copper Development Association (CDA)

23768 www.csaaul.org
Central Station Alarm Association

23769 www.fla-alarms.org
Alarm Association of Florida

23770 www.greyhouse.com
Grey House Publishing
Authoritative reference directories for most business sectors including audio and video markets. Users can search the online databases with varied search criteria allowing for custom searches by product category, geographic area, sales volume, keyword, subject and more. Full Grey House catalog and online ordering also available.

23771 www.nsca.org
National Systems Contractors Association (NSCA)

23772 www.paralink.org
Professional Audio-Video Retailers Association

23773 www.riaa.org
Recording Industry Association of America

23774 www.siaonline.org
Security Industry Association

23775 www.soc.org
Society of Camera Operators

23776 www.tiaonline.org
Telecommunications Industry Association (TIA)

23777 www.vsda.org
Video Software Dealers Association

Associations

23778 Allied Distribution
4839 Sherburn Road
PO Box 607
Eagle River, WI 54521

559-435-5810
FAX 715-479-3551
E-Mail: info@warehousenetwork.com
Home Page: www.warehousenetwork.com
Social Media: *Facebook, Twitter, LinkedIn*

Ernest Brunswick, President
Cyd Brunswick, Customer Service Manager

A sales and marketing association representing
public warehouses and distribution centers in
the United States.
75 Members
Founded in 1933

23779 American Chain of Warehouses
156 Flamingo Dr
Beecher, IL 60401-9725

708-946-9792
FAX 708-946-9793
E-Mail: bjurus@acwi.org
Home Page: www.acwi.org
Social Media: *Facebook, Twitter, LinkedIn*

William J Jurus, VP

Sales and marketing company representing
public warehouses.
50 Members
Founded in 1911

**23780 American Moving & Storage
Association**
1611 Duke St.
Alexandria, VA 22314-3406

888-849-AMSA
FAX 703-683-7527
Home Page: www.moving.org

Organization which provides information and
tips to help with moving.
4000 Members
Founded in 1920

**23781 Automotive Warehouse Distributors
Association**
7101 Wisconsin Avenue
Suite 1300
Bethesda, MD 20814-3415

301-654-6664
FAX 301-654-3299
E-Mail: info@autocare.org
Home Page: www.autocare.org
Social Media: *Facebook, Twitter, LinkedIn,
Youtube, WordPress*

Kathleen Schmatz, MAAP, President/CEO
Susan Medick, CPA, CAE, CFO/COO
Richard D. White, MAAP, SVP
Michael Barratt, CMP, SVP, Meeting & Events
Aaron Lowe, AAP, SVP, Reg. and Gov. Affairs

A trade association consisting of more than 600
members who are manufacturers and warehouse distributors, affiliates, marketing associations and others actively involved in the
production, distribution and installation of motor vehicle parts, tools, services, accessories,
equipment, materials and supplies. A segment
of the Automotive Aftermarket Industry
Association.
600 Members
Founded in 1947

**23782 Burley Auction Warehouse
Association**
620 S Broadway STE 201
Lexington, KY 40508-3150

606-255-4504
FAX 606-255-4534

Denny Wilson, Managing Director

Members are warehouse companies selling burley tobacco at auction in eight burley-produc-
ing states.
225 Members

**23783 Distributors & Consolidators of
America**
2240 Bernays Drive
York, PA 17404

888-519-9195
FAX 717-764-6531
E-Mail: daca@comcast.net
Home Page: www.dacacarriers.com

Andy Delaney, President
Rick Staller, VP
Mike Moran, Secretary
Rich Eberhart, Treasurer
Mike Oliver, Chairman

This organization helps firms and individuals
active in the shipping, warehousing, receiving,
distribution or consolidation of freight
shipments.
39 Members
Founded in 1971

**23784 Distributors and Consolidators of
America**
Home Page: dacacarriers.com
Social Media: *Facebook, Twitter, LinkedIn*

Mike Oliver, Chair
Andy Delaney, President
Rick Staller, Vice President
Mike Moran, Secretary
Rich Eberhart, Treasurer

Association for public warehousing.
Founded in 1971

23785 Engine Service Association
37 Pratt Street
Essex, CT 06426-1159

860-767-1770
FAX 860-767-7932
E-Mail: info@opeesa.com
Home Page: www.opeesa.com
Social Media: *Twitter, LinkedIn*

Nancy Cueroni, Executive Director
Jeff Plotka, President and Director
Steve Purdy, VP, Annual Meeting & Director
Ted Finn, Secretary/Treasurer & Director
Ron Monroe, Past President and Director

Members are central warehouse distributors of
internal combustion engines.
60 Members

23786 Global Cold Chain Alliance
1500 King Street
Ste 201
Alexandria, VA 22314-2730

703-373-4300
FAX 703-373-4301
E-Mail: email@gcca.org
Home Page: www.gcca.org
Social Media: *Facebook, Twitter, LinkedIn*

Corey Rosenbusch, President and CEO
Margot Van Dersal, Controller
Lowell Randel, VP, Gov & Legal Affairs
Richard Tracy, VP, International Programs
Amanda Brondy, Director of International
Projects

Association for the temperature-controlled
products industry.
1300+ Members
Founded in 2007

**23787 Independent Liquid Terminals
Association**
1005 North Glebe Road
Suite 600
Arlington, VA 22201

703-875-2011
FAX 703-875-2018
E-Mail: info@ilta.org
Home Page: www.ilta.org

Wayne N. Driggers, Chairman
Jamie Coleman, Vice Chair
Gregory J. Pound, Secretary/Treasurer
Melinda Whitney, President
Peter Weaver, VP, Government Affairs

We represent bulk liquid terminal companies
that store commercial liquids in aboveground
storage tanks (ASTs) and transfer products to
and from oceangoing tank ships, tank barges,
pipelines, tank trucks and tank rail cars.
400 Members
Founded in 1974

**23788 International Association of
Refrigerated Warehouses**
1500 King Street
Suite 201
Alexandria, VA 22314-2730

703-373-4300
FAX 703-373-4301
E-Mail: email@gcca.org
Home Page: www.gcca.org
Social Media: *Facebook, Twitter, LinkedIn*

Corey Rosenbusch, President and CEO
Margot Van Dersal, Controller
Lowell Randel, VP, Gov & Legal Affairs
Richard Tracy, VP, International Programs
Amanda Brondy, Director of International
Projects

Trade association of public refrigerated warehouses storing all types of perishable
products.
1300+ Members
Founded in 2007

**23789 International Warehouse Logistics
Association**
2800 S River Rd
Suite 260
Des Plaines, IL 60018-6003

847-813-4699
FAX 847-813-0115
E-Mail: mail@IWLA.com
Home Page: www.iwla.com
Social Media: *Facebook, Twitter, LinkedIn,
YouTube*

Rob Doyle, Chairman
Steve DeHaan, President/CEO
Mark DeFabis, Vice Chair
Clifford Otto, Treasurer
Frank Anderson, Secretary

The unified voice of the global logistics
outsourcing industry, representing third party
warehousing, transportation and logistics service providers. Our member companies provide
the most timely and cost-effective global logistics solutions for their customers and are committed to protecting the free flow of products
across international borders.
500 Members
Founded in 1997

**23790 Internationl Warehouse Logistics
Association**
International Warehouse Logistics
Association

2800 S River Road
Suite 260
Des Plains, IL 60018-5764

847-813-4699
FAX 847-813-0115
E-Mail: mail@IWLA.com
Home Page: www.iwla.com
Social Media: *Facebook, Twitter, LinkedIn, YouTube*

Rob Doyle, Chairman
Steve DeHaan, President/CEO
Mark DeFabis, Vice Chair
Clifford Otto, Treasurer
Frank Anderson, Secretary

Trade association of public warehouses.
500+ Members
Founded in 1997

23791 Mobile Self-Storage Association
2001 Jefferson Davis Hwy
Suite 1004
Arlington, VA 22202-3617

703-416-0060
FAX 703-416-0014
E-Mail: bmclean@ms-sa.org
Home Page: www.ms-sa.org

Bob Mclean, CAE, Executive Director

Association for mobile-storage companies.
Founded in 2004

23792 National Portable Storage Association
3312 Broadway
Ste 105
Kansas City, MO 64111

866-777-0635
816-960-6552
FAX 816-960-6575
E-Mail: info@npsa.org
Home Page: www.npsa-us.org
Social Media: *Facebook, Twitter, LinkedIn, YouTube*

Association for portable-storage companies.

23793 RCS Limited
Computer Based Training
1301 Commerce Street
Birmingham, AL 35217

205-841-9955
888-833-1970
FAX 205-841-2106
E-Mail: sales@rcs-limited.co.uk
Home Page: www.rcs-limited.co.uk

Design and build contractor for cold storage warehouses.

23794 Refrigeration Research and Education
World Food Logistics Organization
P.O. Box 6315
Suite 201
Lubbock, TX 79493-6315

703-373-4300
806-789-4078
FAX 703-373-4301
E-Mail: President@larw.org
Home Page: www.larw.org

Barbara Sucsy, President
Ruth Schiermeyer, Press & Media Contact
Val Cochran, WebMaster
Patti Jones, Program Chair
Gretchen Scott, Program Chair

Sponsors graduate-level scientific research in the refrigeration of perishable commodities. Offers annual training institute for public refrigerated warehouse personnel.
1M Members
Founded in 1943

23795 Self Storage Association
1901 N Beauregard St
Suite 110
Alexandria, VA 22311-1738

703-575-8000
888-735-3784
FAX 703-575-8901
E-Mail: ssa@selfstorage.org
Home Page: www.selfstorage.org
Social Media: *Facebook, Twitter, LinkedIn*

John Barry, Chairman/National Director
Marc Smith, Vice Chairman/National Director
John Hutto, Treasurer/National Director
Michael Nunez, Secretary/National Director
Terry Bagley, National Director

Self-storage facility owners/operators and suppliers to the industry.
6000 Members
Founded in 1975

23796 Storage Products Association
572 B Ruger Street
P.O. Box 29920
San Francisco, CA 94129-0920

415-561-6275
FAX 415-561-6120
E-Mail:
LoBue@Storage-Products-Association.org
Home Page:
www.storage-products-association.org
Social Media: *Twitter, RSS*

Theodore Deffenbagh, President
D. Kurt Richarz, Board Member
Raghu Gururangan, Board Member
Michael T. LoBue, CAE, Secretary
Jeff Burke, PhD, Treasurer

Association for storage manufacturers and users.

23797 Warehousing Education and Research Council
1100 Jorie Boulevard
Ste 170
Oak Brook, IL 60523

630-990-0001
FAX 630-990-0256
E-Mail: wercoffice@werc.org
Home Page: www.werc.org
Social Media: *Twitter, LinkedIn, YouTube*

Sheila Benny, President
Tom Nightengale, Vice President
Michael J. Mikitka, CAE, Chief Executive Officer
Angie Silberhorn, CMP, Director of Conference
Dave Pardo, Marketing Manager

Association for logistics and warehouse professionals.

Newsletters

23798 AUA News
American Underground Space Association
1000 Corporate Boulevard
Linthicum, MD 21090

410-689-3700
866-746-4282
FAX 410-689-3800
E-Mail: aua@AUAnet.org
Home Page: www.auanet.org

Thomas O'Neil, President
Elaine Gray, Editor

Offers the latest news on underground space construction development and use in North America. Includes information on infrastruc-

tures.
Cost: $107.00
Frequency: Quarterly
Circulation: 1000
Printed in 4 colors on glossy stock

23799 Affiliated Warehouse Companies Newsletter
Affiliated Warehouse Companies, Inc
PO Box 295
Hazlet, NJ 07730-0295

732-739-2323
FAX 732-739-4154
E-Mail: sales@awco.com
Home Page: www.awco.com

Jim McBride, Publisher
Jim McBride, President
Patrick McBride, Vice President

Assists public warehouse users to gather rates and data, provides information on warehousing and distribution at no charge or obligation for over 100 public warehouse clients in the US, Canada, Mexico and Puerto Rico.
Mailing list available for rent: 8,500 names

23800 Distribution Center Management
Alexander Communications Group
712 Main Street~
Suite 187B
New York, NJ 07005

973-265-2300
800-232-4317
FAX 973-402-6056
E-Mail: info@distributiongroup.com
Home Page: www.distributiongroup.com

Romauld Alexander, President
Margaret Dewitt, Publisher/Marketing Manager

Provides practical strategies and industry news to help distribution center and warehouse professionals improve distribution center efficiency.
Cost: $199.00
8 Pages
Frequency: Monthly
ISBN: 0-894765-1 -
Founded in 1985

Magazines & Journals

23801 Inside Self-Storage
Virgo Publishing LLC
3300 N Central Ave
Suite 300
Phoenix, AZ 85012-2532

480-990-1101
FAX 480-990-0819
E-Mail: troyb@vpico.com
Home Page: www.vpico.com

Jenny Bolton, President
John Siefert, CEO & Director
Kelly Ridley, VP
John LyBarger, Director, Business Development
Troy Bix, Publications Editor

For storage professionals.
Frequency: Monthly
Circulation: 20000
Founded in 1991
Mailing list available for rent

23802 Logistics Management & Distribution Report
Reed Business Information
225 Wyman St
Suite 3
Waltham, MA 02451-1216

781-734-8000
FAX 781-734-8076

E-Mail: fquinn@reedbusiness.com
Home Page: www.reedbusiness.com

Mark Finklestein, President
Mike Levin, Group Editor-in-Chief
Frank Quinn, Editorial Director
Stephen Moylan, President, Divisions

Logistics Management and Distribution Report
is written for managers and professionals in
charge of traffic, transportation, purchasing, inventory control, containerization and warehousing the functions of physical distribution
and business logistics. Covers marketing and
operating strategies, cost reduction opportunities and governmental regulation and law.
Cost: $99.90
Frequency: Monthly
Circulation: 68000
Founded in 1977

23803 Mini-Storage Messenger
MiniCo
2531 W Dunlap Ave
Phoenix, AZ 85021-2730

602-870-1711
800-824-6864
FAX 602-861-1094
E-Mail: publishing@minico.com
Home Page: www.ministoragemessenger.com

Hardy Good, President
Denise Nunez, Director Publishing

As the industry's first trade journal, the
mini-storage messenger has become the leading
trade magazine for anyone involved in
self-storage. This magazine covers rental rates,
marketing trends, and finance.
Cost: $59.95
89 Pages
Frequency: Monthly
Founded in 1979
Printed in 4 colors on glossy stock

23804 Refrigerated Transporter
Primedia
PO Box 66010
Houston, TX 77266

713-513-8124
800-880-0368
FAX 713-523-8384
Home Page: www.refrigeratedtrans.com

Ray Anderson, Advertising
Jay Russel Miller, Editorial
Maria Singletary, Directories
Frequency: Monthly
Circulation: 15000
Founded in 1898

23805 Storage
West World Productions
420 N Camden Dr
Beverly Hills, CA 90210-4507

310-276-9500
FAX 310-276-9874
E-Mail: sinan@kanatsiz.com
Home Page: www.wwpi.com

Yuri R Spiro, Publisher
Laura Klein, Production Manager

Storage is the unique storage-intensive maga-
zine supplement to Computer Technology Re-
view. It is recognized as the bible of the entire
storage industry.
Cost: $10.00
72 Pages
Frequency: Quarterly
Circulation: 72000
ISSN: 0278-9647
Founded in 1981
Printed in 4 colors on glossy stock

23806 Warehousing Management
Reed Business Information

225 Wyman St
Suite 3
Waltham, MA 02451-1216

781-734-8000
FAX 781-734-8076
E-Mail: fquinn@reedbusiness.com
Home Page: www.reedbusiness.com

Mark Finklestein, President
Mike Levin, Group Editor-in-Chief
Frank Quinn, Editorial Director
Stephen Moylan, President, Divisions

Warehousing Management targets warehousing
and distribution center operations managers
with analysis, news, trends, equipment and
events.
Circulation: 47185
Founded in 1977

Trade Shows

23807 Eastpack
Reed Exhibition Companies
255 Wyman Streett
Waltham, MA 02451

781-734-8000
FAX 781-734-8076
E-Mail: fquinn@reedbusiness.com
Home Page: www.reedbusiness.com

Mark Finklestein, President
Mike Levin, Group Editor-in-Chief
Frank Quinn, Editorial Director
Stephen Moylan, President, Divisions
275 booths.
7.5M Attendees
Frequency: March
Founded in 1977

23808 Household Goods Forwarders Association
5904 Richman Avenue
Suite 304
Alexandria, VA 22303-4691

703-684-3780

Belvian Carpinton, Show Manager
Terry Head, President
20 tables.
1M Attendees
Frequency: September

23809 Independent Liquid Terminals Assoc. Annual Operating Conference & Trade Show
Independent Liquid Terminals Association
1005 North Glebe Road
Suite 600
Arlington, VA 20005

703-875-2011
FAX 703-875-2018
E-Mail: info@ilta.org
Home Page: www.ilta.org

E. David Doane, President
Melinda Whitney, Director/Government Affairs

Two-hundred and two booths of products including goods and services designed for the
construction and operation of bulk liquid storage terminals. Includes international
companies.
2,700 Attendees
Frequency: June

23810 Inside Self-Storage World Expo
Virgo Publishing LLC

3300 N Central Ave
Suite 300
Phoenix, AZ 85012-2532

480-675-9925
FAX 480-990-0819
E-Mail: kkennedy@vpico.com
Home Page: www.vpico.com

Jenny Bolton, President

The self-storage industry's largest, most comprehensive conference and tradeshow. The
leading educational and networking event for
facility managers, owners, developers and investors, the ISS Expo provides the resources
professionals need to build, manage and market
their business in a competitive environment.
Circulation: 20000
Founded in 1986
Printed in on glossy stock

23811 International Transportation and Logistics Exhibition and Conference
ILT
1300 Higgins Road
Suite 111
Park Ridge, IL 60068-5764

847-292-1891
FAX 847-823-3901
Home Page: www.warehouselogistics.org

Marge Whalen, Director of Sales
Regan Williams, Trade Show Coordinator

Annual conference and trade show focusing on
public warehousing, distribution, transportation, logistics and systems. Containing 200
exhibits.
3,000 Attendees
Frequency: June

23812 NORPACK
Northern American Expositions Company
33 Rutherford Avenue
Charlestown, MA 02129

617-242-6092
800-225-1577
FAX 617-242-1817
E-Mail: naexpo@hotmail.com
Home Page: naexpo.com

The Northeast's premier trade show for packaging, material handling, warehouse automation,
shipping/receiving, storage and bottling.
4500 Attendees

23813 Northwest Material Handling & Packaging Show
Professional Trade Shows-Division of
Penton Media
47817 Fremont Boulevard
Fremont, CA 94538

510-651-6698
FAX 510-354-3159
Home Page: proshows.com

5,000 Attendees
Frequency: May

23814 Pack Expo
Pakaging Machinery Manufacturers Institute
4350 N Fairfax Drive
Suite 600
Arlington, VA 22203

703-243-8555
888-275-7664
E-Mail: pmmi@pmmi.org
Home Page: www.packexpo.com

Matt Crossn, Communications Director
Sara Kryder, Assistant Communications

Informational meeting and exposition held by
the Packaging Machinery Manufacturers
Institute.
15000 Attendees

23815 Warehousing, Technology & Distribution Show
Industrial Shows of America
164 Lake Front Drive
Hunt Valley, MD 21030-2215

410-771-1445
800-638-6396
FAX 410-771-1158

This show will feature hands-on workshops for the practical applications of new technologies, safety issues and more all designed to improve productivity and cut losses in today's competitive market.
1500 Attendees
Frequency: April

Directories & Databases

23816 Affiliated Warehouse Companies Database of Public Warehouse Users
Affiliated Warehouse Companies, Inc.
PO Box 295
Hazlet, NJ 07730-0295

732-739-2323
FAX 732-739-4154
E-Mail: sales@awco.com
Home Page: www.awco.com

Jim McBride, President
Patrick McBride, Vice President
Jim McBride, Publisher

In excess of 8,000 listings of individuals and companies that use public warehousing, products produced and services required.
Mailing list available for rent: 8,500 names

23817 American Chain of Warehouses Directory
20500 S La Grange Road
Frankfort, IL 60423-1356

703-875-2018
FAX 815-469-2941

Donald R Greenland, Executive VP

Public warehouse listings in the United States are profiled.
50 Pages
Frequency: Annual

23818 American Public Warehouse Register
Reed Business Information
2 Brandywine Way
Sicklerville, NJ 08081-0750

856-728-9745
FAX 630-288-8686
Home Page: www.reedbusiness.com

Laura Masapollo, National Sales Director
Laura MasaPollo, National Sales Director

Worldwide listings of dry, refrigerated, contract and HazMat Public Warehouses Annual.
Cost: $50.00

23819 Associated Warehouses Directory of Services
PO Box 471
Cedar Knolls, NJ 07927-0471

973-539-1277
FAX 973-538-0944
Home Page: www.awilogistics.com

Mark Richards, Editor
Barbara Brown, Circulation Director

A who's who directory of services to the industry.
100 Pages
Frequency: Annual

23820 Directory of Bulk Liquid Terminal and Storage Facilities
ITLA
1133 15th Street NW
Sutie 650
Washington, DC 20005

202-659-2301
FAX 202-466-4166
E-Mail: info@ilta.org
Home Page: www.ilta.org

John Prokop, President
EB Calvert, Director Administration

Locates over 480 bulk liquid terminal/storage facilities. Lists key personnel, addresses, telephone numbers. Lists products handled-petroleum products, crude oil, chemicals, animal fats and oils, vegetable oils, molasses, spirits, etc. Lists storage tanks, modes served, pipeline connections. Other services and capabilities-canning, barreling, bleaching, blending, weighing, warehousing, etc. Subc. available for Directory and Newsletter
Cost: $95.00
300 Pages
Frequency: Annual

23821 Food & Beverage Market Place
Grey House Publishing
4919 Route 22
PO Box 56
Amenia, NY 12501

518-789-8700
800-562-2139
FAX 845-373-6390
E-Mail: books@greyhouse.com
Home Page: www.greyhouse.com
Social Media: *Facebook, Twitter*

Leslie Mackenzie, Publisher
Richard Gottlieb, Editor

This information-packed 3-volume set is the most powerful buying and marketing guide for the US food and beverage industry. Includes thousands of industry freight and transportation listings.
Cost: $595.00
2000 Pages
Frequency: Annual
ISBN: 1-592373-61-5
Founded in 1981

23822 Food & Beverage Marketplace: Online Database
Grey House Publishing
4919 Route 22
PO Box 56
Amenia, NY 12501

518-789-8700
800-562-2139
FAX 845-373-6390
E-Mail: gold@greyhouse.com
Home Page: http://gold.greyhouse.com
Social Media: *Facebook, Twitter*

Richard Gottlieb, President
Leslie Mackenzie, Publisher

This complete updated Food & Beverage Market Place: Online Database is the go-to source for the food and beverage industry. Anyone involved in the food and beverage industry needs this 'industry bible' and the important contacts to develop critical research data that can make for successful business growth.
Frequency: Annual
Founded in 1981

23823 Independent Liquid Terminals Association
1444 Eye St NW
Suite 400
Washington, DC 20005-6538

202-842-9200
FAX 703-875-2018

E-Mail: info@ilta.org
Home Page: www.ilta.org

E David Doane, President
Melinda Whitney, Director/Government Affairs

A 285 page directory, listing 577 for hire, marketing, throughput, and pipeline bulk liquid storage terminals.
Cost: $95.00
285 Pages
Founded in 1975

23824 International Directory of Public Refrigerated Warehouses
1500 King Street
Suite 201
Alexandria, VA 22314

703-373-4300
FAX 703-373-4301
E-Mail: email@iwra.org
Home Page: www.iarw.org

J William Hudson, President/CEO

Offers information on more than 950 member warehouses in 32 countries and on companies supplying products and services to the refrigerated warehouse industry.
Cost: $150.00
232 Pages
Frequency: Annual
Circulation: 6,000

23825 International Warehouse Logistics Directory
1300 Higgins Rd
Suite 111
Park Ridge, IL 60068-5743

847-292-1891
FAX 847-813-0115
E-Mail: bstephens@warehouselogistics.org
Home Page: www.iwla.com

Joel Anderson, President
Ben Stephens, Public Relations/Media Coordinator

The membership directory is published annually in January in book and CD-ROM form.
Frequency: Annually

23826 National Refrigeration Contractors Association
National Refrigeration Contrtactors
1900 Arch Street
Philadelphia, PA 19103-1404

215-564-3484
FAX 215-963-9785
Home Page: www.arcat.com

Elizabeth Barnett, Editor

About 100 member refrigeration contracting companies
Frequency: Annual

23827 Transportation & Distribution Magazine's Integrated Warehousing/Storage
Penton Media
1166 Avenue of the Americas
New York, NY 10036

212-204-4200
FAX 216-696-6662
E-Mail: information@penton.com
Home Page: www.penton.com

Jane Cooper, Marketing

Lists over 1,200 manufacturers of products related to the warehousing and distribution industries.
Frequency: Annual
Circulation: 71,000
Printed in 4 colors on glossy stock

23828 Warehouses Licensed Under US Warehouse Act
Farm Service Agency-US Dept. of Agriculture
PO Box 2415
Washington, DC 20013-2415

FAX 202-690-0014
Home Page: www.fsa.usda.gov/

Agricultural warehouses voluntarily licensed under the US Warehouse Act governing public storage facilities.
Frequency: Annual

23829 Warehousing Distribution Directory
PRIMEDIA Information
3585 Engineering Drive
Suite 100
Norcross, GA 30092

678-421-3000
800-216-1423
FAX 609-371-7819
Home Page: www.primediainfo.com

Amy Middlebrook, Editor
John Capers III, Publisher

List of about 800 warehousing and consolidation companies and firms offering trucking, trailer on flatcar, container on flatcar and pig-

gyback carrier services.
Cost: $55.00
250 Pages
Frequency: SemiAnnual
Circulation: 10,000
Founded in 1949
Printed in 4 colors on glossy stock

Industry Web Sites

23830 http://gold.greyhouse.com
G.O.L.D Grey House OnLine Databases
Grey House Publishing's online database platform, GOLD, offers Quick Search, Keyword Search and Expert Search for most business sectors including warehousing and storage markets. The GOLD platform makes finding the information you need quick and easy - whether you're a novice searcher or an experienced database user. All of Grey House's directory products are available for subscription on the GOLD platform.

23831 www.awco.com
Affiliated Warehouse Companies

Assists public warehouse users to gather rates and data, provides information on warehousing and distribution at no charge or obligation for

over 100 public warehouse clients in the US, Canada, Mexico, Europe and Southeast Asia.

23832 www.greyhouse.com
Grey House Publishing
Authoritative reference directories for direct marketing, demographics, business, research, health care, international trade, food industry and education. Users can search the online databases with varied search criteria allowing for custom searches by product category, geographic area, sales volume, keyword, subject and more. Full Grey House catalog and online ordering also available.

23833 www.larw.org
Refrigeration Research and Education Foundation
Sponsors graduate-level scientific research on the refrigeration of perishable commodities. Offers annual training institute for public refrigerated warehouse personnel.

23834 www.warehouselogistics.org
International Warehouse Logistics Association
For third-party warehousing and related logistics services throughout the world. Collectively, the Association's members ship over 3 trillion pounds annually in North America.

Associations

23835 Alliance for Water Efficiency
33 N. LaSalle Street
Suite 2275
Chicago, IL 60602

773-360-5100
866-730-1493
FAX 773-345-3636
E-Mail: jeffrey@a4we.org
Home Page:
www.allianceforwaterefficiency.org

Mary Ann Dickinson, President/ CEOÿ
Megan Chery, Manager
William Christiansen, Program Manager
Molly Garcia, Accountant/Event Coordinator
Jeffrey Hughes, Director of Operations

An association for water efficient products.
Founded in 2007

23836 American Backflow Prevention Association
3016 Maloney Ave
PO Box 3051
Bryan, TX 77801-3121

979-846-7606
877-227-2127
FAX 979-846-7607
E-Mail: jgraham@calwater.com
Home Page: www.abpa.org

John Graham, International Presidentÿ
Tim Brown, International Vice President
Patti Fauver, Treasurer
Michael Moss, International Past President
Mike Lueck, Director-at-Large

An association dedicated to backflow education
and technical assistance.
Founded in 1984

23837 American Fisheries Society
5410 Grosvenor Lane
Bethesdaÿ, MD 20814

301-897-8616
FAX 301-897-8096
E-Mail: dausten@fisheries.org
Home Page: fisheries.org
Social Media: *x, x, x, Pinterest, Google+,
Vimeo, Fli*

Douglas ÿ Austen, Executive Director
Beth Beard, Strategist, Digital Content
Thomas Bigford, Policy Director
Juanita Flick, Membership Assistant
Sarah Gilbert Fox, Managing Editor, Fisheries
and AFS

Organization dedicated to strengthening the
fisheries profession and advancing fisheries.
Founded in 1870

23838 American Ground Water Trust
50 Pleasant Street
Suite 2
Concord, NH 3301

603-228-5444
800-423-7748
FAX 603-228-6557
E-Mail: trustinfo@agwt.org
Home Page: www.agwt.org
Social Media: *x, x, x*

Kevin McGinnis, Chairman
David Kill, Secretary/Treasurer
Andrew Stone, Executive Director

Promotes public awareness of groundwater.

23839 American Institute of Hydrology
1230 Lincoln Drive
Carbondale, IL 62901

618-453-7809
E-Mail: aih@engr.siu.edu
Home Page: www.aihydrology.org

Mustafa M. Aral, PhD, PE, PH., President
Dr. John L. Nieber, VP for Academic Affairs
John W. Balay, VP for Institute Development
Ed A. Baquerizo, VP for International Affairs
Kurt Hollman, VP for Communication

Promotes hydrology as a science and a profession.
Founded in 1981

23840 American Recreation Coalition
1200 G Street NW
Suite 650
Washington, DC 20005-3832

202-682-9530
FAX 202-682-9529
E-Mail: mmeade@funoutdoors.com
Home Page: www.funoutdoors.com

Derrick Crandall, President
Catherine Ahern, VP
Melinda Meade, Director of Communications

A non-profit Washington based federation that
provides a unified voice for recreation interests
to conserve their full and active participation in
government policy making on issues such as
public land management. ARC works to build
public-private partnerships to enhance and protect
outdoor recreation opportunities and
resources.
100+ Members
Founded in 1979

23841 American Rivers
1101 14th Street NW
Suite 1400
Washington, DC 20005

202-347-7550
877-347-7550
FAX 202-347-9240
E-Mail: akober@americanrivers.org
Home Page: www.americanrivers.org
Social Media: *Facebook, Twitter, YouTube,
Pinterest*

William Robert (Bob) Irvin, President
Georgette Blanchfield, SVP, Advancement
Brendan Mysliwiec, Associate Director, Gov
Relations
Fay Augustyn, Manager
Courtney Barefoot, HR & Board Relations
Director

Nonprofit conservation organization dedicated
to protecting and restoring the rivers of the US.
Founded in 1973

23842 American Society of Irrigation Consultants
4660 S Hagadorn
Suite 195D
East Lansing, MI 48823

508-763-8140
FAX 866-828-5174
E-Mail: carolc@asic.org
Home Page: www.asic.org

Carol Colein, Executive Director
Ivy Munion, President
Corbin Schneider, Vice President
Michael J. Krones, Treasurer
Carly Kardon, Operations and Member
Services

Promotes education skills on data exchange
landscape irrigation. Members are irrigation
consultants, suppliers, and manufacturers.
Founded in 1970

23843 American Water Resources Association
PO Box 1626
Middleburg, VA 20118

540-687-8390
FAX 540-687-8395
E-Mail: info@awra.orgÿ
Home Page: www.awra.org
Social Media: *x, x, x, Blog*

Kenneth D. Reid, CAEÿ, Executive Vice
President
Michael J. Kowalski, CAEÿ, Director of
Operations
Susan Scalia, JAWRA Managing Editor
Patricia A. Reidÿ, Program Coordinatorÿ
Christine McCrehin, Membership Services
Manager

Promotes understanding of water resources and
related issues.
Founded in 1964

23844 American Water Works Association
6666 W. Quincy Ave.
Denver, CO 80235-3098

303-794-7711
800-926-7337
Home Page: www.awwa.org
Social Media: *x, x, x, YouTube, RSS*

Gene C. Koontz, President
Jeanne M. Bennett-Bailey, President-Elect
John J. Donahue, Immediate Past-President
David E. Rager, Treasurer
Jon Eaton, VP/Minnesota Section Director

Nonprofit scientific and education orgaization
dedicated to managind and treating water.
Founded in 1881

23845 American Whitewater
P.O. Box 1540
Cullowhee, NC 28723

828-586-1930
866-262-8429
FAX 828-586-2840
E-Mail: membership@americanwhitewater.org
Home Page: www.americanwhitewater.org
Social Media: *Facebook, Twitter, YouTube,
RSS*

Mark Singleton, Executive Director
Kevin Colburn, National Stewardship Director
Bob Nasdor, Northeast Stewardship Director
Dave Steindorf, California Stewardship
Director
Nathan Fey, Colorado Stewardship Director

Association for whitewaters and rafting.
Founded in 1954

23846 Association of Clean Water Administrators
1634 Eye St. NW
Suite 750
Washington, DC 20006

202-756-0605
FAX 202-793-2600
Home Page: www.acwa-us.org
Social Media: *Twitter*

Julia Anastasio, Executive Director/ General
Counsel
Sean Rolland, Deputy Director
Annette Ivey, Director of Operations
Susan Kirsch, Sr. Environmental Program
Manager
Melissa McCoy, Environmental Program
Manager

Association for the administrators of the clean
water industry.
Founded in 1961

23847 Association of State Drinking Water Administrators

1401 Wilson Blvd
Suite 1225
Arlington, VA 22209

703-812-9505
FAX 703-812-9506
E-Mail: info@asdwa.org
Home Page: www.asdwa.org
Social Media: x, x, YouTube, Blog

John Calkins, President
Steve Sturgess, President-Elect
Jim Taft, Executive Director
Bridget O'Grady, Policy & Legis. Affairs Manager
Deirdre Mason, Project Manager

Professional association serving state drinking water programs.

23848 Association of State Wetland Managers

32 Tandberg Trail
Suite 2A
Windham, ME 04062ÿ

207-892-3399
FAX 207-892-3089
E-Mail: jeanne.christie@aswm.org
Home Page: aswm.org
Social Media: x, LinkedIn, Blog

Jeanne Christie, Executive Director
Peg Bostwick, Senior Staff Policy Analyst
Brenda Zollitsch, Policy Analyst
Marla J. Stelk, Policy Analyst
Dawn Smith, Communications Specialist

A professional association for state wetland managers.
Founded in 1983

23849 Clean Water Action

1444 Eye Street NW
Suite 400
Washington, DC 20005

202-895-0420
FAX 202-895-0438
E-Mail: cwa@cleanwater.org
Home Page: www.cleanwateraction.org
Social Media: Facebook, Twitter, YouTube, Blog

Robert Wendelgass, President/ CEO
Kathy Aterno, National Managing Director
Lynn Thorp, National Campaigns Director
Andrea Herrmann, Director
Chris Bathurst, National Canvass Coordinator

A national citizen's organization working for clean, safe and affordable water and prevention of health-threatening pollution.
Founded in 1960

23850 Coastal & Estuarine Research Federation

2150 North 107th Street
Suite 205
Seattle, WA 98133-9009

206-209-5262
FAX 206-367-8777
E-Mail: info@erf.org
Home Page: www.erf.org
Social Media: Facebook, Twitter, Flickr, Vimeo

Kenneth L. Heck, Jr., President
Robert R. Twilley, President-Elect
Enrique Reyes, Secretary
James Hagy, Treasurer
Mark Wolf-Armstrong, Executive Director (Ex-Officio)

Private nonprofit organization dedicated to advancing the understanging of coastal and estuarine ecosystems.

23851 Ground Water Protection Council

13308 N Macarthur Blvd
Oklahoma City, OK 73142-3021

405-516-4972
FAX 405-516-4973
E-Mail: dan@gwpc.org
Home Page: www.gwpc.org

Mike Paque, Executive Director
Ben Grunewald, Chief of Operations
Paul Jehn, Technical Director
Dan Yates, Associate Executive Director
Mike Nickolaus, Special Projects Director

State ground water and underground injection control agencies whose mission is to promote the protection and conservation of ground water resources for all beneficial uses, recognizing ground water as a component of the ecosystem.
1.75M Members
Founded in 1983

23852 Irrigation Association

8280 Willow Oaks Corporate Drive
Suite 400
Fairfax, VA 22031

703-536-7080
FAX 703-536-7019
E-Mail: info@irrigation.org
Home Page: www.irrigation.org

Aric J. Olson, President
Gregory R. Hunter, Vice President
Deborah M. Hamlin, CAE, FASAE, Chief Executive Officer
John R. Farner, Jr, Government & PA Director
Rebecca J. Bayless, Finance Director

The Irrigation Association is the leading membership organization for irrigation equipment and system manufacturers, dealers, distributors, designers, consultants, contractors and end users.
1600 Members
Founded in 1949

23853 National Aquaculture Association

PO Box 12759
Tallahassee, FL 32317

850-216-2400
FAX 850-216-2480
E-Mail: naa@thenaa.net
Home Page: thenaa.net

Mike Freeze, President
Jim Ekstrom, Vice-President
Adam Hater, Secretary
Rick Martin, Treasurer

A producer-based association dedicated to aquaculture.

23854 National Association of Clean Water Agencies

1816 Jefferson Place N.W.
Washingtonÿ, DC 20036

202-833-2672
FAX 888-267-9505
E-Mail: info@nacwa.org
Home Page: www.nacwa.org
Social Media: Facebook, Twitter, LinkedIn, YouTube

Adam Krantz, Chief Executive Officer
Paula Dannenfeldt, Chief Operating Officer
Shalina Baker, Executive Assistant
Amanda Waters, GC & Director, Public Affairs
Patricia Sinicropi, Senior Dir., Legislative Affairs

Nationally recognized leader in environmental policy and a technical resource on water quality and ecosystem protection.
Founded in 1970

23855 National Drilling Association

4036 Center Rd
Suite B
Brunswick, OH 44212

330-273-5756
877-632-4748
FAX 216-803-9900
E-Mail: info@nda4u.com
Home Page: www.nda4u.com
Social Media: Facebook, LinkedIn

Dan Dunn, President
Larry Gibel, Secretary/Treasurer
Michael Willey, Vice President
Peggy McGee, Immediate Past President

A non-profit trade association of contractors, manufacturers and affiliated members from the drilling industry representing the geotechnical, environmental and mineral exploration sectors of this industry.
250+ Members
Founded in 1972

23856 National Environmental Services Center

Box 6893, West Virginia University
Morgantown, WV 26506-6893

304-293-4191
800-624-8301
FAX 304-293-3161
E-Mail: info@mail.nesc.wvu.edu
Home Page: www.nesc.wvu.edu
Social Media: Facebook, Twitter, WordPress

Gerald Iwan, Ph.D., Director

Helps small, rural communities with their drinking water, wastewater and environmental training needs.
Founded in 1984

23857 National Ground Water Association

601 Dempsey Rd.
Westerville, OH 43081

800-551-7379
FAX 614-898-7786
E-Mail: ngwa@ngwa.org
Home Page: www.ngwa.org
Social Media: Facebook, Twitter, LinkedIn, YouTube

Kevin B. McCray, Chief Executive Officer

International nonprofit organization of groundwater professionals for the responsible use of groundwater.
Founded in 1948

23858 National Institute for Water Resources

University of Massachusetts
Blaisdell House
Amherst, MA 01003

413-545-2842
FAX 413-545-2304
E-Mail: support@niwr.net
Home Page: www.niwr.net

Brian Haggard, President
Sharon Megdal, President Elect
John Tracy, Secretary/Treasurer

Offers information on water resource directions across the nation.
54 Members
Founded in 1974

23859 National Onsite Wastewater Recycling

1199 N. Fairfax St.
Suite 410
Alexandria, VA 22314

703-836-1950
800-966-2942
FAX 703-535-5263
E-Mail: info@nowra.org

Home Page: www.nowra.org
Social Media: *Facebook*

Gregory D Graves, President
Jim Bell, President Elect/VP
Robert B Mayer MSPE, Secretary/Treasurer
Tom Fritts, Past-President

Dedicated solely to educating and representing members within the onsite and decentralized industry. And also to provide leadership and promote the onsite waste water treatment and recycling through education, training, communication and quality tools to support excellence in performance.
3500 Members
Founded in 1992

23860 National Onsite Wastewater Recycling Assoc iation

1199 N. Fairfax St.
Suite 410
Alexandria, VA 22314

703-836-1950
800-966-2942
Home Page: www.nowra.org

Gregory D Graves, President
Jim Bell, President Elect/VP
Robert B Mayer MSPE, Secretary/Treasurer
Tom Fritts, Past-President

Organization dedication to onsite wastewater recycling.
Founded in 1992

23861 National Rural Water Association

2915 S. 13th Street
Duncan, OK 73533

580-252-0629
FAX 580-255-4476
E-Mail: nwra@nwra.org
Home Page: www.nrwa.org
Social Media: *Facebook, Twitter, LinkedIn, YouTube*

Charles A. Hilton, President
Steve Fletcher, Sr. Vice President
Sam Wade, CEO
Matt Holmes, Deputy CEO
Claudette Atwood, CFO

Dedicated to the wise management and use of the nation's water and land resources.
5M+ Members
Founded in 1932

23862 National Water Research Institute

18700 Ward Streetÿ
P.O. Box 8096ÿ
Fountain Valley, CA 92728-8096

714-378-3278
FAX 714-378-3375
E-Mail: jmosher@nwri-usa.org
Home Page: www.nwri-usa.org
Social Media: *Facebook, Twitter, LinkedIn, YouTube*

Jeff Mosher, Executive Directorÿ
Gina Vartanian, Communications and Outreach Manager
Brandi Caskey, Administrative and Events Manager
Suzanne Faubl, Manager
Ken Lanxner, Webmasterÿ

A nonprofit organization devoted to promoting the protection, maintenance and restoration of water supplies.
Founded in 1991

23863 National Water Resources Association

4 E Street Southeast
Washington, DC 20003

202-698-0693
FAX 703-524-1548
E-Mail: nwra@nwra.org

Home Page: www.nwra.org
Social Media: *Twitter*

Dave Koland, President
Ron Thompson, 1st VP
Cheryl Zittle, 2nd VP
Robert Johnson, Secretary
Glenn Johnson, Treasurer

Dedicated to the wise management and use of the nation's water and land resources.
5M+ Members
Founded in 1932

23864 Soil and Water Conservation Society

945 SW Ankeny Rd
Ankeny, IA 50023-9764

515-289-2331
800-843-7645
FAX 515-289-1227
E-Mail: jwpeterson@cox.net
Home Page: www.swcs.org

Jim Guillford, Executive Director
Annie Binder, Director of Publications/Editor
Jody Thompson, Editorial Assistant
Kim Johnson Smith, Professional Development Director
Jody Ogg, Comptroller

SWCS is a nonprofit scientific and educational organization that serves as an advocate for conservation professionals and for science-based conservation practice, programs, and policy.
5000+ Members
Founded in 1943

23865 Submersible Waste Water Pump Association

1866 Sheridan Rd
Suite 212
Highland Park, IL 60035-2545

847-681-1868
FAX 847-681-1869
E-Mail: swpaexdir@sbcglobal.net
Home Page: www.swpa.org

Adam Stolberg, Executive Director
Carol Stolberg, Administrative Director

Represents and serves the manufacturers of submersible pumps for the municipal and industrial wastewater applications. Manufacturers of components and accessory items for those products and companies providing services to users of those products.
Founded in 1976

23866 WateReuse Association

1199 North Fairfax Street
Suite 410ÿ
Alexandria, VA 22314

703-548-0880
FAX 703-548-5085
Home Page: www.watereuse.org
Social Media: *Facebook, Twitter, LinkedIn, YouTube*

Melissa L. Meeker, Executive Director
Maria Greenly, Accounting Manager
Carrie Knooihuizen, Administrative Assistant
Courtney Tharpe, Director of Conferences and Eventsÿ
Erin DiMenna, Director of Membership

An association for advancing the science of water reuse and destination through research.
Founded in 1990

23867 Water Environment Federation

601 Wythe St
Alexandria, VA 22314-1994

703-684-2400
800-666-0206
FAX 703-684-2492
E-Mail: inquiry@wef.org

Home Page: www.wef.org
Social Media: *Facebook, Twitter, LinkedIn*

Eileen O'Neill, Executive Director
Barry Liner, Director
Lisa McFadden, Sr. Program Manager
Steve Harrison, Manager-Technical Programs
Elizabeth Conway, Committee Coordinator

A technical and educational organization with members from varied disciplines who work toward the vision of preservation and enhancement of the global water environment.
34000 Members
Founded in 1928

23868 Water Keeper Alliance

17 Battery Place
Suite 1329ÿ
New York, NY 10004

212-747-0622
FAX 212-747-0611
E-Mail: info@waterkeeper.org
Home Page: waterkeeper.org
Social Media: *Facebook, Twitter, YouTube, Instagram*

Marc A. Yaggi, Executive Director
Mary Beth Postman, Deputy Director
Lesley Adams, Western Regional Coordinator
Peter Cleary, Comm. & Marketing Director
Larry Baldwin, North Carolina CAFO Coordinator

An association using grassroots advocacy to achieve clean waterways.
Founded in 1996

23869 Water Quality Association

4151 Naperville Rd
Lisle, IL 60532-3696

630-505-0160
FAX 630-505-9637
E-Mail: info@mail.wqa.org
Home Page: www.wqa.org
Social Media: *Facebook, Twitter, LinkedIn, Youtube*

Bret P. Tangley, MWS, President
David Westman, MBA, CAE, CPA, Interim Executive Director
Pauli Undesser, MWS, Deputy Executive Director
Susan Barkach, Business Operations Director
Larry Deutsch, Marketing & Comm. Director

An international, nonprofit trade association representing retail/dealers and manufacturer/suppliers in the point of use/entry water quality improvement industry. Membership benefits and services include technical and scientific information, educational seminars and home correspondence course books, professional certification and discount services.
2700+ Members
Founded in 1974

23870 Water and Wastewater Equipment Manufacturers Association

540 Fort Evans Road
Suite 304
Leesburg, VA 20176-3379

703-444-1777
FAX 703-444-1779
E-Mail: info@wwema.org
Home Page: www.wwema.org

Vanessa Leiby, Executive Director
Linda Budzinski, Dir., Membership and Marketing
Octavia Trammell, Office Manager

Represents the interests of companies that manufacture the products that are sold to the portable water and wastewater treatment industries. Also informs, educates and provides leadership

on the issues which affect the worldwide water and wastewater equipment industry.
80 Members
Founded in 1908

Newsletters

23871 Drinking Water and Backflow Prevention
SFA Enterprises
18927 Hickory Creek Drive
Suite 140
Mokena, IL 60448

303-451-0978
888-367-3927
FAX 303-452-9776
E-Mail: backflow@dwbp-online.com
Home Page: www.iapmodwbp.org/

Cindy Most, Managing Editor

Accepts advertising.
Cost: $38.00
24 Pages
Frequency: Monthly
Mailing list available for rent

23872 Jet News
WaterJet Technology Association/Industrial &
Municipal Cleaning Association
906 Olive Street, Suite 1200
Saint Louis, MO 63101-1448

314-241-1445
FAX 314-241-1449
E-Mail: wjta-imca@wjta.org
Home Page: www.wjta.org

George A Savanick PhD, President
Kenneth C Carroll, Association Manager

Provides the latest information on applications, equipment, news from members, new developments, meetings, conferences, and technical information.
Frequency: Bi-Monthly
Circulation: 1000

23873 National Association of Regulatory Utility Commisioners
Natl Assoc of Regulatory Utility Commissioner
1101 Vermont Ave Nw
Suite 200
Washington, DC 20005-3553

202-898-2200
FAX 202-898-2213
E-Mail: admin@naruc.org
Home Page: www.naruc.org

Charles Gray, Executive Director
Diane Munns, Publisher

A national organization that offers valuable information on over 150 consultants and other professionals active in regulated water, sewer and related industries.
Frequency: Monthly
Circulation: 1800
Founded in 1889

23874 National Water Line
National Water Resources Association
3800 Fairfax Dr
Suite 4
Arlington, VA 22203-1703

703-524-1544
FAX 703-524-1548
E-Mail: nrwa@nrwa.org
Home Page: www.nwra.org

Thomas Donnelly, VP

Association news and information.
Frequency: Monthly

23875 US Water News
US Water News
230 Main St
Halstead, KS 67056-1913

316-835-2222
800-251-0046
FAX 316-835-2223
E-Mail: Inquiries@uswaternews.com
Home Page: www.uswaternews.com

Thomas Bell, President/Publisher
Mary DeSana, Editor

Reports news of current events in water resources from across the nation. Accepts advertising.
Cost: $59.00
24 Pages
Frequency: Monthly

23876 Water Newsletter
Water Information Center
1099 18th St
Suite 2600
Denver, CO 80202-1926

303-297-2600
FAX 303-297-2750
Home Page: www.rwolaw.com

Stephen L Waters, Partner

Contents include water supply and waste disposal information, and presents articles on conservation/usage.
Cost: $127.00
Frequency: Monthly
Founded in 1959

Magazines & Journals

23877 APWA Reporter
American Public Works Association
2345 Grand Blvd
Suite 700
Kansas City, MO 64108-2625

816-472-6100
800-848-2792
FAX 816-472-1610
E-Mail: ddancy@apwa.net
Home Page: www.apwa.net

Kaye Sullivan, Executive Director
David Dancy, Marketing Director
Connie Hartline, Publications Manager
Lillie Plowman, Publications/Premiums Marketing Mgr

Circulation to entire membership of American Public Works Association.
Cost: $100.00
Frequency: Monthly
Circulation: 34000
ISBN: 0-092487-3
Founded in 1937
Mailing list available for rent

23878 Bottled Water Reporter
International Bottled Water Association
1700 Diagonal Rd
Suite 650
Alexandria, VA 22314-2870

703-683-5213
800-928-3711
FAX 703-683-4074
E-Mail: ibwainfo@bottledwater.org
Home Page: www.bottledwater.org
Social Media: *Facebook, Twitter, LinkedIn*

Joe Doss, CEO

Provides a vital source of information to bottlers and agencies, consultants and engineers. Also contains statistical data, marketing and management tips and profiles of bottled water

operations and supplier companies.
Cost: $50.00
Circulation: 3000
Founded in 1958

23879 Cleaner Times
Advantage Publishing Company
1000 Nix Rd
Little Rock, AR 72211-3235

501-280-9111
800-525-7038
FAX 501-280-9233
E-Mail: gpuls@adpub.com
Home Page: www.cleanertimes.com

Charlene Yarbrough, Publisher
Gerry Puls, Circulation
Chuck Prieur, Sales Manager
Charlener Yarbrough, Publications/Premiums Marketing Mgr

Application, information, and productivity for persons engaged in the manufacturing, distribution, or the use of high pressure water systems and accessories. The emphasis is on safety, regulatory, which affect the industry as well as cleaning applications.
Cost: $18.00
72 Pages
Frequency: Monthly
Circulation: 10000
ISSN: 1073-9602
Founded in 1989
Printed in 4 colors on glossy stock

23880 Clearwaters
New York Water Environment Association
525 Plum Street
Suite 102
Syracuse, NY 13204

315-422-7811
FAX 315-422-3851
E-Mail: rdh@nywea.org
Home Page: www.nywea.org

Lois Hickey, Editor
Patricia Cerro-Reehil, Executive Director

Contains information on pollution control legislation, regulation, and compliance.
Cost: $25.00
Frequency: Quarterly
Circulation: 3000
Founded in 1929

23881 Drill Bits
National Drilling Association
1545 W 130th St
Suite A2
Hinckley, OH 44233-9121

330-273-5756
877-632-4748
FAX 216-803-9900
E-Mail: info@nda4u.com
Home Page: www.nda4u.com

Peggy McGee, President
Dan Dunn, VP
Jim Howe, Secretary/Treasurer
Tim Cleary, Board of Directors
R. Alan Garrard, Board of Directors

A non-profit trade association of contractors, manufacturers and affiliated members from the drilling industry representing the geotechnical, environmental and mineral exploration sectors of this industry.
250+ Members
Frequency: 2x/Year
Founded in 1972

23882 Ground Water
National Ground Water Association
PO Box 715435
Columbus, OH 43271-5435

614-898-7791
800-551-7379

FAX 614-898-7786
E-Mail: customerservice@ngwa.org
Home Page: www.ngwa.org
Social Media: *Facebook, Twitter, LinkedIn, YouTube*

Paul Humes, VP
Thad Plumley, Publications Director
Shelby Fleck, Advertising
Keviin McKray, Executive Director

Focuses on ground water hydrogeology as a science.
Cost: $395.00
160 Pages
Circulation: 15000
ISSN: 0017-467x
Founded in 1963
Printed in one color

23883 Ground Water Monitoring and Remediation

National Ground Water Association
PO Box 715436
Columbus, OH 43271-5436

614-898-7791
800-551-7379
FAX 614-898-7786
E-Mail: ngwa@ngwa.org
Home Page: www.ngwa.org
Social Media: *Facebook, Twitter, LinkedIn, YouTube*

Paul Humes, VP
Thad Plumley, Publications Director
Kevin McKray, Executive Director

Contains peer-reviewed papers, product and equipment news, EPA updates, industry news, and a mix of original columns authored by industry leaders.
Cost: $195.00
Frequency: Quarterly
Circulation: 15201
ISSN: 1069-3629
Founded in 1981

23884 Industrial Wastewater

Water Environment Federation
601 Wythe St
Alexandria, VA 22314-1994

703-684-2400
FAX 703-684-2492
E-Mail: inquiry@wef.org
Home Page: www.wef.org
Social Media: *Facebook, Twitter, LinkedIn*

Bill Bertera, Executive Director

Provides the information on the practical application of science and technology in the management of water discharges, air emissions, ground water and soil remediation to the industrial personnel, consultants and other involved in all aspects of management, treatment and disposal of industrial wastewater.
Cost: $129.00
Frequency: Bi-Monthly
Circulation: 35500
ISSN: 1067-5337
Founded in 1928

23885 Journal of Soil and Water Conservation

Soil and Water Conservation Society
945 SW Ankeny Road
Ankeny, IA 50023-9764

515-289-2331
800-843-7645
FAX 515-289-1227
E-Mail: pubs@swcs.org
Home Page: www.swcs.org

Oksana Gieseman, Director of Publications

The JSWC is a multidisciplinary journal of natural resource conservation research, practice, policy, and perspectives. The journal has two sections: the A Section containing various de-

partments and features and the Research Section containing peer-reviewed research papers.
Cost: $99.00
Frequency: Bimonthly
Circulation: 2000
ISSN: 0022-4561
Founded in 1945

23886 Journal of the American Water Resources Association

PO Box 1623
Middleburg, VA 20118-1626

540-687-8390
540-687-8390
FAX 540-687-8395
E-Mail: info@awra.org
Home Page: www.awra.org

Kenneth J Lanfear, Editor
Charlene E Young, Publications Production Director
Billy Journell, Manager

Annual directory offering information on all water resources, technologies, systems and services for the water resources industry.
Cost: $205.00
Frequency: Bi-Monthly
ISSN: 1093-474x
Founded in 1964

23887 Landscape & Irrigation

Adams Business Media
PO Box 17349
Chicago, IL 60617-0349

773-221-4223
FAX 773-374-6270
Home Page: www.adamsbrick.com

Karen Adams, President

23888 National Driller

Business News Publishing Company
1050 IL Route 83
Suite 200
Bensenville, IL 60106

800-223-2194
FAX 248-786-1358
Home Page: www.nationaldriller.com

Linda Moffat, Publisher
Greg Ettling, Editor
Lisa Shroeder, Managing Editor

Provides feature articles, timely and valuable industry information, newly developed products and technologies, and quality marketing and business management advice.
Frequency: Monthly
Mailing list available for rent

23889 Operations Forum

Water Environment Federation
601 Wythe St
Alexandria, VA 22314-1994

703-684-2400
800-666-0206
FAX 703-684-2492
Home Page: www.wef.org

Bill Bertera, Executive Director

The emphasis is on process control, plant operations, collection systems and industry news.
Cost: $4995.00
Frequency: Monthly
Circulation: 17005
Founded in 1928

23890 Rural Water Magazine

National Rural Water Association
2915 S 13th St
Duncan, OK 73533-9086

580-252-0629
FAX 580-255-4476

E-Mail: info@nrwa.org
Home Page: www.nrwa.org

Rob Johnson, CEO

Targeted at the operators and board members of rural and small municipal water and wastewater utilities.
56 Pages
Frequency: Quarterly
Circulation: 22800
Founded in 1979

23891 US Water News

US Water News
230 Main St
Halstead, KS 67056-1913

316-835-2222
800-251-0046
FAX 316-835-2223
Home Page: www.uswaternews.com

Thomas Bell, President/Publisher

Reports news of current events from across the nation in the municipal and industrial water and wastewater segments of the water industry.
Cost: $59.00
28 Pages
Frequency: Monthly
Circulation: 20000
Founded in 1984
Printed in on n stock

23892 Water Conditioning and Purification Magazine

Publicom
2800 E Fort Lowell Road
Tucson, AZ 85716

520-323-6144
FAX 520-323-7412
E-Mail: info@wcponline.com
Home Page: www.wcponline.com

Kurt C Peterson, Publisher/Eastern Advertising Exec
Sharon M Peterson, President/Owner
Karen R Smith, Executive Editor
Margo Goldbaum, Circulation Services
Denise M Roberts, Assistant Editor

Comprehensive magazine for all aspects of the water quality improvement industry. Accepts advertising.
Cost: $49.00
100 Pages
Circulation: 20000
ISSN: 1537-1786
Founded in 1959
Mailing list available for rent: 1000 names at $250 per M
Printed in 4 colors on glossy stock

23893 Water Environment & Technology

Water Environment Federation
601 Wythe St
Alexandria, VA 22314-1994

703-684-2400
800-666-0206
FAX 703-684-2492
E-Mail: csc@wef.org
Home Page: www.wef.org
Social Media: *Facebook, Twitter, LinkedIn*

Bill Bertera, Executive Director
Margaret Richards, Editorial Assistant
Tracy Hardwick, Publication Services Manager

Covers a wide range of water quality and municipal wastewater treatment issues, from the design, engineering, and management of domestic wastewater treatment plants to watershed management and wet weather issues.
Cost: $178.00
Frequency: Monthly
Circulation: 27304
Founded in 1928

23894 Water Environment Federation

Water Environment Federation
601 Wythe St
Alexandria, VA 22314-1994

703-684-2400
800-666-0206
FAX 703-684-2492
E-Mail: webfeedback@wef.org
Home Page: www.wef.org

Bill Bertera, Executive Director
David James, Publications Committee

Magazine published monthly for 41,000 members
Cost: $19.00
Founded in 1928

23895 Water Environment Research

Water Environment Federation
601 Wythe St
Alexandria, VA 22314-1994

703-684-2400
FAX 703-684-2492
Home Page: www.wef.org

Bill Bertera, Executive Director
Glenn Reinhardt, Foundation Executive
Director
Tom Wolfe, Advertising

Research journal reviewed by peers and covering the effects of water pollution and the technology and advances used for it's control.
Cost: $158.00
Circulation: 9000
Founded in 1928

23896 Water Resources Research

American Geophysical Union
2000 Florida Ave NW
Washington, DC 20009-1231

202-462-6900
800-966-2481
FAX 202-328-0566
E-Mail: service@agu.org
Home Page: www.agu.org
Social Media: *Facebook, Twitter, LinkedIn*

Fred Spilhaus, Executive Director
Karne Blaususs, Circulation Manager

Presents articles on the social, natural, and physical sciences, with emphasis on geochemistry, hydrology, and groundwater transfer technology.
Cost: $1200.00
Frequency: Monthly
Circulation: 4700
Founded in 1919

23897 Water Technology

National Trade Publications
19 British American Blvd. Wes
Latham, NY 12110

518-783-1281
FAX 518-783-1386
E-Mail: asavino@ntpinc.com
Home Page: www.watertechonline.com
Social Media: *Facebook, Twitter, LinkedIn*

Tracy Ashton-Martin, Vice President of
Business Publishi
Lisa Williman, Marketing Account Executive
Chapman Brown, Advertising Account
Executive
Richard DiPaolo, Editorial Director
Jake Mastroianni, Assistant Editor

Serves the POU/POE water treatment industry.
Accepts advertising.
Cost: $39.00
48 Pages
Frequency: Monthly
Circulation: 21000
Founded in 1981
Mailing list available for rent: 20000 names at $125 per M
Printed in 4 colors on glossy stock

23898 Water Well Journal

Ground Water Publishing Company
601 Dempsey Rd
Westerville, OH 43081-8978

614-882-8179
800-551-7379
FAX 614-898-7786
Home Page: waterwelljournal.org
Social Media: *Facebook, Twitter, LinkedIn*

Kevin McCray, Executive Director
Jennifer Strawn, Associate Editor
Joanne Grant, Manager

A complete publication of the water supply industry. Covers technical issues related to drilling and pump installation, rig maintenance, business management and professional development, well rehabilitation, water treatment and more.
Cost: $95.00
84 Pages
Frequency: Monthly
Founded in 1948

23899 WaterWorld

PennNet
1421 S Sheridan Road
Tulsa, OK 74112

918-835-3161
800-331-4463
FAX 918-831-9415
Home Page: www.pennnet.com
Social Media: *Facebook, Twitter, LinkedIn*

James Laughlin, Editor/Associate Publisher

Gives information about products and services, technology, applications, legislation and regulations to help the water industry pros successfully plan, design, operate and maintain their systems.
Frequency: Monthly
Founded in 1985

23900 World Wastes: the Independent Voice

Communication Channels
6151 Powers Ferry Road NW
Atlanta, GA 30339-2959

770-953-4805
FAX 770-618-0348

Bill Wolpin, Editor
Jerrold France, President Argus Business

Reaches individuals and firms engaged in the removal and disposal of solid wastes.
Cost: $48.00
Frequency: Monthly
Circulation: 36,000

Trade Shows

23901 American Society of Irrigation Consultants Conference

PO Box 426
Byron, CA 94514-0426

925-516-1124
FAX 925-516-1301

Wanda M Sarsfield, Secretary

Irrigation design equipment, supplies, services and seminar.
Frequency: Annual
Founded in 1970

23902 American Water Resources Conference

American Water Resources Association
4 West Federal Street
PO Box 1626
Middleburg, VA 20118-1626

540-687-8390
FAX 540-687-8395

E-Mail: info@awra.org
Home Page: www.awra.org
Social Media: *Facebook, Twitter, LinkedIn, YouTube*

Terry Meyer, Marketing Coordinator
Ken Reid, Executive VP

Show of water resources science and technology.
Frequency: Annual, November
Founded in 1964

23903 American Water Works Association Annual Conference and Exhibition

6666 W Quincy Avenue
Denver, CO 80235

303-794-7711
800-926-7337
FAX 303-347-0804
Home Page: www.awwa.org

Nilaksh Kothari, President
Jack W. Hoffbuhr, Executive Director
Jane M. Johnson, Director of Sales & Research

With more than 500 exhibitors, who are a source of knowledge and information for water professionals who work to improve the supply and quality of water in North America and beyond
12000 Attendees
Frequency: Annual, June
Founded in 1881

23904 Chartmaker

American Recreation Coalition
1225 New York Avenue NW
Suite 450
Washington, DC 20005-6405

202-829-9530
FAX 202-662-7424

Derrick Crandall, President

Triennial exhibits relating to the responsible use of US aquatic resources, including issues such as wetlands conservation, boating safety, sportfish research and enhancement and boating access improvements.

23905 Computers in the Water Industry: The Computer Conference

American Water Works Association
6666 W Quincy Avenue
Denver, CO 80235

303-794-7711
800-926-7337
FAX 303-347-0804
Home Page: www.awwa.org

Nilaksh Kothari, President
Jack W. Hoffbuhr, Executive Director
Jane M. Johnson, Director of Sales & Research

23906 Irrigation Show & Education Conference

6540 Arlington Boulevard
Falls Church, VA 22042-6638

703-536-7080
FAX 703-536-7019
E-Mail: membership@irrigation.org
Home Page: www.irrigation.org

Bob Sears, Executive VP

Four hundred and twenty five booths of the newest in irrigation equipment for the agricultural industry.
3.5M Attendees
Frequency: November

23907 National Ground Water Association Annual Convention and Exposition

National Ground Water Association

601 Dempsey Road
Westerville, OH 43081

614-987-7791
800-551-7379
FAX 614-898-7786
E-Mail: ngwa@ngwa.org
Home Page: www.ngwa.org

Bob Masters, Conference Coordinator
Greg Phelps, Meeting Planner/Expositions Dir
Kevin McKray, Executive Director

Annual show of 4600 manufacturers, suppliers, distributors, consultants and scientists, and contractors/pump installers.
5,100 Attendees
Frequency: December

23908 National Rural Water Association
2915 S 13th Street
Duncan, OK 73533

580-252-0629
FAX 580-255-4476
E-Mail: info@nrwa.org
Home Page: www.nrwa.org

Larissa M Wood, Publications Coordinator
100 booths; 300 exhibitors.
1.5M Attendees
Frequency: September

23909 National Water Resources Association Annual Conference
National Water Resources Association
3800 Fairfax Drive
Suite 4
Arlington, VA 22203

703-524-1544
FAX 703-524-1548
E-Mail: nwra@nwra.org
Home Page: www.nwra.org

Norman Semanko, President
Thomas Donnelly, VP

Annual conference and exhibits relating to the development, control, conservation and utilization of water resources in the reclamation states.
700 Attendees
Frequency: November

23910 North American Lake Management Society International Symposium
North American Lake Management Society
4513 Vernon Boulevard, Suite 103
PO Box 5443
Madison, WI 53705-0443

608-233-2836
FAX 608-233-3186
E-Mail: nalms@nalms.org
Home Page: www.nalms.org

Bev Clark, President

Annual symposium and exhibits related to lake ecology and management.

23911 Soil and Water Conservation Society Annual International Conference
Soil and Water Conservation Society
945 SW Ankeny Road
Ankeny, IA 50021-9764

515-289-2331
800-843-7645
FAX 515-289-1227
Home Page: www.swsc.org

Craig A Cox, Executive VP

Explores ways to improve the linkages among conservation science, policy and application at local, national, and international scales. The conference will provide participants an opportunity to teach skills, learn techniques, compare successes, and improve understanding.
1200 Attendees
Frequency: Annual

23912 Water Environment Federation
Water Environment Federation
601 Wythe Street
Alexandria, VA 22314-1994

703-684-2400
800-666-2492
FAX 703-684-2175
Home Page: www.wef.org

Jenny Grigsby, Advertising
Jack Benson, Association Development

Annual show of 650 manufacturers, suppliers and distributors of water treatment equipment, supplies and services.
14M Attendees
Frequency: October, Chicago

23913 Water Quality Association Convention
Water Quality Association
4151 Naperville Road
Suite 100
Lisle, IL 60532-1088

630-505-0160
FAX 630-505-9637
E-Mail: info@wqa.org
Home Page: www.wqa.org

Peter J Censky, Executive Director
Jeannine Collins, CMP, Convention/Meetings Manager

Annual convention and exhibits of water treatment equipment and related articles.
4,300 Attendees

Directories & Databases

23914 American Water Works Association: Buyers' Guide Issue
American Water Works Association
6666 W Quincy Ave
Denver, CO 80235-3098

303-794-7711
800-926-7337
FAX 303-347-0804
Home Page: www.awwa.org

Andrew Richardson, President
Jack W. Hoffbuhr, Executive Director
Jane M. Johnson, Director of Sales & Research

Member suppliers and distributors of water supply products and services, contractors for water supply projects and engineering consultants.
Frequency: Annual November
Circulation: 80,000

23915 Directory of Water/Sewer and Related Industries Professionals
National Assn of Regulatory Utility Commissioners
1101 Vermont Ave NW
Suite 200
Washington, DC 20005-3553

202-898-2200
FAX 202-898-2213
E-Mail: admin@naruc.org
Home Page: www.naruc.org

Charles Gray, Executive Director

Offers valuable information on over 150 consultants and other professionals active in regulated water, sewer and related industries.
Cost: $25.00
195 Pages
Frequency: Annual

23916 Ground Water Age: Directory of Manufacturers
National Trade Publications

13 Century Hill Drive
Latham, NY 12110-2197

518-831-1281
FAX 518-783-1386

Roslyn Scheib Dahl, Editor

List of over 150 companies that provide products and services to the ground water industry.
Cost: $30.00
Frequency: Annual December
Circulation: 13,448

23917 Ground Water Monitoring & Remediation: Buyers Guide Issue
Ground Water Publishing Company
601 Dempsey Rd
Westerville, OH 43081-8978

614-882-8179
800-332-2104
FAX 614-898-7786
E-Mail: gwpc@ngwa.org
Home Page: www.ngwa.org

Kevin McCray, Executive Director
Thad Plumley, Publications Director

List of companies that provide products used in the ground water monitoring and remediation industry.
Cost: $15.00
Frequency: Annual
Circulation: 12,382
Founded in 1981

23918 Ground Water Monitoring Review: Consultant & Contract Directory
National Ground Water Association
601 Dempsey Rd
Westerville, OH 43081-8978

614-898-7791
800-332-2104
FAX 614-898-7786
Home Page: www.ngwa.org

Paul Humes, VP
Shelby Fleck, Advertising Manager
Kevin McCray, Executive Director

About 400 consultant and contracting firms engaged in ground water monitoring projects.
Cost: $200.00
Frequency: Annual
Circulation: 17,000

23919 Ground Water On-Line
National Ground Water Association
601 Dempsey Rd
Westerville, OH 43081-8978

614-898-7791
800-554-7379
FAX 614-898-7786
E-Mail: ngwa@ngwa.org
Home Page: www.ngwa.org

Paul Humes, VP

Database offers information on more than 90,000 ground water literature citations, which includes information like key words, abstracts, chemical compounds, biological factors, geographic locations, aquifer names, authors, titles, publication source names and a lot more.

23920 Validated Water Treatment Equipment Directory
Water Quality Association
4151 Naperville Rd
Suite 100
Lisle, IL 60532-3696

630-505-0160
FAX 630-505-9637
Home Page: www.wqa.org

Peter Censky, Manager

Over 700 water treatment products tested by the Water Quality Association and their manu-

facturers are listed.
Cost: $6.00
Frequency: SemiAnnual

23921 WATERNET
American Water Works Association
6666 W Quincy Ave
Denver, CO 80235-3098

303-794-7711
800-926-7337
FAX 303-347-0804
Home Page: www.waternetonline.ihe.nl

Andrew Richardson, President
Jack W. Hoffbuhr, Executive Director
Jane M. Johnson, Director of Sales & Research

This database contains more than 23,000 citations, with abstracts, to literature on water
quality, water utility management, analytical
procedures for water quality testing.

**23922 Water Technology: Directory of
Manufacturers and Suppliers Issue**
National Trade Publications
13 Century Hill Drive
Latham, NY 12110-2197

518-783-1281
FAX 518-783-1386
Home Page: www.ntpmedia.com

Mark Wilson, Editor

List of about 250 manufacturers, distributors
and other suppliers of water conditioning and
treatment products.
Cost: $21.00
Frequency: Annual December
Circulation: 17,213

23923 Water Treatability
National Ground Water Information Center
6375 Riverside Drive
Dublin, OH 43017-5045

614-717-2770
FAX 614-761-3446

Offers information on treatment technologies
for the removal of various contaminants from
water supplies.
Frequency: Full-text

**23924 Water Well Journal: Buyer's Guide
Issue**
National Ground Water Association
601 Dempsey Rd
Westerville, OH 43081-8978

614-898-7791
800-332-2104
FAX 614-898-7786
Home Page: www.ngwa.org

Paul Humes, VP
Shelby Fleck, Advertising Manager

List of manufacturers, suppliers and manufacturers' representatives for equipment, machinery and other products for the water well
industry.
Cost: $6.00
Frequency: Annual January
Circulation: 26,000

Industry Web Sites

23925 http://gold.greyhouse.com
G.O.L.D Grey House OnLine Databases
Grey House Publishing's online database platform, GOLD, offers Quick Search, Keyword
Search and Expert Search for most business
sectors including water supply markets. The
GOLD platform makes finding the information
you need quick and easy - whether you're a
novice searcher or an experienced database

user. All of Grey House's directory products
are available for subscription on the GOLD
platform.

23926 www.greyhouse.com
Grey House Publishing
Authoritative reference directories for most
business sectors including water supply markets. Users can search the online databases
with varied search criteria allowing for custom
searches by product category, geographic area,
sales volume, keyword, subject and more. Full
Grey House catalog and online ordering also
available.

23927 www.gwpc.org
Ground Water Protection Council
Provides a forum for dicussing ground water,
watershed and community wallhead protection
and underground injection practices. Conducts
seminars and workshops on these subjects.

23928 www.nda4u.com
National Drilling Association
A non-profit trade association of contractors,
manufacturers and affiliated members from the
drilling industry representing the geotechnical,
environmental and mineral exploration sectors
of this industry.

23929 www.swcs.org
Soil and Water Conservation Society
Promotes erosion control and water quality.
Publishes scholarly journal and practical maga-
zine. Conducts annual conference and trade
show

23930 www.umsu.edu/niwr/
National Institute for Water Resources
Offers information on water resource directions
across the nation.

23931 www.wef.org
Water Environment Federation
A not-for-profit technical and educational organization, consisting of regional association
comprised of air quality professionals concerned with all types of air pollution.

23932 www.wjta.org
WaterJet Technology Association/Industrial
&
Municipal Cleaning Association

Members research for new findings in waterjet
technology.

23933 www.wqa.org
Water Quality Association
For retail/dealers and manufacturer/suppliers in
the point of use/entry water quality improvement industry.

Associations

23934 American Association of Meat Processors

One Meating Place
Elizabethtown, PA 17022

717-367-1168
FAX 717-367-9096
E-Mail: aamp@aamp.com
Home Page: www.aamp.com
Social Media: *Facebook, Twitter, Goole+, YouTube*

Erica Hering, President
Louis Muench, 1st VP
Chad Lottman, 2nd VP
Dwight Ely, 3rd VP
Doug Hankes, Treasurer

Membership consists of small to medium sized meat, poultry and food businesses including, slaughterers, processors, wholesalers, home food service businesses, deli and catering operators and suppliers to the industry. AAMP is affiliated with 32 state, regional and provincial associations.
1400 Members
Founded in 1939

23935 American Machine Tool Distributors Association

7901 Westpark Drive
Suite 320
McLean, MD 22102-4206

703-893-2900
800-524-0475
FAX 703-893-1151
E-Mail: AMT@AMTonline.org
Home Page: www.amtonline.org
Social Media: *Facebook, Twitter, LinkedIn, Youtube*

Douglas K. Woods, President
Amber Thomas, VP
Jeffrey H Traver, VP
Peter R Eelman, VP
Steve Lesnewich, VP

AMTDA will lead distributors of manufacturing technology by providing essential programs and services that help its members gain global recognition from customers and suppliers as the preferred channel of distribution.
300 Members
Founded in 1925

23936 American Supply Association

1200 North Arlington Heights Road
Suite 150
Itasca, IL 60143

630-467-0000
FAX 630-467-0001
E-Mail: info@asa.net
Home Page: www.asa.net
Social Media: *Facebook, Twitter, LinkedIn*

John Strong, Chairman of the Board
Rick Fantham, President
Tim Milford, President-Elect
Steve Cook, Treasurer
Michael Adelizzi, Secretary/EVP

ASA is a not-for-profit national organization serving wholesale distributors and their suppliers in the plumbing, heating, cooling and industrial and mechanical pipe, valves and fittings industries.
Founded in 1969

23937 American Veterinary Distributors Association

3465 Box Hill Corp. Center Drive
Suite H
Abingdon, MD 21009

443-640-1040
FAX 443-640-1086
E-Mail: casey@kingmgmt.org
Home Page: www.avda.net
Social Media: *Facebook, Twitter, LinkedIn*

Bobby Mims, Chairman
Jackie King, Executive Director
Paula Brown, President-Elect
Casey Joseph, Association Coordinator
Debbie Dacre, Director of Finance

The AVDA was established as the national trade organization for businesses engaged in the distribution of animal health products.
Founded in 1976

23938 American Wholesale Marketers Association

11311 Sunset Hills Road
Reston, VA 20190

703-208-3358
800-482-2962
FAX 703-573-5738
E-Mail: info@cdaweb.net
Home Page: cdaweb.net
Social Media: *Facebook, Twitter, LinkedIn, RSS*

Scott Ramminger, President & CEO
Kimberly Bolin, Executive Vice President
Bob Gatty, VP, Communication
Meredith Kimbrell, Director, Education & Communities
Anne Holloway, VP, Government Affairs

A trade organization supporting the confectionary, tobacco and allied industries through programs and services. members include wholesale distributors, manufacturers and other allieds to the industry.
5300 Members
Founded in 1942

23939 AmericanHort

525 9th St. NW
Suite 800
Washington, DC 20004

202-789-2900
FAX 202-789-1893
E-Mail: hello@AmericanHort.org
Home Page: americanhort.org
Social Media: *Facebook, Twitter, LinkedIn, Goole+, YouTube*

David Savoia, CTA, Interim President & CEO
Craig J Regelbrugge, SVP, Industry Advocacy & Research
Carol Baker, Executive Assistant
Sherry L. Johnson, CMP, VP, Knowledge & Bus. Advancement
Steve Carver, Ph.D., Learning Resource Specialist

The American Nursery and Landscape Association serves firms who grow, sell or use plants. ANLA advocates the industry's interests before government and provides its members with unique business knowledge essential to long-term growth and profitability.
2200 Members
Founded in 1876

23940 Appliance Parts Distributors Association

3621 N Oakley Avenue
Chicago, IL 60618

773-230-9851
FAX 888-308-1423
E-Mail: ro@apda.com

Home Page: www.apda.com
Social Media: *Facebook, Twitter, LinkedIn*

Phil F Orazietti, President
Leonard Kremers, Vice President
Ron Clifton, Treasurer
Bob Goldberg, Legal Counsel
Rosemary Jacobshagen, CAE, Association Management

The APDA is an association of independent businesses that aspire to provide the highest level of quality, service, support and information to its customers and suppliers in order to make its value indispensable to the parts distribution channel.

23941 Associated Beer Distributors of Illinois

PO Box 396
Springfield, IL 62705

217-528-4371
FAX 217-528-4376
E-Mail: info@abdi.org
Home Page: www.abdi.org
Social Media: *Facebook, Twitter, LinkedIn*

The ABDI represents, maintains, and improves the interests of its members who are licensed by the State of Illinois to import and distribute beer to licensed retailers.

23942 Associated Equipment Distributors

600 22nd Street
Suite 220
Oak Brook, IL 60523

630-574-0650
800-388-0650
FAX 630-574-0132
E-Mail: info@aednet.org
Home Page: www.aednet.org
Social Media: *Facebook, Twitter, LinkedIn, Goole+, YouTube*

Bob Henderson, EVP & COO
Brian P. McGuire, President/CEO
Jason Blake, SVP/CFO
Jon Cruthers, Vice President of Sales
Phil Riggs, Regional Manager

AED is an international trade association representing companies involved in the distribution, rental and support of equipment used in construction, mining, forestry, power generation, agriculture and industrial applications.
700 Members

23943 Association for High Technology Distribution

N19 W24400 Riverwood Drive
Waukesha, WI 53188

262-696-3645
800-488-4845
FAX 630-574-0132
E-Mail: info@aednet.org
Home Page: www.ahtdmembers.org
Social Media: *Facebook, Twitter, RSS*

Bryan Roesster, Executive Director
Leigha Schatzman, Association Services Manager
Pam Estergard, Financial Services
Cassie Schauer, Association Services Coordinator

The Association for High Technology Distribution has worked to increase the productivity and profitability of the high technology Automation Solutions Providers and Manufacturers who satisfy the automation needs of general industry and OEM manufacturers.
Founded in 1984

23944 Association for Hose and Accessories Distribution

105 Eastern Avenue
Suite 104
Annapolis, MD 21403

410-940-6350
800-624-2227
FAX 410-263-1659
E-Mail: info@nahad.org
Home Page: www.nahad.org
Social Media: *Facebook, Twitter, LinkedIn*

Jim Reilly, President
Skip Bruce, 1st VP
Scott Moss, 2nd VP
Joseph M Thompson Jr., EVP
Mark Fournier, Immediate Past President

The mission of NAHAD is to promote a high standard of professionalism and integrity within the hose and accessories industry by providing a medium for communications, education and training, so that quality is maximized and profitability enhanced.

23945 Association for Suppliers of Printing, Publishing & Converting Tech.

1899 Preston White Drive
Reston, VA 20191

703-264-7200
FAX 703-620-0994
E-Mail: npes@npes.org
Home Page: www.npes.org

Malkon S. Baboyian, Chairman
Ralph J Nappi, President
Greg Safko, VP, Market Data & Research
Mark A. Hischar, Treasurer
Mark J Nuzzaco, Secretary

This association is a trade association of over 400 companies that manufacture and distribute equipment, systems, software, supplies used in printing, publishing and converting.
400 Members
Founded in 1933

23946 Association of Ingersoll-Rand Distributors

1300 Summer Avenue
Cleveland, OH 44115

216-241-7333
FAX 216-241-0105
E-Mail: aird@aird.org
Home Page: www.aird.org

Stu Bassett, President
Brent Darnell, VP
Jonathan Michel, Treasurer
Greg Scott, Secretary

The Association of Ingersoll-Rand Distributors (AIRD) was organized as a central resource for distributors of Ingersoll-Rand compressed air equipment. AIRD is chartered to promote improved business conditions affecting distributors of air compressors, further a better understanding between distributors and equipment suppliers, research ways to lower costs of distributing air compressors, collect and disseminate statistical information and conduct other beneficial activities.
Founded in 1970

23947 Association of Millwork Distributors

10047 Robert Trent Jones Parkway
New Port Richey, FL 34655-4649

727-372-3665
800-786-7274
FAX 727-372-2879
E-Mail: Mail@WorldMillworkAlliance.com
Home Page: www.amdweb.com
Social Media: *Twitter, LinkedIn*

Joe Bayer, President
Dave Ondrasek, 1st VP
Timothy Lyons, 2nd VP

Scott Harder, Associate VP
Simon Sikora, Treasurer

AND provides leadership, education, promotion, networking, and advocacy to, and for, the millwork distribution industry.
Founded in 1963

23948 Association of Pool & Spa Professionals

2111 Eisenhower Avenue
Suite 500
Alexandria, VA 22314-4679

703-838-0083
FAX 703-549-0493
E-Mail: memberservices@apsp.org
Home Page: www.apsp.org
Social Media: *Facebook, Twitter, LinkedIn, Youtube, Flickr, RSS*

Rich Gottwald, President/CEO
Lorna Watkins, Executive Assistant
Jennifer Hatfield, Director, Govt. Affairs
Todd Usher, Manager, Communications
Carvin DiGiovanni, VP, Technical & Standards

APSP is the world's largest international trade association for the swimming pool, spa, and hot tub industry. It works with regulatory and legislative bodies to ensure that their codes, ordinance, and legislation are written to the safest and most current standards. The association's mission is to ensure consumer safety and enhance the business success of its members.
Founded in 1956

23949 Association of Service and Computer Dealers International

131 NW First Avenue
Delray Beach, FL 33444

561-504-8898
FAX 561-431-6302
Home Page: www.ascdi.com
Social Media: *Facebook, Twitter, LinkedIn, YouTube*

Rob Neumeyer, Director
Arthur P Frierman, Associate Counsel
Jerry Roberts, Chairman Emeritus
Joe Marion, President

The ASCDI is a worldwide, nonprofit organization, made up of companies who provide technology business solutions, technical support, and value added services to the business community.
Founded in 1981

23950 Association of Woodworking and Furnishings Suppliers

2400 E Katella Ave
Suite 340
Anaheim, CA 92806

323-838-9440
800-946-2937
FAX 323-838-9443
E-Mail: angelo@awfs.org
Home Page: www.awfs.org
Social Media: *Facebook, Twitter, LinkedIn*

Archie Thompson, VP
Angela Hernandez, Executive Assistant
Nancy Neely, Controller
Angelo Gangone, EVP
Nancy Fister, Education & Conference Director

The Association of Woodworking and Furnishings Suppliers is the largest national trade association in the U.S. representing the interests of the broad array of companies that supply the home and commercial furnishings industry.
Founded in 1911

23951 Automotive Aftermarket Industry Association

7101 Wisconsin Avenue
Suite 1300
Bethesda, MD 20814-3415

301-654-6664
FAX 301-654-3299
E-Mail: info@autocare.org
Home Page: www.autocare.org
Social Media: *Facebook, Twitter, LinkedIn, Youtube, WordPress*

Kathleen Schmatz, MAAP, President/CEO
Susan Medick, CPA, CAE, CFO/COO
Richard D. White, MAAP, SVP
Michael Barratt, CMP, SVP, Meeting & Events
Aaron Lowe, AAP, SVP, Reg. and Gov. Affairs

A trade association consisting of more than 23,000 member companies and affiliates representing over 100,000 repair shops, distribution outlets, and parts stores.
23000 Members
Founded in 1999

23952 Bearing Specialists Association

800 Roosevelt Road
Building C, Suite 312
Glen Ellyn, IL 60137

630-858-3838
FAX 630-790-3095
E-Mail: info@bsahome.org
Home Page: www.bsahome.org
Social Media: *Twitter, LinkedIn, RSS*

Tim Breen, President
John Ruth, VP
Brian Davis, Treasurer

BSA is the forum to enhance networking and knowledge sharing to promote the sale of bearings through authorized distributors.
100 Members
Founded in 1966

23953 Bicycle Product Suppliers Association

740 34th St
Boulder, CO 80303

303-442-2466
FAX 303-552-2060
E-Mail: bpsa@bpsa.org
Home Page: www.bpsa.org

John Nedeau, President
Chris Speyer, Vice President
Patrick Cunnane, Treasurer
Marc Sani, Secretary
Ray Keener, Executive Director

BPSA is an association of suppliers of bicycles, parts, accessories and services who serve the Specialty Bicycle Retailer.

23954 Business Solutions Association

3601 E Joppa Rd.
Baltimore, MD 21234

410-931-8100
FAX 410-931-8111
E-Mail: info@BusinessSolutionsAssociation.com
Home Page: www.opwa.org

Jim O'Brien, President
Bill Cardone, VP
Nick Aronis, Secretary
Alan Goldner, Treasurer

The goal of the Business Solutions Association is to provide a forum for the development of strategic and synergistic solutions to enhance the sale and distribution of business related products and services.

23955 Ceramic Tile Distributors Association

800 Roosevelt Road
Building C, Suite 312
Glen Ellyn, IL 60137

630-545-9415
800-938-2838
FAX 630-790-3095
E-Mail: info@ctdahome.org
Home Page: www.ctdahome.org
Social Media: *Facebook*

Tom Kotel, President
Heidi Martin, VP
Robert DeAngelis, Treasurer
Rick Church, Executive Director
Bill Ives, Legal Counsel

CTDA is an international association of distributors, manufacturers, and allied professionals of ceramic tile and related products.

23956 Cleaning Equipment Trade Association

PO Box 270908
Oklahoma City, OK 73137-0908

704-635-7362
800-441-0111
FAX 704-635-7363
E-Mail: info@ceta.org
Home Page: www.ceta.org

Curtis Braber, President
Aaron Auger, Senior Vice President
Kyle Notch, Vice President
Jimy O'Connell, Secretary
Chad Rasmussen, Treasurer

CETA is dedicated to increasing the awareness and promotion of industry products, while at the same time recognizing the impact on preserving the environment and the opportunity to do business within it.

23957 Commercial Vehicle Solutions Network

3943-2 Baymeadows Road
Jacksonville, FL 32217

904-737-2900
FAX 904-636-9881
E-Mail: info@cvsn.org
Home Page: www.cvsn.org

Dave Willis, President
Edward Neeley, Vice President
Andy Robblee, Treasurer
Angelo Volpe, Executive VP/Secretary
Joe Ward, Director

The Commercial Vehicle Solutions Network (CVSN) is an association of independent parts and service aftermarket distributors serving the transportation industry.
Founded in 2006

23958 Copper and Brass Servicenter Association

6734 W. 121st Street
Overland Park, KS 66209

913-396-0697
FAX 913-345-1006
E-Mail: cbsahq@copper-brass.org
Home Page: www.copper-brass.org
Social Media: *Facebook, Twitter, LinkedIn, YouTube, Flickr*

Susan Avery, CAE, Chief Executive Director
Crystal Roberts, Deputy Exe. Dir./Director of BD
David Blackhurst, Sales Manager
Bonnie Bush, Graphic Designer
Whitney Nelson, Director of Meetings and Events

Distributors (service centers) of fabricated copper and copper alloy products (sheet, plate,

coil, rod, bar tube, etc) and their brass mill suppliers.
78 Members
Founded in 1951

23959 Door & Hardware Institute

14150 Newbrook Drive
Suite 200
Chantilly, VA 20151-2232

703-222-2010
FAX 703-222-2410
Home Page: www.dhi.org
Social Media: *Facebook, Twitter, LinkedIn*

Jerry Heppes, Sr., CAE, Chief Executive Officer
Chuck J. Molina, CTO/Director of IT
Lawrence Beatty, AHC, President
Stephen R. Hildebrand, FDHI, Executive Vice President
Sharon Newport, Director of Operations

The Door & Hardware Institute (DHI) is the only professional association dedicated to the Architectural Openings Industry. DHI represents the North American openings marketplace as the advocate and primary resource for information, professional development and certification.
5000 Members
Founded in 1934

23960 Drycleaning & Laundry Institute International

14700 Sweitzer Lane
Laurel, MD 20707

301-622-1900
800-638-2627
FAX 240-295-0685
E-Mail: techline@dlionline.org
Home Page: www.dlionline.org
Social Media: *Facebook, Twitter, Flickr*

David Machesney, President
Greg Myers, Treasurer
Jan Barlow, Chairman

With its education, research, testing, and professional training, DLI offers solutions that help member businesses provide expert garment care.
2000 Members
Founded in 1907

23961 Electrical Apparatus Service Association Inc

1331 Baur Boulevard
Saint Louis, MO 63132-1903

314-993-2220
FAX 314-993-1269
E-Mail: easainfo@easa.com
Home Page: www.easa.com
Social Media: *Facebook, Twitter, LinkedIn, Youtube*

Mike Dupuis, Chair
James Smith, Vice Chair
Lenwood Ireland, Secretary/Treasurer
Linda J. Raynes, CAE, President & CEO
Anne Vogel, Executive Secretary

Maintains data files on rewinding and repair of electrical equipment. Sponsors seminars
2000 Members
Founded in 1973

23962 Equipment Marketing & Distribution Association (EMDA)

PO Box 1347
Iowa City, IA 52244

319-354-5156
FAX 319-354-5157
E-Mail: pat@emda.net
Home Page: www.emda.net
Social Media: *Facebook, Twitter, LinkedIn*

Patricia A Collins, Executive VP

EMDA is the result of the 2008 merger of FEWA and AIMRA. EMDA members are devtoed to the marketing of specialized equipment: agricultural, outdoor power, light industrial, forestry, irrigation, turf and grounds maintenance, lawn and garden and parts/components for thosesegments of industry.
250 Members
Founded in 1945

23963 Financial & Security Products Association

1024 Mebane Oaks Road #273
Mebane, NC 27302

919-648-0664
800-843-6082
FAX 919-648-0670
E-Mail: info@fspa1.com
Home Page: www.fspa1.com
Social Media: *LinkedIn*

Linda Abell, Chairman
L.A. Smith, President
B.J. Hanson, Executive Director
Gene Polito, Vice President
Kevin Callahan, Secretary-Treasurer

Independent dealers, manufacturers and associates whose outstanding products and services give financial institutions a crucial edge in performance, efficiency and economy.
Founded in 1973

23964 Fluid Power Distributors Association

105 Eastern Avenue
Suite 104
Annapolis, MD 21403

410-940-6347
FAX 410-263-1659
E-Mail: info@fpda.org
Home Page: www.fpda.org

Michael A Hamzey Jr., Chairman & President
Parker Lancaster, VP, Membership
Alex Wheelock, President Elect
Tim Gillig, VP, Finance/Treasurer
Patricia A Lilly, Executive Director

The Fluid Power Distributors Association is a trade association on the move, representing motion solution providers who offer fluid power, automation, and electro-mechanical technologies and distribution services to enhance customer performance and profitability.
300+ Members
Founded in 1974

23965 Food Industry Suppliers Association

1207 Sunset Drive
Greensboro, NC 27408-7215

336-274-6311
FAX 336-691-1839
E-Mail: stella@fisanet.org
Home Page: www.fisanet.org/
Social Media: *LinkedIn*

Bob Morava, President
Brad Myers, VP
David Brink, Vice-President
David Brink, Past President

Member's are distributors and suppliers to the food processing industry.
245 Members
Founded in 1968

23966 Food Marketing Institute

2345 Crystal Drive
Suite 800
Arlington, VA 22202

202-452-8444
FAX 202-429-4519
Home Page: www.fmi.org
Social Media: *Facebook, Twitter, LinkedIn, Youtube, RSS*

Frederick J Morganthall II, Chair
Leslie G Sarasin, President & CEO

Rob Bartels, Vice Chair
Jerry Garland, Vice Chair
Henry Johnson, Vice-Chairman

FMI conducts programs in public affairs, food safety, research, education and industry relations on behalf of its 1,500 member companies in the United States and around the world.
1500 Members

23967 Foodservice Equipment Distributors Association

2250 Point Blvd
Suite 200
Elgin, IL 60123-7887

224-293-6500
800-677-9605
FAX 224-293-6505
E-Mail: feda@feda.com
Home Page: www.feda.com
Social Media: *Facebook, Twitter, LinkedIn*

Raymond Herrick, CAE, Executive VP
Rosie Montanez, Executive Assistant
Stacy Ward, Managing Editor
Adela Ramos, Admin Director/Advertising Manager
Amy Risinger, Membership Services Consultant

Dealers and distributors of foodservice equipment and supplies.
300 Members
Founded in 1933

23968 Gases and Welding Distributors Association

1 Oakwood Blvd.
Suite 195
Hollywood, FL 33020

954-367-7728
844-251-3219
FAX 954-367-7790
E-Mail: gawda@gawda.org
Home Page: www.gawda.org
Social Media: *Facebook, Twitter, LinkedIn, YouTube*

Tom Biedermann, President
Jim Earlbeck, Vice President
Kevin Falconer, Vice President
Mark Raimy, 1st Vice President
Gary Halter, Vice President

GAWDA's mission is to promote the safe operation and economic vitality of distributors of industrial gases and related welding equipment and supplies.
775 Members
Founded in 1945

23969 Global Market Development Center

1275 Lake Plaza Drive
Colorado Springs, CO 80906-3583

719-576-4260
FAX 719-576-2661
E-Mail: info@gmdc.org
Home Page: www.gmdc.com
Social Media: *Facebook, Twitter, LinkedIn, YouTube, Google+, Flickr*

David McConnell, President/CEO
Keith Wypyszynski, VP Business Development/CMO
Ann McConnell, Sr. Director Finance
Michael Winterbottom, VP, IT/Chief Technology Officer

GMDC is the premier non-profit global trade association dedicated to serving General Merchandise and Health Beauty retailers, wholesalers and suppliers. GMDC promotes critical connectivity to grow and expand member companies by uniting members through business building events and opportunities and enriching their thinking through education and training;

consumer and business insights; and information resources.
Founded in 1970

23970 Health Industry Distributors Association

310 Montgomery Street
Alexandria, VA 22314-1516

703-549-4432
FAX 703-549-6495
E-Mail: rowan@hida.org
Home Page: www.hida.org

Matthew J Rowan, President & CEO
Ian Fardey, EVP
Elizabeth Hilla, Executive Director/SVP
Lisa A Queeney, VP, Finance & Operations
Linda Rouse O'Neill, VP, Govt. Affairs

HIDA keeps members current on healthcare reform, government affairs, industry trends and forecasts, provider news, and sales tips.
Founded in 1902

23971 Healthcare Distribution Management Association

901 North Glebe Road
Suite 1000
Arlington, VA 22203

703-787-0000
FAX 703-812-5282
Home Page: www.hdma.net
Social Media: *Twitter, LinkedIn*

Ted Scherr, Chairman
Jon Giacomin, Vice Chair
John M. Gray, President/CEO
Ann W. Bittman, EVP/COO
Patrick M. Kelly, EVP, Gov. Affairs

The Healthcare Distribution Management Association (HDMA) is the national association representing primary, full-service healthcare distributors. HDMA and its members are the vital link in the healthcare system, working daily to provide value, remove costs and develop innovative solutions.
Founded in 1876

23972 Heating, Airconditioning & Refrigeration Distributors International

3455 Mill Run Drive
Suite 820
Columbus, OH 43026

614-345-4328
888-253-2128
FAX 614-345-9161
E-Mail: hardimail@haridnet.org
Home Page: www.hardinet.org
Social Media: *Facebook, Twitter, LinkedIn, Youtube, Instagram, Flickr*

William Bergamini, President
Michael Meier, President-Elect
Tom Roberts, Vice President
Troy Meachum, Secretary/Treasurer
Talbot H. Gee, CEO

This association is a trade organization dedicated to advancing the science of wholesale distribution in the HVACR industry.
750+ Members
Founded in 1960

23973 ISSA

7373 N Lincoln Ave
Lincolnwood, IL 60712-1799

847-982-0800
800-225-4772
FAX 847-982-1012
E-Mail: info@issa.com
Home Page: www.issa.com
Social Media: *Facebook, Twitter, LinkedIn*

Fritz Gast, President
Alan R Tomblin, President Elect/VP

Lydia M Work, International Director
John Swigart, Executive Director
John Barrett, Secretary

The worldwide cleaning industry association.
5700+ Members
Founded in 1923

23974 Industrial Compressor Distributor Association

656 Southern Hills Drive
Eureka, MO 63025

636-938-3957
FAX 636-938-3965
E-Mail: mjgilliam1@aol.com
Home Page: www.icdaonline.com

Margot Gravel, President

The main objectives of the ICDA are to promote for its members the highest standards of production, financial and managerial activities; to act as a vehicle for the solution of common industry problems in an effective and efficient manner; and to increase market volume and profits for its members.

23975 Industrial Supply Association

100 North 20th Street
Suite 400
Philadelphia, PA 19103

215-320-3862
866-460-2360
FAX 215-963-9785
E-Mail: info@isapartners.org
Home Page: www.isapartners.org
Social Media: *Facebook, Twitter, LinkedIn*

Michael Carr, President
Tommy Thompson, VP
Craig Vogel, Treasurer
John Wiborg, Secretary

The primary focus of the Industrial Supply Association is to improve the industrial supply channel through its mission-critical activities including: conventions and forums, gathering and dissemination of critical information, and development and implementation of channel performance initiatives.

23976 International Association of Plastics Distribution

6734 W. 121st Street
Overland Park, KS 66209

913-345-1005
FAX 913-345-1006
E-Mail: iapd@iapd.org
Home Page: www.iapd.org
Social Media: *Facebook, Twitter, LinkedIn, YouTube, Flickr*

Susan E Avery, CAE, CEO
Crystal Roberts, CAE, Deputy Executive Director
Jean McClure, Executive Assistant/HR Manager
Kipp Simmons, Finance Manager
Whitney Nelson, Director, Meetings & Events

The International Association of Plastics Distribution is an international trade association comprised of companies engaged in the distribution and manufacturing of plastics materials.
Founded in 1956

23977 International Foodservice Distributors Association

1410 Spring Hill Road
Suite 210
McLean, VA 22102-3035

703-532-9400
FAX 703-538-4673
Home Page: www.ifdaonline.org
Social Media: *Twitter, LinkedIn*

Thomas A Zatina, Chairman
Mark S. Allen, President/CEO

James A Crawford, Vice Chair
Andy Mercier, Treasurer
Jonathan Eisen, SVP, Gov Relations

Trade association comprised of food distribution companies that supply independent grocers and food service operations throughout the US, Canada and 19 other countries.
135 Members
Founded in 2003

23978 International Sealing Distribution Association

105 Eastern Avenue
Suite 104
Annapolis, MD 21403

410-940-6344
FAX 410-263-1659
E-Mail: info@isd.org
Home Page: www.isd.org
Social Media: *Facebook, Twitter, LinkedIn*

Christy Jaycox, President
John Kates, VP
Steve Luhrs, Treasurer
Deborah B Mitchell, Executive Director
Joseph M Thompson Jr., Associate Director

The International Sealing Distribution Association (ISD) is a not-for-profit trade association formed to enhance the success of members through information, education, and interaction.

23979 International Truck Parts Association

1720 10th Ave. South
Suite 4, PMB 199
Great Falls, MT 59405

202-544-3090
866-346-5692
FAX 301-229-7331
E-Mail: info@itpa.com
Home Page: www.itpa.com

Gerard Zentner, Chairman
Paul Cipolla, Vice Chairman

The International Truck Parts Association was organized as a not-for-profit association to promote, foster, and improve relationships among sellers and buyers of trucks and truck surplus products and other parties.
Founded in 1974

23980 Irrigation Association

8280 Willow Oaks Corporate Drive
Suite 400
Fairfax, VA 22031

703-536-7080
FAX 703-536-7019
E-Mail: info@irrigation.org
Home Page: www.irrigation.org

Aric J. Olson, President
Gregory R. Hunter, Vice President
Deborah M. Hamlin, CAE, FASAE, Chief Executive Officer
John R. Farner, Jr, Government & PA Director
Rebecca J. Bayless, Finance Director

The Irrigation Association is the leading membership organization for irrigation equipment and system manufacturers, dealers, distributors, designers, consultants, contractors and end users.
1600 Members
Founded in 1949

23981 Jewelry Industry Distributors Association

703 Old Route 422 West
Butler, PA 16001

203-254-4492
FAX 513-367-1414
E-Mail: jidainfo@gmail.com

Home Page: www.jidainfo.com
Social Media: *Facebook*

Bill Esslinger, President
Chris Gaber, Vice President
Richard Livesay, Treasurer
Rusty Cooper, Associate Director
Pat Conner, Associate Director

A list of over 130 member firms and their suppliers.
Founded in 1946

23982 Machinery Dealers National Association

315 S Patrick Street
Alexandria, VA 22314

703-836-9300
800-872-7807
FAX 703-836-9303
E-Mail: office@mdna.org
Home Page: www.mdna.org
Social Media: *Facebook, Twitter, LinkedIn, Youtube*

Kim Khoury, CEA, President
Joe Lundvick, CEA, 1st VP
John Greene, CEA, Second Vice President
Terry Yoder, Treasurer
Mark Robinson, Executive Vice President

The Machinery Dealers National Association (MDNA) is an international, nonprofit trade association dedicated to the promotion of the used machinery industry.
Founded in 1941

23983 Material Handling Equipment Distributors Association

201 US Highway 45
Vernon Hills, IL 60061-2398

857-680-3500
FAX 847-362-6989
E-Mail: connect@mheda.org
Home Page: www.mheda.org
Social Media: *Facebook, Twitter, LinkedIn, Google+*

Mark Milovich, President
Liz Richards, Executive Vice President
Anna Mariae Kendall, Marketing Manager
Rebecca Hein, Networking & Comm. Coordinator
Susan Freibrun, Education Manager

The Material Handling Equipment Distributors Association is the only national association dedicated solely to improving the proficiency of the independent material handling equipment distributor.
Founded in 1954

23984 Metals Service Center Institute

4201 Euclid Ave
Rolling Meadows, IL 60008-2025

847-485-3000
800-872-7807
FAX 847-485-3001
E-Mail: info@msci.org
Home Page: www.msci.org/
Social Media: *Facebook, Twitter, LinkedIn*

Bob Weidner, President/CEO
Sharon Hochel, Executive Assistant
Ashley DeVecht, Director, Communications
Ann D'Orazio, VP, Marketing Growth
Jonathan Kalkwarf, VP, Finance & Govt. Affairs

MSCI is a trade association that supports and represents the elements of the metals value chain, including metals producers, distributors and processors.
400 Members
Founded in 1907

23985 Michigan Distributors & Vendors Association

120 N Washington Square
Suite 110 B
Lansing, MI 48933

517-372-2323
FAX 517-372-4404
E-Mail: mdva@mdva.org
Home Page: www.mdva.org

Polly Reber, President
Scott Rorah, Chairman
Amy Klooster, Vice Chairman
Dave Hodson, Secretary/Treasurer
Gerald Abraham, Immediate Past Chairman

The Michigan Distributors and Vendors Association (MDVA) is a non-profit, statewide business association representing two very significant business segments in the grocery and convenience products industry.
100 Members
Founded in 1991

23986 Mississippi Malt Beverage Association

4785 I-55 North, Suite 103
PO Box 1132
Jackson, MS 39215-1132

601-987-9098
FAX 601-981-5566
E-Mail: info@msbeer.com
Home Page: msbeer.com

Richard Brown, President

The MMBA was established to represent and promote the beer wholesalers and beer industry within Mississippi.
12 Members
Founded in 1946

23987 Motorcycle Industry Council

2 Jenner Street
Suite 150
Irvine, CA 92618-3806

949-727-4211
FAX 949-727-3313
E-Mail: ciannello@mic.org
Home Page: www.mic.org

Tom Biedermann, President
Jim Fischbach
Steve Galik
Mark Kearney

The Motorcycle Industry Council (MIC) is a nonprofit, national trade association representing manufacturers and distributors of motorcycles, scooters, motorcycle/ATV parts and accessories and members of allied trades.

23988 Music Distributors Association

14070 Proton Road
Suite 100 LB 9
Dallas, TX 75244-3601

972-233-9107
FAX 972-490-4219
E-Mail: office@musicdistributors.org
Home Page: www.musicdistributors.org
Social Media: *Facebook, Twitter, LinkedIn*

Glenda Plummer, Executive Director

International, nonprofit trade association representing and serving manufacturers, wholesalers, importers and exporters of musical instruments and accessories, sound reinforcement products and published music.
250 Members
Founded in 1939

23989 NPTA Alliance

330 N Wabash Ave
Suite 2000
Chicago, IL 60611

312-321-4092
800-355-6782
FAX 312-673-6736
E-Mail: npta@gonpta.com

Home Page: www.gonpta.com
Social Media: *Twitter, LinkedIn, YouTube*

Hilton Maze, Chairman
Bayard Tynes, 1st Vice Chair
Tom Wernoch, Second Vice Chair
Kevin Gammonley, CEO
Don Clampitt, Treasurer

Representing distributors and suppliers of paper, packaging and facility supplies companies.
220 Members
Founded in 1903

23990 National Association of Chemical Distributors

1555 Wilson Boulevard
Suite 1100
Arlington, VA 22209

703-527-6223
FAX 703-527-7747
E-Mail: nacdpublicaffairs@nacd.com
Home Page: www.nacd.com
Social Media: *Twitter, LinkedIn, Youtube*

Mathew A. Brainerd, Chairman
Douglas A. Brown, Vice Chairman
Thomas M. Corcoran, Treasurer
Eric R. Byer, President
Celeste Clark, Executive Assistant

The National Association of Chemical Distributors (NACD) is an international association of chemical distributor companies that purchase and take title of chemical products from manufacturers.
250 Members
Founded in 1971

23991 National Association of Electrical Distributors

1181 Corporate Lake Drive
St. Louis, MO 63132

314-991-9000
888-791-2512
FAX 314-991-3060
E-Mail: memberservices@naed.org
Home Page: www.naed.org
Social Media: *Facebook, Twitter, LinkedIn, RSS, Youtube*

Tom Naber, President & Chief Executive Officer
Michelle McNamara, SVP
Linda Thurman, Dir., Marketing & Comm.
Ed Orlet, VP, Gov't Affairs
Tim Dencker, VP, Finance

The main goal of the National Association of Electrical Distributors (NAED) is to establish the electrical distributor as an essential force in the electrical industry and the economy.
Founded in 1908

23992 National Association of Flour Distributors

5350 Woodland Place
Canfield, OH 44406

330-718-6563
FAX 877-573-1230
E-Mail: timdove51@gmail.com
Home Page: www.thenafd.com
Social Media: *Facebook, Twitter, LinkedIn*

J Gerard Burns, Chairman
Dominic S. Valente, President
Philip S. Zilka, Jr., 1st VP
Steve Tardella, 2nd VP
Mark R. Munroe, Secretary/Treasurer

The mission of the NAFD is to serve the interests of its members who are engaged in the flour industry and those companies allied thereto by providing educational and networking opportunities.

23993 National Association of Sign Supply Distributors

1001 N Fairfax St.
Suite 301
Alexandria, VA 22314

703-836-4012
FAX 703-836-8353
E-Mail: info@signs.org
Home Page: www.nassd.org
Social Media: *Facebook, Twitter, LinkedIn*

Chris Flejtuch, Chairman
Robert Mattatall, Vice Chair
Jeff Young, Secretary/Treasurer
Lori Anderson, President & CEO
Brandon Hensley, COO

NASSD is a nonprofit trade association for organizations who are engaged in full-line sign supply distribution and who manufacture or supply commercial, neon and electrical sign products.

23994 National Association of Sporting Goods Wholesalers

One Parkview Plaza
Suite 800
Oakbrook Terrace, IL 60181

630-596-9006
FAX 630-544-5055
E-Mail: info@nasgw.org
Home Page: www.nasgw.org
Social Media: *Twitter, LinkedIn, Flickr*

Peter Brownell, Chairman
Brad Burney, Vice Chair
Mike Halleron, Treasurer
Kenyon Gleason, President
Michael Greskiewicz, Director of Business Development

Non-profit trade association of wholesalers, distributors and manufacturers. Serves as a liaison with other sporting goods associations.
400 Members
Founded in 1953

23995 National Association of Wholesaler - Distributors

1325 G Street NW
Suite 1000
Washington, DC 20005-3100

202-872-0885
FAX 202-785-0586
E-Mail: naw@naw.org
Home Page: www.naw.org
Social Media: *Facebook, Twitter, LinkedIn*

Dirk Van Dongen, President
Jade West, SVP - Government Relations
James A Anderson Jr, VP - Government Relations
Ruth Stadius, Director, Communications
Ron Schreibman, SVP - Strategic Direction

The NAW provides members with the opportunity for networking and benchmarking within the entire wholesale distribution industry. NAW also represents the wholesale distribution industry before Congress, the White House, and the judiciary on issues that cross the industry's many lines of trade.

23996 National Beer Wholesalers Association

1101 King Street
Suite 600
Alexandria, VA 22314-2944

703-683-4300
800-300-6417
FAX 703-683-8965
E-Mail: info@nbwa.org
Home Page: www.nbwa.org
Social Media: *Facebook, Twitter, YouTube*

Craig A Purser, President/CEO
Wendy Huerter, Executive Assistant

Rebecca W Spicer, SVP, Comm. & Public Affairs
Paul Pisano, SVP Industry Affairs & Gen. Counsel
Kathleen Joyce, Communications Director

NBWA represents the interests of America's 2,850 independent, licensed beer distributors which service every congressional district and media market in the country.
Founded in 1938

23997 National Electronics Service Dealers Association

3608 Pershing Ave
Fort Worth, TX 76107-4527

817-921-9061
800-797-9197
FAX 817-921-3741
E-Mail: info@nesda.com
Home Page: www.nesda.com

Mack Blakely, Executive Director
Sheila Fredrickson, Dir Communications/Info Technology
Patricia Bohon, Membership & Trade Show Coordinator
James Keesler, Associate Editor/Graphic Designer
Margaret Vazquez, Bookkeeper/Administrative Assistant

Provides educational assistance in electronic training to public schools, compiles statistics, offers certification programs and apprenticeships. Functions as trade association for the electronics service industry.
8 Members
Founded in 1950

23998 National Fastener Distributors Association

10842 Noel Street #107
Los Alamitos, CA 90720

714-484-7858
877-487-6332
FAX 562-684-0695
E-Mail: nfda@nfda-fastener.org
Home Page: www.nfda-fastener.org
Social Media: *Facebook, Twitter, LinkedIn*

Casey McIlhon, President
Marc Strandquist, VP
Kameron Dorsey, Associate Chair
Jeannine Christensen, Meetings & Events
Vickie Lester, MBA, CAE, Executive Management

Develops new uses for fasteners, offers training and educational programs.
250 Members
Founded in 1968

23999 National Frozen & Refrigerated Foods Association

4755 Linglestown Road Suite 300
PO Box 6069
Harrisburg, PA 17112

717-657-8601
FAX 717-657-9862
E-Mail: info@nfraweb.org
Home Page: www.nfraweb.org
Social Media: *Facebook, Twitter, LinkedIn, YouTube, Pinterest*

H V Skip Shaw Jr, President/CEO
Jeff Rumachik, EVP/COO
Dayna Jackson, Director, Membership
Julie W Henderson, VP, Communications
Jessica Kurtz, VP, Finance

NFRA is a non-profit trade association representing all segments of the frozen and refrigerated foods industry. Headquartered in Harrisburg, PA, NFRA is the sponsor of March National Frozen Food Month, June dairy Month, and the Summer Favorites Ice Cream & Novelties promotion as well as the

OctoberCool Food for Kids educational outreach program. NFRA holds the annual National Frozen & Refrigerated Foods Convention in October.
450 Members
Founded in 1945

24000 National Grocers Association

1005 North Glebe Road
Suite 250
Arlington, VA 22201-5758

703-516-0700
FAX 703-516-0115
E-Mail: feedback@nationalgrocers.org
Home Page: www.nationalgrocers.org
Social Media: *Facebook, Twitter, LinkedIn*

Peter J Larkin, President & Chief Executive Officer
Charlie Bray, EVP/COO
Matthew Klein, Director, Finance
Matilda Harvey, Director, Administration
Julia Sullivan, Office Administrator/Receptionist

The National Grocers Association is the national trade association representing the retail and wholesale grocers that comprise the independent sector of the food distribution industry.

24001 National Insulation Association

12100 Sunset Hills Road
Suite 330
Reston, VA 20190

703-464-6422
FAX 703-464-5896
Home Page: www.insulation.org
Social Media: *Facebook, Twitter, YouTube*

J. Kenneth Freeman, President
Kristin V DiDomenico, VP
Erin Freeborn, Director of Meetings
Julie McLaughlin, Senior Director, Publications
Ashley J. Lopez, Senior Manager, Production & Design

The National Insulation Association (NIA) is a trade association representing the mechanical and specialty insulation industry.
Founded in 1953

24002 National Kitchen and Bath Association

687 Willow Grove St
Hackettstown, NJ 07840-1731

908-850-1206
800-843-6522
FAX 908-852-1695
E-Mail: feedback@nkba.org
Home Page: www.nkba.org
Social Media: *Facebook, Twitter, LinkedIn, Pinterest*

Bill Darcy, CEO
Maria Stapperfenne, President
Stephen Graziano, VP, Finance & Operations
Nancy Barnes, Director, Learning and Development
Loren Barrows, Director of Marketing

Protects the interests of members by fostering a better business climate. Awards certification. Conducts training schools and seminars.
60000 Members
Founded in 1963

24003 National Poultry and Food Distributors Association

2014 Osbourne Rd
St. Marys, GA 31558

770-535-9901
877-845-1545
FAX 770-535-7385
E-Mail: kkm@npfda.org

Home Page: www.npfda.org
Social Media: *Facebook, Twitter, LinkedIn*

Lee Wilson, President
Kenny Seeger, VP
Bobby Lipson, Treasurer
Kristin McWhorter, CAE, Executive Director/Corp. Secretary
Kathleen Kerry, Membership Coor./Ex. Assistant

A nationwide association that serves the needs of the poultry and food distribution and processing industries. Provides member services, cost cutting benefits and networking opportunities. Sponsors Poultry Suppliers Showcase every January in Atlanta.
220 Members
Founded in 1967

24004 National School Supply & Equipment Association

8380 Colesville Road
Suite 250
Silver Spring, MD 20910

301-495-0240
800-395-5550
FAX 301-495-3330
E-Mail: memberservices@nssea.org
Home Page: www.edmarket.org
Social Media: *Facebook, Twitter, LinkedIn, Youtube*

Jim McGarry, President/CEO
Adrienne Dayton, VP, Marketing & Communications
Bill Duffy, VP, Operations & Meetings
Joe Tucker, Director, Meetings & Experiences
Karen Prince, Director, Membership

The National School Supply and Equipment Association (NSSEA) is the leading trade organization for the educational products marketplace. NSSEA puts the collective experience of the most successful school industry business in the world at your fingertips.
1400+ Members
Founded in 1916

24005 New York State Beer Wholesalers Association

100 State Street
Suite 400
Albany, NY 12207

518-465-6115
FAX 518-465-1907
E-Mail: nybeer@nycap.rr.com
Home Page: www.nybeer.org

Fred C Dana, Chairman
Steven W Harris, President
Ed Keis, Chairman Elect
Bill Bessette, Treasurer
Deb Boening, Secretary

The New York State Beer Wholesalers Association, Inc. represents and protects the legislative and regulators interests of its members in state and local government. Our primary goal is to uphold the three-tier system in order to safeguard the industry's distribution standards.
44 Members
Founded in 1934

24006 North American Association of Telecommunications Dealers

131 NW First Avenue
DelRay Beach, FL 33444

561-266-9440
FAX 561-266-9017
Home Page: www.natd.com

Rob Neuemeyer, Director
Arthur P Frierman, Associate Counsel

The North American Association of Telecommunications Dealers is a nonprofit organization of companies who provide telecom products to the business community and governments

around the world. The NATD gives you access to the right kind of information, resources and business leaders, and provides you with unique opportunities to help grow your business.

24007 North American Association of Floor Covering Distributors

330 N Wabash Ave
Suite 2000
Chicago, IL 60611-4267

312-321-6836
800-383-3091
FAX 312-673-6962
E-Mail: info@nafcd.org
Home Page: www.nafcd.org
Social Media: *Facebook, Twitter, LinkedIn, Youtube*

Rosana Chaidez, President
Heidi Cronin Mandell, Vice President
Geoff Work, Treasurer
Bryan White, Membership Manager
Kevin Gammonley, Executive Director

The North American Association of Floor Covering Distributors (NAFCD) was organized to foster trade and commerce for those having a business, financial or professional interest as wholesale distributors or manufacturers of floor coverings and allied products.

24008 North American Association of Uniform Manufacturers & Distributors

6800 Jericho Turnpike
Suite 120W
Syosset, NY 11791

516-393-5838
FAX 516-393-5878
E-Mail: rjlerman@naumd.com
Home Page: www.naumd.com

Jim Tewmey, Chair
Richard J. Lerman, CCM, President & CEO
Nancy Marzullo, Bookkeeper & Admin Assistant
Miranda Brock, Social Media & Membership Manager
Jackie Rosselli - Verrico, Director of Communications

An association dedicated to keeping the Uniform & Imagewear Industry strong and healthy.
Founded in 1933

24009 North American Association of Utility Distributors (NAAUD)

3105 Corporate Exchange Court
Bridgeton, MO 63044

314-506-0724
FAX 314-506-0790
E-Mail: director@naaud.org
Home Page: www.naaud.com

Mary Jane Reinhardt, Executive Director
Ralph Knobbe, President
Patrick Novak, Vice President
Jeff Stauffer, Treasurer/Secretary

NAAUD is comprised of select distributors who specialize in supplying products and supply chain services to the electric utility industry. The purpose of NAAUD is to discuss and promote the newest ideas and best concepts for the industry.
Founded in 1988

24010 North American Building Material Distribution Association

330 N Wabash Ave
Suite 2000
Chicago, IL 60611

312-321-6845
888-747-7862
FAX 312-644-0310

E-Mail: info@nbmda.org
Home Page: www.nbmda.org
Social Media: *Facebook, Twitter, LinkedIn, YouTube*

Rick Turk, President
Bill Sauter, President-Elect
Ray Prozzillo, Vice President
Wayne Moriarty, Treasurer
Kevin Gammonley, Executive Vice President

NBMDA develops and promotes the effectiveness of distribution processes to improve member profitability and growth.
Founded in 1952

24011 North American Horticultural Supply Association

100 North 20th Street
4th Floor
Philadelphia, PA 19103-1443

215-320-3877
FAX 215-564-2175
E-Mail: nahsa@fernley.com
Home Page: www.nahsa.org
Social Media: *Facebook, Twitter, LinkedIn*

Sarah Hagy, Executive Director
Jameela Smith, Associate Director
Trudie Rowello, Management Liaison

The North American Horticultural Supply Association's mission is to strengthen and support the distribution and manufacturing of horticultural products and services.
Founded in 1987

24012 North American Meat Processors Association

1150 Connecticut Ave, NW
12th floor
Washington, DC 20036

202-587-4200
800-368-3043
FAX 202-587-4303
E-Mail: info@meatassociation.com
Home Page: www.meatassociation.com
Social Media: *Facebook, Twitter, LinkedIn, YouTube*

Dave McDonald, Chairman
Barry Carpenter, President and CEO
Christl McCarthy, Executive Assistant
Rosemary Mucklow, Director Emeritus
Betsy Booren, VP, Scientific Affairs

Represents processors and distributors of meat, poultry, seafood and game to the food-service industry.
400 Members
Founded in 2012

24013 North American Wholesale Lumber Association

330 N. Wabash
Suite 2000
Chicago, IL 60611

312-321-5133
800-527-8258
FAX 312-673-6838
E-Mail: info@nawla.org
Home Page: www.nawla.org
Social Media: *Facebook, Twitter, LinkedIn*

Scott Elston, Chairman
Jim McGinnis, 1st Vice Chair
Bill Adams, 2nd Vice Chair
John Stockhausen, Secretary/Treasurer
Marc Saracco, Executive Director

Supports the wholesale lumber industry. Publishes monthly NAWLA Bulletin that includes industry and association news, and produces the NAWLA Traders Market, an annual trade show bringing together over 1500 manufacturers and wholesale lumber traders at the premier event in the forest products industry. NAWLA also produces a variety of educational pro-

grams designed to enhance professionalism in the lumber industry.
600+ Members
Founded in 1893

24014 Optical Laboratories Association

225 Reinekers Lane
Suite 700
Alexandria, VA 22314

703-548-4560
866-826-0290
FAX 703-548-4580
E-Mail: info@thevisioncouncil.org
Home Page: www.thevisioncouncil.org
Social Media: *Facebook, Twitter, LinkedIn, YouTube*

Mike Daley, CEO
Brian Carroll, COO/CFO
Maureen Beddis, VP, Marketing & Communications
Greg Chavez, VP, Member Services
Deborah Malakoff-Castor, VP, Shows & Meetings

Independent ophthalmic laboratories and supply houses that manufacture prescription eye glasses.
337 Members
Founded in 1894

24015 Outdoor Power Equipment & Engine Service Association

37 Pratt Street
Essex, CT 06426-1159

860-767-1770
FAX 860-767-7932
E-Mail: info@opeesa.com
Home Page: www.opeesa.com
Social Media: *Facebook, Twitter, LinkedIn*

Jeff Plotka, President & Director
Steve Purdy, VP, Annual Meeting & Director
Ted Finn, Secretary/Treasurer & Director
Ron Monroe, Past President and Director
Nancy Cueroni, Executive Director

The Outdoor Power Equipment and Engine Service Association (OPEESA) consists of more than 140 distributors and manufacturers of outdoor power equipment and air-cooled gas and diesel engines. Their mission is to assist distributors in achieving outstanding channel performance.
140 Members

24016 Outdoor Power Equipment Aftermarket Association

341 South Patrick Street
Suite 1101
Alexandria, VA 22314

703-549-7608
FAX 703-549-7609
E-Mail: jhawes@opeaa.org
Home Page: www.opeaa.org

Franck Sogaard, President
Don Martin, Executive VP
Scott Harris, VP
Jeff Andrews, Immediate Past President
Jim Paugh, Director

Businessmen dedicated to promoting the use of aftermarket parts in outdoor power equipment, as well as trade in the industry.
85 Members
Founded in 1986

24017 Pacific-West Fastener Association

10842 Noel Street #107
Los Alamitos, CA 90720

714-484-4747
877-606-5232
FAX 562-684-0695
E-Mail: info@pac-west.org
Home Page: www.pac-west.org

Social Media: *Facebook, Twitter, LinkedIn, YouTube, Instagram, Google+*

Vickie Lester, Executive Director
Jeannine Christensen, Meetings & Events Manager
Marci Myer, Membership Manager
Claudia Scheutze, Accounting
Tanya Scoralle, Member Services

An organization dedicated to the fastener industry.
Founded in 2009

24018 Pet Industry Distributors Association

3465 Box Hill Corp. Center Drive
Suite H
Abingdon, MD 21009

443-640-1060
FAX 443-640-1086
E-Mail: pida@kingmgmt.org
Home Page: www.pida.org
Social Media: *LinkedIn*

Steven T King, President
Debbie Darce, Director, Finance
Stephanie Kaplan, Director, Online Education
Marci Hickey, Director, Meetings & Member Service
Nina Bull, Association Coordinator

Represents wholesaler-distributors of pet products, providing training and education to members.
190 Members
Founded in 1968

24019 Petroleum Equipment Institute

PO Box 2380
Tulsa, OK 74101-2380

918-494-9696
FAX 918-491-9895
E-Mail: lallen@pei.org
Home Page: www.pei.org
Social Media: *Facebook, Twitter, LinkedIn, Google+*

Kevin McKinney, President
Steve Trabilsy, VP
Robert Peavey, Treasurer
Robert Renkes, EVP
Phil Farrell, Immediate Past President

Members are makers and distributors of equipment used in service stations, bulk plants and other petroleum marketing facilities.
1600+ Members
Founded in 1951
Mailing list available for rent: 1600 names at $275 per M

24020 Power Transmission Distributors Association

230 W. Monroe St
Suite 1410
Chicago, IL 60606-4703

312-516-2100
FAX 312-516-2101
E-Mail: ptda@ptda.org
Home Page: www.ptda.org
Social Media: *Facebook, Twitter, LinkedIn*

Ann Arnott, EVP/CEO
Brenda Holt, Director, Membership
Anna Meyer, Director, Project Management
LeRoy Burcroff, 1st VP
Thomas Clawser, 2nd VP

Members are power transmission/motion control distributors throughout manufacturing firms.
485 Members
Founded in 1960

24021 Professional Beauty Association
15825 N 71st Street
Suite 100
Scottsdale, AZ 85254-1521

480-281-0424
800-468-2274
FAX 480-905-0708
E-Mail: info@probeauty.org
Home Page: www.probeauty.org
Social Media: *Facebook, Twitter, LinkedIn, YouTube, Instagram, Pinterest*

Reuben Carranza, Chairman
Beth Hickey, Vice Chair
Steve Sleeper, Executive Director
Rachel Molepske, Manager of Leadership Operations
Eric Z Horn, CMP, Associate Executive Director

The Professional Beauty Association (PBA) is a nonprofit trade association that represents the interests of the professional beauty industry from manufacturers and distributors to salons and spas. PBA offers business tools, education, advocacy, networking and more to improve individual businesses and the industry as a whole.

24022 Quality Bakers of America Cooperative
1275 Glenlivet Drive
Suite 100
Allentown, PA 18106-3107

973-263-6970
FAX 973-263-0937
E-Mail: info@qba.com
Home Page: www.qba.com

Don Cummings, VP

Members are independent wholesale bakeries and their suppliers.
35 Members
Founded in 1922

24023 Safety Equipment Distributors Association
1901 North Moore Street
Suite 808
Arlington, VA 22209-1762

443-640-1065
FAX 703-528-2148
Home Page: www.safetycentral.org
Social Media: *Facebook, Twitter, LinkedIn*

Daniel K Shipp, President
Lydia Baugh, Communications Director
Ann M Feder, Office Services Manager
Sabra L Decker, QSSP Administrator/Meeting Planner
Dan Glucksman, Public Affairs Director

Trade association comprised of companies that distribute safety equipment & related products and services.
300 Members
Founded in 1968

24024 Security Hardware Distributors Association
105 Eastern Avenue
Suite 104
Annapolis, MD 21403

410-940-6346
FAX 410-263-1659
E-Mail: info@shda.org
Home Page: www.shda.org

Sean Steinmann, President
John Burke, Vice President
David Swartz, Treasurer
Karen Hoffman-Kahl, Immediate Past President
Patricia A. Lilly, Executive Director

The mission of the Security Hardware Distributors Association is to continually improve,

through education and services, the proficiency of Security Distributors in order that they are the most effective and efficient conduit to the marketplace.

24025 Souvenir Wholesale Distributors Association
32770 Arapahoe Rd
#132-155
Lafayette, CO 80026

443-640-1055
888-599-4474
FAX 888-589-7610
E-Mail: info@souvenircentral.org
Home Page: www.souvenircentral.org
Social Media: *Facebook, LinkedIn*

Brenda Taylor, President
Angie Rohnke, Vice President
Libby Smith, Secretary/Treasurer
Matthew Tobin, Immediate Past President

Companies distributing local view scenic post cards and souvenirs in North America and the Caribbean.
110 Members
Founded in 1973

24026 Textile Care Allied Trades Association
271 Route 46 West
Suite C-106
Fairfield, NJ 07004

973-244-1790
FAX 973-244-4455
E-Mail: info@tcata.org
Home Page: www.tcata.org
Social Media: *Facebook, Twitter, LinkedIn*

David Cotter, Chief Executive Officer
Cheryl Paglia, Office Manager

The Textile Care Allied Trades Association (TCATA) is an international trade association representing manufacturers and distributors of dry-cleaning and laundry equipment and supplies. It is the only trade association dedicated exclusively to the interests of the allied trades.

24027 The NPTA Alliance
330 North Wabash Avenue
Suite 200E
Chicago, IL 60611

312-321-4092
800-355-6782
FAX 312-673-6736
E-Mail: webmaster@gonpta.com
Home Page: www.gonpta.com
Social Media: *Twitter, LinkedIn, Youtube*

Kevin Gammonley, CEO
Hilton Maze, Chairman
Bayard Tynes, 1st Vice Chair
Tom Wernoch, Second Vice Chair
Don Clampitt, Treasurer

Wholesale distributors of printing and industrial paper.
2000 Members
Founded in 1903

24028 United Producers Formulators & Distributors Association
PO Box 55
Roswell, GA 30077

770-552-8072
FAX 770-417-1419
E-Mail: Teichler@neogen.com
Home Page: www.upfda.com
Social Media: *Facebook, Twitter*

Tom Eichler, President
Karen Furgiuele, Vice President
Cisse Spragins, Secretary & Treasurer
Valerie Jessee, Executive Director
Tommy Reeves, Immediate Past President

Members are firms which are directly involved in formulating and distributing products or equipment to the pest control industry.

24029 Water & Sewer Distributors of America
100 North 20th Street
Suite 400
Philadelphia, PA 19103-1443

215-320-3882
FAX 215-564-2175
E-Mail: wasda@fernley.com
Home Page: www.wasda.com
Social Media: *Facebook, Twitter, LinkedIn, YouTube*

Kevin A. Murphy, President
Richard Campbell, President-Elect
Bill Driskill, Secretary & Treasurer
Edward Nugent, Past President

WASDA's mission is to promote the water-works/wastewater products distribution industry, and to further improve the image and professionalism of WASDA and its member companies.
100+ Members
Founded in 1979

24030 Wholesale Florists and Florist Suppliers of America
105 Eastern Avenue
Suite 104
Annapolis, MD 21403-3300

410-940-6580
888-289-3372
FAX 410-263-1659
E-Mail: info@wffsa.org
Home Page: www.wffsa.org
Social Media: *Facebook, Twitter, LinkedIn*

Patricia A Lilly, EVP
Joseph Thompson, General Manager
Amy Luckado, Membership Director
Kristin Thompson, Comm. & Conference Director
Lin Guba, Conference Manager

To provide networking and business opportunities to wholesale distributors and floral suppliers.
1.3M+ Members
Founded in 1926

24031 Wine/Spirits Wholesalers of America
805 15th Street NW
Suite 430
Washington, DC 20005

202-371-9792
FAX 202-789-2405
E-Mail: info@wswa.org
Home Page: www.wswa.org
Social Media: *Facebook, Twitter, LinkedIn, YouTube, RSS*

Craig Wolf, President/CEO
Lisa Bockelman, Executive Assistant
Jim Rowland, SVP, Govt. Affairs
Danwson Hobbs, VP, State Affairs
Reilly O'Connor, VP, Govt. Affairs

Two hundred booths for suppliers of alcoholic beverages from around the world.
350+ Members
Founded in 1943

Newsletters

24032 News & Views
Bearing Specialists Association

800 Roosevelt Road
Building C, Suite 312
Glen Ellyn, IL 60137

630-858-3838
FAX 630-790-3095
E-Mail: info@bsahome.org
Home Page: www.bsahome.org
Social Media: *LinkedIn*

Linda Miller, President
Richard W Church, Executive Director
Jerilyn J Church, Executive Secretary

Monthly newsletter of BSA, the forum to enhance networking and knowledge sharing to promote the sale of bearings through authorized distributors. Available to members only.
100 Members
Frequency: E-Newlsetter for Members
Circulation: 400
Founded in 1966

24033 AMD Insider

10047 Robert Trent Jones Parkway
New Port Richey, FL 34655-4649

727-372-3665
800-786-7274
FAX 727-372-2879
Home Page: www.amdweb.com

Rosalie Leone, Chief Executive Officer
Terry Rodimer, Operations and Assistant to the CEO
Jeff Burton, Director of Codes & Standards
Miguel Rivera-Sanchez, Director of Education
William G Simon, Graphics Coordinator

The Association of Millwork Distributors online newsletter providing information for and about the millwork distribution industry.
Frequency: Monthly

24034 APSP SmartBrief

Association of Pool & Spa Professionals
2111 Eisenhower Avenue
Alexandria, VA 22314

703-838-0083
FAX 703-549-0493
E-Mail: memberservices@apsp.org
Home Page: www.apsp.org

Bill Weber, Chief Executive Officer
Terry Brown, Chairman of the Board
Kathleen Carlson, Secretary & Treasurer

APSP SmartBrief is a free weekly e-mail news service available to both APSP members and nonmembers. Each week subscribers are informed of the week's most important news stories for the pool, spa, and hot tub industry.
Frequency: Weekly
Founded in 1956

24035 Creative Marketing Newsletter

Association of Retail Marketing Services
10 DRS james parker BLVD
suite 103
Red Bank, NJ 07701-2003

732-842-5070
FAX 732-219-1938
Home Page: www.goarms.com

Gerri Hopkins, Executive Director
Lisa McCauley, Administrative Director

Retail promotion marketing newsletter for supermarkets, convenience stores, drug chains and suppliers of retail promotions.
Frequency: Quarterly
Founded in 1957
Printed in 3 colors on matte stock

24036 Cutting Edge

Outdoor Power Equipment Aftermarket

341 South Patrick Street
Suite 1101
Alexandria, VA 22314

703-549-7608
FAX 703-549-7609
E-Mail: wsb@opeaa.org
Home Page: www.opeaa.org

Katherine Inslie, President
Susan Dove, Editor

Businessmen dedicated to promoting the use of aftermarket parts in outdoor power equipment, as well as trade in the industry.
Cost: $25.00
Frequency: Quarterly
Founded in 1986

24037 Door & Hardware Industry Watch

Door & Hardware Institute
14150 Newbrook Drive
Chantilly, VA 20151

703-222-2010
FAX 703-222-2410
Home Page: www.dhi.org

Jerry Heppes, Chief Executive Officer
Chuck Molina, Chief Technology Officer
Scott Sabatini, President

Electronic newsletter with the latest industry news and trends.
Frequency: 2 Times/Month
Founded in 1952

24038 Emerging Business

Master Security Company
PO Box 6661
Roanoke, VA 24017-0661

FAX 540-982-8407

Debra Napier, Publisher

Provides summary on articles of interest to small business owners, consultants corner, highlights services available pertaining to alternative financing of growing businesses.
6 Pages
Frequency: Quarterly

24039 FMI Daily Lead

Food Marketing Institute
2345 Crystal Drive
Suite 800
Arlington, VA 22202

202-452-8444
FAX 202-425-4519
Home Page: www.fmi.org
Social Media: *Facebook, Twitter, LinkedIn*

Leslie Sarasin, President; Chief Executive Officer
Pat Shinko, Director
Paul Ryan, Executive Director

Newsletter that provides a daily briefing on top stories in food retailing and wholesaling.
1500 Members
Frequency: Daily
Founded in 1892

24040 ISD Insider

International Sealing Distribution Association
105 Eastern Avenue
Suite 104
Annapolis, MD 21403

410-940-6344
FAX 410-263-1659
E-Mail: info@isd.org
Home Page: www.isd.org

Larry Goode, President
Debbie Mitchess, Executive Director
Joseph Thompson, Associate Director
Marty Lostrom, Conference Manager
Kristin B Thompson, Director of Communications

The association's newsletter is devoted to topics affecting business, training, and technology within the industry, with feature articles from industry experts.
Frequency: Quarterly

24041 Insider

MacLean Hunter
4 Stamford Forum
Stamford, CT 06901-3253

FAX 203-325-8423

Vanessa Grey, Publisher
Adrienne Toth, Editor

A shopping center industry newsweekly. Each issue contains critical information concerning retailer news, new development items, agent announcements and new tenant listings.
Cost: $250.00
6 Pages
Frequency: Monthly

24042 M&E Appraiser

American Society of Appraisers
555 Herndon Pkwy
Suite 125
Herndon, VA 20170-5250

703-478-2228
800-272-8258
FAX 703-742-8471
Home Page: www.appraisers.org

Laurie Saunders, Executive VP
Jackie Montalvo, Editor
J Michael Clarkson, Publisher

Machinery and equipment appraisal information. Accepts advertising.
Cost: $45.00
48 Pages
Frequency: Quarterly
Founded in 1936

24043 MDNA News

Machinery Dealers National Association
315 S Patrick Street
Alexandria, VA 22314

703-836-9300
800-872-7807
FAX 703-836-9303
E-Mail: office@mdna.org
Home Page: www.mdna.org

Michael F Feinstein, President
Paul Lashin, First Vice President
Ron Shuster, Second Vice President
Kim Khoury, Treasurer

This newsletter is a valuable source of information about MDNA events and programs, industry news, updates on chapter activities, government programs, and auctions.
Frequency: 6x/Year
Founded in 1941

24044 MHEDA Connection

Material Handling Equipment Distributors Assoc
201 US Highway 45
Vernon Hills, IL 60061-2398

857-680-3500
FAX 847-362-6989
E-Mail: connect@mheda.org
Home Page: www.mheda.org

Duncan Murphy, President
Liz Richards, Executive Vice President
Kathy Cotter, Marketing Director
Natalie Cobb, Networking & Communications

The MHEDA Connection is a semi-monthly newsletter distributed to members and its associates on the 1st and the 15th of the month.
Frequency: Semi-Monthly
Founded in 1954

24045 NACD News Brief
National Association of Chemical Distributors
1555 Wilson Boulevard
Suite 700
Arlington, VA 22209

703-527-6223
FAX 703-527-7747
E-Mail: nacdpublicaffairs@nacd.com
Home Page: www.nacd.com

Bruce Schechinger, Chairman, Chief Executive Officer
Andrew K Skipp, Vice Chairman
Roger T Harris, Treasurer
Jean-Pierre Baizan, Director at Large

The NACD News Brief is a biweekly e-mail newsletter outlining the key legislative and regulatory actions affecting NACD members and reporting on other key industry activity.
250 Members
Frequency: Bi-Weekly
Founded in 1971

24046 NAW Report
National Association of Wholesalers & Distributors
1325 G Street NW
Suite 1000
Washington, DC 20005-3100

202-872-0885
FAX 202-785-0586
E-Mail: naw@naw.org
Home Page: www.naw.org

Peter L Cook, Executive Director
Dirk VanDongen, Contact

Information on regulation, industry research and programs for distributors and wholesalers.

24047 NBMDA Economic Outlook Report
N.A. Building Material Distribution Association
401 N. Michigan Avenue
Chicago, IL 60611

312-321-6845
888-747-7862
FAX 312-644-0310
E-Mail: info@nbmda.org
Home Page: www.nbmda.org
Social Media: *Facebook, Twitter, LinkedIn*

Duane Lambrecht, President
Bill Delaney, President-Elect
Brian Schell, Vice President
Mark Kasper, Treasurer

This report correlates macroeconomic data to specific product categories directly related to the building material industry
Frequency: Quarterly
Founded in 1952

24048 NSPI News
National Spa and Pool Institute
2111 Eisenhower Ave
Suite 500
Alexandria, VA 22314-4679

703-838-0083
800-323-3996
FAX 703-549-0493
E-Mail: MemberServices@TheAPSP.org
Home Page: www.theapsp.org

Bill Weber, President
Jack Cregol, CEO

24049 National Wholesaler Association
251 W Renner Road
#102
Richardson, TX 75080-1318

FAX 972-470-0134

Don Akerman, Publisher

Offers products, new or old, marketing, distribution expertise, customer analysis, position-

ing, advertising, promotion planning. Accepts advertising.
Frequency: Quarterly

24050 News & Views
Bearing Specialists Association
800 Roosevelt Road
Building C, Suite 312
Glen Ellyn, IL 60137

630-858-3838
FAX 630-790-3095
E-Mail: info@bsahome.org
Home Page: www.bsahome.org
Social Media: *LinkedIn*

Linda Miller, President
Richard W Church, Executive Director
Jerilyn J Church, Executive Secretary

Monthly newlsetter of BSA, the forum to enhance networking and knowledge sharing to promote the sale of bearings through authorized distributors. Available to members only.
100 Members
Frequency: E-Newlsetter for Members
Circulation: 400
Founded in 1966

24051 North American Wholesale Lumber Association Bulletin
North American Wholesale Lumber Association
3601 Algonquin Rd
Suite 400
Rolling Meadows, IL 60008-3181

847-870-7470
800-527-8258
FAX 847-870-0201
E-Mail: info@nawla.org
Home Page: www.nawla.org

Nicholas Kent, President
Stacey Woldt, Meetings Manager

Newsletter published by North American Wholesale Lumber Association.
Frequency: Monthly
Founded in 1892

24052 Unlocked
Security Hardware Distributors Association
105 Eastern Avenue
Suite 104
Annapolis, MD 21403

410-940-6346
FAX 410-263-1659
E-Mail: info@shda.org
Home Page: www.shda.org

Steve Dyson, President
Karen Hoffman, Vice President
Peter Berg, Treasurer
Paul Justen, Immediate Past President

The SHDA newsletter, Unlocked, provides members with the latest news about the association and its educational events and programs as well as trends and news about security hardware distribution.
Frequency: Monthly

24053 Weekly Insights
Global Market Development Center
1275 Lake Plaza Drive
Colorado Springs, CO 80906-3583

719-576-4260
FAX 719-576-2661
E-Mail: info@gmdc.org
Home Page: www.gmdc.com

David T McConnell Jr, President, Chief Executive Officer
Mark Mechelse, Director of Industry Insights
Keith Wypyszynski, VP Business Development
Mike Winterbottom, VP Information Technology, CTO

Weekly Insights addresses important General Merchandise topics, important Health Beauty Wellness topics and news from GMDC.
Frequency: Weekly
Founded in 1970

24054 Winning in Washington-NAW Annual Report
National Association of Wholesalers & Distributors
1725 K St Nw
Washington, DC 20006-1401

202-349-7300
FAX 202-331-7442
Home Page: www.nawc.org

Peter L Cook, Executive Director

Activities of the National Association of Wholesalers and Distributors.

Magazines & Journals

24055 AFI
AFI Communications
2455 E Sunrise Boulevard
Suite 916
Fort Lauderdale, FL 33304-3112

FAX 954-561-4129

Andrew Molchan, President
Bob Lesmeister, Managing Editor

Edited for professional firearm retailers. Editorial emphasis is on new products, new industry and new sales programs for distributors and retailers. Also covers management level trends for manufacturers and wholesalers. Other features include New Products, Archery, Andy's Industry Insights and more.
Circulation: 23,930

24056 AQ Magazine
Association of Pool & Spa Professionals
2111 Eisenhower Avenue
Alexandria, VA 22314

703-838-0083
FAX 703-549-0493
E-Mail: memberservices@apsp.org
Home Page: www.apsp.org

Bill Weber, Chief Executive Officer
Terry Brown, Chairman of the Board
Kathleen Carlson, Secretary & Treasurer

This full-color magazine is written and edited by industry experts with a keen awareness of the issues on the minds of professionals.
Frequency: Quarterly
Founded in 1956

24057 ASA Materials Market Digest
American Supply Association
1200 N. Arlington Heights Rd
Suite 150
Chicago, IL 60654

312-464-0090
FAX 312-464-0091
E-Mail: info@asa.net
Home Page: www.asa.net

Jeff New, Chairman of the Board
Joe Poehling, President
Frank Nisonger, President-Elect
Robert Christiansen, Vice President

Available monthly via e-mail to all members of ASA, the ASA Materials Market Digest is designed to keep readers informed of important trends and recent changes in the industry.
Frequency: Monthly
Founded in 1969

24058 AVEM Resource Guide
Association of Vacuum Equipment
Manufacturers
201 Park Washington Court
Falls Church, VA 22046-4527

703-538-3543
FAX 703-241-5603
E-Mail: aveminfo@avem.org
Home Page: www.avem.org

Dawn M. Shiley, Executive Director

Buyers guide offering products and services
that are offered by AVEM member companies.
Items range from systems, pumps, instrumentation, hardware and deposition components.
49 Members
Frequency: Yearly
Founded in 1969

**24059 American Wholesale Marketers
Association**
Ameican Wholesale Marketers Association
2750 Prosperity Ave
Suite 530
Fairfax, VA 22031-4338

703-208-3358
800-482-2962
FAX 703-573-5738
E-Mail: robertp@awmanet.org
Home Page: www.awmanet.org

Scott Ramminger, President
Traci Carneal, Editor-in-Chief
Joan Fay, Associate Publisher

Information on candy, chewing gum, tobacco,
HBC, general merchandise, snack foods and re-
lated items.
Printed in 4 colors on glossy stock

24060 Beer Perspectives
National Beer Wholesalers Association
1101 King Street
Suite 600
Alexandria, VA 22314-2965

703-683-4300
FAX 703-683-8965
E-Mail: info@nbwa.org
Home Page: www.nbwa.org
Social Media: *Facebook, Twitter*

Craig A Purser, President & CEO
Michael Johnson, EVP/Chief Advisory Officer
Rebecca Spicer, VP Public Affairs/Chief
Paul Pisano, SVP Industry Affairs & Gen.
Counsel

Trade association for beer wholesalers. Provides government and public affairs outreach
as well as education and training for its wholesaler members.
2200 Pages
Founded in 1938

24061 Chemical Distributor
National Association of Chemical
Distributors
1555 Wilson Boulevard
Suite 700
Arlington, VA 22209

703-527-6223
FAX 703-527-7747
E-Mail: nacdpublicaffairs@nacd.com
Home Page: www.nacd.com
Social Media: *Facebook, Twitter, LinkedIn,
YouTube*

Bruce Schechinger, Chairman, Chief Executive
Officer
Andrew K Skipp, Vice Chairman
Roger T Harris, Treasurer
Jean-Pierre Baizan, Director at Large

The industry's magazine that is published nine
times a year and highlights members' news, Association and industry activity, and provides

business information useful to chemical
distributors.
250 Members
Frequency: 9x/Year
Founded in 1971

24062 Cleaner Times
Cleaning Equipment Trade Association
1000 Nix Road
Little Rock, AR 72211-3235

704-635-7362
800-525-7038
FAX 501-280-9233
Home Page: www.cleanertimes.com
Social Media: *Facebook, Twitter, LinkedIn*

Charlene Yarbrough, Publisher
Jim McMurry, Editor
Chris Ragan, Art Director
Chuck Prieur, Advertising Sales

Magazine published by the Cleaning Equipment Trade Association for members.
Frequency: Monthly

24063 Distributor's Link
4297 Corporate Sq
Naples, FL 34104-4754

239-643-2713
800-356-1639
FAX 239-643-5220
E-Mail: leojcoar@linkmagazine.com
Home Page: www.linkmagazine.com

Maryann Marzocchi, President
Tracey Lumia, Advertising Sales
Michael T Wrenn, Marketing Manager

Information aimed at the fastener distributors
nationwide.
Cost: $45.00
300 Pages
Frequency: Quarterly
Circulation: 50000
Founded in 1975

24064 Door & Hardware Magazine
Door & Hardware Institute
14150 Newbrook Drive
Chantilly, VA 20151

703-222-2010
FAX 703-222-2410
Home Page: www.dhi.org
Social Media: *Facebook, Twitter, LinkedIn*

Jerry Heppes, Chief Executive Officer
Chuck Molina, Chief Technology Officer
Scott Sabatini, President

The Door & Hardware magazine offers information and articles from the industry's only
publication dedicated solely to the architectural
openings industry.
Frequency: Monthly

24065 Employment Guide
Bureau of National Affairs
1801 S Bell St
Arlington, VA 22202-4501

703-341-3000
800-372-1033
FAX 800-253-0332
E-Mail: customercare@bna.com
Home Page: www.bnabooks.com
Social Media: *Facebook, Twitter, LinkedIn*

Paul N Wojcik, CEO

An easy-to-read, practical reference guide to a
broad range of employment topics, designed
for the small to medium sized organization.
Cost: $745.00
Founded in 1929

24066 Essentials Magazine
National School Supply & Equipment
Association

8380 Colesville Road
Suite 250
Silver Spring, MD 20910

301-495-0240
800-395-5550
FAX 301-495-3330
Home Page: essentials.nssea.org
Social Media: *Facebook, Twitter, LinkedIn*

Tim Holt, President & Chief Executive Officer
Bill Duffy, VP of Operations & Meetings
DeShuna Spencer, Director of Publications
Adrienne Watts Dayton, VP Marketing &
Communications

Essentials magazine targets all facets of the educational industry from contemporary,
bite-sized studies and statistics, to timely feature articles, as well as NSSEA member interviews, product press releases, and business
updates.
Frequency: Monthly
Founded in 1916

24067 GAWDA Edge
Gases and Welding Distributors Association
100 North 20th Street
4th Floor
Philadelphia, PA 19103

215-564-3484
FAX 215-963-9785
E-Mail: gawda@gawda.org
Home Page: www.gawda.org

Kent Van Amburg, Executive Director
Malvenia Avery, Associate Director
Tawnee Shuey, Meeting Manager
Kate Marlys, Director

Provides relevant news and technology information.
775 Members
Frequency: Quarterly
Founded in 1945

24068 Insulation Outlook
National Insulation Association
12100 Sunset Hills Road
Suite 330
Reston, VA 20190

703-464-6244
FAX 703-464-5896
Home Page: www.insulation.org

Michele M Jones, Executive Vice
President/CEO
Larry Nelles, President
Glenn Frye, President-Elect
Alec Rexroat, Secretary/Treasurer

Insulation Outlook is the only international
publication devoted exclusively to industrial
and commercial insulation applications, products, and materials.
Cost: $65.00
Frequency: Monthly
Founded in 1953

**24069 International Gaming and Wagering
Business**
BNP Media
PO Box 1080
Skokie, IL 60076-9785

847-763-9534
FAX 847-763-9538
E-Mail: igwb@halldata.com
Home Page: www.igwb.com

James Rutherford, Editor
Lynn Davidson, Marketing
Tammie Gizicki, Director

Focuses on business strategy, legislative infor-
mation, food service and promotional concerns.
Frequency: Monthly
Circulation: 25000

24070 Licensing Book
Adventure Publishing Group

1107 Broadway
Suite 1204
New York, NY 10010-1512

212-575-4510
FAX 212-575-4521
Home Page: www.licensingbook.com

Judy Basis, Publisher
Mathew C Scheiner, Editor-in-Chief
Owen Shorts, Owner

Licensing in successful retailing, licensed product merchandising in various aspects.
Cost: $48.00
40 Pages
Frequency: Monthly
Founded in 1983

24071 Licensing International
WFC
3000 Hadley Rd
South Plainfiel, NJ 07080-1183

908-668-4747
FAX 732-769-1711
E-Mail: info@wfcinc.com
Home Page: www.wfcinc.com

Theodore Pytlar, VP
Kimberly Calabrese, Production Manager

Business merchandising magazine serving the licensing industry at all levels. Publishes whole foods magazine.
Cost: $70.00
64 Pages
Frequency: Monthly
Circulation: 14,933

24072 MHEDA Journal
Material Handling Equipment Distributors Assoc
201 US Highway 45
Vernon Hills, IL 60061-2398

857-680-3500
FAX 847-362-6989
E-Mail: connect@mheda.org
Home Page: www.themhedajournal.org
Social Media: *Facebook, Twitter, LinkedIn*

Duncan Murphy, President
Liz Richards, Executive Vice President
Kathy Cotter, Marketing Director
Natalie Cobb, Networking & Communications

The MHEDA journal is the official magazine of the association.
Frequency: Quarterly
Founded in 1954

24073 Material Handling Wholesaler
Specialty Publications International
801 Bluff Street
PO Box 725
Dubuque, IA 52004-725

563-557-4495
877-638-6190
FAX 563-557-4499
E-Mail: circulation@mhwmag.com
Home Page: www.mhwmag.com

Dean Millius, General Manager
Cathy Murphy, Editor
Sharon Dague, Account Executive
Cathy Murphy, Contributing Editor

Published for used and new material handling equipment dealers, parts suppliers, manufacturers reps, repair shops, and brokers includes articles on issues, conventions, products and people that impact the industry.
Cost: $31.00
Frequency: Monthly
Circulation: 27000
Founded in 1979
Printed in 4 colors on newsprint stock

24074 NSPI Business Owners Journal
National Spa and Pool Institute

2111 Eisenhower Ave
Suite 500
Alexandria, VA 22314-4679

703-838-0083
800-323-3996
FAX 703-549-0493
Home Page: www.nspi.org

Bill Weber, President

A resource service offered by the national spa and pool inst. published four times a year. Contains concise, pertinent and useful information of critical importance to business owners throughout the year, this journal delivers information that is easily applied to a business, including more than 100 action alerts and ideas, and 25 to 30 how-to articles, advisories and reports. Covers such topics as ways to cash flows; ways to save and defer taxes; how to sell and buy a business.
Founded in 1956

24075 New Equipment Digest
Penton Media
1300 E 9th St
Suite 316
Cleveland, OH 44114-1503

216-696-7000
FAX 216-696-6662
E-Mail: information@penton.com
Home Page: www.penton.com

Jane Cooper, Marketing
Dave Madonia, Associate Publisher/eMedia
Robert F King, Editor
Garnetta Russell, Ad Services Manager
Bobbie Macy, Circulation Manager

Serves the general industrial field which includes manufacturing, processing, engineering services, construction, transportation, mining, public utilities, wholesale distributors, educational services, libraries and governmental establishments.
Frequency: Monthly
Circulation: 206164
Founded in 1936

24076 Paper & Packaging
NPTA Alliance
401 N Michigan Avenue
Suite 2200
Chicago, IL 60611

312-321-4092
800-355-6782
FAX 312-673-6736
E-Mail: npta@gonpta.com
Home Page: www.gonpta.com

Dennis Coyle, Associate Publisher/Editor

Covers association news, industry news, industry reports, industry events, new products, personnel updates and business articles for management and sales representatives and much more.
Cost: $120.00
Frequency: Quarterly
Circulation: 6000

24077 Plumbing Engineer
TMB Publishing
1838 Techny Ct
Northbrook, IL 60062-5474

847-564-1127
FAX 847-564-1264
E-Mail: tmbpubs@earthlink.net
Home Page: www.tmbpublishing.com

Tom M Brown, President
Cate Brown, Production Manager

Over 400 plumbing products from approximately 250 manufacturers.
Frequency: Monthly
Circulation: 26104
ISSN: 0192-171X

Founded in 1973
Printed in 4 colors

24078 Supply House Times
Reed Business Information
1050 IL Route 83
Suite 200
Bensenville, IL 60106

630-616-0200
800-323-4958
FAX 630-288-8686
E-Mail: leniusp@bnpmedia.com
Home Page: www.supplyht.com

Patricia Lenius, Managing Editor
Scott Franz, Publisher
Kevin Hackney, Marketing Coordinator
Ashley Anderson, Associate Editor
George Zebrowski, Group Publisher

For plumbing, heating, air conditioning and piping wholesalers
Cost: $92.00
62 Pages
Frequency: Monthly
Founded in 1958
Printed in 4 colors on glossy stock

24079 TED Magazine
National Association of Electrical Distributors
1166 Avenue of the Americas
St. Louis, NY 10036

212-204-4200
888-791-2512
FAX 314-991-3060
E-Mail: customerservice@naed.org
Home Page: www.tedmag.com

Tom Naber, President & Chief Executive Officer
Michelle McNamara, Vice President
Becky Burgess, Meetings & Conferences Director

TED magazine (The Electrical Distributor) is NAED's premier trade publication. With the latest industry news as well as articles and research ranging from sales to voice-data-video, TED magazine is necessary reading for all electrical distributors.
Cost: $40.00
Frequency: Monthly
Founded in 1908

24080 Welding & Gases Today
Gases and Welding Distributors Association
8669 Doral Blvd
Suite 130
Philadelphia, PA 33166

215-564-3484
877-382-6440
FAX 305-442-7451
E-Mail: gawda@gawda.org
Home Page: www.gawda.org

Kent Van Amburg, Executive Director
Malvenia Avery, Associate Director
Tawnee Shuey, Meeting Manager
Kate Marlys

The official journal of the Gases and Welding Distributors Association.
775 Members
Frequency: Quarterly
Founded in 1945

Trade Shows

24081 AED Summit
600 22nd~Street
Suite 220
Oak Brook, IL 60523

630-574-0650
800-388-0650
FAX 630-574-0132
E-Mail: info@aednet.org
Home Page: www.aednet.org
Social Media: *Facebook, Twitter, LinkedIn*

Toby Mack, President & CEO
Bob Henderson, Executive Vice President & COO
Dave Gordon, Publisher/Vice President of Sales
Kim Phelan, Executive Editor

The AED Summit provides a pure networking opportunity with both dealers and their manufacturer partners. It also offers high quality, high class, professional education content for executives and managers.
700 Members
Frequency: Annual

24082 ASCDI Winter Conference
Association of Service and Computer Dealers Int'l
131 NW First Avenue
Delray Beach, FL 33444

561-266-9016
FAX 561-266-9017
Home Page: www.ascdi.com
Rob Neumeyer, Director
Bob Boyle, Counsel
Jerry Roberts, Chairman Emeritus
Arthur P Freierman, Treasurer

The ASCDI conferences provide a great forum for networking with others in the industry, meeting old friends, and making new contacts. The winter conference offers an opportunity to learn about the latest technology trends, meet with leading vendors, and gain a competitive edge in the IT market. The conference is conducted by following Green Meeting Practices.
Founded in 1981

24083 AVDA Annual Conference
2105 Laurel Bush Road
Suite 200
Bel Air, MD 21015

443-640-1040
FAX 443-640-1086
E-Mail: kaymie@ksgroup.org
Home Page: www.avda.net
Social Media: *Facebook, Twitter, LinkedIn, YouTube*

George Henriques, Chairman
Mary Pat Thompson, President
Ben Coe, President-Elect

The AVDA annual conference is a three-day program of information and educational sessions featuring industry and outside speakers on a variety of timely business and industry issues and topics.
Frequency: Annual
Founded in 1976

24084 AWFS Fair
Association of Woodworking & Furnishings Suppliers
500 Citadel Drive
Suite 200
Commerce, CA 90040

323-838-9440
800-946-2937

FAX 323-838-9443
E-Mail: info@awfs.org
Home Page: www.awfs.org
Social Media: *Facebook, Twitter, LinkedIn, YouTube*

Joan Kemp, President
Jeff Oliverson, Vice President
Wade Gregory, Secretary/Treasurer
Skip Hem, Immediate Past President

The AWFS Fair is the largest industry show in the United States.
Frequency: Biennial

24085 AWMA Real Deal Expo
American Wholesale Marketers Association
2750 Prosperity Avenue
Suite 530
Fairfax, VA 22031

703-208-3358
800-482-2962
FAX 703-573-5738
E-Mail: info@awmanet.org
Home Page: www.realdealexpo.com

Scott Ramminger, President/CEO
Robert Pignato, VP Marketing/Industry Affairs

Annual show of 4500 manufacturers and suppliers of confectionery, tobacco, snack foods, juice, novelties and technology and allies to the industry.
Frequency: March

24086 American Nursery & Landscape Association Convention
American Nursery & Landscape Association
1000 Vermont Avenue NW
Suite 300
Washington, DC 20005-3922

202-789-2900
FAX 202-789-1893
Home Page: www.anla.org

Peter Orum, President
Robert J Dolibois, Executive Director

Serves firms who grow, sell or use plants. ANLA advocates the industry's interests before government and provides its members with unique business knowledge essential to long-term growth and profitability.
Frequency: July

24087 Annual Business Leadership Summit
Fluid Power Distributors Association
105 Eastern Avenue
Suite 104
Annapolis, MD 21403

410-940-6347
FAX 410-263-1659
E-Mail: info@fpda.org
Home Page: www.fpda.org
Social Media: *Facebook, Twitter, LinkedIn, YouTube*

Richard Neels, President & Chairman of the Board
Steve Schwasnick, President-Elect
Bill Gillies, Vice President - Membership
Hal Kemp, Convention Chair
Mike Hamzey Jr, VP of Finance & Treasurer

This conference is held each spring and is designed especially for industry decision-makers and opinion-leaders, and is focused on business opportunities, economic and industry trends, leadership development and channel efficiencies.
300+ Members
Frequency: Annual
Founded in 1974

24088 Atlantic City Pool & Spa Show
Association of Pool & Spa Professionals

6B South Gold Drive
Hamilton, NJ 08691

609-689-9111
FAX 703-549-0493
E-Mail: memberservices@apsp.org
Home Page: www.nespapool.org

Bill Weber, Chief Executive Officer
Terry Brown, Chairman of the Board
Kathleen Carlson, Secretary & Treasurer

The Atlantic City show is one of the industry's largest, offering a large trade show and business and technical seminars.
10000 Attendees
Frequency: Annual

24089 BSA Convention
Bearing Specialists Association
800 Roosevelt Road
Building C, Suite 312
Glen Ellyn, IL 60137

630-858-3838
FAX 630-790-3095
E-Mail: info@bsahome.org
Home Page: www.bsahome.org
Social Media: *LinkedIn*

Linda Miller, President
Richard W Church, Executive Director
Jerilyn J Church, Executive Secretary
Kathy Fatz, Association Manager
Janet Arden, Publications Editor

The world's premier bearing industry event for authorized distributors of bearing products and services and the manufacturers of those products.
100 Members
Frequency: Annual
Founded in 1966

24090 BSA Winter Meeting
Bearing Specialists Association
800 Roosevelt Road
Building C, Suite 312
Glen Ellyn, IL 60137

630-858-3838
FAX 630-790-3095
E-Mail: info@bsahome.org
Home Page: www.bsahome.org
Social Media: *Facebook, Twitter, LinkedIn*

Eduardo Bichara, President
Richard W Church, Executive Director
Jerilyn J Church, Executive Secretary
Kathy Fatz, Association Manager
Janet Arden, Publications Editor

BSA committees will be addressing many important issues and association projects at the Winter Meeting. Attending this meeting will help to influence the direction the industry takes over the coming years.
Frequency: Annual

24091 CBBD Annual Convention
1415 L Street
Suite 890
Sacramento, CA 95814

916-441-5402
800-952-8308
FAX 916-441-0713
E-Mail: assn@cbbd.com
Home Page: www.cbbd.com
Social Media: *Facebook, Twitter, LinkedIn*

Victoria G Horton, President
Becky Stolberg, Vice President
Rhonda Stevenson, Marketing & Public Affairs Director

The California Beer and Beverage Distributors host this annual convention for professionals in the industry.
100+ Members
Frequency: Annual

24092 CTDA Management Conference

Ceramic Tile Distributors Association
800 Roosevelt Road
Building C, Suite 312
Glen Ellyn, IL 60137

630-545-9415
800-938-2838
FAX 630-790-3095
E-Mail: info@ctdahome.org
Home Page: www.ctdahome.org

Ryan Calkins, President
Frank Donahue, VP
Barbara Vasquez, Treasurer
Bill Ives, Legal Counsel
Rick Church, Executive Director

CTDA Management Conference is host to the biggest industry leaders and features educational sessions and exhibits
450 Attendees
Frequency: Annual

24093 Distribution Management Conference & Technology Expo

Healthcare Distribution Management Association
901 North Glebe Road
Suite 1000
Arlington, VA 22203

703-787-0000
FAX 703-812-5282
Home Page: www.healthcaredistribution.org
Social Media: *Facebook, Twitter, LinkedIn*

Paul Julian, Chairman
David S Moody, Vice Chairman
John M Gray, President & CEO
Albert~ Thomas, Director

Hundreds of healthcare industry thought leaders and supply chain visionaries gather for nearly three days full of networking, business sessions, and an exciting Technology Expo.
Frequency: Annual

24094 EMDA Industry Showcase

FEWA-AIMRA
PO Box 1347
Iowa City, IA 52244

319-354-5156
FAX 319-354-5157
E-Mail: pat@edma.net
Home Page: www.edma.net
Social Media: *Facebook, Twitter, LinkedIn*

Patricia A Collins, Executive VP

Annual convention and 130 exhibits of equipment, supplies and services for independent wholesale-distributors and independent manufacturer's representatives of shortline and specialty farm equipment, light industrial tractors, lawn and garden tractors, turf care equipment, estate and park maintenance equipment.
600 Attendees
Frequency: November

24095 Ed Expo

National School Supply & Equipment Association
8380 Colesville Road
Suite 250
Silver Spring, MD 20910

301-495-0240
800-395-5550
FAX 301-495-3330
Home Page: www.nssea.org
Social Media: *Facebook, Twitter, LinkedIn*

Tim Holt, President & Chief Executive Officer
Bill Duffy, VP of Operations & Meetings
DeShuna Spencer, Director of Publications
Adrienne Watts Dayton, VP Marketing & Communications
Rashad Cheeks, Circulation Manager

Ed Expo is the country's premier back-to-school buying event and is the ideal place for exhibitors to showcase their products to highly-qualified buyers in the educational products marketplace.
Frequency: Annual
Founded in 1916

24096 Executive Conference

Health Industry Distributors Association
310 Montgomery Street
Alexandria, VA 22314-1516

703-549-4432
FAX 703-549-6495
Home Page: www.hida.org

Matthew Rowan, President & CEO
Rochelle Hargraves, Vice President Finance & Operations
Andrew Van Ostrand, Vice President Policy & Research
Amy Michael, Senior Manager Governmental Affairs

Hundreds of distributor and manufacturer executives gather for the Executive Conference, which consists of networking, interactive education, strategic planning, and industry discussions.
Frequency: Annual
Founded in 1902

24097 FPDA Annual Network Symposium

Fluid Power Distributors Association
105 Eastern Avenue
Suite 104
Annapolis, MD 21403

410-940-6347
FAX 410-263-1659
E-Mail: info@fpda.org
Home Page: www.fpda.org

Richard Neels, President & Chairman of the Board
Steve Schwasnick, President-Elect
Bill Gillies, Vice President - Membership
Hal Kemp, Convention Chair
Mike Hamzey Jr, VP of Finance & Treasurer

This meeting is designed for key management and emerging leaders, and focuses on business and product technologies & trends, industry standards & certification, the FPDA Young Executives development and supporting the needs of participants in the FPDA E-Networks program.
300+ Members
Frequency: Annual
Founded in 1974

24098 General Merchandise Marketing Conference

Global Market Development Center
1275 Lake Plaza Drive
Colorado Springs, CO 80906-3583

719-576-4260
FAX 719-576-2661
E-Mail: info@gmdc.org
Home Page: www.gmdc.com

David T McConnell Jr, President/CEO
Mark Deuschle, Chief Marketing Officer
Keith Wypyszynski, VP Business Development
Mike Winterbottom, VP Information Technology/CTO

Annual conference which has Controlled Casual Conference appointments between wholesalers/retailers and the suppliers, business sessions, roundtables and workshops.
Frequency: Annual/June
Founded in 1970

24099 Health Beauty Wellness Marketing Conference

Global Market Development Center

1275 Lake Plaza Drive
Colorado Springs, CO 80906-3583

719-576-4260
FAX 719-576-2661
E-Mail: info@gmdc.org
Home Page: www.gmdc.com

David T McConnell Jr, President, Chief Executive Officer
Mark Deuschle, Chief Marketing Officer
Keith Wypyszynski, VP Business Development
Mike Winterbottom, VP Information Technology, CTO

Annual conference which has Controlled Casual Conference appointments between wholesalers/retailers and the suppliers, Senior Executive Conference appointments, business sessions, roundtables and workshops.
Frequency: Annual
Founded in 1970

24100 IAPD Annual Convention

International Association of Plastics Distribution
6734 W. 121st Street
Overland Park, KS 66209

913-345-1005
FAX 913-345-1006
E-Mail: iapd@iapd.org
Home Page: www.iapd.org

Susan Avery, Executive Director
Cyndy Launchbaugh, Director of Marketing
Denise Rawlings, Member Services Manager
Crystal Roberts, Sales & Advertising Manager
Wendy Schantz, Marketing & Education Manager

This three-day convention is where the best and the brightest of the plastics distribution industry come together to focus on the future of the industry.
Frequency: Annual
Founded in 1956

24101 ISA Product Show & Conference

Industry Supply Association
100 North 20th Street
4th Floor
Philadelphia, PA 19103

215-320-3862
866-460-2360
FAX 215-963-9785
E-Mail: info@isapartners.org
Home Page: www.isaproductshow.org
Social Media: *Facebook, Twitter, LinkedIn, YouTube*

John Buckley, Executive Vice President
Mary Ritchie, Director, Membership Services
Ken Hutton, Managing Director
Christopher Schor, Associate Director

This is the premier event for anyone in the maintenance, repair, operations and production (MROP) industry. Any MROP distributor, manufacturer/supplier, manufacturers' representative or industry service provider is welcome to attend.
Frequency: Annual

24102 ITPA Seasonal Meeting

International Truck Parts Association
1720 10th Ave. South
Suite 4
Bethesda, MD 20817

202-544-3090
866-346-5692
FAX 301-229-7331
E-Mail: info@itpa.com
Home Page: www.itpa.com
Social Media: *Facebook, Twitter, LinkedIn, YouTube*

Andy Reichert, Chairman
Mike Adiletto, Vice Chairman
Venlo Wolfsohn, Executive Director

Meetings are held each Winter, Fall, and Spring and provide outstanding educational programs, one-on-one meetings with the industry's suppliers, and product trade show and excellent networking opportunities.
Frequency: Annual
Founded in 1974

24103 International Foodservice Distributors: Productivity Convention & Expo
201 Park Washington Court
Falls Church, VA 22046-4521

703-532-9400
FAX 703-538-4673
Home Page: www.ifdaonline.org

Mark Allen, President/CEO
Jonathan Eisen, Senior VP Of Government Relations

Workshops, assemblies, facility tours and an exposition are featured. Educational programming features many practitioners who sahre knowledge to be applied to various operations. Practical information for transportation, information technology, human resources and more.
Frequency: October
Founded in 2003

24104 International Pool & Spa Expo
Association of Pool & Spa Professionals
2111 Eisenhower Avenue
Alexandria, VA 22314

703-838-0083
FAX 703-549-0493
E-Mail: jcergol@nspi.org
Home Page: www.poolspapatio.com

Tracy Beaulieu, Conference Manager

The International Pool & Spa Expo is a trade show for the pool, spa and backyard living industry that provides current market updates, info on cutting edge technology and trends.
15M Attendees
Frequency: Annual

24105 Irrigation Show
Irrigation Association
6540 Arlington Boulevard
Falls Church, VA 22042-6638

703-536-7080
FAX 703-536-7019
E-Mail: info@irrigation.org
Home Page: www.irrigation.org

Deborah M Hamlin, Executive Director
Denise Stone, Meetings Director
Kate Baumann, Membership Coordinator
Rebecca Bayless, Finance Director
Marsha Cram, MBA, Foundation & Membership Manager

The Irrigation Show is the industry's one-stop event. Discover innovations on the show floor and in technical sessions, make connections with industry experts, business partners and peers; and build expertise with targeted education and certification.
1600 Members
Founded in 1949

24106 MDVA Convention
Michigan Distributors & Vendors Association
120 N Washington Square
Suite 110 B
Lansing, MI 48933

517-372-2323
FAX 517-372-4404
E-Mail: webmaster@mdva.org
Home Page: www.mdva.org

Polly Reber, President
Russ Nowak, Chairman
Larry Macfirland, Director

Annual meeting for individuals involved in the grocery and convenience products industry.
100 Members
Frequency: Annual

24107 Manufacturers Seminar
Health Industry Distributors Association
310 Montgomery Street
Alexandria, VA 22314-1516

703-549-4432
FAX 703-549-6495
Home Page: www.hida.org
Social Media: *Facebook, Twitter, LinkedIn*

Matthew Rowan, President & CEO
Rochelle Hargraves, Vice President Finance & Operations
Andrew Van Ostrand, Vice President Policy & Research
Amy Michael, Senior Manager Governmental Affairs

The HIDA Educational Foundation Manufacturers Seminar is guaranteed to provide fresh distributor executive perspectives that will allow attendees to formulate solutions that fit their market strategy.
Frequency: Annual
Founded in 1902

24108 Mid-America Pool & Spa Show
Association of Pool & Spa Professionals
2111 Eisenhower Avenue
Alexandria, VA 22314

703-838-0083
FAX 703-549-0493
E-Mail: memberservices@apsp.org
Home Page: www.apsp.org

Bill Weber, Chief Executive Officer
Terry Brown, Chairman of the Board
Kathleen Carlson, Secretary & Treasurer

The Mid-America show offers a large trade show and business and technical seminars.
Frequency: Annual

24109 Midwinter Executive Conference
Food Marketing Institute
2345 Crystal Drive
Suite 800
Arlington, VA 22202

202-452-8444
FAX 202-425-4519
Home Page: www.fmi.org

Leslie Sarasin, President; Chief Executive Officer
Pat Shinko, Director
Paul Ryan, Executive Director

The FMI Midwinter Executive Conference is an extraordinary opportunity for networking and discussion. The event is invitation-only, and it attracts food industry leaders for an outstanding program that addresses the major challenges and opportunities ahead.
1500 Members
Frequency: Annual

24110 NACD Annual Meeting
National Association of Chemical Distributors
1555 Wilson Boulevard
Suite 700
Arlington, VA 22209

703-527-6223
FAX 703-527-7747
E-Mail: nacdpublicaffairs@nacd.com
Home Page: www.nacd.com

Bruce Schechinger, Chairman, Chief Executive Officer
Andrew K Skipp, Vice Chairman
Roger T Harris, Treasurer
Jean-Pierre Baizan, Director at Large

NACD's Annual Meeting is the premier meeting and annual expo for chemical distributor

professionals. It provides an opportunity to exchange ideas with other top executives in the chemical distribution industry, attend sessions that focus on the latest products and trends affecting the industry, and visit with a variety of exhibitors at the Vendor Expo.
250 Members
Founded in 1971

24111 NAFD Annual Convention
National Association of Flour Distributors
5450 Woodland Place
Canfield, OH 44406

330-718-6563
FAX 877-573-1230
E-Mail: timdove51@gmail.com
Home Page: www.thenafd.com
Social Media: *Facebook, Twitter, LinkedIn*

Ted Heim Jr, President
Erin M. Ruhl, CEO
Dominic Valente, VP

The NAFD sponsors an all-industry forum addressing strategic issues impacting the flour distribution supply chain. In addition to manufacturer and distributor decision makers, senior-level ingredient suppliers participate in the NAFD three-day meeting.
Frequency: Annual

24112 NARM Annual Convention
National Association of Recording Merchandisers
9 Eves Drive
Suite 120
Marlton, NJ 08053-3138

856-596-2221
FAX 856-596-3268
Home Page: www.narm.com

Linda M Still, Director Meetings/Conventions
James Donio, President

Containing 39 booths. Featuring AFIM.
2,100 Attendees
Frequency: March

24113 NASSD Annual Meeting
National Association of Sign Supply Distributors
4525 Collins Avenue
Miami Beach
Baltimore, FL 33140

703-836-4012
FAX 703-836-8353
E-Mail: staceyj@clemonsmgmt.com
Home Page: www.nassd.org
Social Media: *Facebook, Twitter, LinkedIn*

Cal Clemons, Executive Director
Stacey Johnson, Association Coordinator

Held each fall, the annual meeting offers all attendees a full schedule of business and social networking activities. The meeting features distributor & manufacturer-only sessions, general speaker sessions, and roundtable discussions. A highlight of the meeting is the executive conferences which are an opportunity for distributors and manufacturers to meet one-on-one to discuss new sales and business opportunities.
Frequency: Annual

24114 NASSD Spring Management Conference
National Association of Sign Supply Distributors
4526 Collins Avenue
Miami Beach
Baltimore, FL 33140

703-836-4013
FAX 703-836-8354
E-Mail: staceyj@clemonsmgmt.com

Home Page: www.nassd.org
Social Media: *Facebook, Twitter, LinkedIn*

Cal Clemons, Executive Director
Stacey Johnson, Association Coordinator

Held each March, this 1-1/2 day conference features general speaker sessions and roundtable discussions. It is the perfect opportunity to get updated on the association's activities and trends in the industry.
Frequency: Annual

24115 NAUMD Convention & Expo

N.A. Association of Uniform Manufacturers & Dist.
336 West 37th Street
Suite 370
New York, NY 10018

212-736-3010
FAX 212-736-3013
E-Mail: rjlerman@naumd.com
Home Page: www.naumd.com
Social Media: *Facebook, Twitter, LinkedIn, you Tube*

Richard J Lerman, President & CEO
Veronica Martin-Bennett, Manager Membership Info Services
John Chwat, Director of Government Affairs
Jeff Rundles, Director of Communications
Lois Miller, Director Expo & Advertising Sales

The NAUMD Convention & Expo provides a tremendous opportunity for attendees to expand their horizons, sales, and profits. Attendees can find new customers and suppliers for every uniform and imagewear need.
Founded in 1933

24116 NBMDA Annual Convention

N.A. Building Material Distribution Association
401 N. Michigan Avenue
Chicago, IL 60611

312-321-6845
888-747-7862
FAX 312-644-0310
E-Mail: info@nbmda.org
Home Page: www.nbmda.org
Social Media: *Facebook, Twitter, LinkedIn, you Tube*

Duane Lambrecht, President
Bill Delaney, President-Elect
Brian Schell, Vice President
Mark Kasper, Treasurer

The NBMDA provides an opportunity to connect with other leaders in the Building Material Distribution industry. This annual convention is designed to be an executive-level interchange between trading partners coupled with stimulating educational opportunities.
Frequency: Annual
Founded in 1952

24117 NBWA Annual Convention

National Beer Wholesalers Association
1101 King Street
Suite 600
Alexandria, VA 22314-8965

703-683-4300
FAX 703-683-8965
E-Mail: info@nbwa.org
Home Page: www.nbwa.org
Social Media: *Facebook, Twitter*

Craig A Purser, President & CEO
Michael Johnson, EVP Fed Aff/Chief Advisory Office
Rebecca Spicer, VP Public Affairs/Chief
Paul Pisano, SVP Industry Affairs & Gen. Counsel

Designed to provide valuable education programs and important networking opportunities for the beer industry. Featuring speakers and

seminars on a number of topics of importance to beer distributors .
2500 Attendees
Frequency: Fall

24118 NGA Annual Convention & Supermarket Synergy Showcase

National Grocers Association
1005 North Glebe Road
Suite 250
Arlington, VA 22201-5758

703-516-0700
FAX 703-516-0115
E-Mail: info@nationalgrocers.org
Home Page: www.nationalgrocers.org
Social Media: *Facebook, Twitter, LinkedIn, you Tube*

Tom Zaucha, President & Chief Executive Officer
Frank DiPasquale, Executive Vice President
Tom Wenning, Executive VP/General Counsel

Each year, attendees are presented with timely and relevant general sessions and workshops, exciting special events and numerous networking opportunities to speak with other industry executives.
Frequency: Annual

24119 NIA Annual Convention

National Insulation Association
12100 Sunset Hills Road
Suite 330
Reston, VA 20190

703-464-6244
FAX 703-464-5896
Home Page: www.insulation.org
Social Media: *Facebook, Twitter, LinkedIn*

Michele M Jones, Executive Vice President/CEO
Larry Nelles, President
Glenn Frye, President-Elect
Alec Rexroat, Secretary/Treasurer

The NIA Annual Convention is the premier gathering for the mechanical and industrial insulation industry, offering valuable and unique educational and industry sessions, networking opportunities, and entertaining evening events.
Frequency: Annual
Founded in 1953

24120 NPTA Annual Convention

NPTA Alliance
330~N.~Wabash Ave
Suite 2000
Chicago, IL 60611

312-321-4092
800-355-6782
FAX 312-673-6736
E-Mail: npta@gonpta.com
Home Page: www.gonpta.com
Social Media: *Facebook, Twitter*

John F Millin, Chairman
Newell Holt, President & CEO
Thomas D O'Connor Jr, Treasurer
Anthony Macleod, Counsel

The NPTA Annual Convention is a prime opportunity to generate business leads, strengthen relationships with trading partners, develop leadership skills and more.
Frequency: Annual
Founded in 1903
Mailing list available for rent

24121 National Frozen & Refrigerated Foods Convention

4755 Linglestown Road Suite 300
PO Box 6069
Harrisburg, PA 17112

717-657-8601
FAX 717-657-9862
E-Mail: info@nfraweb.org

Home Page: www.nfraweb.org
Social Media: *Facebook, LinkedIn*

H V Skip Shaw Jr, President/CEO
Jeff Rumachik, Senior VP
Marlene Barr, VP Membership

NFRA is a non-profit trade association representing all segments of the frozen and refrigerated foods industry. Headquartered in Harrisburg, PA, NFRA is the sponsor of March National Frozen Food Month, June dairy Month, and the Summer Favorites Ice Cream & Novelties promotion as well as the OctoberCool Food for Kids educational outreach program. NFRA holds the annual National Frozen & Refrigerated Foods Convention in October.
450 Members
1200 Attendees
Founded in 1945

24122 PBA Symposium

Professional Beauty Association
15825 N 71st Street
Suite 100
Scottsdale, AZ 85254

480-281-0424
800-468-2274
FAX 480-905-0708
E-Mail: info@probeauty.org
Home Page: www.probeauty.org

Steven Sleeper, Executive Director
Marissa Porcaro, Director - Marketing
Steve Wilkerson, Chief Financial Officer
Christy Weaver, Manager - Finance & Administration

The PBA Symposium is a business education event produced for all sectors of the beauty industry.
Frequency: Annual
Founded in 1953

24123 Paper2011

NPTA
330~N.~Wabash Ave
Suite 2000
Chicago, IL 60611

312-321-4092
800-355-6782
FAX 312-673-6736
E-Mail: npta@gonpta.com
Home Page: www.gonpta.com
Social Media: *Facebook, Twitter*

Greg Savage, Chairman
Kevin Gammonley, CEO
Hilton Maze, Treasurer

Held in conjunction with the American Forest & Paper Association, features timely sessions on emerging issues, corporate suites, and networking opportunities.
Frequency: March
Founded in 1903
Mailing list available for rent

24124 Pet Exposition Trade Show

Pet Industry Distributors Association
2105 Laurel Bush Road
Suite 200
Bel Air, MC 21015

443-640-1060
FAX 443-640-1031
E-Mail: pida@ksgroup.org
Home Page: www.pida.com

Blaine Phillips, President
Donald Fleming, VP

Containing 500 booths and 300 exhibits.
3,000 Attendees
Frequency: March
Founded in 1968

24125 Post Card & Souvenir Distributors Assocation Trade Show
Post Card & Souvenir Distributors Association
2105 Laurel Bush Road
Suite 200
Bel Air, MD 21015

443-640-1055
FAX 443-640-1031
E-Mail: marci@ksgroup.org
Home Page: www.postcardcentral.org

Maria Linton, Manager

Containing 110 booths and 80 exhibits.
175 Attendees
Frequency: September
Founded in 1973

24126 PowerClean Trade Show and Convention
Cleaning Equipment Trade Association
PO Box 1710
Indian Trail, NC 28079

704-635-7362
800-441-0111
FAX 704-635-7363
Home Page: www.ceta.org
Social Media: *Facebook, Twitter, LinkedIn, you Tube*

Tony Tranquill, President
Terry Murray, Senior Vice President
Aaron Auger, Vice President
Judy Bowers, Treasurer

CETA hosts the industry's premier PowerClean annual trade show and convention. PowerClean provides members with the opportunity to showcase new products, technology, and exchange ideas with industry peers, develop and present educational and certification programs, increase awareness and promotion of the industry and products and facilitate the development of unified positions when working with government agencies to set industry standards and policies.

24127 Read Deal Expo Convention
American Wholesale Marketers Association
1128 16th Street NW
Washington, DC 20036-4808

202-463-2124
800-482-2962
FAX 202-467-0559
E-Mail: robertp@awmanet.org
Home Page: www.awmanet.org

Robert Pignato, VP Marketing/Industry Affairs

The AWMA Real Deal Expo and Convention is the country's oldest and largest show for distributors of confections, snacks and convenience products. The AWMA is the only national trade association working on behalf of the convenience products distribution market. AWMA members also include companies and individuals from across the distribution channel, retailers, brokers, manufacturers and others allied to the industry.
Frequency: February

24128 School Equipment Show
National School Supply & Equipment Association
8380 Colesville Road
Suite 250
Silver Spring, MD 20910

301-495-0240
800-395-5550
FAX 301-495-3330
Home Page: www.nssea.org
Social Media: *Facebook, Twitter, LinkedIn, you Tube*

Jim McGarry, President & Chief Executive Officer

Bill Duffy, VP of Operations & Meetings
DeShuna Spencer, Essentials Editor
Adrienne Watts Dayton, VP Marketing & Communications

Industry trade show where attendees can source new products, learn from leading experts in the field, and network with suppliers, distributors and purchasing influencers.
Frequency: Annual
Founded in 1916

24129 Supply Chain Conference
Food Marketing Institute
2345 Crystal Drive
Suite 800
Arlington, VA 22202

202-452-8444
FAX 202-425-4519
Home Page: www.fmi.org
Social Media: *Facebook, Twitter, LinkedIn*

Leslie Sarasin, President; Chief Executive Officer
Pat Shinko, Director
Paul Ryan, Executive Director
Frederick J. Morganthall II~, Chair

Explores the latest trends in distribution, technology and its application, supply chain collaboration, transportation efficiencies, leadership and management skills. Informal discussion groups give attendees an opportunity to discuss ideas and challenges with their peers.
Frequency: Annual

24130 TCATA Annual Management & Educational Conference
Textile Care Allied Trades Association
271 Route 46 West
#D203
Fairfield, NJ 07004

973-244-1790
FAX 973-244-4455
E-Mail: info@tcata.org
Home Page: www.tcata.org
Social Media: *Facebook, Twitter, LinkedIn*

David Cotter, Chief Executive Officer
Cheryl Paglia, Manager

Trade show consisting of well-organized business programs and unique networking opportunities.
Frequency: Annual

Directories & Databases

24131 A-Z Wholesale Source Directory
Sutton Family Communications & Publishing Company
155 Sutton Lane
Fordsville, KY 42343

270-740-0870
E-Mail: jlsutton@apex.net
Home Page: www.fleamarketeer.net

Theresa Sutton, Editor
Lee Sutton, General Manager

Print-out from database of wholesalers, manufacturers, distributors, importers and close-out houses. Database is updated daily to guarantee the most current and up-to-date sources available.
Cost: $550.00
1M Pages

24132 American Warehouse Association and Canadian Association of Warehousing
Association For Logistics Outsourcing

2800 South River Road
Suite 260
Chicago, IL 60018-6003

847-813-4699
FAX 847-813-0115
E-Mail: email@iwla.com
Home Page: www.iwla.com

Joel Hioland, President
Alex Glan, VP/CEO

Nearly 700 warehouse firms with over 2,000 locations specializing in storage, distribution, and third party logistics.

24133 American Wholesalers and Distributors Directory
Gale/Cengage Learning
10650 Toebben Drive
Independence, KY 41051

800-354-9706
800-877-4253
FAX 800-487-8488
E-Mail: gale.galeord@cengage.com
Home Page: www.gale.com
Social Media: *Facebook, Twitter, LinkedIn*

Patrick C Sommers, President

Discover more than 27,000 large and small wholesalers and distributors throughout the US and Puerto Rico.
Frequency: Annual
ISBN: 1-414434-21-9

24134 Complete Directory of Close-outs and Super-buys
Sutton Family Communications & Publishing Company
155 Sutton Lane
Fordsville, KY 42343

270-740-0870
E-Mail: jlsutton@apex.net
Home Page: www.fleamarketeer.net

Theresa Sutton, Editor
Lee Sutton, General Manager

Print-out from database of wholesalers, manufacturers, distributors, importers and close-out houses. Database is updated daily to guarantee the most current and up-to-date sources available.
Cost: $67.50
100+ Pages

24135 Complete Directory of General Flea Market Merchandise
Sutton Family Communications & Publishing Company
155 Sutton Lane
Fordsville, KY 42343

270-740-0870
E-Mail: jlsutton@apex.net
Home Page: www.fleamarketeer.net

Theresa Sutton, Editor
Lee Sutton, General Manager

Print-out from database of wholesalers, manufacturers, distributors, importers and close-out houses. Database is updated daily to guarantee the most current and up-to-date sources available.
Cost: $289.00
100+ Pages

24136 Complete Directory of High Profit Items
Sutton Family Communications & Publishing Company

155 Sutton Lane
Fordsville, KY 42343

270-740-0870
E-Mail: jlsutton@apex.net
Home Page: www.fleamarketeer.net

Theresa Sutton, Editor
Lee Sutton, General Manager

Print-out from database of wholesalers, manufacturers, distributors, importers and close-out houses. Database is updated daily to guarantee the most current and up-to-date sources available.
Cost: $189.00
100+ Pages

24137 Complete Directory of Importers

Sutton Family Communications & Publishing Company
7025 N. Scottsdale Rd #320
Scottsdale, AR 85253

202-595-3101
888-843-0272
FAX 480-245-5000
E-Mail: info@importgenius.com
Home Page: www.importgenius.com

Theresa Sutton, Editor
Lee Sutton, General Manager

Print-out from database of wholesalers, manufacturers, distributors, importers and close-out houses. Database is updated daily to guarantee the most current and up-to-date sources available.
Cost: $109.00
100+ Pages

24138 Complete Directory of Low-Price Merchandise

Sutton Family Communications & Publishing Company
155 Sutton Lane
Fordsville, KY 42343

270-740-0870
E-Mail: jlsutton@apex.net
Home Page: www.fleamarketeer.net

Theresa Sutton, Editor
Lee Sutton, General Manager

Print-out from database of wholesalers, manufacturers, distributors, importers and close-out houses. Database is updated daily to guarantee the most current and up-to-date sources available.
Cost: $72.20
100+ Pages

24139 Complete Directory of Promotional Products

Sutton Family Communications & Publishing Company
155 Sutton Lane
Fordsville, KY 42343

270-740-0870
E-Mail: jlsutton@apex.net
Home Page: www.fleamarketeer.net

Theresa Sutton, Editor
Lee Sutton, General Manager

Print-out from database of wholesalers, manufacturers, distributors, importers and close-out houses. Database is updated daily to guarantee the most current and up-to-date sources available.
Cost: $139.00
100+ Pages

24140 Complete Directory of Stationery Items

Sutton Family Communications & Publishing Company

155 Sutton Lane
Fordsville, KY 42343

270-740-0870
E-Mail: jlsutton@apex.net
Home Page: www.fleamarketeer.net

Theresa Sutton, Editor
Lee Sutton, General Manager

Print-out from database of wholesalers, manufacturers, distributors, importers and close-out houses. Database is updated daily to guarantee the most current and up-to-date sources available.
Cost: $55.20
100+ Pages

24141 Complete Directory of Tabletop Items

Sutton Family Communications & Publishing Company
155 Sutton Lane
Fordsville, KY 42343

270-740-0870
E-Mail: jlsutton@apex.net
Home Page: www.fleamarketeer.net

Theresa Sutton, Editor
Lee Sutton, General Manager

Print-out from database of wholesalers, manufacturers, distributors, importers and close-out houses. Database is updated daily to guarantee the most current and up-to-date sources available.
Cost: $55.20
100+ Pages

24142 Complete Directory of Unusual Items & Fads

Sutton Family Communications & Publishing Company
155 Sutton Lane
Fordsville, KY 42343

270-740-0870
E-Mail: jlsutton@apex.net
Home Page: www.fleamarketeer.net

Theresa Sutton, Editor
Lee Sutton, General Manager

Print-out from database of wholesalers, manufacturers, distributors, importers and close-out houses. Database is updated daily to guarantee the most current and up-to-date sources available.
Cost: $139.00
100+ Pages

24143 Complete Directory of Wholesale Bargains

Sutton Family Communications & Publishing Company
155 Sutton Lane
Fordsville, KY 42343

270-740-0870
E-Mail: jlsutton@apex.net
Home Page: www.fleamarketeer.net

Theresa Sutton, Editor
Lee Sutton, General Manager

Print-out from database of wholesalers, manufacturers, distributors, importers and close-out houses. Database is updated daily to guarantee the most current and up-to-date sources available.
Cost: $92.70
100+ Pages

24144 EMDA Membership Directory

Equipment Marketing & Distribution Associaion
PO Box 1347
Iowa City, IA 52244-1347

319-354-5156
FAX 319-354-5157

E-Mail: pat@emda.net
Home Page: ww.emda.net

Patricia A Collins, Executive VP

Annual directory of FEWA-AIMRA members, includes address, phone, fax, web, e-mail, territory covered (with map) product descriptions, key personnel, and a descriptive paragraph.
Cost: $50.00

24145 Food & Beverage Market Place

Grey House Publishing
4919 Route 22
PO Box 56
Amenia, NY 12501

518-789-8700
800-562-2139
FAX 518-789-0556
E-Mail: gold@greyhouse.com
Home Page: www.greyhouse.com
Social Media: *Facebook, Twitter*

Leslie Mackenzie, Publisher
Richard Gottlieb, Editor
Richard Gottlieb, President

This information packed three-volume set is the most powerful buying and marketing guide for the US food and beverage industry. Includes thousands of wholesale listings.
Cost: $595.00
2000 Pages
Frequency: Annual
ISBN: 1-592373-61-5
Founded in 1981
Mailing list available for rent

24146 Food & Beverage Marketplace: Online Database

Grey House Publishing
4919 Route 22
PO Box 56
Amenia, NY 12501

518-789-8700
800-562-2139
FAX 518-789-0556
E-Mail: gold@greyhouse.com
Home Page: http://gold.greyhouse.com
Social Media: *Facebook, Twitter*

Richard Gottlieb, President
Leslie Mackenzie, Publisher
Richard Gottlieb, Editor

This complete updated Food & Beverage Market Place: Online Database is the go-to source for the food and beverage industry. Anyone involved in the food and beverage industry needs this 'industry bible' and the important contacts to develop critical research data that can make for successful business growth.
Frequency: Annual
Founded in 1981
Mailing list available for rent

24147 Global Logistics & Supply Chain Strategies

Keller International Publishing Corporation
150 Great Neck Rd
Great Neck, NY 11021-3309

516-829-9722
FAX 516-829-9306
E-Mail: jmurph@starpower.net
Home Page: www.supplychainbrain.com

Jerry Keller, President
Brad Berger, Group President/Publisher
Russell Goodman, Editor-in-Chief

Serves manufacturing, wholesale/retail trade, third party logistics, freight forwarding and transportation/warehousing firms.
Cost: $55.00
96 Pages
Frequency: 11 per year
Circulation: 40M
ISSN: 1525-4887

Founded in 1997
Printed in 4 colors on glossy stock

24148 Membership Directory/Buyer's Guide

Naylor Publications
5950 Nw 1st Pl
Gainesville, FL 32607-6018

352-332-1252
800-369-6220
FAX 352-331-3525
E-Mail: chodges@naylor.com
Home Page: www.naylor.com

Michael Moss, President

Provider of integrated communications and image-building solutions for associations.
Circulation: 1,200

24149 Outlet Project Directory

Off-Price Specialists, Value Retail News
29399 US Highway 19 N
Suite 370
Clearwater, FL 33761-2138

727-781-7557
FAX 727-536-4389
Home Page: www.valueretailnews.com

Linda Humphers, Editor-In-Chief
Tom Kirwan, Senior Editor

Offers valuable information on factory outlet projects.
Cost: $225.00
200 Pages
Frequency: Semiannual

24150 Plumbing Engineer: Product Directory Issue

TMB Publishing
1838 Techny Ct
Northbrook, IL 60062-5474

847-564-1127
FAX 847-564-1264
E-Mail: tmbpubs@earthlink.net
Home Page: www.tmbpublishing.com

Tom M Brown, Owner
Cate Brown, Production Manager

Over 400 plumbing products from approximately 250 manufacturers.
Frequency: Annual January
Circulation: 2,6104
ISBN: 0-192171-1 -

24151 Shippers Guide to Department & Chain Stores Nationwide

Shippers Guides
PO Box 112
Duarte, CA 91009-0112

626-357-6430
FAX 248-786-1358

Profiles over 1,000 department stores and chain stores and their traffic managers in the United States.
Cost: $349.00
350 Pages
Frequency: Annual
Circulation: 2,000

24152 Who's Who

Association of Pool & Spa Professionals
2111 Eisenhower Avenue
Alexandria, VA 22314-4679

703-838-0083
FAX 703-549-0493
Home Page: www.theasap.org/

Jack Cergol, Chief Staff Executive
Marianne Kiernan, Executive Secretary

Trade association for pool, spa and hot tub industry. Annual Convention for trade.
Founded in 1956

24153 Who's Who in Beer Wholesaling Directory

National Beer Wholesalers Association
1101 King Street
Suite 600
Alexandria, VA 22314-8965

703-683-4300
FAX 703-683-8965
E-Mail: info@nbwa.org
Home Page: www.nbwa.org
Social Media: *Facebook, Twitter*

Craig A Purser, President & CEO
Michael Johnson, EVP Fed Aff/Chief Advisory Office
Rebecca Spicer, VP Public Affairs/Chief
Paul Pisano, SVP Industry Affairs & Gen. Counsel

A listing of more than 3,000 beer distributors and suppliers in the industry.
Cost: $50.00

24154 Wholesale Grocers

Chain Store Guide
3922 Coconut Palm Dr
Tampa, FL 33619-1389

813-627-6700
800-778-9794
FAX 813-627-7094
E-Mail: info@csgis.com
Home Page: www.csgis.com

Mike Jarvis, Publisher
Shami Choon, Manager

We have uncovered the facts on more than 1,900 grocery suppliers in the U.S. and Canada in this database. This targeted database allows you to reach food wholesalers, cooperatives and voluntary group wholesalers, non-sponsoring wholesalers, and cash and carry operators who serve grocery, convenience, discount and drug stores. You will also find information regarding company headquarters, divisions, branches, and over 11,000 key executives and buyers.
Cost: $335.00
Frequency: Annual

24155 Wholesaler

TMB Publishing
1838 Techny Ct
Northbrook, IL 60062-5474

847-564-1127
FAX 847-564-1264
Home Page: www.tmbpublishing.com

Tom M Brown, Owner

Ranks 100 leading wholesalers of plumbing, heating, air conditioning, refrigeration equipment and industrial pipe, valves and fittings.
Cost: $25.00
Frequency: Annual July
Circulation: 30,000

24156 Wholesaler-Wholesaling 100 Issue

TMB Publishing
1838 Techny Ct
Northbrook, IL 60062-5474

847-564-1127
FAX 847-564-1264
Home Page: www.tmbpublishing.com

Tom M Brown, Owner

Offer information on over 100 leading wholesalers of plumbing-heating equipment and supplies.
Cost: $25.00
Circulation: 25,000

Industry Web Sites

24157 http://gold.greyhouse.com

G.O.L.D Grey House OnLine Databases

Grey House Publishing's online database platform, GOLD, offers Quick Search, Keyword Search and Expert Search for most business sectors, including wholesale markets. The GOLD platform makes finding the information you need quick and easy - whether you're a novice searcher or an experienced database user. All of Grey House's directory products are available for subscription on the GOLD platform.

24158 www.aamp.com

American Association of Meat Processors

For small to medium sized meat, poultry and food businesses including: packers, processors, wholesalers, home food service businesses, retailers, deli and catering operators.

24159 www.adbi.org

Associated Beer Distributors of Illinois

The ABDI represents, maintains, and improves the interests of its members who are licensed by the State of Illinois to import and distribute beer to licensed retailers.

24160 www.aednet.org

Associated Equipment Distributors

AED is an international trade association representing companies involved in the distribution, rental and support of equipment used in construction, mining, forestry, power generation, agriculture and industrial applications.

24161 www.aird.org

Association of Ingersoll-Rand Distributors

The Association of Ingersoll-Rand Distributors (AIRD) was organized as a central resource for distributors of Ingersoll-Rand compressed air equipment. AIRD is chartered to promote improved business conditions affecting distributors of air compressors, further a better understanding between distributors and equipment suppliers, research ways to lower costs of distributing air compressors, collect and disseminate statistical information and conduct other beneficial activities.

24162 www.amdweb.com

Association of Millwork Distributors

AMD provides leadership, education, promotion, networking, and advocacy to, and for, the millwork distribution industry.

24163 www.anla.org

American Nursery & Landscape Association

The American Nursery and Landscape Association serves firms who grow, sell or use plants. ANLA advocates the industry's interests before government and provides its members with unique business knowledge essential to long-term growth and profitability.

24164 www.apda.com

Appliance Parts Distributors Association

The APDA is an association of independent businesses that aspire to provide the highest level of quality, service, support and information to its customers and suppliers in order to make its value indispendable to the parts distribution channel.

24165 www.apsp.org

Association of Pool & Spa Professionals

APSP is the world's largest international trade association for the swimming pool, spa, and hot tub industry. It works with regulatory and legislative bodies to ensure that their codes, ordinance, and legislation are written to the safest and most current standards. The association's mission is to ensure consumer safety and enhance the business success of its members.

24166 www.asa.net
American Supply Association
ASA is a not-for-profit national organization serving wholesale distributors and their suppliers in the plumbing, heating, cooling and industrial and mechanical pipe, valves and fittings industries.

24167 www.ascdi.com
Association of Service and Computer Dealers Int'l
The ASCDI is a worldwide, nonprofit organization, made up of companies who provide technology business solutions, technical suppoer, and value added services to the business community.

24168 www.avda.net
American Veterinary Distributors Association
The AVDA was established as the national trade organization for businesses engaged in the distribution of animal health products.

24169 www.awfs.org
Association of Woodworking & Furnishings Suppliers
The Association of Woodworking and Furnishing Suppliers is the largest national trade association in the U.S. representing the interestes of the broad array of companies that supply the home and commercial furnishings industry.

24170 www.awmanet.org
American Wholesale Marketers Association
An organization supporting the confectionery, tobacco and allied products industries through programs and services.

24171 www.bpsa.org
Bicycle Product Suppliers Association
BPSA is an association of suppliers of bicycles, parts, accessories and services who serve the Specialty Bicycle Retailer.

24172 www.bsahome.org
Bearing Specialists Association
BSA is the forum to enhance networking and knowledge sharing to promote the sale of bearings through authorized distributors.

24173 www.cbbd.com
California Beer & Beverage Distributors
The California Beer and Beverage Distributors is a nonprofit trade association representing over 100 beer distributors and brewer/vendor members.

24174 www.ceta.org
Cleaning Equipment Trade Association
CETA is dedicated to increasing the awareness and promotion of industry products, while at the same time recognizing the impact on preserving the environment and the opportunity to do business within it.

24175 www.ctdahome.org
Ceramic Tile Distributors Association
CTDA is an international association of distributors, manufacturers, and allied professionals of ceramic tile and related products.

24176 www.cvsn.org
Commercial Vehicle Solutions Network
The Commercial Vehicle Solutions Network (CVSN) is an association of independent parts

and service aftermarket distributors serving the transportation industry.

24177 www.dhi.org
Door & Hardware Institute
The Door & Hardware Institute (DHI) is the only professional association dedicated to the Architectural Openings Industry. DHI represents the North American openings marketplace as the advocate and primary resource for information, professional development and certification.

24178 www.easa.com
Electrical Apparatus Service Association Inc
The Electrical Apparatus Service Association (EASA) is an international trade organization of over 2,100 electromechanical sales and service firms in 58 countries. EASA provides members with a means of keeping up-to-date on materials, equipment, and state-of-the-art technology.

24179 www.emda.net
Equipment Marketing & Distribution Association
Trade association dedicated to the marketing of specialized agricultural equipment, outdoor power equipment, light industrial equipment, and forestry equipment.

24180 www.fewa.org
Farm Equipment Wholesalers Association
International trade association of wholesale/distributors of agricultural equipment and related products.

24181 www.fmi.org
Food Marketing Institute
FMI conducts programs in public affairs, food safety, research, education and industry relations on behalf of its 1,500 member companies in the United States and around the world.

24182 www.fpda.org
Fluid Power Distributors Association
Membership is composed of distributors and manufacturers of hydraulic and pneumatic equipment.

24183 www.gawda.org
Gases and Welding Distributors Association
GAWDA's mission is to promote the safe operation and economic vitality of distributors of industrial gases and related welding equipment and supplies.

24184 www.gmdc.com
Global Market Development Center
GMDC is the premier non-profit global trade association dedicated to serving General Merchandise and Health Beauty retailers, wholesalers and suppliers. GMDC promotes critical connectivity to grow and expand member companies by uniting members through business building events and opportunities and enriching their thinking through education and training; consumer and business insights; and information resources.

24185 www.gmdc.org
General Merchandise Distributors Council
International trade association representing pharmacy products to the mass market retail industry.

24186 www.gonpta.com
NPTA Alliance
The NPTA Alliance (formerly the National Paper Trade Association, Inc.) is the association for the $60+ billion paper, packaging and supplies distribution industry. The mission of NPTA is to actively support the success of its

members through the delivery of networking, industry data & research, education and advocacy that focuses on the health of the distribution channel.

24187 www.greyhouse.com
Grey House Publishing
Authoritative reference directories for most business sectors including wholesale service markets. Users can search the online databases with varied search criteria allowing for custom searches by product category, geographic area, sales volume, keyword, subject and more. Full Grey House catalog and online ordering also available.

24188 www.hardinet.org
Heating, Airconditioning & Refrigeration Dist.
This association is a trade organization dedicated to advancing the science of wholesale distribution in the HVACR industry.

24189 www.healthcaredistribution.org
Healthcare Distribution Management Association
The Healthcare Distribution Management Association (HDMA) is the national association representing primary, full-service heatlhcare distributors. HDMA and its members are the vital link in the healthcare system, working daily to provide value, remove costs and develop innovative solutions.

24190 www.hida.org
Health Industry Distributors Association
HIDA keeps members current on healthcare reform, government affairs, industry trends and forecasts, provider news, and sales tips.

24191 www.iapd.org
International Association of Plastics Distribution
The International Association of Plastics Distribution is an international trade association comprised of companies engaged in the distribution and manufacturing of plastics materials.

24192 www.icdaonline.com
Industrial Compressor Distributor Association
The main objetives of the ICDA are to promote for its members the highest standards of production, financial and managerial activities; to act as a vehicle for the solution of common industry problems in an effective and efficient manner; and to increase market volume and profits for its members.

24193 www.insulation.org
National Insulation Association
The National Insulation Association (NIA) is a trade association representing the mechanical and specialty insulation industry.

24194 www.irrigation.org
Irrigation Association
The Irrigation Association is the leading membership organization ffor irrigation equipment and system manufacturers, dealers, distributors, designers, consultants, contractors and end users.

24195 www.isapartners.org
Industrial Supply Association
The primary focus of the Industrial Supply Association is to improve the industrial supply channel through its mission-critical activities including: conventions and forums, gathering and dissemination of critical information, and development and implementation of channel performance initiatives.

24196 www.isd.org
International Sealing Distribution Association

The International Sealing Distribution Association (ISD) is a not-for-profit trade association formed to enhance the success of members through information, education, and interaction.

24197 www.issa.com
International Sanitary Supply Association

Manufacturers, distributors, wholesalers, representatives and publishers engaged in the manufacture and/or distribution of cleaning and maintenance products.

24198 www.itpa.com
International Truck Parts Association

The International Truck Parts Association was organized as a not-for-profit association to promote, foster, and improve relationships among sellers and buyers of trucks and truck surplus products and other parties.

24199 www.lumber.org
North American Wholesale Lumber Association

For lumber and building distributors and manufacturers.

24200 www.mdna.org
Machinery Dealers National Association

The Machinery Dealers National Association (MDNA) is an international, nonprofit trade association dedicated to the promotion of the used machinery industry.

24201 www.mdva.org
Michigan Distributors & Vendors Association

The Michigan Distributors and Vendors Association (MDVA) is a non-profit, statewide business association representing two very significant business segments in the grocery and convenience products industry.

24202 www.mheda.org
Material Handling Equipment Distributors Assoc.

The Material Handling Equipment Distributors Association is the only national association dedicated solely to improving the proficiency of the independent material handling equipment distributor.

24203 www.mic.org
Motorcycle Industry Council

The Motorcycle Industry Council (MIC) is a nonprofit, national trade association representing manufacturers and distributors of motorcycles, scooters, motorcycle/ATV parts and accessories and members of allied trades.

24204 www.msbeer.com
Mississippi Malt Beverage Association

The MMBA was established to represent and promote the beer wholesalers and beer industry within Mississippi.

24205 www.msci.org
Metal Service Center Institute (MSCI)

MSCI is the trade association that supports and represents most elements of the metals value chain, including metals producers, distributors, and processors.

24206 www.naaud.com
North American Association of Utility Distributors

NAAUD is comprised of select distributors who specialize in supplying products and supply chain services to the electric utility industry. The purpose of NAAUD is to discuss and

promote the newest ideas and best concepts for the industry.

24207 www.nacd.com
National Association of Chemical Distributors

The National Association of Chemical Distributors (NACD) is an international association of chemial distributor companies that purchase and take title of chemical products from manufacturers.

24208 www.naed.org
National Association of Electrical Distributors

The main goal of the National Association of Electrical Distributors (NAED) is to establish the electrical distributor as an essential force in the electrical industry and the economy.

24209 www.nafcd.org
North American Association of Floor Covering Dist.

The North American Association of Floor Covering Distributors (NAFCD) was organized to foster trade and commerce for those having a business, financial or professional interest as wholesale distributors or manufacturers of floor coverings and allied products.

24210 www.nahsa.org
North American Horticultural Supply Association

The North American Horticultural Supply Association's mission is to strengthen and support the distribution and manufacturing of horticultural products and services.

24211 www.narm.com
National Association of Recording Merchandisers

Represents the retailers and suppliers of recorded entertainment as well as many suppliers of ancillary products.

24212 www.nassd.org
National Association of Sign Supply Distributors

NASSD is a nonprofit trade association for organizations who are engaged in full-line sign supply distribution and who manufacture or supply commercial, neon and electrical sign products.

24213 www.natd.com
N.A. Association of Telecommunications Dealers

The North American Association of Telecommunications Dealers is a nonprofit organization of companies who provide telecom products to the business community and governments around the world. The NATD gives you access to the right kind of information, resources and business leaders, and provides you with unique opportunities to help grow your business.

24214 www.nationalgrocers.org
National Grocers Association

The National Grocers Association is the national trade association representing the retail and wholesale grocers that comprise the independent sector of the food distribution industry.

24215 www.naumd.com
N.A. Association of Uniform Manufacturers & Dist.

An association dedicated to keeping the Uniform & Imagewear Industry strong and healthy.

24216 www.nbmda.org
N.A. Building Material Distribution Association

NBMDA develops and promotes the effectiveness of distribution processes to improve member profitability and growth.

24217 www.nbwa.org
National Beer Wholesalers Association

Research and development, quality control and ingredients.

24218 www.nesda.com
National Electronics Service Dealers Association

Provides educational assistance in electronic training to public schools, compiles statistics, offers certification programs and apprenticeships. Functions as trade association for the electronics service industry.

24219 www.nfraweb.org
National Frozen & Refrigerated Foods Association

NFRA is a non profit trade association comprised of 650 member companies representing all segments of the frozen and refrigerated foods industry. NFRA has been serving the frozen food industry since 1945 and just recently in 2001 began serving the refrigerated foods industry. The mission of NFRA is to promote the sales and consumption of frozen and refrigerated foods through: education, training, research, sales planning and menu development and providing a forum for industry dialogue.

24220 www.npes.org
NPES Association

This association is a trade association of over 400 companies that manufacture and distribute equipment, systems, software, supplies used in printing, publishing and converting.

24221 www.npfda.org
National Poultry & Food Distributors Association

For poultry and food distribution and processing industries. Provides member services, cost cutting benefits and networking opportunities.

24222 www.nssea.org
National School Supply & Equipment Association

The National School Supply and Equipment Association (NSSEA) is the leading trade organization for the educational products marketplace. NSSEA puts the collective experience of the most successful school industry business in the world at your fingertips.

24223 www.nybeer.org
New York State Beer Wholesalers Association

The New York State Beer Wholesalers Association, Inc. represents and protects the legislative and regulators interests of its members in state and local government. Our primary goal is to uphold the three-tier system in order to safeguard the industry's distribution standards.

24224 www.opeesa.com
Outdoor Power Equipment & Engine Service Assoc.

The Outdoor Power Equipment and Engine Service Association (OPEESA) consists of more than 140 distributors and manufacturers of outdoor power equipment and air-cooled gas and diesel engines. Their mission is to assist distributors in achieving outstanding channel performance.

24225 www.opwa.org
Business Solutions Association

The goal of the Business Solutions Association is to provide a forum for the development of strategic and synergistic solutions to enhance the sale and distribution of business related products and services.

24226 www.pac-west.org

Pacific-West Fastener Association

An organization dedicated to the fastener industry.

24227 www.pida.com

Pet Industry Distributors Association

Represents wholesaler-distributors of pet products, providing training and education to members.

24228 www.probeauty.org

Professional Beauty Association

The Professional Beauty Association (PBA) is a nonprofit trade association that represents the interests of the professional beauty industry from manufacturers and distributors to salons and spas. PBA offers business tools, education, advocacy, networking and more to improve individual businesses and the industry as a whole.

24229 www.ptda.org

Power Transmission Distributors Association

Members are power transmission/motion control distributor throughout manufacturing firms.

24230 www.safetycentral.org

Safety Equipment Distributors Association

Represents wholesale-distributors of safety equipment and works to enhance and improve distribution through excellence in communications, training, education and services.

24231 www.shda.org

Security Hardware Distributors Association

The mission of the Security Hardware Distributors Association is to continually improve, through education and services, the proficiency of Security Distributors in order that they are the most effective and efficient conduit to the marketplace.

24232 www.ssia.info

Shoe Service Institute of America

Shop to shop chat room, links and listings of manufacturers and wholesalers plus shoe care tips.

24233 www.tcata.org

Textile Care Allied Trades Association

The Textile Care Allied Trades Association (TCATA) is an international trade association representing manufacturers and distributors of drycleaning and laundry equipment and supplies. It is the only trade association dedicated exclusively to the interests of the allied trades.

24234 www.wasda.com

Water & Sewer Distributors of America

WASDA's mission is to promote the waterworks/wastewater products distribution industry, and to further improve the image and professionalism of WASDA and its member companies.

C

E

H

I

Q

R

T

U

X

Y

Z

A

ABA Trust & Investments
American Bankers Association, 3218

ABA Washington Letter
American Bar Association Government Affairs Office, 15707

ABA Wealth Management & Trust Conference
American Bankers Association, 3286

ABA Young Lawyers Division
American Bar Association, 15577

ABANA International Conferences
Artist-Blacksmith's Association of North America, 2265

ABC Cruise and Ferry Guide
Reed Travel Group, 23321

ABC Guide to International Travel
Reed Travel Group, 23322

ABC Preferred Flight Planner: Europe- Middle East-Africa
ABC Corporate Services/Reed Travel Group, 23243

ABC Today
Associated Builders and Contractors, 4211

ABCs of Retailing
Hobby Industry Association, 13711

ABD: Aviation Buyer's Directory
Air Service Directory, 3000

ABF E-Buzz
American Beekeeping Federation, 10078

ABF Newsletter
American Beekeeping Federation, 9880

ABI/ADPI Joint Annual Meeting
American Butter Institute, 10409

ABI/INFORM
UMI/Data Courier, 17416

ABIA Insurance News
American Bankers Association, 3145

ABL Insider
American Beverage Licensees Association, 9881, 10079

ABMA Annual Meeting
American Boiler Manufacturers Association, 1927, 13643

ABMA Manufacturers Conference
American Boiler Manufacturers Association, 1928, 13644

ABPA Trade Show Fair
Automotive Body Parts Association, 2576

ABS International Directory of Offices
American Bureau of Shipping, 11586

ABS Magazine
American Bonanza Society, 2826

ACA Annual Conference & Expo
Journal of Counseling and Development, 13208

ACA Annual International Convention & Exposition
American Credit Association International, 9050

ACA Annual Meeting & Exhibition
American Crystallographic Association, 7507

ACA International
Association of Credit and Collection Professionals, 5962, 8597

ACAA Annual Meeting
American Coal Ash Association, 18659

ACAP National Training Conference
American Society of Access Professionals, 12298

ACC Craft Show
American Craft Council, 13758

ACC Docket
American Corporate Counsel Association, 15708

ACCA Annual Meetings
Air Conditioning Contractors of America, 8156

ACCA Conference & Indoor Air Expo
Air Conditioning Contractors of America, 1929

ACCA Contractor Excellence
Air Conditioning Contractors of America, 1911

ACCA Insider
Air Conditioning Contractors of America, 1904, 8008

ACCA Membership Directory
Air Conditioning Contractors of America, 8310

ACCP Report
American College of Clinical Pharmacy, 6360

ACE Annual Conference
Air & Waste Management Association, 8157

ACE Coaster Con
American Coaster Enthusiasts, 1619

ACE News
American Coaster Enthusiasts, 1565

ACF National Convention
American Culinary Federation, 10410

ACF National Convention & Trade Show
American Culinary Federation, 10411

ACF Regional Conference
American Culinary Federation, 10412

ACFSA Directory
American Correctional Food Service Affiliates, 10746

ACFSA International Conference
American Correctional Food Service Affiliates, 15481

ACH Marketing Handbook: A Guide for Financial Institutions &
NACHA: The Electronic Payments Association, 3219

ACH Operating Rules & Guidelines
NACHA: Electronic Payments Association, 3220

ACH Operating Rules, Corporate Edition
NACHA: Electronic Payments Association, 3221

ACH Product & Marketing Handbook for Financial Institutions
NACHA: The Electronic Payments Association, 20631

ACH Settlement Guide
NACHA: Electronic Payments Association, 3222

ACI Materials Journal
American Concrete Institute, 22474

ACI Structural Journal
American Concrete Institute, 22475

ACL Conference
Association of Christian Librarians, 16305

ACLA Annual Meeting
American Clinical Laboratory Association, 6460

ACM Monthly
Composite Market Reports, 20297

ACM SIGGRAPH
Association for Computing Machinery, 12507

ACM-SIGGRAPH Computer Graphics Education Directory
Association for Computing Machinery, 5687

ACMP Conference
Academy of Managed Care Pharmacy, 6461

ACOFP Convention & Scientific Seminar
American College of Osteopathic Family Physicians, 13209

ACOG Clinical Review
American College of Obstetricians/Gynecologists, 12933

ACOMmodate
Association for Convention Operations Management, 8469

ACOS Annual Meeting & Expo
American Oil Chemists' Society, 4725

ACOS News
American College of Osteopathic Surgeons, 12934

ACOS Review
American College of Osteopathic Surgeons, 12935

ACP Sentinel
Association of Contingency Planners, 21693

ACR Standard: Assessment, Cleaning & Restoration of HVAC Sys
National Air Duct Cleaners Association, 1912

ACREL News
American College of Real Estate Lawyers, 20977

ACS Annual Conference and Competition
American Cheese Society, 10413

ACS Mid-Atlantic Regional Meeting
American Chemical Society, 4726

ACS Spring & Fall National Meeting & Expos
American Chemical Society, 4727

ACSH Media Update
American Council on Science and Health, 8311

ACSM Annual Spring Conference
American Congress on Surveying and Mapping, 4343

ACSM Bulletin
American Congress on Surveying and Mapping, 4170

ACSM's Health & Fitness Journal
Lippincott Williams & Wilkins, 12986

ACSM/APLS Annual Conference & Technology Exhibition
American Congress on Surveying & Mapping, 4344

ACSP Annual Meeting
Association of Cosmetology Salon Professionals, 3455

ACT Management of Change Conference
American Council for Technology, 5622

ACT Newsletter
Advertising Communications Times, 386

ACTION Magazine
Mobile Air Conditioning Society Worldwide, 2482

ACUA Annual Conference
Association of College and University Auditors, 240

ACUA Midyear Conference
Association of College and University Auditors, 241

ACUI Conference
Association of College Unions International, 1620

ACUIA Annual Conference & One-Day Seminar
Association of Credit Union Internal Auditors, 242

ACUTA Journal of Communications Technology in Higher Educati
ACUTA, 22610

ADA Courier
American Dietetic Association, 12987

ADA News
American Dental Association, 12988

ADA Today
Americans for Democratic Action, 12145

ADAIC News
Ada Information Clearinghouse, 5300

ADAction News and Notes
Americans for Democratic Action, 12146

ADCLIP
National Research Bureau, 17914

ADDvantage
US Professional Tennis Association, 22146

ADMA Annual Meeting
Alaskan Dog Mushers Association, 21979

ADMA International Fall Conference
Aviation Distributors & Manufacturers Association, 2925

ADMERICA!
American Advertising Federation, 466

ADP Annual Convention and Partners Trade Show
Association of Directory Publishers, 20818

ADP Parts Exchange New
ADP Claims Services Group, 14444

ADPI Weekly Newsletter
American Dairy Products Institute, 9882

ADPI/ABI Annual Conference
American Dairy Products Institute, 10414

AEA Annual Convention
American Electrology Association, 3456

AEA Annual Convention & Trade Show
Aircraft Electronics Association, 7085

AEA International Convention & Trade Show
Aircraft Electronic Association, 2926

AEA Journal of Electrology
American Electrology Association, 3439

AEA Monthly News
American Electronics Association, 7012

AEA National Convention
American Emu Association, 10415

AEA Newsletter
American Electrology Association, 3435

AEA Online Directory
American Electrology Association, 3464

AEA by the Bay
American Electronics Association, 7013

AEA's Californica Monday Morning Report
American Electronics Association, 7014

AEC Automation Newsletter
Technology Automation Services, 5301

Affordable Meetings Exposition and Conference
George Little Management, 8522

Africa-Middle East Petroleum Directory
PennWell Directories, 19938

Africana Librarians Council
African Studies Association, 16195

AfterTouch: New Music Discoveries
Music Discovery Network, 19071

Afterimage
Visual Studies Workshop, 20211

Aftermarket Business Magazine
Advanstar Communications, 2485

Ag Ed Network
ARI Network Services, 1198, 10749

Ag Progress Days
College of Agricultural Sciences, 1051
Penn State University Agricultural Sciences, 10432

AgProfessional Magazine
Agricultural Retailers Association, 10083

Agency Sales Magazine
Manufacturers Agents National Association, 17918

Agri Marketing Magazine
Henderson Communications LLC, 824, 10084, 17919

Agri News Farm Show
Agri News, 1052, 10433

Agri Times Northwest
Sterling Ag, 9891

Agri-Marketing Conference
National Agri-Marketing Association, 10434

Agri-Pulse
International Dairy Foods Association, 9892

AgriMarketing Services Guide
Henderson Communications LLC, 1199, 10750

AgriMarketing Weekly
Henderson Communications LLC, 753

AgriSelling Principles and Practices
Henderson Communications LLC, 825, 17920

Agribusiness Fieldman
Western Agricultural Publishing Company, 826, 10085

Agribusiness Fresh Fruit and Business News
Agribusiness Publications, 10086

Agribusiness Worldwide International Buyer's Guide Issue
Keller International Publishing Corporation, 10751

Agrichemical Age
Farm Progress Publishers, 827

Agricultural & Industrial Manufacturers Membership Directory
Agricultural & Industrial Manufacturers Rep Assn, 17648

Agricultural Aviation
National Agricultural Aviation Association, 828, 2832

Agricultural Aviation Convention
National Agricultural Aviation Association, 2935

Agricultural Comm. Excellence in Ag., Natural Resources and
University of Florida, 4930

Agricultural Education National HQ
National FFA Organization, 9448

Agricultural History
The Sheridan Press, 829

Agricultural Law Update
American Agricultural Law Association, 754, 16083

Agricultural Publications Summit
American Agricultural Editors' Association, 16510

Agricultural Research Institute: Membership Directory
Agricultural Research Institute, 1200, 10752

Agricultural Retailers Association Convention and Expo
Agricultural Retailers Association, 1053, 4731, 10435

Agriculture Research Magazine
Agricultural Research Service, 830

Agro-International Trade Fair for Agricultural Machinery & E
Glahe International, 10436

Agronomy Journal
American Society of Agronomy, 8011

Agweek
Grand Forks Herald, 755, 832

Aidex: Asian International Interior Design Exposition
Reed Exhibition Companies, 14613

Air Beat Magazine
Airborne Law Enforcement Association, 15459

Air Cargo Focus
Cargo Network Services Corporation, 11553

Air Cargo Forum and Exposition
The International Air Cargo Association, 2936

Air Cargo Report
Phillips Publishing, 11547

Air CargoWorld & Traffic World
Knight-Ridder Financial, 23131

Air Classics
Challenge Publications, 2833

Air Conditioning Contractors of America Annual Conference
Air Conditioning Contractors of America, 13647

Air Conditioning Heating & Refrigeration Expo Mexico - AHR
Industrial Shows of America, 13648

Air Conditioning, Heating & Refrigeration News
Business News Publishing Company, 13620

Air Conditioning, Heating & Refrigeration News Directory Iss
The Air-Conditioning, Heating & Refrigeration New, 13664

Air Courier Conference of America
Express Delivery & Logistics Association, 22888

Air Force Magazine
Air Force Association, 2834

Air Freight Directory
Air Cargo, 11587

Air Line Pilot
Air Lines Pilot Association International, 2835

Air Line Pilot Magazine
Airline Pilots Association International, 2836

Air Medical Journal
Elsevier, Health Sciences Division, 2837
Mosby, 12994

Air Medical Transport Conference
Association of Air Medical Services, 2937, 2938, 13230

Air Progress
Challenge Publications, 2838

Air Progress - Warbirds International
Challenge Publications, 2839

Air Quality Measurement Methods and Technology
A&WMA, 8176

Air Safety Week
Phillips Publishing, 2774

Air Show Trade Expo International
Dayton International Airport, 2939

Air Traffic Control Association Convention
Air Traffic Control Association, 2940

Air Transport World
Penton Media, 2840

Air Water Pollution Report's Environment Week
Business Publishers, 7899

Air and Space/Smithsonian
National Air and Space Museum, 2841

Air and Waste Management Association Annual Conference and E
Air and Waste Management Association, 8177

Airborne Law Enforcement Annual Conference & Expo
Airborne Law Enforcement Association, 15484

Airbrush Art and Action
Paisano Publishers, 2224

Aircraft Electronics Association Annual Convention & Trade S
Aircraft Electronics Association, 2941

Aircraft Maintenance Technology
Cygnus Business Media, 2842

Aircraft Owners & Pilots Association Expo
Aircraft Owners & Pilots Association, 2942

Aircraft Owners Pilots Association Expo
Aircraft Owners & Pilots Association, 2943

Airline Catering International
International Inflight Food Service Association, 10087

Airline Financial News
PBI Media, 8731
Phillips Business Information, 17796

Airline Handbook
Air Transport Association, 3004

Airline Pilot Careers
Aviation Information Resources, 2843

Airline, Ship & Catering: Onboard Service Buyer's Guide & Di
International Publishing Company of America, 10753, 23132

Airliners
World Transport Press, 2844

Airliners International
World Airline Historical Society, 2944

Airlines Electronic Engineering Committee Conference
Airlines Electronic Engineering Committee, 2945

Airlines Engineering Committee
Aeronautical Radio, 7539

Airport Business
Cygnus Business Media, 2845

Airport Consultants Council News
Airport Consultants Council, 2775

Airport Journal
Airport Journal, 2847

Airport Operations
Flight Safety Foundation, 2776

Airport Systems Action Planning Meeting
ARINC, 2946

Airports
Aviation Week, 2848
CTB/McGraw Hill, 3006

Airports Council International: North America Convention
Airports Council International-North America, 2947, 2948

Airpower
Sentry Books, 2849

Airways
Airways International, 2850

Aixpert
IBM Corporation, 5397

Akron School Design Institute
American Architectural Foundation, 2119

Alaska Broadcasters Association Conference
Alaska Broadcasters Association, 3936

Alaska Fisherman's Journal
Diversified Business Communications, 10088

Alaska Geology Survey News
Alaska Division of Geological Survey, 18605

Alaska Miner
Alaska Miners Association, 18620

Alaska Miners Association Convention
Alaska Miners Association, 18661

Alaska Miners Association Journal
Alaska Miners Association, 18621

Alcoholic Beverage Control Fast: From the State Capitals
Wakeman Walworth, 9893

Alcoholic Beverage Control: From the State Capitals
Wakeman Walworth, 16589

Alcoholic Beverage Executives' Newsletter International
Patricia Kennedy, 9894

Aldus Magazine
Aldus Corporation, 5398

Alert
Defense Credit Union Council, 8915

Algorithmica
Springer Verlag, 5399

Alimentos Balanceados Para Animales
WATT Publishing Company, 833, 10089

All About Beer
Chautauqua Inc, 16604

All Candy Expo
National Confectioners Association, 10437

All Star Conference
Institute of Internal Auditors, 252

American Forest & Paper Association Report
American Forest & Paper Association, 19312

American Forests
American Forests, 16768

American Forests Magazine
American Forests, 16769

American Fraternal Alliance Annual Meeting
American Fraternal Alliance, 14391

American Fruit Grower
Meister Media Worldwide, 838, 10756
Meister Publishing Company, 10095

American Fruit Grower: Source Book Issue
Meister Media Worldwide, 1202

American Funeral Director
Kates-Boylston Publications, 17539

American Gas Magazine
American Gas Association, 19863, 23589

American Gear Manufacturers Association
American Gear Manufacturers Association, 16923

American Guild Associate News Newsletter
American Guild of Music, 19037

American Hardware Manufacturers Association Newsletter
American Hardware Manufacturers Association, 12601

American Hardwood Export Council
American Hardwood Export Council, 16668

American Health Information Management Association National
American Health Information Management Association, 13299

American Heart Association Scientific Sessions
American Heart Association, 13301

American Herb Association Quarterly Newsletter
American Herb Association, 9898

American Hockey Coaches Association Convention
American Hockey Coaches Association, 22264

American Home Sewing & Craft Association Sewing & Craft Show
American Home Sewing and Craft Association, 22806

American Humane Association Annual Meeting and Training Conf
American Humane Association, 20095

American Humane Association Directory
American Humane Association, 20115

American Hunter
National Rifle Association, 22151

American Imago: Studies In Psychoanalysis and Culture
Johns Hopkins University Press, 12997

American Immigration Lawyers Association Trade Show
American Immigration Lawyers Association, 16056

American Indian Library Association
American Library Association, 16198

American Indian Library Association Conference
American Indian Library Assn Univ. of Pittsburgh, 16308

American Industrial Hygiene Association Conference and Expos
American Industrial Hygiene Association, 21714, 21770

American Industrial Hygiene Conference & Exposition (AIHce)
American Industrial Hygiene Association, 13303

American Industrial Hygiene Conference and Exposition
ACGIH, 12303

American Industrial Real Estate
Pacific Financial Center, 20920

American Industrial Real Estate Association Newsletter
American Industrial Real Estate Association, 20983

American Industry
Publications for Industry, 13993

American InkMaker
Cygnus Publishing, 20502

American Institute for Conservation Annual Meeting
Amer Institute for Conservation of Historic Works, 2269

American Institute of Architects Minn. Convention & Products
American Institute of Architects, Minnesota Chap., 2102

American Institute of Baking Technical Bulletin
American Institute of Baking, 9899

American Institute of Building Design Annual Convention
American Institute of Building Design, 2103, 4356

American Institute of Organbuilders Annual Convention
American Institute of Organ Builders, 19140

American Institute of Timber Construction
American Institute of Timber Construction, 16669

American International Toy Fair Official Directory of Showro
Toy Industry Association, 13765, 13799

American Iron and Steel Institute News
American Iron and Steel Institute, 18337

American Journal of Agricultural Economics (AJAE)
American Agricultural Economics Association, 839

American Journal of Clinical Medicine
American Association of Physician Specialists, Inc, 12998

American Journal of Enology and Viticulture
American Society for Enology and Vinticulture, 10096

American Journal of Health-System Pharmacy
American Society of Health-System Pharmacists, 6404

American Journal of Human Genetics
American Society of Human Genetics, 13001

American Journal of Law & Medicine
American Society of Law, Medicine and Ethics, 14319

American Journal of Managed Care
American Medical Publishing, 13003

American Journal of Medical Quality
American College of Medical Quality, 6405

American Journal of Pharmaceutical Education
American Association of Colleges of Pharmacy, 6406

American Journal of Public Health
American Public Health Association, 6407

American Journal of Roetgenology
American Roentgen Ray Society, 13005

American Journal of Transportation
Fleur de Lis Publishing, 23035

American Laboratory
International Scientific Communications, 4656

American Laboratory Buyers Guide
International Scientific Communications, 4762

American Laundry News
Crain Communications Inc, 4873

American Law Reports Library
Lawyers Co-operative Publishing Company, 16087

American Lawyer
American Lawyer Corporation, 15922

American Lawyers Newspapers Group
American Lawyers Newspapers, 15717

American Lawyers Quarterly
American Lawyers Company, 15923

American League of Financial Institutions Annual Conference
America's Community Bankers, 3290

American Libraries
American Library Association, 16280

American Library Association
American Library Association, 16199

American Library Association Annual Conference
American Library Association, 16309, 20819

American Library Association Handbook
American Library Association, 16326

American Library Association Midwinter Meeting
American Library Association, 16310

American Library Directory
Information Today, 16327, 16517

American Lumber Standard Committee
American Lumber Standard Committee, 16670

American Machine Tool Distributors Association
AMTDA, 17498

American Machinist
Penton Media, 18359

American Machinist Buyers' Guide
Penton Media, 17046

American Management Association
American Management Association, 17086

American Marketing Association
American Marketing Association, 17721

American Meat Institute: Newsletter
American Meat Institute, 9900

American Meat Science Association Directory of Members
American Meat Science Association, 1203, 10757

American Medical Directors Association Annual Symposium
American Medical Directors Association, 13305

American Medical Informatics Association Fall Symposium
American Medical Informatics Association, 13306

American Medical News
American Medical Association, 13006

American Medical Student Association Convention
American Medical Student Association, 13307

American Medical Technologists Convention
American Medical Technologists, 13308

American Medical Writers' Association
American Medical Writers' Association, 16460

American Metal Market
Michael G Botta, 18338
Reed Business Information, 18360

American Meteorological Society Annual Meeting
Renewable Natural Resources Foundation, 8179

American Mold Builders Association/AMBA Membership Directory
American Mold Builders Association, 16924, 20360

American Motorcyclist
American Motorcyclist Association, 18895

American Mover
American Movers Conference, 23036

American Music
University of Illinois Press, 19072

American Music Center Directory
American Music Center, 19174

American Music Center Opportunity Update
American Music Center, 19038

American Music Teacher
Music Teachers National Association, 19073

American Music Therapy Conference
National Music Therapy Association, 19141

American Musical Instrument Society Newsletter
AMIS, 19039

American Musicological Society Annual Meeting
American Musicological Society, 19143

American Musicological Society Inc
University of Iowa, 19040

American Nephrology Nurses Association Symposium
Society of Urologic Nurses and Associates, 13310

American Notary
American Society of Notaries, 15718

American Nurse Today
American Nurses Association, 13007

American Nursery & Landscape Association Convention
American Nursery & Landscape Association, 11817, 24086

American Nurseryman
American Nurseryman Publishing Company, 11784

American Occupational Health Conference & Exhibits
Slack, 8180, 13312

American Occupational Therapy Association Annual Conference
American Occupation Therapy Association, 13313

American Oil and Gas Reporter
National Publishers Group, 19864

American Oil and Gas Reporter Directory
Domestic Petroleum Publishers, 19939

American Oil and Gas Reporter: American Drilling Rig Directo
National Publishers Group, 19940

American Oil and Gas Reporter: Directory of Crude Oil Purcha
Domestic Petroleum Publishers, 19941

American Orff-Schulwerk Association National Conference
American Orff-Schulwerk Association, 19144

American Organist
American Guild of Organists, 19074

American Organization of Nurse Executives Meeting and Exposi
American Hospital Association, 13315

American Orthopaedic Society for Sports Medicine Annual Meet
American Orthopaedic Society for Sports Medicine, 22265

American Orthopsychiatric Association
C/o Clemson University, IFNL, 12788

American Orthotic & Prosthetic Association on National Assem
American Orthotic & Prosthetic Association, 13317

American Osteopathic Association Meeting & Exhibits
American Osteopathic Hospital Association, 13318

American Paddler
American Canoe Association, 22152

American Painting Contractor
Douglas Publications, 4212

American Payroll Association Annual Congress
American Payroll Association, 255

American Payroll Association Fall Forum
American Payroll Association, 256

American Peanut Research and Education Society Annual Meetin
American Peanut Research and Education Society, 10450

American Pharmacists Annual Meeting & Expo
American Pharmacists Association, 6468

American Philatelist
American Philatelic Society, 13713

American Physical Therapy Association Annual Conference
American Physical Therapy Association, 13320

American Planning Association
American Planning Association, 12151

American Plastics Council
American Chemistry Council, 20274

American Printer
American Printer, 20503

American Productivity and Quality Center
American Productivity and Quality Center, 17087

American Psychological Association Annual Convention
American Psychological Association, 13324

American Public Communications Council Conference & Expo
American Public Communications Council, 5170

American Public Health Association Annual Exhibition
American Public Health Association, 13325

American Public Human Services Association Public Human Serv
American Public Human Services Association, 12236

American Public Transit Association Membership Directory
American Public Transit Association, 2634, 23134

American Public Transportation Association Expo
American Public Transit Association, 2584

American Public Warehouse Register
Reed Business Information, 23818

American Public Works Association
American Public Works Association, 23590

American Quarter Horse Journal
American Quarter Horse Association, 22153

American Quilt Study Group
American Quilt Study Group, 13692, 13768

American Real Estate Society Annual Meeting
American Real Estate Society, 21087

American Recovery Association Directory
American Recovery Association, 6056

American Recycling Market: Directory/Reference Manual
Recycling Data Management Corporation, 8316

American Red Angus Magazine
Red Angus Association of America, 10097

American Red Angus: Breeders Directory
Red Angus Association of America, 10758

American Resort Development Association: Membership Director
American Resort Development Association, 21105

American Rifleman
National Rifle Association, 22154

American Rodder
Buckaroo Communications, 2487

American Roentgen Ray Society Meeting
American Roentgen Ray Society, 13326

American Rose Magazine
American Rose Society, 11785

American Safe Deposit Association Conference
American Safe Deposit Association, 3291

American Sailor
US Sailing Association, 3634

American School & University
PRIMEDIA Intertec Publication, 2062

American School Band Directors Association Newsletter
American School Band Directors Association, 19041

American School Health's Annual School Health Conference
American School Health Association, 13327

American Scientific Glassblowers Exhibition
American Scientific Glassblowers Society, 11984

American Shipper
Howard Publications, 11555, 23037, 23441

American Shoemaking
Shoe Trades Publishing Company, 21947

American Shortline Railway Guide
Kalmbach Publishing Company, 23135

American Showcase Illustration
Luerzer's Archive Inc, 5187

American Small Businesses Association
American Small Businesses Association, 17088

American Small Farm Magazine
Back 40 Group, 841

American Society Biochemistry and Molecular Biology Expo
American Society of Biochem & Molecular Biology, 4736

American Society Engineers: Design International
Systems and Design Group, 18432

American Society for Aesthetic Plastic Surgery Conference
American Society for Aesthetic Plastic Surgery, 2104, 2270, 13328

American Society for Dermatologic Surgery Annual Meeting
American Society for Dermatologic Surgery, 13332

American Society for Engineering Education Conference and Ex
American Society for Engineering Education, 7540

American Society for Enology and Vinticulture Annual Meeting
American Society for Enology and Vinticulture, 10451

American Society for Environmental History Annual Conference
Society of Environmental Journalists, 8181

American Society for Health Care Human Resources Administrat
American Hospital Association, 13333

American Society for Healthcare Management Convention
Corcoran Expositions, 13334

American Society for Healthcare Risk Management Convention
American Society for Healthcare Risk Management, 14392

American Society for Industrial Security: Annual Membership
American Society for Industrial Security, 21827

American Society for Information Science
ASIS&T, 16200

American Society for Legal History Annual Meeting
American Society for Legal History, 16057

American Society for Quality
American Society for Quality, 17089, 17499

American Society for Surgery of the Hand Annual Meeting
American Society for Surgery of the Hand, 13339

American Society for Therapeutic Radiology and Oncology Annu
American Society for Therapeutic Radiology & Onc., 13340

American Society for Training & Development Conference & Exp
American Society for Training & Development, 19275

American Society for the Advancement of Project Management
American Society for the Advancement of, 17090

American Society of Agricultural Consultants News
American Society of Agricultural Consultants, 9901

American Society of Anesthesiologists Annual Meeting
American Society of Anesthesiologists, 13342

American Society of Appraisers Directory
American Society of Appraisers, 9132, 21106

American Society of Association Executives Annual Meeting &
American Society of Association Executives, 17091, 17388

American Society of CLU and CHFC Annual Conference
American Society of CLU and CHFC, 14393

American Society of Clinical Oncology Annual Convention
J Spargo & Associates, 13343

American Society of Clinical Pathologists and College of Ame
American Society of Clinical Pathologists, 13344

American Society of Comparative Law
University of Baltimore, 15608

American Society of Composers, Authors and Publishers
American Soc. of Composers, Authors & Publishers, 19175

American Society of Consulting Arborists: Membership Directo
American Society of Consulting Arborists, 1204, 10759

American Society of Electroneurodiagnostic Technologists Con
American Society of Electroneurodiagnostic Tech, 13347

American Society of Farm Managers and Rural Appraisers Newsl
Amer. Society of Farm Managers & Rural Appraisers, 20984

American Society of Hand Therapists Convention
Smith, Bucklin and Associates, 13349

American Society of Human Genetics Annual Meeting
American Society of Human Genetics, 13352

American Society of Indexing
American Society for Indexing, 16201

American Society of Interior Designers National Conference
American Society of Interior Designers, 14614

American Society of International Law Newsletter
American Society of International Law, 15719

American Society of Journalists and Authors Directory
ASJA, 15266
American Society of Journalists and Authors, 16461, 16511, 16518

American Society of Mechanical Engineers
American Society of Mechanical Engineers, 16993

American Society of Media Photgraphers Bulletin
Photo District News, 20198

American Society of Mining and Reclamation
American Society of Mining and Reclamation, 7732

American Society of Nephrology
American Society of Nephrology, 13353

American Society of PeriAnesthesia Nurses
American Gastroenterological Association, 13354

American Society of Plumbing Engineers Meeting
American Society of Plumbing Engineers, 7541

American Society of Post Anesthesia Nurses Meeting
Slack, 13355

American Society of Psychoprophylaxis in Obstetrics/Lamaze C
Smith, Bucklin and Associates, 13356

American Society of Safety Engineers Professional Developmen
American Society of Safety Engineers, 7542, 8182, 21773

American Society of Transplant Physicians Scientific Meeting
Slack, 13357

American Society of Transplant Surgeons Annual Meeting
Wright Organization, 13358

American Society of Travel Agents Membership Directory
NACTA, 23326

American Soybean Association Newsletter
American Soybean Association, 9902

American Space Transportation Association
General Dynamics, 22913

American Speaker
Briefings Publishing Group, 8485

American Speech-Language-Hearing Association Annual Conventi
American Speech- Language Hearing Association, 13360

American Spice Trade Association Membership Roster
American Spice Trade Association, 10760

American Sportfishing
American Sportfishing Association, 9361

American Sports Builders Association
American Sports Builders Association, 16671

American Sportscasters Association Insiders Newsletter
American Sportscasters Association, 3839

American Stamp Dealers Association Newsletter
American Stamp Dealers Association, 13707

American Stock Exchange Fact Book
Publications Department, 9133

American Stock Exchange Guide
CCH, 9134

American String Teachers Journal
American String Teachers Association, 19075

American Sugarbeet Growers Asscociation Annual Meeting
American SugarBeet, 10453

American Textile Machinery Association
American Textile Machinery Association, 16926

American Textile Machinery Exhibition International
Textile Hall Corporation, 22807

American Theatre Magazine
Theatre Communications Group, 19477

American Theological Library Association
The American Theological Library Association, 16202

American Tool, Die & Stamping News
Eagle Publications, 13994, 16994, 18361

American Translators Association
American Translators Association, 16462

American Travel Market Exhibition Company
Reed Exhibition Companies, 23298

American Truck Dealers Convention and Equipment Exposition
National Automobile Dealers Association, 23472

American Trucker
PRIMEDIA Intertec-Technology & Transportation, 23434
Primedia, 23038

American Trucking Association Management Conference and Exhi
American Trucking Association, 23473

American University Business Law Review
American University Washington College of Law, 15924

American University International Law Review
American University Washington College of Law, 15925

American University Journal of Gender, Social Policy & the L
American University Washington College of Law, 15926

American University Law Review
American University Washington College of Law, 15927

American Vegetable Grower
Meister Media Worldwide, 842, 10099

American Veterinary Medical Association Annual Convention
American Veterinary Medical Association, 20100

American Viola Society Journal
American Viola Society, 19076

American Viola Society Newsletter
American Viola Society, 19042

American Walnut Manufacturers Association
American Walnut Manufacturers Association, 16672

American Warehouse Association and Canadian Association of W
Association For Logistics Outsourcing, 24132

American Waste Digest
Charles G Moody, 8014

American Water Resources Association Annual Water Resource C
Renewable Natural Resources Foundation, 8183

American Water Resources Conference
American Water Resources Association, 23902

American Water Works Association: Buyers' Guide Issue
American Water Works Association, 23591, 23914

American Welding Show
American Welding Society, 18433

American Wholesale Marketers Association
Ameican Wholesale Marketers Association, 24059

American Wholesale Marketers Association/ Convenience Distri
American Wholesale Marketers Association, 10100

American Wholesalers and Distributors Directory
Gale/Cengage Learning, 24133

American Window Cleaner Magazine
12 Twelve Publishing Corporation, 4874

American Wood Chip Export Association
Stoel Rives, 16673

American Wood Protection Association Newsletter
American Wood Protection Association, 16747

American Writer
American Independent Writers, 16492

American Zinc Association
American Bearing Manufacturers Association, 18240

American-Turkish Council Annual Meeting
Ideea, 14795

AmericanProfile
Donnelley Marketing Information Services, 18018

Americans For Libraries Council
Americans For Libraries Council, 16203

Americans for the Arts Field Directory
Americans for the Arts, 19549

Americas 1st Freedom
National Rifle Association, 22155

Americover
American First Day Cover Society, 13770

Amusement Business
VNU Business Media, 1575

Amusement Expo
American Amusement Machine Association, 1623

Amusement Industry Expo
I-X Center, 1624

Amusement Park Guide
Globe Pequot Press, 22343

Amusement Showcase International: ASI
William T Glasgow Inc, 1625

Amusement Today
Amusement Today, 1576

Amusement and Music Operators Association International Expo
William T Glasgow Inc, 1626

An Energy Efficient Solution
Alliance for Responsible Atmospheric Policy, 4657

Analysis Solutions
ConnectPress, 5400

Analysis of Class I Railroads
Association of American Railroads, 23039

Analysis of Workers' Compensation Laws
Chamber of Commerce of the United States, 17418

Analytical Chemistry
American Chemical Society, 4626

Anchor Line Newsletter
National Safe Boating Council, 3618

Andrews Report
Report Publications, 20985

Angus Beef Bulletin
American Angus Association, 9903

Angus Journal
American Angus Association, 10101

Animal & Dairy News
American Dairy Science Association, 843

Animal Law Report
American Bar Association, 15928

Animals International
World Society for the Protection of Animals, 20050

Animals' Advocate
Animal Legal Defense Fund, 20051

Animation Magazine
Animation Magazine, 12526, 18802

Annals of Biomedical Engineering
Biomedical Engineering Society, 7361

Annals of Emergency Medicine
Elsevier Publishing, 13010

Annals of Opthalmology
Am. Society of Cont. Medicine, Surgery & Opth., 13011

Annals of Pharmacotherapy
Harvey Whitney Books Company, 6362

Annual AFRDS Convention & Trade Show
Association of Fund-Raising Distributors, 11457

Annual Action Taker Series
Retail Advertising & Marketing International, 478

Annual Advertising Conference
Advertising Women of New York, 479

Annual Algae Biomass Summit
Biomass Power Association, 1450

Annual American Occupational Health Conference
American College of Occupational/Environmental Med, 21774

Annual American and Canadian Sport, Travel and Outdoor Show
Expositions, 23299
Expositions, Inc., 3669

Annual Applied Reliability Engineering and Product Assurance
The University of Arizona, 7543

Annual Automated Imaging Associates Business Conference
Appliance Manufacturer, 12557

Annual Boat & Fishing Show at the Lansing Center
Show Span, Inc, 3670

Annual Boat Show
General Sports Shows/NMMA, 3671

Annual Boat Show & Fishing Exposition
Greenband Enterprises, 3672

Annual Boat, Vacation and Outdoor Show
Showtime Productions, 3673, 23300

Annual Business Leadership Summit
Fluid Power Distributors Association, 24087

Annual Campus Energy Conference
International District Energy Association, 13649

Annual Canadian Conference on Intelligent Systems
Robotics Industris Association, 7544

Annual Capital Sport Fishing, Travel and Outdoor Show
International Sport Show Producers Association, 23301

Annual Chicken Marketing Seminar
National Poultry & Food Distributors, 10456

Annual Clinical Assembly of Osteopathic Specialists
American College of Osteopathic Surgeons, 13362

Annual Community Radio Conference
National Federation of Community Broadcasters, 3937

Annual Conference & Educational Symposia
Society of Accredited Marine Surveyors, 3674

Annual Conference Abstracts
Visitor Studies Association, 8471

Annual Conference Proceedings
Air Traffic Control Association, 2777

Beauty Exposition USA
Beauty Expo USA, 5877

Beauty Fashion
Ledes Group, 5829

Beauty Fashion: Body/Bath/Sun Issue
Beauty Fashion, 5830

Beauty Fashion: CTFA Convention Issue
Beauty Fashion, 5831

Beauty Fashion: Cosmetics Issue
Beauty Fashion, 5832

Beauty Fashion: Men's Issue
Beauty Fashion, 5934

Beauty Fashion: Women's Fragrance Issue
Beauty Fashion, 5833

Beauty Fashion: Women's Treatment Issue
Beauty Fashion, 5834

Beauty Forum NAILPRO
Creative Age Publications, 5835

Beauty Inc.
Fairchild Publications, 5836

Beauty Packaging
Rodman Publishing, 5837

Beauty Store Business
Creative Age Publications, 3440, 5838

Beauty Supply Show: West Coast
West Coast Beauty Supply, 5878

BeautyLink
American Association of Cosmetology Schools, 3441

Bed & Breakfast Home Directory: Homes Away from Home, West C
Knighttime Publications, 13903

Bee Culture
AI Root Company, 10115

Beef Sire Directory
American Breeders Service/Customer Service, 10768

Beef Today
Farm Journal Media, 845

Beer Institute
Beer Institute, 9542

Beer Marketer's Insights Newsletter
Beer Marketer's Insights, 9908, 16590

Beer Perspectives
National Beer Wholesalers Association, 9909, 16608, 24060

Beer Statistics News
Beer Marketer's Insights, 9910, 16591

Beer, Wine & Spirits Beverage Retailer
Oxford Publishing, 10116

Beer, Wine & Spirits Industry Trade Show
Indiana Association of Beverage, 10471, 16629

Before & After: How to Design Cool Stuff
Pagelab, 12527

Before Columbus Foundation
The Raymond House, 16467

Behavioral Health Management
MEDQUEST Communications, 13019

Behavioral Research in Accounting
American Accounting Association, 104

Behind the Seams
National Amateur Baseball Federation, 22127

Belt Pulley
Belt Pulley Pub Company, 846

Beltwide Cotton Conference
National Cotton Council of America, 1067, 10472

Benchmark
Manufacturing Jewelers & Suppliers of America, 15015

Benchmarking: A Practitioner's Guide for Becoming & Staying
Quality & Productivity Management Association, 17300

Benefax
SNL Securities, 8738

Benefits Health Care New York Show
Flagg Management, 13391

Benefits Magazine
International Foundation of Employee Benefit Plans, 14322

Benefits Quarterly
Int'l Society of Certified Employee Benfit Special, 14323

Bentley MicroStation Mail
AEC Systems International/Penton Media, 5636

Berkshire Plastics Network
Downtown Pittsfield Office, 20279

Best Bead Show
Crystal Myths, 15053

Best Employers Association
Best Employers Association, 17102

Best Lawyers in America
Woodward/White, 16090

Best Practices Report
Management Roundtable, 17189

Best of the West
Motorcycle Riders Foundation, 18910

Best's Agents Guide to Life Insurance Companies
AM Best Company, 14281

Best's Directory of Recommended Insurance Attorneys and Adju
AM Best Company, 14446

Best's Insurance News & Analysis
AM Best Company, 14447

Best's Insurance Reports
AM Best Company, 14448

Best's Insurance Reports: International Edition
AM Best Company, 14449

Best's Key Rating Guide
AM Best Company, 14450

Best's Market Guide
AM Best Company, 14451

Best's Review
AM Best Company, 14324

BestWeek
AM Best Company, 14325

Beta Phi Mu
University of South Florida, 16218

Better Buys for Business
Progressive Business Publications, 19259

Better Channel
ABCD: The Microcomputer Industry Association, 5406

Better Crops International Magazine
Potash and Phosphate Institute, 847

Better Homes and Gardens
Meredith Corporation, 14576

Better Roads
WMO DannHausen Corporation, 23041

Better Supervision
Economics Press, 17190

Better Work Supervisor
Clement Communications, 17191

Beverage Digest
Beverage Digest, 9911

Beverage Digest Fact Book
Beverage Digest, 10769

Beverage Digest Soft Drink Atlas
Beverage Digest, 10770

Beverage Dynamics
The Beverage Information Group, 10117, 16609

Beverage Industry
Stagnito Communications, 10118

Beverage Journal
Michigan Licensed Beverage Association, 10119, 16610

Beverage Marketing Directory
Beverage Marketing Corporation, 10771, 16636

Beverage Media
Beverage Media Group, 10120

Beverage Network
Beverage Media Group, 16611

Beverage Retailer Magazine
Oxford Publishing, 10122, 16612

Beverage World Periscope
Keller International Publishing Corporation, 9912

Biennial International Conference on Petroleum Geophysics
Society of Exploration Geophysicists, 8191

Big Ideas Newsletter
Newspaper Association of America, 5081

Big Iron Farm Show and Exhibition
Red River Valley Fair Association, 1068, 10473

Big Show Expo
Big Show Expo, 3459

Big and Tall Men's Apparel Needs Show
Specialty Trade Show, 1769

Biker
Paisano Publishers, 18896

Bill Nelson Newsletter
Nelson Newsletter Publishing Corporation, 13708

Billboard Magazine
Prometheus Global Media, 416, 1580, 19078

Billboard Subscriber File
Edith Roman Associates, 19177

Billcast Archive
George Mason University, Public Choice Center, 12351

Binding Edge
Printing Industry of Illinois, 20492

Binding Industries of America
Printing Industry of Illinois, 20475

Bio & Software and Internet Report
Mary Ann Liebert, 6604

Bio-Mineral Times
Allen C Forter & Son, 8016

BioInterface
Surfaces in Biomaterials Foundation, 8192

BioPharm
Advanstar Communications, 6408

BioWorld Financial Watch
BioWorld, 3531

Biochemistry
American Chemical Society, 4627

Biodiesel Investor Conference
Platts, 23109

Biodiesel Magazine
National Biodiesel Board, 1433

Biodynamics
Biodynamic Farming & Gardening Association, 10123

Bioelectromagnetics - Stun Gun Mini Symposium
Bioelectromagnetics Society, 6837

Bioelectromagnetics - U.S. Air Force Workshop
Bioelectromagnetics Society, 6838

Bioelectromagnetics Journal
John Wiley & Sons, 6783

Bioelectromagnetics Society Meeting
Bioelectromagnetics Society, 6839

Bioenergy Fuels & Products Conference & Expo
Biomass Thermal Energy Council, 1454

Biogas News
American Biogas Council, 1403

Biological & Agricultural Index
HW Wilson Company, 1205, 10772

Biomass Power & Thermal
Biomass Thermal Energy Council, 1434

Biomass Thermal DC Summit
Biomass Thermal Energy Council, 1455

Biomedical Instrumentation & Technology
Assoc for the Advancement of Medical Instrumentat, 13021

Biomedical Market Newsletter
Biomedical Market, 12940

Biomedical Safety & Standards
Aspen Publishers, 13022

Biometrics Technology Expo and Consortium Conference
J Spargo & Associates, 3559

Biophysical Society Annual Meeting
Biophysical Society, 3560

Biosis/Thomson Scientific
BIOSIS, 3564

Biosolids Technical Bulletin
Water Environment Federation, 7905

Biotechnology Investment Conference
Massachusetts Biotechnology Council, 3561

Business Show
INPEX, 19276

Business Solutions
Corry Publishing, 19262

Business Technology Association
Buiness Technology Association, 19263
Business Technology Association, 19277

Business Valuation Monitor
Grant Thornton, 106

Business and Education Conference
Int'l Assoc of Plumbing and Mechanical Officials, 20449

Business and Financial News Media
Larriston Communications, 9145

Business and Health
Medical Economics Publishing, 13026

Business and the Environment: A Resource Guide
Island Press, 8317

Business of Herbs
Northwind Farm Publications, 9917, 10130

Business of Pleasure Boats
National Marine Bankers Association, 3619

Business to Business Exposition
Trade Shows West, 8524

Business to Business Gem Trade Show
Gem & Lapidary Wholesalers, 15054

Business-2-Business Marketer
Business Marketing Association, 17807

Business-to-Business Database Marketing Conference
Interlect Events, 6231

Butane-Propane News
Butane-Propane News, 19867

Buyer's Guide and Member Services Directory
Diesel & Gas Turbine Publications, 6899

Buyers Broker Registry
Who's Who in Creative Real Estate, 21107

Buyers Guide to Outdoor Advertising
DoMedia LLC, 547

By Design
American Society of Golf Course Architects, 22167

Byways
National Motorcoach Network, 23248

C

C/C & Users Journal
Miller Freeman Publications, 5313

C/Net News.Com
CNET, 5314

C2M Consulting to Management
Journal of Management Consulting, 17306

C41SR Journal
Defense News, 12240

CADALYST
Advanstar Communications, 5407

CAE Bulletin
Institute of Internal Auditors, 107

CALICO Annual Conference
Computer Assisted Language Instruction Consortium, 5637

CALICO Journal
Texas State University, 5408

CASE Strategies
Cutter Information Corporation, 5409

CBA Marketplace
Association for Christian Retail, 20785

CBQ-Communication Booknotes Quarterly
Lawrence Erlbaum Associates, 22559

CBSA Capsules
Copper and Brass Servicenter Association, 18341

CBT Solutions
SB Communications, 5410

CCA Newsletter
Coastal Conservation Association, 7907

CCFL Semi-Annual Meetings
Conference on Consumer Finance Law, 9063

CCFMA Annual Convention
Conference Caterers & Food Manufacturers Assoc., 9552

CCHEST Newsletter
Council on Certification of Health, Environmental, 7908

CCM Magazine
Salem Publishing, 19079

CCTI Annual Meeting
Composite Can & Tube Institute, 14044

CD-ROM Databases
Worldwide Videotex, 5690

CD-ROM Enduser
Disc Company, 5411

CD-ROM Librarian
Mecklermedia Corporation, 5412, 16285

CD-ROMs in Print
Thomson Gale, 5691

CDA/Wiesenberger Investment Companies Service
CDA Investment, 9146

CDFA Annual Meeting
Council of Development Finance Agencies, 9064

CDMA Education & Trade Show
Chain Drug Marketing Association, 5879

CDVCA Annual Conference
Community Development Venture Capital Alliance, 9065

CE Pro
EH Publishing, 23735

CE Vision Magazine
Consumer Electronics Association, 23736

CEA Annual Convention
Cosmetology Educators of America, 5880

CEA Industry Forum
Consumer Electronics Association (CEA), 7102

CEA Winter Technology & Standards Forum
Consumer Electronics Association (CEA), 7103

CEB Spring Conference
Council on Employee Benefits, 14398

CED Directory of Engineering and Engineering Technology Prog
Mississippi State University, 7630

CEH On-Line
SRI International, 4764

CEIR - Quarterly National Economic Reports
National Association of Certified Valuation, 8924

CEMA Bulletin
Conveyor Equipment Manufacturers Association, 16980

CEMA Communicator
Computer Event Marketing Association, 8473

CEMA Member Directory and Meeting Planner
Computer Event Marketing Association, 8552

CEMC/ENR Directory of Law Firms
Construction Education Management Corporation, 16092

CEO Connection
Association for Healthcare Philanthropy, 11413

CEO Summit
Consumer Electronics Association (CEA), 7104

CEP Bi-Annual Conference
Center for Effective Philanthropy, 11460

CERCLIS Database of Hazardous Waste Sites
Environmental Protection Agency, 4765

CET Magazine
American Society of Certified Engineering, 7365

CF Industrial Reporter
Clayton-Fillmore, 21031

CFA Digest
CFA Institute, 3240

CFA Fish Farming Trade Show
Catfish Farmers of America, 9409

CFA Institute Annual Conference
CFA Institute, 9066

CFA Magazine
CFA Insitute, 3241

CFESA Conference
Commercial Food Equipment Service Association, 10475

CFMA Annual Conference & Exhibition
Construction Financial Management Association, 4364

CFMA Building Profits
Construction Financial Management Association, 179, 8746

CFO: the Magazine for Chief Financial Officers
CFO Publishing Corporation, 17307

CGAA Signals
Central Station Alarm Association, 15443, 21695

CHANCE: New Directions for Statistics and Computing
Springer Verlag, 5413

CHEMEST
Technical Database Services, 4766

CHPA Annual Executive Conference
Consumer Health Care Products Association, 5881, 13393

CHRIE Communique
Int'l Council on Hotel, Restaurant Institute Edu., 21221

CICA International Conference
Captive Insurance Companies Association, 14328

CID Service
US Department of Agriculture, 10780

CIFA Semi-Annual Meetings
Council of Infrastructure Financing Authorities, 9067

CIM Construction Journal
Construction Industries of Massachusetts, 4228

CIM Magazine
Canadian Inst of Mining, Metallurgy & Petroleum, 18622

CIN: Corporation Index System
Office of Applications & Reports Services, 9147

CIPFA Newsletter
National Association of Independent Public Finance, 8747

CIRB Annual Meeting
Crop Insurance Research Bureau, 14399

CISCO
CISCO, 9148

CLA World Computer and Internet Law Congress Conference
Computer Law Association, 5638

CLAIMS/Comprehensive Data Base
IFI/Plenum Data Corporation, 4767

CLE Guidebook
Law Bulletin Publishing Company, 15730

CLEAR Annual Educational Conference
Council on Legislative Enforcement & Regulation, 12305

CLEO/QELS Conference
Optical Society of America, 7105

CMA Newsletter
College Media Advisers, 5085

CMAA Annual Conference
Club Managers Association of America, 22273

CMAA's World Conference on Club Management & Club Business E
Club Managers Association of America, 10476

CMBA World
Commerical Mortgage Securities Association, 8925

CMM International
Romeland house, 20546

CMM International: FLEX Expo
Bruno Blenheim, 21416

CMP Publications Travel File
CMP Publications, 23327

CMS National Conference
College Music Society, 19146

CMS Newsletter
College Music Society, 19048

CMSA Annual Meeting
Commercial Mortgage Securities Association, 9068

CNA
F+W Media, 2237

CNC West
Arnold Publications, 17541

COAI Annual Spring International Convention
Clowns of America International, 1629

COM Conference of Metallurgists
Minerals, Metals & Materials Society, 7106

COM-AND: Computer Audit News & Developments
Management Advisory Services & Publications, 5315

Chain Restaurant Operators Directory
Chain Store Guide, 10785, 21271

Chain Store Age
Lebhar-Friedman, 21364

Chamber Executive
American Chambers of Congress Exec Communications, 5087

Chamber Executive Magazine
American Chamber of Commerce Executives, 17929

Chamber Music America National Conference
Chamber Music America, 19147

Chamber Music Magazine
Chamber Music America, 19081

Champagne Wines Information Bureau
KCSA, 9926, 16593

Champion Magazine
National Association of Criminal Defense Lawyers, 15940

Channel Magazine
Semiconductor Equipment & Materials International, 7039

Channel Partners Conference & Expo
Virgo Publishing LLC, 488

Chapter 11 Update
Federal Managers Association, 15731

Chapter News
American College of Cardiology, 6363

Chapter Weekly
National Association of Tax Professionals, 109

Charitable Trust Directory
Office of the Secretary of State, 11468

Chartered Property Casualty Underwriters Society Fall Semina
Chartered Property Casualty Underwriter Society, 14403

Chartmaker
American Recreation Coalition, 23904

Cheers
Jobson Publishing Corporation, 10138
The Beverage Information Group, 16613

Cheese Market News
Quarne Publishing, 10139

Cheese Market News: Annual
Quarne Publishing, 10786

Cheese Reporter
Cheese Reporter Publishing Company, 9927

Chef
Talcott Communications Corporation, 10140, 21227

Chek-Chart Service Bulletin
Motor Information Systems/Chek-Chart, 2446

Cheklist
BKB Publications, 3160

Chem Show: Chemical Process Industries Exposition
International Exposition Company, 4739

Chem Source USA
Chemical Sources International, 4768

Chem-Distribution
PennWell Publishing Company, 4740

Chem-Safe
PennWell Conferences and Exhibitions, 4741

ChemEcology
Chemical Manufacturers Association, 4628

ChemStewards
Society of Chemical Manufacturers & Affiliates, 7910

ChemWeek Association
ChemWeek, 4629

Chemcyclopedia
American Chemical Society, 4770

Chemical & Engineering News
American Chemical Society, 7366

Chemical Abstracts
American Chemical Society, 4771

Chemical Bond
American Chemical Society, 4630

Chemical Bulletin
American Chemical Society, 4631

Chemical Distributor
National Association of Chemical Distributors, 24061

Chemical Economics Handbook Program
SRI Consulting, 4632

Chemical Engineering
Chemical Week Associates, 4662

Chemical Engineering Progress
American Institute of Chemical Engineers, 4663

Chemical Equipment
Reed Business Information, 4664

Chemical Equipment Literature Review
Reed Business Information, 4665

Chemical Exposure and Human Health
McFarland & Company Publishers, 4772

Chemical Heritage
Chemical Heritage Foundation, 4666

Chemical Industries Newsletter
SRI International, 4633

Chemical Industry Monitoring
Cyrus J Lawrence, 4634

Chemical Intelligencer
Springer Verlag, 4667

Chemical Management Review
Reed Chemical Publications, 4668

Chemical Market Reporter
Schnell Publishing Company, 4669

Chemical Processing
Putman Media, 4670

Chemical Product News
US Dept. of Commerce, Business & Defense Service, 4635

Chemical Regulation Reporter
Bureau of National Affairs, 4636

Chemical Regulations and Guidelines System
Network Management CRC Systems, 4773

Chemical Times & Trends
Allen Press, 4671

Chemical Week: Financial Survey of the 300 Largest Companies
Chemical Week Associates, 4774

Chemical and Engineering News
American Chemical Society, 4637

Chemical and Pharmaceutical Press
C&P Press, 10141

Chemist
American Institute of Chemists, 4672

Chemistry
American Chemical Society, 6410

Chemistry Research in Technology
American Chemical Society, 4673

Chemweek's Business Daily
Chemical Week/Access Intelligence, 4638

Chicago Auto Show
Chicago Automobile Trade Association, 2596

Chicago Men's Collective: Winter
Merchandise Mart Properties Inc, 1770

Chicken Marketing Seminar
National Chicken Council, 10481

Chief Engineer
Chief Engineers Association of Chicagoland, 23593

Chief Executive
Chief Executive Group, 17311

Chief Executive Officers Newsletter
Center for Entreprenuel Management, 17200

Chief Logistics Officer
Penton Media, 23045

Chief Marketer
Penton Media, Inc., 6208

Chief Officers of State Library Agencies Directory
Chief Officers of State Library Agencies, 16223, 16330

Children's Business
Fairchild Publications, 1732

Children's Writer's and Illustrator's Market
Writer's Market, 16522

Chinese Business in America
Caravel, 14806

Chinese Law and Government
ME Sharpe, 15941

Chlor-Alkali Marketwire
Chemical Week/Access Intelligence, 4639

Chlorine Institute Annual Meeting & Trade Show
Chlorine Institute, 4742

Chlorine Institute Newsletter
Chlorine Institute, 4640

Choice
Association of College and Research Libraries, 16287

Choices
Agricultural & Applied Economics Association, 854, 10142

Choices Magazine
American Agricultural Economics Association, 855

Choral Journal
American Choral Directors Association, 19082

Christian Management Association
Christian Management Association, 17109

Christian Retailing
Strang Communications Company, 20786

Christie's International Magazine
Christies Publications, 2238

Christmas Gift & Hobby Show
HSI Show Productions, 13774

Christmas Gift and Hobby Show
HSI Show Productions, 13775

Christmas Tree Lookout
Pacific Northwest Christmas Tree Association, 856

Christmas Trees
Tree Publishers, 857

Chronos
Golden Bell Press, 15027

Church & Synagogue Libraries Journal
Church and Synagogue Library Association, 16264

Church & Synagogue Libraries Newsletter
Church and Synagogue Library Association, 16265

Cineaste
Cineaste Magazine, 18804

Cinefantastique
CFQ Media, 18805

Cinema Journal
University of Texas Press, 18807

CinemaCon
National Association of Theatre Owners, 1631, 19534

Circle of Champions
Premiere Show Group, 5883

CircuiTree
Business News Publishing Company, 5418

Circuits Assembly
Circuit Assembly, 7040

Circuits Assembly: Buyers' Guide Issue
Miller Freeman Publications, 6900

Circulation
Standard Rate & Data Services, 548

Circulation Management
PRIMEDIA Intertec-Marketing & Professional Service, 20787
Primedia, 17930

Circulation Update E-Newsletter
Newspaper Association of America, 5088

Citograph
Western Agricultural Publishing Company, 10143

Citrus & Vegetable Magazine
Vance Publishing, 858, 10144

Citrus & Vegetable Magazine: Farm Equipment Directory Issue
Vance Publishing, 1206, 10787

Citrus Expo
Southeast AgNet Publications/Citrus Industry Mag, 1072

Citrus Industry
Southeast AgNet Publications, 859

City Visitor
Travelhost, 23249

Civic.com
FCW Government Technology Group, 5419

Civil Air Patrol Annual Conference
Civil Air Patrol, 2960

Computer Journal
Las Vegas Computer Journal, 6610
Oxford University Press, 5434

Computer Law Strategist
Leader Publications, 15948

Computer Link Magazine
Millennium Publishing, 5436

Computer Manager
Story Communications, 5437

Computer Modeling and Simulation in Engineering
Sage Science Press, 5326

Computer Music Journal
MIT Press, 6611

Computer Price Guide
Computer Merchants, 5438

Computer Protocols
Worldwide Videotex, 5327

Computer Reseller News
CMP Publications, 5328

Computer Review
Computer Review, 5695

Computer Security Buyers Guide
Computer Security Institute, 21831

Computer Security Conference & Expo
Computer Security Institute, 21784

Computer Security Journal
Computer Security Institute, 5439, 21719

Computer Security, Auditing and Controls (COM-SAC)
Management Advisory Services & Publications, 5440

Computer Service & Repair Magazine
Searle Publishing Company, 6612

Computer Shopper
Segal Company, 5441

Computer Survival Journal
Enterprise Publishing, 5442

Computer Technology Review
West World Productions, 5443

Computer User Magazine
Key Professional Media, 5444

Computer and Communications Buyer
Technology News of America Company, 5329

Computer and Computer Management News and Developments
Management Advisory Services & Publications, 5330

Computer-Aided Engineering
Penton Media, 2072, 4232, 5446, 7044, 7372

Computerized Investing
American Association of Individual Investors, 8930

Computerized Medical Imaging
National Biomedical Research Foundation, 5265

Computers & Security
Elsevier Science, 5331, 21720

Computers & Structures
Elsevier Science, 5332

Computers and Biomedical Research
Academic Press, 5448

Computers for Contractors and A/E/C Systems Fall
AEC Systems International/Penton Media, 2106

Computers in Accounting
Thomson Reuters, 183

Computers in Libraries
Information Today, 5137

Computers in Libraries: Buyer's Guide & Consultants Director
Mecklermedia Corporation, 16331

Computers in the Schools
Taylor & Francis Group LLC, 5449

Computers in the Water Industry: The Computer Conference
American Water Works Association, 23905

Computers, Foodservice and You
Mike Pappas, 5333

Computers, Informatics, Nursing
Lippincott Williams & Wilkins, 13036

Computertalk
Computertalk Associates, 5450

Computerworld
CW Publishing, 5451

Computing Surveys
Association for Computing Machinery, 5452

Computing in Science & Engineering
American Institute of Physics, 5453, 7373

Concession Profession
National Association of Concessoinaires, 10147

Concession Professsion
National Association of Concessionaires, 10148

Concessionworks Newsletter
National Association of Concessionaires, 9931

Conchem Exhibition and Conference
Reed Exhibition Companies, 4743

Concrete InFocus
National Ready Mixed Concrete Association, 4233
Naylor Publications, 22477

Concrete International
American Concrete Institute, 22478

Concrete Masonry Designs
NCMA, 22479

Concrete Openings
Concrete Sawing and Drilling Association, 22471, 22480

Concrete Pipe News
American Concrete Pipe Association, 4178

Concrete Pressure Pipe Digest
American Concrete Pressure Pipe Association, 4234

Concrete Producer
Hanley Wood, 22481

Concrete Pumping Magazine
American Concrete Pumping Association, 4235

Concrete Sawing and Drilling Association
Polycrystalline Products Association, 16937

Conde Nast Traveler Business Extra
Conde Nast, 23250

Condo Management
Papers, 21035

Condo Vacations: the Complete Guide
Lanier Publishing International, 23329

Conexion Newsletter
Association of Hispanic Advertising Agencies, 389

Conference Board Management Briefing - Marketing
Conference Board, 17815

Conference Executive Summaries
Society for Information Management, 8756

Conference of the Brazilian Association for Aerosol Research
American Association for Aerosol Research, 8195

Conference of the Volunteer Committees of Art Museums of Can
Volunteer Committees of Art Museums, 2277

Conference on New Food & Beverage Concepts Innovators
NorthStar Conferences, 10483

Conference on the Applications of Air Pollution Meteorology
A&WMA, 8196

Confined Space Entry Video and Manual
Shipbuilders Council of America, 3717

Confrontation
CW Post Campus English Department, 19485

Congregational Libraries Today
Church and Synagogue Library Association, 16288

Congress Legislative Directory
American Gas Association, 19945

Congress at Your Fingertips: Congressional Directory
Capitol Advantage, 12362

Congress of Cities & Exposition
National League of Cities, 12307

Congress on Invitro Biology
Society for Invitro Biology, 13398

Congress on Research in Dance
SUNY College of Brockport, 19380

Congressional Digest
Congressional Digest Corporation, 12244

Congressional Staff Directory
Leadership Directories, Inc., 12363

Connect
Media-Mark, 17931

Connect Magazine
American Zoo and Aquarium Association, 9381

Connected
Association of Millwork Distributors, 16751

Connecting to the Grid
Interstate Renewable Energy Council, 1409

Connections
Foundation Center, 11417
National Public Employer Labor Relations Assoc, 12161
Women's Council of Realtors, 21036

Connector
Society of Broadcast Engineers, 1569

Conservation Commission News
New Hampshire Association of Conservation Comm., 7914

Conservation Directory
National Wildlife Federation, 8320

Conservation Education Association
Department of Conservation, 7754

Conservatree Greenline
Greenline Publications, 19313

Consortium of Hospitality Research Information Services
Quanta Press, 13866

Constitution and Membership Roster
National Association of Agricultural Fair Agencies, 8553

Construction Claims Monthly
Business Publishers, 15740

Construction Company Strategist
Brownstone Publishers, 4179

Construction Contractor
Federal Publications, 4180

Construction Dimensions
Association of the Wall and Ceiling Industry, 4237

Construction Distribution
Cygnus Business Media, 4238

Construction Equipment Distribution
Associated Equipment Distributors, 4239

Construction Equipment Monthly
Heartland Communications, 4181

Construction Equipment Operation and Maintenance
Construction Publications, 4240

Construction Equipment: Construction Giants Issue
Reed Business Information, 4425

Construction Executive
Associated Builders and Contractors, 4241

Construction Industry International
Quarto International, 4242

Construction Labor Report
Bureau of National Affairs, 4182

Construction Litigation Reporter
McGraw Hill, 15741

Construction News West
McGraw Hill, 4243

Construction Planning & Scheduling Manual
National Insulation Association, 4426

Construction Specifier: Member Directory Issue
Construction Specifications Institute, 4427

Constructioneer
Associated Construction Publication, 4245

Constructor Magazine
Associated General Contractors of America, 4246

Constructor Newsletter
Associated General Contractors of America, 4183

Constructor: AGC Directory of Membership and Services Issue
Associated General Contractors of America, 4428

Consultant Pharmacist
American Society of Consultant Pharmacists, 13037

Consulting Electrical Engineers(CEE) Technical Forum & Table
Electric Association, 6842

Consulting Magazine
Kennedy Information, 17315

Cosecha Mensual
National Center for Appropriate Technology, 7916

Cosmetic Personal Care Packaging
O&B Communications, 11558

Cosmetic Science Symposium & Expo
Personal Care Products Council, 5884

Cosmetic Surgery Times
Advanstar Communications, 13043

Cosmetic World
Ledes Group, 3442, 5840

Cosmetics & Toiletries
Allured Publishing Corporation, 5841

Cosmetics & Toiletries: Cosmetic Bench Reference
Allured Publishing Corporation, 5937

Cosmetics & Toiletries: Who's Who in R&D Directory Issue
Allured Publishing Corporation, 5938

Cosmoprof North America
Professional Beauty Association, 5885

Cost Control News
Siefer Consultants, 8759

Cost Controller
Siefer Consultants, 17206

Cost Engineering Journal
AACE International, 7377, 8936, 17320

Cost Engineers Notebook
AACE International, 9153

Cost Management Update
Institute of Management Accountants, 8937

Cost Reengineering Report
National Health Information, 13044

Costume Designers Guild Directory
Costumer Designers Guild, 19552

Costume Jewelry Review
Retail Reporting Bureau, 15016

Costume! Business
Gift Basket Review, 1734

Cotton & Quail Antique Gazette
F+W Media, 2208

Cotton Farming
One Grower Publishing, 860, 10152

Council for Agricultural Science and Technology Newsletter
Council For Agricultural Science and Technology, 763

Council of Real Estate Brokerage Managers
Country Radio Broadcaster's Inc, 20933

Council of State Housing Agencies
Hall of States, 12066

Council on Foundations Annual Conference
Council on Foundations, 11461

Council on Library and Information Resources
Council on Library and Information Resources, 16227

Council on National Literatures
Council on National Literatures, 16471

Council on Tall Buildings & Urban Habitat Congress
Lehigh University, 2107

Council on Tall Buildings and Urban Habitat
SR Crown Hall, Illinois Institute of Technology, 2013

Council on Women in Energy and Environmental Leadership News
Association of Energy Engineers, 1410, 7917

Councilor
Safety & Health Council of Northern New England, 21696

Counselor
Advertising Specialty Institute, 390, 420

Counterman
Babcox Publications, 2509

Country Dance and Song Society News
Country Dance and Song Society, 19462

Country Finance
Economist Intelligence Unit, 14737

Country Folks
Lee Publications, 764, 10153

Country Forecasts
Economist Intelligence Unit, 14738

Country Home Product Guide
Meredith Corporation, 14577

Country Inns and Back Roads, North America
HarperCollins, 13907

Country Living
Arens Corporation, 10154
Arens Publications, 861

Country Monitor
Economist Intelligence Unit, 14739

Country Radio Seminar
Country Radio Broadcasters, 19149

Country Reports
Economist Intelligence Unit, 14740

Country Risk Service
Economist Intelligence Unit, 14741

Country Weekly Magazine
American Media Inc, 19086

Country Woman
Reiman Publications, 862, 10155

Country World Newspaper
Echo Publishing Company, 765, 9932

Countryside and Small Stock Journal
Countryside Publications, 863

County Agents
National Association of County Agricultural Agents, 864

Courier
National Tour Association, 23254

Courier Times
Courier Times, 11559

Court Review
American Judges Association, 12250, 15951

Couture International Jeweler
Miller Freeman Publications, 15029

Covering Credit Newsletter
Covering Credit, 6010

Coverings: The Ultimate Tile & Stone Experience
NTP, Coverings Show Management, 4367

Craft Brewers Conference and Brew Expo America
Brewers Association, 10485, 16630

Craft and Needlework Age
F+W Media, 2239

Craftrends
Primedia Enthusiast Group Publishing, 13722

Crafts Magazine
Primedia Enthusiast Group Publishing, 13723

Crafts Report
Crafts Reports Publishing, 13724

Craftsmen's Christmas Classic Arts and Crafts Festival
Gilmore Enterprises, 2279

Craftsmen's Classic Arts and Crafts Festival
Gilmore Enterprises, 2280

Crain's New York Business
Crain Communications, 17321

Cranberries Magazine
Cranberries Magazine, 865

Crane & Hoist Canada
Capamara Communications, 13999

Creative Industry Director
Black Book Inc, 551

Creative Knitting
House of White Birches, 13725

Creative Marketing Newsletter
Association of Retail Marketing Services, 17816, 24035

Creative Selling
Bentley-Hall, 17817

Creativity
Ad Age Group/Division of Crain Communications, 421

Credit
American Financial Services Association, 6061

Credit & Financial Management Review
Credit Research Foundation, 6031

Credit Card Management
Thomson Financial Publishing, 3165, 6032, 8938

Credit Card and Check Fraud: A Stop-Loss Manual
Fraud & Theft Information Bureau, 6062

Credit Collections News
SourceMedia, 8760

Credit Decisioning Study
Credit Research Foundation, 9154

Credit Professional
Credit Professionals International, 6033

Credit Scoring
Credit Research Foundation, 8939

Credit Union Cooperatives
Callahan & Associates, 6063

Credit Union Directory
National Credit Union Administration, 6064

Credit Union Executive Journal
Credit Union National Association, 8940

Credit Union Executives Expo
Credit Union Executives Society, 9072

Credit Union Financial Yearbook
Callahan & Associates, 6065

Credit Union Journal
SourceMedia, 3166, 8761
Thomson Media, 3248

Credit Union Magazine
Credit Union National Association, 6034, 8941

Credit Union Management
Credit Union Executives Society, 8762

Credit Union Management Magazine
Credit Union Executives Society, 3249

Credit Union National Association Governmental Affairs Confe
Credit Union National Association, 6039

Credit Union News Watch
Credit Union National Association, 6011

Credit Union Report
Callahan & Associates, 6012

Credit Union Technology
Credit Union Technology, 8942

Credit and Collection Manager's Letter
Bureau of Business Practice, 8763

Credit and Collection Survey
Broadcast Cable Credit Association, 8943

Crime & Delinquency
Sage Publications, 15464

Crime in America's Top-Rated Cities
Grey House Publishing, 21112

Criminal Justice
American Bar Association, 15952

Criminal Justice Information Exchange Directory
US National Criminal Justice Reference Service, 16096

Criminal Justice Newsletter
Pace Publications, 15446

Criminal Justice Periodical Index
University Microfilms International, 16097

Criminal Law Reporter
Bureau of National Affairs, 15748

Critical Reviews in Food and Nutrition
CRC Press, 10156

Critical Strategies: Psychotherapy in Managed Care
Bill Cohen, 13046

Critique
Neumeier Design Team, 12532

Crittenden Excess & Surplus Insider
Crittenden Publishing, 14333

Crittenden Insurance Markets Newsletter
Crittenden Publishing, 14283

Crittenden's Real Estate Buyers Directory
Crittenden Research, 21113

Crittendon Directory of Real Estate Financing
Crittendon Research, 21114

Crop Insurance Today
National Crop Insurance Services, 866

Crop Life America & RISE Spring Conference
Crop Life America, 10486

Crop Protection Reference
C&P Press, 10798
Vance Communications Corporation, 1209

Design Firm Management & Administration Report
Institute of Management and Administration, 2048

Design Issues
MIT Press, 2075

Design Journal
Journal Communications Group, 2076

Design Lines
American Institute of Building Design, 4257

Design News
Reed Business Information, 7379, 17549

Design Part Show
Job Shop Company, 7557

Design Solutions Magazine
Architectural Woodwork Institute, 2077, 4258, 14579, 16773

Design-Build Project Delivery (ACEC)
American Council of Engineering Companies, 7634

Design/Build Business
Cygnus Publishing, 2078

Designer
HDC Publications, 11677

Designers West
Designers World Corporation, 14580

Designfax
NP Communications, LLC, 5469

Designing with Tile and Stone
Tile & Stone, 14581

Designline
American Institute of Building Design, 2049

Deskbook Encyclopedia of Employment Law
Data Research, 16099

Deskbook Encyclopedia of Public Employment Law
Data Research, 16100

Desktop Engineering
Helmers Publishing, 5470

Desktop Publishers Journal
Desktop Publishing Institute, 12533

Desktop Video Communications
BCR Enterprises, 6617

Destination KC
Show-Me Publishing, 17324

Destinations
American Bus Association, 2511, 23051, 23257

Destinations Showcase
Intl. Association of Convention/Visitors Bureaus, 23304

Detwiler's Directory of Health and Medical Resources
Information Today, 13494

Developing Successful New Products for Foodservice Markets
International Food Service Manufacturers, 10801

Development
National Assn of Industrial & Office Properties, 21040

Development and Alumni Relations Report
LRP Publications, 11421

Developments
American Resort Development Association, 21041

Developments Magazine
American Resort Development Association, 13868

Diabetes Digest Family
Drug Store News Consumer Health Publications, 13057

Diabetes Educator
American Association of Diabetes Educators, 13058

Diagnostic Imaging
Miller Freeman Publications, 13060

Diagnostic Imaging America Latina
Miller Freeman Publications, 13061

Diagnostic Imaging Asia Pacific
Miller Freeman Publications, 13062

Diagnostic Imaging Europe
Miller Freeman Publications, 13063

Diagnostic Testing & Technology Report
Institute of Management and Administration, 12943

Diagnostics Intelligence
CTB International Publishing, 6369

Dialysis and Transplantation
Creative Age Publications, 13064

Diamond Insight
Tryon Mercantile, 15017

Diamond Peacock Club Kebadjian Brothers
Kebadjian Brothers, 14982

Diamond Registry Bulletin
Diamond Registry, 15018

Diamond Report
Rapaport Diamond Corporation, 15091

Diapason
Scranton Gillette Communications, 19088

Dick Davis Digest
Dick Davis Publishing, 9161

Dickens Christmas Show & Festival
Leisure Time Unlimited, 14615

Dictionary of International Trade
World Trade Press, 14812

Die Casting Engineer Magazine
North American Die Casting Association, 18370

Die Casting Management
C-K Publishing, 18371

Diesel & Gas Turbine Worldwide
Diesel & Gas Turbine Publications, 6786, 23595

Diesel Equipment Superintendent
Business Journals, 23443

Diesel Progress: International Edition
Diesel & Gas Turbine Publications, 6902, 23596

Diesel Progress: North American Edition
Diesel & Gas Turbine Publications, 2512, 6903, 16998, 19870

Dietitian's Edge
Rodman Publishing, 10163

Digest
American Bus Association, 23052

Digest for Corporate & Securities Lawyers
Bowne & Company, 3170

Digest of Environmental Law
Strafford Publications, 15751

Digest of Polymer Developments
STR-Specialized Technology Resources, 20314

Digestive Disease Week Meeting & Exhibition
American Gastroenterological Association, 13400

Digital Book Printing Forum
Interquest Ltd., 20826

Digital Content Producer
Prism Business Media, 23738

Digital Directions Report
Computer Economics, 5340

Digital Graphics
National Business Media, 20507

Digital Image Review
Buyers Laboratory, 19253

Digital Imaging
Cygnus Publishing, 12534

Digital Information Network
Buyers Laboratory, 19264

Digital Magic
PennWell Publishing Company, 5138

Digital Output
Rockport Custom Publishing, 20508

Digital Subscriber Line Access Multiplexer Upstarts
Probe Research, 17826

Digital TV/Television Broadcast
United Entertainment Media, 3906

Digital Television
Kagan World Media, 3858

Digital Travel
Jupiter Communications Company, 6618, 23258

Digital Traveler
International Ecotourism Society, 7919

Dimension & Wood Components Buyer's Guide
Miller Publishing Corporation, 16847

Dimension Stone Design Manual
Marble Institute of America, 22498

Dimension Stones of the World: Book of Color Plates
Marble Institute of America, 22499

Dimensions
National Catholic Development Conference, 11422

Dinner Theatre: A Survey and Directory
Greenwood Publishing Group, 1660

Direct
Chief Marketer, 6211
Primedia, 17325, 17939

Direct Connection
Nat'l Council of Architectural Registration Boards, 2050

Direct Deposit Authorization Forms
NACHA: Electronic Payments Association, 3171

Direct Hit
Midwest Direct Marketing Association, 392

Direct Mail Service
Information Resource Group, 6254

Direct Marketing Conference National Conference
DMB Miami, 17991

Direct Marketing Institute
Direct Marketing Association, 492

Direct Marketing Marketplace
National Register Publishing, 18027

Direct Marketing News
Haymarket Media, Inc., 6212

Direct Response
Direct Marketing Center, 6183

Direct Selling Association International Bulletin
World Federation of Direct Selling Associations, 6184

Direct Selling World Directory
World Federation of Direct Selling Association, 6255

Direct-to-Direct Marketing Association Council for Hispanic
Direct Marketing Association, 6167

Direction
American Moving and Storage Association, 23053
Direct Marketing Consultants, 6185

Directions: Looking Ahead in Healthcare
Health Resources Publishing, 12944

Director
NFDA Publications, 17326
National Funeral Director Association, 13065

Directories in Print
Gale/Cengage Learning, 20857

Directors & Trustees Digest
American Bankers Association, 3172

Directors Guild of America Directory of Members
Directors Guild of America, 18845

Directorship
Directorship Search Group, 17212

Directory & Products Guide
Vineyard & Winery Services, 10802, 16639

Directory International Suppliers/Printing Publishing/Conver
Association for Suppliers of Printing, Publishing, 20561

Directory Iron and Steel Plants
Association for Iron & Steel Technology, 18458

Directory Marketplace
Todd Publications, 18028

Directory and Buyer's Guide of the Door and Hardware Institu
Door and Hardware Institute, 12632

Directory for Pediatric Disorders - Online Database
Grey House Publishing, 13495

Directory for People with Chronic Illness - Online Database
Grey House Publishing, 13496

Directory for People with Disabilities - Online Database
Grey House Publishing, 13497

Directory for Small-Scale Agriculture
US Department of Agriculture, 1210

Directory of 2,500 Active Real Estate Lenders
International Wealth Success, 21116

Directory of AFFI Member Companies
American Frozen Food Institute, 10803

Directory of Accredited Engineering & Technology Certificati
Council of Engineer and Scientific Specialty Board, 7635

Directory of Accredited Real Property Appraisers
American Society of Appraisers, 21117

Directory of Active Sportswear
Sutton Family Communications & Publishing Company, 1852

Directory of Actuarial Memberships
Society of Actuaries, 296

Directory of African American Design Firms
San Francisco Redevelopment Agency, 14649

Directory of Alternative Investment Programs
Asset Alternatives, 9162

Directory of American Agriculture
Agricultural Resources & Communications, 1211, 10804

Directory of Animal Care and Control Agencies
American Humane Association, 20116

Directory of Apparel Specialty Stores
AKTRIN Textile Information Center, 1853

Directory of Architectural and Construction Information Reso
Grey House Publishing, 4429

Directory of Bar Associations
American Bar Association, 16101

Directory of Building Codes & Regulations
National Conference of States on Building Codes, 4430

Directory of Bulk Liquid Terminal and Storage Facilities
ITLA, 23820
Independent Liquid Terminals Association, 4777

Directory of Business Information Resources
Grey House Publishing, 17428

Directory of Buyout Financing Sources
Securities Data Publishing, 9163

Directory of Certified Applied Air-Conditioning Products
Air-Conditioning & Refrigeration Institute, 13666

Directory of Certified Business Counselors
Institute of Certified Business Counselors, 16102

Directory of Certified Performance (Online)
Air Conditioning & Refrigeration Institute, 1955

Directory of Certified Unitary Air-Conditioners & Heat Pumps
Air-Conditioning & Refrigeration Institute, 13667

Directory of Chemical Producers: Western Europe
SRI Consulting/IHS Global, 4778, 4779, 4780

Directory of Communications Professionals
National Assn of Regulatory Utility Commissioners, 22700

Directory of Computer and High Technology Grants
Research Grant Guides, 5700

Directory of Contract Packagers and their Facilities
Institute of Packaging Professionals, 11591

Directory of Convenience Stores
Trade Dimensions, 10805, 21438

Directory of Corporate Buyers
Crain Communications Inc, 14458

Directory of Corrugated Plants
Fibre Box Association, 11592, 19342

Directory of Courthouses, Abstract and Title Companies of th
Harbors International, 16103

Directory of Custom Chemical Manufacturers
Delphi Marketing Services, 4781

Directory of Custom Compounders
Delphi Marketing Services, 20457

Directory of Custom Food Processors and Formulators
Delphi Marketing Services, 10806

Directory of Defense Credit Union
Defense Credit Union Council, 9164

Directory of Electric Power Producers and Distributors
McGraw Hill, 23644

Directory of Electric Utility Company Libraries in the Unite
Library Services Committee/Edison Electric Inst, 23645

Directory of Electrical Wholesale Distributors
Penton, 6904

Directory of Employee Assistance Program Providers
Crain Communications Inc, 14459

Directory of Energy Professionals
Assn of Regulatory Utility Commissioners, 23646

Directory of Engineering Document Sources
Global Engineering Documents, 7636

Directory of Engineers in Private Practice
National Society of Professional Engineers, 7637

Directory of Environmental Websites: Online Micro Edition
US Environmental Directories, 8322

Directory of Executive Recruiters
Kennedy Information, 17429

Directory of Field Contacts for the Coordination of the Use
Federal Communications Commission, 3973

Directory of Franchising Organizations
Pilot Books, 18029

Directory of Free Stock Photography
Infosource Publishing, 20250

Directory of Freight Forwarders and Custom House Brokers
International Wealth Success, 11593

Directory of Health Care Group Purchasing Organizations - On
Grey House Publishing, 13498, 13499

Directory of High Discount Merchandise Sources
B Klein Publishers, 21439

Directory of Historic American Theatres
Greenwood Publishing Group, 1661

Directory of Hosiery Manufacturers
Hosiery Association, 1854

Directory of Hospital Personnel - Online Database
Grey House Publishing, 6502, 6503, 13500, 13501

Directory of Hotel & Lodging Companies
American Hotel & Lodging Association, 13908

Directory of International Periodicals & Newsletters on Buil
Division of Mineral Resources, 8323

Directory of Law Enforcement and Criminal
Law Enforcement Standards Office, 15502

Directory of Law-Related CD-ROMs
Infosource Publishing, 16104

Directory of Lawyer Disciplinary Agencies & Lawyers' Funds/C
Center for Professional Responsibility, 16105

Directory of Lawyer Referral Services
American Bar Association, 16106

Directory of Legal Aid & Defender Offices in the United Stat
National Legal Aid and Defender Association, 16107

Directory of Library Automation Software, Systems and Servic
Information Today, 5701

Directory of Listed Plumbing Products
Int'l Assn of Plumbing & Mechanical Officials, 20438, 20450, 20458

Directory of Literary Magazines
Council of Literary Magazines and Presses, 16525

Directory of MA and PhD Programs in Art and Art History
College Art Association, 2300

Directory of Machine Tools and Manufacturing
Association for Manufacturing Technology, 17049

Directory of Mail Drop Addresses and Zip Codes
Fraud & Theft Information Bureau, 21832

Directory of Mail Order Catalogs - Online Database
Grey House Publishing, 1855, 1856, 6256, 6257, 18030, 18031, 19281, 19282, 21440, 21441, 21950, 21951

Directory of Major Mailers
North American Publishing Company, 6258

Directory of Management Consultants
Kennedy Information, 17430

Directory of Management Information Systems Faculty
Management Information Systems Research Center, 17431

Directory of Manufacturer Representatives Service Suppliers
Hobby Industry Association, 13809

Directory of Manufacturers' Sales
Manufacturers' Agents National Association, 9165

Directory of Manufacturing Research Centers
Manufacturing Technology Information, 17649

Directory of Mass Merchandisers
Trade Dimensions, 21443

Directory of Mastercard and Visa Credit Cards
Todd Publications, 9166

Directory of Minority and Women-Owned Investment Bankers
San Francisco Redevelopment Agency, 3353

Directory of Mutual Funds
Investment Company Institute, 9167

Directory of Opportunities in International Law
John Bassett Moore Society of International Law, 16108

Directory of Outplacement & Career Management Firms
Kennedy Information, 17432

Directory of Packaging Consultants
Institute of Packaging Professionals, 11594

Directory of Poetry Publishers
Dustbooks, 16526, 20858

Directory of Private Bar Involvement Programs
American Bar Association, 16109

Directory of Professional Appraisal Services
American Society of Appraisers, 21118

Directory of Property Loss Control Consultants
Crain Communications, 14460

Directory of Public Interest Law Centers
Alliance for Justice, 16110

Directory of Publicly Owned Natural Gas Systems
American Public Gas Association, 23647

Directory of Real Estate Development and Related Education P
Urban Land Institute, 21119

Directory of Religious Media
National Religious Broadcasters, 3974

Directory of Research Grants
Greenwood Publishing Group, 11470

Directory of Selected News Sources Issue
American Journalism Review, 15272

Directory of Shippers
Transportation Technical Services, 23141

Directory of Simulation Software
Society for Modeling and Simulation International, 5702

Directory of Small Magazines Press Magazine Editors & Publis
Dustbooks, 16527, 20859

Directory of Special Libraries and Information Centers
Gale Research, 16333

Directory of Specialty Markets Issue
Insurance Journal, 14461

Directory of State Court Clerks & County Courthouses
WANT Publishing Company, 16111

Directory of State Departments of Agriculture
US Department of Agriculture, 10807

Directory of Suppliers of Services
Independent Liquid Terminals Association, 4782

Directory of Theatre Training Programs
Theatre Directories, 19557

Directory of Top Computer Executives
Applied Computer Research, 5341, 5703

Directory of Transportation Professionals
National Assn of Regulatory Utility Commissioners, 23142

Directory of Truck Dealers
Transportation Technical Services, 23143

Directory of US Exporters
Journal of Commerce, 14813

Directory of US Flexographic Packaging Sources
JPC Directories, 11595

Directory of US Government Software for Mainframes and Micro
US National Technical Information Service, 5704

Directory of US Government: Depository Libraries
Joint Committee on Printing, US Congress, 16334

Electromagnetic News Report
Seven Mountains Scientific, 7054

Electronic Advertising Marketplace Report
Simba Information, 7018

Electronic Business
Reed Business Information, 7055

Electronic Buyers News: Specialized and Local/Regional Direc
CMP Publications, 7155

Electronic Buyers News: Top 50 Distributors Issue
CMP Publications, 7156

Electronic Chemicals News
Chemical Week Associates, 4644

Electronic Commerce Advisor
Thomson Reuters, 6137, 6622

Electronic Commerce News
Phillips Publishing, 6575

Electronic Components
Global Sources, 7056

Electronic Design
Penton Media, 5478, 6801, 7057

Electronic Distribution Directory
Electronic Distribution Show Corporation, 7157

Electronic Distribution Show and Conference
Electronic Distribution Show Corporation, 7116

Electronic Education Report
Simba Information, 5347, 7019

Electronic Imaging East
Miller Freeman Publications, 7117

Electronic Imaging Report
Phillips Publishing, 7020

Electronic Imaging West
Miller Freeman Publications, 7118

Electronic Imaging an Image Processing: An Assessment of Tec
Richard K Mill & Associates, 5705

Electronic Industries Association: Trade Directory and Membe
Electronic Industries Alliance, 7158

Electronic Information Report
Simba Information, 7021

Electronic Mail & Messaging Systems
Business Research Publications, 6623

Electronic Marketing News
Software Assistance International, 5348

Electronic Materials & Process Handbook
International Microelectronics & Electronics, 7159

Electronic Materials Conference
Minerals, Metals & Materials Society, 7119

Electronic Materials Technology News
Business Communications Company, 7022

Electronic Materials and Applications
American Ceramic Society, 11988

Electronic Musician
PRIMEDIA, 19091

Electronic Packaging & Production
Reed Business Information, 7058, 11560

Electronic Payments Journal
NACHA: Electronic Payments Association, 3251

Electronic Payments Review and Buyer's Guide
NACHA: Electronic Payments Association, 3252

Electronic Pesticide Reference: EPR II
C&P Press, 10811
Vance Communications Corporation, 1213

Electronic Products
Hearst Business Communications, 7059

Electronic Publishing
PennWell Publishing Company, 6624, 20510, 20793

Electronic Representatives Directory
Harris Publishing Company, 7160

Electronic Retailer Magazine
Electronic Retailing Association, 6625

Electronic Retailing Association Annual Convention
Electronic Retailing Association, 17992

Electronic West: Annual Western Electrical Exposition Confer
Continental Exhibitions, 7120

Electronics Manufacturers Directory on Diskette
Harris InfoSource International, 7161

Electronics Manufacturing Engineering
Society of Manufacturing Engineers, 7023, 7061

Electronics Payment Journal
NACHA: Electronic Payments Association, 8947

Elevator Escalator Safety Awareness Annual Meeting
Elevator World, 4371

Elevator World
Elevator World, 17000

Email Evolution Conference
Direct Marketing Association, 494, 6234, 17993, 22673

Embedded Systems Conference
CMP Media Headquarters, 5645

Embedded Systems Conference - West
Miller Freeman Publications, 7121

Embedded Systems Programming
Miller Freeman Publications, 5479

Embroidery News
Schiffi Lace & Embroidery Manufacturers Assn, 22787

Embroidery Trade Association Convention
Embroidery Trade Association, 1775

Emediaweekly
Mac Publishing, 6626

Emergency Department Law
Business Publishers, 12947

Emergency Medical Product News
Cygnus Business Media, 21723

Emergency Medical Services
Cygnus Business Media, 21724

Emergency Nurses Association Scientific Assembly & Exhibits
Emergency Nurses Association, 13403

Emergency Preparedness & Response Conference & Exposition: R
National Trade Productions, 21791

Emergency Preparedness News
Business Publishers, 15447, 21697

Emergency Response Conference & Expo
PBI Media, 21792

Emergency Response Directory for Hazardous Materials Acciden
Odin Press, 8331

Emerging Business
Master Security Company, 24038

Emerging Issues Conference
Personal Care Products Council, 5888

Emerging Media Report
Knight MediaCom International, 5096

Emerging Pharmaceuticals
CTB International Publishing, 6371

Emerging Trends
Trends Analysis Group, 13069

Emmy Magazine
Academy of Television Arts & Sciences, 3908

Employee Assistance Program Management Letter
Health Resources Publishing, 12948, 13502, 17214

Employee Benefits Annual Conference
International Foundation of Employee Benefit Plans, 14404

Employee Benefits Cases
Bureau of National Affairs, 15754

Employee Policy for the Public and Private Sector: From the
Wakeman Walworth, 12170

Employee Service Management: NESRA Buyers Directory
National Employee Services & Recreation Assn, 17435

Employers Group
Employers Group, 17117

Employers of America
Employers of America, 17118

Employment Guide
Bureau of National Affairs, 24065

Employment Law Report Strategist
Data Research, 15755

Employment Points
Mailing & Fulfillment Service Association, 396

Employment Sources in the Library and Information Profession
National Center for Information Media & Technology, 16336

Employment, Hours and Earnings
US Department Of Commerce, 17436

Empoyment Points
Mailing & Fulfillment Service Association, 6186, 17831

Encouraging Rejection
Noforehead Press, 2209

Encyclopedia of American Industries
Grey House Publishing, 17651

Encyclopedia of Exhibition
National Association of Theatre Owners, 19562

Encyclopedia of Governmental Advisory Organizations
Gale/Cengage Learning, 12369

Encyclopedia of Sports Business Contacts
Global Sports Productions, 22350

End-User Computing Management
Auerbach Publications, 5349

EndoNurse
Virgo Publishing LLC, 13070

Endocrine Practice
American Association of Clinical Endocrinologists, 13072

Endocrine Reviews
The Endocrine Society, 13073

Endocrine Society Annual Meeting
Scherago International, 13404

Energy
WEFA Group, 1478

Energy - Exhibit Promotions Plus
US Department of Energy/US Dept. of Defense/GSA, 6852
US Dept. of Energy/US Dept. of Defense/GSA, 12309

Energy Daily
King Publishing Group, 23565

Energy Design Update
Aspen Publishers, 2051

Energy Efficiency Journal
NAESCO, 23600

Energy Engineering
Association of Energy Engineers, 1436, 8029, 13627, 23530

Energy Engineering Journal
The Fairmont Press, Association of Energy Engineer, 7381

Energy Engineering: Directory of Software for Energy Manager
Fairmont Press, 7641

Energy Information Administration
National Energy Information Center, 23531

Energy Innovation Summit
National Biodiesel Board, 1457

Energy Insight
Association of Energy Engineers (AEE), 1412

Energy Law Journal
Energy Bar Association, 12254
Federal Energy Bar Association, 1437, 15962

Energy Manager
Primedia, 23601

Energy Markets
Hart Publications, 19873

Energy Network
Gulf Publishing Company, 19874

Energy Process
American Institute of Chemical Engineers, 4679

Energy Report
Pasha Publications, 23566

Energy Science and Technology
US Department of Energy, 1479

Energy Security Expo
EJ Krause & Associates, 21793

Energy Services Marketing Institute News
Association of Energy Engineers, 7382

Energy Statistics Spreadsheets
Institute of Gas Technology, 8332

Energy Today
Trend Publishing, 23602

Energy User News: Energy Technology Buyers Guide
Chilton Company, 8333

Energy and Housing Report
Alan L Frank Associates, 23603

Energy in the News
New York Mercantile Exchange, 23604

EngiNEWS
Production Engine Remanufacturers Association, 2447

Engine Builder
Babcox Publications, 2515

Engine Professional
Automotive Engine Rebuilders Association, 2516

Engineered Systems
Business News Publishing Company, 13628

Engineering & Mining Journal
Primedia Publishing, 18628

Engineering Automation Report
Technology Automation Services, 7383

Engineering Department Management and Administration Report
Institute of Management and Administration, 7331

Engineering News Record
McGraw Hill, 4261, 7384

Engineering Times
National Society of Professional Engineers, 7332

Engineering and Mining Journal
Mining Media, 18373
Primedia Business, 7385

Engineering and Mining Journal: Buying Directory Issue
Primedia, 18679

Engineering with Rubber: How to Design Rubber Components
American Chemical Society: Rubber Division, 21490

Engineers Relay Handbook
Relay and Switch Industry Association, 6909

Engredea
New Hope Natural Media, 5889

Enrollment Management Report
LRP Publications, 17215

Ensign
United States Power Squadrons, 3643

Entelec Conference & Expo
Energy Telecommunications and Electrical Assoc, 5173, 19913, 22674

Enterprise Management Issues
AFCOM, 5480

Enterprise Wireless
Enterprise Wireless Alliance, 22675

Enterprise Wireless Magazine
Enterprise Wireless Association, 22624

Entertainment Marketing Letter
EPM Communications, 1570, 18032

Entertainment and Sports Lawyer
American Bar Association Forum-Entertainment/Sport, 15757

Entertainment, Publishing and the Arts Handbook
Thomson West Publishing, 1588

Entree Travel Newsletter
Entree Publishing, 23233

Enviro Expo
Industrial Shows Northeast, 8211

Environ: A Magazine for Ecologic Living and Health
Environ, 8030

Environment
Helen Dwight Reid Educational Foundation, 8031

Environment Reporter
Bureau of National Affairs, 7926

Environmental & Engineering Geoscience
Geological Society of America, 18629

Environmental & Engineering Geoscience Journal
Association of Engineering Geologists, 8032

Environmental Bankers Association Membership Meeting
Environmental Bankers Association, 3308

Environmental Bibliography
International Academy at Santa Barbara, 8334

Environmental Building News
BuildingGreen, 4187

Environmental Business Journal
Environmental Business International, 8033

Environmental Communicator
North American Association for Environmental, 8034

Environmental Consultant
National Society of Environmental Consultants, 20998

Environmental Cost Estimating Software Report
Donley Technology, 8335

Environmental Design & Construction
Business News Publishing Company, 4262

Environmental Design Research Association Newsletter
Environmental Design Research Association, 7927

Environmental Engineer
American Academy of Environmental Engineers, 7387

Environmental Engineering Science
Mary Ann Liebert, 8035

Environmental Engineers and Managers Institute Newsletter
Association of Energy Engineers, 7928

Environmental Fate Data Bases
Syracuse Research Corporation, 4783

Environmental Forensics
AEHS Foundation Inc, 8036

Environmental Forum
Environmental Law Institute, 15963

Environmental Geochemistry and Health
Society for Environmental Geochemistry and Health, 8037

Environmental Grantmaking Foundations Directory
Resources for Global Sustainability, 11471

Environmental Health & Safety Dictionary
ABS Group, 8336

Environmental Health Newsletter
International Lead Zinc Research Organization, 7929

Environmental Industry Yearbook and The Gallery
Environmental Economics, 4784

Environmental Law Handbook
ABS Group, 8337

Environmental Law Journal
State Bar of Texas, 15964

Environmental Management Association
Vickie Lewis, EMA President, 4847

Environmental Management Conference and Exposition
Environmental Information Association, 4372

Environmental Policy Alert
Inside Washington Publishers, 7931

Environmental Practice
National Association of Environmental Professional, 8039

Environmental Problems & Remediation
InfoTeam, 7932

Environmental Protection
Stevens Publishing Corporation, 8040

Environmental Protection Agency Headquarters Telephone Direc
Environmental Protection Agency, 8338

Environmental Regulatory Advisor
JJ Keller, 7933

Environmental Resource Handbook - Online Database
Grey House Publishing, 8339, 8340

Environmental Science and Technology
American Chemical Society, 8041

Environmental Statutes
Government Institutes, 8341

Environmental Technology Expo
Association of Energy Engineers, 8212

Environmental Times
Environmental Assessment Association, 8042

Environmental Toxicology and Chemistry
Society of Environmental Toxicology and Chemistry, 8043

Environmental Vacations: Volunteer Projects to Save the Plan
John Muir Publications, 23331

Environmental and Engineering Geosciences
Association of Engineering Geologists, 7388

Environmental and Molecular Mutagenesis
Environmental Mutagen Society, 8044

Environotes Newsletter
Federation of Environmental Technologists, 7934

Equestrian Retailer
Morris Communications, 20079

Equip-Mart
Story Communications, 17001

Equipment Distributors Association Annual Meeting
Associated Equipment Distributors, 4373

Equipment Leasing & Finance
Equipment Leasing And Finance Association, 8767

Equipment Manufacturers Conference
American Feed Industry Association, 1080

Equipment Today
Cygnus Business Media, 4263

Esox Angler
Esox Angler, 9382

Essential Rendering
National Renderers Association, 10812

Essentials
Association of Small Foundations/ASF, 11442

Essentials Magazine
National School Supply & Equipment Association, 13729, 24066

Estate Planner's Alert
Thomson Reuters, 15758

Euro Travel Forum
Reed Exhibition Companies, 23306

EuroWatch
WorldTrade Executive, 12171

Europe Agriculture and Trade Report
USDA Economic Research Service, 10168

European Chemical News
Reed Chemical Publications, 4680

European Community
US Council for International Business, 14744

European Investment in United States Real Estate
Mead Ventures, 21121

European Journal of Clinical Chemistry and Clinical Biochemi
Walter De Gruyter, 4681

European Medical Device Manufacturer
Canon Communications, 13074

European PaperMaker
Paper Industry Management Association, 19321

European Sources and News
SSC Group, 5481

European Symposium of the Protein Society
American Institute of Physics, 7561

Evans Economics Analysis and Commentary
Evans Economics, 9176

Event Solutions
Virgo Publishing LLC, 8494

Events World
International Special Events Society: Indiana, 8495

Evergreen Home Show
Westlake Promotions, 11695, 14616

Evergreen Magazine
Evergreen Foundations, 16774

Examiner
Conference of State Bank Supervisors, 3173
Society of Financial Examiners, 8949

Exchange
Association of American University Presses, 20748

Executary
National Association of Executive Secretaries, 19254

Executive Administrator
Seifer Consultants, 17216

Executive Advantage
Briefings Publishing Group, 17217

Executive Brief
Society for Information Management, 8768

Executive Compensation Review for Thrift Institutions
SNL Securities, 8769, 8770, 8771, 8772

Executive Conference
Association of Sales & Marketing Companies, 10495
Health Industry Distributors Association, 24096

Executive Directors Report
Society of Collision Repair Specialists, 2448

Executive Edge
International Association of Fire Chiefs, 8213

Executive Guide to Specialists in Industrial and Office Real
Society of Industrial & Office Realtors, 21122

Executive Guide to World Poultry Trends
WATT Publishing Company, 875, 10169

Executive Housekeeping Today (EHT)
International Executive Housekeepers Association, 13869

Executive Issues
Wharton School, 17219

Executive Leadership Forum
Snack Food Association, 10496

Executive Leadership Forum & Board of Governors Meeting
Electronic Industries Alliance, 7122

Executive Newsline
Electric Power Research Institute, 6767

Executive Protein Institute
Executive Protection Institute, 21588

Executive Recruiter News
Kennedy Information, 17220

Executive Report on Integrated Care & Capitation
Managed Care Information Center, 12949

Executive Report on Managed Care
Health Resources Publishing, 17221
Managed Care Information Center, 12950

Executive Report on Physician Organizations
Health Resources Publishing, 17222
Managed Care Information Center, 12951

Executive Solutions
Dartnell Corporation, 17223

Executive Update
Greater Washington Society of Assn Executives, 17329

Executive Wealth Advisory
National Institute of Business Management, 17224

ExecutiveBrief
Synthetic Organic Chemical Manufacturers Assn, 8045

Exercise Standards and Malpractice Reporter
PRC Publishing, 15759

Exercise and Sport Sicence Reviews
Lippincott Williams & Wilkins, 13075

Exhibit Builder
Exhibit Builder, 8496

Exhibit Ideas Show
Exhibit Builder, 8529

Exhibit Industry Conference & Exposition
Trade Show Exhibitors Association, 8530

Exhibit Marketing Magazine
Eaton Hall Publishing, 8497

Exhibition Perspectives
American Academy of Equine Art, 8475

Exhibitor
Exhibitor Magazine Group, 8498

Exhibitor Conference
Exhibitor Magazine Group, 8531, 17994

Expanded Shale, Clay and Slate Institute Roster of Members
Expanded Shale, Clay and Slate Institute, 18680

Expansion Management
Penton Media, 17330

Experience
American Bar Association, 15965

Experimental Aircraft Association AirVenture
Experimental Aircraft Association, 2964

Experimental Biology
FASEB/OSMC, 13405

Experimental Mechanics
Society for Experimental Mechanics, 7389

Experimental Techniques
Society for Experimental Mechanics, 7390

Expert and the Law
National Forensic Center, 15966

Explore the Net with Internet Explorer
ZD Journals, 6627

Expo Carnes
Consejo Mexicano de la Carne, 10497

Expo of the Americas
EJ Krause & Associates, 10498

Exponent
Iowa Engineering Society, 7391

Export
Adams/Hunter Publishing, 14780

Export Finance Letter
International Business Affairs Corporation, 8773

Export Update
Trade Communications, 14745

Export Yellow Pages
US West Marketing Resources Group, 14815

Exposure
Society for Photographic Education, 20214

Extended Care Product News
HMP Communications, 13076

Extra!
Fairness & Accuracy in Publishing, 5140

Extracts: Essentials for Spa, Home, & Travel
George Little Management, 5890

Extracts: New Discoveries in Beauty and Wellness
George Little Management, 5891

Eye on Design
American Society of Interior Designers, 14583

Eye-Mail Monthly
American Academy of Optometry, 12952

Ezine - WECommerce News
Women in eCommerce, 6628

F

F & I Management Technology
Association of Finance and Insurance Professionals, 8950

FAA Aviation News
Government Printing Office, 2870

FABFORM
Industrial Shows of America, 14047

FABTECH International
Fabricators and Manufacturers Association, 18440

FAMA Flyer
Fire Apparatus Manufacturers' Association, 21698

FASEB Conference Federation for American Societies for Exper
FASEB/OSMC, 13406

FBINAA Conference
FBI National Academy Associates, 15492

FCBA Directory
Federal Communications Bar Association, 16112

FCBA Newsletter
Federal Communications Bar Association, 15760

FCIB
Finance, Credit, International Business Assoc., 5979

FDC Reports: Gold Sheet
FDC Reports, 6372

FDC Reports: Green Sheet
FDC Reports, 6373

FDC Reports: Pink Sheet
FDC Reports, 6374

FDC Reports: Rose Sheet
FDC Reports, 5825

FDC Reports: Tan Sheet
FDC Reports, 6375

FDC Reports: The NDA Pipeline
FDC Reports, 6506

FDIC: Investment Properties Publication
Federal Deposit Insurance Corporation, 21123

FDLI & FDA Annual Conference
Food and Drug Law Institute, 6475

FDLI Prospectus
Food & Drug Law Institute, 6376

FDRS Newsletter
Food Distribution Research Society, 9943

FEDA News & Views
Foodservice Equipment Distributors Association, 10170, 21233

FEI Briefing
Financial Executives Institute, 8774

FEMA Annual Convention
FEMA, 10499

FEMA Winter Committee Meetings
FEMA, 10500

FEMSA Annual Meeting
Fire and Emergency Manufacturers and Services Asso, 15493

FEMSA News
Fire and Emergency Manufacturers and Services Asso, 15448

FENCETECH Convention & Expo
American Fence Association, 4374

FET Annual Meeting
Federation of Environmental Technologists, 8214

FET's Environment Annual Conference & Exhibition
Federation of Environmental Technologists, 8215

FFA National Agricultural Career Show
National FFA Organization, 1082

FFA New Horizons
National FFA Organization, 876, 10171

FFANY Collections
Fashion Footwear Association of New York, 1776

FFTA Annual Forum & INFO FLEX Exhibition
Flexographic Technical Association Inc, 20828

FIAE Annual Convention
Food Industry Association Executives, 10502

FICP Conference
Financial & Insurance Conference Planners, 14405

FLEETSolutions
National Association of Fleet Administrators, 2517

FLEOA Newsletter
Federal Law Enforcement Officers Association, 15449

FLEXO Magazine
Flexographic Technical Association Inc, 20795

FMA Annual Meeting
University of South Florida, 267

FMI Daily Lead
Food Marketing Institute, 24039

FMI/AMI Annual Meat Conference
American Meat Institute, 10503

FMS Annual Meeting
Financial Managers Society, 9075

FOLIO Show
Red 7 Media, LLC, 20829

FOSE
Contingency Planning & Management Conference, 12310
Post Newsweek Tech Media, 5646

FPA Annual Meeting
Financial Planning Association, 9076

FPA Experience: The Annual Conference of the Financial Plann
Financial Planning Association, 9077

FPA Update
Flexible Packaging Association, 9944

FPDA Annual Network Symposium
Fluid Power Distributors Association, 24097

FPSA Annual Conference
Food Processing Suppliers Association, 10504

FRONTIER
Meat & Livestock Australia, 877

FSA Times
Institute of Internal Auditors, 118

Federal Reserve Regulatory Service
Federal Reserve Board Publishers, 3176

Federal Securities Act
Matthew Bender and Company, 8776

Federal Tax Coordinator 2D
Thomson Reuters, 297

Federal Technology Source
Government Executive- National Journal Group, 12375

Federal Travel Directory
Office of Federal Supply & Services, 23332

Federal and Armed Forces Libraries Roundtable Conference
American Library Association, 16231, 16317

Federation of Hospitals Public Policy Conference & Business
Federation of American Health Systems, 13408

Federation of Societies for Coatings Technology
Federation of Societies for Coatings Technology, 14048

Fee Income Report
Siefer Consultants, 8777

Feed & Grain
Cygnus Business Media, 897

Feed Additive Compendium
The Miller Publishing Company, 898, 10813

Feed International
WATT Publishing Company, 899

Feed Management
WATT Publishing Company, 900

Feed and Grain
Cygnus Business Media, 8502

Feedback
Meat & Livestock Australia, 10174

Feedback Theatrebooks and Prospero Press
Feedback Theatrebooks & Prospero Press, 19563

Feedstuffs
The Miller Publishing Company, 773

Fencepost
The Fencepost, 774

Fenestration Magazine
Ashlee Publishing, 4268

Fertilizer Outlook and Technology Conference
Fertilizer Institute, 10508

Fiber Optic Sensors and Systems
IGI Group, 22565

Fiber Optics News
Phillips Business Information, 22566

Fiber Optics Weekly Update
IGI Group, 22567

Fiber Optics and Communications
IGI Group, 22568

Fiberoptic Product News
Reed Business Information, 7393

Fiberoptics Market Intelligence
KMI Corporation, 17832

Fibre Market News
GIE Media, 7936

Fibre Market News: Paper Recycling Markets Directory
Recycling Media Group GIE Publishers, 8342

Fidelity Insight
Mutual Fund Investors Association, 8778

Fidelity and Surety News
American Bar Association, 15972

Fiduciary and Risk Management Association Annual Meeting
Fiduciary and Risk Management Association, 9080

Field Hockey News
US Field Hockey Association, 22129

Film & History
Historians Film Committee, 18810

Film & Video Finder
Information Today, 5193

Film Advisory Board Monthly
Film Advisory Board, 18797

Film Journal International
VNU Business Media, 18812

Film Journal: Distribution Guide Issue
Film Journal International, 18848

Film Journal: Equipment Guide
Film Journal International, 18849

Film Journal: Exhibition Guide
Film Journal International, 18850

Film Superlist: Motion Pictures in the Public Domain
Hollywood Film Archive, 18851

Film Threat
Film Threat International Headquarters, 18813

Films and Videos on Photography
Program for Art on Film, 2301

Filtration News
Eagle Publishers, 14000

Filtration: International Conference & Exposition
INDA Association of Nonwoven Fabrics, 22811

FinEXPO
Miller Freeman Publications, 9081

Finance Company Weekly
SNL Securities, 8779

Finance and Development
International Monetary Fund, 3254

Finance, Credit & International Business Global Conference
Finance, Credit & International Business, 6043

Financial & Security Products Association Annual Conference
Financial & Security Products Association, 3310

Financial Aid for African Americans
Reference Service Press, 11472

Financial Aid for Asian Americans
Reference Service Press, 11473

Financial Aid for Hispanic Americans
Reference Service Press, 11474

Financial Aid for Native Americans
Reference Service Press, 11475

Financial Aid for Veterans, Military Personnel and their Dep
Reference Service Press, 11476

Financial Aid for the Disabled and their Families
Reference Service Press, 11477

Financial Analyst
CFA Institute, 3255

Financial Analysts Journal
CFA Institure, 8952

Financial Bulletin
Grant Thornton, 119

Financial Executive
Financial Executives International, 187, 8953

Financial Management
Financial Management Association International, 189
University of South Florida COBA, 3357

Financial Management Association International Annual Meetin
University of South Florida, 51, 8637, 8780, 9082, 17119, 17226, 17401

Financial Management Journal
Financial Management Association International, 8954, 17332

Financial Management Newsletter
Association of Legal Administrators, 15767

Financial Manager
Broadcast Cable Financial Management Association, 3910, 8955, 17333

Financial Manager/Credit Topics
Broadcast Cable Credit Association, 8956

Financial Managers Update
Financial Managers Society, 8781

Financial NetNews
Institutional Investor, 8782

Financial News
Financial News Corporation, 8783

Financial Performance Profile of Public Consumer Products Ma
Kurt Salmon Associates, 1859, 21952

Financial Planning & Counseling Journal
Association for Financial Counseling and Planning, 8957

Financial Planning Advisory
WPI Communications, 8784

Financial Planning Digest
Harcourt Brace Professional Publishing, 8958

Financial Ratios for Manufacturing Corporations Database
US Department of Commerce, 9177

Financial Review
Blackwell Publishing, 3256

Financial Review Magazine
NFR Communications, 8959

Financial Service Forum
Society of Financial Service Professionals, 14406

Financial Services Canada
Grey House Publishing, 9178

Financial Services Daily
SNL Securities, 3177, 8786

Financial Services M&A Insider
SNL Securities, 8787

Financial Services Quarterly
SNL Securities, 8960

Financial Statistics of Major Investor-Owned Electric Utilit
US Energy Information Administration, 23650

Financial Women International Annual Conference
Financial Women International, 3311, 9083

Financial Women Today
Financial Women International, 8788

Financial Women Today Magazine
Financial Women International, 3257

Financial Yellow Book
Leadership Directories, 9179

Financier
Bank Administration Institute, 8961

Financing Your Business in Eastern Europe
WorldTrade Executive, 9180

Find A Photographer Database
American Society of Media Photographers, 15274

Fine Chemicals Database
Chemron, 4785

Fine Foods Magazine
Griffin Publishing Group, 10175

Fine Gardening
Taunton Press, 11787

Fine Hardwood Veneer Association
American Walnut Manufacturers Association, 16685

Fine Homebuilding
Taunton Press, 4269

Fine Woodworking
Taunton Press, 13732, 16775

Finer Points Magazine
Industrial Diamond Association of America, 14001

Finishers' Management
Publication Management, 18376

Finishing Expo
Society of Manufacturing Engineers, 7562

Fire & Arson Investigator Magazine
International Association of Arson Investigators, 21725

Fire Chief: Equipment and Apparatus Directory Issue
Primedia, 15503

Fire EMS
PennWell, 21726

Fire Engineering
PennWell, 21727

Fire Equipment Manufacturers' Association
Fire Equipment Manufacturers' Association, 16942

Fire Protection Engineering
Society of Fire Protection Engineers, 21728

Fire Protection Equipment Directory
Underwriters Laboratories, 21834

Fire Resistance Directory
Underwriters Laboratories, 21835

Fire Retardant Chemicals Association: Membership Directory
Fire Retardant Chemicals Association, 21836

Food and Agricultural Export Directory
National Technical Information Service, 1216
US Department of Agriculture, 10823

Food and Drug Law Journal
Food & Drug Law Institute, 6420

Food and Drug Letter
FDAnews, 6377

Food for Thought
D/FW Grocers Association, 9958

Food, Beverages & Tobacco in US Industrial Outlook
Superintendent of Documents, 10824

Food, Hunger, Agribusiness: A Directory of Resources
Center For Third World Organizing, 1217
Third World Resources, 10825

FoodService Distributors Database
Chain Store Guide, 10826

FoodService and Hospitality
Kostuch Publications, 10194

FoodTalk
Pike & Fischer, 9959, 10195

Foods ADLIBRA
Foods ADLIBRA Publications, 10827

Foodservice Equipment & Supplies
Reed Europe, 10196

Foodservice Equipment & Supplies Specialist
Reed Business Information, 13870, 21236

Foodservice Equipment Reports
Robin Ashton, 21237

Foodservice Sales and Marketing Association
Grocery Manufactures Association, 9611

Football Officials Association Southwest Convention
Dallas Football Officials Association, 22283

Footprints
Footprint Communications, 20495

Footprints Newsletter
Evangelical Christian Publishers Association, 20749

Footwear Distributors and Retailers of America: Membership D
Footwear Distributors and Retailers of America, 21953

Footwear News
Fairchild Publications, 21931

Footwear Plus
Symphony Publishing, 1738

For Fish Farmers
Mississippi Cooperative Extension Service, 10197

For the President's Eyes Only
Bureau of Business Practice, 21347

Forbes Global
Forbes Media LLC., 8962

Forbes Magazine
Forbes Media LLC., 8963, 17334

Ford Data Base
Ford Investor Services, 9182

Ford's Travel Guides
Ford's Travel Guides, 23333

ForeFront
National Registry of Environmental Professionals, 7937

ForeWord Reviews
ForeWord Magazine, 20797

Forecast International
Forecast International, 2726

Forecaster
Forecaster Publishing Company, 8792

Foreign Affairs
Foreign Affairs, 14781

Foreign Consular Offices in the United States
Bureau of Public Affairs/US Department of State, 12376

Foreign Countries and Plants Certified to Export Meat and Po
US Department of Agriculture, 10829

Foreign Exchange Forecast Data Base
Global Insight, 14816

Foreign Flag Merchant Ships Owned by US Parent Companies
US Department of Transportation, 23144

Foreign Representatives in the US Yellow Book
Leadership Directories, 14817

Foreign Service Journal
American Foreign Service Association, 12257

Forest Expo
Prince George Regional Forest Exhibition Society, 16819

Forest History Society
Forest History Society, 7938

Forest History Today
Forest History Society, 8047

Forest Industries
Miller Freeman Publications, 16776

Forest Landowner Magazine
Forest Landowners Association, 16777

Forest Products Export Directory
Miller Publishing Corporation, 16848

Forest Products Journal
Forest Products Society, 16778

Forest Products Machinery & Equipment Expo
Southern Forest Products Association, 16820

Forestbytes
American Forests, 16752

Forestry Computer Applications
Michaelsen's Micro Magic Publishers, 5351

Forestry Source
Society of American Foresters, 775, 16753

Forestry, Conservation Communications Association Annual Mee
Forestry, Conservation Communications Association, 8217

Forests and People
Louisiana Forestry Association, 16779

Forging
Penton Media, 18377

Forming & Fabricating
Society of Manufacturing Engineers, 17554

Forms & Direct Mail Manufacturer's Marketplace
Bulls-Eye Communications, 20513

Formulary
Advanstar Communications, 6421

Fortified Foods Market
MarketResearch.com, 10830

Fortune Magazine
Time Inc./Time Warner, 17335, 17437

Fortune: Deals of the Year Issue
Time Inc./Time Warner, 17438

Forum
Federal Bar Association, 15768

Foster Travel Publishing Website
Foster Travel Publishing, 23334

Foundation Directory
Foundation Center, 11478

Foundation Directory Online Database
Foundation Center, 11479

Foundation Directory Supplement
Foundation Center, 11480

Foundation Drilling
ADSC, 4271

Foundation Drilling Magazine
Association of Drilled Shaft Contractors, 19755

Foundation Grants Index
Foundation Center, 11481

Foundation Grants to Individuals
Foundation Center, 11482

Foundation News & Commentary
Council on Foundations, 11443

Foundation Operations and Management Report
Association of Small Foundations/ASF, 11483

Foundation Salary & Benefits Report
Association of Small Foundations/ASF, 11484

Foundry Management & Technology
Penton Media, 18378

Foundry Management & Technology: Where to Buy Directory Issu
Penton Publishing Company, 18463

Fragrance Foundation Reference Guide
Fragrance Foundation, 5939

Fragrance and Olfactory Dictionary
Fragrance Foundation, 5940

Frame Building Expo
National Frame Builders Association, 16821

Frame Building News
F+W Media, 4272
National Frame Builders Association, 16780

Franchise Law Journal
American Bar Association, 15974

Fraternal Field Managers' Association
Concordia Mutual Life, 14139

Fred Goss' What's Working in Direct Marketing
United Communications Group, 6187

Fred Hall's Western Fishing Tackle & Boat Show: Delmar
Fred Hall & Associates, 22284

Free US Tourist Attractions
Pilot Books, 23335

Freelance Writer's Report
CNW Publishing, 16496

Fresh Cup Magazine
Fresh Cup Publishing Company, 10198, 21239

Fresh Cut Magazine
Great American Publishing, 904, 10199

Fresh Digest
Fresh Produce & Floral Council, 905

Fresh Summit International Convention & Exposition
Produce Marketing Association, 10519

Freshwater Science
Society for Freshwater Science, 3548

Freshwater and Marine Aquarium Magazine
RC Modeler Corporation, 20080

Friday Flash
Coalition for Government Procurement, 12176

Friday Notes
Council For Agricultural Science and Technology, 776
Council for Agricultural Science and Technology, 9960

Friday Report
Hoke Communications, 6188

Friends of Libraries (FOLUSA)
Association of Library Trustees, Advocates, Friend, 16232

Fringe Ware Review
Fringe Ware, 6802

Fritz and Lavinia Jensen Foundation
Foundation for the Carolinas, 19393

Frohlinger's Marketing Report
Marketing Strategist Communications, 17833

From the Ground Up
Ecology Center, 7939

From the State Capitals
Wakeman Walworth, 12177

Front Page News
Professional Landcare Network, Inc, 11778

Frontline
Computer Security Institute, 5352

Frozen Dinners and Entrees
Leading Edge Reports/Industry Reports, 10831

Fruit Country
Clintron Publishing, 906, 10201

Fuel Line
National Petrochemical & Refiners Association, 19819

Fuel Oil News
Hunter Publishing Limited, 13629, 19875

Fuel Oil News-Source Book Issue
Fuel Oil News, 19951

Fulfillment Management Association
Fulfillment Management Association, 17121

Fulltext Sources Online
Information Today, 6684

Fun Expo
William T Glasgow, 1634

Fund Directions
Financial Communications Company, 8793

Fundamentals of Personnel Law for Managers and Supervisors
Human Resources Council, 17402

Fundamentals of Steel Product Physical Metallurgy
Association for Iron & Steel Technology (AIST), 18464

Funding Alert Newsletter
Society for Nonprofit Organizations, 11425

Funding for Persons with Visual Impairments
Reference Service Press, 11485

Fundraising EDGE
Association of Fund-Raising Distributors, 11444

Fundraising: Hands on Tactics for Nonprofit Groups
McGraw-Hill Trade, 11445

Funds Transfer Report
Bankers Research, 3178

Funworld
Int'l Association of Amusement Parks & Attractions, 22178

Furnaces North America
Metal Treating Institute, 18441

Furniture Executive
American Furniture Manufacturers Association, 11670

Furniture Expo
Glahe International, 11697

Furniture Retailer Resource Guide
Pace Communications, 11732

Furniture Today
Reed Business Information, 11680

Fusion
American Scientific Glassblowers Society, 11969

Fusion Magazine
Newspaper Association of America, 5097, 20750

Fusion Science and Technology
American Nuclear Society, 7394, 8048

Future Actuary
Society of Actuaries, 298

Future Image Report
Future Image, 20201

Futures Industry
Futures Industry Association, 8964

Futures Magazine
Futures Magazine, 907, 10202
Oster Communications, 8965

Futures Magazine Sourcebook
Oster Communications, 9183

Futures Market Alert
Robbins Trading Company, 8794

Futuretech
John Wiley & Sons, 18343

G

G-2 Compliance Report
Institute of Management and Administration, 12953

GAMA Annual Meeting
Gas Appliance Manufacturers Association, 1934

GAMA International Journal
GAMA International, 14335

GAMA Trade Show
Game Manufacturers Association, 1635

GAMP Good Practice Guide
Int'l Society for Pharmaceutical Engineering, 6507

GANA Annual Conference
Glass Association of North America, 11989

GARP Annual Risk Management Convention & Exhibit
Global Association of Risk Professionals, 3312

GATFWORLD Magazine
Graphic Arts Technical Foundation Association, 12536

GAWDA Edge
Gases and Welding Distributors Association, 24067

GBH: Member's Magazine
WGBH Educational Foundation, 3912

GCN Tech Edition
Post Newsweek Tech Media, 5353

GEAPS Operations, Management, & Technology Seminar
Grain Elevator & Processing Society, 1092

GEOWorld
Bel-Av Communciations, 6629
Bel-Av Communications, 5484

GHTA Annual Conference
Gift & Home Trade Association, 11890

GIE+EXPO - Green Industry & Equipment Expo
Professional Lawncare Network, Inc, 1093, 11825

GIN International Database
Global Information Network, 14818

GLDA Gem and Jewelry Show
Gem & Lapidary Dealers Association, 15059

GLOBAL Vantage
Standard & Poor's Corporation, 14819

GMA Update
Gospel Music Association, 19052

GMAil
Gospel Music Association, 19053

GMRS National Repeater Guide
Personal Radio Steering Group, 3976

GOA Membership Directory
Georgia Oilmen Association, 19952

GP Reporter
Star Reporter Publishing Company, 15218

GPS World
Advanstar Communications, 2878

GRAS Flavoring Substances 25
Flavor & Extract Manufacturers Association, 7940, 9961

GRC Bulletin
Geothermal Resources Council, 1413

GSA Today
Geological Society of America, 18630

GTO Annual Convention & Fly In
Pipers Owner Society & Cessna Owner Organization, 2966

GZ (European Jeweler)
JCK International Publishing Group, 15030

Gacs Today
Naylor Publications, 21375

Galante's Venture Capital & Private Equity Directory
Asset Alternatives, 9184

Gale Database of Publications and Broadcast Media
Gale/Cengage Learning, 5194

Gale Directory of Databases
Gale/Cengage Learning, 16337

Gale Directory of Publications and Broadcast Media
Gale/Cengage Learning, 3977

Gale Group Management Contents®
Gale/Cengage Learning, 17439

Gale's Ready Reference Shelf
Gale/Cengage Learning, 5195

Galeria
Decor Magazine, 14618

Game Bird Breeders, Agiculturists, Zoologists and Conservati
Game Bird Breeders, 908

Game Bird Gazette
Allen Publishing, 10203

Game Developer Magazine
Think Services, 5485

Game Manufacturers Association Membership Directory
Game Manufacturers Association, 13810

Games and Entertainment on CD-ROM
Mecklermedia Corporation, 13811

Gaming Conference
Institute of Internal Auditors, 269

Garden Center Magazine
GIE Media, 11790

Garden Center Merchandising & Management
Branch-Smith Publishing, 11791, 21376

Garden Center Products & Supplies
Branch-Smith Publishing, 21377

Garment Manufacturers Index
Klevens Publications, 1860

Gas Industry Training Directory
American Gas Association, 23651

Gas Storage Report
Pasha Publications, 19821

Gas Turbine World
Pequot Publishing, 19876, 23605

Gas Utility Manager
James Informational Media, 19877

Gas and Oil Equipment Directory
Underwriters Laboratories, 19953

Gases & Welding Distributor
Penton Media, 18379

Gasp Report
GASP Engineering, 12537

Gate Way to Oshkosh
Cessna Owner Organization, 2967

Gatlinburg Apparel & Jewelry Market
Norton Shows, 1779

Gear Expo
American Gear Manufacturers Association, 17036

Gear Technology
Randall Publishing Company, 17002

Gebbie Press All-in-One Directory
Gebbie Press, 5196

Gebbie Press: All-In-One Media Directory
Gebbie Press, 16850

Gem & Jewelry Show
International Gem & Jewelry Show, 15060

Gem, Jewelry & Mineral Show
Trade Shows International, 15061

Gemstate Industrial and Construction Show
Trade Shows West, 12618

Genealogical Computing
Ancestry, 5486, 6630

General Audit Management Conference
Institute of Internal Auditors, 270

General Aviation Accident Report
Andrews Communications, 2796, 15769

General Aviation Statistical DataBook
General Aviation Manufacturers Association, 3012

General Bar Law Directory
General Bar, 16115

General Convention
Sigma Phi Delta, 7563

General Encouragement, Motivation and Inspirational Handbook
Economics Press, 6189

General Gifts: A Division of the New York International Gift
George Little Management, 11891

General Ledger
American Institute of Professional Bookkeepers, 121

General Merchandise Marketing Conference
Global Market Development Center, 24098

General Merchandise/Health and Beauty Care Conference
Food Marketing Institute, 5894

Generation Week
Pasha Publications, 23606

Genetic Technology News
John Wiley & Sons, 3534

Genomics Investing
Asset Alternatives, 8795

Geo Outlook
International Ground Source Heat Pump Association, 1438

GeoFlorida
Geo-Institute, American Society of Civil Engineers, 7564

Geoline Expo
Association of Engineering Geologists, 7565

Geology
Geological Society of America, 18631

Geophysical Directory
Geophysical Directory, 18681

Geophysics
Society of Exploration Geophysicists, 8049, 18632

Georgia Petroleum Marketer
Georgia Oilmen Association, 19878

Geospatial Solutions
Advanstar Communications, 6631

Geosphere
Geological Society of America, 18633

Geosynthetics
Industrial Fabrics Association International, 3646, 22812

Geotechnical Fabrics Report
Industrial Fabrics Association International, 7395, 22792

Geotechnical Testing Journal
ASTM International, 7396

Geothermal Energy Expo
Geothermal Energy Association, 1458

Geothermal Energy Weekly
Geothermal Energy Association, 1414

Geothermal Progress Monitor
Office of Geothermal Technologies EE-12, 8344

Geotimes
American Geological Institute, 18634

Getaways for Gourmets in the Northeast
Wood Pond Press, 10832, 21275

Getting Started in Federal Contracting: A Guide Through the
Panoptic Enterprises, 12377

Gift Basket Review
Festivities Publications, 11879

Gifts & Decorative Accessories
Reed Business Information, 11880

Giftware News
Talcott Communications Corporation, 11881

Gilder Technology Report
Gilder Publishing, 5487

Gilmore Shows
Craftsmen's Classic Art & Craft Festivals, 2282

Giving USA
American Association of Fund-Raising Counsel, 11446

Giving USA Update
American Association of Fund-Raising Counsel, 11426

Giving and Receiving Feedback with Grace & Style
American Association of Advertising Agencies, 495

Glass & Ceramic Decorators Annual Seminar & Exposition
Society of Glass & Ceramic Decorators, 11698

Glass & Optical Materials Division Annual Meeting
American Ceramic Society, 11990

Glass Art Society Conference
Glass Art Society, 11991

Glass Craft Exposition
Las Vegas Management, 11992

Glass Craftsman
Arts & Media, 11970

Glass Digest
Ashlee Publishing, 4273

Glass Expo Midwest
US Glass Magazine, 11993

Glass Factory Directory of North America
Glass News, 12009

Glass Magazine
National Glass Association, 2081, 11971

Glass TEXpo
Key Communications, Inc., 11994

GlassBuild America: Glass, Window & Door Expo
National Glass Association, 4375

Glimpsing Kentucky's Forgotten Heroes: Profiles & Lessons fr
Agribusiness Council, 909

Global Business Directory
Women in eCommerce, 6685

Global Connection
Automotive Parts Remanufacturers Association, 2520

Global Cosmetic Industry
Allured Publishing Corporation, 5845

Global Custodian
Asset International, 3258, 8966

Global Dairy Update
DairyBusiness Communications, 777

Global Design News
Reed Business Information, 7397

Global Electronics
Pacific Studies Center, 6768

Global Environmental Change Report
Aspen Publishers, 7941
Cutter Information Corporation, 17227

Global Fire Service Leadership Summit
International Association of Fire Chiefs, 21796

Global Food Marketer
Food Export USA, 9962

Global IT Consulting Report
Kennedy Information, 17336

Global Insight
Motor and Equipment Manufacturers Association, 2521

Global Investment Magazine
Global Investment Technology, 8968

Global Investment Technology
Global Investment Technology, 3179, 8969

Global Leather
American Apparel & Footwear Association, 1780, 21941

Global Logistics & Supply Chain Strategies
Keller International Publishing Corporation, 24147

Global Minor Use Summit
Crop Life America, 10520

Global Money Management
Institutional Investor, 8796

Global Pet Expo
American Pet Products Association, 20102

Global Property Investor
Alexander & Edwards Publishing, 21044

Global Report
Citicorp, 14820

Global Shop Conference
Nielsen Business Media, 496

Global Sourcing Guide
Diesel & Gas Turbine Publications, 6910

Global Survey of Regulatory & Market Developments in Banking
Institute of International Bankers, 3180

Global Technology Business
Global Technology Business Publishing, 5488

Global Techventures Report
Miller Freeman Publications, 5489

Global Telephony
Primedia, 22625

Global Tire News.com
Rubber & Plastic News, 21507

Global Trade
North American Publishing Company, 14782

Global Warming International Conference & Expo
SUPCON International, 8218

GlobalCon Conference & Expo
Association of Energy Engineers, 7566, 8219
Biomass Thermal Energy Council, 1459

Globe Newsletter
International Communications Agency Network, 397

Go-West Magazine
Motor Transport Management Group, 23057

Goats on the Move
Meat & Livestock Australia, 778

Going on Faith
Group Traveler Leader, 23261

Gold Book: AAMP
American Association of Meat Processors, 10833

Gold Newsletter
Blanchard and Company, 8797

Golf Business
National Golf Course Owners Association, 22179

Golf Course Management
Golf Course Superintendents Association of America, 17337, 22180

Golf Course Superintendents Association of America
GCSAA, 22285

Golf Inc Magazine
Cypress Manazines, 22182

Golf Range Times
Forecast Golf Group, 22183

Golf Traveler
Affinity Group, 22351

Golfdom
Questex Medica Group, 22184

Golob's Oil Pollution Bulletin
World Information Systems, 19822

Gospel Music Industry Directory
Gospel Music Association, 19179

Gospel Music Week
Gospel Music Association, 19151

Gospel Today
Gospel Today, 19499

Gourmet News
Oser Communications Group, 9963, 21241

Gourmet Products Show
George Little Management, 10521

Gov't Convention on Emerging Technologies Partnerships for H
National Conference Services, 21797

GovManagement Daily
American Society for Public Administration, 12178

GovSec
National Trade Productions, 6146, 21798

GovSec: The Govenment Security Conference & Expo
1105 Media, 15494

Governance, Risk and Control Conference
Institute of Internal Auditors, 271

Government Accounting and Auditing Update
Thomson Reuters, 122

Government Action Summit
American Frozen Food Institute, 10522

Government Affairs Briefing
North American Die Casting Association, 7567

Government Affairs Bulletin
Financial Services Roundtable, 3259, 8798

Government Affairs Conference
American Advertising Federation, 497
USA Rice Federation, 1094, 10523

Government Affairs Update
American Association for Clinical Chemistry, 4645

Government Assistance Almanac: Guide to all Federal Financia
Omnigraphics, 12378

Government Best Buys
FCW Government Technology Group, 5490

Government Computer News
Reed Business Information, 5354

Government Employee Relations Report
Bureau of National Affairs, 12179

Government Executive
National Journal, 12258

Government Finance Officers Association Newsletter
Government Finance Officers Association, 8799

Government PROcurement
Penton Media, 12180

Government Phone Book USA
Omnigraphics, 12379

Government Product News
Penton Media, 12259

Government Recreation & Fitness
Executive Business Media, 12260, 22185

Government Relations: How To Guide for Clubs & Federations
American Advertising Federation, 422

Government Research Directory
Gale/Cengage Learning, 12380

Government Technology
GT Publications, 12261

Government Video
Miller Freeman Publications, 5142

Government Waste Watch Newspaper
Citizens Against Government Waste, 12181

Governments Canada
Grey House Publishing Canada, 12381

Inspire
Creative Age Publications, 5849

Installer
National Guild of Professional Paperhangers, 14571

Instant and Small Commercial Printer ISCP
Innes Publishing Company, 20522

Institute for Public Relations
University of Florida, 20600

Institute of Business Appraisers
Institute of Business Appraisers, 17126

Institute of Certified Bankers
American Bankers Association, 3104

Institute of Certified Business Counselors
Institute of Certified Business Counselors, 17127

Institute of Federal Taxation
USC Law Center, 16069

Institute of Food Technologists Annual Meeting & Food Expo
Institute of Food Technologists, 10548

Institute of Food and Agricultural Sciences (IFAS)
University of Florida, 9637

Institute of Food and Nutrition
HealthComm International, 10225

Institute of Gas Technology
Institute of Gas Technology, 19828

Institute of Home Office Underwriters
General American Life Insurance Company, 14153

Institute of International Bankers Annual Washington Confere
Institute of International Bankers, 3315

Institute of Investigative Technology
AccuQuest, 15348

Institute of Management & Administration Newsletter
Institute of Management and Administration, 8978, 15979, 17128, 17341

Institute of Management Accountant
Institute of Management Accountant, 17129

Institute of Management Consultants - USA
Institute of Management Consultants - USA, 17130

Institute of Management and Administration
Institute of Management and Administration, 17131

Institute of Police Technology and Management
University of North Florida, 15349

Institute of Textile Technology
North Carolina State University, 22766

Institute of Transportation Engineers Annual Meeting
Institute of Transportation Engineers, 23064, 23112

Institutional Real Estate Letter
Institutional Real Estate, 21048

Instructional Technology for Occupational Safety and Health
Nat. Environmental, Safety & Health Training Assoc, 8231

Instrumentalist
Instrumentalist Company, 19097

Instrumentation Newsletter
National Instruments, 7340

Instrumentation and Automation News
Chilton Company, 13986

Insulation Outlook
National Insulation Association, 4279, 24068

Insurance & Financial Meetings Managment
Coastal Communications Corporation, 8505, 8980, 14340

Insurance & Technology
TechWeb, 14341

Insurance Almanac
Underwriter Printing & Publishing Company, 14468

Insurance Bar Directory
Bar List Publishing Company, 14469

Insurance Companies' Directory List of Mortgage Directors
Communication Network International, 14470

Insurance Conference Planner
Penton Media Inc, 14343
Primedia, 8506

Insurance Daily
SNL Financial, 14288

Insurance Finance & Investment
Institutional Investor, 14289

Insurance Forum
Insurance Forum, 14290

Insurance Insight
Professional Independent Insurance Agents of IL, 14344

Insurance Library Association of Boston
Insurance Library, 16234

Insurance M&A Newsletter
SNL Securities, 8813

Insurance Networking News
SourceMedia, 14346

Insurance Performance Graph
SNL Financial, 14291

Insurance Regulation
Wakeman Walworth Inc, 14292

Insurance Weekly: Life & Health
SNL Financial, 14293

Insurance Weekly: Property & Casualty
SNL Financial, 14294

Int'l Assn of Campus Law Enforcement Administrators Annual C
International Assn of Campus Law Enforcement Admin, 15495

Int'l Conference on Powder Injection Molding of Metals & Cer
Innovative Material Solutions, 17629

Int'l Conference on Southern Hemisphere Meteorology & Oceano
Renewable Natural Resources Foundation, 8232

Int'l Conference on Strategic Business Information in Biotec
Institute for Biotechnology Information, 3562

Int'l. Association of Healthcare Central Services Material M
Int'l. Association of Healthcare, 17132

Int'l. Association of Healthcare Central Svc. Material Manag
IAHCSMM Annual Conference, 17405

Integrated Circuit Manufacturing Synopsis
Semiconductor Equipment & Materials International, 7026

Integrated Environmenal Assessment and Management
SETAC, 8064

Integrated Environmental Assessment and Management
Society of Environmental Toxicology and Chemistry, 7950

Integrated Healthcare News
American Association of Integrated Healthcare, 12965

Integrated Marketing Members Only Conference by Microsoft Ad
Pohly Company, 505

Integrated System Design
Verecom Group, 5517

Intele-Card News
Quality Publishing, 22631

Intellectual Property LAWCAST
Vox Juris, 15779

Intellectual Property Law Review
Clark Boardman Company, 15780

Intellectual Property Litigation Reporter
Andrews Publications, 15781

Intellectual Property Today
Omega Communications, 15782

Intelligence: The Future of Computing
Intelligence, 5361

Intelligent Enterprise
Miller Freeman Publications, 5518

Intelligent Manufacturing
Lionheart Publishing, 16987, 17527

Inter-American Bar Association Newsletter
Inter-American Bar Association, 15783

Inter-American Dialogue on Water Management
Water Environment Federation, 8233

Interactions
Association for Computing Machinery, 5519

Interactive Mobile Investor
Kagan World Media, 3861, 8814

Interactive PR & Marketing News
Phillips Publishing, 20609

Interactive Public Relations
Ragan Communications, 20610

Interactive TV Investor
Kagan World Media, 3862, 8815

Interactive Television
Kagan World Media, 3863

Interagency Council on Information
American Nurses Association Library, 16235

Intercoiffure America-Canada
Creative Age Publications, 5901

Intercom
Society for Technical Communication, 5100

Interface Magazine
Electrochemical Society, 6810, 7407

Interface Newsletter
Society for Environmental Geochemistry and Health, 7952

Interior Construction
Ceilings & Interior Systems Construction Assn, 4280

Interior Decorators Handbook
EW Williams Publications, 14655

Interior Design
Reed Business Information, 14593

Interior Plantscape Symopsium
Professional Landcare Network, 11829

Interior Textiles Fabric Resource Directory
Wool Bureau/Atlanta Merchandise Mart, 22822

Interlibrary Loan Policies Directory
Neal-Schuman Publishers, 16338

Interlocking Concrete Pavement Magazine
Interlocking Concrete Pavement Institute, 4281

Intermountain Contractor
McGraw Hill, 4282

Intermountain Retailer
Utah Food Industry Association, 10226

Internal Auditing
Thomson Reuters, 194

Internal Auditing Report
Thomson Reuters, 131

Internal Auditor Magazine
Institute of Internal Auditors, 195

International Aerospace Abstracts
American Institute of Aeronautics and Astronautics, 3015

International Air Cargo Forum & Exposition
International Air Cargo Association, 2970

International Air Conditioning, Heating & Refrigerating Expo
International Exposition Company, 1938

International Air Conditioning, Heating, & Refrigerating Exp
ASHRAE, 10549, 13652

International Anodizing Conference & Exposition
Aluminum Anodizers Council (AAC), 18442

International Archive Magazine
Luerzer's Archive Inc, 429

International Assoc of Operative Millers Technical Conferenc
International Association of Operative Millers, 10550

International Association for Energy Economics Conference
International Association for Energy Economics, 8234

International Association for Insurance Law: United States C
Chase Communications, 14167

International Association for Worksite Health Promotion
Association for Worksite Health Promotion, 17133

International Association of Amusement Parks and Attractions
Int'l Association of Amusement Parks & Attractions, 1642

International Association of Aquatic & Mar ine Science Libra
The International Association of Aquatic and Marin, 16236

Job Shop Show: Midwest
Edward Publishing LLC, 17041

Job Shop Technology
Edward Publishing, 17560

Job-Site Supervisor
FMI Corporation, 4284

John Bollinger's Capital Growth Letter
Bollinger Capital Management, 8826

John Bollinger's Group Power
Bollinger Capital Management, 8827

John Kremer's Book Marketing Tip of the Week
Open Horizons Publishing, 20756

Joint Airports Environmental/Technical Committee Meeting
Airports Association Council International, 2971

Joint Conference on Decision and Control & European Control
American Automatic Control Council, 6869

Joint ISPA/SCEA Conference & Workshop
Society of Cost Estimating & Analysis, 279

Joint International Conference PBC/ SEGH
Society for Environmental Geochemistry & Health, 8246

Jojoba Happenings
John S Turner Public Relations, 929

Jot and Jolts
Economics Press, 19256

Jots and Jolts
Economics Press, 17249

Journal Of Oncology Management
Alliance Communications Group, 13108

Journal for Insurance Compliance Professionals Newsletter
Association of Insurance Compliance Professionals, 14295

Journal of AOAC International
AOAC International, 4689

Journal of Accountancy
American Institute of Certified Public Accountants, 199

Journal of Accounting Research
University of Chicago Booth School of Business, 200

Journal of Accounting and Public Policy
Elsevier, 201

Journal of Advertising (JA)
American Academy of Advertising, 430

Journal of Advertising Research
World Advertising Research Center Ltd, 431

Journal of Aerospace Engineering
American Society of Civil Engineers, 2882

Journal of Agricultural & Food Chemistry
American Chemical Society, 930

Journal of Air & Waste Management Association
Air & Waste Management Association, 8069

Journal of Air Traffic Control
Air Traffic Control Association, 2883

Journal of Allergy and Clinical Immunology
American Academy of Allergy, Asthma and Immunology, 13110

Journal of American Dietetic Association
American Dietetic Association, 13111

Journal of American Organbuilding
American Institute of Organ Builders, 19101

Journal of American Society for Information Science
John Wiley & Sons, 5524

Journal of Analytical Toxicology
Preston Publications, 4690

Journal of Animal Science
American Society of Animal Science, 10231

Journal of Applied Communications
Agricultural Communicators in Education, 5146
Association for Communications Excellence, 932

Journal of Applied Communications (JAC)
ACE, 933

Journal of Applied Finance
Financial Management Association International, 202, 8983

Journal of Applied Mechanics
American Society of Mechanical Engineers, 7411

Journal of Aquatic Animal Health
American Fisheries Society, 9390

Journal of Arboriculture
International Society of Arboriculture, 11799

Journal of Architectural Education
Blackwell Publishing Inc, 2085

Journal of Architectural and Planning Research
Locke Science Publishing, 2086

Journal of Arts Management, Law, Society
Heldref Publishers, 19502

Journal of Asset Protection
Thomson Reuters, 8984

Journal of Astronautical Sciences
American Astronautical Society, 2884

Journal of Biological Chemistry
American Society for Biochemistry, 3549

Journal of Biomechanical Engineering
American Society of Mechanical Engineers, 7412

Journal of Biomolecular Screening
Sage Publications, 3550

Journal of Broadcasting and Electronic Media
Broadcast Education Association, 3916

Journal of Business Logistics
Council of Supply Chain Management Professionals, 10232

Journal of Cardiovascular Management
Alliance Communications Group, 13112

Journal of Cellular Plastics
Sage Publications, 20318

Journal of Chemical Education
Division of Chemical Education, 4692

Journal of Chemical Information & Computer Sciences
American Chemical Society, 4693

Journal of Chemical Physics
American Institute of Physics, 4694

Journal of Chemical and Engineering Data
American Chemical Society, 4695

Journal of Child Nutrition & Management
School Nutrition Association, 10233

Journal of Chromatographic Science
Preston Publications, 4696

Journal of Clinical Epidemiology
Elsevier Publishing, 13113

Journal of Coatings Technology
Federation of Societies for Coatings Technology, 14016, 17561

Journal of College Radio
Intercollegiate Broadcasting System, 3917

Journal of Colloid & Interface Science
Academic Press, 4697

Journal of Communication
International Communication Association, 22632

Journal of Composite Materials
Sage Publications, 20319

Journal of Computer-Mediated Communication
International Communication Association, 22633

Journal of Construction Accounting & Taxation
Thomson Reuters, 203

Journal of Construction Engineering and Management
American Society of Civil Engineers, 7413

Journal of Corporate Renewal
Turnaround Management Association, 17343

Journal of Cost Analysis and Parametrics
Society of Cost Estimating and Analysis, 204

Journal of Cost Management
Thomson Reuters, 205, 8985

Journal of Court Reporting
National Court Reporters, 15982

Journal of Craniofacial Surgery
Lippencott Williams & Wilkins, 13115

Journal of Current Issues and Research in Advertising
CTC Press, 432

Journal of Dairy Science
American Dairy Science Association, 936, 10234

Journal of Dance Education
National Dance Education Organization, 19503

Journal of Digital Imaging
Society for Imaging Informatics in Medicine, 13116

Journal of Direct Marketing
John Wiley & Sons, 6213

Journal of Education Finance
American Education Finance Association, 8986

Journal of Elastomers and Plastics
Sage Publications, 20320

Journal of Electronic Imaging
International Society for Optical Engineering, 6649

Journal of Electronic Materials
Minerals, Metals & Materials Society, 18637

Journal of Emergency Nursing
Mosby/Professional Opportunities, 13117

Journal of Emerging Technologies in Accounting
American Accounting Association, 206

Journal of Engineered Fibers & Fabrics
INDA Association of Nonwoven Fabrics, 22797

Journal of Engineering Education
American Society for Engineering Education, 7414

Journal of Engineering for Industry
American Society of Mechanical Engineers, 7415, 17010

Journal of Environmental Economics and Management
Association of Environmental and Resource, 8070

Journal of Environmental Education
Heldref Publications, 8071

Journal of Environmental Engineering
American Society of Civil Engineers, 8072

Journal of Environmental Geochemistry and Health
Society for Environmental Geochemistry & Health, 8073

Journal of Environmental Health
National Environmental Health Association, 8074

Journal of Environmental Quality
American Society of Agronomy, 8075, 10235

Journal of Essential Oil Research/JEOR
Allured Publishing Corporation, 5850

Journal of Euromarketing
Taylor & Francis Inc, 433

Journal of ExtraCorporeal Technology
American Society of ExtraCorporeal Technology, 13118

Journal of Family & Consumer Sciences
American Association of Family & Consumer Sciences, 11685

Journal of Film and Video
University Film and Video Association, 18818

Journal of Finance
American Finance Association, 8987

Journal of Fire Sciences
Sage Publications, 21733

Journal of Fixed Income
Institutional Investor, 8989

Journal of Food Distribution Research
Food Distribution Research Society, 10236

Journal of Food Protection
International Association for Food Protection, 8076, 10237, 12264

Journal of Food Science
Institute of Food Technologists, 10238

Journal of Foodservice Business Research
Taylor & Francis, 21242
Taylor & Francis Group LLC, 10239

Journal of Forensic Psychology Practice
Bill Cohen, 13119

Journal of Forensic Sciences
ASTM International, 7416

Journal of Forestry
Society of American Foresters, 938, 16785

Journal of Geophysical Research
American Geophysical Union, 19885

Journal of Gift Planning
National Committee on Planned Giving, 8990, 11451

Journal of Government Financial Management
Association of Government Accountants, 207, 8991

Journal of Guidance, Control & Dynamics
American Institute of Aeronautics and Astronautics, 2885

Local Calling Area Directory
Center for Communications Management, 22703

Local Chambers of Commerce Which Maintain Foreign Trade Serv
US Chamber of Commerce-International Division, 14825

Local Court & County Record Retrievers
BRB Publications, 12393

Locating, Testing and Repairing
Stober Research and Communications, 22635

Locator
John Holmes Publishing Company, 2530

Locator Services
Locator Online, 17013, 18390

Locomotive Engineers Journal
Brotherhood of Locomotive Engineers, 23068

Lodging Hospitality
Penton Media, 13879

Loggers' World
Loggers World Publications, 16786

Logging & Sawmilling Journal
Logging & Sawmilling Journal, 16787

Logging Management
Baum International Media, 16788

Logistics
Retail Industry Leaders Association, 21422

Logistics Journal
Transportation Intermediaries Association, 10256

Logistics Management & Distribution Report
Reed Business Information, 23069, 23802

Long Haul Market
Probe Research, 17848

Long Term Investing
Concept Publishing, 8835

Long-Term Care Insurance Sales Strategies
Sales Creators, 14357

Looking Fit Magazine
Virgo Publishing LLC, 3445

Los Angeles Calendar Motorcycle Show
Breakdown & Legal Assistance for Motorcyclists, 18912

Loss Executives Association
Industrial Risk Insurers, 14190

Loss Prevention Conference & Exhibition
National Retail Federation, 21423

Loss Prevention, Auditing & Safety Conference
Retail Industry Leaders Association, 21424

Lottery, Parimutuel & Casino Regulation: From the State Capi
Wakeman Walworth, 12190

Lubes-N-Greases
LNG Publishing Company, 2531, 14022

Lubricating Engineering
Society of Tribologists & Lubrication Engineers, 14023

Lumber Cooperator
Northeastern Retail Lumber Association, 16789

Lumber and Building Material Expo
Northeastern Retail Lumber Association, 4386

Lumberman's Equipment Digest
Lumbermen Online, 16790

Lumbermen's Red Book
Lumbermens Credit Association, 16858

Lundberg Letter
Lundberg Survey, 19835

Lustre
Cygnus Publishing, 15040

Lynx Global Telecom Database
Lynx Technologies, 22704

M

M Street Radio Directory
M Street Corporation, 5201

M and A Lawyer
Glasser LegalWorks, 16005

M&E Appraiser
American Society of Appraisers, 24042

M-Commerce Security
Probe Research, 17849

M/Tech
AEC Systems International/Penton Media, 2112

M/Tech West
AEC Systems International/Penton Media, 2113

MACS Action!
Mobile Air Conditioning Society Worldwide, 13613

MACS Convention & Trade Show
Mobile Air Conditioning Society Worldwide, 13656

MACS Convention and Trade Show
Mobile Air Conditioning Society Worldwide, 2604

MACS Service Reports
Mobile Air Conditioning Society Worldwide, 13614

MAGIC International Show
MAGIC International, 1795

MAPNetter
Architecture Technology Corporation, 5103

MAR/Hedge
Managed Account Reports, 8836

MB News
Monument Builders of North America, 21052

MBA Newslink
Mortgage Bankers Association, 6016

MBA Research Conclave
MBAResearch and Curriculum Center, 17997

MBCEA Annual Conference
Metal Building Contractors & Erectors Association, 18446

MBCEA Newsletter
Metal Building Contractors & Erectors Association, 18346

MBI World of Modular Conference
Modular Building Institute, 4387

MBR Bookwatch
Midwest Book Review, 20758

MC
National Precast Concrete Association, 22483

MCAA Annual Conference
Mechanical Contractors Association of America, 7586

MCAA Annual Convention & Masonry Showcase
Mason Contractors Association of America, 4388

MCARE: Materials Challenges in Alternative & Renewable Energ
American Ceramic Society, 12001

MD Computing
Springer Verlag, 5534

MDMA Membership and Resource Directory
Midwest Direct Marketing Association, 18040

MDMA's Annual Direct Marketing Conference & Expo
Midwest Direct Marketing Association, 17998

MDNA News
Machinery Dealers National Association, 24043

MDRT Annual Meeting
Million Dollar Round Table, 14421

MDVA Convention
Michigan Distributors & Vendors Association, 24106

MEATXPO
National Meat Association, 10569

MEGA Symposium
A&WMA, 8247

MEGATEX
Industrial Fabrics Association International, 3695

METALFORM
Precision Metalforming Association, 18447

MFMA Annual Conference
Maple Flooring Manufacturers Association, 16832

MFMA/BCCA Annual Conference
Media Financial Management Association, 3945

MFP Report
Bissett Communications, 19257

MFSA Mailing and Fulfillment Expo
Mailing & Fulfillment Service Association, 6237

MFSA Midwinter Executive Conference
Mailing & Fulfillment Service Association, 507, 6238, 17999

MHEDA Connection
Material Handling Equipment Distributors Assoc, 24044

MHEDA Journal
Material Handling Equipment Distributors Assoc, 24072

MIACON Construction, Mining & Waste Management Show
Finocchiaro Enterprises, 4389, 7587, 18667

MILCOM
Armed Forces Communications and Electronics Assn, 5176

MINExpo International
National Mining Association, 18668

MIP-TV: International Television Program Market
Reed Exhibition Companies, 3946

MIPIM
Reed Exhibition Companies, 21094

MISA Buyer's Guide on CD
Meat Industry Suppliers Alliance, 10857

MIXX Conference & Expo
Interactive Advertising Bureau, 508

MJK Commodities Database
MJK Associates, 9198

MJSA Buyers' Guide
Manufacturing Jewelers & Suppliers of America, 15097

MLA Buyer's Guide & Dealer Directory
Mid-America Lumbermens Association, 12635

MLA LINE
Mid-America Lumbermens Association, 12602

MLA Membership Handbook
Music Library Association, 19185

MLA News
Medical Library Association, 16269

MLMIA Annual Corporate Convention and Expo
Multi-Level Marketing International Association, 18000

MMA Annual Meeting and Trade Show
Massachusetts Municipal Association, 12318

MMR/Mass Market Retailers
Racher Press, 21381

MOVE
AAMVA, 2533

MOVE Magazine
American Assn. of Motor Vehicle Administrators, 2534

MPI Membership Directory
Meeting Professionals International, 8558

MPI Semi-Annual Meetings
Meeting Professionals International, 8542

MPMN: Medical Product Manufacturing News
UBM Canon, 6437

MRAA Bearings
Marine Retailers Association of America, 3620

MRC Cyberalert
Media Research Center, 5104

MRF Reports
Motorcycle Riders Foundation, 18894

MRO Today
Pfingsten Publishing, 14024

MS Connection
Lippincott Williams & Wilkins, 13144

MS Quarterly Journal
Society for Information Management, 8999

MSF Guide to Motorcycling Excellence
Motorcycle Safety Foundation, 18916

MSI
Reed Business Information, 17347

MSR Council Matters
MSR Lumber Producers Council, 16755

MSR Lumber Producers Council
MSR Lumber Producers Council, 16701

MSRB Manual
Municipal Securities Rulemaking Board, 3188

MSS Annual Meeting
Manufacturers Standardization Society, 20451

MSW Management
Forester Communications, 8089

MTS TechSurge, Oceans in Action
Marine Technology Society, 8248

MWR Expo
American Logistics Association, 10570

MWorld: Journal of the American Management Association
American Management Association, 17348

Mac News
Mid-Atlantic Council of Shopping Centers, 21005

MacTech
Xplain Corporation, 6654

MacWeek
MacWorld Communications, 5535

MacWorld Conference & Expo
MacWorld 2010, 5664

MacWorld Magazine
Mac Publishing, 5536

Machalek Communications, Inc.
Machalek Communications, 9684

Machine Design Product Locator
Penton Media, 17054

Machine Shop Guide
Worldwide Communications, 17014, 18391

Machinery Dealers National Association
Machinery Dealers National Association, 16951, 18279

Machinery Outlook
Manfredi & Associates, 4192, 16988, 18612

Machinery Trader
Sandhills Publishing, 17015

Machining Technology
Society of Manufacturing Engineers, 16989

Made to Measure
Halper Publishing Company, 1744

Magazine Antiques
Brant Publications, 2248

Magazine Media Factbook (ASME)
American Society of Magazine Editors, 15240, 15256

Magazine Retailer
MetaMedia, 21382

Magazines for Libraries
R R Bowker LLC, 20868

Magic-Unity-Might: MUM Magazine
Society of American Magicians, 1600

Magnet Marketing & Sales
Graham Communications, 17949

Magnetism Conference: Institute of Electrical/Electronics En
Courtesy Associates, 6871

Mail Center Management Report
Institute of Management and Administration, 11549

Mail Order Business Directory
B Klein Publishers, 18041

Mail Order Digest & Washington Newsletter
National Mail Order Association, 6191

Mail Order Product Guide
Todd Publications, 18042

Mail: Journal of Communication Distribution
Excelsior Publications, 19267

Mailcom
The Art & Science of Mail Communications, 5177

Mailer Strategies Conference
Mailing & Fulfillment Service Association, 509, 6239, 18001

Mainly Marketing
Schoonmaker Associates, 17850

Mainsheet
Rhodes 19 Class Association, 3621

Maintenance Sales News
Rankin Publishing Company, 4887

Maintenance Solutions
Trade Press Publishing Corporation, 4888, 7436

Maintenance Supplies
Cygnus Publishing, 4889

Maintenance Technology
Applied Technology Publications, 7437, 14025, 17349, 17566

Maintenance Update
Helicopter Association International, 2890

Major Cities Canada
Grey House Publishing, 21128

Major Orchestra Librarians' Association
MOLA, 16241

Make It Happen
Action Marketing, 17851

Make It Tasty
Prosperity & Profits Unlimited, 9992

Makin' Waves Quarterly Newsletter
Recreational Fishing Alliance, 9371

Making a Difference
National FFA Organization, 9993

Manage
National Management Association, 17350

Managed Care Institute & Display Forum
American Association of Health Plans, 13427

Managed Care Law Conference
American Association of Health Plans, 13428

Managed Care Yearbook
Health Resources Publishing, 13507

Managed Healthcare
Advanstar Communications, 13145

Management & Administration Report (ADMAR)
Institute of Management and Administration, 134

Management Conference & Team Dealer Summit
National Sporting Goods Association, 1796, 22297

Management Consultants International
Kennedy Information, 17351

Management Policies and Personnel Law
Business Research Publications, 17254

Management and Technology
Association of Finance and Insurance Professionals, 9000

Manager's Legal Bulletin
Alexander Hamilton Institute, 17255

Managing 401(k) Plans
Institute of Management and Administration, 8837

Managing Accounts Payable
Institute of Management and Administration, 135

Managing Automation
Thomas Publishing Company, 17016, 17567

Managing Benefits Plans
Institute of Management and Administration, 17256

Managing Credit, Receivable & Collections
Institute of Management and Administration, 8838

Managing Customer Service
Institute of Management and Administration, 17257

Managing Housing Letter
CD Publications, 21006

Managing Human Resource Information Systems
Institute of Management and Administration, 5363

Managing Imports and Exports
Institute of Management and Administration, 14757

Managing Logistics
Institute of Management and Administration, 17258

Managing Media Relations in a Crisis
NACHA: The Electronic Payments Association, 5151, 20637

Managing Today's Federal Employees
LRP Publications, 12191

Managing Training & Development
Institute of Management and Administration, 17259

Managing the General Ledger
Institute of Management and Administration, 136

Manufactured Concrete Products Exposition
National Concrete Masonry Association, 22491

Manufactured Home Merchandiser
RLD Group, 4288

Manufactured Structures Newsletter
Bobbitt Group, 4193

Manufacturer and Repair Directory
National Board of Boiler & Pressure Vessel, 7642

Manufacturers Mart
Philip G Cannon Jr, 17568

Manufacturers Representatives of America: Yearbook and Direc
Manufacturers Representatives of America, 17652

Manufacturers Seminar
Health Industry Distributors Association, 24107

Manufacturers Showcase
Heartland Communications Group, 18392

Manufacturers Wholesalers Outerwear Sportswear Show
I. Spiewak & Sons, 1797

Manufacturing & Distribution USA
Gale/Cengage Learning, 17653

Manufacturing Automation
Vital Information Publications, 6584, 13988

Manufacturing Confectioner
MC Publishing, 10257

Manufacturing Confectioner: Directory of Ingredients, Equipm
Manufacturing Confectioner Publishing Company, 10858

Manufacturing Engineering
Society of Manufacturing Engineers, 17017, 17569, 18393

Manufacturing Market Insider
JBT Communications, 7027

Manufacturing News
Publishers & Producers, 17570

Manufacturing Technology
National Technical Information Service, 16990, 17528

Maple Flooring Manufacturers Association
Maple Flooring Manufacturers Association, 16702

Marcato
MOLA/Editor, 16270

Marina/Dock Age
Preston Publications, 3648

Marinas and Small Craft Harbors
Association of Marina Industries, 3649

Marine Conservation News
Center for Marine Conservation, 7955

Marine Digest & Transportation News
Marine Publishing, 23070

Marine Fabricator
Industrial Fabrics Association International, 3650, 7438, 22799

Marine Log
Simmons-Boardman Publishing Corporation, 3651

Marine News
Maritime Activity Reports, 3652

Marine Products Directory
Underwriters Laboratories, 3720

Marine Retailers Association of America Annual Convention
Marine Regtailers Association of America, 3696

Marine Safety and Security Report
Stamler Publishing Company, 3622

Marine Technology Society Journal
Marine Technology Society, 8090

Marine Textiles
RCM Enterprises, 22788

Marine West Military Expo
Nielsen Business Media, USA, 12319

Marine and Coastal Fisheries: Dynamics, Management, and Ecos
American Fisheries Society, 9391

Markee
HJK Publications, 23739

Market Analysis
Motor and Equipment Manufacturers Association, 2535

Market Europe
PRS Group, 14758

Market Guide for Young Writers: Where and How to Sell What Y
Writer's Market, 16536

Market Maker
Advanstar Communications, 1745

Market News
Meat & Livestock Australia, 9994

Market Research Report
Animal Health Institute, 20117

Market Resource Guide
International Home Furnishings Center, 11736, 14657

Meat Science Journal
American Meat Science Association, 947

Meat and Livestock Weekly
Meat & Livestock Australia, 9996

Meat and Poultry
Sosland Publishing Company, 10260

Meat and Poultry Inspection Directory
US Department of Agriculture, 1227, 10863

Mechanical Contractor Directory Marketing
Mechanical Contractors Association America, 7643

Mechanical Power Transmission Association
Mechanical Power Transmission Association, 16954

Med Ad News
Canon Communicaitons Pharmaceutical Media Group, 6438

MedEsthetics
Creative Age Publications, 5853

Media
Media Index Publishing, 435

Media Access
WGBH Educational Foundation, 5107

Media Communications Association News
Media Communications Association International, 3870

Media Conference & Tradeshow
American Association of Advertising Agencies, 510

Media File
Media Alliance, 5108

Media Law Reporter
Bureau of National Affairs, 5109

Media Mergers & Acquisitions
Kagan World Media, 3871, 5110, 8839

Media Relations Insider
InfoCom Group, 20613

Media Relations Report
Ragan Communications, 20614

Media Reporter
Gay and Lesbian Press Association, 15222

Media Research Directors Association
Ogilvy and Mather, 5015

Media Sports Business
Kagan Research, 22135
Kagan World Media, 3872, 5111

Media Studies Journal
Columbia University, Freedom Forum Media Center, 5152

Media and Account Management Conference
Association of Hispanic Advertising Agencies, 511

MediaQuest
MediaQuest Publishing, 20615

Mediaweek
Prometheus Global Media, 436

Mediaweek Multimedia Directory
Prometheus Global Media, 559

Medical Abbreviations: 24,000
Niel M Davis Associates, 13508

Medical Design & Manufacturing Exhibition East/West
Canon Communications, 13429, 17636

Medical Design and Manufacturing Minneapolis Conference
Canon Communications, 13430

Medical Device Register
Grey House Publishing, 13509

Medical Economics
Advanstar Communicatons, 13147

Medical Equipment Design & Technology Conference
Canon Communications, 17637

Medical Equipment Design & Technology Exhibition & Conferenc
Canon Communications, 13431

Medical Equipment Designer
Adams Business Media, 7443

Medical Group Management Association
Medical Group Management Association, 13432, 17143

Medical Group Management Journal
Medical Group Management Association, 17352

Medical Group Management Update
Medical Group Management Association, 12968, 17260

Medical Liability Advisory Service
Business Publishers, 15840

Medical Malpractice Reports
Matthew Bender and Company, 15841

Medical Marketing and Media
Haymarket Media Inc, 560

Medical Meetings
Penton Media Inc, 13433
Primedia, 8508

Medical Plastics & Biomaterials
Canon Communications, 20330

Medical Reference Services Quarterly
Taylor & Francis, 16298
Taylor & Francis Group LLC, 13148

Medicare and Medicaid Conference
American Association of Health Plans, 13434

Medicine and Science in Sports and Exercise
American College of Sports Medicine, 22196

Meditation Software Market
Probe Research, 17871

Medtrade West
VNU Expositions, 13435

Medtrade/Comtrade
VNU Communications, 13436

Meeting Professionals
Meeting Professionals International, 8509

Meeting of the Acoustical Society of America
Acoustical Society of America, 7588

Meeting of the Electrochemical Society
Appliance Manufacturer, 6872

Meeting the Needs of Employees with Disabilities
Resources for Rehabilitation, 17443

Meetings & Conventions
Reed Business Information, 8510

Meetings Industry
Dunn Enterprises, 8511

Meetings and Conventions: Gavel International Directory Issu
Reed Travel Group, 8559

Member Data Disk
CQ Staff Directories, 12394

Member Directory and Oil & Gas Agencies
Interstate Oil and Gas Compact Commission, 19959

Membership Directory/Buyer's Guide
Naylor Publications, 24148

Membership Directory: Boating Industry Administration
National Association of State Boating Laws, 3721

Membership Roster and Registry of Geothermal Services & Equi
Geothermal Resources Council, 1481

Memo
American Institute of Architects, 2054

Memo to Mailers
US Postal Service, 6197

Memo to the President
American Association State Colleges & Universities, 20616

Memory Makers
F+W Media, 2249

Memphis Gift & Jewelry Show-Fall
Helen Brett Enterprises, 11899

Memphis Gift & Jewelry Show-Spring
Helen Brett Enterprises, 11900

Men's and Boy's Apparel Show
Miami International Merchandise Mart, 1799

Menswear Retailing Magazine
Business Journals Inc, 1746

Mental & Physical Disability Law Reporter
American Bar Association, 16006, 16007

Mental Health Law Reporter
Business Publishers, 16008

Mental and Physical Disability Law Reporter: On-Line
American Bar Association, 15842

Mentor Support Group Directory
National Association of Certified Valuation, 9199

Merchandise Mart Gift/Jewelry/ Resort Show
Denver Merchandise Mart, 15071

Merger & Acquisition Sourcebook Edition
Quality Services Company, 9200

Merger Strategy Report
SNL Securities, 8840

Merger Yearbook
Securities Data Publishing, 9201

Merger and Corporate Transactions Database
Securities Data Publishing, 9202

Mergers & Acquisitions Executive Compensation Review
SNL Securities, 8841

Mergers & Acquisitions Litigation Reporter
Thomson Reuters, 15843

Mergers & Acquisitions Yearbook
American Banker-Bond Buyer, 9203

Mergers and Acquisitions Handbook
National Association of Division Order Analysts, 9204

Messages
Society of Environmental Graphic Designers, 12525

Metal Architecture
Modern Trade Communications, 2089, 18394

Metal Bulletin's Prices and Data Book
Metal Bulletin, 18472

Metal Casting Industry Directory
Penton Media, 18473

Metal Center News
Reed Business Information, 18395

Metal Center News: Metal Distribution Issue
Hitchcock Publishing Company, 18474

Metal Construction Association
MCA Newsletter, 18347

Metal Finishing
Elsevier Science, 18396

Metal Finishing Guidebook Directory
Metal Finishing/Elsevier Science, 18475

Metal Finishing: Guidebook Directory
Metal Finishing/Elsevier Science, 18476

Metal Mecanica
Gardner Publications, 18397

Metal Roofing
F+W Media, 4290

Metal Statistics
American Metal Market, 18477

Metal Statistics: Ferrous Edition
American Metal Market, 18478

MetalForming
Precision Metalforming Association, 18398

Metalcasting Congress
North American Die Casting Association, 7589

Metalcon International
PSMJ Resources, 4390

Metallurgical and Materials Transactions
Minerals, Metals & Materials Society, 18399, 18639

Metals Datafile
Materials Information, 18479

Metalsmith
Society of North American Goldsmiths, 18400

Metalworking Digest
Reed Business Information, 18401

Metalworking Distributor
Penton Media, 18402

Metalworking Machine Tool Expo
Marketing International Corporation, 18448

Metalworking Machinery Mailer
Tade Publishing Group, 17055, 18480

Metropolis
Bellerophon Publications, 11686, 14598

Metropolis Magazine
Bellerophon Publications, 2090

Mexican Forecast
WorldTrade Executive, 14759

Mexican Motor Carrier Directory
Transportation Technical Services, 23152

Mexico Tax, Law,& Business Briefing
WorldTrade Executive, 14826

Michaels Create!
F+W Media, 2250, 14599

Micro Publishing
Cygnus Publishing, 5364

Micro Publishing Report's Directory of Desktop Publishing Su
Cygnus Publishing, 5712

Micro Ticker Report
Waters Information Services, 8842

Microbanker
Microbanker, 3318

Microcomputer Market Place
Random House, 5713

Microprocessor Integrated Circuits
DATA Digest, 5714

Microsoft Applications and Systems Forums
Microsoft Corporation, 5715

Microwave News
Microwave News, 22577

Microwave and RF
Penton Media, 7445

Mid American Beauty Classic
Premiere Show Group, 5906

Mid South Farm Gin Supply Exhibit
Southern Cotton Ginners Association, 1116

Mid South Industrial, Material Handling and Distribution Exp
Industrial Shows of America, 14057

Mid-America Association of Law Libraries
MidAmerican Energy Holdings Company, 16243

Mid-America Association of Law Libraries Convention
Mid-America Association of Law Libraries, 16072

Mid-America Commerce & Industry
Mid-America Commerce & Industry, 17578

Mid-America Farm Show
Salina Area Chamber of Commerce, 1117, 10574

Mid-America Horticulture Trade Show
Mid Am Trade Show, 1118

Mid-America Pool & Spa Show
Association of Pool & Spa Professionals, 24108

Mid-America Resturant, Soft Serve & Pizza Exposition
Exhibition Productions, 10576

Mid-America Sail & Power Boat Show
Lake Erie Marine Trade Association, 3697

Mid-Atlantic Electrical Exposition
S&L Productions, 6873

Mid-Atlantic Food, Beverage & Lodging Expo
Restaurant Association of Maryland, 10577

Mid-Atlantic Group Tour Magazine
Shoreline Creations, 23267

Mid-Atlantic Industrial Woodworking Expo Supply Show
Trade Shows, 11711

Mid-Atlantic Job Shop Show
Edward Publishing, 7590

Mid-Atlantic Nursery Trade Show
Mid Atlantic Nurserymen's Trade Shows, 11837

Mid-Atlantic Plumbing Heating Cooling Expo
Reber-Friel Company, 20452

Mid-Atlantic Regional Library Federation
South Maryland Regional Library, 16319

Mid-Atlantic Retail Food Industry Buyers' Guide
Mid-Atlantic Food Dealers Services, 10865

Mid-South Horn Conference
Central Washington University Music Department, 19158

Mid-South Jewelry & Accessories Fair-Fall
Helen Brett Enterprises, 11901, 11902, 15072, 15073

Mid-West Truck Trader
Heartland Communications, 23451

Mid-Year Technical Conference
National Assn of Government Guaranteed Lenders, 3319

MidAmerican Farmer Grower
MidAmerica Farm Publications, 948

Middle East Business Intelligence
International Executive Reports, 14760

Middle East Executive Reports
International Executive Reports, 14787

Middle East Geosciences Conference & Exhibition
Society of Exploration Geophysicists, 8249

Middle East Librarians' Association
Middle East Librarians Association, 16244

Midrange ERP
MFG Publishing, 17579

Midway USA Food Service and Hospitality Exposition
Kansas Restaurant and Hospitality Association, 10578

Midwest Alternative Dispute Resolution Guide
Law Bulletin Publishing Company, 16009

Midwest Boat Show
Lake Erie Marine Trade Association, 3698

Midwest Contractor
Associated Construction Publication, 4291

Midwest Contractors Expo
Kansas Assn of Plumbing, Heating & Cooling Contr, 13657

Midwest DairyBusiness
DairyBusiness Communications, 949

Midwest Expo: IL
Illinois Fertilizer & Chemical Association, 1120, 10579

Midwest Farm Show
North Country Enterprises, 1121, 10580

Midwest Flyer Magazine
Flyer Publications, 2891

Midwest Food Service News
Pinnacle Publishing, 10261

Midwest Gourmet Exposition
Fairchild Urban Expositions, 10582

Midwest International Band & Orchestra Clinic
Midwest International Band & Orchestra Clinic, 19159

Midwest Jewelry Expo
Wisconsin Jewelry Association, 15074

Midwest Job Shop Show
Edward Publishing, 17638

Midwest Leadership Conference
Indiana Retail Grocers Association, 10583

Midwest Legal Staffing Guide
Law Bulletin Publishing Company, 16010

Midwest Legal Technology Guide
Law Bulletin Publishing Company, 16011

Midwest Petroleum & Convenience Tradeshow
Illinois Petroleum Marketers Association, 19920

Midwest Real Estate News
The Law Bulletin Publishing Company, 21053

Midwest Regional Grape & Wine Conference
Missouri Grape and Wine Board, 10584

Midwest Truck Show
Mid-West Truckers Association, 23477

Midwestern Food Service and Equipment Exposition
Missouri Restaurant Association, 10585

Midwinter Executive Conference
Food Marketing Institute, 24109

Midyear Industry & Technology Issues Conference
American Society for Automation in Pharmacy, 6479

Military & Aerospace Electronics
PennWell Publishing Company, 7028

Military Biographical Profiles
CTB/McGraw Hill, 12395

Military Grocer
Downey Communications, 10262

Military Market
Gannet Company, 21384

Military Trader
F+W Media, 2251, 22197

Military Vehicles
F+W Media, 22198

Milk & Liquid Food Transporter
Brady Company, 23452

Milk and Liquid Food Transporter
Glen Street Publications, 10263

Mill Trade Journal's Recycling Markets
NV Business Publishers Corporation, 19324

Milling and Baking News
Sosland Publishing Company, 10265

Million Dollar Guide to Business and Real Estate Loan Source
International Wealth Success, 21129

Millwork Magazine
Association of Millwork Distributors, 16791

Mine Regulation Reporter
Pasha Publications, 18613

Mine Safety and Health News
Legal Publication Services, 18640

Mine and Quarry Trader
Primedia, 18641

Mineral Exploration Roundup
Assoc for Mineral Exploration British Columbia, 18669

Mineral and Energy Information
Mineral Information Institute, 18481

Minerals Yearbook
US Geological Survey, 18685

Miners News
Miners News, 18642

Mines Magazine
Colorado School of Mines Alumni Association, 18643

Mini Reviews
Cineman Syndicate, 18856

Mini-Storage Messenger
MiniCo, 23803

Mining Directory
Metal Bulletin, 18686

Mining Engineering: SME Membership Directory
Society of Mining, Metallurgy & Exploration, 18687

Mining Record
Mining Record Company, 18644

Mirror News
Market Power, 14572

Missouri Grocer
Missouri Grocers Association, 10266

Missouri Grocers Association Annual Convention & Food Trade
Missouri Grocers Association, 10866

Mix
Prism Business Media, 19109

Mobile Communication Business
Phillips Business Information, 22636

Mobile Internet
Information Gatekeepers, 6588

Mobilehome Parks Report
Thomas P Kerr, 21007

Mobility Magazine
Worldwide ERC, 21054

Model Retailer
Kalmbach Publishing Company, 13739

Modeling Power Devices and Model Validation
Power Sources Manufacturers Association, 7069

Modem Users News
Worldwide Videotex, 22578

Modern Applications News
Nelson Publishing, 17580, 18403

Modern Baking
Penton Media, 10267

Modern Brewery Age
Business Journals, 10268, 16614

Modern Brewery Age: Tabloid Edition
Business Journals, 10269, 16615

Modern Bulk Transporter
Tunnell Publications, 11567, 23453

Modern Bulk Transporter: Buyers Guide
Tunnell Publications, 11599

Modern Car Care
Virgo Publishing LLC, 2536

Modern Casting
American Foundrymen's Society, 18404

Modern Drug Discovery
American Chemical Society, 6439

Modern Drummer
Modern Drummer Publications, 19110

Modern Healthcare
Crain Communications, 13150

Modern Machine Shop
Gardner Publications, 17018, 18405

Modern Machine Shop's Handbook for Metalworkingi Industries
Gardner Publications, 5716

Modern Machine Shop: CNC & Software Guide Software Issue
Gardner Publications, 18482

Modern Materials Handling
Reed Business Information, 7446

Modern Paint & Coatings
Cygnus Publishing, 14027

Modern Plastics
Canon Communications, 20331

Modern Plastics Worldwide
Canon Communications, 20301

Modern Salon
Vance Publishing, 3446

Modern Woodworking
Modern Woodworking, 16792

Molecular Endocrinology
Molecular Society Journals, 13151

Molecular Plant: Microbe Interactions
American Phytopatholgical Society, 3553

Momentum
Metropolitan Life Insurance Company, 14358

Money Laundering Alert
Alert Global Media, 15844

Money Management Letter
Institutional Investor, 8843

Money Market Directory of Pension Funds and their Investment
Money Market Directories, 9205

Money Source Book
Business Information Network, 9206

Money for Film and Video Artists
Americans for the Arts, 19566

Money for International Exchange in the Arts
Americans for the Arts, 19567

Money for Performing Artists
Americans for the Arts, 19568

Money for Visual Arts
Americans for the Arts, 19569

MoneyData
Technical Data, 9207

MoneyWatch
McCarthy, Crisanti & Maffei, 9208

Monitor
Association of Clinical Research Professionals, 6440

Monitoring Times
Grove Enterprises, 3873

Monroe Originals
Karen Monroe, 15042

Montana Green Power Update
National Center for Appropriate Technology, 7959

Monthly Price Review
Urner Barry Publications, 10270

Monthly Resort Real Estate Property Index
MDR Telecom, 21130

More Beef from Pastures
Meat & Livestock Australia, 9997

Morningstar
Morningstar, 9209, 14476

Morristown Antiques Show
Wendy Management, 2285

Mortgage Bankers Association of America
Mortgage Bankers Association, 20944

Mortgage Banking
Mortgage Bankers Association, 3265

Mortgage Banking Performance Report
Mortgage Bankers Association of America, 21131

Mortgage Banking Sourcebook
Mortgage Bankers Association of America, 21132

Mortgage Finance Database
Mortgage Bankers Association of America, 21133

Mortgage Originator
Pfingsten Publishing, 9003

Mortgage Servicing News
Thomson Financial Publishing, 9004
Thomson Media, 3266

Mortgaged Backed Securities Letter
American Banker-Bond Buyer, 8844

Motion Control
ISA Services, 6819, 7447, 17019

Motion Control Technical Reference and Buyers Guide
ISA Services, 17056

Motion Picture Investor
Kagan World Media, 3874, 5112, 8845

Motion Picture TV and Theatre Directory
Motion Picture Enterprises, 18857

Motion System Distributor
Penton Media, 5539, 7448, 17020

Motivation Show
Hall-Erickson, 11903, 23310

Motocross American Reunion and Exhibit Grand Opening
American Motorcyclist Association, 18913

Motor
Hearst Business Communications, 2460

Motor Age
Chilton Company, 2537

Motor Boating
Time4 Media Marine Group, 3653

Motor Carrier Safety Report, HAZMAT Transportation Report
J.J. Keller & Associates, Inc., 7960

Motor Magazine
Hearst Business Communications, 2538

Motor Sports Forum
Racing Information Systems, 22353

Motor Trend
Primedia, 2539

Motor Vehicle Regulation: From the State Capitals
Wakeman Walworth, 12193

Motorcycle Dealer News
Edgell Communications, 18901

Motorcycle Industry Magazine
Industry Shopper Publishing, 18902

Motorcycle Statistical Annual
Motorcycle Industry Council, 18918

Motorcycle and Parts
Glahe International, 18914

Mountain Plains Library Association Annual Conference
Mountain Plains Library Association, 16320

Mouser Report
CAMCO, 21350

Movers News
New York State Movers & Warehousemen's Association, 23072

Movie Collectors World
Arena Publishing, 18822

Movie World Almanac
Hollywood Film Archive, 18858

MovieMaker
MovieMaker Magazine, 18823

Muir's Original Log Home Guide for Builders and Buyers
Gary J Schroder, 4292

MultiMedia & Internet @Schools
Information Today, 20802

Multichannel Merchant
Chief Marketer, 6222

Multicultural Council Meeting
Interactive Advertising Bureau, 512

Multifamily Executive
MGI Publications, 21056

Multilingual Thesaurus of Geosciences
Information Today, 4791

Multimedia & Internet Training Newsletter
Brandon Hall Resources, 6589

Multimedia Monograph Series
SIGDA Multimedia, 17057

Multimedia Strategist
Leader Publications, 17872

Multimedia Telecommunication News
Stoneridge Technical Services, 22637

Municipal Litigation Reporter
Strafford Publications, 15845

Municipal Year Book
ICMA Publications, 12396

Municipal Yellow Book
Leadership Directories, 12397

Museum
American Association of Museums, 2252

Museum Source
George Little Management, 11904

Museum Source: West
George Little Management, 11905

Museum Store
Museum Store Association, 11882

Museum Store Association Trade Show
Museum Store Association, 11906

Museum Store Magazine
Museum Store Association, 21385

Museums & More Specialty Shops Product News
Museums & More Specialty Product News, 21386

Mushroom News
American Mushroom Institute, 951, 10271

Music & Sound Retailer
Testa Communications, 19112

Music Library Association Membership Directory
Music Library Association, 19186

Music Trades Magazine
Music Trades, 19114

Musical America Directory
Musical America, 19187

Musical America International Directory of the Performing Ar
Commonwealth Business Media, 19570

Musical Box Society International
MBSI Member Registration, 19000

Musician's Guide
Billboard Directories, 19188

Mutual Fund Encyclopedia
Dearborn Financial Publishing, 9210

Mutual Fund/Municipal Bond
Interactive Data Corporation, 9211

Mx Newsletter
Professional Aviation Maintenance Association, 2807

Mystery Writer's Market Place and Sourcebook
Writer's Market, 16537

N

N2 Newspaper Next:
American Press Institute, 15223

NAA Annual Convention
Newspaper Association of America, 5178

NAA Record
National Aeronautic Association, 2808

NAAA Annual Conference
National Auto Auction Association, 2605

NAAB Annual Convention
National Association of Animal Breeders, 10586

NAAE Annual Convention
National Association of Agricultural Educators, 10587

NAAEE Annual Meeting
North American Association for Environmental, 8250

NAAFA Newsletter
National Association of Agricultural Fair Agencies, 8479

NEMA Mid-Year Conference
National Emergency Management Association, 12331

NEMRA Annual Conference
Nat'l Electrical Mfgs Representatives Association, 6877

NESHTA Annual Meetings
National Environmental, Safety and Health Training, 8257

NETA World
International Electrical Testing Association, 6820

NEWS 3X/400
Duke Communications International, 5541

NFAIS Annual Conference
National Federation Abstracting & Info Services, 5180

NFAIS e-Notes
National Federation Abstracting & Info Services, 5114

NFBPA FORUM
National Forum for Black Public Administrators, 12332

NFCA National Convention
National Fastpitch Coaches Association, 22303

NFCC Leaders Conference
National Foundation for Credit Counseling, 6047

NFFS Summit Conference
Non-Ferrous Founders' Society, 18449

NFPA Convention
National Federation of Paralegal Associations, 16073

NFPA Journal Update
National Fire Protection Association, 14306

NFPA Journal: Buyers' Guide
National Fire Protection Association, 21844

NFRA Update
National Frozen & Refrigerated Foods Association, 10001

NGA Annual Convention & Supermarket Synergy Showcase
National Grocers Association, 24118

NGI's Daily Gas Price Index
Intelligence Press, 19836

NGPP National Convention & Trade Show
National Guild of Professional Paperhangers, 14629

NGWA Ground Water Summit & GWPC Spring Meeting
Renewable Natural Resources Foundation, 8258

NHA Annual Convention
National Hay Association, 1124

NHA Today
National Hydropower Association, 1416

NHFA Trade Show
National Home Furnishings Association, 11687, 14601

NHLA Annual Convention & Exhibit Showcase North American Har
National Hardwood Lumber Association, 16833

NIA Annual Convention
National Insulation Association, 24119

NICRA Annual Meeting
National Ice Cream Retailers Association, 10613

NICRA Bulletin
National Ice Cream Retailers Association, 10002

NICSA Annual Meeting
National Investment Company Service Association, 9107

NICSA News
National Investment Company Service Association, 8852

NIPA Semi-Annual Meetings
National Institute of Pension Administrators, 9108

NIST Tech Beat
National Institute of Standards & Technology, 12272

NIWR Annual Conference
National Institutes for Water Resources, 8259

NIWR Member Directory
National Institutes for Water Resources, 8354

NJCAA Review
National Junior College Athletic Association, 22199

NLADA Directory of Legal Aid and Defender Offices in the US
National Legal Aid and Defender Association, 16135

NLGI Spokesman
National Lubricating Grease Institute, 19890

NMB Magazine
National Association of Mortgage Brokers, 3270

NMBA Annual Conference
National Marine Bankers Association, 3699

NMEA Convention & Expo
National Marine Electronics Association, 7133

NMRA Membership Directory
National Marine Representative Association, 3722

NOIA Leaders
National Ocean Industries Association, 19960

NORA News
NORA: an Association of Responsible Recyclers, 7963

NORA Semi-Annual Meetings
NORA: Association of Responsible Recyclers, 8260

NORPACK
Northern American Expositions Company, 23812

NORTHCON
Electronic Conventions, 6878

NOx Emissions & Source Monitoring Technical Conference and T
Instrumentation, Systems, and Automation Society, 6879

NPA
National Parking Association, 23118

NPA Annual Meeting
National Pawnbrokers Association, 9109

NPA Annual Parking, Transportation and Services Convention &
National Parking Association, 2610

NPA Fact of the Week
Natural Products Association, 10003

NPA NOW
Natural Products Association, 10004

NPELRA Annual Training Conference
National Public Employer Labor Relations Assoc., 12333

NPELRA Training Conference
National Public Employer Labor Relations Assoc, 12334

NPFDA Annual Convention
National Poultry & Food Distributors, 10614

NPFDA NEWS
National Poultry & Food Distributors, 10005

NPSC Meeting
National Electronics Service Dealers Association, 7134

NPTA Annual Convention
NPTA Alliance, 24120

NRA InSights
National Rifle Association, 22200

NRB Magazine
National Religious Broadcasters, 3922

NRB Shopping Center Directory
Trade Dimensions, 21448

NRB Today
National Religious Broadcasters, 3876, 21969

NRCMA Biweekly Email Bulletin
National Railroad Construction & Maintenance Assoc, 4195

NRCMA Conference
National Railroad Construction & Maintenance Assoc, 4393

NRCMA Membership Directory
National Railroad Construction & Maintenance Assoc, 4442

NRECA's Annual Meeting
National Rural Electric Cooperative Association, 6880

NREP Annual Meetings
National Registry of Environmental Professionals, 8261

NRF Annual Convention & EXPO
Retail Advertising & Marketing International, 514

NRF-BTM Retail Executive Opinion Survey
National Retail Federation, 21351

NRF/BIGresearch Consumer Intentions and Actions Survey
National Retail Federation, 21352

NRLA Annual Conference
National Rural Lenders Association, 6048

NRRA News
National Risk Retention Association, 14359

NSA Annual Meeting
National Shellfisheries Association, 9422

NSA Convention
National Speakers Association, 5181

NSA Directory
National Sheriff's Association, 16136

NSA Newsletter
National Shellfisheries Association, 9372, 10006

NSAA National Convention and Trade Show
National Ski Areas Association, 22304

NSBE Magazine
National Society of Black Engineers, 7449

NSCA Systems Integration Expo
National Systems Contractors Assocaition, 6881

NSCL Legislative Summit
National Conference of State Legislatures, 12335

NSGA Sporting Goods Alert
National Sporting Goods Association, 22137

NSGA Team Line-Up
National Sporting Goods Association, 22138

NSPA Washington Reporter
National Society of Public Accountants, 137

NSPE Annual Convention and Expo
National Society of Professional Engineers, 7593

NSPI Business Owners Journal
National Spa and Pool Institute, 24074

NSPI News
National Spa and Pool Institute, 24048

NSSGA Dredging Seminar & Expo
National Stone, Sand & Gravel Association, 4394

NSSRA Newsletter
National Ski and Snowboard Retailers Association, 21353

NTA Convention
National Tour Association, 23311

NTCA Exchange
National Telephone Cooperative Association, 22638

NTEA Membership Roster & Product Directory
National Truck Equipment Association, 23488

NTIS Alert- Photography & Recording Devices
National Technical Information Service, 20203

NTMA Record
Tooling, 16991

NW Food Manufacturing & Packaging Expo
Northwest Food Processors Association, 10615

NW Stylist and Salon
Porter Publishing, 3447

NWA Annual Education and Networking Conference & Exhibits
National WIC Association, 10617

NWA Newsletter
National Writers Association, 16500

NWA Technology Conference
National WIC Association, 10618

NWA Washington Leadership Conference
National WIC Association, 10619

NWFA Wood Flooring Convention and Expo
National Wood Flooring Association, 16834

NXTcomm
Telecommunications Industry Association/TIA, 22682

NYC/On Stage
Theatre Development Fund, 19571

NaSPA: Association for Corporate Computing Technical Profess
NaSPA, 5281

Nail Manufacturers Council
Professional Beauty Association, 5806

NailPro
Creative Age Publications, 3448

Nails Magazine
Bobit Business Media, 5855
Bobit Publishing Company, 3449

Narrow Fabrics Institute: Buyer's Guide
Narrow Fabrics Institute, 22827

Natinal Pawnbroker Magazine
National Pawnbrokers Association, 9008

National Decorating Product Show
Paint & Decorating Retailers Association, 14630

National Decorating Products Southern Show
Paint & Decorating Retailers Association, 14632

National Defense Magazine
National Defense Industrial Association, 21738

National Demolition Association Conference and Trade Show
National Demolition Association, 4396

National Dipper
US Exposition Corporation, 21246

National Directory of Addresses and Telephone Numbers
Omnigraphics, 18049

National Directory of Budget Motels
Pilot Books, 13912

National Directory of Bulletin Board Systems
Penton Media, 5717

National Directory of Community Newspapers
American Newspaper Representatives, 15276

National Directory of Conservation Land Trusts
Land Trust Alliance, 8355

National Directory of Corporate Giving
Foundation Center, 11490

National Directory of Corporate Public Affairs
Columbia Books, 12398

National Directory of Corrections Construction
National Institute of Justice, 16137

National Directory of Courts of Law
Information Resources, 16138

National Directory of Exchange Groups
Creative Real Estate Magazine, 21138

National Directory of Fire Chiefs & EMS Administrators
National Public Safety Information Bureau, 21845

National Directory of Integrated Healthcare Delivery Systems
Health Resources Publishing, 13510

National Directory of Investment Newsletters
GPS, 9219

National Directory of Law Enforcement Administrators
National Public Safety Information Bureau, 15509, 21846

National Directory of Managed Care Organzatons
Health Resources Publishing, 13511

National Directory of Physician Organizations Database On Cd
Health Resources Publishing, 13512

National Directory of Women Elected Officials
National Women's Political Caucus, 12399

National Dollhouse & Miniatures Trade Show & Convention
Miniatures Association of America, 13789

National Driller
Business News Publishing Company, 23888

National Drug Enforcement Officers Association
Drug Enforcement Administration, 15398

National Dry Stack Conference
Association of Marina Industries, 3702

National Editorial Conference
American Society of Business Publication Editors, 15259

National Education & Training Conference
National Black Police Association, 15497

National Educational Exposition and Conference
Environmental Management Association, 4899

National Electrical Equipment Show
Reed Exhibition Companies, 6882

National Electrical Manufacturers Representatives Associatio
National Electrical Manufacturers Rep Assoc, 6914

National Electrical Wire Processing Technology Expo
Expo Productions, 6883

National Electricity Forum
NARUC, 12338

National Electronic Distributors Association Membership Dire
National Electronic Distributors Association, 6915

National Employee Services and Recreation Association
Employee Services Management Association, 17154

National Employment Listing Service Bulletin
Criminal Justice Center, 15510, 16139

National Environmental Balancing Bureau Meeting
National Environmental Balancing Bureau, 8263

National Environmental Data Referral Service
US National Environmental Data Referral Service, 8356

National Ergonomics Conference & Exposition
Continental Exhibitions, 5667, 21809

National Estimator
Society of Cost Estimating and Analysis, 138

National Farm Machinery Show and Championship Tractor Pull
Kentucky Fair and Exposition Center, 1136, 10633

National Farmers Union News
National Farmers Union, 953, 10278

National Federation of Press Women
National Federation of Press Women, 16479

National Financing Law Digest
Strafford Publications, 15850

National Fire Protection Association Newsletter
National Fire Protection Association, 21739

National Fire Protection World Safety Conference & Expositio
National Fire Protection Association, 21810

National Fish & Wildlife Conservation Congress
Association of Fish & Wildlife Agencies, 8264

National Fisherman
Diversified Business Communications, 9393, 10279

National Flood Risk Management; Flood Risk Summit
Association of State Floodplain Managers, 8265

National FloodProofing Conference and Exposition Levees and
Association of State Floodplain Managers, 8266

National Floor Trends
Business News Publishing Company, 14602

National Fluid Power Association
National Fluid Power Association, 16955

National Food Processors Association Convention
National Food Processors Association, 10280, 10634

National Forensic Center Trade Show
National Forensic Center, 16079

National Frame Builders Association Newsletter
National Frame Builders Association, 16756

National Fraud Issues Conference
Mortgage Bankers Association, 3326, 6050

National Frozen and Refrigerated Foods Convention
National Frozen & Refrigerated Foods Association, 10635

National Golf Cart Manufacturers Association
NGCMA Attn: Fred Somers, Jr., 22048

National Governors' Association
Hall of States, 12119

National Grain Feed Association Annual Convention
National Grain Feed Association, 1138

National Grocer
National Grocers Association, 10281

National Grocers Association Annual Convenience & Supermarke
National Grocers Association, 10637

National Ground Water Association Annual Convention and Expo
National Ground Water Association, 23907

National Guild of Community Schools of the Arts Conference
National Guild of Community Schools of the Arts, 2288

National Halloween & Costume & Party Show
Transworld Exhibits, 1801

National Halloween Convention
Transworld Exhibits, 11907

National Hardware Show
Association Expositions & Services, 12624
Reed Exhibition Companies, 11713
Reed Exhibitions, 4397

National Hardware Show/National Building Products Exposition
Reed Exhibition Companies, 12625

National Hardwood Lumber Association
National Hardwood Lumber Association, 16706

National Hardwood Magazine
Miller Publishing Company, 16793

National Highway Carriers Directory
National Highway Carriers Directory, 23155

National Highway and Airway Carriers Directory
National Highway Carriers Directory, 11601

National Hispanic American Attorney Directory
Hispanic National Bar Association, 16140

National Hispanic Market Trade Show and Media Expo (Se Habla
Hispanic Business, 5182, 18006
Hispanic Business Inc, 20645

National Homebrewers Conference and National Homebrew Compet
Brewers Association, 10638

National Honey Market News
US Department of Agriculture, 10010

National Honey Report
Federal Market News Service, 790

National Hydropower Association Annual Conference
National Hydropower Association, 1466

National Independent Automobile Dealers Association Conventi
National Independent Automobile Dealers Assoc., 2612

National Industrial Automation, Integration & Control Show
Reed Exhibition Companies, 7594

National Industrial Transportation League Reference Manual
National Industrial Transportation League, 23156

National Institute for Golf Management
National Golf Foundation, 22306

National Institute for Water Resources
University of Massachusetts, 23858

National Institute of Justice
US Department Of Justice, 15402

National Institute of Packaging, Handling and Logistic Engin
NIPHLE, 23157

National Insurance Law Service/Insource Insurance
NILS Publishing Company, 14479

National Intelligence Report
Institute of Management and Administration, 12969

National Investment Banking Association Annual Conference
National Investment Banking Association, 3327

National Jeweler: Industry Yellow Pages
Miller Freeman Publications, 15098

National Journal
National Journal, 12274, 20869

National Law Journal: Directory of Current Law & Law-Related
New York Law Publishing Company, 16141

National Lawn & Garden Controlled Marketing Conference
Controlled Marketing Conferences, 21427

National Lawn & Garden Trade Show
Great American Exhibitions, 11840

National Lawn and Garden Show
Controlled Marketing Conferences, 11841

National Leadership Conference
Association of Government Accountants, 281

National League of Postmasters Annual National Convention
National League of Postmasters, 12339

National Library Service for the Blind
Library of Congress, 16250

National Lighting Fair
Dallas Market Center, 6884

National Locksmith
National Publishing Company, 21740

National Magazine Awards
American Society of Magazine Editors, 15260

National Mail Order Merchandise Show
Expo Accessories, 18007

O

One List Directory
MRH Associates, 21144

One Sky
One Sky, 1382

Onion World
Columbia Publishing, 961

Online & CD-ROM Review
Information Today, 6590

Online Advertising Playbook
John Wiley & Sons, 562

Online Audiovisual Catalogers
Minnesota State University, 5284

Online Libraries & Microcomputers
Information Intelligence, 6591

Online MCP
American Concrete Institute, 22500

Online Magazine
Information Today, 22201

Online Marketing Letter
Cyberware Media, 17877

Online Marketplace
Jupiter Communications Company, 17878

Online Networks, Databases & Bulletin Boards on Assistive Te
ERIC Document Reproduction Service, 5719

Online Newsletter
Information Intelligence, 6592, 22581

Online Publishing Update E-Newsletter
Newspaper Association of America, 5116, 20762

Online Reporter
G2 Computer Intelligence, 6133, 6593

Opastco Roundtable
OPASTCO, 22641

Open Systems Economics Letter
Computer Economics, 5368

Opera America Conference
Opera America, 19169

Opera America Membership Directory
Opera America, 19573

Opera America Newsline
Opera America, 19119

Opera News
Metropolitan Opera Guild, 19120

Operations & Fulfillment
Primedia, 6223, 17354

Operations Forum
Water Environment Federation, 23889

Operations Update
Helicopter Association International, 2814

Opportunities for Banks in Life Insurance
American Association of Bank Directors, 3192

Opportunity
Career Skills Press/Brody Communications, 20618

Optical Fiber Communications Conference
Optical Society of America, 5669

Optical Memory News
Phillips Publishing, 5369

Optical Networks and WDM
IGI Group, 22582

Optical Technology 21st Century
Frames Data, 6656

Optics & Photonics News (OPN)
Optical Society of America, 7029

Optics Letters
Optical Society of America, 7070

Optics and Spectroscopy
Optical Society of America, 7457

Optometry's Meeting
American Optometric Association, 13452

Optometry: Journal of the American Optometric Association
American Optometric Association, 13161

Organic Business News
Hotline Printing & Publishing, 10021

Organic Food Mail Order Suppliers
Center for Science in the Public Interest, 10875

Organic Pages Online
Organic Trade Association, 10876

Organic Pages Online North American Resource Directory
Organic Trade Association, 1231

Organic Report
Organic Trade Association, 799

Organic Trade Association Newsletter
Organic Trade Association, 10022

Organic WORLD
John Pappenheimer, 10298

Organic World
Loft Publishing, 962

Organization Charts
Carroll Publishing, 12403

Organization Development Journal
Organization Development Institute, 17355

Organized Executive
Briefings Publishing Group, 17879

Original Equipment Suppliers Association
Original Equipment Suppliers Association, 20602

Origination News
Thomson Financial, 3193

Orion Blue Book: Camera
Orion Research Corporation, 20255

Orion Blue Book: Computer
Orion Research Corporation, 5720, 23753

Orion Blue Book: Copier
Orion Research Corporation, 19283

Orion Blue Book: Guitars and Musical Instruments
Orion Research Corporation, 19190

Orion Blue Book: Guns and Scopes
Orion Research Corporation, 22355

Orion Blue Book: Professional Sound
Orion Research Corporation, 19191

Orion Blue Book: Tools
Orion Research Corporation, 17058

Orion Blue Book: Video and Television
Orion Research Corporation, 23754

Orion Blue Book: Vintage Guitar
Orion Research Corporation, 19192

Orlando Business Journal
Business Journals, 17262

Ornamental and Miscellaneous Metals Fabricator
National Ornamental & Miscellaneous Metals Assn, 18407

Orthopedic Surgical Manufacturers Association
BioMet, 12910

Osteopathic Physicians & Surgeons Annual Convention
Osteopathic Physicians & Surgeons of California, 13453

Ostomy Wound Management
HMP Communications, 13162

Outdoor Advertising Magazine
Outdoor Advertising Magazine, 438

Outdoor America
Isaak Walton League, 8101

Outdoor Electrical Safety Check Booklet
Electrical Safety Foundation International, 6917

Outdoor Journal
American Crappie Association, 9396

Outdoor News Bulletin
Wildlife Management Institute, 7971

Outdoor Photographer
Werner Publshing Corporation, 20218

Outdoor Power Equipment
Adams Business Media, 12611

Outdoor Power Equipment and Engine Service Association
Outdoor Power Equipment and Engine, 16958

Outdoor Retailer Summer Market
Nielsen Sports Group, 1808

Outdoor Retailer Winter Market
VNU Expositions, 1809

Outdoorama Family Sport and Travel Show
Michigan United Conservation Clubs, 22314

Outdoors Magazine
Elk Publishing, 22202

Outerwear
Creative Marketing Plus, 1749

Outerwear Sourcebook: Directory Issue
Creative Marketing Plus, 1865

Outlet Project Directory
Off-Price Specialists, Value Retail News, 24149
Value Retail News, 21449

Outlet Retail Directory
Off-Price Specialists, Value Retail News, 21450

Outlook & Strategies Conference
Paperboard Packaging Council, 11581

Outlook: From the State Capitals
Wakeman Walworth, 12206

Outside Plant
Practical Communications, 22642

Outside Plant: Directory of Outside Plant Contractors Issue
Practical Communications, 22707

Over the Road
Ramp Publishing Group, 23457

Overcoming Objections
Dartnell Corporation, 17880

Overdrive Magazine
Randall Publishing Company, 23458

Overhaul & Maintenance
McGraw Hill, 2898

Overseas Press Club of America Directory
Overseas Press Club of America, 15243; 15279

Owner Operator
Reed Business Information, 23459

Ozark Fall Farmfest
Ozark Empire Fair, 1153

P

P&D Magazine
Motor Transport Management Group, 23075

PA TIMES
American Society for Public Administration, 12207

PACE: Paint and Coatings Expo
Painting and Decorating Contractors of America, 4402

PACK International Expo
Packaging Machinery Manufacturers Institute, 10669

PACex International
Packaging, Food Process and Logistics Exhibition, 10670

PAMA Aviation Maintenance & Management Symposium
Professional Aviation Maintenance Association, 2976

PARCEL
RB Publishing, 11568

PBA Beauty Week
Professional Beauty Association, 5916

PBA Symposium
Professional Beauty Association, 5917, 24122

PC Arcade
Softdisk Publishing, 5546

PC Bridge
Bridge Information Systems, 9221

PC Graphics & Video
Advantstar Communications, 12545

PC Photo
Werner Publishing, 20219

PC Presentations Productions
Pisces Publishing Group, 20527

PC Sources
Ziff Davis Publishing Company, 5547

PC Systems and Support
Technical Enterprises, 5548

PC Techniques
Coriolis Group, 5549

PC Today
Promotional Products Association International, 439

Products for Document Management
Acron Publishing, 5555

Productscan Online
Marketing Intelligence Service, 21452

Professional Advisor
Int'l Society of Speakers, Authors & Consultants, 17269

Professional Agent
Association of Professional Insurance Agents, 14365

Professional Apartment Management
Brownstone Publishers, 21010

Professional Apparel Association Trade
Professional Apparel Association, 1813

Professional Aviation Maintenance Symposium and Trade Show
Professional Aviation Maintenance Association, 2979

Professional Beauty Association Annual Convention
Professional Beauty Association, 5922

Professional BoatBuilder
WoodenBoat Publications, 3657

Professional Boatbuilder: International Boatbuilders Expo an
WoodenBoat Publications, 3706

Professional Builder
Reed Business Information, 2094, 4302, 22486

Professional Carwashing and Detailing
National Trade Publications, 2550

Professional Collector
Pohly & Partners, 9017

Professional Door Dealer Magazine
Virgo Publishing LLC, 4303

Professional Freelance Writers Directory
National Writers Club, 16540

Professional Geologist
American Institute of Professional Geologists, 18650

Professional Golfers Association Golf Show
Sydney Convention and Exhibition Centre, 22318

Professional Golfers Association Merchandise Show
Reed Exhibitions, 22317

Professional Insurance Agents National Annual Conference & E
National Association of Prof. Insurance Agents, 14435

Professional Investor Report
Dow Jones & Company, 9227

Professional Jeweler
Bond Communications, 15044

Professional Journal
AFSM International, 17358

Professional Journal: Sbusiness Publication
AFSM International, 5155

Professional Lawyer
American Bar Association, 16024

Professional Photographer
PPA Publications, 20235

Professional Photographer American Expo
Professional Photographers of America, 20245

Professional Photographers Association
Professional Photographers Assoc. of New England, 20180

Professional Picture Framers Association Show
Professional Picture Framers Association, 2290

Professional Pilot
Queensmith Communications, 2904

Professional Publishing Report
Simba Information, 20766

Professional Relocation and Real Estate Services Directory
Relocation Information Service, 21145

Professional Remodeler
Reed Business Information, 4304

Professional Report
Society of Industrial & Office Realtors, 21064

Professional Roofing
National Roofing Contractors Association, 4305

Professional Safety
American Society of Safety Engineers, 21746

Professional Safety Journal
American Society of Safety Engineering, 7476

Professional Security Alliance Conference & Exhibits
PSA Security Network, 21814

Professional Skater
Professional Skaters Association, 22210

Professional Trade Association Membership
Local Hispanic Chamber of Commerce, 6690

Professional Travelogue Sponsors
El Camino College Foundation, 20183

Professional Truck Driver Institute
Express Carriers Association, 23418

Professional Trucking Services Association
United Truckers Service, 23420

Professional Women Photographers
Metropolitan Opera Guild, 20184

Professional Workers in State Agricultural Experiment Statio
US Department of Agriculture, 1233, 10893

Profile of Pharmacy Faculty
American Association of Colleges of Pharmacy, 6452

Profiles of America
Grey House Publishing, 21146

Profiles of Worldwide Government Leaders
Worldwide Government Directories, 12405

Profiles of...Series - State Handbooks
Grey House Publishing, 21147

Profiles: Health Insurance Edition
National Underwriter Company, 14481

Profiles: Property and Casualty Insurance Edition
National Underwriter Company, 14482

Profit Line
Ernst and Young, 17270

Programming Magazine
National Association for Campus Activities, 8512

Prograzier
Meat & Livestock Australia, 10319

Progress
National Association of Elevator Safety, 21702

Progress Report: The Foundation Newsletter
AAA Foundation for Traffic Safety, 21703

Progressive Architecture
Progressive Scale, 14607

Progressive Architecture: Information Sources Issue
Penton Media, 2122

Progressive Distributor
Pfingsten Publishing, 17594

Progressive Grocer's Marketing Guidebook
Trade Dimensions, 10321

Progressive Periodicals Directory
Progressive Education, 20870

Progressive Railroading
Trade Press Publishing Corporation, 23077

Project Management Journal
Project Management Institute, 17359

Project Management for IT Professionals
CompuMaster, 17410

Projects in Metal
Village Press, 18412

PromaxBDA
PROMAX, 17965

Promo
Chief Marketer, 6225

Promo Expo
Promo Expo Sales, 18011

Promos & Premiums
New World Media, 17888

Promotional Consultant Magazine
Promotional Products Association International, 444

Promowear
National Bussines Media Inc, 1752

Propeller
American Power Boat Association, 3658

Propeller Club Newsletter
Propeller Club of the United States, 3625

Property/Casualty Insurance
National Association of Mutual Insurance Companies, 14366

Prosecutor
National District Attorneys Association, 12280, 16025

Prosound News
United Entertainment Media, 23742

Protecting Intellectual Property in Latin America
WorldTrade Executive, 14831

Protection News
International Foundation for Protection Officers, 21704

Protein Science
Protein Society, 3556

Protocol
Entertainment Services and Technology Association, 1607
Protocol Directory, 8563

Prove It! Measuring Safety Performance Symposium
American Society of Safety Engineers, 21815

Psoriasis Resource
National Psoriasis Foundation, 6395

Psychology of Addictive Behaviors
University of South Florida, 13168

Public Accounting Desk Book
Strafford Publications, 152

Public Accounting Report
CCH, 153

Public Administration Review (PAR)
American Society for Public Administration, 12281

Public Agency Risk Managers Association Convention
Public Agency Risk Managers Association, 14436

Public Broadcasting Report
Warren Communications News, 3879

Public Budgeting and Finance
American Association for Budget and Program, 222

Public Citizen Organizations
Public Citizen, 8360

Public Contract Law Journal
American Bar Association, 16026

Public Contract Newsletter
American Bar Association, 15874

Public Gas News
American Public Gas Association, 19853, 23577

Public Health
State Capitals Newsletters, 12975

Public Health: From the State Capitals
Wakeman Walworth, 12209

Public Human Services Directory
American Public Human Services Association, 12406

Public Integrity
American Society for Public Administration, 12282

Public Library Association
Public Library Association, 16253

Public Library Association National Conference
Public Library Association, 16322

Public Opinion Journal
American Association for Public Opinion Research, 445

Public Power Directory of Local Publicly Owned Electric Util
American Public Power Association, 23663

Public Power Magazine
American Public Power Association, 23619

Public Record Research System
BRB Publications, 12407

Public Records Online
BRB Publications, 12408

Public Relations Career Opportunities
CEO Update, 20627

Public Relations Quarterly
Howard Penn Hudson, 20638

Public Relations Review
Elsevier, 20639

Public Relations Strategist
Public Relations Society of America, 20640

Public Relations Tactics
Public Relations Society of America, 20641, 20657

Public Relations Tactics: Register Issue/The Blue Book
Public Relations Society of America, 20658

V

Validated Water Treatment Equipment Directory
Water Quality Association, 23920

Valley Gazette
Hometown Publications, 18656

Valuation Compilation
National Association of Certified Valuation, 9256

Valuation Insights & Perspectives
Appraisal Institute, 21084

Value Examiner
National Association of Certified Valuation, 9041

Valve Magazine
Valve Manufacturers Association of America, 17029, 20447

Valve Manufacturers Association of America (VMA)
Valve Manufacturers Association of America, 16974

Variety
Reed Business Information, 18832

Variety Merchandise Show
Miller Freeman Publications, 11920, 13796

Varindustry Products
VIPublishing, 5608

Vegetable
US Department of Agriculture, 10383

Vegetable Growers News
Great American Publishing, 1019, 10384

Vegetables
Western Agricultural Publishing Company, 1020, 10385

Vegetarian Journal
Vegetarian Resource Group, 816, 10386

Vegetarian Times
Active Interest Media, 10063

Veggie Life Magazine
EGW, 10387

Velobusiness
Inside Communications, 22246

Velocitus Officers Newsletter
Theta Tau, 7353

Velocity
Strategic Account Management Association, 17982

Vending Times
Vending Times, 1617, 10388

Venture Capital & Health Care Conference
Asset Alternatives, 8902, 9123

Venture Capital Information Technology
Asset Alternatives, 8903

Venture Capital Journal
Securities Data Publishing, 9042

Venture Capital: Where to Find it
National Association of Small Business Investment, 9257

Venture Views & News
Venture Communications, 6205

Verdicts & Settlement
Daily Journal Corporation, 16040

Vertiflite
American Helicopter Society International, 2915

Veterinary Economics
Veterinary Healthcare Communications, 20119

Veterinary Industry Newsletter
Good Communications, 20065

Via Satellite
Phillips Business Information, 3931

Vibration Institute
Vibration Institute, 16975

Vibrations Magazine
Vibration Institute, 17030

Video & Entertainment
Fairchild Publications, 23745

Video Age International
Video Age International, 23746

Video Business
Reed Business Information, 23732

Video Investor
Kagan Research, 23733
Kagan World Media, 3888, 8904

Video Librarian
Video Librarian, 16304, 23747

Video Marketing Newsletter
Outback Group Productions, 17911

Video Networks
Bay Area Video Coalition, 23755

Video Source Book
Gale/Cengage Learning, 23756

Videomaker Magazine
Videomaker, 23749

Vietnam Business Info Track
Vietnam Access, 14767

Vietnam Business Journal
VIAM Communications Group, 14792

Vietnam Market Watch
Vietnam Market Resources, 14768

Vinegar Institute: Basic Reference Manual
Vinegar Institute, 10954

Vineyard & Winery Management Magazine
Vineyard & Winery Services, 10955, 16647

Vineyard and Winery Management Magazine
Vineyard & Winery Management, 10389, 16622

Vinotizie Italian Wine Newsletter
Italian Trade Commission, 10064, 16601

Virginia Farm Show
Lee Publications, 1186

Virus Bulletin
Virus Bulletin, 6659

Vision
Society of Manufacturing Engineers, 6781, 17533

Vision Systems Design
PennWell Publishing Company, 5609

Visitor Studies Today
Visitor Studies Association, 8518

Visual Anthropology Review
American Anthropoligical Association, 2262

Visual Basic Programmer's Journal
Fawcette Technical Publications, 5610

Visual Communications Journal
Graphic Arts Technical Foundation Association, 12554

Visual Merchandising and Store Design
ST Media Group International, 2125

VoIP 2.0
Technology Marketing Corporation, 6679

Vocational Equipment Directory for GMC Truck Dealers
Verbiest Publishing Company, 23492

Voice Mail Reference Manual and Buyer's Guide
Robins Press, 22722

Voice Processing Printed Circuit Cards: A Sourcebook of Supp
Robins Press, 22723

VoiceNews
Stoneridge Technical Services, 22602

Volt Report on Directory Publishing
Volt Directory Marketing, 20814

Volunteer & Combination Officers Section Symposium in the Su
International Association of Fire Chiefs, 17414

Vows Magazine
Peter Grimes, 1757

Vue/Point Conference
Graphic Arts Show Company, 5683, 20558

W

WACRA Annual Conference Research & Application
World Assoc for Case Method Research & Application, 17415

WACRA News
World Assoc for Case Method Research & Application, 17286

WACRA Newsletter
World Assoc for Case Method Research & Application, 17287

WAM: Western Apparel Manufacturers Show
Dallas Market Center, 1823

WATERNET
American Water Works Association, 23921

WATT Poultry Magazine
WATT Poultry USA, 10390

WBCA National Convention
Women's Basketball Coaches Association, 22337

WBMA Annual Convention
Western Building Material Association, 4413

WCRI Annual Issues & Research Conference
Workers Compensation Research Institute, 14442

WDweekly
National Glass Association, 11961

WEF Highlights
Water Environment Federation, 7996

WESTEC-Advanced Productivity Expo
Society of Manufacturing Engineers, 18454

WESTLAW Insurance Library
West Publishing Company, 14489

WESTLAW International Law Library
West Publishing Company, 16156

WESTLAW Legal Services Library
West Publishing Company, 16157

WESTLAW Litigation Library
West Publishing Company, 16158

WESTLAW Transportation Library
West Publishing Company, 23168

WFFC Newsletter
Women in Flavor & Fragrance Commerce, 5828

WFLO/IARW Annual Convention & Trade Show
World Food Logistics Organization, 10724

WINDOWS Magazine
CMP Publications, 5611

WINDPOWER Conference and Exhibition
American Wind Energy Association (AWEA), 8302, 23642

WMC: Western Simulation Multiconference
Society for Modeling and Simulation International, 5684

WMDA Mega Show Annual Convention
WMDA Service Station & Automotive Repair Assoc., 2632

WPMA Convention & Convenience Store Expo
Western Petroleum Marketers Association, 19934

WPMA Weekly Update
Western Petroleum Marketers Association, 19856

WPPI Conference & Expo
Wedding & Portrait Photographers International, 20248

WRC Bulletin
Welding Research Council, 18353

WSA Today
Show Dailies International, 21932

WSA: Western Shoe Associates
Western Shoe Associates, 1824

WSSA Annual Meeting
Weed Science Society of America, 8303

WSSA Newsletter
Weed Science Society of America, 10065

WSWA Annual Convention
Wine and Spirits Wholesalers of America, 10725

WSWA Convention & Exposition
Wine and Spirits Wholesalers of America, 10726

WSWA Executive Committee Meeting
Wine and Spirits Wholesalers of America, 10727

WWD Beauty Biz
Fairchild Publications, 3453, 5865

WWD Buyers Guide: Womens Apparel and Accessories Manufacture
Fairchild Publications, 1866

WWD Magic
MAGIC International, 1825

WWD Suppliers Guide
Fairchild Books and Visuals, 1867

WWWiz Magazine
WWWiz Corporation, 6660

Wafer News Confidential
PennWell Publishing Company, 6782

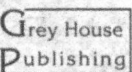

2016 Title List

Visit www.GreyHouse.com for Product Information, Table of Contents, and Sample Pages.

General Reference

An African Biographical Dictionary
America's College Museums
American Environmental Leaders: From Colonial Times to the Present
Encyclopedia of African-American Writing
Encyclopedia of Constitutional Amendments
Encyclopedia of Gun Control & Gun Rights
An Encyclopedia of Human Rights in the United States
Encyclopedia of Invasions & Conquests
Encyclopedia of Prisoners of War & Internment
Encyclopedia of Religion & Law in America
Encyclopedia of Rural America
Encyclopedia of the Continental Congress
Encyclopedia of the United States Cabinet, 1789-2010
Encyclopedia of War Journalism
Encyclopedia of Warrior Peoples & Fighting Groups
The Environmental Debate: A Documentary History
The Evolution Wars: A Guide to the Debates
From Suffrage to the Senate: America's Political Women
Global Terror & Political Risk Assessment
Nations of the World
Political Corruption in America
Privacy Rights in the Digital Era
The Religious Right: A Reference Handbook
Speakers of the House of Representatives, 1789-2009
This is Who We Were: 1880-1900
This is Who We Were: A Companion to the 1940 Census
This is Who We Were: In the 1910s
This is Who We Were: In the 1920s
This is Who We Were: In the 1940s
This is Who We Were: In the 1950s
This is Who We Were: In the 1960s
This is Who We Were: In the 1970s
U.S. Land & Natural Resource Policy
The Value of a Dollar 1600-1865: Colonial Era to the Civil War
The Value of a Dollar: 1860-2014
Working Americans 1770-1869 Vol. IX: Revolutionary War to the Civil War
Working Americans 1880-1999 Vol. I: The Working Class
Working Americans 1880-1999 Vol. II: The Middle Class
Working Americans 1880-1999 Vol. III: The Upper Class
Working Americans 1880-1999 Vol. IV: Their Children
Working Americans 1880-2015 Vol. V: Americans At War
Working Americans 1880-2005 Vol. VI: Women at Work
Working Americans 1880-2006 Vol. VII: Social Movements
Working Americans 1880-2007 Vol. VIII: Immigrants
Working Americans 1880-2009 Vol. X: Sports & Recreation
Working Americans 1880-2010 Vol. XI: Inventors & Entrepreneurs
Working Americans 1880-2011 Vol. XII: Our History through Music
Working Americans 1880-2012 Vol. XIII: Education & Educators
World Cultural Leaders of the 20th & 21st Centuries

Education Information

Charter School Movement
Comparative Guide to American Elementary & Secondary Schools
Complete Learning Disabilities Directory
Educators Resource Directory
Special Education: A Reference Book for Policy and Curriculum Development

Health Information

Comparative Guide to American Hospitals
Complete Directory for Pediatric Disorders
Complete Directory for People with Chronic Illness
Complete Directory for People with Disabilities
Complete Mental Health Directory
Diabetes in America: Analysis of an Epidemic
Directory of Drug & Alcohol Residential Rehab Facilities
Directory of Health Care Group Purchasing Organizations
Directory of Hospital Personnel
HMO/PPO Directory
Medical Device Register
Older Americans Information Directory

Business Information

Complete Television, Radio & Cable Industry Directory
Directory of Business Information Resources
Directory of Mail Order Catalogs
Directory of Venture Capital & Private Equity Firms
Environmental Resource Handbook
Food & Beverage Market Place
Grey House Homeland Security Directory
Grey House Performing Arts Directory
Grey House Safety & Security Directory
Grey House Transportation Security Directory
Hudson's Washington News Media Contacts Directory
New York State Directory
Rauch Market Research Guides
Sports Market Place Directory

Statistics & Demographics

American Tally
America's Top-Rated Cities
America's Top-Rated Smaller Cities
America's Top-Rated Small Towns & Cities
Ancestry & Ethnicity in America
The Asian Databook
Comparative Guide to American Suburbs
The Hispanic Databook
Profiles of America
"Profiles of" Series - State Handbooks
Weather America

Financial Ratings Series

TheStreet Ratings' Guide to Bond & Money Market Mutual Funds
TheStreet Ratings' Guide to Common Stocks
TheStreet Ratings' Guide to Exchange-Traded Funds
TheStreet Ratings' Guide to Stock Mutual Funds
TheStreet Ratings' Ultimate Guided Tour of Stock Investing
Weiss Ratings' Consumer Guides
Weiss Ratings' Guide to Banks
Weiss Ratings' Guide to Credit Unions
Weiss Ratings' Guide to Health Insurers
Weiss Ratings' Guide to Life & Annuity Insurers
Weiss Ratings' Guide to Property & Casualty Insurers

Bowker's Books In Print® Titles

American Book Publishing Record® Annual
American Book Publishing Record® Monthly
Books In Print®
Books In Print® Supplement
Books Out Loud™
Bowker's Complete Video Directory™
Children's Books In Print®
El-Hi Textbooks & Serials In Print®
Forthcoming Books®
Large Print Books & Serials™
Law Books & Serials In Print™
Medical & Health Care Books In Print™
Publishers, Distributors & Wholesalers of the US™
Subject Guide to Books In Print®
Subject Guide to Children's Books In Print®

Canadian General Reference

Associations Canada
Canadian Almanac & Directory
Canadian Environmental Resource Guide
Canadian Parliamentary Guide
Canadian Venture Capital & Private Equity Firms
Financial Post Directory of Directors
Financial Services Canada
Governments Canada
Health Guide Canada
The History of Canada
Libraries Canada
Major Canadian Cities

Grey House Publishing | Salem Press | H.W. Wilson | 4919 Route, 22 PO Box 56, Amenia NY 12501-0056

2016 Title List

Visit **www.SalemPress.com** for Product Information, Table of Contents, and Sample Pages.

Science, Careers & Mathematics

Ancient Creatures
Applied Science
Applied Science: Engineering & Mathematics
Applied Science: Science & Medicine
Applied Science: Technology
Biomes and Ecosystems
Careers in Building Construction
Careers in Business
Careers in Chemistry
Careers in Communications & Media
Careers in Environment & Conservation
Careers in Healthcare
Careers in Hospitality & Tourism
Careers in Human Services
Careers in Law, Criminal Justice & Emergency Services
Careers in Manufacturing
Careers in Physics
Careers in Sales, Insurance & Real Estate
Careers in Science & Engineering
Careers in Technology Services & Repair
Computer Technology Innovators
Contemporary Biographies in Business
Contemporary Biographies in Chemistry
Contemporary Biographies in Communications & Media
Contemporary Biographies in Environment & Conservation
Contemporary Biographies in Healthcare
Contemporary Biographies in Hospitality & Tourism
Contemporary Biographies in Law & Criminal Justice
Contemporary Biographies in Physics
Earth Science
Earth Science: Earth Materials & Resources
Earth Science: Earth's Surface and History
Earth Science: Physics & Chemistry of the Earth
Earth Science: Weather, Water & Atmosphere
Encyclopedia of Energy
Encyclopedia of Environmental Issues
Encyclopedia of Environmental Issues: Atmosphere and Air Pollution
Encyclopedia of Environmental Issues: Ecology and Ecosystems
Encyclopedia of Environmental Issues: Energy and Energy Use
Encyclopedia of Environmental Issues: Policy and Activism
Encyclopedia of Environmental Issues: Preservation/Wilderness Issues
Encyclopedia of Environmental Issues: Water and Water Pollution
Encyclopedia of Global Resources
Encyclopedia of Global Warming
Encyclopedia of Mathematics & Society
Encyclopedia of Mathematics & Society: Engineering, Tech, Medicine
Encyclopedia of Mathematics & Society: Great Mathematicians
Encyclopedia of Mathematics & Society: Math & Social Sciences
Encyclopedia of Mathematics & Society: Math Development/Concepts
Encyclopedia of Mathematics & Society: Math in Culture & Society
Encyclopedia of Mathematics & Society: Space, Science, Environment
Encyclopedia of the Ancient World
Forensic Science
Geography Basics
Internet Innovators
Inventions and Inventors
Magill's Encyclopedia of Science: Animal Life
Magill's Encyclopedia of Science: Plant life
Notable Natural Disasters
Principles of Astronomy
Principles of Chemistry
Principles of Physics
Science and Scientists
Solar System
Solar System: Great Astronomers
Solar System: Study of the Universe
Solar System: The Inner Planets
Solar System: The Moon and Other Small Bodies
Solar System: The Outer Planets
Solar System: The Sun and Other Stars
World Geography

Literature

American Ethnic Writers
Classics of Science Fiction & Fantasy Literature
Critical Insights: Authors
Critical Insights: Film
Critical Insights: Literary Collection Bundles
Critical Insights: Themes
Critical Insights: Works
Critical Survey of Drama
Critical Survey of Graphic Novels: Heroes & Super Heroes
Critical Survey of Graphic Novels: History, Theme & Technique
Critical Survey of Graphic Novels: Independents/Underground Classics
Critical Survey of Graphic Novels: Manga
Critical Survey of Long Fiction
Critical Survey of Mystery & Detective Fiction
Critical Survey of Mythology and Folklore: Heroes and Heroines
Critical Survey of Mythology and Folklore: Love, Sexuality & Desire
Critical Survey of Mythology and Folklore: World Mythology
Critical Survey of Poetry
Critical Survey of Poetry: American Poets
Critical Survey of Poetry: British, Irish & Commonwealth Poets
Critical Survey of Poetry: Cumulative Index
Critical Survey of Poetry: European Poets
Critical Survey of Poetry: Topical Essays
Critical Survey of Poetry: World Poets
Critical Survey of Shakespeare's Plays
Critical Survey of Shakespeare's Sonnets
Critical Survey of Short Fiction
Critical Survey of Short Fiction: American Writers
Critical Survey of Short Fiction: British, Irish, Commonwealth Writers
Critical Survey of Short Fiction: Cumulative Index
Critical Survey of Short Fiction: European Writers
Critical Survey of Short Fiction: Topical Essays
Critical Survey of Short Fiction: World Writers
Critical Survey of Young Adult Literature
Cyclopedia of Literary Characters
Cyclopedia of Literary Places
Holocaust Literature
Introduction to Literary Context: American Poetry of the 20th Century
Introduction to Literary Context: American Post-Modernist Novels
Introduction to Literary Context: American Short Fiction
Introduction to Literary Context: English Literature
Introduction to Literary Context: Plays
Introduction to Literary Context: World Literature
Magill's Literary Annual 2015
Magill's Survey of American Literature
Magill's Survey of World Literature
Masterplots
Masterplots II: African American Literature
Masterplots II: American Fiction Series
Masterplots II: British & Commonwealth Fiction Series
Masterplots II: Christian Literature
Masterplots II: Drama Series
Masterplots II: Juvenile & Young Adult Literature, Supplement
Masterplots II: Nonfiction Series
Masterplots II: Poetry Series
Masterplots II: Short Story Series
Masterplots II: Women's Literature Series
Notable African American Writers
Notable American Novelists
Notable Playwrights
Notable Poets
Recommended Reading: 600 Classics Reviewed
Short Story Writers

Grey House Publishing | Salem Press | H.W. Wilson | 4919 Route, 22 PO Box 56, Amenia NY 12501-0056

2016 Title List

Visit www.SalemPress.com for Product Information, Table of Contents, and Sample Pages.

History and Social Science

The 2000s in America
50 States
African American History
Agriculture in History
American First Ladies
American Heroes
American Indian Culture
American Indian History
American Indian Tribes
American Presidents
American Villains
America's Historic Sites
Ancient Greece
The Bill of Rights
The Civil Rights Movement
The Cold War
Countries, Peoples & Cultures
Countries, Peoples & Cultures: Central & South America
Countries, Peoples & Cultures: Central, South & Southeast Asia
Countries, Peoples & Cultures: East & South Africa
Countries, Peoples & Cultures: East Asia & the Pacific
Countries, Peoples & Cultures: Eastern Europe
Countries, Peoples & Cultures: Middle East & North Africa
Countries, Peoples & Cultures: North America & the Caribbean
Countries, Peoples & Cultures: West & Central Africa
Countries, Peoples & Cultures: Western Europe
Defining Documents: American Revolution
Defining Documents: Civil Rights
Defining Documents: Civil War
Defining Documents: Emergence of Modern America
Defining Documents: Exploration & Colonial America
Defining Documents: Manifest Destiny
Defining Documents: Postwar 1940s
Defining Documents: Reconstruction
Defining Documents: 1920s
Defining Documents: 1930s
Defining Documents: 1950s
Defining Documents: 1960s
Defining Documents: 1970s
Defining Documents: American West
Defining Documents: Ancient World
Defining Documents: Middle Ages
Defining Documents: Vietnam War
Defining Documents: World War I
Defining Documents: World War II
The Eighties in America
Encyclopedia of American Immigration
Encyclopedia of Flight
Encyclopedia of the Ancient World
Fashion Innovators
The Fifties in America
The Forties in America
Great Athletes
Great Athletes: Baseball
Great Athletes: Basketball
Great Athletes: Boxing & Soccer
Great Athletes: Cumulative Index
Great Athletes: Football
Great Athletes: Golf & Tennis
Great Athletes: Olympics
Great Athletes: Racing & Individual Sports
Great Events from History: 17th Century
Great Events from History: 18th Century
Great Events from History: 19th Century
Great Events from History: 20th Century (1901-1940)
Great Events from History: 20th Century (1941-1970)
Great Events from History: 20th Century (1971-2000)
Great Events from History: Ancient World
Great Events from History: Cumulative Indexes
Great Events from History: Gay, Lesbian, Bisexual, Transgender Events

Great Events from History: Middle Ages
Great Events from History: Modern Scandals
Great Events from History: Renaissance & Early Modern Era
Great Lives from History: 17th Century
Great Lives from History: 18th Century
Great Lives from History: 19th Century
Great Lives from History: 20th Century
Great Lives from History: African Americans
Great Lives from History: American Women
Great Lives from History: Ancient World
Great Lives from History: Asian & Pacific Islander Americans
Great Lives from History: Cumulative Indexes
Great Lives from History: Incredibly Wealthy
Great Lives from History: Inventors & Inventions
Great Lives from History: Jewish Americans
Great Lives from History: Latinos
Great Lives from History: Middle Ages
Great Lives from History: Notorious Lives
Great Lives from History: Renaissance & Early Modern Era
Great Lives from History: Scientists & Science
Historical Encyclopedia of American Business
Issues in U.S. Immigration
Magill's Guide to Military History
Milestone Documents in African American History
Milestone Documents in American History
Milestone Documents in World History
Milestone Documents of American Leaders
Milestone Documents of World Religions
Music Innovators
Musicians & Composers 20th Century
The Nineties in America
The Seventies in America
The Sixties in America
Survey of American Industry and Careers
The Thirties in America
The Twenties in America
United States at War
U.S.A. in Space
U.S. Court Cases
U.S. Government Leaders
U.S. Laws, Acts, and Treaties
U.S. Legal System
U.S. Supreme Court
Weapons and Warfare
World Conflicts: Asia and the Middle East
World Political Yearbook

Health

Addictions & Substance Abuse
Adolescent Health & Wellness
Cancer
Complementary & Alternative Medicine
Genetics & Inherited Conditions
Health Issues
Infectious Diseases & Conditions
Magill's Medical Guide
Psychology & Behavioral Health
Psychology Basics

Grey House Publishing | Salem Press | H.W. Wilson | 4919 Route, 22 PO Box 56, Amenia NY 12501-0056

Current Biography
Current Biography Cumulative Index 1946-2013
Current Biography Monthly Magazine
Current Biography Yearbook: 2003
Current Biography Yearbook: 2004
Current Biography Yearbook: 2005
Current Biography Yearbook: 2006
Current Biography Yearbook: 2007
Current Biography Yearbook: 2008
Current Biography Yearbook: 2009
Current Biography Yearbook: 2010
Current Biography Yearbook: 2011
Current Biography Yearbook: 2012
Current Biography Yearbook: 2013
Current Biography Yearbook: 2014
Current Biography Yearbook: 2015

Core Collections
Children's Core Collection
Fiction Core Collection
Graphic Novels Core Collection
Middle & Junior High School Core
Public Library Core Collection: Nonfiction
Senior High Core Collection
Young Adult Fiction Core Collection

The Reference Shelf
Aging in America
American Military Presence Overseas
The Arab Spring
The Brain
The Business of Food
Campaign Trends & Election Law
Conspiracy Theories
The Digital Age
Dinosaurs
Embracing New Paradigms in Education
Faith & Science
Families: Traditional and New Structures
The Future of U.S. Economic Relations: Mexico, Cuba, and Venezuela
Global Climate Change
Graphic Novels and Comic Books
Immigration
Immigration in the U.S.
Internet Safety
Marijuana Reform
The News and its Future
The Paranormal
Politics of the Ocean
Racial Tension in a "Postracial" Age
Reality Television
Representative American Speeches: 2008-2009
Representative American Speeches: 2009-2010
Representative American Speeches: 2010-2011
Representative American Speeches: 2011-2012
Representative American Speeches: 2012-2013
Representative American Speeches: 2013-2014
Representative American Speeches: 2014-2015
Representative American Speeches: 2015-2016
Rethinking Work
Revisiting Gender
Robotics
Russia
Social Networking
Social Services for the Poor
Space Exploration & Development
Sports in America
The Supreme Court
The Transformation of American Cities

U.S. Infrastructure
U.S. National Debate Topic: Surveillance
U.S. National Debate Topic: The Ocean
U.S. National Debate Topic: Transportation Infrastructure
Whistleblowers

Readers' Guide
Abridged Readers' Guide to Periodical Literature
Readers' Guide to Periodical Literature

Indexes
Index to Legal Periodicals & Books
Short Story Index
Book Review Digest

Sears List
Sears List of Subject Headings
Sears: Lista de Encabezamientos de Materia

Facts About Series
Facts About American Immigration
Facts About China
Facts About the 20th Century
Facts About the Presidents
Facts About the World's Languages

Nobel Prize Winners
Nobel Prize Winners: 1901-1986
Nobel Prize Winners: 1987-1991
Nobel Prize Winners: 1992-1996
Nobel Prize Winners: 1997-2001

World Authors
World Authors: 1995-2000
World Authors: 2000-2005

Famous First Facts
Famous First Facts
Famous First Facts About American Politics
Famous First Facts About Sports
Famous First Facts About the Environment
Famous First Facts: International Edition

American Book of Days
The American Book of Days
The International Book of Days

Junior Authors & Illustrators
Eleventh Book of Junior Authors & Illustrations

Monographs
The Barnhart Dictionary of Etymology
Celebrate the World
Guide to the Ancient World
Indexing from A to Z
The Poetry Break
Radical Change: Books for Youth in a Digital Age

Wilson Chronology
Wilson Chronology of Asia and the Pacific
Wilson Chronology of Human Rights
Wilson Chronology of Ideas
Wilson Chronology of the Arts
Wilson Chronology of the World's Religions
Wilson Chronology of Women's Achievements

Grey House Publishing | Salem Press | H.W. Wilson | 4919 Route, 22 PO Box 56, Amenia NY 12501-0056